Legacy Costs

The Story of a Factory Town

Richard Hudelson

HARDBALL

PRESS

REVIEWS

"Union members, activists and leaders can learn much from this engaging book. But it should be read by all who value equality and dignity and seek to understand our society so we can create a new and better world."

— David Newby, Former President, Wisconsin State AFL-CIO

"Legacy Costs is a must read for all organizers and progressives. As a supporter of Senator Sanders, we must find a way to energize the 99%to override the callous destructive 1% who have no vision for our children."

— Rod Ellcessor, Indiana State Teachers Association

"Hudelson's Legacy Costs is a masterful job of writing, a tidy, easy reɛd that tells us how we got to where we are, like it or not. It is an inɩportant, scholarly work, well written for the rank and file."

— Larry Sillanpa, WorkDayMinnesota

"If I were to be asked to suggest one book about the American working class, LEGACY COSTS would be it!"

—Peter Rachleff, Co-Executive Director, East Side Freedom Library

"Readable and concise, a great place to begin exploration of our troubled economy.

—Jim Dash, Union Labor News

"Anyone interested in exploring how the U.S. economy got in the condition it is currently in would do well to begin their exploration with Richard Hudelson's Legacy Costs: The Story of a Factory Town."

—Jim Cavanaugh, Wisconsin Labor History Society Newsletter

"Looking at changes in national labor law here compared to what has happened in Western Europe, Hudelson makes the case that income inequality, poverty and economic insecurity is tied to the weakening of unions and a more insular approach by labor to addressing workers' issues."

— Brooks Johnson, Duluth News-Tribune

"The book traces union victories, the shuttering of the factories and finally some ideas on how unions can regain strength."

—Wisconsin Labor History Society Newsletter

Dedication

To Jonah, Micah and Elise

Equality is the soul of liberty,
There is, in fact, no liberty without it.
Fanny Wright

Legacy Costs - The Story of a Factory Town, by Richard
Hudelson
Copyright © 2017 by Richard Hudelson
Published by Hard Ball Press.
ISBN:978-0-9991358-2-2
Exterior and interior book design by D. Bass.
Information available at: www.hardballpress.com

Library of Congress Cataloging-in-Publication Data
Hudelson, Richard
Legacy Costs - The Story of a Company Town
1. Labor Union—Nonfiction. 2. American labor history. 3. United
Auto Workers history. 4. Chrysler Automobile Company. 5. New
Castle, Indiana - history.

Legacy Costs

The Story of a Factory Town

Richard Hudelson

Contents

MEMORIES OF A FACTORY TOWN   1

HAMMERS IN THE NIGHT   7

NEW CASTLE JOINS THE UAW   17

BUILDING SOLIDARITY   31

WAR BRINGS LABOR PEACE   43

ON THE PICKET LINES   49

THE NEW WAR ON LABOR   61

THE NOT SO PERFECT PERFECT CIRCLE   69

THOSE TROUBLESOME OUTSIDE AGITATORS   83

WHAT IS FREEDOM WITHOUT DIGNITY?   97

PROFITS AND PROSPERITY   109

CAN CAPITALISM BE TAMED?   117

WHEN WALL STREET TAKES OVER THE COMPANY   123

THE WAY NOT TAKEN   137

BURDENS OF THE PAST   149

POSSIBILITIES OF THE PRESENT   157

ABOUT THE AUTHOR   167

ACKNOWLEDGEMENTS   169

SOURCES   171

INDEX   181

MEMORIES OF A FACTORY TOWN

When I was a child my father would come home from his shift at the Chrysler plant and hang his work clothes in the basement. Those work clothes fascinated me. They came from a world I had never seen. They smelled of sweat and oil and were covered with small holes burned by hot sparks of metal. My earliest childhood memories involve those work clothes.

In the basement one day I noticed that Dad's blue denim work jacket was cut into long vertical strips. I came upstairs and asked my mother what happened. She said there had been a long strike at the Chrysler. Since she and Dad had decided they would never make up in wages what they had lost during the strike, they favored abandoning the strike and going back to work. Some men from the union who supported the strike had cut Dad's jacket in order to send him a message.

Such was my introduction to the union.

I grew up in New Castle, Indiana, in the 1950s. My parents, Paul and Charlotte Hudelson, lived in a house in New Castle from late 1941 until 2003. My father and maternal grandfather both worked at the Chrysler, an auto parts plant. A factory town of about twenty-five thousand people, New Castle was a county seat, surrounded by farms and small towns.

My parents had always been frugal. There had been frequent layoffs, which made household finances tight. The cars I remember from my growing up years were a '33 Dodge, a '47 Chevy, and a '50 Plymouth. We seldom ate out.

I remember two family vacations, one to Kentucky and the other to the Smoky Mountains. Mom and Dad gave to the church and helped out some relatives, but just about everything else went for living costs and a modest savings account. The assisted living facility they entered in December 2003 cost more than three thousand dollars a month, increasing as the need for care increased. Their income came from Dad's Chrysler pension and from his Social Security. It was not enough to cover the whole monthly cost, but with their own savings and help from a small inheritance, they got by.

The Chrysler was the largest factory in town, but there were many others. There was a United Auto Workers local at the Chrysler, UAW Local 371, as well as other union locals at many of the other factories in town.

UAW Local 371 was a part of my growing-up years. I remember going with my Dad to the UAW Hall on North Main Street. Local 371 sponsored my older brother's Babe Ruth Baseball team. The Local was a leader in town charity drives, and was often mentioned in the local newspaper. Beyond these bits I remember little about Local 371. While neither my father nor grandfather was opposed to the union, neither was active in it. There were no family stories about the founding of Local 371. There was no grousing or gossip. I rarely heard mention of the union.

Somehow, I became a strong supporter of labor unions. In part this was a result of what I experienced in my youth. Like a bitter strike at the Perfect Circle factory, a chronic cycle of overwork and unemployment, and a persistent undertone of status difference that colored otherwise cooperative relations between families.

My reading was also important in making me a supporter of unions. I became a regular reader of *Solidarity*, the UAW newspaper mailed to our house. I was also impressed by an excerpt on unemployment from Karl Marx's *Capital* that I happened to read. By the time I was a senior in high school I was calling myself a Socialist. I would today call myself a Social Democrat.

The nationally prominent independent journalist I. F. Stone came to New Castle in 1955 to report on the strike at the Perfect Circle factory. In a story on that strike, he called New Castle "a labor citadel." It was, but it was a labor citadel surrounded by hostile territory.

New Castle and surrounding Henry County had roots in the Republican Party of the Civil War era. Republican Ralph Harvey, a farmer from Henry County outside New Castle, represented the region in Congress. The Teetor family from Hagerstown, near New Castle, owned the Perfect Circle Factory. The Teetors played a significant role in state and national efforts to roll back the New Deal and the unions.

In part because of their leadership, in 1957 Indiana became the first northern state to pass a "right-to-work law". Barry Goldwater was popular with many of my high school friends. A large billboard put up by the John Birch Society on Interstate 70 just west of New Castle claimed to show Martin Luther King at a Communist training camp. This would have been around 1963 or 1964. In more recent years, Mitch Daniels, a champion of the Reagan "Revolution", became the most popular Governor in Indiana history.

So, how did New Castle, located as it is within conservative East-Central Indiana, become a labor citadel? This was the first question that started me on the path that led to this book. It is a little bit memoir and a large part labor history, combined with a vigorous defense of labor unions. The first half of the book is an attempt to answer that question. It is primarily a labor history of New Castle informed by early records of UAW Local 371 that are housed in the Reuther Library at Wayne State University, and by subsequent reading in the area of local and national labor history.

The second question that started me down this road was, what enabled mom and dad to enjoy their retirement years together and to survive their last stage of life? In their decline they moved into an assisted living facility. By then Dad was suffering from congestive heart failure and Mom was five years into an Alzheimer's-like decline.

When Mom and Dad were in assisted living I began to hear talk about the "legacy costs" that retirees' pensions supposedly imposed on U.S. automakers and other companies. The prevailing view among the talking heads seemed to be that these legacy costs had to be cut; that the pensions were not sustainable. There were reports of companies in other industries failing to pay promised pensions or paying pensions of reduced amount. Sometimes this was done at court order by companies facing bankruptcy.

There was a lot of talk in the news about Chrysler being in

financial trouble. We were all worried about what would happen to Mom and Dad if the Chrysler pension were reduced or stopped coming. What were they supposed to do? How could my brother, sister and I manage to pay the assisted living bills and take care of our own families?

In March 2007, Dad died in the bed he and Mom bought when they were married in 1940. My brother Dave and I each visited him not long before he died. Mom and my sister Mary were with him when he died.

After Dad's death I found myself thinking about him and his shredded jacket hanging in the basement. When was that? Did that really happen? Neither Dave nor Mary remembered anything about it, and Mom was too far gone to understand what I would have been asking. I got on the computer and did an internet search for "long strike at Chrysler 1950s." I found several references to a 104-day strike at Chrysler in 1950. When I looked into that strike I discovered that the central aim had been to win pensions for Chrysler UAW workers. I was struck by the irony of it all. If my memory is right, my parents had been in favor of abandoning that strike, yet it was the pension won by that strike that was largely responsible for paying the bills in their old age.

Dave, Mary, and I, along with Dave's wife Judy and my wife, Eileen, visited Mom in June 2010. One year earlier we had to move Mom into a nursing home near Dave and Judy in Marion, Indiana, where Mom could receive the higher level of care she needed. Nursing home costs were around six thousand dollars per month. We all sat together on a bench outside in the shade. It was a beautiful day. The birds were singing. Mom was unable to follow the conversation, but she seemed to enjoy the day. She died shortly after that. The remaining value of my parents' estate was a little less than $24,000.

I have been thinking about legacy costs ever since. What would have happened to my parents without Dad's Chrysler pension? What would the talking heads going on about unsustainable pensions have us do? Were those talking heads right in saying that "the new normal" made such pensions unaffordable? How could young people today hope to get through the trials of old age on what they could save from their low wage jobs, if they were able to save at all? What kind of future would I be handing on to my children and grandchildren?

The book that follows is my attempt to talk about these things. I am retired now. For most of my working life I was a college professor. In that role, I gave a lot of thought to the proper role of markets in a just, free, and prosperous society. The book that follows draws on those thoughts, but it also draws on the historical experience from which those thoughts arose. I hope my effort will lead readers to think about and discuss these issues, and I hope this book will help readers understand the historical roots of the anti-union movement that is raging across the country and the world.

HAMMERS IN THE NIGHT

As a boy I shared the front bedroom with my older brother David. Mom, Dad and baby sister Mary slept in the back bedroom on the other side of the wall. Lying in the double bed I shared with Dave waiting for sleep, I could hear the factory where my father worked. There was a constant low roar punctuated by the sound of the massive hammers that formed parts for automobile assembly—BOOM... BOOM... BOOM.

There was no mechanical rhythm to this. Sometimes the pounding booms were close together; sometimes, far apart. Sometimes two would strike more or less simultaneously. It depended on how busy the shop was, how many hammers were in action and how many were silent, awaiting repair, better times, or a change of dies.

There was also a human factor in this rhythm. Each strike of the hammer was initiated by a man pushing a trip. Men are not machines. They have their own rhythms. There were pauses—to exchange a word with another man when you had to shout in his ear to be heard; to wipe away the sweat dripping off a nose; or to check on how the white-hot bars of steel were doing in the oven that fed the hammer.

Lying in bed, I would listen to the roar of the shop and the pounding of the hammers. On some summer nights, with the windows open, a still wind and nothing else happening, the sounds were loud. Each boom rattled my bones. Other nights the sounds were low and far away. Nonetheless, they were always present, night and day. Caught up in the activities of the day, you might not notice them, but if you stopped, they were always there.

The factory was the biggest employer in New Castle, Indiana. Originally built in 1907 to manufacture cars for the Maxwell-Briscoe Company, it was taken over by Chrysler Corporation in 1925, becoming one of Chrysler's six original plants. Located about

7

40 miles east of Indianapolis, the plant produced parts for the auto assembly plants in Detroit. The plant underwent a number of changes and expansions over the years, but its basic structure and function remained the same.

When I worked there summers in the mid-1960s while attending college, I was surprised to see the name "Maxwell" embedded into the frame of the large trimming press I was working on. There were two main parts to the plant: a forge shop where parts were roughly formed out of raw steel, and a machine shop where the roughly formed parts were turned into finished parts suitable for use in the assembly of new cars. In 1934, one of the worst years of the Depression, the plant had 6,700 employees. In the 1950s, when I was a boy, the plant made over 150 different parts. Parts made in New Castle were found in all cars and trucks produced by Chrysler.

My father Paul Hudelson worked in the forge shop. He started there in 1933. He was 18 then, still living with his parents and four sisters on the family farm west of New Castle. For all his life he retained a farmer's awareness of the weather and the conditions of the crops. He was a gardener. When we were kids and he was a young man, Dad kept a large garden on his parents' farm, where he also put in long hours helping with the work in the fields. Used to farm labor, he would work steadily for hours. It was at my grandparents' farm that I learned how much I hated chopping weeds with a hoe in the hot sun. In old age and declining health, my grandparents sold the farm.

My great-grandparents, then tenant farmers, bought this forty-acre farm in 1911.

That was a sad day for all of us. After that, Dad kept a small garden in the backyard on Park Avenue. There were always tomatoes along the sun side of the garage, with grapes, raspberries, green beans, kale, lettuce and other vegetables placed in small well-worked plots. He enjoyed a long, healthy retirement, spending many hours working outside the house, wearing an old straw hat with a plastic sunshade in the rim.

Dad seemed to be always working. When he was on the day shift, he was up early to go off to work at the Chrysler. I remember looking for him walking home from work a little after 2:30 in the afternoon when I was a kid. I would meet him at the corner of Audubon and Park and walk home with him. He was lean and strong. He would come into the house with the smell of the Chrysler on his clothes. He would give my mother a kiss and then clean up, shave, and change clothes. I remember sitting in the bathroom and watching him, admiring the way his biceps wobbled when he shaved.

We were pretty much free-range kids. Mom and Dad were always there if we needed them, but they had chores to do and seemed to be always working. Besides the Chrysler, helping on the farm, gardening, and church responsibilities, Dad did a lot of work around the house—painting, repairing, helping Mom with canning, and so on. We came together for weekday dinners and weekend meals. For much of the 1950s layoffs were common at Chrysler and money was tight. There were five of us. Chickens came with two legs, two thighs and two breasts. Dad always said he liked the back, neck and wings.

Later, when the grandkids came along and Dad was retired with more time for such things, there were bike rides and croquet games with the grandkids. In retirement Dad also liked to travel—usually to visit Dave and Judy and my nephew Jim near Marion, Indiana, Martha and Jim in Florida, Mary and Terry out East, or Eileen and me in Duluth, Minnesota. These were good times. Dad enjoyed travel, playing with the grandkids, and taking us all out to dinner.

There was a gang of boys on the block where I grew up. When we were little we would often pretend to be someone—a baseball player or a fireman. My brother Dave wanted to drive a coal truck.

Legacy Costs

I always said I was Paul Hudelson and I worked at the Chrysler, where I ran a Gogan, like my Dad did. He was my ideal for what a man should be—hard working, kind, and responsible.

Late in life Dad suffered a series of physical problems—a heart attack, a stroke, and gradual loss of vision. I will never forget going with him to a barbershop on Race Street not long after the stroke. He needed a walker then, but he had worked hard and learned to use the walker to get around. Quickly he made his way out of the car and up the step into the barbershop on his own and without any complaint. Inside were two men he had known for a long time. Dick Leitch was one of them. After they greeted Dad and me, we talked the way men do in a barbershop. I was as proud of him that day as I had been as a kid. I enjoyed being with him and talking to the other men. There was nothing special about that day, but for me it kind of stands in as typical of all the others.

Mom grew up in New Castle at 1122 South 17th Street. From there her father, John Henry, walked to work at the Chrysler. She was close to her younger sister, Martha, and to a group of childhood girlfriends, many of whom she knew all her life. She was a good student, always at or near the front of her class. She especially liked music and literature, but was also good at math and science. After high school she went to work as an office girl and bookkeeper in New Castle. In 1940 she married my father. She met him through Dad's sister. When Dad was turned down for World War II service for medical reasons, they picked out a design for a house and had the house built. This was the house at 217 Park Avenue where I grew up. They moved into that house in the fall of 1941 or spring of 1942. They raised a family there and did not leave until age and declining health forced them out in fall, 2003.

There was much hard work for my mom—cooking, cleaning, laundry done by a hand-cranked wringer washer, lugged up the basement stairs and hung on the line outside. There was canning in the summer and three kids to care for. Our house seemed to be kid central for the block. It was not at all uncommon to have a gang of six or seven or more running in and out. There were Kool-Aid popsicles, lemonade and sun tea made in a jar that sat by the back steps. There was PTA and the church where Mom taught Sunday school and put in countless hours in the church kitchen.

Mom had beautiful penmanship. She often served as secretary for the Methodist Women, PTA, or, in her later years, for the local Shakespeare Club, which she greatly enjoyed.

The years of hard work and layoffs at the Chrysler were not easy for her. Mom had a love of learning. When she graduated from high school in 1936 there was a teacher who urged her to go on to college. There was also a small scholarship offer. But this was during the Depression, before it became common for girls to go off to college. Instead of college, Mom worked for a while and then married Dad and raised a family. She often said she loved being a wife and mother, but there was a part of her that longed for the opportunity she had missed. While she never put it this way, she was a victim of the gender roles of her time.

Late in life, when she was struggling with old age and dementia and approaching death, Mom continued to think about her life and her situation. She often talked about Vevay, Indiana, where both of her parents were from and where she often visited relatives in her childhood. She often told a story about seeing Dad for the first time—he sitting straight and tall, driving a horse-drawn wagon up the lane at his parents' farm where Mom was visiting her friend, Dad's sister Dorothy. I think she was thinking about the choice she had made to marry him and about all the consequences that had brought for her life and the opportunities passed by.

She also repeated, over and over, some lines from "Thanitopsis," by William Cullen Bryant. Lines that spoke of meeting death with stoic dignity. Once, in those final years, when Mom and I were walking to the dining room at the assisted living facility, Mom repeated those lines and then said she didn't think she could do that. Even as dementia ate away at her mind, she continued to think about life—with honesty and courage.

We lived at 217 Park Avenue, about six blocks away from the Chrysler where Dad worked. Several of the kids we played with had fathers who worked there. Lots of the fathers of the kids we went to school with worked at the Chrysler. Many of the men in our church worked there, too. The auto industry went through seasonal ups and downs and was highly responsive to economic conditions. During recessions, as people put off buying new cars, there would be layoffs at the Chrysler. Sometimes those layoffs were long. I remember one layoff when Dad tried his hand at selling aluminum siding. That didn't work out very well. People who were laid off were not buying new siding for the house. Eventually Chrysler picked up and Dad and the other men were called back to work.

I remember being troubled by this. There would be men eager to work and people in need of new cars. What was the problem? Why did the factory stand idle? I also remember a troubling sense of my family's position. Our neighbors, the Ruddells, had yearly vacations in Florida. Mr. Ruddell had a lower-level management position at the Chrysler. In the 1950s we didn't go on vacations. We couldn't afford to. This bothered me. It didn't seem fair. My parents worked hard, they deserved a vacation, too. Nonetheless, looking back on it, I have to say that work at the Chrysler was pretty good—better than most other jobs in New Castle.

Although every family is unique, the transition my family experienced from a semi-rural horse-and-buggy world to factory life and a family car was a transition experienced by most of the men and women who worked at the Chrysler. Most of those families had, and many still have, ties to a pre-industrial world. Many of the family names I found in the records of those who worked at the Chrysler and other factories in New Castle are the same as the family names that appear in the surrounding rural cemeteries. Though many others came to New Castle from Kentucky or places even further away, those others usually came from rural or semi-rural backgrounds like those of my family.

Despite the reminders at graduation ceremonies, we all tend to underestimate change. We tend to think the way things are now is pretty much the way they have always been and the way they always will be. This thought impressed itself on William Clement Bond. Writing in 1939, the long-time New Castle native remarked that, "It is impossible to realize the difference in New Castle before 1900 and since." The phrase "impossible to realize" is apt. However much we may intellectually acknowledge change, the full import of it escapes us.

Established in 1822, for the rest of that century New Castle was an agricultural town of no more than three thousand people. People living in town kept horses, cows, hogs and chickens. Bond noted that, "A barn was built with every house," and that on Race Street, just behind the main business district, there were "dilapidated" and "vile smelling" hog pens and outbuildings. There were no paved streets, no plumbers before 1890, and no automobiles.

On June 22, 1907, a crowd of about 18,000 people gathered at a site on "I" Avenue in New Castle, where the cornerstone was laid for the Maxwell-Briscoe automobile factory in New Castle. Charles Fairbanks, the Vice-President of the United States, on hand for the dedication ceremony, told the crowd, "This factory will give employment to many hundreds of wage-earners," adding, "It will open up a new avenue whereby workmen may make provisions for themselves and their families." Intended as an assembly plant for Maxwell cars, the new plant was touted to be the largest automobile manufacturing facility in the world. Within a year production was underway at the plant.

During World War I, the newly developed American auto industry was put to work producing everything from tanks to shells in support of the war effort. After the war there was a period

Maxwell-Briscoe Motor Company was a major automaker in the early twentieth century. After a fire at the New Jersey facility, the company moved production to New Castle, Indiana

Interior Automobile Factory New Castle, Indiana
Maxwell Auto Factory New Castle, IN

A brand new facility with finished Maxell cars awaits installation of machinery for producing parts and assembling new Maxwell cars

Worker drop forging crankshafts, Maxwell Motor Company factory, New Castle, Indiana. Courtesy of the National Automotive History Collection, Detroit Public Library.

of pent-up demand for cars. The auto industry prospered. The plant in New Castle shared in both the wartime effort and the post-war prosperity.

In the early 1920s, the post-war boom exhausted itself and a new period of recession hit the auto industry. Over-extended, deeply in debt, with a large inventory of unsold cars, Maxwell Motor Company faced bankruptcy. The bankers who had invested in Maxwell formed a committee to re-organize the company. They persuaded Walter P. Chrysler, who had been head of the Buick Division of General Motors, to serve as chairman of this committee. By 1925, under Chrysler's leadership, the re-organized Maxwell Motor Company became the Chrysler Corporation. The plant in New Castle became a part of Chrysler Corporation, now producing parts for the Chrysler assembly plants in Detroit. For the next eighty years the factory complex in New Castle would be known as, "The Chrysler."

The Chrysler transformed New Castle.

NEW CASTLE JOINS THE UAW

On April 1, 1937, a story ran in the New Castle *Courier-Times* under the headline, "Little Interest Shown in Union." A meeting at Craig's Garage on South Nineteenth Street, not far from the Chrysler, had drawn only sixty-five "passive" men, down from the two hundred reported at the previous meeting. The *Courier* concluded, "interest shown in the union has obviously waned." Six weeks later, the *Courier* reported, a crowd of "probably 700" gave a "rousing reception" to Homer Martin, national president of the United Auto Workers, when he spoke at the high school gymnasium on Church Street. A UAW Local 371 Record Book claims the crowd that day numbered 2,500. Less than a year later, the *Courier* reported that more than five thousand people turned out for a union rally in Baker Park.

The event in Baker Park was called to celebrate the victories won by the UAW in New Castle and elsewhere in eastern central Indiana. It was a real celebration. The parade, led by the Knights of Pythias band, included a thousand cars. There were flags and speeches by union supporters from cities and towns around the region. Earl Todd, the first president of Local 371, served as master of ceremonies, and Mayor Sidney Baker welcomed the crowd. Similar events were going on all over America as labor organizations and working families celebrated the breakthrough victories of the previous year. America had changed, and millions of Americans welcomed that change.

To understand what had happened, we need to get a sense of what life was like for autoworkers and their families in the years before the union. In 1900, there was no auto industry. Three years after the Maxwell Motor Company began its operations in New Castle, there was one car for every 19,000 people in the United States. By 1930 there was one for every 4.5 persons. In 1929, there were 450,000 people employed in the auto industry. In less than

17

half a lifetime, America had gone from a horse and buggy world to the automotive age. This enormous change rested upon the earlier industrial transformation of America that took root in the years after the Civil War. Without the railroads, coalmines, iron mines, iron and steel industry, and electrical industry, there would have been no automobile. The automotive industry was a part, but a big part, of this greater transformation of America and the wider world.

Before the Civil War manufacturing was small in scale. For the most part it was done for a local or regional market. Small firms each employed a small number of laborers. Skilled laborers supported by a number of apprentices and unskilled helpers did much of this manufacturing work. It was not at all uncommon for the owner of the firm to know his employees personally and to work alongside them. Many of the pioneers in the auto industry had themselves started out working as mechanics or in one of the other skilled trades. John Dodge, one of the pioneering Dodge brothers, was once on his way to a formal social event when he heard about a problem at the Dodge forge shop. On a hot summer day, four consecutive men assigned to a specific foundry job had fainted. Dressed in his tuxedo, Dodge insisted on going to the job site, where he attempted to do the work. After twenty minutes, with his clothes covered with dirt and sweat, he gave up and ordered his engineers to re-think how to get the work done.

By the end of World War I, such shoulder-to-shoulder contact between bosses and workers was a thing of the past. The industry had become much too large for that. In addition, the technology of production had changed in ways that altered the relationship between the boss and the shop-floor worker. In the early days of the automotive industry there were many small companies manufacturing automobiles. These were usually assembly companies that purchased manufactured parts from other companies—often wagon and carriage manufacturing companies, like Studebaker. As the industry moved from small shops to mass production in large industrial facilities, automakers utilized efficiencies of size, control over sources of parts, efficiencies in new technologies and efficiencies in the flow of the production process to produce more cars at lower cost.

Henry Ford is famous for introducing the assembly line to the production of automobiles, but similar changes in the production process were also introduced by Walter P. Chrysler during the time he was head of the Buick Division of General Motors.

In addition, time-study specialists observed specific production processes in order to find ways to increase the efficiency of production. University-trained engineers began to replace self-taught mechanics, bringing a broader understanding of production processes. Research and development teams worked to improve both the ultimate product and the technology of producing it. Rationalized production controlled by management replaced the traditional methods of production, which had been largely under the control of skilled laborers who were doing the work.

As the size and complexity of the production process increased, industry developed a hierarchical management structure that distanced the managers from shop-floor workers. This also had the effect of reducing the need for skilled labor. Someone hired off the street could be trained to do a specific job in the production process in a matter of hours or days. At Ford Motor Company the assembly line method of production more than doubled the number of magnetos produced per worker per day.

The technical and managerial features that made such mass-production industries possible were a mixed blessing for workers. Workers and their bosses always have both shared and opposing interests. While they share an interest in having a company that makes good money, their interests are opposed in how the money made is divided between them. When there is significant unemployment, the bargaining position of the boss is strengthened. It is also true that the boss usually has more resources than the workman, thus enabling the boss to hold out longer in contract negotiations. As the classical economist Adam Smith observed, in disputes between "masters" (employers) and their workmen, "the masters can hold out much longer."

As modern capitalism developed in the nineteenth century, workers formed unions to strengthen their bargaining position against employers. This strategy worked especially well where the work involved skilled labor that could not be readily replaced. In the late nineteenth and early twentieth centuries, with the development of mass-production industries utilizing new technologies that replaced skilled labor, management gained an advantage against the unions. The weakened unions became unable to protect workers' interests. Labor unions survived in the skilled trades—mechanics, carpenters, bricklayers, plumbers, printers and painters—but they largely disappeared in the new mass-production industries

The auto industry was one of these new mass-production industries. Unions continued to represent a small vestige of the nineteenth-century Carriage and Wagon Workers' Union. In addition, some autoworkers doing skilled work, like die makers and machinists, belonged to unions. But the auto industry was, for all practical purposes, a non-union industry. There was no union recognition and no collective bargaining until 1937.

The absence of a union left workers at the mercy of their employers. If the boss wanted you to work overtime, you either did or you lost your job. If there was a downturn in the industry and there were layoffs, who was laid off and who kept working was up to the discretion of the boss. If you thought a foreman had unjustly treated you, there was no grievance procedure.

For most of the auto industry, wages were based on piecework. If you were a machine operator, as most of the employees at New Castle Chrysler were, you would be paid so much for each part you worked on each day. If your machine went down in need of repair, that was your loss. If your foreman assigned you to a machine that was prone to breakdowns, that was your tough luck. Management set the rates for piecework based on the reports of their time-study men. There was almost constant pressure to work faster. If a worker succeeded in exceeding management expectations for production, that worker made money—until management decided to lower the rate per piece. "Rate busters," workers who tried to work fast to make more money, tended to cause management to adjust rates downward, making everyone work faster for the same pay. Workers had no say in any of these production decisions.

Given the loss of unions and consequent loss of power over working conditions, why would anyone work in the auto industry? The short answer is that people needed the work to pay the bills. In the early days of the mass-production auto industry, it was not uncommon for workers to work as little as they could. Absenteeism was high. When asked why he worked only four days a week, one welder replied, "Because I can't get along on three."

Workers were also quick to leave the auto industry whenever they could find something better. Ford Motor Company had a turnover rate of 370 percent. For every 100 employees needed to keep production going, Ford had to make 370 hires every year. In an effort to curb absenteeism and turnover, Ford famously introduced a $5 a day wage for some of their workers in 1914. To qualify for this then high wage, a worker had to pass through a probationary period and continue with reliable work habits. Other automakers soon matched Ford's high wage and Ford's policy of monitoring worker absenteeism. With the auto industry now paying the highest or near-highest wage in the U.S., workers in effect struck a bargain: they would reliably show up for work despite the repetitive monotony, speed, and lack of say, in exchange for high wages.

This bargain held throughout the 1920s. With the end of governmental controls on the economy imposed during World War I, farm prices and wages fell throughout the United States. The auto industry was an exception to this. There, wages remained high. Drawn to these high wages, thousands of rural poor from the South and Midwest joined thousands of new immigrants in heading for Detroit and the auto parts plants of the Midwest. My grandfather was one of the early ones, leaving his home on the Indiana side of the Ohio River to eventually find work at the Maxwell Plant in New Castle. Lots of others came from further south in Kentucky. By the late 1920s many of these autoworkers, like my grandfather, owned their own homes, and some even owned their own cars. While life and health insurance, family vacations, and savings for retirement remained beyond the financial reach of many of these workers, their overall standard of living was high in comparison with the standard for working-class life in other industries. Despite the insecurity of periodic slumps and layoffs, autoworkers were doing pretty well.

Then came the Great Depression of the 1930s. In an economic downturn families must continue to pay for food, housing, and other necessities. They tend to put off discretionary spending, like buying a car. When the Depression hit, auto production dropped sharply. By 1932 it had dropped to the lowest level since 1916. Employment also sharply dropped. Where 450,000 people had been employed nationally in 1929, by 1933 employment had dropped to 243,000, and many of those who continued to work faced frequent layoffs. Only one in three autoworkers worked throughout the year.

A significant number of auto workers who were working at least part of the time during a Depression year took home less than half of what they were making before the Depression. Unable to make ends meet, many autoworkers tried something else. Some returned to live with relatives on farms; others tried whatever paying work they could find. Many became insurance salesmen working on commission, only to discover that there were more people selling insurance than buying it.

Understanding this picture of how things were in the Depression years helps to make sense of some puzzling facts about what was going on in New Castle. For example, I knew that my father hired on at the Chrysler in 1933 in the depths of the Depression. I always wondered how this could be. Wasn't this one of the darkest Depression years? How could anyone get hired at the Chrysler then? Then I heard that 1934 was the year more people worked at the Chrysler than any other year in the entire history of the plant in New Castle. How could this be? Was there something about the work being done at the plant in New Castle that was impervious to the Depression? Having found out a little bit about what was happening with employment in the auto industry during the Depression years, I now have a theory about what was going on in New Castle.

Like elsewhere in the auto industry, the Chrysler plant in New Castle was hit hard by the Depression, with a steep drop in production and a steep drop in steady employment. Laid off workers whose families relied upon their wages were in a difficult situation. Many were unable to continue with rent or house payments. Many who worked at the New Castle plant had come from farms in Indiana and Kentucky. Unable to stay where they were, some returned to those farms or to farms of relatives. Others moved to wherever they were able to find some kind of work to keep their families afloat. When there was a sputter of increased activity at the plant, local management needed to make some new hires to get the work done. In this way my father was offered a job in 1933. Then a single eighteen-year-old living on his parents' farm, my father would have been able to get by with work between layoffs, while a worker with a family to support could not get by.

Ron Lightfoot was also hired at the New Castle plant in 1933. Like my father he was a young man. His father also worked at the Chrysler. Perhaps between the two Depression-era jobs, that family was able to get by. It may be that the reason 1934 was the year more people worked at the Chrysler plant in New Castle than any other year was because people were coming and going— working a little when they got the chance, leaving if they had to, and staying on only if they could afford it. While I cannot say for certain that this is what was happening, Rea Ratcliff, a man who worked at the Chrysler in New Castle from 1926-1972, mentions the way men were treated when work was uncertain as one of the reasons men turned to the union. Men would show up for work only to be sent home and told to come back later and then be sent home again.

During the 1920s unions were in decline throughout the United States. In the mass-production industries like steel and auto, unions were virtually non-existent. Business leaders championed the "American Plan," a paternalistic form of capitalism where able business leaders would manage non-union industries and workers would go along in exchange for a high standard of living. The Depression made the threadbare nature of this promise evident. Employment was insecure. Annual wages fell sharply. Automakers tried to cut costs by speeding up production well above pre-Depression rates. Men laid off would stand for long hours in employment lines only to find that they had been replaced by new men, perhaps younger men, better able to keep up with the increased pace of production and able to work for wages insufficient to support a family. Facing these circumstances, more and more workers began to support unions.

By the mid-1930s, an energized labor movement began to develop across the country. The first convention of the United

Automobile Workers of America met in Detroit in 1935. The union had been granted a probationary charter by the American Federation of Labor (AFL). The UAW's president was Francis Dillon, a man with no experience in the auto industry who had been appointed by the AFL President William Green.

At a second convention in South Bend, Indiana, in 1936, delegates, primarily representing parts plants in the Midwest outside Detroit took the union in a more radical direction, abandoning the AFL for the Congress for Industrial Organization (CIO) and electing officers with roots in the auto industry. The list of delegates for that South Bend convention does not show anyone from New Castle, but it does include Perry Warrun representing Local 146, an early UAW local that then included members working at both Delco Remy and Guide Lamp in Anderson, Indiana. Ron Lightfoot, who along with his father worked at the Chrysler in New Castle, mentions joining the UAW in 1935, through the local in Anderson. A history of the UAW in Anderson also mentions support from the UAW foothold in Anderson for organizing efforts at other cities, including New Castle. It is thus likely that at least some of the workers at the Chrysler plant in New Castle were aware of what had happened in South Bend.

At the South Bend convention, militant midwestern autoworkers put control of the United Auto Workers of America directly into the hands of autoworkers. This action was part of a groundswell of grass-roots activity among previously unorganized workers in mass-production industries, many of them connected to the auto industry. As early as 1934, workers at the Electric Auto-Lite factory in Toledo, Ohio went on strike for the right to bargain collectively with management. When they defied a court injunction against picketing, the police intervened, killing two and injuring hundreds among the picketers and onlookers. Nonetheless, the workers persisted, eventually winning recognition of their union, which became UAW Local 12.

In early 1936, the Goodyear Rubber Company in Akron, Ohio, following the practice common in much of the auto-parts supply industry, attempted to impose wage cuts and speed-ups. Workers staged a sit-down strike, occupying the factory and preventing the company from hiring scabs (replacement workers). In late March they won union recognition for the United Rubber Workers. Later that year, workers at the Bendix plant in South Bend, an auto parts supplier, staged their own sit down strike, winning recognition of the UAW as their agent for collective bargaining. With this strike following so closely on the convention in South Bend earlier that year, the UAW had established its presence in Indiana

Auto workers enjoy a musical interlude during the Bendix Sit-Down Strike, South Bend, Indiana, 1936. This was before the famous sit-down strikes at GM and Chrysler in spring 1937. Walter P. Reuther Library, Archives of Labor and Urban Affairs, Wayne State University.

Riding this wave of labor activism, the UAW mounted a campaign against General Motors, the biggest of the auto companies, in January 1937. By the end of the month, strikes were underway at GM plants throughout the Midwest, including a sit-down strike at the Guide Lamp plant in Anderson and the later dramatic 44-day sit-down strike at the GM Fisher body shop in Flint, Michigan. The GM strike ended with an historic breakthrough when the UAW won the right to represent workers in all GM plants.

On March 8, 1937 the union launched a campaign to win union recognition and seniority rights at Chrysler. Some 17,000 workers sat down at Chrysler plants in the Detroit area. Soon workers at other Chrysler plants joined the struggle. These other Chrysler plants were in Los Angeles, Marysville (Michigan), and New Castle, Indiana. In an agreement reached on April 6, Chrysler Corporation recognized the UAW as representing workers in its plants for collective bargaining.

It took courage for a factory worker to go out on strike in those days. Except for the coal mines, the big mass-production industries were all run on an open-shop (non-union) basis. Management paid men to spy on their fellow workers. Anyone thought to be active in a union would be fired. Beyond that, there was a long history in the United States of the use of violence against attempts to organize unions. Violence had been used against the Auto-Lite strikers and their supporters in 1934. At a Hunger March by Ford workers in 1932, private "servicemen" hired by Ford Motor Company fired into a crowd of almost 3,000 people, killing four.

Detroit auto worker John W. Anderson later recalled what it was like for him and his fellow workers to go out on strike in 1937: "Few of us had ever seen much less walked one [picket line]. The fears of physical injury or even death in those days were deterrents to workers joining a picket line or engaging in other strike activity." Just a few months before workers at the New Castle Chrysler Plant went on strike, workers at the GM plants in Anderson had gone out as part of the UAW campaign there against General Motors. Historian Nelson Lichtenstein describes Anderson then as a "cockpit of GM-sponsored violence and police repression."

With their ties to the Anderson UAW, activists in New Castle had to have known that there was risk in what they were getting into. Their fears were not unfounded. At about that same time, on Memorial Day in 1937, police fired on a marching crowd of strikers and their supporters at Republic Steel in South Chicago. Ten people were killed and many others badly injured.

Beyond the legitimate fears of violence or of being fired, going out on strike also meant doing something that few men working at the Chrysler in New Castle had ever done before. Many of them entered factory work directly from the farm. They had no previous factory experience. They had never belonged to a union or been around anyone who belonged to a union. At first, many of those workers showed little interest in the UAW. So, who were those activists who took that risky step in the spring of 1937, and what led them to do that?

Minutes from the Record Book of early meetings of UAW Local 371 in New Castle give us a partial answer to the question of "who" these activists were. Page one of those minutes records the first meeting of Local 371 after it was officially chartered by the United Auto Workers of America on April 23, 1937. It also provides the names of men serving as temporary officers of the local, pending elections for regular officers. It is highly likely that these were men who had been active in the strike earlier that Spring and in the effort to organize the union that preceded the strike. All of them worked at the Chrysler. New Castle City Directories show that almost all of them lived in neighborhoods within walking distance of the Chrysler in housing they either owned or rented.

One interesting exception to this is Recording Secretary Joe Harris. He lived downtown, probably in a rented room. Federal census data from 1940 indicates that Joe Harris was born in Anderson, about twenty-five miles north of New Castle. This raises the possibility that he knew people active in the UAW in Anderson. By 1940, Harris was married, still working at the Chrysler and living within walking distance of the plant. Harris was one of the early leaders of the UAW in New Castle. His name appears frequently in the early records of the local. He was clearly well liked—often elected by large margins to represent the local at regional conferences and to serve on committees of the local. His opinions clearly carried weight, although he met opposition within the local and did not always prevail.

Another early leader was Earl Todd, the man elected as the first president of UAW Local 371 and a man who continued to play leadership roles within the union into the 1950s. Like many of the other early leaders and activists within Local 371, Todd was originally from Kentucky. Some of the many men working at the Chrysler and other factories in New Castle had experience with the United Mine Workers. Many of those who came from Kentucky came from the southeastern part of the state, near the coalfields of Kentucky and West Virginia, where coal miners connected with the United Mine Workers had fought sometimes-deadly battles with the coal companies. For example, Donnie Pyle, who had relatives working at the Chrysler and other factories in New Castle, mentioned cousins working in coalmines near Hazard, Kentucky.

Besides the group of temporary officers, many other local men were involved in organizing Local 371 and winning union recognition. We know from his interview that Ron Lightfoot had joined the UAW through the Anderson Local as early as 1935. He also mentions secret meetings of pro-union Chrysler workers at Craig's Garage leading up to the 1937 strike and formation of the union. Rea Ratcliff and Goodson Marlow both worked at the Chrysler before and after the formation of the union. Ratcliff mentions being expected to be available for work but not getting straight answers about when work would be available. He also mentions the need for washbasins where men could clean up before going home at the end of a shift. These reasons speak to the conditions that prevailed in the 1920s and the Depression—reasons that no doubt prompted support for the union. Marlow mentions wages and working conditions, and in addition, overtime pay, vacations, pensions, and health insurance. The union would win many of these benefits, but only well into the future. They were not likely to have been on anyone's mind in 1937. In reality, of course, motives for each man or woman (there were some women working at the New Castle Chrysler plant in the 1930s) were specific to his or her working conditions and his or her understanding of the broader world.

In the aftermath of the 1937 strike victory and contract settlement, local enthusiasm for the union swelled. Each week brought another hundred or another seventy-five members into the local. The election for regular officers took place between May 9 and May 11. Results were announced at the mass meeting at the gym mentioned at the opening of this chapter. There were some new names on the list of officers. Jack Gann replaced Earl Todd as President of the Union, but Todd remained an active member of the union who would later serve as its elected president. While the existing minutes for the years that follow show the kind of disagreements and personal rivalries one would expect, they also show that Local 371 was a democratic union with a strong base among Chrysler employees. At that celebration in Baker Park one year after the formation of the union, Mayor Sidney Baker also thanked Local 371 for the peaceful manner with which its members had conducted the organizing drive in New Castle.

While the 1937 national and local union victories made a radical break with the open shop of the past, many predicted that the unions would not survive. The contract signed in 1937 between the Chrysler and the UAW was brief. Chrysler recognized the UAW for purposes of collective bargaining and agreed not to support or sign agreements with other unions. The UAW agreed not to "intimidate" employees into joining. The contract was good for one year. Buoyed by a celebratory sense of the victory following their breakthrough contract, unions across the United States sought to solidify the gains they had won. In a spirit of solidarity they also sought to extend those gains to other working people.

Having won union recognition and a contract, UAW Local 371 in New Castle set to work creating a regular structure for the local. A functioning union local had to be created from scratch. The 1937 Record Book of minutes from its meetings provides a view of what was going on. Officers were elected. A schedule for meetings was established. Committeemen were elected to represent the different departments and shifts. Special committees were formed to deal with particular issues. The new leaders had to make countless decisions, such as voting to prohibit alcohol at meetings and to expel from the meeting any member who was drunk. A ban on smoking at meetings was proposed but failed. Caps and flags were ordered. Efforts were initiated to find a hall for the local. File cabinets and office furniture were ordered. Dances were held. Delegates were elected to represent the local at regional and national meetings of the UAW and the CIO.

Support for the union swelled. The strike victory and the contract won diminished the fears of workers who had previously hung back. Hundreds of new members signed up in a matter of weeks, with significant numbers continuing to join throughout the year.

Still, doubts and even outright opposition to the union

remained among some workers within the plant. Rumors of mal-feasance against national and local leaders surfaced and had to be addressed. There remained interest in continuing a non-UAW company union among some men who worked in the forge shop. There were also some thorny issues involved in working out the relationship between Local 371 and the AFL Die Makers union that had survived in the plant among those skilled workers during the largely non-union history of the plant.

It was often unclear what needed to be done or who was to do it. At early meetings, members of the Executive Committee responded to requests for help with rent or food from members who were laid-off, sick, or injured, by reaching into their own pockets. It was not until fall, 1937 that a Good and Welfare Committee was established to handle such requests and provide support from union funds.

Local 371 moved quickly to strengthen connections with other UAW locals in the area. Representatives from Anderson and Richmond locals spoke at meetings in New Castle. Jack Gann, Frank Popejoy, Joe Harris, William Russell and Curtis White represented Local 371 at a District meeting in Anderson in June 1937. The district meeting opened with a gathering of five thousand UAW members and supporters at Athletic Park in Anderson, where UAW National President Homer Martin was the featured speaker. Afterward, the assembled delegates from the area met at Anderson's Union Hall. The relationship with Anderson was growing particularly strong.

Local 371 also moved quickly to establish relationships with other unions and their supporters in New Castle itself. The national CIO, the Committee for Industrial Organization, had been formed in November 1935 with the purpose of organizing industry-wide unions in the large basic industries that remained unorganized at that time. While originally formed as a "committee" within the American Federation of Labor, leadership of the CIO had from the beginning come from labor leaders like John L. Lewis of the United Mine Workers, who were unhappy with the failure of the AFL to take on this task. When the national president of the AFL, William Green, forced the expulsion of the CIO organized unions from the AFL in spring, 1937, the CIO was reorganized as a separate national federation of labor unions and re-named the Congress of Industrial Organizations.

Since the UAW was one of the CIO unions, it was natural that UAW Local 371 would reach out to other CIO unions in the area. For example, in August 1937, the local approved sending $100 to support a strike in Hartford City by CIO Steel Workers. Local 371 also worked to support CIO activists in New Castle at the Perfect Circle, the Rolling Mill, and Hoosier Kitchen Cabinet factories. Claude Smith, Chairman of United Wood Workers of America Local 616, made up of employees at Hoosier Cabinets, spoke at Local 371 meetings on October 30 and November 6, 1937. Concern for fellow workers at Perfect Circle and the Rolling Mill were evident in the Local 371 Minutes for April and June of 1938. By March 1938, the local had also established a committee to organize community support for the unemployed in New Castle.

In addition, Local 371 sought to support the broader New Castle community of which it was a part. As early as August 1937 the local approved a donation to the respirator fund for Henry County Hospital. In the years that followed, Local 371 would play a leading role in providing financial support for the Community Fund and for special projects, such as establishing the First Aid Unit in New Castle.

Another interesting example of the way the local reached out to the surrounding community involved its ongoing cooperation with Olivet Presbyterian Church. The church was located at the corner of "E" Avenue and South Eighteenth Street in the largely working-class neighborhood situated between the Chrysler and the Perfect Circle plants. Rev. Ralph Felix, pastor at Olivet Presbyterian, came to New Castle in the early 1920s to serve at what was then the Olivet Community Center. The church, founded a year later, continued to offer community service to needy families as part of its mission. During the second winter of the Depression it was feeding more than one thousand persons each week. It also provided clothes and other aid to the needy.

Rev. Felix spoke at a meeting of Local 371 in December 1937 "regarding the serious problems facing the laboring classes at this time." He expressed the desire of Olivet Presbyterian Church to work with the UAW to address these problems. At a meeting in

January 1938, Brother Davis, a member of Local 371, responded, speaking further on the relationship between the CIO and the church. While the membership would later vote down a proposal to close each union meeting with a prayer, the local did support meetings organized by Rev. Felix.

Beginning in the 1880s and 1890s, trade unions within the American Federation of Labor had organized Trades Assemblies in cities across the United States. Delegates representing each trade union in the city—plumbers, painters, carpenters, printers, bricklayers, etc.—would meet periodically to address their common concerns. Following the expulsion of the newly formed CIO unions from the AFL in 1937, these CIO unions began to organize Industrial Union Councils in cities where CIO unions were present. These councils fostered cooperation among CIO locals in each city. By 1938, a CIO Industrial Union Council had been established in New Castle.

Local 371, the largest CIO union in the city, provided support to the other CIO unions in New Castle. The 1938 Record Book of Minutes for Local 371 shows continued concern for the plight of CIO workers at Perfect Circle and the Rolling Mill in particular. At one point serious consideration was given to a proposal to "take-in" CIO workers at these two plants and at Trainer Springs Factory in New Castle. This step was never taken, perhaps because it did not fit the legal structure for collective bargaining established by the National Labor Relations Act. Nevertheless, concern for workers at these and other plants remained high among members of Local 371. Members from these and other CIO unions in New Castle also took part in labor education courses offered by the UAW.

At the Chrysler plant, problems with lingering support for an "independent" union surfaced from time to time, even into the 1950s. This appears to have been connected with unclearly defined seniority rules. As late as 1956 some men with high seniority in the forge shop threatened to form a separate UAW union when they were bumped from choice jobs in the forge shop by men transferring from the machine shop. While everyone agreed that seniority bumps should not happen where specific job skills were necessary, various attempts to solve seniority issues invariably made someone angry.

Richard Hudelson

The first graduating class from night school classes sponsored by UAW Local
371, June 14, 1945. It included UAW members from Perfect Circle and the
Chrysler, United Furniture Workers members from Hoosier Cabinets, and
United Rubber Workers members from World Bestos.
Henry County Historical Society (New Castle, Indiana)

It also appears that because of a lack of clarity in contract language, management felt free to call back laid-off men with less
seniority before it called back men with more seniority. Problems
pertaining to relations between Local 371 and the AFL Die Makers
also persisted.

These thorny issues generated some heat and some headaches
for union leaders, though none of them seriously threatened Local
371. Men from the Forge Division continued to serve in offices and
on committees within the local. Some men doing skilled work
were clearly members of Local 371. Despite the issues that created
difficulties, members of the separate Die Makers union wanted
to cooperate with the local. Floyd Abston, who served eight years
as President of Local 371 over different terms between 1944 and
1963, also served as a Skilled Trades Committeeman within the
local in 1965. On the whole, support for the UAW within Local 371
remained strong.

In the fall of 1939, with all the issues mentioned above

sputtering in the background, the UAW entered into contract negotiations with Chrysler Corporation. The original 1937 agreement between the UAW and Chrysler had been extended until September 1939. Having suffered layoffs and pay cuts as a consequence of the austerity-induced downturn of 1937, the UAW was keen on sharing in the gains resulting from Chrysler's good year in early 1939. The union was also determined to reduce speed-ups throughout Chrysler reported by some of its locals.

Unwilling to give what the UAW wanted, Chrylser was determined to test the strength of the UAW. It was a promising time for such a test. Chrysler had signed one-year agreements with the UAW in 1937 and 1938. Now, in 1939, there was a heated factional battle within the national UAW between supporters of Homer Martin, who was still aligned with the AFL, and other UAW leaders aligned with the CIO. Martin's supporters within the UAW went so far as to organize a "UAW-AFL" chapter to challenge the "UAW-CIO" as the bargaining agent for autoworkers. In 1939, the National Labor Relations Board conducted elections in all Chrysler plants to determine who would represent autoworkers in each plant. Nationally, the UAW-CIO won a strong endorsement in this election. With 92 percent of all eligible employees voting, the UAW-CIO won 81.6% of all votes cast against 9.4% for the UAW-AFL, with 9% voting for the "no representation" (no union) option.

Workers in New Castle, where there was support for an independent local union, were given four choices: the UAW-CIO, the UAW-AFL, an Independent local union or no representation. Over four thousand employees voted. With 79% of the vote cast, the UAW-CIO was the big winner in New Castle, too. The Independent Local union option came in second in New Castle, with 17% of the vote. UAW-AFL and "no representation" each garnered in the 1-3% range. It is worth noting that in the two other Chrysler plants in Indiana, in Kokomo and Evansville, the UAW-CIO did not win an outright majority of votes cast. New Castle was more firmly committed to the CIO than these other plants. Die Sinkers who cast a separate ballot, voting between retaining their affiliation with the AFL, affiliation with the UAW-CIO, and "no union," chose to retain their AFL status by a vote of 71 to 12 to 3. The Die Sinkers would retain their separate union in New

Richard Hudelson

Castle as long as the plant continued to operate there.

With the strong vote of support from Chrysler employees, the UAW-CIO felt secure enough to initiate action against Chrysler. Union workers in Detroit plants staged a deliberate slow down. When Chrysler responded by locking out union workers, the UAW countered the lockout with a strike by Chrysler employees in the Detroit plants. With the labor conflict slowing and then shutting down production in Chrysler plants in Detroit, demand for parts produced at the Chrysler plant in New Castle fell.

By mid-October, workers in New Castle were put on reduced hours. Following this, UAW members in New Castle showed their support for their striking brothers and sisters in Detroit by voting to give the International UAW authority to call a strike in all Chrysler plants.

With neither side giving way, the strike dragged on well into November. Auto sales continued to rebound from the austerity-induced recession of 1937, but Chrysler was missing out on an opportunity to take advantage of the strong demand for cars. Late in November, the company attempted to provoke the UAW into violence by persuading some, mostly African-American workers in Detroit to cross the UAW picket lines and go back to work. Fortunately, a number of African-American leaders in Detroit spoke publicly in support of the UAW, persuading a significant number of the African-Americans involved not to attempt to break the strike. Fortunately as well, union leaders persuaded the massed pickets not to react with violence when some workers, under police protection, did cross the line. There were some minor injuries, but no serious violence.

Finding little support for strikebreaking and a disciplined union response, Chrysler reached an agreement with the union in a matter of days. A summary of the agreement reached provided by Charles Hyde in his history of Chrysler Corporation, describes it this way:

> Chrysler recognized the UAW as the sole bargaining agency in its plants, but it would have been morally, if not legally, obligated to do so anyway because of the NLRB certification elections. The UAW did

37

not get a union shop or paid vacations. While the company still established rates of production, the rates were now subject to a stronger grievance process. Chrysler recognized the shop steward system and agreed to pay stewards while they did their contractual duties, including settling grievances. The union won time-and-a-half pay for overtime, double-time for holiday work, and a minimum of two hours' pay for employees sent home after reporting for work, all significant economic gains. The across-the-board pay raise of 3 cents went to workers who earned, on average, $1 an hour. None of the financial issues were 'deal busters.' And the settlement had little effect on Chrysler's profits. The company estimated that the contract would increase its labor costs about $5 million a year, which turned out to be less than 1 percent of its 1940 sales of $775 million. Even with the increased labor costs, Chrysler enjoyed profits of nearly $38 million that year. The 1939 strike was a test of strength for the UAW and a test of resolve for Chrysler. Both passed.

The 1939 strike was the longest in the history of the auto industry up to that time. The UAW-CIO had shown it had strong support from its members and was capable of united, disciplined action. In recognizing the union as the sole bargaining agent for its production employees, Chrysler Corporation indicated its willingness to work with the union. The settlement reached was a major accomplishment for the UAW.

In New Castle, the UAW had established a powerful base in Local 371 at the Chrysler. UAW activists had established beachheads at the Perfect Circle foundry, the Rolling Mill and a number of other local factories. These UAW activists reached out to activists in other CIO unions working to organize locals in New Castle. Between spring 1937 and the end of 1939, factory workers in New

Richard Hudelson

1939 Contract. Henry County Historical Society
(New Castle, Indiana)

Castle had built a powerful labor movement. Factory workers from
the different local shops were connected to one another. They
were brothers and sisters, fathers and sons, uncles and cousins.
They were neighbors who belonged to the same churches. Their
kids played together. And they were bound together by a sense
of solidarity with all working people and an optimistic vision of
a better world to come. Much had been accomplished and much

more could be done.

My parents married in October 1940. The ceremony was held in the church parsonage on South Main Street. My mother had been forced to quit her office job because her employer didn't believe in married women working. I remember my mother saying that she and my father had reviewed their finances and decided they could get by on the $25/week—good union wages— my father was making at the Chrysler. Living with his parents on the farm west of New Castle while he was working at the plant, my father had been able to save a little nest egg. In 1941 Mom and Dad picked out a house plan and had the house built. Despite war in Europe and growing fear of American involvement, for them the future looked bright.

I never heard my parents say anything at all about the great union victories of the late 1930s. Nor do I remember my grandfather or grandmother saying anything about those union struggles. My grandfather had worked at the Chrysler since 1917—well before the plant was unionized. As a machine repairman at the shop, he held a relatively skilled job and may have been better paid than

Paul Hudelson and Charlotte Henry were married October 12, 1940. Fred Walker and Martha Henry were witnesses. The photo was taken in my maternal grandparents' backyard. My parents are on the viewer's right.

most. Still, he had a friend, Otis Van Bebber, also a machine repairman at the Chrysler, who was an active union man. I wish I knew what was said in the barbershops in New Castle during union campaigns in the fall of 1937 and the spring of '39. I wish I had asked my parents and grandparents about it all, but I was just a kid, and I didn't ask.

In 1940, after the victories of 1937 and 1939, the active supporters of the union must have thought that the years ahead would bring even further battles and further victories. Few then could anticipate the powerful forces that were plotting to destroy the UAW and bring back the days of total management control on the shop floor. Fewer still saw that the coming war would freeze labor's hands, postponing the inevitable battles to come.

World War II was a searing experience for my parents' generation. It was a terrifying, prolonged struggle, separating loved ones and demanding terrible sacrifices. Lives were lost or forever damaged. Like people in every other part of the country, the people of New Castle did their part. Many of the men served in the armed forces. Local women served as well. Everyone pitched in. Expecting to enter into active military service, my father responded to Uncle Sam's call, only to be rejected because of a deviated septum in his nose and consequent loss in his sense of smell. Several of my uncles did serve.

Memorial Day in my growing up years was always a somber occasion. But, it was also a time to reflect on what had been achieved. If people shared pain, they also shared a hard-won victory. Bruce C. Smith, a New Castle native, wrote *The War Comes to Plum Street*. The book tells the story of World War II as it was experienced by a group of neighbors on Plum Street in New Castle. Many people I know from New Castle read and loved that book. Published in 2005, it was one of the last books my father read. It meant a lot to him.

Immediately following the attack on Pearl Harbor and U.S. entry into World War II, UAW leaders in Detroit announced a "no strike" pledge. They promised to discipline any local that violated this pledge. Auto plants and autoworkers were converted to wartime purposes. In New Castle the Chrysler produced shell casings as well as parts for trucks, tanks and planes. With many male autoworkers in active military service, large numbers of women began to work in these plants.

While the contributions of these women to the war effort are generally well known, it is important to note that they were not the first women to work in the auto plants. Mary Wright began working at the Chrysler in New Castle in 1936. Margaret Davis is mentioned in early Local 371 records as an active member. Sometimes she was elected to represent the local at regional meetings or to serve on committees of the local. Helen Griffin was nominated to serve on the board for the local.

All was not smooth sailing for these women. In the years between 1937 and the start of the war, the federal government, frightened by deficits, cut back on some of the stimulus programs aimed at bringing the country out of the Depression. The result was a return to higher levels of unemployment. Some men, even within the union, began to argue that women shouldn't be taking jobs from male wage earners. The question of "the role of women in industry" became a hot topic for consideration in New Castle and in the nation as a whole. At one union meeting, "after much discussion on married women working," member Miss Jean Gibbins called on Local 371 to organize a meeting for all women working in the plant. A motion to do this passed. I have found no further mention of the proposed meeting.

With the coming of the war and the demand for workers in the auto plants, the issue of women working at The Chrysler was temporarily set aside. However, following the end of the war, many women were pressured to relinquish their jobs to returning veterans or to other men who were thought to need them more. It should also be noted that both before and during the war, wages for women in the auto plants were significantly less than for men.

The war also led to extensive recruitment of men to fill jobs in the auto plants now geared up to support the war. Among the men recruited were significant numbers of African-Americans. With the exception of Ford Motor Company, most of the automakers had not actively recruited African-American workers prior to World War II. Those African-Americans who did find jobs in auto plants prior to the war almost always found themselves restricted to the worst jobs—jobs that were low paying, dirty, dangerous, or unhealthy. During the war years, African-Americans were assigned to production jobs where they worked alongside white workers.

Given the prevalence of racism among white autoworkers, as there was among white Americans in general, it is not surprising that some white autoworkers resisted working with African-Americans. There were even some cases where white autoworkers went on strike over this. The most famous of these incidents was a strike at a Packard plant in the Detroit area in June 1943. This strike involved violence directed against African-Americans. Then UAW President R.J. Thomas condemned the strike, both for its racism and for its violation of the UAW "no strike" pledge. Threatened with expulsion from their jobs and from the UAW, the white strikers went back to work.

It is not clear how many African-Americans were working at the Chrysler in New Castle before or during the war. Nor is it clear how well they were accepted within the union. There were at least some African-Americans working there in 1950 and later. My impression is that most African-Americans working at the Chrysler were restricted to janitorial and other non-production jobs. I don't remember a single African-American working in the Heat Treat at the Chrysler when I worked there summers during the mid-1960s. I think it was only in the early 1970s that Chrysler began to address racial discrimination in its plants. Two people I know who worked with my father have told me that he was one of the men in the shop who helped make racial integration of production successful.

VICTORY & PEACE

With victory in Europe in May 1945 and victory in the Pacific in August, World War II finally came to an end. In the months that followed, American workers and their unions sought to reclaim the momentum that had carried them to decisive victories before the war. At the same time, employers launched what would prove to be a protracted campaign to contain and roll back the labor movement. A wave of strikes swept the country following the end of the war, with workers demanding an increase in wages to make up for ground lost during the war and calling for extensions of the ground gained in the pre-war period.

The UAW played an important role in giving direction to the post-war surge among American workers. The UAW pushed for a national health insurance program for all Americans, a proposal supported by President Truman. The UAW also campaigned for a better deal for its members. In late 1945 the UAW led a 99 day strike against Ford to win union security rights. In 1946, the UAW struck General Motors to win vacations, overtime pay, and stronger seniority rights.

The GM strike took on a radical edge with a UAW demand that the company open its books to public scrutiny and grant a large wage increase, based on GM's ability to do so, without raising the price of its cars. Although the campaigns for a national health insurance program and for open book negotiations failed, the strikes at Ford and GM were successful in winning important benefits for UAW members. The union victories were extended to all of the big three automakers, including Chrysler. These struggles brought important benefits to workers at the Chrysler in New Castle and were among the gains Goodson Marlow talked about in his interview many years later.

In that interview, Marlow also mentioned that pensions were one of the most important benefits won by the union. In the years before the New Deal, old age often brought poverty. The vast majority of workers in the mass-production industries had no pensions at all. They either kept working until they died, or, if no longer able to work, were taken in by relatives. There were also county poor farms that took in the destitute elderly. I remember such a poor farm near Memorial Park in New Castle. While the auto industry paid well, a Detroit study done in 1919 concluded that only if insurance, health, and savings were considered "optional" was the standard annual wage for an autoworker adequate to cover all necessary (non-optional) expenses.

An earlier study in Pittsburgh found that a steel worker who worked twelve hours per day, 365 days per year still would not earn enough to provide the barest necessities for a family of five. For the vast majority of American workers, financial security was beyond reach. The Social Security System, which included old-age pensions, was one of the great changes brought by the New Deal. But, while Social Security was a great help to many elderly persons, the old age benefits it offered (prior to increases during the Nixon administration) provided only a meager standard of living.

In the years after World War II, the UAW was one of the first unions to fight for increased Social Security pensions for all workers. When this failed, the UAW and other unions fought to win additional employer-funded pensions for their members. For the UAW, the opening round of the battle for pensions was its contract negotiations with Ford in 1949. John Bugas was chief negotiator for Ford. One of the signs popular among Ford workers marching on picket lines said, "There is a pension in your future, Bugas — How about ours?"

Speaking before a crowd of seven thousand Ford workers, all over sixty, UAW president Walter Reuther drove this point home: "If you make $285 an hour, they give you a pension, but if you make $1.65 an hour, they say you don't need it, you're not entitled to it, and furthermore it's socialistic." Reuther also pounded home the UAW slogan for the strike: "Too Old to Work and Too Young to Die." This slogan spoke to a real problem facing American workers in 1950.

After winning pensions for Ford workers in 1949, the UAW made the demand for pensions a central aim in its contract negotiations with Chrysler in 1950. Furthermore, the union demanded

The battle for pensions came to New Castle in January 1950. Here the union hall is prepared for an evening meeting. Henry County Historical Society (New Castle, Indiana).

that these pensions had to be paid for by regular contributions to a pension fund that made them "actuarially sound." Chrysler refused. Chrysler was willing to commit to pensions for its workers, but it was unwilling to establish an independent fund and make contributions that would pay for the future pensions. Essentially, Chrysler offered a promise. The company asked its employees to accept its word and avoid a strike. The UAW refused, sending the issue to its members for a vote to authorize a strike.

When the votes were tallied, the voice of the rank and file was heard loud and clear.

"STRIKE!"

With the strike deadline approaching, Chrysler put a statement addressed to its employees in the New Castle *Courier Times*, explaining what the company had already offered regarding pensions and other matters. The union replied with a statement explaining why it was saying "no" to this offer. Two days after that, at 10:00 AM on January 25, 1950, production workers in all Chrysler plants walked out. By prior agreement between Chrysler and the UAW, office workers and maintenance workers were allowed to continue working.

In New Castle the exit was orderly and peaceful. Making note of the non-violent work stoppage, the *Courier Times* commented on the strange quiet that followed: "The hum and buzz of the machinery and the constant pound of the hammers in the forge division ceased at the 10 a.m. deadline and the men started filing out."

In a follow-up story the next day, the *Courier* noted that all remained quiet, with "token picket lines" made up of "four to six men in each" around three of the main gates. The *Courier* story also noted that members of the AFL Die Sinkers Union, skilled men who worked in the die shop at the Chrysler, made no effort to cross the token UAW-CIO picket lines. This fact is of some importance, since as we have seen, there had been some tension at the Chrysler between UAW Local 371 and the AFL die makers.

In the past, similar tensions at other plants between CIO and AFL unions had led to significant conflict, some of it marked by violence. Sometimes employers tried to take advantage of such tensions, pitting one group against another. The decisive UAW-CIO victory in the NLRB election in late 1939 put an end to this. In 1950, during the UAW strike at the Chrysler, matters were peacefully managed. Leaders in both Local 371 and in the die makers worked together to prevent difficulties, and Chrysler made no

49

attempt to operate the plant during the strike.

With the strike underway in all Chrysler plants, the press speculated about the possibility that the strike might last as long as a month. The central issue concerned pensions. The UAW wanted regular specified contributions from Chrysler of ten cents per hour per employee to be put into a fund to pay future pensions and medical insurance. The initial demand for ten cents was made with the proviso that adjustments necessary to keep the fund "actuarially sound" would be subject to negotiations between Chrysler and the UAW.

Early in the strike these members of the AFL local union representing motion picture operators and stagehands came out to picket in support of their UAW brothers and sisters. The IATSE's roots go back to the 1890s. In 2016 the union represented some 130,000 members. Henry County Historical Society (New Castle, Indiana).

Chrysler was willing to pay for pensions, but was not willing to agree to such a fund with regular specified contributions. With the auto companies making record profits, the UAW thought it was in a good position to demand the ten cents per hour specified contribution. Chrysler sought to avoid that by persuading its employees to pressure their union into accepting the pension promise Chrysler had already made.

In a statement that appeared in the *Courier Times* on January 26, the day after the strike began, Chrysler ridiculed the union "kitty" fund. The statement went on to say that "Chrysler pays wages regularly. It pays its bill regularly. Its pension and insurance payments would be just as sure and sound." It also criticized UAW leaders, saying that "Calling Chrysler employees on strike, in the face of the pension and insurance benefits Chrysler has offered, shows again how difficult, if not futile, it is to try to do business with people who do such irresponsible things." It concluded by charging UAW leaders with putting its employees through unnecessary hardships.

Another statement appeared one week later, informing its employees and the public about how much Chrysler already paid for employee benefits. Yet another statement from Chrysler appeared two days later. It contrasted the plain language of Chrysler's promise with the "kitty fund" over which the union would share control. A final statement from Chrysler to its employees stressed that "cents per hour don't pay pensions" and insisted that "the strongest assurance of pension payments is Chrysler's guarantee, backed by the full credit and resources of the company." The union held out, demanding the establishment of a pension and insurance fund to which Chrysler would make specific contributions per employee per hour; contributions that would put commitments to future payments on an actuarially sound foundation.

A month passed with no settlement to the strike. A follow-up story in the *Courier Times*, quoted another statement from Chrysler claiming that nationally, Chrysler employees were collectively losing $1,188 per day during the strike. It may have been this statement that persuaded my parents they would never gain enough from the strike to make up for the lost wages. The same article in the *Courier* also pointed out that the UAW had offered to settle if the company would give ten cents per hour raise to each employee. Presumably the union thought such a raise would enable each of its members to begin building an individual nest egg for retirement. With Chrysler refusing to accept the union's offer, the strike dragged on into its second month.

At this point in its history, the UAW did not have a strike fund. The only financial support Chrysler workers received during the strike was meager help from a special assessment of UAW members. Knowing how stressed my own family's finances were, even during short term layoffs, I can understand how, facing a strike with no end in sight, my parents might have come around to the view that it would be best to give up on the strike and go back to work. No doubt other New Castle Chrysler employees were thinking along similar lines as the strike continued.

With grit and determination, Local 371 stood its ground. A strike kitchen was established on "I" Avenue just across from the Chrysler to feed pickets during the strike. Members of New Castle UAW Auxiliary 59, made up of wives of men employed at the Chrysler, worked in the kitchen.

Local 371 also organized meetings for families of members, explaining the purpose of the strike and trying to shore up support.

The strike would last 104 days. A strike kitchen was established across the street from the Chysler. Henry County Historical Society (New Castle, Indiana).

UAW Auxiliary 59 was made up of wives of UAW Local 371 members. They did the work in the strike kitchen during the long strike. Here some members of Auxiliary 59 take a lunch break of their own. Henry County Historical Society (New Castle, Indiana).

Support from families was crucial for winning the strike. Henry County Historical Society (New Castle, Indiana).

Strike supper. Henry County Historical Society
(New Castle, Indiana).

As the strike moved on into warmer weather, the union tried
to draw more people into picket lines around the plant gates, at
least on special occasions.

Pickets by the main gate to the Machine Shop. Henry County Historical
Society (New Castle, Indiana).

Richard Hudelson

A sound car livened things up. Henry County Historical Society (New Castle, Indiana).

The man on the viewer's right, is Earl Todd, President of UAW Local 371 when it was first formed. Henry County Historical Society (New Castle, Indiana).

There is some evidence of intimidation or physical violence by union activists against some who opposed the strike. Evidence to support this can be found in a chapter from a memoir written by Steve Dicken. Mr. Dicken's father, James T. Dicken, worked at the Chrysler and was an early and strong supporter of the union. In conversations with his son, James Dicken talked about a pro-union gang, The Flying Aces, which sometimes fought against anti-union thugs and beat up or threatened Chrysler employees who were not sufficiently supportive of the union. Dicken mentions one incident where a non-union supporter was thrown over the fence surrounding the plant. James Dicken was probably not himself a member of The Flying Aces. But as a strong union supporter he became aware of them. While there is nothing in Steve Dicken's memoir chapter that specifically mentions violence or threats of violence during the pension strike of 1950, the picture it provides of anti-union and pro-union violence is consistent with what is known from other direct witnesses to similar situations in other places and times.

There is no good reason to think New Castle in 1950 would have been free of such tough tactics. In fact, an account of union organization at the Rolling Mill in New Castle in the early 1940s includes mention of "goon squad" activity by UAW supporters there. Then there is also the "evidence" provided by my memory of my father's shredded jacket hanging in our basement and mentioned earlier in this book. Finally, there is an item that appears in *The Imp*, a two-page newsletter produced by UAW Local 371 on May 20, 1949. Under the heading "Scabs Beware!!" the newsletter suggests possible future actions against Chrysler workers not supporting the local. *The Imp* leaves these actions unspecified "for security reasons." In any case, although I am far from certain about this, I think that my father's shredded jacket was linked to the strike for pensions in 1950.

The strike went on for one hundred and four days. With their backs to the wall and their stomachs empty, the UAW rank-and-file held out and won.

In 1961, Frank B. Tuttle, a retired rank-and-file auto worker who had been the first Chrysler pensioner in the United States under the contract won in 1950, wrote a letter to Walter Reuther:

On my 65th birthday in January 1950 I had three important messages before me: from Social Security, telling me that I had an assured life income of exactly $38.69 a month; from Chrysler Corporation, declaring it would never grant the "preposterous"pension demands of our union; and one from you saying that those demands would be won, either at the bargaining table or at the picket line.

Chrysler managed to reverse the sequence— we went to the picket line first and the bargaining table afterwards, but today I am looking at pension checks of $157.46 a month. [This amount included both Tuttle's Social Security check and his Chrysler check.]

This letter shows what a difference the Chrysler pension made and why the struggle to win it was so important.

Chrysler workers had won a pension fund supported by regular payments by Chrysler for each employee. According to historian Nelson Lichtenstein, when the strike was finally settled, Walter Reuther, angry that Chrysler had forced a protracted strike over actually funding a pension fund, "refused to pose for the ritual handshake with Chrysler executives."

Winning pensions was a great victory for UAW workers. That this victory was won by workers, their families, and support received from other unions, neighbors, and friends made the victory all the sweeter. For many years, photographs taken in New Castle during the long battle for pensions at the Chrysler hung on a bulletin board in the UAW union hall there.

Moreover, the significance of that victory extended beyond employees of the Chrysler. In his history of the Ingersoll Rolling Mill in New Castle, Bob Perdue says that, "In looking at all of the information involved here, what really hurt the company's position most was the existence of the Chrysler plant in New Castle. Employees of each facility no doubt socialized and talked about working conditions. If the Chrysler folks got a 5% raise, why not the Ingersoll employees?"

I think Perdue was right about this. What's more, I think that folks from other unions almost certainly felt like they had won something too, like the union stagehands who manned an early picket line in the strike for pensions. In much of working-class New Castle there was a sense of union solidarity that connected union-minded workers in all of the factories. People from various plants lived in the same neighborhoods. Many were relatives by blood or marriage. They went to the same churches. They attended labor education classes sponsored by the UAW in New Castle. They stood with one another on picket lines. They saw themselves as part of a national labor movement and remained supporters of the New Deal program.

Many of these industrial workers were veterans of the Second World War. They saw themselves as Brothers and Sisters fighting for themselves, their families, their neighbors, their city and their country. In recent years we have honored these people as "the greatest generation." It is worth keeping in mind that very many of this greatest generation were union men and women.

In the 1950s, when I was growing up, New Castle was a union town. Many of those unions were products of the labor movement born in the 1930s and of the CIO created by that labor movement. Among those CIO unions were the following:

Communication Workers of America, Local 5804 (Bell Telephone)
Meat Cutters and Packing House Workers, Local 167
New Castle State Hospital Employees, Local 876
UAW Local 370 (Perfect Circle)
UAW Local 371 (Chrysler)
UAW Auxiliary No. 59 (Wives of Chrysler Workers)
UAW Local 466 (Pan American Bridge)
UAW Local 729 (Ingersoll Rolling Mill)
UAW Local 999 (Davis Gray Foundry)
UAW Local 1220 (Trainer Springs)
United Brewery Workers of America, Local 128 (Meadow Gold Dairy)
United Brotherhood of Carpenters and Joiners of America, Local 1910
United Paper Workers, Local 1058 (Hoosier Container)
United Rubber Workers of America, Local 238 (World Bestos)
United Steelworkers of America, Local 2614 (Western Products)

By the mid-1950s, all of these unions had their offices working out of the UAW Hall at 201 North Main.

In the summer of 2011 I traveled to New Castle to meet with some local people who had been leaders in Local 371 or done work on local history. On that trip I heard about the photos of the long strike for pensions at the Chrysler in New Castle. Don Davis, one of a group of local people who have worked on a history of the Chrysler plant, told me about the photos, which were in the New Castle Henry County Historical Society. Many of those photos appear above in this chapter. I regret that I am unable to identify most of the people in the photos. I wish I could. I wish I could thank each of them personally. They won the pensions that kept my parents going in old age.

Five years after those pensions were won, the Perfect Circle Company launched a fight to roll back the gains labor had won. It was part of a fight against labor that raged all across America.

THE NEW WAR ON LABOR

At the heart of the labor movement that spread across the United States in the 1930s was an ethics of solidarity. Workers and their families saw themselves as united in struggle to win a better life for themselves and their families. This ethics of solidarity stood in some tension to an alternative ethical standpoint, one focused on individual freedom, individual rights, and self-reliance.

To be sure, the perspective based on individual rights can be enriched by obligations of charity and love of neighbor. But there is a difference between charity and solidarity. In charity the fortunate help the unfortunate. Solidarity understands itself more as a relationship among equals, each needing the help of the others to win the better life they all seek. From this perspective, the vision of communities of free, self-reliant individuals seems utopian. In the world of modern industry and wage labor, freedom and prosperity can only be won by a united effort. All working people are brothers and sisters. Each has an obligation to aid the others. Each has an obligation not to betray.

In 1955, the tension between the two moral visions—the ethics of individual rights and the ethics of solidarity—came to a head in the Perfect Circle Strike in New Castle. That strike was one of the opening battles in a protracted national war on labor that continues to the present day.

The Perfect Circle Corporation was based in Hagerstown, Indiana, about twelve miles east of New Castle. The company was a family business. In 1894, Charles Teetor, from Hagerstown, worked in a bicycle shop in New Castle. Having invented a cycle designed to ride on railroad rails that could be used by railroad inspectors, Teetor opened a factory to build the cycle in Hagerstown. He later added a gasoline engine to drive the cycle. As the auto industry developed, the Hagerstown factory turned to assembling engines for automakers. With the auto industry growing, Teetor focused on manufacturing piston rings, which required a high level of precision.

In the early 1920s, Lothair Teetor inherited the company from his father Charles. Under Lothair's leadership, the company established a foundry in New Castle to make rough castings for the manufacturing plant in Hagerstown. Lothair Teetor adopted the continuous mass-production technology that had come to dominate the modern auto industry. These changes transformed the shop floor culture of Perfect Circle, replacing the small-scale, craft work atmosphere of the past with modern, efficiency-driven management practices, like those spreading throughout the auto and auto parts industries. Base hourly wages were reduced, but supplemented by piece-rate bonuses. Perfect Circle soon established itself as one of the nation's leading makers of piston rings.

Perfect Circle also adopted the paternalistic management practices popular in some American industries in the 1920s. It provided workers life and accident insurance, paid vacations, profit sharing bonuses, and leisure and recreation programs. However, management unilaterally decided all promotions and transfers without regard to seniority or employee input. When employees staged a walkout in 1929 to protest what they saw as unfair aspects of the piece-rate system, Teetor refused to meet with them.

The slump in the auto industry caused by the Depression put severe economic pressure on the company and its employees. Employees at the Perfect Circle plants in Hagerstown, New Castle, and, later, in Richmond turned to the newly formed United Auto Workers for help.

In March 1937, with support for the UAW growing in the region, Perfect Circle tried to head off the UAW threat by forming "employee councils" in its plants in Hagerstown and New Castle. Faced with the energized labor movement of the 1930s, employers around the country were forming "independent unions" and "employee councils" to head off unions connected to the larger labor organizations external to local control.

During the 1930s and early 1940s, similar so-called "independent" unions appeared at the Chrysler and at the Rolling Mill in New Castle. An article in the New Castle *Courier Times* reporting on the selection of individuals to serve on the employee councils at the Perfect Circle says straightforwardly that the councils were "formed by the Perfect Circle Company." In June 1937, inspired by sit-down strikes by autoworkers elsewhere, UAW supporters at the Perfect Circle foundry in New Castle staged a sit-down strike there. Perfect Circle management responded by offering employees a wage increase and by supporting the "independent" company union competing with the UAW.

As we saw in the previous chapter, in 1939 the UAW was able to win a decisive victory against the "independent" company union at the Chrysler in New Castle. However, the company union at the Perfect Circle foundry had sufficient support among employees in New Castle to defeat UAW Local 370 in NLRB elections in the early 1940s.

As the Perfect Circle Company flourished through the war years, the company was forced to hire many new workers to meet its military contracts. These new workers, many of them from Southeastern Kentucky, tipped the balance away from the company union and toward the UAW. According to historian David Anderson, the federal government, concerned about maintaining war production, "compelled Teetor to sign a union contract with his employees at both the New Castle [Perfect Circle] foundry and the Hagerstown main plant that included maintenance-of-membership clause that amounted to a union shop."

Anderson goes on to say that, "Once covered by a collective bargaining contract, union members at Perfect Circle displayed increasing militancy for the duration of the war, waging several wildcat strikes, protesting management's seniority procedures, demanding a say over piece rates, and then launching a strike that shut down production during the reconversion period [from war to peace] in protest of the company's layoff policy."

It is worth pausing for a moment for a brief reminder of what was in play at Chrysler and Perfect Circle in the period between 1937 and the end of World War II. Industrial America was born in the wake of the Civil War. While some industries began with craft unions inherited from the pre-industrial past, by 1900, most of industrial American was run on an "open shop" basis free of unions and collective bargaining.

By the 1920s "paternalistic capitalism" had become the favored ideology of many of the great leaders of industry. Business leaders saw themselves as men with the vision, knowledge, and character necessary to lead American industry and American workers into a prosperous future. Through organizations like the Chamber of Commerce, the National Association of Manufacturers, and the Citizens' Alliance, leaders in business and industry worked together to insure that government at all levels was friendly to business, that taxes were low, and that businesses were free to operate in a non-union environment. This was the era of labor spies, hired strikebreakers, and hired gunmen. It was also an era of anti-union injunctions, when judges sympathetic to the point of view of business leaders routinely issued injunctions prohibiting pro-union picketing or leafleting around a job site.

For the most part, this system prevailed through the 1920s and into the Depression years of the early 1930s. As the Depression wore on, business leaders sought to survive by cutting wages, increasing piece rates, laying off older workers, and, in general, throwing workers overboard. By the mid-1930s, workers at the grass roots level began to resist. A series of major strikes—including strikes among auto workers at the Auto-Lite plant in Toledo, Teamsters in Minneapolis, and Longshoremen in San Francisco—erupted into violent confrontations between workers on the one side and company "detectives," supported by local law enforcement and the National Guard, on the other side.

This kind of labor violence was not new to America. It had marked earlier labor disputes in the United States—like the railroad strike of 1873, the strike at Homestead Steel in 1892, the Pullman strike of 1896, the iron-mining strikes of 1907 and 1916, the mining wars in the coal fields in 1913-1914, and the steel strike of 1919. One of the things that made the 1930s different was the newly elected administration of Franklin D. Roosevelt, who was promising a "New Deal." By the mid-1930s it was evident to almost everyone that the unregulated capitalism of the post-Civil War era was not working.

In 1934, Congress passed the National Industrial Recovery Act (NIRA) intending to help bring the country out of the Depression. The act included a system of voluntary standards for minimum wages and maximum hours. The idea was to stem the wage cuts, speed-ups and longer hours imposed by employers trying to stay afloat—a downward competition that hurt working families.

The National Industrial Recovery Act of 1933 proposed voluntary standards for wages that would stem the downward spiral of the early depression. By displaying the NRA Blue Eagle businesses indicated that they followed the standards approved by the National Recovery Administration created by that act. The Blue Eagle was retired when the Supreme Court ruled the NIRA unconstitutional..

Employers who adhered to these standards could display the Blue Eagle of the National Recovery Administration. Section 7a of the NIRA gave federal approval for the right of workers to form unions for the purpose of collective bargaining. While some employers willingly cooperated with the NRA, others resisted. Some, like Chrysler and Perfect Circle, attempted to get around the law by promoting company unions as alternatives to unions like the UAW.

In May 1935, the United States Supreme Court ruled that the NIRA was unconstitutional. This ruling left the country in a difficult situation. On the one side, men and women who saw their economic well-being threatened by the arbitrary will of employers were determined to fight back by forming unions for collective bargaining. On the other side employers were determined to maintain their right to manage their own firms. Having promised a New Deal for America, and being sympathetic to the union organizing spreading across the country, Congress responded quickly to the court's ruling. In July 1935, Congress passed the National Labor Relations Act (Wagner Act). That act guaranteed the right of workers (with some tragic exceptions) to form unions for collective bargaining. It required employers to bargain with such unions, gave unions the right to strike, and established the National Labor Relations Board (NLRB) to oversee union-organizing elections and contract negotiations. The act also required the NLRB to enforce fair labor practices on employers.

The United States Supreme Court upheld the act by a five to

four decision on April 12, 1937. This act transformed labor relations in the United States and set the stage for events in New Castle in 1937 and the years that followed.

The court case that upheld the Wagner Act had its origins in actions taken by the Jones & Laughlin Steel Company. The company had fired ten of its employees who were attempting to form a union. The National Labor Relations Board, established by the Wagner Act, ruled that this action by the company violated the Act's guarantee of workers' right to organize. Jones & Laughlin argued that the Wagner Act was an unconstitutional violation of its right to hire or fire whomever it wanted. By upholding the Act, the Supreme Court established the basic constitutionality of the act with respect to hiring and firing.

But what about other practices employers commonly used to resist unionization? Could an employer lay off union members and retain non-union members? Could an employer lay off union members first and call them back last? Could an employer transfer union members to lower paid or less pleasant jobs? Could it reward employees who did not join the union with promotions or transfers to better jobs within the company?

If employers could do these things, being active in a union would become dangerous to a worker's well being, as well as to his or her family. Understandably, unions pressed for a system of seniority rules to govern lay-offs, transfers and promotions.

Could an employer provide financial or other support to a company union? Could it distribute literature in support of a company union to its employees? Could it require employees to attend "educational" meetings where company officials would present a case for a company union and against an "outside" union? Just what practices were "unfair" under the law and what practices were permitted?

It took time to sort all of this out. As we have already seen, issues about lay-offs, callbacks, and transfers arose repeatedly in the dealings between Chrysler and Local 371, with the union complaining about arbitrary actions by the company and pressing for extensions of seniority rights. In general, Chrysler and the UAW dealt with these issues in contract negotiations, gradually spelling out a system of agreed-upon rules. Although this process could not anticipate all difficulties in these areas, it did lay down a way of dealing with issues when they arose, and it did establish a climate of mutual respect within which unanticipated future problems could be handled without undue difficulty. For better or worse, Chrysler had come to accept collective bargaining with the UAW as a fact of life that would govern its management into the future.

Perfect Circle took another approach. It told the UAW to stick it, setting the stage for a ferocious battle of wills.

The Not So Perfect Perfect Circle

Things were different between the UAW and Perfect Circle than they were between the union and Chrysler. Management at Perfect Circle never reconciled itself to collective bargaining, unions, or the New Deal. Lothair Teetor, in charge of Perfect Circle from the late '30s through the war years, saw unions and the New Deal that supported them as "an encroachment on what he and other family members believed was their right to run their local business as they saw fit." Where Chrysler in 1939 had given up on the idea of a company union and accepted the UAW as bargaining agent for its workers, management at Perfect Circle continued to support an "independent" union into the early 1940s, when that sellout union managed to defeat the UAW in NLRB elections.

During the war, the federal government was determined to preserve labor peace in industries sensitive to the war effort. With contracts for production for the military, Perfect Circle expanded production and hired more employees. At some point during the war, whether because of increased support for the UAW resulting from the new hires, or because of an NLRB ruling that the "independent union" was really a "company union" in violation of the National Labor Relations Act, the federal government forced the company to sign a contract with the UAW. Still, even after signing this contract, Perfect Circle continued to protect its prerogatives, resisting efforts to spell out seniority rules to govern promotions and transfers, and refusing to negotiate with the union over piece rates. In short, while Chrysler and the UAW had developed a working relationship, Perfect Circle and the UAW had not.

As early as 1940 Lothair Teetor decided to carry his opposition to the UAW, unions, and the New Deal beyond the Perfect Circle Company. He became active in the Indiana Chamber of Commerce and the National Association of Manufacturers. He served four terms in the Indiana Legislature. Further, President Eisenhower appointed Teetor to a position as Assistant Secretary in the federal Department of Commerce. Having retired from his position as head of Perfect Circle in 1946, Lothair Teetor focused on working for lower federal corporate tax rates and opposing organized labor.

Ralph Teetor, a cousin of Lothair, took over as president of Perfect Circle. He was an able engineer and able businessman who shared the anti-union outlook that had pervaded Perfect Circle management throughout its history. Ralph Teetor led an expansion of the company, opening new facilities in Richmond, Indiana, as well as opening overseas subsidiaries. By the mid-1950s, according to *The Wall Street Journal*, Perfect Circle was "the nation's largest volume producer of piston rings."

Ralph Teetor's conservative view of the world leaned heavily on an idyllic vision of small-town America. Teetor believed that conflict between labor and management grew out of the "friction and petty irritations" caused by the "complicated" nature of modern society. He thought that such conflict was much less likely in small town America, where men in management were "neighbors and friends" of men and women working in the plant. "Our plant towns are such that Perfect Circle people and others are not in the grip of devastating political influences common in large cities," Teetor wrote in "Conversations with Ralph Teetor," his regular column in the employee newsletter. This distrust of cities and celebration of rural and small town life is deeply rooted in American thought. In Teetor's view there were no significant differences of class or hierarchy in the small towns of the Midwest. There, "all of our problems are common problems." There, all problems can be solved if people just willingly deal with one another on "a foundation of mutual respect."

The Teetor family and Perfect Circle undoubtedly felt an attachment to Hagerstown and did much for Hagerstown. A "History of Hagerstown" available on the town's website offers this testimonial to the town's debt to the Teetor family:

> The Teetor's factory brought many good jobs. Youngsters graduating from high school could work in the factory right at home. During the 1930s

depression, Perfect Circle shortened work hours to keep as many employees as possible receiving a paycheck. Perfect Circle was generous to the town and to the area. They gave money to the school, for the public library, and provided machines and tools for the high school industrial Arts classes. In 1956 Perfect Circle gave a large donation to Cambridge City [a nearby town] for their new gymnasium. Camp Wapi-Kamigi, a woods and lake property south of town, was acquired for Hagerstown Girl Scouts with the help of Ralph and Nellie Teetor.

Appreciation for what the Teetors had done for Hagerstown extended to men and women who worked in the Perfect Circle plant there. Sam Selke, an officer in UAW Local 370 who worked at the Perfect Circle foundry in New Castle, said about his own aunt and uncle who lived in Hagerstown and worked at the Perfect Circle plant there: "They thought there was nothing like the Teetors or Perfect Circle. . . . They thought I was crazy [for] being in the union." This sense of gratitude and loyalty to the Teetor family that owned and managed Perfect Circle goes a long way toward explaining why opposition to any union or support for a company union was strong enough within Perfect Circle plants to make it difficult for workers drawn to the UAW to establish strong locals in those plants.

Given their vision of the small-town Midwest and their knowledge of the loyalty to them among a significant number of their employees, management at Perfect Circle blamed attempts to form UAW locals in their plants on "outsiders" and "radicals" who had come to work in their plants, or on UAW staff organizers who, according to management, forced Perfect Circle workers into unions, kept them there through union-shop contracts, and then grew rich off union dues.

While it is understandable that Perfect Circle management might see things this way, it is difficult to square this view of the world with the complex reality at work. There was significant support for Perfect Circle management among workers in their plants, but there was also widespread support for the UAW. This support cannot be explained away as the work of outside radicals or outside union bosses.

One fundamental issue was related to wages. Wages for Perfect Circle workers were significantly less than those paid to factory workers at the Chrysler or to other factory workers across the country employed by major unionized corporations. With living standards for ordinary people rising around them, Perfect Circle workers wanted their families to share in this rising prosperity. One Hagerstown UAW officer put it bluntly, saying that Perfect Circle workers "badly needed" a substantial wage increase "to adequately feed, clothe, and house our families." In New Castle, a significant number of Perfect Circle workers lived in the Belmont neighborhood located just south of the factory. Houses there were built on lots smaller than what was normally required by New Castle city code. They lacked access to city sewer lines and relied on outdoor privies.

There was also that walk-out by workers in the Hagerstown plant in 1929, in protest of what they saw as unfair aspects of the piece rate system in the plant. Perfect Circle management refused even to meet with these workers, insisting on management's prerogative to stipulate these and other matters related to wages, transfers, promotions, and lay-offs. Was this an example of neighborly "mutual respect?" Were there no real problems that needed to be addressed? Is it really surprising that at least some workers in Perfect Circle plants saw the need for a real union?

Carl Evans came from Kentucky to work at Perfect Circle in December 1941. In 1955, he was president of Local 156, the UAW local in the Hagerstown plant. In talking about his decision to support the union, Evans mentioned unsatisfactory shop-floor conditions, low pay, and grievances that were never settled. He also talked about the injustice of a situation where the company could dictate wages and conditions of employment without workers having any real say in the matter. For him, support for the union was a matter of justice and of self-respect. Another worker, a man who grew up in Hagerstown and stood with UAW Local 156 in the Hagerstown plant, said later in life that he and other Perfect Circle workers "owe everything" to the union.

In the years after World War II, there was sufficient support for the UAW in both Hagerstown and New Castle for the UAW to win NLRB certification elections and annual contracts with Perfect Circle in both plants, although, in the words of historian David Anderson, "...it took months of long negotiations, strike threats, and the intervention of federal mediators" to do it. The contracts won addressed long-standing problems at Perfect Circle regarding seniority, transfers, and piece rates. However, in the late 1940s and early 1950s, Perfect Circle continued to resist the UAW's central goals. These were goals the union had won in its negotiations with the big three automakers that contributed to building peaceful relations between labor and management.

One of the union's goals was a company-wide contract with Perfect Circle covering all of its plants. In the case of Perfect Circle this would include the main plant at Hagerstown, the foundry in New Castle, and the two new plants opened in nearby Richmond after the war. Perfect Circle insisted on separate labor contracts with each plant. The separate deals with each plant allowed room for Perfect Circle to play workers at one plant against workers at another. In 1948, Perfect Circle promised workers at its unorganized Richmond plants a wage increase similar to what was won in the unionized Hagerstown and New Castle plants, provided Richmond workers voted against unionization. This meant that Richmond workers would live as "free-riders," sharing any gains won by the UAW in New Castle and Hagerstown without having to bear the costs of union dues or wages lost during strikes. The National Labor Relations Board later ruled that Perfect Circle's explicit promise to Richmond workers was illegal, but that ruling did not prevent the company from insisting on separate contracts at each plant.

A second UAW goal was to achieve pattern bargaining throughout the automotive parts industry. In pre-union days, companies in competitive industries had an incentive to cut labor costs as much as possible as a way of lowering costs of production. Even if an employer thought workers should have sufficient wages, health insurance and pensions, he could not afford to pay that much if his competitors were paying less. Pattern bargaining worked to establish a level playing field, where companies competing in a market faced the same labor costs. Pattern bargaining removed downward competition injurious to workers. By the mid-1950s, pattern bargaining had been established among the big three automakers. Perfect Circle consistently refused to consider pattern bargaining.

A third union goal was establishment of a union shop at Perfect Circle. Contracts including a union shop clause require all men and women working at a plant to be or become members of the union. Where a union shop clause is part of the contract negotiated between management and the union, there can be no free riding by workers within the shop who benefit by contracts won by the union but who pay no union dues. Having a union shop clause significantly strengthens the position of the union within a shop. Chrysler and the other automakers had accepted the union shop in 1950. Perfect Circle consistently refused to accept a union shop clause in any of its union contracts.

Perfect Circle also adopted a "take it or leave it" stance toward the UAW unions within its plants. The National Labor Relations Act required companies to bargain with unions elected by their employees to represent them. When, in 1948, employees at the UAW-organized Hagerstown and New Castle plants went on strike for higher wages, an industry-wide pattern for wages and benefits, and a union shop, Perfect Circle refused to negotiate on these issues. It kept its plants running for the duration of the strike and offered workers willing to cross union picket lines a wage increase, a pension, and increased seniority. Not surprisingly, this resulted in incidents of violence between union pickets and employees willing to cross picket lines. In Hagerstown, local police stepped in to protect employees willing to work during the strike. In New Castle the local police supported the union and refused to protect strikebreakers (scabs) until they were ordered to do so by a court injunction.

In the end, Perfect Circle's intransigent position paid off. In 1948, the company won the showdown with the UAW. Faced with coming cold weather and dwindling support for the strike among Perfect Circle workers, the union settled for what Perfect Circle had already offered to employees willing to cross picket lines.

In the aftermath of that settlement, Perfect Circle's leadership continued its resistance to unions and to the New Deal. Perfect

Circle executives were sent to a "Freedom Forum" seminar in Arkansas, where they attended lectures and films extolling American capitalism. The forum claimed that the achievements of the New Deal led to socialism and tried to show that unions could not help workers. When they returned, the executives toured the region lecturing on the virtues of American capitalism and the evils of the welfare state. Such lectures were also held within Perfect Circle plants, where employee attendance was compulsory.

This "educational" campaign may have had some long-term effect on the thinking of some people in the region, but it had little success in influencing Perfect Circle workers in the short term. Support for the UAW remained strong at the foundry in New Castle. In Hagerstown, where Perfect Circle thought it had gained the upper hand against the UAW, the company demanded a new NLRB certification election. The Taft-Hartley Act, passed in 1947, gave employers the right to demand such elections. In 1951, the NLRB held such an election. The UAW won sixty-eight percent of the votes. In addition, the UAW won representation rights in employee elections run by the NLRB at the two Richmond plants in 1951 and 1952.

Despite this clear indication of majority support for the UAW among employees in all of its plants, Perfect Circle fought on. In May 1955, the company terminated its four separate union contracts at each of its four plants. This action set in motion a series of steps culminating in a bitter strike that summer and fall. During two weeks of negotiations, the company held to a single "take-it-or-leave-it" offer. When the UAW countered with demands that included a union shop, Perfect Circle seized on this issue to force the strike.

Management portrayed its stand as a heroic effort to protect the individual worker's `right to work' from `compulsory unionism.' The company sent a letter to all of its employees. The letter said that Perfect Circle plants would remain open during the strike. It also said that employees had a legal right to continue working during the strike. In addition, it said that Perfect Circle would take all legal steps necessary to protect employees at work.

A strike began on July 25 at all four Perfect Circle plants. All the plants had been under UAW contracts. Employees at each plant had chosen the UAW to represent them and to negotiate for them in secret ballot elections conducted by the National Labor Relations Board. Support for the UAW was strongest at the foundry in New Castle.

On July 26, the first day of the strike, mass picketing by strike supporters prevented anyone from entering the plants. Two days later, the Perfect Circle Company obtained an injunction from the Superior Court of Wayne County, where its Hagerstown and Richmond plants were located, limiting the number of pickets at the Hagerstown and Richmond plants to five people at any one gate. With this injunction in place, workers not in support of the strike and some strikebreakers hired by the company were able to enter these plants, allowing some production to resume.

On August 1, Perfect Circle obtained a similar injunction from the Circuit Court of Henry County against mass picketing at the New Castle plant. However, in New Castle the order of the court was not consistently obeyed. On August 5, a group of pickets threw stones at the cars of workers entering the plant, and on August 15, a large group of pickets stoned a bus carrying strikebreakers into the plant and overturned four cars parked inside the fence surrounding the plant. Other incidents of attempted intimidation of strikebreakers and vandalism against the homes and cars of strikebreakers were reported in New Castle.

On September 19, mass pickets at New Castle prevented anyone from entering the plant. For the next eight days strikers succeeded in shutting down the plant. Perfect Circle responded by firing thirty-five of its striking employees for their role in this mass picketing. Among the fired employees was Carl Batchfield, President of UAW Local 370 in New Castle. In late September, fearing an assault on its plant, Perfect Circle management used a helicopter to transport guns and ammunition into the plant during the night.

On October 1, there was a regularly scheduled meeting of the District Auto Council of the UAW in Indianapolis. These meetings included representatives from UAW locals in Indiana and Kentucky. At this meeting the representatives present heard about the firings of Batchfield and the thirty-four other UAW

With the injunction on mass picketing in place, Perfect Circle tried to run its plants. Strike supporters turned to vandalism to try to discourage scabs. Doug Magers Collection (New Castle, Indiana)

activists at the Perfect Circle foundry in New Castle. After the meeting, a number of representatives from locals in and close to New Castle decided to show support for the strike; they would join the picket line at the foundry in New Castle on October 5.

One such representative was Paul Carper, from UAW Local 662 at the Delco Remy GM plant in Anderson, Indiana. Carper, along with fifteen to twenty-five others from Local 662, drove over to New Castle on the appointed day in private cars. They drove around town a bit, blowing car-horns, along with cars full of people from other UAW locals in the region. Eventually they headed for the Perfect Circle plant, parked their cars on Plum Street, and walked two blocks to the plant. There they found a crowd Carper estimated at between two and four hundred people. William Prosser, a Perfect Circle executive, placed the crowd at between 1,500 and 5,000.

Carper and his friends met people they knew from other UAW locals in the District, began marching around outside the plant gate, and began to sing labor songs, including "Solidarity Forever" and "Old Scabs They Never Die." Suddenly, gunfire erupted from inside the plant. Carper and some other pickets were shot. A single rifle bullet passed through both of Carper's legs. Enraged by the gunfire, pickets who lived near the plant ran home to get guns and returned to fire at those inside the plant. While no one was killed, by the time the gunfight stopped, five strike supporters and three inside the plant had been shot.

After this violent confrontation, New Castle Mayor Paul McCormack contacted Indiana Governor George N. Craig. On October 10, martial law was imposed on the whole of Henry County, of which New Castle is the county seat, and on parts of Wayne County surrounding the Perfect Circle plants in Hagerstown and Richmond. National Guard troops took up positions surrounding the Perfect Circle foundry in New Castle with machine guns and tanks. Guards were posted at other Perfect Circle plants as well.

Following October 5, the National Guard was sent into New Castle and parts of the surrounding area. Tanks and machine guns were positioned around the Perfect Circle foundry. Parts of the Beaumont Neighborhood, where many Perfect Circle workers lived, are visible in the background. Francis Miller/ Time & Life Pictures/Getty Images.

Bars were closed and there was a prohibition on liquor sales in the area under martial law. National Guard checkpoints were set up at key points in and around New Castle.

Overwhelmingly, local media blamed the union, union "thugs," union leaders, and outside agitators for the violence. In the wake of the violence and the blame directed at the unions, workers at the Hagerstown and Richmond plants began to return to work.

Following the violence of October 5, national media sent reporters to cover the strike at the Perfect Circle foundry in New Castle. Here members of UAW Local 370 who worked at the foundry vote. The man in the plaid shirt is Local 370 President, Carl Batchfield. The man in the suit is William Caldwell, staff man for UAW District 3. Caldwell rose to that position from the shop floor at the Chrysler. Francis Miller/Time & Life Pictures/Getty Images.

Despite the media support for the company, the union retained strong support in New Castle. There were municipal elections in New Castle in November 1955. A record voter turnout gave the Democrats a full sweep. Mayor Paul McCormack, the Republican candidate, was defeated by Sidney Baker, a pro-labor Democrat. Baker was a former mayor of New Castle—the mayor who spoke at the giant labor rally in New Castle in 1938. Chelsey Juday, manager of the Perfect Circle foundry in New Castle and the incumbent Republican running for City Council At-Large, received the fewest votes of all candidates running for office.

I had an *Indianapolis News* paper route in New Castle in 1955. Earlier that year I had noticed a splotch of yellow paint on the home of Joe Fisher, one of my customers on "H" Avenue. My mother told me that union supporters were throwing paint on the homes of Perfect Circle employees who did not support the strike. Fisher's wife was a Perfect Circle employee. I don't know if she worked in the plant or in the office. Neither my mother nor my father said anything further to me about the strike, as far as I can remember. There was a lot of tension in the air, with folks in New Castle on both sides.

I do remember feeling conflicted about it. On the one hand it seemed clearly wrong to vandalize someone's home. On the other hand, even then, I had a sense of the importance of solidarity. I also remember coming back to New Castle from my grandparents' farm one evening after the events of October 5. Our 1947 Chevy was stopped at a National Guard checkpoint. Guardsmen with guns approached our car and talked to Dad. They had him open the trunk and searched the car for guns.

National Guard checkpoints were established on roads running into New Castle. Guardsmen searched cars for guns. Doug Magers Collection (New Castle, Indiana).

There was something ominous about the heavy Guard presence and the occasional tank I saw in the street. Like Dad's slashed jacket hanging in the basement, these things seemed to cast a shadow over all of labor's struggles. Still, my heart was with the union. On that day in 1955, a child became a union man.

THOSE TROUBLESOME OUTSIDE AGITATORS

A story covering the first day of the Perfect Circle strike in Hagerstown appeared in the *Chicago Tribune* on July 27, 1955. The story carried the headline: INDIANA GOONS SLUG WORKERS; POLICE WATCH. A few lines below this header, the article went on to say that police had "failed to subdue goon squad violence" and that "a mob of 300 to 500 shouting goons, most of them imported from other Indiana cities, terrorized non-strikers and company executives who sought to enter the plant." The reader who goes beyond the headline and the opening paragraph will find that there were Hagerstown workers among the "mob," and that the "outsiders" came from New Castle, Richmond, Anderson, Connersville and Indianapolis. One car came from Terre Haute.

A map published with the article in the *Chicago Tribune* shows that these places are not far from Hagerstown. They are all places within the UAW District 3 Auto Council, with UAW locals located in each of the towns on the map.

For the duration of the strike, most of the "outsiders" identified in press coverage came from New Castle, Anderson or other nearby towns. They worked at the Chrysler or Rolling Mill in New Castle, or at Delco Remy in Anderson. UAW Locals represented workers in all of those plants. Some of those outsiders would also have been relatives, neighbors or friends of striking Perfect Circle employees. A search of the New Castle City Directories for 1955 and nearby years shows that many of the Chrysler and Rolling Mill employees mentioned in press accounts as active in supporting the Perfect Circle strike have addresses listed on the same streets as the Perfect Circle employees who supported the strike.

UAW activists from Anderson Local 662 undoubtedly had personal connections with people on strike at Perfect Circle. There was an overlapping rural area spotted with several small towns. As we have seen, UAW activists in Anderson had played

83

UAW members from nearby locals supported their union brothers and sisters during the Perfect Circle strike. Most of the men in this photo are from UAW Local 662 in Anderson. Walter P. Reuther Library, Archives of Labor and Urban Affairs, Wayne State University.

something of a leading role in the development of the UAW locals in the area. Activists from Anderson were present at the Second UAW Convention in South Bend. In the crucial spring of 1937, unionists who had experienced a trial by fire in organizing plants in Anderson supported activists in New Castle organizing Local 371. They were also there to support the strike at Perfect Circle.

Paul Carper, the UAW activist from Anderson Local 662, was among the pickets shot at the Perfect Circle Plant in New Castle in October 1955. A trustee and former Sunday school teacher at his Church of the Nazarene in Anderson, Paul was also the father of eight children. In testimony before a U.S. Senate Committee investigating what happened the day he was shot, Carper talked a lot about solidarity. He said that he and others from UAW locals in the region came to New Castle as a result of an informal decision reached by representatives from area locals, following a meeting of the UAW Region Three Auto Council. He said it was an attempt to express solidarity with the struggle there, that no one brought guns, and that no one expected violence. Carper was an "outsider" in the sense that he did not work at the Perfect Circle foundry in New Castle, but only in that sense.

A lot of the "outsiders" on the picket lines at the Perfect Circle plant worked at the Chrysler in New Castle. Rual Vincent was one of those Chrysler employees. His mother had moved from Kentucky to work at the Chrysler before Rual went to work there. Rual would later be elected President of UAW Local 371. There was a history of mutual support between Local 371 at the Chrysler and local 370 at Perfect Circle. As early as 1938, UAW Local 371 at the Chrysler in New Castle had talked about "taking in" UAW locals at Perfect Circle and Ingersoll. These "outsiders" from the Chrysler involved in the Perfect Circle Strike were not so far removed. They were union brothers and sisters, neighbors, relatives, and friends of the striking Perfect Circle workers acting upon their felt moral responsibility of solidarity with fellow workers, not "goons" sent by UAW "bosses" to terrorize local people. Two of the five union pickets shot by gunfire from within the Perfect Circle worked at the Chrysler.

If outsiders were less outside than some reports suggested, insiders were more involved than those same reports suggest. Employees at all four Perfect Circle plants had voted to have the UAW represent them in secret ballot elections conducted by the National Labor Relations Board. Strike votes had been won at all four plants, and significant numbers of workers at all four plants supported the strike. Even at Richmond, where support for the strike was weakest, Perfect Circle management reported that about half the employees at one plant and two thirds at the other were not reporting for work. Following court orders against mass picketing, the number of employees entering plants to work did increase. So, too, did the number of acts of violence involving vandalism of property and threats against working employees. While perpetrators of these acts were often not identified, in cases where they were identified they involved other Perfect Circle employees, not "outsiders."

In New Castle, where support for the strike was strongest, periodic returns to mass picketing in violation of the court order succeeded in shutting down production and led to a significant number of arrests. A comparison of the names of individuals arrested for such "illegal" picketing published in the *Courier Times*, with the New Castle City Directory listing places of employment, shows that most of those arrested were Perfect Circle employees. In one case involving fifty arrests, thirty-one of those arrested were Perfect Circle employees, four were relatives of Perfect Circle employees, three were Chrysler employees, two were Ingersoll employees, and one was identified in the press as an official of the UAW International. That official was William Caldwell, in 1955 serving as Director of UAW Region 3. Caldwell had risen to that position from the shop floor at the Chrysler.

The remaining ten names listed do not appear in the City Directory. They may have been Perfect Circle employees from Anderson, Connersville, or from one of the many small rural towns in the region not listed in the New Castle City Directory. People living in these small towns often worked at factories in the surrounding region, as my father did when he lived on a farm near Cadiz and first worked at the Chrysler.

If the *Chicago Tribune* account of the start of the strike exaggerated the role of outsiders, it also exaggerated the extent of violence. While the Hagerstown Exponent paints a picture of events much like the account in the *Chicago Tribune*, the New Castle *Courier Times* and the *Cincinnati Enquirer* say nothing about mob violence, mentioning only minor charges resulting from picket-line confrontations in Richmond, where Perfect Circle plants were kept in operation, and one incident in Hagerstown where the plant there was not in operation. In New Castle, where the Perfect Circle plant was closed, all was peaceful.

Reports suggesting that mass picketing at the start of the strike and later during the course of the strike involved outside union "goons" and "thugs" terrorizing and intimidating local workers were misleading in several ways. The amount and nature of violence was greatly exaggerated; most of the incidents involved no outsiders; the outsiders that were involved came from geographically close locations and were mainly relatives or neighbors of Perfect Circle workers. These "outsiders" were motivated by a morality of solidarity. They were acting in support of a significant group of workers within the Perfect Circle Plants, where workers had voted in favor of UAW representation and in favor of the strike.

Hagerstown on the first day of the Perfect Circle Strike. Hagerstown was home to the first Perfect Circle plant. The Perfect Circle also had a foundry in New Castle and two other plants in Richmond. All were close to Hagerstown. Walter P. Reuther Library, Archives of Labor and Urban Affairs, Wayne State University.

The *Chicago Tribune* was at that time a leading conservative newspaper openly opposed to the New Deal and to organized labor. Its depiction of striking union members as goons was not untypical. Similar claims had saturated media depiction of unions in the long decades before the breakthrough of the 1930s. They became part of the conceptual furniture in people's minds. These scurrilous stereotypes were still there after World War II, when organized business sought to check and reverse labor's gains of the late 30s. They are still with us today. Even in cases where union organizers employed tough tactics to stop scabs from crossing a picket line, the amount of violence reported in the press is often wildly exaggerated and its causes not explained. Labor organizing and strikes have at times been accompanied by violence, but who initiated the violence often remains unclear.

The National Labor Relations Act (Wagner Act), passed in 1935 and approved by the Supreme Court in 1937, finally institutionalized a compromise that tried to honor both of these moral duties—collective solidarity versus individual rights. The full title to that act was "An act to diminish the causes of labor disputes burdening or obstructing interstate and foreign commerce, to create a National Labor Relations Board, and for other purposes." The act compelled employers to recognize and bargain in good faith with unions elected by their employees to represent them. The act permitted strikes. It also permitted compulsory membership agreements and mass picketing by unions. Labor observers at that time were surely right when they said this legislation paved the way for peaceful formations of the unions.

THE WAGNER ACT

The Wagner Act of 1935 gave legal status to the labor movement bubbling up from within industrial America during the depression of the 1930s. That labor movement was built upon a moral framework of working-class solidarity in struggle against the dominant power of employers. This was a framework inherited from the past—from the struggles of working people in the decades following the Civil War into the decades of the twentieth century—from the Grangers, Populists, Knights of Labor, and IWW to the AFL-CIO. "An Injury to One is a Concern to All" was a principle of the Knights of Labor founded in 1870. "An Injury to One is an Injury to All" was the version of this same principle adopted by the Industrial Workers of the World in the early twentieth century.

The specific contours of this moral framework varied with time and place. Sometimes it involved the struggle of an immigrant ethnic community against the "English" bosses. Sometimes it involved an internationalist, and perhaps utopian, vision of a

Richard Hudelson

socialist future uniting working people in justice, peace, and prosperity for all. The labor movement that emerged from the 1930s was neither utopian nor limited to a particular ethnic community. It understood the exact nature of that New Deal as a work in progress, and saw the unions and the ballot box as the instruments for advancing the cause. Those who embraced this vision saw themselves as brothers and sisters acting in solidarity to overcome the injustices of the past and claim a better life for themselves and all working people.

To be sure, there were often failures of solidarity in this labor movement. Women, African-Americans, Latinos, and Asians, were often excluded, overlooked, or taken for granted, as were farm workers and domestic workers. Still, despite these glaring shortcomings, union minded people lived within a moral framework of solidarity in struggle that placed each individual within a particular moral drama that went beyond the self.

This moral framework of solidarity in struggle against oppressive power of the owners of capital did not fit well with the moral framework of individual rights underlying property law in the United States. The courts were manned by judges, often from the property-owning class, steeped in respect for the law and the legal precedents that protect the propertied class. Many had little interest in fitting powerful unions into the legal framework inherited from the past.

The National Industrial Recovery Act, the first attempt to legitimate union power, was struck down by the Supreme Court as unconstitutional. The Court approved the National Labor Relations Act, the second attempt to make room for union power, by a narrow five to four vote. Subsequent decisions by the Court soon reined in the unions and tipped the balance back toward the labor laws in place before the NLRA.

In 1938, the Court ruled that employers had the right to continue operating struck plants and the right to hire workers to replace workers on strike. In 1939, the Court ruled that sit-down strikes were illegal and employees engaging in them could be fired, even if the sit-down-strike was inspired by unfair labor practices by management. In 1946, Republicans opposed to strong unions gained control of the congress. In 1947, the newly elected Congress passed the Taft-Hartley Act. The Act revised the National Labor Relations Act to further restrict the power of unions and to tip the balance back in favor of the corporate class. It allowed states to pass "right-to-work laws" prohibiting union shops. It also made mass picketing illegal if it became coercive. This undermined the power of a union to enforce a strike vote by its members. Taken together, these changes to federal labor law virtually returned things to the way they were in America's violent pre-NLRA past.

In New Castle, as in all of its other plants, Chrysler had come to accept the kind of collective bargaining envisaged in the National Labor Relations Act of 1935. It signed a contract with the UAW in 1937. After the strike in 1939, it abandoned efforts to organize an "independent" union as an alternative to the UAW. Chrysler management accepted the UAW as the democratically elected representative of its production employees, with a few UAW-sanctioned exceptions. Chrysler did not try to persuade its employees to leave the UAW. It did not call for the NLRB to hold new elections to test whether or not the UAW still had support. It made no effort to operate its plants during the long strike in 1950. And while Chrysler did use local newspapers to try to persuade its employees to pressure the UAW to end that strike, it did not attempt to persuade employees to cross union picket lines.

In 1951, Chrysler signed a union-shop agreement, accepting the overwhelming secret-ballot vote by Chrysler employees, under auspices of the NLRB. As a result, Chrysler did not experience anything like the violence that surfaced during the strikes at Perfect Circle in 1948 and again in 1955. Despite the real drama of the long strike in 1950, things remained peaceful, with strike discipline maintained by only a handful of pickets at factory gates.

Things were different at Perfect Circle. In 1948 and again in 1955, Perfect Circle informed its employees that its plants would be open during strikes approved by vote of its employees, told its employees that each had a right to work during the strike, and promised to do everything it could within the law to protect those employees willing to work. It also offered financial incentives to employees willing to work during the strike.

In 1955, the UAW hoped to keep Perfect Circle plants closed

by having mass pickets at all of its plants. In mass picketing, a large number of strike supporters—union members, families of union members, and other union supporters—gather around the plant where the strike has been called by a vote of the union members. This makes it difficult for scabs or hired strikebreakers to enter the plant.

Mass picketing involves both moral persuasion and an implicit coercive threat. If I try to scab on my fellow workers and I see a crowd of them with their families pleading with me not to betray them, my conscience may bother me enough to cause me to abandon the idea of going to work. If my conscience is too weak to keep me from crossing the picket line, I may abandon the idea of going to work out of fear that I'll be pushed or punched or hit with a rock. Mass picketing played a major role in the late 1930s, when tens of thousands of workers in previously non-union industries managed to win union recognition and conduct successful strikes.

In the 1939 strike against Chrysler, the UAW used mass picketing to prevent the use of scabs to work in the plants. Here we see mass pickets at the Dodge Main plant in Hamtramck in the Detroit area. Walter P. Reuther Library, Archives of Labor and Urban Affairs, Wayne State University.

Monday, July 25 was the first day of the 1955 strike at Perfect Circle plants. Both the company and the union focused efforts on the two Richmond plants, where support for the strike was weakest. Perfect Circle made no attempt to operate the plants in Hagerstown and New Castle. It did attempt to operate the plants in

Richmond that day. Not surprisingly, there were confrontations there between union pickets and workers who crossed the picket lines to work in the plant.

According to a Perfect Circle official, about half of the workers at one plant and one third at the other reported for work that day. According to a union official, the Richmond police force assisted some workers in passing through the massed pickets into the plants. Historian David Anderson's account of the strike says that union pickets effectively closed down all four of the Perfect Circle plants in the first few days of the strike. This suggests that many workers reported for work, but most were dissuaded by the union pickets despite whatever police presence there was that day. In all, four pickets were arrested that day on charges of disorderly conduct.

At Hagerstown, where some newspapers would report massive violence or threats of violence by union "goons," a grand total of two people were arrested. Both were charged with public intoxication. In New Castle, where support for the union was strongest, Perfect Circle made no effort to operate its foundry. There, all was peaceful.

Whatever the level of violence or threat of violence may have been at Richmond and Hagerstown, Perfect Circle thought that level was high enough that it could convince the court to prohibit mass picketing at its plants. Immediately after the incidents at Richmond and Hagerstown, Perfect Circle approached a Wayne County court asking for an injunction against mass picketing at its plants at Richmond and Hagerstown.

The Taft-Hartley change to federal labor law, passed by Congress in 1947, did not prohibit mass picketing, but it did prohibit mass picketing that was coercive in nature. So it would be legal for masses of union members and their supporters to congregate at a plant gate and plead with would-be scabs not to cross the picket line, but it would not be legal for the massed pickets to block, restrain, or strike anyone trying to cross the picket line. In addition, the prohibition against coercive picketing would prohibit coercive threats of injury directed at persons attempting to cross a picket line.

This legal framework attempts to strike a balance between

the right of workers to collectively bargain with their employers and the rights of individual employees and employers. While granting the union the right to represent workers, it also restricts their ability to strike during the terms of a contract, preventing wildcat actions.

Central to the way the law defines that balance is the distinction between persuasion and coercion. Is loud chanting or singing by pickets permitted? Are rousing speeches supporting the strike permitted? What if the speeches exhibit significant anger regarding the possibility of someone crossing the picket line? Is it permissible for pickets to shout at individuals trying to cross a picket line? Is telling someone he ought to be ashamed of himself allowed? Is calling an individual a "scab" allowed? If a single picket pushes an individual trying to cross a picket line does that make the whole picket line illegal? Would such an act be illegal even if strike leaders were trying to restrain aggressive pickets? What if the aggressive act comes from two drunken men whose behavior is not the norm for the pickets? If three muscular union men approach me, coldly look me in the eye, and ask me to "please" not cross the picket line, have I been threatened?

These questions are not easy to answer. A judge uncomfortable with heated disagreement may rule they are coercive threats, where a judge more comfortable with it might not. A judge with little contact with union people may find coercion, where a judge who knows union people personally might not. A judge alarmed by newspaper talk about "union goons" may be quicker to issue an order against mass picketing than a judge skeptical of such a claim. A judge sympathetic to unions may allow more slack than a judge unsympathetic to them. According to one account of the Perfect Circle strike at Richmond in the early days of the strike, several men were arrested "for simply calling a scab a scab."

In Henry County, where Perfect Circle's New Castle foundry was located, strong support for the strike among employees and significant mass picketing kept the plant closed. Despite the absence of violence there, on August 1, Perfect Circle was able to get a temporary restraining order against mass picketing, limiting the number of pickets to five. With incidents occurring at Richmond and Hagerstown, the mere presence of mass pickets at plant gates in New Castle may have had an intimidating effect on workers there who wanted to return to work. Still, the court injunction significantly curtailed the freedom of speech and freedom of assembly of union pickets and their supporters. More importantly, it left the union powerless to prevent scabs and replacement workers hired by Perfect Circle from taking their jobs.

Underlying the increasingly tense situation leading up to the shootings of October 5 were two conflicting moral outlooks. Strike supporters viewed fellow workers willing to work during the strike as traitors who would sell out their fellow workers in exchange for personal gain. Employees willing to work saw the union and union pickets as violating their individual liberty.

The Taft-Harley Act of 1947 prohibited picketing that prevented "replacement workers" from working in the plant. The injunction issued by the courts in Henry and Wayne Counties limited the number of pickets to five. These pickets at the Perfect Circle foundry in New Castle in September 1955 are in defiance of a court order. Soon after this photo was taken, police arrived to disperse the pickets, allowing some workers to enter the plant. Some of the pickets were arrested. Doug Magers Collection (New Castle, Indiana).

There is a difficult moral issue here. Is it morally permissible for union members—even local union members representing a majority of workers in a local plant—to in any way prevent or attempt to prevent fellow workers from entering a plant to go to work? Don't individual workers have a right to liberty—a right to work if they please to do so? Perfect Circle management thought that all workers had such a right to work. They saw their actions in the course of the strike as aimed at protecting that "right to work." William B. Prosser, general manager for Perfect Circle, was clear about this when he testified before the McClellan Commttee:

> "We feel that we are making a contribution to the
> right-to-work cause by the position we have taken
> in this strike. The [non-striking] employees are
> making a personal contribution to the crusade which
> will undoubtedly eventually result in the passage of
> laws establishing the right of an individual to work
> where he pleases without paying tribute to anyone."

During the Perfect Circle strike, similar endorsements of a right to work belonging to each individual worker appeared in a number of letters to the editor. Perfect Circle pushed the idea that each individual has a right to work if he or she chooses to do so. They appealed to the right to liberty—a right that most of us hold dear.

Does the "right-to-work" always override the need for solidarity? Is this kind of "liberty" a bogus proposition or a real principal that deserves a court's protection?

What Is Freedom Without Dignity?

Is democracy coercive? When representatives of companies like Perfect Circle claim that every worker must be free to cross a picket line if he or she chooses, their assertion represents only one side of this moral issue. On the other side is the morality of solidarity, which demands that we not betray those who are engaged in just action. Seen from this side of the dispute, the worker who crosses the union picket line is a traitor to his brothers and sisters who are fighting for fair wages and a safe work environment for everyone.

Most of us believe in democracy—in government of, by, and for the people. For over a century, the idea of extending and deepening democracy has been one of the values underlying the labor movement. Unfortunately for working people, the democratic tide has not extended into corporate practices or governmental economic policies.

With the development of modern industry and modern market systems, the majority of people have no control over economic factors affecting them. Market systems concentrate wealth in the hands of owners of capital. Decisions made in banks and boardrooms far away can shutter a factory and take away a working family's ability to make a living. Recessions, depressions, and market panics over which local people have no control have left them stranded in poverty, their savings exhausted.

The idea of "social democracy" emerged in response to such problems. It called for bringing economic life under democratic control, giving the people—through their elected unions and elected governments—the power to manage markets in order to make them work for the good of the people, and creating social safety nets to protect working people from economic forces beyond their individual power to control. In Europe and elsewhere, Social Democratic political parties emerged, successfully advocating for extending democratic control over economic life.

In the United States, a majority of American voters rejected this Social Democratic model as too "socialist." But, even in the U.S., the need to give people some democratic control over economic forces has affected public policy. The National Labor Relations Act, with its recognition of the right to collective bargaining, was a part of this effort to bring economic forces under democratic control.

Though it fell short of the kind of social democracy institutionalized in other countries, the right to collective bargaining was widely viewed in the 1930s and 40s as an American version of "industrial democracy," a way for the American people to gain at least a degree of control over economic forces affecting them. Through democratic voting, employees could decide if they wanted a union, which union they wanted to represent them, whether or not to call a strike, and whether or not they approved of contracts negotiated on their behalf.

Claims by individual workers to a "right-to-work" during a strike approved by fellow workers conflicts with the principle of majority rule underlying democratic decision-making. Claims by employers to have a right to hire scabs—so called replacement workers—undermines the democratic power of employees to have some say over their working conditions.

There is a further moral problem here that cannot be ignored. In attempting to organize a union or win a strike, workers share a common goal and work together to achieve that goal. In each of these cases, workers engage in collective action. There is a well known collective-action problem confronting all such efforts. It is a problem faced by the labor movement, but also by many other forms of collective action.

Consider, for example, providing for our national defense. This is something that is vitally important to all of us. It is also very expensive. So, how should we pay for it? In the real world, of course, we do it by paying taxes. But for the moment, suppose we live in a society where there are no taxes—what we will discuss later as a "libertarian paradise." If each of us will voluntarily pay a part of the cost of defense, we can manage. Given how important a national defense is to each of us, it seems likely that each of us will be willing to pay our share. But will we?

I might think that if everyone else pays his or her fair share and I don't, there will be enough to provide for the national defense. My family and I will be protected from external aggressors, and it will cost me nothing. But if the others don't pay and I do, there will not be enough money to provide for the national defense. So the rational thing for me to do is to let others pay for the national defense while I enjoy the protection it provides and hold onto the extra cash I didn't spend. In acting this way I become a "free-rider." I enjoy the ride provided by being protected with a national defense without having contributed to it myself. The free-rider problem is found in many situations involving collective action.

How are we going to deal with situations like this? We might have a big campaign to get people to voluntarily contribute to the national defense. David Bergland, the Libertarian Party candidate for President of the United States in 1984, proposed voluntary contributions to do just that. In his book, *Libertarianism in One Lesson*, Bergland opposed all taxation as a form of theft. He called taxation "using force to steal the earnings and property of other people." Bergland favored paying for national defense and police protection by voluntary contributions, holding that, "Most people agree that national defense and protection of constitutional rights are important and would voluntarily support them." Bergland may be right in thinking that most people regard national defense as important, but his thinking ignores the free-rider problem.

In the real world, of course, there must be taxes. Each of us is compelled by law to pay a portion of what it costs to provide for the national defense. Some such coercion is a common way of dealing with free-rider problems. Most of us accept this as a morally legitimate way to deal with them, at least in contexts where the coercion is done by individuals or institutions widely accepted as having legitimate authority. America was not built on pure libertarian foundations. What the American revolution-aries objected to was not coercive taxation as such, but taxation imposed by illegitimate authorities. The slogan was "no taxation without representation," not "no taxation."

Where there is no consensus on what constitutes a legitimate exercise of coercion, free-rider problems are more likely to generate social conflicts involving different moral claims. These conflicts can have tragic outcomes. Consider the American Revolution. Revolutions require collective action. They face the free-rider problem that bedevils any collective action. Since taking part in a revolutionary action is a risky thing, it is tempting to hang back and let others act, even if one agrees with the need for revolution.

In colonial America, each colony thought of itself as having sole power over taxation of its citizens. During the revolutionary war, the army, under the overall command of George Washington, suffered from a chronic lack of arms, ammunition, tents, blankets, shoes, clothing and food. Because the Continental Congress lacked the power to tax, it could only plead with the colonies that each tax its citizens in order to equip the army. This created a collective action problem. Each colony was inclined to hang back, realizing that if the other colonies contributed, success was possible without its own contribution. Each also realized that if others did not contribute, its own payment would fail to be enough and would be wasted. Facing a continued lack of basic supplies (or pay), American soldiers began to drift away. Little by little the American army was disappearing.

Another collective action problem bedeviled Washington. He was having great difficulties purchasing food for American soldiers in winter camp at Valley Forge. Although Washington had some funds on hand, and farmers in the surrounding area had ample food to sell, the British encamped in New York could pay "in solid pounds sterling" while the Americans could pay only in currency of questionable value. This gave even farmers who supported the revolutionary cause a strong economic incentive to sell to the British. If only one farmer sold to the colonial army and others did not, that lone farmer's sacrifice would not help, and the American cause would fail. If other farmers did support the American cause and he did not, the collective end would succeed without his own financial sacrifice.

Reflecting on these problems, George Washington wrote, "We must take the passions of men as nature has given them . . . I do not mean to exclude altogether the idea of patriotism . . . but I will venture to assert that a great and lasting war can never be supported on this principle alone." Washington became a supporter

Richard Hudelson

of the need for a strong central government with the power to raise taxes.

Unions face similar free-rider problems. Consider the task of organizing a union in a non-union shop. That is a shop where the workers' union dues are not mandatory. Suppose wages are low and working conditions are terrible. Suppose that absolutely everyone agrees that having a union to bargain with management would be a good thing. Still, there is a free-rider problem here. Suppose you work to form a union but most of your co-workers don't join in the campaign. You give up time and effort and gain nothing.

Now suppose most others work to form a union and you don't. If enough of the other employees put in the effort, the union is won, you benefit along with each of the others, and you didn't have to put out any effort. Further, in the real world, employers often punish those employees who work to organize a union and reward those who don't. Is it any wonder that workers tend to hang back, to let others do the work? Individual incentives push each employee toward being a free-rider. It takes a strong sense of solidarity to overcome such individual incentives.

Once a union is in place, it faces a second free-rider problem. Suppose you have a union in the place where you work. Suppose the union has successfully negotiated contracts improving pay and working conditions for everyone in the plant. Should you become a member of the union or renew your membership? That costs money. If you pay and others don't, the union doesn't survive and you lose the benefits and your dues. Suppose others pay and you don't. The union survives, you continue to enjoy the benefits, and you save those union dues to spend on something else.

The free-rider issue has long been a problem for the labor movement. Consider this comment from "The Imp," the newsletter of UAW Local 371 at the Chrysler in New Castle. The newsletter was distributed in May 1949, before the UAW won a union shop contract with Chrysler.

SCABS BEWARE ! !

For many, many months the officers of Local

371 have been asked by many of the good Union members to do something about the scabs in our plant who continue to ride our coat tails and benefit by the gains made by the Union. . . . The Union negotiates paid holiday—the scab takes them. The Union negotiates paid vacations—the scab pockets his. The Union negotiates pay increases—the scab gets them also. Any and all of the things you members gain through your Union and for which you pay dues, the scab benefits by also. It is not fair or just that this should be so. The Imp knows that a lot of you good people are sick and tired of carrying these leeches and that you would be glad to see them go elsewhere. . . . If the scab wants to work with us, get his paid vacations, bonuses, pay increases and other things let him pay his part.

How can a union deal with this? In a union shop, employees are required to join a union elected by the employees to represent them. In an agency shop, employees are not required to join the union but must pay a "fair share" to the union. Both of these solutions require all employees to financially support the union democratically elected by their co-workers to represent them.

The problem is clearly addressed in *The Logic of Collective Action*, a classic work by the American economist, Mancur Olson. The book shows how the problem of collective action arises in many different social contexts. In one chapter Olson writes about the issue of coercion facing labor unions. Why is it that coercion often accompanies labor disputes, even labor disputes involving conservative unions? Olson answers:

The correct explanation surely centers around the need for coercion implicit in attempts to provide collective goods to large groups. If some workers in a particular firm go out on strike, the supply function for labor tends to shift to the left; so for those who continue working, or for outside strikebreakers, wages will if anything be higher than they were before. By contrast, for the duration of the conflict the strikers get nothing. Thus all the economic incentives affecting individuals are on the side of those workers who do not respect the picket lines. Should it be surprising, then, that coercion should be applied to keep individual workers from succumbing to the temptation to work during the strike?

Olson goes on to say, "Compulsory membership and picket lines are therefore of the essence of unionism."

A letter to the New Castle, *News Republican* from Evelyn K. Sheffield, a member of UAW Local 156 at the Perfect Circle plant in Hagerstown, addressing fellow workers willing to return to work, nicely states the union point of view regarding such free riders:

> Then you say we need unions. How do you expect your union to settle anything and YOU in there working? Have you ever sat at the bargaining table and heard PC [Perfect Circle] say [about] everything that we ask for that our workers are content with what they have and it is against our principles? Then you ask how long I have worked? I have worked long enough to help the bargaining committee in the past two years get the 5c raise at one time, seniority call back rights to the amount of seniority you had at the time of layoff, longer rest periods, . . . [and]. . . 3 weeks of vacation for people with 15 years of seniority and over...

Can a democratic union function if its members are free to ignore the decisions of the majority of its members, enjoy the benefits won by the union, refuse to pay their share, and refuse to honor a strike called by a vote of the union members? It is no wonder that the demand for a union shop was a central issue at Perfect Circle in 1948 and 1955. It should come as no surprise that attempts of scabs at Perfect Circle to exercise their supposed "right to work" resulted in violence.

One might agree that for unions to function they must exercise some discipline over their members. From this you might conclude that powerful unions have no place in a "free" society. This idea lies at the heart of current libertarian criticisms of union power. Libertarians have no objection to people joining unions. What bothers them are unions' attempts to coerce individuals to join as a condition of employment.

Americans are a liberty-loving people. We do not like to be told what to do. Coercion is abhorrent to us. The current appeal of the libertarian political theory is rooted in this love of liberty. While this appeal is understandable at first glance, libertarianism fails to provide a sensible way of thinking about liberty and why it matters. Libertarianism views the relationship between employer and employee as a voluntary contract entered into by two individuals, each endowed with the right to freely act as he or she sees fit so long as this involves no violation of the rights of others.

For all of the nineteenth and the early part of the twentieth century, this libertarian view shaped the legal approach to employer-employee relations in the United States. Either party was free to enter or not enter into an employment contract with the other for whatever reason. Employers were free to refuse to hire women, African-Americans, Roman Catholics, Jews, or members of unions. They were also free to fire employees who refused to work under dangerous or unhealthy conditions, and to fire employees who refused to work overtime on short notice.

Of course, employees were also free to refuse to work for anyone or under any conditions they disliked. This view treated the employer and the employee as equally free under the law. In reality, the positions of employer and employee were far from equal. As we noted in an earlier chapter, Adam Smith observed long ago, writing about disputes between employers (masters) and their workmen:

> In all such disputes, the masters can hold out much
> longer. A landlord, a farmer, a master manufacturer,
> a merchant, though they did not employ a single
> workman, could generally live a year or two upon

the stocks which they have already acquired. Many
workmen could not subsist a week, few could
subsist a month, and scarce any a year without
employment. In the long-run the workman may be
as necessary to his master as his master is to him;
but the necessity is not so immediate.

The worker and the master may appear to be equally free
agents entering into a free contract, but this appearance masks a
lack of freedom on one side rooted in the unequal positions of the
agents entering the contract.

The working "girl" of the early twentieth century, who des-
perately needed her job, was often prevented from entering into
marriage by a boss who disapproved of married women working.
This happened to my own mother as late as 1940, when she chose
to marry and lost her job.

In the early twentieth century, poor women, coerced by poverty to work in unsafe conditions in New York's textile industry,
died in the Triangle Shirtwaist fire. A century later, over one
hundred poor women, coerced by poverty to work in unsafe conditions, died in a recent fire in a textile factory in Bangladesh. In
other recent news, a major newspaper reported the cases of two
women, working in the United States, both suffering from serious
illnesses, who were told by their employers that they would be
fired if they took sick leave. In another example, a man in Indiana
I know, laid-off in his fifties, now works in a convenience store. He
is expected to be available to work whenever it suits his employer.
He is prohibited from sitting behind the counter. He takes the job
because he needs it to pay the bills and at his age can find nothing
better.

In all of these cases the workers in question would be "free"
by libertarian standards, but such take-it-or-leave it deals are not
expressions of free choice. They reflect an underlying need and an
underlying differential in power that is hostile to real freedom—a
condition well known in the long pre-union era as "wage slavery."

Examples like those above illustrate in different ways an
assault on human dignity. In his discussion of the auto industry
in its pre-union years, historian John Barnard mentions abuse,

humiliation, and insecurity inflicted by arbitrary supervisors as a major problem. He also mentions a young woman who had joined a UAW strike during the early organizing days. When asked why she had joined the union, she responded: "When you join the union, the foreman can't screw you." The choice between sex with the foreman and losing your job is not a free choice. It arises in a condition where real freedom is absent. It rests on a humiliating absence of power that is a permanent feature of wage labor in a non-union world.

Nick DiGaetano was an autoworker in the pre-union era and a union steward in a Chrysler plant after the UAW gained union recognition. In an interview he talked about the difference the union made on the shop floor. Now a worker could "talk to a fore-man on an equal basis." Having the union had changed the factory hand from a "plain, humble, submissive creature into a man. The union made a man out of him."

George Edwards was one of the sit-down strikers in Detroit in 1937, when the UAW won its first contract with General Motors. After union recognition had been won, the sit-down strikers marched out of the plant as a group. Edward described what that moment was like: "It seemed as if every human being in the world was moving in one stream . . . and that they were moving with a unity and spirit of deliverance and joy that was indescribable. It was the most powerful thing I have ever experienced."

Deliverance and joy are the marks of a passage from unfreedom to freedom. The right-to-work, the right-to-scab, is the right to betray this freedom, the right to deliver your fellow workers back to the condition of wage slavery that once held them captive. To some degree, unions do interfere with the freedom of individuals. Unions take collective action. They attempt to advance the freedom and interests of workers through collective bargaining, and, if need be, through strike action. In well-run unions this collective action is democratically controlled. But democratic control, even in the best of circumstances, can involve limitations on the freedom of individuals. For working men and women, real freedom can only be maintained through solidarity and collective action.

The so-called "right-to-work" laws give legal protection to

Richard Hudelson

employers who demand that the workers betray their union's collective decision to strike. This allows the employer to divide workers against each other and break union solidarity. Given these realities, it is not surprising that the demand for a union shop (compulsory membership, dues and support for the union's decisions) is high on the list for union supporters. It is also not surprising that many employers, like Perfect Circle, refused to accept a union shop.

Determined to repeal the National Labor Relations Act and eliminate the union shop, Republicans opposed to strong unions gained control of the congress in 1946. They went on to pass the Taft-Hartley Act, which hobbled the NLRA by permitting states to pass right-to-work laws that made union shop contracts illegal. The Taft-Hartley Act also gave courts the power to issue injunctions restricting picketing, making it easier for companies like Perfect Circle to find employees willing to scab on a strike.

The Taft-Harley Act also included a provision requiring the National Labor Relations Board to conduct special "union-shop authorization polls" before a union-shop agreement could be enforced. Many of organized labor's enemies hoped that such polls would result in workers voting against the union-shop requirements in their contracts, weakening the power of the unions.

In March 1951, the NLRB conducted union shop authorization elections as demanded by the Taft-Hartley Act at all Chrysler plants. Curious to see how strong the support was for the union shop among union members across the country, I looked at the Sixteenth Annual Report of the National Labor Relations Board For the Fiscal Year Ended June 30, 1951. I found there a section (on page ten) entitled "Results of Union-Shop Authorization Polls." The results provided cover the whole period from 1947 to 1951. They include not just Chrysler and the UAW, but all union shop agreements between all firms and all unions. Here are those results:

> During the 4 years and 2 months, from 1947 to 1951, in which a union-shop authorization poll was required by the act [National Labor Relations Act as amended by Taft-Hartley] before a valid

union-shop agreement could be made, the Board conducted 46,119 such polls.

Negotiation of union-shop agreements was authorized by vote of the employees in 44,795 of these polls. This was 97 percent of those conducted.

In the polls conducted, 6,542,564 employees were eligible to vote. Of these, 5,547,478 cast valid ballots. Of those voting, 5,071,988 or 77.5 percent, voted in favor of the union shop.

Unhappy and embarrassed by the strong support for the union-shop among American workers as demonstrated by these authorization polls, the Republican-controlled Congress voted to eliminate the section of the law requiring such authorization polls in the future. Opponents of the union-shop fell back on a campaign to pass state "right-to-work" laws that would forbid union-shop contracts. So much for industrial democracy. So much for an ethics of solidarity.

The battle to break the back of organized labor was building.

The owners and management of Perfect Circle took a stand in opposition to unions. Their stand rested upon two fundamental ideas: that unions interfered with the liberty of employees to work or not work as each saw fit, and that unions prevented free markets from delivering the prosperity that would be their natural outcome. Although each of these ideas was out of fashion in 1955, each has enjoyed a comeback over the last fifty years. In part, this comeback is due to the work of conservatives like Lothair and Ralph Teetor, who labored long and hard in support of their free market ideology.

To labor's dismay, their two fundamental ideas are among the guiding principles embraced by many Americans today. These principles were two of the foundation stones for the Reagan Revolution in 1980. In the previous chapter I considered the libertarian lament that unions interfere with liberty. I argued that unions actually advanced freedom for the vast majority of people. In this chapter I will consider the idea that unions prevent free markets from delivering the prosperity that would be their natural outcome. The central question before us is this: do free markets produce broad-based prosperity?

The idea that free markets will work to advance prosperity is one of the central assertions of Adam Smith's *Wealth of Nations*, first published in 1776. Smith argued that competitive markets provide incentives for each producer to find more efficient methods of production. The producer who does so will lower his costs of production, allowing him (or her) to reap higher-than-average profit. The producer who fails to innovate will eventually be driven out of business by more efficient competitors. In a free-market system, where all markets are competitive, these incentives will affect each producer and will tend to make production of all commodities more efficient. Over time, the outcome of such a system will be an increase in the total amount of goods and services produced—an increase in the wealth of the nation.

While Adam Smith thought that such an increase in the wealth of nations would be broadly shared, not all economists agreed with him. David Ricardo was Smith's great successor in the history of economics. Like Smith, he was a proponent of free-market capitalism. He also agreed with Smith that free markets work to increase the wealth of nations. However, Ricardo did not think this greater wealth would be broadly shared.

In his *Principles of Political Economy*, published in 1817, Ricardo argued that, as the wealth of nations increased, the wages of labor would remain fixed, hovering around the amount required to provide workers with the necessities for survival. In his view, any increased wealth produced above this minimum would be shared as profits on capital and rents on land. Ricardo reached this conclusion based on a general theory of value, one that Smith proposed but did not consistently develop. Ricardo did allow that workers might enjoy some gain in wages as a result of changing moral sensibilities about what wage was necessary for survival, but this was a gain not based on market forces. Indeed, it worked against purely market forces.

In his major work in economic theory, *Capital* (published in 1867), Karl Marx largely agreed with Ricardo. Like Ricardo and Smith, he agreed that free-market systems would work to increase the total wealth produced. Like Ricardo he concluded that free markets would distribute any increase in wealth almost entirely to capitalists and landowners, with none going to wages for workers. Like Ricardo, Marx allowed for some gain in wages to be possible based on changing moral sensibilities external to market forces. Notably however, there was at least one important difference between Ricardo and Marx.

Ricardo thought of market prices as "natural prices" that operated much like natural laws in natural science. In contrast, Marx thought that trade unions, working outside market forces, could compel employers to share the increased wealth produced in the form of higher wages paid to workers. This view is defended in Marx's *Value, Price and Profit* from 1865.

Let us return to the question posed at the start of this discussion: do free-markets tend to produce broad-based prosperity? Smith answers in the affirmative. Ricardo answers in the negative. These two thinkers, Smith and Ricardo, are widely viewed as the greatest of the classical economists. They were both champions of free-market capitalism. They worked from shared fundamental ideas. But from those shared ideas they reached very different answers to the question before us. Because he came first, Smith is usually regarded as the great creative thinker. Because he came later and had the advantage of exposure to criticisms of Smith's reasoning, Ricardo is generally regarded as the more rigorous thinker. Does this mean Ricardo was right?

Ricardo's view that in a free-market system wages for workers would remain at near subsistence levels, no matter how much wealth was produced, was based on a number of fundamental ideas. Among these was the labor theory of value. This is the idea that, in a free-market system, the prices of goods would be determined by the amount of labor time necessary to produce them. In the case of wages, the price of a day of labor would be determined by the labor time necessary to produce the food, housing, and other goods necessary to sustain the worker for a day. In Smith's work this idea is expressed but not consistently worked out. In Ricardo's writings the idea is worked out with greater consistency. However, doing so brought Ricardo, along with Marx and later economists, to see that there were difficulties in using labor time to explain relative prices of commodities in a complex economy. Aware of these difficulties, and perhaps worried about revolutionary uses of Ricardo's theory of wages by Marx and other socialists, several economic theorists began to develop a fundamentally different approach to economic theory.

This different approach to economic theory has come to be known as "marginalist economics." The early developers of marginalism were W. Stanley Jevons (English), Carl Menger (Austrian), and Léon Walrus (French). While the marginalists retained many of Smith's and Ricardo's ideas, they put a new foundation under these ideas. They removed the labor theory of value and replaced it with a theory based on the preferences of individual agents acting within a system of free markets. This marginalist, or neo-classical, approach has been the dominant current in economic theory since its inception around 1870.

Many neo-classical economists share Adam Smith's assumption that an increase in the wealth of nations will benefit the vast majority of human beings; that economic growth will work to the benefit of all or almost all. In the parlance of Ronald Reagan's "trickle down economics," many economists assumed that "a rising tide will lift all boats," that an increase in the wealth of nations will widely distribute the increased wealth created. But what justifies this belief? Producing more is one thing. Sharing broadly is something else.

Suppose I have nothing to sell but my labor, and that I am healthy and willing to work hard. There is nothing in economic theory that says the price for the labor I have to sell will be enough to keep me (or my family) alive. If the price of labor such as mine falls below a subsistence wage, workers and their families will starve or emigrate, the supply of labor will be reduced, and wages will eventually rise. But there is nothing in economic theory to prove that the long-run wage for labor like mine will rise much above subsistence, even if the total amount of wealth produced increases greatly. If increased labor efficiency results in increased profits for the company, the corporate owners are not obligated to share the increased riches with the workers.

While increased economic growth may sometimes increase the demand for labor and therefore increase wages over some period of time, there is no theoretical reason that this will be generally true or continue indefinitely into the future. Erik Brynjalfsson and Andrew McAfree, two professors in the Sloan School of Management at the Massachusetts Institute of Technology, address this point. In their recently published book, *Race Against the Machine*, they consider the impact of technology on the global economy in recent decades. Noting that much of this technology has been used to replace human workers, increasing unemployment, they go on to say, "There is no economic law that says everyone, or even most people, automatically benefit from technological progress." If not economic theory, what then does support the prevailing view that free markets tend to produce broad prosperity?

The philosopher John Hospers, the first Libertarian Party candidate for president of the United States, leaves economic theory behind and answers this question with an appeal to historical experience:

> With the controls taken off business, existing enterprises would expand and new ones would spring into existence satisfying more and more consumer needs; millions more people would be gainfully employed instead of subsisting on welfare, and all kinds of research and production, released from the stranglehold of government, would proliferate, fulfilling man's needs and desires as never before. It has always been so whenever government has permitted men to be free traders on a free market.

This idea that free market systems have a proven track record for promoting broad-based prosperity has a powerful hold on American popular thought. In fact, however, it is very far from true.

Ricardo's *Principles of Political Economy and Taxation* was published in 1817. In that same year, Britain, the epicenter of the emerging free-market capitalist order, saw a hunger march on London made up of desperate wage laborers determined to take the city by storm. Some twenty years later, with the British economic system even more closely approximating a pure free-market system, grain was exported from Ireland while the people of Ireland starved. The harsh conditions experienced by workers then and in the decades that followed seem to confirm Ricardo's view: that the greater wealth produced by free-market capitalism would be unequally shared. As free-market capitalism spread across Europe poverty conditions spread too, giving rise to both hunger and a growing labor movement. From Europe, millions of people left their homes and families for the new world, many of them driven by poverty.

In his Principles of Political Economy, published in 1848 near the high point of unregulated free-market capitalism, the great champion of individual liberty, John Stuart Mill, wrote that, "Hitherto it is questionable if all the mechanical inventions yet made have lightened the day's toil of any human being. They have enabled a greater population to live the same life of drudgery and imprisonment, and an increased number of manufacturers and others to make fortunes."

In the United States during the so-called Giled Age (1870-1900), a period that came closest to Hospers' free market paradise on this side of the Atlantic, wage cuts, longer hours, lay-offs, and unemployment left many working families trapped in grinding poverty.

In the closing decades of the nineteenth century and the early decades of the twentieth century, a movement to abandon pure free market capitalism in favor of a reformed version of capitalism spread throughout the world. The emerging labor movement vigorously supported the reforms, as did many religious leaders, such as Pope Leo XIII and Protestant "social gospel" clergymen in the USA.

Important political leaders also supported reforming capitalism. In the United States, Presidents Theodore Roosevelt and Woodrow Wilson were important proponents of this reform, known as Progressivism. Political leaders in Europe also championed reform versions of capitalism under the banners of "Social Democracy," "Socialism," or some version of a labor party or national party of reform. From country to country, the reform movement varied in details and pace of change, but in general it included such things as limits on child labor, limits on the length of the working day, health and safety regulations, compensation to injured workers and their dependents, unemployment insurance, minimum-wage laws, and the incorporation of unions and collective bargaining into the fabric of economic life.

The labor movement that emerged in Britain, Europe and the United States played an important role in forcing employers and political leaders to accept reform measures. Such reforms provided a degree of economic security and prosperity to workers and their families that had not been experienced during the heyday of free-market capitalism. In this they confirmed the view of Marx that wage slavery and subsistence wages were not the inevitable outcomes of some economic "law." Labor unions could make a difference.

Another departure from free market capitalism had to do with an attempt to control the cycles of boom and bust that had plagued capitalism from its earliest days. These cycles brought the collapse of great enterprises and periods of prolonged depression, unemployment and hard times for millions. The real world cycles of expansion and collapse did not look much like the picture of free-market capitalism as a self-regulating and efficient engine of prosperity painted by the proponents of free market capitalism. While some economic theorists might be content with dismissing such crises as aberrations from what they had proven free markets would produce, business leaders and politicians faced a practical need to find a way to deal with them.

If the free market theory was wrong, where was the problem? Historically, many of these crises were connected to catastrophic failures in the financial sector of the economy. Progressive thinkers pointed to a great capitalist institution as the source of the problem.

The banks.

CAN CAPITALISM BE TAMED?

Banks are in the business of making a profit. They make this profit by investing other people's money and by amassing corporate profits to shape investment policies. Prudent bankers keep some of this money in reserve so they can provide funds for any depositor or investor who wants to withdraw their money along with interest. The rest of the money deposited in the banks is loaned out with the expectation that the bank will make a profit on the loans above what it owes its depositors. But even when the economy is humming along at a steady clip and depositors have confidence in their bank, some banks fail, their assets bought at sale by other banks.

As an economy expands, entrepreneurs and speculators borrow more and more in order to invest in expanding production or to speculate in financial markets where stock prices are rising. Driven to increase profit margins, and infected with the exuberant optimism of such moments, bankers make more and more risky loans, while overconfident investors drive up the share price of the companies they own stock in to unrealistic levels. Eventually the bubble bursts. Debts are called in. Entrepreneurs, speculators, and banks are unable to make payment on their debts. With insufficient funds on hand to satisfy their debts or to provide customer withdrawals, banks fail. The failures ripple throughout the financial sector. Credit dries up. Unable to access needed short-term loans to stay in operation, businesses shut down, individuals lose their savings, and massive unemployment follows.

Responding to yet another financial crisis in 1907, the government created the Federal Reserve System in an effort to manage the financial crises that have occurred since the beginning of capitalism. The Federal Reserve would lend money to banks at risk in order to prevent bank failures and the depressions that follow.

Despite the formation of the Federal Reserve System, a ripple of bank failures plunged the U.S. economy into a deep depression in the early 1930s. Convinced that reckless stock market investments caused these bank failures, and realizing that the profit drive of banks prevented them from regulating themselves, Congress passed the Glass-Steagall Banking Act of 1933. The act divided banks into two categories. Ordinary commercial banks took deposits from and made loans to individuals and businesses. They were prevented from making high-risk investments in stocks and other securities. Investment banks were permitted to provide services to higher-risk investment firms and to make direct investments on their own into securities markets. The Banking Act was paired with creation of the Federal Deposit Insurance Corporation, which provided federal insurance for funds invested in ordinary commercial banks so that individuals who lost their savings when a bank failed could be reimbursed by government insurance.

The Glass-Steagall Act was designed to regulate banking behavior in the hope of preventing future speculative bubbles in financial markets. At the same time the New Deal invested in public infrastructures, such as dams, rural electrification, and the various projects of the Works Progress Administration, in an effort to lift the economy out of the depression. But it was not until the massive deficit spending of World War II that the U.S. economy managed to climb out of the depression, and even then the prospects for the future were unclear.

Would the economy slide back into depression after the end of World War II? Coming out of the war, most economists and public officials were convinced the government needed to play a permanent role in regulating the economy. The idea was that by using the power to tax and spend, along with the Federal Reserve System's power over interest rates, the federal government could manage the business cycle that had plagued the economy in the past. When the economy became too hot, taxes and interest rates should be raised, dampening expansion and preventing destabilizing bubbles. When the economy became too cold, taxes and interest rates should be cut, stimulating demand and investment to prevent the economy from sliding into a depression. From the end of World War II until the mid-1970s, this framework dominated thinking in both academic economics and public policy. It was a framework supported by the theoretical work of the English economist, John Maynard Keynes, and by twenty-five years of stable growth.

In the quarter century following World War II, individuals in the highest income brackets faced income taxes at rates of 70-90%. At the same time, Union density (unionized workers as a percent of the labor force) was higher than at any time in American history, ranging from a high of around 33% in the immediate post-war years to around 25% in 1970. Backed by the labor law reforms of the Wagner Act, unions were able to win a larger share of the wealth produced for employees. While the era was deeply marred by racial discrimination, with good wages won by unions, for many mostly white American families, it was a golden era.

In the late 1960s and early 1970s there was room for hope. It seemed that the means had been found to tame capitalism—to make it a vehicle not just for growth but also for growth widely shared, for broad based prosperity. With a determined effort to end racial discrimination, it seemed possible to extend the tamed capitalism of that era both within the USA and around the world.

Unfortunately, prosperity for working people did not last. By the mid 1970s the US economy was experiencing "stagflation," a combination of stagnant growth and inflation. With stagnant growth came increasing unemployment. With inflation came decreasing real wages. According to prevailing views guiding post-war economic policy, the government could combat unemployment by increasing government spending. But those same views also proposed that to combat inflation you must decrease government spending. The situation was complicated by increasing global competition, in particular from the economies of Germany and Japan, where they had constructed new, more efficient manufacturing facilities that had been destroyed in the war. The US economy also suffered from other competitors, such as the OPEC oil cartel.

With a slack economy and no clear theoretical analysis about how to revitalize the system, free-market proponents called for more market based economic policies. Building on the earlier work of Milton Friedman, F.A. von Hayek, and Richard Mises, champions of free-market economics dominated the academic and public-policy circles from the late 1970s into the next century. Defending the traditional neo-classical ideas of free markets as engines of growth and as self-regulating systems, they argued that the development of new information technologies, mathematically sophisticated investment strategies, and financial products designed to spread risk, together had made financial markets less susceptible to irrational bubbles.

Advocates of greater reliance on markets thought that a large number of private investors, highly motivated by self-interest to make correct assessments of asset values, were much more likely than politically-influenced government bureaucrats to correctly guide investment decisions. While not denying the possibility of external disturbances or temporary problems, these theorists argued that, in general and in the long run, self-regulating markets would greatly out-perform markets regulated by governments.

The basic idea that free markets out-perform regulated markets became widely accepted in the United States and Great Britain. It provided one of the foundations for the program of small government, lower taxes, privatization, greater reliance on markets, and opposition to unions, that came to dominate public policy following the election of Margaret Thatcher in 1979 and Ronald Reagan in 1980. The consensus surrounding these ideas persisted into the next three decades. It was President Clinton who signed the North American Free Trade Agreement in late 1993. And, it was President Clinton who signed the repeal of the Glass-Steagall law in 1999. That was the law that created a firewall between commercial banks and investment banks designed to prevent further depressions. Its repeal by a president of the party of FDR demonstrated how far faith in free markets had been restored.

In the decades that followed, this program was to some extent globalized through the work of institutions like the World Bank, the World Trade Organization, and a series of free-trade agreements. Supporters of the program pointed to rapid growth in China and other Asian countries after they embraced pro-market reforms. Critics pointed out that the Chinese and other

Asian economies involved government planning and regulation to a much greater degree than free-market ideology allowed. Critics also pointed to increasing inequality as a consequence of free-market policies in the U.S, U.K., Latin America, Africa, and the former Communist countries in Eastern Europe where these policies had been tried.

The great economic crisis of 2007, spurred by bogus practices in mortgage lending and high risk investments by the banks, undermined confidence in these resurrected free-market ideas. The meltdown of financial markets in the United States that set off the crisis was a classic example of the sort of crises that have characterized market economies over the last one hundred and fifty years. The rational markets hypothesis—the idea that with current information technologies and current economic modeling capabilities private financial markets could be trusted to avoid a financial crisis—was thoroughly discredited.

So, where does this leave us? The central question that led us to think about the history of economic theory and policy is this: Do free markets produce broad-based prosperity? Clearly, economic theory provides no compelling reason to think that they must have this outcome.

If we turn to John Hospers' claim that the cumulative experiences of humankind show that free-markets do produce such prosperity, it is clear that Hospers is wrong. Free-market capitalism produces great wealth, but by itself it does not bring broad-based prosperity. It distributes income and wealth very unequally, and it produces periodic economic crises. So how do we tame capitalism? What else is needed to create an economy that produces a stable, broad based prosperity?

Leaders in the trade unions have some ideas about this question. Ideas about income equality and democratic rule. But, before we get to that, we'll stop to take a look at how deregulated finance markets worked out for New Castle.

WHEN WALL STREET TAKES OVER THE COMPANY

For the better part of a century, the auto parts industry was big in New Castle. Now it is largely gone. The same thing could be said about a lot of cities and towns across Indiana and the rest of the Midwest. The American auto industry, once one of the flagships of the U.S. economy, has suffered through three decades of decline, narrowly escaping bankruptcy in the steep recession that started in 2007. More than a few people blame the union for that decline.

When I went to New Castle in October 2011 to talk with people there about local history, some blamed the union for their town's decline. These were some of the things I heard: "They got too greedy." "They only worked two hours per day." "Employees played cards when they were supposed to be working." "You would see them outside sitting in the sun all day." "They refused to face reality." "They wouldn't make concessions."

Like many other people in the U.S., some of the people I talked with were convinced that labor unions are special-interest groups looking out only for the wellbeing of their members, that unionized workers are privileged fat cats living off the labor of others, and that the American people would be better off if unions could be eradicated. I think these views serve to mask deeper problems underlying the demise of industrial America and the Chrysler in New Castle; problems that continue to threaten our future. Consideration of what happened at the Chrysler in New Castle will provide an example for some of the other factors at work.

Chrysler emerged from World War II as the second largest automaker in the United States, with nearly twenty-eight percent of the market at a time when there were still close to a dozen carmakers in the U.S. By 1961, before foreign competition became a big factor, Chrysler's market share had dropped to just under eleven percent. A number of factors contributed to this decline.

Chrysler resisted pension agreements like those signed by GM and Ford, leading to the 104-day strike in 1950. That strike caused Chrysler to lose market share to other companies able to deliver new cars.

In the early 1950s, Chrysler also opted for high dividends to stockholders over re-investment in new cost-saving manufacturing methods. That decision left the company with underfunded, outdated, and inefficient plants. Chrysler also spent less on research and development than did General Motors, slowing development of new models and new technologies. Quality problems, explained in part by outdated plants, and unattractive styling throughout much of the fifties contributed to further loss of market share.

Under the leadership of Lynn Townsend, Chrysler Corporation's fortunes improved in the 1960s and early 1970s. But these gains came more from investments in overseas auto manufacturing and from diversification into other industries, like real estate, than from investment in domestic auto-manufacturing facilities. By the late 1970s, Chrysler was in serious financial difficulties, requiring a "fire sale" of many of their overseas investments and a loan guarantee from the federal government for the company to survive.

Lee Iacocca, now in charge of Chrysler Corporation, led an effort to address some of the underlying difficulties facing the company's domestic auto manufacturing core. Between 1978 and 1982, Chrysler worked to modernize its production facilities in order to improve efficiency and raise quality controls. Between 1978 and 1983, the company's workforce was cut by more than half due to more efficient manufacturing technologies. At the very dated plant in New Castle, new transfer machines were introduced that reduced the need for people. In addition, shock absorber production was outsourced to Mexico. By the early 1980s, employment at the plant had dropped from 3,000 to 600.

The economic recession that ran from 1979-1982 brought the deepest downturn in auto sales since the Great Depression. All of the big three automakers in the U.S. were affected by this downturn, Chrysler as much as, if not more than, GM or Ford. Enemies of unions blamed high union wages for the automakers' problems.

Unions themselves have consistently argued that union workers are paid better than non-union workers. Such wage differences do provide a reason to shift production to lower-wage non-union facilities within or outside the United States. This was a factor in the decision, mentioned above, to shift shock absorber production from the Chrysler plant in New Castle to Mexico. However, high union wages do not explain the deindustrialization that characterized the auto industry and the whole American economy from the 1970s into the new century. Other countries, like Germany, had similar high union wages, but Germany and Japan had rebuilt modern efficient production plants, while US automakers and steel producers tried to keep older plants going. The US also paid the cost of the war in Viet Nam, as well as fielding military bases across the globe, trying to produce guns and butter.

Despite union wages and periodic slumps, the American auto industry had long been a very profitable business. But profits in the domestic auto industry declined in the late 1960s and early 1970s. What changed? This decline reflected the restoration in the 1950s and 60s of manufacturing capacity in Japan, Germany and other countries that had been devastated by World War II. Much of this restoration was financed by the overseas investments of American automakers themselves in the 1960s. By 1970, one third of investment by U.S. automakers was overseas rather than in domestic plants, even as domestic auto manufacturing was facing stronger competition.

The changes happening in the auto industry were connected to the "financialization" of the American economy. Historically, most American manufacturing firms were created by people interested in making a particular product. Manufacturing began in a particular location and often stayed in that location for a long period of time. Financing a manufacturing operation was always a necessary part of it. Many firms failed because of their inability to raise money or because of inability to pay debt. Sometimes this led to bank takeovers of firms, as happened when Maxwell Motor Company failed. But in the past, this often led to the financiers finding someone with a background in production to lead the firm, as when Walter P. Chrysler was called in to take the reins at Maxwell. As American corporations developed, some remained firmly under leadership based in production, while others came under leadership based in finance. In the auto industry, for example, Henry Ford and Walter P. Chrysler had their roots on the production side, while Alfred Sloan at General Motors came from the financial side.

In the 1970s control of the auto industry shifted sharply to the financial side. In this time of conglomerates, new companies emerged out of long established manufacturing firms. These new companies were focused on financial investments and maximizing profits for investors. Often this led to a selloff of part or all of the manufacturing base from which the new company had emerged. Sometimes such investment companies were created whole as new firms with new names. They were not created to manufacture a product like automobiles or televisions. They were umbrella investment companies, created to buy and sell a variety of firms engaged in production. Such firms were not tied to any particular product or any particular location. Assets of underperforming companies, even some making a profit, could be sold off to generate capital for investment in more profitable ventures. Old companies, even some generating strong profits, might be used as cash cows to finance other ventures, leaving old established firms to eventually go under for lack of modernization.

The crisis that hit the U.S. auto industry in the late 1970s was partially caused by investments made by American automakers in overseas auto production and in areas not connected to the production of automobiles. This was true of the investments made by Chrysler under the leadership of Lynn Townsend and true of investments at General Motors where GM Finance became a greater source of profits than GM auto manufacturing. From the point of view of a manufacturing firm, there is a certain madness in investing in your competition and neglecting investment in your own firm, but for a diversified finance firm, it doesn't matter where the profits come from.

Even in the past firms historically identified with familiar products have loosened their ties to historic locations. In 1940 RCA moved from its roots in Camden, New Jersey, to Bloomington, Indiana. In the 1960s RCA moved to Memphis, Tennessee. Then, in 1968, RCA moved to Juarez, Mexico. In each case the move was motivated by a quest for cheaper labor and higher profits.

The restructuring of corporations into diversified hold-ing companies, with corporate CEO's shifting the focus of management onto returns on investment disconnected from the production of specific products, further fostered the deindustri-alization of the American economy. In the 1970s and 1980s the movement of production facilities to lower-wage, higher-profit locations, in the non-union United States or overseas, acceler-ated. In the auto industry, General Motors, Chrysler and Ford all shifted much of their production away from their unionized UAW plants. The automakers were also able to use threats of further relocation to force concessions from the UAW.

The decline of the Chrysler in New Castle must be understood within the context of these broader forces. It cannot be explained simply as the product of imagined union intransigence and union refusal to face reality. It is simply not true that the union refused to make any concessions. As early as 1979, the UAW worked with Chrysler Corporation to secure the federal loan guarantees neces-sary to enable the company to avoid bankruptcy. "The UAW led the concessions parade," agreeing to $426.5 million in wage con-cessions. In January 1981, UAW Chrysler employees voted again to approve another $622 million in concessions. Members of UAW Local 371 in New Castle were among those Chrysler employees voting to approve these pay cuts.

The UAW also worked with Chrysler to address some long-standing quality control problems. When the company launched its "Product Quality Control" program, Marc Stepp was the head of the UAW International's Chrysler Department. Stepp's standard message when meeting with UAW locals was, "no quality, no sales . . . no sales, no jobs."

Having survived the threat of bankruptcy with cooperation and concessions from its unionized employees, in 1986 Chrysler Corporation secured an agreement with the UAW designed to increase both efficiency and quality in its production facilities. The "Modern Operating Agreement" incorporated a more col-laborative approach to production. Management relinquished its traditional top-down commanding role. Management employ-ees abandoned coat and tie, traditional symbols of authority, for more casual dress. Work was re-organized into shop floor teams. Job classifications and pay differentials between jobs were reduced, making it easier for shop-floor employees to move from one task to another without loss of pay. Management employees and unionized shop-floor employees met together to discuss how to solve production problems in the most efficient way. Labor-management steering committees were established in each plant and at the national level.

Despite reservations from some members of his local, Noel Blevins, President of UAW Local 371 in New Castle, spoke in support of the new agreement. Blevins directly addressed the need to make the New Castle plant more competitive. Members of Local 371 followed Blevins' lead, volunteering to implement the agreement and becoming the first Chrysler plant to work with local management to establish its work teams.

These collaborative efforts to improve efficiency and quality in production processes paid off. United States Senator Richard Lugar presented a productivity award to the Chrysler plant in New Castle in September 1992. In making the award, Lugar credited the Modern Operating Agreement between Chrysler and the UAW with making possible the gains in productivity. The accomplishments at New Castle were noticed by higher management at Chrysler and elsewhere. Will Ruback, personnel manager at the Chrysler plant in New Castle from 1989 to 1994, noted that over one hundred companies "benchmarked" the plant during the time he was there.

A few years later, in 1998, the internationally-respected Underwriters Laboratory recommended the New Castle Chrysler plant for certification as meeting the QS-9000 quality control standards adopted by the big three automakers in 1994. The New Castle plant was one of the early plants to receive this QS-9000 recommendation. Recognizing the New Castle plant's accomplishment, the state of Indiana presented the plant with its "Indiana Quality Improvement" award in 1999.

With the introduction of well-engineered new models and the cooperation of its UAW workforce, by the mid-1990s Chrysler Corporation had become "the most profitable automotive producer in the world." Recognizing the positive role played by the

Chrysler plant in New Castle and its UAW employees, Chrysler made major investments in the plant in the 1990s, allowing for a call back of laid-off employees and for a significant number of new hires.

Despite this comeback, Bob Eaton, CEO of Chrysler, was deeply worried about challenges of "chronic overcapacity," "empowered buyers," and "environmental concerns that threatened the very existence of the internal combustion engine" facing the global auto industry. Eaton was convinced that for Chrysler to survive it would need to merge with a strong partner. At the same time, Daimler-Benz, the German automaker, saw Chrysler Corporation as a dynamic leader in auto manufacturing. In May 1998, Chrysler and Daimler-Benz announced the planned merger of the two companies.

Three years later, the Chrysler Group within the newly merged company was "on track to hemorrhage $3 billion" for the year. Despite layoffs and closure of several plants, the Chrysler part of DaimlerChrysler continued to lose substantial sums of money. In a short account of the merger between Daimler and Chrysler, Dartmouth business school professor Sydney Finkelstein attributed the failure of the merger to a culture clash between the two firms and the lethargy of Chrysler Group leadership after the merger, which led valuable engineering talent to leave Chrysler. An article in the business journal *Fortune* included both of the CEOs responsible for the merger, Robert Eaton of Chrysler and Jürgen Schrempp of Daimler, on its list of "history's 10 Worst Auto Chiefs."

In May 2007, DaimlerChrysler announced that it was selling eighty percent of Chrysler to the private equity firm Cerberus Capital Management and to some other investors. Two years after the sale to Cerberus, with the U.S. auto industry facing the worst recession since the Great Depression, Chrysler sought bankruptcy protection and help from the federal government.

The demise of the Chrysler in New Castle was in large part due to the failure of the DaimlerChrysler merger. With Chrysler Group leadership seemingly adrift and losses mounting, Daimler leadership took command of the merged company and began selling off assets as a way of cutting losses. American unions and their high union wages were not the problem. By 1994 German wages were already more than fifty percent higher than American wages. In the years that followed, wages in American auto-parts plants fell even further behind. In Germany unions had a say regarding plant closings. In America, unions had no say. A joke popular among autoworkers during the Chrysler/Daimler years went like this: "In Berlin, how do they pronounce the new Chrysler-Daimler company name?" "In German, 'Chrysler' is silent."

In January 2003, partial ownership and management of the New Castle plant was transferred to Metaldyne, an independent company producing parts for automakers in the United States and elsewhere. The agreement between DaimlerChrysler and Metaldyne called for downsizing of the New Castle plant and selling off some of its assets as a way of stemming losses, with Metadyne taking ownership and control of the remaining assets. By 2007, the old plant in New Castle was stripped of its remaining machinery and demolished. Production continued in newer parts of the plant constructed during the DaimlerChrysler years. There were over 1,000 employees as late as 2006.

By 2007 Metaldyne had left behind its connection with DaimlerChrysler and been purchased by Asahi Tech, a Japanese firm. Asahi Tech was interested in selling off some of Metaldyne's assets in order to gain cash for managing its own debt problems. In May, 2009, facing the sharp decline in the auto industry and Asahi Tech's decision to withdraw its support, Metaldyne filed for bankruptcy. Shortly thereafter it announced that the New Castle plant would be closed. Production of auto parts at New Castle Machining and Forge, for a century the backbone for New Castle's economy, came to an end. The hammers stopped. The town was silent. The night was empty.

The loss of the Chrysler was not New Castle's only loss. Perfect Circle led the way. In 1963, Perfect Circle, the company that had successfully faced down the UAW in 1955, became a wholly owned subsidiary of Dana Corporation, a holding company then owning facilities in Argentina, Mexico, Sweden, South Africa and Spain. Dana gradually shifted production operations out of the region. By 1995, it no longer operated in Hagerstown. Dana filed for bankruptcy in 2006. It survived, selling off the foundry in New Castle. At present, Grede Castings operates there as a subsidiary of Metaldyne Performance Group, with non-union wages and high turnover.

The Ingersoll Rolling Mill, a Borg-Warner Company since 1928, was like Chrysler and Perfect Circle a UAW stronghold in New Castle. In the late 1960s Borg-Warner constructed a new facility on the north side of the road opposite the existing rolling mill. The new facility was a cold rolling operation using new technology. In 1971, this new facility was sold to Allegheny Ludlum Steel. While Rolling Mill historian Bob Perdue acknowledged some problems with young employees hired to work at the new facility, he thought a bigger reason for the sale involved quality control problems with materials at the new facility that Borg-Warner was unable to manage. In its facilities elsewhere, Allegheny Ludlum had a history of working with the United Steel Workers of America (USW) and probably, for that reason, workers at the new facility at the New Castle site became a USW local. Allegheny Ludlum continued to operate this plant as a union shop until 2011, when overcapacity in steel production and the deep recession begun in 2007 forced a closure of the plant.

In 1976, Borg-Warner sold the older hot rolling mill on the south side of the road to A. Johnson & Co, of New York. The New Castle plant had $17 million in annual revenues compared to the $400 million of the New York firm. The New York firm was itself a branch of the Axel Johnson Group of Sweden, "a large diversified organization with worldwide gross revenues of approximately $2,500,000,000." The New Castle hot rolling mill was later transferred to Avestia, a Swedish firm with connections to the Axel Johnson Group. In 2001 Avestia merged with Outokumpu, a group of companies headquartered in Espoo, Finland, producing stainless steel. To the best of my knowledge, production continues at Outokumpu in New Castle to this day with UAW Local 729 still representing employees there.

When I set out on this project, I had two questions in mind. First, how did New Castle, that conservative rural Republican place I grew up in, become a labor citadel? Second, what happened to the factory town I grew up in? Where did it go?

In this chapter I made an attempt at answering that second question. What I had found was a bewildering series of business transactions transforming the corporate structures of the Chrysler, the Rolling Mill, the Perfect Circle and the other industrial firms of my youth. It made my head spin. I dutifully recorded these changes as best I could, but they kept coming faster than I could keep track of them.

Then I read a book that shed some needed light. It was *Glass House* by Brian Alexander, published earlier this year. Alexander grew up in Lancaster, Ohio, an "all-American town." Lancaster was home to Anchor Hocking Glass, a long established and financially secure maker of glass tableware. The book told the story of how Anchor Hocking and Lancaster were transformed by a series of corporate transactions that undermined Anchor Hocking and left the residents of Lancaster struggling with economic insecurity and widespread drug addiction.

The central actors in this transformation were a series of private equity investment firms. Among them was Cerberus, the same private equity firm that played a brief part at Chrysler in New Castle. That caught my attention.

Wanting to find out more about what private equity firms were, how they differed from other companies, and why they behaved the way they did, I turned to *Private Equity at Work: When Wall Street Manages Main Street*, a book by two professors in business and economics, Eileen Appelbaum and Rosemary Batt. While I think I have a better idea of what private equity is all about, the reader should not hold Appelbaum and Batt responsible for what follows.

A small group of investors, general partners, form a Private Equity firm. This private equity firm creates a number of private equity funds. They solicit investments in these funds from other investors, who become "limited partners." These private equity funds then buy up existing firms actually making things, turning the money used in the purchase into debt owed by the acquired firms to the investors. The private equity investors also put their people on the boards governing the acquired firms.

The aim of the investors is to maximize return on their investments. Their skills and the skills of the people they put on governing boards of acquired companies, tend to be in finance and investment, not in the technology or management of production. Slicing and dicing, selling off a part of what was acquired and using what's left as a cash cow for further investment, short turn financial gains can be won and reinvested for more gain at the cost of increased debt and weakened production capacity in what is left.

There is an ethical standpoint behind all of this. A common distinction between shareholders and stakeholders helps to understand it. Shareholders are investors. Stakeholders include investors but also employees, consumers, communities where facilities are located, and third parties affected by what firms do. In the Lancaster, Ohio of decades past, management at Anchor Hocking tried to serve the interests of all stakeholders. In the new world of private equity, management is supposed to consider only the interests of shareholders, the capital investors who have, as the saying goes, "skin in the game." The right thing to do is to maximize return on investment. Anything else is an inefficient use of capital resources.

Sometimes what serves shareholders also serves stakeholders, but not always. Consider what Appelbaum and Batt say about what happened to Delphi Automotive Corporation, a mainstay for the economy of Anderson, Indiana in my youth.

> The restructuring of Delphi Automotive Corporation, following the financial crash [of 2007], provides an example in which not only employees but also taxpayers subsidized the outsized returns of private equity and hedge fund owners of Delphi while these owners restructured the company, closed all but four of its twenty-nine operating plants in the United States, and sent all of the twenty-five thousand union jobs to China. Other buyers who lost the bid would have saved American jobs.

Under the ethics of finance capital, management would have been ethically remiss in accepting the lower offer.

Champions of private equity like to say that these firms often rescue struggling companies. Applebaum and Batt agree that this is so, but consider what they have to say about one example of such a rescue. Wilbur Ross has his own private equity investment firm. His firm purchased a number of distressed steel companies and rescued them. But at what price? "In the case of Wilbur Ross, his three year investment netted him $4.5 billion—just equal to what retirees lost in their health and pension plans."

Appelbaum and Bhatt had nothing to say about the role of Cerberus Private Equity in the demise of the Chrysler in New Castle, but they did mention NewPage, a paper manufacturer with a plant in Duluth, my current hometown. When Cerberus purchased NewPage in January 2005 it had six thousand employees, most of them unionized. Cerberus' purchase was heavily leveraged with debt. When NewPage went bankrupt in 2011 it had $3.4 billion in assets and 4.2 billion in debt. The authors also quote Steve Feinberg, co-founder and CEO of Cerberus Capital Management as admitting that, "General partners make absurd amounts of money. We're all overpaid."

Having discovered *Glass House,* and having learned a little bit about the role of private equity capital in Lancaster, New Castle, Anderson, and Duluth, I have come to suspect that private equity investment played a major role in transforming other manufacturing towns, like the Middletown, Ohio of J. D. Vance's *Hillbilly Elegy*, the Dayton, Ohio of Dana Corporation, and a host of other rust belt cities and towns. With that said, I will return to the idea mentioned earlier, that this deindustrialization did not have to happen; that another way was possible.

The New Castle of my growing-up years was a factory town whose working-class neighborhoods were made up mainly of small houses on individual lots. Some neighborhoods were more prosperous than others. There were shabby houses here and there, even in the more prosperous areas. Factory work was monotonous and it had its ups and downs. Lay-offs happened. Nonetheless, for the most part, New Castle was a relatively prosperous town.

Downtown stores were thriving. Downtown streets were crowded on Saturdays. Today, Chrysler, World Bestos, Trainer Springs, Pan American Bridge, the Box Factory, Modernfold Doors, Davis Foundry, and the Slaughter House are all gone. Concrete, weeds, and rusty fences are all that remain. Most of the decent paying factory jobs are gone. Neighborhoods look shabbier. Neighborhood businesses have largely disappeared. Downtown stores are empty, boarded up, or marginally operating. Commercial life is largely relegated to the Highway 3 "bypass," constructed fifty years ago to avoid the congestion downtown. The hammers have stopped. The nights are silent.

New Castle, of course, is not alone in this. Lots of other towns and cities have shared the same fate. There are many people in New Castle and elsewhere who blame the unions for what has happened. My central aim in this chapter has been to argue that there are other forces at work—financialization and globalization—that bear most of the responsibility for what happened. I have tried to support this idea by looking at what happened in New Castle, but we can find evidence elsewhere as well. The truth is that deindustrialization has been as common in the non-union factory towns of the South as it has been in the union towns of the Midwest.

In concluding this chapter I would like to return to some of the things mentioned at the start of the chapter that I have so far ignored—that unionized employees at the Chrysler were only working two hours per day, and that they spent the day playing cards or sitting outside in the sun. When I first heard these things, I thought that people had been misled by baseless, anti-union rumors. It had not been at all like that when I worked at Chrysler. On one of my research trips to New Castle, I had a chance to talk with Gene Ingram. Gene had graduated from Chrysler High School a few years after me. I met him when I came to New Castle to see an exhibit at the Henry County Historical Society that he had helped to create. Gene had worked for thirty some years at the Chrysler—half as a skilled die maker and half on the management side of things. I asked him whether he thought there was any truth to any of these rumors.

To my surprise he said there was. He said these things did

happen for a period in the early 1980s. But, he added, this had nothing to do with a poor work ethic or with the union. He went on to explain that there was a period when the Chrysler was plagued by production problems: broken dies, broken machines, lack of raw materials, or other production-process problems. People were playing cards or sitting in the sun not because they were unwilling to work, but because the work was not ready for them. Of course, in the old pre-union days, employees would have been sent home without pay and told to report back in a few hours to see if problems had been resolved. Under the contract with the UAW the company could not do this. It was not true that the union was protecting slackers.

I suspect that these problems emerged at the Chrysler during the major changes made in the early 1980s. A letter to the editor complaining about Chrysler employees sitting around playing cards appeared in a New Castle newspaper on March 4, 1982. This would have been when Chrysler was moving toward the "lean production" and "low inventory" approach of Japanese automakers. The number of employees at the Chrysler in New Castle had been reduced by more than fifty percent. It would not be surprising that such major changes would result in production difficulties of the kind mentioned by Ingram.

In any case, Chrysler management, with the cooperation of the UAW, was able to address these problems and emerge in the 1990s as a leader in productivity and lean production methods, as we saw above. Whatever the ultimate explanation for New Castle's deindustrialization may be, it can't be blamed on unionized "slacker employees" playing cards.

More importantly, a better outcome than deindustrialization was possible.

The Way Not Taken

While I think it is unfair to blame the demise of the Chrysler plant in New Castle on a poor work ethic among the unionized employees, nonetheless, I think the underlying belief that unions are special-interest groups looking out for their members at a cost to everyone else needs to be examined and debunked.

Unions like to claim that they serve the interests of all workers, but unions never represented more than thirty-five percent of the workforce in the United States. By 1980, when American voters approved the Reagan revolution with its vision of greater reliance on free markets as the pathway to prosperity, unions represented only isolated islands of well-paid workers. It was easy for libertarians and corporate interests to depict them as special interests extorting exorbitant wages and benefits paid for by everyone else. While I can understand how many of the American people came to see unions in this way, I think it was a great mistake to think that doing away with unions would better serve the creation of a broad-based prosperity. There were better alternatives.

The Great Depression and World War II were disasters of global dimension. After the war there was a deliberate effort to prevent the recurrence of war and depression in the future. In the western democracies this effort involved both leaders and the voting public. Institutions like the United Nations, the World Bank and the International Monetary Fund were created to provide tools for addressing problems at the international level. Within each nation-state there was a similar effort to re-shape institutions in ways designed to avoid a relapse into economic depression and better secure a prosperous future. Organized labor played a significant role in this effort.

In Great Britain, the Labour Party won an historic victory in the first post-war national election, leading to the creation of the National Health Service and to a strengthening of the welfare safety net. Similar strengthening of welfare safety nets was accompanied in many Western European countries, along with a restructuring of the institutional role of unions in guiding national economies. In various forms in different countries, co-determination granted nationally organized unions a role in economic planning and decision-making. Working with nationally organized business and industry associations, these unions negotiated frameworks for labor contracts that affect large sectors of the economy and all those who work in those sectors.

There were labor leaders in the U.S. who shared the vision of European labor leaders and sought to restructure the role of organized labor here along similar lines. The most prominent among these were Philip Murray, President of the CIO, and Walter Reuther of the UAW.

Walter Reuther was President of the UAW from 1946 until his death in a plane crash in 1970. He and his brothers, Victor and Roy,

Walter Reuther spoke at the dedication of the new UAW Hall on North Main Street in New Castle in June, 1952. Henry County Historical Society (New Castle, Indiana).

were leaders in the early days of the UAW. The Reuther brothers were sons of Valentine Reuther. They grew up in Wheeling, West Virginia, where Valentine drove a truck for a local brewery and was active in the Socialist Party during the time when the Socialists were led by Eugene Debs, a native of Terre Haute, Indiana. Like Debs, Val Reuther and his sons championed strong trade unions and democracy. The Reuther brothers were also heavily influence by the social gospel Christianity of their grandfather and the Social Democratic politics of Western Europe grounded in the democratic wing of European Marxism. It was Walter Reuther who led the UAW in the late 1940s and early 1950s when a wave of militant unionism led to major gains for unions and their members in the United States.

On August 16, 1945, two days after the Japanese surrender was announced in the United States, Reuther, then head of the UAW's General Motors Division, made public the central demand in the UAW's coming negotiations with General Motors: *a thirty percent wage boost with no increase in the price of cars.* During the war the UAW, like most of the other unions in the USA, had accepted wage-and-price controls designed to support the war effort. The automakers had also done their part, shifting the auto plants to the production of trucks, tanks, planes, and munitions for the military and accepting payments according to the system of wage and price controls in place during the war. In the case of GM, this had meant accepting somewhat less than their normal twenty percent return on invested capital. With the end of the war and the end of wage and price controls, GM leaders were looking forward to a return to higher profits. In effect, Reuther was demanding that they give their workers a huge raise, hold the line on prices, and accept a lower rate of profit. The UAW argued that GM had the ability to pay the thirty percent raise without raising prices and still make an acceptable rate of profit. The union released numbers to support its case. The UAW demand was frankly aimed at redistributing wealth: more for GM's workers and less for GM stockholders.

Reuther and other UAW leaders were motivated by two fundamental concerns. In the first place, they were sympathetic to the idea of creating a more equal distribution of wealth on moral grounds, as a matter of justice. A second concern had to do with preventing a return to the Depression and unemployment of the pre-war years. The wartime demand for production, funded by government deficit spending, had finally stimulated the economy out of the Depression. What would happen now when that spending stopped? Like Reuther and other union leaders, many economists, government officials, and business leaders had become convinced that the key to keeping the economy out of depression was to maintain high levels of demand for goods and services. Raising wages for working families was a way to do that.

An exchange between Walter Reuther, speaking for the UAW, and Harry Coen, speaking for GM, made it pretty clear what the central issue was:

> Reuther: Unless we get a more realistic distribution of America's wealth, we won't get enough to keep this machine [the economy] going.
> Coen: There it is again. You can't talk about this thing without exposing your socialistic desires.
> Reuther: If fighting for a more equal and equitable distribution of wealth in this country is socialistic, I stand guilty of being a Socialist.
> Coen: I think you are convicted.

If socialism is understood as public ownership of the means of production—of the natural resources and machinery used in producing things—then there is nothing "socialist" in Reuther's demand. But, if socialism is understood more loosely—as fundamentally a matter of bringing economic life under democratic control—then Reuther's demand is "socialistic" since it claims a say for organized labor, government, and ultimately the American people, over decisions previously left to private companies and their owners. In this respect, Walter Reuther and his brothers, all sons of a Socialist Party father, stood well within the Social Democratic traditions guiding the restructuring of economic life in Western Europe in the post-war years, developments that also had the support of some Christian leaders both in Europe and in the United States.

Reuther was well informed about how Social Democrats were shaping the future in Western Europe in the post-war years. Here Reuther rows. Waving behind him is Tage Erlander, Prime Minister of Sweden from 1946-69. Seated at the bow is Hubert Humphrey. Willy Brandt, Chancellor of Germany from 1969-74 sits between Humphrey and Reuther. Photo used here courtesy of Sasha Reuther.

Reuther insisted that GM could afford to give a thirty percent raise without any increase in prices and still make a reasonable profit. This was a view supported by a CIO study and by some important people in the Truman administration. General Motors was adamantly opposed to letting its supposed "ability to pay" become the basis for granting a raise to its employees. When Reuther insisted that GM open its books to the public, GM refused. When Reuther insisted that negotiations be open to the press, GM refused. When Reuther called for the creation of a neutral committee of experts to study GM's finances to ascertain whether or not the company had the ability to pay such a raise without raising prices and still make a reasonable profit, GM refused to have anything to do with such a committee. The company refused to enter into any discussion with anyone having to do with its alleged "ability to pay."

Eventually GM did submit a counter offer: a raise of thirteen-and-a-half cents per hour with no promise to hold the line on prices. Reuther rejected the offer because it gave UAW members far less than the union was demanding, but he also rejected the offer for a much deeper reason. Reuther and the UAW saw their fight as a fight for *all workers*. To accept a raise for UAW members funded by increases in prices would be to pass on the cost of higher wages for UAW members to American consumers. It would transform the UAW from a champion of all working families to a special interest group. Reuther denounced the offer as a "conspiracy against the public" and a "bribe offer" the union would reject. The UAW, he said, "will not be a party to sand-bagging the American customer." On November 21, 1945, following an overwhelmingly supportive vote by its GM members, the UAW went on strike against GM. The strike would last 113 days.

Reuther saw the strike as involving much more than GM and its UAW employees. In his view it was a strike about the future of America. Would it be a country where the wealth belonged to a few, where working families did not have enough income to purchase what they produced, and where a return to depression and unemployment might well result? Or would it be a new economy, where wealth was more evenly distributed, prosperity more widely shared, and steady full employment more nearly secured? The UAW took its case to the American public. It published a pamphlet, "Purchasing Power for Prosperity" that argued for "mass purchasing power" based on a more equitable distribution of wealth as the key to avoiding a return to depression.

The UAW's slogan for the strike was, "We fight today for a better tomorrow." The UAW meant to use its power to fight for an economics of prosperity, a fight aimed at lifting up all working families, not just those within the union. It sought to create an "ability to pay" model that could be used to pressure businesses across the United States to provide working families with a greater share of the wealth. The UAW campaign resonated with large numbers of Americans. Support for the strike against GM was strong among GM workers, UAW members as a whole, and the American public.

Veterans also supported the strike. The GM strike, Reuther asserted, was "the fight of every veteran coming home in search of a job and a tangible stake in the future of the country he saved from international fascism." World War II veterans, many of whom had taken part in the breakthrough campaigns of the CIO unions before the war, were eager to renew the struggle to win a better deal for themselves and their families. Unlike the post-WW I period, when many veterans joined anti-union movements, after World War II veterans "remained virtually immune to antilabor political mobilization."

In December 1945, several months after Japan's surrender and just after the start of

PURCHASING POWER
for
PROSPERITY
I

*The Case of the General Motors
Workers for Maintaining
Take-Home Pay*

Presented By
INTERNATIONAL UNION, UAW·CIO, G M DEPARTMENT
WALTER P. REUTHER, Director

Purchasing Power for Prosperity argued that broad based prosperity was necessary for a stable economic future. Walter P. Reuther Library, Wayne State University.

the GM strike, some four thousand U.S. troops in Manila marched on an army headquarters depot there in support of a "bring the boys home" movement. The depot commander ordered them back to their barracks, reminding them that they were "still in the army" and "not working for General Motors."

Back home in the U.S., striking GM workers who were veterans wore their uniforms on the picket lines. When the UAW declared January 12—during the strike—as "Veterans Day," veterans in uniform formed a huge picket line surrounding GM headquarters in Detroit, while smaller groups of uniformed veterans formed picket lines at other GM plants.

The UAW strike against GM was only one of many major strikes by unions within both the CIO and the AFL in the immediate post-war period. Between November 1945, and June 1946, more than three million workers participated in strikes. Returning veterans joined the men and women who had been working in the plants during the war to press for a better deal for workers in the post-war era. Victory in war seems to have left the American people with a sense that other great things were possible. The radicalism of Reuther's call for a redistribution of wealth as the basis for a prosperous future resonated with many Americans. In early December, 1945, polls found that 44 percent of Americans surveyed supported the strikers, while 35 percent supported GM. One month later, a January poll testing opinions about the wider post-war struggle between management and labor over the future, found that by a two to one margin, public opinion thought that labor should have more say over management.

In 1945 Walter Reuther was widely regarded as the most visionary labor leader in the U.S. Prominent figures gave him their support, or at least their praise. Eleanor Roosevelt, theologian Reinhold Niebuhr (widely cited during the Iraq war for his view that war is sometimes the lesser evil and said by President Obama to be his favorite theologian) and Republican Presidential candidate Harold Stassen were among those whose names appeared on the letterhead of a national committee to aid the GM strikers. Articles praising Reuther's vision of a future economy that would give ordinary people a greater share of the wealth appeared in such mainstream magazines as *Life, Fortune,* and *Time.* Speaking for the Automobile Manufacturers' Association, George Romney called Walter Reuther "the most dangerous man in Detroit."

The UAW demand for a thirty percent wage increase without any increase in the price of cars was not an ordinary sort of union demand. Demanding higher wages was ordinary. Demanding no increase in the price of cars was radically different. That's what caused Harry Coen to call Reuther a socialist. That's why George Romney called Reuther dangerous. To understand why Romney said that and what was at stake in the GM strike, we need to put the UAW demand in its historical context.

By 1936, the idea of a "new deal" had gained the overwhelming support of the American people. President Roosevelt nicely formulated that idea in accepting his re-nomination for the presidency:

For too many of us, the political equality we once had was meaningless in the face of economic inequality. A small group had concentrated in their own hands an almost complete control over other people's lives. For too many of us life was no longer free; liberty no longer real; men could no longer follow the pursuit of happiness. Against economic tyranny such as this, the American citizen could appeal only to the organized power of Government. The collapse of 1929 showed up the despotism for what it was. The election of 1932 was the people's mandate to end it. Under that mandate it is being ended.

In reality, Roosevelt's rhetoric exceeded what had been accomplished. Ten years later, in 1946, after the enormous effort and sacrifice of the Second World War, the United States seemed to be at a crossroads. Would the New Deal be strengthened and fortified against the challenges of the future, or would it be weakened by recession, retreat, and gradual erosion? This was one of the central issues facing the American public.

The resolution adopted as the topic for debate in American colleges during the 1946-47 year was this: "That labor should be given a direct share in the management of industry." Reuther and his advisors in the UAW stood firmly on the affirmative side in this debate. They had come to think that only a broad-based prosperity would provide the foundation for strengthening the New Deal and preserving it into the future. They had come to think that a company's ability to pay should guide negotiations between labor and management. And they had come to think that only if labor negotiations became transparent—made open to oversight by unions, government, and the American public, all informed about a companies' ability to pay—could this prosperity be gained.

Reuther and the UAW used the strike against GM to raise this idea for a radical restructuring of the role of organized labor in guiding the American economy. If labor negotiations in the United States came to be conducted in a manner that made clear to the American public what companies could afford to pay, Americans' sense of fairness would support trimming profits in order to raise wages. If General Motors, then one of the largest and most successful companies in America, would agree to this, then other companies might follow. The result would be more disposable income for working families. Alfred Sloan, Chairman of the Board at General Motors, saw clearly what was at stake. If GM were to accept the UAW proposal, he said, "In the final analysis, it gets down to production plus a fixed fee." Sloan was adamantly opposed to the idea, recognizing that such transparent labor negotiations would open the door for unions, government and public opinion to interfere with the prerogatives of private corporations to manage and pursue higher profits than Reuther's "ability to pay" proposal would allow.

At the same time the UAW was launching its strike campaign against General Motors, Philip Murray and other high officials within the national CIO were trying to work out an agreement between the national labor organizations—the Congress of Industrial Organizations and the American Federation of Labor—the Federal Government, and organizations representing the interests of major corporations in the United States, such as the Chamber of Commerce and the National Association of Manufacturers. This agreement would have extended the kind of cooperation between business, labor and government created during the war into the post-war era.

In several ways, Murray's proposal was similar to Reuther's UAW campaign. Both sought to solidify and extend the New Deal into the future. Both aimed to do this by winning higher wages for workers paid for by a lower rate of profit. Both aimed at creating stable, broad-based prosperity by increasing the purchasing power of American families. And both proposals required negotiations between labor and management under conditions of transparency with regard to a company's ability to pay. Had either of these proposals been accepted, they would have worked to push American capitalism toward the emerging European model of an economy jointly managed by corporations, unions and government.

Despite the initial enthusiasm for these ideas in the early

weeks of the UAW strike against General Motors, in the end, both proposals failed. Murray was unable to gain sufficient support from business leaders or from union leaders within the AFL, or even his own CIO. CIO unions ended up accepting wage gains for their members without any basic change in the role of unions in guiding the economy or any promise against rising prices for consumers.

Reuther's plan failed because General Motors refused to open the door to negotiations based on its "ability to pay." As the GM strike dragged on and a wave of strikes swept over one industry after another, opinion in government circles and within the American public began to turn against the UAW and the CIO. In the end Reuther and the UAW were forced to accept a settlement that granted a nineteen-and-a-half cent hourly raise without any commitment from GM about holding the line on prices for cars. General Motors and the rest of corporate America retained freedom to manage without unions or government having a say. This freedom to manage would remain a permanent feature of the economic system in the United States in the decades that followed.

In the elections of 1946, organized labor suffered a major defeat. Republicans, determined to reign in organized labor, won majorities in both houses of Congress. In 1947, the new Congress passed the Taft-Hartley Act, which made changes in labor law that significantly reduced the power of unions. Three years later GM and the UAW negotiated what has come to be known as the "Treaty of Detroit." Fundamentally, the UAW abandoned demands that violated matters GM deemed to be matters of management prerogative, like access to GM financial records or having a say in pricing. In return GM agreed that wages for their workers would rise in line with increased productivity and with inflation. That agreement set a framework that heavily influenced labor/management relations in the United States for several decades.

The decisions made in early 1946 and in the Treaty of Detroit three years later shaped the framework for labor negotiations in the United States and the development of the American economy in the years ahead. The campaign for radical change had been checked. The approach adopted in Western Europe would not be adopted in the United States. The unions in the United States functioned within a narrower context, as agents for their members. Court decisions banning all sit-down strikes and permitting employers to hire permanent replacement workers during strikes made it difficult to organize new unions.

Provisions of the Taft-Hartley Act granting states permission to pass "right to work" laws and permitting injunctions against mass picketing said to be coercive made it even more difficult for unions to organize or conduct a strike. Employers, free to manage, moved production to "right to work" states in the United States and overseas, where unions were often violently repressed. The number of workers covered by union contracts steadily declined. Over time, unions and union wages were relegated to fewer and fewer islands within a sea of non-union, low-wage labor. Unions became the "special interests" conservatives love to attack.

It would have been different if Reuther and Murray's vision had prevailed. Different and better.

History matters. In the years after World War II, many of the countries in Western Europe built economic systems brought under democratic control, enabling working families and the unions that represented them to have a say in decisions that affected their economic well-being. These systems varied from country to country, but they shared some common features: the idea of the nation as a common home for all; an underlying ethics of solidarity; the creation of strong social safety nets; and collaborative planning involving management, labor and government aimed at building a secure economic future. In all of these countries, these post-war systems were built on Social Democratic traditions reaching back into the nineteenth century.

Things were different in the United States. There, an ethics of individual rights, property rights, paternalistic capitalism, and faith in free markets dominated public policy, overriding a series of labor and populist movements from the Civil War until the crisis of the depression in the 1930s. Even then, in the midst of the Depression, with millions of families facing unemployment, homelessness, and poverty, strong opposition to the New Deal and the labor rights that were a part of the New Deal remained, particularly within the right wing of the Republican Party.

Overwhelming popular support for President Franklin D. Roosevelt and the New Deal protected the labor unions during the decade that ran from 1936-1946. However, the tide turned with the elections of November 1946. FDR died in April 1945, World War II ended on September 2, 1945. The battle over the future role of the unions in the United States was fought between December 1945 and the elections in November 1946. Would the labor uprising of the late 1930s expand and deepen or would it be checked or rolled back?

With the war over, the union's "no strike pledge" ended.

Returning veterans joined large numbers of pro-union rank and file, determined to defy management and expand union power. The strike wave of 1946 involved roughly the same number of strikes as the great labor uprising of 1937, but in 1946 more than twice as many workers were involved as in 1937 and the number of strike days in 1946 was nearly three times the number in 1937. A sometimes raucous celebration of the power of ordinary people to chart a new pathway into the future surrounded this labor uprising, reflected in a popular culture that sometimes transgressed the racial and gender boundaries of the past.

Among employers, some, particulary smaller employers more directly and personally challenged by their employees like those at Perfect Circle in New Castle, wanted to get rid of the unions altogether. Big employers, like the big three auto makers, wanted only to set boundaries on what matters were legitimate concerns of the unions, boundaries that would leave corporate leaders free to manage.

Union leaders were also divided about how to respond to the labor uprising from below. Some, like Walter Reuther and Philip Murray, shared the grass-roots goals. They too wanted to expand and deepen the role of unions. Within organized labor, this divide illustrated different versions of the ethics of solidarity. Did worker solidarity include all workers? Black, white, red and yellow? Male and female? Immigrant and native? Or, did it include only members already enrolled in my union? Who are my brothers and sisters? Reuther and Murray worked to claim an institutional role for organized labor that would enable it to serve the interests of all working people. Other labor leaders wanted to stick with a pure and simple trade unionism where the job of the union was to serve the economic interests of its members.

As we saw in the previous chapter, Reuther and Murray's effort to change the role of organized labor in the US to something more like the more encompassing role of organized labor in Western and Northern Europe failed, leaving the unions largely confined to the role of protecting the interests of their members. The Taft-Hartley Act, passed by a Republican-controlled Congress in June, 1947, and the Treaty of Detroit, negotiated between the UAW and General Motors three years later, set the constraints within which unions had power to negotiate for workers; constraints that would prevail in the coming decades.

Sit down strikes were illegal. Massed picketing, often involving men and women from other unions, was for all practical purposes illegal. Companies were free to hire replacement workers and keep operating. Secondary boycotts and strikes, where organized workers could act to support other organized workers, were all illegal. For unions, at least, self-interest was allowed, but solidarity was illegal.

The already established unions struggled on, their power to effectively organize and defend the interests of working families weakened by the changing, conservative legal and political landscapes. The unions focused on defending the interests of their members. State right-to-work laws opened territory for employers to escape unions, whose power depended on worker solidarity. Union density began a several decades-long decline. The powerful spiritual foundation of the unions, an ethics of solidarity and love of neighbor, slowly gave way to a culture of self-interest, individual rights, and personal salvation.

The "Reagan Revolution" embraced these cultural values, proclaiming them to be both the founding principles of the American republic and a sure pathway to a strong and prosperous future. The novelist and autodidactic "philosopher" Ayn Rand became the spiritual guru of much the governing elite. A Republican leader in Congress widely regarded in the media as an intellectual heavyweight, publically proclaimed Rand, the atheist author of *The Virtue of Selfishness*, as fully compatible with the Christianity of St. Thomas Aquinas. No one seemed to question this.

The prevailing orthodoxy of the times lashed the unions as "special interests" extorting "rents," in the form of wages higher than free markets would allow. At the same time orthodox ideologists seemed not to notice the "rents" extracted by the corporations dominating oligopolistic markets, and the "rents" extracted from state governments as corporate welfare in exchange for promised jobs. Republican governors routinely lambasted the federal government for presuming to think that government could wisely invest public money to promote prosperity. At the same time, these same governors presided over strategic tax breaks and other corporate welfare designed to lure jobs from neighboring states. The "conservative" state of Texas led the way, giving in corporate welfare an amount equal to half the state's annual budget.

In the presidential campaign of 1984, an ad for the re-election of President Reagan began with the line, "It is morning again in America." The ad reassured Americans that President Reagan had guided the country back to the path of prosperity and freedom, a path that was claimed to be deeply rooted in America's past. Reagan was able to fool enough voters to win reelection in 1984, although anyone familiar with American history should have known better.

It wasn't long before some people raised some serious doubts. John Gray is an English political philosopher. Like many conservative thinkers, Gray is skeptical of utopian thinking in left-wing political theory, which he thought was dangerous as well as mistaken. By the 1990s, Gray had come to see a different but equally dangerous form of utopian thinking in the free-market capitalism espoused by Margaret Thatcher in Britain and Ronald Reagan in the United States. His book, *False Dawn: The Delusions of Global Capitalism*, published in 1998, contrasts the capitalism of Western Europe, which he views as a pragmatic, humane form of capitalism, with the radical free-market capitalism espoused by Margaret Thatcher and Ronald Reagan.

In Gray's view, the morning in America promised in the Reagan campaign ad is false, both with respect to the dawn that it promises and the past that it claims to love:

> The reactionary utopianism of the Right is a costly and hazardous venture. Peace and stability are the last things to be expected in societies which allow themselves to be ruled by it. Policies of buttressing traditional forms of family life and repressing the worst symptoms of crime can do little to restore the institutions and communities which the free market has desolated. The fate of the Right in the late modern age is to destroy what remains of the past in a vain attempt to recover it.

Gray is especially critical of the United States. He sees a social "breakdown" in America that parallels the world of poverty, gin, and broken families found in 19th Century England described by Charles Dickens. He describes American conservatives as a "crankish and sectarian species of Enlightenment ideology—nineteenth century libertarianism." He sees American conservatives as having embraced "a surreal" understanding of American history that has severed any connection with reality.

Gray is particularly upset about the projection of a free-market past that leaves out tariffs, land grants, slavery, and corporate subsidies. He sees this surreal view as pushing the United States toward "ungovernability," and says that the country has ceased to be "a functioning democracy." He is fearful that, with its faith in itself as a beacon to humankind, America will force its destructive, utopian version of capitalism globally, making it a model "which all societies are fated to emulate." Gray fears that this cutthroat capitalism, championed by far-right conservatives in the United States, will lead to a race to the bottom, forcing the more humane capitalisms of other countries to follow in a downward spiral.

While Gray's description of America may strike some readers as unfair, or at least overstated, I think it needs to be taken seriously. Gray argues that American free-market ideology is based largely on myth and a disregard for history. This laissez-faire ideology traces its roots in American history to the court decisions of the late 1930s, the Taft-Hartley Act, and the long war on organized labor stretching from the post-war period to the present.

Gray's *False Dawn* also brings us back to the contrast between Western European capitalism and the radical free-market capitalism espoused in the United States. In the aftermath of World War II, Western Europe followed one path and the United States followed another. Gray supports the Western European path, viewing it as the kind of pragmatic adaptation to reality that true conservatives favor.

Which version of capitalism has produced the better results? Despite the downward pressure exerted on other counties by competition from anti-union low wage capitalism in the United States and Great Britain, the more humane versions of capitalism in Western Europe have clearly done a better job. In *What Went*

Wrong? George R. Tyler presents a richly supported analysis of the disparities between the cutthroat capitalism of the US and the family friendly capitalism of Western Europe. Between 1985 and 2013 when the book was published, real wages in manufacturing grew by 220% in Denmark; 154% in France; 194% in Germany; 192% in the Netherlands; and 0.47% in the USA. It should be noted here that manufacturing in all of those Western European countries faced the same global competition as that challenging manufacturers in the USA.

A study released by the World Economic Forum in January 2017 provides another view of how well different countries have succeeded in providing economic growth that is also "inclusive," that is to say, broadly shared as opposed to concentrated in the hands of a few. Entitled, "The Inclusive Growth and Development Report," the study includes (Figure 3) an "Inclusive Development Index Top Performers" list. Among developed nations, those top performers are Luxembourg, Switzerland, Iceland, Denmark, Sweden, Netherlands, Australia, New Zealand, and Austria. Low performers among developed nations include: Brazil, Ireland, Japan, Mexico, Nigeria, and the United States.

A recent work on the history of the American standard of living by Robert Gordon of Northwestern University confirms just how bad things really are in the United States. From 1972-2013, real, inflation adjusted income for 90% of American households actually fell. From 1983 to 2013, real wealth for 46% of American households remained virtually flat. For 33% of households, real wealth actually fell, from $11,400 to $9,300. Only for the top 21% of households did real wealth significantly rise. For them it virtually doubled.

For many Americans, life today is economically pinched and insecure. It takes two or more jobs to keep a family afloat. People are working longer hours. Pensions and employer-paid health insurance are becoming increasingly rare, and when they do exist, employees are expected to pay ever-greater shares of the cost. Family life is disrupted by employer demands for short-notice scheduling. Paid vacation time is increasingly rare. Paid family leave is rarely available. About a third of American families are one layoff or one illness away from homelessness. Needing the work to stay afloat, without union contracts to protect them, more and more workers are forced to accept take-it-or-leave-it offers from employers. Of course, they have the right to refuse, just as the unemployed on the street have the right to work for lower wages, but that is about as far as anyone's freedom goes these days.

Aunu Partanen is a Finnish journalist who moved to the United States. In her recent book, *The Nordic Theory of Everything: In Search of a Better Life*, she describes how life in Finland and other Nordic countries differs from life in the USA. Among other things, she notes how much more subservient to employers Americans are than are contemporary Finns.

History matters. Elections matter. Court decisions matter. Even Congress matters. The bleak circumstances facing many American families today are the outcome of a long history of unremitting attacks on labor unions, carried out in elections, court decisions, and Congressional actions.

In Western Europe, unions representing the interests of working families have had and continue to have a say in whether manufacturing plants will be closed. In the United States they never did have such a say, despite the efforts of Walter Reuther and Philip Murray to secure it. In the United States employers retained the right to manage, including the right to sell off even profitable plants in order to invest in overseas manufacturing. In Western Europe, despite the same pressure from global competition and comparable wage and benefit costs, a larger manufacturing sector has been preserved, in large part because unions had a say.

In Western Europe, when companies faced competition that could be met only by adoption of labor saving technologies, displaced workers were supported by strong welfare safety nets and vocational training programs. In the United States, unemployment benefits were often limited and meaningful vocational training not available. In the United States, displaced workers are largely on their own. Individual responsibility is the watchword. In Western Europe, there is a stronger solidarity network supporting working families.

As John Gray feared, cutthroat American capitalism has led a race to the bottom, forcing some "liberalization" of the Western European economies. Here, "liberalization" means adopting more market-driven policies that have had negative impacts on working families. However, European countries have so far managed to retain much of their collaborative and solidarity-based systems, even in the face of such downward pressures. This has allowed those countries to mitigate downward pressures and share the negative impacts of market-driven changes. It has also made it possible for the positive impacts of these same changes to be more widely shared.

During 1945-46, when he was trying to persuade America to restructure the institutional role of organized labor in managing the American economy, Walter Reuther claimed a right for workers to "share in the fruits of advancing technology." As late as 1954, Reuther was still trying to encourage an American response to productivity enhancing technology more like that found in Europe. Speaking before a national conference on economics and collective bargaining, Reuther took a broad perspective:

> Automation must be met sanely and constructively so that the miracle of mass production—and the even greater abundance made possible by automation—can find expression in the lives of people through improved economic security and a fuller share of happiness and human dignity.

It was not to be, at least not in the United States. In Western Europe, where union representation is much higher than it is in the United States and where unions have a say in managing, the benefits of technology have been more broadly shared.

So here we are now, looking back at the path we have travelled and peering across the Atlantic to what lies on the other side. In this case, the grass looks greener on the other side, and it really is. Reuther was right. The American people would be much more secure, much freer, and much richer if they were protected by stronger, more powerful, unions.

POSSIBILITIES OF THE PRESENT

While working on this book, I read *Saving the Republic*, by Mitch Daniels. Daniels was then the second-term Governor of Indiana, the state where I was born and grew up. Daniels had been a participant in the Reagan 'Revolution', both in the campaign and as a highly placed staffer in the Reagan administration. Popular with the voters of Indiana, he was also considered a serious contender for the Republican nomination for president in 2012. In his *Saving the Republic*, published during the run-up to that election, there was a passage where Daniels referred to "the almost unbroken prosperity of the quarter century between the Reagan Recovery of 1983 and the 2008 meltdown."

In 2012, despite a mountain of evidence to the contrary, Daniels' remark was widely accepted as near gospel truth. Somehow the reality of near-stagnant income, economic insecurity, declining wealth, and declining prospects had gone unnoticed by the national media. It took the Occupy Wall Street movement to finally force that reality to light. Today, only someone living in a wealth-bubble can continue to believe that the free market tilt of the Reagan "Revolution" produced "almost unbroken prosperity."

The recent presidential primary campaigns have revealed just how different things are in 2016, compared to where they were in 2012. During the presidential campaign I read this account of an interview with Bernie Sanders:

> The Vermont Senator had just explained his democratic socialism by reminding the host George Stephanopoulos that in the social-democratic countries of Scandinavia, "by and large, government works for ordinary people in the middle class rather than, as is the case right now in our country, for the billionaire class." "I can hear the Republican

attack ad right now," Stephanopoulos, interrupted:
"He wants America to be more like Scandinavia."
That's right," Sanders replied without blinking.
"What's wrong with that?"

This was in the early stage of the primary campaigns. While I agreed with Sanders and found Stephanopoulos' cynicism depressing, at that time I shared Stephanopoulos' view that Sanders' message had no chance with American voters. It often seemed as if we, the American people, were trapped by the burdens of our past, caught in an economic cul-de-sac by a series of historical wrong turns. But the people were no longer buying the old corporate propaganda.

The primary election campaigns revealed the breadth and depth of voter discontent with the insecure and straightened circumstances of their lives. On the Republican side, candidates of the party establishment affirmed their loyalty to the Reagan Revolution without offering anything to address the real problems people faced. Voters flocked to Donald Trump, the man who promised good jobs for all by, so he said, taking them back from immigrants and by personally negotiating better trade deals. On the Democrat side, a surprising tide of millions cast their votes for Bernie Sanders, an avowed socialist. Who could have imagined such a thing even a short two years ago?

There is now an opportunity for real change. The hold of free market ideology on public consciousness has been, if not broken, then at least cracked. Free markets do not provide broad-based prosperity. Tax cuts for the rich will not solve our problems. The rich already have far too much wealth—so much they don't know what to do with it. They may invest it overseas, or in job-destroying automation that will abandon workers on the streets, or in bubble-inflating speculation on the financial markets—speculation that threatens the economic security of the rest of us. Blaming big government is a distraction. We need to restore democracy. Democracy is a form of government—of, for and by the people. Ordinary people need to have a say. They need to have power. We cannot at the same time restore democracy and drown government in a bathtub.

The ideological shell has been cracked. There is an opening here, now, for change. But it is a dangerous moment, too. The insecurity of the times breeds fear and anger. People look for scapegoats. Many, like newly elected President Donald Trump, blame immigrants. However, the problem is not that immigrants have taken good "American" jobs; the problem is that "efficient" capital investment firms, bent on maximizing financial returns for their management and their investors, have dismantled those good "American" jobs.

Workers in the United States need a permanent voice in decisions affecting their lives. They need strong unions with the power to have such a say. Further, if the recent announcements of US corporations about keeping production facilities in America are typical of what is to come, it's clear that these "deals" are not examples of hard bargaining on behalf of American workers so much as sweet subsidies for American companies. What kept some of the at-risk jobs from going to Mexico were financial incentives to be paid to big corporations by the taxpayers in various states. This is just one more example of the kind of corporate welfare given out by state governments over the previous decades. Such handouts reward special interests capable of extracting "rents" through threats, political connections, or bribes. They do not serve the working people as a whole.

In some ways the present resembles the United States of the Depression years. After decades of high-flying capitalism, the country finds itself in a dreary "new normal" with no end in sight. Millions of immigrants, African-Americans, and Latinos are marginally employed in low-wage jobs and vilified by racist right-wing "populists." Outside the United States similar economic conditions around the world give rise to fear, vilification of immigrants and racial minorities, and nationalisms poised to respond with violence. War clouds are everywhere.

The labor rising of the 1930s grew out of similar conditions. The rise of labor power had to overcome long-standing hostile legal, political, and cultural forces. That same union tide could sweep across the country again.

How can an emancipatory labor movement grow out of the present wave of resistance to Republican assaults on the social safety net? As a union activist since the age of eight who has belonged to unions and been active in unions in every decade since, it's clear to me that solidarity is at the foundation of it all. This must be solidarity of the broadest kind—one that is open to all human beings. It flows from a moral imperative to lift up the poor and share the wealth that we produce. Dr. Martin Luther King, Jr. used to say that we are all children of God. We are all brothers and sisters. It is shameful for a wealthy few to horde vast amounts of wealth at the expense of others. Everyone who does socially necessary labor should have a living family wage, as Walter Reuther proposed decades ago.

In the United States, labor solidarity has to be built on respect for workers of diverse racial and ethnic identities. The history of the labor movement in the United States is checkered in this regard. At times it has welcomed minority members who are not "like us," and at times it has turned them away. The way forward clearly requires both an awareness of this checkered past and the resolve to do the right thing.

African-Americans hold a unique place in the history of the United States. They have been a part of that history from the early colonial beginning to the present. Their labor played a large part in building the United States. Slave labor produced the cotton trade, the largest commodity market of its era, creating enormous wealth for plantation owners in the South and bank investors in the North. Their blood was spilled in the Revolutionary War, the Civil War, and every war that followed. Yet, African Americans have been excluded by law and by racial prejudice from full citizenship and from a just share of the wealth that has been produced.

"Jobs and Freedom" was the call for one of the largest demonstrations in American history. It was in Washington D.C. in August of 1963, speaking to the huge crowd rallied there under that banner, that Martin Luther King gave his "I have a Dream" speech. It was in Memphis in April of 1968 that King was murdered. He was in Memphis to support a strike by African-American Sanitation Workers hauling garbage in that city. The overwhelming majority of African-Americans has always been and continues to be a part of the working class in the United States. It is one of the cruelest ironies of our history that it was only in the late 1960s and early

1970s that African-Americans were beginning to be accepted as equals in many American unions. The long decline of good union jobs hurt African-Americans most. Last hired, first fired.

Immigrant workers also need to be included in labor's comeback. They make up around seventeen percent of the workforce in the United States. Many of them are highly educated, with advanced technical skills, while many others labor as "illegals" in low-wage jobs under the arbitrary dictatorship of their employer. Many immigrant workers bring experience building labor unions from their former home countries. Many of them are ready to be active members and leaders of unions. All of them need unions. The labor movement in the United States needs them as well.

Working with these immigrant workers will require working with immigrant community organizations. There is a checkered history between unions and immigrant workers in the United States. White working-class support for Donald Trump in the recent elections is a current addition to that troubling history of racial prejudice. There are also language barriers. As in the pre-World War I era, unions and labor organizers today need to work with immigrant communities that include significant numbers of non-English speaking workers and families. In our time, immigrant community organizations can help existing unions work with immigrant workers, mediating ethnic mistrust and providing needed sympathetic dual-language intermediaries. Unions and the broader labor movement need to work with these organizations to build solidarity with immigrant workers and their families.

Many workers today labor at different jobs for different employers. A labor movement rooted in such working-class communities does not neatly fit the bargaining-unit categories of traditional existing labor law. Precarious, freelance jobs make up an increasingly large segment of the labor market. Labor unions can and should act in solidarity with working-class communities on a variety of issues. These can include matters such as civil rights, gender equality, protection of the environment, public health services, minimum wage laws, and other labor issues. The union movement must understand itself as part of a broader struggle for justice, prosperity, and respect for all people.

It is good for unions and the broader labor movement to be engaged in such ways. But community-based labor movements do have their limits. At best they can put pressure on people with power to exercise that power in just ways. They cannot institutionalize power in working-class hands within the structure of existing labor law.

The National Labor Relations Act (the Wagner Act) often called the "Magna Carta of Labor," sought to give real power to workers, to counterbalance the power of employers. It did so by permitting workers to elect unions to represent them and by requiring employers to bargain in good faith with such elected unions. Under the act, the unions also had the power to strike to prevent plants from operating, forcing employers to bargain. However, as we have seen in previous chapters, subsequent court rulings and changes to labor law have made it difficult to organize unions and have undercut the power of unions to force employers to bargain. Employers' use of outsourcing, subcontracting, part time employment, and franchise arrangements have also resulted in forms of employment that evade provisions of existing labor law, with its narrow definition of bargaining units.

During the period from the end of World War II until the early 1970s, a large number of working families shared in the growing wealth of the nation, although that abundance was not shared equally with people of color or immigrants. For the forty years after that, from the early 1970s to the present, the wealth of the nation has continued to increase, but for the bottom ninety percent of the population, real income declined.

The decades of the 40s, 50s and 60s were the decades of powerful unions like the UAW. The decades from the late 70s on saw outsourcing, loss of jobs, concessions bargaining, short-term management makeovers (from the Chrysler to Acustar to Daimler to Cerberus to Metaldyne) and the final stripping of machinery and destruction of manufacturing plants. Working families remained, but they no longer had a job with a powerful union defending their back.

In this era of permanent replacement workers and mercurially self-changing employers, the Wagner Act of 1935 is as dated as the Magna Carta. Still, the issue of power that the Wagner Act addressed remains. Working families need the power to claim a greater share of the wealth. Strikes against employers who are tied to one location and lack resources to bring in replacement workers continue to make sense. Here the provisions of the Wagner Act can still make possible a real improvement in workers' lives. Otherwise something new is needed—something that community-based organizing and social-issue organizing cannot alone provide.

Collective bargaining as we now have it leaves most workers in the U.S. out. Confined to the representation of Balkanized bargaining units, the unions will remain "special interests" viewed with envy or hostility by many, and vulnerable to the ever-changing economic landscape.

This is not to say that union locals and the national and international organizations with which they are affiliated need to be abandoned or restructured. It is not to say that we need to abandon collective bargaining within the framework of the NLRB. Existing labor relations institutions must be parts of a larger, more encompassing structure and vision. We need a voice backed up with power that will represent the interests of all working people. The only version of this on the horizon, so far as I can see, is something like the Social Democratic model for the institutionalized labor movement in Northern and Western Europe. Walter Reuther and Bernie Sanders are right. We need to be more like Sweden.

The political obstacles to realizing this are great. It will take a national labor and social justice movement. But that does not mean it will take a lifetime, or even a long time. Change can come swiftly when it comes. The AFL-CIO could provide an institutional structure to lead such a movement. The political campaign unfolding over the last year has brought us fear, but also hope. Masses of people understand the need for a major change of direction. They have already taken action to make that change real. We saw it in the four million protesters around the world, mainly women, who marched in protest of President Trump and the Republican Party's racist, anti-immigrant, libertarian agenda.

The millions of voters who supported Bernie Sanders for President and his social democratic platform have clearly shown that many of the American people no longer fall for the idea that free market capitalism will create broad based prosperity. As it turned out, the election was won by a candidate pledged to make America great again, but at the expense of the majority. That platform is a betrayal of the ethics of solidarity. We can make America great only if we also work to make the world great and if we ensure that the bounty of our labor is shared by all.

My father was born in 1915 into a tenant farm family in northern Rush County, Indiana. His ancestors had owned and farmed land in that part of Indiana since the early 1800s. The farmhouse he lived in had no central heat, no electricity, no running water, and no plumbing. He remembered as a boy driving a pony-drawn cart to bring water to the men working in the fields. He remembered herding pigs to market on foot on the national highway, Route 40. His paternal grandparents scraped together enough money to buy a forty-acre farm in nearby Henry County in 1911.

In 1933, at age eighteen, my father began to work at the Chrysler in New Castle. He worked there through layoffs and call-backs until retirement in 1970. A photo of the Chrysler from 1950 is on the cover of this book. My father worked in the forge shop, in the background of the photo. He lived to see two ways of life disappear. The 40-acre farm of his early years is gone, unable to compete with the modern, many thousand acre farming combines that dominate the industry today. The Chrysler plant is gone too, along with the factory life of mid-twentieth century.

The Christianity of my parents was a Christianity of love rather than a Christianity of salvation: "Thou shalt love the Lord thy God with all thy heart...and thy neighbour as thyself." My parents tried to live this teaching. They volunteered to serve the church community and the larger community as well. When the civil rights struggle of the 60s opened our eyes to the evils around us, my parents supported opening our church for a multi-racial day care facility. They supported cooperation between our First Methodist Church and the African Methodist Episcopal Church in New Castle.

Richard Hudelson

When I was driving a Yellow Cab in New Castle, Reverend Calvin Word of AME Church, who was blind, was one of my regular passengers. He talked about my father and working with him at district meetings of the Methodist Men's organization. I also heard that my father was one of the men working at the Chrysler who stepped up to make integration of production lines work in the early 70s. For too many Americans, that Christian love for thy neighbor has also all but disappeared.

My brother and I became strong supporters of unions in part because we grew up in a union town where the value of the union was evident, and in part because unions fit with the love of neighbor central to my parent's Christianity. It also fits with the way our parents took all human beings as neighbors—all races and all religions.

When I was a boy, I always read the UAW newspaper *Solidarity* when it arrived at our house. It fit with the religious teaching at the heart of my upbringing and it expanded my understanding of the world. Walter Reuther was a great hero. I was not surprised to discover later that he grew up in a family with similar religious roots.

Times change. I grew up with a sense that America was changing for the better. The civil rights movement seemed to be a great step forward. As time passed, the sense that America was changing for the better gave way to deepening worries about the future. An expansive love of neighbor gave way to lines dividing us from them. Gradually the circle of solidarity collapsed, beaten down by a long, focused campaign on the part of corporate America promoting an extreme regard for individual rights and individual salvation over a love of neighbor.

As the great global quest for capital accumulation drives us toward ecological disaster, making great piles of wealth for a tiny minority while sentencing the rest of us to wage slavery or unemployment, it becomes clear that we cannot save ourselves alone. We cannot survive living on a planet in the midst of global destruction. Our only salvation lies in the power of the people wisely used, for the good of us all. That way of life can bring much joy. Our union brothers and sisters have tasted that joy in the past. Rebuilding the unions, we can, too.

About the author

Photo: Terry Dunkle

The Perfect Circle Strike in 1955 left Richard Hudelson a supporter of labor unions. Later he taught philosophy at the University of Minnesota Duluth (1977-1996) and at the University of Wisconsin Superior (1996-2011). He is the author of books, articles and reviews in the area of social and political philosophy with a research focus on the history of economics and the proper role of markets. With co-author Carl Ross, he is also the author of *By the Ore Docks: A Working People's History of Duluth*.

ACKNOWLEDGEMENTS

In working on this book I have been helped by many different people. From the Reuther Library at Wayne State, I received extensive help from William LeFevre, an Archivist with the UAW Collection, Mary Wallace, an Audiovisual Archivist, and Anita Sower, a research assistant. Kathie Ward, Coordinator for the Indiana Room at the New Castle-Henry County Public Library, was a great help, pointing me to valuable research materials in that collection and answering numerous questions. Elaine Matthews, from the Public Library in Anderson, Indiana, assisted with valuable information about the UAW in Anderson that had a connection to UAW history in New Castle. From the National Archives and Records Administration in Washington, D.C., Katherine Mollan provided help in locating archival materials related to the Perfect Circle strike. Help in knowing what to do with apples/oranges problems concerning comparisons of international wages and benefits between countries, was provided by Amy Bixler, an Economist with the Bureau of Labor Statistics, and by Linda Ewing, a Special Policy Advisor to then UAW President, Bob King.

Elizabeth Edstene, Gene Ingram, Benjamin Badgley, and Joanne Schell, from the New Castle Henry County Historical Society, have provided help in locating historical documents and photographs over a period of several years. Gene Ingram was also able to explain some features of the history of the Chrysler that puzzled me. Darrel Radford's *New Castle: A Pictorial History* (1992) provided both a rich collection of photographs and a concise but very helpful textual history. Doug Magers kindly allowed me to work with his extensive personal collection of historical materials related to New Castle. I also benefited from several conversations with him.

Don Davis shared valuable work that he has done on the history of the Chrysler in collaboration with Gary Guffey, Kathy Ferrell,

Mary Hall and Dean Harmon. I have also benefited considerably in understanding the history of the Chrysler in its last few decades from *The New Castle Communicator*, a publication written by Beverly Matthews. I would also like to mention *The History of the Indiana Rolling Mill Through 1975*, by Bob Perdue, which has been very helpful for understanding local labor history.

I have been fortunate to have the opportunity to talk with three former presidents of UAW Local 371: Rual Vincent, Noel Blevins, and Luther Ferrell. Each provided unique insights from different time periods. I have also benefited from conversations with Dale Cole and Chuck Jarboe, each with long experience with Chrysler and the UAW. I would also like to thank Donnie Pyle and Gary Drumm for help they have given me in understanding aspects of New Castle's history.

Finally, I would like to thank Tim Sheard, of Hard Ball Press, for his many suggestions that made for a better book, and my wife and author in her own right, Eileen Zeitz Hudelson, for her help in editing the text.

—Richard Hudelson (August 14, 2017)

SOURCES

Front Cover

Image of pickets, courtesy of the Henry County Historical Society, New Castle, Indiana; Image of newspaper clipping from *Courier Times*, New Castle, Indiana

Back Cover

Nick DiGaetano quote from John Barnard, *American Vanguard: The United Auto Workers During the Reuther Years, 1935-1970* (Detroit: Wayne State University Press, 2004) p. 153

Chapter 2: Hammers in the Night

William Clement Bond, *A History of New Castle, Indiana* (1972) New Castle, Indiana Public Library

1817 I Avenue, Video and DVD produced by Don Davis, Gary Guffey, Kathy Ferrell, Mary Hall, and Dean Harmon (February 24, 2009). Available from the Henry County Historical Society located in New Castle, Indiana. Includes Charles Fairbanks quote

Chapter 3: New Castle Joins The UAW

UAW Local 371 Record Books and Correspondence. Reuther Library, Wayne State University (Meeting minutes and corre- spondence in chronological order)

Joyce Shaw Peterson, *American Automobile Workers, 1900-1933* (Albany: State University of New York Press, 1987) John Dodge story, p 59 Turnover rate, p. 10

John Barnard, *American Vanguard: The United Auto Workers*

During the Reuther Years, 1935-70 (Detroit: Wayne State University Press, 2004) Turnover Rate at Ford, pp. 95-96

1817 I Avenue DVD: Interviews with Lightfoot, Marlow, and Ratcliff

Claude Hoffman, *Sit-Down in Anderson: UAW Local 663, Anderson Indiana* (Detroit: Wayne State University Press, 1968) on Anderson and connection between UAW in Anderson and UAW in New Castle

On New Castle Chrysler employees' involvement in UAW strike at Chrysler, spring 1937: http://www.uaw.org/page/uaw-history "Our History"

Nelson Lichtenstein, *The Most Dangerous Man in Detroit* (New York: Basic Books,1995) on events in Anderson,Indiana see p.78

Donnie Pyle: Telephone interview with author

Chapter 4: Building Solidarity

UAW Local 371 Record Books and Correspondence

Charles Hyde, *Riding the Roller Coaster: A History of the Chrysler Corporation* (Detroit: Wayne State University Press, 2008). See summary of 1939 contract

On NLRB conducted Chrysler representation election in 1939: Hyde (pp. 117-118) indicates that all Indiana Chrysler plants failed to give majority support for UAW CIO. Local 371 Record Books indicate strong majority support for UAW CIO. The *Detroit Free Press* "Chrysler Poll Won By CIO," Sept. 29, 1939, which provides results for each plant indicate UAW CIO won strong majority in New Castle

Chapter 5: War Brings Labor Peace

UAW Local 371 Record Books and Correspondence

Barnard: on gendered pre-war wages, p. 24; on African- Americans assigned to production jobs during World War II, p. 14

Marlow Interview: *1817 I Avenue*

Detroit study: Peterson, pp. 75-76

Pittsburgh Steelworkers Study: David Brody, *Steelworkers in America: The Nonunion Era* (Cambridge: Harvard University Press, 1960) p. 98

Quote from Reuther speaking to Ford workers: Lichtenstein, p. 283

Chapter 6: On the Picket Lines

On Flying Squadrons role in UAW strikes: Barnard, p. 94. Barnard mentions such squadrons as made up of strong union supporters willing to fill picket lines where needed, but not necessarily engaged in violence or intimidation

The Imp: The passage quoted is from a single issue found in the UAW Local 371 Record Books and Correspondence collection

Steve Dicken, "Oh, You Can't Scare Me I'm Stickin' To the Union," (unpublished manuscript shared with author)

Tuttle Letter: Victor Reuther, *The Brothers Reuther and the Story of the UAW* (Boston: Houghton Mifflin, 1976) p. 311. Exchange between Walter Reuther and Harry Coen: Victor Reuther, pp. 250-251

Bob Perdue, *The History of the Indiana Rolling Mill Through 1975* nd. Henry County Historical Society (New Castle, Indiana)

Chapter 7: The New War On Labor

David Anderson: "Things Are Different Down Here: The 1955 Perfect Circle Strike, Conservative Civic Identity, and the Roots of the New Right in the 1950s Industrial Heartland," *International*

Labor and Working-Class History No. 74, Fall 2008, pp. 101-123. Anderson provides the history leading up to the events of 1955

Courier Times (New Castle, Indiana) March 19, 1937, p. 1 (on formation of the "independent union" at Perfect Circle)

Chapter 8: The Not So Perfect Perfect Circle

Quote from *Wall Street Journal* from David Anderson, pp. 106-107. Unless otherwise indicated, other quotations in this chapter are from Anderson

Quote on debt to the Teetor family: http://www.hagerstown. in-.gov/pages/about.php

McClellan Committee of the United States Senate: Hearings Before the Select Committee Investigating Improper Activities in the Labor or Management Field (Eighty-Fifth Congress, Second Session, March 31 and April 1, 1958) Part 26. (Testimony of William B. Prosser, P.C. Executive, pp. 10258-10267); (Testimony of Paul Carper, UAW Local 662 Anderson, IN, pp. 10363-10372)

Chapter 9: Those Troublesome Outside Agitators

The account of events in this chapter relies heavily on the work of David Anderson, already cited, and on accounts of these events by the *Courier Times*, a daily newspaper published in New Castle, Indiana

On the claim that a UAW picket was arrested simply for calling a man a "scab," see Robert Kinerk, "Equality for All? Kinerk was an officer and steward for UAW Local 662 in Anderson, who was present on the picket line at Perfect Circle. (UAW Local 662 Collection, Reuther Library, Wayne State University)

Quote fromWilliam Prosser on right to work is from: Mitchel Levitas, "Behind the Violence at Perfect Circle," *The New Leader* (October 31, 1955, p. 13)

Chapter 10: What Is Freedom Without Dignity?

David Bergland, *Libertarianism in One Lesson* 7th ed. (Costa Mesa, CA: Orpheus Publications, 1997) p. 62 and p. 66

Ron Chernow, *Washington: A Life* (New York: Penguin Press, 2010) quotation from Washington, p. 328

Quotation from *The Imp*: UAW Local Record Books and Correspondence

Manure Olson, *The Logic of Collective Action* (Cambridge: Harvard University Press, 1965) p. 71 (both quotations)

Evelyn K. Sheffield letter: UAW Local 662 Collection

Adam Smith, *Wealth of Nations* Book 1, Chapter 8, Section 12

Bangledesh fire: *The Guardian* (UK) Nov. 25, 2012; No sick leave: *New York Times* Oct. 23, 2012 p. A 16

Barnard (four quotations from) p. 27, p. 153, p. 153 again, p. 110

Chapter 11: Profits and Prosperity

Quotations from Ricardo and Lucas: Branko Milanovic, *The Haves and the Have-Nots* (Basic Books: New York, 2011) p. 4

Erik Brynjalfsson and Andrew McAfree, *Race Against the Machine* (Lexington, Massachusetts: Digital Frontier Press)

John Hospers, "What Libertarianism Is," in ed. Tibor Machan, *The Libertarian Alternative* (Chicago: Nelson-Hall, 1974)

Quote from John Stuart Mill: Joel Mokyr, *The Enlightened Economy: An Economic History of Britain 1700-1850* (New Haven: Yale University Press, 2009) p. 469

On roll of economic reforms in bringing broader prosperity in late nineteen century: Norman Rick, *The Age of Reform: 1850-1890* (New York: W.W. Norton, 1977) p. 25 and Mokyr, pp. 484-485

Chapter 12: Can Capitalism Be Tamed?

A well written history of financial crises which became popular in the wake of the financial crisis of 2007 is Charles Kindleberger and Robert Aliber, *Manias, Panics, and Crashes*, 5th Edition (Hoboken, New Jersey: John Wiley and Sons, 2005). Kindleberger was an economist at MIT. The book was originally published in 1978

John Lanchester, *I.O.U. Why Everyone Owes Everyone and No One Can Pay* (New York: Simon and Schuster, 2010)

Ha-Joon Chang, *Things They Don't Tell You About Capitalism* (2010) (New York: Bloomsbury Press, 2011)

The work of Thomas Piketty and his colleagues has provided powerful theoretical and empirical evidence for the view that there is a long run tendency for the rate of return on capital to outpace growth in real wages. Thomas Piketty, *Capital in the Twenty-First Century* (Cambridge: Harvard University Press, 2014)

Chapter 13: When Wall Street Takes Over The Company

Charles K. Hyde, *Riding the Roller Coaster: A History of the Chrysler Corporation* (Detroit: Wayne State University Press) 2003. (Primary source used here.)

Steve Jefferys, *Management and Managed: Fifty Years of Crisis at Chrysler* (Cambridge: Cambridge University Press, 1986)

Barry Bluestone and Bennett Harrison, *The Deindustrialization of America* (New York: Basic Books, 1982)

Jefferson Cowie, *Capital Moves: RCA's Seventy Year Quest for Cheap Labor* (Ithaca, New York: Cornell University Press, 1999)

Beverly Matthews, *The New Castle Communicator* (September 2003) Vol. 2 Issue 4. This is a publication of Chrysler Corporation in New Castle. Unless otherwise noted, information in this chapter about changes at the Chrysler plant in New Castle and what happened there comes from this source.

Quotation from Marc Stepp, Hyde p. 249

Sidney Finkelstein, "The Daimler Chrysler Merger," Tuck School of Business at Dartmouth College, 2002. Includes quotations on Chrysler as most profitable automaker and on Chrysler CEO Bob Eaton's worries

Alex Taylor III, "History's 10 Worst Auto Chiefs," *Fortune Magazine* April 3, 2013

Newspaper Letter of March 4, 1982: Doug Magers Collection, New Castle, Indiana

Brian Alexander, *Glass House: The 1% Economy and the Shattering of the All American Town* (New York: St. Martin's Press, 2017)

Eileen Appelbaum and Rosemary Batt, *Private Equity at Work: When Wall Street Manages Main Street* (New York: Russell Sage Foundation, 2014). On Delphi p. 211; On Wilber Ross, p. 195; from Steve Feinberg, p. 253

Chapter 14: The Way Not Taken

For Overviews of Western European Alternatives See: Richard B. Freeman, *Working Under Different Rules* (New York: Russell Sage Foundation, 1994) Martin Schröder, *Integrating Varieties of Capitalism and Welfare State Research: A Unified Typology of Capitalisms* (New York: Palgrave Macmillan, 2013) David B. Audretsch and Erik E. Lehmann, *The Seven Secrets of Germany: Economic Resilience in an Era of Global Turbulence* (Oxford: Oxford University Press) 2015 and Anu Partanen, *The Nordic Theory of Everything: In Search of a Better Life* (New York: HarperCollins, 2016)

On efforts by Reuther and Murray to re-structure the role of organized labor in the United Sates along Western European lines see: Robert H. Zieger, *The CIO, 1935-1955* (Chapel Hill: University of North Carolina Press, 1955) pp. 213-226 and Nelson Lichten-stein, *The Most Dangerous Man in Detroit: Walter Reuther and the Fate of American Labor* (New York: Basic Books, 1995) pp. 220-247

Exchange between Coen and Reuther: Lichtenstein, p. 231

Support for Reuther and Murray within Truman Administration: Ziegler, p. 215 and p. 218

Quotes including "conspiracy" "bribe" and "sandbagging" against American people: Lichtenstein, p. 232

Support for the GM Strike among veterans: Lichtenstein, p. 234

Sense that "great things were possible" in post-war 1940s: George Lipsitz, *Rainbow at Midnight* (Urbana: University of Illinois Press, 1994) provides a rich account of working class America, leavened by differences of gender, race, and ethnicity, facing a future open with possibilities in the late 1940s

December 1945 poll and January 1946 poll: Lichtenstein, p. 238

Support for Reuther in 1945 and Romney's opposition: Lichten-stein, p. 237. Alfred Sloan quote: Lichtenstein, p. 230

College debate topic 1946-47: http://groups.wfu.edu/NDT/ HistoricalLists/topics.html

On the Treaty of Detroit: Lichtenstein, pp. 271-298 provides an account of the terms of the Treaty of Detroit. A brief statement regarding the part of the agreement regarding wages and the in-fluence of that agreement on wages throughout the US economy, for both union and non-union firms, can be found in Jonathan Schlefer, *The Assumptions Economists Make* (Cambridge, MA: Harvard University Press, 2012) p. 134

Chapter 15: Burdens of the Past

On making solidarity illegal, see: Joe Burns, *Reviving the Strike*

Richard Hudelson

(Brooklyn, NY: Ig Publishing, 2011) pp. 47-70

On corporate welfare, see: Louise Story, "The United States of Subsidies," *New York Times*, December 1, 2012

John Gray, *False Dawn: The Delusions of Global Capitalism* (New York: The Free Press, 1998) (reactionary utopianism, p. 38; breakdown p. 2; crankish and sectarian p. 104; surreal p. 105; ungovernable, p. 109; not a functioning democracy, p. 131, race to the bottom, pp. 78-79

George R. Tyler, *What Went Wrong* (Dallas: Ben Bella Books, 2013) See chart on dust-jacket

World Economic Forum, "The Inclusive Growth and Development Report," January 2017. https://www.weforum.org/ reports/

Robert Gordon, *The Rise and Fall of American Growth* (Princeton: Princeton University Press, 2016) On decline in real income p. 609; On real wealth p. 620

Anu Partanen, *The Nordic Theory of Everything: In Search of a Better Life* (New York: HarperCollins, 2016) pp. 11-46

Two quotes from Walter Reuther: Victor Reuther, *The Brothers Reuther and the Story of the UAW: A Memoir* (Boston: Houghton Mifflin, 1976) (On workers right to share in prosperity: p. 305-306; On the need for a sane approach to automation: p. 318)

Chapter 16: Possibilities of the Present

Quote from Mitch Daniels on "almost unbroken prosperity" (1983-2008): Mitch Daniels, *Keeping the Republic: Saving America by Trusting Americans* (New York: Sentinel, 2011) p. 4

George Stephanopolous Interview with Bernie Sanders: "This Week" (ABC) May 3, 2015

Abston, Floyd: 35

AFL (see American Federation of Labor)

African-Americans: 37, 44-45, 160-161

Allegheny Ludlum Steel: 131

American Federation of Labor: 24, 32-33, 36, 50

Anderson, David: 63, 73, 92, 173-174

Anderson, Indiana: early UAW organizing, 24-26;
support for other UAW locals, 32, 77, 83-84;
private equity in, 133
automation: 112, 156, 158

Baker, Sidney: 17, 29, 79

Batchfield, Carl: 76, 79

Bendix Sit-Down Strike: 25

Bergland, David: 99

Blevins, Noel: 128

capitalism: laissez-faire in theory, 109-112; laissez-faire in practice, 112-115; markets v democracy, 97-98; business cycle, 117-121; reform era, 114-115; varieties of, 137-138, 153-156

Carper, Paul: 77-78, 84-85

Cerberus Capital Management: 129, 132, 134

Christianity: 114, 139, 151, 164-165

Chrysler Corporation: early history, 15, 26; contract (1939), 37-39; pension strike, 49-57; closing of New Castle plant, 124-130

CIO: early history, 24; expelled from AFL, 32-33; industrial union councils, 34; wins

factional fight in UAW, 36-37; locals in New Castle, 58-59

closed shop (see union shop)

co-determination: 138; as industrial democracy, 97-98; post-war public support, 144-146;
check on deindustrialization, 155-156

collective bargaining:
before Wagner Act, 20;
required by Wagner Act, 65-66;
as restriction on management rights, 69;
as democracy, 97-98;
subversion of in recent decades, 151, 163

company unions: 62-63

corporate welfare: 151-152, 159

Dana Corporation: 130, 134

Daniels, Mitch: 3, 157

Davis, Don: 59

Davis, Margaret: 43

Davis Foundry: 58, 135

Debs, Eugene: 139

deindustrialization: 125, 134-136

democracy:
industrial democracy, 97-98;
social democracy, 97-98, 114;
co-determination, 138;
versus right-to-work laws, 98;
versus small government, 158;
power to people, 106, 162-163

Depression (1930s): 8, 11, 21-23, 28, 33, 63-64

Dicken, James: 56

Dicken, Steve: 56

Die Makers at New Castle
  Chrysler: 20, 32, 35, 49
economic theory: classical, 109-111;
  marginalist (neo-classical) 111;
  oligopolies, 151;
  prosperity and, 112
elections: national (1946), 107, 147,
  (1980), 120, 137, (2016), 157-158;
  SNew Castle (1955), 79-80
ethics:
  individual rights v solidarity,
    61, 149-151, 164;
  shareholders and stakeholders, 133
Evans, Carl: 72
Felix, Rev. Ralph: 33-34
financialization: 125-126, 135
free-riders: 73, 99-104
freedom: 61;
  wage-slavery and right-to-work,
    104-106, 109, 165;
  Freedom Forum and Perfect
    Circle, 75
Gann, Jack: 28, 32
Gibbins, Jean: 44
Glass-Steagall Banking Act: 118, 120
globalization: 119-120, 135, 154-156
Grede Castings: 131
Griffin, Helen: 44
Harris, Joe: 27, 32
Hoosier Kitchen Cabinets: 33
Hospers, John: 112, 114, 121
immigrants: 21, 158-159, 162
Imp (UAW Local 371 publication): 56
Ingram, Gene: 135-136
John Birch Society: 3
Juday, Chesley: 79-80
Kentucky: 21-22, 27-28, 63
King, Martin Luther: 3, 160
libertarianism: 98-99, 104-105, 153
Lightfoot, Ron: 23-24, 28
Marlow, Goodson: 28, 46
Martin, Homer: 17, 32, 36

Marx, Karl: 2, 110, 114
mass picketing: 76-77, 85-86,
  88, 90-94, 148, 151
Maxwell Briscoe Company: 7-8, 13-15
McClellan Committee:
  testimony of Paul Carper, 77-78;
  testimony of William Prosser, 95
McCormack, Paul: 78-79
Metaldyne: 130-131, 162
Mill, John Stuart: 113
Modernfold Doors: 135
Murray, Philip: 138, 146, 150, 155
National Health Insurance: 45-46
National Industrial Recovery Act
  (NIRA): 64-65, 89
National Labor Relations Act
  (NLRA): history, 34, 65-66,
  88-89;
  Taft-Hartley revisions, 90, 107;
  current limitations, 162-163
National Labor Relations Board
  (NLRB): history, 65;
  elections at Chrysler, 36-37, 49, 90;
  elections at Perfect Circle, 63,
  69, 73, 75, 85, 90;
  national union shop
  certification elections, 107-108
Occupy Wall Street: 157
Olivet Presbyterian Church: 33
open shop: 26
Outokumpu: 131
Pan American Bridge: 58, 135
pattern bargaining: 73-74
pensions: 3-5;
  strike at Chrysler, 49-59;
  becoming rare, 154
Perdue, Bob: 57-58, 131
Perfect Circle Corporation:
  early history, 61-67;
  ideology, 69-75;
  strike (1955), 75-81, 90-95;
  demise of, 130-131
piece work: 20
Pittsburgh Steelworkers Study: 46

Popejoy, Frank: 32

pre-union era: 64, 73, 105, 136

private equity firms: 129, 132-134

Prosser, William: 77, 95

Pyle, Donnie: 28

racism: 44-45

Ratcliff, Rea: 23, 28

Reagan Revolution: 3, 109, 112, 120, 137, 151-152, 157-158

Republic Steel massacre: 26

Reuther, Walter: 137-148

Ricardo, David: 110-111, 113

Richmond, Indiana: 32, 62, 73-76, 78-79, 85-86, 91-93

right-to-work laws:
open shop past, 20, 63-64;
NLRA permits unionshop, 88;
Taft-Hartley allows states to outlaw union shop, 90;
Perfect Circle supports rtw, 95;
collective action problems, 101-103;
rtw undermines democracy, 98;
rtw supports wage slavery, 106

Rolling Mill and UAW Local 729: 33-34, 38, 56-58;
recent history, 131-132

Romney, George: 144

Ruback, Will: 128

Russell, William: 32

Sanders, Bernie: 157-158, 163

scabs: 24;
in pre-union era, 64;
Supreme Court permits, 89

Selke, Sam: 71

Sheffield, Evelyn: 103

slaughter house: 135

Smith, Adam: optimism regarding Markets, 110;
employers have advantage over employees, 19, 104-105

Smith, Bruce: 43

Smith, Claude: 33

Social Democrats:

idea of, 97-98;
reformed capitalism of, 114;
Reuther as, 139-141

solidarity: 31, 39-40, 58, 61, 88-89;
collective action problems, 101, 106-108;
law and court rulings weaken, 149-151;
solidarity-based capitalisms, 155-156, 160-161, 164

special-interest groups: 123, 137, 147-152

standard of living:
post-war policy, 118-119;
stagnation and decline in recent decades, 154-155, 162-163

Stepp, Marc: 127

Stone, I.F: 2

strikes:
pre-union era, 26, 63-65;
Goodyear and Bendix (1936), 24-25;
GM and Chrysler (1937), 25-26;
Chrysler (1939), 37-39;
Ford (1945), 46;
GM (1945-46), 139-147;
Perfect Circle (1948), 73-74;
Chrysler (1950), 49-57;
Perfect Circle (1955), 75-81, 90-95;
Memphis Sanitation Workers (1968), 160

Sweden: 141, 154, 163

Taft-Hartley Act: 75, 90, 92, 94, 107-108, 147-148

Teetor, Lothair: 62, 69-70, 109

Teetor, Ralph: 70-71, 109

Thatcher, Margaret: 120, 152

Thomas, R.J: 45

Todd, Earl: 17, 27, 28, 55

Trainer Springs: 34, 58, 135

Treaty of Detroit: 147-148

Tyler, George R: 153-154

UAW (see United Auto Workers)

UAW Auxiliary 59: 52-53, 58

UAW Local 156: 72, 103

UAW Local 370: 38, 58, 63, 71, 75-76;
in Perfect Circle Strike, 75-80,

85, 92-94

UAW Local 371:
early history, 17, 26-29;
support for other unions,
32-35, 39-40;
support for New Castle
community, 33-34;
during national UAW factional
fight, 36;
during 1939 strike, 37-39;
during 1950 pension strike, 49-57;
during Perfect Circle Strike,
85-86;
during Chrysler's troubles, 127-129

union density: 119, 151

union shop: 38, 74, 90, 102-103,
107-108

United Auto Workers:
early years, 20-26, 31;
factional battle (1939),36;
strike at Chrysler (1939), 37-38;
Reuther years, 137-148;
during US auto industry
decline, 127-129

United Mine Workers: 32

United Rubber Workers and URW
Local 238: 25, 35, 58, 135

Van Bebber, Otis: 41

Vincent, Rual: 85

violence:
pre-union era, 26, 64;
racist, 45;
anti-strikebreakers, 56, 74;
Wagner Act aims to curb, 88;
in Perfect Circle Strike, 75-81

wages:
pre-union, 20-21;
Depression era, 22-23;
effect of unions, 124-125;
issue in Perfect Circle Strike, 74-81;
international comparisons, 125,
130, 154;
US in recent decades, 154

Wagner Act (see National Labor
Relations Act)

Washington, George: 100-101

Western Europe: 138-141, 149-150,
152-156

White, Curtis: 32

women at New Castle Chrysler:
43, 44

Wood Workers Local 616: 33

World Bestos: 35, 58, 135

World War II veterans' support for
unions: 143-144, 150

Wright, Mary: 43

TITLES FROM HARD BALL PRESS

A Great Vision – A Militant Family's Journey Through the Twentieth Century – by Richard March

Caring – 1199 Nursing Home Workers Tell Their Story

Fight For Your Long Day – Classroom Edition, by Alex Kudera

Love Dies, a thriller, by Timothy Sheard

Murder of a Post Office Manager, A Legal Thriller, by Paul Felton

New York Hustle – Pool Rooms, School Rooms and Street Corners, a memoir, Stan Maron

Passion's Pride – Return to the Dawning, Cathie Wright- Lewis

The Secrets of the Snow, a book of poetry, Hiva Panahi (author & translator)

Sixteen Tons, a Novel, by Kevin Corley

Throw Out the Water, the sequel to *Sixteen Tons*, by Kevin Corley

We Are One – Stories of Work, Life & Love, Elizabeth Gottieb, editor

What Did You Learn at Work Today? The Forbidden Lessons of Labor Education, nonfiction, by Helena Worthen

With Our Loving Hands – 1199 Nursing Home Workers Tell Their Story

Woman Missing, A Mill Town Mystery, by Linda Nordquist

THE LENNY MOSS MYSTERIES by Timothy Sheard

This Won't Hurt A Bit
Some Cuts Never Heal
A Race Against Death
No Place To Be Sick
Slim To None
A Bitter Pill
Someone Has To Die

CHILDREN'S BOOKS

The Cabbage That Came Back, Stephen Pearl (author), Rafael Pearl (Illustrator), Sara Pearl (translator)

Good Guy Jake, *Mark Torres (author), Yana Podrieez (Illustrator)*, Madelin Arroyo (translator)

Hats Off For Gabbie, Marivir Montebon (author), Yana Podriez (illustrator), Madelin Arroyo (translator)
Jimmy's Carwash Adventure, Victor Narro (author & translator), Yana Podriez (illustrator)

Joelito's Big Decision, Ann Berlak (author), Daniel Camacho (Illustrator), José Antonio Galloso (Translator)
Manny & The Mango Tree, Ali R. Bustamante (author), Monica Lunot-Kuker (illustrator), Mauricio Niebla (translator)

Margarito's Forest, Andy Carter (author), Allison Havens (illustrator), Omar Mejia (Translator)

Polar Bear Pete's Ice is Melting! – Timothy Sheard (author), Madelin Arroyo (translator), A FALL 2017 RELEASE

Trailer Park – Jennifer Dillard (author), Madelin Arroyo (translator), Rafael Pearl (illustrator) A SUMMER 2017 RELEASE

AUSTRALIA
DOWNIES Coins Pty. Ltd.
Mr. Ken Downie
P.O. Box 888, ABBOTSFORD, VIC.3067
NOBLE NUMISMATICS Pty Ltd
Mr. Jim Noble
169 Macquarie Street
SYDNEY, NSW 2000
AUSTRIA
HERINEK, Gerhard
Herr Gerhard Herinek
Josefstädterstrasse, 27, 1080 WIEN
BELGIUM
FRANCESCHI & FILS, B.
M. Druso Franceschi
Rue de la Croix-de-Fer, 10
1000 BRUXELLES
VAN DER SCHUEREN, Jean-Luc
M. Jean-Luc Van der Schueren
Rue de la Bourse, 14
1000 BRUXELLES
CANADA
RANDY WEIR NUMISMATICS Ltd
Mr. Randy Weir
P.O. Box 64577
UNIONVILLE, ONT. L3R 0M9
EGYPT
BAJOCCHI JEWELLERS
Cav. Uff. Pietro Bajocchi
Abdel Khalek Sarwat Street, 45
CAIRO 11511
FRANCE
BOURGEY, Sabine
Mme Sabine Bourgey
Rue Drouot, 7, 75009 PARIS
BURGAN, Claude - Maison FLORANGE
M. Claude Burgan
Rue du 4 Septembre, 8
75002 PARIS
LA PARPAÏOLLE
M. Robert Le Guen
B.P. 30036
13251 MARSEILLE
MAISON PLATT S.A.
M. Daniel Renaud
Rue de Richelieu, 49
75001 PARIS
NUMISMATIQUE & CHANGE DE PARIS
Mme Annette Vinchon
Rue de la Bourse, 3
75002 PARIS Cedex 01
O.G.N.
M. Pierre Crinon
Rue de Richelieu, 64
75002 PARIS
Patrick GUILLARD, Eurl
M. Patrick Guillard
B.P. 41
75261 PARIS Cedex 06
POINSIGNON-NUMISMATIQUE (A.)
M. Alain Poinsignon
Rue des Francs Bourgeois, 4
67000 STRASBOURG
SAIVE, Philippe
M. Philippe Saive
Rue Dupont des Loges, 18
57000 METZ
VINCHON Numismatique
Mme Françoise Berthelot-Vinchon
Rue de Richelieu, 77
75002 PARIS
GERMANY
DILLER, Johannes
Herr Johannes Diller
Ohlstadter Strasse 21
81373 MÜNCHEN
FRITZ RUDOLF KÜNKER GmbH & Co. KG
MÜNZENHANDLUNG
Herr Fritz Rudolf Künker
Gutenbergstrasse, 23
49076 OSNABRÜCK
GERHARD HIRSCH NACHF.
Frau Dr. Francisca Bernheimer
Promenadeplatz, 10/II
80333 MÜNCHEN
GORNY & MOSCH, GIESSENER
MÜNZENHANDLUNG GmbH
Maximiliansplatz, 20
80333 MÜNCHEN
JACQUIER, Paul-Francis
Herr Paul-Francis Jacquier
Honsellstrasse, 8
77694 KEHL am RHEIN
KRICHELDORF NACHF. (H.H.)
Herr Volker Kricheldorf
Günterstalstrasse, 16
79102 FREIBURG i. Br.
KURPFÄLZISCHE MÜNZHANDLUNG oHG
- KPM
Herr Helmut Gehrig
Augusta-Anlage, 52
68165 MANNHEIM
LEIPZIGER MÜNZHANDLUNG und
AUKTION
Mrs. Saskia Höhn
Nicolaistrasse 25
04109 LEIPZIG
MANFRED OLDING MÜNZENHANDLUNG
Herr Manfred Olding
Goldbreede 14
49078 OSNABRÜCK
MEISTER, Michael
Herr Michael Meister
Moltkestrasse 6
71634 LUDWIGSBURG

MÜNZEN- UND MEDAILLENHANDLUNG
STUTTGART
Herr Stefan Sonntag
Charlottenstrasse, 4
70182 STUTTGART
NEUMANN GmbH (Ernst)
Herr Ernst Neumann
Wätteplatz, 6
89312 GÜNZBURG
NUMISMATIK LANZ
Dr. Hubert Lanz
Luitpoldblock - Maximiliansplatz 10
80333 MÜNCHEN
PEUS NACHF. (Dr. Busso)
Herr Christoph Raab
Bornwiesenweg, 34
60322 FRANKFURT / M
RITTER MÜNZHANDLUNG GmbH
Herr J. Ritter
Immermannstrasse 19
40210 DÜSSELDORF
Rüdiger KAISER MÜNZEN-FACHGESCHÄFT
Herr Rüdiger Kaiser
Mittelweg, 54
60318 FRANKFURT
TIETJEN + Co
Herr Detlef Tietjen
Spitalerstrasse, 30
20095 HAMBURG
WESTFÄLISCHE
AUKTIONSGESELLSCHAFT
Herr Udo Gans
Nordring 22
59821 ARNSBERG
HUNGARY
Numismatica EREMBOLT
Mr. László Nudelman
Vörösmarty Tèr 6
1051 BUDAPEST
IRELAND
I.C.E Ltd.
Mr. Jérôme Lacroix
Charter House, 5 Pembroke Row
DUBLIN 2
ITALY
BARANOWSKY s.a.s.
Dott. Vincenzo Filonardi
Via del Corso, 184
00187 ROMA
CRIPPA NUMISMATICA S.A.S.
Sign. Paolo Crippa
Via Cavalieri del S. Sepolcro, 10
20121 MILANO
DE FALCO, Alberto
Sign. Alberto de Falco
Corso Umberto, 24
80138 NAPOLI
FALLANI
Dott. Carlo-Maria Fallani
Via del Babuino, 58
00187 ROMA
GIULIO BERNARDI S.R.L.
Sign. Gianni Paoletti
Casella Postale 560
34121 TRIESTE
PAOLUCCI Andrea
Sign. Andrea Paolucci
Via San Francesco, 154
35121 PADOVA
RANIERI Numismatica srl
Sign. Marco Ranieri
Piazza Calderini 2/2
40124 - BOLOGNA
RINALDI, Marco
Sign. Marco Rinaldi
Via Cappello, 23 (Casa di Giulietta)
37121 VERONA
VARESI Numismatica s.a.s.
Sign. Alberto Varesi
Viale Montegrappa 3
27100 PAVIA
JAPAN
DARUMA INTERNATIONAL GALLERIES
Mr. Yuji Otani
2-16-32-701, Takanawa, Minato-ku
TOKYO 108-0074
WORLD COINS JAPAN
Mr. Eiichi Ishii
1-15-5, Hamamatsu-cho, Minato-ku
TOKYO 105-0013
MONACO
EDITIONS VICTOR GADOURY
M. Francesco Pastrone
57 rue Grimaldi, "Le Panorama"
98000 MONTE CARLO
NETHERLANDS
MEVIUS NUMISBOOKS INTERNATIONAL
BV
Mr. Johan Mevius
Oosteinde, 97
7671 AT VRIEZENVEEN
SCHULMAN BV
Mr. Eddy Absil
P.O. Box 346
1400 AH BUSSUM
VERSCHOOR Munthandel
Mr. Dim Verschoor
P.O. Box 5803
3290 AL STRIJEN
WESTERHOF, Jille Binne
Mr. Jille Binne Westerhof
Trekpad, 38-40
8742 KP BURGWERD
NORWAY
OSLO MYNTHANDEL AS
Mr. Gunnar Thesen
Postboks 2745 Solli
0204 OSLO

POLAND
ANTYKWARIAT NUMIZMATYCZNY
Mr. Pawel Niemczyk
ul. Zelazna 67, pawilon 22
00-871 WARSZAWA
PORTUGAL
NUMISPORTO LDA
Mr. Jose Manuel Ferreira Leite
Av. Combatentes Grande Guerra 610 Lj6
4200-186 PORTO
SPAIN
AUREO & CALICO
Mrs. Teresa Siso
Plaza del Angel, 2
08002 BARCELONA
CAYON - JANO S.L.
Mr. Adolfo Cayon
Calle Orfila 10
28010 MADRID
Jesús VICO S.A.
Jorge Juan n 83 Duplicado
28009 MADRID
SEGARRA, Fernando P.
Señor Don Fernando P. Segarra
Calle Mayor 31
Entreplanta Derecha
28012 MADRID
SWEDEN
NORDLINDS MYNTHANDEL AB
Mr. Hans Hirsch
P.O. Box 5132
102 43 STOCKHOLM
SWITZERLAND
ADOLPH HESS AG
Herr H.J. Schramm
Löwenstrasse 55
8001 ZÜRICH
HESS-DIVO AG
Mr. Ulf Künker
Löwenstrasse 55
8001 ZÜRICH
NOMOS AG
Mr. Alan Walker
Zähringerplatz 27
8001 ZÜRICH
NUMISMATICA ARS CLASSICA NAC AG
Mr. Roberto Russo
Löwenstrasse 55
8011 ZÜRICH
NUMISMATICA GENEVENSIS S.A.
Mr. Alain Baron
1 Rond-Point de Plainpalais
1205 GENEVE
THAILAND
HOUSE of COINS, Ltd. Part.
Mr. Jan Olav Aamlid
391/110 Moo 10
Thappraya Road and Soi 13
Thambon, Nongprue, Ampur Banglamung
CHONBURI 20150
UNITED KINGDOM
A.H. BALDWIN & SONS Ltd
Mr. A.H.E. Baldwin
Adelphi Terrace, 11
LONDON, WC2N 6BJ
DAVIES Paul Ltd
Mr. Paul Davies
P.O. Box 17
ILKLEY, W.York., LS29 8TZ
DIX NOONAN WEBB
Mr. Christopher Webb
16 Bolton Street, Piccadilly
LONDON, W1J 8BQ
EIMER, Christopher
Mr. Christopher Eimer
P.O. Box 352
LONDON, NW11 7RF
FORMAT OF BIRMINGHAM Ltd
Mr. Garry Charman
18 Lower Temple Street, Unit K,
Burlington Court
BIRMINGHAM, B2 4JD
KNIGHTSBRIDGE COINS
Mr. Stephen C. Fenton
Duke Street, 43, St. James's
LONDON, SW1Y 6DD
Mark RASMUSSEN "Numismatist"
Mr. Mark Rasmussen
P.O. Box 42
BETCHWORTH, RH3 7YR
RUDD Chris
Mr. Chris Rudd
P. O. Box 222
AYLSHAM, Norfolk, NR11 6TY
Douglas SAVILLE Numismatic Books
Mr. Douglas Saville
Chiltern Thameside, 37c St Peters Avenue,
Caversham
READING, Berkshire, RG4 7DH
SPINK & SON Ltd
Mr. Phil Skingley
69 Southampton Row, Bloomsbury
LONDON, WC1B 4ET
WILKES, TIM
Mr. Tim Wilkes
P.O. Box 150
BATTLE, East Sussex, TN33 0FA
USA
BERK Ltd. (Harlan J.)
Mr. Harlan J. Berk
31 North Clark Street
CHICAGO, IL.60602
BULLOWA, C.E. - COINHUNTER
Mrs. C.E. Bullowa (Mrs. Earl E. Moore)
1616 Walnut Street, Suite 2112
PHILADELPHIA, PA.19103

CEDERLIND, TOM
Mr. Tom Cederalind
P.O. Box 1963
PORTLAND, OR 97207
CLASSICAL NUMISMATIC GROUP
Mr. Victor England
P.O. Box 479
LANCASTER, PA.17608-0479
COIN & CURRENCY INSTITUTE Inc
Mr. Arthur Friedberg
PO Box 399
WILLISTON, VT 05495
DANIEL FRANK SEDWICK, LLC
Mr. Daniel Frank Sedwick
P.O. Box 1964
WINTER PARK, FL 32790
DAVISSON'S LTD.
Allan Davisson, Ph.D.
17862 Big Fish Lake Road
COLD SPRING, MN.56320-1050
Dmitry MARKOV COINS & MEDALS
Mr. Dmitry Markov
P.O. Box 950
NEW YORK, N.Y.10272
DUNIGAN, Mike
Mr. Mike Dunigan
5332 Birchman
FORT WORTH, TX.76107
FREEMAN & SEAR
Mr. Robert D. Freeman
P.O. Box 641352
LOS ANGELES, CA.90064-6352
FROSETH INC. (K.M.)
Mr. Kent Froseth
P.O. Box 23116
MINNEAPOLIS, MN.55423
GILLIO INC. (Ronald J.) - GOLDMÜNZEN
INTERNATIONAL
1103 State Street
SANTA BARBARA, CA.93101
HARVEY, Stephen
Mr. Stephen Harvey
P.O. Box 3778
BEVERLY HILLS, CA.90212
HLS STACKS Rare Coins
Mr. Lawrence R. Stack
18 Arlington Lane
BAYVILLE, N.Y. 11709
JENCEK HISTORICAL ENTERPRISE, INC
205 De Anza Blvd., #149
SAN MATEO, CA 94402
JONATHAN K. KERN Co
Mr. Jonathan K. Kern
441 South Ashland Avenue
LEXINGTON, KY 40502-2114
KREINDLER, B. & H.
Mr. H. Kreindler
236 Altessa Blvd.
MELVILLE, N.Y.11747
MALTER GALLERIES, Inc.
Mr. Michael Malter
P.O. Box 1710
AGOURA HILLS, CA 91376
MARGOLIS, Richard
Mr. Richard Margolis
P.O. Box 2054
TEANECK, NJ 07666
MILCAREK, Dr. Ron
Dr. Ron Milcarek
P.O. Box 1028
GREENFIELD, MA.01302
PEGASI NUMISMATICS
Mr. Eldert Bontekoe
P.O. Box 131040
ANN ARBOR, MI. 48113
PONTERIO & ASSOCIATES, INC.
(a division of Bowers & Merena)
Mr. Richard PONTERIO
18061 Fitch
IRVINE, CA.92614-6018
RARCOA, INC.
Mr. Wayde Milas
6262 South Route 83, Suite 200
WILLOWBROOK, IL.60527-2998
ROSENBLUM, William M./Rare Coins
Mr. William Rosenblum
P.O. Box 785
LITTLETON, CO, 80160-0785
STEPHEN ALBUM Rare Coins
Mr. Joe Lang
P.O. Box 7386
SANTA ROSA, CA 95401
STEPHENS INC. (Karl)
Mr. Karl Stephens
P.O. Box 3038
FALLBROOK, CA.92088
SUBAK INC.
Mr. Carl Subak
22 West Monroe Street, Room 1506
CHICAGO, IL.60603
TELLER NUMISMATIC ENTERPRISES
Mr. M. Louis Teller
16055 Ventura Boulevard, Suite 635
ENCINO, CA.91436
WADDELL, Edward J. Ltd.
Mr. Edward J. Waddell Jr.
P.O. Box 3759
FREDERICK, MD.21705-3759
WORLD-WIDE COINS OF CALIFORNIA
Mr. James F. Elmen
P.O. Box 3684
SANTA ROSA, CA.95402
VENEZUELA
NUMISMATICA GLOBUS
Señor Antonio Alessandrini
Apartado de Correos 50418
VEN - CARACAS 1050

INTRODUCTION

Welcome to the 7th edition of the 21st Century Standard Catalog of World Coins. The most recent annual version of our ever changing and evolving series of comprehensive reference catalogs is designed to meet the needs of those whose interest in coins exceeds the casual jingle of those in your pants pocket or purse. Perhaps you have traveled overseas and still have some coins that came home with you, maybe you read in the news about the Euro circulating commemoratives or issues from recently formed nations, or you are a long-term collector who wants to wade out into the most current of numismatic trends. In all cases, this book is for you.

This book is arranged in alphabetical fashion by country and with grouping for political structure, coinage type and denomination to better help organizes the information. You will find many illustrations, complete listings of metal content, descriptions of the designs and events depicted on the coins as well as date, mint mark varieties and values in multiple grades of preservation. In short, just about all of the information you could want on the most modern coins of the world.

With the information presented in these listings, one can marvel at the ingenuity of today's most inventive world mints, which are striking coins in a variety of shapes, sizes, colors and textures. Enjoy the practicality of coins designed for serious circulation in durable metals. Celebrate the advents of coins made of acrylic materials and those which house precious stones or display selective gold overlays. All are here in this 21st Century edition.

The accuracy of the information offered in this volume is assured through the assistance of a vast number of contributing coin dealers, collectors, manufacturers and researchers who have lent their knowledge to the compiling of this reference by providing our staff with information on new issues, new dates to existing types, accurate mintages and up-to-date pricing. To them all, we offer a heartfelt "Thank You" for their generosity and dedication to the advancement of our shared field of coin collecting.

Coins are issued throughout the year. We endeavor to keep pace with this worldwide information flow with updates to the online version of the Standard Catalog series, found at www.numismaster.com. There you will be able to see the latest issues, additional images and for a small monthly or annual subscription fee, price updates of your favorite issues. You may also find additional coin books and supplies at www.shopnumismaster.com. Thanks for using our services.

Finally, to you the reader, we extend our wishes that you may enjoy using this catalog as much as we enjoyed its production. Look it over, put it to good use and please let us know if you have any comments or questions.

Best Wishes,

The Editorial Staff of the
Standard Catalog of World Coins

ACKNOWLEDGMENTS

Many individuals have contributed countless changes, which have been incorporated into the current edition. While all may not be acknowledged, special appreciation is extended to the following who have exhibited a special enthusiasm for this edition.

Dylan Arthur
Antonio Alessandrini
Paul Baker
Oksana Bandrivska
Albert Beck
Jan Bendix
Richard Benson
Peter N. Berger
Sharon Blocker
Joseph E. Boling
Richard Borek jun.
Al Boulanger
Maruta Brûkle
Mahdi Bseiso
Chris Budesa
John T. Bucek
Fred Colombo
Raymond E. Czahor
Howard A. Daniel III
Konstantinos Dellios
James R. Douglas
Esko Ekman
Andrzej Fischer
Dagmar Flachén
Eugene Freeman
Peter Frei
Arthur Friedburg
Carmen Fuhiniu
Lorraine Gallagher

Tom Galway
David R. Gotkin
Andrew Greatorex
Marcel Häberling
J. Halfpenny
Flemming Lyngbeck Hansen
David Harrison
Martin Rodney Hayter
Emanuel Henry
Jennifer Hird
Teréz Horváth
Serge Huard
Sudhir Humnabadkar
Nelva G. Icaza
Hector Carlos Janson
Alex Kaglyan
Melvyn Kassenoff
Craig Keplinger
Rodolphe Krempp
Aditya Kulkarni
Samson Kin Chiu Lai
Alex Lazarovici
Ma Tak Wo
Runko Mandic
Miguel Angel Pratt Mayans
Bernhard H. Mayer
Derreck Martell
Bill McKay
Juozas Minikevicius

Andy Mirski
Robert Mish
Ing. Benjamin M. Mizrachi R.
Dr. Richard Montrey
Horst-Dieter Müller
Edward Moschetti
Michael G. Nielsen
Janusz Parchimowicz
Dick Parker
Frank Passic
Martin Peeters
Marc Pelletier
Kirsten F. Petersen
Andreas Pitsillides
Gastone Polacco
Jordi Puigdemasa
Martin Purdy
Frank Putrow
Kitty Quan
Yahya Qureshi
Arif Qureshi
Dr. Dennis G. Rainey
Ivan Rakitin
Ilan Rinetzky
William M. Rosenblum
Egon Conti Rossini
Pabitra K. Saha
Remy Said
Jacco Scheper

Dr. Andreas Schikora
Gerhard Schön
George Schumacher
Dr. Wolfgang Schuster
Alexander Shapiro
Ladislav Sin
Ole Sjoelund
Euzan Skuouril
Mira Spijker
Heimo Steriti
Jacek Suchan
Alim A. Sumana
Benjamin Swagerty
Peter Swanston
Steven Tan
Mehmet Tolga Taner
Rivka Toledano
Amelia Travaglini
Anthony Tumonis
Erik J. Van Loon
Natanya van Niekerk
Neil Vance
Carmen Viciedo
Wakim Wakim
Paul Welz
J. Brix Westergaard
J. Hugh Witherow
Joseph Zaffern

AUCTION HOUSES

Dix-Noonan-Webb
Heritage World Coin Auctions
Hess-Divo Ltd.
Gerhard Hirsch

Thomas Høiland Møntauktion
Fritz Rudolf Künker
Leu Numismatik AG
MPO Auctions

Münzenhandlung Harald
   Möller, GmbH
Noble Numismatics, Pty. Ltd.
Ponterio & Associates

Stack's
UBS, AG
World Wide Coins of California

WORLD MINTS, CENTRAL BANKS AND DISTRIBUTORS

Austrian Mint
Banco de Mexico
Banque Centrale Du
   Luxembourg
Black Mountain Coins
Casa de la Moneda de Cuba
Central Bank of D.P.R. Korea -
   Kumbyol Trading Corp.
Central Bank of the Russian
   Federation
CIT
Czech National Bank
Downies
Educational Coin Company
Faude & Huguenin
Global Coins & Medals Ltd. -
   Official Sales Company of
   the Bulgarian Mint

Imprensa Nacional - Casa da
   Moeda, S.A.
Israel Coins & Medals Corp.
Istituto Poligrafico e Zecca
   dello Stato I.p.A.
Jablonex Group - Division of
   Czech Mint
Japan Mint
Kazakhstan Mint
KOMSCO - South Korea
Latvijas Banka
Lietuvos Bankas
Lithuanian Mint
Magyar Penzvero Zrt.
Mayer's Mint GmbH
MDM
Mennica Polska
Mincovna Kremnica

Mint of Finland, Ltd.
Mint of Norway
Monnaie de Paris
Moscow Mint
National Bank of the Republic
   of Belarus
National Bank of Ukraine
New Zealand Mint
Numiscom
Numistrade Gmbh & Co. kg.
Omni Trading B.V.
PandaAmerica
Perth Mint
Pobjoy Mint
Real Casa de la Moneda - Spain
Royal Mint
Royal Australian Mint
Royal Belgian Mint

Royal Canadian Mint
Royal Dutch Mint
Royal Thai Mint
SamlerHuset Group B.V.
Servei D'Emissions Principat
   D'Andorra
Singapore Mint
SoftSky, Inc.
South African Mint
Staatliche Munze Berlin
Staatliche Munze Baden-
   Wurttemberg
Talisman Coins
Thailand Treasury Department
Ufficio Filatelico e Numismatico
   - Vatican
United States Mint

COUNTRY INDEX

Afghanistan	15	Gough Island	820	Papua New Guinea	644
Albania	15	Great Britain	368	Paraguay	644
Alderney	16	Greece	385	Peru	645
Algeria	23	Guatemala	387	Philippines	647
Andorra	24	Guernsey	388	Pitcairn Islands	648
Argentina	31	Guinea	392	Poland	650
Armenia	33	Guyana	392	Portugal	674
Aruba	37	Haiti	392	Qatar	680
Ascension Island	39	Honduras	392	Romania	683
Australia	41	Hong Kong	393	Russia	689
Austria	101	Hungary	393	Rwanda	717
Azerbaijan	111	Iceland	401	Saharawi Arab Democratic Republic	718
Bahamas	112	India	401	Saint Helena	718
Bahrain	112	Indonesia	406	Saint Helena & Ascension	720
Bangladesh	113	Iran	407	Samoa	720
Barbados	114	Iraq	408	San Marino	722
Belarus	115	Ireland	408	Saudi Arabia	725
Belgium	126	Isle of Man	411	Serbia	726
Belgium	131	Israel	431	Seychelles	727
Benin	131	Italy	441	Shawnee Tribal Nation	728
Bermuda	133	Ivory Coast	447	Sierra Leone	729
Bhutan	135	Jamaica	447	Singapore	736
Bolivia	136	Japan	448	Slovakia	742
Bosnia-Herzegovina	136	Jersey	454	Slovenia	747
Botswana	137	Jordan	459	Solomon Islands	751
Brazil	137	Kazakhstan	460	Somalia	754
British Antarctic Territory	139	Kenya	469	Somaliland	762
British Indian Ocean Territory	140	Kiribati	469	South Africa	763
British Virgin Islands	140	Korea, North	470	South Georgia & the Sandwich Islands	776
Brunei	150	Korea, South	498	South Korea	498
Bulgaria	151	Kuwait	500	Spain	778
Burundi	153	Kyrgyzstan	501	Sri Lanka	792
Cambodia	154	Lao	503	Stoltenhoff Island	820
Cameroon	156	Latvia	505	Sudan	794
Canada	157	Lebanon	511	Suriname	794
Cape Verde	198	Lesotho	511	Swaziland	795
Cayman Islands	198	Liberia	511	Sweden	796
Central African States	199	Libya	518	Switzerland	797
Chad	200	Liechtenstein	519	Syria	802
Chile	201	Lithuania	519	Taiwan	225
China, Peoples Republic"	202	Luxembourg	523	Tajikistan	802
China, Repiblic of	225	Macau	525	Tanzania	804
China, Taiwan	225	Macedonia	527	Thailand	804
Colombia	226	Madagascar	528	Timor-Leste	294
Comoros	226	Malawi	529	Togo	810
Congo Democratic Republic	228	Malaysia	533	Tokelau Islands	813
Congo Republic	227	Maldive Islands	537	Tonga	813
Cook Islands	237	Malta	537	Transnistria	814
Costa Rica	268	Mauritania	539	Trinidad & Tobago	817
Croatia	269	Mauritius	540	Tristan da Cunha	817
Cuba	271	Mexico	540	Tunisia	821
Cyprus	279	Moldova	554	Turkey	826
Czech Republic	281	Monaco	557	Turkmenistan	835
Denmark	287	Mongolia	558	Turks & Caicos Islands	836
Djibouti	292	Morocco	563	Tuvalu	837
Dominican Republic	292	Mozambique	565	Uganda	846
East Caribbean States	293	Nagorno-Karabakh	566	Ukraine	850
East Timor	294	Namibia	567	United Arab Emirates	874
Ecuador	295	Nauru	567	United Kingdom	368
Egypt	295	Nepal	569	United States of America	877
Eire	408	Netherlands	571	Uruguay	894
Estonia	298	Netherlands Antilles	578	Uzbekistan	895
Ethiopia	300	New Caledonia	581	Vanuatu	896
Falkland Islands	300	New Zealand	581	Vatican City	897
Fiji	308	Nigeria	590	Venezuela	902
Finland	313	Niue	590	Viet Nam	903
France	320	North Korea	470	West African States	904
French Polynesia	344	Norway	621	Yemen Republic	905
Georgia	345	Oman	622	Yugoslavia	906
Germany	346	Pakistan	624	Zambia	906
Ghana	357	Palau	625	Zimbabwe	909
Gibraltar	357	Panama	642		

HOW TO USE THIS CATALOG

This catalog is designed to serve the needs of both the novice and advanced collectors. It is generally arranged so that persons with no more than a basic knowledge of world history and a casual acquaintance with coin collecting can consult it with confidence and ease. The following explanations summarize the general practices used in preparing this catalog's listings.

ARRANGEMENT

Countries are arranged alphabetically. Political changes within a country are arranged chronologically. In countries where Rulers are the single most significant political entity, a chronological arrangement by Ruler has been employed. Distinctive sub-geographic regions are listed alphabetically following the country's main listings.

Diverse coinage types relating to fabrication methods, revaluations, denomination systems, non-circulating categories and such have been identified, separated and arranged in logical fashion. Chronological arrangement is employed for most circulating coinage. Monetary reforms will flow in order of their institution. Non-circulating types such as Essais, Pieforts, Patterns, Trial Strikes, Mint and Proof sets will follow the main listings.

Within a coinage type coins will be listed by denomination, from smallest to largest. Numbered types within a denomination will be ordered by their first date of issue.

IDENTIFICATION

The most important step in the identification of a coin is the determination of the nation of origin. This is generally easily accomplished where English-speaking lands are concerned, however, use of the country index is sometimes required.

The coins of many countries beyond the English-language realm, such as those of French, Italian or Spanish heritage, are also quite easy to identify through reference to their legends, which appear in the national languages based on Western alphabets. In many instances the name is spelled exactly the same in English as in the national language, such as France; while in other cases it varies only slightly, like Italia for Italy, Belgique or Belgie for Belgium, Brasil for Brazil and Danmark for Denmark.

This is not always the case, however, as in Norge for Norway, Espana for Spain, Sverige for Sweden and Helvetia for Switzerland. Coins bearing Cyrillic lettering are attributable to Bulgaria, Russia, the Slavic states and Mongolia; the Greek script peculiar to Greece, Crete and the Ionian Islands; the Amharic characters of Ethiopia; or Hebrew in the case of Israel.

The toughra monogram, occurs on some of the coins of Afghanistan, Egypt, Sudan, Pakistan, and Turkey. A predominant design feature on the coins of Nepal is the trident; while neighboring Tibet features a lotus blossom or lion on many of their issues.

DATING

Coin dating is the final basic attribution consideration. Here, the problem can be more difficult because the reading of a coin date is subject not only to the vagaries of numeric styling, but to calendar variations caused by the observance of various religious eras or regal periods from country to country, or even within a country. Here again, with the exception of the sphere from North Africa through the Orient, it will be found that most countries rely on Western date numerals and Christian (AD) era reckoning, although in a few instances, coin dating has been tied to the year of a reign or government. The Vatican, for example dates its coinage according to the year of reign of the current pope, in addition to the Christian-era date.

Countries in the Arabic sphere generally date their coins to the Muslim era (AH).

The following table indicates the year dating for the various eras, which correspond to 2009 in Christian calendar reckoning, but it must be remembered that there are overlaps between the eras in some instances.

Christian era (AD)	-2010
Muslim era (AH)	-AH1431
Solar year (SH)	-SH1388
Monarchic Solar era (MS)	-MS2569
Vikrama Samvat (VS)	-VS2067
Saka era (SE)	-SE1932
Buddhist era (BE)	-BE2553
Bangkok era (RS)	-RS229
Chula-Sakarat era (CS)	-CS1372
Ethiopian era (EE)	-EE2003
Korean era	-4343
Javanese Aji Saka era (AS)	-AS1943
Fasli era (FE)	-FE1420
Jewish era (JE)	-JE5770

More detailed guides to less prevalent coin dating systems, which are strictly local in nature, are presented with the appropriate listings.

AH Hejira	AD Christian Date	AH Hejira	AD Christian Date
1420	1999, April 17	1436	2014, October 25
1421	2000, April 6*	1437	2015, October 15*
1422	2001, March 26	1438	2016, October 3
1423	2002, March 15	1439	2017, September 22
1424	2003, March 5	1440	2018, September 12
1425	2004, February 22*	1441	2019, September 11*
1426	2005, February 10	1442	2020, August 20
1427	2006, January 31	1443	2021, August 10
1428	2007, January 20	1444	2022, July 30
1429	2008, January 10*	1445	2023, July 19*
1430	2008, December 29	1446	2024, July 8
1431	2009, December 18	1447	2025, June 27
1432	2010, December 8	1448	2026, June 17
1433	2011, November 27*	1449	2027, June 6*
1434	2012, November 15	1450	2028, May25
1435	2013, November 5		

Some coins carry dates according to both locally observed and Christian eras. This is particularly true in the Arabic world, where the Hejira date may be indicated in Arabic numerals and the Christian date in Western numerals, or both dates in either form.

HEJIRA DATE CONVERSION CHART

HEJIRA (Hijira, Hegira), the name of the Muslim era (A.H. = Anno Hegirae) dates back to the Christian year 622 when Mohammed "fled" from Mecca, escaping to Medina to avoid persecution from the Koreish tribemen. Based on a lunar year the Muslim year is 11 days shorter.

*=Leap Year (Christian Calendar)

The date actually carried on a given coin is generally cataloged here in the first column (Date) to the right of the catalog number. If this date is by a non-Christian dating system, such as 'AH' (Muslim), the Christian equivalent date will appear in parentheses(), for example AH1336(1917). Dates listed alone in the date column which do not actually appear on a given coin, or dates which are known, but do not appear on the coin, are generally enclosed by parentheses with 'ND' at the left, for example ND(2001).

Timing differentials between some era of reckoning, particularly the 354-day Mohammedan and 365-day Christian years, cause situations whereby coins which carry dates for both eras exist bearing two year dates from one calendar combined with a single date from another.

Countermarked Coinage is presented with both 'Countermark Date' and 'Host Coin' date for each type. Actual date representation follows the rules outlined above.

DENOMINATIONS

The second basic consideration to be met in the attribution of a coin is the determination of denomination. Since denominations are usually expressed in numeric rather than word form on a coin, this is usually quite easily accomplished on coins from nations which use Western numerals, except in those instances where issues are devoid of any mention of face value, and denomination must be attributed by size, metallic composition or weight. Coins listed in this volume are generally illustrated in actual size.

The sphere of countries stretching from North Africa through the Orient, on which numeric symbols generally unfamiliar to Westerners are employed, often provide the collector with a much greater challenge. This is particularly true on nearly all pre-20th Century issues. On some of the more modern issues and increasingly so as the years progress, Western-style numerals usually presented in combination with the local numeric system are becoming more commonplace on these coins.

The included table of Standard International Numeral Systems presents charts of the basic numeric designations found on coins of non-Western origin. Although denomination numerals are generally prominently displayed on coins, it must be remembered that these are general representations of characters, which individual coin engravers may have rendered in widely varying styles. Where numeric or script denominations designation forms peculiar to a given coin or country apply, such as the script used on some Persian (Iranian) issues. They are so indicated or illustrated in conjunction with the appropriate listings.

MINTAGES

Quantities minted of each date are indicated where that information is available, generally stated in millions or rounded off to the nearest 10,000 pieces when more exact figures are not available. On quantities of a few thousand or less, actual mintages are generally indicated. For combined mintage figures the abbreviation "Inc. Above" means Included Above, while "Inc. Below" means Included Below. "Est." beside a mintage figure indicates the number given is an estimate or mintage limit.

METALS

Each numbered type listing will contain a description of the coins metallic content. The traditional coinage metals and their symbolic chemical abbreviations sometimes used in this catalog are:

Platinum - (PT)	Copper - (Cu)
Gold - (Au)	Brass -
Silver - (Ag)	Copper-nickel- (CN)
Billion -	Lead - (Pb)
Nickel - (Ni)	Steel -
Zinc - (Zn)	Tin - (Sn)
Bronze - (Ae)	Aluminum - (Al)

Modern commemorative coins have employed still more unusual methods such as bimetallic coins, color applications and precious metal or gem inlays.

PRECIOUS METAL WEIGHTS

Listings of weight, fineness and actual silver (ASW), gold (AGW), platinum or palladium (APW) content of most machine-struck silver, gold, platinum and palladium coins are provided in this edition. This information will be found incorporated in each separate type listing, along with other data related to the coin.

The ASW, AGW or APW figure can be multiplied by the spot price of each precious metal to determine the current intrinsic value of any coin accompanied by these designations.

As the silver and gold bullion markets have advanced and declined sharply over the years, the fineness and total precious metal content of coins has become especially significant where bullion coins - issues which trade on the basis of their intrinsic metallic content rather than numismatic value - are concerned. In many instances, such issues have become worth more in bullion form than their nominal collector values or denominations indicate.

BULLION VALUE

The simplest method for determining the bullion value of a precious metal coin is to multiply the actual precious metal weight by the current spot price for that metal. A silver coin with a .6822 actual silver weight (ASW) would have an intrinsic value of

$8.70 when the spot price of silver is $12.75. If the spot price of silver rose to $17.95 that same coins intrinsic value would rise to $12.25.

PHOTOGRAPHS

To assist the reader in coin identification, every effort has been made to present actual size photographs of every coinage type listed. Obverse and reverse are illustrated, except when a change in design is restricted to one side, and the coin has a diameter of 39mm or larger, in which case only the side required for identification of the type is generally illustrated. All coins up to 60mm are illustrated actual size, to the nearest 1/2mm up to 25mm, and to the nearest 1mm thereafter. Coins larger than 60mm diameter are illustrated in reduced size, with the actual size noted in the descriptive text block. Where slight change in size is important to coin type identification, actual millimeter measurements are stated.

VALUATIONS

Values quoted in this catalog represent the current market and are compiled from recommendations provided and verified through various source documents and specialized consultants. It should be stressed, however, that this book is intended to serve only as an aid for evaluating coins, actual market conditions are constantly changing and additional influences, such as particularly strong local demand for certain coin series, fluctuation of international exchange rates, changes in spot price of precious metals and worldwide collection patterns must also be considered. Publication of this catalog is not intended as a solicitation by the publisher, editors or contributors to buy or sell the coins listed at the prices indicated.

All valuations are stated in U.S. dollars, based on careful assessment of the varied international collector market. Valuations for coins priced below $100.00 are generally stated in full amounts - i.e. 37.50 or 95.00 - while valuations at or above that figure are rounded off in even dollars - i.e. $125.00 is expressed 125. A comma is added to indicate thousands of dollars in value.

For the convenience of overseas collectors and for U.S. collectors doing business with overseas dealers, the base exchange rate for the national currencies of approximately 180 countries are presented in the Foreign Exchange Table.

It should be noted that when particularly select uncirculated or proof-like examples of uncirculated coins become available they can be expected to command proportionally high premiums. Such examples in reference to choice Germanic Thalers are referred to as "erst schlage" or first strikes.

NEW ISSUES

All newly released coins dated up to the year 2006 that have been physically observed by our staff or identified by reliable sources and have been confirmed by press time have been incorporated in this edition. Exceptions exist in some countries where current date coin production lags far behind or information on current issues is less accessible.

SETS

Listings in this catalog for specimen, proof and mint sets are for official, government-produced sets. In many instances privately packaged sets also exist.

Mint Sets/Fleur de Coin Sets: Specially prepared by worldwide mints to provide banks, collectors and government dignitaries with examples of current coinage. Usually subjected to rigorous inspection to insure that top quality specimens of selected business strikes are provided.

Coin Alignment   Medal Alignment

COIN vs MEDAL ALIGNMENT

Some coins are struck with obverse and reverse aligned at a rotation of 180 degrees from each other. When a coin is held for vertical viewing with the obverse design aligned upright and the index finger and thumb at the top and bottom, upon rotation from left to right for viewing the reverse, the latter will be upside down. Such alignment is called "coin rotation." Other coins are struck with the obverse and reverse designs mated on an alignment of zero or 360 degrees. If such an example is held and rotated as described, the reverse will appear upright. This is the alignment, which is generally observed in the striking of medals, and for that reason coins produced in this manner are considered struck in "medal rotation". In some instances, often through error, certain coin issues have been struck to both alignment standards, creating interesting collectible varieties, which will be found noted in some listings. In addition, some countries are now producing coins with other designated obverse to reverse alignments which are considered standard for this type.

Specimen Sets: Forerunners of today's proof sets. In most cases the coins were specially struck, perhaps even double struck, to produce a very soft or matte finish on the effigies and fields, along with high, sharp, "wire" rims. The finish is rather dull to the naked eye.

The original purpose of these sets was to provide VIPs, monarchs and mintmasters around the world with samples of the highest quality workmanship of a particular mint. These were usually housed in elaborate velvet-lined leather and metal cases.

Proof-like Sets are relatively new to the field of numismatics. During the mid 1950s the Royal Canadian Mint furnished the hobby with specially selected early business strike coins that exhibited some qualities similar to proof coinage. However, the "proof-like" fields are generally flawed and the edges are rounded. These pieces are not double struck. These are commonly encountered in cardboard holders, later in soft plastic or pliofilm packaging. Of late, the Royal Canadian Mint packages such sets in rigid plastic cases.

Many worldwide officially issued proof sets would in reality fall into this category upon careful examination of the quality of the coin's finish.

Another term encountered in this category is "Special Select," used to describe the crowns of the Union of South Africa and 100-schilling coins produced for collectors in the late 1970s by the Austrian Mint.

Proof Sets: This is undoubtedly among the most misused terms in the hobby, not only by collectors and dealers, but also by many of the world mints.

A true proof set must be at least double-struck on specially prepared polished planchets and struck using dies (often themselves polished) of the highest quality. Modern-day proof quality consists of frosted effigies surrounded by absolute mirror-like fields.

Listings for proof sets in this catalog are for officially issued proof sets so designated by the issuing authority, and may or may not possess what are considered modern proof quality standards.

It is necessary for collectors to acquire the knowledge to allow them to differentiate true proof sets from would-be proof sets and proof-like sets which may be encountered.

CONDITIONS/GRADING

Wherever possible, coin valuations are given in four or five grades of preservation. For modern commemoratives, which do not circulate, only uncirculated values are usually sufficient. Proof issues are indicated by the word "Proof" next to the date, with valuation proceeded by the word "value" following the mintage. For very recent circulating coins and coins of limited value, one, two or three grade values are presented.

There are almost no grading guides for world coins. What follows is an attempt to help bridge that gap until a detailed, illustrated guide becomes available.

In grading world coins, there are two elements to look for: 1) Overall wear, and 2) loss of design details, such as strands of hair, feathers on eagles, designs on coats of arms, etc.

The age, rarity or type of a coin should not be a consideration in grading.

Grade each coin by the weaker of the two sides. This method appears to give results most nearly consistent with conservative American Numismatic Association standards for U.S. coins. Split grades, i.e., F/VF for obverse and reverse, respectively, are normally no more than one grade apart. If the two sides are more than one grade apart, the series of coins probably wears differently on each side and should then be graded by the weaker side alone.

Grade by the amount of overall wear and loss of design detail evident on each side of the coin. On coins with a moderately small design element, which is prone to early wear, grade by that design alone. For example, the 5-ore (KM#554) of Sweden has a crown above the monogram on which the beads on the arches show wear most clearly. So, grade by the crown alone.

For **Brilliant Uncirculated** (BU) grades there will be no visible signs of wear or handling, even under a 30-power microscope. Full mint luster will be present. Ideally no bags marks will be evident.

For **Uncirculated** (Unc. or MS-60) grades there will be no visible signs of wear or handling, even under a 30-power microscope. Bag marks may be present.

For **Almost Uncirculated** (AU or AU-50), all detail will be visible. There will be wear only on the highest point of the coin. There will often be half or more of the original mint luster present.

On the **Extremely Fine** (EF or XF or XF-40) coin, there will be about 95% of the original detail visible. Or, on a coin with a design with no inner detail to wear down, there will be a light wear over nearly all the coin. If a small design is used as the grading area, about 90% of the original detail will be visible. This latter rule stems from the logic that a smaller amount of detail needs to be present because a small area is being used to grade the whole coin.

The **Very Fine** (VF or VF-20) coin will have about 75% of the original detail visible. Or, on a coin with no inner detail, there will be moderate wear over the entire coin. Corners of letters and numbers may be weak. A small grading area will have about 66% of the original detail.

For **Fine** (F or F-12), there will be about 50% of the original detail visible. Or, on a coin with no inner detail, there will be fairly heavy wear over all of the coin. Sides of letters will be weak. A typically uncleaned coin will often appear as dirty or dull. A small grading area will have just under 50% of the original detail.

On the **Very Good** (VG or VG-8) coin, there will be about 25% of the original detail visible. There will be heavy wear on all of the coin.

The **Good** (G or G-4) coin's design will be clearly outlined but with substantial wear. Some of the larger detail may be visible. The rim may have a few weak spots of wear.

On the **About Good** (AG) coin, there will typically be only a silhouette of a large design. The rim will be worn down into the letters if any.

Strong or weak strikes, partially weak strikes, damage, corrosion, attractive or unattractive toning, dipping or cleaning should be described along with the above grades. These factors affect the quality of the coin just as do wear and loss of detail, but are easier to describe.

STANDARD INTERNATIONAL GRADING TERMINOLOGY AND ABBREVIATIONS

U.S. and ENGLISH SPEAKING LANDS	UNCIRCULATED	EXTREMELY FINE	VERY FINE	FINE	VERY GOOD	GOOD	POOR
Abbreviation	UNC	EF or XF	VF	FF	VG	G	PR
BRAZIL	(1) DW	(3) S	(5) MBC	(7) BC	(8)	(9) R	UTGeG
DENMARK	O	O1	1+	1	1÷	2	3
FINLAND	0	01	1+	1	1?	2	3
FRANCE	NEUF	SUP	TTB or TB	TB or TB	B	TBC	BC
GERMANY	KFR	II / VZGL	III / SS	IV / S	V / S.g.E.	VI / G.e.	G.e.s.
ITALY	FdS	SPL	BB	MB	B	M	—
JAPAN	未 使 用	極 美 品	美 品	並 品	—	—	—
NETHERLANDS	FDC	Pr.	Z.F.	Fr.	Z.g.	G	—
NORWAY	0	01	1+	1	1+	2	3
PORTUGAL	Novo	Soberbo	Muito bo	—	—	—	—
SPAIN	Lujo	SC, IC or EBC	MBC	BC	—	RC	MC
SWEDEN	0	01	1+	1	1?	2	—

BRAZIL

FE	— Flor de Estampa
S	— Soberba
MBC	— Muito Bem Conservada
BC	— Bem Conservada
R	— Regular
UTGeG	— Um Tanto Gasto e Gasto

DENMARK

O	— Uncirkuleret
01	— Meget Paent Eksemplar
1+	— Paent Eksemplar
1	— Acceptabelt Eksemplar
1	—Noget Slidt Eksemplar
2	— Darlight Eksemplar
3	— Meget Darlight Eskemplar

FINLAND

00	— Kiiltolyönti
0	— Lyöntiveres
01	— Erittäin Hyvä
1+	— Hyvä
1?	— Heikko
2	— Huono

FRANCE

NEUF	— New
FDC	— Fleur De Coin
SPL	— Splendide
SUP	— Superbe
TTB	— Très Très Beau
TB	— Très Beau
B	— Beau
TBC	— Tres Bien Conserve
BC	— Bien Conserve

GERMANY

VZGL	— Vorzüglich
SS	— Sehr schön
S	— Schön
S.g.E.	— Sehr gut erhalten
G.e.	— Gut erhalten
G.e.S.	— Gering erhalten Schlecht

ITALY

Fds	— Fior di Stampa
SPL	— Splendid
BB	— Bellissimo
MB	— Molto Bello
B	— Bello
M	— Mediocre

JAPAN

未 使 用	— Mishiyo
極 美 品	— Goku Bihin
美 品	— Bihin
並 品	— Futuhin

NETHERLANDS

Pr.	— Prachtig
Z.F.	— Zeer Fraai
Fr.	— Fraai
Z.g.	— Zeer Goed
G	— Goed

NORWAY

0	— Usirkuleret eks
01	— Meget pent eks
1+	— Pent eks
1	— Fullgodt eks
1-	— Ikke Fullgodt eks
2	— Darlig eks

ROMANIA

NC	— Necirculata (UNC)
FF	— Foarte Frumoasa (VF)
F	— Frumoasa (F)
FBC	— Foarte Bine Conservata (VG)
BC	— Bine Conservata (G)
M	— Mediocru Conservata (POOR)

SPAIN

EBC	— Extraordinariamente Bien Conservada
SC	— Sin Circular
IC	— Incirculante
MBC	— Muy Bien Conservada
BC	— Bien Conservada
RC	— Regular Conservada
MC	— Mala Conservada

SWEDEN

0	— Ocirkulerat
01	— Mycket Vackert
1+	— Vackert
1	— Fullgott
1?	— Ej Fullgott
2	— Dalight

STANDARD INTERNATIONAL NUMERAL SYSTEMS

Prepared especially for the *Standard Catalog of World Coins* © 2012 by Krause Publications

Western	0	½	1	2	3	4	5	6	7	8	9	10	50	100	500	1000
Roman			I	II	III	IV	V	VI	VII	VIII	IX	X	L	C	D	M
Arabic-Turkish	٠	١/٢	١	٢	٣	٤	٥	٦	٧	٨	٩	١٠	٥٠	١٠٠	٥٠٠	١٠٠٠
Malay-Persian	٠	١/٢	١	٢	٣	۴	۵	۶or۷	٧	٨	٩	١٠	۵٠	١٠٠	۵٠٠	١٠٠٠
Eastern Arabic	o	½	l	٢	٣	৪	٤	પ	V	٦	9	lo	٤lo	loo	٤loo	looo
Hyderabad Arabic	o	١/٢	١	٢	٣	๛	٥	५	८	٨	٩	١٠	७٠	١٠٠	७٠٠	١٠٠٠
Indian (Sanskrit)	०	½	१	२	३	४	५	६	७	८	९	१०	५०	१००	५००	१०००
Assamese	০	৵	১	২	৩	৪	৫	৬	৭	৮	৯	১০	৫০	১০০	৫০০	১০০০
Bengali	০	৸	১	২	৩	৪	৫	৬	৭	৮	৯	১০	৫০	১০০	৫০০	১০০০
Gujarati	૦	૧/૨	૧	૨	૩	૪	૫	૬	૭	૮	૯	૧૦	૫૦	૧૦૦	૫૦૦	૧૦૦૦
Kutch	૦	½	૧	૨	૩	૪	૫	૬	૭	૮	૯	૧૦	૫૦	૧૦૦	૫૦૦	૧૦૦૦
Devavnagri	०	९/२	९	२	३	४	५	६ or	७	८	९ or	९०	५०	९००	४००	९०००
Nepalese	०	९/२	९	२	३	४	५	६	७	८	९	९०	५०	९००	४००	९०००
Tibetan	༠	⁷/₂	༡	༢	༣	༤	༥	༦	༧	༨	༩	༧༠	༤༠	༧༠༠	༤༠༠	༧༠༠༠
Mongolian	᠐	᠙/᠒	᠑	᠒	᠓	᠔	᠕	᠖	᠗	᠘	᠙	᠑᠐	᠕᠐	᠑᠐᠐	᠕᠐᠐	᠑᠐᠐᠐
Burmese	၀	၃/၂	၁	၂	၃	၄	၅	၆	၇	၈	၉	၁၀	၅၀	၁၀၀	၅၀၀	၁၀၀၀
Thai-Lao	๐	⁹/₂	๑	๒	๓	๔	๕	๖	๗	๘	๙	๑๐	๕๐	๙๐๐	๕๐๐	๙๐๐๐
Lao-Laotian	໐		໑	໒	໓	໔	໕	໖	໗	໘	໙	໑໐				
Javanese	ꦐ		ꦱ	꧇	ꦲꦠ	ꦕ	ꦏ	ꦭ	ꦩ	ꦴꦮ	�333	ꦩꦴ꧐	꧑꧐	ꦩꦴ꧐꧐	꧑꧐꧐	ꦩꦴ꧐꧐꧐
Ordinary Chinese Japanese-Korean	零	半	一	二	三	四	五	六	七	八	九	十	十五	百	百五	千
Official Chinese			壹	貳	叁	肆	伍	陸	柒	捌	玖	拾	拾伍	佰	佰伍	仟
Commercial Chinese			〡	〢	〣	乂	6	⊥	⊥	三	夂	十	6十	〡百	6百	〡千
Korean		반	일	이	삼	사	오	육	칠	팔	구	십	오십	백	오백	천
Georgian			ა	ბ	გ	დ	ე	ვ	ზ	ჱ	თ	ი	კ	რ	ჳ	ჰ
			11 ია	20 კ	30 ლ	40 მ	60 ჲ	70 ო	80 პ	90 ჟ	200 ს	300 ტ	400 ჳ	600 ფ	700 ქ	800 ღ
Ethiopian	◆		፩	፪	፫	፬	፭	፮	፯	፰	፱	፲	፶	፻	፭፻	፲፻
				20 ፳	30 ፴	40 ፵	60 ፷	70 ፸	80 ፹	90 ፺						
Hebrew			א	ב	ג	ד	ה	ו	ז	ח	ט	י	כ	ק	קת	תת
				20 כ	30 ל	40 מ	60 ס	70 ע	80 פ	90 צ	200 ר	300 ש	400 ת	600 תר	700 תש	800 תת
Greek			A	B	Γ	Δ	E	Z	H	Θ	I	N	P	Φ	A
				20 K	30 Λ	40 M	60 Ξ	70 O	80 Π		200 Σ	300 T	400 Y	600 X	700 Ψ	800 Ω

SILVER BULLION VALUE CHART $25 to $32.50

Oz.	25.00	25.50	26.00	26.50	27.00	27.50	28.00	28.50	29.00	29.50	30.00	30.50	31.00	31.50	32.00	32.50
0.001	0.025	0.026	0.026	0.027	0.027	0.028	0.028	0.029	0.029	0.030	0.030	0.031	0.031	0.032	0.032	0.033
0.002	0.050	0.051	0.052	0.053	0.054	0.055	0.056	0.057	0.058	0.059	0.060	0.061	0.062	0.063	0.064	0.065
0.003	0.075	0.077	0.078	0.080	0.081	0.083	0.084	0.086	0.087	0.089	0.090	0.092	0.093	0.095	0.096	0.098
0.004	0.100	0.102	0.104	0.106	0.108	0.110	0.112	0.114	0.116	0.118	0.120	0.122	0.124	0.126	0.128	0.130
0.005	0.125	0.128	0.130	0.133	0.135	0.138	0.140	0.143	0.145	0.148	0.150	0.153	0.155	0.158	0.160	0.163
0.006	0.150	0.153	0.156	0.159	0.162	0.165	0.168	0.171	0.174	0.177	0.180	0.183	0.186	0.189	0.192	0.195
0.007	0.175	0.179	0.182	0.186	0.189	0.193	0.196	0.200	0.203	0.207	0.210	0.214	0.217	0.221	0.224	0.228
0.008	0.200	0.204	0.208	0.212	0.216	0.220	0.224	0.228	0.232	0.236	0.240	0.244	0.248	0.252	0.256	0.260
0.009	0.225	0.230	0.234	0.239	0.243	0.248	0.252	0.257	0.261	0.266	0.270	0.275	0.279	0.284	0.288	0.293
0.010	0.250	0.255	0.260	0.265	0.270	0.275	0.280	0.285	0.290	0.295	0.300	0.305	0.310	0.315	0.320	0.325
0.020	0.500	0.510	0.520	0.530	0.540	0.550	0.560	0.570	0.580	0.590	0.600	0.610	0.620	0.630	0.640	0.650
0.030	0.750	0.765	0.780	0.795	0.810	0.825	0.840	0.855	0.870	0.885	0.900	0.915	0.930	0.945	0.960	0.975
0.040	1.000	1.020	1.040	1.060	1.080	1.100	1.120	1.140	1.160	1.180	1.200	1.220	1.240	1.260	1.280	1.300
0.050	1.250	1.275	1.300	1.325	1.350	1.375	1.400	1.425	1.450	1.475	1.500	1.525	1.550	1.575	1.600	1.625
0.060	1.500	1.530	1.560	1.590	1.620	1.650	1.680	1.710	1.740	1.770	1.800	1.830	1.860	1.890	1.920	1.950
0.070	1.750	1.785	1.820	1.855	1.890	1.925	1.960	1.995	2.030	2.065	2.100	2.135	2.170	2.205	2.240	2.275
0.080	2.000	2.040	2.080	2.120	2.160	2.200	2.240	2.280	2.320	2.360	2.400	2.440	2.480	2.520	2.560	2.600
0.090	2.250	2.295	2.340	2.385	2.430	2.475	2.520	2.565	2.610	2.655	2.700	2.745	2.790	2.835	2.880	2.925
0.100	2.500	2.550	2.600	2.650	2.700	2.750	2.800	2.850	2.900	2.950	3.000	3.050	3.100	3.150	3.200	3.250
0.110	2.750	2.805	2.860	2.915	2.970	3.025	3.080	3.135	3.190	3.245	3.300	3.355	3.410	3.465	3.520	3.575
0.120	3.000	3.060	3.120	3.180	3.240	3.300	3.360	3.420	3.480	3.540	3.600	3.660	3.720	3.780	3.840	3.900
0.130	3.250	3.315	3.380	3.445	3.510	3.575	3.640	3.705	3.770	3.835	3.900	3.965	4.030	4.095	4.160	4.225
0.140	3.500	3.570	3.640	3.710	3.780	3.850	3.920	3.990	4.060	4.130	4.200	4.270	4.340	4.410	4.480	4.550
0.150	3.750	3.825	3.900	3.975	4.050	4.125	4.200	4.275	4.350	4.425	4.500	4.575	4.650	4.725	4.800	4.875
0.160	4.000	4.080	4.160	4.240	4.320	4.400	4.480	4.560	4.640	4.720	4.800	4.880	4.960	5.040	5.120	5.200
0.170	4.250	4.335	4.420	4.505	4.590	4.675	4.760	4.845	4.930	5.015	5.100	5.185	5.270	5.355	5.440	5.525
0.180	4.500	4.590	4.680	4.770	4.860	4.950	5.040	5.130	5.220	5.310	5.400	5.490	5.580	5.670	5.760	5.850
0.190	4.750	4.845	4.940	5.035	5.130	5.225	5.320	5.415	5.510	5.605	5.700	5.795	5.890	5.985	6.080	6.175
0.200	5.000	5.100	5.200	5.300	5.400	5.500	5.600	5.700	5.800	5.900	6.000	6.100	6.200	6.300	6.400	6.500
0.210	5.250	5.355	5.460	5.565	5.670	5.775	5.880	5.985	6.090	6.195	6.300	6.405	6.510	6.615	6.720	6.825
0.220	5.500	5.610	5.720	5.830	5.940	6.050	6.160	6.270	6.380	6.490	6.600	6.710	6.820	6.930	7.040	7.150
0.230	5.750	5.865	5.980	6.095	6.210	6.325	6.440	6.555	6.670	6.785	6.900	7.015	7.130	7.245	7.360	7.475
0.240	6.000	6.120	6.240	6.360	6.480	6.600	6.720	6.840	6.960	7.080	7.200	7.320	7.440	7.560	7.680	7.800
0.250	6.250	6.375	6.500	6.625	6.750	6.875	7.000	7.125	7.250	7.375	7.500	7.625	7.750	7.875	8.000	8.125
0.260	6.500	6.630	6.760	6.890	7.020	7.150	7.280	7.410	7.540	7.670	7.800	7.930	8.060	8.190	8.320	8.450
0.270	6.750	6.885	7.020	7.155	7.290	7.425	7.560	7.695	7.830	7.965	8.100	8.235	8.370	8.505	8.640	8.775
0.280	7.000	7.140	7.280	7.420	7.560	7.700	7.840	7.980	8.120	8.260	8.400	8.540	8.680	8.820	8.960	9.100
0.290	7.250	7.395	7.540	7.685	7.830	7.975	8.120	8.265	8.410	8.555	8.700	8.845	8.990	9.135	9.280	9.425
0.300	7.500	7.650	7.800	7.950	8.100	8.250	8.400	8.550	8.700	8.850	9.000	9.150	9.300	9.450	9.600	9.750
0.310	7.750	7.905	8.060	8.215	8.370	8.525	8.680	8.835	8.990	9.145	9.300	9.455	9.610	9.765	9.920	10.075
0.320	8.000	8.160	8.320	8.480	8.640	8.800	8.960	9.120	9.280	9.440	9.600	9.760	9.920	10.080	10.240	10.400
0.330	8.250	8.415	8.580	8.745	8.910	9.075	9.240	9.405	9.570	9.735	9.900	10.065	10.230	10.395	10.560	10.725
0.340	8.500	8.670	8.840	9.010	9.180	9.350	9.520	9.690	9.860	10.030	10.200	10.370	10.540	10.710	10.880	11.050
0.350	8.750	8.925	9.100	9.275	9.450	9.625	9.800	9.975	10.150	10.325	10.500	10.675	10.850	11.025	11.200	11.375
0.360	9.000	9.180	9.360	9.540	9.720	9.900	10.080	10.260	10.440	10.620	10.800	10.980	11.160	11.340	11.520	11.700
0.370	9.250	9.435	9.620	9.805	9.990	10.175	10.360	10.545	10.730	10.915	11.100	11.285	11.470	11.655	11.840	12.025
0.380	9.500	9.690	9.880	10.070	10.260	10.450	10.640	10.830	11.020	11.210	11.400	11.590	11.780	11.970	12.160	12.350
0.390	9.750	9.945	10.140	10.335	10.530	10.725	10.920	11.115	11.310	11.505	11.700	11.895	12.090	12.285	12.480	12.675
0.400	10.000	10.200	10.400	10.600	10.800	11.000	11.200	11.400	11.600	11.800	12.000	12.200	12.400	12.600	12.800	13.000
0.410	10.250	10.455	10.660	10.865	11.070	11.275	11.480	11.685	11.890	12.095	12.300	12.505	12.710	12.915	13.120	13.325
0.420	10.500	10.710	10.920	11.130	11.340	11.550	11.760	11.970	12.180	12.390	12.600	12.810	13.020	13.230	13.440	13.650
0.430	10.750	10.965	11.180	11.395	11.610	11.825	12.040	12.255	12.470	12.685	12.900	13.115	13.330	13.545	13.760	13.975
0.440	11.000	11.220	11.440	11.660	11.880	12.100	12.320	12.540	12.760	12.980	13.200	13.420	13.640	13.860	14.080	14.300
0.450	11.250	11.475	11.700	11.925	12.150	12.375	12.600	12.825	13.050	13.275	13.500	13.725	13.950	14.175	14.400	14.625
0.460	11.500	11.730	11.960	12.190	12.420	12.650	12.880	13.110	13.340	13.570	13.800	14.030	14.260	14.490	14.720	14.950

SILVER BULLION VALUE CHART $25 to $32.50

Oz.	25.00	25.50	26.00	26.50	27.00	27.50	28.00	28.50	29.00	29.50	30.00	30.50	31.00	31.50	32.00	32.50
0.470	11.750	11.985	12.220	12.455	12.690	12.925	13.160	13.395	13.630	13.865	14.100	14.335	14.570	14.805	15.040	15.275
0.480	12.000	12.240	12.480	12.720	12.960	13.200	13.440	13.680	13.920	14.160	14.400	14.640	14.880	15.120	15.360	15.600
0.490	12.250	12.495	12.740	12.985	13.230	13.475	13.720	13.965	14.210	14.455	14.700	14.945	15.190	15.435	15.680	15.925
0.500	12.500	12.750	13.000	13.250	13.500	13.750	14.000	14.250	14.500	14.750	15.000	15.250	15.500	15.750	16.000	16.250
0.510	12.750	13.005	13.260	13.515	13.770	14.025	14.280	14.535	14.790	15.045	15.300	15.555	15.810	16.065	16.320	16.575
0.520	13.000	13.260	13.520	13.780	14.040	14.300	14.560	14.820	15.080	15.340	15.600	15.860	16.120	16.380	16.640	16.900
0.530	13.250	13.515	13.780	14.045	14.310	14.575	14.840	15.105	15.370	15.635	15.900	16.165	16.430	16.695	16.960	17.225
0.540	13.500	13.770	14.040	14.310	14.580	14.850	15.120	15.390	15.660	15.930	16.200	16.470	16.740	17.010	17.280	17.550
0.550	13.750	14.025	14.300	14.575	14.850	15.125	15.400	15.675	15.950	16.225	16.500	16.775	17.050	17.325	17.600	17.875
0.560	14.000	14.280	14.560	14.840	15.120	15.400	15.680	15.960	16.240	16.520	16.800	17.080	17.360	17.640	17.920	18.200
0.570	14.250	14.535	14.820	15.105	15.390	15.675	15.960	16.245	16.530	16.815	17.100	17.385	17.670	17.955	18.240	18.525
0.580	14.500	14.790	15.080	15.370	15.660	15.950	16.240	16.530	16.820	17.110	17.400	17.690	17.980	18.270	18.560	18.850
0.590	14.750	15.045	15.340	15.635	15.930	16.225	16.520	16.815	17.110	17.405	17.700	17.995	18.290	18.585	18.880	19.175
0.600	15.000	15.300	15.600	15.900	16.200	16.500	16.800	17.100	17.400	17.700	18.000	18.300	18.600	18.900	19.200	19.500
0.610	15.250	15.555	15.860	16.165	16.470	16.775	17.080	17.385	17.690	17.995	18.300	18.605	18.910	19.215	19.520	19.825
0.620	15.500	15.810	16.120	16.430	16.740	17.050	17.360	17.670	17.980	18.290	18.600	18.910	19.220	19.530	19.840	20.150
0.630	15.750	16.065	16.380	16.695	17.010	17.325	17.640	17.955	18.270	18.585	18.900	19.215	19.530	19.845	20.160	20.475
0.640	16.000	16.320	16.640	16.960	17.280	17.600	17.920	18.240	18.560	18.880	19.200	19.520	19.840	20.160	20.480	20.800
0.650	16.250	16.575	16.900	17.225	17.550	17.875	18.200	18.525	18.850	19.175	19.500	19.825	20.150	20.475	20.800	21.125
0.660	16.500	16.830	17.160	17.490	17.820	18.150	18.480	18.810	19.140	19.470	19.800	20.130	20.460	20.790	21.120	21.450
0.670	16.750	17.085	17.420	17.755	18.090	18.425	18.760	19.095	19.430	19.765	20.100	20.435	20.770	21.105	21.440	21.775
0.680	17.000	17.340	17.680	18.020	18.360	18.700	19.040	19.380	19.720	20.060	20.400	20.740	21.080	21.420	21.760	22.100
0.690	17.250	17.595	17.940	18.285	18.630	18.975	19.320	19.665	20.010	20.355	20.700	21.045	21.390	21.735	22.080	22.425
0.700	17.500	17.850	18.200	18.550	18.900	19.250	19.600	19.950	20.300	20.650	21.000	21.350	21.700	22.050	22.400	22.750
0.710	17.750	18.105	18.460	18.815	19.170	19.525	19.880	20.235	20.590	20.945	21.300	21.655	22.010	22.365	22.720	23.075
0.720	18.000	18.360	18.720	19.080	19.440	19.800	20.160	20.520	20.880	21.240	21.600	21.960	22.320	22.680	23.040	23.400
0.730	18.250	18.615	18.980	19.345	19.710	20.075	20.440	20.805	21.170	21.535	21.900	22.265	22.630	22.995	23.360	23.725
0.740	18.500	18.870	19.240	19.610	19.980	20.350	20.720	21.090	21.460	21.830	22.200	22.570	22.940	23.310	23.680	24.050
0.750	18.750	19.125	19.500	19.875	20.250	20.625	21.000	21.375	21.750	22.125	22.500	22.875	23.250	23.625	24.000	24.375
0.760	19.000	19.380	19.760	20.140	20.520	20.900	21.280	21.660	22.040	22.420	22.800	23.180	23.560	23.940	24.320	24.700
0.770	19.250	19.635	20.020	20.405	20.790	21.175	21.560	21.945	22.330	22.715	23.100	23.485	23.870	24.255	24.640	25.025
0.780	19.500	19.890	20.280	20.670	21.060	21.450	21.840	22.230	22.620	23.010	23.400	23.790	24.180	24.570	24.960	25.350
0.790	19.750	20.145	20.540	20.935	21.330	21.725	22.120	22.515	22.910	23.305	23.700	24.095	24.490	24.885	25.280	25.675
0.800	20.000	20.400	20.800	21.200	21.600	22.000	22.400	22.800	23.200	23.600	24.000	24.400	24.800	25.200	25.600	26.000
0.810	20.250	20.655	21.060	21.465	21.870	22.275	22.680	23.085	23.490	23.895	24.300	24.705	25.110	25.515	25.920	26.325
0.820	20.500	20.910	21.320	21.730	22.140	22.550	22.960	23.370	23.780	24.190	24.600	25.010	25.420	25.830	26.240	26.650
0.830	20.750	21.165	21.580	21.995	22.410	22.825	23.240	23.655	24.070	24.485	24.900	25.315	25.730	26.145	26.560	26.975
0.840	21.000	21.420	21.840	22.260	22.680	23.100	23.520	23.940	24.360	24.780	25.200	25.620	26.040	26.460	26.880	27.300
0.850	21.250	21.675	22.100	22.525	22.950	23.375	23.800	24.225	24.650	25.075	25.500	25.925	26.350	26.775	27.200	27.625
0.860	21.500	21.930	22.360	22.790	23.220	23.650	24.080	24.510	24.940	25.370	25.800	26.230	26.660	27.090	27.520	27.950
0.870	21.750	22.185	22.620	23.055	23.490	23.925	24.360	24.795	25.230	25.665	26.100	26.535	26.970	27.405	27.840	28.275
0.880	22.000	22.440	22.880	23.320	23.760	24.200	24.640	25.080	25.520	25.960	26.400	26.840	27.280	27.720	28.160	28.600
0.890	22.250	22.695	23.140	23.585	24.030	24.475	24.920	25.365	25.810	26.255	26.700	27.145	27.590	28.035	28.480	28.925
0.900	22.500	22.950	23.400	23.850	24.300	24.750	25.200	25.650	26.100	26.550	27.000	27.450	27.900	28.350	28.800	29.250
0.910	22.750	23.205	23.660	24.115	24.570	25.025	25.480	25.935	26.390	26.845	27.300	27.755	28.210	28.665	29.120	29.575
0.920	23.000	23.460	23.920	24.380	24.840	25.300	25.760	26.220	26.680	27.140	27.600	28.060	28.520	28.980	29.440	29.900
0.930	23.250	23.715	24.180	24.645	25.110	25.575	26.040	26.505	26.970	27.435	27.900	28.365	28.830	29.295	29.760	30.225
0.940	23.500	23.970	24.440	24.910	25.380	25.850	26.320	26.790	27.260	27.730	28.200	28.670	29.140	29.610	30.080	30.550
0.950	23.750	24.225	24.700	25.175	25.650	26.125	26.600	27.075	27.550	28.025	28.500	28.975	29.450	29.925	30.400	30.875
0.960	24.000	24.480	24.960	25.440	25.920	26.400	26.880	27.360	27.840	28.320	28.800	29.280	29.760	30.240	30.720	31.200
0.970	24.250	24.735	25.220	25.705	26.190	26.675	27.160	27.645	28.130	28.615	29.100	29.585	30.070	30.555	31.040	31.525
0.980	24.500	24.990	25.480	25.970	26.460	26.950	27.440	27.930	28.420	28.910	29.400	29.890	30.380	30.870	31.360	31.850
0.990	24.750	25.245	25.740	26.235	26.730	27.225	27.720	28.215	28.710	29.205	29.700	30.195	30.690	31.185	31.680	32.175
1.000	25.000	25.500	26.000	26.500	27.000	27.500	28.000	28.500	29.000	29.500	30.000	30.500	31.000	31.500	32.000	32.500

GOLD BULLION VALUE CHART $1,500 to $1,650

Oz.	1500.00	1510.00	1520.00	1530.00	1540.00	1540.00	1550.00	1560.00	1570.00	1580.00	1590.00	1610.00	1620.00	1630.00	1640.00	1650.00
0.001	1.50	1.51	1.52	1.53	1.54	1.54	1.55	1.56	1.57	1.58	1.59	1.61	1.62	1.63	1.64	1.65
0.002	3.00	3.02	3.04	3.06	3.08	3.08	3.10	3.12	3.14	3.16	3.18	3.22	3.24	3.26	3.28	3.30
0.003	4.50	4.53	4.56	4.59	4.62	4.62	4.65	4.68	4.71	4.74	4.77	4.83	4.86	4.89	4.92	4.95
0.004	6.00	6.04	6.08	6.12	6.16	6.16	6.20	6.24	6.28	6.32	6.36	6.44	6.48	6.52	6.56	6.60
0.005	7.50	7.55	7.60	7.65	7.70	7.70	7.75	7.80	7.85	7.90	7.95	8.05	8.10	8.15	8.20	8.25
0.006	9.00	9.06	9.12	9.18	9.24	9.24	9.30	9.36	9.42	9.48	9.54	9.66	9.72	9.78	9.84	9.90
0.007	10.50	10.57	10.64	10.71	10.78	10.78	10.85	10.92	10.99	11.06	11.13	11.27	11.34	11.41	11.48	11.55
0.008	12.00	12.08	12.16	12.24	12.32	12.32	12.40	12.48	12.56	12.64	12.72	12.88	12.96	13.04	13.12	13.20
0.009	13.50	13.59	13.68	13.77	13.86	13.86	13.95	14.04	14.13	14.22	14.31	14.49	14.58	14.67	14.76	14.85
0.010	15.00	15.10	15.20	15.30	15.40	15.40	15.50	15.60	15.70	15.80	15.90	16.10	16.20	16.30	16.40	16.50
0.020	30.00	30.20	30.40	30.60	30.80	30.80	31.00	31.20	31.40	31.60	31.80	32.20	32.40	32.60	32.80	33.00
0.030	45.00	45.30	45.60	45.90	46.20	46.20	46.50	46.80	47.10	47.40	47.70	48.30	48.60	48.90	49.20	49.50
0.040	60.00	60.40	60.80	61.20	61.60	61.60	62.00	62.40	62.80	63.20	63.60	64.40	64.80	65.20	65.60	66.00
0.050	75.00	75.50	76.00	76.50	77.00	77.00	77.50	78.00	78.50	79.00	79.50	80.50	81.00	81.50	82.00	82.50
0.060	90.00	90.60	91.20	91.80	92.40	92.40	93.00	93.60	94.20	94.80	95.40	96.60	97.20	97.80	98.40	99.00
0.070	105.00	105.70	106.40	107.10	107.80	107.80	108.50	109.20	109.90	110.60	111.30	112.70	113.40	114.10	114.80	115.50
0.080	120.00	120.80	121.60	122.40	123.20	123.20	124.00	124.80	125.60	126.40	127.20	128.80	129.60	130.40	131.20	132.00
0.090	135.00	135.90	136.80	137.70	138.60	138.60	139.50	140.40	141.30	142.20	143.10	144.90	145.80	146.70	147.60	148.50
0.100	150.00	151.00	152.00	153.00	154.00	154.00	155.00	156.00	157.00	158.00	159.00	161.00	162.00	163.00	164.00	165.00
0.110	165.00	166.10	167.20	168.30	169.40	169.40	170.50	171.60	172.70	173.80	174.90	177.10	178.20	179.30	180.40	181.50
0.120	180.00	181.20	182.40	183.60	184.80	184.80	186.00	187.20	188.40	189.60	190.80	193.20	194.40	195.60	196.80	198.00
0.130	195.00	196.30	197.60	198.90	200.20	200.20	201.50	202.80	204.10	205.40	206.70	209.30	210.60	211.90	213.20	214.50
0.140	210.00	211.40	212.80	214.20	215.60	215.60	217.00	218.40	219.80	221.20	222.60	225.40	226.80	228.20	229.60	231.00
0.150	225.00	226.50	228.00	229.50	231.00	231.00	232.50	234.00	235.50	237.00	238.50	241.50	243.00	244.50	246.00	247.50
0.160	240.00	241.60	243.20	244.80	246.40	246.40	248.00	249.60	251.20	252.80	254.40	257.60	259.20	260.80	262.40	264.00
0.170	255.00	256.70	258.40	260.10	261.80	261.80	263.50	265.20	266.90	268.60	270.30	273.70	275.40	277.10	278.80	280.50
0.180	270.00	271.80	273.60	275.40	277.20	277.20	279.00	280.80	282.60	284.40	286.20	289.80	291.60	293.40	295.20	297.00
0.190	285.00	286.90	288.80	290.70	292.60	292.60	294.50	296.40	298.30	300.20	302.10	305.90	307.80	309.70	311.60	313.50
0.200	300.00	302.00	304.00	306.00	308.00	308.00	310.00	312.00	314.00	316.00	318.00	322.00	324.00	326.00	328.00	330.00
0.210	315.00	317.10	319.20	321.30	323.40	323.40	325.50	327.60	329.70	331.80	333.90	338.10	340.20	342.30	344.40	346.50
0.220	330.00	332.20	334.40	336.60	338.80	338.80	341.00	343.20	345.40	347.60	349.80	354.20	356.40	358.60	360.80	363.00
0.230	345.00	347.30	349.60	351.90	354.20	354.20	356.50	358.80	361.10	363.40	365.70	370.30	372.60	374.90	377.20	379.50
0.240	360.00	362.40	364.80	367.20	369.60	369.60	372.00	374.40	376.80	379.20	381.60	386.40	388.80	391.20	393.60	396.00
0.250	375.00	377.50	380.00	382.50	385.00	385.00	387.50	390.00	392.50	395.00	397.50	402.50	405.00	407.50	410.00	412.50
0.260	390.00	392.60	395.20	397.80	400.40	400.40	403.00	405.60	408.20	410.80	413.40	418.60	421.20	423.80	426.40	429.00
0.270	405.00	407.70	410.40	413.10	415.80	415.80	418.50	421.20	423.90	426.60	429.30	434.70	437.40	440.10	442.80	445.50
0.280	420.00	422.80	425.60	428.40	431.20	431.20	434.00	436.80	439.60	442.40	445.20	450.80	453.60	456.40	459.20	462.00
0.290	435.00	437.90	440.80	443.70	446.60	446.60	449.50	452.40	455.30	458.20	461.10	466.90	469.80	472.70	475.60	478.50
0.300	450.00	453.00	456.00	459.00	462.00	462.00	465.00	468.00	471.00	474.00	477.00	483.00	486.00	489.00	492.00	495.00
0.310	465.00	468.10	471.20	474.30	477.40	477.40	480.50	483.60	486.70	489.80	492.90	499.10	502.20	505.30	508.40	511.50
0.320	480.00	483.20	486.40	489.60	492.80	492.80	496.00	499.20	502.40	505.60	508.80	515.20	518.40	521.60	524.80	528.00
0.330	495.00	498.30	501.60	504.90	508.20	508.20	511.50	514.80	518.10	521.40	524.70	531.30	534.60	537.90	541.20	544.50
0.340	510.00	513.40	516.80	520.20	523.60	523.60	527.00	530.40	533.80	537.20	540.60	547.40	550.80	554.20	557.60	561.00
0.350	525.00	528.50	532.00	535.50	539.00	539.00	542.50	546.00	549.50	553.00	556.50	563.50	567.00	570.50	574.00	577.50
0.360	540.00	543.60	547.20	550.80	554.40	554.40	558.00	561.60	565.20	568.80	572.40	579.60	583.20	586.80	590.40	594.00
0.370	555.00	558.70	562.40	566.10	569.80	569.80	573.50	577.20	580.90	584.60	588.30	595.70	599.40	603.10	606.80	610.50
0.380	570.00	573.80	577.60	581.40	585.20	585.20	589.00	592.80	596.60	600.40	604.20	611.80	615.60	619.40	623.20	627.00
0.390	585.00	588.90	592.80	596.70	600.60	600.60	604.50	608.40	612.30	616.20	620.10	627.90	631.80	635.70	639.60	643.50
0.400	600.00	604.00	608.00	612.00	616.00	616.00	620.00	624.00	628.00	632.00	636.00	644.00	648.00	652.00	656.00	660.00
0.410	615.00	619.10	623.20	627.30	631.40	631.40	635.50	639.60	643.70	647.80	651.90	660.10	664.20	668.30	672.40	676.50
0.420	630.00	634.20	638.40	642.60	646.80	646.80	651.00	655.20	659.40	663.60	667.80	676.20	680.40	684.60	688.80	693.00
0.430	645.00	649.30	653.60	657.90	662.20	662.20	666.50	670.80	675.10	679.40	683.70	692.30	696.60	700.90	705.20	709.50
0.440	660.00	664.40	668.80	673.20	677.60	677.60	682.00	686.40	690.80	695.20	699.60	708.40	712.80	717.20	721.60	726.00
0.450	675.00	679.50	684.00	688.50	693.00	693.00	697.50	702.00	706.50	711.00	715.50	724.50	729.00	733.50	738.00	742.50

GOLD BULLION VALUE CHART $1,500 to $1,650

Oz.	1500.00	1510.00	1520.00	1530.00	1540.00	1540.00	1550.00	1560.00	1570.00	1580.00	1590.00	1610.00	1620.00	1630.00	1640.00	1650.00
0.460	690.00	694.60	699.20	703.80	708.40	708.40	713.00	717.60	722.20	726.80	731.40	740.60	745.20	749.80	754.40	759.00
0.470	705.00	709.70	714.40	719.10	723.80	723.80	728.50	733.20	737.90	742.60	747.30	756.70	761.40	766.10	770.80	775.50
0.480	720.00	724.80	729.60	734.40	739.20	739.20	744.00	748.80	753.60	758.40	763.20	772.80	777.60	782.40	787.20	792.00
0.490	735.00	739.90	744.80	749.70	754.60	754.60	759.50	764.40	769.30	774.20	779.10	788.90	793.80	798.70	803.60	808.50
0.500	750.00	755.00	760.00	765.00	770.00	770.00	775.00	780.00	785.00	790.00	795.00	805.00	810.00	815.00	820.00	825.00
0.510	765.00	770.10	775.20	780.30	785.40	785.40	790.50	795.60	800.70	805.80	810.90	821.10	826.20	831.30	836.40	841.50
0.520	780.00	785.20	790.40	795.60	800.80	800.80	806.00	811.20	816.40	821.60	826.80	837.20	842.40	847.60	852.80	858.00
0.530	795.00	800.30	805.60	810.90	816.20	816.20	821.50	826.80	832.10	837.40	842.70	853.30	858.60	863.90	869.20	874.50
0.540	810.00	815.40	820.80	826.20	831.60	831.60	837.00	842.40	847.80	853.20	858.60	869.40	874.80	880.20	885.60	891.00
0.550	825.00	830.50	836.00	841.50	847.00	847.00	852.50	858.00	863.50	869.00	874.50	885.50	891.00	896.50	902.00	907.50
0.560	840.00	845.60	851.20	856.80	862.40	862.40	868.00	873.60	879.20	884.80	890.40	901.60	907.20	912.80	918.40	924.00
0.570	855.00	860.70	866.40	872.10	877.80	877.80	883.50	889.20	894.90	900.60	906.30	917.70	923.40	929.10	934.80	940.50
0.580	870.00	875.80	881.60	887.40	893.20	893.20	899.00	904.80	910.60	916.40	922.20	933.80	939.60	945.40	951.20	957.00
0.590	885.00	890.90	896.80	902.70	908.60	908.60	914.50	920.40	926.30	932.20	938.10	949.90	955.80	961.70	967.60	973.50
0.600	900.00	906.00	912.00	918.00	924.00	924.00	930.00	936.00	942.00	948.00	954.00	966.00	972.00	978.00	984.00	990.00
0.610	915.00	921.10	927.20	933.30	939.40	939.40	945.50	951.60	957.70	963.80	969.90	982.10	988.20	994.30	1000.40	1006.50
0.620	930.00	936.20	942.40	948.60	954.80	954.80	961.00	967.20	973.40	979.60	985.80	998.20	1004.40	1010.60	1016.80	1023.00
0.630	945.00	951.30	957.60	963.90	970.20	970.20	976.50	982.80	989.10	995.40	1001.70	1014.30	1020.60	1026.90	1033.20	1039.50
0.640	960.00	966.40	972.80	979.20	985.60	985.60	992.00	998.40	1004.80	1011.20	1017.60	1030.40	1036.80	1043.20	1049.60	1056.00
0.650	975.00	981.50	988.00	994.50	1001.00	1001.00	1007.50	1014.00	1020.50	1027.00	1033.50	1046.50	1053.00	1059.50	1066.00	1072.50
0.660	990.00	996.60	1003.20	1009.80	1016.40	1016.40	1023.00	1029.60	1036.20	1042.80	1049.40	1062.60	1069.20	1075.80	1082.40	1089.00
0.670	1005.00	1011.70	1018.40	1025.10	1031.80	1031.80	1038.50	1045.20	1051.90	1058.60	1065.30	1078.70	1085.40	1092.10	1098.80	1105.50
0.680	1020.00	1026.80	1033.60	1040.40	1047.20	1047.20	1054.00	1060.80	1067.60	1074.40	1081.20	1094.80	1101.60	1108.40	1115.20	1122.00
0.690	1035.00	1041.90	1048.80	1055.70	1062.60	1062.60	1069.50	1076.40	1083.30	1090.20	1097.10	1110.90	1117.80	1124.70	1131.60	1138.50
0.700	1050.00	1057.00	1064.00	1071.00	1078.00	1078.00	1085.00	1092.00	1099.00	1106.00	1113.00	1127.00	1134.00	1141.00	1148.00	1155.00
0.710	1065.00	1072.10	1079.20	1086.30	1093.40	1093.40	1100.50	1107.60	1114.70	1121.80	1128.90	1143.10	1150.20	1157.30	1164.40	1171.50
0.720	1080.00	1087.20	1094.40	1101.60	1108.80	1108.80	1116.00	1123.20	1130.40	1137.60	1144.80	1159.20	1166.40	1173.60	1180.80	1188.00
0.730	1095.00	1102.30	1109.60	1116.90	1124.20	1124.20	1131.50	1138.80	1146.10	1153.40	1160.70	1175.30	1182.60	1189.90	1197.20	1204.50
0.740	1110.00	1117.40	1124.80	1132.20	1139.60	1139.60	1147.00	1154.40	1161.80	1169.20	1176.60	1191.40	1198.80	1206.20	1213.60	1221.00
0.750	1125.00	1132.50	1140.00	1147.50	1155.00	1155.00	1162.50	1170.00	1177.50	1185.00	1192.50	1207.50	1215.00	1222.50	1230.00	1237.50
0.760	1140.00	1147.60	1155.20	1162.80	1170.40	1170.40	1178.00	1185.60	1193.20	1200.80	1208.40	1223.60	1231.20	1238.80	1246.40	1254.00
0.770	1155.00	1162.70	1170.40	1178.10	1185.80	1185.80	1193.50	1201.20	1208.90	1216.60	1224.30	1239.70	1247.40	1255.10	1262.80	1270.50
0.780	1170.00	1177.80	1185.60	1193.40	1201.20	1201.20	1209.00	1216.80	1224.60	1232.40	1240.20	1255.80	1263.60	1271.40	1279.20	1287.00
0.790	1185.00	1192.90	1200.80	1208.70	1216.60	1216.60	1224.50	1232.40	1240.30	1248.20	1256.10	1271.90	1279.80	1287.70	1295.60	1303.50
0.800	1200.00	1208.00	1216.00	1224.00	1232.00	1232.00	1240.00	1248.00	1256.00	1264.00	1272.00	1288.00	1296.00	1304.00	1312.00	1320.00
0.810	1215.00	1223.10	1231.20	1239.30	1247.40	1247.40	1255.50	1263.60	1271.70	1279.80	1287.90	1304.10	1312.20	1320.30	1328.40	1336.50
0.820	1230.00	1238.20	1246.40	1254.60	1262.80	1262.80	1271.00	1279.20	1287.40	1295.60	1303.80	1320.20	1328.40	1336.60	1344.80	1353.00
0.830	1245.00	1253.30	1261.60	1269.90	1278.20	1278.20	1286.50	1294.80	1303.10	1311.40	1319.70	1336.30	1344.60	1352.90	1361.20	1369.50
0.840	1260.00	1268.40	1276.80	1285.20	1293.60	1293.60	1302.00	1310.40	1318.80	1327.20	1335.60	1352.40	1360.80	1369.20	1377.60	1386.00
0.850	1275.00	1283.50	1292.00	1300.50	1309.00	1309.00	1317.50	1326.00	1334.50	1343.00	1351.50	1368.50	1377.00	1385.50	1394.00	1402.50
0.860	1290.00	1298.60	1307.20	1315.80	1324.40	1324.40	1333.00	1341.60	1350.20	1358.80	1367.40	1384.60	1393.20	1401.80	1410.40	1419.00
0.870	1305.00	1313.70	1322.40	1331.10	1339.80	1339.80	1348.50	1357.20	1365.90	1374.60	1383.30	1400.70	1409.40	1418.10	1426.80	1435.50
0.880	1320.00	1328.80	1337.60	1346.40	1355.20	1355.20	1364.00	1372.80	1381.60	1390.40	1399.20	1416.80	1425.60	1434.40	1443.20	1452.00
0.890	1335.00	1343.90	1352.80	1361.70	1370.60	1370.60	1379.50	1388.40	1397.30	1406.20	1415.10	1432.90	1441.80	1450.70	1459.60	1468.50
0.900	1350.00	1359.00	1368.00	1377.00	1386.00	1386.00	1395.00	1404.00	1413.00	1422.00	1431.00	1449.00	1458.00	1467.00	1476.00	1485.00
0.910	1365.00	1374.10	1383.20	1392.30	1401.40	1401.40	1410.50	1419.60	1428.70	1437.80	1446.90	1465.10	1474.20	1483.30	1492.40	1501.50
0.920	1380.00	1389.20	1398.40	1407.60	1416.80	1416.80	1426.00	1435.20	1444.40	1453.60	1462.80	1481.20	1490.40	1499.60	1508.80	1518.00
0.930	1395.00	1404.30	1413.60	1422.90	1432.20	1432.20	1441.50	1450.80	1460.10	1469.40	1478.70	1497.30	1506.60	1515.90	1525.20	1534.50
0.940	1410.00	1419.40	1428.80	1438.20	1447.60	1447.60	1457.00	1466.40	1475.80	1485.20	1494.60	1513.40	1522.80	1532.20	1541.60	1551.00
0.950	1425.00	1434.50	1444.00	1453.50	1463.00	1463.00	1472.50	1482.00	1491.50	1501.00	1510.50	1529.50	1539.00	1548.50	1558.00	1567.50
0.960	1440.00	1449.60	1459.20	1468.80	1478.40	1478.40	1488.00	1497.60	1507.20	1516.80	1526.40	1545.60	1555.20	1564.80	1574.40	1584.00
0.970	1455.00	1464.70	1474.40	1484.10	1493.80	1493.80	1503.50	1513.20	1522.90	1532.60	1542.30	1561.70	1571.40	1581.10	1590.80	1600.50
0.980	1470.00	1479.80	1489.60	1499.40	1509.20	1509.20	1519.00	1528.80	1538.60	1548.40	1558.20	1577.80	1587.60	1597.40	1607.20	1617.00
0.990	1485.00	1494.90	1504.80	1514.70	1524.60	1524.60	1534.50	1544.40	1554.30	1564.20	1574.10	1593.90	1603.80	1613.70	1623.60	1633.50
1.000	1500.00	1510.00	1520.00	1530.00	1540.00	1540.00	1550.00	1560.00	1570.00	1580.00	1590.00	1610.00	1620.00	1630.00	1640.00	1650.00

HEJIRA DATE CONVERSION CHART

HEJIRA (Hijira, Hegira), the name of the Muslim era (A.H. = Anno Hegirae) dates back to the Christian year 622 when Mohammed "fled" from Mecca, escaping to Medina to avoid persecution from the Koreish tribesmen. Based on a lunar year the Muslim year is 11 days shorter.

*=Leap Year (Christian Calendar)

AH Hejira	AD Christian Date
1010	1601, July 2
1011	1602, June 21
1012	1603, June 11
1013	1604, May 30
1014	1605, May 19
1015	1606, May 9
1016	1607, April 28
1017	1608, April 17
1018	1609, April 6
1017	1608, April 28
1018	1609, April 6
1019	1610, March 26
1020	1611, March 16
1021	1612, March 4
1022	1613, February 21
1023	1614, February 11
1024	1615, January 31
1025	1616, January 20
1026	1617, January 9
1027	1617, December 29
1028	1618, December 19
1029	1619, December 8
1030	1620, November 26
1031	1621, November 16
1032	1622, November 5
1033	1623, October 25
1034	1624, October 14
1035	1625, October 3
1036	1626, September 22
1037	1627, September 12
1038	1628, August 31
1039	1629, August 21
1040	1630, August 10
1041	1631, July 30
1042	1632, July 19
1043	1633, July 8
1044	1634, June 27
1045	1635, June 17
1046	1636, June 5
1047	1637, May 26
1048	1638, May 15
1049	1639, May 4
1050	1640, April 23
1051	1641, April 12
1052	1642, April 1
1053	1643, March 22
1054	1644, March 10
1055	1645, February 27
1056	1646, February 17
1057	1647, February 6
1058	1648, January 27
1059	1649, January 15
1060	1650, January 4
1061	1650, December 25
1062	1651, December 14
1063	1652, December 2
1064	1653, November 22
1065	1654, November 11
1066	1655, October 31
1067	1656, October 20
1068	1657, October 9
1069	1658, September 29
1070	1659, September 18
1071	1660, September 6
1072	1661, August 27
1073	1662, August 16
1074	1663, August 5
1075	1664, July 25
1076	1665, July 14
1077	1666, July 4
1078	1667, June 23
1079	1668, June 11
1080	1669, June 1
1081	1670, May 21
1082	1671, May 10
1083	1672, April 29
1084	1673, April 18
1085	1674, April 7

AH Hejira	AD Christian Date
1086	1675, March 28
1087	1676, March 16*
1088	1677, March 6
1089	1678, February 23
1090	1679, February 12
1091	1680, February 2*
1092	1681, January 21
1093	1682, January 10
1094	1682, December 31
1095	1683, December 20
1096	1684, December 8*
1097	1685, November 28
1098	1686, November 17
1099	1687, November 7
1100	1688, October 26*
1101	1689, October 15
1102	1690, October 5
1103	1691, September 24
1104	1692, September 12*
1105	1693, September 2
1106	1694, August 22
1107	1695, August 12
1108	1696, July 31*
1109	1697, July 20
1110	1698, July 10
1111	1699, June 29
1112	1700, June 18
1113	1701, June 8
1114	1702, May 28
1115	1703, May 17
1116	1704, May 6*
1117	1705, April 25
1118	1706, April 15
1119	1707, April 4
1120	1708, March 23*
1121	1709, March 13
1122	1710, March 2
1123	1711, February 19
1124	1712, February 9*
1125	1713, January 28
1126	1714, January 17
1127	1715, January 7
1128	1715, December 27
1129	1716, December 16*
1130	1717, December 5
1131	1718, November 24
1132	1719, November 14
1133	1720, November 2*
1134	1721, October 22
1135	1722, October 12
1136	1723, October 1
1137	1724, September 19
1138	1725, September 9
1139	1726, August 29
1140	1727, August 19
1141	1728, August 7*
1142	1729, July 27
1143	1730, July 17
1144	1731, July 6
1145	1732, June 24*
1146	1733, June 14
1147	1734, June 3
1148	1735, May 24
1149	1736, May 12*
1150	1737, May 1
1151	1738, April 21
1152	1739, April 10
1153	1740, March 29*
1154	1741, March 19
1155	1742, March 8
1156	1743, February 25
1157	1744, February 15*
1158	1745, February 3
1159	1746, January 24
1160	1747, January 13
1161	1748, January 2
1162	1748, December 22*
1163	1749, December 11
1164	1750, November 30
1165	1751, November 20
1166	1752, November 8*
1167	1753, October 29
1168	1754, October 18
1169	1755, October 7
1170	1756, September 26*
1171	1757, September 15
1172	1758, September 4
1173	1759, August 25
1174	1760, August 13*
1175	1761, August 2
1176	1762, July 23

AH Hejira	AD Christian Date
1177	1763, July 12
1178	1764, July 1*
1179	1765, June 20
1180	1766, June 9
1181	1767, May 30
1182	1768, May 18*
1183	1769, May 7
1184	1770, April 27
1185	1771, April 16
1186	1772, April 4*
1187	1773, March 25
1188	1774, March 14
1189	1775, March 4
1190	1776, February 21*
1191	1777, February 1
1192	1778, January 30
1193	1779, January 19
1194	1780, January 8*
1195	1780, December 28*
1196	1781, December 17
1197	1782, December 7
1198	1783, November 26
1199	1784, November 14*
1200	1785, November 4
1201	1786, October 24
1202	1787, October 13
1203	1788, October 2*
1204	1789, September 21
1205	1790, September 10
1206	1791, August 31
1207	1792, August 19*
1208	1793, August 9
1209	1794, July 29
1210	1795, July 18
1211	1796, July 7*
1212	1797, June 26
1213	1798, June 15
1214	1799, June 5
1215	1800, May 25
1216	1801, May 14
1217	1802, May 4
1218	1803, April 23
1219	1804, April 12*
1220	1805, April 1
1221	1806, March 21
1222	1807, March 11
1223	1808, February 28*
1224	1809, February 16
1225	1810, February 6
1226	1811, January 26
1227	1812, January 16*
1228	1813, January 6
1229	1813, December 24
1230	1814, December 14
1231	1815, December 3
1232	1816, November 21*
1233	1817, November 11
1234	1818, October 31
1235	1819, October 20
1236	1820, October 9*
1237	1821, September 28
1238	1822, September 18
1239	1823, September 8
1240	1824, August 26*
1241	1825, August 16
1242	1826, August 5
1243	1827, July 25
1244	1828, July 14*
1245	1829, July 3
1246	1830, June 22
1247	1831, June 12
1248	1832, May 31*
1249	1833, May 21
1250	1834, May 10
1251	1835, April 29
1252	1836, April 18*
1253	1837, April 7
1254	1838, March 27
1255	1839, March 17
1256	1840, March 5*
1257	1841, February 23
1258	1842, February 12
1259	1843, February 1
1260	1844, January 22*
1261	1845, January 10
1262	1845, December 30
1263	1846, December 20
1264	1847, December 9
1265	1848, November 27*
1266	1849, November 17
1267	1850, November 6

AH Hejira	AD Christian Date
1268	1851, October 27
1269	1852, October 15*
1270	1853, October 4
1271	1854, September 24
1272	1855, September 13
1273	1856, September 1*
1274	1857, August 22
1275	1858, August 11
1276	1859, July 31
1277	1860, July 20*
1278	1861, July 9
1279	1862, June 29
1280	1863, June 18
1281	1864, June 6*
1282	1865, May 27
1283	1866, May 16
1284	1867, May 5
1285	1868, April 24*
1286	1869, April 13
1287	1870, April 3
1288	1871, March 23
1289	1872, March 11*
1290	1873, March 1
1291	1874, February 18
1292	1875, February 7
1293	1876, January 28*
1294	1877, January 16
1295	1878, January 5
1296	1878, December 26
1297	1879, December 15
1298	1880, December 4*
1299	1881, November 23
1300	1882, November 12
1301	1883, November 2
1302	1884, October 21*
1303	1885, October 10
1304	1886, September 30
1305	1887, September 19
1306	1888, September 7*
1307	1889, August 28
1308	1890, August 17
1309	1891, August 7
1310	1892, July 26*
1311	1893, July 15
1312	1894, July 5
1313	1895, June 24
1314	1896, June 12*
1315	1897, June 2
1316	1898, May 22
1317	1899, May 12
1318	1900, May 1
1319	1901, April 20
1320	1902, April 10
1321	1903, March 30
1322	1904, March 18*
1323	1905, March 8
1324	1906, February 25
1325	1907, February 14
1326	1908, February 4*
1327	1909, January 23
1328	1910, January 13
1329	1911, January 2
1330	1911, December 22
1331	1912, December 11
1332	1913, November 30
1333	1914, November 19
1334	1915, November 9
1335	1916, October 28*
1336	1917, October 17
1337	1918, October 7
1338	1919, September 26
1339	1920, September 15*
1340	1921, September 4
1341	1922, August 24
1342	1923, August 14
1343	1924, August 2*
1344	1925, July 22
1345	1926, July 12
1346	1927, July 1
1347	1928, June 20*
1348	1929, June 9
1349	1930, May 29
1350	1931, May 19
1351	1932, May 7*
1352	1933, April 26
1353	1934, April 16
1354	1935, April 5
1355	1936, March 24*
1356	1937, March 14
1357	1938, March 3
1358	1939, February 21
1359	1940, February 10*

AH Hejira	AD Christian Date
1360	1941, January 29
1361	1942, January 19
1362	1943, January 8
1363	1943, December 28
1364	1944, December 17*
1365	1945, December 6
1366	1946, November 25
1367	1947, November 15
1368	1948, November 3*
1369	1949, October 24
1370	1950, October 13
1371	1951, October 2
1372	1952, September 21*
1373	1953, September 10
1374	1954, August 30
1375	1955, August 20
1376	1956, August 8*
1377	1957, July 29
1378	1958, July 18
1379	1959, July 7
1380	1960, June 25*
1381	1961, June 14
1382	1962, June 4
1383	1963, May 25
1384	1964, May 13*
1385	1965, May 2
1386	1966, April 22
1387	1967, April 11
1388	1968, March 31*
1389	1969, March 20
1390	1970, March 9
1391	1971, February 27
1392	1972, February 16*
1393	1973, February 4
1394	1974, January 25
1395	1975, January 14
1396	1976, January 3*
1397	1976, December 23*
1398	1977, December 12
1399	1978, December 2
1400	1979, November 21
1401	1980, November 9*
1402	1981, October 30
1403	1982, October 19
1404	1983, October 8
1405	1984, September 27*
1406	1985, September 16
1407	1986, September 6
1408	1987, August 26
1409	1988, August 14*
1410	1989, August 3
1411	1990, July 24
1412	1991, July 13
1413	1992, July 2*
1414	1993, June 21
1415	1994, June 10
1416	1995, May 31
1417	1996, May 19*
1418	1997, May 9
1419	1998, April 28
1420	1999, April 17
1421	2000, April 6*
1422	2001, March 26
1423	2002, March 15
1424	2003, March 5
1425	2004, February 22*
1426	2005, February 10
1427	2006, January 31
1428	2007, January 20
1429	2008, January 10*
1430	2008, December 29
1431	2009, December 18
1432	2010, December 8
1433	2011, November 27*
1434	2012, November 15
1435	2013, November 5
1436	2014, October 25
1437	2015, October 15*
1438	2016, October 3
1439	2017, September 22
1440	2018, September 12
1441	2019, September 1*
1442	2020, August 20
1443	2021, August 10
1444	2022, July 30
1445	2023, July 19*
1446	2024, July 8
1447	2025, June 27
1448	2026, June 17
1449	2027, June 6*
1450	2028, May 25

AFGHANISTAN

The Islamic Republic of Afghanistan, which occupies a mountainous region of Southwest Asia, has an area of 251,825 sq. mi. (652,090 sq. km.) and a population of 25.59 million. Presently, about a fifth of the total population lives in exile as refugees, (mostly in Pakistan). Capital: Kabul. It is bordered by Iran, Pakistan, Turkmenistan, Uzbekistan, Tajikistan, and China's Sinkiang Province. Agriculture and herding are the principal industries; textile mills and cement factories add to the industrial sector. Cotton, wool, fruits, nuts, oil, sheepskin coats and hand-woven carpets are normally exported but foreign trade has been interrupted since 1979.

On September 11, 2001, a terrorist attack on the United States, supported by the Taliban, led to retaliatory strikes by the U.S. Military in coalition with Afghans of a Northern Alliance. The Taliban regime was deposed. During a UN-sponsored conference on Afghanistan that was held in Bonn, Germany, in early November 2001, an agreement was reached for an Interim Authority, under the leadership of Hamid Karzai, to be installed in Afghanistan on December 22, 2001 and to hold power for the following four to six months. A "loya jirga" (Grand Council) then established a Transitional Authority with Hamid Karzai as president to prepare for general elections and a new constitution.

The national symbol on most coins of the kingdom is a stylized mosque, within which is seen the *mihrab*, a niche indicating the direction of Mecca, and the *minbar*, the pulpit, with a flight of steps leading up to it. Inscriptions in Pashtu were first used under the rebel Habibullah, but did not become standard until 1950.

ISLAMIC STATE
SH1373-1381 / 1994-2002AD
STANDARD COINAGE

KM# 1043 500 AFGHANIS
19.8700 g., 0.9990 Silver 0.6382 oz. ASW, 37.9 mm. **Subject:** World Championship of Soccer - 2006 - Germany **Obv:** State Emblem **Rev:** Soccer ball on German map **Edge:** Reeded

Date	Mintage	F	VF	XF	Unc	BU
2001 Proof	—	Value: 50.00				

KM# 1048 500 AFGHANIS
15.0000 g., Silver, 35.08 mm. **Subject:** 100th Anniversary Death of Giuseppe Verdi **Obv:** National arms **Rev:** Bust of Verdi 3/4 left, music score below **Edge:** Plain

Date	Mintage	F	VF	XF	Unc	BU
SH1380(2001) Proof	—	Value: 35.00				

REPUBLIC
SH1381- / 2002- AD
DECIMAL COINAGE

100 Pul = 1 Afghani; 20 Afghani = 1 Amani

KM# 1044 AFGHANI
3.2800 g., Copper Plated Steel, 20 mm. **Obv:** Value, legend above, legend and date below **Rev:** Mosque with flags in wreath

Date	Mintage	F	VF	XF	Unc	BU
SH1383(2004)	—	—	—	—	1.50	2.00
SH1384(2005)	—	—	—	—	1.50	2.00

KM# 1045 2 AFGHANIS
4.1000 g., Stainless Steel, 22 mm. **Obv:** Value, legend above, legend and date below **Rev:** Mosque with flags in wreath

Date	Mintage	F	VF	XF	Unc	BU
SH1383(2004)	—	—	—	—	2.00	2.50
SH1384(2005)	—	—	—	—	2.00	2.50

KM# 1046 5 AFGHANIS
5.0800 g., Brass, 24 mm. **Obv:** Value, legend above, legend and date below **Rev:** Mosque with flags in wreath

Date	Mintage	F	VF	XF	Unc	BU
SH1383(2004)	—	—	—	—	2.50	3.00
SH1384(2005)	—	—	—	—	2.50	3.00

ALBANIA

The Republic of Albania, a Balkan republic bounded by Macedonia, Greece, Montenegro, and the Adriatic Sea, has an area of 11,100 sq. mi. (28,748 sq. km.) and a population of 3.49 million. Capital: Tirane. The country is predominantly agricultural, although recent progress has been made in the manufacturing and mining sectors. Petroleum, chrome, iron, copper, cotton textiles, tobacco and wood products are exported.

MINT MARKS
L – London
R – Rome
V – Vienna

MONETARY SYSTEM
100 Qindar Leku = 1 Lek
100 Qindar Ari = 1 Frang Ar = 5 Lek

REPUBLIC
STANDARD COINAGE

KM# 75 LEK
3.0000 g., Bronze, 18.1 mm. **Obv:** Dalmatian pelican **Rev:** Denomination **Edge:** Plain

Date	Mintage	F	VF	XF	Unc	BU
2008	—	—	—	0.40	1.50	2.00

KM# 93 10 LEKE
3.6000 g., Aluminum-Bronze, 21.25 mm. **Subject:** 85th Anniversary Tirana as capital **Obv:** Archaic tomb **Obv. Legend:** SHQIPERI • ALBANIA **Rev:** Outlined bird above value **Edge:** Reeded

Date	Mintage	F	VF	XF	Unc	BU
2005	—	—	—	—	2.00	3.00

KM# 94 10 LEKE
3.6000 g., Aluminum-Bronze, 21.25 mm. **Subject:** Culture **Obv:** Ornate vest **Obv. Legend:** SHQIPERI • ALBANIA **Rev:** Ornate value **Rev. Legend:** OBJEKTE TE TRASHEGIMISE KULTURORE **Edge:** Reeded

Date	Mintage	F	VF	XF	Unc	BU
2005	—	—	—	—	2.00	3.00

KM# 87 20 LEKE
8.5400 g., Brass, 26.1 mm. **Subject:** Prehistoric art **Obv:** Horseman **Rev:** Ancient coin design with Apollo portrait **Edge:** Reeded

Date	Mintage	F	VF	XF	Unc	BU
2002	—	—	—	—	3.00	4.00

KM# 81 50 LEKE
7.5000 g., Copper-Nickel, 28 mm. **Subject:** Michaelangelo's "David", 500th Anniversary **Obv:** Towered building **Rev:** Statue's head and denomination **Edge:** Plain

Date	Mintage	F	VF	XF	Unc	BU
2001	3,000	—	—	—	6.50	8.00

KM# 88 50 LEKE
12.0000 g., Brass, 28 mm. **Subject:** Declaration of Independence, 90th Anniversary **Obv:** Value within circle **Rev:** Bust facing, dates below **Edge:** Reeded

Date	Mintage	F	VF	XF	Unc	BU
2002	20,000	—	—	—	3.00	4.00

KM# 89 50 LEKE
12.0000 g., Brass, 28 mm. **Subject:** Jeronim de Rada, 100th Anniversary of Death **Obv:** Bust 3/4 facing, dates below, circle surrounds **Rev:** Value within box within circle **Edge:** Plain

Date	Mintage	F	VF	XF	Unc	BU
2003	—	—	—	—	3.00	4.00

KM# 86 50 LEKE
5.5000 g., Copper-Nickel, 24.25 mm. **Obv:** Value and legend **Rev:** Ancient Illyrian helmet **Edge:** Reeded

Date	Mintage	F	VF	XF	Unc	BU
2003 (2004)	200,000	—	—	—	6.00	7.50

KM# 90 50 LEKE
5.5000 g., Copper-Nickel, 24.25 mm. **Subject:** The Beauty of

Durrës **Obv:** Wheel design **Rev:** Ancient bust above value within circle **Edge:** Reeded

Date	Mintage	F	VF	XF	Unc	BU
2004	200,000	—	—	—	3.00	4.00

KM# 91   50 LEKE
5.5000 g., Copper-Nickel, 24.25 mm. **Obv:** Soldier within circle **Rev:** Value within circle **Edge:** Reeded

Date	Mintage	F	VF	XF	Unc	BU
2004	200,000	—	—	—	3.00	4.00

KM# 82   100 LEKE
15.7000 g., 0.9250 Silver 0.4669 oz. ASW, 32.65 mm. **Subject:** Michaelangelo's "David", 500th Anniversary **Obv:** Arch of Triumph **Rev:** Statue's upper half and denomination **Edge:** Plain

Date	Mintage	F	VF	XF	Unc	BU
2001	3,000	—	—	—	32.00	35.00

KM# 84   100 LEKE
15.0000 g., 0.9250 Silver 0.4461 oz. ASW, 32 mm. **Subject:** Albanian-European Integration **Obv:** Dove in flight, stars encircle **Rev:** European and Albanian maps, stars encircle **Edge:** Plain

Date	Mintage	F	VF	XF	Unc	BU
2001	3,000	—	—	—	30.00	32.50

KM# 92   100 LEKE
30.0000 g., 0.9250 Silver 0.8921 oz. ASW, 38 mm. **Subject:** Declaration of Independence, 90th Anniversary **Obv:** Crossed rifle and pistol on manuscript, quill pen **Obv. Legend:** SHQIPERI - ALBANIA **Rev:** Bust of Qemali 3/4 right

Date	Mintage	F	VF	XF	Unc	BU
2002 Proof	7,000	Value: 50.00				

KM# 83   200 LEKE
7.6500 g., 0.9000 Gold 0.2213 oz. AGW, 25.45 mm. **Subject:** Michaelangelo's "David", 500th Anniversary **Obv:** City plaza **Rev:** Statue of "David" and denomination **Edge:** Plain

Date	Mintage	F	VF	XF	Unc	BU
2001	1,000	—	—	—	375	400

KM# 85   200 LEKE
15.0000 g., 0.9250 Silver 0.4461 oz. ASW, 32 mm. **Subject:** Albanian-European Integration **Obv:** Dove in flight within inner circle, stars encircle **Rev:** Adult and infant hand within inner circle, stars encircle **Edge:** Plain

Date	Mintage	F	VF	XF	Unc	BU
2001	1,000	—	—	—	37.50	40.00

MINT SETS

KM#	Date	Mintage	Identification	Issue Price	Mkt Val
MS3	2002-03 (4)	—	KM86, 89 (2003), 87, 88 (2002)	—	22.50

ALDERNEY

Alderney, the northernmost and third largest of the Channel Islands, separated from the coast of France by the dangerous 8-mile-wide tidal channel, has an area of 3 sq. mi. (8 km.) and a population of 1,686. It is a dependency of the British island of Guernsey, to the southwest. Capital: St. Anne. Principal industries are agriculture and raising cattle.

The Channel Islands have never been subject to the British Parliament and are self-governing units under the direct rule of the Crown acting through the Privy Council. Alderney is one of the nine Channel Islands, the only part of the Duchy of Normandy still belonging to the British Crown, and has been a British possession since the Norman Conquest of 1066. Legislation was only recently introduced for the issue of its own coinage, a right it now shares with Jersey and Guernsey.

RULER
British

MONETARY SYSTEM
100 Pence = 1 Pound Sterling

DEPENDENCY
STANDARD COINAGE

KM# 75   50 PENCE
8.0000 g., 0.9250 Silver 0.2379 oz. ASW **Ruler:** Elizabeth II **Subject:** 50th Anniversary of Coronation **Obv:** Crowned head right **Rev:** Royal coach **Edge:** Plain **Shape:** 7-sided

Date	Mintage	F	VF	XF	Unc	BU
2003 Proof	—	Value: 20.00				

KM# 76   50 PENCE
8.0000 g., 0.9250 Silver 0.2379 oz. ASW **Ruler:** Elizabeth II **Subject:** 50th Anniversary of Coronation **Obv:** Crowned head right **Rev:** St. Edward's crown **Edge:** Plain **Shape:** 7-sided

Date	Mintage	F	VF	XF	Unc	BU
2003 Proof	—	Value: 20.00				

KM# 77   50 PENCE
8.0000 g., 0.9250 Silver 0.2379 oz. ASW **Ruler:** Elizabeth II **Subject:** 50th Anniversay of Coronation **Obv:** Crowned head right **Rev:** Elizabeth II horseback **Edge:** Plain **Shape:** 7-sided

Date	Mintage	F	VF	XF	Unc	BU
2003 Proof	—	Value: 20.00				

KM# 78   50 PENCE
8.0000 g., 0.9250 Silver 0.2379 oz. ASW **Ruler:** Elizabeth II **Subject:** 50th Anniversary of Coronation **Obv:** Crowned head right **Rev:** Elizabeth II seated on throne **Edge:** Plain **Shape:** 7-sided

Date	Mintage	F	VF	XF	Unc	BU
2003 Proof	—	Value: 20.00				

KM# 73   POUND
9.5000 g., 0.9250 Silver 0.2825 oz. ASW **Ruler:** Elizabeth II **Subject:** Queen's 75th Birthday **Obv:** Crowned head right

Date	Mintage	F	VF	XF	Unc	BU
2001 Proof	—	Value: 20.00				

KM# 91   POUND
1.2400 g., 0.9990 Gold 0.0398 oz. AGW, 13.92 mm. **Ruler:** Elizabeth II **Rev:** State arms

Date	Mintage	F	VF	XF	Unc	BU
2002 Proof	Est. 50,000	Value: 75.00				

KM# 119   POUND
1.2400 g., 0.9990 Gold 0.0398 oz. AGW, 13.92 mm. **Ruler:** Elizabeth II **Subject:** Trafalgar - Horatio Nelson **Obv:** Head crowned right **Rev:** Bust right in Navy uniform

Date	Mintage	F	VF	XF	Unc	BU
2005 Proof	Est. 20,000	Value: 80.00				

KM# 122   POUND
1.2400 g., 0.9990 Gold 0.0398 oz. AGW, 13.92 mm. **Ruler:** Elizabeth II **Rev:** Queen Elizabeth I

Date	Mintage	F	VF	XF	Unc	BU
2006 Proof	Est. 20,000	Value: 80.00				

KM# 123   POUND
1.2400 g., 0.9990 Gold 0.0398 oz. AGW, 13.92 mm. **Ruler:** Elizabeth II **Rev:** Sir Isaac Newton

Date	Mintage	F	VF	XF	Unc	BU
2006 Proof	Est. 20,000	Value: 80.00				

KM# 124   POUND
1.2400 g., 0.9990 Gold 0.0398 oz. AGW, 13.92 mm. **Ruler:** Elizabeth II **Rev:** William Shakespeare

Date	Mintage	F	VF	XF	Unc	BU
2006 Proof	20,000	Value: 80.00				

KM# 125   POUND
1.2400 g., 0.9990 Gold 0.0398 oz. AGW, 13.92 mm. **Ruler:** Elizabeth II **Rev:** Charles Dickens

Date	Mintage	F	VF	XF	Unc	BU
2006 Proof	Est. 20,000	Value: 80.00				

KM# 130   POUND
1.2400 g., 0.9990 Gold 0.0398 oz. AGW, 13.92 mm. **Ruler:** Elizabeth II **Rev:** Sir Winston Churchill

Date	Mintage	F	VF	XF	Unc	BU
2006 Proof	Est. 20,000	Value: 80.00				

KM# 131   POUND
1.2400 g., 0.9990 Gold 0.0398 oz. AGW, 13.92 mm. **Ruler:** Elizabeth II **Rev:** Elizabeth II corronation

Date	Mintage	F	VF	XF	Unc	BU
2006 Proof	—	Value: 80.00				

KM# 154   POUND
1.2400 g., 0.9990 Gold 0.0398 oz. AGW, 13.92 mm. **Ruler:** Elizabeth II **Rev:** Capt. James Cook

Date	Mintage	F	VF	XF	Unc	BU
2007 Proof	Est. 20,000	Value: 80.00				

KM# 155   POUND
1.2400 g., 0.9990 Gold 0.0398 oz. AGW, 13.92 mm. **Ruler:** Elizabeth II **Rev:** Sir Edward Elgar

Date	Mintage	F	VF	XF	Unc	BU
2007 Proof	Est. 20,000	Value: 80.00				

KM# 156   POUND
1.2400 g., 0.9990 Gold 0.0398 oz. AGW, 13.92 mm. **Ruler:** Elizabeth II **Rev:** Sir Francis Drake

Date	Mintage	F	VF	XF	Unc	BU
2007 Proof	20,000	Value: 80.00				

KM# 157   POUND
1.2400 g., 0.9990 Gold 0.0398 oz. AGW, 13.92 mm. **Ruler:** Elizabeth II **Rev:** John Constable

Date	Mintage	F	VF	XF	Unc	BU
2007 Proof	Est. 20,000	Value: 80.00				

KM# 174   POUND
1.2400 g., 0.9990 Gold 0.0398 oz. AGW, 13.92 mm. **Ruler:** Elizabeth II **Subject:** Princess Diana, 10th Anniversary of Death **Rev:** Bust 3/4 facing left

Date	Mintage	F	VF	XF	Unc	BU
2007 Proof	Est. 20,000	Value: 80.00				

KM# 175a   POUND
28.2800 g., 0.9250 Silver 0.8410 oz. ASW, 38.61 mm. **Ruler:** Elizabeth II

Date	Mintage	F	VF	XF	Unc	BU
2007 Proof	Est. 10,000	Value: 55.00				

KM# 175b   POUND
39.9400 g., 0.9160 Gold 1.1762 oz. AGW, 38.61 mm. **Ruler:** Elizabeth II **Subject:** Princess Diana, 10th Anniversary of Death

Date	Mintage	F	VF	XF	Unc	BU
2007 Proof	—	Value: 2,000				

KM# 189 POUND
1.2400 g., 0.9990 Gold 0.0398 oz. AGW, 13.92 mm. **Ruler:**
Elizabeth II **Rev:** Concord

Date	Mintage	F	VF	XF	Unc	BU
2008 Proof	Est. 1,000				Value: 80.00	

KM# 84 POUND
1.2400 g., 0.9990 Gold 0.0398 oz. AGW, 13.92 mm. **Ruler:**
Elizabeth II **Subject:** Mini Cooper 50th Anniversary **Rev:** Mini
Cooper on tiled floor

Date	Mintage	F	VF	XF	Unc	BU
2009 Proof	5,000				Value: 115	

KM# 59 5 POUNDS
28.2800 g., 0.9250 Silver 0.8410 oz. ASW, 38.6 mm. **Ruler:**
Elizabeth II **Subject:** Queen's 75th Birthday **Obv:** Queen's
portrait right **Rev:** Queen in casual dress surrounded by rose,
thistle, daffodil and pimper nickel

Date	Mintage	F	VF	XF	Unc	BU
2001 Proof	—				Value: 50.00	

KM# 60 5 POUNDS
28.2800 g., Copper-Nickel, 38.6 mm. **Ruler:** Elizabeth II **Subject:**
Queen's 75th Birthday **Obv:** Queen's portrait right **Rev:** Queen in
casual dress surrounded by rose, thistle, daffodil and primper nickel

Date	Mintage	F	VF	XF	Unc	BU
2001	—	—	—	—	13.50	15.00

KM# 24 5 POUNDS
28.2800 g., 0.9250 Copper-Nickel 0.8410 oz., 38.6 mm. **Ruler:**
Elizabeth II **Subject:** Queen Elizabeth II - 50 Years of Reigh **Obv:**
Queen's head right **Rev:** Sword hilt and denomination with royal
arms background **Edge:** Reeded

Date	Mintage	F	VF	XF	Unc	BU
2002 Proof	15,000				Value: 15.00	

KM# 24a 5 POUNDS
28.2800 g., 0.9250 Silver 0.8410 oz. ASW, 38.6 mm. **Ruler:**
Elizabeth II **Subject:** Queen Elizabeth II - 50 Years of Reign **Obv:**
Queen's head right **Rev:** Sword hilt and denomination with royal
arms background **Edge:** Reeded

Date	Mintage	F	VF	XF	Unc	BU
2002 Proof	15,000				Value: 45.00	

KM# 25 5 POUNDS
28.2800 g., 0.9250 Silver 0.8410 oz. ASW, 38.6 mm. **Ruler:**
Elizabeth II **Subject:** Queen's Golden Jubilee **Obv:** Queen's
portrait **Rev:** Honor guard and trumpets **Edge:** Reeded

Date	Mintage	F	VF	XF	Unc	BU
2002 Proof	15,000				Value: 45.00	

KM# 27 5 POUNDS
28.2800 g., Copper-Nickel, 38.6 mm. **Ruler:** Elizabeth II
Subject: 5th Anniversary Death of Princess Diana **Obv:** Crowned
head right **Rev:** Diana accepting flowers from girl **Edge:** Reeded

Date	Mintage	F	VF	XF	Unc	BU
2002	—	—	—	—	13.50	15.00

KM# 27a 5 POUNDS
28.2800 g., 0.9250 Silver 0.8410 oz. ASW, 38.6 mm. **Ruler:**
Elizabeth II **Subject:** 5th Anniversary Death of Princess Diana
Obv: Crowned head right **Rev:** Diana accepting flowers from girl
Edge: Reeded

Date	Mintage	F	VF	XF	Unc	BU
2002 Proof	20,000				Value: 45.00	

KM# 27b 5 POUNDS
39.9400 g., 0.9167 Gold 1.1771 oz. AGW, 38.6 mm. **Ruler:**
Elizabeth II **Subject:** 5th Anniversary Death of Princess Diana
Obv: Crowned head right **Rev:** Diana accepting flowers from girl
Edge: Reeded

Date	Mintage	F	VF	XF	Unc	BU
2002 Proof	100				Value: 2,150	

KM# 29 5 POUNDS
28.2800 g., Copper-Nickel, 38.6 mm. **Ruler:** Elizabeth II
Subject: 150th Anniversary Death of the Duke of Wellington **Obv:**
Queen's portrait **Rev:** Coat of arms, castle and portrait **Edge:**
Reeded

Date	Mintage	F	VF	XF	Unc	BU
2002	—	—	—	—	13.50	15.00

KM# 29a 5 POUNDS
28.2800 g., 0.9250 Silver 0.8410 oz. ASW, 38.6 mm. **Ruler:**
Elizabeth II **Subject:** 150th Anniversary Death of the Duke of
Wellington **Obv:** Queen's portrait **Rev:** Multicolor coat of arms,
portrait and castle **Edge:** Reeded

Date	Mintage	VG	F	VF	XF	Unc
2002 Proof	15,000				Value: 55.00	

KM# 29b 5 POUNDS
39.9400 g., 0.9167 Gold 1.1771 oz. AGW, 38.6 mm. **Ruler:**
Elizabeth II **Subject:** 150th Anniversary Death of the Duke of
Wellington **Obv:** Queen's portrait **Rev:** Coat of arms, castle and
portrait **Edge:** Reeded

Date	Mintage	VG	F	VF	XF	Unc
2002 Proof	200				Value: 2,050	

KM# 44 5 POUNDS
28.2800 g., Copper-Nickel, 38.6 mm. **Ruler:** Elizabeth II **Obv:**
Queen's portrait **Rev:** HMS Mary Rose **Edge:** Reeded

Date	Mintage	F	VF	XF	Unc	BU
2003	—	—	—	—	12.00	13.50

KM# 44a 5 POUNDS
28.2800 g., 0.9250 Silver 0.8410 oz. ASW, 38.6 mm. **Ruler:**
Elizabeth II **Obv:** Queen's portrait **Rev:** HMS Mary Rose below
multicolor flag **Edge:** Reeded

Date	Mintage	F	VF	XF	Unc	BU
2003 Proof	15,000				Value: 60.00	

KM# 45 5 POUNDS
28.2800 g., Copper-Nickel, 38.6 mm. **Ruler:** Elizabeth II **Obv:**
Queen's portrait **Rev:** Alfred the Great on ship **Edge:** Reeded

Date	Mintage	F	VF	XF	Unc	BU
2003	—	—	—	—	12.00	13.50

KM# 45a 5 POUNDS
28.2800 g., 0.9250 Silver 0.8410 oz. ASW, 38.6 mm. **Ruler:**
Elizabeth II **Obv:** Queen's portrait **Rev:** Alfred the Great on ship
below multicolor flag **Edge:** Reeded

Date	Mintage	F	VF	XF	Unc	BU
2003 Proof	15,000				Value: 60.00	

KM# 45b 5 POUNDS
39.9400 g., 0.9167 Gold 1.1771 oz. AGW, 38.6 mm. **Ruler:**
Elizabeth II **Obv:** Queen's portrait **Rev:** Alfred the Great on ship
Edge: Reeded

Date	Mintage	F	VF	XF	Unc	BU
2003 Proof	500				Value: 2,000	

KM# 31 5 POUNDS
28.2800 g., Copper-Nickel, 38.6 mm. **Ruler:** Elizabeth II
Subject: Prince William **Obv:** Queen's portrait **Rev:** Portrait with
open shirt collar **Edge:** Reeded

Date	Mintage	F	VF	XF	Unc	BU
2003	—	—	—	—	16.50	18.00

KM# 31a 5 POUNDS
28.2800 g., 0.9250 Silver 0.8410 oz. ASW, 38.6 mm. **Ruler:**
Elizabeth II **Subject:** Prince William **Obv:** Queen's portrait **Rev:**
Portrait with open shirt collar **Edge:** Reeded

Date	Mintage	F	VF	XF	Unc	BU
2003 Proof	—				Value: 47.50	

KM# 31b 5 POUNDS
39.9400 g., 0.9166 Gold 1.1770 oz. AGW, 38.6 mm. **Ruler:**
Elizabeth II **Subject:** Prince William **Obv:** Queen's portrait **Rev:**
Portrait with open shirt collar **Edge:** Reeded

Date	Mintage	F	VF	XF	Unc	BU
2003 Proof	200				Value: 2,050	

KM# 35 5 POUNDS
28.2800 g., Copper-Nickel, 38.61 mm. **Ruler:** Elizabeth II
Subject: Last Flight of the Concorde, October 24, 2003 **Obv:**
Crowned bust right **Obv. Legend:** ELIZABETH II - ALDERNEY
Rev: Concorde in flight **Rev. Legend:** CONCORDE 1969 - 2003
Edge: Reeded

Date	Mintage	F	VF	XF	Unc	BU
2003	5,000	—	—	—	12.00	15.50

KM# 35a 5 POUNDS
28.2800 g., 0.9250 Silver 0.8410 oz. ASW, 38.61 mm. **Ruler:**
Elizabeth II **Subject:** Last Flight of the Concorde, October 24,
2003 **Obv:** Crowned bust right **Obv. Legend:** ELIZABETH II -
ALDERNEY **Rev:** Concorde in flight **Rev. Legend:** CONCORDE
1969 - 2003 **Edge:** Reeded

Date	Mintage	F	VF	XF	Unc	BU
2003 Proof	5,000				Value: 50.00	

KM# 35b 5 POUNDS
39.9400 g., 0.9166 Gold 1.1770 oz. AGW, 38.6 mm. **Ruler:**
Elizabeth II **Obv:** Queen's portrait **Rev:** Concorde in flight,
October 24, 2003 **Edge:** Reeded

Date	Mintage	F	VF	XF	Unc	BU
2003 Proof	500				Value: 2,000	

KM# 38 5 POUNDS
28.2800 g., Copper-Nickel, 38.6 mm. **Ruler:** Elizabeth II **Obv:**

Queen's portrait **Rev:** Battleship and transports, HMS Belfast
Edge: Reeded **Note:** D-Day

Date	Mintage	F	VF	XF	Unc	BU
2004	—	—	—	—	15.00	17.50

KM# 38a 5 POUNDS
28.2800 g., 0.9250 Silver 0.8410 oz. ASW, 38.6 mm. **Ruler:**
Elizabeth II **Obv:** Queen's portrait **Rev:** Battleship and transports

Date	Mintage	F	VF	XF	Unc	BU
2004 Proof	10,000	Value: 85.00				

KM# 38b 5 POUNDS
39.9400 g., 0.9167 Gold 1.1771 oz. AGW, 38.6 mm. **Ruler:**
Elizabeth II **Obv:** Queen's portrait **Rev:** Battleship and transports

Date	Mintage	F	VF	XF	Unc	BU
2004 Proof	500	Value: 2,000				

KM# 42 5 POUNDS
28.2800 g., Copper-Nickel, 38.6 mm. **Ruler:** Elizabeth II **Obv:**
Crowned head right **Rev:** Florence Nightingale **Edge:** Reeded

Date	Mintage	F	VF	XF	Unc	BU
2004	—	—	—	—	18.00	20.00

KM# 42a 5 POUNDS
28.2800 g., 0.9250 Silver 0.8410 oz. ASW, 38.6 mm. **Ruler:**
Elizabeth II **Obv:** Queen's portrait **Rev:** Florence Nightingale
Edge: Reeded

Date	Mintage	F	VF	XF	Unc	BU
2004 Proof	25,000	Value: 70.00				

KM# 43 5 POUNDS
28.2800 g., Copper-Nickel, 38.6 mm. **Ruler:** Elizabeth II
Subject: 150th Anniversary of the Crimean War **Obv:** Crowned
head right **Rev:** Florence Nightingale head above the Battle of
Inkerman scene with one multicolor soldier **Edge:** Reeded

Date	Mintage	F	VF	XF	Unc	BU
2004 plain	—	—	—	—	25.00	27.50
2004 partial color	—	—	—	—	25.00	27.50

KM# 43a 5 POUNDS
28.2800 g., 0.9250 Silver 0.8410 oz. ASW, 38.6 mm. **Ruler:**
Elizabeth II **Subject:** 150th Anniversary Crimean War **Obv:**
Crowned head right **Rev:** Florence Nightingale head above Battle
of Inkerman scene with one multicolor soldier **Edge:** Reeded

Date	Mintage	F	VF	XF	Unc	BU
2004 Proof	10,000	Value: 85.00				

KM# 43b 5 POUNDS
39.9400 g., 0.9166 Gold 1.1770 oz. AGW, 38.6 mm. **Ruler:**
Elizabeth II **Subject:** 150th Anniversary Crimean War **Obv:**
Crowned head right **Rev:** Florence Nightingale head above Battle
of Inkerman scene with one multicolor soldier **Edge:** Reeded

Date	Mintage	F	VF	XF	Unc	BU
2004 Proof	500	Value: 2,000				

KM# 94 5 POUNDS
28.2800 g., 0.9250 Silver 0.8410 oz. ASW, 38.61 mm. **Ruler:**
Elizabeth II **Subject:** David Beckham **Rev:** Soccer player and
ball as background

Date	Mintage	F	VF	XF	Unc	BU
2004 Proof	—	Value: 45.00				

KM# 95 5 POUNDS
28.2800 g., 0.9250 Silver 0.8410 oz. ASW, 38.61 mm. **Ruler:**
Elizabeth II **Subject:** Michael Owen **Rev:** Soccer player and ball
as background

Date	Mintage	F	VF	XF	Unc	BU
2004 Proof	—	Value: 45.00				

KM# 47 5 POUNDS
28.2800 g., Copper-Nickel, 38.6 mm. **Ruler:** Elizabeth II **Obv:**
Queen's portrait **Rev:** Locomotive,
The Rocket **Edge:** Reeded

Date	Mintage	F	VF	XF	Unc	BU
2004	—	—	—	—	16.00	18.50

KM# 47a 5 POUNDS
28.2800 g., 0.9250 Silver 0.8410 oz. ASW, 38.6 mm. **Ruler:**
Elizabeth II **Obv:** Queen's portrait **Rev:** Locomotive, The Rocket
Edge: Reeded

Date	Mintage	F	VF	XF	Unc	BU
2004 Proof	20,000	Value: 60.00				

KM# 47b 5 POUNDS
39.9400 g., 0.9167 Gold 1.1771 oz. AGW, 38.6 mm. **Ruler:**
Elizabeth II **Obv:** Queen's portrait **Rev:** Locomotive, The Rocket
Edge: Reeded

Date	Mintage	F	VF	XF	Unc	BU
2004 Proof	500	Value: 2,000				

KM# 48 5 POUNDS
28.2800 g., Copper-Nickel, 38.6 mm. **Ruler:** Elizabeth II **Obv:**
Queen's portrait **Rev:** Locomotive, The Royal Scot **Edge:**
Reeded

Date	Mintage	F	VF	XF	Unc	BU
2004	—	—	—	—	16.00	18.50

KM# 48a 5 POUNDS
28.2800 g., 0.9250 Silver 0.8410 oz. ASW, 38.6 mm. **Ruler:**
Elizabeth II **Obv:** Queen's portrait **Rev:** Locomotive, The Royal
Scot **Edge:** Reeded

Date	Mintage	F	VF	XF	Unc	BU
2004 Proof	10,000	Value: 60.00				

KM# 49 5 POUNDS
28.2800 g., Copper-Nickel, 38.6 mm. **Ruler:** Elizabeth II **Obv:**
Queen's portrait **Rev:** Locomotive, The Merchant Navy 21C1
Edge: Reeded

Date	Mintage	F	VF	XF	Unc	BU
2004	—	—	—	—	16.00	18.50

KM# 49a 5 POUNDS
28.2800 g., 0.9250 Silver 0.8410 oz. ASW, 38.6 mm. **Ruler:**
Elizabeth II **Obv:** Queen's portrait **Rev:** Locomotive, The
Merchant Navy 21C1 **Edge:** Reeded

Date	Mintage	F	VF	XF	Unc	BU
2004 Proof	10,000	Value: 60.00				

KM# 53a 5 POUNDS
28.2800 g., 0.9250 Silver 0.8410 oz. ASW, 38.6 mm. **Ruler:**
Elizabeth II **Subject:** End of WWII **Obv:** Elizabeth II by Maklouf
Rev: Flag waving crowd **Edge:** Reeded

Date	Mintage	F	VF	XF	Unc	BU
2005 Proof	5,000	Value: 85.00				

KM# 96 5 POUNDS
28.2800 g., 0.9250 Silver 0.8410 oz. ASW **Ruler:** Elizabeth II
Subject: Locomotives, 200th Anniversary **Rev:** Train station on
a branch line

Date	Mintage	F	VF	XF	Unc	BU
2005 Proof	Est. 10,000	Value: 60.00				
2006 Proof	Est. 25,000	Value: 55.00				

KM# 97 5 POUNDS
28.2800 g., 0.9250 Silver 0.8410 oz. ASW **Ruler:** Elizabeth II
Subject: Locomotives, 200th Anniversary **Rev:** Locomotive
Shop

Date	Mintage	F	VF	XF	Unc	BU
2005 Proof	Est. 10,000	Value: 60.00				
2006 proof	Est. 25,000	Value: 55.00				

KM# 98 5 POUNDS
28.2800 g., 0.9250 Silver 0.8410 oz. ASW **Ruler:** Elizabeth II
Subject: Locomotives, 200th Anniversary **Rev:** Viaduct

Date	Mintage	F	VF	XF	Unc	BU
2005 Proof	Est. 10,000	Value: 60.00				
2006 Proof	Est. 25,000	Value: 55.00				

KM# 53b 5 POUNDS
39.9400 g., 0.9167 Gold 1.1771 oz. AGW, 38.6 mm. **Ruler:**
Elizabeth II **Subject:** 60th Anniversary - End of WWII **Obv:**
Elizabeth II by Maklouf **Rev:** Flag waving crowd **Edge:** Reeded

Date	Mintage	F	VF	XF	Unc	BU
2005 Proof	150	Value: 2,050				

KM# 54b 5 POUNDS
39.9400 g., 0.9167 Gold 1.1771 oz. AGW, 38.6 mm. **Ruler:**
Elizabeth II **Subject:** WWII Liberation **Obv:** Elizabeth II by
Maklouf **Rev:** Churchill flashing the "V" sign **Edge:** Reeded

Date	Mintage	F	VF	XF	Unc	BU
2005 Proof	150	Value: 2,050				

KM# 53 5 POUNDS
Copper-Nickel, 38.61 mm. **Ruler:** Elizabeth II **Subject:** End of
World War II, 60th Anniversary

Date	Mintage	F	VF	XF	Unc	BU
2005	—	—	—	—	15.00	

KM# 54 5 POUNDS
Copper-Nickel **Ruler:** Elizabeth II **Subject:** Winston Churchill

Date	Mintage	F	VF	XF	Unc	BU
2005	Est. 5,000	—	—	—	15.00	

KM# 54a 5 POUNDS
39.9400 g., 0.9160 Silver 1.1762 oz. ASW, 38.61 mm. **Ruler:**
Elizabeth II **Subject:** Sir Winston Churchill

Date	Mintage	F	VF	XF	Unc	BU
2005 Proof	—	Value: 65.00				

KM# 66 5 POUNDS
28.2800 g., Copper-Nickel, 38.6 mm. **Ruler:** Elizabeth II
Subject: Viscount Samuel Hood on his flagship after the Battle
of Saints Passage in 1782 **Obv:** Queen's portrait

Date	Mintage	F	VF	XF	Unc	BU
2005	—	—	—	—	13.50	15.00

KM# 66a 5 POUNDS
28.2800 g., 0.9250 Silver 0.8410 oz. ASW, 38.6 mm. **Ruler:**
Elizabeth II **Subject:** Viscount Samuel Hood on his flagship after
the Battle of Saints Passage in 1782 **Obv:** Queen's portrait **Note:**
Ensign is colored.

Date	Mintage	F	VF	XF	Unc	BU
2005 Proof	—	Value: 50.00				

KM# 68 5 POUNDS
28.2800 g., Copper-Nickel, 38.6 mm. **Ruler:** Elizabeth II **Obv:**
Crowned head right **Rev:** HMS Revenge fighting at Azores, 1591

Date	Mintage	F	VF	XF	Unc	BU
2005	—	—	—	—	12.00	14.00

KM# 68a 5 POUNDS
28.2800 g., 0.9250 Silver 0.8410 oz. ASW, 38.6 mm. **Ruler:**
Elizabeth II **Obv:** Crowned head right **Rev:** HMS Revenge
fighting at Azores, 1591 **Note:** Ensign is colorized.

Date	Mintage	F	VF	XF	Unc	BU
2005 Proof	—	Value: 60.00				

KM# 79 5 POUNDS
Copper-Nickel **Ruler:** Elizabeth II **Subject:** 200th Anniversary
Battle of Trafalgar **Obv:** Crowned head right

Date	Mintage	F	VF	XF	Unc	BU
2005	—	—	—	—	16.00	18.50

KM# 79a 5 POUNDS
28.2800 g., 0.9250 Silver 0.8410 oz. ASW **Ruler:** Elizabeth II
Subject: 200th Anniversary Battle of Trafalgar **Obv:** Crowned
head right

Date	Mintage	F	VF	XF	Unc	BU
2005 Proof	—	Value: 60.00				

KM# 83 5 POUNDS
Copper-Nickel, 38.61 mm. **Subject:** Royal Navy - Admiral Sir John Foster Woodward

Date	Mintage	F	VF	XF	Unc	BU
2005	—	—	—	—	—	15.00

KM# 83a 5 POUNDS
28.4300 g., Silver, 38 mm. **Ruler:** Elizabeth II **Subject:** History of the Royal Navy **Obv:** Heraldic shield **Rev:** Admiral John Woodward, partially colored

Date	Mintage	F	VF	XF	Unc	BU
2005 Proof	— Value: 45.00					

KM# 99 5 POUNDS
28.2800 g., 0.9250 Silver 0.8410 oz. ASW, 38.61 mm. **Ruler:** Elizabeth II **Subject:** Wayne Rooney **Obv:** Shield **Rev:** Soccer player and ball design

Date	Mintage	F	VF	XF	Unc	BU
2005 Proof	— Value: 45.00					

KM# 100 5 POUNDS
28.2800 g., 0.9250 Silver 0.8410 oz. ASW, 38.61 mm. **Ruler:** Elizabeth II **Subject:** Frank Lampard **Obv:** Shield **Rev:** Soccer player and ball design

Date	Mintage	F	VF	XF	Unc	BU
2005 Proof	— Value: 45.00					

KM# 101 5 POUNDS
28.2800 g., 0.9250 Silver 0.8410 oz. ASW, 38.61 mm. **Ruler:** Elizabeth II **Obv:** Shield **Rev:** Soccer player and ball design

Date	Mintage	F	VF	XF	Unc	BU
2005 Proof	— Value: 45.00					

KM# 102 5 POUNDS
28.2800 g., 0.9250 Silver 0.8410 oz. ASW, 38.61 mm. **Ruler:** Elizabeth II **Subject:** Steven Gerrard **Obv:** Shield **Rev:** Soccer player and ball design

Date	Mintage	F	VF	XF	Unc	BU
2005 Proof	— Value: 45.00					

KM# 103 5 POUNDS
28.2800 g., 0.9250 Silver 0.8410 oz. ASW, 38.61 mm. **Ruler:** Elizabeth II **Obv:** Shield **Rev:** Soccer player and ball design

Date	Mintage	F	VF	XF	Unc	BU
2005 Proof	— Value: 45.00					

KM# 104 5 POUNDS
28.2800 g., 0.9250 Silver 0.8410 oz. ASW, 38.61 mm. **Ruler:** Elizabeth II **Obv:** Shield **Rev:** Soccer player and ball design

Date	Mintage	F	VF	XF	Unc	BU
2005 Proof	— Value: 45.00					

KM# 105 5 POUNDS
28.2800 g., 0.9250 Silver 0.8410 oz. ASW, 38.61 mm. **Ruler:** Elizabeth II **Obv:** Shield **Rev:** Soccer player and ball design

Date	Mintage	F	VF	XF	Unc	BU
2005 Proof	— Value: 45.00					

KM# 106 5 POUNDS
28.2800 g., 0.9250 Silver 0.8410 oz. ASW, 38.61 mm. **Ruler:** Elizabeth II **Obv:** Shield **Rev:** Soccer player and ball design

Date	Mintage	F	VF	XF	Unc	BU
2005 Proof	— Value: 45.00					

KM# 107 5 POUNDS
28.2800 g., 0.9250 Silver 0.8410 oz. ASW, 38.61 mm. **Ruler:** Elizabeth II **Obv:** Shield **Rev:** Soccer player and ball design

Date	Mintage	F	VF	XF	Unc	BU
2005 Proof	— Value: 45.00					

KM# 108 5 POUNDS
28.2500 g., 0.9250 Silver 0.8401 oz. ASW, 38.61 mm. **Ruler:** Elizabeth II **Obv:** Shield **Rev:** Soccer player and ball design

Date	Mintage	F	VF	XF	Unc	BU
2005 Proof	— Value: 45.00					

KM# 113 5 POUNDS
Copper-Nickel, 38.61 mm. **Ruler:** Elizabeth II

Date	Mintage	F	VF	XF	Unc	BU
2005	—	—	—	—	—	15.00

KM# 113a 5 POUNDS
28.2800 g., 0.9250 Silver 0.8410 oz. ASW, 38.61 mm. **Ruler:** Elizabeth II **Subject:** Prince William, 21st Birthday

Date	Mintage	F	VF	XF	Unc	BU
2005 Proof	Est. 2,500 Value: 60.00					

KM# 113b 5 POUNDS
39.9400 g., 0.9160 Gold 1.1762 oz. AGW, 38.61 mm. **Ruler:** Elizabeth II **Subject:** Prince William, 21st Birthday

Date	Mintage	F	VF	XF	Unc	BU
2005 Proof	Est. 150 Value: 15.00					

KM# 116 5 POUNDS
Copper-Nickel, 38.61 mm. **Ruler:** Elizabeth II **Subject:** Royal Navy - H.M.S. Warspite

Date	Mintage	F	VF	XF	Unc	BU
2005	—	—	—	—	—	15.00

KM# 116a 5 POUNDS
28.2800 g., 0.9250 Silver 0.8410 oz. ASW, 38.61 mm. **Ruler:** Elizabeth II **Subject:** British Navy - H.M.S. Warspite **Rev:** Multicolor flag

Date	Mintage	F	VF	XF	Unc	BU
2005 Proof	Est. 15,000 Value: 55.00					

KM# 70 5 POUNDS
28.2800 g., 0.9250 Silver 0.8410 oz. ASW, 38.6 mm. **Ruler:** Elizabeth II **Subject:** Queen's 80th Birthday **Obv:** Crowned bust right - gilt **Obv. Legend:** ELIZABETH II - ALDERNARY **Rev:** 1/2 length figures of Queen mother and daughter hugging, facing

Date	Mintage	F	VF	XF	Unc	BU
2006 Proof	— Value: 45.00					

KM# 126 5 POUNDS
Copper-Nickel, 38.61 mm. **Ruler:** Elizabeth II **Rev:** Elizabeth I

Date	Mintage	F	VF	XF	Unc	BU
2006	—	—	—	—	—	12.00

KM# 126a 5 POUNDS
28.2800 g., 0.9250 Silver 0.8410 oz. ASW, 38.61 mm. **Ruler:** Elizabeth II **Rev:** Queen Elizabeth I

Date	Mintage	F	VF	XF	Unc	BU
2006 Proof	Est. 25,000 Value: 55.00					

KM# 126b 5 POUNDS
39.9400 g., 0.9160 Gold 1.1762 oz. AGW, 38.61 mm. **Ruler:** Elizabeth II **Rev:** Queen Elizabeth I

Date	Mintage	F	VF	XF	Unc	BU
2006 Proof	— Value: 2,150					

KM# 127 5 POUNDS
Copper-Nickel, 38.61 mm. **Ruler:** Elizabeth II **Rev:** Sir Isaac Newton

Date	Mintage	F	VF	XF	Unc	BU
2006	—	—	—	—	—	15.00

KM# 127a 5 POUNDS
28.2800 g., 0.9250 Silver 0.8410 oz. ASW, 38.61 mm. **Ruler:** Elizabeth II **Rev:** Sir Isaac Newton

Date	Mintage	F	VF	XF	Unc	BU
2006 Proof	— Value: 55.00					

KM# 127b 5 POUNDS
39.9400 g., 0.9160 Gold 1.1762 oz. AGW, 38.61 mm. **Ruler:** Elizabeth II **Rev:** Sir Isaac Newton

Date	Mintage	F	VF	XF	Unc	BU
2006 Proof	— Value: 2,150					

KM# 128 5 POUNDS
Copper-Nickel, 38.61 mm. **Ruler:** Elizabeth II **Rev:** William Shapeshare

Date	Mintage	F	VF	XF	Unc	BU
2006	—	—	—	—	—	15.00

KM# 128a 5 POUNDS
28.2800 g., 0.9250 Silver 0.8410 oz. ASW, 38.61 mm. **Ruler:** Elizabeth II **Rev:** William Shakespeare

Date	Mintage	F	VF	XF	Unc	BU
2006 Proof	— Value: 55.00					

KM# 128b 5 POUNDS
39.9400 g., 0.9160 Gold 1.1762 oz. AGW, 38.61 mm. **Ruler:** Elizabeth II **Rev:** William Shakespeare

Date	Mintage	F	VF	XF	Unc	BU
2006 Proof	— Value: 2,150					

KM# 129 5 POUNDS
Copper-Nickel, 38.61 mm. **Ruler:** Elizabeth II **Rev:** Charles Dickens

Date	Mintage	F	VF	XF	Unc	BU
2006	—	—	—	—	—	15.00

KM# 129a 5 POUNDS
28.2800 g., 0.9250 Silver 0.8410 oz. ASW, 38.61 mm. **Ruler:** Elizabeth II **Rev:** Charles Dickens

Date	Mintage	F	VF	XF	Unc	BU
2006 Proof	— Value: 55.00					

KM# 129b 5 POUNDS
39.9400 g., 0.9160 Gold 1.1762 oz. AGW, 38.61 mm. **Ruler:** Elizabeth II **Rev:** Charles Dickens

Date	Mintage	F	VF	XF	Unc	BU
2006 Proof	— Value: 2,150					

KM# 132 5 POUNDS
Copper-Nickel, 38.61 mm. **Ruler:** Elizabeth II **Rev:** Elizabeth II Corronation

Date	Mintage	F	VF	XF	Unc	BU
2006	—	—	—	—	—	15.00

KM# 132a 5 POUNDS
28.2800 g., 0.9250 Silver 0.8410 oz. ASW, 38.61 mm. **Ruler:** Elizabeth II **Rev:** Elizabeth II Corronation

Date	Mintage	F	VF	XF	Unc	BU
2006 Proof	Est. 25,000 Value: 55.00					

KM# 133 5 POUNDS
28.2800 g., Copper-Nickel, 38.61 mm. **Ruler:** Elizabeth II **Obv:** Head in tiara right **Rev:** Bust in tiara right

Date	Mintage	F	VF	XF	Unc	BU
2006	—	—	—	—	—	15.00

KM# 133a 5 POUNDS
28.2800 g., 0.9250 Silver 0.8410 oz. ASW, 38.61 mm. **Ruler:** Elizabeth II **Obv:** Head in tiara right **Rev:** Bust in tiara right

Date	Mintage	F	VF	XF	Unc	BU
2006 Proof	— Value: 55.00					

KM# 133b 5 POUNDS
39.9400 g., 0.9160 Gold 1.1762 oz. AGW, 38.61 mm. **Ruler:** Elizabeth II **Obv:** Head in tiara right **Rev:** Bust in tiara right

Date	Mintage	F	VF	XF	Unc	BU
2006 Proof	— Value: 2,150					

KM# 133b.1 5 POUNDS
38.9400 g., 0.9160 Gold with diamonds 1.1467 oz. AGW, 38.61 mm. **Ruler:** Elizabeth II **Obv:** Head in tiara right **Rev:** Bust in tiara right

Date	Mintage	F	VF	XF	Unc	BU
2006 Proof	— Value: 2,300					

KM# 138 5 POUNDS
28.2800 g., 0.9250 Silver 0.8410 oz. ASW, 38.61 mm. **Ruler:** Elizabeth II **Obv:** Shield **Rev:** Soccer player

Date	Mintage	F	VF	XF	Unc	BU
2006 Proof	— Value: 55.00					

KM# 139 5 POUNDS
28.2800 g., 0.9250 Silver 0.8410 oz. ASW, 38.61 mm. **Ruler:** Elizabeth II **Obv:** Shield **Rev:** Soccer player

Date	Mintage	F	VF	XF	Unc	BU
2006 Proof	— Value: 55.00					

KM# 140 5 POUNDS
28.2800 g., 0.9250 Silver 0.8410 oz. ASW, 38.61 mm. **Ruler:** Elizabeth II **Obv:** Shield **Rev:** Soccer player

Date	Mintage	F	VF	XF	Unc	BU
2006 Proof	— Value: 55.00					

KM# 141 5 POUNDS
28.2800 g., 0.9250 Silver 0.8410 oz. ASW, 38.61 mm. **Ruler:** Elizabeth II **Obv:** Shield **Rev:** Soccer player

Date	Mintage	F	VF	XF	Unc	BU
2006 Proof	— Value: 55.00					

KM# 142 5 POUNDS
28.2800 g., 0.9250 Silver 0.8410 oz. ASW, 38.61 mm. **Ruler:** Elizabeth II **Obv:** Shield **Rev:** Soccer player

Date	Mintage	F	VF	XF	Unc	BU
2006 Proof	— Value: 55.00					

KM# 143 5 POUNDS
28.2800 g., 0.9250 Silver 0.8410 oz. ASW, 38.61 mm. **Ruler:** Elizabeth II **Obv:** Shield **Rev:** Soccer player

Date	Mintage	F	VF	XF	Unc	BU
2006 Proof	— Value: 55.00					

KM# 144 5 POUNDS
28.2800 g., 0.9250 Silver 0.8410 oz. ASW, 38.61 mm. **Ruler:** Elizabeth II **Obv:** Shield **Rev:** Soccer player

Date	Mintage	F	VF	XF	Unc	BU
2006 Proof	— Value: 55.00					

KM# 145 5 POUNDS
28.2800 g., 0.9250 Silver 0.8410 oz. ASW, 38.61 mm. **Ruler:** Elizabeth II **Obv:** Shield **Rev:** Soccer player

Date	Mintage	F	VF	XF	Unc	BU
2006 Proof	— Value: 55.00					

KM# 146   5 POUNDS
28.2800 g., 0.9250 Silver 0.8410 oz. ASW, 38.61 mm. **Ruler:**
Elizabeth II **Obv:** Shield **Rev:** Soccer player

Date	Mintage	F	VF	XF	Unc	BU
2006 Proof	—	Value: 55.00				

KM# 147   5 POUNDS
28.2800 g., 0.9250 Silver 0.8410 oz. ASW, 38.61 mm. **Ruler:**
Elizabeth II **Obv:** Shield **Rev:** Soccer player

Date	Mintage	F	VF	XF	Unc	BU
2006 Proof	—	Value: 55.00				

KM# 148   5 POUNDS
Copper-Nickel, 38.61 mm. **Ruler:** Elizabeth II **Subject:** Victoria
Cross, 150th Anniversary **Rev:** Henry Ramage and Victoria Cross
medal

Date	Mintage	F	VF	XF	Unc	BU
2006	—	—	—	—	—	15.00

KM# 148a   5 POUNDS
28.2800 g., 0.9250 Silver 0.8410 oz. ASW, 38.61 mm. **Ruler:**
Elizabeth II **Subject:** Victoria Cross, 150th Anniversary **Rev:**
Henry Ramage and Victoria Cross medal

Date	Mintage	F	VF	XF	Unc	BU
2006 Proof	Est. 30,000	Value: 55.00				

KM# 149   5 POUNDS
28.2800 g., 0.9250 Silver 0.8410 oz. ASW, 38.61 mm. **Ruler:**
Elizabeth II **Subject:** Victoria Cross, 150th Anniversary **Rev:**
Charles Lucas, Victoria Cross medal

Date	Mintage	F	VF	XF	Unc	BU
2006 Proof	Est. 30,000	Value: 55.00				

KM# 150   5 POUNDS
28.2800 g., 0.9250 Silver 0.8410 oz. ASW, 38.61 mm. **Ruler:**
Elizabeth II **Subject:** Victoria Cross, 150th Anniversary **Rev:**
Ernest Smith, Victoria Cross medal

Date	Mintage	F	VF	XF	Unc	BU
2006 Proof	Est. 30,000	Value: 55.00				

KM# 151   5 POUNDS
28.2800 g., 0.9250 Silver 0.8410 oz. ASW, 38.61 mm. **Ruler:**
Elizabeth II **Subject:** Victoria Cross, 150th Anniversary **Rev:**
Stanley Hollis, Victoria Cross medal

Date	Mintage	F	VF	XF	Unc	BU
2006 Proof	Est. 30,000	Value: 55.00				

KM# 152   5 POUNDS
28.2800 g., 0.9250 Silver 0.8410 oz. ASW, 38.61 mm. **Ruler:**
Elizabeth II **Subject:** Victoria Cross, 150th Anniversary **Rev:**
Geoffrey Keyes, Victoria Cross medal

Date	Mintage	F	VF	XF	Unc	BU
2006 Proof	Est. 30,000	Value: 55.00				

KM# 153   5 POUNDS
28.2800 g., 0.9250 Silver 0.8410 oz. ASW, 38.61 mm. **Ruler:**
Elizabeth II **Subject:** Victoria Cross, 150th Anniversary **Rev:**
Daniel Laidlow, Victoria Cross medal

Date	Mintage	F	VF	XF	Unc	BU
2006 Proof	Est. 30,000	Value: 55.00				

KM# 158   5 POUNDS
Copper-Nickel, 38.61 mm. **Ruler:** Elizabeth II **Rev:** Capt. James
Cook

Date	Mintage	F	VF	XF	Unc	BU
2007	—	—	—	—	—	15.00

KM# 158a   5 POUNDS
28.2800 g., 0.9250 Silver 0.8410 oz. ASW, 38.61 mm. **Ruler:**
Elizabeth II **Rev:** Capt. Jmes Cook

Date	Mintage	F	VF	XF	Unc	BU
2007 Proof	Est. 25,000	Value: 55.00				

KM# 158b   5 POUNDS
39.9400 g., 0.9160 Gold 1.1762 oz. AGW, 38.61 mm. **Ruler:**
Elizabeth II **Rev:** Capt. James Cook

Date	Mintage	F	VF	XF	Unc	BU
2007 Proof	—	Value: 2,150				

KM# 159   5 POUNDS
Copper-Nickel, 38.61 mm. **Ruler:** Elizabeth II **Rev:** Sir Edward
Elgar

Date	Mintage	F	VF	XF	Unc	BU
2007	—	—	—	—	—	15.00

KM# 159a   5 POUNDS
28.2800 g., 0.9250 Silver 0.8410 oz. ASW, 38.61 mm. **Ruler:**
Elizabeth II **Rev:** Sir Edward Elgar

Date	Mintage	F	VF	XF	Unc	BU
2007 Proof	Est. 25,000	Value: 55.00				

KM# 159b   5 POUNDS
0.9160 g., 39.9400 Gold 1.1762 oz. AGW, 38.61 mm. **Ruler:**
Elizabeth II **Rev:** Sir Edward Elgar

Date	Mintage	F	VF	XF	Unc	BU
2007 Proof	—	Value: 2,150				

KM# 160   5 POUNDS
Copper-Nickel, 38.61 mm. **Ruler:** Elizabeth II **Rev:** Sir Francis
Drake

Date	Mintage	F	VF	XF	Unc	BU
2007	—	Value: 15.00				

KM# 160a   5 POUNDS
28.2800 g., 0.9250 Silver 0.8410 oz. ASW, 38.61 mm. **Ruler:**
Elizabeth II **Rev:** Sir Francis Drake

Date	Mintage	F	VF	XF	Unc	BU
2007 Proof	Est. 25,000	Value: 55.00				

KM# 160b   5 POUNDS
39.9400 g., 0.9160 Gold 1.1762 oz. AGW, 38.61 mm. **Ruler:**
Elizabeth II **Rev:** Sir Francis Drake

Date	Mintage	F	VF	XF	Unc	BU
2007 Proof	—	Value: 2,150				

KM# 161   5 POUNDS
Copper-Nickel, 38.61 mm. **Ruler:** Elizabeth II **Rev:** John
Constable

Date	Mintage	F	VF	XF	Unc	BU
2007	—	—	—	—	—	15.00

KM# 161a   5 POUNDS
28.2800 g., 0.9260 Silver 0.8419 oz. ASW, 38.61 mm. **Ruler:**
Elizabeth II **Rev:** John Constable

Date	Mintage	F	VF	XF	Unc	BU
2007 Proof	Est. 25,000	Value: 55.00				

KM# 162   5 POUNDS
28.2800 g., 0.9250 Silver partially gilt 0.8410 oz. ASW,
38.61 mm. **Ruler:** Elizabeth II **Rev:** Henry VII

Date	Mintage	F	VF	XF	Unc	BU
2007 Proof	Est. 37,500	Value: 55.00				

KM# 161b   5 POUNDS
39.9400 g., 0.9160 Gold 1.1762 oz. AGW, 39.94 mm. **Ruler:**
Elizabeth II **Rev:** John Constable

Date	Mintage	F	VF	XF	Unc	BU
2007 Proof	—	Value: 2,150				

KM# 163   5 POUNDS
28.2800 g., 0.9250 Silver partially gilt 0.8410 oz. ASW,
38.61 mm. **Ruler:** Elizabeth II **Rev:** Henry VIII

Date	Mintage	F	VF	XF	Unc	BU
2007 Proof	Est. 37,500	Value: 55.00				

KM# 164   5 POUNDS
28.2800 g., 0.9250 Silver partially gilt 0.8410 oz. ASW,
38.61 mm. **Ruler:** Elizabeth II **Rev:** Edward VI

Date	Mintage	F	VF	XF	Unc	BU
2007 Proof	Est. 37,500	Value: 55.00				

KM# 165   5 POUNDS
28.2800 g., 0.9250 Silver partially gilt 0.8410 oz. ASW,
38.61 mm. **Ruler:** Elizabeth II **Rev:** Mary I

Date	Mintage	F	VF	XF	Unc	BU
2007 Proof	Est. 37,500	Value: 55.00				

KM# 166   5 POUNDS
28.2800 g., 0.9250 Silver 0.8410 oz. ASW, 38.61 mm. **Ruler:**
Elizabeth II **Rev:** Elizabeth I

Date	Mintage	F	VF	XF	Unc	BU
2007 Proof	Est. 37,500	Value: 55.00				

KM# 167   5 POUNDS
28.2800 g., 0.9250 Silver partially gilt 0.8410 oz. ASW,
38.61 mm. **Ruler:** Elizabeth II **Rev:** James I

Date	Mintage	F	VF	XF	Unc	BU
2007 Proof	Est. 37,500	Value: 55.00				

KM# 168   5 POUNDS
28.2800 g., 0.9250 Silver 0.8410 oz. ASW, 38.61 mm. **Ruler:**
Elizabeth II **Rev:** Charles I

Date	Mintage	F	VF	XF	Unc	BU
2007 Proof	Est. 37,500	Value: 55.00				

KM# 169   5 POUNDS
28.2800 g., 0.9250 Silver partially gilt 0.8410 oz. ASW,
38.61 mm. **Ruler:** Elizabeth II **Rev:** Charles II

Date	Mintage	F	VF	XF	Unc	BU
2007 Proof	Est. 37,500	Value: 55.00				

KM# 170   5 POUNDS
28.2800 g., 0.9160 Silver partially gilt 0.8328 oz. ASW,
38.61 mm. **Ruler:** Elizabeth II **Rev:** James II

Date	Mintage	F	VF	XF	Unc	BU
2007 Proof	Est. 37,500	Value: 55.00				

KM# 171   5 POUNDS
28.2800 g., 0.9250 Silver partially gilt 0.8410 oz. ASW,
38.61 mm. **Ruler:** Elizabeth II **Rev:** William and Mary

Date	Mintage	F	VF	XF	Unc	BU
2007 Proof	Est. 37,500	Value: 55.00				

KM# 172   5 POUNDS
28.2800 g., 0.9250 Silver partially gilt 0.8410 oz. ASW,
38.61 mm. **Ruler:** Elizabeth II **Rev:** William III

Date	Mintage	F	VF	XF	Unc	BU
2007 Proof	37,500	Value: 55.00				

KM# 173   5 POUNDS
28.2800 g., 0.9250 Silver 0.8410 oz. ASW, 38.61 mm. **Ruler:**
Elizabeth II **Rev:** Anne

Date	Mintage	F	VF	XF	Unc	BU
2007 Proof	Est. 37,500	Value: 55.00				

KM# 175   5 POUNDS
28.2800 g., 0.9250 Copper-Nickel 0.8410 oz., 38.61 mm. **Ruler:**
Elizabeth II **Subject:** Princess Diana, 10th Anniversary of Death

Date	Mintage	F	VF	XF	Unc	BU
2007	—	—	—	—	—	15.00

KM# 177   5 POUNDS
Copper-Nickel, 38.61 mm. **Ruler:** Elizabeth II **Subject:**
Elizabeth II & Prince Philip, 60th Wedding Anniversary **Rev:** 1947
Wedding Portrait

Date	Mintage	F	VF	XF	Unc	BU
2007	—	—	—	—	—	15.00

KM# 177a   5 POUNDS
28.2800 g., 0.9250 Silver 0.8410 oz. ASW, 38.61 mm. **Ruler:**
Elizabeth II **Subject:** Elizabeth II and Prince Philip, 60th Wedding
Anniversary **Rev:** 1947 Wedding Portrait

Date	Mintage	F	VF	XF	Unc	BU
2007 Proof	—	Value: 55.00				

KM# 178   5 POUNDS
Copper-Nickel, 38.61 mm. **Ruler:** Elizabeth II **Subject:**
Elizabeth II and Prince Philip, 60th Wedding Anniversary **Rev:**
State Carriage

Date	Mintage	F	VF	XF	Unc	BU
2007	—	—	—	—	—	15.00

KM# 178a   5 POUNDS
28.2800 g., 0.9250 Silver 0.8410 oz. ASW, 38.61 mm. **Ruler:**
Elizabeth II **Subject:** Elizabeth II and Prince Philip, 60th Wedding
Anniversary **Rev:** State Carriage

Date	Mintage	F	VF	XF	Unc	BU
2007 Proof	—	Value: 55.00				

KM# 179   5 POUNDS
Copper-Nickel, 38.61 mm. **Ruler:** Elizabeth II **Subject:**
Elizabeth II and Prince Philip, 60th Wedding Anniversary **Rev:**
Honeymoon departure

Date	Mintage	F	VF	XF	Unc	BU
2007	—	—	—	—	—	15.00

KM# 179a   5 POUNDS
28.2800 g., 0.9250 Silver 0.8410 oz. ASW, 38.61 mm. **Ruler:**
Elizabeth II **Subject:** Elizabeth II and Prince Philip, 60th Wedding
Anniversary **Rev:** Honeymoon departure

Date	Mintage	F	VF	XF	Unc	BU
2007 Proof	—	Value: 55.00				

KM# 180   5 POUNDS
Copper-Nickel, 38.61 mm. **Ruler:** Elizabeth II **Subject:**
Elizabeth II and Prince Philip, 60th Wedding Anniversary **Rev:**
Portraits

Date	Mintage	F	VF	XF	Unc	BU
2007	—	—	—	—	—	15.00

KM# 180a   5 POUNDS
28.2800 g., 0.9250 Silver 0.8410 oz. ASW, 38.61 mm. **Ruler:**
Elizabeth II **Subject:** Elizabeth II and Prince Philip, 60th Wedding
Anniversary **Rev:** Elizabeth II and Philip portraits

Date	Mintage	F	VF	XF	Unc	BU
2007 Proof	—	Value: 55.00				

KM# 181   5 POUNDS
28.2800 g., 0.9250 Silver 0.8410 oz. ASW, 38.61 mm. **Ruler:**
Elizabeth II **Subject:** Elizabeth II and Prince Philip, 60th Wedding
Anniversary **Rev:** Bridal couple outside Westminster Abbey

Date	Mintage	F	VF	XF	Unc	BU
2007 Proof	Est. 30,000	Value: 55.00				

KM# 182   5 POUNDS
28.2800 g., 0.9250 Silver 0.8410 oz. ASW, 38.61 mm. **Ruler:**
Elizabeth II **Subject:** Elizabeth II and Prince Philip, 60th Wedding
Anniversary **Rev:** Birth of Prince Charles

Date	Mintage	F	VF	XF	Unc	BU
2007 Proof	Est. 30,000	Value: 55.00				

KM# 183   5 POUNDS
28.2800 g., 0.9250 Silver 0.8410 oz. ASW, 38.61 mm. **Ruler:**
Elizabeth II **Subject:** Elizabeth II and Prince Philip, 60th Wedding
Anniversary **Rev:** Modern portrait of Elizabeth and Philip

Date	Mintage	F	VF	XF	Unc	BU
2007 Proof	Est. 30,000	Value: 55.00				

KM# 184   5 POUNDS
28.2800 g., 0.9250 Silver 0.8410 oz. ASW, 38.61 mm. **Ruler:**
Elizabeth II **Subject:** End of World War I, 90th Anniversary **Rev:**
Soldiers and workers, flag in background

Date	Mintage	F	VF	XF	Unc	BU
2008 Proof	Est. 15,000	Value: 55.00				

KM# 184a   5 POUNDS
39.9400 g., 0.9160 Gold 1.1762 oz. AGW, 38.61 mm. **Ruler:**
Elizabeth II **Subject:** End of World War I, 90th Anniversary **Rev:**
Soldiers and workers, flag in background

Date	Mintage	F	VF	XF	Unc	BU
2008 Proof	Est. 250	Value: 2,050				

KM# 185   5 POUNDS
28.2800 g., 0.9250 Silver 0.8410 oz. ASW, 38.61 mm. **Ruler:**
Elizabeth II **Subject:** End of World War I, 90th Anniversary **Rev:**
Tank and soldier

Date	Mintage	F	VF	XF	Unc	BU
2008 Proof	Est. 15,000	Value: 55.00				

KM# 185a   5 POUNDS
39.9400 g., 0.9160 Gold 1.1762 oz. AGW, 38.61 mm. **Ruler:**
Elizabeth II **Subject:** End of World War I, 90th Anniversary **Rev:**
Tank and soldier

Date	Mintage	F	VF	XF	Unc	BU
2008 Proof	Est. 250	Value: 15.00				

KM# 186   5 POUNDS
28.2800 g., 0.9250 Silver 0.8410 oz. ASW, 38.61 mm. **Ruler:**
Elizabeth II **Subject:** End of World War I, 90th Anniversary **Rev:**
Soldiers and gravesites

Date	Mintage	F	VF	XF	Unc	BU
2008 Proof	Est. 15,000	Value: 55.00				

KM# 186a   5 POUNDS
39.9400 g., 0.9160 Gold 1.1762 oz. AGW, 38.61 mm. **Ruler:**
Elizabeth II **Subject:** End of World War I, 90th Anniversary **Rev:**
Soldiers and gravesites

Date	Mintage	F	VF	XF	Unc	BU
2008 Proof	Est. 250	Value: 2,050				

KM# 187   5 POUNDS
28.2800 g., 0.9250 Silver 0.8410 oz. ASW, 38.61 mm. **Ruler:**
Elizabeth II **Subject:** End of World War I, 90th Anniversary **Rev:**
Propaganda

Date	Mintage	F	VF	XF	Unc	BU
2008 Proof	Est. 250	Value: 2,050				

KM# 190   5 POUNDS
Copper-Nickel, 38.61 mm. **Ruler:** Elizabeth II **Rev:** Concorde

Date	Mintage	F	VF	XF	Unc	BU
2008	—	—	—	—	—	15.00

KM# 190a   5 POUNDS
28.2800 g., 0.9250 Silver 0.8410 oz. ASW, 38.61 mm. **Ruler:**
Elizabeth II **Rev:** Concorde

Date	Mintage	F	VF	XF	Unc	BU
2008 Proof	—	Value: 55.00				

KM# 190b   5 POUNDS
1090.8600 g., 0.9160 Gold 32.124 oz. AGW, 38.61 mm.   **Ruler:**
Elizabeth II **Rev:** Concorde

Date	Mintage	F	VF	XF	Unc	BU
2008 Proof	Est. 250			Value: 2,050		

KM# 85   5 POUNDS
28.2800 g., Copper-Nickel, 38.61 mm.   **Ruler:** Elizabeth II
Subject: Mini Cooper 50th Anniversary **Rev:** 1959 Mini Cooper
on tiled floor

Date	Mintage	F	VF	XF	Unc	BU
2009	50,000	—	—	—	—	17.50

KM# 86   5 POUNDS
28.2800 g., 0.9250 Silver 0.8410 oz. ASW, 38.61 mm.   **Ruler:**
Elizabeth II **Subject:** Mini Cooper, 50th Anniversary **Rev:** 1959
Mini Cooper multicolor British flag on roof

Date	Mintage	F	VF	XF	Unc	BU
2009 Proof	—		Value: 75.00			

KM# 87   5 POUNDS
28.2800 g., 0.9250 Silver 0.8410 oz. ASW, 38.61 mm.   **Ruler:**
Elizabeth II **Subject:** Mini Cooper, 50th Anniversary **Rev:** Mini
Cooper, red and pink flowers

Date	Mintage	F	VF	XF	Unc	BU
2009 Proof	2,000		Value: 75.00			

KM# 88   5 POUNDS
28.2800 g., 0.9250 Silver 0.8410 oz. ASW, 38.61 mm.   **Ruler:**
Elizabeth II **Subject:** Mini Cooper, 50th Anniversary **Rev:** Mini
Cooper, 4 views

Date	Mintage	F	VF	XF	Unc	BU
2009 Proof	2,000		Value: 75.00			

KM# 89   5 POUNDS
28.2800 g., 0.9250 Silver 0.8410 oz. ASW, 38.61 mm.   **Ruler:**
Elizabeth II **Subject:** Mini Cooper, 50th Anniversary **Rev:** Rally
Minis

Date	Mintage	F	VF	XF	Unc	BU
2009 Proof	2,000		Value: 75.00			

KM# 193   5 POUNDS
28.2800 g., 0.9250 Silver 0.8410 oz. ASW, 38.61 mm.   **Ruler:**
Elizabeth II **Subject:** British Automobiles **Rev:** Morris Minor

Date	Mintage	F	VF	XF	Unc	BU
2009 Proof	20,000		Value: 55.00			

KM# 194   5 POUNDS
28.2800 g., 0.9250 Silver 0.8410 oz. ASW, 38.61 mm.   **Ruler:**
Elizabeth II **Subject:** British Automobiles **Rev:** Land Rover series
1

Date	Mintage	F	VF	XF	Unc	BU
2009 Proof	Est. 20,000		Value: 55.00			

KM# 195   5 POUNDS
28.2800 g., 0.9250 Silver 0.8410 oz. ASW, 38.61 mm.   **Ruler:**
Elizabeth II **Subject:** British Automobiles **Rev:** Jaguar E type
series 1

Date	Mintage	F	VF	XF	Unc	BU
2009 Proof	Est. 20,000		Value: 55.00			

KM# 196   5 POUNDS
28.2800 g., 0.9250 Silver 0.8410 oz. ASW, 38.61 mm.   **Ruler:**
Elizabeth II **Subject:** British Automobiles **Rev:** Rolls Royce Silver
Ghost

Date	Mintage	F	VF	XF	Unc	BU
2009 Proof	Est. 20,000		Value: 55.00			

KM# 197   5 POUNDS
28.2800 g., 0.9250 Silver 0.8410 oz. ASW, 38.61 mm.   **Ruler:**
Elizabeth II **Subject:** British Automobiles **Rev:** Austrin Seven
"Baby Austin"

Date	Mintage	F	VF	XF	Unc	BU
2009 Proof	Est. 20,000		Value: 55.00			

KM# 198   5 POUNDS
28.2800 g., 0.9250 Silver 0.8410 oz. ASW, 38.61 mm.   **Ruler:**
Elizabeth II **Subject:** British Automobiles **Rev:** Triumph Herald

Date	Mintage	F	VF	XF	Unc	BU
2009 Proof	Est. 20,000		Value: 55.00			

KM# 199   5 POUNDS
28.2800 g., 0.9250 Silver 0.8410 oz. ASW   **Ruler:** Elizabeth II
Subject: British Automobiles **Rev:** Bentley R type Contiental

Date	Mintage	F	VF	XF	Unc	BU
2009 Proof	Est. 20,000		Value: 55.00			

KM# 200   5 POUNDS
28.2800 g., 0.9250 Silver 0.8410 oz. ASW, 38.61 mm.   **Ruler:**
Elizabeth II **Subject:** British Automobiles **Rev:** Lotus Elite (1957)

Date	Mintage	F	VF	XF	Unc	BU
2009 Proof	Est. 20,000		Value: 55.00			

KM# 202   5 POUNDS
28.2800 g., 0.9250 Silver 0.8410 oz. ASW, 38.61 mm.   **Ruler:**
Elizabeth II **Subject:** British Automobiles **Rev:** Austin healey
Sprint MK 1

Date	Mintage	F	VF	XF	Unc	BU
2009 Proof	Est. 20,000		Value: 55.00			

KM# 203   5 POUNDS
28.2800 g., 0.9250 Silver 0.8410 oz. ASW, 38.61 mm.   **Ruler:**
Elizabeth II **Subject:** British Automobiles **Rev:** Bentley 4-1/2 Litre

Date	Mintage	F	VF	XF	Unc	BU
2009 Proof	Est. 20,000		Value: 55.00			

KM# 204   5 POUNDS
28.2800 g., 0.9250 Silver 0.8410 oz. ASW, 38.61 mm.   **Ruler:**
Elizabeth II **Subject:** British Automobiles **Rev:** Hillman Imp

Date	Mintage	F	VF	XF	Unc	BU
2009 Proof	Est. 20,000		Value: 55.00			

KM# 205   5 POUNDS
28.2800 g., 0.9250 Silver 0.8410 oz. ASW, 38.61 mm.   **Ruler:**
Elizabeth II **Subject:** British Automobiles **Rev:** MGB Roadster
MK 1

Date	Mintage	F	VF	XF	Unc	BU
2009 Proof	Est. 20,000		Value: 55.00			

KM# 206   5 POUNDS
28.2800 g., 0.9250 Silver 0.8410 oz. ASW, 38.61 mm.   **Ruler:**
Elizabeth II **Subject:** British Automobiles **Rev:** MG TC Midget

Date	Mintage	F	VF	XF	Unc	BU
2009 Proof	Est. 20,000		Value: 55.00			

KM# 207   5 POUNDS
28.2800 g., 0.9250 Silver 0.8410 oz. ASW, 38.61 mm.   **Ruler:**
Elizabeth II **Subject:** British Automobiles **Rev:** BMC Mini

Date	Mintage	F	VF	XF	Unc	BU
2009 Proof	Est. 20,000		Value: 55.00			

KM# 208   5 POUNDS
28.2800 g., 0.9250 Silver 0.8410 oz. ASW, 38.61 mm.   **Ruler:**
Elizabeth II **Subject:** British Automobiles **Rev:** Morgan Plus Four

Date	Mintage	F	VF	XF	Unc	BU
2009 Proof	Est. 20,000		Value: 55.00			

KM# 209   5 POUNDS
28.2800 g., 0.9250 Silver 0.8410 oz. ASW, 38.61 mm.   **Ruler:**
Elizabeth II **Subject:** British Automobiles **Rev:** Rover P5B

Date	Mintage	F	VF	XF	Unc	BU
2009 Proof	Est. 20,000		Value: 55.00			

KM# 210   5 POUNDS
28.2800 g., 0.9250 Silver 0.8410 oz. ASW, 38.61 mm.   **Ruler:**
Elizabeth II **Subject:** British Automobiles **Rev:** Vauhall - Prince
Henry

Date	Mintage	F	VF	XF	Unc	BU
2009 Proof	Est. 20,000		Value: 55.00			

KM# 201   5 POUNDS
28.2800 g., 0.9250 Silver 0.8410 oz. ASW, 38.61 mm.   **Ruler:**
Elizabeth II **Subject:** British Automobiles **Rev:** Aston Martin DB
5 (1963)

Date	Mintage	F	VF	XF	Unc	BU
2009 Proof	Est. 20,000		Value: 55.00			

KM# 218   5 POUNDS
Copper-Nickel, 38.6 mm.   **Ruler:** Elizabeth II **Subject:** Battle of
Britain, 1940 **Obv:** Head in tiara right **Rev:** Fighter planes

Date	Mintage	F	VF	XF	Unc	BU
2010 Proof	—		Value: 20.00			

KM# 211   5 POUNDS
28.2800 g., Copper-Nickel, 38.61 mm.   **Ruler:** Elizabeth II
Subject: Engagement - Prince William and Catherine Middleton
Obv: Head in tiara right **Rev:** Conjoined busts left

Date	Mintage	F	VF	XF	Unc	BU
2010	100,000	—	—	—	—	20.00

KM# 211a   5 POUNDS
28.2800 g., 0.9250 Silver 0.8410 oz. ASW, 38.61 mm.   **Ruler:**
Elizabeth II **Subject:** Engagement - Prince William and Catherine
Middleton **Obv:** Head in tiara right **Rev:** Conjoined busts left

Date	Mintage	F	VF	XF	Unc	BU
2010 Proof	1,500		Value: 120			

KM# 211b   5 POUNDS
39.9400 g., 0.9167 Gold 1.1771 oz. AGW, 38.61 mm.   **Ruler:**
Elizabeth II **Subject:** Engagement of Prince William and
Catherine Middleton **Obv:** Head in tiara right **Rev:** Conjoined
busts left

Date	Mintage	F	VF	XF	Unc	BU
2010 Proof	1,000		Value: 2,300			

KM# 212   5 POUNDS
28.2800 g., Copper-Nickel, 38.61 mm.   **Ruler:** Elizabeth II
Subject: Royal Wedding **Obv:** Head with tiara right **Rev:**
Catherine and William busts left

Date	Mintage	F	VF	XF	Unc	BU
2011	—	—	—	—	—	17.50

KM# 212a   5 POUNDS
28.2800 g., 0.9250 Silver 0.8410 oz. ASW, 38.61 mm.   **Ruler:**
Elizabeth II **Subject:** Royal Wedding **Obv:** Head with tiara right
Rev: Catherine and William busts left

Date	Mintage	F	VF	XF	Unc	BU
2011 Proof	—		Value: 75.00			

KM# 36   10 POUNDS
155.5170 g., 0.9250 Silver 4.6248 oz. ASW, 65.06 mm.   **Ruler:**
Elizabeth II **Subject:** Last Flight of the Concorde **Obv:** Crowned
bust right **Obv. Legend:** ELIIZABETH II - ALDERNEY **Rev:**
Concorde in flight **Rev. Legend:** CONCORDE 1969 - 2003 **Edge:**
Reeded **Note:** Illustration reduced.

Date	Mintage	F	VF	XF	Unc	BU
2003 Proof	1,969		Value: 200			

KM# 55   10 POUNDS
155.5100 g., 0.9250 Silver 4.6246 oz. ASW, 65 mm.   **Ruler:**
Elizabeth II **Subject:** WWII Liberation **Obv:** Elizabeth II by
Maklouf sign **Rev:** Churchill flashing the "V" **Edge:** Reeded

Date	Mintage	F	VF	XF	Unc	BU
2005 Proof	1,945		Value: 350			

KM# 120   10 POUNDS
155.5000 g., 0.9250 Silver 4.6243 oz. ASW, 65 mm.   **Ruler:**
Elizabeth II **Subject:** Trafalgar - England espects that every man
will do his duty

Date	Mintage	F	VF	XF	Unc	BU
2005 Proof	—		Value: 275			

KM# 82   10 POUNDS
155.5170 g., Silver, 65.03 mm.   **Ruler:** Elizabeth II **Obv:**
Crowned bust right **Obv. Legend:** ELIZABETH II - ALDERNEY
Rev: Four small gilt coinage busts in ornate quadralobe **Rev.
Legend:** + HER MAJESTY QUEEN ELIZABETH II + EIGHTIETH
BIRTHDAY + **Edge:** Reeded, gilt

Date	Mintage	F	VF	XF	Unc	BU
2006 Proof	1,926		Value: 200			

KM# 135   10 POUNDS
155.5000 g., 0.9250 Silver with diamonds 4.6243 oz. ASW,
65 mm.   **Ruler:** Elizabeth II **Obv:** Head in tiara right **Rev:** Bust
in tiara right

Date	Mintage	F	VF	XF	Unc	BU
2006 Proof	Est. 1,000		Value: 250			

KM# 176   10 POUNDS
155.5000 g., 0.9250 Silver 4.6243 oz. ASW, 65 mm.   **Ruler:**
Elizabeth II **Subject:** Princess Diana, 10th Anniversary of Death

Date	Mintage	F	VF	XF	Unc	BU
2007 Proof	Est. 1,500		Value: 275			

KM# 188   10 POUNDS
155.5000 g., 0.9250 Silver 4.6243 oz. ASW, 65 mm.   **Ruler:**
Elizabeth II **Subject:** End of World War I, 90th Anniversary

Date	Mintage	F	VF	XF	Unc	BU
2008 Proof	Est. 150		Value: 350			

KM# 191   10 POUNDS
155.5000 g., 0.9250 Silver 4.6243 oz. ASW, 65 mm.   **Ruler:**
Elizabeth II **Rev:** Corcorde

Date	Mintage	F	VF	XF	Unc	BU
2008 Proof	Est. 750		Value: 275			

KM# 213   10 POUNDS
155.5700 g., 0.9250 Silver 4.6264 oz. ASW, 65 mm. **Ruler:**
Elizabeth II **Subject:** Royal Wedding - Prince William and
Catherine Middleton **Obv:** Head in tiara right **Rev:** Conjoined
busts left, rose window in background

Date	Mintage	F	VF	XF	Unc	BU
2011 Proof	500	Value: 200				

KM# 61   25 POUNDS
7.9800 g., 0.9167 Gold 0.2352 oz. AGW, 22 mm. **Ruler:**
Elizabeth II **Subject:** Queen's 75th Birthday **Obv:** Queen's
portrait right **Rev:** Queen in casual dress surrounded by rose,
thistle, daffodil and pimpernel

Date	Mintage	F	VF	XF	Unc	BU
2001 Proof	—	Value: 450				

KM# 74   25 POUNDS
7.9800 g., 0.9166 Gold 0.2352 oz. AGW. **Ruler:** Elizabeth II
Subject: Queen Elizabet II - Golden Jubilee of Reign **Obv:**
Crowned head right **Rev:** Honor guard and trumpets

Date	Mintage	F	VF	XF	Unc	BU
2002 Proof	—	Value: 450				

KM# 28   25 POUNDS
7.9800 g., 0.9167 Gold 0.2352 oz. AGW, 22.05 mm. **Ruler:**
Elizabeth II **Subject:** 5th Anniversary Death of Princess Diana
Obv: Queen's portrait **Rev:** Diana's cameo portrait left above
denomination **Edge:** Reeded

Date	Mintage	VG	F	VF	XF	Unc
2002 Proof	2,500	Value: 425				

KM# 30   25 POUNDS
7.9800 g., 0.9166 Gold 0.2352 oz. AGW, 22 mm. **Ruler:**
Elizabeth II **Subject:** 150th Anniversary Death of the Duke of
Wellington **Obv:** Queen's portrait **Rev:** Coat of arms, castle and
portrait **Edge:** Reeded

Date	Mintage	VG	F	VF	XF	Unc
2002 Proof	2,500	Value: 425				

KM# 58   25 POUNDS
7.9800 g., 0.9166 Gold 0.2352 oz. AGW, 22 mm. **Ruler:**
Elizabeth II **Subject:** Queen Elizabeth II - Golden Jubilee of Reign
Obv: Crowned head right **Rev:** Sword hilt and denomination with
royal arms in background

Date	Mintage	F	VF	XF	Unc	BU
2002 Proof	2,500	Value: 425				

KM# 32   25 POUNDS
7.9800 g., 0.9166 Gold 0.2352 oz. AGW, 22 mm. **Ruler:**
Elizabeth II **Subject:** Prince William **Obv:** Queen's portrait **Rev:**
Portrait with open shirt collar **Edge:** Reeded

Date	Mintage	F	VF	XF	Unc	BU
2003 Proof	1,500	Value: 450				

KM# 46   25 POUNDS
7.9800 g., 0.9167 Gold 0.2352 oz. AGW, 22 mm. **Ruler:**
Elizabeth II **Obv:** Queen's portrait **Rev:** HMS Mary Rose **Edge:**
Reeded

Date	Mintage	F	VF	XF	Unc	BU
2003 Proof	2,500	Value: 475				

KM# 93   25 POUNDS
7.9800 g., 0.9160 Gold 0.2350 oz. AGW **Ruler:** Elizabeth II
Subject: Royal navy - Alfred the Great

Date	Mintage	F	VF	XF	Unc	BU
2003 Proof	Est. 1,000	Value: 500				

KM# 39   25 POUNDS
7.9800 g., 0.9167 Gold 0.2352 oz. AGW, 22 mm. **Ruler:**
Elizabeth II **Subject:** D-Day **Obv:** Queen's portrait **Rev:**
Battleship and transports **Edge:** Reeded

Date	Mintage	F	VF	XF	Unc	BU
2004 Proof	500	Value: 450				

KM# 50   25 POUNDS
7.9800 g., 0.9167 Gold 0.2352 oz. AGW, 22 mm. **Ruler:**
Elizabeth II **Obv:** Queen's portrait **Rev:** Locomotive, The Rocket
Edge: Reeded

Date	Mintage	F	VF	XF	Unc	BU
2004 Proof	2,500	Value: 475				

KM# 51   25 POUNDS
7.9800 g., 0.9167 Gold 0.2352 oz. AGW, 22 mm. **Ruler:**
Elizabeth II **Obv:** Queen's portrait **Rev:** Locomotive, The
Merchant Navy 21C1 **Edge:** Reeded

Date	Mintage	F	VF	XF	Unc	BU
2004 Proof	1,500	Value: 475				

KM# 67   25 POUNDS
7.9800 g., 0.9167 Gold 0.2352 oz. AGW, 22 mm. **Ruler:**
Elizabeth II **Subject:** Viscount Samuel Hood on his flagship after
the Battle of Saints Passage in 1782 **Obv:** Queen's portrait

Date	Mintage	F	VF	XF	Unc	BU
2005 Proof	—	Value: 425				

KM# 69   25 POUNDS
7.9800 g., 0.9167 Gold 0.2352 oz. AGW, 22 mm. **Ruler:**
Elizabeth II **Obv:** Queen's portrait right **Rev:** HMS Revenge
fighting at Azores, 1591

Date	Mintage	F	VF	XF	Unc	BU
2005 Proof	—	Value: 475				

KM# 109   25 POUNDS
7.9800 g., 0.9160 Gold 0.2350 oz. AGW **Ruler:** Elizabeth II
Subject: David Beckham **Obv:** Shield **Rev:** Soccer player and
ball design

Date	Mintage	F	VF	XF	Unc	BU
2005 Proof	Est. 5,000	Value: 500				

KM# 110   25 POUNDS
7.9800 g., 0.9160 Gold 0.2350 oz. AGW **Ruler:** Elizabeth II
Subject: Michael Owen **Obv:** Shield **Rev:** Soccer player and ball
design

Date	Mintage	F	VF	XF	Unc	BU
2005 Proof	Est. 5,000	Value: 500				

KM# 111   25 POUNDS
7.9800 g., 0.9160 Gold 0.2350 oz. AGW **Ruler:** Elizabeth II
Subject: Lrank Lampard **Obv:** Shield **Rev:** Soccer player and
ball design

Date	Mintage	F	VF	XF	Unc	BU
2005 Proof	Est. 5,000	Value: 500				

KM# 112   25 POUNDS
7.9800 g., 0.9160 Gold 0.2350 oz. AGW **Ruler:** Elizabeth II
Subject: Jeremiah Campbell **Obv:** Shield **Rev:** Soccer player
and ball design.

Date	Mintage	F	VF	XF	Unc	BU
2005 Proof	Est. 5,000	Value: 500				

KM# 117   25 POUNDS
7.9800 g., 0.9160 Gold 0.2350 oz. AGW **Ruler:** Elizabeth II
Subject: Royal Navy - H.M.S. Warspite

Date	Mintage	F	VF	XF	Unc	BU
2005 Proof	Est. 1,500	Value: 500				

KM# 118   25 POUNDS
7.9800 g., 0.9160 Gold 0.2350 oz. AGW **Ruler:** Elizabeth II
Subject: Royal Navy - Admiral Sir John Foster Woodward

Date	Mintage	F	VF	XF	Unc	BU
2005 Proof	Est. 1,500	Value: 500				

KM# 121   25 POUNDS
7.9800 g., 0.9160 Gold 0.2350 oz. AGW **Ruler:** Elizabeth II
Series: Trafalgar - England expects that every man will do his
duty

Date	Mintage	F	VF	XF	Unc	BU
2005 Proof	—	Value: 500				

KM# 92   50 POUNDS
1000.0000 g., Bi-Metallic .925 Silver center in .917 Gold ring,
100 mm. **Ruler:** Elizabeth II **Rev:** Coronation at Westminster

Date	Mintage	F	VF	XF	Unc	BU
2002	Est. 2,002	Value: 1,100				

KM# 62   50 POUNDS
1000.0000 g., 0.9250 Silver 29.738 oz. ASW, 100 mm. **Ruler:**
Elizabeth II **Subject:** 50th Anniversary of Coronation **Obv:**
Queen's portrait right **Rev:** State coach in which the Queen
travelled to and from her coronation

Date	Mintage	F	VF	XF	Unc	BU
2003 Proof	—	Value: 1,150				

KM# 33   50 POUNDS
1000.0000 g., 0.9250 Silver 29.738 oz. ASW, 100 mm. **Ruler:**
Elizabeth II **Subject:** Prince William **Obv:** Queen's portrait **Rev:**
Portrait with open shirt collar **Edge:** Reeded

Date	Mintage	F	VF	XF	Unc	BU
2003 Proof	500	Value: 1,200				

KM# 63   50 POUNDS
1000.0000 g., 0.9250 Silver 29.738 oz. ASW, 100 mm. **Ruler:**
Elizabeth II **Subject:** 50th Anniversary of Coronation **Obv:**
Queen's portrait right **Rev:** St. Edward's crown, royal scepter, orb
of England

Date	Mintage	F	VF	XF	Unc	BU
2003 Proof	—	Value: 1,150				

KM# 64   50 POUNDS
1000.0000 g., 0.9250 Silver 29.738 oz. ASW, 100 mm. **Ruler:**
Elizabeth II **Subject:** 50th Anniversary of Coronation **Obv:**
Queen's portrait right **Rev:** Queen on horseback dressed in the
ceremonial uniform of the Colonel in Chief of the Household
Brigade

Date	Mintage	F	VF	XF	Unc	BU
2003 Proof	—	Value: 1,150				

KM# 65   50 POUNDS
1000.0000 g., 0.9250 Silver 29.738 oz. ASW, 100 mm. **Ruler:**
Elizabeth II **Subject:** 50th Anniversary of Coronation **Obv:**
Queen's portrait right **Rev:** The Queen crowned, seated, holding
the orb and scepter

Date	Mintage	F	VF	XF	Unc	BU
2003 Proof	—	Value: 1,150				

KM# 40   50 POUNDS
1000.0000 g., 0.9250 Silver 29.738 oz. ASW, 100 mm. **Ruler:**
Elizabeth II **Subject:** D-Day **Obv:** Queen's portrait **Rev:** US and
British troops wading ashore **Edge:** Reeded

Date	Mintage	F	VF	XF	Unc	BU
2004 Proof	600	Value: 1,200				

KM# 80   50 POUNDS
1000.0000 g., 0.9250 Silver 29.738 oz. ASW **Ruler:** Elizabeth II
Subject: 200th Anniversary Battle of Trafalgar **Obv:** Crowned
head right

Date	Mintage	F	VF	XF	Unc	BU
2005 Proof	—	Value: 1,200				

KM# 114   50 POUNDS
1000.0000 g., 0.9250 Silver 29.738 oz. ASW, 100 mm. **Ruler:**
Elizabeth II **Subject:** Prince William, 21st Birthday

Date	Mintage	F	VF	XF	Unc	BU
2005 Proof	Est. 100	Value: 1,200				

KM# 136   50 POUNDS
1000.0000 g., 0.9250 Silver partially gilt 29.738 oz. ASW,
100 mm. **Ruler:** Elizabeth II **Rev:** Portraits of Elizabeth II and
cross of 8 floral emblems

Date	Mintage	F	VF	XF	Unc	BU
2006 Proof	Est. 250	Value: 1,150				

KM# 214   50 POUNDS
1000.0000 g., 0.9250 Silver 29.738 oz. ASW, 100 mm. **Ruler:**
Elizabeth II **Subject:** Royal Wedding - Prince William and
Catherine Middleton **Obv:** Head in tiara right **Rev:** Conjoined
busts left, roase window in background

Date	Mintage	F	VF	XF	Unc	BU
2011 Proof	—	Value: 1,150				

KM# 34   100 POUNDS
1000.0000 g., 0.9166 Gold 29.468 oz. AGW, 100 mm. **Ruler:**

Elizabeth II **Subject:** Prince William **Obv:** Queen's portrait **Rev:** Portrait with open shirt collar **Edge:** Reeded

Date	Mintage	F	VF	XF	Unc	BU
2003 Proof	—	Value: 50,000				

KM# 81 100 POUNDS
1000.0000 g., 0.9166 Gold 29.468 oz. AGW **Ruler:** Elizabeth II **Subject:** 200th Anniversary Battle of Trafalgar **Obv:** Crowned head right

Date	Mintage	F	VF	XF	Unc	BU
2005 Proof	—	Value: 50,000				

KM# 37 1000 POUNDS
1090.8600 g., 0.9166 Gold 32.145 oz. AGW, 100 mm. **Ruler:** Elizabeth II **Subject:** Last Flight of the Concorde **Obv:** Queen's portrait **Rev:** Concorde in flight **Edge:** Reeded

Date	Mintage	F	VF	XF	Unc	BU
2003 Proof	34	Value: 54,500				

KM# 41 1000 POUNDS
1000.0000 g., 0.9167 Gold 29.471 oz. AGW, 100 mm. **Ruler:** Elizabeth II **Subject:** D-Day **Obv:** Queen's portrait **Rev:** US and British troops wading ashore **Edge:** Reeded

Date	Mintage	F	VF	XF	Unc	BU
2004 Proof	60	Value: 50,000				

KM# 215 1000 POUNDS
1000.0000 g., 0.9160 Gold 29.448 oz. AGW, 100 mm. **Ruler:** Elizabeth II **Subject:** Royal Wedding - Prince William and Catherine Middleton **Obv:** Head in tiara right **Rev:** Conjoined busts left, rose window in background

Date	Mintage	F	VF	XF	Unc	BU
2011 Proof	—	Value: 57,500				

MINT SETS

KM#	Date	Mintage	Identification	Issue Price	Mkt Val
MS1	2004 (1)	—	Alderney KM#43, Guernsey KM#155, Jersey KM#126, 150th Anniversary of the Crimean War	—	95.00

KM# 216 1000 POUNDS
1090.0000 g., 0.9167 Gold 32.123 oz. AGW, 11 mm. **Ruler:** Elizabeth II **Subject:** Trafalgar, 200th Anniversary

Date	Mintage	F	VF	XF	Unc	BU
2005 Proof	—	Value: 47,500				

KM# 115 1000 POUNDS
1098.8600 g., 0.9160 Gold 32.360 oz. AGW, 38.61 mm. **Ruler:** Elizabeth II **Subject:** Prince William, 21st Birthday

Date	Mintage	F	VF	XF	Unc	BU
2005 Proof	Est. 21	Value: 54,500				

KM# 137 1000 POUNDS
1090.8600 g., 0.9160 Gold 32.124 oz. AGW, 100 mm. **Ruler:** Elizabeth II **Rev:** Portraits of Elizabeth II and cross of 8 floral emblems

Date	Mintage	F	VF	XF	Unc	BU
2006 Proof	—	Value: 54,500				

KM# 192 1000 POUNDS
1090.8600 g., 0.9160 Gold 32.124 oz. AGW, 100 mm. **Ruler:** Elizabeth II **Subject:** Prince Charles, 60th Birthday

Date	Mintage	F	VF	XF	Unc	BU
2008 Proof	Est. 30	Value: 54,500				

ALGERIA

The People's Democratic Republic of Algeria, a North African country fronting on the Mediterranean Sea between Tunisia and Morocco, has an area of 919,595 sq. mi. (2,381,740 sq. km.) and a population of 31.6 million. Capital: Algiers (Alger). Most of the country's working population is engaged in agriculture although a recent industrial diversification, financed by oil revenues, is making steady progress. Wines, fruits, iron and zinc ores, phosphates, tobacco products, liquified natural gas, and petroleum are exported.

MONETARY SYSTEMS
100 Centimes = 1 Franc

REPUBLIC

STANDARD COINAGE

KM# 127 1/4 DINAR
1.1500 g., Aluminum, 16.5 mm. **Subject:** Fennec Fox **Obv:** Value in small circle **Rev:** Head facing

Date	Mintage	F	VF	XF	Unc	BU
2003-AH1423	—	—	1.50	3.00	4.50	5.50

KM# 129 DINAR
4.2400 g., Stainless Steel, 20.6 mm. **Obv:** Value on silhouette of country, within circle **Rev:** African buffalo's head 3/4 left, ancient drawings above **Edge:** Plain

Date	Mintage	F	VF	XF	Unc	BU
AH1422-2002	—	—	1.00	2.00	3.50	6.00
AH1423-2002	—	—	1.00	2.00	3.50	6.00
AH1423-2003	—	—	1.00	2.00	3.50	6.00
AH1424-2003	—	—	1.00	2.00	3.50	6.00
AH1424-2004	—	—	1.00	2.00	3.50	6.00
AH1426-2005	—	—	1.00	2.00	3.50	6.00
AH1427-2006	—	—	1.00	2.00	3.50	6.00
AH1428-2007	—	—	1.00	2.00	3.50	6.00
AH1430-2009	—	—	1.00	2.00	3.50	6.00
AH1431-2010	—	—	1.00	2.00	3.50	6.00

KM# 130 2 DINARS
5.1300 g., Stainless Steel, 22.5 mm. **Obv:** Value on silhouette of country **Rev:** Dromedary camel's head right **Edge:** Plain

Date	Mintage	F	VF	XF	Unc	BU
AH1422-2002	—	—	1.00	2.00	4.00	7.00
AH1423-2002	—	—	1.00	2.00	4.00	7.00
AH1424-2003	—	—	1.00	2.00	4.00	7.00
AH1424-2004	—	—	1.00	2.00	4.00	7.00
AH1426-2005	—	—	1.00	2.00	4.00	7.00
AH1427-2006	—	—	1.00	2.00	4.00	7.00
AH1428-2007	—	—	1.00	2.00	4.00	7.00
AH1430-2009	—	—	1.00	2.00	4.00	7.00
AH1431-2010	—	—	1.00	2.00	4.00	7.00

KM# 123 5 DINARS
6.2000 g., Stainless Steel, 24.5 mm. **Obv:** Denomination within circle **Rev:** Forepart of African elephant right **Edge:** Plain

Date	Mintage	F	VF	XF	Unc	BU
AH1422-2003	—	—	1.50	3.50	6.50	9.50
AH1423-2003	—	—	1.00	3.50	6.50	9.50
AH1424-2003	—	—	1.00	3.00	5.50	8.00
AH1424-2004	—	—	1.00	3.50	6.50	9.50
AH1426-2005	—	—	1.00	3.00	5.50	8.00
AH1426-2006	—	—	1.00	3.50	6.50	9.50
AH1427-2006	—	—	1.00	3.00	5.50	8.00
AH1428-2007	—	—	1.00	3.00	5.50	8.00
AH1430-2009	—	—	1.00	3.00	5.50	8.00
AH1431-2010	—	—	1.00	3.00	5.50	8.00

KM# 124 10 DINARS
4.9500 g., Bi-Metallic Aluminum center in Stainless Steel ring, 26.5 mm. **Obv:** Denomination **Rev:** Barbary falcon's head right **Edge:** Plain

Date	Mintage	F	VF	XF	Unc	BU
AH1422-2002	—	—	1.75	4.00	9.00	—
AH1423-2002	—	—	1.75	4.00	9.00	—
AH1424-2003	—	—	1.75	4.00	9.00	—
AH1425-2004	—	—	1.75	4.00	9.00	—
AH1426-2005	—	—	1.75	4.00	9.00	—
AH1427-2006	—	—	1.75	4.00	9.00	—
AH1428-2007	—	—	1.75	4.00	9.00	—
AH1429-2008	—	—	1.75	4.00	9.00	—
AH1430-2009	—	—	1.75	4.00	9.00	—
AH1431-2010	—	—	1.75	4.00	9.00	—
AH1432-2011	—	—	1.75	4.00	9.00	—

KM# 125   20 DINARS
8.6200 g., Bi-Metallic Aluminum-Bronze center in Stainless Steel ring, 27.5 mm. **Subject:** Lion **Obv:** Denomination **Rev:** Head left

Date	Mintage	F	VF	XF	Unc	BU
AH1424-2004	—	—	4.00	8.00	16.50	20.00
AH1426-2005	—	—	4.00	8.00	16.50	20.00
AH1427-2006	—	—	4.00	8.00	16.50	20.00
AH1428-2007	—	—	4.00	8.00	16.50	20.00
AH1430-2009	—	—	4.00	8.00	16.50	20.00
AH1431-2010	—	—	4.00	8.00	16.50	20.00

KM# 126   50 DINARS
9.2700 g., Bi-Metallic Stainless Steel center in Aluminum-Bronze ring, 28.5 mm. **Obv:** Denomination **Rev:** Dama gazelle with head left

Date	Mintage	F	VF	XF	Unc	BU
AH1424-2003	—	—	4.00	8.00	16.50	—
AH1425-2004	—	—	4.00	8.00	16.50	—
AH1428-2007	—	—	4.00	8.00	16.50	—
AH1429-2008	—	—	4.00	8.00	16.50	—
AH1430-2009	—	—	4.00	8.00	16.50	—

KM# 138   50 DINARS
9.2700 g., Bi-Metallic Stainless Steel center in Aluminum-Bronze ring, 28.5 mm. **Subject:** 50th Anniversary of Liberation **Obv:** Large value **Rev:** Stylized flag and two Moudjahid (revolutionaries)

Date	Mintage	F	VF	XF	Unc	BU
AH1425-2004	3,000,000	—	—	5.00	12.50	15.00
AH1429-2008	—	—	—	5.00	12.50	15.00

KM# 132   100 DINARS
11.0000 g., Bi-Metallic Copper-Nickel center in Stainless Steel ring, 29.5 mm. **Obv:** Denomination stylized with reverse design **Rev:** Horse head right **Edge:** Reeded

Date	Mintage	F	VF	XF	Unc	BU
AH1422-2002	—	—	6.00	12.00	22.00	26.00
AH1423-2002	—	—	6.00	12.00	22.00	26.00
AH1423-2003	—	—	6.00	12.00	22.00	26.00
AH1425-2004	—	—	6.00	12.00	22.00	26.00
AH1428-2007	—	—	6.00	12.00	22.00	26.00
AH1430-2009	—	—	6.00	12.00	22.00	26.00
AH1431-2010	—	—	6.00	12.00	22.00	26.00

KM# 137   100 DINARS
11.0000 g., Bi-Metallic Aluminum-Bronze center in Stainless Steel ring, 29.5 mm. **Subject:** 40th Anniversary of Independence **Obv:** Stylized value using palm tree in doorway and two coins depicting horses' heads **Rev:** Number 40 and stylized face **Edge:** Reeded

Date	Mintage	F	VF	XF	Unc	BU
AH1422-2002	—	—	—	—	25.00	28.00

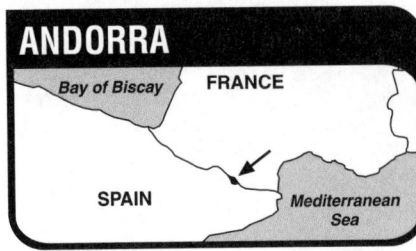

ANDORRA

Bay of Biscay
FRANCE
SPAIN
Mediterranean Sea

Principality of Andorra (Principat d'Andorra), situated on the southern slopes of the Pyrenees Mountains between France and Spain, has an area of 181 sq. mi. (453 sq. km.) and a population of 80,000. Capital: Andorra la Vella. Tourism is the chief source of income. Timber, cattle and derivatives, and furniture are exported.

RULER
Joan D.M. Bisbe D'Urgell I

MONETARY SYSTEM
100 Centims = 1 Diner
NOTE: The Diners have been struck for collectors while the Euro is used in everyday commerce.

MINT MARK
Crowned M = Madrid

PRINCIPALITY
DECIMAL COINAGE

KM# 176   CENTIM
2.1000 g., Aluminum, 27 mm. **Subject:** Charlemagne **Obv:** National arms, date below **Rev:** Crowned head facing, denomination below **Edge:** Plain

Date	Mintage	F	VF	XF	Unc	BU
2002	—	—	—	—	1.50	2.00

KM# 177   CENTIM
2.1300 g., Aluminum, 27 mm. **Subject:** Isard **Obv:** National arms, date below **Rev:** Chamois left facing, denomination at right **Edge:** Plain

Date	Mintage	F	VF	XF	Unc	BU
2002	—	—	—	—	1.50	2.00

KM# 178   CENTIM
2.1400 g., Aluminum, 27 mm. **Subject:** Agnus Dei **Obv:** National arms **Rev:** Lamb of God **Edge:** Plain

Date	Mintage	F	VF	XF	Unc	BU
2002	—	—	—	—	1.00	1.50

KM# 198   CENTIM
Aluminum-Magnesium, 27 mm. **Obv:** National arms **Rev:** A piece of the wall paintings belonging to the 12th century Romanesque church of St. Marti de la Cortinado

Date	Mintage	F	VF	XF	Unc	BU
2003	—	—	—	—	1.25	1.75

KM# 200   CENTIM
Aluminum-Magnesium, 27 mm. **Obv:** National arms **Rev:** Image of the 12th century Romanesque church of St. Miquel d'Engolasters with its bell tower, the Romanesque apse, the small portico and the large Lombard windows

Date	Mintage	F	VF	XF	Unc	BU
2003	—	—	—	—	1.25	1.75

KM# 199   CENTIM
Aluminum-Magnesium, 27 mm. **Obv:** National arms **Rev:** Pont de la Margineda, reproduction of the bridge

Date	Mintage	F	VF	XF	Unc	BU
2003	—	—	—	—	1.25	1.75

KM# 229   CENTIM
Aluminum **Obv:** Crowned arms **Rev:** Santa Coloma

Date	Mintage	F	VF	XF	Unc	BU
2004	—	—	—	—	0.90	1.20

KM# 230   CENTIM
Aluminum **Obv:** Crowned arms **Rev:** Sant Martí de la Cortinada

Date	Mintage	F	VF	XF	Unc	BU
2004	—	—	—	—	0.90	1.20

KM# 231   CENTIM
Aluminum **Obv:** Crowned arms **Rev:** Altar at Santa Coloma

Date	Mintage	F	VF	XF	Unc	BU
2004	—	—	—	—	0.90	1.20

KM# 236   CENTIM
2.8000 g., Brass, 18 mm. **Subject:** Death of Pope John Paul II **Obv:** National arms **Rev:** Karol Wojtyla as priest **Edge:** Reeded

Date	Mintage	F	VF	XF	Unc	BU
2005	15,000	—	—	0.30	0.80	1.20

KM# 245   CENTIM
2.8000 g., Brass, 18 mm. **Obv:** National arms **Rev:** Findern flower - Poet's Daffodil

Date	Mintage	F	VF	XF	Unc	BU
2005	15,000	—	—	—	0.80	1.20
2006	10,000	—	—	—	0.80	1.20
2007	10,000	—	—	—	0.80	1.20
2008	5,000	—	—	—	0.80	1.20

KM# 290   CENTIM
2.8000 g., Brass, 18 mm. **Obv:** National Arms **Rev:** Portrait of Joseph Ratzinger as priest **Edge:** Reeded

Date	Mintage	F	VF	XF	Unc	BU
2006	15,000	—	—	—	—	1.20

KM# 306   CENTIM
2.8000 g., Brass, 18 mm. **Subject:** Popes of the 20th Century **Obv:** National arms **Rev:** Pope Leo XIII **Edge:** Reeded

Date	Mintage	F	VF	XF	Unc	BU
2007	5,000	—	—	—	—	1.20

KM# 179 2 CENTIMS
Brass, 18 mm. **Subject:** Grandalla **Obv:** National arms **Rev:** Edelweiss flower **Edge:** Plain

Date	Mintage	F	VF	XF	Unc	BU
2002	—	—	—	—	1.50	2.00

KM# 201 2 CENTIMS
Copper-Nickel-Zinc, 18.15 mm. **Obv:** National arms **Rev:** Clavell Deltoide, a flower found in Andorra

Date	Mintage	F	VF	XF	Unc	BU
2003	—	—	—	—	1.75	2.50

KM# 232 2 CENTIMS
Brass **Obv:** Crowned arms **Rev:** West Gothic robe

Date	Mintage	F	VF	XF	Unc	BU
2004	—	—	—	—	1.20	1.60

KM# 237 2 CENTIMS
4.0000 g., Brass, 21.3 mm. **Subject:** Death of Pope John-Paul II **Obv:** National arms **Rev:** Karol Wojtyla as priest

Date	Mintage	F	VF	XF	Unc	BU
2005	15,000	—	—	0.50	1.20	1.60

KM# 246 2 CENTIMS
4.0000 g., Brass, 21.3 mm. **Obv:** National arms **Rev:** Pyrenean Chamois **Edge:** Reeded

Date	Mintage	F	VF	XF	Unc	BU
2005	15,000	—	—	—	1.20	1.60
2006	10,000	—	—	—	1.20	1.60
2007	10,000	—	—	—	1.20	1.60
2008	5,000	—	—	—	1.20	1.60

KM# 291 2 CENTIMS
4.0000 g., Brass, 21.3 mm. **Obv:** National Arms **Rev:** Portrait of Joseph Ratzinger as priest

Date	Mintage	F	VF	XF	Unc	BU
2006	15,000	—	—	—	—	1.60

KM# 307 2 CENTIMS
4.0000 g., Brass, 21.3 mm. **Subject:** Popes of the 20th Century **Obv:** National Arms **Rev:** Pope Pius X

Date	Mintage	F	VF	XF	Unc	BU
2007	5,000	—	—	—	—	1.60

KM# 282 2 CENTIMS
0.7300 g., 0.9990 Gold 0.0234 oz. AGW, 11 mm. **Subject:** Berlin Wall, 20th anniversary **Obv:** Shield **Rev:** Brandenburg Gate and brick wall **Edge:** Reeded

Date	Mintage	F	VF	XF	Unc	BU
2009 Proof	5,000	Value: 75.00				

KM# 180 5 CENTIMS
Brass, 21.8 mm. **Subject:** Squirrel **Obv:** National arms **Rev:** Red Squirrel on tree stump **Edge:** Plain

Date	Mintage	F	VF	XF	Unc	BU
2002	—	—	—	—	2.00	2.50

KM# 181 5 CENTIMS
Brass, 21.8 mm. **Subject:** Gall Fer **Obv:** National arms **Rev:** Male Eurasian Capercaillie (grouse) displaying plumage **Edge:** Plain

Date	Mintage	F	VF	XF	Unc	BU
2002	—	—	—	—	2.00	2.50

KM# 203 5 CENTIMS
Brass, 21.8 mm. **Obv:** National arms **Rev:** Wall painting from the 11th century church of Sant Serni de Nagol showing an eagle

Date	Mintage	F	VF	XF	Unc	BU
2003	—	—	—	—	2.25	2.75

KM# 202 5 CENTIMS
Brass, 21.8 mm. **Obv:** National arms **Rev:** The cross of Seven Arms, traditional Gothic cross

Date	Mintage	F	VF	XF	Unc	BU
2003	—	—	—	—	2.25	2.75

KM# 233 5 CENTIMS
Brass **Obv:** Crowned arms **Rev:** Gothic cross

Date	Mintage	F	VF	XF	Unc	BU
2004	—	—	—	—	1.80	2.40

KM# 234 5 CENTIMS
Brass **Obv:** Crowned arms **Rev:** Lady of Canolic

Date	Mintage	F	VF	XF	Unc	BU
2004	—	—	—	—	1.80	2.40

KM# 238 5 CENTIMS
5.5000 g., Brass, 24.5 mm. **Subject:** Death of Pope John-Paul II **Obv:** National arms **Rev:** Karol Wojtyla as bishop **Edge:** Reeded

Date	Mintage	F	VF	XF	Unc	BU
2005	15,000	—	—	0.70	1.80	2.40

KM# 247 5 CENTIMS
5.5000 g., Brass, 24.5 mm. **Obv:** National arms **Rev:** Wall painting from Santa Coloma church **Edge:** Reeded

Date	Mintage	F	VF	XF	Unc	BU
2005	15,000	—	—	—	1.80	2.40
2006	10,000	—	—	—	1.80	2.40
2007	10,000	—	—	—	1.80	2.40
2008	5,000	—	—	—	1.80	2.40

KM# 292 5 CENTIMS
5.5000 g., Brass, 24.5 mm. **Obv:** National Arms **Rev:** Portrait of Joseph Ratzinger as archbishop

Date	Mintage	F	VF	XF	Unc	BU
2006	15,000	—	—	—	—	2.50

KM# 308 5 CENTIMS
5.5000 g., Brass, 24.5 mm. **Subject:** Popes of the 20th Century **Obv:** National Arms **Rev:** Pope Benedict XV

Date	Mintage	F	VF	XF	Unc	BU
2007	5,000	—	—	—	—	2.40

KM# 182 10 CENTIMS
Brass **Subject:** St. Joan de Caselles **Obv:** National arms **Rev:** Tower and building **Edge:** Plain

Date	Mintage	F	VF	XF	Unc	BU
2002	—	—	—	—	3.00	4.00

KM# 204 10 CENTIMS
Nickel Plated Steel, 27.8 mm. **Obv:** National arms **Rev:** 12th century wood carving image from Our Lady of Meritxell

Date	Mintage	F	VF	XF	Unc	BU
2003	—	—	—	—	3.50	4.50

KM# 235 10 CENTIMS
Nickel Plated Steel **Obv:** Crowned arms **Rev:** Casa de la Vall

Date	Mintage	F	VF	XF	Unc	BU
2004	—	—	—	—	3.00	4.00

KM# 239 10 CENTIMS
6.5000 g., Copper-Nickel, 22.2 mm. **Subject:** Death of Pope John-Paul II **Obv:** National arms **Rev:** Karol Wojtyla as archbishop **Edge:** Reeded

Date	Mintage	F	VF	XF	Unc	BU
2005	15,000	—	—	1.00	2.40	3.20

KM# 248 10 CENTIMS
6.5000 g., Copper-Nickel, 22.2 mm. **Obv:** National arms **Rev:** Saint Vicenç d'Enclar church

Date	Mintage	F	VF	XF	Unc	BU
2005	15,000	—	—	—	2.40	3.20
2006	10,000	—	—	—	2.40	3.20
2007	10,000	—	—	—	2.40	3.20
2008	5,000	—	—	—	2.40	3.20

KM# 293 10 CENTIMS
6.5000 g., Copper-Nickel, 22.2 mm. **Obv:** National Arms **Rev:** Portrait of Joseph Ratzinger as archbishop

Date	Mintage	F	VF	XF	Unc	BU
2006	15,000	—	—	—	—	4.00

KM# 309 10 CENTIMS
6.5000 g., Copper-Nickel, 22.2 mm. **Subject:** Popes of the 20th Century **Obv:** National Arms **Rev:** Pope Pius XI

Date	Mintage	F	VF	XF	Unc	BU
2007	5,000	—	—	—	—	3.40

KM# 240 25 CENTIMS
7.7500 g., Copper-Nickel, 24.2 mm. **Subject:** Death of Pope John-Paul II **Obv:** National arms **Rev:** Karol Wojtyla as cardinal

Date	Mintage	F	VF	XF	Unc	BU
2005	15,000	—	—	1.20	3.00	4.00

KM# 249 25 CENTIMS
7.7500 g., Copper-Nickel, 24.2 mm. **Obv:** National arms **Rev:** Our Lady of Meritxell sanctuary

Date	Mintage	F	VF	XF	Unc	BU
2005	15,000	—	—	—	3.00	4.00
2006	10,000	—	—	—	3.00	4.00
2007	10,000	—	—	—	3.00	4.00
2008	5,000	—	—	—	3.00	4.00

KM# 294 25 CENTIMS
7.7500 g., Copper-Nickel, 24.2 mm. **Obv:** National Arms **Rev:** Portrait of Joseph Ratzinger as cardinal

Date	Mintage	F	VF	XF	Unc	BU
2006	15,000	—	—	—	—	4.00

KM# 310 25 CENTIMS
7.7500 g., Copper-Nickel, 24.2 mm. **Subject:** Popes of the 20th Century **Obv:** National Arms **Rev:** Pope Pius XII

Date	Mintage	F	VF	XF	Unc	BU
2007	5,000	—	—	—	—	4.00

KM# 241   50 CENTIMS
9.0000 g., Copper-Nickel, 25.9 mm. **Subject:** Death of Pope John-Paul II **Obv:** National arms **Rev:** Karol Wojtyla as cardinal

Date	Mintage	F	VF	XF	Unc	BU
2005	15,000	—	—	2.70	3.60	4.80

KM# 250   50 CENTIMS
9.0000 g., Copper-Nickel, 25.9 mm. **Obv:** National arms **Rev:** Map of Andorra, 7 towns highlighted

Date	Mintage	F	VF	XF	Unc	BU
2005	15,000	—	—	—	4.00	5.00
2006	10,000	—	—	—	4.00	5.00
2007	10,000	—	—	—	4.00	5.00
2008	5,000	—	—	—	4.00	5.00

KM# 295   50 CENTIMS
9.0000 g., Copper-Nickel, 25.9 mm. **Obv:** National Arms **Rev:** Portrait of Joseph Ratzinger as cardinal

Date	Mintage	F	VF	XF	Unc	BU
2006	15,000	—	—	—	—	4.80

KM# 311   50 CENTIMS
9.0000 g., Copper-Nickel, 25.9 mm. **Subject:** Popes of the 20th Century **Obv:** National Arms **Rev:** Pope John XXIII

Date	Mintage	F	VF	XF	Unc	BU
2007	5,000	—	—	—	—	6.00

KM# 242   DINER
8.5000 g., Bi-Metallic Brass center in Copper-Nickel ring, 24.5 mm. **Subject:** Death of Pope John-Paul II **Obv:** National arms **Rev:** Karol Wojtyla as pope **Edge:** Reeded

Date	Mintage	F	VF	XF	Unc	BU
2005	15,000	—	—	1.60	4.00	6.00

KM# 251   DINER
8.5000 g., Bi-Metallic Brass center in Copper-Nickel ring, 24.5 mm. **Obv:** National arms **Rev:** Our Lady of Meritxell **Edge:** Reeded

Date	Mintage	F	VF	XF	Unc	BU
2005	15,000	—	—	—	4.50	6.00
2006	10,000	—	—	—	4.50	6.00
2007	10,000	—	—	—	4.50	6.00
2008	5,000	—	—	—	4.50	6.00

KM# 296   DINER
8.5000 g., Bi-Metallic Brss center in Copper-Nickel ring, 24.5 mm. **Obv:** National Arms **Rev:** Portrait of Joseph Ratzinger as Pope Benedict XVI

Date	Mintage	F	VF	XF	Unc	BU
2006	15,000	—	—	—	—	6.00

KM# 299   DINER
11.0000 g., Nickel, 25x25 mm. **Subject:** Chess Set **Obv:** National Arms **Rev:** Pawn **Shape:** Square

Date	Mintage	F	VF	XF	Unc	BU
2006	40,000	—	—	—	—	6.00

KM# 299a   DINER
11.0000 g., Brass Gilt, 25x25 mm. **Subject:** Chess Set **Obv:** National Arms **Rev:** Pawn **Shape:** Square

Date	Mintage	F	VF	XF	Unc	BU
2006	40,000	—	—	—	—	6.00

KM# 300   DINER
11.0000 g., Nickel, 25x25 mm. **Subject:** Chess Set **Obv:** National arms **Rev:** Rook **Shape:** Square

Date	Mintage	F	VF	XF	Unc	BU
2006	10,000	—	—	—	—	12.00

KM# 300a   DINER
11.0000 g., Brass Gilt, 25x25 mm. **Subject:** Chess Set **Obv:** National Arms **Rev:** Rook **Shape:** Square

Date	Mintage	F	VF	XF	Unc	BU
2006	10,000	—	—	—	—	12.00

KM# 301   DINER
11.0000 g., Nickel, 25x25 mm. **Subject:** Chess Set **Obv:** National Arms **Rev:** Knight **Shape:** Square

Date	Mintage	F	VF	XF	Unc	BU
2006	10,000	—	—	—	—	12.00

KM# 301a   DINER
11.0000 g., Brass Gilt, 25x25 mm. **Subject:** Chess Set **Obv:** National Arms **Rev:** Knight **Shape:** Square

Date	Mintage	F	VF	XF	Unc	BU
2006	10,000	—	—	—	—	12.00

KM# 302   DINER
11.0000 g., Nickel, 25x25 mm. **Subject:** Chess Set **Obv:** National Arms **Rev:** Bishop **Shape:** Square

Date	Mintage	F	VF	XF	Unc	BU
2006	10,000	—	—	—	—	12.00

KM# 302a   DINER
11.0000 g., Brass Gilt, 25x25 mm. **Subject:** Chess Set **Obv:** National Arms **Rev:** Bishop **Shape:** Square

Date	Mintage	F	VF	XF	Unc	BU
2006	10,000	—	—	—	—	12.00

KM# 303   DINER
11.0000 g., Nickel, 25x25 mm. **Subject:** Chess Set **Obv:** National Arms **Rev:** Queen **Shape:** Square

Date	Mintage	F	VF	XF	Unc	BU
2006	5,000	—	—	—	—	18.00

KM# 303a   DINER
11.0000 g., Brass Gilt, 25x25 mm. **Subject:** Chess Set **Obv:** National Arms **Rev:** Queen **Shape:** Square

Date	Mintage	F	VF	XF	Unc	BU
2006	5,000	—	—	—	—	18.00

KM# 304   DINER
11.0000 g., Nickel, 25x25 mm. **Subject:** Chess Set **Obv:** National Arms **Rev:** King **Shape:** Square

Date	Mintage	F	VF	XF	Unc	BU
2006	5,000	—	—	—	—	18.00

KM# 304a   DINER
11.0000 g., Brass Gilt, 25x25 mm. **Subject:** Chess Set **Obv:** National Arms **Rev:** King **Shape:** Square

Date	Mintage	F	VF	XF	Unc	BU
2006	5,000	—	—	—	—	18.00

KM# 312   DINER
8.5000 g., Bi-Metallic Brass center in Copper-Nickel ring, 24.5 mm. **Subject:** Popes of the 20th Century **Obv:** National Arms **Rev:** Pope Paul VI

Date	Mintage	F	VF	XF	Unc	BU
2007	5,000	—	—	—	—	8.00

KM# 243   2 DINERS
11.2500 g., Bi-Metallic Copper-Nickel center in Brass ring, 28.4 mm. **Subject:** Death of Pope John-Paul II **Obv:** National arms **Rev:** Karol Wojtyla as pope **Edge:** Reeded

Date	Mintage	F	VF	XF	Unc	BU
2005	15,000	—	—	2.40	6.00	8.00

KM# 252   2 DINERS
11.2500 g., Bi-Metallic Copper-Nickel center in Brass ring, 28.4 mm. **Obv:** National arms **Rev:** Signing of the Umpirage between the Bishop of Urgell and Count of Foix **Edge:** Reeded

Date	Mintage	F	VF	XF	Unc	BU
2005	15,000	—	—	—	6.00	8.00
2006	10,000	—	—	—	6.00	8.00
2007	10,000	—	—	—	6.00	8.00
2008	5,000	—	—	—	6.00	8.00

KM# 297   2 DINERS
11.2500 g., Bi-Metallic Copper-Nickel center in Brass ring, 28.4 mm. **Obv:** National Arms **Rev:** Portrait of Joseph Ratzinger as Pope Benedict XVI

Date	Mintage	F	VF	XF	Unc	BU
2006	15,000	—	—	—	—	8.00

KM# 313   2 DINERS
6.0000 g., Bi-Metallic Copper-Nickel center in Brass ring, 28.4 mm. **Subject:** Popes of the 20th Century **Obv:** National Arms **Rev:** Pope John Paul I

Date	Mintage	F	VF	XF	Unc	BU
2007	5,000	—	—	—	—	10.00

KM# 269   2 DINERS
0.7300 g., 0.9990 Gold 0.0234 oz. AGW, 11 mm. **Subject:** von Beethoven **Obv:** National arms **Rev:** Beethoven seated at desk

Date	Mintage	F	VF	XF	Unc	BU
2008 Proof	5,000	Value: 80.00				

KM# 281   2 DINERS
0.7300 g., 0.9990 Gold 0.0234 oz. AGW, 11 mm. **Obv:** Shield **Rev:** Charlemagne **Edge:** Reeded

Date	Mintage	F	VF	XF	Unc	BU
2009 Proof	5,000	Value: 80.00				

KM# 193   5 DINERS
1.2400 g., 0.9990 Gold 0.0398 oz. AGW, 13.92 mm. **Obv:** National arms **Rev:** The Escorial Palace in Madrid **Edge:** Reeded

Date	Mintage	F	VF	XF	Unc	BU
2004 Proof	3,000	Value: 75.00				

KM# 194 5 DINERS
1.2400 g., 0.9990 Gold 0.0398 oz. AGW, 13.92 mm. **Obv:** National arms **Rev:** Eiffel Tower **Edge:** Reeded

Date	Mintage	F	VF	XF	Unc	BU
2004 Proof	3,000	Value: 75.00				

KM# 195 5 DINERS
1.2400 g., 0.9990 Gold 0.0398 oz. AGW, 13.92 mm. **Obv:** National arms **Rev:** Atomic model monument **Edge:** Reeded

Date	Mintage	F	VF	XF	Unc	BU
2004 Proof	3,000	Value: 75.00				

KM# 196 5 DINERS
1.2400 g., 0.9990 Gold 0.0398 oz. AGW, 13.92 mm. **Subject:** Andorran membership in the United Nations **Obv:** National arms **Rev:** Seated woman, world globe and UN logo **Edge:** Reeded

Date	Mintage	F	VF	XF	Unc	BU
2004 Proof	3,000	Value: 80.00				

KM# 315 5 DINERS
15.6000 g., 0.9990 Silver 0.5010 oz. ASW, 35 mm. **Rev:** Bear facing

Date	Mintage	F	VF	XF	Unc	BU
2010 Proof	3,000	Value: 90.00				

KM# 324 5 DINERS
20.0000 g., 0.9250 Silver 0.5948 oz. ASW, 38.6 mm. **Subject:** Beautification of Pope John Paul II **Rev:** Hologram with image of John Paul II at left, St. Peter's facade at right

Date	Mintage	F	VF	XF	Unc	BU
2011 Proof	2,500	Value: 135				

KM# 172 10 DINERS
31.4700 g., 0.9250 Silver 0.9359 oz. ASW, 38.6 mm. **Subject:** Europa **Obv:** National arms **Rev:** Europa in chariot **Edge:** Reeded

Date	Mintage	F	VF	XF	Unc	BU
2001 Proof	15,000	Value: 45.00				

KM# 173 10 DINERS
31.4700 g., 0.9250 Silver 0.9359 oz. ASW, 38.6 mm. **Subject:** Concordia Europea **Obv:** National arms **Rev:** Two crowned women holding hands **Edge:** Reeded

Date	Mintage	F	VF	XF	Unc	BU
2001 Proof	15,000	Value: 45.00				

KM# 175 10 DINERS
31.4700 g., 0.9250 Silver 0.9359 oz. ASW, 38.6 mm. **Subject:** Olympics **Obv:** National arms **Rev:** Snowboarder **Edge:** Reeded

Date	Mintage	F	VF	XF	Unc	BU
2002 Proof	15,000	Value: 45.00				

KM# 183 10 DINERS
31.4700 g., 0.9250 Silver 0.9359 oz. ASW, 38.6 mm. **Subject:** Mouflon **Obv:** National arms **Rev:** Mouflon ram **Edge:** Reeded

Date	Mintage	F	VF	XF	Unc	BU
2002 Proof	15,000	Value: 50.00				

KM# 289 10 DINERS
31.4700 g., 0.9250 Silver 0.9359 oz. ASW, 38.61 mm. **Subject:** FIFA World Cup **Obv:** National Arms **Rev:** Soccer ball, names and years of previous World Cup host countries **Edge:** Reeded

Date	Mintage	F	VF	XF	Unc	BU
2003 Proof	50,000	Value: 85.00				

KM# 188 10 DINERS
31.1035 g., 0.9250 Silver 0.9250 oz. ASW, 38.6 mm. **Obv:** National arms **Rev:** Pope with doves **Edge:** Reeded

Date	Mintage	F	VF	XF	Unc	BU
2004 Proof	9,999	Value: 70.00				

KM# 189 10 DINERS
31.1035 g., 0.9250 Silver 0.9250 oz. ASW, 38.6 mm. **Obv:** National arms **Rev:** Pope holding staff with 2 hands **Edge:** Reeded

Date	Mintage	F	VF	XF	Unc	BU
2004 Proof	9,999	Value: 70.00				

KM# 190 10 DINERS
31.1035 g., 0.9250 Silver 0.9250 oz. ASW, 38.6 mm. **Obv:** National arms **Rev:** Pope raising a chalice **Edge:** Reeded

Date	Mintage	F	VF	XF	Unc	BU
2004 Proof	9,999	Value: 70.00				

KM# 191 10 DINERS
31.1035 g., 0.9250 Silver 0.9250 oz. ASW, 38.6 mm. **Obv:** National arms **Rev:** Pope with hammer **Edge:** Reeded

Date	Mintage	F	VF	XF	Unc	BU
2004 Proof	9,999	Value: 70.00				

KM# 192   10 DINERS
31.1035 g., 0.9250 Silver 0.9250 oz. ASW, 38.6 mm. **Obv:**
National arms **Rev:** Gold-plated Pope writing **Edge:** Reeded

Date	Mintage	F	VF	XF	Unc	BU
2004 Proof	9,999	Value: 70.00				

KM# 205   10 DINERS
31.1000 g., 0.9250 Silver 0.9249 oz. ASW, 38.6 mm. **Rev:** Gold
plated Pope John Paul II wearing mitre and holding crucifix staff
Edge: Reeded

Date	Mintage	F	VF	XF	Unc	BU
2005 Proof	9,999	Value: 70.00				

KM# 206   10 DINERS
31.1000 g., 0.9250 Silver 0.9249 oz. ASW, 38.6 mm. **Obv:**
National arms **Rev:** Pope John Paul II with the Holy Virgin in
background **Edge:** Reeded

Date	Mintage	F	VF	XF	Unc	BU
2005 Proof	9,999	Value: 70.00				

KM# 207   10 DINERS
31.1000 g., 0.9250 Silver 0.9249 oz. ASW, 38.6 mm. **Obv:**
National arms **Rev:** Pope John Paul II in prayer with crucifix at
right **Edge:** Reeded

Date	Mintage	F	VF	XF	Unc	BU
2005 Proof	9,999	Value: 70.00				

KM# 208   10 DINERS
31.1000 g., 0.9250 Silver 0.9249 oz. ASW, 38.6 mm. **Obv:**
National arms **Rev:** Pope John Paul II blessing Vatican crowd
Edge: Reeded

Date	Mintage	F	VF	XF	Unc	BU
2005 Proof	9,999	Value: 70.00				

KM# 209   10 DINERS
31.1000 g., 0.9250 Silver 0.9249 oz. ASW, 38.6 mm. **Obv:**
National arms **Rev:** Pope John Paul II and Mother Teresa **Edge:**
Reeded

Date	Mintage	F	VF	XF	Unc	BU
2005 Proof	9,999	Value: 70.00				

KM# 210   10 DINERS
31.1000 g., 0.9250 Silver 0.9249 oz. ASW, 38.6 mm. **Obv:**
National arms **Rev:** Bearded man above Vatican City **Edge:**
Reeded

Date	Mintage	F	VF	XF	Unc	BU
2005 Proof	9,999	Value: 60.00				

KM# 211   10 DINERS
31.1000 g., 0.9250 Silver 0.9249 oz. ASW, 38.6 mm. **Obv:**
National arms **Rev:** Sad woman above Fatima **Edge:** Reeded

Date	Mintage	F	VF	XF	Unc	BU
2005 Proof	9,999	Value: 60.00				

KM# 212   10 DINERS
31.1000 g., 0.9250 Silver 0.9249 oz. ASW, 38.6 mm. **Obv:**
National arms **Rev:** Radiant woman above Guadalupe Cathedral
Edge: Reeded

Date	Mintage	F	VF	XF	Unc	BU
2005 Proof	9,999	Value: 60.00				

KM# 213   10 DINERS
31.1000 g., 0.9250 Silver 0.9249 oz. ASW, 38.6 mm. **Obv:**
National arms **Rev:** Sea shell above Santiago De Compostel-la
Cathedral **Edge:** Reeded

Date	Mintage	F	VF	XF	Unc	BU
2005 Proof	9,999	Value: 60.00				

KM# 214   10 DINERS
31.1000 g., 0.9250 Silver 0.9249 oz. ASW, 38.6 mm. **Obv:**
National arms **Rev:** Dead man's face with Church of the Holy
Sepulchure in the background **Edge:** Reeded

Date	Mintage	F	VF	XF	Unc	BU
2005 Proof	9,999	Value: 60.00				

KM# 215   10 DINERS
28.8000 g., 0.9250 Silver 0.8565 oz. ASW, 38.61 mm. **Obv:**
National arms **Rev:** 2006 Olympics freestyle skier **Edge:** Reeded

Date	Mintage	F	VF	XF	Unc	BU
2005 Proof	15,000	Value: 50.00				

KM# 217   10 DINERS
3.1100 g., 0.9999 Gold 0.1000 oz. AGW, 20 mm. **Obv:** National
arms **Rev:** Jesus carrying the cross **Edge:** Reeded

Date	Mintage	F	VF	XF	Unc	BU
2006 Proof	9,999	Value: 185				

KM# 218   10 DINERS
31.1035 g., 0.9250 Silver 0.9250 oz. ASW, 38.6 mm. **Obv:**
National arms **Rev:** Birth of Jesus **Edge:** Reeded

Date	Mintage	F	VF	XF	Unc	BU
2006 Proof	9,999	Value: 60.00				

KM# 219   10 DINERS
31.1035 g., 0.9250 Silver 0.9250 oz. ASW, 38.6 mm. **Obv:**
National arms **Rev:** The Last Supper **Edge:** Reeded

Date	Mintage	F	VF	XF	Unc	BU
2006 Proof	9,999	Value: 60.00				

KM# 276   10 DINERS
28.2800 g., 0.9250 Silver 0.8410 oz. ASW, 38.6 mm. **Subject:**
Extreme Sports - Mountain Bike **Obv:** Arms **Rev:** Multicolor biker

Date	Mintage	F	VF	XF	Unc	BU
2007 Proof	5,000	Value: 65.00				

KM# 277   10 DINERS
28.2800 g., 0.9250 Silver 0.8410 oz. ASW, 38.6 mm. **Subject:**
Extreme Sports - Snowboarding **Obv:** Arms **Rev:** Multicolor
snowboarder

Date	Mintage	F	VF	XF	Unc	BU
2007 Proof	5,000	Value: 65.00				

KM# 278   10 DINERS
28.2800 g., 0.9250 Silver 0.8410 oz. ASW, 38.6 mm. **Subject:**
Extreme Sports - Heliskiing **Obv:** Arms **Rev:** Multicolor heliskier

Date	Mintage	F	VF	XF	Unc	BU
2007 Proof	5,000	Value: 65.00				

KM# 244   10 DINERS
28.2800 g., 0.9250 Silver 0.8410 oz. ASW, 28x40 mm. **Subject:**
Great Painters of the World **Obv:** Mona lisa, national arms at
lower left, multicolor **Rev:** Head of Leonardo daVinci at lower left,
study of man in background, multicolor **Edge:** Plain **Shape:**
Vertical rectangular

Date	Mintage	F	VF	XF	Unc	BU
2008	15,000	—	—	—	—	60.00

KM# 271   10 DINERS
28.2800 g., 0.9250 Silver 0.8410 oz. ASW, 28x40 mm. **Obv:**
National arms at left, color painting of ladies at a piano **Rev:**
Renoir facing, female portrait in color in artist's pallet shape
Shape: Vertical rectangle

Date	Mintage	F	VF	XF	Unc	BU
2008 Proof	20,000	Value: 60.00				

KM# 272   10 DINERS
33.0000 g., 0.9250 Silver parially gilt 0.9814 oz. ASW, 38.6 mm.
Subject: Vikings

Date	Mintage	F	VF	XF	Unc	BU
2008	15,000	—	—	—	—	50.00

KM# 273   10 DINERS
28.2800 g., 0.9250 Silver 0.8410 oz. ASW, 38.6 mm. **Subject:**
Cross-country Skiing

Date	Mintage	F	VF	XF	Unc	BU
2008 Proof	10,000	Value: 45.00				

KM# 321   10 DINERS
28.2800 g., 0.9250 Silver 0.8410 oz. ASW, 38.61 mm. **Subject:**
Chopin **Rev:** Portrait pair in ovals, Dresden

Date	Mintage	F	VF	XF	Unc	BU
2009 Proof	—	Value: 45.00				

KM# 280   10 DINERS
28.2800 g., 0.9250 Silver 0.8410 oz. ASW, 38.61 mm. **Subject:** World Cup Football, 2010 **Obv:** Shield **Rev:** Linear and shaded player skicking ball **Edge:** Reeded

Date	Mintage	F	VF	XF	Unc	BU
2009 Proof	10,000	Value: 50.00				

KM# 316   10 DINERS
28.2800 g., 0.9250 Silver 0.8410 oz. ASW, 38.61 mm. **Subject:** Chopin **Rev:** Hand and autograph

Date	Mintage	F	VF	XF	Unc	BU
2009 Proof	—	Value: 50.00				

KM# 317   10 DINERS
28.2800 g., 0.9250 Silver 0.8410 oz. ASW **Subject:** Chopin - Vienna **Rev:** Bust at left, house at right

Date	Mintage	F	VF	XF	Unc	BU
2009 Proof	—	Value: 45.00				

KM# 318   10 DINERS
28.2800 g., 0.9250 Silver 0.8410 oz. ASW, 38.61 mm. **Subject:** Chopin - Paris **Rev:** Party scene, Paris

Date	Mintage	F	VF	XF	Unc	BU
2009 Proof	—	Value: 45.00				

KM# 319   10 DINERS
28.2800 g., 0.9250 Silver 0.8410 oz. ASW, 38.6 mm. **Subject:** Chopin **Rev:** Bust at left, memorial stone at right

Date	Mintage	F	VF	XF	Unc	BU
2009 Proof	—	Value: 45.00				

KM# 320   10 DINERS
28.2800 g., 0.9250 Silver 0.8410 oz. ASW, 38.6 mm. **Subject:** Chopin **Rev:** Portrait pair in ovals, Mallorca

Date	Mintage	F	VF	XF	Unc	BU
2009 Proof	—	Value: 45.00				

KM# 322   10 DINERS
28.2800 g., 0.9250 Silver partially gilt 0.8410 oz. ASW, 38.61 mm. **Subject:** Chopin **Rev:** Chopin at piano left, Gilt profile head at right

Date	Mintage	F	VF	XF	Unc	BU
2009 Proof	—	Value: 45.00				

KM# 323   10 DINERS
28.2800 g., 0.9250 Silver 0.8410 oz. ASW, 38.61 mm. **Subject:** Chopin **Rev:** Two portraits, one in color - Wausau

Date	Mintage	F	VF	XF	Unc	BU
2009 Proof	—	Value: 45.00				

KM# 283   10 DINERS
28.2800 g., 0.9250 Silver 0.8410 oz. ASW, 40x28 mm. **Subject:** Albrecht Durer **Obv:** Adama dn even engraving and shield **Rev:** Durer's Adoration of the Holy Trinity

Date	Mintage	F	VF	XF	Unc	BU
2010 Proof	15,000	Value: 50.00				

KM# 284   10 DINERS
28.2800 g., 0.9250 Silver 0.8410 oz. ASW, 38.61 mm. **Obv:** Shield **Rev:** St. Christopher

Date	Mintage	F	VF	XF	Unc	BU
2010 Proof	5,000	Value: 65.00				

KM# 285   10 DINERS
28.2800 g., 0.9250 Silver 0.8410 oz. ASW, 38.61 mm. **Obv:** Shield **Rev:** St. George **Edge:** Reeded

Date	Mintage	F	VF	XF	Unc	BU
2010 Proof	5,000	Value: 65.00				

KM# 286   10 DINERS
28.2800 g., 0.9250 Silver 0.8410 oz. ASW, 38.61 mm. **Obv:** Shield **Rev:** St. Catherine **Edge:** Reeded

Date	Mintage	F	VF	XF	Unc	BU
2010 Proof	5,000	Value: 65.00				

KM# 287   10 DINERS
28.2800 g., 0.9250 Silver 0.8410 oz. ASW, 38.61 mm. **Obv:** Shield **Rev:** St. Barbara **Edge:** Reeded

Date	Mintage	F	VF	XF	Unc	BU
2010 Proof	5,000	Value: 65.00				

KM# 174   25 DINERS
12.4414 g., 0.9990 Gold 0.3996 oz. AGW, 26 mm. **Subject:** Christmas **Obv:** National arms **Rev:** Nativity scene **Edge:** Reeded

Date	Mintage	F	VF	XF	Unc	BU
2001 Proof	3,000	Value: 725				

KM# 184   25 DINERS
10.0000 g., 0.9999 Gold 0.3215 oz. AGW, 26 mm.   **Subject:**
Christmas **Obv:** National arms **Rev:** Standing Christ child **Edge:**
Reeded

Date	Mintage	F	VF	XF	Unc	BU
2002 Proof	2,000	Value: 625				

KM# 185   25 DINERS
7.7759 g., 0.9990 Gold 0.2497 oz. AGW, 26 mm.   **Subject:**
Christmas **Obv:** National arms **Rev:** Madonna-like mother and
child **Edge:** Reeded

Date	Mintage	F	VF	XF	Unc	BU
2003 Proof	3,000	Value: 450				

KM# 197   25 DINERS
8.0000 g., 0.9990 Gold 0.2569 oz. AGW, 26 mm.   **Subject:**
Christmas **Obv:** National arms **Rev:** Nativity scene **Edge:**
Reeded

Date	Mintage	F	VF	XF	Unc	BU
2004 Proof	5,000	Value: 450				

KM# 216   25 DINERS
6.0000 g., 0.9999 Gold 0.1929 oz. AGW, 26 mm.   **Obv:** National
arms **Rev:** St. Joseph holding infant Jesus **Edge:** Reeded

Date	Mintage	F	VF	XF	Unc	BU
2005 Proof	9,999	Value: 375				

KM# 305   25 DINERS
6.0000 g., 0.9990 Gold 0.1927 oz. AGW, 26 mm.   **Subject:**
Christmas - the Holy Family **Obv:** National Arms **Rev:** St. Joseph,
Mary and Jesus

Date	Mintage	F	VF	XF	Unc	BU
2006 Proof	5,000	Value: 575				

KM# 314   25 DINERS
6.0000 g., 0.9990 Gold 0.1927 oz. AGW, 26 mm.   **Subject:**
Christmas **Obv:** National Arms **Rev:** Angels playing musical
instruments

Date	Mintage	F	VF	XF	Unc	BU
2007 Proof	2,000	Value: 575				

KM# 274   25 DINERS
6.0000 g., 0.9990 Gold 0.1927 oz. AGW, 26 mm.   **Subject:**
Constitution

Date	Mintage	F	VF	XF	Unc	BU
2008 Proof	2,000	Value: 375				

KM# 275   25 DINERS
6.0000 g., 0.9990 Gold 0.1927 oz. AGW, 26 mm.   **Subject:**
Three Kings **Rev:** Magi following star

Date	Mintage	F	VF	XF	Unc	BU
2008 Proof	2,000	Value: 375				

KM# 279   25 DINERS
6.0000 g., 0.9990 Gold 0.1927 oz. AGW, 26 mm.   **Obv:** Shield
Rev: Madonna and child, star of Bethlehem in backgorund **Edge:**
Reeded

Date	Mintage	F	VF	XF	Unc	BU
2009 Proof	1,200	Value: 375				

KM# 288   25 DINERS
6.0000 g., 0.9990 Gold 0.1927 oz. AGW, 26 mm.   **Subject:**
Christmas **Obv:** Shield **Rev:** Archangel Gabriel telling the good
news to Mary

Date	Mintage	F	VF	XF	Unc	BU
2010 Proof	1,200	Value: 375				

KM# 186   50 DINERS
159.5000 g., 0.9990 Bi-Metallic .999 Silver 155.5g coin with .999
Gold 4g, 20x50mm insert 5.1227 oz., 65 mm.   **Subject:** 10th
Anniversary of Constitution **Obv:** National arms **Rev:** Seated
allegorical woman holding scrolled constitution **Edge:** Reeded
Note: Illustration reduced.

Date	Mintage	F	VF	XF	Unc	BU
2003	3,000	—	—	—	325	375

BULLION COINAGE

KM# 268   DINER
31.1050 g., 0.9990 Silver 0.9990 oz. ASW, 38.6 mm.   **Obv:**
Eagle with wings outstretched **Rev:** National Arms **Edge:** Reeded

Date	Mintage	F	VF	XF	Unc	BU
2008	—	—	—	—	—	37.50
2009	—	—	—	—	—	37.50
2010	—	—	—	—	—	37.50
2011	—	—	—	—	—	37.50

KM# 257   5 DINERS
1.5500 g., 0.9990 Gold 0.0498 oz. AGW, 13.92 mm.   **Obv:** Eagle
with wings outstretched **Rev:** National Arms

Date	Mintage	F	VF	XF	Unc	BU
2009	—	—	—	—	—	95.00
2010	—	—	—	—	—	95.00

KM# 258   10 DINERS
3.1100 g., 0.9990 Gold 0.0999 oz. AGW, 16.46 mm.   **Obv:** Eagle
with wings outstretched **Rev:** National Arms

Date	Mintage	F	VF	XF	Unc	BU
2009	—	—	—	—	—	180
2010	—	—	—	—	—	180

KM# 259   25 DINERS
7.7700 g., 0.9990 Gold 0.2496 oz. AGW, 22.5 mm.   **Obv:** Eagle
with wings outstretched **Rev:** National Arms

Date	Mintage	F	VF	XF	Unc	BU
2009	—	—	—	—	—	450
2010	—	—	—	—	—	450

KM# 260   50 DINERS
15.5500 g., 0.9990 Gold 0.4994 oz. AGW, 26 mm.   **Obv:** Eagle
with wings outstretched **Rev:** National Arms

Date	Mintage	F	VF	XF	Unc	BU
2009	—	—	—	—	—	875
2010	—	—	—	—	—	875

KM# 254   50 DINERS
1000.0000 g., 0.9990 Silver 32.117 oz. ASW, 100 mm.   **Obv:**
Eagle with wings outstretched **Rev:** National Arms

Date	Mintage	F	VF	XF	Unc	BU
2010	—	—	—	—	—	1,200

KM# 298   100 DINERS
31.1035 g., 0.9990 Gold 0.9990 oz. AGW, 35 mm. **Obv:** Eagle with open wings **Rev:** Details of National Arms **Edge:** Reeded

Date	Mintage	F	VF	XF	Unc	BU
2006	1,500	—	—	—	—	2,000

KM# 261   100 DINERS
31.1050 g., 0.9990 Gold 0.9990 oz. AGW, 33 mm. **Obv:** Eagle with wings outstretched **Rev:** National Arms

Date	Mintage	F	VF	XF	Unc	BU
2009	—	—	—	—	—	1,700
2010	—	—	—	—	—	1,700

KM# 255   100 DINERS
3110.5000 g., 0.9990 Silver 99.900 oz. ASW, 120 mm. **Obv:** Eagle with wings outstretched **Rev:** National Arms **Note:** 29mm thick

Date	Mintage	F	VF	XF	Unc	BU
2010	—	—	—	—	—	5,000

KM# 256   200 DINERS
6221.0000 g., 0.9990 Silver 199.80 oz. ASW, 140 mm. **Obv:** Eagle with wings outstretched **Rev:** National Arms **Note:** 42mm thick

Date	Mintage	F	VF	XF	Unc	BU
2010	—	—	—	—	—	10,000

ARGENTINA

The Argentine Republic, located in southern South America, has an area of 1,073,518 sq. mi. (3,761,274 sq. km.) and an estimated population of 37.03 million. Capital: Buenos Aires. Its varied topography ranges from the subtropical lowlands of the north to the towering Andean Mountains in the west and the wind-swept Patagonian steppe in the south. The rolling, fertile pampas of central Argentina are ideal for agriculture and grazing, and support most of the republic's population. Meatpacking, flour milling, textiles, sugar refining and dairy products are the principal industries. Oil is found in Patagonia, but most mineral requirements must be imported.

Internal conflict through the first half century of Argentine independence resulted in a provisional national coinage, chiefly of crown-sized silver. Provincial issues mainly of minor denominations supplemented this.

REPUBLIC

REFORM COINAGE
1992; 100 Centavos = 1 Peso

KM# 109   5 CENTAVOS
2.0200 g., Aluminum-Bronze, 17.2 mm. **Obv:** Radiant sunface **Rev:** Large value, date below **Edge:** Reeded **Note:** Prev. KM#84.

Date	Mintage	F	VF	XF	Unc	BU
2004	30,000,000	—	—	—	0.45	0.60
2005	76,000,000	—	—	—	0.45	0.60

KM# 109b   5 CENTAVOS
2.0000 g., Brass Plated Steel, 17.2 mm. **Obv:** Radiant Sunface **Rev:** Large value, date below **Edge:** Plain

Date	Mintage	F	VF	XF	Unc	BU
2006	23,800,000	—	—	—	0.45	0.60
2007	183,000,000	—	—	—	0.45	0.60
2008	114,000,000	—	—	—	0.45	0.60
2009	—	—	—	—	0.45	0.60
2010	—	—	—	—	0.45	0.60

KM# 107   10 CENTAVOS
2.2500 g., Aluminum-Bronze, 18.2 mm. **Obv:** Argentine arms **Rev:** Value, date below **Edge:** Reeded **Note:** Prev. KM#82.

Date	Mintage	F	VF	XF	Unc	BU
2004	190,000,000	—	—	—	0.65	0.85
2005	114,400,000	—	—	—	0.65	0.85

KM# 107a   10 CENTAVOS
2.2000 g., Brass Plated Steel, 18.2 mm. **Obv:** Argentine arms **Rev:** Large value, date below **Edge:** Plain

Date	Mintage	F	VF	XF	Unc	BU
2006	99,600,000	—	—	—	0.65	0.85
2007	204,000,000	—	—	—	0.65	0.85
2008	317,000,000	—	—	—	0.65	0.85
2009	—	—	—	—	0.65	0.85
2010	—	—	—	—	0.65	0.85

KM# 110.1   25 CENTAVOS
5.4000 g., Aluminum-Bronze, 24.2 mm. **Obv:** Buenos Aires City Hall, fine lettering **Rev:** Large value, date below **Edge:** Reeded **Note:** Prev. KM#85.1.

Date	Mintage	F	VF	XF	Unc	BU
2009	—	—	—	—	1.25	1.50
2010	—	—	—	—	1.25	1.50

KM# 110a   25 CENTAVOS
6.1000 g., Copper-Nickel, 24.2 mm. **Obv:** Buenos Aires City Hall, bold lettering **Rev:** Large value, date below **Edge:** Reeded **Note:** Prev. KM#85a.

Date	Mintage	F	VF	XF	Unc	BU
2009	—	—	—	—	1.25	1.50

KM# 111.1   50 CENTAVOS
5.8000 g., Aluminum-Bronze, 25.2 mm. **Obv:** Tucuman Province Capital Building; fine lettering **Rev:** Large value, date below **Edge:** Reeded **Note:** Prev. KM#86.1.

Date	Mintage	F	VF	XF	Unc	BU
2009	—	—	—	—	1.75	2.00
2010	—	—	—	—	1.75	2.00

KM# 111.2   50 CENTAVOS
5.8000 g., Aluminum-Bronze, 25.2 mm. **Obv:** Tucuman Province Capital Building; bold lettering **Rev:** Large value, date below **Edge:** Reeded **Note:** Prev. KM#86.2.

Date	Mintage	F	VF	XF	Unc	BU
2009	—	—	—	—	1.75	2.00

KM# 132.1   PESO
6.3500 g., Bi-Metallic Aluninum-Bronze center in Copper-Nickel ring, 23 mm. **Subject:** General Urquiza **Obv:** Stylized portrait facing **Rev:** Church tower and denomination **Edge:** Reeded

Date	Mintage	F	VF	XF	Unc	BU
2001	995,000	—	—	—	3.75	4.50

KM# 132.2   PESO
6.3500 g., Bi-Metallic Aluminum-Bronze center in Copper-Nickel ring, 23 mm. **Subject:** General Urquiza **Obv:** Stylized portrait facing **Rev:** Church tower and denomination **Edge:** Plain

Date	Mintage	F	VF	XF	Unc	BU
2001	5,000	—	—	—	7.50	8.00

KM# 141   PESO
25.0000 g., 0.9000 Silver 0.7234 oz. ASW, 37 mm. **Obv:** Maria Eva Duarte de Peron **Rev:** "EVITA" audience **Edge:** Reeded

Date	Mintage	F	VF	XF	Unc	BU
ND (2004) Proof	5,000	Value: 45.00				

KM# 140   PESO
25.0000 g., 0.9000 Silver 0.7234 oz. ASW, 37 mm.   **Subject:**
70th Anniversary of Central Bank **Obv:** Bank building **Rev:** Liberty
head in wreath **Edge:** Reeded

Date	Mintage	F	VF	XF	Unc	BU
2005 Proof	2,000	Value: 50.00				

KM# 155   PESO
25.0000 g., 0.9000 Silver 0.7234 oz. ASW, 37 mm.   **Subject:**
Jorge Luis Borges **Obv:** Stylized bust facing **Rev:** Man walking
at street corner

Date	Mintage	F	VF	XF	Unc	BU
2006A	—	—	—	—	—	42.50

KM# 112.1   PESO
6.3500 g., Bi-Metallic Aluminum-Bronze center in Copper-Nickel
ring, 23 mm.   **Obv:** Argentine arms in circle **Rev:** Design of first
Argentine coin in center **Edge:** Plain **Note:** Prev. KM#87.1.

Date	Mintage	F	VF	XF	Unc	BU
2006	30,000,000	—	—	0.50	1.20	1.60
2007	33,000,000	—	—	0.50	1.20	1.60
2008	89,600,000	—	—	0.50	1.20	1.60
2009 D	—	—	—	0.50	1.20	1.60
2010 E	—	—	—	0.50	1.20	1.60

KM# 153   PESO
25.0000 g., 0.9000 Silver 0.7234 oz. ASW, 37 mm.   **Subject:**
25th Anniversary Malvinas Islands Occupation - Heroes **Obv:**
Soldier's bust facing **Obv. Legend:** REPUBLICA ARGENTINA -
1982 - 2007 - LA NACIÓN A SUS HÉROES **Rev:** Outlined map
of islands **Rev. Legend:** MALVINAS ARGENTINAS **Rev.
Inscription:** 2 DE APRIL / 1982 **Edge:** Reeded

Date	Mintage	F	VF	XF	Unc	BU
2007 Proof	3,000	Value: 75.00				

KM# 156   PESO
6.3500 g., Bi-Metallic Aluminum-Bronze center in Copper-Nickel
ring, 23 mm.   **Subject:** Bicentennial - El Palmar **Obv:** Stylized
radiant sun **Rev:** Palm trees

Date	Mintage	F	VF	XF	Unc	BU
2010	—	—	—	—	1.20	1.60

KM# 157   PESO
6.3500 g., Bi-Metallic Aluminum-Bronze center in Copper-Nickel

ring, 23 mm.   **Subject:** Bicentennial - Aconcagua **Obv:** Stylized
radiant run **Rev:** Mountains

Date	Mintage	F	VF	XF	Unc	BU
2010	—	—	—	—	1.20	1.60

KM# 158   PESO
6.3500 g., Bi-Metallic Aluminum-Bronze center in Copper-Nickel
ring, 23 mm.   **Subject:** Bicentennial - Mar del Plata **Obv:** Stylized
radiant sun **Rev:** Elephant seal and fishing boat

Date	Mintage	F	VF	XF	Unc	BU
2010	—	—	—	—	1.20	1.60

KM# 159   PESO
6.3500 g., Bi-Metallic Aluminum-Bronze center in Copper-Nickel
ring, 23 mm.   **Subject:** Bicentennial - Pucara de Tilcara **Obv:**
Stylized radiant sun **Rev:** Cactus and mountains

Date	Mintage	F	VF	XF	Unc	BU
2010	—	—	—	—	1.20	1.60

KM# 160   PESO
6.3500 g., Bi-Metallic Aluminum-Bronze center in Copper-Nickel
ring, 23 mm.   **Subject:** Bicentennial - Glaciar Perito Moreno **Obv:**
Stylized radiant sun **Rev:** Glaciar ice bridge and sea

Date	Mintage	F	VF	XF	Unc	BU
2010	—	—	—	—	1.20	1.60

KM# 135.1   2 PESOS
10.4000 g., Copper-Nickel, 30 mm.   **Subject:** Eva Peron **Obv:**
Head left **Rev:** Stylized crowd scene, value **Rev. Inscription:**
EVITA **Edge:** Reeded

Date	Mintage	F	VF	XF	Unc	BU
2002	1,995,000	—	—	0.85	1.85	2.50

KM# 135.2   2 PESOS
10.4000 g., Copper-Nickel, 30 mm.   **Subject:** Eva Peron **Obv:**
Head left **Rev:** Stylized crowd scene, value **Rev. Inscription:**
EVITA **Edge:** Plain

Date	Mintage	F	VF	XF	Unc	BU
2002	5,000	—	—	—	6.00	8.00

KM# 161   2 PESOS
10.4700 g., Copper-Nickel, 30.35 mm.   **Subject:** Declaration of
Human Rights **Obv:** Legend **Rev:** Female's scarf

Date	Mintage	F	VF	XF	Unc	BU
2006	—	—	—	—	1.85	2.50

KM# 144.1   2 PESOS
10.4000 g., Copper-Nickel, 30 mm.   **Subject:** Malvinas Islands
War, 25th Anniversary **Obv:** Soldier's bust facing **Obv. Legend:**
REPUBLICA ARGENTINA - 1982 - 2007 - LA NACIÓN A SUS
HÉROES **Rev:** Outlined map of islands **Rev. Legend:**
MALVINAS ARGENTINAS **Rev. Inscription:** 2 DE APRIL / 1982
Edge: Reeded

Date	Mintage	F	VF	XF	Unc	BU
2007	1,995,000	—	—	0.85	1.85	2.50

KM# 144.2   2 PESOS
10.4000 g., Copper-Nickel, 30 mm.   **Subject:** Malvinas Islands
War, 25th Anniversary **Obv:** Soldier's bust facing **Obv. Legend:**
REPUBLICA ARGENTINA - 1982 - 2007 - LA NACIÓN A SUS
HÉROES **Rev:** Outlined map of islands **Rev. Legend:**
MALVINAS ARGENTINAS **Rev. Inscription:** 2 DE APRIL / 1982
Edge: Plain

Date	Mintage	F	VF	XF	Unc	BU
2007	5,000	—	—	—	—	9.00

KM# 145   2 PESOS
Copper-Nickel, 30.35 mm.   **Subject:** 100th Anniversary First Oil
Well **Obv:** Oil well **Obv. Legend:** REPÚBLICA ARGENTINA -
DESCUBRIMIENTO DEL PETRÓLEO **Rev:** Modern pump **Rev.
Inscription:** CHUBUT **Edge:** Reeded

Date	Mintage	F	VF	XF	Unc	BU
2007	995,000	—	—	—	6.00	8.00

KM# 162   2 PESOS
10.4700 g., Copper-Nickel, 30.35 mm.   **Subject:** Central Bank,
75th Anniversary **Obv:** Head at right, facing left **Rev:** Bank's main
doors

Date	Mintage	F	VF	XF	Unc	BU
2010	—	—	—	—	1.85	2.50

KM# 133   5 PESOS
8.0640 g., 0.9000 Gold 0.2333 oz. AGW, 22 mm.   **Subject:** Gral.
Justo Jose de Urquiza **Obv:** Stylized portrait facing **Rev:** Church
tower and denomination **Edge:** Reeded

Date	Mintage	F	VF	XF	Unc	BU
2001 Proof	1,000	Value: 400				

KM# 149   5 PESOS
8.0640 g., 0.9000 Gold 0.2333 oz. AGW   **Subject:** 100th
Anniversary City of Comodoro Rivadavia

Date	Mintage	F	VF	XF	Unc	BU
2001 Proof	750	Value: 425				

KM# 143 5 PESOS
27.0000 g., 0.9250 Silver 0.8029 oz. ASW, 40 mm. **Subject:** FIFA
- XVIII World Championship Football - Germany 2006 **Obv:** Football
at right on grass, chaff in background **Obv. Legend:** REPÚBLICA
ARGENTINA **Rev:** Logo **Rev. Legend:** COPA MUNDIAL DE LA
FIFA **Rev. Inscription:** ALEMANIA **Edge:** Reeded

Date	Mintage	F	VF	XF	Unc	BU
2003 Proof	50,000	Value: 55.00				

KM# 146 5 PESOS
27.0000 g., 0.9250 Silver 0.8029 oz. ASW **Subject:** FIFA - XVIII
World Football Championship - Germany 2006 **Obv. Legend:**
REPÚBLICA ARGENTINA **Rev:** Logo **Edge:** Reeded

Date	Mintage	F	VF	XF	Unc	BU
2004 Proof	50,000	Value: 55.00				

KM# 142 5 PESOS
8.0640 g., 0.9000 Gold 0.2333 oz. AGW, 22 mm. **Obv:** Maria
Eva Duarte de Peron **Rev:** "EVITA" and audience

Date	Mintage	F	VF	XF	Unc	BU
ND (2004) Proof	1,000	Value: 400				

KM# 150 5 PESOS
27.0000 g., 0.9250 Silver 0.8029 oz. ASW **Subject:** FIFA - XVIII
World Championship Football - Germany 2006 **Obv:** Forward
player **Rev:** Logo

Date	Mintage	F	VF	XF	Unc	BU
2005 Proof	—	Value: 65.00				

KM# 154 5 PESOS
8.0640 g., 0.9000 Gold 0.2333 oz. AGW, 22 mm. **Subject:** 25th
Anniversary Malvinas Islands Occupation - Heroes **Obv:**
Soldier's bust facing **Obv. Legend:** REPUBLICA ARGENTINA -
1982 - 2007 - LA NACIÓN A SUS HÉROES **Rev:** Outlined map
of islands **Rev. Legend:** MALVINAS ISLANDS **Rev. Inscription:**
2 DE APRIL / 1982 **Edge:** Reeded

Date	Mintage	F	VF	XF	Unc	BU
2007 Proof	1,000	Value: 450				

KM# 147 10 PESOS
6.7500 g., 0.9990 Gold 0.2168 oz. AGW **Subject:** FIFA - XVIII
World Football Championship - Germany 2006 **Obv. Legend:**
REPÚBLICA ARGENTINA **Edge:** Reeded

Date	Mintage	F	VF	XF	Unc	BU
2004 Proof	25,000	Value: 400				

KM# 151 10 PESOS
6.7500 g., 0.9990 Gold 0.2168 oz. AGW **Subject:** FIFA - XVIII
World Championship Football - Germany 2006 **Obv:** Forward
player **Rev:** Logo

Date	Mintage	F	VF	XF	Unc	BU
2005 Proof	—	Value: 400				

KM# 138 25 PESOS
27.0000 g., 0.9250 Silver 0.8029 oz. ASW, 40 mm. **Subject:**
IBERO-AMERICA Series **Obv:** Coats of arms **Rev:** Tall ship
"Presidente Sarmiento" **Edge:** Reeded

Date	Mintage	F	VF	XF	Unc	BU
2002 Proof	—	Value: 60.00				

KM# 139 25 PESOS
27.0000 g., 0.9250 Silver 0.8029 oz. ASW, 40 mm. **Subject:**
Ibero-America **Obv:** National arms in circle of arms **Rev:** Colon
Theater building **Edge:** Reeded

Date	Mintage	F	VF	XF	Unc	BU
2005 Proof	15,500	Value: 55.00				

PROOF SETS

KM#	Date	Mintage	Identification	Issue Price	Mkt Val
PS6	2007 (2)	300	KM#153, 154	475	485

The Republic of Armenia, formerly Armenian S.S.R., is bordered to the north by Georgia, the east by Azerbaijan and the
south and west by Turkey and Iran. It has an area of 11,506 sq.
mi. (29,800 sq. km) and an estimated population of 3.66 million.
Capital: Yerevan. Agriculture including cotton, vineyards and
orchards, hydroelectricity, chemicals - primarily synthetic rubber
and fertilizers, vast mineral deposits of copper, zinc and aluminum, and production of steel and paper are major industries.

Fighting between Christians in Armenia and Muslim forces of
Azerbaijan escalated in 1992 and continued through early 1994.
Each country claimed the Nagorno-Karabakh, an Armenian ethnic enclave, in Azerbaijan. A temporary cease-fire was
announced in May 1994.

MONETARY SYSTEM
100 Luma = 1 Dram

MINT NAME
Revan, (Erevan, now Yerevan)

REPUBLIC
STANDARD COINAGE

KM# 112 10 DRAM
1.3000 g., Aluminum, 20 mm. **Obv:** National arms **Rev:** Value
Edge: Plain

Date	Mintage	F	VF	XF	Unc	BU
2004	—	—	—	—	1.00	1.50

KM# 93 20 DRAM
2.7500 g., Copper Plated Steel, 20.5 mm. **Obv:** National arms
Rev: Denomination **Edge:** Plain

Date	Mintage	F	VF	XF	Unc	BU
2003	—	—	—	—	1.00	1.50
2005	—	—	—	—	1.00	1.50

KM# 94 50 DRAM
3.5000 g., Brass Plated Steel, 21.5 mm. **Obv:** National arms
Rev: Value **Edge:** Reeded

Date	Mintage	F	VF	XF	Unc	BU
2003	—	—	—	—	1.25	1.50

KM# 86 100 DRAM
31.1000 g., 0.9990 Silver 0.9988 oz. ASW, 38 mm. **Obv:**

National arms **Rev:** Bust of General Garegin Nzhdeh facing at right **Edge:** Plain **Edge Lettering:** Serial number

Date	Mintage	F	VF	XF	Unc	BU
2001 Proof	170	Value: 1,000				

KM# 86a   100 DRAM
31.1000 g., 0.9990 Silver Gilt 0.9988 oz. ASW, 38 mm. **Obv:** National arms **Obv. Inscription:** Bust of General Garegin Nzhdeh facing at right **Edge:** Plain **Edge Lettering:** Serial number

Date	Mintage	F	VF	XF	Unc	BU
2001 Proof	30	Value: 3,000				

KM# 87   100 DRAM
31.0400 g., 0.9990 Silver 0.9969 oz. ASW, 38 mm. **Subject:** Armenian Membership in the Council of Europe joined January 1, 2001 **Obv:** National arms **Rev:** Spiral design with star circle **Edge:** Plain **Edge Lettering:** Serial number

Date	Mintage	F	VF	XF	Unc	BU
2001 Proof	200	Value: 300				

KM# 98   100 DRAM
31.1000 g., 0.9250 Silver 0.9249 oz. ASW, 40 mm. **Obv:** National arms **Rev:** Aram Khachatryan, Birth Centennial **Edge:** Reeded

Date	Mintage	F	VF	XF	Unc	BU
2002	300	—	—	—	65.00	100

KM# 99   100 DRAM
31.1000 g., 0.9250 Silver 0.9249 oz. ASW, 40 mm. **Obv:** The Book of Sadness **Rev:** Saint Grigor Narekatsi with book and quill millennium of his poem "The Book of Sadness" **Edge:** Reeded

Date	Mintage	F	VF	XF	Unc	BU
2002 Proof	500	Value: 100				

KM# 110   100 DRAM
33.9200 g., 0.9250 Silver 1.0087 oz. ASW, 39 mm. **Subject:** 110th Anniversary of State Banking in Armenia and 10th Year of National Currency October 7 1893 - November 22, 1993 **Obv:** Building above value **Rev:** State Bank emblem **Edge:** Reeded

Date	Mintage	F	VF	XF	Unc	BU
2003 Proof	300	Value: 200				

KM# 95   100 DRAM
4.0000 g., Nickel Plated Steel, 22.5 mm. **Obv:** National arms **Rev:** Value **Edge:** Reeded

Date	Mintage	F	VF	XF	Unc	BU
2003	—	—	—	—	1.50	2.00

KM# 111   100 DRAM
28.2800 g., 0.9250 Silver 0.8410 oz. ASW, 38.6 mm. **Subject:** FIFA World Cup Soccer Games - Germany **Obv:** National arms **Rev:** Three soccer players

Date	Mintage	F	VF	XF	Unc	BU
2004 Proof	300	Value: 150				

KM# 113   100 DRAM
31.1000 g., 0.9990 Silver 0.9988 oz. ASW, 38 mm. **Subject:** Gandzasar Monastery **Obv:** Monastery **Rev:** Folk art crucifix and denomination

Date	Mintage	F	VF	XF	Unc	BU
2004 Proof	500	Value: 100				

KM# 115   100 DRAM
31.1000 g., 0.9250 Silver 0.9249 oz. ASW, 40 mm. **Subject:** Anania Shirakatsi 1400 Anniversary, Scientist **Obv:** Profile of Shirakatsi, deep in thought **Rev:** Planets and stars, denomination

Date	Mintage	F	VF	XF	Unc	BU
2005 Proof	500	Value: 100				

KM# 123   100 DRAM
31.1000 g., 0.9250 Silver 0.9249 oz. ASW, 40.00 mm. **Subject:** Creation of the Armenian alphabet **Obv:** National arms **Rev:** King Vramshapuh standing at left, alphabet at right

Date	Mintage	F	VF	XF	Unc	BU
2005 Proof	500	Value: 150				

KM# 124   100 DRAM
31.1000 g., 0.9250 Silver 0.9249 oz. ASW, 40.00 mm. **Subject:** Creation of the Armenian alphabet **Obv:** National arms **Rev:** Sahak Partev standing at left, alphabet at right

Date	Mintage	F	VF	XF	Unc	BU
2005 Proof	500	Value: 150				

KM# 125   100 DRAM
31.1000 g., 0.9250 Silver 0.9249 oz. ASW, 40.00 mm. **Subject:** 100th Anniversary - Birth of Artem Mikoyan - Inventor of MIG Jet **Obv:** Three jet airplanes **Rev:** Bust of Mikoyan 3/4 left

Date	Mintage	F	VF	XF	Unc	BU
2005 Proof	500	Value: 125				

KM# 127   100 DRAM
28.2800 g., 0.9250 Silver 0.8410 oz. ASW, 38.61 mm. **Subject:** International Polar Year **Obv:** National arms **Obv. Legend:** REPUBLIC OF ARMENIA **Rev:** Bust of Fridtjof Nansen right at left, ship stuck in ice at lower right, multicolor emblem above

Date	Mintage	F	VF	XF	Unc	BU
2006 Proof	10,000	Value: 100				

KM# 129   100 DRAM
28.2800 g., 0.9250 Silver 0.8410 oz. ASW **Subject:** Hovhannes Aivazovsky **Obv:** National arms at lower left, sailing ship listing at center right multicolor **Rev:** Bust of Aivazovsky 3/4 left at lower left, sailing ships at center right **Shape:** Rectangular, 40 x 28 mm

Date	Mintage	F	VF	XF	Unc	BU
2006 Proof	5,000	Value: 700				

KM# 119   100 DRAM
28.3500 g., 0.9250 Silver 0.8431 oz. ASW, 38.5 mm. **Obv:** National arms **Rev:** Brown bear and two red lines **Edge:** Plain

Date	Mintage	F	VF	XF	Unc	BU
2006 Proof	3,000	Value: 185				

KM# 120   100 DRAM
28.3500 g., 0.9250 Silver 0.8431 oz. ASW, 38.5 mm. **Obv:** National arms **Rev:** Long-eared Hedgehog and two red lines **Edge:** Plain

Date	Mintage	F	VF	XF	Unc	BU
2006 Proof	3,000	Value: 185				

KM# 121   100 DRAM
28.2800 g., 0.9250 Silver 0.8410 oz. ASW, 38.6 mm. **Obv:** National arms, date and value **Rev:** Caucasian Forest Cat **Edge:** Plain

Date	Mintage	F	VF	XF	Unc	BU
2006 Proof	3,000	Value: 100				

KM# 122   100 DRAM
28.2800 g., 0.9250 Silver 0.8410 oz. ASW, 38.6 mm. **Obv:** National arms, date and value **Rev:** Armenian Tortoise **Edge:** Plain

Date	Mintage	F	VF	XF	Unc	BU
2006 Proof	3,000	Value: 135				

KM# 135   100 DRAM
28.2400 g., 0.9250 Silver 0.8398 oz. ASW, 38.53 mm. **Subject:**
Caucasion Leopard **Obv:** National arms **Obv. Legend:**
REPUBLIC OF ARMENIA **Rev:** Leopard walking left **Edge:** Plain

Date	Mintage	F	VF	XF	Unc	BU
2007 Proof	3,000	Value: 110				

KM# 136   100 DRAM
28.2400 g., 0.9250 Silver 0.8398 oz. ASW, 38.5 mm. **Subject:**
Northern Shoveler duck **Obv:** National arms **Obv. Legend:**
REPUBLIC OF ARMENIA **Rev:** Duck standing left **Edge:** Plain

Date	Mintage	F	VF	XF	Unc	BU
2007 Proof	3,000	Value: 85.00				

KM# 141   100 DRAM
28.2800 g., 0.9250 Silver Zircon crystal attached. 0.8410 oz.
ASW, 38.5 mm. **Series:** Signs of the Zodiac **Obv:** National arms
within ring of signs of the Zodiac **Obv. Legend:** REPUBLIC OF
ARMENIA **Rev:** Capricorn with jeweled star at left, multicolor
Edge: Plain

Date	Mintage	F	VF	XF	Unc	BU
2007 Proof	12,000	Value: 85.00				

KM# 153   100 DRAM
28.2800 g., 0.9250 Silver 0.8410 oz. ASW, 38.6 mm. **Obv:**
National arms **Obv. Legend:** REPUBLIC OF ARMENIA **Rev:**
Lake Sevan Salmon

Date	Mintage	F	VF	XF	Unc	BU
2007 Proof	3,000	Value: 100				

KM# 154   100 DRAM
28.2800 g., 0.9250 Silver 0.8410 oz. ASW, 38.6 mm. **Obv:**
National arms **Obv. Legend:** REPUBLIC OF ARMENIA **Rev:**
Armenian viper

Date	Mintage	F	VF	XF	Unc	BU
2007 Proof	3,000	Value: 85.00				

KM# 157   100 DRAM
28.2800 g., 0.9250 Silver 0.8410 oz. ASW, 38.6 mm. **Subject:**
Aquarius

Date	Mintage	F	VF	XF	Unc	BU
2007 Proof	—	Value: 100				

KM# 158   100 DRAM
28.2800 g., 0.9250 Silver 0.8410 oz. ASW, 38.6 mm. **Subject:**
Pisces

Date	Mintage	F	VF	XF	Unc	BU
2007 Proof	—	Value: 100				

KM# 155   100 DRAM
28.2800 g., 0.9250 Silver 0.8410 oz. ASW, 39 mm. **Obv:**
National Arms **Rev:** Caucasian owl on branch, (Aegolius
Funereus Caucasious) red arcs at top and bottom

Date	Mintage	F	VF	XF	Unc	BU
2008 Proof	3,000	Value: 75.00				

KM# 159   100 DRAM
28.2800 g., 0.9250 Silver 0.8410 oz. ASW, 38.6 mm. **Subject:**
Aries

Date	Mintage	F	VF	XF	Unc	BU
2008 Proof	—	Value: 100				

KM# 160   100 DRAM
28.2800 g., 0.9250 Silver 0.8410 oz. ASW, 38.6 mm. **Subject:**
Taurus

Date	Mintage	F	VF	XF	Unc	BU
2008 Proof	—	Value: 100				

KM# 161   100 DRAM
28.2800 g., 0.9250 Silver 0.8410 oz. ASW, 38.6 mm. **Subject:**
Gemini

Date	Mintage	F	VF	XF	Unc	BU
2008 Proof	—	Value: 100				

KM# 162   100 DRAM
28.2800 g., 0.9250 Silver 0.8410 oz. ASW **Subject:** Cancer

Date	Mintage	F	VF	XF	Unc	BU
2008 Proof	—	Value: 100				

KM# 163   100 DRAM
28.2800 g., 0.9250 Silver 0.8410 oz. ASW, 38.6 mm. **Subject:**
Leo

Date	Mintage	F	VF	XF	Unc	BU
2008 Proof	—	Value: 100				

KM# 164   100 DRAM
28.2800 g., 0.9250 Silver 0.8410 oz. ASW, 38.6 mm. **Subject:**
Virgo

Date	Mintage	F	VF	XF	Unc	BU
2008 Proof	—	Value: 100				

KM# 165   100 DRAM
28.2800 g., 0.9250 Silver 0.8410 oz. ASW, 38.6 mm. **Subject:**
Libra

Date	Mintage	F	VF	XF	Unc	BU
2008 Proof	—	Value: 100				

KM# 167   100 DRAM
28.2800 g., 0.9250 Silver 0.8410 oz. ASW, 38.6 mm. **Subject:**
Bezoar

Date	Mintage	F	VF	XF	Unc	BU
2008 Proof	—	Value: 100				

KM# 172   100 DRAM
28.2800 g., 0.9250 Silver 0.8410 oz. ASW, 38.6 mm. **Subject:**
Scorpio

Date	Mintage	F	VF	XF	Unc	BU
2008 Proof	—	Value: 100				

KM# 174   100 DRAM
28.2800 g., 0.9250 Silver 0.8410 oz. ASW, 38.6 mm. **Subject:**
Sagittarius

Date	Mintage	F	VF	XF	Unc	BU
2008 Proof	—	Value: 100				

KM# 177   100 DRAM
28.2800 g., 0.9250 Silver 0.8410 oz. ASW, 38.6 mm. **Subject:**
Armenian Moufflon

Date	Mintage	F	VF	XF	Unc	BU
2008 Proof	—	Value: 75.00				

KM# 178   100 DRAM
28.2800 g., 0.9250 Silver 0.8410 oz. ASW, 38.6 mm. **Subject:**
Toad Agama

Date	Mintage	F	VF	XF	Unc	BU
2008 Proof	—	Value: 75.00				

KM# 182   100 DRAM
28.2800 g., 0.9250 Silver 0.8410 oz. ASW, 38.6 mm. **Subject:**
Pele

Date	Mintage	F	VF	XF	Unc	BU
2008 Proof	—	Value: 60.00				

KM# 183   100 DRAM
28.2800 g., 0.9250 Silver 0.8410 oz. ASW, 38.6 mm. **Subject:**
Eusebio

Date	Mintage	F	VF	XF	Unc	BU
2008 Proof	—	Value: 60.00				

KM# 184   100 DRAM
28.2800 g., 0.9250 Silver 0.8410 oz. ASW, 38.6 mm. **Subject:**
Lev Jashin

Date	Mintage	F	VF	XF	Unc	BU
2008 Proof	—	Value: 60.00				

KM# 187   100 DRAM
28.2800 g., 0.9250 Silver 0.8410 oz. ASW, 38.6 mm. **Subject:** Franz Beckenbauer

Date	Mintage	F	VF	XF	Unc	BU
2008 Proof	—	Value: 60.00				

KM# 156   100 DRAM
28.2800 g., 0.9250 Silver 0.8410 oz. ASW, 38.6 mm. **Subject:** Zbigniew Boniek **Rev:** Portrait facing, multicolor flag

Date	Mintage	F	VF	XF	Unc	BU
2009 Proof	50,000	Value: 85.00				

KM# 96   200 DRAM
4.5000 g., Brass, 24 mm. **Obv:** National arms **Rev:** Value **Edge:** Reeded

Date	Mintage	F	VF	XF	Unc	BU
2003	—	—	—	—	3.00	4.00

KM# 106   500 DRAM
155.5000 g., 0.9250 Silver 4.6243 oz. ASW, 63 mm. **Subject:** 10th Anniversary of Independence **Obv:** National arms **Rev:** Tower with flag, logo at right 9-21-91

Date	Mintage	F	VF	XF	Unc	BU
2001 Proof	200	Value: 400				

KM# 97   500 DRAM
5.0000 g., Bi-Metallic Copper-Nickel center in a Brass ring, 22 mm. **Obv:** National arms **Rev:** Value **Edge:** Segmented reeding

Date	Mintage	F	VF	XF	Unc	BU
2003	—	—	—	—	6.00	8.00

KM# 109   1000 DRAM
15.5500 g., 0.5850 Gold 0.2925 oz. AGW, 26 mm. **Obv:** National arms on ancient coin design **Rev:** Tigran the Great ancient coin portrait

Date	Mintage	F	VF	XF	Unc	BU
2003	500	—	—	—	785	1,200

KM# 128   1000 DRAM
33.6000 g., 0.9250 Silver 0.9992 oz. ASW, 38 mm. **Subject:** 100th Anniversary Birth of Marshal Babajanian **Obv:** National arms **Rev:** Bust of Babajanian 3/4 right

Date	Mintage	F	VF	XF	Unc	BU
2006 Proof	500	Value: 150				

KM# 133   1000 DRAM
33.6000 g., 0.9250 Silver 0.9992 oz. ASW, 40 mm. **Subject:** Armenian grapes **Obv:** National arms **Rev:** Large bunch of grapes at left

Date	Mintage	F	VF	XF	Unc	BU
2007 Proof	5,000	Value: 150				

KM# 169   1000 DRAM
33.6000 g., 0.9250 Silver 0.9992 oz. ASW, 40 mm. **Subject:** Viktor Ambartsumian, 100th Anniversary of Birth **Edge:** Reeded

Date	Mintage	F	VF	XF	Unc	BU
2008 Proof	500	Value: 100				

KM# 171   1000 DRAM
33.6000 g., 0.9250 Silver 0.9992 oz. ASW, 40 mm. **Subject:** A. Spendiaryan Theater of Ballet and Opera, 75th Anniversary

Date	Mintage	F	VF	XF	Unc	BU
2008 Proof	—	Value: 100				

KM# 192   1000 DRAM
33.6000 g., 0.9250 Silver 0.9992 oz. ASW, 40 mm. **Subject:** Mkhitar Gosh - The Codex **Edge:** Reeded

Date	Mintage	F	VF	XF	Unc	BU
2009 Proof	500	Value: 55.00				

KM# 193   1000 DRAM
31.1000 g., 0.9990 Silver 0.9988 oz. ASW, 38 mm. **Subject:** Gladzor University, 750th Anniversary

Date	Mintage	F	VF	XF	Unc	BU
2009 Proof	—	Value: 55.00				

KM# 199   1000 DRAM
33.6000 g., 0.9250 Silver 0.9992 oz. ASW, 40 mm. **Rev:** Poppy plant and flower in color

Date	Mintage	F	VF	XF	Unc	BU
2011 Proof	—	Value: 75.00				

KM# 134   1957 DRAM
33.6000 g., 0.9250 Silver 0.9992 oz. ASW, 40 mm. **Subject:** 50th Anniversary of Matenadaran **Obv:** Small national arms at center surrounded by intricate pattern **Rev:** Building at left center

Date	Mintage	F	VF	XF	Unc	BU
2007 Proof	500	Value: 125				

KM# 117   5000 DRAM
31.1000 g., 0.9250 Silver 0.9249 oz. ASW, 38 mm. **Subject:** Armenian Armed Forces **Obv:** Order of the Combat Cross of the Second Degree and the Emblem of the Ministry of Defense of the Republic of Armenia **Rev:** Arms, date and denomination **Shape:** Octagonal

Date	Mintage	F	VF	XF	Unc	BU
2005 Proof	500	Value: 130				

KM# 126   5000 DRAM
168.1000 g., 0.9250 Silver 4.9990 oz. ASW, 63 mm. **Subject:** 15th Anniversary of Independence **Obv:** National arms **Rev:** Building at center left, multicolor emblem above, mountains in background

Date	Mintage	F	VF	XF	Unc	BU
2006 Proof	300	Value: 400				

KM# 139   5000 DRAM
4.3000 g., 0.9000 Gold 0.1244 oz. AGW, 18 mm. **Subject:** Haik Nahapet **Obv:** Small national arms at upper left, Orion constellation at right **Rev:** 3/4 length classical Archer right

Date	Mintage	F	VF	XF	Unc	BU
2007 Proof	3,000	Value: 400				

KM# 179   5000 DRAM
168.1000 g., 0.9250 Silver partially gold plated 4.9990 oz. ASW, 63 mm. **Subject:** National Currency, 15th Anniversary

Date	Mintage	F	VF	XF	Unc	BU
2008 Proof	—	Value: 150				

KM# 195   5000 DRAM
4.3000 g., 0.9000 Gold 0.1244 oz. AGW, 18 mm. **Subject:** St. Sargis the Commander

Date	Mintage	F	VF	XF	Unc	BU
2009 Proof	—	Value: 225				

KM# 107   10000 DRAM
8.6000 g., 0.9990 Gold 0.2762 oz. AGW, 22 mm. **Obv:** Mesrop Mashtots, creator of the Armenian alphabet **Rev:** Armenian alphabet

Date	Mintage	F	VF	XF	Unc	BU
2002 Proof	1,000	Value: 450				

KM# 108   10000 DRAM
8.6000 g., 0.9990 Gold 0.2762 oz. AGW, 22 mm. **Obv:** Building above value **Rev:** Aram Khachatryan left birth centennial

Date	Mintage	F	VF	XF	Unc	BU
2002 Proof	500	Value: 475				

KM# 114   10000 DRAM
8.6000 g., 0.9990 Gold 0.2762 oz. AGW, 22 mm. **Subject:** Arshile Gorky birth April 15, 1904 **Obv:** Bust of Gorky **Rev:** Denomination

Date	Mintage	F	VF	XF	Unc	BU
2004 Proof	1,000	Value: 450				

KM# 116   10000 DRAM
8.6000 g., 0.9990 Gold 0.2762 oz. AGW, 22 mm.   **Subject:** Martiros Saryan 125th Anniversary of Birth **Obv:** Bust of Saryan **Rev:** Landscape, denomination

Date	Mintage	F	VF	XF	Unc	BU
2005 Proof	1,000		Value: 450			

KM# 130   10000 DRAM
8.6000 g., 0.9990 Gold 0.2762 oz. AGW, 22 mm.   **Subject:** Komitas Vardapet **Obv:** Musical notations and score **Rev:** Bust of Vardapet 3/4 right

Date	Mintage	F	VF	XF	Unc	BU
2006 Proof	1,000		Value: 500			

KM# 131   10000 DRAM
8.6000 g., 0.9000 Gold 0.2488 oz. AGW, 22 mm.   **Subject:** 37th Chess Olympiad **Obv:** Chess piece at right **Rev:** National arms within 6 chess pieces in circle

Date	Mintage	F	VF	XF	Unc	BU
2006 Proof	1,000		Value: 450			

KM# 132   10000 DRAM
8.6000 g., 0.9000 Gold 0.2488 oz. AGW, 22 mm.   **Subject:** Hakob Gurjian **Obv:** Seated female sculpture **Rev:** Head 3/4 right

Date	Mintage	F	VF	XF	Unc	BU
2006 Proof	1,000		Value: 500			

KM# 137   10000 DRAM
8.6000 g., 0.9000 Gold 0.2488 oz. AGW, 22 mm.   **Subject:** Jean Carzou **Obv:** National arms with stylized view of shopping bourse **Rev:** Bust of Carzou 3/4 right at laft center

Date	Mintage	F	VF	XF	Unc	BU
2007 Proof	1,000		Value: 500			

KM# 138   10000 DRAM
8.6000 g., 0.9000 Gold 0.2488 oz. AGW, 22 mm.   **Subject:** 15th Anniversary of Armenian Army **Obv:** National arms **Rev:** Military badge

Date	Mintage	F	VF	XF	Unc	BU
2007 Proof	1,000		Value: 500			

KM# 140   10000 DRAM
8.6000 g., 0.9000 Gold 0.2488 oz. AGW, 22 mm.   **Subject:** 15th Anniversary Liberation of Shusi **Obv:** Bird with wings outspread above two shields **Rev:** Swirl in background

Date	Mintage	F	VF	XF	Unc	BU
2007 Proof	1,000		Value: 500			

KM# 175   10000 DRAM
8.6000 g., 0.9000 Gold 0.2488 oz. AGW, 22 mm.   **Subject:** Sagittarius

Date	Mintage	F	VF	XF	Unc	BU
2008 Proof	—		Value: 425			

KM# 166   10000 DRAM
8.6000 g., 0.9000 Gold 0.2488 oz. AGW, 22 mm.   **Subject:** Libra

Date	Mintage	F	VF	XF	Unc	BU
2008 Proof	—		Value: 425			

KM# 168   10000 DRAM
8.6000 g., 0.9000 Gold 0.2488 oz. AGW, 22 mm.   **Subject:** Court, 10th Anniversary

Date	Mintage	F	VF	XF	Unc	BU
2008 Proof	—		Value: 425			

KM# 170   10000 DRAM
8.6000 g., 0.9000 Gold 0.2488 oz. AGW, 22 mm.   **Subject:** William Saroyan, 100th Anniversary of Birth

Date	Mintage	F	VF	XF	Unc	BU
2008 Proof	—		Value: 425			

KM# 173   10000 DRAM
8.6000 g., 0.9000 Gold 0.2488 oz. AGW, 22 mm.   **Subject:** Scorpio

Date	Mintage	F	VF	XF	Unc	BU
2008 Proof	—		Value: 425			

KM# 176   10000 DRAM
8.6000 g., 0.9000 Gold 0.2488 oz. AGW, 22 mm.   **Subject:** Capricorn

Date	Mintage	F	VF	XF	Unc	BU
2008 Proof	—		Value: 425			

KM# 180   10000 DRAM
8.6000 g., 0.9000 Gold 0.2488 oz. AGW, 22 mm.   **Subject:** Aquarius

Date	Mintage	F	VF	XF	Unc	BU
2008 Proof	—		Value: 425			

KM# 181   10000 DRAM
8.6000 g., 0.9000 Gold 0.2488 oz. AGW, 22 mm.   **Subject:** Pisces

Date	Mintage	F	VF	XF	Unc	BU
2008 Proof	—		Value: 425			

KM# 185   10000 DRAM
8.6000 g., 0.9000 Gold 0.2488 oz. AGW, 22 mm.   **Subject:** Aries

Date	Mintage	F	VF	XF	Unc	BU
2008 Proof	—		Value: 425			

KM# 186   10000 DRAM
8.6000 g., 0.9000 Gold 0.2488 oz. AGW, 22 mm.   **Subject:** Taurus

Date	Mintage	F	VF	XF	Unc	BU
2008 Proof	—		Value: 425			

KM# 188   10000 DRAM
8.6000 g., 0.9000 Gold 0.2488 oz. AGW, 22 mm.   **Subject:** Gemini

Date	Mintage	F	VF	XF	Unc	BU
2008 Proof	—		Value: 425			

KM# 189   10000 DRAM
8.6000 g., 0.9000 Gold 0.2488 oz. AGW, 22 mm.   **Subject:** Cancer

Date	Mintage	F	VF	XF	Unc	BU
2008 Proof	—		Value: 425			

KM# 190   10000 DRAM
8.6000 g., 0.9000 Gold 0.2488 oz. AGW, 22 mm.   **Subject:** Leo

Date	Mintage	F	VF	XF	Unc	BU
2008 Proof	—		Value: 425			

KM# 191   10000 DRAM
8.6000 g., 0.9000 Gold 0.2488 oz. AGW, 22 mm.   **Subject:** Virgo

Date	Mintage	F	VF	XF	Unc	BU
2009 Proof	—		Value: 425			

KM# 194   10000 DRAM
8.6000 g., 0.9000 Gold 0.2488 oz. AGW, 22 mm.   **Subject:** Khachatour Aboryan, 200th Anniversary of Birth

Date	Mintage	F	VF	XF	Unc	BU
2009 Proof	—		Value: 425			

KM# 118   50000 DRAM
8.6000 g., 0.9990 Gold 0.2762 oz. AGW, 22 mm.   **Subject:** Armenian Armed Forces **Obv:** Order of the Combat Cross of the Second Degree and the Emblem of the Ministry of Defense of the Republic of Armenia **Rev:** Arms, date and denomination

Date	Mintage	F	VF	XF	Unc	BU
2005 Proof	1,000		Value: 450			

BULLION COINAGE

KM# 196   500 DRAM
31.1050 g., 0.9990 Silver 0.9990 oz. ASW, 38.6 mm.   **Obv:** National arms **Rev:** Dove, Noah's Ark and sun rise over Mt. Ararat

Date	Mintage	F	VF	XF	Unc	BU
2011LEV	—	—	—	—	—	50.00
2012LEV	—	—	—	—	—	50.00

ARUBA

The second largest island of the former Netherlands Antilles, Aruba is situated near the Venezuelan coast. The island has an area of 74-1/2 sq. mi. (193 sq. km.) and a population of 105,000. Capital: Oranjestad, named after the Dutch royal family. Aruba was important in the processing and transportation of petroleum products in the first part of the twentieth century, but today the chief industry is tourism.

For earlier issues see Curacao and the Netherlands Antilles.

RULER
Dutch

MINT MARKS
(u) Utrecht - Privy marks only
  Wine tendril with grapes, 2001-
  Wine tendril with grapes plus star, 2002-
  Sails of a clipper, 2003-

MONETARY SYSTEM
100 Cents = 1 Florin

DUTCH STATE
"Status Aparte"

DECIMAL COINAGE

KM# 1   5 CENTS
2.0000 g., Nickel Bonded Steel, 16 mm.   **Ruler:** Beatrix **Obv:** National arms **Rev:** Geometric design with value **Edge:** Plain

Date	Mintage	F	VF	XF	Unc	BU
2001(u)	946,900	—	0.10	0.25	0.50	1.00
2002(u)	1,006,000	—	0.10	0.25	0.50	1.00
2003(u)	1,104,100	—	0.10	0.25	0.50	1.00
2004(u)	502,500	—	0.10	0.25	0.50	1.00
2005(u)	602,500	—	0.10	0.25	0.50	1.00
2006(u)	602,000	—	0.10	0.25	0.50	1.00
2007(u)	1,152,000	—	0.10	0.25	0.50	1.00
2008(u)	1,152,000	—	0.10	0.25	0.50	1.00
2009(u)	—	—	0.10	0.25	0.50	1.00
2010(u)	—	—	0.10	0.25	0.50	1.00
2011(u)	—	—	0.10	0.25	0.50	1.00
2012(u)	—	—	0.10	0.25	0.50	1.00

KM# 2   10 CENTS
3.0000 g., Nickel Bonded Steel, 18 mm.   **Ruler:** Beatrix **Obv:** National arms **Rev:** Geometric design with value **Edge:** Reeded

Date	Mintage	F	VF	XF	Unc	BU
2001(u)	1,006,900	—	0.20	0.35	0.60	1.10
2002(u)	1,006,000	—	0.20	0.35	0.60	1.10
2003(u)	1,004,000	—	0.20	0.35	0.60	1.10
2004(u)	402,500	—	0.20	0.35	0.60	1.10
2005(u)	402,500	—	0.20	0.35	0.60	1.10
2006(u)	452,500	—	0.20	0.35	0.60	1.10
2007(u)	1,102,000	—	0.20	0.35	0.60	1.10
2008(u)	1,442,000	—	0.20	0.35	0.60	1.10
2009(u)	—	—	0.20	0.35	0.60	1.10
2009(u)	—	—	0.20	0.35	0.60	1.10
2010(u)	—	—	0.20	0.35	0.60	1.10
2011	—	—	0.20	0.35	0.60	1.10
2012(u)	—	—	0.20	0.35	0.60	1.10

KM# 3   25 CENTS
3.5000 g., Nickel Bonded Steel, 20 mm.   **Ruler:** Beatrix **Obv:** National arms **Rev:** Geometric design with value **Edge:** Plain

Date	Mintage	F	VF	XF	Unc	BU
2001(u)	716,900	—	0.20	0.40	0.75	1.50
2002(u)	806,000	—	0.20	0.40	0.75	1.50
2003(u)	804,000	—	0.20	0.40	0.75	1.50
2004(u)	362,500	—	0.20	0.40	0.75	1.50
2005(u)	302,500	—	0.20	0.40	0.75	1.50
2006(u)	302,000	—	0.20	0.40	0.75	1.50
2007(u)	202,000	—	0.20	0.40	0.75	1.50
2008(u)	202,000	—	0.20	0.40	0.75	1.50
2009(u)	—	—	0.20	0.40	0.75	1.50
2010(u)	—	—	0.20	0.40	0.75	1.50
2011(u)	—	—	0.20	0.40	0.75	1.50
2012(u)	—	—	0.20	0.40	0.75	1.50

KM# 4   50 CENTS
5.0000 g., Nickel Bonded Steel, 20 mm.   **Ruler:** Beatrix **Obv:** National arms **Rev:** Geometric design with value **Edge:** Plain **Shape:** 4-sided

Date	Mintage	F	VF	XF	Unc	BU
2001(u)	506,900	—	0.30	0.50	1.00	1.50
2002(u)	306,000	—	0.30	0.50	1.00	1.50
2003(u)	279,000	—	0.30	0.50	1.00	1.50
2004(u)	402,500	—	0.30	0.50	1.00	1.50
2005(u)	102,500	—	0.30	0.50	1.00	1.50
2006(u)	102,500	—	0.30	0.50	1.00	1.50
2007(u)	32,000	—	0.30	0.60	1.50	2.50
2008(u)	302,000	—	0.30	0.60	1.50	2.50
2009(u)	—	—	0.30	0.60	1.50	2.50
2010(u)	—	—	0.30	0.60	1.50	2.50
2011(u)	—	—	0.30	0.60	1.50	2.50
2012(u)	—	—	0.30	0.60	1.50	2.50

KM# 5   FLORIN
8.5000 g., Nickel Bonded Steel, 26 mm.   **Ruler:** Beatrix **Obv:** Head left **Rev:** National arms and value **Edge:** Lettered **Edge Lettering:** GOD * ZIJ * MET * ONS *

Date	Mintage	F	VF	XF	Unc	BU
2001(u)	406,900	—	0.60	1.00	2.00	3.00
2002(u)	206,000	—	0.60	1.00	2.00	3.00
2003(u)	179,000	—	0.60	1.00	2.00	3.00
2004(u)	410,000	—	0.60	1.00	2.00	3.00
2005(u)	352,500	—	0.60	1.00	2.00	3.00
2006(u)	402,000	—	0.60	1.00	2.00	3.00
2007(u)	502,000	—	0.60	1.00	2.00	3.00
2008(u)	289,000	—	0.60	1.00	2.00	3.00
2009(u)	—	—	0.60	1.00	2.00	3.00
2010(u)	—	—	0.60	1.00	2.00	3.00
2011(u)	—	—	0.60	1.00	2.00	3.00
2012(u)	—	—	0.60	1.00	2.00	3.00

KM# 6   2-1/2 FLORIN
10.3000 g., Nickel Bonded Steel, 30 mm. **Ruler:** Beatrix **Obv:** Head left **Rev:** National arms with value **Edge:** Lettered **Edge Lettering:** GOD * ZIJ * MET * ONS *

Date	Mintage	F	VF	XF	Unc	BU
2001(u) In sets only	6,900	—	—	2.00	3.00	7.00
2002(u) In sets only	6,000	—	—	2.00	3.00	7.00
2003(u) In sets only	4,000	—	—	2.00	3.00	7.00
2004(u) In sets only	2,500	—	—	2.00	3.00	7.00
2005(u) In sets only	2,500	—	—	2.00	3.00	7.00
2006(u) In sets only	2,000	—	—	2.00	3.00	7.00
2007(u) In sets only	2,000	—	—	2.00	3.00	7.00
2008(u) In sets only	2,000	—	—	2.00	3.00	7.00
2009(u) In sets only	2,000	—	—	2.00	3.00	7.00
2010(u) In sets only	—	—	—	2.00	3.00	7.00
2011(u)	—	—	—	2.00	3.00	7.00
2012(u)	—	—	—	2.00	3.00	7.00

KM# 12   5 FLORIN
8.6400 g., Nickel Bonded Steel, 26 mm. **Ruler:** Beatrix **Obv:** Head left **Rev:** National arms with value **Edge:** Plain **Shape:** Square

Date	Mintage	F	VF	XF	Unc	BU
2001(u) In sets only	6,900	—	—	3.00	7.00	9.00
2002(u) In sets only	6,000	—	—	3.00	7.00	9.00
2003(u) In sets only	4,000	—	—	3.00	7.00	9.00
2004(u) In sets only	2,500	—	—	3.00	7.00	9.00
2005(u) In sets only	2,500	—	—	3.00	7.00	9.00

KM# 25   5 FLORIN
11.9000 g., 0.9250 Silver 0.3539 oz. ASW, 29 mm. **Ruler:** Beatrix **Subject:** 50th Anniversary Charter for the Kingdom of the Netherlands including Netherlands Antilles **Obv:** Head left **Rev:** Royal seal **Edge Lettering:** GOD * ZIJ * MET * ONS *

Date	Mintage	F	VF	XF	Unc	BU
2004(u) Proof	4,000	Value: 40.00				

KM# 34   5 FLORIN
11.9000 g., 0.9250 Silver 0.3539 oz. ASW, 29 mm. **Ruler:** Beatrix **Subject:** Queen's Silver Jubilee **Obv:** Head left **Rev:** Flag **Edge:** Lettered **Edge Lettering:** GOD Z'J MET ONS

Date	Mintage	F	VF	XF	Unc	BU
2005(u) Proof	3,100	Value: 32.50				

KM# 38   5 FLORIN
8.4000 g., Aluminum-Bronze, 22.5 mm. **Ruler:** Beatrix **Obv:** Queen with a half crown on face **Rev:** Value and arms **Edge:** Reeded and lettered **Edge Lettering:** GOD * ZIJ * MET * ONS * **Shape:** Round

Date	Mintage	F	VF	XF	Unc	BU
2005(u)	827,500	—	—	—	5.50	7.00
2006(u)	102,000	—	—	—	5.50	10.00
2007(u)	52,000	—	—	—	5.50	10.00
2008(u)	22,000	—	—	—	5.50	10.00
2009(u)	—	—	—	—	5.50	10.00
2010(u)	—	—	—	—	5.50	10.00
2011(u)	—	—	—	—	5.50	10.00
2012(u)	—	—	—	—	5.50	10.00

KM# 41   5 FLORIN
11.9000 g., 0.9250 Silver 0.3539 oz. ASW, 29 mm. **Ruler:** Beatrix **Subject:** Year of the dolphin **Obv:** Head left **Rev:** Two dolphins bounding out of the water **Edge Lettering:** GOD * ZIJ * MET * ONS *

Date	Mintage	F	VF	XF	Unc	BU
2007(u) Proof	1,250	Value: 35.00				

KM# 42   5 FLORIN
11.9000 g., 0.9250 Silver 0.3539 oz. ASW, 29 mm. **Ruler:** Beatrix **Subject:** Fiesta de San Juan **Obv:** Head left **Rev:** Harvesting farmer **Edge Lettering:** GOD * ZIJ * MET * ONS

Date	Mintage	F	VF	XF	Unc	BU
2008(u) Proof	1,250	Value: 40.00				

KM# 43   5 FLORIN
11.9000 g., 0.9250 Silver 0.3539 oz. ASW, 29 mm. **Ruler:** Beatrix **Subject:** Dante at New Year's **Obv:** Head left **Rev:** Dance at New Year's, Hand dropping coins into hat **Edge Lettering:** GOD * ZIJ * MET * ONS

Date	Mintage	F	VF	XF	Unc	BU
2009(u) Proof	1,250	Value: 40.00				

KM# 45   5 FLORIN
11.9000 g., 0.9250 Silver 0.3539 oz. ASW, 29 mm. **Ruler:** Beatrix **Subject:** Olympic Games 2012 **Obv:** Queen Beatrix **Rev:** Two judoka fight men in action **Edge Lettering:** GOD * ZIJ * MET * ONS *

Date	Mintage	F	VF	XF	Unc	BU
2010 Proof	5,000	Value: 35.00				

KM# 46   5 FLORIN
11.9000 g., 0.9250 Silver 0.3539 oz. ASW, 29 mm. **Ruler:** Beatrix **Obv:** Head left **Rev:** California lighthouse and waves **Edge Lettering:** GOD * ZIJ * MET * ONS *

Date	Mintage	F	VF	XF	Unc	BU
2010(u) Proof	1,250	Value: 40.00				

KM# 48   5 FLORIN
11.9000 g., 0.9250 Silver 0.3539 oz. ASW, 29 mm. **Ruler:** Beatrix **Subject:** Royal Vista **Obv:** Shield in wreath above mintmarks **Rev:** Queen Beatrix, Prince Willem-Alexander and Princess Maxima looking left **Edge Lettering:** GOD * ZIJ * MET * ONS * **Note:** Rev: COLOURED, top orange and bottom blue

Date	Mintage	F	VF	XF	Unc	BU
2011(u) Proof	1,250	Value: 50.00				

KM# 47   5 FLORIN
11.9000 g., 0.9250 Silver 0.3539 oz. ASW, 29 mm. **Ruler:** Beatrix **Obv:** Shield in wreath above mintmarks **Rev:** 25 years Status Aparte with Parliament building **Edge Lettering:** GOD * ZIJ * MET * ONS *

Date	Mintage	F	VF	XF	Unc	BU
2011 (u)	1,250	Value: 45.00				

KM# 20   10 FLORIN
25.0000 g., 0.9250 Silver 0.7435 oz. ASW, 38 mm. **Ruler:** Beatrix **Subject:** Green Sea Turtles **Obv:** Head left **Rev:** Seven sea turtles **Edge:** Plain

Date	Mintage	F	VF	XF	Unc	BU
2001(u) Prooflike	2,000	—	—	—	—	80.00

KM# 24   10 FLORIN
17.8000 g., 0.9250 Silver 0.5293 oz. ASW, 33 mm. **Ruler:** Beatrix **Subject:** Crown Prince's Wedding **Obv:** Head left **Rev:** Conjoined busts of prince and princess Maxima, right **Edge Lettering:** GOD ZIJ MET ONS

Date	Mintage	F	VF	XF	Unc	BU
ND(2002)(u) Prooflike	5,000	—	—	—	—	40.00

KM# 27   10 FLORIN
25.0000 g., 0.9250 Silver 0.7435 oz. ASW, 38 mm. **Ruler:** Beatrix **Obv:** Head left **Rev:** Sea shell **Edge:** Plain

Date	Mintage	F	VF	XF	Unc	BU
2003(u) Proof	2,000	Value: 80.00				

KM# 28   10 FLORIN
25.0000 g., 0.9250 Silver 0.7435 oz. ASW, 38 mm. **Ruler:**
Beatrix **Obv:** Head left **Rev:** Snake **Edge:** Plain

Date	Mintage	F	VF	XF	Unc	BU
2003(u) Proof	2,000	Value: 80.00				

KM# 29   10 FLORIN
25.0000 g., 0.9250 Silver 0.7435 oz. ASW, 38 mm. **Ruler:**
Beatrix **Obv:** Head left **Rev:** Owl **Edge:** Plain

Date	Mintage	F	VF	XF	Unc	BU
2003(u) Proof	1,000	Value: 85.00				

KM# 30   10 FLORIN
25.0000 g., 0.9250 Silver 0.7435 oz. ASW, 38 mm. **Ruler:**
Beatrix **Obv:** Head left **Rev:** Tree Frog **Edge:** Plain

Date	Mintage	F	VF	XF	Unc	BU
2004(u) Proof	1,000	Value: 25.00				

KM# 31   10 FLORIN
25.0000 g., 0.9250 Silver 0.7435 oz. ASW, 38 mm. **Ruler:**
Beatrix **Obv:** Head left **Rev:** Fish right **Edge:** Plain

Date	Mintage	F	VF	XF	Unc	BU
2004(u) Proof	1,000	Value: 25.00				

KM# 26   10 FLORIN
6.7200 g., 0.9000 Gold 0.1944 oz. AGW, 22.5 mm. **Ruler:**
Beatrix **Subject:** 20th Anniversary of Autonomy **Obv:** Head left
Rev: Royal seal **Edge:** Reeded

Date	Mintage	F	VF	XF	Unc	BU
2004(u) Proof	1,000	Value: 300				

KM# 33   10 FLORIN
1.2442 g., 0.9990 Gold 0.0400 oz. AGW, 13.9 mm. **Ruler:**
Beatrix **Subject:** Death of Juliana **Obv:** Head left **Rev:** Juliana
in center **Edge:** Reeded

Date	Mintage	F	VF	XF	Unc	BU
ND (2005)(u) Proof	10,000	Value: 75.00				

KM# 35   10 FLORIN
6.7200 g., 0.9000 Gold 0.1944 oz. AGW, 22.5 mm. **Ruler:**
Beatrix **Subject:** Queen's Silver Jubilee **Obv:** Head left **Rev:** Flag
Edge: Reeded

Date	Mintage	F	VF	XF	Unc	BU
2005(u) Proof	750	Value: 350				

KM# 36   10 FLORIN
25.0000 g., 0.9250 Silver 0.7435 oz. ASW, 38 mm. **Ruler:**
Beatrix **Subject:** Status Aparte 20th Anniversary - Flag 30th
Anniversary **Obv:** Queen's portrait **Rev:** Queen standing next to
value and country name **Edge Lettering:** DIOS * TA * CU * NOS *

Date	Mintage	F	VF	XF	Unc	BU
2006(u) Proof	1,250	Value: 45.00				

KM# 44   10 FLORIN
1.2442 g., 0.9990 Gold 0.0400 oz. AGW, 13.9 mm. **Ruler:**
Beatrix **Subject:** Carnival **Obv:** Head left **Rev:** Carnival feathered
facemask

Date	Mintage	F	VF	XF	Unc	BU
2009 Proof	5,000	Value: 75.00				

KM# 49   10 FLORIN
3.3645 g., 0.9000 Gold 0.0973 oz. AGW, 18.5 mm. **Ruler:**
Beatrix **Subject:** Status Aparte **Obv:** Shield in wreath above
mintmarks **Rev:** 25 years Status Aparte with Parliament building
Edge: Reeded

Date	Mintage	F	VF	XF	Unc	BU
2011(u) Proof	1,000	Value: 250				

KM# 22   25 FLORIN
25.0000 g., 0.9250 Silver 0.7435 oz. ASW, 38 mm. **Ruler:**
Beatrix **Subject:** 15th Anniversary of Autonomy **Obv:** Head left
Rev: National arms and inscription **Edge:** Plain

Date	Mintage	F	VF	XF	Unc	BU
2001(u) Proof	3,000	Value: 50.00				

KM# 37   25 FLORIN
6.7200 g., 0.9000 Gold 0.1944 oz. AGW, 22.5 mm. **Ruler:**
Beatrix **Subject:** Status Aparte 20th Anniversary - Flag 30th
Anniversary **Obv:** Queen's portrait **Rev:** Queen standing next to
value and country name **Edge:** Reeded **Note:** Status Aparte

Date	Mintage	F	VF	XF	Unc	BU
2006(u) Proof	1,000	Value: 325				

KM# 23   100 FLORIN
6.7200 g., Gold, 22.5 mm. **Ruler:** Beatrix **Subject:**
Independence **Obv:** Arms, treaty name, dates **Rev:** Head left
Edge: Grained

Date	Mintage	F	VF	XF	Unc	BU
2001(u) Proof	1,000	Value: 400				

MINT SETS

KM#	Date	Mintage	Identification	Issue Price	Mkt Val
MS19	2001 (7)	6,900	KM#1-6, 12	13.25	20.00
MS20	2002 (6)	6,000	KM# 1-6, 12	15.00	20.00
MS21	2003 (7)	4,000	KM# 1-6, 12	15.00	20.00
MS22	2004 (7)	2,500	KM# 1-6, 12	15.00	22.50
MS23	2005 (7)	2,500	KM# 1-6, 12	15.00	22.50
MS24	2006 (7)	2,000	KM# 1-6, 38	15.00	22.50
MS25	2007 (7)	2,500	KM#1-6, 38	20.00	22.50
MS26	2008 (7)	2,000	KM#1-6, 38	26.00	22.50
MS27	2009 (7)	2,000	KM#1-6, 38	26.00	22.50
MS28	2010 (7)	2,000	KM#1-6, 38	26.00	22.50
MS29	2011 (7)	2,000	KM#1-6, 38	26.00	27.50
MS30	2012 (7)	2,000	KM#1-6, 38	28.00	30.00

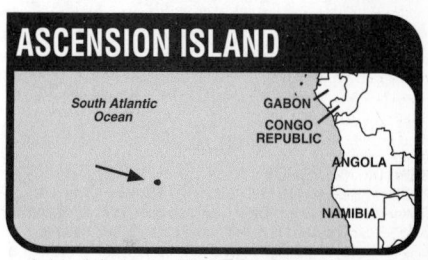

ASCENSION ISLAND

An island of volcanic origin, Ascension Island lies in the South
Atlantic, 700 miles (1,100 km.) northwest of St. Helena. It has an
area of 34 sq. mi. (88 sq. km.) on an island 9 miles (14 km.) long
and 6 miles (10 km.) wide. Approximate population: 1,146.
Although having little vegetation and scant rainfall, the island has
a very healthy climate. The island is the nesting place for a large
number of sea turtles and sooty terns. Phosphates and guano are
the chief natural sources of income. Ascension is a dependency
of the British Colony of St. Helena.

RULER
British

MINT MARKS
PM - Pobjoy Mint

BRITISH ADMINISTRATION
STANDARD COINAGE

KM# 13   50 PENCE
28.6300 g., Copper-Nickel, 38.6 mm. **Subject:** 75th Birthday of
Queen Elizabeth **Obv:** Crowned bust right, denomination below
Rev: Crowned monogram above flowers within circle, date below
Edge: Reeded

Date	Mintage	F	VF	XF	Unc	BU
2001	—	—	—	—	8.00	9.50

KM# 13a   50 PENCE
28.2800 g., 0.9250 Silver 0.8410 oz. ASW, 38.6 mm. **Subject:**
Queen Elizabeth II's 75th Birthday **Obv:** Crowned bust right,
denomination below **Rev:** Crowned monogram above roses
within circle, date below **Edge:** Reeded

Date	Mintage	F	VF	XF	Unc	BU
2001 Proof	10,000	Value: 45.00				

KM# 13b   50 PENCE
47.5400 g., 0.9166 Gold 1.4009 oz. AGW, 38.6 mm. **Subject:**
Queen Elizabeth II's 75th Birthday **Obv:** Crowned bust right,
denomination below **Rev:** Crowned monogram above roses
within circle, date below **Edge:** Reeded

Date	Mintage	F	VF	XF	Unc	BU
2001 Proof	75	Value: 2,600				

KM# 14   50 PENCE
28.6300 g., Copper-Nickel, 38.6 mm. **Subject:** Centennial -
Queen Victoria's Death **Obv:** Crowned bust right, denomination
below **Rev:** Crowned bust left, three dates **Edge:** Reeded

Date	Mintage	F	VF	XF	Unc	BU
2001	—	—	—	—	8.00	9.50

KM# 14a   50 PENCE
28.2800 g., 0.9250 Silver 0.8410 oz. ASW, 38.6 mm. **Subject:**
Centennial of Queen Victoria's Death **Obv:** Crowned bust right,
denomination below **Rev:** Crowned bust left, three dates **Edge:**
Reeded

Date	Mintage	F	VF	XF	Unc	BU
2001 Proof	10,000	Value: 45.00				

KM# 14b   50 PENCE
47.5400 g., 0.9166 Gold 1.4009 oz. AGW, 38.6 mm. **Subject:**
Centennial of Queen Victoria's Death **Obv:** Crowned bust right,
denomination below **Rev:** Crowned bust left, three dates **Edge:**
Reeded

Date	Mintage	F	VF	XF	Unc	BU
2001 Proof	100	Value: 2,600				

KM# 15   50 PENCE
28.3500 g., Copper-Nickel, 38.6 mm. **Subject:** Queen's Golden
Jubilee **Obv:** Crowned bust right, denomination below **Rev:**
Westminster Abby, monogram at left, circle surrounds, two dates
below **Edge:** Reeded

Date	Mintage	F	VF	XF	Unc	BU
ND(2002)	—	—	—	—	8.00	9.50

KM# 15a   50 PENCE
28.2800 g., 0.9250 Silver 0.8410 oz. ASW, 38.6 mm. **Subject:**
Queen Elizabeth II's Golden Jubilee **Obv:** Gold-plated crowned
bust right, denomination below **Rev:** Monogram and Westminster
Abbey within circle, dates below **Edge:** Reeded

Date	Mintage	F	VF	XF	Unc	BU
ND(2002) Proof	10,000	Value: 45.00				

KM# 18   50 PENCE
28.2800 g., Copper-Nickel, 38.6 mm. **Subject:** Death of Queen
Mother **Obv:** Crowned bust right, denomination below **Rev:**
Queen Mother bust right, between her life dates **Edge:** Reeded

Date	Mintage	F	VF	XF	Unc	BU
ND(2002)	—	—	—	—	10.00	12.00

KM# 18a   50 PENCE
28.2800 g., 0.9250 Silver 0.8410 oz. ASW, 38.6 mm. **Subject:**
Death of Queen Mother **Obv:** Crowned bust right, denomination
below **Rev:** Queen Mother bust right, between her life dates
Edge: Reeded

Date	Mintage	F	VF	XF	Unc	BU
ND(2002) Proof	10,000	Value: 45.00				

KM# 16   50 PENCE
28.3600 g., Copper-Nickel, 38.6 mm. **Subject:** Coronation
Jubilee **Obv:** Crowned bust right, denomination below **Rev:**
Crown, two scepters and the ampula **Edge:** Reeded

Date	Mintage	F	VF	XF	Unc	BU
ND (2003) Prooflike	—	—	—	—	10.00	12.00

KM# 16a   50 PENCE
28.2800 g., 0.9250 Silver 0.8410 oz. ASW, 38.6 mm. **Subject:**
Queen Elizabeth II's - 50th Anniversary of Coronation **Obv:**
Crowned bust right, denomination below **Rev:** Crown, two
scepters and the ampula **Edge:** Reeded

Date	Mintage	F	VF	XF	Unc	BU
ND(2003) Proof	5,000	Value: 50.00				

KM# 16b   50 PENCE
39.9400 g., 0.9166 Gold 1.1770 oz. AGW, 38.6 mm. **Subject:**
Queen Elizabeth II's - 50th Anniversary of Coronation **Obv:**
Crowned bust right, denomination below **Rev:** Crown, two
scepters and the ampula **Edge:** Reeded

Date	Mintage	F	VF	XF	Unc	BU
ND(2003) Proof	50	Value: 2,450				

KM# 17   50 PENCE
28.2800 g., Copper-Nickel, 38.6 mm. **Subject:** Queen Elizabeth
II's- 50th Anniversary of Coronation **Obv:** Crowned head right,
denomination below **Rev:** Crowned monogram **Edge:** Reeded

Date	Mintage	F	VF	XF	Unc	BU
ND(2003)	—	—	—	—	10.00	12.00

KM# 17a   50 PENCE
28.2800 g., 0.9250 Silver 0.8410 oz. ASW, 38.6 mm. **Subject:**
Queen Elizabeth II's- 50th Anniversary of Coronation **Obv:**
Crowned head right, denomination below **Rev:** Crowned
monogram **Edge:** Reeded

Date	Mintage	F	VF	XF	Unc	BU
ND(2003) Proof	5,000	Value: 50.00				

KM# 17b   50 PENCE
39.9400 g., 0.9166 Gold 1.1770 oz. AGW, 38.6 mm. **Subject:**
Queen Elizabeth II's - 50th Anniversary of Coronation **Obv:**
Crowned bust right, denomination below **Rev:** Crowned
monogram **Edge:** Reeded

Date	Mintage	F	VF	XF	Unc	BU
ND(2003) Proof	50	Value: 2,450				

KM# 19   2 POUNDS
28.2800 g., Copper-Nickel, 38.6 mm. **Subject:** Royal Wedding,
Prince William and Catherine Middleton **Obv:** Bust in tiara right
Rev: Two bells and two doves

Date	Mintage	F	VF	XF	Unc	BU
2011PM	—	—	—	—	10.00	12.50

KM# 19a   2 POUNDS
28.2800 g., 0.9250 Silver 0.8410 oz. ASW **Subject:** Royal
Wedding of Prince William and Catherine Middleton **Obv:** Bust
in tiara right **Rev:** Two bells and two doves

Date	Mintage	F	VF	XF	Unc	BU
2011PM Proof	—	Value: 65.00				

KM# 20   2 POUNDS
28.2800 g., Copper-Nickel, 38.61 mm. **Subject:** Royal Wedding
of Prince William and Catherine Middleton **Obv:** Bust with tiara right
Rev: Westminster Abbey, profiel portraits conjoined in oval at right

Date	Mintage	F	VF	XF	Unc	BU
2011PM	—	—	—	—	10.00	12.50

KM# 20a   2 POUNDS
28.2800 g., 0.9250 Silver 0.8410 oz. ASW, 38.61 mm. **Subject:**
Royal Wedding of Prince William and Catherine Middleton **Obv:**
Bust in tiara right **Rev:** Westminster Abbey, portraits in oval at
right

Date	Mintage	F	VF	XF	Unc	BU
2011PM Proof	—	Value: 65.00				

KM# 21   2 POUNDS
28.2800 g., Copper-Nickel, 38.61 mm. **Obv:** Conjoined busts
right of 1952 and 2012 portraits **Rev:** 1952 era portrait of Elizabeth
II **Rev. Legend:** Life of Queen Elizabeth II

Date	Mintage	F	VF	XF	Unc	BU
2012PM	—	—	—	—	—	20.00

KM# 22   2 POUNDS
28.2800 g., Copper-Nickel, 38.61 mm. **Subject:** Life of Queen
Elizabeth II **Obv:** Conjoined busts right **Rev:** Elizabeth nursing
Prince Charles

Date	Mintage	F	VF	XF	Unc	BU
2012PM	—	—	—	—	—	15.00

AUSTRALIA

The Commonwealth of Australia, the smallest continent in the world, is located south of Indonesia between the Indian and Pacific oceans. It has an area of 2,967,893 sq. mi. (7,686,850 sq. km.) and an estimated population of 18.84 million. Capital: Canberra. Due to its early and sustained isolation, Australia is the habitat of such curious and unique fauna as the kangaroo, koala, platypus, wombat, echidna and frilled-necked lizard. The continent possesses extensive mineral deposits, the most important of which are iron ore, coal, gold, silver, nickel, uranium, lead and zinc. Raising livestock, mining and manufacturing are the principal industries. Chief exports are wool, meat, wheat, iron ore, coal and nonferrous metals.

Australia is a founding member of the Commonwealth of Nations. Elizabeth II is the Head of State as Queen of Australia; the Prime Minister is Head of Government.

NOTE: Home market grading of Australian coinage is generally stricter than USA practiced standards. The pricing in this catalog reflects strict home market grading standard.

RULER
British until 1942

MONETARY SYSTEM

Decimal Coinage (Commencing 1966)
100 Cents = 1 Dollar

COMMONWEALTH OF AUSTRALIA

MINT MARKS
M – Melbourne
P – Perth
S – Sydney
(sy) - Sydney

DECIMAL COINAGE

KM# 767   CENT
2.6000 g., Bronze, 17.65 mm. **Ruler:** Elizabeth II **Obv:** Head with tiara right **Rev:** Feather-tailed glider and value **Edge:** Plain

Date	Mintage	F	VF	XF	Unc	BU
2006B In sets only	—	—	—	—	—	15.00
2006B Proof	—	Value: 18.00				

KM# 62a   CENT
2.6000 g., 0.9990 Silver 0.0835 oz. ASW, 17.53 mm. **Ruler:** Elizabeth II **Obv:** Young bust right **Rev:** Feather-tailed glider and value **Edge:** Plain

Date	Mintage	F	VF	XF	Unc	BU
2006 Proof	6,500	Value: 15.00				

KM# 767b   CENT
5.6100 g., 0.9990 Gold 0.1802 oz. AGW, 17.53 mm. **Ruler:** Elizabeth II **Obv:** Head with tiara right **Rev:** Feather-tailed glider **Edge:** Plain

Date	Mintage	F	VF	XF	Unc	BU
2006 Proof	300	Value: 650				

KM# 1249   CENT
2.4300 g., 0.9990 Silver 0.0780 oz. ASW, 17.6 mm. **Ruler:** Elizabeth II **Subject:** 1966 Decimal Pattern **Obv:** Head right **Rev:** Waratah, flower of New South Wales

Date	Mintage	F	VF	XF	Unc	BU
2009P Proof	7,500	Value: 15.00				

KM# 767a   CENT
2.9300 g., 0.9990 Silver 0.0941 oz. ASW, 17.53 mm. **Ruler:** Elizabeth II

Date	Mintage	F	VF	XF	Unc	BU
2011B Proof	—	Value: 50.00				

KM# 768   2 CENTS
5.2000 g., Bronze, 21.59 mm. **Ruler:** Elizabeth II **Obv:** Head with tiara right **Rev:** Frill-necked lizard and value

Date	Mintage	F	VF	XF	Unc	BU
2006B	—	—	—	—	15.00	—
2006B Proof	—	Value: 5.00				

KM# 63a   2 CENTS
5.1800 g., 0.9990 Silver 0.1664 oz. ASW, 21.6 mm. **Ruler:** Elizabeth II **Obv:** Young bust right **Rev:** Frill-necked lizard and value **Edge:** Plain

Date	Mintage	F	VF	XF	Unc	BU
2006 Proof	6,500	Value: 15.00				

KM# 768b   2 CENTS
11.3100 g., 0.9990 Gold 0.3632 oz. AGW, 21.6 mm. **Ruler:** Elizabeth II **Obv:** Head with tiara right **Rev:** Frill-necked Lizard and value **Edge:** Plain

Date	Mintage	F	VF	XF	Unc	BU
2006 Proof	300	Value: 700				

KM# 1250   2 CENTS
5.5300 g., 0.9990 Silver 0.1776 oz. ASW, 21.6 mm. **Ruler:** Elizabeth II **Subject:** 1966 Decimal Pattern **Obv:** Head right **Rev:** Wattle, national flower

Date	Mintage	F	VF	XF	Unc	BU
2009P Proof	7,500	Value: 20.00				

KM# 768a   2 CENTS
6.0300 g., 0.9990 Silver 0.1937 oz. ASW, 21.6 mm. **Ruler:** Elizabeth II

Date	Mintage	F	VF	XF	Unc	BU
2011B Proof	—	Value: 100				

KM# 401   5 CENTS
2.8300 g., Copper-Nickel, 19.41 mm. **Ruler:** Elizabeth II **Obv:** Head with tiara right **Rev:** Echidna and value **Edge:** Reeded

Date	Mintage	F	VF	XF	Unc	BU
2001	174,579,000	—	—	—	2.00	3.00
Note: Large obverse head, IRB spaced						
2001	Inc. above	—	—	—	2.00	3.00
Note: Smaller obverse head, RB joined						
2001 Proof	59,569	Value: 15.00				
2002	148,812,000	—	—	—	2.00	3.00
2002 Proof	39,514	Value: 15.00				
2003	115,470,000	—	—	—	2.00	3.00
2003 Proof	39,090	Value: 5.00				
2004	147,658,000	—	—	—	2.00	3.00
Note: Normal sized SD						
2004	Inc. above	—	—	—	2.00	3.00
Note: Smaller SD						
2004 Proof	50,000	Value: 5.00				
2005	194,300,000	—	—	—	2.00	3.00
Note: Normal sized SD						
2005	Inc. above	—	—	—	2.00	3.00
Note: Smaller SD						
2005 Proof	33,520	Value: 5.00				
2006	—	—	—	—	2.00	3.00
2006 Proof	—	Value: 5.00				
2007	—	—	—	—	2.00	3.00
2007 Proof	—	Value: 5.00				
2008	—	—	—	—	2.00	3.00
2008 Proof	—	Value: 5.00				
2009	—	—	—	—	2.00	3.00
2009 Proof	—	Value: 5.00				
2010	—	—	—	—	2.00	3.00
2010 Proof	—	Value: 5.00				
2011	—	—	—	—	2.00	3.00
2011 Proof	—	Value: 5.00				
2012	—	—	—	—	2.00	3.00
2012 Proof	—	Value: 5.00				

KM# 401a   5 CENTS
6.0300 g., 0.9990 Gold 0.1937 oz. AGW, 19.41 mm. **Ruler:** Elizabeth II **Subject:** Federation Centennial **Obv:** Head with tiara right **Rev:** Echidna

Date	Mintage	F	VF	XF	Unc	BU
2001B Proof	650	Value: 650				
2005B Proof	650	Value: 450				
2006B Proof	300	Value: 700				

KM# 401b   5 CENTS
3.2400 g., 0.9999 Silver 0.1042 oz. ASW, 19.41 mm. **Ruler:** Elizabeth II **Obv:** Head with tiara right **Rev:** Echidna **Edge:** Reeded

Date	Mintage	F	VF	XF	Unc	BU
2003B Proof	6,500	Value: 30.00				
2004B Proof	6,500	Value: 20.00				
2005B Proof	6,500	Value: 20.00				
2006B Proof	—	Value: 20.00				
2007B Proof	—	Value: 20.00				
2008B Proof	—	Value: 20.00				
2009B Proof	—	Value: 20.00				
2010B Proof	—	Value: 20.00				
2011B Proof	6,000	Value: 20.00				

KM# 64a   5 CENTS
3.2400 g., 0.9990 Silver 0.1041 oz. ASW, 19.41 mm. **Ruler:** Elizabeth II **Obv:** Young bust right **Rev:** Echidna **Edge:** Reeded

Date	Mintage	F	VF	XF	Unc	BU
2006 Proof	6,500	Value: 20.00				

KM# 1251   5 CENTS
2.7400 g., 0.9990 Silver 0.0880 oz. ASW, 19.6 mm. **Ruler:** Elizabeth II **Subject:** 1966 Decimal Pattern **Obv:** Head right **Rev:** Platypus and yabbie

Date	Mintage	F	VF	XF	Unc	BU
2009P Proof	7,500	Value: 35.00				

KM# 402   10 CENTS
5.6500 g., Copper-Nickel, 23.6 mm.   **Ruler:** Elizabeth II **Obv:** Head with tiara right **Rev:** Lyrebird and value **Edge:** Reeded

Date	Mintage	F	VF	XF	Unc	BU
2001	109,357,000	—	—	—	3.00	4.00
	Note: Large obverse head, IRB spaced					
2001	Inc. above				3.00	4.00
	Note: Smaller obverse head, RB joined					
2001 Proof	59,569	Value: 15.00				
2002	70,329,000	—	—	—	3.00	4.00
2002 Proof	39,514	Value: 5.00				
2003	53,635,000	—	—	—	2.00	3.00
2003 Proof	39,090	Value: 5.00				
2004	89,000,000	—	—	—	3.00	4.00
2004 Proof	50,000	Value: 5.00				
2005	116,700,000	—	—	—	2.00	3.00
2005 Proof	33,520	Value: 5.00				
2006	157,087,000	—	—	—	2.00	3.00
2006 Proof	—	Value: 5.00				
2007	61,096,000	—	—	—	3.00	4.00
2007 Proof	—	Value: 4.00				
2008	82,860,000	—	—	—	3.00	4.00
2008 Proof	—	Value: 5.00				
2009	—	—	—	—	3.00	4.00
2009 Proof	—	Value: 5.00				
2010	—	—	—	—	3.00	4.00
2010 Proof	—	Value: 5.00				
2011	—	—	—	—	3.00	4.00
2011 Proof	—	Value: 5.00				
2012	—	—	—	—	3.00	4.00
2012 Proof	—	Value: 5.00				

KM# 402a   10 CENTS
12.1400 g., 0.9999 Gold 0.3903 oz. AGW, 23.6 mm.   **Ruler:** Elizabeth II **Subject:** Federation Centennial **Obv:** Head with tiara right **Rev:** Lyrebird **Edge:** Reeded

Date	Mintage	F	VF	XF	Unc	BU
2001B Proof	650	Value: 650				
2005B Proof	650	Value: 600				
2006B Proof	300	Value: 750				

KM# 402b   10 CENTS
6.5700 g., 0.9999 Silver 0.2112 oz. ASW, 23.6 mm.   **Ruler:** Elizabeth II **Obv:** Head with tiara right **Rev:** Lyrebird **Edge:** Reeded

Date	Mintage	F	VF	XF	Unc	BU
2003B Proof	6,500	Value: 20.00				
2004B Proof	6,500	Value: 15.00				
2005B Proof	6,500	Value: 15.00				
2006B Proof	—	Value: 15.00				
2007B Proof	—	Value: 15.00				
2008B Proof	—	Value: 15.00				
2009B Proof	—	Value: 15.00				
2010B Proof	—	Value: 15.00				
2011B Proof	6,000	Value: 15.00				

KM# 65a   10 CENTS
6.5700 g., 0.9990 Silver 0.2110 oz. ASW, 23.6 mm.   **Ruler:** Elizabeth II **Obv:** Young bust right **Rev:** Superb Lyrebird **Edge:** Reeded

Date	Mintage	F	VF	XF	Unc	BU
2006 Proof	6,500	Value: 15.00				

KM# 1252   10 CENTS
6.0700 g., 0.9990 Silver 0.1950 oz. ASW, 23.6 mm.   **Ruler:** Elizabeth II **Subject:** 1966 Decimal Pattern **Obv:** Head right **Rev:** Kookabura eating snake

Date	Mintage	F	VF	XF	Unc	BU
2009P Proof	7,500	Value: 45.00				

KM# 403   20 CENTS
11.3000 g., Copper-Nickel, 28.65 mm.   **Ruler:** Elizabeth II **Obv:** Head with tiara right **Rev:** Duckbill Platypus **Edge:** Reeded

Date	Mintage	F	VF	XF	Unc	BU
2001	81,967,000	—	—	—	3.00	4.00
	Note: IRB spaced					
2001	Inc. above				3.00	4.00
	Note: RB joined					
2001	Inc. above				3.00	4.00
	Note: IRB joined					
2001 Proof	59,569	Value: 25.00				
2002	27,244,000	—	—	—	3.00	4.00
2002 Proof	39,514	Value: 2.00				
2004	74,609,000	—	—	—	3.00	4.00
	Note: Small obverse head, flat top A					
2004	Est. 400,000	—	—	—	15.00	20.00
	Note: Large obverse head, pointed A					
2004 Proof	50,000	Value: 10.00				
	Note: Large obverse head, pointed top A					
2004 Proof	Inc. above	Value: 10.00				
	Note: Small obverse head, flat top A					
2005	58,600,000	—	—	—	9.00	10.00
2005 Proof	—	Value: 25.00				
2006	102,462,000	—	—	—	3.00	4.00
2006 Proof	—	Value: 6.00				
2007	42,712,000	—	—	—	3.00	4.00
2007 Proof	—	Value: 25.00				
2008	106,220,000	—	—	—	1.00	2.00
2008 Proof	—	Value: 12.00				
2009	—	—	—	—	1.00	2.00
2009 Proof	—	Value: 12.00				
2010	—	—	—	—	1.00	2.00
2010 Proof	—	Value: 12.00				
2011	—	—	—	—	1.00	2.00
2011 Proof	—	Value: 12.00				
2012	—	—	—	—	1.00	2.00
2012 Proof	—	Value: 12.00				

KM# 532   20 CENTS
11.3000 g., Copper-Nickel, 28.65 mm.   **Ruler:** Elizabeth II **Subject:** Centenary of Federation - Norfolk Island **Obv:** Head with tiara right **Rev:** Norfolk Pine over map of island **Edge:** Reeded

Date	Mintage	F	VF	XF	Unc	BU
2001B	2,000,000	—	—	—	3.50	5.00
2001B Proof	—	Value: 10.00				

KM# 550   20 CENTS
11.3000 g., Copper-Nickel, 28.65 mm.   **Ruler:** Elizabeth II **Series:** Centenary of Federation - New South Wales **Obv:** Head with tiara right **Rev:** Waratah on state map **Edge:** Reeded

Date	Mintage	F	VF	XF	Unc	BU
2001	2,000,000	—	—	—	3.50	5.00
2001 Proof	—	Value: 10.00				

KM# 552   20 CENTS
11.3000 g., Copper-Nickel, 28.65 mm.   **Ruler:** Elizabeth II **Series:** Centenary of Federation - Australian Capital Territory **Obv:** Head with tiara right **Rev:** Parliament House, map, flowers **Edge:** Reeded **Note:** Prev. KM#551.

Date	Mintage	F	VF	XF	Unc	BU
2001	2,000,000	—	—	—	5.00	6.00
2001 Proof	—	Value: 20.00				

KM# 554   20 CENTS
11.3000 g., Copper-Nickel, 28.65 mm.   **Ruler:** Elizabeth II **Series:** Centenary of Federation - Queensland **Obv:** Head with tiara right **Rev:** Jennifer Gray **Edge:** Reeded

Date	Mintage	F	VF	XF	Unc	BU
2001	2,320,000	—	—	—	6.00	8.00
2001 Proof	—	Value: 20.00				

KM# 556   20 CENTS
11.3000 g., Copper-Nickel, 28.65 mm.   **Ruler:** Elizabeth II **Series:** Centenary of Federation - Victoria **Obv:** Head with tiara right **Rev:** Capital building **Edge:** Reeded

Date	Mintage	F	VF	XF	Unc	BU
2001	2,000,000	—	—	—	6.00	8.00
2001 Proof	—	Value: 20.00				

KM# 558   20 CENTS
11.3000 g., Copper-Nickel, 28.65 mm.   **Ruler:** Elizabeth II **Series:** Centenary of Federation - Northern Territory **Obv:** Head with tiara right **Rev:** Two brolga cranes in ritual dance **Edge:** Reeded

Date	Mintage	F	VF	XF	Unc	BU
2001	2,100,000	—	—	—	6.00	9.00
2001 Proof	—	Value: 20.00				

KM# 560   20 CENTS
11.3000 g., Copper-Nickel, 28.65 mm.   **Ruler:** Elizabeth II **Series:** Centenary of Federation - South Australia **Obv:** Head with tiara right **Rev:** Sturt's Desert Pea, landscape and southern cross **Edge:** Reeded

Date	Mintage	F	VF	XF	Unc	BU
2001	2,320,000	—	—	—	6.00	8.00
2001 Proof	—	Value: 20.00				

KM# 562   20 CENTS
11.3000 g., Copper-Nickel, 28.65 mm. **Ruler:** Elizabeth II
Series: Centenary of Federation - Western Australia **Obv:** Head
with tiara right **Rev:** Rabbit-eared Bandicoot (bilby), plant and
map **Edge:** Reeded

Date	Mintage	F	VF	XF	Unc	BU
2001	2,000,000	—	—	—	6.00	10.00
2001 Proof	—	Value: 20.00				

KM# 564   20 CENTS
11.3000 g., Copper-Nickel, 28.65 mm. **Ruler:** Elizabeth II
Series: Centenary of Federation - Tasmania **Obv:** Head with
tiara right **Rev:** Tasmanian Tiger on map **Edge:** Reeded

Date	Mintage	F	VF	XF	Unc	BU
2001	2,000,000	—	—	—	6.00	10.00
2001 Proof	—	Value: 20.00				

KM# 589   20 CENTS
11.3000 g., Copper-Nickel, 28.65 mm. **Ruler:** Elizabeth II
Subject: Sir Donald Bradman **Obv:** Head with tiara right **Rev:**
Sir Donald Bradman **Edge:** Reeded

Date	Mintage	F	VF	XF	Unc	BU
2001B	10,000,000	—	—	—	35.00	40.00

KM# 819   20 CENTS
24.3600 g., 0.9990 Gold 0.7824 oz. AGW, 28.52 mm. **Ruler:**
Elizabeth II **Obv:** Head with tiara right **Rev:** Platypus with
Federation Star **Edge:** Reeded

Date	Mintage	F	VF	XF	Unc	BU
2001 Proof	650	Value: 1,350				

KM# 403a   20 CENTS
13.3600 g., 0.9999 Silver 0.4295 oz. ASW, 28.52 mm. **Ruler:**
Elizabeth II **Obv:** Head with tiara right **Rev:** Platypus **Edge:**
Reeded

Date	Mintage	F	VF	XF	Unc	BU
2003B Proof	6,500	Value: 30.00				
2004B Proof	6,500	Value: 25.00				
2006B Proof	6,500	Value: 25.00				
2007B Proof	—	Value: 25.00				
2008B Proof	—	Value: 25.00				
2009B Proof	—	Value: 25.00				
2010B Proof	—	Value: 25.00				
2011B Proof	6,000	Value: 25.00				

KM# 688   20 CENTS
11.3000 g., Copper-Nickel, 28.65 mm. **Ruler:** Elizabeth II **Obv:**
Head with tiara right **Rev:** Group of Australian Volunteers **Edge:**
Reeded

Date	Mintage	F	VF	XF	Unc	BU
2003B	7,600,000	—	—	—	3.00	4.00
2003B Proof	—	Value: 15.00				

KM# 688a   20 CENTS
11.3000 g., 0.9990 Silver 0.3629 oz. ASW, 28.65 mm. **Ruler:**
Elizabeth II **Obv:** Head right **Rev:** Group of Australian Volunteers
Edge: Reeded

Date	Mintage	F	VF	XF	Unc	BU
2003B Proof	6,500	Value: 35.00				

KM# 688b   20 CENTS
24.3600 g., 0.9990 Gold 0.7824 oz. AGW, 28.65 mm. **Ruler:**
Elizabeth II **Obv:** Head with tiara right **Rev:** Group of Australian
Volunteers **Edge:** Reeded

Date	Mintage	F	VF	XF	Unc	BU
2003B Proof	650	Value: 1,350				

KM# 745   20 CENTS
11.3000 g., Copper-Nickel, 28.65 mm. **Ruler:** Elizabeth II
Subject: 60th Anniversary - End of WWII **Obv:** Head right **Rev:**
Soldier with wife and child **Edge:** Reeded

Date	Mintage	F	VF	XF	Unc	BU
2005B	33,500,000	—	—	—	2.00	3.00
2005B Proof	—	Value: 10.00				

KM# 745a   20 CENTS
13.3600 g., 0.9990 Silver 0.4291 oz. ASW, 28.65 mm. **Ruler:**
Elizabeth II **Obv:** Head right **Rev:** Soldier with wife and child
Edge: Reeded

Date	Mintage	F	VF	XF	Unc	BU
2005B Proof	6,500	Value: 35.00				

KM# 745b   20 CENTS
24.3600 g., 0.9999 Gold 0.7831 oz. AGW, 28.65 mm. **Ruler:**
Elizabeth II **Obv:** Head right **Rev:** Soldier with wife and child
Edge: Reeded

Date	Mintage	F	VF	XF	Unc	BU
2005B Proof	650	Value: 1,350				

KM# 66a   20 CENTS
13.3600 g., 0.9990 Silver 0.4291 oz. ASW, 28.52 mm. **Ruler:**
Elizabeth II **Obv:** Young bust right **Rev:** Platypus **Edge:** Reeded

Date	Mintage	F	VF	XF	Unc	BU
2006 Proof	6,500	Value: 28.00				

KM# 403b   20 CENTS
24.5600 g., 0.9999 Gold 0.7895 oz. AGW, 28.52 mm. **Ruler:**
Elizabeth II **Subject:** Federation Centennial **Obv:** Head with tiara
right **Rev:** Duckbill Platyus **Edge:** Reeded

Date	Mintage	F	VF	XF	Unc	BU
2006B Proof	300	Value: 1,500				

KM# 820   20 CENTS
11.3000 g., Copper-Nickel, 28.65 mm. **Ruler:** Elizabeth II
Subject: Year of the Surf Lifesaver **Obv:** Head with tiara right
Rev: Female lifesaver working line **Edge:** Reeded

Date	Mintage	F	VF	XF	Unc	BU
2007	—	—	—	—	10.00	7.00
2007 Proof	—	Value: 20.00				

KM# 820a   20 CENTS
13.3600 g., 0.9990 Silver 0.4291 oz. ASW, 28.52 mm. **Ruler:**
Elizabeth II **Subject:** Year of the Surfer Lifesaver **Rev:** Female
with rope line

Date	Mintage	F	VF	XF	Unc	BU
2007B Proof	—	Value: 25.00				

KM# 1058   20 CENTS
11.3000 g., Copper-Nickel, 28.65 mm. **Ruler:** Elizabeth II
Subject: Planet earth **Rev:** Map of Australia with water and rocks
around

Date	Mintage	F	VF	XF	Unc	BU
2008	—	—	—	—	12.00	10.00
2008 Proof	—	Value: 12.00				

KM# 1075   20 CENTS
15.5500 g., Copper-Nickel, 28.52 mm. **Ruler:** Elizabeth II
Subject: Year of Astronomy **Rev:** Star gazers

Date	Mintage	F	VF	XF	Unc	BU
2009 Unc	—	—	—	—	10.00	12.00
2009 Proof	—	Value: 25.00				

KM# 1088   20 CENTS
15.5500 g., Copper-Nickel, 28.52 mm. **Ruler:** Elizabeth II **Rev:**
Poppy

Date	Mintage	F	VF	XF	Unc	BU
2009	—	—	—	—	10.00	12.00

KM# 1253   20 CENTS
12.8600 g., 0.9990 Silver 0.4130 oz. ASW, 28.6 mm. **Ruler:**
Elizabeth II **Subject:** 1966 Decimal Pattern **Obv:** Head right **Rev:**
Black swan in flight

Date	Mintage	F	VF	XF	Unc	BU
2009P Proof	10,000	Value: 200				

KM# 1433   20 CENTS
11.3000 g., Copper-Nickel, 28.65 mm. **Ruler:** Elizabeth II
Subject: Nurses **Rev:** Nurse looking over serviceman

Date	Mintage	F	VF	XF	Unc	BU
2009C	—	—	—	—	5.00	7.00

KM# 1430   20 CENTS
11.3000 g., Copper-Nickel, 28.65 mm. **Ruler:** Elizabeth II
Subject: Burke & Wills, 150th Anniversary **Rev:** Burke and Wills
on camels

Date	Mintage	F	VF	XF	Unc	BU
2010C	—	—	—	—	5.00	7.00
2010C Proof	—	Value: 10.00				

KM# 1502   20 CENTS
11.3000 g., Copper-Nickel, 28.65 mm. **Ruler:** Elizabeth II
Subject: Wool Industry **Rev:** Wheel with sheep industry design
in spoke wedges

Date	Mintage	F	VF	XF	Unc	BU
2010C	—	—	—	—	2.00	4.00
2010C Proof	—	Value: 12.00				

KM# 1513   20 CENTS
11.3000 g., Copper-Nickel, 28.65 mm. **Ruler:** Elizabeth II
Subject: Taxation office, 100th Anniversary

Date	Mintage	F	VF	XF	Unc	BU
2010	—	—	—	—	1.50	2.50

KM# 1518   20 CENTS
11.3000 g., Copper-Nickel, 28.65 mm. **Ruler:** Elizabeth II
Subject: Lost Soldiers of Promelles **Rev:** Soldier carrying
another on his shoulder

Date	Mintage	F	VF	XF	Unc	BU
2010	—	—	—	—	1.50	2.50

KM# 1634   20 CENTS
11.3000 g., Copper-Nickel, 28.65 mm. **Ruler:** Elizabeth II
Subject: Year of the Volunteer **Obv:** Head with tiara right **Rev:**
Logo within wreath

Date	Mintage	F	VF	XF	Unc	BU
2011	—	—	—	—	3.00	4.00

KM# 1648   20 CENTS
11.3000 g., Copper-Nickel, 28.65 mm. **Ruler:** Elizabeth II
Subject: War Historians **Obv:** Head with tiara right **Rev:** Man
with tripod taking photograph from atop tank

Date	Mintage	F	VF	XF	Unc	BU
2011	—	—	—	—	3.00	4.00

KM# 1517   20 CENTS
11.3000 g., Copper-Nickel, 28.65 mm. **Ruler:** Elizabeth II
Subject: Ashes Cricket tournament

Date	Mintage	F	VF	XF	Unc	BU
2011	—	—	—	—	1.50	2.50

KM# 1566   20 CENTS
11.3000 g., Copper-Nickel, 28.65 mm. **Ruler:** Elizabeth II
Subject: Royal Wedding **Rev:** Catherine Middleton and Prince
William busts left

Date	Mintage	F	VF	XF	Unc	BU
2011	—	—	—	—	4.00	6.00

KM# 1642   20 CENTS
11.3000 g., Copper-Nickel, 28.65 mm. **Ruler:** Elizabeth II
Subject: International Womens Day, 100th Anniversary **Obv:**
Head with tiara right **Rev:** Three stylized joyful figures

Date	Mintage	F	VF	XF	Unc	BU
2011	—	—	—	—	3.00	4.00

KM# 1625   20 CENTS
11.3000 g., Copper-Nickel, 28.65 mm. **Ruler:** Elizabeth II
Subject: Australian Wheat **Obv:** Head with tiara right **Rev:** Wheat
ear upright

Date	Mintage	F	VF	XF	Unc	BU
2012	—	—	—	—	2.00	2.50
2012 Proof	—	Value: 15.00				

KM# 1742   20 CENTS
11.3000 g., Copper-Nickel, 28.65 mm. **Ruler:** Elizabeth II
Subject: World War II, Bombing of Australia **Obv:** Head with tiara
right **Rev:** People entering air raid shelter

Date	Mintage	F	VF	XF	Unc	BU
2012	—	—	—	—	3.00	4.00

KM# 1743   20 CENTS
11.3000 g., Copper-Nickel, 28.65 mm. **Ruler:** Elizabeth II **Obv:**
Head with tiara right **Rev:** Military lookout

Date	Mintage	F	VF	XF	Unc	BU
2012	—	—	—	—	3.00	5.00

KM# 1743a   20 CENTS
13.3600 g., 0.9990 Silver 0.4291 oz. ASW, 28.65 mm. **Ruler:**
Elizabeth II **Subject:** Bombing of Australia - World War II **Obv:**
Head with tiara right **Rev:** Military lookout

Date	Mintage	F	VF	XF	Unc	BU
2012 Proof	—	Value: 35.00				

KM# 599   25 CENTS
7.7750 g., 0.9990 Silver 0.2497 oz. ASW, 24.8 mm. **Ruler:**
Elizabeth II **Obv:** Head with tiara right **Rev:** Parliament House
Edge: Plain **Shape:** 7-pointed star **Note:** "The Dump" portion of
the "Holey Dollar" KM#598.

Date	Mintage	F	VF	XF	Unc	BU
2001 Prooflike	30,000	—	—	—	—	28.00

KM# 491.1   50 CENTS
15.5500 g., Copper-Nickel, 31.65 mm. **Ruler:** Elizabeth II
Subject: Centenary of Federation, 1901-2001 **Obv:** Head with
tiara right **Rev:** Commonwealth coat of arms **Edge:** Plain **Shape:**
12-sided **Note:** Prev. KM#491.

Date	Mintage	F	VF	XF	Unc	BU
2001B	43,149,600	—	—	—	5.00	6.00
2001B Proof	—	Value: 40.00				

KM# 491.1a   50 CENTS
33.8800 g., 0.9999 Gold 1.0891 oz. AGW, 31.65 mm. **Ruler:**
Elizabeth II **Subject:** Federation Centennial **Obv:** Elizabeth II
Rev: Commonwealth arms above value

Date	Mintage	F	VF	XF	Unc	BU
2001B Proof	650	Value: 1,900				

KM# 491.2   50 CENTS
15.5500 g., Copper-Nickel, 31.65 mm. **Ruler:** Elizabeth II
Subject: Federation Centennial **Obv:** Elizabeth II right **Rev:**
Multicolor arms above value **Edge:** Plain **Shape:** 12-sided

Date	Mintage	F	VF	XF	Unc	BU
2001B Proof	60,000	Value: 50.00				

KM# 491.2a   50 CENTS
15.5500 g., Copper-Nickel, 31.65 mm. **Ruler:** Elizabeth II
Subject: Centenary of Federation, 1901-2001 **Obv:** Head with
tiara right **Rev:** Multicolored Commonwealth coat of arms **Edge:**
Plain **Shape:** 12-sided **Note:** Prev. KM#491a.

Date	Mintage	F	VF	XF	Unc	BU
2001B Proof	—	Value: 50.00				

KM# 533   50 CENTS
15.5500 g., Copper-Nickel, 31.65 mm. **Ruler:** Elizabeth II
Subject: Centennial - Norfolk Island Federation **Obv:** Head with
tiara right **Rev:** Norfolk Island coat of arms **Edge:** Plain **Shape:**
12-sided

Date	Mintage	F	VF	XF	Unc	BU
2001B	2,000,000	—	—	—	6.00	15.00
2001B Proof	—	Value: 70.00				

KM# 535   50 CENTS
16.8860 g., 0.9990 Silver 0.5423 oz. ASW, 32.1 mm. **Ruler:**
Elizabeth II **Subject:** Year of the Snake **Obv:** Head right **Rev:**
Snake with eggs **Edge:** Plain

Date	Mintage	F	VF	XF	Unc	BU
2001	500,000	—	—	—	—	22.00
2001P Proof	5,000	Value: 65.00				

KM# 551   50 CENTS
15.5500 g., Copper-Nickel, 31.65 mm. **Ruler:** Elizabeth II
Series: Centenary of Federation - New South Wales **Obv:** Head
with tiara right **Rev:** New South Wales state arms **Edge:** Plain
Shape: 12-sided

Date	Mintage	F	VF	XF	Unc	BU
2001	3,000,000	—	—	—	6.00	7.00
2001 Proof	—	Value: 40.00				

KM# 553   50 CENTS
15.5500 g., Copper-Nickel, 31.65 mm. **Ruler:** Elizabeth II
Series: Centenary of Federation - Australian Capital Territory
Obv: Head right **Rev:** Australian Capital Territory arms **Edge:**
Plain **Shape:** 12-sided

Date	Mintage	F	VF	XF	Unc	BU
2001	2,000,000	—	—	—	6.00	9.00
2001 Proof	—	Value: 40.00				

KM# 555   50 CENTS
15.5500 g., Copper-Nickel, 31.65 mm. **Ruler:** Elizabeth II
Series: Centenary of Federation - Queensland **Obv:** Head with
tiara right **Rev:** Queensland state arms **Edge:** Plain **Shape:** 12-
sided

Date	Mintage	F	VF	XF	Unc	BU
2001	2,300,000	—	—	—	6.00	9.00
2001 Proof	—	Value: 40.00				

KM# 557   50 CENTS
15.5500 g., Copper-Nickel, 31.65 mm. **Ruler:** Elizabeth II
Series: Centenary of Federation - Victoria **Obv:** Head with tiara
right **Rev:** Victoria state arms **Edge:** Plain **Shape:** 12-sided

Date	Mintage	F	VF	XF	Unc	BU
2001	2,800,000	—	—	—	6.00	8.00
2001 Proof	—	Value: 40.00				

KM# 559   50 CENTS
15.5500 g., Copper-Nickel, 31.65 mm. **Ruler:** Elizabeth II
Series: Centenary of Federation - Northern Territory **Obv:** Head
with tiara right **Rev:** Northern Territory state arms **Edge:** Plain
Shape: 12-sided

Date	Mintage	F	VF	XF	Unc	BU
2001	2,100,000	—	—	—	6.00	10.00
2001 Proof	—	Value: 50.00				

KM# 561   50 CENTS
15.5500 g., Copper-Nickel, 31.65 mm. **Ruler:** Elizabeth II
Series: Centenary of Federation - South Australia **Obv:** Head
with tiara right **Rev:** South Australia state arms **Edge:** Plain
Shape: 12-sided

Date	Mintage	F	VF	XF	Unc	BU
2001	2,400,000	—	—	—	6.00	20.00
2001 Proof	—	Value: 60.00				

KM# 563   50 CENTS
15.5500 g., Copper-Nickel, 31.65 mm. **Ruler:** Elizabeth II

Series: Centenary of Federation - Western Australia **Obv:** Head
with tiara right **Rev:** Western Australia state arms **Edge:** Plain
Shape: 12-sided

Date	Mintage	F	VF	XF	Unc	BU
2001	2,400,000	—	—	—	6.00	15.00
2001 Proof	—	Value: 50.00				

KM# 565   50 CENTS
15.5500 g., Copper-Nickel, 31.65 mm. **Ruler:** Elizabeth II
Series: Centenary of Federation - Tasmania **Obv:** Head with
tiara right **Rev:** Tasmania state arms **Edge:** Plain **Shape:** 12-
sided

Date	Mintage	F	VF	XF	Unc	BU
2001	2,200,000	—	—	—	6.00	10.00
2001 Proof	—	Value: 50.00				

KM# 694   50 CENTS
15.5500 g., Copper-Nickel, 31.65 mm. **Ruler:** Elizabeth II **Obv:**
Head with tiara right **Rev:** Koala, Lorikeet (bird) and Wombat
Edge: Plain **Shape:** 12-sided

Date	Mintage	F	VF	XF	Unc	BU
2001 Proof	—	Value: 9.00				
2004B	10,577,000	—	—	—	3.00	5.00

KM# 602   50 CENTS
15.5500 g., Copper-Nickel, 31.65 mm. **Ruler:** Elizabeth II
Subject: The Outback Region **Obv:** Head right **Rev:** Windmill
Edge: Plain **Shape:** 12-sided

Date	Mintage	F	VF	XF	Unc	BU
2002B	11,507,000	—	—	—	6.00	7.00
2002B Proof	39,000	Value: 25.00				

KM# 645   50 CENTS
15.5500 g., Copper-Nickel, 31.65 mm. **Ruler:** Elizabeth II
Subject: Queen's 50th Anniversary of Accession **Obv:** Head right
Rev: Crown and star **Shape:** 12-sided

Date	Mintage	F	VF	XF	Unc	BU
2002B	32,102	—	—	—	30.00	60.00

Note: Issued only in PNC cover

KM# 645a   50 CENTS
18.2400 g., 0.9990 Silver 0.5858 oz. ASW, 31.65 mm. **Ruler:**
Elizabeth II **Subject:** Queen's 50th Anniversary of Accession
Obv: Head right **Rev:** Crown and star **Shape:** 12-sided

Date	Mintage	F	VF	XF	Unc	BU
2002B Proof	13,500	Value: 60.00				

KM# 404a   50 CENTS
18.2400 g., 0.9999 Silver 0.5863 oz. ASW, 31.65 mm. **Ruler:**
Elizabeth II **Obv:** Head with tiara right **Rev:** Arms **Edge:** Plain
Shape: 12-sided

Date	Mintage	F	VF	XF	Unc	BU
2003B Proof	6,500	Value: 35.00				
2004B Proof	6,500	Value: 35.00				
2005B Proof	6,500	Value: 35.00				
2006B Proof	—	Value: 35.00				
2007B Proof	—	Value: 35.00				
2008B Proof	—	Value: 35.00				
2009B Proof	—	Value: 35.00				
2010B Proof	—	Value: 35.00				
2011B Proof	6,000	Value: 35.00				

KM# 689   50 CENTS
15.5500 g., Copper-Nickel, 31.65 mm. **Ruler:** Elizabeth II **Obv:**
Head right **Rev:** Value within circle of volunteer activities **Edge:**
Plain **Shape:** 12-sided

Date	Mintage	F	VF	XF	Unc	BU
2003B	13,927,000	—	—	—	4.50	5.00
2003B Proof	—	Value: 20.00				

KM# 689a   50 CENTS
15.5500 g., 0.9990 Silver 0.4994 oz. ASW, 31.65 mm. **Ruler:**
Elizabeth II **Obv:** Head right **Rev:** Value within circle of volunteer
activities

Date	Mintage	F	VF	XF	Unc	BU
2003B Proof	6,500	Value: 45.00				

KM# 799   50 CENTS
14.0900 g., Aluminum-Bronze, 31.51 mm. **Ruler:** Elizabeth II
Subject: 50th Anniversary of the Coronation of Elizabeth II **Obv:**
Head with tiara right **Rev:** Crown, Federation star, dates **Edge:**
Plain **Shape:** 12-sided

Date	Mintage	F	VF	XF	Unc	BU
2003	65,003	—	—	—	35.00	40.00

KM# 799a   50 CENTS
18.2400 g., 0.9990 Silver 0.5858 oz. ASW, 31.51 mm. **Ruler:**
Elizabeth II **Subject:** 50th Anniversary of the Coronation of
Elizabeth II **Obv:** Head with tiara right **Rev:** Crown, Federation
star, dates **Edge:** Plain **Shape:** 12-sided

Date	Mintage	F	VF	XF	Unc	BU
2003 Proof	6,967	Value: 60.00				

KM# 404   50 CENTS
15.5500 g., Copper-Nickel, 31.65 mm. **Ruler:** Elizabeth II **Obv:**
Head with tiara right **Rev:** Australian coat of arms with kangaroo
and emu supporters **Edge:** Plain **Shape:** 12-sided

Date	Mintage	F	VF	XF	Unc	BU
2004	17,918,000	—	—	—	9.00	10.00
2004 Proof	—	Value: 25.00				

Date	Mintage	F	VF	XF	Unc	BU
2005	30,000	—	—	—	25.00	40.00
Note: Issued as part of a PNC only						
2005 Proof	—	Value: 10.00				
2006	—	—	—	—	9.00	10.00
2006 Proof	—	Value: 25.00				
2007	—	—	—	—	1.00	1.50
2007 Proof	—	Value: 10.00				
2008	—	—	—	—	7.00	8.00
2008 Proof	—	Value: 10.00				
2009	—	—	—	—	7.00	8.00
2009 Proof	—	Value: 10.00				
2010	—	—	—	—	7.00	8.00
2010 Proof	—	Value: 10.00				
2011	—	—	—	—	7.00	8.00
2011 Proof	—	Value: 10.00				

KM# 694a   50 CENTS
18.2400 g., 0.9990 Silver 0.5858 oz. ASW, 31.65 mm.   **Ruler:** Elizabeth II **Obv:** Head with tiara right **Rev:** Wombat, lorikeet and koala **Edge:** Plain **Shape:** 12-sided

Date	Mintage	F	VF	XF	Unc
2004B Proof	8,203	Value: 75.00			

KM# 746   50 CENTS
15.5500 g., Copper-Nickel, 31.65 mm.   **Ruler:** Elizabeth II **Obv:** Head with tiara right **Rev:** Military cemetery scene **Edge:** Plain **Shape:** 12-sided

Date	Mintage	F	VF	XF	Unc	BU
2005B	11,033,000	—	—	—	3.00	4.00
2005B Proof	—	Value: 20.00				

KM# 746a   50 CENTS
18.2400 g., 0.9990 Silver 0.5858 oz. ASW, 31.65 mm.   **Ruler:** Elizabeth II **Obv:** Head with tiara right **Rev:** Military cemetery scene **Edge:** Plain **Shape:** 12-sided

Date	Mintage	F	VF	XF	Unc	BU
2005B Proof	6,500	Value: 38.00				

KM# 746b   50 CENTS
33.6300 g., 0.9999 Gold 1.0811 oz. AGW, 31.65 mm.   **Ruler:** Elizabeth II **Obv:** Head with tiara right **Rev:** Military cemetery scene **Edge:** Plain **Shape:** 12-sided

Date	Mintage	F	VF	XF	Unc	BU
2005B Proof	650	Value: 1,850				

KM# 769   50 CENTS
15.5500 g., Copper-Nickel, 31.65 mm.   **Ruler:** Elizabeth II **Subject:** Commonweath Games, Secondary School Design Competition **Obv:** Head with tiara right **Rev:** Athletes

Date	Mintage	F	VF	XF	Unc	BU
2005	20,500,000	—	—	—	2.50	3.50
2005 Proof	5,402	Value: 65.00				

KM# 67a   50 CENTS
18.2400 g., 0.9990 Silver 0.5858 oz. ASW, 31.51 mm.   **Ruler:** Elizabeth II **Obv:** Young bust right **Rev:** Australian coat of arms **Edge:** Reeded

Date	Mintage	F	VF	XF	Unc	BU
2006 Proof	6,500	Value: 65.00				

KM# 770   50 CENTS
15.5500 g., Copper-Nickel, 31.65 mm.   **Ruler:** Elizabeth II **Subject:** Basketball **Obv:** Head with tiara right **Obv. Legend:** ELIZABETH II - AUSTRALIA **Rev:** Basketball player shooting basket, Melbourne 2006 logo at left **Rev. Legend:** XVIII COMMONWEALTH GAMES **Shape:** 12-sided

Date	Mintage	F	VF	XF	Unc	BU
2006	5,002	—	—	—	8.50	10.00

KM# 771   50 CENTS
15.5500 g., Copper-Nickel, 31.65 mm.   **Ruler:** Elizabeth II **Subject:** Hockey **Obv:** Head with tiara right **Obv. Legend:** ELIZABETH II - AUSTRALIA **Rev:** Hockey player hitting puck, Melboune 2006 logo at upper left **Rev. Legend:** XVIII COMMONWEALTH GAMES **Shape:** 12-sided

Date	Mintage	F	VF	XF	Unc	BU
2006	4,082	—	—	—	8.50	10.00

KM# 772   50 CENTS
15.5500 g., Copper-Nickel, 31.65 mm.   **Ruler:** Elizabeth II **Subject:** Shooting **Obv:** Head with tiara right **Obv. Legend:** ELIZABETH II - AUSTRALIA **Rev:** Shooter, Melbourne 2006 logo at upper right **Rev. Legend:** XVIII COMMONWEALTH GAMES **Shape:** 12-sided

Date	Mintage	F	VF	XF	Unc	BU
2006	21,070	—	—	—	8.50	10.00

KM# 773   50 CENTS
15.5500 g., Copper-Nickel, 31.65 mm.   **Ruler:** Elizabeth II **Subject:** Weightlifting **Obv:** Head with tiara right **Obv. Legend:** ELIZABETH II - AUSTRALIA **Rev:** Weightlifter holding barbells above head, Melbourne 2006 logo at left **Rev. Legend:** XVIII COMMONWEALTH GAMES **Shape:** 12-sided

Date	Mintage	F	VF	XF	Unc	BU
2006	22,332	—	—	—	8.50	10.00

KM# 774   50 CENTS
15.5500 g., Copper-Nickel, 31.65 mm.   **Ruler:** Elizabeth II **Subject:** Gymnastics **Obv:** Head with tiara right **Obv. Legend:** ELIZABETH II - AUSTRALIA **Rev:** Gymnast standing with right leg up, Melbourne 2006 logo at left **Rev. Legend:** XVIII COMMONWEALTH GAMES **Edge:** Plain **Shape:** 12-sided

Date	Mintage	F	VF	XF	Unc	BU
2006	3,000	—	—	—	8.50	10.00

KM# 775   50 CENTS
15.5500 g., Copper-Nickel, 31.65 mm.   **Ruler:** Elizabeth II **Subject:** Rugby 7's **Obv:** Head with tiara right **Obv. Legend:** ELIZABETH II - AUSTRALIA **Rev:** Rugby player running right, Melbourne 2006 logo at upper left **Rev. Legend:** XVIII COMMONWEALTH GAMES **Shape:** 12-sided

Date	Mintage	F	VF	XF	Unc	BU
2006	24,427	—	—	—	8.50	10.00

KM# 776   50 CENTS
15.5500 g., Copper-Nickel, 31.65 mm.   **Ruler:** Elizabeth II **Subject:** Cycling **Obv:** Head with tiara right **Obv. Legend:** ELIZABETH II - AUSTRALIA **Rev:** Cyclist heading right, Melbourne 2006 logo at upper right **Rev. Legend:** XVIII COMMONWEALTH GAMES **Shape:** 12-sided

Date	Mintage	F	VF	XF	Unc	BU
2006	22,861	—	—	—	8.50	10.00

KM# 777   50 CENTS
15.5500 g., Copper-Nickel, 31.65 mm.   **Ruler:** Elizabeth II **Subject:** Athletics **Obv:** Head with tiara right **Obv. Legend:** ELIZABETH II - AUSTRALIA **Rev:** Runner right, Melbourne 2006 logo at lower right **Rev. Legend:** XVIII COMMONWEALTH GAMES **Shape:** 12-sided

Date	Mintage	F	VF	XF	Unc	BU
2006	22,475	—	—	—	8.50	10.00

KM# 778   50 CENTS
15.5500 g., Copper-Nickel, 31.65 mm.   **Ruler:** Elizabeth II

Subject: Triathlon **Obv:** Head with tiara right **Obv. Legend:** ELIZABETH II - AUSRALIA **Rev:** Bicycle, runner, Melbourne 2006 logo below **Rev. Legend:** XVIII COMMONWEALTH GAMES **Shape:** 12-sided

Date	Mintage	F	VF	XF	Unc	BU
2006	22,302	—	—	—	8.50	10.00

KM# 779   50 CENTS
15.5500 g., Copper-Nickel, 31.65 mm.   **Ruler:** Elizabeth II
Subject: Netball **Obv:** Head with tiara right **Obv. Legend:** ELIZABETH II - AUSTRALIA **Rev:** Player shooting basket, Melbourne 2006 logo at upper left **Rev. Legend:** XVIII COMMONWEALTH GAMES **Shape:** 12-sided

Date	Mintage	F	VF	XF	Unc	BU
2006	22,432	—	—	—	8.50	10.00

KM# 780   50 CENTS
15.5500 g., Copper-Nickel, 31.65 mm.   **Ruler:** Elizabeth II
Subject: Table tennis **Obv:** Head with tiara right **Obv. Legend:** ELIZABETH II - AUSTRALIA **Rev:** Player hitting ball, Melbourne 2006 logo below **Rev. Legend:** XVIII COMMONWEALTH GAMES **Shape:** 12-sided

Date	Mintage	F	VF	XF	Unc	BU
2006	22,070	—	—	—	8.50	10.00

KM# 781   50 CENTS
15.5500 g., Copper-Nickel, 31.65 mm.   **Ruler:** Elizabeth II
Subject: Aquatics **Obv:** Head with tiara right **Obv. Legend:** ELIZABETH II - AUSTRALIA **Rev:** Swimmer, Melbourne 2006 logo **Rev. Legend:** XVIII COMMONWEALTH GAMES **Shape:** 12-sided

Date	Mintage	F	VF	XF	Unc	BU
2006	31,702	—	—	—	8.50	10.00

KM# 801   50 CENTS
15.5500 g., Copper-Nickel, 31.65 mm.   **Ruler:** Elizabeth II
Subject: 80th Birthday of Queen Elizabeth II **Obv:** Head with tiara right **Rev:** Royal Cipher **Shape:** 12-sided

Date	Mintage	F	VF	XF	Unc	BU
2006	28,191	—	—	—	45.00	60.00

KM# 801a   50 CENTS
18.2400 g., 0.9990 Silver partially gilt 0.5858 oz. ASW, 31.65 mm.   **Ruler:** Elizabeth II **Subject:** 80th Birthday of Queen Elizabeth II **Obv:** Head with tiara right **Rev:** Crowned Royal Cipher on large 80, border of alternating British and Australian flags **Shape:** 12-sided

Date	Mintage	F	VF	XF	Unc	BU
2006 Proof	7,500	Value: 85.00				

KM# 802   50 CENTS
15.5500 g., Copper-Nickel, 31.65 mm.   **Ruler:** Elizabeth II
Subject: Visit of Queen Elizabeth II **Obv:** Head with tiara right **Rev:** Australian map and world globe **Shape:** 12-sided

Date	Mintage	F	VF	XF	Unc	BU
2006	—	—	—	—	30.00	45.00

KM# 802a   50 CENTS
18.2400 g., 0.9990 Silver partially gilt 0.5858 oz. ASW, 31.65 mm.   **Ruler:** Elizabeth II **Subject:** Visit of Queen Elizabeth II **Obv:** Head with tiara right **Rev:** Australian map and world globe **Shape:** 12-sided

Date	Mintage	F	VF	XF	Unc	BU
2006 Proof	7,500	Value: 90.00				

KM# 821   50 CENTS
13.2800 g., 0.8000 Silver 0.3416 oz. ASW, 31.51 mm.   **Ruler:** Elizabeth II **Obv:** Head with tiara right **Rev:** Australian coat of arms **Edge:** Reeded

Date	Mintage	F	VF	XF	Unc	BU
2006 Proof	—	Value: 70.00				

KM# 821a   50 CENTS
25.3000 g., 0.9990 Gold 0.8126 oz. AGW, 31.51 mm.   **Ruler:** Elizabeth II **Obv:** Head with tiara right **Rev:** Australian coat of arms **Edge:** Reeded

Date	Mintage	F	VF	XF	Unc	BU
2006 Proof	300	Value: 1,450				

KM# 1001   50 CENTS
15.5500 g., Copper-Nickel, 31.65 mm.   **Ruler:** Elizabeth II
Subject: XVIII COMMONWEALTH GAMES **Obv:** Head with tiara right **Obv. Legend:** ELIZABETH II - AUSTRALIA **Rev:** Squash player, Melbourne 2006 logo **Edge:** Plain **Shape:** 12-sided

Date	Mintage	F	VF	XF	Unc	BU
2006	—	—	—	—	12.50	15.00

KM# 1002   50 CENTS
15.5500 g., Copper-Nickel, 31.65 mm.   **Ruler:** Elizabeth II
Subject: XVIII COMMONWEALTH GAMES **Obv:** Head with tiara right **Obv. Legend:** ELIZABETH II - AUSTRALIA **Rev:** Lawn bowler, Melbourne 2006 logo **Edge:** Plain **Shape:** 12-sided

Date	Mintage	F	VF	XF	Unc	BU
2006	22,602	—	—	—	12.50	15.00

KM# 1003   50 CENTS
15.5500 g., Copper-Nickel, 31.65 mm.   **Ruler:** Elizabeth II
Subject: XVIII COMMONWEALTH GAMES **Obv:** Head with tiara right **Obv. Legend:** ELIZABETH II - AUSTRALIA **Rev:** Boxer, Melbourne 2006 logo **Edge:** Plain **Shape:** 12-sided

Date	Mintage	F	VF	XF	Unc	BU
2006	—	—	—	—	12.50	15.00

KM# 1004   50 CENTS
Aluminum-Bronze, 30 mm.   **Ruler:** Elizabeth II **Obv:** Head with tiara right **Obv. Legend:** ELIZABETH II - AUSTRALIA **Rev:** Everage head facing, multicolor **Rev. Legend:** DAME EDNA EVERAGE - 50TH ANNIVERSARY

Date	Mintage	F	VF	XF	Unc	BU
ND(2006)P	—	—	—	—	20.00	25.00

KM# 1570   50 CENTS
15.5500 g., Copper-Nickel, 31.65 mm.   **Ruler:** Elizabeth II
Subject: Commonwealth Games **Rev:** Badminton

Date	Mintage	F	VF	XF	Unc	BU
2006	—	—	—	—	8.50	10.00

KM# 1041   50 CENTS
15.5500 g., Copper-Nickel, 31.65 mm.   **Ruler:** Elizabeth II
Subject: Elizabeth and Philip Wedding Anniversary **Rev:** Profile portraits and diamond at center of circle of trumpets

Date	Mintage	F	VF	XF	Unc	BU
2007B	60,030	—	—	—	15.00	18.00

KM# 1049   50 CENTS
15.5500 g., Copper-Nickel, 31.65 mm.   **Ruler:** Elizabeth II
Subject: Scouting Centennial in Australia **Rev:** Australian Scout Emblem

Date	Mintage	F	VF	XF	Unc	BU
2008	49,517	—	—	—	10.00	12.00

KM# 1062   50 CENTS
15.5500 g., Copper-Nickel, 31.65 mm.   **Ruler:** Elizabeth II
Subject: 25th Anniversary Australia's Win of the America's Cup **Rev:** Yacht Australia II sailing left **Shape:** 12-sided

Date	Mintage	F	VF	XF	Unc	BU
2008	32,916	—	—	—	15.00	18.00

KM# 1100   50 CENTS
15.5500 g., 0.9990 Silver 0.4994 oz. ASW, 36.6 mm.   **Ruler:**

Elizabeth II **Subject:** Great Barrier Reef **Obv:** Head right **Rev:** Lion fish, multicolor **Edge:** reeded

Date	Mintage	F	VF	XF	Unc	BU
2009P Proof	Est. 10,000	Value: 75.00				

KM# 1101   50 CENTS
15.5500 g., 0.9990 Silver 0.4994 oz. ASW, 36.6 mm. **Ruler:** Elizabeth II **Subject:** Great Barrier Reef **Obv:** Head right **Rev:** Leafy Sea Dragon, multicolor **Edge:** Reeded

Date	Mintage	F	VF	XF	Unc	BU
2009P Proof	Est. 10,000	Value: 75.00				

KM# 1102   50 CENTS
15.5500 g., 0.9990 Silver 0.4994 oz. ASW, 36.6 mm. **Ruler:** Elizabeth II **Subject:** Great Barrier Reef **Rev:** Sea turtle, multicolor

Date	Mintage	F	VF	XF	Unc	BU
2009P Proof	—	Value: 75.00				

KM# 1432   50 CENTS
15.5500 g., Copper-Nickel, 31.65 mm. **Ruler:** Elizabeth II **Subject:** Moon Landing 40th Anniversary **Rev:** Earth, moon and orbiter

Date	Mintage	F	VF	XF	Unc	BU
2009C	—	—	—	—	—	10.00

KM# 1328   50 CENTS
15.5500 g., 0.9990 Silver 0.4994 oz. ASW, 36.6 mm. **Ruler:** Elizabeth II **Subject:** Great Barrier Reef **Obv:** Head right **Rev:** Clownfish, multicolor

Date	Mintage	F	VF	XF	Unc	BU
2010P Proof	—	Value: 60.00				

KM# 1329   50 CENTS
15.5730 g., 0.9990 Silver 0.5002 oz. ASW, 36.6 mm. **Ruler:** Elizabeth II **Subject:** Great Barrier Reef **Rev:** Big belly sea horse in multicolor

Date	Mintage	F	VF	XF	Unc	BU
2010P Proof	—	Value: 75.00				

KM# 1389   50 CENTS
15.5500 g., 0.9990 Silver 0.4994 oz. ASW, 36.6 mm. **Ruler:** Elizabeth II **Subject:** Great Barrier Reef - Morey Eel **Obv:** Hear right **Rev:** Tessellate Moray Eel, multicolor

Date	Mintage	F	VF	XF	Unc	BU
2010(p) Proof	—	Value: 86.00				

KM# 1450   50 CENTS
15.5600 g., 0.9990 Silver 0.4997 oz. ASW **Ruler:** Elizabeth II **Rev:** Australian Sugar Glider, multicolor

Date	Mintage	F	VF	XF	Unc	BU
2010P	—	Value: 45.00				

KM# 1456   50 CENTS
15.5600 g., 0.9990 Silver 0.4997 oz. ASW **Ruler:** Elizabeth II **Rev:** Australian kangaroo, multicolor

Date	Mintage	F	VF	XF	Unc	BU
2010P Proof	—	Value: 25.00				

KM# 1493   50 CENTS
15.5000 g., 0.9990 Silver 0.4978 oz. ASW, 36.6 mm. **Ruler:** Elizabeth II **Rev:** Dingo

Date	Mintage	F	VF	XF	Unc	BU
2010 Proof	—	Value: 50.00				

KM# 1500   50 CENTS
15.5500 g., Copper-Nickel, 31.65 mm. **Ruler:** Elizabeth II **Subject:** Australia Day **Shape:** 12-sided

Date	Mintage	F	VF	XF	Unc	BU
2010	—	—	—	—	2.50	4.50

KM# 1501   50 CENTS
15.5500 g., Copper-Nickel, 31.65 mm. **Ruler:** Elizabeth II **Subject:** Melbourne Cup, 150th Anniversary **Rev:** Horses racing right passing finish pole **Shape:** 12-sided

Date	Mintage	F	VF	XF	Unc	BU
2010	—	—	—	—	2.50	4.50

KM# 1519   50 CENTS
18.2400 g., 0.9990 Silver 0.5858 oz. ASW, 31.5 mm. **Ruler:** Elizabeth II **Subject:** Melbourne Cup, 150th race **Rev:** Trophy, partially gilt **Shape:** 12-sided

Date	Mintage	F	VF	XF	Unc	BU
2010 Proof	—	Value: 80.00				

KM# 1520   50 CENTS
18.2400 g., 0.9990 Silver 0.5858 oz. ASW, 31.5 mm. **Ruler:** Elizabeth II **Subject:** Melbourne Cup **Rev:** Horse and rider, partially gilt **Shape:** 12-sided

Date	Mintage	F	VF	XF	Unc	BU
2010 Proof	—	Value: 80.00				

KM# 1571   50 CENTS
15.5500 g., Copper-Nickel, 31.65 mm. **Ruler:** Elizabeth II **Subject:** Prince William and Catherine Middelton engagement **Rev:** Bundle of roses, Royal arms of Prince William below **Shape:** 12-sided

Date	Mintage	F	VF	XF	Unc	BU
2010	—	—	—	—	4.00	5.00

KM# 1571a   50 CENTS
18.2400 g., 0.9990 Silver partially gilt 0.5858 oz. ASW, 31.65 mm. **Ruler:** Elizabeth II **Subject:** Prince William and Catherine Middelton engagement **Rev:** Bunch of roses, gilt; Royal arms of Prince William below **Shape:** 12-sided

Date	Mintage	F	VF	XF	Unc	BU
2010 Proof	—	Value: 60.00				

KM# 1521   50 CENTS
15.5500 g., Copper-Nickel, 31.65 mm. **Ruler:** Elizabeth II **Subject:** National Service, 60th Anniversary **Shape:** 12-sided

Date	Mintage	F	VF	XF	Unc	BU
2011	—	—	—	—	4.00	5.00

KM# 1525   50 CENTS
15.5500 g., Copper-Nickel, 31.5 mm. **Ruler:** Elizabeth II **Subject:** Australia Day **Rev:** Circle of people clasping hands

Date	Mintage	F	VF	XF	Unc	BU
2011	—	—	—	—	4.00	5.00

KM# 1525a   50 CENTS
18.2400 g., Silver, 31.5 mm. **Ruler:** Elizabeth II **Subject:** Australia day **Rev:** Circle of people clasping hands, partially gilt **Shape:** 12-sided

Date	Mintage	F	VF	XF	Unc	BU
2011 Proof	—	Value: 40.00				

KM# 1532   50 CENTS
15.5500 g., 0.9990 Silver 0.4994 oz. ASW **Ruler:** Elizabeth II **Subject:** Bush Baby **Rev:** Dingo in color

Date	Mintage	F	VF	XF	Unc	BU
2011P Proof	—	Value: 65.00				

KM# 1533   50 CENTS
15.5500 g., 0.9990 Silver 0.4994 oz. ASW **Ruler:** Elizabeth II **Subject:** Bush Babies **Rev:** Bilby in color

Date	Mintage	F	VF	XF	Unc	BU
2011P Proof	—	Value: 65.00				

KM# 1567 50 CENTS
15.5500 g., Copper-Nickel, 31.65 mm. **Ruler:** Elizabeth II
Subject: Royal Wedding **Rev:** Catherine and William busts left
Shape: 12-sided

Date	Mintage	F	VF	XF	Unc	BU
2011	—	—	—	—	3.50	5.00

KM# 1567a 50 CENTS
18.2400 g., 0.9990 Silver partially gilt 0.5858 oz. ASW, 31.65 mm.
Ruler: Elizabeth II **Subject:** Royal Wedding **Rev:** Catherine and
William busts left, gilt flower at bottom **Shape:** 12-sided

Date	Mintage	F	VF	XF	Unc	BU
2011 Proof	—	Value: 60.00				

KM# 1577 50 CENTS
15.5910 g., 0.9990 Silver 0.5007 oz. ASW, 36.6 mm. **Ruler:**
Elizabeth II **Subject:** Australian Sea Life - Starfish **Rev:** Starfish
in color

Date	Mintage	F	VF	XF	Unc	BU
2011P Proof	10,000	Value: 75.00				

KM# 1579 50 CENTS
15.5910 g., 0.9990 Silver 0.5007 oz. ASW, 36.6 mm. **Ruler:**
Elizabeth II **Subject:** Australian sea life - Hawksbill Turtle **Rev:**
Color turtle swimming right

Date	Mintage	F	VF	XF	Unc	BU
2011P Proof	10,000	Value: 70.00				

KM# 1624 50 CENTS
15.5500 g., Copper-Nickel, 31.65 mm. **Ruler:** Elizabeth II
Subject: Triple Zero Code for Emergency, 50th Anniversary **Obv:**
Head with tiara right **Rev:** Telephone handset and 000, in color
Shape: 12-sided

Date	Mintage	F	VF	XF	Unc	BU
2011	—	—	—	—	—	20.00

KM# 404b 50 CENTS
15.5500 g., Copper-Nickel with color, 31.65 mm. **Ruler:**
Elizabeth II **Obv:** Head with tiara right **Rev:** Australian coat-of-
arms with Kangaroo and Emu supporters all in color **Shape:** 12-
sided

Date	Mintage	F	VF	XF	Unc	BU
2012	—	—	—	—	—	25.00

KM# 404c 50 CENTS
18.2400 g., 0.9990 Silver partially gilt 0.5858 oz. ASW,
31.65 mm. **Ruler:** Elizabeth II **Obv:** Head with tiara right **Rev:**
Australian coat-of-arms with Kangaroo and Emu supporters all
gilt **Shape:** 12-sided

Date	Mintage	F	VF	XF	Unc	BU
2012 Proof	—	Value: 75.00				

KM# 1578 50 CENTS
15.5910 g., 0.9990 Silver 0.5007 oz. ASW, 36.6 mm. **Ruler:**
Elizabeth II **Subject:** Australian sea life - Surgeonfish **Rev:**
Surgeonfish in blue, black and yellow colors

Date	Mintage	F	VF	XF	Unc	BU
2012P Proof	10,000	Value: 75.00				

KM# 1697 50 CENTS
15.5910 g., Silver, 36.6 mm. **Ruler:** Elizabeth II **Subject:**
Australian 2012 London Olympic Team **Obv:** Head with tiara right
Rev: Male runner, Syndey Harbor Birdge, Tower of London images

Date	Mintage	F	VF	XF	Unc	BU
2012P Proof	750	Value: 30.00				

KM# 1712 50 CENTS
15.5910 g., 0.9990 Silver 0.5007 oz. ASW, 36.6 mm. **Ruler:**
Elizabeth II **Obv:** Head with tiara right **Rev:** Reef Octopus in color

Date	Mintage	F	VF	XF	Unc	BU
2012P Proof	10,000	Value: 50.00				

KM# 1741 50 CENTS
15.5500 g., Copper-Nickel, 31.65 mm. **Ruler:** Elizabeth II
Subject: Elizabeth II, 60th Anniversary **Obv:** Head with tiara right
Rev: State Crown and floral design **Shape:** 12-sided

Date	Mintage	F	VF	XF	Unc	BU
2012	—	—	—	—	10.00	15.00

KM# 1741a 50 CENTS
18.2400 g., 0.9990 Silver 0.5858 oz. ASW, 31.65 mm. **Ruler:**
Elizabeth II **Subject:** Elizabeth II, 60th Anniversary **Obv:** Head
with tiara right **Rev:** State Crown and floral **Shape:** 12-sided

Date	Mintage	F	VF	XF	Unc	BU
2012 Proof	—	Value: 75.00				

KM# 1744 50 CENTS
15.5500 g., Copper-Nickel, 31.65 mm. **Ruler:** Elizabeth II
Subject: World War II, Bombing of Australia **Obv:** Head with tiara
right **Rev:** Map of Astralia with bombed sites highlighted **Shape:**
12-sided

Date	Mintage	F	VF	XF	Unc	BU
2012	—	—	—	—	7.50	15.00

KM# 1254 55 CENTS
15.5500 g., 0.9990 Silver 0.4994 oz. ASW, 26x38 mm. **Ruler:**
Elizabeth II **Subject:** Postal Service, 200th Anniversary **Obv:**
Head right **Rev:** Early post box **Edge:** Irregular as with a stamp
Shape: Vertical rectangle

Date	Mintage	F	VF	XF	Unc	BU
2009P Proof	8,700	Value: 90.00				

KM# 1255 55 CENTS
15.5500 g., 0.9990 Silver 0.4994 oz. ASW, 26x38 mm. **Ruler:**
Elizabeth II **Subject:** Postal Service, 200th Anniversary **Obv:**
Head right **Rev:** Home delivery **Edge:** Irregular as with a stamp
Shape: Vertical rectangle

Date	Mintage	F	VF	XF	Unc	BU
2009P Proof	8,700	Value: 90.00				

KM# 489 DOLLAR
9.0000 g., Aluminum-Bronze, 25 mm. **Ruler:** Elizabeth II **Obv:**
Head with tiara right **Rev:** Circle of 5 kangaroos **Edge:**
Segmented reeding

Date	Mintage	F	VF	XF	Unc	BU
2001B Proof	1,001,000	Value: 55.00				
2004B	8,800,000	—	—	—	6.00	7.00
2004B Proof	50,000	Value: 75.00				
2005B	5,792,000	—	—	—	6.00	7.00
2005B Proof	33,520	Value: 85.00				
2006B	38,691,000	—	—	—	4.00	5.00
2006B Proof	—	Value: 45.00				
2006B Special Proof	—	Value: 3,500				
Note: Mintage of 25-35 pieces						
2007B	—	—	—	—	20.00	25.00
2007B Proof	—	Value: 45.00				
2008B	30,106,000	—	—	—	3.00	5.00
2008B Proof	—	Value: 45.00				
2009B	4,682,000	—	—	—	4.00	6.00
2009C Mintmaster mark	—	—	—	—	—	25.00
2009B Proof	—	Value: 45.00				
2010B	—	—	—	—	—	5.00
2010B Proof	—	Value: 45.00				
2011B	—	—	—	—	—	5.00
2011B Proof	—	Value: 45.00				
2012B	—	—	—	—	—	5.00
2012B Proof	—	Value: 45.00				

KM# 588 DOLLAR
9.0000 g., Aluminum-Bronze, 25 mm. **Ruler:** Elizabeth II
Subject: 90th Anniversary Royal Australian Navy **Obv:** Head
with tiara right **Rev:** Navy crest **Edge:** Segmented reeding

Date	Mintage	F	VF	XF	Unc	BU
2001	62,429	—	—	—	60.00	65.00

KM# 530 DOLLAR
9.0000 g., Aluminum-Bronze, 25 mm. **Ruler:** Elizabeth II
Subject: Army Centennial **Obv:** Head with tiara right **Rev:** Army
crest **Edge:** Segmented reeding

Date	Mintage	F	VF	XF	Unc	BU
2001C	125,186	—	—	—	18.00	20.00
Note: Large head, IRB spaced						
2001C	Inc. above	—	—	—	18.00	20.00
Note: Small head, IRB joined						
2001S	38,095	—	—	—	25.00	30.00

KM# 530a DOLLAR
11.6600 g., 0.9990 Silver 0.3745 oz. ASW, 24.9 mm. **Ruler:** Elizabeth II **Subject:** Army Centennial **Obv:** Head with tiara right **Rev:** Army crest **Edge:** Segmented reeding

Date	Mintage	F	VF	XF	Unc	BU
2001 Proof	17,839	Value: 50.00				

KM# 531 DOLLAR
9.0000 g., Aluminum-Bronze, 25 mm. **Ruler:** Elizabeth II **Subject:** 80th Anniversary Royal Australian Air Force **Obv:** Head with tiara right **Rev:** Air Force crest **Edge:** Segmented reeding

Date	Mintage	F	VF	XF	Unc	BU
2001B	99,281	—	—	—	18.00	20.00
Note: IRB spaced						
2001B	Inc. above	—	—	—	25.00	30.00
Note: IRB joined						

KM# 534.1 DOLLAR
9.0000 g., Aluminum-Bronze, 25 mm. **Ruler:** Elizabeth II **Subject:** Australian Centenary of Federation - Norfolk Island **Obv:** Head with tiara right **Rev:** Stylized ribbon map of Australia with star **Edge:** Segmented reeding **Note:** Reverse design raised above field. Prev. KM#534.

Date	Mintage	F	VF	XF	Unc	BU
2001B	6,781,200	—	—	—	50.00	55.00
Note: IRB joined						
2001B	Inc. above	—	—	—	50.00	55.00
Note: IRB spaced						
2001B Proof	—	Value: 5.00				

KM# 534.1a DOLLAR
21.7000 g., 0.9999 Gold 0.6976 oz. AGW, 25 mm. **Ruler:** Elizabeth II **Subject:** Federation Centennial **Obv:** Elizabeth II **Rev:** Federation logo

Date	Mintage	F	VF	XF	Unc	BU
2001B Proof	650	Value: 1,250				

KM# 534.2 DOLLAR
9.0000 g., Aluminum-Bronze, 25 mm. **Ruler:** Elizabeth II **Subject:** Australian Centenary of Federation - Norfolk Island **Obv:** Head with tiara right **Rev:** Multicolor ribbon design of Australia with star, printed on the surface. **Edge:** Segmented reeding

Date	Mintage	F	VF	XF	Unc	BU
2001 Proof	—	Value: 12.50				
2001	27,905,000	—	—	—	5.00	—

KM# 594 DOLLAR
31.1035 g., 0.9990 Silver partially gilt 0.9990 oz. ASW, 40 mm. **Ruler:** Elizabeth II **Subject:** Millennium **Obv:** Head with tiara right **Rev:** Gold inset sun on multicolor earth above Egyptian obelisk **Edge:** Reeded

Date	Mintage	F	VF	XF	Unc	BU
2001 Prooflike	30,000	—	—	—	37.00	42.00

KM# 598 DOLLAR
31.1000 g., 0.9990 Silver 0.9988 oz. ASW, 40.4 mm. **Ruler:** Elizabeth II **Subject:** Centenary of Federation "Holey Dollar" **Obv:** Legend around star-shaped center hole **Rev:** Seven coats of arms around star-shaped hole **Edge:** Reeded

Date	Mintage	F	VF	XF	Unc	BU
ND(2001) Prooflike	30,000	—	—	—	35.00	40.00

KM# 682 DOLLAR
9.0000 g., Aluminum-Bronze, 25 mm. **Ruler:** Elizabeth II **Subject:** International Year of Volunteers **Rev:** Volunteers in wreath **Edge:** Segmented reeding

Date	Mintage	F	VF	XF	Unc	BU
2001B	6,000,000	—	—	—	12.00	15.00

KM# 632 DOLLAR
31.1035 g., 0.9990 Silver 0.9990 oz. ASW, 40 mm. **Ruler:** Elizabeth II **Subject:** Queen's Golden Jubilee **Obv:** Head right **Rev:** Queen on horse with multicolor flag background **Edge:** Reeded

Date	Mintage	F	VF	XF	Unc	BU
2002	34,074,000	—	—	—	—	50.00
2002P Proof	40,000	Value: 65.00				

KM# 600.1 DOLLAR
9.0000 g., Aluminum-Bronze, 25 mm. **Ruler:** Elizabeth II **Subject:** Year of the Outback **Obv:** Head with tiara right **Rev:** Stylized map of Australia **Edge:** Segmented reeding **Note:** Prev. KM#600.

Date	Mintage	F	VF	XF	Unc	BU
2002	34,074,000	—	—	—	5.00	7.00
2002 Proof	—	Value: 10.00				
2002C	68,447	—	—	—	7.00	9.00
2002B	32,698	—	—	—	7.00	9.00
2002M	31,694	—	—	—	7.00	9.00
2002S	36,931	—	—	—	7.00	9.00

KM# 600.1a DOLLAR
11.6600 g., 0.9900 Silver 0.3711 oz. ASW, 25 mm. **Ruler:** Elizabeth II **Subject:** Year of the Outback **Obv:** Head with tiara right **Rev:** Stylized map of Australia **Edge:** Segmented reeding

Date	Mintage	F	VF	XF	Unc	BU
2002B Proof	12,500	Value: 65.00				

KM# 600.2 DOLLAR
9.0000 g., Aluminum-Bronze, 25 mm. **Ruler:** Elizabeth II **Subject:** Year of the Outback **Obv:** Head with tiara right **Rev:** Multicolor stylized map of Australia **Edge:** Segmented reeding

Date	Mintage	F	VF	XF	Unc	BU
2002B Proof	39,514	Value: 15.00				

KM# 660 DOLLAR
31.1035 g., 0.9990 Silver partially gilt 0.9990 oz. ASW, 40 mm. **Ruler:** Elizabeth II **Subject:** Melbourne Mint **Obv:** Head with tiara right **Rev:** Mint entrance between two gold foil inserts replicating gold sovereign reverse designs **Edge:** Reeded

Date	Mintage	F	VF	XF	Unc	BU
2002B Proof	13,328	Value: 58.00				

KM# 489a DOLLAR
11.6600 g., 0.9990 Silver 0.3745 oz. ASW, 25 mm. **Ruler:** Elizabeth II **Obv:** Head with tiara right **Rev:** Kangaroos **Edge:** Segmented reeding

Date	Mintage	F	VF	XF	Unc	BU
2003B Proof	6,500	Value: 40.00				
2004B Proof	6,500	Value: 40.00				
2005B Proof	6,500	Value: 40.00				
2006B Proof	—	Value: 40.00				
2007B Proof	—	Value: 40.00				
2008B Proof	—	Value: 40.00				
2009B Proof	—	Value: 40.00				
2010B Proof	—	Value: 40.00				
2011B Proof	6,000	Value: 40.00				

KM# 823 DOLLAR
31.1035 g., 0.9990 Silver 0.9990 oz. ASW, 40 mm. **Ruler:** Elizabeth II **Subject:** 50th Anniversary - Coronation Elizabeth II **Obv:** Head with tiara right **Rev:** Crown in lettered garland **Note:** Colored design.

Date	Mintage	F	VF	XF	Unc	BU
2003P Proof	40,400	Value: 45.00				

KM# 663 DOLLAR
9.0000 g., Aluminum-Bronze, 25 mm. **Ruler:** Elizabeth II
Subject: 50th Anniversary - End of Korean War **Obv:** Head with
tiara right **Rev:** Dove of Peace **Edge:** Segmented reeding

Date	Mintage	F	VF	XF	Unc	BU
2003B	34,949	—	—	—	6.00	8.00
2003C	93,572	—	—	—	6.00	8.00
2003M	36,142	—	—	—	6.00	8.00
2003S	36,091	—	—	—	6.00	8.00

KM# 663a DOLLAR
11.6600 g., 0.9990 Silver 0.3745 oz. ASW, 25 mm. **Ruler:**
Elizabeth II **Subject:** Korean War **Obv:** Queens head right **Rev:**
Dove of Peace **Edge:** Segmented reeding

Date	Mintage	F	VF	XF	Unc	BU
2003B	15,000	Value: 55.00				

KM# 685 DOLLAR
31.1035 g., 0.9990 Silver 0.9990 oz. ASW, 40.6 mm. **Ruler:**
Elizabeth II **Subject:** 21st Birthday of William **Obv:** Head right
Rev: Multicolor Prince William **Edge:** Segmented reeding

Date	Mintage	F	VF	XF	Unc	BU
ND(2003)P Proof	12,500	Value: 45.00				

KM# 690 DOLLAR
9.0000 g., Aluminum-Bronze, 25 mm. **Ruler:** Elizabeth II **Obv:**
Queens head right **Rev:** Australia Volunteers logo **Edge:**
Segmented reeding

Date	Mintage	F	VF	XF	Unc	BU
2003B	4,149,000	—	—	—	15.00	17.00

KM# 690a DOLLAR
9.0000 g., 0.9990 Silver 0.2891 oz. ASW, 25 mm. **Ruler:**
Elizabeth II **Obv:** Queens head right **Rev:** Australia Volunteers
logo

Date	Mintage	F	VF	XF	Unc	BU
2003B Proof	6,500	Value: 30.00				

KM# 690.1 DOLLAR
9.0000 g., Aluminum-Bronze, 25 mm. **Ruler:** Elizabeth II
Subject: Australia's Volunteers **Obv:** Elizabeth II **Rev:** Multicolor
Australia's Volunteers logo **Edge:** Segmented reeding

Date	Mintage	F	VF	XF	Unc	BU
2003B Proof	39,090	Value: 15.00				

KM# 754 DOLLAR
9.0000 g., Aluminum-Bronze, 25 mm. **Ruler:** Elizabeth II
Subject: Womens Suffrage **Obv:** Queens head right **Rev:**
Suffragette talking to Britannia **Edge:** Segmented reeding

Date	Mintage	F	VF	XF	Unc	BU
2003B	10,007,000	—	—	—	5.00	7.00

KM# 763 DOLLAR
13.3600 g., 0.9990 Silver 0.4291 oz. ASW, 28.5 mm. **Ruler:**
Elizabeth II **Series:** Masterpieces in Silver - Port Phillip Patterns
Obv: 1/4 Ounce design **Rev:** Kangaroo design **Edge:** Reeded

Date	Mintage	F	VF	XF	Unc	BU
2003B Proof	10,000	Value: 80.00				

KM# 803 DOLLAR
9.0000 g., Aluminum-Bronze, 25 mm. **Ruler:** Elizabeth II
Subject: Vietnam War Veterans 1962-1973 **Obv:** Head with tiara
right **Rev:** Australian Vietnam Forces National Memorial

Date	Mintage	F	VF	XF	Unc	BU
2003	57,000	—	—	—	45.00	50.00

KM# 822 DOLLAR
54.3000 g., 0.9990 Silver 1.7440 oz. ASW, 50 mm. **Ruler:**
Elizabeth II **Obv:** Superimposed head above replica of Holey
Dollar **Rev:** Replica of Holey Dollar **Edge:** Reeded **Note:** Holey
Dollar replica is embedded in silver collar and comes with replica
Dump also in 0.999 silver.

Date	Mintage	F	VF	XF	Unc	BU
2003 Proof	11,000	Value: 90.00				

KM# 824 DOLLAR
31.1035 g., 0.9990 Silver 0.9990 oz. ASW, 40 mm. **Ruler:**
Elizabeth II **Subject:** Golden Pipeline **Obv:** Head with tiara right
Rev: Charles Yelverton O'Connor, innovative engineer,
multicolor

Date	Mintage	F	VF	XF	Unc	BU
2003P Proof	5,000	Value: 130				

KM# 725 DOLLAR
56.2300 g., 0.9990 Bi-Metallic Copper center in Silver ring
1.8060 oz., 50 mm. **Ruler:** Elizabeth II **Subject:** The Last Penny
Obv: 1964 dated penny obverse **Rev:** 1964 date penny reverse
Edge: Reeded

Date	Mintage	F	VF	XF	Unc	BU
2004B Proof	16,437	Value: 85.00				

KM# 726 DOLLAR
9.0000 g., Aluminum-Bronze, 25 mm. **Ruler:** Elizabeth II
Subject: Eureka Stockade 1854-2004 **Obv:** Head with tiara right
Rev: Stockade and stylized soldiers **Edge:** Segmented reeding

Date	Mintage	F	VF	XF	Unc	BU
2004	—	—	—	—	8.00	10.00
2004B	33,835	—	—	—	5.00	6.00
2004C	70,913	—	—	—	5.00	6.00
2004 E	95,948	—	—	—	5.00	6.00
2004S	45,098	—	—	—	5.00	6.00
2004M	37,526	—	—	—	5.00	6.00
2004 3 known	—	—	—	—	—	1,000

KM# 726a DOLLAR
11.6600 g., 0.9990 Silver 0.3745 oz. ASW, 25 mm. **Ruler:**
Elizabeth II **Subject:** Eureka Stockade **Obv:** Head with tiara right
Rev: Stockade and stylized soldiers **Edge:** Segmented reeding

Date	Mintage	F	VF	XF	Unc	BU
2004B Proof	17,697	Value: 38.00				

KM# 733 DOLLAR
9.0000 g., Aluminum-Bronze, 25 mm. **Ruler:** Elizabeth II **Obv:**
Head with tiara right **Rev:** Multicolor holographic five kangaroos
design **Edge:** Segmented reeding

Date	Mintage	F	VF	XF	Unc	BU
2004B Proof	—	Value: 25.00				

KM# 733.1 DOLLAR
9.0000 g., Aluminum-Bronze, 25 mm. **Ruler:** Elizabeth II **Rev:**
Five kangaroos **Edge:** Segmented reeding

Date	Mintage	F	VF	XF	Unc	BU
2004B	—	—	—	—	—	4.50

KM# 733.1a DOLLAR
11.6600 g., 0.9999 Silver 0.3748 oz. ASW, 25 mm. **Ruler:**
Elizabeth II **Rev:** Five Kangaroos

Date	Mintage	F	VF	XF	Unc	BU
2004B Proof	6,500	Value: 35.00				

KM# 734 DOLLAR
31.1035 g., 0.9990 Silver 0.9990 oz. ASW, 40 mm. **Ruler:**
Elizabeth II **Subject:** First Moon Walk **Obv:** Head with tiara right
Rev: Multicolor rocket in flight **Edge:** Reeded

Date	Mintage	F	VF	XF	Unc	BU
2004P Proof	40,000	Value: 100				

KM# 735   DOLLAR
31.1035 g., 0.9990 Silver 0.9990 oz. ASW, 40 mm.   **Ruler:**
Elizabeth II **Subject:** First Moon Walk **Obv:** Head with tiara right
Rev: Multicolor scene of astronauts planting flag on moon **Edge:**
Reeded

Date	Mintage	F	VF	XF	Unc	BU
2004P Proof	40,000	Value: 110				

KM# 736   DOLLAR
31.1035 g., 0.9990 Silver 0.9990 oz. ASW, 40 mm.   **Ruler:**
Elizabeth II **Subject:** First Moon Walk **Obv:** Head with tiara right
Rev: Multicolor close up of astronaut on moon **Edge:** Reeded

Date	Mintage	F	VF	XF	Unc	BU
2004P Proof	40,000	Value: 95.00				

KM# 737   DOLLAR
31.1035 g., 0.9990 Silver 0.9990 oz. ASW, 40 mm.   **Ruler:**
Elizabeth II **Obv:** Head with tiara right **Rev:** Multicolor Antarctic
view of Mawson Station and penguins **Edge:** Reeded

Date	Mintage	F	VF	XF	Unc	BU
2004P Proof	7,500	Value: 60.00				

KM# 738   DOLLAR
31.1035 g., 0.9990 Silver partially gilt 0.9990 oz. ASW, 40 mm.
Ruler: Elizabeth II **Subject:** 50th Anniversary of Royal Visit **Obv:**
Queens head right **Rev:** Gilt lion and kangaroo **Edge:** Reeded

Date	Mintage	F	VF	XF	Unc	BU
ND (2004) Proof	12,500	Value: 85.00				

KM# 740   DOLLAR
24.3750 g., 0.9990 Silver Encapsulated gold nuggets in center
0.7829 oz. ASW, 40.6 mm.   **Ruler:** Elizabeth II **Obv:** Crowned
head right **Rev:** Eureka Stockade leader, miners and flag **Edge:**
Reeded

Date	Mintage	F	VF	XF	Unc	BU
2004 Proof	12,500	Value: 135				

KM# 747   DOLLAR
9.0000 g., Aluminum-Bronze, 25 mm.   **Ruler:** Elizabeth II
Subject: 60th Anniversary World War II **Obv:** Head with tiara
right **Rev:** Rejoicing serviceman **Edge:** Segmented reeding

Date	Mintage	F	VF	XF	Unc	BU
2005B	31,788,000	—	—	—	3.00	4.00
2005B Proof	—	Value: 35.00				

KM# 747a   DOLLAR
11.6600 g., 0.9990 Silver 0.3745 oz. ASW, 25 mm.   **Ruler:**
Elizabeth II **Obv:** Queen's head right **Rev:** Rejoicing servicemen
Edge: Segmented reeding

Date	Mintage	F	VF	XF	Unc	BU
2005B Proof	6,500	Value: 45.00				

KM# 747b   DOLLAR
21.5200 g., 0.9999 Gold 0.6918 oz. AGW, 25 mm.   **Ruler:**
Elizabeth II **Obv:** Queen's head right **Rev:** Rejoicing servicemen
Edge: Segmented reeding

Date	Mintage	F	VF	XF	Unc	BU
2005B Proof	629	Value: 1,250				

KM# 748   DOLLAR
9.0000 g., Aluminum-Bronze, 25 mm.   **Ruler:** Elizabeth II

Subject: 90th Anniversary Gallipoli Landing 1915-2005 **Obv:**
Head with tiara right **Rev:** Bugler silhouette **Edge:** Segmented
reeding

Date	Mintage	F	VF	XF	Unc	BU
2005	15,000	—	—	—	25.00	30.00
2005B	36,108	—	—	—	5.00	6.00
2005C	76,173	—	—	—	5.00	6.00
2005G	35,452	—	—	—	35.00	40.00
2005M	38,727	—	—	—	5.00	6.00
2005S	39,569	—	—	—	6.00	7.00

KM# 748a   DOLLAR
11.6600 g., 0.9990 Silver 0.3745 oz. ASW, 25 mm.   **Ruler:**
Elizabeth II **Subject:** Gallipoli **Obv:** Queen's head right **Rev:**
Bugler silhouette **Edge:** Segmented reeding

Date	Mintage	F	VF	XF	Unc	BU
2005B Proof	17,749	Value: 45.00				
2005B Proof, 2 known	—	Value: 1,500				

KM# 825   DOLLAR
56.4500 g., 0.9990 Silver partially gilt 1.8130 oz. ASW, 50 mm.
Ruler: Elizabeth II **Obv:** Small head with tiara right superimposed
above replica of Sydney Mint Sovereign **Rev:** Replica of Sydney
Mint Sovereign **Edge:** Reeded

Date	Mintage	F	VF	XF	Unc	BU
2005 Proof	11,845	Value: 90.00				

KM# 830   DOLLAR
31.6000 g., 0.9990 Silver 1.0149 oz. ASW, 40 mm.   **Ruler:**
Elizabeth II **Subject:** Centenary Australian Tennis Open 1905-
2005 **Obv:** Head with tiara right **Rev:** Tennis players

Date	Mintage	F	VF	XF	Unc	BU
2005 Proof	10,000	Value: 50.00				

KM# 831   DOLLAR
31.6000 g., 0.9990 Silver 1.0149 oz. ASW, 40 mm.   **Ruler:**
Elizabeth II **Subject:** Centenary Australian PGA Gold Open
1905-2005 **Obv:** Head with tiara right **Rev:** Golfer

Date	Mintage	F	VF	XF	Unc	BU
2005 Proof	7,500	Value: 85.00				

KM# 832 DOLLAR
31.6000 g., 0.9990 Silver 1.0149 oz. ASW, 40 mm. **Ruler:** Elizabeth II **Subject:** Centenary Rotary 1905-2005 **Obv:** Head with tiara right **Rev:** Rotary International Logo

Date	Mintage	F	VF	XF	Unc	BU
2005 Proof	10,000	Value: 90.00				

KM# 833 DOLLAR
31.1035 g., 0.9990 Silver 0.9990 oz. ASW, 40 mm. **Ruler:** Elizabeth II **Subject:** 90th Anniversary Gallipoli Landings **Obv:** Head with tiara right **Rev:** Multicolor Australian and New Zealand soldiers beneath Australian flag

Date	Mintage	F	VF	XF	Unc	BU
2005 Proof	15,000	Value: 185				

KM# 835 DOLLAR
Aluminum-Bronze, 38.74 mm. **Ruler:** Elizabeth II **Subject:** Living Icons of Australia and New Zealand **Obv:** Head with tiara right **Rev:** Indigenous image of kangaroo

Date	Mintage	F	VF	XF	Unc	BU
2005	20,000	—	—	—	15.00	20.00

KM# 836 DOLLAR
31.1035 g., 0.9990 Silver 0.9990 oz. ASW, 40 mm. **Ruler:** Elizabeth II **Subject:** 21st Birthday Prince Harry of Wales **Obv:** Head with tiara right **Rev:** Prince Harry

Date	Mintage	F	VF	XF	Unc	BU
2005 Proof	12,500	Value: 80.00				

KM# 1015 DOLLAR
31.6000 g., 0.9990 Silver 1.0149 oz. ASW, 40.5 mm. **Ruler:** Elizabeth II **Subject:** 50th Anniversary Australian Territory **Obv:** Head with tiara right **Obv. Legend:** ELIZABETH II • AUSTRALIA **Rev:** Red-footed Booby perched on a branch, multicolor **Rev. Legend:** COCOS (KEELING) ISLANDS **Edge:** Reeded

Date	Mintage	F	VF	XF	Unc	BU
2005P Proof	7,500	Value: 70.00				

KM# 1018 DOLLAR
31.7500 g., 0.9990 Silver 1.0197 oz. ASW, 40.5 mm. **Ruler:** Elizabeth II **Obv:** Head with tiara right **Obv. Legend:** ELIZABETH II - AUSTRALIA **Rev:** Leopard seal with pup on ice, multicolor **Rev. Legend:** Australian Antarctic Territory **Edge:** Reeded

Date	Mintage	F	VF	XF	Unc	BU
2005P Proof	7,500	Value: 60.00				

KM# 838 DOLLAR
31.1035 g., 0.9990 Silver 0.9990 oz. ASW, 40 mm. **Ruler:** Elizabeth II **Subject:** Australain-Japan Year of Exchange **Obv:** Head with tiara right **Rev:** Kangaroo leaping with kangaroo rim decoration

Date	Mintage	F	VF	XF	Unc	BU
2006 Proof	5,000	Value: 45.00				

KM# 77a DOLLAR
11.6600 g., 0.9990 Silver 0.3745 oz. ASW, 25 mm. **Ruler:** Elizabeth II **Obv:** Young bust right **Rev:** Kangaroos **Edge:** Segmented reeding

Date	Mintage	F	VF	XF	Unc	BU
2006 Proof	6,500	Value: 40.00				

KM# 489b DOLLAR
21.5200 g., 0.9990 Gold 0.6912 oz. AGW, 25 mm. **Ruler:** Elizabeth II **Obv:** Head with tiara right **Rev:** Kangaroos **Edge:** Segmented reeding

Date	Mintage	F	VF	XF	Unc	BU
2006 Proof	300	Value: 1,250				

KM# 804 DOLLAR
9.0000 g., Aluminum-Bronze, 25 mm. **Ruler:** Elizabeth II **Subject:** XVIII Commonwealth Games **Obv:** Head with tiara right **Rev:** Graphic at left, logo at right

Date	Mintage	F	VF	XF	Unc	BU
2006	—	—	—	—	3.50	5.00

KM# 805 DOLLAR
9.0000 g., Aluminum-Bronze, 25 mm. **Ruler:** Elizabeth II **Subject:** 50 Years of Television **Obv:** Head with tiara right **Rev:** TV mast and camera **Edge:** Segmented reeding

Date	Mintage	F	VF	XF	Unc	BU
2006B	47,228	—	—	—	5.00	6.00
2006C	135,221	—	—	—	5.00	6.00
2006M	39,600	—	—	—	5.00	6.00
2006S	48,490	—	—	—	5.00	6.00
2006 TV	46,370	—	—	—	15.00	17.00
2006 Without mint mark, 4 known	—	—	—	—	—	1,000

KM# 805a DOLLAR
11.6600 g., 0.9990 Silver 0.3745 oz. ASW, 25 mm. **Ruler:** Elizabeth II **Subject:** 50 Years of Television **Obv:** Head with tiara right **Rev:** TV mast and camera **Edge:** Segmented reeding

Date	Mintage	F	VF	XF	Unc	BU
2006 Proof	10,790	Value: 45.00				
2006A Proof	3,859	Value: 60.00				

KM# 806 DOLLAR
9.0000 g., Aluminum-Bronze Issued in folder., 25 mm. **Ruler:** Elizabeth II **Series:** Colored Oceans **Obv:** Head with tiara right **Rev:** Multicolor jumping Bottlenose dolphins **Edge:** Segmented reeding

Date	Mintage	F	VF	XF	Unc	BU
2006	29,310	—	—	—	—	35.00

KM# 807 DOLLAR
9.0000 g., Aluminum-Bronze, 25 mm. **Ruler:** Elizabeth II **Series:** Colored Oceans **Obv:** Head with tiara right **Rev:** Multicolor clown fish **Edge:** Segmented reeding **Note:** Issued in folder.

Date	Mintage	F	VF	XF	Unc	BU
2006	29,310	—	—	—	25.00	30.00

KM# 826 DOLLAR
60.5000 g., 0.9990 Silver 1.9431 oz. ASW, 50 mm. **Ruler:** Elizabeth II **Obv:** Replica of 1758 Mexico City Mint 8 Reales **Obv. Legend:** ELIZABETH II (small head right) AUSTRALIA **Rev:** Replica of 1758 Mexico City Mint 8 Reales **Rev. Legend:** PILLAR DOLLAR **Edge:** Reeded

Date	Mintage	F	VF	XF	Unc	BU
2006	9,846	—	—	—	115	—

KM# 841 DOLLAR
31.1035 g., 0.9990 Silver Colorized lenticular display. 0.9990 oz. ASW **Ruler:** Elizabeth II **Subject:** 50 Years of Television in Australia 1956-2006 **Obv:** Head with tiara right **Rev:** SIx different historic TV show images **Shape:** Square with rounded corners

Date	Mintage	F	VF	XF	Unc	BU
2006 Proof	12,500	Value: 95.00				

KM# 842 DOLLAR
31.1035 g., 0.9990 Silver 0.9990 oz. ASW, 40 mm. **Ruler:** Elizabeth II **Subject:** 40th Anniversary of Demise of Pre-Decimal Coins **Obv:** Head with tiara right above transparent locket containing small replicas of pre-decimal currency **Rev:** Rim legend about locket

Date	Mintage	F	VF	XF	Unc	BU
2006P Proof	7,500	Value: 150				

KM# 843 DOLLAR
31.1035 g., 0.9990 Silver 0.9990 oz. ASW, 40 mm. **Ruler:** Elizabeth II **Subject:** 80th Birthday of Queen Elizabeth II **Obv:** Head with tiara right **Rev:** Queen Elizabeth II

Date	Mintage	F	VF	XF	Unc	BU
2006P Proof	12,500	Value: 85.00				

KM# 844   DOLLAR
31.1035 g., 0.9990 Silver 0.9990 oz. ASW, 40 mm. **Ruler:**
Elizabeth II **Subject:** Figures of Note **Obv:** Head with tiara
right **Rev:** Queen Elizabeth as portrayed on Australia 1 dollar banknote

Date	Mintage	F	VF	XF	Unc	BU
2006P Proof	1,000	Value: 175				

KM# 845   DOLLAR
31.1035 g., 0.9990 Silver 0.9990 oz. ASW, 40 mm. **Ruler:**
Elizabeth II **Subject:** Figures of Note **Obv:** Head with tiara
right **Rev:** MacArthur and Farrer as portrayed on Australia 2 dollar
banknote

Date	Mintage	F	VF	XF	Unc	BU
2006P Proof	1,000	Value: 95.00				

KM# 846   DOLLAR
31.1035 g., 0.9990 Silver 0.9990 oz. ASW, 40 mm. **Ruler:**
Elizabeth II **Subject:** Figures of Note **Obv:** Head with tiara right
Rev: Banks and Chisholm as portrayed on Australia 5 dollar
banknote

Date	Mintage	F	VF	XF	Unc	BU
2006P Proof	1,000	Value: 95.00				

KM# 847   DOLLAR
31.1035 g., 0.9990 Silver 0.9990 oz. ASW, 40 mm. **Ruler:**
Elizabeth II **Subject:** Figures of Note **Obv:** Head with tiara right
Rev: Greenway and Lawson as portrayed on Australia 10 dollar
banknote

Date	Mintage	F	VF	XF	Unc	BU
2006P Proof	1,000	Value: 95.00				

KM# 848   DOLLAR
31.1035 g., 0.9990 Silver 0.9990 oz. ASW, 40 mm. **Ruler:**
Elizabeth II **Subject:** Figures of Note **Obv:** Head with tiara right
Rev: Kingsford-Smith and Hargrave as portrayed on Australia 20
dollar banknote

Date	Mintage	F	VF	XF	Unc	BU
2006P Proof	1,000	Value: 95.00				

KM# 849   DOLLAR
31.1035 g., 0.9990 Silver 0.9990 oz. ASW, 40 mm. **Ruler:**
Elizabeth II **Subject:** 50th Anniversary of Dame Edna Everage
Obv: Head with tiara right **Rev:** Dame Edna

Date	Mintage	F	VF	XF	Unc	BU
2006P Proof	6,500	Value: 85.00				

KM# 1005   DOLLAR
31.1030 g., 0.9990 Silver 0.9989 oz. ASW, 40 mm. **Ruler:**
Elizabeth II **Obv:** Head with tiara right **Obv. Legend:** ELIZABETH
II - AUSTRALIA **Rev:** Everage head facing, multicolor **Rev.
Legend:** DAME EDNA EVERAGE - 50TH ANNIVERSARY

Date	Mintage	F	VF	XF	Unc	BU
ND(2006)P Proof	6,500	Value: 60.00				

KM# 1008   DOLLAR
31.1030 g., 0.9990 Silver 0.9989 oz. ASW, 40.5 mm. **Ruler:**
Elizabeth II **Subject:** Quadricentennial **Obv:** Head with tiara right
Obv. Legend: ELIZABETH II - AUSTRALIA **Rev:** Sailing ship at
left, early map at right **Rev. Legend:** Australia on the Map

Date	Mintage	F	VF	XF	Unc	BU
2006P	—	—	—	—	—	50.00

KM# 1019   DOLLAR
31.3000 g., 0.9990 Silver 1.0053 oz. ASW, 40.5 mm. **Ruler:**
Elizabeth II **Subject:** 20th Anniversary of base **Obv:** Head with
tiara right **Obv. Legend:** ELIZABETH II - AUSTRALIA **Rev:** Plane
above Albatross and chick on ice, multicolor **Rev. Legend:**
Australian Antarctic Territory - EDGEWORTH DAVID BASE
Edge: Reeded

Date	Mintage	F	VF	XF	Unc	BU
2006P Proof	7,500	Value: 60.00				

KM# 808   DOLLAR
9.0000 g., Aluminum-Bronze, 25 mm. **Ruler:** Elizabeth II
Subject: Ashes Cricket Series 1882-2007 **Obv:** Head with tiara
right **Rev:** Urn with supporters **Edge:** Segmented reeding

Date	Mintage	F	VF	XF	Unc	BU
2007				—	3.00	4.00

KM# 809   DOLLAR
9.0000 g., Aluminum-Bronze, 25 mm. **Ruler:** Elizabeth II
Subject: Year of the Pig **Obv:** Head with tiara right **Rev:** Pig
Edge: Segmented reeding

Date	Mintage	F	VF	XF	Unc	BU
2007	7,500	—	—	—	95.00	—

KM# 809a   DOLLAR
11.6600 g., 0.9990 Silver 0.3745 oz. ASW, 25 mm. **Ruler:**
Elizabeth II **Subject:** Year of the Pig **Obv:** Head with tiara right
Rev: Pig **Edge:** Segmented reeding

Date	Mintage	F	VF	XF	Unc	BU
2007 Proof	—	Value: 28.00				

KM# 828   DOLLAR
9.0000 g., Aluminum-Bronze, 25 mm. **Ruler:** Elizabeth II
Subject: Year of the Surf Lifesaver **Obv:** Head with tiara right
Rev: Three lifesavers carrying rescued person **Edge:**
Segmented reeding

Date	Mintage	F	VF	XF	Unc	BU
2007 Proof	34,500	Value: 20.00				

KM# 828a   DOLLAR
11.6600 g., 0.9990 Silver 0.3745 oz. ASW, 25 mm. **Ruler:**
Elizabeth II **Subject:** Year of the Surfer Lifesaver **Rev:** Three
men saving fourth

Date	Mintage	F	VF	XF	Unc	BU
2007B	—	Value: 40.00				

KM# 829   DOLLAR
9.0000 g., Aluminum-Bronze, 25 mm. **Ruler:** Elizabeth II
Subject: Norman Lindsay and his Magic Pudding **Obv:** Head
with tiara right **Rev:** Lindsay and Pudding characters **Edge:**
Segmented reeding

Date	Mintage	F	VF	XF	Unc	BU
2007	33,690	—	—	—	65.00	—

KM# 850   DOLLAR
27.2200 g., Copper-Nickel, 38.74 mm. **Ruler:** Elizabeth II **Obv:**
Head with tiara right **Rev:** Kangaroo mother and joey **Edge:**
Reeded

Date	Mintage	F	VF	XF	Unc	BU
2007	5,000	—	—	—	275	300

KM# 1009   DOLLAR
31.1030 g., 0.9990 Silver 0.9989 oz. ASW, 40 mm. **Ruler:**
Elizabeth II **Subject:** 75th Anniversary Death of Phar Lap **Obv:**
Head with tiara right **Obv. Legend:** ELIZABETH II - AUSTRALIA
Rev: Horse and rider racing right

Date	Mintage	F	VF	XF	Unc	BU
ND(2007)P Proof	7,500	Value: 95.00				

KM# 1012   DOLLAR
31.1030 g., 0.9990 Silver 0.9989 oz. ASW, 40 mm. **Ruler:**
Elizabeth II **Obv:** Bust with tiara right **Obv. Legend:** ELIZABETH
II - AUSTRALIA **Rev:** Bridge, multicolor fireworks above **Rev.
Legend:** 75th ANNIVERSARY - SYDNEY HARBOUR BRIDGE

Date	Mintage	F	VF	XF	Unc	BU
ND(2007)P Proof	10,000	Value: 85.00				

KM# 1016   DOLLAR
11.6600 g., 0.9990 Silver 0.3745 oz. ASW, 25 mm. **Ruler:**
Elizabeth II **Subject:** 75th Anniversary - Sydney Harbor Bridge
Obv: Head with tiara right **Obv. Legend:** ELIZABETH II _
AUSTRALIA **Rev:** Three men standing at bridge joint **Edge:**
Segmented reeding

Date	Mintage	F	VF	XF	Unc	BU
2007B Proof	12,500	Value: 35.00				

KM# 1016a   DOLLAR
9.0000 g., Aluminum-Bronze, 25 mm. **Ruler:** Elizabeth II
Subject: Sydney Harbor Bridge, 75th Anniversary **Obv:** Head
with tiara right **Rev:** Three men standing at bridge joint

Date	Mintage	F	VF	XF	Unc	BU
2007S	—	—	—	—	3.00	4.00

KM# 1020   DOLLAR
31.4800 g., 0.9990 Silver 1.0111 oz. ASW, 40.5 mm. **Ruler:**
Elizabeth II **Subject:** 50th Anniversary of Station **Obv:** Head with
tiara right **Obv. Legend:** ELIZABETH II - AUSTRALIA **Rev:** Ship
"Kista Dan", multicolor **Rev. Legend:** Australian Antarctic
Territory - DAVIS STATION **Edge:** Reeded

Date	Mintage	F	VF	XF	Unc	BU
2007P Proof	7,500	Value: 60.00				

KM# 1024   DOLLAR
9.0000 g., Aluminum-Bronze, 25 mm. **Ruler:** Elizabeth II
Series: Colored Oceans **Obv:** Head with tiara right **Rev:** Biscuit
Star, multicolor **Edge:** Segmented reeding **Note:** Issued in folder.

Date	Mintage	F	VF	XF	Unc	BU
2007	—	—	—	—	—	22.00

KM# 1025   DOLLAR
9.0000 g., Aluminum-Bronze, 25 mm. **Ruler:** Elizabeth II
Series: Colored Oceans **Obv:** Head with tiara right **Rev:** Longfin
Banner fish, multicolor **Edge:** Segmented reeding

Date	Mintage	F	VF	XF	Unc	BU
2007	25,930	—	—	—	—	22.00

KM# 1026   DOLLAR
9.0000 g., Aluminum-Bronze, 25 mm. **Ruler:** Elizabeth II **Series:**
Colored Oceans **Obv:** Head with tiara right **Rev:** White Shark,
multicolor **Edge:** Segmented reeding **Note:** Issued in folder.

Date	Mintage	F	VF	XF	Unc	BU
2007	30,416	—	—	—	—	22.00

KM# 1027   DOLLAR
9.0000 g., Aluminum-Bronze, 25 mm. **Ruler:** Elizabeth II
Series: Colored Oceans **Obv:** Head with tiara right **Rev:** Big Belly
seahorse **Edge:** Segmented reeding

Date	Mintage	F	VF	XF	Unc	BU
2007	—	—	—	—	—	22.00

KM# 1040   DOLLAR
9.0000 g., Aluminum-Bronze, 25 mm. **Ruler:** Elizabeth II
Subject: APEC **Rev:** Multiple stars

Date	Mintage	F	VF	XF	Unc	BU
2007B	20,108,000	—	—	—	3.00	4.00

KM# 1042   DOLLAR
9.0000 g., Aluminum-Bronze, 25 mm. **Ruler:** Elizabeth II
Subject: 60th Anniversary - Peacekeepers **Rev:** Hand holding
globe within wreath, dove above

Date	Mintage	F	VF	XF	Unc	BU
2007B	31,028	—	—	—	—	15.00

KM# 1437   DOLLAR
Silver partially gilt **Ruler:** Elizabeth II **Subject:** Lunar dollar

Date	Mintage	F	VF	XF	Unc	BU
2007 Proof	—	Value: 50.00				

KM# 1438   DOLLAR
Silver partially gilt **Ruler:** Elizabeth II **Subject:** One Johanna

Date	Mintage	F	VF	XF	Unc	BU
2007 Proof	—	Value: 50.00				

KM# 1653   DOLLAR
9.0000 g., Aluminum-Bronze, 25 mm. **Ruler:** Elizabeth II
Subject: International Polar Year **Obv:** Head with tiara right **Rev:**
Sailing ship in ice

Date	Mintage	F	VF	XF	Unc	BU
2007	—	—	—	—	6.00	8.00

KM# 1682   DOLLAR
13.8000 g., Aluminum-Bronze, 30.6 mm. **Ruler:** Elizabeth II
Subject: World Youth Day **Rev:** Pope Benedict XVI and WYD
logo in color

Date	Mintage	F	VF	XF	Unc	BU
2008	—	—	—	—	—	15.00

KM# 1047   DOLLAR
9.0000 g., Aluminum-Bronze, 25 mm. **Ruler:** Elizabeth II **Rev:**
First coat of arms

Date	Mintage	F	VF	XF	Unc	BU
2008B	32,500	—	—	—	5.00	6.00
2008M	25,202	—	—	—	5.00	6.00
2008C	104,689	—	—	—	15.00	17.00
2008S	32,500	—	—	—	5.00	6.00

KM# 1063   DOLLAR
9.0000 g., Aluminum-Bronze, 25 mm. **Ruler:** Elizabeth II
Subject: Saint Sister Mary Mackillop **Rev:** Nun and three
children, world map in background

Date	Mintage	F	VF	XF	Unc	BU
2008	29,800	—	—	—	15.00	17.00

KM# 1039   DOLLAR
9.0000 g., Aluminum-Bronze, 25 mm. **Ruler:** Elizabeth II
Subject: Boy Scouts, 100th Anniversary

Date	Mintage	F	VF	XF	Unc	BU
2008	—	—	—	—	6.00	7.00

KM# 1047a   DOLLAR
11.6000 g., 0.9990 Silver 0.3726 oz. ASW, 25 mm. **Ruler:**
Elizabeth II **Rev:** First coat of arms

Date	Mintage	F	VF	XF	Unc	BU
2008C Proof	12,500	Value: 45.00				

KM# 1052   DOLLAR
9.0000 g., Aluminum-Bronze, 25 mm. **Ruler:** Elizabeth II **Subject:**
Rugby League Centennial **Rev:** Rugby anniversary logo

Date	Mintage	F	VF	XF	Unc	BU
2008	60,400	—	—	—	15.00	17.00

KM# 1056   DOLLAR
9.0000 g., Aluminum-Bronze, 25 mm. **Ruler:** Elizabeth II
Subject: Year of the Rat

Date	Mintage	F	VF	XF	Unc	BU
2008	—	—	—	—	13.00	15.00

KM# 1056a   DOLLAR
11.6600 g., 0.9990 Silver 0.3745 oz. ASW, 25 mm. **Ruler:**
Elizabeth II **Subject:** Year of the Rat **Rev:** Mouse at center, flora
in arches

Date	Mintage	F	VF	XF	Unc	BU
2008 Proof	10,000	Value: 45.00				

KM# 1059   DOLLAR
9.0000 g., Aluminum-Bronze, 25 mm. **Ruler:** Elizabeth II
Subject: Planet Earth **Rev:** Four hands and elements

Date	Mintage	F	VF	XF	Unc	BU
2008	28,399	—	—	—	20.00	22.00
2008 Proof	—	Value: 25.00				

KM# 1064   DOLLAR
9.0000 g., Aluminum-Bronze, 25 mm. **Ruler:** Elizabeth II
Subject: Centennial of Quarantine **Rev:** Beagle and suitcase like
map of Australia

Date	Mintage	F	VF	XF	Unc	BU
2008	30,094	—	—	—	15.00	17.00

KM# 1068   DOLLAR
9.0000 g., Aluminum-Bronze, 25 mm. **Ruler:** Elizabeth II **Rev:**
Multicolor Echidna

Date	Mintage	F	VF	XF	Unc	BU
2008	20,589	—	—	—	18.00	22.00

KM# 1069   DOLLAR
9.0000 g., Aluminum-Bronze, 25 mm. **Ruler:** Elizabeth II **Rev:**
Multicolor Rock Wallaby

Date	Mintage	F	VF	XF	Unc	BU
2008	24,863	—	—	—	18.00	22.00

KM# 1070   DOLLAR
9.0000 g., Aluminum-Bronze, 25 mm. **Ruler:** Elizabeth II **Rev:**
Multicolor koala

Date	Mintage	F	VF	XF	Unc	BU
2008	27,045	—	—	—	18.00	22.00

KM# 1071   DOLLAR
9.0000 g., Aluminum-Bronze, 25 mm. **Ruler:** Elizabeth II **Rev:**
Multicolor wombat

Date	Mintage	F	VF	XF	Unc	BU
2008	22,295	—	—	—	18.00	22.00

KM# 1076   DOLLAR
9.0000 g., Aluminum-Bronze, 25 mm. **Ruler:** Elizabeth II
Subject: Year of Astronomy **Rev:** Parkes Telescope

Date	Mintage	F	VF	XF	Unc	BU
2008	—	—	—	—	12.00	14.00
2008 Proof	—	Value: 25.00				

KM# 1090   DOLLAR
13.5000 g., Aluminum-Bronze, 29.5 mm. **Ruler:** Elizabeth II
Subject: Ghost Bat **Obv:** Head right **Rev:** Ghost bat against night
sky **Edge:** Reeded

Date	Mintage	F	VF	XF	Unc	BU
2008	—	—	—	—	—	14.00

KM# 1091   DOLLAR
31.1050 g., 0.9990 Silver 0.9990 oz. ASW, 40.6 mm. **Ruler:**
Elizabeth II **Subject:** UNESCO Heritage site - Kakadu National
Park **Rev:** Saltwater crocodile and multicolor swamp

Date	Mintage	F	VF	XF	Unc	BU
2008P Proof	7,500	Value: 75.00				

KM# 1168   DOLLAR
13.5000 g., Aluminum-Bronze, 29.5 mm. **Ruler:** Elizabeth II
Obv: Head right **Rev:** Common wombat

Date	Mintage	F	VF	XF	Unc	BU
2008P	—	—	—	—	—	14.00

KM# 1169   DOLLAR
13.5000 g., Aluminum-Bronze, 29.5 mm. **Ruler:** Elizabeth II
Obv: Head right **Rev:** Echidna

Date	Mintage	F	VF	XF	Unc	BU
2008P	—	—	—	—	—	14.00

KM# 1170   DOLLAR
13.5000 g., Aluminum-Bronze, 29.5 mm. **Ruler:** Elizabeth II
Obv: Head right **Rev:** Frilled-neck lizard

Date	Mintage	F	VF	XF	Unc	BU
2008P	—	—	—	—	—	14.00

KM# 1171   DOLLAR
13.5000 g., Aluminum-Bronze, 29.5 mm. **Ruler:** Elizabeth II
Obv: Head right **Rev:** Grey kangaroo

Date	Mintage	F	VF	XF	Unc	BU
2008P	—	—	—	—	—	14.00

KM# 1172   DOLLAR
13.5000 g., Aluminum-Bronze, 29.5 mm. **Ruler:** Elizabeth II
Obv: Head right **Rev:** Splendid wren

Date	Mintage	F	VF	XF	Unc	BU
2008P	—	—	—	—	—	14.00

KM# 1173   DOLLAR
13.5000 g., Aluminum-Bronze, 29.5 mm. **Ruler:** Elizabeth II
Obv: Head right **Rev:** Palm cockatoo

Date	Mintage	F	VF	XF	Unc	BU
2008P	—	—	—	—	—	14.00

KM# 1174   DOLLAR
13.5000 g., Aluminum-Bronze, 29.5 mm. **Ruler:** Elizabeth II
Obv: Head right **Rev:** Wedge-tailed eagle

Date	Mintage	F	VF	XF	Unc	BU
2008P	—	—	—	—	—	14.00

KM# 1175   DOLLAR
13.5000 g., Aluminum-Bronze, 29.5 mm. **Ruler:** Elizabeth II
Obv: Head right **Rev:** Whale shark

Date	Mintage	F	VF	XF	Unc	BU
2008P	—	—	—	—	—	14.00

KM# 1176   DOLLAR
13.5000 g., Aluminum-Bronze, 29.5 mm. **Ruler:** Elizabeth II
Obv: Head right **Rev:** Green sea turtle

Date	Mintage	F	VF	XF	Unc	BU
2008P	—	—	—	—	—	14.00

KM# 1177   DOLLAR
13.5000 g., Aluminum-Bronze, 29.5 mm. **Ruler:** Elizabeth II
Obv: Head right **Rev:** Platypus

Date	Mintage	F	VF	XF	Unc	BU
2008P	—	—	—	—	—	14.00

KM# 1178   DOLLAR
13.5000 g., Aluminum-Bronze, 29.5 mm. **Ruler:** Elizabeth II
Obv: Head right **Rev:** Australian sea lion

Date	Mintage	F	VF	XF	Unc	BU
2008P	—	—	—	—	—	14.00

KM# 1179 DOLLAR
31.1050 g., 0.9990 Silver 0.9990 oz. ASW, 40.6 mm. **Ruler:**
Elizabeth II **Subject:** 90th Anniversary - End of WWI **Obv:** Head
right **Rev:** Silhouette of bugler, multicolor poppies below

Date	Mintage	F	VF	XF	Unc	BU
2008P Proof	12,500	Value: 90.00				

KM# 1654 DOLLAR
31.1050 g., 0.9990 Silver 0.9990 oz. ASW, 40.6 mm. **Ruler:**
Elizabeth II **Subject:** HMAS Sydney II

Date	Mintage	F	VF	XF	Unc	BU
2008 Proof	—	Value: 90.00				

KM# 1749 DOLLAR
31.1050 g., 0.9990 Silver 0.9990 oz. ASW, 40.6 mm. **Ruler:**
Elizabeth II **Subject:** Treasurers of Australia, Opals **Obv:** Small
head above container of five opals **Rev:** landscape above
container

Date	Mintage	F	VF	XF	Unc	BU
2008P Proof	—	Value: 75.00				

KM# 1428 DOLLAR
13.8000 g., Aluminum-Bronze, 30.6 mm. **Ruler:** Elizabeth II
Subject: Citizenship **Obv:** Head in tiara right **Rev:** National arms

Date	Mintage	F	VF	XF	Unc	BU
2009P	—	—	—	—	—	14.00
2010P	—	—	—	—	—	14.00
2011P	—	—	—	—	—	14.00
2012P	—	—	—	—	—	14.00

KM# 1429 DOLLAR
9.0000 g., Aluminum-Bronze, 25 mm. **Ruler:** Elizabeth II
Subject: Steve Irwin **Rev:** Steve Irwin and animal montage

Date	Mintage	F	VF	XF	Unc	BU
2009(p)	—	—	—	—	—	12.00

KM# 1077 DOLLAR
9.0000 g., Aluminum-Bronze, 25 mm. **Ruler:** Elizabeth II
Subject: Dorothy Wall **Rev:** Portrait and four characters to right

Date	Mintage	F	VF	XF	Unc	BU
2009	—				—	12.00

KM# 1078 DOLLAR
9.0000 g., Aluminum-Bronze, 25 mm. **Ruler:** Elizabeth II
Subject: Year of the Ox **Rev:** V. Gottwald

Date	Mintage	F	VF	XF	Unc	BU
2009	—				12.00	13.00

KM# 1078a DOLLAR
11.6600 g., 0.9990 Silver 0.3745 oz. ASW, 25 mm. **Ruler:**
Elizabeth II **Subject:** Year of the Ox

Date	Mintage	F	VF	XF	Unc	BU
2009 Proof	10,000	Value: 45.00				

KM# 1082 DOLLAR
27.2200 g., Copper-Nickel, 38.74 mm. **Ruler:** Elizabeth II **Rev:**
Kangaroo

Date	Mintage	F	VF	XF	Unc	BU
2009	—				—	25.00

KM# 1087 DOLLAR
9.0000 g., Aluminum-Bronze, 25 mm. **Ruler:** Elizabeth II
Subject: 60th Anniversary - Citizenship **Obv:** Head right **Rev:**
Portraits around globe

Date	Mintage	F	VF	XF	Unc	BU
2009C Proof	—	Value: 28.00				

KM# 1087a DOLLAR
11.9000 g., 0.9990 Silver 0.3822 oz. ASW, 25 mm. **Ruler:**
Elizabeth II **Subject:** 60th Anniversary - Citizenship **Rev:**
Portraits around globe

Date	Mintage	F	VF	XF	Unc	BU
2009C Proof	—	Value: 40.00				

KM# 1089 DOLLAR
Aluminum-Bronze **Ruler:** Elizabeth II **Subject:** Postal Service,
200th Anniversary **Obv:** Head with tiara right **Rev:** Isaac Nichols,
first postman

Date	Mintage	F	VF	XF	Unc	BU
2009	—	—	—	—	—	13.00

KM# 1093 DOLLAR
13.3000 g., Aluminum-Bronze, 30.6 mm. **Ruler:** Elizabeth II
Series: Celebrate Australia - Victoria **Rev:** Little Penguin and
multicolor Melbourne city view

Date	Mintage	F	VF	XF	Unc	BU
2009	—				—	13.00

KM# 1094 DOLLAR
13.3000 g., Aluminum-Bronze, 30.6 mm. **Ruler:** Elizabeth II
Subject: Celebrate Australia - Tasmania **Rev:** Tasmanian Devil
and multicolor Cradle Mountain National Park

Date	Mintage	F	VF	XF	Unc	BU
2009P	—				—	13.00

KM# 1095 DOLLAR
13.3000 g., Aluminum-Bronze, 30.6 mm. **Ruler:** Elizabeth II
Subject: Celebrate Australia - South Australia **Rev:** Wombat and
multicolor cathedral

Date	Mintage	F	VF	XF	Unc	BU
2009P	—				—	13.00

KM# 1096 DOLLAR
13.3000 g., Aluminum-Bronze, 30.6 mm. **Ruler:** Elizabeth II
Subject: Celebrate Australia - Queensland **Rev:** Sea Turtle with
multicolor skyline of Brisbane

Date	Mintage	F	VF	XF	Unc	BU
2009P	—				—	13.00

KM# 1092 DOLLAR
13.3000 g., Aluminum-Bronze, 30.6 mm. **Ruler:** Elizabeth II
Subject: Celebrate Australia - Western Australia **Rev:** Kangaroo
and multicolor Perth city view

Date	Mintage	F	VF	XF	Unc	BU
2009	—				—	13.00

KM# 1097 DOLLAR
13.3000 g., Aluminum-Bronze, 30.6 mm. **Ruler:** Elizabeth II
Subject: Celebrate Australia - Northern Territoty **Rev:** Saltwater
crocodile and multicolor Kakadu National Park

Date	Mintage	F	VF	XF	Unc	BU
2009P	—				—	13.00

KM# 1098   DOLLAR
13.3000 g., Aluminum-Bronze, 30.6 mm. **Ruler:** Elizabeth II
Subject: Celebrate Australia - New South Wales **Rev:** Koala,
multicolor Sydney Opera House and Harbor Bridge

Date	Mintage	F	VF	XF	Unc	BU
2009P	—	—	—	—	—	13.00

KM# 1099   DOLLAR
13.3000 g., Aluminum-Bronze, 30.6 mm. **Ruler:** Elizabeth II
Subject: Celebrate Australia - Capital Territory, Canberra **Rev:**
Cockatoo and multicolor design

Date	Mintage	F	VF	XF	Unc	BU
2009P	—	—	—	—	—	13.00

KM# 1211   DOLLAR
31.1050 g., 0.9990 Silver 0.9990 oz. ASW, 40.6 mm. **Ruler:**
Elizabeth II **Subject:** Antarctic Territory **Obv:** Head right **Rev:**
Douglas Mawson, one of two men standing on magnetic South
Pole

Date	Mintage	F	VF	XF	Unc	BU
2009P Proof	7,500	Value: 85.00				

KM# 1245   DOLLAR
31.1050 g., 0.9990 Silver 0.9990 oz. ASW **Ruler:** Elizabeth II
Subject: 2010 FIFA World Cup, South Africa **Obv:** Head right
Rev: Soccer player and kangaroo in background

Date	Mintage	F	VF	XF	Unc	BU
2009P	15,000	Value: 100				

KM# 1248   DOLLAR
31.1050 g., 0.9990 Silver 0.9990 oz. ASW, 40.6 mm. **Ruler:**
Elizabeth II **Subject:** World Masters Games **Obv:** Head right
Rev: Sydney Harbor Bridge, multicolor logo

Date	Mintage	F	VF	XF	Unc	BU
2009P Proof	5,000	Value: 100				

KM# 1256   DOLLAR
13.8000 g., Aluminum-Bronze, 31 mm. **Ruler:** Elizabeth II
Subject: Space Topics - Astronomers **Obv:** Head right **Rev:**
Galileo Galilei and telescope

Date	Mintage	F	VF	XF	Unc	BU
2009P	—	—	—	—	—	12.00

KM# 1257   DOLLAR
Aluminum-Bronze, 31 mm. **Ruler:** Elizabeth II **Subject:** Space
Topics - Craters **Obv:** Head right **Rev:** Moon crater Daedalus

Date	Mintage	F	VF	XF	Unc	BU
2009P	—	—	—	—	—	12.00

KM# 1258   DOLLAR
Aluminum-Bronze, 31 mm. **Ruler:** Elizabeth II **Subject:** Space
Topics - Moons **Obv:** Head right **Rev:** Apollo astronaut on moon
walk

Date	Mintage	F	VF	XF	Unc	BU
2009P	—	—	—	—	—	12.00

KM# 1259   DOLLAR
Aluminum-Bronze, 31 mm. **Ruler:** Elizabeth II **Subject:** Space
Topics - Observatories **Obv:** Head right **Rev:** Parkes
Observatory, New South Wales

Date	Mintage	F	VF	XF	Unc	BU
2009P	—	—	—	—	—	12.00

KM# 1260   DOLLAR
Aluminum-Bronze, 31 mm. **Ruler:** Elizabeth II **Subject:** Space
Topics - Rockets **Obv:** Head right **Rev:** Saturn V rocket on launch
pad

Date	Mintage	F	VF	XF	Unc	BU
2009P	—	—	—	—	—	12.00

KM# 1261   DOLLAR
Aluminum-Bronze, 31 mm. **Ruler:** Elizabeth II **Subject:** Space
Topics - Rovers **Obv:** Head right **Rev:** Mars rover - Spirit and
Opportunity

Date	Mintage	F	VF	XF	Unc	BU
2009P	—	—	—	—	—	12.00

KM# 1262   DOLLAR
Aluminum-Bronze, 31 mm. **Ruler:** Elizabeth II **Subject:** Space
Topics - Space Shuttles **Obv:** Head right **Rev:** Shuttle Discovery
and Space Exploration

Date	Mintage	F	VF	XF	Unc	BU
2009P	—	—	—	—	—	12.00

KM# 1263   DOLLAR
Aluminum-Bronze, 31 mm. **Ruler:** Elizabeth II **Subject:** Space
Topics - Probes **Obv:** Head right **Rev:** Deep Space Probes -
Pioneer 11 and 11

Date	Mintage	F	VF	XF	Unc	BU
2009P	—	—	—	—	—	12.00

KM# 1264   DOLLAR
Aluminum-Bronze, 31 mm. **Ruler:** Elizabeth II **Subject:** Space
Topics - Space Telescope **Obv:** Head right **Rev:** Hubble Space
Telescope

Date	Mintage	F	VF	XF	Unc	BU
2009P	—	—	—	—	—	12.00

KM# 1265   DOLLAR
31.1050 g., 0.9990 Silver 0.9990 oz. ASW, 27x48 mm. **Ruler:**
Elizabeth II **Subject:** Chinese Mythological Character - Wealth
Obv: Head right **Rev:** Man standing, multicolor **Shape:** Vertical
rectangle

Date	Mintage	F	VF	XF	Unc	BU
2009P	—	—	—	—	—	65.00

KM# 1266   DOLLAR
31.1050 g., 0.9990 Silver 0.9990 oz. ASW, 27x48 mm. **Ruler:**
Elizabeth II **Subject:** Chinese Mythological Character - Longevity
Obv: Head right **Rev:** Man standing with staff, multicolor **Edge
Lettering:** Vertical rectangle

Date	Mintage	F	VF	XF	Unc	BU
2009P	—	—	—	—	—	65.00

KM# 1267   DOLLAR
31.1050 g., 0.9990 Silver 0.9990 oz. ASW, 27x48 mm. **Ruler:**
Elizabeth II **Subject:** Chinese Mythological Character - Success
Obv: Head right **Rev:** Man standing with deer, multicolor **Shape:**
Vertical rectangle

Date	Mintage	F	VF	XF	Unc	BU
2009P	—	—	—	—	—	65.00

KM# 1268   DOLLAR
31.1050 g., 0.9990 Silver 0.9990 oz. ASW, 27x48 mm. **Ruler:**
Elizabeth II **Subject:** Chinese Mythological Character - Fortune
Obv: Head right **Rev:** Man standing with scroll, multicolor **Shape:**
Vertical rectangle

Date	Mintage	F	VF	XF	Unc	BU
2009P	—	—	—	—	—	65.00

KM# 1357   DOLLAR
31.1350 g., 0.9990 Silver 1.0000 oz. ASW, 40.6 mm. **Ruler:**
Elizabeth II **Subject:** International Year of Astronomy **Obv:** Head
right **Rev:** Youth looking through telescope, pointing at universe

Date	Mintage	F	VF	XF	Unc	BU
2009P	7,500	Value: 60.00				

KM# 1358 DOLLAR
30.6000 g., Aluminum-Bronze, 30.6 mm. **Ruler:** Elizabeth II
Subject: Swimming **Obv:** Head light **Rev:** Swimmer

Date	Mintage	F	VF	XF	Unc	BU
2009(p) Proof	7,500	Value: 10.00				

KM# 1359 DOLLAR
32.1350 g., 0.9990 Silver 1.0321 oz. ASW, 40 mm. **Ruler:**
Elizabeth II **Subject:** Swimming **Obv:** Head right **Rev:** Swimmer
with hologram effect added

Date	Mintage	F	VF	XF	Unc	BU
2009(p) Proof	7,500	Value: 70.00				

KM# 1497 DOLLAR
13.8000 g., Aluminum-Bronze, 30.6 mm. **Ruler:** Elizabeth II
Subject: ANZAC **Rev:** Child on lap of grandfather, bugler in
background

Date	Mintage	F	VF	XF	Unc	BU
2009	—	—	—	—	7.50	10.00

KM# 1498 DOLLAR
9.0000 g., Aluminum-Bronze, 25 mm. **Ruler:** Elizabeth II
Subject: Age pensions, 100th Anniversary **Rev:** Extended family
portrait, elder members seated at front center in detail

Date	Mintage	F	VF	XF	Unc	BU
2009	—	—	—	—	7.50	10.00

KM# 1499 DOLLAR
9.0000 g., Aluminum-Bronze, 25 mm. **Ruler:** Elizabeth II
Subject: Girl Guides, 100th Anniversary

Date	Mintage	F	VF	XF	Unc	BU
2009	—	—	—	—	7.50	10.00

KM# 1655 DOLLAR
9.0000 g., Aluminum-Bronze, 25 mm. **Ruler:** Elizabeth II **Obv:**
Head with tiara right **Rev:** Baby bilby in color right

Date	Mintage	F	VF	XF	Unc	BU
2009	—	—	—	—	—	10.00

KM# 1656 DOLLAR
9.0000 g., Aluminum-Bronze, 25 mm. **Ruler:** Elizabeth II **Obv:**
Head with tiara right **Rev:** Frilly lizard in color right

Date	Mintage	F	VF	XF	Unc	BU
2009	—	—	—	—	—	10.00

KM# 1657 DOLLAR
9.0000 g., Aluminum-Bronze, 25 mm. **Ruler:** Elizabeth II
Subject: World Masters Games **Obv:** Head with tiara right **Rev:**
Sydney Harbor Bridge, games logo above

Date	Mintage	F	VF	XF	Unc	BU
2009	—	—	—	—	7.00	10.00

KM# 1324 DOLLAR
31.1050 g., 0.9990 Silver 0.9990 oz. ASW, 41 mm. **Ruler:**
Elizabeth II **Subject:** Lachen Macquarie, Governor of New South
Wales **Obv:** Head right **Rev:** Macquarie, Sydney's "Rum"
Hospital, Holey Dollar

Date	Mintage	F	VF	XF	Unc	BU
2010P Proof	7,500	Value: 90.00				

KM# 1325 DOLLAR
31.1050 g., 0.9990 Silver 0.9990 oz. ASW, 41 mm. **Ruler:**
Elizabeth II **Subject:** 2010 Australian Olympic Team **Obv:** Head
right **Rev:** Downhill skier, multicolor Australian flag

Date	Mintage	F	VF	XF	Unc	BU
2010P Proof	5,000	Value: 100				

KM# 1326 DOLLAR
31.1050 g., 0.9990 Silver 0.9990 oz. ASW, 41 mm. **Ruler:**
Elizabeth II **Subject:** Century of Flight in Australia **Obv:** Head
right **Rev:** Bi-plane, multicolor

Date	Mintage	F	VF	XF	Unc	BU
2010P Proof	7,500	Value: 90.00				

KM# 1380 DOLLAR
13.8000 g., Aluminum-Bronze, 30.6 mm. **Ruler:** Elizabeth II
Subject: Anzac Navy **Obv:** Head right **Rev:** Naval crew member
and ship

Date	Mintage	F	VF	XF	Unc	BU
2010(p)	—	—	—	—	—	12.00

KM# 1381 DOLLAR
31.1030 g., 0.9990 Silver 0.9989 oz. ASW, 40.5 mm. **Ruler:**
Elizabeth II **Subject:** Antarctic - Huskey **Obv:** Head right **Rev:**
Huskey in multicolor

Date	Mintage	F	VF	XF	Unc	BU
2010(p) Proof	7,500	Value: 60.00				

KM# 1382 DOLLAR
13.8000 g., Aluminum-Bronze, 30.6 mm. **Ruler:** Elizabeth II
Subject: Flight Centennial **Obv:** Head right **Rev:** Bi-plane flying
right

Date	Mintage	F	VF	XF	Unc	BU
2010(p)	—	—	—	—	—	13.00

KM# 1383 DOLLAR
31.1035 g., 0.9990 Silver 0.9990 oz. ASW, 40 mm. **Ruler:**
Elizabeth II **Subject:** Edward VII Coinage **Obv:** Head right **Rev:**
Coin designs and Edward VII in multicolor

Date	Mintage	F	VF	XF	Unc	BU
2010(p)	—	—	—	—	—	55.00

KM# 1384 DOLLAR
13.8000 g., Aluminum-Bronze, 30.6 mm. **Ruler:** Elizabeth II
Subject: Celebrate Australia - Barrier Reef **Obv:** Head right **Rev:**
Sea Turtle and multicolor background

Date	Mintage	F	VF	XF	Unc	BU
2010P	—	—	—	—	—	15.00

KM# 1385 DOLLAR
13.8000 g., Aluminum-Bronze, 30.6 mm. **Ruler:** Elizabeth II

Subject: Celebrate Australia - Blue Mountain **Obv:** Head right
Rev: Frog and multicolor background

Date	Mintage	F	VF	XF	Unc	BU
2010P	—	—	—	—	—	15.00

KM# 1386   DOLLAR
13.8000 g., Aluminum-Bronze, 30.6 mm.   **Ruler:** Elizabeth II
Subject: Celebrate Australia - Heard Island **Obv:** Head right **Rev:**
Penguins and multicolor background

Date	Mintage	F	VF	XF	Unc	BU
2010P	—	—	—	—	—	15.00

KM# 1387   DOLLAR
13.8000 g., Aluminum-Bronze, 30.6 mm.   **Ruler:** Elizabeth II
Subject: Celebrate Australia - Shark Bay **Obv:** Head right

Date	Mintage	F	VF	XF	Unc	BU
2010P	—	—	—	—	—	15.00

KM# 1388   DOLLAR
13.8000 g., Aluminum-Bronze, 30.6 mm.   **Ruler:** Elizabeth II
Subject: Celebrate Australia - Tasmanian Wilderness **Obv:**
Head right **Rev:** Animal before multicolor waterfall background

Date	Mintage	F	VF	XF	Unc	BU
2010P	—	—	—	—	—	15.00

KM# 1391   DOLLAR
31.1050 g., 0.9990 Silver 0.9990 oz. ASW   **Ruler:** Elizabeth II
Obv: Head right **Rev:** Panda and koala

Date	Mintage	F	VF	XF	Unc	BU
2010(p)	—	—	—	—	—	45.00

KM# 1392   DOLLAR
31.1050 g., 0.9990 Silver 0.9990 oz. ASW   **Ruler:** Elizabeth II
Subject: World Expo **Obv:** Head right **Rev:** Austrlian Panham

Date	Mintage	F	VF	XF	Unc	BU
2010(p)	—	—	—	—	—	50.00

KM# 1393   DOLLAR
31.1050 g., 0.9990 Silver 0.9990 oz. ASW   **Ruler:** Elizabeth II
Obv: Head right **Rev:** Kookaburra mascot

Date	Mintage	F	VF	XF	Unc	BU
2010(p)	—	—	—	—	—	45.00

KM# 1394   DOLLAR
31.1050 g., 0.9990 Silver 0.9990 oz. ASW   **Ruler:** Elizabeth II
Obv: Head right **Rev:** City scape

Date	Mintage	F	VF	XF	Unc	BU
2010(p)	—	—	—	—	—	45.00

KM# 1395   DOLLAR
Silver, 40x60 mm.   **Ruler:** Elizabeth II **Series:** World Expo **Obv:**
Head right **Shape:** Australian outline

Date	Mintage	F	VF	XF	Unc	BU
2010(p)	—	—	—	—	—	60.00

KM# 1396   DOLLAR
13.8000 g., Aluminum-Bronze, 30.6 mm.   **Ruler:** Elizabeth II
Subject: 2010 Shanghai World Expo **Obv:** Head with tiara right
Rev: Artistic tiger seen from above, advancing forward

Date	Mintage	F	VF	XF	Unc	BU
2010P	—	—	—	—	—	14.00

KM# 1431   DOLLAR
9.0000 g., Aluminum-Bronze, 25 mm.   **Ruler:** Elizabeth II
Subject: Burke and Wills 150th Anniversary **Obv:** Head with tiara
right **Rev:** King seated under dig tree

Date	Mintage	F	VF	XF	Unc	BU
2010C	—	—	—	—	—	12.50
2010C Proof	—	Value: 17.50				

KM# 1434   DOLLAR
31.1350 g., 0.9990 Silver 1.0000 oz. ASW   **Ruler:** Elizabeth II
Subject: Burke & Wills expedition **Rev:** Multicolor scene of
explorers

Date	Mintage	F	VF	XF	Unc	BU
2010P Proof	7,500	Value: 80.00				

KM# 1435   DOLLAR
31.1350 g., 0.9990 Silver 1.0000 oz. ASW, 40.6 mm.   **Ruler:**
Elizabeth II **Subject:** Treasures of Australia - Gold **Rev:** Three
gold nuggets within insert

Date	Mintage	F	VF	XF	Unc	BU
2010P Proof	—	Value: 135				

KM# 1440   DOLLAR
13.3000 g., Aluminum-Bronze, 30.6 mm.   **Ruler:** Elizabeth II
Rev: Blowfly

Date	Mintage	F	VF	XF	Unc	BU
2010P	—	—	—	—	—	12.00

KM# 1441 DOLLAR
13.3000 g., Aluminum-Bronze, 30.6 mm. **Ruler:** Elizabeth II
Rev: Bull Ant

Date	Mintage	F	VF	XF	Unc	BU
2010P	—	—	—	—	—	12.00

KM# 1442 DOLLAR
13.3000 g., Aluminum-Bronze, 30.6 mm. **Ruler:** Elizabeth II
Rev: Burlwing Buttlerfly

Date	Mintage	F	VF	XF	Unc	BU
2010P	—	—	—	—	—	12.00

KM# 1443 DOLLAR
13.3000 g., Aluminum-Bronze, 30.6 mm. **Ruler:** Elizabeth II
Rev: Cicada

Date	Mintage	F	VF	XF	Unc	BU
2010P	—	—	—	—	—	12.00

KM# 1444 DOLLAR
13.3000 g., Aluminum-Bronze, 30.6 mm. **Ruler:** Elizabeth II
Rev: Dragonfly

Date	Mintage	F	VF	XF	Unc	BU
2010P	—	—	—	—	—	12.00

KM# 1445 DOLLAR
13.3000 g., Aluminum-Bronze, 30.6 mm. **Ruler:** Elizabeth II
Rev: Grasshopper

Date	Mintage	F	VF	XF	Unc	BU
2010P	—	—	—	—	—	12.00

KM# 1446 DOLLAR
13.3000 g., Aluminum-Bronze, 30.6 mm. **Ruler:** Elizabeth II
Rev: Ladybug

Date	Mintage	F	VF	XF	Unc	BU
2010P	—	—	—	—	—	12.00

KM# 1447 DOLLAR
13.3000 g., Aluminum-Bronze, 30.6 mm. **Ruler:** Elizabeth II
Rev: Praying mantis

Date	Mintage	F	VF	XF	Unc	BU
2010P	—	—	—	—	—	12.00

KM# 1448 DOLLAR
13.3000 g., Aluminum-Bronze, 30.6 mm. **Ruler:** Elizabeth II
Rev: Red-backed spider

Date	Mintage	F	VF	XF	Unc	BU
2010P	—	—	—	—	—	12.00

KM# 1451 DOLLAR
31.1050 g., 0.9990 Silver 0.9990 oz. ASW **Ruler:** Elizabeth II
Subject: New South Wales - Sidney Coin Show **Rev:** Koala and
multicolor opera house and harbor bridge views

Date	Mintage	F	VF	XF	Unc	BU
2010P Proof	—	Value: 45.00				

KM# 1452 DOLLAR
31.1050 g., 0.9990 Silver 0.9990 oz. ASW **Ruler:** Elizabeth II
Subject: Victoria - Melbourne Coin Show **Rev:** Penguin and
multicolor tram and building

Date	Mintage	F	VF	XF	Unc	BU
2010P Proof	—	Value: 45.00				

KM# 1490 DOLLAR
13.3000 g., Aluminum-Bronze, 30.6 mm. **Ruler:** Elizabeth II
Rev: Burke & Willis statue

Date	Mintage	F	VF	XF	Unc	BU
2010P	—	—	—	—	—	12.00

KM# 1491 DOLLAR
31.1050 g., 0.9990 Silver 0.9990 oz. ASW, 40.6 mm. **Ruler:**
Elizabeth II **Obv:** Head with tiara right **Rev:** Saint Mary Mackillop
in color

Date	Mintage	F	VF	XF	Unc	BU
2010 Proof	—	Value: 60.00				

KM# 1494 DOLLAR
31.1050 g., 0.9990 Silver 0.9990 oz. ASW **Ruler:** Elizabeth II
Subject: New South Wales

Date	Mintage	F	VF	XF	Unc	BU
2010 Proof	—	Value: 50.00				

KM# 1495 DOLLAR
9.0000 g., Aluminum-Bronze, 25 mm. **Ruler:** Elizabeth II
Subject: Australian coinage, 100th Anniversary **Obv:** Head with
tiara right **Rev:** Coinage portraits of Elizabeth II, George VI,
George V and Edward VII

Date	Mintage	F	VF	XF	Unc	BU
2010B	—	—	—	—	4.00	5.00
2010C	—	—	—	—	4.00	5.00
2010M	—	—	—	—	4.00	5.00
2010S	—	—	—	—	4.00	5.00

KM# 1495a DOLLAR
11.6600 g., 0.9990 Silver 0.3745 oz. ASW, 25 mm. **Ruler:**
Elizabeth II **Subject:** Centennial of Commonwealth Coins **Obv:**
Head in tiara right **Rev:** Four portraits

Date	Mintage	F	VF	XF	Unc	BU
2010 Proof	12,500	Value: 50.00				

KM# 1496 DOLLAR
9.0000 g., Aluminum-Bronze, 25 mm. **Ruler:** Elizabeth II
Subject: Fred Hollows - Inspirational Australians

Date	Mintage	F	VF	XF	Unc	BU
2010	—	—	—	—	3.50	5.00

KM# 1503 DOLLAR
9.0000 g., Aluminum-Bronze, 25 mm. **Ruler:** Elizabeth II
Subject: Wool Industry **Rev:** Sheep sheering and map of
Australia

Date	Mintage	F	VF	XF	Unc	BU
2010	—				5.00	6.00
2010 Proof	—	Value: 25.00				

KM# 1505 DOLLAR
31.1050 g., 0.9990 Silver 0.9990 oz. ASW, 40.6 mm. **Ruler:**
Elizabeth II **Subject:** Perth-ANDA Bridge **Rev:** City view

Date	Mintage	F	VF	XF	Unc	BU
2010 Proof	—	Value: 60.00				

KM# 1568 DOLLAR
31.1050 g., 0.9990 Silver 0.9990 oz. ASW, 32.6 mm. **Ruler:**
Elizabeth II **Subject:** Sidney Cove Medallion, Wedgewood theme
Obv: Head with tiara right **Rev:** One female standing on rock
facing three others, seascape in backgorund **Edge:** Reeded
Note: High relief

Date	Mintage	F	VF	XF	Unc	BU
2010P Proof	Est. 5,000	Value: 85.00				

KM# 1659 DOLLAR
9.0000 g., Aluminum-Bronze, 25 mm. **Ruler:** Elizabeth II
Subject: Year of the Tiger **Rev:** Tiger head at center in circle,
floral around

Date	Mintage	F	VF	XF	Unc	BU
2010	—				—	10.00

KM# 1659a DOLLAR
11.6600 g., 0.9990 Silver 0.3745 oz. ASW, 25 mm. **Ruler:**
Elizabeth II **Subject:** Year of the Tiger **Obv:** Head with tiara right
Rev: Tiger head in circle, floral around

Date	Mintage	F	VF	XF	Unc	BU
2010 Proof	—	Value: 30.00				

KM# 1762 DOLLAR
31.1050 g., 0.9990 Silver 0.9990 oz. ASW, 40.6 mm. **Ruler:**
Elizabeth II **Obv:** Head with tiara right **Rev:** Kangaroo bounding
left at sunset

Date	Mintage	F	VF	XF	Unc	BU
2010 F15	7,000	—	—	—	—	125
2010 F15 Proof	5,000	Value: 125				

KM# 1504 DOLLAR
9.0000 g., Aluminum-Bronze, 25 mm. **Ruler:** Elizabeth II
Subject: Historical coin designs **Rev:** Sheep head

Date	Mintage	F	VF	XF	Unc	BU
2011C	—	—	—	—	5.00	6.00

KM# 1523 DOLLAR
31.1035 g., 0.9990 Silver 0.9990 oz. ASW, 40.6 mm. **Ruler:**
Elizabeth II **Subject:** Australia's Bronze Coinagae, 100th
Anniversary **Obv:** Head with tiara right **Rev:** George V and coins,
in color

Date	Mintage	F	VF	XF	Unc	BU
2011 Proof	—	Value: 75.00				

KM# 1528 DOLLAR
31.1050 g., 0.9990 Silver 0.9990 oz. ASW, 40.6 mm. **Ruler:**
Elizabeth II **Subject:** Famous Battles in Australian History **Rev:**
Soldier standing at left, view of Gallipoli, 1915 at right

Date	Mintage	F	VF	XF	Unc	BU
2011P Proof	5,000	Value: 110				

KM# 1529 DOLLAR
13.3000 g., Aluminum-Bronze, 30.6 mm. **Ruler:** Elizabeth II
Subject: ANZAC Day, RAAF **Rev:** Bugler and plane, two airmen
at lower right

Date	Mintage	F	VF	XF	Unc	BU
2011P	—	—	—	—	—	13.00

KM# 1530 DOLLAR
31.1050 g., 0.9990 Silver 0.9990 oz. ASW **Ruler:** Elizabeth II
Subject: Royal Wedding **Rev:** Catherine Middleton and Prince
William in color, Westminster Abbey at left

Date	Mintage	F	VF	XF	Unc	BU
2011P Proof	12,500	Value: 110				

KM# 1531 DOLLAR
31.1050 g., 0.9990 Silver 0.9990 oz. ASW **Ruler:** Elizabeth II
Subject: Naval Battles **Rev:** Battle of Midway

Date	Mintage	F	VF	XF	Unc	BU
2011P Proof	5,000	Value: 110				

KM# 1564 DOLLAR
31.1050 g., 0.9990 Silver 0.9990 oz. ASW **Ruler:** Elizabeth II
Subject: Treasures of Australia **Rev:** Keshi pearl engased in
mother of pearl locket

Date	Mintage	F	VF	XF	Unc	BU
2011P Proof	—	Value: 185				

KM# 1565 DOLLAR
31.1050 g., 0.9990 Silver 0.9990 oz. ASW, 40.6 mm. **Ruler:**
Elizabeth II **Subject:** Antartica **Obv:** Head with tiara right **Rev:**
Killer whale in color

Date	Mintage	F	VF	XF	Unc	BU
2011P Proof	7,500	Value: 115				

KM# 1572 DOLLAR
13.0000 g., Aluminum-Bronze, 30.6 mm. **Ruler:** Elizabeth II
Subject: Bush Babies - Koala **Rev:** Koala lounging at left

Date	Mintage	F	VF	XF	Unc	BU
2011(p)	—	—	—	—	—	15.00

KM# 1573 DOLLAR
13.0000 g., Aluminum-Bronze, 30.6 mm. **Ruler:** Elizabeth II
Subject: Bush babies - Dingo **Rev:** Dingo seated at left

Date	Mintage	F	VF	XF	Unc	BU
2011(p)	—	—	—	—	—	15.00

KM# 1574 DOLLAR
13.0000 g., Aluminum-Bronze, 30.6 mm. **Ruler:** Elizabeth II
Subject: Bush babies - Bilby **Rev:** Bilby at left

Date	Mintage	F	VF	XF	Unc	BU
2011(p)	—	—	—	—	—	15.00

KM# 1575 DOLLAR
13.0000 g., Aluminum-Bronze, 30.6 mm. **Ruler:** Elizabeth II
Subject: Bush babies - Sugar Glider **Rev:** Sugar Glider at left

Date	Mintage	F	VF	XF	Unc	BU
2011(p)	—	—	—	—	—	15.00

KM# 1576 DOLLAR
13.0000 g., Aluminum-Bronze, 30.6 mm. **Ruler:** Elizabeth II
Subject: Bush babies - Kangaroo **Rev:** Kangaroo seated at left

Date	Mintage	F	VF	XF	Unc	BU
2011(p)	—	—	—	—	—	15.00

KM# 1580 DOLLAR
13.8000 g., Aluminum-Bronze, 30.6 mm. **Ruler:** Elizabeth II
Subject: Mythical creatures - Dragon

Date	Mintage	F	VF	XF	Unc	BU
2011P	—	—	—	—	—	12.50

KM# 1581 DOLLAR
13.8000 g., Aluminum-Bronze, 30.6 mm. **Ruler:** Elizabeth II
Subject: Mythical creatures - Fairy

Date	Mintage	F	VF	XF	Unc	BU
2011P	—	—	—	—	—	12.50

KM# 1582 DOLLAR
13.8000 g., Aluminum-Bronze, 30.6 mm. **Ruler:** Elizabeth II
Subject: Mythical creatures - Goblin

Date	Mintage	F	VF	XF	Unc	BU
2011P	—	—	—	—	—	12.50

KM# 1583 DOLLAR
13.8000 g., Aluminum-Bronze, 30.6 mm. **Ruler:** Elizabeth II
Subject: Mythical creatures - Griffin

Date	Mintage	F	VF	XF	Unc	BU
2011P	—	—	—	—	—	12.50

KM# 1584 DOLLAR
13.8000 g., Aluminum-Bronze, 30.6 mm. **Ruler:** Elizabeth II
Subject: Mythical creatures - Mermaid

Date	Mintage	F	VF	XF	Unc	BU
2011P	—	—	—	—	—	12.50

KM# 1585 DOLLAR
13.8000 g., Aluminum-Bronze, 30.6 mm. **Ruler:** Elizabeth II
Subject: Mythical creatures - Tree ent

Date	Mintage	F	VF	XF	Unc	BU
2011P	—	—	—	—	—	12.50

KM# 1586 DOLLAR
13.8000 g., Aluminum-Bronze, 30.6 mm. **Ruler:** Elizabeth II
Subject: Mythical creatures - Ogre

Date	Mintage	F	VF	XF	Unc	BU
2011P	—	—	—	—	—	12.50

KM# 1587 DOLLAR
13.8000 g., Aluminum-Bronze, 30.6 mm. **Ruler:** Elizabeth II
Subject: Mythical creatures - Phoenix

Date	Mintage	F	VF	XF	Unc	BU
2011P	—	—	—	—	—	12.50

KM# 1588 DOLLAR
13.8000 g., Aluminum-Bronze, 30.6 mm. **Ruler:** Elizabeth II
Subject: Mythical creatures - Unicorn

Date	Mintage	F	VF	XF	Unc	BU
2011P	—	—	—	—	—	12.50

KM# 1589 DOLLAR
13.8000 g., Aluminum-Bronze, 30.6 mm. **Ruler:** Elizabeth II
Obv: Head in tiara right **Rev:** Christmas tree decorated in color,
presents below, stars around, holly at bottom flanking **Rev.**
Legend: WISHING YOU A MERRY CHRISTMAS / 2011

Date	Mintage	F	VF	XF	Unc	BU
2011P	—	—	—	—	—	12.50

KM# 1590 DOLLAR
31.1030 g., 0.9990 Silver 0.9989 oz. ASW, 40 mm. **Ruler:**
Elizabeth II **Subject:** Dame Nellie Melba **Obv:** Head with tiara
right **Rev:** Colored bust right, musical notes below, flowers at left

Date	Mintage	F	VF	XF	Unc	BU
2011P Proof	Est. 5,000	Value: 100				

KM# 1591 DOLLAR
13.8000 g., Aluminum-Bronze, 30.6 mm. **Ruler:** Elizabeth II
Subject: Dame Nellie Melba **Obv:** Head with tiara right **Rev:** Bust
at left facing right, flowers at right

Date	Mintage	F	VF	XF	Unc	BU
2011P	—	—	—	—	—	12.50

KM# 1592   DOLLAR
31.1050 g., 0.9990 Silver 0.9990 oz. ASW, 40 mm. **Ruler:**
Elizabeth II **Subject:** Royal Military College - Duntroon; 100th
Anniversary **Obv:** Head with tiara right **Rev:** College emblem gilt
above images of soldiers

Date	Mintage	F	VF	XF	Unc	BU
2011P Proof	Est. 7,500	Value: 100				

KM# 1593   DOLLAR
13.8000 g., Aluminum-Bronze, 30.6 mm. **Ruler:** Elizabeth II
Subject: Royal Military College - Duntroon; 100th Anniversary
Obv: Head with tiara right **Rev:** Military hat badge

Date	Mintage	F	VF	XF	Unc	BU
2011P	—	—	—	—	—	12.50

KM# 1594   DOLLAR
31.1050 g., 0.9990 Silver 0.9990 oz. ASW, 40 mm. **Ruler:**
Elizabeth II **Subject:** Australian Antartic Territory, Killer Whale
Obv: Head with tiara right **Rev:** Killer whale, jumping, and nin the
water with a calf

Date	Mintage	F	VF	XF	Unc	BU
2011P Proof	Est. 7,500	Value: 100				

KM# 1597   DOLLAR
Aluminum-Bronze, 40 mm. **Ruler:** Elizabeth II **Subject:**
Wiggles, 20th Anniversary **Obv:** Head with tiara right **Rev:**
Wiggles characters in Big Red car **Edge:** Reeded

Date	Mintage	F	VF	XF	Unc	BU
2011P	—	—	—	—	—	17.50

KM# 1598   DOLLAR
Aluminum-Bronze, 40 mm. **Ruler:** Elizabeth II **Subject:**
Wiggles, 20th Anniversary **Obv:** Head in tiara right **Rev:** Wiggles
four band members at instruments **Edge:** Reeded

Date	Mintage	F	VF	XF	Unc	BU
2011P	—	—	—	—	—	17.50

KM# 1599   DOLLAR
Aluminum-Bronze, 40 mm. **Ruler:** Elizabeth II **Subject:**
Wiggles, 20th Anniversary **Obv:** Head with tiara right **Rev:**
Wiggles Pirate and animal characters

Date	Mintage	F	VF	XF	Unc	BU
2011P	—	—	—	—	—	17.50

KM# 1600   DOLLAR
Aluminum-Bronze, 40 mm. **Ruler:** Elizabeth II **Subject:**
Wiggles, 20th Anniversary **Obv:** Head with tiara right **Rev:**
Wiggles charactes in starburst

Date	Mintage	F	VF	XF	Unc	BU
2011P	—	—	—	—	—	17.50

KM# 1601   DOLLAR
31.1050 g., 0.9990 Silver 0.9990 oz. ASW, 40 mm. **Ruler:**
Elizabeth II **Subject:** Royal Australian Navy, 100th Anniversary
Obv: Head with tiara right **Rev:** HMAS Yarra, HMAS Anzac and
sailors **Edge:** Reeded

Date	Mintage	F	VF	XF	Unc	BU
2011P Proof	—	Value: 120				

KM# 1602   DOLLAR
13.8000 g., Aluminum-Bronze, 30.6 mm. **Ruler:** Elizabeth II
Subject: Royal Australian Navy, 100th Anniversary **Obv:** Head
with tiara right **Rev:** Navy cap badge

Date	Mintage	F	VF	XF	Unc	BU
2011P	—	—	—	—	—	15.00

KM# 1603   DOLLAR
13.8000 g., Aluminum-Bronze, 30.6 mm. **Ruler:** Elizabeth II
Subject: Elizabeth II's 85th Birthday **Obv:** Head with tiara right

Rev: Elizabeth II in hat at left, birthday legend and emblem below
Edge: Reeded

Date	Mintage	F	VF	XF	Unc	BU
2011P	—	—	—	—	—	15.00

KM# 1604   DOLLAR
31.1050 g., 0.9990 Silver 0.9990 oz. ASW, 40 mm. **Ruler:**
Elizabeth II **Subject:** Wallabies Rugby team **Obv:** Head with tiara
right **Rev:** Wallabies logo in color at left, rugby player at right
Edge: Reeded

Date	Mintage	F	VF	XF	Unc	BU
2011P Proof	Est. 5,000	Value: 100				

KM# 1606   DOLLAR
31.1050 g., 0.9990 Silver 0.9990 oz. ASW, 40 mm. **Ruler:**
Elizabeth II **Subject:** World War II - Siege of Tobruk **Obv:** Head
with tiara right **Rev:** Soldier standing at left, image of solder
carried on stretcher at right; Campaign ribbon below **Edge:**
Reeded

Date	Mintage	F	VF	XF	Unc	BU
2011P Proof	Est. 5,000	Value: 100				

KM# 1607   DOLLAR
31.1050 g., 0.9990 Silver 0.9990 oz. ASW, 40 mm. **Ruler:**
Elizabeth II **Subject:** Ginger Meggs, 90th Birthday **Obv:** Head
with tiara right **Rev:** Cartoon boy riding kangaroo right **Edge:**
Reeded

Date	Mintage	F	VF	XF	Unc	BU
2011P Proof	Est. 3,000	Value: 100				

KM# 1612   DOLLAR
13.8000 g., Aluminum-Bronze, 30.6 mm. **Ruler:** Elizabeth II
Subject: Wet Tropics of Queensland **Obv:** Head with tiara right
Rev: Bird walking right and color fauna background **Edge:**
Reeded

Date	Mintage	F	VF	XF	Unc	BU
2011P	—	—	—	—	—	15.00

KM# 1613   DOLLAR
13.8000 g., Aluminum-Bronze, 30.6 mm. **Ruler:** Elizabeth II
Subject: Macquarie Island **Obv:** Bust with tiara right **Rev:** Sea
lion and color background **Edge:** Reeded

Date	Mintage	F	VF	XF	Unc	BU
2011P	—	—	—	—	—	15.00

KM# 1614   DOLLAR
13.8000 g., Aluminum-Bronze, 30.6 mm. **Ruler:** Elizabeth II
Subject: Goondwana Rainforests **Obv:** Head with tiara right **Rev:**
Bird left with color fauna background **Edge:** Reeded

Date	Mintage	F	VF	XF	Unc	BU
2011P	—	—	—	—	—	15.00

KM# 1615   DOLLAR
13.8000 g., Aluminum-Bronze, 30.6 mm. **Ruler:** Elizabeth II
Subject: Australian Fossil Mammal Sites **Obv:** Head with tiara
right **Rev:** Dingo left with color landscape in background **Edge:**
Reeded

Date	Mintage	F	VF	XF	Unc	BU
2011P	—	—	—	—	—	15.00

KM# 1616   DOLLAR
13.8000 g., Aluminum-Bronze, 30.6 mm. **Ruler:** Elizabeth II
Subject: Purnululu National Park **Obv:** Head with tiara right **Rev:**
Kangaroo right with color background **Edge:** Reeded

Date	Mintage	F	VF	XF	Unc	BU
2011P	—	—	—	—	—	15.00

KM# 1617   DOLLAR
9.0000 g., Aluminum-Bronze, 25 mm. **Ruler:** Elizabeth II **Obv:**
Head with tiara right **Rev:** Crimson Rosella in color

Date	Mintage	F	VF	XF	Unc	BU
2011	—	—	—	—	—	15.00

KM# 1618 DOLLAR

9.0000 g., Aluminum-Bronze, 25 mm. **Ruler:** Elizabeth II **Obv:** Head with tiara right **Rev:** Kookaburra in color

Date	Mintage	F	VF	XF	Unc	BU
2011	—	—	—	—	—	15.00

KM# 1619 DOLLAR

9.0000 g., Aluminum-Bronze, 25 mm. **Ruler:** Elizabeth II **Subject:** CHOGM meeting, Perth **Obv:** Head with tiara right **Rev:** Flags around globe

Date	Mintage	F	VF	XF	Unc	BU
2011	—	—	—	—	—	10.00

KM# 1620 DOLLAR

9.0000 g., Aluminum-Bronze, 25 mm. **Ruler:** Elizabeth II **Subject:** President's Cup **Obv:** Head with tiara right **Rev:** Golfer talking swing

Date	Mintage	F	VF	XF	Unc	BU
2011	—	—	—	—	—	10.00

KM# 1620a DOLLAR

11.9000 g., 0.9990 Silver 0.3822 oz. ASW, 25 mm. **Ruler:** Elizabeth II **Subject:** President's Cup **Obv:** Head with tiara right **Rev:** Gopher taking swing

Date	Mintage	F	VF	XF	Unc	BU
2011 Proof	—	Value: 40.00				

KM# 1621 DOLLAR

31.1050 g., 0.9990 Silver 0.9990 oz. ASW, 40 mm. **Ruler:** Elizabeth II **Subject:** President's Cup **Obv:** Head with tiara right **Rev:** Golf Ball and color trophy and logo, players around edge

Date	Mintage	F	VF	XF	Unc	BU
2011 Proof	—	Value: 100				

KM# 1635 DOLLAR

9.0000 g., Aluminum-Bronze, 25 mm. **Ruler:** Elizabeth II **Subject:** Census, 100th Anniversary **Obv:** Head with tiara right **Rev:** Multiple stylized heads at left, geometric Australia outline at right

Date	Mintage	F	VF	XF	Unc	BU
2011	—	—	—	—	7.00	8.00

KM# 1643 DOLLAR

9.0000 g., Aluminum-Bronze, 25 mm. **Ruler:** Elizabeth II **Obv:** Head with tiara right **Rev:** Mitchell Cockatoo in color

Date	Mintage	F	VF	XF	Unc	BU
2011	—	—	—	—	—	10.00

KM# 1644 DOLLAR

9.0000 g., Aluminum-Bronze, 25 mm. **Ruler:** Elizabeth II **Obv:** Head with tiara right **Rev:** Kingfisher in color

Date	Mintage	F	VF	XF	Unc	BU
2011	—	—	—	—	—	10.00

KM# 1645 DOLLAR

9.0000 g., Aluminum-Bronze, 25 mm. **Ruler:** Elizabeth II **Subject:** Dame Joan Sutherland **Obv:** Head with tiara right **Rev:** Sutherland in opera role facing right

Date	Mintage	F	VF	XF	Unc	BU
2011	—	—	—	—	5.00	7.00

KM# 1647 DOLLAR

9.0000 g., Aluminum-Brass, 25 mm. **Ruler:** Elizabeth II **Obv:** Head with tiara right **Rev:** Flying Fox Bat in color

Date	Mintage	F	VF	XF	Unc	BU
2011	—	—	—	—	—	10.00

KM# 1646 DOLLAR

9.0000 g., Aluminum-Bronze, 25 mm. **Ruler:** Elizabeth II **Obv:** Head with tiara right **Rev:** Birdwing Butterfly in color

Date	Mintage	F	VF	XF	Unc	BU
2011	—	—	—	—	—	10.00

KM# 1661 DOLLAR

9.0000 g., Aluminum-Bronze, 25 mm. **Ruler:** Elizabeth II **Subject:** Year of the Rabbit **Obv:** Head with tiara right **Rev:** Rabbit in circle, floral around

Date	Mintage	F	VF	XF	Unc	BU
2011	—	—	—	—	—	10.00

KM# 1626 DOLLAR

9.0000 g., Aluminum-Bronze, 25 mm. **Ruler:** Elizabeth II **Subject:** Australian Wheat **Obv:** Head with tiara right **Rev:** Stylized wheat field and combine harvester

Date	Mintage	F	VF	XF	Unc	BU
2012	—	—	—	—	6.00	10.00
2012 Proof	—	Value: 40.00				

KM# 1699 DOLLAR

31.1350 g., 0.9990 Silver 1.0000 oz. ASW, 40.6 mm. **Ruler:** Elizabeth II **Subject:** Battle of Kapyong, Korean War **Obv:** Head with tiara right **Rev:** Soldier walking at left, image of soldiers seated at right **Edge:** Reeded

Date	Mintage	F	VF	XF	Unc	BU
2012P Proof	Est. 5,000	Value: 100				

KM# 1680 DOLLAR

9.0000 g., Aluminum-Bronze, 25 mm. **Ruler:** Elizabeth II **Subject:** Year of the Dragon **Rev:** Dragon head within circle, floral around

Date	Mintage	F	VF	XF	Unc	BU
2012	—	—	—	—	—	10.00

KM# 1680a DOLLAR

11.9000 g., 0.9990 Silver 0.3822 oz. ASW, 25 mm. **Ruler:** Elizabeth II **Subject:** Year of the Dragon **Rev:** Dragon head within circle, floral around

Date	Mintage	F	VF	XF	Unc	BU
2012 Proof	—	Value: 40.00				

KM# 1698 DOLLAR

13.8000 g., Aluminum-Bronze, 30.6 mm. **Ruler:** Elizabeth II **Subject:** Australian 2012 London Olympic Team **Obv:** Head with tiara right **Rev:** Kangaroo with boxing gloves raised

Date	Mintage	F	VF	XF	Unc	BU
2012P	750	—	—	—	—	15.00

KM# 1700 DOLLAR

31.1050 g., 0.9990 Silver 0.9990 oz. ASW, 40.6 mm. **Ruler:** Elizabeth II **Subject:** Battle of Kokoda, World War II **Obv:** Head with tiara right **Rev:** Soldier standing at left, image of soldiers walking over bridge at right **Edge:** Reeded

Date	Mintage	F	VF	XF	Unc	BU
2012P Proof	Est. 5,000	Value: 100				

KM# 1701 DOLLAR

31.1350 g., 0.9990 Silver 1.0000 oz. ASW, 40.5 mm. **Ruler:** Elizabeth II **Subject:** Elizabeth II, 60th Anniversary **Obv:** Head with tiara right **Rev:** Dargie's "wattle painting" of Elizabeth II at left, emblem and signature at right **Edge:** Reeded

Date	Mintage	F	VF	XF	Unc	BU
2012P Proof	7,500	Value: 100				

KM# 1661a DOLLAR

11.6600 g., 0.9990 Silver 0.3745 oz. ASW, 25 mm. **Ruler:** Elizabeth II **Subject:** Year of the rabbit **Obv:** Head with tiara right **Rev:** Rabbit in circle, floral around

Date	Mintage	F	VF	XF	Unc	BU
2011 Proof	—	Value: 30.00				

KM# 1704 DOLLAR
13.8000 g., Aluminum-Bronze, 30.6 mm. **Ruler:** Elizabeth II
Subject: Year of the Dragon

Date	Mintage	F	VF	XF	Unc	BU
2012P	—	—	—	—	—	15.00

KM# 1705 DOLLAR
31.1350 g., 0.9990 Silver 1.0000 oz. ASW, 36.6 mm. **Ruler:** Elizabeth II **Obv:** Head with tiara right **Rev:** Koala in a gum tree detailed in an opal at center

Date	Mintage	F	VF	XF	Unc	BU
2012P Proof	8,000	Value: 100				

KM# 1711 DOLLAR
9.0000 g., Aluminum-Bronze, 25 mm. **Ruler:** Elizabeth II
Subject: Ethel C. Pedley **Rev:** Bust facing at left, ncharacters Dot and the Kangaroo at right

Date	Mintage	F	VF	XF	Unc	BU
2012	—	—	—	—	—	12.50

KM# 1714 DOLLAR
13.8000 g., Aluminum-Bronze, 30.6 mm. **Ruler:** Elizabeth II
Subject: ANZAC Day - Nurses **Obv:** Head with tiara right **Rev:** Nurse tending to soldier

Date	Mintage	F	VF	XF	Unc	BU
2012P	—	—	—	—	—	13.50

KM# 1715 DOLLAR
13.8000 g., Aluminum-Bronze, 30.6 mm. **Ruler:** Elizabeth II
Obv: Head with tiara right **Rev:** Two boxing kangaroos on color backgorund

Date	Mintage	F	VF	XF	Unc	BU
2012P	7,500	—	—	—	—	15.00

KM# 1732 DOLLAR
9.0000 g., Aluminum-Bronze, 25 mm. **Ruler:** Elizabeth II **Obv:** Head with tiara right **Rev:** Three wheat ears

Date	Mintage	F	VF	XF	Unc	BU
2012B	—	—	—	—	—	5.00
2012C	—	—	—	—	3.00	5.00
2012C bluebell	—	—	—	—	—	20.00
2012M	—	—	—	—	—	5.00
2012S	—	—	—	—	—	5.00

KM# 1732a DOLLAR
11.6000 g., 0.9990 Silver 0.3726 oz. ASW, 25 mm. **Ruler:** Elizabeth II **Obv:** Head with tiara right **Rev:** Three wheat ears

Date	Mintage	F	VF	XF	Unc	BU
2012 Proof	—	Value: 40.00				

KM# 1734 DOLLAR
9.0000 g., Aluminum-Bronze, 25 mm. **Ruler:** Elizabeth II
Subject: Australian Open **Obv:** Head with tiara right **Rev:** Men's Trophy

Date	Mintage	F	VF	XF	Unc	BU
2012	—	—	—	—	15.00	—

KM# 1735 DOLLAR
9.0000 g., Aluminum-Bronze, 25 mm. **Ruler:** Elizabeth II
Subject: Australian Open **Obv:** Head with tiara right **Rev:** Women's Trophy

Date	Mintage	F	VF	XF	Unc	BU
2012	—	—	—	—	—	15.00

KM# 1736 DOLLAR
9.0000 g., Aluminum-Bronze, 25 mm. **Ruler:** Elizabeth II

Subject: International Year of Cooperatives **Obv:** Head with tiara right **Rev:** Stick figures moving blocks into position

Date	Mintage	F	VF	XF	Unc	BU
2012	—	—	—	—	7.00	10.00

KM# 1738 DOLLAR
9.0000 g., Aluminum-Bronze, 25 mm. **Ruler:** Elizabeth II
Subject: Year of the Farmer **Obv:** Head with tiara right **Rev:** Stylized farm layout with produce and animals

Date	Mintage	F	VF	XF	Unc	BU
2012	—	—	—	—	7.00	10.00

KM# 1745 DOLLAR
9.0000 g., Aluminum-Bronze, 25 mm. **Ruler:** Elizabeth II **Obv:** Head with tiara right **Rev:** Asian Elephant at left in color

Date	Mintage	F	VF	XF	Unc	BU
2012	—	—	—	—	—	15.00

KM# 1746 DOLLAR
9.0000 g., Aluminum-Bronze, 25 mm. **Ruler:** Elizabeth II **Obv:** Head with tiara right **Rev:** Western Lowland Gorilla at right in color

Date	Mintage	F	VF	XF	Unc	BU
2012	—	—	—	—	—	15.00

KM# 1748 DOLLAR
31.1350 g., 0.9990 Silver 1.0000 oz. ASW, 40.6 mm. **Ruler:** Elizabeth II **Subject:** Australian Olympic Team, 2012 London Games **Obv:** Head with tiara right **Rev:** Runner with Big Ben and Sydney Harbor Bridge in color

Date	Mintage	F	VF	XF	Unc	BU
2012P Proof	7,500	Value: 100				

KM# 406a 2 DOLLARS
15.8800 g., 0.9999 Gold 0.5105 oz. AGW, 20.5 mm. **Ruler:** Elizabeth II **Subject:** Federation Centennial **Obv:** Head with tiara right **Rev:** Aboriginal elder **Edge:** Segmented reeding

Date	Mintage	F	VF	XF	Unc	BU
2001B Proof	350	Value: 900				
2005B Proof	650	Value: 875				
2006B Proof	300	Value: 925				

KM# 406 2 DOLLARS
6.6000 g., Aluminum-Bronze, 20.5 mm. **Ruler:** Elizabeth II **Obv:** Head with tiara right **Rev:** Aboriginal elder at left, stars above at right **Edge:** Segmented reeding

Date	Mintage	F	VF	XF	Unc	BU
2001	35,650,000	—	—	—	5.00	6.00
Note: Large obverse head, IRB spaced						
2001	Inc. above	—	—	—	—	—
Note: Smaller obverse head, IRB joined						
2001 Proof	59,569	Value: 8.00				
2002	29,689,000	—	—	—	4.00	6.00
2002 Proof	39,514	Value: 8.00				
2003	13,656,000	—	—	—	4.00	6.00
2003 Proof	39,090	Value: 8.00				
2004	20,084,000	—	—	—	3.50	5.00
2004 Proof	50,000	Value: 7.00				
2005	—	—	—	—	3.50	5.00
2005 Proof	33,520	Value: 7.00				
2006	—	—	—	—	3.50	5.00
2006 Proof	—	Value: 7.00				
2007	—	—	—	—	3.00	4.50
2007 Proof	—	Value: 6.00				
2008	—	—	—	—	3.00	4.50
2008 Proof	—	Value: 6.00				
2009	—	—	—	—	3.00	4.50
2009 Proof	—	Value: 6.00				
2010	—	—	—	—	3.00	4.50
2010 Proof	—	Value: 6.00				
2011	—	—	—	—	3.00	4.50
2011 Proof	—	Value: 6.00				
2012	—	—	—	—	3.00	4.50
2012 Proof	—	Value: 6.00				

KM# 406b 2 DOLLARS
8.5500 g., 0.9999 Silver 0.2748 oz. ASW, 20.5 mm. **Ruler:** Elizabeth II **Obv:** Head with tiara right **Rev:** Aboriginal elder **Edge:** Segmented reeding

Date	Mintage	F	VF	XF	Unc	BU
2003B Proof	6,500	Value: 22.00				
2004B Proof	6,500	Value: 22.00				
2005B Proof	6,500	Value: 22.00				

KM# 764 2 DOLLARS
18.2200 g., 0.9990 Silver 0.5852 oz. ASW, 32.5 mm. **Ruler:** Elizabeth II **Series:** Masterpieces in Silver - Port Phillip Patterns **Obv:** 1/2 ounce design **Rev:** Kangaroo design **Edge:** Reeded

Date	Mintage	F	VF	XF	Unc	BU
2003B Proof	10,000	Value: 35.00				

KM# 755 2 DOLLARS
62.2700 g., 0.9990 Silver 1.9999 oz. ASW, 50 mm. **Ruler:** Elizabeth II **Series:** Australian Peacekeepers **Obv:** Queen's head right **Rev:** Australian army and color insignia **Edge:** Reeded

Date	Mintage	F	VF	XF	Unc	BU
2005P Proof	2,500	Value: 90.00				

KM# 756 2 DOLLARS
62.2700 g., 0.9990 Silver 1.9999 oz. ASW, 50.3 mm. **Ruler:** Elizabeth II **Series:** Australian Peacekeepers **Obv:** Queen's head right **Rev:** Australian navy and color insignia **Edge:** Reeded

Date	Mintage	F	VF	XF	Unc	BU
2005P Proof	2,500	Value: 90.00				

KM# 757 2 DOLLARS
62.2700 g., 0.9990 Silver 1.9999 oz. ASW, 50.3 mm. **Ruler:** Elizabeth II **Subject:** Australian Peacekeepers Set **Obv:** Queen's head right **Rev:** Australian airforce and color insignia **Edge:** Reeded

Date	Mintage	F	VF	XF	Unc	BU
2005P Proof	2,500	Value: 90.00				

KM# 758 2 DOLLARS
62.2700 g., 0.9990 Silver 1.9999 oz. ASW, 50.3 mm. **Ruler:** Elizabeth II **Series:** Australian Peacekeepers **Obv:** Queen's head right **Rev:** Australian federal police and color insignia **Edge:** Reeded

Date	Mintage	F	VF	XF	Unc	BU
2005P Proof	2,500	Value: 90.00				

KM# 759 2 DOLLARS
62.2700 g., 0.9990 Silver 1.9999 oz. ASW, 50.3 mm. **Ruler:** Elizabeth II **Series:** Australian Peacekeepers **Obv:** Queen's head right **Rev:** Australian Agency for International Development and color insignia **Edge:** Reeded

Date	Mintage	F	VF	XF	Unc	BU
2005P Proof	2,500	Value: 90.00				

KM# 852 2 DOLLARS
8.8500 g., 0.9990 Silver 0.2842 oz. ASW, 20.5 mm. **Ruler:** Elizabeth II **Obv:** Young bust right **Rev:** Aboriginal elder **Edge:** Segmented reeding

Date	Mintage	F	VF	XF	Unc	BU
2006 Proof	6,500	Value: 22.00				

KM# 853 2 DOLLARS
1.2441 g., 0.9990 Gold 0.0400 oz. AGW **Ruler:** Elizabeth II **Obv:** Head with tiara right **Rev:** FIFA World Cup

Date	Mintage	F	VF	XF	Unc	BU
2006P Proof	50,000	Value: 75.00				

KM# 1246 2 DOLLARS
0.5000 g., 0.9990 Gold 0.0161 oz. AGW, 12 mm. **Ruler:** Elizabeth II **Subject:** 2010 FIFA World Cup, South Africa **Obv:** Head right **Rev:** Dream kangaroo and soccer ball

Date	Mintage	F	VF	XF	Unc	BU
2009P Proof	7,500	Value: 80.00				

KM# 1627 2 DOLLARS
31.1050 g., 0.9990 Silver 0.9990 oz. ASW, 40.6 mm. **Ruler:** Elizabeth II **Subject:** Royal Australian Navy, 100th Anniversary **Obv:** Head with tiara right **Rev:** HMAS AE 2 submarine

Date	Mintage	F	VF	XF	Unc	BU
2011 Proof	—	Value: 100				

KM# 1628 2 DOLLARS
31.1050 g., 0.9990 Silver 0.9990 oz. ASW, 40.6 mm. **Ruler:** Elizabeth II **Subject:** Royal Australian Navy, 100th Anniversary **Obv:** Head with tiara right **Rev:** HMAS Australia II

Date	Mintage	F	VF	XF	Unc	BU
2011 Proof	—	Value: 100				

KM# 1629 2 DOLLARS
31.1050 g., 0.9990 Silver 0.9990 oz. ASW, 40.6 mm. **Ruler:** Elizabeth II **Subject:** Royal Australian Navy, 100th Anniversary **Obv:** Head with tiara right **Rev:** HMAS Hobart II

Date	Mintage	F	VF	XF	Unc	BU
2011 Proof	—	Value: 100				

KM# 1630 2 DOLLARS
31.1050 g., 0.9990 Silver 0.9990 oz. ASW, 40.6 mm. **Ruler:** Elizabeth II **Subject:** Royal Australian Navy, 100th Anniversary **Obv:** Head with tiara right **Rev:** HMAS Yarra III

Date	Mintage	F	VF	XF	Unc	BU
2011 Proof	—	Value: 100				

KM# 1631 2 DOLLARS
31.1050 g., 0.9990 Silver 0.9990 oz. ASW, 40.6 mm. **Ruler:** Elizabeth II **Subject:** Royal Australian Navy, 100th Anniversary **Obv:** Head with tiara right **Rev:** HMAS Sydney III

Date	Mintage	F	VF	XF	Unc	BU
2011 Proof	—	Value: 100				

KM# 1632 2 DOLLARS
31.1050 g., 0.9990 Silver 0.9990 oz. ASW, 40.6 mm. **Ruler:** Elizabeth II **Subject:** Royal Australian Navy, 100th Anniversary **Obv:** Head with tiara right **Rev:** HMAS Armidale II

Date	Mintage	F	VF	XF	Unc	BU
2011 Proof	—	Value: 100				

KM# 1740 2 DOLLARS
20.0000 g., 0.9990 Silver partially gilt 0.6423 oz. ASW, 34 mm. **Ruler:** Elizabeth II **Subject:** Australian Open **Obv:** Small Queen's portrait above tennis ball **Rev:** Player serving

Date	Mintage	F	VF	XF	Unc	BU
2012 Proof	10,000	Value: 100				

KM# 591 5 DOLLARS
36.3100 g., 0.9990 Silver 1.1662 oz. ASW, 38.74 mm. **Ruler:** Elizabeth II **Subject:** Centennial of Federation Series Finale **Obv:** Queen's head right **Rev:** Multicolor dual hologram: map and rotunda **Edge:** Reeded

Date	Mintage	F	VF	XF	Unc	BU
2001B Proof	—	Value: 55.00				

KM# 592 5 DOLLARS
36.3100 g., 0.9990 Silver 1.1662 oz. ASW, 38.74 mm. **Ruler:** Elizabeth II **Subject:** Barton and Reid **Obv:** Queen's head right **Rev:** Portraits of Dame Flora Reid and Lady Jean Barton **Edge:** Reeded

Date	Mintage	F	VF	XF	Unc	BU
2001B Proof	5,000	Value: 60.00				

KM# 637 5 DOLLARS
36.3100 g., 0.9990 Silver 1.1662 oz. ASW, 38.74 mm. **Ruler:** Elizabeth II **Subject:** Kingston, Barton and Deakin **Obv:** Queen's head right **Rev:** Three rectangular portraits and value **Edge:** Reeded

Date	Mintage	F	VF	XF	Unc	BU
2001B Proof	5,000	Value: 60.00				

KM# 638 5 DOLLARS
36.3100 g., 0.9990 Silver 1.1662 oz. ASW, 38.74 mm. **Ruler:** Elizabeth II **Subject:** Clark, Parkes and Griffith **Obv:** Queen's head right **Rev:** Three rectangular portraits and value **Edge:** Reeded

Date	Mintage	F	VF	XF	Unc	BU
2001B Proof	5,000	Value: 60.00				

KM# 639 5 DOLLARS
36.3100 g., 0.9990 Silver 1.1662 oz. ASW, 38.74 mm. **Ruler:** Elizabeth II **Subject:** Spence, Nicholls and Anderson **Obv:** Queen's head right **Rev:** Three circular portraits and value **Edge:** Reeded

Date	Mintage	F	VF	XF	Unc	BU
2001B Proof	5,000	Value: 60.00				

KM# 640 5 DOLLARS
36.3100 g., 0.9990 Silver 1.1662 oz. ASW, 38.74 mm. **Ruler:** Elizabeth II **Subject:** Reid, Forrest and Quick **Obv:** Queen's head right **Rev:** Three rectangular portraits and value **Edge:** Reeded

Date	Mintage	F	VF	XF	Unc	BU
2001B Proof	5,000	Value: 60.00				

KM# 641 5 DOLLARS
36.3100 g., 0.9990 Silver 1.1662 oz. ASW, 38.74 mm. **Ruler:** Elizabeth II **Subject:** Bathurst Ladies Organizing Committee **Obv:** Queen's head right **Rev:** Circular design with names above value **Edge:** Reeded

Date	Mintage	F	VF	XF	Unc	BU
2001B Proof	5,000	Value: 60.00				

KM# 662   5 DOLLARS
36.3100 g., 0.9990 Silver 1.1662 oz. ASW, 38.74 mm.   **Ruler:**
Elizabeth II **Subject:** Year of the Outback **Obv:** Queen's head
right **Rev:** Multicolor holographic landscape **Edge:** Reeded

Date	Mintage	F	VF	XF	Unc	BU
2002B Proof	15,000	Value: 100				

KM# 761   5 DOLLARS
36.3100 g., 0.9990 Silver 1.1662 oz. ASW   **Ruler:** Elizabeth II
Obv: Queen's head right **Rev:** Sir Donald Bradman

Date	Mintage	F	VF	XF	Unc	BU
2001 Proof	—	Value: 55.00				

KM# 762   5 DOLLARS
20.0000 g., Aluminum-Bronze, 38.74 mm.   **Ruler:** Elizabeth II
Obv: Queen's head right **Rev:** Sir Donald Bradman

Date	Mintage	F	VF	XF	Unc	BU
2001	—	—	—	—	8.50	9.50

KM# 601   5 DOLLARS
10.5200 g., Bi-Metallic Aluminumn-Bronze center in Stainless
Steel ring, 27.8 mm.   **Ruler:** Elizabeth II **Subject:** Battle of Sunda
Strait **Obv:** Head with tiara right **Rev:** Ships bell from the "USS
Houston", denomination below **Shape:** 24-sided **Note:**
Demagnetized.

Date	Mintage	F	VF	XF	Unc	BU
2002B	—	—	—	—	7.50	9.50

KM# 647   5 DOLLARS
28.0000 g., Aluminum-Bronze, 38.74 mm.   **Ruler:** Elizabeth II
Subject: Battle of Sunda Strait **Obv:** Queen's head right **Rev:**
Two ships; USS Houston and HMS Perth **Edge:** Reeded

Date	Mintage	F	VF	XF	Unc	BU
2002B Proof	15,000	Value: 25.00				

KM# 649   5 DOLLARS
20.0000 g., Aluminum-Bronze, 38.74 mm.   **Ruler:** Elizabeth II
Subject: Commonwealth Games **Obv:** Head with tiara right,
denomination below **Rev:** Eight arms, each represents an event
of the games **Edge:** Reeded

Date	Mintage	F	VF	XF	Unc	BU
2002B	11,145	—	—	—	8.50	9.50

KM# 650   5 DOLLARS
20.0000 g., Aluminum-Bronze, 38.74 mm.   **Ruler:** Elizabeth II
Subject: Commonwealth Games **Obv:** Head with tiara right,
denomination below **Rev:** Eight arms, each represents an event
at the games **Edge:** Reeded

Date	Mintage	F	VF	XF	Unc	BU
2002B	11,145	—	—	—	8.50	9.50

KM# 651   5 DOLLARS
20.0000 g., Aluminum-Bronze, 38.74 mm.   **Ruler:** Elizabeth II
Subject: Commonwealth Games **Obv:** Head with tiara right,

denomination below **Rev:** Blue games logo; star above tail of
stylized kangaroo and torch **Edge:** Reeded

Date	Mintage	F	VF	XF	Unc	BU
2002B	11,145	—	—	—	8.50	9.50

KM# 652   5 DOLLARS
36.3100 g., 0.9990 Silver 1.1662 oz. ASW, 38.74 mm.   **Ruler:**
Elizabeth II **Subject:** Commonwealth Games **Obv:** Head with
tiara right, denomination below **Rev:** Victorious athletes **Edge:**
Reeded

Date	Mintage	F	VF	XF	Unc	BU
2002B Proof	7,581	Value: 42.00				

KM# 653   5 DOLLARS
36.3100 g., 0.9990 Silver 1.1662 oz. ASW, 38.74 mm.   **Ruler:**
Elizabeth II **Obv:** Queen's head right **Rev:** Dutch sailing ship,
The Duyfken **Edge:** Reeded

Date	Mintage	F	VF	XF	Unc	BU
2002B Proof	9,096	Value: 40.00				

KM# 654   5 DOLLARS
36.3100 g., 0.9990 Silver 1.1662 oz. ASW, 38.74 mm.   **Ruler:**
Elizabeth II **Obv:** Queen's head right **Rev:** HMS Endeavour
sailing ship **Edge:** Reeded

Date	Mintage	F	VF	XF	Unc	BU
2002B Proof	9,096	Value: 37.50				

KM# 655   5 DOLLARS
36.3100 g., 0.9990 Silver 1.1662 oz. ASW, 38.74 mm.   **Ruler:**
Elizabeth II **Obv:** Queen's head right **Rev:** HMS Sirius sailing
ship **Edge:** Reeded

Date	Mintage	F	VF	XF	Unc	BU
2002B Proof	9,096	Value: 37.50				

KM# 656 5 DOLLARS
36.3100 g., 0.9990 Silver 1.1662 oz. ASW, 38.74 mm. **Ruler:** Elizabeth II **Obv:** Queen's head right **Rev:** HMS Investigator sailing ship **Edge:** Reeded

Date	Mintage	F	VF	XF	Unc	BU
2002B Proof	9,096		Value: 40.00			

KM# 659 5 DOLLARS
31.1035 g., 0.9990 Silver 0.9990 oz. ASW, 40 mm. **Ruler:** Elizabeth II **Subject:** Queen Mother **Obv:** Queen's head right **Rev:** Queen Mother circa 1927 within wreath of roses **Edge:** Reeded

Date	Mintage	F	VF	XF	Unc	BU
2002B Proof	30,000		Value: 35.00			

KM# 765 5 DOLLARS
36.3100 g., 0.9990 Silver 1.1662 oz. ASW, 38.7 mm. **Ruler:** Elizabeth II **Series:** Masterpieces in Silver - Port Phillip Patterns **Obv:** One ounce design **Rev:** Kangaroo design **Edge:** Reeded

Date	Mintage	F	VF	XF	Unc	BU
2003B Proof	10,000		Value: 45.00			

KM# 810 5 DOLLARS
36.3100 g., 0.9950 Silver partially gilt 1.1615 oz. ASW, 40 mm.

Ruler: Elizabeth II **Subject:** Rugby World Cup **Obv:** Head with tiara right **Rev:** Rugby World Cup and official logos **Edge:** Reeded

Date	Mintage	F	VF	XF	Unc	BU
2003 Proof	20,501		Value: 85.00			

KM# 854 5 DOLLARS
20.0000 g., Aluminum-Bronze, 38.74 mm. **Ruler:** Elizabeth II **Subject:** Rugby World Cup **Obv:** Head with tiara right **Rev:** Player kicking ball at posts, official logo **Edge:** Reeded

Date	Mintage	F	VF	XF	Unc	BU
2003	43,802	—	—	—	15.00	16.50

KM# 1017 5 DOLLARS
36.2100 g., 0.9990 Silver 1.1630 oz. ASW, 38.7 mm. **Ruler:** Elizabeth II **Obv:** Head with tiara right **Obv. Legend:** ELIZABETH II - AUSTRALIA **Rev:** Faces in oval hologram in ornate frame **Rev. Legend:** AUSTRALIA'S VOLUNTEERS - MAKING A DIFFERENCE **Edge:** Reeded

Date	Mintage	F	VF	XF	Unc	BU
2003B Proof	15,000		Value: 45.00			

KM# 727 5 DOLLARS
36.3100 g., 0.9990 Silver 1.1662 oz. ASW, 38.74 mm. **Ruler:** Elizabeth II **Subject:** Olympics **Obv:** Queen's head right **Rev:** Parthenon, Sydney Opera House and shield with multicolor flag and rings **Edge:** Reeded

Date	Mintage	F	VF	XF	Unc	BU
2004B Proof	17,500		Value: 40.00			

KM# 728 5 DOLLARS
36.3100 g., 0.9990 Silver 1.1662 oz. ASW, 38.74 mm. **Ruler:** Elizabeth II **Subject:** Tasmania **Obv:** Queen's head right **Rev:** Ship on island map **Edge:** Reeded

Date	Mintage	F	VF	XF	Unc	BU
2004B Proof	7,500		Value: 40.00			

KM# 728a 5 DOLLARS
20.0000 g., Aluminum-Bronze, 38.74 mm. **Ruler:** Elizabeth II **Subject:** Tasmanian Bicentennial **Obv:** Head with tiara right **Rev:** Ship, map, state flower **Edge:** Reeded

Date	Mintage	F	VF	XF	Unc	BU
2004	18,561	—	—	—	12.00	14.00
2004H	2,841	—	—	—	17.50	20.00

KM# 729 5 DOLLARS
31.1035 g., 0.9990 Silver 0.9990 oz. ASW, 40 mm. **Ruler:** Elizabeth II **Subject:** Adelaide to Darwin Railroad **Obv:** Queen's head right **Rev:** Train, tracks and outline map **Edge:** Reeded

Date	Mintage	F	VF	XF	Unc	BU
2004B Proof	12,500		Value: 37.50			

KM# 730 5 DOLLARS
31.1035 g., 0.9990 Silver 0.9990 oz. ASW, 40 mm. **Ruler:** Elizabeth II **Subject:** 150 Years of Australian Steam Railways **Obv:** Queen's head right **Rev:** Old steam train **Edge:** Reeded

Date	Mintage	F	VF	XF	Unc	BU
2004B Proof	15,000		Value: 37.50			

KM# 812 5 DOLLARS
Aluminum-Bronze, 38.74 mm. **Ruler:** Elizabeth II **Subject:** Olympic Games 2000-2004 **Obv:** Head with tiara right

Date	Mintage	F	VF	XF	Unc	BU
2004	—	—	—	—	15.00	16.50

KM# 855   5 DOLLARS
27.2500 g., Copper-Nickel partially gilt, 38.74 mm. **Ruler:**
Elizabeth II **Subject:** Australia's Own Game **Obv:** Head with tiara
right **Rev:** Cup and logos **Edge:** Reeded

Date	Mintage	F	VF	XF	Unc	BU
2004 Proof	16,163	Value: 45.00				

KM# 856   5 DOLLARS
20.0000 g., Aluminum-Bronze, 38.74 mm. **Ruler:** Elizabeth II
Subject: Olympic Games - Sydney To Athens **Obv:** Head with
tiara right **Rev:** Silhouettes ancient Greek athlete and Aboriginal
Edge: Reeded

Date	Mintage	F	VF	XF	Unc	BU
2004	24,376	—	—	—	15.00	16.50

KM# 750   5 DOLLARS
20.0000 g., Aluminum-Bronze, 38.74 mm. **Ruler:** Elizabeth II
Obv: Queen's head right **Rev:** Tennis player **Edge:** Reeded

Date	Mintage	F	VF	XF	Unc	BU
2005B	—	—	—	—	7.50	8.50

KM# 859   5 DOLLARS
36.3100 g., 0.9990 Silver 1.1662 oz. ASW, 38.74 mm. **Ruler:**
Elizabeth II **Subject:** 150 Year of State Government **Obv:** Head
with tiara right **Rev:** Outline map of State of Victoria **Edge:**
Reeded

Date	Mintage	F	VF	XF	Unc	BU
2006 Proof	12,500	Value: 85.00				

KM# 782   5 DOLLARS
36.3100 g., 0.9999 Silver 1.1672 oz. ASW, 38.74 mm. **Ruler:**
Elizabeth II **Subject:** XVIII Commonwealth Games City of Sport
Obv: Head with tiara right, denomination below **Rev:** City skyline
alongside river

Date	Mintage	F	VF	XF	Unc	BU
2006 Proof	10,000	Value: 55.00				

KM# 783   5 DOLLARS
20.0000 g., Aluminum-Bronze, 38.74 mm. **Ruler:** Elizabeth II

Subject: XVIII Commonwealth Games in Melbourne **Obv:** Head
with tiara right, denomination below **Rev:** Games logo and crown
surrounded by stylized athletes **Edge:** Reeded

Date	Mintage	F	VF	XF	Unc	BU
2006	—	—	—	—	15.00	16.50

KM# 786   5 DOLLARS
20.0000 g., Aluminum-Bronze, 38.74 mm. **Ruler:** Elizabeth II
Subject: XVIII Commonwealth Games Queen's Baton Relay **Obv:**
Head with tiara right **Rev:** Stylized baton runner **Edge:** Reeded

Date	Mintage	F	VF	XF	Unc	BU
2006	20,488	—	—	—	15.00	16.50

KM# 786a   5 DOLLARS
36.3100 g., 0.9990 Silver 1.1662 oz. ASW, 38.74 mm. **Ruler:**
Elizabeth II **Subject:** XVIII Commonwealth Games Queen's
Baton Relay **Obv:** Head with tiara right **Rev:** Stylized baton runner
Edge: Reeded

Date	Mintage	F	VF	XF	Unc	BU
2006 Proof	9,100	Value: 75.00				

KM# 787   5 DOLLARS
36.3100 g., 0.9990 Silver 1.1662 oz. ASW, 38.74 mm. **Ruler:**
Elizabeth II **Subject:** Masterpieces in Silver: Australia's Artists
Obv: Head with tiara right **Rev:** Sidney Nolan: Burke & Wills

Date	Mintage	F	VF	XF	Unc	BU
2006 Proof	10,000	Value: 60.00				

KM# 788   5 DOLLARS
36.3100 g., 0.9990 Silver 1.1662 oz. ASW, 38.74 mm. **Ruler:**
Elizabeth II **Subject:** Masters in Art - Siding

Date	Mintage	F	VF	XF	Unc	BU
2006 Proof	10,000	Value: 55.00				

KM# 789   5 DOLLARS
36.3100 g., 0.9990 Silver 1.1662 oz. ASW, 38.74 mm. **Ruler:**
Elizabeth II **Subject:** Masterpieces in Silver: Australia's Artists **Obv:**
Head with tiara right **Rev:** Brett Whitley: Self Portrait in the Studio

Date	Mintage	F	VF	XF	Unc	BU
2006 Proof	10,000	Value: 60.00				

KM# 790   5 DOLLARS
36.3100 g., 0.9990 Silver 1.1662 oz. ASW, 38.74 mm. **Ruler:**
Elizabeth II **Subject:** Masterpieces in Silver: Australia's Artists
Obv: Head with tiara right **Rev:** Russell Drysdale: The Drover's
Wife

Date	Mintage	F	VF	XF	Unc	BU
2006 Proof	10,000	Value: 60.00				

KM# 813   5 DOLLARS
20.0000 g., Aluminum-Bronze, 38.74 mm. **Ruler:** Elizabeth II
Subject: Voyage of Discovery 1606 **Obv:** Head with tiara right
Rev: Dutch yacht Duyfken **Edge:** Reeded **Note:** Mint mark: G.

Date	Mintage	F	VF	XF	Unc	BU
2006	—	—	—	—	15.00	16.50

KM# 813a   5 DOLLARS
36.3100 g., 0.9990 Silver 1.1662 oz. ASW, 38.74 mm. **Ruler:**
Elizabeth II **Subject:** Voyage of Discovery 1606 **Obv:** Head with
tiara right **Rev:** Dutch yacht Duyfken **Edge:** Reeded **Note:** Mint
mark: Tulip.

Date	Mintage	F	VF	XF	Unc	BU
2006P Proof	8,500	Value: 125				

KM# 857   5 DOLLARS
36.3100 g., 0.9999 Silver 1.1672 oz. ASW, 38.74 mm. **Ruler:**
Elizabeth II **Subject:** 150 Year of State Government **Obv:** Head
with tiara right **Rev:** Outline map of State of New South Wales
Edge: Reeded

Date	Mintage	F	VF	XF	Unc	BU
2006 Proof	12,500	Value: 85.00				

KM# 858   5 DOLLARS
36.3100 g., 0.9990 Silver 1.1662 oz. ASW, 38.74 mm. **Ruler:**

Elizabeth II **Subject:** 150 Year of State Government **Obv:** Head with tiara right **Rev:** Outline map of State of Tasmania **Edge:** Reeded

Date	Mintage	F	VF	XF	Unc	BU
2006 Proof	12,500	Value: 85.00				

KM# 860   5 DOLLARS
36.3100 g., 0.9990 Silver 1.1662 oz. ASW, 38.74 mm. **Ruler:** Elizabeth II **Subject:** Masterpieces in Silver: Australia's Artists **Obv:** Ian Rank-Broadley **Rev:** Jeffrey Smart: Keswick Siding

Date	Mintage	F	VF	XF	Unc	BU
2006 Proof	10,000	Value: 60.00				

KM# 1014   5 DOLLARS
1.2441 g., 0.9999 Gold 0.0400 oz. AGW, 19 mm. **Ruler:** Elizabeth II **Obv:** Bust with tiara right **Obv. Legend:** ELIZABETH II - AUSTRALIA **Rev:** Sydney Opera House

Date	Mintage	F	VF	XF	Unc	BU
2006P Proof	100,000	Value: 75.00				

KM# 861   5 DOLLARS
36.3100 g., 0.9990 Silver 1.1662 oz. ASW, 38.74 mm. **Ruler:** Elizabeth II **Subject:** Masterpieces in Silver: Australia's Artists **Obv:** Head with tiara right **Rev:** Grace Cossington-Smith: Curve of the Bridge

Date	Mintage	F	VF	XF	Unc	BU
2007 Proof	10,000	Value: 50.00				

KM# 862   5 DOLLARS
36.3100 g., 0.9990 Silver 1.1662 oz. ASW, 38.74 mm. **Ruler:** Elizabeth II **Subject:** Masterpieces in Silver: Australia's Artists **Obv:** Head with tiara right **Rev:** Clifford Possum Tjpaltjarri: Yuelamu Honey Ant Dreaming

Date	Mintage	F	VF	XF	Unc	BU
2007 Proof	10,000	Value: 50.00				

KM# 863   5 DOLLARS
36.3100 g., 0.9990 Silver 1.1662 oz. ASW, 38.74 mm. **Ruler:** Elizabeth II **Subject:** Masterpieces in Silver: Australia's Artists **Obv:** Head with tiara right **Rev:** William Dobell: Margaret Olley

Date	Mintage	F	VF	XF	Unc	BU
2007 Proof	10,000	Value: 50.00				

KM# 864   5 DOLLARS
36.3100 g., 0.9990 Silver 1.1662 oz. ASW, 38.74 mm. **Ruler:** Elizabeth II **Subject:** Masterpieces in Silver: Australia's Artists **Obv:** Ian Rank-Broadley **Rev:** Margaret Preston: Implement Blue

Date	Mintage	F	VF	XF	Unc	BU
2007 Proof	10,000	Value: 50.00				

KM# 865   5 DOLLARS
36.3100 g., 0.9990 Silver 1.1662 oz. ASW, 38.74 mm. **Ruler:** Elizabeth II **Subject:** Ashes Cricket Series 1882-2007 **Obv:** Head with tiara right **Rev:** Urn with supporters **Edge:** Reeded

Date	Mintage	F	VF	XF	Unc	BU
2007 Proof	12,500	Value: 45.00				

KM# 1013   5 DOLLARS
36.3100 g., 0.9990 Silver 1.1662 oz. ASW, 38.74 mm. **Ruler:** Elizabeth II **Subject:** Sydney Harbour Bridge, 75th Anniversary **Obv:** Bust with tiara right **Obv. Legend:** ELIZABETH II - AUSTRALIA **Rev:** Bridge view **Rev. Inscription:** SYDNEY / HARBOUR / BRIDGE

Date	Mintage	F	VF	XF	Unc	BU
2007 Proof	12,500	Value: 50.00				

KM# 1045   5 DOLLARS
36.3100 g., 0.9990 Silver 1.1662 oz. ASW, 38.74 mm. **Ruler:** Elizabeth II **Subject:** Year of the surfer lifesaver **Rev:** Rowboat in rough seas

Date	Mintage	F	VF	XF	Unc	BU
2007B Proof	12,500	Value: 65.00				

KM# 1046   5 DOLLARS
36.3100 g., 0.9990 Silver 1.1662 oz. ASW, 38.74 mm. **Ruler:** Elizabeth II **Subject:** South Australia State Government **Rev:** Australia map and state enlarged

Date	Mintage	F	VF	XF	Unc	BU
2007B Proof	12,500	Value: 65.00				

KM# 1117   5 DOLLARS
1.2400 g., 0.9990 Gold 0.0398 oz. AGW, 14 mm. **Ruler:** Elizabeth II **Subject:** Sydney Harbor Bridge **Obv:** Head right **Rev:** Bridge view

Date	Mintage	F	VF	XF	Unc	BU
2007P Proof	100,000	Value: 110				

KM# 1050   5 DOLLARS
31.1050 g., 0.9990 oz. ASW, 38.74 mm. **Ruler:** Elizabeth II **Subject:** Scouting Centennial in Australia **Rev:** Scout sign and map

Date	Mintage	F	VF	XF	Unc	BU
2008 Proof	5,000	Value: 65.00				

KM# 1053   5 DOLLARS
36.3100 g., 0.9990 Silver 1.1662 oz. ASW, 38.74 mm. **Ruler:** Elizabeth II **Subject:** Rugby League **Rev:** Two players

Date	Mintage	F	VF	XF	Unc	BU
2008 Proof	10,000	Value: 65.00				

KM# 1055   5 DOLLARS
31.1050 g., 0.9990 Silver 0.9990 oz. ASW, 38.74 mm. **Ruler:** Elizabeth II **Rev:** Antarctic skua in flight over map

Date	Mintage	F	VF	XF	Unc	BU
2008 Proof	12,500	Value: 65.00				

KM# 1065   5 DOLLARS
36.3100 g., 0.9990 Silver 1.1662 oz. ASW, 38.74 mm. **Ruler:** Elizabeth II **Subject:** 30th Anniversary - Northern Territorial Government **Rev:** Territory map and Australia map

Date	Mintage	F	VF	XF	Unc	BU
2008 Proof	12,500	Value: 65.00				

KM# 1066   5 DOLLARS
1.1500 g., 0.9990 Gold 0.0369 oz. AGW, 14 mm. **Ruler:** Elizabeth II **Rev:** Kisp Koala

Date	Mintage	F	VF	XF	Unc	BU
2008 Proof	10,000	Value: 110				

KM# 1067   5 DOLLARS
1.1500 g., 0.9990 Gold 0.0369 oz. AGW, 14 mm. **Ruler:** Elizabeth II **Rev:** Binny Bilby

Date	Mintage	F	VF	XF	Unc	BU
2008 Proof	10,000	Value: 110				

KM# 1072   5 DOLLARS
36.3100 g., 0.9990 Silver 1.1662 oz. ASW, 38.74 mm. **Ruler:** Elizabeth II **Rev:** Avro 504K airplane

Date	Mintage	F	VF	XF	Unc	BU
2008 Proof	10,000	Value: 65.00				

KM# 1073   5 DOLLARS
36.3100 g., 0.9990 Silver 1.1662 oz. ASW, 38.74 mm. **Ruler:** Elizabeth II **Rev:** Airbus A380 airplane

Date	Mintage	F	VF	XF	Unc	BU
2008 Proof	10,000	Value: 65.00				

KM# 1084   5 DOLLARS
Aluminum-Bronze, 38.74 mm. **Ruler:** Elizabeth II **Subject:** Sir Donald Bradman 100th Anniversary of Birth **Rev:** Player with cricket bat

Date	Mintage	F	VF	XF	Unc	BU
2008	—	—	—	—	—	10.00

KM# 1080   5 DOLLARS
36.3100 g., 0.9990 Silver 1.1662 oz. ASW, 38.74 mm. **Ruler:** Elizabeth II **Rev:** Three arctic explorers on map

Date	Mintage	F	VF	XF	Unc	BU
2009 Proof	12,500	Value: 65.00				

KM# 1081   5 DOLLARS
36.3100 g., 0.9990 Silver 1.1662 oz. ASW, 38.74 mm. **Ruler:** Elizabeth II **Subject:** Aurora Australis **Obv:** Head right **Rev:** Sailing ship in Antartic ice in hologram

Date	Mintage	F	VF	XF	Unc	BU
2009 Proof	12,500	Value: 50.00				

KM# 1085   5 DOLLARS
1.2000 g., 0.9990 Gold 0.0385 oz. AGW, 14 mm. **Ruler:** Elizabeth II **Obv:** Head right **Rev:** Lilly Pilly full-neck lizard

Date	Mintage	F	VF	XF	Unc	BU
2009 Proof	10,000	Value: 75.00				

KM# 1086   5 DOLLARS
1.2000 g., 0.9990 Gold 0.0385 oz. AGW, 14 mm. **Ruler:** Elizabeth II **Obv:** Head right **Rev:** Petey Platypus

Date	Mintage	F	VF	XF	Unc	BU
2009 Proof	10,000	Value: 75.00				

KM# 1658   5 DOLLARS
36.3100 g., 0.9990 Silver 1.1662 oz. ASW, 38.74 mm. **Ruler:** Elizabeth II **Subject:** Queensland Government **Rev:** Map of Australian states, Queensland highlighted

Date	Mintage	F	VF	XF	Unc	BU
2009 Proof	—	Value: 85.00				

KM# 1509   5 DOLLARS
36.3100 g., 0.9990 Silver 1.1662 oz. ASW, 38.74 mm. **Ruler:** Elizabeth II **Subject:** Aviation - Constellation L749

Date	Mintage	F	VF	XF	Unc	BU
2010 Proof	—	Value: 60.00				

KM# 1510   5 DOLLARS
36.3100 g., 0.9990 Silver 1.1662 oz. ASW, 37.84 mm. **Ruler:** Elizabeth II **Subject:** Aviation - De Havilland DH 86

Date	Mintage	F	VF	XF	Unc	BU
2010 Proof	—	Value: 60.00				

KM# 1511   5 DOLLARS
36.3100 g., 0.9990 Silver 1.1662 oz. ASW, 38.74 mm. **Ruler:** Elizabeth II **Subject:** Aviation - S.25 Sandringham

Date	Mintage	F	VF	XF	Unc	BU
2010 Proof	—	Value: 60.00				

KM# 1512   5 DOLLARS
36.3100 g., 0.9990 Silver 1.1662 oz. ASW, 38.74 mm. **Ruler:** Elizabeth II **Subject:** Aviation - Boeing 747

Date	Mintage	F	VF	XF	Unc	BU
2010 Proof	—	Value: 60.00				

KM# 1633   5 DOLLARS
Aluminum-Bronze, 38.74 mm. **Ruler:** Elizabeth II **Subject:** Royal Visit **Obv:** Head with tiara right **Rev:** Sixteen crowns

Date	Mintage	F	VF	XF	Unc	BU
2011	—	—	—	—	—	15.00

KM# 1637   5 DOLLARS
1.2400 g., 0.9990 Gold 0.0398 oz. AGW, 14 mm. **Ruler:** Elizabeth II **Subject:** Historic Convict Past - Port Arthur Historic Site

Date	Mintage	F	VF	XF	Unc	BU
2011 Proof	3,000	Value: 125				

KM# 1638   5 DOLLARS
1.2400 g., 0.9990 Gold 0.0398 oz. AGW, 14 mm. **Ruler:** Elizabeth II **Subject:** Historic Convict Past - Cascades Female Factory

Date	Mintage	F	VF	XF	Unc	BU
2011 Proof	3,000	Value: 125				

KM# 1639   5 DOLLARS
1.2400 g., 0.9990 Gold 0.0398 oz. AGW, 14 mm. **Ruler:** Elizabeth II **Subject:** Historic Convict Past - Fremantle Prison

Date	Mintage	F	VF	XF	Unc	BU
2011 Proof	3,000	Value: 125				

KM# 1640   5 DOLLARS
1.2400 g., 0.9990 Gold 0.0398 oz. AGW, 14 mm. **Ruler:**
Elizabeth II **Subject:** Historic Convict Past - Coal Mines Historic
Site

Date	Mintage	F	VF	XF	Unc	BU
2011 Proof	3,000	Value: 125				

KM# 1641   5 DOLLARS
1.2400 g., 0.9990 Gold 0.0398 oz. AGW, 14 mm. **Ruler:**
Elizabeth II **Subject:** Historic Convict Past - Old Government
House and Domain

Date	Mintage	F	VF	XF	Unc	BU
2011 Proof	3,000	Value: 125				

KM# 1652   5 DOLLARS
20.0000 g., Aluminum-Bronze, 38.74 mm. **Ruler:** Elizabeth II
Subject: Remembrance Day, 11.11.11 **Obv:** Head with tiara right
Rev: Poppy in multicolor

Date	Mintage	F	VF	XF	Unc	BU
2011	—	—	—	—	—	17.50

KM# 1739   5 DOLLARS
20.0000 g., Aluminum-Bronze, 38.74 mm. **Ruler:** Elizabeth II
Subject: Australian Open **Obv:** Small Queen's head above
tennis ball **Rev:** Player serving

Date	Mintage	F	VF	XF	Unc	BU
2012	—	—	—	—	—	20.00

KM# 1747   5 DOLLARS
20.0000 g., Aluminum-Bronze, 38.74 mm. **Ruler:** Elizabeth II
Obv: Gead with tiara right **Rev:** Perth Town Hall

Date	Mintage	F	VF	XF	Unc	BU
2012 Antique patina	—	—	—	—	—	20.00

KM# 1269   8 DOLLARS
5.0000 g., 0.9990 Gold 0.1606 oz. AGW, 14x23 mm. **Ruler:**
Elizabeth II **Subject:** Chinese Mythological Character **Obv:** Head
right **Rev:** Man standing, multicolor **Shape:** Vertical rectangle

Date	Mintage	F	VF	XF	Unc	BU
2009P	—	—	—	—	—	435

KM# 1270   8 DOLLARS
5.0000 g., 0.9990 Gold 0.1606 oz. AGW, 14x23 mm. **Ruler:**
Elizabeth II **Subject:** Chinese Mythological Character - Longevity
Obv: Head right **Rev:** Nam standing with staff, multicolor **Shape:**
Vertical rectangle

Date	Mintage	F	VF	XF	Unc	BU
2009P	—	—	—	—	—	435

KM# 1271   8 DOLLARS
5.0000 g., 0.9990 Gold 0.1606 oz. AGW, 14x23 mm. **Ruler:**
Elizabeth II **Subject:** Chinese Mythological Character - Success
Obv: Hand right **Rev:** Man standing with deer, multicolor **Shape:**
Vertical rectangle

Date	Mintage	F	VF	XF	Unc	BU
2009P	—	—	—	—	—	435

KM# 1272   8 DOLLARS
5.0000 g., 0.9990 Gold 0.1606 oz. AGW, 14x23 mm. **Ruler:**
Elizabeth II **Subject:** Mythological Chinese Character - Fortune
Obv: Head right **Rev:** Man standing with scroll, multicolor **Shape:**
Vertical rectangle

Date	Mintage	F	VF	XF	Unc	BU
2009P	—	—	—	—	—	435

KM# 1273   8 DOLLARS
10.0000 g., 0.9990 Gold 0.3212 oz. AGW, 15x25 mm. **Ruler:**
Elizabeth II **Subject:** Mythological Chinese Character - Wealth
Obv: Head right **Rev:** Man standing **Shape:** Vertical rectangle

Date	Mintage	F	VF	XF	Unc	BU
2009P	—	—	—	—	—	800

KM# 593   10 DOLLARS
33.1500 g., Bi-Metallic Gold plated .999 Silver center in Copper
ring, 38.74 mm. **Ruler:** Elizabeth II **Subject:** "The Future" **Obv:**
Queen's portrait **Rev:** Tree, map and denomination **Edge:**
Reeded

Date	Mintage	F	VF	XF	Unc	BU
2001B Proof	20,000	Value: 55.00				

KM# 596   10 DOLLARS
311.0350 g., 0.9990 Silver 9.9896 oz. ASW, 75.5 mm. **Ruler:**
Elizabeth II **Subject:** Calendar Evolution **Obv:** Head with tiara
right, denomination below **Rev:** Multicolor solar system in center,
zodiac symbols in outer circle **Edge:** Segmented reeding **Note:**
Illustration reduced.

Date	Mintage	F	VF	XF	Unc	BU
ND(2001) Proof	15,000	Value: 375				

KM# 633   10 DOLLARS
311.0350 g., 0.9990 Silver 9.9896 oz. ASW, 75.5 mm. **Ruler:**
Elizabeth II **Subject:** Evolution of Time **Obv:** Queen's portrait
right **Rev:** Various time keeping devices **Edge:** Segmented
reeding

Date	Mintage	F	VF	XF	Unc	BU
2002P Proof	1,500	Value: 400				

KM# 661   10 DOLLARS
60.5000 g., 0.9990 Silver 1.9431 oz. ASW, 50 mm. **Ruler:**
Elizabeth II **Subject:** The Adelaide Pound **Obv:** Queen's portrait
above gold-plated coin design **Rev:** Legend around gold-plated
coin design **Edge:** Reeded

Date	Mintage	F	VF	XF	Unc	BU
2002B Proof	10,000	Value: 95.00				

KM# 686   10 DOLLARS
311.0000 g., 0.9990 Silver 9.9885 oz. ASW, 75.5 mm.   **Ruler:**
Elizabeth II **Obv:** Queen's head right **Rev:** Alphabet evolution
design **Edge:** Reeded

Date	Mintage	F	VF	XF	Unc	BU
2003P Proof	1,500	Value: 400				

KM# 751   10 DOLLARS
60.5000 g., 0.9990 Silver Partially gilt 1.9431 oz. ASW, 50 mm.
Ruler: Elizabeth II **Subject:** 150th Anniversary - Sydney Mint
Obv: Head with tiara right above gilt 1853 Sovereign Pattern of
Queen Victoria facing left **Rev:** Gilt reverse of Sovereign Pattern
Edge: Reeded

Date	Mintage	F	VF	XF	Unc	BU
2003B Proof	10,000	Value: 100				
ND(2005)B Proof	10,000	Value: 80.00				

KM# 766   10 DOLLARS
36.3100 g., 0.9990 Silver 1.1662 oz. ASW, 38.7 mm.   **Ruler:**
Elizabeth II **Series:** Masterpieces in Silver - Port Phillip Patterns
Obv: Queen's head right **Rev:** Kangaroo design **Edge:** Reeded

Date	Mintage	F	VF	XF	Unc	BU
2003B Proof	10,000	Value: 90.00				

KM# 1439   10 DOLLARS
Silver partially gilt   **Ruler:** Elizabeth II **Subject:** Sydney Mint,
100th Anniversary

Date	Mintage	F	VF	XF	Unc	BU
2003 Proof	10,000	Value: 85.00				

KM# 739   10 DOLLARS
311.0350 g., 0.9990 Silver 9.9896 oz. ASW, 75.5 mm.   **Ruler:**
Elizabeth II **Subject:** Evolution of Numbers **Obv:** Queen's head
right **Rev:** Numbers, symbols, abacus and calculator **Edge:**
Reeded

Date	Mintage	F	VF	XF	Unc	BU
2004 Proof	1,500	Value: 400				

KM# 744   10 DOLLARS
311.3460 g., 0.9990 Silver 9.9996 oz. ASW, 75.5 mm.   **Ruler:**
Elizabeth II **Obv:** Queen's head right **Rev:** Multicolor symbolic
design **Edge:** Reeded

Date	Mintage	F	VF	XF	Unc	BU
2005 Proof	1,500	Value: 325				

KM# 866   10 DOLLARS
7.7508 g., 0.9990 Gold 0.2489 oz. AGW, 17.53 mm.   **Ruler:**
Elizabeth II **Subject:** 90th Anniversary Gallipoli Landings **Obv:**
Head with tiara right **Rev:** Australian slouch hat on inverted rifle
before memorial

Date	Mintage	F	VF	XF	Unc	BU
2005 Proof	1,000	Value: 750				

KM# 869   10 DOLLARS
7.7759 g., 0.9990 Gold 0.2497 oz. AGW, 17.53 mm.   **Ruler:**
Elizabeth II **Subject:** FIFA World Cup **Obv:** Head with tiara right
Rev: Kangaroo and players on football

Date	Mintage	F	VF	XF	Unc	BU
2006P Proof	25,000	Value: 425				

KM# 867   10 DOLLARS
3.1103 g., 0.9990 Gold 0.0999 oz. AGW   **Ruler:** Elizabeth II
Subject: Ashes Cricket Series 1882-2007 **Obv:** Head with tiara
right **Rev:** Urn and supporters **Edge:** Reeded

Date	Mintage	F	VF	XF	Unc	BU
2007 Proof	—	Value: 195				

KM# 1000   10 DOLLARS
3.1103 g., 0.9990 Gold 0.0999 oz. AGW, 17.53 mm.   **Ruler:**
Elizabeth II **Subject:** Year of the Pig **Obv:** Head with tiara right
Rev: Mother kangaroo with joey **Edge:** Reeded

Date	Mintage	F	VF	XF	Unc	BU
2007 Proof	—	Value: 210				

KM# 1051   10 DOLLARS
3.1000 g., 0.9990 Gold 0.0996 oz. AGW, 17.5 mm.   **Ruler:**
Elizabeth II **Subject:** Scouting Centennial in Australia **Rev:**
Shadow linear portrait of Baden-Powell

Date	Mintage	F	VF	XF	Unc	BU
2008 Proof	1,500	Value: 335				

KM# 1054   10 DOLLARS
3.1100 g., 0.9990 Gold 0.0999 oz. AGW, 17.53 mm.   **Ruler:**
Elizabeth II **Subject:** Rugby League

Date	Mintage	F	VF	XF	Unc	BU
2008 Proof	3,000	Value: 235				

KM# 1622   10 DOLLARS
31.1050 g., 0.9990 Silver partially gilt 0.9990 oz. ASW, 40 mm.
Ruler: Elizabeth II **Subject:** President's Cup **Obv:** Head with
tiara right **Rev:** Trophy, gilt

Date	Mintage	F	VF	XF	Unc	BU
2011 Proof	—	Value: 120				

KM# 1662   10 DOLLARS
3.1100 g., 0.9990 Gold 0.0999 oz. AGW, 17.53 mm.   **Ruler:**
Elizabeth II **Subject:** Year of the Rabbit **Rev:** Rabbit seated left
within circle, floral around

Date	Mintage	F	VF	XF	Unc	BU
2011 Proof	—	Value: 200				

KM# 1660   10 DOLLARS
3.1100 g., 0.9990 Gold 0.0999 oz. AGW, 17.53 mm.   **Ruler:**
Elizabeth II **Subject:** Year of the Tiger **Rev:** Tiger head within
circle, floral around

Date	Mintage	F	VF	XF	Unc	BU
2012 Proof	—	Value: 200				

KM# 1681   10 DOLLARS
3.1103 g., 0.9990 Gold 0.0999 oz. AGW, 17.53 mm.   **Ruler:**
Elizabeth II **Subject:** Year of the Dragon **Rev:** Dragon head within
circle, floral around

Date	Mintage	F	VF	XF	Unc	BU
2012 Proof	—	Value: 200				

KM# 1492   15 DOLLARS
3.1100 g., 0.9990 Gold 0.0999 oz. AGW, 17.53 mm.   **Ruler:**
Elizabeth II **Obv:** Head with tiara right **Rev:** Saint Mary Mackillup
in color

Date	Mintage	F	VF	XF	Unc	BU
2010 Proof	2,010	Value: 215				

KM# 595   20 DOLLARS
14.0300 g., Bi-Metallic .999 4.5287 Silver center in .9999 9.499
Gold ring, 32.1 mm.   **Ruler:** Elizabeth II **Subject:** Gregorian
Millennium **Obv:** Head with tiara right **Rev:** Chronograph watch
face with observatory in center and three depictions of the earth's
rotation **Edge:** Reeded

Date	Mintage	F	VF	XF	Unc	BU
2001 Prooflike	7,500	—	—	—	—	475

KM# 597   20 DOLLARS
19.6300 g., Bi-Metallic .9999 8.8645 Gold center in .9999 10.7618 Silver ring, 32.1 mm. **Ruler:** Elizabeth II **Subject:** Centenary of Federation **Obv:** Head with tiara right within star design **Rev:** National arms on a flowery background **Edge:** Reeded

Date	Mintage	F	VF	XF	Unc	BU
ND(2001) Prooflike	7,500	—	—	—	—	475

KM# 760   20 DOLLARS
Bi-Metallic Gold center in Silver ring **Ruler:** Elizabeth II **Rev:** Sir Donald Bradman portrait

Date	Mintage	F	VF	XF	Unc	BU
2001 Proof	—	Value: 500				

KM# 634   20 DOLLARS
18.3510 g., Bi-Metallic .999 Silver, 4.6655g, breast star shaped center in a .9999 Gold ,13.6855g outer ring, 32.1 mm. **Ruler:** Elizabeth II **Subject:** Queen's Golden Jubilee **Obv:** Queen's head right **Rev:** Queen before Buckingham Palace **Edge:** Reeded

Date	Mintage	F	VF	XF	Unc	BU
2002P Proof	7,500	Value: 675				

KM# 687   20 DOLLARS
13.4056 g., Bi-Metallic .999 Gold 8.3979g Center in a .999 Silver 5.0077g Ring, 32 mm. **Ruler:** Elizabeth II **Subject:** Golden Jubilee of Coronation **Obv:** Head with tiara right **Rev:** Four different coinage portraits of Queen Elizabeth II **Edge:** Reeded

Date	Mintage	F	VF	XF	Unc	BU
2003P Proof	7,500	Value: 625				

KM# 868   25 DOLLARS
7.9881 g., 0.9167 Gold 0.2354 oz. AGW **Ruler:** Elizabeth II **Subject:** 150th Anniversary First Australian Sovereign **Obv:** Head with tiara right

Date	Mintage	F	VF	XF	Unc	BU
2005 Proof	7,500	Value: 475				

KM# 1180   25 DOLLARS
7.7700 g., 0.9990 Gold 0.2496 oz. AGW, 20 mm. **Ruler:** Elizabeth II **Subject:** End of WWI, 90th Anniversary **Obv:** Head right **Rev:** Field cross, multicolor poppies **Rev. Legend:** Ian Rank-Bradley **Edge:** Reeded

Date	Mintage	F	VF	XF	Unc	BU
2008P Proof	1,918	Value: 675				

KM# 1397   25 DOLLARS
7.9880 g., 0.9167 Gold 0.2354 oz. AGW, 22.6 mm. **Ruler:** Elizabeth II **Subject:** Sovereign **Obv:** Head in tiara right **Rev:** National Arms with supporters and flora

Date	Mintage	F	VF	XF	Unc	BU
2009P Proof	2,500	Value: 825				
2010P Proof	—	Value: 825				
2011P Proof	—	Value: 825				
2012P Proof	—	Value: 825				

KM# 1110   25 DOLLARS
10.0000 g., 0.9999 Gold 0.3215 oz. AGW, 15.4x25.4 mm. **Ruler:** Elizabeth II **Rev:** Kangaroo dreaming **Shape:** Vertical rectangle

Date	Mintage	F	VF	XF	Unc	BU
2009 Proof	—	Value: 600				

KM# 1247   25 DOLLARS
7.7700 g., 0.9990 Gold 0.2496 oz. AGW, 21 mm. **Ruler:** Elizabeth II **Subject:** 2010 FIFA World Cup, South Africa **Obv:** Head right **Rev:** Soccer player and kangaroo

Date	Mintage	F	VF	XF	Unc	BU
2009P Proof	7,500	Value: 775				

KM# 1274   25 DOLLARS
10.0000 g., 0.9990 Gold 0.3212 oz. AGW, 15x25 mm. **Ruler:** Elizabeth II **Subject:** Mythological Chinese Character - Longivity **Obv:** Head right **Rev:** Man standing with staff **Shape:** Vertical rectangle

Date	Mintage	F	VF	XF	Unc	BU
2009P	—	—	—	—	—	825

KM# 1275   25 DOLLARS
10.0000 g., 0.9990 Gold 0.3212 oz. AGW, 15x25 mm. **Ruler:** Elizabeth II **Subject:** Mythological Chinese Character - Success **Obv:** Head right **Rev:** Man standing with deer **Shape:** Vertical rectangle

Date	Mintage	F	VF	XF	Unc	BU
2009P	—	—	—	—	—	800

KM# 1276   25 DOLLARS
10.0000 g., 0.9990 Gold 0.3212 oz. AGW, 15x25 mm. **Ruler:** Elizabeth II **Subject:** Mythological Chinese Character - Fortune **Obv:** Head right **Rev:** Man standing with scroll **Shape:** Vertical rectangle

Date	Mintage	F	VF	XF	Unc	BU
2009P	—	—	—	—	—	825

KM# 1623   25 DOLLARS
7.7700 g., 0.9990 Gold 0.2496 oz. AGW, 21 mm. **Ruler:** Elizabeth II **Subject:** President's Cup **Obv:** Head with tiara right **Rev:** Golfer taking swing

Date	Mintage	F	VF	XF	Unc	BU
2011 Proof	—	Value: 600				

KM# 1703   25 DOLLARS
7.7700 g., 0.9999 Gold 0.2498 oz. AGW, 20.6 mm. **Ruler:** Elizabeth II, 60th Anniversary **Obv:** Head with tiara right **Rev:** Young bust right **Edge:** Reeded

Date	Mintage	F	VF	XF	Unc	BU
2012P Proof	Est. 1,000	Value: 500				

KM# 784   30 DOLLARS
1000.0000 g., 0.9990 Silver 32.117 oz. ASW **Ruler:** Elizabeth II **Subject:** Commonwealth Games **Obv:** Head with tiara right **Rev:** Two figures within circle of all the sports

Date	Mintage	F	VF	XF	Unc	BU
2006 Proof	500	Value: 1,250				

KM# 648   50 DOLLARS
36.5100 g., Tri-Metallic .9999 Gold 7.8g, 13.1 mm center in .999 Silver 13.39g, 26.85mm inner ring within a copper 15.32g, 3, 38.74 mm. **Ruler:** Elizabeth II **Subject:** Commonwealth Games **Obv:** Head with tiara right **Rev:** Victorious athletes within inscriptions and runners **Edge:** Reeded

Date	Mintage	F	VF	XF	Unc	BU
2002B Proof	5,000	Value: 600				

KM# 724   50 DOLLARS
36.5100 g., Tri-Metallic .999 Gold 7.8g center in .999 Silver 13.39g ring within .999 Copper 15.32g outer ring, 38.74 mm. **Ruler:** Elizabeth II **Subject:** Olympics - Sydney to Athens **Obv:** Head with tiara right, denomination below **Rev:** Crossed olive and wattle branches about Australian flag and Olympic ring logo **Edge:** Reeded

Date	Mintage	F	VF	XF	Unc	BU
2004B Proof	2,500	Value: 625				

KM# 785   50 DOLLARS
Tri-Metallic Gold center within Silver ring within Copper outer ring, 38.74 mm. **Ruler:** Elizabeth II **Subject:** Melbourne Commonwealth Games **Obv:** Head with tiara right, denomination below **Rev:** Two stylized athletes on central plug surrounded by Games legend and circle of athletes

Date	Mintage	F	VF	XF	Unc	BU
2006 Proof	5,000	Value: 550				

KM# 1696   60 DOLLARS
10.0000 g., 0.9990 Gold 0.3212 oz. AGW, 22.5 mm. **Ruler:** Elizabeth II **Subject:** Australian 2012 London Olympic Team **Obv:** Head with tiara right **Rev:** Athlete standing on platform with flag

Date	Mintage	F	VF	XF	Unc	BU
2012P Proof	2,012					

KM# 643   100 DOLLARS
10.3678 g., 0.9999 Gold 0.3333 oz. AGW, 25 mm. **Ruler:** Elizabeth II **Subject:** Golden Wattle Flower **Obv:** Queen's head right **Rev:** Flower and denomination **Edge:** Reeded

Date	Mintage	F	VF	XF	Unc	BU
2001B	3,000	—	—	—	550	575
2001B Proof	2,500	Value: 600				

KM# 635   100 DOLLARS
31.1035 g., 0.9999 Gold 0.9999 oz. AGW, 32.1 mm. **Ruler:** Elizabeth II **Subject:** Gold Panning **Obv:** Queen's head right **Rev:** Two prospectors dry panning for gold with color highlighted pans and dust **Edge:** Reeded

Date	Mintage	F	VF	XF	Unc	BU
2002P Proof	1,500	Value: 1,750				

KM# 636   100 DOLLARS
31.1035 g., 0.9995 Platinum 0.9995 oz. APW, 32.1 mm. **Ruler:** Elizabeth II **Subject:** Multiculturalism **Obv:** Head with tiara right **Rev:** Six racially diverse portraits against a blue background **Edge:** Reeded

Date	Mintage	F	VF	XF	Unc	BU
2002 Proof	1,000	Value: 1,850				

KM# 646   100 DOLLARS
31.4000 g., 0.9999 Gold 1.0094 oz. AGW, 34.1 mm.   **Ruler:**
Elizabeth II   **Subject:** Queen's 50th Anniversary of Accession
Obv: Queen's head right **Rev:** Silhouette of George VI, queen's
portrait and denomination **Edge:** Reeded

Date	Mintage	F	VF	XF	Unc	BU
2002B Proof	2,002			Value: 1,750		

KM# 657   100 DOLLARS
10.3678 g., 0.9999 Gold 0.3333 oz. AGW, 25 mm.   **Ruler:**
Elizabeth II **Obv:** Queen's head right **Rev:** Sturt's Desert Rose
Edge: Reeded

Date	Mintage	F	VF	XF	Unc	BU
2002B	3,000	—	—	—	550	575
2002B Proof	2,500		Value: 600			

KM# 800   100 DOLLARS
31.1036 g., 0.9990 Gold 0.9990 oz. AGW, 34 mm.   **Ruler:**
Elizabeth II **Subject:** 50th Anniversary of the Coronation of
Elizabeth II **Obv:** Head with tiara right **Rev:** Young portrait of
Queen Elizabeth facing left, royal cipher, crown **Edge:** Plain

Date	Mintage	F	VF	XF	Unc	BU
2003 Proof	660		Value: 1,750			

KM# 870   100 DOLLARS
10.3670 g., 0.9990 Gold 0.3330 oz. AGW, 25 mm.   **Ruler:**
Elizabeth II **Subject:** State Floral Emblems **Obv:** Head with tiara
right **Rev:** Royal Blue Bell flowers **Edge:** Reeded

Date	Mintage	F	VF	XF	Unc	BU
2003 Proof	1,383		Value: 600			

KM# 797   100 DOLLARS
31.1070 g., 0.9990 Gold 0.9991 oz. AGW, 25.1 mm.   **Ruler:**
Elizabeth II **Subject:** 60th Anniversary of end of World War II
Obv: Head with tiara right **Rev:** Latent news real photographic
images of a dancing man celebrating the end of WWII

Date	Mintage	F	VF	XF	Unc	BU
2005P Proof	750		Value: 1,750			

KM# 1243   100 DOLLARS
31.1050 g., 0.9990 Gold 0.9990 oz. AGW, 36 mm.   **Ruler:**
Elizabeth II **Subject:** Treasures of Australia **Obv:** Head right **Rev:**
Mountains **Note:** Insert container with 1 carat of diamonds.

Date	Mintage	F	VF	XF	Unc	BU
2009P Proof	1,000		Value: 2,150			

KM# 1436   100 DOLLARS
Gold   **Ruler:** Elizabeth II

Date	Mintage	F	VF	XF	Unc	BU
2010 Proof	—		Value: 1,750			

KM# 1595   100 DOLLARS
31.1050 g., 0.9990 Gold 0.9990 oz. AGW, 36 mm.   **Ruler:**
Elizabeth II **Subject:** Treasures of Australia **Obv:** Head above
pearl container **Rev:** Landscape above pearl container **Edge:**
Reeded

Date	Mintage	F	VF	XF	Unc	BU
2011P Proof	Est. 1,000		Value: 2,250			

KM# 1596   100 DOLLARS
31.1050 g., 0.9990 Gold 0.9990 oz. AGW, 32 mm.   **Ruler:**
Elizabeth II **Subject:** Gold Coin Program, 25th Anniversary **Obv:**
Head with tiara right **Rev:** Nugget

Date	Mintage	F	VF	XF	Unc	BU
2011P	Est. 1,500		Value: 1,850			

KM# 644   150 DOLLARS
15.5517 g., 0.9999 Gold 0.4999 oz. AGW, 30 mm.   **Ruler:**
Elizabeth II **Obv:** Queen's head right **Rev:** Golden Wattle flower,
value **Edge:** Reeded

Date	Mintage	F	VF	XF	Unc	BU
2001B Proof	1,500		Value: 850			

KM# 658   150 DOLLARS
15.5517 g., 0.9999 Gold 0.4999 oz. AGW, 30 mm.   **Ruler:**
Elizabeth II **Subject:** State Floral Emblems **Obv:** Queen's head
right **Rev:** Sturt's Desert Rose **Edge:** Reeded

Date	Mintage	F	VF	XF	Unc	BU
2002B Proof	1,500		Value: 850			

KM# 872   150 DOLLARS
15.5510 g., 0.9990 Gold 0.4995 oz. AGW, 30 mm.   **Ruler:**
Elizabeth II **Subject:** State Floral Emblems **Obv:** Head with tiara
right **Rev:** Royal Blue Bell flowers **Edge:** Reeded

Date	Mintage	F	VF	XF	Unc	BU
2003	1,105		Value: 850			

KM# 874   150 DOLLARS
15.5510 g., 0.9990 Gold 0.4995 oz. AGW, 30 mm.   **Ruler:**
Elizabeth II **Subject:** Rare Australian Birds **Obv:** Head with tiara
right **Rev:** Red-tailed black cockatoo **Edge:** Reeded

Date	Mintage	F	VF	XF	Unc	BU
2003 Proof	2,500		Value: 850			

KM# 731   150 DOLLARS
10.3670 g., 0.9990 Gold 0.3330 oz. AGW, 25 mm.   **Ruler:**
Elizabeth II **Obv:** Queen's head right **Rev:** Cassowary bird **Edge:**
Reeded

Date	Mintage	F	VF	XF	Unc	BU
2004B Proof	2,500		Value: 600			

KM# 752   150 DOLLARS
10.3678 g., 0.9999 Gold 0.3333 oz. AGW, 25 mm.   **Ruler:**
Elizabeth II **Obv:** Queen's head right **Rev:** Malleefowl bird **Edge:**
Reeded

Date	Mintage	F	VF	XF	Unc	BU
2005B Proof	2,500		Value: 600			

KM# 873   150 DOLLARS
10.3670 g., 0.9990 Gold 0.3330 oz. AGW, 25 mm.   **Ruler:**

Elizabeth II **Subject:** Rare Australian Birds **Obv:** Head with tiara
right **Rev:** Red-tailed black cockatoo **Edge:** Reeded

Date	Mintage	F	VF	XF	Unc	BU
2006	2,500		Value: 625			

KM# 732   200 DOLLARS
15.5518 g., 0.9990 Gold 0.4995 oz. AGW, 30 mm.   **Ruler:**
Elizabeth II **Obv:** Queen's head right **Rev:** Cassowary bird **Edge:**
Reeded

Date	Mintage	F	VF	XF	Unc	BU
2004B Proof	2,500		Value: 850			

KM# 753   200 DOLLARS
15.5518 g., 0.9999 Gold 0.4999 oz. AGW, 30 mm.   **Ruler:**
Elizabeth II **Obv:** Queen's head right **Rev:** Malleefowl bird **Edge:**
Reeded

Date	Mintage	F	VF	XF	Unc	BU
2005B Proof	2,500		Value: 850			

KM# 1695   200 DOLLARS
62.2140 g., 0.9990 Gold 1.9981 oz. AGW   **Ruler:** Elizabeth II
Subject: Australian 2012 London Olympic Team

Date	Mintage	F	VF	XF	Unc	BU
2012	—		Value: 3,600			

KM# 1702   200 DOLLARS
62.2150 g., 0.9990 Gold 1.9982 oz. AGW, 41.1 mm.   **Ruler:**
Elizabeth II **Subject:** Elizabeth II, 60th Anniversary **Obv:** Head
with tiara right **Rev:** Young head portrait right

Date	Mintage	F	VF	XF	Unc	BU
2012P Proof	60		Value: 4,500			

BULLION - KANGAROO

KM# 590   DOLLAR
31.1035 g., 0.9990 Silver 0.9990 oz. ASW, 40 mm.   **Ruler:**
Elizabeth II **Obv:** Queen's portrait **Rev:** Aboriginal-kangaroo
design with dots **Edge:** Reeded

Date	Mintage	F	VF	XF	Unc	BU
2001B Frosted Unc	—	—	—	—	—	35.00
2001B Proof	—		Value: 40.00			

KM# 642   DOLLAR
31.1035 g., 0.9990 Silver 0.9990 oz. ASW, 40 mm.   **Ruler:**
Elizabeth II **Obv:** Head with tiara right, denomination below **Rev:**
Aboriginal-style kangaroo with wavy line background **Edge:**
Reeded

Date	Mintage	F	VF	XF	Unc	BU
2002B	—	—	—	—	35.00	42.00
2002B Proof	—	Value: 50.00				

KM# 798   DOLLAR
31.1035 g., 0.9990 Silver 0.9990 oz. ASW, 40 mm.   **Ruler:**
Elizabeth II **Obv:** Head with tiara right **Rev:** Aboriginal-style
kangaroo design **Edge:** Reeded

Date	Mintage	F	VF	XF	Unc	BU
2003	35,230	—	—	—	—	40.00
2003 Proof	20,400	Value: 45.00				

KM# 798a   DOLLAR
31.1035 g., 0.9990 Silver partially gilt 0.9990 oz. ASW, 40 mm.
Ruler: Elizabeth II **Obv:** Head with tiara right **Rev:** Aboriginal-
style kangaroo design **Edge:** Reeded

Date	Mintage	F	VF	XF	Unc	BU
2003	7,450	—	—	—	—	125

KM# 723   DOLLAR
31.1035 g., 0.9990 Silver 0.9990 oz. ASW, 40 mm.   **Ruler:**
Elizabeth II **Obv:** Head with tiara right, denomination below **Rev:**
Kangaroo with semi-circle background **Edge:** Reeded

Date	Mintage	F	VF	XF	Unc	BU
2004B Frosted Unc	—	—	—	—	—	37.00
2004B Proof	12,500	Value: 42.00				

KM# 723a   DOLLAR
31.1035 g., 0.9990 Silver partially gilt 0.9990 oz. ASW, 40 mm.
Ruler: Elizabeth II **Obv:** Head with tiara right, denomination
below **Rev:** Kangaroo with semi-circle background **Edge:**
Reeded

Date	Mintage	F	VF	XF	Unc	BU
2004B Frosted Unc	—	—	—	—	—	65.00

KM# 749   DOLLAR
31.6000 g., 0.9990 Silver 1.0149 oz. ASW, 40 mm.   **Ruler:**
Elizabeth II **Obv:** Head with tiara right **Rev:** Kangaroo bounding
under Southern Cross and above Federation Star **Edge:** Reeded

Date	Mintage	F	VF	XF	Unc	BU
2005	—	—	—	—	35.00	45.00
2005 Proof	12,500	Value: 50.00				

KM# 749a   DOLLAR
31.1035 g., 0.9990 Silver Partially Gold Plated 0.9990 oz. ASW,
40 mm.   **Ruler:** Elizabeth II **Obv:** Head with tiara right **Rev:**
Kangaroo bounding under Southern Cross and above Federation
Star **Edge:** Reeded

Date	Mintage	F	VF	XF	Unc	BU
2005 Proof	12,500	Value: 60.00				

KM# 837   DOLLAR
31.6000 g., 0.9990 Silver 1.0149 oz. ASW, 40 mm.   **Ruler:**
Elizabeth II **Obv:** Head with tiara right **Rev:** Kangaroo bounding
under Australian sun **Edge:** Reeded

Date	Mintage	F	VF	XF	Unc	BU
2006	—	—	—	—	—	35.00
2006 Proof	12,500	Value: 42.00				

KM# 837a   DOLLAR
31.6000 g., 0.9990 Silver partially gilt 1.0149 oz. ASW, 40 mm.
Ruler: Elizabeth II **Obv:** Head with tiara right **Rev:** Kangaroo
bounding under Australian sun **Edge:** Reeded

Date	Mintage	F	VF	XF	Unc	BU
2006	7,500	—	—	—	—	55.00

KM# 851   DOLLAR
31.6000 g., 0.9990 Silver 1.0149 oz. ASW, 40 mm.   **Ruler:**
Elizabeth II **Obv:** Head with tiara right **Rev:** Kangaroo mother
and joey **Edge:** Reeded

Date	Mintage	F	VF	XF	Unc	BU
2007	15,000	—	—	—	—	45.00
2007 Proof	12,500	Value: 50.00				

KM# 1061   DOLLAR
27.2200 g., Copper-Nickel, 38.74 mm.   **Ruler:** Elizabeth II **Rev:**
Kangaroo holding football

Date	Mintage	F	VF	XF	Unc	BU
2008	9,234	—	—	—	—	25.00

KM# 1061a   DOLLAR
31.1050 g., 0.9990 Silver 0.9990 oz. ASW, 40 mm.   **Ruler:**
Elizabeth II **Rev:** Kangaroo holding football

Date	Mintage	F	VF	XF	Unc	BU
2008	7,500	—	—	—	—	65.00
2008 Proof	10,000	Value: 50.00				

KM# 1061b   DOLLAR
31.1050 g., 0.9990 Silver 0.9990 oz. ASW, 40 mm.   **Ruler:**
Elizabeth II **Rev:** Kangaroo holding football in color

Date	Mintage	F	VF	XF	Unc	BU
2008 Proof	12,500	Value: 95.00				

KM# 1083   DOLLAR
31.1050 g., 0.9990 Silver 0.9990 oz. ASW, 40 mm.   **Ruler:**
Elizabeth II **Rev:** Kangaroo

Date	Mintage	F	VF	XF	Unc	BU
2009	20,000	—	—	—	—	50.00
2009 Proof	20,000	Value: 65.00				

KM# 1083a   DOLLAR
31.1050 g., 0.9990 Silver Partially gilt 0.9990 oz. ASW, 40 mm.
Ruler: Elizabeth II **Rev:** Kangaroo

Date	Mintage	F	VF	XF	Unc	BU
2009	—	—	—	—	—	90.00

KM# 1083b   DOLLAR
31.1035 g., 0.9990 Silver 0.9990 oz. ASW, 40 mm.   **Ruler:**
Elizabeth II **Rev:** Kangaroo in color

Date	Mintage	F	VF	XF	Unc	BU
2009 Proof	—	Value: 75.00				

KM# 1759   DOLLAR
31.1050 g., 0.9990 Silver 0.9990 oz. ASW, 40.6 mm. **Ruler:**
Elizabeth II **Obv:** Head with tiara right **Rev:** Kangaroo and joey

Date	Mintage	F	VF	XF	Unc	BU
2011P	—	—	—	—	—	75.00
2011P Proof	—	Value: 85.00				

KM# 1763   10 DOLLARS
3.1100 g., 0.9990 Gold 0.0999 oz. AGW, 17.53 mm. **Ruler:**
Elizabeth II **Obv:** Head with tiara right **Rev:** Kangaroo right on rocks

Date	Mintage	F	VF	XF	Unc	BU
2010P Proof	1,500	Value: 250				

KM# 1522   10 DOLLARS
3.1100 g., 0.9990 Gold 0.0999 oz. AGW, 17.53 mm. **Ruler:**
Elizabeth II **Rev:** Two kangaroos

Date	Mintage	F	VF	XF	Unc	BU
2011 Proof	1,500	Value: 265				

KM# 1683   10 DOLLARS
3.1100 g., 0.9990 Gold 0.0999 oz. AGW, 17.53 mm. **Ruler:**
Elizabeth II **Rev:** Kangaroo

Date	Mintage	F	VF	XF	Unc	BU
2012P Proof	—	Value: 200				

KM# 1457   DOLLAR
31.1050 g., 0.9990 Silver 0.9990 oz. ASW, 40 mm. **Ruler:**
Elizabeth II **Rev:** Two kangaroos playing

Date	Mintage	F	VF	XF	Unc	BU
2010P Proof	—	Value: 42.00				

KM# 1514   DOLLAR
31.1050 g., 0.9990 Silver 0.9990 oz. ASW, 40. mm. **Ruler:**
Elizabeth II **Rev:** Kangaroo in color

Date	Mintage	F	VF	XF	Unc	BU
2010 Proof	—	Value: 60.00				

KM# 1515   DOLLAR
31.1050 g., 0.9990 Silver 0.9990 oz. ASW, 40 mm. **Ruler:**
Elizabeth II **Rev:** Kangaroo in color

Date	Mintage	F	VF	XF	Unc	BU
2010 Proof	—	Value: 60.00				

KM# 1516   DOLLAR
31.1050 g., 0.9990 Silver 0.9990 oz. ASW, 40 mm. **Ruler:**
Elizabeth II **Rev:** Kangaroo in color

Date	Mintage	F	VF	XF	Unc	BU
2010 Proof	—	Value: 60.00				

KM# 894   15 DOLLARS
3.1101 g., 0.9990 Gold 0.0999 oz. AGW **Ruler:** Elizabeth II
Obv: Head with tiara right **Rev:** Two kangaroos on map of Australia

Date	Mintage	F	VF	XF	Unc	BU
2001	800	—	—	—	—	195

KM# 897   15 DOLLARS
3.1101 g., 0.9990 Gold 0.0999 oz. AGW **Ruler:** Elizabeth II
Obv: Head with tiara right **Rev:** Kangaroo browsing

Date	Mintage	F	VF	XF	Unc	BU
2002	800	—	—	—	—	195

KM# 902   15 DOLLARS
3.1101 g., 0.9990 Gold 0.0999 oz. AGW **Ruler:** Elizabeth II
Obv: Head with tiara right **Rev:** Two kangaroos hopping

Date	Mintage	F	VF	XF	Unc	BU
2003	500	—	—	—	—	195

KM# 907   15 DOLLARS
3.1101 g., 0.9990 Gold 0.0999 oz. AGW **Ruler:** Elizabeth II
Obv: Head with tiara right **Rev:** Crouching kangaroos facing left,
Grass tree plant at right

Date	Mintage	F	VF	XF	Unc	BU
2004	500	—	—	—	—	195

KM# 911   15 DOLLARS
3.1101 g., 0.9990 Gold 0.0999 oz. AGW **Ruler:** Elizabeth II
Obv: Head with tiara right **Rev:** Kangaroo in bush

Date	Mintage	F	VF	XF	Unc	BU
2005	500	—	—	—	—	195

KM# 1737   DOLLAR
31.1350 g., 0.9990 Silver 1.0000 oz. ASW, 40 mm. **Ruler:**
Elizabeth II **Obv:** Head with tiara right **Rev:** Mareeba Rock Wallaby

Date	Mintage	F	VF	XF	Unc	BU
2012	20,000	—	—	—	—	75.00
2012 Proof	20,000	Value: 100				

KM# 1390   2 DOLLARS
0.5000 g., 0.9990 Gold 0.0161 oz. AGW **Ruler:** Elizabeth II
Obv: Head right **Rev:** Kangaroo

Date	Mintage	F	VF	XF	Unc	BU
2010(p)	—	—	—	—	32.00	35.00

KM# 1527   2 DOLLARS
0.5000 g., 0.9990 Gold 0.0161 oz. AGW, 11.6 mm. **Ruler:**
Elizabeth II **Obv:** Head in tiara right **Rev:** Kangaroo bounding left

Date	Mintage	F	VF	XF	Unc	BU
2010P	—	—	—	—	—	50.00

KM# 1649   2 DOLLARS
0.5000 g., 0.9990 Gold 0.0161 oz. AGW, 11.6 mm. **Ruler:**
Elizabeth II **Obv:** Head with tiara right **Rev:** Kangaroo left

Date	Mintage	F	VF	XF	Unc	BU
2011 Proof	—	Value: 50.00				

KM# 893   5 DOLLARS
1.5710 g., 0.9990 Gold 0.0505 oz. AGW **Ruler:** Elizabeth II
Obv: Head with tiara right **Rev:** Two kangaroos on map of Australia

Date	Mintage	F	VF	XF	Unc	BU
2001	10,000	—	—	—	—	115

KM# 1776   10 DOLLARS
3.1100 g., 0.9990 Gold 0.0999 oz. AGW, 17.53 mm. **Ruler:**
Elizabeth II **Rev:** Kangaroo bounding left at sunset

Date	Mintage	F	VF	XF	Unc	BU
2007P	—	—	—	—	—	225

KM# 1772   10 DOLLARS
3.1100 g., 0.9990 Gold 0.0999 oz. AGW, 17.53 mm. **Ruler:**
Elizabeth II **Rev:** Kangaroo bounding right in grassland

Date	Mintage	F	VF	XF	Unc	BU
2008P	—	—	—	—	—	225

KM# 1764   10 DOLLARS
3.1100 g., 0.9990 Gold 0.0999 oz. AGW, 17.53 mm. **Ruler:**
Elizabeth II **Obv:** Head with tiara right **Rev:** Kangaroo left,
constellation in background

Date	Mintage	F	VF	XF	Unc	BU
2009P	—	Value: 250				

KM# 1768   10 DOLLARS
3.1100 g., 0.9990 Gold 0.0999 oz. AGW, 17.53 mm. **Ruler:**
Elizabeth II **Rev:** Kangaroo

Date	Mintage	F	VF	XF	Unc	BU
2010P	—	—	—	—	—	225

KM# 1758   DOLLAR
31.1050 g., 0.9990 Silver 0.9990 oz. ASW, 40.6 mm. **Ruler:**
Elizabeth II **Obv:** Head with tiara right **Rev:** Kangaroo right on rocks

Date	Mintage	F	VF	XF	Unc	BU
2010P	—	—	—	—	—	75.00
2010P Proof	—	Value: 85.00				

KM# 1362   15 DOLLARS
3.1100 g., 0.9990 Gold 0.0999 oz. AGW **Ruler:** Elizabeth II
Obv: Head right **Rev:** Kangaroo

Date	Mintage	F	VF	XF	Unc	BU
2010(p)	—	—	—	—	—	195

KM# 895   25 DOLLARS
7.7508 g., 0.9990 Gold 0.2489 oz. AGW **Ruler:** Elizabeth II
Obv: Head with tiara right **Rev:** Two kangaroos on map of Australia

Date	Mintage	F	VF	XF	Unc	BU
2001	500	—	—	—	—	460

KM# 898   25 DOLLARS
7.7508 g., 0.9990 Gold 0.2489 oz. AGW **Ruler:** Elizabeth II
Obv: Head with tiara right **Rev:** Kangaroo browsing

Date	Mintage	F	VF	XF	Unc	BU
2002	500	—	—	—	—	460

KM# 903   25 DOLLARS
7.7508 g., 0.9990 Gold 0.2489 oz. AGW **Ruler:** Elizabeth II
Obv: Head with tiara right **Rev:** Two kangaroos hopping

Date	Mintage	F	VF	XF	Unc	BU
2003	250	—	—	—	—	460

KM# 908   25 DOLLARS
7.7508 g., 0.9990 Gold 0.2489 oz. AGW **Ruler:** Elizabeth II
Obv: Head with tiara right **Rev:** Crouching kangaroos facing left,
Grass tree plant at right

Date	Mintage	F	VF	XF	Unc	BU
2004	250	—	—	—	—	460

KM# 912   25 DOLLARS
7.7508 g., 0.9990 Gold 0.2489 oz. AGW **Ruler:** Elizabeth II
Obv: Head with tiara right **Rev:** Kangaroo in bush

Date	Mintage	F	VF	XF	Unc	BU
2005	250	—	—	—	—	460

KM# 1605   DOLLAR
31.1050 g., 0.9990 Silver 0.9990 oz. ASW, 33 mm. **Ruler:**
Elizabeth II **Obv:** Head with tiara right **Rev:** Kangaroo left, sun
rays in background **Edge:** Reeded **Note:** Ultra High Relief

Date	Mintage	F	VF	XF	Unc	BU
2011P Proof	Est. 20,000	Value: 110				

KM# 1777   25 DOLLARS
7.7700 g., 0.9990 Gold 0.2496 oz. AGW **Ruler:** Elizabeth II **Rev:** Kangaroo bounding left at sunset

Date	Mintage	F	VF	XF	Unc	BU
2007P	—	—	—	—	—	475

KM# 1773   25 DOLLARS
7.7700 g., 0.9990 Gold 0.2496 oz. AGW **Ruler:** Elizabeth II **Rev:** Kangaroo bounding right in grassland

Date	Mintage	F	VF	XF	Unc	BU
2008P	—	—	—	—	—	475

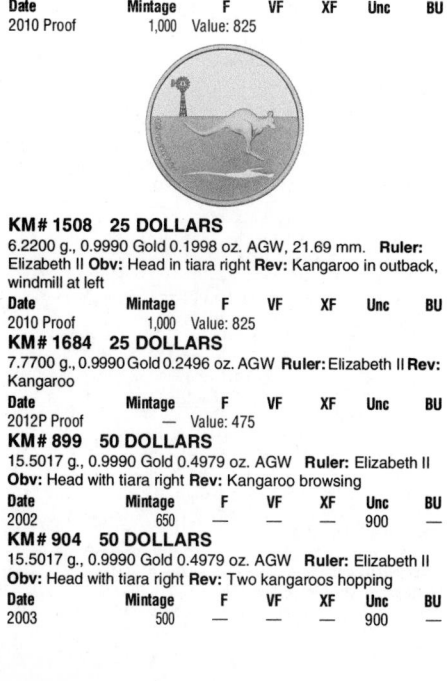

KM# 1765   25 DOLLARS
7.7700 g., 0.9990 Gold 0.2496 oz. AGW, 22 mm. **Ruler:** Elizabeth II **Obv:** Head with tiara right **Rev:** Kangaroo left, constellation in background

Date	Mintage	F	VF	XF	Unc	BU
2009P	—	Value: 475				

KM# 1769   25 DOLLARS
7.7700 g., 0.9990 Gold 0.2496 oz. AGW **Ruler:** Elizabeth II **Rev:** Kangaroo

Date	Mintage	F	VF	XF	Unc	BU
2010P	—	—	—	—	—	475

KM# 1363   25 DOLLARS
7.7500 g., 0.9990 Gold 0.2489 oz. AGW **Ruler:** Elizabeth II **Rev:** Two kangaroos playing

Date	Mintage	F	VF	XF	Unc	BU
2010P	—	—	—	—	—	460

KM# 1506   25 DOLLARS
6.2200 g., 0.9990 Gold 0.1998 oz. AGW, 21.69 mm. **Ruler:** Elizabeth II **Obv:** Head with tiara right **Rev:** Kangaroo in outback, windmill at right

Date	Mintage	F	VF	XF	Unc	BU
2010 Proof	1,000	Value: 825				

KM# 1507   25 DOLLARS
6.2200 g., 0.9990 Gold 0.1998 oz. AGW, 21.69 mm. **Ruler:** Elizabeth II **Obv:** Head in tiara right **Rev:** Kangaroo in outback, windmill at center

Date	Mintage	F	VF	XF	Unc	BU
2010 Proof	1,000	Value: 825				

KM# 1508   25 DOLLARS
6.2200 g., 0.9990 Gold 0.1998 oz. AGW, 21.69 mm. **Ruler:** Elizabeth II **Obv:** Head in tiara right **Rev:** Kangaroo in outback, windmill at left

Date	Mintage	F	VF	XF	Unc	BU
2010 Proof	1,000	Value: 825				

KM# 1684   25 DOLLARS
7.7700 g., 0.9990 Gold 0.2496 oz. AGW **Ruler:** Elizabeth II **Rev:** Kangaroo

Date	Mintage	F	VF	XF	Unc	BU
2012P Proof	—	Value: 475				

KM# 899   50 DOLLARS
15.5017 g., 0.9990 Gold 0.4979 oz. AGW **Ruler:** Elizabeth II **Obv:** Head with tiara right **Rev:** Kangaroo browsing

Date	Mintage	F	VF	XF	Unc	BU
2002	650	—	—	—	900	—

KM# 904   50 DOLLARS
15.5017 g., 0.9990 Gold 0.4979 oz. AGW **Ruler:** Elizabeth II **Obv:** Head with tiara right **Rev:** Two kangaroos hopping

Date	Mintage	F	VF	XF	Unc	BU
2003	500	—	—	—	900	—

KM# 909   50 DOLLARS
15.5017 g., 0.9990 Gold 0.4979 oz. AGW **Ruler:** Elizabeth II **Obv:** Head with tiara right **Rev:** Crouching kangaroos facing left, Grass tree plant at right

Date	Mintage	F	VF	XF	Unc	BU
2004	500	—	—	—	900	—

Note: In sets only

KM# 913   50 DOLLARS
15.5017 g., 0.9990 Gold 0.4979 oz. AGW **Ruler:** Elizabeth II **Obv:** Head with tiara right **Rev:** Kangaroo in bush

Date	Mintage	F	VF	XF	Unc	BU
2005	500	—	—	—	900	—

KM# 1778   50 DOLLARS
15.5500 g., 0.9990 Gold 0.4994 oz. AGW **Ruler:** Elizabeth II **Rev:** Kangaroo bounding left in sunset

Date	Mintage	F	VF	XF	Unc	BU
2007P	—	—	—	—	—	950

KM# 1774   50 DOLLARS
15.5500 g., 0.9990 Gold 0.4994 oz. AGW **Ruler:** Elizabeth II **Rev:** Kangaroo bounding right in grassland

Date	Mintage	F	VF	XF	Unc	BU
2008P	—	—	—	—	—	950

KM# 1766   50 DOLLARS
15.5500 g., 0.9990 Gold 0.4994 oz. AGW, 25 mm. **Ruler:** Elizabeth II **Obv:** Head with tiara right **Rev:** Kangaroo left, constellation in background

Date	Mintage	F	VF	XF	Unc	BU
2009P Proof	—	Value: 950				

KM# 1364   50 DOLLARS
15.5600 g., 0.9990 Gold 0.4997 oz. AGW, 25 mm. **Ruler:** Elizabeth II **Obv:** Head right **Rev:** Two kangaroos playing

Date	Mintage	F	VF	XF	Unc	BU
2010(p)	—	—	—	—	—	900

KM# 1770   50 DOLLARS
15.5500 g., 0.9990 Gold 0.4994 oz. AGW, 25 mm. **Ruler:** Elizabeth II **Rev:** Kangaroo

Date	Mintage	F	VF	XF	Unc	BU
2010P	—	—	—	—	—	950

KM# 1685   50 DOLLARS
15.5500 g., 0.9990 Gold 0.4994 oz. AGW, 25 mm. **Ruler:** Elizabeth II **Rev:** Kangaroo

Date	Mintage	F	VF	XF	Unc	BU
2012P Proof	—	Value: 950				

KM# 1779   100 DOLLARS
31.1050 g., 0.9990 Gold 0.9990 oz. AGW, 32 mm. **Ruler:** Elizabeth II **Rev:** Kangaroo bounding left at sunset

Date	Mintage	F	VF	XF	Unc	BU
2007P	—	—	—	—	—	1,850

KM# 1775   100 DOLLARS
31.1050 g., 0.9990 Gold 0.9990 oz. AGW, 32 mm. **Ruler:** Elizabeth II **Rev:** Kangaroo bounding right in grassland

Date	Mintage	F	VF	XF	Unc	BU
2008P	—	—	—	—	—	1,850

KM# 1767   100 DOLLARS
31.1050 g., 0.9990 Gold 0.9990 oz. AGW, 32 mm. **Ruler:** Elizabeth II **Obv:** Head with tiara right **Rev:** Kangaroo left, constellation in background

Date	Mintage	F	VF	XF	Unc	BU
2009P Proof	—	Value: 1,850				

KM# 1365   100 DOLLARS
31.1035 g., 0.9990 Gold 0.9990 oz. AGW, 32 mm. **Ruler:** Elizabeth II **Obv:** Head right **Rev:** Kangaroo

Date	Mintage	F	VF	XF	Unc	BU
2010(p)	—	—	—	—	—	1,750

KM# 1771   100 DOLLARS
31.1050 g., 0.9990 Gold 0.9990 oz. AGW, 32 mm. **Ruler:** Elizabeth II **Rev:** Kangaroo

Date	Mintage	F	VF	XF	Unc	BU
2010P	—	—	—	—	—	1,850

KM# 1686   100 DOLLARS
31.1050 g., 0.9990 Gold 0.9990 oz. AGW, 32 mm. **Ruler:** Elizabeth II **Rev:** Kangaroo

Date	Mintage	F	VF	XF	Unc	BU
2012P Proof	—	Value: 1,850				

KM# 896   200 DOLLARS
62.2140 g., 0.9990 Gold 1.9981 oz. AGW **Ruler:** Elizabeth II **Obv:** Head with tiara right **Rev:** Two kangaroos on map of Australia

Date	Mintage	F	VF	XF	Unc	BU
2001	300	—	—	—	3,500	—

KM# 901   200 DOLLARS
62.2140 g., 0.9990 Gold 1.9981 oz. AGW **Ruler:** Elizabeth II **Obv:** Head with tiara right **Rev:** Kangaroo browsing

Date	Mintage	F	VF	XF	Unc	BU
2002	300	—	—	—	3,500	—

KM# 905   200 DOLLARS
62.2140 g., 0.9990 Gold 1.9981 oz. AGW **Ruler:** Elizabeth II **Obv:** Head with tiara right **Rev:** Two kangaroos hopping

Date	Mintage	F	VF	XF	Unc	BU
2003	200	—	—	—	3,500	—

KM# 910   200 DOLLARS
62.2140 g., 0.9990 Gold 1.9981 oz. AGW **Ruler:** Elizabeth II **Obv:** Head with tiara right **Rev:** Crouching kangaroos facing left, Grass tree plant at right

Date	Mintage	F	VF	XF	Unc	BU
2004	200	—	—	—	3,500	—

KM# 1462   300 DOLLARS
1000.0000 g., 0.9990 Gold 32.117 oz. AGW **Ruler:** Elizabeth II **Obv:** Head with tiara right **Rev:** Two kangaroos playing

Date	Mintage	F	VF	XF	Unc	BU
2010P	—	—	—	—	—	53,500

KM# 1687   3000 DOLLARS
1000.0000 g., 0.9990 Gold 32.117 oz. AGW **Ruler:** Elizabeth II **Rev:** Kangaroo

Date	Mintage	F	VF	XF	Unc	BU
2012P Proof	—	BV+2%				

KM# 1569   1000000 DOLLARS
1000000.0000 g., 0.9999 Gold 32146. oz. AGW, 800 mm. **Ruler:** Elizabeth II **Obv:** Head with tiara right **Rev:** Red Kangaroo bounding left **Note:** Cast. 120mm thick

Date	Mintage	F	VF	XF	Unc	BU
2012P	1	—	—	—	—	55,500,000

BULLION - KOOKABURRA

KM# 875   50 CENTS
15.5500 g., 0.9990 Silver 0.4994 oz. ASW, 38.74 mm. **Ruler:** Elizabeth II **Obv:** Head with tiara right **Rev:** Kookaburra on branch, tail above, two leaves **Edge:** Reeded **Shape:** Square **Note:** Lenticular technology makes kookaburra appear to move.

Date	Mintage	F	VF	XF	Unc	BU
2002P Proof	75,350	Value: 35.00				

KM# 684   50 CENTS
15.5500 g., 0.9990 Silver 0.4994 oz. ASW, 32.1x32.1 mm. **Ruler:** Elizabeth II **Obv:** Head with tiara right, denomination below **Rev:** Two kookaburras, one in flight **Edge:** Reeded **Shape:** Square

Date	Mintage	F	VF	XF	Unc	BU
2003P Proof	75,350	Value: 32.00				

KM# 876   50 CENTS
15.5500 g., 0.9990 Silver 0.4994 oz. ASW, 38.74 mm. **Ruler:** Elizabeth II **Obv:** Head with tiara right **Rev:** Kookaburra perched on branch, tail below, four leaves **Edge:** Reeded **Shape:** Square with rounded corners

Date	Mintage	F	VF	XF	Unc	BU
2004P Proof	30,350	Value: 32.00				

KM# 877   50 CENTS
15.5500 g., 0.9990 Silver 0.4994 oz. ASW, 25x25 mm. **Ruler:** Elizabeth II **Obv:** Head with tiara right **Rev:** Two kookaburras on branch, one laughing **Edge:** Reeded **Shape:** Square

Date	Mintage	F	VF	XF	Unc	BU
2005P Proof	30,350	Value: 32.00				

KM# 691.1   DOLLAR
31.1035 g., 0.9990 Silver 0.9990 oz. ASW, 40 mm. **Ruler:** Elizabeth II **Obv:** Head with tiara right, denomination below **Rev:** Kookaburra flying over map of Australia **Edge:** Reeded

Date	Mintage	F	VF	XF	Unc	BU
2001P Proof	5,000	Value: 42.00				
2002P	—	—	—	—	35.00	37.00

KM# 479   DOLLAR
31.9700 g., 0.9990 Silver 1.0268 oz. ASW **Ruler:** Elizabeth II **Obv:** Head with tiara right, denomination below **Rev:** Two kookaburras back-to-back on branch

Date	Mintage	F	VF	XF	Unc	BU
2001	—	—	—	—	35.00	—
2001	10,000	—	—	—	45.00	—
Note: Federation star privy mark						
2001	50,000	—	—	—	35.00	—
Note: Santa Claus privy mark						
2001	1,000	—	—	—	125	—
Note: Love token personal message						
2001	75,000	—	—	—	42.00	—
Note: New York State Quarter privy mark						
2001	75,000	—	—	—	42.00	—
Note: North Carolina State Quarter privy mark						
2001	75,000	—	—	—	42.00	—
Note: Rhode Island State Quarter privy mark						
2001	75,000	—	—	—	42.00	—
Note: Vermont State Quarter privy mark						
2001	75,000	—	—	—	42.00	—
Note: Kentucky State Quarter privy mark						

KM# 625   DOLLAR
31.1035 g., 0.9990 Silver 0.9990 oz. ASW, 40.4 mm. **Ruler:** Elizabeth II **Subject:** U.S. State Quarter

Date	Mintage	F	VF	XF	Unc	BU
2002	75,000	—	—	—	45.00	—
Note: Tennessee State Quarter privy mark						
2002	75,000	—	—	—	45.00	—
Note: Ohio State Quarter privy mark						
2002	75,000	—	—	—	45.00	—
Note: Louisiana State Quarter privy mark						

Date	Mintage	F	VF	XF	Unc	BU
2002	75,000	—	—	—	45.00	—
Note: Indiana State Quarter privy mark						
2002	75,000	—	—	—	45.00	—
Note: Mississippi State Quarter privy mark						

KM# 666   DOLLAR
31.6200 g., 0.9990 Silver 1.0155 oz. ASW, 40.3 mm. **Ruler:** Elizabeth II **Obv:** Head with tiara right, denomination below **Rev:** Kookaburra perched on branch **Edge:** Reeded

Date	Mintage	F	VF	XF	Unc	BU
2002	5,000	Value: 37.00				

KM# 691.2   DOLLAR
31.6200 g., 0.9990 Silver 1.0155 oz. ASW, 40.5 mm. **Ruler:** Elizabeth II **Obv:** Head with tiara right, denomination below **Rev:** Multicolor US flag above a kookaburra in flight over Australian map **Edge:** Reeded

Date	Mintage	F	VF	XF	Unc	BU
2002	18,500	—	—	—	35.00	40.00

KM# 683   DOLLAR
31.1035 g., 0.9990 Silver 0.9990 oz. ASW, 40 mm. **Ruler:** Elizabeth II **Obv:** Head with tiara right, denomination below **Rev:** Two kookaburras, one in flight **Edge:** Reeded **Note:** Gilded.

Date	Mintage	F	VF	XF	Unc	BU
2003P Proof	5,000	Value: 37.00				
2004	10,000	—	—	—	—	35.00
2004 Proof	15,000	Value: 45.00				

KM# 1761   DOLLAR
31.1050 g., 0.9990 Silver 0.9990 oz. ASW, 40.6 mm. **Ruler:** Elizabeth II **Obv:** Head with tiara right **Rev:** Kookaburra right on branch

Date	Mintage	F	VF	XF	Unc	BU
2003P	—	—	—	—	—	75.00

KM# 883   DOLLAR
31.1050 g., 0.9990 Silver 0.9990 oz. ASW, 40.5 mm. **Ruler:** Elizabeth II **Obv:** Head with tiara right **Rev:** Kookaburra perched on branch with four leaves **Edge:** Reeded

Date	Mintage	F	VF	XF	Unc	BU
2004P Proof	5,000	Value: 35.00				
2005	5,000	—	—	—	45.00	—
Note: Gemini privy mark						
2005	5,000	—	—	—	45.00	—
Note: Aquarius privy mark						
2005	5,000	—	—	—	45.00	—
Note: Pisces privy mark						
2005	5,000	—	—	—	45.00	—
Note: Aries privy mark						
2005	5,000	—	—	—	45.00	—
Note: Taurus privy mark						
2005	5,000	—	—	—	45.00	—
Note: Cancer privy mark						
2005	5,000	—	—	—	45.00	—
Note: Leo privy mark						
2005	5,000	—	—	—	45.00	—
Note: Virgo privy mark						
2005	5,000	—	—	—	45.00	—
Note: Libra privy mark						
2005	5,000	—	—	—	45.00	—
Note: Scorpio privy mark						
2005	5,000	—	—	—	45.00	—
Note: Sagittarius privy mark						
2005	5,000	—	—	—	45.00	—
Note: Capricorn privy mark						

KM# 883a   DOLLAR
31.1035 g., 0.9990 Silver 0.9990 oz. ASW, 40 mm. **Ruler:** Elizabeth II **Obv:** Head with tiara right **Rev:** Kookaburra perched on branch with four leaves **Note:** Gilded.

Date	Mintage	F	VF	XF	Unc	BU
2004	10,000	—	—	—	55.00	—

KM# 720   DOLLAR
1.0350 g., 0.9990 Silver partially gilt 0.0332 oz. ASW, 40 mm. **Ruler:** Elizabeth II **Obv:** Head with tiara right, denomination below **Rev:** Kookaburra, partially gilt **Edge:** Reeded

Date	Mintage	F	VF	XF	Unc	BU
2005 Proof	—	Value: 65.00				

KM# 886   DOLLAR
31.5600 g., 0.9990 Silver 1.0136 oz. ASW, 40.5 mm. **Ruler:** Elizabeth II **Obv:** Head with tiara right **Rev:** Two kookaburras on branch, one laughing **Edge:** Reeded

Date	Mintage	F	VF	XF	Unc	BU
2005P Proof	5,000	Value: 40.00				

KM# 889   DOLLAR
31.5600 g., 0.9990 Silver 1.0136 oz. ASW, 40.5 mm. **Ruler:** Elizabeth II **Obv:** Head with tiara right **Rev:** Kookaburra on branch, no leaves

Date	Mintage	F	VF	XF	Unc	BU
2007	300,000	—	—	—	35.00	38.00

KM# 1760   DOLLAR
31.1050 g., 0.9990 Silver 0.9990 oz. ASW, 40.6 mm. **Ruler:** Elizabeth II **Obv:** Head with tiara right **Rev:** Kookaburra on branch look at spider web at lower left

Date	Mintage	F	VF	XF	Unc	BU
2008P	—	—	—	—	—	75.00

KM# 1277   DOLLAR
31.1050 g., 0.9990 Silver 0.9990 oz. ASW, 40 mm. **Ruler:** Elizabeth II **Subject:** Kookaburra 20th Anniversary **Obv:** Head right **Rev:** Kookaburra standing right

Date	Mintage	F	VF	XF	Unc	BU
2009 P20 Proof	10,000	Value: 47.00				

KM# 1278   DOLLAR
31.1050 g., 0.9990 Silver 0.9990 oz. ASW, 40 mm. **Ruler:** Elizabeth II **Subject:** Kookaburra 20th Anniversary **Obv:** Head right **Rev:** Kookaburra on branch, head right

Date	Mintage	F	VF	XF	Unc	BU
2009 P20 Proof	10,000	Value: 47.00				

KM# 1279   DOLLAR
31.1050 g., 0.9990 Silver 0.9990 oz. ASW, 40 mm. **Ruler:** Elizabeth II **Subject:** Kookaburra 20th Anniversary **Obv:** Head right **Rev:** Kookaburra on branch left, head upwards

Date	Mintage	F	VF	XF	Unc	BU
2009 P20 Proof	10,000	Value: 47.00				

KM# 1280   DOLLAR
31.1050 g., 0.9990 Silver 0.9990 oz. ASW, 40 mm. **Ruler:** Elizabeth II **Subject:** Kookaburra 20th Anniversary **Obv:** Head right **Rev:** Kookaburra feeding young in nest at right

Date	Mintage	F	VF	XF	Unc	BU
2009 P20 Proof	10,000	Value: 47.00				

KM# 1281   DOLLAR
31.1050 g., 0.9990 Silver 0.9990 oz. ASW, 40 mm. **Ruler:** Elizabeth II **Subject:** Kookaburra 20th Anniversary **Obv:** Head right **Rev:** Kookaburra pair on branch

Date	Mintage	F	VF	XF	Unc	BU
2009 P20 Proof	10,000	Value: 47.00				

KM# 1282   DOLLAR
31.1050 g., 0.9990 Silver 0.9990 oz. ASW, 40 mm. **Ruler:** Elizabeth II **Obv:** Head right **Rev:** Kookaburra on branch, head left

Date	Mintage	F	VF	XF	Unc	BU
2009 P20 Proof	10,000	Value: 47.00				

KM# 1283   DOLLAR
31.1050 g., 0.9990 Silver 0.9990 oz. ASW, 40 mm. **Ruler:** Elizabeth II **Subject:** Kookaburra 20th Anniversary **Obv:** Head right **Rev:** Kookaburra in flight right

Date	Mintage	F	VF	XF	Unc	BU
2009 P20 Proof	10,000	Value: 47.00				

KM# 1284   DOLLAR
31.1050 g., 0.9990 Silver 0.9990 oz. ASW, 40 mm. **Ruler:** Elizabeth II **Subject:** Kookaburra 20th Anniversary **Obv:** Head right **Rev:** Kookaburra by nest at left

Date	Mintage	F	VF	XF	Unc	BU
2009 P20 Proof	10,000	Value: 47.00				

KM# 1285   DOLLAR
31.1050 g., 0.9990 Silver 0.9990 oz. ASW, 40 mm. **Ruler:** Elizabeth II **Subject:** Kookaburra 20th Anniversary **Obv:** Head right **Rev:** Kookaburra on fence post

Date	Mintage	F	VF	XF	Unc	BU
2009 P20 Proof	10,000	Value: 47.00				

KM# 1286   DOLLAR
31.1050 g., 0.9990 Silver 0.9990 oz. ASW, 40 mm. **Ruler:** Elizabeth II **Subject:** Kookaburra 20th Anniversary **Obv:** Head right **Rev:** Kookaburra pair on branch left

Date	Mintage	F	VF	XF	Unc	BU
2009 P20 Proof	10,000	Value: 47.00				

KM# 1287   DOLLAR
31.1050 g., 0.9990 Silver 0.9990 oz. ASW, 40 mm. **Ruler:** Elizabeth II **Subject:** Kookaburra 20th Anniversary **Obv:** Head right **Rev:** Kookaburra on leafy branch left

Date	Mintage	F	VF	XF	Unc	BU
2009 P20 Proof	10,000	Value: 47.00				

KM# 1288   DOLLAR
31.1050 g., 0.9990 Silver 0.9990 oz. ASW, 40 mm. **Ruler:** Elizabeth II **Subject:** Kookaburra 20th Anniversary **Obv:** Head right **Rev:** Kookaburra pair on branch, beaks upward

Date	Mintage	F	VF	XF	Unc	BU
2009 P20 Proof	10,000	Value: 47.00				

KM# 1289   DOLLAR
31.1050 g., 0.9990 Silver 0.9990 oz. ASW, 40 mm. **Ruler:** Elizabeth II **Subject:** Kookaburra 20th Anniversary **Obv:** Head right **Rev:** Kookaburra in flight on map of Australia

Date	Mintage	F	VF	XF	Unc	BU
2009 P20 Proof	10,000	Value: 47.00				

KM# 1290   DOLLAR
31.1050 g., 0.9990 Silver 0.9990 oz. ASW, 40 mm. **Ruler:** Elizabeth II **Subject:** Kookaburra 20th Anniversary **Obv:** Head right **Rev:** Kookaburra on branch right

Date	Mintage	F	VF	XF	Unc	BU
2009 P20 Proof	10,000	Value: 47.00				

KM# 1291   DOLLAR
31.1050 g., 0.9990 Silver 0.9990 oz. ASW, 40 mm. **Ruler:** Elizabeth II **Subject:** Kookaburra 20th Anniversary **Obv:** Head right **Rev:** Two kookaburras, one in flight, one on branch

Date	Mintage	F	VF	XF	Unc	BU
2009 P20 Proof	10,000	Value: 47.00				

KM# 1292   DOLLAR
31.1050 g., 0.9990 Silver 0.9990 oz. ASW, 40 mm. **Ruler:** Elizabeth II **Subject:** Kookaburra 20th Anniversary **Obv:** Head right **Rev:** Kookaburra on branch, head right

Date	Mintage	F	VF	XF	Unc	BU
2009 P20 Proof	10,000	Value: 47.00				

KM# 1293   DOLLAR
31.1050 g., 0.9990 Silver 0.9990 oz. ASW, 40 mm. **Ruler:** Elizabeth II **Subject:** Kookaburra 20th Anniversary **Obv:** Head right **Rev:** Kookaburra pair on branch left

Date	Mintage	F	VF	XF	Unc	BU
2009 P20 Proof	10,000	Value: 47.00				

KM# 1294   DOLLAR
31.1050 g., 0.9990 Silver 0.9990 oz. ASW, 40 mm. **Ruler:** Elizabeth II **Subject:** Kookaburra 20th Anniversary **Obv:** Head right **Rev:** Kookaburra on branch left

Date	Mintage	F	VF	XF	Unc	BU
2009 P20 Proof	10,000	Value: 47.00				

KM# 1295   DOLLAR
31.1050 g., 0.9990 Silver 0.9990 oz. ASW, 40 mm. **Ruler:** Elizabeth II **Subject:** Kookaburra 20th Anniversary **Obv:** Head right **Rev:** Kookaburra admiring spider web

Date	Mintage	F	VF	XF	Unc	BU
2009 P20 Proof	10,000	Value: 47.00				

KM# 1296   DOLLAR
31.1050 g., 0.9990 Silver 0.9990 oz. ASW, 40 mm. **Ruler:** Elizabeth II **Subject:** Kookaburra 20th Anniversary **Obv:** Head right **Rev:** Kookaburra on branch, sunburst in background

Date	Mintage	F	VF	XF	Unc	BU
2009 P20 Proof	10,000	Value: 47.00				

KM# 1471   DOLLAR
31.1050 g., 0.9990 Silver 0.9990 oz. ASW, 40 mm. **Ruler:** Elizabeth II **Rev:** Kookabburra on branch

Date	Mintage	F	VF	XF	Unc	BU
2010P	—	—	—	—	—	45.00

KM# 1692   DOLLAR
31.1050 g., 0.9990 Silver 0.9990 oz. ASW, 40.5 mm. **Ruler:** Elizabeth II **Rev:** Kookaburra

Date	Mintage	F	VF	XF	Unc	BU
2012P	—	—	—	—	—	45.00

KM# 678   2 DOLLARS
62.2070 g., 0.9990 Silver 1.9979 oz. ASW, 40 mm. **Ruler:** Elizabeth II **Obv:** Head with tiara right, denomination below **Rev:** Kookaburra flying over Australian map **Edge:** Reeded

Date	Mintage	F	VF	XF	Unc	BU
2001P Proof	5,000	Value: 90.00				
2002	1,500	—	—	—	82.00	—
Note: 1661 Spanish cob privy mark						
2002	1,500	—	—	—	82.00	—
Note: 1771 Spanish pillar dollar privy mark						
2002	1,500	—	—	—	82.00	—
Note: 1881 Gold sovereign privy mark						
2002	1,500	—	—	—	82.00	—
Note: 1991 Gold Australian nugget privy mark						

KM# 623.1   2 DOLLARS
62.8500 g., 0.9990 Silver 2.0186 oz. ASW, 50 mm. **Ruler:** Elizabeth II **Obv:** Head with tiara right, denomination below **Rev:** Two kookaburras back to back **Edge:** Reeded

Date	Mintage	F	VF	XF	Unc	BU
2001	—	—	—	—	80.00	85.00

KM# 623.2   2 DOLLARS
62.2070 g., 0.9990 Silver 1.9979 oz. ASW **Ruler:** Elizabeth II **Subject:** USA State Quarters - 2001 **Obv:** Head with tiara right, denomination below **Rev:** Two kookaburras on branch with five U.S. State Quarter designs added **Edge:** Segmented reeding **Note:** Prev. KM#623

Date	Mintage	F	VF	XF	Unc	BU
2001	10,000	—	—	—	145	160

KM# 879   2 DOLLARS
62.8500 g., 0.9990 Silver 2.0186 oz. ASW, 40 mm. **Ruler:** Elizabeth II **Obv:** Head with tiara right **Rev:** Kookaburra on branch plus two leaves **Edge:** Reeded

Date	Mintage	F	VF	XF	Unc	BU
2002P Proof	5,000	Value: 90.00				
2003	1,000	—	—	—	115	—
Note: Boer War privy mark						
2003	1,000	—	—	—	115	—
Note: World War I privy mark						
2003	1,000	—	—	—	115	—
Note: World War II privy mark						
2003	1,000	—	—	—	115	—
Note: Korean War privy mark						
2003	1,000	—	—	—	115	—
Note: Vietnam War privy mark						

KM# 881   2 DOLLARS
62.2070 g., 0.9990 Silver 1.9979 oz. ASW, 50 mm. **Ruler:** Elizabeth II **Obv:** Head with tiara right **Rev:** Two kookaburras, one in flight **Edge:** Reeded

Date	Mintage	F	VF	XF	Unc	BU
2003P Proof	800	Value: 90.00				

KM# 884   2 DOLLARS
62.2070 g., 0.9990 Silver 1.9979 oz. ASW, 50 mm. **Ruler:** Elizabeth II **Obv:** Head with tiara right **Rev:** Kookaburra perched on branch with four leaves **Edge:** Reeded

Date	Mintage	F	VF	XF	Unc	BU
2004P Proof	800	Value: 90.00				

KM# 887   2 DOLLARS
62.2070 g., 0.9990 Silver 1.9979 oz. ASW, 50 mm. **Ruler:** Elizabeth II **Obv:** Head with tiara right **Rev:** Two kookaburras on branch, one laughing **Edge:** Reeded

Date	Mintage	F	VF	XF	Unc	BU
2005P Proof	800	Value: 90.00				

KM# 890   2 DOLLARS
62.2070 g., 0.9990 Silver 1.9979 oz. ASW, 50 mm. **Ruler:** Elizabeth II **Obv:** Head with tiara right **Rev:** Kookaburra on branch, no leaves

Date	Mintage	F	VF	XF	Unc	BU
2007	—	—	—	—	85.00	—

KM# 1297   5 DOLLARS
1.5500 g., 0.9990 Gold 0.0498 oz. AGW, 14 mm.   **Ruler:**
Elizabeth II **Subject:** Kookaburra 20th Anniversary **Obv:** Head
right **Rev:** Kookaburra standing on stump right

Date	Mintage	F	VF	XF	Unc	BU
2009 P20 Proof	2,009	Value: 125				

KM# 1298   5 DOLLARS
1.5500 g., 0.9990 Gold 0.0498 oz. AGW, 14 mm.   **Ruler:**
Elizabeth II **Subject:** Kookaburra 20th Anniversary **Obv:** Head
right **Rev:** Kookaburra on branch, head right

Date	Mintage	F	VF	XF	Unc	BU
2009 P20 Proof	2,009	Value: 125				

KM# 1299   5 DOLLARS
1.5500 g., 0.9990 Gold 0.0498 oz. AGW, 14 mm.   **Ruler:**
Elizabeth II **Subject:** Kookaburra 20th Anniversary **Obv:** Head
right **Rev:** Kookaburra on branch left

Date	Mintage	F	VF	XF	Unc	BU
2009 P20 Proof	2,009	Value: 125				

KM# 1300   5 DOLLARS
1.5500 g., 0.9990 Gold 0.0498 oz. AGW, 14 mm.   **Ruler:**
Elizabeth II **Subject:** Kookaburra 20th Anniversary **Obv:** Head
right **Rev:** Kookaburra on branch feeding young at right

Date	Mintage	F	VF	XF	Unc	BU
2009 P20 Proof	2,009	Value: 125				

KM# 1301   5 DOLLARS
1.5500 g., 0.9990 Gold 0.0498 oz. AGW, 14 mm.   **Ruler:**
Elizabeth II **Subject:** Kookaburra 20th Anniversary **Obv:** Head
right **Rev:** Kookaburra pair on branch, heads opposite

Date	Mintage	F	VF	XF	Unc	BU
2009 P20 Proof	2,009	Value: 125				

KM# 1302   5 DOLLARS
1.5500 g., 0.9990 Gold 0.0498 oz. AGW, 14 mm.   **Ruler:**
Elizabeth II **Subject:** Kookaburra 20th Anniversary **Obv:** Head
right **Rev:** Kookaburra on branch, head left

Date	Mintage	F	VF	XF	Unc	BU
2009 P20 Proof	2,009	Value: 125				

KM# 1303   5 DOLLARS
1.5500 g., 0.9990 Gold 0.0498 oz. AGW, 14 mm.   **Ruler:**
Elizabeth II **Subject:** Kookaburra 20th Anniversary **Obv:** Head
right **Rev:** Kookaburra in flight right

Date	Mintage	F	VF	XF	Unc	BU
2009 P20 Proof	2,009	Value: 125				

KM# 1304   5 DOLLARS
1.5500 g., 0.9990 Gold 0.0498 oz. AGW, 14 mm.   **Ruler:**
Elizabeth II **Subject:** Kookaburra 20th Anniversary **Obv:** Head
right **Rev:** Kookaburra at nest left, head right

Date	Mintage	F	VF	XF	Unc	BU
2009 P20 Proof	2,009	Value: 125				

KM# 1305   5 DOLLARS
1.5500 g., 0.9990 Gold 0.0498 oz. AGW, 14 mm.   **Ruler:**
Elizabeth II **Subject:** Kookaburra 20th Anniversary **Obv:** Head
right **Rev:** Kookaburra on fence post

Date	Mintage	F	VF	XF	Unc	BU
2009 P20 Proof	2,009	Value: 125				

KM# 1306   5 DOLLARS
1.5500 g., 0.9990 Gold 0.0498 oz. AGW, 14 mm.   **Ruler:**
Elizabeth II **Subject:** Kookaburra 20th Anniversary **Obv:** Head
right **Rev:** Kookaburra pair left

Date	Mintage	F	VF	XF	Unc	BU
2009 P20 Proof	2,009	Value: 125				

KM# 1307   5 DOLLARS
1.5500 g., 0.9990 Gold 0.0498 oz. AGW, 14 mm.   **Ruler:**
Elizabeth II **Subject:** Kookaburra 20th Anniversary **Obv:** Head
right **Rev:** Kookaburra left on leafy branch

Date	Mintage	F	VF	XF	Unc	BU
2009 P20 Proof	2,009	Value: 125				

KM# 1308   5 DOLLARS
1.5500 g., 0.9990 Gold 0.0498 oz. AGW, 14 mm.   **Ruler:**
Elizabeth II **Subject:** Kookaburra 20th Anniversary **Obv:** Head
right **Rev:** Kookaburra pair facing opposite

Date	Mintage	F	VF	XF	Unc	BU
2009 P20 Proof	2,009	Value: 125				

KM# 1309   5 DOLLARS
1.5500 g., 0.9990 Gold 0.0498 oz. AGW, 14 mm.   **Ruler:**
Elizabeth II **Subject:** Kookaburra 20th Anniversary **Obv:** Head
right **Rev:** Kookaburra in flight on map of Australia

Date	Mintage	F	VF	XF	Unc	BU
2009 P20 Proof	2,009	Value: 125				

KM# 1310   5 DOLLARS
1.5500 g., 0.9990 Gold 0.0498 oz. AGW, 14 mm.   **Ruler:**
Elizabeth II **Subject:** Kookaburra 20th Anniversary **Obv:** Head
right **Rev:** Kookaburra on branch right

Date	Mintage	F	VF	XF	Unc	BU
2009 P20 Proof	2,009	Value: 125				

KM# 1311   5 DOLLARS
1.5500 g., 0.9990 Gold 0.0498 oz. AGW, 14 mm.   **Ruler:**
Elizabeth II **Subject:** Kookaburra 20th Anniversary **Obv:** Head
right **Rev:** Kookaburras, one in flight, one on branch

Date	Mintage	F	VF	XF	Unc	BU
2009 P20 Proof	2,009	Value: 125				

KM# 1312   5 DOLLARS
1.5500 g., 0.9990 Gold 0.0498 oz. AGW, 14 mm.   **Ruler:**
Elizabeth II **Subject:** Kookaburra 20th Anniversary **Obv:** Head
right **Rev:** Kookaburra on branch, head right

Date	Mintage	F	VF	XF	Unc	BU
2009 P20 Proof	2,009	Value: 125				

KM# 1313   5 DOLLARS
1.5500 g., 0.9990 Gold 0.0498 oz. AGW, 14 mm.   **Ruler:**
Elizabeth II **Subject:** Kookaburra 20th Anniversary **Obv:** Head
right **Rev:** Kookaburra pair on branch, one with head upward

Date	Mintage	F	VF	XF	Unc	BU
2009 P20 Proof	2,009	Value: 125				

KM# 1314   5 DOLLARS
1.5500 g., 0.9990 Gold 0.0498 oz. AGW, 14 mm.   **Ruler:**
Elizabeth II **Subject:** Kookaburra 20th Anniversary **Obv:** Head
right **Rev:** Kookaburra on branch left

Date	Mintage	F	VF	XF	Unc	BU
2009 P20 Proof	2,009	Value: 125				

KM# 1315   5 DOLLARS
1.5500 g., 0.9990 Gold 0.0498 oz. AGW, 14 mm.   **Ruler:**
Elizabeth II **Subject:** Kookaburra 20th Anniversary **Obv:** Head
right **Rev:** Kookaburra on branch admiring spider web

Date	Mintage	F	VF	XF	Unc	BU
2009 P20 Proof	2,009	Value: 125				

KM# 1316   5 DOLLARS
1.5500 g., 0.9990 Gold 0.0498 oz. AGW, 14 mm.   **Ruler:**
Elizabeth II **Subject:** Kookaburra 20th Anniversary **Obv:** Head
right **Rev:** Kookaburra on branch, sunburst in background

Date	Mintage	F	VF	XF	Unc	BU
2009 P20 Proof	2,009	Value: 125				

KM# 603   10 DOLLARS
311.0350 g., 0.9990 Silver 9.9896 oz. ASW, 74.9 mm.   **Ruler:**
Elizabeth II **Subject:** Kookaburra **Obv:** Head with tiara right,
denomination below **Rev:** Flying bird over map **Edge:** Reeded

Date	Mintage	F	VF	XF	Unc	BU
2002 Proof	—	Value: 400				

KM# 891   10 DOLLARS
311.0350 g., 0.9990 Silver 9.9896 oz. ASW, 74.9 mm.   **Ruler:**
Elizabeth II **Obv:** Head with tiara right **Rev:** Kookaburra on
branch, no leaves

Date	Mintage	F	VF	XF	Unc	BU
2007					400	—

KM# 1360   10 DOLLARS
311.0350 g., 0.9990 Silver 9.9896 oz. ASW, 75.5 mm.   **Ruler:**
Elizabeth II **Obv:** Head right **Rev:** Kookaburra

Date	Mintage	F	VF	XF	Unc	BU
2010(p) Proof	—	Value: 425				

KM# 1693   10 DOLLARS
311.0350 g., 0.9990 Silver 9.9896 oz. ASW   **Ruler:** Elizabeth II
Rev: Kookaburra

Date	Mintage	F	VF	XF	Unc	BU
2012P Proof	—	Value: 400				

KM# 630   20 DOLLARS
62.2070 g., 0.9990 Silver 1.9979 oz. ASW   **Ruler:** Elizabeth II
Subject: USA State Quarters - 2002 **Obv:** Head with tiara right,
denomination below **Rev:** Kookaburra on branch with five state
quarter designs added below **Edge:** Reeded and plain sections

Date	Mintage	F	VF	XF	Unc	BU
2002	10,000	—	—	—	82.00	85.00

KM# 680   30 DOLLARS
1002.5020 g., 0.9990 Silver 32.197 oz. ASW, 101 mm.   **Ruler:**
Elizabeth II **Obv:** Head with tiara right, denomination below **Rev:**
Kookaburra in flight above Australian map **Edge:** Segmented
reeding

Date	Mintage	F	VF	XF	Unc	BU
2001P Proof	350	Value: 1,200				
2002	—	—	—	—	—	1,250

KM# 624   30 DOLLARS
1002.5020 g., 0.9990 Silver 32.197 oz. ASW, 101 mm.   **Ruler:**
Elizabeth II **Subject:** USA State Quarters - 2001 **Obv:** Head with
tiara right, denomination below **Rev:** Two kookaburras on branch
with five state quarter designs added below **Edge:** Reeded and
plain sections

Date	Mintage	F	VF	XF	Unc	BU
2001	1,000	—	—	—	—	1,200

KM# 631   30 DOLLARS
1002.5020 g., 0.9990 Silver 32.197 oz. ASW, 101 mm.   **Ruler:**
Elizabeth II **Subject:** USA State Quarters - 2002 **Obv:** Head with
tiara right, denomination below **Rev:** Kookaburra on branch with
five state quarter designs added in gold **Edge:** Reeded and plain
sections

Date	Mintage	F	VF	XF	Unc	BU
2002	1,000	—	—	—	—	1,200

KM# 880   30 DOLLARS
1002.5020 g., 0.9990 Silver 32.197 oz. ASW, 101 mm.   **Ruler:**
Elizabeth II **Obv:** Head with tiara right **Rev:** Kookaburra standing
on branch **Edge:** Reeded

Date	Mintage	F	VF	XF	Unc	BU
2002P Proof	350	Value: 1,250				

KM# 882   30 DOLLARS
1002.5020 g., 0.9990 Silver 32.197 oz. ASW, 101 mm.   **Ruler:**
Elizabeth II **Obv:** Head with tiara right **Rev:** Two kookaburras,
one in flight **Edge:** Reeded

Date	Mintage	F	VF	XF	Unc	BU
2003P Proof	350	Value: 1,250				

KM# 885   30 DOLLARS
1002.5020 g., 0.9990 Silver 32.197 oz. ASW, 101 mm.   **Ruler:**
Elizabeth II **Obv:** Head with tiara right **Rev:** Kookaburra perched
on branch with four leaves **Edge:** Reeded

Date	Mintage	F	VF	XF	Unc	BU
2004P Proof	350	Value: 1,250				

KM# 888   30 DOLLARS
1002.5020 g., 0.9990 Silver 32.197 oz. ASW, 101 mm.   **Ruler:**
Elizabeth II **Obv:** Head with tiara right **Rev:** Two kookaburras on
branch, one laughing **Edge:** Reeded

Date	Mintage	F	VF	XF	Unc	BU
2005P Proof	800	Value: 1,250				

KM# 892   30 DOLLARS
1002.5020 g., 0.9990 Silver 32.197 oz. ASW, 101 mm.   **Ruler:**
Elizabeth II **Obv:** Head with tiara right **Rev:** Kookaburras on
branch, no leaves

Date	Mintage	F	VF	XF	Unc	BU
2007	—	—	—	—	1,200	—

KM# 1115   30 DOLLARS
1000.0000 g., 0.9990 Silver 32.117 oz. ASW, 101 mm.   **Ruler:**
Elizabeth II **Rev:** Kookaburra on branch, sunburst background

Date	Mintage	F	VF	XF	Unc	BU
2009P Proof	—	Value: 1,300				

KM# 1361   30 DOLLARS
1000.0000 g., 0.9990 Silver 32.117 oz. ASW, 100 mm.   **Ruler:**
Elizabeth II **Obv:** Head right **Rev:** Kookaburra **Note:** Illustration
reduced.

Date	Mintage	F	VF	XF	Unc	BU
2010(p)	—	—	—	—	—	1,200

KM# 1694   30 DOLLARS
1000.0000 g., 0.9990 Silver 32.117 oz. ASW   **Ruler:** Elizabeth II
Rev: Kookaburra

Date	Mintage	F	VF	XF	Unc	BU
2012P	—	—	—	—	—	1,200

KM# 878   200 DOLLARS
31.6000 g., 0.9990 Silver 1.0149 oz. ASW, 40 mm.   **Ruler:**
Elizabeth II **Obv:** Head with tiara right with denomination **Rev:**
Kookaburra in flight over map of Australia **Note:** Mule.

Date	Mintage	F	VF	XF	Unc	BU
ND(2001) Proof	Est. 20	Value: 2,500				

BULLION - NUGGET

KM# 692   50 DOLLARS
15.5017 g., 0.9999 Gold 0.4983 oz. AGW, 25.1 mm.   **Ruler:**
Elizabeth II **Subject:** Tribute to Liberty **Obv:** Head with tiara right,
denomination below **Rev:** Two kangaroos on map above silver
Liberty Bell insert **Edge:** Reeded

Date	Mintage	F	VF	XF	Unc	BU
2001	650	—	—	—	875	—
2002	1,498	—	—	—	875	—
2002 Proof	—	Value: 900				

KM# 693   100 DOLLARS
31.1035 g., 0.9999 Gold 0.9999 oz. AGW, 32.1 mm.   **Ruler:**
Elizabeth II **Subject:** Tribute to Liberty **Obv:** Head with tiara right,
denomination below **Rev:** Two kangaroos on map above silver
Liberty Bell insert, colored image **Edge:** Reeded

Date	Mintage	F	VF	XF	Unc	BU
2001	1,498	—	—	—	1,735	—
2002	—	—	—	—	—	1,735

KM# 900   100 DOLLARS
31.1035 g., 0.9999 Gold 0.9999 oz. AGW, 32 mm.   **Ruler:**
Elizabeth II **Obv:** Head with tiara right **Rev:** Prospectors dry-
blowing gold dust, colored image

Date	Mintage	F	VF	XF	Unc	BU
2002	1,500	—	—	—	1,735	—

KM# 906   100 DOLLARS
31.1035 g., 0.9990 Gold 0.9990 oz. AGW, 32 mm.   **Ruler:**
Elizabeth II **Obv:** Head with tiara right **Rev:** Prospectors camp,
colored image

Date	Mintage	F	VF	XF	Unc	BU
2003	1,500	—	—	—	1,735	—

KM# 741   100 DOLLARS
31.1035 g., 0.9999 Gold 0.9999 oz. AGW, 32 mm.   **Ruler:**
Elizabeth II **Subject:** Eureka Stockade **Obv:** Head with tiara right,

denomination below **Rev:** Eureka Stockade leader Peter Lalor
and blue flag, colored image **Edge:** Reeded

Date	Mintage	F	VF	XF	Unc	BU
2004	1,500	—	—	—	1,735	—
2004P Proof	1,500	Value: 1,750				

KM# 915   100 DOLLARS
31.1035 g., 0.9990 Gold 0.9990 oz. AGW, 32 mm.   **Ruler:**
Elizabeth II **Subject:** Welcome Stranger Nugget **Obv:** Head with
tiara right **Rev:** Welcome Stranger Nugget surrounded by
Outback setting, colored image

Date	Mintage	F	VF	XF	Unc	BU
2005	1,500	—	—	—	1,735	—

KM# 914   200 DOLLARS
62.2140 g., 0.9990 Gold 1.9981 oz. AGW, 41 mm.   **Ruler:**
Elizabeth II **Obv:** Head with tiara right **Rev:** Kangaroo in
multicolor bush

Date	Mintage	F	VF	XF	Unc	BU
2005	200	—	—	—	3,500	—

BULLION - KOALA

KM# 1366   50 CENTS
15.5500 g., 0.9990 Silver 0.4994 oz. ASW   **Ruler:** Elizabeth II
Obv: Head right **Rev:** Koala

Date	Mintage	F	VF	XF	Unc	BU
2010(p)	—	—	—	—	—	35.00

KM# 1688   50 CENTS
15.5000 g., 0.9990 Silver 0.4978 oz. ASW, 32 mm.   **Ruler:**
Elizabeth II **Rev:** Koala

Date	Mintage	F	VF	XF	Unc	BU
2012P	—	—	—	—	—	20.00

KM# 1111   DOLLAR
31.1050 g., 0.9990 Silver 0.9990 oz. ASW, 40.6 mm.   **Ruler:**
Elizabeth II **Rev:** Koala seated left on branch, shimmer
background

Date	Mintage	F	VF	XF	Unc	BU
2009P	—	—	—	—	—	40.00

KM# 1111a   DOLLAR
31.1050 g., 0.9999 Silver partially gilt 0.9999 oz. ASW, 40.6 mm.
Ruler: Elizabeth II **Rev:** Koala seated left on branch, gilt

Date	Mintage	F	VF	XF	Unc	BU
2009P Proof	10,000	Value: 60.00				

KM# 1464   DOLLAR
31.1050 g., 0.9990 Silver 0.9990 oz. ASW, 40 mm.   **Ruler:**
Elizabeth II **Rev:** Koala on branch

Date	Mintage	F	VF	XF	Unc	BU
2010P	—	—	—	—	—	40.00

KM# 1464a   DOLLAR
31.1050 g., 0.9999 Silver partially gilt 0.9999 oz. ASW   **Ruler:**
Elizabeth II **Rev:** Koala on branch

Date	Mintage	F	VF	XF	Unc	BU
2010P Proof	—	Value: 60.00				

KM# 1689   DOLLAR
31.1050 g., 0.9990 Silver 0.9990 oz. ASW, 40.5 mm.   **Ruler:**
Elizabeth II **Rev:** Koala

Date	Mintage	F	VF	XF	Unc	BU
2012P	—	—	—	—	—	40.00

KM# 916   5 DOLLARS
1.5710 g., 0.9990 Platinum 0.0505 oz. APW   **Ruler:** Elizabeth II
Obv: Head with tiara right **Rev:** Two koalas on branch

Date	Mintage	F	VF	XF	Unc	BU
2001 Proof	5,000	Value: 125				

KM# 1113   5 DOLLARS
1.2440 g., 0.9999 Gold 0.0400 oz. AGW, 14.1 mm.   **Ruler:**
Elizabeth II **Rev:** Koala seated left on branch

Date	Mintage	F	VF	XF	Unc	BU
2009P Proof	15,000	Value: 95.00				

KM# 1467   5 DOLLARS
1.2400 g., 0.9990 Gold 0.0398 oz. AGW   **Ruler:** Elizabeth II **Rev:**
Koala on branch

Date	Mintage	F	VF	XF	Unc	BU
2010P	—	—	—	—	—	90.00

KM# 1368   10 DOLLARS
311.3500 g., 0.9990 Silver 9.9997 oz. ASW   **Ruler:** Elizabeth II
Obv: Head right **Rev:** Koala

Date	Mintage	F	VF	XF	Unc	BU
2010P	—	—	—	—	—	375

KM# 1690   10 DOLLARS
311.3500 g., 0.9990 Silver 9.9997 oz. ASW   **Ruler:** Elizabeth II
Rev: Koala

Date	Mintage	F	VF	XF	Unc	BU
2012P	—	—	—	—	—	400

KM# 917   15 DOLLARS
3.1101 g., 0.9990 Platinum 0.0999 oz. APW   **Ruler:** Elizabeth II
Obv: Head with tiara right **Rev:** Two koalas on a branch

Date	Mintage	F	VF	XF	Unc	BU
2001 Proof	650	Value: 210				

KM# 922   15 DOLLARS
3.1101 g., 0.9990 Platinum 0.0999 oz. APW   **Ruler:** Elizabeth II
Obv: Head with tiara right **Rev:** Koala up a gum tree

Date	Mintage	F	VF	XF	Unc	BU
2002 Proof	650	Value: 210				

KM# 926   15 DOLLARS
3.1101 g., 0.9990 Platinum 0.0999 oz. APW **Ruler:** Elizabeth II
Obv: Head with tiara right **Rev:** Mother and baby koala

Date	Mintage	F	VF	XF	Unc	BU
2003 Proof	500	Value: 210				

KM# 931   15 DOLLARS
3.1101 g., 0.9990 Platinum 0.0999 oz. APW **Ruler:** Elizabeth II
Obv: Head with tiara right **Rev:** Single koala on branch

Date	Mintage	F	VF	XF	Unc	BU
2004 Proof	500	Value: 210				

KM# 935   15 DOLLARS
3.1101 g., 0.9990 Platinum 0.0999 oz. APW **Ruler:** Elizabeth II
Obv: Head with tiara right **Rev:** Single koala with gum leaves

Date	Mintage	F	VF	XF	Unc	BU
2005 Proof	500	Value: 210				

KM# 1114   15 DOLLARS
3.1080 g., 0.9999 Gold 0.0999 oz. AGW, 16.1 mm. **Ruler:**
Elizabeth II **Rev:** Koala seated left on tree branch

Date	Mintage	F	VF	XF	Unc	BU
2009P Proof	5,000	Value: 190				

KM# 1468   15 DOLLARS
3.1101 g., 0.9990 Gold 0.0999 oz. AGW **Ruler:** Elizabeth II **Rev:**
Koala on branch

Date	Mintage	F	VF	XF	Unc	BU
2010P	—	—	—	—	—	190

KM# 918   25 DOLLARS
7.7508 g., 0.9990 Platinum 0.2489 oz. APW **Ruler:** Elizabeth II
Obv: Head with tiara right **Rev:** Two koalas on a branch

Date	Mintage	F	VF	XF	Unc	BU
2001 Proof	275	Value: 485				

KM# 923   25 DOLLARS
7.7508 g., 0.9990 Platinum 0.2489 oz. APW **Ruler:** Elizabeth II
Obv: Head with tiara right **Rev:** Koala up a gum tree

Date	Mintage	F	VF	XF	Unc	BU
2002 Proof	275	Value: 485				

KM# 927   25 DOLLARS
7.7508 g., 0.9990 Platinum 0.2489 oz. APW **Ruler:** Elizabeth II
Obv: Head with tiara right **Rev:** Mother and baby koala

Date	Mintage	F	VF	XF	Unc	BU
2003 Proof	200	Value: 485				

KM# 932   25 DOLLARS
7.7508 g., 0.9990 Platinum 0.2489 oz. APW **Ruler:** Elizabeth II
Obv: Head with tiara right **Rev:** Single koala on branch

Date	Mintage	F	VF	XF	Unc	BU
2004 Proof	200	Value: 485				

KM# 936   25 DOLLARS
7.7508 g., 0.9990 Platinum 0.2489 oz. APW **Ruler:** Elizabeth II
Obv: Head with tiara right **Rev:** Single koala with gum leaves

Date	Mintage	F	VF	XF	Unc	BU
2005 Proof	200	Value: 485				

KM# 1112   30 DOLLARS
1000.0000 g., 0.9999 Silver 32.146 oz. ASW, 100.6 mm. **Ruler:**
Elizabeth II **Rev:** Koala seated left on tree branch

Date	Mintage	F	VF	XF	Unc	BU
2009P Prooflike	—	—	—	—	—	1,150

KM# 1369   30 DOLLARS
1000.0000 g., 0.9990 Silver 32.117 oz. ASW, 100.6 mm. **Ruler:**
Elizabeth II **Obv:** Head light **Rev:** Koala

Date	Mintage	F	VF	XF	Unc	BU
2010(p)	—	—	—	—	—	1,150

KM# 1466   30 DOLLARS
1000.0000 g., 0.9990 Silver 32.117 oz. ASW, 100.6 mm. **Ruler:**
Elizabeth II **Rev:** Koala on branch

Date	Mintage	F	VF	XF	Unc	BU
2010P	—	—	—	—	1,200	

KM# 1691   30 DOLLARS
1000.0000 g., 0.9990 Silver 32.117 oz. ASW, 100.6 mm. **Ruler:**
Elizabeth II **Rev:** Koala

Date	Mintage	F	VF	XF	Unc	BU
2012P	—	—	—	—	1,200	

KM# 919   50 DOLLARS
15.5017 g., 0.9990 Platinum 0.4979 oz. APW **Ruler:** Elizabeth II
Obv: Head with tiara right **Rev:** Two koalas on a branch

Date	Mintage	F	VF	XF	Unc	BU
2001 Proof	350	Value: 960				

KM# 924   50 DOLLARS
15.5017 g., 0.9990 Platinum 0.4979 oz. APW **Ruler:** Elizabeth II
Obv: Head with tiara right **Rev:** Koala up a gum tree

Date	Mintage	F	VF	XF	Unc	BU
2002 Proof	350	Value: 960				

KM# 928   50 DOLLARS
15.5017 g., 0.9990 Platinum 0.4979 oz. APW **Ruler:** Elizabeth II
Obv: Head with tiara right **Rev:** Mother and baby koala

Date	Mintage	F	VF	XF	Unc	BU
2003 Proof	350	Value: 960				

KM# 933   50 DOLLARS
15.5017 g., 0.9990 Platinum 0.4979 oz. APW **Ruler:** Elizabeth II
Obv: Head with tiara right **Rev:** Single koala on branch

Date	Mintage	F	VF	XF	Unc	BU
2004 Proof	350	Value: 960				

KM# 937   50 DOLLARS
15.5017 g., 0.9990 Platinum 0.4979 oz. APW **Ruler:** Elizabeth II
Obv: Head with tiara right **Rev:** Single koala with gum leaves

Date	Mintage	F	VF	XF	Unc	BU
2005 Proof	350	Value: 960				

KM# 921   100 DOLLARS
31.1035 g., 0.9990 Platinum 0.9990 oz. APW **Ruler:** Elizabeth II
Obv: Head with tiara right **Rev:** Federation: Sir Henry Parkes,
flag, parliament house, colored image

Date	Mintage	F	VF	XF	Unc	BU
2001 Proof	1,000	Value: 1,875				

KM# 930   100 DOLLARS
31.1035 g., 0.9990 Platinum 0.9990 oz. APW **Ruler:** Elizabeth II
Obv: Head with tiara right **Rev:** The Arts: Dancers, paint brushes,
opera house, colored image

Date	Mintage	F	VF	XF	Unc	BU
2003 Proof	1,000	Value: 1,875				

KM# 742   100 DOLLARS
31.1035 g., 0.9995 Platinum 0.9995 oz. APW, 32.1 mm. **Ruler:**
Elizabeth II **Obv:** Head with tiara right, denomination below **Rev:**
Sports: Australian sportsmen and women, colored image **Edge:**
Reeded

Date	Mintage	F	VF	XF	Unc	BU
2004P Proof	1,000	Value: 1,875				

KM# 939   100 DOLLARS
31.1035 g., 0.9990 Platinum 0.9990 oz. APW **Ruler:** Elizabeth II
Obv: Head with tiara right **Rev:** Two workers and machine,
colored image

Date	Mintage	F	VF	XF	Unc	BU
2005 Proof	1,000	Value: 1,875				

KM# 1469   100 DOLLARS
31.1050 g., 0.9990 Gold 0.9990 oz. AGW, 32.1 mm. **Ruler:**
Elizabeth II **Rev:** Koala on branch

Date	Mintage	F	VF	XF	Unc	BU
2010P	—	—	—	—	1,500	

KM# 1608   100 DOLLARS
31.1050 g., 0.9990 Gold 0.9990 oz. AGW, 28 mm. **Ruler:**
Elizabeth II **Obv:** Head with tiara right **Rev:** Two pandas seated
in fork of a eucalyptus tree **Edge:** Reeded **Note:** Ultra High Relief

Date	Mintage	F	VF	XF	Unc	BU
2011P Proof	2,000	Value: 1,950				

KM# 920   200 DOLLARS
62.2140 g., 0.9990 Platinum 1.9981 oz. APW **Ruler:** Elizabeth II
Obv: Head with tiara right **Rev:** Two koalas sitting on branch

Date	Mintage	F	VF	XF	Unc	BU
2001	250	Value: 3,700				

KM# 925   200 DOLLARS
62.2140 g., 0.9990 Platinum 1.9981 oz. APW **Ruler:** Elizabeth II
Obv: Head with tiara right **Rev:** Koala up a gum tree

Date	Mintage	F	VF	XF	Unc	BU
2002 Proof	250	Value: 3,700				

KM# 929   200 DOLLARS
62.2140 g., 0.9990 Platinum 1.9981 oz. APW **Ruler:** Elizabeth II
Obv: Head with tiara right **Rev:** Mother and baby koala

Date	Mintage	F	VF	XF	Unc	BU
2003 Proof	200	Value: 3,700				

KM# 934   200 DOLLARS
62.2140 g., 0.9990 Platinum 1.9981 oz. APW **Ruler:** Elizabeth II
Obv: Head with tiara right **Rev:** Single koala on branch

Date	Mintage	F	VF	XF	Unc	BU
2004 Proof	200	Value: 3,700				

KM# 938   200 DOLLARS
62.2140 g., 0.9990 Platinum 1.9981 oz. APW **Ruler:** Elizabeth II
Obv: Head with tiara right **Rev:** Single koala with multicolor gum
leaves

Date	Mintage	F	VF	XF	Unc	BU
2005 Proof	200	Value: 3,700				

KM# 1470   200 DOLLARS
62.2400 g., 0.9990 Gold 1.9990 oz. AGW **Ruler:** Elizabeth II
Rev: Koala on branch

Date	Mintage	F	VF	XF	Unc	BU
2010P	—	—	—	—	—	3,450

BULLION - DISCOVER AUSTRALIA

KM# 940 DOLLAR
31.1035 g., 0.9990 Silver 0.9990 oz. ASW **Ruler:** Elizabeth II **Subject:** Australian Landmarks **Obv:** Head with tiara right **Rev:** Melbourne

Date	Mintage	F	VF	XF	Unc	BU
2006 Proof	7,500	Value: 50.00				

KM# 941 DOLLAR
31.1035 g., 0.9990 Silver 0.9990 oz. ASW **Ruler:** Elizabeth II **Subject:** Australian Landmarks **Obv:** Head with tiara right **Rev:** Uluru

Date	Mintage	F	VF	XF	Unc	BU
2006 Proof	7,500	Value: 50.00				

KM# 942 DOLLAR
31.1035 g., 0.9990 Silver 0.9990 oz. ASW **Ruler:** Elizabeth II **Subject:** Australian Landmarks **Obv:** Head with tiara right **Rev:** Canberra

Date	Mintage	F	VF	XF	Unc	BU
2006 Proof	7,500	Value: 50.00				

KM# 943 DOLLAR
31.1035 g., 0.9990 Silver 0.9990 oz. ASW, 40.6 mm. **Ruler:** Elizabeth II **Subject:** Australian Landmarks **Obv:** Head with tiara right **Rev:** Perth

Date	Mintage	F	VF	XF	Unc	BU
2006 Proof	7,500	Value: 50.00				

KM# 944 DOLLAR
31.1035 g., 0.9990 Silver 0.9990 oz. ASW **Ruler:** Elizabeth II **Subject:** Australian Landmarks **Obv:** Head with tiara right **Rev:** Great Barrier Reef

Date	Mintage	F	VF	XF	Unc	BU
2006 Proof	7,500	Value: 50.00				

KM# 949 DOLLAR
31.1035 g., 0.9990 Silver 0.9990 oz. ASW **Ruler:** Elizabeth II **Subject:** Australian Landmarks **Obv:** Head with tiara right **Rev:** Sydney

Date	Mintage	F	VF	XF	Unc	BU
2007	7,500	Value: 60.00				

KM# 945 DOLLAR
31.1035 g., 0.9990 Silver 0.9990 oz. ASW **Ruler:** Elizabeth II **Subject:** Australian Landmarks **Obv:** Head with tiara right **Rev:** Gold Coast

Date	Mintage	F	VF	XF	Unc	BU
2007 Proof	7,500	Value: 60.00				

KM# 946 DOLLAR
31.1035 g., 0.9990 Silver 0.9990 oz. ASW **Ruler:** Elizabeth II **Subject:** Australian Landmarks **Obv:** Head with tiara right **Rev:** Phillip Island

Date	Mintage	F	VF	XF	Unc	BU
2007 Proof	7,500	Value: 60.00				

KM# 947 DOLLAR
31.1035 g., 0.9990 Silver 0.9990 oz. ASW **Ruler:** Elizabeth II

Subject: Australian Landmarks **Obv:** Head with tiara right **Rev:** Port Arthur

Date	Mintage	F	VF	XF	Unc	BU
2007 Proof	7,500	Value: 60.00				

KM# 948 DOLLAR
31.1035 g., 0.9990 Silver 0.9990 oz. ASW **Ruler:** Elizabeth II **Subject:** Australian Landmarks **Obv:** Head with tiara right **Rev:** Adelaide

Date	Mintage	F	VF	XF	Unc	BU
2007 Proof	7,500	Value: 60.00				

KM# 1021 DOLLAR
31.1050 g., 0.9990 Silver 0.9990 oz. ASW, 40 mm. **Ruler:** Elizabeth II **Subject:** Hobart **Rev:** Buildings and harbor **Rev. Legend:** DISCOVER AUSTRALIA

Date	Mintage	F	VF	XF	Unc	BU
2008P Proof	7,500	Value: 80.00				

KM# 1181 DOLLAR
31.1050 g., 0.9990 Silver 0.9990 oz. ASW, 40 mm. **Ruler:** Elizabeth II **Subject:** Darwin **Obv:** Head right **Rev:** Harbor, multicolor **Rev. Legend:** DISCOVER AUSTRALIA

Date	Mintage	F	VF	XF	Unc	BU
2008P Proof	7,500	Value: 80.00				

KM# 1182 DOLLAR
31.1050 g., 0.9990 Silver 0.9990 oz. ASW, 40 mm. **Ruler:** Elizabeth II **Subject:** Kakadu **Obv:** Head right **Rev:** Crocodile, multicolor **Rev. Legend:** DISCOVER AUSTRALIA

Date	Mintage	F	VF	XF	Unc	BU
2008P Proof	7,500	Value: 80.00				

KM# 1183   DOLLAR
31.1050 g., 0.9990 Silver 0.9990 oz. ASW   **Ruler:** Elizabeth II
Subject: Brisbane **Obv:** Head right **Rev:** Bridge and view **Rev.**
Legend: DISCOVER AUSTRALIA

Date	Mintage	F	VF	XF	Unc	BU
2008P Proof	7,500	Value: 80.00				

KM# 1184   DOLLAR
31.1050 g., 0.9990 Silver 0.9990 oz. ASW   **Ruler:** Elizabeth II
Subject: Broome **Obv:** Head right **Rev:** Seascape, pearls,
multicolor **Rev. Legend:** DISCOVER AUSTRALIA

Date	Mintage	F	VF	XF	Unc	BU
2008P Proof	7,500	Value: 80.00				

KM# 1185   DOLLAR
31.1050 g., 0.9990 Silver 0.9990 oz. ASW   **Ruler:** Elizabeth II
Subject: Sydney **Obv:** Head right **Rev:** Opera House, Harbor
Bridge, multicolor **Rev. Legend:** DISCOVER AUSTRALIA

Date	Mintage	F	VF	XF	Unc	BU
2008P Proof	7,500	Value: 80.00				

KM# 1188   DOLLAR
1.2400 g., 0.9990 Gold 0.0398 oz. AGW, 14 mm.   **Ruler:**
Elizabeth II **Obv:** Head right **Rev:** Brolga **Rev. Legend:**
DISCOVER AUSTRALIA

Date	Mintage	F	VF	XF	Unc	BU
2008P Proof	25,000	Value: 100				

KM# 1103   DOLLAR
31.1050 g., 0.9990 Silver 0.9990 oz. ASW, 27x47 mm.   **Ruler:**
Elizabeth II **Rev:** Turtle Dreaming **Shape:** Rectangle

Date	Mintage	F	VF	XF	Unc	BU
2009 Proof	—	Value: 75.00				

KM# 1107   DOLLAR
31.1050 g., 0.9999 Silver 0.9999 oz. ASW, 27x47 mm.   **Ruler:**
Elizabeth II **Rev:** Kangaroo dreaming **Shape:** Vertical rectangle

Date	Mintage	F	VF	XF	Unc	BU
2009 Proof	—	Value: 75.00				

KM# 1212   DOLLAR
31.1050 g., 0.9990 Silver 0.9990 oz. ASW, 40.6 mm.   **Ruler:**
Elizabeth II **Obv:** Head right **Rev:** Dreaming kangaroo, multicolor
Rev. Legend: DISCOVER AUSTRALIA

Date	Mintage	F	VF	XF	Unc	BU
2009P Proof	10,000	Value: 90.00				

KM# 1213   DOLLAR
31.1050 g., 0.9990 Silver 0.9990 oz. ASW   **Ruler:** Elizabeth II
Obv: Head right **Rev:** Dreaming dolphin, multicolor **Rev. Legend:**
DISCOVER AUSTRALIA **Shape:** 40.6

Date	Mintage	F	VF	XF	Unc	BU
2009P Proof	10,000	Value: 90.00				

KM# 1214   DOLLAR
31.1050 g., 0.9990 Silver 0.9990 oz. ASW, 40.6 mm.   **Ruler:**
Elizabeth II **Obv:** Head right **Rev:** Dreaming king brown snake,
multicolor **Rev. Legend:** DISCOVER AUSTRALIA

Date	Mintage	F	VF	XF	Unc	BU
2009P Proof	10,000	Value: 90.00				

KM# 1215   DOLLAR
31.1050 g., 0.9990 Silver 0.9990 oz. ASW, 40.6 mm.   **Ruler:**
Elizabeth II **Obv:** Head right **Rev:** Dreaming brolga, multicolor

Date	Mintage	F	VF	XF	Unc	BU
2009P Proof	10,000	Value: 90.00				

KM# 1216   DOLLAR
31.1050 g., 0.9990 Silver 0.9990 oz. ASW, 40.6 mm.   **Ruler:**
Elizabeth II **Obv:** Head right **Rev:** Dreaming echidna, multicolor

Date	Mintage	F	VF	XF	Unc	BU
2009P Proof	10,000	Value: 90.00				

KM# 1218   DOLLAR
1.2500 g., 0.9990 Gold 0.0401 oz. AGW, 14 mm.   **Ruler:**
Elizabeth II **Obv:** Head right **Rev:** Dreaming dolphin

Date	Mintage	F	VF	XF	Unc	BU
2009P Proof	25,000	Value: 125				

KM# 1222   DOLLAR
3.1100 g., 0.9990 Gold 0.0999 oz. AGW, 16 mm.   **Ruler:**
Elizabeth II **Obv:** Head right **Rev:** Dreaming kangaroo

Date	Mintage	F	VF	XF	Unc	BU
2009P Proof	2,500	Value: 175				

KM# 1242   DOLLAR
31.1050 g., 0.9990 Silver 0.9990 oz. ASW, 40.6 mm.   **Ruler:**
Elizabeth II **Subject:** Treasures of Australia **Obv:** Head right **Rev:**
Mountains **Note:** Insert container with 1 carat of diamonds.

Date	Mintage	F	VF	XF	Unc	BU
2009P Proof	7,500	Value: 110				

KM# 1403   DOLLAR
31.1050 g., 0.9990 Silver 0.9990 oz. ASW, 40.6 mm.   **Ruler:**
Elizabeth II **Obv:** Head right **Rev:** Frill-neck lizard, multicolor

Date	Mintage	F	VF	XF	Unc	BU
2010(p) Proof	—	Value: 90.00				

KM# 1409   DOLLAR
31.1050 g., 0.9990 Silver 0.9990 oz. ASW, 40.6 mm.   **Ruler:**
Elizabeth II **Obv:** Head right **Rev:** Koala and multicolor

Date	Mintage	F	VF	XF	Unc	BU
2010(p) Proof	—	Value: 90.00				

KM# 1415   DOLLAR
31.1050 g., 0.9990 Silver 0.9990 oz. ASW, 40.6 mm.   **Ruler:**
Elizabeth II **Obv:** Head right **Rev:** Multicolor platypus

Date	Mintage	F	VF	XF	Unc	BU
2010(p) Proof	—	Value: 90.00				

KM# 1421   DOLLAR
31.1050 g., 0.9990 Silver 0.9990 oz. ASW, 40.6 mm.   **Ruler:**
Elizabeth II **Obv:** Head right **Rev:** Multicolor salt water crocodile

Date	Mintage	F	VF	XF	Unc	BU
2010(p) Proof	—	Value: 90.00				

KM# 1427   DOLLAR
31.1050 g., 0.9990 Silver 0.9990 oz. ASW, 40.6 mm.   **Ruler:**
Elizabeth II **Obv:** Head right **Rev:** Multicolor wombat

Date	Mintage	F	VF	XF	Unc	BU
2010(p) Proof	—	Value: 90.00				

KM# 1453   DOLLAR
31.1050 g., 0.9990 Silver 0.9990 oz. ASW, 27x47 mm.   **Ruler:**
Elizabeth II **Rev:** Dreaming dolphin **Shape:** Vertical rectangle

Date	Mintage	F	VF	XF	Unc	BU
2010P Proof	—	—	—	—	—	80.00

KM# 1534   DOLLAR
31.1050 g., 0.9990 Silver 0.9990 oz. ASW   **Ruler:** Elizabeth II
Subject: Dreaming Emu **Rev:** Linear emu in color

Date	Mintage	F	VF	XF	Unc	BU
2011P Proof	—	Value: 105				

KM# 1540   DOLLAR
31.1050 g., 0.9990 Silver 0.9990 oz. ASW   **Ruler:** Elizabeth II
Subject: Dreaming Tasmanian Devil **Rev:** Linear tasmanian
devil in color

Date	Mintage	F	VF	XF	Unc	BU
2011P Proof	—	Value: 105				

KM# 1546   DOLLAR
31.1050 g., 0.9990 Silver 0.9990 oz. ASW   **Ruler:** Elizabeth II
Rev: Linear Kookaburra in color

Date	Mintage	F	VF	XF	Unc	BU
2011P Proof	—					

KM# 1552   DOLLAR
31.1050 g., 0.9990 Silver 0.9990 oz. ASW   **Ruler:** Elizabeth II
Subject: Dreaming Shark **Rev:** Linear shark in color

Date	Mintage	F	VF	XF	Unc	BU
2011P Proof	—	Value: 105				

KM# 1558 DOLLAR
31.1050 g., 0.9990 Silver 0.9990 oz. ASW. **Ruler:** Elizabeth II
Subject: Dreaming Dingo **Rev:** Linear dingo in color

Date	Mintage	F	VF	XF	Unc	BU
2011P Proof	—				Value: 105	

KM# 1609 DOLLAR
31.1050 g., 0.9990 Silver 0.9990 oz. ASW, 27x47 mm. **Ruler:**
Elizabeth II **Obv:** Head with tiara right **Rev:** Dearming Platypus
Shape: Vertical rectangle

Date	Mintage	F	VF	XF	Unc	BU
2011P	—	—	—	—	—	80.00

KM# 1706 DOLLAR
31.1350 g., Silver, 40.6 mm. **Ruler:** Elizabeth II **Obv:** Head with
tiara right **Rev:** Green gold bellfrog, background in color **Edge:**
Reeded

Date	Mintage	F	VF	XF	Unc	BU
2012P Proof	7,500				Value: 100	

KM# 1707 DOLLAR
31.1350 g., 0.9990 Silver 1.0000 oz. ASW, 40.6 mm. **Ruler:**
Elizabeth II **Obv:** Head with tiara right **Rev:** Red kangaroo and
color background

Date	Mintage	F	VF	XF	Unc	BU
2012P Proof	7,500				Value: 100	

KM# 1708 DOLLAR
31.1350 g., 0.9990 Silver 1.0000 oz. ASW, 40.6 mm. **Ruler:**
Elizabeth II **Obv:** Head with tiara right **Rev:** Kookaburra with color
background

Date	Mintage	F	VF	XF	Unc	BU
2012P Proof	7,500				Value: 100	

KM# 1709 DOLLAR
31.1350 g., 0.9990 Silver 1.0000 oz. ASW, 40.6 mm. **Ruler:**
Elizabeth II **Obv:** Head with tiara right **Rev:** Goanna on color
background

Date	Mintage	F	VF	XF	Unc	BU
2012P Proof	7,500				Value: 100	

KM# 1710 DOLLAR
31.1350 g., 0.9990 Silver 1.0000 oz. ASW, 40.6 mm. **Ruler:**
Elizabeth II **Obv:** Head with tiara right **Rev:** Whale shark on color
background

Date	Mintage	F	VF	XF	Unc	BU
2012P Proof	—				Value: 100	

KM# 950 5 DOLLARS
1.2441 g., 0.9990 Gold 0.0400 oz. AGW **Ruler:** Elizabeth II
Subject: Australian Fauna **Obv:** Head with tiara right **Rev:** Salt
water crocodile

Date	Mintage	F	VF	XF	Unc	BU
2006 Proof	25,000				Value: 100	

KM# 953 5 DOLLARS
1.2441 g., 0.9990 Gold 0.0400 oz. AGW **Ruler:** Elizabeth II
Subject: Australian Fauna **Obv:** Head with tiara right **Rev:** Grey
kangaroo

Date	Mintage	F	VF	XF	Unc	BU
2006 Proof	25,000				Value: 100	

KM# 956 5 DOLLARS
1.2441 g., 0.9990 Gold 0.0400 oz. AGW **Ruler:** Elizabeth II
Subject: Australian Fauna **Obv:** Head with tiara right **Rev:** Emu

Date	Mintage	F	VF	XF	Unc	BU
2006 Proof	25,000				Value: 85.00	

KM# 959 5 DOLLARS
1.2441 g., 0.9990 Gold 0.0400 oz. AGW **Ruler:** Elizabeth II
Subject: Australian Fauna **Obv:** Head with tiara right **Rev:** Koala

Date	Mintage	F	VF	XF	Unc	BU
2006 Proof	25,000				Value: 100	

KM# 962 5 DOLLARS
1.2441 g., 0.9990 Gold 0.0400 oz. AGW **Ruler:** Elizabeth II
Subject: Australian Fauna **Obv:** Head with tiara right **Rev:**
Kookaburra

Date	Mintage	F	VF	XF	Unc	BU
2006 Proof	25,000				Value: 100	

KM# 965 5 DOLLARS
1.2441 g., 0.9990 Gold 0.0400 oz. AGW **Ruler:** Elizabeth II
Subject: Australian Fauna **Obv:** Head with tiara right **Rev:**
Echidna

Date	Mintage	F	VF	XF	Unc	BU
2007 Proof	25,000				Value: 100	

KM# 968 5 DOLLARS
1.2441 g., 0.9990 Gold 0.0400 oz. AGW **Ruler:** Elizabeth II
Subject: Australian Fauna **Obv:** Head with tiara right **Rev:**
Common wombat

Date	Mintage	F	VF	XF	Unc	BU
2007 Proof	25,000				Value: 100	

KM# 971 5 DOLLARS
1.2441 g., 0.9990 Gold 0.0400 oz. AGW **Ruler:** Elizabeth II
Subject: Australian Fauna **Obv:** Head with tiara right **Rev:**
Tasmanian devil

Date	Mintage	F	VF	XF	Unc	BU
2007 Proof	25,000				Value: 95.00	

KM# 974 5 DOLLARS
1.2441 g., 0.9990 Gold 0.0400 oz. AGW **Ruler:** Elizabeth II
Subject: Australian Fauna **Obv:** Head with tiara right **Rev:** Great
white shark

Date	Mintage	F	VF	XF	Unc	BU
2007 Proof	25,000				Value: 100	

KM# 977 5 DOLLARS
1.2441 g., 0.9990 Gold 0.0400 oz. AGW **Ruler:** Elizabeth II
Subject: Australian Fauna **Obv:** Head with tiara right **Rev:**
Platypus

Date	Mintage	F	VF	XF	Unc	BU
2007 Proof	25,000				Value: 100	

KM# 1217 5 DOLLARS
1.2500 g., 0.9990 Gold 0.0401 oz. AGW, 14 mm. **Ruler:**
Elizabeth II **Obv:** Head right **Rev:** Dreaming kangaroo

Date	Mintage	F	VF	XF	Unc	BU
2009P Proof	25,000				Value: 125	

KM# 1219 5 DOLLARS
1.2500 g., 0.9990 Gold 0.0401 oz. AGW, 14 mm. **Ruler:**
Elizabeth II **Obv:** Head right **Rev:** Dreaming king brown snake

Date	Mintage	F	VF	XF	Unc	BU
2009P Proof	25,000				Value: 125	

KM# 1220 5 DOLLARS
1.2500 g., 0.9990 Gold 0.0401 oz. AGW, 14 mm. **Ruler:**
Elizabeth II **Obv:** Head right **Rev:** Dreaming brolga

Date	Mintage	F	VF	XF	Unc	BU
2009P Proof	25,000				Value: 125	

KM# 1221 5 DOLLARS
1.2500 g., 0.9990 Gold 0.0401 oz. AGW, 14 mm. **Ruler:**
Elizabeth II **Obv:** Head right **Rev:** Dreaming echidna

Date	Mintage	F	VF	XF	Unc	BU
2009P Proof	25,000				Value: 125	

KM# 1224 5 DOLLARS
3.1100 g., 0.9990 Gold 0.0999 oz. AGW, 14 mm. **Ruler:**
Elizabeth II **Obv:** Head right **Rev:** Dreaming brown snake

Date	Mintage	F	VF	XF	Unc	BU
2009P Proof	2,500				Value: 175	

KM# 1402 5 DOLLARS
1.2400 g., 0.9990 Gold 0.0398 oz. AGW, 14 mm. **Ruler:**
Elizabeth II **Obv:** Head right **Rev:** Frill-neck lizard

Date	Mintage	F	VF	XF	Unc	BU
2010P Proof	25,000				Value: 130	

KM# 1408 5 DOLLARS
1.2400 g., 0.9990 Gold 0.0398 oz. AGW, 14 mm. **Ruler:**
Elizabeth II **Obv:** Head right **Rev:** Koala

Date	Mintage	F	VF	XF	Unc	BU
2010P Proof	25,000				Value: 130	

KM# 1414 5 DOLLARS
1.2400 g., 0.9990 Gold 0.0398 oz. AGW, 14 mm. **Ruler:**
Elizabeth II **Obv:** Head right **Rev:** Platypus

Date	Mintage	F	VF	XF	Unc	BU
2010P Proof	25,000				Value: 130	

KM# 1420 5 DOLLARS
1.2400 g., 0.9990 Gold 0.0398 oz. AGW, 14 mm. **Ruler:**
Elizabeth II **Obv:** Head right **Rev:** Salt water crocodile

Date	Mintage	F	VF	XF	Unc	BU
2010P Proof	25,000				Value: 130	

KM# 1426 5 DOLLARS
1.2400 g., 0.9990 Gold 0.0398 oz. AGW, 14 mm. **Ruler:**
Elizabeth II **Obv:** Head right **Rev:** Wombat

Date	Mintage	F	VF	XF	Unc	BU
2010P Proof	25,000				Value: 130	

KM# 1535 5 DOLLARS
1.2400 g., 0.9990 Gold 0.0398 oz. AGW **Ruler:** Elizabeth II
Subject: Dreaming Emu **Rev:** Linear emu in color

Date	Mintage	F	VF	XF	Unc	BU
2011P Proof	25,000				Value: 125	

KM# 1541 5 DOLLARS
1.2400 g., 0.9990 Gold 0.0398 oz. AGW **Ruler:** Elizabeth II
Subject: Dreaming Tasmanian Devil **Rev:** Linear tasmanian
devil in color

Date	Mintage	F	VF	XF	Unc	BU
2011P Proof	25,000				Value: 125	

KM# 1547 5 DOLLARS
1.2400 g., 0.9990 Gold 0.0398 oz. AGW **Ruler:** Elizabeth II
Obv: Dreaming Kookaburra **Edge:** L:inear Kookaburra in color

Date	Mintage	F	VF	XF	Unc	BU
2011P Proof	250,000				Value: 125	

KM# 1553 5 DOLLARS
1.2400 g., 0.9990 Gold 0.0398 oz. AGW **Ruler:** Elizabeth II
Subject: Dreaming shark **Rev:** Linear shark in color

Date	Mintage	F	VF	XF	Unc	BU
2011P Proof	25,000				Value: 125	

KM# 1559 5 DOLLARS
1.2400 g., 0.9990 Gold 0.0398 oz. AGW **Ruler:** Elizabeth II
Subject: Dreaming Dingo **Rev:** Linear dingo in color

Date	Mintage	F	VF	XF	Unc	BU
2011P Proof	25,000				Value: 125	

KM# 1636 5 DOLLARS
1.2400 g., 0.9990 Gold 0.0398 oz. AGW, 14 mm. **Ruler:**
Elizabeth II **Subject:** Historic Convict Past - Hyde Park Barracks

Date	Mintage	F	VF	XF	Unc	BU
2011 Proof	3,000				Value: 125	

KM# 1716 5 DOLLARS
1.2440 g., 0.9990 Gold 0.0400 oz. AGW, 14.6 mm. **Ruler:**
Elizabeth II **Rev:** Green and Gold Bell Frog in greass

Date	Mintage	F	VF	XF	Unc	BU
2012P Proof	2,500				Value: 100	

KM# 1717 5 DOLLARS
1.2440 g., 0.9990 Gold 0.0400 oz. AGW, 14.6 mm. **Ruler:**
Elizabeth II **Rev:** Kookaburra facing right

Date	Mintage	F	VF	XF	Unc	BU
2012P Proof	2,500				Value: 100	

KM# 1718 5 DOLLARS
1.2440 g., 0.9990 Gold 0.0400 oz. AGW, 14.1 mm. **Ruler:**
Elizabeth II **Rev:** Whale shark swimming right

Date	Mintage	F	VF	XF	Unc	BU
2012P Proof	2,500				Value: 100	

KM# 1719 5 DOLLARS
1.2440 g., 0.9990 Gold 0.0400 oz. AGW, 14.6 mm. **Ruler:**
Elizabeth II **Rev:** Kangaroo bounding right

Date	Mintage	F	VF	XF	Unc	BU
2012P Proof	2,500				Value: 100	

KM# 1720 5 DOLLARS
1.2440 g., 0.9990 Gold 0.0400 oz. AGW, 14.6 mm. **Ruler:**
Elizabeth II **Rev:** Goanna lizard right

Date	Mintage	F	VF	XF	Unc	BU
2012P Proof	2,500				Value: 100	

KM# 1118 10 DOLLARS
1.2400 g., 0.9990 Gold 0.0398 oz. AGW, 14 mm. **Ruler:**
Elizabeth II **Obv:** Bust right **Rev:** Salt water crocodile **Rev.
Legend:** DISCOVER AUSTRALIA

Date	Mintage	F	VF	XF	Unc	BU
2006P Proof	25,000				Value: 110	

KM# 1119 10 DOLLARS
1.2400 g., 0.9990 Gold 0.0398 oz. AGW, 14 mm. **Ruler:**
Elizabeth II **Obv:** Head right **Rev:** Grey kangaroo **Rev. Legend:**
DISCOVER AUSTRALIA

Date	Mintage	F	VF	XF	Unc	BU
2006P Proof	25,000				Value: 110	

KM# 1120 10 DOLLARS
1.2400 g., 0.9990 Gold 0.0398 oz. AGW, 14 mm. **Ruler:**
Elizabeth II **Obv:** Head right **Rev:** Emu **Rev. Legend:**
DISCOVER AUSTRALIA

Date	Mintage	F	VF	XF	Unc	BU
2006P Proof	25,000				Value: 110	

KM# 1121 10 DOLLARS
1.2400 g., 0.9990 Gold 0.0398 oz. AGW, 14 mm. **Ruler:**
Elizabeth II **Obv:** Head right **Rev:** Koala **Rev. Legend:**
DISCOVER AUSTRALIA

Date	Mintage	F	VF	XF	Unc	BU
2006P Proof	25,000				Value: 110	

KM# 1122 10 DOLLARS
1.2400 g., 0.9990 Gold 0.0398 oz. AGW, 14 mm. **Ruler:**
Elizabeth II **Obv:** Head right **Rev:** Kookaburra **Rev. Legend:**
DISCOVER AUSTRALIA

Date	Mintage	F	VF	XF	Unc	BU
2006P Proof	25,000				Value: 110	

KM# 1133 10 DOLLARS
3.1000 g., 0.9990 Platinum 0.0996 oz. APW, 16 mm. **Ruler:**
Elizabeth II **Obv:** Head right **Rev:** Cooktown orchid, multicolor
Rev. Legend: DISCOVER AUSTRALIA

Date	Mintage	F	VF	XF	Unc	BU
2006P Proof	2,500				Value: 300	

KM# 1134 10 DOLLARS
3.1000 g., 0.9990 Platinum 0.0996 oz. APW, 16 mm. **Ruler:**
Elizabeth II **Obv:** Head right **Rev:** Sturt's desert rose, multicolor
Rev. Legend: DISCOVER AUSTRALIA

Date	Mintage	F	VF	XF	Unc	BU
2006P Proof	2,500				Value: 300	

KM# 1135   10 DOLLARS
3.1000 g., 0.9990 Platinum 0.0996 oz. APW, 16 mm. **Ruler:** Elizabeth II **Obv:** Head right **Rev:** Royal Bluebell, multicolor **Rev. Legend:** DISCOVER AUSTRALIA

Date	Mintage	F	VF	XF	Unc	BU
2006P Proof	2,500	Value: 300				

KM# 1136   10 DOLLARS
3.1000 g., 0.9990 Platinum 0.0996 oz. APW, 16 mm. **Ruler:** Elizabeth II **Obv:** Head right **Rev:** Red and green kangaroo paw, multicolor **Rev. Legend:** DISCOVER AUSTRALIA

Date	Mintage	F	VF	XF	Unc	BU
2006P Proof	2,500	Value: 300				

KM# 1137   10 DOLLARS
3.1000 g., 0.9990 Platinum 0.0996 oz. APW, 16 mm. **Ruler:** Elizabeth II **Obv:** Head right **Rev:** Common pink heath, multicolor **Rev. Legend:** DISCOVER AUSTRALIA

Date	Mintage	F	VF	XF	Unc	BU
2006P Proof	2,500	Value: 300				

KM# 1143   10 DOLLARS
1.2400 g., 0.9990 Gold 0.0398 oz. AGW, 14 mm. **Ruler:** Elizabeth II **Obv:** Head right **Rev:** Echidna **Rev. Legend:** DISCOVER AUSTRALIA

Date	Mintage	F	VF	XF	Unc	BU
2007P Proof	25,000	Value: 110				

KM# 1144   10 DOLLARS
1.2400 g., 0.9990 Gold 0.0398 oz. AGW, 14 mm. **Ruler:** Elizabeth II **Obv:** Head right **Rev:** Common wombat **Rev. Legend:** DISCOVER AUSTRALIA

Date	Mintage	F	VF	XF	Unc	BU
2007P Proof	25,000	Value: 110				

KM# 1145   10 DOLLARS
1.2400 g., 0.9990 Gold 0.0398 oz. AGW, 14 mm. **Ruler:** Elizabeth II **Obv:** Head right **Rev:** Tasmanian devil **Rev. Legend:** DISCOVER AUSTRALIA

Date	Mintage	F	VF	XF	Unc	BU
2007P Proof	25,000	Value: 110				

KM# 1146   10 DOLLARS
1.2400 g., 0.9990 Gold 0.0398 oz. AGW, 14 mm. **Ruler:** Elizabeth II **Obv:** Head right **Rev:** Great white shark **Rev. Legend:** DISCOVER AUSTRALIA

Date	Mintage	F	VF	XF	Unc	BU
2007P Proof	25,000	Value: 110				

KM# 1147   10 DOLLARS
1.2400 g., 0.9990 Gold 0.0398 oz. AGW, 14 mm. **Ruler:** Elizabeth II **Obv:** Head right **Rev:** Platypus **Rev. Legend:** DISCOVER AUSTRALIA

Date	Mintage	F	VF	XF	Unc	BU
2007P Proof	25,000	Value: 110				

KM# 1159   10 DOLLARS
3.1000 g., 0.9990 Platinum 0.0996 oz. APW, 16 mm. **Ruler:** Elizabeth II **Obv:** Head right **Rev:** Sturt's desert pea, multicolor **Rev. Legend:** DISCOVER AUSTRALIA

Date	Mintage	F	VF	XF	Unc	BU
2007P Proof	2,500	Value: 300				

KM# 1160   10 DOLLARS
3.1000 g., 0.9990 Platinum 0.0996 oz. APW, 16 mm. **Ruler:** Elizabeth II **Obv:** Head right **Rev:** Tasmanian bluegum, multicolor **Rev. Legend:** DISCOVER AUSTRALIA

Date	Mintage	F	VF	XF	Unc	BU
2007P Proof	2,500	Value: 300				

KM# 1161   10 DOLLARS
3.1000 g., 0.9990 Platinum 0.0996 oz. APW, 16 mm. **Ruler:** Elizabeth II **Obv:** Head right **Rev:** Waratah, multicolor **Rev. Legend:** DISCOVER AUSTRALIA

Date	Mintage	F	VF	XF	Unc	BU
2007P Proof	2,500	Value: 300				

KM# 1162   10 DOLLARS
3.1000 g., 0.9990 Platinum 0.0996 oz. APW, 16 mm. **Ruler:** Elizabeth II **Obv:** Head right **Rev:** Golden wattle, multicolor **Rev. Legend:** DISCOVER AUSTRALIA

Date	Mintage	F	VF	XF	Unc	BU
2007P Proof	2,500	Value: 300				

KM# 1186   10 DOLLARS
1.2400 g., 0.9990 Gold 0.0398 oz. AGW, 14 mm. **Ruler:** Elizabeth II **Obv:** Head right **Rev:** Dolphin **Rev. Legend:** DISCOVER AUSTRALIA

Date	Mintage	F	VF	XF	Unc	BU
2008P Proof	25,000	Value: 110				

KM# 1187   10 DOLLARS
1.2400 g., 0.9990 Gold 0.0398 oz. AGW, 14 mm. **Ruler:** Elizabeth II **Obv:** Head right **Rev:** King brown snake **Rev. Legend:** DISCOVER AUSTRALIA

Date	Mintage	F	VF	XF	Unc	BU
2008P Proof	25,000	Value: 110				

KM# 1189   10 DOLLARS
1.2400 g., 0.9990 Gold 0.0398 oz. AGW, 14 mm. **Ruler:** Elizabeth II **Obv:** Head right **Rev:** Dingo **Rev. Legend:** DISCOVER AUSTRALIA

Date	Mintage	F	VF	XF	Unc	BU
2008P Proof	25,000	Value: 110				

KM# 1190   10 DOLLARS
1.2400 g., 0.9990 Gold 0.0398 oz. AGW, 14 mm. **Ruler:** Elizabeth II **Obv:** Head right **Rev:** Frill-neck lizard **Rev. Legend:** DISCOVER AUSTRALIA

Date	Mintage	F	VF	XF	Unc	BU
2008P Proof	25,000	Value: 110				

KM# 1201   10 DOLLARS
3.1000 g., 0.9990 Platinum 0.0996 oz. APW, 16 mm. **Ruler:** Elizabeth II **Obv:** Head right **Rev:** Black anther fax lilly, multicolor **Rev. Legend:** DISCOVER AUSTRALIA

Date	Mintage	F	VF	XF	Unc	BU
2008P Proof	2,500	Value: 300				

KM# 1202   10 DOLLARS
3.1000 g., 0.9990 Platinum 0.0996 oz. APW, 16 mm. **Ruler:** Elizabeth II **Obv:** Head right **Rev:** Native frangipani, multicolor **Rev. Legend:** DISCOVER AUSTRALIA

Date	Mintage	F	VF	XF	Unc	BU
2008P Proof	2,500	Value: 300				

KM# 1203   10 DOLLARS
3.1000 g., 0.9990 Platinum 0.0996 oz. APW, 16 mm. **Ruler:** Elizabeth II **Obv:** Head right **Rev:** Geraldton wax, multicolor

Date	Mintage	F	VF	XF	Unc	BU
2008P Proof	2,500	Value: 300				

KM# 1204   10 DOLLARS
3.1000 g., 0.9990 Platinum 0.0996 oz. APW, 16 mm. **Ruler:** Elizabeth II **Obv:** Head right **Rev:** Red-flowered kurrajong, multicolor **Rev. Legend:** DISCOVER AUSTRALIA

Date	Mintage	F	VF	XF	Unc	BU
2008P Proof	2,500	Value: 300				

KM# 1205   10 DOLLARS
3.1000 g., 0.9990 Platinum 0.0996 oz. APW, 16 mm. **Ruler:** Elizabeth II **Obv:** Head right **Rev:** Small-leaf lily pilly, multicolor **Rev. Legend:** DISCOVER AUSTRALIA

Date	Mintage	F	VF	XF	Unc	BU
2008P Proof	2,500	Value: 300				

KM# 1206   10 DOLLARS
15.5500 g., 0.9990 Gold 0.4994 oz. AGW, 26 mm. **Ruler:** Elizabeth II **Obv:** Head right **Rev:** Black anther flax lily, multicolor **Rev. Legend:** DISCOVER AUSTRALIA

Date	Mintage	F	VF	XF	Unc	BU
2008P Proof	1,000	Value: 1,500				

KM# 980   15 DOLLARS
3.1101 g., 0.9990 Platinum 0.0999 oz. APW **Ruler:** Elizabeth II **Subject:** Australian Flora **Obv:** Head with tiara right **Rev:** Cooktown orchid

Date	Mintage	F	VF	XF	Unc	BU
2006 Proof	2,500	Value: 220				

KM# 982   15 DOLLARS
3.1101 g., 0.9990 Platinum 0.0999 oz. APW **Ruler:** Elizabeth II **Subject:** Australian Flora **Obv:** Head with tiara right **Rev:** Sturt's desert rose

Date	Mintage	F	VF	XF	Unc	BU
2006 Proof	2,500	Value: 220				

KM# 984   15 DOLLARS
3.1101 g., 0.9990 Platinum 0.0999 oz. APW **Ruler:** Elizabeth II **Subject:** Australian Flora **Obv:** Head with tiara right **Rev:** Royal bluebell

Date	Mintage	F	VF	XF	Unc	BU
2006 Proof	2,500	Value: 220				

KM# 986   15 DOLLARS
3.1101 g., 0.9990 Platinum 0.0999 oz. APW **Ruler:** Elizabeth II **Subject:** Australian Flora **Obv:** Head with tiara right **Rev:** Kangaroo paw

Date	Mintage	F	VF	XF	Unc	BU
2006 Proof	2,500	Value: 220				

KM# 988   15 DOLLARS
3.1101 g., 0.9990 Platinum 0.0999 oz. APW **Ruler:** Elizabeth II **Subject:** Australian Flora **Obv:** Head with tiara right **Rev:** Common pink heath

Date	Mintage	F	VF	XF	Unc	BU
2006 Proof	2,500	Value: 220				

KM# 951   15 DOLLARS
3.1101 g., 0.9990 Gold 0.0999 oz. AGW **Ruler:** Elizabeth II **Subject:** Australian Fauna **Obv:** Head with tiara right **Rev:** Saltwater crocodile

Date	Mintage	F	VF	XF	Unc	BU
2006 Proof	2,500	Value: 195				

KM# 954   15 DOLLARS
3.1101 g., 0.9990 Gold 0.0999 oz. AGW **Ruler:** Elizabeth II **Subject:** Australian Fauna **Obv:** Head with tiara right **Rev:** Grey kangaroo

Date	Mintage	F	VF	XF	Unc	BU
2006 Proof	2,500	Value: 195				

KM# 957   15 DOLLARS
3.1101 g., 0.9990 Gold 0.0999 oz. AGW **Ruler:** Elizabeth II **Subject:** Australian Fauna **Obv:** Head with tiara right **Rev:** Emu

Date	Mintage	F	VF	XF	Unc	BU
2006 Proof	2,500	Value: 195				

KM# 960   15 DOLLARS
3.1101 g., 0.9990 Gold 0.0999 oz. AGW **Ruler:** Elizabeth II **Subject:** Australian Fauna **Obv:** Head with tiara right **Rev:** Koala

Date	Mintage	F	VF	XF	Unc	BU
2006 Proof	2,500	Value: 195				

KM# 963   15 DOLLARS
3.1101 g., 0.9990 Gold 0.0999 oz. AGW **Ruler:** Elizabeth II **Subject:** Australian Fauna **Obv:** Head with tiara right **Rev:** Kookaburra

Date	Mintage	F	VF	XF	Unc	BU
2006 Proof	2,500	Value: 195				

KM# 966   15 DOLLARS
3.1101 g., 0.9990 Gold 0.0999 oz. AGW **Ruler:** Elizabeth II **Subject:** Australian Fauna **Obv:** Head with tiara right **Rev:** Echidna

Date	Mintage	F	VF	XF	Unc	BU
2007 Proof	2,500	Value: 195				

KM# 969   15 DOLLARS
3.1101 g., 0.9990 Gold 0.0999 oz. AGW **Ruler:** Elizabeth II **Subject:** Australian Fauna **Obv:** Head with tiara right **Rev:** Common wombat

Date	Mintage	F	VF	XF	Unc	BU
2007 Proof	2,500	Value: 195				

KM# 972   15 DOLLARS
3.1101 g., 0.9990 Gold 0.0999 oz. AGW **Ruler:** Elizabeth II **Subject:** Australian Fauna **Obv:** Head with tiara right **Rev:** Tasmanian devil

Date	Mintage	F	VF	XF	Unc	BU
2007 Proof	2,500	Value: 195				

KM# 975   15 DOLLARS
3.1101 g., 0.9990 Gold 0.0999 oz. AGW **Ruler:** Elizabeth II **Subject:** Australian Fauna **Obv:** Head with tiara right **Rev:** Great white shark

Date	Mintage	F	VF	XF	Unc	BU
2007 Proof	2,500	Value: 195				

KM# 978   15 DOLLARS
3.1101 g., 0.9990 Gold 0.0999 oz. AGW **Ruler:** Elizabeth II **Subject:** Australian Fauna **Obv:** Head with tiara right **Rev:** Platypus

Date	Mintage	F	VF	XF	Unc	BU
2007 Proof	2,500	Value: 195				

KM# 990   15 DOLLARS
3.1101 g., 0.9990 Platinum 0.0999 oz. APW **Ruler:** Elizabeth II **Subject:** Australian Flora **Obv:** Head with tiara right **Rev:** Anemone buttercup

Date	Mintage	F	VF	XF	Unc	BU
2007 Proof	2,500	Value: 220				

KM# 992   15 DOLLARS
3.1101 g., 0.9990 Platinum 0.0999 oz. APW **Ruler:** Elizabeth II **Subject:** Australian Flora **Obv:** Head with tiara right **Rev:** Sturt's desert pea

Date	Mintage	F	VF	XF	Unc	BU
2007 Proof	2,500	Value: 220				

KM# 994   15 DOLLARS
3.1101 g., 0.9990 Platinum 0.0999 oz. APW **Ruler:** Elizabeth II **Subject:** Australian Flora **Obv:** Head with tiara right **Rev:** Tasmanian bluegum

Date	Mintage	F	VF	XF	Unc	BU
2007 Proof	2,500	Value: 220				

KM# 996   15 DOLLARS
3.1101 g., 0.9990 Platinum 0.0999 oz. APW **Ruler:** Elizabeth II **Subject:** Australian Flora **Obv:** Head with tiara right **Rev:** Waratah

Date	Mintage	F	VF	XF	Unc	BU
2007 Proof	2,500	Value: 220				

KM# 998   15 DOLLARS
3.1101 g., 0.9990 Platinum 0.0999 oz. APW **Ruler:** Elizabeth II **Subject:** Australian Flora **Obv:** Head with tiara right **Rev:** Golden wattle

Date	Mintage	F	VF	XF	Unc	BU
2007 Proof	2,500	Value: 220				

KM# 1104 15 DOLLARS
2.5000 g., 0.9999 Gold 0.0804 oz. AGW, 13x22 mm. **Ruler:**
Elizabeth II **Rev:** Turtle Dreaming **Shape:** Rectangle

Date	Mintage	F	VF	XF	Unc	BU
2009 Proof	—	Value: 175				

KM# 1108 15 DOLLARS
2.5000 g., 0.9999 Gold 0.0804 oz. AGW, 13x22 mm. **Ruler:**
Elizabeth II **Rev:** Kangaroo Dreaming **Shape:** Vertical rectangle

Date	Mintage	Good	VG	F	VF	XF
2009 Proof	—	Value: 175				

KM# 1223 15 DOLLARS
3.1100 g., 0.9990 Gold 0.0999 oz. AGW, 16 mm. **Ruler:**
Elizabeth II **Obv:** Head right **Rev:** Dreaming dolphin

Date	Mintage	F	VF	XF	Unc	BU
2009P Proof	2,500	Value: 195				

KM# 1225 15 DOLLARS
3.1100 g., 0.9990 Gold 0.0999 oz. AGW, 16 mm. **Ruler:**
Elizabeth II **Obv:** Head right **Rev:** Dreaming brolga

Date	Mintage	F	VF	XF	Unc	BU
2009P Proof	2,500	Value: 195				

KM# 1226 15 DOLLARS
3.1100 g., 0.9990 Gold 0.0999 oz. AGW, 16 mm. **Ruler:**
Elizabeth II **Obv:** Head right **Rev:** Dreaming echidna

Date	Mintage	F	VF	XF	Unc	BU
2009P Proof	2,500	Value: 195				

KM# 1228 15 DOLLARS
15.5500 g., 0.9990 Gold 0.4994 oz. AGW, 25 mm. **Ruler:**
Elizabeth II **Obv:** Head right **Rev:** Dreaming dolphin

Date	Mintage	F	VF	XF	Unc	BU
2009P Proof	1,000	Value: 1,100				

KM# 1232 15 DOLLARS
3.1100 g., 0.9990 Platinum 0.0999 oz. APW, 16 mm. **Ruler:**
Elizabeth II **Obv:** Head right **Rev:** Dreaming kangaroo, multicolor

Date	Mintage	F	VF	XF	Unc	BU
2009P Proof	2,500	Value: 400				

KM# 1233 15 DOLLARS
3.1100 g., 0.9990 Platinum 0.0999 oz. APW, 16 mm. **Ruler:**
Elizabeth II **Obv:** Head right **Rev:** Dreaming dolphin, multicolor

Date	Mintage	F	VF	XF	Unc	BU
2009P Proof	2,500	Value: 400				

KM# 1234 15 DOLLARS
3.1100 g., 0.9990 Platinum 0.0999 oz. APW, 16 mm. **Ruler:**
Elizabeth II **Obv:** Head right **Rev:** Dreaming king brown snake,
multicolor

Date	Mintage	F	VF	XF	Unc	BU
2009P Proof	2,500	Value: 400				

KM# 1235 15 DOLLARS
3.1100 g., 0.9990 Platinum 0.0999 oz. APW, 16 mm. **Ruler:**
Elizabeth II **Obv:** Head right **Rev:** Dreaming brolga

Date	Mintage	F	VF	XF	Unc	BU
2009P Proof	2,500	Value: 400				

KM# 1236 15 DOLLARS
3.1100 g., 0.9990 Platinum 0.0999 oz. APW, 16 mm. **Ruler:**
Elizabeth II **Obv:** Head right **Rev:** Dreaming echidna, multicolor

Date	Mintage	F	VF	XF	Unc	BU
2009P Proof	2,500	Value: 400				

KM# 1399 15 DOLLARS
3.1100 g., 0.9990 Platinum 0.0999 oz. APW, 17 mm. **Ruler:**
Elizabeth II **Obv:** Head right **Rev:** Multicolor frill-neck lizard

Date	Mintage	F	VF	XF	Unc	BU
2010(p)	2,500	Value: 335				

KM# 1401 15 DOLLARS
3.1100 g., 0.9990 Gold 0.0999 oz. AGW, 17 mm. **Ruler:**
Elizabeth II **Obv:** Head right **Rev:** Frill-neck lizard

Date	Mintage	F	VF	XF	Unc	BU
2010(p) Proof	2,500	Value: 260				

KM# 1405 15 DOLLARS
3.1100 g., 0.9990 Platinum 0.0999 oz. APW, 17 mm. **Ruler:**
Elizabeth II **Obv:** Head right **Rev:** Multicolor koala

Date	Mintage	F	VF	XF	Unc	BU
2010(p) Proof	2,500	Value: 335				

KM# 1407 15 DOLLARS
3.1100 g., 0.9990 Gold 0.0999 oz. AGW, 16 mm. **Ruler:**
Elizabeth II **Obv:** Head right **Rev:** Koala

Date	Mintage	F	VF	XF	Unc	BU
2010(p) Proof	2,500	Value: 260				

KM# 1411 15 DOLLARS
3.1100 g., 0.9990 Platinum 0.0999 oz. APW, 17 mm. **Ruler:**
Elizabeth II **Obv:** Head right **Rev:** Multicolor platypus

Date	Mintage	F	VF	XF	Unc	BU
2010(p) Proof	2,500	Value: 335				

KM# 1413 15 DOLLARS
0.9990 Gold, 16 mm. **Ruler:** Elizabeth II **Obv:** Head right **Rev:**
Platypus

Date	Mintage	F	VF	XF	Unc	BU
2010(p) Proof	2,500	Value: 260				

KM# 1417 15 DOLLARS
0.9990 Platinum APW, 17 mm. **Ruler:** Elizabeth II **Obv:** Head
right **Rev:** Muticolor saltwater crocodile

Date	Mintage	F	VF	XF	Unc	BU
2010(p) Proof	2,500	Value: 335				

KM# 1419 15 DOLLARS
3.1100 g., 0.9990 Gold 0.0999 oz. AGW, 16 mm. **Ruler:**
Elizabeth II **Obv:** Head right **Rev:** Saltwater crocodile

Date	Mintage	F	VF	XF	Unc	BU
2010(p) Proof	2,500	Value: 260				

KM# 1423 15 DOLLARS
3.1100 g., 0.9990 Platinum 0.0999 oz. APW, 17 mm. **Ruler:**
Elizabeth II **Obv:** Head right **Rev:** Multicolor wombat

Date	Mintage	F	VF	XF	Unc	BU
2010(p) Proof	2,500	Value: 335				

KM# 1425 15 DOLLARS
0.9990 Gold, 16 mm. **Ruler:** Elizabeth II **Obv:** Head right **Rev:**
Wombat

Date	Mintage	F	VF	XF	Unc	BU
2010(p) Proof	2,500	Value: 260				

KM# 1454 15 DOLLARS

2.5000 g., 0.9990 Gold 0.0803 oz. AGW, 13x22 mm. **Ruler:**
Elizabeth II **Rev:** Dolphin dreaming **Shape:** Vertical rectangle

Date	Mintage	F	VF	XF	Unc	BU
2010P Proof	—	Value: 175				

KM# 1536 15 DOLLARS
3.1100 g., 0.9990 Gold 0.0999 oz. AGW **Ruler:** Elizabeth II
Subject: Dreaming Emu **Rev:** Linear emu in color

Date	Mintage	F	VF	XF	Unc	BU
2011P Proof	2,500	Value: 250				

KM# 1538 15 DOLLARS
3.1100 g., 0.9990 Platinum 0.0999 oz. APW **Ruler:** Elizabeth II
Subject: Dreaming Emu **Rev:** Linear emu in color

Date	Mintage	F	VF	XF	Unc	BU
2011P Proof	2,500	Value: 375				

KM# 1542 15 DOLLARS
3.1100 g., 0.9990 Gold 0.0999 oz. AGW **Ruler:** Elizabeth II
Subject: Dreaming Tasmanian Devil **Rev:** Linear tasmanian
devil in color

Date	Mintage	F	VF	XF	Unc	BU
2011P Proof	2,500	Value: 250				

KM# 1544 15 DOLLARS
3.1100 g., 0.9990 Platinum 0.0999 oz. APW **Ruler:** Elizabeth II
Subject: Dreaming Tasmanian Devil **Rev:** Linear tasmanian
devil in color

Date	Mintage	F	VF	XF	Unc	BU
2011P Proof	2,500	Value: 375				

KM# 1548 15 DOLLARS
3.1100 g., 0.9990 Gold 0.0999 oz. AGW **Ruler:** Elizabeth II
Subject: Dreaming Kookaburra **Rev:** Linear kookaburra in color

Date	Mintage	F	VF	XF	Unc	BU
2011P Proof	2,500	Value: 250				

KM# 1550 15 DOLLARS
3.1100 g., 0.9990 Platinum 0.0999 oz. APW **Ruler:** Elizabeth II
Subject: Dreaming Kookaburra **Rev:** Linear kookaburra in color

Date	Mintage	F	VF	XF	Unc	BU
2011P Proof	2,500	Value: 375				

KM# 1554 15 DOLLARS
3.1100 g., 0.9990 Gold 0.0999 oz. AGW **Ruler:** Elizabeth II
Subject: Dreaming Shark **Rev:** Linear shark in color

Date	Mintage	F	VF	XF	Unc	BU
2011P Proof	2,500	Value: 250				

KM# 1556 15 DOLLARS
3.1100 g., 0.9990 Platinum 0.0999 oz. APW **Ruler:** Elizabeth II
Subject: Dreaming Shark **Rev:** Linear shark in color

Date	Mintage	F	VF	XF	Unc	BU
2011P Proof	2,500	Value: 375				

KM# 1560 15 DOLLARS
3.1100 g., 0.9990 Gold 0.0999 oz. AGW **Ruler:** Elizabeth II
Subject: Dreaming Dingo **Rev:** Linear dingo in color

Date	Mintage	F	VF	XF	Unc	BU
2011P Proof	2,500	Value: 250				

KM# 1562 15 DOLLARS
3.1100 g., 0.9990 Platinum 0.0999 oz. APW **Ruler:** Elizabeth II
Subject: Dreaming Dingo **Rev:** Linear dingo in color

Date	Mintage	F	VF	XF	Unc	BU
2011P Proof	2,500	Value: 375				

KM# 1610 15 DOLLARS
2.5000 g., 0.9990 Gold 0.0803 oz. AGW, 13x22 mm. **Ruler:**
Elizabeth II **Obv:** Head with tiara right **Rev:** Platypus dreaming
Shape: Vertical rectangle

Date	Mintage	F	VF	XF	Unc	BU
2011P Proof	—	Value: 175				

KM# 1721 15 DOLLARS
3.1110 g., 0.9990 Gold 0.0999 oz. AGW, 16.6 mm. **Ruler:**
Elizabeth II **Rev:** Green and Gold Bell Frog in grass

Date	Mintage	F	VF	XF	Unc	BU
2012P Proof	1,000	Value: 225				

KM# 1722 15 DOLLARS
3.1110 g., 0.9990 Gold 0.0999 oz. AGW, 16.6 mm. **Ruler:**
Elizabeth II **Rev:** Kookaburra standing right

Date	Mintage	F	VF	XF	Unc	BU
2012P Proof	1,000	Value: 225				

KM# 1723 15 DOLLARS
3.1110 g., 0.9990 Gold 0.0999 oz. AGW, 16.6 mm. **Ruler:**
Elizabeth II **Rev:** Whale Shark swimming right

Date	Mintage	F	VF	XF	Unc	BU
2012P Proof	1,000	Value: 225				

KM# 1724 15 DOLLARS
3.1110 g., 0.9990 Gold 0.0999 oz. AGW, 16.6 mm. **Ruler:**
Elizabeth II **Rev:** Kangaroo bounding right

Date	Mintage	F	VF	XF	Unc	BU
2012P Proof	1,000	Value: 225				

KM# 1725 15 DOLLARS
3.1110 g., 0.9990 Gold 0.0999 oz. AGW, 16.6 mm. **Ruler:**
Elizabeth II **Rev:** Goanna lizard right

Date	Mintage	F	VF	XF	Unc	BU
2012P Proof	1,000	Value: 225				

KM# 1105 20 DOLLARS
5.0000 g., 0.9999 Gold 0.1607 oz. AGW, 14x23.2 mm. **Ruler:**
Elizabeth II **Rev:** Turtle Dreaming **Shape:** Rectangle

Date	Mintage	F	VF	XF	Unc	BU
2009 Proof	—	Value: 325				

KM# 1109 20 DOLLARS
5.0000 g., 0.9999 Gold 0.1607 oz. AGW, 14x23.2 mm. **Ruler:**
Elizabeth II **Rev:** Kangaroo dreaming **Shape:** Vertical rectangle

Date	Mintage	F	VF	XF	Unc	BU
2009 Proof	—	Value: 325				

KM# 1127   25 DOLLARS
3.1000 g., 0.9990 Gold 0.0996 oz. AGW, 15.5 mm.   **Ruler:** Elizabeth II **Obv:** Head right **Rev:** Kookaburra **Rev. Legend:** DISCOVER AUSTRALIA

Date	Mintage	F	VF	XF	Unc	BU
2006P Proof	2,500	Value: 195				

KM# 1123   25 DOLLARS
3.1000 g., 0.9990 Gold 0.0996 oz. AGW, 15.5 mm.   **Ruler:** Elizabeth II **Obv:** Head right **Rev:** Saltwater crocodile **Rev. Legend:** DISCOVER AUSTRALIA

Date	Mintage	F	VF	XF	Unc	BU
2006P Proof	2,500	Value: 195				

KM# 1124   25 DOLLARS
3.1000 g., 0.9990 Gold 0.0996 oz. AGW, 15.5 mm.   **Ruler:** Elizabeth II **Obv:** Head right **Rev:** Grey kangaroo **Rev. Legend:** DISCOVER AUSTRALIA

Date	Mintage	F	VF	XF	Unc	BU
2006P Proof	2,500	Value: 195				

KM# 1125   25 DOLLARS
3.1000 g., 0.9990 Gold 0.0996 oz. AGW, 15.5 mm.   **Ruler:** Elizabeth II **Obv:** Head right **Rev:** Emu **Rev. Legend:** DISCOVER AUSTRALIA

Date	Mintage	F	VF	XF	Unc	BU
2006P Proof	2,500	Value: 195				

KM# 1126   25 DOLLARS
3.1000 g., 0.9990 Gold 0.0996 oz. AGW, 15.5 mm.   **Ruler:** Elizabeth II **Obv:** Head right **Rev:** Koala **Rev. Legend:** DISCOVER AUSTRALIA

Date	Mintage	F	VF	XF	Unc	BU
2006P Proof	2,500	Value: 195				

KM# 1148   25 DOLLARS
3.1000 g., 0.9990 Gold 0.0996 oz. AGW, 15.5 mm.   **Ruler:** Elizabeth II **Obv:** Head right **Rev:** Echinda **Rev. Legend:** DISCOVER AUSTRALIA

Date	Mintage	F	VF	XF	Unc	BU
2007P Proof	2,500	Value: 195				

KM# 1149   25 DOLLARS
3.1000 g., 0.9990 Gold 0.0996 oz. AGW, 15.5 mm.   **Ruler:** Elizabeth II **Obv:** Head right **Rev:** Common wombat **Rev. Legend:** DISCOVER AUSTRALIA

Date	Mintage	F	VF	XF	Unc	BU
2007P Proof	2,500	Value: 195				

KM# 1150   25 DOLLARS
3.1000 g., 0.9990 Gold 0.0996 oz. AGW, 15.5 mm.   **Ruler:** Elizabeth II **Obv:** Head right **Rev:** Tasmanian devil **Rev. Legend:** DISCOVER AUSTRALIA

Date	Mintage	F	VF	XF	Unc	BU
2007P Proof	2,500	Value: 195				

KM# 1151   25 DOLLARS
3.1000 g., 0.9990 Gold 0.0996 oz. AGW, 15.5 mm.   **Ruler:** Elizabeth II **Obv:** Head right **Rev:** Great white shark **Rev. Legend:** DISCOVER AUSTRALIA

Date	Mintage	F	VF	XF	Unc	BU
2007P Proof	2,500	Value: 195				

KM# 1152   25 DOLLARS
3.1000 g., 0.9990 Gold 0.0996 oz. AGW, 15.5 mm.   **Ruler:** Elizabeth II **Obv:** Head right **Rev:** Platypus **Rev. Legend:** DISCOVER AUSTRALIA

Date	Mintage	F	VF	XF	Unc	BU
2007P Proof	2,500	Value: 195				

KM# 1158   25 DOLLARS
3.1000 g., 0.9990 Platinum 0.0996 oz. APW, 16 mm.   **Ruler:** Elizabeth II **Obv:** Head right **Rev:** Anemone buttercup, multicolor **Rev. Legend:** DISCOVER AUSTRALIA

Date	Mintage	F	VF	XF	Unc	BU
2007P Proof	2,500	Value: 325				

KM# 1191   25 DOLLARS
3.1000 g., 0.9990 Gold 0.0996 oz. AGW, 15.5 mm.   **Ruler:** Elizabeth II **Obv:** Head right **Rev:** Dolphin **Rev. Legend:** DISCOVER AUSTRALIA

Date	Mintage	F	VF	XF	Unc	BU
2008P Proof	2,500	Value: 195				

KM# 1192   25 DOLLARS
3.1000 g., 0.9990 Gold 0.0996 oz. AGW, 15.5 mm.   **Ruler:** Elizabeth II **Obv:** Head right **Rev:** King brown snake **Rev. Legend:** DISCOVER AUSTRALIA

Date	Mintage	F	VF	XF	Unc	BU
2008P Proof	2,500	Value: 195				

KM# 1193   25 DOLLARS
3.1000 g., 0.9990 Gold 0.0996 oz. AGW, 15.5 mm.   **Ruler:** Elizabeth II **Obv:** Head right **Rev:** Brolga **Rev. Legend:** DISCOVER AUSTRALIA

Date	Mintage	F	VF	XF	Unc	BU
2008P Proof	2,500	Value: 195				

KM# 1194   25 DOLLARS
3.1000 g., 0.9990 Gold 0.0996 oz. AGW, 15.5 mm.   **Ruler:** Elizabeth II **Obv:** Head right **Rev:** Dingo **Rev. Legend:** DISCOVER AUSTRALIA

Date	Mintage	F	VF	XF	Unc	BU
2008P Proof	2,500	Value: 195				

KM# 1195   25 DOLLARS
3.1000 g., 0.9990 Gold 0.0996 oz. AGW, 15.5 mm.   **Ruler:** Elizabeth II **Obv:** Head right **Rev:** Frill-neck lizard **Rev. Legend:** DISCOVER AUSTRALIA

Date	Mintage	F	VF	XF	Unc	BU
2008P Proof	2,500	Value: 195				

KM# 1106   25 DOLLARS
10.0000 g., 0.9999 Gold 0.3215 oz. AGW, 15.4x25.4 mm.   **Ruler:** Elizabeth II **Rev:** Turtle dreaming **Shape:** Verticle rectangle

Date	Mintage	F	VF	XF	Unc	BU
2009 Proof	—	Value: 625				

KM# 1455   25 DOLLARS
10.0000 g., 0.9990 Gold 0.3212 oz. AGW, 15.4x25.4 mm.   **Ruler:** Elizabeth II **Rev:** Dolphin dreaming **Shape:** Vertical rectangle

Date	Mintage	F	VF	XF	Unc	BU
2010P Proof	—	Value: 600				

KM# 1611   25 DOLLARS
10.0000 g., 0.9990 Gold 0.3212 oz. AGW, 15.4x25.4 mm.   **Ruler:** Elizabeth II **Obv:** Head with tiara right **Rev:** Platypus dreaming **Shape:** Vertical rectangle

Date	Mintage	F	VF	XF	Unc	BU
2011P Proof	—	Value: 625				

KM# 952   50 DOLLARS
15.5017 g., 0.9990 Gold 0.4979 oz. AGW, 25 mm.   **Ruler:** Elizabeth II **Subject:** Australian Fauna **Obv:** Head with tiara right **Rev:** Saltwater crocodile

Date	Mintage	F	VF	XF	Unc	BU
2006 Proof	1,000	Value: 850				

KM# 955   50 DOLLARS
15.5017 g., 0.9990 Gold 0.4979 oz. AGW, 25 mm.   **Ruler:** Elizabeth II **Subject:** Australian Fauna **Obv:** Head with tiara right **Rev:** Grey kangaroo

Date	Mintage	F	VF	XF	Unc	BU
2006 Proof	1,000	Value: 850				

KM# 958   50 DOLLARS
15.5017 g., 0.9990 Gold 0.4979 oz. AGW, 25 mm.   **Ruler:** Elizabeth II **Subject:** Australian Fauna **Obv:** Head with tiara right **Rev:** Emu

Date	Mintage	F	VF	XF	Unc	BU
2006 Proof	1,000	Value: 850				

KM# 961   50 DOLLARS
15.5017 g., 0.9990 Gold 0.4979 oz. AGW, 25 mm.   **Ruler:** Elizabeth II **Subject:** Australian Fauna **Obv:** Head with tiara right **Rev:** Koala

Date	Mintage	F	VF	XF	Unc	BU
2006 Proof	1,000	Value: 850				

KM# 964   50 DOLLARS
15.5017 g., 0.9990 Gold 0.4979 oz. AGW, 25 mm.   **Ruler:** Elizabeth II **Subject:** Australian Fauna **Obv:** Head with tiara right **Rev:** Kookaburra

Date	Mintage	F	VF	XF	Unc	BU
2006 Proof	1,000	Value: 850				

KM# 981   50 DOLLARS
15.5017 g., 0.9990 Platinum 0.4979 oz. APW **Ruler:** Elizabeth II **Subject:** Australian Flora **Obv:** Head with tiara right **Rev:** Cooktown orchid

Date	Mintage	F	VF	XF	Unc	BU
2006 Proof	1,000	Value: 975				

KM# 983   50 DOLLARS
15.5017 g., 0.9990 Platinum 0.4979 oz. APW **Ruler:** Elizabeth II **Subject:** Australian Flora **Obv:** Head with tiara right **Rev:** Sturt's desert rose

Date	Mintage	F	VF	XF	Unc	BU
2006 Proof	1,000	Value: 975				

KM# 985   50 DOLLARS
15.5017 g., 0.9990 Platinum 0.4979 oz. APW **Ruler:** Elizabeth II **Subject:** Australian Flora **Obv:** Head with tiara right **Rev:** Royal bluebell

Date	Mintage	F	VF	XF	Unc	BU
2006 Proof	1,000	Value: 975				

KM# 987   50 DOLLARS
15.5017 g., 0.9990 Platinum 0.4979 oz. APW **Ruler:** Elizabeth II **Subject:** Australian Flora **Obv:** Head with tiara right **Rev:** Kangaroo paw

Date	Mintage	F	VF	XF	Unc	BU
2006 Proof	1,000	Value: 975				

KM# 989   50 DOLLARS
15.5017 g., 0.9990 Platinum 0.4979 oz. APW **Ruler:** Elizabeth II
Subject: Australian Flora **Obv:** Head with tiara right **Rev:**
Common pink heath

Date	Mintage	F	VF	XF	Unc	BU
2006 Proof	1,000	Value: 975				

KM# 967   50 DOLLARS
15.5017 g., 0.9990 Gold 0.4979 oz. AGW, 25 mm. **Ruler:**
Elizabeth II **Subject:** Australian Fauna **Obv:** Head with tiara right
Rev: Echidna

Date	Mintage	F	VF	XF	Unc	BU
2007 Proof	1,000	Value: 850				

KM# 970   50 DOLLARS
15.5017 g., 0.9990 Gold 0.4979 oz. AGW, 25 mm. **Ruler:**
Elizabeth II **Subject:** Australian Fauna **Obv:** Head with tiara right
Rev: Common wombat

Date	Mintage	F	VF	XF	Unc	BU
2007 Proof	1,000	Value: 850				

KM# 973   50 DOLLARS
15.5017 g., 0.9990 Gold 0.4979 oz. AGW, 25 mm. **Ruler:**
Elizabeth II **Subject:** Australian Fauna **Obv:** Head with tiara right
Rev: Tasmanian devil

Date	Mintage	F	VF	XF	Unc	BU
2007 Proof	1,000	Value: 850				

KM# 976   50 DOLLARS
15.5017 g., 0.9990 Gold 0.4979 oz. AGW, 25 mm. **Ruler:**
Elizabeth II **Subject:** Australian Fauna **Obv:** Head with tiara right
Rev: Great white shark

Date	Mintage	F	VF	XF	Unc	BU
2007 Proof	1,000	Value: 850				

KM# 979   50 DOLLARS
15.5017 g., 0.9990 Gold 0.4979 oz. AGW, 25 mm. **Ruler:**
Elizabeth II **Subject:** Australian Fauna **Obv:** Head with tiara right
Rev: Platypus

Date	Mintage	F	VF	XF	Unc	BU
2007 Proof	1,000	Value: 850				

KM# 991   50 DOLLARS
15.5017 g., 0.9990 Platinum 0.4979 oz. APW, 24 mm. **Ruler:**
Elizabeth II **Subject:** Australian Flora **Obv:** Head with tiara right
Rev: Anemone buttercup

Date	Mintage	F	VF	XF	Unc	BU
2007 Proof	1,000	Value: 975				

KM# 993   50 DOLLARS
15.5017 g., 0.9990 Platinum 0.4979 oz. APW **Ruler:** Elizabeth II
Subject: Australian Flora **Obv:** Head with tiara right **Rev:** Sturt's
desert pea

Date	Mintage	F	VF	XF	Unc	BU
2007 Proof	1,000	Value: 975				

KM# 995   50 DOLLARS
15.5017 g., 0.9990 Platinum 0.4979 oz. APW, 24 mm. **Ruler:**
Elizabeth II **Subject:** Australian Flora **Obv:** Head with tiara right
Rev: Tasmanian Bluegum

Date	Mintage	F	VF	XF	Unc	BU
2007 Proof	1,000	Value: 975				

KM# 997   50 DOLLARS
15.5017 g., 0.9990 Platinum 0.4979 oz. APW **Ruler:** Elizabeth II
Subject: Australian Flora **Obv:** Head with tiara right **Rev:**
Waratah

Date	Mintage	F	VF	XF	Unc	BU
2007 Proof	1,000	Value: 975				

KM# 999   50 DOLLARS
15.5017 g., 0.9990 Platinum 0.4979 oz. APW **Ruler:** Elizabeth II
Subject: Australian Flora **Obv:** Head with tiara right **Rev:** Golden
wattle

Date	Mintage	F	VF	XF	Unc	BU
2007 Proof	1,000	Value: 975				

KM# 1167   50 DOLLARS
15.5500 g., 0.9990 Platinum 0.4994 oz. APW, 25 mm. **Ruler:**
Elizabeth II **Subject:** Australian Flora **Rev:** Black-anther flax lily
Rev. Legend: DISCOVER AUSTRALIA

Date	Mintage	F	VF	XF	Unc	BU
2008 Proof	—	Value: 975				

KM# 1196   50 DOLLARS
15.5500 g., 0.9990 Gold 0.4994 oz. AGW, 25 mm. **Ruler:**
Elizabeth II **Obv:** Head right **Rev:** Dolphin **Rev. Legend:**
DISCOVER AUSTRALIA

Date	Mintage	F	VF	XF	Unc	BU
2008P Proof	1,000	Value: 875				

KM# 1197   50 DOLLARS
15.5500 g., 0.9990 Gold 0.4994 oz. AGW, 25 mm. **Ruler:**
Elizabeth II **Obv:** Head right **Rev:** King brown snake **Rev.
Legend:** DISCOVER AUSTRALIA

Date	Mintage	F	VF	XF	Unc	BU
2008P Proof	1,000	Value: 875				

KM# 1198   50 DOLLARS
15.5500 g., 0.9990 Gold 0.4994 oz. AGW, 25 mm. **Ruler:**
Elizabeth II **Obv:** Head right **Rev:** Brogla **Rev. Legend:**
DISCOVER AUSTRALIA

Date	Mintage	F	VF	XF	Unc	BU
2008P Proof	1,000	Value: 875				

KM# 1199   50 DOLLARS
15.5500 g., 0.9990 Gold 0.4994 oz. AGW, 25 mm. **Ruler:**
Elizabeth II **Obv:** Head right **Rev:** Dingo **Rev. Legend:**
DISCOVER AUSTRALIA

Date	Mintage	F	VF	XF	Unc	BU
2008P Proof	1,000	Value: 875				

KM# 1200   50 DOLLARS
15.5500 g., 0.9990 Gold 0.4994 oz. AGW, 25 mm. **Ruler:**
Elizabeth II **Obv:** Head right **Rev:** Frill-neck lizard **Rev. Legend:**
DISCOVER AUSTRALIA

Date	Mintage	F	VF	XF	Unc	BU
2008P Proof	1,000	Value: 875				

KM# 1207   50 DOLLARS
15.5500 g., 0.9990 Platinum 0.4994 oz. APW, 26 mm. **Ruler:**
Elizabeth II **Obv:** Head right **Rev:** Native fragipan, multicolor **Rev.
Legend:** DISCOVER AUSTRALIA

Date	Mintage	F	VF	XF	Unc	BU
2008P Proof	1,000	Value: 1,500				

KM# 1208   50 DOLLARS
15.5500 g., 0.9990 Platinum 0.4994 oz. APW, 26 mm.   **Ruler:**
Elizabeth II **Obv:** Head right **Rev:** Geraldton wax, multicolor **Rev.**
Legend: DISCOVER AUSTRALIA

Date	Mintage	F	VF	XF	Unc	BU
2008P Proof	1,000	Value: 1,500				

KM# 1209   50 DOLLARS
15.5500 g., 0.9990 Platinum 0.4994 oz. APW, 26 mm.   **Ruler:**
Elizabeth II **Obv:** Head right **Rev:** Red-flowered kurrajong,
multicolor **Rev. Legend:** DISCOVER AUSTRALIA

Date	Mintage	F	VF	XF	Unc	BU
2008P Proof	1,000	Value: 1,500				

KM# 1210   50 DOLLARS
15.5500 g., 0.9990 Platinum 0.4994 oz. APW **Ruler:** Elizabeth II
Obv: Head right **Rev:** Small-leaf lilly pilly, multicolor **Rev.**
Legend: DISCOVER AUSTRALIA

Date	Mintage	F	VF	XF	Unc	BU
2008P Proof	1,500	Value: 1,500				

KM# 1229   50 DOLLARS
15.5500 g., 0.9990 Gold 0.4994 oz. AGW, 25 mm.   **Ruler:**
Elizabeth II **Obv:** Head right **Rev:** Dreaming king brown snake

Date	Mintage	F	VF	XF	Unc	BU
2009P Proof	1,000	Value: 1,100				

KM# 1227   50 DOLLARS
15.5500 g., 0.9990 Gold 0.4994 oz. AGW, 25 mm.   **Ruler:**
Elizabeth II **Obv:** Head right **Rev:** Dreaming kangaroo

Date	Mintage	F	VF	XF	Unc	BU
2009P Proof	1,000	Value: 1,100				

KM# 1230   50 DOLLARS
15.5500 g., 0.9990 Gold 0.4994 oz. AGW, 25 mm.   **Ruler:**
Elizabeth II **Obv:** Head right **Rev:** Dreaming brolga

Date	Mintage	F	VF	XF	Unc	BU
2009P Proof	1,000	Value: 1,100				

KM# 1231   50 DOLLARS
15.5500 g., 0.9990 Gold 0.4994 oz. AGW, 25 mm.   **Ruler:**
Elizabeth II **Obv:** Head right **Rev:** Dreaming echidna

Date	Mintage	F	VF	XF	Unc	BU
2009P Proof	1,000	Value: 1,100				

KM# 1237   50 DOLLARS
15.5500 g., 0.9990 Platinum 0.4994 oz. APW, 25 mm.   **Ruler:**
Elizabeth II **Obv:** Head right **Rev:** Dreaming kangaroo, multicolor

Date	Mintage	F	VF	XF	Unc	BU
2009P Proof	1,000	Value: 1,500				

KM# 1238   50 DOLLARS
15.5500 g., 0.9990 Platinum 0.4994 oz. APW, 25 mm.   **Ruler:**
Elizabeth II **Obv:** Head right **Rev:** Dreaming dolphin, multicolor

Date	Mintage	F	VF	XF	Unc	BU
2009P Proof	1,000	Value: 1,500				

KM# 1239   50 DOLLARS
15.5500 g., 0.9990 Platinum 0.4994 oz. APW, 25 mm.   **Ruler:**
Elizabeth II **Obv:** Head right **Rev:** Dreaming king brown snake,
multicolor

Date	Mintage	F	VF	XF	Unc	BU
2009P Proof	1,000	Value: 1,500				

KM# 1240   50 DOLLARS
15.5500 g., 0.9990 Platinum 0.4994 oz. APW, 25 mm.   **Ruler:**
Elizabeth II **Obv:** Head right **Rev:** Dreaming brolga, multicolor

Date	Mintage	F	VF	XF	Unc	BU
2009P Proof	1,000	Value: 1,500				

KM# 1241   50 DOLLARS
15.5500 g., 0.9990 Platinum 0.4994 oz. APW, 25 mm.   **Ruler:**
Elizabeth II **Obv:** Head right **Rev:** Dreaming echidna, multicolor

Date	Mintage	F	VF	XF	Unc	BU
2009P Proof	1,000	Value: 1,500				

KM# 1398   50 DOLLARS
15.5000 g., 0.9990 Platinum 0.4978 oz. APW, 26 mm.   **Ruler:**
Elizabeth II **Obv:** Head right **Rev:** Multicolor frill-neck lizard

Date	Mintage	F	VF	XF	Unc	BU
2010P Proof	1,000	Value: 1,550				

KM# 1400   50 DOLLARS
15.5000 g., 0.9990 Gold 0.4978 oz. AGW, 26 mm.   **Ruler:**
Elizabeth II **Obv:** Head right **Rev:** Frill-neck lizard

Date	Mintage	F	VF	XF	Unc	BU
2010P Proof	1,000	Value: 1,250				

KM# 1404   50 DOLLARS
15.5500 g., 0.9990 Platinum 0.4978 oz. APW, 26 mm.   **Ruler:**
Elizabeth II **Obv:** Head right **Rev:** Multicolor koala

Date	Mintage	F	VF	XF	Unc	BU
2010P Proof	1,000	Value: 1,550				

KM# 1406   50 DOLLARS
15.5000 g., 0.9990 Gold 0.4978 oz. AGW, 26 mm.   **Ruler:**
Elizabeth II **Obv:** Head right **Rev:** Koala

Date	Mintage	F	VF	XF	Unc	BU
2010P Proof	1,000	Value: 1,250				

KM# 1410   50 DOLLARS
15.5000 g., 0.9990 Platinum 0.4978 oz. APW, 26 mm.   **Ruler:**
Elizabeth II **Obv:** Head right **Rev:** Multicolor platypus

Date	Mintage	F	VF	XF	Unc	BU
2010P Proof	1,000	Value: 1,550				

KM# 1412   50 DOLLARS
15.5000 g., 0.9990 Gold 0.4978 oz. AGW **Ruler:** Elizabeth II
Obv: Head right **Rev:** Platypus

Date	Mintage	F	VF	XF	Unc	BU
2010P Proof	1,000	Value: 1,250				

KM# 1416   50 DOLLARS
15.5000 g., 0.9990 Platinum 0.4978 oz. APW, 26 mm.   **Ruler:**
Elizabeth II **Obv:** Head right **Rev:** Multicolor saltwater crocodile

Date	Mintage	F	VF	XF	Unc	BU
2010P Proof	1,000	Value: 1,550				

KM# 1418   50 DOLLARS
15.5000 g., 0.9990 Gold 0.4978 oz. AGW, 26 mm.   **Ruler:**
Elizabeth II **Obv:** Head right **Rev:** Saltwater crocodile

Date	Mintage	F	VF	XF	Unc	BU
2010P Proof	1,000	Value: 1,250				

KM# 1422   50 DOLLARS
15.5000 g., 0.9990 Platinum 0.4978 oz. APW, 26 mm.   **Ruler:**
Elizabeth II **Obv:** Head right **Rev:** Multicolor wombat

Date	Mintage	F	VF	XF	Unc	BU
2010P Proof	1,000	Value: 1,100				

KM# 1424   50 DOLLARS
15.5000 g., 0.9990 Gold 0.4978 oz. AGW, 26 mm.   **Ruler:**
Elizabeth II **Obv:** Head right **Rev:** Wombat

Date	Mintage	F	VF	XF	Unc	BU
2010P Proof	2,500	Value: 1,250				

KM# 1537   50 DOLLARS
15.5500 g., 0.9990 Gold 0.4994 oz. AGW **Ruler:** Elizabeth II
Subject: Dreaming Emu **Rev:** Linear emu in color

Date	Mintage	F	VF	XF	Unc	BU
2011P Proof	—	Value: 1,250				

KM# 1539   50 DOLLARS
15.5500 g., 0.9990 Platinum 0.4994 oz. APW **Ruler:** Elizabeth II
Subject: Dreaming Emu **Rev:** Linear emu in color

Date	Mintage	F	VF	XF	Unc	BU
2011P Proof	1,000	Value: 1,800				

KM# 1543   50 DOLLARS
15.5500 g., 0.9990 Gold 0.4994 oz. AGW **Ruler:** Elizabeth II
Subject: Dreaming Tasmanian Devil **Rev:** Linear tasmanian
devil in color

Date	Mintage	F	VF	XF	Unc	BU
2011P Proof	—	Value: 1,250				

KM# 1545   50 DOLLARS
15.5500 g., 0.9990 Platinum 0.4994 oz. APW **Ruler:** Elizabeth II
Subject: Dreaming Tasmanian Devil **Rev:** Linear tasmanian
devil in color

Date	Mintage	F	VF	XF	Unc	BU
2011P Proof	—	Value: 1,800				

KM# 1549   50 DOLLARS
15.5500 g., 0.9990 Gold 0.4994 oz. AGW **Ruler:** Elizabeth II
Series: Dreaming Kookaburra **Rev:** Linear kookaburra in color

Date	Mintage	F	VF	XF	Unc	BU
2011P Proof	—	Value: 1,250				

KM# 1551   50 DOLLARS
15.5500 g., 0.9990 Platinum 0.4994 oz. APW **Ruler:** Elizabeth II
Subject: Dreaming Kookaburra **Rev:** Linear kookaburra in color

Date	Mintage	F	VF	XF	Unc	BU
2011P Proof	1,000	Value: 1,800				

KM# 1555 50 DOLLARS
15.5500 g., 0.9990 Gold 0.4994 oz. AGW **Ruler:** Elizabeth II
Subject: Dreaming shark **Rev:** Linear shark in color

Date	Mintage	F	VF	XF	Unc	BU
2011P Proof	—	Value: 1,250				

KM# 1557 50 DOLLARS
15.5500 g., 0.9990 Platinum 0.4994 oz. APW **Ruler:** Elizabeth II
Subject: Dreaming shark **Rev:** Linear shark in color

Date	Mintage	F	VF	XF	Unc	BU
2011P Proof	1,000	Value: 1,800				

KM# 1561 50 DOLLARS
15.5500 g., 0.9990 Gold 0.4994 oz. AGW **Ruler:** Elizabeth II
Subject: Dreaming Dingo **Rev:** Linear dingo in color

Date	Mintage	F	VF	XF	Unc	BU
2011P Proof	—	Value: 1,250				

KM# 1563 50 DOLLARS
15.5500 g., 0.9990 Platinum 0.4994 oz. APW **Ruler:** Elizabeth II
Subject: Dreaming Dingo **Rev:** Linear dingo in color

Date	Mintage	F	VF	XF	Unc	BU
2011P Proof	1,000	Value: 1,800				

KM# 1726 50 DOLLARS
15.5540 g., 0.9990 Gold 0.4996 oz. AGW, 25.6 mm. **Ruler:**
Elizabeth II **Rev:** Green and Gold Bell Frog in grass

Date	Mintage	F	VF	XF	Unc	BU
2012P Proof	500	Value: 950				

KM# 1727 50 DOLLARS
15.5540 g., 0.9990 Gold 0.4996 oz. AGW, 25.6 mm. **Ruler:**
Elizabeth II **Rev:** Kookaburra standing right

Date	Mintage	F	VF	XF	Unc	BU
2012P Proof	500	Value: 950				

KM# 1728 50 DOLLARS
15.5540 g., 0.9990 Gold 0.4996 oz. AGW, 25.6 mm. **Ruler:**
Elizabeth II **Rev:** Whale Shark swimming right

Date	Mintage	F	VF	XF	Unc	BU
2012P Proof	500	Value: 950				

KM# 1729 50 DOLLARS
15.5540 g., 0.9990 Gold 0.4996 oz. AGW, 25.6 mm. **Ruler:**
Elizabeth II **Rev:** Kangaroo bounding right

Date	Mintage	F	VF	XF	Unc	BU
2012P Proof	500	Value: 950				

KM# 1730 50 DOLLARS
15.5540 g., 0.9990 Gold 0.4996 oz. AGW, 25.6 mm. **Ruler:**
Elizabeth II **Rev:** Goanna lizard right

Date	Mintage	F	VF	XF	Unc	BU
2012P Proof	500	Value: 950				

KM# 1731 100 DOLLARS
31.1200 g., 0.9995 Platinum 1.0000 oz. APW, 32.6 mm. **Ruler:**
Elizabeth II **Obv:** Head with tiara right **Rev:** Platypus swimming
downward **Edge:** Reeded

Date	Mintage	F	VF	XF	Unc	BU
2012P	30,000	Value: 1,750				

BULLION - LUNAR YEAR

KM# 1010 25 CENTS
0.9990 Silver Gilt, 17.8 mm. **Ruler:** Elizabeth II **Obv:** Bust with
tiara right **Obv. Legend:** ELIZABETH II - AUSTRALIA **Rev:** 4
Chinese characters **Rev. Legend:** LUNAR NEW YEAR - GOOD
FORTUNE & PROSPERITY

Date	Mintage	F	VF	XF	Unc	BU
2007 Proof	8,888	Value: 45.00				

KM# 579 50 CENTS
15.5518 g., 0.9990 Silver 0.4995 oz. ASW, 32.1 mm. **Ruler:**
Elizabeth II **Subject:** Year of the Horse **Obv:** Head with tiara
right, denomination below **Rev:** Horse running left **Edge:** Reeded

Date	Mintage	F	VF	XF	Unc	BU
2002P Proof	5,000	Value: 35.00				

KM# 664 50 CENTS
16.4000 g., 0.9990 Silver 0.5267 oz. ASW, 31.9 mm. **Ruler:**
Elizabeth II **Subject:** Year of the Goat **Obv:** Head with tiara right,
denomination below **Rev:** Two goats **Edge:** Reeded

Date	Mintage	F	VF	XF	Unc	BU
2003	—	—	—	—	20.00	25.00
2003 Proof	—	Value: 35.00				

KM# 673 50 CENTS
15.5518 g., 0.9990 Silver 0.4995 oz. ASW, 32.1 mm. **Ruler:**
Elizabeth II **Subject:** Year of the Monkey **Obv:** Head with tiara right,
denomination below **Rev:** Monkey sitting on branch **Edge:** Reeded

Date	Mintage	F	VF	XF	Unc	BU
2004 Proof	11,000	Value: 35.00				

KM# 791 50 CENTS
15.5680 g., 0.9990 Silver 0.5000 oz. ASW, 32.1 mm. **Ruler:**
Elizabeth II **Subject:** Year of the Rooster **Obv:** Elizabeth II **Rev:**
Standing Rooster looking backwards **Edge:** Reeded

Date	Mintage	F	VF	XF	Unc	BU
2005P Proof	6,000	Value: 50.00				

KM# 814 50 CENTS
15.5500 g., 0.9990 Silver 0.4994 oz. ASW **Ruler:** Elizabeth II
Subject: Bullion Lunar Year - Rooster **Obv:** Head with tiara right

Date	Mintage	F	VF	XF	Unc	BU
2005	—	—	—	—	—	20.00

KM# 1750 50 CENTS
15.5500 g., 0.9990 Silver 0.4994 oz. ASW, 32 mm. **Ruler:**
Elizabeth II **Subject:** Year of the Ox **Obv:** Head with tiara right
Rev: Two oxen standing

Date	Mintage	F	VF	XF	Unc	BU
2009P	—	—	—	—	—	85.00

KM# 1750a 50 CENTS
15.5500 g., 0.9990 Silver 0.4994 oz. ASW, 32 mm. **Ruler:**
Elizabeth II **Subject:** Year of the Ox **Rev:** Two colored oxen
standing

Date	Mintage	F	VF	XF	Unc	BU
2009P	—	—	—	—	—	100

KM# 1370 50 CENTS
15.5500 g., 0.9900 Silver 0.4949 oz. ASW, 32 mm. **Ruler:**
Elizabeth II **Subject:** Year of the Tiger **Obv:** Head right **Rev:**
Tiger at rest left

Date	Mintage	F	VF	XF	Unc	BU
2010P	—	—	—	—	—	20.00

KM# 1474 50 CENTS
15.5600 g., 0.9990 Silver 0.4997 oz. ASW, 32 mm. **Ruler:**
Elizabeth II **Subject:** Year of the Rabbit **Rev:** Mother and baby
rabbit nose to nose

Date	Mintage	F	VF	XF	Unc	BU
2011P Proof	—	Value: 30.00				

KM# 1663 50 CENTS
15.5518 g., 0.9990 Silver 0.4995 oz. ASW, 31.9 mm. **Ruler:**
Elizabeth II **Subject:** Year of the Dragon

Date	Mintage	F	VF	XF	Unc	BU
2012P Proof	—	Value: 25.00				

KM# 1663a   50 CENTS
15.5518 g., 0.9990 Silver 0.4995 oz. ASW, 32.1 mm. **Ruler:**
Elizabeth II **Subject:** Year of the Dragon **Rev:** Dragon in color

Date	Mintage	F	VF	XF	Unc	BU
2012P Proof	—	Value: 30.00				

KM# 536   DOLLAR
31.1035 g., 0.9990 Silver 0.9990 oz. ASW, 40.6 mm. **Ruler:**
Elizabeth II **Subject:** Year of the Snake **Obv:** Head with tiara
right, denomination below **Rev:** Snake with eggs **Edge:** Reeded

Date	Mintage	F	VF	XF	Unc	BU
2001	300,000	—	—	—	80.00	100
2001P Proof	2,500	Value: 100				

KM# 536a   DOLLAR
31.6350 g., 0.9990 Silver partially gilt 1.0160 oz. ASW, 40.6 mm.
Ruler: Elizabeth II **Subject:** Year of the Snake **Obv:** Head with
tiara right, denomination below **Rev:** Gold-plated snake **Edge:**
Reeded

Date	Mintage	F	VF	XF	Unc	BU
2001	50,000	—	—	—	45.00	50.00

KM# 580   DOLLAR
31.1035 g., 0.9990 Silver 0.9990 oz. ASW, 40.6 mm. **Ruler:**
Elizabeth II **Subject:** Year of the Horse **Obv:** Head with tiara
right, denomination below **Rev:** Horse running left **Edge:** Reeded

Date	Mintage	F	VF	XF	Unc	BU
2002P	—	—	—	—	75.00	80.00
2002P Proof	2,500	Value: 75.00				

KM# 580a   DOLLAR
31.6350 g., 0.9990 Silver partially gilt 1.0160 oz. ASW, 40.6 mm.
Ruler: Elizabeth II **Obv:** Head with tiara right **Rev:** Gold-plated
horse **Edge:** Reeded

Date	Mintage	F	VF	XF	Unc	BU
2002	50,000	—	—	—	40.00	45.00

KM# 665   DOLLAR
31.6200 g., 0.9990 Silver 1.0155 oz. ASW, 40.3 mm. **Ruler:**
Elizabeth II **Subject:** Year of the Goat **Obv:** Head with tiara right,
denomination below **Rev:** Two goats **Edge:** Reeded

Date	Mintage	F	VF	XF	Unc	BU
2003	—	—	—	—	50.00	75.00
2003 Proof	—	Value: 75.00				

KM# 665a   DOLLAR
31.6350 g., 0.9990 Silver partially gilt 1.0160 oz. ASW, 40.6 mm.
Ruler: Elizabeth II **Subject:** Year of the Goat **Obv:** Head with tiara
right, denomination below **Rev:** Gold-plated goat **Edge:** Reeded

Date	Mintage	F	VF	XF	Unc	BU
2003	50,000	—	—	—	50.00	55.00

KM# 674a   DOLLAR
31.6350 g., 0.9990 Silver partially gilt 1.0160 oz. ASW, 40.6 mm.
Ruler: Elizabeth II **Subject:** Year of the Monkey **Obv:** Head with
tiara right, denomination below **Rev:** Gold-plated monkey **Edge:**
Reeded

Date	Mintage	F	VF	XF	Unc	BU
2004	50,000	—	—	—	50.00	55.00

KM# 674   DOLLAR
31.1035 g., 0.9990 Silver 0.9990 oz. ASW, 40.6 mm. **Ruler:**
Elizabeth II **Subject:** Year of the Monkey **Obv:** Head with tiara right,
denomination below **Rev:** Monkey sitting on branch **Edge:** Reeded

Date	Mintage	F	VF	XF	Unc	BU
2004	—	—	—	—	40.00	45.00
2004 Proof	8,500	Value: 55.00				

KM# 695   DOLLAR
31.1050 g., 0.9990 Silver 0.9990 oz. ASW, 40.5 mm. **Ruler:**
Elizabeth II **Subject:** Year of the Rooster **Obv:** Head with tiara
right, denomination below **Rev:** Rooster **Edge:** Reeded

Date	Mintage	F	VF	XF	Unc	BU
2005	—	—	—	—	75.00	65.00
2005P Proof	3,500	Value: 80.00				

KM# 695a   DOLLAR
31.6350 g., 0.9990 Silver partially gilt 1.0160 oz. ASW, 40.5 mm.
Ruler: Elizabeth II **Subject:** Year of the Rooster **Obv:** Head with
tiara right, denomination below **Rev:** Gilt rooster **Edge:** Reeded

Date	Mintage	F	VF	XF	Unc	BU
2005 Polished fields	47,200	—	—	—	45.00	50.00
2005 Matte fields	2,800	—	—	—	175	185

KM# 1011   DOLLAR
31.1050 g., 0.9990 Silver 0.9990 oz. ASW, 40 mm. **Ruler:**
Elizabeth II **Obv:** Crowned bust right at top **Obv. Legend:**
ELIZABETH II - AUSTRALIA **Rev:** 12 Lunar figures

Date	Mintage	F	VF	XF	Unc	BU
2007 Proof	8,888	Value: 110				

KM# 1755   DOLLAR
31.1050 g., 0.9990 Silver 0.9990 oz. ASW, 40 mm. **Ruler:**
Elizabeth II **Subject:** Year of the Mouse **Obv:** Head with tiara
right **Rev:** Mouse pair

Date	Mintage	F	VF	XF	Unc	BU
2008P	—	—	—	—	—	75.00

KM# 1755a   DOLLAR
31.1050 g., 0.9990 Silver 0.9990 oz. ASW, 40 mm. **Ruler:**
Elizabeth II **Subject:** Year of the Mouse **Obv:** Head with tiara
right **Rev:** Mouse pair in color

Date	Mintage	F	VF	XF	Unc	BU
2008P	—	—	—	—	—	85.00

KM# 1317   DOLLAR
31.1050 g., 0.9990 Silver 0.9990 oz. ASW, 40.6 mm. **Ruler:**
Elizabeth II **Subject:** Year of the Tiger **Obv:** Head right **Rev:**
Tiger at rest left

Date	Mintage	F	VF	XF	Unc	BU
2010P	—	—	—	—	—	50.00
2010P Proof	1,000	Value: 75.00				

KM# 1317a   DOLLAR
31.1050 g., 0.9990 Silver 0.9990 oz. ASW, 40.6 mm. **Ruler:**
Elizabeth II **Subject:** Year of the Tiger **Obv:** Head right **Rev:**
Tiger at rest left, partially gilt

Date	Mintage	F	VF	XF	Unc	BU
2010P Proof	50,000	Value: 80.00				

KM# 1317b   DOLLAR
31.1050 g., 0.9990 Silver 0.9990 oz. ASW, 40.6 mm. **Ruler:**
Elizabeth II **Subject:** Year of the Tiger **Obv:** Head right **Rev:**
Multicolor tiger at rest left

Date	Mintage	F	VF	XF	Unc	BU
2010P Proof	170,000	Value: 75.00				

KM# 1475   DOLLAR
31.1050 g., 0.9990 Silver 0.9990 oz. ASW, 40 mm. **Ruler:**
Elizabeth II **Subject:** Year of the Rabbit **Rev:** Mother and baby
rabbit nose to nose

Date	Mintage	F	VF	XF	Unc	BU
2011P Proof	—	Value: 50.00				

KM# 1475a DOLLAR
31.1050 g., 0.9990 Silver 0.9990 oz. ASW, 40.5 mm. **Ruler:** Elizabeth II **Subject:** Year of the Rabbit **Rev:** Two rabbits, partially gilt

Date	Mintage	F	VF	XF	Unc	BU
2011P Proof	—	Value: 75.00				

KM# 1475b DOLLAR
31.1050 g., 0.9990 Silver 0.9990 oz. ASW, 40.5 mm. **Ruler:** Elizabeth II **Subject:** Year of the Rabbit **Rev:** Two rabbits in color

Date	Mintage	F	VF	XF	Unc	BU
2011P Proof	—	Value: 75.00				

KM# 1664a DOLLAR
31.1050 g., 0.9990 Silver partially gilt 0.9990 oz. ASW, 40.5 mm. **Ruler:** Elizabeth II **Subject:** Year of the Dragon **Rev:** Dragon gilt

Date	Mintage	F	VF	XF	Unc	BU
2012P Proof	—	Value: 75.00				

KM# 1664 DOLLAR
31.1050 g., 0.9990 Silver 0.9990 oz. ASW, 40.5 mm. **Ruler:** Elizabeth II **Subject:** Year of the Dragon **Rev:** Dragon

Date	Mintage	F	VF	XF	Unc	BU
2012P	—	—	—	—	—	40.00
2012P Proof	—	Value: 45.00				

KM# 1664j DOLLAR
31.1050 g., 0.9990 Silver 0.9990 oz. ASW, 40 mm. **Ruler:**

Elizabeth II **Subject:** Year of the Dragon **Obv:** Head with tiara right **Rev:** Dragon colored brown and orange

Date	Mintage	F	VF	XF	Unc	BU
2012P	—	—	—	—	—	100

KM# 1664b DOLLAR
31.1050 g., 0.9990 Silver 0.9990 oz. ASW, 40.5 mm. **Ruler:** Elizabeth II **Subject:** Year of the Dragon **Rev:** Dragon in black collor

Date	Mintage	F	VF	XF	Unc	BU
2012P	—	—	—	—	—	70.00
2012P Proof	—	Value: 75.00				

KM# 1664c DOLLAR
31.1050 g., 0.9990 Silver 0.9990 oz. ASW, 40 mm. **Ruler:** Elizabeth II **Subject:** Year of the Dragon **Obv:** Head with tiara right **Rev:** Dragon colored red, brown and yellow

Date	Mintage	F	VF	XF	Unc	BU
2012P	20,000	—	—	—	—	100

KM# 1664d DOLLAR
31.1050 g., 0.9990 Silver 0.9990 oz. ASW, 40 mm. **Ruler:** Elizabeth II **Subject:** Year of the Dragon **Obv:** Bust with tiara right **Rev:** Dragon colored black and red

Date	Mintage	F	VF	XF	Unc	BU
2012P	—	—	—	—	—	100

KM# 1664e DOLLAR
31.1050 g., 0.9990 Silver 0.9990 oz. ASW, 40 mm. **Ruler:** Elizabeth II **Subject:** Year of the Dragon **Obv:** Head with tiara right **Rev:** Dragon colored yellow and lavender

Date	Mintage	F	VF	XF	Unc	BU
2012P	—	—	—	—	—	100

KM# 1664f DOLLAR
31.1050 g., 0.9990 Silver 0.9990 oz. ASW, 40 mm. **Ruler:**

Elizabeth II **Subject:** Year of the Dragon **Obv:** Head with tiara right **Rev:** Dragon colored blue and yellow

Date	Mintage	F	VF	XF	Unc	BU
2012P	—	—	—	—	—	100

KM# 1664g DOLLAR
31.1050 g., 0.9990 Silver 0.9990 oz. ASW, 40 mm. **Ruler:** Elizabeth II **Subject:** Year of the Dragon **Obv:** Head with tiara right **Rev:** Dragon colored purple and yellow

Date	Mintage	F	VF	XF	Unc	BU
2012P	—	—	—	—	—	100

KM# 1664h DOLLAR
31.1050 g., 0.9990 Silver 0.9990 oz. ASW, 40 mm. **Ruler:** Elizabeth II **Subject:** Year of the Dragon **Obv:** Head with tiara right **Rev:** Dragon colored orange, brown and yellow

Date	Mintage	F	VF	XF	Unc	BU
2012P	—	—	—	—	—	100

KM# 1664i DOLLAR
31.1050 g., 0.9990 Silver 0.9990 oz. ASW, 40 mm. **Ruler:** Elizabeth II **Subject:** Year of the Dragon **Obv:** Head with tiara right **Rev:** Dragon colored white and blue

Date	Mintage	F	VF	XF	Unc	BU
2012P	—	—	—	—	—	100

KM# 1664k DOLLAR
31.1050 g., 0.9990 Silver 0.9990 oz. ASW, 40 mm. **Ruler:** Elizabeth II **Subject:** Year of the Dragon **Obv:** head with tiara right **Rev:** Dragon colored lavender and grey

Date	Mintage	F	VF	XF	Unc	BU
2012P	—	—	—	—	—	100

KM# 1713 DOLLAR
31.1350 g., 0.9990 Silver 1.0000 oz. ASW, 32.6 mm. **Ruler:** Elizabeth II **Subject:** Year of the Dragon **Obv:** Head with tiara right **Rev:** Dragon **Edge:** Reeded **Note:** High Relief

Date	Mintage	F	VF	XF	Unc	BU
2012P Proof	7,500	Value: 100				

KM# 537 2 DOLLARS
62.2070 g., 0.9990 Silver 1.9979 oz. ASW, 50.3 mm. **Ruler:** Elizabeth II **Subject:** Year of the Snake **Obv:** Head with tiara right, denomination below **Rev:** Snake with eggs **Edge:** Segmented reeding

Date	Mintage	F	VF	XF	Unc	BU
2001	—	—	—	—	75.00	85.00
2001P Proof	1,000	Value: 110				

KM# 581   2 DOLLARS
62.2070 g., 0.9990 Silver 1.9979 oz. ASW, 50 mm. **Ruler:**
Elizabeth II **Subject:** Year of the Horse **Obv:** Head with tiara
right, denomination below **Rev:** Horse running left **Edge:** Reeded

Date	Mintage	F	VF	XF	Unc	BU
2002	—	—	—	—	75.00	85.00
2002P Proof	1,000	Value: 110				

KM# 679   2 DOLLARS
62.8500 g., 0.9990 Silver 2.0186 oz. ASW, 50 mm. **Ruler:**
Elizabeth II **Subject:** Year of the Goat **Obv:** Head with tiara right,
denomination below **Rev:** Two goats **Edge:** Reeded

Date	Mintage	F	VF	XF	Unc	BU
2003	—	—	—	—	75.00	85.00

KM# 675   2 DOLLARS
62.2070 g., 0.9990 Silver 1.9979 oz. ASW, 50 mm. **Ruler:**
Elizabeth II **Subject:** Year of the Monkey **Obv:** Head with tiara
right, denomination below **Rev:** Monkey sitting on branch **Edge:**
Reeded

Date	Mintage	F	VF	XF	Unc	BU
2004	—	—	—	—	75.00	85.00
2004 Proof	7,000	Value: 110				

KM# 793   2 DOLLARS
62.2700 g., 0.9990 Silver 1.9999 oz. ASW, 50.3 mm. **Ruler:**
Elizabeth II **Subject:** Year of the Rooster **Obv:** Elizabeth II **Rev:**
Standing Rooster looking backwards **Edge:** Reeded

Date	Mintage	F	VF	XF	Unc	BU
2005P Proof	2,000	Value: 150				

KM# 1751   2 DOLLARS
62.2700 g., 0.9990 Silver 1.9999 oz. ASW, 50 mm. **Ruler:**
Elizabeth II **Subject:** Year of the Ox **Obv:** Head with tiara right
Rev: Two oxen standing

Date	Mintage	F	VF	XF	Unc	BU
2009P	—	—	—	—	—	125

KM# 1751a   2 DOLLARS
62.2700 g., 0.9990 Silver 1.9999 oz. ASW, 50 mm. **Ruler:**
Elizabeth II **Subject:** Year of the Ox **Obv:** Head with tiara right
Rev: Two colored oxen standing

Date	Mintage	F	VF	XF	Unc	BU
2009P	—	—	—	—	—	125

KM# 1320   2 DOLLARS
62.2100 g., 0.9990 Silver 1.9980 oz. ASW, 50 mm. **Ruler:**
Elizabeth II **Subject:** Year of the Tiger **Obv:** Head right **Rev:**
Tiger seated left

Date	Mintage	F	VF	XF	Unc	BU
2010P Proof	1,000	Value: 160				

KM# 1476   2 DOLLARS
62.2000 g., 0.9990 Silver 1.9977 oz. ASW **Ruler:** Elizabeth II
Subject: Year of the Rabbit **Rev:** Mother and baby rabbit nose
to nose

Date	Mintage	F	VF	XF	Unc	BU
2011P Proof	—	Value: 110				

KM# 1665   2 DOLLARS
62.2700 g., 0.9990 Silver 1.9999 oz. ASW, 50.3 mm. **Ruler:**
Elizabeth II **Subject:** Year of the Dragon

Date	Mintage	F	VF	XF	Unc	BU
2012P Proof	—	Value: 150				

KM# 538   5 DOLLARS
1.5710 g., 0.9990 Gold 0.0505 oz. AGW, 14.1 mm. **Ruler:**
Elizabeth II **Subject:** Year of the Snake **Obv:** Head with tiara
right, denomination below **Rev:** Snake in tree **Edge:** Reeded

Date	Mintage	F	VF	XF	Unc	BU
2001	100,000	—	—	—	—	95.00
2001P Proof	100,000	Value: 100				

KM# 582   5 DOLLARS
1.5552 g., 0.9990 Gold 0.0499 oz. AGW, 14.1 mm. **Ruler:**
Elizabeth II **Subject:** Year of the Horse **Obv:** Head with tiara right,
denomination below **Rev:** Horse galloping left **Edge:** Reeded

Date	Mintage	F	VF	XF	Unc	BU
2002P	100,000	—	—	—	—	95.00

KM# 668   5 DOLLARS
1.5710 g., 0.9999 Gold 0.0505 oz. AGW, 14.1 mm. **Ruler:**
Elizabeth II **Subject:** Year of the Monkey **Obv:** Head with tiara
right, denomination below **Rev:** Monkey **Edge:** Reeded

Date	Mintage	F	VF	XF	Unc	BU
2004P Proof	100,000	Value: 100				

KM# 1022.1   5 DOLLARS
1.5700 g., 0.9999 Gold 0.0505 oz. AGW, 13.93 mm. **Ruler:**
Elizabeth II **Obv:** Head with tiara right **Rev:** Rooster standing
right **Edge:** Reeded **Note:** Polished images with matte fields.

Date	Mintage	F	VF	XF	Unc	BU
2005 Proof	28,000	Value: 110				

KM# 1022.2   5 DOLLARS
1.5700 g., 0.9999 Gold 0.0505 oz. AGW, 13.93 mm. **Ruler:**
Elizabeth II **Subject:** Year of the Rooster **Obv:** Head with tiara
right **Rev:** Rooster standing right, multicolor **Edge:** Reeded

Date	Mintage	F	VF	XF	Unc	BU
2005 Proof	1,000	Value: 120				

KM# 1481   5 DOLLARS
1.5700 g., 0.9999 Gold 0.0505 oz. AGW, 14.1 mm. **Ruler:**
Elizabeth II **Subject:** Year of the Rabbit

Date	Mintage	F	VF	XF	Unc	BU
2011P Proof	—	Value: 100				

KM# 1666   5 DOLLARS
155.5175 g., 0.9990 Silver 4.9948 oz. ASW, 65 mm. **Ruler:**
Elizabeth II **Subject:** Year of the Dragon

Date	Mintage	F	VF	XF	Unc	BU
2012P Proof	—	Value: 225				

KM# 1670   5 DOLLARS
1.5552 g., 0.9990 Gold 0.0499 oz. AGW, 14.1 mm. **Ruler:**
Elizabeth II **Subject:** Year of the Dragon **Rev:** Dragon

Date	Mintage	F	VF	XF	Unc	BU
2012P Proof	—	Value: 110				

KM# 1679   5 DOLLARS
1.5500 g., 0.9990 Gold 0.0498 oz. AGW, 14.1 mm. **Ruler:**
Elizabeth II **Subject:** Year of the Dragon **Rev:** Dragon head
facing in color

Date	Mintage	F	VF	XF	Unc	BU
2012P Proof	—	Value: 125				

KM# 743   8 DOLLARS
155.5175 g., 0.9990 Silver 4.9948 oz. ASW, 65 mm. **Ruler:**
Elizabeth II **Subject:** Year of the Monkey **Obv:** Head with tiara
right, denomination below **Rev:** Gold-plated seated monkey and
multicolored ornamentation **Edge:** Reeded **Note:** Illustration
reduced.

Date	Mintage	F	VF	XF	Unc	BU
2004	6,000	—	—	—	—	220

KM# 1023   8 DOLLARS
155.5150 g., 0.9990 Silver partially gilt 4.9947 oz. ASW, 65 mm.
Ruler: Elizabeth II **Subject:** Year of the Rooster **Obv:** Head with
tiara right **Rev:** Rooster standing left gilt, floral in color **Edge:**
Reeded

Date	Mintage	F	VF	XF	Unc	BU
2005 Proof	10,000	Value: 300				

KM# 1754   8 DOLLARS
155.5150 g., 0.9990 Silver 4.9947 oz. ASW, 65 mm. **Ruler:**
Elizabeth II **Subject:** Year of the Dog **Rev:** German shepard in
color seated

Date	Mintage	F	VF	XF	Unc	BU
2006P	—	—	—	—	—	220

KM# 1756   8 DOLLARS
155.5750 g., 0.9990 Silver 4.9966 oz. ASW, 65 mm. **Ruler:**
Elizabeth II **Subject:** Year of the Pig **Obv:** Head with tiara right
Rev: Pig in color

Date	Mintage	F	VF	XF	Unc	BU
2007P	—	—	—	—	—	225

Year of the Mouse

KM# 1757   8 DOLLARS
155.5750 g., 0.9990 Silver 4.9966 oz. ASW, 65 mm. **Ruler:**
Elizabeth II **Subject:** Year of the Mouse **Obv:** Head with tiara
right **Rev:** Two mice in color

Date	Mintage	F	VF	XF	Unc	BU
2008P	—	—	—	—	—	225

KM# 1371   8 DOLLARS
155.5175 g., 0.9990 Silver 4.9948 oz. ASW, 65 mm. **Ruler:**
Elizabeth II **Subject:** Year of the Tiger **Obv:** Head right **Rev:**
Tiger at rest left

Date	Mintage	F	VF	XF	Unc	BU
2010P	—	—	—	—	—	225

KM# 539   10 DOLLARS
311.0350 g., 0.9990 Silver 9.9896 oz. ASW, 75.5 mm. **Ruler:**
Elizabeth II **Subject:** Year of the Snake **Obv:** Head with tiara
right, denomination below **Rev:** Snake with eggs **Edge:**
Segmented reeding

Date	Mintage	F	VF	XF	Unc	BU
2001	—	—	—	—	375	400
2001P Proof	250	Value: 475				

KM# 583   10 DOLLARS
311.0350 g., 0.9990 Silver 9.9896 oz. ASW, 75.5 mm. **Ruler:**
Elizabeth II **Subject:** Year of the Horse **Obv:** Head with tiara
right, denomination below **Rev:** Horse running left **Edge:**
Segmented reeding

Date	Mintage	F	VF	XF	Unc	BU
2002	—	—	—	—	375	400
2002P Proof	500	Value: 450				

KM# 710   10 DOLLARS
311.0350 g., 0.9990 Silver 9.9896 oz. ASW, 75.5 mm. **Ruler:**
Elizabeth II **Subject:** Year of the Goat **Obv:** Head with tiara right,
denomination below **Rev:** Goat

Date	Mintage	F	VF	XF	Unc	BU
2003	—	—	—	—	375	400
2003 Proof	—	Value: 450				

KM# 1339   10 DOLLARS
311.0350 g., 0.9990 Silver 9.9896 oz. ASW, 75.5 mm. **Ruler:**
Elizabeth II **Subject:** Year of the Goat **Obv:** Head right

Date	Mintage	F	VF	XF	Unc	BU
2003P	—	—	—	—	400	375
2003P Proof	—	Value: 475				

KM# 676   10 DOLLARS
311.0350 g., 0.9990 Silver 9.9896 oz. ASW, 75.5 mm. **Ruler:**
Elizabeth II **Subject:** Year of the Monkey **Obv:** Head with tiara
right, denomination below **Rev:** Monkey sitting on branch **Edge:**
Segmented reeding

Date	Mintage	F	VF	XF	Unc	BU
2004	—	—	—	—	375	400
2004 Proof	5,000	Value: 475				

KM# 696   10 DOLLARS
311.0350 g., 0.9990 Silver 9.9896 oz. ASW, 75.5 mm. **Ruler:**
Elizabeth II **Subject:** Year of the Rooster **Obv:** Head with tiara
right, denomination below **Rev:** Rooster

Date	Mintage	F	VF	XF	Unc	BU
2005	—	—	—	—	375	400
2005 Proof	—	Value: 475				

KM# 1057   10 DOLLARS
3.1100 g., 0.9990 Gold 0.0999 oz. AGW, 17.53 mm. **Ruler:**
Elizabeth II **Subject:** Year of the Rat

Date	Mintage	F	VF	XF	Unc	BU
2008 Proof	2,500	Value: 200				

KM# 1079   10 DOLLARS
3.1100 g., 0.9990 Gold 0.0999 oz. AGW, 17.53 mm. **Ruler:**
Elizabeth II **Subject:** Year of the Ox

Date	Mintage	F	VF	XF	Unc	BU
2009 Proof	2,500	Value: 245				

KM# 1752   10 DOLLARS
311.0350 g., 0.9990 Silver 9.9896 oz. ASW, 75.5 mm. **Ruler:**
Elizabeth II **Subject:** Year of the Ox **Obv:** Head with tiara right
Rev: Two oxen standing

Date	Mintage	F	VF	XF	Unc	BU
2009P	—	—	—	—	—	350

Year of the Ox

KM# 1752a   10 DOLLARS
311.0350 g., 0.9990 Silver 9.9896 oz. ASW, 75.5 mm. **Ruler:**
Elizabeth II **Subject:** Year of the Ox **Obv:** Head with tiara right
Rev: Two colored oxen standing

Date	Mintage	F	VF	XF	Unc	BU
2009P	—	—	—	—	—	150

KM# 1321   10 DOLLARS
3.1100 g., 0.9990 Gold 0.0999 oz. AGW, 19 mm. **Ruler:**
Elizabeth II **Subject:** Year of the Tiger **Obv:** Head right **Rev:**
Tiger head facing

Date	Mintage	F	VF	XF	Unc	BU
2010P Proof	8,000	Value: 260				

Year of the Tiger

KM# 1372   10 DOLLARS
311.0350 g., 0.9990 Silver 9.9896 oz. ASW, 75.5 mm. **Ruler:**
Elizabeth II **Subject:** Year of the Tiger **Obv:** Head right **Rev:**
Tiger at rest left

Date	Mintage	F	VF	XF	Unc	BU
2010P	—	—	—	—	—	400

Year of the Rabbit

KM# 1478   10 DOLLARS
311.0500 g., 0.9990 Silver 9.9901 oz. ASW, 75.5 mm. **Ruler:**
Elizabeth II **Subject:** Year of the Rabbit **Rev:** Two rabbits nestled
under tree

Date	Mintage	F	VF	XF	Unc	BU
2011P Proof	—	Value: 400				

KM# 1667   10 DOLLARS
311.0350 g., 0.9990 Silver 9.9896 oz. ASW, 75.5 mm. **Ruler:**
Elizabeth II **Subject:** Year of the Dragon **Rev:** Dragon

Date	Mintage	F	VF	XF	Unc	BU
2012P Proof	—	Value: 400				

KM# 540   15 DOLLARS
3.1103 g., 0.9990 Gold 0.0999 oz. AGW, 16.1 mm. **Ruler:**
Elizabeth II **Subject:** Year of the Snake **Obv:** Head with tiara
right, denomination below **Rev:** Snake in tree **Edge:** Reeded

Date	Mintage	F	VF	XF	Unc	BU
2001	80,000	—	—	—	—	175
2001P Proof	7,000	Value: 185				

KM# 584   15 DOLLARS
3.1103 g., 0.9990 Gold 0.0999 oz. AGW, 16.1 mm. **Ruler:**
Elizabeth II **Subject:** Year of the Horse **Obv:** Head with tiara
right, denomination below **Rev:** Horse galloping half left **Edge:**
Reeded

Date	Mintage	F	VF	XF	Unc	BU
2002P	—	—	—	—	—	175
2002P Proof	7,000	Value: 185				

KM# 711 15 DOLLARS
3.1100 g., 0.9999 Gold 0.1000 oz. AGW, 16.1 mm. **Ruler:**
Elizabeth II **Subject:** Year of the Goat **Obv:** Head with tiara right,
denomination below **Rev:** Goat

Date	Mintage	F	VF	XF	Unc	BU
2003	—	—	—	—	—	175
2003 Proof	—	Value: 185				

KM# 1340 15 DOLLARS
3.1100 g., 0.9990 Gold 0.0999 oz. AGW, 16.1 mm. **Ruler:**
Elizabeth II **Subject:** Year of the Goat **Obv:** Head right

Date	Mintage	F	VF	XF	Unc	BU
2003P	—	—	—	—	—	175
2003P Proof	—	Value: 195				

KM# 669 15 DOLLARS
3.1103 g., 0.9999 Gold 0.1000 oz. AGW, 16.1 mm. **Ruler:**
Elizabeth II **Subject:** Year of the Monkey **Obv:** Head with tiara
right, denomination below **Rev:** Monkey **Edge:** Reeded

Date	Mintage	F	VF	XF	Unc	BU
2004P	—	—	—	—	—	175
2004P Proof	80,000	Value: 185				

KM# 794 15 DOLLARS
3.1103 g., 0.9999 Gold 0.1000 oz. AGW, 16.1 mm. **Ruler:**
Elizabeth II **Subject:** Year of the Rooster **Obv:** Elizabeth II **Rev:**
Standing rooster right **Edge:** Reeded

Date	Mintage	F	VF	XF	Unc	BU
2005P Proof	7,000	Value: 185				

KM# 794a 15 DOLLARS
31.1030 g., 0.7500 Gold 0.7500 oz. AGW **Ruler:** Elizabeth II
Subject: Year of the Rooster **Obv:** Head with tiara right **Rev:**
Rooster standing right **Edge:** Reeded

Date	Mintage	F	VF	XF	Unc	BU
2005P Proof	15,000	Value: 1,250				

KM# 1373 15 DOLLARS
500.0000 g., 0.9990 Silver 16.058 oz. ASW **Ruler:** Elizabeth II
Subject: Year of the Tiger **Obv:** Head right **Rev:** Tiger at rest left

Date	Mintage	F	VF	XF	Unc	BU
2010P	—	—	—	—	—	650

KM# 1375 15 DOLLARS
3.1100 g., 0.9990 Gold 0.0999 oz. AGW, 16.1 mm. **Ruler:**
Elizabeth II **Subject:** Year of the Tiger **Obv:** Head right

Date	Mintage	F	VF	XF	Unc	BU
2010P	—	—	—	—	—	175

KM# 1482 15 DOLLARS
3.1000 g., 0.9990 Gold 0.0996 oz. AGW, 16.1 mm. **Ruler:**
Elizabeth II **Subject:** Year of the Rabbit **Rev:** Rabbit left

Date	Mintage	F	VF	XF	Unc	BU
2011P Proof	—	Value: 185				

KM# 1671 15 DOLLARS
3.1100 g., 0.9990 Gold 0.0999 oz. AGW, 16.1 mm. **Ruler:**
Elizabeth II **Subject:** Year of the Dragon

Date	Mintage	F	VF	XF	Unc	BU
2012P Proof	—	Value: 225				

KM# 1671a 15 DOLLARS
3.1100 g., 0.9990 Gold 0.0999 oz. AGW, 16.1 mm. **Ruler:**
Elizabeth II **Subject:** Year of the Dragon **Rev:** MUlticolor dragon

Date	Mintage	F	VF	XF	Unc	BU
2012P Proof	—	Value: 225				

KM# 541 25 DOLLARS
7.7508 g., 0.9990 Gold 0.2489 oz. AGW, 20.1 mm. **Ruler:**
Elizabeth II **Subject:** Year of the Snake **Obv:** Head with tiara
right, denomination below **Rev:** Snake in tree **Edge:** Reeded

Date	Mintage	F	VF	XF	Unc	BU
2001	60,000	—	—	—	—	425
2001P Proof	7,000	Value: 450				

KM# 585 25 DOLLARS
7.7759 g., 0.9990 Gold 0.2497 oz. AGW, 20.1 mm. **Ruler:**
Elizabeth II **Subject:** Year of the Horse **Obv:** Head with tiara
right, denomination below **Rev:** Horse galloping half left **Edge:**
Reeded

Date	Mintage	F	VF	XF	Unc	BU
2002P	—	—	—	—	—	425
2002P Proof	7,000	Value: 450				

KM# 712 25 DOLLARS
7.7500 g., 0.9999 Gold 0.2491 oz. AGW **Ruler:** Elizabeth II
Subject: Year of the Goat **Obv:** Head with tiara right,
denomination below **Rev:** Goat

Date	Mintage	F	VF	XF	Unc	BU
2003	—	—	—	—	—	425
2003 Proof	—	Value: 450				

KM# 1341 25 DOLLARS
7.7600 g., 0.9990 Gold 0.2492 oz. AGW, 20 mm. **Ruler:**
Elizabeth II **Subject:** Year of the Goat **Obv:** Head right

Date	Mintage	F	VF	XF	Unc	BU
2003P	—	—	—	—	—	425
2003P Proof	—	Value: 465				

KM# 670 25 DOLLARS
7.7508 g., 0.9999 Gold 0.2492 oz. AGW, 20.1 mm. **Ruler:**
Elizabeth II **Subject:** Year of the Monkey **Obv:** Head with tiara
right, denomination below **Rev:** Monkey **Edge:** Reeded

Date	Mintage	F	VF	XF	Unc	BU
2004P	—	—	—	—	—	425
2004P Proof	60,000	Value: 450				

KM# 795 25 DOLLARS
7.7759 g., 0.9999 Gold 0.2500 oz. AGW, 20.1 mm. **Ruler:**
Elizabeth II **Subject:** Year of the Rooster **Obv:** Elizabeth II **Rev:**
Standing rooster right **Edge:** Reeded

Date	Mintage	F	VF	XF	Unc	BU
2005P Proof	7,000	Value: 450				

KM# 1322 25 DOLLARS
7.7700 g., 0.9990 Gold 0.2496 oz. AGW, 22 mm. **Ruler:**
Elizabeth II **Subject:** Year of the Tiger **Obv:** Head right **Rev:**
Tiger head facing

Date	Mintage	F	VF	XF	Unc	BU
2010P Proof	8,000	Value: 650				

KM# 1483 25 DOLLARS
7.7700 g., 0.9990 Gold 0.2496 oz. AGW **Ruler:** Elizabeth II
Subject: Year of the Rabbit **Rev:** Rabbit left

Date	Mintage	F	VF	XF	Unc	BU
2011P Proof	—	Value: 450				

KM# 1672 25 DOLLARS
7.7700 g., 0.9990 Gold 0.2496 oz. AGW, 22 mm. **Ruler:**
Elizabeth II **Subject:** Year of the Dragon

Date	Mintage	F	VF	XF	Unc	BU
2012P Proof	—	Value: 475				

KM# 1672a 25 DOLLARS
7.7700 g., 0.9990 Gold 0.2496 oz. AGW, 22 mm. **Ruler:**
Elizabeth II **Subject:** Year of the Dragon **Rev:** Multicolor dragon

Date	Mintage	F	VF	XF	Unc	BU
2012P Proof	—	Value: 500				

KM# 542 30 DOLLARS
1002.5020 g., 0.9990 Silver 32.197 oz. ASW, 101 mm. **Ruler:**
Elizabeth II **Subject:** Year of the Snake **Obv:** Head with tiara
right, denomination below **Rev:** Snake with eggs **Edge:**
Segmented reeding

Date	Mintage	F	VF	XF	Unc	BU
2001	—	—	—	—	—	1,150
2001P Proof	250	Value: 1,350				

KM# 586 30 DOLLARS
1002.5020 g., 0.9990 Silver 32.197 oz. ASW, 101 mm. **Ruler:**
Elizabeth II **Subject:** Year of the Horse **Obv:** Head with tiara
right, denomination below **Rev:** Horse running left **Edge:**
Segmented reeding **Note:** Illustration reduced.

Date	Mintage	F	VF	XF	Unc	BU
2002	—	—	—	—	—	1,150
2002P Proof	250	Value: 1,350				

KM# 681 30 DOLLARS
1000.0000 g., 0.9990 Silver 32.117 oz. ASW, 101 mm. **Ruler:**
Elizabeth II **Subject:** Year of the Goat **Obv:** Head with tiara right,
denomination below **Rev:** Nanny goat and kid **Edge:** Segmented
reeding

Date	Mintage	F	VF	XF	Unc	BU
2003	—	—	—	—	—	1,150
2003P Proof	—	Value: 1,350				

KM# 677.1 30 DOLLARS
1000.0000 g., 0.9990 Silver 32.117 oz. ASW, 101 mm. **Ruler:**
Elizabeth II **Subject:** Year of the Monkey **Obv:** Head with tiara
right, denomination below **Rev:** Monkey sitting on branch **Edge:**
Segmented reeding

Date	Mintage	F	VF	XF	Unc	BU
2004	—	—	—	—	—	1,150
2004 Proof	5,250	Value: 1,250				

KM# 677.2 30 DOLLARS
1000.0000 g., 0.9990 Silver 32.117 oz. ASW, 101 mm. **Ruler:**
Elizabeth II **Subject:** Year of the Monkey **Obv:** Head with tiara
right, denomination below **Rev:** Multicolor ornamentation and
monkey with diamond chip eyes sitting on branch **Edge:**
Segmented reeding **Note:** Illustration reduced.

Date	Mintage	F	VF	XF	Unc	BU
2004 Proof	5,000	Value: 1,300				

KM# 697 30 DOLLARS
1000.0000 g., 0.9990 Silver 32.117 oz. ASW, 101 mm. **Ruler:** Elizabeth II **Subject:** Year of the Rooster **Obv:** Head with tiara right, denomination below **Rev:** Rooster, partially gilt and colored **Note:** Illustration reduced.

Date	Mintage	F	VF	XF	Unc	BU
2005 Proof	—	Value: 1,300				

KM# 1374 30 DOLLARS
1000.0000 g., 0.9990 Silver 32.117 oz. ASW, 101 mm. **Ruler:** Elizabeth II **Subject:** Year of the Tiger **Obv:** Head right

Date	Mintage	F	VF	XF	Unc	BU
2010P	—	—	—	—	—	1,150

KM# 1319 30 DOLLARS
1000.0000 g., 0.9990 Silver 32.117 oz. ASW, 101 mm. **Ruler:** Elizabeth II **Subject:** Year of the Tiger **Obv:** Head right **Rev:** Tiger at rest left **Note:** Illustration reduced.

Date	Mintage	F	VF	XF	Unc	BU
2010P Proof	5,000	Value: 1,600				

KM# 1479 30 DOLLARS
1000.0000 g., 0.9990 Silver 32.117 oz. ASW, 101 mm. **Ruler:** Elizabeth II **Subject:** Year of the Rabbit **Rev:** Mother and baby rabbit nose to nose **Note:** Illustration reduced.

Date	Mintage	F	VF	XF	Unc	BU
2010P Proof	—	Value: 1,300				

KM# 1668 30 DOLLARS
1000.0000 g., 0.9990 Silver 32.117 oz. ASW, 101 mm. **Ruler:** Elizabeth II **Subject:** Year of the Dragon **Rev:** Dragon

Date	Mintage	F	VF	XF	Unc	BU
2012P Proof	—	Value: 1,250				

KM# 1668a 30 DOLLARS
1000.0000 g., 0.9990 Silver 32.117 oz. ASW, 101 mm. **Ruler:** Elizabeth II **Obv:** Head with tiara right **Rev:** Dragon in color with gemstone

Date	Mintage	F	VF	XF	Unc	BU
2012P Proof	—	Value: 1,400				

KM# 671 50 DOLLARS
15.5940 g., 0.9999 Gold 0.5013 oz. AGW, 25.1 mm. **Ruler:** Elizabeth II **Subject:** Year of the Monkey **Obv:** Head with tiara right, denomination below **Rev:** Monkey **Edge:** Reeded

Date	Mintage	F	VF	XF	Unc	BU
2004P Proof	40,000	Value: 850				

KM# 1376 50 DOLLARS
15.5940 g., 0.9990 Gold 0.5008 oz. AGW, 25 mm. **Ruler:** Elizabeth II **Subject:** Year of the Tiger **Obv:** Head right

Date	Mintage	F	VF	XF	Unc	BU
2010P Proof	—	Value: 850				

KM# 1484 50 DOLLARS
15.5940 g., 0.9990 Gold 0.5008 oz. AGW, 25.1 mm. **Ruler:** Elizabeth II **Subject:** Year of the Rabbit

Date	Mintage	F	VF	XF	Unc	BU
2011P Proof	—	Value: 950				

KM# 1673 50 DOLLARS
15.5500 g., 0.9990 Gold 0.4994 oz. AGW, 25 mm. **Ruler:** Elizabeth II **Subject:** Year of the dragon

Date	Mintage	F	VF	XF	Unc	BU
2012P Proof	—	Value: 950				

KM# 543 100 DOLLARS
31.1035 g., 0.9990 Gold 0.9990 oz. AGW, 32.1 mm. **Ruler:** Elizabeth II **Subject:** Year of the Snake **Obv:** Head with tiara right, denomination below **Rev:** Snake in tree **Edge:** Reeded

Date	Mintage	F	VF	XF	Unc	BU
2001	30,000	—	—	—	—	1,750
2001P Proof	—	Value: 1,800				

KM# 587 100 DOLLARS
31.1035 g., 0.9990 Gold 0.9990 oz. AGW, 32.1 mm. **Ruler:** Elizabeth II **Subject:** Year of the Horse **Obv:** Head with tiara right, denomination below **Rev:** Horse running left **Edge:** Reeded

Date	Mintage	F	VF	XF	Unc	BU
2002	—	—	—	—	—	1,650
2002P Proof	—	Value: 1,700				

KM# 713 100 DOLLARS
31.1035 g., 0.9999 Gold 0.9999 oz. AGW, 32.1 mm. **Ruler:** Elizabeth II **Subject:** Year of the Goat **Obv:** Head with tiara right, denomination below **Rev:** Goat

Date	Mintage	F	VF	XF	Unc	BU
2003	—	—	—	—	—	1,750
2003 Proof	—	Value: 1,800				

KM# 672 100 DOLLARS
31.1035 g., 0.9999 Gold 0.9999 oz. AGW, 32.1 mm. **Ruler:** Elizabeth II **Subject:** Year of the Monkey **Obv:** Head with tiara right, denomination below **Rev:** Monkey walking left on branch **Edge:** Reeded

Date	Mintage	F	VF	XF	Unc	BU
2004	30,000	—	—	—	—	1,750
2004P Proof	—	Value: 1,800				

KM# 796 100 DOLLARS
31.1035 g., 0.9999 Gold 0.9999 oz. AGW, 32.1 mm. **Ruler:** Elizabeth II **Subject:** Year of the Rooster **Obv:** Elizabeth II **Rev:** Standing rooster right **Edge:** Reeded

Date	Mintage	F	VF	XF	Unc	BU
2005P Proof	3,000	Value: 1,800				

KM# 1323 100 DOLLARS
31.1050 g., 0.9990 Gold 0.9990 oz. AGW, 39.34 mm. **Ruler:**
Elizabeth II **Subject:** Year of the Tiger **Obv:** Head right **Rev:**
Tiger head facing

Date	Mintage	F	VF	XF	Unc	BU
2010P Proof	6,000	Value: 2,650				

KM# 1485 100 DOLLARS
31.1050 g., 0.9990 Gold 0.9990 oz. AGW, 39.34 mm. **Ruler:**
Elizabeth II **Subject:** Year of the Rabbit **Rev:** Rabbit seated left

Date	Mintage	F	VF	XF	Unc	BU
2011P Proof	—	Value: 1,800				

KM# 1674 100 DOLLARS
31.1050 g., 0.9990 Gold 0.9990 oz. AGW, 39.34 mm. **Ruler:**
Elizabeth II **Subject:** Year of the Dragon

Date	Mintage	F	VF	XF	Unc	BU
2012P Proof	—	Value: 1,850				

KM# 1674a 100 DOLLARS
31.1050 g., 0.9990 Gold 0.9990 oz. AGW, 39.34 mm. **Ruler:**
Elizabeth II **Subject:** Year of the Dragon **Rev:** Multicolor dragon

Date	Mintage	F	VF	XF	Unc	BU
2012P Proof	—	Value: 1,875				

KM# 704 200 DOLLARS
62.2140 g., 0.9999 Gold 1.9999 oz. AGW, 41.1 mm. **Ruler:**
Elizabeth II **Subject:** Year of the Snake **Obv:** Head with tiara
right, denomination below **Rev:** Snake

Date	Mintage	F	VF	XF	Unc	BU
2001 Proof	—	Value: 3,450				

KM# 1333 200 DOLLARS
62.2100 g., 0.9990 Gold 1.9980 oz. AGW, 41.1 mm. **Ruler:**
Elizabeth II **Subject:** Year of the Snake **Obv:** Head right

Date	Mintage	F	VF	XF	Unc	BU
2001P Proof	—	Value: 3,450				

KM# 707 200 DOLLARS
62.2140 g., 0.9999 Gold 1.9999 oz. AGW, 41.1 mm. **Ruler:**
Elizabeth II **Subject:** Year of the Horse **Rev:** Horse

Date	Mintage	F	VF	XF	Unc	BU
2002 Proof	—	Value: 3,450				

KM# 1336 200 DOLLARS
62.2100 g., 0.9990 Gold 1.9980 oz. AGW, 41.1 mm. **Ruler:**
Elizabeth II **Subject:** Year of the Horse

Date	Mintage	F	VF	XF	Unc	BU
2002P Proof	—	Value: 3,450				

KM# 714 200 DOLLARS
62.2140 g., 0.9999 Gold 1.9999 oz. AGW, 41.1 mm. **Ruler:**
Elizabeth II **Subject:** Year of the Goat **Obv:** Head with tiara right
Rev: Goat

Date	Mintage	F	VF	XF	Unc	BU
2003 Proof	—	Value: 3,450				

KM# 717 200 DOLLARS
62.2100 g., 0.9999 Gold 1.9998 oz. AGW, 41.1 mm. **Ruler:**
Elizabeth II **Subject:** Year of the Monkey **Obv:** Head with tiara
right **Rev:** Monkey

Date	Mintage	F	VF	XF	Unc	BU
2004 Proof	—	Value: 3,450				

KM# 698 200 DOLLARS
62.2100 g., 0.9999 Gold 1.9998 oz. AGW, 41.1 mm. **Ruler:**
Elizabeth II **Subject:** Year of the Rooster **Obv:** Head with tiara
right **Rev:** Rooster

Date	Mintage	F	VF	XF	Unc	BU
2005 Proof	—	Value: 3,450				

KM# 1377 200 DOLLARS
62.2100 g., 0.9990 Gold 1.9980 oz. AGW, 41.1 mm. **Ruler:**
Elizabeth II **Obv:** Year of the Tiger **Rev:** Tiger head facing

Date	Mintage	F	VF	XF	Unc	BU
2010P	—	—	—	—	—	3,600

KM# 1486 200 DOLLARS
62.2100 g., 0.9990 Gold 1.9980 oz. AGW, 41.1 mm. **Ruler:**
Elizabeth II **Subject:** Year of the Rabbit

Date	Mintage	F	VF	XF	Unc	BU
2011P Proof	—	Value: 3,600				

KM# 1675 200 DOLLARS
62.2140 g., 0.9990 Gold 1.9981 oz. AGW, 41.1 mm. **Ruler:**
Elizabeth II **Subject:** Year of the Dragon

Date	Mintage	F	VF	XF	Unc	BU
2012P Proof	—	Value: 3,550				

KM# 1006 300 DOLLARS
10000.0000 g., 0.9990 Silver 321.17 oz. ASW **Ruler:**
Elizabeth II **Series:** Lunar year **Subject:** Year of the Dog **Obv:**
Head with tiara right **Obv. Legend:** ELIZABETH II - AUSTRALIA
Rev: Dog sitting, facing right

Date	Mintage	F	VF	XF	Unc	BU
2006	—	—	—	—	—	11,500

KM# 1480 300 DOLLARS
10000.0000 g., 0.9990 Silver 321.17 oz. ASW **Ruler:**
Elizabeth II **Subject:** Year of the Rabbit **Rev:** Two rabbits nestled
under tree

Date	Mintage	F	VF	XF	Unc	BU
2011P Proof	—	Value: 11,750				

KM# 1669 300 DOLLARS
10000.0000 g., 0.9990 Silver 321.17 oz. ASW **Ruler:**
Elizabeth II **Subject:** Year of the Dragon **Rev:** Dragon

Date	Mintage	F	VF	XF	Unc	BU
2012P Proof	—	Value: 11,500				

KM# 705 1000 DOLLARS
311.0480 g., 0.9999 Gold 9.9990 oz. AGW, 75.6 mm. **Ruler:**
Elizabeth II **Subject:** Year of the Snake **Obv:** Head with tiara
right, denomination below **Rev:** Snake

Date	Mintage	F	VF	XF	Unc	BU
2001	—	—	—	—	—	17,000

KM# 1334 1000 DOLLARS
311.0480 g., 0.9990 Gold 9.9900 oz. AGW, 75.6 mm. **Ruler:**
Elizabeth II **Subject:** Year of the Snake **Obv:** Head right

Date	Mintage	F	VF	XF	Unc	BU
2001P	—	—	—	—	—	17,000

KM# 708 1000 DOLLARS
311.0480 g., 0.9999 Gold 9.9990 oz. AGW, 75.6 mm. **Ruler:**
Elizabeth II **Subject:** Year of the Horse **Obv:** Head with tiara
right, denomination below **Rev:** Horse

Date	Mintage	F	VF	XF	Unc	BU
2002	—	—	—	—	—	17,000

KM# 1337 1000 DOLLARS
311.0480 g., 0.9990 Gold 9.9900 oz. AGW, 75.6 mm. **Ruler:**
Elizabeth II **Subject:** Year of the Horse **Obv:** Head right

Date	Mintage	F	VF	XF	Unc	BU
2002P	—	—	—	—	—	17,000

KM# 715 1000 DOLLARS
311.0480 g., 0.9999 Gold 9.9990 oz. AGW, 75.6 mm. **Ruler:**
Elizabeth II **Subject:** Year of the Goat **Obv:** Head with tiara right,
denomination below **Rev:** Goat

Date	Mintage	F	VF	XF	Unc	BU
2003	—	—	—	—	—	17,000

KM# 718 1000 DOLLARS
311.0480 g., 0.9999 Gold 9.9990 oz. AGW, 75.6 mm. **Ruler:**
Elizabeth II **Subject:** Year of the Monkey **Obv:** Head with tiara
right, denomination below **Rev:** Monkey

Date	Mintage	F	VF	XF	Unc	BU
2004	—	—	—	—	—	17,000

KM# 699 1000 DOLLARS
311.0480 g., 0.9999 Gold 9.9990 oz. AGW, 75.6 mm. **Ruler:**
Elizabeth II **Subject:** Year of the Rooster **Obv:** Head with tiara
right, denomination below **Rev:** Rooster

Date	Mintage	F	VF	XF	Unc	BU
2005	—	—	—	—	—	17,000

KM# 1378 1000 DOLLARS
311.0480 g., 0.9990 Gold 9.9900 oz. AGW, 75.6 mm. **Ruler:**
Elizabeth II **Subject:** Year of the Tiger **Obv:** Head right

Date	Mintage	F	VF	XF	Unc	BU
2010(p)	—	—	—	—	—	18,000

KM# 1487 1000 DOLLARS
311.0480 g., 0.9990 Gold 9.9900 oz. AGW, 75.6 mm. **Ruler:**
Elizabeth II **Subject:** Year of the Rabbit

Date	Mintage	F	VF	XF	Unc	BU
2011P Proof	—	Value: 18,000				

KM# 1676 1000 DOLLARS
311.0500 g., 0.9990 Gold 9.9901 oz. AGW, 75.6 mm. **Ruler:** Elizabeth II **Subject:** Year of the Dragon

Date	Mintage	F	VF	XF	Unc	BU
2012P Proof	— Value: 18,000					

KM# 706 3000 DOLLARS
1000.0000 g., 0.9999 Gold 32.146 oz. AGW, 100.6 mm. **Ruler:** Elizabeth II **Subject:** Year of the Snake **Obv:** Head with tiara right, denomination below **Rev:** Snake

Date	Mintage	F	VF	XF	Unc	BU
2001	—	—	—	—	—	BV+3%

KM# 1335 3000 DOLLARS
1000.0000 g., 0.9990 Gold 32.117 oz. AGW, 100.6 mm. **Ruler:** Elizabeth II **Subject:** Year of the Snake **Obv:** Head right

Date	Mintage	F	VF	XF	Unc	BU
2001P	—	—	—	—	—	BV+3%

KM# 709 3000 DOLLARS
1000.0000 g., 0.9999 Gold 32.146 oz. AGW, 100.6 mm. **Ruler:** Elizabeth II **Subject:** Year of the Horse **Obv:** Head with tiara right, denomination below **Rev:** Horse

Date	Mintage	F	VF	XF	Unc	BU
2002	—	—	—	—	—	BV+3%

KM# 1338 3000 DOLLARS
1000.0000 g., 0.9990 Gold 32.117 oz. AGW, 100.6 mm. **Ruler:** Elizabeth II **Subject:** Year of the Horse **Obv:** Head right

Date	Mintage	F	VF	XF	Unc	BU
2002P	—	—	—	—	—	BV+3%

KM# 716 3000 DOLLARS
1000.0000 g., 0.9999 Gold 32.146 oz. AGW, 100.6 mm. **Ruler:** Elizabeth II **Subject:** Year of the Goat **Obv:** Head with tiara right, denomination below **Rev:** Goat

Date	Mintage	F	VF	XF	Unc	BU
2003	—	—	—	—	—	BV+3%

KM# 719 3000 DOLLARS
1000.0000 g., 0.9999 Gold 32.146 oz. AGW, 100.6 mm. **Ruler:** Elizabeth II **Subject:** Year of the Monkey **Obv:** Head with tiara right, denomination below **Rev:** Monkey

Date	Mintage	F	VF	XF	Unc	BU
2004	—	—	—	—	—	BV+3%

KM# 700 3000 DOLLARS
1000.0000 g., 0.9999 Gold 32.146 oz. AGW, 100.6 mm. **Ruler:** Elizabeth II **Subject:** Year of the Rooster **Obv:** Head with tiara right, denomination below **Rev:** Rooster

Date	Mintage	F	VF	XF	Unc	BU
2005	—	—	—	—	—	BV+3%

KM# 1379 3000 DOLLARS
1000.0000 g., 0.9990 Gold 32.117 oz. AGW, 100.6 mm. **Ruler:** Elizabeth II **Subject:** Year of the Tiger **Obv:** Head right

Date	Mintage	F	VF	XF	Unc	BU
2010P	—	—	—	—	—	BV+3%

KM# 1488 3000 DOLLARS
1000.0000 g., 0.9990 Gold 32.117 oz. AGW, 100.6 mm. **Ruler:** Elizabeth II **Subject:** Year of the Rabbit

Date	Mintage	F	VF	XF	Unc	BU
2011P Proof	—	BV+3%				

KM# 1677 3000 DOLLARS
1000.0000 g., 0.9990 Gold 32.117 oz. AGW, 100.6 mm. **Ruler:** Elizabeth II **Subject:** Year of the Dragon

Date	Mintage	F	VF	XF	Unc	BU
2012P Proof	—	BV+3%				

KM# 1007 30000 DOLLARS
10000.0000 g., 0.9999 Gold 321.46 oz. AGW, 180.6 mm. **Ruler:** Elizabeth II **Series:** Lunar year **Subject:** Year of the Dog **Obv:** Head with tiara right **Obv. Legend:** ELIZABETH II - AUSTRALIA **Rev:** Dog standing left

Date	Mintage	F	VF	XF	Unc	BU
2006 Proof	100	BV+2%				

KM# 1489 30000 DOLLARS
10000.0000 g., 0.9990 Gold 321.17 oz. AGW, 180.6 mm. **Ruler:** Elizabeth II **Subject:** Year of the Rabbit

Date	Mintage	F	VF	XF	Unc	BU
2011P Proof	100	BV+2%				

KM# 1678 30000 DOLLARS
10000.0000 g., 0.9990 Gold 321.17 oz. AGW, 180.6 mm. **Ruler:** Elizabeth II **Subject:** Year of the Dragon

Date	Mintage	F	VF	XF	Unc	BU
2012P Proof	100	BV+2%				

BABY MINT SETS

KM#	Date	Mintage	Identification	Issue Price	Mkt Val
BMS9	2001 (6)	32,494	KM#401-403, 406, 491.1, 534.1 plus bronze medal	—	110
BMS10	2002 (6)	32,479	KM#401-403, 406, 600.1, 602 plus bronze medal	—	47.50
BMS11	2003 (6)	37,748	KM#401-402, 406, 688-690 plus bronze medal	—	40.00
BMS12	2004 (6)	31,000	KM#401-404, 406, 733.1 plus bronze medal	—	40.00
BMS13	2005 (6)	34,748	KM#401-402, 406, 745-747 plus bronze medal	24.00	27.50
BMS14	2006 (6)	—	KM#401-404, 406, 489 plus bronze medal	24.00	35.00

BABY PROOF SETS

KM#	Date	Mintage	Identification	Issue Price	Mkt Val
BPS7	2001 (6)	15,011	KM#401-403, 406, 491.1, 534.1 plus silver medal	—	165
BPS8	2002 (6)	13,996	KM#401, 403, 406, 600.2, 602 plus silver medal	—	153
BPS9	2003 (6)	14,799	KM#401-402, 406, 688-689, 690.1 plus silver medal	—	125
BPS10	2004 (6)	13,996	KM#401-404, 406, 733 plus silver medal	—	110
BPS11	2005 (6)	—	KM#401-402, 406, 745-747 plus silver medal	—	100
BPS12	2006 (6)	—	KM#401-404, 406, 489 plus silver medal	—	120

MINT SETS

KM#	Date	Mintage	Identification	Issue Price	Mkt Val
MS49	2001 (6)	—	KM#401-403, 406, 491.1, 534.1	—	80.00
MS39	2001 (3)	—	KM532, 533, 534.1	7.80	75.00
MS48	2001 (20)	—	KM532-533, 534.1, 491.1, 550-565	43.68	235
MS40	2001 (3)	—	KM534.1, 550, 551	7.80	70.00
MS41	2001 (3)	—	KM534.1, 552, 553	7.80	70.00
MS42	2001 (3)	—	KM534.1, 554, 555	7.80	75.00
MS43	2001 (3)	—	KM534.1, 556, 557	7.80	72.50
MS44	2001 (3)	—	KM534.1, 558, 559	7.80	75.00
MS45	2001 (3)	—	KM534.1, 560, 561	7.80	85.00
MS46	2001 (3)	—	KM534.1, 562, 563	7.80	80.00
MS47	2001 (3)	—	KM534.1, 564, 565	7.80	70.00
MS51	2002 (3)	—	KM#691.2, 692, 693	—	2,300
MS50	2002 (6)	—	KM#401-403, 406, 600.1, 602	—	65.00
MS52	2003 (5)	—	KM401, 402, 406, 689, 690	—	35.00
MS53	2004 (6)	—	KM401-404, 406, 733.1	—	32.50
MS54	2005 (6)	—	KM#401, 402, 406, 745-747	—	25.00
MS55	2006 (8)	—	KM#401-404, 406, 489, 767-768 40 Years of Decimal Currency	18.50	55.00
MS56	2006 (15)	—	KM#770-781, 1001-1003	80.00	165

PROOF SETS

KM#	Date	Mintage	Identification	Issue Price	Mkt Val
PS107	2001 (3)	—	KM532, 533, 534.2	21.00	95.00
PS108	2001 (3)	—	KM534.2, 550, 551	21.00	65.00
PS109	2001 (3)	—	KM534.2, 552, 553	21.00	75.00
PS110	2001 (3)	—	KM534.2, 554, 555	21.00	75.00
PS111	2001 (3)	—	KM534.2, 556, 557	21.00	75.00
PS112	2001 (3)	—	KM534.2, 558, 559	21.00	85.00
PS113	2001 (3)	—	KM534.2, 560, 561	21.00	95.00
PS114	2001 (3)	—	KM534.2, 562, 563	21.00	85.00
PS115	2001 (3)	—	KM534.2, 564, 565	21.00	85.00
PS116	2001 (20)	—	KM491.2, 532-533, 534.2, 549.2, 550-565	120	665
PS117	2001 (6)	—	KM#401-403, 406, 491.1, 534.1	—	145
PS118	2001 (1)	650	Federation Centennial Set	—	6,000
PS119	2002 (6)	39,513	KM#401-403, 406, 600.2, 602	—	95.00
PS121	2003 (6)	6,500	KM#401b, 402b, 406b, 688a, 689a, 690a	—	180
PS120	2006 (6)	39,090	KM#401-402, 406, 688-689, 690.1	—	70.00
PS122	2003 (4)	10,000	KM763-766	118	250
PS123	2004 (6)	50,000	KM#401-404, 406, 733	—	80.00
PS124	2004 (6)	6,500	KM#401b, 402b, 403b, 404a, 406b, 733.1a	—	150
PS125	2005 (6)	—	KM#401, 402, 406, 745-747	—	85.00
PS126	2005 (6)	6,500	KM#401b, 402b, 406b, 745a, 746a, 747a	—	175
PS127	2005 (6)	650	KM#401a, 402a, 406a, 745a, 746b, 747b	—	5,850
PS128	2006 (8)	—	KM#401-404, 406, 489, 767-768	62.50	120
PS129	2006 (8)	6,500	KM#62a, 63a, 64a, 65a, 66a, 77a, 852	180	220

WEDDING SPECIMEN SETS

KM#	Date	Mintage	Identification	Issue Price	Mkt Val
WSS1	2002 (6)	3,322	KM#401-403, 406, 600.1, 602 Plaque	—	97.50
WSS2	2003 (6)	3,249	KM#401-402, 406, 688-690 Plaque	—	55.00
WSS3	2004 (6)	4,000	KM#401-404, 406, 733.1 Plaque	—	58.50
WSS4	2005 (6)	—	KM#401-402, 406, 745-747 Plaque	60.00	60.00
WSS5	2006 (8)	—	KM#401-404, 406, 489, 767-768 Plaque	60.00	60.00

AUSTRIA

The Commonwealth of Australia, the smallest continent in the world, is located south of Indonesia between the Indian and Pacific oceans. It has an area of 2,967,893 sq. mi. (7,686,850 sq. km.) and an estimated population of 18.84 million. Capital: Canberra. Due to its early and sustained isolation, Australia is the habitat of such curious and unique fauna as the kangaroo, koala, platypus, wombat, echidna and frilled-necked lizard. The continent possesses extensive mineral deposits, the most important of which are iron ore, coal, gold, silver, nickel, uranium, lead and zinc. Raising livestock, mining and manufacturing are the principal industries. Chief exports are wool, meat, wheat, iron ore, coal and nonferrous metals.

Australia is a founding member of the Commonwealth of Nations. Elizabeth II is the Head of State as Queen of Australia; the Prime Minister is Head of Government.

NOTE: Home market grading of Australian coinage is generally stricter than USA practiced standards. The pricing in this catalog reflects strict home market grading standard.

RULER
British until 1942

MONETARY SYSTEM
Decimal Coinage (Commencing 1966)
100 Cents = 1 Dollar

REPUBLIC

POST WWII DECIMAL COINAGE
100 Groschen - 1 Schilling

KM# 2878   10 GROSCHEN
1.1000 g., Aluminum, 20 mm. **Obv:** Small Imperial Eagle with Austrian shield on breast, at top between numbers, scalloped rim, stylized inscription below **Rev:** Large value above date, scalloped rim **Edge:** Plain

Date	Mintage	F	VF	XF	Unc	BU
2001 Special Unc	75,000	—	—	—	—	5.00

KM# 2885   50 GROSCHEN
3.0000 g., Aluminum-Bronze, 19.5 mm. **Obv:** Austrian shield **Rev:** Large value above date **Edge:** Reeded

Date	Mintage	F	VF	XF	Unc	BU
2001 Special Unc	75,000	—	—	—	—	5.00

KM# 2886   SCHILLING
4.2000 g., Aluminum-Bronze, 22.5 mm. **Obv:** Large value above date **Rev:** Edelweiss flower **Edge:** Plain

Date	Mintage	F	VF	XF	Unc	BU
2001 Special Unc	75,000	—	—	—	—	5.00

KM# 2889a   5 SCHILLING
4.8000 g., Copper-Nickel, 23.5 mm. **Obv:** Lippizaner stallion with rider, rearing left **Rev:** Austrian shield divides date, value above, sprays below **Edge:** Plain

Date	Mintage	F	VF	XF	Unc	BU
2001 Special Unc	75,000	—	—	—	—	5.50

KM# 2918   10 SCHILLING
6.2000 g., Copper-Nickel Plated Nickel, 26 mm. **Obv:** Imperial Eagle with Austrian shield on breast, holding hammer and sickle **Rev:** Woman of Wachau left, value and date right of hat **Edge:** Reeded

Date	Mintage	F	VF	XF	Unc	BU
2001 Special Unc	75,000	—	—	—	—	6.00

KM# 3075   20 SCHILLING
8.0000 g., Copper-Aluminum-Nickel, 27.7 mm. **Subject:** Johann Nepomuk Nestroy **Obv:** Denomination within square **Rev:** Bust half left **Edge:** 19 incuse dots

Date	Mintage	F	VF	XF	Unc	BU
2001	225,000	—	—	—	4.50	—
2001 Special Unc	75,000	—	—	—	—	10.00

KM# 3076   50 SCHILLING
8.1500 g., Bi-Metallic Copper-Nickel clad Nickel center in Aluminumn-Bronze ring, 26.5 mm. **Subject:** The Schilling Era **Obv:** Denomination and shields **Rev:** Four old coin designs **Edge:** Plain

Date	Mintage	F	VF	XF	Unc	BU
2001	600,000	—	—	—	7.50	—
2001 Special Unc.	100,000	—	—	—	—	9.50

KM# 3073   100 SCHILLING
13.7000 g., 0.2879 Bi-Metallic Titanium center in 9.95g .900 silver ring. 0.1268 oz., 34 mm. **Subject:** Transportation **Obv:** Automobile engine **Rev:** Car, train, truck, and plane **Edge:** Plain

Date	Mintage	F	VF	XF	Unc	BU
2001 Proof	50,000	Value: 40.00				

KM# 3077   100 SCHILLING
20.0000 g., 0.9000 Silver 0.5787 oz. ASW, 34 mm. **Subject:** Charlemagne **Obv:** Holy Roman Emperor's crown above denomination **Rev:** Bust 3/4 facing with scepter, two shields at right **Edge:** Reeded

Date	Mintage	F	VF	XF	Unc	BU
2001 Proof	50,000	Value: 40.00				

KM# 3079   100 SCHILLING
20.0000 g., 0.9000 Silver 0.5787 oz. ASW, 34 mm. **Subject:** Duke Rudolf IV **Obv:** University teaching scene **Rev:** Bust on right looking left, St. Stephen's Cathedral at left **Edge:** Reeded

Date	Mintage	F	VF	XF	Unc	BU
2001 Proof	50,000	Value: 40.00				

KM# 3074   500 SCHILLING
10.1400 g., 0.9860 Gold 0.3214 oz. AGW, 22 mm. **Subject:** 2000 Years of Christianity - Bible **Obv:** Bible and symbols of the saints: Matthew, Luke, Mark, and John **Rev:** St. Paul reading from a scroll to two listeners

Date	Mintage	F	VF	XF	Unc	BU
2001 Proof	50,000	Value: 600				

KM# 3078   500 SCHILLING
24.0000 g., 0.9250 Silver 0.7137 oz. ASW, 37 mm. **Subject:** Kufstein Castle **Obv:** Castle view above denomination **Rev:** Emperor Maximilian being shown one of his new cannons **Edge:** Plain with engraved lettering

Date	Mintage	F	VF	XF	Unc	BU
2001	50,000	—	—	—	45.00	—
2001 Special Unc.	15,000	—	—	—	—	50.00
2001 Proof	30,000	Value: 60.00				

KM# 3080   500 SCHILLING
24.0000 g., 0.9250 Silver 0.7137 oz. ASW, 37 mm. **Subject:** Schattenburg Castle **Obv:** Castle view **Rev:** Two medieval armourers at work **Edge:** Plain with engraved lettering

Date	Mintage	F	VF	XF	Unc	BU
2001	37,000	—	—	—	42.00	—
2001 Special Unc	15,000	—	—	—	—	50.00
2001 Proof	43,000	Value: 60.00				

KM# 3081   1000 SCHILLING
16.2200 g., 0.9860 Gold 0.5142 oz. AGW, 30 mm. **Subject:** Austrian National Library **Obv:** Archduke Maximilian as a student **Rev:** Library interior view **Edge:** Reeded

Date	Mintage	F	VF	XF	Unc	BU
2001 Proof	30,000	Value: 875				

BULLION COINAGE
Philharmonic Issues

KM# 3004   200 SCHILLING
3.1210 g., 0.9999 Gold 0.1003 oz. AGW, 16 mm. **Series:** Vienna Philharmonic Orchestra **Obv:** The Golden Hall organ **Rev:** Wind and string instruments **Edge:** Reeded

Date	Mintage	F	VF	XF	Unc	BU
2001	26,400	—	—	—	BV+13%	—

KM# 2989   500 SCHILLING
7.7760 g., 0.9999 Gold 0.2500 oz. AGW, 22 mm. **Series:** Vienna Philharmonic Orchestra **Obv:** The Golden Hall organ **Rev:** Wind and string instruments **Edge:** Reeded

Date	Mintage	F	VF	XF	Unc	BU
2001	25,800	—	—	—	BV+10%	—

KM# 3031 1000 SCHILLING
15.5520 g., 0.9999 Gold 0.4999 oz. AGW, 28 mm. **Series:** Vienna Philharmonic Orchestra **Obv:** The Golden Hall organ **Rev:** Wind and string instruments **Edge:** Reeded

Date	Mintage	F	VF	XF	Unc	BU
2001	26,800	—	—	—	BV+8%	—

KM# 2990 2000 SCHILLING
31.1035 g., 0.9999 Gold 0.9999 oz. AGW, 37 mm. **Series:** Vienna Philharmonic Orchestra **Obv:** The Golden Hall organ **Rev:** Wind and string instruments **Edge:** Reeded

Date	Mintage	F	VF	XF	Unc	BU
2001	54,700	—	—	—	BV+4%	—

EURO COINAGE
European Union Issues

KM# 3082 EURO CENT
2.3000 g., Copper Plated Steel, 16.25 mm. **Obv:** Gentian flower **Obv. Legend:** EIN EURO CENT **Rev:** Denomination and globe **Edge:** Plain

Date	Mintage	F	VF	XF	Unc	BU
2002	378,400,000	—	—	—	0.35	—
2002 Special Unc	100,000	—	—	—	—	0.50
2002 Proof	10,000	Value: 15.00				
2003	10,800,000	—	—	—	0.35	—
2003 Special Unc	125,000	—	—	—	—	0.50
2003 Proof	25,000	Value: 3.00				
2004	115,000,000	—	—	—	0.35	—
2004 Special Unc	100,000	—	—	—	—	0.50
2004 Proof	20,000	Value: 3.00				
2005	122,900,000	—	—	—	0.35	—
2005 Special Unc	100,000	—	—	—	—	0.50
2005 Proof	20,000	Value: 4.00				
2006	48,300,000	—	—	—	0.35	—
2006 Special Unc	100,000	—	—	—	—	0.50
2006 Proof	20,000	Value: 4.00				
2007	111,900,000	—	—	—	0.35	—
2007 Special Unc	75,000	—	—	—	—	0.50
2007 Proof	20,000	Value: 4.00				
2008	50,900,000	—	—	—	0.35	—
2008 Special Unc	50,000	—	—	—	—	0.50
2008 Proof	15,000	Value: 4.00				
2009	158,900,000	—	—	—	0.35	—
2009 Special Unc	75,000	—	—	—	—	0.50
2009 Proof	15,000	Value: 4.00				
2010	168,500,000	—	—	—	0.35	—
2010 Special Unc	50,000	—	—	—	—	0.50
2010 Proof	15,000	Value: 4.00				
2011	—	—	—	—	0.35	—
2011 Special Unc	50,000	—	—	—	—	0.50
2011 Proof	15,000	Value: 4.00				
2012	—	—	—	—	0.35	—
2012 Special Unc	—	—	—	—	—	0.50
2012 Proof	—	Value: 4.00				

KM# 3083 2 EURO CENT
3.0600 g., Copper Plated Steel, 18.75 mm. **Obv:** Edelweiss flower in inner circle, stars in outer circle **Obv. Legend:** ZWEI EURO CENT **Rev:** Denomination and globe **Edge:** Grooved

Date	Mintage	F	VF	XF	Unc	BU
2002	326,400,000	—	—	—	0.50	—
2002 Special Unc	100,000	—	—	—	—	0.65
2002 Proof	10,000	Value: 20.00				
2003	118,500,000	—	—	—	0.50	—
2003 Special Unc	125,000	—	—	—	—	0.65
2003 Proof	25,000	Value: 5.00				
2004	156,400,000	—	—	—	0.50	—
2004 Special Unc	100,000	—	—	—	—	0.65
2004 Proof	20,000	Value: 5.00				
2005	113,000,000	—	—	—	0.50	—
2005 Special Unc	100,000	—	—	—	—	0.65
2005 Proof	20,000	Value: 6.00				
2006	39,800,000	—	—	—	0.35	—
2006 Special Unc	100,000	—	—	—	—	0.65
2006 Proof	20,000	Value: 6.00				
2007	72,200,000	—	—	—	0.35	—
2007 Special Unc	75,000	—	—	—	—	0.65
2007 Proof	20,000	Value: 6.00				
2008	125,100,000	—	—	—	0.35	—
2008 Special Unc	50,000	—	—	—	—	0.65
2008 Proof	15,000	Value: 6.00				
2009	120,400,000	—	—	—	0.35	—
2009 Special Unc	75,000	—	—	—	—	0.65
2009 Proof	15,000	Value: 6.00				
2010	104,200,000	—	—	—	0.35	—
2010 Special Unc	50,000	—	—	—	—	0.65
2010 Proof	15,000	Value: 6.00				
2011	—	—	—	—	0.35	—
2011 Special Unc	50,000	—	—	—	—	0.65
2011 Proof	15,000	Value: 6.00				
2012	—	—	—	—	0.35	—
2012 Special Unc	—	—	—	—	—	0.65
2012 Proof	—	Value: 6.00				

KM# 3084 5 EURO CENT
3.9200 g., Copper Plated Steel, 21.25 mm. **Obv:** Alpine prim rose flower in inner ring, stars in outer ring **Obv. Legend:** FUNF EURO CENT **Rev:** Denomination and globe **Edge:** Plain

Date	Mintage	F	VF	XF	Unc	BU
2002	217,000,000	—	—	—	0.75	—
2002 Special Unc	100,000	—	—	—	—	1.00
2002 Proof	10,000	Value: 30.00				
2003	108,500,000	—	—	—	0.75	—
2003 Special Unc	125,000	—	—	—	—	1.00
2003 Proof	25,000	Value: 8.50				
2004	89,300,000	—	—	—	0.75	—
2004 Special Unc	100,000	—	—	—	—	1.00
2004 Proof	20,000	Value: 9.00				
2005	66,100,000	—	—	—	0.75	—
2005 Special Unc	100,000	—	—	—	—	1.00
2005 Proof	20,000	Value: 10.00				
2006	5,600,000	—	—	—	0.75	—
2006 Special Unc	100,000	—	—	—	—	1.00
2006 Proof	20,000	Value: 10.00				
2007	52,700,000	—	—	—	0.75	—
2007 Special Unc	75,000	—	—	—	—	1.00
2007 Proof	20,000	Value: 10.00				
2008	96,700,000	—	—	—	0.75	—
2008 Special Unc	50,000	—	—	—	—	1.00
2008 Proof	15,000	Value: 10.00				
2009	5,800,000	—	—	—	0.75	—
2009 Special Unc	75,000	—	—	—	—	1.00
2009 Proof	15,000	Value: 10.00				
2010	63,700,000	—	—	—	0.75	—
2010 Special Unc	50,000	—	—	—	—	1.00
2010 Proof	15,000	Value: 10.00				
2011	—	—	—	—	0.75	—
2011 Special Unc	50,000	—	—	—	—	1.00
2011 Proof	15,000	Value: 10.00				
2012	—	—	—	—	0.75	—
2012 Special Unc	—	—	—	—	—	1.00
2012 Proof	—	Value: 10.00				

KM# 3085 10 EURO CENT
4.1000 g., Brass, 19.75 mm. **Obv:** St. Stephen's Cathedral spires **Rev:** Relief map of European Union at left, denomination at center right **Edge:** Reeded

Date	Mintage	F	VF	XF	Unc	BU
2002	441,600,000	—	—	—	0.75	—
2002 Special Unc	100,000	—	—	—	—	1.00
2002 Proof	10,000	Value: 45.00				
2003 Special Unc	125,000	—	—	—	—	4.00
2003 Proof	25,000	Value: 8.50				
2004	5,200,000	—	—	—	0.80	—
2004 Special Unc	100,000	—	—	—	—	1.00

KM# 3139 10 EURO CENT
4.1000 g., Brass, 19.75 mm. **Obv:** St. Stephen's Cathedral spires **Rev:** Relief Map of Western Europe, stars, lines and value **Edge:** Reeded

Date	Mintage	F	VF	XF	Unc	BU
2008	70,200,000	—	—	—	0.75	—
2008 Special Unc	50,000	—	—	—	—	1.00
2008 Proof	15,000	Value: 10.00				
2009	15,900,000	—	—	—	0.75	—
2009 Special Unc	75,000	—	—	—	—	1.00
2009 Proof	15,000	Value: 10.00				
2010	42,800,000	—	—	—	0.75	—
2010 Special Unc	50,000	—	—	—	—	1.00
2010 Proof	15,000	Value: 10.00				
2011	—	—	—	—	0.75	—
2011 Special Unc	50,000	—	—	—	—	1.00
2011 Proof	15,000	Value: 10.00				
2012	—	—	—	—	0.75	—
2012 Special Unc	—	—	—	—	—	1.00
2012 Proof	—	Value: 10.00				

The following KM# 2 EURO CENT proof data:
Date	Mintage	F	VF	XF	Unc	BU
2004 Proof	20,000	Value: 9.00				
2005	5,200,000	—	—	—	0.80	—
2005 Special Unc	100,000	—	—	—	—	1.00
2005 Proof	20,000	Value: 10.00				
2006	40,000,000	—	—	—	0.75	—
2006 Special Unc	100,000	—	—	—	—	1.00
2006 Proof	20,000	Value: 10.00				
2007	81,300,000	—	—	—	0.75	—
2007 Special Unc	75,000	—	—	—	—	1.00
2007 Proof	20,000	Value: 10.00				

KM# 3086 20 EURO CENT
5.7400 g., Brass, 22.25 mm. **Obv:** Belvedere Palace gate **Rev:** Relief map of European Union at left, denomination at center right **Edge:** Notched

Date	Mintage	F	VF	XF	Unc	BU
2002	203,400,000	—	—	—	1.00	—
2002 Special Unc	100,000	—	—	—	—	1.25
2002 Proof	10,000	Value: 60.00				
2003	50,900,000	—	—	—	1.00	—
2003 Special Unc	125,000	—	—	—	—	1.25
2003 Proof	25,000	Value: 10.00				
2004	54,800,000	—	—	—	1.00	—
2004 Special Unc	100,000	—	—	—	—	1.25
2004 Proof	20,000	Value: 11.50				
2005	4,100,000	—	—	—	1.10	—
2005 Special Unc	100,000	—	—	—	—	1.25
2005 Proof	20,000	Value: 12.50				
2006	8,200,000	—	—	—	1.00	—
2006 Special Unc	100,000	—	—	—	—	1.25
2006 Proof	20,000	Value: 12.50				
2007	45,000,000	—	—	—	1.00	—
2007 Special Unc	75,000	—	—	—	—	1.25
2007 Proof	20,000	Value: 12.50				

KM# 3140 20 EURO CENT
5.7400 g., Brass, 22.25 mm. **Obv:** Belvedere Palace gate **Rev:** Expanded relief map of European Union at left, denomination at center right **Edge:** Notched

Date	Mintage	F	VF	XF	Unc	BU
2008	45,300,000	—	—	—	1.00	—
2008 Special Unc.	50,000	—	—	—	—	1.50
2008 Proof	15,000	Value: 12.50				
2009	49,800,000	—	—	—	1.00	—
2009 Special Unc	75,000	—	—	—	—	1.50
2009 Proof	15,000	Value: 12.50				
2010	4,200,000	—	—	—	1.00	—
2010 Special Unc	50,000	—	—	—	—	1.50
2010 Proof	15,000	Value: 12.50				
2011	—	—	—	—	1.00	—
2011 Special Unc.	50,000	—	—	—	—	1.50
2011 Proof	15,000	Value: 12.50				
2012	—	—	—	—	1.00	—

Date	Mintage	F	VF	XF	Unc	BU
2012 Special Unc.	—	—	—	—	—	1.50
2012 Proof	—	Value: 12.50				

KM# 3087 50 EURO CENT
7.8000 g., Brass, 24.25 mm. **Obv:** Secession building in Vienna **Rev:** Relief map of European Union at left, denomination at center right **Edge:** Reeded

Date	Mintage	F	VF	XF	Unc	BU
2002	169,100,000	—	—	—	1.25	—
2002 Special Unc	100,000	—	—	—	—	1.50
2002 Proof	10,000	Value: 75.00				
2003	9,100,000	—	—	—	1.25	—
2003 Special Unc	125,000	—	—	—	—	1.50
2003 Proof	25,000	Value: 12.50				
2004	3,100,000	—	—	—	1.25	—
2004 Special Unc	100,000	—	—	—	—	1.50
2004 Proof	20,000	Value: 13.50				
2005	3,100,000	—	—	—	1.25	—
2005 Special Unc	100,000	—	—	—	—	1.50
2005 Proof	20,000	Value: 15.00				
2006	3,200,000	—	—	—	1.25	—
2006 Special Unc	100,000	—	—	—	—	1.50
2006 Proof	20,000	Value: 15.00				
2007	3,000,000	—	—	—	1.25	—
2007 Special Unc	75,000	—	—	—	—	1.50
2007 Proof	20,000	Value: 15.00				

KM# 3141 50 EURO CENT
7.8000 g., Brass, 24.25 mm. **Obv:** Secession building in Vienna **Rev:** Expanded relief map of European Union at left, denomination at right **Edge:** Reeded

Date	Mintage	F	VF	XF	Unc	BU
2008	3,000,000	—	—	—	1.25	—
2008 Special Unc	50,000	—	—	—	—	1.50
2008 Proof	15,000	Value: 15.00				
2009	14,700,000	—	—	—	1.25	—
2009 Special Unc	75,000	—	—	—	—	1.50
2009 Proof	15,000	Value: 15.00				
2010	30,000,000	—	—	—	1.25	—
2010 Special Unc	50,000	—	—	—	—	1.50
2010 Proof	15,000	Value: 15.00				
2011	—	—	—	—	1.25	—
2011 Special Unc	50,000	—	—	—	—	1.50
2011 Proof	15,000	Value: 15.00				
2012	—	—	—	—	1.25	—
2012 Special Unc.	—	—	—	—	—	1.50
2012 Proof	—	Value: 15.00				

KM# 3088 EURO
7.5000 g., Bi-Metallic Copper-Nickel center in Nickel-Brass ring, 23.25 mm. **Obv:** Bust of Mozart right within inner circle, stars in outer circle **Rev:** Value at left, relief map of European Union at right **Edge:** Segmented reeding

Date	Mintage	F	VF	XF	Unc	BU
2002	223,500,000	—	—	—	2.50	—
2002 Special Unc	100,000	—	—	—	—	2.75
2002 Proof	10,000	Value: 100				
2003 Special Unc	125,000	—	—	—	—	5.00
2003 Proof	25,000	Value: 16.50				
2004	2,600,000	—	—	—	2.50	—
2004 Special Unc	100,000	—	—	—	—	2.75
2004 Proof	20,000	Value: 17.50				
2005	2,600,000	—	—	—	2.50	—
2005 Special Unc	100,000	—	—	—	—	2.75
2005 Proof	20,000	Value: 18.50				
2006	7,700,000	—	—	—	2.50	—
2006 Special Unc	100,000	—	—	—	—	2.75
2006 Proof	20,000	Value: 18.50				
2007	41,100,000	—	—	—	2.50	—
2007 Special Unc	75,000	—	—	—	—	2.75
2007 Proof	20,000	Value: 18.50				

KM# 3142 EURO
7.5000 g., Bi-Metallic Copper-Nickel center in Nickel-Brass ring, 23.25 mm. **Obv:** Bust of Mozart right within inner circle, stars in outer circle **Rev:** Value at left, expanded relief map of European Union at right **Edge:** Segmented reeding

Date	Mintage	F	VF	XF	Unc	BU
2008	65,500,000	—	—	—	2.00	—
2008 Special Unc	50,000	—	—	—	—	2.75
2008 Proof	15,000	Value: 15.00				
2009	40,300,000	—	—	—	2.00	—
2009 Special Unc	75,000	—	—	—	—	2.75
2009 Proof	15,000	Value: 15.00				
2010	11,200,000	—	—	—	2.00	—
2010 Special Unc	50,000	—	—	—	—	2.75
2010 Proof	15,000	Value: 15.00				
2011	—	—	—	—	2.00	—
2011 Special Unc	50,000	—	—	—	—	2.75
2011 Proof	15,000	Value: 15.00				
2012	—	—	—	—	2.00	—
2012 Special Unc.	—	—	—	—	—	2.75
2012 Proof	—	Value: 15.00				

KM# 3089 2 EURO
8.5000 g., Bi-Metallic Nickel-Brass center in Copper-Nickel ring, 25.75 mm. **Obv:** Bust of Bertha von Suttner, Novelist and winner of 1905 Peace Prize, facing left within inner circle, stars in outer circle **Rev:** Value at left, relief map of European Union at right **Edge Lettering:** 2 EURO (star) (star) (star) (star)

Date	Mintage	F	VF	XF	Unc	BU
2002	196,400,000	—	—	—	3.75	—
2002 Special Unc	100,000	—	—	—	—	4.00
2002 Proof	10,000	Value: 125				
2003	4,700,000	—	—	—	3.75	—
2003 Special Unc	125,000	—	—	—	—	4.00
2003 Proof	25,000	Value: 25.00				
2004	2,500,000	—	—	—	3.75	—
2004 Special Unc	100,000	—	—	—	—	4.00
2004 Proof	20,000	Value: 27.50				
2006	2,300,000	—	—	—	3.75	—
2006 Special Unc	100,000	—	—	—	—	4.00
2006 Proof	20,000	Value: 27.50				

KM# 3124 2 EURO
8.5000 g., Bi-Metallic Nickel-Brass center in Copper-Nickel ring, 25.75 mm. **Subject:** 50th Anniversary of the State Treaty **Obv:** Treaty seals and signatures **Rev:** Denomination and map **Edge:** Reeding over lettering **Edge Lettering:** "2 EURO" and 3 stars repeated four times

Date	Mintage	F	VF	XF	Unc	BU
2005	6,880,000	—	—	—	5.00	—
2005 Special Unc	100,000	—	—	—	—	6.00
2005 Proof	20,000	Value: 27.50				

KM# 3150 2 EURO
8.5000 g., Bi-Metallic Nickel-Brass center in Copper-Nickel ring, 25.75 mm. **Subject:** 50th Anniversary - Treaty of Rome **Edge:** Reeded and lettered

Date	Mintage	F	VF	XF	Unc	BU
2007	8,905,000	—	—	—	4.00	—

Date	Mintage	F	VF	XF	Unc	BU
2007 Special Unc	75,000	—	—	—	—	5.00
2007 Proof	20,000	Value: 27.50				

KM# 3143 2 EURO
8.5000 g., Bi-Metallic Nickel-Brass center in Copper-Nickel ring, 25.75 mm. **Obv:** Bust of Bertha von Suttner, Novelist and winner of 1905 Peace Prize, at right facing left in inner circle, stars in outer circle **Rev:** Value at left, expanded relief map of European Union at right **Edge Lettering:** 2 EURO ★ ★ ★

Date	Mintage	F	VF	XF	Unc	BU
2008	2,600,000	—	—	—	5.00	—
2008 Special Unc	50,000	—	—	—	—	6.00
2008 Proof	15,000	Value: 25.00				
2009	4,900,000	—	—	—	5.00	—
2009 Special Unc	75,000	—	—	—	—	6.00
2009 Proof	15,000	Value: 25.00				
2010	17,000,000	—	—	—	5.00	—
2010 Special Unc	50,000	—	—	—	—	6.00
2010 Proof	15,000	Value: 25.00				
2011	—	—	—	—	5.00	—
2011 Special Unc	50,000	—	—	—	—	6.00
2011 Proof	15,000	Value: 25.00				
2012	—	—	—	—	5.00	—
2012 Special Unc	—	—	—	—	—	6.00
2012 Proof	—	Value: 25.00				

KM# 3175 2 EURO
8.5000 g., Bi-Metallic Nickel-Brass center in Copper-Nickel ring, 25.75 mm. **Subject:** 10th Anniversary - European Monetary Union **Edge:** Reeded and lettered

Date	Mintage	F	VF	XF	Unc	BU
2009	4,910,000	—	—	—	7.50	—

KM# 3205 2 EURO
8.5000 g., Bi-Metallic Nickel-Brass center in Copper-Nickel ring, 25.75 mm. **Subject:** Euro Coinage, 10th Anniversary **Obv:** Euro symbol on globe at center, child-like rendering around

Date	Mintage	F	VF	XF	Unc	BU
2012	6,000,000	—	—	—	6.00	8.00
2012 Special Unc.	—	—	—	—	—	15.00
2012 Proof	—	Value: 25.00				

KM# 3091 5 EURO
10.0000 g., 0.8000 Silver 0.2572 oz. ASW, 28.5 mm. **Subject:** Schoenbrunn Zoo **Obv:** Denomination within sun design at center, provincial arms surround **Rev:** Building and animals **Edge:** Plain **Shape:** 9-sided

Date	Mintage	F	VF	XF	Unc	BU
ND(2002)	500,000	—	—	—	12.50	—
ND(2002) Special Unc	100,000	—	—	—	—	22.50

KM# 3105 5 EURO
10.0000 g., 0.8000 Silver 0.2572 oz. ASW, 28.5 mm. **Subject:** Water Power **Obv:** Denomination within sun design at center, provincial arms surround **Rev:** Dam with turbine, electric power plant and fish **Edge:** Plain **Shape:** 9-sided

Date	Mintage	F	VF	XF	Unc	BU
2003	500,000	—	—	—	11.50	—
2003 Special Unc	100,000	—	—	—	—	15.00

KM# 3122   5 EURO
10.0000 g., 0.8000 Silver 0.2572 oz. ASW, 28.5 mm. **Subject:** Enlargement of the European Union **Obv:** Denomination within sun design at center, provincial arms surround **Rev:** Map of Europe above country names **Edge:** Plain **Shape:** 9-sided

Date	Mintage	F	VF	XF	Unc	BU
2004	275,000	—	—	—	10.00	—
2004 Special Unc	125,000	—	—	—	—	12.50

KM# 3113   5 EURO
10.0000 g., 0.8000 Silver 0.2572 oz. ASW, 28.5 mm. **Obv:** Denomination within sun design at center, provincial arms surround **Rev:** Soccer player scoring a goal **Edge:** Plain **Shape:** 9-sided **Note:** Centennial of Austrian Soccer

Date	Mintage	F	VF	XF	Unc	BU
2004	600,000	—	—	—	10.00	—
2004 Special Unc	100,000	—	—	—	—	12.50

KM# 3117   5 EURO
10.0000 g., 0.8000 Silver 0.2572 oz. ASW, 28.5 mm. **Subject:** Centennial of Sport Skiing **Obv:** Denomination within sun design at center, provincial arms surround **Rev:** Skier within snowflake design **Edge:** Plain **Shape:** 9-sided

Date	Mintage	F	VF	XF	Unc	BU
2005	500,000	—	—	—	10.00	—
2005 Special Unc	100,000	—	—	—	—	14.50

KM# 3120   5 EURO
10.0000 g., 0.8000 Silver 0.2572 oz. ASW, 28.5 mm. **Subject:** 10th Anniversary of Austrian E U Membership **Obv:** Denomination within sun design at center, provincial arms surround **Rev:** Carinthian Gate Theater and Beethoven cameo portrait **Edge:** Plain **Shape:** 9-sided

Date	Mintage	F	VF	XF	Unc	BU
2005	275,000	—	—	—	12.50	—
2005 Special Unc	125,000	—	—	—	—	14.50

KM# 3131   5 EURO
10.0000 g., 0.8000 Silver 0.2572 oz. ASW, 28.5 mm. **Subject:**

Mozart Obv: Denomination within sun design at center, provincial arms surround **Rev:** Mozart and the Salzburg Cathedral **Edge:** Plain **Shape:** Nine sided

Date	Mintage	F	VF	XF	Unc	BU
2006	375,000	—	—	—	15.00	—
2006 Special Unc	125,000	—	—	—	—	17.50

KM# 3132   5 EURO
10.0000 g., 0.8000 Silver 0.2572 oz. ASW, 28.5 mm. **Subject:** Austrian Presidency of the EU **Obv:** Value in circle of arms **Rev:** Vienna Hofburg and Josefsplatz view **Edge:** Plain **Shape:** Nine sided

Date	Mintage	F	VF	XF	Unc	BU
2006	250,000	—	—	—	12.50	—
2006 Special Unc	100,000	—	—	—	—	14.50

KM# 3144   5 EURO
10.0000 g., 0.8000 Silver 0.2572 oz. ASW, 28.5 mm. **Subject:** Universal Male Suffrage Centennial **Obv:** Value in circle of shields **Rev:** Cameo portraits of Franz Joseph and von Beck on Reichsrat scene **Edge:** Plain **Shape:** 9-sided

Date	Mintage	F	VF	XF	Unc	BU
2007	150,000	—	—	—	13.00	—
2007 Special Unc	100,000	—	—	—	—	15.00

KM# 3145   5 EURO
10.0000 g., 0.8000 Silver 0.2572 oz. ASW, 28.5 mm. **Obv:** Value in circle of shields **Rev:** Mariazell church **Edge:** Plain **Shape:** 9-sided

Date	Mintage	F	VF	XF	Unc	BU
2007	450,000	—	—	—	12.50	—
2007 Special Unc	100,000	—	—	—	—	15.00

KM# 3156   5 EURO
10.0000 g., 0.8000 Silver 0.2572 oz. ASW, 28.5 mm. **Subject:** Herbert Von Karajan, 100th Birth Anniversary **Obv:** Value and nine provincial shields **Rev:** Bust and notes of Beethoven's Ninth Symphony **Shape:** 9-sided

Date	Mintage	F	VF	XF	Unc	BU
2008	150,000	—	—	—	17.00	—
2008 Special Unc	100,000	—	—	—	—	17.50

KM# 3163   5 EURO
10.0000 g., 0.8000 Silver 0.2572 oz. ASW, 28.5 mm. **Obv:**

Value within center of nine shields **Rev:** Two soccer players **Shape:** 9-sided

Date	Mintage	F	VF	XF	Unc	BU
2008	225,000	—	—	—	10.00	—
2008 Special Unc	100,000	—	—	—	—	12.50

KM# 3164   5 EURO
10.0000 g., 0.8000 Silver 0.2572 oz. ASW, 28.5 mm. **Obv:** Value within center of nine shields **Rev:** One soccer player **Shape:** 9-sided

Date	Mintage	F	VF	XF	Unc	BU
2008	225,000	—	—	—	11.50	—
2008 Special Unc	100,000	—	—	—	—	15.00

KM# 3170   5 EURO
10.0000 g., 0.8000 Silver 0.2572 oz. ASW, 28.5 mm. **Subject:** Joseph Haydn, 200th Anniversary of Death **Obv:** Value at center of nine shields **Rev:** Bust facing right at left, pair of violins at right **Shape:** 9-sided

Date	Mintage	F	VF	XF	Unc	BU
2009	450,000	—	—	—	15.00	—
2009 Special Unc	100,000	—	—	—	—	20.00

KM# 3177   5 EURO
10.0000 g., 0.8000 Silver 0.2572 oz. ASW, 28.5 mm. **Subject:** Tyrolean Resistance Fighters, 1809 **Shape:** 9-sided

Date	Mintage	F	VF	XF	Unc	BU
2009	250,000	—	—	—	20.00	—
2009 Special Unc	100,000	—	—	—	—	30.00

KM# 3184   5 EURO
10.0000 g., 0.8000 Silver 0.2572 oz. ASW, 28.5 mm. **Subject:** Grossglockner - High Alpine Road **Shape:** 9-sided

Date	Mintage	F	VF	XF	Unc	BU
2010	250,000	—	—	—	15.00	—
2010 Special Unc	50,000	—	—	—	—	20.00

KM# 3192   5 EURO
10.0000 g., 0.8000 Silver 0.2572 oz. ASW, 28.5 mm. **Subject:** Winter sports **Obv:** Nine provincial shields **Rev:** Snowboarding **Shape:** 9-sided

Date	Mintage	F	VF	XF	Unc	BU
2010	225,000	—	—	—	15.00	—
2010 Special Unc	50,000	—	—	—	—	20.00

KM# 3193   5 EURO
10.0000 g., 0.8000 Silver 0.2572 oz. ASW, 28.5 mm. **Subject:**
Winter Sports **Obv:** Nine provincial shields **Rev:** Ski jumper
Shape: 9-sided

Date	Mintage	F	VF	XF	Unc	BU
2010	225,000	—	—	—	15.00	—
2010 Special Unc	50,000	—	—	—	—	20.00

KM# 3195   5 EURO
10.0000 g., 0.8000 Silver 0.2572 oz. ASW, 28.5 mm. **Subject:**
Pummerin, Bell, 1711-2011 **Obv:** Value within circle of shields
Rev: Large bell **Shape:** 9-sided

Date	Mintage	F	VF	XF	Unc	BU
2011		—	—	—	10.00	—
2011 Special Unc.	50,000	—	—	—	—	12.50

KM# 3196   5 EURO
10.0000 g., 0.8000 Silver 0.2572 oz. ASW, 28.5 mm. **Subject:**
Land of Forests **Shape:** 9-sided

Date	Mintage	F	VF	XF	Unc	BU
2011		—	—	—	10.00	—
2011 Special Unc.	50,000	—	—	—	—	12.50

KM# 3206   5 EURO
8.9000 g., Copper, 28.5 mm. **Subject:** Society of Music Lovers,
200th Anniversary **Obv:** Value at center of circle of nine shields
Rev: Interior of the "Golden Hall" in Vienna **Shape:** 9-sided

Date	Mintage	F	VF	XF	Unc	BU
2012	300,000	—	—	—	—	17.50

KM# 3206a   5 EURO
10.0000 g., 0.8000 Silver 0.2572 oz. ASW, 28.5 mm. **Subject:**
Society of Music Lovers, 200th Anniversary **Obv:** Value in circle
of nine shields **Rev:** Interior of the "Golden Hall" in Vienna **Shape:**
9-sided

Date	Mintage	F	VF	XF	Unc	BU
2012 Special Unc.	50,000	—	—	—	—	30.00

KM# 3096   10 EURO
17.3000 g., 0.9250 Silver 0.5145 oz. ASW, 32 mm. **Subject:**
Ambras Palace **Obv:** Palace, denomination below **Rev:** Three
strolling musicians **Edge:** Reeded

Date	Mintage	F	VF	XF	Unc	BU
2002	130,000	—	—	—	20.00	—
2002 Special Unc	20,000	—	—	—	—	30.00
2002 Proof	50,000	Value: 40.00				

KM# 3099   10 EURO
17.3000 g., 0.9250 Silver 0.5145 oz. ASW, 32 mm. **Subject:**
Eggenberg Palace and Johannes Kepler **Obv:** Palace,
denomination below **Rev:** Half figure seated with tools **Edge:**
Reeded

Date	Mintage	F	VF	XF	Unc	BU
2002	130,000	—	—	—	20.00	—
2002 Special Unc	20,000	—	—	—	—	30.00
2002 Proof	50,000	Value: 32.50				

KM# 3103   10 EURO
17.3000 g., 0.9250 Silver 0.5145 oz. ASW, 32 mm. **Subject:**
Castle of Schlosshof **Obv:** Baroque fountain and palace,
denomination below **Rev:** Two gardeners at work

Date	Mintage	F	VF	XF	Unc	BU
2003	130,000	—	—	—	20.00	—
2003 Special Unc	20,000	—	—	—	—	30.00
2003 Proof	50,000	Value: 32.50				

KM# 3106   10 EURO
17.3000 g., 0.9250 Silver 0.5145 oz. ASW, 32 mm. **Subject:**
Schoenbrunn Palace **Obv:** Fountain with palace background,
denomination below **Rev:** Palmenhaus greenhouse

Date	Mintage	F	VF	XF	Unc	BU
2003	100,000	—	—	—	20.00	—
2003 Special Unc	40,000	—	—	—	—	27.50
2003 Proof	60,000	Value: 30.00				

KM# 3111   10 EURO
17.3000 g., 0.9250 Silver 0.5145 oz. ASW, 32 mm. **Obv:**
Hellbrunn Castle, denomination below **Rev:** Archbishop Marcus
Sitticus and Hellbrunn's "Roman Theatre" **Edge:** Reeded

Date	Mintage	F	VF	XF	Unc	BU
2004	130,000	—	—	—	20.00	—
2004 Special Unc	40,000	—	—	—	—	25.00
2004 Proof	60,000	Value: 30.00				

KM# 3115   10 EURO
17.3000 g., 0.9250 Silver 0.5145 oz. ASW, 32 mm. **Obv:**
Artstetten Castle, denomination below **Rev:** Crypt entrance
behind portraits of Franz Ferdinand and Sophie

Date	Mintage	F	VF	XF	Unc	BU
2004	130,000	—	—	—	20.00	—
2004 Special Unc	40,000	—	—	—	—	25.00
2004 Proof	60,000	Value: 30.00				

KM# 3121   10 EURO
17.3000 g., 0.9250 Silver 0.5145 oz. ASW, 32 mm. **Subject:**
60th Anniversary of the Second Republic **Obv:** Statue of Athena,
nine provincial shields and denomination at right **Rev:** Parliament
building above broken chain, crowd below

Date	Mintage	F	VF	XF	Unc	BU
2005	130,000	—	—	—	20.00	—
2005 Special Unc	40,000	—	—	—	—	25.00
2005 Proof	60,000	Value: 35.00				

KM# 3125   10 EURO
17.3000 g., 0.9250 Silver 0.5145 oz. ASW, 32 mm. **Subject:**
Reopening of the Burg Theater and Opera **Obv:** Two large
buildings, denomination at left **Rev:** Comedy and Tragedy Masks

Date	Mintage	F	VF	XF	Unc	BU
2005	130,000	—	—	—	20.00	—
2005 Special Unc	40,000	—	—	—	—	25.00
2005 Proof	60,000	Value: 35.00				

KM# 3129   10 EURO
17.3000 g., 0.9250 Silver 0.5145 oz. ASW, 32 mm. **Subject:**
Nonnenberg Abbey **Obv:** Abbey view, denomination below **Rev:**
Statue of St. Erentrudis **Edge:** Reeded

Date	Mintage	F	VF	XF	Unc	BU
2006	130,000	—	—	—	20.00	—
2006 Special Unc	40,000	—	—	—	—	25.00
2006 Proof	60,000	Value: 35.00				

KM# 3137   10 EURO
17.3000 g., 0.9250 Silver 0.5145 oz. ASW, 32 mm. **Obv:**
Gottweig Abby above value **Rev:** Charles VI and staircase

Date	Mintage	F	VF	XF	Unc	BU
2006	130,000	—	—	—	20.00	—
2006 Special Unc	40,000	—	—	—	—	30.00
2006 Proof	60,000	Value: 40.00				

KM# 3146   10 EURO
17.3000 g., 0.9250 Silver 0.5145 oz. ASW, 32 mm. **Obv:** Melk
Abbey view **Rev:** Inner view of the Melk Abbey dome

Date	Mintage	F	VF	XF	Unc	BU
2007	130,000	—	—	—	20.00	—
2007 Special Unc	40,000	—	—	—	—	25.00
2007 Proof	60,000	Value: 35.00				

KM# 3148 10 EURO

17.3000 g., 0.9250 Silver 0.5145 oz. ASW, 32 mm. **Obv:** St. Paul's Abbey complex **Obv. Legend:** ST. PAUL IM LAVANTTAL **Obv. Inscription:** REPUBLIK / ÖSTERREICH **Rev:** Entrance facade

Date	Mintage	F	VF	XF	Unc	BU
2007	130,000	—	—	—	20.00	—
2007 Special Unc	60,000	—	—	—	—	25.00
2007 Proof	40,000	Value: 35.00				

KM# 3157 10 EURO

17.3000 g., 0.9250 Silver 0.5145 oz. ASW, 32 mm. **Subject:** Abby of Klosterneuburg **Obv:** Aerial exterior view of church complex **Rev:** Cloister

Date	Mintage	F	VF	XF	Unc	BU
2008	130,000	—	—	—	20.00	—
2008 Special Unc	40,000	—	—	—	—	25.00
2008 Proof	60,000	Value: 45.00				

KM# 3162 10 EURO

17.3000 g., 0.9250 Silver 0.5145 oz. ASW, 32 mm. **Subject:** Seckau Benedict Abbey **Obv:** Exterior of abby, value, date and inscriptions "BENEDIKTINERABTEI SECKAU" and "REPUBLIK OESTERREICH" **Rev:** Interior of abbey

Date	Mintage	F	VF	XF	Unc	BU
2008	130,000	—	—	—	20.00	—
2008 Special Unc	40,000	—	—	—	—	25.00
2008 Proof	60,000	Value: 45.00				

KM# 3176 10 EURO

17.3000 g., 0.9250 Silver 0.5145 oz. ASW, 32 mm. **Series:** Tales and Legends **Subject:** Basilisk of Vienna

Date	Mintage	F	VF	XF	Unc	BU
2009	130,000	—	—	—	20.00	—
2009 Special Unc	30,000	—	—	—	—	25.00
2009 Proof	40,000	Value: 40.00				

KM# 3180 10 EURO

17.3000 g., 0.9250 Silver 0.5145 oz. ASW, 32 mm. **Series:** Tales and Legends **Subject:** Richard the Lionheart in Dürnstein

Date	Mintage	F	VF	XF	Unc	BU
2009	130,000	—	—	—	20.00	—
2009 Special Unc	30,000	—	—	—	—	25.00
2009 Proof	40,000	Value: 45.00				

KM# 3185 10 EURO

17.3000 g., 0.9250 Silver 0.5145 oz. ASW, 32 mm. **Subject:** Erzberg in Styria **Obv:** Iron Mine **Rev:** Two mermen with cloak

Date	Mintage	F	VF	XF	Unc	BU
2010	130,000	—	—	—	25.00	—
2010 Special Unc	30,000	—	—	—	—	28.00
2010 Proof	40,000	Value: 40.00				

KM# 3186 10 EURO

17.3000 g., 0.9250 Silver 0.5145 oz. ASW, 32 mm. **Subject:** Charlemagne in the Undersberg

Date	Mintage	F	VF	XF	Unc	BU
2010(h)	130,000	—	—	—	25.00	—
2010(h) Special Unc	30,000	—	—	—	—	28.00
2010(h) Proof	40,000	Value: 40.00				

KM# 3197 10 EURO

17.3000 g., 0.9250 Silver 0.5145 oz. ASW, 32 mm. **Subject:** The Lindworm in Klagenfurt

Date	Mintage	F	VF	XF	Unc	BU
2011 Special Unc.	30,000	—	—	—	—	25.00
2011 Proof	40,000	Value: 40.00				

KM# 3198 10 EURO

17.3000 g., 0.9250 Silver 0.5145 oz. ASW, 32 mm. **Subject:** My dear old Augustin

Date	Mintage	F	VF	XF	Unc	BU
2011 Special Unc.	30,000	—	—	—	—	25.00
2011 Proof	40,000	Value: 40.00				

KM# 3097 20 EURO

20.0000 g., 0.9000 Silver 0.5787 oz. ASW, 34 mm. **Subject:** Ferdinand I - Renaissance **Obv:** Hofburg Palace "Swiss Gate" with two guards, denomination below **Rev:** Bust looking left, coat of arms at left, dates at right **Edge:** Reeded

Date	Mintage	F	VF	XF	Unc	BU
2002 Proof	50,000	Value: 37.50				

KM# 3098 20 EURO

20.0000 g., 0.9000 Silver 0.5787 oz. ASW, 34 mm. **Subject:** Prince Eugen - Baroque Period **Obv:** Baroque staircase with statues, denomination below **Rev:** Uniformed bust 1/4 left and dates at right, flags above cannons at left **Edge:** Reeded

Date	Mintage	F	VF	XF	Unc	BU
2002 Proof	50,000	Value: 42.00				

KM# 3104 20 EURO

20.0000 g., 0.9000 Silver 0.5787 oz. ASW, 34 mm. **Subject:** Prince Metternich **Obv:** Early steam locomotive, denomination below **Rev:** Portrait with map background **Edge:** Reeded

Date	Mintage	F	VF	XF	Unc	BU
2003 Proof	50,000	Value: 45.00				

KM# 3107 20 EURO

20.0000 g., 0.9000 Silver 0.5787 oz. ASW, 34 mm. **Obv:** Republic of Austria arms, denomination below **Rev:** Four men in a jeep **Edge:** Reeded **Note:** Post War Austrian Reconstruction

Date	Mintage	F	VF	XF	Unc	BU
2003 Proof	50,000	Value: 50.00				

KM# 3112 20 EURO

20.0000 g., 0.9000 Silver 0.5787 oz. ASW, 34 mm. **Obv:** S.M.S Novara under sail in Chinese waters, denomination below **Rev:** Standing figures behind table with globe and microscope **Edge:** Reeded **Note:** First Global Circumnavigation by an Austrian ship.

Date	Mintage	F	VF	XF	Unc	BU
2004 Proof	50,000	Value: 50.00				

KM# 3114 20 EURO

20.0000 g., 0.9000 Silver 0.5787 oz. ASW, 34 mm. **Obv:** SMS Erzherzog Ferdinand Max sailing to the Battle of Lissa, denomination below **Rev:** Sailors at the wheel with Admiral Tegetthof in background **Edge:** Reeded

Date	Mintage	F	VF	XF	Unc	BU
2004 Proof	50,000	Value: 52.50				

KM# 3126   20 EURO
20.0000 g., 0.9000 Silver 0.5787 oz. ASW, 34 mm. **Obv:** Ship, "Admiral Tegetthoff" in arctic waters, denomination below **Rev:** Expedition leaders, von Payer and Weyprecht with their icebound ship behind them **Edge:** Reeded

Date	Mintage	F	VF	XF	Unc	BU
2005 Proof	50,000	Value: 50.00				

KM# 3127   20 EURO
20.0000 g., 0.9000 Silver 0.5787 oz. ASW, 34 mm. **Obv:** SMS St. George sailing past the Statue of Liberty, denomination below **Rev:** Shipyard at Pola, boat on water **Edge:** Reeded

Date	Mintage	F	VF	XF	Unc	BU
2005 Proof	50,000	Value: 50.00				

KM# 3133   20 EURO
20.0000 g., 0.9000 Silver 0.5787 oz. ASW, 34 mm. **Subject:** Austrian Merchant Marine **Obv:** Two passing steam ships **Rev:** 19th Century Triest harbor view **Edge:** Reeded

Date	Mintage	F	VF	XF	Unc	BU
2006 Proof	50,000	Value: 50.00				

KM# 3134   20 EURO
20.0000 g., 0.9000 Silver 0.5787 oz. ASW, 34 mm. **Obv:** SMS Viribus Unitis, flag ship of the Austrian fleet, and other ships steaming left **Rev:** SMS Viribus Unitis, submarine conning tower and seaplane **Edge:** Reeded

Date	Mintage	F	VF	XF	Unc	BU
2006 Proof	50,000	Value: 50.00				

KM# 3149   20 EURO
20.0000 g., 0.9000 Silver 0.5787 oz. ASW, 34 mm. **Series:** Austrian Railways **Obv:** Steam locomotive 1837 with passenger wagons **Obv. Legend:** REPUBLIK ÖSTERREICH **Obv. Inscription:** DAMPFLOKOMOTIVE / AUSTRIA / 1837 **Rev:** People waving at passenger train crossing a trestle **Rev. Legend:** KAISER - FERDINANDS - NORDBAHN **Edge:** Reeded

Date	Mintage	F	VF	XF	Unc	BU
2007 Proof	50,000	Value: 50.00				

KM# 3151   20 EURO
20.0000 g., 0.9000 Silver 0.5787 oz. ASW, 34 mm. **Series:** Austrian Railways **Obv:** Steam locomotive 1848 standing still, viaduct in background **Obv. Legend:** REPUBLIK ÖSTERREICH **Obv. Inscription:** DAMPF-/ LOKOMOTIVE / STEINBROCK / 1848 **Rev:** Steam train traveling right through city **Rev. Legend:** K.K. SÜDBAHN WIEN - TRIEST **Edge:** Reeded

Date	Mintage	F	VF	XF	Unc	BU
2007 Proof	50,000	Value: 50.00				

KM# 3154   20 EURO
20.0000 g., 0.9000 Silver 0.5787 oz. ASW, 34 mm. **Subject:** Southern Railways **Obv:** Steam Locomotive on iron railway bridge **Obv. Inscription:** KOK kkStB 306 **Rev:** Statue of Empress Elizabeth and train platform in Vienna's West Railway station **Rev. Inscription:** KAISERIN-/ ELIZABETH-/ WESTBAHN **Edge:** Reeded

Date	Mintage	F	VF	XF	Unc	BU
2008 Proof	50,000	Value: 70.00				

KM# 3161   20 EURO
20.0000 g., 0.9000 Silver 0.5787 oz. ASW, 34 mm. **Subject:** Imperal - Royal State Railway **Obv:** Locomotive steaming left **Obv. Legend:** Nordbahnhof/Wein **Rev:** Female on platform

Date	Mintage	F	VF	XF	Unc	BU
2008 Proof	50,000	Value: 70.00				

KM# 3178   20 EURO
20.0000 g., 0.9000 Silver 0.5787 oz. ASW, 34 mm. **Subject:** The Electric Railway **Obv:** Locomotive model 1189, the Crocodile **Rev:** Train on the Trisanna Bridge, Wiesburg Castle in background

Date	Mintage	F	VF	XF	Unc	BU
2009 Proof	50,000	Value: 50.00				

KM# 3179   20 EURO
20.0000 g., 0.9000 Silver 0.5787 oz. ASW, 34 mm. **Subject:** Railways of the Future **Obv:** Railjet highspeed OBB train **Rev:** Electric locomotive of the 1063 class in freight yard **Edge:** Reeded

Date	Mintage	F	VF	XF	Unc	BU
2009 Proof	50,000	Value: 50.00				

KM# 3187   20 EURO
20.0000 g., 0.9000 Silver 0.5787 oz. ASW, 34 mm. **Subject:** Rome on the Danube - Virunum **Obv:** Emperor Claudium, 2-horse wagon, gravestone **Rev:** Street scene, wagon and temple facade **Edge:** Reeded

Date	Mintage	F	VF	XF	Unc	BU
2010 Proof	50,000	Value: 75.00				

KM# 3188   20 EURO
20.0000 g., 0.9000 Silver 0.5787 oz. ASW, 34 mm. **Subject:** Rome on the Danube - Vindovona **Edge:** Reeded

Date	Mintage	F	VF	XF	Unc	BU
2010 Proof	50,000	Value: 75.00				

KM# 3199   20 EURO
20.0000 g., 0.9000 Silver 0.5787 oz. ASW, 34 mm. **Subject:** Rome on the Danube - Carnuntum **Edge:** Reeded

Date	Mintage	F	VF	XF	Unc	BU
2011 Proof	50,000	Value: 70.00				

KM# 3200   20 EURO
20.0000 g., 0.9000 Silver 0.5787 oz. ASW, 34 mm. **Subject:** Rome on the Danube - Aguntum

Date	Mintage	F	VF	XF	Unc	BU
2011 Proof	50,000	Value: 70.00				

KM# 3201   20 EURO
20.0000 g., 0.9000 Silver 0.5787 oz. ASW, 34 mm. **Subject:** Nikolaus Joseph von Jacquin **Obv:** Bust at left, flower at right **Rev:** Karibuk Expedition, Jacquin taking notes of plants in book

Date	Mintage	F	VF	XF	Unc	BU
2011 Proof	50,000			Value: 70.00		

KM# 3101   25 EURO
17.1500 g., Bi-Metallic 7.15g pure Niobium (Columbium) blue color center in a 10 g., 0.900 Silver ring, 34 mm. **Subject:** City of Hall in Tyrol **Obv:** Satellite mapping the city from outer space **Rev:** Depiction of the die face used to strike the 1486 guldiner coin **Edge:** Plain

Date	Mintage	F	VF	XF	Unc	BU
2003 Special Unc	50,000	—	—	—	—	125

KM# 3109   25 EURO
17.1500 g., Bi-Metallic 7.15g Niobium center in 10g, 0.900 Silver ring, 34 mm. **Subject:** Semmering Alpine Railway **Obv:** Modern and antique locomotives **Rev:** Steam train **Edge:** Plain

Date	Mintage	F	VF	XF	Unc	BU
2004 Special Unc	50,000	—	—	—	—	100

KM# 3119   25 EURO
17.1500 g., Bi-Metallic Purple color pure Niobium 7.15g center in 10g, 0.900 Silver ring, 34 mm. **Subject:** 50 Years Austrian Television **Obv:** The original test pattern of the 1950's **Rev:** World globe behind "rabbit ear" antenna; television developmental milestones from 7-1 o'clock **Edge:** Plain

Date	Mintage	F	VF	XF	Unc	BU
2005 Special Unc	65,000	—	—	—	—	75.00

KM# 3135   25 EURO
17.1500 g., Bi-Metallic Niobium 7.15g center in 10g, 0.900 Silver ring, 34 mm. **Subject:** European Satellite Navigation **Obv:** Austrian Mint's global location inscribed on a compass face **Rev:** Satellites in orbit around the world globe **Edge:** Plain

Date	Mintage	F	VF	XF	Unc	BU
2006 Special Unc	65,000	—	—	—	—	75.00

KM# 3147   25 EURO
16.5000 g., Bi-Metallic 6.5g Niobium center in 10g, 0.900 Silver ring, 34 mm. **Subject:** Austrian Aviation **Obv:** Interior view of modern cockpit **Rev:** Taube airplane flying above glider and pilot **Edge:** Plain

Date	Mintage	F	VF	XF	Unc	BU
2007 Special Unc	65,000	—	—	—	—	75.00

KM# 3158   25 EURO
16.5000 g., Bi-Metallic 6.5g Niobium center in 10g, 0.900 Silver ring, 34 mm. **Subject:** Carl Baron Auer von Welsbach, 150th Anniversary of Birth **Obv:** Lighting gas lamp before Vienna City Wall **Rev:** Head of Welsbach, development of light bulbs

Date	Mintage	F	VF	XF	Unc	BU
2008 Special Unc	65,000	—	—	—	—	80.00

KM# 3174   25 EURO
16.5000 g., Bi-Metallic 6.5g Niobium center in 10g, 0.900 silver ring, 34 mm. **Subject:** Year of Astronomy **Obv:** Galileo head and instruments **Rev:** Space exploration satellite

Date	Mintage	F	VF	XF	Unc	BU
2009 Special Unc	65,000	—	—	—	—	80.00

KM# 3189   25 EURO
16.5000 g., Bi-Metallic 6.5g Niobium center in 10g, 0.900 Silver ring, 34 mm. **Obv:** Tree and the 4 elements: earth, wind, water, and fire **Rev:** Solar panels, hydroelectric turbine, global thermal energy and wind turbine

Date	Mintage	F	VF	XF	Unc	BU
2010 Special Unc	65,000	—	—	—	—	80.00

KM# 3204   25 EURO

16.5000 g., Bi-Metallic 6.5g Niobium center in 10g, 0.900 Silver ring, 34 mm. **Subject:** Robotics **Rev:** Mars rover

Date	Mintage	F	VF	XF	Unc	BU
2011 Special Unc.	65,000	—				80.00

KM# 3090   50 EURO
10.1400 g., 0.9860 Gold 0.3214 oz. AGW, 22 mm. **Subject:** Saints Benedict and Scholastica **Obv:** St. Benedict and his sister St. Scholastica **Rev:** Monk copying a manuscript **Edge:** Reeded

Date	Mintage	F	VF	XF	Unc	BU
2002 Proof	50,000			Value: 600		

KM# 3102   50 EURO
10.1400 g., 0.9860 Gold 0.3214 oz. AGW, 22 mm. **Subject:** Christian Charity **Obv:** Nursing Sister with hospital patient **Rev:** The Good Samaritan **Edge:** Reeded

Date	Mintage	F	VF	XF	Unc	BU
2003 Proof	50,000			Value: 600		

KM# 3110   50 EURO
10.1400 g., 0.9860 Gold 0.3214 oz. AGW, 22 mm. **Subject:** Great Composers - Joseph Haydn (1732-1809) **Obv:** Esterhazy Palace **Rev:** Bust 3/4 right

Date	Mintage	F	VF	XF	Unc	BU
2004 Proof	50,000			Value: 600		

KM# 3118   50 EURO
10.1400 g., 0.9860 Gold 0.3214 oz. AGW, 22 mm. **Subject:** Great Composers - Ludwig Van Beethoven (1770-1827) **Obv:** Lobkowitz Palace above value and document **Rev:** Bust 3/4 facing, dates at left

Date	Mintage	F	VF	XF	Unc	BU
2005 Proof	50,000			Value: 600		

KM# 3130   50 EURO
10.1400 g., 0.9860 Gold 0.3214 oz. AGW, 22 mm. **Subject:** Great Composers - Mozart **Obv:** Mozart's birthplace, denomination below **Rev:** Leopold and Wolfgang Mozart

Date	Mintage	F	VF	XF	Unc	BU
2006 Proof	50,000			Value: 600		

KM# 3138   50 EURO
10.1400 g., 0.9860 Gold 0.3214 oz. AGW, 22 mm. **Obv:** Gerard Van Swieten holding book and facing left **Rev:** Akademie der Wissenschaften building

Date	Mintage	F	VF	XF	Unc	BU
2007 Proof	50,000			Value: 600		

KM# 3153   50 EURO
10.1400 g., 0.9860 Gold 0.3214 oz. AGW, 22 mm. **Subject:** Ignaz Philipp Sammelweis - Personal Hygiene **Obv:** Bust of Sammelweis 3/4 right, staff of Aesculapius at lower right **Obv. Legend:** REPUBLIK ÖSTERREICH **Rev:** Vienna General Hospital, Sammelweis helping patient wash at lower right **Rev. Legend:** ALLGEMEINES KRANKENHAUS WEIN

Date	Mintage	F	VF	XF	Unc	BU
2008 Proof	50,000	Value: 600				

KM# 3171   50 EURO
10.1400 g., 0.9860 Gold 0.3214 oz. AGW, 22 mm. **Subject:** Theodor Billroth **Obv:** Bust and Aesculapius staff **Rev:** Operation scene

Date	Mintage	F	VF	XF	Unc	BU
2009 Proof	50,000	Value: 600				

KM# 3194   50 EURO
10.1400 g., 0.9860 Gold 0.3214 oz. AGW, 22 mm. **Subject:** Baron Clemens von Pirquet **Obv:** Portrait of von Pirquet **Rev:** Facade of Children's Clinic of Vienna

Date	Mintage	F	VF	XF	Unc	BU
2010 Proof	50,000	Value: 600				

KM# 3202   50 EURO
10.1400 g., 0.9860 Gold 0.3214 oz. AGW, 22 mm. **Subject:** Joanneum Museum **Obv:** Exterior of Art Museum **Rev:** Armor display

Date	Mintage	F	VF	XF	Unc	BU
2011 Proof	50,000	Value: 675				

KM# 3100   100 EURO
16.2270 g., 0.9860 Gold 0.5144 oz. AGW, 30 mm. **Subject:** Raphael Donner **Obv:** Portrait in front of building **Rev:** Providentia Fountain **Edge:** Reeded

Date	Mintage	F	VF	XF	Unc	BU
2002 Proof	30,000	Value: 900				

KM# 3108   100 EURO
16.2270 g., 0.9860 Gold 0.5144 oz. AGW, 30 mm. **Obv:** Gustav Klimt standing **Rev:** Klimt's painting "The Kiss" **Edge:** Reeded

Date	Mintage	F	VF	XF	Unc	BU
2003 Proof	30,000	Value: 900				

KM# 3116   100 EURO
16.2270 g., 0.9860 Gold 0.5144 oz. AGW, 30 mm. **Obv:** Secession Exhibit Hall in Vienna **Rev:** Knight in armor, "strength" with two women, "ambition and sympathy"

Date	Mintage	F	VF	XF	Unc	BU
2004 Proof	30,000	Value: 900				

KM# 3128   100 EURO
16.2270 g., 0.9860 Gold 0.5144 oz. AGW, 30 mm. **Subject:** St. Leopold's Church at Steinhof **Obv:** Domed church building, denomination below **Rev:** Two angels flank stained glass portrait

Date	Mintage	F	VF	XF	Unc	BU
2005 Proof	30,000	Value: 900				

KM# 3136   100 EURO
16.2270 g., 0.9860 Gold 0.5144 oz. AGW, 30 mm. **Subject:** Vienna's River Gate Park **Obv:** Bridge over river scene **Rev:** One of two "sculpted ladies" flanking the park entrance

Date	Mintage	F	VF	XF	Unc	BU
2006 Proof	30,000	Value: 900				

KM# 3155   100 EURO
16.2270 g., 0.9860 Gold 0.5144 oz. AGW, 30 mm. **Obv:** Building at Linke Wienzeile Nr 38 by architect Otto Koloman Wagner **Rev:** Ornate elevator and stairwell

Date	Mintage	F	VF	XF	Unc	BU
2007 Proof	30,000	Value: 865				

KM# 3160   100 EURO
16.2270 g., 0.9860 Gold 0.5144 oz. AGW, 30 mm. **Series:** Crowns of the Habsburgs **Obv:** Crown of the Holy Roman Emperor set upon coronation robe **Rev:** Otto I seated facing and old St. Peter's Bastilica, Rome

Date	Mintage	F	VF	XF	Unc	BU
2008 Proof	30,000	Value: 900				

KM# 3181   100 EURO
16.2270 g., 0.9860 Gold 0.5144 oz. AGW, 30 mm. **Series:** Crowns of the Habsburgs **Subject:** Archducal crown of Austria **Obv:** Crown resting on pillow **Rev:** Procession of the crown, orb and sceptre, Plague memorial column in background

Date	Mintage	F	VF	XF	Unc	BU
2009 Proof	30,000	Value: 900				

KM# 3191   100 EURO
16.2270 g., 0.9860 Gold 0.5144 oz. AGW, 30 mm. **Series:** Crowns of the Habsburgs **Subject:** St. Stephen's Hungarian Crown **Obv:** Crown of St. Stephen **Rev:** Naria Theresa on horseback

Date	Mintage	F	VF	XF	Unc	BU
2010 Proof	30,000	Value: 900				

KM# 3203   100 EURO
16.2270 g., 0.9860 Gold 0.5144 oz. AGW, 30 mm. **Subject:** King Wenceslas

Date	Mintage	F	VF	XF	Unc	BU
2011 Proof	—	Value: 900				

EURO BULLION COINAGE
Philharmonic Issues

KM# 3159   1-1/2 EURO
31.1030 g., 0.9990 Silver 0.9989 oz. ASW, 37 mm. **Obv:** Golden Concert Hall **Rev:** Bouquet of Instruments **Edge:** Plain

Date	Mintage	F	VF	XF	Unc	BU
2008	7,800,000	—	—	—	BV	37.50
2009	9,000,000	—	—	—	BV	37.50
2010	11,300,000	—	—	—	BV	37.50
2011	—	—	—	—	BV	37.50

KM# 3092   10 EURO
3.1210 g., 0.9999 Gold 0.1003 oz. AGW, 16 mm. **Subject:** Vienna Philharmonic **Obv:** The Golden Hall organ **Rev:** Musical instruments **Edge:** Segmented reeding

Date	Mintage	F	VF	XF	Unc	BU
2002	75,789	—	—	—	—BV+13%	
2003	59,654	—	—	—	—BV+13%	
2004	67,994	—	—	—	—BV+13%	
2005	62,071	—	—	—	—BV+13%	
2006	39,892	—	—	—	—BV+13%	
2007	76,325	—	—	—	—BV+13%	
2008	176,700	—	—	—	—BV+13%	
2009	437,700	—	—	—	—BV+13%	
2010	226,700	—	—	—	—BV+13%	
2011	—	—	—	—	—BV+13%	

KM# 3093   25 EURO
7.7760 g., 0.9999 Gold 0.2500 oz. AGW, 22 mm. **Subject:**
Vienna Philharmonic **Obv:** The Golden Hall organ **Rev:** Musical
instruments **Edge:** Segmented reeding

Date	Mintage	F	VF	XF	Unc	BU
2002	40,807	—	—	—	—	BV+10%
2003	34,019	—	—	—	—	BV+10%
2004	32,449	—	—	—	—	BV+10%
2005	32,817	—	—	—	—	BV+10%
2006	29,609	—	—	—	—	BV+10%
2007	34,631	—	—	—	—	BV+10%
2008	97,100	—	—	—	—	BV+10%
2009	172,000	—	—	—	—	BV+10%
2010	84,900	—	—	—	—	BV+10%
2011	—	—	—	—	—	BV+10%

KM# 3094   50 EURO
15.5520 g., 0.9999 Gold 0.4999 oz. AGW, 28 mm. **Subject:**
Vienna Philharmonic **Obv:** The Golden Hall organ **Rev:** Musical
instruments **Edge:** Segmented reeding

Date	Mintage	F	VF	XF	Unc	BU
2002	40,922	—	—	—	—	BV+8%
2003	26,848	—	—	—	—	BV+8%
2004	24,269	—	—	—	—	BV+8%
2005	21,049	—	—	—	—	BV+8%
2006	20,085	—	—	—	—	BV+8%
2007	25,091	—	—	—	—	BV+8%
2008	73,800	—	—	—	—	BV+8%
2009	92,300	—	—	—	—	BV+8%
2010	56,600	—	—	—	—	BV+8%
2011	—	—	—	—	—	BV+8%

KM# 3095   100 EURO
31.1035 g., 0.9999 Gold 0.9999 oz. AGW, 37 mm. **Subject:**
Vienna Philharmonic **Obv:** The Golden Hall organ **Rev:** Musical
instruments **Edge:** Segmented reeding

Date	Mintage	F	VF	XF	Unc	BU
2002	164,105	—	—	—	—	BV+4%
2003	179,881	—	—	—	—	BV+4%
2004	176,319	—	—	—	—	BV+4%
2005	158,564	—	—	—	—	BV+4%
2006	82,174	—	—	—	—	BV+4%
2007	108,675	—	—	—	—	BV+4%
2008	715,800	—	—	—	—	BV+4%
2009	903,000	—	—	—	—	BV+4%
2010	512,000	—	—	—	—	BV+4%
2011	—	—	—	—	—	BV+4%

KM# 3182   2000 EURO
622.1000 g., 0.9999 Gold 19.998 oz. AGW, 74 mm. **Subject:**
Vienna Philharmonic **Obv:** The Golden Hall Organ **Rev:** Musical
instruments **Edge:** Reeded

Date	Mintage	F	VF	XF	Unc	BU
2009	6,027	—	—	—	—	BV+5%

KM# 3123   100000 EURO
31103.5000 g., 0.9999 Gold 999.85 oz. AGW, 370 mm. **Obv:**
The Golden Hall organ **Rev:** Musical instruments **Edge:** Reeded

Date	Mintage	F	VF	XF	Unc	BU
2004 Proof	15	BV+5%				

MINT SETS

KM#	Date	Mintage	Identification	Issue Price	Mkt Val
MS10	2001 (6)	75,000	KM#2878, 2885, 2886, 2889a, 2918, 3075	25.00	40.00
MS11	2002 (8)	100,000	KM#3082-3089, Euro	22.50	25.00
MS12	2003 (8)	125,000	KM#3082-3089, Mozart	22.50	25.00
MS13	2004 (8)	100,000	KM#3082-3089, von Suttner	—	25.00
MS14	2005 (8)	100,000	KM#3082-3088, 3124, State treaty	—	25.00
MS15	2006 (8)	100,000	KM#3082-3089, St. Stephan's Cathedral	—	35.00
MS16	2007 (8)	75,000	KM#3082-3088, 3150, Treaty of Rome	—	25.00
MS17	2008 (8)	50,000	KM#3082-3084, 3139-3143, European Map	—	35.00
MS18	2009 (8)	75,000	KM#3082-3084, 3139-3143	—	25.00
MS19	2010 (8)	—	KM#3082-3084, 3139-3143	—	35.00
MS20	2011 (8)	50,000	KM# 3082-3084, 3139-3143	—	35.00

PROOF SETS

KM#	Date	Mintage	Identification	Issue Price	Mkt Val
PS53	2002 (8)	10,000	KM#3082-3089	85.00	485
PS54	2003 (8)	25,000	KM#3082-3089	85.00	95.00
PS55	2004 (8)	20,000	KM#3082-3089	—	105
PS56	2005 (8)	20,000	KM#3082-3088, 3124	—	110
PS57	2006 (8)	20,000	KM#3082-3089	—	110
PS58	2007 (8)	20,000	KM#3082-3088, 3150	—	110
PS59	2008 (8)	15,000	KM#3082-3084, 3139-3143	—	120
PS60	2009 (8)	15,000	KM#3082-3084, 3139-3143	—	120
PS61	2010 (8)	15,000	KM#3082-3084, 3139-3143	—	100
PS62	2011 (9)	15,000	KM#3082-3084, 3139-3143	—	100

AZERBAIJAN

The Republic of Azerbaijan (formerly Azerbaijan S.S.R.)
includes the Nakhichevan Autonomous Republic. Situated in the
eastern area of Transcaucasia, it is bordered in the west by Armenia, in the north by Georgia and Dagestan, to the east by the Caspian Sea and to the south by Iran. It has an area of 33,430 sq.
mi. (86,600 sq. km.) and a population of 7.8 million. Capital: Baku.
The area is rich in mineral deposits of aluminum, copper, iron,
lead, salt and zinc, with oil as its leading industry. Agriculture and
livestock follow in importance.

MONETARY SYSTEM
100 Qapik = 1 Manat

REPUBLIC
DECIMAL COINAGE

KM# 39   QAPIK
2.8000 g., Copper Plated Steel, 16.25 mm. **Obv:** Map above
value **Rev:** Value and musical instruments **Edge:** Plain

Date	Mintage	F	VF	XF	Unc	BU
ND (2006)	—	—	—	—	—	2.00

KM# 40   3 QAPIK
3.4500 g., Copper Plated Steel, 18 mm. **Obv:** Map above value
Rev: Value above books **Edge:** Grooved

Date	Mintage	F	VF	XF	Unc	BU
ND (2006)	—	—	—	—	—	2.50

KM# 41   5 QAPIK
4.8500 g., Copper Plated Steel, 19.75 mm. **Obv:** Map above
value **Rev:** The Maiden Tower, Baku, above value **Edge:** Reeded

Date	Mintage	F	VF	XF	Unc	BU
ND (2006)	—	—	—	—	—	2.75

KM# 42   10 QAPIK
5.2500 g., Brass Plated Steel, 22.25 mm. **Obv:** Map above value
Rev: Value and Military Helmet, Symbolic of desire to regain
Nagorno-Karabakh **Edge:** Notched

Date	Mintage	F	VF	XF	Unc	BU
ND (2006)	—	—	—	—	—	3.00
2010	—	—	—	—	—	3.00

KM# 43   20 QAPIK
6.6000 g., Brass Plated Steel, 24.25 mm. **Obv:** Map above value
Rev: Value and spiral staircase **Edge:** Segmented reeding

Date	Mintage	F	VF	XF	Unc	BU
ND (2006)	—	—	—	—	—	4.00

KM# 44 50 QAPIK
7.7000 g., Bi-Metallic Brass plated Steel center in Stainless Steel ring, 25.5 mm. **Obv:** Map above value **Rev:** Two oil wells **Edge:** Reeded and lettered

Date	Mintage	F	VF	XF	Unc	BU
ND (2006)	—	—	—	—	—	5.00

KM# 37 50 MANAT
28.3400 g., 0.9250 Silver 0.8428 oz. ASW, 38.6 mm. **Subject:** Heydar Aliyev **Obv:** National map **Rev:** Bust 3/4 right **Edge:** Reeded

Date	Mintage	F	VF	XF	Unc	BU
2004 Proof	2,000	Value: 75.00				

KM# 48 50 MANAT
28.2800 g., 0.9250 Silver 0.8410 oz. ASW, 38.6 mm. **Subject:** FIFA World Cup, 2006 **Edge:** Plain

Date	Mintage	F	VF	XF	Unc	BU
2004 Proof	200	Value: 75.00				

KM# 46 100 MANAT
39.9400 g., 0.9167 Gold 1.1771 oz. AGW **Subject:** Heydar Aliyev **Obv:** National map **Rev:** Bust 3/4 right **Edge:** Reeded

Date	Mintage	F	VF	XF	Unc	BU
2004 Proof	1,000	Value: 2,000				

KM# 47 500 MANAT
50.0000 g., 0.9990 Platinum 1.6059 oz. APW **Subject:** Heydar Aliyev **Obv:** National map **Rev:** Bust 3/4 right **Edge:** Reeded

Date	Mintage	F	VF	XF	Unc	BU
2004 Proof	100	Value: 3,500				

MINT SETS

KM#	Date	Mintage Identification	Issue Price	Mkt Val
MS1	2006 (6)	— KM#39-44.	—	150

BAHAMAS

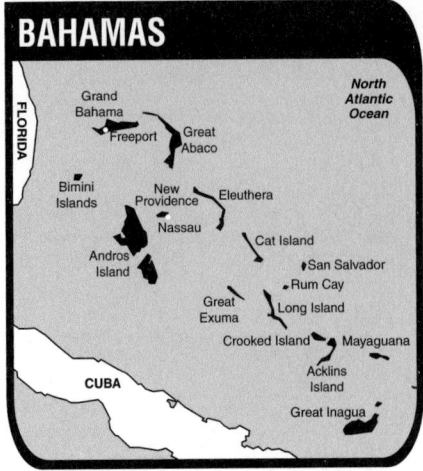

The Commonwealth of the Bahamas is an archipelago of about 3,000 islands, cays and rocks located in the Atlantic Ocean east of Florida and north of Cuba. The total land area of the 800 mile (1,287 km.) long chain of islands is 5,382 sq. mi. (13,935 sq. km.). They have a population of 302,000. Capital: Nassau. The Bahamas import most of their food and manufactured products and export cement, refined oil, pulpwood and lobsters. Tourism is the principal industry. The Bahamas is a member of the Commonwealth of Nations. Elizabeth II is Head of State as Queen of The Bahamas.

The coinage of Great Britain was legal tender in the Bahamas from 1825 to the issuing of a definitive coinage in 1966.

RULER
British

COMMONWEALTH

DECIMAL COINAGE
100 Cents = 1 Dollar

KM# 59a CENT
2.5000 g., Copper Plated Zinc, 19 mm. **Ruler:** Elizabeth II **Obv:** National arms above date **Obv. Legend:** COMMONWEALTH OF THE BAHAMAS **Rev:** Starfish, value at top **Edge:** Plain

Date	Mintage	F	VF	XF	Unc	BU
2000	—	—	—	0.10	0.25	0.75
2001	—	—	—	0.10	0.25	0.75
2004	—	—	—	0.10	0.25	0.75

KM# 218.1 CENT
2.5000 g., Copper Plated Zinc, 19 mm. **Ruler:** Elizabeth II **Obv:** National arms, date below **Rev:** Three starfish

Date	Mintage	F	VF	XF	Unc	BU
2006	—	—	—	—	0.25	0.75
2007	—	—	—	—	0.25	0.75

KM# 218.2 CENT
1.7500 g., Copper Plated Zinc, 17 mm. **Ruler:** Elizabeth II **Obv:** National arms, date below **Rev:** Three starfish

Date	Mintage	F	VF	XF	Unc	BU
2009	—	—	—	—	0.25	0.75

KM# 60 5 CENTS
3.9400 g., Copper-Nickel, 21 mm. **Ruler:** Elizabeth II **Obv:** National arms above date **Obv. Legend:** COMMONWEALTH OF THE BAHAMAS **Rev:** Pineapple above garland divides value at top **Edge:** Smooth

Date	Mintage	F	VF	XF	Unc	BU
2004	—	—	—	0.10	0.25	0.75
2005	—	—	—	0.10	0.25	0.75
2006	—	—	—	0.10	0.25	0.75

KM# 61 10 CENTS
5.1300 g., Copper-Nickel, 23.5 mm. **Ruler:** Elizabeth II **Obv:** National arms, date below, within beaded circle **Rev:** Two bonefish above denomination **Edge:** Plain **Shape:** Scalloped

Date	Mintage	F	VF	XF	Unc	BU
2005	—	—	—	0.25	0.60	0.80

KM# 219 10 CENTS
5.5400 g., Copper-Nickel, 23.5 mm. **Ruler:** Elizabeth II **Obv:** National arms, date below **Rev:** Two fish, value above **Shape:** Scalloped

Date	Mintage	F	VF	XF	Unc	BU
2007	—	—	—	0.25	0.60	0.80

KM# 62 15 CENTS
6.5000 g., Copper-Nickel, 25 mm. **Ruler:** Elizabeth II **Obv:** National arms above date **Rev:** Hibiscus, value divided at bottom **Edge:** Smooth **Shape:** 4-sided

Date	Mintage	F	VF	XF	Unc	BU
2005	—	—	—	0.20	0.50	1.50

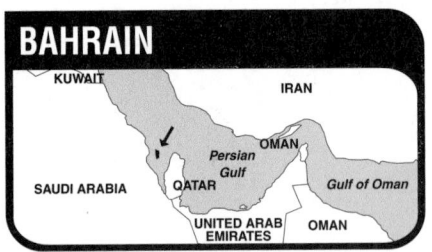

KM# 63.2 25 CENTS
5.7500 g., Copper-Nickel, 24.26 mm. **Ruler:** Elizabeth II **Obv:** National arms, date below **Rev:** Bahamian Sloop, value above **Edge:** Reeded

Date	Mintage	F	VF	XF	Unc	BU
2005	—	—	—	0.30	0.50	1.50

KM# 217 DOLLAR
Silver and gold plated ring **Ruler:** Elizabeth II **Subject:** Queen Mother's 100th Birthday

Date	Mintage	F	VF	XF	Unc	BU
2002 Proof	—	Value: 50.00				

BAHRAIN

The Kingdom of Bahrain, a group of islands in the Persian Gulf off Saudi Arabia, has an area of 268 sq. mi. (622 sq. km.) and a population of 618,000. Capital: Manama. Prior to the depression of the 1930's, the economy was based on pearl fishing. Petroleum and aluminum industries and transit trade are the vital factors in the economy today.

The coinage of the Kingdom of Bahrain was struck at the Royal Mint, London, England.

RULERS

Al Khalifa Dynasty
Hamed Bin Isa, 1999-

TITLES

دولة البحرين

State of Bahrain

مملكة البحرين

Kingdom of Bahrain

KINGDOM
STANDARD COINAGE

KM# 30 5 FILS
2.5000 g., Brass, 19 mm. **Ruler:** Hamed Bin Isa **Obv:** Palm tree
Obv. Legend: KINGDOM OF BAHRAIN **Rev:** Denomination in
chain link border **Edge:** Plain

Date	Mintage	F	VF	XF	Unc	BU
AH1426-2005	—	—	—	—	0.50	0.75
AH1428-2007	—	—	—	—	0.50	0.75
AH1430-2009	—	—	—	—	0.50	0.75
AH1431-2010	—	—	—	—	0.50	0.75

KM# 30a 5 FILS
0.9250 Silver, 19 mm. **Ruler:** Hamed Bin Isa **Obv:** Palm tree
Rev: Denomination in chain link border

Date	Mintage	F	VF	XF	Unc	BU
AH1431-2010 Proof	500	Value: 15.00				

KM# 28 10 FILS
3.3500 g., Brass, 21 mm. **Ruler:** Hamed Bin Isa **Obv:** Palm tree
Obv. Legend: KINGDOM OF BAHRAIN **Rev:** Denomination in
chain link border **Edge:** Plain

Date	Mintage	F	VF	XF	Unc	BU
AH1423-2002	—	—	—	0.30	0.75	1.00
AH1424-2004	—	—	—	0.30	0.75	1.00
AH1426-2005	—	—	—	0.30	0.75	1.00
AH1428-2007	—	—	—	0.30	0.75	1.00
AH1429-2008	—	—	—	0.30	0.75	1.00
AH1431-2010	—	—	—	0.30	0.75	1.00

KM# 28a 10 FILS
0.9250 Silver, 21 mm. **Ruler:** Hamed Bin Isa **Obv:** Palm tree
Rev: Denomination in chain link border

Date	Mintage	F	VF	XF	Unc	BU
AH1431-2010 Proof	500	Value: 25.00				

KM# 24 25 FILS
3.5000 g., Copper-Nickel, 20 mm. **Ruler:** Hamed Bin Isa **Obv:**
Ancient painting **Obv. Legend:** KINGDOM OF BAHRAIN **Rev:**
Denomination in chain link border **Edge:** Reeded

Date	Mintage	F	VF	XF	Unc	BU
AH1423-2002	—	—	—	0.45	1.10	1.50
AH1426-2005	—	—	—	0.45	1.10	1.50
AH1428-2007	—	—	—	0.45	1.10	1.50
AH1429-2008	—	—	—	0.45	1.10	1.50
AH1430-2009	—	—	—	0.45	1.10	1.50

KM# 24a 25 FILS
0.9250 Silver, 20 mm. **Ruler:** Hamed Bin Isa **Obv:** Ancient
painting **Rev:** Denomination in chain link border

Date	Mintage	F	VF	XF	Unc	BU
AH1431-2010 Proof	500	Value: 25.00				

KM# 25 50 FILS
4.5000 g., Copper-Nickel, 22 mm. **Ruler:** Hamed Bin Isa
Subject: Kingdom **Obv:** Stylized sailboats **Obv. Legend:**
KINGDOM OF BAHRAIN **Rev:** Denomination in chain link border
Edge: Reeded

Date	Mintage	F	VF	XF	Unc	BU
AH1423-2002	—	—	—	0.60	1.50	2.00
AH1426-2005	—	—	—	0.60	1.50	2.00
AH1428-2007	—	—	—	0.60	1.50	2.00
AH1429-2008	—	—	—	0.60	1.50	2.00
AH1431-2010	—	—	—	0.60	1.50	2.00

KM# 25a 50 FILS
0.9250 Silver, 22 mm. **Ruler:** Hamed Bin Isa **Obv:** Stylized
sailboats **Rev:** Denomination in chain link border

Date	Mintage	F	VF	XF	Unc	BU
AH1431-2010 Proof	500	Value: 25.00				

KM# 20 100 FILS
6.0000 g., Bi-Metallic Copper-Nickel center in Brass ring, 24 mm.
Obv: Coat of arms within circle, dates at either side **Obv. Legend:**
STATE OF BAHRAIN **Rev:** Numeric denomination back of boxed
denomination within circle, chain surrounds **Edge:** Reeded

Date	Mintage	F	VF	XF	Unc	BU
AH1422-2001	—	—	—	—	3.50	4.00

KM# 26 100 FILS
6.0000 g., Bi-Metallic Copper-Nickel center in Brass ring, 24 mm.
Ruler: Hamed Bin Isa **Subject:** Kingdom **Obv:** National arms
Obv. Legend: KINGDOM OF BAHRAIN **Rev:** Denomination in
chain link border **Edge:** Reeded

Date	Mintage	F	VF	XF	Unc	BU
AH1423-2002	—	—	—	0.90	2.25	3.00
AH1425-2004	—	—	—	0.90	2.25	3.00
AH1426-2005	—	—	—	0.90	2.25	3.00
AH1427-2006	—	—	—	0.90	2.25	3.00
AH1428-2007	—	—	—	0.90	2.25	3.00
AH1429-2008	—	—	—	0.90	2.25	3.00
AH1430-2009	—	—	—	0.90	2.25	3.00
AH1431-2010	—	—	—	0.90	2.25	3.00

KM# 29 100 FILS
6.0000 g., Bi-Metallic Copper-Nickel center in Brass ring, 24 mm.
Ruler: Hamed Bin Isa **Subject:** 1st Bahrain Grand Prix **Obv:**
Maze design within circle **Rev:** Numeric denomination back of
boxed denomination within circle, chain surrounds **Edge:** Reeded

Date	Mintage	F	VF	XF	Unc	BU
AH1425-2004	30,000	—	—	—	30.00	35.00

KM# 26a 100 FILS
0.9250 Silver, 24 mm. **Ruler:** Hamed Bin Isa **Obv:** National
arms **Rev:** Denomination in chain link border

Date	Mintage	F	VF	XF	Unc	BU
AH1431-2010 Proof	500	Value: 30.00				

KM# 22 500 FILS
9.0000 g., Bi-Metallic Brass center in Copper-Nickel ring, 27 mm.
Ruler: Hamed Bin Isa **Obv:** Monument and inscription **Obv.
Inscription:** STATE OF BAHRAIN **Rev:** Denomination **Edge:**
Reeded

Date	Mintage	F	VF	XF	Unc	BU
2001	—	—	—	—	6.00	7.50

KM# 27 500 FILS
9.0000 g., Bi-Metallic Brass center in Copper-Nickel ring, 27 mm.
Ruler: Hamed Bin Isa **Subject:** Kingdom **Obv:** Monument and
inscription **Obv. Legend:** KINGDOM OF BAHRAIN **Rev:**
Denomination **Edge:** Reeded

Date	Mintage	F	VF	XF	Unc	BU
2002	—	—	—	—	6.50	8.00

KM# 27a 500 FILS
0.9250 Silver, 27 mm. **Ruler:** Hamed Bin Isa **Obv:** Monument
and inscription **Rev:** Denomination

Date	Mintage	F	VF	XF	Unc	BU
AH1431-2010 Proof	500	Value: 40.00				

PROOF SETS

KM#	Date	Mintage	Identification	Issue Price	Mkt Val
PS4	2010 (6)	500	KM#30a, 28a, 24a, 25a, 26a, 27a	160	160

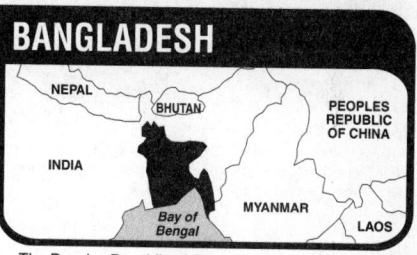

BANGLADESH

The Peoples Republic of Bangladesh (formerly East Pakistan), a parliamentary democracy located on the Bay of Bengal
bordered by India and Burma, has an area of 55,598 sq. mi.
(143,998 sq. km.) and a population of 128.1 million. Capital:
Dhaka. The economy is predominantly agricultural. Jute products, jute and tea are exported.

Bangladesh is a member of the Commonwealth of Nations.
The president is the Head of State and the Government.

MONETARY SYSTEM
100 Poisha = 1 Taka

DATING
Christian era using Bengali numerals.

PEOPLES REPUBLIC
STANDARD COINAGE

KM# 24 50 POISHA
2.6000 g., Stainless Steel, 19.3 mm. **Obv:** National emblem,
Shapla (water lily) within wreath above water **Rev:** Fish, chicken
and produce within inner circle **Edge:** Plain **Shape:** Octagonal

Date	Mintage	F	VF	XF	Unc	BU
2001	—	—	—	—	1.50	2.50

KM# 9c TAKA
4.2500 g., Stainless Steel, 24.91 mm. **Obv:** National emblem,
Shapla (water lily) within wreath above water in octagonal frame
Rev: Stylized family, value at right within octagonal frame **Edge:**
Reeded **Note:** Prev. KM # 9.5.

Date	Mintage	F	VF	XF	Unc	BU
2001	—	—	—	0.80	2.00	3.00
2002	—	—	—	0.80	2.00	3.00
2003	—	—	—	0.80	2.00	3.00
2007	—	—	—	0.80	2.00	3.00

KM# 9b   TAKA
4.0000 g., Brass, 25 mm. **Obv:** National emblem, Shapla (water lily) **Rev:** Stylized family, value at right **Edge:** Reeded **Note:** Prev. KM # 9.3.

Date	Mintage	F	VF	XF	Unc	BU
2003	—	—	0.20	0.55	1.20	1.60

KM# 25   2 TAKA
7.0000 g., Stainless Steel, 26.03 mm. **Obv:** State emblem and "TWO 2 TAKA" within beaded border **Rev:** Two children reading, legend within beaded border **Edge:** Plain

Date	Mintage	F	VF	XF	Unc	BU
2004	—	—	—	1.20	3.00	4.00
2008	—	—	—	1.20	3.00	4.00

KM# 26   5 TAKA
8.1700 g., Steel, 26.8 mm. **Obv:** National emblem, Shapla (water lily) within wreath above water **Rev:** Bridge, date and denomination below **Note:** Prev. KM#18.3.

Date	Mintage	F	VF	XF	Unc	BU
2006	—	—	—	1.00	2.50	3.50
2008	—	—	—	1.00	2.50	3.50

KM# 27   10 TAKA
0.9250 Silver **Subject:** Cricket World Cup **Obv:** Cricket ball logo **Rev:** Trophy

Date	Mintage	F	VF	XF	Unc	BU
2011 Proof	—	Value: 60.00				

BARBADOS

Barbados, a Constitutional Monarchy within the Commonwealth of Nations, is located in the Windward Islands of the West Indies east of St. Vincent. The coral island has an area of 166 sq. mi. (430 sq. km.) and a population of 269,000. Capital: Bridgetown. The economy is based on sugar and tourism. Sugar, petroleum products, molasses, and rum are exported.

MONETARY SYSTEM
100 Cents = 1 Dollar

COMMONWEALTH
DECIMAL COINAGE

KM# 10a   CENT
2.5000 g., Copper Plated Zinc, 19 mm. **Obv:** National arms **Rev:** Trident above value **Edge:** Plain

Date	Mintage	F	VF	XF	Unc	BU
2001	—	—	—	0.10	0.25	0.75
2002	—	—	—	—	0.25	0.75
2003	—	—	—	—	0.25	0.75
2004	—	—	—	—	0.25	0.75
2005	—	—	—	—	0.25	0.75
2006	—	—	—	—	0.25	0.75
2007	—	—	—	—	0.25	0.75

KM# 10b   CENT
2.7800 g., Copper Plated Steel, 18.86 mm. **Obv:** National arms **Rev:** Trident above value

Date	Mintage	F	VF	XF	Unc	BU
2008	—	—	—	—	0.25	0.75
2009	—	—	—	—	0.25	0.75
2010	—	—	—	—	0.25	0.75
2011	—	—	—	—	0.25	0.75

KM# 11   5 CENTS
3.7500 g., Brass, 21 mm. **Obv:** National arms **Rev:** South Point Lighthouse, value below **Edge:** Plain

Date	Mintage	F	VF	XF	Unc	BU
2001	—	—	—	—	0.25	0.75
2002	—	—	—	—	0.25	0.75
2004	—	—	—	—	0.25	0.75
2005	—	—	—	—	0.25	0.75
2006	—	—	—	—	0.25	0.75
2007	—	—	—	—	0.25	0.75

KM# 11a   5 CENTS
3.4600 g., Brass Plated Steel, 21 mm. **Obv:** National arms **Rev:** South Point Lighthouse, value below

Date	Mintage	F	VF	XF	Unc	BU
2008	—	—	—	—	0.25	0.75
2009	—	—	—	—	0.25	0.75
2010	—	—	—	—	0.25	0.75
2011	—	—	—	—	0.25	0.75

KM# 12   10 CENTS
2.2900 g., Copper-Nickel, 17.77 mm. **Obv:** National arms **Rev:** Tern flying left, value below **Edge:** Reeded

Date	Mintage	F	VF	XF	Unc	BU
2001	—	—	—	0.15	0.50	1.50
2003	—	—	—	0.15	0.50	1.50
2004	—	—	—	0.15	0.50	1.50
2005	—	—	—	0.15	0.50	1.50
2007	—	—	—	0.15	0.50	1.50

KM# 12a   10 CENTS
2.0900 g., Nickel Plated Steel, 17.77 mm. **Obv:** National arms **Rev:** Tern flying left, value below **Edge:** Reeded

Date	Mintage	F	VF	XF	Unc	BU
2008	—	—	—	—	0.50	1.50
2009	—	—	—	—	0.50	1.50

KM# 13   25 CENTS
5.6500 g., Copper-Nickel, 23.66 mm. **Obv:** National arms **Rev:** Morgan Lewis Windmill, value above **Edge:** Reeded

Date	Mintage	F	VF	XF	Unc	BU
2001	—	—	—	0.30	0.60	1.60
2003	—	—	—	0.30	0.60	1.60
2004	—	—	—	0.30	0.60	1.60
2005	—	—	—	0.30	0.60	1.60
2006	—	—	—	0.30	0.60	1.60
2007	—	—	—	0.30	0.60	1.60

KM# 13a   25 CENTS
5.1000 g., Nickel Plated Steel, 23.66 mm. **Obv:** National arms **Rev:** Morgan Lewis Windmill, value above **Edge:** Reeded

Date	Mintage	F	VF	XF	Unc	BU
2008	—	—	—	0.30	0.60	1.60
2009	—	—	—	0.30	0.60	1.60
2011	—	—	—	0.30	0.60	1.60

KM# 14.2   DOLLAR
5.9500 g., Copper-Nickel, 25.85 mm. **Obv:** National arms **Rev:** Flying fish left, value below **Shape:** 7-sided **Note:** Thinner planchet.

Date	Mintage	F	VF	XF	Unc	BU
2004	—	—	—	—	2.25	3.00
2005	—	—	—	—	2.25	3.00
2007	—	—	—	—	2.25	3.00

KM# 14.2a   DOLLAR
5.9500 g., Nickel Plated Steel, 25.85 mm. **Obv:** National arms **Rev:** Flying fish left, value below

Date	Mintage	F	VF	XF	Unc	BU
2008	—	—	—	—	2.25	3.00

KM# 69   5 DOLLARS
28.2800 g., 0.9250 Silver 0.8410 oz. ASW, 38.6 mm. **Subject:** UNICEF **Obv:** National arms divide date, denomination below **Rev:** Three boys playing cricket **Edge:** Reeded

Date	Mintage	F	VF	XF	Unc	BU
2001 Proof	—	Value: 45.00				

BELARUS

Belarus (Byelorussia, Belorussia, or White Russia- formerly the Belorussian S.S.R.) is situated along the western Dvina and Dnieper Rivers, bounded in the west by Poland, to the north by Latvia and Lithuania, to the east by Russia and the south by the Ukraine. It has an area of 80,154 sq. mi. (207,600 sq. km.) and a population of 4.8 million. Capital: Minsk. Chief products: peat, salt, and agricultural products including flax, fodder and grasses for cattle breeding and dairy products.

MONETARY SYSTEM
100 Kapeek = 1 Rouble

REPUBLIC

STANDARD COINAGE

KM# 110 ROUBLE
Copper-Nickel, 32 mm. **Subject:** 900th Anniversary of Euphrasinta **Obv:** National arms **Rev:** Euphrasinta of Polatsk

Date	Mintage	F	VF	XF	Unc	BU
2001	Est. 2,000	—	—	—	50.00	—

KM# 112 ROUBLE
Copper-Nickel, 32 mm. **Subject:** Tower of Kamyantes **Obv:** National arms **Rev:** Kamyanets Tower, seal

Date	Mintage	F	VF	XF	Unc	BU
2001	2,000	—	—	—	40.00	—

KM# 47 ROUBLE
13.1400 g., Copper-Nickel, 31.9 mm. **Obv:** National arms **Rev:** European Bison **Edge:** Reeded

Date	Mintage	F	VF	XF	Unc	BU
2001 Proof	5,000	Value: 40.00				

KM# 50 ROUBLE
13.1500 g., Copper-Nickel, 28.7 mm. **Subject:** 2002 Winter Olympics **Obv:** National arms **Rev:** Two freestyle skiers **Edge:** Reeded

Date	Mintage	F	VF	XF	Unc	BU
2001 Prooflike	2,000	—	—	—	—	35.00

KM# 114 ROUBLE
Copper-Nickel, 32 mm. **Subject:** 200th Birthday of Ignatius Dameika **Obv:** National arms **Rev:** Ignatius Dameika, hammer

Date	Mintage	F	VF	XF	Unc	BU
2002 Prooflike	2,000	—	—	—	—	40.00

KM# 116 ROUBLE
33.0000 Copper-Nickel, 33 mm. **Subject:** 120th Birthday of Yanka Kupala **Obv:** National arms **Rev:** Yanka Kupala, 1882-1942

Date	Mintage	F	VF	XF	Unc	BU
2002 Prooflike	2,000	—	—	—	—	40.00

KM# 118 ROUBLE
Copper-Nickel, 33 mm. **Subject:** 120th Birthday of Yakub Kolas **Obv:** National arms **Rev:** Yukab Kolas, 1882-1956

Date	Mintage	F	VF	XF	Unc	BU
2002	2,000	—	—	—	40.00	—

KM# 69 ROUBLE
Copper-Nickel, 33 mm. **Subject:** 80th Anniversary of the Savings Bank **Obv:** Folk art design

Date	Mintage	F	VF	XF	Unc	BU
2002 Prooflike	10,000	—	—	—	15.00	—

KM# 105 ROUBLE
Copper-Nickel, 31.9 mm. **Subject:** Pointer Yanka Kupala 1881-1942

Date	Mintage	F	VF	XF	Unc	BU
2002 Proof	2,000	Value: 35.00				

KM# 106 ROUBLE
Copper-Nickel, 31.9 mm. **Subject:** Jakub Kalas 1881-1956

Date	Mintage	F	VF	XF	Unc	BU
2002 Proof	2,000	Value: 35.00				

KM# 44 ROUBLE
13.1400 g., Copper-Nickel, 31.9 mm. **Obv:** National arms **Rev:** Eurasian Beaver and young **Edge:** Reeded

Date	Mintage	F	VF	XF	Unc	BU
2002 Proof	5,000	Value: 25.00				

KM# 61 ROUBLE
13.1600 g., Copper-Nickel, 32 mm. **Obv:** National arms **Rev:** Wrestlers **Edge:** Reeded

Date	Mintage	F	VF	XF	Unc	BU
2003 Prooflike	5,000	—	—	—	—	10.00

KM# 54 ROUBLE
13.1200 g., Copper-Nickel, 31.9 mm. **Obv:** National arms **Rev:** Mute swans on water with reflections **Edge:** Reeded

Date	Mintage	F	VF	XF	Unc	BU
2003 Proof	5,000	Value: 35.00				

KM# 55 ROUBLE
13.1000 g., Copper-Nickel, 31.9 mm. **Obv:** State arms **Rev:** Herring gull in flight **Edge:** Reeded

Date	Mintage	F	VF	XF	Unc	BU
2003 Proof	5,000	Value: 25.00				

KM# 56 ROUBLE
13.1000 g., Copper-Nickel, 32 mm. **Obv:** National arms **Rev:** Church of the Savior and Transfiguration **Edge:** Reeded

Date	Mintage	F	VF	XF	Unc	BU
2003	2,000	—	—	—	35.00	—

KM# 60 ROUBLE
13.1600 g., Copper-Nickel, 32 mm. **Obv:** National arms **Rev:** Two common cranes **Edge:** Reeded

Date	Mintage	F	VF	XF	Unc	BU
2004 Proof	5,000	Value: 25.00				

KM# 75 ROUBLE
15.9200 g., Copper-Nickel Antiqued Finish, 33 mm. **Subject:** "Kupalle" **Obv:** Folk art cross design **Rev:** Flower above ferns **Edge:** Reeded

Date	Mintage	F	VF	XF	Unc	BU
2004	5,000	—	—	—	40.00	—

KM# 76 ROUBLE
15.9200 g., Copper-Nickel, 33 mm. **Subject:** "Kalyady" **Obv:** Folk art cross design **Rev:** Stylized sunflower **Edge:** Reeded

Date	Mintage	F	VF	XF	Unc	BU
2004	5,000	—	—	—	35.00	—

KM# 78 ROUBLE
15.9000 g., Copper-Nickel, 33 mm. **Obv:** National arms **Rev:** Radziwill's Castle in Neswizh **Edge:** Reeded

Date	Mintage	F	VF	XF	Unc	BU
2004 Prooflike	2,000	—	—	—	—	35.00

KM# 80 ROUBLE
15.9000 g., Copper-Nickel, 33 mm. **Subject:** Defenders of Brest **Obv:** Soviet Patriotic War Order **Rev:** "Courage" monument **Edge:** Reeded

Date	Mintage	F	VF	XF	Unc	BU
2004	5,000	—	—	—	25.00	—

KM# 85 ROUBLE
Copper-Nickel, 33 mm. **Subject:** Soviet Warriors - Liberators **Obv:** Order of the Patriotic War **Rev:** Partisans with blown up railway track

Date	Mintage	F	VF	XF	Unc	BU
2004	3,000	—	—	—	25.00	—

KM# 83 ROUBLE
Copper-Nickel, 33 mm. **Subject:** Memory of Facist Victims **Obv:** National arms **Rev:** Man holding dead

Date	Mintage	F	VF	XF	Unc	BU
2004	3,000	—	—	—	25.00	—

KM# 62 ROUBLE
Copper-Nickel, 31.9 mm. **Subject:** Sculling **Obv:** National arms **Rev:** Two rowers against a background of stylized oars

Date	Mintage	F	VF	XF	Unc	BU
2004	3,000	—	—	—	15.00	—

KM# 81 ROUBLE
Copper-Nickel, 33 mm. **Subject:** 60th Anniversary of Victory **Obv:** Order of the Victory **Rev:** Star and arrows

Date	Mintage	F	VF	XF	Unc	BU
2005	2,000	—	—	—	25.00	—

KM# 127 ROUBLE
Copper-Nickel, 32 mm. **Subject:** 1000th Anniversary of Vaukavysk **Obv:** National arms **Rev:** National arms of Vaukavysk

Date	Mintage	F	VF	XF	Unc	BU
2005	2,000	—	—	—	40.00	—

KM# 130 ROUBLE
Copper-Nickel, 32 mm. **Subject:** Jesnit Roman Catholic Church **Obv:** National arms **Rev:** Jesnit Roman Catholic Church in Neswizh

Date	Mintage	F	VF	XF	Unc	BU
2005	2,000	—	—	—	40.00	—

KM# 104   ROUBLE
Copper-Nickel, 33 mm.   **Subject:** Christmas Egg **Obv:** National arms and folk art cross design **Rev:** Easter egg

Date	Mintage	F	VF	XF	Unc	BU
2005	5,000	—	—	—	35.00	—

KM# 107   ROUBLE
Copper-Nickel, 31.9 mm.   **Subject:** Bagach - Candle in Basket **Obv:** National arms and solar symbol **Rev:** Basket of grain, candle, ear, table, tablecloth

Date	Mintage	F	VF	XF	Unc	BU
2005	5,000	—	—	—	35.00	—

KM# 132   ROUBLE
Copper-Nickel, 33 mm.   **Subject:** Usyaslau of Polatsk **Obv:** Cathedral of St. Sophia **Rev:** Usyaslav of Polatsk, wolf on a solar disk

Date	Mintage	F	VF	XF	Unc	BU
2005 Proof	5,000	Value: 15.00				

KM# 134   ROUBLE
Copper-Nickel, 33 mm.   **Subject:** Tennis **Obv:** National arms **Rev:** Tennis player against racket background

Date	Mintage	F	VF	XF	Unc	BU
2005	5,000	—	—	—	12.00	—

KM# 97   ROUBLE
14.5000 g., Copper-Nickel, 33 mm.   **Subject:** Almany Bogs **Obv:** Blooming plant on frosted design **Rev:** Great Grey Owl **Edge:** Lettered

Date	Mintage	F	VF	XF	Unc	BU
2005 Proof	5,000	Value: 30.00				

KM# 273   ROUBLE
14.5000 g., Copper-Nickel, 33 mm.   **Subject:** Skiing **Edge:** Reeded

Date	Mintage	F	VF	XF	Unc	BU
2006	—	—	—	—	—	20.00

KM# 274   ROUBLE
14.5000 g., Copper-Nickel, 33 mm.   **Subject:** Rogwald

Date	Mintage	F	VF	XF	Unc	BU
2006	—	—	—	—	—	20.00

KM# 275   ROUBLE
13.1600 g., Copper-Nickel, 32 mm.   **Subject:** Commonwealth of Independent States, 15th Anniversary **Edge:** Reeded

Date	Mintage	F	VF	XF	Unc	BU
2006 Prooflike	5,000	—	—	—	—	20.00

KM# 135   ROUBLE
Copper-Nickel, 32 mm.   **Subject:** Vtaselle Wedding **Obv:** National arms, birds, shamrock **Rev:** Loaf of bread, wedding rings, diadem of flowers, background of honeycomb

Date	Mintage	F	VF	XF	Unc	BU
2006	5,000	—	—	—	12.00	—

KM# 138   ROUBLE
Copper-Nickel, 33 mm.   **Subject:** Sophia of Galshany 600th Anniversary **Obv:** Castle of Galshany **Rev:** National arms and Sophia of Galshany

Date	Mintage	F	VF	XF	Unc	BU
2006	5,000	—	—	—	20.00	—

KM# 140   ROUBLE
Copper-Nickel, 33 mm.   **Subject:** Syomukha **Obv:** National arms, solar symbol **Rev:** Chalice, Chaplet of birch, maple, rowan sweet flag leaves

Date	Mintage	F	VF	XF	Unc	BU
2006	5,000	—	—	—	25.00	—

KM# 146   ROUBLE
Copper-Nickel, 33 mm.   **Subject:** Chyrvomy Bar **Obv:** National arms, blooming plant **Rev:** European Mink

Date	Mintage	F	VF	XF	Unc	BU
2006 Proof	5,000	Value: 17.50				

KM# 276   ROUBLE
14.5000 g., Copper-Nickel, 33 mm.   **Subject:** Cycling **Edge:** Plain

Date	Mintage	F	VF	XF	Unc	BU
2006	—	—	—	—	—	20.00

KM# 150   ROUBLE
16.0000 g., Copper-Nickel, 33 mm.   **Subject:** Holidays and Ceremonies **Obv:** Small arms above quilted star design **Rev:** Food, bowl with spoon - Maslenica

Date	Mintage	F	VF	XF	Unc	BU
2007 Antique	5,000	—	—	—	35.00	—

KM# 151   ROUBLE
13.2400 g., Copper-Nickel, 31.86 mm.   **Obv:** Thrush Nightingale in hands in oval **Obv. Legend:** РЭСПУБЛІКА БЕЛАРУСЬ **Rev:** Thrush Nightingale perched on branch in oval **Edge:** Reeded

Date	Mintage	F	VF	XF	Unc	BU
2007 Proof	5,000	Value: 17.50				

KM# 217   ROUBLE
14.3500 g., Copper-Nickel, 33 mm.   **Rev:** Sturgeon

Date	Mintage	F	VF	XF	Unc	BU
2007 Proof	5,000	Value: 15.00				

KM# 215   ROUBLE
13.1800 g., Copper-Nickel, 33 mm.   **Obv:** Sea chart and compose rose **Rev:** Sailing ship Sedov

Date	Mintage	F	VF	XF	Unc	BU
2008 Proof	7,000	Value: 15.00				

KM# 259   ROUBLE
13.1600 g., Copper-Nickel, 32 mm.   **Obv:** Compass **Rev:** Dar Parmoza at sail

Date	Mintage	F	VF	XF	Unc	BU
2009	5,000	—	—	—	—	75.00

KM# 218   ROUBLE
13.1600 g., Copper-Nickel, 32 mm.   **Subject:** Belavezhskaya Pushcha

Date	Mintage	F	VF	XF	Unc	BU
2009 Proof	5,000	Value: 15.00				

KM# 219   ROUBLE
13.1600 g., Copper-Nickel, 32 mm.   **Subject:** Greyleg goose

Date	Mintage	F	VF	XF	Unc	BU
2009 Proof	5,000	Value: 13.00				

KM# 220   ROUBLE
14.3500 g., Copper-Nickel, 32 mm.   **Subject:** Pakatigaroshak **Rev:** Man clubbing dragon

Date	Mintage	F	VF	XF	Unc	BU
2009 Proof	3,500	Value: 13.00				

KM# 221   ROUBLE
15.5000 g., Copper-Nickel, 33 mm.   **Subject:** Legend of the Skylark

Date	Mintage	F	VF	XF	Unc	BU
2009 Prooflike	5,000	—	—	—	—	13.00

KM# 222   ROUBLE
15.5000 g., Copper-Nickel, 33 mm.   **Subject:** Folk Art - Straw Weaving **Rev:** Horse

Date	Mintage	F	VF	XF	Unc	BU
2009 Prooflike	5,000	—	—	—	—	13.00

KM# 264   ROUBLE
15.5000 g., Copper-Nickel, 33 mm.   **Subject:** Metalsmith **Rev:** Horseshoe, house within, small horsemen flanking

Date	Mintage	F	VF	XF	Unc	BU
2010	3,500	Value: 17.50				

KM# 223   ROUBLE
14.3500 g., Copper-Nickel, 33 mm.   **Subject:** EURASEC, 10th Anniversary **Obv:** Folk embroidery pattern **Rev:** Six flags around globe

Date	Mintage	F	VF	XF	Unc	BU
2010 Proof	3,500	Value: 13.00				

KM# 226   ROUBLE
13.1600 g., Copper-Nickel, 33 mm.   **Subject:** 1st Belarus Front **Rev:** Gen. Konstantin Rokossovsky

Date	Mintage	F	VF	XF	Unc	BU
2010 Proof	3,000	Value: 13.00				

KM# 227   ROUBLE
13.1600 g., Copper-Nickel, 33 mm.   **Subject:** 2nd Belarus Front **Rev:** Col. Gen. G.F. Zaharov

Date	Mintage	F	VF	XF	Unc	BU
2010 Proof	3,000	Value: 13.00				

KM# 228   ROUBLE
13.1600 g., Copper-Nickel, 33 mm.   **Subject:** 3rd Belarus Front **Rev:** Col. Gen. Ivan Chernyakhovsky

Date	Mintage	F	VF	XF	Unc	BU
2010 Proof	3,000	Value: 13.00				

KM# 229 ROUBLE
13.1600 g., Copper-Nickel, 33 mm. **Subject:** 1st Baltic Forces
Rev: Gen. Hovhannes Bagramayn

Date	Mintage	F	VF	XF	Unc	BU
2010 Proof	3,000			Value: 13.00		

KM# 236 ROUBLE
15.5000 g., Copper-Nickel, 33 mm. **Subject:** Legend of the Tortoise

Date	Mintage	F	VF	XF	Unc	BU
2010 Prooflike	3,000	—	—	—	—	13.00

KM# 240 ROUBLE
Copper-Nickel, 32 mm. **Subject:** Age of Majority **Rev:** Flowers and folk patterns

Date	Mintage	F	VF	XF	Unc	BU
2010 Proof	4,000			Value: 13.00		

KM# 262 ROUBLE
14.3500 g., Copper-Nickel, 33 mm. **Subject:** End of World War II, 65th Anniversary **Obv:** Broken clock face **Rev:** 5 doves in flight, knitting

Date	Mintage	F	VF	XF	Unc	BU
2010 Proof	3,000			Value: 25.00		

KM# 263 ROUBLE
13.6000 g., Copper-Nickel, 32 mm. **Obv:** Compass and chart **Rev:** Amergo Vespucci sailing ship

Date	Mintage	F	VF	XF	Unc	BU
2010 Proof	4,000			Value: 17.50		

KM# 265 ROUBLE
15.5500 g., Copper-Nickel, 33 mm. **Subject:** Judaism **Rev:** Valozhyn Yeshiva façade, 1806 date

Date	Mintage	F	VF	XF	Unc	BU
2010 Proof	3,000			Value: 15.00		

KM# 270 ROUBLE
13.1600 g., Copper-Nickel, 32 mm. **Obv:** Compass rose and chart **Rev:** Cutty Sark sailing right

Date	Mintage	F	VF	XF	Unc	BU
2010 Proof		—		Value: 13.00		

KM# 234 ROUBLE
13.1600 g., Copper-Nickel, 32 mm. **Rev:** U.S. Frigate Constitution

Date	Mintage	F	VF	XF	Unc	BU
2010 Proof	3,000			Value: 13.00		

KM# 291 ROUBLE
13.1600 g., Copper-Nickel, 32 mm. **Obv:** National arms **Rev:** Curlew bird standing left, oval background

Date	Mintage	F	VF	XF	Unc	BU
2011 Prooflike	2,000	—	—	—	—	20.00

KM# 64 10 ROUBLES
16.8200 g., 0.9250 Silver 0.5002 oz. ASW, 32.9 mm. **Obv:** National arms **Rev:** Jakub Kolas (1882-1956) **Edge:** Reeded

Date	Mintage	F	VF	XF	Unc	BU
2002 Proof	1,000			Value: 150		

KM# 117 10 ROUBLES
15.5500 g., 0.9250 Silver 0.4624 oz. ASW, 33 mm. **Subject:** 120th Birthday of Yanka Kupala **Obv:** National arms **Rev:** Yanka Kupala, 1882-1942

Date	Mintage	F	VF	XF	Unc	BU
2002 Proof	1,000			Value: 150		

KM# 129 10 ROUBLES
1.2400 g., 0.9990 Gold 0.0398 oz. AGW, 13.92 mm. **Subject:** Belarussian Ballet **Obv:** National arms **Rev:** Dancing ballerina

Date	Mintage	F	VF	XF	Unc	BU
2005	25,000	—	—	—	90.00	100

KM# 156 10 ROUBLES
16.8100 g., 0.9250 Silver 0.4999 oz. ASW, 32 mm. **Subject:** Alena Aladana **Rev:** Half-length figure facing, picture in background

Date	Mintage	F	VF	XF	Unc	BU
2007 Proof	4,000			Value: 35.00		

KM# 157 10 ROUBLES
16.8100 g., 0.9250 Silver 0.4999 oz. ASW, 32 mm. **Subject:** Thrush Nightingale **Rev:** Bird standing right on branch

Date	Mintage	F	VF	XF	Unc	BU
2007 Proof	5,000			Value: 40.00		

KM# 172 10 ROUBLES
16.8100 g., 0.9250 Silver 0.4999 oz. ASW, 32 mm. **Subject:** Zair Azgur **Rev:** Profile right

Date	Mintage	F	VF	XF	Unc	BU
2008 Proof	3,000			Value: 40.00		

KM# 173 10 ROUBLES
16.8100 g., 0.9250 Silver 0.4999 oz. ASW, 32 mm. **Subject:** Great White Egret **Rev:** Bird standing left

Date	Mintage	F	VF	XF	Unc	BU
2008 Proof	5,000			Value: 45.00		

KM# 174 10 ROUBLES
16.8100 g., 0.9250 Silver 0.4999 oz. ASW, 32 mm. **Subject:** Vincent Dunin **Rev:** Bust facing

Date	Mintage	F	VF	XF	Unc	BU
2008 Proof	3,000			Value: 35.00		

KM# 175 10 ROUBLES
16.8100 g., 0.9250 Silver 0.4999 oz. ASW, 32 mm. **Subject:** St. Euphrosyne of Polotsk **Rev:** Half-length figure facing within frame

Date	Mintage	F	VF	XF	Unc	BU
2008 Proof	5,000			Value: 40.00		

KM# 176 10 ROUBLES
16.8100 g., 0.9250 Silver 0.4999 oz. ASW, 32 mm. **Subject:** St. Steraphin of Sarov **Rev:** Half-length figure standing within frame

Date	Mintage	F	VF	XF	Unc	BU
2008 Proof	5,000			Value: 40.00		

KM# 177 10 ROUBLES
16.8100 g., 0.9250 Silver 0.4999 oz. ASW, 32 mm. **Subject:** St. Sergii of Radonezh **Rev:** Half-length figure standing within frame

Date	Mintage	F	VF	XF	Unc	BU
2008 Proof	5,000			Value: 40.00		

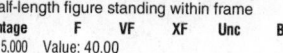

KM# 178 10 ROUBLES
16.8100 g., 0.9250 Silver 0.4999 oz. ASW, 32 mm. **Subject:** St. Nicholas **Rev:** Half-length figure standing within frame

Date	Mintage	F	VF	XF	Unc	BU
2008 Proof	5,000			Value: 40.00		

KM# 179   10 ROUBLES
16.8100 g., 0.9250 Silver 0.4999 oz. ASW, 32 mm.   **Subject:**
St. Panteleimon **Rev:** Half-length figure standing within frame

Date	Mintage	F	VF	XF	Unc	BU
2008 Proof	5,000	Value: 40.00				

KM# 194   10 ROUBLES
16.8100 g., 0.9250 Silver 0.4999 oz. ASW, 32 mm.   **Subject:**
Academy of Science, 80th Anniversary **Rev:** Building

Date	Mintage	F	VF	XF	Unc	BU
2009 Proof	3,000	Value: 40.00				

KM# 195   10 ROUBLES
16.8100 g., 0.9250 Silver 0.4999 oz. ASW, 32 mm.   **Subject:**
Greylag goose **Rev:** Goose swimming left

Date	Mintage	F	VF	XF	Unc	BU
2009 Proof	5,000	Value: 32.00				

KM# 260   10 ROUBLES
16.8100 g., 0.9250 Silver 0.4999 oz. ASW, 32 mm.   **Obv:**
Stylized kestrel in egg **Rev:** Common kestrel

Date	Mintage	F	VF	XF	Unc	BU
2010	2,500	Value: 75.00				

KM# 230   10 ROUBLES
16.8100 g., 0.9250 Silver 0.4999 oz. ASW, 33 mm.   **Subject:**
1st Belarus Front **Rev:** Gen. Konstantin Rokosovsky

Date	Mintage	F	VF	XF	Unc	BU
2010 Proof	2,500	Value: 25.00				

KM# 231   10 ROUBLES
16.8100 g., 0.9250 Silver 0.4999 oz. ASW, 33 mm.   **Subject:**
2nd Belarus Front **Rev:** Col. Gen. G.F. Zakharov

Date	Mintage	F	VF	XF	Unc	BU
2010 Proof	2,500	Value: 25.00				

KM# 232   10 ROUBLES
16.5500 g., 0.9250 Silver 0.4922 oz. ASW, 33 mm.   **Subject:**
3rd Belarus front **Rev:** Col. Gen. Ivan Chernyakovsky

Date	Mintage	F	VF	XF	Unc	BU
2010 Proof	2,500	Value: 25.00				

KM# 233   10 ROUBLES
16.5500 g., 0.9250 Silver 0.4922 oz. ASW, 33 mm.   **Subject:**
1st Baltic Front **Rev:** Gen. Hovhannes Bagramgan

Date	Mintage	F	VF	XF	Unc	BU
2010 Proof	2,500	Value: 25.00				

KM# 111   20 ROUBLES
31.1000 g., 0.9250 Silver 0.9249 oz. ASW, 38.61 mm.   **Subject:**
900th Anniversary of Euphrasinta **Obv:** National arms **Rev:**
Euphrasinta of Polatsk, gold cross

Date	Mintage	F	VF	XF	Unc	BU
2001 Proof	Est. 2,000	Value: 350				

KM# 113   20 ROUBLES
31.1000 g., 0.9250 Silver 0.9249 oz. ASW, 38.61 mm.   **Subject:**
Tower of Kamyantes **Obv:** National arms **Rev:** Kamyanets
Tower, seal

Date	Mintage	F	VF	XF	Unc	BU
2001 Proof	2,000	Value: 100				

KM# 46   20 ROUBLES
33.7300 g., 0.9250 Silver 1.0031 oz. ASW, 38.6 mm.   **Subject:**
Wildlife **Obv:** National arms **Rev:** European Bison **Edge:** Reeded

Date	Mintage	F	VF	XF	Unc	BU
2001 Proof	2,000	Value: 650				

KM# 49   20 ROUBLES
28.3200 g., 0.9250 Silver 0.8422 oz. ASW, 38.6 mm.   **Subject:**
2002 Winter Olympics **Obv:** National arms **Rev:** Marksman
aiming at bullseye **Edge:** Reeded

Date	Mintage	F	VF	XF	Unc	BU
2001 Proof	15,000	Value: 45.00				

KM# 51   20 ROUBLES
33.6500 g., 0.9250 Silver 1.0007 oz. ASW, 38.6 mm.   **Subject:**
2002 Winter Olympics **Obv:** National arms **Rev:** Two freestyle
skiers **Edge:** Reeded

Date	Mintage	F	VF	XF	Unc	BU
2001 Proof	2,000	Value: 60.00				

KM# 45   20 ROUBLES
33.7300 g., 0.9250 Silver 1.0031 oz. ASW, 38.8 mm.   **Obv:**
National arms **Rev:** European beaver and young **Edge:** Reeded

Date	Mintage	F	VF	XF	Unc	BU
2002 Proof	2,000	Value: 200				

KM# 115   20 ROUBLES
31.1000 g., 0.9250 Silver 0.9249 oz. ASW, 38.61 mm.   **Subject:**
200th Birthday of Ignatius Dameika **Obv:** National arms **Rev:**
Ignatius Dameika, hammer and inset with a dameikit stone

Date	Mintage	F	VF	XF	Unc	BU
2002 Proof	1,000	Value: 350				

KM# 119   20 ROUBLES
28.2800 g., 0.9250 Silver 0.8410 oz. ASW, 38.61 mm.   **Subject:**
2006 World Cup Football **Obv:** National arms **Rev:** Stylized 2006,
football

Date	Mintage	F	VF	XF	Unc	BU
2002 Proof	25,000	Value: 75.00				

KM# 59   20 ROUBLES
28.6300 g., 0.9250 Silver 0.8514 oz. ASW, 38.6 mm.   **Obv:**
National arms **Rev:** Brown bear with two cubs **Edge:** Reeded

Date	Mintage	F	VF	XF	Unc	BU
2002 Proof	5,000	Value: 120				

KM# 70   20 ROUBLES
33.8500 g., 0.9250 Silver 1.0066 oz. ASW, 38.61 mm.   **Obv:**
National arms **Rev:** 80th Anniversary - National Savings Bank
Edge: Reeded

Date	Mintage	F	VF	XF	Unc	BU
2002 Proof	1,000	Value: 225				

KM# 120   20 ROUBLES
31.1000 g., 0.9250 Silver 0.9249 oz. ASW, 38.61 mm.   **Subject:**
Freestyle Wrestling **Obv:** National arms **Rev:** Two wrestlers

Date	Mintage	F	VF	XF	Unc	BU
2003 Proof	3,000	Value: 50.00				

KM# 122   20 ROUBLES
31.1000 g., 0.9250 Silver 0.9249 oz. ASW, 38.61 mm.   **Obv:**
National arms **Rev:** Herring gull in flight

Date	Mintage	F	VF	XF	Unc	BU
2003 Proof	2,000	Value: 150				

KM# 149   20 ROUBLES
28.2800 g., 0.9250 Silver 0.8410 oz. ASW, 38.61 mm.   **Subject:**
2004 Olympic Games **Obv:** National arms **Rev:** Female shot-putter

Date	Mintage	F	VF	XF	Unc	BU
2003 Proof	25,000	Value: 32.00				

KM# 53   20 ROUBLES
33.8400 g., 0.9250 Silver 1.0063 oz. ASW, 38.5 mm. **Obv:** State arms **Rev:** Two Mute swans on water with reflections **Edge:** Reeded

Date	Mintage	F	VF	XF	Unc	BU
2003 Proof	2,000	Value: 200				

KM# 57   20 ROUBLES
31.1000 g., 0.9250 Silver 0.9249 oz. ASW, 38.6 mm. **Obv:** National arms **Rev:** Church of the Savior and Transfiguration **Edge:** Reeded

Date	Mintage	F	VF	XF	Unc	BU
2003 Proof	2,000	Value: 100				

KM# 91   20 ROUBLES
31.1000 g., 0.9250 Silver 0.9249 oz. ASW, 38.61 mm. **Subject:** Trade Union Movement Centennial **Obv:** National arms

Date	Mintage	F	VF	XF	Unc	BU
2004 Proof	1,500	Value: 200				

KM# 86   20 ROUBLES
31.1000 g., 0.9250 Silver 0.9249 oz. ASW, 38.61 mm. **Subject:** Soviet Warriors - Liberators **Obv:** Multicolored Order of the Patriotic War **Rev:** Partisans with blown up railway track

Date	Mintage	F	VF	XF	Unc	BU
2004	2,000	—	—	—	100	—

KM# 84   20 ROUBLES
31.1000 g., 0.9250 Silver 0.9249 oz. ASW, 38.61 mm. **Subject:** Memory of Facist Victims **Obv:** Multicolored Order of the Patriotic War **Rev:** Man holding dead

Date	Mintage	F	VF	XF	Unc	BU
2004	2,000	—	—	—	100	—

KM# 124   20 ROUBLES
31.1000 g., 0.9250 Silver 0.9249 oz. ASW, 38.61 mm. **Subject:** Sculling **Obv:** National arms **Rev:** Two rowers against a background of stylized oars

Date	Mintage	F	VF	XF	Unc	BU
2004	3,000	—	—	—	50.00	—

KM# 71   20 ROUBLES
31.1000 g., 0.9250 Silver 0.9249 oz. ASW, 38.6 mm. **Subject:** "Kupalle" **Obv:** Folk art design **Rev:** Fern flower with inset red synthetic crystal **Edge:** Reeded

Date	Mintage	F	VF	XF	Unc	BU
2004 Antique finish	3,000	—	—	—	600	—

KM# 72   20 ROUBLES
31.1000 g., 0.9250 Silver 0.9249 oz. ASW, 38.6 mm. **Subject:** Defense of Brest **Obv:** Multicolor Soviet Order of the Patriotic War **Rev:** "Courage" monument **Edge:** Reeded

Date	Mintage	F	VF	XF	Unc	BU
2004 Proof	3,000	Value: 100				

KM# 73   20 ROUBLES
31.1000 g., 0.9250 Silver 0.9249 oz. ASW, 38.6 mm. **Obv:** National arms **Rev:** Two common cranes **Edge:** Reeded

Date	Mintage	F	VF	XF	Unc	BU
2004 Proof	2,000	Value: 150				

KM# 77   20 ROUBLES
31.1000 g., 0.9250 Silver 0.9249 oz. ASW, 38.6 mm. **Subject:** "Kalyady" **Obv:** Folk art cross design **Rev:** Stylized sunflower with inset blue synthetic crystal **Edge:** Reeded

Date	Mintage	F	VF	XF	Unc	BU
2004 Antique finish	5,000	—	—	—	350	—

KM# 79   20 ROUBLES
31.1000 g., 0.9250 Silver 0.9249 oz. ASW, 38.6 mm. **Obv:** National arms **Rev:** Radziwill's Castle in Neswizh **Edge:** Reeded

Date	Mintage	F	VF	XF	Unc	BU
2004 Proof	2,000	Value: 100				

KM# 82   20 ROUBLES
28.7200 g., 0.9250 Silver 0.8541 oz. ASW, 38.6 mm. **Subject:** WW II Victory **Obv:** Multicolor Soviet Order of Victory **Rev:** Soviet soldiers raising their flag in the Reichstag in Berlin **Edge:** Reeded

Date	Mintage	F	VF	XF	Unc	BU
2005 Proof	12,000	Value: 60.00				

KM# 92   20 ROUBLES
28.6300 g., 0.9250 Silver 0.8514 oz. ASW, 38.6 mm. **Obv:** Two children sitting on crescent moon **Rev:** Symon the Musician and inset orange color glass crystal **Edge:** Plain

Date	Mintage	F	VF	XF	Unc	BU
2005 Antique finish	20,000	—	—	—	65.00	—

KM# 93   20 ROUBLES
28.2800 g., 0.9250 Silver 0.8410 oz. ASW, 38.61 mm. **Subject:** Kalyady's star **Obv:** Two children sitting on a crescent moon **Rev:** Snow Queen, blue glass crystal inset on forehead, flower **Edge:** Plain

Date	Mintage	F	VF	XF	Unc	BU
2005 Antique finish	20,000	—	—	—	65.00	—

KM# 94   20 ROUBLES
28.6300 g., 0.9250 Silver 0.8514 oz. ASW, 38.6 mm. **Obv:** Two children sitting on a crescent moon **Rev:** White glass crystal inset above landscape with fox, the Little Prince **Edge:** Plain

Date	Mintage	F	VF	XF	Unc	BU
2005 Antique finish	20,000	—	—	—	65.00	—

KM# 95   20 ROUBLES
28.6300 g., 0.9250 Silver 0.8514 oz. ASW, 38.61 mm. **Obv:** Two children sitting on a crescent moon **Rev:** The Stone Flower, Yellow glass crystal inset in flower design, heads flank **Edge:** Plain

Date	Mintage	F	VF	XF	Unc	BU
2005 Antique finish	20,000	—	—	—	65.00	—

KM# 96   20 ROUBLES
33.6600 g., 0.9250 Silver 1.0010 oz. ASW, 38.6 mm. **Subject:** Festivals and Rites - Bogach **Obv:** Small national arms above quilted star design **Rev:** Yellow glass crystal inset in candle flame above basket **Edge:** Reeded

Date	Mintage	F	VF	XF	Unc	BU
2005 Antique patina	5,000	—	—	—	170	—

KM# 98   20 ROUBLES
33.6300 g., 0.9250 Silver 1.0000 oz. ASW, 38.6 mm. **Subject:**

Almany Bogs **Obv:** Blooming plant on frosted design **Rev:** Great grey owl in flight **Edge:** Reeded

Date	Mintage	F	VF	XF	Unc	BU
2005 Proof	5,000	Value: 70.00				

KM# 99   20 ROUBLES
31.1000 g., 0.9250 Silver 0.9249 oz. ASW, 38.6 mm. **Series:** Easter Egg **Obv:** Quilted cross design **Rev:** Decorated Easter egg with inset pink glass crystal

Date	Mintage	F	VF	XF	Unc	BU
2005 Antique finish	5,000	—	—	—	250	—

KM# 100   20 ROUBLES
33.6200 g., 0.9250 Silver 0.9998 oz. ASW, 38.6 mm. **Obv:** Large church **Rev:** Usyaslau of Polatsk

Date	Mintage	F	VF	XF	Unc	BU
2005 Proof	5,000	Value: 60.00				

KM# 102   20 ROUBLES
33.9400 g., 0.9250 Silver 1.0093 oz. ASW, 39 mm. **Obv:** National arms **Rev:** Female tennis player

Date	Mintage	F	VF	XF	Unc	BU
2005 Proof	7,000	Value: 60.00				

KM# 128   20 ROUBLES
31.1000 g., 0.9250 Silver 0.9249 oz. ASW, 38.61 mm. **Subject:** 1000th Anniversary of Vaukavysk **Obv:** National arms **Rev:** National arms of Vaukavysk

Date	Mintage	F	VF	XF	Unc	BU
2005 Proof	2,000	Value: 100				

KM# 131   20 ROUBLES
31.1000 g., 0.9250 Silver 0.9249 oz. ASW, 38.61 mm. **Subject:** Jesnit Roman Catholic Church **Obv:** National arms **Rev:** Jesnit Roman Catholic Church in Niasvizh

Date	Mintage	F	VF	XF	Unc	BU
2005 Proof	2,000	Value: 100				

KM# 133   20 ROUBLES
28.2800 g., 0.9250 Silver 0.8410 oz. ASW, 38.61 mm. **Subject:** 2006 Olympic Games **Obv:** National arms **Rev:** Two hockey players

Date	Mintage	F	VF	XF	Unc	BU
2005 Proof	15,000	Value: 40.00				

KM# 101   20 ROUBLES
25.0000 g., 0.9250 Silver 0.7435 oz. ASW, 38.6 mm. **Subject:** 2006 FIFA World Cup Germany **Obv:** National arms **Rev:** Multicolor Europe, Asia and African maps on soccer ball **Note:** 2006 World Cup Soccer

Date	Mintage	F	VF	XF	Unc	BU
2005 Proof	50,000	Value: 50.00				

KM# 148   20 ROUBLES
28.2800 g., 0.9250 Silver 0.8410 oz. ASW, 38.5 mm. **Subject:** Twelve Months **Obv:** Two children sitting on a crescent moon **Rev:** Campfire with inset amber in a circle of produce **Edge:** Plain **Note:** Antiqued finish. Prev. duplicate of KM #137.

Date	Mintage	F	VF	XF	Unc	BU
2006	20,000	—	—	—	65.00	—

KM# 147   20 ROUBLES
33.6300 g., 0.9250 Silver 1.0000 oz. ASW, 38.61 mm. **Subject:** Chyrvomy Bar **Obv:** National arms, blooming plant **Rev:** European mink

Date	Mintage	F	VF	XF	Unc	BU
2006 Proof	5,000	Value: 60.00				

KM# 136   20 ROUBLES
33.6300 g., 0.9250 Silver 1.0000 oz. ASW, 38.61 mm. **Subject:** Vtaselle Wedding **Obv:** National arms, birds, shamrock **Rev:** Loaf of bread, golden wedding rings, diadem of flowers, background of honeycomb

Date	Mintage	F	VF	XF	Unc	BU
2006	25,000	—	—	—	70.00	—

KM# 139   20 ROUBLES
33.6200 g., 0.9250 Silver 0.9998 oz. ASW, 38.61 mm. **Subject:** Sophia of Galshany 600th Anniversary **Obv:** Castle of Galshany **Rev:** National arms and Sophia of Galshany

Date	Mintage	F	VF	XF	Unc	BU
2006 Proof	5,000	Value: 60.00				

KM# 141   20 ROUBLES
33.6200 g., 0.9250 Silver 0.9998 oz. ASW, 38.61 mm. **Subject:** Festivals and Rites - Syomukha **Obv:** National arms, solar symbol **Rev:** Chalice, Chaplet of birch, maple, rowan, sweet flag leaves inserted in green crystal

Date	Mintage	F	VF	XF	Unc	BU
2006 Antique patina	5,000	—	—	—	150	—

KM# 155   20 ROUBLES
33.6200 g., 0.9250 Silver 0.9998 oz. ASW, 36x36 mm. **Subject:** Struve Geodetric Arc **Rev:** Map of Eastern Europe **Shape:** Square

Date	Mintage	F	VF	XF	Unc	BU
2006 Proof	5,000	Value: 55.00				

KM# 166   20 ROUBLES
33.6200 g., 0.9250 Silver 0.9998 oz. ASW, 38.61 mm. **Subject:** Legend of the Stork **Obv:** Woven basket design **Rev:** Stylized bird

Date	Mintage	F	VF	XF	Unc	BU
2007 Proof	5,000	Value: 65.00				

KM# 158   20 ROUBLES
33.6200 g., 0.9250 Silver 0.9998 oz. ASW, 38.61 mm. **Subject:** Belarus - China diplomatic relations **Rev:** Double arches with country scene

Date	Mintage	F	VF	XF	Unc	BU
2007 Proof	2,000	Value: 100				

KM# 159   20 ROUBLES

33.6200 g., 0.9250 Silver 0.9998 oz. ASW, 38.61 mm. **Subject:** Festivals and Rites - Maslenica **Rev:** Pancake and syrup

Date	Mintage	F	VF	XF	Unc	BU
2007 Antique Patina	5,000	—	—	—	—	130

KM# 160   20 ROUBLES
33.6300 g., 0.9250 Silver 1.0000 oz. ASW, 38.61 mm. **Subject:** Napoleon Orda **Rev:** Bust facing, record and musical notes in background

Date	Mintage	F	VF	XF	Unc	BU
2007 Proof	5,000	Value: 45.00				

KM# 161   20 ROUBLES
28.2800 g., 0.9250 Silver 0.8410 oz. ASW, 38.61 mm. **Subject:** Alice in Wonderland **Obv:** Two children sitting on crescent moon reading book **Rev:** Alice and the March Hare

Date	Mintage	F	VF	XF	Unc	BU
2007 Matte Proof	20,000	Value: 60.00				

KM# 162   20 ROUBLES
28.2800 g., 0.9250 Silver 0.8410 oz. ASW, 38.61 mm. **Subject:** Alice Through the Looking Glass **Obv:** Two children sitting on crescent moon reading book **Rev:** Alice and chess board

Date	Mintage	F	VF	XF	Unc	BU
2007 Matte Proof	20,000	Value: 60.00				

KM# 163   20 ROUBLES
31.1050 g., 0.9990 Silver 0.9990 oz. ASW, 40 mm. **Subject:** Belarusian Ballet **Rev:** Ballerina and mirror view

Date	Mintage	F	VF	XF	Unc	BU
2007 Proof	10,000	Value: 50.00				

KM# 164   20 ROUBLES
31.1000 g., 0.9250 Silver 0.9249 oz. ASW, 38.61 mm. **Subject:** International Polar Year **Obv:** IPY logo **Rev:** Antartic map behind two penguins

Date	Mintage	F	VF	XF	Unc	BU
2007 Proof	10,000	Value: 45.00				

KM# 165   20 ROUBLES
33.6200 g., 0.9250 Silver 0.9998 oz. ASW, 38.61 mm. **Subject:** Prince Gleb of Mensk **Obv:** Wood log building **Rev:** Knight seated left

Date	Mintage	F	VF	XF	Unc	BU
2007 Proof	5,000	Value: 60.00				

KM# 167   20 ROUBLES
31.1050 g., 0.9990 Silver 0.9990 oz. ASW, 38.61 mm. **Subject:** Wolf - Canis Lupus **Rev:** Wolf head facing

Date	Mintage	F	VF	XF	Unc	BU
2007 Proof	7,000	Value: 90.00				

KM# 168   20 ROUBLES
31.1050 g., 0.9990 Silver 0.9990 oz. ASW, 38.61 mm. **Subject:** Wolf - Canis Lupis **Rev:** Wolf standing on rock ledge behind second wolf's head facing

Date	Mintage	F	VF	XF	Unc	BU
2007 Proof	7,000	Value: 90.00				

KM# 169   20 ROUBLES
33.6300 g., 0.9250 Silver 1.0000 oz. ASW, 38.61 mm. **Subject:** Dniepra - Sozhsky **Rev:** Sturgeon fish

Date	Mintage	F	VF	XF	Unc	BU
2007 Proof	5,000	Value: 65.00				

KM# 180   20 ROUBLES
33.6300 g., 0.9250 Silver 1.0000 oz. ASW, 38.61 mm. **Subject:** Minsk **Rev:** Old and new city views

Date	Mintage	F	VF	XF	Unc	BU
2008 Proof	7,000	Value: 50.00				

KM# 181   20 ROUBLES
33.6300 g., 0.9250 Silver 1.0000 oz. ASW, 38.61 mm. **Subject:** Financial System, 90th Anniversary **Rev:** Shield

Date	Mintage	F	VF	XF	Unc	BU
2008 Proof	3,000	Value: 60.00				

KM# 182   20 ROUBLES
33.6300 g., 0.9250 Silver 1.0000 oz. ASW, 38.61 mm. **Subject:**
Lipichanskaya Pushcha **Rev:** Kingfisher seated on branch

Date	Mintage	F	VF	XF	Unc	BU
2008 Proof	5,000	Value: 65.00				

KM# 183   20 ROUBLES
33.6200 g., 0.9250 Silver 0.9998 oz. ASW, 38.61 mm. **Subject:**
Festivala and Rites - Dzyady **Rev:** Two angels above table

Date	Mintage	F	VF	XF	Unc	BU
2008 Antique patina	5,000	—	—	—	90.00	—

KM# 184   20 ROUBLES
33.6200 g., 0.9250 Silver 0.9998 oz. ASW, 38.61 mm. **Subject:**
David of Garadzen **Rev:** Half-length figure of knight

Date	Mintage	F	VF	XF	Unc	BU
2008 Proof	5,000	Value: 60.00				

KM# 185   20 ROUBLES
31.1050 g., 0.9990 Silver 0.9990 oz. ASW, 40 mm. **Rev:** Figure
skater

Date	Mintage	F	VF	XF	Unc	BU
2008 Proof	10,000	Value: 50.00				

KM# 186   20 ROUBLES
31.1050 g., 0.9990 Silver 0.9990 oz. ASW, 38.61 mm. **Subject:**
Lynx **Rev:** Lynx head facing

Date	Mintage	F	VF	XF	Unc	BU
2008 Proof	8,000	Value: 95.00				

KM# 187   20 ROUBLES
31.1050 g., 0.9990 Silver 0.9990 oz. ASW, 38.61 mm. **Subject:**
Lynx **Rev:** Adult lynx with cub

Date	Mintage	F	VF	XF	Unc	BU
2008 Proof	8,000	Value: 85.00				

KM# 188   20 ROUBLES
33.6200 g., 0.9250 Silver 0.9998 oz. ASW, 38.61 mm. **Subject:**
Cuckoo Legend **Rev:** Stylized cuckoo

Date	Mintage	F	VF	XF	Unc	BU
2008 Proof	5,000	Value: 60.00				

KM# 189   20 ROUBLES
28.2800 g., 0.9250 Silver 0.8410 oz. ASW, 38.61 mm. **Subject:**
Turandot **Rev:** Female opera character

Date	Mintage	F	VF	XF	Unc	BU
2008 Antique	—	—	—	—	65.00	—

KM# 190   20 ROUBLES
38.6100 g., 0.9250 Silver 1.1482 oz. ASW, 38.61 mm. **Subject:**
House Warming **Obv:** Cat **Rev:** Plated key within house facade

Date	Mintage	F	VF	XF	Unc	BU
2008 Proof	25,000	Value: 50.00				

KM# 191   20 ROUBLES
28.2800 g., 0.9250 Silver 0.8410 oz. ASW, 38.61 mm. **Subject:**
Sedov **Obv:** Compass star, multicolor **Rev:** Sailing ship

Date	Mintage	F	VF	XF	Unc	BU
2008 Proof	25,000	Value: 70.00				

KM# 196   20 ROUBLES
33.6300 g., 0.9250 Silver 1.0000 oz. ASW, 38.61 mm. **Subject:**
65th Anniversary of Liberation **Rev:** Child looking upward to
freeded birds

Date	Mintage	F	VF	XF	Unc	BU
2009 Proof	4,000	Value: 60.00				

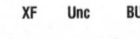

KM# 197   20 ROUBLES
28.2800 g., 0.9250 Silver 0.8410 oz. ASW, 40x28 mm. **Subject:**
Llya Repin **Rev:** Bust and house, artist's palet in corner **Shape:**
Rectangle

Date	Mintage	F	VF	XF	Unc	BU
2009 Proof	1,500	Value: 60.00				

KM# 198 20 ROUBLES
28.2800 g., 0.9250 Silver 0.8410 oz. ASW, 38.61 mm. **Subject:** Sapsy **Rev:** Bee honey comb, apple tree, grain

Date	Mintage	F	VF	XF	Unc	BU
2009 Proof	5,000	Value: 80.00				

KM# 199 20 ROUBLES
33.6300 g., 0.9990 Silver 1.0801 oz. ASW, 38.61 mm. **Subject:** Christening **Rev:** Child in christening gown

Date	Mintage	F	VF	XF	Unc	BU
2009 Proof	5,000	Value: 80.00				

KM# 200 20 ROUBLES
28.2800 g., 0.9250 Silver 0.8410 oz. ASW, 38.61 mm. **Subject:** Dar Pomorza **Rev:** Sail training vessel

Date	Mintage	F	VF	XF	Unc	BU
2009 Proof	25,000	Value: 60.00				

KM# 201 20 ROUBLES
33.6300 g., 0.9250 Silver 1.0000 oz. ASW, 38.61 mm. **Subject:** White stork **Rev:** Bird and nest

Date	Mintage	F	VF	XF	Unc	BU
2009 Proof	7,000	Value: 70.00				

KM# 202 20 ROUBLES
33.6300 g., 0.9250 Silver 1.0000 oz. ASW, 38.61 mm. **Subject:** Belavezhskaya Pushcha **Rev:** Range animals

Date	Mintage	F	VF	XF	Unc	BU
2009 Proof	8,000	Value: 60.00				

KM# 203 20 ROUBLES
28.2800 g., 0.9250 Silver 0.8410 oz. ASW, 38.61 mm. **Series:** Zodiac - Pisces **Rev:** Two fish

Date	Mintage	F	VF	XF	Unc	BU
2009 Matte Proof	25,000	Value: 55.00				

KM# 204 20 ROUBLES
28.2800 g., 0.9250 Silver 0.8410 oz. ASW, 38.61 mm. **Subject:** Zodiac - Aries **Rev:** Ram

Date	Mintage	F	VF	XF	Unc	BU
2009 Matte Proof	25,000	Value: 55.00				

KM# 205 20 ROUBLES
28.2800 g., 0.9250 Silver 0.8410 oz. ASW, 38.61 mm. **Subject:** Zodiac - Taurus **Rev:** Bull

Date	Mintage	F	VF	XF	Unc	BU
2009 Matte Proof	25,000	Value: 55.00				

KM# 206 20 ROUBLES
28.2800 g., 0.9250 Silver 0.8410 oz. ASW, 38.61 mm. **Subject:** Zodiac - Gemini **Rev:** Twins

Date	Mintage	F	VF	XF	Unc	BU
2009 Matte Proof	25,000	Value: 55.00				

KM# 207 20 ROUBLES
28.2800 g., 0.9250 Silver 0.8410 oz. ASW, 38.61 mm. **Subject:** Zodiac - Cancer **Rev:** Crab

Date	Mintage	F	VF	XF	Unc	BU
2009 Matte Proof	25,000	Value: 55.00				

KM# 208 20 ROUBLES
28.2800 g., 0.9250 Silver 0.8410 oz. ASW, 38.61 mm. **Subject:** Zodiac - Leo **Rev:** Lion

Date	Mintage	F	VF	XF	Unc	BU
2009 Matte Proof	25,000	Value: 55.00				

KM# 209 20 ROUBLES
28.2800 g., 0.9250 Silver 0.8410 oz. ASW, 38.61 mm. **Subject:** Zodiac - Virgo **Rev:** Little girl

Date	Mintage	F	VF	XF	Unc	BU
2009 Matte Proof	25,000	Value: 55.00				

KM# 210 20 ROUBLES
28.2800 g., 0.9250 Silver 0.8410 oz. ASW, 38.61 mm. **Subject:** Zodiac - Libra **Rev:** Balance scales

Date	Mintage	F	VF	XF	Unc	BU
2009 Matte Proof	25,000	Value: 55.00				

KM# 211   20 ROUBLES
28.2800 g., 0.9250 Silver 0.8410 oz. ASW, 38.61 mm. **Rev:** Scorpion

Date	Mintage	F	VF	XF	Unc	BU
2009 Matte Proof	25,000	Value: 55.00				

KM# 254   20 ROUBLES
28.2800 g., 0.9250 Silver 0.8410 oz. ASW, 45.3x35.3 mm. **Subject:** Pushkin's stories **Rev:** Tale of Tsar Saltan **Shape:** Vertical oval

Date	Mintage	F	VF	XF	Unc	BU
2010 Proof	7,000	Value: 85.00				

KM# 258   20 ROUBLES
33.6200 g., 0.9250 Silver 0.9998 oz. ASW, 38.61 mm. **Subject:** Expo 2010 **Obv:** Folk pattern **Rev:** Exposition buildings of the past

Date	Mintage	F	VF	XF	Unc	BU
2010 Proof	5,000	Value: 100				

KM# 279   20 ROUBLES
31.1000 g., 0.9990 Silver 0.9988 oz. ASW, 38.61 mm. **Obv:** National arms **Rev:** Two eagle owls, crystals in eyes

Date	Mintage	F	VF	XF	Unc	BU
2010 Proof	5,000	Value: 75.00				

KM# 224   20 ROUBLES
33.6300 g., 0.9250 Silver 1.0000 oz. ASW, 38.61 mm. **Subject:** EURASEC, 10th Anniversary **Obv:** Folk embroidery pattern **Rev:** Six flags around multicolor golbe

Date	Mintage	F	VF	XF	Unc	BU
2010 Proof	3,000	Value: 60.00				

KM# 225   20 ROUBLES
33.6300 g., 0.9250 Silver 1.0000 oz. ASW, 38.6 mm. **Subject:** Syaredniaya Pripyat Reserve **Obv:** Eight ferns forming double cross **Rev:** Marsh turtle

Date	Mintage	F	VF	XF	Unc	BU
2010 Proof	3,000	Value: 60.00				

KM# 235   20 ROUBLES
28.2800 g., 0.9250 Silver 0.8410 oz. ASW, 38.61 mm. **Rev:** U.S. Frigate Constitution

Date	Mintage	F	VF	XF	Unc	BU
2010 Proof	7,000	Value: 75.00				

KM# 237   20 ROUBLES
33.6200 g., 0.9250 Silver 0.9998 oz. ASW, 38.61 mm. **Subject:** Legend of the tortoise

Date	Mintage	F	VF	XF	Unc	BU
2010 Proof	3,000	Value: 55.00				

KM# 239   20 ROUBLES
28.2800 g., 0.9250 Silver 0.8410 oz. ASW, 38.6 mm. **Subject:** Battle of Grunwald **Obv:** Figure with outstretched arms **Rev:** Legend within Fingerprint

Date	Mintage	F	VF	XF	Unc	BU
2010 Proof	2,500	Value: 60.00				

KM# 241   20 ROUBLES
33.6300 g., 0.9250 Silver 1.0000 oz. ASW, 38.61 mm. **Subject:** Age of Majority **Rev:** Multicolor flowers within folk patterns

Date	Mintage	F	VF	XF	Unc	BU
2010 Proof	—	Value: 55.00				

KM# 242   20 ROUBLES
28.2800 g., 0.9250 Silver 0.8410 oz. ASW, 38.61 mm. **Subject:** 3 Musketeers **Rev:** D'Artagnan, with red stone insert

Date	Mintage	F	VF	XF	Unc	BU
2010 Proof	5,000	Value: 85.00				

KM# 243   20 ROUBLES
28.2800 g., 0.9250 Silver 0.8410 oz. ASW, 38.61 mm. **Subject:** The Three Musketeers **Rev:** Aramis, light blue stone insert

Date	Mintage	F	VF	XF	Unc	BU
2010 Proof	5,000	Value: 85.00				

KM# 244   20 ROUBLES
28.2800 g., 0.9250 Silver 0.8410 oz. ASW, 38.61 mm. **Subject:** The Three Musketeers **Rev:** Athos, blue stone insert

Date	Mintage	F	VF	XF	Unc	BU
2010 Proof	5,000	Value: 85.00				

KM# 245   20 ROUBLES
28.2800 g., 0.9250 Silver 0.8410 oz. ASW, 38.61 mm. **Subject:** The Three Musketeers **Rev:** Pathos, red stone insert

Date	Mintage	F	VF	XF	Unc	BU
2010 Proof	5,000	Value: 85.00				

KM# 246   20 ROUBLES
28.2800 g., 0.9250 Silver 0.8410 oz. ASW, 38.61 mm. **Subject:** Orthodox Churches **Rev:** Cathedral of the Assumption

Date	Mintage	F	VF	XF	Unc	BU
2010 Proof	3,000	Value: 75.00				

KM# 247   20 ROUBLES
28.2800 g., 0.9250 Silver 0.8410 oz. ASW, 38.61 mm. **Subject:** Orthodox Churches **Rev:** Cathedral of SS Peter and Paul

Date	Mintage	F	VF	XF	Unc	BU
2010 Proof	3,000	Value: 75.00				

KM# 248   20 ROUBLES
28.2800 g., 0.9250 Silver 0.8410 oz. ASW, 38.61 mm. **Subject:** Orthodox Churches **Rev:** Cathedral of Alexander Nevsky

Date	Mintage	F	VF	XF	Unc	BU
2010 Proof	3,000	Value: 75.00				

KM# 249   20 ROUBLES
28.2800 g., 0.9250 Silver 0.8410 oz. ASW, 38.61 mm. **Subject:** Orthodox Churches **Rev:** Cathedral of St. Nicholas

Date	Mintage	F	VF	XF	Unc	BU
2010 Proof	3,000	Value: 75.00				

KM# 250   20 ROUBLES
28.2800 g., 0.9250 Silver 0.8410 oz. ASW, 45.3x35.3 mm. **Subject:** Pushkin's stories **Rev:** Tale of the Golden Cockerel in multicolor **Shape:** Vertical oval

Date	Mintage	F	VF	XF	Unc	BU
2010 Proof	7,000	Value: 85.00				

KM# 251   20 ROUBLES
28.2800 g., 0.9250 Silver 0.8410 oz. ASW, 45.3x35.3 mm. **Subject:** Pushkin's stories **Rev:** Tale of the fisherman and the fish **Shape:** Vertical oval

Date	Mintage	F	VF	XF	Unc	BU
2010 Proof	7,000	Value: 85.00				

KM# 252   20 ROUBLES
28.2800 g., 0.9250 Silver 0.8410 oz. ASW, 45.3x35.3 mm. **Subject:** Pushkin's stories **Rev:** Tale of one Dead Princess and Seven Knights **Shape:** Vertical oval

Date	Mintage	F	VF	XF	Unc	BU
2010 Proof	7,000	Value: 85.00				

KM# 253   20 ROUBLES
28.2800 g., 0.9250 Silver 0.8410 oz. ASW, 45.3x35.3 mm. **Subject:** Pushkin's stories **Rev:** Ruslan and Ludmila **Shape:** Vertical oval

Date	Mintage	F	VF	XF	Unc	BU
2010 Proof	7,000	Value: 85.00				

KM# 256   20 ROUBLES
31.1000 g., 0.9990 Silver 0.9988 oz. ASW, 38.61 mm. **Rev:** Madonna and child

Date	Mintage	F	VF	XF	Unc	BU
2010 Proof	7,000	—	—	—	—	75.00

KM# 257   20 ROUBLES
28.2800 g., 0.9250 Silver 0.8410 oz. ASW, 28x40 mm. **Subject:** Ivan Khrutsky **Obv:** Color painting of female with fruit basket, arms at lower left **Rev:** Half-length figure of Khrucky, flowers in vase on table **Shape:** Vertical rectangle

Date	Mintage	F	VF	XF	Unc	BU
2010	4,000	—	—	—	—	75.00

KM# 261   20 ROUBLES
Silver **Subject:** End of World War II, 65th Anniversary **Rev:** Five doves in flight, knitting

Date	Mintage	F	VF	XF	Unc	BU
2010 Proof	—	Value: 75.00				

KM# 266   20 ROUBLES
28.2800 g., 0.9250 Silver 0.8410 oz. ASW, 30x45 mm. **Subject:** Minskaya **Rev:** Madonna icon, partially gilt **Shape:** Vertical rectangle

Date	Mintage	F	VF	XF	Unc	BU
2010 Proof	7,000	Value: 150				

KM# 267 20 ROUBLES
28.2800 g., 0.9250 Silver 0.8410 oz. ASW, 30x45 mm. **Subject:** Smalenskaya **Rev:** Madonna Icon, partially gilt **Shape:** Vertical rectangle

Date	Mintage	F	VF	XF	Unc	BU
2010 Prooflike	7,000	—	—	—	—	150

KM# 268 20 ROUBLES
28.2800 g., 0.9250 Silver 0.8410 oz. ASW, 28x40 mm. **Rev:** Nefertiti bust **Shape:** Vertical rectangle

Date	Mintage	F	VF	XF	Unc	BU
2010 Proof	7,000	Value: 100				

KM# 269 20 ROUBLES
28.2800 g., 0.9250 Silver 0.8410 oz. ASW, 28x40 mm. **Rev:** Cupid & Psyche **Shape:** Vertical rectangle

Date	Mintage	F	VF	XF	Unc	BU
2010 Proof	7,000	Value: 100				

KM# 271 20 ROUBLES
28.2800 g., 0.9250 Silver 0.8410 oz. ASW, 38.6 mm. **Obv:** Compass rose and chart **Rev:** Cutty Sark sailing right

Date	Mintage	F	VF	XF	Unc	BU
2010 Proof	—	Value: 50.00				

KM# 272 20 ROUBLES
28.2800 g., 0.9250 Silver 0.8410 oz. ASW, 38.61 mm. **Obv:** Compass rose and chart **Rev:** Amerigo Vespucci sailing left

Date	Mintage	F	VF	XF	Unc	BU
2010 Proof	—	Value: 75.00				

KM# 278 20 ROUBLES
7.7800 g., 0.9990 Gold 0.2499 oz. AGW, 22 mm. **Subject:** Slovyanka **Obv:** Large lis, national arms at top **Rev:** Madonna and Child

Date	Mintage	F	VF	XF	Unc	BU
2010 Proof	Est. 2,500	Value: 475				

KM# 255 20 ROUBLES
28.2800 g., 0.9250 Silver 0.8410 oz. ASW, 38.61 mm. **Subject:** My Love **Rev:** Two cats, red heart shaped crystal insert at top

Date	Mintage	F	VF	XF	Unc	BU
2011 Proof	15,000	Value: 100				

KM# 280 20 ROUBLES
28.2800 g., 0.9250 Silver 0.8410 oz. ASW, 38.61 mm. **Subject:** Krusenstern **Obv:** Compass rose and charts, national arms at top **Rev:** Fully-rigged sailing ship left

Date	Mintage	F	VF	XF	Unc	BU
2011 Proof	7,000	Value: 75.00				

KM# 281 20 ROUBLES
33.6300 g., 0.9250 Silver 1.0000 oz. ASW, 38.61 mm. **Subject:** Motherhood **Obv:** Folk embroidery pattern **Rev:** Mother holding baby, bird

Date	Mintage	F	VF	XF	Unc	BU
2011 Proof	10,000	Value: 75.00				

KM# 281a 20 ROUBLES
33.6300 g., 0.9250 Silver partially gilt 1.0000 oz. ASW, 38.61 mm. **Obv:** Folk embroidery pattern **Rev:** Mother and child, gilt bird

Date	Mintage	F	VF	XF	Unc	BU
2011 Proof	—	Value: 85.00				

KM# 289 20 ROUBLES
26.1600 g., 0.9250 Silver 0.7780 oz. ASW **Subject:** Paleolithic Venus **Obv:** Cave drawing of steer **Rev:** Carved statue of pregnant female **Shape:** Vertical rectangle

Date	Mintage	F	VF	XF	Unc	BU
2011 Proof	Est. 3,500	Value: 75.00				

KM# 290 20 ROUBLES
26.1600 g., 0.9250 Silver 0.7780 oz. ASW **Subject:** Voltaire **Obv:** Carved portrait bust **Rev:** Statue of seated Voltaire **Shape:** Vertical rectangle

Date	Mintage	F	VF	XF	Unc	BU
2011 Proof	Est. 3,500	Value: 85.00				

KM# 121 50 ROUBLES
4.4500 g., 0.9990 Gold 0.1429 oz. AGW, 25 mm. **Subject:** Fox **Obv:** National arms **Rev:** Red fox with inset diamond eyes

Date	Mintage	F	VF	XF	Unc	BU
2002	Est. 2,000	—	—	—	1,000	—

KM# 126 50 ROUBLES
62.2000 g., 0.9250 Silver 1.8497 oz. ASW, 50 mm. **Subject:** 60th Anniversary of Victory **Obv:** Order of the Victory, multicolored **Rev:** Stars and arrows

Date	Mintage	F	VF	XF	Unc	BU
2005	2,000	—	—	—	—	—
2005 Proof	—	Value: 220				

KM# 142 50 ROUBLES
7.7800 g., 0.9990 Gold 0.2499 oz. AGW, 25 mm. **Subject:** Peregrine Falcon **Obv:** National arms **Rev:** Peregrine falcon with inset diamond eye

Date	Mintage	F	VF	XF	Unc	BU
2006	2,000	—	—	750	1,000	—

KM# 143 50 ROUBLES
8.0000 g., 0.9000 Gold 0.2315 oz. AGW, 21 mm. **Subject:** Bison **Obv:** National arms **Rev:** European bison

Date	Mintage	F	VF	XF	Unc	BU
2006	3,000	Value: 600				

KM# 144 50 ROUBLES
8.0000 g., 0.9000 Gold 0.2315 oz. AGW, 21 mm. **Subject:** Beaver **Obv:** National arms **Rev:** Family of Eurasian beavers

Date	Mintage	F	VF	XF	Unc	BU
2006 Proof	3,000	Value: 600				

KM# 145 50 ROUBLES
8.0000 g., 0.9000 Gold 0.2315 oz. AGW, 21 mm. **Subject:** Mute Swan **Obv:** National arms **Rev:** Pair of mute swans

Date	Mintage	F	VF	XF	Unc	BU
2006	3,000	Value: 600				

KM# 123 50 ROUBLES
8.0000 g., 0.9000 Gold 0.2315 oz. AGW, 21 mm. **Subject:** Herring Gull **Obv:** National arms **Rev:** Herring gull in flight

Date	Mintage	F	VF	XF	Unc	BU
2006	3,000	Value: 600				

KM# 125 50 ROUBLES
8.0000 g., 0.9000 Gold 0.2315 oz. AGW, 21 mm. **Obv:** National arms **Rev:** Pair of common cranes

Date	Mintage	F	VF	XF	Unc	BU
2006	3,000	Value: 600				

KM# 277 50 ROUBLES
7.7800 g., 0.9990 Gold 0.2499 oz. AGW, 25 mm. **Obv:** National arms **Rev:** Owl head facing

Date	Mintage	F	VF	XF	Unc	BU
2010 Proof	Est. 2,000	Value: 475				

KM# 286 50 ROUBLES
7.7800 g., 0.9990 Gold 0.2499 oz. AGW, 25 mm. **Obv:** National arms **Rev:** Hedgehog

Date	Mintage	F	VF	XF	Unc	BU
2011 Proof	Est. 1,000	Value: 475				

KM# 58 100 ROUBLES
155.5000 g., 0.9250 Silver 4.6243 oz. ASW, 64 mm. **Obv:** Theater building **Rev:** Two ballet dancers **Edge:** Reeded **Note:** Illustration reduced.

Date	Mintage	F	VF	XF	Unc	BU
2003 Proof	1,000	Value: 750				

KM# 216 100 ROUBLES
17.2800 g., 0.9000 Gold 0.5000 oz. AGW, 32 mm. **Subject:** China - Belarus relations, 15th Anniversary **Obv:** National arms **Rev:** Two archways, forest in left, Great Wall on right

Date	Mintage	F	VF	XF	Unc	BU
2007 Proof	1,000	Value: 1,000				

KM# 192   100 ROUBLES
155.5000 g., 0.9990 Silver 4.9942 oz. ASW, 65 mm. **Subject:**
Figure skating **Rev:** Pair of skates and snowflakes **Note:**
Illustration reduced.

Date	Mintage	F	VF	XF	Unc	BU
2008 Proof	500	Value: 450				

KM# 193   100 ROUBLES
155.5000 g., 0.9990 Silver 4.9942 oz. ASW, 65 mm. **Subject:**
White Stork Legend **Rev:** Stylized stork

Date	Mintage	F	VF	XF	Unc	BU
2008 Proof	500	Value: 350				

KM# 103   200 ROUBLES
31.1050 g., 0.9990 Gold 0.9990 oz. AGW, 40 mm. **Obv:**
National arms **Rev:** Belarussian ballerina

Date	Mintage	F	VF	XF	Unc	BU
2005 Proof	1,500	Value: 2,000				

KM# 74   1000 ROUBLES
1000.0000 g., 0.9990 Silver 32.117 oz. ASW, 100 mm. **Subject:**
2004 Olympics **Obv:** National arms **Rev:** Ancient charioteer
Note: Illustration reduced.

Date	Mintage	F	VF	XF	Unc	BU
2004 Proof	650	Value: 1,500				

KM# 170   1000 ROUBLES
1000.0000 g., 0.9990 Silver 32.117 oz. ASW, 100 mm. **Subject:**
Belarussian Ballet **Rev:** Ballerina and mirror image **Note:**
Illustration reduced.

Date	Mintage	F	VF	XF	Unc	BU
2007 Proof	300	Value: 1,500				

KM# 171   1000 ROUBLES
1000.0000 g., 0.9990 Silver partially gilt 32.117 oz. ASW,
100 mm. **Subject:** Cross of St. Euphrosyne of Polotsk **Obv:**
Church facade **Rev:** Gold-plated pectorial cross **Note:** Illustration
reduced.

Date	Mintage	F	VF	XF	Unc	BU
2007 Proof-like	2,000	Value: 2,000				

BELGIUM

The Kingdom of Belgium, a constitutional monarchy in northwest Europe, has an area of 11,780 sq. mi. (30,519 sq. km.) and
a population of 10.1 million, chiefly Dutch-speaking Flemish and
French-speaking Walloons. Capital: Brussels. Agriculture, dairy
farming, and the processing of raw materials for re-export are the
principal industries. Beurs voor Diamant in Antwerp is the world's
largest diamond trading center. Iron and steel, machinery motor
vehicles, chemicals, textile yarns and fabrics comprise the principal exports.

RULER
Albert II, 1993-

MINT MARK
Angel head - Brussels

MINTMASTERS' INITIALS & PRIVY MARKS
Pair of scales – Romain Coenen (1987 -)
Goose feather – Serge Lesens (2010)
   NOTE: Beginning in 1987, the letters "qp" (quality proof)
appear on non-circulating coins

MONETARY SYSTEM
100 Centimes = 1 Franc
1 Euro = 100 Cents

LEGENDS
   Belgian coins are usually inscribed either in Dutch, French
or both. However some modern coins are being inscribed in Latin
or German. The language used is best told by noting the spelling
of the name of the country.
(Fr) French: BELGIQUE or BELGES
(Du) Dutch: BELGIE or BELGEN
(La) Latin: BELGICA
(Ge) German: BELGIEN

KINGDOM
DECIMAL COINAGE

KM# 148.1   50 CENTIMES
2.7000 g., Bronze, 19 mm. **Ruler:** Baudouin I **Obv:** Crowned
denomination divides date, legend in French **Obv. Legend:**
BELGIQUE **Rev:** Helmeted mine worker left, miner's lamp at right,
large head, tip of neck 1/2 mm from rim **Edge:** Plain

Date	Mintage	F	VF	XF	Unc	BU
2001 In sets only	60,000	—	—	—	2.00	
2001 Proof	5,000	Value: 25.00				

   Note: Medal alignment

KM# 149.1   50 CENTIMES
2.7500 g., Bronze, 19 mm. **Ruler:** Baudouin I **Obv:** Crowned
denomination divides date, legend in Dutch **Obv. Legend:**
BELGIE **Rev:** Helmeted mine worker left, miner's lamp at right,
large head **Edge:** Plain

Date	Mintage	F	VF	XF	Unc	BU
2001 In sets only	60,000	—	—	—	3.00	
2001 Proof	5,000	Value: 25.00				

   Note: Medal alignment

Date	Mintage	F	VF	XF	Unc	BU
2007 In sets only	60,000	—	—	—	2.00	

KM# 148.2   50 CENTIMES
2.7500 g., Bronze, 19 mm. **Ruler:** Baudouin I **Obv:** Crowned
denomination divides date, legend in French **Obv. Legend:**
BELGIQUE **Rev:** Helmeted mine worker left, miner's lamp at right,
large head, tip of neck 1/2 mm from rim **Edge:** Plain **Note:** Medal
alignment.

Date	Mintage	F	VF	XF	Unc	BU
2001 Proof	—	Value: 30.00				

KM# 149.2   50 CENTIMES
2.7500 g., Bronze, 19 mm. **Ruler:** Baudouin I **Obv:** Crowned
denomination divides date, legend in French **Obv. Legend:**
BELGIQUE **Rev:** Helmeted mine worker left, miner's lamp at right,
large head, tip of neck 1/2 mm from rim **Edge:** Plain **Note:** Medal
alignment.

Date	Mintage	F	VF	XF	Unc	BU
2001 Proof	—	Value: 30.00				

KM# 188 FRANC
2.7500 g., Nickel Plated Iron, 18 mm. **Ruler:** Albert II **Obv:** Head left, outline around back of head **Rev:** Vertical line divides date and large denomination, legend in Dutch **Rev. Legend:** BELGIE **Edge:** Plain

Date	Mintage	F	VF	XF	Unc	BU
2001 In sets only	60,000	—	—	—	3.00	—
2001 Proof	5,000	Value: 25.00				

Note: Medal alignment

KM# 187 FRANC
2.7500 g., Nickel Plated Iron, 18 mm. **Ruler:** Albert II **Obv:** Head left, outline around back of head **Rev:** Vertical line divides date and large denomination, legend in French **Rev. Legend:** BELGIQUE **Note:** Mint mark: angel head. Unknown mintmaster's privy mark: scales.

Date	Mintage	F	VF	XF	Unc	BU
2001 In sets only	60,000	—	—	—	3.00	—
2001 Proof	5,000	Value: 25.00				

Note: Medal alignment

KM# 189 5 FRANCS (5 Frank)
5.5000 g., Aluminum-Bronze, 24 mm. **Ruler:** Albert II **Obv:** Head left, outline around back of head **Rev:** Vertical line divides date and denomination, legend in French **Rev. Legend:** BELGIQUE **Note:** Mint mark: angel head. Mintmaster R. Coenen's privy mark: scale.

Date	Mintage	F	VF	XF	Unc	BU
2001 In sets only	60,000	—	—	—	4.00	—
2001 Proof	5,000	Value: 25.00				

Note: Medal alignment

KM# 190 5 FRANCS (5 Frank)
5.5000 g., Aluminum-Bronze, 24 mm. **Ruler:** Albert II **Obv:** Head left, outline around back of head **Rev:** Vertical line divides date and large denomination, legend in Dutch **Rev. Legend:** BELGIE **Note:** Mint mark: angel head. Mintmaster R. Coenen's privy mark: scale.

Date	Mintage	F	VF	XF	Unc	BU
2001 In sets only	60,000	—	—	—	4.00	—
2001 Proof	5,000	Value: 25.00				

Note: Medal alignment

KM# 191 20 FRANCS (20 Frank)
8.5000 g., Nickel-Bronze, 25.65 mm. **Ruler:** Albert II **Obv:** Head left, outline around back of head **Rev:** Vertical line divides date and large denomination, legend in French **Rev. Legend:** BELGIQUE **Note:** Mint mark: angel head. Mintmaster R. Coenen's privy mark: scale.

Date	Mintage	F	VF	XF	Unc	BU
2001 In sets only	60,000	—	—	—	4.00	—
2001 Proof	5,000	Value: 25.00				

Note: Medal alignment

KM# 192 20 FRANCS (20 Frank)
8.5000 g., Nickel-Bronze, 25.7 mm. **Ruler:** Albert II **Obv:** Head left, outline around back of head **Rev:** Vertical line divides date and large denomination, legend in Dutch **Rev. Legend:** BELGIE **Note:** Mint mark: angel head. Mintmaster R. Coenen's privy mark: scale.

Date	Mintage	F	VF	XF	Unc	BU
2001 In sets only	60,000	—	—	—	5.00	—
2001 Proof	5,000	Value: 25.00				

Note: Medal alignment

KM# 193 50 FRANCS (50 Frank)
7.0000 g., Nickel, 22.7 mm. **Ruler:** Albert II **Obv:** Head left, outline around back of head **Rev:** Vertical line divides large denomination and date, legend in French **Rev. Legend:** BELGIQUE **Note:** Mint mark: angel head. Mintmaster R. Coenen's privy mark: scale.

Date	Mintage	F	VF	XF	Unc	BU
2001 In sets only	60,000	—	—	—	8.00	—
2001 Proof	5,000	Value: 25.00				

Note: Medal alignment

KM# 194 50 FRANCS (50 Frank)
7.0000 g., Nickel, 22.75 mm. **Ruler:** Albert II **Obv:** Head left, outline around back of head **Rev:** Vertical line divides large denomination and date, legend in Dutch **Rev. Legend:** BELGIE **Note:** Mint mark: angel head. Mintmaster R. Coenen's privy mark: scale.

Date	Mintage	F	VF	XF	Unc	BU
2001 In sets only	60,000	—	—	—	8.00	—
2001 Proof	5,000	Value: 25.00				

Note: Medal alignment

KM# 222 500 FRANCS (500 Frank)
22.8500 g., 0.9250 Silver 0.6795 oz. ASW, 37 mm. **Ruler:** Albert II **Subject:** Europe: Europa and the Bull **Obv:** Map and denomination **Rev:** Europa sitting on a bull **Edge:** Plain

Date	Mintage	F	VF	XF	Unc	BU
2001 (qp) Proof	40,000	Value: 50.00				

KM# 223 5000 FRANCS
15.5500 g., 0.9990 Gold 0.4994 oz. AGW, 29 mm. **Ruler:** Albert II **Subject:** Europe: Europa and the Bull **Obv:** Map and denomination **Rev:** Europa sitting on a bull **Edge:** Plain

Date	Mintage	F	VF	XF	Unc	BU
2001 (qp) Proof	2,000	Value: 875				

EURO COINAGE
European Union Issues

KM# 307 100 ECU
15.5500 g., 0.9990 Gold 0.4994 oz. AGW, 29 mm. **Ruler:** Albert II **Subject:** Prince Philippe, 50th Birthday

Date	Mintage	F	VF	XF	Unc	BU
2010 Proof	—	Value: 900				

KM# 224 EURO CENT
2.3000 g., Copper Plated Steel, 16.25 mm. **Ruler:** Albert II **Obv:** Head left within inner circle, stars 3/4 surround, date below **Rev:** Denomination and globe **Edge:** Plain

Date	Mintage	F	VF	XF	Unc	BU
2001	99,840,000	—	—	0.30	0.75	1.00
2001 Proof	15,000	Value: 12.00				
2002 In sets only	140,000	—	—	—	18.50	25.00
2002 Proof	15,000	Value: 15.00				
2003	10,135,000	—	—	0.25	0.60	0.80
2003 Proof	15,000	Value: 12.00				
2004	180,000,000	—	—	0.25	0.60	0.80
2004 Proof	—	Value: 12.00				
2005 In sets only	—	—	—	—	—	18.50
2005 Proof	3,000	Value: 12.00				
2006	15,000,000	—	—	0.25	0.60	0.80
2006 Proof	—	Value: 12.00				
2007	60,000,000	—	—	0.25	0.60	0.80
2007 Proof	—	Value: 12.00				

KM# 274 EURO CENT
2.3000 g., Copper Plated Steel, 16.25 mm. **Ruler:** Albert II **Obv:** Head of Albert II left, crowned monogram at right, date below

Date	Mintage	F	VF	XF	Unc	BU
2008	50,000,000	—	—	—	0.35	0.75
2008 Proof	—	Value: 12.00				
2009	19,950,000	—	—	—	0.35	0.75
2009 Proof	1,500	Value: 12.00				
2010	30,000,000	—	—	—	0.35	0.75
2010 Proof	1,850	Value: 12.00				
2011	—	—	—	—	—	0.75
2011 Proof	1,850	Value: 12.00				
2012	—	—	—	—	—	0.75
2012 Proof	1,850	Value: 12.00				

KM# 225 2 EURO CENT
3.0600 g., Copper Plated Steel, 18.75 mm. **Ruler:** Albert II **Obv:** Head left within circle, stars 3/4 surround, date below **Rev:** Denomination and globe **Edge:** Grooved

Date	Mintage	F	VF	XF	Unc	BU
2001 In sets only	40,000	—	—	—	—	—

Note: Only available in sets at present, circulation strikes not yet released

Date	Mintage	F	VF	XF	Unc	BU
2001 Proof	15,000	Value: 15.00				
2002 In sets only	140,000	—	—	—	—	6.50
2002 Proof	15,000	Value: 12.00				
2003	40,135,000	—	—	0.30	0.75	1.00
2003 Proof	15,000	Value: 12.00				
2004	140,000,000	—	—	0.30	0.75	1.00
2004 Proof	15,000	Value: 12.00				
2005 In sets only	—	—	—	—	—	1.00
2005 Proof	—	Value: 12.00				
2006	30,000,000	—	—	0.30	0.75	1.00
2006 Proof	—	Value: 12.00				
2007	70,000,000	—	—	0.30	0.75	1.00
2007 Proof	—	Value: 12.00				

KM# 275 2 EURO CENT
3.0600 g., Copper Plated Steel, 18.75 mm. **Ruler:** Albert II **Obv:** Head of Albert II left, crowned monogram at right, date below **Edge:** Grooved

Date	Mintage	F	VF	XF	Unc	BU
2008	40,000,000	—	—	—	0.75	1.00
2008 Proof	—	Value: 12.00				
2009	10,000,000	—	—	—	0.75	1.00
2009 Proof	1,500	Value: 12.00				
2010	20,000,000	—	—	—	0.75	1.00
2010 Proof	1,850	Value: 12.00				
2011	—	—	—	—	—	1.00
2011 Proof	1,850	Value: 12.00				
2012	—	—	—	—	—	1.00
2012 Proof	1,850	Value: 12.00				

KM# 226 5 EURO CENT
3.9200 g., Copper Plated Steel, 21.25 mm. **Ruler:** Albert II **Obv:** Head left within circle, stars 3/4 surround, date below **Rev:** Denomination and globe **Edge:** Plain

Date	Mintage	F	VF	XF	Unc	BU
2001 In sets only	40,000	—	—	—	—	12.50
2001 Proof	15,000	Value: 15.00				
2002 In sets only	140,000	—	—	—	—	8.00
2002 Proof	15,000	Value: 15.00				
2003	30,135,000	—	—	0.30	0.80	1.20
2003 Proof	15,000	Value: 12.00				
2004	75,000,000	—	—	0.30	0.80	1.20
2004 Proof	—	Value: 12.00				
2005	110,000,000	—	—	0.30	0.80	1.20
2005 Proof	3,000	Value: 12.00				
2006	35,000,000	—	—	0.30	0.80	1.20
2006 Proof	—	Value: 12.00				
2007 In sets only	—	—	—	—	—	8.00
2007 Proof	—	Value: 12.00				

KM# 276 5 EURO CENT
3.9200 g., Copper Plated Steel, 21.25 mm. **Ruler:** Albert II **Obv:** Redesigned head of Albert II left

Date	Mintage	F	VF	XF	Unc	BU
2008	—	—	—	—	—	2.00
2008 Proof	—	Value: 12.00				
2009	—	—	—	—	—	1.20
2009 Proof	1,500	Value: 12.00				
2010	25,000,000	—	—	—	0.75	1.20
2010 Proof	1,850	Value: 12.00				
2011	—	—	—	—	—	1.20
2011 Proof	1,850	Value: 12.00				
2012	—	—	—	—	—	1.20
2012 Proof	1,850	Value: 12.00				

KM# 227 10 EURO CENT
4.1000 g., Brass, 19.75 mm. **Ruler:** Albert II **Obv:** Head left within inner circle, stars 3/4 surround, date below **Rev:** Denomination and map **Edge:** Reeded

Date	Mintage	F	VF	XF	Unc	BU
2001	145,790,000	—	—	—	0.75	1.25
2001 Proof	15,000	Value: 12.00				

Date	Mintage	F	VF	XF	Unc	BU
2002 In sets only	140,000	—	—	—	6.00	8.00
2002 Proof	15,000	Value: 15.00				
2003 In sets only	135,000	—	—	—	6.00	8.00
2003 Proof	15,000	Value: 15.00				
2004	20,000,000	—	—	—	1.00	1.50
2004 Proof	—	Value: 12.00				
2005	10,000,000	—	—	—	1.00	1.50
2005 Proof	3,000	Value: 12.00				
2006 In sets only	—	—	—	—	1.00	1.50
2006 Proof	—	Value: 12.00				

KM# 242 10 EURO CENT
4.1000 g., Brass, 19.75 mm. **Ruler:** Albert II **Obv:** King's portrait **Rev:** Relief map of Western Europe, stars, lines and value **Edge:** Reeded

Date	Mintage	F	VF	XF	Unc	BU
2007	—	—	—	—	1.00	1.50
2007 Proof	—	Value: 12.00				

KM# 277 10 EURO CENT
4.1000 g., Brass, 19.75 mm. **Ruler:** Albert II **Obv:** Head of Albert II left, crowned monogram right, date below **Edge:** Reeded

Date	Mintage	F	VF	XF	Unc	BU
2008	—	—	—	—	—	6.00
2008 Proof	—	Value: 12.00				
2009	—	—	—	—	—	1.50
2009 Proof	1,500	Value: 12.00				
2010	20,000,000	—	—	—	1.00	1.50
2010 Proof	1,850	Value: 12.00				
2011	—	—	—	—	1.00	1.50
2011 Proof	1,850	Value: 12.00				
2012	—	—	—	—	—	1.50
2012 Proof	1,850	Value: 12.00				

KM# 228 20 EURO CENT
5.7400 g., Brass, 22.25 mm. **Ruler:** Albert II **Obv:** Head left within circle, stars 3/4 surround, date below **Rev:** Denomination and map **Edge:** Notched

Date	Mintage	F	VF	XF	Unc	BU
2001 In sets only	40,000	—	—	—	10.00	12.50

Note: Only available in sets at present, circulation strikes not yet released

Date	Mintage	F	VF	XF	Unc	BU
2001 Proof	15,000	Value: 15.00				
2002	104,140,000	—	—	—	1.00	1.50
2002 Proof	15,000	Value: 12.00				
2003	30,135,000	—	—	—	1.25	1.75
2003 Proof	15,000	Value: 12.00				
2004	109,550,000	—	—	—	1.25	1.75
2004 Proof	—	Value: 12.00				
2005	10,000,000	—	—	—	1.25	1.75
2005 Proof	3,000	Value: 12.00				
2006	40,000,000	—	—	—	1.25	1.75
2006 Proof	—	Value: 12.00				

KM# 243 20 EURO CENT
5.7400 g., Brass, 22.25 mm. **Ruler:** Albert II **Obv:** King's portrait **Rev:** Relief map of Western Europe, stars, lines and value **Edge:** Notched

Date	Mintage	F	VF	XF	Unc	BU
2007	—	—	—	—	1.25	1.75
2007 Proof	—	Value: 12.00				

KM# 278 20 EURO CENT
5.7400 g., Brass, 22.25 mm. **Ruler:** Albert II **Obv:** Redesigned head of Albert II left **Edge:** Notched

Date	Mintage	F	VF	XF	Unc	BU
2008	—	—	—	—	—	2.00
2008 Proof	—	Value: 12.00				
2009	30,100,000	—	—	—	1.25	1.75
2009 Proof	1,500	Value: 12.00				
2010	15,000,000	—	—	—	1.25	1.75
2010 Proof	1,850	Value: 12.00				
2011	—	—	—	—	1.25	1.75
2011 Proof	1,850	Value: 12.00				
2012	—	—	—	—	—	1.75
2012 Proof	1,850	Value: 12.00				

KM# 229 50 EURO CENT
7.8000 g., Brass, 24.25 mm. **Ruler:** Albert II **Obv:** Head left within circle, stars 3/4 surround, date below **Rev:** Denomination and map **Edge:** Reeded

Date	Mintage	F	VF	XF	Unc	BU
2001 In sets only	40,000	—	—	—	10.00	12.50
2001 Proof	15,000	Value: 15.00				
2002	50,040,000	—	—	—	1.00	1.50
2002 Proof	15,000	Value: 12.00				
2003 In sets only	135,000	—	—	—	—	12.50
2003 Proof	15,000	Value: 12.00				
2004	8,000,000	—	—	—	1.25	1.75
2004 Proof	—	Value: 12.00				
2005 In sets only	—	—	—	—	—	12.50
2005 Proof	3,000	Value: 12.00				
2006 In sets only	—	—	—	—	—	12.50
2006 Proof	—	Value: 12.00				

KM# 244 50 EURO CENT
7.8000 g., Brass, 24.25 mm. **Ruler:** Albert II **Obv:** King's portrait **Rev:** Relief map of Western Europe, stars, lines and value **Edge:** Reeded

Date	Mintage	F	VF	XF	Unc	BU
2007	—	—	—	—	1.25	1.75
2007 Proof	—	Value: 12.00				

KM# 279 50 EURO CENT
7.8000 g., Brass, 24.25 mm. **Ruler:** Albert II **Obv:** Redesigned head of Albert II left **Edge:** Reeded

Date	Mintage	F	VF	XF	Unc	BU
2008	25,000,000	—	—	—	—	4.00
2008 Proof	—	Value: 12.00				
2009	30,000,000	—	—	—	2.00	3.00
2009 Proof	1,500	Value: 12.00				
2010	—	—	—	—	—	3.00
2010 Proof	1,850	Value: 12.00				
2011	—	—	—	—	—	3.00
2011 Proof	1,850	Value: 12.00				
2012	—	—	—	—	—	3.00
2012 Proof	1,850	Value: 12.00				

KM# 230 EURO
7.5000 g., Bi-Metallic Copper-Nickel center in Nickel-Brass ring, 23.25 mm. **Ruler:** Albert II **Obv:** Head left within circle, stars 3/4 surround, date below **Rev:** Denomination and map **Edge:** Segmented reeding

Date	Mintage	F	VF	XF	Unc	BU
2001 In sets only	40,000	—	—	—	—	15.00

Note: Only available in sets at present, circulation strikes not yet released

Date	Mintage	F	VF	XF	Unc	BU
2001 Proof	15,000	Value: 18.00				
2002	90,640,000	—	—	—	3.00	5.00

Note: Only a fraction of the mintage released at present

Date	Mintage	F	VF	XF	Unc	BU
2002 Proof	15,000	Value: 15.00				
2003	6,000,000	—	—	—	3.00	5.00
2003 Proof	15,000	Value: 15.00				
2004	15,000,000	—	—	—	3.00	5.00
2004 Proof	—	Value: 15.00				
2005 In sets only	—	—	—	—	—	15.00
2005 Proof	3,000	Value: 15.00				
2006 In sets only	—	—	—	—	—	15.00
2006 Proof	—	Value: 15.00				

KM# 245 EURO
7.5000 g., Bi-Metallic Copper-Nickel center in Nickel-Brass ring, 23.25 mm. **Ruler:** Albert II **Obv:** King's portrait **Rev:** Relief map of Western Europe, stars, lines and value **Edge:** Segmented reeding

Date	Mintage	F	VF	XF	Unc	BU
2007	—	—	—	—	3.00	5.00
2007 Proof	—	Value: 15.00				

KM# 280 EURO
7.5000 g., Bi-Metallic Copper-Nickel center in Nickel-Brass ring, 23.25 mm. **Ruler:** Albert II **Obv:** Redesigned head of Albert II left **Edge:** Segmented reeding

Date	Mintage	F	VF	XF	Unc	BU
2008	—	—	—	—	—	6.00
2008 Proof	—	Value: 15.00				
2009	10,000,000	—	—	—	3.00	5.00
2009 Proof	1,500	Value: 15.00				
2010	—	—	—	—	—	5.00
2010 Proof	1,850	Value: 15.00				
2011	—	—	—	—	—	5.00
2011 Proof	1,850	Value: 15.00				
2012	—	—	—	—	—	5.00
2012 Proof	1,850	Value: 15.00				

KM# 231 2 EURO
8.5000 g., Bi-Metallic Nickel-Brass center in Copper-Nickel ring, 25.75 mm. **Ruler:** Albert II **Obv:** Head left within circle, stars 3/4 surround, date below **Rev:** Denomination and map **Edge:** Reeded with 2's and stars

Date	Mintage	F	VF	XF	Unc	BU
2001 In sets only	40,000	—	—	—	12.50	15.00

Note: Only available in sets at present, circulation strikes not yet released

Date	Mintage	F	VF	XF	Unc	BU
2001 Proof	15,000	Value: 20.00				
2002	50,140,000	—	—	—	3.75	6.00
2002 Proof	15,000	Value: 18.00				
2003	30,135,000	—	—	—	3.75	6.00
2003 Proof	15,000	Value: 18.00				
2004	65,500,000	—	—	—	3.75	6.00
2004 Proof	—	Value: 18.00				
2005	10,500,000	—	—	—	3.75	6.00
2005 Proof	3,000	Value: 18.00				
2006	20,000,000	—	—	—	3.75	6.00
2006 Proof	—	Value: 18.00				

KM# 240 2 EURO
8.5000 g., Bi-Metallic Nickel-Brass center in Copper-Nickel ring, 25.75 mm. **Ruler:** Albert II **Subject:** Schengen Agreement **Obv:** Albert II of Belgium and Henri of Luxembourg **Rev:** Value and map **Edge:** Reeded with 2's and stars

Date	Mintage	F	VF	XF	Unc	BU
2005	5,977,000	—	—	—	5.00	7.50
2005 Prooflike	20,000	—	—	—	—	20.00
2005 Proof	3,000	Value: 25.00				

KM# 241   2 EURO
8.5000 g., Bi-Metallic Nickel-Brass center in Copper-Nickel ring, 25.75 mm.   **Ruler:** Albert II **Obv:** Atomic model **Rev:** Value and map **Edge:** Reeded with 2's and stars

Date	Mintage	F	VF	XF	Unc	BU
2006	4,977,000	—	—	—	4.00	6.00
2006 Prooflike	20,000	—	—	—	—	25.00
2006 Proof	3,000	Value: 100				

KM# 246   2 EURO
8.5000 g., Bi-Metallic Nickel-Brass center in Copper-Nickel ring, 25.75 mm.   **Ruler:** Albert II **Obv:** King's portrait **Rev:** Relief map of Western Europe, stars, lines and value **Edge:** Reeded with 2's and stars

Date	Mintage	F	VF	XF	Unc	BU
2007	—	—	—	—	3.75	6.00
2007 Proof	—	Value: 25.00				

KM# 247   2 EURO
8.5000 g., Bi-Metallic Nickel-Brass center in Copper-Nickel ring, 25.75 mm.   **Ruler:** Albert II **Subject:** 50th Anniversary Treaty of Rome **Obv:** Open treaty book **Rev:** Large value at left, modified outline of Europe at right **Edge:** Reeded with stars and 2's

Date	Mintage	F	VF	XF	Unc	BU
2007	4,960,000	—	—	—	—	9.00
2007 Prooflike	35,000	—	—	—	—	25.00
2007 Proof	10,000	Value: 75.00				

KM# 248   2 EURO
8.5000 g., Bi-Metallic Nickel-Brass center in Copper-Nickel ring, 25.75 mm.   **Ruler:** Albert II **Subject:** Universal Declaration of Human Rights **Obv:** Book in bow **Rev:** Large value "2" at left, modified map of Europe at right **Edge:** Reeded with 2's and stars

Date	Mintage	F	VF	XF	Unc	BU
2008	—	—	—	—	—	6.00

KM# 281   2 EURO
8.5000 g., Bi-Metallic Nickel-Brass center in Copper-Nickel ring, 25.75 mm.   **Ruler:** Albert II **Obv:** Head of Albert II left, crowned monogram right, date below **Edge:** Reeded with 2's and stars

Date	Mintage	F	VF	XF	Unc	BU
2008	—	—	—	—	—	7.50
2008 Proof	—	Value: 18.00				
2009	—	—	—	—	4.00	6.00
2009 Proof	—	Value: 18.00				
2010	—	—	—	—	4.00	6.00
2010 Proof	—	Value: 18.00				
2011	—	—	—	—	4.00	6.00
2011 Proof	—	Value: 18.00				

KM# 282   2 EURO
8.5000 g., Bi-Metallic Nickel-Brass center in Copper-Nickel ring, 25.75 mm.   **Ruler:** Albert II **Subject:** 10th Anniversary of EMU **Obv:** Stick figure and E symbol **Edge:** Reeded with 2's and stars

Date	Mintage	F	VF	XF	Unc	BU
2009	5,000,000	—	—	—	15.00	
2009 Prooflike	—	—	—	—	—	20.00
2009 Proof	—	Value: 70.00				

KM# 288   2 EURO
8.5000 g., Bi-Metallic Nickel-Brass center in Copper-Nickel ring, 25.75 mm.   **Ruler:** Albert II **Subject:** Louis Braille, 200th Anniversary of Birth **Obv:** Bust right with braile text **Edge:** Reeded with 2's and stars

Date	Mintage	F	VF	XF	Unc	BU
2009	5,000,000	—	—	—	—	5.00

KM# 289   2 EURO
8.5000 g., Bi-Metallic Nickel-Brass center in Copper-Nickel ring, 25.75 mm.   **Ruler:** Albert II **Subject:** EU Council Presidency **Rev:** eu in script **Edge:** Reeded with 2's and stars

Date	Mintage	F	VF	XF	Unc	BU
2010	—	—	—	—	3.00	7.50

KM# 308   2 EURO
8.5000 g., Bi-Metallic Nickel-Brass center in Copper-Nickel ring, 25.75 mm.   **Ruler:** Albert II **Subject:** International Women's Day, 100th Anniversary **Obv:** Portraits of I. van Diest and M. Popelin

Date	Mintage	F	VF	XF	Unc	BU
2011	5,000,000	—	—	—	9.00	12.50
2011 Special Unc.	6,000	—	—	—	—	15.00
2011 Proof	7,500	Value: 25.00				

KM# 315   2 EURO
8.5000 g., Bi-Metallic Nickel-Brass center in Copper-Nickel ring, 25.75 mm.   **Ruler:** Albert II **Subject:** Euro coinage, 10th Anniversary **Obv:** Euro symbol on globe, child-like rendering around

Date	Mintage	F	VF	XF	Unc	BU
2012	6,000,000	—	—	—	6.00	8.00
2012 Special Unc.	—	—	—	—	—	15.00
2012 Proof	—	Value: 25.00				

KM# 270   5 EURO
14.6000 g., 0.9250 Silver 0.4342 oz. ASW, 30 mm.   **Ruler:** Albert II **Subject:** Smurfs - 50th Anniversary **Obv:** Map of Western Europe **Rev:** Smurf

Date	Mintage	F	VF	XF	Unc	BU
2008 Proof	25,000	Value: 50.00				

KM# 270a   5 EURO
14.6000 g., 0.9250 Silver 0.4342 oz. ASW, 30 mm.   **Ruler:** Albert II **Subject:** Smurf - 50th Anniversary **Obv:** Map of Western Europe **Rev:** Multicolor 50 and Smurf

Date	Mintage	F	VF	XF	Unc	BU
2008 Proof	—	Value: 75.00				

KM# 303   5 EURO
14.6000 g., 0.9250 Silver 0.4342 oz. ASW, 30 mm.   **Ruler:** Albert II **Subject:** Belgian Railways, 175th Anniversary

Date	Mintage	F	VF	XF	Unc	BU
2010 Proof	—	Value: 50.00				

KM# 313   5 EURO
14.6000 g., 0.9250 Silver 0.4342 oz. ASW, 30 mm.   **Ruler:** Albert II **Subject:** Helene Dutrieu, Belgium's first female aviator **Obv:** Euro zone map **Rev:** Female portrait at left, biplane at right

Date	Mintage	F	VF	XF	Unc	BU
2011 Proof	—	Value: 50.00				

KM# 233   10 EURO
18.9300 g., 0.9250 Silver 0.5629 oz. ASW, 32.9 mm.   **Ruler:** Albert II **Subject:** Belgian Railway System **Obv:** Value, head at right transposed on map **Rev:** Train exiting tunnel **Edge:** Reeded

Date	Mintage	F	VF	XF	Unc	BU
ND (2002) Proof	50,000	Value: 50.00				

KM# 235   10 EURO
18.9300 g., 0.9250 Silver 0.5629 oz. ASW, 32.9 mm.   **Ruler:** Albert II **Subject:** "Simenon" **Edge:** Reeded

Date	Mintage	F	VF	XF	Unc	BU
2003 Proof	50,000	Value: 40.00				

KM# 236   10 EURO
18.9300 g., 0.9250 Silver 0.5629 oz. ASW, 32.9 mm.   **Ruler:** Albert II **Subject:** "Tintin" **Edge:** Reeded

Date	Mintage	F	VF	XF	Unc	BU
2004 Proof	50,000	Value: 85.00				

KM# 234   10 EURO
18.7500 g., 0.9250 Silver 0.5576 oz. ASW, 33 mm.   **Ruler:** Albert II **Obv:** Value **Rev:** Western Europe map and Goddess Europa riding a bull **Edge:** Reeded

Date	Mintage	F	VF	XF	Unc	BU
2004 Proof	50,000	Value: 40.00				

KM# 252   10 EURO
18.7500 g., 0.9250 Silver 0.5576 oz. ASW, 33 mm.   **Ruler:** Albert II **Subject:** 60th Anniversary of Liberation **Obv:** Map of Western Europe and stars **Rev:** Phoenix

Date	Mintage	F	VF	XF	Unc	BU
2005 Proof	50,000	Value: 50.00				

KM# 251   10 EURO
18.7500 g., 0.9250 Silver 0.5576 oz. ASW, 33 mm.   **Ruler:** Albert II **Subject:** Netherland-Belgium Soccer, 75th Anniversary **Obv:** Map of Western Europe and stars **Rev:** Soccer Player

Date	Mintage	F	VF	XF	Unc	BU
2005 Proof	50,000	Value: 45.00				

KM# 255   10 EURO
18.7500 g., 0.9250 Silver 0.5576 oz. ASW, 33 mm.   **Ruler:** Albert II **Subject:** Justus Lipsius, 400th Anniversary of Death

Obv: Map of Western Europe and stars **Rev:** Half-length figure of Justus Lipsius

Date	Mintage	F	VF	XF	Unc	BU
2006 Proof	50,000		Value: 45.00			

KM# 257 10 EURO
18.7500 g., 0.9250 Silver 0.5576 oz. ASW, 33 mm. **Ruler:** Albert II **Subject:** 50th Anniversary - Mine Accident in Marcinelle **Obv:** Map of Western Europe and stars **Rev:** Male head and industrial mine scene

Date	Mintage	F	VF	XF	Unc	BU
2006 Proof	50,000		Value: 45.00			

KM# 257a 10 EURO
18.7500 g., 0.9250 Silver 0.5576 oz. ASW, 33 mm. **Ruler:** Albert II **Subject:** 50th Anniversary, Mine Accident in Marcinelle **Obv:** Map of Western Europe and stars **Rev:** Multicolor male head and industrial mine scene

Date	Mintage	F	VF	XF	Unc	BU
2006 Proof	2,000		Value: 75.00			

KM# 260 10 EURO
18.7500 g., 0.9250 Silver 0.5576 oz. ASW, 33 mm. **Ruler:** Albert II **Subject:** Treaty of Rome, 50th Anniversary **Obv:** Map of Western Europe **Rev:** Document and feather pen

Date	Mintage	F	VF	XF	Unc	BU
2007 Proof	40,000		Value: 45.00			

KM# 263 10 EURO
18.7500 g., 0.9250 Silver 0.5576 oz. ASW, 33 mm. **Ruler:** Albert II **Subject:** International Polar Year **Obv:** Map of Western Europe **Rev:** Wind farm and polar station

Date	Mintage	F	VF	XF	Unc	BU
2007 Proof	40,000		Value: 50.00			

KM# 266 10 EURO
18.7500 g., 0.9250 Silver 0.5576 oz. ASW, 33 mm. **Ruler:** Albert II **Subject:** 100th Anniversary Maurice Maeterlinck **Obv:** Map of Western Europe **Rev:** Gateway and dome in blue

Date	Mintage	F	VF	XF	Unc	BU
2008 Proof	20,000		Value: 75.00			

KM# 268 10 EURO
18.7500 g., 0.9250 Silver 0.5576 oz. ASW, 33 mm. **Ruler:** Albert II **Subject:** Beijing Olympics **Obv:** Map of Western Europe **Rev:** Sport events, logo and torch

Date	Mintage	F	VF	XF	Unc	BU
2008 Proof	20,000		Value: 50.00			

KM# 284 10 EURO
18.7500 g., 0.9250 Silver 0.5576 oz. ASW **Ruler:** Albert II **Subject:** 75th Birthday of the King **Obv:** Head at left, laurel sprigs

Date	Mintage	F	VF	XF	Unc	BU
2009	—	—	—	—	—	50.00

KM# 285 10 EURO
18.7500 g., 0.9250 Silver 0.5576 oz. ASW **Ruler:** Albert II **Subject:** Erasmus

Date	Mintage	F	VF	XF	Unc	BU
2009	—	—	—	—	—	50.00

KM# 290 10 EURO
18.7500 g., 0.9250 Silver 0.5576 oz. ASW, 33 mm. **Ruler:** Albert II **Subject:** Royal Museum for Central Asia 100th Anniversary

Date	Mintage	F	VF	XF	Unc	BU
2010	—	—	—	—	—	45.00

KM# 291 10 EURO
18.7500 g., 0.9250 Silver 0.5576 oz. ASW, 33 mm. **Ruler:** Albert II **Subject:** Jean Django' Reinhart Birth Centennial

Date	Mintage	F	VF	XF	Unc	BU
2010 Proof	—		Value: 45.00			

KM# 304 10 EURO
18.7500 g., 0.9250 Silver 0.5576 oz. ASW, 33 mm. **Ruler:** Albert II **Subject:** Jean "Django" Reinhardt, 100th Anniversary of Birth

Date	Mintage	F	VF	XF	Unc	BU
2010 Proof	—		Value: 50.00			

KM# 309 10 EURO
18.7500 g., 0.9250 Silver 0.5576 oz. ASW, 33 mm. **Ruler:** Albert II **Subject:** Discovery of the South Pole **Obv:** Euro zone map **Rev:** Map, dog sled, Roald Amundsen

Date	Mintage	F	VF	XF	Unc	BU
2011 Proof	—		Value: 50.00			

KM# 311 10 EURO
18.7500 g., 0.9250 Silver 0.5576 oz. ASW, 33 mm. **Ruler:** Albert II **Obv:** Euro zone map, partially gilt **Rev:** Belgian deep sea exploration

Date	Mintage	F	VF	XF	Unc	BU
2011 Proof	—		Value: 50.00			

KM# 259 12 1/2 EURO
1.2500 g., 0.9990 Gold 0.0401 oz. AGW, 13.92 mm. **Ruler:** Albert II **Subject:** Saxe-Coburg-Gotha, 175th Anniversary **Obv:** Lion and tablet with constitution **Rev:** Head of Leopold I left

Date	Mintage	F	VF	XF	Unc	BU
2006 Proof	15,000		Value: 75.00			

KM# 265 12 1/2 EURO
1.2500 g., 0.9990 Gold 0.0401 oz. AGW, 13.92 mm. **Subject:** 175th Anniversary Saxe-Coburg-Gotha **Obv:** Lion and tablet **Rev:** Leopold II head left

Date	Mintage	F	VF	XF	Unc	BU
2007 Proof	15,000		Value: 75.00			

KM# 271 12 1/2 EURO
1.2500 g., 0.9990 Gold 0.0401 oz. AGW, 13.92 mm. **Ruler:** Albert II **Subject:** 175th Anniversary - Saxe-Coburg-Gotha **Obv:** Lion and tablet **Rev:** Albert I bust right

Date	Mintage	F	VF	XF	Unc	BU
2008 Proof	15,000		Value: 75.00			

KM# 292 12 1/2 EURO
1.2440 g., 0.9990 Gold 0.0400 oz. AGW, 14 mm. **Ruler:** Albert II **Subject:** Leopold III

Date	Mintage	F	VF	XF	Unc	BU
2009 Proof	—		Value: 85.00			

KM# 293 12 1/2 EURO
0.9990 Gold, 14 mm. **Ruler:** Albert II

Date	Mintage	F	VF	XF	Unc	BU
2010 Proof	—		Value: 85.00			

KM# 254 20 EURO
22.8500 g., 0.9990 Silver 0.7339 oz. ASW, 37 mm. **Ruler:** Albert II **Subject:** FIFA World Cup in Germany **Obv:** Albert II head left **Rev:** Soccer player with ball

Date	Mintage	F	VF	XF	Unc	BU
2005 Proof	25,000		Value: 65.00			

KM# 262 20 EURO
22.8500 g., 0.9250 Silver 0.6795 oz. ASW, 37 mm. **Ruler:** Albert II **Subject:** Georges Remi, 100th Anniversary of Birth **Obv:** Map of Western Europe and stars **Rev:** Profile of Georges Renir and his character Tin Tin right

Date	Mintage	F	VF	XF	Unc	BU
2007 Proof	50,000		Value: 75.00			

KM# 287 20 EURO
22.8500 g., 0.9500 Silver 0.6979 oz. ASW, 37 mm. **Ruler:** Albert II **Obv:** Value and map of euro countries **Rev:** Fr. Damien and churches in Tremblo and Molokai, date of canionization below

Date	Mintage	F	VF	XF	Unc	BU
2009 Proof	15,000		Value: 75.00			

KM# 305 20 EURO
22.8500 g., 0.9250 Silver 0.6795 oz. ASW, 37 mm. **Ruler:** Albert II **Subject:** A Dog of Flanders

Date	Mintage	F	VF	XF	Unc	BU
2010 Proof	—		Value: 75.00			

KM# 269 25 EURO
3.1100 g., 0.9990 Gold 0.0999 oz. AGW, 18 mm. **Ruler:** Albert II **Subject:** Beijing Olympics **Obv:** Map of Western Europe **Rev:** Sport events, logo, torch

Date	Mintage	F	VF	XF	Unc	BU
2008 Proof	5,000		Value: 200			

KM# 294 25 EURO
3.1100 g., 0.9990 Gold 0.0999 oz. AGW, 18 mm. **Ruler:** Albert II **Subject:** Bejing Olympics

Date	Mintage	F	VF	XF	Unc	BU
2008 Proof	4,050		Value: 250			

KM# 250 50 EURO
6.2200 g., 0.9990 Gold 0.1998 oz. AGW, 21 mm. **Ruler:** Albert II **Subject:** Albert II, 70th Birthday **Obv:** Map of Western Europe and stars **Rev:** Portrait of Albert II

Date	Mintage	F	VF	XF	Unc	BU
2004 Proof	10,000		Value: 350			

KM# 256 50 EURO
6.2200 g., 0.9990 Gold 0.1998 oz. AGW, 21 mm. **Ruler:** Albert II **Subject:** Justus Lipsius, 400th Anniversary of Death **Obv:** Map of Western Europe and stars **Rev:** Half-length figure of Justus Lipius right

Date	Mintage	F	VF	XF	Unc	BU
2006 Proof	2,500		Value: 365			

KM# 261 50 EURO
6.2200 g., 0.9990 Gold 0.1998 oz. AGW, 21 mm. **Ruler:** Albert II **Subject:** Treaty of Rome, 50th Anniversary **Obv:** Map of Western Europe **Rev:** Document and feather pen

Date	Mintage	F	VF	XF	Unc	BU
2007 Proof	2,500		Value: 365			

KM# 267 50 EURO
6.2200 g., 0.9990 Gold 0.1998 oz. AGW, 21 mm. **Ruler:** Albert II **Subject:** 100th Anniversary Maurice Maeterlinck **Obv:** Map of Western Europe **Rev:** Gate and dove

Date	Mintage	F	VF	XF	Unc	BU
2008 Proof	2,500		Value: 400			

KM# 286 50 EURO
8.4500 g., 0.9990 Gold 0.2714 oz. AGW **Ruler:** Albert II **Subject:** Erasmus

Date	Mintage	F	VF	XF	Unc	BU
2009	—	—	—	—	—	425

KM# 306 50 EURO
6.2200 g., 0.9990 Gold 0.1998 oz. AGW, 22 mm. **Ruler:** Albert II **Subject:** Royal Museum for Central Africa

Date	Mintage	F	VF	XF	Unc	BU
2010 Proof	—		Value: 400			

KM# 310 50 EURO
8.4500 g., 0.9990 Gold 0.2714 oz. AGW, 22 mm. **Ruler:** Albert II **Obv:** Euro zone map **Rev:** Four men standing around flag, Roald Amundsen profile at right

Date	Mintage	F	VF	XF	Unc	BU
2011 Proof	—		Value: 550			

KM# 312 50 EURO
6.2200 g., 0.9990 Gold 0.1998 oz. AGW, 22 mm. **Ruler:** Albert II **Obv:** Euro zone map **Rev:** Belgian deep sea exploration

Date	Mintage	F	VF	XF	Unc	BU
2011 Proof	2,500		Value: 550			

KM# 237 100 EURO
15.5500 g., 0.9990 Gold 0.4994 oz. AGW, 29 mm. **Ruler:** Albert II **Subject:** Founding Fathers

Date	Mintage	F	VF	XF	Unc	BU
2002 Proof	5,000		Value: 850			

KM# 238 100 EURO
15.5500 g., 0.9990 Gold 0.4994 oz. AGW, 29 mm. **Ruler:** Albert II **Subject:** 10th Anniversary of Reign

Date	Mintage	F	VF	XF	Unc	BU
2003 Proof	5,000		Value: 850			

KM# 239 100 EURO
15.5500 g., 0.9990 Gold 0.4994 oz. AGW, 29 mm. **Ruler:** Albert II **Subject:** Franc Germinal

Date	Mintage	F	VF	XF	Unc	BU
2004 Proof	5,000		Value: 850			

KM# 253 100 EURO
15.5500 g., 0.9990 Gold 0.4994 oz. AGW, 29 mm. **Ruler:** Albert II **Subject:** 175th Anniversary of Liberty **Obv:** Albert II head left **Rev:** Scene of the 1830 Revolution

Date	Mintage	F	VF	XF	Unc	BU
2005 Proof	5,000		Value: 850			

KM# 258 100 EURO
15.5500 g., 0.9990 Gold 0.4994 oz. AGW, 29 mm. **Ruler:** Albert II **Subject:** Saxe-Coburg-Gotha, 175th Anniversary **Obv:** Map of Western Europe and stars **Rev:** Church in Laeken, Kings monogram around

Date	Mintage	F	VF	XF	Unc	BU
2006 Proof	5,000		Value: 850			

KM# 264 100 EURO
15.5500 g., 0.9990 Gold 0.4994 oz. AGW, 29 mm. **Ruler:** Albert II **Subject:** Belgian Coins 175th Anniversary **Obv:** Map of Western Europe **Rev:** Screw press, coin designs

Date	Mintage	F	VF	XF	Unc	BU
2007 Proof	5,000		Value: 850			

KM# 272 100 EURO
15.5500 g., 0.9990 Gold 0.4994 oz. AGW, 29 mm. **Ruler:** Albert II **Subject:** 50th Anniversary: Brussels Exposition **Obv:** Map of Western Europe

Date	Mintage	F	VF	XF	Unc	BU
2008 Proof	5,000	Value: 850				

KM# 283 100 EURO
15.5500 g., 0.9990 Gold 0.4994 oz. AGW **Ruler:** Albert II **Subject:** Royal Wedding Anniversary **Obv:** Conjoined leads at right

Date	Mintage	F	VF	XF	Unc	BU
2009 Proof	—	Value: 850				

KM# 314 100 EURO
15.5500 g., 0.9990 Gold 0.4994 oz. AGW, 29 mm. **Ruler:** Albert II **Subject:** Victor Horta **Obv:** Euro zone map **Rev:** Bust at left, flora

Date	Mintage	F	VF	XF	Unc	BU
2011 Proof	—	Value: 950				

MINT SETS

KM#	Date	Mintage	Identification	Issue Price	Mkt Val
MS14	2001 (10)	60,000	KM#148.1, 149.1, 187-194	15.00	45.00
MS15	1999/2000/2001 (24)	40,000	Euro Intro	—	250
MS16	2002 (8)	100,000	KM#224-231, 700th Anniversary	—	62.50
MS17	2002 (8)	20,000	KM#224-231, Cycling	—	62.50
MS18	2002 (8)	20,000	KM#224-231, Euros plus waffle francs	—	62.50
MS19	2003 (8)	100,000	KM#224-231, Television 50th	—	37.50
MS20	2003 (8)	15,000	KM#224-231, Ford Production in Belgium Centennial	—	37.50
MS21	2003 (8)	10,000	KM#224-231, Rose	—	37.50
MS22	2003 (8)	10,000	KM#224-231, Baby	—	37.50
MS23.1	2004 (9)	60,000	KM#224-231, Belgian Red Cross, plain medal	—	25.00
MS23.2	2004 (9)	2,000	KM#224-231, Belgian Red Cross, enameled medal	—	175
MS24	2004 (9)	5,000	KM#224-231, Love, medal for engraving	—	37.50
MS25	2004 (9)	5,000	KM#224-231, Baby, medal for engraving	—	37.50
MS26.1	2005 (9)	38,000	KM#224-231, Grand Palace, UNESCO site, plain medal	—	60.00
MS26.2	2005 (9)	2,000	KM#224-231, Grand Palace, UNESCO site, gilt medal	—	85.00
MS27.1	2006 (9)	38,000	KM#224-231, Flemish Houses, UNESCO site, plain medal	—	40.00
MS27.2	2006 (9)	2,000	KM#224-231, Flemish Houses, UNESCO site, colored medal	—	75.00
MS28.1	2007 (9)	38,000	KM#224-226, 242-246, Canal, UNESCO site, plain medal	—	27.50
MS28.2	2007 (9)	2,000	KM#224-226, 242-246, Canal, UNESCO site, colored medal	—	70.00
MS29.1	2008 (9)	25,000	KM#274-281, Belltower, UNESCO site, plain medal	—	75.00
MS29.2	2008 (9)	2,000	KM#274-281, Belltower, UNESCO site, colored medal	—	85.00
MS30	2009 (8)	25,000	KM#274-281, plus medal	—	45.00
MS31	2010 (8)	30,000	KM#274-281, plus medal	—	45.00
MS32	2011 (8)	30,000	KM#274-281, plus medal	—	45.00

PROOF SETS

KM#	Date	Mintage	Identification	Issue Price	Mkt Val
PS10	2001 (8)	15,000	KM#224-231	80.00	125
PS11	2002 (8)	3,240	KM#224-231	80.00	115
PS12	2003 (8)	3,241	KM#224-231	80.00	110
PS13	2004 (8)	3,006	KM#224-231	80.00	105
PS14	2005 (8)	3,006	KM#224-231	—	110
PS15	2006 (8)	3,006	KM#224-231	—	115
PS17	2007 (8)	3,000	KM#224-226, 242-247	—	175
PS18	2008 (8)	2,500	KM#224-227, 276-278, 280-281	—	100
PS19	2009 (8)	1,500	KM#274-281	—	100
PS20	2010 (8)	1,850	KM#274-281	—	100
PS21	2011 (8)	1,850	KM#274-281	—	100

BELIZE

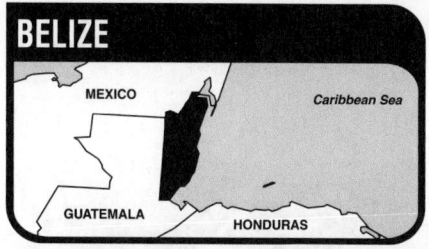

Belize, formerly British Honduras, but now a Constitutional Monarchy within the Commonwealth of Nations, is situated in Central America south of Mexico and east and north of Guatemala, with an area of 8,867 sq. mi. (22,960 sq. km.) and a population of *242,000. Capital: Belmopan. Tourism now augments Belize's economy, in addition to sugar, citrus fruits, chicle and hardwoods, which are exported.

MONETARY SYSTEM

Commencing 1864
100 Cents = 1 Dollar

COMMONWEALTH

DECIMAL COINAGE

KM# 33a CENT
0.8000 g., Aluminum, 19.5 mm. **Obv:** Bust of Queen Elizabeth right **Rev:** Denomination within circle **Edge:** Smooth, scalloped

Date	Mintage	F	VF	XF	Unc	BU
2002	—	—	—	0.10	0.15	0.45
2005	—	—	—	0.10	0.15	0.45
2007	—	—	—	0.10	0.15	0.45
2010	—	—	—	0.10	0.15	0.45

KM# 34a 5 CENTS
1.0400 g., Aluminum, 20.2 mm. **Obv:** Bust of Queen Elizabeth II right **Rev:** Denomination within circle **Edge:** Plain

Date	Mintage	F	VF	XF	Unc	BU
2002	—	—	—	0.10	0.20	0.45
2003	—	—	—	0.10	0.20	0.45
2005	—	—	—	0.10	0.20	0.45
2006	—	—	—	0.10	0.20	0.45
2009	—	—	—	0.10	0.20	0.45

KM# 115 5 CENTS
1.0500 g., Aluminum, 20.2 mm.

Date	Mintage	F	VF	XF	Unc	BU
2002	—	—	—	0.10	0.20	0.40

KM# 36 25 CENTS
5.6550 g., Copper-Nickel, 23.6 mm. **Obv:** Crowned bust of Queen Elizabeth II right **Rev:** Denomination within circle, date below **Edge:** Reeded

Date	Mintage	F	VF	XF	Unc	BU
2003	—	—	—	0.35	0.75	1.50
2007	—	—	—	0.35	0.75	1.50

KM# 37 50 CENTS
9.0700 g., Copper-Nickel, 27.74 mm. **Obv:** Crowned bust of

Queen Elizabeth right **Rev:** Denomination within circle, date below **Edge:** Reeded

Date	Mintage	F	VF	XF	Unc	BU
2010	—	—	—	1.00	2.00	3.00

KM# 134 DOLLAR
30.9400 g., 0.9990 Silver 0.9937 oz. ASW, 39.9 mm. **Subject:** Mayan King **Obv:** National arms **Rev:** Mayan portrait in ornate headdress **Edge:** Reeded

Date	Mintage	F	VF	XF	Unc	BU
2002	—	—	—	—	37.50	40.00

KM# 99 DOLLAR
8.9000 g., Nickel-Brass, 27 mm. **Obv:** Crowned bust of Queen Elizabeth II right **Rev:** Columbus' three ships, denomination above, date below **Edge:** Alternating reeded and plain **Shape:** 10-sided

Date	Mintage	F	VF	XF	Unc	BU
2003	—	—	—	—	2.25	3.00
2007	—	—	—	—	2.25	3.00

BENIN

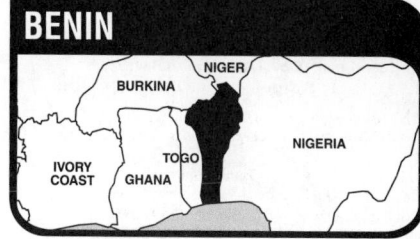

The Republic of Benin (formerly the Republic of Dahomey), located on the south side of the African bulge between Togo and Nigeria, has an area of 43,500 sq. mi. (112,620 sq. km.) and a population of 5.5 million. Capital: Porto-Novo. The principal industry of Benin, one of the poorest countries of West Africa, is the processing of palm oil products. Palm kernel oil, peanuts, cotton, and coffee are exported.

PEOPLES REPUBLIC

STANDARD COINAGE

KM# 53 100 CFA FRANCS
27.0000 g., Copper-Nickel Silver plated, 38.61 mm. **Rev:** Multicolor Cannabis Sativa, Aeromatic

Date	Mintage	F	VF	XF	Unc	BU
2010 Proof	2,500	Value: 60.00				

KM# 71   100 FRANCS
20.0000 g., 0.9990 Silver 0.6423 oz. ASW, 36 mm. **Obv:** State arms **Rev:** Steam train in colored forest scene

Date	Mintage	F	VF	XF	Unc	BU
2010 Proof	—				Value: 35.00	

KM# 63   500 FRANCS
Silver, 38.61 mm. **Obv:** National arms **Rev:** Euro coin motifs

Date	Mintage	F	VF	XF	Unc	BU
2002	—				Value: 45.00	

KM# 64   1000 FRANCS
Silver, 38.61 mm. **Obv:** National arms **Rev:** Zebra

Date	Mintage	F	VF	XF	Unc	BU
2001 Proof	—				Value: 45.00	

KM# 65   1000 FRANCS
Silver, 38.61 mm. **Obv:** National arms **Rev:** Giraffe

Date	Mintage	F	VF	XF	Unc	BU
2001 Proof	—				Value: 45.00	

KM# 66   1000 FRANCS
Silver, 38.61 mm. **Obv:** National arms **Rev:** Whale

Date	Mintage	F	VF	XF	Unc	BU
2001 Proof	—				Value: 65.00	

KM# 54   1000 FRANCS
20.0000 g., 0.9990 Silver 0.6423 oz. ASW, 36 mm. **Rev:** Multicolor Lockheed Orion

Date	Mintage	F	VF	XF	Unc	BU
2002 Proof	—				Value: 35.00	

KM# 55   1000 FRANCS
20.0000 g., 0.9990 Silver 0.6423 oz. ASW, 36 mm. **Rev:** Multicolor Convair 990 Coronado over mountains

Date	Mintage	F	VF	XF	Unc	BU
2002 Proof	—				Value: 35.00	

KM# 60   1000 FRANCS
Silver **Subject:** Sir Francis Drake and the Golden Hind

Date	Mintage	F	VF	XF	Unc	BU
2003 Proof	—				Value: 37.50	

KM# 62   1000 FRANCS
Silver **Rev:** Klaus Stortebeker and ship

Date	Mintage	F	VF	XF	Unc	BU
2003 Proof	—				Value: 37.50	

KM# 56   1000 FRANCS
20.0000 g., 0.9990 Silver 0.6423 oz. ASW, 36 mm. **Rev:** Multicolor Douglas DC-8 at airport

Date	Mintage	F	VF	XF	Unc	BU
2003 Proof	—				Value: 35.00	

KM# 57   1000 FRANCS
20.0000 g., 0.9990 Silver 0.6423 oz. ASW, 36 mm. **Rev:** Multicolor Fokker 100 left

Date	Mintage	F	VF	XF	Unc	BU
2003 Proof	—				Value: 35.00	

KM# 58   1000 FRANCS
20.0000 g., 0.9990 Silver 0.6423 oz. ASW, 36 mm. **Rev:** Multicolor Douglas DC-4 right

Date	Mintage	F	VF	XF	Unc	BU
2004 Proof	—				Value: 35.00	

KM# 59   1000 FRANCS
20.0000 g., 0.9990 Silver 0.6423 oz. ASW, 36 mm. **Rev:** Multicolor General Aviation GA-43 against blue sky

Date	Mintage	F	VF	XF	Unc	BU
2004 Proof	—				Value: 45.00	

KM# 67   1000 FRANCS
20.0000 g., 0.9990 Silver 0.6423 oz. ASW, 36 mm. **Obv:** National arms **Rev:** Blue plane at airport in color

Date	Mintage	F	VF	XF	Unc	BU
2005 Proof	—				Value: 45.00	

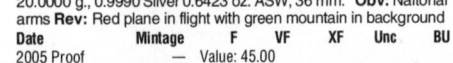

KM# 68   1000 FRANCS
20.0000 g., 0.9990 Silver 0.6423 oz. ASW, 36 mm. **Obv:** Naitonal arms **Rev:** Red plane in flight with green mountain in background

Date	Mintage	F	VF	XF	Unc	BU
2005 Proof	—				Value: 45.00	

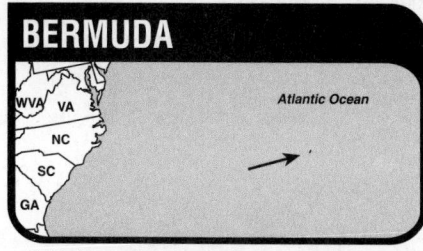

BERMUDA

The Parliamentary British Colony of Bermuda, situated in the western Atlantic Ocean 660 miles (1,062 km.) east of North Carolina, has an area of 20.6 sq. mi. (53 sq. km.) and a population of 61,600. Capital: Hamilton. Concentrated essences, beauty preparations, and cut flowers are exported. Most Bermudians derive their livelihood from tourism. The British monarch is the head of state and is represented by a governor. U.S. Currency circulates in common with the Eastern Caribbean Dollar.

RULER
British

BRITISH COLONY
DECIMAL COINAGE

100 Cents = 1 Dollar

KM# 107 CENT
2.5000 g., Copper Plated Zinc, 19 mm. **Ruler:** Elizabeth II **Obv:** Head with tiara right **Rev:** Wild boar left **Edge:** Plain

Date	Mintage	F	VF	XF	Unc	BU
2001	1,600,000	—	—	—	0.50	0.75
2002	1,120,000	—	—	—	0.50	0.75
2003	800,000	—	—	—	0.50	0.75
2004	1,600,000	—	—	—	0.25	0.50
2005	3,200,000	—	—	—	0.25	0.50
2006	800,000	—	—	—	0.25	0.50
2007	—	—	—	—	0.25	0.50
2008	—	—	—	—	0.25	0.50

KM# 107a CENT
2.5000 g., Copper Plated Steel **Ruler:** Elizabeth II

Date	Mintage	F	VF	XF	Unc	BU
2008	2,400,000	—	—	—	0.25	0.50
2009	4,000,000	—	—	—	0.25	0.50

KM# 108 5 CENTS
5.0000 g., Copper-Nickel, 21.2 mm. **Ruler:** Elizabeth II **Obv:** Head with tiara right **Rev:** Queen angel fish left **Edge:** Plain

Date	Mintage	F	VF	XF	Unc	BU
2001	1,000,000	—	—	—	0.75	1.00
2002	700,000	—	—	—	0.75	1.00
2003	700,000	—	—	—	0.75	1.00
2004	700,000	—	—	—	0.75	1.00
2005	600,000	—	—	—	0.75	1.00
2008	500,000	—	—	—	0.75	1.00
2009	1,500,000	—	—	—	0.50	0.75

KM# 109 10 CENTS
2.5000 g., Copper-Nickel, 17.8 mm. **Ruler:** Elizabeth II **Obv:** Head with tiara right **Rev:** Bermuda lily **Edge:** Reeded

Date	Mintage	F	VF	XF	Unc	BU
2001	1,400,000	—	—	—	0.85	1.00
2002	800,000	—	—	—	0.85	1.00
2003	600,000	—	—	—	0.85	1.00
2004	800,000	—	—	—	0.85	1.00
2005	800,000	—	—	—	0.85	1.00
2008	2,000,000	—	—	—	0.50	0.75
2009	2,000,000	—	—	—	0.50	0.75

KM# 110 25 CENTS
Copper-Nickel, 24 mm. **Ruler:** Elizabeth II **Obv:** Head with tiara right **Rev:** Yellow-billed tropical bird right **Edge:** Reeded

Date	Mintage	F	VF	XF	Unc	BU
2001	800,000	—	—	—	1.50	2.00
2002	800,000	—	—	—	1.50	2.00
2003	800,000	—	—	—	1.50	2.00
2004	800,000	—	—	—	1.50	2.00
2005	1,440,000	—	—	—	1.50	2.00
2006	320,000	—	—	—	1.50	2.00
2007	—	—	—	—	1.50	2.00
2008	1,200,000	—	—	—	1.00	1.50
2009	2,000,000	—	—	—	1.00	1.50

KM# 111 DOLLAR
Nickel-Brass, 26 mm. **Ruler:** Elizabeth II **Obv:** Head with tiara right **Rev:** Sailboat

Date	Mintage	F	VF	XF	Unc	BU
2001	12,000	—	—	—	3.00	3.50
2002	12,000	—	—	—	3.00	3.50
2003	12,000	—	—	—	3.00	3.50
2004	12,000	—	—	—	3.00	3.50
2005	240,000	—	—	—	2.00	3.00
2008	300,000	—	—	—	2.00	3.00
2009	600,000	—	—	—	2.00	3.00

KM# 139 DOLLAR
28.2800 g., Copper-Nickel, 38.6 mm. **Ruler:** Elizabeth II **Obv:** Head with tiara right **Rev:** 4 Gombey dancers **Edge:** Reeded

Date	Mintage	F	VF	XF	Unc	BU
2001	—	—	—	—	12.00	14.00

KM# 124 DOLLAR
28.4100 g., Copper-Nickel, 38.5 mm. **Ruler:** Elizabeth II **Subject:** Queen's Golden Jubilee **Obv:** Head with tiara right **Rev:** Stylized trumpeters above monogram and date **Edge:** Reeded

Date	Mintage	F	VF	XF	Unc	BU
2002	—	—	—	—	10.00	12.00

KM# 380 2 DOLLARS
31.6040 g., 0.9990 Silver 1.0150 oz. ASW, 38.61 mm. **Ruler:** Elizabeth II **Subject:** Bermuda Hawksbill Turtle **Obv:** Bust right **Rev:** Turtle **Rev. Legend:** BERMUDA HAWKSBILL TURTLE / TWO DOLLARS

Date	Mintage	F	VF	XF	Unc	BU
2008 Proof	2,500	Value: 50.00				

KM# 157 3 DOLLARS
33.6300 g., 0.9250 Silver 1.0000 oz. ASW, 35 mm. **Ruler:** Elizabeth II **Subject:** Shipwrecks Series **Obv:** Elizabeth II **Rev:** Gold-plated image of the Hunter Galley **Edge:** Plain

Date	Mintage	F	VF	XF	Unc	BU
2006 Proof	15,000	Value: 90.00				

KM# 158 3 DOLLARS
33.6300 g., 0.9250 Silver 1.0000 oz. ASW, 35 mm. **Ruler:** Elizabeth II **Subject:** Shipwrecks Series **Obv:** Elizabeth II **Rev:** Gold-plated image of the North Carolina **Edge:** Plain

Date	Mintage	F	VF	XF	Unc	BU
2006 Proof	15,000	Value: 90.00				

KM# 159 3 DOLLARS
33.6300 g., 0.9250 Silver 1.0000 oz. ASW, 35 mm. **Ruler:** Elizabeth II **Subject:** Shipwrecks Series **Obv:** Elizabeth II **Rev:** Gold-plated image of the Pollockshields **Edge:** Plain

Date	Mintage	F	VF	XF	Unc	BU
2006 Proof	15,000	Value: 90.00				

KM# 140 3 DOLLARS
33.6300 g., 0.9250 Silver 1.0000 oz. ASW, 35 mm. **Ruler:** Elizabeth II **Subject:** Shipwrecks Series **Obv:** Elizabeth II **Rev:** The Mary Celestia gold-plated image **Edge:** Plain **Shape:** Triangular

Date	Mintage	F	VF	XF	Unc	BU
2006 Proof	15,000	Value: 90.00				

KM# 141 3 DOLLARS
1.5550 g., 0.9990 Gold 0.0499 oz. AGW, 15 mm. **Ruler:** Elizabeth II **Subject:** Shipwreck Series **Obv:** Elizabeth II **Rev:** The Mary Celestia **Edge:** Plain **Shape:** Triangular

Date	Mintage	F	VF	XF	Unc	BU
2006 Proof	15,000	Value: 100				

KM# 148   3 DOLLARS
33.6300 g., 0.9250 Silver 1.0000 oz. ASW, 35 mm. **Ruler:**
Elizabeth II **Subject:** Shipwreck Series **Obv:** Elizabeth II **Rev:**
The Constellation in gold-plated image **Edge:** Plain **Shape:**
Triangular

Date	Mintage	F	VF	XF	Unc	BU
2006 Proof	15,000	Value: 90.00				

KM# 149   3 DOLLARS
1.5550 g., 0.9990 Gold 0.0499 oz. AGW, 15 mm. **Ruler:**
Elizabeth II **Subject:** Shipwreck Series **Obv:** Elizabeth II **Rev:**
The Constellation **Edge:** Plain **Shape:** Triangular

Date	Mintage	F	VF	XF	Unc	BU
2006 Proof	15,000	Value: 100				

KM# 156   3 DOLLARS
33.6300 g., 0.9250 Silver 1.0000 oz. ASW, 35 mm. **Ruler:**
Elizabeth II **Subject:** Shipwrecks Series **Obv:** Elizabeth II **Rev:**
Gold-plated image of the Sea Venture **Edge:** Plain

Date	Mintage	F	VF	XF	Unc	BU
2007 Proof	15,000	Value: 90.00				

KM# 164   3 DOLLARS
33.6300 g., 0.9250 Silver 1.0000 oz. ASW, 35 mm. **Ruler:**
Elizabeth II **Series:** Bermuda Shipwrecks **Obv:** Head with tiara
right, gilt **Rev:** Dutchman sailing ship "Manilla", gilt, 1739 **Edge:**
Plain, gilt **Shape:** Triangular

Date	Mintage	F	VF	XF	Unc	BU
2007 Proof	15,000	Value: 85.00				

KM# 165   3 DOLLARS
33.6300 g., 0.9250 Silver 1.0000 oz. ASW, 35 mm. **Ruler:**
Elizabeth II **Series:** Bermuda Shipwrecks **Obv:** Head with tiara
right, gilt **Rev:** 16th century Spanish sailing ship "Santa Lucia",
gilt, 1584 **Edge:** Plain, gilt **Shape:** Triangular

Date	Mintage	F	VF	XF	Unc	BU
2007 Proof	15,000	Value: 85.00				

KM# 166   3 DOLLARS
33.6300 g., 0.9250 Silver 1.0000 oz. ASW **Ruler:** Elizabeth II
Series: Bermuda Shipwrecks **Obv:** Head with tiara right, gilt **Rev:**
Spanish luxury steamship "Cristobal Colon", gilt, 1936 **Edge:** Plain

Date	Mintage	F	VF	XF	Unc	BU
2007 Proof	15,000	Value: 85.00				

KM# 167   3 DOLLARS
33.6300 g., 0.9250 Silver 1.0000 oz. ASW, 35 mm. **Ruler:**
Elizabeth II **Series:** Bermuda Shipwrecks **Obv:** Head with tiara
right, gilt **Rev:** English iron-hulled steamer with sails "Kate", gilt,
1878 **Edge:** Plain **Shape:** Triangular

Date	Mintage	F	VF	XF	Unc	BU
2007 Proof	15,000	Value: 85.00				

KM# 168   3 DOLLARS
33.6300 g., 0.9250 Silver 1.0000 oz. ASW, 35 mm. **Ruler:**
Elizabeth II **Series:** Bermuda Shipwrecks **Obv:** Head with tiara
right, gilt **Rev:** 16th century Spanish sailing ship "San Pedro", gilt,
1596 **Edge:** Plain, gilt **Shape:** Triangular

Date	Mintage	F	VF	XF	Unc	BU
2007 Proof	15,000	Value: 85.00				

KM# 169   3 DOLLARS
33.6300 g., 0.9250 Silver 1.0000 oz. ASW, 35 mm. **Ruler:**
Elizabeth II **Series:** Bermuda Shipwrecks **Obv:** Head with tiara
right, gilt **Rev:** American luxury yacht "Col. William G. Ball", gilt,
1943 **Edge:** Plain, gilt **Shape:** Triangular

Date	Mintage	F	VF	XF	Unc	BU
2007 Proof	15,000	Value: 85.00				

KM# 381   4 DOLLARS
34.0000 g., 0.9250 Silver 1.0111 oz. ASW, 40 mm. **Ruler:**
Elizabeth II **Obv:** Bust right **Obv. Legend:** Elizabeth II, Value,
BERMUDA **Rev:** Sea venture sailing ship **Rev. Legend:** 1609-
2009 400th ANNIVERSARY OF THE SETTLEMENT OF
BERMUDA **Shape:** Square

Date	Mintage	F	VF	XF	Unc	BU
ND(2009) Proof	2,000	Value: 55.00				

KM# 120   5 DOLLARS
28.2800 g., 0.9250 Silver 0.8410 oz. ASW, 38.6 mm. **Ruler:**
Elizabeth II **Subject:** Gombey Dancers **Obv:** Head with tiara right
Rev: Multicolor costumed dancers **Edge:** Reeded

Date	Mintage	F	VF	XF	Unc	BU
2001 Proof	3,500	Value: 60.00				

KM# 161   5 DOLLARS
28.2800 g., 0.9250 Silver 0.8410 oz. ASW, 38.6 mm. **Ruler:**
Elizabeth II **Obv:** Bust with tiara right **Rev:** Statehouse facade,
St. George's **Edge:** Reeded

Date	Mintage	F	VF	XF	Unc	BU
2001 Proof	3,500	Value: 45.00				

KM# 129   5 DOLLARS
28.2800 g., 0.9250 Silver 0.8410 oz. ASW, 38.6 mm. **Ruler:**
Elizabeth II **Subject:** Queen's Jubilee **Obv:** Gold-plated head
with tiara right, denomination below **Rev:** Trumpeters, monogram
and date below **Edge:** Reeded

Date	Mintage	F	VF	XF	Unc	BU
2002 Proof	20,000	Value: 42.00				

KM# 162   5 DOLLARS
28.2800 g., 0.9250 Silver 0.8410 oz. ASW, 38.6 mm. **Ruler:**
Elizabeth II **Subject:** 100th Anniversary Cup Match - Cricket
Obv: Head with tiara right **Rev:** Two players with caps and teams
shields below, multicolor **Edge:** Reeded

Date	Mintage	F	VF	XF	Unc	BU
2002 Proof	3,500	Value: 45.00				

KM# 171 5 DOLLARS
28.2800 g., 0.9250 Silver 0.8410 oz. ASW, 38.6 mm. **Ruler:**
Elizabeth II **Subject:** Queen's Golden Jubilee **Obv:** Head with
tiara right **Rev:** Stylized trumpeters above monogram and date
Edge: Reeded

Date	Mintage	F	VF	XF	Unc	BU
2002 Proof	3,500	Value: 50.00				

KM# 170 5 DOLLARS
28.2800 g., 0.9250 Silver 0.8410 oz. ASW, 38.6 mm. **Ruler:**
Elizabeth II **Subject:** 100th Anniversary Fitted Dinghy Racing
Obv: Head with tiara right **Rev:** Two dinghies, multicolor sails
Edge: Reeded

Date	Mintage	F	VF	XF	Unc	BU
ND(2003) Proof	3,500	Value: 50.00				

KM# 130 5 DOLLARS
28.2800 g., 0.9250 Silver 0.8410 oz. ASW, 38.6 mm. **Ruler:**
Elizabeth II **Subject:** Queen's Jubilee **Obv:** Gold-plated head
with tiara right **Rev:** Royal visit scene **Edge:** Reeded

Date	Mintage	F	VF	XF	Unc	BU
2003 Proof	20,000	Value: 42.00				

KM# 131 5 DOLLARS
28.2800 g., 0.9250 Silver 0.8410 oz. ASW, 38.6 mm. **Ruler:**
Elizabeth II **Obv:** Head with tiara right **Rev:** Bermudan stone
quarry scene **Edge:** Reeded

Date	Mintage	F	VF	XF	Unc	BU
2004 Proof	3,500	Value: 60.00				

KM# 160 5 DOLLARS
14.5000 g., 0.9250 Silver partially gilt 0.4312 oz. ASW, 30.9 mm.
Ruler: Elizabeth II **Subject:** Bermuda Quincentennial **Obv:** Head
with tiara right, partially gold-plated **Rev:** Caravel sailing ship
partially gold-plated compass face **Edge:** Plain **Shape:**
Pentagonal

Date	Mintage	F	VF	XF	Unc	BU
2005 Proof	2,500	Value: 45.00				

KM# 142 9 DOLLARS
155.5200 g., 0.9990 Silver 4.9949 oz. ASW, 65 mm. **Ruler:**
Elizabeth II **Subject:** Shipwreck Series **Obv:** Elizabeth II **Rev:**
The Mary Celestia **Edge:** Plain **Shape:** Triangular

Date	Mintage	F	VF	XF	Unc	BU
2007 Proof	1,000	Value: 210				

KM# 150 9 DOLLARS
155.5200 g., 0.9990 Silver 4.9949 oz. ASW, 65 mm. **Ruler:**
Elizabeth II **Subject:** Shipwreck Series **Obv:** Elizabeth II **Rev:**
The Constellation **Edge:** Plain **Shape:** Triangular

Date	Mintage	F	VF	XF	Unc	BU
2007 Proof	1,000	Value: 210				

KM# 143 30 DOLLARS
31.4890 g., 0.9990 Gold 1.0113 oz. AGW, 35 mm. **Ruler:**
Elizabeth II **Subject:** Shipwreck Series **Obv:** Elizabeth II **Rev:**
The Mary Celestia **Edge:** Plain **Shape:** Triangular

Date	Mintage	F	VF	XF	Unc	BU
2006 Proof	750	Value: 1,800				

KM# 151 30 DOLLARS
31.4890 g., 0.9990 Gold 1.0113 oz. AGW, 35 mm. **Ruler:**
Elizabeth II **Subject:** Shipwreck Series **Obv:** Elizabeth II **Rev:**
The Constellation **Edge:** Plain **Shape:** Triangular

Date	Mintage	F	VF	XF	Unc	BU
2006 Proof	750	Value: 1,800				

KM# 144 60 DOLLARS
1000.0000 g., 0.9990 Silver 32.117 oz. ASW, 100 mm. **Ruler:**
Elizabeth II **Subject:** Shipwreck Series **Obv:** Elizabeth II **Rev:**
The Mary Celestia **Edge:** Plain

Date	Mintage	F	VF	XF	Unc	BU
2007 Proof	300	Value: 1,250				

KM# 152 60 DOLLARS
1000.0000 g., 0.9990 Silver 32.117 oz. ASW, 100 mm. **Ruler:**
Elizabeth II **Subject:** Shipwreck Series **Obv:** Elizabeth II **Rev:**
The Constellation **Edge:** Plain **Shape:** Triangular

Date	Mintage	F	VF	XF	Unc	BU
2007 Proof	300	Value: 1,250				

KM# 145 90 DOLLARS
155.5200 g., 0.9990 Gold 4.9949 oz. AGW, 65 mm. **Ruler:**
Elizabeth II **Subject:** Shipwreck Series **Obv:** Elizabeth II **Rev:**
The Mary Celestia **Edge:** Plain **Shape:** Triangular

Date	Mintage	F	VF	XF	Unc	BU
2006 Proof	90	Value: 8,750				

KM# 153 90 DOLLARS
155.5200 g., 0.9990 Gold 4.9949 oz. AGW, 65 mm. **Ruler:**
Elizabeth II **Subject:** Shipwreck Series **Obv:** Elizabeth II **Rev:**
The Constellation **Edge:** Plain **Shape:** Triangular

Date	Mintage	F	VF	XF	Unc	BU
2006 Proof	90	Value: 8,750				

KM# 174 90 DOLLARS
155.5200 g., 0.9990 Gold 4.9949 oz. AGW, 65 mm. **Ruler:**
Elizabeth II **Subject:** Sea Venture, 1609 **Obv:** Head with tiara
right **Rev:** Sailing ship left **Shape:** Triangle

Date	Mintage	F	VF	XF	Unc	BU
2006 Proof	—	Value: 9,000				

KM# 173 100 DOLLARS
1000.0000 g., 0.9250 Silver selective gold plating 29.738 oz.
ASW, 100 mm. **Ruler:** Elizabeth II **Subject:** 500th Anniversary
of Discovery **Obv:** Head right **Rev:** Caraval within compass
Shape: 5-sided

Date	Mintage	F	VF	XF	Unc	BU
2005 Proof	250	Value: 1,150				

KM# 146 300 DOLLARS
155.5200 g., 0.9995 Platinum 4.9974 oz. APW, 65 mm. **Ruler:**
Elizabeth II **Subject:** Shipwrecks Series **Obv:** Elizabeth II **Rev:**
The Mary Celestia **Edge:** Plain **Shape:** Triangular

Date	Mintage	F	VF	XF	Unc	BU
2006 Proof	60	Value: 9,500				

KM# 154 300 DOLLARS
155.5200 g., 0.9995 Platinum 4.9974 oz. APW, 65 mm. **Ruler:**
Elizabeth II **Subject:** Shipwreck Series **Obv:** Elizabeth II **Rev:**
The Constellation **Edge:** Plain **Shape:** Triangular

Date	Mintage	F	VF	XF	Unc	BU
2006 Proof	60	Value: 9,500				

KM# 172 500 DOLLARS
31.1050 g., 0.9990 Gold with selective silver plating 0.9990 oz.
AGW, 30.89 mm. **Ruler:** Elizabeth II **Obv:** Queen Elizabeth II
Rev: Caravel sailing ship in compass face **Edge:** Plain **Shape:**
5-sided **Note:** Bermuda Quincentennial. Prev. KM#160a.

Date	Mintage	F	VF	XF	Unc	BU
2005 Proof	—	Value: 1,800				

KM# 147 600 DOLLARS
1096.0000 g., 0.9180 Gold 32.346 oz. AGW, 100 mm. **Ruler:**
Elizabeth II **Subject:** Shipwreck Series **Obv:** Elizabeth II **Rev:**
The Mary Celestia **Edge:** Plain **Shape:** Triangular

Date	Mintage	F	VF	XF	Unc	BU
2007 Proof	300	Value: 57,000				

KM# 155 600 DOLLARS
1096.0000 g., 0.9180 Gold 32.346 oz. AGW, 100 mm. **Ruler:**
Elizabeth II **Subject:** Shipwreck Series **Obv:** Elizabeth II **Rev:**
The Constellation **Edge:** Plain **Shape:** Triangular

Date	Mintage	F	VF	XF	Unc	BU
2007 Proof	300	Value: 57,000				

PIEDFORT

KM#	Date	Mintage	Identification	Mkt Val
P3	2005	250	5 Dollars. 0.9250 Silver. 29.0000 g. 30.89 mm. Gold plated bust and rim. Caravel type sailing ship in partially gold plated compass face and rim. Plain, gold plated edge.	—

MINT SETS

KM#	Date	Mintage	Identification	Issue Price	Mkt Val
MS8	2004 (5)	2,300	KM#107-111.	—	10.00

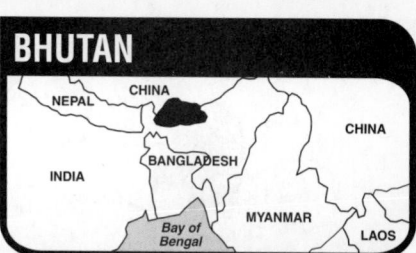

BHUTAN

The Kingdom of Bhutan, a landlocked Himalayan country
bordered by Tibet and India, has an area of 18,150 sq. mi. (38,394
sq. km.) and a population of 675,000. Capital: Thimphu. Virtually
the entire population is engaged in agricultural and pastoral activities. Rice, wheat, barley, and yak butter are produced in sufficient quantity to make the country self-sufficient in food. The
economy of Bhutan is primitive and many transactions are conducted on a barter basis.

RULER
Jigme Singye Wangchuck, 1972-2006
King Jigme Khesar Namgyel Wangchuck, 2006-

KINGDOM
REFORM COINAGE

Commencing 1974; 100 Chetrums (Paisa) = 1 Ngultrum
(Rupee); 100 Ngultrums = 1 Sertum

KM# 105 5 CHETRUMS
3.8600 g., Brass, 21.9 mm. **Obv:** Monkey right, date below **Rev:**
Effigy of the old "Ma-tam", value below **Edge:** Plain

Date	Mintage	F	VF	XF	Unc	BU
2003	—	—	—	0.25	0.50	

KM# 116 NGULTRUM
8.1000 g., Nickel Plated Steel **Ruler:**
Jigme Khesar Namgyel Wangchuck

Date	Mintage	F	VF	XF	Unc	BU
2008	—	—	—	3.00	4.00	

KM# 115 100 NGULTRUMS
20.2000 g., Silver, 38 mm. **Ruler:**
Jigme Khesar Namgyel Wangchuck **Subject:** Coronation **Obv:**
Portrait left **Rev:** Seal

Date	Mintage	F	VF	XF	Unc	BU
2008 Proof	—	Value: 60.00				

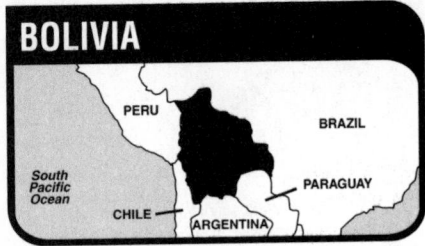

BOLIVIA

The Plurinational State of Bolivia, a landlocked country in west central South America, has an area of 424,165 sq. mi. (1,098,580 sq. km.) and a population of *8.33 million. Its capitals are: La Paz (administrative) and Sucre (constitutional). Principal exports are tin, zinc, antimony, tungsten, petroleum, natural gas, cotton and coffee.

MINT MARKS
A - Paris
(a) - Paris, privy marks only
CHI - Valcambia
H - Heaton
KN - Kings' Norton

REPUBLIC

REFORM COINAGE
1987-; 1,000,000 Peso Bolivianos = 1 Boliviano;
100 Centavos = 1 Boliviano

KM# 213   10 CENTAVOS
1.8500 g., Copper Clad Steel, 19 mm. **Obv:** National arms **Rev:** Value

Date	Mintage	F	VF	XF	Unc	BU
2001	—	—	—	—	0.50	1.00
2006	—	—	—	—	0.50	1.00
2008	—	—	—	—	0.50	1.00

KM# 202   10 CENTAVOS
1.8500 g., Stainless Steel, 19 mm. **Obv:** National arms, star below **Rev:** Denomination within circle, date below

Date	Mintage	F	VF	XF	Unc	BU
2006	—	—	—	0.20	0.50	0.70

KM# 214   10 CENTAVOS
1.8500 g., Copper Plated Steel, 19 mm. **Obv:** National arms **Obv. Legend:** ESTADO PLURINACIONAL DE BOLIVIA **Rev:** Value

Date	Mintage	F	VF	XF	Unc	BU
2010	—	—	—	—	0.10	0.20

KM# 203   20 CENTAVOS
3.2500 g., Stainless Steel, 22 mm. **Obv:** National arms, star below **Obv. Legend:** REPUBLICA DE BOLIVIA **Rev:** Denomination within circle, date below **Rev. Legend:** LA UNION ES LA FUERZA **Edge:** Plain

Date	Mintage	F	VF	XF	Unc	BU
2001	—	—	—	0.25	0.60	0.80
2006	—	—	—	0.25	0.60	0.80
2008	—	—	—	0.25	0.60	0.80

KM# 215   20 CENTAVOS
3.2500 g., Stainless Steel, 22 mm. **Obv:** National arms **Obv. Legend:** ESTADO PLURINACIONAL DE BOLIVIA **Rev:** Value

Date	Mintage	F	VF	XF	Unc	BU
2010	—	—	—	—	0.15	0.25

KM# 204   50 CENTAVOS
3.7500 g., Stainless Steel, 24 mm. **Obv:** National arms, star below **Obv. Legend:** REPUBLICA DE BOLIVIA **Rev:** Denomination within circle, date below **Rev. Legend:** LA UNION ES LA FUERZA **Edge:** Plain

Date	Mintage	F	VF	XF	Unc	BU
2001	—	—	—	0.30	0.75	1.00
2006	—	—	—	0.30	0.75	1.00
2008	—	—	—	0.30	0.75	1.00

KM# 216   50 CENTAVOS
3.7500 g., Stainless Steel, 24 mm. **Obv:** National arms **Obv. Legend:** ESTADO PLURINACIONAL DE BOLIVIA **Rev:** Value

Date	Mintage	F	VF	XF	Unc	BU
2010	—	—	—	—	0.50	1.00

KM# 205   BOLIVIANO
5.0000 g., Stainless Steel, 27 mm. **Obv:** National arms, star below **Obv. Legend:** REPUBLICA DE BOLIVIA **Rev:** Denomination within circle, date below sprays **Rev. Legend:** LA UNION ES LA FUERZA **Edge:** Plain

Date	Mintage	F	VF	XF	Unc	BU
2001	—	—	—	0.35	0.90	1.20
2004	—	—	—	0.35	0.90	1.20
2008	—	—	—	0.35	0.90	1.20

KM# 217   BOLIVIANO
5.0000 g., Stainless Steel, 27 mm. **Obv:** National arms **Obv. Legend:** ESTADO PLURINACIONAL DE BOLIVIA **Rev:** Value

Date	Mintage	F	VF	XF	Unc	BU
2010	—	—	—	—	1.50	2.00

KM# 206.2   2 BOLIVIANOS
6.2500 g., Stainless Steel, 27 mm. **Obv:** National arms, star below **Rev:** Denomination within circle, date below **Note:** Increased size.

Date	Mintage	F	VF	XF	Unc	BU
2008	—	—	—	—	2.00	3.00

KM# 218   2 BOLIVIANOS
6.2500 g., Stainless Steel, 27 mm. **Obv:** National arms **Obv. Legend:** ESTADO PLURINACIONAL DE BOLIVIA **Rev:** Value

Date	Mintage	F	VF	XF	Unc	BU
2010	—	—	—	—	1.50	2.00

KM# 212   5 BOLIVIANOS
5.0000 g., Bi-Metallic Bronze Plated Steel center in Stainless Steel ring, 23 mm. **Obv:** National arms **Obv. Legend:** REPUBLICA DE BOLIVIA **Rev:** Denomination **Rev. Legend:** LA UNION ES LA FUERZA **Edge:** Reeded

Date	Mintage	F	VF	XF	Unc	BU
2001	—	—	—	0.90	2.25	3.00
2004	—	—	—	0.90	2.25	3.00

KM# 219   5 BOLIVIANOS
5.0000 g., Bi-Metallic Bronze Plated Steel center in Stainless Steel ring, 23 mm. **Obv:** National arms **Obv. Legend:** ESTADO PLURINACIONAL DE BOLIVIA **Rev:** Value **Edge:** Reeded

Date	Mintage	F	VF	XF	Unc	BU
2010	—	—	—	—	4.00	5.00

BOSNIA - HERZEGOVINA

The Republic of Bosnia and Herzegovina borders Croatia to the north and west, Serbia to the east and Montenegro in the southeast with only 12.4 mi. of coastline. The total land area is 19,735 sq. mi. (51,129 sq. km.). They have a population of *4.34 million. Capital: Sarajevo. Electricity, mining and agriculture are leading industries.

MONETARY SYSTEM
1 Convertible Marka = 100 Convertible Feniga =
1 Deutschemark 1998-
NOTE: German Euros circulate freely.

REPUBLIC

REFORM COINAGE
1998-

KM# 121   5 FENINGA
2.6600 g., Nickel Plated Steel, 18 mm. **Obv:** Denomination on map **Rev:** Triangle and stars **Edge:** Reeded

Date	Mintage	F	VF	XF	Unc	BU
2005	—	—	—	—	1.00	1.25
2008	—	—	—	—	1.00	1.25
2011	—	—	—	—	1.00	1.25

KM# 115   10 FENINGA
3.9000 g., Copper Plated Steel, 20 mm. **Obv:** Denomination on map within circle **Rev:** Triangle and stars, date at left within circle **Edge:** Plain

Date	Mintage	F	VF	XF	Unc	BU
2004	—	—	—	—	0.50	0.75
2007	—	—	—	—	0.50	0.75
2008	—	—	—	—	0.50	0.75
2011	—	—	—	—	0.50	0.75

KM# 116 20 FENINGA
4.5000 g., Copper Plated Steel, 22 mm. **Obv:** Denomination on map within circle **Rev:** Triangle and stars, date at left within circle **Edge:** Reeded

Date	Mintage	F	VF	XF	Unc	BU
2004	—				1.00	1.25
2007	—				1.00	1.25
2008	—				1.00	1.25
2009	—				1.00	1.25

KM# 117 50 FENINGA
5.1500 g., Copper Plated Steel, 24 mm. **Obv:** Denomination on map within circle **Rev:** Triangle and stars, date at left within circle

Date	Mintage	F	VF	XF	Unc	BU
2007	—				—	3.00

KM# 118 KONVERTIBLE MARKA
4.9500 g., Nickel Plated Steel, 23.23 mm. **Obv:** Denomination **Rev:** Coat of arms above date **Edge:** Segmented reeding

Date	Mintage	F	VF	XF	Unc	BU
2002	—	—	—	—	5.50	6.00
2003	—	—	—	—	5.50	6.00
2004	—	—	—	—	5.50	6.00
2006	—	—	—	—	4.00	5.00
2007	—	—	—	—	4.00	5.00
2008	—	—	—	—	4.00	5.00
2009	—	—	—	—	4.00	5.00

KM# 119 2 KONVERTIBLE MARKA
6.9000 g., Bi-Metallic Copper-Nickel center in Nickel-Brass ring, 25.75 mm. **Obv:** Denomination within circle **Rev:** Dove of Peace, date at right within circle **Edge:** Segmented reeding

Date	Mintage	F	VF	XF	Unc	BU
2002	—	—	—	—	13.50	15.00
2003	—	—	—	—	13.50	15.00
2008	—	—	—	—	13.50	15.00

KM# 120 5 KONVERTIBLE MARKA
10.3500 g., Bi-Metallic Nickel-Brass center in Copper-Nickel ring, 30 mm. **Obv:** Denomination within circle **Rev:** Dove of Peace in flight **Edge:** Reeded

Date	Mintage	F	VF	XF	Unc	BU
2005	—	—	—	—	17.50	20.00
2009	—	—	—	—	17.50	20.00

BOTSWANA

The Republic of Botswana (formerly Bechuanaland), located in south central Africa between Namibia and Zimbabwe, has an area of 224,607 sq. mi. (600,370 sq. km.) and a population of *1.62 million. Capital: Gaborone. Botswana is a member of a Customs Union with South Africa, Lesotho, and Swaziland. The economy is primarily pastoral with a rapidly developing mining industry, of which diamonds, copper and nickel are the chief elements. Meat products and diamonds comprise 85 percent of the exports.

Botswana is a member of the Commonwealth of Nations. The president is Chief of State and Head of government.

MINT MARK
B - Berne

MONETARY SYSTEM
100 Cents = 1 Thebe

REPUBLIC

REFORM COINAGE
100 Thebe = 1 Pula

KM# 26 5 THEBE
2.4100 g., Copper Plated Steel, 16.9 mm. **Obv:** National arms, date below **Rev:** Toko bird left, value above **Edge:** Plain **Shape:** 7-sided

Date	Mintage	F	VF	XF	Unc	BU
2002	—			0.25	0.50	1.00
2007	—			0.25	0.50	1.00
2009	—			0.25	0.50	1.00

KM# 27 10 THEBE
2.8000 g., Nickel Plated Steel, 18 mm. **Obv:** National arms above date **Rev:** South African Oryx right, value above

Date	Mintage	F	VF	XF	Unc	BU
2002	—	—	—	0.30	0.75	1.25
2008	—	—	—	0.30	0.75	1.25

KM# 28 25 THEBE
3.5000 g., Nickel Plated Steel, 21 mm. **Obv:** National arms, date below **Rev:** Zebu left, value above **Shape:** 7-sided

Date	Mintage	F	VF	XF	Unc	BU
2007	—		0.30	0.60	1.50	2.00
2009	—		0.30	0.60	1.50	2.00

KM# 29 50 THEBE
4.8200 g., Nickel Plated Steel, 21.5 mm. **Obv:** National arms, date below **Rev:** African Fish Eagle left, value above

Date	Mintage	F	VF	XF	Unc	BU
2001	—		0.50	1.00	2.00	2.50

KM# 24 PULA
8.7000 g., Nickel-Brass, 23.5 mm. **Obv:** National arms, date below **Rev:** Zebra left, denomination above **Shape:** 7-sided

Date	Mintage	F	VF	XF	Unc	BU
2007	—		1.00	1.75	3.50	6.00

KM# 25a 2 PULA
6.0000 g., Brass Plated Steel, 24.5 mm. **Subject:** Wildlife **Obv:** National arms, date below **Rev:** Rhinoceros left, denomination above **Shape:** 7-sided

Date	Mintage	F	VF	XF	Unc	BU
2004	—				2.75	3.50

KM# 30 5 PULA
6.2000 g., Bi-Metallic Copper-Nickel center in Brass ring, 23.4 mm. **Obv:** National arms, date below **Rev:** Mophane worm on a mophane leaf, denomination below within circle **Edge:** Reeded

Date	Mintage	F	VF	XF	Unc	BU
2007	—				6.50	10.00

BRAZIL

The Federative Republic of Brazil, which comprises half the continent of South America and is the only Latin American country deriving its culture and language from Portugal, has an area of 3,286,488 sq. mi. (8,511,965 sq. km.) and a population of *169.2 million. Capital: Brasilia. The economy of Brazil is as varied and complex as any in the developing world. Agriculture is a mainstay of the economy, while only 4 percent of the area is under cultivation. Known mineral resources are almost unlimited in variety and size of reserves. A large, relatively sophisticated industry ranges from basic steel and chemical production to finished consumer goods. Coffee, cotton, iron ore and cocoa are the chief exports.

MINT MARKS
(a) - Paris, privy marks only
B - Bahia

REPUBLIC

REFORM COINAGE

2750 Cruzeiros Reais = 1 Real; 100 Centavos = 1 Real

KM# 647   CENTAVO

2.4300 g., Copper Plated Steel, 17 mm. **Obv:** Cabral bust at right **Rev:** Denomination on linear design at left, 3/4 globe with sash on right, date below **Edge:** Plain

Date	Mintage	F	VF	XF	Unc	BU
2001	242,924,000	—	—	—	0.10	0.20
2002	161,824,000	—	—	—	0.10	0.20
2003	250,000,000	—	—	—	0.10	0.20
2004	167,232,000	—	—	—	0.10	0.20

KM# 648   5 CENTAVOS

4.1000 g., Copper Plated Steel, 22 mm. **Obv:** Tiradente bust at right, dove at left **Rev:** Denomination on linear design at left, 3/4 globe with sash on right, date below **Edge:** Plain

Date	Mintage	F	VF	XF	Unc	BU
2001	175,940,000	—	—	—	0.45	0.65
2002	153,088,000	—	—	—	0.45	0.65
2003	260,000,000	—	—	—	0.45	0.65
2004	262,656,000	—	—	—	0.45	0.65
2005	230,144,000	—	—	—	0.45	0.65
2006	255,488,000	—	—	—	0.45	0.65
2007	403,968,000	—	—	—	0.45	0.65
2008	28,672,000	—	—	—	0.45	0.65
2009	400,128,000	—	—	—	0.30	0.50
2010	550,144,000	—	—	—	0.30	0.50
2011	—	—	—	—	0.30	0.50

KM# 649.2   10 CENTAVOS

4.8000 g., Bronze Plated Steel, 20 mm. **Obv:** Bust of Pedro at right, horseman with sword in right hand at left **Rev:** Denomination on linear design at left, 3/4 globe with sash on right, date below **Edge:** Reeded

Date	Mintage	F	VF	XF	Unc	BU
2001	134,701,000	—	—	—	0.60	0.80
2002	172,032,000	—	—	—	0.60	0.80
2003	252,666,000	—	—	—	0.60	0.80
2004	348,480,000	—	—	—	0.60	0.80
2005	362,112,000	—	—	—	0.60	0.80
2006	265,728,000	—	—	—	0.60	0.80
2007	316,800,000	—	—	—	0.60	0.80
2008	534,412,000	—	—	—	0.50	0.75
2009	205,748,000	—	—	—	0.50	0.75
2010	520,128,000	—	—	—	0.50	0.75
2011	—	—	—	—	0.50	0.75

KM# 650   25 CENTAVOS

7.5500 g., Bronze Plated Steel, 25 mm. **Obv:** Deodoro bust at right, national arms at left **Rev:** Denomination on linear design at left, 3/4 globe with sash on right, date below **Edge:** Reeded

Date	Mintage	F	VF	XF	Unc	BU
2001	92,642,000	—	—	—	0.75	1.00
2002	100,096,000	—	—	—	0.75	1.00
2003	147,200,000	—	—	—	0.75	1.00
2004	160,000,000	—	—	—	0.75	1.00
2005	100,096,000	—	—	—	0.75	1.00
2006	110,720,000	—	—	—	0.75	1.00
2007	118,784,000	—	—	—	0.75	1.00
2008	269,031,000	—	—	—	0.60	0.75
2009	200,985,000	—	—	—	0.60	0.75
2010	240,000,000	—	—	—	0.60	0.75
2011	—	—	—	—	0.60	0.75

KM# 651   50 CENTAVOS

9.2500 g., Copper-Nickel, 23 mm. **Obv:** Rio Branco bust at right, map at left **Rev:** Denomination on linear design at left, 3/4 globe with sash on right, date below **Edge Lettering:** BRASIL ORDEM E PROGRESSO

Date	Mintage	F	VF	XF	Unc	BU
2001	14,735,000	—	—	—	1.50	1.75

KM# 651a   50 CENTAVOS

6.8000 g., Stainless Steel, 23 mm. **Obv:** Rio Branco bust at right, map at left **Rev:** Denomination on linear design at left, 3/4 globe with sash on right, date below **Edge Lettering:** BRASIL ORDEM E PROGRESSO

Date	Mintage	F	VF	XF	Unc	BU
2002	189,952,000	—	—	—	1.25	1.50
2003	143,696,000	—	—	—	1.25	1.50
2005	122,416,000	—	—	—	1.25	1.50
2006	39,984,000	—	—	—	1.25	1.50
2007	130,032,000	—	—	—	1.25	1.50
2008	290,080,000	—	—	—	1.25	1.50
2009	300,048,000	—	—	—	1.25	1.50
2010	170,016,000	—	—	—	1.25	1.50
2011	—	—	—	—	1.25	1.50

KM# 652a   REAL

7.0000 g., Bi-Metallic Stainless Steel center in Bronze Plated Steel ring, 27 mm. **Obv:** Allegorical portrait **Rev:** Denomination on linear design at left, 3/4 globe with sash on right, date below **Edge:** Segmented reeding

Date	Mintage	F	VF	XF	Unc	BU
2002	54,192,000	—	—	—	3.50	4.50
2003	100,000,000	—	—	—	3.50	4.50
2004	150,016,000	—	—	—	3.50	4.50
2005	43,776,000	—	—	—	3.50	4.50
2006	179,968,000	—	—	—	3.50	4.50
2007	275,712,000	—	—	—	3.50	4.50
2008	664,833,000	—	—	—	3.50	4.50
2009	245,247,000	—	—	—	2.00	2.50
2010	220,032,000	—	—	—	2.00	2.50
2011	—	—	—	—	2.00	2.50

KM# 656   REAL

7.0000 g., Bi-Metallic Stainless Steel center in Bronze Plated Steel ring, 27 mm. **Subject:** Centennial of Juscelino Kubitschek, president **Obv:** Head left **Rev:** Denomination on linear design at left, 3/4 globe with sash on right, date below **Edge:** Segmented reeding

Date	Mintage	F	VF	XF	Unc	BU
2002	50,000,000	—	—	—	3.50	4.50

KM# 668   REAL

7.0000 g., Bi-Metallic Stainless Steel center in Bronze Plated Steel ring, 27 mm. **Subject:** 40th Anniversary of Central Bank **Obv:** Monument **Rev:** Value on flag **Edge:** Segmented reeding

Date	Mintage	F	VF	XF	Unc	BU
2005	40,000,000	—	—	—	5.00	6.50

KM# 657   2 REAIS

28.0000 g., 0.9990 Silver 0.8993 oz. ASW, 40 mm. **Subject:** Centennial - Carlos Drummond de Andrade **Obv:** Denomination and writer **Rev:** Stylized portrait **Edge:** Reeded

Date	Mintage	F	VF	XF	Unc	BU
ND(2002) Proof	6,999	Value: 60.00				

KM# 658   2 REAIS

28.0000 g., 0.9990 Silver 0.8993 oz. ASW, 40 mm. **Subject:** Centennial - Juscelino Kubitschek **Obv:** Bust facing in upper right, initials at left **Rev:** Denomination **Edge:** Reeded

Date	Mintage	F	VF	XF	Unc	BU
2002 Proof	12,999	Value: 55.00				

KM# 663   2 REAIS

27.0000 g., 0.9250 Silver 0.8029 oz. ASW, 40 mm. **Obv:** Value and piano player **Rev:** Ary Barroso singing **Edge:** Reeded

Date	Mintage	F	VF	XF	Unc	BU
2003 Proof	7,000	Value: 60.00				

KM# 665   2 REAIS

27.0000 g., 0.9250 Silver 0.8029 oz. ASW, 40 mm. **Subject:** Centennial - Cándido Con Portinari **Obv:** Starving family scene, value and country name **Rev:** Portinari's portrait, stars in squares design **Edge:** Reeded

Date	Mintage	F	VF	XF	Unc	BU
ND(2003) Proof	2,000	Value: 75.00				

KM# 666   2 REAIS
27.0000 g., 0.9250 Silver 0.8029 oz. ASW, 40 mm. **Subject:**
FIFA Centennial **Obv:** Soccer ball and value **Rev:** Center part of
a Brazilian flag and stars **Edge:** Reeded

Date	Mintage	F	VF	XF	Unc	BU
2004 Proof	12,166	Value: 75.00				

KM# 671   2 REAIS
27.0000 g., 0.9250 Silver 0.8029 oz. ASW, 40 mm. **Subject:**
Centennial of Flight 14 bis **Obv:** Image of 14 Bis **Obv. Legend:**
"Centenario Do Voo Do 14 Bis Brasil 1906-2006" **Rev:** Image
and signature of Santos Dumont and value **Edge:** Reeded

Date	Mintage	F	VF	XF	Unc	BU
2006 Proof	4,000	Value: 65.00				

KM# 672   2 REAIS
10.1700 g., Copper-Nickel, 30 mm. **Subject:** Pan-American
Games XV **Obv:** Official logo of Pan-American Games XV **Rev:**
Image of running athlete, XV Jogos Pan-Americanos, value,
Brasil and date. **Edge:** Reeded

Date	Mintage	F	VF	XF	Unc	BU
2007	10,000	—	—	—	—	12.00

KM# 675   2 REAIS
10.1700 g., Copper-Nickel, 30 mm. **Subject:** Japanese
immigration to Brazil, 100th Anniversary **Obv:** Farmer and
persimmon crop **Rev:** Ship "Kasato Maru" **Edge:** Reeded

Date	Mintage	F	VF	XF	Unc	BU
2008	10,000	—	—	—	—	16.00

KM# 661   5 REAIS
28.0000 g., 0.9990 Silver 0.8993 oz. ASW, 40 mm. **Subject:**
World Cup 2000 **Obv:** Soccer player and Brazilian flag **Rev:**
Soccer ball and value **Edge:** Reeded

Date	Mintage	F	VF	XF	Unc	BU
2002 Proof	10,149	Value: 60.00				

KM# 673   5 REAIS
27.0000 g., 0.9250 Silver 0.8029 oz. ASW, 40 mm. **Subject:**
Pan-American Games XV **Obv:** Official logo of Pan-American
Games XV **Rev:** Sugar Loaf, lines of Copacabana sidewalk, "XV
Jogos Pan-Americanos", value, Brasil and date. **Edge:** Reeded

Date	Mintage	F	VF	XF	Unc	BU
2007 Proof	4,000	Value: 65.00				

KM# 674   5 REAIS
27.0000 g., 0.9250 Silver 0.8029 oz. ASW, 40 mm. **Subject:**
Royal Family's arrival in Brazil, 200th Anniversary **Obv:** Ship
"Martim de Freitas" **Rev:** Names and dates of institutions created
by Dom John **Edge:** Reeded

Date	Mintage	F	VF	XF	Unc	BU
2008 Proof	2,000	Value: 75.00				

KM# 676   5 REAIS
27.0000 g., 0.9250 Silver 0.8029 oz. ASW, 40 mm. **Subject:**
World Heritage Sites, Brasilia, 50th Anniversary **Obv:** Schematic
city plan **Rev:** Brasilia's architecture montage: Congress,
Cathedral, Presidential palace and Warriors sculpture **Edge:**
Reeded

Date	Mintage	F	VF	XF	Unc	BU
2010 Proof	6,000	Value: 65.00				

KM# 677   5 REAIS
27.0000 g., 0.9250 Silver 0.8029 oz. ASW, 40 mm. **Subject:**
2010 World Cup, South Africa **Obv:** Two players with scoccer
ball, Brazil flag in background **Rev:** Map of Africa, South african
savannah, soccer player at left **Edge:** Reeded

Date	Mintage	F	VF	XF	Unc	BU
2010 Proof	9,000	Value: 65.00				

KM# 678   5 REAIS
27.0000 g., 0.9250 Silver 0.8029 oz. ASW, 40 mm. **Subject:**
UNESCO World Heritage site. 300th Anniversary of the Foundling
of the Pilar Vila Rica of Ouro Preto **Obv:** Houses and churches
representing the city's architecture **Obv. Legend:** OURO PRETO
Rev: Three angels, baroque scrolls and BRAZIL **Rev. Legend:**
PATRIMONIO DA HUMANIDADE • UNESCO **Edge:** Reeded

Date	Mintage	F	VF	XF	Unc	BU
2011 Proof	2,000	Value: 65.00				

KM# 659   20 REAIS
8.0000 g., 0.9000 Gold 0.2315 oz. AGW, 22 mm. **Obv:** Juscelino
Kubitschek de Oliveira's portrait **Rev:** Value **Edge:** Reeded

Date	Mintage	F	VF	XF	Unc	BU
2002 Proof	2,499	Value: 450				

KM# 660   20 REAIS
8.0000 g., 0.9000 Gold 0.2315 oz. AGW, 22 mm. **Obv:** Carlos
Drummond de Andrade portrait and value **Rev:** Andrade
caricature, name and dates **Edge:** Reeded

Date	Mintage	F	VF	XF	Unc	BU
ND(2002) Proof	2,499	Value: 450				

KM# 662   20 REAIS
8.0000 g., 0.9000 Gold 0.2315 oz. AGW, 22 mm. **Subject:**
World Cup 2002 **Obv:** Soccer player **Rev:** Value, inscription and
shooting stars **Edge:** Reeded

Date	Mintage	F	VF	XF	Unc	BU
2002 Proof	2,499	Value: 450				

KM# 664   20 REAIS
8.0000 g., 0.9000 Gold 0.2315 oz. AGW, 22 mm. **Subject:**
Centennial - Ary Barroso **Obv:** Piano keyboard and musical notes
above value **Rev:** Caricature of Ary Barroso **Edge:** Reeded

Date	Mintage	F	VF	XF	Unc	BU
2003 Proof	2,500	Value: 450				

KM# 670   20 REAIS
8.0000 g., 0.9000 Gold 0.2315 oz. AGW, 22 mm. **Subject:** FIFA
Centennial **Obv:** Soccer ball, value, date **Obv. Legend:** BRAZIL
Rev: Christ Redeemer, sugar loaf **Rev. Legend:** FUTBUL
MONDIAL CENTENARIO DA FIFA **Edge:** Reeded

Date	Mintage	F	VF	XF	Unc	BU
2004 Proof	4,060	Value: 450				

BRITISH ANTARCTIC TERRITORY

BRITISH TERRITORY
DECIMAL COINAGE

KM# 1   2 POUNDS
Copper-Nickel, 38.6 mm. **Ruler:** Elizabeth II **Subject:** 200th
Anniversary of the Granting of Letters Patent **Obv:** Elizabeth II
bust facing right **Rev:** Arms with denomination below **Rev.
Legend:** 1908 . CENTENARY OF GRANTING OF LETTERS
PATENT . 2008

Date	Mintage	F	VF	XF	Unc	BU
2008	Est. 50,000	—	—	—	17.50	20.00

KM# 1a   2 POUNDS
28.2800 g., 0.9250 Silver 0.8410 oz. ASW **Ruler:** Elizabeth II
Obv: Bust right **Rev:** Supported arms

Date	Mintage	F	VF	XF	Unc	BU
2008 Proof	Est. 10,000	Value: 60.00				

KM# 5   2 POUNDS
28.2800 g., Copper-Nickel **Ruler:** Elizabeth II **Subject:** Antarctic
treaty **Obv:** Bust right **Rev:** Whale and other Antarctic wildlife
Shape: 38.6

Date	Mintage	F	VF	XF	Unc	BU
2009	50,000	—	—	—	15.00	18.00

KM# 5a   2 POUNDS
28.2800 g., 0.9250 Silver 0.8410 oz. ASW, 38.6 mm. **Ruler:**
Elizabeth II **Obv:** Bust right **Rev:** Whale and other Antarctic
wildlife

Date	Mintage	F	VF	XF	Unc	BU
2009 Proof	10,000	Value: 45.00				

KM# 6   2 POUNDS
28.2800 g., Copper-Nickel, 38.61 mm. **Ruler:** Elizabeth II
Subject: Scott's Terra Nova Expedition **Obv:** Bust in tiara right
Rev: Captain scott, ship and men on ice flow

Date	Mintage	F	VF	XF	Unc	BU
2012	—	—	—	—	17.50	20.00

KM# 2   4 POUNDS
1.2400 g., 0.9999 Gold 0.0399 oz. AGW, 13.92 mm. **Ruler:** Elizabeth II **Obv:** Bust right **Rev:** Supported arms

Date	Mintage	F	VF	XF	Unc	BU
2008 Proof	Est. 10,000				Value: 100	

KM# 3   20 POUNDS
6.2200 g., 0.9999 Gold 0.1999 oz. AGW   **Ruler:** Elizabeth II **Obv:** Bust right **Rev:** Supported arms

Date	Mintage	F	VF	XF	Unc	BU
2008 Proof	Est. 2,000				Value: 350	

BRITISH INDIAN OCEAN TERRITORY

TERRITORY
DECIMAL COINAGE

KM# 1   2 POUNDS
28.2800 g., Copper-Nickel, 38.61 mm. **Ruler:** Elizabeth II **Obv:** Bust with tiara right **Rev:** Arms with supporters

Date	Mintage	F	VF	XF	Unc	BU
2009PM Proof	—				Value: 25.00	

KM# 2   2 POUNDS
28.2800 g., Copper-Nickel with glass insert, 38.61 mm. **Ruler:** Elizabeth II **Obv:** Small head at top, sea turtle insert **Rev:** Circle of life of the sea turtle

Date	Mintage	F	VF	XF	Unc	BU
2009PM Proof	—				Value: 40.00	

KM# 5   2 POUNDS
28.2800 g., Copper-Nickel, 38.61 mm. **Ruler:** Elizabeth II **Subject:** Royal Wedding **Obv:** Bust with tiara right **Rev:** Conjoined busts left of Catherine Middleton and Prince William

Date	Mintage	F	VF	XF	Unc	BU
2011PM	—	—	—	—	10.00	12.50

KM# 6   2 POUNDS
28.2800 g., Copper-Nickel, 38.61 mm. **Ruler:** Elizabeth II **Subject:** 60th Wedding anniversary **Obv:** Bust in tiara right **Rev:** Crowned EP cipher within circle of crosses and anchors

Date	Mintage	F	VF	XF	Unc	BU
2011PM	—	—	—	—	17.50	20.00

KM# 9   2 POUNDS
28.2800 g., Copper-Nickel, 38.61 mm. **Ruler:** Elizabeth II **Subject:** Life of Queen Elizabeth II **Obv:** Conjoined busts right, young and current portraits **Rev:** Queen Mother waving at left, Queen Elizabeth at right

Date	Mintage	F	VF	XF	Unc	BU
2012PM Proof	—				Value: 20.00	

KM# 8   2 POUNDS
28.2800 g., Copper-Nickel, 38.6 mm. **Ruler:** Elizabeth II **Subject:** Life of Queen Elizabeth II **Obv:** Conjoined busts left **Rev:** Elizabeth and Margaret as children riding ponies

Date	Mintage	F	VF	XF	Unc	BU
2012PM	—	—	—	—	—	15.00

BRITISH VIRGIN ISLANDS

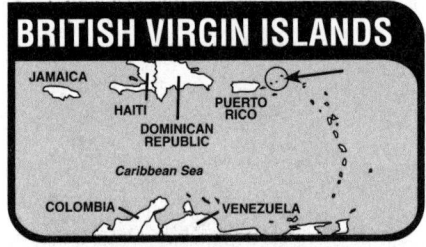

The Colony of the Virgin Islands, a British colony situated in the Caribbean Sea northeast of Puerto Rico and west of the Leeward Islands, has an area of 59 sq. mi. (155 sq. km.) and a population of 13,000. Capital: Road Town. The principal islands of the 36-island group are Tortola, Virgin Gorda, Anegada, and Jost Van Dyke. The chief industries are fishing and stock raising. Fish, livestock and bananas are exported. U.S. currency and Sterling circulate in common with the East Caribbean Dollar.

BRITISH COLONY
STANDARD COINAGE

KM# 196   DOLLAR
28.2800 g., Copper-Nickel, 38.6 mm. **Subject:** Queen's Golden Jubilee **Obv:** Queen's bust right **Rev:** Carnival dancers **Edge:** Reeded

Date	Mintage	F	VF	XF	Unc	BU
2002	—	—	—	—	7.50	9.50

KM# 180   DOLLAR
28.2800 g., Copper-Nickel, 25.7 mm. **Subject:** Sir Francis Drake **Obv:** Queen's bust right **Rev:** Ship, portrait and map **Edge:** Reeded

Date	Mintage	F	VF	XF	Unc	BU
2002	—	—	—	—	7.50	9.50

KM# 183   DOLLAR
28.2800 g., Copper-Nickel, 38.6 mm. **Subject:** Sir Walter Raleigh **Obv:** Queen's bust right **Rev:** Ship, portrait and map **Edge:** Reeded

Date	Mintage	F	VF	XF	Unc	BU
2002	—	—	—	—	7.50	9.50

KM# 187   DOLLAR
28.2800 g., Copper-Nickel, 38.6 mm. **Subject:** Queen's Golden Jubilee **Obv:** Queen's bust right **Rev:** Queen on horse **Edge:** Reeded

Date	Mintage	F	VF	XF	Unc	BU
2002	—	—	—	—	7.50	9.50

KM# 190   DOLLAR
28.2800 g., Copper-Nickel, 38.6 mm. **Subject:** Queen's Golden Jubilee **Obv:** Queen's bust right **Rev:** Queen on throne **Edge:** Reeded

Date	Mintage	F	VF	XF	Unc	BU
2002	—	—	—	—	7.50	9.50

KM# 193   DOLLAR
28.2800 g., Copper-Nickel, 38.6 mm. **Subject:** Queen's Golden Jubilee **Obv:** Queen's bust right **Rev:** Queen with President Ronald Reagan and First Lady Nancy Reagan **Edge:** Reeded

Date	Mintage	F	VF	XF	Unc	BU
2002	—	—	—	—	7.50	9.50

KM# 199   DOLLAR
28.2800 g., Copper-Nickel, 38.6 mm. **Subject:** Teddy Bear Centennial **Obv:** Queen's bust right **Rev:** Teddy bear **Edge:** Reeded

Date	Mintage	F	VF	XF	Unc	BU
2002	—	—	—	—	8.50	15.00

KM# 204   DOLLAR
28.2800 g., Copper-Nickel, 38.6 mm. **Subject:** Princess Diana **Obv:** Queen's bust right **Rev:** Diana's portrait **Edge:** Reeded

Date	Mintage	F	VF	XF	Unc	BU
2002	—	—	—	—	7.50	9.50

KM# 207   DOLLAR
28.2800 g., Copper-Nickel, 38.6 mm. **Subject:** September 11, 2001 **Obv:** Queen's bust right **Rev:** World Trade Center twin towers **Edge:** Reeded

Date	Mintage	F	VF	XF	Unc	BU
2002	—	—	—	—	12.00	13.50

KM# 210   DOLLAR
28.2800 g., Copper-Nickel, 38.6 mm. **Subject:** September 11, 2001 **Obv:** Queen's bust right **Rev:** Statue of Liberty **Edge:** Reeded

Date	Mintage	F	VF	XF	Unc	BU
2002	—	—	—	—	12.00	13.50

KM# 213 DOLLAR
28.2800 g., Copper-Nickel, 38.6 mm. **Subject:** Queen Mother **Obv:** Queen's bust right **Rev:** Queen Mother and a young Prince Charles **Edge:** Reeded

Date	Mintage	F	VF	XF	Unc	BU
2002PM	—	—	—	—	10.00	12.00

KM# 216 DOLLAR
28.2800 g., Copper-Nickel, 38.6 mm. **Subject:** Queen Mother **Obv:** Queen's bust right **Rev:** Queen Mother with four grandchildren **Edge:** Reeded

Date	Mintage	F	VF	XF	Unc	BU
2002PM	—	—	—	—	10.00	12.00

KM# 219 DOLLAR
28.2800 g., Copper-Nickel, 38.6 mm. **Subject:** Queen Mother Series **Obv:** Queen's bust right **Rev:** Queen Mother with uniformed Prince Charles **Edge:** Reeded

Date	Mintage	F	VF	XF	Unc	BU
2002PM	—	—	—	—	10.00	12.00

KM# 222 DOLLAR
28.2800 g., Copper-Nickel, 38.6 mm. **Subject:** Queen Mother Series **Obv:** Queen's bust right **Rev:** Queen Mother's coffin **Edge:** Reeded

Date	Mintage	F	VF	XF	Unc	BU
2002PM	—	—	—	—	10.00	12.00

KM# 225 DOLLAR
28.4400 g., Copper-Nickel, 38.6 mm. **Subject:** Kennedy Assassination **Obv:** Queen's bust right **Rev:** President Kennedy's portrait left **Edge:** Reeded

Date	Mintage	F	VF	XF	Unc	BU
2003	—	—	—	—	10.00	12.00

KM# 229 DOLLAR
28.2800 g., Copper-Nickel, 38.6 mm. **Subject:** Powered Flight Centennial **Obv:** Queen's bust right **Rev:** Three historic airplanes and rocket **Edge:** Reeded

Date	Mintage	F	VF	XF	Unc	BU
2003	—	—	—	—	10.00	12.00

KM# 232 DOLLAR
28.2800 g., Copper-Nickel, 38.6 mm. **Obv:** Queen's bust right **Rev:** Henry VIII and Elizabeth I **Edge:** Reeded

Date	Mintage	F	VF	XF	Unc	BU
2003	—	—	—	—	10.00	12.00

KM# 235 DOLLAR
28.2800 g., Copper-Nickel, 38.6 mm. **Obv:** Queen's bust right **Rev:** Matthew Parker, Archbishop of Canterbury **Edge:** Reeded

Date	Mintage	F	VF	XF	Unc	BU
2003	—	—	—	—	10.00	12.00

KM# 238 DOLLAR
28.2800 g., Copper-Nickel, 38.6 mm. **Obv:** Queen's bust right **Rev:** Sir Francis Drake and ships **Edge:** Reeded

Date	Mintage	F	VF	XF	Unc	BU
2003	—	—	—	—	10.00	12.00

KM# 241 DOLLAR
28.2800 g., Copper-Nickel, 38.6 mm. **Obv:** Queen's bust right **Rev:** Sir Walter Raleigh **Edge:** Reeded

Date	Mintage	F	VF	XF	Unc	BU
2003	—	—	—	—	10.00	12.00

KM# 244 DOLLAR
28.2800 g., Copper-Nickel, 38.6 mm. **Obv:** Queen's bust right **Rev:** Sir William Shakespeare **Edge:** Reeded

Date	Mintage	F	VF	XF	Unc	BU
2003	—	—	—	—	10.00	12.00

KM# 247 DOLLAR
28.2800 g., Copper-Nickel, 38.6 mm. **Obv:** Queen's bust right **Rev:** Elizabeth I above her funeral procession **Edge:** Reeded

Date	Mintage	F	VF	XF	Unc	BU
2003	—	—	—	—	10.00	12.00

KM# 250 DOLLAR
28.2800 g., Copper-Nickel, 38.6 mm. **Subject:** Olympics **Obv:** Queen's bust right **Rev:** Ancient bust, runners and coin **Edge:** Reeded

Date	Mintage	F	VF	XF	Unc	BU
2003	—	—	—	—	10.00	12.00

KM# 253 DOLLAR
28.2800 g., Copper-Nickel, 38.6 mm. **Subject:** Olympics **Obv:** Queen's bust right **Rev:** Ancient bust, charioteer and coin **Edge:** Reeded

Date	Mintage	F	VF	XF	Unc	BU
2003	—	—	—	—	10.00	12.00

KM# 303 DOLLAR
28.2800 g., Copper-Nickel, 38.6 mm. **Subject:** 2004 Athens Olympics **Obv:** Queen's bust right **Rev:** Ancient athlete's bust

right, runners at lower right, ancient coin with owl at upper right **Edge:** Reeded

Date	Mintage	F	VF	XF	Unc	BU
2003	—	—	—	—	10.00	12.00

KM# 306 DOLLAR
28.2800 g., Copper-Nickel, 38.6 mm. **Subject:** 2004 Athens Olympics **Obv:** Queen's bust right **Rev:** Ancient athlete bust left, chariot race at lower left, ancient coin at upper left **Edge:** Reeded

Date	Mintage	F	VF	XF	Unc	BU
2003	—	—	—	—	10.00	12.00

KM# 310 DOLLAR
28.2800 g., Copper-Nickel, 38.6 mm. **Subject:** Queen Elizabeth's Golden Coronation Jubilee **Obv:** Elizabeth II **Rev:** Cameo portraits above the ship "Gothic" **Edge:** Reeded

Date	Mintage	F	VF	XF	Unc	BU
2003	—	—	—	—	7.50	9.50

KM# 319 DOLLAR
28.2800 g., Copper-Nickel **Subject:** 50th Anniversary of Coronation **Rev:** Queen riding in automobile

Date	Mintage	F	VF	XF	Unc	BU
2003	—	—	—	—	12.00	15.00

KM# 320 DOLLAR
28.2800 g., Copper-Nickel **Subject:** Golden Jubilee of Coronation **Rev:** Sir. Edmond Hillary on Mt. Everest, Queen II above mountain climbers

Date	Mintage	F	VF	XF	Unc	BU
2003	—	—	—	—	12.00	15.00

KM# 321 DOLLAR
28.2800 g., Copper-Nickel **Rev:** Queen presenting Ascot Horse Racing prize

Date	Mintage	F	VF	XF	Unc	BU
2003	—	—	—	—	10.00	12.00

KM# 265   DOLLAR
28.2800 g., Copper-Nickel, 38.6 mm.   **Obv:** Queen's bust right
Rev: Sir Francis Drake, ship and map **Edge:** Reeded

Date	Mintage	F	VF	XF	Unc	BU
2004	—			—	10.00	12.00

KM# 267.1   DOLLAR
28.2800 g., Copper-Nickel, 38.6 mm.   **Obv:** Queen's bust right
Rev: Peter Rabbit **Edge:** Reeded

Date	Mintage	F	VF	XF	Unc	BU
2004	—			—	15.00	17.00

KM# 267.2   DOLLAR
28.2800 g., Copper-Nickel, 38.6 mm.   **Obv:** Queen's bust right
Rev: Multicolor Peter Rabbit **Edge:** Reeded

Date	Mintage	F	VF	XF	Unc	BU
2004	—			—	20.00	22.00

KM# 268   DOLLAR
3.1100 g., 0.9990 Silver 0.0999 oz. ASW, 18 mm.   **Obv:** Queen's
bust right **Rev:** Peter Rabbit **Edge:** Reeded

Date	Mintage	F	VF	XF	Unc	BU
2004 Proof	10,000	Value: 25.00				

KM# 281   DOLLAR
28.2800 g., Copper-Nickel, 38.6 mm.   **Obv:** Queen's bust right
Rev: Sailor above two D-Day landing craft **Edge:** Reeded

Date	Mintage	F	VF	XF	Unc	BU
2004	—			—	10.00	12.00

KM# 286   DOLLAR
28.2800 g., Copper-Nickel, 38.6 mm.   **Obv:** Queen's bust right
Rev: Dolphin **Edge:** Reeded

Date	Mintage	F	VF	XF	Unc	BU
2004	—			—	12.00	14.00

KM# 297   DOLLAR
28.2800 g., Copper-Nickel, 38.6 mm.   **Obv:** Queen's bust right
Rev: Soldier above tank and jeeps **Edge:** Reeded

Date	Mintage	F	VF	XF	Unc	BU
2004	—			—	10.00	12.00

KM# 300   DOLLAR
28.2800 g., Copper-Nickel, 38.6 mm.   **Obv:** Queen's bust right
Rev: Pilot and planes above D-Day landing **Edge:** Reeded

Date	Mintage	F	VF	XF	Unc	BU
2004	—			—	10.00	12.00

KM# 330   DOLLAR
Copper-Nickel   **Ruler:** Elizabeth II **Rev:** Battle of Britain

Date	Mintage	F	VF	XF	Unc	BU
2005	—			—	15.00	17.00

KM# 331   DOLLAR
Copper-Nickel   **Ruler:** Elizabeth II **Rev:** Battle of Berlin

Date	Mintage	F	VF	XF	Unc	BU
2005	—			—	15.00	17.00

KM# 312   DOLLAR
28.2800 g., Copper-Nickel, 38.6 mm.   **Obv:** Bust of Queen
Elizabeth II right **Rev:** Mother and baby dolphins **Edge:** Reeded

Date	Mintage	F	VF	XF	Unc	BU
2005	—			—	12.00	14.00

KM# 322   DOLLAR
28.2800 g., Copper-Nickel   **Rev:** VJ Day, McArthur and U.S.S.
Missiouri Battleship

Date	Mintage	F	VF	XF	Unc	BU
2005	—			—	10.00	12.00

KM# 323   DOLLAR
28.2800 g., Copper-Nickel   **Rev:** Warships near Atlantic coast,
West Indies islands

Date	Mintage	F	VF	XF	Unc	BU
2005	—			—	10.00	12.00

KM# 324   DOLLAR
28.2800 g., Copper-Nickel   **Rev:** Death of Nelson

Date	Mintage	F	VF	XF	Unc	BU
2005	—			—	10.00	12.00

KM# 325   DOLLAR
28.2800 g., Copper-Nickel   **Rev:** Nelson and Order Star above
ships

Date	Mintage	F	VF	XF	Unc	BU
2005	—			—	10.00	12.00

KM# 326   DOLLAR
28.2800 g., Copper-Nickel   **Rev:** Nelson and Napoleon

Date	Mintage	F	VF	XF	Unc	BU
2005	—			—	10.00	12.00

KM# 327   DOLLAR
28.2800 g., Copper-Nickel   **Rev:** Nelson's Column, statue and
ships

Date	Mintage	F	VF	XF	Unc	BU
2005	—			—	10.00	12.00

KM# 328   DOLLAR
28.2800 g., Copper-Nickel   **Rev:** V.E. Day, Montgomery and
Eisenhower

Date	Mintage	F	VF	XF	Unc	BU
2005	—			—	10.00	12.00

KM# 403   DOLLAR
28.2800 g., Copper-Nickel, 38.61 mm.   **Ruler:** Elizabeth II **Obv:**
Bust in tiara right **Rev:** Inverted Swan postage stamp

Date	Mintage	F	VF	XF	Unc	BU
2005PM	—			—	17.50	20.00

KM# 349   DOLLAR
28.2800 g., Copper-Nickel, 38.60 mm.   **Ruler:** Elizabeth II
Subject: 5th Anniversary Attack on Twin Towers, New York City
Obv: Crowned bust right **Obv. Legend:** BRITISH VIRGIN
ISLANDS - QUEEN ELIZABETH II **Rev:** Twin Towers in sprays,
remembrance ribbon privy mark at upper right **Rev. Inscription:**
LEST WE FORGET **Edge:** Reeded

Date	Mintage	F	VF	XF	Unc	BU
2006	—			—	15.00	17.00

KM# 329 DOLLAR
Copper-Nickel **Rev:** Two dolphins

Date	Mintage	F	VF	XF	Unc	BU
2006	—	—	—	—	10.00	12.00

KM# 332 DOLLAR
28.2800 g., Copper-Nickel, 38.60 mm. **Ruler:** Elizabeth II
Subject: 400th Anniversary Founding of Jamestown **Obv:** Bust
with tiara right **Obv. Legend:** BRITISH VIRGIN ISLANDS -
QUEEN ELIZABETH II **Rev:** British lion laying, American eagle
perched on sprays **Rev. Legend:** UNITED IN FRIENDSHIP
Edge: Reeded

Date	Mintage	F	VF	XF	Unc	BU
2007	—	—	—	—	16.50	18.50

KM# 404 DOLLAR
28.2800 g., Copper-Nickel, 38.61 mm. **Ruler:** Elizabeth II **Obv:**
Bust in tiara right **Rev:** George Washington 5 cent postage stamp

Date	Mintage	F	VF	XF	Unc	BU
2007PM	—	—	—	—	17.50	20.00

KM# 370 DOLLAR
28.2800 g., Copper-Nickel, 38.6 mm. **Ruler:** Elizabeth II **Obv:**
Bust right **Rev:** Two soccer players and leopard

Date	Mintage	F	VF	XF	Unc	BU
2009	—	—	—	—	12.00	15.00

KM# 373 DOLLAR
28.2800 g., Copper-Nickel, 38.6 mm. **Ruler:** Elizabeth II **Obv:**
Bust right **Rev:** Queen Elizabeth I aboard ship

Date	Mintage	F	VF	XF	Unc	BU
2009	—	—	—	—	12.00	15.00

KM# 375 DOLLAR
28.2800 g., Copper-Nickel, 38.6 mm. **Ruler:** Elizabeth II **Obv:**
Bust right **Rev:** Elizabeth I between two columns

Date	Mintage	F	VF	XF	Unc	BU
2009	—	—	—	—	12.00	15.00

KM# 393 DOLLAR
28.2800 g., Copper-Nickel, 38.6 mm. **Ruler:** Elizabeth II
Subject: Peanuts 60th Anniversary **Rev:** Snoopy sleeping atop
doghouse

Date	Mintage	F	VF	XF	Unc	BU
2010PM	—	—	—	—	—	25.00

KM# 396 DOLLAR
28.2800 g., Bronze with antique patina, 38.6 mm. **Ruler:**
Elizabeth II **Subject:** Elgin Marbles **Rev:** Two horsemen

Date	Mintage	F	VF	XF	Unc	BU
2010PM	—	—	—	—	25.00	

KM# 402 DOLLAR
28.2800 g., Copper-Nickel, 38.61 mm. **Ruler:** Elizabeth II
Subject: Birth of Venus

Date	Mintage	F	VF	XF	Unc	BU
2010PM	—	—	—	—	—	15.00

KM# 278 2 DOLLARS
58.0000 g., Bronze, 50 mm. **Obv:** Queen's bust right **Rev:** 1896
Olympic medal design **Edge:** Reeded

Date	Mintage	F	VF	XF	Unc	BU
2004 Proof	3,500	Value: 20.00				

KM# 380 2 DOLLARS
Bronze with patina, 50 mm. **Ruler:** Elizabeth II **Rev:** Turtle

Date	Mintage	F	VF	XF	Unc	BU
2008PM	—	—	—	—	—	20.00

KM# 269.1 2.50 DOLLARS
7.7758 g., 0.9990 Silver 0.2497 oz. ASW, 26 mm. **Obv:** Queen's
bust right **Rev:** Peter Rabbit **Edge:** Reeded

Date	Mintage	F	VF	XF	Unc	BU
2004 Proof	—	Value: 18.00				

KM# 269.2 2.50 DOLLARS
7.7758 g., 0.9990 Silver 0.2497 oz. ASW, 26 mm. **Obv:** Queen's
bust right **Rev:** Multicolor Peter Rabbit **Edge:** Reeded

Date	Mintage	F	VF	XF	Unc	BU
2004 Proof	7,500	Value: 25.00				

KM# 381 4 DOLLARS
Silver **Ruler:** Elizabeth II **Subject:** 400th Anniversary of
Settlement

Date	Mintage	F	VF	XF	Unc	BU
2009PM	—	—	—	—	—	35.00

KM# 284 5 DOLLARS
10.0000 g., 0.9900 Titanium 0.3183 oz., 36.1 mm. **Obv:**
Queen's bust right **Rev:** British Guiana stamp design **Edge:**
Reeded

Date	Mintage	F	VF	XF	Unc	BU
2004 Proof	7,500	Value: 95.00				

KM# 340 5 DOLLARS
0.9999 Bi-Metallic Silver center in Gold ring. **Ruler:** Elizabeth II
Obv: Conjoined busts with Philip right, within gold ring **Obv.
Legend:** BRITISH VIRGIN ISLANDS — QUEEN ELIZABETH II
Rev: Conjoined busts of Princess Elizabeth and Prince Philip
right within gold ring **Rev. Legend:** WITH THIS RING, I THEE
WED **Edge:** Reeded

Date	Mintage	F	VF	XF	Unc	BU
2007 Proof	—	Value: 500				

KM# 405 5 DOLLARS
28.2800 g., Copper-Nickel gilt, 38.61 mm. **Ruler:** Elizabeth II
Obv: Bust in tiara right **Rev:** Benjamin Franklin postage stamp

Date	Mintage	F	VF	XF	Unc	BU
2007PM	—	—	—	—	17.50	20.00

KM# 414 5 DOLLARS
28.2800 g., Copper-Nickel gilt, 38.61 mm. **Ruler:** Elizabeth II
Subject: Bejing Olympics **Obv:** Bust in tiara right **Rev:** Tennis
plays against Great Wall background

Date	Mintage	F	VF	XF	Unc	BU
2008PM Proof	—	Value: 25.00				

KM# 414a 5 DOLLARS
28.2800 g., Silver with gilt center, 38.61 mm. **Ruler:** Elizabeth II
Subject: Bejing Olympics **Obv:** Bust in tiara right **Rev:** Tennis
plays against Great Wall background

Date	Mintage	F	VF	XF	Unc	BU
2008PM Proof	—	Value: 50.00				

KM# 383 5 DOLLARS
Titanium **Ruler:** Elizabeth II **Subject:** Bejing Olympics - Tennis

Date	Mintage	F	VF	XF	Unc	BU
2009PM Proof	—	Value: 55.00				

KM# 384 5 DOLLARS
Titanium **Ruler:** Elizabeth II **Subject:** Bejing Olympics -
Swimming

Date	Mintage	F	VF	XF	Unc	BU
2009PM Proof	—	Value: 55.00				

KM# 385 5 DOLLARS
Titanium **Ruler:** Elizabeth II **Subject:** Bejing Olympics

Date	Mintage	F	VF	XF	Unc	BU
2009PM Proof	—	Value: 55.00				

KM# 386 5 DOLLARS
Titanium **Ruler:** Elizabeth II **Subject:** Bejing Olympics

Date	Mintage	F	VF	XF	Unc	BU
2009PM Proof	—	Value: 55.00				

KM# 387 5 DOLLARS
Titanium **Ruler:** Elizabeth II **Subject:** Bejing Olympics

Date	Mintage	F	VF	XF	Unc	BU
2009PM Proof	—	Value: 55.00				

KM# 399   5 DOLLARS
7.0000 g., Bi-Metallic Gold and Titanium, 38.6 mm.   **Ruler:** Elizabeth II **Subject:** 175th Anniversary of Publication of Hans Christian Anderson's first book **Rev:** Scene from the Little Mermaid

Date	Mintage	F	VF	XF	Unc	BU
2010PM Proof	Est. 5,000	Value: 120				

KM# 400   5 DOLLARS
10.0000 g., Tri-Metallic Silver, Gold and Titanium, 38.6 mm. **Ruler:** Elizabeth II **Subject:** 175th Anniversary of Publication of Hans Christian Andersen's first book **Rev:** Scene from the Little Mermaid

Date	Mintage	F	VF	XF	Unc	BU
2010PM Proof	Est. 7,500	Value: 120				

KM# 181   10 DOLLARS
28.2800 g., 0.9250 Silver 0.8410 oz. ASW, 38.6 mm.   **Subject:** Sir Francis Drake **Obv:** Queen's bust right **Rev:** Ship, portrait and map **Edge:** Reeded

Date	Mintage	F	VF	XF	Unc	BU
2002 Proof	—	Value: 45.00				

KM# 184   10 DOLLARS
28.2800 g., 0.9250 Silver 0.8410 oz. ASW, 38.6 mm.   **Subject:**

Sir Walter Raleigh **Obv:** Queen's bust right **Rev:** Ship, portrait and map **Edge:** Reeded

Date	Mintage	F	VF	XF	Unc	BU
2002 Proof	—	Value: 45.00				

KM# 188   10 DOLLARS
28.2800 g., 0.9250 Gold Clad Silver 0.8410 oz., 38.6 mm. **Subject:** Queen's Golden Jubilee **Obv:** Queen's bust right **Rev:** Queen on horse trotting left **Edge:** Reeded

Date	Mintage	F	VF	XF	Unc	BU
2002 Proof	10,000	Value: 42.50				

KM# 191   10 DOLLARS
28.2800 g., 0.9250 Gold Clad Silver 0.8410 oz., 38.6 mm. **Subject:** Queen's Golden Jubilee **Obv:** Queen's bust right **Rev:** 3/4-length Queen seated on throne **Edge:** Reeded

Date	Mintage	F	VF	XF	Unc	BU
2002 Proof	10,000	Value: 45.00				

KM# 194   10 DOLLARS
28.2800 g., 0.9250 Gold Clad Silver 0.8410 oz., 38.6 mm. **Subject:** Queen's Golden Jubilee **Obv:** Queen's bust right **Rev:** Queen with President Ronald Reagan and First Lady Nancy Reagan **Edge:** Reeded

Date	Mintage	F	VF	XF	Unc	BU
2002 Proof	10,000	Value: 45.00				

KM# 197   10 DOLLARS
28.2800 g., 0.9250 Gold Clad Silver 0.8410 oz., 38.6 mm. **Subject:** Queen's Golden Jubilee **Obv:** Queen's bust right **Rev:** Carnival dancers **Edge:** Reeded

Date	Mintage	F	VF	XF	Unc	BU
2002 Proof	10,000	Value: 45.00				

KM# 200   10 DOLLARS
28.2800 g., 0.9250 Silver 0.8410 oz. ASW, 38.6 mm.   **Subject:** Teddy Bear Centennial **Obv:** Queen's bust right **Rev:** Teddy bear **Edge:** Reeded

Date	Mintage	F	VF	XF	Unc	BU
2002 Proof	10,000	Value: 40.00				

KM# 205   10 DOLLARS
28.2800 g., 0.9250 Silver 0.8410 oz. ASW, 38.6 mm.   **Subject:** Princess Diana **Obv:** Queen's bust right **Rev:** Diana's portrait **Edge:** Reeded

Date	Mintage	F	VF	XF	Unc	BU
2002 Proof	10,000	Value: 40.00				

KM# 208.1   10 DOLLARS
28.2800 g., 0.9250 Silver 0.8410 oz. ASW, 38.6 mm.   **Subject:** September 11, 2001 **Obv:** Queen's bust right **Rev:** World Trade Center twin towers **Edge:** Reeded

Date	Mintage	F	VF	XF	Unc	BU
2002 Proof	10,000	Value: 50.00				

KM# 208.2   10 DOLLARS
28.2800 g., 0.9250 Silver 0.8410 oz. ASW, 38.6 mm.   **Subject:** September 11, 2001 **Obv:** Queen's bust right **Rev:** Holographic multicolor World Trade Center twin towers **Edge:** Reeded

Date	Mintage	F	VF	XF	Unc	BU
2002 Proof	10,000	Value: 45.00				

KM# 211   10 DOLLARS
28.2800 g., 0.9250 Silver 0.8410 oz. ASW, 38.6 mm.   **Subject:** September 11, 2001 **Obv:** Queen's bust right **Rev:** Statue of Liberty **Edge:** Reeded

Date	Mintage	F	VF	XF	Unc	BU
2002 Proof	10,000	Value: 40.00				

KM# 214   10 DOLLARS
28.2800 g., 0.9250 Silver 0.8410 oz. ASW, 38.6 mm. **Subject:**
Queen Mother **Obv:** Queen's bust right **Rev:** Queen Mother with
young Prince Charles **Edge:** Reeded

Date	Mintage	F	VF	XF	Unc	BU
2002PM Proof	10,000	Value: 40.00				

KM# 217   10 DOLLARS
28.2800 g., 0.9250 Silver 0.8410 oz. ASW, 38.6 mm. **Subject:**
Queen Mother Series **Obv:** Queen's bust right **Rev:** Queen
Mother with four grandchildren **Edge:** Reeded

Date	Mintage	F	VF	XF	Unc	BU
2002PM Proof	10,000	Value: 40.00				

KM# 220   10 DOLLARS
28.2800 g., 0.9250 Silver 0.8410 oz. ASW, 38.6 mm. **Subject:**
Queen Mother Series **Obv:** Queen's bust right **Rev:** Queen
Mother with uniformed Prince Charles **Edge:** Reeded

Date	Mintage	F	VF	XF	Unc	BU
2002PM Proof	10,000	Value: 40.00				

KM# 223   10 DOLLARS
28.2800 g., 0.9250 Silver 0.8410 oz. ASW, 38.6 mm. **Subject:**
Queen Mother Series **Obv:** Queen's bust right **Rev:** Queen
Mother's coffin **Edge:** Reeded

Date	Mintage	F	VF	XF	Unc	BU
2002PM Proof	10,000	Value: 40.00				

KM# 226   10 DOLLARS
28.2800 g., 0.9250 Silver 0.8410 oz. ASW, 38.6 mm. **Subject:**
Kennedy Assassination **Obv:** Queen's bust right **Rev:** President
Kennedy's head left **Edge:** Reeded

Date	Mintage	F	VF	XF	Unc	BU
2003 Proof	10,000	Value: 50.00				

KM# 230   10 DOLLARS
28.2800 g., 0.9250 Silver 0.8410 oz. ASW, 38.6 mm. **Subject:**
Powered Flight Centennial **Obv:** Queen's bust right **Rev:** Three
historic airplanes and rocket **Edge:** Reeded

Date	Mintage	F	VF	XF	Unc	BU
2003 Proof	10,000	Value: 45.00				

KM# 233   10 DOLLARS
28.2800 g., 0.9250 Silver 0.8410 oz. ASW, 38.6 mm. **Obv:**
Queen's bust right **Rev:** Henry VIII and Elizabeth I **Edge:** Reeded

Date	Mintage	F	VF	XF	Unc	BU
2003 Proof	10,000	Value: 42.00				

KM# 236   10 DOLLARS
28.2800 g., 0.9250 Silver 0.8410 oz. ASW, 38.6 mm. **Obv:**
Queen's bust right **Rev:** Matthew Parker, Archbishop of
Canterbury **Edge:** Reeded

Date	Mintage	F	VF	XF	Unc	BU
2003 Proof	10,000	Value: 42.00				

KM# 239   10 DOLLARS
28.2800 g., 0.9250 Silver 0.8410 oz. ASW, 38.6 mm. **Obv:**
Queen's bust right **Rev:** Sir Francis Drake and ships **Edge:**
Reeded

Date	Mintage	F	VF	XF	Unc	BU
2003 Proof	10,000	Value: 42.00				

KM# 242   10 DOLLARS
28.2800 g., 0.9250 Silver 0.8410 oz. ASW, 38.6 mm. **Obv:**
Queen's bust right **Rev:** Sir Walter Raleigh **Edge:** Reeded

Date	Mintage	F	VF	XF	Unc	BU
2003 Proof	10,000	Value: 42.00				

KM# 245   10 DOLLARS
28.2800 g., 0.9250 Silver 0.8410 oz. ASW, 38.6 mm. **Obv:**
Queen's bust right **Rev:** Sir William Shakespeare **Edge:** Reeded

Date	Mintage	F	VF	XF	Unc	BU
2003 Proof	10,000	Value: 42.00				

KM# 248   10 DOLLARS
28.2800 g., 0.9250 Silver 0.8410 oz. ASW, 38.6 mm. **Obv:**
Queen's bust right **Rev:** Elizabeth I above her funeral procession
Edge: Reeded

Date	Mintage	F	VF	XF	Unc	BU
2003 Proof	10,000	Value: 42.00				

KM# 251   10 DOLLARS
28.2800 g., 0.9250 Silver 0.8410 oz. ASW, 38.6 mm. **Subject:**
Olympics **Obv:** Queen's bust right **Rev:** Ancient bust, runners
and coin **Edge:** Reeded

Date	Mintage	F	VF	XF	Unc	BU
2003 Proof	10,000	Value: 42.00				

KM# 254   10 DOLLARS
28.2800 g., 0.9250 Silver 0.8410 oz. ASW, 38.6 mm. **Subject:** Olympics **Obv:** Queen's bust right **Rev:** Ancient bust, charioteer and coin **Edge:** Reeded

Date	Mintage	F	VF	XF	Unc	BU
2003 Proof	10,000	Value: 42.00				

KM# 311   10 DOLLARS
28.3000 g., 0.9250 Gold Clad Silver 0.8416 oz., 38.6 mm.
Subject: Queen Elizabeth's Golden Coronation Jubilee **Obv:** Elizabeth II **Rev:** Cameo portrait above ship "Gothic" **Edge:** Reeded

Date	Mintage	F	VF	XF	Unc	BU
2003 Proof	—	Value: 50.00				

KM# 266   10 DOLLARS
28.2800 g., 0.9250 Silver 0.8410 oz. ASW, 38.6 mm. **Obv:** Queen's bust right **Rev:** Sir Francis Drake, ship and map **Edge:** Reeded

Date	Mintage	F	VF	XF	Unc	BU
2004 Proof	10,000	Value: 45.00				

KM# 270.1   10 DOLLARS
28.2800 g., 0.9250 Silver 0.8410 oz. ASW, 38.6 mm. **Obv:** Queen's bust right **Rev:** Peter Rabbit **Edge:** Reeded

Date	Mintage	F	VF	XF	Unc	BU
2004 Proof	5,000	Value: 47.50				

KM# 270.2   10 DOLLARS
28.2800 g., 0.9250 Silver 0.8410 oz. ASW, 38.6 mm. **Obv:** Queen's bust right **Rev:** Multicolor Peter Rabbit **Edge:** Reeded

Date	Mintage	F	VF	XF	Unc	BU
2004 Proof	—	Value: 65.00				

KM# 274   10 DOLLARS
1.2440 g., 0.9999 Gold 0.0400 oz. AGW, 14 mm. **Obv:** Queen's bust right **Rev:** Hernando Pizarro **Edge:** Reeded

Date	Mintage	F	VF	XF	Unc	BU
2004 Proof	350	Value: 85.00				

KM# 282   10 DOLLARS
28.2800 g., 0.9250 Silver 0.8410 oz. ASW, 38.6 mm. **Obv:** Queen's bust right **Rev:** Sailor above two D-Day landing craft **Edge:** Reeded

Date	Mintage	F	VF	XF	Unc	BU
2004 Proof	10,000	Value: 50.00				

KM# 287   10 DOLLARS
31.1035 g., 0.9990 Silver 0.9990 oz. ASW, 38.6 mm. **Obv:** Queen's bust right **Rev:** Dolphin **Edge:** Reeded

Date	Mintage	F	VF	XF	Unc	BU
2004 Proof	10,000	Value: 55.00				

KM# 288   10 DOLLARS
1.2440 g., 0.9999 Gold 0.0400 oz. AGW, 14 mm. **Obv:** Queen's bust right **Rev:** Dolphin **Edge:** Reeded

Date	Mintage	F	VF	XF	Unc	BU
2004 Proof	10,000	Value: 75.00				

KM# 298   10 DOLLARS
28.2800 g., 0.9250 Silver 0.8410 oz. ASW, 38.6 mm. **Obv:** Queen's bust right **Rev:** Soldier above tank and jeeps **Edge:** Reeded

Date	Mintage	F	VF	XF	Unc	BU
2004 Proof	10,000	Value: 50.00				

KM# 301   10 DOLLARS
28.2800 g., 0.9250 Silver 0.8410 oz. ASW, 38.6 mm. **Obv:** Queen's bust right **Rev:** Pilot and planes above D-Day landing **Edge:** Reeded

Date	Mintage	F	VF	XF	Unc	BU
2004 Proof	10,000	Value: 50.00				

KM# 304   10 DOLLARS
28.2800 g., 0.9250 Silver 0.8410 oz. ASW, 38.6 mm. **Obv:** Queen's bust right **Rev:** Ancient Olympic bust, runners and owl coin **Edge:** Reeded

Date	Mintage	F	VF	XF	Unc	BU
2004 Proof	10,000	Value: 50.00				

KM# 307   10 DOLLARS
28.2800 g., 0.9250 Silver 0.8410 oz. ASW, 38.6 mm. **Obv:** Queen's bust right **Rev:** Ancient Olympic bust, charioteer and Zeus coin **Edge:** Reeded

Date	Mintage	F	VF	XF	Unc	BU
2004 Proof	10,000	Value: 50.00				

KM# 313   10 DOLLARS
31.1030 g., 0.9990 Silver 0.9989 oz. ASW, 38.6 mm. **Obv:** Bust of Queen Elizabeth II right **Rev:** Mother and baby dolphin **Edge:** Reeded

Date	Mintage	F	VF	XF	Unc	BU
2005 Proof	10,000	Value: 55.00				

KM# 314   10 DOLLARS
1.2440 g., 0.9999 Gold 0.0400 oz. AGW, 13.92 mm. **Obv:** Bust of Queen Elizabeth II right **Rev:** Mother and baby dolphin **Edge:** Reeded

Date	Mintage	F	VF	XF	Unc	BU
2005 Proof	10,000	Value: 70.00				

KM# 350   10 DOLLARS
28.2800 g., 0.9250 Silver 0.8410 oz. ASW, 38.60 mm. **Ruler:** Elizabeth II **Subject:** 5th Anniversary - Attack on Twin Towers, New York City **Obv:** Crowned bust right **Obv. Legend:** BRITISH VIRGIN ISLANDS — QUEEN ELIZABETH II **Rev:** Twin Towers in sprays, remembrance ribbon privy mark at upper right **Rev. Inscription:** LEST WE FORGET **Edge:** Reeded

Date	Mintage	F	VF	XF	Unc	BU
2006 Proof	10,000	Value: 77.50				

KM# 333   10 DOLLARS
28.2800 g., 0.9167 Silver 0.8334 oz. ASW, 38.60 mm. **Ruler:** Elizabeth II **Subject:** 400th Anniversary Founding of Jamestown **Obv:** Bust with tiara right **Obv. Legend:** BRITISH VIRGIN ISLANDS — QUEEN ELIZABETH II **Rev:** British lion laying, American eagle perched on sprays **Rev. Legend:** UNITED IN FRIENDSHIP **Edge:** Reeded

Date	Mintage	F	VF	XF	Unc	BU
2007 Proof	25,000	Value: 75.00				

KM# 334   10 DOLLARS
1.2444 g., 0.9999 Gold 0.0400 oz. AGW, 13.92 mm. **Ruler:** Elizabeth II **Subject:** 400th Anniversary Founding of Jamestown **Obv:** Bust with tiara right **Obv. Legend:** BRITISH VIRGIN ISLANDS — QUEEN ELIZABETH II **Rev:** British lion laying, American eagle perched on sprays **Rev. Legend:** UNITED IN FRIENDSHIP **Edge:** Reeded

Date	Mintage	F	VF	XF	Unc	BU
2007 Proof	20,000	Value: 75.00				

KM# 339   10 DOLLARS
28.2800 g., Copper-Nickel **Ruler:** Elizabeth II **Subject:** 10th Anniversary Death of Princess Diana **Obv:** Bust with tiara right **Obv. Legend:** BRITISH VIRGIN ISLANDS — QUEEN ELIZABETH II **Rev:** Mother Teresa at left, Princess Diana at right **Rev. Legend:** MOTHER TERESA • IN LOVING MEMORY • PRINCESS DIANA **Edge:** Reeded

Date	Mintage	F	VF	XF	Unc	BU
2007	—	—	—	—	18.50	

KM# 339a   10 DOLLARS
0.9167 Silver **Ruler:** Elizabeth II **Subject:** 10th Anniversary - Death of Princess Diana **Obv:** Bust with tiara right **Obv. Legend:** BRITISH VIRGIN ISLANDS — QUEEN ELIZABETH II **Rev:** Mother Teresa at left, Princess Diana at right **Rev. Legend:** MOTHER TERESA • IN LOVING MEMORY • PRINCESS DIANA **Edge:** Reeded

Date	Mintage	F	VF	XF	Unc	BU
2007 Proof	—	Value: 75.00				

KM# 341   10 DOLLARS
28.2800 g., Copper-Nickel **Ruler:** Elizabeth II **Subject:** Diamond Wedding Anniversary **Obv:** Conjoined busts with Philip right **Obv. Legend:** BRITISH VIRGIN ISLANDS — QUEEN ELIZABETH II **Rev:** Bride to be and King George VI standing facing **Rev. Legend:** Diamond Wedding of H.M. Queen Elizabeth II & H.R.H. Prince Philip **Rev. Inscription:** THE GIVING AWAY **Edge:** Reeded

Date	Mintage	F	VF	XF	Unc	BU
2007	—	—	—	—	16.50	18.50

KM# 341a   10 DOLLARS
28.2800 g., 0.9250 Silver 0.8410 oz. ASW **Ruler:** Elizabeth II **Subject:** Diamond Wedding Anniversary **Obv:** Conjoined busts with Philip right **Obv. Legend:** BRITISH VIRGIN ISLANDS — QUEEN ELIZABETH II **Rev:** Bride to be and King George VI standing facing **Rev. Legend:** Diamond Wedding of H.M. Queen Elizabeth II & H.R.H. Prince Philip **Rev. Inscription:** THE GIVING AWAY **Edge:** Reeded

Date	Mintage	F	VF	XF	Unc	BU
2007 Proof	—	Value: 75.00				

KM# 342   10 DOLLARS
28.2800 g., Copper-Nickel **Ruler:** Elizabeth II **Subject:** Diamond Wedding Anniversary **Obv:** Conjoined busts with Philip right **Obv. Legend:** BRITISH VIRGIN ISLANDS — QUEEN ELIZABETH II **Rev. Legend:** Diamond Wedding of H.M. Queen Elizabeth II & H.R.H. Prince Philip **Rev. Inscription:** THE GLASS COACH **Edge:** Reeded

Date	Mintage	F	VF	XF	Unc	BU
2007	—	—	—	—	16.50	18.50

KM# 342a   10 DOLLARS
28.2800 g., 0.9250 Silver 0.8410 oz. ASW **Ruler:** Elizabeth II **Subject:** Diamond Wedding Anniversary **Obv:** Conjoined busts with Philip right **Obv. Legend:** BRITISH VIRGIN ISLANDS — QUEEN ELIZABETH II **Rev. Legend:** Diamond Wedding of H.M. Queen Elizabeth II & H.R.H. Prince Philip **Rev. Inscription:** THE GLASS COACH **Edge:** Reeded

Date	Mintage	F	VF	XF	Unc	BU
2007 Proof	—	Value: 75.00				

KM# 343   10 DOLLARS
28.2800 g., Copper-Nickel **Ruler:** Elizabeth II **Subject:** Diamond Wedding Anniversary **Obv:** Conjoined busts with Philip right **Obv. Legend:** BRITISH VIRGIN ISLANDS — QUEEN ELIZABETH II **Rev. Legend:** Diamond Wedding of H.M. Queen Elizabeth II & H.R.H. Prince Philip **Rev. Inscription:** THE HONEYMOON **Edge:** Reeded

Date	Mintage	F	VF	XF	Unc	BU
2007	—	—	—	—	16.50	18.50

KM# 343a   10 DOLLARS
28.2800 g., 0.9250 Silver 0.8410 oz. ASW **Ruler:** Elizabeth II **Subject:** Diamond Wedding Anniversary **Obv:** Conjoined busts with Philip right **Obv. Legend:** BRITISH VIRGIN ISLANDS — QUEEN ELIZABETH II **Rev. Legend:** Diamond Wedding of H.M. Queen Elizabeth II & H.R.H. Prince Philip **Rev. Inscription:** THE HONEYMOON **Edge:** Reeded

Date	Mintage	F	VF	XF	Unc	BU
2007 Proof	—	Value: 75.00				

KM# 344   10 DOLLARS
28.2800 g., Copper-Nickel **Ruler:** Elizabeth II **Subject:** Diamond Wedding Anniversary **Obv:** Conjoined busts with Philip right **Obv. Legend:** BRITISH VIRGIN ISLANDS — QUEEN ELIZABETH II **Rev. Legend:** Diamond Wedding of H.M. Queen Elizabeth II & H.R.H. Prince Philip **Rev. Inscription:** THE WEDDING PROGRAM **Edge:** Reeded

Date	Mintage	F	VF	XF	Unc	BU
2007	—	—	—	—	16.50	18.50

KM# 344a   10 DOLLARS
28.2800 g., 0.9250 Silver 0.8410 oz. ASW **Ruler:** Elizabeth II **Subject:** Diamond Wedding Anniversary **Obv:** Conjoined busts with Philip right **Obv. Legend:** BRITISH VIRGIN ISLANDS — QUEEN ELIZABETH II **Rev. Legend:** Diamond Wedding of H.M. Queen Elizabeth II & H.R.H. Prince Philip **Rev. Inscription:** THE WEDDING PROGRAM **Edge:** Reeded

Date	Mintage	F	VF	XF	Unc	BU
2007 Proof	—	Value: 75.00				

KM# 411   10 DOLLARS
28.2800 g., 0.9250 Silver 0.8410 oz. ASW, 38.61 mm. **Ruler:** Elizabeth II **Subject:** Act of Union, 300th Anniversary **Obv:** Bust in tiara right **Rev:** Flags above Queen Anne's portrait, lion and unicorn supporters flanking

Date	Mintage	F	VF	XF	Unc	BU
2007PM Proof	—	Value: 42.00				

KM# 371   10 DOLLARS
28.2800 g., 0.9250 Silver 0.8410 oz. ASW, 38.6 mm. **Ruler:** Elizabeth II **Obv:** Bust right **Rev:** Two soccer players and leopard

Date	Mintage	F	VF	XF	Unc	BU
2009 Proof	10,000	Value: 40.00				
2010	—	Value: 40.00				

KM# 372 10 DOLLARS
1.2400 g., 0.9990 Gold 0.0398 oz. AGW, 13.92 mm. **Ruler:** Elizabeth II **Obv:** Bust right **Rev:** Henry VIII facing

Date	Mintage	F	VF	XF	Unc	BU
2009PM Proof	5,000				Value: 80.00	

KM# 374 10 DOLLARS
28.2800 g., 0.9250 Silver 0.8410 oz. ASW, 38.6 mm. **Ruler:** Elizabeth II **Obv:** Bust right **Rev:** Elizabeth I aboard ship

Date	Mintage	F	VF	XF	Unc	BU
2009 Proof	10,000				Value: 42.00	

KM# 376 10 DOLLARS
28.2800 g., 0.9250 Silver 0.8410 oz. ASW, 38.6 mm. **Ruler:** Elizabeth II **Obv:** Bust right **Rev:** Elizabeth I between two columns

Date	Mintage	F	VF	XF	Unc	BU
2009 Proof	10,000				Value: 42.00	

KM# 382 10 DOLLARS
28.2800 g., Copper-Nickel, 38.6 mm. **Ruler:** Elizabeth II **Subject:** Centennial of Naval Aviation **Rev:** 1936 Fairey Swordfish returning to carrier HMS Fencer

Date	Mintage	F	VF	XF	Unc	BU
2009	—	—	—	—	—	7.50

KM# 382a 10 DOLLARS
28.2800 g., Silver, 38.6 mm. **Ruler:** Elizabeth II **Subject:** Centennial of Naval Aviation **Rev:** 1936 Fairey Swordfish returing to carrier HMS Fencer

Date	Mintage	F	VF	XF	Unc	BU
2009 Proof	10,000				Value: 40.00	

KM# 394 10 DOLLARS
28.2800 g., 0.9250 Silver 0.8410 oz. ASW, 38.6 mm. **Ruler:** Elizabeth II **Subject:** Peanuts 60th Anniversary **Rev:** Multicolor Snoopy asleep atop doghouse

Date	Mintage	F	VF	XF	Unc	BU
2010PM Proof	10,000				Value: 40.00	

KM# 395 10 DOLLARS
1.2400 g., 0.9990 Gold 0.0398 oz. AGW, 13.92 mm. **Ruler:** Elizabeth II **Series:** Peanuts 60th Anniversary **Rev:** Snoopy asleep atop doghouse

Date	Mintage	F	VF	XF	Unc	BU
2010PM Proof	10,000				Value: 100	

KM# 397 10 DOLLARS
31.1060 g., 0.9990 Silver 0.9990 oz. ASW, 38.6 mm. **Ruler:** Elizabeth II **Subject:** Elgin Marbles **Rev:** Two horsemen

Date	Mintage	F	VF	XF	Unc	BU
2010PM Proof	10,000				Value: 50.00	

KM# 398 10 DOLLARS
1.2200 g., 0.9990 Gold 0.0392 oz. AGW, 13.92 mm. **Ruler:** Elizabeth II **Subject:** Birth of Venus

Date	Mintage	F	VF	XF	Unc	BU
2010PM Proof	Est. 10,000				Value: 100	

KM# 401 10 DOLLARS
28.2800 g., 0.9250 Silver 0.8410 oz. ASW, 38.6 mm. **Ruler:** Elizabeth II **Subject:** Birth of Venus

Date	Mintage	F	VF	XF	Unc	BU
2010 Proof	Est. 10,000				Value: 50.00	

KM# 406 10 DOLLARS
28.2800 g., 0.9250 Silver 0.8410 oz. ASW, 38.61 mm. **Ruler:** Elizabeth II **Obv:** Bust in tiara right **Rev:** World Trade Center complex

Date	Mintage	F	VF	XF	Unc	BU
2011PM Proof					Value: 45.00	

KM# 407 10 DOLLARS
28.2800 g., 0.9250 Silver 0.8410 oz. ASW, 38.61 mm. **Ruler:** Elizabeth II **Subject:** Queen Elizabeth II's 85th Birthday **Obv:** Older and young busts conjoined right **Rev:** Queen on horseback left

Date	Mintage	F	VF	XF	Unc	BU
2011PM Proof					Value: 42.00	

KM# 408 10 DOLLARS
28.2800 g., 0.9250 Silver 0.8410 oz. ASW, 38.61 mm. **Ruler:** Elizabeth II **Subject:** Royal Wedding - Prince William and Catherine Middleton **Obv:** Bust in tiara right **Rev:** Busts of Catherine and William

Date	Mintage	F	VF	XF	Unc	BU
2011PM Proof					Value: 42.00	

KM# 409 10 DOLLARS
1.2200 g., 0.9990 Gold 0.0392 oz. AGW, 13.92 mm. **Ruler:** Elizabeth II **Obv:** Bust in tiara right **Rev:** Anne Boylen bust 1/4 left

Date	Mintage	F	VF	XF	Unc	BU
2011PM					Value: 100	

KM# 410 10 DOLLARS
28.2800 g., Silver with insert, 38.61 mm. **Ruler:** Elizabeth II **Subject:** Life cycle of a tree frog **Obv:** Frog at center **Rev:** Life cycle of a tree frog

Date	Mintage	F	VF	XF	Unc	BU
2011PM Proof					Value: 120	

KM# 417 10 DOLLARS
28.2800 g., Copper-Nickel, 38.61 mm. **Ruler:** Elizabeth II **Subject:** Life of Queen Elizabeth II **Obv:** Current and young busts conjoined right **Rev:** Half length bust facing wearing Order sash and tiara

Date	Mintage	F	VF	XF	Unc	BU
2012PM Proof					Value: 20.00	

KM# 418 10 DOLLARS
28.2800 g., Copper-Nickel, 38.6 mm. **Ruler:** Elizabeth II **Subject:** Life of Queen Elizabeth II **Obv:** Conjoined busts right **Rev:** Elizabeth II on horseback as if reviewing troops

Date	Mintage	F	VF	XF	Unc	BU
2012PM	—	—	—	—	—	15.00

KM# 419 10 DOLLARS
28.2800 g., Copper-Nickel, 38.6 mm. **Ruler:** Elizabeth II **Subject:** Valentine's day **Obv:** Conjoined busts right **Rev:** Crescent moon and pixi

Date	Mintage	F	VF	XF	Unc	BU
2012PM	—	—	—	—	—	15.00

KM# 420 10 DOLLARS
28.2800 g., 0.9250 Silver 0.8410 oz. ASW, 38.6 mm. **Ruler:** Elizabeth II **Subject:** Summer Olympics, London **Obv:** Conjoined busts right **Rev:** Gymnast on pommel horse, Union Jack in color below

Date	Mintage	F	VF	XF	Unc	BU
2012PM Proof					Value: 50.00	

KM# 421 10 DOLLARS
28.2800 g., 0.9250 Silver 0.8410 oz. ASW, 38.6 mm. **Ruler:** Elizabeth II **Subject:** Summer Olympics, London **Obv:** Conjoined busts right **Rev:** Dressage, Union Jack in color below

Date	Mintage	F	VF	XF	Unc	BU
2012PM Proof					Value: 50.00	

KM# 422 10 DOLLARS
28.2800 g., 0.9250 Silver 0.8410 oz. ASW, 38.6 mm. **Ruler:** Elizabeth II **Subject:** Summer Olympics, London **Obv:** Conjoined busts right **Rev:** Fencing, Union Jack in color below

Date	Mintage	F	VF	XF	Unc	BU
2012PM Proof					Value: 50.00	

KM# 423 10 DOLLARS
28.2800 g., 0.9250 Silver 0.8410 oz. ASW, 38.6 mm. **Ruler:** Elizabeth II **Subject:** Summer Olympics, London **Obv:** Conjoined busts right **Rev:** Soccer players, Union Jack in color below

Date	Mintage	F	VF	XF	Unc	BU
2012PM Proof					Value: 50.00	

KM# 201   20 DOLLARS
1.2441 g., 0.9999 Gold 0.0400 oz. AGW, 13.92 mm. **Subject:**
Teddy Bear Centennial **Obv:** Queen's bust right **Rev:** Teddy bear
Edge: Reeded

Date	Mintage	F	VF	XF	Unc	BU
2002 Proof	10,000	Value: 70.00				

KM# 227   20 DOLLARS
1.2400 g., 0.9999 Gold 0.0399 oz. AGW, 13.92 mm. **Subject:**
Kennedy Assassination **Obv:** Queen's bust right **Rev:** President
Kennedy's portrait **Edge:** Reeded

Date	Mintage	F	VF	XF	Unc	BU
2003 Proof	10,000	Value: 70.00				

KM# 279a   20 DOLLARS
63.5900 g., 0.9990 Silver Gilt 2.0423 oz. ASW, 49.93 mm.
Ruler: Elizabeth II **Subject:** XXVII Olympic Games **Obv:** Bust
with tiara right **Rev:** 1896 Olympic medal design **Edge:** Reeded

Date	Mintage	F	VF	XF	Unc	BU
2004PM Proof	—	Value: 100				

KM# 271   20 DOLLARS
1.2440 g., 0.9999 Gold 0.0400 oz. AGW, 14 mm. **Obv:** Queen's
bust right **Rev:** Peter Rabbit **Edge:** Reeded

Date	Mintage	F	VF	XF	Unc	BU
2004 Proof	5,000	Value: 75.00				

KM# 279   20 DOLLARS
58.0000 g., 0.9990 Silver 1.8628 oz. ASW, 50 mm. **Subject:**
XXVIII Olympic Games **Obv:** Bust with tiara right **Rev:** 1896
Olympic medal design **Edge:** Reeded

Date	Mintage	F	VF	XF	Unc	BU
2004PM Proof	2,004	Value: 90.00				

KM# 345   20 DOLLARS
3.9600 g., 0.7500 Gold 0.0955 oz. AGW, 21.78 mm. **Ruler:**
Elizabeth II **Subject:** 500th Anniversary - Death of Columbus
Obv: Crowned bust right **Obv. Legend:** BRITISH VIRGIN
ISLANDS - QUEEN ELIZABETH II **Rev:** Bust of Columbus facing
3/4 left at right, outlined map of the Americas at left **Rev. Legend:**
1451 - CHRISTOPHER COLUMBUS - 1506 **Edge:** Reeded **Note:**
Struck in white gold.

Date	Mintage	F	VF	XF	Unc	BU
2006 Proof	1,506	Value: 165				

KM# 346   20 DOLLARS
4.0200 g., 0.7500 Gold 0.0969 oz. AGW, 21.78 mm. **Ruler:**
Elizabeth II **Subject:** 500th Anniversary - Death of Columbus
Obv: Crowned bust right **Obv. Legend:** BRITISH VIRGIN
ISLANDS - QUEEN ELIZABETH II **Rev:** Sailing ship "Santa

Maria" **Rev. Legend:** 1451-CHRISTOPHER COLUMBUS-1506
Edge: Reeded **Note:** Struck in rose gold.

Date	Mintage	F	VF	XF	Unc	BU
2006 Proof	1,506	Value: 165				

KM# 347   20 DOLLARS
3.9900 g., 0.7500 Gold 0.0962 oz. AGW, 21.78 mm. **Ruler:**
Elizabeth II **Subject:** 500th Anniversary - Death of Columbus
Obv: Crowned bust right **Obv. Legend:** BRITISH VIRGIN
ISLANDS - QUEEN ELIZABETH II **Rev:** Sailing ships "Niña" and
"Pinta" **Rev. Legend:** 1451 - CHRISTOPHER COLUMBUS -
1506 **Edge:** Reeded **Note:** Struck in yellow gold.

Date	Mintage	F	VF	XF	Unc	BU
2006 Proof	1,506	Value: 165				

KM# 379   30 DOLLARS
155.5000 g., 0.9990 Silver 4.9942 oz. ASW **Ruler:** Elizabeth II
Subject: Nelson's Victory at Trafalgar **Rev:** Two ships

Date	Mintage	F	VF	XF	Unc	BU
2008 Proof	—	Value: 250				

KM# 275   25 DOLLARS
3.1100 g., 0.9999 Gold 0.1000 oz. AGW, 18 mm. **Obv:** Queen's
bust right **Rev:** Hernando Pizarro portrait and life events pictorial
Edge: Reeded

Date	Mintage	F	VF	XF	Unc	BU
2004 Proof	350	Value: 185				

KM# 289   25 DOLLARS
3.1100 g., 0.9999 Gold 0.1000 oz. AGW, 18 mm. **Obv:** Queen's
bust right **Rev:** Dolphin **Edge:** Reeded

Date	Mintage	F	VF	XF	Unc	BU
2004 Proof	6,000	Value: 170				

KM# 315   25 DOLLARS
3.1100 g., 0.9999 Gold 0.1000 oz. AGW, 18 mm. **Obv:** Bust of
Queen Elizabeth II right **Rev:** Mother and baby dolphins **Edge:**
Reeded

Date	Mintage	F	VF	XF	Unc	BU
2005 Proof	6,000	Value: 170				

KM# 335   25 DOLLARS
3.1120 g., 0.9999 Gold AGW 0.1004 0.1000 oz. AGW,
17.95 mm. **Ruler:** Elizabeth II **Subject:** 400th Anniversary
Founding of Jamestown **Obv:** Bust with tiara right **Obv. Legend:**
BRITISH VIRGIN ISLANDS - QUEEN ELIZABETH II **Rev:** British
lion laying, American eagle perched on sprays **Rev. Legend:**
UNITED IN FRIENDSHIP **Edge:** Reeded

Date	Mintage	VG	F	VF	XF	Unc
2007 Proof	7,500	Value: 170				

KM# 412   25 DOLLARS
6.2200 g., 0.9990 Gold 0.1998 oz. AGW, 22 mm. **Ruler:**
Elizabeth II **Subject:** Nelson's victory at Trafalgar **Obv:** Bust in
tiara right **Rev:** Victory crowned Britannia standing on prow

Date	Mintage	F	VF	XF	Unc	BU
2008PM Proof	—	Value: 450				

KM# 202   50 DOLLARS
3.1100 g., 0.9999 Gold 0.1000 oz. AGW, 17.95 mm. **Subject:**
Teddy Bear Centennial **Obv:** Queen's bust right **Rev:** Teddy bear
Edge: Reeded

Date	Mintage	F	VF	XF	Unc	BU
2002 Proof	7,000	Value: 175				

KM# 272   50 DOLLARS
3.1100 g., 0.9999 Gold 0.1000 oz. AGW, 18 mm. **Obv:** Queen's
bust right **Rev:** Peter Rabbit **Edge:** Reeded

Date	Mintage	F	VF	XF	Unc	BU
2004 Proof	3,000	Value: 180				

KM# 276   50 DOLLARS
6.2200 g., 0.9999 Gold 0.1999 oz. AGW, 22 mm. **Obv:** Queen's
bust right **Rev:** Treasure ship with blue color sail **Edge:** Reeded

Date	Mintage	F	VF	XF	Unc	BU
2004 Proof	350	Value: 375				

KM# 290   50 DOLLARS
6.2200 g., 0.9999 Gold 0.1999 oz. AGW, 22 mm. **Obv:** Queen's
bust right **Rev:** Dolphin **Edge:** Reeded

Date	Mintage	F	VF	XF	Unc	BU
2004 Proof	3,500	Value: 325				

KM# 316   50 DOLLARS
6.2200 g., 0.9999 Gold 0.1999 oz. AGW, 22 mm. **Obv:** Bust of
Queen Elizabeth II right **Rev:** Large and small dolphins **Edge:**
Reeded

Date	Mintage	F	VF	XF	Unc	BU
2005	3,500	Value: 350				

KM# 351   50 DOLLARS
6.2200 g., 0.9999 Gold 0.1999 oz. AGW, 22.00 mm. **Ruler:**
Elizabeth II **Subject:** 5th Anniversary - Attack on Twin Towers,
New York City **Obv:** Crowned bust right **Obv. Legend:** BRISH
VIRGIN ISLANDS - QUEEN ELIZABETH II **Rev:** Twin Towers in
sprays, remembrance ribbon privy mark at upper right **Rev.
Inscription:** LEST WE FORGET **Edge:** Reeded

Date	Mintage	F	VF	XF	Unc	BU
2006 Proof	2,000	Value: 365				

KM# 413   50 DOLLARS
6.2200 g., 0.9999 Gold 0.1998 oz. AGW, 22 mm. **Ruler:**
Elizabeth II **Subject:** Color photography, 100th Anniversary **Obv:**
Bust in tiara right **Rev:** Conjoined portraits right in photo frame

Date	Mintage	F	VF	XF	Unc	BU
2007PM Proof	—	Value: 450				

KM# 336   50 DOLLARS
6.2230 g., 0.9999 Gold AGW 0.1999 0.2000 oz. AGW,
22.00 mm. **Ruler:** Elizabeth II **Subject:** 400th Anniversary
Founding of Jamestown **Obv:** Bust with tiara right **Obv. Legend:**
BRITISH VIRGIN ISLANDS - QUEEN ELIZABETH II **Rev:** British
lion laying, American eagle perched on sprays **Rev. Legend:**
UNITED IN FRIENDSHIP **Edge:** Reeded

Date	Mintage	F	VF	XF	Unc	BU
2007 Proof	5,000	Value: 350				

KM# 377   50 DOLLARS
6.2200 g., 0.9999 Gold 0.1998 oz. AGW, 22 mm. **Ruler:**
Elizabeth II **Obv:** Bust right **Rev:** Elizabeth II aboard ship with
1mm pearl

Date	Mintage	F	VF	XF	Unc	BU
2009 Proof	750	Value: 375				

KM# 378 50 DOLLARS
6.2200 g., 0.9990 Gold 0.1998 oz. AGW, 22 mm. **Ruler:** Elizabeth II **Obv:** Bust right **Rev:** Elizabeth II between two columns, .01ct ruby insert

Date	Mintage	F	VF	XF	Unc	BU
2009 Proof	750	Value: 375				

KM# 285 75 DOLLARS
11.0000 g., Bi-Metallic .990 Titanium 2g center in .9999 Gold 9g ring, 36.5 mm. **Obv:** Queen's bust right **Rev:** British Guiana stamp design **Edge:** Reeded

Date	Mintage	F	VF	XF	Unc	BU
2004 Proof	2,500	Value: 450				

KM# 389 75 DOLLARS
Bi-Metallic Titanium and gold **Ruler:** Elizabeth II **Subject:** Mozart

Date	Mintage	F	VF	XF	Unc	BU
2006PM Proof	—	Value: 450				

KM# 388 75 DOLLARS
Bi-Metallic Titanium and gold, 36.5 mm. **Ruler:** Elizabeth II **Subject:** Bejing Olympics **Obv:** Bust in tiara right **Rev:** Tennis plays against Great Wall background

Date	Mintage	F	VF	XF	Unc	BU
2009PM Proof	—	Value: 450				

KM# 182 100 DOLLARS
6.2200 g., 0.9990 Gold 0.1998 oz. AGW, 22 mm. **Subject:** Sir Francis Drake **Obv:** Queen's bust right **Rev:** Ship, portrait and map **Edge:** Reeded

Date	Mintage	F	VF	XF	Unc	BU
2002 Proof	5,000	Value: 345				

KM# 185 100 DOLLARS
6.2200 g., 0.9990 Gold 0.1998 oz. AGW, 22 mm. **Subject:** Sir Walter Raleigh **Obv:** Queen's bust right **Rev:** Ship, portrait and map **Edge:** Reeded

Date	Mintage	F	VF	XF	Unc	BU
2002 Proof	5,000	Value: 345				

KM# 189 100 DOLLARS
6.2208 g., 0.9999 Gold 0.2000 oz. AGW, 22 mm. **Subject:** Queen's Golden Jubilee **Obv:** Queen's bust right **Rev:** Queen on horse **Edge:** Reeded

Date	Mintage	F	VF	XF	Unc	BU
2002 Proof	2,002	Value: 355				

KM# 192 100 DOLLARS
6.2208 g., 0.9999 Gold 0.2000 oz. AGW, 22 mm. **Subject:** Queen's Golden Jubilee **Obv:** Queen's bust right **Rev:** Queen on throne **Edge:** Reeded

Date	Mintage	F	VF	XF	Unc	BU
2002 Proof	2,002	Value: 355				

KM# 195 100 DOLLARS
6.2208 g., 0.9999 Gold 0.2000 oz. AGW, 22 mm. **Subject:** Queen's Golden Jubilee **Obv:** Queen's bust right **Rev:** Queen with President Ronald Reagan and Mrs. Nancy Reagan **Edge:** Reeded

Date	Mintage	F	VF	XF	Unc	BU
2002 Proof	2,002	Value: 355				

KM# 198 100 DOLLARS
6.2208 g., 0.9999 Gold 0.2000 oz. AGW, 22 mm. **Subject:** Queen's Golden Jubilee **Obv:** Queen's bust right **Rev:** Carnival dancers **Edge:** Reeded

Date	Mintage	F	VF	XF	Unc	BU
2002 Proof	2,002	Value: 355				

KM# 203 100 DOLLARS
6.2200 g., 0.9999 Gold 0.1999 oz. AGW, 22 mm. **Subject:** Teddy Bear Centennial **Obv:** Queen's bust right **Rev:** Teddy bear **Edge:** Reeded

Date	Mintage	F	VF	XF	Unc	BU
2002 Proof	5,000	Value: 345				

KM# 206 100 DOLLARS
6.2200 g., 0.9999 Gold 0.1999 oz. AGW, 22 mm. **Subject:** Princess Diana **Obv:** Queen's bust right **Rev:** Diana's portrait **Edge:** Reeded

Date	Mintage	F	VF	XF	Unc	BU
2002 Proof	5,000	Value: 345				

KM# 209.1 100 DOLLARS
6.2200 g., 0.9999 Gold 0.1999 oz. AGW, 22 mm. **Subject:** September 11, 2001 **Obv:** Queen's bust right **Rev:** World Trade Center twin towers **Edge:** Reeded

Date	Mintage	F	VF	XF	Unc	BU
2002 Proof	5,000	Value: 345				

KM# 209.2 100 DOLLARS
6.2200 g., 0.9999 Gold 0.1999 oz. AGW, 22 mm. **Subject:** September 11, 2001 **Obv:** Queen's bust right **Rev:** Holographic multicolor World Trade Center twin towers **Edge:** Reeded

Date	Mintage	F	VF	XF	Unc	BU
2002 Proof	5,000	Value: 345				

KM# 212 100 DOLLARS
6.2200 g., 0.9999 Gold 0.1999 oz. AGW, 22 mm. **Subject:** September 11, 2001 **Obv:** Queen's bust right **Rev:** Statue of Liberty **Edge:** Reeded

Date	Mintage	F	VF	XF	Unc	BU
2002 Proof	5,000	Value: 345				

KM# 215 100 DOLLARS
6.2200 g., 0.9999 Gold 0.1999 oz. AGW, 22 mm. **Subject:** Queen Mother Series **Obv:** Queen's bust right **Rev:** Queen Mother with young Prince Charles **Edge:** Reeded

Date	Mintage	F	VF	XF	Unc	BU
2002PM Proof	5,000	Value: 345				

KM# 218 100 DOLLARS
6.2200 g., 0.9999 Gold 0.1999 oz. AGW, 22 mm. **Subject:** Queen Mother Series **Obv:** Queen's bust right **Rev:** Queen Mother with four grandchildren **Edge:** Reeded

Date	Mintage	F	VF	XF	Unc	BU
2002PM Proof	5,000	Value: 345				

KM# 221 100 DOLLARS
6.2200 g., 0.9999 Gold 0.1999 oz. AGW, 22 mm. **Subject:** Queen Mother Series **Obv:** Queen's bust right **Rev:** Queen Mother with uniformed Prince Charles **Edge:** Reeded

Date	Mintage	F	VF	XF	Unc	BU
2002PM Proof	5,000	Value: 345				

KM# 224 100 DOLLARS
6.2200 g., 0.9999 Gold 0.1999 oz. AGW, 22 mm. **Subject:** Queen Mother Series **Obv:** Queen's bust right **Rev:** Queen Mother's coffin **Edge:** Reeded

Date	Mintage	F	VF	XF	Unc	BU
2002PM Proof	5,000	Value: 345				

KM# 228 100 DOLLARS
6.2200 g., 0.9999 Gold 0.1999 oz. AGW, 22 mm. **Subject:** Kennedy Assassination **Obv:** Queen's bust right **Rev:** President Kennedy's portrait **Edge:** Reeded

Date	Mintage	F	VF	XF	Unc	BU
2003 Proof	5,000	Value: 345				

KM# 231 100 DOLLARS
15.5500 g., 0.9999 Gold 0.4999 oz. AGW, 30 mm. **Subject:** Powered Flight Centennial **Obv:** Queen's bust right **Rev:** Three historic airplanes and rocket **Edge:** Reeded

Date	Mintage	F	VF	XF	Unc	BU
2003 Proof	—	Value: 850				

KM# 234 100 DOLLARS
6.2200 g., 0.9999 Gold 0.1999 oz. AGW, 22 mm. **Obv:** Queen's bust right **Rev:** Henry VIII and Elizabeth I **Edge:** Reeded

Date	Mintage	F	VF	XF	Unc	BU
2003 Proof	5,000	Value: 345				

KM# 237 100 DOLLARS
6.2200 g., 0.9999 Gold 0.1999 oz. AGW, 22 mm. **Obv:** Queen's bust right **Rev:** Matthew Parker, Archbishop of Canterbury **Edge:** Reeded

Date	Mintage	F	VF	XF	Unc	BU
2003 Proof	5,000	Value: 345				

KM# 240 100 DOLLARS
6.2200 g., 0.9999 Gold 0.1999 oz. AGW, 22 mm. **Obv:** Queen's bust right **Rev:** Sir Francis Drake and ships **Edge:** Reeded

Date	Mintage	F	VF	XF	Unc	BU
2003 Proof	5,000	Value: 345				

KM# 243 100 DOLLARS
6.2200 g., 0.9999 Gold 0.1999 oz. AGW, 22 mm. **Obv:** Queen's bust right **Rev:** Sir Walter Raleigh **Edge:** Reeded

Date	Mintage	F	VF	XF	Unc	BU
2003 Proof	5,000	Value: 345				

KM# 246 100 DOLLARS
6.2200 g., 0.9999 Gold 0.1999 oz. AGW, 22 mm. **Obv:** Queen's bust right **Rev:** Sir William Shakespeare **Edge:** Reeded

Date	Mintage	F	VF	XF	Unc	BU
2003 Proof	5,000	Value: 345				

KM# 249 100 DOLLARS
6.2200 g., 0.9999 Gold 0.1999 oz. AGW, 22 mm. **Obv:** Queen's bust right **Rev:** Elizabeth I above her funeral procession **Edge:** Reeded

Date	Mintage	F	VF	XF	Unc	BU
2003 Proof	5,000	Value: 345				

KM# 252 100 DOLLARS
6.2200 g., 0.9999 Gold 0.1999 oz. AGW, 22 mm. **Subject:** Olympics **Obv:** Queen's bust right **Rev:** Ancient Olympic bust, runners in background and coin upper right **Edge:** Reeded

Date	Mintage	F	VF	XF	Unc	BU
2003 Proof	5,000	Value: 345				

KM# 255 100 DOLLARS
6.2200 g., 0.9999 Gold 0.1999 oz. AGW, 22 mm. **Subject:** Olympics **Obv:** Queen's bust right **Rev:** Ancient bust, charioteer and coin **Edge:** Reeded

Date	Mintage	F	VF	XF	Unc	BU
2003 Proof	5,000	Value: 345				

KM# 273.1 100 DOLLARS
6.2200 g., 0.9999 Gold 0.1999 oz. AGW, 22 mm. **Obv:** Queen's bust right **Rev:** Peter Rabbit **Edge:** Reeded

Date	Mintage	F	VF	XF	Unc	BU
2004 Proof	2,000	Value: 355				

KM# 273.2 100 DOLLARS
6.2200 g., 0.9999 Gold 0.1999 oz. AGW, 22 mm. **Obv:** Queen's bust right **Rev:** Multicolor Peter Rabbit **Edge:** Reeded

Date	Mintage	F	VF	XF	Unc	BU
2004 Proof	—	Value: 355				

KM# 283 100 DOLLARS
6.2200 g., 0.9999 Gold 0.1999 oz. AGW, 22 mm. **Obv:** Queen's bust right **Rev:** Sailor above two D-Day landing craft **Edge:** Reeded

Date	Mintage	F	VF	XF	Unc	BU
2004 Proof	5,000	Value: 345				

KM# 299 100 DOLLARS
6.2200 g., 0.9999 Gold 0.1999 oz. AGW, 22 mm. **Obv:** Queen's bust right **Rev:** Soldier above tank and jeeps **Edge:** Reeded

Date	Mintage	F	VF	XF	Unc	BU
2004 Proof	5,000	Value: 345				

KM# 302 100 DOLLARS
6.2200 g., 0.9999 Gold 0.1999 oz. AGW, 22 mm. **Obv:** Queen's bust right **Rev:** Pilot and planes above D-Day landing **Edge:** Reeded

Date	Mintage	F	VF	XF	Unc	BU
2004 Proof	5,000	Value: 345				

KM# 305 100 DOLLARS
6.2200 g., 0.9999 Gold 0.1999 oz. AGW, 22 mm. **Obv:** Queen's bust right **Rev:** Ancient Olympic bust, runners and owl coin **Edge:** Reeded

Date	Mintage	F	VF	XF	Unc	BU
2004 Proof	5,000	Value: 345				

KM# 308 100 DOLLARS
6.2200 g., 0.9999 Gold 0.1999 oz. AGW, 22 mm. **Obv:** Queen's bust right **Rev:** Ancient Olympic bust, charioteer and Zeus coin **Edge:** Reeded

Date	Mintage	F	VF	XF	Unc	BU
2004 Proof	5,000	Value: 345				

KM# 317 125 DOLLARS
15.5510 g., 0.9999 Gold 0.4999 oz. AGW, 30 mm. **Obv:** Bust of Queen Elizabeth II right **Rev:** Mother and baby dolphin **Edge:** Reeded

Date	Mintage	F	VF	XF	Unc	BU
2005	1,500	Value: 875				

KM# 337 125 DOLLARS
15.5590 g., 0.9999 Gold AGW 0.5000 0.5002 oz. AGW, 30.00 mm. **Ruler:** Elizabeth II **Subject:** 400th Anniversary Founding of Jamestown **Obv:** Bust with tiara right **Obv. Legend:** BRITISH VIRGIN ISLANDS - QUEEN ELIZABETH II **Rev:** British lion laying, American eagle perched on sprays **Rev. Legend:** UNITED IN FRIENDSHIP **Edge:** Reeded

Date	Mintage	F	VF	XF	Unc	BU
2007 Proof	3,000	Value: 850				

KM# 309 250 DOLLARS
15.5517 g., 0.9990 Gold 0.4995 oz. AGW, 30 mm. **Obv:** Queen's bust right **Rev:** Statue of Liberty and the date "11 Sept. 2001" **Edge:** Reeded

Date	Mintage	F	VF	XF	Unc	BU
2002	250	Value: 850				

KM# 280 250 DOLLARS
58.0000 g., 0.5000 Gold 0.9323 oz. AGW, 50 mm. **Obv:** Queen's bust right **Rev:** 1896 Olympic medal design **Edge:** Reeded

Date	Mintage	F	VF	XF	Unc	BU
2004 Proof	1,000	Value: 1,600				

KM# 318 250 DOLLARS
31.1030 g., 0.9999 Gold 0.9998 oz. AGW, 32.7 mm. **Obv:** Bust of Queen Elizabeth II right **Rev:** Mother and baby dolphin **Edge:** Reeded

Date	Mintage	F	VF	XF	Unc	BU
2005 Proof	750	Value: 1,700				

KM# 390 250 DOLLARS
Gold **Ruler:** Elizabeth II **Subject:** Mozart

Date	Mintage	F	VF	XF	Unc	BU
2006PM Proof	—	Value: 1,700				

KM# 338 250 DOLLARS
31.1030 g., 0.9999 Gold AGW 0.9999 0.9998 oz. AGW, 32.70 mm. **Ruler:** Elizabeth II **Subject:** 400th Anniversary Founding of Jamestown **Obv:** Bust with tiara right **Obv. Legend:** BRITISH VIRGIN ISLANDS - QUEEN ELIZABETH II **Rev:** British lion laying, American eagle perched on sprays **Rev. Legend:** UNITED IN FRIENDSHIP **Edge:** Reeded

Date	Mintage	F	VF	XF	Unc	BU
2007 Proof	1,000	Value: 1,700				

KM# 277 500 DOLLARS

160.7562 g., 0.9990 Gold 5.1630 oz. AGW, 150 mm. **Obv:** Queen's bust right **Rev:** Gold-plated portrait of Hernando Pizarro, small inset emerald above Pizarro's life events pictoral **Edge:** Reeded **Note:** Photo reduced.

Date	Mintage	F	VF	XF	Unc	BU
2004 Proof	500	Value: 8,750				

KM# 348 500 DOLLARS

160.7562 g., 0.9990 Gold 5.1630 oz. AGW, 150.00 mm. **Ruler:** Elizabeth II **Subject:** 500th Anniversary - Death of Columbus **Obv:** Crowned bust right **Obv. Legend:** BRITISH VIRGIN ISLANDS - QUEEN ELIZABETH II **Rev:** Ship in background at left, Columbus standing at right with right arm outstreched looking right, compass below. **Rev. Legend:** 1451 - DISCOVERER OF AMERICA - CHRISTOPHER COLUMBUS - 1506 **Edge:** Reeded

Date	Mintage	F	VF	XF	Unc	BU
2006 Proof	1,506	Value: 8,600				

KM# 392 500 DOLLARS

160.7560 g., 0.9990 Silver 5.1630 oz. ASW, 150 mm. **Ruler:** Elizabeth II **Subject:** Battle of Trafalgar **Rev:** Two naval ships in battle

Date	Mintage	F	VF	XF	Unc	BU
2008PM Proof	—	Value: 250				

MINT SETS

KM#	Date	Mintage Identification	Issue Price	Mkt Val
MS12	2007 (4)	— KM# 341 - 344	65.00	80.00

PROOF SETS

KM#	Date	Mintage Identification	Issue Price	Mkt Val
PS20	2007 (4)	— KM# 341a - 344a	300	300

BRUNEI

Negara Brunei Darussalam (State of Brunei), an independent sultanate on the northwest coast of the island of Borneo, has an area of 2,226 sq. mi. (5,765 sq. km.) and a population of *326,000. Capital: Bandar Seri Begawan. Crude oil and rubber are exported.

TITLES

نكري بروني

Negri Brunei

RULERS

Sultan Hassanal Bolkiah I, 1967-

SULTANATE

DECIMAL COINAGE

100 Sen = 1 Dollar (Ringgit)

KM# 34 SEN

1.7500 g., Copper Clad Steel, 17.7 mm. **Ruler:** Sultan Hassanal Bolkiah **Obv:** Uniformed bust facing **Rev:** Native design, denomination below, date at right **Edge:** Plain

Date	Mintage	F	VF	XF	Unc	BU
2001	576,000	—	—	0.15	0.40	0.50
2002	804,900	—	—	0.15	0.40	0.50
2004	—	—	—	0.15	0.40	0.50
2005	—	—	—	0.15	0.40	0.50
2006	—	—	—	0.15	0.40	0.50

KM# 34b SEN

1.7000 g., Brass, 17.7 mm. **Ruler:** Sultan Hassanal Bolkiah **Obv:** Uniformed bust facing **Rev:** Native design, denomination below, date at right

Date	Mintage	F	VF	XF	Unc	BU
2008	—	—	—	—	0.40	0.50
2009	—	—	—	—	0.40	0.50
2010	—	—	—	—	0.40	0.50

KM# 35 5 SEN

1.4100 g., Copper-Nickel, 16.26 mm. **Ruler:** Sultan Hassanal Bolkiah **Obv:** Uniformed bust facing **Rev:** Native design, denomination below, date at right **Edge:** Reeded

Date	Mintage	F	VF	XF	Unc	BU
2001	808,000	—	—	0.20	0.50	0.75
2002	1,418,178	—	—	0.20	0.50	0.75
2004	—	—	—	0.20	0.50	0.75
2005	—	—	—	0.20	0.50	0.75
2006	—	—	—	0.20	0.50	0.75
2007	—	—	—	0.20	0.50	0.75
2008	—	—	—	0.20	0.50	0.75
2009	—	—	—	0.20	0.50	0.75
2010	—	—	—	0.20	0.50	0.75

KM# 36 10 SEN

2.8200 g., Copper-Nickel, 19.4 mm. **Ruler:** Sultan Hassanal Bolkiah **Obv:** Uniformed bust facing **Rev:** Native design, denomination below, date at right **Edge:** Reeded

Date	Mintage	F	VF	XF	Unc	BU
2001	164,000	—	—	0.30	0.75	1.00

Date	Mintage	F	VF	XF	Unc	BU
2002	476,452	—	—	0.30	0.75	1.00
2004	—	—	—	0.30	0.75	1.00
2005	—	—	—	0.30	0.75	1.00
2006	—	—	—	0.30	0.75	1.00
2007	—	—	—	0.30	0.75	1.00
2008	—	—	—	0.30	0.75	1.00

KM# 37 20 SEN

5.6500 g., Copper-Nickel, 23.5 mm. **Ruler:** Sultan Hassanal Bolkiah **Obv:** Uniformed bust facing **Rev:** Native design, denomination below, date at right **Edge:** Reeded

Date	Mintage	F	VF	XF	Unc	BU
2001	270,647	—	—	0.45	1.10	1.50
2002	597,272	—	—	0.45	1.10	1.50
2004	—	—	—	0.45	1.10	1.50
2005	—	—	—	0.45	1.10	1.50
2008	—	—	—	0.45	1.10	1.50
2009	—	—	—	0.45	1.10	1.50
2010	—	—	—	0.45	1.10	1.50

KM# 38 50 SEN

9.3300 g., Copper-Nickel, 27.7 mm. **Ruler:** Sultan Hassanal Bolkiah **Obv:** Uniformed bust facing **Rev:** National arms within circle, denomination below, date at right **Edge:** Security

Date	Mintage	F	VF	XF	Unc	BU
2001	50,000	—	—	1.00	2.50	3.00
2002	1,325	—	—	1.40	3.50	5.00
2004	—	—	—	0.75	1.80	2.50
2005	—	—	—	0.75	1.80	2.50
2006	—	—	—	0.75	1.80	2.50
2007	—	—	—	0.75	1.80	2.50
2008	—	—	—	0.75	1.80	2.50
2009	—	—	—	0.75	1.80	2.50
2010	—	—	—	0.75	1.80	2.50

KM# 80 2 DOLLARS

31.1000 g., Copper-Nickel, 40.7 mm. **Ruler:** Sultan Hassanal Bolkiah **Subject:** 20th Anniversary of Independence **Obv:** Bust 3/4 left, facing **Obv. Legend:** SULTAN HAJI HASSANAL BOLKIAH **Rev:** National arms **Rev. Legend:** NEGARI BRUNEI DARUSSALAM

Date	Mintage	F	VF	XF	Unc	BU
2004 Proof	4,000	Value: 65.00				

KM# 86 2 DOLLARS

31.1000 g., Copper-Nickel, 40.7 mm. **Ruler:** Sultan Hassanal Bolkiah **Subject:** 60th Birthday **Obv:** Bust 3/4 left, facing **Obv. Legend:** SULTAN HAJI HASSANAL BOLKIAH **Rev:** Multicolor 1/2-length figure in civilian clothes, facing

Date	Mintage	F	VF	XF	Unc	BU
2006 Proof	200	Value: 120				

KM# 77 3 DOLLARS

24.0000 g., Copper-Nickel, 40 mm. **Ruler:** Sultan Hassanal Bolkiah **Obv:** Uniformed bust facing **Obv. Legend:** SULTAN HAJI HASSANAL BOLKIAH **Rev:** Logo at center **Rev. Legend:** COMMONWEALTH FINANCE MINISTERS MEETING **Edge:** Reeded

Date	Mintage	F	VF	XF	Unc	BU
2003 Proof	4,000	Value: 40.00				

KM# 83 3 DOLLARS

31.1000 g., Copper-Nickel, 40.7 mm. **Ruler:** Sultan Hassanal Bolkiah **Subject:** Royal Wedding **Obv:** Multicolor portraits of Royal couple

Date	Mintage	F	VF	XF	Unc	BU
2004 Proof	5,000	Value: 50.00				

KM# 81   20 DOLLARS
31.1000 g., 0.9990 Silver 0.9988 oz. ASW, 40.7 mm. **Ruler:** Sultan Hassanal Bolkiah **Subject:** 20th Anniversary of Independence **Obv:** Bust 3/4 left, facing **Obv. Legend:** SULTAN HAJI HASSANAL BOLKIAH **Rev:** National arms **Rev. Legend:** NEGARI BRUNEI DARUSSALAM

Date	Mintage	F	VF	XF	Unc	BU
2004 Proof	1,000	Value: 120				

KM# 87   20 DOLLARS
31.1000 g., 0.9990 Silver 0.9988 oz. ASW, 40.7 mm. **Ruler:** Sultan Hassanal Bolkiah **Subject:** 60th Birthday **Obv:** Bust 3/4 left, facing **Obv. Legend:** SULTAN HAJI HASSANAL BOLKIAH **Rev:** Multicolor 1/2-length figure in civilian clothes, facing

Date	Mintage	F	VF	XF	Unc	BU
2006 Proof	200	Value: 275				

KM# 78   30 DOLLARS
62.2000 g., 0.9990 Silver 1.9977 oz. ASW **Ruler:** Sultan Hassanal Bolkiah **Subject:** Commonwealth Finance Ministers' Meeting **Obv:** Logo at upper left, multicolor bust of Sultan 3/4, facing at right **Obv. Legend:** SULTAN HAJI HASSANAL BOLKIAH **Rev:** World map at left - center, national arms at upper right **Shape:** Rectangular, 65 x 31 mm

Date	Mintage	F	VF	XF	Unc	BU
2003 Proof	1,000	Value: 210				

KM# 84   30 DOLLARS
31.1000 g., 0.9990 Silver 0.9988 oz. ASW, 40.7 mm. **Ruler:** Sultan Hassanal Bolkiah **Subject:** Royal Wedding **Obv:** Multicolor portraits of Royal couple

Date	Mintage	F	VF	XF	Unc	BU
2004 Proof	1,000	Value: 180				

KM# 82   200 DOLLARS
31.1000 g., 0.9999 Gold 0.9997 oz. AGW, 32.1 mm. **Ruler:** Sultan Hassanal Bolkiah **Subject:** 20th Anniversary of Independence **Obv:** Bust 3/4 left, facing **Obv. Legend:** SULTAN HAJI HASSANAL BOLKIAH **Rev:** National arms **Rev. Legend:** NEGARI BRUNEI DARUSSALAM

Date	Mintage	F	VF	XF	Unc	BU
2004 Proof	200	Value: 2,400				

KM# 85   200 DOLLARS
31.1000 g., 0.9999 Gold 0.9997 oz. AGW, 32 mm. **Ruler:** Sultan Hassanal Bolkiah **Subject:** Royal Wedding **Obv:** Multicolor portraits of Royal couple

Date	Mintage	F	VF	XF	Unc	BU
2004 Proof	200	Value: 2,400				

KM# 88   200 DOLLARS
31.1000 g., 0.9999 Gold 0.9997 oz. AGW, 32.1 mm. **Ruler:** Sultan Hassanal Bolkiah **Subject:** 60th Birthday **Obv:** Bust 3/4 left, facing **Obv. Legend:** SULTAN HAJI HASSANAL BOLKIAH **Rev:** Multicolor 1/2-length figure in civilian clothes, facing

Date	Mintage	F	VF	XF	Unc	BU
2006 Proof	200	Value: 2,500				

PROOF SETS

KM#	Date	Mintage	Identification	Issue Price	Mkt Val
PS20	2003 (2)	500	KM#77-78	—	250
PS21	2004 (3)	200	KM80-82	—	1,800
PS22	2004 (3)	200	KM83-85	—	1,850
PS23	2006 (3)	200	KM86-88	—	2,200

BULGARIA

The Republic of Bulgaria, formerly the Peoples Republic of Bulgaria, a Balkan country on the Black Sea in southeastern Europe, has an area of 42,855 sq. mi. (110,910 sq. km.) and a population of *8.31 million. Capital: Sofia. Agriculture remains a key component of the economy but industrialization, particularly heavy industry, has been emphasized since the late 1940s. Machinery, tobacco and cigarettes, wines and spirits, clothing and metals are the chief exports. Bulgaria joined the European Union in January 2007.

MONETARY SYSTEM
100 Stotinki = 1 Lev

REPUBLIC
REFORM COINAGE

KM# 237   STOTINKA
1.8000 g., Aluminum-Bronze, 16 mm. **Obv:** Madara horseman right, animal below **Rev:** Denomination above date **Edge:** Plain

Date	Mintage	F	VF	XF	Unc	BU
2002 Proof	10,000	Value: 1.00				

KM# 237a   STOTINKA
1.8000 g., Brass Plated Steel, 16 mm. **Obv:** Madara horseman right **Rev:** Denomination above date

Date	Mintage	F	VF	XF	Unc	BU
2002 Proof	10,000	Value: 1.00				

KM# 238   2 STOTINKI
2.5000 g., Aluminum-Bronze, 18 mm. **Obv:** Madara horseman right, animal below **Rev:** Denomination above date **Edge:** Plain

Date	Mintage	F	VF	XF	Unc	BU
2002 Proof	10,000	Value: 1.50				

KM# 238a   2 STOTINKI
2.5000 g., Brass Plated Steel, 18 mm. **Obv:** Madara horseman right **Rev:** Denomination above date

Date	Mintage	F	VF	XF	Unc	BU
2002 Proof	10,000	Value: 1.50				

KM# 239a   5 STOTINKI
3.5000 g., Brass Plated Steel, 20 mm. **Obv:** Madara horseman right **Rev:** Denomination above date

Date	Mintage	F	VF	XF	Unc	BU
2002 Proof	10,000	Value: 2.00				

KM# 239   5 STOTINKI
3.5000 g., Aluminum-Bronze, 20 mm. **Obv:** Madara horseman right, animal below **Rev:** Denomination above date **Edge:** Plain **Note:** Prev. KM#A239.

Date	Mintage	F	VF	XF	Unc	BU
2002 Proof	10,000	Value: 2.00				

KM# 240   10 STOTINKI
3.0000 g., Copper-Nickel-Zinc, 18.5 mm. **Obv:** Madara horseman right, animal below **Rev:** Denomination above date **Edge:** Reeded

Date	Mintage	F	VF	XF	Unc	BU
2002 Proof	10,000	Value: 2.50				

KM# 241   20 STOTINKI
4.0000 g., Copper-Nickel-Zinc, 20.5 mm. **Obv:** Madara horseman right, animal below **Rev:** Denomination above date **Edge:** Reeded

Date	Mintage	F	VF	XF	Unc	BU
2002 Proof	10,000	Value: 3.00				

KM# 242   50 STOTINKI
5.0000 g., Copper-Nickel-Zinc, 22.5 mm. **Obv:** Madara horseman right, animal below **Rev:** Denomination above date **Edge:** Reeded

Date	Mintage	F	VF	XF	Unc	BU
2002 Proof	10,000	Value: 5.00				

KM# 272   50 STOTINKI
5.0000 g., Copper-Nickel-Zinc, 22.5 mm. **Obv:** Stylized Bulgarian arms, lion left, NATO - 2004 under lion **Rev:** Denomination above date **Edge:** Reeded

Date	Mintage	F	VF	XF	Unc	BU
2004	—	—	—	—	2.00	3.00

KM# 282   50 STOTINKI
5.0000 g., Copper-Nickel-Zinc, 22.5 mm. **Obv:** European Union seated woman allegory **Rev:** Value above date **Edge:** Reeded **Note:** Prev. KM#274.

Date	Mintage	F	VF	XF	Unc	BU
2005	—	—	—	—	1.25	1.75

KM# 291   50 STOTINKI
5.0000 g., Copper-Nickel-Zinc, 22.5 mm. **Obv:** Value **Rev:** Pillar behind open book **Edge:** Reeded **Note:** Prev. KM#276.

Date	Mintage	F	VF	XF	Unc	BU
2007	500,000	—	—	—	—	1.50

KM# 254   LEV
7.0000 g., Bi-Metallic Copper-Nickel center in Brass ring, 24.5 mm. **Obv:** St. Ivan of Rila **Rev:** Denomination **Edge:** Segmented reeding

Date	Mintage	F	VF	XF	Unc	BU
2002	24,842,000	—	—	—	3.00	4.00
2002 Proof	10,000	Value: 10.00				

KM# 257   LEV
15.5500 g., 0.9990 Gold 0.4994 oz. AGW **Obv:** St. Ivan of Rila **Rev:** Large number one **Edge:** Plain

Date	Mintage	F	VF	XF	Unc	BU
2002 Proof	2,000	Value: 850				

KM# 281   1.95583 LEVA
20.0000 g., 0.9990 Silver 0.6423 oz. ASW, 40 mm.   **Subject:** Bulgaria - EU **Obv:** National Arms, vlaue below **Rev:** Female seated within stars

Date	Mintage	F	VF	XF	Unc	BU
2005 Proof	14,000	Value: 500				

KM# 290   1.95583 LEVA
20.0000 g., 0.9990 Silver Partially gold plated 0.6423 oz. ASW, 40 mm.   **Subject:** Bulgaria in the EU **Obv:** National Arms **Rev:** Column and open window design

Date	Mintage	F	VF	XF	Unc	BU
2007 Proof	14,000	Value: 45.00				

KM# 304   2 LEVA
16.4000 g., 0.9990 Copper 0.5267 oz., 34.2 mm.   **Subject:** Dechko, Uzunov 110th Anniversary of Birth **Obv:** National arms **Rev:** Petar Stoikov

Date	Mintage	F	VF	XF	Unc	BU
2009 Proof	8,000	Value: 15.00				

KM# 310   2 LEVA
16.4000 g., Copper-Nickel, 34.2 mm.   **Obv:** National arms, value below **Rev:** Zahariy Zograf's self-portriat

Date	Mintage	F	VF	XF	Unc	BU
2010 Proof	—	Value: 25.00				

KM# 258   5 LEVA
1.2400 g., 0.9990 Gold 0.0398 oz. AGW   **Obv:** Denomination **Rev:** Olympic archer **Edge:** Plain

Date	Mintage	F	VF	XF	Unc	BU
2002 Proof	12,000	Value: 75.00				

KM# 259   5 LEVA
1.2400 g., 0.9990 Gold 0.0398 oz. AGW   **Obv:** Denomination **Rev:** Olympic cyclist **Edge:** Plain

Date	Mintage	F	VF	XF	Unc	BU
2002 Proof	12,000	Value: 75.00				

KM# 260   5 LEVA
1.2400 g., 0.9990 Gold 0.0398 oz. AGW   **Obv:** Denomination **Rev:** Olympic fencing **Edge:** Plain

Date	Mintage	F	VF	XF	Unc	BU
2002 Proof	12,000	Value: 75.00				

KM# 261   5 LEVA
1.2400 g., 0.9990 Gold 0.0398 oz. AGW   **Obv:** Denomination **Rev:** Olympic wrestling **Edge:** Plain

Date	Mintage	F	VF	XF	Unc	BU
2002 Proof	12,000	Value: 75.00				

KM# 262   5 LEVA
1.2400 g., 0.9990 Gold 0.0398 oz. AGW, 14 mm.   **Obv:** Denomination **Rev:** Olympic gymnastics **Edge:** Plain

Date	Mintage	F	VF	XF	Unc	BU
2002 Proof	12,000	Value: 75.00				

KM# 263   5 LEVA
1.2400 g., 0.9990 Gold 0.0398 oz. AGW, 14 mm.   **Obv:** Denomination **Rev:** Olympics founder Pierre du Coubertin **Edge:** Plain

Date	Mintage	F	VF	XF	Unc	BU
2002 Proof	17,000	Value: 75.00				

KM# 264   5 LEVA
1.2400 g., 0.9990 Gold 0.0398 oz. AGW, 14 mm.   **Obv:** Denomination **Rev:** Olympic running **Edge:** Plain

Date	Mintage	F	VF	XF	Unc	BU
2002 Proof	12,000	Value: 75.00				

KM# 265   5 LEVA
1.2400 g., 0.9990 Gold 0.0398 oz. AGW, 14 mm.   **Obv:** Denomination **Rev:** Olympic swimming **Edge:** Plain

Date	Mintage	F	VF	XF	Unc	BU
2002 Proof	12,000	Value: 75.00				

KM# 266   5 LEVA
1.2400 g., 0.9990 Gold 0.0398 oz. AGW, 14 mm.   **Obv:** Denomination **Rev:** Olympic tennis **Edge:** Plain

Date	Mintage	F	VF	XF	Unc	BU
2002 Proof	12,000	Value: 75.00				

KM# 267   5 LEVA
1.2400 g., 0.9990 Gold 0.0398 oz. AGW, 14 mm.   **Obv:** Denomination **Rev:** Olympic weight lifting **Edge:** Plain

Date	Mintage	F	VF	XF	Unc	BU
2002 Proof	12,000	Value: 75.00				

KM# 274   5 LEVA
15.0000 g., Copper-Nickel, 34.2 mm.   **Subject:** Sourvakari **Obv:** National arms **Rev:** Multicolor children in winter clothes

Date	Mintage	F	VF	XF	Unc	BU
2002 Proof	5,000	Value: 15.00				

KM# 276   5 LEVA
15.0000 g., Copper-Nickel, 34.2 mm.   **Obv:** National arms, date and denomination below **Rev:** Multicolor child on rocking horse **Edge:** Plain **Note:** Prev. KM#275.

Date	Mintage	F	VF	XF	Unc	BU
2003 Proof	10,000	Value: 35.00				

KM# 268   5 LEVA
28.2800 g., 0.9250 Silver 0.8410 oz. ASW, 38.5 mm.   **Obv:** Denomination **Rev:** FIFA Soccer trophy cup **Edge:** reeded

Date	Mintage	F	VF	XF	Unc	BU
2003 Proof	50,000	Value: 42.00				

KM# 277   5 LEVA
15.0000 g., Copper-Nickel, 34.2 mm.   **Subject:** Palm Sunday **Obv:** National Arms **Rev:** Bogomil Nikolov and Elena Dimitrova

Date	Mintage	F	VF	XF	Unc	BU
2004 Proof	10,000	Value: 15.00				

KM# 279   5 LEVA
15.0000 g., Copper-Nickel, 34.2 mm.   **Subject:** Baba Marta **Obv:** National Arms **Rev:** Multicolor flora and butterfly

Date	Mintage	F	VF	XF	Unc	BU
2005 Proof	10,000	Value: 15.00				

KM# 284   5 LEVA
23.3000 g., 0.5000 Silver 0.3745 oz. ASW, 38.6 mm.   **Subject:** Bulgaria Crafts - winemaking **Obv:** National Arms **Rev:** Multicolor grapes - wine caraffe

Date	Mintage	F	VF	XF	Unc	BU
2006 Proof	10,000	Value: 30.00				

KM# 296   5 LEVA
23.3000 g., 0.5000 Silver 0.3745 oz. ASW, 38.6 mm.   **Subject:** Bulgarian Crafts - Carpet Weaving **Obv:** National Arms **Rev:** Ivan Todorov and Plamen Dzhermanov

Date	Mintage	F	VF	XF	Unc	BU
2007 Proof	7,000	Value: 30.00				

KM# 305   5 LEVA
23.3000 g., 0.9990 Silver 0.7483 oz. ASW, 38.6 mm.   **Subject:** Bulgarian National Bank, 130th Anniversary **Obv:** Bank emblem **Rev:** Multicolor lion mozaic, fragment of stained glass

Date	Mintage	F	VF	XF	Unc	BU
2009 Proof	4,000	Value: 45.00				

KM# 306   5 LEVA
0.5000 Silver   **Subject:** Traditional Bulgarian Crafts - Pottery **Rev:** Color pot and design

Date	Mintage	F	VF	XF	Unc	BU
2009	—	—	—	—	—	35.00

KM# 247   10 LEVA
23.3300 g., 0.9250 Silver 0.6938 oz. ASW, 38.5 mm.   **Subject:** Olympics **Obv:** National arms, date and denomination below **Rev:** Ski jumper **Edge:** Plain with serial number

Date	Mintage	F	VF	XF	Unc	BU
2001 Proof	25,000	Value: 45.00				

KM# 246   10 LEVA
23.6000 g., 0.9250 Silver 0.7018 oz. ASW, 38.5 mm.   **Subject:** Higher Education **Obv:** National arms, date and denomination below **Rev:** Graduate before building **Edge:** Plain

Date	Mintage	F	VF	XF	Unc	BU
2001 Proof	10,000	Value: 45.00				

KM# 275   10 LEVA
23.3000 g., 0.9250 Silver 0.6929 oz. ASW, 38.6 mm.   **Obv:** National arms **Rev:** Head and Star of David

Date	Mintage	F	VF	XF	Unc	BU
2003 Proof	2,000	Value: 40.00				

KM# 270   10 LEVA
23.3300 g., 0.9990 Silver 0.7493 oz. ASW, 38.6 mm.   **Subject:** National Theater Centennial **Edge:** Plain

Date	Mintage	F	VF	XF	Unc	BU
2004 Proof	5,000	Value: 50.00				

KM# 273   10 LEVA
23.2000 g., 0.9250 Silver 0.6899 oz. ASW, 38.5 mm.   **Obv:** National arms, date and denomination below **Rev:** St. Nikolay Mirlikiisky Chudofvorez with gold-plated crosses and halo **Edge:** Plain

Date	Mintage	F	VF	XF	Unc	BU
2004 Proof	10,000	Value: 45.00				

KM# 280 10 LEVA
23.3000 g., 0.9250 Silver 0.6929 oz. ASW, 38.6 mm. **Subject:** XX Olympic Games - Turino, Italy **Obv:** National arms **Rev:** Short track speed skater

Date	Mintage	F	VF	XF	Unc	BU
2005 Proof	4,000				Value: 40.00	

KM# 283 10 LEVA
20.0000 g., 0.9990 Silver Partially gold plated 0.6423 oz. ASW, 40 mm. **Obv:** National arms **Rev:** Ancient sculpture

Date	Mintage	F	VF	XF	Unc	BU
2005 Proof	10,000				Value: 45.00	

KM# 285 10 LEVA
23.3000 g., 0.9250 Silver 0.6929 oz. ASW, 38.6 mm. **Subject:** National Parks - Black Sea Coast **Obv:** National arms **Rev:** Map and three circular motifs

Date	Mintage	F	VF	XF	Unc	BU
2006 Proof	7,000				Value: 40.00	

KM# 286 10 LEVA
20.0000 g., 0.9990 Silver 0.6423 oz. ASW, 40 mm. **Subject:** Treasures of Bulgaria - Letnitsa **Obv:** National arms **Rev:** Horseman statue

Date	Mintage	F	VF	XF	Unc	BU
2006 Proof	10,000				Value: 40.00	

KM# 295 10 LEVA
23.3000 g., 0.9250 Silver 0.6929 oz. ASW, 38.6 mm. **Subject:** National Parks - Pirin Mountain **Obv:** National arms **Rev:** Vanya Dimitrova

Date	Mintage	F	VF	XF	Unc	BU
2007 Proof	6,000				Value: 40.00	

KM# 297 10 LEVA
20.0000 g., 0.9990 Silver Partially gold plated 0.6423 oz. ASW, 40 mm. **Subject:** Treasures of Bulgaria - Pegasus from Vayovo **Obv:** National arms **Rev:** Pegasus forepart

Date	Mintage	F	VF	XF	Unc	BU
2007 Proof	10,000				Value: 45.00	

KM# 292 10 LEVA
31.1000 g., 0.9990 Silver 0.9988 oz. ASW, 40 mm. **Subject:** Boris Christov **Obv:** National arms **Obv. Legend:** БЪЛГАРСКА НАРОДНА БАНКА **Rev:** Early regal 1/2-length male figure facing holding orb **Rev. Legend:** ИМЕНИТИ БЪЛГАРСКИ ГЛАСОВЕ **Note:** Prev. KM#277.

Date	Mintage	F	VF	XF	Unc	BU
2007 Proof	10,000				Value: 50.00	

KM# 298 10 LEVA
23.3000 g., 0.9250 Silver 0.6929 oz. ASW, 38.6 mm. **Subject:** 130th Anniversary Bulgarian Liberation **Obv:** National arms **Rev:** Two figures in 19th century coats

Date	Mintage	F	VF	XF	Unc	BU
2008 Proof	10,000				Value: 40.00	

KM# 299 10 LEVA
23.3000 g., 0.9250 Silver 0.6929 oz. ASW, 38.6 mm. **Subject:** Shooting sports **Obv:** National Arms **Rev:** Target, bowhunter, rifleman

Date	Mintage	F	VF	XF	Unc	BU
2008 Proof	5,000				Value: 40.00	

KM# 300 10 LEVA
20.0000 g., 0.9990 Silver Partially gold plated 0.6423 oz. ASW, 40 mm. **Subject:** Treasures of Bulgaria - Sevt III **Obv:** Statue head of King Sevt III **Rev:** Elena Todorova and Todor Todorav

Date	Mintage	F	VF	XF	Unc	BU
2008 Proof	8,000				Value: 45.00	

KM# 301 10 LEVA
23.3000 g., 0.9250 Silver 0.6929 oz. ASW, 38.6 mm. **Subject:** Bulgarian Independence - 100th Anniversary **Rev:** Crowned shield

Date	Mintage	F	VF	XF	Unc	BU
2008 Proof	5,000				Value: 40.00	

KM# 302 10 LEVA
31.1000 g., 0.9990 Silver Partially gold plated 0.9988 oz. ASW, 40 mm. **Subject:** Great Bulgarian Voices: Nikolay Gyaurov **Obv:** National arms **Rev:** Elena Todorov and Todor Todorov

Date	Mintage	F	VF	XF	Unc	BU
2008 Proof	6,000				Value: 50.00	

KM# 308 10 LEVA
31.1050 g., 0.9990 Silver 0.9990 oz. ASW, 40 mm. **Obv:** National arms **Rev:** Belogradchick rock formations

Date	Mintage	F	VF	XF	Unc	BU
2010 Proof	—				Value: 50.00	

KM# 309 10 LEVA
31.1050 g., 0.9990 Silver 0.9990 oz. ASW, 40 mm. **Subject:** 125th Anniversary of Unifacation **Obv:** National arms **Rev:** Document seal gilt

Date	Mintage	F	VF	XF	Unc	BU
2010 Proof	—				Value: 50.00	

KM# 312 10 LEVA
23.3300 g., 0.9250 Silver 0.6938 oz. ASW, 38.61 mm. **Obv:** St. Geroge Zograf at right, National arms and value at left **Rev:** St. George Zograf Monastery

Date	Mintage	F	VF	XF	Unc	BU
2011 Proof	6,000				Value: 75.00	

KM# 313 10 LEVA
31.1050 g., 0.9990 Silver 0.9990 oz. ASW, 40 mm. **Obv:** National arms **Rev:** Gena Dimitrova as Princess Turnadot

Date	Mintage	F	VF	XF	Unc	BU
2011 Proof	4,000				Value: 75.00	

KM# 314 10 LEVA
23.3300 g., 0.9250 Silver partially gilt 0.6938 oz. ASW, 23.33 mm. **Subject:** Khan Krum **Obv:** Fragment miniture from Constantine Manasses' Chronicle, Khan Krum drinks a toast **Rev:** Khan Krum pursuing the Byzantines

Date	Mintage	F	VF	XF	Unc	BU
2011 Proof	5,000				Value: 75.00	

KM# 269 20 LEVA
1.5500 g., 0.9990 Gold 0.0498 oz. AGW, 16 mm. **Obv:** Denomination **Rev:** Mother of God **Edge:** Plain

Date	Mintage	F	VF	XF	Unc	BU
2003 Proof	20,000				Value: 90.00	

KM# 287 20 LEVA
1.5500 g., 0.9990 Gold 0.0498 oz. AGW, 13.9 mm. **Subject:** Iconography St John the Baptist **Obv:** National arms **Rev:** Saint facing

Date	Mintage	F	VF	XF	Unc	BU
2006 Proof	12,000				Value: 90.00	

KM# 294 20 LEVA
1.5500 g., 0.9990 Gold 0.0498 oz. AGW, 13.9 mm. **Subject:** Iconography - St. George the Victorious **Rev:** St. George slaying dragon

Date	Mintage	F	VF	XF	Unc	BU
2007 Proof	8,000				Value: 90.00	

KM# 303 20 LEVA
1.5500 g., 0.9990 Gold 0.0498 oz. AGW, 13.9 mm. **Subject:** Tsar Boris I, the Baptist **Obv:** Half-length figure facing **Rev:** Krassimir Angelov, Borislav Kyossev, Razvigov Kolev

Date	Mintage	F	VF	XF	Unc	BU
2008 Proof	8,000				Value: 90.00	

KM# 293 100 LEVA
8.6400 g., 0.9990 Gold 0.2775 oz. AGW **Subject:** Iconography - St. George the Victorious **Obv:** National arms **Rev:** Plamen Chernev

Date	Mintage	F	VF	XF	Unc	BU
2007 Proof	1,500				Value: 475	

KM# 307 100 LEVA
7.7700 g., 0.9990 Gold 0.2496 oz. AGW, 22 mm. **Subject:** Bulgarian Iconography - St. Dimitar the Wonder Worker

Date	Mintage	F	VF	XF	Unc	BU
2009 Proof	—				Value: 425	

KM# 311 100 LEVA
8.6400 g., 0.9990 Gold 0.2775 oz. AGW, 24 mm. **Obv:** National arms, value below **Rev:** St. Naum and Monastery of St. Naum in Ohrid

Date	Mintage	F	VF	XF	Unc	BU
2010 Proof	3,000				Value: 500	

KM# 271 125 LEVA
7.7800 g., 0.9990 Gold 0.2499 oz. AGW, 21 mm. **Subject:** Bulgarian National Bank 125th Anniversary

Date	Mintage	F	VF	XF	Unc	BU
2004 Proof	3,000				Value: 425	

PIEDFORT

KM#	Date	Mintage	Identification	Mkt Val
P4	2004	5,000	10 Leva. 0.9990 Silver. 46.6600 g. 100 Years - National Theatre, 38.61mm.	75.00

PROOF SETS

KM#	Date	Mintage	Identification	Issue Price	Mkt Val
PS8	2002 (7)	10,000	KM#237-242, 254	—	25.00

BURUNDI

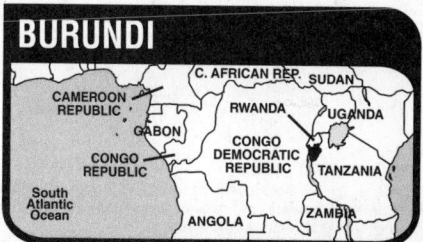

The Republic of Burundi, a landlocked country in central Africa, was a kingdom with a feudalistic society, caste system and Mwami (king) for more than 400 years before independence. It has an area of 10,740 sq. mi. (27,830 sq. km.) and a population of 6.3 million. Capital: Bujumbura. Plagued by poor soil, irregular rainfall and a single-crop economy, coffee, Burundi is barely able to feed itself. Coffee and tea are exported.

Although the area was visited by European explorers and missionaries in the latter half of the 19th century, it wasn't until the 1890s that it, together with Rwanda, fell under European domination as part of German East Africa. Following World War I, the territory was mandated to Belgium by the League of Nations and administered with the Belgian Congo. After World War II it became a U.N. Trust Territory. Limited self-government was established by U.N.-supervised elections in 1961. Burundi gained independence as a kingdom under Mwami Mwambutsa IV on July 1, 1962. The republic was established by military coup in 1966.

NOTE: For earlier coinage see Belgian Congo, and Rwanda and Burundi. For previously listed coinage dated 1966, coins of Mwambutsa IV and Ntare V, refer to *UNUSUAL WORLD COINS*, 5th edition, Krause Publications, 2007.

RULERS
Mwambutsa IV, 1962-1966
Ntare V, 1966

MINT MARKS
PM - Pobjoy Mint
(b) - Privy Marks, Brussels

MONETARY SYSTEM
100 Centimes = 1 Franc

REPUBLIC
1966-
STANDARD COINAGE

KM# 19 FRANC
0.8700 g., Aluminum, 18.91 mm. **Obv:** Denomination **Rev:** Arms above date **Edge:** Reeded

Date	Mintage	F	VF	XF	Unc	BU
2003PM	—			0.50	1.50	2.00

The Kingdom of Cambodia, formerly Democratic Kampu-chea and the Khmer Republic, a land of paddy fields and forest-clad hills located on the Indo-Chinese peninsula, fronting on the Gulf of Thailand, has an area of 70,238 sq. mi. (181,040 sq. km.) and a population of *11.21 million. Capital: Phnom Penh. Agri-culture is the basis of the economy, with rice the chief crop. Native industries include cattle breeding, weaving and rice milling. Rub-ber, cattle, corn, and timber are exported.

RULERS

Kings of Cambodia
Norodom Sihanouk, 1991-1993
  Chairman, Supreme National Council
  King, 1993-

KINGDOM
1993 -

DECIMAL COINAGE

KM# 98   500 RIELS
19.9200 g., Brass, 38.7 mm. **Subject:** Angkor Wat **Obv:** Armless statue of Jayavarman VII **Rev:** View of Angkor Wat in center **Edge:** Reeded

Date	Mintage	F	VF	XF	Unc	BU
2001	28,000	—	—	—	7.50	10.00

KM# 99   3000 RIELS
1.2441 g., 0.9999 Gold 0.0400 oz. AGW, 13.92 mm. **Subject:** Angkor Wat **Obv:** Armless statue of Jayavarman VII **Rev:** View of Angkor Wat in center **Edge:** Reeded

Date	Mintage	F	VF	XF	Unc	BU
2001	28,000	—	—	—	70.00	80.00

KM# 100   3000 RIELS
20.0000 g., 0.9250 Silver 0.5948 oz. ASW, 38.7 mm. **Subject:** Buddha **Obv:** Armless statue of Jayavarman VII **Rev:** Radiant Buddha next to a carved Buddha face **Edge:** Reeded

Date	Mintage	F	VF	XF	Unc	BU
2001 Proof	10,000	Value: 55.00				

KM# 101   3000 RIELS
20.0000 g., 0.9250 Silver 0.5948 oz. ASW, 38.7 mm. **Subject:** Apsara Dance **Obv:** Armless statue of Jayavarman VII **Rev:** Dancer next to multicolor carpet pattern **Edge:** Reeded

Date	Mintage	F	VF	XF	Unc	BU
2001 Proof	10,000	Value: 60.00				

KM# 103   3000 RIELS
20.0000 g., 0.9990 Silver 0.6423 oz. ASW, 38.7 mm. **Obv:** King Jayavarman VII (1162-1201) **Rev:** Multicolor Tutankhamen's mask **Edge:** Reeded

Date	Mintage	F	VF	XF	Unc	BU
2004 Proof	9,100	Value: 65.00				

KM# 104   3000 RIELS
1.2440 g., 0.9990 Gold 0.0400 oz. AGW, 13.92 mm. **Obv:** King Jayavarman VII (1162-1201) **Rev:** Sphinx and pyramid **Edge:** Reeded

Date	Mintage	F	VF	XF	Unc	BU
2004 Proof	27,900	Value: 95.00				

KM# 124   3000 RIELS
1.2400 g., 0.9990 Gold 0.0398 oz. AGW, 13.92 mm. **Rev:** Pyramids

Date	Mintage	F	VF	XF	Unc	BU
2004	—	—	—	—	70.00	80.00

KM# 139   3000 RIELS
31.1050 g., 0.9990 Silver 0.9990 oz. ASW **Subject:** 2006 FIFA World Cup - Germany **Obv:** King Jayavarman VII **Rev:** Temple above half of a soccer ball

Date	Mintage	F	VF	XF	Unc	BU
2004 Proof	—	Value: 80.00				

KM# 126   3000 RIELS
1.2200 g., 0.9990 Gold 0.0392 oz. AGW, 13.92 mm. **Rev:** Taj Mahal

Date	Mintage	F	VF	XF	Unc	BU
2005	—	—	—	—	70.00	80.00

KM# 127   3000 RIELS
31.1050 g., Silver, 38.7 mm. **Rev:** Indian Dancer, multicolor

Date	Mintage	F	VF	XF	Unc	BU
2005	—	Value: 65.00				

KM# 129   3000 RIELS
1.2200 g., 0.9990 Gold 0.0392 oz. AGW, 13.92 mm. **Rev:** Colosseum in Rome

Date	Mintage	F	VF	XF	Unc	BU
2006	—	—	—	—	70.00	80.00

KM# 130   3000 RIELS
Silver, 38.7 mm. **Rev:** Multicolor Roman soldier

Date	Mintage	F	VF	XF	Unc	BU
2006 Proof	—	Value: 80.00				

KM# 110   3000 RIELS
31.1050 g., 0.9990 Silver 0.9990 oz. ASW, 40.7 mm. **Subject:** Year of the Dog **Rev:** Multicolor St. Bernard

Date	Mintage	F	VF	XF	Unc	BU
2006 Prooflike	4,000	—	—	—	—	80.00

KM# 111   3000 RIELS
31.1050 g., 0.9990 Silver 0.9990 oz. ASW, 40.7 mm. **Subject:** Year of the Dog **Rev:** Multicolor Bloodhound

Date	Mintage	F	VF	XF	Unc	BU
2006 Prooflike	4,000	—	—	—	—	80.00

KM# 112   3000 RIELS
31.1050 g., 0.9990 Silver 0.9990 oz. ASW, 40.7 mm. **Subject:** Year of the Dog **Rev:** Multicolor Siberian Husky

Date	Mintage	F	VF	XF	Unc	BU
2006 Prooflike	4,000	—	—	—	—	80.00

KM# 113   3000 RIELS
31.1050 g., 0.9990 Silver 0.9990 oz. ASW, 40.7 mm. **Subject:** Year of the Dog **Rev:** Multicolor Shar Pei

Date	Mintage	F	VF	XF	Unc	BU
2006 Prooflike	4,000	—	—	—	—	80.00

KM# 114   3000 RIELS
31.1050 g., 0.9990 Silver 0.9990 oz. ASW, 40.7 mm. **Subject:** Year of the Dog **Rev:** Multicolor Borzaya

Date	Mintage	F	VF	XF	Unc	BU
2006 Prooflike	51,000	—	—	—	—	80.00

KM# 115   3000 RIELS
31.1050 g., 0.9990 Silver 0.9990 oz. ASW, 40.7 mm. **Subject:** Year of the Dog **Rev:** Multicolor Labrador

Date	Mintage	F	VF	XF	Unc	BU
2006 Prooflike	51,000	—	—	—	—	80.00

KM# 116   3000 RIELS
31.1050 g., 0.9990 Silver 0.9990 oz. ASW, 40.7 mm. **Subject:** Year of the Dog **Rev:** Multicolor Russian Spaniel

Date	Mintage	F	VF	XF	Unc	BU
2006 Prooflike	51,000	—	—	—	—	80.00

KM# 117   3000 RIELS
31.1050 g., 0.9990 Silver 0.9990 oz. ASW, 40.7 mm. **Subject:** Year of the Dog **Rev:** Multicolor Newfoundland

Date	Mintage	F	VF	XF	Unc	BU
2006 Prooflike	51,000	—	—	—	—	80.00

KM# 132   3000 RIELS
1.2200 g., 0.9990 Gold 0.0392 oz. AGW, 13.92 mm. **Rev:** Borobudur Temple, Indonesia

Date	Mintage	F	VF	XF	Unc	BU
2007	28,000	—	—	—	70.00	80.00

KM# 133 3000 RIELS
31.1050 g., 0.9990 Silver 0.9990 oz. ASW, 38.7 mm. **Rev:**
Legomo dancer, multicolor

Date	Mintage	F	VF	XF	Unc	BU
2007 Proof	10,000	Value: 80.00				

KM# 118 3000 RIELS
31.1050 g., 0.9990 Silver 0.9990 oz. ASW, 40.7 mm. **Subject:**
Year of the Pig **Rev:** Multicolor pig

Date	Mintage	F	VF	XF	Unc	BU
2007 Prooflike	—	—	—	—	—	80.00

KM# 135 3000 RIELS
31.1050 g., 0.9990 Silver 0.9990 oz. ASW, 40.7 mm. **Subject:**
Year of the Pig **Rev:** Multicolor pig

Date	Mintage	F	VF	XF	Unc	BU
2007 Prooflike	30,000	—	—	—	—	90.00

KM# 136 3000 RIELS
31.1050 g., 0.9990 Silver 0.9990 oz. ASW, 40.7 mm. **Subject:**
Year of the Pig **Rev:** Multicolor pig

Date	Mintage	F	VF	XF	Unc	BU
2007 Prooflike	30,000	—	—	—	—	90.00

KM# 137 3000 RIELS
31.1050 g., 0.9990 Silver 0.9990 oz. ASW, 40.7 mm. **Subject:**
Year of the Pig **Rev:** Multicolor pig

Date	Mintage	F	VF	XF	Unc	BU
2007 Prooflike	30,000	—	—	—	—	90.00

KM# 138 3000 RIELS
31.1050 g., 0.9990 Silver 0.9990 oz. ASW, 40.7 mm. **Subject:**
Year of the Pig **Rev:** Multicolor pig

Date	Mintage	F	VF	XF	Unc	BU
2007 Prooflike	30,000	—	—	—	—	90.00

KM# 121 3000 RIELS
1.2400 g., 0.9990 Gold 0.0398 oz. AGW, 13.9 mm. **Subject:**
Statue torso **Rev:** Shwe Dragon Pagoda, Mynamar

Date	Mintage	F	VF	XF	Unc	BU
2008 Proof	—	Value: 75.00				

KM# 123 3000 RIELS
31.1035 g., 0.9990 Silver 0.9990 oz. ASW, 40.7 mm. **Obv:**
Statue torso **Rev:** Multicolor Padaung

Date	Mintage	F	VF	XF	Unc	BU
2009 Proof	—	Value: 75.00				

KM# 102 10000 RIELS
31.1035 g., 0.9990 Bi-Metallic Gold center in silver ring.
0.9990 oz., 40.7 mm. **Subject:** Angkor Wat **Obv:** Armless statue
of Jayavarman **Rev:** Multicolor holographic view of Angkor Wat
in center **Edge:** Reeded

Date	Mintage	F	VF	XF	Unc	BU
2001 Proof	3,000	Value: 350				

KM# 125 10000 RIELS
31.1050 g., 0.9990 Silver 0.9990 oz. ASW, 40.7 mm. **Rev:** Great
Wall of China, holographic insert

Date	Mintage	F	VF	XF	Unc	BU
2003 Proof	—	Value: 300				

KM# 105 10000 RIELS
31.1035 g., 0.9990 Silver 0.9990 oz. ASW, 40.7 mm. **Obv:** King
Jayavarman VII (1162-1201) **Rev:** Sphinx and pyramid on
holographic gold insert **Edge:** Reeded

Date	Mintage	F	VF	XF	Unc	BU
2004 Proof	2,100	Value: 300				

KM# 119 10000 RIELS
31.1050 g., 0.9990 Silver 0.9990 oz. ASW, 38.7 mm. **Subject:**
Zheng He 600th Anniversary **Rev:** Sailing ship with latent image

Date	Mintage	F	VF	XF	Unc	BU
2005 Proof	200	Value: 150				

KM# 120 10000 RIELS
31.1050 g., 0.9990 Silver 0.9990 oz. ASW, 38.7 mm. **Subject:**
Zheng He 600th Anniversary **Rev:** Multicolor figure standing

Date	Mintage	F	VF	XF	Unc	BU
2005 Proof	200	Value: 150				

KM# 128 10000 RIELS
31.1050 g., 0.9990 Silver 0.9990 oz. ASW, 40.7 mm. **Rev:** Taj
Mahal in multicolor hologram at center

Date	Mintage	F	VF	XF	Unc	BU
2005 Proof	—	Value: 300				

KM# 131 10000 RIELS
31.1050 g., 0.9990 Silver 0.9990 oz. ASW, 40.7 mm. **Rev:**
Colosseum in multicolor hologram

Date	Mintage	F	VF	XF	Unc	BU
2006 Proof	—	Value: 300				

KM# 134   10000 RIELS
31.1050 g., 0.9990 Silver 0.9990 oz. ASW, 40.7 mm. **Rev:**
Boraburdur temple, Indonesia

Date	Mintage	F	VF	XF	Unc	BU
2007 Proof	300	Value: 300				

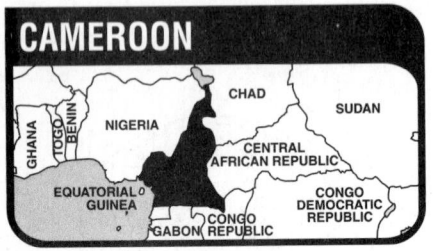

KM# 122   10000 RIELS
31.1035 g., 0.9990 Silver 0.9990 oz. ASW, 40.7 mm. **Obv:**
Statue torso **Rev:** Hologram of Shwe Dragon Pagoda, Mynamar

Date	Mintage	F	VF	XF	Unc	BU
2009 Proof	—	Value: 150				

CAMEROON

The Republic of Cameroon, located in west-central Africa on the Gulf of Guinea, has an area of 183,569 sq. mi. (475,445 sq. km.) and a population of *15.13 million. Capital: Yaounde. About 90 percent of the labor force is employed on the land; cash crops account for 80 percent of the country's export revenue. Cocoa, coffee, aluminum, cotton, rubber, and timber are exported. Cameroon is a member of the Commonwealth of Nations. The President is the Head of State; the Prime Minister is the Head of Government.

MINT MARKS
(a) - Paris, privy marks only
SA - Pretoria, 1943

MONETARY SYSTEM
100 Centimes = 1 Franc

REPUBLIC

STANDARD COINAGE

KM# 28   500 FRANCS
15.5500 g., 0.9250 Silver 0.4624 oz. ASW, 33 mm. **Subject:**
Zodiac - Cancer **Obv:** National arms

Date	Mintage	F	VF	XF	Unc	BU
2010	3,000	—	—	—	—	50.00

KM# 29   500 FRANCS
15.5500 g., 0.9250 Silver 0.4624 oz. ASW **Subject:** Zodiac -
Leo **Obv:** National arms

Date	Mintage	F	VF	XF	Unc	BU
2010	3,000	—	—	—	—	50.00

KM# 30   500 FRANCS
15.5500 g., 0.9250 Silver 0.4624 oz. ASW, 33 mm. **Subject:**
Zodiac - Virgo **Obv:** National arms

Date	Mintage	F	VF	XF	Unc	BU
2010	3,000	—	—	—	—	50.00

KM# 31   500 FRANCS
15.5500 g., 0.9250 Silver 0.4624 oz. ASW, 33 mm. **Subject:**
Zodiac - Libra **Obv:** National arms

Date	Mintage	F	VF	XF	Unc	BU
2010	3,000	—	—	—	—	50.00

KM# 32   500 FRANCS
15.5500 g., 0.9990 Silver 0.4994 oz. ASW, 33 mm. **Subject:**
Zodiac - Scorpius **Obv:** National arms

Date	Mintage	F	VF	XF	Unc	BU
2010	3,000	—	—	—	—	50.00

KM# 33   500 FRANCS
15.5500 g., 0.9250 Silver 0.4624 oz. ASW, 33 mm. **Subject:**
Zodiac - Sagittarius **Obv:** National arms

Date	Mintage	F	VF	XF	Unc	BU
2010	3,000	—	—	—	—	50.00

KM# 34   500 FRANCS
15.5500 g., 0.9250 Silver 0.4624 oz. ASW, 33 mm. **Subject:**
Zodiac - Capricorn **Obv:** National Arms

Date	Mintage	F	VF	XF	Unc	BU
2010	3,000	—	—	—	—	50.00

KM# 35   500 FRANCS
15.5500 g., 0.9250 Silver 0.4624 oz. ASW, 33 mm. **Subject:**
Zodiac - Aquarius **Obv:** National arms

Date	Mintage	F	VF	XF	Unc	BU
2010	3,000	—	—	—	—	50.00

KM# 25   500 FRANCS
15.5500 g., 0.9250 Silver 0.4624 oz. ASW, 33 mm. **Subject:**
Zodiac - Aries **Obv:** National arms

Date	Mintage	F	VF	XF	Unc	BU
2010	3,000	—	—	—	—	50.00

KM# 26   500 FRANCS
15.5500 g., 0.9250 Silver 0.4624 oz. ASW, 33 mm. **Subject:**
Zodiac - Taurus **Obv:** National arms

Date	Mintage	F	VF	XF	Unc	BU
2010	3,000	—	—	—	—	50.00

KM# 36   500 FRANCS
15.5500 g., 0.9250 Silver 0.4624 oz. ASW, 33 mm. **Subject:**
Zodiac - Pisces **Obv:** National arms

Date	Mintage	F	VF	XF	Unc	BU
2010	3,000	—	—	—	—	50.00

KM# 27   500 FRANCS
15.5500 g., 0.9250 Silver 0.4624 oz. ASW, 33 mm. **Subject:**
Zodiac - Gemini **Obv:** National arms

Date	Mintage	F	VF	XF	Unc	BU
2010	3,000	—	—	—	—	50.00

KM# 40   1500 FRANCS
62.2000 g., 0.9990 Silver 1.9977 oz. ASW, 40x40 mm. **Obv:**
National arms **Rev:** Black Rhinoceros head profile facing right

Date	Mintage	F	VF	XF	Unc	BU
2010 Proof	—	Value: 85.00				

KM# 24   1000 FRANCS
25.0000 g., 0.9250 Copper-Nickel 0.7435 oz., 38.61 mm. **Obv:**
Arms **Rev:** Papillons D'Amour butterfly **Edge:** Reeded

Date	Mintage	F	VF	XF	Unc	BU
2010 Proof	2,500	Value: 65.00				

KM# 37   1000 FRANCS
25.0000 g., 0.9990 Silver 0.8029 oz. ASW, 38.61 mm. **Subject:**
Ange de l'amour **Obv:** National arms **Rev:** Cupuid

Date	Mintage	F	VF	XF	Unc	BU
2010 Proof	2,500	Value: 80.00				

KM# 38   1000 FRANCS
20.0000 g., 0.9250 Silver 0.5948 oz. ASW, 38.61 mm. **Obv:**
National arms **Rev:** Heat sensetive image of the Shroud of Turin

Date	Mintage	F	VF	XF	Unc	BU
2010 Proof	2,010	Value: 75.00				

KM# 49   1000 FRANCS
25.0000 g., Copper-Nickel, 39 mm. **Obv:** National arms **Rev:**
Two swans, hologram between them

Date	Mintage	F	VF	XF	Unc	BU
2011 Antique Finish	—	—	—	—	—	65.00
2011 Proof	—	Value: 65.00				

KM# 50   1000 FRANCS
25.0000 g., Copper-Nickel, 39 mm. **Obv:** National arms **Rev:**
Monarch Butterfly in 3-D and color

Date	Mintage	F	VF	XF	Unc	BU
2011 Proof	—	Value: 100				

CANADA

Canada is located to the north of the United States, and spans the full breadth of the northern portion of North America from Atlantic to Pacific oceans, except for the State of Alaska. It has a total area of 3,850,000 sq. mi. (9,971,550 sq. km.) and a population of 30.29 million. Capital: Ottawa.

Canada is a member of the Commonwealth of Nations. Elizabeth II is Head of State as Queen of Canada.

RULER
British 1763-

MONETARY SYSTEM
1 Dollar = 100 Cents

CONFEDERATION

CIRCULATION COINAGE

KM# 289 CENT
2.2500 g., Copper Plated Steel, 19.05 mm. **Ruler:** Elizabeth II **Obv:** Crowned head right **Obv. Designer:** Dora dePédery-Hunt **Rev:** Maple twig design **Rev. Designer:** George E. Kruger-Gray **Edge:** Round and plain

Date	Mintage	MS-63	Proof
2001	919,358,000	0.30	—
2001P Proof	—	—	5.00
2003	92,219,775	0.30	—
2003P Proof	—	—	5.00
2003P	235,936,799	1.50	—

KM# 445 CENT
2.2500 g., Copper Plated Steel, 19.1 mm. **Ruler:** Elizabeth II **Subject:** Elizabeth II Golden Jubilee **Obv:** Crowned head right, Jubilee commemorative dates 1952-2002 **Obv. Designer:** Dora dePédery-Hunt **Rev:** Denomination above maple leaves **Rev. Designer:** George E. Kruger-Gray **Edge:** Plain

Date	Mintage	MS-63	Proof
1952-2002	716,366,000	0.75	—
1952-2002P	114,212,000	1.00	—
1952-2002P Proof	32,642	—	5.00

KM# 445a CENT
0.9250 Silver **Ruler:** Elizabeth II **Subject:** Elizabeth II Golden Jubilee **Obv:** Crowned head right, Jubilee commemorative dates 1952-2002 **Obv. Designer:** Dora dePédery-Hunt **Rev:** Denomination above maple leaves **Rev. Designer:** George E. Kruger-Gray

Date	Mintage	MS-63	Proof
1952-2002	21,537	—	3.00

KM# 490 CENT
2.2500 g., Copper Plated Zinc, 19.05 mm. **Ruler:** Elizabeth II **Obv:** New effigy of Queen Elizabeth II right **Obv. Designer:** Susanna Blunt **Rev:** Two maple leaves **Edge:** Plain

Date	Mintage	MS-63	Proof
2003	56,877,144	0.25	—
2004	653,317,000	0.25	—
2004 Proof	—	—	2.50
2005	759,658,000	0.25	—
2005 Proof	—	—	2.50
2006	886,275,000	0.25	—
2006 Proof	—	—	2.50

KM# 490a CENT
2.2500 g., Copper Plated Steel, 19.05 mm. **Ruler:** Elizabeth II **Obv:** Bust right **Obv. Designer:** Susanna Blunt **Rev:** Two maple leaves **Rev. Designer:** G. E. Kruger-Gray

Date	Mintage	MS-63	Proof
2003P	591,257,000	0.25	—
2003 WP	Inc. above	0.25	—
2004P	134,906,000	0.25	—
2005P	30,525,000	0.25	—
2006P	137,733,000	0.25	—
2006(ml)	Inc. above	0.25	—
2007(ml)	938,270,000	0.25	—
2007(ml) Proof	—	—	2.50
2008(ml)	787,625,000	0.25	—
2008(ml) Proof	—	—	2.50
2009(ml)	455,680,000	0.25	—
2009(ml) Proof	—	—	2.50
2010(ml)	—	0.25	—
2010(ml) Proof	—	—	2.50
2011(ml)	—	0.25	—
2011(ml) Proof	—	—	2.50
2012(ml)	—	0.25	—
2012(ml) Proof	—	—	2.50

KM# 468 CENT
2.5000 g., Copper **Ruler:** Elizabeth II **Subject:** 50th Anniversary of the Coronation of Elizabeth II **Obv:** 1953 Effigy of the Queen, Jubilee commemorative dates 1953-2003 **Obv. Designer:** Mary Gillick

Date	Mintage	MS-63	Proof
1953-2003 Proof	—	—	2.50

KM# 490b CENT
2.2500 g., Copper Plated Zinc **Ruler:** Elizabeth II **Obv:** Head right **Rev:** Maple leaf, selectively gold plated **Note:** Bound into Annual Report.

Date	Mintage	MS-63	Proof
2003 Proof	7,746	—	35.00

KM# 1023 CENT
Copper, 19.1 mm. **Ruler:** Elizabeth II **Obv:** George V bust left **Rev:** Value within wreath, dual dates below

Date	Mintage	MS-63	Proof
1935-2010 Proof	—	—	10.00

KM# 1153 CENT
Copper, 19.1 mm. **Ruler:** Elizabeth II

Date	Mintage	MS-63	Proof
1911-2011 Proof	—	—	10.00

KM# 410 3 CENTS
3.1100 g., 0.9250 Silver Gilt 0.0925 oz. ASW, 21.3 mm. **Ruler:** Elizabeth II **Subject:** 1st Canadian Postage Stamp **Obv:** Crowned head right **Obv. Designer:** Dora dePédery-Hunt **Rev:** Partial stamp design **Rev. Designer:** Sandford Fleming **Edge:** Plain

Date	Mintage	MS-63	Proof
2001 Proof	59,573	—	12.50

KM# 182 5 CENTS
4.6000 g., Copper-Nickel, 19.55 mm. **Ruler:** Elizabeth II **Obv:** Crowned head right **Obv. Designer:** Dora dePedery-Hunt **Rev:** Beaver on rock divides dates and denomination **Rev. Designer:** George E. Kruger-Gray **Edge:** Plain

Date	Mintage	MS-63	Proof
2001	30,035,000	12.50	—
2001P Proof	—	—	10.00
2003	—	0.30	—

KM# 182b 5 CENTS
3.9000 g., Nickel Plated Steel, 21.2 mm. **Ruler:** Elizabeth II **Obv:** Crowned head right **Obv. Designer:** Dora dePedery-Hunt **Rev:** Beaver on rock divides date and denomination **Rev. Designer:** George E. Kruger-Gray **Edge:** Plain

Date	Mintage	MS-63	Proof
2001 P	136,650,000	0.35	—
2003 P	32,986,921	0.35	—

KM# 182a 5 CENTS
5.3500 g., 0.9250 Silver 0.1591 oz. ASW, 21.2 mm. **Ruler:** Elizabeth II **Obv:** Crowned head right **Obv. Designer:** Dora dePedery-Hunt **Rev:** Beaver on rock divides date and denomination **Rev. Designer:** George E. Kruger-Gray

Date	Mintage	MS-63	Proof
2001 Proof	—	—	5.00
2003 Proof	—	—	5.00

KM# 413 5 CENTS
5.3500 g., 0.9250 Silver 0.1591 oz. ASW, 21.2 mm. **Ruler:** Elizabeth II **Subject:** Royal Military College **Obv:** Crowned head right **Rev:** Marching cadets and arch **Rev. Designer:** Gerald T. Locklin **Edge:** Plain

Date	Mintage	MS-63	Proof
2001 Proof	25,834	—	7.00

KM# 446 5 CENTS
3.9500 g., Nickel Plated Steel, 21.2 mm. **Ruler:** Elizabeth II **Subject:** Elizabeth II Golden Jubilee **Obv:** Crowned head right, Jubilee commemorative dates 1952-2002 **Obv. Designer:** Dora dePedery-Hunt **Rev. Designer:** George E. Kruger-Gray **Note:** Magnetic.

Date	Mintage	MS-63	Proof
1952-2002P	135,960,000	0.45	—
1952-2002P Proof	32,642	—	10.00

KM# 446a 5 CENTS
5.3500 g., 0.9250 Silver 0.1591 oz. ASW, 21.2 mm. **Ruler:** Elizabeth II **Subject:** Elizabeth II Golden Jubilee **Obv:** Queen, Jubilee commemorative dates 1952-2002

Date	Mintage	MS-63	Proof
1952-2002 Proof	21,573	—	11.50

KM# 453 5 CENTS
5.3500 g., 0.9250 Silver 0.1591 oz. ASW, 21.2 mm. **Ruler:** Elizabeth II **Subject:** Vimy Ridge - WWI **Obv:** Crowned head right **Rev:** Vimy Ridge Memorial, allegorical figure and dates 1917-2002 **Rev. Designer:** S. A. Allward

Date	Mintage	MS-63	Proof
2002 Proof	22,646	—	11.50

KM# 491   5 CENTS
3.9500 g., Nickel Plated Steel, 21.2 mm.   **Ruler:** Elizabeth II **Obv:** Bare head right **Obv. Designer:** Susanna Blunt **Rev:** Beaver divides date and denomination **Rev. Designer:** George E. Kruger-Gray **Note:** Magnetic.

Date	Mintage	MS-63	Proof
2003P	61,392,180	0.45	—
2004P	132,097,000	0.45	—
2004P Proof	—	—	2.50
2005P	89,664,000	0.45	—
2005P Proof	—	—	2.50
2006P	139,308,000	0.50	—
2006P Proof	—	—	2.50
2006(ml)	184,874,000	0.45	—
2006(ml) Proof	—	—	2.50
2007(ml)	221,472,000	0.45	—
2007(ml) Proof	—	—	2.50
2008(ml)	278,530,000	0.45	—
2008(ml) Proof	—	—	2.50
2009(ml)	266,488,000	0.45	—
2009(ml) Proof	—	—	2.50
2010(ml)	—	0.45	—
2010(ml) Proof	—	—	2.50
2011(ml)	—	0.45	—
2011(ml) Proof	—	—	2.50
2012(ml)	—	0.45	—
2012(ml) Proof	—	—	2.50

KM# 469   5 CENTS
5.3500 g., 0.9250 Silver 0.1591 oz. ASW, 21.2 mm.   **Ruler:** Elizabeth II **Subject:** 50th Anniversary of the Coronation of Elizabeth II **Obv:** Crowned head right, Jubilee commemorative dates 1953-2003 **Obv. Designer:** Mary Gillick

Date	Mintage	MS-63	Proof
1953-2003 Proof	21,573	—	11.50

KM# 491a   5 CENTS
5.3500 g., 0.9250 Silver 0.1591 oz. ASW, 21.1 mm.   **Ruler:** Elizabeth II **Obv:** Crowned head right **Obv. Designer:** Susanna Blunt **Rev:** Beaver divides date and denomination **Edge:** Plain

Date	Mintage	MS-63	Proof
2004 Proof	—	—	3.50

KM# 506   5 CENTS
5.3500 g., 0.9250 Silver 0.1591 oz. ASW, 21.3 mm.   **Ruler:** Elizabeth II **Obv:** Bare head right **Rev:** "Victory" design of the KM-40 reverse **Edge:** Plain **Shape:** 12-sided

Date	Mintage	MS-63	Proof
1944-2004 Proof	20,019	—	15.00

KM# 627   5 CENTS
3.9500 g., Nickel Plated Steel, 21.2 mm.   **Ruler:** Elizabeth II **Subject:** 60th Anniversary, Victory in Europe 1945-2005 **Obv:** Head right **Rev:** Large V **Edge:** Plain

Date	Mintage	MS-63	Proof
2005P	59,269,192	4.50	—

KM# 758   5 CENTS
5.3000 g., 0.9250 Silver 0.1576 oz. ASW   **Ruler:** Elizabeth II **Obv:** George VI head left **Rev:** Torch and large V

Date	Mintage	MS-63	Proof
2005 Proof	42,792	—	35.00

KM# 758a   5 CENTS
5.3000 g., 0.9250 Silver selectively gold plated 0.1576 oz. ASW   **Ruler:** Elizabeth II **Obv:** George VI head left **Rev:** Torch and large V **Note:** Bound into Annual Report.

Date	Mintage	MS-63	Proof
2005 Proof	6,065	—	40.00

KM# 491b   5 CENTS
4.6000 g., Copper-Nickel   **Ruler:** Elizabeth II **Obv:** Bust right **Rev:** Beaver

Date	Mintage	MS-63	Proof
2006	43,008,000	5.00	—

KM# 1024   5 CENTS
Nickel, 21.2 mm.   **Ruler:** Elizabeth II **Obv:** George V bust left **Rev:** Denomination and 1935-2010 anniversary dates, two maple leaves below

Date	Mintage	MS-63	Proof
1935-2010 Proof	—	—	15.00

KM# 1154   5 CENTS
Nickel, 21.2 mm.   **Ruler:** Elizabeth II

Date	Mintage	MS-63	Proof
1911-2011 Proof	—	—	15.00

KM# 412a   10 CENTS
2.4000 g., 0.9250 Silver 0.0714 oz. ASW, 18 mm.   **Ruler:** Elizabeth II **Subject:** Year of the Volunteer **Obv:** Crowned head right **Rev:** Three portraits left above banner, radiant sun below **Edge:** Reeded

Date	Mintage	MS-63	Proof
2001P Proof	40,634	—	9.00

KM# 183b   10 CENTS
1.7700 g., Nickel Plated Steel, 18.03 mm.   **Ruler:** Elizabeth II **Obv:** Crowned head right **Obv. Designer:** Dora dePedery-Hunt **Rev:** Bluenose sailing left, date at right, denomination below **Rev. Designer:** Emanuel Hahn **Edge:** Reeded

Date	Mintage	MS-63	Proof
2001 P	266,000,000	0.45	—
2003 P	162,398,000	0.20	—

KM# 183a   10 CENTS
2.4000 g., 0.9250 Silver 0.0714 oz. ASW, 18.03 mm.   **Ruler:** Elizabeth II **Obv:** Crowned head right **Rev:** Bluenose sailing left, date at right, denomination below

Date	Mintage	MS-63	Proof
2001 Proof	—	—	5.00
2002 Proof	—	—	7.50
2003 Proof	—	—	7.50

KM# 412   10 CENTS
1.7700 g., Nickel Plated Steel, 18 mm.   **Ruler:** Elizabeth II **Subject:** Year of the Volunteer **Obv:** Crowned head right **Rev:** Three portraits left and radiant sun **Edge:** Reeded

Date	Mintage	MS-63	Proof
2001P	224,714,000	4.50	—

KM# 447   10 CENTS
1.7700 g., Nickel Plated Steel, 18 mm.   **Ruler:** Elizabeth II **Subject:** Elizabeth II Golden Jubilee **Obv:** Crowned head right, Jubilee commemorative dates 1952-2002

Date	Mintage	MS-63	Proof
1952-2002P	252,563,000	1.00	—
1952-2002 Proof	32,642	—	2.50

KM# 447a   10 CENTS
2.3200 g., 0.9250 Silver 0.0690 oz. ASW, 18 mm.   **Ruler:** Elizabeth II **Subject:** Elizabeth II Golden Jubilee **Obv:** Crowned head right, Jubilee commemorative dates 1952-2002

Date	Mintage	MS-63	Proof
2002 Proof	21,537	—	12.50

KM# 492   10 CENTS
1.7700 g., Nickel Plated Steel, 18 mm.   **Ruler:** Elizabeth II **Obv:** Head right **Obv. Designer:** Susanna Blunt **Rev:** Bluenose sailing left

Date	Mintage	MS-63	Proof
2003P	—	1.25	—
2004P	211,924,000	0.60	—
2004P Proof	—	—	2.50
2005P	212,175,000	0.60	—
2005P Proof	—	—	2.50
2006P	312,122,000	0.60	—
2006P Proof	—	—	2.50
2007(ml) Straight 7	304,110,000	0.60	—
2007(ml) Curved 7	Inc. above	0.60	—

Date	Mintage	MS-63	Proof
2007(ml) Proof	—	—	2.50
2008(ml)	467,495,000	0.60	—
2008(ml) Proof	—	—	2.50
2009(ml)	370,700,000	0.60	—
2009(ml) Proof	—	—	2.50
2010(ml)	—	0.60	—
2010(ml) Proof	—	—	2.50
2011(ml)	—	0.60	—
2011(ml) Proof	—	—	2.50
2012(ml)	—	0.60	—
2012(ml) Proof	—	—	2.50

KM# 470   10 CENTS
2.3200 g., 0.9250 Silver 0.0690 oz. ASW   **Ruler:** Elizabeth II **Subject:** 50th Anniversary of the Coronation of Elizabeth II **Obv:** Head right **Rev:** Bluenose sailing left

Date	Mintage	MS-63	Proof
1953-2003 Proof	21,537	—	12.00

KM# 492a   10 CENTS
2.4000 g., 0.9250 Silver 0.0714 oz. ASW, 18 mm.   **Ruler:** Elizabeth II **Obv:** Bare head right **Obv. Designer:** Susanna Blunt **Rev:** Sailboat **Edge:** Reeded

Date	Mintage	MS-63	Proof
2004 Proof	—	—	5.00

KM# 524   10 CENTS
2.4000 g., 0.9250 Silver 0.0714 oz. ASW, 18 mm.   **Ruler:** Elizabeth II **Subject:** Golf, Championship of Canada, Centennial. **Obv:** Head right

Date	Mintage	MS-63	Proof
2004	39,486	12.50	—

KM# 1025   10 CENTS
Silver, 18.03 mm.   **Ruler:** Elizabeth II **Obv:** George V bust left **Rev:** Value within wreath, dual dates below

Date	Mintage	MS-63	Proof
1935-2010 Proof	—	—	20.00

KM# 1155   10 CENTS
Silver, 18.03 mm.   **Ruler:** Elizabeth II

Date	Mintage	MS-63	Proof
1911-2011 Proof	—	—	20.00

KM# 184   25 CENTS
5.0700 g., Nickel, 23.88 mm.   **Ruler:** Elizabeth II **Obv:** Crowned head right **Obv. Designer:** Dora dePedery-Hunt **Rev:** Caribou left, denomination above, date at right **Rev. Designer:** Emanuel Hahn

Date	Mintage	MS-63	Proof
2001	8,415,000	5.00	—
2001 Proof	—	—	7.50

KM# 184b   25 CENTS
4.4000 g., Nickel Plated Steel, 23.88 mm.   **Ruler:** Elizabeth II **Obv:** Crowned head right **Rev:** Caribou left, denomination above, date at right

Date	Mintage	MS-63	Proof
2001 P	55,773,000	0.95	—
2001 P Proof	—	—	5.00
2002 P	156,105,000	2.50	—
2002 P Proof	—	—	5.00
2003 P	87,647,000	2.50	—
2003 P Proof	—	—	5.00

KM# 184a   25 CENTS
5.9000 g., 0.9250 Silver 0.1755 oz. ASW, 23.88 mm.   **Ruler:** Elizabeth II **Obv:** Crowned head right **Rev:** Caribou left, denomination above, date at right

Date	Mintage	MS-63	Proof
2001 Proof	—	—	9.50
2003 Proof	—	—	9.50

KM# 419   25 CENTS
4.4000 g., Nickel Plated Steel, 23.9 mm.   **Ruler:** Elizabeth II **Subject:** Canada Day **Obv:** Crowned head right **Rev:** Maple leaf at center, children holding hands below **Rev. Designer:** Silke Ware **Edge:** Reeded

Date	Mintage	MS-63	Proof
2001	96,352	7.00	—

KM# 448 25 CENTS
4.4000 g., Nickel Plated Steel, 23.9 mm. **Ruler:** Elizabeth II
Subject: Elizabeth II Golden Jubilee **Obv:** Crowned head right
Rev: Caribou left

Date	Mintage	MS-63	Proof
1952-2002P	152,485,000	2.00	—
1952-2002P Proof 32,642		—	6.00

KM# 448a 25 CENTS
5.9000 g., 0.9250 Silver 0.1755 oz. ASW, 23.9 mm. **Ruler:**
Elizabeth II **Subject:** Elizabeth II Golden Jubilee **Obv:** Crowned
head right, Jubilee commemorative dates 1952-2002

Date	Mintage	MS-63	Proof
1952-2002 Proof	100,000	—	12.50

KM# 451 25 CENTS
4.4000 g., Nickel Plated Steel, 23.9 mm. **Ruler:** Elizabeth II **Rev:**
Small human figures supporting large maple leaf

Date	Mintage	MS-63	Proof
2002P	30,627,000	5.00	—

KM# 451a 25 CENTS
4.4000 g., Nickel Plated Steel, 23.9 mm. **Ruler:** Elizabeth II
Subject: Canada Day **Obv:** Crowned head right **Rev:** Human
figures supporting large red maple leaf **Edge:** Reeded

Date	Mintage	MS-63	Proof
2002P	49,901	6.00	—

KM# 493 25 CENTS
4.4000 g., Nickel Plated Steel, 23.9 mm. **Ruler:** Elizabeth II
Obv: Bare head right **Obv. Designer:** Susanna Blunt **Rev:**
Caribou left, denomination above, date at right

Date	Mintage	MS-63	Proof
2003P	66,861,633	2.00	—
2003P W	—	—	—
2004P	177,466,000	2.50	—
2004P Proof	—	—	5.00
2005P	206,346,000	2.50	—
2005P Proof	—	—	5.00
2006P	423,189,000	2.50	—
2006P Proof	—	—	5.00
2007(ml)	386,763,000	2.50	—
2007(ml) Proof	—	—	5.00
2008(ml)	387,222,000	2.50	—
2008(ml) Proof	—	—	5.00
2009(ml)	266,766,000	2.50	—
2009(ml) Proof	—	—	5.00
2010(ml)	—	2.50	—
2010(ml) Proof	—	—	5.00
2011(ml)	—	2.50	—
2011(ml) Proof	—	—	5.00
2012(ml)	—	2.50	—
2012(ml) Proof	—	—	5.00

KM# 471 25 CENTS
5.9000 g., 0.9250 Silver 0.1755 oz. ASW, 23.9 mm. **Ruler:**
Elizabeth II **Subject:** 50th Anniversary of the Coronation of
Elizabeth II **Obv:** 1953 Effigy of the Queen, Coronation Jubilee
dates 1953-2003 **Obv. Designer:** Mary Gillick

Date	Mintage	MS-63	Proof
1953-2003 Proof	21,537	—	12.50

KM# 474 25 CENTS
4.4000 g., 0.9250 Silver 0.1308 oz. ASW, 23.9 mm. **Ruler:**
Elizabeth II **Subject:** Canada Day **Obv:** Queen's head right **Rev:**
Polar bear and red colored maple leaves

Date	Mintage	MS-63	Proof
2003 Proof	63,511	—	12.00

KM# 493a 25 CENTS
5.9000 g., 0.9250 Silver 0.1755 oz. ASW, 23.9 mm. **Ruler:**
Elizabeth II **Obv:** Bare head right **Obv. Designer:** Suanne Blunt
Rev: Caribou **Edge:** Reeded

Date	Mintage	MS-63	Proof
2004 Proof	—	—	6.50

KM# 510 25 CENTS
4.4000 g., Nickel Plated Steel, 23.9 mm. **Ruler:** Elizabeth II
Obv: Bare head right **Rev:** Red poppy in center of maple leaf
Edge: Reeded

Date	Mintage	MS-63	Proof
2004	28,500,000	5.00	—

KM# 510a 25 CENTS
5.9000 g., 0.9250 Silver 0.1755 oz. ASW, 23.9 mm. **Ruler:**
Elizabeth II **Obv:** Bare head right **Rev:** Poppy at center of maple
leaf, selectively gold plated **Edge:** Reeded **Note:** Housed in
Annual Report.

Date	Mintage	MS-63	Proof
2004 Proof	12,677	—	20.00

KM# 525 25 CENTS
4.4000 g., Nickel Plated Steel, 23.9 mm. **Ruler:** Elizabeth II
Obv: Bare head right **Rev:** Maple leaf, colorized

Date	Mintage	MS-63	Proof
2004	16,028	8.00	—

KM# 628 25 CENTS
4.4000 g., Nickel Plated Steel, 23.9 mm. **Ruler:** Elizabeth II
Subject: First Settlement, Ile Ste Croix 1604-2004 **Obv:** Bare
head right **Rev:** Sailing ship Bonne-Renommee

Date	Mintage	MS-63	Proof
2004P	15,400,000	5.00	—

KM# 698 25 CENTS
4.4000 g., Nickel Plated Steel **Ruler:** Elizabeth II **Rev:** Santa,
colorized

Date	Mintage	MS-63	Proof
2004	62,777	5.00	—

KM# 699 25 CENTS
4.4000 g., Nickel Plated Steel, 23.9 mm. **Ruler:** Elizabeth II
Series: Canada Day **Rev:** Moose head, humorous

Date	Mintage	MS-63	Proof
2004	44,752	5.00	—

KM# 529 25 CENTS
4.4000 g., Nickel Plated Steel, 23.9 mm. **Ruler:** Elizabeth II
Subject: WWII, 60th Anniversary **Obv:** Head right **Rev:** Three
soldiers and flag

Date	Mintage	MS-63	Proof
1945-2005	3,500	20.00	—

KM# 530 25 CENTS
4.4000 g., Nickel Plated Steel, 23.9 mm. **Ruler:** Elizabeth II
Subject: Alberta **Obv:** Head right

Date	Mintage	MS-63	Proof
2005P	20,640,000	7.00	—

KM# 531 25 CENTS
4.4000 g., Nickel Plated Steel, 23.9 mm. **Ruler:** Elizabeth II
Subject: Canada Day **Obv:** Head right **Rev:** Beaver, colorized

Date	Mintage	MS-63	Proof
2005P	58,370	8.50	—

KM# 532 25 CENTS
4.4000 g., Nickel Plated Steel, 23.9 mm. **Ruler:** Elizabeth II
Subject: Saskatchewan **Obv:** Head right

Date	Mintage	MS-63	Proof
2005P	19,290,000	7.00	—

KM# 533 25 CENTS
4.4000 g., Nickel Plated Steel, 23.9 mm. **Ruler:** Elizabeth II
Obv: Head right **Rev:** Stuffed bear in Christmas stocking,
colorized

Date	Mintage	MS-63	Proof
2005P	72,831	10.00	—

KM# 535 25 CENTS
4.4000 g., Nickel Plated Steel, 23.9 mm. **Ruler:** Elizabeth II
Subject: Year of the Veteran **Obv:** Head right **Rev:** Conjoined
busts of young and veteran left **Edge:** Reeded

Date	Mintage	MS-63	Proof
2005P	29,390,000	7.00	—

KM# 576 25 CENTS
4.4000 g., Nickel Plated Steel, 23.9 mm. **Ruler:** Elizabeth II
Subject: Quebec Winter Carnival **Obv:** Head right **Rev:**
Snowman, colorized

Date	Mintage	MS-63	Proof
2006	8,200	10.00	—

KM# 534 25 CENTS
4.4000 g., Nickel Plated Steel, 23.9 mm. **Ruler:** Elizabeth II
Subject: Toronto Maple Leafs **Obv:** Head right **Rev:** Colorized
team logo

Date	Mintage	MS-63	Proof
2006P	11,765	12.50	—

KM# 575 25 CENTS
4.4000 g., Nickel Plated Steel, 23.9 mm. **Ruler:** Elizabeth II
Subject: Montreal Canadiens **Obv:** Head right **Rev:** Colorized logo

Date	Mintage	MS-63	Proof
2006P	11,765	12.50	—

KM# 629 25 CENTS
4.4000 g., Nickel Plated Steel, 23.9 mm. **Ruler:** Elizabeth II
Obv: Head right **Rev:** Medal of Bravery **Edge:** Reeded

Date	Mintage	MS-63	Proof
2006(ml)	20,040,000	2.50	—

KM# 632 25 CENTS
12.6100 g., Nickel Plated Steel, 35 mm. **Ruler:** Elizabeth II
Subject: Queen Elizabeth II 80th Birthday **Rev:** Crown, colorized

Date	Mintage	MS-63	Proof
1926-2006 Specimen	24,977		25.00

KM# 633 25 CENTS
4.4300 g., Nickel Plated Steel, 23.9 mm. **Ruler:** Elizabeth II
Subject: Canada Day **Obv:** Crowned head right **Rev:** Boy
marching with flag, colorized

Date	Mintage	MS-63	Proof
2006P	30,328	6.00	—

KM# 634   25 CENTS
4.4300 g., Nickel Plated Steel **Ruler:** Elizabeth II **Subject:** Breast Cancer **Rev:** Four ribbons, all colorized **Note:** Sold housed in a bookmark.

Date	Mintage	MS-63	Proof
2006P	40,911	10.00	—

KM# 635   25 CENTS
4.4300 g., Nickel Plated Steel **Ruler:** Elizabeth II **Subject:** Breast Cancer **Rev:** Colorized pink ribbon applique in center.

Date	Mintage	MS-63	Proof
2006P	29,798,000	1.50	—

KM# 636   25 CENTS
4.4000 g., Nickel Plated Steel **Ruler:** Elizabeth II **Obv:** Head right **Obv. Designer:** Susana Blunt **Rev:** Medal of Bravery design (maple leaf within wreath)

Date	Mintage	MS-63	Proof
2006	20,045,111	7.00	—

KM# 637   25 CENTS
4.4300 g., Nickel Plated Steel **Ruler:** Elizabeth II **Subject:** Wedding **Rev:** Colorized bouquet of flowers

Date	Mintage	MS-63	Proof
2007(ml)	10,318	5.00	—

KM# 642   25 CENTS
4.4300 g., Nickel Plated Steel **Ruler:** Elizabeth II **Subject:** Ottawa Senators **Obv:** Head right **Rev:** Logo

Date	Mintage	MS-63	Proof
2006P	11,765	12.50	—

KM# 644   25 CENTS
4.4300 g., Nickel Plated Steel **Ruler:** Elizabeth II **Subject:** Calgary Flames **Obv:** Head right **Rev:** Logo

Date	Mintage	MS-63	Proof
2007(ml)	1,082	12.50	—

KM# 645   25 CENTS
4.4300 g., Nickel Plated Steel **Ruler:** Elizabeth II **Subject:** Edmonton Oilers **Obv:** Head right **Rev:** Logo

Date	Mintage	MS-63	Proof
2007(ml)	2,214	12.50	—

KM# 647   25 CENTS
4.4300 g., Nickel Plated Steel **Ruler:** Elizabeth II **Subject:** Santa and Rudolph **Rev:** Colorized Santa in sled lead by Rudolph

Date	Mintage	MS-63	Proof
2006P	99,258	5.00	—

KM# 682   25 CENTS
4.4300 g., Nickel Plated Steel **Ruler:** Elizabeth II **Subject:** Curling **Obv:** Head right

Date	Mintage	MS-63	Proof
2007	22,400,000	7.50	—
2008 Mule	—	—	—

KM# 683   25 CENTS
4.4300 g., Nickel Plated Steel **Ruler:** Elizabeth II **Subject:** Ice Hockey **Obv:** Head right

Date	Mintage	MS-63	Proof
2007	22,400,000	7.50	—
2008 Mule	—	—	—

KM# 684   25 CENTS
4.4300 g., Nickel Plated Steel, 23.8 mm. **Ruler:** Elizabeth II **Subject:** Paraolympic Winter Games **Obv:** Head right **Rev:** Wheelchair curling

Date	Mintage	MS-63	Proof
2007	22,400,000	7.50	—
2008 Mule	—	—	—

KM# 685   25 CENTS
4.4300 g., Nickel Plated Steel **Ruler:** Elizabeth II **Subject:** Biathlon **Obv:** Head right

Date	Mintage	MS-63	Proof
2007	22,400,000	7.50	—
2008 Mule	—	—	—

KM# 638   25 CENTS
4.4300 g., Nickel Plated Steel **Ruler:** Elizabeth II **Subject:** Birthday **Rev:** Colorized baloons

Date	Mintage	MS-63	Proof
2007(ml)	24,531	5.00	—

KM# 639   25 CENTS
4.4300 g., Nickel Plated Steel **Ruler:** Elizabeth II **Subject:** Baby birth **Rev:** Colorized baby rattle **Edge:** Reeded

Date	Mintage	MS-63	Proof
2007(ml)	30,090	5.00	—

KM# 640   25 CENTS
4.4300 g., Nickel Plated Steel **Ruler:** Elizabeth II **Subject:** Oh Canada **Obv:** Head right **Rev:** Maple leaf, colorized

Date	Mintage	MS-63	Proof
2006(ml)	23,582	8.50	—

KM# 641   25 CENTS
4.4300 g., Nickel Plated Steel **Ruler:** Elizabeth II **Subject:** Congratulations **Obv:** Head right **Rev:** Fireworks, colorized

Date	Mintage	MS-63	Proof
2006(ml)	9,671	8.00	—

KM# 643   25 CENTS
4.4300 g., Nickel Plated Steel **Ruler:** Elizabeth II **Subject:** Vancouver Canucks **Obv:** Head right **Rev:** Logo

Date	Mintage	MS-63	Proof
2007(ml)	1,526	12.50	—

KM# 686   25 CENTS
4.4300 g., Nickel Plated Steel, 23.8 mm. **Ruler:** Elizabeth II **Subject:** Alpine Skiing **Obv:** Head right

Date	Mintage	MS-63	Proof
2007	22,400,000	7.50	—
2008 Mule	—	—	—

KM# 701   25 CENTS
4.4300 g., Nickel Plated Steel **Ruler:** Elizabeth II **Subject:** Birthday **Rev:** Party hat, multicolor

Date	Mintage	MS-63	Proof
2007	11,376	8.00	—

KM# 702   25 CENTS
4.4300 g., Nickel Plated Steel **Ruler:** Elizabeth II **Subject:** Congratulations **Rev:** Trophy, multicolor

Date	Mintage	MS-63	Proof
2007	—	8.00	—

KM# 703   25 CENTS
4.4300 g., Nickel Plated Steel **Ruler:** Elizabeth II **Subject:** Wedding **Rev:** Cake, multicolor

Date	Mintage	MS-63	Proof
2007	—	8.00	—

KM# 704   25 CENTS
4.4300 g., Nickel Plated Steel **Ruler:** Elizabeth II **Subject:** Canada Day **Rev:** Mountie, colorized

Date	Mintage	MS-63	Proof
2007(ml)	27,743	8.00	—

KM# 705   25 CENTS
4.4300 g., Nickel Plated Steel **Ruler:** Elizabeth II **Subject:** Christmas **Rev:** Multicolor tree

Date	Mintage	MS-63	Proof
2007	66,267	8.00	—

KM# 706   25 CENTS
12.6100 g., Nickel Plated Steel, 35.0 mm. **Ruler:** Elizabeth II **Subject:** Red-breasted Nuthatch **Obv:** Head right **Obv. Legend:** ELIZABETH II - D • G • REGINA **Obv. Designer:** Susanna Blunt **Rev:** Nuthatch perched on pine branch multicolor **Rev. Legend:** CANADA **Rev. Designer:** Arnold Nogy **Edge:** Plain

Date	Mintage	MS-63	Proof
2007(ml) Specimen	11,909	25.00	—

KM# 707   25 CENTS
12.6100 g., Nickel Plated Steel, 35 mm. **Ruler:** Elizabeth II **Obv:** Elizabeth II **Rev:** Multicolor ruby-throated hummingbird and flower **Edge:** Plain

Date	Mintage	MS-63	Proof
2007 Specimen	17,174	—	25.00

KM# 708   25 CENTS
12.6100 g., Nickel Plated Steel, 35 mm. **Ruler:** Elizabeth II **Subject:** Queen's 60th Wedding Anniversary **Rev:** Royal carriage in color

Date	Mintage	MS-63	Proof
1947-2007 Specimen	15,235	—	24.00

KM# 713 25 CENTS
4.4000 g., Nickel Plated Steel **Ruler:** Elizabeth II **Rev:** Toronto Maple Leaf logo, colorized

Date	Mintage	MS-63	Proof
2007(ml)	5,365	5.00	—

KM# 714 25 CENTS
4.4000 g., Nickel Plated Steel **Ruler:** Elizabeth II **Rev:** Ottawa Senators logo, colorized

Date	Mintage	MS-63	Proof
2007(ml)	2,474	5.00	—

KM# 723 25 CENTS
4.4000 g., Nickel Plated Steel **Ruler:** Elizabeth II **Rev:** Montreal Canadiens logo, colorized

Date	Mintage	MS-63	Proof
2007(ml)	4,091	5.00	—

KM# 1039 25 CENTS
4.4300 g., Nickel Plated Steel, 23.9 mm. **Ruler:** Elizabeth II **Subject:** Canada Day **Rev:** Colorized moose head

Date	Mintage	MS-63	Proof
2008	11,538	12.50	—

KM# 760 25 CENTS
4.4300 g., Nickel Plated Steel **Ruler:** Elizabeth II **Subject:** Baby **Rev:** Multicolor blue teddy bear

Date	Mintage	MS-63	Proof
2008	29,639	8.00	—

KM# 761 25 CENTS
4.4300 g., Nickel Plated Steel **Ruler:** Elizabeth II **Subject:** Birthday **Rev:** Multicolor party hat

Date	Mintage	MS-63	Proof
2008	11,376	8.00	—

KM# 762 25 CENTS
4.4300 g., Nickel Plated Steel **Ruler:** Elizabeth II **Subject:** Congratulations **Rev:** Multicolor trophy

Date	Mintage	MS-63	Proof
2008	6,821	8.00	—

KM# 763 25 CENTS
4.4300 g., Nickel Plated Steel **Ruler:** Elizabeth II **Subject:** Wedding **Rev:** Multicolor wedding cake

Date	Mintage	MS-63	Proof
2008	7,407	8.00	—

KM# 764 25 CENTS
4.4300 g., Nickel Plated Steel **Ruler:** Elizabeth II **Subject:** Santa Claus **Rev:** Multicolor Santa

Date	Mintage	MS-63	Proof
2008	42,344	8.00	—

KM# 765 25 CENTS
4.4300 g., Nickel Plated Steel, 23.9 mm. **Ruler:** Elizabeth II **Subject:** Vancouver Olympics **Rev:** Freestyle skiing

Date	Mintage	MS-63	Proof
2008	—	2.00	—

KM# 766 25 CENTS
4.4300 g., Nickel Plated Steel, 23.8 mm. **Ruler:** Elizabeth II **Subject:** Vancouver Olympics **Rev:** Figure skating

Date	Mintage	MS-63	Proof
2008	—	2.00	—

KM# 768 25 CENTS
4.4300 g., Nickel Plated Steel, 23.9 mm. **Ruler:** Elizabeth II **Subject:** Vancouver Olympics **Rev:** Snow boarding

Date	Mintage	MS-63	Proof
2008	—	2.00	—

KM# 769 25 CENTS
4.4300 g., Nickel Plated Steel **Ruler:** Elizabeth II **Subject:** Vancouver Olympics **Rev:** Olympic mascott - Miga

Date	Mintage	MS-63	Proof
2008	—	3.00	—

KM# 770 25 CENTS
4.4300 g., Nickel Plated Steel **Ruler:** Elizabeth II **Subject:** Vancouver Olympics **Rev:** Olympic mascott - Quatchi

Date	Mintage	MS-63	Proof
2008	—	3.00	—

KM# 771 25 CENTS
4.4300 g., Nickel Plated Steel **Ruler:** Elizabeth II **Subject:** Vancouver Olympics **Rev:** Olympic mascott - Sumi

Date	Mintage	MS-63	Proof
2008	—	3.00	—

KM# 772 25 CENTS
4.4300 g., Nickel Plated Steel **Ruler:** Elizabeth II **Subject:** Oh Canada **Rev:** Multicolor red flag

Date	Mintage	MS-63	Proof
2008	—	8.00	—

KM# 773 25 CENTS
12.6100 g., Nickel Plated Steel, 35 mm. **Ruler:** Elizabeth II **Obv:** Bust right **Obv. Designer:** Susanna Blunt **Rev:** Downy woodpecker in tree, multicolor **Rev. Designer:** Arnold Nogy **Edge:** Plain **Note:** Prev. KM#717.

Date	Mintage	MS-63	Proof
2008(ml)	14,282	24.00	—

KM# 774 25 CENTS
12.6100 g., Nickel Plated Steel, 35 mm. **Ruler:** Elizabeth II **Obv:** Bust right **Obv. Designer:** Susanna Blunt **Rev:** Northern cardinal perched on branch - multicolor **Rev. Designer:** Arnold Nogy **Edge:** Plain **Note:** Prev. KM#718.

Date	Mintage	MS-63	Proof
2008(ml)	11,604	25.00	—

KM# 775 25 CENTS
4.4300 g., Nickel Plated Steel, 23.8 mm. **Ruler:** Elizabeth II **Subject:** End of WWI, 90th Anniversary **Rev:** Multicolor poppy

Date	Mintage	MS-63	Proof
1918-2008	10,167	8.00	—

KM# 776 25 CENTS
12.6100 g., Nickel Plated Steel, 35 mm. **Ruler:** Elizabeth II **Subject:** Anne of Green Gables **Rev:** Image of young girl, multicolor **Rev. Designer:** Ben Stahl

Date	Mintage	MS-63	Proof
1908-2008	32,795	20.00	—

KM# 841 25 CENTS
4.4300 g., Nickel Plated Steel **Ruler:** Elizabeth II **Subject:** Vancouver Olympics **Rev:** Bobsleigh **Shape:** 23.8

Date	Mintage	MS-63	Proof
2008	—	3.00	—

KM# 1041 25 CENTS
4.4300 g., Nickel Plated Steel **Ruler:** Elizabeth II **Subject:** WWI **Rev:** Three military men standing over tomb

Date	Mintage	MS-63	Proof
2008(ml)	10,167	12.50	—

KM# 840 25 CENTS
4.4300 g., Nickel Plated Steel, 23.8 mm. **Ruler:** Elizabeth II **Subject:** Valcouver 2010 Olympics **Rev:** Cross-country skiing

Date	Mintage	MS-63	Proof
2009	—	3.00	—

KM# 842   25 CENTS
4.4300 g., Nickel Plated Steel, 23.9 mm.   **Ruler:** Elizabeth II
Subject: Edmonton Olympics **Rev:** Speed skating

Date	Mintage	MS-63	Proof
2009		3.00	—

KM# 885   25 CENTS
4.4000 g., Nickel Plated Steel, 35 mm.   **Ruler:** Elizabeth II
Subject: Canada Day **Rev:** Animals in boat with flag **Rev. Legend:** Canada 25 cents

Date	Mintage	MS-63	Proof
2009	11,091	5.00	—

KM# 886   25 CENTS
12.6100 g., Nickel Plated Steel, 35 mm.   **Ruler:** Elizabeth II
Subject: Notre-Dame-Du-Saguenay **Obv:** Bust right **Obv. Legend:** Elizabeth II DG Regina **Obv. Designer:** Susanna Blunt **Rev:** Color photo of fjord and statue **Rev. Legend:** Canada 25 cents

Date	Mintage	MS-63	Proof
2009 Specimen	16,653	—	25.00

KM# 915   25 CENTS
4.4300 g., Nickel Plated Steel, 23.9 mm.   **Ruler:** Elizabeth II
Subject: Surprise Birthday **Obv:** Bust right **Obv. Designer:** Susanna Blunt **Rev:** Colorized

Date	Mintage	MS-63	Proof
2009	9,663	12.50	—

KM# 916   25 CENTS
4.4300 g., Nickel Plated Steel, 23.9 mm.   **Ruler:** Elizabeth II
Subject: Share the Excitement **Obv:** Bust right **Obv. Designer:** Susanna Blunt **Rev:** Colorized

Date	Mintage	MS-63	Proof
2009	4,126	12.50	—

KM# 917   25 CENTS
4.4300 g., Nickel Plated Steel, 23.9 mm.   **Ruler:** Elizabeth II
Subject: Share the Love **Obv:** Bust right **Obv. Designer:** Susanna Blunt **Rev:** Two doves, coolored

Date	Mintage	MS-63	Proof
2009	7,571	12.50	—

KM# 918   25 CENTS
4.4300 g., Nickel Plated Steel, 23.9 mm.   **Ruler:** Elizabeth II
Subject: Thank You **Obv:** Bust right **Obv. Designer:** Susanna Blunt **Rev:** Colorized

Date	Mintage	MS-63	Proof
2009	4,415	12.50	—

KM# 933   25 CENTS
4.4000 g., Nickel Plated Steel, 23.9 mm.   **Ruler:** Elizabeth II **Rev:** Santa Claus, multicolor

Date	Mintage	MS-63	Proof
2009	933	16.50	—

KM# 934   25 CENTS
4.4000 g., Nickel Plated Steel, 23.9 mm.   **Ruler:** Elizabeth II **Rev:** Multicolor teddy bear, crescent moon

Date	Mintage	MS-63	Proof
2009	25,182	16.50	—

KM# 935   25 CENTS
4.4000 g., Nickel Plated Steel, 23.9 mm.   **Ruler:** Elizabeth II
Subject: Oh Canada **Rev:** Maple leaves, yellow color

Date	Mintage	MS-63	Proof
2009	14,451	16.50	—

KM# 952   25 CENTS
4.4000 g., Nickel Plated Steel, 23.9 mm.   **Ruler:** Elizabeth II **Rev:** Sledge hockey

Date	Mintage	MS-63	Proof
2009		3.00	—

KM# 1063   25 CENTS
Nickel Plated Steel   **Ruler:** Elizabeth II **Subject:** Men's Hockey **Rev:** Hockey player and maple leaf outline

Date	Mintage	MS-63	Proof
2009	—	2.50	—

KM# 1063a   25 CENTS
Nickel Plated Steel   **Ruler:** Elizabeth II **Subject:** Men's Hockey **Rev:** Hockey player and maple leaf outline in red

Date	Mintage	MS-63	Proof
2009	—	7.50	—

KM# 1064   25 CENTS
Nickel Plated Steel   **Ruler:** Elizabeth II **Subject:** Women's Hockey **Rev:** Hockey player and maple leaf outline

Date	Mintage	MS-63	Proof
2009	—	2.50	—

KM# 1064a   25 CENTS
Nickel Plated Steel   **Ruler:** Elizabeth II **Subject:** Women's Hockey **Rev:** Hockey player and male leaf outline in red

Date	Mintage	MS-63	Proof
2009	—	7.50	—

KM# 1065   25 CENTS
Nickel Plated Steel   **Ruler:** Elizabeth II **Subject:** Klassen - Female hockey player **Rev:** Skater and maple leaf outline

Date	Mintage	MS-63	Proof
2009	—	2.50	—

KM# 1065a   25 CENTS
Nickel Plated Steel   **Ruler:** Elizabeth II **Subject:** Klassen - female skater **Rev:** Skater and maple leaf outline in red

Date	Mintage	MS-63	Proof
2009	—	7.50	—

KM# 880   25 CENTS
4.4000 g., Nickel Plated Steel, 23.88 mm.   **Ruler:** Elizabeth II
Subject: Miga Mascot Vancouver Olympics **Rev:** Mica Mascot - color **Rev. Legend:** Vancouver 2010 25 cents

Date	Mintage	MS-63	Proof
2010	14,654	3.00	—

KM# 881   25 CENTS
4.4000 g., Nickel Plated Steel, 23.88 mm.   **Ruler:** Elizabeth II
Subject: Quatchi Mascot - Vancouver Olympics **Obv:** Bust right **Rev:** Quatchi Mascot color **Rev. Legend:** Vancouver 2010 25 cents

Date	Mintage	MS-63	Proof
2010	15,310	3.00	—

KM# 882   25 CENTS
4.4000 g., Nickel Plated Steel, 23.88 mm.   **Ruler:** Elizabeth II
Subject: Sumi Mascot **Rev:** Sumi Mascot color **Rev. Legend:** Vancouver 2010 25 cents

Date	Mintage	MS-63	Proof
2010	15,333	3.00	—

KM# 953   25 CENTS
4.4000 g., Nickel Plated Steel, 23.9 mm.   **Ruler:** Elizabeth II **Rev:** Ice hockey

Date	Mintage	MS-63	Proof
2010	—	3.00	—

KM# 953a   25 CENTS
4.4000 g., Nickel Plated Steel, 23.9 mm.   **Ruler:** Elizabeth II **Rev:** Ice Hockey - red enamel

Date	Mintage	MS-63	Proof
2010	—	8.00	—

KM# 954   25 CENTS
4.4000 g., Nickel Plated Steel, 23.9 mm.   **Ruler:** Elizabeth II **Rev:** Curling

Date	Mintage	MS-63	Proof
2010	—	3.00	—

KM# 954a   25 CENTS
4.4000 g., Nickel Plated Steel, 23.9 mm.   **Ruler:** Elizabeth II **Rev:** Curling red enamel

Date	Mintage	MS-63	Proof
2010	—	8.00	—

KM# 955   25 CENTS
4.4000 g., Nickel Plated Steel, 23.9 mm.   **Ruler:** Elizabeth II **Rev:** Wheelchair curling

Date	Mintage	MS-63	Proof
2010	—	3.00	—

KM# 955a   25 CENTS
4.4000 g., Nickel Plated Steel, 23.9 mm.   **Ruler:** Elizabeth II **Rev:** Wheelchair curling - red enamel

Date	Mintage	MS-63	Proof
2010	—	8.00	—

KM# 956   25 CENTS
4.4000 g., Nickel Plated Steel, 23.9 mm.   **Ruler:** Elizabeth II **Rev:** Biathlon

Date	Mintage	MS-63	Proof
2010	—	3.00	—

KM# 956a   25 CENTS
4.4000 g., Nickel Plated Steel, 23.9 mm.   **Ruler:** Elizabeth II **Rev:** Biathlon - red enamel

Date	Mintage	MS-63	Proof
2010	—	8.00	—

KM# 957   25 CENTS
4.4000 g., Nickel Plated Steel, 23.9 mm.   **Ruler:** Elizabeth II **Rev:** Alpine skiing

Date	Mintage	MS-63	Proof
2010	—	3.00	—

KM# 957a   25 CENTS
4.4000 g., Nickel Plated Steel, 23.9 mm.   **Ruler:** Elizabeth II **Rev:** Alpine skiing - red enamel

Date	Mintage	MS-63	Proof
2010	—	8.00	—

KM# 958   25 CENTS
4.4000 g., Nickel Plated Steel, 23.9 mm.   **Ruler:** Elizabeth II **Rev:** Snowboarding

Date	Mintage	MS-63	Proof
2010	—	3.00	—

KM# 958a   25 CENTS
4.4000 g., Nickel Plated Steel, 23.9 mm.   **Ruler:** Elizabeth II **Rev:** Snowboarding - red enamel

Date	Mintage	MS-63	Proof
2010	—	8.00	—

KM# 959   25 CENTS
23.9000 g., Nickel Plated Steel, 23.9 mm.   **Ruler:** Elizabeth II
Rev: Free-style skiing

Date	Mintage	MS-63	Proof
2010	—	3.00	—

KM# 959a 25 CENTS
4.4000 g., Nickel Plated Steel, 23.9 mm. **Ruler:** Elizabeth II **Rev:** Free-style skiing - red enamel

Date	Mintage	MS-63	Proof
2010	—	8.00	—

KM# 960 25 CENTS
4.4000 g., Nickel Plated Steel, 23.9 mm. **Ruler:** Elizabeth II **Rev:** Alpine skiing

Date	Mintage	MS-63	Proof
2010	—	3.00	—

KM# 960a 25 CENTS
4.4000 g., Nickel Plated Steel, 23.9 mm. **Ruler:** Elizabeth II **Rev:** Alpine skiing - red enamel

Date	Mintage	MS-63	Proof
2010	—	8.00	—

KM# 988 25 CENTS
4.4000 g., Multi-Ply Plated Steel, 23.88 mm. **Ruler:** Elizabeth II **Rev:** Blue baby carriage

Date	Mintage	MS-63	Proof
2010	—	10.00	—

KM# 989 25 CENTS
4.4000 g., Nickel Plated Steel, 23.9 mm. **Ruler:** Elizabeth II **Rev:** Purple gift box

Date	Mintage	MS-63	Proof
2010	—	10.00	—

KM# 990 25 CENTS
4.4000 g., Nickel Plated Steel, 23.9 mm. **Ruler:** Elizabeth II **Rev:** Four stars

Date	Mintage	MS-63	Proof
2010	—	10.00	—

KM# 991 25 CENTS
4.4000 g., Nickel Plated Steel, 23.9 mm. **Ruler:** Elizabeth II **Rev:** Three maple leaves

Date	Mintage	MS-63	Proof
2010	—	12.50	—

KM# 992 25 CENTS
4.4000 g., Nickel Plated Steel, 23.9 mm. **Ruler:** Elizabeth II **Rev:** Three zinnias

Date	Mintage	MS-63	Proof
2010	—	12.50	—

KM# 993 25 CENTS
23.9000 g., Nickel Plated Steel, 23.9 mm. **Ruler:** Elizabeth II **Rev:** Pink hearts and roses

Date	Mintage	MS-63	Proof
2010	—	10.00	—

KM# 994 25 CENTS
12.6100 g., Nickel Plated Steel, 35 mm. **Ruler:** Elizabeth II **Rev:** Goldfinch, multicolor **Rev. Designer:** Arnold Nogy

Date	Mintage	MS-63	Proof
2010 Proof	Est. 14,000	—	25.00

KM# 1001 25 CENTS
12.6100 g., Nickel Plated Steel, 35 mm. **Ruler:** Elizabeth II **Subject:** Blue Jay **Rev:** Multicolor blue jay on yellow maple leaves

Date	Mintage	MS-63	Proof
2010	Est. 14,000		25.00

KM# 1006 25 CENTS
0.5000 g., 0.9990 Gold 0.0161 oz. AGW, 11 mm. **Ruler:** Elizabeth II **Rev:** Caribou head left

Date	Mintage	MS-63	Proof
2010 Proof	15,000		80.00

KM# 1021 25 CENTS
Nickel Plated Steel, 23.9 mm. **Ruler:** Elizabeth II **Rev:** Santa Claus in color

Date	Mintage	MS-63	Proof
2010	—	15.00	—

KM# 1026 25 CENTS
Silver, 23.8 mm. **Ruler:** Elizabeth II **Obv:** George V bust left **Rev:** Value within wreath, dual dates below

Date	Mintage	MS-63	Proof
1935-2010 Proof	—	—	25.00

KM# 1028 25 CENTS
4.4000 g., Nickel Plated Steel, 23.9 mm. **Ruler:** Elizabeth II **Rev:** Soldier standing, two red poppies, large maple leaf behind

Date	Mintage	MS-63	Proof
2010	—	15.00	—

KM# 1110 25 CENTS
12.6100 g., Nickel Plated Steel, 35 mm. **Ruler:** Elizabeth II **Subject:** Royal Wedding **Rev:** Colored portraits left of William and Katherine

Date	Mintage	MS-63	Proof
2011 Proof	—		25.00

KM# 1156 25 CENTS
Silver, 23.8 mm. **Ruler:** Elizabeth II

Date	Mintage	MS-63	Proof
1911-2011			25.00

KM# 1079 25 CENTS
12.6100 g., Nickel Plated Steel, 35 mm. **Ruler:** Elizabeth II **Rev:** Barn Swallow in color **Rev. Designer:** Arnold Nagy

Date	Mintage	MS-63	Proof
2011	Est. 14,000	—	25.00

KM# 1080 25 CENTS
4.4300 g., Nickel Plated Steel, 23.88 mm. **Ruler:** Elizabeth II **Subject:** Oh Canada! **Rev:** Maple leaf and circular legend

Date	Mintage	MS-63	Proof
2011	—	2.50	—

KM# 1081 25 CENTS
4.4300 g., Nickel Plated Steel, 23.88 mm. **Ruler:** Elizabeth II **Subject:** Wedding **Rev:** Two rings

Date	Mintage	MS-63	Proof
2011	—	2.50	—

KM# 1082 25 CENTS
4.4300 g., Nickel Plated Steel, 23.88 mm. **Ruler:** Elizabeth II **Subject:** Birthday **Rev:** Year in four baloons

Date	Mintage	MS-63	Proof
2011	—	2.50	—

KM# 1083 25 CENTS
4.4300 g., Nickel Plated Steel, 23.88 mm. **Ruler:** Elizabeth II **Subject:** New Baby! **Rev:** Baby's feet

Date	Mintage	MS-63	Proof
2011	—	2.50	—

KM# 1084 25 CENTS
4.4300 g., Nickel Plated Steel, 23.88 mm. **Ruler:** Elizabeth II **Rev:** Tooth Fairy

Date	Mintage	MS-63	Proof
2011	—	2.50	—

KM# 1113 25 CENTS
12.6100 g., Nickel Plated Steel, 35 mm. **Ruler:** Elizabeth II **Rev:** Fantasy Furry Woods creature in color

Date	Mintage	MS-63	Proof
2011	—	20.00	—

KM# 1114   25 CENTS
12.6100 g., Nickel Plated Steel, 35 mm. **Ruler:** Elizabeth II **Rev:** Fantasy sea serpent in color

Date	Mintage	MS-63	Proof
2011	—	20.00	—

KM# 1115   25 CENTS
12.6100 g., Nickel Plated Steel, 35 mm. **Ruler:** Elizabeth II **Rev:** Tulip and ladybug in color

Date	Mintage	MS-63	Proof
2011	—	25.00	—

KM# 1116   25 CENTS
12.6100 g., Nickel Plated Steel, 35 mm. **Ruler:** Elizabeth II **Rev:** Black capped chickadee in color

Date	Mintage	MS-63	Proof
2011 Proof	—	—	25.00

KM# 1148   25 CENTS
4.4300 g., Nickel Plated Steel, 23.9 mm. **Ruler:** Elizabeth II **Obv:** Bust right **Rev:** Snowflake

Date	Mintage	MS-63	Proof
2011	—	7.50	—

KM# 1168   25 CENTS
4.4000 g., Nickel Plated Steel, 23.9 mm. **Ruler:** Elizabeth II **Obv:** Bust right **Rev:** Stylized bison

Date	Mintage	MS-63	Proof
2011	—	2.50	—

KM# 1168a   25 CENTS
4.4000 g., Nickel Plated Steel with color, 23.9 mm. **Ruler:** Elizabeth II **Obv:** Bust right **Rev:** Stylized bison, green circle in background

Date	Mintage	MS-63	Proof
2011	—	9.50	—

KM# 1169   25 CENTS
4.4000 g., Nickel Plated Steel, 23.9 mm. **Ruler:** Elizabeth II **Obv:** Bust right **Rev:** Stylized falcon

Date	Mintage	MS-63	Proof
2011	—	2.50	—

KM# 1169a   25 CENTS
4.4000 g., Nickel Plated Steel with color, 23.9 mm. **Ruler:** Elizabeth II **Obv:** Bust right **Rev:** Stylized falcon with yellow circle in background

Date	Mintage	MS-63	Proof
2011	—	9.50	—

KM# 1170   25 CENTS
4.4000 g., Nickel Plated Steel, 23.9 mm. **Ruler:** Elizabeth II **Obv:** Bust right **Rev:** Stylized orca whale

Date	Mintage	MS-63	Proof
2011	—	2.50	—

KM# 1170a   25 CENTS
4.4000 g., Nickel Plated Steel with color, 23.9 mm. **Ruler:** Elizabeth II **Obv:** Bust right **Rev:** Stylized orca whale with blue circle in background

Date	Mintage	MS-63	Proof
2011	—	9.50	—

KM# 1171   25 CENTS
0.5000 g., 0.9990 Gold 0.0161 oz. AGW, 11 mm. **Ruler:** Elizabeth II **Obv:** Bust right **Rev:** Cougar head left

Date	Mintage	MS-63	Proof
2011 Proof	—	—	80.00

KM# 1172   25 CENTS
12.6100 g., Copper Plated Silver gold plated, 35 mm. **Ruler:** Elizabeth II **Obv:** Bust right **Rev:** Wayne Greskey in hockey helmet left

Date	Mintage	MS-63	Proof
2011 Proof	—	—	35.00

KM# 1192   25 CENTS
4.4300 g., Nickel Plated Steel, 23.9 mm. **Ruler:** Elizabeth II **Subject:** Canadian Broadcasting Company, 75th Anniversary **Obv:** Bust right **Rev:** Old-time radio microphone

Date	Mintage	MS-63	Proof
2011	—	2.50	—

KM# 1193   25 CENTS
12.6100 g., Nickel Plated Steel, 35 mm. **Ruler:** Elizabeth II **Subject:** Mythical Creature - Mishepishu **Obv:** Bust right **Rev:** Horned lizard in color

Date	Mintage	MS-63	Proof
2011	—	15.00	—

KM# 1227   25 CENTS
4.4300 g., Nickel Plated Steel, 23.9 mm. **Ruler:** Elizabeth II **Obv:** Bust right **Rev:** Tooth Fairy in flight

Date	Mintage	MS-63	Proof
2012	—	2.50	—

KM# 1228   25 CENTS
4.4300 g., Nickel Plated Steel, 23.9 mm. **Ruler:** Elizabeth II **Subject:** Baby **Rev:** Baby's mobile

Date	Mintage	MS-63	Proof
2012	—	2.50	—

KM# 1229   25 CENTS
4.4300 g., Nickel Plated Steel, 23.9 mm. **Ruler:** Elizabeth II **Subject:** Wedding **Rev:** Two wedding rings with small feet

Date	Mintage	MS-63	Proof
2012	—	2.50	—

KM# 1230   25 CENTS
4.4300 g., Nickel Plated Steel, 23.9 mm. **Ruler:** Elizabeth II **Subject:** Birthday **Rev:** Cone with character face

Date	Mintage	MS-63	Proof
2012	—	2.50	—

KM# 1231   25 CENTS
4.4300 g., Nickel Plated Steel, 23.9 mm. **Ruler:** Elizabeth II **Subject:** Oh, Canada ! **Rev:** Maple leaves with character faces

Date	Mintage	MS-63	Proof
2012	—	2.50	—

KM# 1232   25 CENTS
4.4300 g., Nickel Plated Steel, 23.88 mm. **Ruler:** Elizabeth II **Subject:** Winnipeg Jets **Rev:** Jet superimposed on Maple leaf

Date	Mintage	MS-63	Proof
2012	—	2.50	—

KM# 1233   25 CENTS
12.6100 g., Nickel Plated Steel, 35 mm. **Ruler:** Elizabeth II **Subject:** Titanic, 100th Anniversary **Obv:** Bust right **Rev:** Two views of Titanic, one at dockside, one nighttime at sea

Date	Mintage	MS-63	Proof
2012	—	20.00	—

KM# 290   50 CENTS
8.1000 g., Nickel, 27.1 mm. **Ruler:** Elizabeth II **Obv:** Crowned head right **Obv. Designer:** Dora dePedery-Hunt **Rev:** Redesigned arms **Rev. Designer:** Cathy Bursey-Sabourin **Edge:** Reeded

Date	Mintage	MS-63	Proof
2001P	—	1.50	—
2001P Proof	—	—	5.00
2003P	—	1.50	—
2003P Proof	—	—	5.00

KM# 290b   50 CENTS
6.9000 g., Nickel Plated Steel, 27.13 mm. **Ruler:** Elizabeth II **Obv:** Crowned head right **Obv. Designer:** Dora dePedery-Hunt **Rev:** Redesigned arms **Rev. Designer:** Cathy Bursey-Sabourin **Edge:** Reeded

Date	Mintage	MS-63	Proof
2001 P	389,000	1.50	—
2003 P	—	5.00	—

KM# 290a   50 CENTS
11.6640 g., 0.9250 Silver 0.3469 oz. ASW, 27.13 mm. **Ruler:** Elizabeth II **Obv:** Crowned head right **Obv. Designer:** Dora dePedery-Hunt **Rev:** Redesigned arms **Rev. Designer:** Cathy Bursey-Sabourin **Edge:** Reeded

Date	Mintage	MS-63	Proof
2001 Proof	—	—	12.00
2003 Proof	—	—	12.00

KM# 420 50 CENTS
9.3000 g., 0.9250 Silver 0.2766 oz. ASW, 27.13 mm. **Ruler:** Elizabeth II **Series:** Festivals - Quebec **Obv:** Crowned head right **Rev:** Snowman and Chateau Frontenac **Rev. Designer:** Sylvie Daigneault **Edge:** Reeded

Date	Mintage	MS-63	Proof
2001 Proof	58,123	—	8.50

KM# 421 50 CENTS
9.3000 g., 0.9250 Silver 0.2766 oz. ASW, 27.13 mm. **Ruler:** Elizabeth II **Series:** Festivals - Nunavut **Obv:** Crowned head right **Rev:** Dancer, dog sled and snowmobiles **Rev. Designer:** John Mardon **Edge:** Reeded

Date	Mintage	MS-63	Proof
2001 Proof	58,123	—	8.50

KM# 422 50 CENTS
9.3000 g., 0.9250 Silver 0.2766 oz. ASW, 27.13 mm. **Ruler:** Elizabeth II **Series:** Festivals - Newfoundland **Obv:** Crowned head right **Rev:** Sailor and musical people **Rev. Designer:** David Craig **Edge:** Reeded

Date	Mintage	MS-63	Proof
2001 Proof	58,123	—	8.50

KM# 423 50 CENTS
9.3000 g., 0.9250 Silver 0.2766 oz. ASW, 27.13 mm. **Ruler:** Elizabeth II **Series:** Festivals - Prince Edward Island **Obv:** Crowned head right **Rev:** Family, juggler and building **Rev. Designer:** Brenda Whiteway **Edge:** Reeded

Date	Mintage	MS-63	Proof
2001 Proof	58,123	—	8.50

KM# 424 50 CENTS
9.3000 g., 0.9250 Silver 0.2766 oz. ASW, 27.13 mm. **Ruler:** Elizabeth II **Series:** Folklore - The Sled **Obv:** Crowned head right **Rev:** Family scene **Rev. Designer:** Valentina Hotz-Entin **Edge:** Reeded

Date	Mintage	MS-63	Proof
2001 Proof	28,979	—	9.00

KM# 425 50 CENTS
9.3000 g., 0.9250 Silver 0.2766 oz. ASW, 27.13 mm. **Ruler:** Elizabeth II **Series:** Folklore - The Maiden's Cave **Obv:** Crowned head right **Rev:** Woman shouting **Rev. Designer:** Peter Kiss **Edge:** Reeded

Date	Mintage	MS-63	Proof
2001 Proof	28,979	—	9.00

KM# 426 50 CENTS
9.3000 g., 0.9250 Silver 0.2766 oz. ASW, 27.13 mm. **Ruler:** Elizabeth II **Series:** Folklore - The Small Jumpers **Obv:** Crowned head right **Rev:** Jumping children on seashore **Rev. Designer:** Miynki Tanobe **Edge:** Reeded

Date	Mintage	MS-63	Proof
2001 Proof	28,979	—	9.00

KM# 509 50 CENTS
6.9000 g., Nickel Plated Steel, 27.13 mm. **Ruler:** Elizabeth II **Obv:** Crowned head right **Rev:** National arms **Edge:** Reeded

Date	Mintage	MS-63	Proof
2001 P		1.50	

KM# 444 50 CENTS
6.9000 g., Nickel Plated Steel, 27.13 mm. **Ruler:** Elizabeth II **Subject:** Queen's Golden Jubilee **Obv:** Coronation crowned head right and monogram **Rev:** Canadian arms **Rev. Designer:** Bursey Sabourin **Edge:** Reeded

Date	Mintage	MS-63	Proof
1952-2002P	14,440,000	2.50	—

KM# 444a 50 CENTS
9.3000 g., 0.9250 Silver 0.2766 oz. ASW, 27.13 mm. **Ruler:** Elizabeth II **Subject:** Elizabeth II Golden Jubilee **Obv:** Crowned head right, Jubilee commemorative dates 1952-2002

Date	Mintage	MS-63	Proof
1952-2002 Proof	100,000	—	17.50

KM# 444b 50 CENTS
9.3000 g., 0.9250 Silver Gilt 0.2766 oz. ASW, 27.13 mm. **Ruler:** Elizabeth II **Subject:** Queen's Golden Jubilee **Obv:** Crowned head right and monogram **Rev:** Canadian arms **Edge:** Reeded **Note:** Special 24 karat gold-plated issue of KM#444.

Date	Mintage	MS-63	Proof
1952-2002 Proof	32,642	—	35.00

KM# 454 50 CENTS
9.3000 g., 0.9250 Silver 0.2766 oz. ASW, 27.13 mm. **Ruler:** Elizabeth II **Subject:** Nova Scotia Annapolis Valley Apple Blossom Festival **Obv:** Crowned head right **Rev. Designer:** Bonnie Ross

Date	Mintage	MS-63	Proof
2002 Proof	59,998	—	8.50

KM# 455 50 CENTS
9.3000 g., 0.9250 Silver 0.2766 oz. ASW, 27.13 mm. **Ruler:** Elizabeth II **Subject:** Stratford Festival **Obv:** Crowned head right **Rev:** Couple with building in background **Rev. Designer:** Laurie McGaw

Date	Mintage	MS-63	Proof
2002 Proof	59,998	—	8.50

KM# 456 50 CENTS
9.3000 g., 0.9250 Silver 0.2766 oz. ASW, 27.13 mm. **Ruler:** Elizabeth II **Subject:** Folklorama **Obv:** Crowned head right **Rev. Designer:** William Woodruff

Date	Mintage	MS-63	Proof
2002 Proof	59,998	—	8.50

KM# 457 50 CENTS
9.3000 g., 0.9250 Silver 0.2766 oz. ASW, 27.13 mm. **Ruler:** Elizabeth II **Subject:** Calgary Stampede **Obv:** Crowned head right **Rev. Designer:** Stan Witten

Date	Mintage	MS-63	Proof
2002 Proof	59,998	—	8.50

KM# 458 50 CENTS
9.3000 g., 0.9250 Silver 0.2766 oz. ASW, 27.13 mm. **Ruler:** Elizabeth II **Subject:** Squamish Days Logger Sports **Obv:** Crowned head right **Rev. Designer:** Jose Osio

Date	Mintage	MS-63	Proof
2002 Proof	59,998	—	8.50

KM# 459 50 CENTS
9.3000 g., 0.9250 Silver 0.2766 oz. ASW, 27.13 mm. **Ruler:** Elizabeth II **Series:** Folklore and Legends **Obv:** Crowned head right **Rev:** The Shoemaker in Heaven **Rev. Designer:** Francine Gravel

Date	Mintage	MS-63	Proof
2002 Proof	19,267	—	9.50

KM# 460 50 CENTS
9.3000 g., 0.9250 Silver 0.2766 oz. ASW, 27.13 mm. **Ruler:** Elizabeth II **Series:** Folklore and Legends **Subject:** The Ghost Ship **Obv:** Crowned head right **Rev. Designer:** Colette Boivin

Date	Mintage	MS-63	Proof
2002 Proof	19,267	—	9.50

KM# 461 50 CENTS
9.3000 g., 0.9250 Silver 0.2766 oz. ASW, 27.13 mm. **Ruler:** Elizabeth II **Series:** Folklore and Legends **Subject:** The Pig That Wouldn't Get Over the Stile **Obv:** Crowned head right **Rev. Designer:** Laura Jolicoeur

Date	Mintage	MS-63	Proof
2002 Proof	19,267	—	9.50

KM# 494 50 CENTS
6.9000 g., Nickel Plated Steel, 27.13 mm. **Ruler:** Elizabeth II **Obv:** Crowned head right **Obv. Designer:** Susanna Blunt **Rev:** National arms **Rev. Designer:** Cathy Bursey-Sabourin **Edge:** Reeded

Date	Mintage	MS-63	Proof
2003P W	—	5.00	—
2003P W Proof	—	—	7.50
2004P	—	5.00	—
2004P Proof	—	—	7.50
2005P	200,000	1.50	—
2005P Proof	—	—	5.00
2006P	98,000	1.50	—
2006P Proof	—	—	5.00
2007(ml)	250,000	1.50	—
2007(ml) Proof	—	—	5.00
2008(ml)	211,000	1.50	—
2008(ml) Proof	—	—	5.00
2009(ml)	150,000	1.50	—
2009(ml) Proof	—	—	5.00
2010(ml)	—	1.50	—
2010(ml) Proof	—	—	5.00
2011(ml)	—	1.50	—
2011(ml) Proof	—	—	5.00
2012(ml)	—	1.50	—
2012(ml) Proof	—	—	5.00

KM# 472 50 CENTS
11.6200 g., 0.9250 Silver 0.3456 oz. ASW, 27.13 mm. **Ruler:** Elizabeth II **Subject:** 50th Anniversary of the Coronation of Elizabeth II **Obv:** Crowned head right, Jubilee commemorative dates 1952-2002 **Obv. Designer:** Mary Gillick

Date	Mintage	MS-63	Proof
2003 Proof	30,000	—	15.00

KM# 475 50 CENTS
9.3000 g., 0.9250 Silver 0.2766 oz. ASW, 27.13 mm. **Ruler:** Elizabeth II **Obv:** Crowned head right **Obv. Designer:** Dora dePédery-Hunt **Rev:** Golden daffodil **Rev. Designer:** Christie Paquet, Stan Witten

Date	Mintage	MS-63	Proof
2003 Proof	36,293	—	25.00

KM# 476 50 CENTS
9.3000 g., 0.9250 Silver 0.2766 oz. ASW, 27.13 mm. **Ruler:** Elizabeth II **Subject:** Yukon International Storytelling Festival **Obv:** Crowned head right **Obv. Designer:** Dora dePédery-Hunt **Rev. Designer:** Ken Anderson, Jose Oslo

Date	Mintage	MS-63	Proof
2003 Proof	—	—	11.00

KM# 477 50 CENTS
9.3000 g., 0.9250 Silver 0.2766 oz. ASW, 27.13 mm. **Ruler:** Elizabeth II **Subject:** Festival Acadien de Caraquet **Obv:** Crowned head right **Obv. Designer:** Dora dePédery-Hunt **Rev:** Sailboat and couple **Rev. Designer:** Susan Taylor, Hudson Design Group

Date	Mintage	MS-63	Proof
2003 Proof	—	—	11.00

KM# 478 50 CENTS
9.3000 g., 0.9250 Silver 0.2766 oz. ASW, 27.13 mm. **Ruler:** Elizabeth II **Subject:** Back to Batoche **Obv:** Crowned head right **Obv. Designer:** Dora dePédery-Hunt **Rev. Designer:** David Hannan, Stan Witten

Date	Mintage	MS-63	Proof
2003 Proof	—	—	11.00

KM# 479   50 CENTS
9.3000 g., 0.9250 Silver 0.2766 oz. ASW, 27.13 mm. **Ruler:**
Elizabeth II **Subject:** Great Northern Arts Festival **Obv:** Crowned
head right **Obv. Designer:** Dora dePédery-Hunt **Rev. Designer:**
Dawn Oman, Susan Taylor

Date	Mintage	MS-63	Proof
2003 Proof	—	—	11.00

KM# 494a   50 CENTS
9.3000 g., 0.9250 Silver 0.2766 oz. ASW, 27.13 mm. **Ruler:**
Elizabeth II **Obv:** Crowned head right **Obv. Designer:** Susanna
Blunt **Rev:** Canadian coat of arms **Edge:** Reeded

Date	Mintage	MS-63	Proof
2004 Proof	—	—	7.50

KM# 526   50 CENTS
1.2700 g., 0.9999 Gold 0.0408 oz. AGW, 14 mm. **Ruler:**
Elizabeth II **Subject:** Moose **Obv:** Head right **Rev:** Moose head
facing right

Date	Mintage	MS-63	Proof
2004 Proof	—	—	85.00

KM# 606   50 CENTS
9.3000 g., 0.9250 Silver 0.2766 oz. ASW, 27.13 mm. **Ruler:**
Elizabeth II **Obv:** Head right **Obv. Designer:** Susanna Blunt **Rev:**
Clouded Sulphur Butterfly, hologram **Rev. Designer:** Susan
Taylor

Date	Mintage	MS-63	Proof
2004 Proof	15,281	—	30.00

KM# 712   50 CENTS
9.3000 g., 0.9250 Silver 0.2766 oz. ASW, 27.13 mm. **Ruler:**
Elizabeth II **Rev:** Hologram of Tiger Swallowtail butterfly

Date	Mintage	MS-63	Proof
2004 Proof	20,462	—	30.00

KM# 536   50 CENTS
9.3000 g., 0.9250 Silver with partial gold plating 0.2766 oz. ASW,
27.13 mm. **Ruler:** Elizabeth II **Subject:** Golden rose **Obv:** Head
right **Obv. Designer:** Susanna Blunt **Rev. Designer:** Christie
Paquet

Date	Mintage	MS-63	Proof
2005 Proof	17,418	—	19.00

KM# 537   50 CENTS
9.3000 g., 0.9250 Silver 0.2766 oz. ASW, 27.13 mm. **Ruler:**
Elizabeth II **Obv:** Head right **Obv. Designer:** Susanna Blunt **Rev:**
Great Spangled Fritillary butterfly, hologram **Rev. Designer:**
Jianping Yan

Date	Mintage	MS-63	Proof
2005 Proof	20,000	—	35.00

KM# 538   50 CENTS
9.3000 g., 0.9250 Silver 0.2766 oz. ASW, 27.13 mm. **Ruler:**
Elizabeth II **Subject:** Toronto Maple Leafs **Obv:** Head right **Obv.
Designer:** Susanna Blunt **Rev:** Darryl Sittler

Date	Mintage	MS-63	Proof
2005 Specimen	25,000	—	16.00

KM# 539   50 CENTS
9.3000 g., 0.9250 Silver 0.2766 oz. ASW, 27.13 mm. **Ruler:**
Elizabeth II **Subject:** Toronto Maple Leafs **Obv:** Head right **Obv.
Designer:** Susanna Blunt **Rev:** Dave Keon

Date	Mintage	MS-63	Proof
2005 Specimen	25,000	—	16.00

KM# 540   50 CENTS
9.3000 g., 0.9250 Silver 0.2766 oz. ASW, 27.13 mm. **Ruler:**
Elizabeth II **Subject:** Toronto Maple Leafs **Obv:** Head right **Obv.
Designer:** Susanna Blunt **Rev:** Jonny Bover

Date	Mintage	MS-63	Proof
2005 Specimen	25,000	—	16.00

KM# 541   50 CENTS
9.3000 g., 0.9250 Silver 0.2766 oz. ASW, 27.13 mm. **Ruler:**
Elizabeth II **Subject:** Toronto Maple Leafs **Obv:** Head right **Obv.
Designer:** Susanna Blunt **Rev:** Tim Horton

Date	Mintage	MS-63	Proof
2005 Specimen	25,000	—	16.00

KM# 543   50 CENTS
9.3000 g., 0.9250 Silver 0.2766 oz. ASW **Ruler:** Elizabeth II
Subject: WWII - Battle of Britain **Obv:** Head right **Rev:** Fighter
plane in sky

Date	Mintage	MS-63	Proof
2005 Specimen	20,000	—	22.50

KM# 544   50 CENTS
9.3000 g., 0.9250 Silver 0.2766 oz. ASW, 27.13 mm. **Ruler:**
Elizabeth II **Subject:** WWII - Battle of Scheldt **Obv:** Head right
Obv. Designer: Susanna Blunt **Rev:** Four soldiers walking down
road **Rev. Designer:** Peter Mossman

Date	Mintage	MS-63	Proof
2005 Specimen	20,000	—	19.00

KM# 545   50 CENTS
9.3000 g., 0.9250 Silver 0.2766 oz. ASW, 27.13 mm. **Ruler:**
Elizabeth II **Subject:** WWII - Battle of the Atlantic **Obv:** Head right
Obv. Designer: Susanna Blunt **Rev:** Merchant ship sinking **Rev.
Designer:** Peter Mossman

Date	Mintage	MS-63	Proof
2005 Specimen	20,000	—	19.00

KM# 546   50 CENTS
9.3000 g., 0.9250 Silver 0.2766 oz. ASW, 27.13 mm. **Ruler:**
Elizabeth II **Subject:** WWII - Conquest of Sicily **Obv:** Head right
Obv. Designer: Susanna Blunt **Rev:** Tank among town ruins
Rev. Designer: Peter Mossman

Date	Mintage	MS-63	Proof
2005 Specimen	20,000	—	19.00

KM# 547   50 CENTS
9.3000 g., 0.9250 Silver 0.2766 oz. ASW, 27.13 mm. **Ruler:**
Elizabeth II **Subject:** WWII - Liberation of the Netherlands **Obv:**
Head right **Obv. Designer:** Susanna Blunt **Rev:** Soldiers in
parade, one holding flag **Rev. Designer:** Peter Mossman

Date	Mintage	MS-63	Proof
2005 Specimen	20,000	—	19.00

KM# 548   50 CENTS
9.3000 g., 0.9250 Silver 0.2766 oz. ASW, 27.13 mm. **Ruler:**
Elizabeth II **Subject:** WWII - Raid of Dieppe **Obv:** Head right
Obv. Designer: Susanna Blunt **Rev:** Three soldiers exiting
landing craft **Rev. Designer:** Peter Mossman

Date	Mintage	MS-63	Proof
2005 Specimen	20,000	—	19.00

KM# 577   50 CENTS
9.3000 g., 0.9250 Silver 0.2766 oz. ASW, 27.13 mm. **Ruler:**
Elizabeth II **Subject:** Montreal Canadiens **Obv:** Head right **Obv.
Designer:** Susanna Blunt **Rev:** Guy LaFleur

Date	Mintage	MS-63	Proof
2005 Specimen	25,000	—	17.50

KM# 578   50 CENTS
9.3000 g., 0.9250 Silver 0.2766 oz. ASW, 27.13 mm. **Ruler:**
Elizabeth II **Subject:** Montreal Canadiens **Obv:** Head right **Obv.
Designer:** Susanna Blunt **Rev:** Jaque Plante

Date	Mintage	MS-63	Proof
2005 Specimen	25,000	—	17.50

KM# 579   50 CENTS
9.3000 g., 0.9250 Silver 0.2766 oz. ASW, 27.13 mm. **Ruler:**
Elizabeth II **Subject:** Montreal Canadiens **Obv:** Head right **Obv.
Designer:** Susanna Blunt **Rev:** Jean Beliveau

Date	Mintage	MS-63	Proof
2005 Specimen	25,000	—	17.50

KM# 580   50 CENTS
9.3000 g., 0.9250 Silver 0.2766 oz. ASW, 27.13 mm. **Ruler:**
Elizabeth II **Subject:** Montreal Canadiens **Obv:** Head right **Obv.
Designer:** Susanna Blunt **Rev:** Maurice Richard

Date	Mintage	MS-63	Proof
2005 Specimen	25,000	—	17.50

KM# 599   50 CENTS
9.3000 g., 0.9250 Silver 0.2766 oz. ASW, 27.13 mm. **Ruler:**
Elizabeth II **Obv:** Head right **Obv. Designer:** Susanna Blunt **Rev:**
Monarch butterfly, colorized **Rev. Designer:** Susan Taylor

Date	Mintage	MS-63	Proof
2005 Proof	20,000	—	35.00

KM# 542   50 CENTS
1.2700 g., 0.9990 Gold 0.0408 oz. AGW, 13.92 mm. **Ruler:**
Elizabeth II **Rev:** Voyagers with northern lights above **Rev.
Designer:** Emanuel Hahn

Date	Mintage	MS-63	Proof
2005 Proof	Est. 25,000	—	100

KM# 648   50 CENTS
9.3000 g., 0.9250 Silver With Partial Gold Plating 0.2766 oz.
ASW **Ruler:** Elizabeth II **Subject:** Golden Daisy **Obv:** Head right

Date	Mintage	MS-63	Proof
2006	18,190	22.00	—

KM# 649   50 CENTS
9.3000 g., 0.9250 Silver 0.2766 oz. ASW **Ruler:** Elizabeth II
Subject: Short-tailed swallowtail **Obv:** Head right **Rev:** Colorized
butterfly

Date	Mintage	MS-63	Proof
2006	24,568	25.00	—

KM# 650   50 CENTS
9.3000 g., 0.9250 Silver 0.2766 oz. ASW **Ruler:** Elizabeth II
Obv: Head right **Rev:** Silvery blue hologram

Date	Mintage	MS-63	Proof
2006	16,000	25.00	—

KM# 651   50 CENTS
9.3000 g., 0.9250 Silver 0.2766 oz. ASW **Ruler:** Elizabeth II
Subject: Cowboy **Obv:** Head right

Date	Mintage	MS-63	Proof
2006	—	17.50	

KM# 494b   50 CENTS
6.9000 g., Nickel Plated Steel partially gilt, 27.13 mm. **Ruler:**
Elizabeth II **Rev:** State Arms, gilt **Note:** Housed in Mint Annual
Report

Date	Mintage	MS-63	Proof
2006	—	15.00	

KM# 716   50 CENTS
9.3000 g., 0.9250 Silver 0.2766 oz. ASW **Ruler:** Elizabeth II
Rev: Multicolor holiday ornaments

Date	Mintage	MS-63	Proof
2006	16,989	17.50	—

KM# 717   50 CENTS
1.2400 g., 0.9990 Gold 0.0398 oz. AGW, 13.9 mm. **Ruler:**
Elizabeth II **Rev:** Wolf

Date	Mintage	MS-63	Proof
2006 Proof	—	—	100

KM# 926   50 CENTS
1.2400 g., 0.9990 Gold 0.0398 oz. AGW, 13.9 mm. **Ruler:**
Elizabeth II **Rev:** Cowboy and bronco rider

Date	Mintage	MS-63	Proof
2006 Proof	—	—	100

KM# 715   50 CENTS
9.3000 g., 0.9250 Silver with partial gold plating 0.2766 oz. ASW,
27.12 mm. **Ruler:** Elizabeth II **Rev:** Forget-me-not flower

Date	Mintage	MS-63	Proof
2007 Proof	22,882	—	29.00

KM# 927   50 CENTS
1.2400 g., 0.9990 Gold 0.0398 oz. AGW, 13.9 mm. **Ruler:**
Elizabeth II **Subject:** Gold Louis

Date	Mintage	MS-63	Proof
2007 Proof	—	—	100

KM# 777 50 CENTS
1.2400 g., 0.9990 Gold 0.0398 oz. AGW, 13.9 mm. **Ruler:** Elizabeth II **Subject:** DeHavilland beaver

Date	Mintage	MS-63	Proof
2008 Proof	20,000	—	100

KM# 778 50 CENTS
20.0000 g., 0.9250 Silver colorized green 0.5948 oz. ASW, 34.06 mm. **Ruler:** Elizabeth II **Subject:** Milk delivery **Obv:** Bust right **Rev:** Cow head and milk can **Shape:** Triangle

Date	Mintage	MS-63	Proof
2008 Proof	24,448	—	35.00

KM# 779 50 CENTS
9.3000 g., 0.9250 Silver 0.2766 oz. ASW, 35 mm. **Ruler:** Elizabeth II **Rev:** Multicolor snowman

Date	Mintage	MS-63	Proof
2008	21,679	17.50	—

KM# 780 50 CENTS
9.3000 g., 0.9250 Silver 0.2766 oz. ASW **Ruler:** Elizabeth II **Subject:** Ottawa Mint Centennial 1908-2008

Date	Mintage	MS-63	Proof
2008 Proof	3,248	—	20.00

KM# 845 50 CENTS
9.3000 g., 0.9250 Silver 0.2766 oz. ASW, 27.13 mm. **Ruler:** Elizabeth II **Rev:** Calgary Flames lenticular design, old and new logos

Date	Mintage	MS-63	Proof
2009		15.00	—

KM# 846 50 CENTS
9.3000 g., 0.9250 Silver 0.2766 oz. ASW, 27.13 mm. **Ruler:** Elizabeth II **Rev:** Edmonton Oiler's lenticular design, old and new logos

Date	Mintage	MS-63	Proof
2009		15.00	—

KM# 847 50 CENTS
9.3000 g., 0.9250 Silver 0.2766 oz. ASW, 27.13 mm. **Ruler:** Elizabeth II **Rev:** Montreal Canadiens lenticular design, old and new logos

Date	Mintage	MS-63	Proof
2009		15.00	—

KM# 848 50 CENTS
9.3000 g., 0.9250 Silver 0.2766 oz. ASW, 27.13 mm. **Ruler:** Elizabeth II **Rev:** Ottawa Senators lenticular design, old and new logos

Date	Mintage	MS-63	Proof
2009	—	15.00	—

KM# 849 50 CENTS
9.3000 g., 0.9250 Silver 0.2766 oz. ASW, 27.13 mm. **Ruler:** Elizabeth II **Rev:** Toronto Maple Leafs lenticular design, old and new logos

Date	Mintage	MS-63	Proof
2009		15.00	—

KM# 850 50 CENTS
9.3000 g., 0.9250 Silver 0.2766 oz. ASW, 27.13 mm. **Ruler:** Elizabeth II **Rev:** Vancouver Canucks lenticular design, old and new logos

Date	Mintage	MS-63	Proof
2009		15.00	—

KM# 857 50 CENTS
6.9000 g., Nickel Plated Steel, 35 mm. **Ruler:** Elizabeth II **Rev:** Calgary Flames lenticular old and new logos

Date	Mintage	MS-63	Proof
2009		25.00	—

KM# 858 50 CENTS
6.9000 g., Nickel Plated Steel, 35 mm. **Ruler:** Elizabeth II **Rev:** Edmonton Oilers lenticular old and new logos

Date	Mintage	MS-63	Proof
2009		25.00	—

KM# 859 50 CENTS
35.0000 g., Nickel Plated Steel, 35 mm. **Ruler:** Elizabeth II **Rev:** Montreal Canadians lenticular old and new logo

Date	Mintage	MS-63	Proof
2009		25.00	—

KM# 860 50 CENTS
6.9000 g., Nickel Plated Steel, 35 mm. **Ruler:** Elizabeth II **Rev:** Ottawa Senators lenticular old and new logos

Date	Mintage	MS-63	Proof
2009		25.00	—

KM# 861 50 CENTS
6.9000 g., Nickel Plated Steel, 35 mm. **Ruler:** Elizabeth II **Rev:** Toronto Maple Leafs lenticular old and new logos

Date	Mintage	MS-63	Proof
2009		25.00	—

KM# 862 50 CENTS
6.9000 g., Nickel Plated Steel, 35 mm. **Ruler:** Elizabeth II **Rev:** Vancouver Canucks lenticular old and new logos

Date	Mintage	MS-63	Proof
2009		25.00	—

KM# 887 50 CENTS
19.1000 g., Copper-Nickel, 34.06 mm. **Ruler:** Elizabeth II **Subject:** Six-string national guitar **Obv:** Bust right **Obv. Legend:** Elizabeth II DG Regina **Obv. Designer:** Susanna Blunt **Rev:** Hologram with 6 "strings" **Rev. Legend:** 50 CENTS Canada **Shape:** Triangle

Date	Mintage	MS-63	Proof
2009 Proof	13,602	—	50.00

KM# 936 50 CENTS
9.3000 g., Nickel **Ruler:** Elizabeth II **Rev:** Vancouver Canucks goalie jersey

Date	Mintage	MS-63	Proof
2009	3,563	15.00	—

KM# 937 50 CENTS
6.9000 g., Nickel Plated Steel, 35 mm. **Ruler:** Elizabeth II **Rev:** Calgary Flames player - colorized

Date	Mintage	MS-63	Proof
2009	3,518	15.00	—

KM# 938 50 CENTS
6.9000 g., Nickel Plated Steel, 35 mm. **Ruler:** Elizabeth II **Rev:** Edmonton Oilers player

Date	Mintage	MS-63	Proof
2009	3,562	15.00	—

KM# 939 50 CENTS
6.9000 g., Nickel Plated Steel, 35 mm. **Ruler:** Elizabeth II **Rev:** Toronto Maple Leafs player

Date	Mintage	MS-63	Proof
2009	5,918	15.00	—

KM# 940 50 CENTS
6.9000 g., Nickel Plated Steel, 35 mm. **Ruler:** Elizabeth II **Rev:** Montreal Canadiens player

Date	Mintage	MS-63	Proof
2009	9,865	15.00	—

KM# 941 50 CENTS
6.9000 g., Nickel Plated Steel, 35 mm. **Ruler:** Elizabeth II **Rev:** Ottawa Senators player

Date	Mintage	MS-63	Proof
2009	3,293	15.00	—

KM# 1035 50 CENTS
12.6100 g., Brass Plated Steel, 35 mm. **Ruler:** Elizabeth II **Subject:** Christmas toy train **Rev:** movement from far to close

Date	Mintage	MS-63	Proof
2009	19,103	17.50	—

KM# 961 50 CENTS
6.9000 g., Nickel Plated Steel, 35 mm. **Ruler:** Elizabeth II **Rev:** Bob sleigh

Date	Mintage	MS-63	Proof
2010	—	15.00	—

KM# 961a 50 CENTS
6.9000 g., Nickel Plated Steel, 35 mm. **Ruler:** Elizabeth II **Rev:** Bob sleigh - red enamel

Date	Mintage	MS-63	Proof
2010		15.00	—

KM# 962 50 CENTS
6.9000 g., Nickel Plated Steel, 35 mm. **Ruler:** Elizabeth II **Rev:** Speed skating

Date	Mintage	MS-63	Proof
2010	—	15.00	—

KM# 962a 50 CENTS
6.9000 g., Nickel Plated Steel, 35 mm. **Ruler:** Elizabeth II **Rev:** Speed skating - red enamel

Date	Mintage	MS-63	Proof
2010		15.00	—

KM# 963 50 CENTS
6.9000 g., Nickel Plated Steel, 35 mm. **Ruler:** Elizabeth II **Rev:** Miga in bob sleigh

Date	Mintage	MS-63	Proof
2010	2,119	15.00	—

KM# 964 50 CENTS
6.9000 g., Nickel Plated Steel, 35 mm. **Ruler:** Elizabeth II **Rev:** Miga in hockey

Date	Mintage	MS-63	Proof
2010	5,275	15.00	—

KM# 965 50 CENTS
6.9000 g., Nickel Plated Steel, 35 mm. **Ruler:** Elizabeth II **Rev:** Quatchi in ice hockey

Date	Mintage	MS-63	Proof
2010	5,614	15.00	—

KM# 966 50 CENTS
6.9000 g., Nickel Plated Steel, 35 mm. **Ruler:** Elizabeth II **Rev:** Sumi Para Sledge

Date	Mintage	MS-63	Proof
2010	3,707	15.00	—

KM# 967 50 CENTS
6.9000 g., Nickel Plated Steel, 35 mm. **Ruler:** Elizabeth II **Rev:** Figure-skating mascot **Edge:** Reeded

Date	Mintage	MS-63	Proof
2010	2,981	15.00	—

KM# 968 50 CENTS
6.9000 g., Nickel Plated Steel, 35 mm. **Ruler:** Elizabeth II **Rev:** Free-style mascot

Date	Mintage	MS-63	Proof
2010	2,114	15.00	—

KM# 969 50 CENTS
6.9000 g., Nickel Plated Steel, 35 mm. **Ruler:** Elizabeth II **Rev:** Skeleton mascot

Date	Mintage	MS-63	Proof
2010	1,672	15.00	—

KM# 970 50 CENTS
6.9000 g., Nickel Plated Steel, 35 mm. **Ruler:** Elizabeth II **Rev:** Parallel giant slalom mascot

Date	Mintage	MS-63	Proof
2010	1,730	15.00	—

KM# 971 50 CENTS
6.9000 g., Nickel Plated Steel, 35 mm. **Ruler:** Elizabeth II **Rev:** Alpine skiing mascot

Date	Mintage	MS-63	Proof
2010	2,309	15.00	—

KM# 972   50 CENTS
6.9000 g., Nickel Plated Steel, 35 mm. **Ruler:** Elizabeth II **Rev:** Para Olympic alpine skiing mascott

Date	Mintage	MS-63	Proof
2010	1,902	15.00	—

KM# 973   50 CENTS
6.9000 g., Nickel Plated Steel, 35 mm. **Ruler:** Elizabeth II **Rev:** Snowboard mascot

Date	Mintage	MS-63	Proof
2010	2,090	15.00	—

KM# 974   50 CENTS
6.9000 g., Nickel Plated Steel, 35 mm. **Ruler:** Elizabeth II **Rev:** Speed-skating mascott

Date	Mintage	MS-63	Proof
2010	1,825	15.00	—

KM# 985   50 CENTS
1.2400 g., 0.9990 Gold 0.0398 oz. AGW, 13.92 mm. **Ruler:** Elizabeth II **Subject:** RCMP **Rev:** Mountie on horseback **Rev. Designer:** Janet Griffin-Scott

Date	Mintage	MS-63	Proof
2010 Proof	Est. 14,000	—	100

KM# 986   50 CENTS
12.6100 g., Brass Plated Steel, 35 mm. **Ruler:** Elizabeth II **Rev:** Dasplerosaurus Torosus - 3-D lenticular movement

Date	Mintage	MS-63	Proof
2010	—	—	40.00

KM# 1015   50 CENTS
12.6100 g., Brass Plated Steel, 35 mm. **Ruler:** Elizabeth II **Rev:** Sinosauropteryx

Date	Mintage	MS-63	Proof
2010	—	25.00	—

KM# 1016   50 CENTS
12.6100 g., Brass Plated Steel, 35 mm. **Ruler:** Elizabeth II **Rev:** Albertosaurus

Date	Mintage	MS-63	Proof
2010	—	25.00	—

KM# 1043   50 CENTS
Nickel Plated Steel, 34 mm. **Ruler:** Elizabeth II **Rev:** Santa Claus transforms into Rudolf the red-nosed reindeer

Date	Mintage	MS-63	Proof
2010	—	17.50	—

KM# 1157   50 CENTS
Silver **Ruler:** Elizabeth II

Date	Mintage	MS-63	Proof
1911-2011	—	—	45.00

KM# 1180   50 CENTS
6.9000 g., Nickel Plated Steel, 27.13 mm. **Ruler:** Elizabeth II **Obv:** Bust right **Rev:** Winnipeg Jets Logo, jet over maple leaf **Edge:** Reeded

Date	Mintage	MS-63	Proof
2011	—	15.00	—

KM# 1191   50 CENTS
12.6100 g., Copper Plated Steel, 35 mm. **Ruler:** Elizabeth II **Obv:** Bust right **Rev:** Santa Claus checking list, and in sled over house

Date	Mintage	MS-63	Proof
2011	—	27.50	—

KM# 1202   50 CENTS
1.2700 g., 0.9999 Gold 0.0408 oz. AGW, 13.92 mm. **Ruler:** Elizabeth II **Rev:** Wood Bison **Rev. Designer:** Corrine Hunt **Edge:** Reeded

Date	Mintage	MS-63	Proof
2011 Proof	Est. 2,500	—	100

KM# 1204   50 CENTS
1.2700 g., 0.9999 Gold 0.0408 oz. AGW, 13.92 mm. **Ruler:** Elizabeth II **Subject:** Boreal Forest **Rev:** Bird and tree **Rev. Designer:** Corrine Hunt **Edge:** Reeded

Date	Mintage	MS-63	Proof
2011 Proof	Est. 2,500	—	100

KM# 1206   50 CENTS
1.2700 g., 0.9999 Gold 0.0408 oz. AGW, 13.92 mm. **Ruler:** Elizabeth II **Rev:** Peregrine Falcon perched on branch **Rev. Designer:** Corrine Hunt

Date	Mintage	MS-63	Proof
2011 Proof	Est. 2,500	—	100

KM# 1208   50 CENTS
1.2700 g., 0.9999 Gold 0.0408 oz. AGW, 13.92 mm. **Ruler:** Elizabeth II **Rev:** Orca Whale **Rev. Designer:** Corrine Hunt **Edge:** Reeded

Date	Mintage	MS-63	Proof
2011 Proof	Est. 2,500	—	100

KM# 1218   50 CENTS
1.2700 g., 0.9999 Gold 0.0408 oz. AGW, 13.92 mm. **Ruler:** Elizabeth II **Obv:** Bust right **Rev:** Schooner sailing left

Date	Mintage	MS-63	Proof
2012 Proof	—	—	90.00

KM# 1234   50 CENTS
12.6100 g., Nickel Plated Steel, 35 mm. **Ruler:** Elizabeth II **Subject:** Titanic, 100th Anniversary **Obv:** Bust right **Rev:** Titanic sailing forward towards iceberg, colored sea

Date	Mintage	MS-63	Proof
2012 Proof	—	—	40.00

KM# 186   DOLLAR
7.0000 g., Aureate-Bronze Plated Nickel, 26.5 mm. **Ruler:** Elizabeth II **Obv:** Crowned head right **Obv. Designer:** Dora dePedery-Hunt **Rev:** Loon right, date and denomination **Rev. Designer:** Robert R. Carmichael **Shape:** 11-sided

Date	Mintage	MS-63	Proof
2001	—	2.50	—
2001 Proof	74,194	—	8.00
2002	—	4.50	—
2002 Proof	65,315	—	7.50
2003	—	5.50	—

Note: Mintage of 5,101,000 includes both KM186 and KM495 examples.

2003 Proof	—	—	12.00

KM# 414   DOLLAR
25.1750 g., 0.9250 Silver 0.7487 oz. ASW, 36 mm. **Ruler:** Elizabeth II **Subject:** National Ballet **Obv:** Crowned head right **Rev:** Ballet dancers **Rev. Designer:** Scott McKowen **Edge:** Reeded

Date	Mintage	MS-63	Proof
2001	65,000	27.50	—
2001 Proof	225,000	—	35.00

KM# 434   DOLLAR
25.1750 g., 0.9250 Silver 0.7487 oz. ASW, 36 mm. **Ruler:** Elizabeth II **Obv:** Crowned head right **Rev:** Recycled 1911 pattern dollar design: denomination, country name and dates in crowned wreath **Edge:** Reeded

Date	Mintage	MS-63	Proof
1911-2001 Proof	24,996	—	55.00

KM# 186a   DOLLAR
Gilt Aureate-Bronze Plated Nickel, 26.5 mm. **Ruler:** Elizabeth II **Subject:** Olympic Win

Date	Mintage	MS-63	Proof
2002 Proof	—	—	40.00

KM# 443   DOLLAR
25.1750 g., 0.9250 Silver 0.7487 oz. ASW, 36 mm. **Ruler:** Elizabeth II **Subject:** Queen's Golden Jubilee **Obv:** Crowned

head right, with anniversary date at left **Obv. Designer:** Dora dePédery-Hunt **Rev:** Queen in her coach and a view of the coach, denomination below **Edge:** Reeded

Date	Mintage	MS-63	Proof
1952-2002	65,140	28.50	—
1952-2002 Proof	29,688	—	40.00

KM# 443a DOLLAR

25.1800 g., 0.9250 Silver Gilt 0.7488 oz. ASW, 36 mm. **Ruler:** Elizabeth II **Subject:** Queen's Golden Jubilee **Obv:** Crowned head right with anniversary date **Rev:** Queen in her coach and a view of the coach **Edge:** Reeded **Note:** Special 24 karat gold plated issue of KM#443.

Date	Mintage	MS-63	Proof
2002 Proof	32,642	—	45.00

KM# 462 DOLLAR

7.0000 g., Aureate-Bronze Plated Nickel **Ruler:** Elizabeth II **Obv:** Commemorative dates 1952-2002 **Obv. Designer:** Dora dePédery-Hunt **Rev:** Family of Loons

Date	Mintage	MS-63	Proof
2002 Specimen	67,672	—	35.00

KM# 467 DOLLAR

7.0000 g., Aureate-Bronze Plated Nickel **Ruler:** Elizabeth II **Subject:** Elizabeth II Golden Jubilee **Obv:** Crowned head right, Jubilee commemorative dates 1952-2002 **Obv. Designer:** Dora dePédery-Hunt

Date	Mintage	MS-63	Proof
2002	2,302,000	2.50	—
2002 Proof	—	—	8.00

KM# 467a DOLLAR

Gold **Ruler:** Elizabeth II **Subject:** 50th Anniversary, Accession to the Throne **Obv:** Crowned head right **Note:** Sold on the internet.

Date	Mintage	MS-63	Proof
2002	1	—	55,500

KM# 503 DOLLAR

25.1750 g., 0.9250 Silver 0.7487 oz. ASW, 36 mm. **Ruler:** Elizabeth II **Subject:** Queen Mother **Obv:** Crowned head right **Obv. Designer:** Dora de Pedery-Hunt **Rev:** Queen Mother facing

Date	Mintage	MS-63	Proof
2002 Proof	9,994	—	250

KM# 495 DOLLAR

7.0000 g., Aureate-Bronze Plated Nickel, 26.5 mm. **Ruler:** Elizabeth II **Obv:** Bare head right **Obv. Designer:** Susanna Blunt **Rev:** Loon right **Rev. Designer:** Robert R. Carmichael **Shape:** 11-sided

Date	Mintage	MS-63	Proof
2003	5,102,000	5.50	—

Note: Mintage of 5,101,000 includes both KM 186 and 495 examples.

Date	Mintage	MS-63	Proof
2003W Prooflike	—	—	—
2003 Proof	62,507	—	7.50
2004	10,894,000	1.75	—
2004 Proof	—	—	12.00
2005	44,375,000	3.00	—
2005 Proof	—	—	7.50
2006	49,111,000	3.00	—
2006 Proof	—	—	7.50
2006(ml)	49,111,000	3.00	—
2006(ml) Proof	—	—	7.50
2007(ml)	38,045,000	3.00	—
2007(ml) Proof	—	—	7.50
2008(ml)	29,561,000	3.00	—
2008(ml) Proof	—	—	7.50
2009(ml)	39,601,000	3.00	—
2009(ml) Proof	—	—	7.50
2010(ml)	—	3.00	—
2010(ml) Proof	—	—	7.50
2011(ml)	—	3.00	—
2011(ml) Proof	—	—	7.50
2012(ml)	—	3.00	—
2012(ml) Proof	—	—	7.50

KM# 450 DOLLAR

25.1750 g., 0.9999 Silver 0.8093 oz. ASW, 36 mm. **Ruler:**

Elizabeth II **Subject:** Cobalt Mining Centennial **Obv:** Queens portrait right **Obv. Designer:** Dora dePédery-Hunt **Rev:** Mine tower and fox **Edge:** Reeded

Date	Mintage	MS-63	Proof
2003	51,130	30.00	—
2003 Proof	88,536	—	45.00

KM# 473 DOLLAR

25.1750 g., 0.9999 Silver 0.8093 oz. ASW **Ruler:** Elizabeth II **Subject:** 50th Anniversary of the Coronation of Elizabeth II **Obv:** 1953 effigy of the Queen, Jubilee dates 1953-2003 **Obv. Designer:** Mary Gillick **Rev:** Voyageur, date and denomination below

Date	Mintage	MS-63	Proof
1953-2003 Proof	21,537	—	45.00

KM# 480 DOLLAR

25.1750 g., 0.9999 Silver 0.8093 oz. ASW **Ruler:** Elizabeth II **Subject:** Coronation of Queen Elizabeth II **Obv:** Head right **Rev:** Voyaguers **Rev. Designer:** Emanuel Hahn

Date	Mintage	MS-63	Proof
1953-2003 Proof	29,586	—	50.00

KM# 480a DOLLAR

Gold **Ruler:** Elizabeth II **Subject:** 50th Anniversary of Coronation **Obv. Designer:** Mary Gilick **Rev:** Voyageur **Note:** Sold on the internet.

Date	Mintage	MS-63	Proof
1953-2003	1	—	62,750

KM# 511 DOLLAR

25.1750 g., 0.9999 Silver 0.8093 oz. ASW, 36 mm. **Ruler:** Elizabeth II **Obv:** Elizabeth II **Rev:** Poppy on maple leaf **Edge:** Reeded

Date	Mintage	MS-63	Proof
2004 Proof	24,527	—	50.00

KM# 507 DOLLAR

7.0000 g., Aureate-Bronze Plated Nickel, 26.5 mm. **Ruler:** Elizabeth II **Obv:** Bare head right, date below **Obv. Designer:** Susanna Blunt **Rev:** Loon **Edge:** Plain **Shape:** 11-sided

Date	Mintage	MS-63	Proof
2004 Proof	25,105	—	75.00

KM# 512 DOLLAR

25.1750 g., 0.9999 Silver 0.8093 oz. ASW, 36 mm. **Ruler:** Elizabeth II **Subject:** First French Settlement in America **Obv:** Crowned head right **Rev:** Sailing ship **Edge:** Reeded

Date	Mintage	MS-63	Proof
2004	42,582	30.00	—
2004 Fleur-dis-lis privy mark	8,315	60.00	—
2004 Proof	106,974	—	50.00

KM# 513 DOLLAR

7.0000 g., Aureate-Bronze Plated Nickel, 26.5 mm. **Ruler:** Elizabeth II **Subject:** Olympics **Obv:** Bare head right **Rev:** Maple leaf, Olympic flame and rings above loon **Edge:** Plain **Shape:** 11-sided

Date	Mintage	MS-63	Proof
2004	6,526,000	8.00	—

KM# 513a DOLLAR

9.3100 g., 0.9250 Silver 0.2769 oz. ASW, 26.5 mm. **Ruler:** Elizabeth II **Subject:** Olympics **Obv:** Bare head right **Rev:** Multicolor maple leaf, Olympic flame and rings above loon **Edge:** Plain **Shape:** 11-sided

Date	Mintage	MS-63	Proof
2004 Proof	19,994	—	50.00

KM# 549 DOLLAR

25.1750 g., 0.9250 Silver 0.7487 oz. ASW, 36.07 mm. **Ruler:** Elizabeth II **Subject:** 40th Anniversary of National Flag **Obv:** Head right **Obv. Designer:** Susanna Blunt **Rev. Designer:** William Woodruff

Date	Mintage	MS-63	Proof
2005	50,948	27.50	—
2005 Proof	95,431	—	40.00

KM# 549a DOLLAR

25.1750 g., 0.9250 Silver partially gilt 0.7487 oz. ASW, 36.07 mm. **Ruler:** Elizabeth II **Subject:** 40th Anniversary of National Flag **Obv:** Head right

Date	Mintage	MS-63	Proof
2005	62,562	75.00	—

KM# 549b DOLLAR

25.1800 g., 0.9250 Silver 0.7488 oz. ASW, 36.07 mm. **Ruler:** Elizabeth II **Subject:** 40th Anniversary National Flag **Rev:** National flag, colorized

Date	Mintage	MS-63	Proof
2005 Proof	4,898	—	350

KM# 552 DOLLAR

7.0000 g., Aureate-Bronze Plated Nickel, 26.5 mm. **Ruler:** Elizabeth II **Subject:** Terry Fox **Obv:** Head right

Date	Mintage	MS-63	Proof
2005	1,290,900	3.50	—

KM# 553 DOLLAR

7.0000 g., Aureate-Bronze Plated Nickel **Ruler:** Elizabeth II **Subject:** Tuffed Puffin **Obv:** Head right **Obv. Designer:** Susanna Blunt

Date	Mintage	MS-63	Proof
2005	39,818	—	30.00

KM# 581 DOLLAR

9.3100 g., 0.9250 Silver 0.2769 oz. ASW **Ruler:** Elizabeth II **Subject:** Lullabies Loonie **Obv:** Head right **Obv. Designer:** Susanna Blunt **Rev:** Loon and moon, teddy bear in stars

Date	Mintage	MS-63	Proof
2006	18,103	4.50	—

KM# 582 DOLLAR

7.0000 g., Aureate-Bronze Plated Nickel, 26.5 mm. **Ruler:** Elizabeth II **Subject:** Snowy owl **Obv:** Head right **Obv. Designer:** Susanna Blunt **Rev:** Snowy owl with year above

Date	Mintage	MS-63	Proof
2006 Specimen	39,935	—	30.00

KM# 583 DOLLAR
25.1750 g., 0.9250 Silver 0.7487 oz. ASW, 36 mm. **Ruler:**
Elizabeth II **Obv:** Head right **Rev:** Victoria Cross

Date	Mintage	MS-63	Proof
2006	27,254	25.00	—
2006 Proof	53,822	—	45.00

KM# 583a DOLLAR
25.1750 g., 0.9250 Silver partially gilt 0.7487 oz. ASW, 36 mm.
Ruler: Elizabeth II **Obv:** Head right **Rev:** Victoria Cross gilt

Date	Mintage	MS-63	Proof
2006 Proof	53,822	—	75.00

KM# 630 DOLLAR
9.3100 g., 0.9250 Silver with enamel 0.2769 oz. ASW **Ruler:**
Elizabeth II **Subject:** Olympic Games **Obv:** Crowned head right
Rev: Loon in flight, colored olympic logo above

Date	Mintage	MS-63	Proof
2006	19,956	30.00	—

KM# 654 DOLLAR
7.0000 g., 0.9250 Silver 0.2082 oz. ASW **Ruler:** Elizabeth II
Obv: Head right **Rev:** Snowflake, colorized **Note:** Sold in a CD
package.

Date	Mintage	MS-63	Proof
2006(ml)	34,014	35.00	—

KM# 655 DOLLAR
7.0000 g., 0.9250 Silver 0.2082 oz. ASW **Ruler:** Elizabeth II
Subject: Baby Rattle **Obv:** Head right **Rev:** Baby rattle

Date	Mintage	MS-63	Proof
2006	3,207	20.00	—

KM# 655a DOLLAR
7.0000 g., 0.9250 Silver 0.2082 oz. ASW **Ruler:** Elizabeth II
Obv: Bust right **Rev:** Baby Rattle, partially gilt

Date	Mintage	MS-63	Proof
2006	1,911	15.00	—

KM# 656 DOLLAR
28.1750 g., 0.9250 Silver 0.8379 oz. ASW **Ruler:** Elizabeth II
Subject: Medal of Bravery **Obv:** Head right

Date	Mintage	MS-63	Proof
2006 Proof	8,343	—	50.00

KM# 656a DOLLAR
28.1750 g., 0.9250 Silver with multicolor enamel 0.8379 oz. ASW
Ruler: Elizabeth II **Subject:** Medal of Bravery **Obv:** Head right
Rev: Maple leaf within wreath. Colorized.

Date	Mintage	MS-63	Proof
2006 Proof	4,999	—	150

KM# 688 DOLLAR

7.0000 g., Aureate Bronze, 26.5 mm. **Ruler:** Elizabeth II **Obv:**
Head right **Rev:** Trumpeter Swan

Date	Mintage	MS-63	Proof
2007(ml)	40,000	20.00	—

KM# 653 DOLLAR
25.1750 g., 0.9250 Silver 0.7487 oz. ASW, 36.07 mm. **Ruler:**
Elizabeth II **Subject:** Thayendanegea **Obv:** Head right **Rev:** Bust
3/4 facing right

Date	Mintage	MS-63	Proof
2007	16,378	30.00	—
2007 Proof	—	—	40.00

KM# 653a DOLLAR
25.1750 g., 0.9250 Silver partially gilt 0.7487 oz. ASW,
36.07 mm. **Ruler:** Elizabeth II **Subject:** Thayendanega **Rev:**
Bust 3/4 right, partially gold plated

Date	Mintage	MS-63	Proof
2007 Proof	60,000	—	125

KM# 720 DOLLAR
25.1800 g., 0.9250 Silver 0.7488 oz. ASW, 36.07 mm. **Ruler:**
Elizabeth II **Obv:** Bust right **Rev:** Thayendanega multicolor

Date	Mintage	MS-63	Proof
2007 Proof	4,760	—	120

KM# 700 DOLLAR
7.0000 g., 0.9250 Silver 0.2082 oz. ASW **Ruler:** Elizabeth II
Rev: Alphabet Letter Blocks

Date	Mintage	MS-63	Proof
2007	3,207	—	25.00

KM# 719 DOLLAR
25.1800 g., 0.9250 Silver 0.7488 oz. ASW, 36.07 mm. **Ruler:**
Elizabeth II **Subject:** Celebration of the Arts **Rev:** Book, TV set,
musical instruments, film montage **Rev. Designer:** Friedrich
Peter **Edge:** Reeded

Date	Mintage	MS-63	Proof
2007	6,466	—	55.00

KM# A727 DOLLAR
7.0000 g., Aureate Bronze, 26.5 mm. **Ruler:** Elizabeth II
Subject: Vancouver Olympic Games **Rev:** Loon splashing in
water, Olympics logo at right

Date	Mintage	MS-63	Proof
2007(ml)	19,973	3.00	—

KM# 721 DOLLAR
7.0000 g., Nickel-Bronze, 26.5 mm. **Ruler:** Elizabeth II **Obv:**
Bust right **Rev:** Calgary flames, multicolor in circle

Date	Mintage	MS-63	Proof
2008		25.00	—

KM# 722 DOLLAR
7.0000 g., Nickel-Bronze, 26.5 mm. **Ruler:** Elizabeth II **Obv:**
Bust **Rev:** Edmonton Oilers logo, multicolor in logo

Date	Mintage	MS-63	Proof
2008	1,584	25.00	—

KM# 723A DOLLAR
7.0000 g., Nickel-Bronze, 26.5 mm. **Ruler:** Elizabeth II **Obv:**
Bust right **Rev:** Montreal Canadians, multicolor logo in circle

Date	Mintage	MS-63	Proof
2008	2,659	25.00	—

KM# 724 DOLLAR
7.0000 g., Nickel, 26.5 mm. **Ruler:** Elizabeth II **Rev:** Ottowa
Senators, multicolor logo in circle

Date	Mintage	MS-63	Proof
2008	1,633	25.00	—

KM# 725 DOLLAR
7.0000 g., Nickel-Bronze, 26.5 mm. **Ruler:** Elizabeth II **Obv:**
Bust right **Rev:** Toronto Maple Leafs, multicolor logo in circle

Date	Mintage	MS-63	Proof
2008		25.00	—

KM# 726 DOLLAR
7.0000 g., Nickel-Bronze, 26.5 mm. **Ruler:** Elizabeth II **Obv:**
Bust left **Rev:** Vancouver Canucks, logo in center

Date	Mintage	MS-63	Proof
2008	1,302	25.00	—

KM# 767 DOLLAR
25.1800 g., 0.9250 Silver 0.7488 oz. ASW, 36.07 mm. **Ruler:**
Elizabeth II **Rev:** Poppy at center of large maple leaf

Date	Mintage	MS-63	Proof
2008 Proof	—	—	50.00

KM# 781 DOLLAR
25.1800 g., 0.9250 Silver partially gilt 0.7488 oz. ASW,
36.07 mm. **Ruler:** Elizabeth II **Subject:** Ottawa Mint Centennial
1908-2008 **Rev:** Maple leaf transforming into a common loon, gilt
rim and 100 **Rev. Designer:** Jason Bowman

Date	Mintage	MS-63	Proof
2008 Proof	15,000	—	65.00

KM# 784 DOLLAR
7.0000 g., Nickel-Bronze, 26.5 mm. **Ruler:** Elizabeth II **Rev:**
Common elder

Date	Mintage	MS-63	Proof
2008 Specimen	21,227	—	50.00

KM# 785 DOLLAR
25.1800 g., 0.9250 Silver 0.7488 oz. ASW, 36.07 mm. **Ruler:**
Elizabeth II **Subject:** Founding of Quebec 400th Anniversary
Rev: Samuel de Champlain, ship and town view **Rev. Designer:**
Susanne Duranceau

Date	Mintage	MS-63	Proof
2008	35,000	25.00	—
2008 Proof	65,000	—	40.00

KM# 785a DOLLAR
25.1800 g., 0.9250 Silver partially gilt. 0.7488 oz. ASW,
36.07 mm. **Ruler:** Elizabeth II **Subject:** Founding of Quebec
400th Anniversary **Rev:** Samuel de Champlain selectively gold
plated, ship, town view **Rev. Designer:** Susanne Duranceau

Date	Mintage	MS-63	Proof
2008 Proof	38,630	—	75.00

KM# 787 DOLLAR
7.0000 g., Nickel-Bronze, 26.5 mm. **Ruler:** Elizabeth II **Subject:**
Lucky Loonie **Rev:** Loon splashing and Olympic logo at right **Rev.
Designer:** Steve Hepurn

Date	Mintage	MS-63	Proof
2008	—	20.00	—

KM# 787a DOLLAR
9.3100 g., 0.9250 Silver 0.2769 oz. ASW, 26.5 mm. **Ruler:** Elizabeth II **Rev:** Loon splashing with Olympic logo and maple leaf in color above **Rev. Designer:** Steve Hepurn

Date	Mintage	MS-63	Proof
2008 Proof	52,987	—	25.00

KM# 790 DOLLAR
6.5000 g., Nickel, 26.5 mm. **Ruler:** Elizabeth II **Rev:** Calgary Flames

Date	Mintage	MS-63	Proof
2008		25.00	—

KM# 791 DOLLAR
6.5000 g., Nickel, 26.5 mm. **Ruler:** Elizabeth II **Rev:** Edmonton Oilers

Date	Mintage	MS-63	Proof
2008	—	25.00	—

KM# 792 DOLLAR
6.5000 g., Nickel, 26.5 mm. **Ruler:** Elizabeth II **Rev:** Montreal Canadiens

Date	Mintage	MS-63	Proof
2008	—	25.00	—

KM# 793 DOLLAR
6.5000 g., Nickel, 26.5 mm. **Ruler:** Elizabeth II **Rev:** Ottawa Senators

Date	Mintage	MS-63	Proof
2008		25.00	—

KM# 794 DOLLAR
6.5000 g., Nickel, 26.5 mm. **Ruler:** Elizabeth II **Rev:** Toronto Maple Leafs

Date	Mintage	MS-63	Proof
2008	—	25.00	—

KM# 795 DOLLAR
6.5000 g., Nickel, 26.5 mm. **Ruler:** Elizabeth II **Rev:** Vancouver Canucks

Date	Mintage	MS-63	Proof
2008	—	25.00	—

KM# 851 DOLLAR
33.6500 g., Nickel, 26.5 mm. **Ruler:** Elizabeth II **Rev:** Calgary Flames Road Jersey

Date	Mintage	MS-63	Proof
2009	382	25.00	—

KM# 852 DOLLAR
33.6500 g., 0.9990 Nickel 1.0807 oz., 26.5 mm. **Ruler:** Elizabeth II **Rev:** Edmonton Oilers Road Jersey

Date	Mintage	MS-63	Proof
2009	472	25.00	—

KM# 853 DOLLAR
33.6500 g., Nickel, 26.5 mm. **Ruler:** Elizabeth II **Rev:** Montreal Canadiens Road Jersey

Date	Mintage	MS-63	Proof
2009	4,857	25.00	—

KM# 854 DOLLAR
33.6500 g., Nickel, 26.5 mm. **Ruler:** Elizabeth II **Rev:** Ottawa Senators Road Jersey

Date	Mintage	MS-63	Proof
2009	387	25.00	—

KM# 855 DOLLAR
33.6500 g., Nickel, 26.5 mm. **Ruler:** Elizabeth II **Rev:** Toronto Maple Leafs Road Jersey

Date	Mintage	MS-63	Proof
2009	1,328	25.00	—

KM# 856 DOLLAR
33.6500 g., Nickel, 26.5 mm. **Ruler:** Elizabeth II **Rev:** Vancouver Canucks Road Jersey

Date	Mintage	MS-63	Proof
2009	794	25.00	—

KM# 864 DOLLAR
7.0000 g., Aureate Bronze, 26.5 mm. **Ruler:** Elizabeth II **Subject:** Montreal Canadiens, 100th Anniversary **Rev:** Montreal Canadiens logo and large 100 **Shape:** 11-sided

Date	Mintage	MS-63	Proof
2009	—	25.00	—

KM# 865 DOLLAR
25.1700 g., 0.9250 Silver 0.7485 oz. ASW, 36.07 mm. **Ruler:** Elizabeth II **Subject:** Montreal Canadiens 100th Anniversary **Obv:** Bust right **Obv. Designer:** Susanna Blunt **Rev:** Montreal Canadiens logo partially gilt

Date	Mintage	MS-63	Proof
2009 Proof in black case	15,000	—	75.00
2009 Proof in acrillic stand	5,000		150

KM# 889 DOLLAR
25.1800 g., 0.9250 Silver 0.7488 oz. ASW, 36.07 mm. **Ruler:** Elizabeth II **Subject:** 100th Anniversary of flight in Canada **Obv:** Bust right **Obv. Legend:** Elizabeth II DG Regina **Obv. Designer:** Susanna Blunt **Rev:** Silhouette with arms spread, 3 planes, plane cutout **Rev. Legend:** Canada Dollar 1909-2009 **Rev. Designer:** Jason Bouwman

Date	Mintage	MS-63	Proof
2009	13,074	35.00	—
2009 Proof	52,549	—	55.00

KM# 889a DOLLAR
25.1800 g., 0.9250 Silver partially gilt. 0.7488 oz. ASW, 36.07 mm. **Ruler:** Elizabeth II **Obv:** Bust right **Rev:** Silouette with arms spread, 3 planes, plane shadow partially gilt

Date	Mintage	MS-63	Proof
2009(ml) Proof	27,549	—	50.00

KM# 914 DOLLAR
7.0000 g., Aureate-Bronze Plated Nickel, 26.5 mm. **Ruler:** Elizabeth II **Obv:** Bust right **Obv. Designer:** Susanna Blunt **Rev:** Blue heron in flight

Date	Mintage	MS-63	Proof
2009 Specimen	21,677	50.00	—

KM# 883 DOLLAR
7.0000 g., Aureate-Bronze Plated Nickel, 26.5 mm. **Ruler:** Elizabeth II **Subject:** Lucky Loonie **Obv:** Bust right **Obv. Legend:** Elizabeth II DG Regina **Rev:** Canadian Olympic logo **Rev. Legend:** Canada Dollar

Date	Mintage	MS-63	Proof
2010	12,000	20.00	—

KM# 883a DOLLAR
9.3100 g., 0.9250 Silver 0.2769 oz. ASW, 26.5 mm. **Ruler:** Elizabeth II **Subject:** Lucky Loonie **Obv:** Bust right **Obv. Legend:** Elizabeth II DG Regina **Rev:** Canadian Olympic logo in color **Rev. Legend:** Vancouver 2010 Canada Dollar **Shape:** 11-sided

Date	Mintage	MS-63	Proof
2010 Proof	40,000	—	55.00

KM# 1046 DOLLAR
Aureate Bronze, 26.5 mm. **Ruler:** Elizabeth II **Subject:** Roughriders **Rev:** S logo **Shape:** 11-sided

Date	Mintage	MS-63	Proof
2010(ml)		7.50	

KM# 975 DOLLAR
0.9250 Silver, 36 mm. **Ruler:** Elizabeth II **Rev:** Sun mask **Rev. Designer:** Xwa lack Tun

Date	Mintage	MS-63	Proof
2010 Proof	1,278	—	200

KM# 995 DOLLAR
25.1700 g., 0.9250 Silver 0.7485 oz. ASW, 36.07 mm. **Ruler:**
Elizabeth II **Rev:** HMCS Sackville **Rev. Designer:** Yves Berube

Date	Mintage	MS-63	Proof
2010 Proof	Est. 50,000	—	50.00

KM# 995a DOLLAR
25.1700 g., 0.9250 Silver partially gilt 0.7485 oz. ASW,
36.07 mm. **Ruler:** Elizabeth II **Subject:** Navy Centennial **Rev:**
HMCS Sackville, sea waves in gilt

Date	Mintage	MS-63	Proof
2010	—	—	110

KM# 996 DOLLAR
7.0000 g., Aureate Bronze, 26.5 mm. **Ruler:** Elizabeth II **Rev:**
Northern Harrier Hawk

Date	Mintage	MS-63	Proof
2010	35,000	30.00	—
2010(ml)	—	—	50.00

KM# 1017 DOLLAR
7.0000 g., Aureate Bronze, 26.5 mm. **Ruler:** Elizabeth II **Rev:**
Male and female sailors saluting, HMCS Halifax and anchor
above

Date	Mintage	MS-63	Proof
2010	—	5.00	—

KM# 1017a DOLLAR
7.0000 g., Aureate Bronze gilt, 26.5 mm. **Ruler:** Elizabeth II
Rev: Male and female sailors saluting, HMCS Halifax in
background and anchor above

Date	Mintage	MS-63	Proof
2010 Proof	—	—	50.00

KM# 1027 DOLLAR
25.1800 g., 0.9250 Silver 0.7488 oz. ASW, 36.07 mm. **Ruler:**
Elizabeth II **Obv:** George V bust left **Rev:** Voyaguers, dual dates
below

Date	Mintage	MS-63	Proof
2010 Proof	7,500	—	70.00

KM# 1050 DOLLAR
25.1800 g., 0.9250 Silver 0.7488 oz. ASW, 36.07 mm. **Ruler:**
Elizabeth II **Rev:** Red poppy in large field of poppies **Edge:**
Reeded

Date	Mintage	MS-63	Proof
2010 Proof	5,000	—	55.00

KM# 1086 DOLLAR
7.0000 g., Aureate-Bronze Plated Nickel, 26.5 mm. **Ruler:**
Elizabeth II **Rev:** Great Grey Owl **Rev. Designer:** Arnold Nagy

Date	Mintage	MS-63	Proof
2011	35,000	13.50	—

KM# 1087 DOLLAR
25.1800 g., 0.9250 Silver 0.7488 oz. ASW, 36.07 mm. **Ruler:**
Elizabeth II **Subject:** Parks Canada, 100th Anniversary **Rev:**
Female head looking downward into hands holding nature scene
Rev. Designer: Luc Normandin

Date	Mintage	MS-63	Proof
2011	25,000	50.00	—
2011 Proof	—	—	60.00

KM# 1087a DOLLAR
25.1800 g., 0.9250 Silver partially gilt 0.7488 oz. ASW,
36.07 mm. **Ruler:** Elizabeth II **Subject:** Parks Canada, 100th
Anniversary **Rev:** Female head looking downward to hands
holding nature scene, partially gilt **Rev. Designer:** Luc
Normandin

Date	Mintage	MS-63	Proof
2011 Proof	45,000	—	75.00

KM# 1112 DOLLAR
25.1700 g., 0.9250 Silver 0.7485 oz. ASW, 36.07 mm. **Ruler:**
Elizabeth II **Obv:** Crowned bust left of George V **Obv. Designer:**
E. B. MacKennal **Rev:** Value and date within maple wreath **Rev.**
Designer: W.H.J. Blakemore

Date	Mintage	MS-63	Proof
2011 Proof	Est. 15,000	—	115

KM# 1166 DOLLAR
7.0000 g., Aureate-Bronze Plated Nickel, 26.5 mm. **Ruler:**
Elizabeth II **Subject:** Canada Parks **Obv:** Bust right **Rev:** Stylized
animals

Date	Mintage	MS-63	Proof
2011	—	—	5.00

KM# 1216 DOLLAR
9.3100 g., 0.9250 Silver 0.2769 oz. ASW, 26.5 mm. **Ruler:**
Elizabeth II **Obv:** Bust right, SP/PA below **Rev:** Loon, 1987-2012
below

Date	Mintage	MS-63	Proof
2012 Specimen	—	—	55.00

KM# 1222 DOLLAR
7.0000 g., Aureate-Bronze Plated Nickel, 26.5 mm. **Ruler:**
Elizabeth II **Obv:** Bust right **Rev:** Loon and two young, 1987-2012
dates

Date	Mintage	MS-63	Proof
2012 Specimen	—	—	40.00

KM# 1225 DOLLAR
25.1800 g., 0.9250 Silver 0.7488 oz. ASW, 36.07 mm. **Ruler:**
Elizabeth II **Subject:** War of 1812, 200th Anniversary **Obv:** Bust
right **Rev:** Two soldiers and guide on patrol

Date	Mintage	MS-63	Proof
2012	—	50.00	—
2012 Proof	—	—	60.00

KM# 1225a DOLLAR
25.1800 g., 0.9250 Silver partially gilt 0.7488 oz. ASW,
36.07 mm. **Ruler:** Elizabeth II **Subject:** War of 1812, 200th
Anniversary **Obv:** Bust right, gilt rim **Rev:** Two solders and guide,
partially gilt

Date	Mintage	MS-63	Proof
2012 Proof	—	—	65.00

KM# 652 DOLLAR (Louis)
1.5000 g., 0.9990 Gold 0.0482 oz. AGW, 14.1 mm. **Ruler:**
Elizabeth II **Subject:** Gold Louis **Obv:** Bust right **Obv. Designer:**
Susanna Blunt **Rev:** Crowned double L monogram within wreath

Date	Mintage	MS-63	Proof
2006 Proof	5,648	—	110

KM# 756 DOLLAR (Louis)
1.5550 g., 0.9990 Gold 0.0499 oz. AGW, 14.1 mm. **Ruler:**
Elizabeth II **Obv:** Bust right **Obv. Designer:** Susanna Blunt **Rev:**
Crown above two oval shields

Date	Mintage	MS-63	Proof
2007 Proof	4,023	—	110

KM# 834 DOLLAR (Louis)
1.5550 g., 0.9990 Gold 0.0499 oz. AGW, 14.1 mm. **Ruler:** Elizabeth II **Obv:** Bust right **Obv. Designer:** Susanna Blunt **Rev:** Crowned double L monogram, three lis around

Date	Mintage	MS-63	Proof
2008 Proof	3,793	—	110

KM# 270c 2 DOLLARS
8.8300 g., 0.9250 Silver gold plated center 0.2626 oz. ASW, 28 mm. **Ruler:** Elizabeth II **Obv:** Crowned head right within circle, date below **Rev:** Polar bear right within circle, denomination below **Note:** 1.9mm thick.

Date	Mintage	MS-63	Proof
2001 Proof	—	—	12.00

KM# 270 2 DOLLARS
7.3000 g., Bi-Metallic Aluminum-Bronze center in Nickel ring, 28 mm. **Ruler:** Elizabeth II **Obv:** Crowned head right within circle, date below **Obv. Designer:** Dora dePedery-Hunt **Rev:** Polar bear right within circle, denomination below **Rev. Designer:** Brent Townsend **Edge:** Segmented reeding

Date	Mintage	MS-63	Proof
2001	27,008,000	5.00	—
2001 Proof	74,944	—	12.50
2002	11,910,000	5.00	—
2002 Proof	65,315	—	12.50
2003	7,123,697	5.00	—
2003 Proof	62,007	—	12.50

KM# 449 2 DOLLARS
7.3000 g., Bi-Metallic Aluminum-Bronze center in Nickel ring, 28 mm. **Ruler:** Elizabeth II **Subject:** Elizabeth II Golden Jubilee **Obv:** Crowned head right, jubilee commemorative dates 1952-2002 **Edge:** Segmented reeding

Date	Mintage	MS-63	Proof
2002	27,020,000	4.00	—

KM# 449a 2 DOLLARS
8.8300 g., 0.9250 Silver gold plated center 0.2626 oz. ASW **Ruler:** Elizabeth II **Subject:** Elizabeth II Golden Jubilee **Obv:** Crowned head right, jubilee commemorative dates 1952-2002

Date	Mintage	MS-63	Proof
2002 Proof	100,000	—	14.00

KM# 496 2 DOLLARS
7.3000 g., Bi-Metallic Aluminum-Bronze center in Nickel ring, 28 mm. **Ruler:** Elizabeth II **Obv:** Head right **Obv. Designer:** Susanna Blunt **Rev:** Polar bear advancing right **Rev. Designer:** Brent Townsend **Edge:** Segmented reeding

Date	Mintage	MS-63	Proof
2003	11,244,000	5.00	—
2003W	71,142	25.00	—
2004	12,908,000	5.00	—
2004 Proof	—	—	12.50
2005	38,317,000	5.00	—
2005 Proof	—	—	12.50
2006(ml)	35,319,000	5.00	—
2006(ml) Proof	—	—	12.50
2007(ml)	38,957,000	5.00	—
2007(ml) Proof	—	—	12.50
2008(ml)	18,400,000	5.00	—
2008(ml) Proof	—	—	12.50
2009(ml)	38,430,000	5.00	—

Date	Mintage	MS-63	Proof
2009(ml) Proof	—	—	12.50
2010(ml)	—	5.00	—
2010(ml) Proof	—	—	12.50
2011(ml)	—	5.00	—
2011(ml) Proof	—	—	12.50
2012(ml)	—	5.00	—
2012(ml) Proof	—	—	12.50

KM# 270d 2 DOLLARS
8.8300 g., 0.9250 Silver gold plated center 0.2626 oz. ASW **Ruler:** Elizabeth II **Subject:** 100th Anniversary of the Cobalt Silver Strike **Obv:** Crowned head right, within circle, date below **Rev:** Polar bear right, within circle, denomination below

Date	Mintage	MS-63	Proof
2003 Proof	100,000	—	25.00

KM# 496a 2 DOLLARS
10.8414 g., 0.9250 Bi-Metallic Gold plated Silver center in Silver ring 0.3224 oz., 28 mm. **Ruler:** Elizabeth II **Obv:** Head right **Obv. Designer:** Susanna Blunt **Rev:** Polar Bear **Edge:** Segmented reeding

Date	Mintage	MS-63	Proof
2004 Proof	—	—	25.00

KM# 835 2 DOLLARS
8.8000 g., 0.9250 Silver 0.2617 oz. ASW, 27.95 mm. **Ruler:** Elizabeth II **Rev:** Proud Polar Bear advancing right

Date	Mintage	MS-63	Proof
2004 Proof	12,607	—	40.00

KM# 837 2 DOLLARS
7.3000 g., Bi-Metallic Aluminum-Bronze center in Nickel ring **Ruler:** Elizabeth II **Obv:** Bust left, date at top **Rev:** Polar Bear advancing right

Date	Mintage	MS-63	Proof
2006(ml)	—	7.50	—
2007(ml)	38,957,000	7.50	—

KM# 631 2 DOLLARS
7.3000 g., Bi-Metallic Aluminum-Bronze center in Nickel ring, 28 mm. **Ruler:** Elizabeth II **Subject:** 10th Anniversary of $2 coin **Obv:** Crowned head right **Edge:** Segmented reeding

Date	Mintage	MS-63	Proof
2006(ml)	5,005,000	25.00	—
2006(ml) Proof	—	—	40.00

KM# 631a 2 DOLLARS
Bi-Metallic 22 Kt Gold ring around 4.1 Kt. Gold core **Ruler:** Elizabeth II **Subject:** 10th Anniversary of $2 coin **Obv:** Crowned head right **Rev:** Polar bear

Date	Mintage	MS-63	Proof
2006 Proof	2,068	—	400

KM# 836 2 DOLLARS
7.3000 g., Bi-Metallic Aluminum-Bronze center in Nickel ring, 28 mm. **Ruler:** Elizabeth II **Subject:** $2 coin, 10th Anniversary **Rev:** "Churchill" Polar Bear, northern lights **Edge:** Segmented reeding

Date	Mintage	MS-63	Proof
2006(ml)	31,636	7.50	—

KM# 796 2 DOLLARS
8.8300 g., 0.9250 Silver 0.2626 oz. ASW, 28.07 mm. **Ruler:** Elizabeth II **Rev:** Bear, gold plated center

Date	Mintage	MS-63	Proof
2008	—	25.00	—

KM# 1040 2 DOLLARS
7.3000 g., Bi-Metallic Aluminum-Bronze center in Nickel ring, 28 mm. **Ruler:** Elizabeth II **Subject:** Quebec 400th Anniversary **Rev:** Lis and small sailing ship **Edge:** Segmented reeding

Date	Mintage	MS-63	Proof
2008	—	7.50	—

KM# 1020 2 DOLLARS
7.3000 g., Bi-Metallic Aluminum-Bronze center in Nickel ring, 28 mm. **Ruler:** Elizabeth II **Rev:** Two lynx cubs **Rev. Designer:** Christie Paquet **Edge:** Segmented reeding

Date	Mintage	MS-63	Proof
2010 Specimen	15,000	—	40.00

KM# 1088 2 DOLLARS
7.3000 g., Bi-Metallic Aluminum-Bronze center in Nickel ring, 28 mm. **Ruler:** Elizabeth II **Rev:** Elk Calf **Rev. Designer:** Christine Paquet **Edge:** Segmented reeding

Date	Mintage	MS-63	Proof
2011	—	7.50	—

KM# 1167 2 DOLLARS
7.3000 g., Bi-Metallic Aluminum-Bronze center in Nickel ring, 28 mm. **Ruler:** Elizabeth II **Subject:** Canada Parks **Obv:** Bust right **Rev:** Stylized trees

Date	Mintage	MS-63	Proof
2011	—	7.50	—

KM# 657 3 DOLLARS
11.7200 g., 0.9250 Silver gilt 0.3485 oz. ASW, 27x27 mm. **Ruler:** Elizabeth II **Rev:** Beaver within wreath **Shape:** Square

Date	Mintage	MS-63	Proof
2006 Proof	19,963	—	225

KM# 1051 3 DOLLARS
11.6000 g., 0.9250 Silver gilt 0.3450 oz. ASW, 27x27 mm. **Ruler:** Elizabeth II **Subject:** Wildlife conservation **Rev:** Stylized polar bear and northern lights **Shape:** square

Date	Mintage	MS-63	Proof
2010 Specimen	15,000	55.00	—

KM# 978 3 DOLLARS
7.9600 g., Silver Partially Gilt, 27 mm. **Ruler:** Elizabeth II **Rev:** Return of the Tyee (giant salmon)

Date	Mintage	MS-63	Proof
2010 Proof	15,000	—	50.00

KM# 1011   3 DOLLARS
11.6000 g., 0.9250 Silver gilt 0.3450 oz. ASW, 27x27 mm.
Ruler: Elizabeth II **Rev:** Barn Owl **Rev. Designer:** Jason
Bouwman **Shape:** Square

Date	Mintage	MS-63	Proof
2010 Proof	15,000	—	65.00

KM# 1089   3 DOLLARS
11.6000 g., 0.9250 Silver gilt 0.3450 oz. ASW, 27x27 mm.
Ruler: Elizabeth II **Rev:** Orca Whale **Rev. Designer:** Jason
Bouwman **Shape:** Square

Date	Mintage	MS-63	Proof
2011 Proof	15,000	—	65.00

KM# 1090   3 DOLLARS
7.9600 g., 0.9999 Silver with red and yellow partial gilding
0.2557 oz. ASW, 27 mm.   **Ruler:** Elizabeth II **Obv:** Bust right
Rev: Eskimo mother kneeling, child on back, partially gilt **Rev.
Designer:** Andrew Oappik

Date	Mintage	MS-63	Proof
2011 Proof	10,000	—	65.00

KM# 1117   3 DOLLARS
7.9600 g., 0.9999 Silver 0.2559 oz. ASW, 27 mm.   **Ruler:**
Elizabeth II **Subject:** January birthstone, Garnet **Obv:** Bust left
Rev: Birthstone at cener of artistic sunburst **Edge:** Reeded

Date	Mintage	MS-63	Proof
2011 Proof	—	—	65.00

KM# 1118   3 DOLLARS
7.9600 g., 0.9999 Silver 0.2559 oz. ASW, 27 mm.   **Ruler:**
Elizabeth II **Subject:** February birthstone, Amythest **Obv:** Bust
right **Rev:** Birthstone at cener of artistic sunburst **Edge:** Reeded

Date	Mintage	MS-63	Proof
2011 Proof	—	—	65.00

KM# 1119   3 DOLLARS
7.9600 g., 0.9999 Silver 0.2559 oz. ASW, 27 mm.   **Ruler:**
Elizabeth II **Subject:** March birthstone, Aquamarine **Obv:** Bust
right **Rev:** Birthstone at cener of artistic sunburst **Edge:** Reeded

Date	Mintage	MS-63	Proof
2011 Proof	—	—	65.00

KM# 1120   3 DOLLARS
7.9600 g., 0.9999 Silver 0.2559 oz. ASW, 27 mm.   **Ruler:**
Elizabeth II **Subject:** April birthstone, diamond **Obv:** Bust right
Rev: Birthstone at cener of artistic sunburst **Edge:** Reeded

Date	Mintage	MS-63	Proof
2011 Proof	—	—	65.00

KM# 1121   3 DOLLARS
7.9600 g., 0.9999 Silver 0.2559 oz. ASW, 27 mm.   **Ruler:**
Elizabeth II **Subject:** May birthstone **Obv:** Bust right **Rev:**
Birthstone at cener of artistic sunburst **Edge:** Reeded

Date	Mintage	MS-63	Proof
2011 Proof	—	—	65.00

KM# 1122   3 DOLLARS
7.9600 g., 0.9999 Silver 0.2559 oz. ASW, 27 mm.   **Ruler:**
Elizabeth II **Subject:** June birthstone, Alexandrite **Obv:** Bust right
Rev: Birthstone at cener of artistic sunburst

Date	Mintage	MS-63	Proof
2011 Proof	—		65.00

KM# 1123   3 DOLLARS
7.9600 g., 0.9999 Silver 0.2559 oz. ASW, 27 mm.   **Ruler:**
Elizabeth II **Subject:** July birthstone, Ruby **Obv:** Bust right **Rev:**
Birthstone at cener of artistic sunburst

Date	Mintage	MS-63	Proof
2011 Proof	—	—	65.00

KM# 1124   3 DOLLARS
7.9600 g., 0.9999 Silver 0.2559 oz. ASW, 27 mm.   **Ruler:**
Elizabeth II **Subject:** August birthstone, Priedot **Obv:** Bust right
Rev: Birthstone at cener of artistic sunburst

Date	Mintage	MS-63	Proof
2011 Proof	—	—	65.00

KM# 1125   3 DOLLARS
7.9600 g., 0.9999 Silver 0.2559 oz. ASW, 27 mm.   **Ruler:**
Elizabeth II **Subject:** September birhtstone **Obv:** Bust right **Rev:**
Birthstone at cener of artistic sunburst **Edge:** Reeded

Date	Mintage	MS-63	Proof
2011 Proof	—	—	65.00

KM# 1126   3 DOLLARS
7.9600 g., 0.9999 Silver 0.2559 oz. ASW, 27 mm.   **Ruler:**
Elizabeth II **Subject:** October birthstone **Obv:** Bust right **Rev:**
Birthstone at cener of artistic sunburst

Date	Mintage	MS-63	Proof
2011 Proof	—	—	65.00

KM# 1127   3 DOLLARS
7.9600 g., 0.9999 Silver 0.2559 oz. ASW, 27 mm.   **Ruler:**
Elizabeth II **Subject:** November birthstone **Obv:** Bust right **Rev:**
Birthstone at cener of artistic sunburst

Date	Mintage	MS-63	Proof
2011 Proof	—	—	65.00

KM# 1128   3 DOLLARS
7.9600 g., 0.9999 Silver 0.2559 oz. ASW, 27 mm.   **Ruler:**
Elizabeth II **Subject:** December birhtstone **Obv:** Bust right **Rev:**
Birthstone at cener of artistic sunburst

Date	Mintage	MS-63	Proof
2011 Proof	—	—	65.00

KM# 1151   3 DOLLARS
11.8000 g., 0.9250 Silver gold plated 0.3509 oz. ASW,
27x27 mm. **Ruler:** Elizabeth II **Obv:** Bust right **Rev:** Black footed
ferret

Date	Mintage	MS-63	Proof
2011 Proof	Est. 15,000	—	65.00

KM# 728   4 DOLLARS
15.8700 g., 0.9250 Silver 0.4719 oz. ASW, 34 mm.   **Ruler:**
Elizabeth II **Subject:** Dinosaur fossil **Obv:** Bust right **Rev:**
Parasaurolophus, selective enameling

Date	Mintage	MS-63	Proof
2007 Proof	14,946	—	125

KM# 797   4 DOLLARS
15.8700 g., 0.9990 Silver 0.5097 oz. ASW, 34 mm.   **Ruler:**
Elizabeth II **Subject:** Dinosaur fossil **Obv:** Bust right **Rev:**
Triceratops, enameled **Rev. Designer:** Kerri Burnett

Date	Mintage	MS-63	Proof
2008 Proof	13,046	—	75.00

KM# 890   4 DOLLARS
15.8700 g., 0.9990 Silver 0.5097 oz. ASW, 34 mm.   **Ruler:**
Elizabeth II **Subject:** Tyrannosaurus Rex **Obv:** Bust right **Obv.
Legend:** Elizabeth II DG Regina **Obv. Designer:** Susanna Blunt
Rev: T-Rex skeleton in selective aging **Rev. Legend:** Canada 4
Dollars **Rev. Designer:** Kerri Burnette

Date	Mintage	MS-63	Proof
2009 Proof	13,572	—	55.00

KM# 942   4 DOLLARS
15.8700 g., Silver, 34 mm. **Ruler:** Elizabeth II **Rev:** Kids hanging
stocking on fireplace, Christmas tree on right

Date	Mintage	MS-63	Proof
2009 Proof	6,011	—	45.00

KM# 1014   4 DOLLARS
15.8700 g., 0.9990 Silver selectively plated 0.5097 oz. ASW,
34 mm.   **Ruler:** Elizabeth II **Rev:** Euoplocephalus **Rev.
Designer:** Kerri Burnett

Date	Mintage	MS-63	Proof
2010 Proof	Est. 13,000	—	55.00

KM# 1022   4 DOLLARS
Silver selective plating **Ruler:** Elizabeth II **Rev:** Dromaeosaurus

Date	Mintage	MS-63	Proof
2010 Proof	8,982	—	55.00

KM# 1129   4 DOLLARS
15.8700 g., 0.9999 Silver 0.5102 oz. ASW, 34 mm.   **Ruler:**
Elizabeth II **Obv:** Bust right **Rev:** Baby's footprint **Edge:** Reeded

Date	Mintage	MS-63	Proof
2011 Proof	Est. 10,000	—	60.00

KM# 435   5 DOLLARS
16.8600 g., 0.9250 Silver 0.5014 oz. ASW, 28.4 mm.   **Ruler:**
Elizabeth II **Subject:** Guglielmo Marconi **Obv:** Crowned head

right **Rev:** Gold-plated cameo portrait of Marconi **Rev. Designer:** Cosme Saffioti **Edge:** Reeded **Note:** Only issued in two coin set with British 2 pounds KM#1014a.

Date	Mintage	MS-63	Proof
2001 Proof	15,011	—	30.00

KM# 519   5 DOLLARS
8.3600 g., 0.9000 Gold 0.2419 oz. AGW, 21.6 mm. **Ruler:** Elizabeth II **Obv:** Crowned head right **Rev:** National arms **Edge:** Reeded

Date	Mintage	MS-63	Proof
1912-2002 Proof	2,002		450

KM# 603   5 DOLLARS
31.1050 g., 0.9999 Silver 0.9999 oz. ASW **Ruler:** Elizabeth II **Obv:** Head right **Rev:** Loon splashing in the water, hologram

Date	Mintage	MS-63	Proof
2002 Satin Proof	30,000	—	45.00

KM# 518   5 DOLLARS
31.1200 g., 0.9999 Silver 1.0004 oz. ASW, 38 mm. **Ruler:** Elizabeth II **Subject:** F.I.F.A. World Cup Soccer , Germany 2006 **Obv:** Crowned head right, denomination **Rev:** Goalie on knees **Edge:** Reeded

Date	Mintage	MS-63	Proof
2003 Proof	21,542	—	40.00

KM# 514   5 DOLLARS
31.1200 g., 0.9999 Silver 1.0004 oz. ASW, 38 mm. **Ruler:** Elizabeth II **Obv:** Crowned head right **Rev:** Moose **Edge:** Reeded

Date	Mintage	MS-63	Proof
2004 Proof	12,822	—	175

KM# 527   5 DOLLARS
31.1200 g., 0.9999 Silver 1.0004 oz. ASW **Ruler:** Elizabeth II **Subject:** Golf, Championship of Canada, Centennial **Obv:** Head right

Date	Mintage	MS-63	Proof
2004 Proof	18,750	—	30.00

KM# 554   5 DOLLARS
31.1200 g., 0.9999 Silver 1.0004 oz. ASW **Ruler:** Elizabeth II **Subject:** Alberta **Obv. Designer:** Head right **Rev. Designer:** Michelle Grant

Date	Mintage	MS-63	Proof
2005 Proof	20,000		35.00

KM# 555   5 DOLLARS
31.1200 g., 0.9999 Silver 1.0004 oz. ASW **Ruler:** Elizabeth II **Subject:** Saskatchewan **Obv:** Head right **Obv. Designer:** Susanna Blunt **Rev. Designer:** Paulett Sapergia

Date	Mintage	MS-63	Proof
2005 Proof	20,000		35.00

KM# 556.1   5 DOLLARS
31.1200 g., 0.9990 Silver 0.9995 oz. ASW, 38.02 mm. **Ruler:** Elizabeth II **Subject:** 60th Anniversay Victory WWII - Veterans **Obv:** Bust right **Rev:** Large V and heads of sailor, soldier and aviator on large maple leaf **Edge:** Reeded

Date	Mintage	MS-63	Proof
2005	25,000	32.00	

KM# 556.2   5 DOLLARS
31.1200 g., 0.9999 Silver 1.0004 oz. ASW, 38.02 mm. **Ruler:** Elizabeth II **Subject:** 60th Anniversary Victory WW II - Veterans **Obv:** Bust right **Rev:** Large V and heads of sailor, soldier and aviator on maple leaf with small maple leaf added at left and right **Edge:** Reeded

Date	Mintage	MS-63	Proof
2005	10,000	125	—

KM# 557   5 DOLLARS
31.1200 g., 0.9999 Silver 1.0004 oz. ASW, 36 mm. **Ruler:** Elizabeth II **Subject:** Walrus and calf **Obv:** Head right **Obv. Designer:** Susanna Blunt **Rev:** Two walruses and calf **Rev. Designer:** Pierre Leduc

Date	Mintage	MS-63	Proof
2005 Proof	5,519	—	40.00

KM# 558   5 DOLLARS
31.1200 g., 0.9999 Silver 1.0004 oz. ASW, 36 mm. **Ruler:** Elizabeth II **Subject:** White tailed deer **Obv:** Head right **Obv. Designer:** Susanna Blunt **Rev:** Two deer standing **Rev. Designer:** Xerxes Irani

Date	Mintage	MS-63	Proof
2005 Proof	6,439	—	40.00

KM# 585   5 DOLLARS
31.1200 g., 0.9999 Silver 1.0004 oz. ASW, 36 mm. **Ruler:** Elizabeth II **Obv:** Head right **Obv. Designer:** Susanna Blunt **Rev:** Peregrine Falcon feeding young ones **Rev. Designer:** Dwayne Harty

Date	Mintage	MS-63	Proof
2006 Proof	7,226	—	45.00

KM# 586   5 DOLLARS
31.1200 g., 0.9999 Silver 1.0004 oz. ASW, 36 mm. **Ruler:** Elizabeth II **Subject:** Sable Island horses **Obv:** Head right **Obv. Designer:** Susanna Blunt **Rev:** Horse and foal standing **Rev. Designer:** Christie Paquet

Date	Mintage	MS-63	Proof
2006 Proof	10,108	—	45.00

KM# 658   5 DOLLARS
31.1200 g., 0.9999 Silver 1.0004 oz. ASW, 36.07 mm. **Ruler:** Elizabeth II **Subject:** Breast Cancer Awareness **Rev:** Colorized pink ribbon

Date	Mintage	MS-63	Proof
2006 Proof	11,048	—	50.00

KM# 659   5 DOLLARS
31.1200 g., 0.9999 Silver 1.0004 oz. ASW **Ruler:** Elizabeth II **Subject:** C.A.F. Snowbirds Acrobatic Jet Flying Team **Rev:** Image of fighter jets and piolt

Date	Mintage	MS-63	Proof
2006 Proof	10,034	—	50.00

KM# 1036   5 DOLLARS
31.1200 g., 0.9990 Silver 0.9995 oz. ASW **Ruler:** Elizabeth II **Subject:** 80th Anniversary **Rev:** Two deer standing, one eating branch

Date	Mintage	MS-63	Proof
2009 Proof	27,872	—	70.00

KM# 1130   5 DOLLARS
8.5000 g., Bi-Metallic Niobium center in .925 Silver ring, 28 mm. **Ruler:** Elizabeth II **Subject:** Summer - Buck Moon **Obv:** Bust right **Rev:** Buck against summer moon

Date	Mintage	MS-63	Proof
2011 Proof	7,500	—	125

KM# 1131   5 DOLLARS
8.5000 g., Bi-Metallic Niobium center in .925 Silver ring, 28 mm. **Ruler:** Elizabeth II **Subject:** Fall Moon **Obv:** Bust right **Rev:** Native American hunter seated tracking prey before Harvest Moon

Date	Mintage	MS-63	Proof
2011 Proof	7,500	—	125

KM# 1132   5 DOLLARS
8.5000 g., Bi-Metallic Niobium center in .925 Silver ring, 28 mm.
Ruler: Elizabeth II **Subject:** Winter Moon **Obv:** Bust right **Rev:**
Wolf howling before Winter Moon

Date	Mintage	MS-63	Proof
2011 Proof	7,500	—	125

KM# 1133   5 DOLLARS
8.5000 g., Bi-Metallic Niobium center in .925 Silver ring, 28 mm.
Ruler: Elizabeth II **Subject:** Spring Moon **Obv:** Bust right **Rev:**
Phlox blossoming agains a Spring Moon

Date	Mintage	MS-63	Proof
2011 Proof	7,500	—	125

KM# 1149   5 DOLLARS
3.1300 g., 0.9999 Gold 0.1006 oz. AGW, 16 mm. **Ruler:**
Elizabeth II **Subject:** Norman Bethune **Obv:** Bust right **Rev:** Half-
length figure at right, looking left

Date	Mintage	MS-63	Proof
2011 Proof	Est. 5,000	—	300

KM# 1236   5 DOLLARS
8.3600 g., 0.9000 Gold 0.2419 oz. AGW, 21.6 mm. **Ruler:**
Elizabeth II **Obv:** Bust right **Rev:** Crowned monogram in wreath

Date	Mintage	MS-63	Proof
1952-2012 Proof	—	—	500

KM# 1194   5 DOLLARS
Gold **Ruler:** Elizabeth II **Obv:** Bust right **Rev:** Royal Cypher,
wreath below

Date	Mintage	MS-63	Proof
2012 Proof	—	—	200

KM# 1220   5 DOLLARS
3.1300 g., 0.9999 Gold 0.1006 oz. AGW, 16 mm. **Ruler:**
Elizabeth II **Subject:** Year of the Dragon **Obv:** Bust right **Rev:**
Dragon forpart right

Date	Mintage	MS-63	Proof
2012 Specimen	Est. 38,888	—	225

KM# 515   8 DOLLARS
28.8000 g., 0.9250 Silver 0.8565 oz. ASW, 39 mm. **Ruler:**
Elizabeth II **Obv:** Head right **Obv. Designer:** Susanna Blunt **Rev:**
Grizzly bear walking left **Edge:** Reeded

Date	Mintage	MS-63	Proof
2004 Proof	12,942	—	85.00

KM# 597   8 DOLLARS
32.1500 g., 0.9999 Silver partially gilt 1.0335 oz. ASW **Ruler:**
Elizabeth II **Subject:** Canadian Pacific Railway, 120th
Anniversary **Obv:** Head right **Obv. Designer:** Susanna Blunt
Rev: Railway bridge, center is gilt

Date	Mintage	MS-63	Proof
2005 Proof	9,892	—	65.00

KM# 598   8 DOLLARS
32.1500 g., 0.9999 Silver partially gilt 1.0335 oz. ASW **Ruler:**
Elizabeth II **Subject:** Canadian Pacific Railway, 120th
Anniversary **Obv:** Head right **Rev:** Railway memorial to the
Chinese workers, center gilt

Date	Mintage	MS-63	Proof
2005 Proof	9,892	—	65.00

KM# 730   8 DOLLARS
25.1800 g., 0.9999 Silver 0.8094 oz. ASW, 36.07 mm. **Ruler:**
Elizabeth II **Obv:** Queens's head at top in circle, three Chinese
characters **Rev:** Dragon and other creatures

Date	Mintage	MS-63	Proof
2007 Proof	19,996	—	55.00

KM# 731   8 DOLLARS
0.9990 Silver **Ruler:** Elizabeth II **Rev:** Maple leaf, long life
hologram

Date	Mintage	MS-63	Proof
2007	15,000	—	60.00

KM# 943   8 DOLLARS
25.1800 g., Silver, 36.1 mm. **Ruler:** Elizabeth II **Rev:** Hologram
maple of wisdom at top left, crystal in center, dragons around

Date	Mintage	MS-63	Proof
2009 Proof	7,273	—	90.00

KM# 1012   8 DOLLARS
25.3000 g., 0.9250 Silver 0.7524 oz. ASW, 36.07 mm. **Ruler:**
Elizabeth II **Rev:** Horses around central maple leaf hologram
Rev. Designer: Simon Ng

Date	Mintage	MS-63	Proof
2010 Proof	8,888	—	100

KM# 520   10 DOLLARS
16.7200 g., 0.9000 Gold 0.4838 oz. AGW, 26.92 mm. **Ruler:**
Elizabeth II **Obv:** Crowned head right **Rev:** National arms **Edge:**
Reeded

Date	Mintage	MS-63	Proof
1912-2002 Proof	2,002	—	850

KM# 559   10 DOLLARS
25.1750 g., 0.9999 Silver 0.8093 oz. ASW, 36 mm. **Ruler:**
Elizabeth II **Subject:** Pope John Paul II **Obv:** Head right

Date	Mintage	MS-63	Proof
2005 Proof	24,716	—	45.00

KM# 757   10 DOLLARS
25.1750 g., 0.9999 Silver 0.8093 oz. ASW **Ruler:** Elizabeth II
Subject: Year of the Veteran **Rev:** Profile left of young and old
veteran

Date	Mintage	MS-63	Proof
2005 Proof	6,549	—	225

KM# 661   10 DOLLARS
25.1750 g., 0.9999 Silver 0.8093 oz. ASW **Ruler:** Elizabeth II
Subject: National Historic Sites **Obv:** Head right **Rev:** Fortress
of Louisbourg

Date	Mintage	MS-63	Proof
2006 Proof	5,544	—	40.00

KM# 1010   10 DOLLARS
0.9990 Silver **Ruler:** Elizabeth II **Subject:** 75th Anniversary
Canadian Bank Notes **Rev:** Female seated

Date	Mintage	MS-63	Proof
2010 Proof	7,500	—	80.00

KM# 1096   10 DOLLARS
27.7800 g., 0.9250 Silver 0.8261 oz. ASW, 40 mm. **Ruler:**
Elizabeth II **Obv:** Bust right **Rev:** Blue whale diving in sea

Date	Mintage	MS-63	Proof
2010 Proof	10,000	—	85.00

KM# 1199   10 DOLLARS
15.8700 g., 0.9999 Silver 0.5102 oz. ASW, 34 mm. **Ruler:** Elizabeth II **Subject:** Winter Scene - Skating **Rev:** Three kids skating on pond, colored holly at left

Date	Mintage	MS-63	Proof
2011 Proof	Est. 8,000	—	40.00

KM# 1198   10 DOLLARS
15.8700 g., 0.9990 Silver 0.5097 oz. ASW, 34 mm. **Ruler:** Elizabeth II **Subject:** Highway of Heroes **Obv:** Bust right **Obv. Designer:** Susanna Blunt **Rev:** Citizens on Highway 401 overpass with signs and flags, large maple leaf in background, Memorial Cross medal at top left. **Rev. Designer:** Stan Witten and Major Carl Gauthier **Edge:** Reeded

Date	Mintage	MS-63	Proof
2011	25,000	—	70.00

KM# 1200   10 DOLLARS
15.8700 g., 0.9999 Silver 0.5102 oz. ASW, 34 mm. **Ruler:** Elizabeth II **Subject:** Winter scene - Two houses **Rev:** Two houses in snowy lane, colored holly flanking

Date	Mintage	MS-63	Proof
2011 Proof	Est. 8,000	—	40.00

KM# 1201   10 DOLLARS
15.8700 g., 0.9999 Silver 0.5102 oz. ASW, 34 mm. **Ruler:** Elizabeth II **Obv:** Bust right **Rev. Designer:** Corrine Hunt

Date	Mintage	MS-63	Proof
2011 Proof	Est. 10,000	—	50.00

KM# 1203   10 DOLLARS
15.8700 g., 0.9999 Silver 0.5102 oz. ASW, 34 mm. **Ruler:** Elizabeth II **Subject:** Boreal Forest **Rev:** Bird and tree **Rev. Designer:** Corrine Hunt

Date	Mintage	MS-63	Proof
2011 Proof	Est. 10,000	—	50.00

KM# 1205   10 DOLLARS
15.8700 g., 0.9999 Silver 0.5102 oz. ASW, 34 mm. **Ruler:** Elizabeth II **Obv:** Bust right **Rev:** Peregrine Falcon perched on branch **Rev. Designer:** Corrine Hunt

Date	Mintage	MS-63	Proof
2011 Proof	Est. 10,000	—	50.00

KM# 1207   10 DOLLARS
15.8700 g., 0.9999 Silver 0.5102 oz. ASW, 34 mm. **Ruler:** Elizabeth II **Obv:** Bust right **Rev:** Orca Whale **Rev. Designer:** Corrine Hunt

Date	Mintage	MS-63	Proof
2011 Proof	Est. 10,000	—	50.00

KM# 1221   10 DOLLARS
15.8700 g., 0.9990 Silver 0.5097 oz. ASW, 34 mm. **Ruler:** Elizabeth II **Subject:** Year of the Dragon **Obv:** Bust right **Rev:** Dragon forepart right

Date	Mintage	MS-63	Proof
2012 Specimen	58,888	—	40.00

KM# 1235   10 DOLLARS
25.1750 g., 0.9990 Silver 0.8086 oz. ASW, 36 mm. **Ruler:** Elizabeth II **Obv:** Bust right **Rev:** Titanic sailing at right, map of Eastern Canada at left

Date	Mintage	MS-63	Proof
2012 Proof	—	—	100

KM# 415   15 DOLLARS
33.6300 g., 0.9250 Silver with gold insert 1.0000 oz. ASW, 40 mm. **Ruler:** Elizabeth II **Subject:** Year of the Snake **Obv:** Crowned head right **Rev:** Snake within circle of lunar calendar signs **Rev. Designer:** Harvey Chain **Edge:** Reeded

Date	Mintage	MS-63	Proof
2001 Proof	60,754	—	85.00

KM# 463   15 DOLLARS
33.6300 g., 0.9250 Silver with gold insert 1.0000 oz. ASW **Ruler:** Elizabeth II **Subject:** Year of the Horse **Obv:** Crowned head right **Obv. Designer:** Dora dePédery-Hunt **Rev:** Horse in center with Chinese Lunar calendar around **Rev. Designer:** Harvey Chain

Date	Mintage	MS-63	Proof
2002 Proof	59,395	—	85.00

KM# 481   15 DOLLARS
33.6300 g., 0.9250 Silver with gold insert 1.0000 oz. ASW, 40 mm. **Ruler:** Elizabeth II **Subject:** Year of the Sheep **Obv:** Crowned head right **Rev:** Sheep in center with Chinese Lunar calendar around **Rev. Designer:** Harvey Chain

Date	Mintage	MS-63	Proof
2003 Proof	53,714	—	85.00

KM# 610   15 DOLLARS
33.6300 g., 0.9250 Silver Gold octagon applique in center 1.0000 oz. ASW **Ruler:** Elizabeth II **Subject:** Year of the Monkey **Obv:** Crowned head right **Rev:** Monkey in center with Chinese Lunar calendar around

Date	Mintage	MS-63	Proof
2004 Proof	46,175	—	150

KM# 560   15 DOLLARS
33.6300 g., 0.9250 Silver with gold insert 1.0000 oz. ASW **Ruler:** Elizabeth II **Subject:** Year of the Rooster **Obv:** Crowned head right **Rev:** Rooster in center with Chinese Lunar calendar around

Date	Mintage	MS-63	Proof
2005 Proof	44,690	—	125

KM# 587   15 DOLLARS
33.6300 g., 0.9250 Silver with gold insert 1.0000 oz. ASW **Ruler:** Elizabeth II **Subject:** Year of the Dog **Obv:** Crowned head left **Rev:** Dog in center with Chinese Lunar calendar around

Date	Mintage	MS-63	Proof
2006 Proof	41,617	—	100

KM# 732   15 DOLLARS
33.6300 g., 0.9250 Silver with gold insert 1.0000 oz. ASW, 40 mm. **Ruler:** Elizabeth II **Subject:** Year of the Pig **Rev:** Pig at center of lunar characters

Date	Mintage	MS-63	Proof
2007 Proof	48,888	—	100

KM# 801   15 DOLLARS
33.6300 g., 0.9250 Silver with gold insert 1.0000 oz. ASW, 40 mm. **Ruler:** Elizabeth II **Subject:** Year of the Rat **Rev:** Rat, gold octagonal insert at center

Date	Mintage	MS-63	Proof
2008 Proof	48,888	—	90.00

KM# 803   15 DOLLARS
30.0000 g., 0.9250 Silver 0.8921 oz. ASW, 36.15 mm. **Ruler:** Elizabeth II **Rev:** Queen Victoria's coinage portrait

Date	Mintage	MS-63	Proof
2008	3,442	100	—

KM# 804   15 DOLLARS
30.0000 g., 0.9250 Silver 0.8921 oz. ASW, 36.15 mm. **Ruler:** Elizabeth II **Rev:** Edward VII coinage portrait **Rev. Designer:** G. W. DeSaulles

Date	Mintage	MS-63	Proof
2008	6,261	100	—

KM# 805   15 DOLLARS
20.0000 g., 0.9250 Silver 0.5948 oz. ASW, 36.15 mm. **Ruler:** Elizabeth II **Rev:** George V coinage portrait

Date	Mintage	MS-63	Proof
2008		100	—

KM# 806   15 DOLLARS
31.5600 g., 0.9250 Silver 0.9385 oz. ASW, 49.8 x 28.6 mm. **Ruler:** Elizabeth II **Rev:** Queen of Spades, multicolor playing card

Date	Mintage	MS-63	Proof
2008 Proof	8,714	—	90.00

KM# 807   15 DOLLARS
31.5600 g., 0.9250 Silver 0.9385 oz. ASW, 28.6x49.8 mm. **Ruler:** Elizabeth II **Rev:** Jack of Hearts, multicolor playing card

Date	Mintage	MS-63	Proof
2008 Proof	11,362	—	90.00

KM# 919   15 DOLLARS
31.5600 g., 0.9250 Silver 0.9385 oz. ASW, 49.8 x 28.6 mm.

Ruler: Elizabeth II **Obv:** Bust right **Obv. Designer:** Susanna Blunt **Rev:** Ten of spades, multicolor **Shape:** rectangle

Date	Mintage	MS-63	Proof
2009 Proof	5,921	—	90.00

KM# 920   15 DOLLARS
31.5600 g., 0.9250 Silver 0.9385 oz. ASW, 49.8 x 28.6 mm. **Ruler:** Elizabeth II **Obv:** Bust right **Obv. Designer:** Susanna Blunt **Rev:** King of hearts, multicolor **Shape:** Rectangle

Date	Mintage	MS-63	Proof
2009 Proof	5,798	—	90.00

KM# 866   15 DOLLARS
33.6300 g., 0.9250 Silver with gold insert 1.0000 oz. ASW, 40 mm. **Ruler:** Elizabeth II **Subject:** Year of the Ox **Rev:** Ox, octagon gold insert

Date	Mintage	MS-63	Proof
2009 Proof	48,888	—	90.00

KM# 922   15 DOLLARS
30.0000 g., 0.9250 Silver 0.8921 oz. ASW, 36.15 mm. **Ruler:** Elizabeth II **Obv:** Bust right **Obv. Designer:** Susanna Blunt **Rev:** Paget portrait of George VI

Date	Mintage	MS-63	Proof
2009(ml) Prooflike	—	100	—

KM# 923   15 DOLLARS
30.0000 g., 0.9250 Silver 0.8921 oz. ASW, 36.15 mm. **Ruler:** Elizabeth II **Obv:** Bust right **Obv. Designer:** Susanna Blunt **Rev:** Gillick portrait of Queen Elizabeth II

Date	Mintage	MS-63	Proof
2009(ml) Prooflike	2,643	100	—

KM# 1038   15 DOLLARS
Silver, 38 mm. **Ruler:** Elizabeth II **Subject:** Year of the tiger **Rev:** Tiger in forest **Shape:** scalloped

Date	Mintage	MS-63	Proof
2009 Proof	10,268	—	85.00

KM# 980   15 DOLLARS
34.0000 g., 0.9250 Silver 1.0111 oz. ASW, 40 mm. **Ruler:** Elizabeth II **Rev:** Tiger in gold insert

Date	Mintage	MS-63	Proof
2010 Proof	48,888	—	100

KM# 1032   15 DOLLARS
0.9990 Silver **Ruler:** Elizabeth II **Subject:** Year of the tiger **Rev:** Tiger walking tiger

Date	Mintage	MS-63	Proof
2010 Proof	9,999	—	85.00

KM# 1055   15 DOLLARS
31.1050 g., 0.9990 Silver 0.9990 oz. ASW, 38 mm. **Ruler:** Elizabeth II **Rev:** Rabbit sitting, head turned left **Shape:** scalloped

Date	Mintage	MS-63	Proof
2011 Proof	19,888	—	85.00

KM# 1091   15 DOLLARS
25.1100 g., 0.9250 Silver 0.7467 oz. ASW, 36.15 mm. **Ruler:** Elizabeth II **Rev:** Prince Charles bust **Rev. Designer:** Laurie McGaw

Date	Mintage	MS-63	Proof
2011 Prooflike	10,000	100	—

KM# 1092   15 DOLLARS
25.1100 g., 0.9250 Silver 0.7467 oz. ASW, 36.15 mm. **Ruler:** Elizabeth II **Rev:** Prince William **Rev. Designer:** Laurie McGaw

Date	Mintage	MS-63	Proof
2011 Prooflike	10,000	100	—

KM# 1093   15 DOLLARS
25.1800 g., 0.9250 Silver 0.7488 oz. ASW, 36.15 mm. **Ruler:** Elizabeth II **Rev:** Prince Harry bust 1/4 right **Rev. Designer:** Laurie McGaw

Date	Mintage	MS-63	Proof
2011 Prooflike	10,000	100	—

KM# 1094   15 DOLLARS
31.3900 g., 0.9990 Silver 1.0082 oz. ASW, 38 mm. **Ruler:** Elizabeth II **Rev:** Rabbit bounding left **Rev. Designer:** Aries Cheung

Date	Mintage	MS-63	Proof
2011 Proof	9,999	—	100

KM# 1152   15 DOLLARS
31.3900 g., 0.9999 Silver 1.0091 oz. ASW, 38 mm. **Ruler:** Elizabeth II **Obv:** Bust right **Rev:** Magpie, bird of happyness in flight at top, lotus flowers at bottom, maple leaf hologram at center

Date	Mintage	MS-63	Proof
2011 Proof	Est. 8,888	—	100

KM# 1183   15 DOLLARS
31.1050 g., 0.9990 Silver 0.9990 oz. ASW, 36.5 mm. **Ruler:** Elizabeth II **Subject:** Year of the Dragon **Obv:** Bust right **Rev:** Dragon right

Date	Mintage	MS-63	Proof
2012 Proof	—	—	75.00

KM# 1186   15 DOLLARS
31.1050 g., 0.9990 Silver 0.9990 oz. ASW, 36.5 mm. **Ruler:** Elizabeth II **Subject:** Year of the Dragon **Obv:** Bust right **Rev:** Dragon left **Shape:** Scalloped

Date	Mintage	MS-63	Proof
2012 Proof	—	—	75.00

KM# 411 20 DOLLARS
31.1035 g., 0.9250 Silver 0.9250 oz. ASW, 38 mm. **Ruler:** Elizabeth II **Subject:** Transportation - Steam Locomotive **Obv:** Crowned head right **Obv. Designer:** Dora dePédery-Hunt **Rev:** First Canadian Steel Steam Locomotive and cameo hologram **Rev. Designer:** Don Curely **Edge:** Segmented reeding

Date	Mintage	MS-63	Proof
2001 Proof	15,000	—	45.00

KM# 427 20 DOLLARS
31.1030 g., 0.9250 Silver 0.9249 oz. ASW, 38 mm. **Ruler:** Elizabeth II **Series:** Transportation - The Marco Polo **Obv:** Crowned head right **Rev:** Sailship with hologram cameo **Rev. Designer:** J. Franklin Wright **Edge:** Segmented reeding

Date	Mintage	MS-63	Proof
2001 Proof	15,000	—	45.00

KM# 428 20 DOLLARS
31.1030 g., 0.9250 Silver 0.9249 oz. ASW, 38 mm. **Ruler:** Elizabeth II **Series:** Transportation - Russell Touring Car **Obv:** Crowned head right **Rev:** Russell touring car with hologram cameo **Rev. Designer:** John Mardon **Edge:** Segmented reeding

Date	Mintage	MS-63	Proof
2001 Proof	15,000	—	45.00

KM# 464 20 DOLLARS
31.1030 g., 0.9250 Silver 0.9249 oz. ASW **Ruler:** Elizabeth II **Obv:** Crowned head right **Obv. Designer:** Dora dePédery-Hunt **Rev:** Gray-Dort Model 25-SM with cameo hologram **Rev. Designer:** John Mardon

Date	Mintage	MS-63	Proof
2002 Proof	15,000	—	45.00

KM# 465 20 DOLLARS
31.1030 g., 0.9250 Silver 0.9249 oz. ASW **Ruler:** Elizabeth II **Obv:** Crowned head right **Obv. Designer:** Dora dePédery-Hunt **Rev:** Sailing ship William D. Lawrence **Rev. Designer:** Bonnie Ross

Date	Mintage	MS-63	Proof
2002 Proof	15,000	—	45.00

KM# 523 20 DOLLARS
31.3900 g., 0.9990 Silver 1.0082 oz. ASW, 38 mm. **Ruler:** Elizabeth II **Obv:** Crowned head right **Obv. Designer:** Dora dePédery-Hunt **Rev:** Canadian Rockies, multicolor

Date	Mintage	MS-63	Proof
2003 Proof	29,967	—	50.00

KM# 483 20 DOLLARS
31.1030 g., 0.9250 Silver with selective gold plating 0.9249 oz. ASW **Ruler:** Elizabeth II **Subject:** The HMCS Bras d'or (FHE-400) **Obv:** Crowned head right **Obv. Designer:** Dora dePédery-Hunt **Rev:** Ship in water **Rev. Designer:** Donald Curley, Stan Witten

Date	Mintage	MS-63	Proof
2003 Proof	15,000	—	45.00

KM# 482 20 DOLLARS
31.3900 g., 0.9999 Silver 1.0091 oz. ASW, 38 mm. **Ruler:** Elizabeth II **Obv:** Crowned head right **Obv. Designer:** Dora dePédery-Hunt **Rev:** Niagara Falls hologram **Rev. Designer:** Gary Corcoran

Date	Mintage	MS-63	Proof
2003 Proof	29,967	—	75.00

KM# 484 20 DOLLARS
31.1030 g., 0.9250 Silver with selective gold plating 0.9249 oz. ASW **Ruler:** Elizabeth II **Subject:** Canadian National FA-1 diesel-electric locomotive **Obv:** Crowned head right **Obv. Designer:** Dora dePédery-Hunt **Rev. Designer:** John Mardon, William Woodruff

Date	Mintage	MS-63	Proof
2003 Proof	15,000	—	45.00

KM# 485 20 DOLLARS
31.1030 g., 0.9250 Silver with selective gold plating 0.9249 oz. ASW **Ruler:** Elizabeth II **Obv:** Crowned head right **Obv. Designer:** Dora dePédery-Hunt **Rev:** The Bricklin SV-1 **Rev. Designer:** Brian Hughes, José Oslo

Date	Mintage	MS-63	Proof
2003 Proof	15,000	—	45.00

KM# 611 20 DOLLARS
31.3900 g., 0.9999 Silver 1.0091 oz. ASW, 38 mm. **Ruler:** Elizabeth II **Obv:** Head right **Obv. Designer:** Susanna Blunt **Rev:** Iceberg, hologram

Date	Mintage	MS-63	Proof
2004 Proof	24,879	—	45.00

KM# 838 20 DOLLARS
31.3900 g., 0.9999 Silver partially gilt 1.0091 oz. ASW, 38 mm. **Ruler:** Elizabeth II **Rev:** Hopewell Rocks, gilt

Date	Mintage	MS-63	Proof
2004 Proof	16,918	—	45.00

KM# 561 20 DOLLARS
31.3900 g., 0.9999 Silver 1.0091 oz. ASW, 38 mm. **Ruler:** Elizabeth II **Obv:** Head right **Obv. Designer:** Susanna Blunt **Rev:** Three-masted sailing ship, hologram of the sea **Rev. Designer:** Bonnie Ross

Date	Mintage	MS-63	Proof
2005 Proof	18,276	—	55.00

KM# 562 20 DOLLARS
31.3900 g., 0.9999 Silver 1.0091 oz. ASW, 38 mm. **Ruler:** Elizabeth II **Subject:** Northwest Territories Diamonds **Obv:** Head right **Obv. Designer:** Susanna Blunt **Rev:** Multicolor diamond hologram on landscape **Rev. Designer:** José Oslo **Edge:** Reeded

Date	Mintage	MS-63	Proof
2005 Proof	35,000	—	45.00

KM# 563 20 DOLLARS
31.3900 g., 0.9999 Silver 1.0091 oz. ASW **Ruler:** Elizabeth II **Subject:** Mingan Archepelago **Obv:** Head right **Obv. Designer:** Susanna Blunt **Rev:** Cliffs with whale tail out of water **Rev. Designer:** Pierre Leduc

Date	Mintage	MS-63	Proof
2005 Proof	—	—	45.00

KM# 564 20 DOLLARS
31.3900 g., 0.9999 Silver 1.0091 oz. ASW **Ruler:** Elizabeth II **Subject:** Rainforests of the Pacific Northwest **Obv:** Head right **Rev:** Open winged bird **Designer:** Susanna Blunt

Date	Mintage	MS-63	Proof
2005 Proof	—	—	45.00

KM# 565 20 DOLLARS
31.3900 g., 0.9999 Silver 1.0091 oz. ASW, 38 mm. **Ruler:** Elizabeth II **Subject:** Toronto Island National Park **Obv:** Head right **Rev:** Toronto Island Lighthouse, Toronto skyline in background

Date	Mintage	MS-63	Proof
2005 Proof	—	—	45.00

KM# 588 20 DOLLARS
31.3900 g., 0.9999 Silver 1.0091 oz. ASW **Ruler:** Elizabeth II **Subject:** Georgian Bay National Park **Obv:** Head right **Rev:** Canoe and small trees on island

Date	Mintage	MS-63	Proof
2006 Proof		—	60.00

KM# 589 20 DOLLARS
31.1000 g., 0.9999 Silver 0.9997 oz. ASW, 38 mm. **Ruler:** Elizabeth II **Obv:** Head right **Rev:** Notre Dame Basilica, Montreal, as a hologram

Date	Mintage	MS-63	Proof
2006 Proof	15,000	—	50.00

KM# 663   20 DOLLARS
31.3900 g., 0.9999 Silver 1.0091 oz. ASW, 38 mm.   **Ruler:**
Elizabeth II **Subject:** Nahanni National Park **Obv:** Head right
Rev: Bear walking along stream, cliff in background

Date	Mintage	MS-63	Proof
2006 Proof	—	—	60.00

KM# 664   20 DOLLARS
31.3900 g., 0.9999 Silver 1.0091 oz. ASW, 38 mm.   **Ruler:**
Elizabeth II **Subject:** Jasper National Park **Obv:** Head right **Rev:**
Cowboy on horseback in majestic scene

Date	Mintage	MS-63	Proof
2006 Proof	—	—	60.00

KM# 665   20 DOLLARS
31.1000 g., 0.9999 Silver 0.9997 oz. ASW, 38 mm.   **Ruler:**
Elizabeth II **Obv:** Head right **Rev:** Holographic rendering of CN
Tower

Date	Mintage	MS-63	Proof
2006 Proof	15,000	—	60.00

KM# 666   20 DOLLARS
31.1000 g., 0.9999 Silver 0.9997 oz. ASW   **Ruler:** Elizabeth II
Obv: Head right **Rev:** Holographic view of Pengrowth
Saddledome in Calgary

Date	Mintage	MS-63	Proof
2006 Proof	15,000	—	55.00

KM# 667   20 DOLLARS
31.3900 g., 0.9999 Silver 1.0091 oz. ASW   **Ruler:** Elizabeth II
Subject: Tall Ship **Obv:** Head right **Rev:** Ketch and holographic
image of thunderstorm in sky

Date	Mintage	MS-63	Proof
2006 Proof	10,299	—	60.00

KM# 734   20 DOLLARS
31.1000 g., 0.9990 Silver 0.9988 oz. ASW, 38 mm.   **Ruler:**
Elizabeth II **Rev:** Holiday sleigh ride

Date	Mintage	MS-63	Proof
2007 Proof	6,804	—	70.00

KM# 735   20 DOLLARS
31.1000 g., 0.9990 Silver 0.9988 oz. ASW, 38 mm.   **Ruler:**
Elizabeth II **Rev:** Snowflake, aquamarine crystal

Date	Mintage	MS-63	Proof
2007 Proof	4,989	—	175

KM# 737   20 DOLLARS
31.1000 g., 0.9990 Silver 0.9988 oz. ASW, 38 mm.   **Ruler:**
Elizabeth II **Subject:** International Polar Year

Date	Mintage	MS-63	Proof
2007 Proof	9,164	—	65.00

KM# 737a   20 DOLLARS
31.1000 g., 0.9990 Silver 0.9988 oz. ASW, 38 mm.   **Ruler:**
Elizabeth II **Subject:** International Polar Year **Rev:** Blue plasma
coating

Date	Mintage	MS-63	Proof
2007 Proof	3,005	—	250

KM# 738   20 DOLLARS
31.3900 g., 0.9990 Silver 1.0091 oz. ASW, 38 mm.   **Ruler:**
Elizabeth II **Subject:** Tall ships **Rev:** Brigantine in harbor,
hologram

Date	Mintage	MS-63	Proof
2007 Proof	16,000	—	60.00

KM# 839   20 DOLLARS
31.3900 g., 0.9999 Silver 1.0091 oz. ASW   **Ruler:** Elizabeth II
Rev: Northern lights in hologram

Date	Mintage	MS-63	Proof
2007		35.00	—

KM# 808   20 DOLLARS
31.5000 g., 0.9250 Silver 0.9368 oz. ASW, 38 mm.   **Ruler:**
Elizabeth II **Subject:** Agriculture trade **Rev:** Team of horses
plowing

Date	Mintage	MS-63	Proof
2008 Proof	5,802	—	70.00

KM# 809   20 DOLLARS
31.1050 g., 0.9990 Silver 0.9990 oz. ASW, 38 mm.   **Ruler:**
Elizabeth II **Rev:** Royal Hudson Steam locomotive

Date	Mintage	MS-63	Proof
2008 Proof	8,345	—	70.00

KM# 810   20 DOLLARS
31.3900 g., 0.9990 Silver 1.0082 oz. ASW, 38 mm.   **Ruler:**
Elizabeth II **Rev:** Green leaf and crystal raindrop **Rev. Designer:**
Stanley Witten

Date	Mintage	MS-63	Proof
2008 Proof	15,000	—	110

KM# 811   20 DOLLARS
31.1050 g., 0.9999 Silver 0.9990 oz. ASW   **Ruler:** Elizabeth II
Rev: Snowflake, amethyst crystal

Date	Mintage	MS-63	Proof
2008 Proof	7,172	—	90.00

KM# 813   20 DOLLARS
31.1050 g., 0.9990 Silver 0.9990 oz. ASW, 38 mm. **Ruler:**
Elizabeth II **Rev:** Carolers around tree

Date	Mintage	MS-63	Proof
2008 Proof	10,000	—	70.00

KM# 872   20 DOLLARS
31.1050 g., 0.9990 Silver 0.9990 oz. ASW, 38 mm. **Ruler:**
Elizabeth II **Rev:** Snowflake, sapphire crystal

Date	Mintage	MS-63	Proof
2008 Proof	7,765	—	85.00

KM# 893   20 DOLLARS
31.3900 g., 0.9990 Silver 1.0082 oz. ASW, 38 mm. **Ruler:**
Elizabeth II **Subject:** Coal mining trade **Obv:** Bust right **Obv.**
Legend: Elizabeth II DG Regina **Obv. Designer:** Susanna Blunt
Rev: Miner pushing cart with coal **Rev. Legend:** Canada 20
Dollars **Rev. Designer:** John Marder

Date	Mintage	MS-63	Proof
2009 Proof	10,000	—	75.00

KM# 891   20 DOLLARS
31.3900 g., 0.9990 Silver 1.0082 oz. ASW, 38 mm. **Ruler:**
Elizabeth II **Subject:** Great Canadian Locomotives - Jubilee
Obv: Bust right **Obv. Legend:** Elizabeth II DG Regina **Obv.**
Designer: Susanna Blunt **Rev:** Jubilee locomotive side view **Rev.**
Legend: Canada 20 Dollars **Edge Lettering:** Jubilee

Date	Mintage	MS-63	Proof
2009 Proof	6,036	—	70.00

KM# 870   20 DOLLARS
27.7800 g., 0.9250 Silver 0.8261 oz. ASW, 40 mm. **Ruler:**
Elizabeth II **Rev:** Calgary Flames goalie mask multicolor on goal net

Date	Mintage	MS-63	Proof
2009 Proof	10,000	—	70.00

KM# 871   20 DOLLARS
27.7800 g., 0.9250 Silver 0.8261 oz. ASW, 40 mm. **Ruler:**
Elizabeth II **Rev:** Edmonton Oilers goalie mask, multicolor on goal
net

Date	Mintage	MS-63	Proof
2009 Proof	10,000	—	70.00

KM# 872A   20 DOLLARS
27.7800 g., 0.9250 Silver 0.8261 oz. ASW, 40 mm. **Ruler:**
Elizabeth II **Rev:** Montreal Canadians goalie mask multicolor

Date	Mintage	MS-63	Proof
2009 Proof	10,000	—	70.00

KM# 873   20 DOLLARS
27.7800 g., 0.9250 Silver 0.8261 oz. ASW, 40 mm. **Ruler:**
Elizabeth II **Rev:** Ottawa Senators goalie mask on goal net

Date	Mintage	MS-63	Proof
2009 Proof	10,000	—	70.00

KM# 874   20 DOLLARS
27.7800 g., 0.9250 Silver 0.8261 oz. ASW, 40 mm. **Ruler:**
Elizabeth II **Rev:** Toronto Maple Leafs goalie mask, multicolor on
goal net

Date	Mintage	MS-63	Proof
2009 Proof	10,000	—	70.00

KM# 875   20 DOLLARS
27.7800 g., 0.9250 Silver 0.8261 oz. ASW, 40 mm. **Ruler:**
Elizabeth II **Rev:** Vancouver Canucks goalie mask, multicolor on
goal net

Date	Mintage	MS-63	Proof
2009 Proof	10,000	—	70.00

KM# 876   20 DOLLARS
31.5000 g., 0.9250 Silver 0.9368 oz. ASW, 40 mm. **Ruler:**
Elizabeth II **Rev:** Summer moon mask

Date	Mintage	MS-63	Proof
2009 Proof	2,834	—	75.00

KM# 944   20 DOLLARS
31.1050 g., 0.9990 Silver 0.9990 oz. ASW, 38 mm. **Ruler:**
Elizabeth II **Rev:** Snowflake - light blue crystal

Date	Mintage	MS-63	Proof
2009 Proof	7,477	—	95.00

KM# 945   20 DOLLARS
31.1050 g., 0.9990 Silver 0.9990 oz. ASW, 38 mm. **Ruler:**
Elizabeth II **Rev:** Snowflake - light red crystal

Date	Mintage	MS-63	Proof
2009 Proof	7,004	—	95.00

KM# 892   20 DOLLARS
31.3900 g., 0.9990 Silver 1.0082 oz. ASW, 38 mm. **Ruler:**
Elizabeth II **Subject:** Crystal raindrop **Obv:** Bust right **Rev:** Maple
leaf and rain drop - fall colors **Rev. Designer:** Celia Godkin

Date	Mintage	MS-63	Proof
2009 Proof	9,998	—	75.00

KM# 987   20 DOLLARS
31.3900 g., 0.9999 Silver 1.0091 oz. ASW, 38 mm. **Ruler:**
Elizabeth II **Rev:** Lotus Water Lilly in multicolor and crystal **Rev.**
Designer: Cladio D'Angelo

Date	Mintage	MS-63	Proof
2010 Proof	10,000	—	100

KM# 1009   20 DOLLARS
31.3900 g., 0.9990 Silver 1.0082 oz. ASW **Ruler:** Elizabeth II
Subject: 75th Anniversary of Canadian Bank Notes **Rev:** Female
and farmer seated

Date	Mintage	MS-63	Proof
2010 Proof	7,500	—	70.00

KM# 1013   20 DOLLARS
31.3900 g., 0.9990 Silver 1.0082 oz. ASW, 38 mm. **Ruler:**
Elizabeth II **Rev:** Maple leaf and crystal **Rev. Designer:** Celia
Godkin

Date	Mintage	MS-63	Proof
2010 Proof	10,000	—	95.00

KM# 1018   20 DOLLARS
31.3900 g., 0.9990 Silver 1.0082 oz. ASW, 38 mm. **Ruler:**
Elizabeth II **Rev:** Steam Locomotive Selkirk

Date	Mintage	MS-63	Proof
2010 Proof	10,000	—	80.00

KM# 1048   20 DOLLARS
31.1050 g., 0.9999 Silver 0.9999 oz. ASW, 38 mm. **Ruler:**
Elizabeth II **Rev:** Snowflake, blue crystals

Date	Mintage	MS-63	Proof
2010 Proof	7,500	—	85.00

KM# 1049   20 DOLLARS
31.1050 g., 0.9999 Silver 0.9999 oz. ASW, 38 mm. **Ruler:**
Elizabeth II **Rev:** Snowflake, tanzanite crystals

Date	Mintage	MS-63	Proof
2010 Proof	7,500	—	85.00

KM# 1066   20 DOLLARS
31.9900 g., 0.9990 Silver 1.0274 oz. ASW, 38 mm. **Ruler:**
Elizabeth II **Rev:** Pinecone with ruby crystals **Rev. Designer:**
Susan Taylor

Date	Mintage	MS-63	Proof
2010 Proof	5,000	—	120

KM# 1067   20 DOLLARS
31.9900 g., 0.9990 Silver 1.0274 oz. ASW, 38 mm. **Ruler:**
Elizabeth II **Rev:** Pinecone with moonlight blue crystals **Rev.
Designer:** Susan Taylor

Date	Mintage	MS-63	Proof
2010 Proof	5,000	—	120

KM# 1075   20 DOLLARS
27.7800 g., 0.9250 Silver 0.8261 oz. ASW, 40 mm. **Ruler:**
Elizabeth II **Subject:** Winter Scene **Rev:** Horse pulling cut
Christmas Tree **Rev. Designer:** Rene Clark

Date	Mintage	MS-63	Proof
2011 Proof	8,000	—	70.00

KM# 1111   20 DOLLARS
31.3900 g., 0.9990 Silver 1.0082 oz. ASW, 40 mm. **Ruler:**
Elizabeth II **Subject:** Royal Wedding **Rev:** Portraits of Katherine
and William facing each other, crystal insert

Date	Mintage	MS-63	Proof
2011 Proof	—	—	85.00

KM# 1134   20 DOLLARS
31.3900 g., 0.9999 Silver 1.0091 oz. ASW, 38 mm. **Ruler:**
Elizabeth II **Subject:** Canadian Pacific's D-10 Steam Locomotive
Obv: Bust right **Rev:** Steam locomotive right **Edge:** Lettered

Date	Mintage	MS-63	Proof
2011 Proof	10,000	—	80.00

KM# 1135   20 DOLLARS
31.3900 g., 0.9999 Silver 1.0091 oz. ASW, 38 mm. **Ruler:**
Elizabeth II **Obv:** Bust right **Rev:** Tulip in color and Vienitian glass
lady bug

Date	Mintage	MS-63	Proof
2011 Proof	—	—	140

KM# 1145   20 DOLLARS
31.3900 g., 0.9999 Silver 1.0091 oz. ASW, 38 mm. **Ruler:**
Elizabeth II **Obv:** Bust right **Rev:** Wild rose in color, swarovski
crystrals

Date	Mintage	MS-63	Proof
2011 Proof	Est. 10,000	—	110

KM# 1147   20 DOLLARS
31.3900 g., 0.9999 Silver 1.0091 oz. ASW, 38 mm. **Ruler:**
Elizabeth II **Obv:** Bust right **Rev:** Maple leaves, seeds in color,
swarovski crystal drop

Date	Mintage	MS-63	Proof
2011 Proof	—	—	110

KM# 1181   20 DOLLARS
31.3900 g., 0.9990 Silver 1.0082 oz. ASW, 38 mm. **Ruler:**
Elizabeth II **Obv:** Bust right **Rev:** Winnipeg Jets Logo, jet over
maple leaf

Date	Mintage	MS-63	Proof
2011 Proof	15,000	—	95.00

KM# 1182   20 DOLLARS
31.9900 g., 0.9999 Silver 1.0284 oz. ASW, 38 mm. **Ruler:**
Elizabeth II **Obv:** Bust right **Rev:** Christmas tree with six crystals

Date	Mintage	MS-63	Proof
2011 Proof	—	—	75.00

KM# 1187   20 DOLLARS
31.3900 g., 0.9990 Silver 1.0082 oz. ASW, 38 mm. **Ruler:**
Elizabeth II **Obv:** Bust right **Rev:** Snowflake with emerald crystals

Date	Mintage	MS-63	Proof
2011 Proof	15,000	—	85.00

KM# 1188   20 DOLLARS
31.8900 g., 0.9990 Silver 1.0242 oz. ASW, 38 mm. **Ruler:**
Elizabeth II **Obv:** Bust right **Rev:** Snowflake with topaz crystals

Date	Mintage	MS-63	Proof
2011 Proof	15,000	—	95.00

KM# 1189   20 DOLLARS
31.8900 g., 0.9990 Silver 1.0242 oz. ASW, 38 mm. **Ruler:**
Elizabeth II **Obv:** Bust right **Rev:** Three snowflakes with three
Hyacinth red crystals

Date	Mintage	MS-63	Proof
2011 Proof	15,000	—	115

KM# 1190   20 DOLLARS
31.8900 g., 0.9990 Silver 1.0242 oz. ASW, 38 mm. **Ruler:**
Elizabeth II **Obv:** Bust right **Rev:** Three snowflakes with three
Montana blue crystals

Date	Mintage	MS-63	Proof
2011 Proof	15,000	—	115

KM# 1237 20 DOLLARS
31.1050 g., 0.9990 Silver 0.9990 oz. ASW, 38 mm. **Ruler:** Elizabeth II **Subject:** Elizabeth II, Diamond Jubilee **Obv:** Bust right **Rev:** Conjoined busts right of Elizabeth II with crown and Philip II in Naval uniform

Date	Mintage	MS-63	Proof
2012 Proof	—	—	75.00

KM# 1238 20 DOLLARS
31.1050 g., 0.9990 Silver 0.9990 oz. ASW, 38 mm. **Ruler:** Elizabeth II **Subject:** Elizabeth II, Diamond Jubilee **Obv:** Bust right **Rev:** Crowned monogram within wreath

Date	Mintage	MS-63	Proof
1952-2012 Proof	—	—	75.00

KM# 1137 20 DOLLARS
31.3900 g., 0.9990 Silver 1.0082 oz. ASW, 38 mm. **Ruler:** Elizabeth II **Subject:** Elizabeth II, 60th Anniversary of reign **Obv:** Bust right **Rev:** Crowned bust right with swarovski crystal insert **Edge:** Reeded

Date	Mintage	MS-63	Proof
2012 Proof	15,000	—	105

KM# 1177 20 DOLLARS
27.7800 g., 0.9250 Silver 0.8261 oz. ASW, 38 mm. **Ruler:** Elizabeth II **Obv:** Bust right **Rev:** Youthful busts right of Elizabeth II and Prince Philip

Date	Mintage	MS-63	Proof
2012 Proof	—	—	85.00

KM# 1178 20 DOLLARS
27.7800 g., 0.9250 Silver 0.8261 oz. ASW, 38 mm. **Ruler:** Elizabeth II **Obv:** Bust right **Rev:** Royal cypher, wreath below

Date	Mintage	MS-63	Proof
2012 Proof	—	—	85.00

KM# 742 25 DOLLARS
27.7800 g., 0.9250 Silver 0.8261 oz. ASW, 40 mm. **Ruler:** Elizabeth II **Subject:** Vancouver Olympics **Rev:** Alpine skiing, hologram

Date	Mintage	MS-63	Proof
2007 Proof	45,000	—	65.00

KM# 743 25 DOLLARS
27.7800 g., 0.9250 Silver 0.8261 oz. ASW, 40 mm. **Ruler:** Elizabeth II **Subject:** Vancouver Olympics **Rev:** Athletics pride hologram

Date	Mintage	MS-63	Proof
2007 Proof	45,000	—	65.00

KM# 744 25 DOLLARS
27.7500 g., 0.9250 Silver 0.8252 oz. ASW, 40 mm. **Ruler:** Elizabeth II **Subject:** Vancouver Olympics **Rev:** Biathleon hologram

Date	Mintage	MS-63	Proof
2007 Proof	54,000	—	65.00

KM# 745 25 DOLLARS
27.7800 g., 0.9250 Silver 0.8261 oz. ASW, 40 mm. **Ruler:** Elizabeth II **Subject:** Vancouver Olympics **Rev:** Curling hologram

Date	Mintage	MS-63	Proof
2007 Proof	—	—	65.00

KM# 746 25 DOLLARS
27.7800 g., 0.9250 Silver 0.8261 oz. ASW, 40 mm. **Ruler:** Elizabeth II **Subject:** Vancouver Olympics **Rev:** Hockey, hologram

Date	Mintage	MS-63	Proof
2007 Proof	45,000	—	65.00

KM# 814 25 DOLLARS
27.7800 g., 0.9250 Silver 0.8261 oz. ASW, 40 mm. **Ruler:**

Elizabeth II **Subject:** Vancouver Olympics **Rev:** Bobsleigh, hologram

Date	Mintage	MS-63	Proof
2008 Proof	45,000	—	65.00

KM# 815 25 DOLLARS
27.7800 g., 0.9250 Silver 0.8261 oz. ASW, 40 mm. **Ruler:** Elizabeth II **Subject:** Vancouver Olympics **Rev:** Figure skating, hologram

Date	Mintage	MS-63	Proof
2008 Proof	45,000	—	65.00

KM# 816 25 DOLLARS
27.7800 g., 0.9250 Silver 0.8261 oz. ASW, 40 mm. **Ruler:** Elizabeth II **Subject:** Vancouver Olympics **Rev:** Freestyle skating, hologram

Date	Mintage	MS-63	Proof
2008 Proof	45,000	—	65.00

KM# 817 25 DOLLARS
27.7800 g., 0.9250 Silver 0.8261 oz. ASW, 40 mm. **Ruler:** Elizabeth II **Subject:** Vancouver Olympics **Rev:** Snowboarding, hologram

Date	Mintage	MS-63	Proof
2008 Proof	45,000	—	65.00

KM# 818 25 DOLLARS
27.7800 g., 0.9250 Silver 0.8261 oz. ASW, 40 mm. **Ruler:** Elizabeth II **Subject:** Vancouver Olympics **Rev:** Home of the 2010 Olympics

Date	Mintage	MS-63	Proof
2008 Proof	45,000	—	65.00

KM# 903 25 DOLLARS
27.7800 g., 0.9250 Silver 0.8261 oz. ASW, 40 mm. **Ruler:** Elizabeth II **Subject:** 2010 Vancouver Olympics **Obv:** Bust right **Obv. Designer:** Susanna Blunt **Rev:** Cross Country Skiing and hologram at left

Date	Mintage	MS-63	Proof
2009 Proof	45,000	—	65.00

KM# 904 25 DOLLARS
27.7800 g., 0.9250 Silver 0.8261 oz. ASW, 40 mm. **Ruler:** Elizabeth II **Subject:** 2010 Vancouver Olympics **Obv:** Bust right **Obv. Designer:** Susanna Blunt **Rev:** Olympians holding torch, hologram at left

Date	Mintage	MS-63	Proof
2009 Proof	45,000	—	65.00

KM# 905   25 DOLLARS
27.7800 g., 0.9250 Silver 0.8261 oz. ASW, 40 mm. **Ruler:**
Elizabeth II **Subject:** 2010 Vancouver Olympics **Obv:** Bust right
Obv. Designer: Susanna Blunt **Rev:** Sled, hologram at left

Date	Mintage	MS-63	Proof
2009 Proof	45,000	—	65.00

KM# 906   25 DOLLARS
27.7800 g., 0.9250 Silver 0.8261 oz. ASW, 40 mm. **Ruler:**
Elizabeth II **Subject:** 2010 Vancouver Olympics **Obv:** Bust right
Obv. Designer: Susanna Blunt **Rev:** Ski Jumper, hologram at left

Date	Mintage	MS-63	Proof
2009 Proof	45,000	—	65.00

KM# 907   25 DOLLARS
27.7800 g., 0.9250 Silver 0.8261 oz. ASW, 40 mm. **Ruler:**
Elizabeth II **Subject:** 2010 Vancouver Olympics **Obv:** Bust right
Obv. Designer: Susanna Blunt **Rev:** Speed Skaters, hologram
at left

Date	Mintage	MS-63	Proof
2009 Proof	45,000	—	65.00

KM# 1146   25 DOLLARS
62.4100 g., 0.9999 Silver selectively gilt 2.0062 oz. ASW, 60 mm.
Ruler: Elizabeth II **Obv:** Bust right **Rev:** Toronto map and skyline,
partilly gilt **Edge:** Reeded

Date	Mintage	MS-63	Proof
2011 Proof	Est. 7,500	—	180

KM# 1173   25 DOLLARS
31.3900 g., 0.9999 Silver 1.0091 oz. ASW, 38 mm. **Ruler:**
Elizabeth II **Obv:** Bust right **Rev:** Wayne Greskey skating right,
father's portrait in circle at right, 99 in hologram at lower right

Date	Mintage	MS-63	Proof
2011 Proof	—	—	85.00

KM# 590   30 DOLLARS
31.5000 g., 0.9250 Silver 0.9368 oz. ASW **Ruler:** Elizabeth II
Subject: Pacific Northwest Wood Carvings **Obv:** Head right **Rev:**
Welcome figure totem pole

Date	Mintage	MS-63	Proof
2006 Proof	9,904	—	75.00

KM# 668   30 DOLLARS
31.5000 g., 0.9250 Silver 0.9368 oz. ASW **Ruler:** Elizabeth II
Subject: Canadarm and Col. C. Hadfield **Obv:** Head right **Rev:**
Hologram of Canadarm

Date	Mintage	MS-63	Proof
2006 Proof	9,357	—	90.00

KM# 669   30 DOLLARS
31.5000 g., 0.9250 Silver 0.9368 oz. ASW **Ruler:** Elizabeth II
Subject: National War Memorial **Obv:** Head right **Rev:** Statue of
three soldiers

Date	Mintage	MS-63	Proof
2006 Proof	8,876	—	85.00

KM# 670   30 DOLLARS
31.5000 g., 0.9250 Silver 0.9368 oz. ASW **Ruler:** Elizabeth II
Subject: Beaumont Hamel Newfoundland **Obv:** Head right **Rev:**
Caribou statue on rock outcrop

Date	Mintage	MS-63	Proof
2006 Proof	15,325	—	95.00

KM# 671   30 DOLLARS
31.5000 g., 0.9250 Silver 0.9368 oz. ASW **Ruler:** Elizabeth II
Obv: Head right **Rev:** Dog Sled Team in color

Date	Mintage	MS-63	Proof
2006 Proof	7,384	—	85.00

KM# 739   30 DOLLARS
31.5000 g., 0.9250 Silver 0.9368 oz. ASW, 40 mm. **Ruler:**
Elizabeth II **Rev:** Niagra Falls panoramic hologram

Date	Mintage	MS-63	Proof
2007 Proof	7,384	—	85.00

KM# 741   30 DOLLARS
31.5000 g., 0.9250 Silver 0.9368 oz. ASW, 40 mm. **Ruler:**
Elizabeth II **Rev:** War Memorial, Vimy Ridge

Date	Mintage	MS-63	Proof
2007 Proof	5,335	—	85.00

KM# 819   30 DOLLARS
31.5000 g., 0.9250 Silver 0.9368 oz. ASW, 40 mm. **Ruler:**
Elizabeth II **Subject:** IMAX **Rev:** Youth reaching out to shark on
large screen

Date	Mintage	MS-63	Proof
2008 Proof	3,861	—	75.00

KM# 895   30 DOLLARS
33.7500 g., 0.9250 Silver 1.0037 oz. ASW, 40 mm. **Ruler:**
Elizabeth II **Subject:** International year of astronomy **Obv:** Bust
right **Obv. Legend:** Elizabeth II 30 Dollars DG Regina **Obv.**
Designer: Susanna Blunt **Rev:** Observatory with planets and
colored sky **Rev. Legend:** Canada **Rev. Designer:** Colin Mayne

Date	Mintage	MS-63	Proof
2009 Proof	7,174	—	90.00

KM# 566   50 DOLLARS
12.0000 g., 0.5833 Gold 0.2250 oz. AGW, 27 mm. **Ruler:**
Elizabeth II **Subject:** End of World War II, 60th Anniversary **Obv:**
Head right **Rev:** Large V and three portraits

Date	Mintage	MS-63	Proof
2005 Specimen	4,000	—	375

KM# 672   50 DOLLARS
31.1600 g., 0.9995 Palladium 1.0013 oz. **Ruler:** Elizabeth II
Subject: Constellation in Spring sky position **Rev:** Large Bear at
top

Date	Mintage	MS-63	Proof
2006 Proof	297	—	1,200

KM# 673   50 DOLLARS
31.1600 g., 0.9995 Palladium 1.0013 oz. **Ruler:** Elizabeth II
Subject: Constellation in Summer sky position **Rev:** Large Bear
at left

Date	Mintage	MS-63	Proof
2006 Proof	296	—	1,200

KM# 674   50 DOLLARS
31.1600 g., 0.9995 Palladium 1.0013 oz. **Ruler:** Elizabeth II
Subject: Constellation in Autumn sky position **Rev:** Large Bear
towards bottom

Date	Mintage	MS-63	Proof
2006 Proof	296	—	1,200

KM# 675   50 DOLLARS
31.1600 g., 0.9995 Palladium 1.0013 oz. **Ruler:** Elizabeth II
Subject: Constellation in Winter sky position **Rev:** Large Bear
towards right

Date	Mintage	MS-63	Proof
2006 Proof	293	—	1,200

KM# 709   50 DOLLARS
155.5000 g., 0.9999 Silver 4.9987 oz. ASW **Ruler:** Elizabeth II
Subject: Queen's 60th Wedding Anniversary **Rev:** Coat of Arms and Mascots of Elizabeth and Philip

Date	Mintage	MS-63	Proof
2007 Proof	1,957	—	350

KM# 783   50 DOLLARS
156.7700 g., 0.9990 Silver 5.0350 oz. ASW, 65 mm. **Ruler:** Elizabeth II **Subject:** Ottawa Mint Centennial 1908-2008 **Rev:** Mint building facade **Note:** Photo reduced.

Date	Mintage	MS-63	Proof
2008 Proof	2,078	—	400

KM# 896   50 DOLLARS
156.7700 g., 0.9990 Silver 5.0350 oz. ASW, 65.25 mm. **Ruler:** Elizabeth II **Subject:** 150 Anniversary of the start of construction of the parliament buildings **Obv:** Bust right **Obv. Legend:** Elizabeth II Canada DG Regina **Obv. Designer:** Susanna Blunt **Rev:** Incomplete west block, original architecture **Rev. Legend:** 50 Dollars 1859-2009

Date	Mintage	MS-63	Proof
2009 Proof	910	—	450

KM# 1008   50 DOLLARS
157.6000 g., 0.9990 Silver 5.0617 oz. ASW, 65.25 mm. **Ruler:** Elizabeth II **Subject:** 75th Anniversary of Canadian Bank Notes **Rev:** Female seated speaking into microphone **Note:** Photo reduced.

Date	Mintage	MS-63	Proof
2010 Proof	2,000	—	450

KM# 567   75 DOLLARS
31.4400 g., 0.4166 Gold 0.4211 oz. AGW, 36.07 mm. **Ruler:** Elizabeth II **Subject:** Pope John Paul II **Obv:** Head right **Rev:** Pope giving blessing

Date	Mintage	MS-63	Proof
2005 Proof	1,870	—	825

KM# 747   75 DOLLARS
12.0000 g., 0.5830 Gold 0.2249 oz. AGW, 27 mm. **Ruler:** Elizabeth II **Subject:** Vancouver Olympics - Athletics Pride **Rev:** Athletics celebrating, holding flag aloft

Date	Mintage	MS-63	Proof
2007 Proof	4,524	—	440

KM# 748   75 DOLLARS
12.0000 g., 0.5830 Gold 0.2249 oz. AGW, 27 mm. **Ruler:** Elizabeth II **Obv:** Bust right **Obv. Designer:** Susanna Blunt **Rev:** Canada geese in flight left, multicolor

Date	Mintage	MS-63	Proof
2007 Proof	4,418	—	440

KM# 749   75 DOLLARS
12.0000 g., 0.5830 Gold 0.2249 oz. AGW, 27 mm. **Ruler:** Elizabeth II **Rev:** Mountie, multicolor

Date	Mintage	MS-63	Proof
2007 Proof	6,687	—	440

KM# 820   75 DOLLARS
12.0000 g., 0.5830 Gold partially silver plated 0.2249 oz. AGW, 27 mm. **Ruler:** Elizabeth II **Rev:** 2010 Olympic Inukshuk Stone man, partially silver plated

Date	Mintage	MS-63	Proof
2008 Proof	—	—	420

KM# 821   75 DOLLARS
12.0000 g., 0.5830 Gold 0.2249 oz. AGW, 27 mm. **Ruler:** Elizabeth II **Rev:** Four Host Nations mask emblems, colored **Rev. Designer:** Jody Broomfield

Date	Mintage	MS-63	Proof
2008 Proof	8,000	—	440

KM# 947   75 DOLLARS
12.0000 g., 0.5830 Gold 0.2249 oz. AGW, 27 mm. **Ruler:** Elizabeth II **Subject:** Vancouver Olympics **Rev:** Tent building at Olympic site, color

Date	Mintage	MS-63	Proof
2008 Proof	8,000	—	440

KM# 908   75 DOLLARS
12.0000 g., 0.5830 Gold 0.2249 oz. AGW, 27 mm. **Ruler:** Elizabeth II **Subject:** 2010 Vancouver Olympics **Obv:** Bust right **Obv. Designer:** Susana Blunt **Rev:** Multicolor moose

Date	Mintage	MS-63	Proof
2009 Proof	4,075	—	440

KM# 909   75 DOLLARS
12.0000 g., 0.5830 Gold 0.2249 oz. AGW, 27 mm. **Ruler:** Elizabeth II **Subject:** 2010 Vancouver Olympics **Obv:** Bust right **Obv. Designer:** Susanna Blunt **Rev:** Multicolor athletics and torch

Date	Mintage	MS-63	Proof
2009 Proof	4,479	—	440

KM# 910   75 DOLLARS
12.0000 g., 0.5830 Gold 0.2249 oz. AGW, 27 mm. **Ruler:**
Elizabeth II **Subject:** 2010 Vancouver Olympics **Obv:** Bust right
Obv. Designer: Susanna Blunt **Rev:** Wolf, multicolor

Date	Mintage	MS-63	Proof
2009 Proof	4,161	—	440

KM# 1002   75 DOLLARS
12.0000 g., 0.5830 Gold 0.2249 oz. AGW, 27 mm. **Ruler:**
Elizabeth II **Rev:** Spring color maple leaves

Date	Mintage	MS-63	Proof
2010 Proof	1,000	—	500

KM# 1003   75 DOLLARS
12.0000 g., 0.5830 Gold 0.2249 oz. AGW, 27 mm. **Ruler:**
Elizabeth II **Rev:** Summer color maple leaves

Date	Mintage	MS-63	Proof
2010 Proof	1,000	—	500

KM# 1004   75 DOLLARS
12.0000 g., 0.5830 Gold 0.2249 oz. AGW, 27 mm. **Ruler:**
Elizabeth II **Rev:** Fall color maple leaves

Date	Mintage	MS-63	Proof
2010 Proof	1,000	—	500

KM# 1005   75 DOLLARS
12.0000 g., 0.5830 Gold 0.2249 oz. AGW, 27 mm. **Ruler:**
Elizabeth II **Rev:** Winter color maple leaves

Date	Mintage	MS-63	Proof
2010 Proof	1,000	—	500

KM# 416   100 DOLLARS
13.3375 g., 0.5830 Gold alloyed with 5.5579 g of .999 Silver,
.1787 oz ASW 0.2500 oz. AGW, 27 mm. **Ruler:** Elizabeth II

Subject: Library of Parliament **Obv:** Crowned head right **Obv.**
Designer: Dora dePedery-Hunt **Rev:** Statue in domed building
Rev. Designer: Robert R. Carmichael **Edge:** Reeded

Date	Mintage	MS-63	Proof
2001 Proof	8,080	—	475

KM# 452   100 DOLLARS
13.3375 g., 0.5830 Gold 0.2500 oz. AGW, 27 mm. **Ruler:**
Elizabeth II **Subject:** Discovery of Oil in Alberta **Obv:** Crowned
head right **Rev:** Oil well with black oil spill on ground **Rev.**
Designer: John Marden **Edge:** Reeded

Date	Mintage	MS-63	Proof
2002 Proof	9,994	—	475

KM# 486   100 DOLLARS
13.3375 g., 0.5830 Gold 0.2500 oz. AGW **Ruler:** Elizabeth II
Subject: 100th Anniversary of the Discovery of Marquis Wheat
Obv: Head right

Date	Mintage	MS-63	Proof
2003 Proof	9,993	—	475

KM# 528   100 DOLLARS
12.0000 g., 0.5830 Gold 0.2249 oz. AGW **Ruler:** Elizabeth II
Subject: St. Lawrence Seaway, 50th Anniversary **Obv:** Head
right

Date	Mintage	MS-63	Proof
2004 Proof	7,454	—	425

KM# 593   100 DOLLARS
12.0000 g., 0.5833 Gold 0.2250 oz. AGW **Ruler:** Elizabeth II
Subject: 130th Anniversary, Supreme Court **Obv:** Head right

Date	Mintage	MS-63	Proof
2005 Proof	5,092	—	425

KM# 591   100 DOLLARS
12.0000 g., 0.5833 Gold 0.2250 oz. AGW **Ruler:** Elizabeth II
Subject: 75th Anniversary, Hockey Classic between Royal
Military College and U.S. Military Academy **Obv:** Head right

Date	Mintage	MS-63	Proof
2006 Proof	5,439	—	425

KM# 689   100 DOLLARS
12.0000 g., 0.5833 Gold 0.2250 oz. AGW, 27 mm. **Ruler:**
Elizabeth II **Subject:** 140th Anniversary Dominion **Obv:** Head
right

Date	Mintage	MS-63	Proof
2007 Proof	4,453	—	425

KM# 823   100 DOLLARS
12.0000 g., 0.5830 Gold 0.2249 oz. AGW, 27 mm. **Ruler:**
Elizabeth II **Rev:** Fraser River

Date	Mintage	MS-63	Proof
2008 Proof	3,089	—	425

KM# 898   100 DOLLARS
12.0000 g., 0.5830 Gold 0.2249 oz. AGW, 27 mm. **Ruler:**
Elizabeth II **Subject:** 10th Anniversary of Nunavut **Obv:** Bust right
Obv. Legend: Elizabeth II DG Regina **Obv. Designer:** Susanna
Blunt **Rev:** Inuit dancer with 3 faces behind **Rev. Legend:** Canada
100 Dollars 1999-2009

Date	Mintage	MS-63	Proof
2009 Proof	2,309	—	425

KM# 997   100 DOLLARS
12.0000 g., 0.5830 Gold 0.2249 oz. AGW, 27 mm. **Ruler:**
Elizabeth II **Rev:** Henry Hudson, Map of Hudson's Bay **Rev.**
Designer: John Mantha

Date	Mintage	MS-63	Proof
2010 Proof	Est. 5,000	—	425

KM# 1073   100 DOLLARS
12.0000 g., 0.5830 Gold 0.2249 oz. AGW, 27 mm. **Ruler:**
Elizabeth II **Subject:** Canadian Railroads, 175th Anniversary
Rev: Early steam locomotive

Date	Mintage	MS-63	Proof
2011	3,000	—	425

KM# 417   150 DOLLARS
13.6100 g., 0.7500 Gold 0.3282 oz. AGW, 28 mm. **Ruler:**
Elizabeth II **Subject:** Year of the Snake **Obv:** Crowned head right
Obv. Designer: Dora dePedery-Hunt **Rev:** Multicolor snake
hologram **Edge:** Reeded

Date	Mintage	MS-63	Proof
2001 Proof	6,571	—	625

KM# 604   150 DOLLARS
13.6100 g., 0.7500 Gold 0.3282 oz. AGW **Ruler:** Elizabeth II
Obv: Head right **Rev:** Stylized horse left

Date	Mintage	MS-63	Proof
2002 Proof	6,843	—	625

KM# 487   150 DOLLARS
13.6100 g., 0.7500 Gold 0.3282 oz. AGW, 28 mm. **Ruler:**
Elizabeth II **Subject:** Year of the Ram **Obv:** Crowned head right
Rev: Stylized ram left, hologram **Rev. Designer:** Harvey Chan

Date	Mintage	MS-63	Proof
2003 Proof	3,927	—	625

KM# 614   150 DOLLARS
13.6100 g., 0.7500 Gold 0.3282 oz. AGW **Ruler:** Elizabeth II
Obv: Head right **Rev:** Year of the Monkey, hologram

Date	Mintage	MS-63	Proof
2004 Proof	3,392	—	625

KM# 568   150 DOLLARS
13.6100 g., 0.7500 Gold 0.3282 oz. AGW **Ruler:** Elizabeth II
Subject: Year of the Rooster **Obv:** Head right **Rev:** Rooster left, hologram

Date	Mintage	MS-63	Proof
2005 Proof	3,731	—	625

KM# 592   150 DOLLARS
13.6100 g., 0.7500 Gold 0.3282 oz. AGW, 28 mm. **Ruler:** Elizabeth II **Subject:** Year of the Dog, hologram **Obv:** Head right **Rev:** Stylized dog left

Date	Mintage	MS-63	Proof
2006 Proof	2,604	—	625

KM# 733   150 DOLLARS
13.6100 g., 0.7500 Gold 0.3282 oz. AGW, 28 mm. **Ruler:** Elizabeth II **Subject:** Year of the Pig **Obv:** Head right **Rev:** Pig in center with Chinese lunar calendar around, hologram

Date	Mintage	MS-63	Proof
2007 Proof	826	—	733

KM# 802   150 DOLLARS
11.8400 g., 0.7500 Gold 0.2855 oz. AGW, 28 mm. **Ruler:** Elizabeth II **Subject:** Year of the Rat **Rev:** Rat, hologram

Date	Mintage	MS-63	Proof
2008 Proof	582	—	550

KM# 899   150 DOLLARS
10.4000 g., 0.9990 Gold 0.3340 oz. AGW, 22.5 mm. **Ruler:** Elizabeth II **Subject:** Blessings of wealth **Obv:** Bust right **Obv. Legend:** Elizabeth II, DG Regina, Fine Gold 99999 or PUR **Obv. Designer:** Susanna Blunt **Rev:** Three goldfish surround peony, clouds **Rev. Legend:** Canada 150 Dollars (Chinese symbols of good fortune) **Rev. Designer:** Harvey Chan **Edge:** Scalloped

Date	Mintage	MS-63	Proof
2009 Proof	1,273	—	650

KM# 867   150 DOLLARS
11.8400 g., 0.7500 Gold 0.2855 oz. AGW, 28 mm. **Ruler:** Elizabeth II **Subject:** Year of the Ox **Rev:** Ox, hologram

Date	Mintage	MS-63	Proof
2009 Proof	486	—	550

KM# 979   150 DOLLARS
11.8400 g., 0.7500 Gold 0.2855 oz. AGW, 28 mm. **Ruler:** Elizabeth II **Rev:** Year of the Tiger **Rev:** Tiger in hologram

Date	Mintage	MS-63	Proof
2010 Proof	1,507	—	550

KM# 1030   150 DOLLARS
10.4000 g., 0.9999 Gold 0.3343 oz. AGW **Ruler:** Elizabeth II **Subject:** Blessing of Wealth **Shape:** Scalloped

Date	Mintage	MS-63	Proof
2010 Proof	1,388	—	650

KM# 1031   150 DOLLARS
Gold **Ruler:** Elizabeth II **Subject:** Year of the Tiger **Rev:** Tiger walking

Date	Mintage	MS-63	Proof
2010 Proof	2,500	—	600

KM# 1054   150 DOLLARS
Gold **Ruler:** Elizabeth II **Subject:** Year of the rabbit **Rev:** Rabbit hopping left, character at left

Date	Mintage	MS-63	Proof
2011 Proof	2,500	—	600

KM# 1053   150 DOLLARS
13.6100 g., 0.7500 Gold 0.3282 oz. AGW, 28 mm. **Ruler:** Elizabeth II **Subject:** Year of the rabbit **Rev:** Rabbit hologram

Date	Mintage	MS-63	Proof
2011 Proof	Est. 4,888	—	600

KM# 1184   150 DOLLARS
13.6100 g., 0.7500 Gold 0.3282 oz. AGW, 28 mm. **Ruler:** Elizabeth II **Subject:** Year of the Dragon **Obv:** Bust right **Rev:** Dragon left

Date	Mintage	MS-63	Proof
2012 Proof	—	—	650

KM# 418   200 DOLLARS
17.1350 g., 0.9166 Gold 0.5049 oz. AGW, 29 mm. **Ruler:** Elizabeth II **Subject:** Cornelius D. Krieghoff's "The Habitant farm" **Obv:** Queens head right **Edge:** Reeded

Date	Mintage	MS-63	Proof
2001 Proof	5,406	—	975

KM# 466   200 DOLLARS
17.1350 g., 0.9166 Gold 0.5049 oz. AGW, 29 mm. **Ruler:** Elizabeth II **Subject:** Thomas Thompson "The Jack Pine" (1916-17) **Obv:** Crowned head right

Date	Mintage	MS-63	Proof
2002 Proof	5,264	—	975

KM# 488   200 DOLLARS
17.1350 g., 0.9166 Gold 0.5049 oz. AGW **Ruler:** Elizabeth II **Subject:** Fitzgerald's "Houses" (1929) **Obv:** Crowned head right **Rev:** House with trees

Date	Mintage	MS-63	Proof
2003 Proof	4,118	—	975

KM# 516   200 DOLLARS
16.0000 g., 0.9166 Gold 0.4715 oz. AGW, 29 mm. **Ruler:** Elizabeth II **Subject:** "Fragments" **Obv:** Crowned head right **Rev:** Fragmented face **Edge:** Reeded

Date	Mintage	MS-63	Proof
2004 Proof	3,917	—	900

KM# 569   200 DOLLARS
16.0000 g., 0.9166 Gold 0.4715 oz. AGW **Ruler:** Elizabeth II **Subject:** Fur traders **Obv:** Head right **Rev:** Men in canoe riding wave

Date	Mintage	MS-63	Proof
2005 Proof	3,669	—	900

KM# 594   200 DOLLARS
16.0000 g., 0.9166 Gold 0.4715 oz. AGW **Ruler:** Elizabeth II **Subject:** Timber trade **Obv:** Head right **Rev:** Lumberjacks felling tree

Date	Mintage	MS-63	Proof
2006 Proof	3,218	—	900

KM# 691   200 DOLLARS
16.0000 g., 0.9166 Gold 0.4715 oz. AGW, 29 mm. **Ruler:** Elizabeth II **Subject:** Fishing Trade **Obv:** Head right **Rev:** Two fishermen hauling net

Date	Mintage	MS-63	Proof
2007 Proof	2,137	—	900

KM# 824   200 DOLLARS
16.0000 g., 0.9170 Gold 0.4717 oz. AGW, 29 mm. **Ruler:** Elizabeth II **Subject:** Commerce **Rev:** Horse drawn plow

Date	Mintage	MS-63	Proof
2008 Proof	1,951	—	900

KM# 894   200 DOLLARS
16.0000 g., 0.9160 Gold 0.4712 oz. AGW, 29 mm. **Ruler:**
Elizabeth II **Subject:** Coal mining trade **Obv:** Bust right **Obv.**
Legend: Elizabeth II DG Regina **Obv. Designer:** Susanna Blunt
Rev: Miner pushing cart with black coal **Rev. Legend:** Canada
200 Dollars **Rev. Designer:** John Marder

Date	Mintage	MS-63	Proof
2009 Proof	2,241	—	900

KM# 1000   200 DOLLARS
16.0000 g., 0.9160 Gold 0.4712 oz. AGW, 29 mm. **Ruler:**
Elizabeth II **Subject:** Petroleum and Oil Trade **Rev:** Oil railcar
and well head

Date	Mintage	MS-63	Proof
2010 Proof	Est. 4,000	—	900

KM# 1060   200 DOLLARS
16.0000 g., 0.9167 Gold 0.4715 oz. AGW, 29 mm. **Ruler:**
Elizabeth II **Rev:** Olympic athletics with medal, flag and flowers

Date	Mintage	MS-63	Proof
2010 Proof	—	—	900

KM# 1074   200 DOLLARS
16.0000 g., 0.9167 Gold 0.4715 oz. AGW, 29 mm. **Ruler:**
Elizabeth II **Rev:** SS Beaver - Seam Sail ship **Rev. Designer:**
John Mardon

Date	Mintage	MS-63	Proof
2011 Proof	2,800	—	900

KM# 1143   200 DOLLARS
16.0000 g., 0.9167 Gold 0.4715 oz. AGW, 27 mm. **Ruler:**
Elizabeth II **Subject:** Wedding, Prince William and Katherine
Middleton **Obv:** Bust right **Rev:** Half-length figures facing,
swarovski crystal **Edge:** Reeded

Date	Mintage	MS-63	Proof
2011 Proof	2,000	—	900

KM# 1174   200 DOLLARS
16.0000 g., 0.9160 Gold 0.4712 oz. AGW, 29 mm. **Ruler:**
Elizabeth II **Obv:** Bust right **Rev:** Wayne Greskey skating right,
father's portrait in circle at right, 99 in color at lower right **Rev.**
Designer: Glen Green

Date	Mintage	MS-63	Proof
2011 Proof	999	—	900

KM# 1219   200 DOLLARS
16.0000 g., 0.9167 Gold 0.4715 oz. AGW, 29 mm. **Ruler:**
Elizabeth II **Obv:** Bust right **Rev:** Prospector panning for gold in
stream

Date	Mintage	MS-63	Proof
2012 Proof	—	—	900

KM# 1223   200 DOLLARS
16.0000 g., 0.9167 Gold 0.4715 oz. AGW, 29 mm. **Ruler:**
Elizabeth II **Obv:** Bust right **Rev:** Vikings and ship

Date	Mintage	MS-63	Proof
2012 Proof	—	—	900

KM# 677   250 DOLLARS
45.0000 g., 0.5833 Gold 0.8439 oz. AGW, 40 mm. **Ruler:**
Elizabeth II **Rev:** Dog Sled Team

Date	Mintage	MS-63	Proof
2006 Proof	953	—	1,625

KM# 751   250 DOLLARS
1000.0000 g., 0.9999 Silver 32.146 oz. ASW, 101.6 mm. **Ruler:**
Elizabeth II **Subject:** Vancouver Olympics, 2010 **Rev:** Early
Canada motif **Note:** Illustration reduced.

Date	Mintage	MS-63	Proof
2007 Proof	2,500	—	1,250

KM# 833   250 DOLLARS
1000.0000 g., 0.9990 Silver 32.117 oz. ASW, 101.6 mm. **Ruler:**
Elizabeth II **Subject:** Vancouver Olympics 2010 **Rev:** Towards
confederation **Note:** Illustration reduced.

Date	Mintage	MS-63	Proof
2008 Proof	2,500	—	1,350

KM# 913   250 DOLLARS
1000.0000 g., 0.9999 Silver 32.146 oz. ASW, 101.5 mm. **Ruler:**
Elizabeth II **Obv:** Bust right **Obv. Designer:** Susanna Blunt **Rev:**
Mask with fish - Surviving the flood **Note:** Illustration reduced.

Date	Mintage	MS-63	Proof
2009 Proof	815	—	1,350

KM# 949   250 DOLLARS
1000.0000 g., 0.9990 Silver 32.117 oz. ASW, 101.6 mm. **Ruler:**
Elizabeth II **Rev:** Modern Canada

Date	Mintage	MS-63	Proof
2009 Proof	905	—	1,350

KM# 981   250 DOLLARS
1000.0000 g., 0.9990 Silver 32.117 oz. ASW, 101.6 mm. **Ruler:**
Elizabeth II **Rev:** Eagle head

Date	Mintage	MS-63	Proof
2010 Antique Patina	500	1,350	—
2010 Proof	500	—	1,400

KM# 981a   250 DOLLARS
1000.0000 g., 0.9990 Silver 32.117 oz. ASW, 101.6 mm. **Ruler:**
Elizabeth II **Rev:** Eagle head, blue enamel

Date	Mintage	MS-63	Proof
2010 Proof	500	—	1,400

KM# 1044   250 DOLLARS
1000.0000 g., 0.9990 Silver 32.117 oz. ASW, 101.6 mm. **Ruler:**
Elizabeth II **Subject:** Baniff, 125th Anniversary of resort founding
Rev: Features of Baniff

Date	Mintage	MS-63	Proof
2010 Proof	750	—	1,650

KM# 1150   250 DOLLARS
1000.0000 g., 0.9999 Silver 32.146 oz. ASW, 100 mm. **Ruler:**
Elizabeth II **Rev:** Lacrosse

Date	Mintage	MS-63	Proof
2011 Proof	—	—	1,350

KM# 1185   250 DOLLARS
1000.0000 g., 0.9990 Silver 32.117 oz. ASW, 101.6 mm. **Ruler:**
Elizabeth II **Subject:** Year of the Dragon **Obv:** Bust left **Rev:**
Dragon left

Date	Mintage	MS-63	Proof
2012 Proof	—	—	1,350

KM# 501   300 DOLLARS
60.0000 g., 0.5833 Gold 1.1252 oz. AGW, 50 mm. **Ruler:**
Elizabeth II **Obv:** Triple cameo portraits of Queen Elizabeth II by
Gillick, Machin and de Pedery-Hunt, each in 14K gold, rose in
center **Rev:** Dates "1952-2002" and denomination in legend, rose
in center **Note:** Housed in anodized gold-colored aluminum box
with cherrywood stained siding

Date	Mintage	MS-63	Proof
1952-2002 Proof	999	—	2,150

KM# 517   300 DOLLARS
60.0000 g., 0.5833 Gold 1.1252 oz. AGW, 50 mm. **Ruler:**
Elizabeth II **Obv:** Four coinage portraits of Elizabeth II **Rev:**
Canadian arms above value **Edge:** Plain

Date	Mintage	MS-63	Proof
2004 Proof	998	—	2,150

KM# 600   300 DOLLARS
60.0000 g., 0.5833 Gold 1.1252 oz. AGW, 40 mm. **Ruler:**
Elizabeth II **Subject:** Welcome Figure Totem Pole **Obv:** Head
right **Rev:** Men with totem pole

Date	Mintage	MS-63	Proof
2005 Proof	948	—	2,150

KM# 570.1   300 DOLLARS
45.0000 g., 0.5833 Gold 0.8439 oz. AGW, 40 mm. **Ruler:**
Elizabeth II **Subject:** Standard Time - 4 AM Pacific **Obv:** Head
right **Rev:** Roman numeral clock with world inside

Date	Mintage	MS-63	Proof
2005 Proof	200	—	1,650

KM# 570.2   300 DOLLARS
45.0000 g., 0.5830 Gold 0.8434 oz. AGW, 40 mm. **Ruler:**
Elizabeth II **Subject:** Standard Time - Mountian 5 AM **Obv:** Head
right **Rev:** Roman numeral clock with world inside.

Date	Mintage	MS-63	Proof
2005 Proof	200	—	1,650

KM# 570.3   300 DOLLARS
45.0000 g., 0.5830 Gold 0.8434 oz. AGW, 40 mm. **Ruler:**
Elizabeth II **Subject:** Standard Time - Central 6 PM **Obv:** Head
right **Rev:** Roman numeral clock with world inside

Date	Mintage	MS-63	Proof
2005 Proof	200	—	1,650

KM# 570.4   300 DOLLARS
45.0000 g., 0.5830 Gold 0.8434 oz. AGW, 40 mm. **Ruler:**
Elizabeth II **Subject:** Standard Time - Eastern 7 AM **Obv:** Head
right **Rev:** Roman numeral clock with world inside

Date	Mintage	MS-63	Proof
2005 Proof	200	—	1,650

KM# 570.5   300 DOLLARS
45.0000 g., 0.5830 Gold 0.8434 oz. AGW, 40 mm. **Ruler:**
Elizabeth II **Subject:** Standard Time - Atlantic 8 AM **Obv:** Head
right **Rev:** Roman numeral clock with world inside

Date	Mintage	MS-63	Proof
2005 Proof	200	—	1,650

KM# 570.6   300 DOLLARS
45.0000 g., 0.5830 Gold 0.8434 oz. AGW, 40 mm. **Ruler:**
Elizabeth II **Subject:** Standard Time - Newfoundland 8:30 **Obv:**
Head right **Rev:** Roman numeral clock with world inside

Date	Mintage	MS-63	Proof
2005 Proof	200	—	1,650

KM# 596   300 DOLLARS
60.0000 g., 0.5833 Gold 1.1252 oz. AGW, 50 mm. **Ruler:**
Elizabeth II **Subject:** Shinplaster **Obv:** Head right **Rev:** Britannia
bust, spear over shoulder

Date	Mintage	MS-63	Proof
2005 Proof	994	—	2,150

KM# 678   300 DOLLARS
45.0000 g., 0.5833 Gold 0.8439 oz. AGW, 40 mm. **Ruler:**
Elizabeth II **Rev:** Hologram of Canadarm, Col. C. Hadfield in
spacewalk

Date	Mintage	MS-63	Proof
2006 Proof	581	—	1,650

KM# 679   300 DOLLARS
60.0000 g., 0.5833 Gold 1.1252 oz. AGW, 50 mm. **Ruler:**
Elizabeth II **Subject:** Queen Elizabeth's 80th Birthday **Rev:** State
Crown, colorized

Date	Mintage	MS-63	Proof
2006 Proof	996	—	2,150

KM# 680   300 DOLLARS
60.0000 g., 0.5833 Gold 1.1252 oz. AGW, 50 mm. **Ruler:**
Elizabeth II **Subject:** Crystal Snowflake

Date	Mintage	MS-63	Proof
2006 Proof	998	—	2,150

KM# 595   300 DOLLARS
60.0000 g., 0.5833 Gold 1.1252 oz. AGW, 50 mm. **Ruler:**
Elizabeth II **Subject:** Shinplaster **Obv:** Head right **Rev:** Seated
Britannia with shield

Date	Mintage	MS-63	Proof
2006 Proof	940	—	2,150

KM# 692   300 DOLLARS
60.0000 g., 0.5833 Gold 1.1252 oz. AGW, 50 mm. **Ruler:**
Elizabeth II **Subject:** Shinplaster **Rev:** 1923 25 cent bank note

Date	Mintage	MS-63	Proof
2007 Proof	778	—	2,150

KM# 740   300 DOLLARS
45.0000 g., 0.5830 Gold 0.8434 oz. AGW, 40 mm. **Ruler:**
Elizabeth II **Rev:** Canadian Rockies panoramic hologram

Date	Mintage	MS-63	Proof
2007 Proof	511	—	1,650

KM# 752   300 DOLLARS
60.0000 g., 0.5830 Gold 1.1246 oz. AGW, 50 mm. **Ruler:**
Elizabeth II **Subject:** Vancouver Olympics **Rev:** Olympic ideals,
classic figures and torch

Date	Mintage	MS-63	Proof
2007 Proof	953	—	2,150

KM# 825   300 DOLLARS
45.0000 g., 0.5830 Gold 0.8434 oz. AGW, 50 mm. **Ruler:**
Elizabeth II **Rev:** Alberta Coat of Arms

Date	Mintage	MS-63	Proof
2008 Proof	344	—	1,650

KM# 826   300 DOLLARS
60.0000 g., 0.5830 Gold 1.1246 oz. AGW, 50 mm. **Ruler:**
Elizabeth II **Rev:** Newfoundland and Labrador Coat of Arms

Date	Mintage	MS-63	Proof
2008 Proof	472	—	2,150

KM# 827   300 DOLLARS
45.0000 g., 0.5830 Gold 0.8434 oz. AGW, 40 mm. **Ruler:**
Elizabeth II **Subject:** Canadian achievements IMAX **Rev:** Kid in
audience reaching out to shark on big screen

Date	Mintage	MS-63	Proof
2008 Proof	—	—	1,650

KM# 828   300 DOLLARS
60.0000 g., 0.5830 Gold 1.1246 oz. AGW, 50 mm. **Ruler:**
Elizabeth II **Rev:** Four seasons moon mask in color, blue design
in border

Date	Mintage	MS-63	Proof
2008 Proof	544	—	2,150

KM# 830   300 DOLLARS
60.0000 g., 0.5830 Gold 1.1246 oz. AGW, 50 mm. **Ruler:**
Elizabeth II **Subject:** Vancouver Olympics **Rev:** Olympic
competition, athletics and torch

Date	Mintage	MS-63	Proof
2008 Proof	334	—	2,150

KM# 900   300 DOLLARS
60.0000 g., 0.5830 Gold 1.1246 oz. AGW, 50 mm. **Ruler:**
Elizabeth II **Subject:** Yukon Coat of Arms **Obv:** Bust right **Obv.
Legend:** Elizabeth II DG Regina **Obv. Designer:** Susanna Blunt
Rev: Yukon Coat of Arms **Rev. Legend:** Canada 300 Dollars

Date	Mintage	MS-63	Proof
2009 Proof	325	—	2,150

KM# 877   300 DOLLARS
60.0000 g., 0.5830 Gold 1.1246 oz. AGW, 50 mm. **Ruler:**
Elizabeth II **Rev:** Summer moon mask, enameled

Date	Mintage	MS-63	Proof
2009 Proof	—	—	2,150

KM# 911   300 DOLLARS
60.0000 g., 0.5830 Gold 1.1246 oz. AGW, 50 mm. **Ruler:**
Elizabeth II **Subject:** 2010 Vancouver Olympics **Obv:** Bust right
Obv. Designer: Susanna Blunt **Rev:** Athletics with torch -
Olympic firendship

Date	Mintage	MS-63	Proof
2009 Proof	880	—	2,150

KM# 999   300 DOLLARS
54.0000 g., 0.5830 Gold 1.0121 oz. AGW, 50 mm. **Ruler:**
Elizabeth II **Rev:** British Columbia Arms

Date	Mintage	MS-63	Proof
2010 Proof	500	—	1,900

KM# 1047   300 DOLLARS
60.0000 g., 0.5830 Gold 1.1246 oz. AGW, 50 mm. **Ruler:**
Elizabeth II **Rev:** Snowflake, white crystals

Date	Mintage	MS-63	Proof
2010 Proof	750	—	2,150

KM# 1078   300 DOLLARS
60.0000 g., 0.5830 Gold 1.1246 oz. AGW, 50 mm. **Ruler:**
Elizabeth II **Rev:** New Brunswick Coat of arms

Date	Mintage	MS-63	Proof
2010 Proof	500	—	2,150

KM# 1095   300 DOLLARS
60.0000 g., 0.9167 Gold 1.7683 oz. AGW, 50 mm. **Ruler:**
Elizabeth II **Rev:** Manitoba Coat of arms

Date	Mintage	MS-63	Proof
2011 Proof	500	—	3,300

KM# 1215 300 DOLLARS
60.0000 g., 0.9170 Gold 1.7689 oz. AGW, 50 mm. **Ruler:** Elizabeth II **Obv:** Bust right **Rev:** Arms of Nova Scotia

Date	Mintage	MS-63	Proof
2011 Proof	—	—	3,300

KM# 1240 300 DOLLARS
45.0000 g., 0.5830 Gold 0.8434 oz. AGW, 40 mm. **Ruler:** Elizabeth II **Subject:** Elizabeth II, Diamond Jubilee **Obv:** Bust right **Rev:** Youthful bust with crown right, insert crystal at right

Date	Mintage	MS-63	Proof
1952-2012 Proof	—	—	1,600

KM# 1195 300 DOLLARS
Gold **Ruler:** Elizabeth II **Obv:** Bust right **Rev:** Youthful Elizabeth II right, hands uplifted, crystal

Date	Mintage	MS-63	Proof
2012 Proof	—	—	1,650

KM# 1224 300 DOLLARS
60.0000 g., 0.9167 Gold 1.7683 oz. AGW, 50 mm. **Ruler:** Elizabeth II **Obv:** Bust right **Rev:** Shield of Quebec

Date	Mintage	MS-63	Proof
2012 Proof	—	—	3,300

KM# 433 350 DOLLARS
38.0500 g., 0.9999 Gold 1.2232 oz. AGW, 34 mm. **Ruler:** Elizabeth II **Subject:** The Mayflower Flower **Obv:** Crowned head right **Rev:** Two flowers **Rev. Designer:** Bonnie Ross **Edge:** Reeded

Date	Mintage	MS-63	Proof
2001 Proof	1,988	—	2,350

KM# 502 350 DOLLARS
38.0500 g., 0.9999 Gold 1.2232 oz. AGW, 34 mm. **Ruler:** Elizabeth II **Subject:** The Wild Rose **Obv:** Crowned head right **Obv. Designer:** Dora de Pedery-Hunt **Rev:** Wild rose plant **Rev. Designer:** Dr. Andreas Kare Hellum

Date	Mintage	MS-63	Proof
2002 Proof	2,001	—	2,350

KM# 504 350 DOLLARS
38.0500 g., 0.9999 Gold 1.2232 oz. AGW, 34 mm. **Ruler:** Elizabeth II **Subject:** The White Trillium **Obv:** Crowned head right **Obv. Designer:** Dora de Pedery-Hunt **Rev:** White Trillium

Date	Mintage	MS-63	Proof
2003 Proof	1,865	—	2,350

KM# 601 350 DOLLARS
38.0500 g., 0.9999 Gold 1.2232 oz. AGW **Ruler:** Elizabeth II **Subject:** Western Red Lily **Obv:** Head right **Rev:** Western Red Lilies

Date	Mintage	MS-63	Proof
2005 Proof	1,634	—	2,350

KM# 626 350 DOLLARS
38.0500 g., 0.9999 Gold 1.2232 oz. AGW, 34 mm. **Ruler:** Elizabeth II **Subject:** Iris Vericolor **Obv:** Crowned head right **Rev:** Iris

Date	Mintage	MS-63	Proof
2006 Proof	1,995	—	2,350

KM# 754 350 DOLLARS
35.0000 g., 0.9999 Gold 1.1251 oz. AGW, 34 mm. **Ruler:** Elizabeth II **Rev:** Purple violet

Date	Mintage	MS-63	Proof
2007 Proof	1,392	—	2,200

KM# 832 350 DOLLARS
35.0000 g., 0.9999 Gold 1.1251 oz. AGW, 34 mm. **Ruler:** Elizabeth II **Rev:** Purple saxifrage

Date	Mintage	MS-63	Proof
2008 Proof	1,313	—	2,200

KM# 901 350 DOLLARS
35.0000 g., 0.9990 Gold 1.1241 oz. AGW, 34 mm. **Ruler:** Elizabeth II **Subject:** Pitcher plant **Obv:** Bust right **Obv. Legend:** Elizabeth II Canada DG Regina Fine Gold 350 Dollars or PUR 99999 **Obv. Designer:** Susana Blunt **Rev:** Cluster of pitcher flowers **Rev. Legend:** Julie Wilson

Date	Mintage	MS-63	Proof
2009 Proof	1,003	—	2,200

KM# 1019 350 DOLLARS
35.0000 g., 0.9990 Gold 1.1241 oz. AGW, 34 mm. **Ruler:** Elizabeth II **Rev:** Praire Crocus **Rev. Designer:** Celia Godkin

Date	Mintage	MS-63	Proof
2010 Proof	Est. 1,400	—	2,200

KM# 1136 350 DOLLARS
35.0000 g., 0.9999 Gold 1.1251 oz. AGW, 34 mm. **Ruler:** Elizabeth II **Obv:** Bust right **Rev:** Mountain Avens in bloom **Edge:** Reeded

Date	Mintage	MS-63	Proof
2011 Proof	1,300	—	2,200

KM# 710 500 DOLLARS
156.5000 g., 0.9999 Gold 5.0309 oz. AGW, 60 mm. **Ruler:** Elizabeth II **Subject:** Queen's 60th Wedding **Rev:** Coat of Arms and Mascots of Elizabeth and Philip

Date	Mintage	MS-63	Proof
2007	198	9,150	—

KM# 782 500 DOLLARS
155.7600 g., 0.9990 Gold 5.0026 oz. AGW, 60 mm. **Ruler:** Elizabeth II **Subject:** Ottawa Mint Centennial 1908-2008 **Rev:** Mint building facade **Note:** Illustration reduced.

Date	Mintage	MS-63	Proof
2008	248	9,150	—

KM# 897 500 DOLLARS
156.0500 g., 0.9990 Gold 5.0119 oz. AGW, 60 mm. **Ruler:** Elizabeth II **Subject:** 150th Anniversary of the start of construction of the Parliament Buildings **Obv:** Bust right **Rev:** Incomplete west block, original architecture **Rev. Legend:** 500 Dollars 1859-2009

Date	Mintage	MS-63	Proof
2009 Proof	77	—	9,150

KM# 1007 500 DOLLARS
156.5000 g., 0.9990 Gold 5.0263 oz. AGW, 60 mm. **Ruler:** Elizabeth II **Subject:** 75th Anniversary of Canadian Bank Notes **Rev:** Abundance seated under tree

Date	Mintage	MS-63	Proof
2010 Proof	200	—	9,150

KM# 1179 500 DOLLARS
156.5000 g., 0.9999 Gold 5.0309 oz. AGW, 60 mm. **Ruler:** Elizabeth II **Obv:** Crowned bust of George V **Rev:** Arms of Canada, dual dates and denomination below **Edge:** Serially numbered

Date	Mintage	MS-63	Proof
1912-2012 Proof	200	—	9,150

KM# 681 2500 DOLLARS
1000.0000 g., 0.9999 Gold 32.146 oz. AGW, 101.6 mm. **Ruler:**

Elizabeth II **Subject:** Kilo **Rev:** Common Characters, Early Canada **Note:** Illustration reduced.

Date	Mintage	MS-63	Proof
2007	20	57,000	—

KM# 902   2500 DOLLARS
1000.0000 g., 0.9990 Silver 32.117 oz. ASW, 101.6 mm. **Ruler:** Elizabeth II **Series:** History and Culture Collection **Subject:** Modern Canada **Obv:** Bust right **Obv. Legend:** Vancouver 2010, 2500 Dollars, Elizabeth II **Obv. Designer:** Susanna Blunt **Rev:** Canadian landscape with modern elements **Note:** Illustration reduced.

Date	Mintage	MS-63	Proof
2009 Proof	2,500	—	1,250

KM# 902a   2500 DOLLARS
1000.0000 g., 0.9990 Gold 32.117 oz. AGW, 101.6 mm. **Ruler:** Elizabeth II **Series:** History and Culture Collection **Subject:** Modern Canada **Obv:** Bust right **Obv. Legend:** Vancouver 2010, 2500 Dollars, Elizabeth II **Obv. Designer:** Susana Blunt **Rev:** Canadian landscape with modern elements

Date	Mintage	MS-63	Proof
2009 Proof	50	—	57,000

KM# 912   2500 DOLLARS
1000.0000 g., 0.9999 Gold 32.146 oz. AGW, 101 mm. **Ruler:** Elizabeth II **Obv:** Bust right **Obv. Designer:** Susanna Blunt **Rev:** Mask with fish - Surviving the flood **Note:** Illustration reduced.

Date	Mintage	MS-63	Proof
2009 Proof	40	—	57,000

KM# 984   2500 DOLLARS
1000.0000 g., 0.9990 Gold 32.117 oz. AGW, 101 mm. **Ruler:** Elizabeth II **Note:** Illustration reduced.

Date	Mintage	MS-63	Proof
2010 Proof	20	—	57,000

KM# 1045   2500 DOLLARS
1000.0000 g., 0.9999 Gold 32.146 oz. AGW, 101 mm. **Ruler:** Elizabeth II **Subject:** Baniff, 125th Anniversary **Rev:** Highlights of Baniff **Note:** Illustration reduced.

Date	Mintage	MS-63	Proof
2010	—	—	57,000

KM# 1197   2500 DOLLARS
1000.0000 g., 0.9990 Gold 32.117 oz. AGW, 101.6 mm. **Ruler:** Elizabeth II **Subject:** LaCrosse, 350th Anniversary **Obv:** Bust right **Rev:** LaCrosse players

Date	Mintage	MS-63	Proof
2011 Proof	35	—	57,000

KM# 1217   2500 DOLLARS
1000.0000 g., 0.9999 Gold 32.146 oz. AGW, 101 mm. **Ruler:** Elizabeth II **Obv:** Bust right **Rev:** Early lacrosse game

Date	Mintage	MS-63	Proof
2011 Proof	—	—	57,000

KM# 1209   100000 DOLLARS
10000.0000 g., 1.0000 Gold 321.49 oz. AGW **Ruler:** Elizabeth II **Obv:** Bust right **Rev:** Bill Reid's sculpture: Spirit of Haida Gwaii **Note:** The sculpture is at the Canadian Embassy in Washington, D.C.

Date	Mintage	MS-63	Proof
2011 Proof	—	—	565,000

SILVER BULLION COINAGE

KM# 617   DOLLAR
1.5550 g., 0.9999 Silver 0.0500 oz. ASW, 16 mm. **Ruler:** Elizabeth II **Obv:** Crowned head right **Rev:** Holographic Maple leaf **Edge:** Reeded

Date	Mintage	MS-63	Proof
2003 Proof	—	—	4.50

KM# 621   DOLLAR
1.5550 g., 0.9999 Silver 0.0500 oz. ASW, 17 mm. **Ruler:** Elizabeth II **Obv:** Crowned head right **Rev:** Maple leaf **Edge:** Reeded

Date	Mintage	MS-63	Proof
2004 Mint logo privy mark Proof	13,859	—	4.50

KM# 718   DOLLAR
15.5500 g., 0.9990 Silver 0.4994 oz. ASW, 32 mm. **Ruler:** Elizabeth II **Obv:** Bust right **Rev:** Grey Wolf standing with moon in background **Rev. Designer:** William Woodruff **Edge:** Reeded

Date	Mintage	MS-63	Proof
2005	106,800	40.00	—
2006 WW	—	40.00	—
2007	—	40.00	—

KM# 618   2 DOLLARS
3.1100 g., 0.9999 Silver 0.1000 oz. ASW, 20.1 mm. **Ruler:** Elizabeth II **Obv:** Crowned head right **Rev:** Holographic Maple leaf **Edge:** Reeded

Date	Mintage	MS-63	Proof
2003 Proof	—	—	7.50

KM# 622   2 DOLLARS
3.1100 g., 0.9999 Silver 0.1000 oz. ASW, 21 mm. **Ruler:** Elizabeth II **Obv:** Crowned head right **Rev:** Maple leaf **Edge:** Reeded

Date	Mintage	MS-63	Proof
2004 Mint logo privy mark Proof	13,859	—	7.50

KM# 571   2 DOLLARS
3.1100 g., 0.9999 Silver 0.1000 oz. ASW, 21 mm. **Ruler:** Elizabeth II **Obv:** Head right **Rev:** Lynx

Date	Mintage	MS-63	Proof
2005 Proof	—	—	7.50

KM# 619   3 DOLLARS
7.7760 g., 0.9999 Silver 0.2500 oz. ASW, 26.9 mm. **Ruler:** Elizabeth II **Obv:** Crowned head right **Rev:** Holographic Maple leaf **Edge:** Reeded

Date	Mintage	MS-63	Proof
2003 Proof	—	—	15.00

KM# 623   3 DOLLARS
7.7760 g., 0.9999 Silver 0.2500 oz. ASW, 27 mm. **Ruler:** Elizabeth II **Obv:** Crowned head right **Rev:** Maple leaf **Edge:** Reeded

Date	Mintage	MS-63	Proof
2004 Mint logo privy mark Proof	13,859	—	12.50

KM# 572 3 DOLLARS
7.7760 g., 0.9999 Silver 0.2500 oz. ASW, 27 mm. **Ruler:** Elizabeth II **Obv:** Head right **Rev:** Lynx

Date	Mintage	MS-63	Proof
2005 Proof	—	—	12.50

KM# 620 4 DOLLARS
15.5500 g., 0.9999 Silver 0.4999 oz. ASW, 33.9 mm. **Ruler:** Elizabeth II **Obv:** Crowned head right **Rev:** Holographic Maple leaf **Edge:** Reeded

Date	Mintage	MS-63	Proof
2003 Proof	—	—	25.00

KM# 624 4 DOLLARS
15.5500 g., 0.9999 Silver 0.4999 oz. ASW, 34 mm. **Ruler:** Elizabeth II **Obv:** Crowned head right **Rev:** Maple leaf **Edge:** Reeded

Date	Mintage	MS-63	Proof
2004 Mint logo privy mark Proof	13,859	—	22.50

KM# 573 4 DOLLARS
15.5500 g., 0.9999 Silver 0.4999 oz. ASW, 34 mm. **Ruler:** Elizabeth II **Obv:** Head right **Rev:** Lynx

Date	Mintage	MS-63	Proof
2005 Proof	—	—	22.50

KM# 437 5 DOLLARS
31.1035 g., 0.9999 Silver 0.9999 oz. ASW, 38 mm. **Ruler:** Elizabeth II **Obv:** Crowned head right, date and denomination below **Rev:** Radiant maple leaf hologram **Edge:** Reeded

Date	Mintage	MS-63	Proof
2001 Good fortune privy mark	29,906	75.00	

KM# 187 5 DOLLARS
31.1000 g., 0.9999 Silver 0.9997 oz. ASW **Ruler:** Elizabeth II **Obv:** Crowned head right, date and denomination below **Obv. Designer:** Dora de Pedery-Hunt **Rev:** Maple leaf flanked by 9999

Date	Mintage	MS-63	Proof
2001	398,563	35.00	—
2001 Reverse proof, Snake privy mark	25,000	—	45.00
2002	576,196	35.00	—
2002 Reverse proof, Horse privy mark	25,000	—	45.00
2003	—	35.00	—
2003 Reverse proof, sheep privy mark	25,000	—	45.00

KM# 436 5 DOLLARS
31.1035 g., 0.9999 Silver 0.9999 oz. ASW, 38 mm. **Ruler:** Elizabeth II **Obv:** Crowned head right, date and denomination below **Rev:** Three maple leaves in autumn colors, 9999 flanks **Rev. Designer:** Debbie Adams **Edge:** Reeded

Date	Mintage	MS-63	Proof
2001 Proof	49,709	—	40.00

KM# 505 5 DOLLARS
31.1035 g., 0.9999 Silver 0.9999 oz. ASW, 38 mm. **Ruler:** Elizabeth II **Obv:** Crowned head right, date and denomination below **Rev:** Two maple leaves in spring color (green) **Edge:** Reeded

Date	Mintage	MS-63	Proof
2002	29,509	37.50	—

KM# 521 5 DOLLARS
31.1035 g., 0.9999 Silver 0.9999 oz. ASW **Ruler:** Elizabeth II **Obv:** Head right **Rev:** Maple leaf, summer colors **Rev. Designer:** Stan Witten

Date	Mintage	MS-63	Proof
2003	29,416	37.50	—

KM# 607 5 DOLLARS
31.1200 g., 0.9999 Silver 1.0004 oz. ASW **Ruler:** Elizabeth II **Obv:** Head right **Rev:** Maple leaf, winter colors

Date	Mintage	MS-63	Proof
2004	—	37.50	—

KM# 625 5 DOLLARS
31.1035 g., 0.9999 Silver 0.9999 oz. ASW, 38 mm. **Ruler:** Elizabeth II **Obv:** Bust right **Obv. Designer:** Susanna Blunt **Rev:** Maple leaf **Edge:** Reeded

Date	Mintage	MS-63	Proof
2004 Mint logo privy mark Specimen	13,859	—	37.50
2004 Monkey privy mark Specimen	25,000	—	37.50
2004 D-Day privy mark Specimen	11,698	—	37.50
2004 Desjardins privy mark	15,000	37.50	—
2004 Capricorn privy Mark Reverse proof	5,000	—	37.50

Date	Mintage	MS-63	Proof
2004 Aquarius privy mark Reverse proof	5,000	—	37.50
2004 Pisces privy mark Reverse proof	5,000	—	37.50
2004 Aries privy mark Reverse proof	5,000	—	37.50
2004 Taurus privy mark Reverse proof	5,000	—	37.50
2004 Gemini privy mark Reverse proof	5,000	—	37.50
2004 Cancer privy mark Reverse proof	5,000	—	37.50
2004 Leo privy mark Reverse proof	5,000	—	37.50
2004 Virgo privy mark Reverse proof	5,000	—	37.50
2004 Libra privy mark Reverse proof	5,000	—	37.50
2004 Scorpio privy mark Reverse proof	5,000	—	37.50
2004 Sagittarius privy mark Reverse proof	5,000	—	37.50
2005	—	35.00	—
2005 Tulip privy mark Reverse proof	3,500	—	40.00
2005 Tank privy mark Reverse proof	7,000	—	60.00
2005 USS Missouri privy mark Reverse proof	7,000	—	60.00
2005 Rooster privy mark Reverse proof	15,000	—	50.00
2006	—	35.00	—
2006 Dog privy mark Reverse proof	—	—	50.00
2007	—	35.00	—
2007 F12 privy mark Reverse proof	—	—	130
2007 Pig privy mark Reverse proof	—	—	40.00
2008	—	35.00	—
2008 F12 privy mark Reverse proof	—	—	130
2008 Rat privy mark Reverse proof	—	—	40.00
2009	—	35.00	—
2009 Brandenberg Gate privy mark Reverse proof	—	—	50.00
2009 Tower Bridge privy mark Reverse proof	—	—	40.00
2009 Ox Privy mark Reverse proof	—	—	37.50
2010	—	35.00	—
2011	—	35.00	—
2012	—	35.00	—

KM# 508 5 DOLLARS
31.1035 g., 0.9999 Silver 0.9999 oz. ASW, 38 mm. **Ruler:** Elizabeth II **Obv:** Crowned head right, date and denomination below **Obv. Designer:** Dora de Pedery-Hunt **Rev:** Holographic Maple leaf flanked by 9999 **Edge:** Reeded

Date	Mintage	MS-63	Proof
2003 Proof	—	—	37.50

KM# 522 5 DOLLARS
31.1050 g., 0.9999 Silver 0.9999 oz. ASW **Ruler:** Elizabeth II **Obv:** Head right **Rev:** Maple leaf, winter color **Rev. Designer:** Stan Witten

Date	Mintage	MS-63	Proof
2004	26,763	35.00	—

KM# 574 5 DOLLARS
31.1035 g., 0.9999 Silver 0.9999 oz. ASW, 38 mm. **Ruler:** Elizabeth II **Obv:** Head right **Rev:** Lynx

Date	Mintage	MS-63	Proof
2005 Proof	—	—	37.50

KM# 924   5 DOLLARS
31.1050 g., 0.9999 Silver 0.9999 oz. ASW **Ruler:** Elizabeth II
Rev: Maple Leaf, laser engraved **Rev. Designer:** Joan Nguyen

Date	Mintage	MS-63	Proof
2005 Proof	25,000	—	60.00

KM# 550   5 DOLLARS
31.1035 g., 0.9999 Silver 0.9999 oz. ASW **Ruler:** Elizabeth II
Obv: Head right **Rev:** Big Leaf Maple, colorized **Rev. Designer:** Stan Witten

Date	Mintage	MS-63	Proof
2005	21,233	35.00	

KM# 660   5 DOLLARS
31.1050 g., 0.9990 Silver 0.9990 oz. ASW **Ruler:** Elizabeth II
Obv: Bust right **Obv. Designer:** Susanna Blunt **Rev:** Silver maple, colorized **Rev. Designer:** Stan Witten

Date	Mintage	MS-63	Proof
2006	14,157	37.50	

KM# 625a   5 DOLLARS
31.1050 g., 0.9999 Silver 0.9999 oz. ASW, 38 mm. **Ruler:** Elizabeth II **Rev:** Maple leaf, gilt

Date	Mintage	MS-63	Proof
2007	—	75.00	—
2008	—	75.00	—
2009	—	75.00	—
2009 Tower Bridge Privy Mark	—	75.00	—
2010	—	75.00	—

KM# 729   5 DOLLARS
31.1050 g., 0.9990 Silver 0.9990 oz. ASW, 38 mm. **Ruler:** Elizabeth II **Obv:** Bust right **Rev:** Maple leaf orange multicolor

Date	Mintage	MS-63	Proof
2007 Proof	—	—	45.00

KM# 925   5 DOLLARS
31.1050 g., 0.9990 Silver 0.9990 oz. ASW **Ruler:** Elizabeth II
Obv: Bust right **Obv. Designer:** Susanna Blunt **Rev:** Sugar maple, colorized **Rev. Designer:** Stan Witten

Date	Mintage	MS-63	Proof
2007	11,495	37.50	—

KM# 928   5 DOLLARS
31.3900 g., 0.9990 Silver 1.0082 oz. ASW, 38 mm. **Ruler:** Elizabeth II **Rev:** Orange sugar maple leaf **Rev. Designer:** Stan Witten

Date	Mintage	MS-63	Proof
2007 Specimen	20,000	—	75.00

KM# 800   5 DOLLARS
31.1050 g., 0.9990 Silver 0.9990 oz. ASW, 38 mm. **Ruler:** Elizabeth II **Subject:** Vancouver Olympics **Obv:** Bust right **Obv. Designer:** Susanna Blunt **Rev:** Maple leaf, Olympic logo at left, turtle

Date	Mintage	MS-63	Proof
2008	—	37.50	—
2009	—	37.50	—
2010	—	37.50	—

KM# 798   5 DOLLARS
31.1050 g., 0.9990 Silver 0.9990 oz. ASW, 38 mm. **Ruler:** Elizabeth II **Subject:** Maple Leaf 20th Anniversary **Rev:** Maple Leaf, selective gold plating

Date	Mintage	MS-63	Proof
2008 Proof	10,000	—	75.00

KM# 799   5 DOLLARS
31.1050 g., 0.9990 Silver 0.9990 oz. ASW, 38 mm. **Ruler:** Elizabeth II **Subject:** Breast Cancer Awareness **Rev:** Multicolor, green maple leaf and pink ribbon

Date	Mintage	MS-63	Proof
2008	11,048	85.00	—

KM# 800a   5 DOLLARS
31.1050 g., 0.9999 Silver partially gilt 0.9999 oz. ASW, 38 mm. **Ruler:** Elizabeth II **Rev:** Maple leaf gilt, olympic logo at left

Date	Mintage	MS-63	Proof
2008		50.00	—

KM# 1056   5 DOLLARS
31.1050 g., 0.9999 Silver 0.9999 oz. ASW, 38 mm. **Ruler:** Elizabeth II **Rev:** Maple leaf in brown color, card diamond

Date	Mintage	MS-63	Proof
2008	—	50.00	—

KM# 1057   5 DOLLARS
31.1050 g., 0.9999 Silver 0.9999 oz. ASW, 38 mm. **Ruler:** Elizabeth II **Rev:** Maple Leaf in green color, card heart

Date	Mintage	MS-63	Proof
2008	—	50.00	—

KM# 1058   5 DOLLARS
31.1050 g., 0.9999 Silver 0.9999 oz. ASW, 38 mm. **Ruler:** Elizabeth II **Rev:** Maple leaf in green color, card club

Date	Mintage	MS-63	Proof
2008	—	50.00	—

KM# 1059   5 DOLLARS
31.1050 g., 0.9999 Silver 0.9999 oz. ASW, 38 mm. **Ruler:** Elizabeth II **Rev:** Maple Leaf in red color, card spade

Date	Mintage	MS-63	Proof
2008	—	50.00	—

KM# 863   5 DOLLARS
31.1050 g., 0.9999 Silver 0.9999 oz. ASW, 38 mm. **Ruler:**
Elizabeth II **Subject:** Vancouver Olympics **Rev:** Thunderbird
Totem **Rev. Designer:** Rick Harry

Date	Mintage	MS-63	Proof
2009	—	50.00	—

KM# 863a   5 DOLLARS
31.1050 g., 0.9999 Silver partially gilt 0.9999 oz. ASW, 38 mm.
Ruler: Elizabeth II **Rev:** Thunderbird, gilt

Date	Mintage	MS-63	Proof
2009	—	60.00	—

KM# 1061   5 DOLLARS
31.1050 g., 0.9999 Silver 0.9999 oz. ASW, 38 mm. **Ruler:**
Elizabeth II **Rev:** Maple leaf in red color, support our troops yellow
ribbon

Date	Mintage	MS-63	Proof
2009	—	70.00	—

KM# 998   5 DOLLARS
31.1200 g., 0.9990 Silver 0.9995 oz. ASW, 38 mm. **Ruler:**
Elizabeth II **Rev:** Olympic Hockey

Date	Mintage	MS-63	Proof
2010 Proof	—	—	42.50

KM# 998a   5 DOLLARS
31.1050 g., 0.9999 Silver partially gilt 0.9999 oz. ASW, 38 mm.
Ruler: Elizabeth II **Rev:** Hockey player, gilt maple leaves flanking

Date	Mintage	MS-63	Proof
2010	—	50.00	—

KM# 1077   5 DOLLARS
31.3900 g., 0.9990 Silver 1.0082 oz. ASW, 34 mm. **Ruler:**
Elizabeth II **Rev:** Maple leaf on 45 degree angle left

Date	Mintage	MS-63	Proof
2010 Proof	9,000	—	80.00

KM# 1052   5 DOLLARS
31.1050 g., 0.9999 Silver 0.9999 oz. ASW, 38 mm. **Ruler:**
Elizabeth II **Rev:** Wolf standing with moonlight in background

Date	Mintage	MS-63	Proof
2011	1,000,000	40.00	—

KM# 1109   5 DOLLARS
31.1050 g., 0.9990 Silver 0.9990 oz. ASW, 38 mm. **Ruler:**
Elizabeth II **Rev:** Grizzly Bear walking right

Date	Mintage	MS-63	Proof
2011	—	40.00	—

KM# 1164   5 DOLLARS
31.1050 g., 0.9990 Silver 0.9990 oz. ASW, 38 mm. **Ruler:**
Elizabeth II **Obv. Designer:** Susanna Blunt **Rev:** Cougar **Rev.
Designer:** William Woodruff

Date	Mintage	MS-63	Proof
2012	1,000,000	40.00	—

KM# 1158   10 DOLLARS
31.1050 g., 0.9999 Silver 0.9999 oz. ASW, 38 mm. **Ruler:**
Elizabeth II **Obv:** Bust right **Rev:** Branch with three maple leaves

Date	Mintage	MS-63	Proof
2011 Proof	—	—	50.00

KM# 1062   20 DOLLARS
7.9600 g., 0.9999 Silver 0.2559 oz. ASW, 27 mm. **Ruler:**
Elizabeth II **Rev:** Five Maple leaves at left **Note:** Thick planchet

Date	Mintage	MS-63	Proof
2011	200,000	25.00	—

KM# 1176   20 DOLLARS
7.9600 g., 0.9999 Silver 0.2559 oz. ASW, 27 mm. **Ruler:**
Elizabeth II **Obv:** Bust right **Rev:** Canoe and reflection **Rev.
Designer:** Jason Bouwman **Edge:** Reeded **Note:** Thick planchet.

Date	Mintage	MS-63	Proof
2011	200,000	25.00	—

KM# 1226   20 DOLLARS
7.9600 g., 0.9999 Silver 0.2559 oz. ASW, 27 mm. **Ruler:**
Elizabeth II **Obv:** Bust right **Rev:** Waterline view of polar bear
swimming **Edge:** Reeded

Date	Mintage	MS-63	Proof
2012	250,000	25.00	—

KM# 1239   20 DOLLARS
31.3900 g., 0.9990 Silver 1.0082 oz. ASW, 38 mm. **Ruler:**
Elizabeth II **Subject:** Elizabeth II, Diamond Jubilee **Obv:** Bust
right **Rev:** Youthful bust with crown right, crystal insert

Date	Mintage	MS-63	Proof
1952-2012 Proof	—	—	100

KM# 676   250 DOLLARS
1000.0000 g., 0.9999 Silver 32.146 oz. ASW **Ruler:** Elizabeth II
Subject: Kilo

Date	Mintage	MS-63	Proof
2006	—	1,350	—

KM# 1160   250 DOLLARS
1000.0000 g., 0.9999 Silver 32.146 oz. ASW, 101 mm. **Ruler:**
Elizabeth II **Rev:** Three maple leaves on branch

Date	Mintage	MS-63	Proof
2011	—	—	1,350

GOLD BULLION COINAGE

KM# 888   50 CENTS
1.2700 g., 0.9990 Gold 0.0408 oz. AGW, 13.92 mm. **Ruler:**
Elizabeth II **Subject:** Red maple **Obv:** Bust right **Obv. Legend:**
Elizabeth II 50 cents **Obv. Designer:** Susanna Blunt **Rev:** Two
maple leaves **Rev. Legend:** Canada, Fine gold 1/25 oz or PUR 9999

Date	Mintage	MS-63	Proof
2009 Proof	150,000	—	90.00

KM# 1085   50 CENTS
1.2700 g., 0.9990 Gold 0.0408 oz. AGW, 13.92 mm. **Ruler:**
Elizabeth II **Rev:** Geese in flight left **Rev. Designer:** Emily
Damstra

Date	Mintage	MS-63	Proof
2011 Proof	10,000	—	90.00

KM# 1214   50 CENTS
1.2700 g., 1.0000 Gold 0.0408 oz. AGW, 13.92 mm. **Ruler:**
Elizabeth II **Obv:** Bust right **Rev:** Three maple leaves, 2007-2012
above

Date	Mintage	MS-63	Proof
2012 Proof	—	—	90.00

KM# 438   DOLLAR
1.5810 g., 0.9990 Gold 0.0508 oz. AGW, 14.1 mm. **Ruler:**
Elizabeth II **Subject:** Holographic Maple Leaves **Obv:** Crowned
head right **Rev:** Three maple leaves multicolor hologram **Edge:**
Reeded

Date	Mintage	MS-63	Proof
2001	600	85.00	—

KM# 1138   DOLLAR
1.5600 g., 0.9999 Gold 0.0501 oz. AGW, 14 mm. **Ruler:**
Elizabeth II **Obv:** Bust right **Rev:** Maple leaf

Date	Mintage	MS-63	Proof
1911-2011	—	—	100

KM# 1213   DOLLAR
1.5810 g., 1.0000 Gold 0.0508 oz. AGW, 14.1 mm.   **Ruler:**
Elizabeth II **Obv:** Bust right **Rev:** Three maple leaves, 2007-2012
above

Date	Mintage	MS-63	Proof
2012 Proof	—	—	110

KM# 439   5 DOLLARS
3.1310 g., 0.9999 Gold 0.1006 oz. AGW, 16 mm.   **Ruler:**
Elizabeth II **Subject:** Holographic Maple Leaves **Obv:** Crowned
head right **Rev:** Three maple leaves multicolor hologram **Edge:**
Reeded

Date	Mintage	MS-63	Proof
2001	600	200	—

KM# 929   5 DOLLARS
3.1300 g., 0.9990 Gold 0.1005 oz. AGW, 16 mm.   **Ruler:**
Elizabeth II **Obv. Designer:** Susan Blunt **Rev:** Maple leaf **Rev.
Designer:** Walter Ott

Date	Mintage	MS-63	Proof
2007	—	—	200
2008	—	—	200
2009	—	—	200
2010	—	—	200
2011	—	—	200

KM# 1139   5 DOLLARS
3.1300 g., 0.9990 Gold 0.1005 oz. AGW, 16 mm.   **Ruler:**
Elizabeth II **Obv:** Bust right **Rev:** Maple leaf

Date	Mintage	MS-63	Proof
1911-2011	—	225	—

KM# 1212   5 DOLLARS
3.1300 g., 1.0000 Gold 0.1006 oz. AGW, 16 mm.   **Ruler:**
Elizabeth II **Obv:** Bust right **Rev:** Three maple leaves, 2007-2012
above

Date	Mintage	MS-63	Proof
2012 Proof	—	—	200

KM# 440   10 DOLLARS
7.7970 g., 0.9999 Gold 0.2506 oz. AGW, 20 mm.   **Ruler:**
Elizabeth II **Subject:** Holographic Maples Leaves **Obv:** Crowned
head right **Rev:** Three maple leaves multicolor hologram **Edge:**
Reeded

Date	Mintage	MS-63	Proof
2001	15,000	475	—

KM# 1140   10 DOLLARS
7.7970 g., 0.9999 Gold 0.2506 oz. AGW, 20 mm.   **Ruler:**
Elizabeth II **Obv:** Bust right **Rev:** Maple leaf

Date	Mintage	MS-63	Proof
1911-2011	—	475	—

KM# 1211   10 DOLLARS
7.7970 g., 1.0000 Gold 0.2507 oz. AGW, 20 mm.   **Ruler:**
Elizabeth II **Obv:** Bust right **Rev:** Three maple leaves, 2007-2012
above

Date	Mintage	MS-63	Proof
2012 Proof	—	—	475

KM# 441   20 DOLLARS
15.5840 g., 0.9999 Gold 0.5010 oz. AGW, 25 mm.   **Ruler:**
Elizabeth II **Subject:** Holographic Maples Leaves **Obv:** Crowned
head right **Rev:** Three maple leaves multicolor hologram **Edge:**
Reeded

Date	Mintage	MS-63	Proof
2001	600	925	—

KM# 442   50 DOLLARS
31.1500 g., 0.9999 Gold 1.0014 oz. AGW, 30 mm.   **Ruler:**
Elizabeth II **Subject:** Holographic Maples Leaves **Obv:** Crowned
head right **Rev:** Three maple leaves multicolor hologram **Edge:**
Reeded

Date	Mintage	MS-63	Proof
2001	600	1,850	—

KM# 1042   50 DOLLARS
31.1050 g., 0.9990 Gold 0.9990 oz. AGW, 30 mm.   **Ruler:**
Elizabeth II **Rev:** Vancouver logo and maple leaf **Edge:** Reeded

Date	Mintage	MS-63	Proof
2008P	—	1,850	—

KM# 1042a   50 DOLLARS
31.1050 g., 0.9999 Gold partially enameled 0.9999 oz. AGW,
30 mm.   **Ruler:** Elizabeth II **Rev:** Maple leaf in red enamel,
olympic logo at left

Date	Mintage	MS-63	Proof
2008	—	1,850	—

KM# 1037   50 DOLLARS
31.1050 g., 0.9999 Gold 0.9999 oz. AGW, 30 mm.   **Ruler:**
Elizabeth II **Rev:** Thunderbird **Edge:** Reeded

Date	Mintage	MS-63	Proof
2009	—	1,850	—

KM# 1037a   50 DOLLARS
31.1050 g., 0.9999 Gold 0.9999 oz. AGW, 30 mm.   **Ruler:**
Elizabeth II **Rev:** Thunderbird, stars in red enamel highlights

Date	Mintage	MS-63	Proof
2009	—	1,850	—

KM# 1029   50 DOLLARS
31.1050 g., 0.9999 Gold 0.9999 oz. AGW, 30 mm.   **Ruler:**
Elizabeth II **Rev:** Hockey player flanked by maple leaves

Date	Mintage	MS-63	Proof
2010	—	1,850	—

KM# 1029a   50 DOLLARS
31.1050 g., 0.9999 Gold 0.9999 oz. AGW, 30 mm.   **Ruler:**
Elizabeth II **Rev:** Hockey player, red enameled maple leaves
flanking

Date	Mintage	MS-63	Proof
2010	—	1,850	—

KM# 1141   50 DOLLARS
31.1050 g., 0.9999 Gold 0.9999 oz. AGW, 30 mm.   **Ruler:**
Elizabeth II **Obv:** Bust right **Rev:** Maple leaf

Date	Mintage	MS-63	Proof
1911-2011	—	1,850	—

KM# 1210   50 DOLLARS
31.1050 g., 1.0000 Gold 100000 oz. AGW   **Ruler:** Elizabeth II
Obv: Bust right **Rev:** Three maple leaves, 2007-2012 above

Date	Mintage	MS-63	Proof
2012 Proof	—	—	1,850

KM# 750   200 DOLLARS
31.1050 g., 1.0000 Gold 100000 oz. AGW, 30 mm.   **Ruler:**
Elizabeth II **Rev:** Three maple leaves

Date	Mintage	MS-63	Proof
2007 Proof, T/E privy mark	500	—	1,850

KM# 786 200 DOLLARS
31.1050 g., 1.0000 Gold 100000 oz. AGW, 30 mm. **Ruler:** Elizabeth II **Obv:** Bust right on lathe-work background **Rev:** Two maple leaves on lathe-work background

Date	Mintage	MS-63	Proof
2008 Proof	—	—	1,850

KM# 1162 200 DOLLARS
31.1050 g., 1.0000 Gold 100000 oz. AGW **Ruler:** Elizabeth II **Rev:** Maple leaf with lathe backgound

Date	Mintage	MS-63	Proof
2009 Proof	—	—	1,850

KM# 1163 200 DOLLARS
31.1050 g., 0.9990 Gold 0.9990 oz. AGW **Ruler:** Elizabeth II **Subject:** Celebrating win **Rev:** Three athletics with hands raised

Date	Mintage	MS-63	Proof
2010 Proof	—	—	1,850

KM# 1165 200 DOLLARS
31.1050 g., 1.0000 Gold 100000 oz. AGW **Ruler:** Elizabeth II **Obv. Designer:** Susanna Blunt **Rev:** Mountie on horseback, lathe backgound **Rev. Designer:** Ago Aarand

Date	Mintage	MS-63	Proof
2011	—	1,850	—

KM# 1161 2500 DOLLARS
1000.0000 g., 0.9999 Gold 32.146 oz. AGW, 101 mm. **Ruler:** Elizabeth II **Rev:** Three maple leaves on branch

Date	Mintage	MS-63	Proof
2011	—	—	56,000

KM# 755 1000000 DOLLARS
100000.0000 g., 0.9999 Gold 3214.6 oz. AGW **Ruler:** Elizabeth II **Obv:** Bust right **Rev:** Three maple leaves **Note:** Cast

Date	Mintage	MS-63	Proof
2007	10	5,630,000	—

PLATINUM BULLION COINAGE

KM# 429 30 DOLLARS
3.1100 g., 0.9995 Platinum 0.0999 oz. APW, 16 mm. **Ruler:** Elizabeth II **Obv:** Crowned head right **Rev:** Harlequin duck's head **Rev. Designer:** Cosme Saffioti and Susan Taylor **Edge:** Reeded

Date	Mintage	MS-63	Proof
2001 Proof	448	—	200

KM# 1097 30 DOLLARS
3.1100 g., 0.9995 Platinum 0.0999 oz. APW, 16 mm. **Ruler:** Elizabeth II **Rev:** Great Blue Heron

Date	Mintage	MS-63	Proof
2002 Proof	344	—	200

KM# 1101 30 DOLLARS
3.1100 g., 0.9995 Platinum 0.0999 oz. APW, 16 mm. **Ruler:** Elizabeth II **Rev:** Atlantic Walrus

Date	Mintage	MS-63	Proof
2003	365	—	250

KM# 1105 30 DOLLARS
3.1100 g., 0.9995 Platinum 0.0999 oz. APW, 16 mm. **Ruler:** Elizabeth II **Rev:** Grizzly Bear

Date	Mintage	MS-63	Proof
2004 Proof	380	—	250

KM# 430 75 DOLLARS
7.7760 g., 0.9995 Platinum 0.2499 oz. APW, 20 mm. **Ruler:** Elizabeth II **Obv:** Crowned head right **Rev.** Harlequin duck in flight **Rev. Designer:** Cosme Saffioti and Susan Taylor **Edge:** Reeded

Date	Mintage	MS-63	Proof
2001 Proof	448	—	500

KM# 1098 75 DOLLARS
7.7700 g., 0.9995 Platinum 0.2497 oz. APW, 20 mm. **Ruler:** Elizabeth II **Rev:** Great Blue Heron

Date	Mintage	MS-63	Proof
2002 Proof	344	—	525

KM# 1102 75 DOLLARS
7.7700 g., 0.9995 Platinum 0.2497 oz. APW, 20 mm. **Ruler:** Elizabeth II **Rev:** Atlantic Walrus

Date	Mintage	MS-63	Proof
2003 Proof	365	—	550

KM# 1106 75 DOLLARS
7.7700 g., 0.9995 Platinum 0.2497 oz. APW, 20 mm. **Ruler:** Elizabeth II **Rev:** Grizzly Bear

Date	Mintage	MS-63	Proof
2004 Proof	380	—	550

KM# 431 150 DOLLARS
15.5500 g., 0.9995 Platinum 0.4997 oz. APW, 25 mm. **Ruler:** Elizabeth II **Obv:** Crowned head right **Rev:** Two harlequin ducks **Rev. Designer:** Cosme Saffioti and Susan Taylor **Edge:** Reeded

Date	Mintage	MS-63	Proof
2001 Proof	448	—	1,000

KM# 1099 150 DOLLARS
15.5500 g., 0.9995 Platinum 0.4997 oz. APW, 25 mm. **Ruler:** Elizabeth II **Rev:** Great Blue Heron

Date	Mintage	MS-63	Proof
2002 Proof	344	—	1,000

KM# 1103 150 DOLLARS
15.5500 g., 0.9995 Platinum 0.4997 oz. APW, 25 mm. **Ruler:** Elizabeth II **Rev:** Atlantic Walrus

Date	Mintage	MS-63	Proof
2003 Proof	365	—	1,000

KM# 1107 150 DOLLARS
15.5500 g., 0.9995 Platinum 0.4997 oz. APW, 25 mm. **Ruler:** Elizabeth II **Rev:** Grizzly Bear

Date	Mintage	MS-63	Proof
2004 Proof	380	—	1,000

KM# 432 300 DOLLARS
31.1035 g., 0.9995 Platinum 0.9995 oz. APW, 30 mm. **Ruler:** Elizabeth II **Obv:** Crowned head right **Rev:** Two standing harlequin ducks **Rev. Designer:** Cosme Saffioti and Susan Taylor **Edge:** Reeded

Date	Mintage	MS-63	Proof
2001 Proof	448	—	1,900

KM# 1100 300 DOLLARS
31.1050 g., 0.9995 Platinum 0.9995 oz. APW, 30 mm. **Ruler:** Elizabeth II **Rev:** Great Blue Heron

Date	Mintage	MS-63	Proof
2002 Proof	344	—	1,950

KM# 1104 300 DOLLARS
31.1050 g., 0.9995 Platinum 0.9995 oz. APW, 30 mm. **Ruler:** Elizabeth II **Rev:** Atlantic Walrus

Date	Mintage	MS-63	Proof
2003 Proof	365	—	1,950

KM# 1108 300 DOLLARS
31.1050 g., 0.9995 Platinum 0.9995 oz. APW, 30 mm. **Ruler:** Elizabeth II **Rev:** Grizzly Bear

Date	Mintage	MS-63	Proof
2004 Proof	380	—	1,950

KM# 753 300 DOLLARS
31.1050 g., 0.9999 Platinum 0.9999 oz. APW **Ruler:** Elizabeth II **Rev:** Wooly mammoth

Date	Mintage	MS-63	Proof
2007 Proof	400	—	3,200

KM# 831 300 DOLLARS
31.1050 g., 0.9990 Platinum 0.9990 oz. APW **Ruler:** Elizabeth II **Rev:** Saber Tooth Scimitar cat

Date	Mintage	MS-63	Proof
2008 Proof	200	—	3,500

KM# 951 300 DOLLARS
31.1600 g., 0.9999 Platinum 1.0008 oz. APW, 30 mm. **Ruler:** Elizabeth II **Rev:** Steppe Bison

Date	Mintage	MS-63	Proof
2009 Proof	200	—	3,500

KM# 1159 300 DOLLARS
31.1050 g., 0.9990 Platinum 0.9990 oz. APW, 30 mm. **Ruler:** Elizabeth II **Rev:** Ground Sloth

Date	Mintage	MS-63	Proof
2010 Proof	—	—	1,900

KM# 1175 300 DOLLARS
31.1050 g., 0.9995 Platinum 0.9995 oz. APW, 30 mm. **Ruler:** Elizabeth II **Obv:** Bust right **Rev:** Cougar head left

Date	Mintage	MS-63	Proof
2011 Proof	—	—	1,950

MINT SETS

KM#	Date	Mintage	Identification	Issue Price	Mkt Val
MS8	2001 (5)	600	KM438-442	1,996	2,950
MS10	2002 (7)	—	KM#444-449, 467, Oh! Canada! 135th Birthday Gift set.	17.00	16.00
MS11	2002 (7)	—	KM#444-449, 467, Tiny Treasures Uncirculated Gift Set	17.00	16.00
MS9	2002 (7)	135,000	Double-dated 1952-2002, KM#444-449, 467 Elizabeth II Golden Jubilee	11.75	16.00
MS12	2003 (7)	135,000	KM#289, 182b, 183b, 184b, 290, 186, 270	12.00	16.00
MS13	2003 (7)	75,000	KM490-496	13.25	20.00
MS14	2003 (7)	—	KM289, 182-184, 290, 186, 270, Oh! Canada!	17.75	16.00
MS15	2003 (7)	—	KM289, 182-184, 290, 186, 270, Tiny Treasures Uncirculated Gift Set	17.75	16.00

PROOF SETS

KM#	Date	Mintage	Identification	Issue Price	Mkt Val
PS51	2001 (4)	—	KM429, 430, 431, 432	—	3,600
PS54	2002 (2)	—	KM#519, 520	750	1,125
PS52	2002 (8)	100,000	KM#443, 444a,445,446a-449a, 467 Elizabeth II Golden Jubilee	60.00	125
PS53	2002 (3)	—	KM#459-461 Canadian Folklore and Legends Collection	57.50	35.00
PS55	2003 (8)	100,000	KM#182a,183a,184a, 186, 270d, 289, 290a, 450 100th Anniversary of the Cobalt Silver Strike	62.50	125
PS56	2003 (6)	30,000	KM#468-473 50th Anniversary of the Coronation of Elizabeth II	75.00	100
PS57	2004 (8)	—	KM#490, 491a-494a, 495, 496a, 512	—	115
PS58	2004 (5)	25,000	KM#621-625	—	100

SPECIMEN SETS (SS)

KM#	Date	Mintage	Identification	Issue Price	Mkt Val
SS90	2002 (7)	75,000	KM#444-449,462 Elizabeth II Golden Jubilee	30.00	65.00
SS91	2003 (3)	75,000	KM#(uncertain), 270, 289, 290	30.00	50.00

CAPE VERDE

The Republic of Cape Verde, Africa's smallest republic, is located in the Atlantic Ocean, about 370 miles (595 km.) west of Dakar, Senegal, off the coast of Africa. The 14-island republic has an area of 1,557 sq. mi. (4,033 sq. km.) and a population of 435,983. Capital: Praia. The refueling of ships and aircraft is the chief economic function of the country. Fishing is important and agriculture is widely practiced, but the Cape Verdes are not self-sufficient in food. Fish products, salt, bananas, and shellfish are exported.

After 500 years of Portuguese rule, the Cape Verdes became independent on July 5, 1975. At the first general election, all seats of the new national assembly were won by the Party for the Independence of Guinea-Bissau and Cape Verde (PAIGC). The PAIGC linked the two former colonies into one state. Antonio Mascarenhas Monteiro won the first free presidential election in 1991.

RULER
Portuguese, until 1975

MONETARY SYSTEM
100 Centavos = 1 Escudo

REPUBLIC
DECIMAL COINAGE

KM# 46   25 ESCUDOS
15.5517 g., 0.9990 Silver 0.4995 oz. ASW, 30.4 mm. **Obv:** Value above national arms **Rev:** Jesus **Edge:** Plain

Date	Mintage	F	VF	XF	Unc	BU
2006 Proof	—	Value: 40.00				

KM# 47   50 ESCUDOS
1.5550 g., 0.9990 Gold 0.0499 oz. AGW, 16 mm. **Obv:** Value above national arms **Rev:** Jesus **Edge:** Plain

Date	Mintage	F	VF	XF	Unc	BU
2006 Proof	—	Value: 100				

KM# 48   50 ESCUDOS
25.0000 g., 0.9250 Silver 0.7435 oz. ASW, 38.8 mm. **Subject:** 500th Anniversary Death of Christopher Columbus **Obv:** National arms **Obv. Legend:** CABO VERDE **Rev:** Sailing ship "Santa Maria" **Rev. Legend:** A SANTA MARIA DE CHRIST?V?O COLOMBO **Edge:** Reeded

Date	Mintage	F	VF	XF	Unc	BU
2006 Proof	—	Value: 55.00				

KM# 49   50 ESCUDOS
25.0000 g., 0.9250 Silver 0.7435 oz. ASW, 38.6 mm. **Subject:** Appearance in Grotto **Obv:** National arms **Obv. Legend:** CABO VERDE **Rev:** Maria standing facing 3/4 left at right **Rev. Legend:** AVE MARIA - LOURDES **Edge:** Reeded

Date	Mintage	F	VF	XF	Unc	BU
2006 Proof	—	Value: 65.00				

KM# 50   50 ESCUDOS
25.0000 g., 0.9250 Silver 0.7435 oz. ASW **Obv:** National arms **Rev:** Red Kite bird

Date	Mintage	F	VF	XF	Unc	BU
2006 Proof	—	Value: 65.00				

KM# 52   50 ESCUDOS
25.0000 g., 0.9250 Silver 0.7435 oz. ASW, 38.6 mm. **Rev:** East India Company's Princess Louisa and 1/2 real from shipwreck

Date	Mintage	F	VF	XF	Unc	BU
2006 Proof	Est. 1,500	Value: 75.00				

KM# 53   50 ESCUDOS
25.0000 g., 0.9250 Silver 0.7435 oz. ASW, 38.6 mm. **Rev:** Princess Louisa hitting the reef, 1/2 real from shipwreck

Date	Mintage	F	VF	XF	Unc	BU
2006 Proof	Est. 1,500	Value: 75.00				

KM# 45   200 ESCUDOS
7.8000 g., Copper-Nickel, 29.5 mm. **Subject:** 30th Anniversary of Independence **Obv:** National arms in number 2 of 200 **Rev:** Symbolic education design **Edge:** Reeded **Shape:** Round

Date	Mintage	F	VF	XF	Unc	BU
2005	—	—	—	—	8.50	10.00

KM# 45a   200 ESCUDOS
18.2800 g., 0.9250 Silver 0.5436 oz. ASW **Subject:** 30th Anniversary of Independence **Obv:** National arms in number 2 of 200 **Rev:** Symbolic education design **Edge:** Reeded **Shape:** Round

Date	Mintage	F	VF	XF	Unc	BU
2005 Proof	—	Value: 70.00				

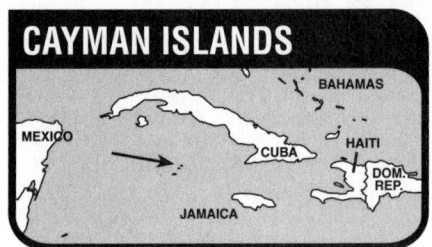

KM# 51   250 ESCUDOS
Copper-Nickel **Subject:** Independence, 35th Anniversary **Obv:** Ship sailing forward **Rev:** Arms

Date	Mintage	F	VF	XF	Unc	BU
2010	—	—	—	—	—	15.00

CAYMAN ISLANDS

The Cayman Islands are a British Crown Colony situated about 180 miles (280 km) northwest of Jamaica. It consists of three islands: Grand Cayman, Little Cayman, and Cayman Brac. The islands have an area of 102 sq. mi. (259 sq. km.) and a population of 33,200. Capital: George Town. Seafaring, commerce, banking, and tourism are the principal industries. Rope, turtle shells, and sharkskins are exported.

RULER
British

MINT MARKS
CHI - Valcambi

MONETARY SYSTEM
100 Cents = 1 Dollar

BRITISH COLONY
DECIMAL COINAGE

KM# 131   CENT
2.5500 g., Copper Plated Steel, 17 mm. **Ruler:** Elizabeth II **Obv:** Crowned head right **Rev:** Grand Caiman thrush **Edge:** Plain

Date	Mintage	F	VF	XF	Unc	BU
2002	10,000,000	—	—	0.15	0.35	0.75
2005	16,220,000	—	—	0.15	0.35	0.75
2008	12,000,000	—	—	0.15	0.35	0.75

KM# 132   5 CENTS
2.0000 g., Nickel Plated Steel, 18 mm. **Ruler:** Elizabeth II **Obv:** Crowned head right **Rev:** Pink-spotted shrimp **Edge:** Plain

Date	Mintage	F	VF	XF	Unc	BU
2002	2,500,000	—	—	0.15	0.35	1.00
2005	2,500,000	—	—	0.15	0.35	1.00
2008	300,000	—	—	0.15	0.35	1.00

KM# 133   10 CENTS
3.4500 g., Nickel Plated Steel, 21 mm. **Ruler:** Elizabeth II **Obv:** Head with tiara right **Rev:** Green turtle surfacing **Edge:** Reeded

Date	Mintage	F	VF	XF	Unc	BU
2002	3,000,000	—	0.25	0.40	1.00	1.25
2005	3,000,000	—	0.25	0.40	1.00	1.25
2008	3,500,000	—	0.25	0.40	1.00	1.25

KM# 134   25 CENTS
5.1000 g., Nickel Plated Steel, 24.26 mm. **Ruler:** Elizabeth II **Obv:** Head with tiara right **Rev:** Schooner sailing right **Edge:** Reeded

Date	Mintage	F	VF	XF	Unc	BU
2002	2,500,000	—	—	0.75	1.25	1.50
2005	2,500,000	—	—	0.75	1.25	1.50
2008	2,500,000	—	—	0.75	1.25	1.50

KM# 136 2 DOLLARS
28.3400 g., 0.9250 Silver 0.8428 oz. ASW, 38.6 mm. **Ruler:** Elizabeth II **Obv:** Gold plated Queen Elizabeth II **Rev:** British crown and value **Edge:** Reeded

Date	Mintage	F	VF	XF	Unc	BU
2002 Proof	—	Value: 45.00				

KM# 135 2 DOLLARS
28.2800 g., 0.9250 Silver 0.8410 oz. ASW, 38.6 mm. **Ruler:** Elizabeth II **Subject:** 500th Anniversary - Christopher Columbus First Recorded Sighting of the Cayman Islands **Obv:** Crowned head right **Rev:** Quincentennial Celebrations Logo in color

Date	Mintage	F	VF	XF	Unc	BU
2003 Proof	1,500	Value: 55.00				

KM# 138 2 DOLLARS
28.2800 g., 0.9250 Silver 0.8410 oz. ASW, 38.61 mm. **Ruler:** Elizabeth II **Subject:** Royal Horticulture Society **Obv:** Head right, gilt portrait **Rev:** RHS Tent and flowers

Date	Mintage	F	VF	XF	Unc	BU
2003 Proof	—	Value: 45.00				

KM# 137 5 DOLLARS
28.2800 g., 0.9250 Silver 0.8410 oz. ASW, 38.6 mm. **Ruler:** Elizabeth II **Subject:** Elizabeth II's 80th Birthday **Obv:** Crowned head right - gilt **Obv. Legend:** CAYMAN ISLANDS - ELIZABETH II **Rev:** Queen crowning Charles as Prince of Wales

Date	Mintage	F	VF	XF	Unc	BU
2006 Proof	25,000	Value: 50.00				

KM# 145 5 DOLLARS
28.2800 g., 0.9250 Silver 0.8410 oz. ASW, 38.61 mm. **Ruler:** Elizabeth II **Subject:** Queen Elizabeth, 80th Birthday **Rev:** Elizabeth and Philip in the state coach

Date	Mintage	F	VF	XF	Unc	BU
2006 Proof	Est. 25,000	Value: 50.00				

KM# 149 5 DOLLARS
28.2800 g., 0.9250 Silver 0.8410 oz. ASW, 38.6 mm. **Ruler:** Elizabeth II **Obv:** Head in tiara right, gilt face and rim **Rev:** Queen and Prince Philip in carriage, gilt 80 above

Date	Mintage	F	VF	XF	Unc	BU
2006 Proof	—	Value: 50.00				

KM# 139 5 DOLLARS
28.2800 g., 0.9250 Silver 0.8410 oz. ASW, 38.61 mm. **Ruler:** Elizabeth II **Subject:** Cayman Islands Monetary Authority, 10th Anniversary **Obv:** Bust right **Rev:** Island's coat of arms

Date	Mintage	F	VF	XF	Unc	BU
2007 Proof	200	Value: 110				

KM# 146 5 DOLLARS
28.2800 g., 0.9250 Silver 0.8410 oz. ASW, 38.61 mm. **Ruler:** Elizabeth II **Subject:** End of World War I, 90th Anniversary

Date	Mintage	F	VF	XF	Unc	BU
2008 Proof	—	Value: 50.00				

KM# 147 5 DOLLARS
28.2800 g., 0.9250 Silver 0.8410 oz. ASW, 38.61 mm. **Ruler:** Elizabeth II **Subject:** End of World War I, 90th Anniversary

Date	Mintage	F	VF	XF	Unc	BU
2008 Proof	—	Value: 50.00				

KM# 141 5 DOLLARS
28.2800 g., 0.9250 Silver 0.8410 oz. ASW, 38.6 mm. **Ruler:** Elizabeth II **Subject:** Constitutional Government, 50th Anniversary **Obv:** Bust right **Rev:** Coat of arms

Date	Mintage	F	VF	XF	Unc	BU
2009 Proof	300	Value: 75.00				

KM# 140 10 DOLLARS
7.9880 g., 0.9167 Gold 0.2354 oz. AGW, 22.1 mm. **Ruler:** Elizabeth II **Subject:** Cayman Islands Monetary Authority, 10th Anniversary **Obv:** Bust right **Rev:** Island's coat of arms

Date	Mintage	F	VF	XF	Unc	BU
2007 Proof	75	Value: 475				

KM# 142 10 DOLLARS
7.9880 g., 0.9167 Gold 0.2354 oz. AGW, 22.1 mm. **Ruler:** Elizabeth II **Subject:** Constitutional Government, 50th Anniversary **Obv:** Bust right **Rev:** Coat of Arms

Date	Mintage	F	VF	XF	Unc	BU
2009 Proof	125	Value: 475				

KM# 148 50 DOLLARS
155.5000 g., 0.9250 Silver 4.6243 oz. ASW, 65 mm. **Ruler:** Elizabeth II **Subject:** End of World War I, 90th Anniversary **Rev:** Soldier in the field with barbed wire

Date	Mintage	F	VF	XF	Unc	BU
2008 Proof	Est. 150	Value: 300				

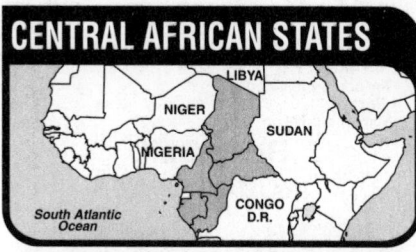

CENTRAL AFRICAN STATES

The Central African States, a monetary union comprised of Equatorial Guinea (a former Spanish possession), the former French possessions and now independent states of the Republic of Congo (Brazzaville), Gabon, Central African Republic, Chad and Cameroon, issues a common currency for the member states from a common central bank. The monetary unit, the African Financial Community franc, is tied to and supported by the French franc.

In 1960, an attempt was made to form a union of the newly independent republics of Chad, Congo, Central Africa and Gabon. The proposal was discarded when Chad refused to become a constituent member. The four countries then linked into an Equatorial Customs Unit, to which Cameroon became an associate member in 1961. A more extensive cooperation of the five republics, identified as the Central African Customs and Economic Union, was entered into force at the beginning of 1966.

In 1974 the Central Bank of the Equatorial African States, which had issued coins and paper currency in its own name and with the names of the constituent member nations, changed its name to the Bank of the Central African States. Equatorial Guinea converted to the CFA currency system issuing its first 100 Franc in 1985.

For earlier coinage see French Equatorial Africa.

Country Code Letters
To observe the movement of coinage throughout the states, the country of origin in which the coin is intended to circulate is designated by the following additional code letters:
A = Chad
B = Central African Republic
C = Congo

D = Gabon
E = Cameroon

By 1992 this practice was discontinued as the strategy had proved to be inconclusive.

MONETARY UNION
STANDARD COINAGE

KM# 8 FRANC
1.3000 g., Aluminum, 23 mm. **Obv:** Three giant eland left, date below **Rev:** Denomination within wreath

Date	Mintage	F	VF	XF	Unc	BU
2003	—	0.20	0.40	0.80	2.00	—

KM# 16 FRANC
1.6100 g., Stainless Steel, 14.9 mm. **Obv:** Value **Rev:** Value above produce **Edge:** Plain

Date	Mintage	F	VF	XF	Unc	BU
2006(a)	—	—	—	—	0.15	0.25

KM# 17 2 FRANCS
2.4300 g., Stainless Steel, 17.9 mm. **Obv:** Value **Rev:** Value above produce **Edge:** Plain

Date	Mintage	F	VF	XF	Unc	BU
2006(a)	—	—	—	—	0.25	0.35

KM# 7 5 FRANCS
3.0000 g., Aluminum-Bronze, 20 mm. **Obv:** Three giant eland left, date below **Rev:** Denomination within wreath

Date	Mintage	F	VF	XF	Unc	BU
2003	—	0.15	0.30	0.60	1.25	—

KM# 18 5 FRANCS
2.4100 g., Brass, 15.9 mm. **Obv:** Value **Rev:** Value above produce **Edge:** Reeded

Date	Mintage	F	VF	XF	Unc	BU
2006(a)	—	—	—	—	0.50	0.65

KM# 9 10 FRANCS
4.0000 g., Aluminum-Bronze, 23 mm. **Obv:** Three giant eland left, date below **Rev:** Denomination within wreath

Date	Mintage	F	VF	XF	Unc	BU
2003(a)	—	0.20	0.35	0.75	1.50	—

KM# 19 10 FRANCS

3.0000 g., Brass, 17.9 mm. **Obv:** Value **Rev:** Value above produce **Edge:** Reeded

Date	Mintage	F	VF	XF	Unc	BU
2006(a)	—	—	—	—	0.75	1.00

KM# 10   25 FRANCS
8.0000 g., Aluminum-Bronze, 27.2 mm. **Obv:** Three giant eland left, date below **Rev:** Denomination within wreath

Date	Mintage	F	VF	XF	Unc	BU
2003(a)	—	0.25	0.50	1.00	2.00	—

KM# 20   25 FRANCS
4.2000 g., Brass, 22.7 mm. **Obv:** Value **Rev:** Value above produce **Edge:** Reeded

Date	Mintage	F	VF	XF	Unc	BU
2006(a)	—	—	—	—	1.00	1.25

KM# 11   50 FRANCS
4.7000 g., Nickel, 21.5 mm. **Obv:** Three giant eland left, date below **Rev:** Denomination within flower design **Edge:** Reeded
Note: Starting in 1996 an extra flora item was added where the mintmark was formerly located.

Date	Mintage	F	VF	XF	Unc	BU
2003(a)	—	0.75	1.50	3.50	6.00	—

KM# 21   50 FRANCS
4.9000 g., Stainless Steel, 22 mm. **Obv:** Value **Rev:** Value above produce **Edge:** Reeded

Date	Mintage	F	VF	XF	Unc	BU
2006(a)	—	—	—	—	1.25	1.50

KM# 13   100 FRANCS
7.0500 g., Nickel, 25.5 mm. **Obv:** Three giant eland **Rev:** Denomination

Date	Mintage	F	VF	XF	Unc	BU
2003	—	—	—	—	4.50	6.00

KM# 15   100 FRANCS
6.0000 g., Bi-Metallic Stainless Steel center in Brass ring, 23.9 mm. **Obv:** Denomination above initials within beaded circle **Rev:** Value above produce **Edge:** Reeded

Date	Mintage	F	VF	XF	Unc	BU
2006(a)	—	—	—	—	5.00	6.50

KM# 22   500 FRANCS
8.1000 g., Copper-Nickel, 26 mm. **Obv:** Value above produce **Rev:** Value **Edge:** Segmented reeding and lettering

Date	Mintage	F	VF	XF	Unc	BU
2006(a)	—	—	—	—	8.00	10.00

KM# 23   1000 FRANCS
Silver, 37 mm. **Subject:** FIFA World Cup, England, 2004 **Edge:** Plain

Date	Mintage	F	VF	XF	Unc	BU
2004(a)	—	—	—	—	—	20.00

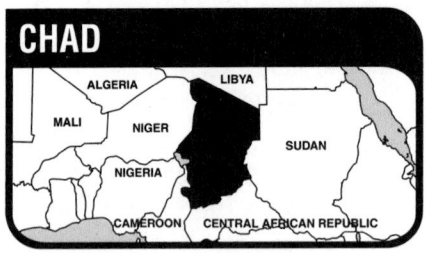

CHAD

The Republic of Chad, a landlocked country of central Africa, is the largest country of former French Equatorial Africa. It has an area of 495,755 sq. mi. (1,284,000 sq. km.) and a population of *7.27 million. Capital: N'Djamena. An expanding livestock industry produces camels, cattle and sheep. Cotton (the chief product), ivory and palm oil are important exports.

NOTE: For earlier and related coinage see French Equatorial Africa and the Equatorial African States. For later coinage see Central African States.

MINT MARKS
(a) - Paris, privy marks only
(b) - Brussels
NI - Numismatic Italiana, Arezzo, Italy

REPUBLIC
DECIMAL COINAGE

KM# 30   500 FRANCS
Silver, 31 mm. **Obv:** Native portrait within circle **Rev:** Rhino mom and baby

Date	Mintage	F	VF	XF	Unc	BU
2001 Proof	—	Value: 30.00				

KM# 20   1000 FRANCS
15.0000 g., 0.9990 Silver 0.4818 oz. ASW, 35 mm. **Obv:** Native portrait within circle, denomination below **Rev:** Ancient Arabic war ship **Edge:** Plain

Date	Mintage	F	VF	XF	Unc	BU
2001 Proof	—	Value: 40.00				

KM# 21   1000 FRANCS
25.1000 g., 0.9990 Silver 0.8061 oz. ASW, 40 mm. **Obv:** Native portrait within circle, denomination below **Rev:** Soccer player and stadium **Edge:** Reeded

Date	Mintage	F	VF	XF	Unc	BU
2001 Proof	—	Value: 50.00				

KM# 35   1000 FRANCS
20.0000 g., Silver, 40 mm. **Subject:** African Fauna **Obv:** Native portrait within circle **Rev:** Balearica Pavonina (two birds)

Date	Mintage	F	VF	XF	Unc	BU
2001 Proof	—	Value: 45.00				

KM# 29   1000 FRANCS
15.0000 g., 0.9990 Silver 0.4818 oz. ASW, 36 mm. **Obv:** Native portrait within circle **Rev:** Multicolor orang-outan

Date	Mintage	F	VF	XF	Unc	BU
2001 Proof	—	Value: 35.00				

KM# 22   1000 FRANCS
20.0000 g., 0.9990 Silver 0.6423 oz. ASW, 40 mm. **Obv:** Native portrait within circle, denomination below **Rev:** Horizontal soccer player above stadium **Edge:** Reeded

Date	Mintage	F	VF	XF	Unc	BU
2002 Proof	5,000	Value: 45.00				

KM# 23   1000 FRANCS
20.1500 g., 0.9990 Silver 0.6472 oz. ASW, 40 mm. **Obv:** Native portrait within circle, denomination below **Rev:** Soccer player and Arch of Triumph **Edge:** Reeded

Date	Mintage	F	VF	XF	Unc	BU
2002 Proof	—	Value: 40.00				

KM# 31   1000 FRANCS
15.0000 g., 0.9850 Silver 0.4750 oz. ASW, 34 mm. **Rev:** Multicolor McDonnell-Douglass DC-10 landing left

Date	Mintage	F	VF	XF	Unc	BU
2002 Proof	—	Value: 35.00				

KM# 32   1000 FRANCS
15.0000 g., 0.9850 Silver 0.4750 oz. ASW, 34 mm. **Rev:** Multicolor Boeing 747 taking-off right

Date	Mintage	F	VF	XF	Unc	BU
2002 Proof	—	Value: 35.00				

KM# 36   1000 FRANCS
20.0000 g., Silver, 40 mm. **Subject:** Animals in Peril **Obv:** Native portrait within circle **Rev:** Leopard

Date	Mintage	F	VF	XF	Unc	BU
2003 Proof	—	Value: 20.00				

KM# 33   1000 FRANCS
15.0000 g., 0.9850 Silver 0.4750 oz. ASW, 34 mm. **Rev:** Multicolor McDonnell-Douglass DC-9 over mountains

Date	Mintage	F	VF	XF	Unc	BU
2003 Proof	—	Value: 35.00				

KM# 34   1000 FRANCS
15.0000 g., 0.9850 Silver 0.4750 oz. ASW, 34 mm. **Rev:** Multicolor Fokker F-7a top wing

Date	Mintage	F	VF	XF	Unc	BU
2003 Proof	—	Value: 35.00				

The Republic of Chile, a ribbon-like country on the Pacific coast of southern South America, has an area of 292,135 sq. mi. (756,950 sq. km.) and a population of *15.21 million. Capital: Santiago. Historically, the economic base of Chile has been the rich mineral deposits of its northern provinces. Copper has accounted for more than 75 percent of Chile's export earnings in recent years. Other important mineral exports are iron ore, iodine and nitrate of soda. Fresh fruits and vegetables, as well as wine are increasingly significant in inter-hemispheric trade.

MINT MARK
So – Santiago
(ml) – Maple leaf – Royal Canadian Mint (RCM)

REPUBLIC

REFORM COINAGE
100 Centavos = 1 Peso; 1000 Old Escudos = 1 Peso

KM# 231   PESO
0.7000 g., Aluminum, 15.5 mm. **Obv:** Gen. Bernardo O'Higgins bust right **Obv. Legend:** REPUBLICA - DE CHILE **Rev:** Denomination above date within wreath **Edge:** Plain **Shape:** 8-sided **Note:** Varieties exist.

Date	Mintage	F	VF	XF	Unc	BU
2001So Narrow date	—	—	—	—	0.10	0.20
2002So Narrow date	—	—	—	—	0.10	0.20
2003So Narrow date	—	—	—	—	0.10	0.20
2004So Wide date	—	—	—	—	0.10	0.20
2005So Wide date	—	—	—	—	0.10	0.20
2006So Wide date	—	—	—	—	0.10	0.20
2008So Wide date	—	—	—	—	0.10	0.20
2009So Wide date	—	—	—	—	0.10	0.20

KM# 232   5 PESOS
2.2000 g., Aluminum-Bronze, 15.5 mm. **Obv:** Gen. Bernardo O'Higgins bust right **Obv. Legend:** REPUBLICA - DE CHILE **Rev:** Denomination above date within wreath **Edge:** Plain **Shape:** 8-sided **Note:** Varieties exist.

Date	Mintage	F	VF	XF	Unc	BU
2001So Narrow date	—	—	—	0.10	0.35	0.60
2001So (sa) Wide date	—	—	—	0.15	0.50	0.75

Note: Without name of sculptor

2002So Narrow date	—	—	—	0.15	0.50	0.75
2002So Wide date	—	—	—	0.10	0.35	0.60
2003So	—	—	—	0.10	0.35	0.60
2004So	—	—	—	0.10	0.35	0.60
2005So	—	—	—	0.10	0.35	0.60
2006So	—	—	—	0.10	0.35	0.60
2007So	—	—	—	0.10	0.35	0.60
2008So	—	—	—	0.10	0.35	0.60
2009So	—	—	—	0.10	0.35	0.60
2010So	—	—	—	0.10	0.35	0.60
2011So	—	—	—	0.10	0.35	60.00

KM# 228.2   10 PESOS
3.5000 g., Aluminum-Bronze, 21 mm. **Obv:** Bust of Gen. Bernardo O'Higgins right **Obv. Legend:** REPUBLICA - DE CHILE **Rev:** Denomination above date within sprays **Edge:** Reeded **Note:** All 9's are curl tail 9's except for the 1999 date, these are straight tail 9's. Normal rim.

Date	Mintage	F	VF	XF	Unc	BU
2001So	—	—	0.10	0.20	0.50	0.65
2002So	—	—	0.10	0.20	0.50	0.65
2003So	—	—	0.10	0.20	0.50	0.65
2004So	—	—	0.10	0.20	0.50	0.65
2005So	—	—	0.10	0.20	0.50	0.65
2006So	—	—	0.10	0.20	0.50	0.65
2007	—	—	0.10	0.20	0.50	0.65

Note: Struck in Canada

2008So	—	—	0.10	0.20	0.50	0.65
2009So	—	—	0.10	0.20	0.50	0.65
2010So	—	—	0.10	0.20	0.50	0.65
2011So	—	—	0.10	0.20	0.50	0.65

KM# 219.2   50 PESOS
7.0000 g., Aluminum-Bronze, 25 mm. **Obv:** Bust of Gen. Bernardo O'Higgins right **Obv. Legend:** REPUBLICA - DE CHILE **Rev:** Denomination above date within sprays **Edge:** Ornamented **Shape:** 10-sided **Note:** Narrow date.

Date	Mintage	F	VF	XF	Unc	BU
2001So	—	—	0.25	0.50	1.25	1.50
2002So	—	—	0.25	0.50	1.25	1.50
2005So	—	—	0.25	0.50	1.00	1.25
2006So	—	—	0.25	0.50	1.00	1.25
2007	—	—	0.25	0.50	1.00	1.25

Note: Struck in Canada

2009So	—	—	0.25	0.50	1.00	1.25
2010So	—	—	0.25	0.50	1.00	1.25

KM# 219.3   50 PESOS
7.0000 g., Aluminum-Bronze, 25 mm. **Obv:** Bust of Gen. Bernardo O'Higgins right **Obv. Legend:** REPUBLICA - DE CHIIE **Rev:** Denomination above date within sprays **Note:** Error spelling in legend of CHILE.

Date	Mintage	F	VF	XF	Unc	BU
2008	—	—	—	—	1.50	2.50
2009	—	—	—	—	—	2.50

KM# 236   100 PESOS
7.5800 g., Bi-Metallic Copper-Nickel-Zinc center in Aluminum-Bronze ring, 23.5 mm. **Subject:** Native people **Obv:** Bust of native Mapuche girl facing **Obv. Legend:** REPUBLICA DE CHILE - PUEBLOS ORIGINARIOS **Rev:** National arms above denomination **Edge:** Segmented reeding

Date	Mintage	F	VF	XF	Unc	BU
2001So	—	—	0.35	0.90	2.25	3.00
2003So	—	—	0.35	0.90	2.25	3.00
2004So	—	—	0.35	0.90	2.25	3.00
2005So	—	—	0.35	0.90	2.25	3.00
2006So	—	—	0.35	0.90	2.25	3.00
2008So	—	—	0.35	0.90	2.25	3.00
2009So	—	—	0.35	0.90	2.25	3.00
2010So	—	—	0.35	0.90	2.25	3.00

KM# 235   500 PESOS

6.5000 g., Bi-Metallic Aluminum-Bronze center in Copper-Nickel-Zinc ring, 26 mm.   **Subject:** Cardinal Raul Silva Henriquez **Obv:** Bust of cardinal within inner ring facing left **Rev:** Denomination above date within wreath **Edge:** Reeded

Date	Mintage	F	VF	XF	Unc	BU
2001So	—	—	—	—	6.00	6.50
2002So 4.1mm date	—	—	—	—	6.00	6.50
2002So 5.2mm date	—	—	—	—	6.00	6.50
2003So	—	—	—	—	6.00	6.50
2008So	—	—	—	—	6.00	6.50
2009So	—	—	—	—	6.00	6.50
2010So	—	—	—	—	6.00	6.50
2011So	—	—	—	—	6.00	6.50

CHINA / Peoples Republic

The Peoples Republic of China, located in eastern Asia, has an area of 3,696,100 sq. mi. (9,596,960 sq. km.) (including Manchuria and Tibet) and a population of *1.20 billion. Capital: Peking (Beijing). The economy is based on agriculture, mining, and manufacturing. Textiles, clothing, metal ores, tea and rice are exported.

MONETARY SYSTEM

After 1949

10 Fen (Cents) = 1 Jiao
10 Jiao = 1 Renminbi Yuan

MINT MARKS
(b) - Beijing (Peking)
(s) - Shanghai
(y) - Shenyang (Mukden)

OBVERSE LEGENDS

中华人民共和国

ZHONGHUA RENMIN GONGHEGUO
(Peoples Republic of China)

中国人民银行

ZHONGGUO RENMIN YINHANG
(Peoples Bank of China)

PEOPLES REPUBLIC

STANDARD COINAGE

KM# 1   FEN

0.7000 g., Aluminum, 18 mm.   **Obv:** National emblem **Rev:** Value in wreath, date below **Edge:** Reeded **Note:** Prev. Y#1.

Date	Mintage	F	VF	XF	Unc	BU
2005	—	—	—	—	0.15	0.25
2006	—	—	—	—	0.15	0.25
2007	—	—	—	—	0.15	0.25
2008	—	—	—	—	0.15	0.25

Date	Mintage	F	VF	XF	Unc	BU
2009	—	—	—	—	0.15	0.25
2010	—	—	—	—	0.15	0.25
2011	—	—	—	—	0.15	0.25

KM# 1210   JIAO

1.1200 g., Aluminum, 19 mm.   **Obv:** Denomination, date below **Rev:** Orchid **Rev. Legend:** ZHONGGUA RENMIN YINHANG **Edge:** Plain **Note:** Prev. Y#1068.

Date	Mintage	F	VF	XF	Unc	BU
2001	—	—	—	—	0.50	0.75
2002	—	—	—	—	0.50	0.75
2003	—	—	—	—	0.50	0.75

KM# 1210a   JIAO

Copper-Nickel, 19 mm.   **Obv:** Denomination, date below **Note:** Prev. Y#1068a.

Date	Mintage	F	VF	XF	Unc	BU
2005	—	—	—	—	0.50	0.75

KM# 1210b   JIAO

3.2000 g., Stainless Steel, 19 mm.   **Obv:** Value, date below **Rev:** Orchid **Rev. Legend:** ZHONGGUA RENMIN YINHANG **Edge:** Plain **Note:** Prev. Y#1068b.

Date	Mintage	F	VF	XF	Unc	BU
2005	—	—	—	—	—	0.25
2006	—	—	—	—	—	0.25
2007	—	—	—	—	—	0.25
2008	—	—	—	—	—	0.25
2009	—	—	—	—	—	0.25
2010	—	—	—	—	—	0.25
2011	—	—	—	—	—	0.25

KM# 336   5 JIAO

3.8000 g., Brass, 20.5 mm.   **Obv:** National emblem, date below **Rev:** Denomination above flowers **Edge:** Segmented reeding **Note:** Prev. Y#329.

Date	Mintage	F	VF	XF	Unc	BU
2001	—	—	—	—	1.00	1.25

KM# 1411   5 JIAO

3.8000 g., Brass, 20.5 mm.   **Obv:** Denomination **Rev:** Flower **Rev. Legend:** ZHONGGUA RENMIN YINHANG **Edge:** Segmented reeding **Note:** Prev. Y#1106.

Date	Mintage	F	VF	XF	Unc	BU
2002	—	—	—	—	1.50	1.75
2003	—	—	—	—	1.50	1.75
2004	—	—	—	—	1.50	1.75
2005	—	—	—	—	1.50	1.75
2006	—	—	—	—	1.50	1.75
2007	—	—	—	—	1.50	1.75
2008	—	—	—	—	1.50	1.75
2009	—	—	—	—	1.50	1.75
2010	—	—	—	—	1.50	1.75
2011	—	—	—	—	1.50	1.75

KM# 1212   YUAN

6.1000 g., Nickel Plated Steel, 24.9 mm.   **Obv:** Denomination, date below **Rev:** Chrysanthemum **Rev. Legend:** ZHONGGUA RENMIN YINHANG **Edge:** "RMB" three times **Note:** Prev. Y#1069.

Date	Mintage	F	VF	XF	Unc	BU
2001	—	—	—	—	2.00	2.50
2002	—	—	—	—	2.00	2.50
2003	—	—	—	—	2.00	2.50
2004	—	—	—	—	2.00	2.50
2005	—	—	—	—	2.00	2.50
2006	—	—	—	—	2.00	2.50
2007	—	—	—	—	2.00	2.50
2008	—	—	—	—	2.00	2.50
2009	—	—	—	—	2.00	2.50
2010	—	—	—	—	2.00	2.50
2011	—	—	—	—	2.00	2.50
2012	—	—	—	—	2.00	2.50

KM# 1465   YUAN

6.8500 g., Brass, 25 mm.   **Obv:** Value **Rev:** Celebrating child and ram **Edge:** Lettered **Edge Lettering:** "RMB" three times **Note:** Prev. Y#1125.

Date	Mintage	F	VF	XF	Unc	BU
2003	—	—	—	—	5.00	6.00

KM# 1521   YUAN

Brass **Obv:** Denomination **Rev:** Celebrating Child **Note:** Prev. Y#1247.

Date	Mintage	F	VF	XF	Unc	BU
2004	—	—	—	—	2.50	3.00

KM# 1522   YUAN

Nickel Clad Steel **Obv:** Palace **Rev:** Deng Xiao Ping 1904-2004 **Note:** Prev. Y#1248.

Date	Mintage	F	VF	XF	Unc	BU
2004	—	—	—	—	3.50	4.00

KM# 1523   YUAN

Nickel Clad Steel **Subject:** 50th Year of Peoples Congress **Obv:** Congress building **Note:** Prev. Y#1249.

Date	Mintage	F	VF	XF	Unc	BU
2004	—	—	—	—	3.50	4.00

KM# 1574   YUAN

5.9600 g., Nickel Clad Steel, 25 mm.   **Obv:** Building **Rev:** Bust of Chenyun **Edge:** Lettered **Note:** Prev. Y#1208.

Date	Mintage	F	VF	XF	Unc	BU
2005	—	—	—	—	3.50	4.00

KM# 1575   YUAN

Brass **Subject:** Year of the Rooster **Obv:** Denomination **Rev:** Celebrating Child **Note:** Prev. Y#1250.

Date	Mintage	F	VF	XF	Unc	BU
2005	—	—	—	—	3.00	3.50

KM# 1650   YUAN

Brass **Subject:** Year of the Dog **Obv:** Denomination **Rev:** Celebrating Child **Note:** Prev. Y#1251.

Date	Mintage	F	VF	XF	Unc	BU
2006	—	—	—	—	7.00	8.00

KM# 1775   YUAN

6.7500 g., Brass, 25 mm.   **Subject:** 29th Olympics **Obv:** Stylized Olympics logo **Rev:** Cartoon swimmer **Edge:** Reeded **Note:** Prev. Y#1256.

Date	Mintage	F	VF	XF	Unc	BU
2008 (2006)(y)	—	—	—	—	5.00	6.00

KM# 1776 YUAN
6.7500 g., Brass, 25 mm. **Subject:** 29th Olympics **Obv:** Stylized Olympics logo **Rev:** Cartoon Weight Lifter **Edge:** Reeded **Note:** Prev. Y#1257.

Date	Mintage	F	VF	XF	Unc	BU
2008 (2006)	—	—	—	—	5.00	6.00

KM# 1810 YUAN
Brass, 25 mm. **Obv:** Beijing Olympic logo **Rev:** Character playing ping-pong

Date	Mintage	F	VF	XF	Unc	BU
2008	—	—	—	—	2.50	3.00

KM# 1811 YUAN
Brass, 25 mm. **Obv:** Beijing Olympic logo **Rev:** Character fencing with bow and arrow

Date	Mintage	F	VF	XF	Unc	BU
2008	—	—	—	—	2.50	3.00

KM# 1812 YUAN
Brass, 25 mm. **Obv:** Beijing Olympic logo **Rev:** Character on horseback

Date	Mintage	F	VF	XF	Unc	BU
2008	—	—	—	—	2.50	3.00

KM# 1813 YUAN
Brass, 25 mm. **Obv:** Large value **Rev:** Boy with rat pattern chinese knot & cluster of fireworks

Date	Mintage	F	VF	XF	Unc	BU
2008	10,000,000	—	—	—	2.50	3.00

KM# 1988 YUAN
Nickel Plated Brass, 25 mm. **Subject:** Shanghai Expo **Obv:** Expo logo **Rev:** Skyline and expo mascot

Date	Mintage	F	VF	XF	Unc	BU
2010	60,000,000	—	—	—	6.00	8.00

KM# 1989 YUAN
Brass, 25 mm. **Subject:** Year of the Tiger **Obv:** Large value **Rev:** Child dancing

Date	Mintage	F	VF	XF	Unc	BU
2010	60,000,000	—	—	—	5.00	7.50

KM# 1990 YUAN
Brass, 25 mm. **Subject:** Enviornmental protection **Obv:** State emblem **Rev:** Caligraphy - Peace-Harmony

Date	Mintage	F	VF	XF	Unc	BU
2010	10,000,000	—	—	—	6.00	8.00

KM# 1991 YUAN
Brass, 25 mm. **Subject:** Environmental protection **Obv:** National emblem **Rev:** Family dancing, globe

Date	Mintage	F	VF	XF	Unc	BU
2010	10,000,000	—	—	—	6.00	8.00

KM# 1993 YUAN
Brass, 25 mm. **Subject:** Year of the Rabbit **Obv:** Large value **Rev:** Child playing

Date	Mintage	F	VF	XF	Unc	BU
2011	60,000,000	—	—	—	6.00	8.00

KM# 1363 5 YUAN
12.8000 g., Brass, 30 mm. **Subject:** 50th Anniversary - Chinese Occupation of Tibet **Obv:** National emblem **Rev:** Potala Palace, value and two dancers **Edge:** Reeded **Note:** Prev. Y#1126.

Date	Mintage	F	VF	XF	Unc	BU
2001(y)	10,000,000	—	—	—	8.00	—

KM# 1364 5 YUAN
12.8000 g., Brass, 30 mm. **Subject:** Revolution: 90th Anniversary **Obv:** National emblem **Rev:** Battle scene **Edge:** Reeded **Note:** Prev. Y#1109.

Date	Mintage	F	VF	XF	Unc	BU
2001		—	—	—	7.50	8.50

KM# 1412 5 YUAN
12.8000 g., Brass, 30 mm. **Subject:** The Great Wall **Obv:** State arms, icroscopic inscription repeated four times on the inner raised rim **Obv. Inscription:** SHI JIE WEN HUA YI CHAN **Rev:** Two views of the Great Wall **Edge:** Reeded **Note:** Prev. Y#1107.

Date	Mintage	F	VF	XF	Unc	BU
2002	—	—	—	—	7.00	8.00

KM# 1413 5 YUAN
12.8000 g., Brass, 30 mm. **Subject:** Terra Cotta Army **Obv:** State arms and the microscopic inscription repeated four times on the raised inner rim. **Obv. Inscription:** SHI JIE WEN HUA YI CHAN **Rev:** Terra Cotta Soldier close-up with many more in background **Edge:** Reeded **Note:** Prev. Y#1108.

Date	Mintage	F	VF	XF	Unc	BU
2002	—	—	—	—	7.00	8.00

KM# 1461 5 YUAN
12.8000 g., Brass, 30 mm. **Obv:** National emblem **Rev:** Chaotian Temple in Beigang Taiwan **Edge:** Reeded **Note:** Prev. Y#1127.

Date	Mintage	F	VF	XF	Unc	BU
2003	10,000,000	—	—	—	7.00	8.00

KM# 1462 5 YUAN
12.8000 g., Brass, 30 mm. **Obv:** National emblem **Rev:** Chikan Tower on Treasure Island Taiwan **Edge:** Reeded **Note:** Prev. Y#1128.

Date	Mintage	F	VF	XF	Unc	BU
2003(y)	10,000,000	—	—	—	7.00	8.00

KM# 1463 5 YUAN
12.8000 g., Brass, 30 mm. **Subject:** Chaotian Temple in Beijing **Obv:** State emblem **Rev:** Buildings **Edge:** Reeded **Note:** Prev. Y#1230.

Date	Mintage	F	VF	XF	Unc	BU
2003	10,000,000	—	—	—	7.00	8.00

KM# 1464 5 YUAN
Brass, 30 mm. **Obv:** National emblem **Rev:** Imperial Palace **Note:** Prev. Y#1252.

Date	Mintage	F	VF	XF	Unc	BU
2003	—	—	—	—	7.00	8.00

KM# 1524 5 YUAN
Brass, 30 mm. **Obv:** National emblem **Rev:** Island scene **Note:** Prev. Y#1253.

Date	Mintage	F	VF	XF	Unc	BU
2004	—	—	—	—	6.00	7.00

KM# 1525 5 YUAN
Brass, 30 mm. **Obv:** National emblem **Rev:** Lighthouse **Note:** Prev. Y#1254.

Date	Mintage	F	VF	XF	Unc	BU
2004	—	—	—	—	6.00	7.00

KM# 1526 5 YUAN
12.7000 g., Brass, 30 mm. **Obv:** National emblem **Rev:** Peking Man bust and discovery site view **Edge:** Reeded **Note:** Prev. Y#1201.

Date	Mintage	F	VF	XF	Unc	BU
2004	6,000,000	—	—	—	6.00	7.00

KM# 1527 5 YUAN
12.7000 g., Brass, 30 mm. **Obv:** National emblem **Rev:** Pavillion and bridge **Edge:** Reeded **Note:** Prev. Y#1202.

Date	Mintage	F	VF	XF	Unc	BU
2004	6,000,000	—	—	—	6.00	7.00

KM# 1068 5 YUAN
22.0000 g., 0.9000 Silver 0.6366 oz. ASW, 36 mm. **Obv:** Great Wall **Rev:** Gymnast, denomination at right **Edge:** Reeded **Note:** Prev. Y#1189.

Date	Mintage	F	VF	XF	Unc	BU
2005(y)	—	—	—	—	75.00	85.00

KM# 1576 5 YUAN
12.9200 g., Brass, 30 mm. **Obv:** National emblem **Rev:** Lijiang building **Edge:** Reeded **Note:** Prev. Y#1209.

Date	Mintage	F	VF	XF	Unc	BU
2005	—	—	—	—	6.00	7.00

KM# 1577 5 YUAN
12.8000 g., Brass, 30 mm. **Subject:** "Taiwan" **Obv:** State emblem **Rev:** Tower and terrace **Edge:** Reeded **Note:** Prev. Y#1231.

Date	Mintage	F	VF	XF	Unc	BU
2005	—	—	—	—	6.00	7.00

KM# 1578   5 YUAN
12.9200 g., Brass, 30 mm. **Obv:** National emblem **Rev:** Green City Hall **Edge:** Reeded **Note:** Prev. Y#1210.

Date	Mintage	F	VF	XF	Unc	BU
2005	—	—	—	—	6.00	7.00

KM# 1731   5 YUAN
Brass, 30 mm.   **Obv:** State emblem **Rev:** Large statue head

Date	Mintage	F	VF	XF	Unc	BU
2006 Proof	10,000,000	Value: 3.00				

KM# 1992   5 YUAN
Brass, 30 mm.   **Subject:** Chinese Communist Party, 90th Anniversary **Obv:** National emblem **Rev:** Banner, hammer and sythe, stars, birds in flight

Date	Mintage	F	VF	XF	Unc	BU
2011	60,000,000	—	—	—	7.50	9.00

KM# 1395   10 YUAN
31.1035 g., 0.9990 Silver 0.9990 oz. ASW, 40 mm.   **Subject:** 2008 Olympics Beijing bid **Obv:** Gold-plated "V" design **Rev:** Radiant Temple of Heaven **Edge:** Reeded **Note:** Prev. Y#1103.

Date	Mintage	F	VF	XF	Unc	BU
2001 Proof	60,000	Value: 50.00				

KM# 1384   10 YUAN
31.1035 g., 0.9990 Silver 0.9990 oz. ASW   **Series:** Folk Fairy Tales **Rev:** Heroic figure putting ax to mountains

Date	Mintage	F	VF	XF	Unc	BU
2001 Proof	30,000	Value: 120				

KM# 1385   10 YUAN
31.1035 g., 0.9990 Silver 0.9990 oz. ASW, 40 mm.   **Series:** Folk Fairy Tales **Rev:** Multicolor angelic figure

Date	Mintage	F	VF	XF	Unc	BU
2001 Proof	30,000	Value: 120				

KM# 1396   10 YUAN
31.1035 g., 0.9990 Silver 0.9990 oz. ASW, 40 mm.   **Series:** Folk customs - Mid Autumn Festival **Rev:** Flora and sun

Date	Mintage	F	VF	XF	Unc	BU
2001 Proof	40,000	Value: 180				

KM# 1397   10 YUAN
31.1035 g., 0.9990 Silver 0.9990 oz. ASW, 32 mm.   **Subject:** Bejing International Coin Expo **Obv:** Globe hemisphere view **Rev:** Bejing city view

Date	Mintage	F	VF	XF	Unc	BU
2001 Proof	40,000	Value: 125				

KM# 1398   10 YUAN
31.1035 g., 0.9990 Silver 0.9990 oz. ASW, 40 mm.   **Subject:** Bejing opera **Rev:** Two multicolor actors, one with hankie

Date	Mintage	F	VF	XF	Unc	BU
2001 Proof	38,000	Value: 100				

KM# 1399   10 YUAN
31.1035 g., 0.9990 Silver 0.9990 oz. ASW, 40 mm.   **Subject:** Bejing opera **Rev:** Two actors, one with blue ribbon

Date	Mintage	F	VF	XF	Unc	BU
2001 Proof	38,000	Value: 120				

KM# 1400   10 YUAN
31.1035 g., 0.9990 Silver 0.9990 oz. ASW, 40 mm.   **Subject:** Bejing opera **Rev:** Two multicolor actors, one with tassles

Date	Mintage	F	VF	XF	Unc	BU
2001 Proof	38,000	Value: 60.00				

KM# 1401   10 YUAN
31.1035 g., 0.9990 Silver 0.9990 oz. ASW, 40 mm.   **Subject:** Bejing opera **Rev:** Two multicolor actors, white or black beard

Date	Mintage	F	VF	XF	Unc	BU
2001 Proof	38,000	Value: 120				

KM# 1428   10 YUAN
31.1035 g., 0.9990 Silver 0.9990 oz. ASW, 40 mm.   **Series:** Folk Fairy Tales **Rev:** Multicolor male figure seated

Date	Mintage	F	VF	XF	Unc	BU
2002 Proof	30,000	Value: 120				

KM# 1429   10 YUAN
31.1035 g., 0.9990 Silver Colorized 0.9990 oz. ASW, 40 mm.   **Series:** Folk fairy tails **Rev:** Male figure brandishing sword

Date	Mintage	F	VF	XF	Unc	BU
2002 Proof	30,000	Value: 120				

KM# 1438   10 YUAN
31.1035 g., 0.9990 Silver 0.9990 oz. ASW, 40 mm.   **Series:** Folk customs **Rev:** Dragon boat

Date	Mintage	F	VF	XF	Unc	BU
2002 Proof	40,000	Value: 120				

KM# 1441   10 YUAN
31.1035 g., 0.9990 Silver Colorized 0.9990 oz. ASW, 40 mm.   **Series:** Classic literature **Rev:** Black and red dressed women seated **Shape:** Octagon

Date	Mintage	F	VF	XF	Unc	BU
2002 Proof	38,000	Value: 100				

KM# 1442   10 YUAN
31.1035 g., 0.9990 Silver 0.9990 oz. ASW, 40 mm.   **Series:** Classic literature **Rev:** Multicolor white dressed woman standing **Shape:** Octagon

Date	Mintage	F	VF	XF	Unc	BU
2002 Proof	38,000	Value: 100				

KM# 1443   10 YUAN
31.1035 g., 0.9990 Silver 0.9990 oz. ASW, 40 mm.   **Series:** Classic literature **Rev:** Multicolor yellow dressed woman walking left **Shape:** Octagon

Date	Mintage	F	VF	XF	Unc	BU
2002 Proof	38,000	Value: 100				

KM# 1444   10 YUAN
31.1035 g., 0.9990 Silver 0.9990 oz. ASW, 40 mm.   **Series:** Classic literature **Obv:** Multicolor purple dressed woman **Shape:** Octagon

Date	Mintage	F	VF	XF	Unc	BU
2002 Proof	38,000	Value: 100				

KM# 1447   10 YUAN
31.1035 g., 0.9990 Silver 0.9990 oz. ASW, 40 mm.   **Subject:** Bejing Coin and Stamp Fair **Obv:** Hemisphere map **Rev:** Highway design

Date	Mintage	F	VF	XF	Unc	BU
2002 Proof	40,000	Value: 95.00				

KM# 1448   10 YUAN
31.1035 g., 0.9990 Silver 0.9990 oz. ASW, 40 mm.   **Subject:** Table tennis, 50th anniversary **Rev:** Trophies, flag

Date	Mintage	F	VF	XF	Unc	BU
2002 Proof	50,000	Value: 100				

KM# 1449   10 YUAN
31.1035 g., 0.9990 Silver 0.9990 oz. ASW   **Series:** Bejing opera **Rev:** Two multicolor characters, one seated **Shape:** 40

Date	Mintage	F	VF	XF	Unc	BU
2002 Proof	38,000	Value: 50.00				

KM# 1450   10 YUAN
31.1035 g., 0.9990 Silver 0.9990 oz. ASW, 40 mm.   **Series:** Bejing opera **Rev:** Two multicolor characters, white and green

Date	Mintage	F	VF	XF	Unc	BU
2002 Proof	38,000	Value: 125				

KM# 1451   10 YUAN
31.1035 g., 0.9990 Silver 0.9990 oz. ASW, 40 mm.   **Series:** Bejing opera **Rev:** Bearded character, black

Date	Mintage	F	VF	XF	Unc	BU
2002 Proof	38,000	Value: 125				

KM# 1452   10 YUAN
31.1035 g., 0.9990 Silver 0.9990 oz. ASW, 40 mm.   **Series:** Bejing opera **Rev:** Multicolor bearded character, red

Date	Mintage	F	VF	XF	Unc	BU
2002 Proof	38,000	Value: 125				

KM# A1455   10 YUAN
31.1035 g., 0.9990 Silver 0.9990 oz. ASW, 40 mm.   **Subject:** World Expo 2010 **Rev:** Tower

Date	Mintage	F	VF	XF	Unc	BU
2002 Proof	50,000	Value: 100				

KM# 1455   10 YUAN
31.1035 g., 0.9990 Silver 0.9990 oz. ASW, 40 mm.   **Subject:** Shanghai World Expo of 2010 **Obv:** Flower design with inset pearl **Rev:** 2010 Logo incorporating a tower **Edge:** Reeded **Note:** Prev. Y#1233.

Date	Mintage	F	VF	XF	Unc	BU
2002 Proof	50,000	Value: 125				

KM# 1507   10 YUAN
31.1035 g., 0.9990 Silver 0.9990 oz. ASW, 40 mm.   **Obv:** Stylized forest **Rev:** Cyclists in forest **Edge:** Reeded **Note:** Prev. Y#1132.

Date	Mintage	F	VF	XF	Unc	BU
2003 Proof	30,000	Value: 125				

KM# 1508   10 YUAN
31.1035 g., 0.9990 Silver 0.9990 oz. ASW, 40 mm.   **Obv:** Stylized forest **Rev:** Birds flying over forest **Edge:** Reeded **Note:** Prev. Y#1133.

Date	Mintage	F	VF	XF	Unc	BU
2003(y) Proof	30,000	Value: 125				

KM# 1510   10 YUAN
31.1035 g., 0.9990 Silver 0.9990 oz. ASW, 40 mm.   **Obv:** Solar system design **Rev:** Multicolor Chinese Astronaut **Edge:** Reeded **Note:** Prev. Y#1134.

Date	Mintage	F	VF	XF	Unc	BU
2003(y) Proof	60,000	Value: 90.00				

KM# 1487   10 YUAN
31.1035 g., 0.9990 Silver 0.9990 oz. ASW, 40 mm.   **Rev:** Two Koi

Date	Mintage	F	VF	XF	Unc	BU
2003 Proof	100,000	Value: 90.00				

KM# 1489   10 YUAN
31.1035 g., 0.9990 Silver 0.9990 oz. ASW, 40 mm.   **Subject:** Arbor Day **Rev:** Trees with bike riders

Date	Mintage	F	VF	XF	Unc	BU
2003 Proof	30,000	Value: 90.00				

KM# 1490   10 YUAN
31.1035 g., 0.9990 Silver 0.9990 oz. ASW, 40 mm.   **Subject:** Arbor Day **Rev:** Close-up of leaves, birds in flight

Date	Mintage	F	VF	XF	Unc	BU
2003 Proof	30,000	Value: 120				

KM# 1491   10 YUAN
31.1035 g., 0.9990 Silver 0.9990 oz. ASW, 40 mm.   **Series:** Fairy tails **Rev:** Multicolor blue female

Date	Mintage	F	VF	XF	Unc	BU
2003 Proof	30,000	Value: 120				

KM# 1492   10 YUAN
31.1035 g., 0.9990 Silver 0.9990 oz. ASW, 40 mm.   **Subject:** Fairy tails **Rev:** Multicolor red bloused girl

Date	Mintage	F	VF	XF	Unc	BU
2003 Proof	30,000	Value: 120				

KM# 1496   10 YUAN
31.1035 g., 0.9990 Silver 0.9990 oz. ASW, 40 mm.   **Series:** Class literature **Rev:** Multicolor purple cloaked man and monkey

Date	Mintage	F	VF	XF	Unc	BU
2003 Proof	38,000	Value: 120				

KM# 1497   10 YUAN
31.1035 g., 0.9990 Silver 0.9990 oz. ASW, 40 mm.   **Series:** Classic literature **Rev:** Two multicolor men fighting in clouds

Date	Mintage	F	VF	XF	Unc	BU
2003 Proof	38,000	Value: 120				

KM# 1498 10 YUAN
31.1035 g., 0.9990 Silver 0.9990 oz. ASW, 40 mm. **Rev:**
Multicolor female standing, black dress **Shape:** Octagon

Date	Mintage	F	VF	XF	Unc	BU
2003 Proof	38,000		Value: 120			

KM# 1499 10 YUAN
31.1035 g., 0.9990 Silver 0.9990 oz. ASW, 40 mm. **Series:**
Classic Literature **Rev:** Multicolor female kneeling **Shape:**
Octagon

Date	Mintage	F	VF	XF	Unc	BU
2003 Proof	38,000		Value: 120			

KM# 1500 10 YUAN
31.1035 g., 0.9990 Silver 0.9990 oz. ASW, 40 mm. **Series:**
Classic literature **Rev:** Multicolor female walking, rose dress
Shape: Octagon

Date	Mintage	F	VF	XF	Unc	BU
2003 Proof	—		Value: 120			

KM# 1501 10 YUAN
31.1035 g., 0.9990 Silver 0.9990 oz. ASW, 40 mm. **Series:**
Classic literature **Rev:** Multicolor female kneeling, red dress
Shape: Octagon

Date	Mintage	F	VF	XF	Unc	BU
2003 Proof	—		Value: 120			

KM# 1570 10 YUAN
31.1035 g., 0.9990 Silver 0.9990 oz. ASW, 40 mm. **Obv:**
National arms above People's Congress Hall and ornamental
column **Rev:** Multicolor hologram depicting the hall's overhead
lighting **Edge:** Reeded **Note:** Prev. KM#1212.

Date	Mintage	F	VF	XF	Unc	BU
2004 Proof	50,000		Value: 100			

KM# 1559 10 YUAN
31.1035 g., 0.9990 Silver 0.9990 oz. ASW, 40 mm. **Obv:**
Monkey King leading the Master over bridge **Rev:** Multicolor
Monkey King fighting the "Ox Fiend" **Edge:** Reeded **Note:** Prev.
Y#1214.

Date	Mintage	F	VF	XF	Unc	BU
2004 Proof	38,000		Value: 110			

KM# 1558 10 YUAN
31.1035 g., 0.9990 Silver 0.9990 oz. ASW, 40 mm. **Obv:**
Monkey King leading the Master over bridge **Rev:** Multicolor Pig
carrying Monkey King piggy-back style **Edge:** Reeded **Note:**
Prev. Y#1215.

Date	Mintage	F	VF	XF	Unc	BU
2004 Proof	38,000		Value: 110			

KM# 1566 10 YUAN
31.1035 g., 0.9990 Silver 0.9990 oz. ASW, 40 mm. **Obv:**
Guangan Exposition Hall **Rev:** Deng Xiaoping and value **Edge:**
Reeded **Note:** Prev. Y#1240. Photo reduced.

Date	Mintage	F	VF	XF	Unc	BU
2004 Proof	80,000		Value: 90.00			

KM# 1539 10 YUAN
31.1035 g., 0.9990 Silver 0.9990 oz. ASW, 40 mm. **Subject:**
20th Anniversary / Bank of China Industrial and Commercial **Rev:**
Panda walking with cub

Date	Mintage	F	VF	XF	Unc	BU
2004 Proof	120,000		Value: 90.00			

KM# 1541 10 YUAN
31.1035 g., 0.9990 Silver 0.9990 oz. ASW, 40 mm. **Subject:**
50th Anniversary China Construction Bank **Rev:** Panda walking
with cub

Date	Mintage	F	VF	XF	Unc	BU
2004 Proof	170,000		Value: 90.00			

KM# 1543 10 YUAN
31.1035 g., 0.9990 Silver 0.9990 oz. ASW, 40 mm. **Subject:**
Bejing International Coin Expo **Rev:** Panda walking with cub, gold
plated center

Date	Mintage	F	VF	XF	Unc	BU
2004 Proof	30,000		Value: 120			

KM# 1557 10 YUAN
31.1035 g., 0.9990 Silver 0.9990 oz. ASW, 40 mm. **Series:** Folk
customs **Subject:** Lantern Festival **Rev:** Boy holding lantern
Note: Colorized

Date	Mintage	F	VF	XF	Unc	BU
2004 Proof	60,000		Value: 100			

KM# 1555 10 YUAN
31.1035 g., 0.9990 Silver 0.9990 oz. ASW, 40 mm. **Subject:**
100th Anniversary Red Cross **Obv:** Red Cross within wreath **Rev:**
Dove **Note:** Colorized

Date	Mintage	F	VF	XF	Unc	BU
2004 Proof	60,000		Value: 85.00			

KM# 1580 10 YUAN
31.1035 g., 0.9990 Silver 0.9990 oz. ASW, 40 mm. **Subject:**
600th Anniversary of Zheng He's voyage **Obv:** Multicolor stylized
sailboat on water **Rev:** Ancient Chinese navigational instruments
Edge: Reeded **Note:** Prev. Y#1239.

Date	Mintage	F	VF	XF	Unc	BU
2005(y) Proof	—		Value: 100			

KM# 1592   10 YUAN
31.1050 g., 0.9990 Silver gilt rim 0.9990 oz. ASW, 40 mm.   **Obv:** Temple of Heaven **Rev:** Panda cub and mom seated in bamboo
Note: Gilt rim

Date	Mintage	F	VF	XF	Unc	BU
2005 Proof	30,000	Value: 85.00				

KM# 1601   10 YUAN
31.1050 g., 0.9990 Silver 0.9990 oz. ASW, 40 mm.   **Subject:** Foundation of Industrial & Commercial Bank **Obv:** Temple of Heaven, gilt rim **Rev:** Panda cub and mom seated in bamboo

Date	Mintage	F	VF	XF	Unc	BU
2005 Proof	100,000	Value: 70.00				

KM# 1603   10 YUAN
31.1050 g., 0.9990 Silver 0.9990 oz. ASW, 40 mm.   **Subject:** 100th Anniversary of Bank of Shanghai **Obv:** Temple of Heaven **Rev:** Panda cub and mom seated in bamboo

Date	Mintage	F	VF	XF	Unc	BU
2005 Proof	50,000	Value: 80.00				

KM# 1618   10 YUAN
31.1050 g., 0.9990 Silver 0.9990 oz. ASW, 40 mm.   **Subject:** 2006 World Cup - Germany **Obv:** Multicolor logo **Rev:** Classical soccer player and goal net **Note:** Prev - Y1255, KM1670

Date	Mintage	F	VF	XF	Unc	BU
2005 Proof	50,000	Value: 90.00				

KM# 1626   10 YUAN
31.1050 g., 0.9990 Silver 0.9990 oz. ASW, 40 mm.   **Subject:** 600th Anniversary - Zheng He's Voyages **Obv:** Multicolor logo **Rev:** Nautical invention

Date	Mintage	F	VF	XF	Unc	BU
2005 Proof	60,000	Value: 85.00				

KM# 1628   10 YUAN
31.1050 g., 0.9990 Silver 0.9990 oz. ASW, 40 mm.   **Subject:** Chen Yun Birth Centennial **Obv:** House **Rev:** Half-length figure facing

Date	Mintage	F	VF	XF	Unc	BU
2005 Proof	15,000	Value: 140				

KM# 1629   10 YUAN
31.1050 g., 0.9990 Silver 0.9990 oz. ASW, 40 mm.   **Subject:** Chen Yun Birth Centennial **Obv:** House **Rev:** Figure seated in chair, arm outstretched

Date	Mintage	F	VF	XF	Unc	BU
2005 Proof	15,000	Value: 140				

KM# 1631   10 YUAN
31.1050 g., 0.9990 Silver 0.9990 oz. ASW, 40 mm.   **Subject:** 60th Anniversary of Victory - War of Resistance **Obv:** Monument **Rev:** People celebrating

Date	Mintage	F	VF	XF	Unc	BU
2005 Proof	30,000	Value: 140				

KM# 1636   10 YUAN
31.1050 g., 0.9990 Silver 0.9990 oz. ASW, 40 mm.   **Series:**

Classical Literature **Obv:** Horseman on arch bridge **Rev:** Multicolor monkey and female

Date	Mintage	F	VF	XF	Unc	BU
2005 Proof	38,000	Value: 130				

KM# 1637   10 YUAN
31.1050 g., 0.9990 Silver 0.9990 oz. ASW, 40 mm.   **Series:** Classical Literature **Obv:** Horseman on arch bridge **Rev:** Multicolor man slaying spider on web

Date	Mintage	F	VF	XF	Unc	BU
2005 Proof	38,000	Value: 130				

KM# 1639   10 YUAN
31.1050 g., 0.9990 Silver 0.9990 oz. ASW, 40 mm.   **Subject:** Chinese Movie Centennial **Obv:** Winged column **Rev:** Old time movie camera

Date	Mintage	F	VF	XF	Unc	BU
2005 Proof	60,000	Value: 85.00				

KM# 1670   10 YUAN
31.1035 g., 0.9990 Silver 0.9990 oz. ASW   **Subject:** World Cup Soccer **Obv:** Colorized logo **Rev:** Classically dressed athlete scoring goal **Note:** Prev. Y#1255.

Date	Mintage	F	VF	XF	Unc	BU
2006 Proof	—	Value: 100				

KM# 1666   10 YUAN
31.1050 g., 0.9990 Silver 0.9990 oz. ASW, 40 mm.   **Obv:** Temple of Heaven **Rev:** Two pandas seated with bamboo

Date	Mintage	F	VF	XF	Unc	BU
2006 Proof	50,000	Value: 75.00				

KM# 1668   10 YUAN
31.1050 g., 0.9990 Silver 0.9990 oz. ASW, 40 mm.   **Subject:** 10th Anniversary of China Minsheng Banking Corp **Obv:** Temple of Heaven **Rev:** Two pandas seated with bamboo

Date	Mintage	F	VF	XF	Unc	BU
2006 Proof	70,000	Value: 85.00				

KM# A1670   10 YUAN
31.1050 g., 0.9990 Silver 0.9990 oz. ASW, 40 mm.   **Subject:**
Shengang Horticultural Expo **Obv:** Temple of Heaven **Rev:** Two
pandas seated with bamboo

Date	Mintage	F	VF	XF	Unc	BU
2006 Proof	30,000	Value: 85.00				

KM# 1675   10 YUAN
31.1050 g., 0.9990 Silver 0.9990 oz. ASW, 40 mm.   **Subject:**
10th Anniversary Jinan City Commercial Bank **Obv:** Temple of
Heaven **Rev:** Two pandas seated with bamboo

Date	Mintage	F	VF	XF	Unc	BU
2006 Proof	20,000	Value: 85.00				

KM# 1676   10 YUAN
31.1050 g., 0.9990 Silver Gold plated outer ring 0.9990 oz. ASW,
40 mm.   **Subject:** Beijing International Stamp and Coin Expo
Obv: Temple of Heaven **Rev:** Two pandas seated with bamboo

Date	Mintage	F	VF	XF	Unc	BU
2006 Proof	20,000	Value: 100				

KM# 1690   10 YUAN
31.1050 g., 0.9990 Silver 0.9990 oz. ASW, 40 mm.   **Subject:**
Yvelv Academy **Obv:** Front door of Academy **Rev:** Exterior view

Date	Mintage	F	VF	XF	Unc	BU
2006 Proof	40,000	Value: 85.00				

KM# 1691   10 YUAN
31.1050 g., 0.9990 Silver 0.9990 oz. ASW, 40 mm.   **Subject:**
Qinghai - Tibet Railway Opening **Obv:** Lhasa Railway Station
with mountains in background **Rev:** Yvante Bridge over the
Yangtze River and tibetan antelope and yak

Date	Mintage	F	VF	XF	Unc	BU
2006 Proof	36,000	Value: 150				

KM# 1693   10 YUAN
31.1050 g., 0.9990 Silver 0.9990 oz. ASW, 40 mm.   **Obv:** Map
of marches and hammer and sickle **Rev:** Group of marchers in
snow

Date	Mintage	F	VF	XF	Unc	BU
2006 Proof	25,000	Value: 110				

KM# 1729   10 YUAN
31.1050 g., 0.9990 Silver 0.9990 oz. ASW, 40 mm.   **Subject:**
60th Anniversary - Foundry of Mongolia Autonomous Region
Obv: Wheel of Mongolian Lele Cart **Rev:** Grassland view of
Mongolia, huts and horsemen

Date	Mintage	F	VF	XF	Unc	BU
2007 Proof	20,000	Value: 110				

KM# 1702   10 YUAN
31.1050 g., 0.9990 Silver 0.9990 oz. ASW   **Subject:** 2007
Summer Olympics **Obv:** Beijing Olympic logo **Rev:** Child with
kite, multicolor design **Shape:** 40 **Note:** Issued in 2006

Date	Mintage	F	VF	XF	Unc	BU
2008 Proof	160,000	Value: 45.00				

KM# 1703   10 YUAN
31.1050 g., 0.9990 Silver 0.9990 oz. ASW, 40 mm.   **Subject:**
2007 Summer Olympics **Obv:** Beijing Olympics logo **Rev:** Two
children playing leapfrog, multicolor **Note:** Issued in 2006

Date	Mintage	F	VF	XF	Unc	BU
2008 Proof	16,000	Value: 65.00				

KM# 1704   10 YUAN
31.1050 g., 0.9990 Silver 0.9990 oz. ASW, 40 mm.   **Subject:**
2007 Summer Olympics **Obv:** Beijing Olympics logo **Rev:** Child
rolling ring with stick, multicolor **Note:** Issued in 2006

Date	Mintage	F	VF	XF	Unc	BU
2008 Proof	160,000	Value: 55.00				

KM# 1705   10 YUAN
31.1050 g., 0.9990 Silver 0.9990 oz. ASW, 40 mm.   **Subject:**
2007 Summer Olympics **Obv:** Beijing Olympic's logo **Rev:** Young
girl dancing, multicolor **Note:** Issued in 2006

Date	Mintage	F	VF	XF	Unc	BU
2008 Proof	160,000	Value: 55.00				

KM# 1825   10 YUAN
31.1050 g., 0.9990 Silver 0.9990 oz. ASW, 40 mm.   **Subject:**
Bank of Communications, Centennial

Date	Mintage	F	VF	XF	Unc	BU
2008 Proof	—	Value: 85.00				

KM# 1843   10 YUAN
31.1050 g., 0.9990 Silver 0.9990 oz. ASW, 40 mm.   **Subject:**
Beijing Olympics **Rev:** Multicolor mask, stall tea scene

Date	Mintage	F	VF	XF	Unc	BU
2008 Proof	160,000	Value: 55.00				

KM# 1844   10 YUAN
31.1050 g., 0.9990 Silver 0.9990 oz. ASW, 40 mm.   **Subject:**
Beijing Olympics **Rev:** Multicolor mask, lion dancer

Date	Mintage	F	VF	XF	Unc	BU
2008 Proof	160,000	Value: 55.00				

KM# 1845   10 YUAN
31.1050 g., 0.9990 Silver 0.9990 oz. ASW, 40 mm.   **Subject:** Beijing Olympics **Rev:** Multicolor mask, Yangtze dancer

Date	Mintage	F	VF	XF	Unc	BU
2008 Proof	160,000	Value: 55.00				

KM# 1846   10 YUAN
31.1050 g., 0.9990 Silver 0.9990 oz. ASW, 40 mm.   **Subject:** Beijing Olympics **Rev:** Multicolor mask, Beijing Opera

Date	Mintage	F	VF	XF	Unc	BU
2008 Proof	160,000	Value: 45.00				

KM# 1852   10 YUAN
31.1050 g., 0.9990 Silver 0.9990 oz. ASW, 40 mm.   **Subject:** Hainan Special Economic Zone

Date	Mintage	F	VF	XF	Unc	BU
2008 Proof	20,000	Value: 90.00				

KM# 1854   10 YUAN
31.1050 g., 0.9990 Silver 0.9990 oz. ASW, 40 mm.   **Subject:** Para Olympics

Date	Mintage	F	VF	XF	Unc	BU
2008 Proof	30,000	Value: 100				

KM# 1856   10 YUAN
31.1050 g., 0.9990 Silver 0.9990 oz. ASW, 40 mm.   **Subject:** Ningxia Hui Autonomous Region

Date	Mintage	F	VF	XF	Unc	BU
2008 Proof	20,000	Value: 105				

KM# 1858   10 YUAN
31.1050 g., 0.9990 Silver 0.9990 oz. ASW, 40 mm.   **Subject:** Beijing Coin and Stamp Expo

Date	Mintage	F	VF	XF	Unc	BU
2008 Proof	30,000	Value: 75.00				

KM# 1859   10 YUAN
31.1050 g., 0.9990 Silver 0.9990 oz. ASW, 40 mm.   **Subject:** Guangxi Zhuang Autonomous Region

Date	Mintage	F	VF	XF	Unc	BU
2008 Proof	20,000	Value: 90.00				

KM# 1907   10 YUAN
31.1050 g., 0.9990 Silver 0.9990 oz. ASW, 40 mm.   **Subject:** Shanghai Expo

Date	Mintage	F	VF	XF	Unc	BU
2009 Proof	—	Value: 60.00				

KM# 1891   10 YUAN
31.1050 g., 0.9990 Silver 0.9990 oz. ASW, 40 mm.   **Subject:** Precious Metal Commemoratives, 30th Anniversary

Date	Mintage	F	VF	XF	Unc	BU
2009	300,000	—	—	—	—	40.00

KM# 1892   10 YUAN
31.1050 g., 0.9990 Silver 0.9990 oz. ASW, 40 mm.   **Subject:** Beijing International Coin & Stamp Show

Date	Mintage	F	VF	XF	Unc	BU
2009	30,000	—	—	—	—	60.00

KM# 1896   10 YUAN
31.1050 g., 0.9990 Silver 0.9990 oz. ASW, 40 mm.   **Subject:** P.R.C. 60th Anniversary

Date	Mintage	F	VF	XF	Unc	BU
2009 Proof	100,000	Value: 50.00				

KM# 1898   10 YUAN
31.1050 g., 0.9990 Silver 0.9990 oz. ASW, 40 mm.   **Subject:** P.R.C. 60th Anniversary **Rev:** Multicolor

Date	Mintage	F	VF	XF	Unc	BU
2009 Proof	100,000	Value: 55.00				

KM# 1902   10 YUAN
31.1050 g., 0.9990 Silver 0.9990 oz. ASW, 40 mm.   **Subject:** Outlaws of the Marsh, series 1 **Rev:** Multicolor

Date	Mintage	F	VF	XF	Unc	BU
2009 Proof	60,000	Value: 60.00				

KM# 1903   10 YUAN
31.1050 g., 0.9990 Silver 0.9990 oz. ASW, 40 mm.   **Subject:** Outlaws of the Marsh, series 1 **Rev:** Multicolor

Date	Mintage	F	VF	XF	Unc	BU
2009 Proof	60,000	Value: 60.00				

KM# 1905   10 YUAN
31.1050 g., 0.9990 Silver 0.9990 oz. ASW, 40 mm.   **Subject:** 16th Asian Games

Date	Mintage	F	VF	XF	Unc	BU
2009 Proof	60,000	Value: 48.00				

KM# 1908   10 YUAN
31.1050 g., 0.9990 Silver 0.9990 oz. ASW, 40 mm.   **Subject:** Shanghai Expo

Date	Mintage	F	VF	XF	Unc	BU
2009 Proof	—	Value: 48.00				

KM# 1910   10 YUAN
31.1050 g., 0.9990 Silver 0.9990 oz. ASW, 40 mm.   **Subject:** China Agricultural Bank

Date	Mintage	F	VF	XF	Unc	BU
2009	100,000	—	—	—	—	40.00

KM# 1939   10 YUAN
31.1050 g., 0.9990 Silver 0.9990 oz. ASW, 40 mm.   **Series:** Outlaws of the Marsh, series 2 **Rev:** Multicolor

Date	Mintage	F	VF	XF	Unc	BU
2010 Proof	70,000	Value: 60.00				

KM# 1940   10 YUAN
31.1050 g., 0.9990 Silver 0.9990 oz. ASW, 40 mm.   **Series:** Outlaws of the Marsh, series 2 **Rev:** Multicolor

Date	Mintage	F	VF	XF	Unc	BU
2010 Proof	70,000	Value: 60.00				

KM# 1942   10 YUAN
10.3600 g., 0.9990 Gold 0.3327 oz. AGW   **Subject:** Shanghai World Expo, 2010

Date	Mintage	F	VF	XF	Unc	BU
2010 Proof	60,000	Value: 550				

KM# 1943   10 YUAN
31.1050 g., 0.9990 Silver 0.9990 oz. ASW, 40 mm.   **Subject:** Shanghai World Expo, 2010

Date	Mintage	F	VF	XF	Unc	BU
2010 Proof	80,000	Value: 60.00				

KM# 1944   10 YUAN
31.1050 g., 0.9990 Silver 0.9990 oz. ASW, 40 mm.   **Subject:** Shanghai World Expo, 2010

Date	Mintage	F	VF	XF	Unc	BU
2010 Proof	80,000	Value: 60.00				

KM# 1946   10 YUAN
31.1050 g., 0.9990 Silver 0.9990 oz. ASW, 40 mm.   **Subject:** Wudang Mountain

Date	Mintage	F	VF	XF	Unc	BU
2010 Proof	60,000	Value: 60.00				

KM# 1953   10 YUAN
31.1050 g., 0.9990 Silver 0.9990 oz. ASW   **Subject:** Shenzhen Economic Zone

Date	Mintage	F	VF	XF	Unc	BU
2010 Proof	30,000	Value: 60.00				

KM# 1955   10 YUAN
31.1050 g., 0.9990 Silver 0.9990 oz. ASW, 40 mm.   **Subject:** 16th Asian Games

Date	Mintage	F	VF	XF	Unc	BU
2010 Proof	60,000	Value: 60.00				

KM# 1957   10 YUAN
31.1050 g., 0.9990 Silver 0.9990 oz. ASW, 40 mm.   **Subject:** Bejing Opera, series 1 **Rev:** Multicolor face mask

Date	Mintage	F	VF	XF	Unc	BU
2010 Proof	50,000	Value: 60.00				

KM# 1958   10 YUAN
31.1050 g., 0.9990 Silver 0.9990 oz. ASW, 40 mm.   **Subject:** Bejing Opera, series 1 **Rev:** Multicolor face mask

Date	Mintage	F	VF	XF	Unc	BU
2010 Proof	50,000	Value: 60.00				

KM# 1959   10 YUAN
31.1050 g., 0.9990 Silver 0.9990 oz. ASW, 40 mm.   **Subject:** Bejing Stamp & Coin Expo

Date	Mintage	F	VF	XF	Unc	BU
2010 Proof	30,000	Value: 60.00				

KM# 1985   10 YUAN
31.1050 g., 0.9990 Silver 0.9990 oz. ASW, 40 mm.   **Subject:** Peking Opera art **Rev:** Lu Zhishen, the "Flowery Monk" character from Water Margin

Date	Mintage	F	VF	XF	Unc	BU
2011 Proof	50,000	Value: 75.00				

KM# 1986   10 YUAN
31.1050 g., 0.9990 Silver 0.9990 oz. ASW, 40 mm.   **Subject:** Peking Opera art **Rev:** Shan Ziongxin

Date	Mintage	F	VF	XF	Unc	BU
2011 Proof	50,000	Value: 75.00				

KM# 1994   10 YUAN
31.1050 g., 0.9990 Silver 0.9990 oz. ASW, 40 mm.   **Subject:** Bejing-Shanghai High Speed Rail **Obv:** Temple of Heaven **Rev:** Two pandas

Date	Mintage	F	VF	XF	Unc	BU
2011 Proof	30,000	Value: 200				

KM# 1996   10 YUAN
31.1050 g., 0.9990 Silver 0.9990 oz. ASW, 40 mm.   **Subject:** Xi-an Hortaculture Exposition **Obv:** Temple of Heaven **Rev:** Two pandas

Date	Mintage	F	VF	XF	Unc	BU
2011 Proof	20,000	Value: 235				

KM# 1998   10 YUAN
31.1050 g., 0.9990 Silver 0.9990 oz. ASW, 40 mm.   **Subject:** 26th Summer Universade, Shezhuan **Obv:** Colored wreath logo **Rev:** Cubic building

Date	Mintage	F	VF	XF	Unc	BU
2011 Proof	30,000	Value: 200				

KM# 2000   10 YUAN
31.1050 g., 0.9990 Silver 0.9990 oz. ASW, 40 mm.   **Subject:** Peaceful liberation, 60th Anniversary **Obv:** National emblem **Rev:** Ornate design

Date	Mintage	F	VF	XF	Unc	BU
2011 Proof	30,000	—	—	—	—	200

KM# 2002   10 YUAN
31.1050 g., 0.9990 Silver 0.9990 oz. ASW, 40 mm.   **Subject:** 100th Anniversary of the Revolution **Obv:** National emblem **Rev:** Revolutionary army advancing right - Wuchang Uprising

Date	Mintage	F	VF	XF	Unc	BU
2011 Proof	160,000	Value: 100				

KM# 2004   10 YUAN
31.1050 g., 0.9990 Silver 0.9990 oz. ASW, 40 mm.   **Subject:** Avation Industry in the P.R.C., 60th Anniversary **Obv:** Temple of Heaven **Rev:** Two pandas

Date	Mintage	F	VF	XF	Unc	BU
2011 Proof	20,000	Value: 200				

KM# 2007   10 YUAN
31.1050 g., 0.9990 Silver 0.9990 oz. ASW, 40 mm.   **Subject:** World Heritage Site **Obv:** National emblem **Rev:** Songyue Temple Pagoda

Date	Mintage	F	VF	XF	Unc	BU
2011 Proof	60,000	Value: 150				

KM# 1388   20 YUAN
62.2070 g., 0.9990 Silver 1.9979 oz. ASW, 40 mm.   **Subject:** Mogao Grottos **Obv:** 8-story building **Rev:** Buddha-like statue **Edge:** Reeded **Note:** Prev. Y#1082.

Date	Mintage	F	VF	XF	Unc	BU
2001 Proof	30,000	Value: 150				

KM# 1432   20 YUAN
62.2070 g., 0.9990 Silver 1.9979 oz. ASW, 40 mm.   **Rev:** Buddha-like statue

Date	Mintage	F	VF	XF	Unc	BU
2002 Proof	30,000	Value: 150				

KM# 1563   20 YUAN
31.1035 g., 0.9990 Silver 0.9990 oz. ASW, 40 mm.   **Series:** Maijishan grotto art **Rev:** Two figures standing

Date	Mintage	F	VF	XF	Unc	BU
2004 Proof	20,000	Value: 90.00				

KM# 1390   50 YUAN
155.5175 g., 0.9990 Silver 4.9948 oz. ASW, 70 mm.   **Subject:** Mogao Grottoes **Obv:** Eight story building **Rev:** Four musicians **Edge:** Reeded. **Note:** Prev. Y#1083.

Date	Mintage	F	VF	XF	Unc	BU
2001 Proof	8,000	Value: 300				

KM# 1389   50 YUAN
3.1104 g., 0.9990 Gold 0.0999 oz. AGW   **Subject:** Mogao Grottoes **Obv:** Eight story building **Rev:** Buddha-like statue **Edge:** Reeded. **Note:** Prev. Y#1084.

Date	Mintage	F	VF	XF	Unc	BU
2001 Proof	50,000	Value: 250				

KM# 1394 50 YUAN
155.5175 g., 0.9990 Silver 4.9948 oz. ASW, 90 x 40 mm.
Subject: Han Xizai's Dinner Party **Obv:** Tang Dynasty buildings
Rev: Multicolor "Five Dynasties" painting **Edge:** Plain **Shape:**
Rectangular **Note:** Prev. Y#1104.

Date	Mintage	F	VF	XF	Unc	BU
2001 Proof	18,800	Value: 275				

KM# 1386 50 YUAN
155.5175 g., 0.9990 Silver 4.9948 oz. ASW, 90 x 40 mm. **Series:**
Folk fairy tails **Rev:** Seven multicolor figures on beach **Shape:**
Rectangle

Date	Mintage	F	VF	XF	Unc	BU
2001 Proof	10,000	Value: 300				

KM# 1402 50 YUAN
155.5190 g., 0.9990 Silver 4.9948 oz. ASW, 90 x 50 mm.
Subject: Bejing opera **Rev:** Four multicolor actors **Shape:**
Rectangle

Date	Mintage	F	VF	XF	Unc	BU
2001 Proof	11,800	Value: 300				

KM# 1433 50 YUAN
155.5190 g., 0.9990 Silver 4.9948 oz. ASW, 70 mm. **Series:**
Long men grottoes **Rev:** Two figures

Date	Mintage	F	VF	XF	Unc	BU
2002 Proof	8,000	Value: 300				

KM# 1445 50 YUAN
155.5190 g., 0.9990 Silver 4.9948 oz. ASW, 65 x 26 mm. **Series:**
Classic literature **Rev:** Multicolor crowd of women **Shape:** Fan-like

Date	Mintage	F	VF	XF	Unc	BU
2002 Proof	11,800	Value: 200				

KM# 1430 50 YUAN
155.7900 g., 0.9990 Silver 5.0035 oz. ASW, 90 x 40 mm. **Series:**
Folk fairy tails **Rev:** Multicolor female with red ribbon **Shape:**
Rectangle

Date	Mintage	F	VF	XF	Unc	BU
2002 Proof	—	Value: 375				

KM# 1437 50 YUAN
3.1100 g., 0.9990 Gold 0.0999 oz. AGW, 18 mm. **Subject:** Kuan yin

Date	Mintage	F	VF	XF	Unc	BU
2002 Proof	33,000	Value: 225				

KM# 1453 50 YUAN
155.5190 g., 0.9990 Silver 4.9948 oz. ASW, 90 x 40 mm. **Series:**
Bejing opera **Rev:** Three multicolor characters one with spikes
in costume **Shape:** Rectangle

Date	Mintage	F	VF	XF	Unc	BU
2002 Proof	11,800	Value: 300				

KM# 1493 50 YUAN
155.3500 g., 0.9990 Silver 4.9894 oz. ASW, 90 x 40 mm. **Series:**
Fairy tails **Rev:** Multicolor man with two boys in buckets, jenole
in flight at left **Shape:** Rectangle

Date	Mintage	F	VF	XF	Unc	BU
2003 Proof	10,000	Value: 350				

KM# 1512 50 YUAN
3.1104 g., 0.9990 Gold 0.0999 oz. AGW, 18 mm. **Obv:** Putuo
Mountain Pilgrimage Gate **Rev:** Seated Kuanyin with holographic
background **Edge:** Reeded **Note:** Prev. Y#1234.

Date	Mintage	F	VF	XF	Unc	BU
2003 Proof	33,000	Value: 225				

KM# 1502 50 YUAN
155.5000 g., 0.9990 Silver 4.9942 oz. ASW, 80 x 50 mm. **Series:**
Class literature **Rev:** Multicolor man lying on couch **Shape:**
Rectangle

Date	Mintage	F	VF	XF	Unc	BU
2003 Proof	10,000	Value: 350				

KM# 1503 50 YUAN
155.1500 g., 0.9990 Silver 4.9830 oz. ASW, 65 x 125 mm.
Series: Class literature **Rev:** Six people **Shape:** Arc **Note:**
Colorized

Date	Mintage	F	VF	XF	Unc	BU
2003 Proof	11,800	Value: 350				

KM# 1572 50 YUAN
3.1100 g., 0.9990 Gold 0.0999 oz. AGW, 18 mm. **Obv:** Putuo
Mountain Pilgrimage Gate **Rev:** Kuanyin and value **Edge:**
Reeded **Note:** Prev. Y#1237.

Date	Mintage	F	VF	XF	Unc	BU
2004 Proof	33,000	Value: 225				

KM# 1560 50 YUAN
155.5175 g., 0.9990 Silver 4.9948 oz. ASW, 80 x 50 mm. **Obv:**
Monkey King leading the Master over bridge **Rev:** Multicolor
Monkey King fighting the Pig Demon of Bones **Edge:** Plain
Shape: Rectangle **Note:** Prev. Y#1216.

Date	Mintage	F	VF	XF	Unc	BU
2004 Proof	10,000	Value: 375				

KM# 1635 50 YUAN
155.0000 g., 0.9990 Silver 4.9782 oz. ASW, 80 x 50 mm. **Series:**
Classical Literature **Obv:** Horseman on arch bridge **Rev:**
Multicolor female and lion **Shape:** Rectangle **Note:** Illustration
reduced.

Date	Mintage	F	VF	XF	Unc	BU
2005 Proof	10,000	Value: 350				

KM# 1901 50 YUAN
155.5000 g., 0.9990 Silver 4.9942 oz. ASW, 80x50 mm.
Subject: Outlaws of the Marsh, series 1 **Rev:** Multicolor **Shape:**
Rectangle

Date	Mintage	F	VF	XF	Unc	BU
2009 Proof	10,000	Value: 250				

KM# 1938 50 YUAN
155.5000 g., 0.9990 Silver 4.9942 oz. ASW, 80x50 mm.
Subject: Outlaws of the Marsh, series 2 **Rev:** Multicolor **Shape:**
Regtangle

Date	Mintage	F	VF	XF	Unc	BU
2010 Proof	12,000	Value: 225				

KM# 1951 50 YUAN
62.1000 g., 0.9990 Silver 1.9945 oz. ASW **Subject:** Yungang
Grotto Art

Date	Mintage	F	VF	XF	Unc	BU
2010 Proof	20,000	Value: 120				

KM# 1514 100 YUAN
3.1013 g., 0.9990 Platinum 0.0996 oz. APW, 18 mm. **Series:**
Guan Yi

Date	Mintage	F	VF	XF	Unc	BU
2003 Proof	33,000	Value: 225				

KM# 1534 100 YUAN
15.5500 g., 0.9990 Palladium 0.4994 oz., 27 mm. **Obv:** Temple
of Heaven **Rev:** Panda mother and cub, "kissing pandas" **Edge:**
Reeded **Note:** Prev. Y#1211.

Date	Mintage	F	VF	XF	Unc	BU
2004 Proof	8,000	Value: 550				

KM# 1573 100 YUAN
3.1100 g., 0.9995 Platinum 0.0999 oz. APW, 18 mm. **Obv:**
Putuo Mountain Pilgrimage Gate **Rev:** Kuanyin and value **Edge:**
Reeded **Note:** Prev. Y#1238.

Date	Mintage	F	VF	XF	Unc	BU
2004 Proof	33,000	Value: 225				

KM# 1540 100 YUAN
7.8500 g., 0.9990 Gold 0.2521 oz. AGW, 22 mm. **Subject:** 20th
Anniversary / Bank of China Industrial and Commercial **Rev:**
Panda walking with cub

Date	Mintage	F	VF	XF	Unc	BU
2004 Proof	50,000	Value: 425				

KM# 1542 100 YUAN
7.8400 g., 0.9990 Gold 0.2518 oz. AGW, 22 mm. **Subject:** 50th
Anniversary China Construction Bank **Rev:** Panda walking with
cub

Date	Mintage	F	VF	XF	Unc	BU
2004 Proof	60,000	Value: 400				

KM# 1600 100 YUAN
7.7700 g., 0.9990 Gold 0.2496 oz. AGW, 22 mm. **Subject:** Foundation of Industrial & Commercial Bank **Obv:** Temple of Heaven **Rev:** Panda cub and mom seated in bamboo

Date	Mintage	F	VF	XF	Unc	BU
2005 Proof	40,000	Value: 500				

KM# 1602 100 YUAN
7.7700 g., 0.9990 Gold 0.2496 oz. AGW, 22 mm. **Subject:** 100th Anniversary of Bank of Shanghai **Obv:** Temple of Heaven **Rev:** Panda cub and mom seated in bamboo

Date	Mintage	F	VF	XF	Unc	BU
2005 Proof	40,000	Value: 500				

KM# 1616 100 YUAN
7.7000 g., 0.9990 Gold 0.2473 oz. AGW, 22 mm. **Subject:** 2006 World Cup - Germany **Obv:** Multicolor logo **Rev:** Temple of Heaven and soccer ball

Date	Mintage	F	VF	XF	Unc	BU
2005 Proof	10,000	Value: 550				

KM# A979 100 YUAN
8.5000 g., 0.9990 Gold 0.2730 oz. AGW, 22 mm. **Subject:** 10th Anniversary Bank of Beijing **Obv:** Temple of Heaven **Rev:** Two pandas

Date	Mintage	F	VF	XF	Unc	BU
2006	100	—	—	—	—	800

KM# A980 100 YUAN
8.5000 g., 0.9990 Gold 0.2730 oz. AGW, 22 mm. **Subject:** 10th Anniversary China Minsheng Banking Corp. **Obv:** Temple of Heaven **Rev:** Two Pandas munching on bamboo

Date	Mintage	F	VF	XF	Unc	BU
2006	100	—	—	—	—	800

KM# 1665 100 YUAN
7.7700 g., 0.9990 Gold 0.2496 oz. AGW, 22 mm. **Subject:** 10th Anniversary Bank of Beijing **Obv:** Temple of Heaven **Rev:** Two pandas seated with bamboo

Date	Mintage	F	VF	XF	Unc	BU
2006 Proof	150,000	Value: 375				

KM# 1667 100 YUAN
7.7700 g., 0.9990 Silver 0.2496 oz. ASW, 22 mm. **Subject:** 10th Anniversary - China Minsheng Banking Corp **Obv:** Temple of Heaven **Rev:** Two pandas seated with bamboo

Date	Mintage	F	VF	XF	Unc	BU
2006 Proof	20,000	Value: 550				

KM# 1669 100 YUAN
7.7700 g., 0.9990 Gold 0.2496 oz. AGW, 22 mm. **Subject:** Shenyang Horticultural Expo **Obv:** Temple of Heaven **Rev:** Two pandas seated with bamboo

Date	Mintage	F	VF	XF	Unc	BU
2006 Proof	10,000	Value: 550				

KM# 1694 100 YUAN
7.7700 g., 0.9990 Gold 0.2496 oz. AGW, 22 mm. **Subject:** Qinghai - Tibet Railway Opening **Obv:** Map of railway route and track layer **Rev:** Kun Lun Tunnel Portal

Date	Mintage	F	VF	XF	Unc	BU
2006 Proof	16,000	Value: 550				

KM# 1730 100 YUAN
7.7700 g., 0.9990 Gold 0.2496 oz. AGW, 22 mm. **Subject:** 60th Anniversary - Foundry of Mongolia Autonomous Region **Obv:** Wheel of Mongolian Lele Cart **Rev:** Female Mongolian in posture of welcome

Date	Mintage	F	VF	XF	Unc	BU
2007 Proof	10,000	Value: 550				

KM# 1824 100 YUAN
7.7700 g., 0.9990 Gold 0.2496 oz. AGW, 23 mm. **Subject:** Bank of Communications, Centennial **Rev:** Panda

Date	Mintage	F	VF	XF	Unc	BU
2008 Proof	10,000	Value: 550				

KM# 1853 100 YUAN
7.7700 g., 0.9990 Gold 0.2496 oz. AGW **Subject:** Hainan Special Economic Zone

Date	Mintage	F	VF	XF	Unc	BU
2008 Proof	10,000	Value: 550				

KM# 1857 100 YUAN
7.7700 g., 0.9990 Gold 0.2496 oz. AGW **Subject:** Ningxia Hui Autonomous Region

Date	Mintage	F	VF	XF	Unc	BU
2008 Proof	10,000	Value: 550				

KM# 1860 100 YUAN
7.7700 g., 0.9990 Gold 0.2496 oz. AGW **Subject:** Guangzi Zhuang Autonomous Region

Date	Mintage	F	VF	XF	Unc	BU
2008 Proof	10,000	Value: 550				

KM# 1890 100 YUAN
7.7700 g., 0.9990 Gold 0.2496 oz. AGW, 23 mm. **Subject:** Precious Metal Commemoratives, 30th Anniversary **Obv:** Temple of Heaven **Rev:** Two pandas seated

Date	Mintage	F	VF	XF	Unc	BU
2009	10,000	—	—	—	—	550

KM# 1895 100 YUAN
7.7700 g., 0.9990 Gold 0.2496 oz. AGW, 22 mm. **Subject:** P.R.C. 60th Anniversary

Date	Mintage	F	VF	XF	Unc	BU
2009 Proof	100,000	Value: 400				

KM# 1904 100 YUAN
7.7700 g., 0.9990 Gold 0.2496 oz. AGW, 22 mm. **Subject:** 16th Asian Games

Date	Mintage	F	VF	XF	Unc	BU
2009 Proof	30,000	Value: 500				

KM# 1909 100 YUAN
7.7700 g., 0.9990 Gold 0.2496 oz. AGW, 22 mm. **Subject:** China Agricultural Bank

Date	Mintage	F	VF	XF	Unc	BU
2009	100,000	—	—	—	—	400

KM# 1945 100 YUAN
7.7700 g., 0.9990 Gold 0.2496 oz. AGW **Subject:** Wudang Mountain

Date	Mintage	F	VF	XF	Unc	BU
2010 Proof	30,000	Value: 500				

KM# 1952 100 YUAN
7.7700 g., 0.9990 Gold 0.2496 oz. AGW **Subject:** Shenzhen Economic Zone

Date	Mintage	F	VF	XF	Unc	BU
2010 Proof	20,000	Value: 500				

KM# 1954 100 YUAN
7.7700 g., 0.9990 Gold 0.2496 oz. AGW **Subject:** 16th Asian Games

Date	Mintage	F	VF	XF	Unc	BU
2010 Proof	30,000	Value: 500				

KM# 1956 100 YUAN
7.7700 g., 0.9990 Gold 0.2496 oz. AGW **Subject:** Beijing Opera, series 1 **Rev:** Multicolor

Date	Mintage	F	VF	XF	Unc	BU
2010 Proof	30,000	Value: 500				

KM# 1987 100 YUAN
7.7700 g., 0.9990 Gold 0.2496 oz. AGW, 22 mm. **Subject:** Peking Opera art **Rev:** Mask of Guan Yu

Date	Mintage	F	VF	XF	Unc	BU
2011 Proof	30,000	Value: 500				

KM# 1995 100 YUAN
7.7700 g., 0.9990 Gold 0.2496 oz. AGW, 22 mm. **Subject:** Beijing-Shanghai High Speed Rail **Obv:** Temple of Heaven **Rev:** Two pandas

Date	Mintage	F	VF	XF	Unc	BU
2011 Proof	10,000	Value: 600				

KM# 1997 100 YUAN
7.7700 g., 0.9990 Gold 0.2496 oz. AGW, 22 mm. **Subject:** Xi-an Horticulture Exposition **Obv:** Temple of Heaven **Rev:** Two pandas

Date	Mintage	F	VF	XF	Unc	BU
2011 Proof	3,000	Value: 750				

KM# 1999 100 YUAN
7.7700 g., 0.9990 Gold 0.2496 oz. AGW, 22 mm. **Subject:** 26th Summer Universade, Shezhuan **Obv:** Colored wreath logo **Rev:** Rays and smile face design

Date	Mintage	F	VF	XF	Unc	BU
2011 Proof	20,000	Value: 750				

KM# 2001 100 YUAN
7.7700 g., 0.9990 Gold 0.2496 oz. AGW, 22 mm. **Subject:** Peaceful Liberation, 60th Anniversary **Obv:** National emblem **Rev:** Ornate design

Date	Mintage	F	VF	XF	Unc	BU
2011 Proof	20,000	Value: 750				

KM# 2003 100 YUAN
7.7700 g., 0.9990 Gold 0.2496 oz. AGW, 22 mm. **Subject:** 100th Anniversary of the Revolution **Obv:** National emblem **Rev:** Sun Yat-sen bust facing

Date	Mintage	F	VF	XF	Unc	BU
2011 Proof	100,000	Value: 650				

KM# 2005 100 YUAN
7.7700 g., 0.9990 Gold 0.2496 oz. AGW, 22 mm. **Subject:** Avation Industry in the P.R.C., 60th Anniversary **Obv:** Temple of Heaven **Rev:** Two pandas

Date	Mintage	F	VF	XF	Unc	BU
2011 Proof	5,000	Value: 750				

KM# 2008 100 YUAN
7.7700 g., 0.9990 Gold 0.2496 oz. AGW, 22 mm. **Subject:** World Heritage Site **Obv:** National emblem **Rev:** Gate of the Shaolin Temple

Date	Mintage	F	VF	XF	Unc	BU
2011 Proof	30,000	Value: 650				

KM# 1488 150 YUAN
10.0500 g., 0.9990 Gold 0.3228 oz. AGW, 23 mm. **Subject:** Spring festival **Obv:** Tree with berries **Rev:** Two Koi in ribbon sea

Date	Mintage	F	VF	XF	Unc	BU
2003 Proof	50,000	Value: 600				

KM# 1511 150 YUAN
10.1300 g., 0.9990 Gold 0.3253 oz. AGW, 23 mm. **Subject:** Space flight **Rev:** Multicolor astronaut and ship

Date	Mintage	F	VF	XF	Unc	BU
2003 Proof	30,000	Value: 625				

KM# 1556 150 YUAN
10.5000 g., 0.9990 Gold 0.3372 oz. AGW, 23 mm. **Series:** Folk customs **Subject:** Lantern Festival **Rev:** Boy holding lantern **Note:** Colorized

Date	Mintage	F	VF	XF	Unc	BU
2004 Proof	20,000	Value: 650				

KM# 1638   150 YUAN
10.0500 g., 0.9990 Gold 0.3228 oz. AGW, 23 mm. **Subject:** Chinese Movie Centennial **Obv:** Winged column **Rev:** Movie clipboard

Date	Mintage	F	VF	XF	Unc	BU
2005 Proof	20,000	Value: 650				

KM# 1848   150 YUAN
10.1000 g., 0.9990 Gold 0.3244 oz. AGW, 23 mm. **Subject:** Beijing Olympics **Obv:** Beijing Olympics **Rev:** Classical soccer player

Date	Mintage	F	VF	XF	Unc	BU
2008 Proof	60,000	Value: 600				

KM# 1847   150 YUAN
10.1000 g., 0.9990 Gold 0.3244 oz. AGW, 23 mm. **Subject:** Beijing Olympics **Rev:** Classical wrestlers

Date	Mintage	F	VF	XF	Unc	BU
2008 Proof	60,000	Value: 600				

KM# 1700   150 YUAN
10.0500 g., 0.9990 Gold 0.3228 oz. AGW, 23 mm. **Subject:** 29th Summer Olympics **Obv:** Beijing Olympic logo **Rev:** Ancient horsemaid and new logo **Note:** Issued in 2006

Date	Mintage	F	VF	XF	Unc	BU
2008 Proof	60,000	Value: 600				

KM# 1701   150 YUAN
10.0500 g., 0.9990 Gold 0.3228 oz. AGW, 23 mm. **Subject:** 29th Summer Olympics **Obv:** Beijing Olympic logo **Rev:** Ancient archer and new logo **Note:** Issued in 2006

Date	Mintage	F	VF	XF	Unc	BU
2008 Proof	60,000	Value: 600				

KM# 1855   150 YUAN
10.1000 g., 0.9990 Gold 0.3244 oz. AGW **Subject:** Para Olympics

Date	Mintage	F	VF	XF	Unc	BU
2008 Proof	15,000	Value: 700				

KM# 1900   150 YUAN
10.3600 g., 0.9990 Gold 0.3327 oz. AGW, 23 mm. **Subject:** Outlaws of the Marsh, series 1 **Rev:** Multicolor

Date	Mintage	F	VF	XF	Unc	BU
2009 Proof	30,000	Value: 650				

KM# 1906   150 YUAN
10.3500 g., 0.9990 Gold 0.3324 oz. AGW **Subject:** Shanghai Expo

Date	Mintage	F	VF	XF	Unc	BU
2009 Proof	—	Value: 650				

KM# 1937   150 YUAN
10.3500 g., 0.9990 Gold 0.3324 oz. AGW **Subject:** Outlaws of the Marsh, series 2 **Rev:** Multicolor

Date	Mintage	F	VF	XF	Unc	BU
2010 Proof	35,000	Value: 650				

KM# 1941   150 YUAN
155.5500 g., 0.9990 Gold 4.9958 oz. AGW **Subject:** Shanghai World Expo, 2010

Date	Mintage	F	VF	XF	Unc	BU
2010 Proof	1,000	Value: 8,500				

KM# 1387   200 YUAN
15.5519 g., 0.9990 Gold 0.4995 oz. AGW, 27 mm. **Series:** Folk fairy tails **Rev:** Multicolor heroic figure putting ax to clouds

Date	Mintage	F	VF	XF	Unc	BU
2001 Proof	8,800	Value: 1,050				

KM# 1391   200 YUAN
15.5518 g., 0.9990 Gold 0.4995 oz. AGW, 27 mm. **Subject:** Mogao Grottoes **Obv:** Eight story building **Rev:** Dancing drummer **Edge:** Reeded. **Note:** Prev. Y#1085.

Date	Mintage	F	VF	XF	Unc	BU
2001 Proof	8,800	Value: 1,050				

KM# 1393   200 YUAN
15.5518 g., 0.9990 Gold 0.4995 oz. AGW, 27 mm. **Subject:** 50th Anniversary Chinese Occupation of Tibet **Obv:** Five stars **Rev:** Denomination in flower **Edge:** Reeded **Note:** Prev. Y#1087.

Date	Mintage	F	VF	XF	Unc	BU
2001 Proof	15,000	Value: 950				

KM# 1403   200 YUAN
15.5520 g., 0.9990 Gold 0.4995 oz. AGW, 27 mm. **Subject:** Bejing opera **Rev:** Multicolor ribbon dancer

Date	Mintage	F	VF	XF	Unc	BU
2001 Proof	8,000	Value: 1,100				

KM# 1431   200 YUAN
15.5000 g., 0.9990 Gold 0.4978 oz. AGW **Subject:** Art **Rev:** Multicolor male with snake and staff **Note:** Prev. Y#1148.

Date	Mintage	F	VF	XF	Unc	BU
2002 Proof	8,800	Value: 1,050				

KM# 1434   200 YUAN
15.5500 g., 0.9990 Gold 0.4994 oz. AGW, 27 mm. **Subject:** Buddha **Note:** Prev. Y#1145.

Date	Mintage	F	VF	XF	Unc	BU
2002 Proof	8,800	Value: 1,050				

KM# 1439   200 YUAN
15.5190 g., 0.9990 Gold 0.4984 oz. AGW, 27 mm. **Subject:** Sichuan Sanxingdui relics **Obv:** Museum building **Rev:** Face mask

Date	Mintage	F	VF	XF	Unc	BU
2002 Proof	8,800	Value: 1,050				

KM# 1440   200 YUAN
15.5000 g., 0.9990 Gold 0.4978 oz. AGW **Subject:** Ceremonial Mask **Note:** Prev. Y#1149.

Date	Mintage	F	VF	XF	Unc	BU
2002 Proof	5,000	Value: 1,100				

KM# 1446   200 YUAN
15.5000 g., 0.9990 Gold 0.4978 oz. AGW **Subject:** Dream of the Red Mansion **Shape:** Octagon **Note:** Prev. Y#1147.

Date	Mintage	F	VF	XF	Unc	BU
2002 Proof	8,000	Value: 1,100				

KM# 1454   200 YUAN
15.5000 g., 0.9990 Gold 0.4978 oz. AGW **Subject:** Peking Opera **Note:** Prev. Y#1146.

Date	Mintage	F	VF	XF	Unc	BU
2002 Proof	8,000	Value: 1,050				

KM# 1456   200 YUAN
15.5190 g., 0.9990 Gold 0.4984 oz. AGW, 27 mm. **Subject:** World Expo 2010 **Rev:** Skyline

Date	Mintage	F	VF	XF	Unc	BU
2002 Proof	5,000	Value: 1,100				

KM# 1494   200 YUAN
15.5519 g., 0.9999 Gold 0.4999 oz. AGW **Subject:** Chinese Mythical Folk Tales **Note:** Prev. Y#1160.

Date	Mintage	F	VF	XF	Unc	BU
2003 Proof	8,800	Value: 1,050				

KM# 1495   200 YUAN
15.5150 g., 0.9990 Gold 0.4983 oz. AGW, 27 mm. **Subject:** Finger Sarira of Sakyanmunt **Obv:** Tall tower **Rev:** Flora design

Date	Mintage	F	VF	XF	Unc	BU
2003 Proof	12,000	Value: 950				

KM# 1504   200 YUAN
15.5519 g., 0.9999 Gold 0.4999 oz. AGW **Subject:** Pilgrimage to the West **Note:** Prev. Y#1159.

Date	Mintage	F	VF	XF	Unc	BU
2003 Proof	11,800	Value: 950				

KM# 1506   200 YUAN
15.5130 g., 0.9990 Gold 0.4982 oz. AGW, 40 mm. **Series:** Classical literature **Rev:** Multicolor blue seated female **Shape:** Hexagon

Date	Mintage	F	VF	XF	Unc	BU
2003 Proof	8,000	Value: 1,050				

KM# 1509   200 YUAN
15.5150 g., 0.9990 Gold 0.4983 oz. AGW, 27 mm. **Series:** Wulingyan Scenic Resort

Date	Mintage	F	VF	XF	Unc	BU
2003 Proof	8,000	Value: 950				

KM# 1561   200 YUAN
15.5500 g., 0.9990 Gold 0.4994 oz. AGW, 27 mm. **Obv:** Monkey King leading the Master over bridge **Rev:** Multicolor Monkey King on one knee meeting the Master **Edge:** Reeded **Note:** Prev. Y#1217.

Date	Mintage	F	VF	XF	Unc	BU
2004 Proof	11,800	Value: 950				

KM# 1564   200 YUAN
15.5600 g., 0.9990 Gold 0.4997 oz. AGW, 27 mm. **Series:** Maijishan grotto art **Rev:** Buddha statue

Date	Mintage	F	VF	XF	Unc	BU
2004 Proof	8,800	Value: 1,050				

KM# 1567   200 YUAN
15.5518 g., 0.9990 Gold 0.4995 oz. AGW, 27 mm. **Obv:** Guangan Exposition Hall **Rev:** Deng Xiaoping and value **Edge:** Reeded **Note:** Prev. Y#1241.

Date	Mintage	F	VF	XF	Unc	BU
2004 Proof	10,000	Value: 950				

KM# 1571   200 YUAN
15.5500 g., 0.9990 Gold 0.4994 oz. AGW, 27 mm. **Obv:** National arms above People's Congress Hall and ornamental column **Rev:** Multicolor hologram depicting the hall's overhead lighting **Edge:** Reeded **Note:** Prev. Y#1213.

Date	Mintage	F	VF	XF	Unc	BU
2004 Proof	5,000	Value: 1,050				

KM# 1625   200 YUAN
15.5500 g., 0.9990 Gold 0.4994 oz. AGW, 27 mm. **Subject:** 600th Anniversary of Zheng He's Voyages **Obv:** Multicolor logo **Rev:** Zheng He portrait in linear form

Date	Mintage	F	VF	XF	Unc	BU
2005 Proof	6,000	Value: 950				

KM# 1627   200 YUAN
15.5500 g., 0.9990 Gold 0.4994 oz. AGW, 27 mm. **Subject:** Chen Yun Birth Centennial **Obv:** House **Rev:** Head 3/4 right

Date	Mintage	F	VF	XF	Unc	BU
2005 Proof	5,000	Value: 1,100				

KM# 1630   200 YUAN
15.5500 g., 0.9990 Gold 0.4994 oz. AGW, 27 mm. **Subject:** 60th Anniverasary of Victory - War of Resistance **Obv:** Monument **Rev:** Mob of Peoples Army

Date	Mintage	F	VF	XF	Unc	BU
2005 Proof	5,000	Value: 1,100				

KM# 1633   200 YUAN
15.5500 g., 0.9990 Gold 0.4994 oz. AGW, 27 mm. **Series:** Classical Literature **Obv:** Horseman on arch bridge **Rev:** Two multicolor women, one with monkey, other with rabbit

Date	Mintage	F	VF	XF	Unc	BU
2005 Proof	11,800	Value: 950				

KM# 1689   200 YUAN
15.5500 g., 0.9990 Gold 0.4994 oz. AGW, 27 mm. **Subject:** Yvelv Academy **Obv:** Front door of Academy **Rev:** Interior room

Date	Mintage	F	VF	XF	Unc	BU
2006 Proof	7,000	Value: 950				

KM# 1692   200 YUAN
15.5500 g., 0.9990 Gold 0.4994 oz. AGW, 27 mm. **Subject:** 70th Anniversary of Long March **Obv:** Route of the marches, hammer and sickle symbol **Rev:** Group of marchers advancing with rifles

Date	Mintage	F	VF	XF	Unc	BU
2006 Proof	10,000	Value: 950				

KM# 1949   200 YUAN
15.5500 g., 0.9990 Gold 0.4994 oz. AGW **Subject:** Yungang Grotto Art

Date	Mintage	F	VF	XF	Unc	BU
2010 Proof	10,000	Value: 975				

KM# 1435   300 YUAN
1000.0000 g., 0.9990 Silver 32.117 oz. ASW, 100 mm. **Series:** Long men grottoes **Rev:** Large female statue

Date	Mintage	F	VF	XF	Unc	BU
2002 Proof	8,000	Value: 1,750				

KM# 1513   300 YUAN
1000.0000 g., 0.9990 Silver 32.117 oz. ASW, 100 mm. **Series:** Guan Yi

Date	Mintage	F	VF	XF	Unc	BU
2003 Proof	3,800	Value: 3,500				

KM# 1568   300 YUAN
1000.0000 g., 0.9990 Silver 32.117 oz. ASW, 100 mm. **Obv:** Guangan Exposition Hall **Rev:** Deng Xiaoping and value **Edge:** Reeded **Note:** Prev. Y#1242.

Date	Mintage	F	VF	XF	Unc	BU
2004 Proof	5,000	Value: 1,850				

KM# 1579   300 YUAN
1000.0000 g., 0.9990 Silver 32.117 oz. ASW, 100 mm. **Series:** Kuan Yin **Rev:** Female seated holding flower

Date	Mintage	F	VF	XF	Unc	BU
2004 Proof	3,800	Value: 2,000				

KM# 1617   300 YUAN
1000.0000 g., 0.9990 Silver 32.117 oz. ASW, 100 mm. **Subject:** 2006 World Cup - Germany **Obv:** Multicolor logo **Rev:** World Cup Trophy

Date	Mintage	F	VF	XF	Unc	BU
2005 Proof	3,000	Value: 2,250				

KM# 1634   300 YUAN
1000.0000 g., 0.9990 Silver 32.117 oz. ASW, 100 mm. **Series:** Classical Literature **Obv:** Horseman on arch bridge **Rev:** Multicolor heavenly buddha

Date	Mintage	F	VF	XF	Unc	BU
2005 Proof	5,000	Value: 2,250				

KM# 1849   300 YUAN
1000.0000 g., 0.9990 Silver 32.117 oz. ASW, 100 mm. **Subject:** Beijing Olympics **Obv:** Multicolor logo **Rev:** Classical tug of war **Note:** Photo reduced.

Date	Mintage	F	VF	XF	Unc	BU
2008 Proof	20,008	Value: 2,250				

KM# 1897   300 YUAN
1000.0000 g., 0.9990 Silver 32.117 oz. ASW, 100 mm. **Subject:** P.R.C. 60th Anniversary

Date	Mintage	F	VF	XF	Unc	BU
2009 Proof	6,000	Value: 2,100				

KM# 1950   300 YUAN
1000.0000 g., 0.9990 Silver 32.117 oz. ASW **Subject:** Yungang Grotto Art

Date	Mintage	F	VF	XF	Unc	BU
2010 Proof	3,800	Value: 2,100				

KM# 2006   300 YUAN
1000.0000 g., 0.9990 Silver 32.117 oz. ASW, 100 mm. **Subject:** World Heritage Site **Obv:** National emblem **Rev:** Tianzhong Pavillon at the Zhongyue Temple

Date	Mintage	F	VF	XF	Unc	BU
2011 Proof	5,000	Value: 1,500				

KM# 1392   2000 YUAN
155.5175 g., 0.9990 Gold 4.9948 oz. AGW, 60 mm. **Subject:** Mogao Grottoes **Obv:** Eight story building **Rev:** Two dancers **Edge:** Reeded **Note:** Prev. #Y1086.

Date	Mintage	F	VF	XF	Unc	BU
2001 Proof	288	Value: 25,000				

KM# 1436   2000 YUAN
155.5175 g., 0.9990 Gold 4.9948 oz. AGW, 60 mm. **Subject:** Chinese grottos art - Longmen **Note:** Prev. #Y1151.

Date	Mintage	F	VF	XF	Unc	BU
2002	288	Value: 13,500				

KM# 1505   2000 YUAN
155.5000 g., 0.9990 Gold 4.9942 oz. AGW, 64 x 40 mm. **Series:**
Class literature **Rev:** Two multicolor monkey kings **Shape:**
Rectangle **Note:** Illustration reduced.

Date	Mintage	F	VF	XF	Unc	BU
2003 Proof	500	Value: 11,500				

KM# 1562   2000 YUAN
155.5175 g., 0.9990 Gold 4.9948 oz. AGW, 64x40 mm. **Obv:**
Monkey King leading Master over bridge **Rev:** Multicolor Monkey
King fighting the Pig "Demon of Bones" **Edge:** Plain **Shape:** Ingot
Note: Prev. #Y1218. Illustration reduced.

Date	Mintage	F	VF	XF	Unc	BU
2004 Proof	500	Value: 11,500				

KM# 1565   2000 YUAN
155.5175 g., 0.9990 Gold 4.9948 oz. AGW, 60 mm. **Subject:**
Maijishan Grottos **Obv:** Grotto view **Rev:** Buddha portrait within
halo of flying devatas **Edge:** Reeded **Note:** Prev. #Y1206.

Date	Mintage	F	VF	XF	Unc	BU
2004(y) Proof	288	Value: 14,500				

KM# 1569   2000 YUAN
155.5175 g., 0.9990 Gold 4.9948 oz. AGW, 60 mm. **Obv:**
Guangan Exposition Hall **Rev:** Deng Xiaoping and value **Edge:**
Reeded **Note:** Prev. #Y1243.

Date	Mintage	F	VF	XF	Unc	BU
2004 Proof	600	Value: 13,500				

KM# 1632   2000 YUAN
155.0000 g., 0.9990 Gold 4.9782 oz. AGW, 64 x 40 mm. **Series:**
Classic Literature Pilgrimage To The West **Obv:** Horseback rider
on arch bridge **Rev:** Multicolor court scene **Shape:** Rectangle

Date	Mintage	F	VF	XF	Unc	BU
2005 Proof	500	Value: 13,500				

KM# 1850   2000 YUAN
155.5500 g., 0.9990 Gold 4.9958 oz. AGW, 60 mm. **Subject:**
Beijing Olympics **Obv:** Multicolor logo **Rev:** Four sports

Date	Mintage	F	VF	XF	Unc	BU
2008 Proof	—	Value: 16,500				

KM# 1894   2000 YUAN
155.5000 g., 0.9990 Gold 4.9942 oz. AGW, 60 mm. **Subject:**
P.R.C. 60th Anniversary

Date	Mintage	F	VF	XF	Unc	BU
2009 Proof	600	Value: 12,000				

KM# 1899   2000 YUAN
155.5000 g., 0.9990 Gold 4.9942 oz. AGW, 64c40 mm.
Subject: Outlaws of the Marsh, series 1 **Rev:** Multicolor **Shape:**
Rectangle

Date	Mintage	F	VF	XF	Unc	BU
2009 Proof	800	Value: 12,000				

KM# 1936   2000 YUAN
155.5500 g., 0.9990 Gold 4.9958 oz. AGW, 64x40 mm. **Series:**
Outlaws of the Marsh, series 2 **Rev:** Multicolor **Shape:** Rectangle

Date	Mintage	F	VF	XF	Unc	BU
2010 Proof	900	Value: 12,000				

KM# 1948   2000 YUAN
155.5000 g., 0.9990 Gold 4.9942 oz. AGW **Subject:** Yungang
Grotto Art

Date	Mintage	F	VF	XF	Unc	BU
2010 Proof	800	Value: 12,000				

KM# 1893   10000 YUAN
1000.0000 g., 0.9990 Gold 32.117 oz. AGW, 90 mm. **Subject:**
P.R.C. 60th Anniversary

Date	Mintage	F	VF	XF	Unc	BU
2009 Proof	100	Value: 50,000				

KM# 1947   10000 YUAN
1000.0000 g., 0.9990 Gold 32.117 oz. AGW **Subject:** Yungang
Grotto Art

Date	Mintage	F	VF	XF	Unc	BU
2010 Proof	100	Value: 50,000				

KM# 1851   100000 YUAN
10000.0000 g., 0.9990 Gold 321.17 oz. AGW, 180 mm.
Subject: Beijing Olympics **Obv:** Multicolor logo **Rev:** Sports
montage, Temple of Heaven

Date	Mintage	F	VF	XF	Unc	BU
2008 Proof	29	Value: 650,000				

SILVER BULLION COINAGE
Lunar Series

KM# 1379   10 YUAN
30.8400 g., 0.9990 Silver 0.9905 oz. ASW, 39.9 mm. **Subject:**
Year of the Snake **Obv:** Traditional style building **Rev:** Snake
Shape: Scalloped **Note:** Prev. Y#1041.

Date	Mintage	F	VF	XF	Unc	BU
2001 Proof	6,800	Value: 165				

KM# 1382   10 YUAN
31.1035 g., 0.9990 Silver 0.9990 oz. ASW **Subject:** Year of the
Snake **Shape:** Fan-like **Note:** Prev. Y#1042.

Date	Mintage	F	VF	XF	Unc	BU
2001	66,000	—	—	—	100	115

KM# 1375   10 YUAN
31.1035 g., 0.9990 Silver 0.9990 oz. ASW, 40 mm. **Subject:**
Year of the Snake **Rev:** Multicolor

Date	Mintage	F	VF	XF	Unc	BU
2001 Proof	6,800	Value: 150				

KM# 1418   10 YUAN
31.1035 g., 0.9990 Silver 0.9990 oz. ASW, 40 mm. **Subject:**
Year of the Horse **Obv:** Da Zheng Hall **Rev:** Stylized horse head
Edge: Reeded **Note:** Prev. Y#1232.

Date	Mintage	F	VF	XF	Unc	BU
2002	50,000					140

KM# 1414   10 YUAN
31.1035 g., 0.9990 Silver 0.9990 oz. ASW, 40 mm. **Subject:**
Year of the Horse **Rev:** Multicolor horse prancing right

Date	Mintage	F	VF	XF	Unc	BU
2002 Proof	10,000	Value: 150				

KM# 1423   10 YUAN
31.1035 g., 0.9990 Silver 0.9990 oz. ASW, 40 mm. **Subject:**
Year of the Horse **Shape:** Fan-like

Date	Mintage	F	VF	XF	Unc	BU
2002 Proof	50,000	Value: 175				

KM# 1425   10 YUAN
31.1035 g., 0.9990 Silver 0.9990 oz. ASW, 40 mm. **Subject:**
Year of the Horse **Shape:** Scalloped

Date	Mintage	F	VF	XF	Unc	BU
2002 Proof	6,800	Value: 400				

KM# A1477   10 YUAN
31.1035 g., 0.9990 Silver 0.9990 oz. ASW, 40 mm. **Subject:**
Year of the Sheep

Date	Mintage	F	VF	XF	Unc	BU
2003 Proof	66,000	Value: 150				

KM# 1477   10 YUAN
31.1035 g., 0.9990 Silver 0.9990 oz. ASW, 40 mm. **Subject:**
Year of the Sheep **Rev:** Multicolor

Date	Mintage	F	VF	XF	Unc	BU
2003 Proof	6,800	Value: 150				

KM# 1480   10 YUAN
31.1035 g., 0.9990 Silver 0.9990 oz. ASW, 40 mm. **Subject:**
Year of the sheep **Shape:** Scalloped

Date	Mintage	F	VF	XF	Unc	BU
2003 Proof	50,000	Value: 60.00				

KM# 1485   10 YUAN
31.1035 g., 0.9990 Silver 0.9990 oz. ASW, 30 x 85 mm.
Subject: Year of the Sheep **Shape:** Fan-like

Date	Mintage	F	VF	XF	Unc	BU
2003 Proof	66,000	Value: 175				

KM# A1545   10 YUAN
31.1035 g., 0.9990 Silver 0.9990 oz. ASW, 40 mm. **Series:**
Lunar New Year **Subject:** Year of the Monkey **Rev:** Multicolor
monkey

Date	Mintage	F	VF	XF	Unc	BU
2004 Proof	—	Value: 150				

KM# 1545   10 YUAN
31.1035 g., 0.9990 Silver 0.9990 oz. ASW, 40 mm. **Series:**
Lunar New Year **Subject:** Year of the Monkey

Date	Mintage	F	VF	XF	Unc	BU
2004 Proof	80,000	Value: 150				

KM# 1548   10 YUAN
31.1035 g., 0.9990 Silver 0.9990 oz. ASW, 40 mm. **Subject:**
Lunar New Year **Rev:** Monkey **Shape:** Scalloped

Date	Mintage	F	VF	XF	Unc	BU
2004 Proof	6,800	Value: 190				

KM# 1553   10 YUAN
31.1035 g., 0.9990 Silver 0.9990 oz. ASW, 30 x 85 mm. **Series:**
Lunar New Year **Subject:** Year of the Monkey **Rev:** Monkey
Shape: Fan-like

Date	Mintage	F	VF	XF	Unc	BU
2004 Proof	66,000	Value: 175				

KM# 1612   10 YUAN
31.1050 g., 0.9990 Silver 0.9990 oz. ASW, 40 mm. **Subject:**
Year of the rooster **Obv:** Classical rooster **Rev:** Multicolor rooster

Date	Mintage	F	VF	XF	Unc	BU
2005 Proof	100,000	Value: 190				

KM# 1613   10 YUAN
31.1050 g., 0.9990 Silver 0.9990 oz. ASW, 40 mm. **Subject:**
Year of the rooster **Obv:** Classical rooster **Rev:** Rooster, hen and
chicks **Shape:** Scallop

Date	Mintage	F	VF	XF	Unc	BU
2005 Proof	60,000	Value: 125				

KM# 1614   10 YUAN
31.1050 g., 0.9990 Silver 0.9990 oz. ASW, 40 mm. **Subject:**

Year of the rooster **Obv:** Classical rooster **Rev:** Rooster, hen and
chicks

Date	Mintage	F	VF	XF	Unc	BU
2005 Proof	8,000	Value: 150				

KM# 1615   10 YUAN
31.1050 g., 0.9990 Silver 0.9990 oz. ASW, 30 x 85 mm.
Subject: Year of the rooster **Obv:** Temple **Rev:** Rooster, hen
and chicks **Shape:** Fan-like **Note:** Photo reduced.

Date	Mintage	F	VF	XF	Unc	BU
2005 Proof	66,000	Value: 190				

KM# 1684   10 YUAN
31.1035 g., 0.9990 Silver 0.9990 oz. ASW, 40 mm. **Obv:** Dog-
shaped belt-hook from ancient Chinese bronze ware, decorative
design of dog tail-shaped plant leaves **Rev:** 2 smart dogs **Note:**
Prev. Y#1225; 1657.

Date	Mintage	F	VF	XF	Unc	BU
2006	80,000	—	—	—	—	125

KM# 1685   10 YUAN
31.1035 g., 0.9990 Silver 0.9990 oz. ASW, 40 mm. **Obv:** Dog-
shaped belt-hook depicted from ancient Chinese bronze ware
and a decorative design of dog tail-shaped plant leaves **Rev:** 2
smart dogs **Shape:** Scalloped **Note:** Prev. Y#1223; KM#1655.

Date	Mintage	F	VF	XF	Unc	BU
2006 Proof	60,000	Value: 140				

KM# 1686   10 YUAN
31.1035 g., 0.9990 Silver 0.9990 oz. ASW **Obv:** Qing Yuan Gate of the China Great Wall **Rev:** 2 dogs at play **Shape:** Fan-like **Note:** Prev. Y#1219; KM#1651. Photo reduced.

Date	Mintage	F	VF	XF	Unc	BU
2006 Proof	66,000	Value: 165				

KM# 1687   10 YUAN
31.1035 g., 0.9990 Silver 0.9990 oz. ASW, 40 mm. **Obv:** Belt-hook in dog shape from Chinese ancient bronze ware and a decorative design of dog tail-shaped plant leaves **Rev:** 2 dogs at play **Note:** Prev. Y#1221; KM#1653.

Date	Mintage	F	VF	XF	Unc	BU
2006 Proof	100,000	Value: 125				

KM# 1716   10 YUAN
31.1050 g., 0.9990 Silver 0.9990 oz. ASW, 40 mm. **Subject:** Year of the Pig **Obv:** Classical pig **Rev:** Pig walking right

Date	Mintage	F	VF	XF	Unc	BU
2007 Proof	80,000	Value: 140				

KM# 1717   10 YUAN
31.1050 g., 0.9990 Silver 0.9990 oz. ASW, 40 mm. **Subject:** Year of the Pig **Obv:** Classical pig **Rev:** Multicolor sow and four piglets sucking

Date	Mintage	F	VF	XF	Unc	BU
2007 Proof	100,000	Value: 125				

KM# 1718   10 YUAN
31.1050 g., 0.9990 Silver 0.9990 oz. ASW, 85 x 60 mm. **Subject:** Year of the Pig **Obv:** Temple **Rev:** Sow and four pigletts **Shape:** Fan-like

Date	Mintage	F	VF	XF	Unc	BU
2007 Proof	66,000	Value: 190				

KM# 1719   10 YUAN
31.1050 g., 0.9990 Silver 0.9990 oz. ASW, 40 mm. **Subject:** Year of the Pig **Obv:** Classical pig **Rev:** Pig walking right **Shape:** Scalloped

Date	Mintage	F	VF	XF	Unc	BU
2007 Proof	60,000	Value: 140				

KM# 1830   10 YUAN
31.1050 g., 0.9990 Silver 0.9990 oz. ASW, 40 mm. **Rev:** Multicolor

Date	Mintage	F	VF	XF	Unc	BU
2008 Proof	—	Value: 55.00				

KM# 1831   10 YUAN
31.1050 g., 0.9990 Silver 0.9990 oz. ASW, 40 mm. **Subject:** Year of the Rat

Date	Mintage	F	VF	XF	Unc	BU
2008 Proof	—	Value: 140				

KM# 1832   10 YUAN
31.1050 g., 0.9990 Silver 0.9990 oz. ASW, 40 mm. **Subject:** Year of the Rat **Shape:** Scallop

Date	Mintage	F	VF	XF	Unc	BU
2008 Proof	—	Value: 140				

KM# 1833   10 YUAN
31.1050 g., 0.9990 Silver 0.9990 oz. ASW, 85 x 60 mm. **Subject:** Year of the Rat **Shape:** Fan-like

Date	Mintage	F	VF	XF	Unc	BU
2008 Proof	—	Value: 190				

KM# 1875   10 YUAN
31.1050 g., 0.9990 Silver 0.9990 oz. ASW, 40 mm. **Rev:** Multicolor

Date	Mintage	F	VF	XF	Unc	BU
2009 Proof	—	Value: 125				

KM# 1876   10 YUAN
31.1050 g., 0.9990 Silver 0.9990 oz. ASW, 40 mm. **Subject:** Year of the Ox

Date	Mintage	F	VF	XF	Unc	BU
2009 Proof	100,000	Value: 125				

KM# 1877   10 YUAN
31.1050 g., 0.9990 Silver 0.9990 oz. ASW **Subject:** Year of the Ox

Date	Mintage	F	VF	XF	Unc	BU
2009 Proof	66,000	Value: 140				

KM# 1878   10 YUAN
31.1050 g., 0.9990 Silver 0.9990 oz. ASW **Shape:** Fan-like

Date	Mintage	F	VF	XF	Unc	BU
2009 Proof	66,000	Value: 190				

KM# 1922   10 YUAN
31.1050 g., 0.9990 Silver 0.9990 oz. ASW **Subject:** Year of the Tiger **Shape:** Arc

Date	Mintage	F	VF	XF	Unc	BU
2010	66,000	—	—	—	—	100

KM# 1923   10 YUAN
31.1050 g., 0.9990 Silver 0.9990 oz. ASW **Subject:** Year of the Tiger **Shape:** Scalloped

Date	Mintage	F	VF	XF	Unc	BU
2010 Proof	60,000	Value: 100				

KM# 1924   10 YUAN
31.1050 g., 0.9990 Silver 0.9990 oz. ASW **Subject:** Year of the Tiger

Date	Mintage	F	VF	XF	Unc	BU
2010 Proof	100,000	Value: 100				

KM# 1925   10 YUAN
31.1050 g., 0.9990 Silver 0.9990 oz. ASW **Subject:** Year of the Tiger **Rev:** Multicolor

Date	Mintage	F	VF	XF	Unc	BU
2010 Proof	100,000	Value: 125				

KM# 1971   10 YUAN
31.1050 g., 0.9990 Silver 0.9990 oz. ASW **Subject:** Year of the Rabbit **Shape:** Arc

Date	Mintage	F	VF	XF	Unc	BU
2011	66,000	—	—	—	—	100

KM# 1972   10 YUAN
31.1050 g., 0.9990 Silver 0.9990 oz. ASW **Subject:** Year of the Rabbit **Shape:** Scalloped

Date	Mintage	F	VF	XF	Unc	BU
2011 Proof	60,000	Value: 100				

KM# 1973   10 YUAN
31.1050 g., 0.9990 Silver 0.9990 oz. ASW, 40 mm. **Subject:** Year of the Rabbit

Date	Mintage	F	VF	XF	Unc	BU
2011 Proof	100,000	Value: 100				

KM# 1974   10 YUAN
31.1050 g., 0.9990 Silver 0.9990 oz. ASW **Subject:** Year of the Rabbit **Rev:** Multicolor

Date	Mintage	F	VF	XF	Unc	BU
2011 Proof	100,000	Value: 100				

KM# 2020   10 YUAN
31.1050 g., 0.9990 Silver 0.9990 oz. ASW **Subject:** Year of the Dragon **Shape:** Fan

Date	Mintage	F	VF	XF	Unc	BU
2012 Proof	—	Value: 100				

KM# 2021   10 YUAN
31.1050 g., 0.9990 Silver 0.9990 oz. ASW, 40 mm. **Subject:** Year of the Dragon **Shape:** Scalloped

Date	Mintage	F	VF	XF	Unc	BU
2012 proof	—	Value: 100				

KM# 2022   10 YUAN
31.1050 g., 0.9990 Silver 0.9990 oz. ASW, 40 mm. **Subject:** Year of the Dragon

Date	Mintage	F	VF	XF	Unc	BU
2012 Proof	—	Value: 45.00				

KM# 2023   10 YUAN
31.1050 g., 0.9990 Silver 0.9990 oz. ASW **Subject:** Year of the Dragon **Rev:** Colored dragon

Date	Mintage	F	VF	XF	Unc	BU
2012 Proof	—	Value: 100				

KM# 1377   50 YUAN
155.4400 g., 0.9990 Silver 4.9923 oz. ASW, 80.6 x 50.5 mm. **Subject:** Year of the Snake **Obv:** Traditional style building **Rev:** Snake **Edge:** Plain **Shape:** Rectangle **Note:** Illustration reduced. Prev. Y#1040.

Date	Mintage	F	VF	XF	Unc	BU
2001 Proof	1,888	Value: 1,250				

KM# 1421 50 YUAN
155.5190 g., 0.9990 Silver 4.9948 oz. ASW, 80 x 50 mm.
Subject: Year of the Horse **Rev:** Three horses running left
Shape: Rectangle

Date	Mintage	F	VF	XF	Unc	BU
2002 Proof	1,888	Value: 2,000				

KM# 1484 50 YUAN
155.5000 g., 0.9990 Silver 4.9942 oz. ASW, 80 x 50 mm.
Subject: Year of the Sheep **Shape:** Rectangle

Date	Mintage	F	VF	XF	Unc	BU
2003 Proof	1,888	Value: 1,250				

KM# 1551 50 YUAN
155.5000 g., 0.9990 Silver 4.9942 oz. ASW, 80 x 50 mm. **Series:**
Lunar New Year **Subject:** Year of the Monkey **Rev:** Monkey
Shape: Rectangle **Note:** Photo reduced.

Date	Mintage	F	VF	XF	Unc	BU
2004 Proof	1,888	Value: 1,250				

KM# 1611 50 YUAN
155.0000 g., 0.9990 Silver 4.9782 oz. ASW, 80 x 50 mm.
Subject: Year of the Rooster **Obv:** Classical rooster **Rev:**
Rooster, hen and chicks **Shape:** Rectangle **Note:** Photo reduced.

Date	Mintage	F	VF	XF	Unc	BU
2005 Proof	1,888	Value: 1,250				

KM# 1683 50 YUAN
155.4400 g., 0.9990 Silver 4.9923 oz. ASW, 60 x 50 mm.
Subject: Year of the Dog **Obv:** Classical dog **Rev:** Two dogs
Shape: Rectangle **Note:** Photo reduced.

Date	Mintage	F	VF	XF	Unc	BU
2006 Proof	1,888	Value: 1,250				

KM# 1720 50 YUAN
155.5500 g., 0.9990 Silver 4.9958 oz. ASW, 80 x 50 mm.
Subject: Year of the Pig **Obv:** Classical pig **Rev:** Sow and four
pigletts **Shape:** Rectangle

Date	Mintage	F	VF	XF	Unc	BU
2007 Proof	1,888	Value: 1,250				

KM# 1834 50 YUAN
155.5000 g., 0.9990 Silver 4.9942 oz. ASW, 80 x 50 mm.
Subject: Year of the Rat **Shape:** Rectangle

Date	Mintage	F	VF	XF	Unc	BU
2008 Proof	—	Value: 1,250				

KM# 1879 50 YUAN
Silver **Subject:** Year of the Ox

Date	Mintage	F	VF	XF	Unc	BU
2009 Proof	1,888	Value: 1,250				

KM# 1920 50 YUAN
155.5000 g., 0.9990 Silver 4.9942 oz. ASW **Subject:** Year of
the Tiger **Shape:** Rectangle

Date	Mintage	F	VF	XF	Unc	BU
2010 Proof	1,888	Value: 1,250				

KM# 1921 50 YUAN
155.5000 g., 0.9990 Silver 4.9942 oz. ASW **Subject:** Year of
the Tiger

Date	Mintage	F	VF	XF	Unc	BU
2010 Proof	8,800	Value: 850				

KM# 1969 50 YUAN
155.5000 g., 0.9990 Silver 4.9942 oz. ASW, 80x50 mm.
Subject: Year of the Rabbit **Shape:** Rectangle **Note:** Photo
reduced.

Date	Mintage	F	VF	XF	Unc	BU
2011 Proof	1,888	Value: 1,250				

KM# 1970 50 YUAN
155.5000 g., 0.9990 Silver 4.9942 oz. ASW **Subject:** Year of
the Rabbit **Rev:** Multicolor

Date	Mintage	F	VF	XF	Unc	BU
2011 Proof	8,800	Value: 750				

KM# 2018 50 YUAN
155.5500 g., 0.9990 Silver 4.9958 oz. ASW, 80x50 mm.
Subject: Year of the Dragon **Shape:** Rectangle

Date	Mintage	F	VF	XF	Unc	BU
2012 Proof	—	Value: 850				

KM# 2019 50 YUAN
155.5500 g., 0.9990 Silver 4.9958 oz. ASW **Subject:** Year of
the Dragon **Rev:** Colored dragon

Date	Mintage	F	VF	XF	Unc	BU
2012 proof	—	Value: 750				

KM# 1420 300 YUAN
1000.0000 g., 0.9990 Silver 32.117 oz. ASW, 100 mm. **Series:**
Lunar **Subject:** Year of the Horse

Date	Mintage	F	VF	XF	Unc	BU
2002 Proof	3,800	Value: 6,500				

KM# 1479 300 YUAN
1000.0000 g., 0.9990 Silver 32.117 oz. ASW, 100 mm. **Subject:**
Year of the Sheep

Date	Mintage	F	VF	XF	Unc	BU
2003 Proof	3,800	Value: 7,500				

KM# 1547 300 YUAN
1000.0000 g., 0.9990 Silver 32.117 oz. ASW, 100 mm. **Series:**
Lunar New Year **Subject:** Year of the Monkey **Rev:** Monkey

Date	Mintage	F	VF	XF	Unc	BU
2004 Proof	3,800	Value: 9,000				

KM# 1610 300 YUAN
1000.0000 g., 0.9990 Silver 32.117 oz. ASW, 100 mm. **Subject:**
Year of the Rooster **Obv:** Classical rooster **Rev:** Rooster strutting
Note: Photo reduced.

Date	Mintage	F	VF	XF	Unc	BU
2005 Proof	3,800	Value: 5,000				

KM# 1682   300 YUAN
1000.0000 g., 0.9990 Silver 32.117 oz. ASW, 100 mm. **Obv:** Dog-shaped belt-hook from ancient Chinese bronze ware, decorative design of dog tail-shaped plant leaves **Rev:** 2 dogs **Note:** Prev. Y#1227; KM#1659. Photo reduced.

Date	Mintage	F	VF	XF	Unc	BU
2006 Proof	3,800	Value: 4,500				

KM# 1725   300 YUAN
1000.0000 g., 0.9990 Silver 32.117 oz. ASW, 100 mm. **Subject:** Year of the Pig **Obv:** Classical pig **Rev:** Three pigs

Date	Mintage	F	VF	XF	Unc	BU
2007 Proof	3,800	Value: 5,000				

KM# 1839   300 YUAN
1000.0000 g., 0.9990 Silver 32.117 oz. ASW, 100 mm. **Subject:** Year of the Rat

Date	Mintage	F	VF	XF	Unc	BU
2008 Proof	—	Value: 5,000				

KM# 1884   300 YUAN
1000.0000 g., 0.9990 Silver 32.117 oz. ASW **Subject:** Year of the Ox

Date	Mintage	F	VF	XF	Unc	BU
2009 Proof	3,800	Value: 5,000				

KM# 1919   300 YUAN
1000.0000 g., 0.9990 Silver 32.117 oz. ASW **Subject:** Year of the Tiger

Date	Mintage	F	VF	XF	Unc	BU
2010 Proof	3,800	Value: 4,500				

KM# 1968   300 YUAN
1000.0000 g., 0.9990 Silver 32.117 oz. ASW, 100 mm. **Subject:** Year of the Rabbit **Note:** Photo reduced.

Date	Mintage	F	VF	XF	Unc	BU
2011 Proof	1,888	Value: 4,500				

KM# 2017   300 YUAN
1000.0000 g., 0.9990 Silver 32.117 oz. ASW, 100 mm. **Subject:** Year of the Dragon

Date	Mintage	F	VF	XF	Unc	BU
2012 Proof	—	Value: 1,250				

Panda Series

KM# 1772   3 YUAN
7.7700 g., 0.9990 Silver 0.2496 oz. ASW, 25 mm. **Obv:** Temple of Heaven **Rev:** Panda seated on rock

Date	Mintage	F	VF	XF	Unc	BU
2007 Proof	30,000	Value: 30.00				

KM# 1780   3 YUAN
7.7700 g., 0.9990 Silver 0.2496 oz. ASW, 25 mm. **Obv:** Temple of Heaven **Rev:** Panda looking forward

Date	Mintage	F	VF	XF	Unc	BU
2007 Proof	30,000	Value: 30.00				

KM# 1740   3 YUAN
7.7700 g., 0.9990 Silver 0.2496 oz. ASW, 25 mm. **Obv:** Temple of Heaven **Rev:** Panda seated with branch

Date	Mintage	F	VF	XF	Unc	BU
2007 Proof	30,000	Value: 30.00				

KM# 1742   3 YUAN
7.7700 g., 0.9990 Silver 0.2496 oz. ASW, 25 mm. **Obv:** Temple of Heaven **Rev:** Panda walking right

Date	Mintage	F	VF	XF	Unc	BU
2007 Proof	30,000	Value: 30.00				

KM# 1744   3 YUAN
7.7700 g., 0.9990 Silver 0.2496 oz. ASW, 25 mm. **Obv:** Temple of Heaven **Rev:** Panda seated with bamboo branch

Date	Mintage	F	VF	XF	Unc	BU
2007 Proof	30,000	Value: 30.00				

KM# 1746   3 YUAN
7.7700 g., 0.9990 Silver 0.2496 oz. ASW **Obv:** Temple of Heaven **Rev:** Panda hanging from branch

Date	Mintage	F	VF	XF	Unc	BU
2007 Proof	30,000	Value: 30.00				

KM# 1748   3 YUAN
7.7700 g., 0.9990 Silver 0.2496 oz. ASW, 25 mm. **Obv:** Temple of Heaven **Rev:** Panda walking forward

Date	Mintage	F	VF	XF	Unc	BU
2007 Proof	30,000	Value: 30.00				

KM# 1750   3 YUAN
7.7700 g., 0.9990 Silver 0.2496 oz. ASW, 25 mm. **Obv:** Temple of Heaven **Rev:** Panda drinking water

Date	Mintage	F	VF	XF	Unc	BU
2007 Proof	30,000	Value: 30.00				

KM# 1752   3 YUAN
7.7700 g., 0.9990 Silver 0.2496 oz. ASW, 25 mm. **Obv:** Tample of Heaven **Rev:** Panda seated in oval with branch

Date	Mintage	F	VF	XF	Unc	BU
2007 Proof	30,000	Value: 30.00				

KM# 1754   3 YUAN
7.7700 g., 0.9990 Silver 0.2496 oz. ASW, 25 mm. **Obv:** Temple of Heaven **Rev:** Panda seated on geometric background

Date	Mintage	F	VF	XF	Unc	BU
2007 Proof	30,000	Value: 30.00				

KM# 1756   3 YUAN
7.7700 g., 0.9990 Silver 0.2496 oz. ASW, 10 mm. **Obv:** Temple of Heaven **Rev:** Panda on rock

Date	Mintage	F	VF	XF	Unc	BU
2007 Proof	30,000	Value: 30.00				

KM# 1758   3 YUAN
7.7700 g., 0.9990 Silver 0.2496 oz. ASW, 25 mm. **Obv:** Temple of Heaven **Rev:** Panda seated on river bank

Date	Mintage	F	VF	XF	Unc	BU
2007 Proof	30,000	Value: 30.00				

KM# 1760   3 YUAN
7.7700 g., 0.9990 Silver 0.2496 oz. ASW, 25 mm. **Obv:** Temple of Heaven **Rev:** Panda on tree branch

Date	Mintage	F	VF	XF	Unc	BU
2007 Proof	30,000	Value: 30.00				

KM# 1762   3 YUAN
7.7700 g., 0.9990 Silver 0.2496 oz. ASW, 25 mm. **Obv:** Temple of Heaven **Rev:** Panda on rock ledge

Date	Mintage	F	VF	XF	Unc	BU
2007 Proof	30,000	Value: 30.00				

KM# 1764   3 YUAN
7.7700 g., 0.9990 Silver 0.2496 oz. ASW, 25 mm. **Obv:** Temple of Heaven **Rev:** Panda seated munching bamboo

Date	Mintage	F	VF	XF	Unc	BU
2007 Proof	30,000	Value: 30.00				

KM# 1766   3 YUAN
7.7700 g., 0.9990 Silver 0.2496 oz. ASW, 25 mm. **Obv:** Temple of Heaven **Rev:** Panda pulling bamboo

Date	Mintage	F	VF	XF	Unc	BU
2007 Proof	30,000	Value: 30.00				

KM# 1768   3 YUAN
7.7700 g., 0.9990 Silver 0.2496 oz. ASW, 25 mm. **Obv:** Temple of Heaven **Rev:** Panda in tree

Date	Mintage	F	VF	XF	Unc	BU
2007 Proof	30,000	Value: 30.00				

KM# 1770   3 YUAN
7.7700 g., 0.9990 Silver 0.2496 oz. ASW, 25 mm. **Obv:** Temple of Heaven **Rev:** Panda looking over branch

Date	Mintage	F	VF	XF	Unc	BU
2007 Proof	30,000	Value: 30.00				

KM# 1774   3 YUAN
7.7700 g., 0.9990 Silver 0.2496 oz. ASW, 25 mm. **Obv:** Temple of Heaven **Rev:** Panda looking out over rock

Date	Mintage	F	VF	XF	Unc	BU
2007 Proof	30,000	Value: 30.00				

KM# A1776   3 YUAN
7.7700 g., 0.9990 Silver 0.2496 oz. ASW, 25 mm. **Obv:** Temple of Heaven **Rev:** Panda seated on frosted background

Date	Mintage	F	VF	XF	Unc	BU
2007 Proof	30,000	Value: 30.00				

KM# 1778   3 YUAN
7.7700 g., 0.9990 Silver 0.2496 oz. ASW, 25 mm. **Obv:** Temple of Heaven **Rev:** Panda walking amongst bamboo

Date	Mintage	F	VF	XF	Unc	BU
2007 Proof	30,000	Value: 30.00				

KM# 1782   3 YUAN
7.7700 g., 0.9990 Silver 0.2496 oz. ASW, 25 mm. **Obv:** Temple of Heaven **Rev:** Panda and cub walking right

Date	Mintage	F	VF	XF	Unc	BU
2007 Proof	30,000	Value: 30.00				

KM# 1784   3 YUAN
7.7700 g., 0.9990 Silver 0.2496 oz. ASW, 25 mm. **Obv:** Temple of Heaven **Rev:** Panda seated with cub on left

Date	Mintage	F	VF	XF	Unc	BU
2007 Proof	30,000	Value: 30.00				

KM# 1786   3 YUAN
7.7700 g., 0.9990 Silver 0.2496 oz. ASW, 25 mm. **Obv:** Temple of Heaven **Rev:** Panda seated with cub on right

Date	Mintage	F	VF	XF	Unc	BU
2007 Proof	30,000	Value: 30.00				

KM# 1788   3 YUAN
7.7700 g., 0.9990 Silver 0.2496 oz. ASW, 25 mm. **Obv:** Temple of Heaven **Rev:** Panda seated with cub, both munching bamboo

Date	Mintage	F	VF	XF	Unc	BU
2007 Proof	30,000	Value: 30.00				

KM# 1365   10 YUAN
31.1035 g., 0.9990 Silver 0.9990 oz. ASW, 40.1 mm. **Obv:** Temple of Heaven with incuse legend **Rev:** Panda walking left through bamboo **Edge:** Oblique reeding **Note:** Large and small date varieties exist. Prev. Y#1111.

Date	Mintage	F	VF	XF	Unc	BU
2001	250,000			—	41.25	48.75
2001 D Proof	—	Value: 75.00				
2002 Proof	—	Value: 75.00				

KM# A1365   10 YUAN
31.2300 g., 0.9990 Silver 1.0030 oz. ASW, 40 mm. **Obv:** Temple of Heaven, incuse legend **Rev:** Multicolor panda walking in bamboo **Edge:** Slanted reeding **Note:** Large and small date varieties exist.

Date	Mintage	F	VF	XF	Unc	BU
2002 Proof	—	Value: 90.00				

Note: Privately colored

KM# 1466   10 YUAN
31.1035 g., 0.9990 Silver 0.9990 oz. ASW, 40 mm. **Obv:** Temple of Heaven **Rev:** Panda eating bamboo in a frosted circle **Edge:** Slant reeded **Note:** Prev. Y#1244.

Date	Mintage	F	VF	XF	Unc	BU
2003 Proof	—	Value: 90.00				

KM# 1528   10 YUAN
31.1035 g., 0.9990 Silver 0.9990 oz. ASW, 40 mm. **Obv:** Temple of Heaven **Rev:** Panda nuzzling her cub **Edge:** Slant reeded **Note:** Prev. Y#1245.

Date	Mintage	F	VF	XF	Unc	BU
2004 Proof	—	Value: 90.00				

KM# 1589   10 YUAN
31.1050 g., 0.9990 Silver 0.9990 oz. ASW, 40 mm. **Obv:** Temple of Heaven **Rev:** Panda cub and mom seated in bamboo

Date	Mintage	F	VF	XF	Unc	BU
2005 Proof	60,000	Value: 90.00				

KM# 1664   10 YUAN
31.1050 g., 0.9990 Silver 0.9990 oz. ASW, 40 mm. **Obv:** Temple of Heaven **Rev:** Two pandas seated with bamboo

Date	Mintage	F	VF	XF	Unc	BU
2006 Proof	600,000	Value: 75.00				

KM# 1706   10 YUAN
31.1050 g., 0.9990 Silver 0.9990 oz. ASW, 40 mm. **Obv:** Temple of Heaven **Rev:** Two pandas, one walking, one seated

Date	Mintage	F	VF	XF	Unc	BU
2007 Proof	600,000	Value: 75.00				

KM# 1865   10 YUAN
31.1050 g., 0.9990 Silver 0.9990 oz. ASW, 40 mm. **Obv:** Temple of Heaven **Rev:** Adult panda at left, facing left, cub on right facing left, cub seated

Date	Mintage	F	VF	XF	Unc	BU
2008 Proof	—	Value: 60.00				

KM# 1814   10 YUAN
31.1050 g., 0.9990 Silver 0.9990 oz. ASW, 40 mm. **Rev:** Panda cub pawing mom

Date	Mintage	F	VF	XF	Unc	BU
2008 Proof	—	Value: 60.00				

KM# 1931   10 YUAN
31.1050 g., 0.9990 Silver 0.9990 oz. ASW, 40 mm. **Obv:** Temple of Heaven **Rev:** Two pandas, one lying on back

Date	Mintage	F	VF	XF	Unc	BU
2010	800,000	—	—	—	—	60.00

KM# 1980   10 YUAN
31.1050 g., 0.9990 Silver 0.9990 oz. ASW, 40 mm.

Date	Mintage	F	VF	XF	Unc	BU
2011	—	—	—	—	—	45.00

KM# 2029   10 YUAN
31.1050 g., 0.9990 Silver 0.9990 oz. ASW, 40 mm.

Date	Mintage
—	

KM# 1468   50 YUAN
151.5000 g., 0.9990 Silver 4.8658 oz. ASW, 80 x 50 mm. **Shape:** Rectangle

Date	Mintage	F	VF	XF	Unc	BU
2003 Proof	1,888	Value: 1,150				

KM# 1530   50 YUAN
155.5000 g., 0.9990 Silver 4.9942 oz. ASW, 70 mm. **Rev:** Panda walking with cub **Note:** Illustration reduced.

Date	Mintage	F	VF	XF	Unc	BU
2004 Proof	10,000	Value: 600				

KM# 1588   50 YUAN
155.0000 g., 0.9990 Silver 4.9782 oz. ASW, 70 mm. **Obv:** Temple of Heaven **Rev:** Panda cub and mom seated in bamboo

Date	Mintage	F	VF	XF	Unc	BU
2005 Proof	10,000	Value: 550				

KM# 1663   50 YUAN
155.5500 g., 0.9990 Silver 4.9958 oz. ASW, 70 mm. **Obv:** Temple of Heaven **Rev:** Two pandas seated with bamboo

Date	Mintage	F	VF	XF	Unc	BU
2006 Proof	10,000	Value: 550				

KM# 1708   50 YUAN
155.5500 g., 0.9990 Silver 4.9958 oz. ASW, 70 mm. **Obv:** Temple of Heaven **Rev:** Two pandas, one walking, one seated

Date	Mintage	F	VF	XF	Unc	BU
2007 Proof	10,000	Value: 550				

KM# 1867   50 YUAN
155.5000 g., 0.9990 Silver 4.9942 oz. ASW

Date	Mintage	F	VF	XF	Unc	BU
2008 Proof	—	Value: 550				

KM# 1816   50 YUAN
155.5500 g., Silver, 70 mm. **Rev:** Panda cub pawing mom

Date	Mintage	F	VF	XF	Unc	BU
2008 Proof	—	Value: 550				

KM# 1935   50 YUAN
155.5500 g., 0.9990 Silver 4.9958 oz. ASW **Obv:** Temple of Heaven **Rev:** Two pandas, one lying on back

Date	Mintage	F	VF	XF	Unc	BU
2010 Proof	10,000	Value: 650				

KM# 1984   50 YUAN
155.5500 g., 0.9990 Silver 4.9958 oz. ASW

Date	Mintage	F	VF	XF	Unc	BU
2011 Proof	—	Value: 200				

KM# 2033   50 YUAN
155.5500 g., 0.9990 Silver 4.9958 oz. ASW, 70 mm.

Date	Mintage	F	VF	XF	Unc	BU
2012 Proof	—	Value: 650				

KM# 1370   300 YUAN
1000.0000 g., 0.9990 Silver 32.117 oz. ASW, 100 mm. **Rev:** Panda walking thru bamboo

Date	Mintage	F	VF	XF	Unc	BU
2001 D Proof	2,000	Value: 2,500				

KM# 1416   300 YUAN
1000.0000 g., 0.9990 Silver 32.117 oz. ASW, 100 mm. **Subject:** Panda Coinage 20th Anniversary **Obv:** Temple of Heaven **Rev:** Two gold inserts with the 1982 and 2002 panda designs on bamboo leaves **Edge:** Plain **Note:** Large and small date varieties exist. Prev. Y#1116.

Date	Mintage	F	VF	XF	Unc	BU
2002 Proof	6,000	Value: 3,000				

KM# 1473   300 YUAN
1000.0000 g., 0.9990 Silver 32.117 oz. ASW **Rev:** Panda and bamboo **Shape:** 100

Date	Mintage	F	VF	XF	Unc	BU
2003 Proof	7,500	Value: 2,000				

KM# 1536 300 YUAN
1000.0000 g., 0.9990 Silver 32.117 oz. ASW, 100 mm. **Rev:**
Panda walking with cub

Date	Mintage	F	VF	XF	Unc	BU
2004 Proof	4,000	Value: 2,000				

KM# 1587 300 YUAN
1000.0000 g., 0.9990 Silver 32.117 oz. ASW, 100 mm. **Obv:**
Temple of Heaven **Rev:** Panda cub and mom seated in bamboo
Note: Photo reduced.

Date	Mintage	F	VF	XF	Unc	BU
2005 Proof	4,000	Value: 2,250				

KM# 1662 300 YUAN
1000.0000 g., 0.9990 Silver 32.117 oz. ASW, 100 mm. **Obv:**
Temple of Heaven **Rev:** Two pandas seated with bamboo **Note:**
Photo reduced.

Date	Mintage	F	VF	XF	Unc	BU
2006 Proof	4,000	Value: 2,250				

KM# 1712 300 YUAN
1000.0000 g., 0.9990 Silver 32.117 oz. ASW, 100 mm. **Obv:**
Temple of Heaven **Rev:** Two pandas, one walking, one seated

Date	Mintage	F	VF	XF	Unc	BU
2007 Proof	4,000	Value: 2,250				

KM# 1820 300 YUAN
1000.0000 g., 0.9990 Silver 32.117 oz. ASW, 100 mm. **Rev:**
Panda cub pawing mom

Date	Mintage	F	VF	XF	Unc	BU
2008 Proof	—	Value: 2,000				

KM# 1871 300 YUAN
1000.0000 g., 0.9990 Silver 32.117 oz. ASW

Date	Mintage	F	VF	XF	Unc	BU
2008 Proof	—	Value: 2,000				

KM# 1934 300 YUAN
1000.0000 g., 0.9990 Silver 32.117 oz. ASW **Obv:** Temple of
Heaven **Rev:** Two pandas, one lying on back

Date	Mintage	F	VF	XF	Unc	BU
2010 Proof	4,000	Value: 1,500				

KM# 1983 300 YUAN
1000.0000 g., 0.9990 Silver 32.117 oz. ASW, 100 mm.

Date	Mintage	F	VF	XF	Unc	BU
2011 Proof	—	Value: 1,250				

KM# 2032 300 YUAN
1000.0000 g., 0.9990 Silver 32.117 oz. ASW, 100 mm.

Date	Mintage	F	VF	XF	Unc	BU
2012 Proof	—	Value: 1,500				

GOLD BULLION COINAGE
Panda Series

KM# 1779 15 YUAN
1.2400 g., 0.9990 Gold 0.0398 oz. AGW, 12 mm. **Obv:** Temple
of Heaven **Rev:** Panda walking amongst bamboo

Date	Mintage	F	VF	XF	Unc	BU
2007 Proof	18,000	Value: 95.00				

KM# 1741 15 YUAN
1.2400 g., 0.9990 Gold 0.0398 oz. AGW, 12 mm. **Obv:** Temple
of Heaven **Rev:** Panda seated with branch

Date	Mintage	F	VF	XF	Unc	BU
2007 Proof	18,000	Value: 95.00				

KM# 1743 15 YUAN
1.2400 g., 0.9990 Gold 0.0398 oz. AGW, 12 mm. **Obv:** Temple
of heaven **Rev:** Panda walking right

Date	Mintage	F	VF	XF	Unc	BU
2007 Proof	18,000	Value: 95.00				

KM# 1745 15 YUAN
1.2400 g., 0.9990 Gold 0.0398 oz. AGW, 12 mm. **Obv:** Temple
of heaven **Rev:** Panda seated with bamboo branch

Date	Mintage	F	VF	XF	Unc	BU
2007 Proof	18,000	Value: 95.00				

KM# 1747 15 YUAN
1.2400 g., 0.9990 Gold 0.0398 oz. AGW, 12 mm. **Obv:** Temple
of Heaven **Rev:** Panda hanging from branch

Date	Mintage	F	VF	XF	Unc	BU
2007 Proof	18,000	Value: 95.00				

KM# 1749 15 YUAN
1.2400 g., 0.9990 Gold 0.0398 oz. AGW, 12 mm. **Obv:** Temple
of Heaven **Rev:** Panda walking forward

Date	Mintage	F	VF	XF	Unc	BU
2007 Proof	18,000	Value: 95.00				

KM# 1751 15 YUAN
1.2400 g., 0.9990 Gold 0.0398 oz. AGW, 12 mm. **Obv:** Temple
of Heaven **Rev:** Panda drinking water

Date	Mintage	F	VF	XF	Unc	BU
2007 Proof	18,000	Value: 95.00				

KM# 1753 15 YUAN
1.2400 g., 0.9990 Gold 0.0398 oz. AGW, 12 mm. **Obv:** Temple
of Heaven **Rev:** Panda seated in oval with branch

Date	Mintage	F	VF	XF	Unc	BU
2007 Proof	18,000	Value: 95.00				

KM# 1755 15 YUAN
1.2400 g., 0.9990 Gold 0.0398 oz. AGW, 12 mm. **Rev:** Panda
seated on geometric background

Date	Mintage	F	VF	XF	Unc	BU
2007 Proof	18,000	Value: 95.00				

KM# 1757 15 YUAN
1.2400 g., 0.9990 Gold 0.0398 oz. AGW, 12 mm. **Obv:** Temple
of Heaven **Rev:** Panda on rock

Date	Mintage	F	VF	XF	Unc	BU
2007 Proof	18,000	Value: 95.00				

KM# 1759 15 YUAN
1.2400 g., 0.9990 Gold 0.0398 oz. AGW, 12 mm. **Obv:** Temple
of Heaven **Rev:** Panda seated on river bank

Date	Mintage	F	VF	XF	Unc	BU
2007 Proof	18,000	Value: 95.00				

KM# 1761 15 YUAN
1.2400 g., 0.9990 Gold 0.0398 oz. AGW, 12 mm. **Obv:** Temple
of Heaven **Rev:** Panda on tree branch

Date	Mintage	F	VF	XF	Unc	BU
2007 Proof	18,000	Value: 95.00				

KM# 1763 15 YUAN
1.2400 g., 0.9990 Gold 0.0398 oz. AGW, 12 mm. **Obv:** Temple
of Heaven **Rev:** Panda on rock ledge

Date	Mintage	F	VF	XF	Unc	BU
2007 Proof	18,000	Value: 95.00				

KM# 1765 15 YUAN
1.2400 g., 0.9990 Gold 0.0398 oz. AGW, 12 mm. **Obv:** Temple
of Heaven **Rev:** Panda seated munching bamboo

Date	Mintage	F	VF	XF	Unc	BU
2007 Proof	18,000	Value: 95.00				

KM# 1767 15 YUAN
1.2400 g., 0.9990 Gold 0.0398 oz. AGW **Obv:** Temple of Heaven
Rev: Panda pulling bamboo **Shape:** 12

Date	Mintage	F	VF	XF	Unc	BU
2007 Proof	1,800	Value: 95.00				

KM# 1769 15 YUAN
1.2400 g., 0.9990 Gold 0.0398 oz. AGW, 12 mm. **Obv:** Temple
of Heaven **Rev:** Panda in tree

Date	Mintage	F	VF	XF	Unc	BU
2007 Proof	18,000	Value: 95.00				

KM# 1771 15 YUAN
1.2400 g., 0.9990 Gold 0.0398 oz. AGW **Obv:** Temple of Heaven
Rev: Panda looking over branch

Date	Mintage	F	VF	XF	Unc	BU
2007 Proof	18,000	Value: 95.00				

KM# 1773 15 YUAN
1.2400 g., 0.9990 Gold 0.0398 oz. AGW, 12 mm. **Obv:** Temple
of Heaven **Rev:** Panda seated on rock

Date	Mintage	F	VF	XF	Unc	BU
2007 Proof	18,000	Value: 95.00				

KM# A1775 15 YUAN
1.2400 g., 0.9990 Gold 0.0398 oz. AGW, 12 mm. **Obv:** Temple
of Heaven **Rev:** Panda looking out from rock

Date	Mintage	F	VF	XF	Unc	BU
2007 Proof	18,000	Value: 95.00				

KM# 1777 15 YUAN
1.2400 g., 0.9990 Gold 0.0398 oz. AGW, 12 mm. **Obv:** Temple
of Heaven **Rev:** Panda seated on frosted background

Date	Mintage	F	VF	XF	Unc	BU
2007 Proof	18,000	Value: 95.00				

KM# 1781 15 YUAN
1.2400 g., 0.9990 Gold 0.0398 oz. AGW, 12 mm. **Obv:** Temple
of Heaven **Rev:** Panda looking forward

Date	Mintage	F	VF	XF	Unc	BU
2007 Proof	18,000	Value: 95.00				

KM# 1783 15 YUAN
1.2400 g., 0.9990 Gold 0.0398 oz. AGW, 12 mm. **Obv:** Temple
of Heaven **Rev:** Panda and cub walking right

Date	Mintage	F	VF	XF	Unc	BU
2007 Proof	18,000	Value: 95.00				

KM# 1785 15 YUAN
1.2400 g., 0.9990 Gold 0.0398 oz. AGW, 12 mm. **Obv:** Temple
of Heaven **Rev:** Panda seated with cub on left

Date	Mintage	F	VF	XF	Unc	BU
2007 Proof	18,000	Value: 95.00				

KM# 1787 15 YUAN
1.2400 g., 0.9990 Gold 0.0398 oz. AGW, 12 mm. **Obv:** Temple
of Heaven **Rev:** Panda seated with cub on right

Date	Mintage	F	VF	XF	Unc	BU
2007 Proof	18,000	Value: 95.00				

KM# 1789 15 YUAN
1.2400 g., 0.9990 Gold 0.0398 oz. AGW, 12 mm. **Obv:** Temple
of Heaven **Rev:** Panda seated with cub, both munching bamboo

Date	Mintage	F	VF	XF	Unc	BU
2007 Proof	18,000	Value: 95.00				

KM# 1366 20 YUAN
1.5600 g., 0.9990 Gold 0.0501 oz. AGW, 14 mm. **Obv:** Temple
of Heaven **Rev:** Panda walking left through bamboo **Edge:**
Reeded **Note:** Large and small date varieties exist. Prev. Y#1112.

Date	Mintage	F	VF	XF	Unc	BU
2001	200,000	—	—	—	95.00	115
2001 D	Inc. above	—	—	—	95.00	115
2002	74,601	—	—	—	95.00	115

KM# 1467 20 YUAN
1.5552 g., 0.9999 Gold 0.0500 oz. AGW, 14.5 mm. **Subject:**
Panda **Obv:** Temple of Heaven **Rev:** Panda facing, walking
through bamboo **Edge:** Reeded **Note:** Large and small date
varieties exist. Prev. Y#1154.

Date	Mintage	F	VF	XF	Unc	BU
2003	117,000	—	—	—	—	110

KM# 1529 20 YUAN
1.5552 g., 0.9999 Gold 0.0500 oz. AGW, 14 mm. **Rev:** Panda
walking with cub **Note:** Large and small date varieties exist. Prev.
Y#1172.

Date	Mintage	F	VF	XF	Unc	BU
2004	101,000	—	—	—	—	120

KM# 1586 20 YUAN
1.5500 g., 0.9990 Gold 0.0498 oz. AGW, 14 mm. **Obv:** Temple
of Heaven **Rev:** Panda cub and mom seated in bamboo

Date	Mintage	F	VF	XF	Unc	BU
2005 Proof	89,500	Value: 125				

KM# 1661   20 YUAN
1.5552 g., 0.9990 Gold 0.0499 oz. AGW, 14 mm. **Obv:** Temple of Heaven **Rev:** Two pandas seated with bamboo

Date	Mintage	F	VF	XF	Unc	BU
2006 Proof	62,000	Value: 145				

KM# 1707   20 YUAN
1.5552 g., 0.9990 Gold 0.0499 oz. AGW, 14 mm. **Obv:** Temple of Heaven **Rev:** Two pandas, one walking, one seated

Date	Mintage	F	VF	XF	Unc	BU
2007 Proof	200,000	Value: 95.00				

KM# 1815   20 YUAN
1.5552 g., 0.9990 Gold 0.0499 oz. AGW, 14 mm. **Rev:** Panda cut pawing mom

Date	Mintage	F	VF	XF	Unc	BU
2008 Proof	—	Value: 95.00				

KM# 1866   20 YUAN
1.5552 g., 0.9990 Gold 0.0499 oz. AGW

Date	Mintage	F	VF	XF	Unc	BU
2008 Proof	—	Value: 95.00				

KM# 1930   20 YUAN
1.5500 g., 0.9990 Gold 0.0498 oz. AGW **Obv:** Temple of Heaven **Rev:** Two pandas, one lying on back

Date	Mintage	F	VF	XF	Unc	BU
2010	120,000	—	—	—	—	100

KM# 1979   20 YUAN
1.5500 g., 0.9990 Gold 0.0498 oz. AGW, 14 mm.

Date	Mintage	F	VF	XF	Unc	BU
2011	—	—	—	—	—	100

KM# 2028   20 YUAN
1.5500 g., 0.9990 Gold 0.0498 oz. AGW, 14 mm.

Date	Mintage	F	VF	XF	Unc	BU
2012	—	—	—	—	—	100

KM# 1817   30 YUAN
3.1100 g., 0.9990 Gold 0.0999 oz. AGW, 18 mm. **Rev:** Panda cub pawing mom

Date	Mintage	F	VF	XF	Unc	BU
2008 Proof	—	Value: 215				

KM# 1367   50 YUAN
3.1103 g., 0.9990 Gold 0.0999 oz. AGW, 18 mm. **Obv:** Temple of Heaven **Rev:** Panda walking left through bamboo **Edge:** Reeded **Note:** Large and small date varieties exist. Prev. Y#1113.

Date	Mintage	F	VF	XF	Unc	BU
2001	50,000	—	—	—	—	200
2001 D	150,000	—	—	—	—	250

KM# 1457   50 YUAN
3.1103 g., 0.9999 Gold 0.1000 oz. AGW **Subject:** Temple of Heaven **Rev:** Panda walking

Date	Mintage	F	VF	XF	Unc	BU
2002	36,092	—	—	—	—	225

KM# 1469   50 YUAN
3.1103 g., 0.9999 Gold 0.1000 oz. AGW **Subject:** Panda **Note:** Large and small date varieties exist. Prev. Y#1157.

Date	Mintage	F	VF	XF	Unc	BU
2003	47,500	—	—	—	—	215

KM# 1531   50 YUAN
3.1103 g., 0.9999 Gold 0.1000 oz. AGW **Subject:** Panda **Note:** Large and small date varieties exist. Prev. Y#1173.

Date	Mintage	F	VF	XF	Unc	BU
2004	—	—	—	—	—	200

KM# 1585   50 YUAN
3.1100 g., 0.9990 Gold 0.0999 oz. AGW, 18 mm. **Obv:** Temple of Heaven **Rev:** Panda cub and mom seated in bamboo

Date	Mintage	F	VF	XF	Unc	BU
2005	150,000	—	—	—	—	200

KM# 1660   50 YUAN
3.1100 g., 0.9990 Gold 0.0999 oz. AGW, 18 mm. **Obv:** Temple of Heaven **Rev:** Two pandas seated with bamboo

Date	Mintage	F	VF	XF	Unc	BU
2006	150,000	—	—	—	—	200

KM# 1709   50 YUAN
3.1100 g., 0.9990 Gold 0.0999 oz. AGW, 18 mm. **Obv:** Temple of Heaven **Rev:** Two pandas, one walking, one seated

Date	Mintage	F	VF	XF	Unc	BU
2007	150,000	—	—	—	—	200

KM# 1868   50 YUAN
3.1000 g., 0.9990 Gold 0.0996 oz. AGW, 18 mm. **Rev:** Panda cub pawing mom

Date	Mintage	F	VF	XF	Unc	BU
2008	—	—	—	—	—	200

KM# 1929   50 YUAN
3.1100 g., 0.9990 Gold 0.0999 oz. AGW **Obv:** Temple of Heaven **Rev:** Two pandas, one lying on back

Date	Mintage	F	VF	XF	Unc	BU
2010	120,000	—	—	—	—	200

KM# 1978   50 YUAN
3.1100 g., 0.9990 Gold 0.0999 oz. AGW, 18 mm.

Date	Mintage	F	VF	XF	Unc	BU
2011	—	—	—	—	—	200

KM# 2027   50 YUAN
3.1100 g., 0.9990 Gold 0.0999 oz. AGW, 18 mm.

Date	Mintage	F	VF	XF	Unc	BU
2012	—	—	—	—	—	200

KM# 1368   100 YUAN
7.7759 g., 0.9990 Gold 0.2497 oz. AGW, 22 mm. **Obv:** Temple of Heaven **Rev:** Panda walking left through bamboo **Edge:** Reeded **Note:** Large and small date varieties exist. Prev. Y#1114.

Date	Mintage	F	VF	XF	Unc	BU
2001	85,010	—	—	—	—	425
2001 D	Inc. above	—	—	—	—	475

KM# 1458   100 YUAN
7.7759 g., 0.9999 Gold 0.2500 oz. AGW **Obv:** Temple of Heaven **Rev:** Panda walking

Date	Mintage	F	VF	XF	Unc	BU
2002	19,205	—	—	—	—	450

KM# 1471   100 YUAN
7.7759 g., 0.9999 Gold 0.2500 oz. AGW **Subject:** Panda **Note:** Large and small date varieties exist. Prev. Y#1158.

Date	Mintage	F	VF	XF	Unc	BU
2003	28,000	—	—	—	—	425

KM# 1533   100 YUAN
7.7759 g., 0.9999 Gold 0.2500 oz. AGW **Subject:** Panda **Note:** Large and small date varieties exist. Prev. Y#1174. Photo reduced.

Date	Mintage	F	VF	XF	Unc	BU
2004	41,000	—	—	—	—	425

KM# 1584   100 YUAN
7.7700 g., 0.9990 Gold 0.2496 oz. AGW, 22 mm. **Obv:** Temple of Heaven **Rev:** Panda cub and mom seated in bamboo

Date	Mintage	F	VF	XF	Unc	BU
2005	40,000	—	—	—	—	425

KM# 1659   100 YUAN
7.7700 g., 0.9990 Gold 0.2496 oz. AGW, 22 mm. **Obv:** Temple of Heaven **Rev:** Two pandas seated with bamboo

Date	Mintage	F	VF	XF	Unc	BU
2006	28,500	—	—	—	—	450

KM# 1710   100 YUAN
7.7700 g., 0.9990 Gold 0.2496 oz. AGW, 22 mm. **Obv:** Temple of Heaven **Rev:** Two pandas, one walking, one seated

Date	Mintage	F	VF	XF	Unc	BU
2007	60,000	—	—	—	—	425

KM# 1818   100 YUAN
7.7700 g., 0.9990 Gold 0.2496 oz. AGW, 22 mm. **Rev:** Panda cub pawing mom

Date	Mintage	F	VF	XF	Unc	BU
2008	—	—	—	—	—	425

KM# 1928   100 YUAN
7.7700 g., 0.9990 Gold 0.2496 oz. AGW **Obv:** Temple of Heaven **Rev:** Two panda, one lying on back

Date	Mintage	F	VF	XF	Unc	BU
2010	120,000	—	—	—	—	450

KM# 1977   100 YUAN
7.7700 g., 0.9990 Gold 0.2496 oz. AGW, 22 mm.

Date	Mintage	F	VF	XF	Unc	BU
2011	—	—	—	—	—	450

KM# 2026   100 YUAN
7.7700 g., 0.9990 Gold 0.2496 oz. AGW, 22 mm.

Date	Mintage	F	VF	XF	Unc	BU
2012	—	—	—	—	—	450

KM# 1369   200 YUAN
15.5518 g., 0.9990 Gold 0.4995 oz. AGW, 27 mm. **Obv:** Temple of Heaven **Rev:** Panda in bamboo forest **Edge:** Slanted reeding **Note:** Illustration reduced. Large and small date varieties exist. Prev. Y#1105.

Date	Mintage	F	VF	XF	Unc	BU
2001	33,215	—	—	—	—	875
2001 D	100,000	—	—	—	—	850

KM# 1459   200 YUAN
15.5518 g., 0.9999 Gold 0.4999 oz. AGW **Rev:** Panda

Date	Mintage	F	VF	XF	Unc	BU
2002	28,514	—	—	—	—	875

KM# 1472   200 YUAN
15.5519 g., 0.9999 Gold 0.4999 oz. AGW **Subject:** Panda **Note:** Large and small date varieties exist. Prev. Y#1162.

Date	Mintage	F	VF	XF	Unc	BU
2003	25,000	—	—	—	—	875

KM# 1535   200 YUAN
15.5519 g., 0.9990 Gold 0.4995 oz. AGW **Subject:** Panda **Note:** Large and small date varieties exist. Prev. Y#1175.

Date	Mintage	F	VF	XF	Unc	BU
2004	42,000	—	—	—	—	850

KM# 1583   200 YUAN
15.5518 g., 0.9990 Gold 0.4995 oz. AGW, 27 mm. **Obv:** Temple of Heaven **Rev:** Panda cub and mom seated in bamboo

Date	Mintage	F	VF	XF	Unc	BU
2005	36,410	—	—	—	—	850

KM# 1658   200 YUAN
15.5500 g., 0.9990 Gold 0.4994 oz. AGW, 27 mm. **Obv:** Temple of Heaven **Rev:** Two pandas seated with bamboo

Date	Mintage	F	VF	XF	Unc	BU
2006	25,600	—	—	—	—	875

KM# 1711   200 YUAN
15.5500 g., 0.9990 Gold 0.4994 oz. AGW **Obv:** Temple of Heaven **Rev:** Two pandas, one walking, one seated

Date	Mintage	F	VF	XF	Unc	BU
2007	60,000	—	—	—	—	850

KM# 1870   200 YUAN
15.5000 g., 0.9990 Gold 0.4978 oz. AGW

Date	Mintage	F	VF	XF	Unc	BU
2009	—	—	—	—	—	850

KM# 1927   200 YUAN
15.5500 g., 0.9990 Gold 0.4994 oz. AGW **Obv:** Temple of Heaven **Rev:** Two pandas, one lying on back

Date	Mintage	F	VF	XF	Unc	BU
2010	120,000	—	—	—	—	900

KM# 1976   200 YUAN
15.5500 g., 0.9990 Gold 0.4994 oz. AGW

Date	Mintage	F	VF	XF	Unc	BU
2011	—	—	—	—	—	—BV+20%

KM# 2025   200 YUAN
15.5500 g., 0.9990 Gold 0.4994 oz. AGW, 27 mm.

Date	Mintage	F	VF	XF	Unc	BU
2012	—	—	—	—	—	900

KM# 1371   500 YUAN
31.1035 g., 0.9990 Gold 0.9990 oz. AGW, 32 mm. **Obv:** Temple of Heaven **Rev:** Panda walking through bamboo **Edge:** Reeded **Note:** Prev. Y#1088.

Date	Mintage	F	VF	XF	Unc	BU
2001	—	—	—	—	—	—BV+15%
2001 D	150,000	—	—	—	—	—BV+15%

KM# 1405   500 YUAN
31.1050 g., 0.9999 Gold 0.9999 oz. AGW **Rev:** Panda

Date	Mintage	F	VF	XF	Unc	BU
2001	41,411	—	—	—	—	—BV+15%

KM# 1460   500 YUAN
31.1050 g., 0.9999 Gold 0.9999 oz. AGW **Rev:** Panda

Date	Mintage	F	VF	XF	Unc	BU
2002	28,345	—	—	—	—	—BV+20%

KM# 1474   500 YUAN
31.1320 g., 0.9999 Gold 1.0008 oz. AGW **Subject:** Panda **Note:** Large and small date varieties exist. Prev. Y#1164.

Date	Mintage	F	VF	XF	Unc	BU
2003	36,300	—	—	—	—	—BV+15%

KM# 1537   500 YUAN
31.1035 g., 0.9999 Gold 0.9999 oz. AGW **Subject:** Panda **Note:** Large and small date varieties exist. Prev. Y#1176.

Date	Mintage	F	VF	XF	Unc	BU
2004	55,000	—	—	—	—	—BV+10%

KM# 1582   500 YUAN
31.1050 g., 0.9990 Gold 0.9990 oz. AGW, 32 mm. **Obv:** Temple of Heaven **Rev:** Panda cub and mom seated in bamboo

Date	Mintage	F	VF	XF	Unc	BU
2005	50,300	BV+10%				

KM# 1657   500 YUAN
31.1050 g., 0.9990 Gold 0.9990 oz. AGW, 32 mm. **Obv:** Temple of Heaven **Rev:** Two panda's seated with bamboo

Date	Mintage	F	VF	XF	Unc	BU
2006	115,600	BV+10%				

KM# 1713   500 YUAN
31.1050 g., 0.9990 Gold 0.9990 oz. AGW, 32 mm. **Obv:** Temple of Heaven **Rev:** Two pandas, one walking, one seated

Date	Mintage	F	VF	XF	Unc	BU
2007	150,000	BV+10%				

KM# 1821   500 YUAN
31.1050 g., 0.9990 Gold 0.9990 oz. AGW, 32 mm. **Rev:** Panda cub pawing mom

Date	Mintage	F	VF	XF	Unc	BU
2008	—	BV+10%				

KM# 1872   500 YUAN
31.1050 g., 0.9990 Gold 0.9990 oz. AGW

Date	Mintage	F	VF	XF	Unc	BU
2009	—	BV+10%				

KM# 1926   500 YUAN
31.1050 g., 0.9990 Gold 0.9990 oz. AGW **Obv:** Temple of Heaven **Rev:** Two pandas, one lying on back

Date	Mintage	F	VF	XF	Unc	BU
2010	300,000	—	—	—	—	1,550

KM# 1975   500 YUAN
31.1050 g., 0.9990 Gold 0.9990 oz. AGW

Date	Mintage	F	VF	XF	Unc	BU
2011	—	—	—	—	—	—BV+10%

KM# 2024   500 YUAN
31.1050 g., 0.9990 Gold 0.9990 oz. AGW, 32 mm.

Date	Mintage	F	VF	XF	Unc	BU
2012	—	—	—	—	—	—BV+10%

KM# 1581   2000 YUAN
155.0000 g., 0.9990 Gold 4.9782 oz. AGW, 60 mm. **Obv:** Temple of Heaven **Rev:** Panda cub and mom seated in bamboo **Note:** Photo reduced.

Date	Mintage	F	VF	XF	Unc	BU
2005 Proof	1,000	BV+25%				

KM# 1656   2000 YUAN
155.5500 g., 0.9990 Gold 4.9958 oz. AGW, 60 mm. **Obv:** Temple of Heaven **Rev:** Two pandas seated with bamboo **Note:** Photo reduced.

Date	Mintage	F	VF	XF	Unc	BU
2006 Proof	1,000	BV+25%				

KM# 1714   2000 YUAN
155.5500 g., 0.9990 Gold 4.9958 oz. AGW, 60 mm. **Obv:** Temple of Heaven **Rev:** Two pandas, one walking, one seated

Date	Mintage	F	VF	XF	Unc	BU
2007 Proof	1,000	BV+25%				

KM# 1822   2000 YUAN
155.5000 g., 0.9990 Gold 4.9942 oz. AGW, 60 mm. **Rev:** Panda cub pawing mom

Date	Mintage	F	VF	XF	Unc	BU
2008 Proof	1,000	BV+25%				

KM# 1873   2000 YUAN
155.5000 g., 0.9990 Gold 4.9942 oz. AGW

Date	Mintage	F	VF	XF	Unc	BU
2009 Proof	1,000	BV+25%				

KM# 1914   2000 YUAN
155.5000 g., 0.9990 Gold 4.9942 oz. AGW **Subject:** Year of the Tiger **Rev:** Multicolor

Date	Mintage	F	VF	XF	Unc	BU
2010 Proof	1,800	Value: 8,500				

KM# 1933   2000 YUAN
155.5000 g., 0.9990 Gold 4.9942 oz. AGW **Obv:** Temple of Heaven **Rev:** Two pandas, one lying on back

Date	Mintage	F	VF	XF	Unc	BU
2010 Proof	1,000	Value: 8,750				

KM# 1982   2000 YUAN
155.5500 g., 0.9990 Gold 4.9958 oz. AGW, 60 mm.

Date	Mintage	F	VF	XF	Unc	BU
2011	—	Value: 8,500				

KM# 1372   10000 YUAN
1000.0000 g., 0.9990 Gold 32.117 oz. AGW **Subject:** Panda **Note:** Large and small date varieties exist. Prev. #Y1138.

Date	Mintage	F	VF	XF	Unc	BU
2001	68	—	—	—	—	—BV+35%

KM# A1475   10000 YUAN
1000.0000 g., 0.9990 Gold 32.146 oz. AGW **Subject:** Panda **Note:** Large and small date varieties exist. Prev. #Y1165.

Date	Mintage	F	VF	XF	Unc	BU
2002	68	—	—	—	—	—BV+35%

KM# 1475   10000 YUAN
1000.0000 g., 0.9990 Gold 32.117 oz. AGW, 100 mm. **Rev:** Panda and bamboo

Date	Mintage	F	VF	XF	Unc	BU
2003 Proof	68	BV+35%				

KM# 1538   10000 YUAN
1000.0000 g., 0.9999 Gold 32.146 oz. AGW **Subject:** Panda **Note:** Large and small date varieties exist. Prev. #Y1177.

Date	Mintage	F	VF	XF	Unc	BU
2004	68	—	—	—	—	—BV+35%

KM# A1580   10000 YUAN
1000.0000 g., 0.9990 Gold 32.117 oz. AGW, 90 mm. **Obv:**

Temple of Heaven **Rev:** Panda cub and mom seated in bamboo **Note:** Photo reduced.

Date	Mintage	F	VF	XF	Unc	BU
2005 Proof	100	BV+25%				

KM# 1655 10000 YUAN
1000.0000 g., 0.9990 Gold 32.117 oz. AGW, 90 mm. **Obv:**
Temple of Heaven **Rev:** Two pandas seated with bamboo **Note:** Photo reduced.

Date	Mintage	F	VF	XF	Unc	BU
2006 Proof	200	BV+20%				

KM# 1715 10000 YUAN
1000.0000 g., 0.9990 Gold 32.117 oz. AGW **Obv:** Temple of Heaven **Rev:** Two pandas, one walking, one seated

Date	Mintage	F	VF	XF	Unc	BU
2007 Proof	200	BV+20%				

KM# 1823 10000 YUAN
1000.0000 g., 0.9990 Gold 32.117 oz. AGW. **Rev:** Panda cub pawing mom

Date	Mintage	F	VF	XF	Unc	BU
2008 Proof	200	BV+20%				

KM# 1874 10000 YUAN
1000.0000 g., 0.9990 Gold 32.117 oz. AGW

Date	Mintage	F	VF	XF	Unc	BU
2009 Proof	200	BV+20%				

KM# 1932 10000 YUAN
1000.0000 g., 0.9990 Gold 32.117 oz. AGW **Obv:** Temple of Heaven **Rev:** Two pandas, one lying on back

Date	Mintage	F	VF	XF	Unc	BU
2010 Proof	200	Value: 47,500				

KM# 1981 10000 YUAN
1000.0000 g., 0.9990 Gold 32.117 oz. AGW, 90 mm.

Date	Mintage	F	VF	XF	Unc	BU
2011 Proof	—	Value: 62,500				

KM# 2030 10000 YUAN
1000.0000 g., 0.9990 Gold 32.117 oz. AGW, 90 mm.

Date	Mintage	F	VF	XF	Unc	BU
2012 Proof	—	BV+20%				

Lunar Series

KM# 1967 20 YUAN
3.1100 g., 0.9990 Gold 0.0999 oz. AGW, 18 mm. **Subject:** Year of the Rabbit **Rev:** Multicolor

Date	Mintage	F	VF	XF	Unc	BU
2011 Proof	80,000	Value: 225				

KM# 1374 50 YUAN
3.1103 g., 0.9990 Gold 0.0999 oz. AGW, 18 mm. **Subject:** Year of the Snake **Note:** Prev. Y#1141.1; 1043.

Date	Mintage	F	VF	XF	Unc	BU
2001	48,000	—	—	—	—	265

KM# 1376 50 YUAN
3.1105 g., 0.9999 Gold 0.1000 oz. AGW **Subject:** Year of the Snake **Rev:** Multicolor. **Note:** Prev. Y#1141.2.

Date	Mintage	F	VF	XF	Unc	BU
2001	30,000	—	—	—	—	350

KM# 1419 50 YUAN
3.1050 g., 0.9999 Gold 0.0998 oz. AGW **Subject:** Year of the Horse **Rev:** Dramatic horse profile right **Note:** Prev. Y#1143.1.

Date	Mintage	F	VF	XF	Unc	BU
2002	48,000	—	—	—	—	240

KM# 1417 50 YUAN
3.1050 g., 0.9999 Gold 0.0998 oz. AGW **Subject:** Year of the Horse **Rev:** Multicolor horse prancing forward **Note:** Prev. Y#1143.2.

Date	Mintage	F	VF	XF	Unc	BU
2002	30,000	—	—	—	—	425

KM# 1478 50 YUAN
3.1103 g., 0.9999 Gold 0.1000 oz. AGW **Subject:** Year of the Goat **Note:** Prev. Y#1155.1.

Date	Mintage	F	VF	XF	Unc	BU
2003	48,000	—	—	—	—	275

KM# A1478 50 YUAN
3.1105 g., 0.9999 Gold 0.1000 oz. AGW **Subject:** Year of the Goat **Rev:** Multicolor. **Note:** Prev. Y#1155.2

Date	Mintage	F	VF	XF	Unc	BU
2003	30,000	—	—	—	—	400

KM# 1544 50 YUAN
3.1103 g., 0.9999 Gold 0.1000 oz. AGW, 18 mm. **Subject:** Year of the Monkey **Note:** Prev. Y#1167.1.

Date	Mintage	F	VF	XF	Unc	BU
2004	48,000	—	—	—	—	275

KM# 1546 50 YUAN
3.1103 g., 0.9999 Gold 0.1000 oz. AGW **Subject:** Year of the Monkey **Rev:** Multicolor monkey and baby **Note:** Prev. Y#1167.2

Date	Mintage	F	VF	XF	Unc	BU
2004	30,000	—	—	—	—	425

KM# 1608 50 YUAN
3.1100 g., 0.9990 Gold 0.0999 oz. AGW, 18 mm. **Subject:** Year of the Rooster **Obv:** Classical rooster **Rev:** Multicolor rooster

Date	Mintage	F	VF	XF	Unc	BU
2005 Proof	30,000	Value: 375				

KM# 1609 50 YUAN
3.1100 g., 0.9990 Gold 0.0999 oz. AGW, 18 mm. **Subject:** Year of the Rooster **Obv:** Classical rooster **Rev:** Rooster, hen and chicks

Date	Mintage	F	VF	XF	Unc	BU
2005 Proof	60,000	Value: 300				

KM# 1680 50 YUAN
3.1103 g., 0.9990 Gold 0.0999 oz. AGW, 18 mm. **Obv:** Dog-shaped belt-hook from ancient Chinese bronze ware, decorative design of dog tail-shaped plant leaves **Rev:** 2 smart dogs **Note:** Prev. Y#1226; KM#1658.

Date	Mintage	F	VF	XF	Unc	BU
2006	60,000	—	—	—	—	225

KM# 1681 50 YUAN
3.1103 g., 0.9990 Gold 0.0999 oz. AGW, 18 mm. **Obv:** Dog-shaped belt-hook , an ancient Chinese bronze ware, decorative disign of dog tail-shaped plant leaves **Rev:** 2 dogs at play **Note:** Prev. Y#1222; KM#1654.

Date	Mintage	F	VF	XF	Unc	BU
2006 Proof	30,000	Value: 220				

KM# 1721 50 YUAN
3.1000 g., 0.9990 Gold 0.0996 oz. AGW, 18 mm. **Subject:** Year of the Pig **Obv:** Classical pig **Rev:** Pig walking right

Date	Mintage	F	VF	XF	Unc	BU
2007 Proof	—	Value: 225				

KM# 1722 50 YUAN
3.1000 g., 0.9990 Gold 0.0996 oz. AGW, 18 mm. **Subject:** Year of the Pig **Obv:** Classical pig **Rev:** Multicolor sow and piglets sucking

Date	Mintage	F	VF	XF	Unc	BU
2007 Proof	30,000	Value: 550				

KM# 1835 50 YUAN
3.1100 g., 0.9990 Gold 0.0999 oz. AGW **Subject:** Year of the Rat **Rev:** Multicolor **Shape:** 18

Date	Mintage	F	VF	XF	Unc	BU
2008 Proof	30,000	Value: 350				

KM# 1836 50 YUAN
3.1100 g., 0.9990 Gold 0.0999 oz. AGW, 18 mm. **Subject:** Year of the Rat

Date	Mintage	F	VF	XF	Unc	BU
2008 Proof	60,000	Value: 225				

KM# 1880 50 YUAN
3.1100 g., 0.9990 Gold 0.0999 oz. AGW **Subject:** Year of the Ox colorized

Date	Mintage	F	VF	XF	Unc	BU
2009 Proof	30,000	Value: 400				

KM# 1881 50 YUAN
3.1100 g., 0.9990 Gold 0.0999 oz. AGW **Subject:** Year of the Ox

Date	Mintage	F	VF	XF	Unc	BU
2009 Proof	80,000	Value: 180				

KM# 1917 50 YUAN
3.1100 g., 0.9990 Gold 0.0999 oz. AGW **Subject:** Year of the Tiger

Date	Mintage	F	VF	XF	Unc	BU
2010 Proof	80,000	Value: 225				

KM# 1918 50 YUAN
3.1100 g., 0.9990 Gold 0.0999 oz. AGW **Subject:** Year of the Tiger **Rev:** Multicolor

Date	Mintage	F	VF	XF	Unc	BU
2010 Proof	80,000	Value: 225				

KM# 1966 50 YUAN
3.1100 g., 0.9990 Gold 0.0999 oz. AGW, 18 mm. **Subject:** Year of the Rabbit

Date	Mintage	F	VF	XF	Unc	BU
2011 Proof	80,000	Value: 225				

KM# 2015 50 YUAN
3.1050 g., 0.9990 Gold 0.0997 oz. AGW, 18 mm. **Subject:** Year of the Dragon

Date	Mintage	F	VF	XF	Unc	BU
2012 Proof	—	Value: 225				

KM# 2016 50 YUAN
3.1050 g., 0.9990 Gold 0.0997 oz. AGW, 18 mm. **Subject:** Year of the Dragon **Rev:** Colored

Date	Mintage	F	VF	XF	Unc	BU
2012 Proof	—	Value: 225				

KM# 1380 200 YUAN
15.5518 g., 0.9990 Gold 0.4995 oz. AGW **Subject:** Year of the Snake **Shape:** Flower **Note:** Prev. Y#1045.

Date	Mintage	F	VF	XF	Unc	BU
2001 Proof	2,300	Value: 1,250				

KM# 1383 200 YUAN
15.5518 g., 0.9990 Gold 0.4995 oz. AGW **Subject:** Year of the Snake **Rev:** Fan **Note:** Prev. Y#1044.

Date	Mintage	F	VF	XF	Unc	BU
2001	6,600	—	—	—	—	950

KM# 1424 200 YUAN
15.5500 g., 0.9990 Gold 0.4994 oz. AGW **Subject:** Year of the Horse **Shape:** Fan

Date	Mintage	F	VF	XF	Unc	BU
2002	6,600	—	—	—	—	1,000

KM# 1426 200 YUAN
15.5000 g., 0.9990 Gold 0.4978 oz. AGW **Subject:** Year of the Horse **Shape:** Flower **Note:** Prev. Y#1150.

Date	Mintage	F	VF	XF	Unc	BU
2002	2,300	—	—	—	—	1,350

KM# 1475.1 200 YUAN
15.5517 g., 0.9999 Gold 0.4999 oz. AGW **Subject:** Year of the Goat **Shape:** Fan

Date	Mintage	F	VF	XF	Unc	BU
2003	6,600	—	—	—	—	900

KM# 1481 200 YUAN
15.5519 g., 0.9999 Gold 0.4999 oz. AGW **Subject:** Year of the Goat **Shape:** Flower **Note:** Prev. Y#1161.

Date	Mintage	F	VF	XF	Unc	BU
2003	2,300	—	—	—	—	1,350

KM# 1486 200 YUAN
15.5130 g., 0.9990 Gold 0.4982 oz. AGW, 58 x 30 mm. **Subject:** Year of the Sheep **Shape:** Fan

Date	Mintage	F	VF	XF	Unc	BU
2003 Proof	6,600	Value: 1,100				

KM# 1549   200 YUAN
15.5519 g., 0.9999 Gold 0.4999 oz. AGW **Subject:** Year of the Monkey **Shape:** Flower **Note:** Prev. Y#1169.

Date	Mintage	F	VF	XF	Unc	BU
2004	2,300	—	—	—	—	1,350

KM# 1554   200 YUAN
15.5519 g., 0.9999 Gold 0.4999 oz. AGW **Subject:** Year of the Monkey **Shape:** Fan **Note:** Illustration reduced. Prev. Y#1168.

Date	Mintage	F	VF	XF	Unc	BU
2004	6,600	—	—	—	—	1,100

KM# 1606   200 YUAN
15.5500 g., 0.9990 Gold 0.4994 oz. AGW, 27 mm. **Series:** Classical rooster **Subject:** Year of the Rooster **Obv:** Rooster, hen and chicks **Shape:** Scallops

Date	Mintage	F	VF	XF	Unc	BU
2005 Proof	8,000	Value: 925				

KM# 1607   200 YUAN
15.5500 g., 0.9990 Gold 0.4994 oz. AGW, 58 x 30 mm. **Subject:** Year of the Rooster **Obv:** Temple **Rev:** Rooster, hen and chicks **Shape:** Fan **Note:** Illustration reduced.

Date	Mintage	F	VF	XF	Unc	BU
2005 Proof	6,600	Value: 950				

KM# 1677   200 YUAN
15.6300 g., 0.9990 Gold 0.5020 oz. AGW, 27 mm. **Subject:** Year of the Dog **Obv:** Dog-shaped belt-hook from ancient Chinese bronze ware, decorative design of dog tail-shaped plant leaves **Rev:** 2 smart dogs **Shape:** Scalloped **Note:** Prev. Y#1224; KM#1656.

Date	Mintage	F	VF	XF	Unc	BU
2006 Proof	8,000	Value: 1,350				

KM# 1679   200 YUAN
15.6300 g., 0.9990 Gold 0.5020 oz. AGW **Subject:** Year of the Dog **Obv:** Qing Yuan Gate of the China Great Wall **Rev:** 2 dogs at play **Shape:** 30° Fan **Note:** Illustration reduced. Prev. Y#1220; KM#1652.

Date	Mintage	F	VF	XF	Unc	BU
2006 Proof	6,600	Value: 1,100				

KM# 1723   200 YUAN
15.5000 g., 0.9990 Gold 0.4978 oz. AGW, 58 x 39 mm. **Subject:** Year of the Pig **Obv:** Temple **Rev:** Sow and four pigletts **Shape:** Fan

Date	Mintage	F	VF	XF	Unc	BU
2007 Proof	6,600	Value: 1,150				

KM# 1724   200 YUAN
15.5500 g., 0.9990 Gold 0.4994 oz. AGW, 27 mm. **Subject:** Year of the Pig **Obv:** Classical pig **Rev:** Pig walking right **Shape:** Flower

Date	Mintage	F	VF	XF	Unc	BU
2007 Proof	8,000	Value: 950				

KM# 1837   200 YUAN
15.5000 g., 0.9990 Gold 0.4978 oz. AGW, 27 mm. **Subject:** Year of the Rat **Shape:** Flower

Date	Mintage	F	VF	XF	Unc	BU
2008 Proof	8,000	Value: 950				

KM# 1838   200 YUAN
15.5000 g., 0.9990 Gold 0.4978 oz. AGW, 58 x 39 mm. **Subject:** Year of the Rat **Shape:** Fan

Date	Mintage	F	VF	XF	Unc	BU
2008 Proof	6,600	Value: 1,000				

KM# 1883   200 YUAN
15.5000 g., 0.9990 Gold 0.4978 oz. AGW **Subject:** Year of the Ox **Shape:** Fan

Date	Mintage	F	VF	XF	Unc	BU
2009 Proof	6,600	Value: 1,000				

KM# 1882   200 YUAN
15.5000 g., 0.9990 Gold 0.4978 oz. AGW **Subject:** Year of the Ox **Shape:** Flower

Date	Mintage	F	VF	XF	Unc	BU
2009 Proof	8,000	Value: 950				

KM# 1915   200 YUAN
15.5500 g., 0.9990 Gold 0.4994 oz. AGW **Subject:** Year of the Tiger **Shape:** Arc

Date	Mintage	F	VF	XF	Unc	BU
2010	6,600	—	—	—	—	900

KM# 1916   200 YUAN
15.5500 g., 0.9990 Gold 0.4994 oz. AGW **Subject:** Year of the Tiger **Shape:** Scalloped

Date	Mintage	F	VF	XF	Unc	BU
2010 Proof	8,000	Value: 900				

KM# 1964   200 YUAN
15.5000 g., 0.9990 Gold 0.4978 oz. AGW **Subject:** Year of the Rabbit **Shape:** Arc **Note:** Photo reduced.

Date	Mintage	F	VF	XF	Unc	BU
2011	6,600	—	—	—	—	950

KM# 1965   200 YUAN
15.5500 g., 0.9990 Gold 0.4994 oz. AGW, 27 mm. **Subject:** Year of the Rabbit **Shape:** Scallop

Date	Mintage	F	VF	XF	Unc	BU
2011 Proof	8,000	Value: 900				

KM# 2013   200 YUAN
15.5500 g., 0.9990 Gold 0.4994 oz. AGW **Subject:** Year of the Dragon **Shape:** Fan

Date	Mintage	F	VF	XF	Unc	BU
2012 Proof	—	Value: 950				

KM# 2014   200 YUAN
15.5500 g., 0.9990 Gold 0.4994 oz. AGW, 27 mm. **Subject:** Year of the Dragon **Shape:** Scalloped

Date	Mintage	F	VF	XF	Unc	BU
2012 Proof	—	Value: 950				

KM# 1378   2000 YUAN
155.5175 g., 0.9990 Gold 4.9948 oz. AGW, 80 x 50 mm. **Subject:** Year of the Snake **Shape:** Rectangle **Note:** Prev. #Y1046.

Date	Mintage	F	VF	XF	Unc	BU
2001 Proof	118	Value: 22,500				

KM# 1422   2000 YUAN
155.5175 g., 0.9999 Gold 4.9993 oz. AGW **Subject:** Year of the Horse **Shape:** Rectangle **Note:** Prev. #Y1152.

Date	Mintage	F	VF	XF	Unc	BU
2002 Proof	118	Value: 22,500				

KM# 1483   2000 YUAN
155.5190 g., 0.9999 Gold 4.9993 oz. AGW **Subject:** Year of the Goat **Note:** Prev. #Y1163.

Date	Mintage	F	VF	XF	Unc	BU
2003 Proof	118	Value: 22,500				

KM# 1552   2000 YUAN
155.1750 g., 0.9999 Gold 4.9883 oz. AGW **Subject:** Year of the Monkey **Note:** Prev. #Y1170. **Note:** Illustration reduced.

Date	Mintage	F	VF	XF	Unc	BU
2004 Proof	118	Value: 22,500				

KM# 1605   2000 YUAN
155.5500 g., 0.9990 Gold 4.9958 oz. AGW, 64 x 40 mm.
Subject: Year of the Rooster **Obv:** Classical rooster **Rev:**
Rooster, hen and chicks **Shape:** Rectangle **Note:** Photo reduced.

Date	Mintage	F	VF	XF	Unc	BU
2005 Proof	118	Value: 22,500				

KM# 1678   2000 YUAN
155.5500 g., 0.9990 Gold 4.9958 oz. AGW, 64 x 40 mm.
Subject: Year of the Dog **Obv:** Classical dog **Rev:** Two dogs
Note: Photo reduced.

Date	Mintage	F	VF	XF	Unc	BU
2006 Proof	118	Value: 22,500				

KM# 1726   2000 YUAN
155.5500 g., 0.9990 Gold 4.9958 oz. AGW, 64 x 40 mm.
Subject: Year of the Pig **Obv:** Classical pig **Rev:** Sow and four
pigletts **Shape:** Rectangle

Date	Mintage	F	VF	XF	Unc	BU
2007 Proof	118	Value: 22,500				

KM# 1840   2000 YUAN
155.0000 g., 0.9990 Gold 4.9782 oz. AGW, 64 x 40 mm.
Subject: Year of the Rat **Shape:** Rectangle

Date	Mintage	F	VF	XF	Unc	BU
2008 Proof	118	Value: 22,500				

KM# 1885   2000 YUAN
155.5000 g., 0.9990 Gold 4.9942 oz. AGW, 64x40 mm.
Subject: Year of the Ox **Shape:** Rectangle

Date	Mintage	F	VF	XF	Unc	BU
2009 Proof	118	Value: 22,500				

KM# 1913   2000 YUAN
155.2000 g., 0.9990 Gold 4.9846 oz. AGW, 64x40 mm.
Subject: Year of the Tiger **Shape:** Rectangle

Date	Mintage	F	VF	XF	Unc	BU
2010 Proof	118	Value: 20,000				

KM# 1962   2000 YUAN
155.5000 g., 0.9990 Gold 4.9942 oz. AGW, 64x40 mm.
Subject: Year of the Rabbit **Shape:** Rectangle **Note:** Photo
reduced.

Date	Mintage	F	VF	XF	Unc	BU
2011 Proof	118	Value: 20,000				

KM# 1963   2000 YUAN
155.5000 g., 0.9990 Gold 4.9942 oz. AGW **Subject:** Year of
the Rabbit **Rev:** Multicolor **Note:** Photo reduced.

Date	Mintage	F	VF	XF	Unc	BU
2011 Proof	1,800	Value: 9,500				

KM# 2011   2000 YUAN
155.5500 g., 0.9990 Gold 4.9958 oz. AGW, 64x40 mm.
Subject: Year of the Dragon **Shape:** Rectangle

Date	Mintage	F	VF	XF	Unc	BU
2012 Proof	—	Value: 20,000				

KM# 2012   2000 YUAN
155.5500 g., 0.9990 Gold 4.9958 oz. AGW **Subject:** Year of
the Dragon **Rev:** Colored Dragon

Date	Mintage	F	VF	XF	Unc	BU
2012 Proof	—	Value: 9,500				

KM# 2031   2000 YUAN
155.5500 g., 0.9990 Gold 4.9958 oz. AGW, 60 mm.

Date	Mintage	F	VF	XF	Unc	BU
2012 Proof	—	BV+25%				

KM# 1381   10000 YUAN
1000.0000 g., 0.9990 Gold 32.117 oz. AGW **Subject:** Year of
the Snake **Shape:** Scalloped **Note:** Prev. #Y1047.

Date	Mintage	F	VF	XF	Unc	BU
2001 Proof	15	Value: 125,000				

KM# 1427   10000 YUAN
1000.0000 g., 0.9999 Gold 32.146 oz. AGW **Subject:** Year of
the Horse **Shape:** Scalloped **Note:** Prev. #Y1153.

Date	Mintage	F	VF	XF	Unc	BU
2002 Proof	15	Value: 90,000				

KM# 1482   10000 YUAN
1000.0000 g., 0.9999 Gold 32.146 oz. AGW, 100 mm. **Subject:**
Year of the Goat **Shape:** Scalloped **Note:** Prev. #Y1166.

Date	Mintage	F	VF	XF	Unc	BU
2003 Proof	15	Value: 75,000				

KM# 1550   10000 YUAN
1000.0000 g., 0.9999 Gold 32.146 oz. AGW, 100 mm. **Subject:**
Year of the Monkey **Shape:** Scalloped **Note:** Prev. #Y1171.

Date	Mintage	F	VF	XF	Unc	BU
2004 Proof	15	Value: 90,000				

KM# 1604   10000 YUAN
1000.0000 g., 0.9990 Gold 32.117 oz. AGW, 100 mm. **Obv:**
Classical rooster **Rev:** Rooster strutting **Edge:** Scalloped **Note:**
Photo reduced.

Date	Mintage	F	VF	XF	Unc	BU
2005 Proof	15	Value: 75,000				

KM# 1727   10000 YUAN
1000.0000 g., 0.9990 Gold 32.117 oz. AGW, 100 mm. **Subject:**
Year of the Pig **Obv:** Classical pig **Rev:** Three pigs **Shape:**
Scalloped

Date	Mintage	F	VF	XF	Unc	BU
2007 Proof	118	Value: 70,000				

KM# 1841   10000 YUAN
1000.0000 g., 0.9990 Gold 32.117 oz. AGW, 100 mm. **Subject:**
Year of the Rat **Shape:** Scalloped

Date	Mintage	F	VF	XF	Unc	BU
2008 Proof	118	Value: 70,000				

KM# 1912   10000 YUAN
1000.0000 g., 0.9990 Gold 32.117 oz. AGW, 100 mm. **Subject:**
Year of the Tiger **Shape:** Scalloped

Date	Mintage	F	VF	XF	Unc	BU
2010 Proof	118	Value: 65,000				

KM# 1961   10000 YUAN
1000.0000 g., 0.9990 Gold 32.117 oz. AGW, 100 mm. **Subject:**
Year of the Rabbit **Shape:** Scalloped **Note:** Photo reduced.

Date	Mintage	F	VF	XF	Unc	BU
2011 Proof	118	Value: 65,000				

KM# 2010   10000 YUAN
1000.0000 g., 0.9990 Gold 32.117 oz. AGW, 100 mm. **Subject:**
Year of the Dragon

Date	Mintage	F	VF	XF	Unc	BU
2012 Proof	—	Value: 75,000				

KM# 1728   100000 YUAN
10000.0000 g., 0.9990 Gold 321.17 oz. AGW, 180 mm.
Subject: Year of the Pig **Obv:** Classical pig **Rev:** Sow with four
pigletts sucking

Date	Mintage	F	VF	XF	Unc	BU
2007 Proof	18	Value: 500,000				

KM# 1842 100000 YUAN
10000.0000 g., 0.9990 Gold 321.17 oz. AGW, 180 mm.

Date	Mintage	F	VF	XF	Unc	BU
2008 Proof	18	Value: 500,000				

KM# 1886 100000 YUAN
1000.0000 g., 0.9990 Gold 32.117 oz. AGW, 180 mm. **Subject:** Year of the Ox

Date	Mintage	F	VF	XF	Unc	BU
2009 Proof	118	Value: 70,000				

KM# 1887 100000 YUAN
10000.0000 g., 0.9990 Gold 321.17 oz. AGW, 180 mm.
Subject: Year of the Ox

Date	Mintage	F	VF	XF	Unc	BU
2009 Proof	—	Value: 700,000				

KM# 1911 100000 YUAN
10000.0000 g., 0.9990 Gold 321.17 oz. AGW, 180 mm.
Subject: Year of the Tiger

Date	Mintage	F	VF	XF	Unc	BU
2010 Proof	18	Value: 700,000				

KM# 1960 100000 YUAN
10000.0000 g., 0.9990 Gold 321.17 oz. AGW, 180 mm.
Subject: Year of the Rabbit **Note:** Photo reduced.

Date	Mintage	F	VF	XF	Unc	BU
2011 Proof	18	Value: 700,000				

KM# 2009 100000 YUAN
10000.0000 g., 0.9990 Gold 321.17 oz. AGW, 180 mm.
Subject: Year of the Dragon

Date	Mintage	F	VF	XF	Unc	BU
2012 Proof	—	Value: 700,000				

PALLADIUM BULLION COINAGE
Panda Series

KM# A1531 100 YUAN
15.5590 g., 0.9990 Palladium 0.4997 oz., 14 mm. **Rev:** Panda walking with cub

Date	Mintage	F	VF	XF	Unc	BU
2004 Proof	8,000	Value: 500				

KM# 1590 100 YUAN
15.5500 g., 0.9990 Palladium 0.4994 oz., 30 mm. **Obv:** Temple of Heaven **Rev:** Panda cub and mom seated in bamboo

Date	Mintage	F	VF	XF	Unc	BU
2005 Proof	8,000	Value: 530				

PLATINUM BULLION COINAGE
Panda Series

KM# 1470 50 YUAN
1.5500 g., 0.9995 Platinum 0.0498 oz. APW, 14.03 mm. **Obv:** Temple of Heaven, incuse legend **Rev:** Panda standing facing eating bamboo **Edge:** Reeded

Date	Mintage	F	VF	XF	Unc	BU
2003 Proof	50,000	Value: 135				

KM# 1532 50 YUAN
1.4500 g., 0.9995 Platinum 0.0466 oz. APW, 14 mm. **Obv:** Temple of Heaven, incuse legend **Rev:** Panda standing facing with cub **Edge:** Reeded

Date	Mintage	F	VF	XF	Unc	BU
2004 Proof	50,000	Value: 135				

KM# 1415 100 YUAN
3.1103 g., 0.9995 Platinum 0.0999 oz. APW, 18 mm. **Subject:** Panda Coinage 20th Anniversary **Obv:** Seated panda design of 1982 **Rev:** Walking panda design of 2002 **Edge:** Reeded **Note:** Prev. Y#1115.

Date	Mintage	F	VF	XF	Unc	BU
2002 Proof	20,000	Value: 250				

KM# 1591 100 YUAN
3.1100 g., 0.9990 Platinum 0.0999 oz. APW, 18 mm. **Obv:** Temple of Heaven **Rev:** Panda cub and mom seated in bamboo

Date	Mintage	F	VF	XF	Unc	BU
2005 Proof	30,000	Value: 200				

TAIWAN
REPUBLIC
STANDARD COINAGE

Y# 550 1/2 YUAN
3.0000 g., Bronze, 18 mm. **Obv:** Orchid **Rev:** Value and Chinese symbols **Edge:** Plain

Date	Mintage	F	VF	XF	Unc	BU
90(2001) Proof	—	Value: 10.00				
92(2003)	—	—	0.15	0.30	1.00	1.25
92(2003) Proof	—	Value: 10.00				

Y# 551 YUAN
3.8000 g., Aluminum-Bronze, 20 mm. **Obv:** Bust of Chiang Kai-shek left **Rev:** Chinese value in center, 1 below **Edge:** Reeded

Date	Mintage	F	VF	XF	Unc	BU
90(2001) Proof	—	Value: 12.50				
92(2003)	—	—	0.15	0.30	0.45	
92(2003) Proof	—	Value: 12.50				
94 (2005)	—	—	0.15	0.30	0.45	
95(2006)	—	—	0.15	0.30	0.45	
96(2007)	—	—	0.15	0.30	0.45	
97(2008)	—	—	0.15	0.30	0.45	
98(2009)	—	—	0.15	0.30	0.45	

Date	Mintage	F	VF	XF	Unc	BU
99(2010)	—	—	—	0.15	0.30	0.45
100(2011)	—	—	—	0.15	0.30	0.45

Y# 552 5 YUAN
4.4000 g., Copper-Nickel, 22 mm. **Obv:** Bust of Chiang Kai-shek left **Rev:** Chinese value in center, 5 below **Edge:** Reeded

Date	Mintage	F	VF	XF	Unc	BU
90(2001) Proof	—	Value: 12.50				
92(2003)	—	—	0.15	0.25	0.50	0.75
92(2003) Proof	—	Value: 12.50				

Y# 553 10 YUAN
7.5000 g., Copper-Nickel, 26 mm. **Obv:** Bust of Chiang Kai-shek left **Rev:** Chinese value in center, 10 below **Edge:** Reeded

Date	Mintage	F	VF	XF	Unc	BU
90(2001) Proof	—	Value: 15.00				
92(2003)	—	—	0.25	0.45	0.75	1.00
92(2003) Proof	—	Value: 15.00				
93(2004)	—	—	0.25	0.45	0.75	1.00
94(2005)	—	—	0.25	0.45	0.75	1.00
95(2006)	—	—	0.25	0.45	0.75	1.00
96(2007)	—	—	0.25	0.45	0.75	1.00
96(2007) Proof	—	Value: 15.00				
97(2008)	—	—	0.25	0.45	0.75	1.00
98(2009)	—	—	0.25	0.45	0.75	1.00
99(2010)	—	—	0.25	0.45	0.75	1.00

Y# 567 10 YUAN
7.4300 g., Copper-Nickel, 26 mm. **Subject:** 90th Anniversary of the Republic **Obv:** Bust of Sun Yat-sen facing **Rev:** Holographic design and denomination **Edge:** Reeded

Date	Mintage	F	VF	XF	Unc	BU
90 (2001)	30,000,000	—	—	—	2.50	3.00

Y# 572 10 YUAN
7.5000 g., Copper-Nickel, 26 mm. **Subject:** Chiang Ching-kuo, president **Obv:** Portrait facing **Rev:** Two legends in latent format, large value below

Date	Mintage	F	VF	XF	Unc	BU
2010	—	—	—	—	2.00	3.00

Y# 573 10 YUAN
7.5000 g., Copper-Nickel, 26 mm. **Subject:** Chiang Wei-shui **Obv:** Portrait facing **Rev:** Two legends as latent images, large value below

Date	Mintage	F	VF	XF	Unc	BU
2010	—	—	—	—	2.00	3.00

Y# 574 10 YUAN
7.5000 g., Copper-Nickel, 26 mm. **Subject:** Dr. Sun Yat-sen **Obv:** Bust facing **Rev:** Two legends as latent images, large value below

Date	Mintage	F	VF	XF	Unc	BU
2010	—	—	—	—	2.00	3.00

Y# 565   20 YUAN

8.5000 g., Bi-Metallic Copper-Nickel center in Aluminum-Bronze ring., 26.85 mm. **Subject:** Mona Rudao, Sediq chieftain **Obv:** Male portrait **Rev:** Three boats **Edge:** Reeded

Date	Mintage	F	VF	XF	Unc	BU
90(2001)	—	—	—	—	3.50	4.50
90(2001) Proof	—	Value: 18.00				
92(2003)	—	—	—	—	3.50	4.50
92(2003) Proof	—	Value: 18.00				

Y# 568   50 YUAN

10.0000 g., Aluminum-Bronze, 28 mm. **Obv:** Bust **Rev:** Denomination above latent image denomination **Edge:** Reeding and denomination

Date	Mintage	F	VF	XF	Unc	BU
90-2001 Proof	—	Value: 20.00				
91-2002	—	—	—	—	7.50	10.00
92-2003	—	—	—	—	7.50	10.00
92-2003 Proof	—	Value: 20.00				
93-2004	—	—	—	—	7.50	10.00
94-2005	—	—	—	—	7.50	10.00
95-2006	—	—	—	—	7.50	10.00

Y# 570   50 YUAN

15.5680 g., 0.9990 Silver 0.5000 oz. ASW, 33 mm. **Subject:** World Cup Baseball **Obv:** Player at bat with ball background **Rev:** Mount Jade above denomination **Edge:** Reeded

Date	Mintage	F	VF	XF	Unc	BU
90(2001)	130,000	—	—	—	25.00	27.50

Y# 569   50 YUAN

15.5680 g., 0.9990 Silver 0.5000 oz. ASW, 33 mm. **Subject:** 90th Anniversary of the Republic **Obv:** Portrait of Sun Yat-sen **Rev:** Latent image above denomination **Edge:** Reeded

Date	Mintage	F	VF	XF	Unc	BU
90(2001)	230,000	—	—	—	25.00	27.50

Y# 571   50 YUAN

31.1035 g., 0.9990 Silver 0.9990 oz. ASW, 38 mm. **Subject:** Third National Expressway **Obv:** Multicolor island map **Rev:** Kao Ping Hsi bridge **Edge:** Reeded

Date	Mintage	F	VF	XF	Unc	BU
93-2004	20,000	—	—	—	45.00	50.00

MINT SETS

KM#	Date	Mintage Identification	Issue Price	Mkt Val
MS9	92(2003) (6)	— Y550-553, 565, 568 plus C-N Year of the Goat medal	—	20.00

PROOF SETS

KM#	Date	Mintage Identification	Issue Price	Mkt Val
PS10	90(2001) (6)	210,000 Y#550-553, 565, 568 plus medal	29.40	90.00
PS12	92(2003) (6)	— Y550-553, 565, 568 plus silver Year of the Goat Medal	—	100

COLOMBIA

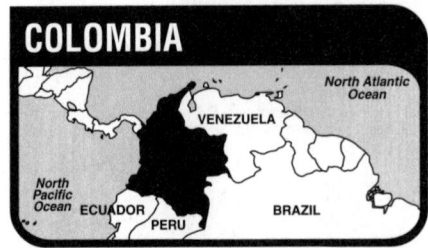

The Republic of Colombia, in the northwestern corner of South America, has an area of 440,831 sq. mi. (1,138,910 sq. km.) and a population of *42.3 million. Capital: Bogota. The economy is primarily agricultural with a mild, rich coffee being the chief crop. Colombia has the world's largest platinum deposits and important reserves of coal, iron ore, petroleum and limestone; other precious metals and emeralds are also mined. Coffee, crude oil, bananas, sugar and emeralds are exported.

MINT MARKS
A, M – Medellin (capital), Antioquia (state)
B - BOGOTA
(D) Denver, USA
H – Birmingham (Heaton & Sons)
(m) - Medellin, w/o mint mark
(Mo) - Mexico City
NI - Numismatica Italiana, Arezzo, Italy
    mint marks stylized in wreath
(P) - Philadelphia
(S) - San Francisco, USA.
(W) - Waterbury, CT (USA, Scoville mint)

REPUBLIC

DECIMAL COINAGE
100 Centavos = 1 Peso

KM# 282.2   20 PESOS
3.6000 g., Aluminum-Bronze, 20.25 mm. **Obv:** Flagged arms, 68 beads circle around the rim **Rev:** Denomination within wreath

Date	Mintage	F	VF	XF	Unc	BU
2003	15,900,000	—	—	—	0.50	0.75

KM# 294   20 PESOS
2.0000 g., Brass, 17.2 mm. **Obv:** Head of Simon Bolivar left **Rev:** Value **Edge:** Reeded

Date	Mintage	F	VF	XF	Unc	BU
2004	22,700,000	—	—	—	0.15	0.25
2005	56,100,000	—	—	—	0.15	0.25
2006	63,012,500	—	—	—	0.15	0.25
2007	87,300,000	—	—	—	0.15	0.25
2008	5,850,000	—	—	—	0.20	0.30

KM# 283.2   50 PESOS
4.6000 g., Copper-Nickel-Zinc, 21.8 mm. **Obv:** National arms, date below **Rev:** Denomination within wreath, 72 beads circle around rim **Edge:** Reeded

Date	Mintage	F	VF	XF	Unc	BU
2003	59,842,620	—	—	0.30	0.80	1.20
2004	51,700,000	—	—	0.30	0.80	1.20
2005	47,200,000	—	—	0.30	0.80	1.20
2006	22,000,000	—	—	0.30	0.80	1.20
2007	29,324,000	—	—	0.30	0.80	1.20
2008	67,500,000	—	—	0.30	0.80	1.20
2009	3,000,000	—	—	0.40	1.00	1.25
2010	55,100,000	—	—	0.25	0.75	1.00
2011	—	—	—	0.25	0.75	1.00

KM# 283.2a   50 PESOS
Stainless Steel, 21.8 mm. **Obv:** National Arms **Rev:** Denomination within wreath, 72 beads circle around rim **Edge:** Reeded

Date	Mintage	F	VF	XF	Unc	BU
2007	—	—	—	—	0.80	1.20
2008	—	—	—	—	0.80	1.20
2009	—	—	—	—	0.80	1.20
2010	—	—	—	—	0.80	1.20

KM# 285.2   100 PESOS
5.3100 g., Aluminum-Bronze, 23 mm. **Obv:** Flagged arms above date **Rev:** Denomination within wreath, numerals 6mm tall **Edge:** Segmented reeding and lettered **Edge Lettering:** CIEN PESOS (twice) **Note:** Edge varieties exist.

Date	Mintage	F	VF	XF	Unc	BU
2006	59,000,000	—	—	0.60	1.50	2.00
2007	55,000,000	—	—	0.60	1.50	2.00

Date	Mintage	F	VF	XF	Unc	BU
2008	120,200,000	—	—	0.60	1.50	2.00
2009	41,800,000	—	—	0.60	1.50	2.00
2010	85,400,000	—	—	0.50	1.25	1.50
2011	—	—	—	0.50	1.25	1.50

KM# 287   200 PESOS
7.0800 g., Copper-Nickel-Zinc, 24.4 mm. **Obv:** Denomination within lined circle, date below **Rev:** Quimbaya artwork **Edge Lettering:** MOTIVO QUIMBAYA - 200 PESOS

Date	Mintage	F	VF	XF	Unc	BU
2003	26,600,000	—	—	0.60	1.50	2.00
2004	31,200,000	—	—	0.60	1.50	2.00
2005	49,700,000	—	—	0.60	1.50	2.00
2006	75,462,500	—	—	0.60	1.50	2.00
2007	85,000,000	—	—	0.60	1.50	2.00
2008	110,400,000	—	—	0.60	1.50	2.00
2009	42,200,000	—	—	0.60	1.50	2.00
2010	85,600,000	—	—	0.60	1.50	2.00
2011	—	—	—	0.60	1.50	2.00

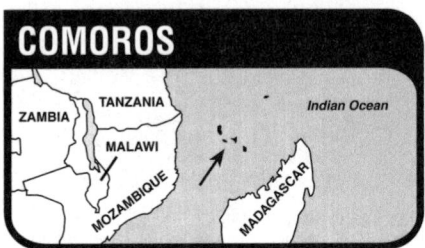

KM# 286   500 PESOS
7.1400 g., Bi-Metallic Aluminum-Bronze center in Copper-Zinc-Nickel ring, 23.7 mm. **Obv:** Guacari tree within circle **Rev:** Denomination within circle, date below **Edge:** Segmented reeding

Date	Mintage	F	VF	XF	Unc	BU
2002	38,800,000	—	—	1.20	3.00	4.00
2003	26,410,000	—	—	1.20	3.00	4.00
2004	90,454,000	—	—	1.20	3.00	4.00
2005	97,664,000	—	—	1.20	3.00	4.00
2006	70,700,000	—	—	1.20	3.00	4.00
2007	109,624,000	—	—	1.20	3.00	4.00
2008	132,400,000	—	—	1.20	3.00	4.00
2009	39,700,000	—	—	1.20	3.00	4.00
2010	35,800,000	—	—	1.00	2.00	3.00
2011	—	—	—	1.00	2.00	3.00

COMOROS

The Federal Islamic Republic of the Comoros, a volcanic archipelago located in the Mozambique Channel of the Indian Ocean 300 miles (483 km.) northwest of Madagascar, has an area of 719 sq. mi. (2,171 sq. km.) and a population of *714,000. Capital: Moroni. The economy of the islands is based on agriculture. There are practically no mineral resources. Vanilla, essence or perfumes, copra, and sisal are exported.

Ancient Phoenician traders were probably the first visitors to the Comoro Islands, but the first detailed knowledge of the area was gathered by Arab sailors. Arab dominion and culture were firmly established when the Portuguese, Dutch, and French arrived in the 16th century. In 1843 a Malagasy ruler ceded the island of Mayotte to France; the other three principal islands of the archipelago-Anjouan, Moheli, and Grand Comore came under French protection in 1886. The islands were joined administratively with Madagascar in 1912. The Comoros became partially autonomous, with the status of a French overseas territory, in 1946, and achieved complete internal autonomy in 1961. On Dec. 31, 1975, after 133 years of French association, the Comoro Islands became the independent Republic of the Comoros.

Mayotte retained the option of determining its future ties and in 1976 voted to remain French. Its present status is that of a French Territorial Collectivity. French currency now circulates there.

MINT MARKS
(a) - Paris, privy marks only
A - Paris

MONETARY SYSTEM
100 Centimes = 1 Franc

FEDERAL ISLAMIC REPUBLIC

BANQUE CENTRAL COINAGE

KM# 19   10 FRANCS
2.4000 g., Steel, 17 mm. **Obv:** Crescent and four stars **Rev:** Value

Date	Mintage	F	VF	XF	Unc	BU
2001(a)	—	—	—	—	7.50	15.00

KM# 14a   25 FRANCS
3.9700 g., Steel, 20 mm. **Series:** F.A.O. **Obv:** Chickens **Rev:** Denomination above date

Date	Mintage	F	VF	XF	Unc	BU
2001(a) Horseshoe	—	0.20	0.40	0.80	2.00	—

KM# 16   50 FRANCS
5.6000 g., Nickel, 23.93 mm. **Obv:** Crescent and stars above denomination, date below **Rev:** Building with tall tower **Edge:** Reeded

Date	Mintage	F	VF	XF	Unc	BU
2001(a) horseshoe	—	—	—	—	2.50	3.50

KM# 16a   50 FRANCS
Nickel Plated Steel, 23.9 mm. **Obv:** Crescent and stars above denomination, date below **Rev:** Building with tall tower **Edge:** Reeded

Date	Mintage	F	VF	XF	Unc	BU
2001(a)	—	0.25	0.50	1.00	2.50	3.50

KM# 18a   100 FRANCS
10.2000 g., Copper-Nickel, 28 mm. **Obv:** Crescent and stars above denomination, date below **Rev:** Boat and fish

Date	Mintage	F	VF	XF	Unc	BU
2003(a)	—	—	—	—	3.50	5.00

KM# 20   1000 FRANCS
22.2000 g., 0.9000 Silver 0.6423 oz. ASW, 37 mm. **Obv:** Crescent and four stars **Rev:** Mosque of the Sultans

Date	Mintage	F	VF	XF	Unc	BU
2002 Proof	500	Value: 150				

CONGO REPUBLIC

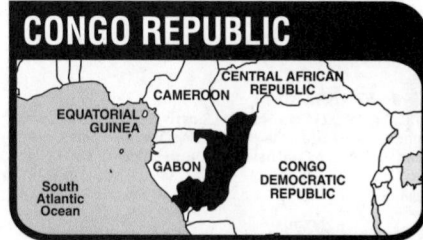

The Republic of the Congo (formerly the Peoples Republic of the Congo), located on the equator in west-central Africa, has an area of 132,047 sq. mi. (342,000 sq. km.) and a population of *2.98 million. Capital: Brazzaville. Agriculture forestry, mining, and food processing are the principal industries. Timber, industrial diamonds, potash, peanuts, and cocoa beans are exported.

NOTE: For earlier and related coinage see French Equatorial Africa and the Equatorial African States. For later coinage see Central African States.

RULER
French until 1960
MINT MARK
(a) - Paris, privy marks only
MONETARY SYSTEM
100 Centimes = 1 Franc

REPUBLIC

Republique du Congo

DECIMAL COINAGE

KM# 110   500 FRANCS
Silver **Subject:** History of aviation **Rev:** Swiss Air jet over mountains, 1931-2001, in color

Date	Mintage	F	VF	XF	Unc	BU
2002 Proof	—	Value: 40.00				

KM# 47   1000 FRANCS
15.0000 g., 0.9990 Silver 0.4818 oz. ASW, 35 mm. **Obv:** Seated woman with tablet **Rev:** Two soccer players and colosseum **Edge:** Plain

Date	Mintage	F	VF	XF	Unc	BU
2001 Proof	—	Value: 40.00				

KM# 48   1000 FRANCS
20.0000 g., 0.9990 Silver 0.6423 oz. ASW, 38 mm. **Obv:** Seated woman with tablet **Rev:** Two soccer players and Mexican pyramid **Edge:** Reeded

Date	Mintage	F	VF	XF	Unc	BU
2001 Proof	—	Value: 45.00				

KM# 112   1000 FRANCS
Silver, 38 mm. **Subject:** Thomas W. Lawson **Obv:** Female holding tablets **Rev:** Seven-masted Great Lakes Sconner sailing right

Date	Mintage	F	VF	XF	Unc	BU
2001 Proof	—	Value: 40.00				

KM# 113   1000 FRANCS
Silver, 38 mm. **Obv:** Female with tablets **Rev:** Hohenzollern castle

Date	Mintage	F	VF	XF	Unc	BU
2002 Proof	—	Value: 40.00				

KM# 114   1000 FRANCS
Silver, 38 mm. **Obv:** Female seated with tablets **Rev:** Nymphenburg palace

Date	Mintage	F	VF	XF	Unc	BU
2002 Proof	—	Value: 40.00				

KM# 109   1000 FRANCS
20.0000 g., 0.9990 Silver 0.6423 oz. ASW, 38.6 mm. **Obv:** Seated woman with tablets **Rev:** Portuguese merchant ship

Date	Mintage	F	VF	XF	Unc	BU
2002 Proof	—	Value: 45.00				

KM# 67   1000 FRANCS
31.1050 g., 0.9990 Silver 0.9990 oz. ASW, 40 mm. **Rev:** Eifle tower and franc coin in color

Date	Mintage	F	VF	XF	Unc	BU
2002 Proof	Est. 2,001	Value: 90.00				

KM# 68   1000 FRANCS
Silver **Subject:** African Wildlife **Shape:** Rectangle

Date	Mintage	F	VF	XF	Unc	BU
2002 Proof						

KM# 50   1000 FRANCS
20.2000 g., Silver, 40 mm. **Series:** Endangered Wildlife **Obv:** Seated woman with tablet **Obv. Legend:** REPUBLIQUE DU CONGO **Rev:** Gorilla seated with infant **Rev. Legend:** - LE MONDE ANIMAL EN PERIL **Edge:** Reeded

Date	Mintage	F	VF	XF	Unc	BU
2003 Proof	—	Value: 50.00				

KM# 108   1000 FRANCS
20.0000 g., 0.9990 Silver 0.6423 oz. ASW, 38.6 mm. **Obv:** Seated woman with two tablets **Rev:** James Cook and the Endeavour

Date	Mintage	F	VF	XF	Unc	BU
2003 Proof	—	Value: 45.00				

KM# 111   1000 FRANCS
Silver, 38 mm. **Subject:** Konrad Duden **Obv:** Female holding tablets **Rev:** Bust facing, writing

Date	Mintage	F	VF	XF	Unc	BU
2004 Proof	—	Value: 40.00				

KM# 51   1000 FRANCS
15.5000 g., Silver, 35.02 mm. **Obv:** Seated woman with tablet **Obv. Legend:** REPUBLIQUE DU CONGO **Rev:** Head of Michelangelo 3/4 right **Edge:** Plain

Date	Mintage	F	VF	XF	Unc	BU
2005 Proof	—	Value: 37.50				

KM# 72   1000 FRANCS
0.9990 Silver **Obv:** National Arms **Rev:** Steam locomotive Limmat and Spanish Bon trasport (1847) from Baden to Zurich

Date	Mintage	F	VF	XF	Unc	BU
2007 Proof	—	Value: 75.00				

KM# 69   1500 FRANCS
1.2400 g., 0.9990 Gold 0.0398 oz. AGW, 13.92 mm. **Rev:** Ferdinand Graf von Zeppelin

Date	Mintage	F	VF	XF	Unc	BU
2005 Proof	—	Value: 100				

KM# 70   1500 FRANCS
1.2400 g., 0.9990 Gold 0.0398 oz. AGW, 13.92 mm. **Rev:** Spinx and Pyramids

Date	Mintage	F	VF	XF	Unc	BU
2005 Proof	—	Value: 100				

KM# 71   1500 FRANCS
1.2400 g., 0.9990 Gold 0.0398 oz. AGW, 13.94 mm. **Rev:** Neuschwanstein castle

Date	Mintage	F	VF	XF	Unc	BU
2005 Proof	—	Value: 100				

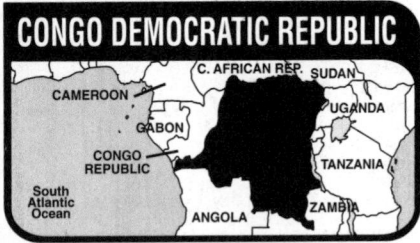

CONGO DEMOCRATIC REPUBLIC

The Democratic Republic of the Congo (formerly the Republic of Zaire, and earlier the Belgian Congo), located in the south-central part of Africa, has an area of 905,568 sq. mi. (2,345,410 sq. km.) and a population of *47.4 million. Capital: Kinshasa. The mineral-rich country produces copper, tin, diamonds, gold, zinc, cobalt and uranium.

DEMOCRATIC REPUBLIC
1998 -

REFORM COINAGE
Congo Francs; July 1998

KM# 76   25 CENTIMES
0.8800 g., Aluminum, 19.90 mm. **Obv:** Lion left **Rev:** Mongoose **Edge:** Plain

Date	Mintage	F	VF	XF	Unc	BU
2002	—	—	—	—	0.75	1.00

KM# 77   25 CENTIMES
0.8500 g., Aluminum, 20 mm. **Obv:** Lion left **Rev:** Ram right, looking left **Edge:** Plain

Date	Mintage	F	VF	XF	Unc	BU
2002	—	—	—	—	0.75	1.00

KM# 83   25 CENTIMES
1.3000 g., Aluminum, 20 mm. **Obv:** Lion left **Rev:** Wild leaping dog right **Edge:** Plain

Date	Mintage	F	VF	XF	Unc	BU
2002	—	—	—	—	0.75	1.00

KM# 75   50 CENTIMES
2.2000 g., Aluminum, 26.97 mm. **Obv:** Lion left **Rev:** Soccer player right, bumping ball with head **Edge:** Plain

Date	Mintage	F	VF	XF	Unc	BU
2002	—	—	—	—	1.25	1.50

KM# 78   50 CENTIMES
2.1600 g., Aluminum, 27 mm. **Obv:** Lion left **Rev:** Giraffe right, looking left **Edge:** Plain

Date	Mintage	F	VF	XF	Unc	BU
2002	—	—	—	—	1.25	1.50

KM# 79   50 CENTIMES
2.2000 g., Aluminum, 26.92 mm. **Obv:** Lion left **Rev:** Gorilla facing, looking left **Edge:** Plain

Date	Mintage	F	VF	XF	Unc	BU
2002	—	—	—	—	1.00	1.25

KM# 80   50 CENTIMES
2.1600 g., Aluminum, 27 mm. **Obv:** Lion left **Rev:** Butterfly **Edge:** Plain

Date	Mintage	F	VF	XF	Unc	BU
2002	—	—	—	—	1.50	1.75

KM# 123   50 CENTIMES
3.9200 g., Stainless Steel, 22.3 mm. **Obv:** Lion left above denomination **Rev:** Verney L. Camereon **Edge:** Plain

Date	Mintage	F	VF	XF	Unc	BU
2002	—	—	—	—	1.00	1.25

KM# 81   FRANC
4.5700 g., Brass, 20.31 mm. **Obv:** Lion left **Rev:** Turtle **Edge:** Plain

Date	Mintage	F	VF	XF	Unc	BU
2002	—	—	—	—	1.25	1.50

KM# 82   FRANC
4.5200 g., Brass, 20.32 mm. **Obv:** Lion left **Rev:** Chicken **Edge:** Plain

Date	Mintage	F	VF	XF	Unc	BU
2002	—	—	—	—	1.50	1.75

KM# 156   FRANC
5.0000 g., Nickel Clad Steel, 24.8 mm. **Subject:** 25th Anniversary - Pope John Paul II's Visit **Obv:** Lion left **Rev:** Pope John Paul II as a priest in 1946 **Edge:** Plain

Date	Mintage	F	VF	XF	Unc	BU
2004	—	—	—	—	2.00	2.50

KM# 157   FRANC
5.0000 g., Nickel Clad Steel, 24.8 mm. **Subject:** 25th Anniversary - Pope John Paul II's Visit **Obv:** Lion left **Rev:** Pope John Paul II as a Cardinal in 1967 **Edge:** Plain

Date	Mintage	F	VF	XF	Unc	BU
2004	—	—	—	—	2.00	2.50

KM# 158   FRANC
5.0000 g., Nickel Clad Steel, 24.8 mm. **Subject:** 25th Anniversary - Pope John Paul II's Visit **Obv:** Lion left **Rev:** Pope John Paul II as newly elected pope in 1978 **Edge:** Plain

Date	Mintage	F	VF	XF	Unc	BU
2004	—	—	—	—	2.00	2.50

KM# 159 FRANC

5.0000 g., Nickel Clad Steel, 24.8 mm. **Subject:** 25th Anniversary - Pope John Paul II's Visit **Obv:** Lion left **Rev:** Pope John Paul II wearing a mitre **Edge:** Plain

Date	Mintage	F	VF	XF	Unc	BU
2004	—	—	—	—	2.00	2.50

KM# 174 FRANC

6.0000 g., Copper-Nickel, 21 mm. **Obv:** Lion left **Rev:** African Golden Cat right **Edge:** Plain

Date	Mintage	F	VF	XF	Unc	BU
2004	5,000	—	—	—	7.25	9.00

KM# 174a FRANC

8.0000 g., 0.9990 Silver 0.2569 oz. ASW, 21 mm. **Obv:** Lion left **Rev:** African Golden Cat right **Edge:** Plain

Date	Mintage	F	VF	XF	Unc	BU
2004	25	—	—	—	270	300

KM# 56 5 FRANCS

22.4000 g., Copper-Nickel, 39.8 mm. **Series:** Wild Life Protection **Obv:** Lion left **Rev:** Multicolor swallowtail butterfly hologram **Edge:** Reeded **Note:** Prev. KM#79.

Date	Mintage	F	VF	XF	Unc	BU
2002(2001)	20,000	—	—	—	35.00	40.00

KM# 57 5 FRANCS

22.4000 g., Copper-Nickel, 39.8 mm. **Series:** Wild Life Protection **Obv:** Lion left **Rev:** Multicolor dark greenish butterfly hologram **Edge:** Reeded **Note:** Prev. KM#80.

Date	Mintage	F	VF	XF	Unc	BU
2002(2001)	20,000	—	—	—	35.00	40.00

KM# 58 5 FRANCS

22.4000 g., Copper-Nickel, 39.8 mm. **Series:** Wild Life Protection **Obv:** Lion left **Rev:** Multicolor red and black butterfly hologram **Edge:** Reeded **Note:** Prev. KM#81.

Date	Mintage	F	VF	XF	Unc	BU
2002(2001)	20,000	—	—	—	35.00	40.00

KM# 170 5 FRANCS

24.3000 g., Copper-Nickel, 38.5 mm. **Obv:** Lion left **Rev:** Multicolor German 1 mark coin dated 2001 **Edge:** Reeded

Date	Mintage	F	VF	XF	Unc	BU
2002	—	—	—	—	15.00	20.00

KM# 198 5 FRANCS

Copper-Nickel, 38.6 mm. **Obv:** Lion left **Rev:** Cameleon on branch in color

Date	Mintage	F	VF	XF	Unc	BU
2003	—	—	—	—	—	25.00

KM# 128 5 FRANCS

8.0000 g., Iron, 27.26x14.13 mm. **Obv:** Country name, lion and date in the bowl part of the spoon; value on the handle part **Edge:** Reeded **Note:** This is the Spoon part of the Compass and Spoon set. See also KM#127 (The spoon is the compass needle.)

Date	Mintage	F	VF	XF	Unc	BU
2004	5,000	—	—	—	15.00	—

KM# 146 5 FRANCS

27.0000 g., Copper-Nickel, 38.6 mm. **Obv:** Lion left **Rev:** Multicolor Quetzal bird **Edge:** Reeded

Date	Mintage	F	VF	XF	Unc	BU
2004 Proof	5,000	Value: 45.00				

KM# 147 5 FRANCS

27.0000 g., Copper-Nickel, 38.6 mm. **Obv:** Lion left **Rev:** Multicolor Bird of Paradise **Edge:** Reeded

Date	Mintage	F	VF	XF	Unc	BU
2004 Proof	5,000	Value: 45.00				

KM# 148 5 FRANCS

27.0000 g., Copper-Nickel, 38.6 mm. **Obv:** Lion left **Rev:** Multicolor Kingfisher bird **Edge:** Reeded

Date	Mintage	F	VF	XF	Unc	BU
2004 Proof	5,000	Value: 45.00				

KM# 164 5 FRANCS

25.4000 g., Copper-Nickel, 38.8 mm. **Subject:** Papal Visit **Obv:** Lion left **Rev:** Pope John Paul II with staff and mitre **Edge:** Reeded

Date	Mintage	F	VF	XF	Unc	BU
ND (2004) Proof	—	Value: 25.00				

KM# 165 5 FRANCS

49.5000 g., Copper-Nickel, 45.1 mm. **Obv:** Lion left **Rev:** Rotating 50 year calender **Edge:** Reeded

Date	Mintage	F	VF	XF	Unc	BU
ND(2004) Matte	—	—	—	—	75.00	—

KM# 166 5 FRANCS

2.1600 g., Wood Maple wood, 39.4 mm. **Obv:** Lion, brown ink **Rev:** Gorilla, brown ink **Edge:** Plain

Date	Mintage	F	VF	XF	Unc	BU
2005	2,000	—	—	—	21.00	—

KM# 181 5 FRANCS

25.9200 g., Copper-Nickel, 38.58 mm. **Series:** Wildlife Protection **Obv:** Lion standing laft **Obv. Legend:** REPUBLIQUE DENOCRATIQUE DU CONGO **Rev:** Red Perch, multicolor **Edge:** Reeded

Date	Mintage	F	VF	XF	Unc	BU
2005	5,000	—	—	—	—	20.00

KM# 182 5 FRANCS

Copper-Nickel Gilt **Obv:** Lion standing left **Rev:** Two cupids embracing, roses - multicolor **Rev. Legend:** *Endless Love* **Edge:** Reeded **Shape:** Heart

Date	Mintage	F	VF	XF	Unc	BU
2005 Proof	5,000	Value: 35.00				

KM# 179 5 FRANCS

25.9200 g., Copper-Nickel, 38.58 mm. **Series:** Wildlife Protection **Obv:** Lion standing left **Obv. Legend:** REPUBLIQUE DEMOCRATIQUE DU CONGO **Rev:** Butterfly Fish, multicolor **Edge:** Reeded

Date	Mintage	F	VF	XF	Unc	BU
2005	5,000	—	—	—	—	26.00

KM# 180 5 FRANCS

25.9200 g., Copper-Nickel, 38.58 mm. **Series:** Wildlife Protection **Obv:** Lion standing left **Obv. Legend:** REPUBLIQUE DEMOCRATIQYE DU CONGO **Rev:** African Moony Fish, multicolor **Edge:** Reeded

Date	Mintage	F	VF	XF	Unc	BU
2005	5,000	—	—	—	—	26.00

KM# 178 5 FRANCS

26.3000 g., Silver Plated Bronze, 38.6 mm. **Obv:** Lion **Rev:** Multicolor Pope John Paul II wearing a mitre **Edge:** Reeded

Date	Mintage	F	VF	XF	Unc	BU
2007 Proof	—	Value: 40.00				

KM# 72   10 FRANCS
20.0000 g., 0.9250 Silver 0.5948 oz. ASW, 40.1 mm. **Series:**
Airplanes **Obv:** Lion left **Rev:** Mikoyan-Gurevich Mig 21 fighter
flying left **Edge:** Reeded

Date	Mintage	F	VF	XF	Unc	BU
2001 Proof	—				Value: 40.00	

KM# 74   10 FRANCS
31.1035 g., 0.9990 Silver 0.9990 oz. ASW, 40 mm. **Subject:**
2004 Olympics **Obv:** Lion left **Rev:** Convex chariot **Edge:** Reeded

Date	Mintage	F	VF	XF	Unc	BU
2001 Antique Finish	15,000	—	—	—	45.00	—

KM# 167   10 FRANCS
20.0000 g., 0.9250 Silver 0.5948 oz. ASW, 40.1 mm. **Obv:** Lion
left **Rev:** SS Bremen ship at sea **Edge:** Reeded

Date	Mintage	F	VF	XF	Unc	BU
2001 Proof	—				Value: 35.00	

KM# 168   10 FRANCS
20.0000 g., 0.9250 Silver 0.5948 oz. ASW, 40.1 mm. **Obv:** Lion
left **Rev:** RMS Queen Elizabeth 2 at sea **Edge:** Reeded

Date	Mintage	F	VF	XF	Unc	BU
2001 Proof	—				Value: 35.00	

KM# 169   10 FRANCS
20.0000 g., 0.9250 Silver 0.5948 oz. ASW, 30 mm. **Obv:** Lion
left **Rev:** Sail Ship America **Edge:** Reeded

Date	Mintage	F	VF	XF	Unc	BU
2001 Proof	—				Value: 35.00	

KM# 197   10 FRANCS
20.0000 g., 0.5948 Silver 0.3824 oz. ASW, 40.1 mm. **Obv:** Lion
left **Rev:** SS Andrea Doria sailing left

Date	Mintage	F	VF	XF	Unc	BU
2001 Proof	—				Value: 45.00	

KM# 199   10 FRANCS
Silver, 40.1 mm. **Obv:** Lion left **Rev:** M.S. Voyager of the Seas
sailing left

Date	Mintage	F	VF	XF	Unc	BU
2001 Proof	—				Value: 45.00	

KM# 175   10 FRANCS
25.8300 g., Silver, 40 mm. **Obv:** Lion left **Rev:** 3 players **Edge:**
Reeded

Date	Mintage	F	VF	XF	Unc	BU
2001	—	—	—	—	—	50.00

KM# 38   10 FRANCS
31.3000 g., 0.9250 Silver 0.9308 oz. ASW, 27 x 47.1 mm.
Subject: Illusion **Obv:** Lion left **Rev:** Multicolor couple in flower
picture **Edge:** Plain **Shape:** Rectangular **Note:** Prev. KM#61.

Date	Mintage	F	VF	XF	Unc	BU
2001 Proof	—				Value: 50.00	

KM# 59   10 FRANCS
25.9500 g., 0.9250 Silver 0.7717 oz. ASW, 39.9 mm. **Series:**
Wild Life Protection **Obv:** Lion left **Rev:** Multicolor swallowtail
butterfly hologram **Edge:** Reeded **Note:** Prev. KM#82.

Date	Mintage	F	VF	XF	Unc	BU
2002 (2001) Proof	15,000				Value: 65.00	

KM# 60   10 FRANCS
25.9500 g., 0.9250 Silver 0.7717 oz. ASW, 39.9 mm. **Series:**
Wild Life Protection **Obv:** Lion left **Rev:** Multicolor dark greenish
butterfly hologram **Edge:** Reeded **Note:** Prev. KM#83.

Date	Mintage	F	VF	XF	Unc	BU
2002 (2001) Proof	15,000				Value: 65.00	

KM# 61   10 FRANCS
25.9500 g., 0.9250 Silver 0.7717 oz. ASW, 39.9 mm. **Series:**
Wild Life Protection **Obv:** Lion left **Rev:** Multicolor red and black
butterfly hologram **Edge:** Reeded **Note:** Prev. KM#84.

Date	Mintage	F	VF	XF	Unc	BU
2002 (2001) Proof	15,000				Value: 65.00	

KM# 65   10 FRANCS
20.0000 g., 0.9250 Silver 0.5948 oz. ASW, 40.1 mm.   **Series:**
Airplanes **Obv:** Lion left **Rev:** Vickers Vimy twin engine biplane
flying left **Edge:** Reeded **Note:** Prev. KM#88.

Date	Mintage	F	VF	XF	Unc	BU
2001 Proof	—	Value: 40.00				

KM# 66   10 FRANCS
20.0000 g., 0.9250 Silver 0.5948 oz. ASW, 40.1 mm.   **Series:**
Airplanes **Obv:** Lion left **Rev:** Fokker DR1 triplane flying left **Edge:**
Reeded **Note:** Prev. KM#89.

Date	Mintage	F	VF	XF	Unc	BU
2001 Proof	—	Value: 40.00				

KM# 67   10 FRANCS
20.0000 g., 0.9250 Silver 0.5948 oz. ASW, 40.1 mm.   **Series:**
Airplanes **Obv:** Lion left **Rev:** Lockheed Vega flying left **Edge:**
Reeded **Note:** Prev. KM#90.

Date	Mintage	F	VF	XF	Unc	BU
2001 Proof	—	Value: 40.00				

KM# 68   10 FRANCS
20.0000 g., 0.9250 Silver 0.5948 oz. ASW, 40.1 mm.   **Series:**
Airplanes **Obv:** Lion left **Rev:** Boeing 314 Clipper flying left **Edge:**
Reeded **Note:** Prev. KM#91.

Date	Mintage	F	VF	XF	Unc	BU
2001 Proof	—	Value: 40.00				

KM# 69   10 FRANCS
20.0000 g., 0.9250 Silver 0.5948 oz. ASW, 40.1 mm.   **Series:**
Airplanes **Obv:** Lion left **Rev:** Junkers JU-87 Stuka in a dive
Edge: Reeded **Note:** Prev. KM#92.

Date	Mintage	F	VF	XF	Unc	BU
2001 Proof	—	Value: 40.00				

KM# 70   10 FRANCS
20.0000 g., 0.9250 Silver 0.5948 oz. ASW, 40.1 mm.   **Series:**
Airplanes **Obv:** Lion left **Rev:** B-29 Enola Gay flying left **Edge:**
Reeded **Note:** Prev. KM#93.

Date	Mintage	F	VF	XF	Unc	BU
2001 Proof	—	Value: 45.00				

KM# 71   10 FRANCS
20.0000 g., 0.9250 Silver 0.5948 oz. ASW, 40.1 mm.   **Series:**
Airplanes **Obv:** Lion left **Rev:** Bell X-1 rocket plane flying left
Edge: Reeded **Note:** Prev. KM#94.

Date	Mintage	F	VF	XF	Unc	BU
2001 Proof	—	Value: 40.00				

KM# 91   10 FRANCS
31.1000 g., 0.9990 Silver 0.9988 oz. ASW, 40 mm.   **Subject:**
Olympics **Obv:** Lion left **Rev:** Ancient athlete incuse design **Edge:**
Plain **Note:** Design hubs with the design of the 500 sika coin KM-
42 of Ghana

Date	Mintage	F	VF	XF	Unc	BU
2002 Antiqued finish	—	—	—	—	40.00	—

KM# 124   10 FRANCS
26.0000 g., 0.9250 Silver 0.7732 oz. ASW, 40 mm.   **Subject:**
Field Marshal Erwin Rommel **Obv:** Lion left above value **Rev:**
Rommel, tank and map **Edge:** Reeded

Date	Mintage	F	VF	XF	Unc	BU
2002 Proof	15,000	Value: 42.50				

KM# 125   10 FRANCS
26.0000 g., 0.9250 Silver 0.7732 oz. ASW, 40 mm.   **Subject:**
George S. Patton **Obv:** Lion left above value **Rev:** Patton, tank
and map **Edge:** Reeded

Date	Mintage	F	VF	XF	Unc	BU
2002 Proof	15,000	Value: 42.50				

KM# 162   10 FRANCS
20.2000 g., 0.9990 Silver 0.6488 oz. ASW, 40 mm.   **Obv:** Lion
left **Rev:** Space shuttle and five astronauts **Edge:** Reeded

Date	Mintage	F	VF	XF	Unc	BU
2002 Proof	—	Value: 40.00				

KM# 189   10 FRANCS
26.1500 g., Copper-Nickel, 40.3 mm.   **Series:** Automobiles **Obv:**
Lion standing left **Rev:** Rolls Royce **Edge:** Reeded

Date	Mintage	F	VF	XF	Unc	BU
2002 Proof	—	Value: 18.00				

KM# 190   10 FRANCS
26.1500 g., Copper-Nickel, 40.3 mm.   **Series:** Automobiles **Obv:**
Lion standing left **Rev:** Peujeot

Date	Mintage	F	VF	XF	Unc	BU
2002 Proof	—	Value: 18.00				

KM# 191   10 FRANCS
26.1500 g., Copper-Nickel, 40.3 mm.   **Series:** Automobiles **Obv:**
Lion standing left **Rev:** Opel **Edge:** Reeded

Date	Mintage	F	VF	XF	Unc	BU
2002 Proof	—	Value: 18.00				

KM# 192   10 FRANCS
26.1500 g., Copper-Nickel, 40.3 mm.   **Series:** Automobiles **Obv:**
Lion standing left **Rev:** Cadillac

Date	Mintage	F	VF	XF	Unc	BU
2002 Proof	—	Value: 18.00				

KM# 93   10 FRANCS
31.2300 g., 0.9990 Silver 1.0030 oz. ASW, 38.7 mm. **Obv:** Lion
left **Rev:** Bearded portrait of Verney L. Camereon **Edge:** Reeded

Date	Mintage	F	VF	XF	Unc	BU
2002	—			—	45.00	50.00

KM# 94   10 FRANCS
26.1500 g., Copper-Nickel, 40.3 mm. **Subject:** Historic
Automobiles **Obv:** Lion left **Rev:** 1908 Berliet car **Edge:** Reeded

Date	Mintage	F	VF	XF	Unc	BU
2002 Proof	—	Value: 18.00				

KM# 95   10 FRANCS
26.1500 g., Copper-Nickel, 40.3 mm. **Subject:** Historic
Automobiles **Obv:** Lion left **Rev:** 1919 Hispano Suiza H6 car right
Edge: Reeded

Date	Mintage	F	VF	XF	Unc	BU
2002 Proof	—	Value: 18.00				

KM# 96   10 FRANCS
32.0000 g., Silver Plated Copper, 40 mm. **Subject:** World Cup
Soccer **Obv:** Lion left **Rev:** Soccer player and multicolor
American flag **Edge:** Reeded

Date	Mintage	F	VF	XF	Unc	BU
2002 Proof	20,000	Value: 50.00				

KM# 97   10 FRANCS
32.0000 g., Silver Plated Copper, 40 mm. **Subject:** World Cup
Soccer **Obv:** Lion left **Rev:** Two soccer players and multicolor
flag of Ecuador **Edge:** Reeded

Date	Mintage	F	VF	XF	Unc	BU
2002 Proof	20,000	Value: 50.00				

KM# 103   10 FRANCS
19.0000 g., 0.9990 Silver 0.6102 oz. ASW, 40 mm. **Series:**
Airplanes **Obv:** Lion left **Rev:** WWI German Gotha Ursinus G
bomber flying left at 8 o'clock **Edge:** Reeded

Date	Mintage	F	VF	XF	Unc	BU
2002 Proof	—	Value: 40.00				

KM# 104   10 FRANCS
19.0000 g., 0.9990 Silver 0.6102 oz. ASW, 40 mm. **Series:**
Airplanes **Obv:** Lion left **Rev:** WWII ME 109 German fighter plane
flying left **Edge:** Reeded

Date	Mintage	F	VF	XF	Unc	BU
2002 Proof	—	Value: 40.00				

KM# 105   10 FRANCS
19.0000 g., 0.9990 Silver 0.6102 oz. ASW, 40 mm. **Series:**
Airplanes **Obv:** Lion left **Rev:** Savoia-Marchetti S 55 seaplane
flying left **Edge:** Reeded

Date	Mintage	F	VF	XF	Unc	BU
2002 Proof	—	Value: 40.00				

KM# 106   10 FRANCS
19.0000 g., 0.9990 Silver 0.6102 oz. ASW, 40 mm. **Series:**
Airplanes **Obv:** Lion left **Rev:** B-58 Hustler Delta wing bomber
flying left at 8 o'clock **Edge:** Reeded

Date	Mintage	F	VF	XF	Unc	BU
2002 Proof	—	Value: 40.00				

KM# 107   10 FRANCS
19.0000 g., 0.9990 Silver 0.6102 oz. ASW, 40 mm. **Series:**
Airplanes **Obv:** Lion left **Rev:** CF-105 Arrow jet fighter plane flying
right, nose up **Edge:** Reeded

Date	Mintage	F	VF	XF	Unc	BU
2002 Proof	—	Value: 40.00				

KM# 108   10 FRANCS
19.0000 g., 0.9990 Silver 0.6102 oz. ASW, 40 mm. **Series:**
Airplanes **Obv:** Lion left **Rev:** XB-70 Valkyrie experimental jet
bomber flying right **Edge:** Reeded

Date	Mintage	F	VF	XF	Unc	BU
2002 Proof	—	Value: 40.00				

KM# 187   10 FRANCS
26.1500 g., Copper-Nickel, 40.3 mm. **Series:** Automobiles **Obv:**
Lion standing left **Rev:** Buick **Edge:** Reeded

Date	Mintage	F	VF	XF	Unc	BU
2002 Proof	—	Value: 18.00				

KM# 188   10 FRANCS
26.1500 g., Copper-Nickel, 40.3 mm. **Series:** Automobiles **Obv:**
Lion standing left **Rev:** Land Rover **Edge:** Reeded

Date	Mintage	F	VF	XF	Unc	BU
2002 Proof	—	Value: 18.00				

KM# 193   10 FRANCS
26.1500 g., Copper-Nickel, 40.3 mm. **Series:** Automobiles **Obv:**
Lion standing left **Rev:** Benz **Shape:** Reeded

Date	Mintage	F	VF	XF	Unc	BU
2002 Proof	—	Value: 18.00				

KM# 194   10 FRANCS
26.1500 g., Copper-Nickel, 40.3 mm. **Series:** Automobiles **Obv:**
Lion standing left **Rev:** Audi **Edge:** Reeded

Date	Mintage	F	VF	XF	Unc	BU
2002 Proof	—	Value: 18.00				

KM# 195   10 FRANCS
26.1500 g., Copper-Nickel, 40.3 mm. **Series:** Automobiles **Obv:**
Lion standing left **Rev:** Alfa Romero

Date	Mintage	F	VF	XF	Unc	BU
2002 Proof	—	Value: 18.00				

KM# 196   10 FRANCS
26.1500 g., Copper-Nickel, 40.3 mm. **Series:** Automobiles **Obv:**
Lion standing left **Rev:** Ford Model 'T' **Edge:** Reeded

Date	Mintage	F	VF	XF	Unc	BU
2002 Proof	—	Value: 18.00				

KM# 163 10 FRANCS
39.1000 g., Acrylic, 49.9 mm. **Obv:** Old World Swallowtail
butterfly above lion and value **Rev:** Rear view of the obverse
Edge: Plain

Date	Mintage	F	VF	XF	Unc	BU
2003	—	—	—	—	75.00	—

KM# 171 10 FRANCS
39.1000 g., Acrylic, 49.9 mm. **Obv:** Gorch Fock sail ship above
lion and value **Rev:** Rear view of the obverse design **Edge:** Plain

Date	Mintage	F	VF	XF	Unc	BU
2003	1,000	—	—	—	75.00	—

KM# 109 10 FRANCS
19.0000 g., 0.9990 Silver 0.6102 oz. ASW, 40 mm. **Obv:** Lion
left **Rev:** 14 BIS early aircraft in flight **Edge:** Reeded

Date	Mintage	F	VF	XF	Unc	BU
2003 Proof	—	Value: 40.00				

KM# 110 10 FRANCS
19.0000 g., 0.9990 Silver 0.6102 oz. ASW, 40 mm. **Obv:** Lion
left **Rev:** WWI Sopwith Camel fighter plane flying right **Edge:**
Reeded

Date	Mintage	F	VF	XF	Unc	BU
2003 Proof	—	Value: 40.00				

KM# 111 10 FRANCS
19.0000 g., 0.9990 Silver 0.6102 oz. ASW, 40 mm. **Obv:** Lion
left **Rev:** Curtiss NC-4 early seaplane flying left **Edge:** Reeded

Date	Mintage	F	VF	XF	Unc	BU
2003 Proof	—	Value: 40.00				

KM# 112 10 FRANCS
19.0000 g., 0.9990 Silver 0.6102 oz. ASW, 40 mm. **Obv:** Lion
left **Rev:** Macchi-Castoldi MC-72 seaplane flying left at 8 o'clock
Edge: Reeded

Date	Mintage	F	VF	XF	Unc	BU
2003 Proof	—	Value: 40.00				

KM# 113 10 FRANCS
19.0000 g., 0.9990 Silver 0.6102 oz. ASW, 40 mm. **Obv:** Lion
left **Rev:** WWII CA-12 Boomerang fighter plane flying above map
at 10 o'clock **Edge:** Reeded

Date	Mintage	F	VF	XF	Unc	BU
2003 Proof	—	Value: 40.00				

KM# 114 10 FRANCS
19.0000 g., 0.9990 Silver 0.6102 oz. ASW, 40 mm. **Obv:** Lion
left **Rev:** B-50A Superfortress bomber flying left **Edge:** Reeded

Date	Mintage	F	VF	XF	Unc	BU
2003 Proof	—	Value: 40.00				

KM# 115 10 FRANCS
19.0000 g., 0.9990 Silver 0.6102 oz. ASW, 40 mm. **Obv:** Lion
left **Rev:** WWII Heinkel-178 German jet plane flying left **Edge:**
Reeded

Date	Mintage	F	VF	XF	Unc	BU
2003 Proof	—	Value: 40.00				

KM# 116 10 FRANCS
19.0000 g., 0.9990 Silver 0.6102 oz. ASW, 40 mm. **Obv:** Lion
left **Rev:** Early De Havilland Comet jet liner flying left **Edge:**
Reeded

Date	Mintage	F	VF	XF	Unc	BU
2003 Proof	—	Value: 40.00				

KM# 117 10 FRANCS
19.0000 g., 0.9990 Silver 0.6102 oz. ASW, 40 mm. **Obv:** Lion
left **Rev:** Panavia Tornado jet fighter-bomber flying left **Edge:**
Reeded

Date	Mintage	F	VF	XF	Unc	BU
2003 Proof	—	Value: 40.00				

KM# 118 10 FRANCS
19.0000 g., 0.9990 Silver 0.6102 oz. ASW, 40 mm. **Obv:** Lion
left **Rev:** Hindustan HF24 jet fighter flying left **Edge:** Reeded

Date	Mintage	F	VF	XF	Unc	BU
2003 Proof	—	Value: 40.00				

KM# 119 10 FRANCS
19.0000 g., 0.9990 Silver 0.6102 oz. ASW, 40 mm. **Obv:** Lion
left **Rev:** Lockheed F-117 Stealth fighter flying left **Edge:** Reeded

Date	Mintage	F	VF	XF	Unc	BU
2003 Proof	—	Value: 40.00				

KM# 120   10 FRANCS
19.0000 g., 0.9990 Silver 0.6102 oz. ASW, 40 mm. **Obv:** Lion left **Rev:** North American X-15 experimental rocket plane flying right at 1 o'clock **Edge:** Reeded

Date	Mintage	F	VF	XF	Unc	BU
2003 Proof	— Value: 40.00					

KM# 122   10 FRANCS
25.0000 g., 0.9250 Silver 0.7435 oz. ASW, 38.6 mm. **Obv:** Lion left **Rev:** Multicolor 3D hologram view of Victoria Falls **Edge:** Reeded

Date	Mintage	F	VF	XF	Unc	BU
2003 Proof	5,000 Value: 50.00					

KM# 99.1   10 FRANCS
24.9100 g., 0.9250 Silver 0.7408 oz. ASW, 38.6 mm. **Obv:** Lion left **Rev:** Chameleon **Edge:** Reeded

Date	Mintage	F	VF	XF	Unc	BU
2003 Proof	— Value: 45.00					

KM# 99.2   10 FRANCS
24.9100 g., 0.9250 Silver 0.7408 oz. ASW, 38.6 mm. **Obv:** Lion left **Rev:** Multicolor chameleon **Edge:** Reeded

Date	Mintage	F	VF	XF	Unc	BU
2003 Proof	— Value: 50.00					

KM# 100   10 FRANCS
24.9100 g., 0.9250 Silver 0.7408 oz. ASW, 38.6 mm. **Obv:** Lion left **Rev:** Striped skunk **Edge:** Reeded

Date	Mintage	F	VF	XF	Unc	BU
2003 Proof	— Value: 45.00					

KM# 101   10 FRANCS
24.9100 g., 0.9250 Silver 0.7408 oz. ASW, 38.6 mm. **Obv:** Lion left **Rev:** Porcupine on rock, right **Edge:** Reeded

Date	Mintage	F	VF	XF	Unc	BU
2003 Proof	— Value: 47.50					

KM# 102   10 FRANCS
24.9100 g., 0.9250 Silver 0.7408 oz. ASW, 38.6 mm. **Obv:** Lion left **Rev:** Giant Pangolin on rock right **Edge:** Reeded

Date	Mintage	F	VF	XF	Unc	BU
2003 Proof	— Value: 45.00					

KM# 132   10 FRANCS
25.0000 g., 0.9000 Silver 0.7234 oz. ASW, 40 mm. **Obv:** Lion left **Rev:** Multicolor dolphin leaping left **Edge:** Reeded

Date	Mintage	F	VF	XF	Unc	BU
2003 Proof	5,000 Value: 50.00					

KM# 133   10 FRANCS
25.0000 g., 0.9000 Silver 0.7234 oz. ASW, 40 mm. **Obv:** Lion left **Rev:** Multicolor sea turtle left **Edge:** Reeded

Date	Mintage	F	VF	XF	Unc	BU
2003 Proof	5,000 Value: 50.00					

KM# 134   10 FRANCS
25.0000 g., 0.9000 Silver 0.7234 oz. ASW, 40 mm. **Obv:** Lion left **Rev:** Multicolor killer whale jumping right **Edge:** Reeded

Date	Mintage	F	VF	XF	Unc	BU
2003 Proof	5,000 Value: 50.00					

KM# 135   10 FRANCS
26.0000 g., 0.9990 Silver 0.8350 oz. ASW, 40 mm. **Obv:** Lion left **Rev:** Pope John Paul II with staff and mitre, waving **Edge:** Reeded

Date	Mintage	F	VF	XF	Unc	BU
2003 Proof	— Value: 55.00					

KM# 141   10 FRANCS
25.0000 g., 0.9250 Silver 0.7435 oz. ASW, 38.6 mm. **Obv:** Lion left **Rev:** Multicolor Emperor fish swimming left **Edge:** Reeded

Date	Mintage	F	VF	XF	Unc	BU
2004 Proof	5,000 Value: 55.00					

KM# 142   10 FRANCS
25.0000 g., 0.9250 Silver 0.7435 oz. ASW, 38.6 mm. **Obv:** Lion left **Rev:** Multicolor octopus facing **Edge:** Reeded

Date	Mintage	F	VF	XF	Unc	BU
2004 Proof	5,000 Value: 75.00					

KM# 143   10 FRANCS
25.0000 g., 0.9250 Silver 0.7435 oz. ASW, 38.6 mm. **Obv:** Lion left **Rev:** Formula 1 and GT race cars **Edge:** Reeded

Date	Mintage	F	VF	XF	Unc	BU
2004 Proof	5,000 Value: 45.00					

KM# 145   10 FRANCS
25.0000 g., 0.9250 Silver 0.7435 oz. ASW, 27x47 mm. **Obv:** Lion left **Rev:** Pope with crucifix **Edge:** Plain **Shape:** Rectangular

Date	Mintage	F	VF	XF	Unc	BU
2004 Proof	5,000 Value: 50.00					

KM# 149   10 FRANCS
25.0000 g., 0.9250 Silver 0.7435 oz. ASW, 38.6 mm. **Obv:** Lion left **Rev:** Multicolor Quetzal bird **Edge:** Reeded

Date	Mintage	F	VF	XF	Unc	BU
2004 Proof	5,000	Value: 50.00				

KM# 150   10 FRANCS
25.0000 g., 0.9250 Silver 0.7435 oz. ASW, 38.6 mm. **Obv:** Lion left **Rev:** Multicolor Bird of Paradise on branch left **Edge:** Reeded

Date	Mintage	F	VF	XF	Unc	BU
2004 Proof	5,000	Value: 55.00				

KM# 151   10 FRANCS
25.0000 g., 0.9250 Silver 0.7435 oz. ASW, 38.6 mm. **Obv:** Lion left **Rev:** Multicolor Kingfisher bird left **Edge:** Reeded

Date	Mintage	F	VF	XF	Unc	BU
2004 Proof	5,000	Value: 55.00				

KM# 155   10 FRANCS
Acrylic Clear, 50 mm. **Obv:** Etched nine-masted sailing junk above lion, value and country name **Edge:** Plain

Date	Mintage	F	VF	XF	Unc	BU
2004	2,000	—	—	—	55.00	—

KM# 126   10 FRANCS
25.0000 g., 0.9250 Silver 0.7435 oz. ASW, 38.6 mm. **Obv:** Lion left above value **Rev:** Sundial face with collapsible gnomon **Edge:** Reeded

Date	Mintage	F	VF	XF	Unc	BU
2004 Proof	5,000	Value: 50.00				

KM# 127   10 FRANCS
25.0000 g., 0.9250 Silver 0.7435 oz. ASW, 38.6 mm. **Obv:** Lion left above value **Rev:** Compass face **Edge:** Reeded **Note:** Compass part of the Compass and Spoon set

Date	Mintage	F	VF	XF	Unc	BU
2004 Proof	5,000	Value: 50.00				

KM# 172   10 FRANCS
25.0000 g., Silver, 38.6 mm. **Obv:** Lion left **Rev:** Pope waving half facing at left, cross at upper right, Vatican at lower right

Date	Mintage	F	VF	XF	Unc	BU
2005 Proof	3,000	Value: 50.00				

KM# 179a   10 FRANCS
25.0000 g., 0.9250 Silver 0.7435 oz. ASW, 38.58 mm. **Series:** Wildlife Protection **Obv:** Lion standing left **Obv. Legend:** REPUBLIQUE DEMOCRATIQUE DU CONGO **Rev:** Butterfly Fish, multicolor **Edge:** Reeded

Date	Mintage	F	VF	XF	Unc	BU
2005 Proof	5,000	Value: 45.00				

KM# 180a   10 FRANCS
25.0000 g., 0.9250 Silver 0.7435 oz. ASW, 38.58 mm. **Series:** Wildlife Protection **Obv:** Lion standing left **Obv. Legend:** REPUBLIQUE DEMOCRATIQUE DU CONGO **Rev:** African Moony Fish, multicolor **Edge:** Reeded

Date	Mintage	F	VF	XF	Unc	BU
2005 Proof	5,000	Value: 45.00				

KM# 181a   10 FRANCS
25.0000 g., 0.9250 Silver 0.7435 oz. ASW, 38.58 mm. **Series:** Wildlife Protection **Obv:** Lion standing left **Obv. Legend:** REPUBLIQUE DEMOCRATIQUE DU CONGO **Rev:** Red Perch, multicolor **Edge:** Reeded

Date	Mintage	F	VF	XF	Unc	BU
2005 Proof	5,000	Value: 45.00				

KM# 176   10 FRANCS
32.0000 g., 0.9990 Silver 1.0278 oz. ASW, 40 mm. **Obv:** Lion standing left **Obv. Legend:** REPUBLIQUE DEMOCRATIQUE DU CONGO **Rev:** World Trade Center Twin Towers as they were before 9-11 **Edge:** Reeded

Date	Mintage	F	VF	XF	Unc	BU
2006 Proof	—	Value: 50.00				

KM# 200   10 FRANCS
Silver Plated Copper, 40 mm. **Subject:** Aviation Centennial 1903-2003 **Obv:** National arms **Rev:** Early aircraft and bust

Date	Mintage	F	VF	XF	Unc	BU
2008 Proof	—	Value: 15.00				

KM# 201   10 FRANCS
Silver Plated Copper, 40 mm. **Subject:** Warriors of the World **Obv:** National arms **Rev:** Spartan standing

Date	Mintage	F	VF	XF	Unc	BU
2010 Proof	—	Value: 20.00				

KM# 202   10 FRANCS
Silver Plated Copper, 40 mm. **Subject:** Warriors of the World **Obv:** National arms **Rev:** Centurian

Date	Mintage	F	VF	XF	Unc	BU
2010 Proof	—	Value: 20.00				

KM# 203   10 FRANCS
Silver Plated Copper, 40 mm. **Subject:** Warriors of the World **Obv:** National arms **Rev:** Gladiator standing

Date	Mintage	F	VF	XF	Unc	BU
2010 Proof	—	Value: 20.00				

KM# 204   10 FRANCS
Silver Plated Copper, 40 mm. **Subject:** Warriors of the World **Obv:** Naitonal arms **Rev:** Chinese warrior

Date	Mintage	F	VF	XF	Unc	BU
2010 Proof	—	Value: 20.00				

KM# 205   10 FRANCS
Silver Plated Copper, 40 mm.   **Subject:** Warriors of the World
Obv: Naitonal Arms **Rev:** Celtic Warrior

Date	Mintage	F	VF	XF	Unc	BU
2010 Proof	—	Value: 20.00				

KM# 206   10 FRANCS
Silver Plated Copper, 40 mm.   **Subject:** Warriors of the World
Obv: National arms **Rev:** Mongolian warrior on horseback

Date	Mintage	F	VF	XF	Unc	BU
2010 Proof	—	Value: 20.00				

KM# 207   10 FRANCS
Silver Plated Copper, 40 mm.   **Subject:** Warriors of the World
Obv: National arms **Rev:** Viking standing

Date	Mintage	F	VF	XF	Unc	BU
2010 Proof	—	Value: 20.00				

KM# 208   10 FRANCS
Silver Plated Copper, 40 mm.   **Subject:** Warriors of the World
Obv: National arms **Rev:** English Archer

Date	Mintage	F	VF	XF	Unc	BU
2010 Proof	—	Value: 20.00				

KM# 209   10 FRANCS
Silver Plated Copper, 40 mm.   **Subject:** Warriors of the World
Obv: National arms **Rev:** Templar Knight on horseback

Date	Mintage	F	VF	XF	Unc	BU
2010 Proof	—	Value: 20.00				

KM# 210   10 FRANCS
Silver Plated Copper, 40 mm.   **Subject:** Warriors of the World
Obv: National arms **Rev:** Ninja standing

Date	Mintage	F	VF	XF	Unc	BU
2010 Proof	—	Value: 20.00				

KM# 211   10 FRANCS
Silver Plated Copper, 40 mm.   **Subject:** Warriors of the World
Obv: National arms **Rev:** Samurai warrior standing

Date	Mintage	F	VF	XF	Unc	BU
2010 Proof	—	Value: 20.00				

KM# 212   10 FRANCS
Silver Plated Copper, 40 mm.   **Subject:** Warriors of the World
Obv: National arms **Rev:** Zulu warrior standing

Date	Mintage	F	VF	XF	Unc	BU
2010 Proof	—	Value: 20.00				

KM# 136   20 FRANCS
1.2440 g., 0.9999 Gold 0.0400 oz. AGW, 13.92 mm.   **Obv:** Lion
left **Rev:** Pope John Paul II with staff and mitre, waving **Edge:**
Plain

Date	Mintage	F	VF	XF	Unc	BU
2003 Proof	—	Value: 70.00				

KM# 137   20 FRANCS
1.2440 g., 0.9999 Gold 0.0400 oz. AGW, 13.92 mm.   **Obv:** Lion
left **Rev:** Skunk **Edge:** Plain

Date	Mintage	F	VF	XF	Unc	BU
2003 Proof	25,000	Value: 70.00				

KM# 138   20 FRANCS
1.2440 g., 0.9999 Gold 0.0400 oz. AGW, 13.92 mm.   **Obv:** Lion
left **Rev:** Giant anteater right **Edge:** Plain

Date	Mintage	F	VF	XF	Unc	BU
2003 Proof	25,000	Value: 70.00				

KM# 139   20 FRANCS
1.2440 g., 0.9999 Gold 0.0400 oz. AGW, 13.92 mm.   **Obv:** Lion
left **Rev:** Porcupine right **Edge:** Plain

Date	Mintage	F	VF	XF	Unc	BU
2003 Proof	25,000	Value: 70.00				

KM# 140   20 FRANCS
1.2440 g., 0.9999 Gold 0.0400 oz. AGW, 13.92 mm.   **Obv:** Lion
left **Rev:** Chameleon **Edge:** Plain

Date	Mintage	F	VF	XF	Unc	BU
2003 Proof	25,000	Value: 70.00				

KM# 184   20 FRANCS
1.2200 g., 0.9999 Gold 0.0392 oz. AGW, 13.74 mm.   **Subject:**
XXVIII Summer Olympics - Athens **Obv:** Lion standing right **Rev:**
Athenian tetradrachm featuring owl perched **Edge:** Reeded

Date	Mintage	F	VF	XF	Unc	BU
2003 Proof	25,000	Value: 70.00				

KM# 186   20 FRANCS
1.2441 g., 0.9999 Gold 0.0400 oz. AGW, 13.92 mm.   **Subject:**
Christmas **Obv:** Lion standing left **Rev:** Jesus lying in manger

Date	Mintage	F	VF	XF	Unc	BU
ND(2004) Proof	25,000	Value: 70.00				

KM# 144   20 FRANCS
1.2440 g., 0.9999 Gold 0.0400 oz. AGW, 13.92 mm.   **Obv:** Lion
left **Rev:** Ferrari coat of arms **Edge:** Plain

Date	Mintage	F	VF	XF	Unc	BU
2004 Proof	5,000	Value: 75.00				

KM# 173   20 FRANCS
1.5300 g., 0.9990 Gold 0.0491 oz. AGW, 13.9 mm.   **Obv:** Lion left
Rev: Pope waving at left, cross at upper right, Vatican at lower right

Date	Mintage	F	VF	XF	Unc	BU
2005 Proof	25,000	Value: 90.00				

KM# 213   25 FRANCS
Acrylic, 50mm mm.   **Rev:** H.M. Bark Endeavour at center;

Captian James Cook bust at top left, National arms at bottom center

Date	Mintage	F	VF	XF	Unc	BU
2009	—				—	55.00

KM# 185   75 FRANCS
15.5500 g., 0.9999 Gold 0.4999 oz. AGW **Subject:** XXVIII Summer Olympics - Athens **Obv:** Lion standing right **Rev:** Athenian tetradrachm featuring owl perched **Edge:** Reeded

Date	Mintage	F	VF	XF	Unc	BU
2003 Proof	500 Value: 850					

KM# 129   100 FRANCS
31.1000 g., 0.9999 Gold 0.9997 oz. AGW, 40 mm. **Series:** Wild Life Protection **Obv:** Lion left **Rev:** Reflective multicolor swallowtail butterfly **Edge:** Reeded

Date	Mintage	F	VF	XF	Unc	BU
2002 Proof	50 Value: 1,700					

KM# 130   100 FRANCS
31.1000 g., 0.9999 Gold 0.9997 oz. AGW, 40 mm. **Series:** Wild Life Protection **Obv:** Lion left **Rev:** Reflective multicolor dark greenish butterfly **Edge:** Reeded

Date	Mintage	F	VF	XF	Unc	BU
2002 Proof	50 Value: 1,700					

KM# 131   100 FRANCS
31.1000 g., 0.9999 Gold 0.9997 oz. AGW, 40 mm. **Series:** Wild Life Protection **Obv:** Lion left **Rev:** Reflective multicolor red and black butterfly **Edge:** Reeded

Date	Mintage	F	VF	XF	Unc	BU
2002 Proof	50 Value: 1,700					

KM# 152   100 FRANCS
31.1035 g., 0.9999 Gold 0.9999 oz. AGW, 38.6 mm. **Obv:** Lion left **Rev:** Multicolor Quetzal bird **Edge:** Reeded

Date	Mintage	F	VF	XF	Unc	BU
2004 Proof	25 Value: 1,800					

KM# 153   100 FRANCS
31.1035 g., 0.9999 Gold 0.9999 oz. AGW, 38.6 mm. **Obv:** Lion left **Rev:** Multicolor Bird of Paradise left **Edge:** Reeded

Date	Mintage	F	VF	XF	Unc	BU
2004 Proof	25 Value: 1,800					

KM# 154   100 FRANCS
31.1035 g., 0.9999 Gold 0.9999 oz. AGW, 38.6 mm. **Obv:** Lion left **Rev:** Multicolor Kingfisher bird **Edge:** Reeded

Date	Mintage	F	VF	XF	Unc	BU
2004 Proof	25 Value: 1,800					

KM# 179b   100 FRANCS
31.1000 g., 0.9990 Gold 0.9988 oz. AGW, 38.58 mm. **Series:** Wildlife Protection **Obv:** Lion standing left **Obv. Legend:** REPUBLIQUE DEMOCRATIQUE DU CONGO **Rev:** Butterfly Fish, multicolor **Edge:** Reeded

Date	Mintage	F	VF	XF	Unc	BU
2005 Proof	25 Value: 1,800					

KM# 180b   100 FRANCS
31.1000 g., 0.9990 Gold 0.9988 oz. AGW, 38.58 mm. **Series:** Wildlife Protection **Obv:** Lion standing left **Obv. Legend:** REPUBLIQUE DEMOCRATIQUE DU CONGO **Rev:** African Mooney Fish, muticolor **Edge:** Reeded

Date	Mintage	F	VF	XF	Unc	BU
2005 Proof	25 Value: 1,800					

KM# 181b   100 FRANCS
31.1000 g., 0.9990 Gold 0.9988 oz. AGW, 38.58 mm. **Series:** Wildlife Protection **Obv:** Lion standing left **Obv. Legend:** REPUBLIQUE DEMOCRATIQUE DU CONGO **Rev:** Red Perch, multicolor **Edge:** Reeded

Date	Mintage	F	VF	XF	Unc	BU
2005 Proof	25 Value: 1,800					

MINT SETS

KM#	Date	Mintage	Identification	Issue Price	Mkt Val
MS2	2004 (4)	—	KM#156-159	—	12.50

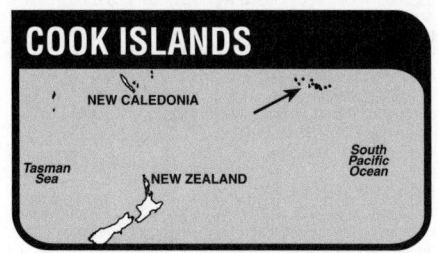

Cook Islands, a self-governing dependency of New Zealand consisting of 15 islands, is located in the South Pacific Ocean about 2,000 miles (3,218 km.) northeast of New Zealand. It has an area of 93 sq. mi. (234 sq. km.) and a population of 17,185. Capital: Avarua. The United States claims the islands of Danger, Manahiki, Penrhyn, and Rakahanga atolls. Citrus and canned fruits and juices, copra, clothing, jewelry, and mother-of-pearl shell are exported.

RULER
British

MINT MARK
PM - Pobjoy Mint

MONETARY SYSTEM
100 Cents = 1 Dollar

DEPENDENCY OF NEW ZEALAND
DECIMAL COINAGE

KM# 419   CENT
1.4400 g., Aluminum, 21.9 mm. **Ruler:** Elizabeth II **Obv:** Crowned head right, date below **Rev:** Bust of Capt. James Cook right, denomination below **Edge:** Plain

Date	Mintage	F	VF	XF	Unc	BU
2003	—	—	—	—	1.25	1.50

KM# 420   CENT
1.4400 g., Aluminum, 21.9 mm. **Ruler:** Elizabeth II **Obv:** Crowned head right, date below **Rev:** Collie dog right, denomination below **Edge:** Plain

Date	Mintage	F	VF	XF	Unc	BU
2003	—	—	—	—	0.75	1.00

KM# 421   CENT
1.4400 g., Aluminum, 21.9 mm. **Ruler:** Elizabeth II **Obv:** Crowned head right, date below **Rev:** Pointer dog right, denomination above **Edge:** Plain

Date	Mintage	F	VF	XF	Unc	BU
2003	—	—	—	—	0.75	1.00

KM# 422   CENT
1.4400 g., Aluminum, 21.9 mm. **Ruler:** Elizabeth II **Obv:** Crowned head right, date below **Rev:** Rooster right, denomination above **Edge:** Plain

Date	Mintage	F	VF	XF	Unc	BU
2003	—	—	—	—	0.75	1.00

KM# 423   CENT
1.4400 g., Aluminum, 22 mm. **Ruler:** Elizabeth II **Obv:** Crowned head right, date below **Rev:** Monkey on branch, denomination at left **Edge:** Plain

Date	Mintage	F	VF	XF	Unc	BU
2003	—	—	—	—	0.75	1.00

KM# 756   CENT
3.6400 g., Brass Plated Steel, 11.8 mm. **Ruler:** Elizabeth II **Obv:** Bust right **Rev:** Female Hula dancer

Date	Mintage	F	VF	XF	Unc	BU
2010	—	—	—	—	0.75	1.00

KM# 757   2 CENTS
5.1000 g., Brass Plated Steel, 19.8 mm. **Ruler:** Elizabeth II **Obv:** Bust right **Rev:** The Endeavor

Date	Mintage	F	VF	XF	Unc	BU
2010	—	—	—	—	0.75	1.00

KM# 758   5 CENTS
6.1500 g., Brass Plated Steel, 21.7 mm. **Ruler:** Elizabeth II **Obv:** Bust right **Rev:** Tiare Maori flower

Date	Mintage	F	VF	XF	Unc	BU
2010	—	—	—	—	1.00	1.50

KM# 759   10 CENTS
11.5000 g., Nickel Plated Steel, 20.5 mm. **Ruler:** Elizabeth II **Obv:** Bust right **Rev:** Yellowfin tuna

Date	Mintage	F	VF	XF	Unc	BU
2010	—	—	—	—	1.00	1.50

KM# 760   20 CENTS
14.1300 g., Nickel Plated Steel, 21.75 mm. **Ruler:** Elizabeth II **Obv:** Bust right **Rev:** Bird

Date	Mintage	F	VF	XF	Unc	BU
2010	—	—	—	—	1.50	2.00

KM# 1116 50 CENTS
28.2800 g., Copper-Nickel, 38.61 mm. **Ruler:** Elizabeth II
Subject: Elizabeth II Corronation, 50th Anniversary

Date	Mintage	F	VF	XF	Unc	BU
2002	—					20.00

KM# 1144 50 CENTS
Copper-Nickel **Ruler:** Elizabeth II **Rev:** Edward "Ned" Kelley in color

Date	Mintage	F	VF	XF	Unc	BU
2004 Proof	Est. 10,000	Value: 15.00				

KM# 761 50 CENTS
Nickel Plated Steel, 24.75 mm. **Ruler:** Elizabeth II **Obv:** Bust right **Rev:** The Endeavor

Date	Mintage	F	VF	XF	Unc	BU
2010	—	—	—	—	2.00	2.50

KM# 1114 DOLLAR
32.0000 g., Copper-Nickel, 40 mm. **Ruler:** Elizabeth II **Subject:** 2002 Winter Olympics, Salt Lake City

Date	Mintage	F	VF	XF	Unc	BU
2001	Est. 20,000	—	—	—	—	15.00

KM# 1115 DOLLAR
9.5000 g., 0.9990 Silver 0.3051 oz. ASW, 22.5 mm. **Ruler:** Elizabeth II **Series:** 2002 Commonwealth Games, Manchester **Rev:** Track field and medals on ribbons

Date	Mintage	F	VF	XF	Unc	BU
2001 Proof	Est. 5,000	Value: 20.00				

KM# 396 DOLLAR
24.8828 g., 0.9990 Silver with Acrylic capsule center containing tiny rubies, sapphires and cubic zirconias 0.7992 oz. ASW, 40.6 mm. **Ruler:** Elizabeth II **Subject:** Crown Jewels **Obv:** Crowned head right, legend **Rev:** Crowns and royal regalia **Edge:** Reeded

Date	Mintage	F	VF	XF	Unc	BU
2002 Proof	50,000	Value: 32.50				

KM# 1117 DOLLAR
0.9990 Silver **Ruler:** Elizabeth II **Subject:** 2002 Winter Olumpics, Salt Lake City **Rev:** Figure skating

Date	Mintage	F	VF	XF	Unc	BU
2002 Proof	—	Value: 37.50				

KM# 1118 DOLLAR
Copper-Nickel **Ruler:** Elizabeth II **Subject:** XVII World Cup, Korea and Japan **Rev:** Soccer player and ball

Date	Mintage	F	VF	XF	Unc	BU
2002 Proof	—	Value: 15.00				

KM# 416 DOLLAR
10.7500 g., Copper-Nickel, 28.5 mm. **Ruler:** Elizabeth II **Obv:** Queen's new portrait **Rev:** Tangaroa statue and value **Edge:** Scalloped

Date	Mintage	F	VF	XF	Unc	BU
2003	—	—	—	—	2.50	3.00

KM# 455 DOLLAR
23.9000 g., Copper-Nickel, 38.5 mm. **Ruler:** Elizabeth II **Obv:** Queen Elizabeth II **Rev:** 50th Anniversary - Playboy magazine logo **Edge:** Reeded

Date	Mintage	F	VF	XF	Unc	BU
2003	—	—	—	—	7.00	9.00

KM# 455a DOLLAR
25.2700 g., Copper-Nickel partiall gilt, 38.3 mm. **Ruler:** Elizabeth II **Obv:** Elizabeth II **Rev:** Playboy magazine's 50th Anniversary logo **Edge:** Reeded

Date	Mintage	F	VF	XF	Unc	BU
2003 Proof	50,000	Value: 20.00				

KM# 455b DOLLAR
25.2700 g., 0.9990 Silver 0.8116 oz. ASW, 38.3 mm. **Ruler:** Elizabeth II **Obv:** Elizabeth II **Rev:** Playboy magazine's 50th Anniversary logo **Edge:** Reeded

Date	Mintage	F	VF	XF	Unc	BU
2003 Proof	—	Value: 40.00				

KM# 455c DOLLAR
25.2700 g., 0.9990 Silver Gilt 0.8116 oz. ASW, 38.3 mm. **Ruler:** Elizabeth II **Obv:** Elizabeth II **Rev:** Playboy magazine's 50th Anniversary logo **Edge:** Reeded

Date	Mintage	F	VF	XF	Unc	BU
2003 Proof	—	Value: 50.00				

KM# 462 DOLLAR
Copper-Nickel, 41 mm. **Ruler:** Elizabeth II **Rev:** Face of 5 Euro Banknote

Date	Mintage	F	VF	XF	Unc	BU
2003	—	—	—	—	7.00	9.00

KM# 463 DOLLAR
Copper-Nickel, 41 mm. **Ruler:** Elizabeth II **Rev:** Face of 10 Euro Banknote

Date	Mintage	F	VF	XF	Unc	BU
2003	—	—	—	—	7.00	9.00

KM# 464 DOLLAR
Copper-Nickel, 41 mm. **Ruler:** Elizabeth II **Rev:** Face of 20 Euro Banknote

Date	Mintage	F	VF	XF	Unc	BU
2003	—	—	—	—	7.00	9.00

KM# 465 DOLLAR
Copper-Nickel, 41 mm. **Ruler:** Elizabeth II **Rev:** Face of 50 Euro Banknote

Date	Mintage	F	VF	XF	Unc	BU
2003	—	—	—	—	7.00	9.00

KM# 466 DOLLAR
Copper-Nickel, 41 mm. **Ruler:** Elizabeth II **Rev:** Face of 100 Euro Banknote

Date	Mintage	F	VF	XF	Unc	BU
2003	—	—	—	—	7.00	9.00

KM# 467 DOLLAR
Copper-Nickel, 41 mm. **Ruler:** Elizabeth II **Rev:** Face of 500 Euro Banknote

Date	Mintage	F	VF	XF	Unc	BU
2003	—	—	—	—	7.00	9.00

KM# 424 DOLLAR
8.5000 g., 0.9990 Silver 0.2730 oz. ASW, 25.1 mm. **Ruler:** Elizabeth II **Subject:** Zodiac Gemstones - Cancer **Obv:** Crowned head above ornamental center **Rev:** Encapsulated emeralds above Crab (Cancer) **Edge:** Reeded

Date	Mintage	F	VF	XF	Unc	BU
ND(2003) Proof	10,000	Value: 25.00				

KM# 424a DOLLAR
8.5000 g., 0.9990 Silver Gilt 0.2730 oz. ASW, 25.1 mm. **Ruler:** Elizabeth II **Obv:** Crowned head above ornamental center **Rev:** Encapsulated emeralds above Crab (cancer)

Date	Mintage	F	VF	XF	Unc	BU
ND(2003) Proof	10,000	Value: 60.00				

KM# 425 DOLLAR
8.5000 g., 0.9990 Silver 0.2730 oz. ASW, 25.1 mm. **Ruler:** Elizabeth II **Subject:** Zodiac Gemstones - Aquarius **Obv:** Crowned head above ornamental center **Rev:** Encapsulated garnets with Aquarius in background **Edge:** Reeded

Date	Mintage	F	VF	XF	Unc	BU
ND(2004) Proof	—	Value: 25.00				

KM# 425a DOLLAR
8.5000 g., 0.9990 Silver Gilt 0.2730 oz. ASW, 25.1 mm. **Ruler:** Elizabeth II **Obv:** Crowned head above ornamental center **Rev:** Encapsulated garnets with Aquarius in background

Date	Mintage	F	VF	XF	Unc	BU
ND(2003) Proof	10,000	Value: 60.00				

KM# 426 DOLLAR
8.5000 g., 0.9990 Silver 0.2730 oz. ASW, 25.1 mm. **Ruler:** Elizabeth II **Subject:** Zodiac Gemstones - Aries **Obv:** Crowned head above ornamental center **Rev:** Encapsulated Bloodstones in center with ram at left **Edge:** Reeded

Date	Mintage	F	VF	XF	Unc	BU
ND(2003) Proof	10,000	Value: 25.00				

KM# 426a DOLLAR
8.5000 g., 0.9990 Silver Gilt 0.2730 oz. ASW, 25.1 mm. **Ruler:** Elizabeth II **Obv:** Crowned head above ornamental center **Rev:** Encapsulated Bloodstones in center with ram at left

Date	Mintage	F	VF	XF	Unc	BU
ND(2003) Proof	10,000	Value: 60.00				

KM# 427 DOLLAR
8.5000 g., 0.9990 Silver 0.2730 oz. ASW, 25.1 mm. **Ruler:** Elizabeth II **Subject:** Zodiac Gemstones - Taurus **Obv:** Crowned head above ornamental center **Rev:** Encapsulated Sapphires with bull in background **Edge:** Reeded

Date	Mintage	F	VF	XF	Unc	BU
ND(2003) Proof	10,000	Value: 25.00				

KM# 427a DOLLAR
8.5000 g., 0.9990 Silver Gilt 0.2730 oz. ASW, 25.1 mm. **Ruler:** Elizabeth II **Subject:** Zodiac Gemstones - Taurus **Obv:** Crowned head above ornamental center **Rev:** Encapsulated Sapphires with bull in background **Edge:** Reeded

Date	Mintage	F	VF	XF	Unc	BU
ND(2003) Proof	10,000	Value: 60.00				

KM# 428 DOLLAR
8.5000 g., 0.9990 Silver 0.2730 oz. ASW, 25.1 mm. **Ruler:** Elizabeth II **Obv:** Crowned head above ornamental center **Rev:** Encapsulated Agates between twins **Edge:** Reeded

Date	Mintage	F	VF	XF	Unc	BU
ND(2003) Proof	10,000	Value: 25.00				

KM# 428a DOLLAR
8.5000 g., 0.9990 Silver Gilt 0.2730 oz. ASW, 25.1 mm. **Ruler:** Elizabeth II **Obv:** Crowned head above ornamental center **Rev:** Encapsulated Agates between twins **Edge:** Reeded

Date	Mintage	F	VF	XF	Unc	BU
ND(2003) Proof	10,000	Value: 60.00				

KM# 429 DOLLAR
8.5000 g., 0.9990 Silver 0.2730 oz. ASW, 25.1 mm. **Ruler:**

Elizabeth II **Obv:** Crowned head above ornamental center **Rev:** Encapsulated Onyx stones with lion at right **Edge:** Reeded

Date	Mintage	F	VF	XF	Unc	BU
ND(2003) Proof	10,000	Value: 25.00				

KM# 429a DOLLAR

8.5000 g., 0.9990 Silver 0.2730 oz. ASW, 25.1 mm. **Ruler:** Elizabeth II **Obv:** Crowned head above ornamental center **Rev:** Encapsulated Onyx stones with lion at right **Edge:** Reeded

Date	Mintage	F	VF	XF	Unc	BU
ND(2003) Proof	10,000	Value: 60.00				

KM# 430 DOLLAR

8.5000 g., 0.9990 Silver 0.2730 oz. ASW, 25.1 mm. **Ruler:** Elizabeth II **Subject:** Zodiac Gemstones - Virgo **Obv:** Crowned head above ornamented center **Rev:** Encapsulated Carnelian stones with woman at right **Edge:** Reeded

Date	Mintage	F	VF	XF	Unc	BU
ND(2003) Proof	10,000	Value: 25.00				

KM# 430a DOLLAR

8.5000 g., 0.9990 Silver Gilt 0.2730 oz. ASW, 25.1 mm. **Ruler:** Elizabeth II **Subject:** Zodiac Gemstones - Virgo **Obv:** Crowned head above ornamented center **Rev:** Encapsulated Carnelian stones with Virgo at right **Edge:** Reeded

Date	Mintage	F	VF	XF	Unc	BU
ND(2003) Proof	10,000	Value: 60.00				

KM# 431 DOLLAR

8.5000 g., 0.9990 Silver 0.2730 oz. ASW, 25.1 mm. **Ruler:** Elizabeth II **Subject:** Zodiac Gemstones - Libra **Obv:** Crowned head above ornamented center **Rev:** Encapsulated Peridot stones with balance scale **Edge:** Reeded

Date	Mintage	F	VF	XF	Unc	BU
ND(2003) Proof	10,000	Value: 25.00				

KM# 431a DOLLAR

8.5000 g., 0.9990 Silver Gilt 0.2730 oz. ASW, 25.1 mm. **Ruler:** Elizabeth II **Subject:** Zodiac Gemstones - Libra **Obv:** Crowned head above ornamented center **Rev:** Encapsulated Peridot stones with balance scale **Edge:** Reeded

Date	Mintage	F	VF	XF	Unc	BU
ND(2003) Proof	10,000	Value: 60.00				

KM# 432 DOLLAR

8.5000 g., 0.9990 Silver 0.2730 oz. ASW, 25.1 mm. **Ruler:** Elizabeth II **Subject:** Zodiac Gemstones - Scorpio **Obv:** Crowned head above ornamented center **Rev:** Encapsulated Aquamarine stones with scorpion at lower right **Edge:** Reeded

Date	Mintage	F	VF	XF	Unc	BU
ND(2003) Proof	10,000	Value: 25.00				

KM# 432a DOLLAR

8.5000 g., 0.9990 Silver Gilt 0.2730 oz. ASW, 25.1 mm. **Ruler:** Elizabeth II **Subject:** Zodiac Gemstones - Scorpio **Obv:** Crowned head above ornamented center **Rev:** Encapsulated Aquamarine stones with scorpion at lower right **Edge:** Reeded

Date	Mintage	F	VF	XF	Unc	BU
ND(2003) Proof	10,000	Value: 60.00				

KM# 433 DOLLAR

8.5000 g., 0.9990 Silver 0.2730 oz. ASW, 25.1 mm. **Ruler:**

Elizabeth II **Subject:** Zodiac Gemstones - Sagittarius **Obv:** Crowned head above ornamented center **Rev:** Encapsulated Topaz stones with centaur at right **Edge:** Reeded

Date	Mintage	F	VF	XF	Unc	BU
ND(2003) Proof	10,000	Value: 25.00				

KM# 433a DOLLAR

8.5000 g., 0.9990 Silver Gilt 0.2730 oz. ASW, 25.1 mm. **Ruler:** Elizabeth II **Subject:** Zodiac Gemstones - Sagittarius **Obv:** Crowned head above ornamented center **Rev:** Encapsulated Topaz stones with centaur at right **Edge:** Reeded

Date	Mintage	F	VF	XF	Unc	BU
ND(2003) Proof	10,000	Value: 60.00				

KM# 434 DOLLAR

8.5000 g., 0.9990 Silver 0.2730 oz. ASW, 25.1 mm. **Ruler:** Elizabeth II **Subject:** Zodiac Gemstones - Capricorn **Obv:** Crowned head above ornamental center **Rev:** Encapsulated rubies with goat at right **Edge:** Reeded

Date	Mintage	F	VF	XF	Unc	BU
ND(2003) Proof	10,000	Value: 25.00				

KM# 434a DOLLAR

8.5000 g., 0.9990 Silver Gilt 0.2730 oz. ASW, 25.1 mm. **Ruler:** Elizabeth II **Subject:** Zodiac Gemstones - Capricorn **Obv:** Crowned head above ornamented center **Rev:** Encapsulated Rubies with goat at right **Edge:** Reeded

Date	Mintage	F	VF	XF	Unc	BU
ND(2003) Proof	10,000	Value: 60.00				

KM# 435 DOLLAR

8.5000 g., 0.9990 Silver 0.2730 oz. ASW, 25.1 mm. **Ruler:** Elizabeth II **Subject:** Zodiac Gemstones - Pices **Obv:** Crowned head above ornamented center **Rev:** Encapsulated Amethyst stones and two fish **Edge:** Reeded

Date	Mintage	F	VF	XF	Unc	BU
ND(2003) Proof	10,000	Value: 25.00				

KM# 435a DOLLAR

8.5000 g., 0.9990 Silver Gilt 0.2730 oz. ASW, 25.1 mm. **Ruler:** Elizabeth II **Subject:** Zodiac Gemstones - Pices **Obv:** Crowned head above ornamented center **Rev:** Encapsulated Amethyst stones and 2 fish **Edge:** Reeded

Date	Mintage	F	VF	XF	Unc	BU
ND(2003) Proof	10,000	Value: 60.00				

KM# 746 DOLLAR

24.9000 g., Copper-Nickel **Ruler:** Elizabeth II **Subject:** Historic ships - Espusi **Shape:** 38

Date	Mintage	F	VF	XF	Unc	BU
2003	—	—	—	—	15.00	20.00

KM# 747 DOLLAR

24.9000 g., Copper-Nickel, 38 mm. **Ruler:** Elizabeth II **Subject:** Historic ships - Gorch Foch

Date	Mintage	F	VF	XF	Unc	BU
2003	—	—	—	—	15.00	20.00

KM# 748 DOLLAR

24.9000 g., Copper-Nickel, 38 mm. **Ruler:** Elizabeth II **Subject:** Historic ships - Constitution

Date	Mintage	F	VF	XF	Unc	BU
2003	—	—	—	—	15.00	20.00

KM# 749 DOLLAR

24.9000 g., Copper-Nickel, 38 mm. **Ruler:** Elizabeth II **Subject:** Historic ships - Beagle

Date	Mintage	F	VF	XF	Unc	BU
2003	—	—	—	—	15.00	20.00

KM# 750 DOLLAR

24.9000 g., Copper-Nickel, 38 mm. **Ruler:** Elizabeth II **Subject:** Historic ship - Endeavour

Date	Mintage	F	VF	XF	Unc	BU
2003	—	—	—	—	15.00	20.00

KM# 751 DOLLAR

24.9000 g., Copper-Nickel, 38 mm. **Ruler:** Elizabeth II **Subject:** Historic Ship - Vasa

Date	Mintage	F	VF	XF	Unc	BU
2003	—	—	—	—	15.00	20.00

KM# 1127 DOLLAR

31.6350 g., 0.9990 Silver 1.0160 oz. ASW, 40.5 mm. **Ruler:** Elizabeth II **Rev:** James Cook and siling ship

Date	Mintage	F	VF	XF	Unc	BU
2003 Proof	Est. 4,999	Value: 50.00				

KM# 1130 DOLLAR

31.1050 g., 0.9990 Silver 0.9990 oz. ASW, 38.6 mm. **Ruler:** Elizabeth II **Subject:** Full Gospel Business Men's Fellowship, 50th Anniversary

Date	Mintage	F	VF	XF	Unc	BU
2003 Proof	Est. 4,999	Value: 55.00				

KM# 1143   DOLLAR
28.2800 g., 0.9250 Silver partially gilt 0.8410 oz. ASW,
38.61 mm.   **Ruler:** Elizabeth II **Series:** Elizabeth II, 50th
Anniversary of Corronation

Date	Mintage	F	VF	XF	Unc	BU
2003 Proof	Est. 20,000	—	—	—	—	45.00

KM# 438   DOLLAR
31.1035 g., 0.9990 Silver 0.9990 oz. ASW, 40.5 mm.   **Ruler:**
Elizabeth II **Obv:** Crowned head right **Rev:** Multicolor Deng
Xiaoping on Chinese map **Edge:** Plain **Shape:** As a map

Date	Mintage	F	VF	XF	Unc	BU
2004	20,000	—	—	—	45.00	50.00

KM# 454   DOLLAR
27.5300 g., 0.9990 Silver Clad Copper-Nickel 0.8842 oz. ASW,
38.6 mm.   **Ruler:** Elizabeth II **Subject:** 60th Anniversary - D-
Day Invasion **Obv:** Crowned bust right, new portrait **Rev:** Invasion
scene of soldiers storming the beaches (Sword, Gold, Juno,
Omaha, and Utah) of Normandy

Date	Mintage	F	VF	XF	Unc	BU
2004	—	—	—	—	15.00	18.00

KM# 1146   DOLLAR
31.6350 g., 0.9990 Silver 1.0160 oz. ASW   **Ruler:** Elizabeth II
Subject: Cobb & Co. 150th Anniversary **Rev:** Hackney Cab in
color

Date	Mintage	F	VF	XF	Unc	BU
2004 Proof	Est. 5,000	Value: 55.00				

KM# 1147   DOLLAR
31.6350 g., 0.9990 Silver 1.0160 oz. ASW   **Ruler:** Elizabeth II
Subject: 90th Anniversary, Battle of the Emden and Sydney I

Date	Mintage	F	VF	XF	Unc	BU
2004 Proof	Est. 5,000	Value: 55.00				

KM# 1148   DOLLAR
10.7500 g., Copper-Nickel, 28.28 mm.   **Ruler:** Elizabeth II **Rev:**
Elvis Presley

Date	Mintage	F	VF	XF	Unc	BU
2004	—	—	—	—	—	15.00

KM# 1150   DOLLAR
31.1050 g., 0.9990 Silver 0.9990 oz. ASW, 45 mm.   **Ruler:**
Elizabeth II **Subject:** XXVIII Summer Olympics, Athens **Rev:**
Cyclist in color

Date	Mintage	F	VF	XF	Unc	BU
2004	Est. 5,000	—	—	—	—	45.00

KM# 1151   DOLLAR
31.1050 g., 0.9990 Silver 0.9990 oz. ASW, 45 mm.   **Ruler:**
Elizabeth II **Rev:** Gymnast

Date	Mintage	F	VF	XF	Unc	BU
2004	Est. 5,000	—	—	—	—	45.00

KM# 1152   DOLLAR
31.1050 g., 0.9990 Silver 0.9990 oz. ASW, 45 mm.   **Ruler:**
Elizabeth II **Subject:** XXVIII Summer Olympics, Athens **Rev:**
Two basketball players in color

Date	Mintage	F	VF	XF	Unc	BU
2004	Est. 5,000	—	—	—	—	45.00

KM# 1153   DOLLAR
31.1050 g., 0.9990 Silver 0.9990 oz. ASW, 45 mm.   **Ruler:**
Elizabeth II **Subject:** XVIII Summer Olympics, Athens **Rev:**
Sprinter in color

Date	Mintage	F	VF	XF	Unc	BU
2004	Est. 5,000	—	—	—	—	45.00

KM# 1154   DOLLAR
31.1050 g., 0.9990 Silver 0.9990 oz. ASW, 45 mm.   **Ruler:**
Elizabeth II **Subject:** XXVIII Summer Olympics, Athens **Rev:**
Archer in color

Date	Mintage	F	VF	XF	Unc	BU
2004	Est. 5,000	—	—	—	—	45.00

KM# 1155   DOLLAR
31.1050 g., 0.9990 Silver 0.9990 oz. ASW, 45 mm.   **Ruler:**
Elizabeth II **Subject:** XXVIII Summer Olympics, Athens **Rev:**
Weightlifter in color

Date	Mintage	F	VF	XF	Unc	BU
2004 Proof	Est. 5,000	—	—	—	—	45.00

KM# 1156   DOLLAR
24.0000 g., Copper-Nickel, 38 mm.   **Ruler:** Elizabeth II **Rev:**
Mohandas Ghandhi

Date	Mintage	F	VF	XF	Unc	BU
2004	—	—	—	—	—	15.00

KM# 443   DOLLAR
23.9000 g., Copper-Nickel, 38.5 mm.   **Ruler:** Elizabeth II
Subject: Battle of Trafalgar **Obv:** Crowned bust right, new portrait
Rev: HMS Victory and color portrait of Nelson **Edge:** Reeded

Date	Mintage	F	VF	XF	Unc	BU
2005	—	—	—	—	12.00	14.00

KM# 470   DOLLAR
31.1600 g., 0.9990 Silver 1.0008 oz. ASW, 39.02 mm.   **Ruler:**
Elizabeth II **Obv:** Twin Towers and Statue of Liberty, Queens
Head below **Obv. Legend:** COOK ISLANDS / WE WILL NEVER
FORGET **Rev:** Freedoom Tower and Statue of Liberty **Rev.
Inscription:** LET / FREEDOM / RING - FREEDOM TOWER
Edge: Reeded and plain with lettering **Edge Lettering:** 1 TROY
OZ. .999 FINE SILVER

Date	Mintage	F	VF	XF	Unc	BU
2005 Proof	—	Value: 45.00				
2006 Proof	—	Value: 40.00				

KM# 1107   DOLLAR
31.1050 g., 0.9990 Silver partially gilt 0.9990 oz. ASW, 40 mm.
Ruler: Elizabeth II **Rev:** Pope Benedict XVI partially gilt

Date	Mintage	F	VF	XF	Unc	BU
2005 Proof	—	Value: 45.00				

KM# 1133   DOLLAR
Copper-Nickel, 38.6 mm.   **Ruler:** Elizabeth II **Subject:** Star
Wars, 30th Anniversary

Date	Mintage	F	VF	XF	Unc	BU
2005 Proof	Est. 9,999	Value: 30.00				

KM# 1157   DOLLAR
31.6350 g., 0.9990 Silver 1.0160 oz. ASW   **Ruler:** Elizabeth II
Subject: Australian Automobiles

Date	Mintage	F	VF	XF	Unc	BU
2005 Proof	Est. 1,500	Value: 55.00				

KM# 1158   DOLLAR
31.6350 g., 0.9990 Silver 1.0160 oz. ASW   **Ruler:** Elizabeth II
Subject: Australian Automobiles

Date	Mintage	F	VF	XF	Unc	BU
2005 Proof	Est. 1,500	Value: 55.00				

KM# 1159   DOLLAR
31.6350 g., 0.9990 Silver 1.0160 oz. ASW   **Ruler:** Elizabeth II
Subject: Australian Automobiles

Date	Mintage	F	VF	XF	Unc	BU
2005 Proof	Est. 1,500	Value: 55.00				

KM# 1160   DOLLAR
31.6350 g., 0.9990 Silver 1.0160 oz. ASW   **Ruler:** Elizabeth II
Subject: Australian Automobiles

Date	Mintage	F	VF	XF	Unc	BU
2005 Proof	Est. 1,500	Value: 55.00				

KM# 1161   DOLLAR
31.6350 g., 0.9990 Silver 1.0160 oz. ASW   **Ruler:** Elizabeth II
Subject: Australian Automobiles

Date	Mintage	F	VF	XF	Unc	BU
2005 Proof	Est. 1,500	Value: 55.00				

KM# 1162   DOLLAR
31.6350 g., 0.9990 Silver 1.0160 oz. ASW   **Ruler:** Elizabeth II
Subject: Australian Automobiles

Date	Mintage	F	VF	XF	Unc	BU
2005 Proof	Est. 1,500	Value: 55.00				

KM# 1163   DOLLAR
31.6350 g., 0.9990 Silver 1.0160 oz. ASW   **Ruler:** Elizabeth II
Subject: Australian Automobiles

Date	Mintage	F	VF	XF	Unc	BU
2005 Proof	Est. 1,500	Value: 55.00				

KM# 1164   DOLLAR
31.6350 g., 0.9990 Silver 1.0160 oz. ASW   **Ruler:** Elizabeth II
Subject: Australian Automobiles

Date	Mintage	F	VF	XF	Unc	BU
2005 Proof	Est. 1,500	Value: 55.00				

KM# 1165   DOLLAR
31.6350 g., 0.9990 Silver 1.0160 oz. ASW   **Ruler:** Elizabeth II
Subject: Australian Automobiles

Date	Mintage	F	VF	XF	Unc	BU
2005 Proof	Est. 1,500	Value: 55.00				

KM# 1166   DOLLAR
31.6350 g., 0.9990 Silver 1.0160 oz. ASW   **Ruler:** Elizabeth II
Subject: Australian Automobiles

Date	Mintage	F	VF	XF	Unc	BU
2005 Proof	1,500	Value: 55.00				

KM# 1167   DOLLAR
31.6350 g., 0.9990 Silver 1.0160 oz. ASW   **Ruler:** Elizabeth II
Subject: Australian Automobiles

Date	Mintage	F	VF	XF	Unc	BU
2005 Proof	Est. 1,500	Value: 55.00				

KM# 1168   DOLLAR
31.6350 g., 0.9990 Silver 1.0160 oz. ASW   **Ruler:** Elizabeth II
Subject: Australian Automobiles

Date	Mintage	F	VF	XF	Unc	BU
2005 Proof	Est. 1,500	Value: 55.00				

KM# 1173   DOLLAR
32.0000 g., Copper-Nickel, 40 mm.   **Ruler:** Elizabeth II **Rev:**
Snowflake, building tower hockey play and figure skater

Date	Mintage	F	VF	XF	Unc	BU
2005	20,000	—	—	—	—	15.00

KM# 1174   DOLLAR
Copper-Nickel   **Ruler:** Elizabeth II **Subject:** Marriage of Prince
Charles and Camilla Parker-Bowles

Date	Mintage	F	VF	XF	Unc	BU
2005	Est. 5,000	—	—	—	—	15.00

KM# 1177   DOLLAR
31.6350 g., 0.9990 Silver 1.0160 oz. ASW   **Ruler:** Elizabeth II
Rev: Pope John Paul II in color

Date	Mintage	F	VF	XF	Unc	BU
2005 Proof	5,000	Value: 125				

KM# 479   DOLLAR
Copper-Nickel, 38.6 mm.   **Ruler:** Elizabeth II **Subject:** Gun ships
of the world **Rev:** HMS Redoutable

Date	Mintage	F	VF	XF	Unc	BU
2006	—	—	—	—	—	25.00

KM# 480 DOLLAR
24.9000 g., Copper-Nickel, 38 mm. **Ruler:** Elizabeth II **Subject:** Gunships of the world **Obv:** Crowned bust right **Rev:** Ark Royal in color **Edge:** Reeded

Date	Mintage	F	VF	XF	Unc	BU
2006	—	—	—	—	—	25.00

KM# 752 DOLLAR
24.9000 g., Copper-Nickel, 38 mm. **Ruler:** Elizabeth II **Subject:** Gun ships - Chesapeak **Rev:** Multicolor naval ship

Date	Mintage	F	VF	XF	Unc	BU
2006	—	—	—	—	15.00	20.00

KM# 753 DOLLAR
24.9000 g., Copper-Nickel, 38 mm. **Ruler:** Elizabeth II **Subject:** Gun ships - Syvende **Rev:** Multicolor naval ship

Date	Mintage	F	VF	XF	Unc	BU
2006	—	—	—	—	15.00	20.00

KM# 754 DOLLAR
24.9000 g., Copper-Nickel, 38 mm. **Ruler:** Elizabeth II **Rev:** Multicolor Naval ship

Date	Mintage	F	VF	XF	Unc	BU
2006	—	—	—	—	15.00	20.00

KM# 755 DOLLAR
24.9000 g., Copper-Nickel, 38 mm. **Ruler:** Elizabeth II **Subject:** Gun Ships - Mary Rose **Rev:** Multicolor Naval ship

Date	Mintage	F	VF	XF	Unc	BU
2006	—	—	—	—	15.00	20.00

KM# 1137 DOLLAR
31.6350 g., 0.9990 Silver 1.0160 oz. ASW **Ruler:** Elizabeth II **Subject:** 1923 New South Wales Garford Fire

Date	Mintage	F	VF	XF	Unc	BU
2006 Proof	Est. 5,000	Value: 55.00				

KM# 1169 DOLLAR
0.5000 g., 0.9990 Gold 0.0161 oz. AGW **Ruler:** Elizabeth II **Rev:** Pope Benedict XVI

Date	Mintage	F	VF	XF	Unc	BU
2006 Proof	—	Value: 45.00				

KM# 1179 DOLLAR
Silver **Ruler:** Elizabeth II **Subject:** David Livingstone

Date	Mintage	F	VF	XF	Unc	BU
2006 Proof	—	Value: 45.00				

KM# 1180 DOLLAR
Silver **Ruler:** Elizabeth II **Subject:** Ferdinanad Magellan

Date	Mintage	F	VF	XF	Unc	BU
2006 Proof	—	Value: 45.00				

KM# 1181 DOLLAR
Silver **Ruler:** Elizabeth II **Subject:** Roald Amundsen

Date	Mintage	F	VF	XF	Unc	BU
2006 Proof	—	Value: 45.00				

KM# 1182 DOLLAR
Silver **Ruler:** Elizabeth II **Subject:** Christopher Columbus

Date	Mintage	F	VF	XF	Unc	BU
2006 Proof	—	Value: 45.00				

KM# 1183 DOLLAR
Silver **Ruler:** Elizabeth II **Subject:** Juan Sebastian de Elcano

Date	Mintage	F	VF	XF	Unc	BU
2006 Proof	—	Value: 45.00				

KM# 733 DOLLAR
25.0900 g., Copper-Nickel, 38.8 mm. **Ruler:** Elizabeth II **Rev:** HMS Victory **Rev. Legend:** England expects that every man will do his duty

Date	Mintage	F	VF	XF	Unc	BU
2007	—	—	—	—	—	15.00

KM# 734 DOLLAR
25.0900 g., Copper-Nickel, 38.8 mm. **Ruler:** Elizabeth II **Rev:** Admiral Nelson and two naval vessels **Rev. Legend:** England expects that every man will do his duty

Date	Mintage	F	VF	XF	Unc	BU
2007	—	—	—	—	—	15.00

KM# 735 DOLLAR
0.5000 g., 0.9990 Gold 0.0161 oz. AGW, 11 mm. **Ruler:** Elizabeth II **Rev:** Treaty of Rome - Slovenia

Date	Mintage	F	VF	XF	Unc	BU
2007 Proof	—	Value: 40.00				

KM# 736 DOLLAR
0.5000 g., 0.9990 Gold 0.0161 oz. AGW **Ruler:** Elizabeth II **Rev:** Benedict XVI's 2 Euro Coin

Date	Mintage	F	VF	XF	Unc	BU
2007 Proof	—	Value: 40.00				

KM# 471 DOLLAR
35.8000 g., 0.9990 Silver 1.1498 oz. ASW **Ruler:** Elizabeth II **Subject:** Sputnik 50th Anniversary - 1957-2007 **Obv:** Small bust divides legend above, center globe with color applique **Rev:** Satellite orbiting Earth with color applique **Rev. Legend:** SPUTNIK 50th ANNIVERSARY 1957 - 2007 **Edge:** Plain **Note:** Center piece rotates freely

Date	Mintage	F	VF	XF	Unc	BU
ND2007 Proof	—	Value: 95.00				

KM# 490 DOLLAR
31.1030 g., 0.9990 Silver 0.9989 oz. ASW, 40.6 mm. **Ruler:** Elizabeth II **Subject:** Historical Australian Coins **Obv:** Head with tiara right **Rev:** 1757 New South Wales Holey Dollar **Edge:** Reeded

Date	Mintage	F	VF	XF	Unc	BU
2007 Proof	1,500	Value: 125				

KM# 491 DOLLAR
31.1030 g., 0.9990 Silver 0.9989 oz. ASW, 40.6 mm. **Ruler:** Elizabeth II **Subject:** Historical Australian Coins **Obv:** Head with tiara right **Rev:** Gilt 1857 Sydney Mint Sovereign **Edge:** Reeded

Date	Mintage	F	VF	XF	Unc	BU
2007 Proof	1,500	Value: 125				

KM# 492   DOLLAR
31.1030 g., 0.9990 Silver Selective copper plating 0.9989 oz.
ASW, 40.6 mm.   **Ruler:** Elizabeth II **Subject:** Historical
Australian Coins **Obv:** Head with tiarra right **Rev:** Copper 1937
pattern penny **Edge:** Reeded

Date	Mintage	F	VF	XF	Unc	BU
2007 Proof	1,500	Value: 125				

KM# 1138   DOLLAR
0.5000 g., 0.9990 Gold 0.0161 oz. AGW, 11 mm.   **Ruler:**
Elizabeth II **Subject:** Treaty of Rome, 50th Anniversary **Rev:** San
Marino

Date	Mintage	F	VF	XF	Unc	BU
2007 Proof	Est. 5,000	Value: 50.00				

KM# 1196   DOLLAR
25.0000 g., Copper-Nickel, 38.6 mm.   **Ruler:** Elizabeth II **Rev:**
Elizabeth II and Prince Philip in color

Date	Mintage	F	VF	XF	Unc	BU
2007 Proof	Est. 50,000	Value: 17.50				

KM# 1197   DOLLAR
25.0000 g., Copper-Nickel, 38.6 mm.   **Ruler:** Elizabeth II **Rev:**
Elizabeth II and Prince Philip in color

Date	Mintage	F	VF	XF	Unc	BU
2007 Proof	Est. 50,000	Value: 17.50				

KM# 1198   DOLLAR
25.0000 g., Copper-Nickel, 38.6 mm.   **Ruler:** Elizabeth II **Rev:**
Elizabeth II and Prince Philip in color

Date	Mintage	F	VF	XF	Unc	BU
2007 Proof	Est. 50,000	Value: 17.50				

KM# 1199   DOLLAR
25.0000 g., Copper-Nickel, 38.6 mm.   **Ruler:** Elizabeth II **Rev:**
Elizabeth II and Prince Philip in color

Date	Mintage	F	VF	XF	Unc	BU
2007 Proof	Est. 50,000	Value: 17.50				

KM# 1200   DOLLAR
25.0000 g., Copper-Nickel, 38.6 mm.   **Ruler:** Elizabeth II **Rev:**
Elizabth and Prince Philip in color

Date	Mintage	F	VF	XF	Unc	BU
2007 Proof	Est. 50,000	Value: 17.50				

KM# 493   DOLLAR
31.1030 g., 0.9990 Silver 0.9989 oz. ASW, 40.6 mm.   **Ruler:**
Elizabeth II **Subject:** Historical Australian Coins **Obv:** Head with
tiara right **Rev:** 1823 MacIntosh and Degraves Shilling **Edge:**
Reeded

Date	Mintage	F	VF	XF	Unc	BU
2008 Proof	1,500	Value: 125				

KM# 494   DOLLAR
31.1030 g., 0.9990 Silver Selective gold plating 0.9989 oz. ASW,
40.6 mm.   **Ruler:** Elizabeth II **Subject:** Historic Australian Coins

Obv: Head with tiara right **Rev:** Gilt 1788 George III Spade
Guinea **Edge:** Reeded

Date	Mintage	F	VF	XF	Unc	BU
2008 Proof	1,500	Value: 125				

KM# 495   DOLLAR
31.1030 g., 0.9990 Silver 0.9989 oz. ASW, 40.6 mm.   **Ruler:**
Elizabeth II **Subject:** Historic Australian Coins **Obv:** Head with
tiara right **Rev:** Australian 1910 Florin **Edge:** Reeded

Date	Mintage	F	VF	XF	Unc	BU
2008 Proof	1,500	Value: 125				

KM# 496   DOLLAR
31.1030 g., 0.9990 Silver Selective gold plating 0.9989 oz. ASW,
40.6 mm.   **Ruler:** Elizabeth II **Subject:** Historic Australian Coins
Obv: Head with tiara right **Rev:** Gilt 1808-1815 Gold Pagoda
Edge: Reeded

Date	Mintage	F	VF	XF	Unc	BU
2008 Proof	1,500	Value: 125				

KM# 497   DOLLAR
31.1030 g., 0.9990 Silver 0.9989 oz. ASW, 40.6 mm.   **Ruler:**
Elizabeth II **Subject:** Historic Australian Coins **Obv:** Head with
tiara right **Rev:** 1850's Taylor's sixpence pattern **Edge:** Reeded

Date	Mintage	F	VF	XF	Unc	BU
2008 Proof	1,500	Value: 125				

KM# 498   DOLLAR
31.1050 g., 0.9990 Silver Selective copper plating 0.9990 oz.
ASW, 40.6 mm.   **Ruler:** Elizabeth II **Subject:** Historic Australian
Coins **Obv:** Head with tiara right **Rev:** Copper Australian WWII
Interment Camp Token **Edge:** Reeded

Date	Mintage	F	VF	XF	Unc	BU
2008 Proof	1,500	Value: 125				

KM# 499   DOLLAR
31.1030 g., 0.9990 Silver 0.9989 oz. ASW, 40.6 mm.   **Ruler:**
Elizabeth II **Subject:** Historic Australian Coins **Obv:** Head with
tiara right **Rev:** Australian 1946 Perth Mint Shilling **Edge:** Reeded

Date	Mintage	F	VF	XF	Unc	BU
2008 Proof	1,500	Value: 125				

KM# 500   DOLLAR
31.1030 g., 0.9990 Silver 0.9989 oz. ASW, 40.6 mm.   **Ruler:**
Elizabeth II **Subject:** Historic Australian Coins **Obv:** Head with
tiara right **Rev:** Australian 1938 Crown **Edge:** Reeded

Date	Mintage	F	VF	XF	Unc	BU
2008 Proof	1,500	Value: 125				

KM# 501   DOLLAR
31.1030 g., 0.9990 Silver 0.9989 oz. ASW, 40.6 mm.   **Ruler:**
Elizabeth II **Subject:** Historic Australian Coins **Obv:** Head with
tiara right **Rev:** Copper Australian 1930 Penny **Edge:** Reeded

Date	Mintage	F	VF	XF	Unc	BU
2008 Proof	1,500	Value: 125				

KM# 502   DOLLAR
31.1030 g., 0.9990 Silver 0.9989 oz. ASW, 40.6 mm.   **Ruler:**
Elizabeth II **Subject:** World War I **Obv:** Head with tiara right **Rev:**
Multicolor image of Australian WWI soldier in Europe **Edge:**
Reeded

Date	Mintage	F	VF	XF	Unc	BU
2008 Proof	1,918	Value: 85.00				

KM# 504 DOLLAR
31.1030 g., 0.9990 Silver 0.9989 oz. ASW, 40.6 mm. **Ruler:**
Elizabeth II **Subject:** WWI **Obv:** Head with tiara right **Rev:**
Multicolor image of Australian WWI soldier in Mid-East scene
Edge: Reeded

Date	Mintage	F	VF	XF	Unc	BU
2008 Proof	1,918	Value: 85.00				

KM# 506 DOLLAR
31.1030 g., 0.9990 Silver 0.9989 oz. ASW, 40.6 mm. **Ruler:**
Elizabeth II **Subject:** Captain Cook **Obv:** Head with tiara right
Rev: Multicolor image of James Cook within letter C **Edge:**
Reeded

Date	Mintage	F	VF	XF	Unc	BU
2008 Proof	1,779	Value: 100				

KM# 507 DOLLAR
31.1030 g., 0.9990 Silver 0.9989 oz. ASW, 40.6 mm. **Ruler:**
Elizabeth II **Subject:** Captain Cook **Obv:** Head with tiara right
Rev: Multicolor image of James Cook, Bottany Bay all within letter
O **Edge:** Reeded

Date	Mintage	F	VF	XF	Unc	BU
2008 Proof	1,779	Value: 100				

KM# 508 DOLLAR
31.1030 g., 0.9990 Silver 0.9989 oz. ASW, 40.6 mm. **Ruler:**
Elizabeth II **Subject:** Captain Cook **Obv:** Head with tiara right
Rev: Multicolor image of James Cook, a new world all within letter
O **Edge:** Reeded

Date	Mintage	F	VF	XF	Unc	BU
2008 Proof	1,779	Value: 100				

KM# 509 DOLLAR
31.1030 g., 0.9990 Silver 0.9989 oz. ASW, 40.6 mm. **Ruler:**
Elizabeth II **Subject:** Captain Cook **Obv:** Head with tiara right
Rev: Multicolor image of James Cook, striking the reef, large
letter K in background **Edge:** Reeded

Date	Mintage	F	VF	XF	Unc	BU
2008 Proof	1,779	Value: 100				

KM# 765 DOLLAR
35.8000 g., 0.9990 Silver 1.1498 oz. ASW, 40 mm. **Ruler:**
Elizabeth II **Subject:** 1961 First man in Space

Date	Mintage	F	VF	XF	Unc	BU
2008 Proof	—	Value: 115				

KM# 801 DOLLAR
31.1050 g., 0.9990 Silver 0.9990 oz. ASW, 40 mm. **Ruler:**
Elizabeth II **Rev:** An-2, partially gilt

Date	Mintage	F	VF	XF	Unc	BU
2008 Proof	—	Value: 50.00				

KM# 802 DOLLAR
31.1050 g., 0.9990 Silver 0.9990 oz. ASW, 40 mm. **Ruler:**
Elizabeth II **Rev:** An-74, partially gilt

Date	Mintage	F	VF	XF	Unc	BU
2008 Proof	—	Value: 50.00				

KM# 803 DOLLAR
31.1050 g., 0.9990 Silver 0.9990 oz. ASW, 40 mm. **Ruler:**
Elizabeth II **Rev:** An-124, partially gilt

Date	Mintage	F	VF	XF	Unc	BU
2008 Proof	—	Value: 50.00				

KM# 804 DOLLAR
31.1050 g., 0.9990 Silver 0.9990 oz. ASW, 40 mm. **Ruler:**
Elizabeth II **Rev:** An-148, partially gilt

Date	Mintage	F	VF	XF	Unc	BU
2008 Proof	—	Value: 50.00				

KM# 805 DOLLAR
31.1050 g., 0.9990 Silver 0.9990 oz. ASW, 40 mm. **Ruler:**
Elizabeth II **Rev:** An-225, partially gilt

Date	Mintage	F	VF	XF	Unc	BU
2008 Proof	—	Value: 50.00				

KM# 1208 DOLLAR
0.5000 g., 0.9990 Gold 0.0161 oz. AGW, 11 mm. **Ruler:**
Elizabeth II **Subject:** British Monarchs - Henry V

Date	Mintage	F	VF	XF	Unc	BU
2008 Proof	Est. 14,500	Value: 35.00				

KM# 1209 DOLLAR
0.5000 g., 0.9990 Gold 0.0161 oz. AGW, 11 mm. **Ruler:**
Elizabeth II **Subject:** British Monarchs - Henry VIII

Date	Mintage	F	VF	XF	Unc	BU
2008 Proof	Est. 50,000	Value: 35.00				

KM# 1209a DOLLAR
0.5000 g., 0.9990 Platinum 0.0161 oz. APW, 11 mm. **Ruler:**
Elizabeth II **Subject:** British Monarchs - Henry VIII

Date	Mintage	F	VF	XF	Unc	BU
2008 Proof	Est. 50,000	Value: 50.00				

KM# 1210 DOLLAR
0.5000 g., 0.9990 Gold 0.0161 oz. AGW, 11 mm. **Ruler:**
Elizabeth II **Subject:** British Monarchs - Elizabeth II

Date	Mintage	F	VF	XF	Unc	BU
2008 Proof	Est. 50,000	Value: 35.00				

KM# 701 DOLLAR
31.1050 g., 0.9990 Silver 0.9990 oz. ASW, 39 mm. **Ruler:**
Elizabeth II **Subject:** First Man on the Moon, 40th Anniversary
Obv: Head right at top, multicolor moon in center **Rev:** Rocket,
orbiter, moon walk. moon in multicolor at center

Date	Mintage	F	VF	XF	Unc	BU
2009 Proof	25,000	Value: 110				

KM# 702 DOLLAR
31.1050 g., 0.9990 Silver 0.9990 oz. ASW, 33x33 mm. **Ruler:**
Elizabeth II **Subject:** Cook's Cottage, 75th Anniversary of
relocation **Obv:** Head right **Rev:** Cottage and multicolor Captain
Cook image **Shape:** Square

Date	Mintage	F	VF	XF	Unc	BU
2009 Proof	5,000	Value: 95.00				

KM# 706 DOLLAR
0.5000 g., 0.9990 Gold 0.0161 oz. AGW, 11 mm. **Ruler:**
Elizabeth II **Subject:** Pope Benedict XVI visits the Holy Land **Rev:**
Dome of the Rock

Date	Mintage	F	VF	XF	Unc	BU
2009 Proof	25,000	Value: 35.00				

KM# 772 DOLLAR
27.0000 g., Copper silver plated, 40 mm. **Ruler:** Elizabeth II
Subject: Year of Astronomy **Rev:** Sun, multicolor

Date	Mintage	F	VF	XF	Unc	BU
2009	—	—	—	—	—	20.00

KM# 773 DOLLAR
27.0000 g., Copper silver plated, 40 mm. **Ruler:** Elizabeth II
Subject: Year of Astronomy **Rev:** Mercury, multicolor

Date	Mintage	F	VF	XF	Unc	BU
2009	—	—	—	—	—	20.00

KM# 774   DOLLAR
27.0000 g., Copper silver plated, 40 mm. **Ruler:** Elizabeth II
Subject: Year of Astronomy **Rev:** Venus, multicolor

Date	Mintage	F	VF	XF	Unc	BU
2009	—	—	—	—	—	25.00

KM# 775   DOLLAR
27.0000 g., Copper silver plated, 40 mm. **Ruler:** Elizabeth II
Subject: Year of Astronomy **Rev:** Earth, multicolor

Date	Mintage	F	VF	XF	Unc	BU
2009	—	—	—	—	—	22.00

KM# 776   DOLLAR
27.0000 g., Copper silver plated, 40 mm. **Ruler:** Elizabeth II
Subject: Year of Astronomy **Rev:** Mars, multicolor

Date	Mintage	F	VF	XF	Unc	BU
2009	—	—	—	—	—	22.00

KM# 777   DOLLAR
27.0000 g., Copper silver plated, 40 mm. **Ruler:** Elizabeth II
Subject: Year of Astronomy **Rev:** Jupiter, multicolor

Date	Mintage	F	VF	XF	Unc	BU
2009	—	—	—	—	—	22.00

KM# 778   DOLLAR
27.0000 g., Copper silver plated, 40 mm. **Ruler:** Elizabeth II
Subject: Year of Astronomy **Rev:** Saturn, multicolor

Date	Mintage	F	VF	XF	Unc	BU
2009	—	—	—	—	—	22.00

KM# 779   DOLLAR
27.0000 g., Copper silver plated, 40 mm. **Ruler:** Elizabeth II
Subject: Year of Astronomy **Rev:** Uranus, multicolor

Date	Mintage	F	VF	XF	Unc	BU
2009	—	—	—	—	—	22.00

KM# 780   DOLLAR
27.0000 g., Copper silver plated, 40 mm. **Ruler:** Elizabeth II
Subject: Year of Astronomy **Rev:** Neptune, multicolor

Date	Mintage	F	VF	XF	Unc	BU
2009	—	—	—	—	—	22.00

KM# 781   DOLLAR
27.0000 g., Copper silver plated, 40 mm. **Ruler:** Elizabeth II
Subject: Year of Astronomy **Rev:** Solar System, multicolor

Date	Mintage	F	VF	XF	Unc	BU
2009	—	—	—	—	—	22.00

KM# 794   DOLLAR
Copper-Nickel silver plated, 40 mm. **Ruler:** Elizabeth II **Rev:**
Nessie, multicolor

Date	Mintage	F	VF	XF	Unc	BU
2009	—	—	—	—	—	22.00

KM# 795   DOLLAR
Copper-Nickel silver plated, 40 mm. **Ruler:** Elizabeth II **Rev:**
Bigfoot, multicolor

Date	Mintage	F	VF	XF	Unc	BU
2009	—	—	—	—	—	22.00

KM# 796   DOLLAR
Copper-Nickel, 40 mm. **Ruler:** Elizabeth II **Rev:** Medussa,
multicolor

Date	Mintage	F	VF	XF	Unc	BU
2009	—	—	—	—	—	22.00

KM# 797   DOLLAR
Copper-Nickel, 40 mm. **Ruler:** Elizabeth II **Rev:** Pegasus,
multicolor

Date	Mintage	F	VF	XF	Unc	BU
2009	—	—	—	—	—	22.00

KM# 798   DOLLAR
Silver, 40 mm. **Ruler:** Elizabeth II **Rev:** Baba Yaga, multicolor

Date	Mintage	F	VF	XF	Unc	BU
2009	—	—	—	—	—	22.00

KM# 799   DOLLAR
Copper-Nickel, 40 mm. **Ruler:** Elizabeth II **Rev:** Phoenix,
multicolor

Date	Mintage	F	VF	XF	Unc	BU
2009	—	—	—	—	—	22.00

KM# 1172   DOLLAR
27.0000 g., Copper-Nickel, 38.6 mm.   **Ruler:** Elizabeth II
Subject: Moon Landing, 40th Anniversary **Rev:** Landing module
Eagle and moon in color

Date	Mintage	F	VF	XF	Unc	BU
2009	—	—	—	—	—	17.50

KM# 1231   DOLLAR
25.0000 g., Copper-Nickel partially gilt, 38.6 mm.   **Ruler:**
Elizabeth II **Subject:** British Monarchs - Henry VIII

Date	Mintage	F	VF	XF	Unc	BU
2009	Est. 50,000	—	—	—	—	17.50

KM# 1241   DOLLAR
31.1350 g., 0.9990 Silver 1.0000 oz. ASW, 38.61 mm.   **Ruler:**
Elizabeth II **Subject:** Battle of Gettysburg and General Meade
Rev: Battle scene at left, Meade in color at right

Date	Mintage	F	VF	XF	Unc	BU
2009 Proof	—	Value: 75.00				

KM# 1327   DOLLAR
Silver   **Ruler:** Elizabeth II **Subject:** Mystical creatures - Drago
Rev: Dragon in color

Date	Mintage	F	VF	XF	Unc	BU
2009 Proof	—	Value: 75.00				

KM# 1328   DOLLAR
Copper-Nickel   **Ruler:** Elizabeth II **Subject:** Wonders of the
World **Rev:** Ayers Rock in color

Date	Mintage	F	VF	XF	Unc	BU
2009	—	—	—	—	—	20.00

KM# 762   DOLLAR
10.9300 g., Bi-Metallic Copper Nickel center in Aluminum-Bronze
ring.   **Ruler:** Elizabeth II **Obv:** Bust right **Rev:** Carved Maori
figure (Tangaroa)

Date	Mintage	F	VF	XF	Unc	BU
2010	—	—	—	—	5.00	6.00

KM# 720   DOLLAR
0.1200 g., 0.9990 Silver 0.0039 oz. ASW, 4 mm.   **Ruler:**
Elizabeth II **Rev:** Fisherman's God statue **Note:** Illustration
enlarged.

Date	Mintage	F	VF	XF	Unc	BU
2010 Prooflike	5,000	—	—	—	—	7.00

KM# 739   DOLLAR
31.1050 g., 0.9990 Silver 0.9990 oz. ASW, 37.65 mm.   **Ruler:**
Elizabeth II **Subject:** Niko & the way to the stars **Obv:** Head
crowned left **Rev:** Multicolor deer **Shape:** 7-sided

Date	Mintage	F	VF	XF	Unc	BU
2010 Proof	3,500	Value: 60.00				

KM# 740   DOLLAR
31.1050 g., 0.9990 Silver 0.9990 oz. ASW, 37.65 mm.   **Ruler:**
Elizabeth II **Subject:** Niko & the way to the stars **Obv:** Head
crowned left **Rev:** Multicolor wolf **Shape:** 7-sided

Date	Mintage	F	VF	XF	Unc	BU
2010 Proof	3,500	Value: 60.00				

KM# 741   DOLLAR
31.1050 g., 0.9990 Silver 0.9990 oz. ASW, 37.65 mm.   **Ruler:**
Elizabeth II **Subject:** Niko & the way to the stars **Obv:** Head
crowned left **Rev:** Multicolor flying squirrel **Shape:** 7-sided

Date	Mintage	F	VF	XF	Unc	BU
2010 Proof	3,500	Value: 60.00				

KM# 742   DOLLAR
31.1050 g., 0.9990 Silver 0.9990 oz. ASW, 37.65 mm.   **Ruler:**
Elizabeth II **Subject:** Niko and the way to the stars **Obv:** Head
crowned right **Rev:** Multicolor Ermine **Shape:** 7-sided

Date	Mintage	F	VF	XF	Unc	BU
2010 Proof	3,500	Value: 60.00				

KM# 743   DOLLAR
31.1050 g., 0.9990 Silver 0.9990 oz. ASW, 37.65 mm.   **Ruler:**
Elizabeth II **Subject:** Niko and the way to the stars **Obv:** Head
crowned right **Rev:** Multicolor deer, flying squirrel and ermine
Shape: 7-sided

Date	Mintage	F	VF	XF	Unc	BU
2010 Proof	3,500	Value: 60.00				

KM# 744   DOLLAR
31.1350 g., 0.9990 Silver 1.0000 oz. ASW, 40.6 mm.   **Ruler:**
Elizabeth II **Subject:** Battle of Trafalgar, 1805 **Rev:** Multicolor
battle scene, HMS Victory

Date	Mintage	F	VF	XF	Unc	BU
2010 Proof	5,000	Value: 80.00				

KM# 770   DOLLAR
31.1050 g., 0.9990 Silver 0.9990 oz. ASW, 40 mm.   **Ruler:**
Elizabeth II **Subject:** Battle of Hampton Roads, Va. **Rev:** Monitor,
multicolor background

Date	Mintage	F	VF	XF	Unc	BU
2010 Proof	5,000	Value: 80.00				

KM# 771   DOLLAR
31.1050 g., 0.9990 Silver 0.9990 oz. ASW, 40 mm.   **Ruler:**
Elizabeth II **Subject:** Battle of Salams **Rev:** Trireame, multicolor
insert

Date	Mintage	F	VF	XF	Unc	BU
2010 Proof	5,000	Value: 100				

KM# 1243   DOLLAR
31.1350 g., 0.9990 Silver 1.0000 oz. ASW, 40.6 mm. **Ruler:**
Elizabeth II **Subject:** Battle of Midway **Rev:** Aircraft carrier

Date	Mintage	F	VF	XF	Unc	BU
2010 Proof	5,000	Value: 100				

KM# 1256   DOLLAR
31.1350 g., 0.9990 Silver 1.0000 oz. ASW, 40.6 mm. **Ruler:**
Elizabeth II **Subject:** Battle of Grunwald

Date	Mintage	F	VF	XF	Unc	BU
2010 Proof	—	Value: 50.00				

KM# 1257   DOLLAR
31.1050 g., 0.9990 Silver 0.9990 oz. ASW, 40.6 mm. **Ruler:**
Elizabeth II **Subject:** Trafalgar **Rev:** H.M.S. Victory and Battle
scene in color

Date	Mintage	F	VF	XF	Unc	BU
2010 Proof	5,000	Value: 80.00				

KM# 1295   DOLLAR
0.5000 g., 0.9990 Gold 0.0161 oz. AGW, 11 mm. **Ruler:**
Elizabeth II **Rev:** Martin Luther King

Date	Mintage	F	VF	XF	Unc	BU
2010 Proof	—	Value: 50.00				

KM# 1313   DOLLAR
27.0000 g., Silver Plated Copper, 38.61 mm. **Ruler:** Elizabeth II
Subject: Marilyn Monroe, 85th Birthday

Date	Mintage	F	VF	XF	Unc	BU
2011 Proof	2,500	Value: 25.00				

KM# 1283   DOLLAR
31.1000 g., 0.9990 Silver 0.9988 oz. ASW, 40.6 mm. **Ruler:**
Elizabeth II **Subject:** Florin - 1927 design

Date	Mintage	F	VF	XF	Unc	BU
2011 Proof	1,500	Value: 75.00				

KM# 1235   DOLLAR
31.1350 g., 0.9990 Silver 1.0000 oz. ASW, 40.6 mm. **Ruler:**
Elizabeth II **Subject:** Battle of Jutland, 1916 **Rev:** Multicolor
battleship

Date	Mintage	F	VF	XF	Unc	BU
2011 Proof	5,000	Value: 85.00				

KM# 1269   DOLLAR
31.1350 g., 0.9990 Silver 1.0000 oz. ASW, 47.6x27.6 mm.
Ruler: Elizabeth II **Subject:** Year of the Rabbit **Rev:** Two brown
rabbits **Shape:** Rectangle

Date	Mintage	F	VF	XF	Unc	BU
2011 Proof	3,000	Value: 100				

KM# 1270   DOLLAR
31.1350 g., 0.9990 Silver 1.0000 oz. ASW, 47.6x27.6 mm.
Ruler: Elizabeth II **Subject:** Year of the Rabbit **Rev:** Two white
rabbits **Shape:** Rectangle

Date	Mintage	F	VF	XF	Unc	BU
2011 Proof	3,000	Value: 100				

KM# 1271   DOLLAR
31.1350 g., 0.9990 Silver 1.0000 oz. ASW, 47.6x27.6 mm.
Ruler: Elizabeth II **Subject:** Year of the Rabbit **Rev:** One black
rabbit **Shape:** Rectangle

Date	Mintage	F	VF	XF	Unc	BU
2011 Proof	3,000	Value: 100				

KM# 1272   DOLLAR
31.1350 g., 0.9990 Silver 1.0000 oz. ASW, 47.6x27.6 mm.
Ruler: Elizabeth II **Subject:** Year of the Rabbit **Rev:** One black
rabbit **Shape:** Rectangle

Date	Mintage	F	VF	XF	Unc	BU
2011 Proof	3,000	Value: 100				

KM# 1284   DOLLAR
31.1000 g., 0.9990 Silver 0.9988 oz. ASW, 40.6 mm. **Ruler:**
Elizabeth II **Subject:** Florin - 1934-35 Centenary

Date	Mintage	F	VF	XF	Unc	BU
2011 Proof	1,500	Value: 75.00				

KM# 1285   DOLLAR
31.1000 g., 0.9990 Silver 0.9988 oz. ASW, 40.6 mm. **Ruler:**
Elizabeth II **Subject:** Florin - 1901-51 Jubilee

Date	Mintage	F	VF	XF	Unc	BU
2011 Proof	1,500	Value: 75.00				

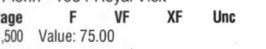

KM# 1286   DOLLAR
31.1000 g., 0.9990 Silver 0.9988 oz. ASW, 40.6 mm. **Ruler:**
Elizabeth II **Subject:** Florin - 1954 Royal Visit

Date	Mintage	F	VF	XF	Unc	BU
2011 Proof	1,500	Value: 75.00				

KM# 1342 DOLLAR
31.1050 g., 0.9990 Silver 0.9990 oz. ASW, 38.61 mm. **Ruler:** Elizabeth II **Subject:** Planets - Mercury **Rev:** with color

Date	Mintage	F	VF	XF	Unc	BU
2011 Proof	—	Value: 75.00				

KM# 1343 DOLLAR
31.1050 g., 0.9990 Silver 0.9990 oz. ASW, 38.61 mm. **Ruler:** Elizabeth II **Subject:** Plants - Venus **Rev:** with color

Date	Mintage	F	VF	XF	Unc	BU
2011 Proof	—	Value: 75.00				

KM# 1344 DOLLAR
31.1050 g., 0.9990 Silver 0.9990 oz. ASW, 38.61 mm. **Ruler:** Elizabeth II **Subject:** Planets - Earth **Rev:** with color

Date	Mintage	F	VF	XF	Unc	BU
2011 Proof	—	Value: 75.00				

KM# 1345 DOLLAR
31.1050 g., 0.9990 Silver 0.9990 oz. ASW, 38.61 mm. **Ruler:** Elizabeth II **Subject:** Plants - Mars **Rev:** with color

Date	Mintage	F	VF	XF	Unc	BU
2011 Proof	—	Value: 75.00				

KM# 1346 DOLLAR
31.1050 g., 0.9990 Silver 0.9990 oz. ASW, 38.61 mm. **Ruler:** Elizabeth II **Subject:** Planets - Jupiter **Rev:** Jupiter and Sagittarius with color

Date	Mintage	F	VF	XF	Unc	BU
2011 Proof	—	Value: 75.00				

KM# 1347 DOLLAR
31.1050 g., 0.9990 Silver 0.9990 oz. ASW, 38.61 mm. **Ruler:** Elizabeth II **Subject:** Planets - Saturn **Rev:** Saturn and Capricorn with color

Date	Mintage	F	VF	XF	Unc	BU
2011 Proof	—	Value: 75.00				

KM# 1348 DOLLAR
31.1050 g., 0.9990 Silver 0.9990 oz. ASW, 38.61 mm. **Ruler:** Elizabeth II **Subject:** Planets - Uranis **Rev:** Uranis and Aquarius with color

Date	Mintage	F	VF	XF	Unc	BU
2011 Proof	—	Value: 75.00				

KM# 1385 DOLLAR
31.1050 g., 0.9990 Silver 0.9990 oz. ASW, 38.61 mm. **Ruler:** Elizabeth II **Subject:** Marylin Monroe, 80th Birthday **Rev:** Marylin Monroe in color pose

Date	Mintage	F	VF	XF	Unc	BU
2011 Proof	—	Value: 125				

KM# 1396 DOLLAR
31.1050 g., 0.9990 Silver 0.9990 oz. ASW, 38.61 mm. **Ruler:** Elizabeth II **Subject:** Hollywood Legends - Elizabeth Taylor **Rev:** Elizabeth Taylor facing photo

Date	Mintage	F	VF	XF	Unc	BU
2011 Proof	—	Value: 125				

KM# 1375 DOLLAR
0.5000 g., 0.9990 Gold 0.0161 oz. AGW, 11 mm. **Ruler:** Elizabeth II **Obv:** Head with tiara right **Rev:** Titanic sailing left

Date	Mintage	F	VF	XF	Unc	BU
2012 Proof	—	Value: 50.00				

KM# 1391 DOLLAR
31.1050 g., 0.9990 Silver 0.9990 oz. ASW, 47.6x27.6 mm. **Ruler:** Elizabeth II **Obv:** Head with crown right **Rev:** Orange dragon at right

Date	Mintage	F	VF	XF	Unc	BU
2012 Proof	3,000	Value: 125				

KM# 1392 DOLLAR
31.1050 g., 0.9990 Silver 0.9990 oz. ASW, 47.6x27.6 mm. **Ruler:** Elizabeth II **Obv:** Head with crown right **Rev:** Blue dragon at left center

Date	Mintage	F	VF	XF	Unc	BU
2012 Proof	3,000	Value: 125				

KM# 1393 DOLLAR
31.1050 g., 0.9990 Silver 0.9990 oz. ASW, 47.6x27.6 mm. **Ruler:** Elizabeth II **Obv:** Head with crown right **Rev:** Brown dragon at center

Date	Mintage	F	VF	XF	Unc	BU
2012 Proof	3,000	Value: 125				

KM# 1394 DOLLAR
31.1050 g., 0.9990 Silver 0.9990 oz. ASW, 47.6x27.6 mm. **Ruler:** Elizabeth II **Obv:** Head with crown right **Rev:** Orange dragon at left

Date	Mintage	F	VF	XF	Unc	BU
2012 Proof	3,000	Value: 125				

KM# 554 2 DOLLARS
31.1050 g., 0.9990 Silver 0.9990 oz. ASW, 40.5 mm. **Ruler:** Elizabeth II **Subject:** Asian wildlife **Rev:** Multicolored pheasant-tailed Jacana

Date	Mintage	F	VF	XF	Unc	BU
2001 Proof	3,000	Value: 85.00				

KM# 551 2 DOLLARS
31.1050 g., 0.9990 Silver 0.9990 oz. ASW, 40.5 mm. **Ruler:** Elizabeth II **Subject:** Asian wildlife **Rev:** Multicolor Mikado Pheasant

Date	Mintage	F	VF	XF	Unc	BU
2001 Proof	5,000	Value: 85.00				

KM# 552 2 DOLLARS
31.1050 g., 0.9990 Silver 0.9990 oz. ASW, 40.5 mm. **Ruler:** Elizabeth II **Subject:** Asian wildlife **Rev:** Multicolor black-faced spoonbill

Date	Mintage	F	VF	XF	Unc	BU
2001 Proof	5,000	Value: 85.00				

KM# 553 2 DOLLARS
31.1050 g., 0.9990 Silver 0.9990 oz. ASW, 40.5 mm. **Ruler:** Elizabeth II **Subject:** Asian wildlife **Rev:** Multicolor Indian Pitta

Date	Mintage	F	VF	XF	Unc	BU
2001 Proof	3,000	Value: 85.00				

KM# 468 2 DOLLARS
Copper-Nickel **Ruler:** Elizabeth II **Rev:** Football championship

Date	Mintage	F	VF	XF	Unc	BU
2002	—	—	—	—	5.00	7.00

KM# 1119 2 DOLLARS
Copper-Nickel, 30 mm. **Ruler:** Elizabeth II **Subject:** XXVIII Summer Olympics, Athens **Rev:** Discus thrower

Date	Mintage	F	VF	XF	Unc	BU
2002 Proof	—	Value: 15.00				

KM# 1120 2 DOLLARS
Silver **Ruler:** Elizabeth II **Subject:** Endangered Wildlife **Rev:** Lion family

Date	Mintage	F	VF	XF	Unc	BU
2002 Proof	—	Value: 25.00				

KM# 1282 2 DOLLARS
31.1350 g., 0.9990 Silver 1.0000 oz. ASW, 40.6 mm. **Ruler:** Elizabeth II **Subject:** Taiwan New Koala Family **Obv:** Head crowned right **Rev:** Multicolor Koala seated with leaves

Date	Mintage	F	VF	XF	Unc	BU
2002 Proof	—	Value: 135				

KM# 417 2 DOLLARS
7.5500 g., Copper-Nickel, 26 mm. **Ruler:** Elizabeth II **Obv:** Crowned bust right, new portrait **Rev:** Mortar and pestle from Atiu Island **Edge:** Triangular

Date	Mintage	F	VF	XF	Unc	BU
2003	—	—	—	—	3.00	3.50

KM# 1123 2 DOLLARS
62.7700 g., 0.9990 Silver 2.0160 oz. ASW, 50 mm. **Ruler:** Elizabeth II **Rev:** Edward "Ned" Kelly in color

Date	Mintage	F	VF	XF	Unc	BU
2003 Proof	Est. 2,500	Value: 100				

KM# 1124 2 DOLLARS
62.7700 g., 0.9990 Silver 2.0160 oz. ASW, 50 mm. **Ruler:** Elizabeth II **Rev:** Daniel Morgan in color

Date	Mintage	F	VF	XF	Unc	BU
2003 Proof	Est. 2,500	Value: 100				

KM# 1125 2 DOLLARS
62.7700 g., 0.9990 Silver 2.0160 oz. ASW **Ruler:** Elizabeth II **Rev:** Ben Hall in color

Date	Mintage	F	VF	XF	Unc	BU
2003 Proof	Est. 2,500	Value: 100				

KM# 1126 2 DOLLARS
62.7700 g., 0.9990 Silver 2.0160 oz. ASW, 50 mm. **Ruler:** Elizabeth II **Rev:** Fred Ward "Captain Thunderbolt" in color

Date	Mintage	F	VF	XF	Unc	BU
2003 Proof	Est. 2,500	Value: 100				

KM# 1139 2 DOLLARS
0.9990 Silver, 30 mm. **Ruler:** Elizabeth II **Subject:** John F. Kennedy, 40th Anniversary of Death

Date	Mintage	F	VF	XF	Unc	BU
2003 Proof	—	Value: 45.00				

KM# 1141 2 DOLLARS
Gold **Ruler:** Elizabeth II **Rev:** Bird in color

Date	Mintage	F	VF	XF	Unc	BU
2003 Proof	Est. 5,000	Value: 85.00				

KM# 1142 2 DOLLARS
Gold **Ruler:** Elizabeth II **Subject:** Love swing **Rev:** Bird in color

Date	Mintage	F	VF	XF	Unc	BU
2003 Proof	Est. 5,000	Value: 85.00				

KM# 536 2 DOLLARS
31.1050 g., 0.9990 Silver 0.9990 oz. ASW, 40.7 mm. **Ruler:** Elizabeth II **Subject:** Birds of New Zealand **Rev:** Multicolor tui

Date	Mintage	F	VF	XF	Unc	BU
2005 Prooflike	8,000	—	—	—	—	90.00

KM# 537 2 DOLLARS
31.1050 g., 0.9990 Silver 0.9990 oz. ASW, 40.7 mm. **Ruler:** Elizabeth II **Subject:** Birds of New Zealand **Rev:** Multicolor bell bird

Date	Mintage	F	VF	XF	Unc	BU
2005 Prooflike	8,000	—	—	—	—	90.00

KM# 538 2 DOLLARS
31.1050 g., 0.9990 Silver 0.9990 oz. ASW, 40.7 mm. **Ruler:** Elizabeth II **Subject:** Birds of New Zealand **Rev:** Multicolor New Zealand Pigeon

Date	Mintage	F	VF	XF	Unc	BU
2005 Prooflike	8,000	—	—	—	—	90.00

KM# 539 2 DOLLARS
31.1050 g., 0.9990 Silver 0.9990 oz. ASW, 40.7 mm. **Ruler:** Elizabeth II **Subject:** Birds of New Zealand **Rev:** Multicolor yellow crowned parakeet

Date	Mintage	F	VF	XF	Unc	BU
2005 Prooflike	8,000	—	—	—	—	90.00

KM# 524 2 DOLLARS
31.1050 g., 0.9990 Silver 0.9990 oz. ASW, 40.7 mm. **Ruler:** Elizabeth II **Subject:** Classic Speedsters from the 1930's **Rev:** Multicolor 1935 Auburn 851 Speedster

Date	Mintage	F	VF	XF	Unc	BU
2006 Prooflike	6,000	—	—	—	—	80.00

KM# 525 2 DOLLARS
31.1050 g., 0.9990 Silver 0.9990 oz. ASW, 40.7 mm. **Ruler:** Elizabeth II **Subject:** Classic Speedsters from the 1930's **Rev:** Multicolor 1935 Bugatti Type 57SC Atlantic Speedster

Date	Mintage	F	VF	XF	Unc	BU
2006 Prooflike	6,000	—	—	—	—	80.00

KM# 526 2 DOLLARS
31.1050 g., 0.9990 Silver 0.9990 oz. ASW, 40.7 mm. **Ruler:** Elizabeth II **Subject:** Speedsters from the 1930's **Rev:** Multicolor 1936 Duesenberg SSJ Speedster

Date	Mintage	F	VF	XF	Unc	BU
2006 Prooflike	6,000	—	—	—	—	80.00

KM# 527 2 DOLLARS
31.1050 g., 0.9990 Silver 0.9990 oz. ASW, 40.7 mm. **Ruler:** Elizabeth II **Subject:** Speedsters from the 1930's **Rev:** Multicolor 1930 Packard 734 Boattail Speedster

Date	Mintage	F	VF	XF	Unc	BU
2006 Prooflike	6,000	—	—	—	—	80.00

KM# 1170   2 DOLLARS
10.0000 g., 0.9250 Silver 0.2974 oz. ASW, 30 mm. **Ruler:**
Elizabeth II **Rev:** Motion Pictures, 100th Anniversary

Date	Mintage	F	VF	XF	Unc	BU
2006	Est. 2,500	—	—	—	—	35.00

KM# 1288   2 DOLLARS
31.1050 g., 0.9990 Silver 0.9990 oz. ASW, 40.7 mm. **Ruler:**
Elizabeth II **Rev:** Supermarine S-6B race plane in color

Date	Mintage	F	VF	XF	Unc	BU
2006 Prooflike	6,000	—	—	—	—	75.00

KM# 1289   2 DOLLARS
31.1050 g., 0.9990 Silver 0.9990 oz. ASW, 40.7 mm. **Ruler:**
Elizabeth II **Rev:** GeeBee race plane in color

Date	Mintage	F	VF	XF	Unc	BU
2006 Prooflike	6,000	—	—	—	—	75.00

KM# 1290   2 DOLLARS
31.1050 g., 0.9990 Silver 0.9990 oz. ASW, 40.7 mm. **Ruler:**
Elizabeth II **Rev:** Hughes H-1 race plane in color

Date	Mintage	F	VF	XF	Unc	BU
2006 Prooflike	6,000	—	—	—	—	75.00

KM# 1291   2 DOLLARS
31.1050 g., 0.9990 Silver 0.9990 oz. ASW, 40.7 mm. **Ruler:**
Elizabeth II **Rev:** Polikarpov I-16 race plane in color

Date	Mintage	F	VF	XF	Unc	BU
2006 Prooflike	6,000	—	—	—	—	75.00

KM# 1316   2 DOLLARS
Silver **Ruler:** Elizabeth II **Rev:** Motorcycle - Brough in color

Date	Mintage	F	VF	XF	Unc	BU
2007 Proof	—	Value: 45.00				

KM# 1317   2 DOLLARS
Silver **Ruler:** Elizabeth II **Rev:** Motorcycle - BSA Sloper in color

Date	Mintage	F	VF	XF	Unc	BU
2007 Proof	—	Value: 45.00				

KM# 1318   2 DOLLARS
Silver **Ruler:** Elizabeth II **Rev:** Motorcycle - IZH 8

Date	Mintage	F	VF	XF	Unc	BU
2007 Proof	—	Value: 45.00				

KM# 514   2 DOLLARS
31.1050 g., 0.9990 Silver 0.9990 oz. ASW, 40.7 mm. **Ruler:**
Elizabeth II **Subject:** Great Motorcycles from the 1930's **Rev:**
Multicolor 1930 BSA Sloper

Date	Mintage	F	VF	XF	Unc	BU
2007 Prooflike	6,000	—	—	—	—	70.00

KM# 515   2 DOLLARS
31.1050 g., 0.9990 Silver 0.9990 oz. ASW, 40.7 mm. **Ruler:**
Elizabeth II **Subject:** Great motorcycles from the 1930's **Rev:**
Multicolor 1937 Ariel 1000 Squarefour

Date	Mintage	F	VF	XF	Unc	BU
2007 Prooflike	6,000	—	—	—	—	70.00

KM# 516   2 DOLLARS
31.1050 g., 0.9990 Silver 0.9990 oz. ASW, 40.7 mm. **Ruler:**
Elizabeth II **Subject:** Great motorcycles from the 1930's **Rev:**
Multicolor 1938 12H 8

Date	Mintage	F	VF	XF	Unc	BU
2007 Prooflike	6,000	—	—	—	—	70.00

KM# 517   2 DOLLARS
31.1050 g., 0.9990 Silver 0.9990 oz. ASW, 40.7 mm. **Ruler:**
Elizabeth II **Subject:** Great motorcycles from the 1930's **Rev:**
Multicolor 1931 Matchless Silver Hawk

Date	Mintage	F	VF	XF	Unc	BU
2007 Prooflike	6,000	—	—	—	—	70.00

KM# 518   2 DOLLARS
31.1050 g., 0.9990 Silver 0.9990 oz. ASW, 40.7 mm. **Ruler:**
Elizabeth II **Subject:** Great motocycles from the 1930's **Rev:**
Multicolor 1932 Brough Superior SS100

Date	Mintage	F	VF	XF	Unc	BU
2007 Prooflike	6,000	—	—	—	—	70.00

KM# 529   2 DOLLARS
31.1050 g., 0.9990 Silver 0.9990 oz. ASW, 40.7 mm. **Ruler:**
Elizabeth II **Subject:** International Women's Day **Rev:** Multicolor
tulips, large 8

Date	Mintage	F	VF	XF	Unc	BU
2007 Prooflike	4,000	—	—	—	—	65.00

KM# 532   2 DOLLARS
31.1050 g., 0.9990 Silver 0.9990 oz. ASW, 40.7 mm. **Ruler:**
Elizabeth II **Subject:** Sherlock Holmes **Rev:** Multicolor portrait

Date	Mintage	F	VF	XF	Unc	BU
2007 Prooflike	8,000	—	—	—	—	100

KM# 1184   2 DOLLARS
31.1050 g., 0.9990 Silver 0.9990 oz. ASW, 40.7 mm. **Ruler:**
Elizabeth II **Subject:** Birds of Fiji **Rev:** Island Thrush in color

Date	Mintage	F	VF	XF	Unc	BU
2007	Est. 4,000	—	—	—	—	45.00

KM# 1185   2 DOLLARS
31.1050 g., 0.9990 Silver 0.9990 oz. ASW, 40.7 mm. **Ruler:**
Elizabeth II **Subject:** Birds of Fiji **Rev:** Vampire Bat in color

Date	Mintage	F	VF	XF	Unc	BU
2007	Est. 4,000	—	—	—	—	45.00

KM# 1186   2 DOLLARS
31.1050 g., 0.9990 Silver 0.9990 oz. ASW, 40.7 mm. **Ruler:**
Elizabeth II **Subject:** Birds of Fiji **Rev:** Kingfisher in color

Date	Mintage	F	VF	XF	Unc	BU
2007	4,000	—	—	—	—	45.00

KM# 1187   2 DOLLARS
31.1050 g., 0.9990 Silver 0.9990 oz. ASW, 40.7 mm. **Ruler:**
Elizabeth II **Subject:** Birds of Fiji **Rev:** Lori in color

Date	Mintage	F	VF	XF	Unc	BU
2007	4,000	—	—	—	—	45.00

KM# 510   2 DOLLARS
31.1050 g., 0.9990 Silver 0.9990 oz. ASW, 40.7 mm. **Ruler:**
Elizabeth II **Subject:** Year of the Rat **Rev:** Multicolor scene of
little girl from Russian animated cartoon

Date	Mintage	F	VF	XF	Unc	BU
2008 Prooflike	10,000	—	—	—	—	80.00

KM# 511   2 DOLLARS
31.1050 g., 0.9990 Silver 0.9990 oz. ASW, 40.7 mm. **Ruler:**
Elizabeth II **Subject:** Year of the Rat **Rev:** Multicolor scene of
nutcracker from Russian animated cartoon

Date	Mintage	F	VF	XF	Unc	BU
2008 Prooflike	10,000	—	—	—	—	80.00

KM# 512   2 DOLLARS
39.1050 g., 0.9990 Silver 1.2559 oz. ASW, 40.7 mm. **Ruler:**
Elizabeth II **Rev:** Multicolor scene of Adventure of Cat Leopold
Russian animated cartoon

Date	Mintage	F	VF	XF	Unc	BU
2008 Prooflike	10,000	—	—	—	—	80.00

KM# 513   2 DOLLARS
31.1050 g., 0.9990 Silver 0.9990 oz. ASW, 40.7 mm. **Ruler:**
Elizabeth II **Subject:** Year of the Rat **Rev:** Multicolor scene of
tough toy soldier from Russian animated cartoon

Date	Mintage	F	VF	XF	Unc	BU
2008 Prooflike	10,000	—	—	—	—	80.00

KM# 519   2 DOLLARS
31.1050 g., 0.9990 Silver 0.9990 oz. ASW, 40.7 mm. **Ruler:**
Elizabeth II **Subject:** Racers from the 1930's **Rev:** Multicolor Gee
Bee

Date	Mintage	F	VF	XF	Unc	BU
2008 Prooflike	6,000	—	—	—	—	70.00

KM# 520   2 DOLLARS
31.1050 g., 0.9990 Silver 0.9990 oz. ASW, 40.7 mm. **Ruler:**
Elizabeth II **Subject:** Racers from the 1930's **Rev:** Multicolor,
Hughes H-1 Racer

Date	Mintage	F	VF	XF	Unc	BU
2008 Prooflike	6,000	—	—	—	—	70.00

KM# 521   2 DOLLARS
31.1050 g., 0.9990 Silver 0.9990 oz. ASW, 40.7 mm. **Ruler:**
Elizabeth II **Subject:** Racers from the 1930's **Rev:** Multicolor
Laird Turner LTR-14 Meteor

Date	Mintage	F	VF	XF	Unc	BU
2008 Prooflike	6,000	—	—	—	—	70.00

KM# 522 2 DOLLARS
31.1050 g., 0.9990 Silver 0.9990 oz. ASW, 40.7 mm. **Ruler:** Elizabeth II **Subject:** Racers from the 1930's **Rev:** Multicolor Spuermarine S.6B Floatplane

Date	Mintage	F	VF	XF	Unc	BU
2008 Prooflike	6,000	—	—	—	—	70.00

KM# 523 2 DOLLARS
31.1050 g., 0.9990 Silver 0.9990 oz. ASW, 40.7 mm. **Ruler:** Elizabeth II **Subject:** Racers from the 1930's **Rev:** Multicolor Polikarpov I-16

Date	Mintage	F	VF	XF	Unc	BU
2008 Prooflike	6,000	—	—	—	—	70.00

KM# 528 2 DOLLARS
31.1050 g., 0.9990 Silver 0.9990 oz. ASW, 40.7 mm. **Ruler:** Elizabeth II **Subject:** Valentines (Love) **Rev:** Multicolor pair of swans **Rev. Legend:** Love is precious

Date	Mintage	F	VF	XF	Unc	BU
2008 Prooflike	16,000	—	—	—	—	90.00

KM# 530 2 DOLLARS
31.1050 g., 0.9990 Silver 0.9990 oz. ASW, 40.7 mm. **Ruler:** Elizabeth II **Subject:** Mikhail Kalasknikov **Rev:** Multicolor portrait in uniform with siver gun

Date	Mintage	F	VF	XF	Unc	BU
2008 Prooflike	20,000	—	—	—	—	100

KM# 531 2 DOLLARS
31.1050 g., 0.9990 Silver 0.9990 oz. ASW, 40.7 mm. **Ruler:** Elizabeth II **Subject:** Mikhail Kalasknikov **Rev:** Multicolor red star, soldier and gun

Date	Mintage	F	VF	XF	Unc	BU
2008 Prooflike	20,000	—	—	—	—	100

KM# 533 2 DOLLARS
31.1050 g., 0.9990 Silver 0.9990 oz. ASW, 40.7 mm. **Ruler:** Elizabeth II **Subject:** Sherlock Holmes **Rev:** Multicolor scene from Hound of the Baskervilles

Date	Mintage	F	VF	XF	Unc	BU
2008 Prooflike	8,000	—	—	—	—	100

KM# 534 2 DOLLARS
31.1050 g., 0.9990 Silver 0.9990 oz. ASW, 40.7 mm. **Ruler:** Elizabeth II **Subject:** Sherlock Holmes **Rev:** Multicolor scehe from the Final Problem

Date	Mintage	F	VF	XF	Unc	BU
2008 Prooflike	8,000	—	—	—	—	100

KM# 535 2 DOLLARS
31.1050 g., 0.9990 Silver 0.9990 oz. ASW, 40.7 mm. **Ruler:** Elizabeth II **Subject:** Sherlock Holmes **Rev:** Multicolor scene from the Sign of the Four

Date	Mintage	F	VF	XF	Unc	BU
2008 Prooflike	8,000	—	—	—	—	100

KM# 540 2 DOLLARS
31.1050 g., 0.9990 Silver 0.9990 oz. ASW, 40.7 mm. **Ruler:** Elizabeth II **Subject:** Ballet dancers **Rev:** Multicolor Vasley Nijinnsky

Date	Mintage	F	VF	XF	Unc	BU
2008 Prooflike	8,000	—	—	—	—	85.00

KM# 541 2 DOLLARS
31.1050 g., 0.9990 Silver 0.9990 oz. ASW, 40.7 mm. **Ruler:** Elizabeth II **Subject:** Ballet Dancers **Rev:** Multicolor Matuilda Kshesinskaya

Date	Mintage	F	VF	XF	Unc	BU
2008 Prooflike	8,000	—	—	—	—	85.00

KM# 542 2 DOLLARS
31.1050 g., 0.9990 Silver 0.9990 oz. ASW, 40.7 mm. **Ruler:** Elizabeth II **Subject:** Ballet dancers **Rev:** Multicolor Sergey Lifar

Date	Mintage	F	VF	XF	Unc	BU
2008 Prooflike	8,000	—	—	—	—	85.00

KM# 543 2 DOLLARS
31.1050 g., 0.9990 Silver 0.9990 oz. ASW, 40.7 mm. **Ruler:** Elizabeth II **Subject:** Ballet dancers **Rev:** Multicolor Anna Pavlova

Date	Mintage	F	VF	XF	Unc	BU
2008 Prooflike	—	—	—	—	—	85.00

KM# 544 2 DOLLARS
31.1050 g., 0.9990 Silver 0.9990 oz. ASW, 40.7 mm. **Ruler:** Elizabeth II **Subject:** White Army **Rev:** Multicolor Anton Denkin

Date	Mintage	F	VF	XF	Unc	BU
2008 Prooflike	6,000	—	—	—	—	85.00

KM# 545 2 DOLLARS
31.1050 g., 0.9990 Silver 0.9990 oz. ASW, 40.7 mm. **Ruler:** Elizabeth II **Subject:** White Army **Rev:** Multicolor Pytor Vrangel

Date	Mintage	F	VF	XF	Unc	BU
2008 Prooflike	6,000	—	—	—	—	85.00

KM# 546 2 DOLLARS
31.1050 g., 0.9990 Silver 0.9990 oz. ASW, 40.7 mm. **Ruler:** Elizabeth II **Subject:** White Army **Rev:** Multicolor Alexander Kutepov

Date	Mintage	F	VF	XF	Unc	BU
2008 Prooflike	6,000	—	—	—	—	85.00

KM# 547 2 DOLLARS
31.1050 g., 0.9990 Silver 0.9990 oz. ASW, 40.7 mm. **Ruler:** Elizabeth II **Subject:** White Army **Rev:** Multicolor Alexander Kolchak

Date	Mintage	F	VF	XF	Unc	BU
2008 Prooflike	6,000	—	—	—	—	85.00

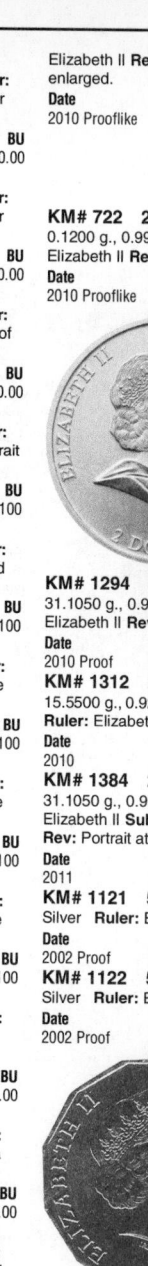

KM# 721 2 DOLLARS
0.1200 g., 0.9990 Gold 0.0039 oz. AGW, 4 mm. **Ruler:**

Elizabeth II **Rev:** Lady Penrhyn sailing ship **Note:** Illustration enlarged.

Date	Mintage	F	VF	XF	Unc	BU
2010 Prooflike	5,000	—	—	—	—	12.00

KM# 722 2 DOLLARS
0.1200 g., 0.9950 Platinum 0.0038 oz. APW, 4 mm. **Ruler:** Elizabeth II **Rev:** Humpback whale **Note:** Illustration enlarged.

Date	Mintage	F	VF	XF	Unc	BU
2010 Prooflike	5,000	—	—	—	—	15.00

KM# 1294 2 DOLLARS
31.1050 g., 0.9990 Silver 0.9990 oz. ASW, 33 mm. **Ruler:** Elizabeth II **Rev:** Fish with crown partially gilt

Date	Mintage	F	VF	XF	Unc	BU
2010 Proof	—	Value: 55.00				

KM# 1312 2 DOLLARS
15.5500 g., 0.9250 Silver partially gilt 0.4624 oz. ASW, 33 mm. **Ruler:** Elizabeth II **Subject:** Good Luck

Date	Mintage	F	VF	XF	Unc	BU
2010	1,000	—	—	—	—	45.00

KM# 1384 2 DOLLARS
31.1050 g., 0.9990 Silver 0.9990 oz. ASW, 40.7 mm. **Ruler:** Elizabeth II **Subject:** Polish President's death, 1st Anniversary **Rev:** Portrait at right, plane crash site in color at left

Date	Mintage	F	VF	XF	Unc	BU
2011	—	—	—	—	—	75.00

KM# 1121 5 DOLLARS
Silver **Ruler:** Elizabeth II **Rev:** Sir Francis Drake

Date	Mintage	F	VF	XF	Unc	BU
2002 Proof	—	Value: 35.00				

KM# 1122 5 DOLLARS
Silver **Ruler:** Elizabeth II **Rev:** Kon Tiki and Thor Heyerdahl

Date	Mintage	F	VF	XF	Unc	BU
2002 Proof	—	Value: 45.00				

KM# 418 5 DOLLARS
14.0000 g., Aluminum-Bronze, 31.5 mm. **Ruler:** Elizabeth II **Obv:** Crowned bust right, new portrait **Rev:** Conch shell and value **Shape:** 12-sided

Date	Mintage	F	VF	XF	Unc	BU
2003	—	—	—	—	6.00	8.00

KM# 1140 5 DOLLARS
20.0000 g., 0.9990 Silver 0.6423 oz. ASW **Ruler:** Elizabeth II **Subject:** Vincent van Gogh, 150th Anniversary of Birth

Date	Mintage	F	VF	XF	Unc	BU
2003 Proof	Est. 5,000	Value: 35.00				

KM# 469 5 DOLLARS
Copper-Nickel, 40 mm. **Ruler:** Elizabeth II **Obv:** USPS logo, Queens head above **Rev:** 5 cent 1847 Benjamin Franklin stamp

Date	Mintage	F	VF	XF	Unc	BU
2004	—	—	—	—	10.00	12.00

KM# 469a 5 DOLLARS
Silver, 40 mm. **Ruler:** Elizabeth II **Obv:** USPS logo, Queens head above **Rev:** 5 cent 1847 Benjamin Franklin stamp **Edge:** Reeded

Date	Mintage	F	VF	XF	Unc	BU
2004 Proof	—	Value: 35.00				

KM# 1149 5 DOLLARS
31.6350 g., 0.9990 Silver 1.0160 oz. ASW **Ruler:** Elizabeth II **Subject:** Apollo Moon Landing, 35th Anniversary **Rev:** Astronaut in Solar System

Date	Mintage	F	VF	XF	Unc	BU
2004 Proof	Est. 10,000	Value: 55.00				

KM# 1108 5 DOLLARS
25.0000 g., 0.9250 Silver 0.7435 oz. ASW **Ruler:** Elizabeth II **Subject:** Ferrari F2

Date	Mintage	F	VF	XF	Unc	BU
2005 Proof	Est. 8,000	Value: 45.00				

KM# 1109 5 DOLLARS
25.0000 g., 0.9250 Silver 0.7435 oz. ASW **Ruler:** Elizabeth II **Rev:** Ferrari F 2004 in color

Date	Mintage	F	VF	XF	Unc	BU
2005 Proof	Est. 8,000	Value: 45.00				

KM# 1134 5 DOLLARS
31.1050 g., 0.9990 Silver 0.9990 oz. ASW, 38.6 mm. **Ruler:** Elizabeth II **Subject:** Star Wars, 30th Anniversary

Date	Mintage	F	VF	XF	Unc	BU
2005 Proof	Est. 9,999	Value: 45.00				

KM# 1135 5 DOLLARS
31.1050 g., 0.9990 Silver 0.9990 oz. ASW, 38.6 mm. **Ruler:** Elizabeth II **Subject:** Star Wars, 30th Anniversary

Date	Mintage	F	VF	XF	Unc	BU
2005 Proof	Est. 9,999	Value: 45.00				

KM# 1175 5 DOLLARS
25.0000 g., 0.9250 Silver 0.7435 oz. ASW **Ruler:** Elizabeth II **Subject:** Marriage of Prince Charles and Camilla Parker-Bowles

Date	Mintage	F	VF	XF	Unc	BU
2005 Proof	Est. 5,000	Value: 45.00				

KM# 478 5 DOLLARS
Silver Gilt **Ruler:** Elizabeth II **Subject:** Pope Benedict XVI's visit to Valencia, Spain **Obv:** Bust right **Rev:** Valencia Cathedral **Shape:** Cathedral outline **Note:** Jeweled cathedral.

Date	Mintage	F	VF	XF	Unc	BU
2006 Proof	2,500	Value: 100				

KM# 560 5 DOLLARS
25.0000 g., 0.9250 Silver partially gilt 0.7435 oz. ASW, 35x31 mm. **Ruler:** Elizabeth II **Subject:** Benedict XVI Annus Secundus **Rev:** Cross in crystals and gilt Papal Arms **Shape:** 6-sided

Date	Mintage	F	VF	XF	Unc	BU
2006 Proof	5,000	Value: 95.00				

KM# 561 5 DOLLARS
25.0000 g., 0.9990 Silver partially gilt 0.8029 oz. ASW, 42x49 mm. **Ruler:** Elizabeth II **Subject:** Benedict XVI visits Germany **Rev:** Cathedral gilt, crystal inserts **Shape:** oval

Date	Mintage	F	VF	XF	Unc	BU
2006 Proof	5,000	Value: 95.00				

KM# 562   5 DOLLARS
25.0000 g., 0.9990 Silver 0.8029 oz. ASW, 35x35 mm.   **Ruler:**
Elizabeth II **Subject:** Benedict XVI **Rev:** Profile at left, cross in
crystal inserts **Shape:** Square

Date	Mintage	F	VF	XF	Unc	BU
2006 Proof	5,000	Value: 95.00				

KM# 563   5 DOLLARS
25.0000 g., 0.9990 Silver partially gilt 0.8029 oz. ASW,
35x38 mm. **Ruler:** Elizabeth II **Subject:** Christmas in St. Peter's
Square **Rev:** St. Peter's partially gilt, star crystal insert **Shape:**
Triange

Date	Mintage	F	VF	XF	Unc	BU
2006 Proof	5,000	Value: 95.00				

KM# 564   5 DOLLARS
25.0000 g., 0.9990 Silver 0.8029 oz. ASW, 20x44 mm.   **Ruler:**
Elizabeth II **Subject:** benedict XVI visits Poland **Rev:** Polish icon,
partially gilt, crystal insert **Shape:** Candle

Date	Mintage	F	VF	XF	Unc	BU
2006 Proof	564	Value: 95.00				

KM# 565   5 DOLLARS
25.0000 g., 0.9990 Silver partially gilt 0.8029 oz. ASW, 38.6 mm.
Ruler: Elizabeth II **Rev:** St. Peter's Basilica, partially gilt, crystals
as stars

Date	Mintage	F	VF	XF	Unc	BU
2006 Proof	5,000	Value: 95.00				

KM# 566   5 DOLLARS
25.0000 g., 0.9990 Silver partially gilt 0.8029 oz. ASW,
35x35 mm. **Ruler:** Elizabeth II **Subject:** Swiss Guards, 500th
Anniversary **Rev:** Four Swiss guards, partially gilt, crystal insert
Shape: Diamond

Date	Mintage	F	VF	XF	Unc	BU
2006 Proof	5,000	Value: 95.00				

KM# 567   5 DOLLARS
25.0000 g., 0.9990 Silver 0.8029 oz. ASW, 40x25 mm.   **Ruler:**
Elizabeth II **Subject:** Benedict XVI visits Turkey **Rev:** Pope and
Patrarch, partially gilt, crystal insert **Shape:** Rectangle

Date	Mintage	F	VF	XF	Unc	BU
2006 Proof	5,000	Value: 95.00				

KM# 568   5 DOLLARS
25.0000 g., 0.9990 Silver 0.8029 oz. ASW, 40x25 mm.   **Ruler:**
Elizabeth II **Subject:** Urbi et Orbi message **Rev:** Benedict XVI
giving blessing, partially gilt, crystal insert **Shape:** Rectangle

Date	Mintage	F	VF	XF	Unc	BU
2006 Proof	5,000	Value: 95.00				

KM# 569   5 DOLLARS
0.2500 g., 0.9990 Silver partially gilt 0.0080 oz. ASW, 29x42 mm.
Ruler: Elizabeth II **Subject:** Benedict XVI visits Vallencia **Rev:**
Valencia cathedral facade, partially gilt, crystal inserts **Shape:**
Irregular

Date	Mintage	F	VF	XF	Unc	BU
2006 Proof	5,000	Value: 85.00				

KM# 570   5 DOLLARS
31.1000 g., 0.9990 Silver 0.9988 oz. ASW, 38.6 mm.   **Ruler:**
Elizabeth II **Rev:** Statue of Liberty gilt pop-up

Date	Mintage	F	VF	XF	Unc	BU
2006 Proof	5,000	Value: 100				

KM# 571   5 DOLLARS
31.1000 g., 0.9990 Silver 0.9988 oz. ASW, 38.6 mm.   **Ruler:**
Elizabeth II **Rev:** Ludwig's castle gilt pop-up

Date	Mintage	F	VF	XF	Unc	BU
2006 Proof	5,000	Value: 100				

KM# 572   5 DOLLARS
25.0000 g., 0.9990 Silver partially gilt 0.8029 oz. ASW,
35x35 mm. **Ruler:** Elizabeth II **Subject:** Benedict XVI visits
Marianzell **Rev:** Our Lady or Marianzell, partially gilt, crystal
inserts **Shape:** Tablet

Date	Mintage	F	VF	XF	Unc	BU
2007 Proof	5,000	Value: 95.00				

KM# 573   5 DOLLARS
25.0000 g., 0.9990 Silver 0.8029 oz. ASW, 35x35 mm.   **Ruler:**
Elizabeth II **Rev:** St. Francis, tau cross, partially gilt, crystal insert
Shape: Dove

Date	Mintage	F	VF	XF	Unc	BU
2007 Proof	5,000	Value: 95.00				

KM# 574   5 DOLLARS
25.0000 g., 0.9990 Silver 0.8029 oz. ASW, 31x40 mm.   **Ruler:**
Elizabeth II **Rev:** Benedict XVI bust left, partially gilt, crystal insert
Shape: Irregular

Date	Mintage	F	VF	XF	Unc	BU
2007 Proof	5,000	Value: 95.00				

KM# 575   5 DOLLARS
25.0000 g., 0.9990 Silver 0.8029 oz. ASW, 35x45 mm.   **Ruler:**
Elizabeth II **Subject:** Benedict XVI visits Brazil **Rev:** Christ statue
in Rio, partially gilt, crystal insert **Shape:** Diamond

Date	Mintage	F	VF	XF	Unc	BU
2007 Proof	5,000	Value: 95.00				

KM# 576   5 DOLLARS
25.0000 g., 0.9990 Silver 0.8029 oz. ASW, 37 mm.   **Ruler:**
Elizabeth II **Subject:** Princess Diana, 10th Anniversary of death
Rev: Bust at left, multicolored rose **Shape:** Heart

Date	Mintage	F	VF	XF	Unc	BU
2007 Proof	1,997	Value: 75.00				

KM# 577   5 DOLLARS
25.0000 g., 0.9990 Silver partially gilt 0.8029 oz. ASW,
39x24 mm. **Ruler:** Elizabeth II **Subject:** Docrine of the
Immaculate Conception **Rev:** Virgin Mary and cathedral, partially
gilt, crystal insert **Shape:** Rectangle

Date	Mintage	F	VF	XF	Unc	BU
2007 Proof	5,000	Value: 95.00				

KM# 578   5 DOLLARS
25.0000 g., 0.9990 Silver 0.8029 oz. ASW, 31x35 mm.   **Ruler:**
Elizabeth II **Subject:** Benedict XVI visits Loredo **Rev:** Pope
blessing crowd, cathedral, partially gilt, crystal insert **Shape:** 6-
sided

Date	Mintage	F	VF	XF	Unc	BU
2007 Proof	5,000	Value: 95.00				

KM# 579   5 DOLLARS
25.0000 g., 0.9990 Silver partially gilt 0.8029 oz. ASW, 35x35 mm.   **Ruler:**
Elizabeth II **Subject:** Santo Subito **Rev:** Pope John Paul II,
partially gilt, crystal insert **Shape:** Cross

Date	Mintage	F	VF	XF	Unc	BU
2007 Proof	5,000	Value: 100				

KM# 580   5 DOLLARS
25.0000 g., 0.9990 Silver 0.8029 oz. ASW, 30x45 mm.   **Ruler:**
Elizabeth II **Subject:** Way of the Cross **Rev:** Benedict XVI holdign
cross, collesum in background, partially gilt, crystal insert **Shape:**
Vertical oval

Date	Mintage	F	VF	XF	Unc	BU
2007 Proof	5,000	Value: 95.00				

KM# 581   5 DOLLARS
31.1000 g., 0.9990 Silver 0.9988 oz. ASW, 38.6 mm.   **Ruler:**
Elizabeth II **Rev:** Parthenon gilt pop-up

Date	Mintage	F	VF	XF	Unc	BU
2007 Proof	5,000	Value: 100				

KM# 583   5 DOLLARS
31.1000 g., 0.9990 Silver 0.9988 oz. ASW, 38.6 mm.   **Ruler:**
Elizabeth II **Rev:** Rio's Christ statue gilt pop-up

Date	Mintage	F	VF	XF	Unc	BU
2007 Proof	5,000	Value: 100				

KM# 584   5 DOLLARS
31.1000 g., 0.9990 Silver 0.9988 oz. ASW, 38.6 mm.   **Ruler:**
Elizabeth II **Rev:** Colleseum gilt pop-up

Date	Mintage	F	VF	XF	Unc	BU
2007 Proof	5,000	Value: 100				

KM# 586 5 DOLLARS
31.1000 g., 0.9990 Silver 0.9988 oz. ASW, 38.6 mm. **Ruler:**
Elizabeth II **Rev:** Eifle Tower gilt pop-up

Date	Mintage	F	VF	XF	Unc	BU
2007 Proof	5,000	Value: 100				

KM# 763 5 DOLLARS
20.0000 g., Silver, 38.61 mm. **Ruler:** Elizabeth II **Subject:**
Brenham Meteor **Obv:** Bust right **Rev:** Meteorite and fragment
inset

Date	Mintage	F	VF	XF	Unc	BU
2007 Proof	2,500	Value: 100				

KM# 1188 5 DOLLARS
20.0000 g., 0.9250 Silver 0.5948 oz. ASW, 38.61 mm. **Ruler:**
Elizabeth II **Subject:** Elvis Presley, 30th Anniversary of death

Date	Mintage	F	VF	XF	Unc	BU
2007 Proof	Est. 50,000	Value: 70.00				

KM# 1189 5 DOLLARS
20.0000 g., 0.9250 Silver 0.5948 oz. ASW, 38.61 mm. **Ruler:**
Elizabeth II **Subject:** Elvis Presely, 30th Anniversary of Death
Rev: Love me Tender, 1956

Date	Mintage	F	VF	XF	Unc	BU
2007 Proof	Est. 50,000	Value: 70.00				

KM# 1201 5 DOLLARS
25.0000 g., Copper-Nickel partially gilt, 38.6 mm. **Ruler:**
Elizabeth II **Subject:** Lady Diana, 10th Anniversary of Death **Rev:**
Diana partially gilt

Date	Mintage	F	VF	XF	Unc	BU
2007 Proof	Est. 50,000	Value: 22.50				

KM# 1202 5 DOLLARS
25.0000 g., Copper-Nickel partially gilt, 38.6 mm. **Ruler:**
Elizabeth II **Subject:** Princess Diana, 10th Anniversary of Death
Rev: Diana in wedding dress, partially gilt

Date	Mintage	F	VF	XF	Unc	BU
2007 Proof	Est. 14,500	Value: 22.50				

KM# 1203 5 DOLLARS
155.5000 g., Copper-Nickel partially gilt, 65 mm. **Ruler:**
Elizabeth II **Subject:** Princess Diana, 10th Anniversary of Death
Rev: Lady Diana, partially gilt

Date	Mintage	F	VF	XF	Unc	BU
2007 Proof	Est. 1,961	Value: 85.00				

KM# 1320 5 DOLLARS
Silver **Ruler:** Elizabeth II **Rev:** Copernicus with solar system,
partially gilt

Date	Mintage	F	VF	XF	Unc	BU
2008 Proof	—	Value: 50.00				

KM# 594 5 DOLLARS
25.0000 g., 0.9990 Silver 0.8029 oz. ASW, 35x35 mm. **Ruler:**
Elizabeth II **Subject:** Pope John Paul II Election 30th Anniversary
Rev: John Paul II coat-of-arms, aprtially gilt, crystal insert **Shape:**
Diamond

Date	Mintage	F	VF	XF	Unc	BU
2008 Proof	5,000	Value: 120				

KM# 595 5 DOLLARS
25.0000 g., 0.9990 Silver 0.8029 oz. ASW, 30x45 mm. **Ruler:**
Elizabeth II **Subject:** Lourdes, 150th Anniversary **Rev:** Statue of
Our Lady of Lourdes, partially gilt, crystal insert **Shape:** Vertical
oval

Date	Mintage	F	VF	XF	Unc	BU
2008 Proof	5,000	Value: 110				

KM# 596 5 DOLLARS
25.0000 g., 0.9990 Silver 0.8029 oz. ASW, 30x45 mm. **Ruler:**
Elizabeth II **Subject:** Lourdes, 150th Anniversary **Rev:** Our Lady
of Lourdes, holigram, partially gilt, crystal insert **Shape:** Vertical
oval

Date	Mintage	F	VF	XF	Unc	BU
2008 Proof	5,000	Value: 120				

KM# 597 5 DOLLARS
25.0000 g., 0.9990 Silver 0.8029 oz. ASW, 40x25 mm. **Ruler:**
Elizabeth II **Subject:** Benedict XVI Annus Novas **Rev:** Benedict
XVI and dove **Shape:** Oval

Date	Mintage	F	VF	XF	Unc	BU
2008 Proof	5,000	Value: 100				

KM# 598 5 DOLLARS
25.0000 g., 0.9990 Silver 0.8029 oz. ASW, 32x41 mm. **Ruler:**
Elizabeth II **Rev:** St. Peter's Square, cresch and christmas tree,
partially gilt, crystal insert **Shape:** Triangle

Date	Mintage	F	VF	XF	Unc	BU
2008 Proof	5,000	Value: 100				

KM# 599 5 DOLLARS
25.0000 g., 0.9990 Silver 0.8029 oz. ASW, 35x35 mm. **Ruler:**
Elizabeth II **Subject:** Crufifixio Domini **Rev:** Benedict XVI before
cross, partially gilt, crystal inserts **Shape:** Cross

Date	Mintage	F	VF	XF	Unc	BU
2008 Proof	5,000	Value: 100				

KM# 600 5 DOLLARS
25.0000 g., 0.9990 Silver 0.8029 oz. ASW, 29x42 mm. **Ruler:**
Elizabeth II **Subject:** Paulus year **Rev:** Benedict XVI in Basicilica,
partially gilt, crystal insert **Shape:** Vertical rectangle

Date	Mintage	F	VF	XF	Unc	BU
2008 Proof	5,000	Value: 100				

KM# 601 5 DOLLARS
25.0000 g., 0.9990 Silver 0.8029 oz. ASW, 40x25 mm. **Ruler:**
Elizabeth II **Subject:** Sistine Chapel, 500th Anniversary **Rev:**
Adam and god, Sistine Chapel ceiling, partially gilt, crystal insert
Shape: Rectangle

Date	Mintage	F	VF	XF	Unc	BU
2008 Proof	5,000	Value: 120				

KM# 602 5 DOLLARS
25.0000 g., 0.9990 Silver 0.8029 oz. ASW, 40x42 mm. **Ruler:**
Elizabeth II **Rev:** St Martin on horseback, partially gilt, crystal
insert **Shape:** 8-sided

Date	Mintage	F	VF	XF	Unc	BU
2008 Proof	5,000	Value: 100				

KM# 603 5 DOLLARS
25.0000 g., 0.9990 Silver 0.8029 oz. ASW, 45x34 mm. **Ruler:**
Elizabeth II **Subject:** Benedict XVI visits Sydney **Rev:** Sydney
Harbor Bridge and Sydney Opera House, partially gilt, crystal
insert **Shape:** Irregular oval

Date	Mintage	F	VF	XF	Unc	BU
2008 Proof	5,000	Value: 100				

KM# 604 5 DOLLARS
25.0000 g., 0.9990 Silver 0.8029 oz. ASW, 35x35 mm. **Ruler:**
Elizabeth II **Subject:** Tu Es Peterus **Rev:** Cross Keys, Christ
handing keys to kneeling St. Peter. Partially gilt, crystal insert.
Shape: Square

Date	Mintage	F	VF	XF	Unc	BU
2008 Proof	5,000	Value: 120				

KM# 605 5 DOLLARS
25.0000 g., 0.9990 Silver 0.8029 oz. ASW, 38.6 mm. **Ruler:**
Elizabeth II **Rev:** Pope blessing crowd, partially gilt, crystal inserts

Date	Mintage	F	VF	XF	Unc	BU
2008 Proof	5,000	Value: 110				

KM# 606 5 DOLLARS
25.0000 g., 0.9990 Silver 0.8029 oz. ASW, 42x29 mm. **Ruler:**
Elizabeth II **Subject:** Benedict XVI visits the United States **Rev:**
Benedict XVI, the White House, Statue of Liberty, UN Building,
partially gilt, crystal inserts **Shape:** Irregular US Map shape

Date	Mintage	F	VF	XF	Unc	BU
2008 Proof	5,000	Value: 110				

KM# 607 5 DOLLARS
25.0000 g., 0.9990 Silver 0.8029 oz. ASW, 40x42 mm. **Ruler:**
Elizabeth II **Rev:** St. George slaying dragon, partially gilt, crystal
insert **Shape:** 8-sided

Date	Mintage	F	VF	XF	Unc	BU
2008 Proof	5,000	Value: 100				

KM# 608 5 DOLLARS
31.1050 g., 0.9990 Silver 0.9990 oz. ASW, 38.6 mm. **Ruler:**
Elizabeth II **Subject:** Conversion of Russia, 1000th Anniversary
Rev: Baptism scene **Note:** Exclusive to the Russian Market.

Date	Mintage	F	VF	XF	Unc	BU
2008 Proof	500	Value: 120				

KM# 609 5 DOLLARS
31.1050 g., 0.9990 Silver 0.9990 oz. ASW, 47x27 mm. **Ruler:**
Elizabeth II **Subject:** Orthodox Communication **Rev:** Patriarch's
meeting **Shape:** Rectangle **Note:** Exclusive to the Russian
Market.

Date	Mintage	F	VF	XF	Unc	BU
2008 Proof	500	Value: 120				

KM# 610 5 DOLLARS
25.0000 g., 0.9990 Silver 0.8029 oz. ASW, 30x38 mm. **Ruler:**
Elizabeth II **Rev:** Icon - Theotokos of Vladimir, wood insert
Shape: Rectangle **Note:** Exclusive to the Russian Market.

Date	Mintage	F	VF	XF	Unc	BU
2008 Proof	2,500	Value: 120				

KM# 611   5 DOLLARS
31.1050 g., 0.9990 Silver 0.9990 oz. ASW, 38.6 mm.   **Ruler:** Elizabeth II **Subject:** Kiev Churches **Rev:** Church of All Saints **Note:** Exclusive to the Russian Market.

Date	Mintage	F	VF	XF	Unc	BU
2008 Proof	500	Value: 120				

KM# 612   5 DOLLARS
31.1050 g., 0.9990 Silver 0.9990 oz. ASW, 38.6 mm.   **Ruler:** Elizabeth II **Subject:** Kiev Churches **Rev:** Dormotion of Theotokos **Note:** Exclusive to the Russian Market.

Date	Mintage	F	VF	XF	Unc	BU
2008 Proof	500	Value: 120				

KM# 613   5 DOLLARS
31.1050 g., 0.9990 Silver 0.9990 oz. ASW   **Ruler:** Elizabeth II **Subject:** Kiev Churches **Rev:** Refractory of Pechersky **Shape:** 38.6 **Note:** Exclusive to the Russian Market.

Date	Mintage	F	VF	XF	Unc	BU
2008 Proof	500	Value: 120				

KM# 614   5 DOLLARS
31.1050 g., 0.9990 Silver 0.9990 oz. ASW, 38.6 mm.   **Ruler:** Elizabeth II **Subject:** Kiev Churches **Rev:** Troitskaya Barbican **Note:** Exclusive to the Russian Market.

Date	Mintage	F	VF	XF	Unc	BU
2008 Proof	500	Value: 120				

KM# 615   5 DOLLARS
25.0000 g., 0.9250 Silver 0.7435 oz. ASW, 37 mm.   **Ruler:** Elizabeth II **Rev:** Cupid and roses **Rev. Legend:** My Everlasting Love **Shape:** Heart

Date	Mintage	F	VF	XF	Unc	BU
2008 Proof	2,500	Value: 70.00				

KM# 616   5 DOLLARS
25.0000 g., 0.9250 Silver 0.7435 oz. ASW, 38.6 mm.   **Ruler:** Elizabeth II **Subject:** Endangered Wildlife - Arctic **Rev:** Polar bear and cubs, crystal inserts

Date	Mintage	F	VF	XF	Unc	BU
2008 Proof	2,500	Value: 70.00				

KM# 617   5 DOLLARS
25.0000 g., 0.9250 Silver 0.7435 oz. ASW, 38.6 mm.   **Ruler:** Elizabeth II **Subject:** Engangered wildlife - Antarctic **Rev:** Penguin, crystal insert

Date	Mintage	F	VF	XF	Unc	BU
2008 Proof	2,500	Value: 70.00				

KM# 618   5 DOLLARS
25.0000 g., 0.9250 Silver 0.7435 oz. ASW, 38.6 mm.   **Ruler:** Elizabeth II **Subject:** Pultusk Meteorite **Rev:** Earth and Meteorite fragment insert

Date	Mintage	F	VF	XF	Unc	BU
2008 Proof	2,500	Value: 85.00				

KM# 666   5 DOLLARS
141.4000 g., 0.9990 Silver 4.5414 oz. ASW, 65 mm.   **Ruler:** Elizabeth II **Subject:** Tall ships **Obv:** Bust right **Rev:** Germany's Preussen, 5-masted square rigger

Date	Mintage	F	VF	XF	Unc	BU
2008 Proof	—	Value: 285				

KM# 667   5 DOLLARS
141.4000 g., 0.9990 Silver 4.5414 oz. ASW, 65 mm.   **Ruler:** Elizabeth II **Subject:** Tall ships **Rev:** France's France II

Date	Mintage	F	VF	XF	Unc	BU
2008 Proof	—	Value: 285				

KM# 668   5 DOLLARS
141.4000 g., 0.9990 Silver 4.5414 oz. ASW, 65 mm.   **Ruler:** Elizabeth II **Subject:** Tall Ships **Rev:** America's Thomas W. Lawson, 7-masted schooner

Date	Mintage	F	VF	XF	Unc	BU
2008 Proof	—	Value: 285				

KM# 669 5 DOLLARS
141.4000 g., 0.9990 Silver 4.5414 oz. ASW, 65 mm. **Ruler:**
Elizabeth II **Subject:** Tall Ships **Rev:** Russia's Sedov, 4-masted
barque

Date	Mintage	F	VF	XF	Unc	BU
2008 Proof	—	Value: 285				

KM# 670 5 DOLLARS
141.4000 g., 0.9990 Silver 4.5414 oz. ASW, 65 mm. **Ruler:**
Elizabeth II **Subject:** Tall Ships **Rev:** Norway's Christian Radich

Date	Mintage	F	VF	XF	Unc	BU
2008 Proof	—	Value: 285				

KM# 671 5 DOLLARS
141.4000 g., 0.9990 Silver 4.5414 oz. ASW, 65 mm. **Ruler:**
Elizabeth II **Subject:** Tall Ships **Rev:** Russian 4-masted barque
Kruzenshtern

Date	Mintage	F	VF	XF	Unc	BU
2008 Proof	—	Value: 285				

KM# 766 5 DOLLARS
31.1050 g., 0.9990 Silver 0.9990 oz. ASW, 40 mm. **Ruler:**
Elizabeth II **Subject:** First man on the Moon **Rev:** Moon and rock
fragment

Date	Mintage	F	VF	XF	Unc	BU
2008 Proof	—	Value: 120				

KM# 1207 5 DOLLARS
0.5000 g., 0.9990 Gold 0.0161 oz. AGW, 11 mm. **Ruler:**
Elizabeth II **Rev:** American Bison

Date	Mintage	F	VF	XF	Unc	BU
2008 Proof	Est. 5,000	Value: 40.00				

KM# 1211 5 DOLLARS
155.5000 g., Copper-Nickel partially gilt, 65 mm. **Ruler:**
Elizabeth II **Subject:** British Monarchs - Elizabeth I

Date	Mintage	F	VF	XF	Unc	BU
2008 Proof	Est. 450	Value: 85.00				

KM# 1330 5 DOLLARS
Silver **Ruler:** Elizabeth II **Rev:** European Bison, partially gilt

Date	Mintage	F	VF	XF	Unc	BU
2009 Proof	—	Value: 50.00				

KM# 640 5 DOLLARS
25.0000 g., 0.9990 Silver 0.8029 oz. ASW, 38.6 mm. **Ruler:**
Elizabeth II **Rev:** Papal Tiara above crossed keys, partially gilt,
crystal inserts

Date	Mintage	F	VF	XF	Unc	BU
2009 Proof	5,000	Value: 120				

KM# 641 5 DOLLARS
25.0000 g., 0.9990 Silver 0.8029 oz. ASW **Ruler:** Elizabeth II
Subject: Benedict XVI visits Israel **Rev:** Benedict XVI and "Dome
of the Rock", partially gilt, crystal inserts **Shape:** Diamond

Date	Mintage	F	VF	XF	Unc	BU
2009 Proof	5,000	Value: 115				

KM# 642 5 DOLLARS
25.0000 g., 0.9990 Silver 0.8029 oz. ASW **Ruler:** Elizabeth II
Subject: Benedict XVI visits Africa **Rev:** Bust at left, partially gilt,
crystal inserts **Shape:** Irregular, Africa shape

Date	Mintage	F	VF	XF	Unc	BU
2009 Proof	5,000	Value: 115				

KM# 643 5 DOLLARS
25.0000 g., 0.9990 Silver 0.8029 oz. ASW **Ruler:** Elizabeth II
Subject: Easter 2009 **Rev:** Statue of the risen Christ, partially
gilt, crystal inserts **Shape:** Fish

Date	Mintage	F	VF	XF	Unc	BU
2009 Proof	5,000	Value: 115				

KM# 644 5 DOLLARS
25.0000 g., 0.9990 Silver 0.8029 oz. ASW, 35 mm. **Ruler:**
Elizabeth II **Rev:** Star of the Magi, partially gilt, crystal inserts
Shape: Star

Date	Mintage	F	VF	XF	Unc	BU
2009 Proof	5,000	Value: 115				

KM# 645 5 DOLLARS
25.0000 g., 0.9990 Silver 0.8029 oz. ASW, 35x35 mm. **Ruler:**
Elizabeth II **Rev:** Cathedral of Santiago de Compostela, partially
gilt, crystal inserts

Date	Mintage	F	VF	XF	Unc	BU
2009 Proof	5,000	Value: 120				

KM# 646 5 DOLLARS
25.0000 g., 0.9990 Silver 0.8029 oz. ASW, 25x35 mm. **Ruler:**
Elizabeth II **Rev:** Michangelo's Pieta, partially gilt, crystal inserts
Shape: Rectangle

Date	Mintage	F	VF	XF	Unc	BU
2009 Proof	5,000	Value: 115				

KM# 647 5 DOLLARS
25.0000 g., 0.9990 Silver 0.8029 oz. ASW, 30x34 mm. **Ruler:**
Elizabeth II **Rev:** St. Christopher, partially gilt, crystal inserts
Shape: Oval

Date	Mintage	F	VF	XF	Unc	BU
2009 Proof	5,000	Value: 115				

KM# 648 5 DOLLARS
25.0000 g., 0.9990 Silver 0.8029 oz. ASW, 40x25 mm. **Ruler:**
Elizabeth II **Subject:** Benedict XVI visits the Czech Republic **Rev:**
Benedict XVI in Wenceleses square, partially gilt, crystal inserts
Shape: Rectangle

Date	Mintage	F	VF	XF	Unc	BU
2009 Proof	5,000	Value: 115				

KM# 649 5 DOLLARS
25.0000 g., 0.9990 Silver 0.8029 oz. ASW **Ruler:** Elizabeth II
Rev: Christmas, village scene, partially gilt, crystal inserts **Shape:**
Diamond

Date	Mintage	F	VF	XF	Unc	BU
2009 Proof	5,000	Value: 115				

KM# 650 5 DOLLARS
31.1050 g., 0.9990 Silver 0.9990 oz. ASW, 38.6 mm. **Ruler:**
Elizabeth II **Subject:** Kiev Churches **Rev:** Andreevskaya Church
Note: Exclusive to the Russian Market.

Date	Mintage	F	VF	XF	Unc	BU
2009 Proof	500	Value: 125				

KM# 651 5 DOLLARS
31.1050 g., 0.9990 Silver 0.9990 oz. ASW, 38.6 mm. **Ruler:**
Elizabeth II **Subject:** Kiev Churches **Rev:** Kirillovskaya Church
Note: Exclusive to the Russian Market.

Date	Mintage	F	VF	XF	Unc	BU
2009 Proof	500	Value: 125				

KM# 652 5 DOLLARS
31.1050 g., 0.9990 Silver 0.9990 oz. ASW, 38.6 mm. **Ruler:**
Elizabeth II **Subject:** Kiev Chruches **Rev:** Mikailovsky Monastery
Note: Exclusive to the Russian Market.

Date	Mintage	F	VF	XF	Unc	BU
2009 Proof	500	Value: 125				

KM# 653 5 DOLLARS
31.1050 g., 0.9990 Silver 0.9990 oz. ASW, 38.6 mm. **Ruler:**
Elizabeth II **Subject:** Kiev Churches **Rev:** Cathedral of St. Sophia
Note: Exclusive to the Russian Market.

Date	Mintage	F	VF	XF	Unc	BU
2009 Proof	500	Value: 125				

KM# 654   5 DOLLARS
31.1050 g., 0.9990 Silver 0.9990 oz. ASW, 38.61 mm.   **Ruler:**
Elizabeth II **Subject:** Ukraine Landmarks - Bendrological park,
Sofiyivka **Rev:** Statue and gardens **Note:** Exclusive to the
Russian Market.

Date	Mintage	F	VF	XF	Unc	BU
2009 Proof	500	Value: 120				

KM# 655   5 DOLLARS
31.1050 g., 0.9990 Silver 0.9990 oz. ASW, 38.61 mm.   **Ruler:**
Elizabeth II **Subject:** Ukraine Landmarks - Holy Dormition Kiev
Pechersk Lavra **Rev:** Churches **Note:** Exclusive to the Russian
Market.

Date	Mintage	F	VF	XF	Unc	BU
2009 Proof	500	Value: 120				

KM# 656   5 DOLLARS
31.1050 g., 0.9990 Silver 0.9990 oz. ASW, 38.61 mm.   **Ruler:**
Elizabeth II **Subject:** Ukraine Landmarks - Holy Dormition
Pochayiv Lavra **Rev:** Buildings **Note:** Exclusive to the Russian
Market.

Date	Mintage	F	VF	XF	Unc	BU
2009 Proof	500	Value: 120				

KM# 657   5 DOLLARS
31.1050 g., 0.9990 Silver 0.9990 oz. ASW, 38.61 mm.   **Ruler:**
Elizabeth II **Subject:** Ukraine Landmarks - Holy Dormition
Sviatohirsk Lavra **Rev:** Virgin Mary and Church **Note:** Exclusive
to the Russian Market.

Date	Mintage	F	VF	XF	Unc	BU
2009 Proof	500	Value: 120				

KM# 658   5 DOLLARS
31.1050 g., 0.9990 Silver 0.9990 oz. ASW, 38.61 mm.   **Ruler:**
Elizabeth II **Subject:** Ukraine Landmarks - Kamyanets National
Reserve **Rev:** Fortress **Note:** Exclusive to the Russian Market.

Date	Mintage	F	VF	XF	Unc	BU
2009 Proof	500	Value: 120				

KM# 659   5 DOLLARS
31.1050 g., 0.9990 Silver 0.9990 oz. ASW, 38.6 mm.   **Ruler:**
Elizabeth II **Subject:** Ukraine Landmarks - Khersones Tavrijsky
National Reserve **Rev:** Roman ruins **Note:** Exclusive to the
Russian Market.

Date	Mintage	F	VF	XF	Unc	BU
2009 Proof	500	Value: 120				

KM# 660   5 DOLLARS
31.1050 g., 0.9990 Silver 0.9990 oz. ASW, 38.6 mm.   **Ruler:**
Elizabeth II **Subject:** Ukraine Landmarks - Khortytsia National
Reserve **Rev:** Stone carvings and bridge **Note:** Exclusive to the
Russian Market.

Date	Mintage	F	VF	XF	Unc	BU
2009 Proof	500	Value: 120				

KM# 661   5 DOLLARS
31.1050 g., 0.9990 Silver 0.9990 oz. ASW, 38.6 mm.   **Ruler:**
Elizabeth II **Subject:** Ukraine Landmarks - National Theatre of
Odessa **Rev:** Opera House **Note:** Exclusive to the Russian
Market.

Date	Mintage	F	VF	XF	Unc	BU
2009 Proof	500	Value: 120				

KM# 662   5 DOLLARS
31.1050 g., 0.9990 Silver 0.9990 oz. ASW, 38.6 mm.   **Ruler:**
Elizabeth II **Subject:** Ukraine Landmarks - Olesko Castle **Rev:**
Hillside dwelling **Note:** Exclusive to the Russian Market.

Date	Mintage	F	VF	XF	Unc	BU
2009 Proof	500	Value: 120				

KM# 663   5 DOLLARS
31.1050 g., 0.9990 Silver 0.9990 oz. ASW, 38.6 mm.   **Ruler:**
Elizabeth II **Subject:** Ukraine Landmarks - Palanok Castle in
Mukachevo **Rev:** Hilltop fortress **Note:** Exclusive to the Russian
Market.

Date	Mintage	F	VF	XF	Unc	BU
2009 Proof	500	Value: 120				

KM# 664   5 DOLLARS
31.1050 g., 0.9990 Silver 0.9990 oz. ASW, 38.6 mm.   **Ruler:**
Elizabeth II **Subject:** Ukraine Landmarks - Khotyn Fortress
Reserve **Rev:** Road to castle **Note:** Exclusive to the Russian
Market.

Date	Mintage	F	VF	XF	Unc	BU
2009 Proof	500	Value: 120				

KM# 665   5 DOLLARS
31.1050 g., 0.9990 Silver 0.9990 oz. ASW, 38.6 mm.   **Ruler:**
Elizabeth II **Subject:** Ukraine Landmarks - Upper Castle of Lutsk
Rev: Tower **Note:** Exclusive to the Russian Market.

Date	Mintage	F	VF	XF	Unc	BU
2009 Proof	500	Value: 120				

KM# 672 5 DOLLARS
25.0000 g., 0.9250 Silver 0.7435 oz. ASW, 38.6 mm. **Ruler:** Elizabeth II **Rev:** HMS Endeavour and James Cook portrait

Date	Mintage	F	VF	XF	Unc	BU
2009 Proof	2,500	Value: 45.00				

KM# 673 5 DOLLARS
25.0000 g., 0.5000 Silver 0.4019 oz. ASW, 38.6 mm. **Ruler:** Elizabeth II **Rev:** Ferrari F-2008 Carbon

Date	Mintage	F	VF	XF	Unc	BU
2009 Proof	2,008	Value: 60.00				

KM# 674 5 DOLLARS
20.0000 g., 0.9250 Silver 0.5948 oz. ASW, 38.61 mm. **Ruler:** Elizabeth II **Subject:** Endangered Wildlife **Rev:** Giant Anteater

Date	Mintage	F	VF	XF	Unc	BU
2009 Proof	5,000	Value: 50.00				

KM# 675 5 DOLLARS
31.1050 g., 0.9250 Silver 0.9250 oz. ASW, 38.6 mm. **Ruler:** Elizabeth II **Series:** International Womens Day **Rev:** Roses and butterfly **Note:** Exclusive to the Russian Market

Date	Mintage	F	VF	XF	Unc	BU
2009 Proof	500	Value: 120				

KM# 676 5 DOLLARS
25.0000 g., 0.9250 Silver 0.7435 oz. ASW, 38.6 mm. **Ruler:** Elizabeth II **Rev:** Sir Lancelot, multicolor

Date	Mintage	F	VF	XF	Unc	BU
2009 Proof	2,500	Value: 75.00				

KM# 677 5 DOLLARS
0.9250 Silver **Ruler:** Elizabeth II **Subject:** Masters of Europe - Vermeer **Rev:** Girl with a pearl earing, multicolor **Shape:** Vertical rectangle

Date	Mintage	F	VF	XF	Unc	BU
2009 Proof	—	Value: 85.00				

KM# 678 5 DOLLARS
0.9250 Silver **Ruler:** Elizabeth II **Subject:** Masters of Europe - DaVinci **Rev:** Lady with an ermine, multicolor **Shape:** Vertical rectangle

Date	Mintage	F	VF	XF	Unc	BU
2009 Proof	—	Value: 95.00				

KM# 679 5 DOLLARS
0.9250 Silver **Ruler:** Elizabeth II **Subject:** Masters of Europe - Jan Matejko **Rev:** Wernyhora, multicolor **Shape:** Vertical rectangle

Date	Mintage	F	VF	XF	Unc	BU
2009 Proof	—	Value: 85.00				

KM# 680 5 DOLLARS
Silver **Ruler:** Elizabeth II **Subject:** 50th Anniversary of Space exploration, 40th Anniversary of Apollo 11 **Obv:** Moon **Rev:** Moonscape and moon rock implant

Date	Mintage	F	VF	XF	Unc	BU
2009 Matte	1,969	—	—	—	—	180

KM# 681 5 DOLLARS
25.0000 g., 0.9250 Silver copper plated 0.7435 oz. ASW **Ruler:** Elizabeth II **Subject:** 400th Anniversary of Mars observations **Obv:** Bust with tiara right **Rev:** Mars landscape

Date	Mintage	F	VF	XF	Unc	BU
2009 Matte	2,500	—	—	—	—	160

KM# 682 5 DOLLARS
25.0000 g., 0.9250 Silver 0.7435 oz. ASW, 38.61 mm. **Ruler:** Elizabeth II **Subject:** Year of the Ox **Rev:** Child riding oxen, partially gilt **Note:** Exclusive to the Russian market

Date	Mintage	F	VF	XF	Unc	BU
2009 Proof	1,000	Value: 200				

KM# 683   5 DOLLARS
25.0000 g., 0.9990 Silver 0.8029 oz. ASW   **Ruler:** Elizabeth II
Subject: World of Flowers - Pansey **Rev:** Pansey, multicolor
cloisonne

Date	Mintage	F	VF	XF	Unc	BU
2009 Proof	2,500	Value: 85.00				

KM# 684   5 DOLLARS
25.0000 g., 0.9990 Silver 0.8029 oz. ASW, 38.6 mm.   **Ruler:**
Elizabeth II **Subject:** World of flowers - Poppy **Rev:** Poppy,
multicolor closinne

Date	Mintage	F	VF	XF	Unc	BU
2009 Proof	2,500	Value: 85.00				

KM# 685   5 DOLLARS
25.0000 g., 0.9250 Silver 0.7435 oz. ASW, 30x43 mm.   **Ruler:**
Elizabeth II **Obv:** Bust right **Rev:** Easter chick, thermal image
changing **Shape:** Egg

Date	Mintage	F	VF	XF	Unc	BU
2009 Proof	2,500	Value: 70.00				

KM# 686   5 DOLLARS
25.0000 g., 0.9250 Silver 0.7435 oz. ASW, 35x35 mm.   **Ruler:**
Elizabeth II **Rev:** Season's greetings, rocking horse **Shape:**
Square

Date	Mintage	F	VF	XF	Unc	BU
2009 Proof	2,500	Value: 60.00				

KM# 687   5 DOLLARS
25.0000 g., 0.9990 Silver 0.8029 oz. ASW, 30x38 mm.   **Ruler:**
Elizabeth II **Rev:** Kazan Virgin icon **Shape:** Vertical rectangle
Note: Exclusive to the Russian market

Date	Mintage	F	VF	XF	Unc	BU
2009 Proof	2,500	Value: 125				

KM# 764   5 DOLLARS
Silver, 25x40 mm.   **Ruler:** Elizabeth II **Subject:** Ferrari, the
Legend **Rev:** Car and enameled shield **Shape:** Vertical rectangle

Date	Mintage	F	VF	XF	Unc	BU
2009 Proof	—	Value: 125				

KM# 782   5 DOLLARS
20.0000 g., 0.9990 Silver 0.6423 oz. ASW, 40 mm.   **Ruler:**
Elizabeth II **Subject:** Year of Astronomy **Rev:** Sun, multicolor

Date	Mintage	F	VF	XF	Unc	BU
2009	—	—	—	—	—	50.00

KM# 783   5 DOLLARS
20.0000 g., 0.9990 Silver 0.6423 oz. ASW, 40 mm.   **Ruler:**
Elizabeth II **Subject:** Year of Astronomy **Rev:** Mercury, multicolor

Date	Mintage	F	VF	XF	Unc	BU
2009	—	—	—	—	—	50.00

KM# 784   5 DOLLARS
20.0000 g., 0.9990 Silver 0.6423 oz. ASW, 40 mm.   **Ruler:**
Elizabeth II **Subject:** Year of Astronomy **Rev:** Venus, multicolor

Date	Mintage	F	VF	XF	Unc	BU
2009	—	—	—	—	—	55.00

KM# 785   5 DOLLARS
20.0000 g., 0.9990 Silver 0.6423 oz. ASW, 40 mm.   **Ruler:**
Elizabeth II **Subject:** Year of Astronomy **Rev:** Earth, multicolor

Date	Mintage	F	VF	XF	Unc	BU
2009	—	—	—	—	—	50.00

KM# 786   5 DOLLARS
20.0000 g., 0.9990 Silver 0.6423 oz. ASW, 40 mm.   **Ruler:**
Elizabeth II **Subject:** Year of Astronomy **Rev:** Mars, multicolor

Date	Mintage	F	VF	XF	Unc	BU
2009	—	—	—	—	—	50.00

KM# 787   5 DOLLARS
20.0000 g., 0.9990 Silver 0.6423 oz. ASW, 40 mm.   **Ruler:**
Elizabeth II **Subject:** Year of Astronomy **Rev:** Jupiter, multicolor

Date	Mintage	F	VF	XF	Unc	BU
2009	—	—	—	—	—	50.00

KM# 788   5 DOLLARS
20.0000 g., 0.9990 Silver 0.6423 oz. ASW, 40 mm.   **Ruler:**
Elizabeth II **Subject:** Year of Astronomy **Rev:** Saturn, multicolor

Date	Mintage	F	VF	XF	Unc	BU
2009	—	—	—	—	—	50.00

KM# 789   5 DOLLARS
20.0000 g., 0.9990 Silver 0.6423 oz. ASW, 40 mm.   **Ruler:**
Elizabeth II **Subject:** Year of Astronomy **Rev:** Uranus, multicolor

Date	Mintage	F	VF	XF	Unc	BU
2009	—	—	—	—	—	50.00

KM# 790   5 DOLLARS
20.0000 g., 0.9990 Silver 0.6423 oz. ASW, 40 mm. **Ruler:**
Elizabeth II **Subject:** Year of Astronomy **Rev:** Neptune,
multicolor

Date	Mintage	F	VF	XF	Unc	BU
2009	—	—	—	—	—	50.00

KM# 791   5 DOLLARS
20.0000 g., 0.9990 Silver 0.6423 oz. ASW, 40 mm. **Ruler:**
Elizabeth II **Subject:** Year of Astronomy **Rev:** Solar System,
multicolor

Date	Mintage	F	VF	XF	Unc	BU
2009	—	—	—	—	—	50.00

KM# 1225   5 DOLLARS
28.2800 g., 0.9250 Silver 0.8410 oz. ASW, 38.6 mm. **Ruler:**
Elizabeth II **Subject:** Ikuko Shimizu's Hello Kitty **Rev:** Kitty and
London Buss in multicolor

Date	Mintage	F	VF	XF	Unc	BU
2009 Proof	Est. 3,000 Value: 115					

KM# 1226   5 DOLLARS
28.2800 g., 0.9250 Silver 0.8410 oz. ASW, 38.6 mm. **Ruler:**
Elizabeth II **Subject:** Ikuko Shimizu's Hello Kitty **Rev:** Kitty
playing polo in multicolor

Date	Mintage	F	VF	XF	Unc	BU
2009 Proof	Est. 3,000 Value: 115					

KM# 1227   5 DOLLARS
28.2800 g., 0.9250 Silver 0.8410 oz. ASW, 38.6 mm. **Ruler:**
Elizabeth II **Subject:** Ikuko Shimizu's Hello Kitty **Rev:** Kitty and
Daniel with Tower Bridge in multicolor

Date	Mintage	F	VF	XF	Unc	BU
2009 Proof	Est. 3,000 Value: 115					

KM# 1236   5 DOLLARS
25.0000 g., 0.9250 Silver 0.7435 oz. ASW, 38.61 mm. **Ruler:**
Elizabeth II **Subject:** Lady of the Lake

Date	Mintage	F	VF	XF	Unc	BU
2009 Proof	2,500 Value: 75.00					

KM# 1237   5 DOLLARS
25.0000 g., 0.9250 Silver 0.7435 oz. ASW, 38.61 mm. **Ruler:**
Elizabeth II **Rev:** Excalibur set into rock in color

Date	Mintage	F	VF	XF	Unc	BU
2009 Proof	2,500 Value: 75.00					

KM# 1238   5 DOLLARS
25.0000 g., 0.9250 Silver 0.7435 oz. ASW, 38.61 mm. **Ruler:**
Elizabeth II **Subject:** King Arthur

Date	Mintage	F	VF	XF	Unc	BU
2009 Proof	2,500 Value: 75.00					

KM# 1239   5 DOLLARS
25.0000 g., 0.9250 Silver 0.7435 oz. ASW, 38.61 mm. **Ruler:**
Elizabeth II **Subject:** Sir Galahad

Date	Mintage	F	VF	XF	Unc	BU
2009 Proof	2,500 Value: 75.00					

KM# 1240   5 DOLLARS
25.0000 g., 0.9250 Silver 0.7435 oz. ASW, 38.61 mm. **Ruler:**
Elizabeth II **Subject:** Knights of the Round table theme

Date	Mintage	F	VF	XF	Unc	BU
2009 Proof	2,500 Value: 75.00					

KM# 1329   5 DOLLARS
Silver **Ruler:** Elizabeth II **Subject:** Banker's Day **Rev:** Map of
Ukraine, locations pinpointed

Date	Mintage	F	VF	XF	Unc	BU
2009 Antique patina	—	—	—	—	—	85.00

KM# 1331   5 DOLLARS
Silver **Ruler:** Elizabeth II **Rev:** Napoleon on horseback in battle
in color

Date	Mintage	F	VF	XF	Unc	BU
2009	—	Value: 80.00				

KM# 1340   5 DOLLARS
Silver **Ruler:** Elizabeth II **Subject:** Trafalgar **Rev:** HMS Victory
in color

Date	Mintage	F	VF	XF	Unc	BU
2010 Proof	—	Value: 80.00				

KM# 1337   5 DOLLARS
Silver **Ruler:** Elizabeth II **Subject:** Clothed and nude Maya
Shape: Rectangle **Note:** Detachable clothing over image.

Date	Mintage	F	VF	XF	Unc	BU
2010 Proof	—	Value: 80.00				

KM# 723   5 DOLLARS
31.1050 g., 0.9990 Silver 0.9990 oz. ASW, 24x47 mm. **Ruler:**
Elizabeth II **Subject:** War of 1812 **Rev:** Peter Bagraton

Date	Mintage	F	VF	XF	Unc	BU
2010 Antique patina	2,000	—	—	—	—	55.00

KM# 724   5 DOLLARS
31.1050 g., 0.9990 Silver 0.9990 oz. ASW **Ruler:** Elizabeth II
Subject: War of 1812 **Rev:** Mikhail Kutuzov **Shape:** 24x47

Date	Mintage	F	VF	XF	Unc	BU
2010 Antique patina	2,000	—	—	—	—	55.00

KM# 725   5 DOLLARS
31.1050 g., 0.9990 Silver 0.9990 oz. ASW, 27x47 mm. **Ruler:**
Elizabeth II **Subject:** War of 1812 **Rev:** Bikoly Raevsky

Date	Mintage	F	VF	XF	Unc	BU
2010 Antique finish	2,000	—	—	—	—	55.00

KM# 726   5 DOLLARS
20.0000 g., 0.9990 Silver 0.6423 oz. ASW, 30x43 mm. **Ruler:**
Elizabeth II **Subject:** Imperial Eggs **Rev:** Blue egg

Date	Mintage	F	VF	XF	Unc	BU
2010 Proof	2,500 Value: 70.00					

KM# 727   5 DOLLARS
20.0000 g., 0.9990 Silver 0.6423 oz. ASW, 30x43 mm. **Ruler:**
Elizabeth II **Subject:** Imperial Egg **Rev:** Green cloisonne

Date	Mintage	F	VF	XF	Unc	BU
2010 Proof	2,500 Value: 70.00					

KM# 728   5 DOLLARS
20.0000 g., 0.9990 Silver 0.6423 oz. ASW, 30x43 mm.   **Ruler:**
Elizabeth II **Subject:** Imperial Egg **Rev:** Yellow cloisonne and
Bohemian crystals

Date	Mintage	F	VF	XF	Unc	BU
2010 Proof	2,500	Value: 70.00				

KM# 729   5 DOLLARS
25.0000 g., 0.9990 Silver 0.8029 oz. ASW, 38.6 mm.   **Ruler:**
Elizabeth II **Rev:** Martin Luther King, pointing **Note:** Fits together
with KM#730.

Date	Mintage	F	VF	XF	Unc	BU
2010 Antique finish	2,500	—	—	—	—	60.00

KM# 730   5 DOLLARS
25.0000 g., 0.9990 Silver 0.8029 oz. ASW, 38.6 mm.   **Ruler:**
Elizabeth II **Rev:** Barack Obama, pointing **Note:** Fits together
with KM#729.

Date	Mintage	F	VF	XF	Unc	BU
2010 Antique finish	2,500	—	—	—	—	60.00

KM# 731   5 DOLLARS
25.0000 g., 0.9250 Silver 0.7435 oz. ASW, 38.6 mm.   **Ruler:**
Elizabeth II **Subject:** Tender Love **Rev:** Rose in relief hologram

Date	Mintage	F	VF	XF	Unc	BU
2010 Proof	2,500	Value: 50.00				

KM# 732   5 DOLLARS
25.0000 g., 0.9250 Silver 0.7435 oz. ASW, 30x38 mm.   **Ruler:**
Elizabeth II **Rev:** Holy Trinity icon

Date	Mintage	F	VF	XF	Unc	BU
2010 Proof	2,500	Value: 65.00				

KM# 1244   5 DOLLARS
25.0000 g., 0.9250 Silver 0.7435 oz. ASW, 30x38 mm.   **Ruler:**
Elizabeth II **Subject:** Vasily Tropinin, 1776-1857 **Rev:** The
Lacemaker, multicolor **Shape:** Vertical rectangle

Date	Mintage	F	VF	XF	Unc	BU
2010 Proof	2,500	Value: 65.00				

KM# 1245   5 DOLLARS
25.0000 g., 0.9250 Silver 0.7435 oz. ASW, 40.6 mm.   **Ruler:**
Elizabeth II **Subject:** Don Juan, Battle of Lepanto

Date	Mintage	F	VF	XF	Unc	BU
2010 Proof	1,000	Value: 75.00				

KM# 1250   5 DOLLARS
26.0000 g., 0.9250 Silver 0.7732 oz. ASW, 30x38 mm.   **Ruler:**
Elizabeth II **Subject:** Peter Brandl **Shape:** Vertical rectangle

Date	Mintage	F	VF	XF	Unc	BU
2010 Proof	2,500	Value: 60.00				

KM# 1251   5 DOLLARS
25.0000 g., 0.9250 Silver 0.7435 oz. ASW, 30x38 mm.   **Ruler:**
Elizabeth II **Subject:** Michangelo's David **Shape:** Vertical
rectangle

Date	Mintage	F	VF	XF	Unc	BU
2010 Proof	2,500	Value: 55.00				

KM# 1252   5 DOLLARS
25.0000 g., 0.9250 Silver 0.7435 oz. ASW, 38.61 mm.   **Ruler:**
Elizabeth II **Subject:** Hollywood Stars - Ginger Rogers

Date	Mintage	F	VF	XF	Unc	BU
2010 Proof	2,500	Value: 75.00				

KM# 1254   5 DOLLARS
25.0000 g., 0.9250 Silver 0.7435 oz. ASW, 38.61 mm.   **Ruler:**
Elizabeth II **Subject:** Hollywood Stars - Clark Gable

Date	Mintage	F	VF	XF	Unc	BU
2010 Proof	2,500	Value: 75.00				

KM# 1255   5 DOLLARS
25.0000 g., 0.9250 Silver 0.7435 oz. ASW, 38.61 mm.   **Ruler:**
Elizabeth II **Subject:** Gdansk **Rev:** Town view, statue in copper
Note: Antique patina.

Date	Mintage	F	VF	XF	Unc	BU
2010	1,000	Value: 60.00				

KM# 1281 5 DOLLARS
Silver, 27x47 mm. **Ruler:** Elizabeth II **Subject:** Ferrari 250 GTO and 599 GTO **Rev:** Car at top and bottom, yellow logo at center **Shape:** Vertical rectangle

Date	Mintage	F	VF	XF	Unc	BU
2010 Proof	1,010	Value: 135				

KM# 1253 5 DOLLARS
25.0000 g., 0.9250 Silver 0.7435 oz. ASW, 38.61 mm. **Ruler:** Elizabeth II **Subject:** Hollywood Stars - John Wayne

Date	Mintage	F	VF	XF	Unc	BU
2010 Proof	2,500	Value: 75.00				

KM# 1292 5 DOLLARS
25.0000 g., 0.9990 Silver 0.8029 oz. ASW, 30x38 mm. **Ruler:** Elizabeth II **Subject:** Russian Icons **Rev:** Icon of St. Nicolas **Shape:** Vertical rectangle

Date	Mintage	F	VF	XF	Unc	BU
2010 Proof	—	Value: 120				

KM# 1299 5 DOLLARS
25.0000 g., 0.9250 Silver 0.7435 oz. ASW, 38.61 mm. **Ruler:** Elizabeth II **Rev:** HAH 280 Meteorite in color

Date	Mintage	F	VF	XF	Unc	BU
2010 Antique Patina	2,500					100

KM# 1300 5 DOLLARS
31.1050 g., 0.9250 Silver 0.9250 oz. ASW, 38.61 mm. **Ruler:** Elizabeth II **Subject:** Yugra district **Rev:** Bear

Date	Mintage	F	VF	XF	Unc	BU
2010 Proof	2,000	Value: 75.00				

KM# 1301 5 DOLLARS
31.1050 g., 0.9250 Silver 0.9250 oz. ASW, 38.61 mm. **Ruler:** Elizabeth II **Subject:** Yugra District **Rev:** Crude Oil

Date	Mintage	F	VF	XF	Unc	BU
2010 Proof	2,000	Value: 75.00				

KM# 1302 5 DOLLARS
31.1050 g., 0.9250 Silver 0.9250 oz. ASW, 38.61 mm. **Ruler:** Elizabeth II **Subject:** Yugra District **Rev:** Sledge Jump

Date	Mintage	F	VF	XF	Unc	BU
2010 Proof	2,000	Value: 75.00				

KM# 1303 5 DOLLARS
31.1050 g., 0.9990 Silver 0.9990 oz. ASW, 38.61 mm. **Ruler:** Elizabeth II **Subject:** Day of Prudence

Date	Mintage	F	VF	XF	Unc	BU
2010 Antique patina	500	—	—	—	—	75.00

KM# 1304 5 DOLLARS
25.0000 g., 0.9990 Silver 0.8029 oz. ASW, 30x38 mm. **Ruler:** Elizabeth II **Subject:** Russian Icons **Rev:** The Holy Face of Christ **Shape:** Vertical rectangle

Date	Mintage	F	VF	XF	Unc	BU
2010 Proof	2,500	Value: 75.00				

KM# 1305 5 DOLLARS
25.0000 g., 0.9990 Silver 0.8029 oz. ASW, 30x38 mm. **Ruler:** Elizabeth II **Subject:** Russian Icons **Rev:** St. Sergius of Radonezh **Shape:** Vertical rectangle

Date	Mintage	F	VF	XF	Unc	BU
2010 Proof	2,500	Value: 75.00				

KM# 1307 5 DOLLARS
25.0000 g., 0.9250 Silver 0.7435 oz. ASW, 38.61 mm. **Ruler:** Elizabeth II **Rev:** Wedding day, color and partially gilt

Date	Mintage	F	VF	XF	Unc	BU
2010 Proof	2,000	Value: 75.00				

KM# 1308 5 DOLLARS
31.1050 g., 0.9990 Silver 0.9990 oz. ASW, 38.61 mm. **Ruler:** Elizabeth II **Subject:** Dear Grandmother

Date	Mintage	F	VF	XF	Unc	BU
2010 Proof	500	Value: 75.00				

KM# 1309 5 DOLLARS
25.0000 g., 0.9250 Silver 0.7435 oz. ASW, 38.61 mm. **Ruler:** Elizabeth II **Rev:** Cats at night

Date	Mintage	F	VF	XF	Unc	BU
2010 Proof	2,000	Value: 75.00				

KM# 1310 5 DOLLARS
25.0000 g., 0.9990 Silver 0.8029 oz. ASW, 30x38 mm. **Ruler:** Elizabeth II **Subject:** Patron saints **Rev:** St. Helena **Shape:** Vertical rectangle

Date	Mintage	F	VF	XF	Unc	BU
2010 Proof	2,500	Value: 75.00				

KM# 1311 5 DOLLARS
25.0000 g., 0.9990 Silver 0.8029 oz. ASW, 30x38 mm. **Ruler:** Elizabeth II **Subject:** Patron Saints **Rev:** St. Constantine **Shape:** Vertical rectangle

Date	Mintage	F	VF	XF	Unc	BU
2010 Proof	2,500	Value: 75.00				

KM# 1334 5 DOLLARS
Silver, 40 mm. **Ruler:** Elizabeth II **Subject:** 2nd Crusade

Date	Mintage	F	VF	XF	Unc	BU
2010 Antique patina	—	—	—	—	—	100

KM# 1335 5 DOLLARS
Silver, 40 mm. **Ruler:** Elizabeth II **Subject:** 3rd Crusade

Date	Mintage	F	VF	XF	Unc	BU
2010 Antique patina	—	—	—	—	—	100

KM# 1336 5 DOLLARS
Silver **Ruler:** Elizabeth II **Subject:** 4th Crusade

Date	Mintage	F	VF	XF	Unc	BU
2010 Antique patina	—	—	—	—	—	100

KM# 1338 5 DOLLARS
Silver **Ruler:** Elizabeth II **Subject:** Lubek

Date	Mintage	F	VF	XF	Unc	BU
2010 Antique patina	—	—	—	—	—	100

KM# 1339 5 DOLLARS
Silver **Ruler:** Elizabeth II **Subject:** Zutphen

Date	Mintage	F	VF	XF	Unc	BU
2010 Antque patina	—	—	—	—	—	100

KM# 1314 5 DOLLARS
25.0000 g., 0.9250 Silver 0.7435 oz. ASW, 38.61 mm. **Ruler:** Elizabeth II **Subject:** Marilyn Monroe, 85th Birthday

Date	Mintage	F	VF	XF	Unc	BU
2011 Proof	1,926	Value: 75.00				

KM# 1380   5 DOLLARS
Silver, 30x28.5 mm. **Ruler:** Elizabeth II **Subject:** Seeds of Love
Rev: Vine and half of a heart shaped red crystal

Date	Mintage	F	VF	XF	Unc	BU
2011 Antique patina	—	Value: 75.00				

KM# 1261   5 DOLLARS
25.0000 g., 0.9250 Silver 0.7435 oz. ASW, 38.61 mm. **Ruler:**
Elizabeth II **Subject:** Flowers - Daisy

Date	Mintage	F	VF	XF	Unc	BU
2011 Proof	2,500	Value: 56.00				

KM# 1262   5 DOLLARS
25.0000 g., 0.9250 Silver 0.7435 oz. ASW, 38.61 mm. **Ruler:**
Elizabeth II **Subject:** Hollywood Stars - Sophia Loren

Date	Mintage	F	VF	XF	Unc	BU
2011 Proof	2,500	Value: 75.00				

KM# 1263   5 DOLLARS
25.0000 g., 0.9250 Silver 0.7435 oz. ASW, 38.61 mm. **Ruler:**
Elizabeth II **Subject:** Hollywood Stars - Elizabeth Taylor

Date	Mintage	F	VF	XF	Unc	BU
2011 Proof	2,500	Value: 75.00				

KM# 1264   5 DOLLARS
25.0000 g., 0.9250 Silver 0.7435 oz. ASW, 38.61 mm. **Ruler:**
Elizabeth II **Subject:** Hollywood Stars - Marylin Monroe

Date	Mintage	F	VF	XF	Unc	BU
2011 Proof	2,500	Value: 75.00				

KM# 1265   5 DOLLARS
25.0000 g., 0.9250 Silver 0.7435 oz. ASW, 38.61 mm. **Ruler:**
Elizabeth II **Subject:** Terminator-2, 20th Anniversary **Rev:**
Walking through flames

Date	Mintage	F	VF	XF	Unc	BU
2011 Proof	—	Value: 80.00				

KM# 1266   5 DOLLARS
25.0000 g., 0.9250 Silver 0.7435 oz. ASW, 38.61 mm. **Ruler:**
Elizabeth II **Subject:** Terminator-2, 20th Anniversary **Rev:** Riding
motorcycle

Date	Mintage	F	VF	XF	Unc	BU
2011 Proof	—	Value: 80.00				

KM# 1267   5 DOLLARS
25.0000 g., 0.9250 Silver 0.7435 oz. ASW **Ruler:** Elizabeth II
Subject: Terminator-2, 20th Anniversary **Rev:** Head shot **Shape:**
38.61

Date	Mintage	F	VF	XF	Unc	BU
2011 Proof	—	Value: 80.00				

KM# 1287   5 DOLLARS
31.1000 g., 0.9250 Silver 0.9249 oz. ASW, 38.6 mm. **Ruler:**
Elizabeth II **Subject:** Scent of Austalia - Eucalyptus **Rev:** Koala,
eucalyptus leaves and gum berries

Date	Mintage	F	VF	XF	Unc	BU
2011	2,500	—	—	—	—	100

KM# 1353   5 DOLLARS
25.0000 g., 0.9250 Silver 0.7435 oz. ASW, 30x38 mm. **Ruler:**
Elizabeth II **Subject:** Patron Saints **Rev:** St. Mary Magalene
Shape: Vertical rectangle

Date	Mintage	F	VF	XF	Unc	BU
2011 Proof	—	Value: 75.00				

KM# 1355   5 DOLLARS
25.0000 g., 0.9250 Silver 0.7435 oz. ASW, 30x38 mm. **Ruler:**
Elizabeth II **Subject:** Patron Saints **Rev:** St. Catherine Icon
Shape: Vertical rectangle

Date	Mintage	F	VF	XF	Unc	BU
2011 Proof	—	Value: 75.00				

KM# 1357   5 DOLLARS
25.0000 g., Silver, 30x38 mm. **Ruler:** Elizabeth II **Subject:**
Patrol Saints **Rev:** St. Oleg Icon **Shape:** Vertical rectangle

Date	Mintage	F	VF	XF	Unc	BU
2011 Proof	—	Value: 75.00				

KM# 1358   5 DOLLARS
25.0000 g., 0.9250 Silver 0.7435 oz. ASW, 30x38 mm. **Ruler:**
Elizabeth II **Subject:** Patron Saints **Rev:** St. Vladimir Icon **Shape:**
Vertical rectangle

Date	Mintage	F	VF	XF	Unc	BU
2011 Proof	—	Value: 75.00				

KM# 1361   5 DOLLARS
31.1050 g., 0.9990 Silver 0.9990 oz. ASW, 38.61 mm. **Ruler:**
Elizabeth II **Subject:** Soyuzmultfilm 75th Anniversary - Winnie
the Pooh **Rev:** Winnie the Pooh in color **Edge:** Reeded

Date	Mintage	F	VF	XF	Unc	BU
2011 Proof	2,000	Value: 80.00				

KM# 1362   5 DOLLARS
31.1050 g., 0.9990 Silver 0.9990 oz. ASW, 38.61 mm. **Ruler:**
Elizabeth II **Subject:** Soyuzmultfilm 75th Anniversary - Winnie
the Pooh **Rev:** Piglet in color **Edge:** Reeded

Date	Mintage	F	VF	XF	Unc	BU
2011 Proof	2,000	Value: 80.00				

KM# 1363   5 DOLLARS
31.1050 g., 0.9990 Silver 0.9990 oz. ASW, 38.61 mm. **Ruler:**
Elizabeth II **Subject:** Soyuzmultfilm 75th Anniversary - Winnie
the Pooh **Rev:** Owl in color **Edge:** Reeded

Date	Mintage	F	VF	XF	Unc	BU
2011 Proof	2,000	Value: 80.00				

KM# 1364   5 DOLLARS
31.1050 g., 0.9990 Silver 0.9990 oz. ASW, 38.61 mm. **Ruler:**
Elizabeth II **Subject:** Soyuzmultfilm 75th Anniversary - Winnie
the Pooh **Rev:** Eyore in color **Edge:** Reeded

Date	Mintage	F	VF	XF	Unc	BU
2011 Proof	2,000	Value: 80.00				

KM# 1365   5 DOLLARS
31.1050 g., 0.9990 Silver 0.9990 oz. ASW, 38.61 mm. **Ruler:**
Elizabeth II **Subject:** Soyuzmultfilm 75th Anniversary - Winnie
the Pooh **Rev:** Rabbit in color **Edge:** Reeded

Date	Mintage	F	VF	XF	Unc	BU
2011 Proof	2,000	Value: 80.00				

KM# 1367   5 DOLLARS
31.1050 g., 0.9990 Silver 0.9990 oz. ASW, 38.61 mm. **Ruler:**
Elizabeth II **Subject:** Soyuzmultfilm 75th Anniversary - Little Boy
and Karlsson-on-the-Roof **Rev:** Little Boy and dog in color **Edge:**
Reeded

Date	Mintage	F	VF	XF	Unc	BU
2011 Proof	2,000	Value: 80.00				

KM# 1368   5 DOLLARS
31.1050 g., 0.9990 Silver 0.9990 oz. ASW, 38.61 mm. **Ruler:**
Elizabeth II **Subject:** Soyuzmultfilm 75th Anniversary - Little Boy
and Karlsson-on-the-Roof **Rev:** Karlsson in color **Edge:** Reeded

Date	Mintage	F	VF	XF	Unc	BU
2011 Proof	2,000	Value: 80.00				

KM# 1369   5 DOLLARS
31.1050 g., 0.9990 Silver 0.9990 oz. ASW, 38.61 mm.   **Ruler:** Elizabeth II **Subject:** Soyuzmultfilm 75th Anniversary - Little Boy and Karlsson-on-the-Roof **Rev:** Freken Bok in color **Edge:** Reeded

Date	Mintage	F	VF	XF	Unc	BU
2011 Proof	2,000	Value: 80.00				

KM# 1371   5 DOLLARS
31.1050 g., 0.9990 Silver 0.9990 oz. ASW, 38.61 mm.   **Ruler:** Elizabeth II **Subject:** Soyuzmultfilm 75th Anniversary - Cheburashka and Crocodile Gena **Rev:** Cheburashka with orange in color **Edge:** Reeded

Date	Mintage	F	VF	XF	Unc	BU
2011 Proof	2,000	Value: 80.00				

KM# 1372   5 DOLLARS
31.1050 g., 0.9990 Silver 0.9990 oz. ASW, 38.61 mm.   **Ruler:** Elizabeth II **Subject:** Soyuzmultfilm 75th Anniversary - Cheburashka and Crocodile Gena **Rev:** Madame Shapoklyak and dog in color **Edge:** Reeded

Date	Mintage	F	VF	XF	Unc	BU
2011 Proof	2,000	Value: 80.00				

KM# 1373   5 DOLLARS
31.1050 g., 0.9990 Silver 0.9990 oz. ASW, 38.61 mm.   **Ruler:** Elizabeth II **Subject:** Soyuzmultfilm 75th Anniversary - Cheburashka and Crocodile Gena **Rev:** Crocodile Gena in color **Edge:** Reeded

Date	Mintage	F	VF	XF	Unc	BU
2011 Proof	2,000	Value: 80.00				

KM# 1374   5 DOLLARS
31.1050 g., 0.9990 Silver 0.9990 oz. ASW, 38.61 mm.   **Ruler:** Elizabeth II **Subject:** Soyuzmultfilm 75th Anniversary - Hedgehog in a fog **Rev:** Hedgehog in a fog in color **Edge:** Reeded

Date	Mintage	F	VF	XF	Unc	BU
2011 Proof	2,000	Value: 80.00				

KM# 1381   5 DOLLARS
Silver, 40 mm.   **Ruler:** Elizabeth II **Subject:** Muonionalusta Meteor **Obv:** Head with tiara right **Rev:** View of meteor falling and fragment insert

Date	Mintage	F	VF	XF	Unc	BU
2011 Proof	—	Value: 100				

KM# 1386   5 DOLLARS
25.0000 g., 0.9250 Silver 0.7435 oz. ASW, 38.61 mm.   **Ruler:** Elizabeth II **Subject:** Marylin Monroe, 80th Birthday **Rev:** Color image of Marylin Monroe

Date	Mintage	F	VF	XF	Unc	BU
2011 Proof	2,500	Value: 125				

KM# 1376   5 DOLLARS
25.0000 g., 0.9250 Silver 0.7435 oz. ASW, 45x30 mm.   **Ruler:** Elizabeth II **Obv:** Head with tiara right **Rev:** Titanic sailing left in color, coal fragment insert **Shape:** Horizontal oval

Date	Mintage	F	VF	XF	Unc	BU
2012 Proof	2,012	Value: 100				

KM# 1377   5 DOLLARS
20.0000 g., 0.9990 Silver 0.6423 oz. ASW, 30x43 mm.   **Ruler:** Elizabeth II **Subject:** Imperial Egg - Swan **Obv:** Head with tiara right **Rev:** Pink coloring

Date	Mintage	F	VF	XF	Unc	BU
2012 Proof	—	Value: 75.00				

KM# 1378   5 DOLLARS
20.0000 g., 0.9990 Silver 0.6423 oz. ASW, 30x43 mm.   **Ruler:** Elizabeth II **Subject:** Imperial egg - Elephant **Obv:** Head with tiara right **Rev:** Blue coloring

Date	Mintage	F	VF	XF	Unc	BU
2012 Proof	—	Value: 75.00				

KM# 1379   5 DOLLARS
20.0000 g., 0.9990 Silver 0.6423 oz. ASW, 30x43 mm.   **Ruler:** Elizabeth II **Subject:** Imperial egg **Obv:** Head in tiara right **Rev:** Multicolor closonne

Date	Mintage	F	VF	XF	Unc	BU
2012 Proof	—	Value: 75.00				

KM# 1382   5 DOLLARS
31.1050 g., 0.9990 Silver 0.9990 oz. ASW, 38.61 mm.   **Ruler:** Elizabeth II **Subject:** History of Egypt **Rev:** Tutankhamun's gold mask in color

Date	Mintage	F	VF	XF	Unc	BU
2012 Proof	—	Value: 125				

KM# 1390   5 DOLLARS
31.1050 g., 0.9990 Silver 0.9990 oz. ASW, 38.61 mm.   **Ruler:** Elizabeth II **Subject:** Titanic, 100th Anniversary **Rev:** Titanic side view sailing left, recovered coal fragment insert

Date	Mintage	F	VF	XF	Unc	BU
2012 Proof	—	Value: 125				

KM# 1395   5 DOLLARS
31.1050 g., 0.9990 Silver 0.9990 oz. ASW, 38.61 mm.   **Ruler:** Elizabeth II **Obv:** Head with tiara right **Rev:** Cherry Blossom in color

Date	Mintage	F	VF	XF	Unc	BU
2012 Proof	—	Value: 100				

KM# 473   10 DOLLARS
20.1200 g., Silver, 38.62 mm.   **Ruler:** Elizabeth II **Subject:** 2004 Summer Olympics - Athens **Obv:** Crowned bust right **Rev:** Male discus thrower **Edge:** Reeded

Date	Mintage	F	VF	XF	Unc	BU
2001 Proof	—	Value: 37.50				

KM# 549   10 DOLLARS
10.0000 g., 0.9999 Gold 0.3215 oz. AGW, 25 mm.   **Ruler:** Elizabeth II **Rev:** Multicolored Mikado Pheasant

Date	Mintage	F	VF	XF	Unc	BU
2001 Proof	1,000	Value: 550				

KM# 550   10 DOLLARS
10.0000 g., 0.9999 Gold 0.3215 oz. AGW, 25 mm.   **Ruler:** Elizabeth II **Rev:** Multicolor black-faced spoonbill

Date	Mintage	F	VF	XF	Unc	BU
2001 Proof	1,000	Value: 550				

KM# 453   10 DOLLARS
186.8300 g., 0.9990 Silver Gilt 6.0005 oz. ASW, 89 mm. **Ruler:** Elizabeth II **Obv:** Crowned bust right, unique portrait for Cook Is. **Rev:** Queen Victoria standing with lion **Edge:** Reeded

Date	Mintage	F	VF	XF	Unc	BU
2003 Proof	198	Value: 350				

KM# 1110   10 DOLLARS
1.2400 g., 0.9990 Gold 0.0398 oz. AGW **Ruler:** Elizabeth II **Rev:** Emblem

Date	Mintage	F	VF	XF	Unc	BU
2005 Proof	Est. 8,000	Value: 85.00				

KM# 1136   10 DOLLARS
1.2400 g., 0.9990 Gold 0.0398 oz. AGW, 13.92 mm. **Ruler:** Elizabeth II **Subject:** Star Wars, 30th Anniversary

Date	Mintage	F	VF	XF	Unc	BU
2005 Proof	9,999	Value: 85.00				

KM# 1176   10 DOLLARS
1.2400 g., 0.9990 Gold 0.0398 oz. AGW **Ruler:** Elizabeth II **Subject:** Marriage of Prince Charles and Camilla Parker-Bowles

Date	Mintage	F	VF	XF	Unc	BU
2005 Proof	Est. 25,000	Value: 85.00				

KM# 1178   10 DOLLARS
1.2400 g., 0.9990 Gold 0.0398 oz. AGW, 13.92 mm. **Ruler:** Elizabeth II **Rev:** Pope John Paul II

Date	Mintage	F	VF	XF	Unc	BU
2005 Proof	Est. 25,000	Value: 85.00				

KM# 582   10 DOLLARS
31.1000 g., 0.9990 Silver 0.9988 oz. ASW, 38.6 mm. **Ruler:** Elizabeth II **Rev:** Chichen Itza gilt pop-up

Date	Mintage	F	VF	XF	Unc	BU
2007 Proof	5,000	Value: 65.00				

KM# 585   10 DOLLARS
31.1000 g., 0.9990 Silver 0.9988 oz. ASW, 38.6 mm. **Ruler:** Elizabeth II **Rev:** Easter Island status gilt pop-up

Date	Mintage	F	VF	XF	Unc	BU
2007 Proof	5,000	Value: 100				

KM# 587   10 DOLLARS
31.1000 g., 0.9990 Silver 0.9988 oz. ASW, 38.6 mm. **Ruler:** Elizabeth II **Rev:** Pyrmids gilt pop-up

Date	Mintage	F	VF	XF	Unc	BU
2007 Proof	5,000	Value: 65.00				

KM# 588   10 DOLLARS
31.1000 g., 0.9990 Silver 0.9988 oz. ASW, 38.6 mm. **Ruler:** Elizabeth II **Rev:** Golden Gate Bridge gilt pop-up

Date	Mintage	F	VF	XF	Unc	BU
2007 Proof	5,000	Value: 65.00				

KM# 589   10 DOLLARS
31.1000 g., 0.9990 Silver 0.9988 oz. ASW, 38.6 mm. **Ruler:** Elizabeth II **Rev:** Great Wall of China gilt pop-up

Date	Mintage	F	VF	XF	Unc	BU
2007 Proof	5,000	Value: 65.00				

KM# 590   10 DOLLARS
31.1000 g., 0.9990 Silver 0.9988 oz. ASW, 38.6 mm. **Ruler:** Elizabeth II **Rev:** Sydney Harbor Bridge gilt pop-up

Date	Mintage	F	VF	XF	Unc	BU
2007 Proof	5,000	Value: 65.00				

KM# 592   10 DOLLARS
31.1000 g., 0.9990 Silver 0.9988 oz. ASW, 38.6 mm. **Ruler:** Elizabeth II **Rev:** Petra Treasury gilt pop-up

Date	Mintage	F	VF	XF	Unc	BU
2007 Proof	5,000	Value: 65.00				

KM# 593   10 DOLLARS
31.1000 g., 0.9990 Silver 0.9988 oz. ASW, 38.6 mm. **Ruler:** Elizabeth II **Rev:** Taj mahal gilt pop-up

Date	Mintage	F	VF	XF	Unc	BU
2007 Proof	5,000	Value: 65.00				

KM# 1113   10 DOLLARS
0.5000 g., 0.9990 Gold 0.0161 oz. AGW, 11 mm. **Ruler:** Elizabeth II **Subject:** Treaty of rome, 50th Anniversary **Rev:** Monaco

Date	Mintage	F	VF	XF	Unc	BU
2007 Proof	Est. 5,000	Value: 50.00				

KM# 1171   10 DOLLARS
0.5000 g., 0.9990 Gold 0.0161 oz. AGW, 11 mm. **Ruler:** Elizabeth II **Subject:** Treaty of Rome, 50th Anniversary **Rev:** Vatican City

Date	Mintage	F	VF	XF	Unc	BU
2007 Proof	Est. 5,000	Value: 50.00				

KM# 1192   10 DOLLARS
1.2400 g., 0.9990 Gold 0.0398 oz. AGW, 13.92 mm. **Ruler:** Elizabeth II **Subject:** European Monarchs **Rev:** Elizabeth II

Date	Mintage	F	VF	XF	Unc	BU
2007 Proof	Est. 10,000	Value: 85.00				

KM# 1193   10 DOLLARS
1.2400 g., 0.9990 Gold 0.0398 oz. AGW **Ruler:** Elizabeth II **Subject:** European Monarchs **Rev:** Juan Carlos I

Date	Mintage	F	VF	XF	Unc	BU
2007 Proof	Est. 10,000	Value: 85.00				

KM# 1195   10 DOLLARS
1.2400 g., Gold, 13.92 mm. **Ruler:** Elizabeth II **Subject:** European Monarchs **Rev:** Beatrix

Date	Mintage	F	VF	XF	Unc	BU
2007 Proof	Est. 10,000	Value: 85.00				

KM# 1204   10 DOLLARS
1.2400 g., 0.9990 Gold 0.0398 oz. AGW, 13.92 mm. **Ruler:** Elizabeth II **Subject:** Christmas **Rev:** Cherib seated on rock

Date	Mintage	F	VF	XF	Unc	BU
2007 proof	Est. 15,000	Value: 85.00				

KM# 1194   10 DOLLARS
1.2400 g., 0.9990 Gold 0.0398 oz. AGW **Ruler:** Elizabeth II **Subject:** European Monarchs **Rev:** Carl XVI Gustaf

Date	Mintage	F	VF	XF	Unc	BU
2007 Proof	Est. 10,000	Value: 85.00				

KM# 619   10 DOLLARS
31.1000 g., 0.9990 Silver 0.9988 oz. ASW, 38.6 mm. **Ruler:** Elizabeth II **Rev:** Angor Wat temple gilt pop-up

Date	Mintage	F	VF	XF	Unc	BU
2008 Proof	5,000	Value: 65.00				

KM# 620   10 DOLLARS
31.1000 g., 0.9990 Silver 0.9988 oz. ASW, 38.6 mm. **Ruler:** Elizabeth II **Rev:** Ayer's Rock gilt pop-up

Date	Mintage	F	VF	XF	Unc	BU
2008 Proof	5,000	Value: 65.00				

KM# 621   10 DOLLARS
31.1000 g., 0.9990 Silver 0.9988 oz. ASW, 38.6 mm. **Ruler:** Elizabeth II **Rev:** Parliament Buildings and Big Ben pop-up

Date	Mintage	F	VF	XF	Unc	BU
2008 Proof	5,000	Value: 65.00				

KM# 622   10 DOLLARS
31.1000 g., 0.9990 Silver 0.9988 oz. ASW, 38.6 mm. **Ruler:** Elizabeth II **Rev:** Mt. Rushmore figures gilt pop-up

Date	Mintage	F	VF	XF	Unc	BU
2008 Proof	5,000	Value: 65.00				

KM# 623   10 DOLLARS
31.1000 g., 0.9990 Silver 0.9988 oz. ASW, 38.6 mm. **Ruler:** Elizabeth II **Rev:** Sydney Opera House gilt pop-up

Date	Mintage	F	VF	XF	Unc	BU
2008 Proof	5,000	Value: 65.00				

KM# 624   10 DOLLARS
31.1000 g., 0.9990 Silver 0.9988 oz. ASW, 38.6 mm. **Ruler:** Elizabeth II **Rev:** Malaysian Twin Towers gilt pop-up

Date	Mintage	F	VF	XF	Unc	BU
2008 Proof	5,000	Value: 65.00				

KM# 625   10 DOLLARS
31.1000 g., 0.9990 Silver 0.9988 oz. ASW, 38.6 mm. **Ruler:** Elizabeth II **Rev:** Sphinx gilt pop-up

Date	Mintage	F	VF	XF	Unc	BU
2008 Proof	5,000	Value: 65.00				

KM# 626   10 DOLLARS
31.1000 g., 0.9990 Silver 0.9988 oz. ASW, 38.6 mm. **Ruler:** Elizabeth II **Rev:** Stonehedge gilt pop-up

Date	Mintage	F	VF	XF	Unc	BU
2008 Proof	5,000	Value: 65.00				

KM# 627   10 DOLLARS
62.2050 g., 0.9990 Silver 1.9979 oz. ASW, 50 mm. **Ruler:** Elizabeth II **Rev:** Tsar Alexander II, multicolor **Note:** Exclusive to the Russian Market.

Date	Mintage	F	VF	XF	Unc	BU
2008 Proof	500	Value: 350				

KM# 628   10 DOLLARS
62.2050 g., 0.9990 Silver 1.9979 oz. ASW **Ruler:** Elizabeth II **Rev:** Tsar Alexi, multicolor **Note:** Exclusive to the Russian Market.

Date	Mintage	F	VF	XF	Unc	BU
2008 Proof	500	Value: 350				

KM# 629   10 DOLLARS
62.2050 g., 0.9990 Silver 1.9979 oz. ASW, 50 mm. **Ruler:** Elizabeth II **Rev:** Tsarina Anna, multicolor

Date	Mintage	F	VF	XF	Unc	BU
2008 Proof	500	Value: 350				

KM# 630   10 DOLLARS
62.2050 g., 0.9990 Silver 1.9979 oz. ASW, 50 mm. **Ruler:** Elizabeth II **Rev:** Tsarina Elizabeth, multicolor

Date	Mintage	F	VF	XF	Unc	BU
2008 Proof	500	Value: 350				

KM# 631   10 DOLLARS
62.2050 g., 0.9990 Silver 1.9979 oz. ASW, 50 mm. **Ruler:** Elizabeth II **Rev:** Tsar Mikhail, multicolor

Date	Mintage	F	VF	XF	Unc	BU
2008 Proof	500	Value: 350				

KM# 632   10 DOLLARS
62.2050 g., 0.9990 Silver 1.9979 oz. ASW, 50 mm. **Ruler:** Elizabeth II **Rev:** Tsar Paul I, multicolor

Date	Mintage	F	VF	XF	Unc	BU
2008 Proof	500	Value: 350				

KM# 633   10 DOLLARS
31.1000 g., 0.9990 Silver 0.9988 oz. ASW, 40 mm. **Ruler:** Elizabeth II **Rev:** Nathan Rothschild bust at right, partially gilt

Date	Mintage	F	VF	XF	Unc	BU
2008 Proof	10,000	Value: 55.00				

KM# 634   10 DOLLARS
31.1050 g., 0.9990 Silver 0.9990 oz. ASW, 40 mm. **Ruler:** Elizabeth II **Rev:** Henry Ford at left and Model-A car at right, partially gilt

Date	Mintage	F	VF	XF	Unc	BU
2008 Proof	10,000	Value: 55.00				

KM# 635   10 DOLLARS
31.1000 g., 0.9990 Silver 0.9988 oz. ASW, 40 mm. **Ruler:** Elizabeth II **Rev:** John D. Rockefeller Sr., bust right, oil derrick partially gilt.

Date	Mintage	F	VF	XF	Unc	BU
2008 Proof	10,000	Value: 60.00				

KM# 704   10 DOLLARS
1.0000 g., 0.9990 Gold 0.0321 oz. AGW, 13.9 mm. **Ruler:** Elizabeth II **Subject:** Gorch Fock **Rev:** Sailing vessel right

Date	Mintage	F	VF	XF	Unc	BU
2008 Proof	15,000	Value: 70.00				

KM# 705   10 DOLLARS
62.2100 g., 0.9990 Silver 1.9980 oz. ASW, 50 mm. **Ruler:**
Elizabeth II **Subject:** Kiev Churches **Rev:** Lavra bell tower

Date	Mintage	F	VF	XF	Unc	BU
2008 Proof	500				—	125

KM# 1205   10 DOLLARS
1.0000 g., 0.9990 Gold 0.0321 oz. AGW, 13.92 mm. **Ruler:**
Elizabeth II **Rev:** Gorch Fock I, 1933

Date	Mintage	F	VF	XF	Unc	BU
2008 Proof	—	Value: 70.00				

KM# 1206   10 DOLLARS
1.0000 g., 0.9990 Gold 0.0321 oz. AGW, 13.92 mm. **Ruler:**
Elizabeth II **Subject:** Endangered Wildlife **Rev:** Polar Bear

Date	Mintage	F	VF	XF	Unc	BU
2008 Proof	Est. 25,000	Value: 70.00				

KM# 688   10 DOLLARS
31.1050 g., 0.9990 Silver 0.9990 oz. ASW, 38.6 mm. **Ruler:**
Elizabeth II **Rev:** Statues of Ramesses II at Abu Simbel gilt pop-up

Date	Mintage	F	VF	XF	Unc	BU
2009 Proof	5,000	Value: 65.00				

KM# 689   10 DOLLARS
31.1050 g., 0.9990 Silver 0.9990 oz. ASW, 38.6 mm. **Ruler:**
Elizabeth II **Rev:** Arc de Triumph gilt pop-up

Date	Mintage	F	VF	XF	Unc	BU
2009 Proof	5,000	Value: 65.00				

KM# 690   10 DOLLARS
31.1050 g., 0.9990 Silver 0.9990 oz. ASW, 38.6 mm. **Ruler:**
Elizabeth II **Rev:** Hagia Sofia gilt pop-up

Date	Mintage	F	VF	XF	Unc	BU
2009 Proof	5,000	Value: 65.00				

KM# 691   10 DOLLARS
31.1050 g., 0.9990 Silver 0.9990 oz. ASW, 38.6 mm. **Ruler:**
Elizabeth II **Rev:** Temple of Heaven gilt pop-up

Date	Mintage	F	VF	XF	Unc	BU
2009 Proof	5,000	Value: 65.00				

KM# 692   10 DOLLARS
31.1050 g., 0.9990 Silver 0.9990 oz. ASW, 38.6 mm. **Ruler:**
Elizabeth II **Rev:** Holstein Gate gilt pop-up

Date	Mintage	F	VF	XF	Unc	BU
2009 Proof	5,000	Value: 65.00				

KM# 693   10 DOLLARS
31.1050 g., 0.9990 Silver 0.9990 oz. ASW, 38.6 mm. **Ruler:**
Elizabeth II **Rev:** Ruins of Kaiser Church in Berlin, gilt pop-up

Date	Mintage	F	VF	XF	Unc	BU
2009 Proof	5,000	Value: 65.00				

KM# 694   10 DOLLARS
31.1050 g., 0.9990 Silver 0.9990 oz. ASW, 38.6 mm. **Ruler:**
Elizabeth II **Rev:** Statue of Peter I gilt pop-up

Date	Mintage	F	VF	XF	Unc	BU
2009 Proof	5,000	Value: 65.00				

KM# 695   10 DOLLARS
31.1050 g., 0.9990 Silver 0.9990 oz. ASW, 38.6 mm. **Ruler:**
Elizabeth II **Rev:** Bridge in Venice, gilt pop-up

Date	Mintage	F	VF	XF	Unc	BU
2009 Proof	5,000	Value: 65.00				

KM# 696   10 DOLLARS
31.1050 g., 0.9990 Silver 0.9990 oz. ASW, 38.6 mm. **Ruler:**
Elizabeth II **Rev:** Opera house, gilt pop-up

Date	Mintage	F	VF	XF	Unc	BU
2009 Proof	—	Value: 65.00				

KM# 703   10 DOLLARS
25.0000 g., 0.9990 Silver 0.8029 oz. ASW, 38.6 mm. **Ruler:**
Elizabeth II **Subject:** Nicolaus Copernicus **Rev:** Bust facing and
orbit of the planets, crystal insert, partially gold plated

Date	Mintage	F	VF	XF	Unc	BU
2009 Proof	7,500	Value: 75.00				

KM# 708   10 DOLLARS
1.0000 g., 0.9990 Gold 0.0321 oz. AGW, 13.9 mm. **Ruler:**
Elizabeth II **Rev:** Bridge

Date	Mintage	F	VF	XF	Unc	BU
2009 Proof	250	Value: 70.00				

KM# 709   10 DOLLARS
1.0000 g., 0.9990 Gold 0.0321 oz. AGW, 13.9 mm. **Ruler:**
Elizabeth II **Rev:** Statue and gardens

Date	Mintage	F	VF	XF	Unc	BU
2009 Proof	250	Value: 70.00				

KM# 710   10 DOLLARS
1.0000 g., 0.9990 Gold 0.0321 oz. AGW, 13.9 mm. **Ruler:**
Elizabeth II **Rev:** City Gate tower

Date	Mintage	F	VF	XF	Unc	BU
2009 Proof	250	Value: 70.00				

KM# 711   10 DOLLARS
1.0000 g., 0.9990 Gold 0.0321 oz. AGW, 13.9 mm. **Ruler:**
Elizabeth II **Rev:** Virgin Mary statue and church in background

Date	Mintage	F	VF	XF	Unc	BU
2009 Proof	250	Value: 70.00				

KM# 712   10 DOLLARS
1.0000 g., 0.9990 Gold 0.0321 oz. AGW, 13.9 mm. **Ruler:**
Elizabeth II **Rev:** Multiple church spires

Date	Mintage	F	VF	XF	Unc	BU
2009 Proof	250	Value: 70.00				

KM# 713   10 DOLLARS
1.0000 g., 0.9990 Gold 0.0321 oz. AGW, 13.9 mm. **Ruler:**
Elizabeth II **Rev:** National Theater

Date	Mintage	F	VF	XF	Unc	BU
2009 Proof	250	Value: 70.00				

KM# 714   10 DOLLARS
1.0000 g., 0.9990 Gold 0.0321 oz. AGW, 13.9 mm. **Ruler:**
Elizabeth II **Rev:** Castle

Date	Mintage	F	VF	XF	Unc	BU
2009 Proof	250	Value: 70.00				

KM# 715   10 DOLLARS
1.0000 g., 0.9990 Gold 0.0321 oz. AGW, 13.9 mm. **Ruler:**
Elizabeth II **Rev:** Castle on a hill

Date	Mintage	F	VF	XF	Unc	BU
2009 Proof	250	Value: 70.00				

KM# 716   10 DOLLARS
1.0000 g., 0.9990 Gold 0.0321 oz. AGW, 13.9 mm. **Ruler:**
Elizabeth II **Rev:** Castle

Date	Mintage	F	VF	XF	Unc	BU
2009 Proof	250	Value: 70.00				

KM# 717   10 DOLLARS
1.0000 g., 0.9990 Gold 0.0321 oz. AGW, 13.9 mm. **Ruler:**
Elizabeth II **Rev:** Castle

Date	Mintage	F	VF	XF	Unc	BU
2009 Proof	250	Value: 65.00				

KM# 718   10 DOLLARS
1.0000 g., 0.9990 Gold 0.0321 oz. AGW, 13.9 mm. **Ruler:**
Elizabeth II **Rev:** Church

Date	Mintage	F	VF	XF	Unc	BU
2009 Proof	250	Value: 65.00				

KM# 719   10 DOLLARS
1.0000 g., 0.9990 Gold 0.0321 oz. AGW, 13.9 mm. **Ruler:**
Elizabeth II **Rev:** Ancient ruins

Date	Mintage	F	VF	XF	Unc	BU
2009 Proof	250	Value: 65.00				

KM# 792   10 DOLLARS
31.1050 g., 0.9990 Silver 0.9990 oz. ASW, 40 mm. **Ruler:**
Elizabeth II **Subject:** Tycoons - Alfred Nobel **Rev:** Nobel bust at
right, Prize Medal partially gilt at right

Date	Mintage	F	VF	XF	Unc	BU
2009 Proof	10,000	Value: 55.00				

KM# 793   10 DOLLARS
31.1050 g., 0.9990 Silver 0.9990 oz. ASW, 40 mm. **Ruler:**
Elizabeth II **Subject:** Tycoons **Rev:** Cecil Rhodes, partially gilt

Date	Mintage	F	VF	XF	Unc	BU
2009 Proof	10,000	Value: 55.00				

KM# 1228   10 DOLLARS
155.5000 g., 0.9250 Silver 4.6243 oz. ASW, 65 mm. **Ruler:**
Elizabeth II **Subject:** Ikuko Shimizu's Hello Kitty **Rev:** Kitty and
Buckingham Palace in multicolor

Date	Mintage	F	VF	XF	Unc	BU
2009 Proof	Est. 1,500	Value: 350				

KM# 1232   10 DOLLARS
1.2400 g., 0.9990 Gold 0.0398 oz. AGW, 13.92 mm. **Ruler:**
Elizabeth II **Subject:** Knut Hamsun, 150th Anniversary of Birth

Date	Mintage	F	VF	XF	Unc	BU
2009 Proof	Est. 1,000	Value: 85.00				

KM# 1233   10 DOLLARS
1.2400 g., 0.9990 Gold 0.0398 oz. AGW, 13.92 mm. **Ruler:**
Elizabeth II **Subject:** Sweedish King Oscar II

Date	Mintage	F	VF	XF	Unc	BU
2009 Proof	Est. 10,000	Value: 85.00				

KM# 1332   10 DOLLARS
1.2400 g., 0.9990 Gold 0.0398 oz. AGW, 13.92 mm. **Ruler:**
Elizabeth II **Subject:** 40th Anniversary of Moon landing

Date	Mintage	F	VF	XF	Unc	BU
2009 Proof	—	Value: 100				

KM# 1333   10 DOLLARS
1.2400 g., 0.9990 Gold 0.0398 oz. AGW, 13.92 mm. **Ruler:**
Elizabeth II **Subject:** James Cook and the H.M.S Endeavor

Date	Mintage	F	VF	XF	Unc	BU
2009 Proof	—	Value: 100				

KM# 1249   10 DOLLARS
31.1350 g., 0.9990 Silver 1.0000 oz. ASW, 45 mm. **Ruler:**
Elizabeth II **Subject:** Albert Durer **Rev:** Rabbit illustration with
crystals

Date	Mintage	F	VF	XF	Unc	BU
2010 Proof	3,000	Value: 75.00				

KM# 1258   10 DOLLARS
50.0000 g., 0.9250 Silver 1.4869 oz. ASW, 50 mm. **Ruler:**
Elizabeth II **Subject:** Windows of Heaven **Rev:** Cologne
Cathedral, stained glass windows, facade and ceiling arch plan

Date	Mintage	F	VF	XF	Unc	BU
2010 Proof	2,000	Value: 250				

KM# 1293   10 DOLLARS
31.1050 g., 0.9990 Silver 0.9990 oz. ASW, 45 mm. **Ruler:**
Elizabeth II **Subject:** Oberg **Rev:** Rural Russian folk scene

Date	Mintage	F	VF	XF	Unc	BU
2010 Proof	—	Value: 75.00				

KM# 1296   10 DOLLARS
0.5000 g., 0.9990 Gold 0.0161 oz. AGW, 11 mm. **Ruler:**
Elizabeth II **Rev:** Barack Obama

Date	Mintage	F	VF	XF	Unc	BU
2010 Proof	—	Value: 50.00				

KM# 1297   10 DOLLARS
1.0000 g., 0.9990 Gold 0.0321 oz. AGW, 13.92 mm. **Ruler:**
Elizabeth II **Rev:** Martin Luther King

Date	Mintage	F	VF	XF	Unc	BU
2010 Proof	—	Value: 75.00				

KM# 1298   10 DOLLARS
1.0000 g., 0.9990 Gold 0.0321 oz. AGW, 13.92 mm. **Ruler:**
Elizabeth II **Rev:** Barack Obama

Date	Mintage	F	VF	XF	Unc	BU
2010 Proof	—	Value: 75.00				

KM# 1259   10 DOLLARS
50.0000 g., 0.9990 Silver 1.6059 oz. ASW, 50 mm. **Ruler:**
Elizabeth II **Subject:** Windows of Heaven **Rev:** Westminister
Abbey, stained glass windows, floor plan and facade

Date	Mintage	F	VF	XF	Unc	BU
2011 Proof	2,000	Value: 300				

KM# 1388   10 DOLLARS
50.0000 g., 0.9990 Silver 1.6059 oz. ASW, 50 mm. **Ruler:**
Elizabeth II **Subject:** St. Issac's Cathedral, St. Petersburg **Rev:**
Stained glass window and floor plan

Date	Mintage	F	VF	XF	Unc	BU
2011 Proof	2,000	Value: 300				

KM# 1389   10 DOLLARS
50.0000 g., 0.9990 Silver 1.6059 oz. ASW, 50 mm. **Ruler:**
Elizabeth II **Subject:** Seville Cathedral **Rev:** Stained glass
window, floor plan and façade

Date	Mintage	F	VF	XF	Unc	BU
2011 Proof	2,000	Value: 300				

KM# 1131   12 DOLLARS
10.0000 g., 0.9999 Gold 0.3215 oz. AGW, 26 mm. **Ruler:**
Elizabeth II **Subject:** Full Gospel Business Men's Fellowship,
50th Anniversary **Rev:** Jesus Christ

Date	Mintage	F	VF	XF	Unc	BU
2003 Proof	Est. 4,999	Value: 550				

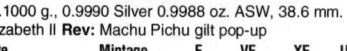

KM# 591   20 DOLLARS
31.1000 g., 0.9990 Silver 0.9988 oz. ASW, 38.6 mm. **Ruler:**
Elizabeth II **Rev:** Machu Pichu gilt pop-up

Date	Mintage	F	VF	XF	Unc	BU
2007 Proof	5,000	Value: 65.00				

KM# 636   20 DOLLARS
93.3000 g., 0.9990 Silver 2.9965 oz. ASW, 55 mm. **Ruler:**
Elizabeth II **Rev:** Michangelo, Creation of Adam, multicolor with
crystal inserts

Date	Mintage	F	VF	XF	Unc	BU
2008 Proof	1,000	Value: 550				

KM# 637   20 DOLLARS
93.3000 g., 0.9990 Silver 2.9965 oz. ASW, 55 mm. **Ruler:**
Elizabeth II **Rev:** DaVinci, Last Supper, multicolor with crystal
inserts

Date	Mintage	F	VF	XF	Unc	BU
2008 Proof	1,000	Value: 650				

KM# 638   20 DOLLARS
93.3000 g., 0.9990 Silver 2.9965 oz. ASW, 55 mm. **Ruler:**
Elizabeth II **Rev:** Raffaello, School of Athens, multicolor with
crystal inserts

Date	Mintage	F	VF	XF	Unc	BU
2008 Proof	1,000	Value: 450				

KM# 639   20 DOLLARS
93.3000 g., 0.9990 Silver 2.9965 oz. ASW, 55 mm. **Ruler:**
Elizabeth II **Rev:** Botticelli, Birth of Venus, multicolor with crystal
inserts

Date	Mintage	F	VF	XF	Unc	BU
2008 Proof	1,458	Value: 375				

KM# 699   20 DOLLARS
93.3150 g., 0.9990 Silver 2.9970 oz. ASW, 55 mm. **Ruler:**
Elizabeth II **Subject:** European Masters - Raffaelo **Rev:** Sistine
Chapel Madonna, crystals embedded

Date	Mintage	F	VF	XF	Unc	BU
2009 Proof	1,512	Value: 375				

KM# 697   20 DOLLARS
93.3150 g., 0.9990 Silver 2.9970 oz. ASW, 55 mm. **Ruler:**
Elizabeth II **Subject:** European Masters - DaVinci **Rev:** Mona
Lisa, 12 crystals imbedded

Date	Mintage	F	VF	XF	Unc	BU
2009 Proof	999	Value: 1,350				

KM# 700   20 DOLLARS
93.3150 g., 0.9990 Silver 2.9970 oz. ASW, 55 mm. **Ruler:**
Elizabeth II **Subject:** European Masters - Spitzwig **Rev:** The Poor
Poet, crystals embedded

Date	Mintage	F	VF	XF	Unc	BU
2009 Proof	—	Value: 550				

KM# 769   20 DOLLARS
93.3150 g., 0.9990 Silver partially gilt 2.9970 oz. ASW, 55 mm.
Ruler: Elizabeth II **Rev:** Vetruvian man

Date	Mintage	F	VF	XF	Unc	BU
2010 Proof	—	Value: 550				

KM# 1246   20 DOLLARS
93.3000 g., 0.9990 Silver 2.9965 oz. ASW, 55 mm. **Ruler:**
Elizabeth II **Subject:** Carlo Maratta **Rev:** Holy Night, color image
of Mary and child, crystals

Date	Mintage	F	VF	XF	Unc	BU
2010	1,655	—	—	—	—	300

KM# 1248   20 DOLLARS
93.3000 g., 0.9990 Silver 2.9965 oz. ASW, 55 mm. **Ruler:**
Elizabeth II **Subject:** Rembrandt **Rev:** Man in a Golden Helmet,
plus crystals

Date	Mintage	F	VF	XF	Unc	BU
2010 Proof	1,655	Value: 300				

KM# 698   20 DOLLARS
93.3150 g., 0.9990 Silver 2.9970 oz. ASW, 55 mm. **Ruler:**
Elizabeth II **Subject:** European Masters - Rembrandt **Rev:** The
Night watch, crystals embedded

Date	Mintage	F	VF	XF	Unc	BU
2009 Proof	1,642	Value: 375				

KM# 1341   20 DOLLARS
93.1350 g., 0.9990 Silver 2.9912 oz. ASW, 55 mm. **Ruler:**
Elizabeth II **Subject:** Van Gogh, Sunflowers

Date	Mintage	F	VF	XF	Unc	BU
2010 Proof	—	Value: 375				

KM# 1387   20 DOLLARS
93.1350 g., 0.9990 Silver 2.9912 oz. ASW, 55 mm. **Ruler:**
Elizabeth II **Obv:** Head with tiara right **Rev:** Brun painting **Edge:**
Reeded

Date	Mintage	F	VF	XF	Unc	BU
2011 Proof	—	Value: 150				

KM# 1397   20 DOLLARS
93.3000 g., 0.9990 Silver 2.9965 oz. ASW, 55 mm. **Ruler:**
Elizabeth II **Obv:** Bust with tiara right **Rev:** Nefertiti head in color
at center, crystal frame around

Date	Mintage	F	VF	XF	Unc	BU
2012 Proof	—	Value: 350				

KM# 1145   25 DOLLARS
7.8700 g., 0.9999 Gold 0.2530 oz. AGW **Ruler:** Elizabeth II **Rev:**
Edward "Ned"Kelley in color

Date	Mintage	F	VF	XF	Unc	BU
2004 proof	Est. 1,000	Value: 475				

KM# 1190   25 DOLLARS
155.5000 g., 0.9250 Silver 4.6243 oz. ASW, 65 mm. **Ruler:**
Elizabeth II **Subject:** Elvis Presely, 30th Anniversary of death
Rev: That's All right, Mama

Date	Mintage	F	VF	XF	Unc	BU
2007 Proof	Est. 1,977	Value: 350				

KM# 1321   25 DOLLARS
Silver **Ruler:** Elizabeth II **Rev:** Christian Radish

Date	Mintage	F	VF	XF	Unc	BU
2008 Proof	—	Value: 85.00				

KM# 1322   25 DOLLARS
Silver **Ruler:** Elizabeth II **Rev:** France II

Date	Mintage	F	VF	XF	Unc	BU
2008 Proof	—	Value: 85.00				

KM# 1325   25 DOLLARS
Silver **Ruler:** Elizabeth II **Rev:** Sedov

Date	Mintage	F	VF	XF	Unc	BU
2008 Proof	—	Value: 85.00				

KM# 1326   25 DOLLARS
Silver **Ruler:** Elizabeth II **Rev:** Thomas Lawson

Date	Mintage	F	VF	XF	Unc	BU
2008 Proof	—	Value: 85.00				

KM# 767   25 DOLLARS
155.5000 g., 0.9990 Silver 4.9942 oz. ASW, 65 mm. **Ruler:**
Elizabeth II **Subject:** Year of the Ox **Rev:** Child riding back of ox,
partially gilt

Date	Mintage	F	VF	XF	Unc	BU
2009 Proof	—	Value: 675				

KM# 1229   25 DOLLARS
7.9800 g., 0.9160 Gold 0.2350 oz. AGW, 22.05 mm. **Ruler:**
Elizabeth II **Subject:** Ikuko Shimizu's Hello Kitty **Rev:** Kitty and
Union Jack flag in multicolor

Date	Mintage	F	VF	XF	Unc	BU
2009 Proof	Est. 1,000	Value: 700				

KM# 1242   25 DOLLARS
4.0000 g., 0.9990 Gold 0.1285 oz. AGW, 14x23.3 mm. **Ruler:**
Elizabeth II **Subject:** Shroud of Turin **Rev:** Image of the face of
Jesus, 3 red crystals

Date	Mintage	F	VF	XF	Unc	BU
2010 Proof	2,000	Value: 500				

KM# 1323   25 DOLLARS
Silver **Ruler:** Elizabeth II **Rev:** Krulzernen

Date	Mintage	F	VF	XF	Unc	BU
2011 Proof	—	Value: 85.00				

KM# 1324   25 DOLLARS
Silver **Ruler:** Elizabeth II **Rev:** Preussen

Date	Mintage	F	VF	XF	Unc	BU
2011 Proof	—	Value: 85.00				

KM# 1360 25 DOLLARS
155.5000 g., 0.9990 Silver 4.9942 oz. ASW, 65 mm. **Ruler:** Elizabeth II **Subject:** Soyuzmultfilm 75th Anniversary - Winnie the Pooh **Rev:** Winnie the Pooh characters in color **Edge:** Reeded

Date	Mintage	F	VF	XF	Unc	BU
2011 Proof	500	Value: 400				

KM# 1366 25 DOLLARS
155.5000 g., 0.9990 Silver 4.9942 oz. ASW, 65 mm. **Ruler:** Elizabeth II **Subject:** Soyuzmultfilm 75th Anniversary - Little Boy and Karlsson-on-the-Roof **Rev:** Little Boy, Karlsson and Freken Bok in color **Edge:** Reeded

Date	Mintage	F	VF	XF	Unc	BU
2011 Proof	500	Value: 400				

KM# 1370 25 DOLLARS
155.5000 g., 0.9990 Silver 4.9942 oz. ASW, 65 mm. **Ruler:** Elizabeth II **Subject:** Soyuzmultfilm 75th Anniversary - Cheburashka and Crocodile Gena **Rev:** Cheburashka, Crocodile Gena and Madame Shapoklyak in color **Edge:** Reeded

Date	Mintage	F	VF	XF	Unc	BU
2011 Proof	500	Value: 400				

KM# 439 30 DOLLARS
10.0000 g., 0.9999 Gold 0.3215 oz. AGW, 16.1 mm. **Ruler:** Elizabeth II **Obv:** Crowned head right, date below **Rev:** Multicolor Peony flower and denomination **Edge:** Reeded

Date	Mintage	F	VF	XF	Unc	BU
2004	10,000	—	—	—	—	550

KM# 1128 35 DOLLARS
10.0210 g., 0.9990 Gold 0.3218 oz. AGW, 25 mm. **Ruler:** Elizabeth II **Rev:** James Cook and sailing ship

Date	Mintage	F	VF	XF	Unc	BU
2003 Proof	Est. 4,999	Value: 570				

KM# 440 35 DOLLARS
10.0000 g., 0.9999 Gold 0.3215 oz. AGW, 16.1 mm. **Ruler:** Elizabeth II **Obv:** Crowned head right, date below **Rev:** Multicolor Chinese man beating a tiger and denomination **Edge:** Reeded

Date	Mintage	F	VF	XF	Unc	BU
2004	6,000	—	—	—	—	550

KM# 441 35 DOLLARS
10.0000 g., 0.9999 Gold 0.3215 oz. AGW, 16.1 mm. **Ruler:** Elizabeth II **Obv:** Crowned head right, date below **Rev:** Multicolor Chinese man riding a horse and denomination **Edge:** Reeded

Date	Mintage	F	VF	XF	Unc	BU
2004	10,000	—	—	—	—	550

KM# 442 35 DOLLARS
10.0000 g., 0.9999 Gold 0.3215 oz. AGW, 25 x 15 mm. **Ruler:** Elizabeth II **Obv:** Crowned head right, date below **Rev:** Multicolor "Eight immortals crossing the sea" and denomination **Edge:** Plain **Shape:** Ingot

Date	Mintage	F	VF	XF	Unc	BU
2004	3,000	—	—	—	—	575

KM# 1132 50 DOLLARS
31.1050 g., 0.9999 Gold 0.9999 oz. AGW, 38.6 mm. **Ruler:** Elizabeth II **Subject:** Full Gospel Business Men's Fellowship, 50th Anniversary **Rev:** Jesus Christ

Date	Mintage	F	VF	XF	Unc	BU
2003 Proof	Est. 2,999	Value: 1,700				

KM# 1319 50 DOLLARS
Silver **Ruler:** Elizabeth II **Subject:** Worlf Wildlife Fund **Rev:** Two deer

Date	Mintage	F	VF	XF	Unc	BU
2007 Proof	—	Value: 100				

KM# 1191 50 DOLLARS
7.7800 g., 0.7500 Gold 0.1876 oz. AGW, 26 mm. **Ruler:** Elizabeth II **Subject:** Elvis Presley, 30th Anniversary of death

Date	Mintage	F	VF	XF	Unc	BU
2007 Proof	500	Value: 420				

KM# 800 50 DOLLARS
155.5000 g., 0.9990 Silver 4.9942 oz. ASW, 65 mm. **Ruler:** Elizabeth II **Subject:** Tales of the Carribean **Rev:** Sea monster atacking Pirate ship

Date	Mintage	F	VF	XF	Unc	BU
2008	500	—	—	—	—	1,500

KM# 1230 50 DOLLARS
15.6100 g., 0.9990 Gold 0.5014 oz. AGW, 26.5 mm. **Ruler:** Elizabeth II **Subject:** Ikuko Shimizu's Hello Kitty **Rev:** Kitty and Daniel in automobile near Westminster and Big Ben in multicolor

Date	Mintage	F	VF	XF	Unc	BU
2009 Proof	Est. 1,000	Value: 900				

KM# 1234 50 DOLLARS
31.1050 g., 0.9990 Palladium 0.9990 oz., 38.6 mm. **Ruler:** Elizabeth II **Rev:** H.M.A.V. Bounty, as full hull model

Date	Mintage	F	VF	XF	Unc	BU
2009 Proof	—	—	—	—	—	1,000

KM# 738 50 DOLLARS
31.1050 g., 0.9999 Palladium 0.9999 oz. **Ruler:** Elizabeth II **Rev:** Ship model left

Date	Mintage	F	VF	XF	Unc	BU
2010	—	—	—	—	—	900

KM# 397 100 DOLLARS
23.3276 g., 0.9999 Gold Acrylic capsule center containing tiny diamonds, rubies and sapphires 0.7499 oz. AGW, 32.1 mm. **Ruler:** Elizabeth II **Subject:** Crown Jewels **Obv:** Crowned bust right, legend **Rev:** Crowns and royal regalia **Edge:** Reeded

Date	Mintage	F	VF	XF	Unc	BU
2002 Proof	5,000	Value: 1,350				

KM# 1129 100 DOLLARS
31.1620 g., 0.9990 Gold 1.0008 oz. AGW, 32 mm. **Ruler:** Elizabeth II **Rev:** James Cook and sailing ship

Date	Mintage	F	VF	XF	Unc	BU
2003 Proof	Est. 2,999	Value: 1,600				

KM# 503 100 DOLLARS
31.1030 g., 0.9999 Gold 0.9998 oz. AGW, 40.6 mm. **Ruler:** Elizabeth II **Subject:** WWI **Obv:** Head with tiara right **Rev:** Multicolor image of Australian WWI soldier in Europe **Edge:** Reeded

Date	Mintage	F	VF	XF	Unc	BU
2008 Proof	90	Value: 2,000				

KM# 505 100 DOLLARS
31.1030 g., 0.9999 Gold 0.9998 oz. AGW, 40.6 mm. **Ruler:** Elizabeth II **Subject:** WWI **Obv:** Head with tiara right **Rev:** Multicolor image of Australian WWI soldier in Mid-East scene **Edge:** Reeded

Date	Mintage	F	VF	XF	Unc	BU
2008 Proof	90	Value: 2,000				

KM# 737 100 DOLLARS
31.1050 g., 0.9999 Platinum 0.9999 oz. APW **Ruler:** Elizabeth II **Rev:** Ship model left

Date	Mintage	F	VF	XF	Unc	BU
2010	—	—	—	—	—	2,250

KM# 1212 200 DOLLARS
31.1620 g., 0.9990 Gold 1.0017 oz. AGW, 32 mm. **Ruler:** Elizabeth II **Subject:** John Marshall's Cow Parade **Rev:** Cow in multicolor

Date	Mintage	F	VF	XF	Unc	BU
2008	Est. 100	—	—	—	—	1,800

KM# 1213 200 DOLLARS
31.1620 g., 0.9990 Gold 1.0008 oz. AGW, 32 mm. **Ruler:** Elizabeth II **Subject:** John Marshall's Cow Parade **Rev:** African Moonlight Cow in multicolor

Date	Mintage	F	VF	XF	Unc	BU
2008	Est. 100	—	—	—	—	1,800

KM# 1214 200 DOLLARS
31.1650 g., 0.9990 Gold 1.0009 oz. AGW, 32 mm. **Ruler:** Elizabeth II **Subject:** John Marshall's Cow Parade **Rev:** Discownt Motivated in multicolor

Date	Mintage	F	VF	XF	Unc	BU
2008	Est. 100	—	—	—	—	1,800

KM# 1215 200 DOLLARS
31.1650 g., 0.9990 Gold 1.0018 oz. AGW **Ruler:** Elizabeth II **Subject:** John Marshall's Cow Parade **Rev:** Moodonna in multicolor

Date	Mintage	F	VF	XF	Unc	BU
2008	Est. 100	—	—	—	—	1,800

KM# 1216 200 DOLLARS
31.1650 g., 0.9990 Gold 1.0009 oz. AGW, 32 mm. **Ruler:** Elizabeth II **Subject:** John Marshall's Cow Parade **Rev:** Moodiba in multicolor

Date	Mintage	F	VF	XF	Unc	BU
2008	Est. 100	—	—	—	—	1,800

KM# 1217 200 DOLLARS
31.1650 g., 0.9999 Gold 1.0018 oz. AGW, 32 mm. **Ruler:** Elizabeth II **Subject:** John Marshall's Cow Parade **Rev:** Railbow Cowwow in multicolor

Date	Mintage	F	VF	XF	Unc	BU
2008	Est. 100	—	—	—	—	1,800

KM# 1218   200 DOLLARS
31.1650 g., 0.9999 Gold 1.0018 oz. AGW, 32 mm. **Ruler:** Elizabeth II **Subject:** John Marshall's Cow Parade **Rev:** Picowso in multicolor

Date	Mintage	F	VF	XF	Unc	BU
2008	Est. 100	—	—	—	—	1,800

KM# 1219   200 DOLLARS
31.1650 g., 0.9990 Gold 1.0009 oz. AGW, 32 mm. **Ruler:** Elizabeth II **Subject:** John Marshall's Cow Parade **Rev:** Location Cow in multicolor

Date	Mintage	F	VF	XF	Unc	BU
2008	Est. 100	—	—	—	—	1,800

KM# 1220   200 DOLLARS
31.1650 g., 0.9999 Gold 1.0018 oz. AGW, 32 mm. **Ruler:** Elizabeth II **Subject:** John Marshall's Cow Parade **Rev:** Milking in the Farmhouse in multicolor

Date	Mintage	F	VF	XF	Unc	BU
2008	Est. 100	—	—	—	—	1,800

KM# 1221   200 DOLLARS
31.1650 g., 0.9999 Gold 1.0018 oz. AGW, 32 mm. **Ruler:** Elizabeth II **Subject:** John Marshall's Cow Parade **Rev:** Evening Cows in multicolor

Date	Mintage	F	VF	XF	Unc	BU
2008	Est. 100	—	—	—	—	1,800

KM# 1222   200 DOLLARS
31.1650 g., 0.9999 Gold 1.0018 oz. AGW, 32 mm. **Ruler:** Elizabeth II **Subject:** John Marshall's Cow Parade **Rev:** Cultural Moosic Cow in multicolor

Date	Mintage	F	VF	XF	Unc	BU
2008	Est. 100	—	—	—	—	1,800

KM# 1223   200 DOLLARS
31.1650 g., 0.9999 Gold 1.0018 oz. AGW, 32 mm. **Ruler:** Elizabeth II **Subject:** John Marshall's Cow Parade **Rev:** Freedomoo Cow in multicolor

Date	Mintage	F	VF	XF	Unc	BU
2008	Est. 100	—	—	—	—	1,800

KM# 1224   200 DOLLARS
31.1650 g., 0.9999 Gold 1.0018 oz. AGW, 32 mm. **Ruler:** Elizabeth II **Subject:** John Marshall's Cow Parade **Rev:** Bovingham Palace Cow in multicolor

Date	Mintage	F	VF	XF	Unc	BU
2008	Est. 100	—	—	—	—	1,800

KM# 768   200 DOLLARS
31.1050 g., 0.9990 Gold 0.9990 oz. AGW, 40.6 mm. **Ruler:** Elizabeth II **Subject:** Year of the Ox **Rev:** Child riding back of ox

Date	Mintage	F	VF	XF	Unc	BU
2009 Proof	—	Value: 1,750				

KM# 389   500 DOLLARS
2000.0000 g., 0.9990 Silver 64.234 oz. ASW, 105 mm. **Ruler:** Elizabeth II **Subject:** Moby Dick **Obv:** Crowned head right **Rev:**

Whale jumping over a six-man rowboat **Edge:** Plain **Note:** Illustration reduced.

Date	Mintage	F	VF	XF	Unc	BU
2001 Proof	—	Value: 2,500				

KM# 548   500 DOLLARS
113.0000 g., 1.0000 Gold 3.6328 oz. AGW, 50 mm. **Ruler:** Elizabeth II **Subject:** Jack Nicklaus **Rev:** Portrait facing - two golf poses flanking

Date	Mintage	F	VF	XF	Unc	BU
2006 Proof	113	Value: 6,500				

MAUNDY MONEY
Ceremonial Sterling Pence

KM# 449   PENNY
0.4800 g., 0.9990 Silver 0.0154 oz. ASW, 11.1 mm. **Ruler:** Elizabeth II **Subject:** Maundy **Obv:** Crowned bust right **Rev:** Crowned denomination divides date within wreath **Edge:** Plain

Date	Mintage	F	VF	XF	Unc	BU
2002 Proof	5,000	Value: 8.00				

KM# 450   2 PENCE
0.9400 g., 0.9990 Silver 0.0302 oz. ASW, 13.4 mm. **Ruler:** Elizabeth II **Subject:** Maundy **Obv:** Crowned bust right **Rev:** Crowned denomination divides date within wreath **Edge:** Plain

Date	Mintage	F	VF	XF	Unc	BU
2002 Proof	5,000	Value: 10.00				

KM# 451   3 PENCE
1.4400 g., 0.9990 Silver 0.0462 oz. ASW, 16.1 mm. **Ruler:** Elizabeth II **Subject:** Maundy **Obv:** Crowned bust right **Rev:** Crowned denomination divides date within wreath **Edge:** Plain

Date	Mintage	F	VF	XF	Unc	BU
2002 Proof	5,000	Value: 12.00				

KM# 452   4 PENCE
1.9300 g., 0.9990 Silver 0.0620 oz. ASW, 17.5 mm. **Ruler:** Elizabeth II **Subject:** Maundy **Obv:** Crowned bust right **Rev:** Crowned denomination divides date within wreath **Edge:** Plain

Date	Mintage	F	VF	XF	Unc	BU
2002 Proof	5,000	Value: 15.00				

PROOF SETS

KM#	Date	Mintage	Identification	Issue Price	Mkt Val
PS25	2002 (4)	5,000	KM#449-452 Maundy Set	—	45.00

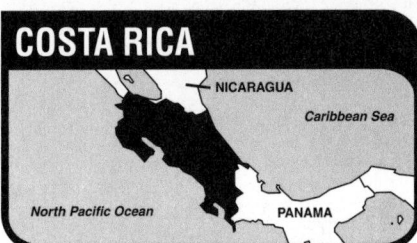

COSTA RICA

The Republic of Costa Rica, located in southern Central America between Nicaragua and Panama, has an area of 19,730 sq. mi. (51,100 sq. km.) and a population of 3.4 million. Capital: San Jose. Agriculture predominates; tourism and coffee, bananas, beef and sugar contribute heavily to the country's export earnings.

KEY TO MINT IDENTIFICATION

Key Letter	Mint
(a)	Armant Metalurgica, Santiago, Chile
(c)	Casa de Moneda, Mexico City Mint
(cc)	Casa de Moneda, Brazil
(co)	Colombia Republican Banko
(g)	Guatemala Mint
(i)	Italcambio Mint
(p) or (P)	Philadelphia Mint, USA
(r)	RCM – Royal Canadian Mint
(rm)	Royal Mint, London
(s)	San Francisco
(sj)	San Jose
(sm)	Sherrit Mint, Toronto
(v)	Vereingte Deutsche Metallwerke, Karlsruhe
(w)	Westain, Toronto

REPUBLIC

REFORM COINAGE
1920, 100 Centimos = 1 Colon

KM# 227a.2   5 COLONES
4.0000 g., Brass, 21.6 mm. **Obv:** National arms, date below, large letters in legend, large date, shield is not outlined **Rev:** Denomination above spray, B.C.C.R. below, thin '5' **Edge:** Segmented reeding

Date	Mintage	F	VF	XF	Unc	BU
2001(a)	—	—	—	—	0.65	1.00

KM# 227b   5 COLONES
0.9000 g., Aluminum, 21.4 mm. **Obv:** National arms **Obv. Legend:** REPUBLICA DE COSTA RICA **Rev:** Denomination above sprays, B.C.C.R. **Edge:** Plain

Date	Mintage	F	VF	XF	Unc	BU
2005	—	—	—	—	0.35	0.50
2008	—	—	—	—	0.35	0.50

KM# 228.2   10 COLONES
5.0000 g., Brass, 23.5 mm. **Obv:** National arms, date below, large legend and date, shield not outlined **Rev:** Denomination above spray, B.C.C.R. below, thick '1' **Edge:** Segmented reeding

Date	Mintage	F	VF	XF	Unc	BU
2002(a)	—	—	—	—	1.25	1.50

KM# 228b   10 COLONES
1.1300 g., Aluminum, 22.97 mm. **Obv:** National arms **Obv. Legend:** REPUBLICA DE COSTA RICA **Rev:** Denomination above sprays, B.C.C.R. **Edge:** Reeded

Date	Mintage	F	VF	XF	Unc	BU
2005	—	—	—	—	0.50	0.75
2008	—	—	—	—	0.50	0.75

KM# 229a   25 COLONES
7.0000 g., Brass, 25.4 mm. **Obv:** National arms **Obv. Legend:**

REPUBLICA DE COSTA RICA **Rev:** Value above sprays, B.C.C.R. below **Edge:** Segmented reeding

Date	Mintage	F	VF	XF	Unc	BU
2001(a)	—	—	—	—	2.50	3.00
2003	—	—	—	—	2.50	3.00
2007	—	—	—	—	2.50	3.00

KM# 229a.1 25 COLONES
7.0000 g., Brass **Obv:** National arms, date below **Rev:** Value above sprays, B.C.C.R. below **Edge:** Plain

Date	Mintage	F	VF	XF	Unc	BU
2005	—	—	—	—	2.50	3.00

KM# 231.1a 50 COLONES
7.9200 g., Aluminum-Bronze, 27.5 mm. **Obv:** National arms, date below **Rev:** Value with spray below **Rev. Legend:** B. C. C. R. **Edge:** Segmented reeding

Date	Mintage	F	VF	XF	Unc	BU
2002	—	—	—	—	3.00	4.00

KM# 231.1b 50 COLONES
7.8400 g., Brass Plated Steel, 27.5 mm. **Obv:** National arms above date **Rev:** Value above sprays, B.C.C.R. below **Edge:** Segmented reeding

Date	Mintage	F	VF	XF	Unc	BU
2006	—	—	—	—	3.50	5.00
2007	—	—	—	—	3.50	5.00

KM# 230a 100 COLONES
Brass, 29.5 mm. **Obv:** National arms, date below, large letters in legend and date, shield outlined **Rev:** Value above spray, B.C.C.R. below **Edge:** Segmented reeding

Date	Mintage	F	VF	XF	Unc	BU
2006(a)	—	—	—	—	4.50	6.00

KM# 240a 100 COLONES
8.8000 g., Brass Plated Steel, 29.4 mm. **Obv:** National arms above date **Rev:** Value above sprays **Edge:** Reeded

Date	Mintage	F	VF	XF	Unc	BU
2006	—	—	—	—	4.50	6.00
2007	—	—	—	—	4.50	6.00

KM# 239.1 500 COLONES
11.0000 g., Copper-Aluminum-Nickel, 32.9 mm. **Obv:** National arms **Obv. Legend:** REPUBLICA DE COSTA RICA **Rev:** Value above sprays, B.C.C.R. below, thick numerals **Edge:** Segmented reeding

Date	Mintage	F	VF	XF	Unc	BU
2003(a)	—	—	—	2.00	3.00	5.00
2005	—	—	—	2.00	3.00	5.00
2006	—	—	—	2.00	3.00	5.00

KM# 239.2 500 COLONES
Brass, 32.9 mm. **Obv:** National arms, date below **Obv. Legend:** REPUBLICA DE COSTA RICA **Rev:** Denomination above sprays, B.C.C.R. below, thin numerals **Edge:** Segmented reeding

Date	Mintage	F	VF	XF	Unc	BU
2003 Rare	100	—	—	—	—	250

KM# 239.1a 500 COLONES
10.8800 g., Brass Plated Steel, 33 mm. **Obv:** National arms, date below **Rev:** Value above sprays, B.C.C.R. below **Edge:** Segmented reeding

Date	Mintage	F	VF	XF	Unc	BU
2006	—	—	—	—	2.00	5.00
2007	—	—	—	—	2.00	5.00

CROATIA

The Republic of Croatia, (Hrvatska) bordered on the west by the Adriatic Sea and the northeast by Hungary, has an area of 21,829 sq. mi. (56,538 sq. km.) and a population of 4.7 million. Capital: Zagreb.

NOTE: Coin dates starting with 1994 are followed with a period. Example: 1994.

REPUBLIC

REFORM COINAGE
May 30, 1994 - 1000 Dinara = 1 Kuna; 100 Lipa = 1 Kuna

For the circulating minor coins, the reverse legend (name of item) is in Croatian for odd dated years and Latin for even dated years.

KM# 3 LIPA
0.7000 g., Aluminum, 17 mm. **Obv:** Denomination above crowned arms **Obv. Legend:** REPUBLIKA HRVATSKA **Rev:** Ears of corn, date below **Rev. Legend:** KUKURUZ **Edge:** Plain

Date	Mintage	F	VF	XF	Unc	BU
2001.	2,000,000	—	—	0.20	0.50	—
2001. Proof	1,000	Value: 2.50				
2003	1,500,000	—	—	0.20	0.50	—
2003. Proof	1,000	Value: 2.50				
2005.	—	—	—	0.20	0.50	—
2005. Proof	—	Value: 2.00				
2007.	—	—	—	0.20	0.50	—
2007. Proof	—	Value: 2.00				
2009. In sets only	—	—	—	—	—	—

KM# 12 LIPA
0.7000 g., Aluminum, 17 mm. **Obv:** Denomination above crowned arms **Obv. Legend:** REPUBLIKA HRVATSKA **Rev:** Ears of corn, date below **Rev. Legend:** ZEA MAYS **Edge:** Plain

Date	Mintage	F	VF	XF	Unc	BU
2002.	3,000,000	—	—	0.40	1.00	—
2002. Proof	1,000	Value: 2.50				
2004.	2,000,000	—	—	0.40	1.00	—
2004. Proof	2,000	Value: 1.50				
2006.	—	—	—	0.40	1.00	—
2006. Proof	—	Value: 1.50				
2008.	—	—	—	0.40	1.00	—
2008. Proof	—	Value: 1.50				

KM# 4 2 LIPE
0.9200 g., Aluminum, 19 mm. **Obv:** Denomination above crowned arms on half braid **Obv. Legend:** REPUBLIKA HRVATSKA **Rev:** Grapevine, date below **Rev. Legend:** VINOVA LOZA **Edge:** Plain

Date	Mintage	F	VF	XF	Unc	BU
2001.	2,986,000	—	—	0.40	1.00	—
2001. Proof	1,000	Value: 3.00				
2003.	2,000,000	—	—	0.40	1.00	—
2003. Proof	1,000	Value: 3.00				
2005.	—	—	—	0.40	1.00	—
2005. Proof	—	Value: 3.00				
2007.	—	—	—	0.40	1.00	—
2007. Proof	—	Value: 3.00				
2009. In sets only	—	—	—	—	—	—

KM# 14 2 LIPE
0.9200 g., Aluminum, 19 mm. **Obv:** Denomination above crowned arms on half braid **Obv. Legend:** REPUBLIKA HRVATSKA **Rev:** Grapevine, date below **Rev. Legend:** VITIS VINIFERA **Edge:** Plain

Date	Mintage	F	VF	XF	Unc	BU
2002.	2,000,000	—	—	0.80	2.00	—
2002. Proof	1,000	Value: 3.00				
2004.	2,000,000	—	—	0.80	2.00	—
2004. Proof	2,000	Value: 2.50				
2006.	—	—	—	0.80	2.00	—
2006. Proof	—	Value: 2.50				
2008.	—	—	—	0.80	2.00	—
2008. Proof	—	Value: 2.50				

KM# 5 5 LIPA
2.5000 g., Brass Plated Steel, 18 mm. **Obv:** Denomination above crowned arms **Obv. Legend:** REPUBLIKA HRVATSKA **Rev:** Oak leaves, date below **Rev. Legend:** HRAST LUZNJAK **Edge:** Plain

Date	Mintage	F	VF	XF	Unc	BU
2001.	6,598,000	—	—	0.40	1.00	—
2001. Proof	1,000	Value: 4.00				
2003.	13,000,000	—	—	0.40	1.00	—
2003. Proof	2,000	Value: 3.50				
2005.	—	—	—	0.40	1.00	—
2005. Proof	—	Value: 3.50				
2007.	—	—	—	0.40	1.00	—
2007. Proof	—	Value: 3.50				
2009.	—	—	—	0.40	1.00	—
2011.	—	—	—	0.40	1.00	—

KM# 15 5 LIPA
2.5000 g., Brass Plated Steel, 18 mm. **Obv:** Denomination

above crowned arms **Obv. Legend:** REPUBLIKA HRVATSKA **Rev:** Oak leaves, date below **Rev. Legend:** QUERCUS ROBUR **Edge:** Plain

Date	Mintage	F	VF	XF	Unc	BU
2002.	3,500,000	—	—	0.80	2.00	—
2002. Proof	1,000	Value: 4.00				
2004.	2,000,000	—	—	0.80	2.00	—
2004. Proof	2,000	Value: 3.00				
2006.	—	—	—	0.80	2.00	—
2006. Proof	—	Value: 3.00				
2008	—	—	—	0.80	2.00	—
2008. Proof	—	Value: 3.00				

KM# 6   10 LIPA
3.2500 g., Brass Plated Steel, 20 mm. **Obv:** Denomination above crowned arms **Obv. Legend:** REPUBLIKA HRVATSKA **Rev:** Tobacco plant, date below **Rev. Legend:** DUHAN **Edge:** Plain

Date	Mintage	F	VF	XF	Unc	BU
2001.	31,500,000	—	—	0.40	1.50	—
2001. Proof	1,000	Value: 5.00				
2003.	12,000,000	—	—	0.40	1.50	—
2003. Proof	1,000	Value: 5.00				
2005.	—	—	—	0.40	1.50	—
2005. Proof	—	Value: 5.00				
2007.	—	—	—	0.40	1.50	—
2007. Proof	—	Value: 5.00				
2009.	—	—	—	0.40	1.50	—
2011.	—	—	—	0.40	1.50	—

KM# 16   10 LIPA
3.2500 g., Brass Plated Steel, 20 mm. **Obv:** Denomination above crowned arms on half braid **Obv. Legend:** REPUBLIKA HRVATSKA **Rev:** Tobacco plant, date below **Rev. Legend:** NICOTIANA TABACUM **Edge:** Plain

Date	Mintage	F	VF	XF	Unc	BU
2002.	2,000,000	—	—	0.80	2.50	—
2002. Proof	1,000	Value: 5.00				
2004.	2,000,000	—	—	0.80	2.50	—
2004. Proof	2,000	Value: 4.50				
2006.	—	—	—	0.80	2.50	—
2006. Proof	—	Value: 4.50				
2008.	—	—	—	0.80	2.50	—
2008. Proof	—	Value: 4.50				
2010.	—	—	—	0.80	2.50	—

KM# 7   20 LIPA
2.9000 g., Nickel Plated Steel, 18.5 mm. **Obv:** Denomination above crowned arms **Obv. Legend:** REPUBLIKA HRVATSKA **Rev:** Olive branch, date below **Rev. Legend:** MASLINA **Edge:** Plain

Date	Mintage	F	VF	XF	Unc	BU
2001.	23,000,000	—	—	0.45	1.50	—
2001. Proof	1,000	Value: 5.00				
2003.	12,500,000	—	—	0.45	1.50	—
2003. Proof	1,000	Value: 5.00				
2005.	—	—	—	0.45	1.50	—
2005. Proof	—	Value: 5.00				
2007.	—	—	—	0.45	1.50	—
2007. Proof	—	Value: 5.00				
2009.	—	—	—	0.45	1.50	—
2011.	—	—	—	0.45	1.50	—

KM# 17   20 LIPA
2.9000 g., Nickel Plated Steel, 18.5 mm. **Obv:** Denomination above crowned arms on half braid **Obv. Legend:** REPUBLIKA HRVATSKA **Rev:** Olive branch, date below **Rev. Legend:** OLEA EUROPAEA **Edge:** Plain

Date	Mintage	F	VF	XF	Unc	BU
2002.	2,000,000	—	—	0.80	2.50	—
2002. Proof	1,000	Value: 5.00				
2004.	2,000,000	—	—	0.80	2.50	—
2004. Proof	2,000	Value: 4.50				
2006.	—	—	—	0.80	2.50	—
2006. Proof	—	Value: 4.50				
2008.	—	—	—	0.80	2.50	—
2008. Proof	—	Value: 4.50				
2010.	—	—	—	0.80	2.50	—

KM# 8   50 LIPA
3.6500 g., Nickel Plated Steel, 20.5 mm. **Obv:** Denomination above crowned arms on half braid **Obv. Legend:** REPUBLIKA HRVATSKA **Rev:** Flowers, date below **Rev. Legend:** VELEBITSKA DEGENIJA **Edge:** Plain

Date	Mintage	F	VF	XF	Unc	BU
2001.	5,500,000	—	—	0.60	1.50	—
2001. Proof	1,000	Value: 5.50				
2003.	8,000,000	—	—	0.60	1.50	—
2003. Proof	1,000	Value: 5.50				
2005.	—	—	—	0.60	1.50	—
2005. Proof	—	Value: 5.00				
2007.	—	—	—	0.60	1.50	—
2007. Proof	—	Value: 5.00				
2009.	—	—	—	0.60	1.50	—
2011.	—	—	—	0.60	1.50	—

KM# 19   50 LIPA
3.6500 g., Nickel Plated Steel, 20.5 mm. **Obv:** Denomination above crowned arms on half braid **Obv. Legend:** REPUBLIKA HRVATSKA **Rev:** Flowers, date below **Rev. Legend:** DEGENIA VELEBITICA **Edge:** Plain

Date	Mintage	F	VF	XF	Unc	BU
2002.	2,000,000	—	—	0.80	2.50	—
2002. Proof	1,000	Value: 5.00				
2004.	2,000,000	—	—	0.80	2.50	—
2004. Proof	2,000	Value: 4.50				
2006.	—	—	—	0.80	2.50	—
2006. Proof	—	Value: 4.50				
2008.	—	—	—	0.80	2.50	—
2008. Proof	—	Value: 4.50				
2010.	—	—	—	0.80	2.50	—

KM# 9.1   KUNA
5.0000 g., Copper-Nickel-Zinc, 22.5 mm. **Obv:** Marten back of numeral, arms divide branches below **Obv. Legend:** REPUBLIKA HRVATSKA **Rev:** Nightingale left, two dates **Rev. Legend:** SLAVUJ **Edge:** Reeded

Date	Mintage	F	VF	XF	Unc	BU
2001.	1,000,000	—	—	0.75	1.65	2.00
2001. Proof	1,000	Value: 4.50				
2003.	2,000,000	—	—	0.75	1.65	2.00
2003. Proof	1,000	Value: 4.50				
2005.	—	—	—	0.75	1.65	2.00
2005. Proof	—	Value: 4.50				
2007.	—	—	—	0.75	1.65	2.00
2007. Proof	—	Value: 4.50				
2009.	—	—	—	0.75	1.65	2.00
2011.	—	—	—	0.75	1.65	2.00

KM# 9.2   KUNA
5.0000 g., Copper-Nickel-Zinc, 22.5 mm. **Obv:** Crowned arms flanked by sprays, denomination above on marten **Rev:** Nightingale, left, '1994' above, date below **Edge:** Reeded

Date	Mintage	F	VF	XF	Unc	BU
2001 Proof	—	Value: 4.00				

KM# 20.1   KUNA
5.0000 g., Copper-Nickel-Zinc, 22.5 mm. **Obv:** Marten back of numeral, arms divide branches below **Rev:** Nightingale left, date below **Rev. Legend:** Error spelling "LUSCINNIA" MEGARHYNCHOS **Edge:** Reeded **Note:** Formerly KM-20

Date	Mintage	F	VF	XF	Unc	BU
2002.	—	—	—	—	—	2.00

KM# 20.2   KUNA
5.0000 g., Copper-Nickel-Zinc, 22.5 mm. **Obv:** Marten back of numeral, arms divide branches below **Obv. Legend:** REPUBLIKA HRVATSKA **Rev:** Nightingale left, date below **Rev. Legend:** Correct spelling "LUSCINIA" MEGARHYNCHOS **Edge:** Reeded

Date	Mintage	F	VF	XF	Unc	BU
2002.	1,000,000	—	—	1.00	3.00	—
2002. Proof	1,000	Value: 5.00				
2006.	—	—	—	1.00	3.00	—
2006. Proof	—	Value: 5.00				
2008.	—	—	—	1.00	3.00	—
2008. Proof	—	Value: 5.00				
2010.	—	—	—	1.00	3.00	—

KM# 79   KUNA
5.0000 g., Copper-Nickel-Zinc, 22.5 mm. **Subject:** 10th Anniversary of National Currency **Obv:** Crowned arms flanked by sprays, denomination above on marten **Obv. Legend:** REPUBLIKA HRVATSKA **Rev:** Nightingale left, date below **Rev. Legend:** MEGARHYNCHOS **Edge:** Reeded

Date	Mintage	F	VF	XF	Unc	BU
ND(2004)	30,000	—	—	1.00	3.00	—
ND(2004) Proof	2,000	Value: 5.00				

KM# 10   2 KUNE
6.2000 g., Copper-Nickel-Zinc, 24.5 mm. **Obv:** Marten back of numeral, arms divide branches below **Obv. Legend:** REPUBLIKA HRVATSKA **Rev:** Bluefin tuna right, date below **Rev. Legend:** TUNJ **Edge:** Reeded

Date	Mintage	F	VF	XF	Unc	BU
2001.	1,250,000	—	—	1.00	2.00	—
2001. Proof	1,000	Value: 6.50				
2003.	7,250,000	—	—	1.00	2.00	—
2003. Proof	1,000	Value: 6.50				
2005.	—	—	—	1.00	2.00	—
2005. Proof	—	Value: 6.50				
2007.	—	—	—	1.00	2.00	—
2007. Proof	—	Value: 6.50				
2009.	—	—	—	1.00	2.00	—
2011.	—	—	—	1.00	2.00	—

KM# 21   2 KUNE
6.2000 g., Copper-Nickel-Zinc, 24.5 mm. **Obv:** Marten back of numeral, arms divide branches below **Obv. Legend:**

REPUBLIKA HRVATSKA **Rev:** Bluefin tuna right, date below
Rev. Legend: THUNNUS - THYNNUS **Edge:** Reeded

Date	Mintage	F	VF	XF	Unc	BU
2002.	1,000,000	—	—	1.50	3.00	—
2002. Proof	1,000	Value: 6.00				
2004.	2,000,000	—	—	1.50	3.00	—
2004. Proof	2,000	Value: 5.50				
2006.	—	—	—	1.50	3.00	—
2006. Proof	—	Value: 5.50				
2008.	—	—	—	1.50	3.00	—
2008. Proof	—	Value: 5.50				
2010.	—	—	—	1.50	3.00	—

KM# 11   5 KUNA
7.4500 g., Copper-Nickel-Zinc, 26.7 mm. **Obv:** Marten back of
numeral, arms divide branches below **Obv. Legend:**
REPUBLIKA HRVATSKA **Rev:** Brown bear left, date below **Rev.
Legend:** MRKI MEDVJED **Edge:** Reeded

Date	Mintage	F	VF	XF	Unc	BU
2001.	17,300,000	—	—	1.50	5.00	10.00
2001. Proof	1,000	Value: 9.00				
2003.	1,000,000	—	—	1.50	5.00	10.00
2003. Proof	1,000	Value: 9.00				
2005.	—	—	—	1.50	5.00	10.00
2005. Proof	—	Value: 9.00				
2007.	—	—	—	1.50	5.00	10.00
2007. Proof	—	Value: 9.00				
2009.	—	—	—	1.50	5.00	10.00
2011	—	—	—	1.50	5.00	10.00

KM# 23   5 KUNA
7.4500 g., Copper-Nickel-Zinc, 26.5 mm. **Obv:** Marten back of
numeral, arms divide branches below **Obv. Legend:**
REPUBLIKA HRVATSKA **Rev:** Brown bear left, date below **Rev.
Legend:** URSUS ARCTOS **Edge:** Reeded

Date	Mintage	F	VF	XF	Unc	BU
2002.	2,000,000	—	—	2.00	5.00	9.00
2002. Proof	1,000	Value: 9.00				
2004.	2,000,000	—	—	2.00	5.00	9.00
2004. Proof	2,000	Value: 8.00				
2006.	—	—	—	2.00	5.00	9.00
2006. Proof	—	Value: 8.00				
2008.	—	—	—	2.00	5.00	9.00
2008. Proof	—	Value: 8.00				
2010.	—	—	—	2.00	5.00	9.00

KM# 66   25 KUNA
12.7500 g., Bi-Metallic Brass center in Copper-Nickel ring,
32 mm. **Subject:** 10th Anniversary of International Recognition
Obv: Denomination in 3-D on outlined marten within circle, arms
divide sprays below **Rev:** National map **Edge:** Plain **Shape:** 12-
sided

Date	Mintage	F	VF	XF	Unc	BU
ND(2002)	200,000	—	—	—	8.50	—

KM# 78   25 KUNA
12.7500 g., Bi-Metallic Brass center in Copper-Nickel ring,
32 mm. **Subject:** Croatian European Union Candidacy **Obv:**
Denomination in 3-D on outlined marten within circle, arms divide
sprays below **Rev:** Joined squares within circle of stars **Edge:**
Plain **Shape:** 12-sided

Date	Mintage	F	VF	XF	Unc	BU
ND (2004)	30,000	—	—	—	10.00	—
ND (2004) Proof		Value: 25.00				

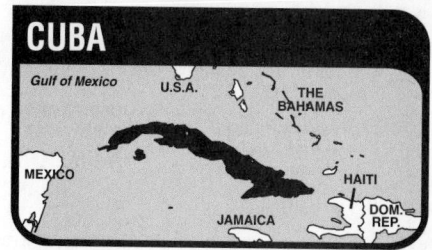

KM# 93   25 KUNA
12.7500 g., Bi-Metallic Brass center in Copper-Nickel ring,
32 mm. **Subject:** EBRD Annual Meeting, Zagreb **Obv:** Large
value at center **Rev:** Stylized old and new skyline

Date	Mintage	F	VF	XF	Unc	BU
2010	—	—	—	—	—	10.00

KM# 83   150 KUNA
24.0000 g., 0.9250 Silver 0.7137 oz. ASW, 37 mm. **Subject:**
2006 Winter Olympics - Italy **Obv:** National arms below
denomination **Rev:** Slalom skiing

Date	Mintage	F	VF	XF	Unc	BU
ND(2006) Proof	15,000	Value: 40.00				

KM# 84   150 KUNA
24.0000 g., 0.9250 Silver 0.7137 oz. ASW, 37 mm. **Subject:**
2006 World Soccer Championship - Germany **Obv:** National
arms below denomination **Rev:** Soccer player

Date	Mintage	F	VF	XF	Unc	BU
ND(2006) Proof	50,000	Value: 35.00				

KM# 85   150 KUNA
24.0000 g., 0.9250 Silver 0.7137 oz. ASW, 37 mm. **Subject:**
2006 World Soccer Championship - Germany **Obv:** National
arms above denomination **Rev:** Vignette

Date	Mintage	F	VF	XF	Unc	BU
ND(2006) Proof	10,000	Value: 45.00				

KM# 86   150 KUNA
24.0000 g., 0.9250 Silver 0.7137 oz. ASW, 37 mm. **Subject:**
150th Anniversary - Birth of Nikola Tesla **Obv:** National arms
above induction motor and denomination **Rev:** Bust of Tesla

Date	Mintage	F	VF	XF	Unc	BU
ND(2006) Proof	5,000	Value: 50.00				

KM# 87   150 KUNA
24.0000 g., 0.9250 Silver 0.7137 oz. ASW, 37 mm. **Issuer:**
Croatian National Bank **Subject:** 2008 Olympic Games - Peoples
Republic of China **Obv:** National arms, value in laurel wreath
Rev: T'ai-ho Tien gate in Beijing, athlete **Edge:** Plain **Edge
Lettering:** Ag 925/1000 24 g 37 mm PP HNZ

Date	Mintage	F	VF	XF	Unc	BU
ND(2006) Proof	20,000	Value: 40.00				

KM# 88   150 KUNA
24.0000 g., 0.9250 Silver 0.7137 oz. ASW, 37 mm. **Subject:**
Ican Mestrovic **Obv:** Squares and shamrocks **Rev:** Female
kneeling with Irish harp

Date	Mintage	F	VF	XF	Unc	BU
2007	4,000	—	—	—	—	45.00

KM# 89   150 KUNA
24.0000 g., 0.9250 Silver 0.7137 oz. ASW, 37 mm. **Subject:**
Benedikt Kotruljevic **Obv:** Pile of coins **Rev:** Bust right

Date	Mintage	F	VF	XF	Unc	BU
2007	10,000	—	—	—	—	40.00

KM# 90   150 KUNA
24.0000 g., 0.9250 Silver 0.7137 oz. ASW, 37 mm. **Subject:**
Historic Ships - Dubrovnik Karaka **Obv:** Sail within compass **Rev:**
Ship

Date	Mintage	F	VF	XF	Unc	BU
2007	10,000	—	—	—	—	40.00

KM# 91   1000 KUNA
7.0000 g., 0.9860 Gold 0.2219 oz. AGW, 22 mm. **Subject:**
Andrija Monorovicic, 150th Anniversary of Birth **Obv:** Globe
bisected showing layers **Rev:** Bust facing

Date	Mintage	F	VF	XF	Unc	BU
2007	2,000	—	—	—	—	375

KM# 92   1000 KUNA
7.0000 g., 0.9860 Gold 0.2219 oz. AGW, 22 mm. **Subject:** Marin
Drzic **Obv:** Shield flanked by comedy and tragedy masks **Rev:**
Half-length figure right

Date	Mintage	F	VF	XF	Unc	BU
2008	2,000	—	—	—	—	375

MINT SETS

KM#	Date	Mintage	Identification	Issue Price	Mkt Val
MS2	2002 (9)	—	KM#12, 14-17, 19, 20.1, 21, 23	—	25.00

PROOF SETS

KM#	Date	Mintage	Identification	Issue Price	Mkt Val
PS32	2001 (9)	—	KM#3-8, 9.2, 10, 11	—	45.00
PS33	2003 (9)	—	KM#3-8, 9.1, 10, 11	—	45.00
PS34	2004 (9)	—	KM#12, 14-17, 19, 21, 23, 79	—	40.00
PS35	2005 (9)	—	KM#3-8, 9.1, 10-11	—	40.00
PS36	2006 (9)	—	KM#12, 14-17, 19, 20.2, 21, 23	—	40.00
PS37	2007 (9)	—	KM#3-8, 9.1, 10-11	—	45.00
PS38	2008 (9)	—	KM#12, 14-17, 19, 20.2, 21, 23	—	40.00

CUBA

The Republic of Cuba, situated at the northern edge of the
Caribbean Sea about 90 miles (145 km.) south of Florida, has an
area of 42,804 sq. mi. (110,860 sq. km.) and a population of *11.2
million. Capital: Havana. The Cuban economy is based on the
cultivation and refining of sugar, which provides 80 percent of
export earnings.

MINT MARK
Key - Havana, 1977-

MONETARY SYSTEM
100 Centavos = 1 Peso

SECOND REPUBLIC
1962 - Present
DECIMAL COINAGE

KM# 33.3   CENTAVO
0.7500 g., Aluminum, 16.76 mm. **Obv:** Cuban arms within
wreath, denomination below **Rev:** Roman denomination within
circle of star, date below **Edge:** Plain **Note:** Shield varieties exist.

Date	Mintage	F	VF	XF	Unc	BU
2001	—	—	—	0.40	0.80	1.75
2003	—	—	—	0.40	0.80	1.75
2004	—	—	—	0.40	0.80	1.75
2005	—	—	—	0.40	0.80	1.75
2006	—	—	—	—	0.80	1.75
2007	—	—	—	—	0.80	1.75
2008	—	—	—	—	0.80	1.75
2010	—	—	—	—	0.80	1.75

KM# 34   5 CENTAVOS
1.5600 g., Aluminum, 21 mm. **Obv:** National arms within wreath,
denomination below **Rev:** Roman denomination within circle of
star, date below **Note:** Shield varieties exist.

Date	Mintage	F	VF	XF	Unc	BU
2001	6,703,331	—	0.10	0.25	0.75	1.50
2002	14,830,000	—	0.10	0.25	0.75	1.50
Note: High or low dates exist.						
2003	62,520,000	—	0.10	0.25	0.75	1.50
2004	62,520,000	—	0.10	0.25	0.75	1.50
2006	62,520,000	—	0.10	0.25	0.75	1.50
2007	62,520,000	—	0.10	0.25	0.75	1.50
2008	—	—	0.10	0.25	0.75	1.50
2009	—	—	0.10	0.25	0.75	1.50

KM# 35.2   20 CENTAVOS
Aluminum, 24 mm. **Obv:** National arms, revised shield **Rev:**
Roman denomination within circle of star

Date	Mintage	F	VF	XF	Unc	BU
2002	—	4.00	7.00	10.00	15.00	—
Note: Large and small dates exist.						

Date	Mintage	F	VF	XF	Unc	BU
2003	—	4.00	7.00	10.00	15.00	—
2005	—	4.00	7.00	10.00	15.00	—
2006	—	4.00	7.00	10.00	15.00	—

KM# 35.1 20 CENTAVOS
2.0000 g., Aluminum, 24 mm. **Obv:** Cuban arms within wreath, denomination below **Rev:** Roman denomination within circle of star, date below **Note:** Shield varieties exist.

Date	Mintage	F	VF	XF	Unc	BU
2002	25,000,000	—	0.50	1.00	2.00	4.00
2003	11,911,000	—	0.50	1.00	2.00	4.00
2005	—	—	0.50	1.00	2.00	4.00
2006	—	—	0.50	1.00	2.00	4.00
2007	—	—	0.50	1.00	2.00	4.00

KM# 834 PESO
Copper-Nickel, 32.65 mm. **Obv:** National arms **Rev:** Butterfly - multicolor **Rev. Legend:** FAUNA CUBANA - PAJERO CARPINTERO

Date	Mintage	F	VF	XF	Unc	BU
2001	—	—	—	—	—	15.00

KM# 844 PESO
26.0000 g., Copper-Nickel, 38 mm. **Subject:** Bolivar, 175th Anniversary of Liberation **Rev:** Bust

Date	Mintage	F	VF	XF	Unc	BU
2001	—	—	—	—	—	15.00

KM# 845 PESO
26.0000 g., Copper-Nickel, 38 mm. **Subject:** Bolivar - 175th Anniversary of Liberation **Rev:** Birthplace

Date	Mintage	F	VF	XF	Unc	BU
2001	—	—	—	—	—	15.00

KM# 846 PESO
Copper-Nickel, 38 mm. **Subject:** Boliver, 175th Anniversary of Liberation **Rev:** Battle scene

Date	Mintage	F	VF	XF	Unc	BU
2001	—	—	—	—	—	15.00

KM# 847 PESO
26.0000 g., Copper-Nickel, 38 mm. **Subject:** Cuban Fauna - Avellaneda Butterfly **Rev:** Butterfly

Date	Mintage	F	VF	XF	Unc	BU
2001	—	—	—	—	—	15.00

KM# 848 PESO
26.0000 g., Copper-Nickel, 38 mm. **Subject:** Global Conference Three

Date	Mintage	F	VF	XF	Unc	BU
2001	200	—	—	—	—	50.00

KM# 849 PESO
26.0000 g., Copper-Nickel, 38 mm. **Subject:** Monuments of Cuba **Rev:** Havana Cathedral

Date	Mintage	F	VF	XF	Unc	BU
2001	—	—	—	—	—	15.00

KM# 850 PESO
26.0000 g., Copper-Nickel, 38 mm. **Subject:** Monuments of Cuba **Rev:** Trinidad Cathedral

Date	Mintage	F	VF	XF	Unc	BU
2001	—	—	—	—	—	15.00

KM# 851 PESO
Copper-Nickel, 38 mm. **Subject:** Monuments of Cuba **Rev:** Templete

Date	Mintage	F	VF	XF	Unc	BU
2001	—	—	—	—	—	15.00

KM# 852 PESO
26.0000 g., Copper-Nickel, 38 mm. **Subject:** Playa Giron

Date	Mintage	F	VF	XF	Unc	BU
2001	—	—	—	—	—	15.00

KM# 829 PESO
13.0000 g., Copper-Nickel, 32.65 mm. **Obv:** National arms **Rev:** Carpenter bird perched - multicolor **Rev. Legend:** FAUNA CUBANA - PAJERO CARPINTERO **Edge:** Plain

Date	Mintage	F	VF	XF	Unc	BU
2001	—	—	—	—	15.00	—

KM# 347 PESO
5.5200 g., Brass Plated Steel, 24.5 mm. **Subject:** Jose Marti **Obv:** National arms within wreath, denomination below **Rev:** Smaller Bust facing, denomination at left **Rev. Legend:** PATRIA O MUERTE **Note:** Rim varieties exist.

Date	Mintage	F	VF	XF	Unc	BU
2001	—	—	—	1.00	2.00	4.00
2002	—	—	—	1.00	2.00	4.00

KM# 830 PESO
13.0000 g., Copper-Nickel, 32.65 mm. **Obv:** National arms **Rev:** Parrot perched - multicolor **Rev. Legend:** FAUNA CUBANA - COTORRA **Edge:** Plain

Date	Mintage	F	VF	XF	Unc	BU
2001	—	—	—	—	15.00	—

KM# 831 PESO
12.7000 g., Copper-Nickel, 32.5 mm. **Obv:** National arms **Rev:** Pink orchid - multicolor **Rev. Legend:** FLORA CUBANA - ORQUIDEAS **Edge:** Plain

Date	Mintage	F	VF	XF	Unc	BU
2001	—	—	—	—	20.00	—

KM# 832 PESO
12.7000 g., Copper-Nickel, 32.5 mm. **Obv:** National arms **Rev:** Yellow orchid - multicolor **Rev. Legend:** FLORA CUBANA - ORQUIDEAS **Edge:** Plain

Date	Mintage	F	VF	XF	Unc	BU
2001	—	—	—	—	20.00	—

KM# 833 PESO
12.7000 g., Copper-Nickel, 32.5 mm. **Obv:** National arms **Rev:** White orchid - multicolor **Rev. Legend:** FLORA CUBANA - ORQUIDEAS **Edge:** Plain

Date	Mintage	F	VF	XF	Unc	BU
2001	—	—	—	—	20.00	—

KM# 853 PESO
26.0000 g., Copper-Nickel, 38 mm. **Subject:** Federico Engels

Date	Mintage	F	VF	XF	Unc	BU
2002	—	—	—	—	—	15.00

KM# 854 PESO
26.0000 g., Copper-Nickel, 38 mm. **Subject:** Lenin

Date	Mintage	F	VF	XF	Unc	BU
2002	—	—	—	—	—	15.00

KM# 855 PESO
26.0000 g., Copper-Nickel, 38 mm. **Subject:** Mao Tse Tung

Date	Mintage	F	VF	XF	Unc	BU
2002	—	—	—	—	—	15.00

KM# 856 PESO
26.0000 g., Copper-Nickel, 38 mm. **Subject:** Karl Marx

Date	Mintage	F	VF	XF	Unc	BU
2002	—	—	—	—	—	15.00

KM# 951 PESO
Copper-Nickel **Rev:** Birds in color

Date	Mintage	F	VF	XF	Unc	BU
2002 Proof	— Value: 60.00					

KM# 953 PESO
Copper **Subject:** "Ernesto "Che" Guevara, 75th Birthday **Rev:** Bust **Shape:** 38

Date	Mintage	F	VF	XF	Unc	BU
2003	—	—	—	—	—	50.00

KM# 857 PESO
26.0000 g., Copper-Nickel, 38 mm. **Subject:** Che Guevara, 75th Anniversary of Birth

Date	Mintage	F	VF	XF	Unc	BU
2003	—	—	—	—	—	15.00

KM# 858 PESO
26.0000 g., Copper-Nickel, 38 mm. **Subject:** Che Guevara, 75th Anniversary of Birth

Date	Mintage	F	VF	XF	Unc	BU
2003	—	—	—	—	—	15.00

KM# 728 PESO
Silver **Subject:** Endangered Wildlife **Rev:** Crocodile

Date	Mintage	F	VF	XF	Unc	BU
2003	— Value: 45.00					

KM# 859 PESO
26.0000 g., Copper-Nickel, 38 mm. **Subject:** Fauna - Hawk Pilgrin

Date	Mintage	F	VF	XF	Unc	BU
2004	—	—	—	—	—	17.00

KM# 860 PESO
26.0000 g., Copper-Nickel, 38 mm. **Subject:** Fauna Iberian Lynx

Date	Mintage	F	VF	XF	Unc	BU
2004	—	—	—	—	—	17.00

KM# 861 PESO
26.0000 g., Copper-Nickel, 38 mm. **Subject:** Fauna - Imperial Eagle

Date	Mintage	F	VF	XF	Unc	BU
2004	—	—	—	—	—	17.00

KM# 862 PESO
26.0000 g., Copper-Nickel, 38 mm. **Subject:** Fauna Lobo Gris

Date	Mintage	F	VF	XF	Unc	BU
2004	—	—	—	—	—	17.00

KM# 863 PESO
26.0000 g., Copper-Nickel, 38 mm. **Subject:** Fauna - Oso Pards

Date	Mintage	F	VF	XF	Unc	BU
2004	—	—	—	—	—	17.00

KM# 864 PESO
26.0000 g., Copper-Nickel, 38 mm. **Subject:** Fauna - Osprey

Date	Mintage	F	VF	XF	Unc	BU
2004	—	—	—	—	—	17.00

KM# 865 PESO
Copper-Nickel, 38 mm. **Subject:** Cuban Tobacco

Date	Mintage	F	VF	XF	Unc	BU
2005	—	—	—	—	—	17.00

KM# 866 PESO
26.0000 g., Copper-Nickel, 32.8 mm. **Subject:** Tropical Fish - Pygolites **Obv:** National arms within wreath **Rev:** Pyglopites dicanthus

Date	Mintage	F	VF	XF	Unc	BU
2005	—	—	—	—	—	15.00

KM# 867 PESO
26.0000 g., Copper-Nickel, 32.8 mm. **Subject:** Tropical Fish - Zanclus **Obv:** National arms within wreath **Rev:** Zanclus canescens

Date	Mintage	F	VF	XF	Unc	BU
2005	—	—	—	—	—	15.00

KM# 868 PESO
26.0000 g., Copper-Nickel, 32.8 mm. **Subject:** Tropical Fish - Rhinecanthus **Obv:** National arms

Date	Mintage	F	VF	XF	Unc	BU
2005	—	—	—	—	—	15.00

KM# 924 PESO
Nickel Plated Steel **Subject:** Cuban Tobacco, 500th Anniversary **Rev:** Tobacco traders before caraval sailing ship

Date	Mintage	F	VF	XF	Unc	BU
2005 Proof	—	—	—	—	—	10.00

KM# 869 PESO
26.0000 g., Copper-Nickel, 38 mm. **Obv:** National arms within wreath **Rev:** Toucan

Date	Mintage	F	VF	XF	Unc	BU
2006	—	—	—	—	—	15.00

KM# 870 PESO
26.0000 g., Copper-Nickel, 38 mm. **Subject:** 29th Summer Olympics

Date	Mintage	F	VF	XF	Unc	BU
2006	—	—	—	—	—	15.00

KM# 871 PESO
26.0000 g., Copper-Nickel, 38 mm. **Subject:** Che Guevara, 40th Anniversary of his Death **Obv:** National arms within wreath **Rev:** Bust facing

Date	Mintage	F	VF	XF	Unc	BU
2007	—	—	—	—	—	15.00

KM# 871a PESO
26.0000 g., Copper, 38 mm. **Obv:** Che Guevara, 40th Anniversary of his Death

Date	Mintage	F	VF	XF	Unc	BU
2007	—	—	—	—	—	15.00

KM# 873 PESO
26.0000 g., Copper-Nickel **Subject:** Fauna - Buitre (Condor)

Date	Mintage	F	VF	XF	Unc	BU
2007	—	—	—	—	—	17.00

KM# 874 PESO
26.0000 g., Copper-Nickel, 38 mm. **Subject:** Fauna - Burro

Date	Mintage	F	VF	XF	Unc	BU
2007	—	—	—	—	—	17.00

KM# 875 PESO
26.0000 g., Copper-Nickel, 38 mm. **Subject:** Fauna - Cobra Montesa

Date	Mintage	F	VF	XF	Unc	BU
2007	—	—	—	—	—	17.00

KM# 876 PESO
26.0000 g., Copper-Nickel **Subject:** Fauna - Gato Montes

Date	Mintage	F	VF	XF	Unc	BU
2007	—	—	—	—	—	17.00

KM# 877 PESO
26.0000 g., Copper-Nickel, 38 mm. **Subject:** Fauma - Mastin Espanol

Date	Mintage	F	VF	XF	Unc	BU
2007	—	—	—	—	—	17.00

KM# 878 PESO
26.0000 g., Copper-Nickel, 26 mm. **Subject:** Fauna - Urogallo

Date	Mintage	F	VF	XF	Unc	BU
2007	—	—	—	—	—	17.00

KM# 879 PESO
26.0000 g., Copper-Nickel, 38 mm. **Subject:** Fortress - El Morro

Date	Mintage	F	VF	XF	Unc	BU
2007	—	—	—	—	—	17.00

KM# 880 PESO
26.0000 g., Copper-Nickel, 38 mm. **Subject:** Fortress - La Fuerza

Date	Mintage	F	VF	XF	Unc	BU
2007	—	—	—	—	—	15.00

KM# 881 PESO
26.0000 g., Copper-Nickel, 38 mm. **Subject:** Fortress - La Punta

Date	Mintage	F	VF	XF	Unc	BU
2007	—	—	—	—	—	15.00

KM# 882 PESO
26.0000 g., Copper-Nickel, 38 mm. **Subject:** Garibaldi

Date	Mintage	F	VF	XF	Unc	BU
2007	—	—	—	—	—	15.00

KM# 883 PESO
26.0000 g., Copper-Nickel, 38 mm. **Subject:** Santa Ana Ship

Date	Mintage	F	VF	XF	Unc	BU
2007	—	—	—	—	—	15.00

KM# 884 PESO
26.0000 g., Copper-Nickel, 38 mm. **Subject:** Sputnik

Date	Mintage	F	VF	XF	Unc	BU
2007	—	—	—	—	—	15.00

KM# 901   PESO
38.0000 g., Copper-Nickel, 38 mm. **Subject:** Ship - Principe Asturias

Date	Mintage	F	VF	XF	Unc	BU
2008	—	—	—	—	15.00	—

KM# 902   PESO
26.0000 g., Copper-Nickel, 38 mm. **Subject:** Ship San Carlos

Date	Mintage	F	VF	XF	Unc	BU
2008	—	—	—	—	15.00	—

KM# 903   PESO
38.0000 g., Copper-Nickel, 38 mm. **Subject:** Ship- San Hermene

Date	Mintage	F	VF	XF	Unc	BU
2008	—	—	—	—	—	15.00

KM# 907   PESO
41.0000 g., Copper, 45 mm. **Subject:** Revolution, 50th Anniversary **Obv:** National arms within wreath **Rev:** Five scenes in medallions

Date	Mintage	F	VF	XF	Unc	BU
2009 Antique patina	2,009	—	—	—	—	15.00

KM# 908   PESO
26.0000 g., Copper-Nickel, 38 mm. **Subject:** Fidel & Raul Castro **Obv:** National arms within wreath

Date	Mintage	F	VF	XF	Unc	BU
2009	5,000	—	—	—	—	15.00

KM# 908a   PESO
26.0000 g., Copper, 38 mm. **Subject:** Fidel and Raul Castro

Date	Mintage	F	VF	XF	Unc	BU
2009	5,000	—	—	—	—	15.00

KM# 910   PESO
26.0000 g., Copper-Nickel, 38 mm. **Subject:** Manatee

Date	Mintage	F	VF	XF	Unc	BU
2009	—	—	—	—	—	15.00

KM# 956   PESO
Gold, 45 mm. **Subject:** Revolution, 50th Anniversary

Date	Mintage	F	VF	XF	Unc	BU
2009 Proof	50	Value: 2,000				

KM# 954   PESO
26.0000 g., Copper-Nickel, 38 mm. **Obv:** National arms within wreath **Rev:** Castro and Hemingway

Date	Mintage	F	VF	XF	Unc	BU
2010	5,000	—	—	—	—	15.00

KM# 954a   PESO
26.0000 g., Copper, 38 mm. **Obv:** National arms within wreath **Rev:** Castro and Hemingway

Date	Mintage	F	VF	XF	Unc	BU
2010	5,000	—	—	—	—	15.00

KM# 954b   PESO
20.0000 g., 0.9990 Silver 0.6423 oz. ASW, 38 mm. **Obv:** National arms within wreath **Rev:** Castro and Hemingway

Date	Mintage	F	VF	XF	Unc	BU
2010 Proof	5,000	Value: 45.00				

KM# 955   PESO
26.0000 g., Copper-Nickel, 38 mm. **Subject:** Independence of the Americas, 200th Anniversary **Obv:** National arms at left and legend at right **Rev:** Sunburst and map of the Americas

Date	Mintage	F	VF	XF	Unc	BU
2011	—	—	—	—	—	15.00

KM# 955a   PESO
26.0000 g., Copper, 38 mm. **Subject:** Independence of the Americas, 200th Anniversary **Obv:** National arms within wreath at left, legend at right **Rev:** Sunburst and map of the Americas

Date	Mintage	F	VF	XF	Unc	BU
2011	—	—	—	—	—	15.00

KM# 955b   PESO
20.0000 g., 0.9990 Silver 0.6423 oz. ASW, 38 mm. **Subject:** Independence of the Americas, 200th Anniversary **Obv:** National arms at left, legend at right **Rev:** Sunburst and map of the Americas

Date	Mintage	F	VF	XF	Unc	BU
2011 Proof	1,810	Value: 45.00				

KM# 346a   3 PESOS
8.2000 g., Nickel Clad Steel, 26.3 mm. **Obv:** National arms within wreath, denomination below **Rev:** Head facing, date below **Note:** Shield varieties exist.

Date	Mintage	F	VF	XF	Unc	BU
2002	—	—	—	2.50	5.00	7.00

KM# 739   5 PESOS
1.2400 g., Gold, 14 mm. **Subject:** Wonders of the Ancient World **Obv:** Cuban arms **Rev:** Ancient lighthouse of Alexandria

Date	Mintage	F	VF	XF	Unc	BU
2005 Proof	5,000	Value: 85.00				

KM# 740   5 PESOS
1.2400 g., Gold, 14 mm. **Subject:** Wonders of the Ancient World **Obv:** Cuban arms **Rev:** Colossus of Rhodes

Date	Mintage	F	VF	XF	Unc	BU
2005 Proof	5,000	Value: 75.00				

KM# 741   5 PESOS
1.2400 g., Gold, 14 mm. **Subject:** Wonders of the Ancient World **Obv:** Cuban arms **Rev:** Hanging Gardens of Babylon

Date	Mintage	F	VF	XF	Unc	BU
2005 Proof	5,000	Value: 75.00				

KM# 742   5 PESOS
1.2400 g., Gold, 14 mm. **Subject:** Wonders of the Ancient World **Obv:** Cuban arms **Rev:** Egyptian Pyramids

Date	Mintage	F	VF	XF	Unc	BU
2005	5,000	Value: 75.00				

KM# 743   5 PESOS
1.2400 g., Gold, 14 mm. **Subject:** Wonders of the Ancient World **Obv:** Cuban arms **Rev:** Temple of Artemis

Date	Mintage	F	VF	XF	Unc	BU
2005 Proof	5,000	Value: 75.00				

KM# 744   5 PESOS
1.2400 g., Gold, 14 mm. **Subject:** Wonders of the Ancient World **Obv:** Cuban arms **Rev:** Statue of Jupiter

Date	Mintage	F	VF	XF	Unc	BU
2005	5,000	Value: 75.00				

KM# 745   5 PESOS
1.2400 g., Gold, 14 mm. **Subject:** Wonders of the Ancient World **Obv:** Cuban arms **Rev:** Mausoleum of Halicarnas

Date	Mintage	F	VF	XF	Unc	BU
2005 Proof	5,000	Value: 75.00				

KM# 746   5 PESOS
1.2400 g., Gold, 14 mm. **Obv:** Cuban arms **Rev:** Cortes, Montezuma and Aztec Pyramid

Date	Mintage	F	VF	XF	Unc	BU
2005 Proof	15,000	Value: 75.00				

KM# 885   5 PESOS
12.0000 g., Silver, 30 mm. **Subject:** Che Guevara, 40th Anniversary of his Death

Date	Mintage	F	VF	XF	Unc	BU
2007 Proof	—	Value: 45.00				

KM# 763   10 PESOS
20.0000 g., 0.9990 Silver 0.6423 oz. ASW, 38 mm. **Subject:** Third Globalization Conference **Obv:** Cuban arms **Rev:** World map

Date	Mintage	F	VF	XF	Unc	BU
2001 Proof	100	Value: 200				

KM# 764   10 PESOS
20.0000 g., 0.9990 Silver 0.6423 oz. ASW, 38 mm. **Subject:** 40th Anniversary - Battle of Giron **Obv:** Cuban arms **Rev:** Soldiers on tank

Date	Mintage	F	VF	XF	Unc	BU
2001 Proof	3,000	Value: 45.00				

KM# 765   10 PESOS
31.1035 g., 0.9990 Silver 0.9990 oz. ASW, 38 mm. **Subject:** 106th Anniversary - Jose Marti's **Obv:** Cuban arms **Rev:** Monument

Date	Mintage	F	VF	XF	Unc	BU
2001 Proof	2,000	Value: 50.00				

KM# 762   10 PESOS
31.1035 g., 0.9990 Silver 0.9990 oz. ASW, 38 mm. **Obv:** Cuban arms **Rev:** Two Bee hummingbirds

Date	Mintage	F	VF	XF	Unc	BU
2001 Proof	20,000	Value: 45.00				

KM# 766   10 PESOS
15.0000 g., 0.9990 Silver 0.4818 oz. ASW, 35 mm. **Subject:** Cuban Fauna **Obv:** Cuban arms **Rev:** Red-splashed Sulphur butterfly

Date	Mintage	F	VF	XF	Unc	BU
2001 Proof	5,000	Value: 40.00				

KM# 767   10 PESOS
15.0000 g., 0.9990 Silver 0.4818 oz. ASW, 35 mm. **Subject:**

Cuban Fauna **Obv:** Cuban arms **Rev:** Cuban Parrot

Date	Mintage	F	VF	XF	Unc	BU
2001 Proof	5,000	Value: 40.00				

KM# 768 10 PESOS
15.0000 g., 0.9990 Silver 0.4818 oz. ASW, 35 mm. **Obv:** National arms **Rev:** Cuban (Green) woodpecker

Date	Mintage	F	VF	XF	Unc	BU
2001 Proof	5,000	Value: 40.00				

KM# 769 10 PESOS
15.0000 g., 0.9990 Silver 0.4818 oz. ASW, 35 mm. **Obv:** Cuban arms **Rev:** Multicolor white orchid

Date	Mintage	F	VF	XF	Unc	BU
2001 Proof	5,000	Value: 35.00				

KM# 770 10 PESOS
15.0000 g., 0.9990 Silver 0.4818 oz. ASW, 35 mm. **Subject:** Cuban Flora **Obv:** Cuban arms **Rev:** Multicolor yellow orchid

Date	Mintage	F	VF	XF	Unc	BU
2001 Proof	5,000	Value: 35.00				

KM# 771 10 PESOS
15.0000 g., 0.9990 Silver 0.4818 oz. ASW, 35 mm. **Subject:** Cuban Flora **Obv:** Cuban arms **Rev:** Multicolor pink orchid

Date	Mintage	F	VF	XF	Unc	BU
2001 Proof	5,000	Value: 35.00				

KM# 772 10 PESOS

31.1035 g., 0.9990 Silver 0.9990 oz. ASW, 42 mm. **Obv:** Cuban arms **Rev:** Multicolor Santa Maria

Date	Mintage	F	VF	XF	Unc	BU
2001 Proof	4,000	Value: 55.00				

KM# 773 10 PESOS
15.0000 g., 0.9990 Silver 0.4818 oz. ASW, 35 mm. **Subject:** World Cup Soccer Champions **Obv:** Cuban arms **Rev:** Soccer player and stadium

Date	Mintage	F	VF	XF	Unc	BU
2001 Proof	7,500	Value: 35.00				

KM# 774 10 PESOS
20.0000 g., 0.9990 Silver 0.6423 oz. ASW, 38 mm. **Subject:** Cuban Monuments **Obv:** Cuban arms **Rev:** Trinidad street view

Date	Mintage	F	VF	XF	Unc	BU
2001 Proof	5,000	Value: 45.00				

KM# 775 10 PESOS
20.0000 g., 0.9990 Silver 0.6423 oz. ASW, 38 mm. **Subject:** Cuban Monuments **Obv:** Cuban arms **Rev:** Havana Cathedral

Date	Mintage	F	VF	XF	Unc	BU
2001 Proof	5,000	Value: 45.00				

KM# 776 10 PESOS
20.0000 g., 0.9990 Silver 0.6423 oz. ASW, 38 mm. **Subject:** Cuban Monuments **Obv:** Cuban arms **Rev:** Template building

Date	Mintage	F	VF	XF	Unc	BU
2001 Proof	5,000	Value: 45.00				

KM# 777 10 PESOS
31.1035 g., 0.9990 Silver 0.9990 oz. ASW, 38 mm. **Obv:** Cuban arms **Rev:** Bolivar standing at his birthplace

Date	Mintage	F	VF	XF	Unc	BU
2001 Proof	5,000	Value: 50.00				

KM# 828 10 PESOS
20.0000 g., 0.9990 Silver 0.6423 oz. ASW **Subject:** XVII World Soccer Championship - Korea and Japan 2002 **Obv:** National arms

Date	Mintage	F	VF	XF	Unc	BU
2001 proof	—	Value: 50.00				

KM# 778 10 PESOS
31.1035 g., 0.9990 Silver 0.9990 oz. ASW, 38 mm. **Obv:** Cuban arms **Rev:** Bolivar and map of South America

Date	Mintage	F	VF	XF	Unc	BU
2001 Proof	5,000	Value: 50.00				

KM# 779 10 PESOS
31.1035 g., 0.9990 Silver 0.9990 oz. ASW, 38 mm. **Subject:** 180th Anniversary of the Battle of Carabobo **Obv:** Cuban arms **Rev:** Bolivar leading troops

Date	Mintage	F	VF	XF	Unc	BU
2001 Proof	5,000	Value: 50.00				

KM# 734 10 PESOS
20.0000 g., 0.9990 Silver 0.6423 oz. ASW, 37.9 mm. **Subject:** Olympics **Obv:** Cuban arms **Rev:** Runner and ancient ruins **Edge:** Reeded

Date	Mintage	F	VF	XF	Unc	BU
2002 Proof	—	Value: 40.00				

KM# 780 10 PESOS
20.0000 g., 0.9990 Silver 0.6423 oz. ASW, 38 mm. **Subject:** World Cup Soccer Champions **Obv:** Cuban arms **Rev:** Soccer player and map above "CHILE 1962"

Date	Mintage	F	VF	XF	Unc	BU
2002 Proof	7,500	Value: 40.00				

KM# 781 10 PESOS
20.0000 g., 0.9990 Silver 0.6423 oz. ASW, 38 mm. **Subject:**
World Cup Soccer Champions **Obv:** Cuban arms **Rev:** Soccer
player and Cuauhtemoc head below MEXICO 1970

Date	Mintage	F	VF	XF	Unc	BU
2002 Proof	7,500	Value: 40.00				

KM# 782 10 PESOS
20.0000 g., 0.9990 Silver 0.6423 oz. ASW, 38 mm. **Obv:** Cuban
arms **Rev:** Vasco De Gama and ship

Date	Mintage	F	VF	XF	Unc	BU
2002 Proof	5,000	Value: 45.00				

KM# 783 10 PESOS
20.0000 g., 0.9990 Silver 0.6423 oz. ASW, 38 mm. **Obv:** Cuban
arms **Rev:** Americo Vespucio and ship

Date	Mintage	F	VF	XF	Unc	BU
2002 Proof	5,000	Value: 45.00				

KM# 784 10 PESOS
31.1035 g., 0.9990 Silver 0.9990 oz. ASW, 38 mm. **Subject:**
Leaders of Communism **Obv:** Cuban arms **Rev:** Head of Mao
Tse Tung left

Date	Mintage	F	VF	XF	Unc	BU
2002 Proof	2,000	Value: 55.00				

KM# 785 10 PESOS
31.1035 g., 0.9990 Silver 0.9990 oz. ASW, 38 mm. **Subject:**
Leaders of Communism **Obv:** Cuban arms **Rev:** Head of Karl
Marx 3/4 left

Date	Mintage	F	VF	XF	Unc	BU
2002 Proof	2,000	Value: 55.00				

KM# 786 10 PESOS
31.1035 g., 0.9990 Silver 0.9990 oz. ASW, 38 mm. **Subject:**
Leaders of Communism **Obv:** Cuban arms **Rev:** Head of Vladimir
Lenin right

Date	Mintage	F	VF	XF	Unc	BU
2002 Proof	2,000	Value: 65.00				

KM# 787 10 PESOS
31.1035 g., 0.9990 Silver 0.9990 oz. ASW, 38 mm. **Subject:**
Leaders of Communism **Obv:** Cuban arms **Rev:** Head of
Federico Engels 3/4 right

Date	Mintage	F	VF	XF	Unc	BU
2002 Proof	2,000	Value: 55.00				

KM# 788 10 PESOS
27.0000 g., 0.9990 Silver 0.8672 oz. ASW, 40 mm. **Subject:**
IBERO-AMERICA Series **Obv:** Circle of arms around Cuban
arms **Rev:** Santisima Trinidad ship

Date	Mintage	F	VF	XF	Unc	BU
2002 Proof	14,000	Value: 50.00				

KM# 952 10 PESOS
27.0000 g., 0.9250 Silver 0.8029 oz. ASW **Obv:** National Arms
surrounded by 10 older arms **Rev:** Santisima Trinidad, sailing
ship

Date	Mintage	F	VF	XF	Unc	BU
2002 Proof	—	Value: 60.00				

KM# 793 10 PESOS
31.1000 g., 0.9990 Silver 0.9988 oz. ASW, 38 mm. **Subject:**
World Cup Soccer - Germany 2006 **Obv:** Cuban arms **Rev:** 5
soccer players

Date	Mintage	F	VF	XF	Unc	BU
2003 Proof	50,000	Value: 45.00				

KM# 789 10 PESOS
31.1035 g., 0.9990 Silver 0.9990 oz. ASW, 38 mm. **Subject:**
Jose Marti's 150th Birthday **Obv:** Cuban arms **Rev:** Numbered
infield behind head right

Date	Mintage	F	VF	XF	Unc	BU
2003 Proof	150	Value: 150				

KM# 794 10 PESOS
20.0000 g., 0.9990 Silver 0.6423 oz. ASW, 38 mm. **Subject:**
Endangered Wildlife **Obv:** Cuban arms **Rev:** Cuban Crocodile

Date	Mintage	F	VF	XF	Unc	BU
2003 Proof	5,000	Value: 50.00				

KM# 795 10 PESOS
20.0000 g., 0.9990 Silver 0.6423 oz. ASW, 38 mm. **Subject:**
Endangered Wildlife **Obv:** Cuban arms **Rev:** Ocelot

Date	Mintage	F	VF	XF	Unc	BU
2003 Proof	5,000	Value: 50.00				

KM# 792 10 PESOS
20.0000 g., 0.9990 Silver 0.6423 oz. ASW, 38 mm. **Obv:** Cuban
arms **Rev:** Che Guevara, 75th Anniversary of Birth

Date	Mintage	F	VF	XF	Unc	BU
2003 Proof	5,000	Value: 45.00				

KM# 791 10 PESOS

20.0000 g., 0.9990 Silver 0.6423 oz. ASW, 38 mm. **Obv:** Cuban arms **Rev:** Sailing ship, Sovereign of the Seas

Date	Mintage	F	VF	XF	Unc	BU
2003 Proof	5,000	Value: 45.00				

KM# 790 10 PESOS
20.0000 g., 0.9990 Silver 0.6423 oz. ASW, 38 mm. **Obv:** Cuban arms **Rev:** Ferdinand Magellan, ship, and astrolab

Date	Mintage	F	VF	XF	Unc	BU
2003 Proof	5,000	Value: 45.00				

KM# 727 10 PESOS
Silver **Subject:** Endangered wildlife **Rev:** Iguana

Date	Mintage	F	VF	XF	Unc	BU
2003 Proof	—	Value: 45.00				

KM# 921 10 PESOS
Silver **Subject:** World Cup, Germany **Rev:** Five soccer players

Date	Mintage	F	VF	XF	Unc	BU
2003 Proof	50,000	Value: 60.00				

KM# 796 10 PESOS
20.0000 g., 0.9990 Silver 0.6423 oz. ASW, 38 mm. **Obv:** Cuban arms **Rev:** John Cabot's portrait in cameo above ship

Date	Mintage	F	VF	XF	Unc	BU
2004 Proof	5,000	Value: 45.00				

KM# 797 10 PESOS
15.0000 g., 0.9990 Silver 0.4818 oz. ASW, 35 mm. **Subject:** Hippocampus Kuda **Obv:** Cuban arms **Rev:** Spotted seahorse

Date	Mintage	F	VF	XF	Unc	BU
2004 Proof	5,000	Value: 50.00				

KM# 798 10 PESOS
20.0000 g., 0.9990 Silver 0.6423 oz. ASW, 38 mm. **Obv:** Cuban arms **Rev:** Murphy's Petrel bird on rock

Date	Mintage	F	VF	XF	Unc	BU
2004 Proof	5,000	Value: 50.00				

KM# 799 10 PESOS
20.0000 g., 0.9990 Silver 0.6423 oz. ASW, 38 mm. **Obv:** Cuban arms **Rev:** Cuban Rock Iguana on branch

Date	Mintage	F	VF	XF	Unc	BU
2004 Proof	5,000	Value: 50.00				

KM# 800 10 PESOS
31.1000 g., 0.9990 Silver 0.9988 oz. ASW, 38 mm. **Obv:** Cuban arms **Rev:** Imperial eagle perched on branch

Date	Mintage	F	VF	XF	Unc	BU
2004 Proof	1,000	Value: 60.00				

KM# 801 10 PESOS
31.1000 g., 0.9990 Silver 0.9988 oz. ASW, 38 mm. **Obv:** Cuban arms **Rev:** Bearded vulture in flight

Date	Mintage	F	VF	XF	Unc	BU
2004 Proof	1,000	Value: 60.00				

KM# 802 10 PESOS
31.1000 g., 0.9990 Silver 0.9988 oz. ASW, 38 mm. **Obv:** Cuban arms **Rev:** Iberian Lynx

Date	Mintage	F	VF	XF	Unc	BU
2004 Proof	1,000	Value: 60.00				

KM# 803 10 PESOS
31.1000 g., 0.9990 Silver 0.9988 oz. ASW, 38 mm. **Obv:** Cuban arms **Rev:** 2 grey wolves

Date	Mintage	F	VF	XF	Unc	BU
2004 Proof	1,000	Value: 65.00				

KM# 804 10 PESOS
31.1000 g., 0.9990 Silver 0.9988 oz. ASW, 38 mm. **Obv:** Cuban arms **Rev:** Brown bear

Date	Mintage	F	VF	XF	Unc	BU
2004	—	—	—	—		35.00
2004 Proof	1,000	Value: 65.00				

KM# 805 10 PESOS
31.1000 g., 0.9990 Silver 0.9988 oz. ASW, 38 mm. **Obv:** Cuban arms **Rev:** Peregrine Falcon perches on branch

Date	Mintage	F	VF	XF	Unc	BU
2004 Proof	1,000	Value: 65.00				

KM# 806 10 PESOS
20.0000 g., 0.9990 Silver 0.6423 oz. ASW, 38 mm. **Subject:** Monuments of Cuba **Obv:** Cuban arms **Rev:** University of Havana building

Date	Mintage	F	VF	XF	Unc	BU
2004 Proof	1,500	Value: 50.00				

KM# 807 10 PESOS
20.0000 g., 0.9990 Silver 0.6423 oz. ASW, 38 mm. **Subject:** Monuments of Cuba **Obv:** Cuban arms **Rev:** Fountain of India

Date	Mintage	F	VF	XF	Unc	BU
2004 Proof	1,500	Value: 50.00				

KM# 808 10 PESOS
20.0000 g., 0.9990 Silver 0.6423 oz. ASW, 38 mm. **Subject:** Monuments of Cuba **Obv:** Cuban arms **Rev:** Plaza building

Date	Mintage	F	VF	XF	Unc	BU
2004 Proof	1,500	Value: 50.00				

KM# 923 10 PESOS
15.0000 g., 0.9990 Silver 0.4818 oz. ASW **Rev:** Sea Horse and coral reef in color

Date	Mintage	F	VF	XF	Unc	BU
2004 Proof	—	Value: 40.00				

KM# 809 10 PESOS
27.0000 g., 0.9250 Silver 0.8029 oz. ASW, 40 mm. **Obv:** Cuban arms within circle of arms **Rev:** Portions of the old Havana Wall

Date	Mintage	F	VF	XF	Unc	BU
2005 Proof	12,000	Value: 75.00				

KM# 810 10 PESOS
20.0000 g., 0.9990 Silver 0.6423 oz. ASW, 38 mm. **Subject:** Tobacco **Obv:** Cuban arms **Rev:** Indian showing tobacco to Columbus, ship in background

Date	Mintage	F	VF	XF	Unc	BU
2005 Proof	2,000	Value: 50.00				

KM# 811 10 PESOS
20.0000 g., 0.9250 Silver 0.5948 oz. ASW, 38 mm. **Subject:** Columbus' Ships **Obv:** Cuban arms **Rev:** The Santa Maria under sail

Date	Mintage	F	VF	XF	Unc	BU
2005 Proof	5,000	Value: 45.00				

KM# 812 10 PESOS
20.0000 g., 0.9250 Silver 0.5948 oz. ASW, 38 mm. **Subject:** Columbus' Ships **Obv:** Cuban arms **Rev:** The Nina under sail

Date	Mintage	F	VF	XF	Unc	BU
2005 Proof	5,000	Value: 45.00				

KM# 813 10 PESOS
20.0000 g., 0.9250 Silver 0.5948 oz. ASW, 38 mm. **Subject:** Columbus' Ships **Obv:** Cuban arms **Rev:** The Pinta under sail

Date	Mintage	F	VF	XF	Unc	BU
2005 Proof	5,000	Value: 45.00				

KM# 814 10 PESOS
20.0000 g., 0.9250 Silver 0.5948 oz. ASW, 38 mm. **Obv:** Cuban arms **Rev:** Cuban Solenodon on branch

Date	Mintage	F	VF	XF	Unc	BU
2005 Proof	5,000	Value: 45.00				

KM# 815 10 PESOS
15.0000 g., 0.9990 Silver 0.4818 oz. ASW, 35 mm. **Obv:** Cuban arms **Rev:** Multicolor Solenodon on branch

Date	Mintage	F	VF	XF	Unc	BU
2005 Proof	5,000	Value: 40.00				

KM# 816 10 PESOS
15.0000 g., 0.9250 Silver 0.4461 oz. ASW, 35 mm. **Subject:** Tropical Fish **Obv:** Cuban arms **Rev:** Picassofish (triggerfish)

Date	Mintage	F	VF	XF	Unc	BU
2005 Proof	2,000	Value: 40.00				

KM# 817 10 PESOS
15.0000 g., 0.9250 Silver 0.4461 oz. ASW, 35 mm. **Subject:** Tropical Fish **Obv:** Cuban arms **Rev:** Moorish Idol fish

Date	Mintage	F	VF	XF	Unc	BU
2005 Proof	2,000	Value: 40.00				

KM# 818 10 PESOS
15.0000 g., 0.9250 Silver 0.4461 oz. ASW, 35 mm. **Subject:** Tropical Fish **Obv:** Cuban arms **Rev:** Regal Angel fish

Date	Mintage	F	VF	XF	Unc	BU
2005 Proof	2,000	Value: 40.00				

KM# 819 10 PESOS
20.0000 g., 0.9990 Silver 0.6423 oz. ASW, 38 mm. **Subject:** Don Quijote, 400th Anniversary **Obv:** Cuban arms **Rev:** Don Quijote and Sancho looking at two windmills

Date	Mintage	F	VF	XF	Unc	BU
2005 Proof	5,000	Value: 50.00				

KM# 820 10 PESOS
31.1000 g., 0.9990 Silver 0.9988 oz. ASW, 38 mm. **Subject:** Maximo Gomez Centennial of Death **Obv:** Cuban arms **Rev:** Bust 3/4 left, numbered behind neck

Date	Mintage	F	VF	XF	Unc	BU
2005 Proof	100	Value: 220				

KM# 925 10 PESOS
27.0000 g., 0.9250 Silver 0.8029 oz. ASW, 40 mm. **Subject:** Ibero American sites **Rev:** Old City Wall

Date	Mintage	F	VF	XF	Unc	BU
2005	—	Value: 60.00				

KM# 821 10 PESOS
20.0000 g., 0.9250 Silver 0.5948 oz. ASW, 38 mm. **Subject:** XXIX Olympics **Obv:** Cuban arms **Rev:** Baseball player with bat, baseball background

Date	Mintage	F	VF	XF	Unc	BU
2006 Proof	15,000	Value: 45.00				

KM# 897 10 PESOS
27.0000 g., 0.9250 Silver 0.8029 oz. ASW, 40 mm. **Subject:** Ibero - American Series - Javelin

Date	Mintage	F	VF	XF	Unc	BU
2007 Proof	—	Value: 45.00				

KM# 898 10 PESOS
20.0000 g., Silver, 38 mm. **Subject:** Spitnik

Date	Mintage	F	VF	XF	Unc	BU
2007 Proof	—	Value: 45.00				

KM# 886 10 PESOS
20.0000 g., Silver, 38 mm. **Subject:** Che Guevara, 40th Anniversary of his Death

Date	Mintage	F	VF	XF	Unc	BU
2007 Proof	—	Value: 45.00				

KM# 887 10 PESOS
20.0000 g., Silver, 38 mm. **Subject:** Fauna - Buitre (Condor)

Date	Mintage	F	VF	XF	Unc	BU
2007 Proof	—	Value: 45.00				

KM# 888 10 PESOS
20.0000 g., Silver **Subject:** Fauna Burro

Date	Mintage	F	VF	XF	Unc	BU
2007 Proof	—	Value: 45.00				

KM# 889 10 PESOS
20.0000 g., Silver, 38 mm. **Subject:** Fauna - Cobra Montesa

Date	Mintage	F	VF	XF	Unc	BU
2007 Proof	—				Value: 45.00	

KM# 890 10 PESOS
20.0000 g., Silver, 38 mm. **Subject:** Fauna - Gato Montes

Date	Mintage	F	VF	XF	Unc	BU
2007 Proof	—				—	45.00

KM# 891 10 PESOS
20.0000 g., Silver, 38 mm. **Subject:** Fauna - Mastin Espanol

Date	Mintage	F	VF	XF	Unc	BU
2007 Proof	—				Value: 40.00	

KM# 892 10 PESOS
20.0000 g., Silver, 38 mm. **Subject:** Fauna - Urogallo

Date	Mintage	F	VF	XF	Unc	BU
2007 Proof	—				Value: 45.00	

KM# 893 10 PESOS
20.0000 g., Silver, 38 mm. **Subject:** Fortress - El Morro

Date	Mintage	F	VF	XF	Unc	BU
2007 Proof	—				Value: 45.00	

KM# 894 10 PESOS
20.0000 g., Silver, 38 mm. **Subject:** Fortress - La Fuerza

Date	Mintage	F	VF	XF	Unc	BU
2007 Proof	—				Value: 45.00	

KM# 895 10 PESOS
20.0000 g., Silver, 38 mm. **Subject:** La Punta

Date	Mintage	F	VF	XF	Unc	BU
2007 Proof	—				Value: 45.00	

KM# 896 10 PESOS
20.0000 g., Silver, 20 mm. **Subject:** Garabaldi

Date	Mintage	F	VF	XF	Unc	BU
2007 Proof	—				Value: 45.00	

KM# 899 10 PESOS
20.0000 g., Silver, 38 mm. **Subject:** World Championship Soccer England

Date	Mintage	F	VF	XF	Unc	BU
2007 Proof	—				Value: 45.00	

KM# 904 10 PESOS
20.0000 g., 0.9990 Silver 0.6423 oz. ASW, 38 mm. **Subject:** Ship Principe Asturias

Date	Mintage	F	VF	XF	Unc	BU
2008 Proof	—				Value: 45.00	

KM# 905 10 PESOS
20.0000 g., 0.9990 Silver 0.6423 oz. ASW, 40 mm. **Subject:** Ship - San Carlos **Obv:** National arms within wreath

Date	Mintage	F	VF	XF	Unc	BU
2008 Proof	—				Value: 45.00	

KM# 906 10 PESOS
20.0000 g., 0.9990 Silver 0.6423 oz. ASW, 38 mm. **Subject:** Ship - San Hermene

Date	Mintage	F	VF	XF	Unc	BU
2008 Proof	—				Value: 45.00	

KM# 911 10 PESOS
20.0000 g., 0.9990 Silver 0.6423 oz. ASW, 38 mm. **Subject:** Fidel and Raul Castro

Date	Mintage	F	VF	XF	Unc	BU
2009 Proof	5,000				Value: 45.00	

KM# 912 10 PESOS
20.0000 g., 0.9990 Silver 0.6423 oz. ASW, 38 mm. **Subject:** Manatee **Obv:** National arms in wreath

Date	Mintage	F	VF	XF	Unc	BU
2009 Proof	—				Value: 45.00	

KM# 926 10 PESOS
27.0000 g., 0.9250 Silver 0.8029 oz. ASW, 40 mm. **Subject:** Ibero-American series - Historic coins **Obv:** Cuban arms at center of circle of other national arms **Rev:** Historic coin

Date	Mintage	F	VF	XF	Unc	BU
2010 Proof	12,000				Value: 60.00	

KM# 900 20 PESOS
62.2000 g., 0.9990 Silver 1.9977 oz. ASW, 45 mm. **Subject:** Che Guevara - 40th Anniversary of Death

Date	Mintage	F	VF	XF	Unc	BU
2007 Proof	—				Value: 100	

KM# 913 20 PESOS
62.2100 g., 0.9990 Silver 1.9980 oz. ASW, 45 mm. **Subject:** Revolution 50th Anniversary

Date	Mintage	F	VF	XF	Unc	BU
2009 Proof	1,959				Value: 150	

KM# 922 25 PESOS
7.7800 g., 0.9990 Gold 0.2499 oz. AGW **Subject:** Wold Cup, Germany **Rev:** Soccer player and globe

Date	Mintage	F	VF	XF	Unc	BU
2004 Proof	25,000				Value: 450	

KM# 822 100 PESOS
31.1000 g., 0.9990 Gold 0.9988 oz. AGW, 38 mm. **Subject:** 100th Anniversary - Death of Marti **Obv:** Cuban arms **Rev:** Monument

Date	Mintage	F	VF	XF	Unc	BU
2001 Proof	100				Value: 1,750	

PESO CONVERTIBLE SERIES

KM# 733 CENTAVO
0.7500 g., Aluminum, 16.75 mm. **Obv:** Cuban arms **Rev:** Tower and denomination **Edge:** Plain

Date	Mintage	F	VF	XF	Unc	BU
2001	—	—	—	—	2.00	—
2002	—	—	—	—	2.00	—
2003	—	—	—	—	2.00	—
2005	—	—	—	—	2.00	—
2007	—	—	—	—	2.00	—

KM# 729 CENTAVO
1.7000 g., Copper Plated Steel, 15 mm. **Obv:** National arms within wreath, denomination below **Rev:** Tower and denomination **Edge:** Reeded

Date	Mintage	F	VF	XF	Unc	BU
2002	—	—	—	—	3.00	—
2006	—	—	—	—	3.00	—
2007	—	—	—	—	3.00	—

KM# 575.2 5 CENTAVOS
2.6500 g., Nickel Plated Steel, 18 mm. **Obv:** National arms **Rev:** Casa Colonial **Note:** Coin alignment, recut designs.

Date	Mintage	F	VF	XF	Unc	BU
2001	—	—	—	—	1.00	—
2002	—	—	—	—	1.00	—
2003	—	—	—	—	1.00	—
2004	—	—	—	—	1.00	—
2006	—	—	—	—	1.00	—
2007	—	—	—	—	1.00	—
2008	—	—	—	—	1.00	—

KM# 576.2 10 CENTAVOS
3.9400 g., Nickel Plated Steel, 20 mm. **Obv:** National arms **Rev:** Castillo de la Fuerza **Note:** Coin alignment, recut designs.

Date	Mintage	F	VF	XF	Unc	BU
2002	—	—	—	—	2.00	—
2003	—	—	—	—	2.00	—
2008	—	—	—	—	2.00	—
2009	—	—	—	—	2.00	—

KM# 577.2 25 CENTAVOS
5.7000 g., Nickel Plated Steel, 23 mm. **Obv:** National arms **Rev:** Trinidad **Note:** Coin alignment.

Date	Mintage	F	VF	XF	Unc	BU
2001	—	—	—	—	3.00	—
2002	—	—	—	—	3.00	—
2003	—	—	—	—	3.00	—
2006	—	—	—	—	3.00	—
2007	—	—	—	—	3.00	—
2008	—	—	—	—	3.00	—

KM# 578.2 50 CENTAVOS
7.5000 g., Nickel Plated Steel, 25 mm. **Obv:** Cuban arms **Rev:** Havana Cathedral **Note:** Coin alignment.

Date	Mintage	F	VF	XF	Unc	BU
2002	—	—	—	—	5.00	—
2007	—	—	—	—	5.00	—

KM# 579.2 PESO
8.5000 g., Nickel Plated Steel, 27 mm. **Obv:** National arms **Rev:** Guama **Note:** Coin alignment.

Date	Mintage	F	VF	XF	Unc	BU
2001	—	—	—	—	5.00	—
2007	—	—	—	—	5.00	—

MINT SETS

KM#	Date	Mintage	Identification	Issue Price	Mkt Val
MS3	2001 (3)	—	KM#831-833	—	62.50

CYPRUS

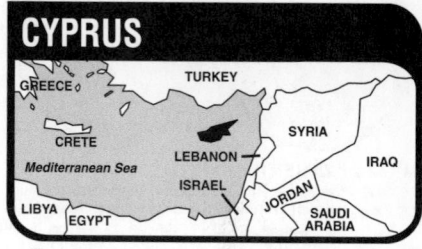

The island of Cyprus lies in the eastern Mediterranean Sea 44 miles (71 km.) south of Turkey and 60 miles (97 km.) off the Syrian coast. It is the third largest island in the Mediterranean Sea, having an area of 3,572 sq. mi. (9,251 sq. km.) and a population of 736,636. Capital: Nicosia. Agriculture, light manufacturing and tourism are the chief industries. Citrus fruit, potatoes, footwear and clothing are exported

Cyprus is a member of the Commonwealth of Nations. The president is Chief of State and Head of Government. Cyprus is also a member of the European Union since May 2004.

MINT MARKS
no mint mark - Royal Mint, London, England
H - Birmingham, England

REPUBLIC

REFORM COINAGE
100 Cents = 1 Pound

KM# 53.3 CENT
2.0000 g., Nickel-Brass, 16.5 mm. **Obv:** Shielded arms within altered wreath, date below **Rev:** Stylized bird on a branch, denomination at left **Edge:** Plain

Date	Mintage	F	VF	XF	Unc	BU
2003	5,000,000	—	—	0.10	0.20	0.30
2004 Narrow figures	12,000,000	—	—	0.10	0.20	0.30

KM# 54.3 2 CENTS
2.5000 g., Nickel-Brass, 19 mm. **Obv:** Shielded arms within altered wreath, date below **Rev:** Stylized goats, denomination upper right **Edge:** Plain

Date	Mintage	F	VF	XF	Unc	BU
2003	5,000,000	—	—	0.15	0.25	0.35
2004	7,000,000	—	—	0.15	0.25	0.35

KM# 55.3 5 CENTS
3.7500 g., Nickel-Brass, 22 mm. **Obv:** Altered wreath around arms **Rev:** Stylized bull's head above denomination **Edge:** Plain

Date	Mintage	F	VF	XF	Unc	BU
2001	15,000,000	—	—	0.20	0.50	0.75
2004	15,000,000	—	—	0.20	0.50	0.75

KM# 56.3 10 CENTS
5.5000 g., Nickel-Brass, 24.5 mm. **Obv:** Altered wreath around arms **Rev:** Decorative vase, denomination above **Edge:** Reeded

Date	Mintage	F	VF	XF	Unc	BU
2002	10,000,000	—	—	0.35	0.75	1.00
2004 Narrow figures	7,000,000	—	—	0.35	0.75	1.00

KM# 62.2 20 CENTS
7.7500 g., Nickel-Brass, 27.25 mm. **Obv:** Altered wreath around arms **Rev:** Head left, denomination at right **Edge:** Reeded

Date	Mintage	F	VF	XF	Unc	BU
2001	15,000,000	—	—	—	1.00	1.50
2004	4,000,000	—	—	—	1.00	1.50

KM# 66 50 CENTS
7.0000 g., Copper-Nickel, 26 mm. **Subject:** Abduction of Europa **Obv:** National arms, date below **Rev:** Female figure riding bull right within square, denomination below **Edge:** Plain **Shape:** 7-sided

Date	Mintage	F	VF	XF	Unc	BU
2002	7,000,000	—	—	—	2.50	3.25
2004	5,000,000	—	—	—	2.50	3.25

KM# 96 POUND
28.2800 g., Copper-Nickel, 38.6 mm. **Obv:** National arms **Rev:** Butterfly on branch

Date	Mintage	F	VF	XF	Unc	BU
2002 Proof	—	Value: 50.00				

KM# 75 POUND
28.2800 g., Copper-Nickel, 38.6 mm. **Subject:** Cyprus Joins the European Union **Obv:** National arms **Rev:** Map in center with Triton trumpeting through a seashell **Edge:** Plain

Date	Mintage	F	VF	XF	Unc	BU
2004	3,000				25.00	50.00

KM# 75a POUND
28.2800 g., 0.9250 Silver 0.8410 oz. ASW, 38.6 mm. **Subject:** Cyprus Joins the European Union **Obv:** National arms **Rev:** Map and Triton trumpeting through a sea shell **Edge:** Plain

Date	Mintage	F	VF	XF	Unc	BU
2004 Proof	3,000	Value: 80.00				

KM# 76 POUND
28.2700 g., Copper-Nickel, 38.5 mm. **Obv:** National arms **Rev:** Mediterranean Monk Seal **Edge:** Plain

Date	Mintage	F	VF	XF	Unc	BU
2005 Proof	4,000	Value: 50.00				

KM# 76a POUND
28.2800 g., 0.9250 Silver 0.8410 oz. ASW **Obv:** National arms **Rev:** Mediterranean Monk Seal **Edge:** Plain

Date	Mintage	F	VF	XF	Unc	BU
2005	4,000	Value: 60.00				

KM# 77 POUND
28.2800 g., Copper-Nickel, 38.6 mm. **Obv:** National arms **Rev:** Akamas Centaurea flowers **Edge:** Plain

Date	Mintage	F	VF	XF	Unc	BU
2006 Prooflike	6,000	Value: 30.00				

KM# 77a POUND
28.2800 g., 0.9250 Silver 0.8410 oz. ASW **Obv:** National arms **Rev:** Akamas Centaurea flowers **Edge:** Plain

Date	Mintage	F	VF	XF	Unc	BU
2006	3,000	Value: 75.00				

KM# 86 POUND
28.2800 g., Copper-Nickel, 38.6 mm. **Subject:** 50th Anniversary Treaty of Rome **Obv:** National arms **Rev:** Open Treaty Book **Edge:** Plain

Date	Mintage	F	VF	XF	Unc	BU
2007 Prooflike	10,000	Value: 28.00				

KM# 87 20 POUNDS
7.9880 g., Gold, 22.05 mm. **Obv:** National arms **Rev:** Greek god Triton, trumpeter (messenger) of the deep sea below outlined map of Cyprus

Date	Mintage	F	VF	XF	Unc	BU
2004 Proof	1,500	Value: 1,000				

EURO COINAGE
European Union Issues

KM# 78 EURO CENT
2.3000 g., Copper Plated Steel, 16.25 mm. **Obv:** Two Mouflons **Rev:** Large value at left, globe at lower right **Edge:** Plain

Date	Mintage	F	VF	XF	Unc	BU
2008	40,000,000	—	—	—	0.35	0.50
2009	20,000,000	—	—	—	0.35	0.50
2010	200,000	—	—	—	0.35	0.50
2011	—	—	—	—	0.35	0.50
2012	—	—	—	—	0.35	0.50

KM# 79 2 EURO CENT
3.0600 g., Copper Plated Steel, 18.75 mm. **Obv:** Two Mouflons **Rev:** Large value at left, globe at lower right **Edge:** Grooved

Date	Mintage	F	VF	XF	Unc	BU
2008	100,000,000	—	—	—	0.50	0.75
2009	1,000,000	—	—	—	0.50	0.75
2010	200,000	—	—	—	0.50	0.75
2011	—	—	—	—	0.50	0.75
2012	—	—	—	—	0.50	0.75

KM# 80 5 EURO CENT
3.9200 g., Copper Plated Steel, 21.25 mm. **Obv:** Two Mouflons **Rev:** Large value at left, globe at lower right **Edge:** Plain

Date	Mintage	F	VF	XF	Unc	BU
2008	60,000,000	—	—	—	1.00	1.25
2009	6,000,000	—	—	—	1.00	1.25
2010	200,000	—	—	—	1.00	1.25
2011	—	—	—	—	1.00	1.25
2012	—	—	—	—	1.00	1.25

KM# 81 10 EURO CENT
4.1000 g., Brass, 19.75 mm. **Obv:** Early sailing boat **Rev:** Modified outline of Europe at left, large value at right **Edge:** Reeded

Date	Mintage	F	VF	XF	Unc	BU
2008	70,000,000	—	—	—	1.25	1.50
2009	1,000,000	—	—	—	1.25	1.50
2010	200,000	—	—	—	1.25	1.50
2011	—	—	—	—	1.25	1.50
2012	—	—	—	—	1.25	1.50

KM# 82 20 EURO CENT
5.7400 g., Brass, 22.25 mm. **Obv:** Early sailing boat **Rev:** Modified outline of Europe at left, large value at right **Edge:** Notched

Date	Mintage	F	VF	XF	Unc	BU
2008	65,000,000	—	—	—	1.50	2.00
2009	1,000,000	—	—	—	1.50	2.00
2010	200,000	—	—	—	1.50	2.00
2011	—	—	—	—	1.50	2.00
2012	—	—	—	—	1.50	2.00

KM# 83 50 EURO CENT
7.8000 g., Brass, 24.25 mm. **Obv:** Early sailing boat **Rev:** Modified outline of Europe at left, large value at right **Edge:** Reeded

Date	Mintage	F	VF	XF	Unc	BU
2008	30,000,000	—	—	—	2.00	2.50
2009	1,000,000	—	—	—	2.00	2.50
2010	200,000	—	—	—	2.00	2.50
2011	—	—	—	—	2.00	2.50
2012	—	—	—	—	2.00	2.50

KM# 84 EURO
7.5000 g., Bi-Metallic Copper-Nickel center in Nickel-Brass ring, 23.25 mm. **Obv:** Ancient cross shaped idol discovered in the village of Pomos in the distrct of Paphos. **Rev:** Large value at left, modified outline of Europe at right **Edge:** Segmented reeding

Date	Mintage	F	VF	XF	Unc	BU
2008	28,000,000	—	—	—	3.50	5.00
2009	4,000,000	—	—	—	3.50	5.00
2010	200,000	—	—	—	3.50	5.00
2011	—	—	—	—	3.50	5.00
2012	—	—	—	—	3.50	5.00

KM# 85 2 EURO
8.5000 g., Bi-Metallic Nickel-Brass center in Copper-Nickel ring, 25.75 mm. **Obv:** Ancient cross shaped idol discovered in the village of Pomos in the distrct of Paphos. **Rev:** Large value at left, modified outline of Europe at right

Date	Mintage	F	VF	XF	Unc	BU
2008	25,000,000	—	—	—	5.00	7.00
2009	5,000,000	—	—	—	5.00	7.00
2010	200,000	—	—	—	5.00	7.00
2011	—	—	—	—	5.00	7.00
2012	—	—	—	—	5.00	7.00

KM# 89 2 EURO
8.5000 g., Bi-Metallic Nickel-Brass center in Copper-Nickel ring, 25.75 mm. **Subject:** 10th Anniversary of Euro **Obv:** Ancient statue wearing a cross found in Solol **Rev:** Childs drawing of a stick figure and 2E

Date	Mintage	F	VF	XF	Unc	BU
2009	980,000	—	—	—	5.00	7.00
2009 Special Unc.	20,000	—	—	—	—	15.00
2009 Proof	—	Value: 25.00				

KM# 97 2 EURO
8.5000 g., Bi-Metallic Nickel-Brass center in Copper-Nickel ring, 25.75 mm. **Subject:** Euro Coinage, 10th Anniversary **Obv:** Euro symbol on globe, child-like rendering around

Date	Mintage	F	VF	XF	Unc	BU
2012	1,000,000	—	—	—	6.00	8.00
2012 Special Unc.	5,000	—	—	—	—	15.00
2012 Proof	8,000	Value: 25.00				

KM# 88 5 EURO
28.2800 g., 0.9250 Silver 0.8410 oz. ASW, 38.61 mm. **Subject:** Entry into Euro Zone **Obv:** National arms **Rev:** Euro band around outlined Europe and Cyprus **Edge:** Reeded

Date	Mintage	F	VF	XF	Unc	BU
2008 Proof	15,000	Value: 75.00				

KM# 94 5 EURO
28.2800 g., 0.9250 Silver 0.8410 oz. ASW, 38.61 mm. **Subject:** Republic of Cyprus, 50th Anniversary **Obv:** National arms **Rev:** Bird in stylized tree

Date	Mintage	F	VF	XF	Unc	BU
2010 Proof	5,000	Value: 65.00				

KM# 95 20 EURO
7.9900 g., 0.9000 Gold 0.2312 oz. AGW, 22 mm. **Subject:** Republic of Cyprus, 50th Anniversary **Obv:** National arms **Rev:** Bird in stylized tree **Edge:** Reeded

Date	Mintage	F	VF	XF	Unc	BU
2010 Proof	750	Value: 400				

CZECH REPUBLIC

The Czech Republic was formerly united with Slovakia as Czechoslovakia. It is bordered in the west by Germany, to the north by Poland, to the east by Slovakia and to the south by Austria. It consists of 3 major regions: Bohemia, Moravia and Silesia and has an area of 30,450 sq. mi. (78,864 sq. km.) and a population of 10.4 million. Capital: Prague (Praha). Agriculture and livestock are chief occupations while coal deposits are the main mineral resources.

MINT MARKS
(c) - castle = Hamburg
(cr) - cross = British Royal Mint
(l) - leaf = Royal Canadian
(m) - crowned *b* or *CM* = Jablonec nad Nisou
(mk) - *MK* in circle = Kremnica
(o) - broken circle = Vienna (Wien)

MONETARY SYSTEM
1 Czechoslovak Koruna (Kcs) = 1 Czech Koruna (Kc)
1 Koruna = 100 Haleru

REPUBLIC
STANDARD COINAGE

KM# 6 10 HALERU
0.6000 g., Aluminum, 15.5 mm. **Obv:** Crowned Czech lion left, date below **Rev:** Denomination and stylized river **Edge:** Plain **Note:** Two varieties of mint marks exist for 1994.

Date	Mintage	F	VF	XF	Unc	BU
2001(m)	40,525,000	—	—	—	0.20	—
2001(m) Proof	2,500	Value: 10.00				
2002(m)	81,496,000	—	—	—	0.20	—
2002(m) Proof	3,490	Value: 10.00				
2003(m)	3,022,350	—	—	—	0.20	—
2003(m) Proof	3,000	Value: 7.00				
2004(m)	—	—	—	—	0.20	—
2004(m) Proof	—	Value: 7.00				
2005(m)	—	—	—	—	0.20	—

KM# 2.3 20 HALERU
0.7400 g., Aluminum, 17 mm. **Obv:** Crowned Czech lion left, date above **Rev:** Open 2 in denomination, "h" above angle line **Edge:** Reeded **Note:** Medal alignment.

Date	Mintage	F	VF	XF	Unc	BU
2001(m)	44,425,000	—	—	—	0.30	—
2001(m) Proof	2,500	Value: 12.50				
2002(m)	20,000	—	—	—	0.30	—
2002(m) Proof	3,490	Value: 12.50				
2003(m)	22,200	—	—	—	0.30	—
2003(m) Proof	3,000	Value: 7.50				
2004(m)	—	—	—	—	0.30	—
2004(m) Proof	—	Value: 7.50				

KM# 3.2 50 HALERU
0.9000 g., Aluminum, 19 mm. **Obv:** Crowned Czech lion left, date below **Rev:** Large denomination **Edge:** Segmented reeding **Note:** Outlined lettering and larger mint mark

Date	Mintage	F	VF	XF	Unc	BU
2001(m)	21,425,000	—	—	—	0.50	—
2001(m) Proof	2,500	Value: 12.50				
2002(m)	26,246,298	—	—	—	0.50	—
2002(m) Proof	3,490	Value: 12.50				
2003(m)	41,548,000	—	—	—	0.50	—
2003(m) Proof	3,000	Value: 7.50				
2004(m)	931,145	—	—	—	0.50	—
2004(m) Proof	4,000	Value: 7.50				
2005(m)	36,814,000	—	—	—	0.50	—
2005(m) Proof	3,000	Value: 7.50				
2006(m)	40,030,500	—	—	—	0.50	—
2006(m) Proof	2,500	Value: 7.50				
2007(m)	35,020,500	—	—	—	0.50	—
2007(m) Proof	2,500	Value: 7.50				
2008(m)	17,000	—	—	—	0.50	—
2008(m) Proof	2,500	Value: 3.00				
2009(m)	—	—	—	—	0.50	—
2009(m) Proof	2,500	Value: 3.00				

KM# 3.1 50 HALERU
0.9000 g., Aluminum, 19 mm. **Obv:** Crowned Czech lion left, date below **Rev:** Large denomination **Edge:** Segmented reeding **Note:** Prev. KM#3.

Date	Mintage	F	VF	XF	Unc	BU
2001(m)	21,425,000	—	—	—	0.50	—
2001(m) Proof	2,500	Value: 12.50				

KM# 7 KORUNA
3.6000 g., Nickel Plated Steel, 20 mm. **Obv:** Crowned Czech lion left, date below **Rev:** Denomination above crown **Edge:** Reeded **Note:** Two varieties of mint marks exist for 1996. 2000-03 have two varieties in the artist monogram.

Date	Mintage	F	VF	XF	Unc	BU
2001(m)	15,938,353	—	—	—	0.60	—
2001(m) Proof	2,500	Value: 20.00				
2002(m)	26,244,666	—	—	—	0.60	—
2002(m) Proof	3,490	Value: 20.00				
2003(m)	36,877,440	—	—	—	0.60	—
2003(m) Proof	3,000	Value: 10.00				
2004(m)	30,500	—	—	—	0.60	—
2004(m) Proof	4,000	Value: 10.00				
2005(m)	14,000	—	—	—	0.60	—
2005(m) Proof	3,000	Value: 10.00				
2006(m)	27,097,500	—	—	—	0.60	—
2006(m) Proof	2,500	Value: 10.00				
2007(m)	14,170,500	—	—	—	0.60	—
2007(m) Proof	2,500	Value: 10.00				
2008(m)	29,617,000	—	—	—	0.60	—
2008(m) Proof	2,500	Value: 6.00				
2009(m)	38,367,400	—	—	—	0.60	—

Date	Mintage	F	VF	XF	Unc	BU
2009(m) Proof	3,200	Value: 6.00				
2010(m)	15,004,602	—	—	—	0.60	—
2010(m) Proof	3,200	Value: 6.00				
2011(m)	4,000,600	—	—	—	0.60	—
2011(m) Proof	2,500	Value: 6.00				
2012(m)	19,000,000	—	—	—	0.60	—

KM# 9 2 KORUNY
3.7000 g., Nickel Plated Steel, 21.5 mm. **Obv:** Crowned Czech lion left, date below **Rev:** Large denomination, pendant design at left **Edge:** Plain **Shape:** 11-sided **Note:** Two varieties of designer monograms exist for 2001-04.

Date	Mintage	F	VF	XF	Unc	BU
2001(m)	26,117,000	—	—	—	0.65	—
2001(m) Proof	2,500	Value: 20.00				
2002(m)	20,941,084	—	—	—	0.65	—
2002(m) Proof	3,490	Value: 20.00				
2003(m)	20,955,000	—	—	—	0.65	—
2003(m) Proof	3,000	Value: 12.50				
2004(m)	15,658,556	—	—	—	0.65	—
2004(m) Proof	4,000	Value: 10.00				
2005(m)	14,000	—	—	—	0.65	—
2005(m) Proof	3,000	Value: 7.50				
2006(m)	30,500	—	—	—	0.65	—
2006(m) Proof	2,500	Value: 7.50				
2007(m)	30,020,500	—	—	—	0.65	—
2007(m) Proof	2,500	Value: 7.50				
2008(m)	26,267,000	—	—	—	0.65	—
2008(m) Proof	2,500	Value: 5.00				
2009(m)	25,418,000	—	—	—	0.65	—
2009(m) Proof	3,200	Value: 5.00				
2010(m)	26,054,000	—	—	—	0.65	—
2010(m) Proof	3,200	Value: 5.00				
2011(m)	12,000,000	—	—	—	0.65	—
2011(m) Proof	2,500	Value: 5.00				
2012(m)	13,000,000	—	—	—	0.65	—

KM# 8 5 KORUN
4.8000 g., Nickel Plated Steel, 23 mm. **Obv:** Crowned Czech lion left, date below **Rev:** Large denomination, Charles bridge and linden leaf **Edge:** Plain

Date	Mintage	F	VF	XF	Unc	BU
2001(m)	25,000	—	—	—	1.00	—
2001(m) Proof	2,500	Value: 27.50				
2002(m)	21,344,995	—	—	—	1.00	—
2002(m) Proof	3,490	Value: 27.50				
2003(m)	22,000	—	—	—	1.00	—
2003(m) Proof	3,000	Value: 15.00				
2004(m)	34,940	—	—	—	1.00	—
2004(m) Proof	4,000	Value: 12.00				
2005(m)	14,000	—	—	—	1.00	—
2005(m) Proof	3,000	Value: 10.00				
2006(m)	25,030,500	—	—	—	1.00	—
2006(m) Proof	2,500	Value: 10.00				
2007(m)	20,500	—	—	—	1.00	—
2007(m) Proof	2,500	Value: 10.00				
2008(m)	11,617,000	—	—	—	1.00	—
2008(m) Proof	2,500	Value: 6.00				
2009(m)	19,911,000	—	—	—	1.00	—
2009(m) Proof	3,200	Value: 6.00				
2010(m)	14,711,000	—	—	—	1.00	—
2010(m) Proof	3,200	Value: 6.00				
2011(m)	—	—	—	—	1.00	—
2011(m) Proof	5,500	Value: 6.00				

KM# 4 10 KORUN
7.6200 g., Copper Plated Steel, 24.5 mm. **Obv:** Crowned Czech lion left, date below **Rev:** Brno Cathedral, denomination below **Edge:** Reeded **Note:** Position of designer's initials on reverse change during the 1995 strike.

Date	Mintage	F	VF	XF	Unc	BU
2001(m)	25,000	—	—	—	1.50	—
2001(m) Proof	2,500	Value: 28.00				
2002(m)	20,156	—	—	—	1.50	—
2002(m) Proof	3,490	Value: 28.00				
2003(m)	18,747,000	—	—	—	1.50	—
2003(m) Proof	3,000	Value: 17.50				
2004(m)	2,255,740	—	—	—	1.50	—
2004(m) Proof	4,000	Value: 14.00				
2005(m)	14,000	—	—	—	1.50	—
2005(m) Proof	3,000	Value: 10.00				
2006(m)	30,500	—	—	—	1.50	—
2006(m) Proof	2,500	Value: 10.00				

Date	Mintage	F	VF	XF	Unc	BU
2007(m)	20,500	—	—	—	1.50	—
2007(m) Proof	2,500	Value: 10.00				
2008(m)	10,092,000	—	—	—	1.50	—
2008(m) Proof	2,500	Value: 7.00				
2009(m)	10,511,000	—	—	—	1.50	—
2009(m) Proof	3,200	Value: 7.00				
2010(m)	16,811,000	—	—	—	1.50	—
2010(m) Proof	3,200	Value: 7.00				
2011(m)	—	—	—	—	1.50	—
2011(m) Proof	5,500	Value: 7.00				

KM# 5 20 KORUN
8.4300 g., Brass Plated Steel, 26 mm. **Obv:** Crowned Czech lion left, date below **Rev:** St. Wenceslas (Duke Vaclav) on horse **Edge:** Plain **Shape:** 13-sided **Note:** Two varieties of mint marks and style of 9's exist for 1997.

Date	Mintage	F	VF	XF	Unc	BU
2001(m)	25,000	—	—	—	2.50	—
2001(m) Proof	2,500	Value: 40.00				
2002(m)	20,996,500	—	—	—	2.50	—
2002(m) Proof	3,490	Value: 40.00				
2003(m)	22,000	—	—	—	2.50	—
2003(m) Proof	3,000	Value: 25.00				
2004(m)	8,249,507	—	—	—	2.50	—
2004(m) Proof	4,000	Value: 22.50				
2005(m)	9,866,778	—	—	—	2.50	—
2005(m) Proof	3,000	Value: 22.50				
2006(m)	2,096,500	—	—	—	2.50	—
2006(m) Proof	2,500	Value: 22.50				
2007(m)	20,500	—	—	—	2.50	—
2007(m) Proof	2,500	Value: 22.50				
2008(m)	17,000	—	—	—	2.50	—
2008(m) Proof	2,500	Value: 10.00				
2009(m)	11,000	—	—	—	2.50	—
2009(m) Proof	3,200	Value: 10.00				
2010(m)	11,000	—	—	—	2.50	—
2010(m) Proof	3,200	Value: 10.00				
2011(m)	8,000,000	—	—	—	2.50	—
2011(m) Proof	5,500	Value: 10.00				
2012(m)	8,000,000	—	—	—	2.50	—

KM# 1 50 KORUN
9.7000 g., Bi-Metallic Brass Plated Steel center in Copper Plated Steel ring, 27.5 mm. **Obv:** Crowned Czech lion left **Rev:** Prague city view **Edge:** Plain

Date	Mintage	F	VF	XF	Unc	BU
2001(m)	16,000	—	—	—	9.00	—
2001(m) Proof	2,500	Value: 80.00				
2002(m)	16,771	—	—	—	9.00	—
2002(m) Proof	3,490	Value: 80.00				
2003(m)	22,000	—	—	—	9.00	—
2003(m) Proof	3,000	Value: 50.00				
2004(m)	34,555	—	—	—	9.00	—
2004(m) Proof	4,000	Value: 40.00				
2005(m)	14,000	—	—	—	9.00	—
2005(m) Proof	3,000	Value: 25.00				
2006(m)	30,500	—	—	—	9.00	—
2006(m) Proof	2,500	Value: 25.00				
2007(m)	20,500	—	—	—	9.00	—
2007(m) Proof	2,500	Value: 25.00				
2008(m)	9,528,300	—	—	—	9.00	—
2008(m) Proof	2,500	Value: 20.00				
2009(m)	36,719,050	—	—	—	9.00	—
2009(m) Proof	3,200	Value: 20.00				
2010(m)	17,210,000	—	—	—	9.00	—
2010(m) Proof	32,000	Value: 20.00				
2011(m)	10,000,000	—	—	—	9.00	—
2011(m) Proof	5,500	Value: 20.00				
2012(m)	10,000,000	—	—	—	9.00	—

KM# 58 200 KORUN
13.0000 g., 0.9000 Silver 0.3761 oz. ASW, 31 mm. **Subject:** Frantisek Skroup **Obv:** Quartered, elongated arms above date **Rev:** Portrait and name **Note:** 1,480 pieces uncirculated and 13 proof remelted.

Date	Mintage	F	VF	XF	Unc	BU
ND(2001)	11,944	—	—	—	16.00	18.00
Note: Milled edge						
ND(2001) Proof	3,179	Value: 35.00				
Note: Plain edge with CESKA NARODNI BANKA *0.900* 13g						

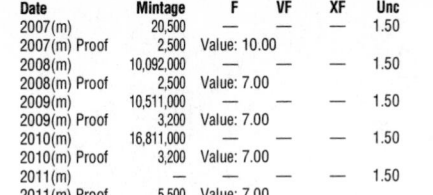

KM# 51 200 KORUN
13.0000 g., 0.9000 Silver 0.3761 oz. ASW, 31 mm. **Subject:** Jaroslav Seifert **Obv:** Quartered arms above denomination **Rev:** Head right, dates at left **Note:** 1,680 pieces uncirculated and 2 proof remelted.

Date	Mintage	F	VF	XF	Unc	BU
ND(2001)	11,746	—	—	—	16.00	18.00
Note: Milled edge						
ND(2001) Proof	3,186	Value: 35.00				
Note: Plain edge with CESKA NARODNI BANKA *0.900* 13g						

KM# 53 200 KORUN
13.0000 g., 0.9000 Silver 0.3761 oz. ASW, 31 mm. **Subject:** 250th Anniversary - Death of Kilian Ignac Dientzenhofer **Obv:** Quartered arms, denomination at right **Rev:** Doorway and caliper **Note:** 1,840 pieces uncirculated and 104 proof remelted.

Date	Mintage	F	VF	XF	Unc	BU
ND(2001)	11,565	—	—	—	16.00	18.00
Note: Milled edge						
ND(2001) Proof	3,282	Value: 35.00				
Note: Plain edge with CESKA NARODNI BANKA *0.900* 13g						

KM# 54 200 KORUN
13.0000 g., 0.9000 Silver 0.3761 oz. ASW, 31 mm. **Subject:** Euro Currency System **Obv:** National arms **Rev:** Prague gros coin design **Note:** 134 pieces uncirculated and 1 proof remelted.

Date	Mintage	F	VF	XF	Unc	BU
ND(2001)	13,730	—	—	—	16.00	18.00
Note: Milled edge						
ND(2001) Proof	3,995	Value: 30.00				
Note: Plain edge with CESKA NARODNI BANKA *0.900* 13g						

KM# 52 200 KORUN
13.0000 g., 0.9000 Silver 0.3761 oz. ASW, 31 mm. **Subject:** Soccer **Obv:** Quartered arms on square, denomination below **Rev:** Rampant lion on soccer ball **Note:** 2,350 pieces uncirculated and 1 proof remelted.

Date	Mintage	F	VF	XF	Unc	BU
ND(2001)	12,050	—	—	—	16.00	18.00
Note: Milled edge						
ND(2001) Proof	3,896	Value: 30.00				
Note: Plain edge with CESKA NARODNI BANKA *0.900* 13g						

KM# 59 200 KORUN
13.0000 g., 0.9000 Silver 0.3761 oz. ASW, 31 mm. **Subject:** Mikolas Ales **Obv:** Four coats of arms above denomination **Rev:** Horse and rider **Note:** 573 pieces uncirculated and 139 proof remelted.

Date	Mintage	F	VF	XF	Unc	BU
ND(2002)	11,879	—	—	—	16.00	18.00
Note: Milled edge						
ND(2002)(m) Proof	4,258	Value: 30.00				
Note: Plain edge with CESKA NARODNI BANKA *0.900* 13g						

KM# 57   200 KORUN
13.0000 g., 0.9000 Silver 0.3761 oz. ASW, 30.9 mm. **Subject:**
Jiri of Podebrady **Obv:** Overlapped arms **Rev:** Head right **Note:**
1,200 pieces uncirculated and 5 proof remelted.

Date	Mintage	F	VF	XF	Unc	BU
ND(2002)	11,729	—	—	—	16.00	18.00

Note: Milled edge
ND(2002) Proof   3,591   Value: 30.00
Note: Plain edge with CESKA NARODNI BANKA *0.900* 13g

KM# 56   200 KORUN
13.0000 g., 0.9000 Silver 0.3761 oz. ASW, 30.9 mm. **Subject:**
Emil Holub **Obv:** National arms, eagles and lions, denomination
below **Rev:** Traveler and African dancers **Note:** 1,350 pieces
uncirculated and 7 proof remelted.

Date	Mintage	F	VF	XF	Unc	BU
ND(2002)	11,602	—	—	—	16.00	18.00

Note: Milled edge
ND(2002) Proof   3,588   Value: 30.00
Note: Plain edge with CESKA NARODNI BANKA *0.900* 13g

KM# 55   200 KORUN
13.0000 g., 0.9000 Silver 0.3761 oz. ASW, 31 mm. **Subject:**
St. Zdislava **Obv:** Old and new arms form diamond above
denomination **Rev:** Saint feeding sick person **Note:** 865 pieces
uncirculated remelted.

Date	Mintage	F	VF	XF	Unc	BU
ND(2002)	12,083	—	—	—	16.00	18.00

Note: Milled edge
ND(2002) Proof   3,596   Value: 30.00
Note: Plain edge with CESKA NARODNI BANKA *0.900* 13g

KM# 60   200 KORUN
13.1400 g., 0.9000 Silver 0.3802 oz. ASW, 31 mm. **Subject:**
Jaroslav Vrchlicky **Obv:** Denomination and quill **Rev:** Bust with
hat facing **Note:** 889 pieces uncirculated and 5 proof remelted.

Date	Mintage	F	VF	XF	Unc	BU
ND(2003)	10,583	—	—	—	16.00	18.00

Note: Milled edge
ND(2003) Proof   3,692   Value: 30.00
Note: Plain edge with CESKA NARODNI BANKA *0.900* 13g

KM# 62   200 KORUN
13.0000 g., 0.9000 Silver 0.3761 oz. ASW, 30.9 mm. **Subject:**
Josef Thomayer **Obv:** National arms **Rev:** Portrait **Note:** 783
uncirculated and 12 proof were remelted.

Date	Mintage	F	VF	XF	Unc	BU
ND(2003)	10,525	—	—	—	16.00	18.00

Note: Milled edge
ND(2003) Proof   3,981   Value: 30.00
Note: Plain edge with CESKA NARODNI BANKA *0.900* 13g

KM# 63   200 KORUN
13.0000 g., 0.9000 Silver 0.3761 oz. ASW, 31 mm. **Subject:**
Tabor-Bechyne Electric Railway **Obv:** Head left **Rev:** Railroad
station scene **Note:** 808 Uncirculated were remelted.

Date	Mintage	F	VF	XF	Unc	BU
ND(2003)	10,986	—	—	—	16.00	18.00

Note: Milled edge
ND(2003) Proof   4,097   Value: 30.00
Note: Plain edge with CESKA NARODNI BANKA *0.900* 13g

KM# 64   200 KORUN
13.0000 g., 0.9000 Silver 0.3761 oz. ASW, 31 mm. **Subject:**
Bohemian Skiers' Union **Obv:** Head 3/4 left **Rev:** Skier **Note:** 680
Uncirculated and 13 proof were remelted.

Date	Mintage	F	VF	XF	Unc	BU
ND(2003)	10,801	—	—	—	16.00	18.00

Note: Milled edge
ND(2003) Proof   4,284   Value: 30.00
Note: Plain edge with CESKA NARODNI BANKA *0.900* 13g

KM# 70   200 KORUN
13.1000 g., 0.9000 Silver 0.3790 oz. ASW, 30.8 mm. **Subject:**
300th Anniversary - Death of pond builder Jakub Krcin **Obv:** Coat
of arms above value with reflected design below **Rev:** Two
fishermen in boat with reflection on water below **Note:** 656
uncirculated remelted.

Date	Mintage	F	VF	XF	Unc	BU
ND(2004)(m)	10,685	—	—	—	16.00	18.00

Note: Milled edge
ND(2004) Proof   3,995   Value: 30.00
Note: Plain edge with CESKA NARODNI BANKA *0.900* 13g

KM# 71   200 KORUN
13.0000 g., 0.9000 Silver 0.3761 oz. ASW **Subject:** Entry into
the European Union **Rev:** State emblems of 15 members of the
European Union

Date	Mintage	F	VF	XF	Unc	BU
2004	13,918	—	—	—	16.00	18.00

Note: Plain edge with codes for EU countries
2004 Proof   9,994   Value: 30.00
Note: Plain edge with CESKA NARODNI BANKA *0.900* 13g

KM# 72   200 KORUN
13.0000 g., 0.9000 Silver 0.3761 oz. ASW, 31 mm. **Subject:**
Prokop Diviš **Obv:** Lighting conductor modulator **Rev:** Head of Diviš

Date	Mintage	F	VF	XF	Unc	BU
2004	10,145	—	—	—	16.00	18.00

Note: Milled edge
2004 Proof   3,897   Value: 30.00
Note: Plain edge with CESKA NARODNI BANKA *0.900* 13g

KM# 73   200 KORUN
13.0000 g., 0.9000 Silver 0.3761 oz. ASW **Subject:** Leos
Janacek **Rev:** Head of Janacek

Date	Mintage	F	VF	XF	Unc	BU
2004	10,143	—	—	—	16.00	18.00

Note: Milled edge
2004 Proof   4,100   Value: 30.00
Note: Plain edge with CESKA NARODNI BANKA *0.900* 13g

KM# 74   200 KORUN
13.0000 g., 0.9000 Silver 0.3761 oz. ASW **Subject:** Kralice Bible
Obv: Enlargement of bible page **Rev:** Bible page

Date	Mintage	F	VF	XF	Unc	BU
2004	10,975	—	—	—	16.00	18.00

Note: Reeded
2004 Proof   5,000   Value: 30.00

KM# 77   200 KORUN
13.0000 g., 0.9000 Silver 0.3761 oz. ASW, 31 mm. **Obv:** Prokop
Divis **Rev:** Lightning conductor

Date	Mintage	F	VF	XF	Unc	BU
2004	—	—	—	—	16.00	18.00

Note: Reeded
2004 Proof   —   Value: 30.00
Note: Plain edge with CESKA NARODNI BANKA * Ag 0.900 * 13g *

KM# 78   200 KORUN
13.0000 g., 0.9000 Silver 0.3761 oz. ASW, 31 mm. **Subject:**
100th Anniversary of Jan Werich and Jiri Voskovec

Date	Mintage	F	VF	XF	Unc	BU
2005	10,884	—	—	—	16.00	18.00

Note: Milled edge
2005 Proof   4,997   Value: 30.00
Note: Plain edge with CESKA NARODNI BANKA *0.900* 13g

KM# 79   200 KORUN
13.0000 g., 0.9000 Silver 0.3761 oz. ASW, 31 mm. **Subject:**

100th Anniversary of Production of 1st Car in Mlada Boleslav
Rev: 1st car of LK factory

Date	Mintage	F	VF	XF	Unc	BU
2005	13,225	—	—	—	16.00	18.00
2005 Proof	10,797	Value: 30.00				

Note: Plain edge with CESKA NARODNI BANKA *0.900* 13g

KM# 80   200 KORUN
13.0000 g., 0.9000 Silver 0.3761 oz. ASW, 31 mm.   **Subject:** 450th Anniversary - Birth of Mikulas Dacicky **Obv:** Arms of Dacicky **Rev:** Head of Mikulas Dacicky z Heslova

Date	Mintage	F	VF	XF	Unc	BU
2005	10,076	—	—	—	16.00	18.00
2005 Proof	5,597	Value: 30.00				

Note: Milled edge

Note: Plain edge with CESKA NARODNI BANKA *0.900* 13g

KM# 84   200 KORUN
13.0000 g., 0.9000 Silver 0.3761 oz. ASW, 31 mm.   **Subject:** 700th Anniversary - Death of Vaclav III **Obv:** Sword between two shields positioned top-to-top **Rev:** King Vaclav III between shields of Bohemia and Moravia

Date	Mintage	F	VF	XF	Unc	BU
2006	10,471	—	—	—	16.00	18.00
2006 Proof	7,497	Value: 30.00				

Note: Milled edge

Note: Plain edge with CESKA NARODNI BANKA *0.900* 13g

KM# 85   200 KORUN
13.0000 g., 0.9000 Silver 0.3761 oz. ASW, 31 mm.   **Subject:** 100th Anniversary - Birth of Jaroslav Jezek **Obv:** Musical score **Rev:** Caricature looking at score

Date	Mintage	F	VF	XF	Unc	BU
2006(m)	10,192	—	—	—	16.00	18.00
2006(m) Proof	15,442	Value: 30.00				

Note: Milled edge

Note: Plain edge with CESKA NARODNI BANKA *0.900* 13g

KM# 81   200 KORUN
13.0000 g., 0.9000 Silver 0.3761 oz. ASW, 31 mm.   **Subject:** 250th Anniversary - Birth of F.J. Gerstner

Date	Mintage	F	VF	XF	Unc	BU
2006	11,101	—	—	—	16.00	18.00
2006 Proof	6,194	Value: 30.00				

Note: Milled edge

Note: Plain edge with CESKA NARODNI BANKA *0.900* 13g

KM# 82   200 KORUN
13.0000 g., 0.9000 Silver 0.3761 oz. ASW, 31 mm.   **Subject:** 150th Anniversary - School of Glass Making in Kamenicky Senov **Obv:** Image of National Arms within glass cube **Rev:** Artistic image within glass cube

Date	Mintage	F	VF	XF	Unc	BU
2006	9,546	—	—	—	16.00	18.00

Note: Milled edge

| 2006 | 6,494 | | | | | Value: 30.00 |

Note: Plain edge with CESKA NARODNI BANKA *0.900* 13g

KM# 83   200 KORUN
13.0000 g., 0.9000 Silver 0.3761 oz. ASW, 31 mm.   **Subject:** 500th Anniversary - Death of Matej Rejsek **Obv:** Pulpit in the church of St. Laurer in Kank **Rev:** Portrait of Rejsek on the Prasna gate in Prague

Date	Mintage	F	VF	XF	Unc	BU
2006	9,594	—	—	—	16.00	18.00
2006 Proof	6,494	Value: 30.00				

Note: Milled edge

Note: Plain edge with CESKA NARODNI BANKA *0.900* 13g

KM# 91   200 KORUN
13.0000 g., 0.9000 Silver 0.3761 oz. ASW, 31 mm.   **Subject:** Founding of Jednota Bratrska, 550th Anniversary **Obv:** Emblem of Jednota Bratrska, tree, ram with flag. **Rev:** Chalice with ram with flag

Date	Mintage	F	VF	XF	Unc	BU
2007	10,471	—	—	—	20.00	22.00
2007 Proof	8,297	Value: 32.00				

Note: Milled edge

Note: Plain edge with CESKA NARODNI BANKA *0.900* 13g

KM# 92   200 KORUN
13.0000 g., 0.9000 Silver 0.3761 oz. ASW, 31 mm.   **Subject:** Charles Bridge cornerstone, 650th anniversary

Date	Mintage	F	VF	XF	Unc	BU
2007	10,772	—	—	—	20.00	22.00
2007 Proof	18,746	Value: 32.00				

Note: Milled edge

Note: Plain edge with CESKA NARODNI BANKA *0.900* 13g

KM# 93   200 KORUN
13.0000 g., 0.9000 Silver 0.3761 oz. ASW, 31 mm.   **Subject:** Jarmila Novotná, 100th Anniversary of Birth **Obv:** Names of the operas in which Novotna sang **Rev:** Head of Novotna

Date	Mintage	F	VF	XF	Unc	BU
2007	9,584	—	—	—	20.00	22.00
2007 Proof	12,788	Value: 32.00				

Note: Milled edge

Note: Plain edge with CESKA NARODNI BANKA *0.900* 13g

KM# 94   200 KORUN
13.0000 g., 0.9000 Silver 0.3761 oz. ASW, 31 mm.   **Subject:** Earth Satelite Launch, 50th Anniversary **Obv:** Satelite and sound signal of satelite **Rev:** Plentary system with satelite

Date	Mintage	F	VF	XF	Unc	BU
2007	10,148	—	—	—	20.00	22.00
2007 Proof	14,797	Value: 32.00				

Note: Milled edge

Note: Plain edge with CESKA NARODNI BANKA *0.900* 13g

KM# 97   200 KORUN
13.0000 g., 0.9000 Silver 0.3761 oz. ASW, 31 mm.   **Subject:** Charles IV Vineyard Planting decree

Date	Mintage	F	VF	XF	Unc	BU
2008	9,768	—	—	—	20.00	22.00
2008 Proof	16,997	Value: 32.00				

Note: Milled edge

Note: Plain edge with CESKA NARODNI BANKA *0.900* 13g

KM# 98   200 KORUN
13.0000 g., 0.9000 Silver 0.3761 oz. ASW   **Subject:** Josef Hlavka, 100th Anniversary of Death **Obv:** Wing over architectural element **Rev:** Facing portrait of Hlavka

Date	Mintage	F	VF	XF	Unc	BU
2008	9,559	—	—	—	20.00	22.00
2008 Proof	15,976	Value: 32.00				

Note: Milled edge

Note: Plain edge with CESKA NARODNI BANKA *0.900* 13g

KM# 99   200 KORUN
13.0000 g., 0.9000 Silver 0.3761 oz. ASW, 31 mm.   **Subject:** Schengen Convention **Obv:** Arms **Rev:** Opening of the frontiers

Date	Mintage	F	VF	XF	Unc	BU
2008	9,739	—	—	—	20.00	22.00
2008 Proof	15,743	Value: 32.00				

Note: Milled edge

Note: Plain edge with CESKA NARODNI BANKA *0.900* 13g

KM# 100   200 KORUN
13.0000 g., 0.9000 Silver 0.3761 oz. ASW, 31 mm.   **Subject:** Viktor Ponrepo,150th Anniversary **Obv:** Tripod camera **Rev:** Mustache and top hat

Date	Mintage	F	VF	XF	Unc	BU
2008	9,572	—	—	—	20.00	22.00
2008 Proof	14,997	Value: 32.00				

Note: Milled edge

Note: Plain edge with CESKA NARODNI BANKA *0.900* 13g

KM# 101   200 KORUN
13.0000 g., 0.9000 Silver 0.3761 oz. ASW, 31 mm.   **Subject:** National Technical Museum **Obv:** Steam Locomotive and driving wheel **Rev:** Museum façade and clock face

Date	Mintage	F	VF	XF	Unc	BU
2008	9,972	—	—	—	22.00	25.00
2008 Proof	14,997	Value: 35.00				

Note: Milled edge

Note: Plain edge with CESKA NARODNI BANKA *0.900* 13g

KM# 102   200 KORUN
13.0000 g., 0.9000 Silver 0.3761 oz. ASW, 31 mm.   **Subject:** Czech Ice Hockey Association - 100th Anniversary **Obv:** Hockey Player **Rev:** Logo

Date	Mintage	F	VF	XF	Unc	BU
2008	10,272	—	—	—	20.00	22.00
2008 Proof	15,097	Value: 32.00				

Note: Milled edge

Note: Plain edge with CESKA NARODNI BANKA *0.900* 13g

KM# 105   200 KORUN
13.0000 g., 0.9000 Silver 0.3761 oz. ASW, 31 mm.   **Subject:** Czech Presidency to Council of the European Union **Obv:** Arms in circle **Rev:** Czech flag and circle of stars

Date	Mintage	F	VF	XF	Unc	BU
2009	13,172	—	—	—	20.00	22.00
2009 Proof	19,697	Value: 32.00				

Note: Milled edge

Note: Plain edge with CESKA NARODNI BANKA *0.900* 13g

KM# 106   200 KORUN
13.0000 g., 0.9000 Silver 0.3761 oz. ASW, 31 mm.   **Subject:** Nordic World Ski Championships in Liberec **Obv:** Logo with skis **Rev:** Cross country skiers and ski jumpers

Date	Mintage	F	VF	XF	Unc	BU
2009	10,772	—	—	—	20.00	22.00
2009 Proof	15,197	Value: 32.00				

Note: Milled edge

Note: Plain edge with CESKA NARODNI BANKA *0.900* 13g

KM# 107   200 KORUN
13.0000 g., 0.9000 Silver 0.3761 oz. ASW, 31 mm.   **Subject:** North Pole Exploration **Obv:** Facing Explorer **Rev:** Sled and Northern Lights

Date	Mintage	F	VF	XF	Unc	BU
2009	10,172	—	—	—	20.00	22.00
2009 Proof	16,767	Value: 32.00				

Note: Milled edge

Note: Plain edge with CESKA NARODNI BANKA *0.900* 13g

KM# 108 200 KORUN
13.0000 g., 0.9000 Silver 0.3761 oz. ASW, 31 mm. **Subject:** Rabbi Jehuda Löw **Obv:** Star of David and dates **Rev:** Symbols of Rabbi Low

Date	Mintage	F	VF	XF	Unc	BU
2009	11,275	—	—	—	20.00	22.00
Note: Milled edge						
2009 Proof	18,100	Value: 32.00				
Note: Plain edge with CESKA NARODNI BANKA *0.900* 13g						

KM# 109 200 KORUN
13.0000 g., 0.9000 Silver 0.3761 oz. ASW, 31 mm. **Subject:** Kepler's Planetary Motion Laws **Obv:** Kepler's plan of Mars **Rev:** Portrait of Kepler

Date	Mintage	F	VF	XF	Unc	BU
2009	10,472	—	—	—	20.00	22.00
Note: Milled edge						
2009 Proof	19,687	Value: 32.00				
Note: Plain edge with CESKA NARODNI BANKA *0.900* 13g						

KM# 112 200 KORUN
13.0000 g., 0.9000 Silver 0.3761 oz. ASW, 31 mm. **Subject:** Astronomical Clock, Prague **Obv:** Figures of four apostles and rooster **Rev:** Clock works

Date	Mintage	F	VF	XF	Unc	BU
2010	10,372	—	—	—	18.00	20.00
Note: Milled edge						
2010 Proof	16,097	Value: 30.00				
Note: Plain edge with CESKA NARODNI BANKA *0.900* 13g						

KM# 113 200 KORUN
13.0000 g., 0.9250 Silver 0.3866 oz. ASW, 31 mm. **Subject:** Gustav Mahler **Obv:** Part of Mahler's 5th symphony **Rev:** Portrait of Mahler

Date	Mintage	F	VF	XF	Unc	BU
2010	9,672	—	—	—	18.00	20.00
Note: Milled edge						
2010 Proof	15,047	Value: 30.00				
Note: Plain edge with CESKA NARODNI BANKA *0.900* 13g						

KM# 114 200 KORUN
13.0000 g., 0.9000 Silver 0.3761 oz. ASW, 31 mm. **Subject:** Alfons Mucha **Obv:** Print of Music by Mucha **Rev:** Facing portrait of Mucha

Date	Mintage	F	VF	XF	Unc	BU
2010	10,072	—	—	—	18.00	20.00
Note: Milled edge						
2010 Proof	15,897	Value: 30.00				
Note: Plain edge with CESKA NARODNI BANKA *0.900* 13g						

KM# 115 200 KORUN
13.0000 g., 0.9250 Silver 0.3866 oz. ASW, 31 mm. **Subject:** John of Luxembourg, 700th Wedding Anniversary **Obv:** Czech lion on tapestry background **Rev:** John and wife standing

Date	Mintage	F	VF	XF	Unc	BU
2010	9,572	—	—	—	18.00	20.00
Note: Milled edge						
2010 Proof	13,897	Value: 32.00				
Note: Plain edge with CESKA NARODNI BANKA *0.900* 13g						

KM# 116 200 KORUN
13.0000 g., 0.9000 Silver 0.3761 oz. ASW, 31 mm. **Subject:** Karel Zeman, 100th Anniversary of Birth **Obv:** Marionettes of Zeman's cinemas **Rev:** Submarine, airship, octopus of Zeman's cinemas

Date	Mintage	F	VF	XF	Unc	BU
2010	9,275	—	—	—	18.00	20.00
Note: Milled edge						
2010 Proof	13,000	Value: 32.00				
Note: Plain edge with CESKA NARODNI BANKA *0.900* 13g						

KM# 119 200 KORUN
13.0000 g., 0.9250 Silver 0.3866 oz. ASW, 31 mm. **Subject:** Prague Conservatory, 200th Anniversary

Date	Mintage	F	VF	XF	Unc	BU
2011	7,777	—	—	—	18.00	20.00
Note: Milled edge						
2011 Proof	11,500	Value: 32.00				
Note: Plain edge with CESKA NARODNI BANKA *0.925* 13g						

KM# 120 200 KORUN
13.0000 g., 0.9250 Silver 0.3866 oz. ASW, 31 mm. **Subject:** Jan Kaspar, 100th Anniversary of First Flight

Date	Mintage	F	VF	XF	Unc	BU
2011	7,777	—	—	—	18.00	20.00
Note: Milled edge						
2011 Proof	11,600	Value: 32.00				
Note: Plain edge with CESKA NARODNI BANKA *0.925* 13g						

KM# 121 200 KORUN
13.0000 g., 0.9250 Silver 0.3866 oz. ASW, 31 mm. **Subject:** Jiri Melantrich, 500th Anniversary of Birth

Date	Mintage	F	VF	XF	Unc	BU
2011	7,877	—	—	—	18.00	20.00
Note: Milled edge						
2011 Proof	11,600	Value: 32.00				
Note: Plain edge with CESKA NARODNI BANKA *0.925* 13g						

KM# 122 200 KORUN
13.0000 g., 0.9250 Silver 0.3866 oz. ASW, 31 mm. **Subject:** Petr Vok, 400th Anniversary of Death

Date	Mintage	F	VF	XF	Unc	BU
2011	8,200	—	—	—	18.00	20.00
Note: Milled edge						
2011 Proof	12,200	Value: 32.00				
Note: Plain edge with CESKA NARODNI BANKA *0.925* 13g						

KM# 126 200 KORUN
13.0000 g., 0.9250 Silver 0.3866 oz. ASW, 31 mm. **Subject:** Emperor Rudolf II, 400th Anniversary of Death

Date	Mintage	F	VF	XF	Unc	BU
2012	—	—	—	—	—	25.00
Note: Milled edge						
2012 Proof	—	Value: 32.00				

KM# 127 200 KORUN
13.0000 g., 0.9250 Silver 0.3866 oz. ASW, 31 mm. **Subject:** Sokol, 150th Anniversary

Date	Mintage	F	VF	XF	Unc	BU
2012	—	—	—	—	—	25.00
2012 Proof	—	Value: 32.00				

KM# 128 200 KORUN
13.0000 g., 0.9250 Silver 0.3866 oz. ASW **Subject:** Czech Scouts - Junak, 100th Anniversary

Date	Mintage	F	VF	XF	Unc	BU
2012	—	—	—	—	—	25.00
2012 Proof	—	Value: 32.00				

KM# 129 200 KORUN
13.0000 g., 0.9250 Silver 0.3866 oz. ASW, 31 mm. **Subject:** Kamil Lhotak, 100th Anniversary of Birth

Date	Mintage	F	VF	XF	Unc	BU
2012	—	—	—	—	—	25.00
2012 Proof	—	Value: 32.00				

KM# 123 500 KORUN
25.0000 g., 0.9250 Silver 0.7435 oz. ASW, 40 mm. **Subject:** Karel Jaromir Erben, 200th Anniversary of Birth

Date	Mintage	F	VF	XF	Unc	BU
2011	7,200	—	—	—	30.00	35.00
Note: Milled edge						
2011 Proof	10,600	Value: 45.00				
Note: Plain edge with CESKA NARODNI BANKA *0.925* 13g						

KM# 130 500 KORUN
25.0000 g., 0.9250 Silver 0.7435 oz. ASW, 40 mm. **Subject:** Prague Municipal House, 100th Anniversary

Date	Mintage	F	VF	XF	Unc	BU
2012	—	—	—	—	—	30.00
2012 Proof	—	Value: 35.00				

KM# 131 500 KORUN
25.0000 g., 0.9250 Silver 0.7435 oz. ASW, 40 mm. **Subject:** Jiri Truka, 100th Anniversary of Birth

Date	Mintage	F	VF	XF	Unc	BU
2012	—	—	—	—	—	30.00
2012 Proof	—	Value: 35.00				

GOLD BULLION COINAGE

KM# 65 2000 KORUN
6.2200 g., 0.9999 Gold 0.1999 oz. AGW, 20 mm. **Subject:** Romanesque - Znojmo Rotunda **Obv:** Three heraldic animals **Rev:** Farmer and round building

Date	Mintage	F	VF	XF	Unc	BU
ND(2001)	2,197	—	—	—	—	350
Note: Milled edge						
ND(2001) Proof	2,997	Value: 375				
Note: Plain edge						

KM# 66 2000 KORUN
6.2200 g., 0.9999 Gold 0.1999 oz. AGW, 20 mm. **Subject:** Gothic - Cloister of the Vyssi Brod Monastery **Obv:** Three heraldic animals above Gothic design **Rev:** Man holding church building model

Date	Mintage	F	VF	XF	Unc	BU
2001	2,195	—	—	—	—	350
Note: Milled edge						
2001 Proof	2,997	Value: 375				
Note: Plain edge						

KM# 67 2000 KORUN
6.2200 g., 0.9999 Gold 0.1999 oz. AGW, 20 mm. **Subject:** Gothic - Fountain in Kutna Hora **Obv:** Three heraldic animals **Rev:** Fountain enclosure

Date	Mintage	F	VF	XF	Unc	BU
2002	2,195	—	—	—	—	350
Note: Milled edge						

Date	Mintage	F	VF	XF	Unc	BU
2002 Proof	2,997	Value: 375				

Note: Plain edge

KM# 61   2000 KORUN
6.2200 g., 0.9999 Gold 0.1999 oz. AGW, 20 mm. **Subject:** Renaissance - Litomysl Castle **Obv:** Three heraldic animals above mermaid **Rev:** Aerial castle view and mythical creature

Date	Mintage	F	VF	XF	Unc	BU
2002	2,094	—	—	—	—	350

Note: Milled edge

Date	Mintage	F	VF	XF	Unc	BU
2002 Proof	3,097	Value: 375				

Note: Plain edge

KM# 68   2000 KORUN
6.2200 g., 0.9999 Gold 0.1999 oz. AGW, 20 mm. **Subject:** Renaissance - Slavonice House Gables **Obv:** Three heraldic animals above city view **Rev:** City arms

Date	Mintage	F	VF	XF	Unc	BU
2003	1,994	—	—	—	—	350

Note: Milled edge

Date	Mintage	F	VF	XF	Unc	BU
2003 Proof	2,996	Value: 375				

Note: Plain edge

KM# 69   2000 KORUN
6.2200 g., 0.9999 Gold 0.1999 oz. AGW, 20 mm. **Subject:** Baroque - Buchlovice Palace **Obv:** Three heraldic animals above palace **Rev:** Palace view

Date	Mintage	F	VF	XF	Unc	BU
2003	1,994	—	—	—	—	350

Note: Milled edge

Date	Mintage	F	VF	XF	Unc	BU
2003 Proof	3,197	Value: 375				

Note: Plain edge

KM# 75   2000 KORUN
6.2200 g., 0.9999 Gold 0.1999 oz. AGW, 20 mm. **Obv:** Ornamental porch below three heraldic animals **Rev:** Hluboka Castle with coat of arms in foreground

Date	Mintage	F	VF	XF	Unc	BU
2004	1,994	—	—	—	—	350

Note: Milled edge

Date	Mintage	F	VF	XF	Unc	BU
2004 Proof	2,997	Value: 375				

Note: Plain edge

KM# 86   2000 KORUN
6.2200 g., 0.9990 Gold 0.1998 oz. AGW, 20 mm. **Subject:** Kacina Castle

Date	Mintage	F	VF	XF	Unc	BU
2004	1,994	—	—	—	—	350

Note: Milled edge

Date	Mintage	F	VF	XF	Unc	BU
2004 Proof	2,996	Value: 375				

Note: Plain edge

KM# 87   2000 KORUN
6.2200 g., 0.9990 Gold 0.1998 oz. AGW, 20 mm. **Subject:** Lazne Bohdanec Spa **Obv:** Gocar Spa Pavillion, full facade **Rev:** Gocar Spa Pavillion central area

Date	Mintage	F	VF	XF	Unc	BU
2005	1,997	—	—	—	—	350

Note: Milled edge

Date	Mintage	F	VF	XF	Unc	BU
2005 Proof	2,996	Value: 375				

Note: Plain edge

KM# 88   2000 KORUN
6.2200 g., 0.9990 Gold 0.1998 oz. AGW, 20 mm. **Subject:** Dancing House in Prague **Rev:** Exterior view of Dancing House

Date	Mintage	F	VF	XF	Unc	BU
2005	1,996	—	—	—	—	350

Note: Milled edge

Date	Mintage	F	VF	XF	Unc	BU
2005 Proof	3,297	Value: 375				

Note: Plain edge

KM# 76   2500 KORUN
31.1040 g., Bi-Metallic .9999 Gold 7.776g center in .999 Silver 23.328g ring, 40 mm. **Subject:** Czech entry into the European Union **Obv:** Value within circle of shields **Rev:** "1.5.2004" within circle of dates and text **Edge:** Lettered **Edge Lettering:** CNB * Ag 0.999 * 23,328 g CNB Au 999.9 * 7,776g *

Date	Mintage	F	VF	XF	Unc	BU
ND (2004) Proof	8,117	Value: 500				

KM# 89   2500 KORUN
7.7770 g., 0.9990 Gold 0.2498 oz. AGW, 22 mm. **Subject:** Hand Paper Mill at Velke Losiny

Date	Mintage	F	VF	XF	Unc	BU
2006	1,800	—	—	—	1,500	—

Note: Milled edge

Date	Mintage	F	VF	XF	Unc	BU
2006	3,000	Value: 3,000				

Note: Plain edge

KM# 90   2500 KORUN
7.7850 g., 0.9990 Gold 0.2500 oz. AGW, 22 mm. **Subject:** Observatory at Prague Klementinum **Obv:** Sun's rays thru clouds **Rev:** Building tower, rays and moon **Note:** Prev. KM #86.

Date	Mintage	F	VF	XF	Unc	BU
2006	1,897	—	—	—	—	700

Note: Milled edge

Date	Mintage	F	VF	XF	Unc	BU
2006 Proof	3,797	Value: 1,000				

Note: Plain edge

KM# 95   2500 KORUN
7.7770 g., 0.9990 Gold 0.2498 oz. AGW, 22 mm. **Subject:** Sevcinsky Mine at Pribram-Brezove Hory **Rev:** Head-gear tower at mine

Date	Mintage	F	VF	XF	Unc	BU
2007	2,097	—	—	—	—	425

Note: Milled edge

Date	Mintage	F	VF	XF	Unc	BU
2007 Proof	5,097	Value: 450				

Note: Plain edge

KM# 96   2500 KORUN
7.7770 g., 0.9990 Gold 0.2498 oz. AGW, 22 mm. **Subject:** Water mill at Slup **Obv:** Water Mill **Rev:** Water Mill

Date	Mintage	F	VF	XF	Unc	BU
2007	2,297	—	—	—	—	425
2007 Proof	6,297	Value: 450				

KM# 103   2500 KORUN
7.7800 g., 0.9990 Gold 0.2499 oz. AGW, 22 mm. **Subject:** Stadlec Suspension Bridge **Obv:** Side view of bridge **Rev:** View of bridge thru arch

Date	Mintage	F	VF	XF	Unc	BU
2008	3,097	—	—	—	—	425

Note: Milled edge

Date	Mintage	F	VF	XF	Unc	BU
2008 Proof	10,897	Value: 450				

Note: Plain edge

KM# 104   2500 KORUN
7.7800 g., 0.9990 Gold 0.2499 oz. AGW, 22 mm. **Subject:** Plsen Brewery **Obv:** Copper vats **Rev:** Plsen Brewery façade and wooden barrels

Date	Mintage	F	VF	XF	Unc	BU
2008	3,197	—	—	—	—	425

Note: Milled edge

Date	Mintage	F	VF	XF	Unc	BU
2008 Proof	10,797	Value: 450				

Note: Plain edge

KM# 110   2500 KORUN
7.7770 g., 0.9990 Gold 0.2498 oz. AGW, 22 mm. **Subject:** Elbe Sluice under Strekov Castle **Obv:** Turbine in sluice in the Labe (Elbe) river **Rev:** Sluice under Strekov castle

Date	Mintage	F	VF	XF	Unc	BU
2009	3,497	—	—	—	—	425

Note: Milled edge

Date	Mintage	F	VF	XF	Unc	BU
2009 Proof	10,497	Value: 450				

Note: Plain edge

KM# 111   2500 KORUN
7.7770 g., 0.9990 Gold 0.2498 oz. AGW, 22 mm. **Subject:** Windmill at Ruprechtov

Date	Mintage	F	VF	XF	Unc	BU
2009	3,497	—	—	—	—	425
2009 Proof	10,497	Value: 450				

KM# 117   2500 KORUN
7.7700 g., 0.9990 Gold 0.2496 oz. AGW, 22 mm. **Subject:** Hammer Mill in Dobriv

Date	Mintage	F	VF	XF	Unc	BU
2010	3,797	—	—	—	—	425

Note: Milled edge

Date	Mintage	F	VF	XF	Unc	BU
2010 Proof	9,997	Value: 450				

Note: Plain edge

KM# 118 2500 KORUN
7.7700 g., 0.9990 Gold 0.2496 oz. AGW, 22 mm. **Subject:** Michael Mine in Ostrana **Obv:** Turbine **Rev:** Mine shaft

Date	Mintage	F	VF	XF	Unc	BU
2010	3,697	—	—	—	—	425

Note: Milled edge

Date	Mintage	F	VF	XF	Unc	BU
2010 Proof	9,097	Value: 450				

Note: Plain edge

KM# 124 5000 KORUN
15.5530 g., 0.9999 Gold 0.5000 oz. AGW, 28 mm. **Subject:** Gothic Bridge in Pisek

Date	Mintage	F	VF	XF	Unc	BU
2011	2,600	—	—	—	—	850
2011 Proof	6,900	Value: 900				

KM# 125 5000 KORUN
15.5530 g., 0.9999 Gold 0.5000 oz. AGW, 28 mm. **Subject:** Renaissance Bridge in Stribro

Date	Mintage	F	VF	XF	Unc	BU
2011	2,700	—	—	—	—	850

Note: Milled edge

Date	Mintage	F	VF	XF	Unc	BU
2011 Proof	7,300	Value: 900				

Note: Plain edge

KM# 132 5000 KORUN
15.5530 g., 0.9999 Gold 0.5000 oz. AGW, 28 mm. **Subject:** Banocco Bridge in Namest nad Oslavou

Date	Mintage	F	VF	XF	Unc	BU
2012	—	—	—	—	—	900
2012 Proof	—	Value: 950				

KM# 133 5000 KORUN
15.5530 g., 0.9999 Gold 0.5000 oz. AGW, 28 mm. **Subject:** Negrelli viaduct in Prague

Date	Mintage	F	VF	XF	Unc	BU
2012	—	—	—	—	—	950
2012 Proof	—	Value: 1,000				

KM# 134 10000 KORUN
31.1070 g., 0.9999 Gold 1.0000 oz. AGW, 34 mm. **Subject:** Gold Bulla of Sicily, 800th Anniversary

Date	Mintage	F	VF	XF	Unc	BU
2012 Proof	—	Value: 2,000				

MINT SETS

KM#	Date	Mintage	Identification	Issue Price	Mkt Val
MS14	2001 (9)	11,500	KM#1, 2.3, 3.2, 4-9, Tyn Church folder	—	17.50
MS15	2002 (9)	11,885	KM#1, 2.3, 3.2, 4-9, Castles	—	60.00
MS16	2002 (9)	5,115	KM#1, 2.3, 3.2, 4-9, NATO Summit folder	—	17.50
MS17	2003 (9)	22,000	KM#1, 2.3, 3.2, 4-9, CNB 10th Anniversary	—	30.00
MS18	2004 (7)	7,500	KM#1, 3.2, 4-5, 7-9, Football	—	30.00
MS19	2004 (7)	13,000	KM#1, 3.2, 4-5, 7-9, EU Entry	—	40.00
MS20	2004 (7)	10,000	KM#1, 3.2, 4-5, 7-9 IIHF Hockey Year	—	16.00
MS21	2005 (8)	13,015	KM#1, 3.2, 4-5, 7-9, plus Smetna/Dvorak Medal and CD	—	17.50
MS22	2006 (7)	9,000	KM#1, 3.2, 4-5, 7-9, UNESCO Folder	—	16.00
MS23	2006 (7)	5,139	KM#1, 3.2, 4-5, 7-9, Football Championship	—	40.00
MS24	2006 (7)	9,784	KM#1, 3.2, 4-5, 7-9, plus Euro Medal	—	45.00
MS25	2007 (7)	8,500	KM#1, 3.2, 4-5, 7-9, UNESCO Kunta Hora folder	—	25.00
MS26	2007 (14)	10,000	KM#1, 3.2, 4-5, 7-9. Natural beauties with Slovakia coins	—	35.00
MS27	2008 (7)	9,000	KM#1, 3.2, 4-5, 7-9, plus UNESCO Medal	—	30.00
MS28	2008 (8)	6,000	KM#1, 3.2, 4-5, 7-9. Soccer medal and package	—	17.50
MS29	2009 (8)	10,000	KM#1, 3.2, 4-5, 7-9 plus brass Southern Bohemia Medal	—	17.50
MS30	2010 (6)	10,000	KM#1, 3.2, 4-5, 7-9, Zlin Region folder	—	17.50
MS31	2011 (6)	10,000	KM#1, 4-5, 7-9, Plzen Region folder	—	17.50
MS32	2011 (6)	5,000	KM#1, 4-5, 7-9. Baby set.	—	17.50
MS33	2011 (6)	450	KM# 1, 4-5, 7-9. ENA and CNB official distribution	12.00	—

PROOF SETS

KM#	Date	Mintage	Identification	Issue Price	Mkt Val
PS6	2001 (9)	2,500	KM#1, 2.3, 3.1, 4-9	35.00	250
PS7	2002 (9)	3,490	KM#1, 2.3, 3.2, 4-9	35.00	250
PS8	2003 (9)	3,000	KM#1, 2.3, 3.2, 4-9	35.00	150
PS9	2004 (7)	4,000	KM#1, 3.2, 4-5, 7-9	35.00	100
PS10	2005 (7)	3,000	KM#1, 3.2, 4-5, 7-9, and silver strike of Czechoslovakia KM#4	—	100
PS11	2006 (7)	2,500	KM#1, 3.2, 4-5, 7-9, and silver strike of Czechoslovakia KM#2	—	120
PS12	2007 (7)	2,500	KM#1, 3.2, 4-5, 7-9, and silver Unesco medal	—	120
PS13	2008 (7)	2,500	KM#1, 3.2, 4-5, 7-9 and silver medal	—	85.00
PS14	2009 (8)	3,200	KM#1, 3.2, 4-5, 7-9 and silver medal	—	85.00
PS15	2010 (6)	3,200	KM#1, 4-5, 7-9	—	85.00
PS16	2011 (6)	3,500	KM#1, 4-5, 7-9, velvet case	—	85.00
PS17	2011 (6)	2,000	KM#1, 4-5, 7-9 leather case	—	120

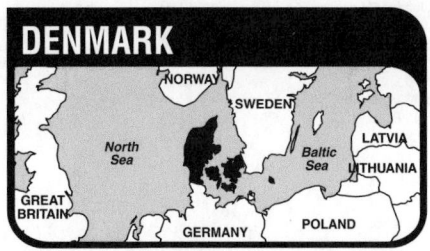

DENMARK

The Kingdom of Denmark (Danmark), a constitutional monarchy located at the mouth of the Baltic Sea, has an area of 16,639 sq. mi. (43,070 sq. km.) and a population of 5.2 million. Capital: Copenhagen. Most of the country is arable. Agriculture is conducted by large farms served by cooperatives. The largest industries are food processing, iron and metal, and shipping. Machinery, meats (chiefly bacon), dairy products and chemicals are exported.

As a result of a referendum held September 28, 2000, the currency of the European Monetary Union, the Euro, will not be introduced in Denmark in the foreseeable future.

RULER
Margrethe II, 1972—

MINT MARKS
(h) - Copenhagen, heart

MINT OFFICIALS' INITIALS
Copenhagen Mint

Letter	Date	Name
LG	1989-2001	Laust Grove

MONEYERS' INITIALS
Copenhagen Mint

Letter	Date	Name
A	1986-	Johan Alkjaer (designer)
HV	1986-	Hanne Varming (sculptor)
JP	1989-	Jan Petersen

MONETARY SYSTEM
100 Øre = 1 Krone

KINGDOM
DECIMAL COINAGE

KM# 868.1 25 ORE
2.8000 g., Bronze, 17.5 mm. **Ruler:** Margrethe II **Obv:** Large crown divides date above, initial to right of country **Rev:** Denomination, small heart above, mint mark and initials LG-JP below **Note:** Beginning in 1996 and ending with 1998, the words "DANMARK" and "ØRE" have raised edges. Heart mint mark under "ØRE"; Prev. KM#868.

Date	Mintage	F	VF	XF	Unc	BU
2001 LG; JP; A	10,530,000	—	—	—	0.15	—

KM# 868.2 25 ORE
2.8000 g., Bronze, 17.5 mm. **Ruler:** Margrethe II **Obv:** Large crown divides date above **Rev:** Denomination, small heart above **Edge:** Plain **Note:** Without initials

Date	Mintage	F	VF	XF	Unc	BU
2002	12,000,000	—	—	—	0.15	—
2003	17,590,000	—	—	—	0.15	—
2004	7,040,304	—	—	—	0.15	1.50
2004 Proof	3,000	Value: 12.00				
2005	19,039,000	—	—	—	0.15	1.50
2005 Proof	2,650	Value: 12.00				
2006	16,796,000	—	—	—	0.15	1.50
2006 Proof	1,800	Value: 12.00				
2007	20,592,000	—	—	—	0.15	1.50
2007 Proof	1,400	Value: 12.00				
2008	2,049,000	—	—	—	1.50	2.25
2008 Proof	1,000	Value: 20.00				

KM# 866.2 50 ORE
4.3000 g., Bronze, 21.5 mm. **Ruler:** Margrethe II **Obv:** Large crown divides date above, initial to right of country name **Rev:** Large heart above value, mint mark and initials LG-JP below **Note:** Beginning in 1996 and ending in 1998, the words "DANMARK" and "ØRE" have raised edges. Heart mint mark under the word "ØRE".

Date	Mintage	F	VF	XF	Unc	BU
2001 LG; JP; A	12,270,000	—	—	—	0.25	—

KM# 866.3 50 ORE
4.3000 g., Bronze, 21.5 mm. **Ruler:** Margrethe II **Obv:** Large crown divides date above **Rev:** Small heart above denomination **Edge:** Plain **Note:** No initials

Date	Mintage	F	VF	XF	Unc	BU
2002	3,900,000	—	—	—	0.20	—
2003	8,817,000	—	—	—	0.15	—
2004	10,040,706	—	—	—	0.15	2.25
2004 Proof	3,000	Value: 15.00				
2005	12,037,000	—	—	—	0.15	2.25
2005 Proof	2,650	Value: 15.00				
2006	14,843,000	—	—	—	0.15	2.25
2006 Proof	1,800	Value: 15.00				
2007	10,198,000	—	—	—	0.15	2.25
2007 Proof	1,400	Value: 15.00				
2008	2,573,000	—	—	—	0.15	2.25
2008 Proof	1,000	Value: 15.00				
2009 In sets only	25,700	—	—	—	0.15	3.00
2009 Proof	1,050	Value: 15.00				
2010 In sets only	24,300	—	—	—	0.15	2.25
2010 Proof	1,010	Value: 15.00				
2011 In sets only	—	—	—	—	0.15	2.25
2011 Proof	—	Value: 15.00				

KM# 873.1 KRONE
3.6000 g., Copper-Nickel, 20.25 mm. **Ruler:** Margrethe II **Obv:** 3 crowned MII monograms around center hole, date, mint mark, and initials LG-JP-A below **Rev:** Wave design surrounds center hole, value above, hearts flank **Edge:** Reeded **Note:** Prev. KM#873.

Date	Mintage	F	VF	XF	Unc	BU
2001 LG; JP; A	14,640,000	—	—	—	0.50	—

KM# 873.2 KRONE
3.6000 g., Copper-Nickel, 20.25 mm. **Ruler:** Margrethe II **Obv:** 3 crowned MII monograms around center hole, date below **Rev:** Design surrounds center hole, value above, hearts flank **Edge:** Reeded **Note:** Without initials

Date	Mintage	F	VF	XF	Unc	BU
2002	9,000,000	—	—	—	0.45	—
2003	5,231,000	—	—	—	0.45	—

Date	Mintage	F	VF	XF	Unc	BU
2004	16,139,596	—	—	—	0.45	3.00
2004 Proof	3,000	Value: 18.00				
2005	16,757,000	—	—	—	0.45	3.00
2005 Proof	2,650	Value: 18.00				
2006	21,026,000	—	—	—	0.45	3.00
2006 Proof	1,800	Value: 18.00				
2007	11,729,000	—	—	—	0.45	3.00
2007 Proof	1,400	Value: 18.00				
2008	13,339,000	—	—	—	0.45	3.00
2008 Proof	1,000	Value: 18.00				
2009	624,000	—	—	—	1.00	4.00
2009 Proof	1,050	Value: 18.00				
2010 In sets only	26,000	—	—	—	0.45	3.00
2010 Proof	1,010	Value: 18.00				
2011 In sets only	—	—	—	—	—	4.00
2011 Proof	—	Value: 18.00				

KM# 874.1   2 KRONER
5.9000 g., Copper-Nickel, 24.5 mm.   **Ruler:** Margrethe II **Obv:** 3 crowned MII monograms around center hole, date and initials LG-JP-A below **Rev:** Design surrounds center hole, denomination above, hearts flank **Edge:** Segmented reeding **Note:** Prev. KM#874.

Date	Mintage	F	VF	XF	Unc	BU
2001 LG; JP; A	11,180,000	—	—	—	0.60	—

KM# 874.2   2 KRONER
5.9000 g., Copper-Nickel, 24.5 mm.   **Ruler:** Margrethe II **Obv:** 3 crowned MII monograms around center hole, date and initials LGpJP-A below **Rev:** Wave design surrounds center hole, denomination above, hearts flank **Edge:** Segmented reeding **Note:** Without initials

Date	Mintage	F	VF	XF	Unc	BU
2002	60,159,000	—	—	—	0.60	—
2004	7,381,531	—	—	—	0.60	3.00
2004 Proof	3,000	Value: 22.00				
2005	16,681,000	—	—	—	0.60	3.00
2005 Proof	2,650	Value: 22.00				
2006	7,329,000	—	—	—	0.60	3.00
2006 Proof	1,800	Value: 22.00				
2007	22,059,000	—	—	—	0.60	3.00
2007 Proof	1,400	Value: 22.00				
2008	2,622,000	—	—	—	0.60	3.00
2008 Proof	1,000	Value: 22.00				
2009 In sets only	25,700	—	—	—	—	4.50
2009 Proof	1,050	Value: 22.00				
2010 In sets only	24,300	—	—	—	3.00	6.00
2010 Proof	1,010	Value: 22.00				
2011	—	—	—	—	0.80	4.00
2011 Proof	—	Value: 22.00				

KM# 869.1   5 KRONER
9.2000 g., Copper-Nickel, 28.5 mm.   **Ruler:** Margrethe II **Obv:** 3 crowned MII monograms around center hole, date and initials LG-JP-A below **Rev:** Wave design surrounds center hole, denomination above, hearts flank **Edge:** Reeded **Note:** Large and small date varieties exist.

Date	Mintage	F	VF	XF	Unc	BU
2001 LG; JP; A	5,700,000	—	—	—	1.50	—

KM# 869.2   5 KRONER
9.2000 g., Copper-Nickel, 28.5 mm.   **Ruler:** Margrethe II **Obv:** 3 crowned MII monograms around center hole, date below **Rev:** Wave design surrounds center hole, denomination above, hearts flank **Edge:** Reeded **Note:** Without initials

Date	Mintage	F	VF	XF	Unc	BU
2002	5,980,000	—	—	—	1.50	—
2004	1,415,925	—	—	—	1.50	4.00
2004 Proof	3,000	Value: 30.00				
2005	7,073,000	—	—	—	1.50	4.00
2005 Proof	2,650	Value: 30.00				
2006	3,431,000	—	—	—	1.50	4.00
2006 Proof	1,800	Value: 30.00				
2007	4,983,000	—	—	—	1.50	4.00
2007 Proof	1,400	Value: 30.00				
2008	7,506,000	—	—	—	1.50	4.00
2008 Proof	1,000	Value: 30.00				
2009 In sets only	25,700	—	—	—	—	6.00
2009 Proof	1,050	Value: 30.00				
2010 In sets only	24,300	—	—	—	1.50	4.00
2010 Proof	1,010	Value: 30.00				
2011 In sets only	—	—	—	—	—	8.00
2011 Proof	—	Value: 30.00				

KM# 887.1   10 KRONER
7.0000 g., Aluminum-Bronze, 23.35 mm.   **Ruler:** Margrethe II **Obv:** Crowned head right within inner circle, date, initials LG-JP-A below, mint mark after II in title **Obv. Legend:** MARGRETHE II - DANMARKS DRONNING **Rev:** Crowned arms within inner circle above denomination **Edge:** Plain

Date	Mintage	F	VF	XF	Unc	BU
2001(h) LG; JP; A	4,800,000	—	—	—	3.00	—

KM# 887.2   10 KRONER
7.1000 g., Aluminum-Bronze, 23.35 mm.   **Ruler:** Margrethe II **Obv:** Crowned bust right, mint mark after II in title **Obv. Legend:** MARGRETHE II - DANMARKS DRONNING **Rev:** Crowned arms and denomination **Edge:** Plain **Note:** Without initials

Date	Mintage	F	VF	XF	Unc	BU
2002(h)	7,299,900	—	—	—	3.00	—

KM# 896   10 KRONER
7.0000 g., Aluminum-Bronze, 23.35 mm.   **Ruler:** Margrethe II **Obv:** Crowned bust right within circle, date below **Obv. Legend:** MARGRETHE II - DANMARKS DRONNING **Rev:** Crowned arms above denomination **Edge:** Plain

Date	Mintage	F	VF	XF	Unc	BU
2004(h)	5,835,426	—	—	—	3.00	5.50
2004(h) Proof	3,000	Value: 35.00				
2005(h)	2,614,000	—	—	—	3.00	5.50
2005(h) Proof	2,650	Value: 35.00				
2006(h)	3,530,000	—	—	—	3.00	5.50
2006(h) Proof	1,800	Value: 35.00				
2007(h)	3,294,000	—	—	—	2.50	5.50
2007(h) Proof	1,400	Value: 35.00				
2008(h)	2,258,000	—	—	—	2.50	5.50
2008(h) Proof	1,000	Value: 35.00				
2009(h)	1,701,000	—	—	—	2.50	5.50
2009(h) Proof	1,050	Value: 35.00				
2010(h) In sets only	—	—	—	—	2.50	5.50
2010(h) Proof	—	Value: 35.00				

KM# 898   10 KRONER
7.0000 g., Aluminum-Bronze, 23.35 mm.   **Ruler:** Margrethe II **Series:** Fairy Tales **Subject:** Hans Christian Andersen's Ugly duckling story **Obv:** Crowned bust right within circle, date below **Obv. Legend:** MARGRETHE II - DANMARKS DRONNING **Rev:** Swan and reflection on water within circle, value below **Edge:** Plain

Date	Mintage	F	VF	XF	Unc	BU
2005(h)	1,206,675	—	—	—	3.00	8.00

KM# 906   10 KRONER
31.1000 g., 0.9990 Silver 0.9988 oz. ASW, 38 mm.   **Ruler:** Margrethe II **Series:** Fairy Tales **Subject:** Hans Christian Andersen's The Ugly Duckling **Obv:** Crowned bust right **Obv. Legend:** MARGRETHE II - DANMARKS DRONNING **Rev:** Swan and reflection on water

Date	Mintage	F	VF	XF	Unc	BU
2005(h)	75,000	—	—	—	—	40.00

KM# 907   10 KRONER
8.6500 g., 0.9000 Gold 0.2503 oz. AGW, 22 mm.   **Ruler:** Margrethe II **Series:** Fairy Tales **Subject:** Hans Christian Andersen's The Ugly Duckling **Obv:** Crowned bust right **Obv. Legend:** MARGRETHE II - DANMARKS DRONNING **Rev:** Swan and reflection on water

Date	Mintage	F	VF	XF	Unc	BU
2005(h)	7,000	—	—	—	—	450

KM# 900   10 KRONER
7.0000 g., Aluminum-Bronze, 23.35 mm.   **Ruler:** Margrethe II **Series:** Fairy Tales **Subject:** Hans Christian Andersen's Little Mermaid **Obv:** Crowned bust right within circle, date below **Obv. Legend:** MARGRETHE II - DANMARKS DRONNING **Rev:** Little Mermaid **Edge:** Plain

Date	Mintage	F	VF	XF	Unc	BU
2005(h)	1,206,675	—	—	—	3.00	8.00

KM# 908   10 KRONER
31.1000 g., 0.9990 Silver 0.9988 oz. ASW, 38 mm.   **Ruler:** Margrethe II **Series:** Fairy Tales **Subject:** Hans Christian Andersen's Little Mermaid **Obv:** Crowned bust right, date below **Obv. Legend:** MARGRETHE II - DANMARKS DRONNING **Rev:** Little Mermaid

Date	Mintage	F	VF	XF	Unc	BU
2005(h)	40,220	—	—	—	—	40.00

KM# 911   10 KRONER
8.6500 g., 0.9000 Gold 0.2503 oz. AGW, 22 mm.   **Ruler:** Margrethe II **Series:** Fairy Tales **Subject:** Hans Christian Andersen's Little Mermaid **Obv:** Crowned bust right **Obv. Legend:** MARGRETHE II - DANMARKS DRONNING **Rev:** Little Mermaid

Date	Mintage	F	VF	XF	Unc	BU
2005(h)	4,220	—	—	—	—	500

KM# 903   10 KRONER
7.1000 g., Aluminum-Bronze, 23.35 mm.   **Ruler:** Margrethe II **Series:** Fairy Tales **Subject:** H.C. Andersen's "The Shadow" **Obv:** Crowned bust right within circle, date below **Obv. Legend:** MARGRETHE II - DANMARKS DRONNING **Rev:** Stylized figures **Edge:** Plain

Date	Mintage	F	VF	XF	Unc	BU
2006(h)	1,206,675	—	—	—	3.00	8.00

KM# 909   10 KRONER
31.1000 g., 0.9990 Silver 0.9988 oz. ASW, 38 mm.   **Ruler:** Margrethe II **Series:** Fairy Tales **Subject:** H.C. Andersen's "Skyggen" (The Shadow) **Obv:** Crowned bust right **Obv. Legend:** MARGRETHE II - DANMARKS DRONNING **Rev:** Stylized figures

Date	Mintage	F	VF	XF	Unc	BU
2006(h)	22,317	—	—	—	—	40.00

KM# 910   10 KRONER
8.6500 g., 0.9000 Gold 0.2503 oz. AGW, 22 mm.   **Ruler:** Margrethe II **Series:** Fairy Tales **Subject:** H.C. Andersen's "Skyggen" (The Shadow) **Obv:** Crowned bust right **Obv. Legend:** MARGRETHE II - DANMARKS DRONNING **Rev:** Stylized figures

Date	Mintage	F	VF	XF	Unc	BU
2006(h)	3,070	—	—	—	—	450

KM# 914a   10 KRONER
31.1000 g., 0.9990 Silver 0.9988 oz. ASW, 38 mm. **Ruler:**
Margrethe II **Series:** Fairy Tales **Subject:** Hans Christian
Andersen's Snow Queen **Obv:** Crowned bust right **Obv. Legend:**
MARGRETHE II - DANMARKS DRONNING **Rev:** Ice pieces

Date	Mintage	F	VF	XF	Unc	BU
2006(h)	25,758	—	—	—	—	40.00

KM# 914b   10 KRONER
8.6500 g., 0.9000 Gold 0.2503 oz. AGW, 22 mm. **Ruler:**
Margrethe II **Series:** Fairy Tales **Subject:** The Snow Queen **Obv:**
Crowned bust right **Obv. Legend:** MARGRETHE II - DANMARKS
DRONNING **Rev:** Ice pieces

Date	Mintage	F	VF	XF	Unc	BU
2006(h)	3,075	—	—	—	—	450

KM# 914   10 KRONER
7.1000 g., Aluminum-Bronze, 23.35 mm. **Ruler:** Margrethe II
Series: Fairy Tales **Subject:** Hans Christian Andersen's Snow
Queen **Obv:** Crowned bust right **Obv. Legend:** MARGRETHE II
- DANMARKS DRONNING **Rev:** Ice pieces

Date	Mintage	F	VF	XF	Unc	BU
2006(h)	1,206,675	—	—	—	4.00	10.00

KM# 923a   10 KRONER
31.1000 g., 0.9990 Silver 0.9988 oz. ASW, 38 mm. **Ruler:**
Margrethe II **Series:** Fairy Tales **Subject:** H.C. Anderson's 'The
Nightingale' **Rev:** Bird

Date	Mintage	F	VF	XF	Unc	BU
2007 Proof	18,117	Value: 40.00				

KM# 916   10 KRONER
7.1000 g., Aluminum-Bronze, 23.35 mm. **Ruler:** Margrethe II
Subject: International Polar Year 2007-2009 **Obv:** Head with
tiara right **Obv. Legend:** MARGRETHE II - DANMARKS
DRONNING **Rev:** Polar bear facing, walking on ice flow **Rev.
Legend:** POLARÅR 2007-2009 **Edge:** Plain

Date	Mintage	F	VF	XF	Unc	BU
2007(h)	1,200,000	—	—	—	4.00	10.00

KM# 923   10 KRONER
7.1000 g., Aluminum-Bronze, 23.35 mm. **Ruler:** Margrethe II
Series: Fairy Tales **Subject:** H.C. Anderson's 'The Nightingale'
Rev: Bird

Date	Mintage	F	VF	XF	Unc	BU
2007	1,206,675	—	—	—	4.00	10.00

KM# 923b   10 KRONER
8.6500 g., 0.9000 Gold 0.2503 oz. AGW, 22 mm. **Ruler:**
Margrethe II **Series:** Fairy Tales **Subject:** H.C. Anderson's 'The
Nightingale' **Rev:** Bird

Date	Mintage	F	VF	XF	Unc	BU
2007	2,964	—	—	—	—	450

KM# 925   10 KRONER
7.2000 g., Aluminum-Bronze, 23.35 mm. **Ruler:** Margrethe II
Series: International Polar Year 2007-2009 **Obv:** Head with tiara
right **Rev:** Outlined globe **Rev. Legend:** POLARÅR 2007-2009
Edge: Plain

Date	Mintage	F	VF	XF	Unc	BU
2008(h)	1,200,000	—	—	—	3.00	10.00

KM# 932   10 KRONER
7.1000 g., Aluminum-Bronze, 23.5 mm. **Ruler:** Margrethe II
Rev: Ice scape, Northern Lights

Date	Mintage	F	VF	XF	Unc	BU
2009	1,200,000	—	—	—	3.00	10.00

KM# 943   10 KRONER
7.0000 g., Aluminum-Bronze, 23.35 mm. **Ruler:** Margrethe II
Obv: Head right **Obv. Legend:** MARGRETHE II DANMARKS
DRONNING **Rev:** Crowned shield and value **Edge:** Plain

Date	Mintage	F	VF	XF	Unc	BU
2011(h)	—	—	—	—	3.50	
2011(h) Proof	—	Value: 25.00				

KM# 888.1   20 KRONER
9.3000 g., Aluminum-Bronze, 27 mm. **Ruler:** Margrethe II **Obv:**
Crowned bust right within circle, date and initials LG-JP-A below,
mint mark after II in legend **Obv. Legend:** MARGRETHE II -
DANMARKS DRONNING **Rev:** Crowned arms within ornaments
and value **Edge:** Alternating reeded and plain sections

Date	Mintage	F	VF	XF	Unc	BU
2001(h) LG; JP; A	2,900,000	—	—	—	5.50	9.00

KM# 889   20 KRONER
9.3000 g., Aluminum-Bronze, 27 mm. **Ruler:** Margrethe II
Series: Danish Towers **Obv:** Crowned bust right within circle
date below, mint mark after II in legend **Obv. Legend:**
MARGRETHE II - DANMARKS DRONNING **Rev:** Aarhus City
Hall **Edge:** Reeded and plain sections

Date	Mintage	F	VF	XF	Unc	BU
2002(h)	1,208,600	—	—	—	6.50	10.00

KM# 888.2   20 KRONER
9.3000 g., Aluminum-Bronze, 27 mm. **Ruler:** Margrethe II **Obv:**
Crowned bust right within circle, mint mark after II in legend **Obv.
Legend:** MARGRETHE II - DANMARKS DRONNING **Rev:**
Crowned arms within ornaments and value **Edge:** Alternate
reeded and plain sections **Note:** Without initials.

Date	Mintage	F	VF	XF	Unc	BU
2002(h)	5,500,000	—	—	—	6.00	10.00

KM# 890   20 KRONER
9.3000 g., Aluminum-Bronze, 27 mm. **Ruler:** Margrethe II **Series:**
Danish towers **Obv:** Crowned bust right within circle, mint mark and
date **Obv. Legend:** MARGRETHE II - DANMARKS DRONNING
Rev: Copenhagen Old Stock Exchange spire with four intertwined
dragon tails **Edge:** Alternate reeded and plain sections

Date	Mintage	F	VF	XF	Unc	BU
2003(h)	1,208,600	—	—	—	6.00	10.00

KM# 891   20 KRONER
9.3000 g., Aluminum-Bronze, 27 mm. **Ruler:** Margrethe II **Obv:**
Crowned bust right within circle, mint mark and date **Obv.
Legend:** MARGRETHE II - DANMARKS DRONNING **Rev:**
Crowned arms above denomination **Edge:** Alternate reeded and
plain sections

Date	Mintage	F	VF	XF	Unc	BU
2003(h)	5,720,000	—	—	—	6.00	10.00
2004(h)	6,922,182	—	—	—	6.00	10.00
2004(h) Proof	3,000	Value: 50.00				
2005(h)	4,194,000	—	—	—	6.00	10.00
2005(h) Proof	2,650	Value: 50.00				
2006(h)	3,051,000	—	—	—	6.00	10.00
2006(h) Proof	1,800	Value: 50.00				
2007(h)	2,409,000	—	—	—	5.00	10.00
2007(h) Proof	1,400	Value: 50.00				
2008(h)	1,982,000	—	—	—	5.00	10.00
2008(h) Proof	1,000	Value: 50.00				
2009(h)	2,021,000	—	—	—	5.00	10.00
2009(h) Proof	1,050	Value: 50.00				
2010(h) In sets only	—	—	—	—	5.00	
2010(h) Proof	—	Value: 50.00				

KM# 892   20 KRONER
9.3100 g., Aluminum-Bronze, 27 mm. **Ruler:** Margrethe II
Series: Danish towers **Obv:** Crowned bust right within circle, mint
mark and date **Obv. Legend:** MARGRETHE II - DANMARKS
DRONNING **Rev:** Christiansborg Castle (parliament) tower and
Danish flag **Edge:** Alternate reeded and plain sections

Date	Mintage	F	VF	XF	Unc	BU
2003(h)	1,208,600	—	—	—	6.00	10.00

KM# 893   20 KRONER
9.3100 g., Aluminum-Bronze, 27 mm. **Ruler:** Margrethe II
Series: Danish Towers **Obv:** Crowned bust right within circle,
date below **Obv. Legend:** MARGRETHE II - DANMARKS
DRONNING **Rev:** Gåsetårnet tower **Edge:** Alternate reeded and
plain sections

Date	Mintage	F	VF	XF	Unc	BU
2004(h)	1,208,600	—	—	—	6.00	10.00

KM# 894   20 KRONER
9.3100 g., Aluminum-Bronze, 27 mm. **Ruler:** Margrethe II
Subject: Crown Prince's Wedding **Obv:** Crowned bust right
within circle, date below **Obv. Legend:** MARGRETHE II -
DANMARKS DRONNING **Rev:** Crown Prince Frederik and
Crown Princess Mary **Edge:** Alternate reeded and plain sections

Date	Mintage	F	VF	XF	Unc	BU
2004(h)	1,200,000	—	—	—	7.00	10.00

KM# 897   20 KRONER
9.3100 g., Aluminum-Bronze, 27 mm. **Ruler:** Margrethe II
Series: Danish Towers **Obv:** Crowned bust right within circle,
date below **Obv. Legend:** MARGRETHE II - DANMARKS
DRONNING **Rev:** Svaneke water tower, Bornholm **Edge:**
Alternate reeded and plain sections

Date	Mintage	F	VF	XF	Unc	BU
2004(h)	1,208,600	—	—	—	6.00	10.00

KM# 899   20 KRONER
9.3000 g., Aluminum-Bronze, 27 mm.   **Ruler:** Margrethe II   **Series:** Danish Towers **Obv:** Crowned bust right within circle, date below **Obv. Legend:** MARGRETHE II - DANMARKS DRONNING **Rev:** Landet Kirke, with elements from the story of Elvira Madigan and Sixten Sparre, including a revolver among leaves of chestnut-trees **Edge:** Segmented reeding

Date	Mintage	F	VF	XF	Unc	BU
2005(h)	1,208,600	—	—	—	6.00	10.00

KM# 901   20 KRONER
9.3000 g., Aluminum-Bronze, 27 mm.   **Ruler:** Margrethe II   **Series:** Danish Towers **Obv:** Crowned bust right within circle, date below **Obv. Legend:** MARGRETHE II - DANMARKS DRONNING **Rev:** Lighthouse of Nolsoy (Faeroe Islands) **Edge:** Alternate plain and reeded segments

Date	Mintage	F	VF	XF	Unc	BU
2005(h)	1,208,600	—	—	—	6.00	10.00

KM# 902   20 KRONER
9.3300 g., Aluminum-Bronze, 27 mm.   **Ruler:** Margrethe II **Series:** Danish Towers **Obv:** Crowned bust right within circle, date below **Obv. Legend:** MARGRETHE II - DANMARKS DRONNING **Rev:** Gråsten Castle Bell Tower **Edge:** Segmented reeding

Date	Mintage	F	VF	XF	Unc	BU
2006(h)	1,208,600	—	—	—	6.00	10.00

KM# 913   20 KRONER
9.3000 g., Aluminum-Bronze, 27 mm.   **Ruler:** Margrethe II   **Series:** Danish Towers **Obv:** Crowned bust right within circle, date below **Obv. Legend:** MARGRETHE II - DANMARKS DRONNING **Rev:** The Greenland Cairns: Nukaritt/Three Brothers **Rev. Legend:** TRE BRØDRE **Edge:** Alternate plain and reeded segments

Date	Mintage	F	VF	XF	Unc	BU
2006(h)	1,208,600	—	—	—	6.00	10.00

KM# 919   20 KRONER
9.3000 g., Aluminum-Bronze, 27 mm.   **Ruler:** Margrethe II   **Series:** Danish Towers **Obv:** Bust with tiarra right **Obv. Legend:** MARGRETHE II - DANMARKS DRONNING **Rev:** City Hall in Copenhagen **Rev. Legend:** KØBENHAVNS RÅDHUS **Edge:** Alternate plain and reeded segments

Date	Mintage	F	VF	XF	Unc	BU
2007(h)	1,208,600	—	—	—	6.00	10.00

KM# 920   20 KRONER
9.3000 g., Aluminum-Bronze, 27 mm.   **Ruler:** Margrethe II   **Series:** Danish Ships **Obv:** Crowned bust right **Obv. Legend:** MARGRETHE II - DANMARKS DRONNING **Rev:** Sailing ship Jylland **Rev. Legend:** FREGATTEN - JYLLAND **Edge:** Segmented reeding

Date	Mintage	F	VF	XF	Unc	BU
2007(h)	1,200,000	—	—	—	7.00	10.00

KM# 921   20 KRONER
9.3000 g., Aluminum-Bronze, 27 mm.   **Ruler:** Margrethe II   **Series:** Danish ships **Subject:** The Galathea 3 expedition **Obv:** Crowned bust right **Obv. Legend:** MARGRETHE II - DANMARKS DRONNING **Rev:** Ship Vaedderen, route map in background **Rev. Legend:** VAEDDEREN **Edge:** Segmented reeding

Date	Mintage	F	VF	XF	Unc	BU
2007(h)	1,200,000	—	—	—	6.00	10.00

KM# 926   20 KRONER
9.3000 g., Aluminum-Bronze, 27 mm.   **Ruler:** Margrethe II   **Series:** Danish Ships **Obv:** Head with tiara right **Rev:** World's first ocean-going diesel-engine merchant ship, built 1912 **Rev. Legend:** SELANDIA **Edge:** Segmented reeding

Date	Mintage	F	VF	XF	Unc	BU
2008(h)	1,200,000	—	—	—	6.00	9.00
2008(h) Proof	1,500	Value: 85.00				

KM# 927   20 KRONER
9.3000 g., Aluminum-Bronze, 27 mm.   **Ruler:** Margrethe II   **Series:** Danish Ships **Subject:** Voyage to Dublin, Ireland, with full size replica Viking ship, HAVHINGSTEN **Obv:** Crowned bust right **Obv. Legend:** MARGRETHE II - DANMARKS DRONNING **Rev:** Sailing vessel at sea **Rev. Legend:** HAVHINGSTEN / 20 KRONER **Edge:** Segmented reeding

Date	Mintage	F	VF	XF	Unc	BU
2008	1,200,000	—	—	—	6.00	9.00
2008 Proof	1,500	Value: 85.00				

KM# 928   20 KRONER
9.3000 g., Aluminum-Bronze, 27 mm.   **Ruler:** Margrethe II   **Series:** Danish Ships **Rev:** Royal Yacht Dannebrog **Edge:** Segmented reeding

Date	Mintage	F	VF	XF	Unc	BU
2008	1,200,000	—	—	—	5.00	9.00
2008 Proof	1,500	Value: 85.00				

KM# 935   20 KRONER
9.3000 g., Aluminum-Bronze, 27 mm.   **Ruler:** Margrethe II   **Series:** Danish Ships **Obv:** Crowned bust right **Obv. Legend:** MARGRETHE II - DANMARKS DRONNING **Rev:** Lightship XVII (built 1895) on duty **Edge:** Segmented reeding

Date	Mintage	F	VF	XF	Unc	BU
2009	1,100,000	—	—	—	5.00	9.00
2009 Proof	1,500	Value: 85.00				

KM# 936   20 KRONER
9.3000 g., Aluminum-Bronze, 27 mm.   **Ruler:** Margrethe II   **Series:** Danish Ships **Obv:** Crowned bust facing right **Rev:** FAERØBÅD (Boat of Faeroe Islands) **Edge:** Segmented reeding

Date	Mintage	F	VF	XF	Unc	BU
2009	900,000	—	—	—	5.00	9.00
2009 Proof	2,825	Value: 85.00				

KM# 937   20 KRONER
9.3000 g., Aluminum-Bronze, 27 mm.   **Ruler:** Margrethe II   **Subject:** Queen's 70th Birthday **Obv:** Head right **Rev:** Crowned shield against background of daisies

Date	Mintage	F	VF	XF	Unc	BU
2010	1,440,000	—	—	—	6.50	9.00
2010 Proof	4,100	Value: 25.00				

KM# 940   20 KRONER
9.3000 g., Aluminum-Bronze, 27 mm.   **Ruler:** Margrethe II   **Series:** Danish Ships **Subject:** Greenland kayak - women's ship **Obv:** Bust facing right **Rev. Legend:** "KAJAK • KONEBÅD" **Edge:** Segmented reeding

Date	Mintage	F	VF	XF	Unc	BU
2010	972,000	—	—	—	5.00	
2010 Proof	1,877	—	—	—		

KM# 941   20 KRONER
9.3000 g., Aluminum-Bronze, 27 mm.   **Ruler:** Margrethe II   **Series:** Danish Ships **Subject:** The Hjejlen, a paddle steamer **Obv:** Head right **Obv. Legend:** MARGRETHE II DANMARKS DRONNING **Rev:** The Hjejlen and value **Edge:** Segmented reeding

Date	Mintage	F	VF	XF	Unc	BU
2011	700,000	—	—	—	6.00	
2011 Proof	2,262	Value: 30.00				

KM# 942   20 KRONER
9.3000 g., Aluminum-Bronze, 27 mm. **Ruler:** Margrethe II
Subject: The Emma Maersk, a container ship **Obv:** Head right
Obv. Legend: MARGRETHE II DANMARKS DRONNING **Rev:**
Emma Maersk, container ship, right **Edge:** Segmented reeding

Date	Mintage	F	VF	XF	Unc	BU
2011	800,000	—	—	—	6.00	—
2011 Proof	3,810	Value: 30.00				

KM# 944   20 KRONER
9.3000 g., Aluminum-Bronze, 27 mm. **Ruler:** Margrethe II **Obv:**
Head right **Obv. Legend:** MARGRETHE II DANMARKS
DRONNING **Rev:** Crowned shield and value **Edge:** Segmented
reeding

Date	Mintage	F	VF	XF	Unc	BU
2011(h)	—	—	—	—	6.00	—
2011(h) Proof	—	Value: 50.00				

KM# 917   100 KRONER
31.0000 g., 0.9990 Silver 0.9956 oz. ASW, 38 mm. **Ruler:**
Margrethe II **Subject:** International Polar Year 2007-2009 **Obv:**
Crowned bust right **Obv. Legend:** MARGRETHE II - DANMARKS
DRONNING **Rev:** Polar bear facing, walking on ice flow **Rev.
Legend:** POLARÅR 2007-2009

Date	Mintage	F	VF	XF	Unc	BU
2007(h)	43,048	—	—	—	—	50.00

KM# 930   100 KRONER
31.1000 g., 0.9990 Silver 0.9988 oz. ASW, 38 mm. **Ruler:**
Margrethe II **Subject:** International Polar Year 2007-2009 **Rev:**
Globe and dog sled

Date	Mintage	F	VF	XF	Unc	BU
2008	15,631	—	—	—	—	50.00

KM# 933   100 KRONER
31.1000 g., 0.9990 Silver 0.9988 oz. ASW, 38 mm. **Ruler:**
Margrethe II **Subject:** International Polar Year 2007-2009 **Rev:**
Ice scape, Northern Lights

Date	Mintage	F	VF	XF	Unc	BU
2009	10,600	—	—	—	—	50.00

KM# 895   200 KRONER
31.1000 g., 0.9990 Silver 0.9988 oz. ASW, 38.3 mm. **Ruler:**
Margrethe II **Subject:** Wedding of Crown Prince **Obv:** Crowned
bust right within circle, date below **Obv. Legend:** MARGRETHE
II - DANMARKS DRONNING **Rev:** Crown Prince Frederik and
Crown Princess Mary **Edge:** Plain **Note:** No initials.

Date	Mintage	F	VF	XF	Unc	BU
2004(h)	125,000	—	—	—	—	60.00

KM# 929   500 KRONER
31.1000 g., 0.9990 Silver 0.9988 oz. ASW, 38 mm. **Ruler:**
Margrethe II **Rev:** Royal Yacht Dannebrog

Date	Mintage	F	VF	XF	Unc	BU
2008	31,700	—	—	—	—	100

KM# 938   500 KRONER
31.1000 g., 0.9990 Silver 0.9988 oz. ASW, 38 mm. **Ruler:**
Margrethe II **Subject:** Queen's 70th Birthday **Obv:** Head right
Rev: Crowned shield against a background of daisies

Date	Mintage	F	VF	XF	Unc	BU
2010	—	—	—	—	—	95.00

KM# 918   1000 KRONER
8.6500 g., 0.9000 Gold 0.2503 oz. AGW, 22 mm. **Ruler:**
Margrethe II **Subject:** International Polar Year 2007-2009 **Obv:**
Crowned bust right **Obv. Legend:** MARGRETHE II - DANMARKS
DRONNING **Rev:** Polar bear facing, walking on ice flow **Rev.
Legend:** POLARÅR 2007-2009 **Note:** Struck from gold from
Greenland having a small polar bear to right of denomination.

Date	Mintage	F	VF	XF	Unc	BU
2007(h) Proof	6,000	Value: 450				

KM# 931   1000 KRONER
8.6500 g., 0.9000 Gold 0.2503 oz. AGW, 22 mm. **Ruler:**
Margrethe II **Subject:** International Polar Year 2007-2009 **Rev:**
Globe and dog sled

Date	Mintage	F	VF	XF	Unc	BU
2008 Proof	3,604	Value: 450				

KM# 934   1000 KRONER
8.6500 g., 0.9000 Gold 0.2503 oz. AGW, 22 mm. **Ruler:**
Margrethe II **Subject:** International Polar Year 2007-2009 **Rev:**
Ice scape, Northern Lights

Date	Mintage	F	VF	XF	Unc	BU
2009 Proof	2,400	Value: 450				

KM# 939   1000 KRONER
8.6500 g., 0.9000 Gold 0.2503 oz. AGW, 22 mm. **Ruler:**
Margrethe II **Subject:** Queen's 70th Birthday **Obv:** Bust right
Rev: Crowned shield against background of daisies

Date	Mintage	F	VF	XF	Unc	BU
2010	—	—	—	—	—	500

MINT SETS

KM#	Date	Mintage	Identification	Issue Price	Mkt Val
MS46	2001 (5)	28,000	KM866.2, 868, 869, 873, 874, 887, 888	15.00	37.50
MS47	2002 (7)	28,000	KM866.3, 868.2, 869.2, 873.2, 874.2, 887.2, 888.2	17.50	35.00
MS48	2003 (6)	30,000	KM866.3, 868.2, 873.2, 889, 890, 891	17.50	35.00
MS49	2004 (8)	33,000	KM866.3, 868.2, 869.2, 873.2, 874.2, 891, 894, 896, plus Battle of Køge Bay medal in Nordic gold	34.50	75.00
MS50	2005 (8)	26,700	KM866.3, 868.2, 869.2, 873.2, 874.2, 891, 896, 898, plus Battle of Copenhagen medal in Nordic gold	34.50	50.00
MS51	2006 (8)	25,000	KM#866.3, 868.2, 869.2, 873.2, 874.2, 891, 896, plus Floating Dock medal in Copenhagen sound medal in Nordic gold	40.00	42.00
MS52	2006 (8)	5,000	KM#866.3, 868.2, 869.2, 873.2, 874.2, 891, 896 plus children's medal in Nordic gold. (Children's coin set)	—	48.00
MS53	2002-07 (9)	8,600	KM#889, 890, 892, 893, 897, 899, 901, 902, 913, 919. (Tower coin set)	—	100
MS54	2005-07 (6)	6,675	KM#898, 900, 903, 914, 923 plus Hans Christian Anderson medal in Nordic gold (Fairy tale coin set)	—	55.00
MS55	2007 (8)	23,000	KM#866.3, 868.2, 869.2, 873.2, 874.2, 891, 896 plus Galathea medal in Nordic gold.	—	42.00
MS56	2007 (7)	2,700	KM#866.3, 868.2, 869.2, 873.2, 874.2, 891, 896 plus Children's medal in Nordic gold (Children's coin set)	46.00	50.00
MS57	2008 (7)	1,000	KM#866.3, 868.2, 869.2, 873.2, 874.2, 891, 896 plus Children's medal in Nordic gold (Children's coin set).	—	50.00
MS58	2008 (8)	20,350	KM#866.3, 868.2, 869.2, 873.2, 874.2, 891, 896 plus Battle of Kronberg Castle Coast (Elsinore) medal in Nordic gold.	—	45.00
MS59	2009 (6)	1,450	KM#866.3, 869.2, 873.2, 874.2, 891, 896 plus Children's medal in Nordic gold (Children's coin set)	—	65.00
MS60	2009 (7)	24,250	KM#866.3, 869.2, 873.2, 874.2, 891, 896 plus Neptune admiring Naval fleet medal in Nordic gold.	—	60.00
MS61	2010 (7)	1,300	KM#866.3, 869.2, 873.2, 874.2, 891, 896 plus children's medal in Nordic gold (Children's coin set).	—	45.00
MS62	2010 (7)	—	KM#866.3, 869.2, 873.2, 874.2, 891, 896 plus Danish Navy's first dry dock medal in Nordic gold	—	45.00
MS63	2011 (6)	—	KM#866.3, 869.2, 873.2, 874.2, 943-944 & Children's Metal.	—	45.00
MS64	2011 (6)	—	KM#866.3, 869.2, 873.2, 874.2, 943-944	—	185

PROOF SETS

KM#	Date	Mintage	Identification	Issue Price	Mkt Val
PS1	2004 (8)	3,000	KM#866.3, 868.2, 869.2, 873.2, 874.2, 891, 896, plus Royal Wedding medal in .925 Silver	150	250
PS2	2005 (8)	2,650	KM866.3, 868.2, 869.2, 873.2, 874.2, 896, 891 plus 1801 Battle of Copenhagen medal in .925 Silver	150	185
PS3	2006 (8)	1,800	KM#866.3, 868.2, 869.2, 873.2, 874.2, 896, 891 plus 1691 Floating Dock medal in .925 Silver	160	185
PS4	2007 (8)	1,400	KM#866.3, 868.2, 869.2, 873.2, 874.2, 896, 891, plus Galathea medal in .925 silver	160	185
PS5	2008 (8)	1,000	KM#866.3, 868.2, 869.2, 873.2, 874.2, 896, 891, plus medal in .925 Silver	—	200
PS6	2009 (7)	1,050	KM#866.3, 869.2, 873.2, 874.2, 891, 896 plus Nepture admiring Naval fleet medal in .925 Silver.	—	250
PS7	2010 (7)	1,010	KM#866.3, 869.2, 873.2, 874.2, 891, 896 plus Danish Navy's first dry dock medal in .925 Silver.	—	185
PS8	2011 (2)	3,010	KM#943-944	—	28.00
PS9	2011 (6)	—	KM#866.3, 869.2, 873.2, 874.2, 943-944	—	185

DJIBOUTI

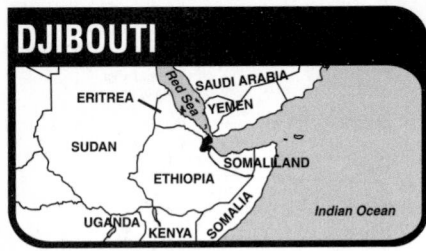

The Republic of Djibouti (formerly French Somaliland and the French Overseas Territory of Afars and Issas), located in northeast Africa at the Bab el Mandeb Strait connecting the Suez Canal and the Red Sea with the Gulf of Aden and the Indian Ocean, has an area of 8,950 sq. mi. (22,000 sq. km.) and a population of 421,320. Capital: Djibouti. The tiny nation has less than one sq. mi. of arable land, and no natural resources except salt, sand, and camels. The commercial activities of the transshipment port of Djibouti and the Addis Abada-Djibouti railroad are the basis of the economy. Salt, fish and hides are exported.

REPUBLIC
STANDARD COINAGE

KM# 34 10 FRANCS
3.4000 g., Copper-Nickel, 20.9 mm. **Obv:** National arms **Rev:** Chimpanzee **Edge:** Plain

Date	Mintage	F	VF	XF	Unc	BU
2003	—			—	2.00	4.00

KM# 23 10 FRANCS
3.0000 g., Aluminum-Bronze, 20 mm. **Obv:** National arms within wreath, date below **Rev:** Boats on water, denomination above **Note:** Varieties exist.

Date	Mintage	F	VF	XF	Unc	BU
2004(a)	—			—	2.50	4.50
2007(a)	—				2.50	4.50
2010(a)	—				2.50	4.50

KM# 24 20 FRANCS
4.0000 g., Aluminum-Bronze, 23.5 mm. **Obv:** National arms within wreath, date below **Rev:** Boats on water, denomination above **Note:** Varieties exist.

Date	Mintage	F	VF	XF	Unc	BU
2007(a)	—			—	2.50	4.50
2010(a)	—			—	2.50	4.50

KM# 25 50 FRANCS
7.0500 g., Copper-Nickel, 25.7 mm. **Obv:** National arms within wreath, date below **Rev:** Pair of dromedary camels right, denomination above

Date	Mintage	F	VF	XF	Unc	BU
2007(a)	—			—	6.00	9.00
2010(a)	—			—	6.00	9.00

KM# 38 100 FRANCS
Nickel Possibly Copper-Nickel-Zinc, confirmation of magnetic quality requested, 35 mm. **Subject:** 25th Anniversary of Independence **Obv:** Small national arms on state flag **Obv. Legend:** REPUBLIQUE DE DJIBOUTI **Rev:** UNITÉ in color **Rev. Legend:** UNITÉ ... ÉGALITÉ ... PAIX

Date	Mintage	F	VF	XF	Unc	BU
ND(2002)	—			—	—	145

KM# 39 100 FRANCS
Nickel Possibly Copper-Nickel-Zinc, confirmation of magnetic quality requested, 35 mm. **Subject:** 25th Anniversary of Independence **Obv:** Small national arms on state flag **Obv. Legend:** REPUBLIQUE DE DJIBOUTI **Rev:** É/GAL/ITÉ in color **Rev. Legend:** UNITÉ ... ÉGALITÉ ... PAIX

Date	Mintage	F	VF	XF	Unc	BU
AH(2002)	—			—	—	145

KM# 40 100 FRANCS
Nickel Possibly Copper-Nickel-Zinc, confirmation of magnetic quality requested, 35 mm. **Subject:** 25th Anniversary of Independence **Obv:** Small national arms on state flag **Obv. Legend:** REPUBLIQUE DE DJIBOUTI **Rev:** PAI/X in color **Rev. Legend:** UNITÉ ... ÉGALITÉ ... PAIX

Date	Mintage	F	VF	XF	Unc	BU
ND(2002)	—			—	—	145

KM# 26 100 FRANCS
12.0000 g., Copper-Nickel, 30 mm. **Obv:** National arms within wreath, date below **Rev:** Pair of dromedary camels right, denomination above

Date	Mintage	F	VF	XF	Unc	BU
2004(a)	—		—	2.50	7.00	9.00
2007(a)	—		—	2.50	7.00	9.00
2010(a)	—		—	2.50	7.00	9.00

KM# 41 250 FRANCS
22.2000 g., 0.9000 Silver 0.6423 oz. ASW **Obv:** National arms **Obv. Legend:** REPUBLIQUE DE DJIBOUTI **Rev:** Two dromedary camels right **Rev. Legend:** UNITÉ - ÉGALITÉ - PAIX

Date	Mintage	F	VF	XF	Unc	BU
2002(a) Proof	—					

 Note: Confirmation requested

KM# 27 500 FRANCS
Aluminum-Bronze **Obv:** National arms within wreath, date below **Rev:** Denomination within sprays

Date	Mintage	F	VF	XF	Unc	BU
2010(a)	—		—	6.00	12.00	15.00

DOMINICAN REPUBLIC

The Dominican Republic, which occupies the eastern two-thirds of the island of Hispaniola, has an area of 18,704 sq. mi. (48,734 sq. km.) and a population of 7.9 million. Capital: Santo Domingo. The largely agricultural economy produces sugar, coffee, tobacco and cocoa. Tourism and casino gaming are also a rising source of revenue.

REPUBLIC
REFORM COINAGE
1937

100 Centavos = 1 Peso Oro

KM# 80.2 PESO
6.4900 g., Brass, 25 mm. **Subject:** Juan Pablo Duarte **Obv:** National arms and denomination **Rev:** DUARTE below bust, date below **Note:** Medal die alignment.

Date	Mintage	F	VF	XF	Unc	BU
2002	—			—	2.00	2.50
2005	—			—	2.00	2.50
2008	—			—	2.00	2.50

KM# 90 PESO
12.5000 g., Copper-Nickel, 30.6 mm. **Obv:** Pan American Games logo **Rev:** National arms and denomination **Edge:** Reeded

Date	Mintage	F	VF	XF	Unc	BU
2003 Proof	—	Value: 15.00				

KM# 89 5 PESOS
6.0600 g., Bi-Metallic Stainless Steel center in Brass ring, 23 mm. **Subject:** Sanchez **Obv:** National arms and denomination **Rev:** Portrait facing within circle, date below **Edge:** Segmented reeding

Date	Mintage	F	VF	XF	Unc	BU
2002	—			—	2.50	3.00
2005	—			—	2.50	3.00
2007	—			—	2.50	3.00
2008	—			—	2.50	3.00

KM# 106 10 PESOS
8.2000 g., Bi-Metallic Brass center in Copper-Nickel ring, 27 mm. **Obv:** Value at left of national arms **Obv. Legend:** • REPUBLICA

DOMINICANA • **Rev:** Bust of General Mella facing **Rev. Legend:** BANCO CENTRAL DE LA REPUBLICA DOMINICANA **Edge:** Segmented reeding

Date	Mintage	F	VF	XF	Unc	BU
2005	—	—	—	—	6.00	8.00
2007	—	—	—	—	6.00	8.00
2008	—	—	—	—	6.00	8.00

KM# 107   25 PESOS

8.5600 g., Copper-Nickel, 28.82 mm.   **Obv:** Value at left of national arms **Obv. Legend:** REPUBLICA DOMINICANA **Rev:** Bust of General Luperon facing **Rev. Legend:** BANCO CENTRAL DE LA REPUBLICA DOMINICANA **Rev. Inscription:** HEROE DE LA RESTAURACION **Edge:** Reeded

Date	Mintage	F	VF	XF	Unc	BU
2005	—	—	—	—	5.00	7.00
2008	—	—	—	—	5.00	7.00

EAST CARIBBEAN STATES

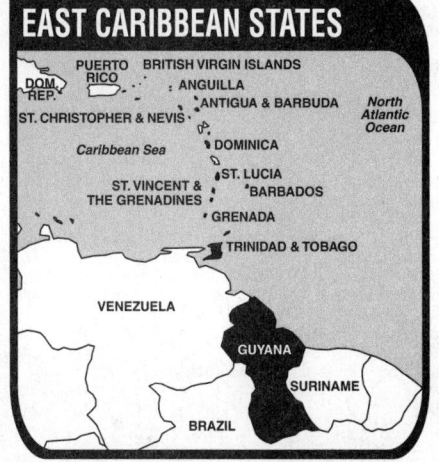

The East Caribbean States, formerly the British Caribbean Territories (Eastern Group), formed a currency board in 1950 to provide the constituent territories of Trinidad & Tobago, Barbados, British Guiana (now Guyana), British Virgin Islands, Anguilla, St. Kitts, Nevis, Antigua, Dominica, St. Lucia, St. Vincent and Grenada with a common currency, thereby permitting withdrawal of the regular British Pound currency. This was dissolved in 1965 and after the breakup, the East Caribbean Territories, a grouping including Barbados, the Leeward and Windward Islands, came into being. Coinage of the dissolved 'Eastern Group' continues to circulate. Paper currency of the East Caribbean Authority was first issued in 1965 and although Barbados withdrew from the group they continued using them prior to 1973 when Barbados issued a decimal coinage.

A series of 4-dollar coins tied to the FAO coinage program were released in 1970 under the name of the Caribbean Development Bank by eight loosely federated island groupings in the eastern Caribbean. These issues are listed individually in this volume under Antigua, Barbados, Dominica, Grenada, Montserrat, St. Kitts, St. Lucia and St. Vincent.

STANDARD COINAGE
100 Cents = 1 Dollar

KM# 10   CENT

0.9000 g., Aluminum, 18.4 mm.   **Ruler:** Elizabeth II **Obv:** Young bust right **Rev:** Wreath divides denomination, date upper right **Shape:** Scalloped **Note:** Prev. KM#1.

Date	Mintage	F	VF	XF	Unc	BU
2001	—	—	—	—	0.20	0.30

KM# 34   CENT

1.0300 g., Aluminum, 18.42 mm.   **Ruler:** Elizabeth II **Obv:** Crowned head right **Rev:** Denomination **Edge:** Plain

Date	Mintage	F	VF	XF	Unc	BU
2002	—	—	—	—	0.20	0.30
2004	—	—	—	—	0.20	0.30
2008	—	—	—	—	0.20	0.30
2011	—	—	—	—	0.20	0.30

KM# 35   2 CENTS

1.4200 g., Aluminum, 21.46 mm.   **Ruler:** Elizabeth II **Obv:** Crowned head right **Rev:** Denomination **Edge:** Plain

Date	Mintage	F	VF	XF	Unc	BU
2002	—	—	—	—	0.25	0.35
2004	—	—	—	—	0.25	0.35
2008	—	—	—	—	0.25	0.35

KM# 36   5 CENTS

1.7400 g., Aluminum, 23.11 mm.   **Ruler:** Elizabeth II **Obv:** Crowned head right **Rev:** Denomination **Edge:** Plain

Date	Mintage	F	VF	XF	Unc	BU
2002	—	—	—	—	0.30	0.45
2004	—	—	—	—	0.30	0.45
2008	—	—	—	—	0.30	0.45
2010	—	—	—	—	0.30	0.45

KM# 37   10 CENTS

2.5900 g., Copper-Nickel, 18.06 mm.   **Ruler:** Elizabeth II **Obv:** Crowned head right **Rev:** Sir Francis Drake's Golden Hind and denomination **Edge:** Reeded

Date	Mintage	F	VF	XF	Unc	BU
2002	—	—	—	—	0.40	0.60
2004	—	—	—	—	0.40	0.60
2007	—	—	—	—	0.40	0.60

KM# 37a   10 CENTS

Nickel Plated Steel, 18 mm.   **Ruler:** Elizabeth II **Obv:** Crowned head right **Rev:** Sir Francis Drake's Golden Hind and denomination **Edge:** Reeded

Date	Mintage	F	VF	XF	Unc	BU
2009	—	—	—	—	0.40	0.60

KM# 38   25 CENTS

6.4800 g., Copper-Nickel, 23.98 mm.   **Ruler:** Elizabeth II **Obv:** Crowned head right **Rev:** Sir Francis Drake's Golden Hind and denomination **Edge:** Reeded

Date	Mintage	F	VF	XF	Unc	BU
2002	—	—	—	—	0.50	0.75
2004	—	—	—	—	0.50	0.75
2007	—	—	—	—	0.50	0.75

KM# 38a   25 CENTS

Nickel Plated Steel, 24 mm.   **Ruler:** Elizabeth II **Obv:** Crowned head right **Rev:** Sir Francis Drake's Golden Hind and denomination **Edge:** Reeded

Date	Mintage	F	VF	XF	Unc	BU
2010	—	—	—	—	0.50	0.75

KM# 39   DOLLAR

7.9800 g., Copper-Nickel, 26.5 mm.   **Ruler:** Elizabeth II **Obv:** Crowned head right **Rev:** Sir Francis Drake's Golden Hind and denomination **Edge:** Segmented reeding

Date	Mintage	F	VF	XF	Unc	BU
2002	—	—	—	—	2.00	3.00
2004	—	—	—	—	2.00	3.00
2007	—	—	—	—	2.00	3.00

KM# 40   DOLLAR

28.2800 g., Copper-Nickel Gilt, 38.6 mm.   **Ruler:** Elizabeth II **Subject:** Golden Jubilee Monarchs **Obv:** Crowned head right **Rev:** Henry III (1216-1277) **Edge:** Reeded

Date	Mintage	F	VF	XF	Unc	BU
2002	5,000	—	—	—	22.50	25.00

KM# 42   DOLLAR

28.2800 g., Copper-Nickel Gilt, 38.6 mm.   **Ruler:** Elizabeth II **Subject:** Golden Jubilee Monarchs **Obv:** Crowned head right **Rev:** Edward III (1327-1377) **Edge:** Reeded

Date	Mintage	F	VF	XF	Unc	BU
2002	5,000	—	—	—	22.50	25.00

KM# 44   DOLLAR

28.2800 g., Copper-Nickel Gilt, 38.6 mm.   **Ruler:** Elizabeth II **Subject:** Golden Jubilee Monarchs **Obv:** Crowned head right **Rev:** George III (1760-1820) **Edge:** Reeded

Date	Mintage	F	VF	XF	Unc	BU
2002	5,000	—	—	—	22.50	25.00

KM# 46   DOLLAR

28.2800 g., Copper-Nickel Gilt, 38.6 mm.   **Ruler:** Elizabeth II **Subject:** Golden Jubilee Monarchs **Obv:** Crowned head right **Rev:** Queen Victoria (1837-1901) **Edge:** Reeded

Date	Mintage	F	VF	XF	Unc	BU
2002	5,000	—	—	—	22.50	25.00

KM# 48   DOLLAR

28.2800 g., Copper-Nickel Gilt, 38.6 mm.   **Ruler:** Elizabeth II **Subject:** Golden Jubilee Monarchs **Obv:** Crowned head right **Rev:** Queen Elizabeth II (1952-) **Edge:** Reeded

Date	Mintage	F	VF	XF	Unc	BU
2002	5,000	—	—	—	22.50	25.00

KM# 86   DOLLAR

27.7300 g., Copper-Nickel, 38.5 mm.   **Ruler:** Elizabeth II **Subject:** Coronation Jubilee **Obv:** Crowned head right **Rev:** Fireworks display above building **Edge:** Reeded

Date	Mintage	F	VF	XF	Unc	BU
2002	—	—	—	—	10.00	12.00

KM# 58   DOLLAR

7.9800 g., Copper-Nickel, 26.5 mm.   **Ruler:** Elizabeth II **Subject:** 25th Anniversary **Obv:** Head right **Rev:** Motto within wreath

Date	Mintage	F	VF	XF	Unc	BU
2008	500,000	—	—	—	—	5.00

KM# 51   2 DOLLARS

56.5600 g., Copper-Nickel Gilt, 38.6 mm.   **Ruler:** Elizabeth II **Subject:** British Military Leaders **Obv:** Crowned head right **Rev:** Wellington's portrait and battle scene **Edge:** Reeded

Date	Mintage	F	VF	XF	Unc	BU
2002 Proof	10,000	Value: 45.00				

KM# 54   2 DOLLARS

56.5600 g., Copper-Nickel Gilt, 38.6 mm.   **Ruler:** Elizabeth II **Subject:** British Military Leaders **Obv:** Crowned head right **Rev:** Admiral Nelson's portrait and naval battle scene **Edge:** Reeded

Date	Mintage	F	VF	XF	Unc	BU
2003 Proof	10,000	Value: 45.00				

KM# 57   2 DOLLARS

56.5600 g., Copper-Nickel Gilt, 38.6 mm.   **Ruler:** Elizabeth II **Subject:** British Military Leaders **Obv:** Crowned head right **Rev:** Churchill's portrait and air battle scene **Edge:** Reeded

Date	Mintage	F	VF	XF	Unc	BU
2003 Proof	10,000	Value: 45.00				

KM# 41   10 DOLLARS
28.2800 g., 0.9250 Silver with gold cameo 0.8410 oz. ASW, 38.6 mm. **Ruler:** Elizabeth II **Subject:** Golden Jubilee Monarchs **Obv:** Crowned head right **Rev:** Henry III (1216-1272) **Edge:** Reeded

Date	Mintage	F	VF	XF	Unc	BU
2002 Proof	10,000	Value: 65.00				

KM# 41a   10 DOLLARS
39.9400 g., 0.9166 Gold 1.1770 oz. AGW, 38.6 mm. **Ruler:** Elizabeth II **Subject:** Golden Jubilee Monarchs **Obv:** Crowned head right **Rev:** Henry III (1216-1272) **Edge:** Reeded

Date	Mintage	F	VF	XF	Unc	BU
2002 Proof	100	Value: 2,000				

KM# 43   10 DOLLARS
28.2800 g., 0.9250 Silver 0.8410 oz. ASW, 38.6 mm. **Ruler:** Elizabeth II **Subject:** Golden Jubile Monarchs **Obv:** Crowned head right **Rev:** Edward III (1327-1377) **Edge:** Reeded

Date	Mintage	F	VF	XF	Unc	BU
2002 Proof	10,000	Value: 65.00				

KM# 43a   10 DOLLARS
39.9400 g., 0.9166 Gold 1.1770 oz. AGW, 38.6 mm. **Ruler:** Elizabeth II **Subject:** Golden Jubilee Monarchs **Obv:** Crowned head right **Rev:** Edward III (1327-1377) **Edge:** Reeded

Date	Mintage	F	VF	XF	Unc	BU
2002 Proof	100	Value: 2,000				

KM# 45   10 DOLLARS
28.2800 g., 0.9250 Silver with gold cameo 0.8410 oz. ASW, 38.6 mm. **Subject:** Golden Jubilee Monarchs **Obv:** Crowned head right **Rev:** George III (1760-1820) **Edge:** Reeded

Date	Mintage	F	VF	XF	Unc	BU
2002 Proof	10,000	Value: 65.00				

KM# 45a   10 DOLLARS
39.9400 g., 0.9166 Gold 1.1770 oz. AGW, 38.6 mm. **Ruler:** Elizabeth II **Subject:** Golden Jubilee Monarchs **Obv:** Crowned head right **Rev:** George III (1760-1820) **Edge:** Reeded

Date	Mintage	F	VF	XF	Unc	BU
2002 Proof	100	Value: 2,000				

KM# 47   10 DOLLARS
28.2800 g., 0.9250 Silver with partial gold plating 0.8410 oz. ASW, 38.6 mm. **Ruler:** Elizabeth II **Subject:** Golden Jubilee Monarchs **Obv:** Crowned head right **Rev:** Queen Victoria (1837-1901) **Edge:** Reeded

Date	Mintage	F	VF	XF	Unc	BU
2002 Proof	10,000	Value: 65.00				

KM# 47a   10 DOLLARS
39.9400 g., 0.9166 Gold 1.1770 oz. AGW, 38.6 mm. **Ruler:** Elizabeth II **Subject:** Golden Jubilee Monarchs **Obv:** Crowned head right **Rev:** Queen Victoria (1837-1901) **Edge:** Reeded

Date	Mintage	F	VF	XF	Unc	BU
2002 Proof	100	Value: 2,000				

KM# 49   10 DOLLARS
28.2800 g., 0.9250 Silver with gold cameo 0.8410 oz. ASW, 38.6 mm. **Ruler:** Elizabeth II **Subject:** Golden Jubilee Monarchs **Obv:** Crowned head right **Rev:** Queen Elizabeth II (1952-) **Edge:** Reeded

Date	Mintage	F	VF	XF	Unc	BU
2002 Proof	10,000	Value: 65.00				

KM# 49a   10 DOLLARS
39.9400 g., 0.9166 Gold 1.1770 oz. AGW, 38.6 mm. **Ruler:** Elizabeth II **Subject:** Golden Jubilee Monarchs **Obv:** Crowned head right **Rev:** Queen Elizabeth II (1952-) **Edge:** Reeded

Date	Mintage	F	VF	XF	Unc	BU
2002 Proof	100	Value: 2,000				

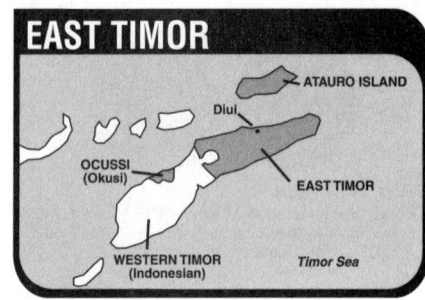

KM# 59   10 DOLLARS
Silver partially gilt, 39 mm. **Ruler:** Elizabeth II **Obv:** Head right, partially gilt **Rev:** Fireworks display above Buckingham Palace

Date	Mintage	F	VF	XF	Unc	BU
2002 Proof	—	Value: 50.00				

EAST TIMOR

East Timor, population: 522,433, area: 7332 sq. miles, capital: Dili, is primarily located on the eastern half of the island of Timor, just northwest of Australia at the eastern end of the Indonesian archipelago. Formerly a Portuguese colony, Timor declared its independence from Portugal on November 28, 1975. After nine short days of fledgling autonomy, a guerilla faction sympathetic to the Indonesian territorial claim to East Timor seized the government. On July 17, 1976 the Provisional government enacted a law, which dissolved the free republic and made East Timor the 24th province of Indonesia. Violent rule and civil unrest plagued the province, with great loss of life and extreme damage to property and natural resources until independence was again achieved with United Nations assistance during a period from 1999 to 2002. Emerging as the Democratic Republic of Timor-Leste and commonly known as East Timor the country has worked, with international assistance to rebuild its decimated infrastructure. Natural resources waiting to be tapped include rich oil reserves, though current exports are most dependent on coffee, sandalwood and marble. The first coins of the new republic were issued in 2003.

DEMOCRATIC REPUBLIC OF TIMOR-LESTE

DECIMAL COINAGE

KM# 1   CENTAVO
3.1000 g., Nickel Clad Steel, 17 mm. **Obv:** Nautilus above date **Rev:** Denomination within circle **Edge:** Plain

Date	Mintage	F	VF	XF	Unc	BU
2003	1,500,000	—	—	—	1.50	2.50
2003 Proof	12,500	Value: 8.00				
2004	1,500,000	—	—	—	1.50	2.50

KM# 2   5 CENTAVOS
4.1000 g., Nickel Clad Steel, 18.75 mm. **Obv:** Rice plant above date **Rev:** Denomination within circle **Edge:** Plain

Date	Mintage	F	VF	XF	Unc	BU
2003	1,500,000	—	—	—	2.00	3.00
2003 Proof	12,500	Value: 10.00				
2004	1,500,000	—	—	—	2.00	3.00
2006	—	—	—	—	2.00	3.00

KM# 3   10 CENTAVOS
5.2000 g., Nickel Clad Steel, 20.75 mm. **Obv:** Rooster left above date **Rev:** Denomination within circle **Edge:** Plain

Date	Mintage	F	VF	XF	Unc	BU
2003	2,500,000	—	—	—	2.50	4.00
2003 Proof	12,500	Value: 12.00				
2004	2,500,000	—	—	—	2.50	4.00
2006	—	—	—	—	2.50	4.00

KM# 4   25 CENTAVOS
5.8500 g., Nickel-Brass, 21.25 mm. **Obv:** Sail boat above date **Rev:** Denomination within circle **Edge:** Reeded

Date	Mintage	F	VF	XF	Unc	BU
2003	1,500,000	—	—	—	3.50	5.00
2003 Proof	12,500	Value: 16.00				
2004	1,500,000	—	—	—	3.50	5.00
2006	—	—	—	—	3.50	5.00

KM# 5   50 CENTAVOS
6.5000 g., Nickel-Brass, 25 mm. **Obv:** Coffee plant with beans above date **Rev:** Denomination within circle **Edge:** Reeded

Date	Mintage	F	VF	XF	Unc	BU
2003	1,000,000	—	—	—	5.00	7.00
2003 Proof	12,500	Value: 22.00				
2004	1,000,000	—	—	—	5.00	7.00
2006	—	—	—	—	5.00	7.00

MINT SETS

KM#	Date	Mintage	Identification	Issue Price	Mkt Val
MS1	2003 (5)	25,000	KM#1-5	27.84	35.00

PROOF SETS

KM#	Date	Mintage	Identification	Issue Price	Mkt Val
PS1	2003 (5)	12,500	KM#1-5	57.25	70.00

ECUADOR

The Republic of Ecuador, located astride the equator on the Pacific Coast of South America, has an area of 105,037 sq. mi. (283,560 sq. km.) and a population of 10.9 million. Capital: Quito. Agriculture is the mainstay of the economy but there are appreciable deposits of minerals and petroleum. It is one of the world's largest exporters of bananas and balsa wood. Coffee, cacao, sugar and petroleum are also valuable exports.

REPUBLIC

REFORM COINAGE
100 Centavos = 1 Dollar

KM# 104   CENTAVO (Un)
2.5200 g., Brass, 19 mm. **Obv:** Map of the Americas within circle **Rev:** Denomination **Edge:** Plain

Date	Mintage	F	VF	XF	Unc	BU
2003	—	—	—	—	0.20	0.40
2004	—	—	—	—	0.20	0.40

KM# 104a   CENTAVO (Un)
2.4200 g., Copper Plated Steel, 19 mm. **Obv:** Map of the Americas **Rev:** Denomination **Edge:** Plain

Date	Mintage	F	VF	XF	Unc	BU
2003	—	—	—	—	0.30	0.50

KM# 105   5 CENTAVOS (Cinco)
5.0000 g., Steel, 21.2 mm. **Subject:** Juan Montalvo **Obv:** Bust 3/4 facing and arms **Rev:** Denomination **Edge:** Plain

Date	Mintage	F	VF	XF	Unc	BU
2003	—	—	—	—	0.50	0.75

KM# 115   SUCRE (Un)
8.3600 g., 0.9000 Gold 0.2419 oz. AGW, 22 mm. **Subject:** Homage to Jefferson Pérez Quezada **Obv:** National arms **Obv. Legend:** BANCO CENTRAL DEL ECUADOR **Rev:** 3/4 length figure of Perez running **Rev. Legend:** BICAMPEON MUNDIAL - CAMPEON OLIMPICO ATLANTA 1996

Date	Mintage	F	VF	XF	Unc	BU
2006	—	Value: 450				

KM# 112   25000 SUCRES
27.1000 g., 0.9250 Silver 0.8059 oz. ASW, 40 mm. **Subject:** IBERO-AMERICA Series **Obv:** Coats of arms **Rev:** Balsawood sailing raft **Edge:** Reeded

Date	Mintage	F	VF	XF	Unc	BU
2002 Proof	—	Value: 65.00				

KM# 113   25000 SUCRES
27.0000 g., 0.9250 Silver 0.8029 oz. ASW, 40 mm. **Obv:** National arms **Rev:** Capital building in Quito **Edge:** Reeded

Date	Mintage	F	VF	XF	Unc	BU
2004 Proof	1,000	Value: 60.00				

KM# 114   25000 SUCRES
27.2000 g., 0.9250 Silver 0.8089 oz. ASW, 40 mm. **Subject:** 2006 World Cup Soccer **Obv:** National arms **Rev:** Ecuadorian Soccer player torso holding a soccer ball **Edge:** Reeded

Date	Mintage	F	VF	XF	Unc	BU
ND(2006) Proof	—	Value: 50.00				

EGYPT

The Arab Republic of Egypt, located on the northeastern corner of Africa, has an area of 385,229 sq. mi. (1,1001,450 sq. km.) and a population of 62.4 million. Capital: Cairo. Although Egypt is an almost rainless expanse of desert, its economy is predominantly agricultural. Cotton, rice and petroleum are exported. Other main sources of income are revenues from the Suez Canal, remittances of Egyptian workers abroad and tourism.

ARAB REPUBLIC
AH1391- / 1971- AD
DECIMAL COINAGE

KM# 941   5 PIASTRES
1.9500 g., Brass, 18 mm. **Obv:** Denomination divides dates below, legend above **Rev:** Antique pottery vase **Edge:** Plain

Date	Mintage	F	VF	XF	Unc	BU
AH1425-2004	—	—	—	—	1.50	2.00

KM# 941a   5 PIASTRES
1.5000 g., Brass Plated Steel, 18 mm. **Obv:** Denomination divides dates below, legend above **Rev:** Antique pottery vase

Date	Mintage	F	VF	XF	Unc	BU
AH1429/2008	—	—	—	—	1.50	2.00

KM# 922   10 PIASTRES
4.5200 g., Copper-Nickel, 24.8 mm. **Subject:** National Women's

Council **Obv:** Value **Rev:** Woman standing next to Sphinx **Edge:** Reeded

Date	Mintage	F	VF	XF	Unc	BU
AH1425-2004	—	—	—	—	1.50	2.00

KM# 990   10 PIASTRES
3.4100 g., Nickel Plated Steel, 19.03 mm. **Obv:** Text, date and value **Rev:** Mosque

Date	Mintage	F	VF	XF	Unc	BU
AH1429 (2008)	—	—	—	—	1.00	1.50

KM# 923   20 PIASTRES
6.0000 g., Copper-Nickel, 26.8 mm. **Subject:** National Women's Council **Obv:** Value **Rev:** Woman standing next to Sphinx **Edge:** Reeded

Date	Mintage	F	VF	XF	Unc	BU
AH1425-2004	—	—	—	—	2.50	3.50

KM# 991   25 PIASTRES
4.5000 g., Nickel Plated Steel, 21 mm. **Obv:** Value at center, Arabic legend at top, dates below **Rev:** Value at center, Arabic at top, English value below **Edge:** Reeded

Date	Mintage	F	VF	XF	Unc	BU
AH1429-2008	—	—	—	—	2.50	3.50
AH1430-2009	—	—	—	—	2.50	3.50
AH1431-2010	—	—	—	—	2.50	3.50

KM# 942.1   50 PIASTRES
6.5000 g., Brass, 25 mm. **Obv:** Value **Rev:** Bust of Cleopatra left **Edge:** Reeded **Note:** Non-magnetic.

Date	Mintage	F	VF	XF	Unc	BU
AH1426-2005	—	—	—	1.20	3.00	4.00
AH1427-2006	—	—	—	1.20	3.00	4.00

KM# 942.2   50 PIASTRES
6.5000 g., Brass Plated Steel, 23 mm. **Obv:** Value **Rev:** Bust of Cleopatra left **Edge:** Reeded **Note:** Magnetic

Date	Mintage	F	VF	XF	Unc	BU
AH1428-2007	—	—	—	—	1.00	1.50
AH1429-2008	—	—	—	—	1.00	1.50
AH1430-2009	—	—	—	—	1.00	1.50
AH1431-2010	—	—	—	—	1.00	1.50

KM# 903   1/2 POUND
4.0000 g., 0.8750 Gold 0.1125 oz. AGW, 18 mm. **Subject:** Egyptian Museum Centennial **Obv:** Value **Rev:** Building **Edge:** Reeded

Date	Mintage	F	VF	XF	Unc	BU
AH1423-2002	—	—	—	—	250	270

KM# 930   POUND
15.0000 g., 0.7200 Silver 0.3472 oz. ASW, 35 mm. **Subject:** National Women's Council **Obv:** Value **Rev:** Woman standing next to Sphinx **Edge:** Reeded

Date	Mintage	F	VF	XF	Unc	BU
AH1421-2001	600	—	—	—	45.00	50.00

KM# 936   POUND
8.0000 g., 0.8750 Gold 0.2250 oz. AGW, 24 mm. **Subject:** 50th Anniversary of Egyptian Revolution **Obv:** Value **Rev:** Soldier with flag, pyramids and radiant sun **Edge:** Reeded

Date	Mintage	F	VF	XF	Unc	BU
AH1423-2002	400	—	—	—	415	425

KM# 938 POUND
8.0000 g., 0.8750 Gold 0.2250 oz. AGW, 24 mm. **Subject:** Alexandria Library **Obv:** Cufic text in center **Rev:** Arched inscription above slanted library roof **Edge:** Reeded

Date	Mintage	F	VF	XF	Unc	BU
AH1423-2002	750	—	—	—	415	425

KM# 904 POUND
15.0000 g., 0.7200 Silver 0.3472 oz. ASW, 35 mm. **Subject:** Egyptian Museum Centennial **Obv:** Value **Rev:** Building, centennial numerals in background **Edge:** Reeded

Date	Mintage	F	VF	XF	Unc	BU
AH1423-2002	1,500	—	—	—	35.00	40.00

KM# 905 POUND
8.0000 g., 0.8750 Gold 0.2250 oz. AGW, 24 mm. **Subject:** Egyptian Museum Centennial **Obv:** Value **Rev:** Building, centennial numerals in background **Edge:** Reeded

Date	Mintage	F	VF	XF	Unc	BU
AH1423-2002	300	—	—	—	415	425

KM# 909 POUND
15.0000 g., 0.7200 Silver 0.3472 oz. ASW, 35 mm. **Subject:** International Ear, Nose and Throat Conference **Obv:** King Tut's Gold Mask **Rev:** "IFOS" on world map **Edge:** Reeded

Date	Mintage	F	VF	XF	Unc	BU
AH1423-2002	2,500	—	—	—	30.00	35.00

KM# 910 POUND
15.0000 g., 0.7200 Silver 0.3472 oz. ASW, 35 mm. **Subject:** 50th Anniversary of Egyptian Revolution **Obv:** Value **Rev:** Soldier with flag **Edge:** Reeded

Date	Mintage	F	VF	XF	Unc	BU
AH1423-2002	1,500	—	—	—	35.00	40.00

KM# 912 POUND
15.0000 g., 0.7200 Silver 0.3472 oz. ASW, 35 mm. **Subject:** Alexandria Library **Obv:** Legend and inscription **Rev:** Inscribed arches above library roof **Edge:** Reeded

Date	Mintage	F	VF	XF	Unc	BU
AH1423-2002	8,000	—	—	—	30.00	35.00

KM# 913 POUND
15.0000 g., 0.7200 Silver 0.3472 oz. ASW, 35 mm. **Subject:** Body Building Championships **Obv:** Arabic and English legends **Rev:** Mr. Universe cartoon **Edge:** Reeded

Date	Mintage	F	VF	XF	Unc	BU
AH1423-2002	1,000	—	—	—	30.00	35.00

KM# 955 POUND
8.0000 g., 0.8750 Gold 0.2250 oz. AGW, 24 mm. **Subject:** Golden Jubilee Ein Shams University **Obv:** Value **Rev:** Obelisk with bird standing at left and right **Edge:** Reeded

Date	Mintage	F	VF	XF	Unc	BU
AH1422-2002	400	—	—	—	400	420

KM# 956 POUND
8.0000 g., 0.8750 Gold 0.2250 oz. AGW, 24 mm. **Subject:** Police Day **Obv:** Police eagle with wings spread, value **Rev:** Police badge **Edge:** Reeded

Date	Mintage	F	VF	XF	Unc	BU
AH1422-2002	400	—	—	—	400	420

KM# 957 POUND
8.0000 g., 0.8750 Gold 0.2250 oz. AGW, 24 mm. **Subject:** 30th Anniversary October War Victory **Obv:** Value **Rev:** Soldier holding flag on top of pyramid **Edge:** Reeded

Date	Mintage	F	VF	XF	Unc	BU
AH1424-2003	200	—	—	—	415	425

KM# 958 POUND
8.0000 g., 0.8750 Gold 0.2250 oz. AGW, 24 mm. **Series:** Value **Subject:** Radio and Television Festival **Obv:** Modern abstract design **Edge:** Reeded

Date	Mintage	F	VF	XF	Unc	BU
AH1424-2003	1,000	—	—	—	385	400

KM# 959 POUND
8.0000 g., 0.8750 Gold 0.2250 oz. AGW, 24 mm. **Subject:** 50th Anniversary El Gomhoreya Newspaper - Hosni Mubarak **Obv:** Value **Rev:** Bust facing at left, building in background **Edge:** Reeded

Date	Mintage	F	VF	XF	Unc	BU
AH1424-2003	400	—	—	—	400	420

KM# 915 POUND
15.0000 g., 0.7200 Silver 0.3472 oz. ASW, 35 mm. **Subject:** 30th Anniversary of the October War **Obv:** Value, dates and legend **Rev:** Soldier with flag above pyramids **Edge:** Reeded

Date	Mintage	F	VF	XF	Unc	BU
AH1424-2003	1,000	—	—	—	30.00	35.00

KM# 917 POUND
15.0000 g., 0.7200 Silver 0.3472 oz. ASW, 35 mm. **Subject:** 25th Anniversary of the Commerce Society **Obv:** Value, dates and legend **Rev:** Radiant sun above lattice work **Edge:** Reeded

Date	Mintage	F	VF	XF	Unc	BU
AH1424-2003	1,200	—	—	—	30.00	35.00

KM# 924 POUND
15.0000 g., 0.7200 Silver 0.3472 oz. ASW, 35 mm. **Subject:** 90th Anniversary Scouts **Obv:** Value **Rev:** Combined scouting badge **Edge:** Reeded

Date	Mintage	F	VF	XF	Unc	BU
AH1425-2004	2,000	—	—	—	30.00	35.00

KM# 960 POUND
8.0000 g., 0.8750 Gold 0.2250 oz. AGW, 24 mm. **Subject:** Golden Jubilee Military Production **Obv:** Value **Rev:** Ancient chariot, horse and rider left **Edge:** Reeded

Date	Mintage	F	VF	XF	Unc	BU
AH1425-2004	750	—	—	—	385	400

KM# 934 POUND
15.0000 g., 0.7250 Silver 0.3496 oz. ASW, 35 mm. **Subject:** Golden Jubilee - Military Production **Obv:** Value **Rev:** Ancient chariot, horse and rider **Edge:** Reeded

Date	Mintage	F	VF	XF	Unc	BU
AH1425-2004	1,000	—	—	—	30.00	35.00

KM# 940 POUND
8.5000 g., Bi-Metallic Brass center in Copper-Nickel ring, 25.1 mm. **Obv:** Value **Rev:** King Tutankhaman's gold mask **Edge:** Reeded

Date	Mintage	F	VF	XF	Unc	BU
AH1426-2005	—	—	—	—	3.00	5.00
AH1427-2006	—	—	—	—	3.00	5.00

KM# 940a POUND
8.5000 g., Bi-Metallic Brass Plated Steel center in Nickel Plated Steel ring, 25.1 mm. **Obv:** Value at center **Rev:** King Tutankhaman's gold mask **Edge:** Reeded **Note:** Magnetic

Date	Mintage	F	VF	XF	Unc	BU
AH1428-2007	—	—	—	—	3.00	5.00
AH1429-2008	—	—	—	—	3.00	4.00
AH1430-2009	—	—	—	—	3.00	4.00
AH1431-2010	—	—	—	—	3.00	4.00

KM# 965 POUND
15.0000 g., 0.7200 Silver 0.3472 oz. ASW, 35 mm. **Subject:** Golden Jubilee Suez Canal Nationalization **Obv:** Value **Rev:** Large "50" above government buildings **Edge:** Reeded

Date	Mintage	F	VF	XF	Unc	BU
AH1427-2006	1,750	—	—	—	35.00	40.00

KM# 966 POUND
15.0000 g., 0.7200 Silver 0.3472 oz. ASW, 35 mm. **Subject:** 60th Anniversary UNESCO **Obv:** Value **Rev:** Logo **Edge:** Reeded

Date	Mintage	F	VF	XF	Unc	BU
AH1427-2006	800	—	—	—	100	125

KM# 967 POUND
15.0000 g., 0.7200 Silver 0.3472 oz. ASW, 35 mm. **Subject:** 13th General Population Census **Obv:** Value **Rev:** Stylized couple leaning left at left **Edge:** Reeded

Date	Mintage	F	VF	XF	Unc	BU
AH1427-2006	2,000	—	—	—	45.00	50.00

KM# 961 POUND
8.0000 g., 0.8750 Gold 0.2250 oz. AGW, 24 mm. **Subject:** World Environment Day **Obv:** Value **Rev:** Stylized tree, emblem at left, bird standing at right **Edge:** Reeded

Date	Mintage	F	VF	XF	Unc	BU
AH1427-2006	200	—	—	—	415	425

KM# 962 POUND
8.0000 g., 0.8750 Gold 0.2250 oz. AGW, 24 mm. **Subject:** Golden Jubilee Suez Canal Nationalization **Obv:** Value **Rev:** Large "50" above government buildings **Edge:** Reeded

Date	Mintage	F	VF	XF	Unc	BU
AH1427-2006	1,000	—	—	—	385	400

KM# 963 POUND
8.0000 g., 0.8750 Gold 0.2250 oz. AGW, 24 mm. **Subject:** Silver Jubilee Egyptian Enviromental Protection **Obv:** Value **Rev:** World globe **Edge:** Reeded

Date	Mintage	F	VF	XF	Unc	BU
AH1428-2007	300	—	—	—	400	420

KM# 964 POUND
8.0000 g., 0.8750 Gold 0.2250 oz. AGW, 24 mm. **Subject:** Diamond Jubilee Air Force **Obv:** Value **Rev:** Air Force emblem **Edge:** Reeded

Date	Mintage	F	VF	XF	Unc	BU
AH1428-2007	130	—	—	—	550	—

KM# 968 POUND
15.0000 g., 0.7200 Silver 0.3472 oz. ASW, 35 mm. **Subject:** 100th Anniversary Ahly Club **Obv:** Value **Rev:** Large "100" with linked zeroes **Edge:** Reeded

Date	Mintage	F	VF	XF	Unc	BU
AH1428-2007	5,000	—	—	—	45.00	50.00

KM# 944 POUND
15.0000 g., 0.7200 Silver 0.3472 oz. ASW, 35.00 mm. **Subject:** Air Force Diamond Jubilee **Obv:** Value **Rev:** Air Force insignia **Edge:** Reeded

Date	Mintage	F	VF	XF	Unc	BU
AH1428-2007		—	—	—	45.00	50.00

KM# 931 5 POUNDS
17.5000 g., 0.7200 Silver 0.4051 oz. ASW, 37 mm. **Subject:** National Women's Council **Obv:** Value **Rev:** Woman standing next to Sphinx **Edge:** Reeded

Date	Mintage	F	VF	XF	Unc	BU
AH1421-2001	600	—	—	—	55.00	60.00

KM# 932 5 POUNDS
17.5000 g., 0.7200 Silver 0.4051 oz. ASW, 37 mm. **Subject:** 50th Anniversary of the National Police **Obv:** Value and police logo **Rev:** Ceremonial design **Edge:** Reeded

Date	Mintage	F	VF	XF	Unc	BU
AH1422-2002	750	—	—	—	45.00	50.00

KM# 906 5 POUNDS
17.5000 g., 0.7200 Silver 0.4051 oz. ASW, 37 mm. **Subject:** Egyptian Museum Centennial **Obv:** Value **Rev:** Building, centennial numerals in background **Edge:** Reeded

Date	Mintage	F	VF	XF	Unc	BU
AH1423-2002	1,500	—	—	—	45.00	48.00

KM# 907 5 POUNDS
26.0000 g., 0.8750 Gold 0.7314 oz. AGW, 33 mm. **Subject:** Egyptian Museum Centennial **Obv:** Value **Rev:** Building, centennial numerals in background **Edge:** Reeded

Date	Mintage	F	VF	XF	Unc	BU
AH1423-2002	250	—	—	—	1,250	1,300

KM# 911 5 POUNDS
17.5500 g., 0.9250 Silver 0.5219 oz. ASW, 37 mm. **Subject:** 50th Anniversary of the Egyptian Revolution **Obv:** Value **Rev:** Soldier with flag **Edge:** Reeded

Date	Mintage	F	VF	XF	Unc	BU
AH1423-2002	1,500	—	—	—	45.00	48.00

KM# 914 5 POUNDS
17.5000 g., 0.7200 Silver 0.4051 oz. ASW, 37 mm. **Subject:** Body Building Championships **Obv:** Arabic and English legends **Rev:** Mr. Universe cartoon **Edge:** Reeded

Date	Mintage	F	VF	XF	Unc	BU
AH1423-2002	800	—	—	—	40.00	45.00

KM# 916 5 POUNDS
17.5000 g., 0.7200 Silver 0.4051 oz. ASW, 37 mm. **Subject:** 30th Anniversary of the October War **Obv:** Value and legend **Rev:** Soldier with flag above pyramids **Edge:** Reeded

Date	Mintage	F	VF	XF	Unc	BU
AH1424-2003	800	—	—	—	40.00	45.00

KM# 918 5 POUNDS
17.5000 g., 0.7200 Silver 0.4051 oz. ASW, 37 mm. **Obv:** Value and legend **Rev:** Geo-Physical Institute **Edge:** Reeded

Date	Mintage	F	VF	XF	Unc	BU
AH1424-2003	800	—	—	—	40.00	45.00

KM# 919 5 POUNDS
17.5000 g., 0.7200 Silver 0.4051 oz. ASW, 37 mm. **Subject:** 50th Anniversary of the Republic **Obv:** Value and legend **Rev:** Portrait and building **Edge:** Reeded

Date	Mintage	F	VF	XF	Unc	BU
AH1424-2003	3,000	—	—	—	37.00	42.00

KM# 920 5 POUNDS
17.5000 g., 0.7200 Silver 0.4051 oz. ASW, 37 mm. **Subject:** 25th Anniversary of the Delta Bank **Obv:** Value and legend **Rev:** Delta on world globe **Edge:** Reeded

Date	Mintage	F	VF	XF	Unc	BU
AH1424-2004	1,500	—	—	—	37.00	42.00

KM# 925 5 POUNDS
17.5000 g., 0.7200 Silver 0.4051 oz. ASW, 37 mm. **Obv:** Value **Rev:** Balance scale **Edge:** Reeded

Date	Mintage	F	VF	XF	Unc	BU
AH1425-2004	3,300	—	—	—	37.00	42.00

KM# 974 5 POUNDS
17.5000 g., 0.7200 Silver 0.4051 oz. ASW, 37 mm. **Subject:** Golden Jubilee Cairo Mint **Obv:** Value **Rev:** National arms above mint building **Edge:** Reeded

Date	Mintage	F	VF	XF	Unc	BU
AH1425-2004	1,750	—	—	—	45.00	50.00

KM# 933 5 POUNDS
17.5000 g., 0.7200 Silver 0.4051 oz. ASW, 37 mm. **Subject:** 90th Anniversary - Egyptian Scouts Organization - 1914-2004 **Obv:** Value **Rev:** Combined scouting emblem **Edge:** Reeded

Date	Mintage	F	VF	XF	Unc	BU
AH1425-2004	—	—	—	—	37.00	42.00

KM# 935 5 POUNDS
17.5000 g., 0.7200 Silver 0.4051 oz. ASW, 37 mm. **Subject:** Golden Jubilee - Military Production **Obv:** Value **Rev:** Ancient chariot, horse and rider left **Edge:** Reeded

Date	Mintage	F	VF	XF	Unc	BU
AH1425-2004	800	—	—	—	40.00	45.00

KM# 975 5 POUNDS
17.5000 g., 0.7200 Silver 0.4051 oz. ASW, 37 mm. **Subject:** 60th Anniversary Arab League **Obv:** Value **Rev:** Logo in center of ornate background **Edge:** Reeded

Date	Mintage	F	VF	XF	Unc	BU
AH1426-2005	2,000	—	—	—	55.00	60.00

KM# 976 5 POUNDS
17.5000 g., 0.7200 Silver 0.4051 oz. ASW, 37 mm. **Subject:** World Environment Day **Obv:** Value **Rev:** Stylized tree with logo at left, bird at right **Edge:** Reeded

Date	Mintage	F	VF	XF	Unc	BU
AH1427-2006	1,000	—	—	—	70.00	80.00

KM# 977 5 POUNDS
17.5000 g., 0.7200 Silver 0.4051 oz. ASW, 35 mm. **Subject:** Golden jubilee Suez Canal Nationalization **Obv:** Value **Rev:** Large "50" above government buildings **Edge:** Reeded

Date	Mintage	F	VF	XF	Unc	BU
AH1427-2006	1,750	—	—	—	45.00	50.00

KM# 978 5 POUNDS
17.5000 g., 0.7200 Silver 0.4051 oz. ASW, 37 mm. **Subject:** 60th Anniversary UNESCO **Obv:** Value **Rev:** Logo **Edge:** Reeded

Date	Mintage	F	VF	XF	Unc	BU
AH1427-2006	800	—	—	—	100	125

KM# 979 5 POUNDS
17.5000 g., 0.7200 Silver 0.4051 oz. ASW, 37 mm. **Subject:** Diamond Jubilee Academy of Arab Language **Obv:** Value **Rev:** Globe on open book **Edge:** Reeded

Date	Mintage	F	VF	XF	Unc	BU
AH1427-2006	1,000	—	—	—	70.00	80.00

KM# 980 5 POUNDS
17.5000 g., 0.7200 Silver 0.4051 oz. ASW, 37 mm. **Subject:** 13th General Population Census **Obv:** Circle with inscription in center **Rev:** Stylized couple leaning left at left **Edge:** Reeded

Date	Mintage	F	VF	XF	Unc	BU
AH1427-2006	1,500	—	—	—	65.00	75.00

KM# 981 5 POUNDS
17.5000 g., 0.7200 Silver 0.4051 oz. ASW, 37 mm. **Subject:** 100th Anniversary Ahly Club **Obv:** Value **Rev:** Large "100" With linked zeroes **Edge:** Reeded

Date	Mintage	F	VF	XF	Unc	BU
AH1428-2007	3,000	—	—	—	45.00	50.00

KM# 982 5 POUNDS
17.5000 g., 0.7200 Silver 0.4051 oz. ASW, 37 mm. **Subject:** Diamond Jubilee Court of Cassation **Obv:** Balance scale above inscriptions **Rev:** Court building **Edge:** Reeded

Date	Mintage	F	VF	XF	Unc	BU
AH1428-2007	450	—	—	—	125	150

KM# 983 5 POUNDS
17.5000 g., 0.7200 Silver 0.4051 oz. ASW, 37 mm. **Subject:** Silver Jubilee Enviromental Protection Agency **Obv:** Value **Rev:** World globe **Edge:** Reeded

Date	Mintage	F	VF	XF	Unc	BU
AH1428-2007	1,300	—	—	—	55.00	60.00

KM# 984 5 POUNDS
17.5000 g., 0.7200 Silver 0.4051 oz. ASW, 37 mm. **Subject:** 11th Arab Sports Championship - Egypt **Obv:** Value **Rev:** Stylized player on map of Arab countries **Edge:** Reeded

Date	Mintage	F	VF	XF	Unc	BU
AH1428-2007	6,300	—	—	—	45.00	50.00

KM# 943 5 POUNDS
17.5000 g., 0.7200 Silver 0.4051 oz. ASW, 37 mm. **Subject:** 11th Pan-Arab Games **Obv:** Value **Rev:** Logo with outlined map of Arab nations in background **Edge:** Reeded

Date	Mintage	F	VF	XF	Unc	BU
AH1428-2007	6,300	—	—	—	30.00	35.00

KM# 945 5 POUNDS
17.5000 g., 0.7200 Silver 0.4051 oz. ASW, 37 mm. **Subject:** Air Force Diamond Jubilee **Obv:** Value **Rev:** Air Force insignia **Edge:** Reeded

Date	Mintage	F	VF	XF	Unc	BU
AH1428-2007	600	—	—	—	55.00	60.00

KM# 908 10 POUNDS
40.0000 g., 0.8750 Gold 1.1252 oz. AGW, 37 mm. **Subject:** Egyptian Museum Centennial **Obv:** Denomination **Rev:** Building, centennial numerals in background **Edge:** Reeded

Date	Mintage	F	VF	XF	Unc	BU
AH1423-2002	150	—	—	—	2,000	2,100

KM# 989 10 POUNDS
40.0000 g., 0.8750 Gold 1.1252 oz. AGW, 37 mm. **Subject:** Golden Jubilee Police Day **Obv:** Eagle left with wings spread **Rev:** Police emblem **Edge:** Reeded

Date	Mintage	F	VF	XF	Unc	BU
AH1422-2002	150	—	—	—	2,000	2,100

KM# 985 10 POUNDS
40.0000 g., 0.8750 Gold 1.1252 oz. AGW, 37 mm. **Subject:** 50th Anniversary El Gomhoreya News **Obv:** Value **Rev:** Bust of Hosni Mubarak facing at left, building in background **Edge:** Reeded

Date	Mintage	F	VF	XF	Unc	BU
AH1424-2003	50	—	—	—	2,100	2,200

KM# 986 10 POUNDS
40.0000 g., 0.8750 Gold 1.1252 oz. AGW, 37 mm. **Subject:** Golden Jubilee Military Production **Obv:** Value **Rev:** Ancient chariot, horse and rider left **Edge:** Reeded

Date	Mintage	F	VF	XF	Unc	BU
AH1425-2004	85	—	—	—	2,100	2,200

KM# 987 10 POUNDS
40.0000 g., 0.8750 Gold 1.1252 oz. AGW, 37 mm. **Subject:** 60th Anniversary Arab League **Obv:** Value **Rev:** Emblem at center, ornate background **Edge:** Reeded

Date	Mintage	F	VF	XF	Unc	BU
AH1426-2005	50	—	—	—	2,100	2,200

KM# 988 10 POUNDS
40.0000 g., 0.8750 Gold 1.1252 oz. AGW, 37 mm. **Subject:** Diamond Jubilee Air Force **Obv:** Value **Rev:** Air Force emblem **Edge:** Reeded

Date	Mintage	F	VF	XF	Unc	BU
AH1428-2007	25	—	—	—	2,150	2,250

ESTONIA

The Republic of Estonia (formerly the Estonian Soviet Socialist Republic of the U.S.S.R.) is the northernmost of the three Baltic States in Eastern Europe. It has an area of 17,462 sq. mi. (45,100 sq. km.) and a population of 1.6 million. Capital: Tallinn. Agriculture and dairy farming are the principal industries. Butter, eggs, bacon, timber and petroleum are exported.

MODERN REPUBLIC
1991 - present
STANDARD COINAGE

KM# 22   10 SENTI
1.8500 g., Aluminum-Bronze, 17.1 mm.   **Obv:** Three lions left divide date **Rev:** Denomination **Rev. Legend:** EESTI VABARIIK **Edge:** Plain

Date	Mintage	F	VF	XF	Unc	BU
2002	30,000,000	—	—	0.20	0.50	0.80
2006	31,000,000	—	—	0.20	0.50	0.80
2008	15,000,000	—	—	0.20	0.50	0.80

KM# 23a   20 SENTI
2.0000 g., Nickel Plated Steel, 18.9 mm.   **Obv:** National arms divide date **Rev:** Denomination **Rev. Legend:** EESTI VABARIIK **Edge:** Plain

Date	Mintage	F	VF	XF	Unc	BU
2003	11,100,000	—	—	—	0.60	1.00
2004	20,000,000	—	—	—	0.60	1.00
2006	2,000,000	—	—	—	0.60	1.00
2008	12,000,000	—	—	—	0.60	1.00

KM# 24   50 SENTI
2.9000 g., Aluminum-Bronze, 19.5 mm.   **Obv:** National arms divide date **Rev:** Denomination **Rev. Legend:** EESTI VABARIIK **Edge:** Plain

Date	Mintage	F	VF	XF	Unc	BU
2004	10,000,000	—	—	—	1.00	1.50
2006	7,000,000	—	—	—	1.00	1.50
2007	17,000,000	—	—	—	1.00	1.50

KM# 35   KROON
5.0000 g., Aluminum-Bronze, 23.5 mm.   **Obv:** National arms **Rev:** Large, thick denomination **Rev. Legend:** EESTI VABARIIK **Edge:** Segmented reeding

Date	Mintage	F	VF	XF	Unc	BU
2001	15,000,000	—	—	0.50	1.00	1.50
2003	15,000,000	—	—	0.50	1.00	1.50
2006	15,170,000	—	—	0.50	1.00	1.50

KM# 44   KROON
4.8000 g., Brass, 23.21 mm.   **Obv:** National arms **Rev:** Stylized plant in circle **Rev. Legend:** EESTI VABARIIK **Edge:** Segmented reeding

Date	Mintage	F	VF	XF	Unc	BU
2008	20,000,000	—	—	0.50	1.50	2.00

KM# 38   10 KROONI
28.2800 g., 0.9990 Silver 0.9083 oz. ASW, 38.6 mm.   **Subject:** Tartu University **Obv:** National arms **Rev:** Building in oval, value at left **Edge:** Reeded

Date	Mintage	F	VF	XF	Unc	BU
2002 Proof	10,000	Value: 40.00				

KM# 40   10 KROONI
28.2800 g., 0.9990 Silver 0.9083 oz. ASW, 38.6 mm.   **Subject:** Estonian Flag **Obv:** National arms **Rev:** Round multicolor flag design **Edge:** Reeded

Date	Mintage	F	VF	XF	Unc	BU
2004 Proof	10,000	Value: 40.00				

KM# 42   10 KROONI
28.2800 g., 0.9990 Silver 0.9083 oz. ASW, 38.6 mm.   **Subject:** Torino Winter Olympics **Obv:** National arms **Rev:** Gold inset cross country skier in semi circle above Olympic flame **Edge:** Reeded

Date	Mintage	F	VF	XF	Unc	BU
2006 Proof	5,000	Value: 45.00				

KM# 46   10 KROONI
28.2800 g., 0.9990 Silver 0.9083 oz. ASW, 38.61 mm.   **Subject:** 90th Anniversary of Independence **Obv:** National arms **Obv. Legend:** EESTI VABARIIK **Rev:** Wiiralt oak tree **Edge:** Plain

Date	Mintage	F	VF	XF	Unc	BU
2008 Proof	10,000	Value: 50.00				

KM# 48   10 KROONI
28.2800 g., 0.9990 Silver 0.9083 oz. ASW, 38.61 mm.   **Subject:** Olympics **Obv:** Arms **Rev:** Torch and geometric patterns

Date	Mintage	F	VF	XF	Unc	BU
2008 Proof	—	Value: 42.50				

KM# 49   10 KROONI
24.1000 g., 0.9990 Silver 0.7740 oz. ASW, 38.61 mm.   **Subject:** National Museum **Obv:** National arms within starburst **Rev:** Design in star

Date	Mintage	F	VF	XF	Unc	BU
2008 Proof	—	Value: 42.50				

KM# 51   10 KROONI
31.1050 g., 0.9990 Silver 0.9990 oz. ASW, 40.6 mm.   **Subject:** Song and Dance Festival **Obv:** National Arms **Rev:** Circle of dancers

Date	Mintage	F	VF	XF	Unc	BU
2009 Proof	—	Value: 45.00				

KM# 53   10 KROONI
28.2800 g., 0.9990 Silver 0.9083 oz. ASW, 38.61 mm.   **Subject:**

Vancouver Winter Olympics **Obv:** National arms within wreath, date below **Rev:** Two stylized cross county skiers right

Date	Mintage	F	VF	XF	Unc	BU
2010 Proof	—	Value: 45.00				

KM# 55 25 KROONI
24.1000 g., 0.9999 Silver 0.7747 oz. ASW, 38.61 mm.

Date	Mintage	F	VF	XF	Unc	BU
2010 Proof	—	Value: 50.00				

KM# 50 50 KROONI
8.6400 g., 0.9990 Gold 0.2775 oz. AGW, 22 mm. **Obv:** National Arms and laurel branch **Rev:** Windmill

Date	Mintage	F	VF	XF	Unc	BU
2008 Proof	—	Value: 475				

KM# 54 50 KROONI
24.5000 g., 0.9990 Silver with Wood insert 0.7869 oz. ASW, 38.61 mm. **Subject:** Estonian Nature **Obv:** Arms and legend

Date	Mintage	F	VF	XF	Unc	BU
2010 Proof	—	Value: 50.00				

KM# 39 100 KROONI
7.7760 g., 0.9999 Gold 0.2500 oz. AGW **Subject:** Monetary Reform **Obv:** National arms **Rev:** Cross design **Edge:** Reeded

Date	Mintage	F	VF	XF	Unc	BU
2002	2,000	—	—	—	—	450

KM# 41 100 KROONI
7.7760 g., 0.9999 Gold 0.2500 oz. AGW, 22 mm. **Subject:** Olympic Games **Obv:** National arms within wreath **Rev:** Olympic flame above rings in center **Edge:** Reeded

Date	Mintage	F	VF	XF	Unc	BU
2004	5,000	—	—	—	—	425

KM# 43 100 KROONI
28.2800 g., 0.9990 Silver 0.9083 oz. ASW, 38.6 mm. **Subject:** National Opera **Obv:** National arms **Rev:** Building front **Edge:** Plain

Date	Mintage	F	VF	XF	Unc	BU
2006 Proof	10,000	Value: 45.00				

KM# 45 100 KROONI
7.7800 g., 0.9999 Gold 0.2501 oz. AGW **Subject:** 15th Anniversary Reintroduction of the Estonian Kroon **Obv:** National arms **Obv. Legend:** EESTI VARBARIIK **Rev:** Cornflower **Rev. Legend:** KROONI TAAS- / KEHTESTAMISE / 15. AASTAPAEV **Edge:** Plain **Shape:** Triangular

Date	Mintage	F	VF	XF	Unc	BU
2007 Prooflike	6,000	—	—	—	—	500

KM# 47 100 KROONI
7.7750 g., 0.9990 Platinum 0.2497 oz. APW, 18 mm. **Subject:** 90th Anniversary of Republic **Rev:** Three birds on wire

Date	Mintage	F	VF	XF	Unc	BU
2008 Proof	3,000	Value: 600				

KM# 52 100 KROONI
7.7800 g., 0.9990 Gold 0.2499 oz. AGW, 22 mm. **Subject:** Song and dance festival **Obv:** Arms **Rev:** Stylized chorus on stage

Date	Mintage	F	VF	XF	Unc	BU
2009 Proof	—	Value: 435				

KM# 56 100 KROONI
7.7800 g., 0.9990 Gold 0.2499 oz. AGW, 22 mm.

Date	Mintage	F	VF	XF	Unc	BU
2010 Proof	—	Value: 435				

EURO COINAGE

KM# 61 EURO CENT
2.3000 g., Copper Plated Steel, 16.25 mm. **Obv:** Map of Estonia **Rev:** Denomination and globe

Date	Mintage	F	VF	XF	Unc	BU
2011	—	—	—	—	0.35	0.50

KM# 62 2 EURO CENT
3.0600 g., Copper Plated Steel, 18.75 mm. **Obv:** Map of Estonia **Rev:** Denomination and globe **Edge:** Grooved

Date	Mintage	F	VF	XF	Unc	BU
2011	—	—	—	—	0.50	0.75

KM# 63 5 EURO CENT
3.9200 g., Copper Plated Steel, 21.25 mm. **Obv:** Map of Estonia **Rev:** Denomination and globe

Date	Mintage	F	VF	XF	Unc	BU
2011	—	—	—	—	0.75	1.25

KM# 64 10 EURO CENT
4.1000 g., Brass, 19.75 mm. **Obv:** Map of Estonia **Rev:** Relief map of Western Europe, stars, line and value **Edge:** Reeded

Date	Mintage	F	VF	XF	Unc	BU
2011	—	—	—	—	1.25	2.00

KM# 65 20 EURO CENT
5.7400 g., Brass, 22.25 mm. **Obv:** Map of Estonia **Rev:** Relief map of Western Europe, stars, line and value **Edge:** Notched

Date	Mintage	F	VF	XF	Unc	BU
2011	—	—	—	—	1.00	1.50

KM# 66 50 EURO CENT
7.8000 g., Brass, 24.25 mm. **Obv:** Map of Estonia **Rev:** Relief map of Western Europe, stars, line and value **Edge:** Reeded

Date	Mintage	F	VF	XF	Unc	BU
2011	—	—	—	—	1.25	2.00

KM# 67 EURO
7.5000 g., Bi-Metallic Copper-Nickel center in Nickel-Brass ring, 23.35 mm. **Obv:** Map of Estonia **Rev:** Relief map of Western Europe, stars, lines and value **Edge:** Segmented reeding

Date	Mintage	F	VF	XF	Unc	BU
2011	—	—	—	—	2.75	4.00

KM# 68 2 EURO
8.5000 g., Bi-Metallic Nickel-Brass center in Copper-Nickel ring, 25.75 mm. **Obv:** Map of Estonia **Rev:** Relief map of Western Europe, stars, lines and value **Edge:** Reeded and lettered

Date	Mintage	F	VF	XF	Unc	BU
2011	—	—	—	—	3.75	6.00

KM# 70 2 EURO
8.5000 g., Bi-Metallic Nickel-Brass center in Copper-Nickel ring, 25.75 mm. **Subject:** Euro Coinage, 10th Anniversary **Obv:** Euro symbol on globe at center, child-like rendering around

Date	Mintage	F	VF	XF	Unc	BU
2012	2,000,000	—	—	—	3.75	6.00

KM# 71   10 EURO
28.8000 g., 0.9999 Silver 0.9258 oz. ASW, 38.61 mm. **Subject:** Estonia's Future **Obv:** National arms **Rev:** Two dancing figures, value at top **Edge Lettering:** Ag 999.9

Date	Mintage	F	VF	XF	Unc	BU
2011 Proof	30,000	Value: 75.00				

KM# 69   20 EURO
14.6000 g., Bi-Metallic .9999 Gold center in .9999 Silver ring, 27.25 mm. **Subject:** Estonia's entry into Eurozone **Obv:** National arms **Rev:** Lace

Date	Mintage	F	VF	XF	Unc	BU
2011 Proof	10,000	Value: 475				

ETHIOPIA

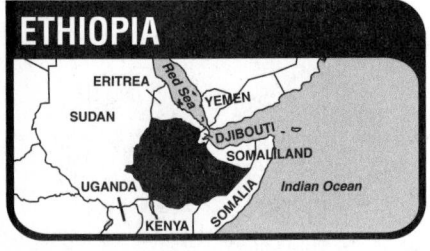

The People's Federal Republic of Ethiopia (formerly the Peoples Democratic Republic and the Empire of Ethiopia), Africa's oldest independent nation, faces the Red Sea in East-Central Africa. The country has an area of 424,214 sq. mi. (1,004,390 sq. km.) and a population of 56 million people who are divided among 40 tribes that speak some 270 languages and dialects. Capital: Addis Ababa. The economy is predominantly agricultural and pastoral. Gold and platinum are mined and petroleum fields are being developed. Coffee, oilseeds, hides and cereals are exported.

DATING
Ethiopian coinage is dated by the Ethiopian Era calendar (E.E.), which commenced 7 years and 8 months after the advent of A.D. dating.

EXAMPLE
1900   (10 and 9 = 19 x 100)
  36   (Add 30 and 6)
1936 E.E.
   8   (Add)
1943/4 AD

PEOPLES DEMOCRATIC REPUBLIC

DECIMAL COINAGE

100 Santeems (Cents) = 1 Birr (Dollar)
100 Matonas = 100 Santeems

KM# 44.3   5 CENTS
3.0000 g., Brass, 20 mm. **Obv:** Large lion head, right **Rev:** Denomination left of figure

Date	Mintage	F	VF	XF	Unc	BU
EE1996 (2004)	—	—	—	—	—	1.00
EE1998 (2006)	—	—	—	—	—	1.00
EE1999 (2007)	—	—	—	—	—	1.00
EE2000 (2008)	—	—	—	—	—	1.00

KM# 45.3   10 CENTS
4.5000 g., Brass, 23 mm. **Obv:** Large lion head right **Rev:** Mountain Nyala, denomination at right

Date	Mintage	F	VF	XF	Unc	BU
EE1996 (2004)	—	—	—	—	—	1.25
EE1997 (2005)	—	—	—	—	—	1.25
EE1998 (2006)	—	—	—	—	—	1.25
EE2000 (2008)	—	—	—	—	—	1.25

KM# 46.3   25 CENTS
3.7000 g., Copper-Nickel, 21.45 mm. **Obv:** Large lion head right **Rev:** Man and woman with arms raised divide denomination

Date	Mintage	F	VF	XF	Unc	BU
EE1996 (2004)	—	—	—	—	—	1.25
EE1997 (2005)	—	—	—	—	—	1.25
EE2000 (2008)	—	—	—	—	—	1.25

KM# 47.2   50 CENTS
6.0000 g., Copper-Nickel, 25 mm. **Obv:** Small lion head, two long chin whiskers at left nearly touch date **Rev:** People of the republic, denomination above

Date	Mintage	F	VF	XF	Unc	BU
EE1996 (2004)	—	—	—	1.50	3.00	—
EE1997 (2005)	—	—	—	1.50	3.00	—
EE2000 (2008)	—	—	—	1.50	3.00	—

FEDERAL DEMOCRATIC REPUBLIC

DECIMAL COINAGE

KM# 78   BIRR
Bi-Metallic Brass Plated Steel center in Nickel Plated Steel ring, 28 mm. **Obv:** Large lion right in center **Rev:** Balance scale

Date	Mintage	F	VF	XF	Unc	BU
EE2003/2010	411,600,000	—	—	—	2.25	5.00

KM# 79   BIRR
Bi-Metallic Nickel-Brass center in Copper-Nickel ring, 25 mm. **Obv:** Large lion head r. **Rev:** Balance scale

Date	Mintage	F	VF	XF	Unc	BU
EE2002 (2010)	—	—	—	—	—	5.00

KM# 76   20 BIRR
30.0000 g., 0.9000 Silver 0.8680 oz. ASW, 40 mm. **Obv:** Vertical symbol with ribbon **Rev:** Reconstructed skeleton

Date	Mintage	F	VF	XF	Unc	BU
EE2000 (2007) Proof	Est. 50,000	Value: 75.00				

KM# 77   600 BIRR
20.0000 g., Gold, 34 mm. **Rev:** Selam Skull

Date	Mintage	F	VF	XF	Unc	BU
EE2000 (2007) Proof	Est. 1,000	Value: 1,250				

FALKLAND ISLANDS

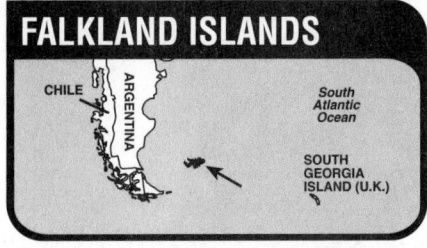

The Colony of the Falkland Islands and Dependencies, a British colony located in the South Atlantic about 500 miles northeast of Cape Horn, has an area of 4,700 sq. mi. (12,170 sq. km.) and a population of 2,121. East Falkland, West Falkland, South Georgia, and South Sandwich are the largest of the 200 islands. Capital: Stanley. Sheep grazing is the main industry. Wool, whale oil, and seal oil are exported.

RULER
British

MONETARY SYSTEM
100 Pence = 1 Pound

BRITISH COLONY

DECIMAL COINAGE

KM# 130   PENNY
Bronze Plated Steel, 20.3 mm. **Ruler:** Elizabeth II **Obv:** Head with tiara right **Obv. Legend:** QUEEN ELIZABETH THE SECOND **Rev:** Two Gentoo penguins flank value **Rev. Legend:** FALKLAND ISLANDS **Edge:** Plain

Date	Mintage	F	VF	XF	Unc	BU
2004	—	—	—	—	0.50	0.75

KM# 131   2 PENCE
Bronze Plated Steel, 25.9 mm. **Ruler:** Elizabeth II **Obv:** Head with tiara right **Obv. Legend:** QUEEN ELIZABETH THE SECOND **Rev:** Upland goose alighting, value above **Rev. Legend:** FALKLAND ISLANDS **Edge:** Plain

Date	Mintage	F	VF	XF	Unc	BU
2004	—	—	—	—	0.50	1.00

KM# 132   5 PENCE
Copper-Nickel, 18 mm. **Ruler:** Elizabeth II **Obv:** Head with tiara right **Obv. Legend:** QUEEN ELIZABETH THE SECOND **Rev:** Black-browed Albatross in flight, value below **Rev. Legend:** FALKLAND - ISLANDS **Edge:** Reeded

Date	Mintage	F	VF	XF	Unc	BU
2004	—	—	—	—	0.75	1.00

KM# 133   10 PENCE
Copper-Nickel, 24.5 mm. **Ruler:** Elizabeth II **Obv:** Head with tiara right **Obv. Legend:** QUEEN ELIZABETH THE SECOND **Rev:** Ursine seal with cub, value below **Rev. Legend:** FALKLAND ISLANDS

Date	Mintage	F	VF	XF	Unc	BU
2004	—	—	—	—	1.50	3.00

KM# 134   20 PENCE
Copper-Nickel, 21.4 mm. **Ruler:** Elizabeth II **Obv:** Head with tiara right **Obv. Legend:** QUEEN ELIZABETH THE SECOND **Rev:** Romney marsh sheep standing left, value above **Rev. Legend:** FALKLAND ISLANDS **Edge:** Plain **Shape:** 7-sided

Date	Mintage	F	VF	XF	Unc	BU
2004	—	—	—	—	2.00	4.00

KM# 70   50 PENCE
29.1000 g., Copper-Nickel, 38.6 mm. **Ruler:** Elizabeth II **Subject:** Centennial of Queen Victoria's Death **Obv:** Crowned bust right, denomination below **Rev:** Crowned head left, three dates **Edge:** Reeded

Date	Mintage	F	VF	XF	Unc	BU
2001	—	—	—	—	6.00	7.00

KM# 70a   50 PENCE
28.2800 g., 0.9250 Silver 0.8410 oz. ASW, 38.6 mm. **Ruler:** Elizabeth II **Obv:** Crowned bust right, denomination below **Rev:** Crowned head left, three dates **Edge:** Reeded

Date	Mintage	F	VF	XF	Unc	BU
2001 Proof	10,000	Value: 50.00				

KM# 70b   50 PENCE
47.5400 g., 0.9170 Gold 1.4015 oz. AGW, 38.61 mm. **Ruler:** Elizabeth II **Subject:** Centennial of Queen Victoria's Death **Obv:** Crowned bust right, denomination below **Rev:** Victoria's crowned bust left, three dates **Edge:** Reeded

Date	Mintage	F	VF	XF	Unc	BU
2001 Proof	100	Value: 2,500				

KM# 71   50 PENCE
29.1000 g., Copper-Nickel, 38.6 mm. **Ruler:** Elizabeth II **Subject:** Queen Elizabeth's 75th Birthday **Obv:** Crowned bust right, denomination below **Rev:** Bust of Queen Elizabeth II left **Edge:** Reeded

Date	Mintage	F	VF	XF	Unc	BU
2001	—	—	—	—	6.00	7.00

KM# 71b   50 PENCE
47.5400 g., 0.9170 Gold 1.4015 oz. AGW, 38.61 mm. **Ruler:** Elizabeth II **Subject:** Queen Elizabeth's 75th Birthday **Obv:** Crowned bust right, denomination below **Rev:** Bust of Queen Elizabeth II left

Date	Mintage	F	VF	XF	Unc	BU
2001 Proof	Est. 100	Value: 2,500				

KM# 86   50 PENCE
28.2800 g., Copper-Nickel, 38.6 mm. **Ruler:** Elizabeth II **Obv:** Crowned bust right, denomination below **Rev:** Edward IV (1461-83) with Rose Ryal gold coin design **Edge:** Reeded

Date	Mintage	F	VF	XF	Unc	BU
2001	—	—	—	—	9.00	10.00

KM# 86a   50 PENCE
28.2800 g., 0.9250 Silver 0.8410 oz. ASW, 38.6 mm. **Ruler:** Elizabeth II **Obv:** Crowned bust right, denomination below **Rev:** Edward IV (1461-83) with gold-plated Rose Ryal gold coin design **Edge:** Reeded

Date	Mintage	F	VF	XF	Unc	BU
2001 Proof	5,000	Value: 50.00				

KM# 87   50 PENCE
28.2800 g., Copper-Nickel, 38.6 mm. **Ruler:** Elizabeth II **Obv:** Crowned bust right, denomination below **Rev:** Henry VII (1485-1509) with 1489 Gold Sovereign coin design **Edge:** Reeded

Date	Mintage	F	VF	XF	Unc	BU
2001	—	—	—	—	9.00	10.00

KM# 87a   50 PENCE
28.2800 g., 0.9250 Silver 0.8410 oz. ASW, 38.6 mm. **Ruler:** Elizabeth II **Obv:** Crowned bust right, denomination below **Rev:** Henry VII (1485-1509) with gold-plated 1489 gold Sovereign coin design **Edge:** Reeded

Date	Mintage	F	VF	XF	Unc	BU
2001 Proof	5,000	Value: 50.00				

KM# 88   50 PENCE
28.2800 g., Copper-Nickel, 38.6 mm. **Ruler:** Elizabeth II **Obv:** Crowned bust right, denomination below **Rev:** Charles II (1660-85) with 1663 gold Guinea coin design **Edge:** Reeded

Date	Mintage	F	VF	XF	Unc	BU
2001	—	—	—	—	9.00	10.00

KM# 88a   50 PENCE
28.2800 g., 0.9250 Silver 0.8410 oz. ASW, 38.6 mm. **Ruler:** Elizabeth II **Obv:** Crowned bust right, denomination below **Rev:** Charles II (1660-85) with gold-plated Gold Guinea coin design **Edge:** Reeded

Date	Mintage	F	VF	XF	Unc	BU
2001 Proof	5,000	Value: 50.00				

KM# 89   50 PENCE
28.2800 g., Copper-Nickel, 38.6 mm. **Ruler:** Elizabeth II **Obv:** Crowned bust right, denomination below **Rev:** Queen Victoria with Gold Sovereign coin design **Edge:** Reeded

Date	Mintage	F	VF	XF	Unc	BU
2001	—	—	—	—	9.00	10.00

KM# 89a   50 PENCE
28.2800 g., 0.9250 Silver 0.8410 oz. ASW, 38.6 mm. **Ruler:** Elizabeth II **Obv:** Crowned bust right, denomination below **Rev:** Queen Victoria with gold-plated Gold Sovereign coin design **Edge:** Reeded

Date	Mintage	F	VF	XF	Unc	BU
2001 Proof	5,000	Value: 50.00				

KM# 73.1   50 PENCE
28.1300 g., Copper-Nickel, 38.6 mm. **Ruler:** Elizabeth II **Subject:** Queen's Golden Jubilee **Obv:** Crowned head right, denomination below **Rev:** Queen Elizabeth II on throne in inner circle below multicolor bunting **Edge:** Reeded

Date	Mintage	F	VF	XF	Unc	BU
2002(2001) Proof	—	Value: 8.00				

KM# 73.2   50 PENCE
Copper-Nickel **Ruler:** Elizabeth II **Subject:** Queen's Golden Jubilee **Obv:** Crowned bust right, denomination below **Rev:** With plain bunting

Date	Mintage	F	VF	XF	Unc	BU
2002	—	—	—	—	6.00	7.00

KM# 73a.1   50 PENCE
28.2800 g., 0.9250 Silver 0.8410 oz. ASW, 38.6 mm. **Ruler:** Elizabeth II **Subject:** Queen's Golden Jubilee **Obv:** Crowned bust right, denomination below **Rev:** Queen on throne below multicolor bunting **Edge:** Reeded

Date	Mintage	F	VF	XF	Unc	BU
2002 Proof	25,000	Value: 45.00				

KM# 73a.2   50 PENCE
28.2800 g., 0.9250 Silver 0.8410 oz. ASW, 38.61 mm. **Ruler:** Elizabeth II **Obv:** Crowned bust right, denomination below **Rev:** With plain bunting

Date	Mintage	F	VF	XF	Unc	BU
2002 Proof	—	Value: 45.00				

KM# 73b.1   50 PENCE
39.9400 g., 0.9170 Gold 1.1775 oz. AGW, 38.61 mm. **Ruler:** Elizabeth II **Obv:** Crowned bust right, denomination below **Rev:** Crowned queen with scepter and orb below multicolor bunting **Edge:** Reeded

Date	Mintage	F	VF	XF	Unc	BU
2002 Proof	150	Value: 2,000				

KM# 74.1   50 PENCE
28.1300 g., Copper-Nickel, 38.6 mm. **Ruler:** Elizabeth II
Subject: Queen's Golden Jubilee **Obv:** Crowned bust right,
denomination below **Rev:** Queen on horse half left in inner circle
below multicolor bunting **Edge:** Reeded

Date	Mintage	F	VF	XF	Unc	BU
2002(2001) Proof	—				Value: 8.00	

KM# 74.2   50 PENCE
Copper-Nickel **Ruler:** Elizabeth II **Subject:** Queen's Golden
Jubilee **Obv:** Crowned bust right, denomination below **Rev:** With
plain bunting

Date	Mintage	F	VF	XF	Unc	BU
2002	—	—	—	—	7.00	8.00

KM# 74a.1   50 PENCE
28.2800 g., 0.9250 Silver 0.8410 oz. ASW, 38.6 mm. **Ruler:**
Elizabeth II **Subject:** Queen's Golden Jubilee **Obv:** Crowned
bust right, denomination below **Edge:** Reeded

Date	Mintage	F	VF	XF	Unc	BU
2002 Proof	25,000				Value: 45.00	

KM# 74a.2   50 PENCE
28.2800 g., 0.9250 Silver 0.8410 oz. ASW, 38.61 mm. **Ruler:**
Elizabeth II **Subject:** Queen's Golden Jubilee **Obv:** Crowned
bust right, denomination below **Rev:** With plain bunting

Date	Mintage	F	VF	XF	Unc	BU
2002 Proof	—				Value: 45.00	

KM# 74b.1   50 PENCE
39.9400 g., 0.9170 Gold 1.1775 oz. AGW, 38.61 mm. **Ruler:**
Elizabeth II **Subject:** Queen's Golden Jubilee **Obv:** Crowned
bust right, denomination below **Rev:** Queen on horseback below
multicolored bunting **Edge:** Reeded

Date	Mintage	F	VF	XF	Unc	BU
2002 Proof	150				Value: 2,050	

KM# 74b.2   50 PENCE
39.9400 g., 0.9170 Gold 1.1775 oz. AGW, 38.61 mm. **Ruler:**
Elizabeth II **Subject:** Queen's Golden Jubilee **Obv:** Crowned
bust right, denomination below **Rev:** With plain bunting

Date	Mintage	F	VF	XF	Unc	BU
2002 Proof	—				Value: 2,000	

KM# 75.1   50 PENCE
28.1300 g., Copper-Nickel, 38.6 mm. **Ruler:** Elizabeth II
Subject: Queen's Golden Jubilee **Obv:** Crowned bust right,
denomination below **Rev:** Queen Elizabeth II talking into
microphone below multicolor bunting **Edge:** Reeded

Date	Mintage	F	VF	XF	Unc	BU
2002(2001) Proof	—				Value: 8.00	

KM# 75.2   50 PENCE
Copper-Nickel **Ruler:** Elizabeth II **Subject:** Queen's Golden
Jubilee **Obv:** Crowned bust right, denomination below **Rev:** With
plain bunting

Date	Mintage	F	VF	XF	Unc	BU
2002	—	—	—	—	6.00	7.00

KM# 75a.1   50 PENCE
28.2800 g., 0.9250 Silver 0.8410 oz. ASW, 38.6 mm. **Ruler:**
Elizabeth II **Subject:** Queen's Golden Jubilee **Obv:** Crowned
bust right, denomination below **Rev:** Queen speaking into a radio
microphone below multicolored bunting **Edge:** Reeded

Date	Mintage	F	VF	XF	Unc	BU
2002 Proof	25,000				Value: 45.00	

KM# 75a.2   50 PENCE
28.2800 g., 0.9250 Silver 0.8410 oz. ASW, 38.61 mm. **Ruler:**
Elizabeth II **Subject:** Queen's Golden Jubilee **Obv:** Crowned
bust right, denomination below **Rev:** With plain bunting

Date	Mintage	F	VF	XF	Unc	BU
2002 Proof	—				Value: 45.00	

KM# 75b.1   50 PENCE
39.9400 g., 0.9170 Gold 1.1775 oz. AGW, 38.61 mm. **Ruler:**
Elizabeth II **Subject:** Queen's Golden Jubilee **Obv:** Crowned
bust right, denomination below **Rev:** Elizabeth speaking into a
radio microphone below multicolored bunting **Edge:** Reeded

Date	Mintage	F	VF	XF	Unc	BU
2002 Proof	50				Value: 2,050	

KM# 75b.2   50 PENCE
39.9400 g., 0.9170 Gold 1.1775 oz. AGW, 38.61 mm. **Ruler:**
Elizabeth II **Subject:** Queen's Golden Jubilee **Obv:** Crowned
bust right, denomination below **Rev:** With plain bunting

Date	Mintage	F	VF	XF	Unc	BU
2002 Proof	—				Value: 2,000	

KM# 76.1   50 PENCE
28.1300 g., Copper-Nickel, 38.6 mm. **Ruler:** Elizabeth II
Subject: Queen's Golden Jubilee **Obv:** Crowned bust right,
denomination below **Rev:** Queen walking to left in front of a crowd
below multicolored bunting **Edge:** Reeded

Date	Mintage	F	VF	XF	Unc	BU
2002(2001) Proof	—				Value: 8.00	

KM# 76.2   50 PENCE
Copper-Nickel **Ruler:** Elizabeth II **Subject:** Queen's Golden
Jubilee **Obv:** Crowned bust right, denomination below **Rev:** With
plain bunting

Date	Mintage	F	VF	XF	Unc	BU
2002	—	—	—	—	6.00	7.00

KM# 76a.1   50 PENCE
28.2800 g., 0.9250 Silver 0.8410 oz. ASW, 38.6 mm. **Ruler:**
Elizabeth II **Subject:** Queen's Golden Jubilee **Obv:** Crowned
bust right, denomination below **Rev:** Queen standing before
crowd below multicolored bunting **Edge:** Reeded

Date	Mintage	F	VF	XF	Unc	BU
2002 Proof	15,000				Value: 45.00	

KM# 76a.2   50 PENCE
28.2800 g., 0.9250 Silver 0.8410 oz. ASW, 38.61 mm. **Ruler:**
Elizabeth II **Subject:** Queen's Golden Jubilee **Obv:** Crowned
bust right, denomination below **Rev:** With plain bunting

Date	Mintage	F	VF	XF	Unc	BU
2002 Proof	—				Value: 45.00	

KM# 76b.1   50 PENCE
39.9400 g., 0.9170 Gold 1.1775 oz. AGW, 38.61 mm. **Ruler:**
Elizabeth II **Subject:** Queen's Golden Jubilee **Obv:** Crowned
bust right, denomination below **Rev:** Queen standing before a
crowd below multicolored bunting **Edge:** Reeded

Date	Mintage	F	VF	XF	Unc	BU
2002 Proof	50				Value: 2,050	

KM# 76b.2   50 PENCE
39.9400 g., 0.9170 Gold 1.1775 oz. AGW, 38.61 mm. **Ruler:**
Elizabeth II **Subject:** Queen's Golden Jubilee **Obv:** Crowned
bust right, denomination below **Rev:** With plain bunting

Date	Mintage	F	VF	XF	Unc	BU
2002 Proof	—				Value: 2,000	

KM# 77.1   50 PENCE
28.1300 g., Copper-Nickel, 38.6 mm. **Ruler:** Elizabeth II
Subject: Queen's Golden Jubilee **Obv:** Crowned bust right,
denomination below **Rev:** Conjoined busts of Queen Elizabeth,
Prince Charles, Prince William facing left in inner circle below
multicolor bunting **Edge:** Reeded

Date	Mintage	F	VF	XF	Unc	BU
2002(2001) Proof	—				Value: 8.00	

KM# 77.2   50 PENCE
Copper-Nickel **Ruler:** Elizabeth II **Subject:** Queen's Golden
Jubilee **Obv:** Crowned bust right, denomination below **Rev:** With
plain bunting

Date	Mintage	F	VF	XF	Unc	BU
2002	—	—	—	—	6.00	7.00

KM# 77a.1   50 PENCE
28.2800 g., 0.9250 Silver 0.8410 oz. ASW, 38.6 mm. **Ruler:**
Elizabeth II **Subject:** Queen's Golden Jubilee **Obv:** Crowned
bust right, denomination below **Rev:** Queen, Prince Charles and
Prince William below multicolor bunting **Edge:** Reeded

Date	Mintage	F	VF	XF	Unc	BU
2002 Proof	15,000				Value: 45.00	

KM# 77a.2   50 PENCE
28.2800 g., 0.9250 Silver 0.8410 oz. ASW, 38.61 mm. **Ruler:**
Elizabeth II **Subject:** Queen's Golden Jubilee **Obv:** Crowned
bust right, denomination below **Rev:** With plain bunting

Date	Mintage	F	VF	XF	Unc	BU
2002 Proof	—				Value: 45.00	

KM# 77b.1   50 PENCE
39.9400 g., 0.9170 Gold 1.1775 oz. AGW, 38.61 mm. **Ruler:**
Elizabeth II **Subject:** Queen's Golden Jubilee **Obv:** Crowned
bust right, denomination below **Rev:** Elizabeth II, Prince Charles
and his son William below multicolored bunting **Edge:** Reeded

Date	Mintage	F	VF	XF	Unc	BU
2002 Proof	50				Value: 2,050	

KM# 77b.2   50 PENCE
39.9400 g., 0.9170 Gold 1.1775 oz. AGW, 38.61 mm. **Ruler:**
Elizabeth II **Subject:** Queen's Golden Jubilee **Obv:** Crowned
bust right, denomination below **Rev:** With plain bunting

Date	Mintage	F	VF	XF	Unc	BU
2002 Proof	—				Value: 2,000	

KM# 78.1   50 PENCE
28.1300 g., Copper-Nickel, 38.6 mm. **Ruler:** Elizabeth II
Subject: Queen's Golden Jubilee **Obv:** Crowned bust right,
denomination below **Rev:** Royal coach below multicolor bunting
Edge: Reeded

Date	Mintage	F	VF	XF	Unc	BU
2002 Proof	—				Value: 8.00	

KM# 78.2   50 PENCE
Copper-Nickel **Ruler:** Elizabeth II **Subject:** Queen's Golden
Jubilee **Obv:** Crowned bust right, denomination below **Rev:** With
plain bunting

Date	Mintage	F	VF	XF	Unc	BU
2002	—	—	—	—	6.00	7.00

KM# 78a.1   50 PENCE
28.2800 g., 0.9250 Silver 0.8410 oz. ASW, 38.6 mm. **Ruler:**
Elizabeth II **Subject:** Queen's Golden Jubilee **Obv:** Crowned
bust right, denomination below **Rev:** Coronation coach below
multicolor bunting **Edge:** Reeded

Date	Mintage	F	VF	XF	Unc	BU
2002 Proof	15,000	Value: 45.00				

KM# 78b.1   50 PENCE
39.9400 g., 0.9170 Gold 1.1775 oz. AGW, 38.61 mm. **Ruler:**
Elizabeth II **Subject:** Queen's Golden Jubilee **Obv:** Crowned
bust right, denomination below **Rev:** Coronation coach below
multicolor bunting **Edge:** Reeded

Date	Mintage	F	VF	XF	Unc	BU
2002 Proof	150	Value: 2,050				

KM# 78b.2   50 PENCE
39.9400 g., 0.9170 Gold 1.1775 oz. AGW, 38.61 mm. **Ruler:**
Elizabeth II **Subject:** Queen's Golden Jubilee **Obv:** Crowned
bust right, denomination below **Rev:** With plain bunting

Date	Mintage	F	VF	XF	Unc	BU
2002 Proof	—	Value: 2,000				

KM# 79.1   50 PENCE
28.1300 g., Copper-Nickel, 38.6 mm. **Ruler:** Elizabeth II
Subject: Queen's Golden Jubilee **Obv:** Crowned bust right,
denomination below **Rev:** Scepter and orb below multicolor
bunting **Edge:** Reeded

Date	Mintage	F	VF	XF	Unc	BU
2002 Proof	—	Value: 8.00				

KM# 79.2   50 PENCE
Copper-Nickel **Ruler:** Elizabeth II **Subject:** Queen's Golden
Jubilee **Obv:** Crowned bust right, denomination below **Rev:** With
plain bunting

Date	Mintage	F	VF	XF	Unc	BU
2002	—	—	—	—	6.00	7.00

KM# 79a.1   50 PENCE
28.2800 g., 0.9250 Silver 0.8410 oz. ASW, 38.6 mm. **Ruler:**
Elizabeth II **Subject:** Queen's Golden Jubilee **Obv:** Crowned
bust right, denomination below **Rev:** Orb and scepter below
multicolor bunting **Edge:** Reeded

Date	Mintage	F	VF	XF	Unc	BU
2002 Proof	15,000	Value: 45.00				

KM# 79a.2   50 PENCE
28.2800 g., 0.9250 Silver 0.8410 oz. ASW, 38.61 mm. **Ruler:**
Elizabeth II **Subject:** Queen's Golden Jubilee **Obv:** Crowned
bust right, denomination below **Rev:** With plain bunting

Date	Mintage	F	VF	XF	Unc	BU
2002 Proof	—	Value: 45.00				

KM# 79b.1   50 PENCE
39.9400 g., 0.9170 Gold 1.1775 oz. AGW, 38.61 mm. **Ruler:**
Elizabeth II **Subject:** Queen's Golden Jubilee **Obv:** Crowned
bust right, denomination below **Rev:** Orb and scepter below
multicolor bunting **Edge:** Reeded

Date	Mintage	F	VF	XF	Unc	BU
2002 Proof	150	Value: 1,800				

KM# 79b.2   50 PENCE
39.9400 g., 0.9170 Gold 1.1775 oz. AGW, 38.61 mm. **Ruler:**
Elizabeth II **Subject:** Queen's Golden Jubilee **Obv:** Crowned
bust right, denomination below **Rev:** With plain bunting

Date	Mintage	F	VF	XF	Unc	BU
2002 Proof	—	Value: 2,000				

KM# 80.1   50 PENCE
28.1300 g., Copper-Nickel, 38.6 mm. **Ruler:** Elizabeth II **Subject:**
Queen's Golden Jubilee **Obv:** Crowned bust right, denomination
below **Rev:** Crown below multicolor bunting **Edge:** Reeded

Date	Mintage	F	VF	XF	Unc	BU
2002 Proof	—	Value: 8.00				

KM# 80.2   50 PENCE
Copper-Nickel **Ruler:** Elizabeth II **Subject:** Queen's Golden
Jubilee **Obv:** Crowned bust right, denomination below **Rev:** With
plain bunting

Date	Mintage	F	VF	XF	Unc	BU
2002	—	—	—	—	6.00	7.00

KM# 80a.1   50 PENCE
28.2800 g., 0.9250 Silver 0.8410 oz. ASW, 38.6 mm. **Ruler:**
Elizabeth II **Subject:** Queen's Golden Jubilee **Obv:** Crowned
bust right, denomination below **Rev:** Crown below multicolor
bunting **Edge:** Reeded

Date	Mintage	F	VF	XF	Unc	BU
2002 Proof	15,000	Value: 45.00				

KM# 80a.2   50 PENCE
28.2800 g., 0.9250 Silver 0.8410 oz. ASW, 38.61 mm. **Ruler:**
Elizabeth II **Subject:** Queen's Golden Jubilee **Obv:** Crowned
bust right, denomination below **Rev:** With plain bunting

Date	Mintage	F	VF	XF	Unc	BU
2002 Proof	—	Value: 45.00				

KM# 80b.1   50 PENCE
39.9400 g., 0.9170 Gold 1.1775 oz. AGW, 38.61 mm. **Ruler:**
Elizabeth II **Subject:** Queen's Golden Jubilee **Obv:** Crowned
bust right, denomination below **Rev:** Crown below multicolor
bunting **Edge:** Reeded

Date	Mintage	F	VF	XF	Unc	BU
2002 Proof	150	Value: 2,050				

KM# 80b.2   50 PENCE
39.9400 g., 0.9170 Gold 1.1775 oz. AGW, 38.61 mm. **Ruler:**
Elizabeth II **Subject:** Queen's Golden Jubilee **Obv:** Crowned
bust right, denomination below **Rev:** With plain bunting

Date	Mintage	F	VF	XF	Unc	BU
2002 Proof	—	Value: 2,000				

KM# 81.1   50 PENCE
28.1300 g., Copper-Nickel, 38.6 mm. **Ruler:** Elizabeth II
Subject: Queen's Golden Jubilee **Obv:** Crowned bust right,
denomination below **Rev:** Throne below multicolor bunting **Edge:**
Reeded

Date	Mintage	F	VF	XF	Unc	BU
2002 Proof	—	Value: 8.00				

KM# 81.2   50 PENCE
Copper-Nickel **Ruler:** Elizabeth II **Subject:** Queen's Golden
Jubilee **Obv:** Crowned bust right, denomination below **Rev:** With
plain bunting

Date	Mintage	F	VF	XF	Unc	BU
2002	—	—	—	—	6.00	7.00

KM# 81a.1   50 PENCE
28.2800 g., 0.9250 Silver 0.8410 oz. ASW, 38.6 mm. **Ruler:**
Elizabeth II **Subject:** Queen's Golden Jubilee **Obv:** Crowned
bust right, denomination below **Rev:** Coronation throne below
multicolor bunting **Edge:** Reeded

Date	Mintage	F	VF	XF	Unc	BU
2002 Proof	15,000	Value: 45.00				

KM# 81a.2   50 PENCE
28.2800 g., 0.9250 Silver 0.8410 oz. ASW, 38.61 mm. **Ruler:**
Elizabeth II **Subject:** Queen's Golden Jubilee **Obv:** Crowned
bust right, denomination below **Rev:** With plain bunting

Date	Mintage	F	VF	XF	Unc	BU
2002 Proof	—	Value: 45.00				

KM# 81b.1   50 PENCE
39.9400 g., 0.9170 Gold 1.1775 oz. AGW, 38.61 mm. **Ruler:**
Elizabeth II **Subject:** Queen's Golden Jubilee **Obv:** Crowned
bust right, denomination below **Rev:** Coronation Throne below
multicolored bunting **Edge:** Reeded

Date	Mintage	F	VF	XF	Unc	BU
2002 Proof	150	Value: 2,050				

KM# 81b.2   50 PENCE
39.9400 g., 0.9170 Gold 1.1775 oz. AGW, 38.61 mm. **Ruler:**
Elizabeth II **Subject:** Queen's Golden Jubilee **Obv:** Crowned
bust right, denomination below **Rev:** With plain bunting

Date	Mintage	F	VF	XF	Unc	BU
2002 Proof	—	Value: 2,000				

KM# 82.1   50 PENCE
28.1300 g., Copper-Nickel, 38.6 mm. **Ruler:** Elizabeth II
Subject: Queen's Golden Jubilee **Obv:** Crowned bust right,
denomination below **Rev:** Queen on throne below multicolor
bunting **Edge:** Reeded

Date	Mintage	F	VF	XF	Unc	BU
2002 Proof	—	—	—	—	6.00	7.00

KM# 82.2   50 PENCE
Copper-Nickel **Ruler:** Elizabeth II **Subject:** Queen's Golden
Jubilee **Obv:** Crowned bust right, denomination below **Rev:** With
plain bunting

Date	Mintage	F	VF	XF	Unc	BU
2002	—	—	—	—	6.00	7.00

KM# 82a.1   50 PENCE
28.2800 g., 0.9250 Silver 0.8410 oz. ASW, 38.6 mm. **Ruler:**
Elizabeth II **Subject:** Queen's Golden Jubilee **Obv:** Crowned
bust right, denomination below **Rev:** Queen on throne below
multicolor bunting **Edge:** Reeded

Date	Mintage	F	VF	XF	Unc	BU
2002 Proof	15,000	Value: 45.00				

KM# 82a.2   50 PENCE
28.2800 g., 0.9250 Silver 0.8410 oz. ASW, 38.61 mm. **Ruler:**
Elizabeth II **Subject:** Queen's Golden Jubilee **Obv:** Crowned
bust right, denomination below **Rev:** With plain bunting

Date	Mintage	F	VF	XF	Unc	BU
2002 Proof	—	Value: 45.00				

KM# 82b.1   50 PENCE
39.9400 g., 0.9170 Gold 1.1775 oz. AGW, 38.61 mm.   **Ruler:**
Elizabeth II **Subject:** Queen's Golden Jubilee **Obv:** Crowned
bust right, denomination below **Rev:** Queen seated on throne
below multicolor bunting **Edge:** Reeded

Date	Mintage	F	VF	XF	Unc	BU
2002 Proof	50	Value: 1,800				

KM# 82b.2   50 PENCE
39.9400 g., 0.9170 Gold 1.1775 oz. AGW, 38.61 mm.   **Ruler:**
Elizabeth II **Subject:** Queen's Golden Jubilee **Obv:** Crowned
bust right, denomination below **Rev:** With plain bunting
Edge: Reeded

Date	Mintage	F	VF	XF	Unc	BU
2002 Proof	—	Value: 2,000				

KM# 83.1   50 PENCE
28.1300 g., Copper-Nickel, 38.6 mm.   **Ruler:** Elizabeth II
Subject: Queen's Golden Jubilee **Obv:** Crowned bust right,
denomination below **Rev:** Queen and young family below
multicolor bunting **Edge:** Reeded

Date	Mintage	F	VF	XF	Unc	BU
2002 Proof	—	—	—	—	6.00	7.00

KM# 83a.1   50 PENCE
28.2800 g., 0.9250 Silver 0.8410 oz. ASW, 38.6 mm.   **Ruler:**
Elizabeth II **Subject:** Queen's Golden Jubilee **Obv:** Crowned
bust right, denomination below **Rev:** Royal family below
multicolor bunting **Edge:** Reeded

Date	Mintage	F	VF	XF	Unc	BU
2002 Proof	15,000	Value: 45.00				

KM# 83a.2   50 PENCE
28.2800 g., 0.9250 Silver 0.8410 oz. ASW, 38.61 mm.   **Ruler:**
Elizabeth II **Subject:** Queen's Golden Jubilee **Obv:** Crowned
bust right, denomination below **Rev:** With plain bunting

Date	Mintage	F	VF	XF	Unc	BU
2002 Proof	—	Value: 45.00				

KM# 83b.1   50 PENCE
39.9400 g., 0.9170 Gold 1.1775 oz. AGW, 38.61 mm.   **Ruler:**
Elizabeth II **Subject:** Queen's Golden Jubilee **Obv:** Crowned
bust right, denomination below **Rev:** Royal Family below
multicolor bunting **Edge:** Reeded

Date	Mintage	F	VF	XF	Unc	BU
2002 Proof	50	Value: 2,050				

KM# 83b.2   50 PENCE
39.9400 g., 0.9170 Gold 1.1775 oz. AGW, 38.61 mm.   **Ruler:**
Elizabeth II **Subject:** Queen's Golden Jubilee **Obv:** Crowned
bust right, denomination below **Rev:** With plain bunting

Date	Mintage	F	VF	XF	Unc	BU
2002 Proof	—	Value: 2,000				

KM# 84.1   50 PENCE
28.1300 g., Copper-Nickel, 38.6 mm.   **Ruler:** Elizabeth II
Subject: Queen's Golden Jubilee **Obv:** Crowned bust right,
denomination below **Rev:** Queens head and tree house below
multicolor bunting **Edge:** Reeded

Date	Mintage	F	VF	XF	Unc	BU
2002 Proof	—	Value: 8.00				

KM# 84.2   50 PENCE
Copper-Nickel   **Ruler:** Elizabeth II **Subject:** Queen's Golden
Jubilee **Obv:** Crowned bust right, denomination below **Rev:** With
plain bunting

Date	Mintage	F	VF	XF	Unc	BU
2002	—	—	—	—	6.00	7.00

KM# 84a.1   50 PENCE
28.2800 g., 0.9250 Silver 0.8410 oz. ASW, 38.6 mm.   **Ruler:**
Elizabeth II **Subject:** Queen's Golden Jubilee **Obv:** Crowned
bust right, denomination below **Rev:** Queen and tree house below
multicolor bunting **Edge:** Reeded

Date	Mintage	F	VF	XF	Unc	BU
2002 Proof	25,000	Value: 45.00				

KM# 84a.2   50 PENCE
28.2800 g., 0.9250 Silver 0.8410 oz. ASW, 38.61 mm.   **Ruler:**
Elizabeth II **Subject:** Queen's Golden Jubilee **Obv:** Crowned
bust right, denomination below **Rev:** With plain bunting

Date	Mintage	F	VF	XF	Unc	BU
2002 Proof	—	Value: 45.00				

KM# 84b.1   50 PENCE
39.9400 g., 0.9170 Gold 1.1775 oz. AGW, 38.61 mm.   **Ruler:**
Elizabeth II **Subject:** Queen's Golden Jubilee **Obv:** Crowned
bust right, denomination below **Rev:** Queen and tree house below
multicolor bunting **Edge:** Reeded

Date	Mintage	F	VF	XF	Unc	BU
2002 Proof	50	Value: 2,050				

KM# 84b.2   50 PENCE
39.9400 g., 0.9170 Gold 1.1775 oz. AGW, 38.61 mm.   **Ruler:**
Elizabeth II **Subject:** Queen's Golden Jubilee **Obv:** Crowned
bust right, denomination below **Rev:** With plain bunting

Date	Mintage	F	VF	XF	Unc	BU
2002 Proof	—	Value: 2,000				

KM# 90   50 PENCE
28.2800 g., Copper-Nickel, 38.6 mm.   **Ruler:** Elizabeth II **Obv:**
Crowned bust right, denomination below **Rev:** Conjoined busts
of Elizabeth and Philip below multicolor bunting **Edge:** Reeded

Date	Mintage	F	VF	XF	Unc	BU
2002	—	—	—	—	6.00	7.00

KM# 90a.1   50 PENCE
28.2800 g., 0.9250 Silver 0.8410 oz. ASW, 38.6 mm.   **Ruler:**
Elizabeth II **Obv:** Crowned bust right, denomination below **Rev:**
Elizabeth and Philip below multicolor bunting **Edge:** Reeded

Date	Mintage	F	VF	XF	Unc	BU
2002 Proof	15,000	Value: 45.00				

KM# 90a.2   50 PENCE
28.2800 g., 0.9250 Silver 0.8410 oz. ASW, 38.6 mm.   **Ruler:**
Elizabeth II **Obv:** Crowned bust right, denomination below **Rev:**
With plain bunting

Date	Mintage	F	VF	XF	Unc	BU
2002 Proof	—	Value: 45.00				

KM# 90b.1   50 PENCE
39.9400 g., 0.9170 Gold 1.1775 oz. AGW, 38.61 mm.   **Ruler:**
Elizabeth II **Obv:** Crowned bust right, denomination below **Rev:**
Elizabeth and Philip below multicolor bunting

Date	Mintage	F	VF	XF	Unc	BU
2002 Proof	50	Value: 2,050				

KM# 90b.2   50 PENCE
39.9400 g., 0.9170 Gold 1.1775 oz. AGW, 38.61 mm.   **Ruler:**
Elizabeth II **Obv:** Crowned bust right, denomination below **Rev:**
With plain bunting **Edge:** Reeded

Date	Mintage	F	VF	XF	Unc	BU
2002 Proof	—	Value: 2,000				

KM# 91   50 PENCE
28.2800 g., Copper-Nickel, 38.6 mm.   **Ruler:** Elizabeth II **Obv:**
Crowned bust right, denomination below **Rev:** Queen and
Aborigine dancers below multicolor bunting **Edge:** Reeded

Date	Mintage	F	VF	XF	Unc	BU
2002	—	—	—	—	6.00	7.00

KM# 91a.1   50 PENCE
28.2800 g., 0.9250 Silver 0.8410 oz. ASW, 38.6 mm.   **Ruler:**
Elizabeth II **Obv:** Crowned bust right, denomination below **Rev:**
Queen and Aborigine dancers below multicolor bunting **Edge:**
Reeded

Date	Mintage	F	VF	XF	Unc	BU
2002 Proof	15,000	Value: 45.00				

KM# 91a.2   50 PENCE
28.2800 g., 0.9250 Silver 0.8410 oz. ASW, 38.6 mm.   **Ruler:**
Elizabeth II **Obv:** Crowned bust right, denomination below **Rev:**
With plain bunting **Edge:** Reeded

Date	Mintage	F	VF	XF	Unc	BU
2002 Proof	—	Value: 45.00				

KM# 91b.1   50 PENCE
39.9400 g., 0.9170 Gold 1.1775 oz. AGW, 38.61 mm.   **Ruler:**
Elizabeth II **Obv:** Crowned bust right, denomination below **Rev:**
Queen and Aborigine dancers below multicolor bunting **Edge:**
Reeded

Date	Mintage	F	VF	XF	Unc	BU
2002 Proof	50	Value: 2,050				

KM# 91b.2   50 PENCE
39.9400 g., 0.9170 Gold 1.1775 oz. AGW, 38.61 mm.   **Ruler:**
Elizabeth II **Obv:** Crowned bust right, denomination below **Rev:**
With plain bunting **Edge:** Reeded

Date	Mintage	F	VF	XF	Unc	BU
2002 Proof	—	Value: 2,000				

KM# 92   50 PENCE
28.2800 g., Copper-Nickel, 38.6 mm.   **Ruler:** Elizabeth II **Obv:**
Crowned bust right, denomination below **Rev:** Queen and St.
Paul's Cathedral dome below multicolor bunting **Edge:** Reeded

Date	Mintage	F	VF	XF	Unc	BU
2002	—	—	—	—	6.00	7.00

KM# 92a.1   50 PENCE
28.2800 g., 0.9250 Silver 0.8410 oz. ASW, 38.6 mm.   **Ruler:**
Elizabeth II **Obv:** Crowned bust right, denomination below **Rev:**
Queen and St. Paul's Cathedral dome below multicolor bunting
Edge: Reeded

Date	Mintage	F	VF	XF	Unc	BU
2002 Proof	15,000	Value: 45.00				

KM# 92a.2   50 PENCE
28.2800 g., 0.9250 Silver 0.8410 oz. ASW, 38.6 mm.   **Ruler:**
Elizabeth II **Obv:** Crowned bust right, denomination below **Rev:**
With plain bunting **Edge:** Reeded

Date	Mintage	F	VF	XF	Unc	BU
2002 Proof	—	Value: 45.00				

KM# 92b.1   50 PENCE
39.9400 g., 0.9170 Gold 1.1775 oz. AGW, 38.61 mm. **Ruler:**
Elizabeth II **Obv:** Crowned bust right, denomination below **Rev:**
Queen and St. Paul's Cathedral dome below multicolor bunting
Edge: Reeded

Date	Mintage	F	VF	XF	Unc	BU
2002 Proof	50	Value: 2,050				

KM# 92b.2   50 PENCE
39.9400 g., 0.9170 Gold 1.1775 oz. AGW, 38.61 mm. **Ruler:**
Elizabeth II **Obv:** Crowned bust right, denomination below **Rev:**
With plain bunting **Edge:** Reeded

Date	Mintage	F	VF	XF	Unc	BU
2002 Proof	—	Value: 2,000				

KM# 93   50 PENCE
28.2800 g., Copper-Nickel, 38.6 mm. **Ruler:** Elizabeth II **Obv:**
Crowned bust right, denomination below **Rev:** Elizabeth and
Philip in coronation coach below multicolor bunting **Edge:**
Reeded

Date	Mintage	F	VF	XF	Unc	BU
2002	—	—	—	—	6.00	7.00

KM# 93a.1   50 PENCE
28.2800 g., 0.9250 Silver 0.8410 oz. ASW, 38.6 mm. **Ruler:**
Elizabeth II **Obv:** Crowned bust right, denomination below **Rev:**
Elizabeth and Philip in coronation coach below multicolor bunting
Edge: Reeded

Date	Mintage	F	VF	XF	Unc	BU
2002 Proof	15,000	Value: 45.00				

KM# 93a.2   50 PENCE
28.2800 g., 0.9250 Silver 0.8410 oz. ASW, 38.6 mm. **Ruler:**
Elizabeth II **Obv:** Crowned bust right, denomination below **Rev:**
With plain bunting **Edge:** Reeded

Date	Mintage	F	VF	XF	Unc	BU
2002 Proof	—	Value: 45.00				

KM# 93b.1   50 PENCE
39.9400 g., 0.9170 Gold 1.1775 oz. AGW, 38.61 mm. **Ruler:**
Elizabeth II **Obv:** Crowned bust right, denomination below **Rev:**
Elizabeth and Philip in coronation coach below multicolor bunting
Edge: Reeded

Date	Mintage	F	VF	XF	Unc	BU
2002 Proof	50	Value: 2,050				

KM# 93b.2   50 PENCE
39.9400 g., 0.9170 Gold 1.1775 oz. AGW, 38.61 mm. **Ruler:**
Elizabeth II **Obv:** Crowned bust right, denomination below **Rev:**
With plain bunting **Edge:** Reeded

Date	Mintage	F	VF	XF	Unc	BU
2002 Proof	—	Value: 2,000				

KM# 94   50 PENCE
28.2800 g., Copper-Nickel, 38.6 mm. **Ruler:** Elizabeth II **Obv:**
Crowned bust right, denomination below **Rev:** Elizabeth and
Prince Charles at flower show below multicolor bunting **Edge:**
Reeded

Date	Mintage	F	VF	XF	Unc	BU
2002	—	—	—	—	6.00	7.00

KM# 94a.1   50 PENCE
28.2800 g., 0.9250 Silver 0.8410 oz. ASW, 38.6 mm. **Ruler:**
Elizabeth II **Obv:** Crowned bust right, denomination below **Rev:**
Queen and Prince Charles at flower show below multicolor
bunting **Edge:** Reeded

Date	Mintage	F	VF	XF	Unc	BU
2002 Proof	15,000	Value: 45.00				

KM# 94a.2   50 PENCE
28.2800 g., 0.9250 Silver 0.8410 oz. ASW, 38.6 mm. **Ruler:**
Elizabeth II **Obv:** Crowned bust right, denomination below **Rev:**
With plain bunting **Edge:** Reeded

Date	Mintage	F	VF	XF	Unc	BU
2002 Proof	—	Value: 45.00				

KM# 94b.1   50 PENCE
39.9400 g., 0.9170 Gold 1.1775 oz. AGW, 38.61 mm. **Ruler:**
Elizabeth II **Obv:** Crowned bust right, denomination below **Rev:**
Queen and Prince Charles at flower show below multicolor
bunting **Edge:** Reeded

Date	Mintage	F	VF	XF	Unc	BU
2002 Proof	50	Value: 2,050				

KM# 94b.2   50 PENCE
39.9400 g., 0.9170 Gold 1.1775 oz. AGW, 38.61 mm. **Ruler:**
Elizabeth II **Obv:** Crowned bust right, denomination below **Rev:**
With plain bunting **Edge:** Reeded

Date	Mintage	F	VF	XF	Unc	BU
2002 Proof	—	Value: 2,000				

KM# 95   50 PENCE
28.2800 g., Copper-Nickel, 38.6 mm. **Ruler:** Elizabeth II **Obv:**
Crowned bust right, denomination below **Rev:** Elizabeth and
Philip on balcony below multicolor bunting **Edge:** Reeded

Date	Mintage	F	VF	XF	Unc	BU
2002	—	—	—	—	6.00	7.00

KM# 95a.1   50 PENCE
28.2800 g., 0.9250 Silver 0.8410 oz. ASW, 38.6 mm. **Ruler:**
Elizabeth II **Obv:** Crowned bust right, denomination below **Rev:**
Elizabeth and Philip on balcony below colored bunting **Edge:**
Reeded

Date	Mintage	F	VF	XF	Unc	BU
2002 Proof	15,000	Value: 45.00				

KM# 95a.2   50 PENCE
28.2800 g., 0.9250 Silver 0.8410 oz. ASW, 38.6 mm. **Ruler:**
Elizabeth II **Obv:** Crowned bust right, denomination below **Rev:**
With plain bunting **Edge:** Reeded

Date	Mintage	F	VF	XF	Unc	BU
2002 Proof	—	Value: 45.00				

KM# 95b.1   50 PENCE
39.9400 g., 0.9170 Gold 1.1775 oz. AGW, 38.61 mm. **Ruler:**
Elizabeth II **Obv:** Crowned bust right, denomination below **Rev:**
Elizabeth and Philip on balcony below multicolor bunting **Edge:**
Reeded

Date	Mintage	F	VF	XF	Unc	BU
2002 Proof	50	Value: 2,050				

KM# 95b.2   50 PENCE
39.9400 g., 0.9170 Gold 1.1775 oz. AGW, 38.61 mm. **Ruler:**
Elizabeth II **Obv:** Crowned bust right, denomination below **Rev:**
With plain bunting **Edge:** Reeded

Date	Mintage	F	VF	XF	Unc	BU
2002 Proof	—	Value: 2,000				

KM# 96   50 PENCE
28.2800 g., Copper-Nickel, 38.6 mm. **Ruler:** Elizabeth II **Obv:**
Crowned bust right, denomination below **Rev:** Multicolor jets
below multicolor bunting **Edge:** Reeded

Date	Mintage	F	VF	XF	Unc	BU
2002	—	—	—	—	6.00	7.00

KM# 96a.1   50 PENCE
28.2800 g., 0.9250 Silver 0.8410 oz. ASW, 38.6 mm. **Ruler:**
Elizabeth II **Obv:** Crowned bust right, denomination below **Rev:**
Multicolor jets below multicolor bunting **Edge:** Reeded

Date	Mintage	F	VF	XF	Unc	BU
2002 Proof	15,000	Value: 45.00				

KM# 96a.2   50 PENCE
28.2800 g., 0.9250 Silver 0.8410 oz. ASW, 38.6 mm. **Ruler:**
Elizabeth II **Obv:** Crowned bust right, denomination below **Rev:**
With plain bunting **Edge:** Reeded

Date	Mintage	F	VF	XF	Unc	BU
2002 Proof	—	Value: 45.00				

KM# 96b.1   50 PENCE
39.9400 g., 0.9170 Gold 1.1775 oz. AGW, 38.61 mm. **Ruler:**
Elizabeth II **Obv:** Crowned bust right, denomination below **Rev:**
Multicolor jets below multicolor bunting **Edge:** Reeded

Date	Mintage	F	VF	XF	Unc	BU
2002 Proof	50	Value: 2,050				

KM# 96b.2   50 PENCE
39.9400 g., 0.9170 Gold 1.1775 oz. AGW, 38.61 mm. **Ruler:**
Elizabeth II **Obv:** Crowned bust right, denomination below **Rev:**
With plain bunting **Edge:** Reeded

Date	Mintage	F	VF	XF	Unc	BU
2002 Proof	—	Value: 2,000				

KM# 97   50 PENCE
28.2800 g., Copper-Nickel, 38.6 mm. **Ruler:** Elizabeth II **Obv:**
Crowned bust right, denomination below **Rev:** Queen and
fireworks below multicolor bunting **Edge:** Reeded

Date	Mintage	F	VF	XF	Unc	BU
2002	—	—	—	—	6.00	7.00

KM# 97a.1   50 PENCE
28.2800 g., 0.9250 Silver 0.8410 oz. ASW, 38.61 mm. **Ruler:**
Elizabeth II **Obv:** Crowned bust right, denomination below **Rev:**
Queen and fireworks below multicolor bunting **Edge:** Reeded

Date	Mintage	F	VF	XF	Unc	BU
2002 Proof	15,000	Value: 45.00				

KM# 97a.2   50 PENCE
28.2800 g., 0.9250 Silver 0.8410 oz. ASW, 38.6 mm. **Ruler:**
Elizabeth II **Obv:** Crowned bust right, denomination below **Rev:**
With plain bunting **Edge:** Reeded

Date	Mintage	F	VF	XF	Unc	BU
2002 Proof	—	Value: 45.00				

KM# 97b.1   50 PENCE
39.9400 g., 0.9170 Gold 1.1775 oz. AGW, 38.61 mm. **Ruler:**
Elizabeth II **Obv:** Crowned bust right, denomination below **Rev:**
Queen and fireworks below multicolor bunting **Edge:** Reeded

Date	Mintage	F	VF	XF	Unc	BU
2002 Proof	50	Value: 2,050				

KM# 97b.2   50 PENCE
39.9400 g., 0.9170 Gold 1.1775 oz. AGW, 38.61 mm. **Ruler:**
Elizabeth II **Obv:** Crowned bust right, denomination below **Rev:**
With plain bunting **Edge:** Reeded

Date	Mintage	F	VF	XF	Unc	BU
2002 Proof	—	Value: 2,000				

KM# 98   50 PENCE
28.2800 g., Copper-Nickel, 38.6 mm. **Ruler:** Elizabeth II **Obv:**
Crowned bust right, denomination below **Rev:** UK map and flags
below multicolor bunting **Edge:** Reeded

Date	Mintage	F	VF	XF	Unc	BU
2002	—	—	—	—	6.00	7.00

KM# 98a.1   50 PENCE
28.2800 g., 0.9250 Silver 0.8410 oz. ASW, 38.6 mm. **Ruler:**
Elizabeth II **Obv:** Crowned bust right, denomination below **Rev:**
UK and four flags below multicolor bunting **Edge:** Reeded

Date	Mintage	F	VF	XF	Unc	BU
2002 Proof	15,000	Value: 45.00				

KM# 98a.2   50 PENCE
28.2800 g., 0.9250 Silver 0.8410 oz. ASW, 38.6 mm. **Ruler:**
Elizabeth II **Obv:** Crowned bust right, denomination below **Rev:**
With plain bunting **Edge:** Reeded

Date	Mintage	F	VF	XF	Unc	BU
2002 Proof	—	Value: 45.00				

KM# 98b.1   50 PENCE
39.9400 g., 0.9170 Gold 1.1775 oz. AGW, 38.61 mm. **Ruler:**
Elizabeth II **Obv:** Crowned bust right, denomination below **Rev:**
UK map and four flags below multicolor bunting **Edge:** Reeded

Date	Mintage	F	VF	XF	Unc	BU
2002 Proof	50	Value: 2,050				

KM# 98b.2   50 PENCE
39.9400 g., 0.9170 Gold 1.1775 oz. AGW, 38.61 mm. **Ruler:**
Elizabeth II **Obv:** Crowned bust right, denomination below **Rev:**
With plain bunting **Edge:** Reeded

Date	Mintage	F	VF	XF	Unc	BU
2002 Proof	—	Value: 2,000				

KM# 99   50 PENCE
28.2800 g., Copper-Nickel, 38.6 mm. **Ruler:** Elizabeth II **Obv:**
Crowned bust right, denomination below **Rev:** Queen and two
Commonwealth Games athletes below multicolor bunting **Edge:**
Reeded

Date	Mintage	F	VF	XF	Unc	BU
2002	—	—	—	—	6.00	7.00

KM# 99a.1   50 PENCE
28.2800 g., 0.9250 Silver 0.8410 oz. ASW, 38.6 mm. **Ruler:**
Elizabeth II **Obv:** Crowned bust right, denomination below **Rev:**
Queen and two Commonwealth Games athletes below multicolor
bunting **Edge:** Reeded

Date	Mintage	F	VF	XF	Unc	BU
2002 Proof	15,000	Value: 45.00				

KM# 99a.2   50 PENCE
28.2800 g., 0.9250 Silver 0.8410 oz. ASW, 38.6 mm. **Ruler:**
Elizabeth II **Obv:** Crowned bust right, denomination below **Rev:**
With plain bunting **Edge:** Reeded

Date	Mintage	F	VF	XF	Unc	BU
2002 Proof	—	Value: 45.00				

KM# 99b.1   50 PENCE
39.9400 g., 0.9170 Gold 1.1775 oz. AGW, 38.61 mm. **Ruler:**
Elizabeth II **Obv:** Crowned bust right, denomination below **Rev:**
Queen and two Commonwealth Games athletes below multicolor
bunting **Edge:** Reeded

Date	Mintage	F	VF	XF	Unc	BU
2002 Proof	50	Value: 2,050				

KM# 99b.2   50 PENCE
39.9400 g., 0.9170 Gold 1.1775 oz. AGW, 38.61 mm. **Ruler:**
Elizabeth II **Obv:** Crowned bust right, denomination below **Rev:**
With plain bunting **Edge:** Reeded

Date	Mintage	F	VF	XF	Unc	BU
2002 Proof	—	Value: 2,000				

KM# 100   50 PENCE
28.2800 g., Copper-Nickel, 38.6 mm. **Ruler:** Elizabeth II **Obv:**
Crowned bust right, denomination below **Rev:** Royal Ascot
Carriage scene below multicolor bunting **Edge:** Reeded

Date	Mintage	F	VF	XF	Unc	BU
2002	—	—	—	—	6.00	7.00

KM# 100a.1   50 PENCE
28.2800 g., 0.9250 Silver 0.8410 oz. ASW, 38.6 mm. **Ruler:**
Elizabeth II **Obv:** Crowned bust right, denomination below **Rev:**
Royal Ascot Carriage scene below multicolor bunting **Edge:**
Reeded

Date	Mintage	F	VF	XF	Unc	BU
2002 Proof	15,000	Value: 45.00				

KM# 100a.2   50 PENCE
28.2800 g., 0.9250 Silver 0.8410 oz. ASW, 38.6 mm. **Ruler:**
Elizabeth II **Obv:** Crowned bust right, denomination below **Rev:**
With plain bunting **Edge:** Reeded

Date	Mintage	F	VF	XF	Unc	BU
2002 Proof	—	Value: 45.00				

KM# 100b.1   50 PENCE
39.9400 g., 0.9170 Gold 1.1775 oz. AGW, 38.61 mm. **Ruler:**
Elizabeth II **Obv:** Crowned bust right, denomination below **Rev:**
Royal Ascot Carriage scene below multicolor bunting **Edge:** Reeded

Date	Mintage	F	VF	XF	Unc	BU
2002 Proof	50	Value: 2,050				

KM# 100b.2   50 PENCE
39.9400 g., 0.9170 Gold 1.1775 oz. AGW, 38.61 mm. **Ruler:**
Elizabeth II **Obv:** Crowned bust right, denomination below **Rev:**
With plain bunting **Edge:** Reeded

Date	Mintage	F	VF	XF	Unc	BU
2002 Proof	—	Value: 2,000				

KM# 101   50 PENCE
28.2800 g., Copper-Nickel, 38.6 mm. **Ruler:** Elizabeth II **Obv:**
Crowned bust right, denomination below **Rev:** Queen and two
hockey players below multicolor bunting **Edge:** Reeded

Date	Mintage	F	VF	XF	Unc	BU
2002	—	—	—	—	6.00	7.00

KM# 101a.1   50 PENCE
28.2800 g., 0.9250 Silver 0.8410 oz. ASW, 38.6 mm. **Ruler:**
Elizabeth II **Obv:** Crowned bust right, denomination below **Rev:**
Queen and two hockey players below multicolor bunting **Edge:**
Reeded

Date	Mintage	F	VF	XF	Unc	BU
2002 Proof	15,000	Value: 45.00				

KM# 101a.2   50 PENCE
28.2800 g., 0.9250 Silver 0.8410 oz. ASW, 38.6 mm. **Ruler:**
Elizabeth II **Obv:** Crowned bust right, denomination below **Rev:**
With plain bunting **Edge:** Reeded

Date	Mintage	F	VF	XF	Unc	BU
2002 Proof	—	Value: 45.00				

KM# 101b.1   50 PENCE
39.9400 g., 0.9170 Gold 1.1775 oz. AGW, 38.61 mm. **Ruler:**
Elizabeth II **Obv:** Crowned bust right, denomination below **Rev:**
Queen and two hockey players below multicolor bunting **Edge:**
Reeded

Date	Mintage	F	VF	XF	Unc	BU
2002 Proof	50	Value: 2,050				

KM# 101b.2   50 PENCE
39.9400 g., 0.9170 Gold 1.1775 oz. AGW, 38.61 mm. **Ruler:**
Elizabeth II **Obv:** Crowned bust right, denomination below **Rev:**
With plain bunting **Edge:** Reeded

Date	Mintage	F	VF	XF	Unc	BU
2002 Proof	—	Value: 2,000				

KM# 102   50 PENCE
28.2800 g., Copper-Nickel, 38.6 mm. **Ruler:** Elizabeth II **Obv:**
Crowned bust right, denomination below **Rev:** Queen Mother as
a young lady and as an elderly lady **Edge:** Reeded

Date	Mintage	F	VF	XF	Unc	BU
ND(2002)	—	—	—	—	9.00	10.00

KM# 102a   50 PENCE
28.2800 g., 0.9250 Silver 0.8410 oz. ASW, 38.6 mm. **Ruler:**
Elizabeth II **Obv:** Crowned bust right, denomination below **Rev:**
Queen Mother as a young lady and as an elderly lady **Edge:** Reeded

Date	Mintage	F	VF	XF	Unc	BU
ND(2002) Proof	10,000	Value: 45.00				

KM# 135   50 PENCE
Copper-Nickel, 27.3 mm. **Ruler:** Elizabeth II **Obv:** Crowned bust
right **Rev:** Fox standing right **Shape:** 7-sided

Date	Mintage	F	VF	XF	Unc	BU
2004	—	—	—	—	5.00	7.50

KM# 149   50 PENCE
28.2800 g., 0.9250 Silver 0.8410 oz. ASW, 38.6 mm. **Ruler:**
Elizabeth II **Subject:** Queen's 80th Birthday **Obv:** Head with tiara
right - gilt **Obv. Legend:** QUEEN ELIZABETH II - FALKLAND
ISLANDS **Rev:** Elizabeth seated at left, Queen Mother at right
holding baby

Date	Mintage	F	VF	XF	Unc	BU
2006 Proof	—	Value: 45.00				

KM# 163   50 PENCE
Copper-Nickel, 27.3 mm. **Ruler:** Elizabeth II **Subject:** 25th
Annivery of Liberation **Obv:** Head in tiara right **Rev:** Soldier in
full gear standing before map of Falklands

Date	Mintage	F	VF	XF	Unc	BU
2007PM	—	—	—	—	5.00	7.50

KM# 136   POUND
Nickel-Brass, 22.5 mm. **Ruler:** Elizabeth II **Obv:** Crowned bust
right **Rev:** Shield

Date	Mintage	F	VF	XF	Unc	BU
2004	—	—	—	—	3.50	5.00

KM# 137   2 POUNDS
11.9800 g., Bi-Metallic Copper-Nickel center in Nickel-Brass ring,
28.4 mm. **Ruler:** Elizabeth II **Obv:** Head with tiara right **Obv.
Legend:** QUEEN ELIZABETH THE SECOND **Rev:** Sun and map
surrounded by wildlife **Edge:** Reeded and lettered **Edge
Lettering:** 30 YEARS OF FALKLAND ISLANDS COINAGE

Date	Mintage	F	VF	XF	Unc	BU
2004	—	—	—	5.00	10.00	12.00

KM# 103   25 POUNDS
7.8100 g., 0.9999 Gold 0.2511 oz. AGW, 22 mm. **Ruler:**
Elizabeth II **Obv:** Crowned bust right, denomination below **Rev:**
Queen Mother as a young lady and as an elderly lady **Edge:**
Reeded

Date	Mintage	F	VF	XF	Unc	BU
ND(2002) Proof	1,000	Value: 450				

CROWN COINAGE

KM# 161 1/25 CROWN
0.5000 g., 0.9990 Gold 0.0161 oz. AGW, 11 mm. **Ruler:** Elizabeth II **Subject:** Henry Dunant, Founder, International Red Cross and 1901 Nobel Peace Prize winner **Obv:** Bust with tiara right **Rev:** Dunant bust facing

Date	Mintage	F	VF	XF	Unc	BU
2010PM Proof	—	Value: 80.00				

KM# 141 1/5 CROWN
6.2200 g., 0.9999 Gold 0.1999 oz. AGW **Ruler:** Elizabeth II **Subject:** Diamond Wedding Anniversary **Obv:** Conjoined busts with Prince Philip right **Obv. Legend:** QUEEN ELIZABETH II - FALKLAND ISLANDS **Rev:** Bride and groom standing facing at wedding cake; .01 carat x 1.3mm diamond embedded at top **Rev. Legend:** Diamond Wedding of H.M. Queen Elizabeth II & H.R.H. Prince Philip **Edge:** Reeded

Date	Mintage	F	VF	XF	Unc	BU
2007PM Proof	—	Value: 450				

KM# 129 CROWN
Copper-Nickel **Ruler:** Elizabeth II **Rev:** Nelson and the H.M.S. Victory

Date	Mintage	F	VF	XF	Unc	BU
2005	—	—	—	—	10.00	12.00

KM# 151 CROWN
Copper-Nickel, 38.61 mm. **Ruler:** Elizabeth II **Subject:** I. K. Burnel **Rev:** S. S. Great Britain sailing right

Date	Mintage	F	VF	XF	Unc	BU
2006PM	—	—	—	—	—	15.00

KM# 152 CROWN
Copper-Nickel, 38.61 mm. **Ruler:** Elizabeth II **Subject:** Artic and Antarctic - John Ross and James Clark Ross **Rev:** Ships Victory and Erebus

Date	Mintage	F	VF	XF	Unc	BU
2006PM	—	—	—	—	—	15.00

KM# 143a CROWN
0.9167 Silver **Ruler:** Elizabeth II **Subject:** Diamond Wedding Anniversary **Obv:** Conjoined busts with Prince Philip right **Obv. Legend:** QUEEN ELIZABETH II - FALKLAND ISLANDS **Rev:** Bride and groom standing facing at wedding cake **Rev. Legend:** Diamond Wedding of H.M. Queen Elizabeth II & H.R.H. Prince Philip **Edge:** Reeded

Date	Mintage	VG	F	VF	XF	Unc
2007PM Proof	—	Value: 40.00				

KM# 138 CROWN
Copper-Nickel **Ruler:** Elizabeth II **Rev:** Winston Churchill

Date	Mintage	F	VF	XF	Unc	BU
2007	—	—	—	—	15.00	17.50

KM# 139 CROWN
Copper-Nickel **Ruler:** Elizabeth II **Rev:** Queen Elizabeth I

Date	Mintage	F	VF	XF	Unc	BU
2007	—	—	—	—	15.00	17.50

KM# 140 CROWN
Copper-Nickel **Ruler:** Elizabeth II **Rev:** Charles Darwin

Date	Mintage	F	VF	XF	Unc	BU
2007	—	—	—	—	15.00	17.50

KM# 142 CROWN
Copper-Nickel **Ruler:** Elizabeth II **Subject:** Diamond Wedding Anniversary **Obv:** Conjoined busts with Prince Philip right **Obv. Legend:** QUEEN ELIZABETH II - FALKLAND ISLANDS **Rev:** King George VI standing at left giving Philip standing at right his consent to a contract of matrimony **Rev. Legend:** Diamond Wedding of H.M. Queen Elizabeth II & H.R.H. Prince Philip **Edge:** Reeded

Date	Mintage	F	VF	XF	Unc	BU
2007PM	—	—	—	—	17.00	20.00

KM# 142a CROWN
0.9167 Silver **Ruler:** Elizabeth II **Subject:** Diamond Wedding Anniversary **Obv:** Conjoined busts with Prince Philip right **Obv. Legend:** QUEEN ELIZABETH II - FALKLAND ISLANDS **Rev:** King George VI, standing at left, giving Philip, standing at right, his consent to a contract of matrimony. **Rev. Legend:** Diamond Wedding of H.M. Queen Elizabeth II & H.R.H. Prince Philip **Edge:** Reeded

Date	Mintage	F	VF	XF	Unc	BU
2007PM	—	Value: 40.00				

KM# 143 CROWN
Copper-Nickel **Ruler:** Elizabeth II **Subject:** Diamond Wedding Anniversary **Obv:** Conjoined busts with Prince Philip right **Obv. Legend:** QUEEN ELIZABETH II - FALKLAND ISLANDS **Rev:** Bride and groom standing at wedding cake **Rev. Legend:** Diamond Wedding of H.M. Queen Elizabeth II & H.R.H. Prince Philip **Edge:** Reeded

Date	Mintage	F	VF	XF	Unc	BU
2007PM	—	—	—	—	17.00	20.00

KM# 144 CROWN
Copper-Nickel **Ruler:** Elizabeth II **Subject:** Diamond Wedding Anniversary **Obv:** Conjoined busts with Prince Philip right **Obv. Legend:** QUEEN ELIZABETH II - FALKLAND ISLANDS **Rev:** Bridesmaids and Page Boys **Rev. Legend:** Diamond Wedding of H.M. Queen Elizabeth II & H.R.H. Prince Philip **Edge:** Reeded

Date	Mintage	F	VF	XF	Unc	BU
2007PM	—	—	—	—	17.00	20.00

KM# 144a CROWN
0.9167 Silver **Ruler:** Elizabeth II **Subject:** Diamond Wedding Anniversary **Obv:** Conjoined busts with Prince Philip right **Obv. Legend:** QUEEN ELIZABETH II - FALKLAND ISLANDS **Rev:** Bridesmaids and Page Boys **Rev. Legend:** Diamond Wedding of H.M. Queen Elizabeth II & H.R.H. Prince Philip **Edge:** Reeded

Date	Mintage	F	VF	XF	Unc	BU
2007PM Proof	—	Value: 40.00				

KM# 145 CROWN
Copper-Nickel **Ruler:** Elizabeth II **Subject:** Diamond Wedding Anniversary **Obv:** Conjoined busts with Prince Philip right **Obv. Legend:** QUEEN ELIZABETH II - FALKLAND ISLANDS **Rev:** Buckingham Palace facade **Rev. Legend:** Diamond Wedding of H.M. Queen Elizabeth II & H.R.H. Prince Philip **Edge:** Reeded

Date	Mintage	F	VF	XF	Unc	BU
2007PM	—	—	—	—	17.00	20.00

KM# 145a CROWN
0.9167 Silver **Ruler:** Elizabeth II **Subject:** Diamond Wedding Anniversary **Obv:** Conjoined busts with Prince Philip right **Obv. Legend:** QUEEN ELIZABETH II - FALKLAND ISLANDS **Rev:** Buckingham Palace facade **Rev. Legend:** Diamond Wedding of H.M. Queen Elizabeth II & H.R.H. Prince Philip **Edge:** Reeded

Date	Mintage	F	VF	XF	Unc	BU
2007PM Proof	—	Value: 35.00				

KM# 146 CROWN
Copper-Nickel **Ruler:** Elizabeth II **Subject:** 10th Anniversary - Death of Princess Diana **Obv:** Bust with tiara right **Obv. Legend:** QUEEN ELIZABETH II - FALKLAND ISLANDS **Rev:** Bust of Princess Diana facing 3/4 right **Rev. Legend:** 1961 - 1997 • DIANA — PRINCESS OF WALES **Edge:** Reeded

Date	Mintage	F	VF	XF	Unc	BU
2007PM	—	—	—	—	17.00	20.00

KM# 146a CROWN
0.9167 Silver **Ruler:** Elizabeth II **Subject:** 10th Anniversary Death of Princess Diana **Obv:** Bust with tiara right **Obv. Legend:** QUEEN ELIZABETH II - FALKLAND ISLANDS **Rev:** Bust of Princess Diana facing 3/4 right **Rev. Legend:** 1961 - 1997 ? DIANA ? PRINCESS OF WALES **Edge:** Reeded

Date	Mintage	F	VF	XF	Unc	BU
2007PM Proof	—	Value: 75.00				

KM# 147 CROWN
Copper-Nickel, 38 mm. **Ruler:** Elizabeth II **Subject:** 20th Anniversary - Falkland Islands Fishery **Obv:** Bust right of Queen Elizabeth II **Rev:** Shortfin Squid (Illex Argentinca) **Edge:** Reeded

Date	Mintage	F	VF	XF	Unc	BU
2007PM	—	—	—	—	17.00	20.00

KM# 148 CROWN
Copper-Nickel, 39 mm. **Ruler:** Elizabeth II **Subject:** Scouting Centennial **Obv:** Crowned bust right **Obv. Legend:** QUEEN ELIZABETH II FALKLAND ISLANDS 2007 **Rev:** Baden-Powell bust 3/4 left, scout saluting, tent flanking within circle on animal tracks **Rev. Legend:** 1857 ROBERT BADEN-POWELL 1941 ONE CROWN **Edge:** Reeded

Date	Mintage	F	VF	XF	Unc	BU
2007PM	—	—	—	—	12.50	15.00

KM# 148a CROWN
28.2800 g., 0.9250 Silver 0.8410 oz. ASW, 38.5 mm. **Ruler:** Elizabeth II **Subject:** Scouting Centennial **Obv:** Crowned bust right **Obv. Legend:** QUEEN ELIZABETH II FALKLAND ISLANDS 2007 **Rev:** Baden-Powell bust 3/4 facing left, scout saluting and tent flanking, within circle of animal tracks and rope **Rev. Legend:** 1857 ROBERT BADEN-POWELL 1941 ONE CROWN **Edge:** Reeded

Date	Mintage	F	VF	XF	Unc	BU
2007PM Proof	10,000	Value: 65.00				

KM# 156 CROWN
28.2800 g., Copper-Nickel, 38.61 mm. **Ruler:** Elizabeth II **Subject:** International Polar Year - Discovery **Obv:** Bust in tiara right **Rev:** Icebound ship

Date	Mintage	F	VF	XF	Unc	BU
2007PM	—	—	—	—	17.50	20.00

KM# 157 CROWN
Copper-Nickel, 38.61 mm. **Ruler:** Elizabeth II **Subject:** 25th Anniversary of Liberation **Obv:** Bust in tiara right **Rev:** Britannia standing before map of the Falkland Islands

Date	Mintage	F	VF	XF	Unc	BU
2007PM	—	—	—	—	17.50	20.00

KM# 150 CROWN
28.2800 g., Copper-Nickel, 38.6 mm. **Ruler:** Elizabeth II **Subject:** Royal Air Force, 90th anniversary

Date	Mintage	F	VF	XF	Unc	BU
2008	—	—	—	—	—	12.00

KM# 153 CROWN
Copper-Nickel, 38.61 mm. **Ruler:** Elizabeth II **Subject:** Spitfire
Obv: Bust in tiara right **Rev:** Two planes in flight

Date	Mintage	F	VF	XF	Unc	BU
2008	—	—	—	—	12.50	15.00

KM# 154 CROWN
Copper-Nickel, 38.61 mm. **Ruler:** Elizabeth II **Subject:** Port
Louis **Obv:** Bust in tiara right **Rev:** Flag raising over fort

Date	Mintage	F	VF	XF	Unc	BU
2008	—	—	—	—	12.50	15.00

KM# 162 CROWN
Copper-Nickel, 38.61 mm. **Ruler:** Elizabeth II **Obv:** Bust in tiara
right **Rev:** Charles Darwin bust left

Date	Mintage	F	VF	XF	Unc	BU
2009PM	—	—	—	—	17.50	20.00

KM# 158 CROWN
28.2800 g., Copper-Nickel, 38.61 mm. **Ruler:** Elizabeth II
Subject: Race for the South Pole **Obv:** Bust in tiara right **Rev:**
Portraits of Scott and Amundsen, dog-sleds, and man-pulled sleds.

Date	Mintage	F	VF	XF	Unc	BU
2011PM	—	—	—	—	17.50	20.00

KM# 159 CROWN
Copper-Nickel, 38.61 mm. **Ruler:** Elizabeth II **Subject:** RAF
Search and Rescue 70th anniversary **Obv:** Bust in tiara right **Rev:**
RAF Search and Rescue Helicopter

Date	Mintage	F	VF	XF	Unc	BU
2011PM	—	—	—	—	17.50	20.00

KM# 160 CROWN
Copper-Nickel, 38.61 mm. **Ruler:** Elizabeth II **Subject:** Royal
Wedding - Prince William and Catherine Middleton **Obv:** Bust in
tiara right **Rev:** Busts left

Date	Mintage	F	VF	XF	Unc	BU
2011PM	—	—	—	—	17.50	20.00

KM# 164 CROWN
Copper-Nickel, 38.61 mm. **Ruler:** Elizabeth II **Subject:**
Elizabeth and Philip 60th Wedding anniversary **Obv:** Bust in tiara
right **Rev:** Lion on crown and Plumes

Date	Mintage	F	VF	XF	Unc	BU
2011PM	—	—	—	—	17.50	20.00

KM# 165 CROWN
28.2800 g., Copper-Nickel, 38.6 mm. **Ruler:** Elizabeth II
Subject: Life of Queen Elizabeth II **Obv:** Conjoined busts right
Rev: Elizabeth, the Queen mother in robes of the Order of the
Garter

Date	Mintage	F	VF	XF	Unc	BU
2012PM	—	—	—	—	—	15.00

KM# 166 CROWN
28.2800 g., Copper-Nickel, 38.6 mm. **Ruler:** Elizabeth II
Subject: Life of Queen Elizabeth II **Obv:** Conjoined busts right
Rev: Elizabeth as WWII nurse

Date	Mintage	F	VF	XF	Unc	BU
2012PM	—	—	—	—	—	15.00

KM# 167 CROWN
Silver with glass insert, 38.6 mm. **Ruler:** Elizabeth II **Obv:** Head
at top, butterfly in glass **Rev:** Life of the butterfly around central
image

Date	Mintage	F	VF	XF	Unc	BU
2012PM Proof	—	Value: 75.00				

PIEDFORT

KM#	Date	Mintage	Identification	Mkt Val
P4	2001	500	50 Pence. 0.9250 Silver. 56.5600 g. 38.6 mm. Reeded edge. Proof KM#86a.	95.00
P5	2001	500	50 Pence. 0.9250 Silver. 56.5600 g. 38.6 mm. Reeded edge. Proof KM#70a.	110
P6	2001	—	50 Pence. 0.9250 Silver. 56.5600 g. 38.6 mm. Queen's portrait. Edward's portrait with two gold plated coin designs. Reeded edge.	—
P7	2001	—	50 Pence. 0.9250 Silver. 56.5600 g. 38.6 mm. Queen's portrait. Henry's portrait with two gold plated coin designs. Reeded edge.	—

KM#	Date	Mintage	Identification	Mkt Val
P8	2001	—	50 Pence. 0.9250 Silver. 56.5600 g. 38.6 mm. Queen's portrait. Charles' portrait with two gold plated coin designs. Reeded edge.	—
P9	2001	—	50 Pence. 0.9250 Silver. 56.5600 g. 38.6 mm. Queen's portrait. Victoria's portrait with two gold plated coin designs. Reeded edge.	—
P10	2001	500	50 Pence. 0.9250 Silver. 56.5600 g. 38.6 mm. Reeded edge.	90.00
P11	2001	500	50 Pence. 0.9250 Silver. 56.5600 g. 38.6 mm. Reeded edge.	95.00
P12	2001	500	50 Pence. 0.9250 Silver. 56.5600 g. 38.6 mm. Reeded edge.	95.00
P13	2001	500	50 Pence. 0.9250 Silver. 56.5600 g. 38.6 mm. Reeded edge.	110
P14	2002	500	50 Pence. 0.9250 Silver. 56.5600 g. 38.6 mm. Reeded edge. Proof KM#73a.	95.00
P15	2002	500	50 Pence. 0.9250 Silver. 56.5600 g. 38.6 mm. Reeded edge. Proof KM#74a.	110
P16	2002	500	50 Pence. 0.9250 Silver. 56.5600 g. 38.6 mm. Reeded edge. Proof KM#75a.	95.00
P17	2002	500	50 Pence. 0.9250 Silver. 56.5600 g. 38.6 mm. Reeded edge. Proof KM#76a.	95.00
P18	2002	500	50 Pence. 0.9250 Silver. 56.5600 g. 38.6 mm. Reeded edge. Proof KM#77a.	95.00
P19	2002	500	50 Pence. 0.9250 Silver. 56.5600 g. 38.6 mm. Reeded edge. Proof KM#78a.	95.00
P20	2002	500	50 Pence. 0.9250 Silver. 56.5600 g. 38.6 mm. Reeded edge. Proof KM#79a.	95.00
P21	2002	500	50 Pence. 0.9250 Silver. 56.5600 g. 38.6 mm. Reeded edge. Proof KM#80a.	95.00
P22	2002	500	50 Pence. 0.9250 Silver. 56.5600 g. 38.6 mm. Reeded edge. Proof KM#81a.	95.00
P23	2002	500	50 Pence. 0.9250 Silver. 56.5600 g. 38.6 mm. Reeded edge. Proof KM#82a.	95.00
P24	2002	500	50 Pence. 0.9250 Silver. 56.5600 g. 38.6 mm. Reeded edge. Proof KM#83a.	95.00
P25	2002	500	50 Pence. 0.9250 Silver. 56.5600 g. 38.6 mm. Reeded edge. Proof KM#84a.	95.00
P26	ND(2002)	500	50 Pence. 0.9250 Silver. 56.5600 g. 38.6 mm. Reeded edge. Proof KM#102a.	95.00

FIJI

The Republic of Fiji consists of about 320 islands located in
the southwestern Pacific 1,100 miles (1,770 km.) north of New
Zealand. The islands have a combined area of 7,056 sq. mi.
(18,274 sq. km.) and a population of 772,891. Capital: Suva. Fiji's
economy is based on agriculture and mining. Sugar, coconut
products, manganese, and gold are exported. Fiji is a member of
the Commonwealth of Nations, but has been subject to periodic
short suspensions.

MINT MARK
(o) - Royal Canadian Mint, Ottawa

REPUBLIC
British Administration until 1970

DECIMAL COINAGE
100 Cents = 1 Dollar

KM# 49a CENT
1.5800 g., Copper Plated Zinc, 17.53 mm. **Ruler:** Elizabeth II
Obv: Crowned head right, date at right **Rev:** Tanoa kava bowl
divides denomination

Date	Mintage	F	VF	XF	Unc	BU
2001(o)	—	—	—	—	0.20	0.65
2002(o)	5,880,000	—	—	—	0.20	0.65
2003(o)	8,030,000	—	—	—	0.20	0.65
2004(o)	8,840,000	—	—	—	0.20	0.65
2005(o)	9,720,000	—	—	—	0.20	0.65

KM# 50a 2 CENTS
3.1600 g., Copper Plated Zinc, 21.08 mm. **Ruler:** Elizabeth II
Obv: Crowned head right, date at right **Rev:** Palm fan and
denomination

Date	Mintage	F	VF	XF	Unc	BU
2001(o)	2,830,000	—	—	—	0.30	0.85
2002(o)	5,000,000	—	—	—	0.30	0.85
2003(o)	6,410,000	—	—	—	0.30	0.85
2004(o)	7,050,000	—	—	—	0.30	0.85
2005(o)	7,760,000	—	—	—	0.30	0.85

KM# 51a 5 CENTS
2.3400 g., Nickel Plated Steel, 19.41 mm. **Ruler:** Elizabeth II **Obv:** Crowned head right **Rev:** Fijian drum - lali divides denomination **Edge:** Reeded

Date	Mintage	F	VF	XF	Unc	BU
2006(I)	—	—	—	—	0.75	1.00

KM# 119 5 CENTS
2.3400 g., Nickel Plated Steel, 19.5 mm. **Ruler:** Elizabeth II **Obv:** Crowned head right **Rev:** Fijian drum - Lali divides denomination **Edge:** Plain

Date	Mintage	F	VF	XF	Unc	BU
2009	—	—	—	—	0.75	1.00
2010	—	—	—	—	0.75	1.00

KM# 52a 10 CENTS
4.7500 g., Nickel Plated Steel, 23.6 mm. **Ruler:** Elizabeth II **Obv:** Crowned head right **Rev:** Throwing club - ula tava tava divides value **Edge:** Reeded

Date	Mintage	F	VF	XF	Unc	BU
2006	—	—	—	—	1.00	1.25

KM# 120 10 CENTS
3.5500 g., Nickel Plated Steel, 21.5 mm. **Ruler:** Elizabeth II **Obv:** Crowned head right **Rev:** Throwing club - ula tava tava divides value **Edge:** Reeded

Date	Mintage	F	VF	XF	Unc	BU
2009	—	—	—	—	1.00	1.25

KM# 95 20 CENTS
11.2400 g., Copper-Nickel, 28.5 mm. **Ruler:** Elizabeth II **Obv:** Crowned head right, date at right **Rev:** South Pacific Games flame logo **Edge:** Reeded **Note:** Prooflike examples issued in special cards.

Date	Mintage	F	VF	XF	Unc	BU
2003	1,540,000	—	—	—	1.50	2.50
2003 Prooflike	—	—	—	—	—	6.00

KM# 53a 20 CENTS
10.5000 g., Nickel Plated Steel, 28.5 mm. **Ruler:** Elizabeth II **Obv:** Crowned head right **Rev:** Tabua on braided sennit cord divides denomination **Edge:** Reeded

Date	Mintage	F	VF	XF	Unc	BU
2006(I)	—	—	0.20	0.35	1.25	1.50

KM# 121 20 CENTS
4.6800 g., Nickel Plated Steel, 24 mm. **Ruler:** Elizabeth II **Obv:** Crowned head right **Rev:** Tabua, a ceremonial whale's tooth divides denomination **Edge:** Segmented reeding

Date	Mintage	F	VF	XF	Unc	BU
2009	—	—	—	0.35	1.25	1.50

KM# 122 50 CENTS
6.5000 g., Nickel Plated Steel, 26.5 mm. **Ruler:** Elizabeth II **Obv:** Crowned head right **Rev:** Sailing canoe - Takia, denomination below **Edge:** Reeded

Date	Mintage	F	VF	XF	Unc	BU
2009	—	—	—	—	1.00	2.00

KM# 164 50 CENTS
27.2200 g., Copper-Nickel, 38.74 mm. **Ruler:** Elizabeth II **Subject:** Year of the Tiger **Obv:** Female goddess facing **Rev:** Multicolor Formosan Tiger

Date	Mintage	F	VF	XF	Unc	BU
2010(c)	6,000	—	—	—	—	50.00

KM# 114 DOLLAR
31.1050 g., 0.9990 Silver 0.9990 oz. ASW, 40.7 mm. **Ruler:** Elizabeth II **Subject:** Sputnik I, 50th Anniversary **Rev:** Multicolor earth, satellite rocket

Date	Mintage	F	VF	XF	Unc	BU
2007 Prooflike	6,000	—	—	—	—	100

KM# 115 DOLLAR
31.1050 g., 0.9990 Silver 0.9990 oz. ASW **Ruler:** Elizabeth II **Subject:** Birds of Fiji **Rev:** Multicolor - blue crested broadbill

Date	Mintage	F	VF	XF	Unc	BU
2008 Prooflike	4,000	—	—	—	—	90.00

KM# 116 DOLLAR
31.1050 g., 0.9990 Silver 0.9990 oz. ASW **Ruler:** Elizabeth II **Subject:** Birds of Fiji **Rev:** Multicolor collared lory

Date	Mintage	F	VF	XF	Unc	BU
2008 Prooflike	4,000	—	—	—	—	90.00

KM# 117 DOLLAR
31.1050 g., 0.9990 Silver 0.9990 oz. ASW **Ruler:** Elizabeth II **Subject:** Birds of Fiji **Rev:** Multicolor - Island Thrush

Date	Mintage	F	VF	XF	Unc	BU
2008 Prooflike	4,000	—	—	—	—	90.00

KM# 118 DOLLAR
31.1050 g., 0.9990 Silver 0.9990 oz. ASW **Ruler:** Elizabeth II **Subject:** Birds of Fiji **Rev:** Multicolor white collared kingfisher

Date	Mintage	F	VF	XF	Unc	BU
2008 Prooflike	4,000	—	—	—	—	90.00

KM# 124 DOLLAR
Copper-Nickel **Ruler:** Elizabeth II **Subject:** Barack Obama elected U.S. President

Date	Mintage	F	VF	XF	Unc	BU
2009	—	—	—	—	—	15.00

KM# 130 DOLLAR
Copper-Nickel partially gilt, 40 mm. **Ruler:** Elizabeth II **Subject:** Pacific Explorers - Sir Francis Drake **Rev:** Ship, portrait in oval

Date	Mintage	F	VF	XF	Unc	BU
2009 Proof	—	Value: 15.00				

KM# 131 DOLLAR
Copper-Nickel partially gilt, 40 mm. **Ruler:** Elizabeth II **Subject:** Pacific Explorers - Ferdinand Magellan **Rev:** Ship, portrait in oval

Date	Mintage	F	VF	XF	Unc	BU
2009 Proof	—	Value: 15.00				

KM# 132 DOLLAR
Copper-Nickel partially gilt, 40 mm. **Ruler:** Elizabeth II **Subject:** Pacific Explorers - James Cook **Rev:** Ship, portrait in oval

Date	Mintage	F	VF	XF	Unc	BU
2009 Proof	—	Value: 15.00				

KM# 133 DOLLAR
Copper-Nickel partially gilt, 40 mm. **Ruler:** Elizabeth II **Subject:** Pacific Explorers - Abel Tasman **Rev:** Ship, portrait in oval

Date	Mintage	F	VF	XF	Unc	BU
2009 Proof	—	Value: 15.00				

KM# 134 DOLLAR
Copper-Nickel partially gilt **Ruler:** Elizabeth II **Subject:** Pacific Explorers - Jacob DeMare & William Schouten **Rev:** Ship, portraits in oval

Date	Mintage	F	VF	XF	Unc	BU
2009 Proof	—	Value: 15.00				

KM# 135 DOLLAR
Copper-Nickel partially gilt **Ruler:** Elizabeth II **Subject:** Pacific Explorers - William Bligh **Rev:** Ship, portrait in oval

Date	Mintage	F	VF	XF	Unc	BU
2009	—	—	—	—	—	15.00

KM# 137 DOLLAR
Copper-Nickel, 38.61 mm. **Ruler:** Elizabeth II **Subject:** Great animals of the World - Panda **Rev:** Panda seated, fur pattern as background

Date	Mintage	F	VF	XF	Unc	BU
2009	—	—	—	—	—	15.00

KM# 137a DOLLAR
Copper-Nickel gilt **Ruler:** Elizabeth II **Subject:** Great animals of the World - Panda

Date	Mintage	F	VF	XF	Unc	BU
2009	—	—	—	—	—	15.00

KM# 138 DOLLAR
Copper-Nickel, 38.61 mm. **Ruler:** Elizabeth II **Subject:** Great animals of the World - Koi **Rev:** Koi fish swimming right, scale pattern as background

Date	Mintage	F	VF	XF	Unc	BU
2009	—	—	—	—	—	15.00

KM# 138a DOLLAR
Copper-Nickel gilt **Ruler:** Elizabeth II **Subject:** Great animals of the World - Koi

Date	Mintage	F	VF	XF	Unc	BU
2009	—	—	—	—	—	15.00

KM# 139 DOLLAR
Copper-Nickel **Ruler:** Elizabeth II **Subject:** Great animals of the World - Zebra

Date	Mintage	F	VF	XF	Unc	BU
2009	—	—	—	—	—	15.00

KM# 139a DOLLAR
Copper-Nickel gilt, 38.61 mm. **Ruler:** Elizabeth II **Subject:** Great animals of the World - Zebra

Date	Mintage	F	VF	XF	Unc	BU
2009	—	—	—	—	—	15.00

KM# 140 DOLLAR
Copper-Nickel **Ruler:** Elizabeth II **Subject:** Great animals of the World - Elephant

Date	Mintage	F	VF	XF	Unc	BU
2009	—	—	—	—	—	15.00

KM# 140a DOLLAR
Copper-Nickel gilt **Ruler:** Elizabeth II **Subject:** Great animals of the World - Elephant

Date	Mintage	F	VF	XF	Unc	BU
2009	—	—	—	—	—	15.00

KM# 141 DOLLAR
Copper-Nickel, 38.61 mm. **Ruler:** Elizabeth II **Subject:** Great animals of the world - Cheeta **Rev:** Cheets standing left, fur pattern background

Date	Mintage	F	VF	XF	Unc	BU
2009	—	Value: 15.00				

KM# 141a DOLLAR
Copper-Nickel gilt **Ruler:** Elizabeth II **Subject:** Great animals of the World - Cheeta

Date	Mintage	F	VF	XF	Unc	BU
2009	—	—	—	—	—	15.00

KM# 142 DOLLAR
Copper-Nickel, 38.61 mm. **Ruler:** Elizabeth II **Subject:** Great animals of teh World - Leopard **Rev:** Leopard walking left, leopard skin background

Date	Mintage	F	VF	XF	Unc	BU
2009	—	—	—	—	—	15.00

KM# 142a DOLLAR
Copper-Nickel gilt **Ruler:** Elizabeth II **Subject:** Great animals of the World - Leopard

Date	Mintage	F	VF	XF	Unc	BU
2009	—	—	—	—	—	15.00

KM# 143 DOLLAR
Copper-Nickel **Ruler:** Elizabeth II **Subject:** Great animals of the World - Giraffe

Date	Mintage	F	VF	XF	Unc	BU
2009	—	—	—	—	—	15.00

KM# 143a DOLLAR
Copper-Nickel gilt **Ruler:** Elizabeth II **Subject:** Great animals of the World - Giraffe

Date	Mintage	F	VF	XF	Unc	BU
2009	—	—	—	—	—	15.00

KM# 144 DOLLAR
Copper-Nickel, 38.61 mm. **Ruler:** Elizabeth II **Subject:** Great animals of the World - Tiger **Rev:** Tiger advancing right, fur pattern as background

Date	Mintage	F	VF	XF	Unc	BU
2009	—	—	—	—	—	15.00

KM# 144a DOLLAR
Copper-Nickel gilt **Ruler:** Elizabeth II **Subject:** Great animals of the World - Tiger

Date	Mintage	F	VF	XF	Unc	BU
2009	—	—	—	—	—	15.00

KM# 145 DOLLAR
Copper-Nickel silver plated **Ruler:** Elizabeth II **Subject:** Tropical fish - Yellow pointed nose

Date	Mintage	F	VF	XF	Unc	BU
2009	—	—	—	—	—	15.00

KM# 146 DOLLAR
Copper-Nickel silver plated **Ruler:** Elizabeth II **Subject:** Tropical fish - Albino yellow fish

Date	Mintage	F	VF	XF	Unc	BU
2009	—	—	—	—	—	15.00

KM# 147 DOLLAR
Copper-Nickel silver plated **Ruler:** Elizabeth II **Subject:** Tropical fish - Striped Butterfly fish

Date	Mintage	F	VF	XF	Unc	BU
2009	—	—	—	—	—	15.00

KM# 148 DOLLAR
Copper-Nickel silver plated **Ruler:** Elizabeth II **Subject:** Tropical fish - Damsel fish

Date	Mintage	F	VF	XF	Unc	BU
2009	—	—	—	—	—	15.00

KM# 149 DOLLAR
Copper-Nickel silver plated **Ruler:** Elizabeth II **Subject:** Tropical fish - Surgern fish

Date	Mintage	F	VF	XF	Unc	BU
2009	—	—	—	—	—	15.00

KM# 150 DOLLAR
Copper-Nickel silver plated **Ruler:** Elizabeth II **Subject:** Tropical fish - Clown fish

Date	Mintage	F	VF	XF	Unc	BU
2009	—	—	—	—	—	15.00

KM# 126 DOLLAR
Silver **Ruler:** Elizabeth II **Subject:** H.C. Andersen - Steadfast Tin Soldier **Rev:** Multicolor toy soldier in flames

Date	Mintage	F	VF	XF	Unc	BU
2010 Proof	—	Value: 50.00				

KM# 127 DOLLAR
Silver **Ruler:** Elizabeth II **Subject:** H.C. Andersen - The Nightengale **Rev:** Multicolor bird

Date	Mintage	F	VF	XF	Unc	BU
2010 Proof	—	Value: 60.00				

KM# 128 DOLLAR
Silver **Ruler:** Elizabeth II **Subject:** H.C. Andersen - Thumbelina **Rev:** Multicolor Pixi

Date	Mintage	F	VF	XF	Unc	BU
2010 Proof	—	Value: 50.00				

KM# 129 DOLLAR
Silver **Ruler:** Elizabeth II **Subject:** H.C. Andersen - The little match girl **Rev:** Multicolor girl with match

Date	Mintage	F	VF	XF	Unc	BU
2010 Proof	—	Value: 50.00				

KM# 152 DOLLAR
31.1050 g., 0.9990 Silver 0.9990 oz. ASW, 46x29 mm. **Ruler:** Elizabeth II **Subject:** Siberian Tiger **Shape:** Irregular

Date	Mintage	F	VF	XF	Unc	BU
2010 Proof	10,000	Value: 50.00				

KM# 153 DOLLAR
31.1050 g., 0.9990 Silver 0.9990 oz. ASW, 46x29 mm. **Ruler:** Elizabeth II **Subject:** Bengal Tiger **Shape:** Irregular

Date	Mintage	F	VF	XF	Unc	BU
2010 Proof	10,000	Value: 50.00				

KM# 154 DOLLAR
Tri-Metallic Copper center, Brass inner ring, Copper-Nickel outer ring., 40 mm. **Ruler:** Elizabeth II **Subject:** FIAA World Cup - South Africa **Rev:** Pretoria stadium and antelopes

Date	Mintage	F	VF	XF	Unc	BU
2010	—	—	—	—	—	20.00

KM# 155 DOLLAR
Tri-Metallic Copper center, Brass inner ring, Copper-Nickel outer ring., 40 mm. **Ruler:** Elizabeth II **Subject:** FIAA World Cup - South Africa **Rev:** Kapstadt stadium and Zebra

Date	Mintage	F	VF	XF	Unc	BU
2010	—	—	—	—	—	20.00

KM# 156 DOLLAR
Tri-Metallic Copper center, Brass inner ring, Copper-Nickel outer ring., 40 mm. **Ruler:** Elizabeth II **Subject:** FIAA World Cup - South Africa **Rev:** Johannesburg Stadium and Rhinos

Date	Mintage	F	VF	XF	Unc	BU
2010	—	—	—	—	—	20.00

KM# 157 DOLLAR
Tri-Metallic Copper center, Brass inner ring, Copper-Nickel outer ring., 40 mm. **Ruler:** Elizabeth II **Subject:** FIAA World Cup - South Africa **Rev:** Johannesburg Stadium and Leopard

Date	Mintage	F	VF	XF	Unc	BU
2010	—	—	—	—	—	20.00

KM# 158 DOLLAR
Tri-Metallic Copper center, Brass inner ring, Copper-Nickel outer ring., 40 mm. **Ruler:** Elizabeth II **Subject:** FIAA World Cup - South Africa **Rev:** Rustenburg Stadium and Lion

Date	Mintage	F	VF	XF	Unc	BU
2010	—	—	—	—	—	20.00

KM# 159 DOLLAR
Tri-Metallic Copper center, Brass inner ring, Copper-Nickel outer ring., 40 mm. **Ruler:** Elizabeth II **Subject:** FIAA World Cup - South Africa **Rev:** Durban Stadium and Giraffes

Date	Mintage	F	VF	XF	Unc	BU
2010	—	—	—	—	—	20.00

KM# 160 DOLLAR
Tri-Metallic Copper center, Brass inner ring, Copper-Nickel outer ring., 40 mm. **Ruler:** Elizabeth II **Subject:** FIAA World Cup - South Africa **Rev:** Polokwane Stadium and Elephant

Date	Mintage	F	VF	XF	Unc	BU
2010	—	—	—	—	—	20.00

KM# 161 DOLLAR
Tri-Metallic Copper center, Brass inner ring, Copper-Nickel outer ring., 40 mm. **Ruler:** Elizabeth II **Subject:** FIAA World Cup - South Africa **Rev:** Nelspruit stadium and Water buffalo

Date	Mintage	F	VF	XF	Unc	BU
2010	—	—	—	—	—	20.00

KM# 162 DOLLAR
Tri-Metallic Copper center, Brass inner ring, Copper-Nickel outer ring., 40 mm. **Ruler:** Elizabeth II **Subject:** FIAA World Cup - South Africa **Rev:** Bloemfontein stadium and Lemurs

Date	Mintage	F	VF	XF	Unc	BU
2010	—	—	—	—	—	20.00

KM# 163 DOLLAR
Tri-Metallic Copper center, Brass inner ring, Copper-Nickel outer ring., 40 mm. **Ruler:** Elizabeth II **Subject:** FIAA World Cup - South Africa **Rev:** Port Elizabeth stadium and Animal

Date	Mintage	F	VF	XF	Unc	BU
2010	—	—	—	—	—	20.00

KM# 181   DOLLAR
31.1050 g., 0.9990 Silver 0.9990 oz. ASW, 38.61 mm. **Ruler:**
Elizabeth II **Subject:** Year of the Tiger **Obv:** Head with crown
right **Rev:** Bengal Tiger in color **Shape:** Yin-Yang

Date	Mintage	F	VF	XF	Unc	BU
2010 Proof	—				Value: 50.00	

KM# 182   DOLLAR
31.1050 g., 0.9990 Silver 0.9990 oz. ASW, 38.61 mm. **Ruler:**
Elizabeth II **Obv:** Head with crown right **Rev:** Siberian tiger in
color **Shape:** Yin-Yang

Date	Mintage	F	VF	XF	Unc	BU
2010 Proof	—				Value: 50.00	

KM# 170   DOLLAR
31.1050 g., 0.9990 Silver 0.9990 oz. ASW, 38.6 mm. **Ruler:**
Elizabeth II **Subject:** Year of the Dragon **Obv:** Characters,
Filigree center **Rev:** Characters, Filigree center

Date	Mintage	F	VF	XF	Unc	BU
2011 Proof	10,000			Value: 70.00		

KM# 176   DOLLAR
31.1050 g., 0.9990 Silver 0.9990 oz. ASW, 38.61 mm. **Ruler:**
Elizabeth II **Subject:** Year of the Rabbit **Obv:** Head with crown
right **Rev:** Rabbit eating carrot, carrots in color

Date	Mintage	F	VF	XF	Unc	BU
2011 Proof	—				Value: 50.00	

KM# 177   DOLLAR
31.1050 g., 0.9990 Silver 0.9990 oz. ASW, 38.61 mm. **Ruler:**
Elizabeth II **Subject:** Year of the Rabbit **Obv:** Head at left, rabbit
in center cut-out **Rev:** Rabbit in center, leatuce leaves around

Date	Mintage	F	VF	XF	Unc	BU
2011 Proof	—				Value: 50.00	

KM# 179   DOLLAR
31.1050 g., 0.9990 Silver 0.9990 oz. ASW, 38.61 mm. **Ruler:**

Elizabeth II **Subject:** Year of the Rabbit **Obv:** Head in crown right
Rev: Snow rabbit in color **Shape:** Yin-Yang

Date	Mintage	F	VF	XF	Unc	BU
2011 Proof					Value: 50.00	

KM# 180   DOLLAR
31.1050 g., 0.9990 Silver 0.9990 oz. ASW, 38.61 mm. **Ruler:**
Elizabeth II **Subject:** Year of the Rabbit **Obv:** Head with crown
right **Rev:** Summer rabbit **Shape:** Yin-Yang

Date	Mintage	F	VF	XF	Unc	BU
2011 Proof	—				Value: 50.00	

KM# 171   DOLLAR
15.5500 g., 0.9990 Silver with color. 0.4994 oz. ASW, 38.6 mm.
Ruler: Elizabeth II **Subject:** Year of the Dragon **Rev:** Red dragon
Shape: Yin

Date	Mintage	F	VF	XF	Unc	BU
2012 Proof	10,000			Value: 70.00		

KM# 172   DOLLAR
15.5500 g., 0.9990 Silver with color. 0.4994 oz. ASW, 38.6 mm.
Ruler: Elizabeth II **Subject:** Year of the Dragon **Rev:** Blue dragon
Shape: Yang

Date	Mintage	F	VF	XF	Unc	BU
2012 Proof	—			Value: 50.00		

KM# 108   2 DOLLARS
10.0000 g., 0.9250 Silver 0.2974 oz. ASW **Ruler:** Elizabeth II
Subject: XVIII FIFA World Rootball Championship - Germany
2006 **Obv:** Crowned head right **Obv. Legend:** ELIZABETH II -
FIJI **Rev:** World cup

Date	Mintage	F	VF	XF	Unc	BU
2004 Proof	50,000			Value: 22.00		

KM# 151   2 DOLLARS
31.1050 g., 0.9990 Silver 0.9990 oz. ASW, 40.5 mm. **Ruler:**
Elizabeth II **Rev:** Hawksbill Taku Turtle

Date	Mintage	F	VF	XF	Unc	BU
2010 Prooflike	—	—	—	—	—	50.00
2011 Prooflike	—	—	—	—	—	50.00

KM# 151a   2 DOLLARS
31.1050 g., 0.9990 Silver partially gilt 0.9990 oz. ASW, 40 mm.
Ruler: Elizabeth II **Rev:** Hawksbill Taku Turtle, gilt

Date	Mintage	F	VF	XF	Unc	BU
2010 Proof	Est. 5,000			Value: 65.00		

KM# 166   2 DOLLARS
31.1050 g., 0.9990 Silver 0.9990 oz. ASW, 45x31 mm. **Ruler:**
Elizabeth II **Rev:** Submarine Ohio in color **Shape:** Oval

Date	Mintage	F	VF	XF	Unc	BU
2010 Prooflike	15,000	—	—	—	—	90.00

KM# 167   2 DOLLARS
31.1050 g., 0.9990 Silver 0.9990 oz. ASW, 45x31 mm. **Ruler:**
Elizabeth II **Rev:** Submarine Triomphant in color **Shape:** Oval

Date	Mintage	F	VF	XF	Unc	BU
2010 Prooflike	15,000	—	—	—	—	90.00

KM# 168   2 DOLLARS
31.1050 g., 0.9990 Silver 0.9990 oz. ASW, 45x31 mm. **Ruler:**
Elizabeth II **Rev:** Submarine Typhoon in color **Shape:** Oval

Date	Mintage	F	VF	XF	Unc	BU
2010 Prooflike	15,000	—	—	—	—	90.00

KM# 169   2 DOLLARS
31.1050 g., 0.9990 Silver 0.9990 oz. ASW, 45x31 mm. **Ruler:**
Elizabeth II **Rev:** Submarine Vanguard in color **Shape:** Oval

Date	Mintage	F	VF	XF	Unc	BU
2010 Prooflike	15,000	—	—	—	—	90.00

KM# 165   2 DOLLARS

31.1050 g., 0.9990 Silver partially gilt 0.9990 oz. ASW, 40.7 mm. **Ruler:** Elizabeth II **Rev:** Pacific Swordfish gilt

Date	Mintage	F	VF	XF	Unc	BU
2011 Prooflike	5,000	—	—	—	—	80.00

KM# 93   5 DOLLARS
1.5550 g., 0.9999 Gold 0.0500 oz. AGW **Ruler:** Elizabeth II **Obv:** Crowned head right, date at right **Rev:** Arms

Date	Mintage	F	VF	XF	Unc	BU
2002	3,000	Value: 95.00				

KM# 115A   5 DOLLARS
1.5600 g., 0.9999 Gold 0.0501 oz. AGW, 13.9 mm. **Ruler:** Elizabeth II **Rev:** Coat of Arms

Date	Mintage	F	VF	XF	Unc	BU
2002 Proof	3,000	Value: 220				

KM# 173   5 DOLLARS
Silver partially gilt, 39 mm. **Ruler:** Elizabeth II **Subject:** Queen Elizabeth II, 80th Birthday

Date	Mintage	F	VF	XF	Unc	BU
2006	—	Value: 50.00				

KM# 82   10 DOLLARS
31.6200 g., 0.9250 Silver 0.9403 oz. ASW, 38.6 mm. **Ruler:** Elizabeth II **Obv:** Crowned head right, date at right **Rev:** William Bligh's - HMS Providence **Edge:** Reeded

Date	Mintage	F	VF	XF	Unc	BU
2001 Proof	—	Value: 40.00				

KM# 83   10 DOLLARS
28.2800 g., 0.9250 Silver 0.8410 oz. ASW, 38.6 mm. **Ruler:** Elizabeth II **Subject:** Queen Elizabeth II - 50 Years of Reign **Obv:** Queen's head right, gilded **Rev:** Cloth draped sword hilt, legend and denomination **Rev. Legend:** Defender of the Faith... **Edge:** Reeded

Date	Mintage	F	VF	XF	Unc	BU
2002 Proof	15,000	Value: 40.00				

KM# 84   10 DOLLARS
28.2800 g., 0.9250 Silver 0.8410 oz. ASW, 38.6 mm. **Ruler:**

Elizabeth II **Subject:** Queen Elizabeth II - 50th Year of Reign **Obv:** Head right, gilded **Rev:** Four man chorus, legend, and denomination **Rev. Legend:** Westminster Abbey June 1953. **Edge:** Reeded

Date	Mintage	F	VF	XF	Unc	BU
2002 Proof	15,000	Value: 40.00				

KM# 94   10 DOLLARS
3.1100 g., 0.9999 Gold 0.1000 oz. AGW **Ruler:** Elizabeth II **Obv:** Crowned head right, date at right **Rev:** Arms **Edge:** Reeded

Date	Mintage	F	VF	XF	Unc	BU
2002 Proof	2,000	Value: 185				

KM# 101   10 DOLLARS
31.1000 g., 0.9990 Silver 0.9988 oz. ASW, 40 mm. **Ruler:** Elizabeth II **Series:** Save the Whales **Obv:** Crowned head right, date at right **Obv. Legend:** ELIZABETH II - FIJI **Rev:** Sperm Whale on mother-of-pearl inset **Edge:** Plain

Date	Mintage	F	VF	XF	Unc	BU
2002 Proof	2,000	Value: 85.00				

KM# 104   10 DOLLARS
28.2800 g., 0.9250 Silver 0.8410 oz. ASW, 38.6 mm. **Ruler:** Elizabeth II **Series:** Endangered Wildlife **Obv:** Crowned head right **Obv. Legend:** ELIZABETH II - FIJI **Rev:** Head of Peregrine Falcon right

Date	Mintage	F	VF	XF	Unc	BU
2002 Proof	—	Value: 45.00				

KM# 105   10 DOLLARS
28.2800 g., 0.9250 Silver 0.8410 oz. ASW, 38.6 mm. **Ruler:** Elizabeth II **Obv:** Crowned head right **Obv. Legend:** ELIZABETH II - FIJI **Rev:** Sailing ship "Vostok"

Date	Mintage	F	VF	XF	Unc	BU
2002 Proof	—	Value: 40.00				

KM# 106   10 DOLLARS
1.2400 g., 0.9999 Gold 0.0399 oz. AGW, 13.88 mm. **Ruler:** Elizabeth II **Obv:** Crowned head right **Obv. Legend:** ELIZABETH II - FIJI **Rev:** Sailing ship at left, naval bust 3/4 left at right **Rev. Legend:** HMS INVESTIGATOR * MATTHEW FLINDERS **Edge:** Reeded

Date	Mintage	F	VF	XF	Unc	BU
2002 Proof	—	Value: 75.00				

KM# 114A   10 DOLLARS
3.1100 g., 0.9999 Gold 0.1000 oz. AGW, 16 mm. **Ruler:** Elizabeth II **Rev:** Coat of Arms

Date	Mintage	F	VF	XF	Unc	BU
2002 Proof	2,000	Value: 350				

KM# 113   10 DOLLARS
1.2400 g., Gold, 13.91 mm. **Ruler:** Elizabeth II **Subject:** Lost Treasure of King Richard **Obv:** Crowned head right **Rev:** Bust of King Richard facing **Edge:** Reeded

Date	Mintage	F	VF	XF	Unc	BU
2003 Proof	—	Value: 70.00				

KM# 107   10 DOLLARS
28.2600 g., 0.9250 Silver 0.8404 oz. ASW, 38.61 mm. **Ruler:** Elizabeth II **Obv:** Crowned head right **Obv. Legend:** ELIZABETH II - FIJI **Rev:** Sailing ship at left, naval bust 3/4 left at right **Rev.**

Legend: HMS INVESTIGATOR * MATTHEW FLINDERS **Edge:** Reeded

Date	Mintage	F	VF	XF	Unc	BU
2003 Proof	—	Value: 40.00				

KM# 109   10 DOLLARS
Silver **Ruler:** Elizabeth II **Subject:** XXVIII Summer Olympics - Athens 2004 **Obv:** Crowned head right **Obv. Legend:** ELIZABETH II - FIJI **Rev:** Regatta

Date	Mintage	F	VF	XF	Unc	BU
2004 Proof	—	Value: 40.00				

KM# 110   10 DOLLARS
Copper-Nickel-Zinc, 38.6 mm. **Ruler:** Elizabeth II **Subject:** XVIII FIFA World Football Championship - Germany 2006 **Obv:** Crowned head right **Obv. Legend:** ELIZABETH II - FIJI **Rev:** Digital countdown clock

Date	Mintage	F	VF	XF	Unc	BU
2005	50,000	—	—	—	—	45.00

KM# 111   10 DOLLARS
1.2400 g., 0.9999 Gold 0.0399 oz. AGW **Ruler:** Elizabeth II **Subject:** 500th Anniversary Death of Christopher Columbus **Obv:** Crowned head right **Obv. Legend:** ELIZABETH II - FIJI **Rev:** Sailing ship "Santa Maria"

Date	Mintage	F	VF	XF	Unc	BU
2006 Proof	15,000	Value: 70.00				

KM# 125   10 DOLLARS
31.1050 g., 0.9990 Silver 0.9990 oz. ASW **Ruler:** Elizabeth II **Obv:** Crowned head right **Rev:** Yes we can!

Date	Mintage	F	VF	XF	Unc	BU
2009 Proof	—	Value: 50.00				

KM# 178   10 DOLLARS
28.2800 g., 0.9250 Silver 0.8410 oz. ASW, 38.61 mm. **Ruler:** Elizabeth II **Obv:** Head with tiara right **Rev:** Barak Obama at left

Date	Mintage	F	VF	XF	Unc	BU
2009 Proof	—	Value: 50.00				

KM# 112   25 DOLLARS
155.5000 g., 0.9990 Silver 4.9942 oz. ASW **Ruler:** Elizabeth II **Obv:** Crowned head right **Obv. Legend:** ELIZABETH II - FIJI **Rev:** Sailing ship "Vostok"

Date	Mintage	F	VF	XF	Unc	BU
2002 Proof	—	Value: 200				

KM# 99   100 DOLLARS
7.7800 g., 0.5850 Gold 0.1463 oz. AGW **Ruler:** Elizabeth II **Subject:** 2006 FIFA World Cup - Germany **Obv:** Crowned head right, date at right **Rev:** World Cup **Edge:** Reeded

Date	Mintage	F	VF	XF	Unc	BU
2003 Proof	25,000	Value: 250				

KM# 136   100 DOLLARS
31.1050 g., 0.9990 Gold 0.9990 oz. AGW, 32 mm. **Ruler:** Elizabeth II **Rev:** Beach scene

Date	Mintage	F	VF	XF	Unc	BU
2009 Proof-like	—	—	—	—	—	1,700

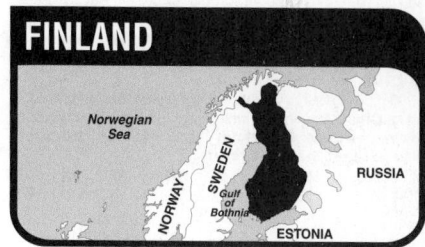

FINLAND

The Republic of Finland, the third most northerly state of the European continent, has an area of 130,559 sq. mi. (338,127 sq. km.) and a population of 5.1 million. Capital: Helsinki. Lumbering, shipbuilding, metal and woodworking are the leading industries. Paper, timber, wood pulp, plywood and metal products are exported.

MONETARY SYSTEM
100 Pennia = 1 Markka

MINT MARKS
H - Birmingham 1921
Heart (h) - Copenhagen 1922
No mm – Helsinki
M – 1987-2006
FI – FINLAND – 2007-
Rampant lion in a circle – 2010-

MINT OFFICIALS' INITIALS

Letter	Date	Name
J-M	2002	Toivo Jaatinen & Raimo Makkonen
L-M	2000-03	Maija Lavonen & Raimo Makkonen
K-M	2004	Heli Kauhanen & Raimo Makkonen
K-M	2005-2006	Tapio Kettunen & Raimo Makkonen
M-M	2002-2006	Pertti Mäkinen & Raimo Makkonen
N-M	2001	Antti Neuvonen & Raimo Makkonen
P-M	2003	Matti Peltokangas & Raimo Makkonen
P-M	2001, 2005-2007	Reijo Paavilainen & Raimo Makkonen
S-M	2003	Anneli Sigriläinen & Raimo Makkonen
VV-M	2002	Erkki Vainio & Hannu Veijalainen & Raimo Makkonen

REPUBLIC

REFORM COINAGE

KM# 65   10 PENNIA
1.8000 g., Copper-Nickel, 16.3 mm. **Obv:** Flower pods and stems, date at right **Rev:** Denomination to right of honeycombs

Date	Mintage	F	VF	XF	Unc	BU
2001 M	25,000,000	—	—	—	1.00	1.50
2001 M Proof	—	Value: 7.00				

KM# 66   50 PENNIA
3.3000 g., Copper-Nickel, 19.7 mm. **Obv:** Polar bear, date below **Rev:** Denomination above flower heads **Edge:** Reeded

Date	Mintage	F	VF	XF	Unc	BU
2001 M	200,000	—	—	0.20	1.00	1.50
2001 M Proof	—	Value: 8.00				

KM# 76   MARKKA
5.0000 g., Aluminum-Bronze, 22.2 mm. **Obv:** Rampant lion left within circle, date below **Rev:** Ornaments flank denomination within circle

Date	Mintage	F	VF	XF	Unc	BU
2001 M	200,000	—	—	0.35	0.75	1.00
2001 M Proof	—	Value: 10.00				

KM# 95   MARKKA
8.6400 g., 0.7500 Gold 0.2083 oz. AGW, 22 mm. **Subject:** Last Markka Coin **Obv:** Rampant lion with sword left **Rev:** Stylized tree with roots **Edge:** Reeded

Date	Mintage	F	VF	XF	Unc	BU
2001M P-M Proof	55,000	Value: 350				

KM# 106   MARKKA
6.1000 g., Copper-Nickel, 24 mm. **Subject:** Remembrance Markka **Obv:** Rampant lion with sword left **Rev:** Denomination and pine tree **Edge:** Plain **Note:** This coin is encased in acrylic resin and sealed in a display card.

Date	Mintage	F	VF	XF	Unc	BU
2001M N-M	500,000	—	—	—	5.00	6.50

KM# 73   5 MARKKAA
5.5000 g., Copper-Aluminum-Nickel, 24.5 mm. **Obv:** Lake Saimaa ringed seal, date below **Rev:** Denomination, dragonfly and lily pad leaves

Date	Mintage	F	VF	XF	Unc	BU
2001 M	200,000	—	—	—	4.00	6.00
2001 M Proof	—	Value: 12.00				

KM# 77   10 MARKKAA
8.8000 g., Bi-Metallic Brass center in Copper-Nickel ring, 27.25 mm. **Obv:** Capercaillie bird within circle, date above **Rev:** Denomination and branches

Date	Mintage	F	VF	XF	Unc	BU
2001 M	200,000	—	—	3.00	5.00	6.00
2001 M Proof	—	Value: 18.00				

KM# 96   25 MARKKAA
20.2000 g., Bi-Metallic Brass center in Copper-Nickel ring, 35 mm. **Subject:** First Nordic Ski Championship, "Lahti 2001" **Obv:** Stylized woman's face **Rev:** Female torso, landscape **Edge:** Plain

Date	Mintage	F	VF	XF	Unc	BU
2001M Prooflike	100,000	—	—	20.00	30.00	

KM# 97   100 MARKKAA
31.0000 g., 0.9250 Silver 0.9219 oz. ASW, 35 mm. **Subject:** Aino Ackte **Obv:** Partial portrait **Rev:** High heel boot and trouser bottom **Edge:** Plain

Date	Mintage	F	VF	XF	Unc	BU
2001M	33,000	—	—	—	35.00	45.00
2001M Proof	12,000	Value: 60.00				

EURO COINAGE
European Union Issues

KM# 98   EURO CENT
2.3000 g., Copper Plated Steel, 16.25 mm. **Obv:** Rampant lion left surrounded by stars, date at left **Rev:** Denomination and globe **Edge:** Plain

Date	Mintage	F	VF	XF	Unc	BU
2001M	500,000	—	—	—	10.00	—
2001M Proof	15,000	—	—	—	—	—
2002M	659,000	—	—	—	5.00	—
2002M Proof	13,000	Value: 15.00				
2003M	6,790,000	—	—	—	1.00	—
2003M Proof	14,500	Value: 15.00				
2004M	9,690,000	—	—	—	1.00	—
2004M Proof	5,000	Value: 15.00				
2005M	5,800,000	—	—	—	1.00	—
2005M Proof	3,000	Value: 15.00				
2006M	4,000,000	—	—	—	1.00	—
2006M Proof	3,300	Value: 15.00				
2007FI	3,000,000	—	—	—	1.00	—
2007FI Proof	—	Value: 15.00				
2008FI	1,500,000	—	—	—	1.00	—
2008FI Proof	2,500	Value: 15.00				
2009FI	—	—	—	—	1.00	—
2009FI Proof	2,500	Value: 15.00				
2010FI	—	—	—	—	1.00	—
2010FI Proof	2,000	Value: 15.00				
2011FI	—	—	—	—	1.00	—
2011FI Proof	—	Value: 15.00				
2012FI	—	—	—	—	1.00	—
2012FI Proof	—	Value: 15.00				

KM# 99   2 EURO CENT
3.0600 g., Copper Plated Steel, 18.75 mm. **Obv:** Rampant lion surrounded by stars, date at left **Rev:** Denomination and globe **Edge:** Grooved

Date	Mintage	F	VF	XF	Unc	BU
2001M	500,000	—	—	—	10.00	—
2001M Proof	15,000	Value: 15.00				
2002M	659,000	—	—	—	5.00	—
2002M Proof	13,000	Value: 15.00				
2003M	6,790,000	—	—	—	5.00	—
2003M Proof	14,500	Value: 15.00				
2004M	8,024,000	—	—	—	5.00	—
2004M Proof	5,000	Value: 15.00				
2005M	5,800,000	—	—	—	5.00	—
2005M Proof	3,000	Value: 15.00				
2006M	4,000,000	—	—	—	5.00	—
2006M Proof	3,300	Value: 15.00				
2007FI	3,000,000	—	—	—	5.00	—
2007FI Proof	—	Value: 15.00				
2008FI	1,500,000	—	—	—	5.00	—
2008FI Proof	2,500	Value: 15.00				
2009FI	—	—	—	—	5.00	—
2009FI Proof	2,500	Value: 15.00				
2010FI	—	—	—	—	5.00	—
2010FI Proof	2,000	Value: 15.00				
2011FI	—	—	—	—	5.00	—
2011FI Proof	—	Value: 15.00				
2012FI	—	—	—	—	5.00	—
2012FI Proof	—	Value: 15.00				

KM# 100   5 EURO CENT
3.9200 g., Copper Plated Steel, 21.25 mm. **Obv:** Rampant lion left surrounded by stars, date at left **Rev:** Denomination and globe **Edge:** Plain

Date	Mintage	F	VF	XF	Unc	BU
2001M	213,756,000	—	—	—	0.50	—
2001M Proof	15,000	Value: 15.00				
2002M	101,824,000	—	—	—	0.50	—
2002M Proof	13,000	Value: 15.00				
2003M	790,000	—	—	—	1.00	—
2003M Proof	14,500	Value: 15.00				
2004M	629,000	—	—	—	1.00	—
2004M Proof	5,000	Value: 15.00				
2005M	800,000	—	—	—	1.00	—
2005M Proof	3,000	Value: 15.00				
2006M	1,000,000	—	—	—	1.00	—
2006M Proof	3,000	Value: 15.00				
2007FI	1,000,000	—	—	—	1.00	—
2007FI Proof	—	Value: 15.00				
2008FI	1,000,000	—	—	—	1.00	—
2008FI Proof	2,500	Value: 15.00				
2009FI	—	—	—	—	1.00	—
2009FI Proof	2,500	Value: 15.00				
2010FI	—	—	—	—	1.00	—
2010FI Proof	2,000	Value: 15.00				
2011FI	—	—	—	—	1.00	—
2011FI Proof	—	Value: 15.00				
2012FI	—	—	—	—	1.00	—
2012FI Proof	—	Value: 15.00				

KM# 101   10 EURO CENT
4.1000 g., Brass, 19.75 mm. **Obv:** Rampant lion left surrounded by stars, date at left **Rev:** Denomination and map **Edge:** Reeded

Date	Mintage	F	VF	XF	Unc	BU
2001M	14,730,000	—	—	—	10.00	—
2001M Proof	15,000	Value: 18.00				
2002M	1,499,000	—	—	—	2.50	—
2002M Proof	13,000	Value: 18.00				
2003M	790,000	—	—	—	2.50	—
2003M Proof	14,500	Value: 18.00				
2004M	629,000	—	—	—	2.50	—
2004M Proof	5,000	Value: 18.00				
2005M	800,000	—	—	—	2.50	—
2005M Proof	3,000	Value: 18.00				
2006M	1,000,000	—	—	—	2.50	—
2006M Proof	3,300	Value: 18.00				

KM# 126   10 EURO CENT
4.1000 g., Brass, 19.75 mm. **Obv:** Rampant lion surrounded by stars **Rev:** Relief map of Western Europe, stars, lines and value **Edge:** Reeded

Date	Mintage	F	VF	XF	Unc	BU
2007FI	1,000,000	—	—	—	2.50	—
2007FI Proof	—	Value: 18.00				
2008FI	1,000,000	—	—	—	2.50	—
2008FI Proof	2,500	Value: 18.00				
2009FI	—	—	—	—	2.50	—
2009FI Proof	2,500	Value: 18.00				
2010FI	—	—	—	—	2.50	—
2010FI Proof	2,000	Value: 18.00				
2011FI	—	—	—	—	2.50	—
2011FI Proof	—	Value: 18.00				
2012FI	—	—	—	—	2.50	—
2012FI Proof	—	Value: 18.00				

KM# 102   20 EURO CENT
5.7400 g., Brass, 22.25 mm.   **Obv:** Rampant lion left surrounded by stars, date at left **Rev:** Denomination and map **Edge:** Notched

Date	Mintage	F	VF	XF	Unc	BU
2001M	121,763,000	—	—	—	1.75	—
2001M Proof	15,000	Value: 20.00				
2002M	100,759,000	—	—	—	1.75	—
2002M Proof	13,000	Value: 20.00				
2003M	790,000	—	—	—	1.75	—
2003M Proof	14,500	Value: 20.00				
2004M	629,000	—	—	—	1.75	—
2004M Proof	5,000	Value: 20.00				
2005M	800,000	—	—	—	1.75	—
2005M Proof	3,000	Value: 20.00				
2006M	1,000,000	—	—	—	1.75	—
2006M Proof	3,300	Value: 20.00				

KM# 127   20 EURO CENT
5.7400 g., Brass, 22.25 mm.   **Obv:** Rampant lion surrounded by stars **Rev:** Relief map of Western Europe, stars, lines and value **Edge:** Notched

Date	Mintage	F	VF	XF	Unc	BU
2007FI	1,000,000	—	—	—	1.75	—
2007FI Proof	—	Value: 20.00				
2008FI	1,000,000	—	—	—	1.75	—
2008FI Proof	2,500	Value: 20.00				
2009FI	—	—	—	—	1.75	—
2009FI Proof	2,500	Value: 20.00				
2010FI	—	—	—	—	1.75	—
2010FI Proof	2,000	Value: 20.00				
2011FI	—	—	—	—	1.75	—
2011FI Proof	—	Value: 20.00				
2012FI	—	—	—	—	1.75	—
2012FI Proof	—	Value: 20.00				

KM# 103   50 EURO CENT
7.8000 g., Brass, 24.25 mm.   **Obv:** Rampant lion left surrounded by stars, date at left **Rev:** Denomination and map **Edge:** Reeded

Date	Mintage	F	VF	XF	Unc	BU
2001M	4,432,000	—	—	—	7.50	—
2001M Proof	15,000	Value: 22.00				
2002M	1,147,000	—	—	—	5.00	—
2002M Proof	13,000	Value: 22.00				
2003M	790,000	—	—	—	5.00	—
2003M Proof	14,500	Value: 22.00				
2004M	629,000	—	—	—	5.00	—
2004M Proof	5,000	Value: 22.00				
2005M	4,800,000	—	—	—	5.00	—
2005M Proof	3,000	Value: 22.00				
2006M	6,850,000	—	—	—	5.00	—
2006M Proof	3,300	Value: 22.00				

KM# 128   50 EURO CENT
7.8000 g., Brass, 24.25 mm.   **Obv:** Rampant lion surrounded by stars **Rev:** Relief map of Western Europe, stars, lines and value **Edge:** Reeded

Date	Mintage	F	VF	XF	Unc	BU
2007FI	1,000,000	—	—	—	5.00	—
2007FI Proof	—	Value: 22.00				
2008FI	8,000,000	—	—	—	5.00	—
2008FI Proof	2,500	Value: 22.00				
2009FI	—	—	—	—	5.00	—

Date	Mintage	F	VF	XF	Unc	BU
2009FI Proof	2,500	Value: 22.00				
2010FI	—	—	—	—	5.00	—
2010FI Proof	2,000	Value: 22.00				
2011FI	—	—	—	—	5.00	—
2011FI Proof	—	Value: 22.00				
2012FI	—	—	—	—	5.00	—
2012FI Proof	—	Value: 22.00				

KM# 104   EURO
7.5000 g., Bi-Metallic Copper-Nickel center in Nickel-Brass ring, 23.25 mm.   **Obv:** 2 flying swans, date below, surrounded by stars on outer ring **Rev:** Denomination and map **Edge:** Segmented reeding

Date	Mintage	F	VF	XF	Unc	BU
2001M	13,862,000	—	—	—	3.00	—
2001M Proof	15,000	Value: 25.00				
2002M	14,114,000	—	—	—	6.50	—
2002M Proof	13,000	Value: 25.00				
2003M	790,000	—	—	—	6.50	—
2003M Proof	14,500	Value: 25.00				
2004M	5,529,000	—	—	—	6.50	—
2004M Proof	5,000	Value: 25.00				
2005M	7,935,000	—	—	—	6.50	—
2005M Proof	3,000	Value: 25.00				
2006M	1,705,000	—	—	—	6.50	—
2006M Proof	3,300	Value: 25.00				

KM# 129   EURO
7.5000 g., Bi-Metallic Copper-Nickel center in Nickel-Brass ring, 23.25 mm.   **Obv:** 2 flying swans surrounded by stars on outer ring **Rev:** Relief map of western Europe, stars, lines and value **Edge:** Segmented reeding

Date	Mintage	F	VF	XF	Unc	BU
2007FI	1,000,000	—	—	—	6.50	—
2007FI Proof	—	Value: 25.00				
2008FI	1,000,000	—	—	—	6.50	—
2008FI Proof	2,500	Value: 25.00				
2009FI	—	—	—	—	6.50	—
2009FI Proof	2,500	Value: 25.00				
2010FI	—	—	—	—	6.50	—
2010FI Proof	2,000	Value: 25.00				
2011FI	—	—	—	—	6.50	—
2011FI Proof	—	Value: 25.00				
2012FI	—	—	—	—	6.50	—
2012FI Proof	—	Value: 25.00				

KM# 105   2 EURO
8.5000 g., Bi-Metallic Nickel-Brass center in Copper-Nickel ring, 25.75 mm.   **Obv:** 2 cloudberry flowers surrounded by stars on outer ring **Rev:** Denomination and map **Edge:** Reeded and lettered **Edge Lettering:** SUOMI FINLAND

Date	Mintage	F	VF	XF	Unc	BU
2001M	29,132,000	—	—	—	4.00	—
2001M Proof	15,000	Value: 30.00				
2002M	1,386,000	—	—	—	7.50	—
2002M Proof	13,000	Value: 30.00				
2003M	9,080,000	—	—	—	5.00	—
2003M Proof	14,500	Value: 30.00				
2004M	10,029,000	—	—	—	5.00	—
2004M Proof	5,000	Value: 30.00				
2005M	10,800,000	—	—	—	5.00	—
2005M Proof	3,000	Value: 30.00				
2006M	11,000,000	—	—	—	5.00	—
2006M Proof	3,300	Value: 30.00				

KM# 114   2 EURO
8.5000 g., Bi-Metallic Nickel-Brass center in Copper-Nickel ring, 25.75 mm.   **Subject:** EU Expansion **Obv:** Stylized flower **Rev:** Denomination and map **Edge:** Reeded and lettered

Date	Mintage	F	VF	XF	Unc	BU
2004M M	1,000,000	—	—	—	10.00	11.50
2004M M Proof	—	—	—	—	—	—

KM# 119   2 EURO
8.5000 g., Bi-Metallic Nickel-Brass center in Copper-Nickel ring, 25.75 mm.   **Subject:** 60th Anniversary - Finland - UN **Obv:** Dove on a puzzle **Rev:** Denomination over map **Edge Lettering:** YK 1945-2005 FN

Date	Mintage	F	VF	XF	Unc	BU
2005M K	2,000,000	—	—	—	6.00	7.50

KM# 125   2 EURO
8.5000 g., Bi-Metallic Nickel-Brass center in Copper-Nickel ring, 25.75 mm.   **Subject:** Centennial of Universal Suffrage **Obv:** Two faces **Rev:** Value and map **Edge Lettering:** SUOMI FINLAND

Date	Mintage	F	VF	XF	Unc	BU
2006M M	2,500,000	—	—	—	6.00	7.50

KM# 130   2 EURO
8.5000 g., Bi-Metallic Nickel-Brass center in Copper-Nickel ring, 25.75 mm.   **Obv:** 2 cloudberry flowers surrounded by stars on outer ring **Rev:** Relief map of Western Europe, stars, lines and value **Edge:** Reeded and lettered **Edge Lettering:** SUOMI FINLAND

Date	Mintage	F	VF	XF	Unc	BU
2006M Error die pairing	Est. 55,000	—	—	50.00	75.00	100
2007FI	8,600,000	—	—	—	6.00	7.50
2007FI Proof	—	Value: 30.00				
2008FI	9,800,000	—	—	—	6.00	7.50
2008FI Proof	2,500	Value: 30.00				
2009FI	—	—	—	—	6.00	7.50
2009FI Proof	2,500	Value: 30.00				
2010FI	—	—	—	—	6.00	7.50
2010FI Proof	2,000	Value: 30.00				
2011FI	—	—	—	—	6.00	7.50
2011FI Proof	—	Value: 30.00				
2012FI	—	—	—	—	6.00	7.50
2012FI Proof	—	Value: 30.00				

KM# 138   2 EURO
8.5000 g., Bi-Metallic Nickel-Brass center in Copper-Nickel ring, 25.75 mm.   **Subject:** 50th Anniversary Treaty of Rome **Obv:**

Open treaty book **Rev:** Large value at left, modified outline of Europe at right **Edge:** Reeded and lettered

Date	Mintage	F	VF	XF	Unc	BU
2007	—				7.00	9.00
2007 Proof	—	Value: 75.00				

KM# 139   2 EURO
8.5000 g., Bi-Metallic Nickel-Brass center in Copper-Nickel ring, 25.75 mm. **Subject:** 90th Anniversary of Independence **Obv:** Longboat rowing together **Edge:** Reeded and lettered

Date	Mintage	F	VF	XF	Unc	BU
2007M	2,000,000	—	—	—	—	6.00
2007M Proof	20,000	Value: 20.00				

KM# 143   2 EURO
8.5000 g., Bi-Metallic Nickel-Brass center in Copper-Nickel ring, 25.75 mm. **Subject:** Universal Declaration of Human Rights **Obv:** Human figure within heart in landscape **Rev:** Segmented reeding

Date	Mintage	F	VF	XF	Unc	BU
2008	2,500,000	—	—	—	6.00	7.50
2008 Proof	2,500	Value: 25.00				

KM# 144   2 EURO
8.5000 g., Bi-Metallic Nickel-Brass center in Copper-Nickel ring, 25.75 mm. **Subject:** EMU 10th Anniversary **Obv:** Stick figure and E symbol **Edge:** Reeded and lettered

Date	Mintage	F	VF	XF	Unc	BU
2009	1,400,000	—	—	—	6.00	7.50
2009 Proof	25,000	Value: 30.00				

KM# 149   2 EURO
8.5000 g., Bi-Metallic Nickel-Brass center in Copper-Nickel ring, 25.75 mm. **Subject:** Finnish Autonomy, 200th Anniversary **Obv:** Classical Pyramid **Edge:** Lettered

Date	Mintage	F	VF	XF	Unc	BU
2009	1,600,000	—	—	—	6.00	7.50
2009 Proof	2,500	Value: 30.00				

KM# 154   2 EURO
8.5000 g., Bi-Metallic Nickel-Brass center in Copper-Nickel ring, 25.75 mm. **Subject:** Finnish Currency, 150th Anniversary

Date	Mintage	F	VF	XF	Unc	BU
2010	—	—	—	—	6.00	7.50
2010 Proof	2,000	Value: 30.00				

KM# 163   2 EURO
8.5000 g., Bi-Metallic Nickel-Brass center in Copper-Nickel ring, 25.75 mm. **Subject:** Bank of Finland, 200th Anniversary

Date	Mintage	F	VF	XF	Unc	BU
2011	—	—	—	—	6.00	7.50
2011 Proof	—	Value: 30.00				

KM# 178   2 EURO
8.5000 g., Bi-Metallic Nickel-Brass center in Copper-Nickel ring, 25.75 mm. **Subject:** Euro coinage, 10th Anniversary **Obv:** Euro symbol on globe at center, child-like rendering around

Date	Mintage	F	VF	XF	Unc	BU
2012M	1,500,000	—	—	—	6.00	8.00
2012M Special Unc.	—	—	—	—	—	15.00
2012 Proof	—	Value: 25.00				

KM# 111   5 EURO
20.1000 g., Bi-Metallic Copper-Nickel center in Brass ring, 34.9 mm. **Subject:** Ice Hockey World Championships **Obv:** Summer landscape and denomination **Rev:** Three hockey sticks and a puck **Edge:** Plain

Date	Mintage	F	VF	XF	Unc	BU
2003M M-M	150,000	—	—	—	27.50	35.00

KM# 118   5 EURO
19.8000 g., Bi-Metallic Brass center in Copper-Nickel ring, 35 mm. **Subject:** 10th Anniversary - IAAF World Championships in Athletics **Obv:** Female javelin thrower, denomination **Rev:** Running feet **Edge:** Plain

Date	Mintage	F	VF	XF	Unc	BU
2005M K-M	170,000	—	—	—	15.00	20.00
2005M K-M Proof	5,000	Value: 30.00				

KM# 123   5 EURO
18.7000 g., Brass, 35 mm. **Subject:** 150th Anniversary - Demilitarization of Aland **Obv:** Boat, Dove of Peace on the helm **Rev:** Tree **Edge Lettering:** AHVENANMAAN DEMILITARISOINTI 150 VUOTTA*

Date	Mintage	F	VF	XF	Unc	BU
2006 M-M	55,000	—	—	—	20.00	25.00

KM# 131   5 EURO
9.8100 g., Bi-Metallic Copper-Nickel center in Aluminum-Bronze ring, 27.25 mm. **Subject:** Finland Presidency of European Union **Obv:** Letter decorations with 2006 and SUOMI-FINLAND **Rev:** 5 EURO below letter decoration

Date	Mintage	F	VF	XF	Unc	BU
2006M P-M	100,000	—	—	—	15.00	20.00

KM# 135   5 EURO
19.8100 g., Bi-Metallic Aluminum-Bronze center in Copper-Nickel ring, 35 mm. **Subject:** 90th Anniversary of Finland's Independence

Date	Mintage	F	VF	XF	Unc	BU
2007 P	130,000	—	—	—	15.00	20.00
2007 P Proof	20,000	Value: 30.00				

KM# 146   5 EURO
19.8100 g., Bi-Metallic Aluminum-Bronze center in Copper-Nickel ring, 35 mm. **Subject:** Independence, 90th Anniversary **Obv:** Petroglif of a longboat

Date	Mintage	F	VF	XF	Unc	BU
2007	130,000	—	—	—	—	15.00
2007 Proof	20,000	Value: 35.00				

KM# 141   5 EURO
19.8100 g., Bi-Metallic Copper-Nickel center in Aluminum-Bronze ring, 35 mm. **Subject:** Science and Research

Date	Mintage	F	VF	XF	Unc	BU
2008	25,000	—	—	—	15.00	20.00
2008 Proof	20,000	Value: 30.00				

KM# 158   5 EURO
9.8000 g., Bi-Metallic Copper-Nickel center in Aluminum-Bronze ring, 27.5 mm. **Subject:** Provinces - Finland proper

Date	Mintage	F	VF	XF	Unc	BU
2010	90,000	—	—	—	—	15.00
2010 Proof	30,000	Value: 40.00				

KM# 156   5 EURO
9.8000 g., Bi-Metallic Copper-Nickel center in Aluminum-Bronze ring, 27.25 mm. **Subject:** Historical Provinces - Satakunta

Date	Mintage	F	VF	XF	Unc	BU
2010	—	—	—	—	—	20.00

KM# 159   5 EURO
9.8000 g., Bi-Metallic Copper-Nickel center in Aluminum-Bronze ring, 27.25 mm. **Subject:** Provinces - Karelia **Rev:** Shield

Date	Mintage	F	VF	XF	Unc	BU
2011	100,000	—	—	—	15.00	20.00
2011 Proof	20,000	Value: 30.00				

KM# 160 5 EURO
9.8000 g., Bi-Metallic Copper-Nickel center in Aluminum-Bronze ring, 27.5 mm. **Subject:** Provinces - Uusimaa

Date	Mintage	F	VF	XF	Unc	BU
2011	100,000	—	—	—	15.00	20.00
2011 Proof	20,000	Value: 30.00				

KM# 161 5 EURO
9.8000 g., Bi-Metallic Copper-Nickel center in Aluminum-Bronze ring, 27.5 mm. **Subject:** Provinces - Tavastia

Date	Mintage	F	VF	XF	Unc	BU
2011	—	—	—	—	—	15.00

KM# 162 5 EURO
9.8000 g., Bi-Metallic Copper-Nickel center in Aluminum-Bronze ring, 27.5 mm. **Subject:** Provinces - Savonia

Date	Mintage	F	VF	XF	Unc	BU
2011	100,000	—	—	—	15.00	20.00
2011 Proof	20,000	Value: 30.00				

KM# 170 5 EURO
9.8000 g., Bi-Metallic Copper-Nickel center in Aluminum-Bronze ring, 27.25 mm. **Subject:** Provinces: Lapland **Obv:** Shield **Rev:** Antler

Date	Mintage	F	VF	XF	Unc	BU
2011	100,000	—	—	—	15.00	20.00
2011 Proof	20,000	Value: 30.00				

KM# 171 5 EURO
9.8000 g., Bi-Metallic Copper-Nickel center in Aluminum-Bronze ring, 27.25 mm. **Subject:** Provinces: Ostrobuthnia **Obv:** Shield **Rev:** Wood

Date	Mintage	F	VF	XF	Unc	BU
2011	—	—	—	—	—	15.00
2011 Proof		Value: 40.00				

KM# 175 5 EURO
9.8000 g., Bi-Metallic Copper-Nickel center in Nickel-Brass ring, 27.25 mm. **Subject:** Provinces - Hame **Rev:** Shield

Date	Mintage	F	VF	XF	Unc	BU
2011	100,000	—	—	—	—	25.00
2011 Proof	20,000	Value: 35.00				

KM# 176 5 EURO
9.8000 g., Bi-Metallic Copper-Nickel center in Nickel-Brass ring, 27.25 mm. **Subject:** Provinces Pohjois-Karjalan **Rev:** Shield

Date	Mintage	F	VF	XF	Unc	BU
2011	100,000	—	—	—	—	25.00
2011 Proof	20,000	Value: 35.00				

KM# 177 5 EURO
9.8000 g., Bi-Metallic Copper-Nickel center in Aluminum-Bronze ring., 27.25 mm. **Series:** Provinces - Åland **Obv:** Needle sewing fishing net **Rev:** Shield

Date	Mintage	F	VF	XF	Unc	BU
2011	100,000	—	—	—	—	25.00
2011 Proof	20,000	Value: 35.00				

KM# 107 10 EURO
27.4000 g., 0.9250 Silver 0.8148 oz. ASW, 38.6 mm. **Subject:** 50th Anniversary - Helsinki Olympics **Obv:** Flames and denomination above globe with map of Finland **Rev:** Tower and partial coin design **Edge:** Plain

Date	Mintage	F	VF	XF	Unc	BU
2002M VV-M	10,000	—	—	—	30.00	32.00
2002M VV-M Proof	34,800	Value: 35.00				

KM# 108 10 EURO
27.4000 g., 0.9250 Silver 0.8148 oz. ASW, 38.6 mm. **Subject:** Elias Lönnrot **Obv:** Ribbon with stars **Rev:** Quill and signature **Edge:** Plain

Date	Mintage	F	VF	XF	Unc	BU
2002M M-M	40,000	—	—	—	30.00	32.00
2002M M-M Proof	40,000	Value: 35.00				

KM# 110 10 EURO
27.4000 g., 0.9250 Silver 0.8148 oz. ASW, 38.6 mm. **Subject:** Anders Chydenius **Obv:** Stylized design **Rev:** Name and book **Edge:** Plain

Date	Mintage	F	VF	XF	Unc	BU
2003M L-M	30,000	—	—	—	32.00	35.00
2003M Proof	30,000	Value: 40.00				

KM# 112 10 EURO
27.4000 g., 0.9250 Silver 0.8148 oz. ASW, 38.6 mm. **Subject:** Mannerheim and St. Petersburg **Obv:** Head 3/4 facing **Rev:** Fortress, denomination at right

Date	Mintage	F	VF	XF	Unc	BU
2003 S-M	6,000	—	—	—	35.00	37.50
2003 S-M Proof	29,000	Value: 55.00				

KM# 115 10 EURO
27.4000 g., 0.9250 Silver 0.8148 oz. ASW, 38.6 mm. **Subject:** 200th Birthday of Johan Ludwig Runeberg **Obv:** Head of Runeberg **Rev:** Text of 1831 Helsingfors Tidningar newspaper

Date	Mintage	F	VF	XF	Unc	BU
2004 K-M	5,600	—	—	—	32.00	35.00
2004 K-M Proof	22,750	Value: 45.00				

KM# 116 10 EURO
27.4000 g., 0.9250 Silver 0.8148 oz. ASW, 38.6 mm. **Subject:** Tove Jansson **Obv:** Three "muumi" figures **Rev:** Head of Tove Jansson

Date	Mintage	F	VF	XF	Unc	BU
2004 M-M	50,000	—	—	—	32.00	35.00
2004 M-M Proof	20,000	Value: 45.00				

KM# 120 10 EURO
25.5000 g., 0.9250 Silver 0.7583 oz. ASW, 38.6 mm. **Subject:** 60 years of Peace **Obv:** Dove of peace **Rev:** Flowering plant

Date	Mintage	F	VF	XF	Unc	BU
2005 M-M	55,000	—	—	—	32.00	35.00
2005 Proof	5,000	Value: 45.00				

KM# 122 10 EURO
25.5000 g., 0.9250 Silver 0.7583 oz. ASW, 38.6 mm. **Subject:** Unknown Soldier and Finnish Film Art **Obv:** Trench **Rev:** Soldier with helmet on top of a film

Date	Mintage	F	VF	XF	Unc	BU
2005 P-M	25,000	—	—	—	35.00	37.50
2005 P-M Proof	15,000	Value: 50.00				

KM# 124 10 EURO
25.5000 g., 0.9250 Silver 0.7583 oz. ASW, 38.6 mm. **Subject:** 200th Birthday - Johan Vilhelm Snellman **Obv:** Sun rising over the lake **Rev:** Snellman

Date	Mintage	F	VF	XF	Unc	BU
2006 K-M	—	—	—	—	32.00	35.00
2006 K-M Proof	—	Value: 45.00				

KM# 132   10 EURO
25.5000 g., 0.9250 Silver 0.7583 oz. ASW, 38.6 mm. **Subject:**
100th Anniversary of Parliamentary Reform **Obv:** Two stylist
heads female and male with text SUOMI FINLAND 10 EURO
Rev: Male and female fingers inserting ballot paper into ballot
box with text 100V EDUSKUNTAUUDISTUS 2006 **Edge**
Lettering: LANTDAGSREFORMEN 1906

Date	Mintage	F	VF	XF	Unc	BU
2006M M-M	40,000	—	—	—	32.00	35.00
2006M M-M Proof	20,000	Value: 45.00				

KM# 134   10 EURO
25.5000 g., 0.9250 Silver 0.7583 oz. ASW, 38.6 mm. **Subject:**
A.E. Nordenskiöld and the Northeast Passage **Rev:** Sailor at
ship's wheel during foul weather

Date	Mintage	F	VF	XF	Unc	BU
2007M P	7,000	—	—	—	32.00	35.00
2007M P Proof	33,000	Value: 45.00				

KM# 136   10 EURO
25.5000 g., 0.9250 Silver 0.7583 oz. ASW, 38.6 mm. **Subject:**
Mikael Agricola - Finnish Language **Obv:** Quill pen and lettering
Rev: Alphabet Letters

Date	Mintage	F	VF	XF	Unc	BU
2007 P	6,000	—	—	—	32.00	35.00
2007 P Proof	24,000	Value: 45.00				

KM# 140   10 EURO
25.5000 g., 0.9250 Silver 0.7583 oz. ASW, 38.6 mm. **Subject:**
Finnish Flag

Date	Mintage	F	VF	XF	Unc	BU
2008	9,000	—	—	—	32.00	30.00
2008 Proof	26,000	Value: 35.00				

KM# 142   10 EURO
25.5000 g., 0.9250 Silver 0.7583 oz. ASW, 38.6 mm. **Subject:**
Mika Waltari

Date	Mintage	F	VF	XF	Unc	BU
2008	5,000	—	—	—	30.00	32.00
2008 Proof	15,000	Value: 35.00				

KM# 148   10 EURO
25.5000 g., 0.9250 Silver 0.7583 oz. ASW, 38.6 mm. **Subject:**
Fredrik Pacius **Obv:** Opening notes to Kung Karls Jakt, first opera
of Pacius **Rev:** Stage curtian opening

Date	Mintage	F	VF	XF	Unc	BU
2009	7,000	—	—	—	35.00	37.50
2009 Proof	28,000	Value: 50.00				

KM# 173   10 EURO
25.5000 g., 0.9250 Silver 0.7583 oz. ASW **Subject:** Council of
State, 200th Anniversary

Date	Mintage	F	VF	XF	Unc	BU
2009	5,000	—	—	—	—	50.00
2009 Proof	15,000	Value: 60.00				

KM# 151   10 EURO
25.5000 g., 0.9250 Silver 0.7583 oz. ASW, 38.6 mm. **Subject:**
Eero Saarinen, 100th Anniversary of Birth **Rev:** St. Louis Arch

Date	Mintage	F	VF	XF	Unc	BU
2010	6,000	—	—	—	—	40.00
2010 Proof	20,000	Value: 50.00				

KM# 152   10 EURO
25.5000 g., 0.9250 Silver 0.7583 oz. ASW, 38.6 mm. **Subject:**
Minna Carth, author

Date	Mintage	F	VF	XF	Unc	BU
2010	4,000	—	—	—	—	45.00
2010 Proof	16,000	Value: 55.00				

KM# 157   10 EURO
25.5000 g., 0.9250 Silver 0.7583 oz. ASW, 38.6 mm. **Subject:**
Konsta Jylhan, 100th Anniversary of Birth

Date	Mintage	F	VF	XF	Unc	BU
2010	—	—	—	—	32.00	35.00
2010 Proof	—	Value: 50.00				

KM# 165   10 EURO
25.5000 g., 0.9250 Silver 0.7583 oz. ASW, 38.6 mm. **Subject:**
Hella Wuolijiki and Equality

Date	Mintage	F	VF	XF	Unc	BU
2011	5,000	—	—	—	30.00	35.00
2011 Proof	7,000	Value: 50.00				

KM# 166   10 EURO
25.5000 g., 0.9250 Silver 0.7583 oz. ASW, 38.6 mm. **Subject:**
Kaj Franck and industrial art **Obv:** Franck's signature

Date	Mintage	F	VF	XF	Unc	BU
2011	5,000	—	—	—	30.00	35.00
2011 Proof	10,000	Value: 50.00				

KM# 167   10 EURO
25.5000 g., 0.9250 Silver 0.7583 oz. ASW, 38.6 mm. **Subject:**
Pehr Kalm and European Explorers **Obv:** Mountain laurel - kalmia
latifolia **Rev:** Surveyor before Niagara Falls

Date	Mintage	F	VF	XF	Unc	BU
2011	6,000	—	—	—	30.00	35.00
2011 Proof	14,000	Value: 50.00				

KM# 168   10 EURO
25.5000 g., 0.5000 Silver 0.4099 oz. ASW, 38.6 mm. **Subject:**
Juhani Aho and Finnish Literature **Rev:** Pen point and manuscript

Date	Mintage	F	VF	XF	Unc	BU
2011	8,000	—	—	—	—	50.00

KM# 168a   10 EURO
25.5000 g., 0.9250 Silver 0.7583 oz. ASW, 38.6 mm. **Subject:**
Juhani Aho and Finnish Literature

Date	Mintage	F	VF	XF	Unc	BU
2011 Proof	7,000	Value: 60.00				

KM# 179   10 EURO
25.5000 g., 0.9250 Silver 0.7583 oz. ASW, 38.6 mm. **Subject:**
Henrik Wigstrom, 150th Anniversary of Birth **Obv:** Swan
swimming left, lilly pads nearby **Rev:** Floral egg ball

Date	Mintage	F	VF	XF	Unc	BU
2012	—	—	—	—	30.00	35.00
2012 Proof	—	Value: 50.00				

KM# 121 20 EURO
1.7300 g., 0.9000 Gold 0.0501 oz. AGW, 13.9 mm. **Subject:**
10th Anniversary - IAAF World Championships in Athletics **Obv:**
Helsinki Stadium **Rev:** Two faces

Date	Mintage	F	VF	XF	Unc	BU
2005 M-M Proof	30,000				Value: 100	

KM# 172 20 EURO
25.5000 g., 0.9250 Silver 0.7583 oz. ASW, 38.6 mm. **Subject:**
Peace and security **Obv:** Two peace doves with a twig

Date	Mintage	F	VF	XF	Unc	BU
2009	3,500	—	—	—	32.00	40.00
2009 Proof	11,500				Value: 60.00	

KM# 153 20 EURO
33.6200 g., 0.9250 Silver 0.9998 oz. ASW, 38.61 mm. **Subject:**
Children's creativity

Date	Mintage	F	VF	XF	Unc	BU
2010	3,500	—	—	—	—	40.00
2010 Proof	10,000				Value: 50.00	

KM# 169 20 EURO
33.6200 g., 0.5000 Silver 0.5404 oz. ASW, 38.6 mm. **Subject:**
Baltic Sea

Date	Mintage	F	VF	XF	Unc	BU
2011	7,000					50.00

KM# 169a 20 EURO
33.6200 g., 0.9250 Silver 0.9998 oz. ASW, 38.6 mm. **Subject:**
Protecting the Baltic **Obv:** Seal and fish **Rev:** Fishing boat and
map of the Baltic Sea

Date	Mintage	F	VF	XF	Unc	BU
2011 Proof	8,000				Value: 50.00	

KM# 113 50 EURO
13.2000 g., Bi-Metallic .75 Gold center in .925 Silver ring,
27.25 mm. **Subject:** Finnish art and design **Obv:** Snowflake
design within box, beaded circle surrounds **Rev:** Snowflake
design within beaded circle

Date	Mintage	F	VF	XF	Unc	BU
2003 P-M Proof	10,600				Value: 350	

KM# 133 50 EURO
12.8000 g., Bi-Metallic .75 Gold center in .925 Silver ring,
27.25 mm. **Subject:** Finland Presidency of European Union
Obv: Letter decorations with 2006 and SUOMI-FINLAND **Rev:**
50 EURO below letter decoration

Date	Mintage	F	VF	XF	Unc	BU
2006M P-M Proof	8,000				Value: 400	

KM# 180 50 EURO
Bi-Metallic 5g .75 gold center in 5.8 g .925 Silver ring, 27.25 mm.
Obv: Angular patterns **Rev:** Angular patterns

Date	Mintage	F	VF	XF	Unc	BU
2012 Proof	5,000				Value: 500	

KM# 109 100 EURO
8.6400 g., 0.9000 Gold 0.2500 oz. AGW, 22 mm. **Subject:**
Lapland **Obv:** Small tree and mountain stream **Rev:** Lake
landscape beneath the midnight sun **Edge:** Plain with serial
number

Date	Mintage	F	VF	XF	Unc	BU
2002M J-M Proof	25,000				Value: 425	

KM# 117 100 EURO
8.6400 g., 0.9000 Gold 0.2500 oz. AGW, 22 mm. **Subject:** 150th
Birthday of Albert Edelfelt **Obv:** Flower **Rev:** Head of Edelfelt

Date	Mintage	F	VF	XF	Unc	BU
2004 M-M Proof	8,500				Value: 450	

KM# 137 100 EURO
8.4800 g., 0.9170 Gold 0.2500 oz. AGW **Subject:** 90th
Anniversary of Finland's Independence **Obv:** Finland and the
years of independence **Rev:** Abstract composition

Date	Mintage	F	VF	XF	Unc	BU
2007 P	—	—	—	—	450	425
2007 P Proof					Value: 450	

KM# 174 100 EURO
8.4800 g., 0.9170 Gold 0.2500 oz. AGW, 22 mm. **Subject:**
Finnish War, Birth of Autonomy **Obv:** Half of an Eagle at left **Rev:**
Half of a Crown at right

Date	Mintage	F	VF	XF	Unc	BU
2008 Proof	9,000				Value: 625	

KM# 145 100 EURO
6.7800 g., 0.9170 Gold 0.1999 oz. AGW, 22 mm. **Subject:** Diet
of Porvoo

Date	Mintage	F	VF	XF	Unc	BU
2009 Proof	7,500				Value: 350	

KM# 150 100 EURO
5.6500 g., 0.9170 Gold 0.1666 oz. AGW, 22 mm. **Subject:**
Finnish Currency, 150th Anniversary

Date	Mintage	F	VF	XF	Unc	BU
2010 Proof	—				Value: 450	

KM# 164 100 EURO
5.6500 g., 0.9170 Gold 0.1666 oz. AGW, 22 mm. **Subject:** Bank
of Finland, 200th Anniversary **Obv:** Swan in flight

Date	Mintage	F	VF	XF	Unc	BU
2011 Proof	8,000				Value: 525	

MINT SETS

KM#	Date	Mintage	Identification	Issue Price	Mkt Val
MS58	2001 (5)	20,000	KM#65, 66, 73, 76, 77 plus 1865 coin design medal	18.00	22.50
MS59	2001 (5)	—	KM#65, 66, 73, 76, 77, medal (Johan Vilhelm Snellman)	—	22.50
MS60	2002 (8)	130,000	KM#98-105, Church medal	—	40.00
MS61	2003 (8)	170,000	KM#98-105, Golden Medal, goldpanning in Lappland	—	37.50
MS62	2002 (8)	2,000	KM#98-105, Baby	—	100
MS63	2003 (9)	8,000	KM#98-105, Silver medal, goldpanning in Lappland	—	125
MS64	2003 (8)	15,000	KM#98-105, Ice Hockey	—	60.00
MS65	2003 (9)	3,000	KM#98-105, medal and teddy bear	—	—
MS66	2003 (9)	5,000	KM#98-105, Baby, medal	—	37.50
MS67	2003 (9)	4,000	KM#98-105, Rose, medal	—	60.00
MS68	2003 (9)	30,000	KM#98-105, Christmas, golden medal	—	37.50
MS69	2004 (8)	55,000	KM#98-105, Euro zone, medal	—	40.00
MS70	2004 (8)	5,000	KM#98-105, 114, baby, medal	—	35.00
MS71	2004 (8)	18,000	KM#98-105, Tove Jansson, 90th Birthday	—	42.50
MS72	2004 (9)	4,000	KM#98-105, Music, medal	—	60.00
MS73	2005 (8)	40,000	KM#98-105, Wildlife, medal	—	42.50
MS74	2005 (9)	30,000	KM#98-105, 118, Paraolympics	—	55.00
MS75	2005 (9)	4,000	KM#98-105, Baby, medal	—	45.00
MS76	2005 (9)	3,000	KM#98-105, Music, medal	—	55.00
MS77	2006 (9)	40,000	KM#98-105, 119, Lighthouse	—	45.00
MS78	2006 (9)	20,000	KM#98-105, 125, Centennial of Parlament reform, suffrage	—	55.00
MS79	2006 (9)	3,200	KM#98-105, Music, medal	—	55.00
MS80	2006 (9)	4,000	KM#98-105, Wedding, medal	—	55.00
MS81	2006 (9)	4,600	KM#98-105, Baby, medal	—	55.00
MS82	2006 (9)	4,000	KM#98-105, Aland	—	45.00
MS83	2007 (9)	30,000	KM#98-100, 126-130, Lighthouse, medal	—	30.00
MS84	2007 (9)	3,000	KM#98-100, 126-130, Rose, medal	—	70.00
MS85	2007 (9)	3,000	KM#98-100, 126-130, Marriage, medal	—	55.00
MS86	2007 (9)	4,000	KM#98-100, 126-130, Baby, medal	—	65.00
MS87	2007 (10)	20,000	KM#98-100, 126-130, 138, European Song Festival, medal	—	45.00
MS88	2007 (8)	4,000	KM#98-100, 126-130, Aland	—	40.00
MS89	2007 (9)	20,000	KM#98-100, 126-130, 139, Swans	—	50.00
MS90	2007 (3)	—	KM98-100	—	10.00
MS91	2008 (9)	30,000	KM#98-100, 126-130, Lighthouse, medal	—	35.00
MS92	2008 (9)	3,000	KM#98-100, 126-130, Rose, medal	—	55.00
MS93	2008 (9)	3,000	KM#98-100, 126-130, Wedding, medal	—	45.00
MS94	2008 (9)	4,000	KM#98-100, 126-130, Baby, medal	—	50.00
MS95	2008 (9)	4,000	KM#98-100, 126-130, Aland medal	—	25.00
MS96	2008 (9)	30,000	KM#98-100, 126-130, 143	—	25.00
MS97	2009 (10)	20,000	KM#98-100, 126-130, 149 plus medal	—	40.00
MS98	2009 (10)	30,000	KM#98-100, 126-130, 149 plus lighthouse medal	—	45.00
MS99	2009 (10)	2,200	KM#98-100, 126-130, 149 Aland	—	40.00
MS100	2009 (10)	1,500	KM#98-100, 126-130, 149, Wedding, plus medal	—	45.00
MS101	2009 (10)	3,000	KM#98-100, 126-130, 149, Music plus medal	—	45.00
MS102	2009 (10)	4,000	KM#98-100, 126-130, 149, Baby, plus medal	—	45.00

KM#	Date	Mintage	Identification	Issue Price	Mkt Val
MS103	2010 (10)	30,000	KM#98-100, 126-130, 154 and Lighthouse medal	—	45.00
MS104	2010 (10)	15,000	KM#98-100, 126-130, 154 plus Biology medal	—	45.00
MS105	2010 (10)	2,500	KM#98-100, 126-130, 154 plus Music medal	—	45.00
MS106	2010 (10)	2	KM#98-100, 126-130, 154 plus Wedding medal	—	45.00
MS107	2010 (10)	3,000	KM#98-100, 126-130, 154 plus Kids medal	—	45.00
MS108	2010 (3)	7,000	KM#98-100	—	12.50
MS109	2011 (10)	20,000	KM#98-100, 126-130, 163 plus Lighthouse medal	—	45.00
MS110	2011 (10)	15,000	KM#98-100, 126-130, 163 plus Nature medal	—	45.00
MS111	2011 (10)	3,000	KM#98-100, 126-130, 163 plus Kids medal	—	45.00
MS112	2011 (10)	2,500	KM#98-100, 126-130, 163 plus Music medal	—	45.00
MS113	2011 (10)	2,500	KM#98-100, 126-130, 163 plus Wedding medal	—	45.00
MS114	2011 (3)	10,000	KM#98-100	—	15.00

PROOF SETS

KM#	Date	Mintage	Identification	Issue Price	Mkt Val
PS9	2001 (6)	—	KM#65-66, 73, 76-77, medal (Suomen Markka 1864-2001)	—	60.00
PS10	2002 (9)	5,000	KM#98-105, European Union gold medal	—	550
PS11	2002 (9)	8,000	KM#98-105, National Theater silver medal	—	185
PS12	2003 (9)	500	KM#98-105, Gold medal	—	350
PS13	2003 (9)	5,000	KM#98-105, Gold medal with diamond chip	—	500
PS14	2003 (9)	1,000	KM#98-105, Silver medal	—	400
PS15	2003 (9)	8,000	KM#98-105, Silver medal with diamond chip	—	150
PS16	2004 (10)	5,000	KM#98-105, 114, Silver medal	—	225
PS17	2005 (10)	3,000	KM#98-105, 118, Silver medal	—	200
PS18	2005 (4)	2,005	KM#118, 121 plus 2 older coins.	—	225
PS19	2006 (10)	3,300	KM#98-105, 125, Salmon medal	—	200
PS20	2007 (10)	2,500	KM#98-100, 126-130, 138, Silver medal.	—	150
PS21	2008 (10)	2,500	KM#98-100, 126-130, 143 plus medal	—	185
PS22	2009 (11)	2,500	KM#98-100, 126-130, 144, 149, plus medal	—	225
PS23	2010 (10)	2,000	KM#98-100, 126-130, 154 plus medal	—	200
PS24	2011 (10)	—	KM#98-100, 126-130, 163 plus medal	—	200
PS25	2010 (3)	7,000	KM#150 plus Russian 1863 Kopek and Finnish 1864 Pennia	—	475

FRANCE

The French Republic, largest of the West European nations, has an area of 210,026 sq. mi. (547,030 sq. km.) and a population of 58.1 million. Capital: Paris. Agriculture, manufacturing, tourist industry and financial services are the most important elements of France's diversified economy. Textiles and clothing, steel products, machinery and transportation equipment, chemicals, pharmaceuticals, nuclear electricity, agricultural products and wine are exported.

ENGRAVER GENERALS' PRIVY MARKS

Mark	Desc.	Date	Name
ϱ	Horseshoe	2000-2002	Gérard Buquoy
♡	SL Heart-shaped monogram	2002-2003	Serge Levet
🐚	French horn w/starfish in water	2003	Hubert Lariviére

MINT DIRECTORS' PRIVY MARKS

Some modern coins struck from dies produced at the Paris Mint have the 'A' mint mark. In the absence of a mint mark, the cornucopia privy mark serves to attribute a coin to Paris design.

A – Paris, Central Mint

MODERN REPUBLICS
1870-

REFORM COINAGE
Commencing 1960

1 Old Franc = 1 New Centime;
100 New Centimes = 1 New Franc

KM# 928   CENTIME
1.6500 g., Stainless Steel, 15 mm. **Obv:** Cursive legend surrounds grain sprig **Rev:** Cursive denomination, date at top **Edge:** Plain **Note:** 1991-1993 dated coins, non-Proof, exist in both coin and medal alignment. Values given here are for medal alignment examples. Pieces struck in coin alignment have been traded for as much as $50.00.

Date	Mintage	F	VF	XF	Unc	BU
2001 In sets only	—	—	—	—	—	1.50
2001 Proof	—	Value: 2.00				

KM# 928a   CENTIME
2.5000 g., 0.7500 Gold 0.0603 oz. AGW **Obv:** Cursive legend surrounds grain sprig, medallic alignment **Rev:** Cursive denomination, date above, medallic alignment **Edge:** Plain **Note:** Last Centime.

Date	Mintage	F	VF	XF	Unc	BU
2001	Est. 7,492	—	—	—	—	175

KM# 933   5 CENTIMES
2.0000 g., Aluminum-Bronze, 17 mm. **Obv:** Liberty bust left **Rev:** Denomination above date, grain sprig below, laurel branch at left **Edge:** Plain **Note:** 1991-1993 dated coins, non-Proof exist in both coin and medal alignment.

Date	Mintage	F	VF	XF	Unc	BU
2001 In sets only	—	—	—	—	1.50	2.50
2001 Proof	—	Value: 1.00				

KM# 929   10 CENTIMES
3.0000 g., Aluminum-Bronze, 20 mm. **Obv:** Liberty bust left **Rev:** Denomination above date, grain sprig below, laurel branch at left **Edge:** Plain **Note:** Without mint mark. 1991-1993 dated coins, non-Proof, exist in both coin and medal alignment.

Date	Mintage	F	VF	XF	Unc	BU
2001 In sets only	—	—	—	—	—	3.00
2001 Proof	—	Value: 1.00				

KM# 930   20 CENTIMES
4.0000 g., Aluminum-Bronze, 23.5 mm. **Obv:** Liberty bust left **Rev:** Denomination above date, grain sprig below, laurel branch at left **Edge:** Plain **Note:** Without mint mark. 1991-1993 dated coins, non-Proof, exist in both coin and medal alignment.

Date	Mintage	F	VF	XF	Unc	BU
2001 In sets only	—	—	—	—	—	3.00
2001 Proof	—	Value: 1.00				

KM# 931.1   1/2 FRANC
4.5000 g., Nickel, 19.5 mm. **Obv:** The Seed Sower **Rev:** Laurel divides denomination and date **Edge:** Reeded **Note:** Without mint mark.

Date	Mintage	F	VF	XF	Unc	BU
2001 In sets only	—	—	—	—	2.00	3.00

KM# 931.2   1/2 FRANC
4.5000 g., Nickel, 19.5 mm. **Obv:** Modified sower, engraver's signature: "O. ROTY" preceded by "D'AP" **Rev:** Laurel divides date and denomination **Edge:** Plain

Date	Mintage	F	VF	XF	Unc	BU
2001	—	—	—	—	0.40	0.60
2001 Proof	—	Value: 1.50				

KM# 925.2   FRANC
6.0000 g., Nickel, 24 mm. **Obv:** Modified sower, engraver's signature: O. ROTY, preceded by D'AP **Rev:** Laurel divides date and denomination **Edge:** Plain

Date	Mintage	F	VF	XF	Unc	BU
2001	—	—	—	—	0.40	0.60
2001 Proof	—	Value: 2.50				

KM# 925.1a   FRANC
8.0000 g., 0.7500 Gold 0.1929 oz. AGW, 24 mm. **Obv:** The Seed Sower **Rev:** Laurel divides date and denomination **Edge:** Reeded **Note:** Medallic alignment.

Date	Mintage	F	VF	XF	Unc	BU
2001	Est. 9,941	—	—	—	BV	365

KM# 1290   FRANC
17.7700 g., 0.9800 Silver 0.5599 oz. ASW **Subject:** The Last Franc **Obv:** Legend on polished field **Obv. Legend:** UN ULTIME FRANC **Rev:** Number "1" on polished field **Edge Lettering:** REPUBLIQUE FRANCAISE STARCK LIBERTE EGALITE FRATERNITE (2001). **Note:** The coin is intentionally warped and the edge inscription is very faint. Struck at Paris Mint.

Date	Mintage	F	VF	XF	Unc	BU
2001 Matte	49,838	Value: 100				

KM# 1290a FRANC
26.1000 g., 0.7500 Gold 0.6293 oz. AGW **Subject:** The Last Franc **Obv:** Legend on polished field **Obv. Legend:** UN ULTIME FRANC **Rev:** Number "1" on polished field **Edge Lettering:** REPUBLIQUE FRANCAISE. STARCK. LIBERTE. EGALITE. FRATERNITE (cornucopia) 2001 **Note:** This coin has an intentionally warped surface and the edge inscription is very weak.

Date	Mintage	F	VF	XF	Unc	BU
2001 Matte	4,963	—	—	—	1,200	1,600

KM# 925.1 FRANC
6.0000 g., Nickel, 24 mm. **Obv:** The Seed Sower **Rev:** Laurel branch divides denomination and date **Edge:** Reeded **Note:** Without mint mark.

Date	Mintage	F	VF	XF	Unc	BU
2001	20,000,000	—	—	—	0.40	0.60

KM# 942.1 2 FRANCS
7.5000 g., Nickel, 26.5 mm. **Obv:** The Seed Sower **Rev:** Denomination on branches, date below **Edge:** Wide reeded

Date	Mintage	F	VF	XF	Unc	BU
2001 Bee	—	—	—	—	0.75	1.25

KM# 942.2 2 FRANCS
7.5000 g., Nickel, 26.5 mm. **Obv:** The Seed Sower **Rev:** Denomination on branches, date below **Edge:** Plain

Date	Mintage	F	VF	XF	Unc	BU
2001	—	—	—	—	0.75	1.25
2001 Proof	—	Value: 3.50				

KM# 926a.1 5 FRANCS
10.0000 g., Nickel Clad Copper-Nickel, 29 mm. **Obv:** The Seed Sower **Rev:** Branches divide denomination and date **Edge:** Reeded

Date	Mintage	F	VF	XF	Unc	BU
2001 In sets only	—	—	—	—	5.00	7.50

KM# 926a.2 5 FRANCS
10.0000 g., Nickel Clad Copper-Nickel, 29 mm. **Obv:** Modified sower, engraver's signature: "O. ROTY" preceded by "D'AP" **Rev:** Branches divide date and denomination **Edge:** Plain

Date	Mintage	F	VF	XF	Unc	BU
2001	—	—	—	—	1.65	2.50
2001 Proof	—	Value: 6.50				

KM# 1309 5 FRANCS
12.0000 g., 0.9000 Silver 0.3472 oz. ASW. **Subject:** Last Year of the Franc **Obv:** The Seed Sower **Rev:** Denomination and date **Edge:** Lettered **Edge Lettering:** " * LIBERTY * EGALITE * FRATERNITE * "

Date	Mintage	F	VF	XF	Unc	BU
2001	25,000	—	—	—	22.50	25.00

KM# 1265.1 6.55957 FRANCS
13.0000 g., 0.9000 Silver 0.3761 oz. ASW **Subject:** Last Year of the French Franc **Obv:** French and other European euro currency equivalents **Rev:** Europa allegorical portrait, date below, "last year of the franc" logo after the date **Edge:** Reeded

Date	Mintage	F	VF	XF	Unc	BU
2001	Est. 20,000	—	—	—	25.00	35.00

KM# 1265.2 6.55957 FRANCS
22.2000 g., 0.9000 Silver 0.6423 oz. ASW **Obv:** French and other European euro currency equivalents **Rev:** Europa allegorical portrait, date below, "last year of the franc" logo after the date **Edge:** Plain

Date	Mintage	F	VF	XF	Unc	BU
2001 Proof	Est. 10,000	Value: 45.00				

KM# 1276 6.55957 FRANCS
22.2000 g., 0.9000 Silver 0.6423 oz. ASW **Subject:** Mottos **Obv:** Denomination **Rev:** FRATERNITE in red letters **Edge:** Reeded

Date	Mintage	F	VF	XF	Unc	BU
2001 Proof	2,171	Value: 50.00				

KM# 1277 6.55957 FRANCS
22.2000 g., 0.9000 Silver 0.6423 oz. ASW **Subject:** Mottos **Obv:** Denomination **Rev:** EGALITE in white letters

Date	Mintage	F	VF	XF	Unc	BU
2001 Proof	2,190	Value: 50.00				

KM# 1278 6.55957 FRANCS
22.2000 g., 0.9000 Silver 0.6423 oz. ASW **Subject:** Mottos **Obv:** Denomination **Rev:** LIBERTE in white letters

Date	Mintage	F	VF	XF	Unc	BU
2001 Proof	2,259	Value: 50.00				

KM# 964.2 10 FRANCS
Aluminum-Bronze, 23 mm. **Obv:** Winged figure divides RF **Rev:** Patterned denomination above date **Edge:** Plain

Date	Mintage	F	VF	XF	Unc	BU
2001	—	—	—	—	6.00	7.50
2001 Proof	—	Value: 15.00				

KM# 1268 10 FRANCS
22.2000 g., 0.9000 Silver 0.6423 oz. ASW **Subject:** Monuments of France - Palace of Versailles **Obv:** Stylized French map **Rev:** 1/2 bust of Louis XIV at right, internal and external palace views at left **Edge:** Plain

Date	Mintage	F	VF	XF	Unc	BU
2001 Proof	Est. 2,561	Value: 50.00				

KM# 1270 10 FRANCS
22.2000 g., 0.9000 Silver 0.6423 oz. ASW **Subject:** Monuments of France - Arch of Triumph **Obv:** Stylized French map **Rev:** Arch of Triumph on the Champs Elysees partial close up and aerial views

Date	Mintage	F	VF	XF	Unc	BU
2001 Proof	Est. 2,882	Value: 50.00				

KM# 1272 10 FRANCS
22.2000 g., 0.9000 Silver 0.6423 oz. ASW **Subject:** Monuments of France - Notre Dame Cathedral **Obv:** Stylized French map **Rev:** Gargoyle at left, cathedral views at right

Date	Mintage	F	VF	XF	Unc	BU
2001 Proof	Est. 2,877	Value: 50.00				

KM# 1274 10 FRANCS
22.2000 g., 0.9000 Silver 0.6423 oz. ASW **Subject:** Monuments of France - Eiffel Tower **Obv:** Stylized French map **Rev:** Two tower views

Date	Mintage	F	VF	XF	Unc	BU
2001 Proof	—	Value: 45.00				

KM# 1008.2 20 FRANCS
9.0000 g., Tri-Metallic Copper-Aluminum-Nickel center, Nickel inner ring, Copper-Aluminum-Nickel outer ring, 27 mm. **Obv:** Mont St. Michel **Rev:** Patterned denomination above date **Edge:** 5 milled bands, reeded or plain

Date	Mintage	F	VF	XF	Unc	BU
2001	—	—	—	—	8.00	10.00
2001 Proof	—	Value: 25.00				

KM# 1266 65.5997 FRANCS
8.4500 g., 0.9200 Gold 0.2499 oz. AGW **Subject:** Last Year of the French Franc **Obv:** French and other European euro currency equivalents **Rev:** Europa allegorical portrait, date below, "last year of the franc" logo after the date **Edge:** Reeded

Date	Mintage	F	VF	XF	Unc	BU
2001 Proof	3,000	Value: 600				

KM# 1269 100 FRANCS
17.0000 g., 0.9200 Gold 0.5028 oz. AGW **Subject:** Palace of Versailles **Obv:** Stylized French map **Rev:** Louis XIV with internal and external palace views **Edge:** Plain

Date	Mintage	F	VF	XF	Unc	BU
2001 Proof	105	Value: 875				

KM# 1271 100 FRANCS
17.0000 g., 0.9200 Gold 0.5028 oz. AGW **Obv:** Champs-Elysees **Rev:** Arch of Triumph partial close up and aerial views

Date	Mintage	F	VF	XF	Unc	BU
2001 Proof	115	Value: 871				

KM# 1273 100 FRANCS
17.0000 g., 0.9200 Gold 0.5028 oz. AGW **Obv:** Notre-Dame Cathedral **Rev:** Gargoyle and cathedral views

Date	Mintage	F	VF	XF	Unc	BU
2001 Proof	116	Value: 875				

KM# 1275 100 FRANCS
17.0000 g., 0.9200 Gold 0.5028 oz. AGW **Obv:** Eiffel Tower **Rev:** Two tower views

Date	Mintage	F	VF	XF	Unc	BU
2001 Proof	170	Value: 875				

KM# 1267 655.957 FRANCS
31.1035 g., 0.9990 Gold 0.9990 oz. AGW **Subject:** Last Year of the French Franc **Obv:** French and other European euro currency equivalents **Rev:** Europa allegorical portrait, date below, "last year of the franc" logo after the date **Edge:** Plain

Date	Mintage	F	VF	XF	Unc	BU
2001 Proof	2,000	Value: 875				

KM# 1267.1 655.957 FRANCS
155.5175 g., 0.9990 Gold 4.9948 oz. AGW **Obv:** French and other European euro currency equivalents **Rev:** Europa allegorical portrait, date below, "last year of the franc" after the date **Edge:** Plain

Date	Mintage	F	VF	XF	Unc	BU
2001 Proof	99	Value: 8,450				

KM# 1279 655.957 FRANCS
17.0000 g., 0.9200 Gold 0.5028 oz. AGW **Subject:** Motto Series **Obv:** Denomination **Rev:** FRATERNITE **Edge:** Reeded

Date	Mintage	F	VF	XF	Unc	BU
2001 Proof	62	Value: 875				

KM# 1280 655.957 FRANCS
17.0000 g., 0.9200 Gold 0.5028 oz. AGW **Subject:** Motto Series **Obv:** Denomination **Rev:** EGALITE

Date	Mintage	F	VF	XF	Unc	BU
2001 Proof	64	Value: 875				

KM# 1281 655.957 FRANCS
17.0000 g., 0.9200 Gold 0.5028 oz. AGW **Subject:** Motto Series **Obv:** Denomination **Rev:** LIBERTE

Date	Mintage	F	VF	XF	Unc	BU
2001 Proof	63	Value: 875				

KM# 1617 20 EURO
163.8000 g., 0.9500 Silver 5.0028 oz. ASW, 50 mm. **Subject:** Unesco site - The Kremlin in Moscow **Obv:** Wall Tower and cathedral

Date	Mintage	F	VF	XF	Unc	BU
2009P Proof	500	Value: 250				

EURO COINAGE
European Union Issues

KM# 1282 EURO CENT
2.2700 g., Copper Plated Steel, 16.3 mm. **Obv:** Human face **Rev:** Denomination and globe **Edge:** Plain

Date	Mintage	F	VF	XF	Unc	BU
2001	300,681,580	—	—	—	0.35	0.50
2001 Proof	15,000	Value: 10.00				
2002	200,000	—	—	—	—	10.00
2002 Proof	21,453	Value: 8.00				
2003	160,017,000	—	—	—	1.00	1.50
2003 Proof	40,000	Value: 8.00				
2004	400,032,000	—	—	—	0.35	0.50

Date	Mintage	F	VF	XF	Unc	BU
2004 Proof	20,000	Value: 10.00				
2005	240,320,000	—	—	—	0.35	0.50
2005 Proof	10,000	Value: 12.00				
2006	343,078,000	—	—	—	0.35	0.50
2006 Proof	10,000	Value: 12.00				
2007	300,058,000	—	—	—	0.35	0.50
2007 Proof	7,500	Value: 14.00				
2008	462,757,000	—	—	—	0.35	0.50
2008 Proof	7,500	Value: 14.00				
2009	404,050,500	—	—	—	0.35	0.50
2009 Proof	7,500	Value: 14.00				
2010	—	—	—	—	0.35	0.50
2010 Proof	—	Value: 15.00				
2011	—	—	—	—	0.35	0.50
2011 Proof	—	Value: 15.00				
2012	—	—	—	—	0.35	0.50
2012 Proof	—	Value: 15.00				

KM# 1283 2 EURO CENT
3.0300 g., Copper Plated Steel, 18.7 mm. **Obv:** Human face **Rev:** Denomination and globe **Edge:** Grooved

Date	Mintage	F	VF	XF	Unc	BU
2001	249,101,580	—	—	—	0.50	0.75
2001 Proof	15,000	Value: 10.00				
2002 In sets only	100,000	—	—	—	—	12.50
2002 Proof	21,453	Value: 8.00				
2003	160,175,000	—	—	—	1.25	2.00
2003 Proof	40,000	Value: 8.00				
2004	300,024,000	—	—	—	—	1.00
2004 Proof	20,000	Value: 10.00				
2005	2,603,202,000	—	—	—	—	1.00
2005 Proof	10,000	Value: 12.00				
2006	283,278,000	—	—	—	—	1.00
2006 Proof	10,000	Value: 12.00				
2007	213,258,000	—	—	—	—	1.00
2007 Proof	7,500	Value: 14.00				
2008	386,557,000	—	—	—	—	1.00
2008 Proof	7,500	Value: 14.00				
2009	317,050,500	—	—	—	—	1.00
2009 Proof	7,500	Value: 14.00				
2010	—	—	—	—	—	1.00
2010 Proof	—	Value: 14.00				
2011	—	—	—	—	—	1.00
2011 Proof	—	Value: 14.00				
2012	—	—	—	—	—	1.00
2012 Proof	—	Value: 14.00				

KM# 1284 5 EURO CENT
3.8600 g., Copper Plated Steel, 21.2 mm. **Obv:** Human face **Rev:** Denomination and globe **Edge:** Plain

Date	Mintage	F	VF	XF	Unc	BU
2001	217,324,477	—	—	—	0.75	1.25
2001 Proof	15,000	Value: 12.00				
2002	186,400,000	—	—	—	0.75	1.25
2002 Proof	21,453	Value: 10.00				
2003	101,175,000	—	—	—	1.00	1.50
2003 Proof	40,000	Value: 10.00				
2004	60,162,000	—	—	—	—	1.25
2004 Proof	20,000	Value: 12.00				
2005	20,320,000	—	—	—	—	1.25
2005 Proof	10,000	Value: 14.00				
2006	132,078,000	—	—	—	—	1.25
2006 Proof	10,000	Value: 14.00				
2007	130,058,000	—	—	—	—	1.25
2007 Proof	7,500	Value: 16.00				
2008	218,257,000	—	—	—	—	1.25
2008 Proof	7,500	Value: 16.00				
2009	184,550,500	—	—	—	—	1.25
2009 Proof	7,500	Value: 16.00				
2010	—	—	—	—	—	1.25
2010 Proof	—	Value: 16.00				
2011	—	—	—	—	—	1.25
2011 Proof	—	Value: 16.00				
2012	—	—	—	—	—	1.25
2012 Proof	—	Value: 16.00				

KM# 1285 10 EURO CENT
4.0700 g., Brass, 19.7 mm. **Obv:** The seed sower divides date and RF **Rev:** Denomination and map **Edge:** Reeded

Date	Mintage	F	VF	XF	Unc	BU
2001	144,513,261	—	—	—	1.25	2.00
2001 Proof	15,000	Value: 12.00				
2002	206,700,000	—	—	—	0.75	1.25
2002 Proof	21,453	Value: 10.00				
2003	180,875,000	—	—	—	1.25	2.00
2003 Proof	40,000	Value: 10.00				
2004	5,000,000	—	—	—	—	1.50
2004 In sets only	140,000	—	—	—	—	—
2004 Proof	20,000	Value: 12.00				
2005	45,120,000	—	—	—	—	1.50
2005 Proof	10,000	Value: 14.00				
2006	60,278,000	—	—	—	—	1.50
2006 Proof	10,000	Value: 14.00				

KM# 1410 10 EURO CENT
4.0700 g., Brass, 19.7 mm. **Obv:** Sower **Rev:** Relief map of Western Europe, stars, lines and value **Edge:** Reeded

Date	Mintage	F	VF	XF	Unc	BU
2007	90,158,000	—	—	—	—	1.50
2007 Proof	7,500	Value: 14.00				
2008	178,757,000	—	—	—	—	1.50
2008 Proof	7,500	Value: 14.00				
2009	142,550,500	—	—	—	—	1.50
2009 Proof	7,500	Value: 14.00				
2010	—	—	—	—	—	1.50
2010 Proof	—	Value: 14.00				
2011	—	—	—	—	—	1.50
2011 Proof	—	Value: 14.00				
2012	—	—	—	—	—	1.50
2012 Proof	—	Value: 14.00				

KM# 1286 20 EURO CENT
5.7300 g., Brass, 22.2 mm. **Obv:** The seed sower divides date and RF **Rev:** Denomination and map **Edge:** Notched

Date	Mintage	F	VF	XF	Unc	BU
2001	256,342,108	—	—	—	1.00	1.50
2001 Proof	15,000	Value: 14.00				
2002	192,100,000	—	—	—	1.00	1.50
2002 Proof	21,453	Value: 12.00				
2003 In sets only	180,000	—	—	—	—	9.50
2003 Proof	40,000	Value: 12.00				
2004 In sets only	160,000	—	—	—	—	9.50
2004 Proof	20,000	Value: 14.00				
2005 In sets only	120,000	—	—	—	—	9.50
2005 Proof	10,000	Value: 16.00				
2006 In sets only	67,600	—	—	—	—	9.50
2006 Proof	10,000	Value: 16.00				

KM# 1411 20 EURO CENT
5.7300 g., Brass, 22.2 mm. **Obv:** Sower **Rev:** Relief map of Western Europe, stars, lines and value **Edge:** Notched

Date	Mintage	F	VF	XF	Unc	BU
2007	40,258,000	—	—	—	—	1.50
2007 Proof	7,500	Value: 14.00				
2008	25,557,000	—	—	—	—	1.50
2008 Proof	7,500	Value: 14.00				
2009	82,550,500	—	—	—	—	1.50
2009 Proof	7,500	Value: 14.00				
2010	—	—	—	—	—	1.50
2010 Proof	—	Value: 14.00				
2011	—	—	—	—	—	1.50
2011 Proof	—	Value: 14.00				
2012	—	—	—	—	—	1.50
2012 Proof	—	Value: 14.00				

KM# 1293 1/4 EURO
12.5000 g., Aluminum-Bronze, 30 mm. **Subject:** Childrens Design **Obv:** Euro globe with children **Rev:** Denomination and stars **Edge:** Plain

Date	Mintage	F	VF	XF	Unc	BU
2002	1,000,000	—	—	—	6.50	8.50

KM# 1300 1/4 EURO
13.0000 g., 0.9000 Silver 0.3761 oz. ASW, 30 mm. **Subject:** Europa **Obv:** Eight French euro coin designs **Rev:** Portrait and flags design of 6.55957 francs coin KM-1265 **Edge:** Reeded

Date	Mintage	F	VF	XF	Unc	BU
2002	20,000	—	—	—	20.00	22.00

KM# 1293a 1/4 EURO
13.0000 g., 0.9000 Silver 0.3761 oz. ASW, 30 mm. **Subject:** Childrens Design **Obv:** Euro globe with children **Rev:** Denomination **Edge:** Plain

Date	Mintage	F	VF	XF	Unc	BU
2002 Proof	10,000	Value: 45.00				

KM# 1331 1/4 EURO
3.1100 g., 0.9990 Gold 0.0999 oz. AGW, 15 mm. **Subject:** Children's Design **Obv:** Euro globe with children **Rev:** Denomination **Edge:** Plain

Date	Mintage	F	VF	XF	Unc	BU
2002 Proof	5,000	Value: 185				

KM# 1350 1/4 EURO
3.1100 g., 0.9999 Gold 0.1000 oz. AGW, 15 mm. **Obv:** Obverse design of first one franc coin **Rev:** Reverse design of first one franc coin **Edge:** Plain

Date	Mintage	F	VF	XF	Unc	BU
2003 Proof	5,000	Value: 185				

KM# 1372 1/4 EURO
22.2000 g., 0.900 Silver 0.6423 oz. ASW, 37 mm. **Obv:** Samuel de Champlain **Rev:** Sail ship **Edge:** Plain

Date	Mintage	F	VF	XF	Unc	BU
2004	20,000	—	—	—	27.50	32.50

KM# 1390 1/4 EURO
13.0000 g., 0.9000 Silver 0.3761 oz. ASW, 30 mm. **Subject:** European Union Expansion **Obv:** Partial face and flags **Rev:** Puzzle map **Edge:** Plain

Date	Mintage	F	VF	XF	Unc	BU
2004	20,000	—	—	—	22.00	25.00

KM# 1402 1/4 EURO
11.0000 g., Aluminum-Bronze, 30 mm. **Subject:** Jules Verne **Obv:** Various scenes from Jules Verne's novels **Rev:** Jules Verne's portrait left of value and date

Date	Mintage	F	VF	XF	Unc	BU
2005	50,000	—	—	—	—	10.00

KM# 1442 1/4 EURO
22.2000 g., 0.9000 Silver 0.6423 oz. ASW, 37 mm. **Obv:** Bust of Franklin facing slightly right at left, his diplomatic and technical successes at right **Obv. Legend:** BENJAMIN FRANKLIN 1706-2006 **Obv. Inscription:** AMI DE LA FRANCE **Rev:** French flag at left, American flag at right **Rev. Inscription:** PHILOSOPHE / DIPLOMATE / ÉCRIVAIN / SAVANT

Date	Mintage	F	VF	XF	Unc	BU
2006	15,000	—	—	—	32.00	35.00

KM# 1445 1/4 EURO
22.2000 g., 0.9000 Silver 0.6423 oz. ASW, 37 mm. **Subject:** Marshall Bernadotte under Napoleon **Rev:** Military bust facing 3/4 right at left, building in backgound at right **Rev. Legend:** LIBERTÉ / ÉGALITÉ / FRATERNITÉ - KARL XIV JOHAN ROI DE SUÈDE

Date	Mintage	F	VF	XF	Unc	BU
2006 Proof	10,000	—	—	—	32.00	35.00

KM# 1457 1/4 EURO
22.2000 g., 0.9000 Silver 0.6423 oz. ASW, 37 mm. **Subject:** Hèpitaux de France Foundation **Obv:** Foundation logo **Rev:** TGV train, money box on outlined map of France

Date	Mintage	F	VF	XF	Unc	BU
2006	50,000	—	—	—	28.00	30.00

KM# 1415 1/4 EURO
22.2000 g., 0.9000 Silver 0.6423 oz. ASW, 37 mm. **Obv:** Jean de la Fontaine, value, Chinese astrological animals, date, Paris mint privy marks but without national identification **Rev:** Dog in wreath **Edge:** Reeded **Note:** Anonymous coinage

Date	Mintage	F	VF	XF	Unc	BU
2006	10,000	—	—	—	32.00	35.00

KM# 1417 1/4 EURO
22.2000 g., 0.9000 Silver 0.6423 oz. ASW, 37 mm. **Obv:** Jean de la Fontaine, value, Chinese astrological animals, date, Paris mint privy marks but without national identification **Rev:** Pig in wreath **Edge:** Reeded **Note:** Anonymous issue.

Date	Mintage	F	VF	XF	Unc	BU
2007	10,000	—	—	—	32.00	35.00

KM# 1419 1/4 EURO
13.0000 g., 0.9000 Silver 0.3761 oz. ASW, 30 mm. **Obv:** Military bust of Lafayette facing 3/4 left **Obv. Legend:** LA FAYETTE. HÉROS DE LA RÉVOLUTION AMÉRICAINE **Obv. Inscription:** 1757/1854 at left, RF monogram at right **Rev:** Sailing ship L' Hermione **Rev. Legend:** LA FAYETTE, HERO OF THE AMERICAN REVOLUTION **Edge:** Plain

Date	Mintage	F	VF	XF	Unc	BU
2007 (a) Proof-like	5,000	—	—	—	32.00	35.00

KM# 1421 1/4 EURO
15.0000 g., 0.9000 Silver 0.4340 oz. ASW **Subject:** 90th Anniversary Death of Degas **Obv:** Ballerina "The Star" at left **Obv. Inscription:** Degas **Rev:** Paint brushes and oils multicolor at left, self portrait at right **Rev. Inscription:** LIBERTÉ / ÉGALITÉ / FRATERNITÉ **Shape:** rectangular, 30 x 21 mm

Date	Mintage	F	VF	XF	Unc	BU
2007	5,000	—	—	—	42.00	45.00

KM# 1461 1/4 EURO
13.0000 g., 0.9000 Silver 0.3761 oz. ASW, 30 mm. **Subject:** Sebastien Le Prestre de Vauban, 300th Anniversary of Death **Obv:** Arms above funeral coach, book at left **Rev:** Vauban standing; plans of fortress

Date	Mintage	F	VF	XF	Unc	BU
2007 Proof	5,000	Value: 22.00				

KM# 1483 1/4 EURO
13.0000 g., 0.9000 Silver 0.3761 oz. ASW, 37 mm. **Subject:** 2007 Rugby World Cup **Obv:** Two Rugby players **Rev:** Logo and goal

Date	Mintage	F	VF	XF	Unc	BU
2007	5,000	—	—	—	32.00	35.00

KM# 1570 1/4 EURO
15.0000 g., 0.9000 Silver 0.4340 oz. ASW, 30 x 21 mm. **Subject:** Edward Manet **Obv:** Manet's "Olympia" painting **Rev:** Multicolor paint brushes and Manet's portrait **Shape:** Rectangle

Date	Mintage	F	VF	XF	Unc	BU
2008	10,000	—	—	—	—	65.00

KM# 1572 1/4 EURO
22.2000 g., 0.9000 Silver 0.6423 oz. ASW, 37 mm. **Subject:** Lunar New Year - Year of the Rat **Obv:** Bust of Jean de la Fontaine and twelve awards **Rev:** Rat within border

Date	Mintage	F	VF	XF	Unc	BU
2008	10,000	—	—	—	32.00	35.00

KM# 1287 50 EURO CENT
7.8100 g., Brass, 24.2 mm. **Obv:** The Seed Sower divides date and RF **Rev:** Denomination and map **Edge:** Reeded

Date	Mintage	F	VF	XF	Unc	BU
2001	276,287,274	—	—	—	1.25	2.00
2001 Proof	15,000	Value: 15.00				
2002	226,500,000	—	—	—	1.25	2.00
2002 Proof	21,453	Value: 14.00				
2003 In sets only	180,000	—	—	—	—	11.50
2003 Proof	40,000	Value: 14.00				
2004 In sets only	160,000	—	—	—	—	11.50
2004 Proof	20,000	Value: 15.00				
2005 In sets only	120,000	—	—	—	—	11.50
2005 Proof	10,000	Value: 17.00				
2006 In sets only	67,600	—	—	—	—	11.50
2006 Proof	10,000	Value: 17.00				

KM# 1412 50 EURO CENT
7.8100 g., Brass, 24.2 mm. **Obv:** Sower **Rev:** Relief map of Western Europe, stars, lines and value **Edge:** Reeded

Date	Mintage	F	VF	XF	Unc	BU
2007 In sets only	58,000	—	—	—	—	11.50
2007 Proof	7,500	Value: 16.00				
2008 In sets only	57,000	—	—	—	—	2.00
2008 Proof	7,500	Value: 16.00				
2009 In sets only	50,500	—	—	—	—	2.00
2009 Proof	7,500	Value: 16.00				
2010	—	—	—	—	—	2.00
2010 Proof	—	Value: 16.00				
2011	—	—	—	—	—	2.00
2011 Proof	—	Value: 16.00				
2012	—	—	—	—	—	2.00
2012 Proof	—	Value: 16.00				

KM# 1288 EURO
7.5000 g., Bi-Metallic Copper-Nickel center in Nickel-Brass ring, 23.25 mm. **Obv:** Stylized tree divides RF within circle, date below **Rev:** Denomination and map **Edge:** Segmented reeding

Date	Mintage	F	VF	XF	Unc	BU
2001	150,251,624	—	—	—	2.75	4.00
2001 Proof	15,000	Value: 18.00				
2002	129,400,000	—	—	—	2.50	3.75
2002 Proof	21,453	Value: 16.00				
2003 In sets only	100,000	—	—	—	8.00	12.50
2003 Proof	20,000	Value: 18.00				
2004 In sets only	160,000	—	—	—	—	2.50
2004 Proof	20,000	Value: 18.00				
2005 In sets only	120,000	—	—	—	—	2.50
2005 Proof	10,000	Value: 20.00				
2006 In sets only	78,000	—	—	—	—	2.50
2006 Proof	10,000	Value: 20.00				

KM# 1413 EURO
7.5000 g., Bi-Metallic Copper-Nickel center in Nickel-Brass ring, 23.25 mm. **Obv:** Stylized tree **Rev:** Relief map of Western Europe, stars, lines and value **Edge:** Segmented reeding

Date	Mintage	F	VF	XF	Unc	BU
2007 In sets only	58,000	—	—	—	—	11.50
2007 Proof	7,500	Value: 20.00				
2008 In sets only	57,000	—	—	—	—	2.50
2008 Proof	7,500	Value: 20.00				
2009 In sets only	50,500	—	—	—	—	2.50
2009 Proof	7,500	Value: 20.00				
2010	—	—	—	—	—	2.50
2010 Proof	—	Value: 20.00				
2011	—	—	—	—	—	2.50
2011 Proof	—	Value: 20.00				
2012	—	—	—	—	—	2.50
2012 Proof	—	Value: 20.00				

KM# 1464 EURO
155.5500 g., 0.9500 Silver 4.7508 oz. ASW, 50 mm. **Subject:** Sebastien Le Prestre de Vauban, 300th Anniversary of Death

Date	Mintage	F	VF	XF	Unc	BU
2007 Proof	500	Value: 325				

KM# 1470 EURO
17.0000 g., 0.9200 Gold 0.5028 oz. AGW, 31 mm. **Subject:** Le Petit Prince, 60th Anniversary **Obv:** Prince standing with rabbit

Date	Mintage	F	VF	XF	Unc	BU
2007 Proof	2,000	Value: 875				

KM# 1486 EURO
17.0000 g., 0.9200 Gold 0.5028 oz. AGW, 31 mm. **Subject:** 2007 Rugby World Cup **Obv:** Two players and goal **Rev:** Logo and goal

Date	Mintage	F	VF	XF	Unc	BU
2007 Proof	500	Value: 875				

KM# 1490 EURO
22.0000 g., 0.9000 Silver 0.6366 oz. ASW **Subject:** Unesco **Obv:** Great Wall of China

Date	Mintage	F	VF	XF	Unc	BU
2007 Proof	5,000	Value: 60.00				

KM# 1491 EURO
8.4500 g., 0.9200 Gold 0.2499 oz. AGW, 22 mm. **Subject:** Unesco **Obv:** Crest Wall of China **Rev:** Unesco Building and emblem

Date	Mintage	F	VF	XF	Unc	BU
2007 Proof	500	Value: 450				

KM# 1492 EURO
22.0000 g., 0.9000 Silver 0.6423 oz. ASW, 37 mm. **Subject:** Point Neuf 400th Anniversary **Obv:** Monuments of France logo **Rev:** Point Neuf Bridge, Paris Mint Museum

Date	Mintage	F	VF	XF	Unc	BU
2007 Proof	3,000	Value: 80.00				

KM# 1493 EURO
8.4500 g., 0.9200 Gold 0.2499 oz. AGW, 22 mm. **Subject:** Point Neuf, 400th Anniversary **Obv:** Monuments of France logo **Rev:** Point Neuf Brudge, Paris Mint Building

Date	Mintage	F	VF	XF	Unc	BU
2007 Proof	500	Value: 450				

KM# 1495 EURO
8.4500 g., 0.9200 Gold 0.2499 oz. AGW, 22 mm. **Subject:** Cannes Film Festival **Obv:** Cinema screen and stage, Golden Palm Award

Date	Mintage	F	VF	XF	Unc	BU
2007 Proof	500	Value: 450				

KM# 1514 EURO
17.0000 g., 0.9200 Gold 0.5028 oz. AGW, 31 mm. **Subject:** Stanislas Lesczynski **Obv:** Bust, shield **Rev:** Palac Stanislas - Nancy

Date	Mintage	F	VF	XF	Unc	BU
2007 Proof	500	Value: 875				

KM# 1587 EURO
8.4500 g., 0.9200 Gold 0.2499 oz. AGW, 22 mm. **Subject:** Court of Human Rights, 50th Anniversary **Obv:** Sower left **Rev:** Text

Date	Mintage	F	VF	XF	Unc	BU
2009P Proof	500	Value: 450				

KM# 1332 1-1/2 EURO
22.2000 g., 0.9000 Silver 0.6423 oz. ASW, 37 mm. **Obv:** Victor Hugo, denomination and map **Rev:** Multicolor "Gavroche" **Edge:** Plain

Date	Mintage	F	VF	XF	Unc	BU
2002 Proof	10,000	Value: 55.00				

KM# 1301 1-1/2 EURO
22.2000 g., 0.9000 Silver 0.6423 oz. ASW, 37 mm. **Subject:** Europa **Obv:** Eight French euro coins design **Rev:** Portrait and flags design of 6.55957 francs KM-1265 **Edge:** Plain

Date	Mintage	F	VF	XF	Unc	BU
2002 Proof	50,000	Value: 45.00				

KM# 1305   1-1/2 EURO
22.2000 g., 0.9000 Silver 0.6423 oz. ASW, 37 mm.   **Subject:**
French Landmarks **Obv:** French map **Rev:** Le Mont St. Michel
Edge: Plain

Date	Mintage	F	VF	XF	Unc	BU
2002 Proof	10,000	Value: 50.00				

KM# 1307   1-1/2 EURO
22.2000 g., 0.9000 Silver 0.6423 oz. ASW, 37 mm.   **Subject:**
French Landmarks **Obv:** French map **Rev:** La Butte Montmartre
Edge: Plain

Date	Mintage	F	VF	XF	Unc	BU
2002 Proof	10,000	Value: 47.50				

KM# 1310   1-1/2 EURO
22.2000 g., 0.9000 Silver 0.6423 oz. ASW, 37 mm.   **Subject:**
First West to East Transatlantic Flight **Obv:** Denomination, map
and Lindbergh portrait **Rev:** Spirit of St. Louis (airplane) and map
Edge: Plain

Date	Mintage	F	VF	XF	Unc	BU
2002 Proof	10,000	Value: 50.00				

KM# 1840   1-1/2 EURO
22.2000 g., 0.9000 Silver 0.6423 oz. ASW, 37 mm.   **Subject:**
Snow White **Rev:** Scenes from the book, color

Date	Mintage	F	VF	XF	Unc	BU
2002 Proof	—	Value: 55.00				

KM# 1843   1-1/2 EURO
22.2000 g., 0.9000 Silver 0.6423 oz. ASW, 37 mm.   **Subject:**
Athletic Games **Rev:** Shot Put athlete and stadium

Date	Mintage	F	VF	XF	Unc	BU
2002 Proof	—	Value: 55.00				

KM# 1841   1-1/2 EURO
22.2000 g., 0.9000 Silver 0.6423 oz. ASW, 37 mm.   **Subject:**
Cinderella **Rev:** Scenes from the book, color

Date	Mintage	F	VF	XF	Unc	BU
2002 Proof	—	Value: 55.00				

KM# 1842   1-1/2 EURO
22.2000 g., 0.9000 Silver 0.6423 oz. ASW, 37 mm.   **Subject:**
Pinocchio **Rev:** Scenes form the book, color

Date	Mintage	F	VF	XF	Unc	BU
2002 Proof	—	Value: 55.00				

KM# 1321   1-1/2 EURO
22.2000 g., 0.9000 Silver 0.6423 oz. ASW, 37 mm.   **Obv:** Tour
de France logo **Rev:** Cyclist going left **Edge:** Plain

Date	Mintage	F	VF	XF	Unc	BU
2003 Proof	150,000	Value: 50.00				

KM# 1322   1-1/2 EURO
22.2000 g., 0.9000 Silver 0.6423 oz. ASW, 37 mm.   **Obv:** Tour
de France logo **Rev:** Group of cyclists and Arch de Triumph **Edge:**
Plain

Date	Mintage	F	VF	XF	Unc	BU
2003 (Ht) Proof	150,000	Value: 50.00				

KM# 1323   1-1/2 EURO
22.2000 g., 0.9000 Silver 0.6423 oz. ASW, 37 mm.   **Obv:** Tour
de France logo **Rev:** Two cyclists and spectators **Edge:** Plain

Date	Mintage	F	VF	XF	Unc	BU
2003 (Ht) Proof	150,000	Value: 50.00				

KM# 1324   1-1/2 EURO
22.2000 g., 0.9000 Silver 0.6423 oz. ASW, 37 mm.   **Obv:** Tour
de France logo **Rev:** Two groups of cyclists **Edge:** Plain

Date	Mintage	F	VF	XF	Unc	BU
2003 (Ht) Proof	150,000	Value: 50.00				

KM# 1325   1-1/2 EURO
22.2000 g., 0.9000 Silver 0.6423 oz. ASW, 37 mm.   **Obv:** Tour
de France logo **Rev:** Cyclists, stopwatch and gears **Edge:** Plain

Date	Mintage	F	VF	XF	Unc	BU
2003 (Ht) Proof	150,000	Value: 50.00				

KM# 1336   1-1/2 EURO
22.2000 g., 0.9000 Silver 0.6423 oz. ASW, 37 mm.   **Obv:**
Jefferson and Napoleon with Louisiana Purchase map **Rev:** Jazz
musician, mansion and river boat **Edge:** Plain

Date	Mintage	F	VF	XF	Unc	BU
2003 Proof	10,000	Value: 55.00				

KM# 1338   1-1/2 EURO
22.2000 g., 0.9000 Silver 0.6423 oz. ASW, 37 mm.   **Obv:** Curved
cross design with multiple values **Rev:** Goddess Europa and flags
Edge: Plain

Date	Mintage	F	VF	XF	Unc	BU
2003 Proof	40,000	Value: 50.00				

KM# 1341   1-1/2 EURO
22.2000 g., 0.9000 Silver 0.6423 oz. ASW, 37 mm.   **Obv:**
Denomination and compass face **Rev:** SS Normandie and New
York City **Edge:** Plain

Date	Mintage	F	VF	XF	Unc	BU
2003 Proof	15,000	Value: 55.00				

KM# 1343   1-1/2 EURO
22.2000 g., 0.9000 Silver 0.6423 oz. ASW, 37 mm.   **Obv:**
Denomination and compass face **Rev:** Airplane and Tokyo
Geisha **Edge:** Plain

Date	Mintage	F	VF	XF	Unc	BU
2003 Proof	15,000	Value: 55.00				

KM# 1345   1-1/2 EURO
22.2000 g., 0.9000 Silver 0.6423 oz. ASW, 37 mm.   **Obv:** Paul
Gauguin **Rev:** Native woman **Edge:** Plain

Date	Mintage	F	VF	XF	Unc	BU
2003 Proof	15,000	Value: 55.00				

KM# 1351   1-1/2 EURO
22.2000 g., 0.9000 Silver 0.6423 oz. ASW, 37 mm.   **Obv:**
Obverse design of first one franc coin **Rev:** Reverse design of
first one franc coin **Edge:** Plain

Date	Mintage	F	VF	XF	Unc	BU
2003 Proof	15,000	Value: 50.00				

KM# 1353   1-1/2 EURO
22.2000 g., 0.9000 Silver 0.6423 oz. ASW, 37 mm.   **Obv:** Mona
Lisa **Rev:** Leonardo da Vinci **Edge:** Plain

Date	Mintage	F	VF	XF	Unc	BU
2003 Proof	10,000	Value: 55.00				

KM# 1355   1-1/2 EURO
22.2000 g., 0.9000 Silver 0.6423 oz. ASW, 37 mm.   **Obv:** Map
and denomination **Rev:** Chateau Chambord **Edge:** Plain

Date	Mintage	F	VF	XF	Unc	BU
2003 Proof	10,000	Value: 50.00				

KM# 1357   1-1/2 EURO
22.2000 g., 0.9000 Silver 0.6423 oz. ASW, 37 mm.   **Obv:**
Denomination in swirling design **Rev:** Multicolor Hansel and
Gretel, witch and house **Edge:** Plain

Date	Mintage	F	VF	XF	Unc	BU
2003 Proof	10,000	Value: 55.00				

KM# 1359   1-1/2 EURO
22.2000 g., 0.9000 Silver 0.6423 oz. ASW, 37 mm.   **Obv:**
Denomination in swirling design **Rev:** Multicolor Alice in
Wonderland **Edge:** Plain

Date	Mintage	F	VF	XF	Unc	BU
2003 Proof	10,000	Value: 55.00				

KM# 1361   1-1/2 EURO
22.2000 g., 0.9000 Silver 0.6423 oz. ASW, 37 mm.   **Obv:** Pierre
de Coubertin **Rev:** Olympic runners **Edge:** Plain

Date	Mintage	F	VF	XF	Unc	BU
2003 Proof	50,000	Value: 50.00				

KM# 1364   1-1/2 EURO
22.2000 g., 0.9000 Silver 0.6423 oz. ASW, 37 mm.   **Obv:** Map
with denomination **Rev:** Avignon Popes Palace **Edge:** Plain

Date	Mintage	F	VF	XF	Unc	BU
2004 Proof	10,000	Value: 50.00				

KM# 1373   1-1/2 EURO
22.2000 g., 0.9000 Silver 0.6423 oz. ASW, 37 mm. **Obv:** Emile Loubet and King Edward VII **Rev:** Marianne and Britannia **Edge:** Plain

Date	Mintage	F	VF	XF	Unc	BU
2004 Proof	10,000	Value: 50.00				

KM# 1374   1-1/2 EURO
22.2000 g., 0.9000 Silver 0.6423 oz. ASW, 37 mm. **Obv:** Soccer ball and denomination **Rev:** Rooster and quill **Edge:** Plain

Date	Mintage	F	VF	XF	Unc	BU
2004 Proof	25,000	Value: 55.00				

KM# 1378   1-1/2 EURO
22.2000 g., 0.9000 Silver 0.6423 oz. ASW, 37 mm. **Obv:** Compass rose **Rev:** Ocean liner **Edge:** Plain

Date	Mintage	F	VF	XF	Unc	BU
2004 Proof	10,000	Value: 50.00				

KM# 1380   1-1/2 EURO
22.2000 g., 0.9000 Silver 0.6423 oz. ASW, 37 mm. **Obv:** Compass rose **Rev:** Trans-Siberian Railroad **Edge:** Plain

Date	Mintage	F	VF	XF	Unc	BU
2004 Proof	10,000	Value: 50.00				

KM# 1382   1-1/2 EURO
22.2000 g., 0.9000 Silver 0.6423 oz. ASW, 37 mm. **Obv:** Compass rose **Rev:** Half-track vehicle **Edge:** Plain

Date	Mintage	F	VF	XF	Unc	BU
2004 Proof	10,000	Value: 47.50				

KM# 1384   1-1/2 EURO
22.2000 g., 0.9000 Silver 0.6423 oz. ASW, 37 mm. **Obv:** Compass rose **Rev:** Biplane airliner **Edge:** Plain

Date	Mintage	F	VF	XF	Unc	BU
2004 Proof	10,000	Value: 47.50				

KM# 1386   1-1/2 EURO
22.2000 g., 0.9000 Silver 0.6423 oz. ASW, 37 mm. **Obv:** F.A. Bartholdi **Rev:** Statue of Liberty **Edge:** Plain

Date	Mintage	F	VF	XF	Unc	BU
2004 Proof	15,000	Value: 47.50				

KM# 1391   1-1/2 EURO
22.2000 g., 0.9000 Silver 0.6423 oz. ASW, 37 mm. **Subject:** European Union Expansion **Obv:** Puzzle map of Europe **Rev:** Partial face and flags **Edge:** Plain

Date	Mintage	F	VF	XF	Unc	BU
2004 Proof	40,000	Value: 42.50				

KM# 1366   1-1/2 EURO
22.2000 g., 0.9000 Silver 0.6423 oz. ASW, 37 mm. **Obv:** Book, eagle and denomination **Rev:** Napoleon and coronation scene in background **Edge:** Plain

Date	Mintage	F	VF	XF	Unc	BU
2004 Proof	20,000	Value: 45.00				

KM# 1369   1-1/2 EURO
22.2000 g., 0.9000 Silver 0.6423 oz. ASW, 37 mm. **Obv:** Soldiers and Normandy invasion scene **Rev:** "D-DAY" above denomination **Edge:** Plain

Date	Mintage	F	VF	XF	Unc	BU
2004 Proof	20,000	Value: 50.00				

KM# 1844   1-1/2 EURO
22.2000 g., 0.9000 Silver 0.6423 oz. ASW, 37 mm. **Obv:** Sower advancing left within stars **Rev:** Head at left, stars at right

Date	Mintage	F	VF	XF	Unc	BU
2004 Proof	—	Value: 55.00				

KM# 1423   1-1/2 EURO
22.2000 g., 0.9000 Silver 0.6423 oz. ASW, 37 mm. **Subject:** Biathlon **Rev:** Skier at right facing 3/4 left, mountain peaks in background **Rev. Inscription:** JEUX D'HIVER

Date	Mintage	F	VF	XF	Unc	BU
2005 Proof	30,000	Value: 45.00				

KM# 1425   1-1/2 EURO
22.2000 g., 0.9000 Silver 0.6423 oz. ASW, 37 mm. **Series:** Jules Verne **Subject:** From the Earth to the Moon **Rev:** Crowd observing at lower left, volcano erupting above, moon at upper right, Verne in spaceship at lower right, factory chimneys belching smoke in background **Rev. Legend:** DE LA TERRE… LA LUNE

Date	Mintage	F	VF	XF	Unc	BU
2005 Proof	5,000	Value: 65.00				

KM# 1427   1-1/2 EURO
22.2000 g., 0.9000 Silver 0.6423 oz. ASW, 37 mm. **Rev:** Kitty and poodle at table at cafe, multicolor **Rev. Legend:** Hello Kitty

Date	Mintage	F	VF	XF	Unc	BU
2005 Proof	4,000	Value: 65.00				

KM# 1428   1-1/2 EURO
22.2000 g., 0.9000 Silver 0.6423 oz. ASW, 37 mm. **Rev:** Kitty on the Champs-Elysees, multicolor **Rev. Legend:** Hello Kitty

Date	Mintage	F	VF	XF	Unc	BU
2005 Proof	4,000	Value: 65.00				

KM# 1431   1-1/2 EURO
22.2000 g., 0.9000 Silver 0.6423 oz. ASW, 37 mm. **Subject:** Bicentennial Victory at Austerlitz **Rev:** Battle scene **Rev. Legend:** LIBERTÉ ÉGALITÉ FRATERNITÉ

Date	Mintage	F	VF	XF	Unc	BU
2005 Proof	15,000	Value: 50.00				

KM# 1434   1-1/2 EURO
22.2000 g., 0.9000 Silver 0.6423 oz. ASW, 37 mm. **Subject:** 50th Anniversary of the Europe flag **Rev:** Stars at left, partial flag at center right

Date	Mintage	F	VF	XF	Unc	BU
2005 Proof	15,000	Value: 50.00				

KM# 1436   1-1/2 EURO
22.2000 g., 0.9000 Silver 0.6423 oz. ASW, 37 mm. **Subject:** Centenary Law of Dec. 9, 1905 **Obv:** "Sower" left in ring of stars

Date	Mintage	F	VF	XF	Unc	BU
2005 Proof	15,000	Value: 50.00				
2006 Proof	10,000	Value: 50.00				

KM# 1438   1-1/2 EURO
22.2000 g., 0.9000 Silver 0.6423 oz. ASW, 37 mm. **Series:** Jules Verne **Subject:** 20,000 Leagues Under the Sea **Rev:** Submarine above plants and divers **Rev. Legend:** VINGT MILLE LIEUES SOUS LES MERS

Date	Mintage	F	VF	XF	Unc	BU
2005 Proof	5,000	Value: 65.00				

KM# 1440   1-1/2 EURO
22.2000 g., 0.9000 Silver 0.6423 oz. ASW, 37 mm. **Subject:** 150th Anniversary of Classification of Bordeax Wines **Rev:** Stylized female with grapes between various names of wines at her feet

Date	Mintage	F	VF	XF	Unc	BU
2005 Proof	5,000	Value: 65.00				

KM# 1441   1-1/2 EURO
22.2000 g., 0.9000 Silver 0.6423 oz. ASW, 37 mm. **Subject:** 60th Anniversary - End of World War II **Rev:** Doves in flight **Rev. Inscription:** L'EUROPE FAIT LA PAIX

Date	Mintage	F	VF	XF	Unc	BU
2005 Proof	50,000	Value: 45.00				

KM# 1453 1-1/2 EURO
22.2000 g., 0.9000 Silver 0.6423 oz. ASW, 37 mm. **Subject:**
100th Anniversary - Death of Paul Cézanne **Obv:** Self portrait
Obv. Inscription: PAUL / CÉZANNE **Rev:** "The Card Players"
Rev. Legend: LIBERTÉ ÉGALITÉ FRATERNITÉ

Date	Mintage	F	VF	XF	Unc	BU
2006 Proof	5,000	Value: 65.00				

KM# 1455 1-1/2 EURO
22.2000 g., 0.9000 Silver 0.6423 oz. ASW, 37 mm. **Obv:** Map
of the Basilica **Rev:** Bust of Pope Benoît with arms outstretched
facing 3/4 right at lower left, Basilica in background **Rev. Legend:**
500 ANS de la BASILIQUE SAINT-PIERRE

Date	Mintage	F	VF	XF	Unc	BU
2006 Proof	5,000	Value: 65.00				

KM# 1456 1-1/2 EURO
22.2000 g., 0.9000 Silver 0.6423 oz. ASW, 37 mm. **Rev:** Half
of Arc at left, eternal flame above WW I plaque at right **Rev.
Legend:** ARC DE TRIOMPHE

Date	Mintage	F	VF	XF	Unc	BU
2006 Proof	10,000	Value: 50.00				

KM# 1458 1-1/2 EURO
22.2000 g., 0.9000 Silver 0.6423 oz. ASW, 37 mm. **Subject:**
300th Anniversary - Completion of the Dome of Les Invalides
Rev: Dome between Jules-Hardouin Mansart at left, Louis XIV
at right **Rev. Legend:** SAINT-LOUIS - DES INVALIDES **Rev.
Inscription:** 28/AOÛT - 1706

Date	Mintage	F	VF	XF	Unc	BU
2006 Proof	10,000	Value: 50.00				

KM# 1444 1-1/2 EURO
22.2000 g., 0.9000 Silver 0.6423 oz. ASW, 37 mm. **Subject:**
100th Anniversary - French Grand Prix **Obv:** Steering wheel with
early race car in upper segment, two gauges at lower left, R / F
at lower right **Obv. Legend:** LE MANS 1906 - CENTENAIRE du
1er GRAND PRIX de l'AUTOMOBILE CLUB de FRANCE **Rev:**
Modern racing car's steering wheel **Rev. Legend:** MAGNY-
COURS

Date	Mintage	F	VF	XF	Unc	BU
2006 Proof	5,000	Value: 65.00				

KM# 1447 1-1/2 EURO
22.2000 g., 0.9000 Silver 0.6423 oz. ASW, 37 mm. **Obv:**
Strogoff on horseback wielding sword, city at left, soldiers at lower
left, calvalry at right **Obv. Legend:** MICHEL STROGOFF **Rev:**
Head of Verne facing 3/4 right at left center, instruments and
anchor in curved band **Rev. Legend:** 1828 JULES VERNE 1905
- LIBERTÉ . ÉGALITÉ . FRATERNITÉ

Date	Mintage	F	VF	XF	Unc	BU
2006 Proof	500	Value: 100				

KM# 1450 1-1/2 EURO
22.2000 g., 0.9000 Silver 0.6423 oz. ASW, 37 mm. **Subject:**
Jules Verne **Obv:** Hot air balloon, parrots at left, native masks at
lower left, foliage at right, native huts below, map of Africa in
background **Obv. Legend:** CINQ SEMAINES EN BAILON **Rev:**
Head of Verne facing 3/4 right at left center, instruments and
anchor in curved band **Rev. Legend:** 1828 JULES VERNE 1905

Date	Mintage	F	VF	XF	Unc	BU
2006 Proof	5,000	Value: 65.00				

KM# 1452 1-1/2 EURO
22.2000 g., 0.9000 Silver 0.6423 oz. ASW, 37 mm. **Subject:**
Formula 1 World Championship **Obv:** Race car outline on
checker board background **Obv. Legend:** LIBERTÉ ÉGALITÉ
FRATERNITÉ **Rev:** Race car outline in victory sprays with star
Rev. Legend: RENAULT - CHAMPION DU MONDE FIA 2005
DES CONSTRUCTEURS DE FORMULE 1

Date	Mintage	F	VF	XF	Unc	BU
2006 Proof	10,000	Value: 50.00				

KM# 1501 1-1/2 EURO
22.2000 g., 0.9000 Silver 0.6423 oz. ASW, 37 mm. **Subject:**
Georges Pompendev Center, 30th Anniversary

Date	Mintage	F	VF	XF	Unc	BU
2007 Proof	—	Value: 50.00				

KM# 1484 1-1/2 EURO
22.2000 g., 0.9000 Silver 0.6423 oz. ASW, 37 mm. **Subject:**
2007 Rugby World Cup **Obv:** Two players and goal **Rev:** Logo
and goal

Date	Mintage	F	VF	XF	Unc	BU
2007 Proof	5,000	Value: 50.00				

KM# 1462 1-1/2 EURO
22.0000 g., 0.9000 Silver 0.6366 oz. ASW, 37 mm. **Subject:**
Sebastien Le Prestre de Vauban, 300th Anniversary of Death

Date	Mintage	F	VF	XF	Unc	BU
2007 Proof	30,000	Value: 40.00				

KM# 1465 1-1/2 EURO
22.2000 g., 0.9000 Silver 0.6423 oz. ASW, 37 mm. **Subject:** Le
Petit Prince, 60th Anniversary **Obv:** Prince standing, multicolor

Date	Mintage	F	VF	XF	Unc	BU
2007 Proof	3,000	Value: 55.00				

KM# 1467 1-1/2 EURO
22.2000 g., 0.9000 Silver 0.6423 oz. ASW, 37 mm. **Subject:** Le
Petit Prince, 60th Anniversary **Obv:** Prince lying in field, multicolor

Date	Mintage	F	VF	XF	Unc	BU
2007 Proof	3,000	Value: 55.00				

KM# 1469 1-1/2 EURO
22.2000 g., 0.9000 Silver 0.6423 oz. ASW, 37 mm. **Subject:** Le
Petite Prince, 60th Anniversary **Obv:** Prince standing with rabbit,
multicolor

Date	Mintage	F	VF	XF	Unc	BU
		—	Value: 55.00			

KM# 1473 1-1/2 EURO
22.2000 g., 0.9000 Silver 0.6423 oz. ASW, 37 mm. **Subject:**
Paul E. Victor, 100th Birthday **Obv:** International Polar Year Logo
Rev: Bust at left, Islands

Date	Mintage	F	VF	XF	Unc	BU
2007 Proof	5,000	Value: 55.00				

KM# 1475 1-1/2 EURO
22.2000 g., 0.9000 Silver 0.6423 oz. ASW, 37 mm. **Obv:**
Formula 1 race car on checkered background **Rev:** Legend in
wreath on checkered background

Date	Mintage	F	VF	XF	Unc	BU
2007//2006 Proof	5,000	Value: 55.00				

KM# 1477 1-1/2 EURO
22.2000 g., 0.9000 Silver 0.6423 oz. ASW, 37 mm. **Subject:**
29th Summer Olympic Games Beijing **Obv:** Rider on horseback,
globe map of China **Rev:** Equestrian jump over orienteal fence

Date	Mintage	F	VF	XF	Unc	BU
2007 Proof	10,000	Value: 50.00				

KM# 1479 1-1/2 EURO
22.2000 g., 0.9000 Silver 0.6423 oz. ASW, 37 mm. **Subject:**
Airbus A380 **Obv:** Airplane **Rev:** Europa head and flags

Date	Mintage	F	VF	XF	Unc	BU
2007 Proof	5,000	Value: 50.00				

KM# 1488 1-1/2 EURO
22.2000 g., 0.9000 Silver 0.6423 oz. ASW, 37 mm. **Obv:**
Christian Dior bust **Rev:** Dior Museum building

Date	Mintage	F	VF	XF	Unc	BU
2007 Proof	3,000	Value: 75.00				

KM# 1505 1-1/2 EURO
22.2000 g., 0.9000 Silver 0.6423 oz. ASW, 37 mm. **Subject:**
George Remir Centennial **Obv:** Wand and sparkles **Rev:** Tin Tin
and the Professor calculus in multicolor

Date	Mintage	F	VF	XF	Unc	BU
2007 Proof	10,000	Value: 60.00				

KM# 1506 1-1/2 EURO
22.2000 g., 0.9000 Silver 0.6423 oz. ASW, 37 mm. **Subject:**
Georges Remi Centennial **Obv:** Wand and sparkles **Rev:** Tin Tin
and Captain Haddock in multicolor

Date	Mintage	F	VF	XF	Unc	BU
2007 Proof	10,000	Value: 65.00				

KM# 1507 1-1/2 EURO
22.2000 g., 0.9000 Silver 0.6423 oz. ASW, 37 mm. **Subject:**
Georges Remi Centennial **Obv:** Wand and sparkles **Rev:** Tin Tin
and Chang in multicolor

Date	Mintage	F	VF	XF	Unc	BU
2007 Proof	10,000	Value: 65.00				

KM# 1511 1-1/2 EURO
22.2000 g., 0.9000 Silver 0.6423 oz. ASW, 37 mm. **Subject:**
Aristides de Sousa Mendes, Portuguese diplomat **Obv:** Bust right
Rev: Plaque

Date	Mintage	F	VF	XF	Unc	BU
2007 Proof	3,000	Value: 55.00				

KM# 1516 1-1/2 EURO
22.2000 g., 0.9000 Silver 0.6423 oz. ASW, 37 mm. **Subject:**
Asterix **Rev:** The Banquet

Date	Mintage	F	VF	XF	Unc	BU
2007 Proof	3,000	Value: 55.00				

KM# 1517 1-1/2 EURO
22.2000 g., 0.9000 Silver 0.6423 oz. ASW, 37 mm. **Subject:**
Asterix **Rev:** The posion

Date	Mintage	F	VF	XF	Unc	BU
2007 Proof	3,000	Value: 55.00				

KM# 1518 1-1/2 EURO
22.2000 g., 0.9000 Silver 0.6423 oz. ASW, 37 mm. **Subject:**
Asterix **Rev:** The Chase

Date	Mintage	F	VF	XF	Unc	BU
2007 Proof	3,000	Value: 55.00				

KM# 1527 1-1/2 EURO
22.2000 g., 0.9000 Silver 0.6423 oz. ASW, 37 mm. **Subject:**
French Presidency of European Union **Obv:** Text written stars
Rev: Europa head and flags

Date	Mintage	F	VF	XF	Unc	BU
2008 Proof	10,000	Value: 50.00				

KM# 1532 1-1/2 EURO
22.2000 g., 0.9000 Silver 0.6423 oz. ASW **Subject:** Eurpean
Parliament, 50th Anniversary **Obv:** Map of EU within stars **Rev:**
European Parliament Building in Strasboury **Shape:** 37

Date	Mintage	F	VF	XF	Unc	BU
2008 Proof	30,000	Value: 50.00				

KM# 1537 1-1/2 EURO
22.2000 g., 0.9000 Silver 0.6423 oz. ASW, 37 mm. **Subject:** 5th
Republic, 50th Anniversasry **Obv:** Sower **Rev:** deGaulle head right

Date	Mintage	F	VF	XF	Unc	BU
2008 Proof	10,000	Value: 50.00				

KM# 1543 1-1/2 EURO
22.2000 g., 0.9000 Silver 0.6423 oz. ASW, 37 mm. **Subject:**
29th Summer Olympic Games - Beijing **Obv:** Swimmer and globe
Rev: Diver and oriental screen

Date	Mintage	F	VF	XF	Unc	BU
2008 Proof	10,000	Value: 65.00				

KM# 1546 1-1/2 EURO
22.2000 g., 0.9000 Silver 0.6423 oz. ASW, 37 mm. **Subject:**
UEFA **Obv:** French soccer team **Rev:** UEFA logo

Date	Mintage	F	VF	XF	Unc	BU
2008 Proof	5,000	Value: 55.00				

KM# 1548 1-1/2 EURO
22.2000 g., 0.9000 Silver 0.6423 oz. ASW, 37 mm. **Subject:**
Franco - Japanese Relators, 150th Anniversary **Obv:** Eiffel Tower
and Kimono forming logo **Rev:** Delacroix "La Liberte"

Date	Mintage	F	VF	XF	Unc	BU
2008 Proof	5,000	Value: 65.00				

KM# 1549 1-1/2 EURO
22.2000 g., 0.9000 Silver 0.6423 oz. ASW, 37 mm. **Subject:**
Franco - Japanese Relators - 150th Anniversary **Obv:** Eillfel
Tower and Kimono forming logo **Rev:** Ichikawa Ebizo IV portrait
painting

Date	Mintage	F	VF	XF	Unc	BU
2008 Proof	5,000	Value: 65.00				

KM# 1550 1-1/2 EURO
22.2000 g., 0.9000 Silver 0.6423 oz. ASW, 37 mm. **Subject:**
Franco - Japanese Relators - 150th Anniversary **Obv:** Eillfel
Tower and Kimono forming logo **Rev:** Scenes of Paris and Tokyo
- Eillfel Tower and Pagoda Sensoji

Date	Mintage	F	VF	XF	Unc	BU
2008 Proof	5,000	Value: 65.00				

KM# 1551 1-1/2 EURO
22.2000 g., 0.9000 Silver 0.6423 oz. ASW, 37 mm. **Subject:**
Franco - Japanese Relators - 150th Anniversary **Obv:** Eillfel
Tower and Kimono forming logo **Rev:** Japanese cash coin of
"Kanei Tsuho"

Date	Mintage	F	VF	XF	Unc	BU
2008 Proof	5,000	Value: 65.00				

KM# 1555 1-1/2 EURO
22.2000 g., 0.9000 Silver 0.6423 oz. ASW, 37 mm. **Subject:**
André Citronën **Obv:** First front wheel drive auto **Rev:** Bust 1/4 left

Date	Mintage	F	VF	XF	Unc	BU
2008 Proof	5,000	Value: 65.00				

KM# 1558 1-1/2 EURO
22.2000 g., 0.9000 Silver 0.6423 oz. ASW, 37 mm. **Subject:**
Rouen Armada **Obv:** Cape Horn, sextant, hour glass **Rev:** Sailing
ship

Date	Mintage	F	VF	XF	Unc	BU
2008 Proof	5,000	Value: 65.00				

KM# 1561 1-1/2 EURO
22.2000 g., 0.9000 Silver 0.6423 oz. ASW **Subject:** Lourdes,
150th Anniversary **Obv:** Church of Notre Dame at Lourdes **Rev:**
Cross with Pope John Paul II, Pope Benedict XVI and Bernadette
Soubirous in quadrants

Date	Mintage	F	VF	XF	Unc	BU
2008 Proof	15,000	Value: 60.00				

KM# 1574 1-1/2 EURO
22.2000 g., 0.9000 Silver 0.6423 oz. ASW, 37 mm. **Subject:**
UNESCO - Grand Canyon **Obv:** Grand Canyon **Rev:** UNESCO
logos

Date	Mintage	F	VF	XF	Unc	BU
2008 Proof	5,000	Value: 65.00				

KM# 1576 1-1/2 EURO
22.2000 g., 0.9000 Silver 0.6423 oz. ASW, 37 mm. **Subject:**
International Polar Year **Obv:** IPY logo **Rev:** Emperor Penguin
and map of Antartica

Date	Mintage	F	VF	XF	Unc	BU
2008 Proof	5,000	Value: 65.00				

KM# 1578 1-1/2 EURO
22.2000 g., 0.9000 Silver 0.6423 oz. ASW, 37 mm. **Subject:** Spirou, 70th Anniversary **Obv:** Character Spirou in thought **Rev:** 70th Anniversary logo

Date	Mintage	F	VF	XF	Unc	BU
2008 Proof	10,000	Value: 60.00				

KM# 1633 1-1/2 EURO
11.0000 g., Aluminum-Bronze, 30 mm. **Obv:** Stadium view, soccer player **Rev:** Shield of Olympique Lyonnais

Date	Mintage	F	VF	XF	Unc	BU
2009	25,000	—	—	—	15.00	20.00

KM# 1723 1-1/2 EURO
11.0000 g., Aluminum-Bronze, 30 mm. **Obv:** Soccer player **Rev:** Girondins de Bordeaux logo

Date	Mintage	F	VF	XF	Unc	BU
2010	25,000	—	—	—	15.00	20.00

KM# 1754 1-1/2 EURO
11.0000 g., Aluminum-Bronze, 30 mm. **Subject:** Olympique de Marseille **Obv:** Soccer player **Rev:** OM logo

Date	Mintage	F	VF	XF	Unc	BU
2011	25,000	—	—	—	—	15.00

KM# 1918 1-1/2 EURO
11.0000 g., Aluminum-Bronze, 30 mm. **Subject:** Paris Saint Germain **Obv:** Stadium and player **Rev:** Team logo

Date	Mintage	F	VF	XF	Unc	BU
2012(a)	25,000	—	—	—	—	15.00

KM# 1289 2 EURO
8.5000 g., Bi-Metallic Nickel-Brass center in Copper-Nickel ring, 25.75 mm. **Obv:** Stylized tree divides RF within circle, date below **Rev:** Denomination and map **Edge:** Reeded with 2's and stars

Date	Mintage	F	VF	XF	Unc	BU
2001	237,950,793	—	—	—	3.75	6.00
2001 Proof	15,000	Value: 20.00				
2002	153,700,000	—	—	—	3.75	6.00
2002 Proof	21,453	Value: 18.00				
2003 In sets only	180,000	—	—	—	—	13.50
2003 Proof	40,000	Value: 20.00				
2004 In sets only	160,000	—	—	—	—	13.50
2004 Proof	20,000	Value: 20.00				
2005 In sets only	120,000	—	—	—	—	13.50
2005 Proof	10,000	Value: 20.00				
2006 In sets only	67,600	—	—	—	—	13.50
2006 Proof	10,000	Value: 20.00				

KM# 1414 2 EURO
8.5000 g., Bi-Metallic Nickel-Brass center in Copper-Nickel ring, 25.75 mm. **Obv:** Stylized tree divides RF within circle, date below **Rev:** Relief map of Western Europe, stars, lines and value **Edge:** Reeded with 2's and stars

Date	Mintage	F	VF	XF	Unc	BU
2007 In sets only	58,000	—	—	—	—	15.00
2007 Proof	7,500	Value: 25.00				
2008 In sets only	57,000	—	—	—	—	6.00
2008 Proof	7,500	Value: 25.00				
2009 In sets only	50,500	—	—	—	—	6.00
2009 Proof	7,500	Value: 25.00				
2010		—	—	—	—	6.00
2010 Proof		Value: 25.00				
2011		—	—	—	—	6.00
2011 Proof		Value: 25.00				

Date	Mintage	F	VF	XF	Unc	BU
2012		—	—	—	—	6.00
2012 Proof		Value: 25.00				

KM# 1460 2 EURO
8.5000 g., Bi-Metallic Nickel-Brass center in Copper-Nickel ring, 25.75 mm. **Subject:** Treaty of Rome 50th Anniversary **Edge:** Reeded with 2's and stars

Date	Mintage	F	VF	XF	Unc	BU
2007	9,600,000	—	—	—	5.50	6.50

KM# 1459 2 EURO
8.5000 g., Bi-Metallic Nickel-Brass center in Copper-Nickel ring, 25.75 mm. **Subject:** European Union Presidency **Obv:** Inscription **Obv. Inscription:** PRÉSIDENCE / FRANÇAISE / UNION / EUROPÉENNE / RF **Rev:** Large value "2" at left, modified map of Europe at right **Edge:** Reeded with 2's and stars

Date	Mintage	F	VF	XF	Unc	BU
2008(a)	20,100,000	—	—	—	5.50	6.50

KM# 1542 2 EURO
8.5000 g., Bi-Metallic Nickel-Brass center in Copper-Nickel ring, 25.75 mm. **Subject:** 5th Republic, 50th Anniversary **Obv:** Text within stars **Rev:** Value at left, relief map of the EU at right **Edge:** Reeded with 2's and stars

Date	Mintage	F	VF	XF	Unc	BU
2008(a)	10,000,000	—	—	—	6.50	7.50
2008(a) Sets only	20,000	—	—	—	—	20.00
2008(a) Proof	10,000	Value: 40.00				

KM# 1590 2 EURO
8.5000 g., Bi-Metallic Nickel-Brass center in Copper-Nickel ring, 25.75 mm. **Subject:** EMU 10th Anniversary **Obv:** Stick figure and E design **Edge:** Reeded with 2's and stars

Date	Mintage	F	VF	XF	Unc	BU
2009		—	—	—	8.00	10.00
2009 Proof	10,000	Value: 15.00				

KM# 1676 2 EURO
8.5000 g., Bi-Metallic Nickel-Brass center in Copper-Nickel ring, 25.75 mm. **Subject:** 70th Anniversary, June 18th Appeal **Obv:** General Charles DeGaulle giving BBC speech **Rev:** Value and map **Edge:** Reeded with 2's and stars

Date	Mintage	F	VF	XF	Unc	BU
2010	20,000	—	—	—	8.00	10.00
2010 Proof	10,000	Value: 15.00				

KM# 1789 2 EURO
8.5000 g., Bi-Metallic Nickel-Brass center in Copper-Nickel ring,

25.75 mm. **Subject:** International Music Day, 30th Anniversary **Obv:** Youth jamming **Rev:** Value and map of Western Europe **Edge:** Reeded with 2's and stars

Date	Mintage	F	VF	XF	Unc	BU
2011	10,000,000	—	—	—	5.00	—
2011 Special Unc.		—	—	—	—	8.00
2011 Proof	10,000	Value: 15.00				

KM# 1847 2 EURO
22.2000 g., 0.9000 Silver 0.6423 oz. ASW, 37 mm. **Obv:** Sailing ship L'Hermione **Rev:** Ship figurehead at right, ship's wheel at bottom

Date	Mintage	F	VF	XF	Unc	BU
2012(a) Proof	10,000	Value: 35.00				

KM# 1846 2 EURO
8.5000 g., Bi-Metallic Nickel-Brass center in Copper-Nickel ring, 25.75 mm. **Subject:** Euro coinage, 10th Anniversary **Obv:** Euro symbol on globe, child-like drawing around

Date	Mintage	F	VF	XF	Unc	BU
2012(a)	10,000,000	—	—	—	6.50	7.50
2012(a) Special Unc.		—	—	—	—	10.00
2012(a) Proof		Value: 15.00				

KM# 1894 2 EURO
8.5000 g., Bi-Metallic Nickel-Brass center in Copper-Nickel ring, 25.75 mm. **Subject:** abbé Pierre, 100th anniversary of Birth **Obv:** Portrait facing of abbé Pierre, wearing beret

Date	Mintage	F	VF	XF	Unc	BU
2012(a)	1,000,000	—	—	—	6.00	7.00
2012(a) Special Unc.	10,000	—	—	—	—	10.00
2012(a) Proof	10,000	Value: 25.00				

KM# 1347 5 EURO
24.9000 g., 0.9000 Bi-Metallic .900 Silver 22.2g planchet with .750 Gold 2.7g insert 0.7205 oz., 37 mm. **Obv:** The Seed Sower on gold insert **Rev:** Denomination and map **Edge:** Plain

Date	Mintage	F	VF	XF	Unc	BU
2002 Proof	10,000	Value: 550				

KM# 1371 5 EURO
24.9000 g., Bi-Metallic .750 Gold 2.7 g insert on .900 Silver 22.2g planchet, 37 mm. **Obv:** The Seed Sower on gold insert **Rev:** French face map and denomination **Edge:** Plain

Date	Mintage	F	VF	XF	Unc	BU
2004 Proof	3,000	Value: 550				

KM# 1523 5 EURO
22.2000 g., 0.9000 Silver 0.6423 oz. ASW, 37 mm. **Subject:** Euro - 5th Anniversary **Obv:** The Seed Sower

Date	Mintage	F	VF	XF	Unc	BU
2007 Proof	5,000	Value: 55.00				

KM# 1524 5 EURO
163.8000 g., 0.9500 Silver 5.0028 oz. ASW, 50 mm. **Subject:** Euro 5th Anniversary **Obv:** Sower

Date	Mintage	F	VF	XF	Unc	BU
2007 Proof	500	Value: 325				

KM# 1525 5 EURO
1.2400 g., 0.9990 Gold 0.0398 oz. AGW, 14 mm. **Subject:** Euro 5th Anniversary **Obv:** The Seed Sower

Date	Mintage	F	VF	XF	Unc	BU
2007 Proof	2,000	Value: 75.00				

KM# 1526 5 EURO
31.1050 g., 0.9200 Gold 0.9200 oz. AGW, 31 mm. **Subject:** Euro 5th Anniversary **Obv:** The Seed Sower

Date	Mintage	F	VF	XF	Unc	BU
2007 Proof	500	Value: 1,500				

KM# 1534 5 EURO
10.0000 g., 0.5000 Silver 0.1607 oz. ASW, 27 mm. **Obv:** Sower, full length **Rev:** Value within hexagon design

Date	Mintage	F	VF	XF	Unc	BU
2008 Proof	2,000,000	Value: 15.00				

KM# 1538 5 EURO
1.2400 g., 0.9990 Gold 0.0398 oz. AGW, 13.9 mm. **Subject:** 5th Republic, 50th Anniversary **Obv:** Sower **Rev:** de Gaulle head right

Date	Mintage	F	VF	XF	Unc	BU
2008 Proof	20,000	Value: 75.00				

KM# 1566 5 EURO
22.2000 g., 0.9000 Silver 0.6423 oz. ASW, 37 mm. **Subject:** Gabrielle Chanel **Obv:** Bust right in hat **Rev:** Value on "Matelassé" pattern

Date	Mintage	F	VF	XF	Unc	BU
2008 Proof	10,000	Value: 65.00				

KM# 1567 5 EURO
8.4500 g., 0.9200 Gold 0.2499 oz. AGW, 22 mm. **Subject:** Gabrielle Chanel **Obv:** Portrait in hat, right **Rev:** Value on "Matelassé" pattern

Date	Mintage	F	VF	XF	Unc	BU
2008 Proof	500	Value: 475				

KM# 1568 5 EURO
163.8000 g., 0.9500 Silver 5.0028 oz. ASW, 50 mm. **Subject:** Gabrielle Chanel **Obv:** Portrait in hat, right **Rev:** Vlaue on "Matelassé" pattern

Date	Mintage	F	VF	XF	Unc	BU
2008 Proof	500	Value: 350				

KM# 1586   5 EURO
1.2400 g., 0.9990 Gold 0.0398 oz. AGW, 13.9 mm. **Subject:** Court of Human Rights, 50th Anniversary **Obv:** The Seed Sower left **Rev:** Text

Date	Mintage	F	VF	XF	Unc	BU
2009P Proof	10,000	Value: 70.00				

KM# 1625   5 EURO
15.0000 g., 0.9000 Silver 0.4340 oz. ASW, 30 x 21 mm. **Subject:** Monet **Obv:** Le Bassin Aux Nympheas, 1900 painting **Rev:** Multicolor pallet and brushes, portrait **Shape:** Rectangle

Date	Mintage	F	VF	XF	Unc	BU
2009P Proof	20,000	Value: 35.00				

KM# 1627   5 EURO
22.2000 g., 0.9000 Silver 0.6423 oz. ASW, 37 mm. **Subject:** Year of the Ox **Obv:** Oxen within Asia screen garden **Rev:** Portrait of La Fontaine

Date	Mintage	F	VF	XF	Unc	BU
2009P Proof	10,000	Value: 35.00				

KM# 1674   5 EURO
1.2400 g., 0.9990 Gold 0.0398 oz. AGW, 13.9 mm. **Obv:** The Seed Sower left **Rev:** Wheat and olive branch

Date	Mintage	F	VF	XF	Unc	BU
2010 Proof	10,000	Value: 75.00				

KM# 1680   5 EURO
0.5000 g., 0.9990 Gold 0.0161 oz. AGW, 11 mm. **Subject:** Cluny Abbey, 1100th Anniversary **Obv:** Europa head facing **Rev:** Cluny Abbey

Date	Mintage	F	VF	XF	Unc	BU
2010 Proof	20,000	Value: 45.00				

KM# 1715   5 EURO
22.2000 g., 0.9000 Silver 0.6423 oz. ASW, 37 mm. **Obv:** Tiger within border **Rev:** La Fontaine bust at left, animals at right

Date	Mintage	F	VF	XF	Unc	BU
2010 Proof	10,000	Value: 65.00				

KM# 1785   5 EURO
1.2440 g., 0.9990 Gold 0.0400 oz. AGW, 13.9 mm. **Subject:** Euro Starter Kit, 10th Anniversary **Obv:** Sower **Rev:** Euro starter kit

Date	Mintage	F	VF	XF	Unc	BU
2011 Proof	10,000	Value: 100				

KM# 1791   5 EURO
0.5000 g., 0.9990 Gold 0.0161 oz. AGW, 11 mm. **Subject:** International Music Day, 30th Anniversary **Obv:** Europa **Rev:** Youth jamming

Date	Mintage	F	VF	XF	Unc	BU
2011 Proof	20,000	Value: 100				

KM# 1810   5 EURO
0.5000 g., 0.9990 Gold 0.0161 oz. AGW, 11 mm. **Subject:** UNESCO World Heritage Site - Palace of Versailles

Date	Mintage	F	VF	XF	Unc	BU
2011 Proof	20,000	Value: 100				

KM# 1833   5 EURO
22.2000 g., 0.9000 Silver 0.6423 oz. ASW, 37 mm. **Subject:** Year of the Rabbit **Obv:** Rabbit seated facing right **Rev:** Fontaine and animals

Date	Mintage	F	VF	XF	Unc	BU
2011 Proof	10,000	Value: 50.00				

KM# 1851   5 EURO
0.5000 g., 0.9990 Gold 0.0161 oz. AGW, 11 mm. **Subject:** Eurocorps, 20th Anniversary **Obv:** Mitterrand and Kohl standing clasping hands **Rev:** Europa facing

Date	Mintage	F	VF	XF	Unc	BU
2012(a) Proof	10,000	Value: 65.00				

KM# 1890   5 EURO
0.5000 g., 0.9990 Gold 0.0161 oz. AGW, 11 mm. **Subject:** Euro, 10th Anniversary **Obv:** The Sower advancing left **Rev:** Value on globe with child-like renderings around

Date	Mintage	F	VF	XF	Unc	BU
2012(a) Proof	10,000	Value: 75.00				

KM# 1896   5 EURO
1.2440 g., 0.9990 Gold 0.0400 oz. AGW, 13.9 mm. **Subject:** abbé Pierre, 100th anniversary of Birth **Obv:** Pierre's bust at left, shaddow figure at right **Rev:** Emmaus International logo and quote

Date	Mintage	F	VF	XF	Unc	BU
2012(a) Proof	10,000	Value: 100				

KM# 1907   5 EURO
0.5000 g., 0.9990 Gold 0.0161 oz. AGW, 11 mm. **Subject:** UNESCO - World Heritage Site **Obv:** Abu Simbel temple **Rev:** Sphinx and Pyramids

Date	Mintage	F	VF	XF	Unc	BU
2012(a) Proof	10,000	Value: 75.00				

KM# 1302   10 EURO
8.4500 g., 0.9990 Gold 0.2714 oz. AGW, 22 mm. **Subject:** Europa **Obv:** Eight French euro coin designs **Rev:** Portrait and flags design of 6.55957 francs KM-1265 **Edge:** Reeded

Date	Mintage	F	VF	XF	Unc	BU
2002 Proof	3,000	Value: 475				

KM# 1326   10 EURO
8.4500 g., 0.9200 Gold 0.2499 oz. AGW, 22 mm. **Obv:** Tour de France logo **Rev:** Cyclist going left **Edge:** Reeded

Date	Mintage	F	VF	XF	Unc	BU
2003 (Ht) Proof	5,000	Value: 400				

KM# 1348   10 EURO
8.4500 g., 0.9200 Gold 0.2499 oz. AGW, 22 mm. **Obv:** The seed sower **Rev:** Denomination and map **Edge:** Plain

Date	Mintage	F	VF	XF	Unc	BU
2003 Proof	15,000	Value: 475				

KM# 1352   10 EURO
8.4500 g., 0.9200 Gold 0.2499 oz. AGW, 22 mm. **Obv:** Obverse design of first one franc coin **Rev:** Reverse design of first one franc coin **Edge:** Plain

Date	Mintage	F	VF	XF	Unc	BU
2003 Proof	10,000	Value: 475				

KM# 1362   10 EURO
8.4500 g., 0.9200 Gold 0.2499 oz. AGW, 22 mm. **Obv:** Pierre de Coubertin **Rev:** Olympic runners **Edge:** Plain

Date	Mintage	F	VF	XF	Unc	BU
2003 Proof	15,000	Value: 475				

KM# 1367   10 EURO
6.4100 g., 0.9000 Gold 0.1855 oz. AGW, 22 mm. **Obv:** Book, denomination and eagle **Rev:** Napoleon and coronation scene **Edge:** Plain

Date	Mintage	F	VF	XF	Unc	BU
2004 Proof	5,000	Value: 400				

KM# 1375   10 EURO
8.4500 g., 0.9200 Gold 0.2499 oz. AGW, 22 mm. **Obv:** Half soccer ball and denomination **Rev:** Eiffel tower and soccer balls **Edge:** Plain

Date	Mintage	F	VF	XF	Unc	BU
2004 Proof	10,000	Value: 475				

KM# 1392   10 EURO
8.4500 g., 0.9200 Gold 0.2499 oz. AGW, 22 mm. **Subject:** European Union Expansion **Obv:** Partial face and flags **Rev:** Puzzle map **Edge:** Reeded

Date	Mintage	F	VF	XF	Unc	BU
2004 Proof	5,000	Value: 475				

KM# 1403   10 EURO
8.4500 g., 0.9200 Gold 0.2499 oz. AGW, 22 mm. **Subject:** Jules Verne **Obv:** Various scenes from Verne's novel "Around The World in 80 Days" **Rev:** Jules Verne's portrait left of value and date

Date	Mintage	F	VF	XF	Unc	BU
2005 Proof	2,000	Value: 475				

KM# 1424   10 EURO
8.4500 g., 0.9200 Gold 0.2499 oz. AGW, 22 mm. **Subject:** Biathlon **Rev:** Skier at right facing 3/4 left, mountain peaks in background **Rev. Inscription:** JEUX D'HIVER

Date	Mintage	F	VF	XF	Unc	BU
2005 Proof	—	Value: 475				

KM# 1426   10 EURO
8.4500 g., 0.9200 Gold 0.2499 oz. AGW, 22 mm. **Series:** Jules Verne **Subject:** From the earth to the moon **Rev:** Crowd observing at lower left, volcano erupting above, moon at upper right, Verne in spaceship at lower right, chimneys belching smoke in backgrond **Rev. Legend:** DE LA TERRE À LA LUNE

Date	Mintage	F	VF	XF	Unc	BU
2005 Proof	2,000	Value: 475				

KM# 1429   10 EURO
8.4500 g., 0.9200 Gold 0.2499 oz. AGW, 22 mm. **Rev:** Kitty at the Spectacle, multicolor **Rev. Legend:** Hello Kitty

Date	Mintage	F	VF	XF	Unc	BU
2005 Proof	1,000	Value: 425				

KM# 1432 10 EURO
6.4100 g., 0.9000 Gold 0.1855 oz. AGW, 21 mm. **Subject:** Bicentennial - Victory at Austerlitz **Rev:** Battle scene **Rev. Legend:** LIBERTÉ ÉGALITÉ FRATERNITÉ

Date	Mintage	F	VF	XF	Unc	BU
2005 Proof	3,000	Value: 400				

KM# 1435 10 EURO
8.4500 g., 0.9200 Gold 0.2499 oz. AGW, 22 mm. **Subject:** 50th Anniversary - Flag of Europe **Rev:** Stars at left, partial flag at center right

Date	Mintage	F	VF	XF	Unc	BU
2005 Proof	3,000	Value: 475				

KM# 1439 10 EURO
8.4500 g., 0.9200 Gold 0.2499 oz. AGW, 22 mm. **Series:** Jules Verne **Subject:** 20,000 Leagues Under the Sea **Rev:** Submarine above plants and divers **Rev. Legend:** VINGT MILLE LIEUES SOUS LES MERS

Date	Mintage	F	VF	XF	Unc	BU
2005 Proof	2,000	Value: 475				

KM# 1446 10 EURO
8.4500 g., 0.9200 Gold 0.2499 oz. AGW, 22 mm. **Subject:** Marshal Bernadotte under Napoleon **Rev:** Military bust facing 3/4 right at left, building in backgound at right **Rev. Legend:** LIBERTÉ GALITÉ FRATERNITÉ - KARL XIV JOHAN ROI DE SUÉDE

Date	Mintage	F	VF	XF	Unc	BU
2006 Proof	1,000	Value: 475				

KM# 1416 10 EURO
8.4500 g., 0.9200 Gold 0.2499 oz. AGW, 22 mm. **Obv:** Jean de la Fontaine, value, Chinese astrological animals, date, Paris mint privy marks but without national identification **Rev:** Dog in wreath **Edge:** Reeded

Date	Mintage	F	VF	XF	Unc	BU
2006 Proof	500	Value: 475				

KM# 1448 10 EURO
8.4500 g., 0.9200 Gold 0.2499 oz. AGW, 22 mm. **Subject:** 20,000 Leagues Under the Sea **Obv:** Strogoff horseback wielding a sword, city at left, soldiers at lower left, calvary at right - the Tartars, Siberia and the Tsar's Army **Obv. Legend:** MICHEL STROGOFF **Rev:** Head of Verne facing 3/4 right at left center, instruments and anchor in curved band **Rev. Legend:** 1828 JULES VERNE 1905

Date	Mintage	F	VF	XF	Unc	BU
2006 Proof	500	Value: 475				

KM# 1449 10 EURO
8.4500 g., 0.9200 Gold 0.2499 oz. AGW, 22 mm. **Subject:** 20,000 Leagues Under the Sea **Obv:** Hot air balloon, parrots at left, native masks below left, foliage at right, huts below, map of Africa in background. **Obv. Legend:** CINQ SEMAINES EN BALLON **Rev:** Head of Verne facing 3/4 right at left center, instruments and anchor in curved band **Rev. Legend:** 1828 JULES VERNE 1905 - LIBERTÉ . ÉGALITÉ . FRATERNITÉ

Date	Mintage	F	VF	XF	Unc	BU
2006 Proof	500	Value: 475				

KM# 1451 10 EURO
8.4500 g., 0.9200 Gold 0.2499 oz. AGW, 22 mm. **Subject:** 100th Anniversary - French Grand Prix **Obv:** Steering wheel with early race car in upper segment, two gauges at lower left, R / F at lower right **Obv. Legend:** LE MANS 1906 - CENTENAIRE du 1er GRAND PRIX de l'AUTOMOBILE CLUB de FRANCE **Rev. Legend:** MAGNY-COURS

Date	Mintage	F	VF	XF	Unc	BU
2006 Proof	500	Value: 475				

KM# 1418 10 EURO
8.4500 g., 0.9200 Gold 0.2499 oz. AGW, 22 mm. **Obv:** Jean de la Fontaine, value, Chinese astrological animals, date, Paris mint privy marks but without national identification **Rev:** Pig in wreath **Edge:** Reeded **Note:** anonymous issue

Date	Mintage	F	VF	XF	Unc	BU
2007 Proof	500	Value: 475				

KM# 1420 10 EURO
8.4500 g., 0.9200 Gold 0.2499 oz. AGW, 22 mm. **Obv:** Military bust of Lafayette facing 3/4 left **Obv. Legend:** LA FAYETTE. HÉROS DELA RÉVOLUTION AMÉRICAINE **Obv. Inscription:** 1757/1854 at left, RF monogram at right **Rev:** Sailing ship L'Hermione **Rev. Legend:** LA FAYETTE, HERO OF THE AMERICAN REVOLUTION **Edge:** Plain

Date	Mintage	F	VF	XF	Unc	BU
2007 (a) Proof	500	Value: 475				

KM# 1502 10 EURO
8.4500 g., 0.9200 Gold 0.2499 oz. AGW, 22 mm. **Subject:** Georges Pompidou Center, 30th Anniversary

Date	Mintage	F	VF	XF	Unc	BU
2007 Proof	—	Value: 475				

KM# 1463 10 EURO
8.4500 g., 0.9200 Gold 0.2499 oz. AGW, 22 mm. **Subject:** Sebastien Le Prestre de Vauban, 300th Anniversary of Death

Date	Mintage	F	VF	XF	Unc	BU
2007 Proof	3,000	Value: 475				

KM# 1474 10 EURO
8.4500 g., 0.9200 Gold 0.2499 oz. AGW, 22 mm. **Subject:** Paul E. Victor, 100th birthday **Obv:** International polar year logo **Rev:** Bust at left, Islands

Date	Mintage	F	VF	XF	Unc	BU
2007	500	—	—	—	—	475

KM# 1476 10 EURO
8.4500 g., 0.9200 Gold 0.2499 oz. AGW, 22 mm. **Obv:** Formula 1 race car on checkered background **Rev:** Legend in wreath on checkered background

Date	Mintage	F	VF	XF	Unc	BU
2007//2006 Proof	500	Value: 475				

KM# 1478 10 EURO
8.4500 g., 0.9200 Gold 0.2499 oz. AGW, 22 mm. **Subject:** 29th Summer Olympic Games Beijing **Obv:** Rider on horseback, globe map of China **Rev:** Equestrian jump over oriental fence

Date	Mintage	F	VF	XF	Unc	BU
2007 Proof	500	Value: 475				

KM# 1480 10 EURO
8.4500 g., 0.9200 Gold 0.2499 oz. AGW, 22 mm. **Subject:** Airbus A380 **Obv:** Airplane **Rev:** Europa head and flags

Date	Mintage	F	VF	XF	Unc	BU
2007 Proof	1,000	Value: 475				

KM# 1485 10 EURO
8.4500 g., 0.9200 Gold 0.2499 oz. AGW, 22 mm. **Subject:** 2007 Rugby World Cup **Obv:** Two players and goal **Rev:** Logo and goal

Date	Mintage	F	VF	XF	Unc	BU
2007 Proof	500	Value: 475				

KM# 1489 10 EURO
8.4500 g., 0.9200 Gold 0.2499 oz. AGW, 22 mm. **Obv:** Christian Dior **Rev:** Dior Museum building

Date	Mintage	F	VF	XF	Unc	BU
2007 Proof	1,000	Value: 475				

KM# 1508 10 EURO
8.4500 g., 0.9200 Gold 0.2499 oz. AGW, 22 mm. **Subject:** Georges Remi Centennial **Obv:** Wand and sparkles **Rev:** Tin Tin raising cap

Date	Mintage	F	VF	XF	Unc	BU
2007 Proof	1,000	Value: 475				

KM# 1512 10 EURO
8.4500 g., 0.9200 Gold 0.2499 oz. AGW, 22 mm. **Subject:** Aristides de Sousa Mendes, Portuguese diplomat **Obv:** Bust right **Rev:** Plaque

Date	Mintage	F	VF	XF	Unc	BU
2007 Proof	500	Value: 475				

KM# 1519 10 EURO
8.4500 g., 0.9200 Gold 0.2499 oz. AGW, 22 mm. **Subject:** Asterix **Rev:** Character with torch

Date	Mintage	F	VF	XF	Unc	BU
2007 Proof	500	Value: 475				

KM# 1544 10 EURO
8.4500 g., 0.9200 Gold 0.2499 oz. AGW, 22 mm. **Subject:** 29th Summer Olympic Games - Beijing **Obv:** Swimmer and globe **Rev:** Diver and oriental screen

Date	Mintage	F	VF	XF	Unc	BU
2008 Proof	1,000	Value: 475				

KM# 1528 10 EURO
8.4500 g., 0.9200 Gold 0.2499 oz. AGW, 22 mm. **Subject:** French Presidency of European Union **Obv:** Text within stars **Rev:** Europa head and flags

Date	Mintage	F	VF	XF	Unc	BU
2008 Proof	1,000	Value: 475				

KM# 1533 10 EURO
8.4500 g., 0.9200 Gold 0.2499 oz. AGW, 22 mm. **Subject:** European Parliament, 50th Anniversary **Obv:** Map of EU within stars **Rev:** European Parliament Building in Strasbourg

Date	Mintage	F	VF	XF	Unc	BU
2008 Proof	3,000	Value: 475				

KM# 1539 10 EURO
8.4500 g., 0.9990 Gold 0.2714 oz. AGW, 22 mm. **Subject:** 5th Republic, 50th Anniversary **Obv:** The Seed Sower **Rev:** de Gaulle head right

Date	Mintage	F	VF	XF	Unc	BU
2008 Proof	1,000	Value: 475				

KM# 1547 10 EURO
8.4500 g., 0.9200 Gold 0.2499 oz. AGW, 22 mm. **Subject:** UEFA **Obv:** French soccer team **Rev:** UEFA logo

Date	Mintage	F	VF	XF	Unc	BU
2008 Proof	500	Value: 475				

KM# 1552 10 EURO
8.4500 g., 0.9200 Gold 0.2499 oz. AGW, 22 mm. **Subject:** Franco - Japanese Relators - 150th Anniversary **Obv:** Eiffel Tower and Kimono forming logo **Rev:** Delacroix's "La Liberte"

Date	Mintage	F	VF	XF	Unc	BU
2008 Proof	3,000	Value: 475				

KM# 1553 10 EURO
8.4500 g., 0.9200 Gold 0.2499 oz. AGW, 22 mm. **Subject:** Franco - Japanese Relators - 150th Anniversary **Obv:** Eiffel Tower and Kimono forming logo **Rev:** "Ichikawa Ebizo IV" portrait painting

Date	Mintage	F	VF	XF	Unc	BU
2008 Proof	3,000	Value: 475				

KM# 1554 10 EURO
8.4500 g., 0.9200 Gold 0.2499 oz. AGW, 22 mm. **Subject:** Franco - Japanese Relators - 150th Anniversary **Obv:** Eiffel Tower and Kimono forming logo **Rev:** Japanese cash coin from "Kanci Tsuho"

Date	Mintage	F	VF	XF	Unc	BU
2008 Proof	3,000	Value: 475				

KM# 1556 10 EURO
0.4500 g., 0.9200 Gold 0.0133 oz. AGW, 22 mm. **Subject:** André Citronë **Obv:** First front wheel drive auto **Rev:** Bust 1/4 left

Date	Mintage	F	VF	XF	Unc	BU
2008 Proof	500	Value: 475				

KM# 1559 10 EURO
8.4500 g., 0.9200 Gold 0.2499 oz. AGW, 22 mm. **Subject:** Rouen Armada **Obv:** Cape Hown, sextant, hour glass **Edge:** Sailing ship

Date	Mintage	F	VF	XF	Unc	BU
2008 Proof	500	Value: 475				

KM# 1562 10 EURO
8.4500 g., 0.9200 Gold 0.2499 oz. AGW, 22 mm. **Subject:** Lourdes, 150th Anniversary **Obv:** Church of Notre Dame at Lourdes **Rev:** Cross with Pope John Paul II, Pope Benedict XVI and Bernadette Soubirous in quadrants

Date	Mintage	F	VF	XF	Unc	BU
2008 Proof	1,000	Value: 475				

KM# 1573 10 EURO
8.4500 g., 0.9200 Gold 0.2499 oz. AGW, 22 mm. **Subject:** Lunar New Year - Year of the Rat **Obv:** Bust of Jean de la Fontaine and twelve awards **Rev:** Rat within border

Date	Mintage	F	VF	XF	Unc	BU
2008 Proof	500	Value: 475				

KM# 1575 10 EURO
8.4500 g., 0.9200 Gold 0.2499 oz. AGW, 22 mm. **Subject:** UNESCO - Grand Canyon **Obv:** Grand Canyon **Rev:** UNESCO logos

Date	Mintage	F	VF	XF	Unc	BU
2008 Proof	500	Value: 475				

KM# 1577 10 EURO
8.4500 g., 0.9200 Gold 0.2499 oz. AGW, 22 mm. **Subject:** International Polar Year **Obv:** IPY logo **Rev:** Emperor Penguin and map of Antartica

Date	Mintage	F	VF	XF	Unc	BU
2008 Proof	500	Value: 475				

KM# 1579 10 EURO
8.4500 g., 0.9200 Gold 0.2499 oz. AGW, 22 mm. **Subject:** Spirou, 70th Anniversary **Obv:** Character Spirou in thought **Rev:** 70th Aniversary logo

Date	Mintage	F	VF	XF	Unc	BU
2008 Proof	500	Value: 475				

KM# 1675 10 EURO
22.2000 g., 0.9000 Silver 0.6423 oz. ASW, 37 mm. **Obv:** Sower left **Rev:** Wheat and olive branch

Date	Mintage	F	VF	XF	Unc	BU
2009	—	—	—	—	30.00	
2010 Proof	10,000	Value: 35.00				

KM# 1591 10 EURO
27.2000 g., 0.9000 Silver 0.7870 oz. ASW, 37 mm. **Subject:** Europa - Fall of Berlin Wall **Obv:** Brandenburg gate and doves in flight **Rev:** Head facing and flags

Date	Mintage	F	VF	XF	Unc	BU
2009P Proof	10,000	Value: 37.50				

KM# 1580 10 EURO
12.0000 g., 0.9000 Silver 0.3472 oz. ASW, 29 mm. **Obv:** Modernistic sower advancing right **Rev:** Wreath and value

Date	Mintage	F	VF	XF	Unc	BU
2009P	2,000,000	—	—	—	—	17.50

KM# 1584 10 EURO
22.2000 g., 0.9000 Silver 0.6423 oz. ASW, 37 mm. **Subject:** Court of Human Rights, 50th Anniversary **Obv:** Sower left **Rev:** Text

Date	Mintage	F	VF	XF	Unc	BU
2009P Proof	10,000	Value: 35.00				

KM# 1596 10 EURO
22.2000 g., 0.9000 Silver 0.6423 oz. ASW, 37 mm. **Subject:** Concorde 40th Anniversary **Obv:** Concorde in flight **Rev:** Tail emblems

Date	Mintage	F	VF	XF	Unc	BU
2009P Proof	3,000	Value: 40.00				

KM# 1601   10 EURO
20.8900 g., 0.9000 Silver 0.6044 oz. ASW, 37 mm. **Obv:** Eiffel
Tower Structure **Rev:** Gustave Eiffel at left

Date	Mintage	F	VF	XF	Unc	BU
2009P Proof	10,000	Value: 35.00				

KM# 1606   10 EURO
27.2000 g., 0.9000 Silver 0.7870 oz. ASW, 37 mm. **Subject:**
Bugatti 100th Anniversary **Obv:** Ettore Bugatti at left **Rev:** Race
car and quilt motif

Date	Mintage	F	VF	XF	Unc	BU
2009P Proof	10,000	Value: 32.50				

KM# 1611   10 EURO
22.2000 g., 0.9000 Silver 0.6423 oz. ASW, 37 mm. **Subject:**
Curie Institute, 100th Anniversary

Date	Mintage	F	VF	XF	Unc	BU
2009P Proof	10,000	Value: 35.00				

KM# 1616   10 EURO
27.2000 g., 0.9000 Silver 0.7870 oz. ASW, 37 mm. **Subject:**
Unesco site - The Kremlin in Moscow **Obv:** Wall Tower and
cathedral

Date	Mintage	F	VF	XF	Unc	BU
2009P Proof	20,000	Value: 37.50				

KM# 1621   10 EURO
22.2000 g., 0.9000 Silver 0.6423 oz. ASW, 37 mm. **Subject:**
First Moon Landing, 40th Anniversary **Obv:** Footprint on the moon

Date	Mintage	F	VF	XF	Unc	BU
2009P Proof	10,000	Value: 35.00				

KM# 1629   10 EURO
22.2000 g., 0.9000 Silver 0.6423 oz. ASW, 37 mm. **Subject:**
Comic strip heroes **Obv:** Wanted posted **Rev:** Lucky Luke on
horseback

Date	Mintage	F	VF	XF	Unc	BU
2009P Proof	5,000	Value: 40.00				

KM# 1631   10 EURO
22.2000 g., 0.9000 Silver 0.6423 oz. ASW, 37 mm. **Obv:** Soccer
player **Rev:** Shield of Stade Francais in color

Date	Mintage	F	VF	XF	Unc	BU
2009P Proof	5,000	Value: 40.00				

KM# 1634   10 EURO
27.2000 g., 0.9000 Silver 0.7870 oz. ASW, 37 mm. **Subject:**
Alpine skiing **Obv:** Globe and downhill skier **Rev:** Downhill skier
on mountainside

Date	Mintage	F	VF	XF	Unc	BU
2009P Proof	10,000	Value: 37.50				

KM# 1636   10 EURO
22.2000 g., 0.9000 Silver 0.6423 oz. ASW, 37 mm. **Subject:**
FIFA World Cup, South Africa **Obv:** Soccer player on field **Rev:**
Soccerball, map of Africa, Prorea flower

Date	Mintage	F	VF	XF	Unc	BU
2009P Proof	15,000	Value: 35.00				

KM# 1645   10 EURO
12.0000 g., 0.9000 Silver 0.3472 oz. ASW, 29 mm. **Subject:**
Aquitaine **Rev:** Value at center, wreath horizontal

Date	Mintage	F	VF	XF	Unc	BU
2010	7,690	—	—	—	—	22.50

KM# 1646   10 EURO
12.0000 g., 0.9000 Silver 0.3472 oz. ASW, 29 mm. **Subject:**
Auvergne **Rev:** Value at center, wreath horizontal

Date	Mintage	F	VF	XF	Unc	BU
2010	7,690					

KM# 1647   10 EURO
12.0000 g., 0.9000 Silver 0.3472 oz. ASW, 29 mm. **Subject:**
Basse - Normandie **Rev:** Value at center, wreath horizontal

Date	Mintage	F	VF	XF	Unc	BU
2010	7,690	—	—	—	—	22.50

KM# 1648   10 EURO
12.0000 g., 0.9000 Silver 0.3472 oz. ASW, 29 mm. **Subject:**
Bretagne **Rev:** Value at center, wreath horizontal

Date	Mintage	F	VF	XF	Unc	BU
2010	7,690	—	—	—	—	22.50

KM# 1649   10 EURO
12.0000 g., 0.9000 Silver 0.3472 oz. ASW, 29 mm. **Subject:**
Burgundy **Rev:** Value at center, wreath horizontal

Date	Mintage	F	VF	XF	Unc	BU
2010	7,690	—	—	—	—	22.50

KM# 1650   10 EURO
12.0000 g., 0.9000 Silver 0.3472 oz. ASW, 29 mm. **Subject:**
Centre **Rev:** Value at center, wreath horizontal

Date	Mintage	F	VF	XF	Unc	BU
2010	7,690	—	—	—	—	22.50

KM# 1651   10 EURO
12.0000 g., 0.9000 Silver 0.3472 oz. ASW, 29 mm. **Subject:**
Champagne - Ardenne **Rev:** Value at center, wreath horizontal

Date	Mintage	F	VF	XF	Unc	BU
2010	7,690	—	—	—	—	22.50

KM# 1652   10 EURO
12.0000 g., 0.9000 Silver 0.3472 oz. ASW, 29 mm. **Subject:**
Alsace **Rev:** Value at center, wreath horizontal

Date	Mintage	F	VF	XF	Unc	BU
2010	7,690	—	—	—	—	22.50

KM# 1653   10 EURO
12.0000 g., 0.9000 Silver 0.3472 oz. ASW, 29 mm. **Subject:**
French - Comte **Rev:** Value at center, wreath horizontal

Date	Mintage	F	VF	XF	Unc	BU
2010	7,690	—	—	—	—	22.50

KM# 1654   10 EURO
12.0000 g., 0.9000 Silver 0.3472 oz. ASW, 29 mm. **Subject:**
French Guiana **Rev:** Value at center, wreath horizontal

Date	Mintage	F	VF	XF	Unc	BU
2010	7,690	—	—	—	—	22.50

KM# 1655   10 EURO
12.0000 g., 0.9000 Silver 0.3472 oz. ASW, 29 mm. **Subject:**
Guadeloupe **Rev:** Value at center, wreath horizontal

Date	Mintage	F	VF	XF	Unc	BU
2010	7,690	—	—	—	—	22.50

KM# 1656   10 EURO
12.0000 g., 0.9000 Silver 0.3472 oz. ASW, 29 mm. **Subject:**
Haute - Normandie **Rev:** Value at center, wreath horizontal

Date	Mintage	F	VF	XF	Unc	BU
2010	7,690	—	—	—	—	22.50

KM# 1657   10 EURO
12.0000 g., 0.9000 Silver 0.3472 oz. ASW, 29 mm. **Subject:**
Ile-de-France **Rev:** Value at center, wreath horizontal

Date	Mintage	F	VF	XF	Unc	BU
2010	7,690	—	—	—	—	22.50

KM# 1658   10 EURO
12.0000 g., 0.9000 Silver 0.3472 oz. ASW, 29 mm. **Subject:**
Corsica **Rev:** Value at center, wreath horizontal

Date	Mintage	F	VF	XF	Unc	BU
2010	7,690	—	—	—	—	22.50

KM# 1659   10 EURO
12.0000 g., 0.9000 Silver 0.3472 oz. ASW, 29 mm. **Subject:**
Languedoc - Roussillon **Rev:** Value at center, wreath horizontal

Date	Mintage	F	VF	XF	Unc	BU
2010	7,690	—	—	—	—	22.50

KM# 1660   10 EURO
12.0000 g., 0.9000 Silver 0.3472 oz. ASW, 29 mm. **Subject:**
Limousin **Rev:** Value at center, wreath horizontal

Date	Mintage	F	VF	XF	Unc	BU
2010	7,690	—	—	—	—	22.50

KM# 1661   10 EURO
12.0000 g., 0.9000 Silver 0.3472 oz. ASW, 29 mm. **Subject:**
Lorroaine **Rev:** Value at center, wreath horizontal

Date	Mintage	F	VF	XF	Unc	BU
2010	7,690	—	—	—	—	22.50

KM# 1662   10 EURO
12.0000 g., 0.9000 Silver 0.3472 oz. ASW, 29 mm. **Subject:**
Martinique **Rev:** Value at center, wreath horizontal

Date	Mintage	F	VF	XF	Unc	BU
2010	7,690	—	—	—	—	22.50

KM# 1663   10 EURO
12.0000 g., 0.9000 Silver 0.3472 oz. ASW, 29 mm. **Subject:**
Midi - Pyrenees **Rev:** Value at center, wreath horizontal

Date	Mintage	F	VF	XF	Unc	BU
2010	7,690	—	—	—	—	—

KM# 1664   10 EURO
12.0000 g., 0.9000 Silver 0.3472 oz. ASW, 29 mm. **Subject:**
Nord - Pas de - Calais **Rev:** Value at center, wreath horizontal

Date	Mintage	F	VF	XF	Unc	BU
2010	7,690	—	—	—	—	22.50

KM# 1665   10 EURO
12.0000 g., 0.9000 Silver 0.3472 oz. ASW, 29 mm. **Subject:**
Pays de la Loire **Rev:** Value at center, wreath horizontal

Date	Mintage	F	VF	XF	Unc	BU
2010	7,690	—	—	—	—	22.50

KM# 1666   10 EURO
12.0000 g., 0.9000 Silver 0.3472 oz. ASW, 29 mm. **Subject:**
Picardie **Rev:** Value at center, wreath horizontal

Date	Mintage	F	VF	XF	Unc	BU
2010	7,690	—	—	—	—	22.50

KM# 1667   10 EURO
12.0000 g., 0.9000 Silver 0.3472 oz. ASW, 29 mm. **Subject:**
Poitou - Charentes **Rev:** Value at center, wreath horizontal

Date	Mintage	F	VF	XF	Unc	BU
2010	7,690	—	—	—	—	22.50

KM# 1668   10 EURO
12.0000 g., 0.9000 Silver 0.3472 oz. ASW, 29 mm. **Subject:**
Provence - Alpes - Cote d'Azur **Rev:** Value at center, wreath
horizontal

Date	Mintage	F	VF	XF	Unc	BU
2010	7,690	—	—	—	—	22.50

KM# 1669   10 EURO
12.0000 g., 0.9000 Silver 0.3472 oz. ASW, 29 mm. **Subject:**
Reunion **Rev:** Value at center, wreath horizontal

Date	Mintage	F	VF	XF	Unc	BU
2010	7,690	—	—	—	—	22.50

KM# 1670   10 EURO
12.0000 g., 0.9000 Silver 0.3472 oz. ASW, 29 mm. **Subject:**
Rhone - Alpes **Rev:** Value at center, wreath horizontal

Date	Mintage	F	VF	XF	Unc	BU
2010	7,690	—	—	—	—	22.50

KM# 1681   10 EURO
22.2000 g., 0.9990 Silver 0.7130 oz. ASW, 37 mm. **Subject:**
Cluny Abbey, 1100th Anniversary **Obv:** Europa head facing **Rev:**
Cluny Abbey

Date	Mintage	F	VF	XF	Unc	BU
2010 Proof	10,000	Value: 50.00				

KM# 1686   10 EURO
22.2000 g., 0.9000 Silver 0.6423 oz. ASW, 37 mm. **Obv:**
Georges Pompidou Center design **Rev:** Design detail

Date	Mintage	F	VF	XF	Unc	BU
2010 Proof	30,000	Value: 40.00				

KM# 1691   10 EURO
22.2000 g., Nickel-Copper Aeronotical alloy, 37 mm. **Obv:**
Marcel Dassault **Rev:** Mirage III plane

Date	Mintage	F	VF	XF	Unc	BU
2010 Proof	20,000	Value: 45.00				

KM# 1695   10 EURO
22.2000 g., 0.9000 Silver 0.6423 oz. ASW, 37 mm. **Obv:** Mother
Teresa and child **Rev:** Mother Teresa and Pope John Paul II

Date	Mintage	F	VF	XF	Unc	BU
2010 Proof	20,000	Value: 40.00				

KM# 1700   10 EURO
22.2000 g., 0.9000 Silver 0.6423 oz. ASW, 37 mm. **Obv:** Taj
Mahal **Rev:** UNESCO offices

Date	Mintage	F	VF	XF	Unc	BU
2010 Proof	10,000	Value: 55.00				

KM# 1705   10 EURO
22.2000 g., 0.9000 Silver 0.6423 oz. ASW, 37 mm. **Obv:** Lille
station and route map **Rev:** Three TGV trains

Date	Mintage	F	VF	XF	Unc	BU
2010 Proof	30,000	Value: 35.00				

KM# 1708   10 EURO
15.0000 g., 0.9000 Silver 0.4340 oz. ASW, 30x21 mm. **Rev:**
Georges Braque **Shape:** Rectangle

Date	Mintage	F	VF	XF	Unc	BU
2010 Proof	20,000	Value: 50.00				

KM# 1713   10 EURO
15.0000 g., 0.9000 Silver 0.4340 oz. ASW, 30x21 mm. **Rev:**
Picasso **Shape:** Rectangle

Date	Mintage	F	VF	XF	Unc	BU
2010 Proof	20,000	Value: 60.00				

KM# 1717   10 EURO
22.2000 g., 0.9000 Silver 0.6423 oz. ASW, 37 mm. **Obv:** Blake
and Mortimer **Rev:** "Secret of the Swordfish" scene, arrest of Col.
Olrik.

Date	Mintage	F	VF	XF	Unc	BU
2010 Proof	10,000	Value: 50.00				

KM# 1720   10 EURO
22.2000 g., 0.9000 Silver 0.6423 oz. ASW, 37 mm. **Obv:**
Handball player and globe **Rev:** Handball player, net and Big Ben

Date	Mintage	F	VF	XF	Unc	BU
2010 Proof	10,000	Value: 40.00				

KM# 1722   10 EURO
22.2000 g., 0.9000 Silver 0.6423 oz. ASW, 37 mm. **Obv:** Soccer
player **Rev:** Stade Toulousain logo, multicolor

Date	Mintage	F	VF	XF	Unc	BU
2010 Proof	5,000	Value: 50.00				

KM# 1726   10 EURO
10.0000 g., 0.5000 Silver 0.1607 oz. ASW, 29 mm. **Subject:**
Mayotte **Obv:** Value at center, wreath horizontal

Date	Mintage	F	VF	XF	Unc	BU
2011	—	—	—	—	—	20.00

KM# 1727   10 EURO
10.0000 g., 0.5000 Silver 0.1607 oz. ASW, 29 mm. **Subject:**
Aquitaine

Date	Mintage	F	VF	XF	Unc	BU
2011	—	—	—	—	—	20.00

KM# 1728   10 EURO
10.0000 g., 0.5000 Silver 0.1607 oz. ASW, 29 mm. **Subject:**
Auvergne

Date	Mintage	F	VF	XF	Unc	BU
2011	—	—	—	—	—	20.00

KM# 1729   10 EURO
10.0000 g., 0.5000 Silver 0.1607 oz. ASW, 29 mm. **Subject:**
Basse - Normindie

Date	Mintage	F	VF	XF	Unc	BU
2011	—	—	—	—	—	20.00

KM# 1730   10 EURO
10.0000 g., 0.5000 Silver 0.1607 oz. ASW, 29 mm. **Subject:**
Bretagne

Date	Mintage	F	VF	XF	Unc	BU
2011	—	—	—	—	—	20.00

KM# 1731   10 EURO
10.0000 g., 0.5000 Silver 0.1607 oz. ASW, 29 mm. **Subject:** Burgundy

Date	Mintage	F	VF	XF	Unc	BU
2011	—	—	—	—	—	20.00

KM# 1732   10 EURO
10.0000 g., 0.5000 Silver 0.1607 oz. ASW, 29 mm. **Subject:** Centre

Date	Mintage	F	VF	XF	Unc	BU
2011	—	—	—	—	—	20.00

KM# 1733   10 EURO
10.0000 g., 0.5000 Silver 0.1607 oz. ASW, 29 mm. **Subject:** Campagne - Ardenne

Date	Mintage	F	VF	XF	Unc	BU
2011	—	—	—	—	—	20.00

KM# 1734   10 EURO
10.0000 g., 0.5000 Silver 0.1607 oz. ASW, 29 mm. **Subject:** Alsace

Date	Mintage	F	VF	XF	Unc	BU
2011	—	—	—	—	—	20.00

KM# 1735   10 EURO
10.0000 g., 0.5000 Silver 0.1607 oz. ASW, 29 mm. **Subject:** France - Comte

Date	Mintage	F	VF	XF	Unc	BU
2011	—	—	—	—	—	20.00

KM# 1736   10 EURO
10.0000 g., 0.5000 Silver 0.1607 oz. ASW, 29 mm. **Subject:** French Guiana

Date	Mintage	F	VF	XF	Unc	BU
2011	—	—	—	—	—	20.00

KM# 1737   10 EURO
10.0000 g., 0.5000 Silver 0.1607 oz. ASW, 29 mm. **Subject:** Guadeloupe

Date	Mintage	F	VF	XF	Unc	BU
2011	—	—	—	—	—	20.00

KM# 1738   10 EURO
10.0000 g., 0.5000 Silver 0.1607 oz. ASW, 29 mm. **Subject:** Haute - Normandie

Date	Mintage	F	VF	XF	Unc	BU
2011	—	—	—	—	—	20.00

KM# 1739   10 EURO
10.0000 g., 0.5000 Silver 0.1607 oz. ASW, 29 mm. **Subject:** Ile de France

Date	Mintage	F	VF	XF	Unc	BU
2011	—	—	—	—	—	20.00

KM# 1740   10 EURO
10.0000 g., 0.5000 Silver 0.1607 oz. ASW, 29 mm. **Subject:** Corsica

Date	Mintage	F	VF	XF	Unc	BU
2011	—	—	—	—	—	20.00

KM# 1741   10 EURO
10.0000 g., 0.5000 Silver 0.1607 oz. ASW, 29 mm. **Subject:** Lansuedoc - Rossillon

Date	Mintage	F	VF	XF	Unc	BU
2011	—	—	—	—	—	20.00

KM# 1742   10 EURO
10.0000 g., 0.5000 Silver 0.1607 oz. ASW, 29 mm. **Subject:** Limousin

Date	Mintage	F	VF	XF	Unc	BU
2011	—	—	—	—	—	20.00

KM# 1743   10 EURO
10.0000 g., 0.5000 Silver 0.1607 oz. ASW, 29 mm. **Subject:** Lorroaine

Date	Mintage	F	VF	XF	Unc	BU
2011	—	—	—	—	—	20.00

KM# 1744   10 EURO
10.0000 g., 0.5000 Silver 0.1607 oz. ASW, 29 mm. **Subject:** Martinique

Date	Mintage	F	VF	XF	Unc	BU
2011	—	—	—	—	—	20.00

KM# 1745   10 EURO
10.0000 g., 0.5000 Silver 0.1607 oz. ASW, 29 mm. **Subject:** Nord Pas de Calais

Date	Mintage	F	VF	XF	Unc	BU
2011	—	—	—	—	—	20.00

KM# 1746   10 EURO
10.0000 g., 0.5000 Silver 0.1607 oz. ASW, 29 mm. **Subject:** Pays de la Loire

Date	Mintage	F	VF	XF	Unc	BU
2011	—	—	—	—	—	20.00

KM# 1747   10 EURO
10.0000 g., 0.5000 Silver 0.1607 oz. ASW, 29 mm. **Subject:** Picardie

Date	Mintage	F	VF	XF	Unc	BU
2011	—	—	—	—	—	20.00

KM# 1748   10 EURO
10.0000 g., 0.5000 Silver 0.1607 oz. ASW, 29 mm. **Subject:** Poitou - Charentes

Date	Mintage	F	VF	XF	Unc	BU
2011	—	—	—	—	—	20.00

KM# 1749   10 EURO
10.0000 g., 0.5000 Silver 0.1607 oz. ASW, 29 mm. **Subject:** Province - Alpes - Cote d'Azur

Date	Mintage	F	VF	XF	Unc	BU
2011	—	—	—	—	—	20.00

KM# 1750   10 EURO
10.0000 g., 0.5000 Silver 0.1607 oz. ASW, 29 mm. **Subject:** Reunion

Date	Mintage	F	VF	XF	Unc	BU
2011	—	—	—	—	—	20.00

KM# 1751   10 EURO
10.0000 g., 0.5000 Silver 0.1607 oz. ASW, 29 mm. **Subject:** Phone - Alpes

Date	Mintage	F	VF	XF	Unc	BU
2011	—	—	—	—	—	20.00

KM# 1752   10 EURO
10.0000 g., 0.5000 Silver 0.1607 oz. ASW, 29 mm. **Subject:** Midi - Pyreneis

Date	Mintage	F	VF	XF	Unc	BU
2011	—	—	—	—	—	20.00

KM# 1784   10 EURO
22.2000 g., 0.9000 Silver 0.6423 oz. ASW, 37 mm. **Subject:** Euro Starter Kit, 10th Anniversary **Obv:** Sower left **Rev:** Euro starter kit

Date	Mintage	F	VF	XF	Unc	BU
2011 Proof	10,000	Value: 40.00				

KM# 1790   10 EURO
22.2000 g., 0.9000 Silver 0.6423 oz. ASW, 37 mm. **Subject:** International Music Day, 30th Anniversary **Obv:** Europa **Rev:** Youth jamming

Date	Mintage	F	VF	XF	Unc	BU
2011 Proof	10,000	Value: 40.00				

KM# 1795   10 EURO
22.2000 g., 0.9000 Silver 0.6423 oz. ASW, 37 mm. **Subject:** Great Explorers - Jacques Cartier **Obv:** The Grand Hermine sailing away **Rev:** Cartier, globe and compass rose

Date	Mintage	F	VF	XF	Unc	BU
2011 Proof	30,000	Value: 50.00				

KM# 1800   10 EURO
22.2000 g., 0.9000 Silver 0.6423 oz. ASW, 37 mm. **Subject:** Colvis, 481-511 **Obv:** Hands over chalice, reign dates at left, value at right **Rev:** Crowned head left

Date	Mintage	F	VF	XF	Unc	BU
2011 Proof	20,000	Value: 50.00				

KM# 1802   10 EURO
22.2000 g., 0.9000 Silver 0.6423 oz. ASW, 37 mm. **Subject:** Charlemagne, 768-814 **Obv:** Cross on orb, reight dates at left, value at right **Rev:** Crowned head left

Date	Mintage	F	VF	XF	Unc	BU
2011 Proof	20,000	Value: 50.00				

KM# 1804   10 EURO
22.2000 g., 0.9000 Silver 0.6423 oz. ASW, 37 mm. **Subject:** Charles II, 840-877 **Obv:** KARLOS monogram **Rev:** Crowned head left

Date	Mintage	F	VF	XF	Unc	BU
2011 Proof	20,000	Value: 50.00				

KM# 1806   10 EURO
22.2000 g., 0.9000 Silver 0.6423 oz. ASW, 37 mm. **Subject:** WWF - Audouin's Gull **Obv:** Gull in flight right **Rev:** Gull standing right, WWF panda logo

Date	Mintage	F	VF	XF	Unc	BU
2011 Proof	20,000	Value: 50.00				

KM# 1809   10 EURO
22.2000 g., 0.9000 Silver 0.6423 oz. ASW, 37 mm. **Subject:** UNESCO World Heritage Site - Palace of Versailles **Obv:** Building and garden plan **Rev:** Top view of UNESCO's Paris headquarters

Date	Mintage	F	VF	XF	Unc	BU
2011 Proof	20,000	Value: 50.00				

KM# 1814   10 EURO
22.2000 g., 0.9000 Silver 0.6423 oz. ASW, 37 mm. **Obv:** Metz
railroad station **Rev:** TGV and ICE trains

Date	Mintage	F	VF	XF	Unc	BU
2011 Proof	10,000	Value: 50.00				

KM# 1819   10 EURO
15.0000 g., 0.9000 Silver 0.4340 oz. ASW, 30x21 mm. **Subject:**
Vassily Kandinsky **Shape:** Rectangle

Date	Mintage	F	VF	XF	Unc	BU
2011 Proof	10,000	Value: 60.00				

KM# 1823   10 EURO
15.0000 g., 0.9000 Silver 0.4340 oz. ASW, 31 mm. **Subject:**
Andy Warhol **Obv:** Portrait facing **Rev:** Dollar sign in color

Date	Mintage	F	VF	XF	Unc	BU
2011 Proof	10,000	Value: 60.00				

KM# 1827   10 EURO
22.2000 g., 0.9000 Silver 0.6423 oz. ASW, 37 mm. **Obv:**
Cosette - Les Miserables **Rev:** Victor Hugo

Date	Mintage	F	VF	XF	Unc	BU
2011 Proof	10,000	Value: 50.00				

KM# 1829   10 EURO
22.2000 g., 0.9000 Silver 0.6423 oz. ASW, 37 mm. **Obv:** Nana
Rev: Emile Zola

Date	Mintage	F	VF	XF	Unc	BU
2011 Proof	5,000	Value: 50.00				

KM# 1831   10 EURO
22.2000 g., 0.9000 Silver 0.6423 oz. ASW, 37 mm. **Obv:** The
Stranger **Rev:** Albert Camus

Date	Mintage	F	VF	XF	Unc	BU
2011 Proof	—	Value: 50.00				

KM# 1835   10 EURO
22.2000 g., 0.9000 Silver 0.6423 oz. ASW, 37 mm. **Subject:**
Comic Strip XIII **Obv:** Montage of characters **Rev:** Profile left and
large XIII

Date	Mintage	F	VF	XF	Unc	BU
2011 Proof	10,000	Value: 50.00				

KM# 1755   10 EURO
22.2000 g., 0.9000 Silver 0.6423 oz. ASW, 37 mm. **Obv:** Bicycle
racer **Rev:** Metro 92 logo

Date	Mintage	F	VF	XF	Unc	BU
2011 Proof	5,000	Value: 50.00				

KM# 1838   10 EURO
22.2000 g., 0.9000 Silver 0.6423 oz. ASW, 37 mm. **Obv:** Female
figure skater and globe **Rev:** Figure skating pair

Date	Mintage	F	VF	XF	Unc	BU
2011 Proof	10,000	Value: 50.00				

KM# 1850   10 EURO
22.2000 g., 0.9000 Silver 0.6423 oz. ASW, 27 mm. **Subject:**
Eurocorps, 20th Anniversary **Obv:** Mitterrand and Kohl standing
clasping hands **Rev:** Europa facing

Date	Mintage	F	VF	XF	Unc	BU
2012(a) Proof	10,000	Value: 35.00				

KM# 1856   10 EURO
22.2000 g., 0.9000 Silver 0.6423 oz. ASW, 37 mm. **Subject:**
Hugues Capet **Obv:** Crowned head faicing **Rev:** Right hand
raised in benidiction

Date	Mintage	F	VF	XF	Unc	BU
2012(a) Proof	20,000	Value: 35.00				

KM# 1857   10 EURO
22.2000 g., 0.9000 Silver 0.6423 oz. ASW, 37 mm. **Subject:**
Saint Louis **Obv:** Crowned head facing **Rev:** Oak tree

Date	Mintage	F	VF	XF	Unc	BU
2012(a) Proof	20,000	Value: 35.00				

KM# 1859   10 EURO
22.2000 g., 0.9000 Silver 0.6423 oz. ASW, 37 mm. **Subject:**
The Three Musketeers **Obv:** D'Artagnan, cross emblem and
three musketeers standing with swords raised **Rev:** Musketeers
motto: "Un pour tours…" at left, Alexandre Dumas portrait at right

Date	Mintage	F	VF	XF	Unc	BU
2012(a) Proof	5,000	Value: 35.00				

KM# 1862   10 EURO
10.0000 g., 0.5000 Silver 0.1607 oz. ASW, 29 mm. **Subject:**
Mayotte **Obv:** Value at center, wreath horizontal

Date	Mintage	F	VF	XF	Unc	BU
2012(a)	—	—	—	—	—	20.00

KM# 1863   10 EURO
10.0000 g., 0.5000 Silver 0.1607 oz. ASW, 29 mm. **Subject:**
Aquitaine **Obv:** Value at center, wreath horizontal

Date	Mintage	F	VF	XF	Unc	BU
2012(a)	—	—	—	—	—	20.00

KM# 1864   10 EURO
10.0000 g., 0.5000 Silver 0.1607 oz. ASW, 29 mm. **Subject:**
Auvergne **Obv:** Value at center, wreath horizontal

Date	Mintage	F	VF	XF	Unc	BU
2012(a)	—	—	—	—	—	20.00

KM# 1865   10 EURO
10.0000 g., 0.5000 Silver 0.1607 oz. ASW, 29 mm. **Subject:**
Basse - Normandie **Obv:** Value at center, wreath horizontal

Date	Mintage	F	VF	XF	Unc	BU
2012(a)	—	—	—	—	—	20.00

KM# 1866   10 EURO
10.0000 g., 0.5000 Silver 0.1607 oz. ASW, 29 mm. **Subject:**
Bretagne **Obv:** Value at center, wreath horizontal

Date	Mintage	F	VF	XF	Unc	BU
2012(a)	—	—	—	—	—	20.00

KM# 1867   10 EURO
10.0000 g., 0.5000 Silver 0.1607 oz. ASW, 29 mm. **Subject:**
Burgundy **Obv:** Value at center, wreath horizontal

Date	Mintage	F	VF	XF	Unc	BU
2012(a)	—	—	—	—	—	20.00

KM# 1868   10 EURO
10.0000 g., 0.5000 Silver 0.1607 oz. ASW, 29 mm. **Subject:**
Centre **Obv:** Value at center, wreath horizontal

Date	Mintage	F	VF	XF	Unc	BU
2012(a)	—	—	—	—	—	20.00

KM# 1869   10 EURO
10.0000 g., 0.5000 Silver 0.1607 oz. ASW, 29 mm. **Subject:**
Champagne - Ardenne **Obv:** Value at center, wreath horizontal

Date	Mintage	F	VF	XF	Unc	BU
2012(a)	—	—	—	—	—	20.00

KM# 1870   10 EURO
10.0000 g., 0.5000 Silver 0.1607 oz. ASW, 29 mm. **Subject:**
Alsace **Obv:** Value at center, wreath horizontal

Date	Mintage	F	VF	XF	Unc	BU
2012(a)	—	—	—	—	—	20.00

KM# 1871   10 EURO
10.0000 g., 0.5000 Silver 0.1607 oz. ASW, 29 mm. **Subject:**
France - Comte

Date	Mintage	F	VF	XF	Unc	BU
2012(a)	—	—	—	—	—	20.00

KM# 1872   10 EURO
10.0000 g., 0.5000 Silver 0.1607 oz. ASW, 29 mm. **Subject:**
French Guiana **Obv:** Value at center, wreath horizontal

Date	Mintage	F	VF	XF	Unc	BU
2012(a)	—	—	—	—	—	20.00

KM# 1873   10 EURO
10.0000 g., 0.5000 Silver 0.1607 oz. ASW, 29 mm. **Subject:**
Guadeloupe **Obv:** Value at center, wreath horizontal

Date	Mintage	F	VF	XF	Unc	BU
2012(a)	—	—	—	—	—	20.00

KM# 1874   10 EURO
10.0000 g., 0.5000 Silver 0.1607 oz. ASW, 29 mm. **Subject:**
Haute - Normandie **Obv:** Value at center, wreath horizontal

Date	Mintage	F	VF	XF	Unc	BU
2012(a)	—	—	—	—	—	20.00

KM# 1875   10 EURO
10.0000 g., 0.5000 Silver 0.1607 oz. ASW, 29 mm. **Subject:** Ile
de France **Obv:** Value at center, wreath horizontal

Date	Mintage	F	VF	XF	Unc	BU
2012(a)	—	—	—	—	—	20.00

KM# 1876   10 EURO
10.0000 g., 0.5000 Silver 0.1607 oz. ASW, 29 mm. **Subject:**
Corsica **Obv:** Value at center, wreath horizontal

Date	Mintage	F	VF	XF	Unc	BU
2012(a)	—	—	—	—	—	20.00

KM# 1877   10 EURO
10.0000 g., 0.5000 Silver 0.1607 oz. ASW, 29 mm. **Subject:**
Lansuedoc - Rossillon **Obv:** Value at center, wreath horizontal

Date	Mintage	F	VF	XF	Unc	BU
2012(a)	—	—	—	—	—	20.00

KM# 1878   10 EURO
10.0000 g., 0.5000 Silver 0.1607 oz. ASW, 29 mm. **Subject:**
Limousin **Obv:** Value at center, wreath horizontal

Date	Mintage	F	VF	XF	Unc	BU
2012(a)	—	—	—	—	—	20.00

KM# 1879   10 EURO
10.0000 g., 0.5000 Silver 0.1607 oz. ASW, 29 mm. **Subject:**
Martinique **Obv:** Value at center, wreath horizontal

Date	Mintage	F	VF	XF	Unc	BU
2012(a)	—	—	—	—	—	20.00

KM# 1880   10 EURO
10.0000 g., 0.5000 Silver 0.1607 oz. ASW, 29 mm. **Subject:**
Nord Pas de Calais **Obv:** Value at center, wreath horizontal

Date	Mintage	F	VF	XF	Unc	BU
2012(a)	—	—	—	—	—	20.00

KM# 1881   10 EURO
10.0000 g., 0.5000 Silver 0.1607 oz. ASW, 29 mm. **Subject:**
Pays de la Loire **Obv:** Value at center, wreath horizontal

Date	Mintage	F	VF	XF	Unc	BU
2012(a)	—	—	—	—	—	20.00

KM# 1882   10 EURO
10.0000 g., 0.5000 Silver 0.1607 oz. ASW, 29 mm. **Subject:**
Picardie **Obv:** Value at center, wreath horizontal

Date	Mintage	F	VF	XF	Unc	BU
2012(a)	—	—	—	—	—	20.00

KM# 1883   10 EURO
10.0000 g., 0.5000 Silver 0.1607 oz. ASW, 29 mm. **Subject:**
Poitou - Charentes **Obv:** Value at center, wreath horizontal

Date	Mintage	F	VF	XF	Unc	BU
2012(a)	—	—	—	—	—	20.00

KM# 1884   10 EURO
10.0000 g., 0.5000 Silver 0.1607 oz. ASW, 29 mm. **Subject:**
Province - Alpes - Cote d'Azur **Obv:** Value at center, wreath
horizontal

Date	Mintage	F	VF	XF	Unc	BU
2012(a)	—	—	—	—	—	20.00

KM# 1885   10 EURO
10.0000 g., 0.5000 Silver 0.1607 oz. ASW, 29 mm. **Subject:**
Reunion **Obv:** Value at center, wreath horizontal

Date	Mintage	F	VF	XF	Unc	BU
2012(a)	—	—	—	—	—	20.00

KM# 1886 10 EURO
10.0000 g., 0.5000 Silver 0.1607 oz. ASW, 29 mm. **Subject:** Phone - Alpes **Obv:** Value at center, wreath horizontal

Date	Mintage	F	VF	XF	Unc	BU
2012(a)	—	—	—	—	—	20.00

KM# 1887 10 EURO
10.0000 g., 0.5000 Silver 0.1607 oz. ASW, 29 mm. **Subject:** Midi - Pyreneis **Obv:** Value at center, wreath horizontal

Date	Mintage	F	VF	XF	Unc	BU
2012(a)	—	—	—	—	—	20.00

KM# 1888 10 EURO
10.0000 g., 0.5000 Silver 0.1607 oz. ASW, 29 mm. **Subject:** Lorroaine **Obv:** Value at center, wreath horizontal

Date	Mintage	F	VF	XF	Unc	BU
2012(a)	—	—	—	—	—	20.00

KM# 1889 10 EURO
22.2000 g., 0.9000 Silver 0.6423 oz. ASW, 37 mm. **Subject:** Euro, 10th Anniversary **Obv:** The Sower advaning left **Rev:** Value at center on globe, child-like drawings around

Date	Mintage	F	VF	XF	Unc	BU
2012(a) Proof	15,000	Value: 35.00				

KM# 1895 10 EURO
22.2000 g., 0.9000 Silver 0.6423 oz. ASW, 37 mm. **Subject:** abbé Pierre, 100th anniversary of Birth **Obv:** Pierre at left, shadow at right **Rev:** Emmaus Internaitonal logo and quote

Date	Mintage	F	VF	XF	Unc	BU
2012(a) Proof	10,000	Value: 35.00				

KM# 1905 10 EURO
22.2000 g., 0.9000 Silver 0.6423 oz. ASW, 37 mm. **Subject:** UNESCO - World Heritage Site **Obv:** Abu Simbel temple **Rev:** Sphinx and Pyramids

Date	Mintage	F	VF	XF	Unc	BU
2012(a) Proof	10,000	Value: 35.00				

KM# 1911 10 EURO
22.2000 g., 0.9000 Silver 0.6423 oz. ASW, 37 mm. **Subject:** TGV South-East **Obv:** Lyon Saint-Exupery station **Rev:** Two modern locomotives

Date	Mintage	F	VF	XF	Unc	BU
2012(a) Proof	5,000	Value: 35.00				

KM# 1916 10 EURO
22.2000 g., 0.9000 Silver 0.6423 oz. ASW, 37 mm. **Subject:** Comic strip hero **Obv:** Largo Winch and building **Rev:** Winch riding motorcycle being chased by two cars

Date	Mintage	F	VF	XF	Unc	BU
2012(a) Proof	5,000	Value: 35.00				

KM# 1919 10 EURO
22.2000 g., 0.9000 Silver 0.6423 oz. ASW, 37 mm. **Subject:** Toulonnais Rugby Club **Obv:** Value and Stadium field view **Rev:** Colored shield and portrait Felix Mayol

Date	Mintage	F	VF	XF	Unc	BU
2012(a) Proof	5,000	Value: 45.00				

KM# 1921 10 EURO
22.2000 g., 0.9000 Silver 0.6423 oz. ASW, 37 mm. **Subject:** 2012 Summer Olympics, London **Obv:** Two judo athletes and map of Europe **Rev:** Two judo athletes

Date	Mintage	F	VF	XF	Unc	BU
2012(a) Proof	10,000	Value: 35.00				

KM# 1924 10 EURO
22.2000 g., 0.9000 Silver 0.6423 oz. ASW **Subject:** Year of the Dragon **Obv:** Dragon **Rev:** La Fontaine and zodiac animals **Shape:** 37

Date	Mintage	F	VF	XF	Unc	BU
2012(a) Proof	10,000	Value: 45.00				

KM# A1450 15 EURO
31.0000 g., 0.9000 Silver 0.8970 oz. ASW, 31 mm. **Rev:** Pantheon

Date	Mintage	F	VF	XF	Unc	BU
2007 Proof	7,500	Value: 75.00				

KM# 1535 15 EURO
15.0000 g., 0.9000 Silver 0.4340 oz. ASW, 31 mm. **Obv:** Sower, half length advancing right **Rev:** Value within hexagon

Date	Mintage	F	VF	XF	Unc	BU
2008	500,000	—	—	—	45.00	
2008 Proof	7,500	Value: 55.00				
2009 Proof	7,500	Value: 55.00				

KM# 1333 20 EURO
17.0000 g., 0.9200 Gold 0.5028 oz. AGW, 31 mm. **Obv:** Victor Hugo, denomination and map **Rev:** "Gavroche" **Edge:** Plain

Date	Mintage	F	VF	XF	Unc	BU
2002 Proof	2,000	Value: 875				

KM# 1306 20 EURO
17.0000 g., 0.9200 Gold 0.5028 oz. AGW, 31 mm. **Subject:** French Landmarks **Obv:** French map **Rev:** Le Mont St. Michel **Edge:** Plain

Date	Mintage	F	VF	XF	Unc	BU
2002 Proof	1,000	Value: 875				

KM# 1308 20 EURO
17.0000 g., 0.9200 Gold 0.5028 oz. AGW, 31 mm. **Subject:** French Landmarks **Obv:** French map **Rev:** La Butte Montmartre **Edge:** Plain

Date	Mintage	F	VF	XF	Unc	BU
2002 Proof	1,000	Value: 875				

KM# 1327 20 EURO
8.4500 g., 0.9200 Gold 0.2499 oz. AGW, 31 mm. **Obv:** Tour de France logo **Rev:** Group of cyclists and Arch de Triumph **Edge:** Reeded

Date	Mintage	F	VF	XF	Unc	BU
2003A Proof	5,000	Value: 475				

KM# 1328 20 EURO
8.4500 g., 0.9200 Gold 0.2499 oz. AGW, 31 mm. **Obv:** Tour de France logo **Rev:** Two cyclists and spectators **Edge:** Reeded

Date	Mintage	F	VF	XF	Unc	BU
2003A Proof	5,000	Value: 475				

KM# 1329 20 EURO
8.4500 g., 0.9200 Gold 0.2499 oz. AGW, 31 mm. **Obv:** Tour de France logo **Rev:** Two groups of cyclists **Edge:** Reeded

Date	Mintage	F	VF	XF	Unc	BU
2003A Proof	5,000	Value: 475				

KM# 1330 20 EURO
8.4500 g., 0.9200 Gold 0.2499 oz. AGW, 31 mm. **Obv:** Tour de France logo **Rev:** Cyclist, stop watch and gears **Edge:** Reeded

Date	Mintage	F	VF	XF	Unc	BU
2003A Proof	5,000	Value: 4.75				

KM# 1334 20 EURO
17.0000 g., 0.9200 Gold 0.5028 oz. AGW, 31 mm. **Obv:** Tour de France logo **Rev:** Cyclist going left **Edge:** Plain

Date	Mintage	F	VF	XF	Unc	BU
2003 Proof	5,000	Value: 875				

KM# 1337 20 EURO
17.0000 g., 0.9200 Gold 0.5028 oz. AGW, 31 mm. **Obv:** Jefferson and Napoleon with Louisiana Purchase map **Rev:** Jazz musician, mansion and river boat **Edge:** Plain

Date	Mintage	F	VF	XF	Unc	BU
2003 Proof	1,000	Value: 875				

KM# 1339 20 EURO
17.0000 g., 0.9200 Gold 0.5028 oz. AGW, 31 mm. **Obv:** Curved cross design with multiple values **Rev:** Goddess Europa and flags **Edge:** Plain

Date	Mintage	F	VF	XF	Unc	BU
2003 Proof	3,000	Value: 875				

KM# 1342 20 EURO
17.0000 g., 0.9200 Gold 0.5028 oz. AGW, 31 mm. **Obv:** Denomination and compass face **Rev:** SS Normandie and New York City skyline **Edge:** Plain

Date	Mintage	F	VF	XF	Unc	BU
2003 Proof	1,000	Value: 875				

KM# 1344 20 EURO
17.0000 g., 0.9200 Gold 0.5028 oz. AGW, 31 mm. **Obv:** Denomination and compass face **Rev:** Airplane and Tokyo Geisha **Edge:** Plain

Date	Mintage	F	VF	XF	Unc	BU
2003 Proof	1,000	Value: 875				

KM# 1346 20 EURO
17.0000 g., 0.9200 Gold 0.5028 oz. AGW, 31 mm. **Obv:** Paul Gauguin **Rev:** Native woman **Edge:** Plain

Date	Mintage	F	VF	XF	Unc	BU
2003 Proof	2,000	Value: 875				

KM# 1349 20 EURO
17.0000 g., 0.9200 Gold 0.5028 oz. AGW, 31 mm. **Obv:** The Seed Sower **Rev:** Denomination and map **Edge:** Plain

Date	Mintage	F	VF	XF	Unc	BU
2003 Proof	5,000	Value: 875				

KM# 1354 20 EURO
17.0000 g., 0.9200 Gold 0.5028 oz. AGW, 31 mm. **Obv:** Mona Lisa **Rev:** Leonardo da Vinci and denomination **Edge:** Plain

Date	Mintage	F	VF	XF	Unc	BU
2003 Proof	1,000	Value: 875				

KM# 1356 20 EURO
17.0000 g., 0.9200 Gold 0.5028 oz. AGW, 31 mm. **Obv:** Map and denomination **Rev:** Chateau Chambord **Edge:** Plain

Date	Mintage	F	VF	XF	Unc	BU
2003 Proof	1,000	Value: 875				

KM# 1358 20 EURO
17.0000 g., 0.9200 Gold 0.5028 oz. AGW, 31 mm. **Obv:** Denomination in swirling design **Rev:** Hansel and Gretel, witch and house **Edge:** Plain

Date	Mintage	F	VF	XF	Unc	BU
2003 Proof	1,000	Value: 875				

KM# 1360 20 EURO
17.0000 g., 0.9200 Gold 0.5028 oz. AGW, 31 mm. **Obv:** Denomination in swirling design **Rev:** Alice in Wonderland **Edge:** Plain

Date	Mintage	F	VF	XF	Unc	BU
2003 Proof	1,000	Value: 875				

KM# 1363 20 EURO
17.0000 g., 0.9200 Gold 0.5028 oz. AGW, 31 mm. **Obv:** Pierre de Coubertin **Rev:** Olympic runners **Edge:** Plain

Date	Mintage	F	VF	XF	Unc	BU
2003 Proof	3,000	Value: 875				

KM# 1365 20 EURO
17.0000 g., 0.9200 Gold 0.5028 oz. AGW, 31 mm. **Obv:** Map with denomination **Rev:** Avignon Popes Palace **Edge:** Plain

Date	Mintage	F	VF	XF	Unc	BU
2004 Proof	1,000	Value: 875				

KM# 1370 20 EURO
17.0000 g., 0.9200 Gold 0.5028 oz. AGW, 31 mm. **Obv:** Soldiers and Normandy invasion scene **Rev:** "D-DAY" above denomination **Edge:** Plain

Date	Mintage	F	VF	XF	Unc	BU
2004 Proof	2,000	Value: 875				

KM# 1376 20 EURO
17.0000 g., 0.9200 Gold 0.5028 oz. AGW, 31 mm. **Subject:** Centenary Law of Dec. 9, 1905 **Obv:** "Sower" left in ring of stars **Rev:** Denomination and French map face design **Edge:** Plain

Date	Mintage	F	VF	XF	Unc	BU
2004 Proof	3,000	Value: 875				
2006 Proof	1,000	Value: 875				

KM# 1379 20 EURO
17.0000 g., 0.9200 Gold 0.5028 oz. AGW, 31 mm. **Obv:** Compass rose **Rev:** Ocean liner **Edge:** Plain

Date	Mintage	F	VF	XF	Unc	BU
2004 Proof	1,000	Value: 875				

KM# 1381 20 EURO
17.0000 g., 0.9200 Gold 0.5028 oz. AGW, 31 mm. **Obv:** Compass rose **Rev:** Trans-Siberian Railroad **Edge:** Plain

Date	Mintage	F	VF	XF	Unc	BU
2004 Proof	1,000	Value: 875				

KM# 1383 20 EURO
17.0000 g., 0.9200 Gold 0.5028 oz. AGW, 31 mm. **Obv:** Compass rose **Rev:** Half-track vehicle **Edge:** Plain

Date	Mintage	F	VF	XF	Unc	BU
2004 Proof	1,000	Value: 875				

KM# 1385 20 EURO
17.0000 g., 0.9200 Gold 0.5028 oz. AGW, 31 mm. **Obv:** Compass rose **Rev:** Biplane airliner **Edge:** Plain

Date	Mintage	F	VF	XF	Unc	BU
2004 Proof	1,000	Value: 875				

KM# 1387 20 EURO
155.5000 g., 0.9500 Silver 4.7493 oz. ASW, 50 mm. **Obv:** Statue of Liberty **Rev:** F. A. Bartholdi **Edge:** Plain

Date	Mintage	F	VF	XF	Unc	BU
2004 Proof	999	Value: 200				

KM# 1388   20 EURO
17.0000 g., 0.9200 Gold 0.5028 oz. AGW, 31 mm. **Obv:** Statue of Liberty **Rev:** F. A. Bartholdi **Edge:** Plain

Date	Mintage	F	VF	XF	Unc	BU
2004 Proof	2,000	Value: 875				

KM# 1393   20 EURO
17.0000 g., 0.9200 Gold 0.5028 oz. AGW, 31 mm. **Subject:** European Union Expansion **Obv:** Partial face and flags **Rev:** Puzzle map **Edge:** Plain

Date	Mintage	F	VF	XF	Unc	BU
2004 Proof	3,000	Value: 875				

KM# 1433   20 EURO
17.0000 g., 0.9200 Gold 0.5028 oz. AGW, 31 mm. **Subject:** Bicentennial Victory at Austerlitz **Rev:** Battle scene **Rev. Legend:** LIBERTÉ ÉGALITÉ FRATERNITÉ

Date	Mintage	F	VF	XF	Unc	BU
2005 Proof	5,000	Value: 875				

KM# 1437   20 EURO
17.0000 g., 0.9200 Gold 0.5028 oz. AGW, 31 mm. **Subject:** Centenary - Law of Dec. 9, 1905 **Obv:** "Sower" at left in ring of stars

Date	Mintage	F	VF	XF	Unc	BU
2005 Proof	1,500	Value: 875				

KM# 1454   20 EURO
155.5000 g., 0.9500 Silver 4.7493 oz. ASW, 50 mm. **Subject:** 100th Anniversary - Paul Cézanne's death **Obv:** Self portrait **Rev:** "The Card Players" **Rev. Legend:** LIBERTÉ ÉGALITÉ FRATERNITÉ

Date	Mintage	F	VF	XF	Unc	BU
2006 Proof	500	Value: 225				

KM# 1443   20 EURO
155.5200 g., 0.9500 Silver 4.7499 oz. ASW, 50 mm. **Obv:** Bust of Franklin facing slightly right at left, his diplomatic and technical successes at right **Obv. Legend:** BENJAMIN FRANKLIN 1706-2006 **Obv. Inscription:** AMI DE LA FRANCE

Date	Mintage	F	VF	XF	Unc	BU
2006 Proof	500	Value: 225				

KM# 1520   20 EURO
155.5000 g., 0.9500 Silver 4.7493 oz. ASW, 50 mm. **Subject:** Asterix **Rev:** Character running downhill

Date	Mintage	F	VF	XF	Unc	BU
2007 Proof	500	Value: 325				

KM# 1468   20 EURO
17.0000 g., 0.9200 Gold 0.5028 oz. AGW, 31 mm. **Subject:** Le Petit Prince, 60th Anniversary **Obv:** Prince lying in field

Date	Mintage	F	VF	XF	Unc	BU
2007 Proof	2,000	Value: 875				

KM# 1471   20 EURO
155.5500 g., 0.9500 Silver 4.7508 oz. ASW, 50 mm. **Obv:** Two dragons in flight **Rev:** Merlin and Excalibur

Date	Mintage	F	VF	XF	Unc	BU
2007 Proof	500	Value: 300				

KM# 1472   20 EURO
17.0000 g., 0.9200 Gold 0.5028 oz. AGW, 31 mm. **Obv:** Two dragons in flight **Rev:** Merlin & Excalibur

Date	Mintage	F	VF	XF	Unc	BU
2007 Proof	500	Value: 875				

KM# 1494   20 EURO
155.5500 g., 0.9500 Silver 4.7508 oz. ASW, 50 mm. **Subject:** Point Neuf - 400th Anniversary **Obv:** Moments of France logo **Rev:** Point Neuf Bridge and Paris Mint Building

Date	Mintage	F	VF	XF	Unc	BU
2007 Proof	500	Value: 300				

KM# 1496   20 EURO
155.5500 g., 0.9500 Silver 4.7508 oz. ASW, 50 mm. **Subject:** Cannes Film Festival, 60th Anniversary **Obv:** Cinema screen and stage, Golden Palm Award

Date	Mintage	F	VF	XF	Unc	BU
2007 Proof	500	Value: 300				

KM# 1499   20 EURO
17.0000 g., 0.9200 Gold 0.5028 oz. AGW, 30 x 21 mm. **Subject:** Edgar Degas, 90th Anniversary of Seuth **Obv:** Degas painting of dancer **Rev:** Brushes and Degas portrait **Shape:** Rectangle

Date	Mintage	F	VF	XF	Unc	BU
2007 Proof	500	Value: 1,000				

KM# 1509   20 EURO
100.0000 g., 0.9500 Silver 3.0542 oz. ASW, 49 mm. **Subject:** Georges Remi Centennial **Rev:** Tin Tin and Snowy

Date	Mintage	F	VF	XF	Unc	BU
2007 Proof	500	Value: 325				

KM# 1513   20 EURO
155.5000 g., 0.9500 Silver 4.7493 oz. ASW, 50 mm. **Subject:** Stanislas Leszczynski **Obv:** Bust and shield **Rev:** Palace Stanislas - Nancy

Date	Mintage	F	VF	XF	Unc	BU
2007 Proof	500	Value: 325				

KM# 1521   20 EURO
17.0000 g., 0.9200 Gold 0.5028 oz. AGW, 31 mm. **Subject:** Asterix **Rev:** Asterix and Cleopatria

Date	Mintage	F	VF	XF	Unc	BU
2007 Proof	500	Value: 875				

KM# 1529   20 EURO
163.8000 g., 0.9500 Silver 5.0028 oz. ASW, 50 mm. **Subject:** French Presidency of European Union **Obv:** Text within stars **Rev:** Europa head and flags

Date	Mintage	F	VF	XF	Unc	BU
2008 Proof	500	Value: 250				

KM# 1540   20 EURO
163.8000 g., 0.9500 Silver 5.0028 oz. ASW, 50 mm. **Subject:** 5th Republic, 50th Anniversary **Obv:** Sower **Rev:** de Gaulle head right

Date	Mintage	F	VF	XF	Unc	BU
2008 Proof	500	Value: 250				

KM# 1541   20 EURO
17.0000 g., 0.9205 Gold 0.5031 oz. AGW, 31 mm. **Subject:** 5th Republic, 50th Anniversary **Obv:** Sower **Rev:** de Gaulle head right

Date	Mintage	F	VF	XF	Unc	BU
2008 Proof	500	Value: 875				

KM# 1557   20 EURO
163.8000 g., 0.9500 Silver 5.0028 oz. ASW, 50 mm. **Subject:** André Citronë **Obv:** First front wheel drive auto **Rev:** Bust 1/4 left

Date	Mintage	F	VF	XF	Unc	BU
2008 Proof	500	Value: 325				

KM# 1560   20 EURO
163.8000 g., 0.9500 Silver 5.0028 oz. ASW, 50 mm. **Subject:** Rouen Armada **Obv:** Cape Horn, sextant, hour glass **Rev:** Sailing ship

Date	Mintage	F	VF	XF	Unc	BU
2008 Proof	—	Value: 350				

KM# 1563   20 EURO
163.8000 g., 0.9500 Silver 5.0028 oz. ASW, 50 mm. **Subject:** Lourdes, 150th Anniversary **Obv:** Church of Notre Dame at Lourdes **Rev:** Cross with Pope John Paul II, Pope Benedict XVI and Bernadette Soubirous in quadrants

Date	Mintage	F	VF	XF	Unc	BU
2008 Proof	500	Value: 300				

KM# 1571   20 EURO
17.0000 g., 0.9200 Gold 0.5028 oz. AGW, 30 x 21 mm. **Subject:** Edward Manet **Obv:** Manet's "Olympia" painting **Rev:** Paint brushes and Manet's portrait **Shape:** Rectangle

Date	Mintage	F	VF	XF	Unc	BU
2008 Proof	500	Value: 875				

KM# 1602   20 EURO
44.4000 g., 0.9000 Silver 1.2847 oz. ASW, 37 mm. **Obv:** Eiffel Tower Structure **Rev:** Gustave Eiffel at left

Date	Mintage	F	VF	XF	Unc	BU
2009P Proof	5,000	Value: 100				

KM# 1607   20 EURO
44.4000 g., 0.9000 Silver 1.2847 oz. ASW, 37 mm. **Subject:** Bugatti 100th Anniversary **Obv:** Ettore Bugatti at left **Rev:** Race car and grill motif

Date	Mintage	F	VF	XF	Unc	BU
2009P Proof	5,000	Value: 100				

KM# 1612   20 EURO
44.4000 g., 0.9000 Silver 1.2847 oz. ASW, 37 mm. **Subject:** Curie Institute, 100th Anniversary

Date	Mintage	F	VF	XF	Unc	BU
2009P Proof	5,000	Value: 70.00				

KM# 1690   20 EURO
44.4000 g., 0.9000 Silver 1.2847 oz. ASW, 37 mm. **Obv:** Marcel Dassault **Rev:** Mirage III plane

Date	Mintage	F	VF	XF	Unc	BU
2010 Proof	2,000	Value: 75.00				

KM# 1704   20 EURO
44.4000 g., 0.9000 Silver 1.2847 oz. ASW, 37 mm. **Obv:** Lille station and route map **Rev:** Three TGV trains

Date	Mintage	F	VF	XF	Unc	BU
2010 Proof	2,000	Value: 75.00				

KM# 1815   20 EURO
44.4000 g., 0.9000 Silver 1.2847 oz. ASW, 37 mm. **Obv:** Metz railroad station **Rev:** TGV and ICE trains

Date	Mintage	F	VF	XF	Unc	BU
2011 Proof	1,000	Value: 100				

KM# 1912   20 EURO
44.4000 g., 0.9000 Silver 1.2847 oz. ASW, 37 mm. **Subject:** TGV South East **Obv:** Lyon Saint-Exupery station **Rev:** Two modern locomotives

Date	Mintage	F	VF	XF	Unc	BU
2012(a) Proof	1,000	Value: 75.00				

KM# 1581   25 EURO
18.0000 g., 0.9000 Silver 0.5208 oz. ASW, 33 mm. **Obv:** Modernistic sower advancing right **Rev:** Value and wreath

Date	Mintage	F	VF	XF	Unc	BU
2009P	250,000	—	—	—	—	35.00

KM# 1303   50 EURO
31.0000 g., 0.9990 Gold 0.9956 oz. AGW, 37 mm. **Subject:** Europa **Obv:** Eight French euro coin designs **Rev:** Portrait and flags design of 6.55957 francs KM-1265 **Edge:** Plain

Date	Mintage	F	VF	XF	Unc	BU
2002 Proof	2,000	Value: 1,700				

KM# 1335   50 EURO
31.1000 g., 0.9990 Gold 0.9988 oz. AGW, 37 mm. **Obv:** Tour de France logo **Rev:** Cyclist going left **Edge:** Plain

Date	Mintage	F	VF	XF	Unc	BU
2003 Proof	1,500	Value: 1,700				

KM# 1340   50 EURO
1000.0000 g., 0.9500 Silver 30.541 oz. ASW, 100 mm. **Obv:** Curved cross design with multiple values **Rev:** Goddess Europa and flags **Edge:** Plain with three line inscription at six o'clock

Date	Mintage	F	VF	XF	Unc	BU
2003 Proof	2,000	Value: 1,150				

KM# 1368   50 EURO
31.1000 g., 0.9990 Gold 0.9988 oz. AGW, 37 mm. **Obv:** Book, denomination and eagle **Rev:** Napoleon and coronation scene **Edge:** Plain

Date	Mintage	F	VF	XF	Unc	BU
2004 Proof	2,000	Value: 1,700				

KM# 1394   50 EURO
31.1040 g., 0.9990 Gold 0.9990 oz. AGW, 37 mm. **Subject:** European Union Expansion **Obv:** Partial face and flags **Rev:** Puzzle map **Edge:** Plain

Date	Mintage	F	VF	XF	Unc	BU
2004 Proof	2,000	Value: 1,700				

KM# 1430   50 EURO
31.1040 g., 0.9990 Gold 0.9990 oz. AGW, 37 mm. **Rev:** Kitty and Daniel in Versailles **Rev. Legend:** Hello Kitty

Date	Mintage	F	VF	XF	Unc	BU
2005 Proof	1,000	Value: 1,700				

KM# 1466   50 EURO
31.1050 g., 0.9990 Gold 0.9990 oz. AGW, 37 mm. **Subject:** Le Petit Prince, 60th Anniversary **Obv:** Prince standing

Date	Mintage	F	VF	XF	Unc	BU
2007 Proof	2,000	Value: 1,700				

KM# 1481   50 EURO
31.1040 g., 0.9990 Gold 0.9988 oz. AGW, 37 mm. **Subject:** Airbus A380 **Obv:** Airplane **Rev:** Europa and flags

Date	Mintage	F	VF	XF	Unc	BU
2007 Proof	500	Value: 1,700				

KM# 1487   50 EURO
1000.0000 g., 0.9500 Silver 30.541 oz. ASW **Subject:** 2007 Rugby World Cup **Obv:** Two players and goal **Rev:** Logo and goal **Shape:** Oval

Date	Mintage	F	VF	XF	Unc	BU
2007 Proof	299	Value: 1,250				

KM# 1510   50 EURO
31.1050 g., 0.9990 Gold 0.9990 oz. AGW, 37 mm. **Subject:** Georges Remi Centennial **Obv:** Wand and sparkles **Rev:** Tin Tin and dog Snowy

Date	Mintage	F	VF	XF	Unc	BU
2007 Proof	500	Value: 1,700				

KM# 1522   50 EURO
31.0500 g., 0.9990 Gold 0.9972 oz. AGW, 37 mm. **Subject:** Asterix **Rev:** Asterix and the Butcher of Arverne

Date	Mintage	F	VF	XF	Unc	BU
2007 Proof	500	Value: 1,700				

KM# 1530   50 EURO
31.1040 g., 0.9990 Gold 0.9990 oz. AGW, 37 mm. **Subject:** French Presidency of the Euopean Union **Obv:** Text within stars **Rev:** Europa head within flags

Date	Mintage	F	VF	XF	Unc	BU
2008 Proof	500	Value: 1,700				

KM# 1564   50 EURO
31.1040 g., 0.9990 Gold 0.9990 oz. AGW, 37 mm. **Subject:** Lourdes, 150th Anniversary **Obv:** Church of Notre Dame at Lourdes **Rev:** Cross with Pope John Paul II, Pope Benedict XVI and Bernadette Soubirous in quadrants

Date	Mintage	F	VF	XF	Unc	BU
2008 Proof	500	Value: 1,700				

KM# 1603   50 EURO
163.8000 g., 0.9500 Silver 5.0028 oz. ASW, 50 mm. **Obv:** Eiffel Tower Structure **Rev:** Gustave Eiffel at left

Date	Mintage	F	VF	XF	Unc	BU
2009P Proof	1,000	Value: 250				

KM# 1597   50 EURO
163.8000 g., 0.9500 Silver 5.0028 oz. ASW, 50 mm. **Subject:** Concorde 40th Anniversary **Obv:** Concorde in flight **Rev:** Tail emblems

Date	Mintage	F	VF	XF	Unc	BU
2009P Proof	1,000	Value: 250				

KM# 1585   50 EURO
163.8000 g., 0.9500 Silver 5.0028 oz. ASW, 50 mm. **Subject:** Court of Human Rights, 50th Anniversary **Obv:** Sower left **Rev:** Text

Date	Mintage	F	VF	XF	Unc	BU
2009P Proof	500	Value: 275				

KM# 1592   50 EURO
8.4500 g., 0.9200 Gold 0.2499 oz. AGW, 22 mm. **Subject:** Europa - Fall of Berlin Wall **Obv:** Brandenburg gate and doves in flight **Rev:** Head facing and flags

Date	Mintage	F	VF	XF	Unc	BU
2009P	1,000	Value: 475				

KM# 1598   50 EURO
8.4500 g., 0.9200 Gold 0.2499 oz. AGW, 22 mm. **Subject:** Concorde 40th Anniversary **Obv:** Concorde in flight **Rev:** Tail emblems

Date	Mintage	F	VF	XF	Unc	BU
2009P Proof	3,000	Value: 475				

KM# 1604   50 EURO
8.4500 g., 0.9200 Gold 0.2499 oz. AGW, 22 mm. **Obv:** Eiffel Tower Structure **Rev:** Gustave Eiffel at left

Date	Mintage	F	VF	XF	Unc	BU
2009P Proof	1,000	Value: 475				

KM# 1608   50 EURO
163.8000 g., 0.9500 Silver 5.0028 oz. ASW, 50 mm. **Subject:** Bugatti 100th Anniverary **Obv:** Ettore Bugatti at left **Rev:** Race car and grill motif

Date	Mintage	F	VF	XF	Unc	BU
2009P Proof	500	Value: 275				

KM# 1609   50 EURO
8.4500 g., 0.9200 Gold 0.2499 oz. AGW, 22 mm. **Subject:** Bugatti 100th Anniversary **Obv:** Ettore Bugatti at left **Rev:** Race car and grill motif

Date	Mintage	F	VF	XF	Unc	BU
2009P Proof	1,000	Value: 475				

KM# 1613   50 EURO
163.8000 g., 0.9500 Silver 5.0028 oz. ASW, 50 mm. **Subject:** Curie Institute, 100th Anniversary

Date	Mintage	F	VF	XF	Unc	BU
2009P Proof	500	Value: 275				

KM# 1614   50 EURO
8.4500 g., 0.9200 Gold 0.2499 oz. AGW, 22 mm. **Subject:** Curie Institute, 100th Anniversary

Date	Mintage	F	VF	XF	Unc	BU
2009P Proof	1,000	Value: 475				

KM# 1618   50 EURO
8.4500 g., 0.9200 Gold 0.2499 oz. AGW, 22 mm. **Subject:** Unesco site - the Kremlin in Moscow **Obv:** Wall Tower and cathedral

Date	Mintage	F	VF	XF	Unc	BU
2009P Proof	1,000	Value: 475				

KM# 1622   50 EURO
163.8000 g., 0.9500 Silver 5.0028 oz. ASW, 50 mm. **Subject:** First Moon Landing, 40th Anniversary **Obv:** Footprint on the moon

Date	Mintage	F	VF	XF	Unc	BU
2009P Proof	500	Value: 275				

KM# 1623   50 EURO
8.4500 g., 0.9200 Gold 0.2499 oz. AGW, 22 mm. **Subject:** First Moon Landing, 40th Anniversary **Obv:** Footprint on the moon

Date	Mintage	F	VF	XF	Unc	BU
2009P Proof	1,000	Value: 475				

KM# 1628   50 EURO
8.4500 g., 0.9200 Gold 0.2499 oz. AGW, 22 mm. **Subject:** Year of the Ox **Obv:** Oxen within Asian screen **Rev:** Portrait of LaFontaine

Date	Mintage	F	VF	XF	Unc	BU
2009P Proof	500	Value: 475				

KM# 1630   50 EURO
8.4500 g., 0.9200 Gold 0.2499 oz. AGW, 22 mm. **Subject:** Comic strip heroes **Obv:** Wanted Poster **Rev:** Lucky Luke on horseback

Date	Mintage	F	VF	XF	Unc	BU
2009P Proof	1,000	Value: 475				

KM# 1632   50 EURO
8.4500 g., 0.9200 Gold 0.2499 oz. AGW, 22 mm. **Obv:** Rugby player **Rev:** State Francais

Date	Mintage	F	VF	XF	Unc	BU
2009P Proof	500	Value: 475				

KM# 1635   50 EURO
8.4500 g., 0.9200 Gold 0.2499 oz. AGW, 22 mm. **Subject:** Alpine skiing **Obv:** Globe and downhill skier **Rev:** Downhill skier on mountainside

Date	Mintage	F	VF	XF	Unc	BU
2009P Proof	1,000	Value: 475				

KM# 1637   50 EURO
163.8000 g., 0.9500 Silver 5.0028 oz. ASW, 50 mm. **Subject:**

FIFA World Cup, South Africa 2010 **Obv:** Soccer player on field **Rev:** Soccerball, Map of Africa, Protrea flower

Date	Mintage	F	VF	XF	Unc	BU
2009P Proof	500	Value: 275				

KM# 1638   50 EURO
8.4500 g., 0.9200 Gold 0.2499 oz. AGW, 22 mm. **Subject:** FIFA World Cup, South Africa 2010 **Obv:** Soccer Player on field **Rev:** Soccerball, Map of Africa, Protea flower

Date	Mintage	F	VF	XF	Unc	BU
2009P Proof	7,500	Value: 475				

KM# 1845   50 EURO
163.8000 g., 0.9500 Silver 5.0028 oz. ASW, 50 mm. **Subject:** UNESCO Site - The Kremlin in Moscow

Date	Mintage	F	VF	XF	Unc	BU
2009 Proof	—	Value: 275				

KM# 1644   50 EURO
36.0000 g., 0.9000 Silver 1.0416 oz. ASW, 36 mm. **Obv:** The Seed Sower advancing right, sun rays from above **Rev:** Value at center, wreath horizontal

Date	Mintage	F	VF	XF	Unc	BU
2010	100,000	—	—	—	—	45.00

KM# 1673   50 EURO
8.4500 g., 0.9200 Gold 0.2499 oz. AGW, 22 mm. **Obv:** The Seed Sower left **Rev:** Wheat and olive branch

Date	Mintage	F	VF	XF	Unc	BU
2010 Proof	500	Value: 475				

KM# 1679   50 EURO
8.4500 g., 0.9250 Gold 0.2513 oz. AGW, 22 mm. **Subject:** Cluny Abbey, 1100th Anniversary **Obv:** Europa head facing **Rev:** Cluney Abbey

Date	Mintage	F	VF	XF	Unc	BU
2010 Proof	1,000	Value: 475				

KM# 1684   50 EURO
8.4500 g., 0.9200 Gold 0.2499 oz. AGW, 22 mm. **Obv:** Georges Pompidou Center design **Rev:** Design detail

Date	Mintage	F	VF	XF	Unc	BU
2010 Proof	3,000	Value: 475				

KM# 1685   50 EURO
163.8000 g., 0.9500 Silver 5.0028 oz. ASW, 50 mm. **Obv:** Georges Pompidou Center design **Rev:** Design detail

Date	Mintage	F	VF	XF	Unc	BU
2010 Proof	1,000	Value: 225				

KM# 1688   50 EURO
8.4500 g., 0.9200 Gold 0.2499 oz. AGW, 22 mm. **Obv:** Marcel Dassault **Rev:** Mirage III plane

Date	Mintage	F	VF	XF	Unc	BU
2010 Proof	1,000	Value: 475				

KM# 1694   50 EURO
8.4500 g., 0.9200 Gold 0.2499 oz. AGW, 22 mm. **Obv:** Mother Teresa and child **Rev:** Mother Teresa and Pope John Paul II

Date	Mintage	F	VF	XF	Unc	BU
2010 Proof	1,000	Value: 475				

KM# 1699   50 EURO
8.4500 g., 0.9200 Gold 0.2499 oz. AGW, 22 mm. **Obv:** Taj Mahal **Rev:** UNESCO offices

Date	Mintage	F	VF	XF	Unc	BU
2010 Proof	1,000	Value: 475				

338 FRANCE

KM# 1702 50 EURO
8.4500 g., 0.9200 Gold 0.2499 oz. AGW, 22 mm. Obv: Lille station and route map Rev: Three TGV trains

Date	Mintage	F	VF	XF	Unc	BU
2010 Proof	1,000	Value: 475				

KM# 1703 50 EURO
163.8000 g., 0.9500 Silver 5.0028 oz. ASW, 50 mm. Obv: Lille station and route map Rev: Three TGV trains

Date	Mintage	F	VF	XF	Unc	BU
2010 Proof	500	Value: 275				

KM# 1714 50 EURO
8.4500 g., 0.9200 Gold 0.2499 oz. AGW, 22 mm. Obv: Tiger within border Rev: La Fontaine bust at left, animals at right

Date	Mintage	F	VF	XF	Unc	BU
2010 Proof	500	Value: 475				

KM# 1716 50 EURO
8.4500 g., 0.9200 Gold 0.2499 oz. AGW, 22 mm. Obv: Blake and Mortimer Rev: "Secret of the Swordfish" scene, the arrest of Col. Olrik

Date	Mintage	F	VF	XF	Unc	BU
2010 Proof	500	Value: 475				

KM# 1719 50 EURO
8.4500 g., 0.9200 Gold 0.2499 oz. AGW, 22 mm. Obv: Handball player on globe Rev: Handball player, net, Big Ben

Date	Mintage	F	VF	XF	Unc	BU
2010 Proof	1,000	Value: 475				

KM# 1721 50 EURO
8.4500 g., 0.9200 Gold 0.2499 oz. AGW, 22 mm. Obv: Soccer player Rev: Stade Toulousain logo, multicolor

Date	Mintage	F	VF	XF	Unc	BU
2010 Proof	500	Value: 475				

KM# 1786 50 EURO
8.4500 g., 0.9200 Gold 0.2499 oz. AGW, 22 mm. Subject: Euro Starter Kit, 10th Anniversary Obv: Sower Rev: Euro starter kit

Date	Mintage	F	VF	XF	Unc	BU
2011 Proof	3,000	Value: 475				

KM# 1792 50 EURO
8.4500 g., 0.9200 Gold 0.2499 oz. AGW, 22 mm. Subject: International Music Day, 30th Anniversary Obv: Europa Rev: Youth jamming

Date	Mintage	F	VF	XF	Unc	BU
2011 Proof	3,000	Value: 475				

KM# 1796 50 EURO
8.4500 g., 0.9200 Gold 0.2499 oz. AGW, 22 mm. Subject: Great Explorers - Jacques Cartier Obv: The Grande Hermine sailing away Rev: Carter, globe and compass rose

Date	Mintage	F	VF	XF	Unc	BU
2011 Proof	3,000	Value: 1,475				

KM# 1801 50 EURO
8.4500 g., 0.9200 Gold 0.2499 oz. AGW, 22 mm. Subject: Clovis, 481-511 Obv: Hands over chalice, reign dates at left, value at right Rev: Crowned head left

Date	Mintage	F	VF	XF	Unc	BU
2011 Proof	1,500	Value: 475				

KM# 1803 50 EURO
8.4500 g., 0.9200 Gold 0.2499 oz. AGW, 22 mm. Subject: Charlemagne, 768-814 Obv: Cross on orb, reight dates at left, value at right Rev: Crowned head left

Date	Mintage	F	VF	XF	Unc	BU
2011 Proof	1,500	Value: 475				

KM# 1805 50 EURO
8.4500 g., 0.9200 Gold 0.2499 oz. AGW, 22 mm. Subject: Charles II, 840-877 Obv: KARLOS monogram Rev: Crowned head left

Date	Mintage	F	VF	XF	Unc	BU
2011 Proof	1,500	Value: 475				

KM# 1807 50 EURO
8.4500 g., 0.9200 Gold 0.2499 oz. AGW, 22 mm. Subject: WWF - Audouin's Gull Obv: Gull in flight right Rev: Gull standing right, WWF logo at right

Date	Mintage	F	VF	XF	Unc	BU
2011 Proof	1,000	Value: 475				

KM# 1811 50 EURO
8.4500 g., 0.9200 Gold 0.2499 oz. AGW, 22 mm. Subject: UNESCO World Heritage Site - Palace of Versailles

Date	Mintage	F	VF	XF	Unc	BU
2011 Proof	1,000	Value: 475				

KM# 1816 50 EURO
163.8000 g., 0.9500 Silver 5.0028 oz. ASW, 50 mm. Obv: Metz railroad station Rev: TGV and ICE trains

Date	Mintage	F	VF	XF	Unc	BU
2011 Proof	500	Value: 250				

KM# 1817 50 EURO
8.4500 g., 0.9200 Gold 0.2499 oz. AGW, 22 mm. Obv: Metz railroad station Rev: TGV and ICE trains

Date	Mintage	F	VF	XF	Unc	BU
2011 Proof	1,000	Value: 475				

KM# 1828 50 EURO
8.4500 g., 0.9200 Gold 0.2499 oz. AGW, 22 mm. Obv: Cosette - Les Miserables Rev: Victor Hugo

Date	Mintage	F	VF	XF	Unc	BU
2011 Proof	3,000	Value: 475				

KM# 1830 50 EURO
8.4500 g., 0.9200 Gold 0.2499 oz. AGW, 22 mm. Obv: Nana Rev: Emile Zola

Date	Mintage	F	VF	XF	Unc	BU
2011 Proof	1,000	Value: 475				

KM# 1832 50 EURO
8.4500 g., 0.9200 Gold 0.2499 oz. AGW, 22 mm. Obv: The Stranger Rev: Albert Camus

Date	Mintage	F	VF	XF	Unc	BU
2011 Proof	—	Value: 475				

KM# 1834 50 EURO
8.4500 g., 0.9200 Gold 0.2499 oz. AGW, 22 mm. **Subject:** Year of the Rabbit **Obv:** Rabbit seated facing right **Rev:** Fontaine and animals

Date	Mintage	F	VF	XF	Unc	BU
2011 Proof	500	Value: 475				

KM# 1837 50 EURO
8.4500 g., 0.9200 Gold 0.2499 oz. AGW, 22 mm. **Obv:** Comic Characters **Rev:** Profile left and large XIII

Date	Mintage	F	VF	XF	Unc	BU
2011 Proof	1,000	Value: 475				

KM# 1839 50 EURO
8.4500 g., 0.9200 Gold 0.2499 oz. AGW, 22 mm. **Obv:** Female figure skater on globe **Rev:** Figure skating pair

Date	Mintage	F	VF	XF	Unc	BU
2011 Proof	1,000	Value: 475				

KM# 1756 50 EURO
8.4500 g., 0.9200 Gold 0.2499 oz. AGW, 22 mm. **Obv:** Bicycle racer **Rev:** Metro 92 logo

Date	Mintage	F	VF	XF	Unc	BU
2011 Proof	500	Value: 475				

KM# 1848 50 EURO
163.8000 g., 0.9250 Silver gilt 4.8711 oz. ASW, 50 mm. **Obv:** Battleship Jeanne de Arc **Rev:** WWII convoy image, anchor chain below

Date	Mintage	F	VF	XF	Unc	BU
2012(a) Proof	500	Value: 275				

KM# 1849 50 EURO
8.4500 g., 0.9200 Gold 0.2499 oz. AGW, 22 mm. **Obv:** SS France waterline view **Rev:** Winged funnels, porthole detail below

Date	Mintage	F	VF	XF	Unc	BU
2012(a) Proof	1,500	Value: 475				

KM# 1852 50 EURO
8.4500 g., 0.9200 Gold 0.2499 oz. AGW, 22 mm. **Subject:** Eurocorps, 20th Anniversary **Obv:** Mitterrand and Kohl standing clasping hands **Rev:** Europa facing

Date	Mintage	F	VF	XF	Unc	BU
2012(a) Proof	1,500	Value: 475				

KM# 1858 50 EURO
8.4500 g., 0.9200 Gold 0.2499 oz. AGW, 22 mm. **Subject:** Philippe II Auguste **Obv:** Crowned head facing **Rev:** The Louvre's original design

Date	Mintage	F	VF	XF	Unc	BU
2012(a) Proof	1,500	Value: 475				

KM# 1860 50 EURO
8.4500 g., 0.9200 Gold 0.2499 oz. AGW, 22 mm. **Subject:** Savinien Cyrano de Bergerac **Obv:** Half-length figure of Cyrano at left, Roxane on balcony at top right **Rev:** Quote at left, Edmond Rostand portrait at right

Date	Mintage	F	VF	XF	Unc	BU
2012(a) Proof	1,000	Value: 475				

KM# 1861 50 EURO
8.4500 g., 0.9200 Gold 0.2499 oz. AGW, 22 mm. **Subject:** Puss in boots **Obv:** Puss in boots stasnding, castle in background **Rev:** Quote at left, Charles Perrault portrait at right

Date	Mintage	F	VF	XF	Unc	BU
2012(a) Proof	1,000	Value: 475				

KM# 1891 50 EURO
8.4500 g., 0.9200 Gold 0.2499 oz. AGW, 22 mm. **Subject:** Euro, 10th Anniversary **Obv:** The Sower advancing left **Rev:** Value on globe, child-like renderings around

Date	Mintage	F	VF	XF	Unc	BU
2012(a) Proof	1,000	Value: 475				

KM# 1897 50 EURO
8.4500 g., 0.9200 Gold 0.2499 oz. AGW, 22 mm. **Subject:** abbé Pierre, 100th anniversary of Birth **Obv:** Pierre's bust at left, shaddow figure at right **Rev:** Emmaus International logo and quote

Date	Mintage	F	VF	XF	Unc	BU
2012(a) Proof	1,000	Value: 475				

KM# 1906 50 EURO
163.8000 g., 0.9500 Silver 5.0028 oz. ASW, 50 mm. **Subject:** UNESCO - World Heritage Site **Obv:** Abu Simbel temple **Rev:** Sphinx and Pyramids

Date	Mintage	F	VF	XF	Unc	BU
2012(a) Proof	500	Value: 250				

KM# 1908 50 EURO
8.4500 g., 0.9200 Gold 0.2499 oz. AGW, 22 mm. **Subject:** UNESCO - World Heritage Site **Obv:** Abu Simbel temple **Rev:** Sphinx and Pyramids

Date	Mintage	F	VF	XF	Unc	BU
2012(a) Proof	1,500	Value: 475				

KM# 1913 50 EURO
163.8000 g., 0.9500 Silver 5.0028 oz. ASW, 50 mm. **Subject:** TGV South-East **Obv:** Lyon Saint-Exupery station **Rev:** Two modern locomotives

Date	Mintage	F	VF	XF	Unc	BU
2012(a) Proof	500	Value: 250				

KM# 1914 50 EURO
8.4500 g., 0.9200 Gold 0.2499 oz. AGW, 22 mm. **Subject:** TGV Sud-East **Obv:** Lyon Saint-Exupery station **Rev:** Two modern locomotives

Date	Mintage	F	VF	XF	Unc	BU
2012(a) Proof	1,000	Value: 475				

KM# 1917 50 EURO
8.4500 g., 0.9200 Gold 0.2499 oz. AGW, 22 mm. **Subject:** Comic strip hero **Obv:** Largo Winch and building **Rev:** Winch riding motocycle being chased by two cars

Date	Mintage	F	VF	XF	Unc	BU
2012(a) Proof	500	Value: 475				

KM# 1920 50 EURO
8.4500 g., 0.9200 Gold 0.2499 oz. AGW, 22 mm. **Subject:** Toulonnais Rugby Club **Obv:** Value and stadium field view **Rev:** Shield and portrait of Felix Mayol

Date	Mintage	F	VF	XF	Unc	BU
2012(a) Proof	500	Value: 475				

KM# 1922 50 EURO
8.4500 g., 0.9200 Gold 0.2499 oz. AGW, 22 mm. **Subject:** 2012 Summer Olympics, London **Obv:** Two judo athletes and map of Europe **Rev:** Two judo athletes

Date	Mintage	F	VF	XF	Unc	BU
2012(a) Proof	1,000	Value: 475				

KM# 1925 50 EURO
8.4500 g., 0.9200 Gold 0.2499 oz. AGW, 22 mm. **Subject:** Year of the Dragon **Obv:** Dragon **Rev:** La Fontaine and zodiac animals

Date	Mintage	F	VF	XF	Unc	BU
2012(a) Proof	1,000	Value: 475				

KM# 1304 100 EURO
155.5175 g., 0.9990 Gold 4.9948 oz. AGW, 50 mm. **Subject:** Europa **Obv:** Eight French euro coin designs **Rev:** Portrait and flags design of 6.55957 francs KM-1265 **Edge:** Plain

Date	Mintage	F	VF	XF	Unc	BU
2002 Proof	99	Value: 8,400				

KM# 1377 100 EURO
155.5175 g., 0.9990 Gold 4.9948 oz. AGW, 50 mm. **Subject:** D-Day 60th Anniversary **Obv:** Soldiers and Normandy invasion scene **Rev:** "D-Day" inscription above denomination **Edge:** Plain

Date	Mintage	F	VF	XF	Unc	BU
2004 Proof	299	Value: 8,400				

KM# 1389 100 EURO
155.5000 g., 0.9990 Gold 4.9942 oz. AGW, 50 mm. **Obv:** Statue of Liberty **Rev:** F. A. Bartholdi **Edge:** Plain

Date	Mintage	F	VF	XF	Unc	BU
2004 Proof	99	Value: 8,400				

KM# 1395 100 EURO
155.5000 g., 0.9990 Gold 4.9958 oz. AGW, 50 mm. **Subject:** European Union Expansion **Obv:** Partial face and flags **Rev:** Puzzle map **Edge:** Plain

Date	Mintage	F	VF	XF	Unc	BU
2004 Proof	99	Value: 8,400				

KM# 1482 100 EURO
155.5500 g., 0.9990 Gold 4.9958 oz. AGW, 50 mm. **Subject:** Airbus A380 **Rev:** Europa head and flags

Date	Mintage	F	VF	XF	Unc	BU
2007 Proof	99	Value: 8,450				

KM# 1497 100 EURO
155.5000 g., 0.9990 Gold 4.9942 oz. AGW, 50 mm. **Subject:** Cannes Film Festival, 60th Anniversary **Obv:** Cinema screen and stage, Golden Palm Award

Date	Mintage	F	VF	XF	Unc	BU
2007 Proof	99	Value: 8,450				

KM# 1582 100 EURO
3.1000 g., 0.9990 Gold 0.0996 oz. AGW, 15 mm. **Obv:** Modernistic sower advancing right **Rev:** Value and wreath

Date	Mintage	F	VF	XF	Unc	BU
2008P	50,000	—	—	—	—	175
2009P	50,000	—	—	—	—	175
2010P	50,000	—	—	—	—	175

KM# 1531 100 EURO
155.5000 g., 0.9990 Gold 4.9942 oz. AGW, 50 mm. **Subject:** French Presidency of the European Union **Obv:** Text within stars **Rev:** Europa head and flags

Date	Mintage	F	VF	XF	Unc	BU
2008 Proof	99	Value: 8,400				

KM# 1536 100 EURO
3.1000 g., 0.9990 Gold 0.0996 oz. AGW, 15 mm. **Obv:** The Seed Sower, full length **Rev:** Hexagon

Date	Mintage	F	VF	XF	Unc	BU
2008 Proof	—	Value: 175				

KM# 1545 100 EURO
155.5000 g., 0.9990 Gold 4.9942 oz. AGW, 50 mm. **Subject:** 29th Summer Olympic Games - Beijing **Obv:** Swimmer and globe **Rev:** Diver and oriental screen

Date	Mintage	F	VF	XF	Unc	BU
2008 Proof	99	Value: 8,450				

KM# 1565 100 EURO
155.5000 g., 0.9990 Gold 4.9942 oz. AGW, 50 mm. **Subject:** Lourdes, 150th Anniversary **Obv:** Church of Notre Dame at Lourdes **Rev:** Cross with Pope John Paul II, Pope Benedict XVI and Bernadette Soubirous in quadrants

Date	Mintage	F	VF	XF	Unc	BU
2008 Proof	99	Value: 8,450				

KM# 1588 100 EURO
31.1050 g., 0.9200 Gold 0.9200 oz. AGW, 47 mm. **Subject:**

Court of Human Rights, 50th Anniversary **Obv:** The Seed Sower left **Rev:** Text

Date	Mintage	F	VF	XF	Unc	BU
2009P Proof	500	Value: 875				

KM# 1626   100 EURO
17.0000 g., 0.9200 Gold 0.5028 oz. AGW, 30 x 21 mm. **Subject:** Renoir **Obv:** Le dejuner des canotiers, 1881 painting **Rev:** Brushes and portrait **Shape:** Rectangle

Date	Mintage	F	VF	XF	Unc	BU
2009P Proof	500	Value: 875				

KM# 1643   100 EURO
3.1000 g., 0.9990 Gold 0.0996 oz. AGW, 15 mm. **Obv:** The Seed Sower advancing right, sun rays from above **Rev:** Value in center, wreath horizontal

Date	Mintage	F	VF	XF	Unc	BU
2010	50,000	—	—	—	—	175

KM# 1672   100 EURO
17.0000 g., 0.9200 Gold 0.5028 oz. AGW, 18 mm. **Obv:** The Seed Sower left **Rev:** Wheat and olive branch

Date	Mintage	F	VF	XF	Unc	BU
2010 Proof	500	Value: 900				

KM# 1689   100 EURO
327.6000 g., 0.9500 Silver 10.005 oz. ASW, 65 mm. **Obv:** Marcel Dassault **Rev:** Mirage III plane

Date	Mintage	F	VF	XF	Unc	BU
2010 Proof	500	Value: 375				

KM# 1707   100 EURO
17.0000 g., 0.9200 Gold 0.5028 oz. AGW, 30x21 mm. **Rev:** Georges Braque **Shape:** Rectangle

Date	Mintage	F	VF	XF	Unc	BU
2010 Proof	500	Value: 875				

KM# 1711   100 EURO
17.0000 g., 0.9200 Gold 0.5028 oz. AGW, 30x21 mm. **Rev:** Picasso **Shape:** Rectangle

Date	Mintage	F	VF	XF	Unc	BU
2010 Proof	500	Value: 875				

KM# 1724   100 EURO
50.0000 g., 0.9000 Silver 1.4467 oz. ASW, 47 mm. **Obv:** Value at center, wreath horizontal **Rev:** Hercules goup

Date	Mintage	F	VF	XF	Unc	BU
2011	50,000	—	—	—	—	150
2012	50,000	—	—	—	—	150

KM# 1787   100 EURO
17.0000 g., 0.9200 Gold 0.5028 oz. AGW, 31 mm. **Subject:** Euro Starter Kit, 10th Anniversary **Obv:** Sower **Rev:** Euro starter kit

Date	Mintage	F	VF	XF	Unc	BU
2011 Proof	500	Value: 875				

KM# 1820   100 EURO
17.0000 g., 0.9200 Gold 0.5028 oz. AGW, 30x21 mm. **Subject:** Vassily Kandinsky **Shape:** Rectangle

Date	Mintage	F	VF	XF	Unc	BU
2011 Proof	500	Value: 875				

KM# 1824   100 EURO
17.0000 g., 0.9200 Gold 0.5028 oz. AGW, 31 mm. **Subject:** Andy Warhol **Obv:** Portrait facing **Rev:** Dollar Sign

Date	Mintage	F	VF	XF	Unc	BU
2011 Proof	500	Value: 875				

KM# 1836   100 EURO
327.6000 g., 0.9500 Silver 10.005 oz. ASW, 75 mm. **Obv:** Commic characters **Rev:** Profile left and large XIII

Date	Mintage	F	VF	XF	Unc	BU
2011 Proof	500	Value: 400				

KM# 1892   100 EURO
17.0000 g., 0.9200 Gold 0.5028 oz. AGW, 31 mm. **Subject:** Euro, 10th Anniversary **Obv:** The Sower advancing left **Rev:** Value on globe at center, child-like renderings around

Date	Mintage	F	VF	XF	Unc	BU
2012(a) Proof	500	Value: 950				

KM# 1589   200 EURO
31.1040 g., 0.9990 Gold 0.9990 oz. AGW, 37 mm. **Subject:** Court of Human Rights - 50th Anniversary **Obv:** The Seed Sower left **Rev:** Text

Date	Mintage	F	VF	XF	Unc	BU
2009P Proof	500	Value: 1,700				

KM# 1593 200 EURO
31.1040 g., 0.9990 Gold 0.9990 oz. AGW, 37 mm. **Subject:**
Europa - Fall of Berlin Wall **Obv:** Brandenburg gate and doves
in flight **Rev:** Head facing and flags

Date	Mintage	F	VF	XF	Unc	BU
2009P Proof	500	Value: 1,700				

KM# 1624 200 EURO
31.1040 g., 0.9990 Gold 0.9990 oz. AGW, 37 mm. **Subject:**
First Moon Landing, 40th Anniversary **Obv:** Footprint on the moon

Date	Mintage	F	VF	XF	Unc	BU
2009P Proof	1,000	Value: 1,700				

KM# 1639 200 EURO
31.1040 g., 0.9990 Gold 0.9990 oz. AGW, 37 mm. **Subject:**
FIFA World Cup, South Africa 2010 **Obv:** Soccer player on field
Rev: Soccerball, Map of Africa, Protea flower **Shape:** 37

Date	Mintage	F	VF	XF	Unc	BU
2009P Proof	500	Value: 1,700				

KM# 1678 200 EURO
31.1040 g., 0.9990 Gold 0.9990 oz. AGW, 37 mm. **Subject:**
Cluny Abbey, 1100th Anniversary **Obv:** Europa head facing **Rev:**
Cluny Abbey

Date	Mintage	F	VF	XF	Unc	BU
2010 Proof	500	Value: 1,700				

KM# 1683 200 EURO
31.1040 g., 0.9990 Gold 0.9990 oz. AGW, 37 mm. **Obv:**
Georges Pompidou Center design **Rev:** Design detail

Date	Mintage	F	VF	XF	Unc	BU
2010 Proof	500	Value: 1,700				

KM# 1693 200 EURO
31.1040 g., 0.9990 Gold 0.9990 oz. AGW, 37 mm. **Obv:** Mother
Teresa and child **Rev:** Mother Teresa and Pope John Paul II

Date	Mintage	F	VF	XF	Unc	BU
2010 Proof	500	Value: 1,700				

KM# 1698 200 EURO
31.1040 g., 0.9990 Gold 0.9990 oz. AGW, 37 mm. **Obv:** Taj
Mahal **Rev:** UNESCO offices

Date	Mintage	F	VF	XF	Unc	BU
2010 Proof	1,000	Value: 1,700				

KM# 1701 200 EURO
31.1040 g., 0.9990 Gold 0.9990 oz. AGW, 37 mm. **Obv:** Lille
station and route map **Rev:** Three TGV trains

Date	Mintage	F	VF	XF	Unc	BU
2010 Proof	500	Value: 1,700				

KM# 1818 200 EURO
31.1040 g., 0.9990 Gold 0.9990 oz. AGW, 37 mm. **Obv:** Metz
railroad station **Rev:** TGV and ICE trains

Date	Mintage	F	VF	XF	Unc	BU
2011 Proof	—	Value: 1,700				

KM# 1757 200 EURO
4.0000 g., 0.9990 Gold 0.1285 oz. AGW, 21 mm. **Obv:** French
region names around RF **Rev:** Value within wreath

Date	Mintage	F	VF	XF	Unc	BU
2011(a) Proof	—	—	—	—	—	250

KM# 1793 200 EURO
31.1040 g., 0.9990 Gold 0.9990 oz. AGW, 37 mm. **Subject:**
International Music Day, 30th Anniversary **Obv:** Europa **Rev:**
Youth jamming

Date	Mintage	F	VF	XF	Unc	BU
2011 Proof	500	Value: 1,750				

KM# 1797 200 EURO
31.1040 g., 0.9990 Gold 0.9990 oz. AGW, 37 mm. **Subject:**
Great Explorers - Jacques Cartier **Obv:** The Grande Hermine
sailing away **Rev:** Cartier, globe and compass rose

Date	Mintage	F	VF	XF	Unc	BU
2011 Proof	500	Value: 1,700				

KM# 1808 200 EURO
31.1040 g., 0.9990 Gold 0.9990 oz. AGW, 37 mm. **Subject:**
WWF - Audouin's Gull **Obv:** Gull in flight right **Rev:** Gull standing
right, WWF logo right

Date	Mintage	F	VF	XF	Unc	BU
2011 Proof	500	Value: 1,700				

KM# 1853 200 EURO
31.1040 g., 0.9990 Gold 0.9990 oz. AGW, 37 mm. **Subject:**
Eurocorps, 20th Anniversary **Obv:** Mitterrand and Kohl standing
clasping hands **Rev:** Europa facing

Date	Mintage	F	VF	XF	Unc	BU
2012(a) Proof	500	Value: 1,850				

KM# 1898 200 EURO
31.1040 g., 0.9990 Gold 0.9990 oz. AGW **Subject:** abbé Pierre,
100th anniversary of Birth **Obv:** Pierre's bust at left, shaddow
figure at right **Rev:** Emmaus International logo, quote below
Shape: 37

Date	Mintage	F	VF	XF	Unc	BU
2012(a) Proof	500	Value: 1,850				

KM# 1915 200 EURO
31.1040 g., 0.9990 Gold 0.9990 oz. AGW, 37 mm. **Subject:**
TGV South-East **Obv:** Lyon Saint-Exupery station **Rev:** Two
modern locomotives

Date	Mintage	F	VF	XF	Unc	BU
2012(a) Proof	500	Value: 1,850				

KM# 1923 200 EURO
31.1040 g., 0.9990 Gold 0.9990 oz. AGW, 37 mm. **Subject:**
2012 Summer Olympics, London **Obv:** Two judo athletes and
map of Europe **Rev:** Two judo athletes

Date	Mintage	F	VF	XF	Unc	BU
2012(a) Proof	500	Value: 1,850				

KM# 1926 200 EURO
31.1040 g., 0.9990 Gold 0.9990 oz. AGW, 37 mm. **Subject:**
Year of the Dragon **Obv:** Dragon **Rev:** La Fontaine and zodiac
animals

Date	Mintage	F	VF	XF	Unc	BU
2012(a) Proof	500	Value: 1,850				

KM# 1583   250 EURO
8.4500 g., 0.9200 Gold 0.2499 oz. AGW, 22 mm. **Obv:** Modernistic sower advancing right **Rev:** Value and wreath

Date	Mintage	F	VF	XF	Unc	BU
2009P	25,000	—	—	—	—	475

KM# 1671   250 EURO
62.2080 g., 0.9990 Gold 1.9979 oz. AGW, 37 mm. **Obv:** The Seed Sower left **Rev:** Wheat and olive branch

Date	Mintage	F	VF	XF	Unc	BU
2010 Proof	500	Value: 3,400				

KM# 1788   250 EURO
62.2080 g., 0.9990 Gold 1.9979 oz. AGW, 37 mm. **Subject:** Euro Starter Kit, 10th Anniversary **Obv:** Sower **Rev:** Euro starter kit **Note:** Thick planchet.

Date	Mintage	F	VF	XF	Unc	BU
2011 Proof	500	Value: 3,400				

KM# 1893   250 EURO
62.2080 g., 0.9990 Gold 1.9979 oz. AGW, 37 mm. **Subject:** Euro, 10th Anniversary **Obv:** The Sower advancing left **Rev:** Value on globe at center, child-like renderings around

Date	Mintage	F	VF	XF	Unc	BU
2012(a) Proof	500	Value: 3,600				

KM# 1396   500 EURO
1000.0000 g., 0.9990 Gold 32.117 oz. AGW, 85 mm. **Subject:** European Union Expansion **Obv:** Partial face and flags **Rev:** Puzzle map **Edge:** Plain **Note:** Illustration reduced.

Date	Mintage	F	VF	XF	Unc	BU
2004 Proof	20	Value: 53,500				

KM# 1594   500 EURO
155.5000 g., 0.9990 Gold 4.9942 oz. AGW, 50 mm. **Subject:** Europa - Fall of Berlin Wall **Obv:** Brandenburg gate and doves in flight **Rev:** Head facing and flags

Date	Mintage	F	VF	XF	Unc	BU
2009P Proof	99	Value: 8,400				

KM# 1599   500 EURO
155.5000 g., 0.9990 Gold 4.9942 oz. AGW, 50 mm. **Subject:** Concorde 40th Anniversary **Obv:** Concorde in flight **Rev:** Tail emblems

Date	Mintage	F	VF	XF	Unc	BU
2009P Proof	99	Value: 8,400				

KM# 1605   500 EURO
155.5000 g., 0.9990 Gold 4.9942 oz. AGW, 50 mm. **Obv:** Eiffel Tower Structure **Rev:** Gustave Eiffel at left

Date	Mintage	F	VF	XF	Unc	BU
2009P Proof	99	Value: 8,400				

KM# 1610   500 EURO
155.5000 g., 0.9990 Gold 4.9942 oz. AGW, 50 mm. **Subject:** Bugatti 100th Anniversary **Obv:** Ettore Bugatti at left **Rev:** Race car and grill motif

Date	Mintage	F	VF	XF	Unc	BU
2009P Proof	99	Value: 8,400				

KM# 1615   500 EURO
155.5000 g., 0.9990 Gold 4.9942 oz. AGW, 50 mm. **Subject:** Curie Institute, 100th Anniversary

Date	Mintage	F	VF	XF	Unc	BU
2009P Proof	99	Value: 8,400				

KM# 1619   500 EURO
155.5000 g., 0.9990 Gold 4.9942 oz. AGW, 50 mm. **Subject:** Unesco site - The Kremlin in Moscow **Obv:** Wall Tower and cathedral

Date	Mintage	F	VF	XF	Unc	BU
2009P Proof	99	Value: 8,400				

KM# 1640   500 EURO
155.5000 g., 0.9990 Gold 4.9942 oz. AGW, 50 mm. **Subject:** FIFA World Cup, South Africa 2010 **Obv:** Soccer player on field **Rev:** Soccerball, Map of Africa, Protea flower

Date	Mintage	F	VF	XF	Unc	BU
2009P Proof	99	Value: 8,400				

KM# 1642   500 EURO
12.0000 g., 0.9990 Gold 0.3854 oz. AGW, 31 mm. **Obv:** The Seed Sower advancing right, sun rays from below **Rev:** Value in center, wreath horizontal

Date	Mintage	F	VF	XF	Unc	BU
2010	25,000	—	—	—	—	675

KM# 1687   500 EURO
155.5000 g., 0.9990 Gold 4.9942 oz. AGW, 50 mm. **Obv:** Marcel Dassault **Rev:** Mirage III plane

Date	Mintage	F	VF	XF	Unc	BU
2010 Proof	99	Value: 8,450				

KM# 1692   500 EURO
155.5000 g., 0.9990 Gold 4.9942 oz. AGW, 50 mm. **Obv:** Mother Teresa and child **Rev:** Mother Teresa and Pope John Paul II

Date	Mintage	F	VF	XF	Unc	BU
2010 Proof	99	Value: 8,400				

KM# 1697   500 EURO
155.5000 g., 0.9990 Gold 4.9942 oz. AGW, 50 mm. **Obv:** Taj Mahal **Rev:** UNESCO offices

Date	Mintage	F	VF	XF	Unc	BU
2010 Proof	99	Value: 8,400				

KM# 1706   500 EURO
155.5000 g., 0.9990 Gold 4.9942 oz. AGW **Obv:** Doves **Rev:** Georges Baraque **Shape:** 50

Date	Mintage	F	VF	XF	Unc	BU
2010 Proof	99	Value: 8,400				

KM# 1710   500 EURO
155.5000 g., 0.9990 Gold 4.9942 oz. AGW, 50 mm. **Rev:** Picasso

Date	Mintage	F	VF	XF	Unc	BU
2010 Proof	99	Value: 8,400				

KM# 1712   500 EURO
1000.0000 g., 0.9500 Silver 30.541 oz. ASW, 100 mm. **Rev:** Picasso

Date	Mintage	F	VF	XF	Unc	BU
2010 Proof	500	Value: 10,000				

KM# 1718   500 EURO
155.5000 g., 0.9990 Gold 4.9942 oz. AGW, 50 mm. **Obv:** Handball player on globe **Rev:** Handball player, net, Big Ben

Date	Mintage	F	VF	XF	Unc	BU
2010 Proof	99	Value: 8,400				

KM# 1798   500 EURO
155.5000 g., 0.9990 Gold 4.9942 oz. AGW, 50 mm. **Subject:** Great Explorers - Jacques Cartier **Obv:** The Grande Hermine sailing away **Rev:** Cartier, globe and compass rose

Date	Mintage	F	VF	XF	Unc	BU
2011 Proof	99	Value: 8,400				

KM# 1812   500 EURO
155.5000 g., 0.9990 Gold 4.9942 oz. AGW, 50 mm. **Subject:** UNESCO World Heritage Site - Palace of Versailles

Date	Mintage	F	VF	XF	Unc	BU
2011 Proof	99	Value: 8,400				

KM# 1821   500 EURO
155.5000 g., 0.9990 Gold 4.9942 oz. AGW, 53x37 mm. **Subject:** Vassily Kandinsky **Shape:** Rectangle

Date	Mintage	F	VF	XF	Unc	BU
2011 Proof	99	Value: 8,400				

KM# 1825   500 EURO
155.5000 g., 0.9990 Gold 4.9942 oz. AGW, 53x37 mm. **Subject:** Andy Warhol **Shape:** Rectangle

Date	Mintage	F	VF	XF	Unc	BU
2011 Proof	99	Value: 8,400				

KM# 1854 500 EURO
155.5900 g., 0.9990 Gold 4.9971 oz. AGW, 50 mm. **Subject:** Eurocorps, 20th Anniversary **Obv:** Mitterrand and Kohl standing clasping hands **Rev:** Europa facing

Date	Mintage	F	VF	XF	Unc	BU
2012(a) Proof	99	Value: 9,250				

KM# 1899 500 EURO
155.5000 g., 0.9990 Gold 4.9942 oz. AGW, 50 mm. **Subject:** abbé Pierre, 100th anniversary of Birth **Obv:** Pierre's bust at left, shadow at right **Rev:** Emmaus International logo, quote below

Date	Mintage	F	VF	XF	Unc	BU
2012(a) Proof	99	Value: 9,250				

KM# 1909 500 EURO
155.5000 g., 0.9990 Gold 4.9942 oz. AGW, 50 mm. **Subject:** UNESCO - World Heritage Site **Obv:** Abu Simbel temple **Rev:** Sphinx and Pyramids

Date	Mintage	F	VF	XF	Unc	BU
2012(a) Proof	99	Value: 9,250				

KM# 1927 500 EURO
155.5000 g., 0.9990 Gold 4.9942 oz. AGW, 50 mm. **Subject:** Year of the Dragon **Obv:** Dragon **Rev:** La Fontaine and zodiac animals

Date	Mintage	F	VF	XF	Unc	BU
2012(a) Proof	99	Value: 9,250				

KM# 1595 1000 EURO
311.0000 g., 0.9990 Gold 9.9885 oz. AGW, 65 mm. **Subject:** Europa - Fall of Berlin Wall **Obv:** Brandenburg gate and doves in flight **Rev:** Head facing and flags

Date	Mintage	F	VF	XF	Unc	BU
2009P Proof	20	Value: 17,000				

KM# 1600 1000 EURO
311.0000 g., 0.9990 Gold 9.9885 oz. AGW, 65 mm. **Subject:** Concorde 40 Anniversary **Obv:** Concorde in flight **Rev:** Tail emblems

Date	Mintage	F	VF	XF	Unc	BU
2009P Proof	20	Value: 17,000				

KM# 1677 1000 EURO
31.1000 g., 0.9990 Gold 0.9988 oz. AGW, 65 mm. **Subject:** Cluny Abbey, 1100th Anniversary **Obv:** Europa head facing **Rev:** Cluny Abby view

Date	Mintage	F	VF	XF	Unc	BU
2010 Proof	39	Value: 17,000				

KM# 1682 1000 EURO
311.0000 g., 0.9990 Gold 9.9885 oz. AGW, 65 mm. **Obv:** Georges Pompidou Center design **Rev:** Design detail

Date	Mintage	F	VF	XF	Unc	BU
2010 Proof	39	Value: 17,000				

KM# 1725 1000 EURO
20.0000 g., 0.9990 Gold 0.6423 oz. AGW, 39 mm. **Obv:** Value at center, wreath horizontal **Rev:** Hercules goup

Date	Mintage	F	VF	XF	Unc	BU
2011	10,000	—	—	—	—	1,150
2012	10,000	—	—	—	—	1,150

KM# 1794 1000 EURO
311.0000 g., 0.9990 Gold 9.9885 oz. AGW, 65 mm. **Subject:** International Music Day, 30th Anniversary **Obv:** Europa **Rev:** Youth jamming

Date	Mintage	F	VF	XF	Unc	BU
2011 Proof	39	Value: 17,000				

KM# 1799 1000 EURO
311.0000 g., 0.9990 Gold 9.9885 oz. AGW, 65 mm. **Subject:** Great Explorers - Jacques Cartier **Obv:** The Grande Hermine sailing away **Rev:** Cartier, globe and compass rose

Date	Mintage	F	VF	XF	Unc	BU
2011 Proof	39	Value: 17,000				

KM# 1855 1000 EURO
311.0000 g., 0.9990 Gold 9.9885 oz. AGW, 65 mm. **Subject:** Eurocorps, 20th Anniversary **Obv:** Mitterrand and Kohl standing clasping hands **Rev:** Europa facing

Date	Mintage	F	VF	XF	Unc	BU
2012(a) Proof	39	Value: 18,000				

KM# 1620 5000 EURO
1000.0000 g., 0.9990 Gold 32.117 oz. AGW, 85 mm. **Subject:** Unesco site - The Kremlin in Moscow **Obv:** Wall Tower and cathedral

Date	Mintage	F	VF	XF	Unc	BU
2009P Proof	39	Value: 53,500				

KM# 1696 5000 EURO
1000.0000 g., 0.9990 Gold 32.117 oz. AGW, 85 mm. **Obv:** Taj Mahal and diamond inserts **Rev:** UNESCO offices

Date	Mintage	F	VF	XF	Unc	BU
2010 Proof	29	Value: 53,500				

KM# 1709 5000 EURO
1000.0000 g., 0.9990 Gold 32.117 oz. AGW, 85 mm. **Rev:** Picasso

Date	Mintage	F	VF	XF	Unc	BU
2010 Proof	29	Value: 53,500				

KM# 1813 5000 EURO
1000.0000 g., 0.9990 Gold 32.117 oz. AGW, 85 mm. **Subject:** UNESCO World Heritage Site - Palace of Versailles

Date	Mintage	F	VF	XF	Unc	BU
2011 Proof	29	Value: 53,500				

KM# 1822 5000 EURO
1000.0000 g., 0.9990 Gold 32.117 oz. AGW, 90x63 mm. **Subject:** Vassily Kandinsky **Shape:** Rectangle

Date	Mintage	F	VF	XF	Unc	BU
2011 Proof	29	Value: 53,500				

KM# 1826 5000 EURO
1000.0000 g., 0.9990 Gold 32.117 oz. AGW, 90x63 mm. **Subject:** Andy Warhol **Shape:** Rectangle

Date	Mintage	F	VF	XF	Unc	BU
2011 Proof	29	Value: 53,500				

KM# 1910 5000 EURO
1000.0000 g., 0.9990 Gold 32.117 oz. AGW, 85 mm. **Subject:** UNESCO - World Heritage Site **Obv:** Abu Simbel temple **Rev:** Sphinx and Pyramids

Date	Mintage	F	VF	XF	Unc	BU
2012(a) Proof	29	Value: 57,000				

KM# 1928 5000 EURO
75.0000 g., 0.9990 Gold 2.4088 oz. AGW, 45 mm. **Obv:** Value at center, wreath horizontal **Rev:** Hercules group

Date	Mintage	F	VF	XF	Unc	BU
2012(a)	2,000	—	—	—	—	4,500

MINT SETS

KM#	Date	Mintage	Identification	Issue Price	Mkt Val
MS20	2001 (2)	10,000	KM#925.1a, 928a	—	475
MS21	2001 (8)	35,000	KM#1282-1289	20.25	20.00
MS22	2002 (8)	35,000	KM#1282-1289	20.25	40.00
MS23	2003 (8)	—	KM#1282-89	—	55.00
MS24	2004 (8)	—	KM#1282-1289	—	45.00
MS25	2005 (8)	—	KM#1282-1289	—	45.00
MS26	2005 (8)	40,000	KM#1282-1289 Moebius set plus token	45.00	45.00
MS27	2005 (8)	10,000	KM1282-1289, French Memories - Bordeaux	45.00	45.00
MS28	2006 (8)	70,000	KM#1282-1289	36.50	42.50
MS29	2006 (8)	500	KM#1282-1289, Denver, Colorado special ANA Coin Convention Set	45.00	70.00
MS30	2006 (8)	500	KM#1282-1289, Berlin Coin Fair set	45.00	55.00
MS31	2006 (8)	500	KM1282-1289, Pierre Curie set	45.00	50.00
MS32	2006 (8)	500	KM#1282-1289, Musee de la Monnaie set	45.00	50.00
MS33	2006 (8)	500	KM#1282-1289, Journees du Patrimoine set	45.00	50.00
MS34	2006 (8)	500	KM#1282-1289, Bourgogne set	45.00	50.00
MS35	2006 (8)	500	KM#1282-1289, "Coree set" (Korea)	45.00	50.00
MS36	2006 (8)	500	KM#1282-1289, Nord Pas-de-Calais set	45.00	50.00
MS37	2006 (8)	500	KM#1282-1289, Jacques Chirac set	45.00	50.00
MS38	2006 (8)	500	KM#1282-1289, Mitterrand & Khol	45.00	50.00
MS39	2006 (8)	500	KM#1282-1289, Birthday 1 set	45.00	45.00
MS40	2006 (8)	500	KM#1282-1289, Birthday 2 set	45.00	45.00
MS41	2006 (8)	500	KM#1282-1289, Tokyo set	45.00	50.00
MS42	2006 (8)	500	KM#1282-1289, Viaduc de Millau set	45.00	50.00
MS43	2006 (8)	500	KM#1282-1289, Ile-de-France set	45.00	50.00

PROOF SETS

KM#	Date	Mintage	Identification	Issue Price	Mkt Val
PS21	2001 (8)	15,000	KM#1282-1289	59.00	125
PS22	2002 (8)	40,000	KM#1282-1289	59.00	110
PS23	2003 (5)	150,000	KM#1321, 1322, 1323, 1324, 1325	—	260
PS24	2003 (5)	5,000	KM#1326, 1327, 1328, 1329, 1330	—	1,900
PS25	2003 (8)	—	KM#1282-1289	—	110
PS26	2004 (9)	20,000	KM#1282-1289 plus Pantheon 5 Euro	—	150
PS27	2005 (9)	10,000	KM#1282-1289 plus Pantheon 5 Euro	—	150
PS28	2006 (9)	10,000	KM#1282-1289 plus Pantheon 5 Euro	—	150
PS29	2007 (9)	7,500	KM#1282-84, 1410-1414 plus 15 Euro	—	150
PS30	2008 (10)	7,500	KM#1282-84, 1410-1414, 1535	—	200
PS31	2009 (10)	7,500	KM#1282-84, 1410-1414, 1535	—	200
PS32	2010 (9)	9,000	KM#1282-84, 1410-1414 plus 15 Euro	—	150
PS33	2011 (9)	9,000	KM#1282-84, 1410-1414, 1795	—	200
PS34	2012 (9)	10,000	KM#1282-84, 1410-1414 plus Hercules 10 Euro	—	200

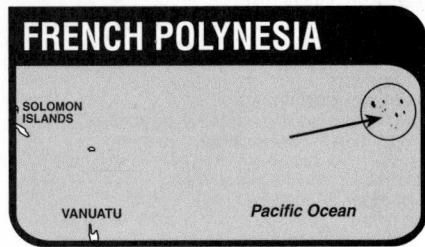

FRENCH POLYNESIA

SOLOMON
ISLANDS

VANUATU   *Pacific Ocean*

The Territory of French Polynesia (formerly French Oceania) has an area of 1,544 sq. mi. (3,941 sq. km.) and a population of 220,000. It is comprised of the same five archipelagoes that were grouped administratively to form French Oceania.

The colony of French Oceania became the Territory of French Polynesia by act of the French National Assembly in March, 1957. In Sept. of 1958 it voted in favor of the new constitution of the Fifth Republic, thereby electing to remain within the new French Community.

Picturesque, mountainous Tahiti, the setting of many tales of adventure and romance, is one of the most inspiringly beautiful islands in the world. Robert Louis Stevenson called it 'God's sweetest works'. It was there that Paul Gaugin, one of the pioneers of the Impressionist movement, painted the brilliant, exotic pictures that later made him famous. The arid coral atolls of Tuamotu comprise the most economically valuable area of French Polynesia. Pearl oysters thrive in the warm, limpid lagoons, and extensive portions of the atolls are valuable phosphate rock.

RULER
French

MINT MARK
(a) - Paris, privy marks only

MONETARY SYSTEM
100 Centimes = 1 Franc

FRENCH OVERSEAS TERRITORY

DECIMAL COINAGE

KM# 11   FRANC
1.3000 g., Aluminum, 23 mm. **Obv:** Seated Liberty with torch and cornucopia right, date below, legend added flanking figure's feet **Obv. Legend:** I. E. O. M. **Rev:** Legend and island scene divide denomination

Date	Mintage	F	VF	XF	Unc	BU
2001(a)	2,900,000	—	—	—	0.50	1.00
2002(a)	1,600,000	—	—	—	0.50	1.00
2003(a)	4,200,000	—	—	—	0.50	1.00
2004(a)	2,400,000	—	—	—	0.50	1.00
2005(a)	—	—	—	—	0.50	1.00
2006(a)	2,100,000	—	—	—	0.50	1.00
2007(a) Coin rotation	3,400,000	—	—	—	0.50	1.00
2007(a) Medal rotation	Inc. above	—	—	—	—	30.00
2008(a)	4,800,000	—	—	—	0.50	1.00
2009(a)	3,200,000	—	—	—	0.50	1.00
2010(a)	2,100,000	—	—	—	0.50	1.00
2011(a)	—	—	—	—	0.50	1.00

KM# 10   2 FRANCS
2.3000 g., Aluminum, 27 mm. **Obv:** Seated Liberty with torch and cornucopia right, date below, legend added flanking figure's feet **Obv. Legend:** I. E. O. M. **Rev:** Legend and island scene divide denomination

Date	Mintage	F	VF	XF	Unc	BU
2001(a)	2,400,000	—	—	—	0.75	1.50
2002(a)	2,500,000	—	—	—	0.75	1.50
2003(a)	3,200,000	—	—	—	0.75	1.50
2004(a)	3,000,000	—	—	—	0.75	1.50
2005(a)	900,000	—	—	—	0.75	1.50
2006(a)	1,600,000	—	—	—	0.75	1.50
2007(a)	640,000	—	—	—	0.75	1.50
2008(a)	1,900,000	—	—	—	0.75	1.50

Date	Mintage	F	VF	XF	Unc	BU
2009(a)	1,600,000	—	—	—	0.75	1.50
2010(a)	2,400,000	—	—	—	0.75	1.50
2011(a)	1,600,000	—	—	—	0.75	1.50

KM# 12   5 FRANCS
3.7500 g., Aluminum, 31 mm. **Obv:** Seated Liberty with torch and cornucopia right, date below, legend added flanking figure's feet **Obv. Legend:** I. E. O. M. **Rev:** Legend and island divide denomination

Date	Mintage	F	VF	XF	Unc	BU
2001(a)	1,600,000	—	—	—	1.00	2.00
2002(a)	400,000	—	—	—	1.00	2.00
2003(a)	1,000,000	—	—	—	1.00	2.00
2004(a)	600,000	—	—	—	1.00	2.00
2005(a)	600,000	—	—	—	1.00	2.00
2006(a)	720,000	—	—	—	1.00	2.00
2007(a)	1,000,000	—	—	—	1.00	2.00
2008(a)	1,060,000	—	—	—	1.00	2.00
2009(a)	900,000	—	—	—	1.00	2.00
2010(a)	700,000	—	—	—	1.00	2.00
2011(a)	900,000	—	—	—	1.00	2.00

KM# 8   10 FRANCS
6.0000 g., Nickel, 24 mm. **Obv:** Capped head left, date and legend below **Obv. Legend:** I. E. O. M. **Rev:** Native art, denomination below **Edge:** Reeded

Date	Mintage	F	VF	XF	Unc	BU
2001(a)	500,000	—	—	—	1.25	2.75
2002(a)	600,000	—	—	—	1.25	2.75
2003(a)	1,000,000	—	—	—	1.25	2.75
2004(a)	600,000	—	—	—	1.25	2.75
2005(a)	200,000	—	—	—	1.25	2.75

KM# 8a   10 FRANCS
6.0000 g., Copper-Nickel, 24 mm. **Obv:** Capped head left, date and legend below **Obv. Legend:** I. E. O. M. **Rev:** Native art, denomination below **Edge:** Reeded

Date	Mintage	F	VF	XF	Unc	BU
2006(a)	620,000	—	—	—	1.25	2.75
2007(a)	800,000	—	—	—	1.25	2.75
2008(a)	820,000	—	—	—	1.25	2.75
2009(a)	1,000,000	—	—	—	1.25	2.75
2010(a)	500,000	—	—	—	1.25	2.75
2011(a)	200,000	—	—	—	1.25	2.75

KM# 9   20 FRANCS
10.0000 g., Nickel, 28.3 mm. **Obv:** Capped head left, date and legend below **Obv. Legend:** I. E. O. M. **Rev:** Flowers, vanilla shoots, bread fruit **Edge:** Reeded

Date	Mintage	F	VF	XF	Unc	BU
2001(a)	500,000	—	—	—	1.75	3.25
2002(a)	300,000	—	—	—	1.75	3.25
2003(a)	700,000	—	—	—	1.75	3.00
2004(a)	600,000	—	—	—	1.75	3.00
2005(a)	30,000	—	—	—	20.00	30.00

KM# 9a   20 FRANCS
10.0000 g., Copper-Nickel, 28.3 mm. **Obv:** Capped head left, date and legend below **Obv. Legend:** I. E. O. M. **Rev:** Flowers, vanilla shoots, bread fruit **Edge:** Reeded

Date	Mintage	F	VF	XF	Unc	BU
2006(a)	300,000	—	—	—	1.75	3.00
2007(a)	450,000	—	—	—	1.75	3.00
2008(a)	610,000	—	—	—	1.75	3.00
2009(a)	750,000	—	—	—	1.75	3.00
2010(a)	200,000	—	—	—	1.75	3.00
2011(a)	400,000	—	—	—	1.75	3.00

KM# 13   50 FRANCS
15.0000 g., Nickel, 33 mm. **Obv:** Capped head left, date and legend below **Obv. Legend:** I. E. O. M. **Rev:** Denomination above Moorea Harbor **Edge:** Reeded

Date	Mintage	F	VF	XF	Unc	BU
2001(a)	300,000	—	—	—	2.00	4.00
2002(a)	—	—	—	—	2.00	4.00
2003(a)	240,000	—	—	—	2.00	4.00
2004(a)	100,000	—	—	—	2.00	4.00
2005(a)	100,000	—	—	—	2.00	4.00

KM# 13a   50 FRANCS
15.0000 g., Copper-Nickel, 33 mm. **Obv:** Capped head left, date and legend below **Obv. Legend:** I. E. O. M. **Rev:** Denomination above Moorea Harbor **Edge:** Reeded

Date	Mintage	F	VF	XF	Unc	BU
2006(a)	15,000	—	—	—	3.00	5.00
2007(a)	310,000	—	—	—	2.00	4.00
2008(a)	200,000	—	—	—	2.00	4.00
2009(a)	300,000	—	—	—	2.00	4.00
2010(a)	120,000	—	—	—	2.00	4.00
2011(a)	130,000	—	—	—	2.00	4.00

KM# 14   100 FRANCS
10.0000 g., Nickel-Bronze, 30 mm. **Obv:** Capped head left, date below **Rev:** Denomination above Moorea Harbor **Edge:** Reeded

Date	Mintage	F	VF	XF	Unc	BU
2001(a)	200,000	—	—	—	3.00	5.00
2002(a)	—	—	—	—	3.00	5.00
2003(a)	600,000	—	—	—	2.75	5.00
2004(a)	450,000	—	—	—	2.75	5.00
2005(a)	300,000	—	—	—	2.75	5.00

KM# 14a   100 FRANCS
10.0000 g., Aluminum-Bronze, 30 mm. **Obv:** Capped head left, date below **Obv. Legend:** I. E. O. M. **Rev:** Denomination above Moorea Harbor **Edge:** Reeded

Date	Mintage	F	VF	XF	Unc	BU
2006(a)	200,000	—	—	—	2.75	5.00
2007(a)	650,000	—	—	—	2.75	5.00
2008(a)	690,000	—	—	—	2.75	5.00
2009(a)	—	—	—	—	2.75	5.00
2010(a)	—	—	—	—	2.75	5.00
2011(a)	—	—	—	—	2.75	5.00

MINT SETS

KM#	Date	Mintage	Identification	Issue Price	Mkt Val
MS1	2001 (7)	3,000	KM#8-14	—	22.50
MS2	2002 (7)	5,000	KM#8-14	—	22.50
MS3	2003 (7)	3,000	KM#8-14	—	22.50

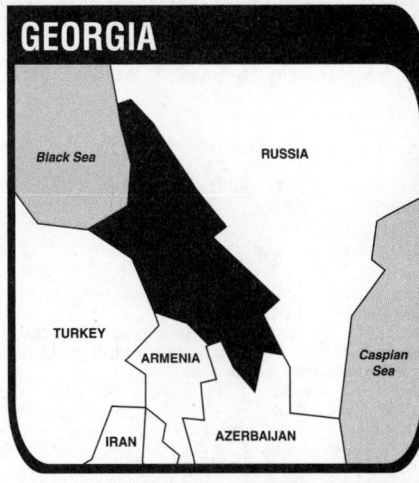

GEORGIA

Georgia (formerly the Georgian Social Democratic Republic under the U.S.S.R.), is bounded by the Black Sea to the west and by Turkey, Armenia and Azerbaijan. It occupies the western part of Transcaucasia covering an area of 26,900 sq. mi. (69,700 sq. km.) and a population of 5.7 million. Capitol: Tbilisi. Hydro-electricity, minerals, forestry and agriculture are the chief industries.

Germano-- Georgian treaty was signed on May 28, 1918, followed by a Turko-Georgian peace treaty on June 4. The end of WW I and the collapse of the central powers allowed free The collapse of the U.S.S.R. allowed full transition to independence and on April 9, 1991 a unanimous vote declared the republic an independent state based on its original treaty of independence of May 1918.

MONETARY SYSTEM
100 Thetri = 1 Lari

INDEPENDENT STATE (C.I.S.)

STANDARD COINAGE
100 Thetri = 1 Lari

KM# 89 50 THETRI
6.5000 g., Copper-Nickel, 24 mm. **Obv:** National arms **Rev:** Value **Edge:** Reeded and lettered

Date	Mintage	F	VF	XF	Unc	BU
2006	—	—	—	—	3.00	4.00

KM# 95 LARI
28.2800 g., 0.9990 Silver 0.9083 oz. ASW, 38.61 mm. **Subject:** World Cup Soccer, 2006 Germany **Obv:** Map of Georgia, flag **Rev:** World Cup trophy, two soccer players

Date	Mintage	F	VF	XF	Unc	BU
2004 Proof	50,000	Value: 45.00				

KM# 90 LARI
7.8000 g., Copper-Nickel, 26.2 mm. **Obv:** National arms **Rev:** Value **Edge:** Reeded and lettered

Date	Mintage	F	VF	XF	Unc	BU
2006	—	—	—	—	5.00	6.50

KM# 92 2 LARI
12.9200 g., Copper-Nickel, 31 mm. **Obv:** Trophy cup, value and date **Rev:** UFFA Winners Cup and soccer player **Edge:** Plain

Date	Mintage	F	VF	XF	Unc	BU
2006	10,000	—	—	—	—	18.00

KM# 94 2 LARI
8.0000 g., Bi-Metallic Aluminum-Bronze center in Copper-Nickel ring, 27 mm. **Obv:** National arms **Rev:** Large value **Edge:** Reeded and lettered

Date	Mintage	F	VF	XF	Unc	BU
2006	—	—	—	—	7.50	9.00

KM# 103 2 LARI
28.2800 g., 0.9250 Silver 0.8410 oz. ASW, 38.61 mm. **Obv:** Trophy cup, value and date **Rev:** UEFA Winners Cup and soccer player

Date	Mintage	F	VF	XF	Unc	BU
2006 Proof	6,000	Value: 50.00				

KM# 93 3 LARI
12.8000 g., Copper-Nickel, 31 mm. **Obv:** Three oil wells **Rev:** Map with "Baku-Tbilisi-Ceyhan" route **Edge:** Lettered

Date	Mintage	F	VF	XF	Unc	BU
2006	3,000	—	—	—	—	25.00

KM# 102 3 LARI
28.2800 g., Silver, 38.61 mm. **Obv:** Three oil wells **Rev:** Map with "Baku-Tbilisi-Ceyhan" route

Date	Mintage	F	VF	XF	Unc	BU
2006 Proof	5,000	Value: 50.00				

KM# 106 10 LARI
28.2800 g., 0.9250 Silver 0.8410 oz. ASW, 38.61 mm. **Subject:** St. George's Day **Obv:** Drawing of church by Don Christoforo de Castelli **Rev:** Church of St. george in Ilora

Date	Mintage	F	VF	XF	Unc	BU
2009 Proof	1,500	Value: 50.00				

KM# 104 20 LARI
28.2800 g., 0.9250 Silver 0.8410 oz. ASW, 38.61 mm. **Obv:** Two classical runners **Rev:** Exterior of Bird's Nest Stadium, torch

Date	Mintage	F	VF	XF	Unc	BU
2008 Proof	1,500	Value: 50.00				

KM# 105 20 LARI
8.5000 g., 0.9000 Gold 0.2459 oz. AGW, 25 mm. **Obv:** Two classical runners **Rev:** Exterior of Bird's Nest Stadium, torch

Date	Mintage	F	VF	XF	Unc	BU
2008 Proof	—	Value: 450				

BULLION COINAGE

KM# 96 10 LARI
3.1100 g., 0.9990 Gold 0.0999 oz. AGW, 16 mm. **Obv:** Ancient sailing vessel, trade route **Rev:** Golden Fleece

Date	Mintage	F	VF	XF	Unc	BU
2006	4,000	—	—	—	—	175

KM# 97 25 LARI
7.7800 g., 0.9990 Gold 0.2499 oz. AGW, 22 mm. **Obv:** Ancient sailing ship trade route map **Rev:** Golden Feece

Date	Mintage	F	VF	XF	Unc	BU
2006	—	—	—	—	—	450

KM# 98 50 LARI
28.0000 g., 0.9990 Gold 0.8993 oz. AGW, 28 mm. **Obv:** Ancient sailing ship, trade route map **Rev:** Golden Fleece

Date	Mintage	F	VF	XF	Unc	BU
2006	—	—	—	—	—	1,500

KM# 99 100 LARI
31.1050 g., 0.9990 Gold 0.9990 oz. AGW, 37 mm. **Obv:** Ancient sailing ship, trade route map **Rev:** Golden Fleece

Date	Mintage	F	VF	XF	Unc	BU
2006	—	—	—	—	—	1,650

KM# 100 300 LARI
155.5000 g., 0.9990 Gold 4.9942 oz. AGW, 50 mm. **Obv:** Ancient sailing ship, trade route map **Rev:** Golden Fleece

Date	Mintage	F	VF	XF	Unc	BU
2006	—	—	—	—	—	8,500

KM# 101 1000 LARI
311.0000 g., 0.9990 Gold 9.9885 oz. AGW, 60 mm. **Obv:** Ancient sailing ship, trade route map **Rev:** Golden Fleece

Date	Mintage	F	VF	XF	Unc	BU
2006	—	—	—	—	—	16,500

GERMANY-FEDERAL REPUBLIC

1949-

The Federal Republic of Germany, located in north-central Europe, has an area of 137,744 sq. mi. (356,910sq. km.) and a population of 81.1 million. Capital: Berlin. The economy centers about one of the world's foremost industrial establishments. Machinery, motor vehicles, iron, steel, yarns and fabrics are exported.

MINT MARKS
A - Berlin
D - Munich
F - Stuttgart
G - Karlsruhe
J - Hamburg

MONETARY SYSTEM
100 Pfennig = 1 Deutsche Mark (DM)

FEDERAL REPUBLIC

STANDARD COINAGE

KM# 105   PFENNIG
2.0000 g., Copper Plated Steel, 16.5 mm. **Obv:** Five oak leaves, date below **Obv. Legend:** BUNDESREPUBLIK DEUTSCHLAND **Rev:** Denomination

Date	Mintage	F	VF	XF	Unc	BU
2001A In sets only	130,000	—	—	—	5.00	—
2001A Proof	78,000	Value: 5.00				
2001D In sets only	130,000	—	—	—	5.00	—
2001D Proof	78,000	Value: 5.00				
2001F In sets only	130,000	—	—	—	5.00	—
2001F Proof	78,000	Value: 5.00				
2001G In sets only	130,000	—	—	—	5.00	—
2001G Proof	78,000	Value: 5.00				
2001J In sets only	130,000	—	—	—	5.00	—
2001J Proof	78,000	Value: 5.00				

KM# 106a   2 PFENNIG
2.9000 g., Copper Plated Steel, 19.25 mm. **Obv:** Five oak leaves, date below **Rev:** Denomination

Date	Mintage	F	VF	XF	Unc	BU
2001A In sets only	130,000	—	—	—	5.00	—
2001A Proof	78,000	Value: 5.00				
2001D In sets only	130,000	—	—	—	5.00	—
2001D Proof	78,000	Value: 5.00				
2001F In sets only	130,000	—	—	—	5.00	—
2001F Proof	78,000	Value: 5.00				
2001G In sets only	130,000	—	—	—	5.00	—
2001G Proof	78,000	Value: 5.00				
2001J In sets only	130,000	—	—	—	5.00	—
2001J Proof	78,000	Value: 5.00				

KM# 107   5 PFENNIG
3.0000 g., Brass Clad Steel, 18.5 mm. **Obv:** Five oak leaves, date below **Obv. Legend:** BUNDESREPUBLIK DEUTSCHLAND **Rev:** Denomination

Date	Mintage	F	VF	XF	Unc	BU
2001A In sets only	130,000	—	—	—	5.00	—
2001A Proof	78,000	Value: 5.00				
2001D In sets only	130,000	—	—	—	5.00	—
2001D Proof	78,000	Value: 5.00				
2001F In sets only	130,000	—	—	—	5.00	—
2001F Proof	78,000	Value: 5.00				
2001G In sets only	130,000	—	—	—	5.00	—
2001G Proof	78,000	Value: 5.00				
2001J In sets only	130,000	—	—	—	5.00	—
2001J Proof	78,000	Value: 5.00				

KM# 108   10 PFENNIG
4.0000 g., Brass Clad Steel, 21.5 mm. **Obv:** Five oak leaves, date below **Obv. Legend:** BUNDESREPUBLIK DEUTSCHLAND **Rev:** Denomination **Edge:** Plain

Date	Mintage	F	VF	XF	Unc	BU
2001A In sets only	130,000	—	—	—	5.00	—
2001A Proof	78,000	Value: 5.00				
2001D In sets only	130,000	—	—	—	5.00	—
2001D Proof	78,000	Value: 5.00				

Date	Mintage	F	VF	XF	Unc	BU
2001F In sets only	130,000	—	—	—	5.00	—
2001F Proof	78,000	Value: 5.00				
2001G In sets only	130,000	—	—	—	5.00	—
2001G Proof	78,000	Value: 5.00				
2001J In sets only	130,000	—	—	—	5.00	—
2001J Proof	78,000	Value: 5.00				

KM# 109.2   50 PFENNIG
3.5000 g., Copper-Nickel, 20 mm. **Obv:** Denomination **Obv. Legend:** BUNDESREPUBLIK DEUTSCHLAND **Rev:** Woman planting an oak seedling **Edge:** Plain

Date	Mintage	F	VF	XF	Unc	BU
2001A In sets only	130,000	—	—	—	10.00	—
2001A Proof	78,000	Value: 10.00				
2001D In sets only	130,000	—	—	—	10.00	—
2001D Proof	78,000	Value: 10.00				
2001F In sets only	130,000	—	—	—	10.00	—
2001F Proof	78,000	Value: 10.00				
2001G In sets only	130,000	—	—	—	10.00	—
2001G Proof	78,000	Value: 10.00				
2001J In sets only	130,000	—	—	—	10.00	—
2001J Proof	78,000	Value: 10.00				

KM# 110   MARK
5.5000 g., Copper-Nickel, 23.5 mm. **Obv:** Eagle **Rev:** Denomination flanked by oak leaves, date below

Date	Mintage	F	VF	XF	Unc	BU
2001A In sets only	130,000	—	—	—	15.00	—
2001A Proof	78,000	Value: 15.00				
2001D In sets only	130,000	—	—	—	15.00	—
2001D Proof	78,000	Value: 15.00				
2001F In sets only	130,000	—	—	—	15.00	—
2001F Proof	78,000	Value: 15.00				
2001G In sets only	130,000	—	—	—	15.00	—
2001G Proof	78,000	Value: 15.00				
2001J In sets only	130,000	—	—	—	15.00	—
2001J Proof	78,000	Value: 15.00				

KM# 203   MARK
12.0000 g., 0.9999 Gold 0.3858 oz. AGW, 23.5 mm. **Subject:** Retirement of the Mark Currency **Obv:** Eagle **Rev:** Denomination flanked by oak leaves, date below **Edge:** Arabeskes

Date	Mintage	F	VF	XF	Unc	BU
2001A Proof	200,000	Value: 750				
2001D Proof	200,000	Value: 750				
2001G Proof	200,000	Value: 750				
2001J Proof	200,000	Value: 750				
2001F Proof	200,000	Value: 750				

KM# 170   2 MARK
7.0000 g., Copper-Nickel Clad Nickel, 26.75 mm. **Subject:** Ludwig Erhard **Obv:** Eagle above denomination **Rev:** Head facing divides dates **Edge Lettering:** EINIGKEIT UND RECHT UND FREIHEIT

Date	Mintage	F	VF	XF	Unc	BU
2001A In sets only	130,000	—	—	—	10.00	—
2001A Proof	78,000	Value: 10.00				
2001D In sets only	130,000	—	—	—	10.00	—
2001D Proof	78,000	Value: 10.00				
2001F In sets only	130,000	—	—	—	10.00	—
2001F Proof	78,000	Value: 10.00				
2001G In sets only	130,000	—	—	—	10.00	—

Date	Mintage	F	VF	XF	Unc	BU
2001G Proof	78,000	Value: 10.00				
2001J In sets only	130,000	—	—	—	10.00	—
2001J Proof	78,000	Value: 10.00				

KM# 175   2 MARK
7.0400 g., Copper-Nickel Clad Nickel, 26.8 mm. **Subject:** Franz Joseph Strauss **Obv:** Eagle above denomination **Rev:** Head left divides dates **Edge Lettering:** EINIGKEIT UND RECHT UND FREIHEIT

Date	Mintage	F	VF	XF	Unc	BU
2001A In sets only	130,000	—	—	—	10.00	—
2001A Proof	78,000	Value: 10.00				
2001D In sets only	130,000	—	—	—	10.00	—
2001D Proof	78,000	Value: 10.00				
2001F In sets only	130,000	—	—	—	10.00	—
2001F Proof	78,000	Value: 10.00				
2001G In sets only	130,000	—	—	—	10.00	—
2001G Proof	78,000	Value: 10.00				
2001J In sets only	130,000	—	—	—	10.00	—
2001J Proof	78,000	Value: 10.00				

KM# 183   2 MARK
7.0000 g., Copper-Nickel Clad Nickel, 26.75 mm. **Subject:** Willy Brandt **Obv:** Eagle above denomination **Rev:** Head facing divides dates **Edge Lettering:** EINIGKEIT UND RECHT UND FREIHEIT

Date	Mintage	F	VF	XF	Unc	BU
2001A In sets only	130,000	—	—	—	10.00	—
2001A Proof	78,000	Value: 10.00				
2001D In sets only	130,000	—	—	—	10.00	—
2001D Proof	78,000	Value: 10.00				
2001F In sets only	130,000	—	—	—	10.00	—
2001F Proof	78,000	Value: 10.00				
2001G In sets only	130,000	—	—	—	10.00	—
2001G Proof	78,000	Value: 10.00				
2001J In sets only	130,000	—	—	—	10.00	—
2001J Proof	78,000	Value: 10.00				

KM# 140.1   5 MARK
10.0000 g., Copper-Nickel Clad Nickel, 29 mm. **Obv:** Denomination within rounded square therefore nicknamed "TV-Fives" **Rev:** Eagle above date **Edge Lettering:** EINIGKEIT UND RECHT UND FREIHEIT

Date	Mintage	F	VF	XF	Unc	BU
2001A In sets only	130,000	—	—	—	30.00	—
2001A Proof	78,000	Value: 30.00				
2001D In sets only	130,000	—	—	—	30.00	—
2001D Proof	78,000	Value: 30.00				
2001F In sets only	130,000	—	—	—	30.00	—
2001F Proof	78,000	Value: 30.00				
2001G In sets only	130,000	—	—	—	30.00	—
2001G Proof	78,000	Value: 30.00				
2001J In sets only	130,000	—	—	—	30.00	—
2001J Proof	78,000	Value: 30.00				

COMMEMORATIVE COINAGE

KM# 204   10 MARK
15.5000 g., 0.9250 Silver 0.4609 oz. ASW, 32.5 mm. **Obv:** Imperial eagle above denomination **Rev:** Naval Museum, Stralsund **Edge Lettering:** "OHNE WASSER KEIN LEBEN"

Date	Mintage	F	VF	XF	Unc	BU
2001A	2,500,000	—	—	—	17.50	18.50
2001A Proof	826,300	Value: 22.00				

KM# 206   10 MARK
15.5000 g., 0.9250 Silver 0.4609 oz. ASW, 32.5 mm. **Subject:** Federal Court of Constitution: 50th Anniversary **Obv:** Stylized eagle above denomination **Rev:** Justice holding books and scale **Edge:** Lettered **Edge Lettering:** FÜR DAS GESAMTE DEUTSCHE VOLK

Date	Mintage	F	VF	XF	Unc	BU
2001G	2,000,000	—	—	—	17.50	18.50
2001G Proof	766,300	Value: 22.00				

KM# 205   10 MARK
15.5000 g., 0.9250 Silver 0.4609 oz. ASW, 32.5 mm. **Subject:** 200th Anniversary - Birth of Albert Gustav Lortzing **Obv:** Stylized eagle above denomination **Rev:** Portrait and music **Edge Lettering:** * WILDSCHUETZ * UNDINE * ZAR UND ZIMMERMANN *

Date	Mintage	F	VF	XF	Unc	BU
2001J	2,500,000	—	—	—	17.50	18.50
2001J Proof	826,300	Value: 22.00				

EURO COINAGE
European Union Issues

KM# 207   EURO CENT
2.3000 g., Copper Plated Steel, 16.25 mm. **Obv:** Oak leaves **Rev:** Denomination and globe **Edge:** Plain

Date	Mintage	F	VF	XF	Unc	BU
2002A	800,090,000	—	—	—	0.35	—
2002A Proof	75,000	Value: 1.00				
2002D	840,090,000	—	—	—	0.35	—
2002D Proof	75,000	Value: 1.00				
2002F	960,090,000	—	—	—	0.35	—
2002F Proof	75,000	Value: 1.00				
2002G	560,090,000	—	—	—	0.35	—
2002G Proof	75,000	Value: 1.00				

Date	Mintage	F	VF	XF	Unc	BU
2002J	840,090,000	—	—	—	0.35	—
2002J Proof	75,000	Value: 1.00				
2003A In sets only	90,000	—	—	—	4.50	—
2003A Proof	75,000	Value: 1.00				
2003D In sets only	90,000	—	—	—	4.50	—
2003D Proof	75,000	Value: 1.00				
2003F In sets only	90,000	—	—	—	4.50	—
2003F Proof	75,000	Value: 1.00				
2003G In sets only	90,000	—	—	—	4.50	—
2003G Proof	75,000	Value: 1.00				
2003J In sets only	90,000	—	—	—	4.50	—
2003J Proof	75,000	Value: 1.00				
2004A	280,090,000	—	—	—	0.35	—
2004A Proof	75,000	Value: 1.00				
2004D	294,090,000	—	—	—	0.35	—
2004D Proof	75,000	Value: 1.00				
2004F	336,090,000	—	—	—	0.35	—
2004F Proof	75,000	Value: 1.00				
2004G	196,090,000	—	—	—	0.35	—
2004G Proof	75,000	Value: 1.00				
2004J	294,090,000	—	—	—	0.35	—
2004J Proof	75,000	Value: 1.00				
2005A	120,090,000	—	—	—	0.35	—
2005A Proof	75,000	Value: 1.00				
2005D	126,090,000	—	—	—	0.35	—
2005D Proof	75,000	Value: 1.00				
2005F	144,090,000	—	—	—	0.35	—
2005F Proof	75,000	Value: 1.00				
2005G	84,090,000	—	—	—	0.35	—
2005G Proof	75,000	Value: 1.00				
2005J	126,090,000	—	—	—	0.35	—
2005J Proof	75,000	Value: 1.00				
2006A In sets only	90,000	—	—	—	4.50	—
2006A Proof	75,000	Value: 1.00				
2006D In sets only	90,000	—	—	—	4.50	—
2006D Proof	75,000	Value: 1.00				
2006F In sets only	90,000	—	—	—	4.50	—
2006F Proof	75,000	Value: 1.00				
2006G In sets only	90,000	—	—	—	4.50	—
2006G Proof	75,000	Value: 1.00				
2006J In sets only	90,000	—	—	—	4.50	—
2006J Proof	75,000	Value: 1.00				
2007A	119,490,000	—	—	—	0.35	—
2007A Proof	75,000	Value: 1.00				
2007D	125,460,000	—	—	—	0.35	—
2007D Proof	75,000	Value: 1.00				
2007F	143,370,000	—	—	—	0.35	—
2007F Proof	75,000	Value: 1.00				
2007G	83,670,000	—	—	—	0.35	—
2007G Proof	75,000	Value: 1.00				
2007J	125,460,000	—	—	—	0.35	—
2007J Proof	75,000	Value: 1.00				
2008A	101,280,000	—	—	—	0.35	—
2008A Proof	70,000	Value: 1.00				
2008D	106,340,000	—	—	—	0.35	—
2008D Proof	70,000	Value: 1.00				
2008F	121,520,000	—	—	—	0.35	—
2008F Proof	70,000	Value: 1.00				
2008G	70,920,000	—	—	—	0.35	—
2008G Proof	70,000	Value: 1.00				
2008J	106,340,000	—	—	—	0.35	—
2008J Proof	70,000	Value: 1.00				
2009A	100,060,000	—	—	—	0.35	—
2009A Proof	50,000	Value: 1.00				
2009D	105,060,000	—	—	—	0.35	—
2009D Proof	50,000	Value: 1.00				
2009F	120,060,000	—	—	—	0.35	—
2009F Proof	50,000	Value: 1.00				
2009G	70,060,000	—	—	—	0.35	—
2009G Proof	50,000	Value: 1.00				
2009J	105,060,000	—	—	—	0.35	—
2009J Proof	50,000	Value: 1.00				
2010A	94,454,000	—	—	—	0.35	—
2010A Proof	45,150	Value: 1.00				
2010D	99,167,000	—	—	—	0.35	—
2010D Proof	40,120	Value: 1.00				
2010F	113,327,000	—	—	—	0.35	—
2010F Proof	40,120	Value: 1.00				
2010G	66,127,000	—	—	—	0.35	—
2010G Proof	40,120	Value: 1.00				
2010J	99,167,000	—	—	—	0.35	—
2010J Proof	40,120	Value: 1.00				
2011A	118,400,000	—	—	—	0.35	—
2011A Proof	Est. 50,000	Value: 1.25				
2011D	124,375,000	—	—	—	0.35	—
2011D Proof	Est. 50,000	Value: 1.25				
2011F	142,135,000	—	—	—	0.35	—
2011F Proof	Est. 50,000	Value: 1.25				
2011G	82,935,000	—	—	—	0.35	—
2011G Proof	Est. 50,000	Value: 1.25				
2011J	124,375,000	—	—	—	0.35	—
2011J Proof	Est. 50,000	Value: 1.25				
2012A	—	—	—	—	0.35	—
2012A Proof	Est. 40,000	Value: 1.25				
2012D	—	—	—	—	0.35	—
2012D Proof	Est. 40,000	Value: 1.25				
2012F	—	—	—	—	0.35	—
2012F Proof	Est. 40,000	Value: 1.25				
2012G	—	—	—	—	0.35	—
2012G Proof	Est. 40,000	Value: 1.25				
2012J	—	—	—	—	0.35	—
2012J Proof	Est. 40,000	Value: 1.25				

KM# 208   2 EURO CENT
3.0600 g., Copper Plated Steel, 18.75 mm. **Obv:** Oak leaves
Rev: Denomination and globe **Edge:** Grooved

Date	Mintage	F	VF	XF	Unc	BU
2002A	480,090,000	—	—	—	0.50	—
2002A Proof	75,000	Value: 1.50				
2002D	504,090,000	—	—	—	0.50	—
2002D Proof	75,000	Value: 1.50				
2002F	576,090,000	—	—	—	0.50	—
2002F Proof	75,000	Value: 1.50				
2002G	336,090,000	—	—	—	0.50	—
2002G Proof	75,000	Value: 1.50				
2002J	504,090,000	—	—	—	0.50	—
2002J Proof	75,000	Value: 1.50				
2003A	90,000	—	—	—	0.50	—
2003A Proof	75,000	Value: 1.50				
2003D	90,000	—	—	—	0.50	—
2003D Proof	75,000	Value: 1.50				
2003F	90,000	—	—	—	0.50	—
2003F Proof	75,000	Value: 1.50				
2003G	90,000	—	—	—	0.50	—
2003G Proof	75,000	Value: 1.50				
2003J	90,000	—	—	—	0.50	—
2003J Proof	75,000	Value: 1.50				
2004A	112,090,000	—	—	—	0.50	—
2004A Proof	75,000	Value: 1.50				
2004D	117,690,000	—	—	—	0.50	—
2004D Proof	75,000	Value: 1.50				
2004F	134,490,000	—	—	—	0.50	—
2004F Proof	75,000	Value: 1.50				
2004G	78,490,000	—	—	—	0.50	—
2004G Proof	75,000	Value: 1.50				
2004J	117,690,000	—	—	—	0.50	—
2004J Proof	75,000	Value: 1.50				
2005A	44,090,000	—	—	—	0.50	—
2005A Proof	75,000	Value: 1.50				
2005D	46,290,000	—	—	—	0.50	—
2005D Proof	75,000	Value: 1.50				
2005F	52,890,000	—	—	—	0.50	—
2005F Proof	75,000	Value: 1.50				
2005G	30,890,000	—	—	—	0.50	—
2005G Proof	75,000	Value: 1.50				
2005J	46,290,000	—	—	—	0.50	—
2005J Proof	75,000	Value: 1.50				
2006A	27,090,000	—	—	—	0.50	—
2006A Proof	75,000	Value: 1.50				
2006D	28,440,000	—	—	—	0.50	—
2006D Proof	75,000	Value: 1.50				
2006F	32,490,000	—	—	—	0.50	—
2006F Proof	75,000	Value: 1.50				
2006G	18,990,000	—	—	—	0.50	—
2006G Proof	75,000	Value: 1.50				
2006J	28,440,000	—	—	—	0.50	—
2006J Proof	75,000	Value: 1.50				
2007A	52,490,000	—	—	—	0.50	—
2007A Proof	75,000	Value: 1.50				
2007D	55,110,000	—	—	—	0.50	—
2007D Proof	75,000	Value: 1.50				
2007F	62,970,000	—	—	—	0.50	—
2007F Proof	75,000	Value: 1.50				
2007G	36,770,000	—	—	—	0.50	—
2007G Proof	75,000	Value: 1.50				
2007J	55,110,000	—	—	—	0.50	—
2007J Proof	75,000	Value: 1.50				
2008A	29,280,000	—	—	—	0.50	—
2008A Proof	70,000	Value: 1.50				
2008D	30,740,000	—	—	—	0.50	—
2008D Proof	70,000	Value: 1.50				
2008F	35,120,000	—	—	—	0.50	—
2008F Proof	70,000	Value: 1.50				
2008G	20,520,000	—	—	—	0.50	—
2008G Proof	70,000	Value: 1.50				
2008J	30,740,000	—	—	—	0.50	—
2008J Proof	70,000	Value: 1.50				
2009A	39,660,000	—	—	—	0.50	—
2009A Proof	50,000	Value: 1.50				
2009D	41,640,000	—	—	—	0.50	—
2009D Proof	50,000	Value: 1.50				
2009F	47,580,000	—	—	—	0.50	—
2009F Proof	50,000	Value: 1.50				
2009G	27,780,000	—	—	—	0.50	—
2009G Proof	50,000	Value: 1.50				
2009J	41,640,000	—	—	—	0.50	—
2009J Proof	50,000	Value: 1.50				
2010A	39,854,000	—	—	—	0.50	—
2010A Proof	45,150	Value: 1.50				
2010D	41,837,000	—	—	—	0.50	—
2010D Proof	40,120	Value: 1.50				
2010F	47,807,000	—	—	—	0.50	—
2010F Proof	40,120	Value: 1.50				
2010G	20,903,000	—	—	—	0.50	—
2010G Proof	40,120	Value: 1.50				
2010J	41,837,000	—	—	—	0.50	—
2010J Proof	40,120	Value: 1.50				

Date	Mintage	F	VF	XF	Unc	BU
2011A	100,455,000	—	—	—	0.50	—
2011A Proof	Est. 50,000	Value: 1.50				
2011D	105,475,000	—	—	—	0.50	—
2011D Proof	50,000	Value: 1.50				
2011F	120,535,000	—	—	—	0.50	—
2011F Proof	Est. 50,000	Value: 1.50				
2011G	70,335,000	—	—	—	0.50	—
2011G Proof	50,000	Value: 1.50				
2011G	105,475,000	—	—	—	0.50	—
2011J Proof	Est. 50,000	Value: 1.50				
2012A	—	—	—	—	0.50	—
2012A Proof	Est. 40,000	Value: 1.75				
2012D	—	—	—	—	0.50	—
2012D Proof	Est. 40,000	Value: 1.75				
2012F	—	—	—	—	0.50	—
2012F Proof	Est. 40,000	Value: 1.75				
2012G	—	—	—	—	0.50	—
2012G Proof	Est. 40,000	Value: 1.75				
2012J	—	—	—	—	0.50	—
2012J Proof	Est. 40,000	Value: 1.75				

KM# 209   5 EURO CENT
3.9200 g., Copper Plated Steel, 21.25 mm. **Obv:** Oak leaves
Rev: Denomination and globe **Edge:** Plain

Date	Mintage	F	VF	XF	Unc	BU
2002A	475,000,000	—	—	—	0.75	—
2002A Proof	130,000	Value: 2.00				
2002D	495,700,000	—	—	—	0.75	—
2002D Proof	130,000	Value: 2.00				
2002F	563,710,000	—	—	—	0.75	—
2002F Proof	130,000	Value: 2.00				
2002G	328,400,000	—	—	—	0.75	—
2002G Proof	130,000	Value: 2.00				
2002J	501,850,000	—	—	—	0.75	—
2002J Proof	130,000	Value: 2.00				
2003A In sets only	180,000	—	—	—	4.50	—
2003A Proof	150,000	Value: 2.00				
2003D In sets only	180,000	—	—	—	4.50	—
2003D Proof	150,000	Value: 2.00				
2003F In sets only	180,000	—	—	—	4.50	—
2003F Proof	150,000	Value: 2.00				
2003G In sets only	180,000	—	—	—	4.50	—
2003G Proof	150,000	Value: 2.00				
2003J In sets only	180,000	—	—	—	4.50	—
2003J Proof	150,000	Value: 2.00				
2004A	112,000,000	—	—	—	0.75	—
2004A Proof	—	Value: 2.00				
2004D	117,600,000	—	—	—	0.75	—
2004D Proof	—	Value: 2.00				
2004F	134,400,000	—	—	—	0.75	—
2004F Proof	—	Value: 2.00				
2004G	78,400,000	—	—	—	0.75	—
2004G Proof	—	Value: 2.00				
2004J	117,600,000	—	—	—	0.75	—
2004J Proof	—	Value: 2.00				
2005A	44,000,000	—	—	—	0.75	—
2005A Proof	—	Value: 2.00				
2005D	46,200,000	—	—	—	0.75	—
2005D Proof	—	Value: 2.00				
2005F	52,800,000	—	—	—	0.75	—
2005F Proof	—	Value: 2.00				
2005G	30,800,000	—	—	—	0.75	—
2005G Proof	—	Value: 2.00				
2005J	46,200,000	—	—	—	0.75	—
2005J Proof	—	Value: 2.00				
2006A	27,000,000	—	—	—	0.75	—
2006A Proof	—	Value: 2.00				
2006D	28,350,000	—	—	—	0.75	—
2006D Proof	—	Value: 2.00				
2006F	32,400,000	—	—	—	0.75	—
2006F Proof	—	Value: 2.00				
2006G	18,900,000	—	—	—	0.75	—
2006G Proof	—	Value: 2.00				
2006J	28,350,000	—	—	—	0.75	—
2006J Proof	—	Value: 2.00				
2007A	52,400,000	—	—	—	0.75	—
2007A Proof	—	Value: 2.00				
2007D	55,020,000	—	—	—	0.75	—
2007D Proof	—	Value: 2.00				
2007F	62,880,000	—	—	—	0.75	—
2007F Proof	—	Value: 2.00				
2007G	38,680,000	—	—	—	0.75	—
2007G Proof	—	Value: 2.00				
2007J	55,020,000	—	—	—	0.75	—
2007J Proof	—	Value: 2.00				
2008A	29,200,000	—	—	—	0.75	—
2008A Proof	—	Value: 2.00				
2008D	30,700,000	—	—	—	0.75	—
2008D Proof	—	Value: 2.00				
2008F	35,000,000	—	—	—	0.75	—
2008F Proof	—	Value: 2.00				
2008G	20,400,000	—	—	—	0.75	—
2008G Proof	—	Value: 2.00				

Date	Mintage	F	VF	XF	Unc	BU
2008J	30,700,000	—	—	—	0.75	—
2008J Proof	—	Value: 2.00				
2009A	—	—	—	—	0.75	—
2009A Proof	—	Value: 2.00				
2009D	—	—	—	—	0.75	—
2009D Proof	—	Value: 2.00				
2009F	—	—	—	—	0.75	—
2009F Proof	—	Value: 2.00				
2009G	—	—	—	—	0.75	—
2009G Proof	—	Value: 2.00				
2009J	—	—	—	—	0.75	—
2009J Proof	—	Value: 2.00				
2010A	—	—	—	—	0.75	—
2010A Proof	—	Value: 2.00				
2010D	—	—	—	—	0.75	—
2010D Proof	—	Value: 2.00				
2010F	—	—	—	—	0.75	—
2010F Proof	—	Value: 2.00				
2010G	—	—	—	—	0.75	—
2010G Proof	—	Value: 2.00				
2010J	—	—	—	—	0.75	—
2010J Proof	—	Value: 2.00				
2011A	59,275,000	—	—	—	0.75	—
2011A Proof	Est. 50,000	Value: 2.25				
2011D	62,215,000	—	—	—	0.75	—
2011D Proof	Est. 50,000	Value: 2.25				
2011F	71,095,000	—	—	—	0.75	—
2011F Proof	Est. 50,000	Value: 2.25				
2011G	41,495,000	—	—	—	0.75	—
2011G Proof	Est. 50,000	Value: 2.25				
2011J	62,215,000	—	—	—	0.75	—
2011J Proof	Est. 50,000	Value: 2.25				
2012A	—	—	—	—	0.75	—
2012A Proof	Est. 40,000	Value: 2.25				
2012D	—	—	—	—	0.75	—
2012D Proof	Est. 40,000	Value: 2.25				
2012F	—	—	—	—	0.75	—
2012F Proof	Est. 40,000	Value: 2.25				
2012G	—	—	—	—	0.75	—
2012G Proof	Est. 40,000	Value: 2.25				
2012J	—	—	—	—	0.75	—
2012J Proof	Est. 40,000	Value: 2.25				

KM# 210   10 EURO CENT
4.0000 g., Brass, 19.7 mm. **Obv:** Brandenburg Gate **Rev:** Denomination and map **Edge:** Reeded

Date	Mintage	F	VF	XF	Unc	BU
2002A	696,240,000	—	—	—	0.75	—
2002A Proof	75,000	Value: 2.00				
2002D	722,040,000	—	—	—	0.75	—
2002D Proof	75,000	Value: 2.00				
2002F	838,890,000	—	—	—	0.75	—
2002F Proof	75,000	Value: 2.00				
2002G	494,390,000	—	—	—	0.75	—
2002G Proof	75,000	Value: 2.00				
2002J	758,730,000	—	—	—	0.75	—
2002J Proof	75,000	Value: 2.00				
2003A	50,750,000	—	—	—	1.25	—
2003A Proof	75,000	Value: 2.00				
2003D	50,940,000	—	—	—	1.25	—
2003D Proof	75,000	Value: 2.00				
2003F	6,090,000	—	—	—	2.00	—
2003F Proof	75,000	Value: 2.00				
2003G	13,090,000	—	—	—	1.25	—
2003G Proof	75,000	Value: 2.00				
2003J	25,590,000	—	—	—	1.25	—
2003J Proof	75,000	Value: 2.00				
2004A In sets only	99,000	—	—	—	4.50	—
2004A Proof	75,000	Value: 2.00				
2004D	11,290,000	—	—	—	1.25	—
2004D Proof	75,000	Value: 2.00				
2004F	51,450,000	—	—	—	1.25	—
2004F Proof	75,000	Value: 2.00				
2004G	15,550,000	—	—	—	1.25	—
2004G Proof	75,000	Value: 2.00				
2004J In sets only	90,000	—	—	—	4.50	—
2004J Proof	75,000	Value: 2.00				
2005A In sets only	90,000	—	—	—	4.50	—
2005A Proof	75,000	Value: 2.00				
2005D In sets only	90,000	—	—	—	4.50	—
2005D Proof	75,000	Value: 2.00				
2005F In sets only	90,000	—	—	—	4.50	—
2005F Proof	75,000	Value: 2.00				
2005G In sets only	90,000	—	—	—	4.50	—
2005G Proof	75,000	Value: 2.00				
2005J In sets only	90,000	—	—	—	4.50	—
2005J Proof	75,000	Value: 2.00				
2006A In sets only	90,000	—	—	—	4.50	—
2006A Proof	75,000	Value: 2.00				
2006D In sets only	90,000	—	—	—	4.50	—
2006D Proof	75,000	Value: 2.00				
2006F In sets only	90,000	—	—	—	4.50	—
2006F Proof	75,000	Value: 2.00				

Date	Mintage	F	VF	XF	Unc	BU
2006G In sets only	90,000	—	—	—	4.50	—
2006G Proof	75,000	Value: 2.00				
2006J In sets only	90,000	—	—	—	4.50	—
2006J Proof	75,000	Value: 2.00				

KM# 254   10 EURO CENT
4.1000 g., Brass, 19.75 mm.   **Obv:** Brandenburg Gate **Rev:** Relief map of Western Europe, stars, lines and value **Edge:** Reeded

Date	Mintage	F	VF	XF	Unc	BU
2007A In sets only	90,000	—	—	—	4.50	—
2007A Proof	75,000	Value: 2.00				
2007D In sets only	90,000	—	—	—	4.50	—
2007D Proof	75,000	Value: 2.00				
2007F In sets only	90,000	—	—	—	4.50	—
2007F Proof	75,000	Value: 2.00				
2007G In sets only	90,000	—	—	—	4.50	—
2007G Proof	75,000	Value: 2.00				
2007J In sets only	90,000	—	—	—	4.50	—
2007J Proof	75,000	Value: 2.00				
2008A In sets only	80,000	—	—	—	4.50	—
2008A Proof	70,000	Value: 2.00				
2008D In sets only	80,000	—	—	—	4.50	—
2008D Proof	70,000	Value: 2.00				
2008F In sets only	80,000	—	—	—	4.50	—
2008F Proof	70,000	Value: 2.00				
2008G In sets only	80,000	—	—	—	4.50	—
2008G Proof	70,000	Value: 2.00				
2008J In sets only	80,000	—	—	—	4.50	—
2008J Proof	70,000	Value: 2.00				
2009A In sets only	60,000	—	—	—	4.50	—
2009A Proof	50,000	Value: 2.00				
2009D In sets only	60,000	—	—	—	4.50	—
2009D Proof	50,000	Value: 2.00				
2009F Proof	50,000	Value: 2.00				
2009G In sets only	60,000	—	—	—	4.50	—
2009G Proof	50,000	Value: 2.00				
2009J In sets only	60,000	—	—	—	4.50	—
2009J Proof	50,000	Value: 2.00				
2010A In sets only	53,800	—	—	—	3.00	—
2010A Proof	45,150	Value: 2.00				
2010D In sets only	46,800	—	—	—	3.00	—
2010D Proof	40,120	Value: 2.00				
2010F In sets only	46,800	—	—	—	3.00	—
2010F Proof	40,120	Value: 2.00				
2010G In sets only	46,800	—	—	—	3.00	—
2010G Proof	40,120	Value: 2.00				
2010J In sets only	46,800	—	—	—	3.00	—
2010J Proof	40,120	Value: 2.00				
2011A In sets only	Est. 55,000	—	—	—	3.00	—
2011A Proof	Est. 50,000	Value: 2.75				
2011D In sets only	Est. 55,000	—	—	—	3.00	—
2011D Proof	Est. 50,000	Value: 2.75				
2011F In sets only	Est. 55,000	—	—	—	3.00	—
2011F Proof	Est. 50,000	Value: 2.75				
2011G In sets only	Est. 55,000	—	—	—	3.00	—
2011G Proof	Est. 50,000	Value: 2.75				
2011J In sets only	Est. 55,000	—	—	—	3.00	—
2011J Proof	Est. 50,000	Value: 2.75				
2012A	—	—	—	—	3.00	—
2012A Proof	Est. 40,000	Value: 2.75				
2012D	—	—	—	—	3.00	—
2012D Proof	Est. 40,000	Value: 2.75				
2012F	—	—	—	—	3.00	—
2012F Proof	Est. 40,000	Value: 2.75				
2012G	—	—	—	—	3.00	—
2012G Proof	Est. 40,000	Value: 2.75				
2012J	—	—	—	—	3.00	—
2012J Proof	Est. 40,000	Value: 2.75				

KM# 211   20 EURO CENT
5.7400 g., Brass, 22.2 mm.   **Obv:** Brandenburg Gate **Rev:** Denomination and map **Edge:** Notched

Date	Mintage	F	VF	XF	Unc	BU
2002A	378,240,000	—	—	—	1.00	—
2002A Proof	75,000	Value: 3.00				
2002D	367,090,000	—	—	—	1.00	—
2002D Proof	75,000	Value: 3.00				
2002F	421,690,000	—	—	—	1.00	—
2002F Proof	75,000	Value: 3.00				
2002G	251,990,000	—	—	—	1.00	—
2002G Proof	75,000	Value: 3.00				
2002J	441,090,000	—	—	—	1.00	—
2002J Proof	75,000	Value: 3.00				
2003A	41,950,000	—	—	—	1.00	—
2003A Proof	75,000	Value: 3.00				
2003D	24,190,000	—	—	—	1.00	—
2003D Proof	75,000	Value: 3.00				
2003F	82,490,000	—	—	—	1.00	—
2003F Proof	75,000	Value: 3.00				
2003G	42,190,000	—	—	—	1.00	—
2003G Proof	75,000	Value: 3.00				
2003J In sets only	90,000	—	—	—	4.50	—

Date	Mintage	F	VF	XF	Unc	BU
2003J Proof	75,000	Value: 3.00				
2004A In sets only	90,000	—	—	—	4.50	—
2004A Proof	75,000	Value: 3.00				
2004D	49,850,000	—	—	—	2.50	—
2004D Proof	75,000	Value: 3.00				
2004F In sets only	90,000	—	—	—	4.50	—
2004F Proof	75,000	Value: 3.00				
2004G In sets only	90,000	—	—	—	4.50	—
2004G Proof	75,000	Value: 3.00				
2004J In sets only	90,000	—	—	—	4.50	—
2004J Proof	75,000	Value: 3.00				
2005A	8,090,000	—	—	—	1.00	—
2005A Proof	75,000	Value: 3.00				
2005D	8,490,000	—	—	—	1.00	—
2005D Proof	75,000	Value: 3.00				
2005F	9,690,000	—	—	—	1.00	—
2005F Proof	75,000	Value: 3.00				
2005G	5,690,000	—	—	—	1.00	—
2005G Proof	75,000	Value: 3.00				
2005J	8,490,000	—	—	—	1.00	—
2005J Proof	75,000	Value: 3.00				
2006A	39,090,000	—	—	—	1.00	—
2006A Proof	75,000	Value: 3.00				
2006D	41,040,000	—	—	—	1.00	—
2006D Proof	75,000	Value: 3.00				
2006F	46,890,000	—	—	—	1.00	—
2006F Proof	75,000	Value: 3.00				
2006G	27,390,000	—	—	—	1.00	—
2006G Proof	75,000	Value: 3.00				
2006J	41,040,000	—	—	—	1.00	—
2006J Proof	75,000	Value: 3.00				
2007F Error die paring		—	—	—	60.00	75.00

KM# 255   20 EURO CENT
5.7400 g., Brass, 22.25 mm.   **Obv:** Brandenburg Gate **Rev:** Relief map of Western Europe, stars, lines and value **Edge:** Notched

Date	Mintage	F	VF	XF	Unc	BU
2007A	21,690,000	—	—	—	1.00	—
2007A Proof	75,000	Value: 3.00				
2007D	22,770,000	—	—	—	1.00	—
2007D Proof	75,000	Value: 3.00				
2007F	26,010,000	—	—	—	1.00	—
2007F Proof	75,000	Value: 3.00				
2007G	15,210,000	—	—	—	1.00	—
2007G Proof	75,000	Value: 3.00				
2007J	23,020,000	—	—	—	1.00	—
2007J Proof	75,000	Value: 3.00				
2008A	15,880,000	—	—	—	1.00	—
2008A Proof	70,000	Value: 3.00				
2008D	16,670,000	—	—	—	1.00	—
2008D Proof	70,000	Value: 3.00				
2008F	19,040,000	—	—	—	1.00	—
2008F Proof	70,000	Value: 3.00				
2008G	11,140,000	—	—	—	1.00	—
2008G Proof	70,000	Value: 3.00				
2008J	16,420,000	—	—	—	1.00	—
2008J Proof	70,000	Value: 3.00				
2009A	21,660,000	—	—	—	1.00	—
2009A Proof	50,000	Value: 3.00				
2009D	22,740,000	—	—	—	1.00	—
2009D Proof	50,000	Value: 3.00				
2009F	25,980,000	—	—	—	1.00	—
2009F Proof	50,000	Value: 3.00				
2009G	15,180,000	—	—	—	1.00	—
2009G Proof	50,000	Value: 3.00				
2009J	22,740,000	—	—	—	1.00	—
2009J Proof	50,000	Value: 3.00				
2010A	33,055,000	—	—	—	1.00	—
2010A Proof	Est. 50,000	Value: 3.00				
2010D	34,705,000	—	—	—	1.00	—
2010D Proof	Est. 50,000	Value: 3.00				
2010F	39,655,000	—	—	—	1.00	—
2010F Proof	Est. 50,000	Value: 3.00				
2010G	23,155,000	—	—	—	1.00	—
2010G Proof	50,000	Value: 3.00				
2010J	34,705,000	—	—	—	1.00	—
2010J Proof	50,000	Value: 3.00				
2011A	—	—	—	—	1.00	—
2011A Proof	Est. 40,000	Value: 3.00				
2011D	—	—	—	—	1.00	—
2011D Proof	Est. 40,000	Value: 3.00				
2011F	—	—	—	—	1.00	—
2011F Proof	Est. 40,000	Value: 3.00				
2011G	—	—	—	—	1.00	—
2011F Proof	Est. 40,000	Value: 3.00				
2011J	—	—	—	—	1.00	—
2011J Proof	Est. 40,000	Value: 3.00				
2012A	—	—	—	—	1.00	—
2012A Proof	—	Value: 3.00				
2012D	—	—	—	—	1.00	—
2012D Proof	—	Value: 3.00				

Date	Mintage	F	VF	XF	Unc	BU
2012F	—	—	—	—	1.00	—
2012F Proof	—	Value: 3.00				
2012G	—	—	—	—	1.00	—
2012G Proof	—	Value: 3.00				
2012J	—	—	—	—	1.00	—
2012J Proof	—	Value: 3.00				

KM# 212   50 EURO CENT
7.8100 g., Brass, 24.2 mm.   **Obv:** Brandenburg Gate **Rev:** Denomination and map **Edge:** Reeded

Date	Mintage	F	VF	XF	Unc	BU
2002A	337,840,000	—	—	—	1.75	—
2002A Proof	75,000	Value: 4.00				
2002D	370,330,000	—	—	—	1.75	—
2002D Proof	75,000	Value: 4.00				
2002F	430,570,000	—	—	—	1.75	—
2002F Proof	75,000	Value: 4.00				
2002G	256,650,000	—	—	—	1.75	—
2002G Proof	75,000	Value: 4.00				
2002J	401,490,000	—	—	—	1.75	—
2002J Proof	75,000	Value: 4.00				
2003A In sets only	90,000	—	—	—	4.50	—
2003A Proof	75,000	Value: 4.00				
2003D	70,710,000	—	—	—	4.50	—
2003D Proof	75,000	Value: 4.00				
2003F In sets only	99,000	—	—	—	4.50	—
2003F Proof	75,000	Value: 4.00				
2003G In sets only	99,000	—	—	—	4.50	—
2003G Proof	75,000	Value: 4.00				
2003J	39,690,000	—	—	—	1.75	—
2003J Proof	75,000	Value: 4.00				
2004A	82,350,000	—	—	—	1.75	—
2004A Proof	75,000	Value: 4.00				
2004D In sets only	90,000	—	—	—	4.50	—
2004D Proof	75,000	Value: 4.00				
2004F	73,610,000	—	—	—	1.75	—
2004F Proof	75,000	Value: 4.00				
2004G	37,530,000	—	—	—	1.75	—
2004G Proof	75,000	Value: 4.00				
2004J In sets only	90,000	—	—	—	4.50	—
2004J Proof	75,000	Value: 4.00				
2005A In sets only	90,000	—	—	—	4.50	—
2005A Proof	75,000	Value: 4.00				
2005D In sets only	90,000	—	—	—	4.50	—
2005D Proof	75,000	Value: 4.00				
2005F In sets only	90,000	—	—	—	4.50	—
2005F Proof	75,000	Value: 4.00				
2005G In sets only	90,000	—	—	—	4.50	—
2005G Proof	75,000	Value: 4.00				
2005J In sets only	90,000	—	—	—	4.50	—
2005J Proof	75,000	Value: 4.00				
2006A In sets only	90,000	—	—	—	4.50	—
2006A Proof	75,000	Value: 4.00				
2006D In sets only	90,000	—	—	—	4.50	—
2006D Proof	75,000	Value: 4.00				
2006F In sets only	90,000	—	—	—	4.50	—
2006F Proof	75,000	Value: 4.00				
2006G In sets only	90,000	—	—	—	4.50	—
2006G Proof	75,000	Value: 4.00				
2006J In sets only	90,000	—	—	—	4.50	—
2006J Proof	75,000	Value: 4.00				

KM# 256   50 EURO CENT
7.8000 g., Brass, 24.25 mm.   **Obv:** Brandenburg Gate **Rev:** Relief map of Western Europe, stars, lines and value **Edge:** Reeded

Date	Mintage	F	VF	XF	Unc	BU
2007A In sets only	90,000	—	—	—	4.50	—
2007A Proof	75,000	Value: 4.00				
2007D In sets only	90,000	—	—	—	4.50	—
2007D Proof	75,000	Value: 4.00				
2007F In sets only	90,000	—	—	—	4.50	—
2007F Proof	75,000	Value: 4.00				
2007G In sets only	90,000	—	—	—	4.50	—
2007G Proof	75,000	Value: 4.00				
2007J In sets only	90,000	—	—	—	4.50	—
2007J Proof	75,000	Value: 4.00				
2008A In sets only	80,000	—	—	—	4.50	—
2008A Proof	70,000	Value: 4.00				
2008D In sets only	80,000	—	—	—	4.50	—
2008D Proof	70,000	Value: 4.00				
2008F In sets only	80,000	—	—	—	4.50	—
2008F Proof	70,000	Value: 4.00				
2008G In sets only	80,000	—	—	—	4.50	—
2008G Proof	70,000	Value: 4.00				
2008J In sets only	80,000	—	—	—	4.50	—
2008J Proof	70,000	Value: 4.00				
2009A In sets only	60,000	—	—	—	4.50	—
2009A Proof	50,000	Value: 4.00				
2009D In sets only	60,000	—	—	—	4.50	—
2009D Proof	50,000	Value: 4.00				
2009F In sets only	60,000	—	—	—	4.50	—

Date	Mintage	F	VF	XF	Unc	BU
2009F Proof	50,000	Value: 4.00				
2009G In sets only	60,000	—	—	—	4.50	—
2009G Proof	50,000	Value: 4.00				
2009J In sets only	60,000	—	—	—	4.50	—
2009J Proof	50,000	Value: 4.00				
2010A In sets only	53,800	—	—	—	3.00	—
2010A Proof	45,150	Value: 4.00				
2010D In sets only	46,800	—	—	—	3.00	—
2010D Proof	40,120	Value: 4.00				
2010F In sets only	46,800	—	—	—	3.00	—
2010F Proof	40,120	Value: 4.00				
2010G In sets only	46,800	—	—	—	3.00	—
2010G Proof	40,120	Value: 4.00				
2010J In sets only	46,800	—	—	—	3.00	—
2010J Proof	40,120	Value: 4.00				
2011A In sets only	Est. 55,000	—	—	—	3.00	—
2011A Proof	Est. 50,000	Value: 4.00				
2011D In sets only	Est. 55,000	—	—	—	3.00	—
2011D Proof	Est. 50,000	Value: 4.00				
2011F In sets only	Est. 55,000	—	—	—	3.00	—
2011F Proof	Est. 50,000	Value: 4.00				
2011G In sets only	Est. 55,000	—	—	—	3.00	—
2011G Proof	Est. 50,000	Value: 4.00				
2011J In sets only	Est. 55,000	—	—	—	3.00	—
2011J Proof	Est. 50,000	Value: 4.00				
2012A	—	—	—	—	3.00	—
2012A Proof	Est. 40,000	Value: 4.00				
2012D	—	—	—	—	3.00	—
2012D Proof	Est. 40,000	Value: 4.00				
2012F	—	—	—	—	3.00	—
2012F Proof	Est. 40,000	Value: 4.00				
2012G	—	—	—	—	3.00	—
2012G Proof	Est. 40,000	Value: 4.00				
2012J	—	—	—	—	3.00	—
2012J Proof	Est. 40,000	Value: 4.00				

KM# 213   EURO
7.5000 g., Bi-Metallic Copper-Nickel center in Nickel-Brass ring, 23.25 mm. **Obv:** Stylized eagle **Rev:** Denomination over map **Edge:** Segmented reeding

Date	Mintage	F	VF	XF	Unc	BU
2002A	367,990,000	—	—	—	2.50	—
2002A Proof	75,000	Value: 6.50				
2002D	372,690,000	—	—	—	2.50	—
2002D Proof	75,000	Value: 6.50				
2002F	739,890,000	—	—	—	2.50	—
2002F Proof	75,000	Value: 6.50				
2002G	266,440,000	—	—	—	2.50	—
2002G Proof	75,000	Value: 6.50				
2002J	372,400,000	—	—	—	2.50	—
2002J Proof	75,000	Value: 6.50				
2003A	50,340,000	—	—	—	2.50	—
2003A Proof	75,000	Value: 6.50				
2003D In sets only	90,000	—	—	—	5.50	—
2003D Proof	75,000	Value: 6.50				
2003F In sets only	90,000	—	—	—	5.50	—
2003F Proof	75,000	Value: 6.50				
2003G In sets only	90,000	—	—	—	5.50	—
2003G Proof	75,000	Value: 6.50				
2003J	29,940,000	—	—	—	2.50	—
2003J Proof	75,000	Value: 6.50				
2004A	21,950,000	—	—	—	2.50	—
2004A Proof	75,000	Value: 6.50				
2004D	89,350,000	—	—	—	2.50	—
2004D Proof	75,000	Value: 6.50				
2004F	88,290,000	—	—	—	2.50	—
2004F Proof	75,000	Value: 6.50				
2004G	41,740,000	—	—	—	2.50	—
2004G Proof	75,000	Value: 6.50				
2004J In sets only	90,000	—	—	—	5.50	—
2004J Proof	75,000	Value: 6.50				
2005A In sets only	99,000	—	—	—	5.50	—
2005A Proof	75,000	Value: 5.00				
2005D In sets only	90,000	—	—	—	5.50	—
2005D Proof	75,000	Value: 5.00				
2005F In sets only	90,000	—	—	—	5.50	—
2005F Proof	75,000	Value: 5.00				
2005G In sets only	90,000	—	—	—	5.50	—
2005G Proof	75,000	Value: 5.00				
2005J	59,930,000	—	—	—	2.50	—
2005J Proof	75,000	Value: 5.00				
2006A In sets only	90,000	—	—	—	5.50	—
2006A Proof	75,000	Value: 5.00				
2006D In sets only	90,000	—	—	—	5.50	—
2006D Proof	75,000	Value: 5.00				
2006F In sets only	90,000	—	—	—	5.50	—
2006F Proof	75,000	Value: 5.00				
2006G In sets only	90,000	—	—	—	5.50	—
2006G Proof	75,000	Value: 5.00				
2006J In sets only	90,000	—	—	—	5.50	—
2006J Proof	75,000	Value: 5.00				

KM# 257   EURO
7.5000 g., Bi-Metallic Copper-Nickel center in Nickel-Brass ring, 23.25 mm. **Obv:** Stylized eagle **Rev:** Relief map of Western Europe, stars, lines and value **Edge:** Segmented reeding

Date	Mintage	F	VF	XF	Unc	BU
2007A In sets only	90,000	—	—	—	5.50	—
2007A Proof	75,000	Value: 5.00				
2007D In sets only	90,000	—	—	—	5.50	—
2007D Proof	75,000	Value: 5.00				
2007F In sets only	90,000	—	—	—	5.50	—
2007F Proof	75,000	Value: 5.00				
2007G In sets only	90,000	—	—	—	5.50	—
2007G Proof	75,000	Value: 5.00				
2007J In sets only	90,000	—	—	—	5.50	—
2007J Proof	75,000	Value: 5.00				
2008A In sets only	80,000	—	—	—	5.50	—
2008A Proof	70,000	Value: 5.00				
2008D In sets only	80,000	—	—	—	5.50	—
2008D Proof	70,000	Value: 5.00				
2008F In sets only	80,000	—	—	—	5.50	—
2008F Proof	70,000	Value: 5.00				
2008G In sets only	80,000	—	—	—	5.50	—
2008G Proof	70,000	Value: 5.00				
2008J In sets only	80,000	—	—	—	5.50	—
2008J Proof	70,000	Value: 5.00				
2009A In sets only	60,000	—	—	—	5.50	—
2009A Proof	50,000	Value: 5.00				
2009D In sets only	60,000	—	—	—	5.50	—
2009D Proof	50,000	Value: 5.00				
2009F In sets only	60,000	—	—	—	5.50	—
2009F Proof	50,000	Value: 5.00				
2009G In sets only	60,000	—	—	—	5.50	—
2009G Proof	50,000	Value: 5.00				
2009J In sets only	60,000	—	—	—	5.50	—
2009J Proof	50,000	Value: 5.00				
2010A In sets only	53,800	—	—	—	4.00	—
2010A Proof	45,150	Value: 5.00				
2010D In sets only	46,800	—	—	—	4.00	—
2010D Proof	40,120	Value: 5.00				
2010F In sets only	46,800	—	—	—	4.00	—
2010F Proof	40,120	Value: 5.00				
2010G In sets only	46,800	—	—	—	4.00	—
2010G Proof	40,120	Value: 5.00				
2010J In sets only	46,800	—	—	—	4.00	—
2010J Proof	40,120	Value: 5.00				
2011A In sets only	Est. 55,000	—	—	—	4.00	—
2011A Proof	Est. 50,000	Value: 5.00				
2011D In sets only	Est. 55,000	—	—	—	4.00	—
2011D Proof	Est. 50,000	Value: 5.00				
2011F In sets only	Est. 55,000	—	—	—	4.00	—
2011F Proof	Est. 50,000	Value: 5.00				
2011G In sets only	Est. 55,000	—	—	—	4.00	—
2011G Proof	Est. 50,000	Value: 5.00				
2011J In sets only	Est. 55,000	—	—	—	4.00	—
2011J Proof	Est. 50,000	Value: 5.00				
2012A	—	—	—	—	4.00	—
2012A Proof	Est. 40,000	Value: 5.00				
2012D	—	—	—	—	4.00	—
2012D Proof	Est. 40,000	Value: 5.00				
2012F	—	—	—	—	4.00	—
2012F Proof	Est. 40,000	Value: 5.00				
2012G	—	—	—	—	4.00	—
2012G Proof	Est. 40,000	Value: 5.00				
2012J	—	—	—	—	4.00	—
2012J Proof	Est. 40,000	Value: 5.00				

KM# 214   2 EURO
8.5000 g., Bi-Metallic Nickel-Brass center in Copper-Nickel ring, 25.75 mm. **Obv:** Stylized eagle **Rev:** Denomination and map **Edge:** Reeded and "EINIGKEIT UND RECHT UND FREIHEIT"

Date	Mintage	F	VF	XF	Unc	BU
2002A	239,010,000	—	—	—	4.50	—
2002A Proof	75,000	Value: 12.50				
2002D	231,390,000	—	—	—	4.50	—
2002D Proof	75,000	Value: 12.50				
2002F	281,180,000	—	—	—	4.50	—
2002F Proof	75,000	Value: 12.50				
2002G	181,040,000	—	—	—	4.50	—
2002G Proof	75,000	Value: 12.50				
2002J	257,910,000	—	—	—	4.50	—
2002J Proof	75,000	Value: 12.50				
2003A	20,560,000	—	—	—	4.50	—
2003A Proof	75,000	Value: 12.50				
2003D	22,260,000	—	—	—	4.50	—
2003D Proof	75,000	Value: 12.50				
2003F	24,550,000	—	—	—	4.50	—
2003F Proof	75,000	Value: 12.50				
2003G	29,238,000	—	—	—	4.50	—

Date	Mintage	F	VF	XF	Unc	BU
2003G Proof	75,000	Value: 12.50				
2003J	19,590,000	—	—	—	4.50	—
2003J Proof	75,000	Value: 12.50				
2004A	31,660,000	—	—	—	4.50	—
2004A Proof	75,000	Value: 12.50				
2004D	19,930,000	—	—	—	4.50	—
2004D Proof	75,000	Value: 12.50				
2004F In sets only	90,000	—	—	—	5.50	—
2004F Proof	75,000	Value: 12.50				
2004G In sets only	90,000	—	—	—	5.50	—
2004G Proof	75,000	Value: 12.50				
2004J	22,600,000	—	—	—	4.50	—
2004J Proof	75,000	Value: 12.50				
2005A In sets only	90,000	—	—	—	5.50	—
2005A Proof	75,000	Value: 10.00				
2005D In sets only	90,000	—	—	—	5.50	—
2005D Proof	75,000	Value: 10.00				
2005F In sets only	90,000	—	—	—	5.50	—
2005F Proof	75,000	Value: 10.00				
2005G In sets only	90,000	—	—	—	5.50	—
2005G Proof	75,000	Value: 10.00				
2005J In sets only	90,000	—	—	—	5.50	—
2005J Proof	75,000	Value: 10.00				
2006A In sets only	90,000	—	—	—	5.50	—
2006A Proof	75,000	Value: 10.00				
2006D In sets only	90,000	—	—	—	5.50	—
2006D Proof	75,000	Value: 10.00				
2006F In sets only	90,000	—	—	—	5.50	—
2006F Proof	75,000	Value: 10.00				
2006G In sets only	90,000	—	—	—	5.50	—
2006G Proof	75,000	Value: 10.00				
2006J In sets only	90,000	—	—	—	5.50	—
2006J Proof	75,000	Value: 10.00				

KM# 253   2 EURO
8.5000 g., Bi-Metallic Nickel-Brass center in Copper-Nickel ring, 25.75 mm. **Obv:** Schleswig Holstein castle **Obv. Legend:** BUNDESREPULIK DEUTSCHLAND **Obv. Inscription:** SCHLESWIG- / HOLSTEIN **Rev:** Denomination over map

Date	Mintage	F	VF	XF	Unc	BU
2006A	6,170,000	—	—	—	5.00	6.00
2006A Proof	145,000	Value: 10.00				
2006D	6,470,000	—	—	—	5.00	6.00
2006D Proof	145,000	Value: 10.00				
2006F	7,370,000	—	—	—	5.00	6.00
2006F Proof	145,000	Value: 10.00				
2006G	4,370,000	—	—	—	5.00	6.00
2006G Proof	145,000	Value: 10.00				
2006J	6,470,000	—	—	—	5.00	6.00
2006J Proof	145,000	Value: 10.00				

KM# 259   2 EURO
8.5000 g., Bi-Metallic Nickel-Brass center in Copper-Nickel ring, 25.75 mm. **Subject:** 50th Anniversary Treaty of Rome **Obv:** Open treaty book **Obv. Legend:** BUNDESREPUBLIK DEUTSCHLAND **Rev:** Large value at left, modified outline of Europe at right **Edge Lettering:** EINIGKEIT UND RECHT UND FREIHEIT

Date	Mintage	F	VF	XF	Unc	BU
2007A	1,090,000	—	—	—	4.00	5.00
2007A Proof	125,000	Value: 10.00				
2007D	14,590,000	—	—	—	4.00	5.50
2007D Proof	125,000	Value: 10.00				
2007F	8,090,000	—	—	—	4.00	5.50
2007F Proof	125,000	Value: 10.00				
2007G	5,090,000	—	—	—	4.00	5.50
2007G Proof	125,000	Value: 10.00				
2007J	1,590,000	—	—	—	4.00	5.50
2007J Proof	125,000	Value: 10.00				

KM# 260   2 EURO
8.5000 g., Bi-Metallic Nickel-Brass center in Copper-Nickel ring, 25.75 mm. **Obv:** City buildings, Mecklenburg's Schwerin Castle **Obv. Legend:** BUNDESREPUBLIK DEUTSCHLAND **Obv. Inscription:** MECKLENBURG- / VORPOMMERN **Rev:** Large value at left, modified map of Europe at right **Edge Lettering:** EINIGKEIT UND RECHT UND FREIHEIT

Date	Mintage	F	VF	XF	Unc	BU
2007A	1,210,000	—	—	—	4.00	5.50
2007A Proof	145,000	Value: 10.00				
2007D	12,010,000	—	—	—	4.00	5.50

Date	Mintage	F	VF	XF	Unc	BU
2007D Proof	145,000	Value: 10.00				
2007F	12,110,000	—	—	—	4.00	5.50
2007F Proof	145,000	Value: 10.00				
2007G	4,370,000	—	—	—	4.00	5.50
2007G Proof	145,000	Value: 10.00				
2007J	1,240,000	—	—	—	4.00	5.50
2007J Proof	145,000	Value: 10.00				

KM# 261   2 EURO
8.5000 g., Bi-Metallic Nickel-Brass center in Copper-Nickel ring, 25.75 mm. **Obv:** Hamburg Cathedral **Obv. Legend:** BUNDESREPUBLIK DEUTSCHLAND **Obv. Inscription:** HAMBURG **Rev:** Large value at left, modified outline of Europe at right **Edge Lettering:** EINIGKEIT UND RECHT UND FREIHEIT

Date	Mintage	F	VF	XF	Unc	BU
2008A	1,160,000	—	—	—	4.00	5.50
2008A Proof	140,000	Value: 10.00				
2008D	9,060,000	—	—	—	4.00	5.50
2008D Proof	140,000	Value: 10.00				
2008F	9,760,000	—	—	—	4.00	5.50
2008F Proof	140,000	Value: 10.00				
2008G	9,760,000	—	—	—	4.00	5.50
2008G Proof	4,360,000	Value: 10.00				
2008J	6,460,000	—	—	—	4.00	5.50
2008J Proof	140,000	Value: 10.00				

KM# 258   2 EURO
8.5000 g., Bi-Metallic Nickel-Brass center in Copper-Nickel ring, 25.75 mm. **Obv:** Stylized eagle **Rev:** Relief map of Western Europe, stars, lines and value **Edge Lettering:** EINIGKEIT UND RECHT UND FREIHEIT

Date	Mintage	F	VF	XF	Unc	BU
2008A	11,480,000	—	—	—	4.50	—
2008A Proof	20,000	Value: 10.00				
2008D	12,050,000	—	—	—	4.50	—
2008D Proof	70,000	Value: 10.00				
2008F	13,760,000	—	—	—	4.50	—
2008F Proof	70,000	Value: 10.00				
2008G	8,060,000	—	—	—	4.50	—
2008G Proof	70,000	Value: 10.00				
2008J	12,050,000	—	—	—	4.50	—
2008J Proof	70,000	Value: 10.00				
2009A In sets only	—	—	—	—	4.50	—
2009A Proof	50,000	Value: 10.00				
2009D In sets only	—	—	—	—	4.50	—
2009D Proof	50,000	Value: 10.00				
2009F In sets only	—	—	—	—	4.50	—
2009F Proof	50,000	Value: 10.00				
2009G In sets only	—	—	—	—	4.50	—
2009G Proof	50,000	Value: 10.00				
2009J In sets only	—	—	—	—	4.50	—
2009J Proof	50,000	Value: 10.00				
2010A	19,654,000	—	—	—	4.50	—
2010A Proof	45,150	Value: 10.00				
2010D	20,627,000	—	—	—	4.50	—
2010D Proof	40,120	Value: 10.00				
2010F	23,567,000	—	—	—	4.50	—
2010F Proof	40,120	Value: 10.00				
2010G	13,767,000	—	—	—	4.50	—
2010G Proof	40,120	Value: 10.00				
2010J	20,627,000	—	—	—	4.50	—
2010J Proof	40,120	Value: 10.00				
2011A	20,175,000	—	—	—	4.50	—
2011A Proof	Est. 50,000	Value: 10.00				
2011D	21,265,000	—	—	—	4.50	—
2011D Proof	Est. 50,000	Value: 10.00				
2011F	24,295,000	—	—	—	4.50	—
2011F Proof	Est. 50,000	Value: 10.00				
2011G	Est. 14,195,000	—	—	—	4.50	—
2011G Proof	Est. 50,000	Value: 10.00				
2011J	21,265,000	—	—	—	4.50	—
2011J Proof	Est. 50,000	Value: 10.00				

KM# 277   2 EURO
8.5000 g., Bi-Metallic Nickel-Brass center in Copper-Nickel ring, 25.75 mm. **Subject:** EMU, 10th Anniversary **Obv:** Stick figure and E symbol

Date	Mintage	F	VF	XF	Unc	BU
2009A	6,060,000	—	—	—	4.50	5.00

Date	Mintage	F	VF	XF	Unc	BU
2009A Proof	80,000	Value: 10.00				
2009D	7,360,000	—	—	—	4.50	5.00
2009D Proof	80,000	Value: 10.00				
2009F	7,260,000	—	—	—	4.50	5.00
2009F Proof	80,000	Value: 10.00				
2009G	4,260,000	—	—	—	4.50	5.00
2009G Proof	80,000	Value: 10.00				
2009J	6,360,000	—	—	—	4.50	5.00
2009J Proof	80,000	Value: 10.00				

KM# 276   2 EURO
8.5000 g., Bi-Metallic Nickel-Brass center in Copper-Nickel ring, 25.75 mm. **Obv:** Building in Saarland **Rev:** Value and map

Date	Mintage	F	VF	XF	Unc	BU
2009A	6,110,000	—	—	—	4.50	5.00
2009A Proof	100,000	Value: 10.00				
2009D	6,410,000	—	—	—	4.50	5.00
2009D Proof	100,000	Value: 10.00				
2009F	7,310,000	—	—	—	4.50	5.00
2009F Proof	100,000	Value: 10.00				
2009G	4,310,000	—	—	—	4.50	5.00
2009G Proof	100,000	Value: 10.00				
2009J	6,410,000	—	—	—	4.50	5.00
2009J Proof	100,000	Value: 10.00				

KM# 285   2 EURO
8.5000 g., Bi-Metallic Nickel-Brass center in Copper-Nickel ring, 25.75 mm. **Obv:** Bremen town hall and statue and knight statue **Rev:** Value and map

Date	Mintage	F	VF	XF	Unc	BU
2010A	6,104,000	—	—	—	4.50	5.00
2010A Proof	100,000	Value: 10.00				
2010D	6,397,000	—	—	—	4.50	5.00
2010D Proof	100,000	Value: 10.00				
2010F	7,297,000	—	—	—	4.50	5.00
2010F Proof	100,000	Value: 10.00				
2010G	4,297,000	—	—	—	4.50	5.00
2010G Proof	100,000	Value: 10.00				
2010J	6,397,000	—	—	—	4.50	5.00
2010J Proof	100,000	Value: 10.00				

KM# 293   2 EURO
8.5000 g., Bi-Metallic Nickel-Brass center in Copper-Nickel ring, 25.75 mm. **Obv:** Cologne Cathedral

Date	Mintage	F	VF	XF	Unc	BU
2011A	6,102,000	—	—	—	5.00	7.50
2011A Proof	102,000	Value: 10.00				
2011D	6,402,000	—	—	—	5.00	7.50
2011D Proof	102,000	Value: 10.00				
2011F	7,302,000	—	—	—	5.00	7.50
2011F Proof	102,000	Value: 10.00				
2011G	4,302,000	—	—	—	5.00	7.50
2011G Proof	102,000	Value: 10.00				
2011J	6,402,000	—	—	—	5.00	7.50
2011J Proof	102,000	Value: 10.00				

KM# 305   2 EURO
8.5000 g., Bi-Metallic Nickel-Brass center in Copper-Nickel ring, 25.75 mm. **Series:** German States **Subject:** Bavaria, Neuschwanstein Castle **Rev:** Relief map of Europe, stars, lines and value **Edge Lettering:** EINIGKEIT UND RECHT UND FREIHEIT

Date	Mintage	F	VF	XF	Unc	BU
2012A	Est. 6,100,000	—	—	—	4.00	5.00
2012A Proof	—	Value: 10.00				
2012D	Est. 6,400,000	—	—	—	4.00	5.00
2012D Proof	—	Value: 10.00				
2012F	Est. 7,300,000	—	—	—	4.00	5.00
2012F Proof	—	Value: 10.00				
2012G	Est. 4,300,000	—	—	—	4.00	5.00
2012G Proof	—	Value: 10.00				
2012J	Est. 6,400,000	—	—	—	4.00	5.00
2012J Proof	—	Value: 10.00				

KM# 306   2 EURO
8.5000 g., Bi-Metallic Nickel-Brass center in Copper-Nickel ring, 25.75 mm. **Subject:** Euro coinage, 10th Anniversary **Obv:** Euro symbol on globe at center, child-like rendering around **Rev:** Reliev map of Europe, stars, lines and value **Edge Lettering:** EINIGKEIT UND RECHT UND FREIHEIT

Date	Mintage	F	VF	XF	Unc	BU
2012A	Est. 6,100,000	—	—	—	4.00	5.00
2012A Proof	—	Value: 10.00				

Date	Mintage	F	VF	XF	Unc	BU
2012D	Est. 6,400,000	—	—	—	4.00	5.00
2012D Proof	—	Value: 10.00				
2012F	Est. 7,300,000	—	—	—	4.00	5.00
2012F Proof	—	Value: 10.00				
2012G	Est. 4,300,000	—	—	—	4.00	5.00
2012G Proof	—	Value: 10.00				
2012J	Est. 6,400,000	—	—	—	4.00	5.00
2012J Proof	—	Value: 10.00				

KM# 215   10 EURO
18.0000 g., 0.9250 Silver 0.5353 oz. ASW, 32.5 mm. **Subject:** Introduction of the Euro Currency **Obv:** Stylized round eagle **Rev:** Euro symbol and map **Edge Lettering:** IM ZEICHEN DER EINIGUNG EUROPAS

Date	Mintage	F	VF	XF	Unc	BU
2002F	2,000,000	—	—	—	22.00	25.00
2002F Proof	400,000	Value: 30.00				

KM# 216   10 EURO
18.0000 g., 0.9250 Silver 0.5353 oz. ASW, 32.5 mm. **Subject:** Berlin Subway Centennial **Obv:** Stylized squarish eagle **Rev:** Elevated and subterranean train views **Edge Lettering:** HISTORISCH UND ZUKUNFTS WEISEND

Date	Mintage	F	VF	XF	Unc	BU
2002D	2,000,000	—	—	—	22.00	25.00
2002D Proof	400,000	Value: 30.00				

KM# 217   10 EURO
18.0000 g., 0.9250 Silver 0.5353 oz. ASW, 32.5 mm. **Subject:** Documenta Kassel Art Exposition **Obv:** Stylized eagle above inscription **Rev:** Exposition logo **Edge Lettering:** ART (in nine languages)

Date	Mintage	F	VF	XF	Unc	BU
2002J	2,000,000	—	—	—	22.00	25.00
2002J Proof	300,000	Value: 30.00				

KM# 218   10 EURO
18.0000 g., 0.9250 Silver 0.5353 oz. ASW, 32.5 mm. **Subject:** Museum Island, Berlin **Obv:** Stylized eagle **Rev:** Aerial view of museum complex **Edge Lettering:** FREISTÄTTE FUR KÜNST UND WISSENSCHAFT

Date	Mintage	F	VF	XF	Unc	BU
2002A	2,000,000	—	—	—	22.00	25.00
2002A Proof	280,000	Value: 30.00				

KM# 219   10 EURO

18.0000 g., 0.9250 Silver 0.5353 oz. ASW, 32.5 mm. **Subject:** 50 Years - German Television **Obv:** Stylized eagle silhouette **Rev:** Television screen silhouette **Edge Lettering:** BILDUNG UNTERHALTUNG INFORMATION

Date	Mintage	F	VF	XF	Unc	BU
2002G	2,000,000	—	—	—	22.00	25.00
2002G Proof	290,000	Value: 32.00				

KM# 222   10 EURO

18.0000 g., 0.9250 Silver 0.5353 oz. ASW, 32.5 mm. **Subject:** Justus von Liebig **Obv:** Eagle above denomination **Rev:** Liebig's portrait **Edge Lettering:** FORSCHEN • LEHREN • ANWENDEN •

Date	Mintage	F	VF	XF	Unc	BU
2003J	2,050,000	—	—	—	22.00	25.00
2003J Proof	350,000	Value: 30.00				

KM# 227   10 EURO

18.0000 g., 0.9250 Silver 0.5353 oz. ASW, 32.5 mm. **Obv:** Stylized eagle above denomination **Rev:** Gottfried Semper and floor plan **Edge Lettering:** ARCHITEKT • FORSCHER • KOSMOPOLIT • DEMOKRAT •

Date	Mintage	F	VF	XF	Unc	BU
2003G	2,050,000	—	—	—	22.00	25.00
2003G Proof	350,000	Value: 30.00				

KM# 223   10 EURO

18.0000 g., 0.9250 Silver 0.5353 oz. ASW, 32.5 mm. **Subject:** World Cup Soccer **Obv:** Stylized round eagle above denomination **Rev:** German map on soccer ball **Edge Lettering:** DIE WELT ZU GAST BEI FREUNDEN A • D • F • G • J • **Note:** Mint is determined by which letter "E" in the edge inscription has a short center bar. If the first letter "E" has the short center bar the coin is from the Berlin mint. Second "E"= Munich, third "E"=Stuttgart, fourth "E"=Karlsruhe, fifth "E"=Hamburg

Date	Mintage	F	VF	XF	Unc	BU
2003A	710,000	—	—	—	22.00	25.00
2003A Proof	80,000	Value: 32.00				
2003D	710,000	—	—	—	22.00	25.00
2003D Proof	80,000	Value: 32.00				
2003F	710,000	—	—	—	22.00	25.00
2003F Proof	80,000	Value: 32.00				
2003G	710,000	—	—	—	22.00	25.00
2003G Proof	80,000	Value: 32.00				
2003J	710,000	—	—	—	22.00	25.00
2003J Proof	80,000	Value: 32.00				

KM# 224   10 EURO

18.0000 g., 0.9250 Silver 0.5353 oz. ASW, 32.5 mm. **Subject:** Ruhr Industrial District **Obv:** Stylized eagle, denomination below **Rev:** Various city views **Edge Lettering:** RUHRPOTT KULTURLANDSCHAFT

Date	Mintage	F	VF	XF	Unc	BU
2003F	2,050,000	—	—	—	22.00	25.00
2003F Proof	350,000	Value: 30.00				

KM# 226   10 EURO

18.0000 g., 0.9250 Silver 0.5353 oz. ASW, 32.5 mm. **Subject:** 50th Anniversary of the Ill-fated East German Revolution **Obv:** Stylized eagle, denomination at left **Rev:** Tank tracks over slogans **Edge Lettering:** ERINNERUNG AN DEN VOLKSAUFSTAND IN DER DDR

Date	Mintage	F	VF	XF	Unc	BU
2003A	2,050,000	—	—	—	22.00	25.00
2003A Proof	350,000	Value: 30.00				

KM# 225   10 EURO

18.0000 g., 0.9250 Silver 0.5353 oz. ASW, 32.5 mm. **Subject:** German Museum München Centennial **Obv:** Stylized eagle, denomination at left **Rev:** Abstract design **Edge Lettering:** SAMMELN • AUSSTELLEN • FORSCHEN • BILDEN •

Date	Mintage	F	VF	XF	Unc	BU
2003D	2,050,000	—	—	—	22.00	25.00
2003D Proof	350,000	Value: 30.00				

KM# 230   10 EURO

18.0000 g., 0.9250 Silver 0.5353 oz. ASW, 32.5 mm. **Obv:** Stylized eagle, stars and denomination **Rev:** Bauhaus Dessau geometric shapes design **Edge Lettering:** KUNST TECHNIK LEHRE

Date	Mintage	F	VF	XF	Unc	BU
2004A	1,800,000	—	—	—	22.00	25.00
2004A Proof	300,000	Value: 30.00				

KM# 232   10 EURO

18.0000 g., 0.9250 Silver 0.5353 oz. ASW, 32.5 mm. **Obv:** Stylized eagle and denomination **Rev:** Geese flying over Wattenmeer National Park **Edge Lettering:** MEERESGRUND TRIFFT HORIZONT

Date	Mintage	F	VF	XF	Unc	BU
2004J	1,800,000	—	—	—	22.00	25.00
2004J Proof	300,000	Value: 30.00				

KM# 233   10 EURO

18.0000 g., 0.9250 Silver 0.5353 oz. ASW, 32.5 mm. **Obv:** Stylized eagle **Rev:** Eduard Moerike **Edge Lettering:** OHNE DAS SCHÖNE WAS SOLL DER GEWINN

Date	Mintage	F	VF	XF	Unc	BU
2004F	1,800,000	—	—	—	22.00	25.00
2004F Proof	300,000	Value: 30.00				

KM# 234   10 EURO

18.0000 g., 0.9250 Silver 0.5353 oz. ASW, 32.5 mm. **Obv:** Stylized eagle, denomination below **Rev:** Space station above the earth **Edge Lettering:** RAUMFAHRT VERBINDET DIE WELT

Date	Mintage	F	VF	XF	Unc	BU
2004D	1,800,000	—	—	—	22.00	25.00
2004D Proof	300,000	Value: 30.00				

KM# 231   10 EURO

18.0000 g., 0.9250 Silver 0.5353 oz. ASW, 32.5 mm. **Obv:** Stylized eagle above denomination **Rev:** European Union country names and dates **Edge Lettering:** FREUDE SCHÖNER GÖTTERFUNKEN

Date	Mintage	F	VF	XF	Unc	BU
2004F	—	—	—	—	22.00	25.00
2004F Proof	—	Value: 30.00				
2004G	1,800,000	—	—	—	22.00	25.00
2004G Proof	300,000	Value: 30.00				

KM# 229   10 EURO

18.0000 g., 0.9250 Silver 0.5353 oz. ASW, 32.5 mm. **Obv:** Stylized eagle, denomination below **Rev:** Soccer ball orbiting the earth **Edge Lettering:** DIE WELT ZU GAST BEI FREUNDEN A D F G J **Note:** Soccer Series: Mint determination same as KM-223

Date	Mintage	F	VF	XF	Unc	BU
2004A	800,000	—	—	—	22.00	25.00
2004A Proof	80,000	Value: 30.00				
2004D	800,000	—	—	—	22.00	25.00
2004D Proof	80,000	Value: 30.00				
2004F	800,000	—	—	—	22.00	25.00
2004F Proof	80,000	Value: 30.00				
2004G	800,000	—	—	—	22.00	25.00
2004G Proof	80,000	Value: 30.00				
2004J	800,000	—	—	—	22.00	25.00
2004J Proof	80,000	Value: 30.00				

KM# 238   10 EURO
18.0000 g., 0.9250 Silver 0.5353 oz. ASW, 32.5 mm. **Subject:** Albert Einstein **Obv:** Stylized eagle within circle, denomination below **Rev:** E=mc2 on a sphere resting on a net **Edge Lettering:** NICHT AUFHOREN ZU FRAGEN

Date	Mintage	F	VF	XF	Unc	BU
2005J	1,800,000	—	—	—	22.00	25.00
2005J Proof	300,000	Value: 30.00				

KM# 239   10 EURO
18.0000 g., 0.9250 Silver 0.5353 oz. ASW, 32.5 mm. **Subject:** Friedrich von Schiller **Obv:** Stylized eagle **Rev:** Schiller portrait **Edge Lettering:** ERNST IST DAS LEBEN. HEITER IST DIE KUNST

Date	Mintage	F	VF	XF	Unc	BU
2005G	1,800,000	—	—	—	20.00	22.00
2005G Proof	300,000	Value: 30.00				

KM# 240   10 EURO
18.0000 g., 0.9250 Silver 0.5353 oz. ASW, 32.5 mm. **Subject:** Magdeburg **Obv:** Stylized eagle, denomination below **Rev:** Church flanked by landmarks and objects **Edge Lettering:** MAGADOBURG 805 • MAGDEBURG 2005

Date	Mintage	F	VF	XF	Unc	BU
2005A	1,800,000	—	—	—	22.00	25.00
2005A Proof	300,000	Value: 30.00				

KM# 241   10 EURO
18.0000 g., 0.9250 Silver 0.5353 oz. ASW, 32.5 mm. **Subject:** Bavarian Forest National Park **Obv:** Stylized eagle **Rev:** Various park scenes **Edge:** Lettered

Date	Mintage	F	VF	XF	Unc	BU
2005D	1,800,000	—	—	—	22.00	25.00
2005D Proof	300,000	Value: 30.00				

KM# 242   10 EURO
18.0000 g., 0.9250 Silver 0.5353 oz. ASW, 32.5 mm. **Subject:** Bertha von Suttner **Obv:** Stylized eagle above stars **Rev:** Suttner's portrait **Edge Lettering:** EIPHNH PAX FRIEDEN twice

Date	Mintage	F	VF	XF	Unc	BU
2005F	1,800,000	—	—	—	22.00	25.00
2005F Proof	300,000	Value: 30.00				

KM# 243   10 EURO
18.0000 g., 0.9250 Silver 0.5353 oz. ASW, 32.5 mm. **Subject:** World Cup Soccer **Obv:** Round stylized eagle **Rev:** Ball and legs seen through a net **Edge Lettering:** DIE WELT ZU GAST BEI FREUNDEN

Date	Mintage	F	VF	XF	Unc	BU
2005A	800,000	—	—	—	22.00	25.00
2005A Proof	80,000	Value: 32.00				
2005D	800,000	—	—	—	22.00	25.00
2005D Proof	80,000	Value: 32.00				
2005F	800,000	—	—	—	22.00	25.00
2005F Proof	80,000	Value: 32.00				
2005G	800,000	—	—	—	22.00	25.00
2005G Proof	80,000	Value: 32.00				
2005J	800,000	—	—	—	22.00	25.00
2005J Proof	80,000	Value: 32.00				

KM# 245   10 EURO
18.0000 g., 0.9250 Silver 0.5353 oz. ASW, 32.5 mm. **Subject:** Karl Friedrich Schinkel **Obv:** Stylized eagle **Rev:** Kneeling brick layer **Edge Lettering:** DER MENSCH BILDE SICH IN ALLEM SCHÖN

Date	Mintage	F	VF	XF	Unc	BU
2006F	1,600,000	—	—	—	22.00	25.00
2006F Proof	300,000	Value: 30.00				

KM# 246   10 EURO
18.0000 g., 0.9250 Silver 0.5353 oz. ASW, 32.5 mm. **Subject:** Dresden **Obv:** Stylized eagle **Rev:** City view and reflection **Edge Lettering:** 1206 1485 1547 1697 1832 1945 1989 2006

Date	Mintage	F	VF	XF	Unc	BU
2006A	1,600,000	—	—	—	22.00	25.00
2006A Proof	300,000	Value: 25.00				

KM# 247   10 EURO
18.0000 g., 0.9250 Silver 0.5353 oz. ASW, 32.5 mm. **Subject:** Hanseatic League **Obv:** Stylized eagle **Rev:** Old sail boat **Edge Lettering:** Wandel durch Handel - von der Hanse nach Europa

Date	Mintage	F	VF	XF	Unc	BU
2006J	1,600,000	—	—	—	20.00	22.00
2006J Proof	300,000	Value: 25.00				

KM# 248   10 EURO
18.0000 g., 0.9250 Silver 0.5353 oz. ASW, 32.5 mm. **Subject:** Mozart **Obv:** Stylized eagle, music and denomination above **Rev:** Bust left, dates above **Edge Lettering:** -- MOZART -- DIE WELT HAT EINEN SINN

Date	Mintage	F	VF	XF	Unc	BU
2006D	1,600,000	—	—	—	20.00	22.00
2006D Proof	300,000	Value: 25.00				

KM# 249   10 EURO
18.0000 g., 0.9250 Silver 0.5353 oz. ASW, 32.5 mm. **Subject:** World Cup Soccer **Obv:** Stylized eagle **Rev:** Brandenburg Gate on ball on globe **Edge Lettering:** DIE WELT ZU GAST BEI FREUNDEN - ADFGJ **Note:** Mint is determined by which letter "E" in the edge inscription has a short center bar. If the first letter "E" has the short center bar the coin is from the Berlin mint. Second "E"= Munich, third "E"=Stuttgart, fourth "E"=Karlsruhe, fifth "E"=Hamburg

Date	Mintage	F	VF	XF	Unc	BU
2006A	800,000	—	—	—	20.00	22.00
2006A Proof	80,000	Value: 25.00				
2006D	800,000	—	—	—	20.00	22.00
2006D Proof	80,000	Value: 25.00				
2006F	800,000	—	—	—	20.00	22.00
2006F Proof	80,000	Value: 25.00				
2006G	800,000	—	—	—	20.00	22.00
2006G Proof	80,000	Value: 25.00				
2006J	800,000	—	—	—	20.00	22.00
2006J Proof	80,000	Value: 25.00				

KM# 263   10 EURO
18.0000 g., 0.9250 Silver 0.5353 oz. ASW, 32.5 mm. **Subject:** Saarland, 50th Anniversary of German control **Obv:** Eagle **Rev:** Modern town view, four stylized heads

Date	Mintage	F	VF	XF	Unc	BU
2007G	1,600,000	—	—	—	22.00	25.00
2007G Proof	300,000	Value: 30.00				

KM# 264   10 EURO
18.0000 g., 0.9250 Silver 0.5353 oz. ASW, 32.5 mm. **Subject:** Treaty of Rome, 50th Anniversary **Obv:** Eagle **Rev:** Map of Central Europe and stars

Date	Mintage	F	VF	XF	Unc	BU
2007F	1,600,000	—	—	—	22.00	25.00
2007F	300,000	Value: 30.00				

KM# 265   10 EURO
18.0000 g., 0.9250 Silver 0.5353 oz. ASW, 32.5 mm. **Subject:**
Wilhelm Busch, 175th Anniversary of Birth **Obv:** Eagle within
square **Rev:** Portrait of Busch, characters Helene, Max and Moritz
flanking

Date	Mintage	F	VF	XF	Unc	BU
2007D	1,600,000	—	—	—	22.00	25.00
2007D	300,000	Value: 30.00				

KM# 266   10 EURO
18.0000 g., 0.9250 Silver 0.5353 oz. ASW, 32.5 mm. **Subject:**
Deutsche Bundesbank, 50th Aniversary **Obv:** Eagle on rectangle
design **Rev:** Buildings on graph

Date	Mintage	F	VF	XF	Unc	BU
2007J	1,600,000	—	—	—	22.00	25.00
2007J Proof	300,000	Value: 30.00				

KM# 268   10 EURO
18.0000 g., 0.9250 Silver 0.5353 oz. ASW, 32.5 mm. **Subject:**
Eagle **Rev:** St. Elisabeth von Thuringen

Date	Mintage	F	VF	XF	Unc	BU
2007A	1,160,000	—	—	—	22.00	25.00
2007A	300,000	Value: 30.00				

KM# 271   10 EURO
18.0000 g., 0.9250 Silver 0.5353 oz. ASW, 32.5 mm. **Subject:**
Franz Kafka, 125th Anniversary of Birth **Obv:** Eagle **Rev:** Prague
Cathedral, writings & portrait **Edge Lettering:** EIN KÄFIG GING
EINEN VOGEL SUCHENS

Date	Mintage	F	VF	XF	Unc	BU
2008G	1,500,000	—	—	—	22.00	25.00
2008G Proof	260,000	Value: 30.00				

KM# 272   10 EURO
18.0000 g., 0.9250 Silver 0.5353 oz. ASW, 32.5 mm. **Subject:**

Max Planck, 150th Anniversary of Birth **Obv:** Eagle **Rev:** Graph
and portrait **Edge Lettering:** DEM ANWENDEN MUSS DAS +
ERENNEN VORAUSGEHEN

Date	Mintage	F	VF	XF	Unc	BU
2008F	1,500,000	—	—	—	22.00	25.00
2008F Proof	260,000	Value: 30.00				

KM# 273   10 EURO
18.0000 g., 0.9250 Silver 0.5353 oz. ASW **Subject:** Carl
Spitzweg - 200th Anniversary of Birth **Obv:** Eagle **Rev:** Spitzweg
reclining in bed with books, umbrella above **Edge Lettering:**
ACH, DIE VERGANGENHEIT ÌST SCHÖN **Shape:** 32.5

Date	Mintage	F	VF	XF	Unc	BU
2008D	1,500,000	—	—	—	22.00	25.00
2008D Proof	260,000	Value: 30.00				

KM# 274   10 EURO
18.0000 g., 0.9250 Silver 0.5353 oz. ASW, 32.5 mm. **Subject:**
Gorch Fock II, 50th Anniversary **Obv:** Eagle **Rev:** Naval training
sailing ship Gorch Fock II **Edge Lettering:** SEEFAHRT ÌST NOT

Date	Mintage	F	VF	XF	Unc	BU
2008J	1,500,000	—	—	—	22.00	25.00
2008J Proof	260,000	Value: 30.00				

KM# 294   10 EURO
18.0000 g., 0.9250 Silver 0.5353 oz. ASW, 32.5 mm. **Subject:**
Archaology in Germany **Obv:** Eagle, stars flanking **Rev:** Sun,
moon and star shield

Date	Mintage	F	VF	XF	Unc	BU
2008A	1,500,000	—	—	—	22.00	25.00
2008A Proof	260,000	Value: 30.00				

KM# 279   10 EURO
18.0000 g., 0.9250 Silver 0.5353 oz. ASW, 32.5 mm. **Subject:**
IAAF World Championships - Berlin **Obv:** Eagle and value **Rev:**
Female javelin thrower in stadium **Note:** Mint Marks letters are
in Morse Code.

Date	Mintage	F	VF	XF	Unc	BU
2009A	—	—	—	—	22.00	25.00
2009A Proof	40,000	Value: 30.00				
2009D	—	—	—	—	22.00	25.00
2009D Proof	40,000	Value: 30.00				
2009F	—	—	—	—	22.00	25.00
2009F Proof	40,000	Value: 30.00				
2009G	—	—	—	—	22.00	25.00
2009G Proof	40,000	Value: 30.00				
2009J	—	—	—	—	22.00	25.00
2009J Proof	40,000	Value: 30.00				

KM# 280   10 EURO
18.0000 g., 0.9250 Silver 0.5353 oz. ASW, 32.5 mm. **Subject:**
Kepler's Laws - 400th Anniversary **Obv:** Eagle above value **Rev:**
Portrait and geometric diagram demonstrating planetary orbits

Date	Mintage	F	VF	XF	Unc	BU
2009F	1,500,000	—	—	—	22.00	25.00
2009F Proof	200,000	Value: 25.00				

KM# 281   10 EURO
18.0000 g., 0.9250 Silver 0.5353 oz. ASW, 32.5 mm. **Subject:**
International Aerospace Expo, 100th Anniversary **Obv:** Eagle
above value **Rev:** Plane landing, montage of plane development

Date	Mintage	F	VF	XF	Unc	BU
2009D	1,500,000	—	—	—	22.00	25.00
2009D Proof	200,000	Value: 25.00				

KM# 282   10 EURO
18.0000 g., 0.9250 Silver 0.5353 oz. ASW, 32.5 mm. **Subject:**
Leipzig University - 600th Anniversary **Obv:** Eagle above value
Rev: University seal, portrait of Gottfried Wilhelm Leibniz

Date	Mintage	F	VF	XF	Unc	BU
2009A	1,610,000	—	—	—	22.00	25.00
2009G Proof	200,000	Value: 25.00				

KM# 284   10 EURO
18.0000 g., 0.9250 Silver 0.5353 oz. ASW, 32.5 mm. **Subject:**
Marion Countess Donhoff - 100th Anniversary of Birth **Obv:** Eagle
and value **Rev:** Profile right

Date	Mintage	F	VF	XF	Unc	BU
2009J	1,500,000	—	—	—	22.00	25.00
2009J Proof	200,000	Value: 25.00				

KM# 281a   10 EURO
18.0000 g., 0.9250 Silver partially gilt 0.5353 oz. ASW, 32.5 mm.
Subject: International Air Travel, 100th Anniversary **Obv:**
Stylized eagle **Rev:** Airplanes, partially gilt

Date	Mintage	F	VF	XF	Unc	BU
2009D	1,650,000	—	—	—	22.00	25.00
2009D Proof	20,000	Value: 30.00				

KM# 283   10 EURO
18.0000 g., 0.9250 Silver 0.5353 oz. ASW, 32.5 mm. **Subject:**
Youth hostels - 100th Anniversary **Obv:** Eagle and value **Rev:**
Stylized mountain, Alternal hostel in Westphalia

Date	Mintage	F	VF	XF	Unc	BU
2009G	1,500,000	—	—	—	22.00	25.00
2009G Proof	200,000	Value: 25.00				

KM# 290   10 EURO
18.0000 g., 0.9250 Silver 0.5353 oz. ASW, 32.5 mm. **Subject:**
German Unification, 20th Anniversary **Edge Lettering:**
EINIGKGIT UND RECHT UND PREIFEIT

Date	Mintage	F	VF	XF	Unc	BU
2010A	1,500,000	—	—	—	20.00	22.00
2010A Proof	184,200	Value: 25.00				

KM# 291   10 EURO
18.0000 g., 0.9250 Silver 0.5353 oz. ASW **Subject:** 175th
Anniversary of German Railroads **Edge Lettering:** AUF
VEREINTEN GLEISEN 1835-2010

Date	Mintage	F	VF	XF	Unc	BU
2010	Est. 1,900,000	—	—	—	21.00	23.00
2010 Proof	186,000	Value: 30.00				

KM# 287   10 EURO
18.0000 g., 0.9250 Silver 0.5353 oz. ASW, 32.5 mm. **Subject:**
Porcelain Production in Germany, 300th Anniversary

Date	Mintage	F	VF	XF	Unc	BU
2010F	1,500,000	—	—	—	20.00	22.00
2010F Proof	182,900	Value: 25.00				

KM# 288   10 EURO
18.0000 g., 0.9250 Silver 0.5353 oz. ASW, 32.5 mm. **Subject:**
Robert Schumann - 200th Birth Anniversary

Date	Mintage	F	VF	XF	Unc	BU
2010J	1,500,000	—	—	—	20.00	22.00
2010J Proof	182,900	Value: 25.00				

KM# 289   10 EURO
18.0000 g., 0.9250 Silver 0.5353 oz. ASW, 32.5 mm. **Subject:**
Konrad Zuse, 100th Birth Anniversary

Date	Mintage	F	VF	XF	Unc	BU
2010G	1,500,000	—	—	—	20.00	22.00
2010G Proof	18,290	Value: 25.00				

KM# 298   10 EURO
18.0000 g., 0.9250 Silver 0.5353 oz. ASW, 32.5 mm. **Subject:**
FIS World Alpine Ski Championships **Edge Lettering:**
FESTSPIELE IM SHNEE (Issued in 2010)

Date	Mintage	F	VF	XF	Unc	BU
2011A	Est. 400,000	—	—	—	21.00	23.00
2011A	Est. 41,820	Value: 30.00				
2011D	Est. 400,000	—	—	—	21.00	23.00
2011D	Est. 41,820	Value: 30.00				
2011F	Est. 400,000	—	—	—	21.00	23.00
2011F	Est. 41,820	Value: 30.00				
2011G	Est. 400,000	—	—	—	21.00	23.00
2011G	Est. 41,820	Value: 30.00				
2011J	Est. 400,000	—	—	—	21.00	23.00
2011J	Est. 41,820	Value: 30.00				

KM# 299   10 EURO
14.0000 g., Copper-Nickel, 32.5 mm. **Subject:** Soccer
(Football) Women's World Cup in Germany **Edge Lettering:** DIE
ZUKUNFT DES FUSSBALLS 1ST WEIBLICH

Date	Mintage	F	VF	XF	Unc	BU
2011A	Est. 360,000	—	—	—	14.50	15.00
2011D	Est. 360,000	—	—	—	14.50	15.00
2011F	Est. 360,000	—	—	—	14.50	15.00
2011G	Est. 360,000	—	—	—	14.50	15.00
2011J	Est. 360,000	—	—	—	14.50	15.00

KM# 299a   10 EURO
16.0000 g., 0.6250 Silver 0.3215 oz. ASW, 32.5 mm. **Subject:**
Soccer (Football) Women's World Cup in Germany **Edge
Lettering:** DIE ZUKUNFT DES FUSSBALLS 1ST WEIBLICH

Date	Mintage	F	VF	XF	Unc	BU
2011A Proof	Est. 40,000	Value: 30.00				
2011D Proof	Est. 40,000	Value: 30.00				
2011F Proof	Est. 40,000	Value: 30.00				
2011G Proof	Est. 40,000	Value: 30.00				
2011J Proof	Est. 40,000	Value: 30.00				

KM# 295   10 EURO
16.0000 g., 0.6250 Silver 0.3215 oz. ASW, 32.5 mm. **Subject:**
Franz Liszt, 200th Anniversary of Birth **Edge Lettering:** CGME
OBLICE - GENIE VEPPUCHIT

Date	Mintage	F	VF	XF	Unc	BU
2011G	Est. 2,200,000	—	—	—	15.00	16.00
2011G Proof	Est. 200,000	Value: 30.00				

KM# 296   10 EURO
16.0000 g., 0.6250 Silver 0.3215 oz. ASW, 32.5 mm. **Subject:**
125th Anniversary of the Automobile **Obv:** Stylized eage **Rev:**
Hand on steering wheel, zig-sag roadway **Edge Lettering:** WAS
UNS BEWEGT

Date	Mintage	F	VF	XF	Unc	BU
2011F	Est. 1,800,000	—	—	—	16.00	18.00
2011F Proof	Est. 200,000	Value: 30.00				

KM# 300   10 EURO
14.0000 g., Copper-Nickel, 32.5 mm. **Subject:** Till Eulenspiegel,
500th Anniversary **Edge Lettering:** SO BIN ICH DOCH HIE
GEWESEN

Date	Mintage	F	VF	XF	Unc	BU
2011D	Est. 1,800,000	—	—	—	14.50	15.00

KM# 300a   10 EURO
16.0000 g., 0.6250 Silver 0.3215 oz. ASW, 32.5 mm. **Subject:**
Til Eulenspiegel, 500th Anniversary **Edge Lettering:** SO BIN ICH
DOCH HIE GEWESEN

Date	Mintage	F	VF	XF	Unc	BU
2011D Proof	Est. 200,000	Value: 30.00				

KM# 301   10 EURO
Copper-Nickel, 32.5 mm. **Subject:** Discovery of the
Archaeopteryx, 150th Anniversary **Edge Lettering:**
ARCHAEOPTERYX - ZEUGE DER EVOLUTION

Date	Mintage	F	VF	XF	Unc	BU
2011A	Est. 1,800,000	—	—	—	14.50	15.00

KM# 301a   10 EURO
16.0000 g., 0.6250 Silver 0.3215 oz. ASW, 32.5 mm. **Subject:**
Discovery of the Archaeopteryx, 150th Anniversary **Edge
Lettering:** ARCHAEOPTERYX - ZEUGE DER EVOLUTION

Date	Mintage	F	VF	XF	Unc	BU
2011A Proof	200,000	Value: 30.00				

KM# 302   10 EURO
14.0000 g., Copper-Nickel, 32.5 mm. **Subject:** Elbe Tunnel,
Hamburg, 100th Anniversary **Edge Lettering:** VERBINDUNG
VON STADT UND HAFEN

Date	Mintage	F	VF	XF	Unc	BU
2011J	—	—	—	—	14.50	15.00

KM# 302a   10 EURO
16.0000 g., 0.6250 Silver 0.3215 oz. ASW, 32.5 mm. **Subject:**
Elbe Tunnel, Hamburg, 100th Anniversary **Edge Lettering:**
VERBINDUNG VON STADT UND HAFEN

Date	Mintage	F	VF	XF	Unc	BU
2011J Proof	Est. 200,000	Value: 30.00				

KM# 308   10 EURO
18.0000 g., 0.9250 Silver 0.5353 oz. ASW, 32.5 mm. **Subject:**
Freidreich der Grosse, 300th Anniversary of Birth **Obv:** Eagle
Rev: Bust facing 1/4 left

Date	Mintage	F	VF	XF	Unc	BU
2012A Proof	—	Value: 25.00				

KM# 309   10 EURO
18.0000 g., 0.9250 Silver 0.5353 oz. ASW, 32.5 mm. **Obv:**
Eagle **Rev:** Seedling sprouting form dried earth

Date	Mintage	F	VF	XF	Unc	BU
2012G Proof	—	Value: 30.00				

KM# 310   10 EURO
18.0000 g., 0.9250 Silver 0.5353 oz. ASW, 32.5 mm. **Subject:**
Borthers Grimm, 200th Anniversary **Obv:** Eagle **Rev:** Conjoined
portriats left

Date	Mintage	F	VF	XF	Unc	BU
2012F Proof	—	Value: 30.00				

KM# 311   10 EURO
18.0000 g., 0.9250 Silver 0.5353 oz. ASW, 32.5 mm. **Subject:**
National Library, 100th Anniversary **Obv:** Eagle **Rev:** Young mind
with inventions and ideas

Date	Mintage	F	VF	XF	Unc	BU
2012D Proof	—	Value: 30.00				

KM# 312   10 EURO
18.0000 g., 0.9250 Silver 0.5353 oz. ASW, 32.5 mm. **Subject:**
Gerhart Hauptmann, 150th Anniversary of Birth **Obv:** Eagle **Rev:**
Stylized portrait at right facing left and a manuscript at left

Date	Mintage	F	VF	XF	Unc	BU
2012J Proof	—	Value: 30.00				

KM# 297   20 EURO
3.8900 g., 0.9999 Gold 0.1250 oz. AGW, 17.5 mm. **Series:**
German Forst **Subject:** Oak Tree **Obv:** Stylized eagle, stars,
legend "BUNDERSREPUBLIK DEUTSCHLAND", date and value
Rev: Oak leaf and legends "DEUTSCHER WALD" and "EICHE"
Edge: Reeded

Date	Mintage	F	VF	XF	Unc	BU
2010A	40,000	—	—	—	—	275
2010D	40,000	—	—	—	—	275
2010F	40,000	—	—	—	—	275
2010G	40,000	—	—	—	—	275
2010J	40,000	—	—	—	—	275

KM# 303   20 EURO
3.8900 g., 0.9999 Gold 0.1250 oz. AGW, 17.5 mm. **Series:**
German Forest **Subject:** Beech Tree **Obv:** Stylized eagle, stars,
legend, date and value **Obv. Legend:** BUNDERSREPUBLIK
DEUTSCHLAND **Rev:** Beech leaf and legends **Rev. Legend:**
DEUTSCHER WALD / BUCHE **Edge:** Reeded

Date	Mintage	F	VF	XF	Unc	BU
2011A	40,000	—	—	—	—	275
2011D	40,000	—	—	—	—	275
2011F	40,000	—	—	—	—	275
2011G	40,000	—	—	—	—	275
2011J	40,000	—	—	—	—	275

KM# 307   20 EURO
3.8900 g., 0.9999 Gold 0.1250 oz. AGW, 17.5 mm. **Series:**
German Forest **Subject:** Spruce Tree **Obv:** Stylized eagle, stars,
date and value **Obv. Legend:** BUNDESREPUBLIK
DEUTSCHLAND **Rev:** Spruce branch end and legends **Rev.
Legend:** DEUTSCHER WALD / FICHTE **Edge:** Reeded

Date	Mintage	F	VF	XF	Unc	BU
2012A	Est. 40,000	—	—	—	—	275
2012D	Est. 40,000	—	—	—	—	275
2012F	Est. 40,000	—	—	—	—	275
2012G	Est. 40,000	—	—	—	—	275
2012J	Est. 40,000	—	—	—	—	275

KM# 220   100 EURO
15.5500 g., 0.9990 Gold 0.4994 oz. AGW, 28 mm. **Subject:**
Introduction of the Euro Currency **Obv:** Stylized round eagle **Rev:**
Euro symbol and arches **Edge:** Reeded

Date	Mintage	F	VF	XF	Unc	BU
2002A Proof	100,000	Value: 975				
2002D Proof	100,000	Value: 975				
2002F Proof	100,000	Value: 975				
2002G Proof	100,000	Value: 975				
2002J Proof	100,000	Value: 975				

KM# 228   100 EURO
15.5500 g., 0.9999 Gold 0.4983 oz. AGW, 28 mm. **Obv:** Stylized
eagle, denomination below **Rev:** Quedlinburg Abbey in
monogram **Edge:** Reeded

Date	Mintage	F	VF	XF	Unc	BU
2003A Proof	80,000	Value: 975				
2003D Proof	80,000	Value: 975				
2003F Proof	80,000	Value: 975				
2003G Proof	80,000	Value: 975				
2003J Proof	80,000	Value: 975				

KM# 235   100 EURO
15.5500 g., 0.9999 Gold 0.4999 oz. AGW, 28 mm. **Obv:** Stylized eagle, denomination below **Rev:** Bamberg city view **Edge:** Reeded

Date	Mintage	F	VF	XF	Unc	BU
2004A Proof	80,000	Value: 975				
2004D Proof	80,000	Value: 975				
2004F Proof	80,000	Value: 975				
2004G Proof	80,000	Value: 975				
2004J Proof	80,000	Value: 975				

KM# 236   100 EURO
15.5500 g., 0.9990 Gold 0.4994 oz. AGW **Subject:** UNESCO - Weimar **Obv:** Stylized eagle **Rev:** Historical City of Weimar buildings **Edge:** Reeded

Date	Mintage	F	VF	XF	Unc	BU
2006A Proof	70,000	Value: 975				
2006D Proof	70,000	Value: 975				
2006F Proof	70,000	Value: 975				
2006G Proof	70,000	Value: 975				
2006J Proof	70,000	Value: 975				

KM# 237   100 EURO
15.5500 g., 0.9990 Gold 0.4994 oz. AGW, 28 mm. **Subject:** Soccer - Germany 2006 **Obv:** Round stylized eagle **Rev:** Aerial view of stadium

Date	Mintage	F	VF	XF	Unc	BU
2005A Proof	70,000	Value: 975				
2005D Proof	70,000	Value: 975				
2005F Proof	70,000	Value: 975				
2005G Proof	70,000	Value: 975				
2005J Proof	70,000	Value: 975				

KM# 267   100 EURO
15.5500 g., 0.9990 Gold 0.4994 oz. AGW, 28 mm. **Subject:** Lubeck - UNESCO Heritage site **Obv:** Eagle **Rev:** City view

Date	Mintage	F	VF	XF	Unc	BU
2007A	66,000	Value: 975				
2007D	66,000	Value: 975				
2007F	66,000	Value: 975				
2007G	66,000	Value: 975				
2007J	66,000	Value: 975				

KM# 270   100 EURO
15.5500 g., 0.9990 Gold 0.4994 oz. AGW, 28 mm. **Subject:** Goslar - UNESCO Heritage site **Obv:** Eagle **Edge:** Reeded

Date	Mintage	F	VF	XF	Unc	BU
2008A	64,000	Value: 975				
2008D	64,000	Value: 975				
2008F	64,000	Value: 975				
2008G	64,000	Value: 975				
2008J	64,000	Value: 975				

KM# 278   100 EURO
15.5500 g., 0.9990 Gold 0.4994 oz. AGW, 28 mm. **Subject:** Trier - UNESCO Heritage site **Obv:** Eagle and denomination **Rev:** Riverside montage of buildings **Edge:** Reeded

Date	Mintage	F	VF	XF	Unc	BU
2009A Proof	64,000	Value: 975				
2009D Proof	64,000	Value: 975				
2009F Proof	64,000	Value: 975				
2009G Proof	64,000	Value: 975				
2009J Proof	64,000	Value: 975				

KM# 286   100 EURO
15.5500 g., 0.9990 Gold 0.4994 oz. AGW, 28 mm. **Subject:** Wurzburg - UNESCO Heritage site **Rev:** Wurzburg residence and court garden

Date	Mintage	F	VF	XF	Unc	BU
2010A Proof	64,000	Value: 975				
2010D Proof	64,000	Value: 975				
2010F Proof	64,000	Value: 975				
2010G Proof	64,000	Value: 975				
2010J Proof	64,000	Value: 975				

KM# 304   100 EURO
15.5500 g., 0.9999 Gold 0.4999 oz. AGW **Subject:** UNESCO World Heritage Site - Wartburg Castle **Obv:** Stylized eagle, stars, legend date and value **Obv. Legend:** BUNDERSREPUBLIK DEUTSCHLAND **Rev:** Wartburg Castle and legends **Rev. Legend:** UNESCO WELTERB WARTBURG / GEGR 1067 LUDWIG DER SPRINGER HERMANN I... **Edge:** Reeded

Date	Mintage	F	VF	XF	Unc	BU
2011A Proof	60,000	Value: 975				
2011D Proof	60,000	Value: 975				
2011F Proof	60,000	Value: 975				
2011G Proof	60,000	Value: 975				
2011J Proof	60,000	Value: 975				

KM# 313   100 EURO
15.5500 g., 0.9999 Gold 0.4999 oz. AGW, 28 mm. **Subject:** UNESCO - Aachen Cathedral **Obv:** Eagle **Rev:** Side view of Cathedral

Date	Mintage	F	VF	XF	Unc	BU
2012A Proof	—	Value: 875				
2012D Proof	—	Value: 875				
2012F Proof	—	Value: 875				
2012G Proof	—	Value: 875				
2012J Proof	—	Value: 875				

KM# 221   200 EURO
31.1000 g., 0.9990 Gold 0.9988 oz. AGW, 32.5 mm. **Subject:** Introduction of the Euro Currency **Obv:** Stylized round eagle **Rev:** Euro symbol and arches **Edge Lettering:** IM ... ZEICHEN ... DER ... EINIGUNG ... EUROPAS

Date	Mintage	F	VF	XF	Unc	BU
2002A Proof	20,000	Value: 1,950				
2002D Proof	20,000	Value: 1,950				
2002F Proof	20,000	Value: 1,950				
2002G Proof	20,000	Value: 1,950				
2002J Proof	20,000	Value: 1,950				

MINT SETS

KM#	Date	Mintage	Identification	Issue Price	Mkt Val
MS119	2001A (10)	130,000	KM105,106a,107-108,109.2,110,140.1,170,175,183	—	40.00
MS120	2001D (10)	130,000	KM105,106a,107-108,109.2,110,140.1,170,175,183	—	40.00
MS121	2001F (10)	130,000	KM105,106a,107-108,109.2,110,140.1,170,175,183	—	40.00
MS122	2001G (10)	130,000	KM105,106a,107-108,109.2,110,140.1,170,175,183	—	40.00
MS123	2001J (10)	130,000	KM105,106a,107-108,109.2,110,140.1,170,175,183	—	40.00
MS124	2002A (8)	90,000	KM#207-214	—	20.00
MS125	2002D (8)	90,000	KM#207-214	—	20.00
MS126	2002F (8)	90,000	KM#207-214	—	20.00
MS127	2002G (8)	90,000	KM#207-214	—	20.00
MS128	2002J (8)	90,000	KM#207-214	—	20.00
MS129	2003A (8)	90,000	KM#207-214	—	25.00
MS130	2003D (8)	90,000	KM#207-214	—	27.50
MS131	2003F (8)	90,000	KM#207-214	—	27.50
MS132	2003G (8)	90,000	KM#207-214	—	27.50
MS133	2003J (8)	90,000	KM#207-214	—	25.00
MS134	2004A (8)	90,000	KM#207-214	—	24.00
MS135	2004D (8)	90,000	KM#207-214	—	22.00
MS136	2004F (8)	90,000	KM#207-214	—	24.00
MS137	2004G (8)	90,000	KM#207-214	—	24.00
MS138	2004J (8)	90,000	KM#207-214	—	28.00
MS139	2005A (8)	90,000	KM#207-214	—	28.00
MS140	2005D (8)	90,000	KM#207-214	—	28.00
MS142	2005G (1)	90,000	KM#207-214	—	28.00
MS141	2005F (8)	90,000	KM#207-214	—	28.00
MS143	2005J (8)	90,000	KM#207-214	—	26.00
MS144	2006A (9)	90,000	KM#207-214, 253	—	35.00
MS149	2006 (5)	80,000	KM#253 (A, D, F, G and J)	—	23.00
MS145	2006D (9)	90,000	KM#207-214, 253	—	35.00
MS146	2006F (9)	90,000	KM#207-214, 253	—	35.00
MS147	2006G (9)	90,000	KM#207-214, 253	—	35.00
MS148	2006J (9)	90,000	KM#207-214, 253	—	35.00
MS150	2007A (9)	—	KM#207-209, 254-257, 259, 260	—	27.00
MS151	2007D (9)	90,000	KM#207-209, 254-257, 259, 260	—	27.00
MS152	2007F (9)	90,000	KM#207-209, 254-257, 259, 260	—	27.00
MS153	2007G (9)	90,000	KM#207-209, 254-257, 259, 260	—	27.00
MS154	2007J (9)	90,000	KM#207-209, 254-257, 259, 260	—	27.00
MS155	2007 (5)	80,000	KM#260 (A, D, F, G and J)	—	23.00
MS156	2008A (9)	70,000	KM#207-209, 254-258, 260	—	27.50
MS159	2008 (9)	70,000	KM#207-209, 254-258, 261	—	27.50
MS161	2008 (5)	55,000	KM#261 (A, D, F, G, J)	—	30.00
MS157	2008D (9)	70,000	KM#207-209, 254-258, 261	—	27.50
MS158	2008F (9)	70,000	KM#207-209, 254-258, 261	—	27.50
MS160	2008J (9)	70,000	KM#207-209, 254-258, 261	—	27.50
MS162	2009A (9)	60,000	KM#207-209, 254-258, 276	—	27.50
MS163	2009D (9)	60,000	KM#207-209, 254-258, 276	—	27.50
MS164	2009F (9)	60,000	KM#207-209, 254-258, 276	—	27.50
MS165	2009G (9)	60,000	KM#207-209, 254-258, 276	—	27.50
MS166	2009J (9)	60,000	KM#207-209, 254-258, 276	—	27.50
MS167	2009 (5)	—	KM#276 (A, D, F, G, J)	—	27.50
MS168	2010A (9)	53,800	KM#207-209, 254-258, 285	—	25.00
MS169	2010D (9)	53,800	KM#207-209, 254-258, 285	—	25.00
MS170	2010F (9)	53,800	KM#207-209, 254-258, 285	—	25.00
MS171	2010G (9)	53,800	KM#207-209, 254-258, 285	—	25.00
MS172	2010J (9)	53,800	KM#207-209, 254-258, 285	—	25.00
MS173	2010 (5)	—	KM#285 (A, D, F, G, J)	—	27.50
MS174	2011A (9)	54,000	KM#207-209, 254-258, 293	—	25.00
MS175	2011D (9)	47,000	KM#207-209, 254-258, 293	—	25.00
MS176	2011F (9)	47,000	KM#207-209, 254-258, 293	—	25.00
MS177	2011G (9)	47,000	KM#207-209, 254-258, 293	—	25.00
MS178	2011J (9)	47,000	KM#207-209, 254-258, 293	—	25.00
MS179	2011 (5)	—	KM#293 (A, D, F, G, J)	—	27.50

PROOF SETS

KM#	Date	Mintage	Identification	Issue Price	Mkt Val
PS150	2001A (10)	78,000	KM105,106a,107-108,109.2,110,140.1,170,175,183	—	110
PS151	2001D (10)	78,000	KM105,106a,107-108,109.2,110,140.1,170,175,183	—	110
PS152	2001F (10)	78,000	KM105,106a,107-108,110,140.1,170,175,183	—	110
PS153	2001G (10)	78,000	KM105,106a,107-108,109.2,110,140.1,170,175,183	—	110
PS154	2001J (10)	78,000	KM105,106a,107-108,109.2,110,140.1,170,175,183	—	110
PS155	2002A (8)	75,000	KM#207-214	—	35.00
PS156	2002D (8)	75,000	KM#207-214	—	35.00
PS157	2002F (8)	75,000	KM#207-214	—	35.00
PS158	2002G (8)	75,000	KM#207-214	—	35.00
PS159	2002J (8)	75,000	KM#207-214	—	35.00
PS160	2003A (8)	75,000	KM#207-214	—	35.00
PS161	2003D (8)	75,000	KM#207-214	—	35.00
PS162	2003F (8)	75,000	KM#207-214	—	35.00
PS163	2003G (8)	75,000	KM#207-214	—	35.00
PS164	2003J (8)	75,000	KM#207-214	—	35.00
PS165	2004A (8)	75,000	KM#207-214	—	35.00
PS166	2004D (8)	75,000	KM#207-214	—	35.00
PS167	2004F (8)	75,000	KM#207-214	—	35.00
PS168	2004G (8)	75,000	KM#207-214	—	35.00
PS169	2004J (8)	75,000	KM#207-214	—	35.00
PS170	2005A (8)	75,000	KM#207-214	—	30.00
PS171	2005D (8)	75,000	KM#207-214	—	30.00
PS172	2005F (8)	75,000	KM#207-214	—	30.00
PS173	2005G (8)	75,000	KM#207-214	—	30.00
PS174	2005J (8)	75,000	KM#207-214	—	30.00
PS175	2006A (9)	75,000	KM#207-214, 253	—	40.00
PS176	2006D (9)	75,000	KM#207-214, 253	—	40.00
PS177	2006E (9)	75,000	KM#207-214, 253	—	40.00
PS178	2006G (9)	75,000	KM#207-214, 253	—	40.00
PS179	2006G (9)	75,000	KM#207-214, 253	—	40.00
PS180	2006 (5)	—	KM#253 (A, D, E, G, J)	—	30.00
PS181	2007A (9)	70,000	KM#207-209, 254-257, 259, 260	—	40.00
PS182	2007D (9)	70,000	KM#207-209, 254-257, 259, 260	—	40.00
PS183	2007E (9)	70,000	KM#207-209, 254-257, 259, 260	—	40.00
PS184	2007G (9)	70,000	KM#207-209, 254-257, 259, 260	—	40.00
PS185	2007G (9)	70,000	KM#207-209, 254-257, 259, 260	—	40.00
PS186	2007 (5)	—	KM#260 (A, D, E, G, J)	—	40.00
PS187	2008A (9)	—	KM#207-209, 254-258, 261	—	40.00
PS188	2008D (9)	—	KM#207-209, 254-258, 261	—	40.00
PS194	2009D (9)	—	KM#207-209, 254-258, 276	—	40.00
PS189	2008E (9)	—	KM#207-209, 254-258, 261	—	40.00
PS190	2008G (9)	—	KM#207-209, 254-258, 261	—	40.00
PS191	2008J (9)	—	KM#207-209, 254-258, 261	—	40.00
PS192	2008 (5)	—	KM#261 (A, D, E, G, J)	—	40.00
PS193	2009A (9)	—	KM#207-209, 254-258, 276	—	40.00
PS195	2009E (9)	—	KM#207-209, 254-258, 276	—	40.00
PS196	2009G (9)	—	KM#207-209, 254-258, 276	—	40.00
PS197	2009J (9)	—	KM#207-209, 254-258, 276	—	40.00
PS198	2009 (5)	—	KM#276 (A, D, E, G, J)	—	40.00
PS199	2010A (9)	—	KM#207-209, 254-258, 285	—	40.00
PS200	2010D (9)	—	KM#207-209, 254-258, 285	—	40.00
PS201	2010E (9)	—	KM#207-209, 254-258, 285	—	40.00
PS202	2010G (9)	—	KM#207-209, 254-258, 285	—	40.00
PS203	2010J (9)	—	KM#207-209, 254-258, 285	—	40.00
PS204	2010 (5)	—	KM#285 (A, D, E, G, J)	—	40.00
PS205	2011A (9)	—	KM#207-209, 254-258, 293	—	40.00
PS206	2011D (9)	—	KM#207-209, 254-258, 293	—	40.00
PS207	2011E (9)	—	KM#207-209, 254-258, 293	—	40.00
PS208	2011G (9)	—	KM#207-209, 254-258, 293	—	40.00
PS209	2011J (9)	—	KM#207-209, 254-258, 293	—	40.00
PS210	2011 (5)	—	KM#293 (A, D, E, G, J)	—	40.00

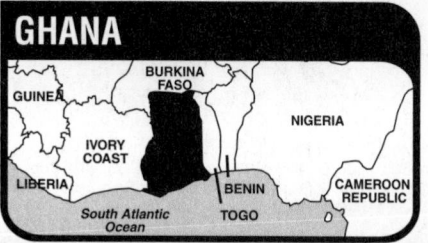

GHANA

The Republic of Ghana, a member of the Commonwealth of Nations situated on the West Coast of Africa between Ivory Coast and Togo, has an area of 92,100 sq. mi. (238,540 sq. km.) and a population of 14 million, almost entirely African. Capital: Accra. Cocoa (the major crop), coconuts, palm kernels and coffee are exported. Mining, second in importance to agriculture, is concentrated on gold, manganese and industrial diamonds.

MONETARY SYSTEM
1 Cedi = 100 Pesewas, 1965-2007
1 (new) Cedi = 10,000 (old) Cedis, 2007-

REPUBLIC

DECIMAL COINAGE

KM# 36   10 CEDIS
4.4100 g., Copper-Nickel, 22.9 mm. **Obv:** National arms divides date and denomination **Rev:** Gorilla family **Edge:** Plain

Date	Mintage	F	VF	XF	Unc	BU
2003	—	—	—	—	1.50	2.00

REFORM COINAGE
2007-

KM# 37   PESEWA
1.8200 g., Copper Plated Steel, 17 mm. **Obv:** National arms **Obv. Legend:** GHANA **Rev:** Adomi Bridge **Edge:** Plain

Date	Mintage	F	VF	XF	Unc	BU
2007	—	—	—	—	—	0.75

KM# 38   5 PESEWAS
2.5000 g., Nickel Clad Steel, 18 mm. **Obv:** National arms **Obv. Legend:** GHANA **Rev:** Native male blowing horn **Edge:** Plain

Date	Mintage	F	VF	XF	Unc	BU
2007	—	—	—	—	—	1.25

KM# 39   10 PESEWAS
3.2300 g., Nickel Clad Steel, 20.4 mm. **Obv:** National arms **Obv. Legend:** GHANA **Rev:** Open book, pen **Edge:** Reeded

Date	Mintage	F	VF	XF	Unc	BU
2007	—	—	—	—	—	2.50

KM# 40   20 PESEWAS
4.4000 g., Nickel Plated Steel, 23.5 mm. **Obv:** National arms **Obv. Legend:** GHANA **Rev:** Split open cocoa pod **Edge:** Plain

Date	Mintage	F	VF	XF	Unc	BU
2007	—	—	—	—	—	3.50

KM# 41   50 PESEWAS
6.0800 g., Nickel Plated Steel, 26.4 mm. **Obv:** National arms **Obv. Legend:** GHANA **Rev:** 1/2 length figure of market woman facing **Edge:** Reeded

Date	Mintage	F	VF	XF	Unc	BU
2007	—	—	—	—	—	6.00

KM# 42   CEDI
7.4000 g., Bi-Metallic Brass center in Nickel Plated Steel ring, 28 mm. **Obv:** National arms **Obv. Legend:** GHANA **Rev:** Scale of Justice in sprays **Edge:** Segmented reeding

Date	Mintage	F	VF	XF	Unc	BU
2007	—	—	—	—	—	10.00

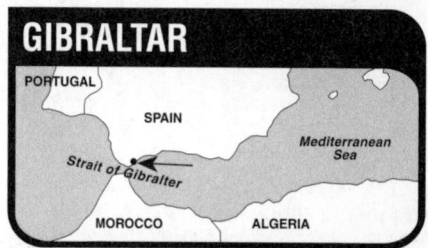

GIBRALTAR

The British Colony of Gibraltar, located at the southernmost point of the Iberian Peninsula, has an area of 2.25 sq. mi. (6.5 sq. km.) and a population of 29,651. Capital (and only town): Gibraltar. Aside from its strategic importance as guardian of the western entrance to the Mediterranean Sea, Gibraltar is also a free port and a British naval base.

RULERS
British

MINT MARKS
PM - Pobjoy Mint
PMM – Pobjoy Mint (only appears on coins dated 2000)

NOTE: ALL coins for 1988 –2003 include the PM mint mark except the 2000 dated circulation pieces which instead have PMM.

MINT PRIVY MARKS
U - Unc finish

MONETARY SYSTEM
100 Pence = 1 Pound

BRITISH COLONY

DECIMAL COINAGE
100 Pence = 1 Pound

KM# 773   PENNY
3.5200 g., Bronze Plated Steel, 20.4 mm. **Ruler:** Elizabeth II **Obv:** Head with tiara right **Rev:** Barbary partridge left divides denomination

Date	Mintage	F	VF	XF	Unc	BU
2001 AA	—	—	—	—	0.35	0.50
2002 AA	—	—	—	—	0.35	0.50
2003 AA	—	—	—	—	0.35	0.50

KM# 1046   PENNY
3.5400 g., Copper Plated Steel, 20.02 mm. **Ruler:** Elizabeth II **Subject:** 300th Anniversary **Obv:** Crowned bust right **Rev:** Monkey **Edge:** Plain

Date	Mintage	F	VF	XF	Unc	BU
2004	—	—	—	—	0.30	0.50

KM# 1079   PENNY
3.5400 g., Copper Plated Steel, 20.02 mm.   **Ruler:** Elizabeth II
Obv: Bust right **Rev:** Sceptre

Date	Mintage	F	VF	XF	Unc	BU
2005	—	—	—	—	0.35	0.50
2006	—	—	—	—	0.35	0.50
2007	—	—	—	—	0.35	0.50
2008	—	—	—	—	0.35	0.50
2009	—	—	—	—	0.35	0.50
2010	—	—	—	—	0.35	0.50

KM# 774   2 PENCE
Bronze Plated Steel, 20.4 mm.   **Ruler:** Elizabeth II **Obv:** Head
with tiara right

Date	Mintage	F	VF	XF	Unc	BU
2001 AA	—	—	—	—	0.50	0.85
2001 PM AB	—	—	—	—	0.50	0.85
2002	—	—	—	—	0.50	0.85
2003 AA	—	—	—	—	0.50	0.85

KM# 1044   2 PENCE
7.0400 g., Copper Plated Steel, 25.4 mm.   **Ruler:** Elizabeth II
Subject: 300th Anniversary **Obv:** Crowned bust right **Rev:** Four
old keys **Edge:** Plain

Date	Mintage	F	VF	XF	Unc	BU
2004	—	—	—	—	0.50	0.65

KM# 1065   2 PENCE
7.2000 g., Copper Plated Steel, 25.9 mm.   **Ruler:** Elizabeth II
Subject: Operation Torch, 1942 **Rev:** Three soldiers

Date	Mintage	F	VF	XF	Unc	BU
2005	—	—	—	—	0.50	0.65
2006	—	—	—	—	0.50	0.65
2007	—	—	—	—	0.50	0.65
2008	—	—	—	—	0.50	0.65
2009	—	—	—	—	0.50	0.65
2010	—	—	—	—	0.50	0.65
2011	—	—	—	—	0.50	0.65

KM# 1080   2 PENCE
25.4000 g., Copper Plated Steel, 25.4 mm.   **Ruler:** Elizabeth II
Subject: Diamond Wedding **Rev:** Conjoined busts of Elizabeth
II and Philip

Date	Mintage	F	VF	XF	Unc	BU
2007	—	—	—	—	0.50	0.65

KM# 775   5 PENCE
3.1000 g., Copper-Nickel, 18 mm. **Ruler:** Elizabeth II **Obv:** Head
with tiara right **Rev:** Barbary Ape left divides denomination

Date	Mintage	F	VF	XF	Unc	BU
2001 AB	—	—	—	—	0.60	0.75
2002 AB	—	—	—	—	0.60	0.75
2003 AA	—	—	—	—	0.60	0.75

KM# 1049   5 PENCE
3.2500 g., Copper-Nickel, 18 mm. **Ruler:** Elizabeth II **Subject:**
Tercentenary 1704-2004 **Obv:** Elizabeth II **Rev:** British Royal
Sceptre **Edge:** Reeded

Date	Mintage	F	VF	XF	Unc	BU
2004	—	—	—	—	—	1.50

KM# 1081   5 PENCE
3.1000 g., Copper-Nickel, 18 mm. **Ruler:** Elizabeth II **Obv:** Bust
in diadem right **Rev:** Barbary ape seated

Date	Mintage	F	VF	XF	Unc	BU
2005	—	—	—	—	0.60	0.75
2006	—	—	—	—	0.60	0.75
2007	—	—	—	—	0.60	0.75
2008	—	—	—	—	0.60	0.75
2009	—	—	—	—	0.60	0.75
2010	—	—	—	—	0.60	0.75
2011	—	—	—	—	0.60	0.75

KM# 776   10 PENCE
6.5000 g., Copper-Nickel, 24.5 mm.   **Ruler:** Elizabeth II **Obv:**
Head with tiara right, date below **Rev:** Denomination below
building

Date	Mintage	F	VF	XF	Unc	BU
2001 AA	—	—	—	—	1.00	1.25
2001 AB	—	—	—	—	1.00	1.25
2001 AC	—	—	—	—	1.00	1.25
2001 AE	—	—	—	—	1.00	1.25
2002 AC	—	—	—	—	1.00	1.25
2003 AA	—	—	—	—	1.00	1.25

KM# 1047   10 PENCE
6.4200 g., Copper-Nickel, 24.4 mm.   **Ruler:** Elizabeth II **Subject:**
300th Anniversary **Obv:** Elizabeth II **Rev:** Three military officers
planning Operation Torch 1942 **Edge:** Reeded

Date	Mintage	F	VF	XF	Unc	BU
2004	—	—	—	—	0.75	1.00

KM# 1082   10 PENCE
6.4200 g., Copper-Nickel, 24.4 mm.   **Ruler:** Elizabeth II **Subject:**
The Great Siege, 1779-1793 **Obv:** Bust in diadem right **Rev:**
Cannon left

Date	Mintage	F	VF	XF	Unc	BU
2005	—	—	—	—	0.75	1.00
2006	—	—	—	—	0.75	1.00
2007	—	—	—	—	0.75	1.00
2008	—	—	—	—	0.75	1.00
2009	—	—	—	—	0.75	1.00
2010	—	—	—	—	0.75	1.00
2011	—	—	—	—	0.75	1.00

KM# 777   20 PENCE
5.0000 g., Copper-Nickel, 21.4 mm.   **Ruler:** Elizabeth II **Obv:**
Head with tiara right, date below **Rev:** Our Lady of Europa,
denomination below and right **Shape:** 7-sided

Date	Mintage	F	VF	XF	Unc	BU
2001 AA	—	—	—	—	1.50	2.00

KM# 1048   20 PENCE
4.9400 g., Copper-Nickel, 21.4 mm.   **Ruler:** Elizabeth II **Subject:**
300th Anniversary **Obv:** Crowned buat right **Rev:** Neanderthal
skull found in Gibraltar in 1848 **Edge:** Plain **Shape:** 7-sided

Date	Mintage	F	VF	XF	Unc	BU
2004	—	—	—	—	1.00	1.50

KM# 1083   20 PENCE
4.9400 g., Copper-Nickel, 21.4 mm.   **Ruler:** Elizabeth II **Obv:**
Bust in diadem right **Rev:** Keyring with four keys **Shape:** 7-sided

Date	Mintage	F	VF	XF	Unc	BU
2005	—	—	—	—	1.50	2.00
2006	—	—	—	—	1.50	2.00
2007	—	—	—	—	1.50	2.00
2008	—	—	—	—	1.50	2.00
2009	—	—	—	—	1.50	2.00
2010	—	—	—	—	1.50	2.00
2011	—	—	—	—	1.50	2.00

KM# 971   50 PENCE
8.0000 g., Copper-Nickel, 27.3 mm. **Ruler:** Elizabeth II **Subject:**
Christmas **Obv:** Head with tiara right, date below **Rev:** Three
wise men **Edge:** Plain **Shape:** 7-sided

Date	Mintage	F	VF	XF	Unc	BU
2001 BB	30,000	—	—	—	10.00	12.00

KM# 971a   50 PENCE
8.0000 g., 0.9250 Silver 0.2379 oz. ASW, 27.3 mm.   **Ruler:**
Elizabeth II **Obv:** Head with tiara right, date below **Rev:** Three
wise men **Edge:** Plain **Shape:** 7-sided

Date	Mintage	F	VF	XF	Unc	BU
2001 Proof	5,000	Value: 35.00				

KM# 971b   50 PENCE
8.0000 g., 0.9167 Gold 0.2358 oz. AGW, 27.3 mm.   **Ruler:**
Elizabeth II **Obv:** Head with tiara right, date below **Rev:** Three
wise men **Edge:** Plain **Shape:** 7-sided

Date	Mintage	F	VF	XF	Unc	BU
2001 Proof	250	Value: 645				

KM# 778   50 PENCE
8.0000 g., Copper-Nickel, 27.3 mm. **Ruler:** Elizabeth II **Obv:**
Head with tiara right **Rev:** Dolphins surround denomination **Edge:**
Plain **Shape:** 7-sided

Date	Mintage	F	VF	XF	Unc	BU
2001 AA	—	—	—	—	4.50	5.50
2001 AB	—	—	—	—	4.50	5.50
2003 AB	—	—	—	—	4.50	5.50

KM# 1026   50 PENCE
8.0000 g., Copper-Nickel, 27.3 mm. **Ruler:** Elizabeth II **Subject:**
Christmas **Obv:** Head with tiara right, date below **Rev:** Shepherds
Edge: Plain **Shape:** 7-sided

Date	Mintage	F	VF	XF	Unc	BU
2002PM BB	30,000	—	—	—	10.00	12.00

KM# 1026a   50 PENCE
8.0000 g., 0.9250 Silver 0.2379 oz. ASW, 27.3 mm.   **Ruler:**
Elizabeth II **Subject:** Christmas **Obv:** Head with tiara right, date
below **Rev:** Two shepherds **Edge:** Plain **Shape:** 7-sided

Date	Mintage	F	VF	XF	Unc	BU
2002PM Proof	2,002	Value: 35.00				

KM# 1063a 50 PENCE
8.0000 g., 0.9250 Silver 0.2379 oz. ASW, 27.3 mm. **Ruler:**
Elizabeth II **Subject:** Christmas **Rev:** Joseph & Mary

Date	Mintage	F	VF	XF	Unc	BU
2003PM BB	—			—	12.00	14.00

KM# 1063 50 PENCE
8.0000 g., Copper-Nickel **Ruler:** Elizabeth II **Series:** Christmas
Obv: Head with tiara right, date below **Rev:** Joseph & Mary
Shape: 27.3

Date	Mintage	F	VF	XF	Unc	BU
2003PM BB	—			—	10.00	12.00

KM# 1050 50 PENCE
8.0000 g., Copper-Nickel, 27.3 mm. **Ruler:** Elizabeth II **Subject:**
Tercentenary 1704-2004 **Obv:** Elizabeth II **Rev:** HMS Victory
sailing past Gibraltar **Edge:** Plain **Shape:** 7-sided

Date	Mintage	F	VF	XF	Unc	BU
2004	—			—	—	3.00

KM# 1066 50 PENCE
8.0000 g., Copper-Nickel, 27.3 mm. **Ruler:** Elizabeth II **Subject:**
Christmas **Rev:** Santa Claus walking left with sack over shoulder
and waving **Shape:** 7-sided

Date	Mintage	F	VF	XF	Unc	BU
2004	—			—	10.00	12.00

KM# 1084 50 PENCE
8.0000 g., Copper-Nickel, 27.3 mm. **Ruler:** Elizabeth II **Subject:**
Glorious 1st of June, 1794 **Rev:** Marines firing from deck of Naval
ship **Shape:** 7-sided

Date	Mintage	F	VF	XF	Unc	BU
2004	—			—	10.00	12.00

KM# 1085 50 PENCE
8.0000 g., Copper-Nickel, 27.3 mm. **Ruler:** Elizabeth II **Subject:**
Siege of Sebastopol, 1854 **Rev:** Troops in the Crimea **Shape:** 7-
sided

Date	Mintage	F	VF	XF	Unc	BU
2004	—			—	10.00	12.00

KM# 1086 50 PENCE
8.0000 g., Copper-Nickel, 27.3 mm. **Ruler:** Elizabeth II **Subject:**
World War I **Rev:** Troops advancing right **Shape:** 7-sided

Date	Mintage	F	VF	XF	Unc	BU
2004	—			—	10.00	12.00

KM# 1087 50 PENCE
8.0000 g., Copper-Nickel, 27.3 mm. **Ruler:** Elizabeth II **Subject:**
World War II **Rev:** Troops in fox hole **Shape:** 7-sided

Date	Mintage	F	VF	XF	Unc	BU
2004	—			—	10.00	12.00

KM# 1088 50 PENCE
8.0000 g., Copper-Nickel, 27.3 mm. **Ruler:** Elizabeth II **Subject:**
The Falklands, 1982 **Rev:** Troops advancing forward **Shape:** 7-
sided

Date	Mintage	F	VF	XF	Unc	BU
2004	—			—	10.00	12.00

KM# 1067 50 PENCE
8.0000 g., Copper-Nickel, 27.3 mm. **Ruler:** Elizabeth II **Subject:**
Christmas **Rev:** Mary and child **Shape:** 7-sided

Date	Mintage	F	VF	XF	Unc	BU
2005	—			—	10.00	12.00

KM# 1074 50 PENCE
28.2800 g., Copper-Nickel, 27.13 mm. **Ruler:** Elizabeth II
Subject: Capture of Gibraltar **Rev:** Naval Battle **Shape:** 7-sided

Date	Mintage	F	VF	XF	Unc	BU
2005	—			—	7.50	10.00

KM# 1089 50 PENCE
8.0000 g., Copper-Nickel, 27.3 mm. **Ruler:** Elizabeth II **Subject:**
Capture of Gibraltar, 1704 **Rev:** Naval Battle **Shape:** 7-sided

Date	Mintage	F	VF	XF	Unc	BU
2006	—	—	—	—	4.50	5.50
2007	—	—	—	—	4.50	5.50
2008	—	—	—	—	4.50	5.50
2009	—	—	—	—	4.50	5.50
2010	—	—	—	—	4.50	5.50

KM# 1068 50 PENCE
8.0000 g., Copper-Nickel, 27.3 mm. **Ruler:** Elizabeth II **Subject:**
Christmas **Rev:** Tree **Shape:** 7-sided

Date	Mintage	F	VF	XF	Unc	BU
2006	—	—	—	—	10.00	12.00

KM# 1069 50 PENCE
8.0000 g., Copper-Nickel, 27.3 mm. **Ruler:** Elizabeth II **Subject:**
Christmas **Rev:** Santa, large face **Shape:** 7-sided

Date	Mintage	F	VF	XF	Unc	BU
2007	—			—	10.00	12.00

KM# 1070 50 PENCE
8.0000 g., Copper-Nickel, 27.3 mm. **Ruler:** Elizabeth II **Subject:**
Christmas **Shape:** 7-sided

Date	Mintage	F	VF	XF	Unc	BU
2008	—			—	10.00	12.00

KM# 1090 50 PENCE
8.0000 g., Copper-Nickel, 27.3 mm. **Ruler:** Elizabeth II **Subject:**
Our Lady of Europe **Rev:** Madonna and Child seated **Shape:** 7-
sided

Date	Mintage	F	VF	XF	Unc	BU
2008	—			—	7.50	9.00

KM# 1071 50 PENCE
8.0000 g., Copper-Nickel, 27.3 mm. **Ruler:** Elizabeth II **Subject:**
Christmas **Shape:** 7-sided

Date	Mintage	F	VF	XF	Unc	BU
2009	—			—	10.00	12.00

KM# 988 1/25 CROWN
1.2240 g., 0.9990 Gold 0.0393 oz. AGW, 13.92 mm. **Ruler:**
Elizabeth II **Subject:** Peter Rabbit Centennial **Obv:** Crowned
bust right **Rev:** Peter Rabbit **Edge:** Reeded

Date	Mintage	F	VF	XF	Unc	BU
2002 Proof	5,000	Value: 70.00				

KM# 988a 1/25 CROWN
1.2240 g., 0.9990 Platinum 0.0393 oz. APW, 13.92 mm. **Ruler:**
Elizabeth II **Subject:** Peter Rabbit Centennial **Obv:** Crowned
bust right **Rev:** Peter Rabbit **Edge:** Reeded

Date	Mintage	F	VF	XF	Unc	BU
2002 Proof	3,000	Value: 80.00				

KM# 1016 1/25 CROWN
1.2441 g., 0.9999 Gold 0.0400 oz. AGW, 13.92 mm. **Ruler:**
Elizabeth II **Subject:** Peter Pan **Obv:** Crowned bust right **Rev:**
Peter Pan and Tinkerbell flying above city **Edge:** Reeded

Date	Mintage	F	VF	XF	Unc	BU
2002 Proof	10,000	Value: 70.00				

KM# 989 1/10 CROWN
3.1100 g., 0.9990 Gold 0.0999 oz. AGW, 17.95 mm. **Ruler:**
Elizabeth II **Subject:** Peter Rabbit Centennial **Obv:** Crowned
bust right **Rev:** Peter Rabbit **Edge:** Reeded

Date	Mintage	F	VF	XF	Unc	BU
2002 Proof	5,000	Value: 180				

KM# 989a 1/10 CROWN
3.1100 g., 0.9990 Platinum 0.0999 oz. APW, 17395 mm. **Ruler:**
Elizabeth II **Subject:** Peter Rabbit Centennial **Obv:** Crowned
bust right **Rev:** Peter Rabbit **Edge:** Reeded

Date	Mintage	F	VF	XF	Unc	BU
2002 Proof	2,000	Value: 215				

KM# 1017   1/10 CROWN
3.1104 g., 0.9999 Gold 0.1000 oz. AGW, 17.95 mm. **Ruler:**
Elizabeth II **Subject:** Peter Pan **Obv:** Crowned bust right **Rev:**
Peter Pan and Tinkerbell flying above city **Edge:** Reeded

Date	Mintage	F	VF	XF	Unc	BU
2002 Proof	7,500	Value: 180				

KM# 902   1/5 CROWN
6.2200 g., 0.9999 Gold 0.1999 oz. AGW, 22 mm. **Ruler:**
Elizabeth II **Subject:** Queen Mother **Obv:** Bust with tiara right
Rev: 1953 Coronation scene **Edge:** Reeded

Date	Mintage	F	VF	XF	Unc	BU
2001 Proof	5,000	Value: 355				

KM# 903   1/5 CROWN
6.2200 g., 0.9999 Gold 0.1999 oz. AGW **Ruler:** Elizabeth II
Obv: Bust with tiara right **Rev:** Queen Mother and Prince Charles
in 1954

Date	Mintage	F	VF	XF	Unc	BU
2001 Proof	5,000	Value: 355				

KM# 909   1/5 CROWN
6.2200 g., 0.9999 Gold 0.1999 oz. AGW, 22 mm. **Ruler:**
Elizabeth II **Series:** Victorian Era - Victoria's Coronation 1838
Obv: Bust with tiara right **Rev:** 1838 Coronation scene **Edge:**
Reeded

Date	Mintage	F	VF	XF	Unc	BU
2001 Proof	5,000	Value: 355				

KM# 909.1   1/5 CROWN
6.2200 g., 0.9999 Gold 0.1999 oz. AGW, 22 mm. **Ruler:**
Elizabeth II **Series:** Victorian Era **Obv:** Bust with tiara right **Rev:**
1838 Coronation scene with a tiny emerald set in the field below
the 1838 date **Edge:** Reeded

Date	Mintage	F	VF	XF	Unc	BU
2001 Proof	2,001	Value: 355				

KM# 911.1   1/5 CROWN
6.2200 g., 0.9999 Gold 0.1999 oz. AGW, 22 mm. **Ruler:**
Elizabeth II **Series:** Victorian Era - Empress of India 1876 **Obv:**
Bust with tiara right **Rev:** Crowned portrait of Victoria and two
elephants **Edge:** Reeded

Date	Mintage	F	VF	XF	Unc	BU
2001 Proof	5,000	Value: 355				

KM# 911.2   1/5 CROWN
6.2200 g., 0.9999 Gold 0.1999 oz. AGW, 22 mm. **Ruler:**
Elizabeth II **Series:** Victorian Era - Empress of India 1876 **Obv:**
Bust with tiara right **Rev:** Tiny ruby set in the field behind Victoria's
head **Edge:** Reeded

Date	Mintage	F	VF	XF	Unc	BU
2001 Proof	2,001	Value: 355				

KM# 913.1   1/5 CROWN
6.2200 g., 0.9999 Gold 0.1999 oz. AGW, 22 mm. **Ruler:**
Elizabeth II **Series:** Victorian Era - Diamond Jubilee 1897 **Obv:**
Bust with tiara right **Rev:** Victoria's cameo portrait above naval
ships **Edge:** Reeded

Date	Mintage	F	VF	XF	Unc	BU
2001 Proof	5,000	Value: 355				

KM# 913.2   1/5 CROWN
6.2200 g., 0.9999 Gold 0.1999 oz. AGW, 22 mm. **Ruler:**
Elizabeth II **Series:** Victorian Era - Diamond Jubilee 1897 **Obv:**
Bust with tiara right **Rev:** Tiny diamond set at the top of the fourth
mast **Edge:** Reeded

Date	Mintage	F	VF	XF	Unc	BU
2001 Proof	2,001	Value: 355				

KM# 915.1   1/5 CROWN
6.2200 g., 0.9999 Gold 0.1999 oz. AGW, 22 mm. **Ruler:**
Elizabeth II **Series:** Victorian Era - Victoria's Death 1901 **Obv:**
Bust with tiara right **Rev:** Victoria's cameo portrait and Osborne
Manor **Edge:** Reeded

Date	Mintage	F	VF	XF	Unc	BU
2001 Proof	5,000	Value: 355				

KM# 915.2   1/5 CROWN
6.2200 g., 0.9999 Gold 0.1999 oz. AGW, 22 mm. **Ruler:**
Elizabeth II **Series:** Victorian Era - Victoria's Death 1901 **Obv:**
Bust with tiara right **Rev:** Tiny sapphire set in the field between
the towers **Edge:** Reeded

Date	Mintage	F	VF	XF	Unc	BU
2001 Proof	2,001	Value: 355				

KM# 917   1/5 CROWN
6.2200 g., 0.9999 Gold 0.1999 oz. AGW, 22 mm. **Ruler:**
Elizabeth II **Series:** Victorian Era - Prince Albert and the Great
Exhibition 1851 **Obv:** Bust with tiara right **Rev:** Albert's cameo
portrait and the exhibit hall **Edge:** Reeded

Date	Mintage	F	VF	XF	Unc	BU
2001 Proof	5,000	Value: 355				

KM# 919   1/5 CROWN
6.2200 g., 0.9999 Gold 0.1999 oz. AGW, 22 mm. **Ruler:**
Elizabeth II **Series:** Victorian Era - Isambard K. Brunel **Obv:** Bust
with tiara right **Rev:** Portrait in top hat and railroad bridge **Edge:**
Reeded

Date	Mintage	F	VF	XF	Unc	BU
2001 Proof	5,000	Value: 355				

KM# 921   1/5 CROWN
6.2200 g., 0.9999 Gold 0.1999 oz. AGW, 22 mm. **Ruler:**
Elizabeth II **Series:** Victorian Era - Charles Dickens **Obv:** Bust
with tiara right **Rev:** Portrait and scene from "Oliver Twist" **Edge:**
Reeded

Date	Mintage	F	VF	XF	Unc	BU
2001 Proof	5,000	Value: 355				

KM# 923   1/5 CROWN
6.2200 g., 0.9999 Gold 0.1999 oz. AGW, 22 mm. **Ruler:**
Elizabeth II **Series:** Victorian Era - Charles Darwin **Obv:** Bust
with tiara right **Rev:** Portrait, ship and a squatting aboriginal figure
Edge: Reeded

Date	Mintage	F	VF	XF	Unc	BU
2001 Proof	5,000	Value: 355				

KM# 925   1/5 CROWN
6.2200 g., 0.9999 Gold 0.1999 oz. AGW, 22 mm. **Ruler:**
Elizabeth II **Series:** Mythology of the Solar System **Obv:** Queens
portrait **Rev:** Standing goddess with snake basket **Edge:** Reeded

Date	Mintage	F	VF	XF	Unc	BU
2001 Proof	5,000	Value: 355				

KM# 926   1/5 CROWN
Bi-Metallic 0.925 Silver center in 0.999 Gold ring, 32.25 mm.
Ruler: Elizabeth II **Series:** Mythology of the Solar System **Obv:**
Bust with tiara right **Rev:** Standing goddess with snake basket
Edge: Reeded

Date	Mintage	F	VF	XF	Unc	BU
2001 In Proof sets only	999	Value: 500				

KM# 929.1   1/5 CROWN
6.2200 g., 0.9999 Gold 0.1999 oz. AGW, 22 mm. **Ruler:**
Elizabeth II **Series:** Mythology of the Solar System - Sun **Obv:**
Bust with tiara right **Rev:** Helios in chariot and the sun **Edge:**
Reeded

Date	Mintage	F	VF	XF	Unc	BU
2001 Proof	5,000	Value: 355				

KM# 929.2   1/5 CROWN
6.2200 g., 0.9999 Gold 0.1999 oz. AGW, 22 mm. **Ruler:**
Elizabeth II **Series:** Mythology of the Solar System **Obv:** Bust
with tiara right **Rev:** Fiery hologram in the sun **Edge:** Reeded

Date	Mintage	F	VF	XF	Unc	BU
2001 In Proof sets only	999	Value: 355				

KM# 931.1   1/5 CROWN
6.2200 g., 0.9999 Gold 0.1999 oz. AGW, 22 mm. **Ruler:**
Elizabeth II **Series:** Mythology of the Solar System - Moon **Obv:**
Bust with tiara right **Rev:** Goddess Diana and the moon **Edge:**
Reeded

Date	Mintage	F	VF	XF	Unc	BU
2001 Proof	5,000	Value: 355				

KM# 931.2   1/5 CROWN
6.2200 g., 0.9999 Gold 0.1999 oz. AGW, 22 mm. **Ruler:**
Elizabeth II **Series:** Mythology of the Solar System - Moon **Obv:**
Bust with tiara right **Rev:** Small pearl set in the moon **Edge:**
Reeded

Date	Mintage	F	VF	XF	Unc	BU
2001 In Proof sets only	999	Value: 355				

KM# 933.1   1/5 CROWN
6.2200 g., 0.9999 Gold 0.1999 oz. AGW, 22 mm. **Ruler:**
Elizabeth II **Series:** Mythology of the Solar System - Atlas **Obv:**
Bust with tiara right **Rev:** Atlas carrying the earth **Edge:** Reeded

Date	Mintage	F	VF	XF	Unc	BU
2001 Proof	5,000	Value: 355				

KM# 933.2   1/5 CROWN
6.2200 g., 0.9999 Gold 0.1999 oz. AGW, 22 mm. **Ruler:**
Elizabeth II **Series:** Mythology of the Solar System - Atlas **Obv:**
Bust with tiara right **Rev:** Tiny diamond set in the earth **Edge:**
Reeded

Date	Mintage	F	VF	XF	Unc	BU
2001 In Proof sets only	999	Value: 355				

KM# 935   1/5 CROWN
6.2200 g., 0.9999 Gold 0.1999 oz. AGW, 22 mm. **Ruler:**
Elizabeth II **Series:** Mythology of the Solar System - Neptune
Obv: Bust with tiara right **Rev:** Seated god with trident and ringed
planet **Edge:** Reeded

Date	Mintage	F	VF	XF	Unc	BU
2001 Proof	5,000	Value: 355				

KM# 937   1/5 CROWN
6.2200 g., 0.9999 Gold 0.1999 oz. AGW, 22 mm. **Ruler:**
Elizabeth II **Series:** Mythology of the Solar System - Jupiter **Obv:**
Bust with tiara right **Rev:** Seated god with lightning bolts and a
planet **Edge:** Reeded

Date	Mintage	F	VF	XF	Unc	BU
2001 Proof	5,000	Value: 355				

KM# 939   1/5 CROWN
6.2200 g., 0.9999 Gold 0.1999 oz. AGW, 22 mm. **Ruler:**
Elizabeth II **Series:** Mythology of the Solar System - Mars **Obv:**
Bust with tiara right **Rev:** Standing Roman solider and a planet
Edge: Reeded

Date	Mintage	F	VF	XF	Unc	BU
2001 Proof	5,000	Value: 355				

KM# 941   1/5 CROWN
6.2200 g., 0.9999 Gold 0.1999 oz. AGW, 22 mm. **Ruler:**
Elizabeth II **Series:** Mythology of the Solar System - Mercury
Obv: Bust with tiara right **Rev:** Seated god with caduceus and a
planet **Edge:** Reeded

Date	Mintage	F	VF	XF	Unc	BU
2001 Proof	5,000	Value: 355				

KM# 943   1/5 CROWN
6.2200 g., 0.9999 Gold 0.1999 oz. AGW, 22 mm. **Ruler:**
Elizabeth II **Series:** Mythology of the Solar System - Uranus **Obv:**
Bust with tiara right **Rev:** Seated god with scepter **Edge:** Reeded

Date	Mintage	F	VF	XF	Unc	BU
2001 Proof	5,000	Value: 355				

KM# 945   1/5 CROWN
6.2200 g., 0.9999 Gold 0.1999 oz. AGW, 22 mm. **Ruler:**
Elizabeth II **Series:** Mythology of the Solar System - Saturn **Obv:**
Bust with tiara right **Rev:** Seated god with long handled sickle
and a ringed planet **Edge:** Reeded

Date	Mintage	F	VF	XF	Unc	BU
2001 Proof	5,000	Value: 355				

KM# 947   1/5 CROWN
6.2200 g., 0.9999 Gold 0.1999 oz. AGW, 22 mm. **Ruler:**
Elizabeth II **Series:** Mythology of the Solar System - Pluto **Obv:**
Bust with tiara right **Rev:** Seated god with dogs and a planet
Edge: Reeded

Date	Mintage	F	VF	XF	Unc	BU
2001 Proof	5,000	Value: 355				

KM# 949   1/5 CROWN
6.2200 g., 0.9999 Gold 0.1999 oz. AGW, 22 mm. **Ruler:**
Elizabeth II **Series:** Mythology of the Solar System - Venus **Obv:**
Bust with tiara right **Rev:** Goddess seated on a half shell **Edge:**
Reeded

Date	Mintage	F	VF	XF	Unc	BU
2001 Proof	5,000	Value: 355				

KM# 951   1/5 CROWN
6.2200 g., 0.9999 Gold 0.1999 oz. AGW, 22 mm. **Ruler:**
Elizabeth II **Subject:** Queen's 76th Birthday **Obv:** Bust with tiara
right **Rev:** Queen in Order of the Garter robes with a tiny inset
diamond **Edge:** Reeded

Date	Mintage	F	VF	XF	Unc	BU
2001 Proof	2,001	Value: 355				

KM# 954   1/5 CROWN
6.2200 g., 0.9999 Gold 0.1999 oz. AGW, 22 mm. **Ruler:**
Elizabeth II **Series:** Victorian Age Part II - Victoria's Accession
to the Throne **Obv:** Bust with tiara right **Rev:** Victoria learning of
her accession **Edge:** Reeded

Date	Mintage	F	VF	XF	Unc	BU
2001 Proof	5,000	Value: 355				

KM# 956   1/5 CROWN
6.2200 g., 0.9999 Gold 0.1999 oz. AGW, 22 mm. **Ruler:**
Elizabeth II **Series:** Victorian Age Part II - Royal Family **Rev:**
Victoria and Albert seated with children **Edge:** Reeded

Date	Mintage	F	VF	XF	Unc	BU
2001 Proof	5,000	Value: 355				

KM# 958   1/5 CROWN
6.2200 g., 0.9999 Gold 0.1999 oz. AGW, 22 mm. **Ruler:**
Elizabeth II **Series:** Victorian Age Part II - Victoria in Scotland
Obv: Bust with tiara right **Rev:** Victoria on horse and servant
Edge: Reeded

Date	Mintage	F	VF	XF	Unc	BU
2001 Proof	5,000	Value: 355				

KM# 960   1/5 CROWN
6.2200 g., 0.9999 Gold 0.1999 oz. AGW, 22 mm. **Ruler:**
Elizabeth II **Series:** Victorian Age Part II **Obv:** Bust with tiara right
Rev: Portraits of Gladstone and Disaraeli **Edge:** Reeded

Date	Mintage	F	VF	XF	Unc	BU
2001 Proof	5,000	Value: 355				

KM# 962   1/5 CROWN
6.2200 g., 0.9999 Gold 0.1999 oz. AGW, 22 mm. **Ruler:**
Elizabeth II **Series:** Victorian Age Part II **Obv:** Bust with tiara right
Rev: Florence Nightingale holding lantern **Edge:** Reeded

Date	Mintage	F	VF	XF	Unc	BU
2001 Proof	5,000	Value: 355				

KM# 964   1/5 CROWN
6.2200 g., 0.9999 Gold 0.1999 oz. AGW, 22 mm. **Ruler:**
Elizabeth II **Series:** Victorian Age Part II **Obv:** Bust with tiara right
Rev: Lord Tennyson with the Light Brigade in background **Edge:**
Reeded

Date	Mintage	F	VF	XF	Unc	BU
2001 Proof	5,000	Value: 355				

KM# 966   1/5 CROWN
6.2200 g., 0.9999 Gold 0.1999 oz. AGW, 22 mm. **Ruler:**
Elizabeth II **Series:** Victorian Age Part II **Obv:** Bust with tiara right
Rev: Stanley meeting Dr. Livingstone **Edge:** Reeded

Date	Mintage	F	VF	XF	Unc	BU
2001 Proof	5,000	Value: 355				

KM# 968   1/5 CROWN
6.2200 g., 0.9999 Gold 0.1999 oz. AGW, 22 mm. **Ruler:**
Elizabeth II **Series:** Victorian Age Part II **Obv:** Bust with tiara right
Rev: Bronte sisters **Edge:** Reeded

Date	Mintage	F	VF	XF	Unc	BU
2001 Proof	5,000	Value: 355				

KM# 978   1/5 CROWN
6.2200 g., 0.9990 Gold 0.1998 oz. AGW, 22 mm. **Ruler:**
Elizabeth II **Subject:** Queen Mother's Life **Obv:** Bust right **Rev:**
Prince William's christening scene **Edge:** Reeded

Date	Mintage	F	VF	XF	Unc	BU
2002 Proof	5,000	Value: 355				

KM# 980   1/5 CROWN
6.2200 g., 0.9999 Gold 0.1999 oz. AGW, 22 mm. **Ruler:**
Elizabeth II **Subject:** World Cup Soccer **Obv:** Bust right **Rev:**
Two players about to collide **Edge:** Reeded

Date	Mintage	F	VF	XF	Unc	BU
2002 Proof	5,000	Value: 355				

KM# 982   1/5 CROWN
6.2200 g., 0.9999 Gold 0.1999 oz. AGW, 22 mm. **Ruler:**
Elizabeth II **Subject:** World Cup Soccer **Obv:** Bust right **Rev:**
Two players facing viewer **Edge:** Reeded

Date	Mintage	F	VF	XF	Unc	BU
2002 Proof	5,000	Value: 355				

KM# 984 1/5 CROWN
6.2200 g., 0.9999 Gold 0.1999 oz. AGW, 22 mm. **Ruler:** Elizabeth II **Subject:** World Cup Soccer **Obv:** Bust right **Rev:** Two horizontal players **Edge:** Reeded

Date	Mintage	F	VF	XF	Unc	BU
2002 Proof	5,000	Value: 355				

KM# 986 1/5 CROWN
6.2200 g., 0.9999 Gold 0.1999 oz. AGW, 22 mm. **Ruler:** Elizabeth II **Subject:** World Cup Soccer **Obv:** Bust right **Rev:** Two players moving to the left **Edge:** Reeded

Date	Mintage	F	VF	XF	Unc	BU
2002 Proof	5,000	Value: 355				

KM# 990 1/5 CROWN
6.2200 g., 0.9990 Gold 0.1998 oz. AGW, 22 mm. **Ruler:** Elizabeth II **Subject:** Peter Rabbit Centennial **Obv:** Bust right **Rev:** Peter Rabbit **Edge:** Reeded

Date	Mintage	F	VF	XF	Unc	BU
2002 Proof	3,500	Value: 355				

KM# 990a 1/5 CROWN
6.2200 g., 0.9990 Platinum 0.1998 oz. APW, 22 mm. **Ruler:** Elizabeth II **Subject:** Peter Rabbit Centennial **Obv:** Bust right **Rev:** Peter Rabbit **Edge:** Reeded

Date	Mintage	F	VF	XF	Unc	BU
2002 Proof	1,500	Value: 400				

KM# 993 1/5 CROWN
6.2200 g., 0.3750 Gold 0.0750 oz. AGW, 22 mm. **Ruler:** Elizabeth II **Subject:** Queen's Golden Jubilee **Obv:** Bust with tiara right **Rev:** Royal couple and tree house **Edge:** Reeded

Date	Mintage	F	VF	XF	Unc	BU
2002 Proof	5,000	Value: 140				

KM# 993a 1/5 CROWN
6.2200 g., 0.9999 Gold 0.1999 oz. AGW, 22 mm. **Ruler:** Elizabeth II **Subject:** Queen's Golden Jubilee **Obv:** Bust with tiara right **Rev:** Royal couple and tree house **Edge:** Reeded

Date	Mintage	F	VF	XF	Unc	BU
2002 Proof	2,002	Value: 355				

KM# 995 1/5 CROWN
6.2200 g., 0.3750 Gold 0.0750 oz. AGW, 22 mm. **Ruler:** Elizabeth II **Subject:** Queen's Golden Jubilee **Obv:** Bust with tiara right **Rev:** Royal coach **Edge:** Reeded

Date	Mintage	F	VF	XF	Unc	BU
2002 Proof	5,000	Value: 140				

KM# 995a 1/5 CROWN
6.2200 g., 0.9999 Gold 0.1999 oz. AGW, 22 mm. **Ruler:** Elizabeth II **Subject:** Queen's Golden Jubilee **Obv:** Bust with tiara right **Rev:** Royal coach **Edge:** Reeded

Date	Mintage	F	VF	XF	Unc	BU
2002 Proof	2,002	Value: 355				

KM# 997 1/5 CROWN
6.2200 g., 0.3750 Gold 0.0750 oz. AGW, 22 mm. **Ruler:** Elizabeth II **Subject:** Queen's Golden Jubilee **Obv:** Bust with tiara right **Rev:** Queen holding baby **Edge:** Reeded

Date	Mintage	F	VF	XF	Unc	BU
2002 Proof	5,000	Value: 140				

KM# 997a 1/5 CROWN
6.2200 g., 0.9999 Gold 0.1999 oz. AGW, 22 mm. **Ruler:** Elizabeth II **Subject:** Queen's Golden Jubilee **Obv:** Bust with tiara right **Rev:** Queen holding baby **Edge:** Reeded

Date	Mintage	F	VF	XF	Unc	BU
2002 Proof	2,002	Value: 355				

KM# 999 1/5 CROWN
6.2200 g., 0.3750 Gold 0.0750 oz. AGW, 22 mm. **Ruler:** Elizabeth II **Subject:** Queen's Golden Jubilee **Obv:** Bust with tiara right **Rev:** Yacht under Tower bridge **Edge:** Reeded

Date	Mintage	F	VF	XF	Unc	BU
2002 Proof	5,000	Value: 140				

KM# 999a 1/5 CROWN
6.2200 g., 0.9999 Gold 0.1999 oz. AGW, 22 mm. **Ruler:** Elizabeth II **Subject:** Queen's Golden Jubilee **Obv:** Bust with tiara right **Rev:** Yacht under Tower bridge **Edge:** Reeded

Date	Mintage	F	VF	XF	Unc	BU
2002 Proof	2,002	Value: 355				

KM# 1001 1/5 CROWN
6.2200 g., 0.9999 Gold 0.1999 oz. AGW, 22 mm. **Ruler:** Elizabeth II **Subject:** Queen's Golden Jubilee **Obv:** Bust with tiara right **Rev:** Crown jewels inset with a tiny diamond, ruby, sapphire and emerald **Edge:** Reeded

Date	Mintage	F	VF	XF	Unc	BU
2002 Proof	2,002	Value: 355				

KM# 1003 1/5 CROWN
6.2200 g., Electrum Special alloy of equal parts of gold and silver, 22 mm. **Ruler:** Elizabeth II **Series:** Ancient Coins **Obv:** Bust with tiara right **Rev:** Head of Athena left **Edge:** Reeded **Note:** From a Mysia electrum coin c.520BC.

Date	Mintage	F	VF	XF	Unc	BU
2002 Proof	3,500	Value: 175				

KM# 1005 1/5 CROWN
6.2200 g., Electrum Special alloy of equal parts of gold and silver., 22 mm. **Ruler:** Elizabeth II **Series:** Ancient Coins **Obv:** Bust with tiara right **Rev:** Head of Hercules right **Edge:** Reeded **Note:** From a Lesbos coin c. 480-450 BC.

Date	Mintage	F	VF	XF	Unc	BU
2002 Proof	3,500	Value: 175				

KM# 1007 1/5 CROWN
6.2200 g., 0.9990 Electrum Special alloy of equal parts of gold and silver. 0.1998 oz., 22 mm. **Ruler:** Elizabeth II **Series:** Ancient Coins **Obv:** Bust with tiara right **Rev:** Pegasus **Edge:** Reeded **Note:** From a Lampsakos electrum coin c. 450 BC.

Date	Mintage	F	VF	XF	Unc	BU
2002 Proof	3,500	Value: 175				

KM# 1009 1/5 CROWN
6.2200 g., Electrum Special Alloy of equal parts of gold and silver., 22 mm. **Ruler:** Elizabeth II **Series:** Ancient Coins **Obv:** Bust with tiara right **Rev:** Lion and bull facing **Edge:** Reeded **Note:** From a Kroisos "sic" coin c. 560-546 BC.

Date	Mintage	F	VF	XF	Unc	BU
2002 Proof	3,500	Value: 175				

KM# 1012 1/5 CROWN
6.2200 g., 0.9999 Gold 0.1999 oz. AGW, 22 mm. **Ruler:** Elizabeth II **Subject:** Queen Mother **Obv:** Bust with tiara right **Rev:** Queen Mother trout fishing **Edge:** Reeded

Date	Mintage	F	VF	XF	Unc	BU
2002 Proof	5,000	Value: 355				

KM# 1014 1/5 CROWN
6.2200 g., 0.9999 Gold 0.1999 oz. AGW, 22 mm. **Ruler:** Elizabeth II **Subject:** Princess Diana **Obv:** Bust right **Rev:** Diana's portrait **Edge:** Reeded

Date	Mintage	F	VF	XF	Unc	BU
2002 Proof	5,000	Value: 355				

KM# 1018 1/5 CROWN
6.2200 g., 0.9999 Gold 0.1999 oz. AGW, 22 mm. **Ruler:** Elizabeth II **Subject:** Peter Pan **Obv:** Bust right **Rev:** Peter Pan and Tinkerbell flying above city **Edge:** Reeded

Date	Mintage	F	VF	XF	Unc	BU
2002 Proof	5,000	Value: 355				

KM# 1020 1/5 CROWN
6.2200 g., 0.9999 Gold 0.1999 oz. AGW, 22 mm. **Ruler:** Elizabeth II **Subject:** Grand Masonic Lodge **Obv:** Bust right **Rev:** Masonic seal above Gibraltar **Edge:** Reeded

Date	Mintage	F	VF	XF	Unc	BU
2002 Proof	5,000	Value: 355				

KM# 991 1/2 CROWN
15.5500 g., 0.9990 Gold 0.4994 oz. AGW, 30 mm. **Ruler:** Elizabeth II **Subject:** Peter Rabbit Centennial **Obv:** Bust right **Rev:** Peter Rabbit **Edge:** Reeded

Date	Mintage	F	VF	XF	Unc	BU
2002 Proof	1,000	Value: 875				

KM# 1002 1/2 CROWN
15.5500 g., 0.9999 Gold 0.4999 oz. AGW, 30 mm. **Ruler:** Elizabeth II **Subject:** Queen's Golden Jubilee **Obv:** Bust with tiara right **Rev:** Crown jewels inset with a tiny diamond, ruby, sapphire and emerald **Edge:** Reeded

Date	Mintage	F	VF	XF	Unc	BU
2002 Proof	999	Value: 875				

KM# 1004 1/2 CROWN
15.5500 g., Electrum Special alloy of equal parts of gold and silver., 32.2 mm. **Ruler:** Elizabeth II **Series:** Ancient Coins **Obv:** Bust with tiara right **Rev:** Head of Athena left **Edge:** Reeded **Note:** From a Mysia electrum coin c. 520 BC.

Date	Mintage	F	VF	XF	Unc	BU
2002 Proof	2,000	Value: 300				

KM# 1006 1/2 CROWN
15.5500 g., Electrum Special alloy of equal parts of gold and silver., 32.2 mm. **Ruler:** Elizabeth II **Series:** Ancient Coins **Obv:** Bust with tiara right **Rev:** Head of Hercules right **Edge:** Reeded **Note:** From a Lesbos coin c. 480-450 BC.

Date	Mintage	F	VF	XF	Unc	BU
2002 Proof	2,000	Value: 300				

KM# 1008 1/2 CROWN
15.5500 g., Gold With Silver Special alloy of equal parts of gold and silver., 32.2 mm. **Ruler:** Elizabeth II **Series:** Ancient Coins **Obv:** Bust with tiara right **Rev:** Pegasus **Edge:** Reeded **Note:** From a Lampsakos electrum coin c. 450 BC.

Date	Mintage	F	VF	XF	Unc	BU
2002 Proof	2,000	Value: 300				

KM# 1010 1/2 CROWN
15.5500 g., Electrum Special alloy of equal parts of gold and silver., 32.2 mm. **Ruler:** Elizabeth II **Series:** Ancient Coins **Obv:** Bust with tiara right **Rev:** Lion and bull facing **Edge:** Reeded **Note:** From a Kroisos [sic] coin c. 560-546 BC.

Date	Mintage	F	VF	XF	Unc	BU
2002 Proof	2,000	Value: 300				

KM# 1056 CROWN
31.1000 g., 0.9990 Tri-Metallic Center: silver, Ring: silver-gilt, Outer ring: silver-pearl black 0.9988 oz., 38.60 mm. **Ruler:** Elizabeth II **Series:** 21st Century **Obv:** Crowned bust right **Obv. Legend:** GIBRALTER • ELIZABETH II **Rev:** Helmeted cross at center flanked by satellites, archaic sailing ship below **Rev. Legend:** 21st CENTURY **Edge:** Reeded

Date	Mintage	F	VF	XF	Unc	BU
2001 Proof	2,001	Value: 700				

KM# 904 CROWN
28.2800 g., Copper-Nickel, 38.6 mm. **Ruler:** Elizabeth II **Subject:** The Life of Queen Elizabeth - The Queen Mother **Obv:** Bust with tiara right **Rev:** 1953 Coronation scene **Edge:** Reeded

Date	Mintage	F	VF	XF	Unc	BU
2001	—	—	—	—	10.00	12.00

KM# 904a CROWN
28.2800 g., 0.9250 Silver 0.8410 oz. ASW, 38.6 mm. **Ruler:** Elizabeth II **Subject:** The Life of Queen Elizabeth - The Queen Mother **Obv:** Bust with tiara right **Rev:** 1953 Coronation scene **Edge:** Reeded

Date	Mintage	F	VF	XF	Unc	BU
2001 Proof	10,000	Value: 47.50				

KM# 905   CROWN
28.2800 g., Copper-Nickel, 38.6 mm.   **Ruler:** Elizabeth II
Subject: The Life of Queen Elizabeth - The Queen Mother **Obv:**
Bust with tiara right **Rev:** Queen Mother with Prince Charles in
1954 **Edge:** Reeded

Date	Mintage	F	VF	XF	Unc	BU
2001	—	—	—	—	10.00	12.00

KM# 905a   CROWN
28.2800 g., 0.9250 Silver 0.8410 oz. ASW, 38.6 mm.   **Ruler:**
Elizabeth II **Subject:** The Life of Queen Elizabeth - The Queen
Mother **Obv:** Bust with tiara right **Rev:** Queen Mother with Prince
Charles in 1954 **Edge:** Reeded

Date	Mintage	F	VF	XF	Unc	BU
2001 Proof	10,000 Value: 47.50					

KM# 906   CROWN
28.2800 g., Copper-Nickel, 38.6 mm.   **Ruler:** Elizabeth II
Subject: 21st Century **Obv:** Crowned bust right, date below **Rev:**
Celtic cross, Viking ship and modern technological items **Edge:**
Reeded

Date	Mintage	F	VF	XF	Unc	BU
2001	—	—	—	—	10.00	12.00

KM# 906a   CROWN
31.1035 g., 0.9990 Silver 0.9990 oz. ASW, 38.6 mm.   **Ruler:**
Elizabeth II **Subject:** 21st Century **Obv:** Crowned bust right, date
below **Rev:** Celtic cross, Viking ship and modern technological
items **Edge:** Reeded **Note:** 31.1035 .999 Silver, 1.0000 ASW
with a gold plated inner ring and a blackened outer ring.

Date	Mintage	F	VF	XF	Unc	BU
2001 Proof	2,001 Value: 75.00					

KM# 906b   CROWN
31.1000 g., Tri-Metallic Center .9995 Platinum 5.2g. Inner Ring
.9999 Gold 14.2g. Outer Ring .999 Silver 11.7g   **Ruler:**
Elizabeth II **Subject:** 21st Century **Obv:** Crowned bust right, date
below **Rev:** Celtic cross, Viking ship and modern technological
items

Date	Mintage	F	VF	XF	Unc	BU
2001 Proof	999 Value: 750					

KM# 910   CROWN
28.2800 g., Copper-Nickel, 38.6 mm.   **Ruler:** Elizabeth II **Series:**
The Victorian Age **Obv:** Bust with tiara right **Rev:** 1838 Coronation
of Queen Victoria **Edge:** Reeded

Date	Mintage	F	VF	XF	Unc	BU
2001	—	—	—	—	10.00	12.00

KM# 910a   CROWN
28.2800 g., 0.9250 Silver 0.8410 oz. ASW, 38.6 mm.   **Ruler:**
Elizabeth II **Series:** Victorian Era **Obv:** Bust with tiara right **Rev:**
1838 Coronation scene **Edge:** Reeded

Date	Mintage	F	VF	XF	Unc	BU
2001 Proof	10,000 Value: 47.50					

KM# 912   CROWN
Copper-Nickel, 38.6 mm.   **Ruler:** Elizabeth II **Series:** Victorian
Era - Empress of India 1876 **Obv:** Bust with tiara right **Rev:**
Crowned portrait of Victoria and two elephants

Date	Mintage	F	VF	XF	Unc	BU
2001					10.00	12.00

KM# 912a   CROWN
28.2800 g., 0.9250 Silver 0.8410 oz. ASW   **Ruler:** Elizabeth II
Series: The Victorian Age - Empress of India 1876 **Obv:** Bust
with tiara right **Rev:** Crowned portrait of Victoria and two
elephants

Date	Mintage	F	VF	XF	Unc	BU
2001 Proof	10,000 Value: 47.50					

KM# 914   CROWN
Copper-Nickel, 38.6 mm.   **Ruler:** Elizabeth II **Series:** Victorian
Era - Diamond Jubilee **Obv:** Bust with tiara right **Rev:** Victoria's
cameo portrait above naval ships

Date	Mintage	F	VF	XF	Unc	BU
2001					10.00	12.00

KM# 914a   CROWN
28.2800 g., 0.9250 Silver 0.8410 oz. ASW   **Ruler:** Elizabeth II
Series: The Victorian Age - Diamond Jubilee 1897 **Obv:** Bust
with tiara right **Rev:** Victoria's cameo above naval ships, Spithead
Review

Date	Mintage	F	VF	XF	Unc	BU
2001 Proof	10,000 Value: 47.50					

KM# 916   CROWN
Copper-Nickel, 38.6 mm.   **Ruler:** Elizabeth II **Series:** The
Victorian Age - Victoria's Death 1901 **Obv:** Bust with tiara right
Rev: Victoria's cameo portrait and Osborne Manor

Date	Mintage	F	VF	XF	Unc	BU
2001					10.00	12.00

KM# 916a   CROWN
28.2800 g., 0.9250 Silver 0.8410 oz. ASW, 38.6 mm.   **Ruler:**
Elizabeth II **Series:** The Victorian Age - Victoria's Death 1901
Obv: Bust with tiara right **Rev:** Victoria's cameo portrait and
Osborne Manor

Date	Mintage	F	VF	XF	Unc	BU
2001 Proof	10,000 Value: 47.50					

KM# 918   CROWN
Copper-Nickel, 38.6 mm.   **Ruler:** Elizabeth II **Series:** The
Victorian Age - Prince Albert and the Great Exhibition 1851 **Obv:**
Bust with tiara right **Rev:** Albert's cameo portrait and the exhibit
hall

Date	Mintage	F	VF	XF	Unc	BU
2001 Proof	5,000 Value: 175					

KM# 918a   CROWN
28.2800 g., 0.9250 Silver 0.8410 oz. ASW, 38.6 mm.   **Ruler:**
Elizabeth II **Series:** The Victorian Age - Prince Albert and the
Great Exhibition 1851 **Obv:** Bust with tiara right **Rev:** Albert's
cameo portrait and the exhibit hall

Date	Mintage	F	VF	XF	Unc	BU
2001 Proof	10,000 Value: 47.50					

KM# 920   CROWN
Copper-Nickel, 38.6 mm.   **Ruler:** Elizabeth II **Series:** The
Victorian Age **Obv:** Bust with tiara right **Rev:** 1/2 bust of Isambard
K. Brunel half left in front of railroad bridge

Date	Mintage	F	VF	XF	Unc	BU
2001					10.00	12.00

KM# 920a   CROWN
28.2800 g., 0.9250 Silver 0.8410 oz. ASW, 38.6 mm.   **Ruler:**
Elizabeth II **Series:** Victorian Era **Obv:** Bust with tiara right **Rev:**
1/2 bust of Isambard K. Brunel half left in front of railroad bridge

Date	Mintage	F	VF	XF	Unc	BU
2001 Proof	10,000 Value: 47.50					

KM# 922   CROWN
Copper-Nickel, 38.6 mm.   **Ruler:** Elizabeth II **Series:** The
Victorian Age **Obv:** Bust with tiara right **Rev:** 1/2 length bust of
Charles Dickens half left, scene from "Oliver Twist" in background

Date	Mintage	F	VF	XF	Unc	BU
2001					10.00	12.00

KM# 922a   CROWN
28.2800 g., 0.9250 Silver 0.8410 oz. ASW, 38.6 mm.   **Series:**
The Victorian Age **Obv:** Bust with tiara right **Rev:** 1/2 length bust
of Charles Dickens half left, scene from "Oliver Twist" in
background

Date	Mintage	F	VF	XF	Unc	BU
2001 Proof	10,000 Value: 47.50					

KM# 924   CROWN
Copper-Nickel, 38.6 mm.   **Ruler:** Elizabeth II **Series:** The
Victorian Age **Obv:** Bust with tiara right **Rev:** 3/4-length figure of
Charles Darwin right, ship and a squatting aboriginal figure

Date	Mintage	F	VF	XF	Unc	BU
2001					10.00	12.00

KM# 924a   CROWN
28.2800 g., 0.9250 Silver 0.8410 oz. ASW, 38.6 mm.   **Ruler:**
Elizabeth II **Series:** The Victorian Age **Obv:** Bust with tiara right
Rev: 3/4-length figure of Charles Darwin right, ship and a
squatting aboriginal figure

Date	Mintage	F	VF	XF	Unc	BU
2001 Proof	10,000 Value: 47.50					

KM# 927   CROWN
28.2800 g., Copper-Nickel, 38.6 mm.   **Ruler:** Elizabeth II **Series:**
Mythology of the Solar System **Obv:** Bust with tiara right **Rev:**
Standing goddess with snake basket **Edge:** Reeded

Date	Mintage	F	VF	XF	Unc	BU
2001	—	—	—	—	10.00	12.00

KM# 927a   CROWN
28.2800 g., 0.9250 Silver 0.8410 oz. ASW, 38.6 mm.   **Ruler:**
Elizabeth II **Series:** Mythology of the Solar System **Obv:** Bust
with tiara right **Rev:** Standing goddess with snake basket **Edge:**
Reeded

Date	Mintage	F	VF	XF	Unc	BU
2001 Proof	10,000 Value: 47.50					

KM# 928   CROWN
Bi-Metallic Titanium center in Silver ring, 32.25 mm.   **Ruler:**
Elizabeth II **Series:** Mythology of the Solar System **Obv:** Bust
with tiara right **Rev:** Standing goddess with snake basket **Edge:**
Reeded

Date	Mintage	F	VF	XF	Unc	BU
2001 In Proof sets only	2,001 Value: 150					

KM# 930   CROWN
Copper-Nickel, 38.6 mm.   **Ruler:** Elizabeth II **Series:** Mythology

of the Solar System - Sun **Obv:** Bust with tiara right **Rev:** Helios in chariot and the sun

Date	Mintage	F	VF	XF	Unc	BU
2001	—	—	—	—	10.00	12.00

KM# 930a CROWN
28.2800 g., 0.9250 Silver 0.8410 oz. ASW, 38.6 mm. **Ruler:** Elizabeth II **Series:** Mythology of the Solar System - Sun **Obv:** Bust with tiara right **Rev:** Helios in chariot and the sun

Date	Mintage	F	VF	XF	Unc	BU
2001 Proof	10,000	Value: 47.50				

KM# 930a.1 CROWN
28.2800 g., 0.9250 Silver 0.8410 oz. ASW **Ruler:** Elizabeth II **Series:** Mythology of the Solar System - Sun **Obv:** Bust with tiara right **Rev:** Fiery hologram in the sun

Date	Mintage	F	VF	XF	Unc	BU
2001 Proof	2,001	Value: 87.50				

KM# 932 CROWN
Copper-Nickel, 38.6 mm. **Ruler:** Elizabeth II **Series:** Mythology of the Solar System - Moon **Obv:** Bust with tiara right **Rev:** Goddess Diana and the moon

Date	Mintage	F	VF	XF	Unc	BU
2001	—	—	—	—	10.00	12.00

KM# 932a CROWN
28.2800 g., 0.9250 Silver 0.8410 oz. ASW, 38.6 mm. **Ruler:** Elizabeth II **Series:** Mythology of the Solar System - Moon **Obv:** Bust with tiara right **Rev:** Goddess Diana and the moon

Date	Mintage	F	VF	XF	Unc	BU
2001 Proof	10,000	Value: 47.50				

KM# 932a.1 CROWN
28.2800 g., 0.9250 Silver 0.8410 oz. ASW, 38.6 mm. **Ruler:** Elizabeth II **Series:** Mythology of the Solar System - Moon **Obv:** Bust with tiara right **Rev:** Small pearl set in the moon

Date	Mintage	F	VF	XF	Unc	BU
2001 Proof	2,001	Value: 87.50				

KM# 934 CROWN
Copper-Nickel **Ruler:** Elizabeth II **Series:** Mythology of the Solar System - Atlas **Obv:** Bust with tiara right **Rev:** Atlas carrying the earth

Date	Mintage	F	VF	XF	Unc	BU
2001	—	—	—	—	10.00	12.00

KM# 934a CROWN
28.2800 g., 0.9250 Silver 0.8410 oz. ASW, 38.6 mm. **Ruler:** Elizabeth II **Series:** Mythology of the Solar System - Atlas **Obv:** Bust with tiara right **Rev:** Atlas carrying the earth

Date	Mintage	F	VF	XF	Unc	BU
2001 Proof	10,000	Value: 47.50				

KM# 934a.1 CROWN
28.2800 g., 0.9250 Silver 0.8410 oz. ASW, 38.6 mm. **Ruler:** Elizabeth II **Series:** Mythology of the Solar System - Atlas **Obv:** Bust with tiara right **Rev:** Fancy diamond set in the earth

Date	Mintage	F	VF	XF	Unc	BU
2001 Proof	2,001	Value: 87.50				

KM# 936 CROWN
Copper-Nickel, 38.6 mm. **Ruler:** Elizabeth II **Series:** Mythology of the Solar System **Obv:** Bust with tiara right **Rev:** Seated Neptune with trident and ringed planet

Date	Mintage	F	VF	XF	Unc	BU
2001	—	—	—	—	10.00	12.00

KM# 936a CROWN
28.2800 g., 0.9250 Silver 0.8410 oz. ASW, 38.6 mm. **Ruler:** Elizabeth II **Series:** Mythology of the Solar System **Obv:** Bust with tiara right **Rev:** Seated Neptune with trident and ringed planet

Date	Mintage	F	VF	XF	Unc	BU
2001 Proof	10,000	Value: 47.50				

KM# 938 CROWN
Copper-Nickel, 38.6 mm. **Ruler:** Elizabeth II **Series:** Mythology

of the Solar System **Obv:** Bust with tiara right **Rev:** Seated Jupiter with lightening bolts and a planet

Date	Mintage	F	VF	XF	Unc	BU
2001	—	—	—	—	10.00	12.00

KM# 938a CROWN
28.2800 g., 0.9250 Silver 0.8410 oz. ASW, 38.6 mm. **Ruler:** Elizabeth II **Series:** Mythology of the Solar System **Obv:** Bust with tiara right **Rev:** Seated Jupiter with lightening bolts and a planet

Date	Mintage	F	VF	XF	Unc	BU
2001 Proof	10,000	Value: 47.50				

KM# 940 CROWN
Copper-Nickel, 38.6 mm. **Ruler:** Elizabeth II **Series:** Mythology of the Solar System - Mars **Obv:** Bust with tiara right **Rev:** Standing Roman soldier and a planet

Date	Mintage	F	VF	XF	Unc	BU
2001	—	—	—	—	10.00	12.00

KM# 940a CROWN
28.2800 g., 0.9250 Silver 0.8410 oz. ASW, 38.6 mm. **Ruler:** Elizabeth II **Series:** Mythology of the Solar System - Mars **Obv:** Bust with tiara right **Rev:** Standing Roman soldier and a planet

Date	Mintage	F	VF	XF	Unc	BU
2001 Proof	10,000	Value: 47.50				

KM# 942 CROWN
Copper-Nickel, 38.6 mm. **Ruler:** Elizabeth II **Series:** Mythology of the Solar System **Obv:** Bust with tiara right **Rev:** Seated Mercury with caduceus and a planet

Date	Mintage	F	VF	XF	Unc	BU
2001	—	—	—	—	10.00	12.00

KM# 942a CROWN
28.2800 g., 0.9250 Silver 0.8410 oz. ASW, 38.6 mm. **Ruler:** Elizabeth II **Series:** Mythology of the Solar System **Obv:** Bust with tiara right **Rev:** Seated Mercury with caduceus and a planet

Date	Mintage	F	VF	XF	Unc	BU
2001 Proof	10,000	Value: 47.50				

KM# 944 CROWN
Copper-Nickel, 38.6 mm. **Ruler:** Elizabeth II **Series:** Mythology of the Solar System **Obv:** Bust with tiara right **Rev:** Seated Uranus with scepter

Date	Mintage	F	VF	XF	Unc	BU
2001	—	—	—	—	10.00	12.00

KM# 944a CROWN
28.2800 g., 0.9250 Silver 0.8410 oz. ASW, 38.6 mm. **Ruler:** Elizabeth II **Series:** Mythology of the Solar System **Obv:** Bust with tiara right **Rev:** Seated Uranus with scepter

Date	Mintage	F	VF	XF	Unc	BU
2001 Proof	10,000	Value: 47.50				

KM# 946 CROWN
Copper-Nickel, 38.6 mm. **Ruler:** Elizabeth II **Series:** Mythology of the Solar System **Obv:** Bust with tiara right **Rev:** Seated Saturn with long handled sickle and a ringed planet

Date	Mintage	F	VF	XF	Unc	BU
2001	—	—	—	—	10.00	12.00

KM# 946a CROWN
28.2800 g., 0.9250 Silver 0.8410 oz. ASW, 38.6 mm. **Ruler:** Elizabeth II **Series:** Mythology of the Solar System **Obv:** Bust with tiara right **Rev:** Seated Saturn with long handled sickle and a ringed planet

Date	Mintage	F	VF	XF	Unc	BU
2001 Proof	10,000	Value: 47.50				

KM# 948 CROWN
Copper-Nickel, 38.6 mm. **Ruler:** Elizabeth II **Series:** Mythology of the Solar System **Obv:** Bust with tiara right **Rev:** Seated Pluto with dogs and planet

Date	Mintage	F	VF	XF	Unc	BU
2001	—	—	—	—	10.00	12.00

KM# 948a CROWN
28.2800 g., 0.9250 Silver 0.8410 oz. ASW, 38.6 mm. **Ruler:** Elizabeth II **Series:** Mythology of the Solar System **Obv:** Bust with tiara right **Rev:** Seated Pluto with dogs and planet

Date	Mintage	F	VF	XF	Unc	BU
2001 Proof	10,000	Value: 47.50				

KM# 950 CROWN
Copper-Nickel, 38.6 mm. **Ruler:** Elizabeth II **Series:** Mythology of the Solar System **Obv:** Bust with tiara right **Rev:** Venus seated on a half shell

Date	Mintage	F	VF	XF	Unc	BU
2001	—	—	—	—	10.00	12.00

KM# 950a CROWN
28.2800 g., 0.9250 Silver 0.8410 oz. ASW, 38.6 mm. **Ruler:** Elizabeth II **Series:** Mythology of the Solar System **Obv:** Bust with tiara right **Rev:** Venus seated on a half shell

Date	Mintage	F	VF	XF	Unc	BU
2001 Proof	10,000	Value: 47.50				

KM# 952 CROWN
28.2800 g., Copper-Nickel, 38.6 mm. **Ruler:** Elizabeth II **Subject:** Queen's 75th Birthday **Obv:** Bust with tiara right **Rev:** Queen in Order of Garter robes **Edge:** Reeded

Date	Mintage	F	VF	XF	Unc	BU
2001	—	—	—	—	10.00	12.00

KM# 952a CROWN
28.2800 g., 0.9250 Silver 0.8410 oz. ASW, 38.6 mm. **Ruler:** Elizabeth II **Subject:** Queen's 75th Birthday **Obv:** Bust with tiara right **Rev:** Queen in Order of Garter robes **Edge:** Reeded

Date	Mintage	F	VF	XF	Unc	BU
2001 Proof	10,000	Value: 47.50				

KM# 955 CROWN
28.2800 g., Copper-Nickel, 38.6 mm. **Ruler:** Elizabeth II **Series:** Victorian Age Part II **Obv:** Bust with tiara right **Rev:** Victoria learning of her accession **Edge:** Reeded

Date	Mintage	F	VF	XF	Unc	BU
2001	—	—	—	—	10.00	12.00

KM# 955a CROWN
28.2800 g., 0.9250 Silver 0.8410 oz. ASW, 38.6 mm. **Ruler:** Elizabeth II **Series:** Victorian Age Part II **Obv:** Bust with tiara right **Rev:** Victoria learning of her accession **Edge:** Reeded

Date	Mintage	F	VF	XF	Unc	BU
2001 Proof	10,000	Value: 47.50				

KM# 957 CROWN
Copper-Nickel, 38.6 mm. **Ruler:** Elizabeth II **Series:** Victorian Age Part II - Royal Family **Obv:** Bust with tiara right **Rev:** Victoria and Albert seated with children **Edge:** Reeded

Date	Mintage	F	VF	XF	Unc	BU
2001	—	—	—	—	10.00	12.00

KM# 957a CROWN
28.2800 g., 0.9250 Silver 0.8410 oz. ASW, 38.6 mm. **Ruler:** Elizabeth II **Series:** Victorian Age Part II - Royal Family **Obv:** Bust with tiara right **Rev:** Victoria and Albert seated with children **Edge:** Reeded

Date	Mintage	F	VF	XF	Unc	BU
2001 Proof	10,000	Value: 47.50				

KM# 959 CROWN
Copper-Nickel, 38.6 mm. **Ruler:** Elizabeth II **Series:** Victorian Age Part II - Victoria in Scotland **Obv:** Bust with tiara right **Rev:** Victoria on horse with servant **Edge:** Reeded

Date	Mintage	F	VF	XF	Unc	BU
2001	2,001	—	—	—	10.00	12.00

KM# 959a CROWN
28.2800 g., 0.9250 Silver 0.8410 oz. ASW, 38.6 mm. **Ruler:** Elizabeth II **Series:** Victorian Age Part II - Victoria in Scotland **Obv:** Bust with tiara right **Rev:** Victoria on horse with servant **Edge:** Reeded

Date	Mintage	F	VF	XF	Unc	BU
2001 Proof	10,000	Value: 47.50				

KM# 961   CROWN
Copper-Nickel, 38.6 mm. **Ruler:** Elizabeth II **Series:** Victorian
Age Part II - Gladstone and Disraeli **Obv:** Bust with tiara right
Rev: Portraits of both politicians **Edge:** Reeded

Date	Mintage	F	VF	XF	Unc	BU
2001	—			—	10.00	12.00

KM# 961a   CROWN
28.2800 g., 0.9250 Silver 0.8410 oz. ASW, 38.6 mm. **Ruler:**
Elizabeth II **Series:** Victorian Age Part II - Gladstone and Disraeli
Obv: Bust with tiara right **Rev:** Portraits of both politicians **Edge:**
Reeded

Date	Mintage	F	VF	XF	Unc	BU
2001 Proof	10,000	Value: 47.50				

KM# 963   CROWN
Copper-Nickel, 38.6 mm. **Ruler:** Elizabeth II **Series:** Victorian
Age Part II **Obv:** Bust with tiara right **Rev:** Florence Nightingale
holding lantern **Edge:** Reeded

Date	Mintage	F	VF	XF	Unc	BU
2001	—			—	10.00	12.00

KM# 963a   CROWN
28.2800 g., 0.9250 Silver 0.8410 oz. ASW, 38.6 mm. **Ruler:**
Elizabeth II **Series:** Victorian Age Part II **Obv:** Bust with tiara right
Rev: Florence Nightingale holding lantern **Edge:** Reeded

Date	Mintage	F	VF	XF	Unc	BU
2001 Proof	10,000	Value: 47.50				

KM# 965   CROWN
Copper-Nickel, 38.6 mm. **Ruler:** Elizabeth II **Series:** Victorian
Age Part II **Obv:** Bust with tiara right **Rev:** Lord Tennyson with
the Light Brigade in background **Edge:** Reeded

Date	Mintage	F	VF	XF	Unc	BU
2001	—			—	10.00	12.00

KM# 965a   CROWN
28.2800 g., 0.9250 Silver 0.8410 oz. ASW, 38.6 mm. **Ruler:**
Elizabeth II **Series:** Victorian Age Part II **Obv:** Bust with tiara right
Rev: Lord Tennyson with the Light Brigade in background **Edge:**
Reeded

Date	Mintage	F	VF	XF	Unc	BU
2001 Proof	10,000	Value: 47.50				

KM# 967   CROWN
Copper-Nickel, 38.6 mm. **Ruler:** Elizabeth II **Series:** Victorian
Age Part II **Obv:** Bust with tiara right **Rev:** Stanley meeting Dr.
Livingstone **Edge:** Reeded

Date	Mintage	F	VF	XF	Unc	BU
2001	—			—	10.00	12.00

KM# 967a   CROWN
28.2800 g., 0.9250 Silver 0.8410 oz. ASW, 38.6 mm. **Ruler:**
Elizabeth II **Series:** Victorian Age Part II **Obv:** Bust with tiara right
Rev: Stanley meeting Dr. Livingstone **Edge:** Reeded

Date	Mintage	F	VF	XF	Unc	BU
2001 Proof	10,000	Value: 47.50				

KM# 969   CROWN
Copper-Nickel, 38.6 mm. **Ruler:** Elizabeth II **Series:** Victorian
Age Part II **Obv:** Bust with tiara right **Rev:** Bronte sisters **Edge:**
Reeded

Date	Mintage	F	VF	XF	Unc	BU
2001	—			—	10.00	12.00

KM# 969a   CROWN
28.2800 g., 0.9250 Silver 0.8410 oz. ASW, 38.6 mm. **Ruler:**
Elizabeth II **Series:** Victorian Age Part II **Obv:** Bust with tiara right
Rev: Bronte sisters **Edge:** Reeded

Date	Mintage	F	VF	XF	Unc	BU
2001 Proof	10,000	Value: 47.50				

KM# 1061   CROWN
31.1000 g., Electrum Special alloy of equal parts of gold and
silver. **Ruler:** Elizabeth II **Series:** Ancient Coins **Obv:** Crowned
bust right **Rev:** Lion and bull facing **Note:** From a Kroisos [sic]
coin c. 560-546 BC.

Date	Mintage	F	VF	XF	Unc	BU
2002 Proof	—	Value: 700				

KM# 1060   CROWN
31.1000 g., Electrum Special alloy of equal parts of gold and
silver. **Ruler:** Elizabeth II **Series:** Ancient Coins. **Obv:** Crowned
bust right **Rev:** Lion and bull facing **Note:** From a Lampsakos
electrum coin c. 450 BC.

Date	Mintage	F	VF	XF	Unc	BU
2002 Proof	—	Value: 700				

KM# 1059   CROWN
31.1000 g., Electrum Special alloy of equal parts of gold and
silver. **Ruler:** Elizabeth II **Series:** Ancient Coins **Obv:** Crowned
bust right **Rev:** Head of Hercules right **Note:** From a Lesbos coin
c. 480-450

Date	Mintage	F	VF	XF	Unc	BU
2002 Proof	—	Value: 700				

KM# 1058   CROWN
31.1000 g., 1.0000 Electrum Special alloy of equal parts of gold
and silver. 0.9998 oz. **Ruler:** Elizabeth II **Series:** Ancient Coins
Obv: Crowned head right **Rev:** Head of Athena left **Note:** From
a Mysia electrum coin c. 520 BC.

Date	Mintage	F	VF	XF	Unc	BU
2002 Proof	—	Value: 700				

KM# 979   CROWN
28.2800 g., Copper-Nickel, 38.6 mm. **Ruler:** Elizabeth II
Subject: Queen Mother's Life **Obv:** Bust with tiara right **Rev:**
Christening of Prince William **Edge:** Reeded

Date	Mintage	F	VF	XF	Unc	BU
2002	—			—	10.00	12.00

KM# 979a   CROWN
28.2800 g., 0.9250 Silver 0.8410 oz. ASW, 38.6 mm. **Ruler:**
Elizabeth II **Subject:** Queen Mother's Life **Obv:** Bust with tiara
right **Rev:** Prince William's christening **Edge:** Reeded

Date	Mintage	F	VF	XF	Unc	BU
2002 Proof	10,000	Value: 47.50				

KM# 981   CROWN
28.2800 g., Copper-Nickel, 38.6 mm. **Ruler:** Elizabeth II
Subject: World Cup Soccer **Obv:** Bust with tiara right **Rev:** Two
players about to collide **Edge:** Reeded

Date	Mintage	F	VF	XF	Unc	BU
2002	—			—	10.00	11.50

KM# 981a   CROWN
28.2800 g., 0.9250 Silver 0.8410 oz. ASW, 38.6 mm. **Ruler:**
Elizabeth II **Subject:** World Cup Soccer **Obv:** Bust with tiara right
Rev: Two players about to collide **Edge:** Reeded

Date	Mintage	F	VF	XF	Unc	BU
2002 Proof	10,000	Value: 47.50				

KM# 983   CROWN
28.2800 g., Copper-Nickel, 38.6 mm. **Ruler:** Elizabeth II
Subject: World Cup Soccer **Obv:** Bust with tiara right **Rev:** Two
players facing viewer **Edge:** Reeded

Date	Mintage	F	VF	XF	Unc	BU
2002	—			—	10.00	11.50

KM# 983a   CROWN
28.2800 g., 0.9250 Silver 0.8410 oz. ASW, 38.6 mm. **Ruler:**
Elizabeth II **Subject:** World Cup Soccer **Obv:** Bust with tiara right
Rev: Two players facing viewer **Edge:** Reeded

Date	Mintage	F	VF	XF	Unc	BU
2002 Proof	10,000	Value: 47.50				

KM# 985   CROWN
28.2800 g., Copper-Nickel, 38.6 mm. **Ruler:** Elizabeth II
Subject: World Cup Soccer **Obv:** Bust with tiara right **Rev:** Two
horizontal players **Edge:** Reeded

Date	Mintage	F	VF	XF	Unc	BU
2002	—			—	10.00	11.50

KM# 985a   CROWN
28.2800 g., 0.9250 Silver 0.8410 oz. ASW, 38.6 mm. **Ruler:**
Elizabeth II **Subject:** World Cup Soccer **Obv:** Bust with tiara right
Rev: Two horizontal players **Edge:** Reeded

Date	Mintage	F	VF	XF	Unc	BU
2002 Proof	10,000	Value: 47.50				

KM# 987   CROWN
28.2800 g., Copper-Nickel, 38.6 mm. **Ruler:** Elizabeth II
Subject: World Cup Soccer **Obv:** Bust with tiara right **Rev:** Two
players moving to left **Edge:** Reeded

Date	Mintage	F	VF	XF	Unc	BU
2002	—			—	10.00	11.50

KM# 987a   CROWN
28.2800 g., 0.9250 Silver 0.8410 oz. ASW, 38.6 mm. **Ruler:**
Elizabeth II **Subject:** World Cup Soccer **Obv:** Bust with tiara right
Rev: Two players moving to left **Edge:** Reeded

Date	Mintage	F	VF	XF	Unc	BU
2002 Proof	10,000	Value: 47.50				

KM# 992.1   CROWN
28.2800 g., Copper-Nickel, 38.6 mm. **Ruler:** Elizabeth II
Subject: Peter Rabbit Centennial **Obv:** Bust with tiara right **Rev:**
Peter Rabbit **Edge:** Reeded

Date	Mintage	F	VF	XF	Unc	BU
2002	—			—	10.00	12.00

KM# 992a   CROWN
28.2800 g., 0.9250 Silver 0.8410 oz. ASW, 38.6 mm. **Ruler:**
Elizabeth II **Subject:** Peter Rabbit Centennial **Obv:** Bust with
tiara right **Rev:** Peter Rabbit **Edge:** Reeded

Date	Mintage	F	VF	XF	Unc	BU
2002 Proof	10,000	Value: 47.50				

KM# 992.2   CROWN
Copper-Nickel **Ruler:** Elizabeth II **Obv:** Bust with tiara right **Rev:**
Peter Rabbit in multi-color

Date	Mintage	F	VF	XF	Unc	BU
2002	—			—	10.00	12.00

KM# 994 CROWN
28.2800 g., Copper-Nickel, 38.6 mm. **Ruler:** Elizabeth II
Subject: Queen's Golden Jubilee **Obv:** Bust with tiara right **Rev:**
Royal couple and tree house **Edge:** Reeded

Date	Mintage	F	VF	XF	Unc	BU
2002	—	—	—	—	10.00	12.00

KM# 994a CROWN
Yellow Brass, 38.6 mm. **Ruler:** Elizabeth II **Subject:** Queen's
Golden Jubilee **Obv:** Bust with tiara right **Rev:** Royal couple and
tree house **Edge:** Reeded

Date	Mintage	F	VF	XF	Unc	BU
2002 Proof	15,000	Value: 20.00				

KM# 994b CROWN
28.2800 g., 0.9250 Gold Clad Silver 0.8410 oz., 38.6 mm. **Ruler:**
Elizabeth II **Subject:** Queen's Golden Jubilee **Obv:** Bust with
tiara right **Rev:** Royal couple and tree house **Edge:** Reeded

Date	Mintage	F	VF	XF	Unc	BU
2002 Proof	10,000	Value: 55.00				

KM# 996 CROWN
28.2800 g., Copper-Nickel, 38.6 mm. **Ruler:** Elizabeth II
Subject: Queen's Golden Jubilee **Obv:** Bust with tiara right **Rev:**
Royal coach **Edge:** Reeded

Date	Mintage	F	VF	XF	Unc	BU
2002	—	—	—	—	10.00	12.00

KM# 996a CROWN
Yellow Brass, 38.6 mm. **Ruler:** Elizabeth II **Subject:** Queen's
Golden Jubilee **Obv:** Bust with tiara right **Rev:** Royal coach **Edge:**
Reeded

Date	Mintage	F	VF	XF	Unc	BU
2002 Proof	15,000	Value: 20.00				

KM# 996b CROWN
28.2800 g., 0.9250 Gold Clad Silver 0.8410 oz., 38.6 mm. **Ruler:**
Elizabeth II **Subject:** Queen's Golden Jubilee **Obv:** Bust with
tiara right **Rev:** Royal coach **Edge:** Reeded

Date	Mintage	F	VF	XF	Unc	BU
2002 Proof	10,000	Value: 55.00				

KM# 998 CROWN
28.2800 g., Copper-Nickel, 38.6 mm. **Ruler:** Elizabeth II
Subject: Queen's Golden Jubilee **Obv:** Bust with tiara right **Rev:**
Royal couple with baby **Edge:** Reeded

Date	Mintage	F	VF	XF	Unc	BU
2002	—	—	—	—	10.00	12.00

KM# 998a CROWN
Yellow Brass, 38.6 mm. **Ruler:** Elizabeth II **Subject:** Queen's
Golden Jubilee **Obv:** Bust with tiara right **Rev:** Royal couple with
baby **Edge:** Reeded

Date	Mintage	F	VF	XF	Unc	BU
2002 Proof	15,000	Value: 20.00				

KM# 998b CROWN
28.2800 g., 0.9250 Gold Clad Silver 0.8410 oz., 38.6 mm. **Ruler:**
Elizabeth II **Subject:** Queen's Golden Jubilee **Obv:** Bust with
tiara right **Rev:** Royal couple with baby **Edge:** Reeded

Date	Mintage	F	VF	XF	Unc	BU
2002 Proof	1,000	Value: 55.00				

KM# 1000 CROWN
28.2800 g., Copper-Nickel, 38.6 mm. **Ruler:** Elizabeth II
Subject: Queen's Golden Jubilee **Obv:** Bust with tiara right **Rev:**
Royal yacht under Tower bridge **Edge:** Reeded

Date	Mintage	F	VF	XF	Unc	BU
2002	—	—	—	—	10.00	12.00

KM# 1000a CROWN
Yellow Brass, 38.6 mm. **Ruler:** Elizabeth II **Subject:** Queen's
Golden Jubilee **Obv:** Bust with tiara right **Rev:** Royal yacht under
Tower bridge **Edge:** Reeded

Date	Mintage	F	VF	XF	Unc	BU
2002 Proof	15,000	Value: 20.00				

KM# 1000b CROWN
28.2800 g., 0.9250 Gold Clad Silver 0.8410 oz., 38.6 mm. **Ruler:**
Elizabeth II **Subject:** Queen's Golden Jubilee **Obv:** Bust with
tiara right **Rev:** Royal yacht under Tower bridge **Edge:** Reeded

Date	Mintage	F	VF	XF	Unc	BU
2002 Proof	10,000	Value: 55.00				

KM# 1013 CROWN
28.2800 g., Copper-Nickel dark patina, 38.6 mm. **Ruler:**
Elizabeth II **Subject:** Death of Queen Mother **Obv:** Bust with tiara
right **Rev:** Queen Mother trout fishing **Edge:** Reeded

Date	Mintage	F	VF	XF	Unc	BU
2002	—	—	—	—	10.00	12.00

KM# 1013a CROWN
28.2800 g., 0.9250 Silver 0.8410 oz. ASW, 38.6 mm. **Ruler:**
Elizabeth II **Subject:** Queen Mother **Obv:** Bust with tiara right
Rev: Queen Mother trout fishing **Edge:** Reeded **Note:** Obv. and
rev. have blackened legends.

Date	Mintage	F	VF	XF	Unc	BU
2002 Proof	5,000	Value: 175				

KM# 1015 CROWN
28.2800 g., Copper-Nickel, 38.6 mm. **Ruler:** Elizabeth II
Subject: Princess Diana **Obv:** Bust with tiara right **Rev:** Diana's
portrait **Edge:** Reeded

Date	Mintage	F	VF	XF	Unc	BU
2002	—	—	—	—	10.00	12.00

KM# 1015a CROWN
28.2800 g., 0.9250 Silver 0.8410 oz. ASW, 38.6 mm. **Ruler:**
Elizabeth II **Subject:** Princess Diana **Obv:** Bust with tiara right
Rev: Diana's portrait **Edge:** Reeded

Date	Mintage	F	VF	XF	Unc	BU
2002 Proof	10,000	Value: 47.50				

KM# 1019 CROWN
28.2800 g., Copper-Nickel, 38.6 mm. **Ruler:** Elizabeth II
Subject: Peter Pan **Obv:** Bust with tiara right **Rev:** Peter Pan
and Tinkerbell flying above city **Edge:** Reeded

Date	Mintage	F	VF	XF	Unc	BU
2002	—	—	—	—	10.00	12.00

KM# 1019a CROWN
28.2800 g., 0.9250 Silver 0.8410 oz. ASW, 38.6 mm. **Ruler:**
Elizabeth II **Subject:** Peter Pan **Obv:** Bust with tiara right **Rev:**
Peter Pan and Tinkerbell flying above city **Edge:** Reeded

Date	Mintage	F	VF	XF	Unc	BU
2002 Proof	10,000	Value: 47.50				

KM# 1021 CROWN
28.2800 g., Copper-Nickel, 38.6 mm. **Ruler:** Elizabeth II
Subject: Grand Masonic Lodge **Obv:** Bust with tiara right **Rev:**
Masonic seal above Gibraltar **Edge:** Reeded

Date	Mintage	F	VF	XF	Unc	BU
2002 Proof	5,000	Value: 12.00				

KM# 1021a CROWN
28.2800 g., 0.9250 Silver 0.8410 oz. ASW, 38.6 mm. **Ruler:**
Elizabeth II **Subject:** Grand Masonic Lodge **Obv:** Bust with tiara
right **Rev:** Masonic seal above Gibraltar **Edge:** Reeded

Date	Mintage	F	VF	XF	Unc	BU
2002 Proof	10,000	Value: 47.50				

KM# 1025 CROWN
28.2800 g., Copper-Nickel, 38.6 mm. **Ruler:** Elizabeth II
Subject: Calpe Conference **Obv:** Bust with tiara right **Rev:**
Crossed flags and arms **Edge:** Reeded

Date	Mintage	F	VF	XF	Unc	BU
2002PM	—	—	—	—	10.00	12.00

KM# 1025a CROWN
28.2800 g., 0.9250 Silver 0.8410 oz. ASW, 38.6 mm. **Ruler:**
Elizabeth II **Subject:** Calpe Conference **Obv:** Bust with tiara right
Rev: Crossed flags and arms **Edge:** Reeded

Date	Mintage	F	VF	XF	Unc	BU
2002PM Proof	10,000	Value: 47.50				

KM# 1052 CROWN
Copper-Nickel **Ruler:** Elizabeth II **Subject:** 2004 Athens
Olympics **Rev:** Horse jumping left

Date	Mintage	F	VF	XF	Unc	BU
2003	—	—	—	—	10.00	12.00

KM# 1053 CROWN
Copper-Nickel **Ruler:** Elizabeth II **Subject:** 2004 Athens
Olympics **Rev:** Javelin thrower

Date	Mintage	F	VF	XF	Unc	BU
2003	—	—	—	—	10.00	12.00

KM# 1054 CROWN
Copper-Nickel **Ruler:** Elizabeth II **Subject:** 2004 Athens
Olympics **Rev:** Field Hockey

Date	Mintage	F	VF	XF	Unc	BU
2003	—	—	—	—	10.00	12.00

KM# 1055 CROWN
Copper-Nickel **Ruler:** Elizabeth II **Subject:** 2004 Athens
Olympics **Rev:** Wrestlers

Date	Mintage	F	VF	XF	Unc	BU
2003	—	—	—	—	10.00	12.00

KM# 1035 CROWN
28.2800 g., Copper-Nickel, 38.6 mm. **Ruler:** Elizabeth II
Subject: 1700th Anniversary - Death of St. George **Obv:** Bust
with tiara right **Rev:** St. George and the dragon **Edge:** Reeded

Date	Mintage	F	VF	XF	Unc	BU
2003	—	—	—	—	9.00	10.00

KM# 1035a CROWN
28.2800 g., 0.9250 Silver 0.8410 oz. ASW, 38.6 mm. **Ruler:**
Elizabeth II **Subject:** 1700th Anniversary - Death of St. George
Obv: Bust with tiara right **Rev:** St. George and the dragon **Edge:**
Reeded

Date	Mintage	F	VF	XF	Unc	BU
2003 Proof	10,000	Value: 47.50				

KM# 1039 CROWN
28.3000 g., Copper-Nickel, 38.6 mm. **Ruler:** Elizabeth II
Subject: Peter Rabbit **Obv:** Bust with tiara right **Rev:** Peter Rabbit
holding carrot **Edge:** Reeded

Date	Mintage	F	VF	XF	Unc	BU
2003PM	—	—	—	—	9.00	10.00

KM# 1040 CROWN
28.2800 g., Copper-Nickel, 38.6 mm. **Ruler:** Elizabeth II
Subject: Centennial of Powered Flight **Obv:** Queens portrait
Rev: Stealth bomber within circles of WWI and WWII planes
Edge: Reeded

Date	Mintage	F	VF	XF	Unc	BU
2003PM	—	—	—	—	10.00	12.00

KM# 1040a CROWN
31.1000 g., Tri-Metallic .9995 Platinum 5.2g center in .9999 Gold
14.2 g ring within .999 Silver 11.7 g outer ring, 38.6 mm. **Ruler:**
Elizabeth II **Subject:** Centennial of Powered Flight **Obv:** Queens
portrait **Rev:** Stealth bomber within circles of WWI and WWII
planes **Edge:** Reeded

Date	Mintage	F	VF	XF	Unc	BU
2003PM Proof	999	Value: 1,750				

KM# 1041 CROWN
28.2800 g., Copper-Nickel, 38.6 mm. **Ruler:** Elizabeth II
Subject: 50th Anniversary of Coronation **Obv:** Queens portrait
Rev: Buckingham Palace **Edge:** Reeded

Date	Mintage	F	VF	XF	Unc	BU
2003PM	—	—	—	—	10.00	12.00

KM# 1094 CROWN
28.2800 g., Copper-Nickel, 38.6 mm. **Ruler:** Elizabeth II **Rev:**
Battleship Bismark under fire, colored poppy below

Date	Mintage	F	VF	XF	Unc	BU
2004	—	—	—	—	10.00	12.00

KM# 1075 CROWN
28.2800 g., Copper-Nickel, 38.6 mm. **Ruler:** Elizabeth II
Subject: Trafalgar - First Shot **Rev:** Naval battle scene

Date	Mintage	F	VF	XF	Unc	BU
2005	—	—	—	—	10.00	12.00

KM# 1076 CROWN
28.2800 g., Copper-Nickel, 38.6 mm. **Ruler:** Elizabeth II
Subject: Trafalgar - Breaking the line **Rev:** Naval battle

Date	Mintage	F	VF	XF	Unc	BU
2005	—	—	—	—	10.00	12.00

KM# 1077 CROWN
28.2800 g., Copper-Nickel, 38.6 mm. **Ruler:** Elizabeth II
Subject: Trafalgar - Hardy **Rev:** Bust facing

Date	Mintage	F	VF	XF	Unc	BU
2005	—	—	—	—	10.00	12.00

KM# 1078 CROWN
28.2800 g., Copper-Nickel, 38.6 mm. **Ruler:** Elizabeth II
Subject: Trafalgar - Nelson **Rev:** Bust facing

Date	Mintage	F	VF	XF	Unc	BU
2005	—	—	—	—	10.00	12.00

KM# 1034 2 CROWN
41.5000 g., Bi-Metallic .999 Silver 11.5g. star shaped center in
Copper outer ring, 50 mm. **Ruler:** Elizabeth II **Subject:** Euro's
First Anniversary **Obv:** Crowned bust right within star silhouette
Rev: Europa riding a bull, stars and star silhouette in background
Edge: Reeded

Date	Mintage	F	VF	XF	Unc	BU
2003PM Proof	3,500	Value: 125				

KM# 1034a 2 CROWN
50.0000 g., Bi-Metallic .9999 Gold 20g star shaped center in
Copper outer ring, 50 mm. **Ruler:** Elizabeth II **Subject:** 1st
Anniversary - Euro **Obv:** Crowned bust right within star silhouette
Rev: Europa riding the bull, stars and star silhouette in
background **Edge:** Reeded

Date	Mintage	F	VF	XF	Unc	BU
2003PM Proof	2,003	Value: 850				

KM# 1034b 2 CROWN
56.3000 g., Bi-Metallic .9999 Gold 20.8g star shaped center in a
.999 Silver 35.5g outer ring, 50 mm. **Ruler:** Elizabeth II **Subject:**
1st Anniversary - Euro **Obv:** Crowned bust right within star
silhouette **Rev:** Europa riding the bull, stars and star silhouette
in background **Edge:** Reeded

Date	Mintage	F	VF	XF	Unc	BU
2003PM Proof	2,003	Value: 900				

KM# 907 5 CROWN
Tri-Metallic Center .9995 Platinum 26.9g. Inner Ring .9999 Gold
73.41g. Outer Ring .999 Silver 55.19g, 50 mm. **Ruler:**
Elizabeth II **Subject:** 21st Century **Obv:** Crowned bust right, date
below **Rev:** Celtic cross, Viking ship and modern technological
items **Edge:** Reeded

Date	Mintage	F	VF	XF	Unc	BU
2001 Proof	199	Value: 6,500				

KM# 1042 5 CROWN
155.5500 g., 0.9990 Silver 4.9958 oz. ASW, 65 mm. **Ruler:**
Elizabeth II **Subject:** 50th Anniversary of Coronation **Obv:**
Queens portrait **Rev:** Buckingham Palace with tiny .01ct ruby,
diamond and sapphire inserts above the main entrance **Edge:**
Reeded

Date	Mintage	F	VF	XF	Unc	BU
2003PM Proof	2,003	Value: 225				

KM# 1045 32 CROWNS
1000.0000 g., 0.9990 Silver 32.117 oz. ASW **Ruler:** Elizabeth II
Subject: Beatrix Potter's Peter Rabbit **Obv:** Bust with tiara right
Rev: Multicolor Peter Rabbit holding carrot, with blue coat and
red slippers

Date	Mintage	F	VF	XF	Unc	BU
2003 Proof	1,000	Value: 1,150				

KM# 869 POUND
9.5000 g., Nickel-Brass, 22.5 mm. **Ruler:** Elizabeth II **Obv:**
Head with tiara right **Rev:** Gibraltar coat of arms - castle and key

Date	Mintage	F	VF	XF	Unc	BU
2001 AA	—	—	—	—	3.50	4.50
2001 AB	—	—	—	—	3.50	4.50
2002 AC	—	—	—	—	3.50	4.50

KM# 1036 POUND
9.5000 g., Nickel-Brass, 22 mm. **Ruler:** Elizabeth II **Subject:** 1700th Anniversary - Death of St. George **Obv:** Bust with tiara right **Rev:** St. George and the dragon **Edge:** Reeded

Date	Mintage	F	VF	XF	Unc	BU
2003	—	—	—	—	9.00	10.00

KM# 1051 POUND
9.5000 g., Nickel-Brass, 22.5 mm. **Ruler:** Elizabeth II **Subject:** Tercentenary 1704-2004 **Obv:** Elizabeth II **Rev:** Old cannon set for a downhill target **Edge:** Reeded

Date	Mintage	F	VF	XF	Unc	BU
2004PM	—	—	—	—	—	4.00

KM# 1091 POUND
9.5000 g., Nickel-Brass, 22.5 mm. **Ruler:** Elizabeth II **Obv:** Bust in diadem right **Rev:** Neanderthal Skull

Date	Mintage	F	VF	XF	Unc	BU
2005	—	—	—	—	3.50	4.50
2006	—	—	—	—	3.50	4.50
2007	—	—	—	—	3.50	4.50
2008	—	—	—	—	3.50	4.50
2009	—	—	—	—	3.50	4.50
2010	—	—	—	—	3.50	4.50
2011	—	—	—	—	3.50	4.50

KM# 970 2 POUNDS
12.0000 g., Bi-Metallic Copper-Nickel center in Nickel-Brass ring, 28.4 mm. **Ruler:** Elizabeth II **Subject:** Bicentennial of the Union Jack **Obv:** Head with tiara right **Rev:** Standing Britannia wearing flag as a cape **Edge:** Reeded

Date	Mintage	F	VF	XF	Unc	BU
2001 AA	—	—	—	—	10.00	12.00

KM# 970a 2 POUNDS
12.0000 g., 0.9990 Bi-Metallic Silver center in Gold plated Silver ring 0.3854 oz., 28.4 mm. **Ruler:** Elizabeth II **Subject:** Bicentennial of the Union Jack **Obv:** Head with tiara right **Rev:** Standing Britannia wearing flag as a cape **Edge:** Reeded

Date	Mintage	F	VF	XF	Unc	BU
2001	7,500	—	—	—	35.00	40.00

KM# 1043 2 POUNDS
12.0000 g., Bi-Metallic Copper-Nickel center in Nickel-Brass ring, 28.4 mm. **Ruler:** Elizabeth II **Obv:** Head with tiara right **Rev:** Old cannon **Edge:** Reeded

Date	Mintage	F	VF	XF	Unc	BU
2003PM	—	—	—	—	10.00	12.00

KM# 1057 2 POUNDS
12.0000 g., Bi-Metallic Copper-Nickel center in Nickel-Brass ring, 28.4 mm. **Ruler:** Elizabeth II **Subject:** Tercentenary 1704-2004 **Obv:** Elizabeth II **Rev:** Naval Battle, capture of Gibraltar **Edge:** Reeded

Date	Mintage	F	VF	XF	Unc	BU
2004PM	—	—	—	—	10.00	12.00

KM# 1072 2 POUNDS
12.0000 g., Bi-Metallic Copper-Nickel center in Nickel-Brass ring, 28.4 mm. **Ruler:** Elizabeth II **Subject:** Capture of Gibraltar **Rev:** Sea Battle

Date	Mintage	F	VF	XF	Unc	BU
2004	—	—	—	—	10.00	12.00

KM# 1092 2 POUNDS
12.0000 g., Bi-Metallic Copper-Nickel center in Nickel-Brass ring, 28.4 mm. **Ruler:** Elizabeth II **Subject:** Battle of Trafalgar **Rev:** Two Naval vessels and rock in backbround

Date	Mintage	F	VF	XF	Unc	BU
2005	—	—	—	—	10.00	12.00
2006	—	—	—	—	10.00	12.00
2007	—	—	—	—	10.00	12.00
2008	—	—	—	—	10.00	12.00
2009	—	—	—	—	10.00	12.00
2010	—	—	—	—	10.00	12.00
2011	—	—	—	—	10.00	12.00

KM# 1073 2 POUNDS
12.0000 g., Bi-Metallic Copper-Nickel center in Nickel-Brass ring, 28.4 mm. **Ruler:** Elizabeth II **Subject:** Battle of Trafalgar **Rev:** Sea Battle

Date	Mintage	F	VF	XF	Unc	BU
2005	—	—	—	—	10.00	12.00

KM# 1093 2 POUNDS
12.0000 g., Bi-Metallic Copper-Nickel center in Nickel-Brass ring, 28.4 mm. **Ruler:** Elizabeth II **Subject:** Diamond Wedding Anniversary **Obv:** Bust in diadem right **Rev:** Conjoined busts of Elizabeth and Philip

Date	Mintage	F	VF	XF	Unc	BU
2007	—	—	—	—	10.00	12.00

KM# 953 5 POUNDS
20.0000 g., Virenium, 36.1 mm. **Ruler:** Elizabeth II **Subject:** Gibraltar Chronicle 200 Years **Obv:** Head with tiara right **Rev:** Naval battle scene with newspaper in background **Edge:** Reeded

Date	Mintage	F	VF	XF	Unc	BU
2001	—	—	—	—	17.00	20.00

KM# 953a 5 POUNDS
23.5000 g., 0.9250 Silver 0.6988 oz. ASW, 36.1 mm. **Ruler:** Elizabeth II **Subject:** Gibraltar Chronicle 200 Years **Obv:** Head with tiara right **Rev:** Naval battle scene with newspaper in background **Edge:** Reeded

Date	Mintage	F	VF	XF	Unc	BU
2001 Proof	10,000	Value: 50.00				

KM# 953b 5 POUNDS
39.8300 g., 0.9167 Gold 1.1738 oz. AGW, 36.1 mm. **Ruler:** Elizabeth II **Subject:** Gibraltar Chronicle 200 Years **Obv:** Head with tiara right **Rev:** Naval battle scene with newspaper in background **Edge:** Reeded

Date	Mintage	F	VF	XF	Unc	BU
2001 Proof	850	Value: 2,000				

KM# 1011 5 POUNDS
20.0000 g., Virenium, 36.1 mm. **Ruler:** Elizabeth II **Subject:** Queen's Golden Jubilee **Obv:** Head with tiara right **Rev:** Coronation scene **Edge:** Reeded

Date	Mintage	F	VF	XF	Unc	BU
2002	—	—	—	—	17.00	20.00

KM# 1011a 5 POUNDS
23.5000 g., 0.9250 Silver 0.6988 oz. ASW, 36.1 mm. **Ruler:** Elizabeth II **Subject:** Queen's Golden Jubilee **Obv:** Head with tiara right **Rev:** Coronation scene **Edge:** Reeded

Date	Mintage	F	VF	XF	Unc	BU
2002 Proof	10,000	Value: 50.00				

KM# 1011b 5 POUNDS
39.8300 g., 0.9166 Gold 1.1737 oz. AGW, 36.1 mm. **Ruler:** Elizabeth II **Subject:** Queen's Golden Jubilee **Obv:** Head with tiara right **Rev:** Coronation scene **Edge:** Reeded

Date	Mintage	F	VF	XF	Unc	BU
2002 Proof	850	Value: 2,000				

KM# 1064 5 POUNDS
Silver, 38 mm. **Ruler:** Elizabeth II **Subject:** 200th Anniversary, Battle of Trafalgar **Rev:** Two naval vessels **Edge:** Reeded

Date	Mintage	F	VF	XF	Unc	BU
2005 Proof	—	Value: 45.00				

KM# 1095 5 POUNDS
Silver, 38.6 mm. **Ruler:** Elizabeth II **Subject:** History fo the RAF - Flypast **Obv:** Bust in crown right **Rev:** Bomber and two planes in flight

Date	Mintage	F	VF	XF	Unc	BU
2007 Proof	—	Value: 50.00				

KM# 1096 5 POUNDS
Silver, 38.61 mm. **Ruler:** Elizabeth II **Subject:** History of the

RAF - Avro Lancaster **Obv:** Bust in crown right **Rev:** Lancaster bomber flying right

Date	Mintage	F	VF	XF	Unc	BU
2007 Proof	—	Value: 50.00				

CROWN COINAGE
1991 - Present

KM# 1037   1/5 SOVEREIGN
1.2200 g., 0.9999 Gold 0.0392 oz. AGW, 13.92 mm. **Ruler:** Elizabeth II **Subject:** Death of St. George **Obv:** Bust with tiara right **Rev:** St. George and the dragon **Edge:** Reeded

Date	Mintage	F	VF	XF	Unc	BU
2003 Proof	10,000	Value: 70.00				

KM# 1038   SOVEREIGN
6.2200 g., 0.9999 Gold 0.1999 oz. AGW, 22 mm. **Ruler:** Elizabeth II **Subject:** Death of St. George **Obv:** Bust with tiara right **Rev:** St. George and the dragon **Edge:** Reeded

Date	Mintage	F	VF	XF	Unc	BU
2003 Proof	5,000	Value: 355				

ROYAL COINAGE

KM# 896   1/25 ROYAL
1.2441 g., 0.9999 Gold 0.0400 oz. AGW, 13.92 mm. **Ruler:** Elizabeth II **Subject:** Bullion **Obv:** Bust with tiara right **Rev:** Two cherubs **Edge:** Reeded

Date	Mintage	F	VF	XF	Unc	BU
2001	—	—	—	—	—	75.00
2001 Proof	1,000	Value: 76.50				

KM# 972   1/25 ROYAL
1.2440 g., 0.9990 Gold 0.0400 oz. AGW, 13.92 mm. **Ruler:** Elizabeth II **Subject:** Cherubs **Obv:** Bust with tiara right **Rev:** Two cherubs shooting arrrows **Edge:** Reeded

Date	Mintage	F	VF	XF	Unc	BU
2002	—	—	—	—	—	75.00
2002 Proof	1,000	Value: 76.50				

KM# 1027   1/25 ROYAL
1.2440 g., 0.9999 Gold 0.0400 oz. AGW, 13.92 mm. **Ruler:** Elizabeth II **Obv:** Bust with tiara right **Rev:** Cherub with crossed arms **Edge:** Reeded

Date	Mintage	F	VF	XF	Unc	BU
2003PM	—	—	—	—	—	75.00
2003PM Proof	—	Value: 76.50				

KM# 897   1/10 ROYAL
3.1100 g., 0.9999 Gold 0.1000 oz. AGW, 18 mm. **Ruler:** Elizabeth II **Subject:** Bullion **Obv:** Bust with tiara right **Rev:** Two cherubs **Edge:** Reeded

Date	Mintage	F	VF	XF	Unc	BU
2001	—	—	—	—	—	175
2001 Proof	1,000	Value: 180				

KM# 973   1/10 ROYAL
3.1100 g., 0.9990 Gold 0.0999 oz. AGW, 17.95 mm. **Ruler:** Elizabeth II **Subject:** Cherubs **Obv:** Bust with tiara right **Rev:** Two cherubs shooting arrows **Edge:** Reeded

Date	Mintage	F	VF	XF	Unc	BU
2002	—	—	—	—	—	175
2002 Proof	1,000	Value: 180				

KM# 1028   1/10 ROYAL
3.1100 g., 0.9999 Gold 0.1000 oz. AGW, 17.95 mm. **Ruler:** Elizabeth II **Obv:** Bust with tiara right **Rev:** Cherub with crossed arms **Edge:** Reeded

Date	Mintage	F	VF	XF	Unc	BU
2003PM	—	—	—	—	—	175
2003PM Proof	—	Value: 180				

KM# 898   1/5 ROYAL
6.2200 g., 0.9990 Gold 0.1998 oz. AGW, 22 mm. **Ruler:** Elizabeth II **Subject:** Bullion **Obv:** Bust with tiara right **Rev:** Two cherubs **Edge:** Reeded

Date	Mintage	F	VF	XF	Unc	BU
2001	—	—	—	—	—	350
2001 Proof	1,000	Value: 355				

KM# 974   1/5 ROYAL
6.2200 g., 0.9990 Gold 0.1998 oz. AGW, 22 mm. **Ruler:** Elizabeth II **Obv:** Bust with tiara right **Rev:** Two cherubs shooting arrows **Edge:** Reeded

Date	Mintage	F	VF	XF	Unc	BU
2002	—	—	—	—	—	350
2002 Proof	1,000	Value: 355				

KM# 1029   1/5 ROYAL
6.2200 g., 0.9999 Gold 0.1999 oz. AGW, 22 mm. **Ruler:** Elizabeth II **Obv:** Bust with tiara right **Rev:** Cherub with crossed arms **Edge:** Reeded

Date	Mintage	F	VF	XF	Unc	BU
2003PM	—	—	—	—	—	350
2003PM Proof	—	Value: 355				

KM# 899   1/2 ROYAL
15.5517 g., 0.9999 Gold 0.4999 oz. AGW, 30 mm. **Ruler:** Elizabeth II **Subject:** Bullion **Obv:** Bust with tiara right **Rev:** Two cherubs **Edge:** Reeded

Date	Mintage	F	VF	XF	Unc	BU
2001	—	—	—	—	—	875
2001 Proof	1,000	Value: 880				

KM# 975   1/2 ROYAL
15.5510 g., 0.9990 Gold 0.4995 oz. AGW, 30 mm. **Ruler:** Elizabeth II **Obv:** Bust with tiara right **Rev:** Two cherubs shooting arrows **Edge:** Reeded

Date	Mintage	F	VF	XF	Unc	BU
2002	—	—	—	—	—	875
2002 Proof	1,000	Value: 880				

KM# 1030   1/2 ROYAL
15.5510 g., 0.9999 Gold 0.4999 oz. AGW, 30 mm. **Ruler:** Elizabeth II **Obv:** Bust with tiara right **Rev:** Cherub with crossed arms **Edge:** Reeded

Date	Mintage	F	VF	XF	Unc	BU
2003PM	—	—	—	—	—	875
2003PM Proof	—	Value: 880				

KM# 900   ROYAL
28.2800 g., Copper-Nickel, 38.6 mm. **Ruler:** Elizabeth II **Obv:** Bust with tiara right **Rev:** Two cherubs **Edge:** Reeded

Date	Mintage	F	VF	XF	Unc	BU
2001	—	—	—	—	10.00	12.00

KM# 900a   ROYAL
31.1035 g., 0.9990 Silver 0.9990 oz. ASW **Ruler:** Elizabeth II **Obv:** Bust with tiara right **Rev:** Two cherubs

Date	Mintage	F	VF	XF	Unc	BU
2001 Proof	10,000	Value: 47.50				

KM# 901   ROYAL
31.1035 g., 0.9999 Gold 0.9999 oz. AGW, 32.7 mm. **Ruler:** Elizabeth II **Subject:** Bullion **Obv:** Bust with tiara right **Rev:** Two cherubs **Edge:** Reeded

Date	Mintage	F	VF	XF	Unc	BU
2001	—	—	—	—	—	1,700
2001 Proof	1,000	Value: 1,700				

KM# 976   ROYAL
28.2800 g., Copper-Nickel, 38.6 mm. **Ruler:** Elizabeth II **Obv:** Bust with tiara right **Rev:** Two cherubs shooting arrows **Edge:** Reeded

Date	Mintage	F	VF	XF	Unc	BU
2002	—	—	—	—	10.00	12.00

KM# 976a   ROYAL
31.1035 g., 0.9990 Silver 0.9990 oz. ASW **Ruler:** Elizabeth II **Obv:** Bust with tiara right **Rev:** Two cherubs shooting arrows **Edge:** Reeded

Date	Mintage	F	VF	XF	Unc	BU
2002 Proof	1,000	Value: 47.50				

KM# 977   ROYAL
31.1035 g., 0.9990 Gold 0.9990 oz. AGW, 32.7 mm. **Ruler:** Elizabeth II **Obv:** Bust with tiara right **Rev:** Two cherubs shooting arrows **Edge:** Reeded

Date	Mintage	F	VF	XF	Unc	BU
2002	—	—	—	—	—	1,700
2002 Proof	1,000	Value: 1,700				

KM# 1031   ROYAL
28.2800 g., Copper-Nickel, 38.6 mm. **Ruler:** Elizabeth II **Obv:** Bust with tiara right **Rev:** Cherub with crossed arms **Edge:** Reeded

Date	Mintage	F	VF	XF	Unc	BU
2003PM	—	—	—	—	10.00	12.00

KM# 1031a   ROYAL
28.2800 g., 0.9990 Silver 0.9083 oz. ASW, 38.6 mm. **Ruler:** Elizabeth II **Obv:** Bust with tiara right **Rev:** Cherub with crossed arms **Edge:** Reeded

Date	Mintage	F	VF	XF	Unc	BU
2003PM Proof	10,000	Value: 47.50				

KM# 1032   ROYAL
31.1035 g., 0.9999 Gold 0.9999 oz. AGW, 32.7 mm. **Ruler:** Elizabeth II **Obv:** Bust with tiara right **Rev:** Cherub with crossed arms **Edge:** Reeded

Date	Mintage	F	VF	XF	Unc	BU
2003PM	—	—	—	—	—	1,700
2003PM Proof	—	Value: 1,700				

PROOF SETS

KM#	Date	Mintage	Identification	Issue Price	Mkt Val
PS29	2001 (5)	1,000	KM#896-899, 901	—	3,225
PS30	2003 (5)	1,000	KM#1027-30, 1032	—	3,225

GREAT BRITAIN

The United Kingdom of Great Britain and Northern Ireland, located off the northwest coast of the European continent, has an area of 94,227 sq. mi. (244,820 sq. km.) and a population of 54 million. Capital: London. The economy is based on industrial activity and trading. Machinery, motor vehicles, chemicals, and textile yarns and fabrics are exported.

By the mid-20th century, most of the territories formerly comprising the British Empire had gained independence, and the empire had evolved into the Commonwealth of Nations, an association of equal and autonomous states, which enjoy special trade interests. The Commonwealth is presently composed of 54 member nations, including the United Kingdom. All recognize the British monarch as head of the Commonwealth. Sixteen continue to recognize the British monarch as Head of State. They are: United Kingdom, Antigua and Barbuda, Australia, Bahamas, Barbados, Belize, Canada, Grenada, Jamaica, New Zealand, Papua New Guinea, St. Christopher & Nevis, Saint Lucia, Saint Vincent and the Grenadines, Solomon Islands, and Tuvalu. Elizabeth II is personally, and separately, the Queen of the sovereign, independent countries just mentioned. There is no other British connection between the several individual, national sovereignties, except that High Commissioners represent them each instead of ambassadors in each other's countries.

RULERS
Elizabeth II, 1952--

KINGDOM
PRE-DECIMAL COINAGE

KM# 898   PENNY
0.4713 g., 0.9250 Silver 0.0140 oz. ASW, 11 mm. **Ruler:** Elizabeth II **Obv:** Laureate bust right **Rev:** Crowned value in sprays divides date within wreath **Edge:** Reeded

Date	Mintage	F	VF	XF	Unc	BU
2001 Prooflike	1,132	—	—	45.00	50.00	55.00
2002 Prooflike	1,681	—	—	45.00	50.00	55.00
2003 Prooflike	1,608	—	—	50.00	55.00	60.00
2004 Prooflike	1,613	—	—	50.00	55.00	60.00
2005 Prooflike	1,685	—	—	50.00	55.00	60.00
2006 Prooflike	1,811	—	—	50.00	55.00	60.00
2006 Proof	6,394	—	—	—	—	—
2007 Prooflike	1,985	—	—	50.00	55.00	60.00
2008 Prooflike	1,833	—	—	50.00	55.00	60.00
2009 Prooflike	1,602	—	—	50.00	55.00	60.00
2010 Prooflike	1,617	—	—	50.00	55.00	60.00
2011 Prooflike	—	—	—	50.00	55.00	60.00

KM# 898a   PENNY
0.9167 Gold, 11 mm. **Ruler:** Elizabeth II **Obv:** Laureate bust right **Rev:** Crowned denomination divides date within wreath

Date	Mintage	F	VF	XF	Unc	BU
2002 Proof	2,002	Value: 1,000				

KM# 899   2 PENCE
0.9426 g., 0.9250 Silver 0.0280 oz. ASW, 13 mm. **Ruler:** Elizabeth II **Obv:** Laureate bust right **Obv. Legend:** Without BRITT OMN **Rev:** Crowned value in sprays divides date within wreath **Edge:** Reeded

Date	Mintage	F	VF	XF	Unc	BU
2001 Prooflike	1,132	—	—	45.00	70.00	60.00
2002 Prooflike	1,681	—	—	45.00	70.00	60.00
2003 Prooflike	1,608	—	—	50.00	75.00	65.00
2004 Prooflike	1,613	—	—	50.00	75.00	65.00
2005 Prooflike	1,685	—	—	50.00	75.00	65.00

Date	Mintage	F	VF	XF	Unc	BU
2006 Prooflike	1,811	—	—	50.00	75.00	65.00
2006 Proof	6,394	—	—	—	—	—
2007 Prooflike	1,822	—	—	50.00	75.00	65.00
2008 Prooflike	1,999	—	—	50.00	75.00	65.00
2009 Prooflike	1,602	—	—	50.00	75.00	65.00
2010 Prooflike	1,617	—	—	50.00	75.00	65.00
2011 Prooflike	—	—	—	50.00	75.00	65.00

KM# 899a 2 PENCE
0.9167 Gold, 13 mm. **Ruler:** Elizabeth II **Series:** Maundy Sets **Obv:** Laureate bust right **Obv. Legend:** Without BRITT OMN **Rev:** Crowned denomination divides date within wreath

Date	Mintage	F	VF	XF	Unc	BU
2002 Proof	2,002	Value: 1,100				

KM# 901 3 PENCE
1.4138 g., 0.9250 Silver 0.0420 oz. ASW, 16 mm. **Ruler:** Elizabeth II **Obv:** Laureate bust right **Obv. Legend:** without BRITT OMN **Rev:** Crowned value in sprays divides date within wreath **Edge:** Reeded

Date	Mintage	F	VF	XF	Unc	BU
2001 Prooflike	1,132	—	—	50.00	75.00	65.00
2002 Prooflike	1,681	—	—	50.00	75.00	65.00
2003 Prooflike	1,608	—	—	55.00	80.00	70.00
2004 Prooflike	1,613	—	—	55.00	80.00	70.00
2005 Prooflike	1,685	—	—	55.00	80.00	70.00
2006 Prooflike	1,811	—	—	55.00	80.00	70.00
2006 Proof	6,394	—	—	—	—	—
2007 Prooflike	1,822	—	—	55.00	80.00	70.00
2008 Prooflike	1,833	—	—	55.00	80.00	70.00
2009 Prooflike	1,794	—	—	55.00	80.00	70.00
2010 Prooflike	1,617	—	—	55.00	80.00	70.00
2011 Prooflike	—	—	—	55.00	80.00	70.00

KM# 901a 3 PENCE
0.9167 Gold, 16 mm. **Ruler:** Elizabeth II **Obv:** Laureate bust right **Obv. Legend:** Without RITT OMN **Rev:** Crowned denomination divides date within wreath

Date	Mintage	F	VF	XF	Unc	BU
2002 Proof	2,002	Value: 1,150				

KM# 902 4 PENCE (Groat)
1.8851 g., 0.9250 Silver 0.0561 oz. ASW, 18 mm. **Ruler:** Elizabeth II **Obv:** Laureate bust right **Obv. Legend:** without BRITT OMN **Rev:** Crowned value in sprays divides date within wreath **Edge:** Reeded

Date	Mintage	F	VF	XF	Unc	BU
2001 Prooflike	1,132	—	—	50.00	75.00	65.00
2002 Prooflike	1,681	—	—	50.00	75.00	65.00
2003 Prooflike	1,608	—	—	50.00	75.00	65.00
2004 Prooflike	1,613	—	—	50.00	75.00	65.00
2005 Prooflike	1,685	—	—	50.00	75.00	65.00
2006 Prooflike	1,811	—	—	50.00	75.00	65.00
2006 Proof	6,394	—	—	—	—	—
2007 Prooflike	1,822	—	—	50.00	75.00	65.00
2008 Prooflike	1,833	—	—	50.00	75.00	65.00
2009 Prooflike	1,602	—	—	50.00	75.00	65.00
2010 Prooflike	1,787	—	—	50.00	75.00	65.00
2011 Prooflike	—	—	—	50.00	75.00	65.00

KM# 902a 4 PENCE
0.9167 Gold, 18 mm. **Ruler:** Elizabeth II **Obv:** Laureate bust right **Obv. Legend:** Without BRITT OMN **Rev:** Crowned denomination divides date within wreath

Date	Mintage	F	VF	XF	Unc	BU
2002 Proof	2,002	Value: 1,250				

DECIMAL COINAGE

1971-1981: 100 New Pence = 1 Pound; 1982-present: 100 Pence = 1 Pound

KM# 986 PENNY
3.5600 g., Copper Plated Steel, 20.32 mm. **Ruler:** Elizabeth II **Subject:** Badge of Henry VII **Obv:** Head with tiara right **Rev:** Crowned portcullis with chains **Edge:** Plain

Date	Mintage	F	VF	XF	Unc	BU
2001	928,698,000	—	—	0.15	1.75	2.50
2001 Proof	—	Value: 3.25				
2002	601,446,000	—	—	0.15	1.75	2.50
2002 Proof	60,770	Value: 3.25				
2003	539,436,000	—	—	0.15	1.75	2.50
2003 Proof	43,513	Value: 3.25				
2004	739,764,000	—	—	0.15	1.75	2.50
2004 Proof	35,020	Value: 3.25				
2005	536,318,000	—	—	0.15	1.75	2.50
2005 Proof	40,563	Value: 3.25				
2006	524,605,000	—	—	0.15	1.75	2.50
2006 Proof	37,689	Value: 3.25				
2007	548,002,000	—	—	0.15	1.75	2.50
2007 Proof	38,215	Value: 3.25				
2008	180,600,000	—	—	0.25	2.50	3.00
2008 Proof	36,333	Value: 3.25				

KM# 986c PENNY
0.9167 Gold **Ruler:** Elizabeth II **Obv:** Head with tiara right **Rev:** Crowned portcullis

Date	Mintage	F	VF	XF	Unc	BU
2002 Proof	—	Value: 750				
2008 Proof	2,008	Value: 550				

KM# 1107 PENNY
3.5900 g., Copper Plated Steel, 20.3 mm. **Ruler:** Elizabeth II **Obv:** Head with tiara right **Rev:** Section of the Royal Arms - Lion and Harp

Date	Mintage	F	VF	XF	Unc	BU
2008	507,952,000	—	—	—	—	0.20
2008 Proof	—	Value: 3.50				
2009	556,412,000	—	—	—	—	0.20
2009 Proof	—	Value: 3.50				
2010	421,002,000	—	—	—	—	0.20
2010 Proof	—	Value: 3.50				
2011	—	—	—	—	—	0.20
2011 Proof	—	Value: 3.50				
2012	—	—	—	—	—	0.20
2012 Proof	—	Value: 3.50				

KM# 1107a PENNY
3.5600 g., 0.9250 Silver 0.1059 oz. ASW, 20.3 mm. **Ruler:** Elizabeth II **Obv:** Head with tiara right **Rev:** Section of the Royal Arms - Lion and Harp

Date	Mintage	F	VF	XF	Unc	BU
2008 Proof	—	Value: 13.50				
2009	—	—	—	—	—	25.00
2009 Proof	—	Value: 25.00				
2010	—	—	—	—	—	25.00
2010 Proof	3,500	Value: 25.00				

KM# 986b PENNY
3.5600 g., 0.9250 Silver 0.1059 oz. ASW, 20.3 mm. **Ruler:** Elizabeth II **Obv:** Head with tiara right **Rev:** Crowned portcullis **Edge:** Plain

Date	Mintage	F	VF	XF	Unc	BU
2008 Proof	10,000	Value: 16.50				

KM# 1107b PENNY
0.9167 Gold, 20.3 mm. **Ruler:** Elizabeth II **Obv:** Head with tiara right **Rev:** Section of the Royal Arms - Lion and Harp

Date	Mintage	F	VF	XF	Unc	BU
2008 Proof	—	Value: 350				

KM# 1107c PENNY
Platinum APW, 20.3 mm. **Ruler:** Elizabeth II **Obv:** Head with tiara right **Rev:** Section of the Royal Arms - Lion and Harp

Date	Mintage	F	VF	XF	Unc	BU
2008 Proof	—	Value: 600				

KM# 1107a.1 PENNY
3.5600 g., 0.9250 Silver partially gilt 0.1059 oz. ASW, 20.3 mm. **Ruler:** Elizabeth II **Obv:** Head with tiara right **Rev:** Section of the Royal Arms - Lion and Harp, gilt

Date	Mintage	F	VF	XF	Unc	BU
2012 Proof	—	Value: 25.00				

KM# 987 2 PENCE
7.1400 g., Copper Plated Steel, 25.86 mm. **Ruler:** Elizabeth II **Obv:** Head with tiara right **Rev:** Welsh plumes and crown **Edge:** Plain

Date	Mintage	F	VF	XF	Unc	BU
2001	551,880,000	—	—	0.15	1.75	2.50
2002	168,556,000	—	—	0.15	1.75	2.50
2003	260,225,000	—	—	0.15	1.75	2.50
2003 Proof	43,513	Value: 3.25				
2004	356,396,000	—	—	0.15	1.75	2.50
2004 Proof	35,020	Value: 3.25				
2005	280,396,000	—	—	0.15	1.75	2.50
2005 Proof	40,563	Value: 3.25				
2006	170,637,000	—	—	0.15	1.75	2.50
2006 Proof	37,689	Value: 3.25				
2007	254,500,000	—	—	0.15	1.75	2.50
2007 Proof	38,215	Value: 3.25				
2008	10,600,000	—	—	0.25	3.00	3.50

KM# 987a 2 PENCE
Bronze, 25.91 mm. **Ruler:** Elizabeth II **Obv:** Head with tiara right **Rev:** Welsh plumes and crown

Date	Mintage	F	VF	XF	Unc	BU
2002 Proof	60,770	Value: 2.50				
2003 Proof	43,513	Value: 2.50				
2004 Proof	35,020	Value: 2.50				

KM# 987c 2 PENCE
0.9167 Gold, 25.91 mm. **Ruler:** Elizabeth II **Subject:** Queen's Golden Jubilee - 1952-2002 **Obv:** Head with tiara right **Rev:** Welsh plumes and crown

Date	Mintage	F	VF	XF	Unc	BU
2002 Proof	—	Value: 850				
2008 Proof	2,008	Value: 650				

KM# 1108 2 PENCE
7.1000 g., Copper Plated Steel, 25.86 mm. **Ruler:** Elizabeth II **Obv:** Head with tiara right **Rev:** Section of the Royal Arms - Lion

Date	Mintage	F	VF	XF	Unc	BU
2008	241,679,000	—	—	0.15	2.50	1.75
2008 Proof	36,333	Value: 3.25				
2009	150,400,500	—	—	0.15	2.50	1.75
2009 Proof	—	Value: 3.25				
2010	38,000,000	—	—	0.15	2.50	1.75
2010 Proof	40,000	Value: 3.25				
2011	—	—	—	0.15	2.50	1.75
2011 Proof	—	Value: 3.25				
2012	—	—	—	0.15	2.50	1.75
2012 Proof	—	Value: 3.25				

KM# 1108a 2 PENCE
7.1200 g., 0.9250 Silver 0.2117 oz. ASW, 25.86 mm. **Ruler:** Elizabeth II **Obv:** Head in tiara right **Rev:** Section of the Royal Arms - Lion

Date	Mintage	F	VF	XF	Unc	BU
2008 Proof	—	Value: 17.50				
2009 Proof	—	Value: 17.50				
2010 Proof	3,500	Value: 17.50				
2011 Proof	—	Value: 25.00				

Note: Also exists as a Piedfort, P78.

KM# 987b 2 PENCE
7.1200 g., 0.9250 Silver 0.2117 oz. ASW, 25.9 mm. **Ruler:** Elizabeth II **Obv:** Head with tiara right **Rev:** Welsh plumes and crown **Edge:** Plain

Date	Mintage	F	VF	XF	Unc	BU
2008 Proof	10,000	Value: 18.50				

KM# 1108b 2 PENCE
0.9167 Gold, 25.9 mm. **Ruler:** Elizabeth II **Obv:** Head in tiara right **Rev:** Section of the Royal Arms - Lion

Date	Mintage	F	VF	XF	Unc	BU
2008 Proof	—	Value: 700				

KM# 1108c 2 PENCE
Platinum APW, 25.9 mm. **Ruler:** Elizabeth II **Obv:** Head in tiara right **Rev:** Section of Royal Arms - Lion

Date	Mintage	F	VF	XF	Unc	BU
2008 Proof	—	Value: 1,100				

KM# 1108a.1 2 PENCE
7.1200 g., 0.9250 Silver partially gilt 0.2117 oz. ASW, 25.86 mm. **Ruler:** Elizabeth II **Obv:** Head with tiara right **Rev:** Section of the Royal Arms - Lion

Date	Mintage	F	VF	XF	Unc	BU
2012 Proof	—	Value: 17.50				

KM# 988 5 PENCE
3.2500 g., Copper-Nickel, 18 mm. **Ruler:** Elizabeth II **Obv:** Head with tiara right **Rev:** Crowned thistle

Date	Mintage	F	VF	XF	Unc	BU
2001	337,930,000	—	—	0.25	2.00	2.50
2001 Proof	45,617	Value: 3.00				

Date	Mintage	F	VF	XF	Unc	BU
2002	219,258,000	—	—	0.25	2.00	2.50
2002 Proof	60,770	Value: 3.00				
2003	333,230,000	—	—	0.25	2.00	2.50
2003 Proof	43,513	Value: 3.00				
2004	271,810,000	—	—	0.25	2.00	2.50
2004 Proof	35,020	Value: 3.00				
2005	236,212,000	—	—	0.25	2.00	2.50
2005 Proof	40,563	Value: 3.00				
2006	317,697,000	—	—	0.25	2.00	2.50
2006 Proof	37,689	Value: 3.00				
2007	246,720,000	—	—	0.25	2.00	2.50
2007 Proof	38,215	Value: 3.00				
2008	92,880,000	—	—	—	4.50	5.00

KM# 988b 5 PENCE
0.9167 Gold, 18 mm. **Ruler:** Elizabeth II **Obv:** Head with tiara right **Rev:** Crowned thistle

Date	Mintage	F	VF	XF	Unc	BU
2002 Proof	—	Value: 450				
2008 Proof	—	Value: 400				

KM# 1109 5 PENCE
3.2500 g., Copper-Nickel, 18 mm. **Ruler:** Elizabeth II **Obv:** Head with tiara right **Rev:** Section of the Royal Arms - Center of shield

Date	Mintage	F	VF	XF	Unc	BU
2008	165,172,000	—	—	0.25	2.00	2.50
2008 Proof	36,333	Value: 3.00				
2009	132,960,300	—	—	0.25	2.00	2.50
2009 Proof	40,000	Value: 3.00				
2010	180,250,500	—	—	0.25	2.00	2.50
2010 Proof	40,000	Value: 3.00				

KM# 1109a 5 PENCE
3.2500 g., 0.9250 Silver 0.0966 oz. ASW, 18 mm. **Ruler:** Elizabeth II **Obv:** Head in tiara right **Rev:** Section of Royal Arms - Center of shield

Date	Mintage	F	VF	XF	Unc	BU
2008 Proof	—	Value: 20.00				
2009 Proof	—	Value: 20.00				
2010 Proof	3,500	Value: 20.00				
2011 Proof	—	Value: 35.00				

Note: Also exists as a Piedfort, P79.

KM# 988a 5 PENCE
3.2500 g., 0.9250 Silver 0.0966 oz. ASW, 18 mm. **Ruler:** Elizabeth II **Obv:** Head with tiara right **Rev:** Crowned thistle **Edge:** Reeded

Date	Mintage	F	VF	XF	Unc	BU
2008 Proof	10,000	Value: 22.50				

KM# 1109b 5 PENCE
0.9167 Gold, 18 mm. **Ruler:** Elizabeth II **Obv:** Head in tiara right **Rev:** Section of Royal Arms - Center

Date	Mintage	F	VF	XF	Unc	BU
2008 Proof	—	Value: 500				

KM# 1109c 5 PENCE
Platinum APW, 18 mm. **Ruler:** Elizabeth II **Obv:** Head in tiara right **Rev:** Section of Royal Arms - Center

Date	Mintage	F	VF	XF	Unc	BU
2008 Proof	—	Value: 800				

KM# 1109d 5 PENCE
3.2500 g., Nickel Plated Steel, 18 mm. **Ruler:** Elizabeth II **Obv:** Head with tiara right **Rev:** Section of Royal Arms - Center of shield

Date	Mintage	F	VF	XF	Unc	BU
2011	—	—	—	0.25	2.00	2.50
2011 Proof	—	Value: 3.00				
2012	—	—	—	0.25	2.00	2.50
2012 Proof	—	Value: 3.00				

KM# 1109a.1 5 PENCE
3.2500 g., 0.9250 Silver with fully gilt reverse 0.0966 oz. ASW, 18 mm. **Ruler:** Elizabeth II **Obv:** Head with tiara right **Rev:** Section of the Royal Arms - Center of shield

Date	Mintage	F	VF	XF	Unc	BU
2012 Proof	—	Value: 20.00				

KM# 989 10 PENCE
6.5000 g., Copper-Nickel, 24.5 mm. **Ruler:** Elizabeth II **Obv:** Head with tiara right **Rev:** Crowned lion passant left

Date	Mintage	F	VF	XF	Unc	BU
2001	129,281,000	—	—	0.50	3.50	4.00
2001 Proof	45,617	Value: 3.50				
2002	80,934,000	—	—	0.50	3.50	4.00
2002 Proof	60,770	Value: 3.50				
2003	88,118,000	—	—	0.50	3.50	4.00
2003 Proof	43,513	Value: 3.50				
2004	99,602,000	—	—	0.50	3.50	4.00
2004 Proof	35,020	Value: 3.50				
2005	69,604,000	—	—	0.50	3.50	4.00
2005 Proof	40,563	Value: 3.50				
2006	118,803,000	—	—	0.50	3.50	4.00
2006 Proof	37,689	Value: 3.50				
2007	72,720,000	—	—	0.50	3.50	4.00
2007 Proof	38,215	Value: 3.50				
2008	9,720,000	—	—	0.50	3.50	4.00

KM# 989b 10 PENCE
0.9167 Gold, 24.5 mm. **Ruler:** Elizabeth II **Obv:** Head with tiara right **Rev:** Crowned lion prancing left

Date	Mintage	F	VF	XF	Unc	BU
2002 Proof	—	Value: 650				
2008 Proof	2,008	Value: 550				

KM# 1110 10 PENCE
6.5000 g., Copper-Nickel, 24.5 mm. **Ruler:** Elizabeth II **Obv:** Head with tiara right **Rev:** Section of the Royal Arms - two lions

Date	Mintage	F	VF	XF	Unc	BU
2008	71,447,000	—	—	0.50	4.00	3.50
2008 Proof	36,333	Value: 3.50				
2009	84,360,000	—	—	0.50	4.00	3.50
2009 Proof	40,000	Value: 3.50				
2010	25,320,500	—	—	0.50	4.00	3.50
2010 Proof	40,000	Value: 3.50				

KM# 1110a 10 PENCE
6.5000 g., 0.9250 Silver 0.1933 oz. ASW, 24.5 mm. **Ruler:** Elizabeth II **Obv:** Head with tiara right **Rev:** Section of the Royal Arms - two lions

Date	Mintage	F	VF	XF	Unc	BU
2008 Proof	—	Value: 25.00				
2009 proof	—	Value: 25.00				
2010 Proof	3,500	Value: 25.00				
2011 Proof	—	Value: 80.00				

Note: Also exists as a Piedfort, P80.

KM# 989a 10 PENCE
6.5000 g., 0.9250 Silver 0.1933 oz. ASW, 24.5 mm. **Ruler:** Elizabeth II **Obv:** Head with tiara right **Rev:** Crowned lion prancing left **Edge:** Reeded

Date	Mintage	F	VF	XF	Unc	BU
2008 Proof	10,000	Value: 20.00				

KM# 1110b 10 PENCE
0.9167 Gold, 24.5 mm. **Ruler:** Elizabeth II **Obv:** Head in tiara right **Rev:** Section of Royal Arms - two lions

Date	Mintage	F	VF	XF	Unc	BU
2008 Proof	—	Value: 950				

KM# 1110c 10 PENCE
Platinum APW, 24.5 mm. **Ruler:** Elizabeth II **Obv:** Head in tiara right **Rev:** Section of Royal Arms - two lions

Date	Mintage	F	VF	XF	Unc	BU
2008 Proof	—	Value: 1,600				

KM# 1110d 10 PENCE
6.5000 g., Nickel Plated Steel, 24.5 mm. **Ruler:** Elizabeth II **Obv:** Head with tiara right **Rev:** Section of Royal Arms - two lions

Date	Mintage	F	VF	XF	Unc	BU
2011	—	—	—	0.50	3.50	4.00
2011 Proof	—	Value: 3.50				
2012	—	—	—	0.50	3.50	4.00
2012 Proof	—	Value: 0.30				

KM# 1110a.1 10 PENCE
6.5000 g., 0.9250 Silver 0.1933 oz. ASW, 24.5 mm. **Ruler:** Elizabeth II **Obv:** Head with tiara right **Rev:** Section of the Royal Arms - two lions

Date	Mintage	F	VF	XF	Unc	BU
2012 Proof	—	Value: 25.00				

KM# 990 20 PENCE
5.0000 g., Copper-Nickel, 21.4 mm. **Ruler:** Elizabeth II **Obv:** Head with tiara right **Rev:** Crowned double rose **Shape:** 7-sided

Date	Mintage	F	VF	XF	Unc	BU
2001	148,122,500	—	—	0.50	3.50	4.00
2001 Proof	45,617	Value: 4.50				
2002	93,360,000	—	—	0.50	3.50	4.00
2002 Proof	60,770	Value: 4.50				
2003	153,383,750	—	—	0.50	3.50	4.00
2003 Proof	43,513	Value: 4.50				
2004	120,212,500	—	—	0.50	3.50	4.00
2004 Proof	35,020	Value: 4.50				
2005	124,488,750	—	—	0.50	3.50	4.00
2005 Proof	40,563	Value: 4.50				
2006	114,800,000	—	—	0.50	3.50	4.00
2006 Proof	37,689	Value: 4.50				
2007	117,075,000	—	—	0.50	3.50	4.00
2007 Proof	38,215	Value: 4.50				
2008	11,900,000	—	—	0.50	3.50	4.00

KM# 990b 20 PENCE
0.9167 Gold, 21.4 mm. **Ruler:** Elizabeth II **Obv:** Head with tiara right **Rev:** Crowned double rose **Shape:** 7-sided

Date	Mintage	F	VF	XF	Unc	BU
2002 Proof	—	Value: 550				
2008 Proof	2,008	Value: 500				

KM# 1111 20 PENCE
5.0000 g., Copper-Nickel, 21.4 mm. **Ruler:** Elizabeth II **Obv:** Head with tiara right **Rev:** Section of the Royal Arms - lion's tails **Shape:** 7-sided

Date	Mintage	F	VF	XF	Unc	BU
2008	115,022,000	—	—	0.50	3.50	4.00
2008 Proof	36,333	Value: 4.50				
2009	121,625,300	—	—	0.50	3.50	4.00
2009 Proof	40,000	Value: 4.50				
2010	91,700,500	—	—	0.50	3.35	4.00
2010 Proof	40,000	Value: 4.50				
2011	—	—	—	5.00	3.50	4.00
2011 Proof	—	Value: 4.50				
2012	—	—	—	0.50	3.50	4.00
2012 Proof	—	Value: 4.50				

KM# 1111a 20 PENCE
5.0000 g., 0.9250 Silver 0.1487 oz. ASW, 21.4 mm. **Ruler:** Elizabeth II **Obv:** Head in tiara right **Rev:** Section of the Royal Arms - lion's tails **Shape:** 7-sided

Date	Mintage	F	VF	XF	Unc	BU
2008 Proof	—	Value: 35.00				
2009 Proof	—	Value: 35.00				
2010 Proof	—	Value: 35.00				
2011 Proof	—	Value: 80.00				

Note: Also exists as a Piedfort, P81.

KM# 990a 20 PENCE
5.0000 g., 0.9250 Silver 0.1487 oz. ASW, 21.4 mm. **Ruler:** Elizabeth II **Obv:** Head with tiara right **Rev:** Crowned double rose **Edge:** Plain **Shape:** 7-sided

Date	Mintage	F	VF	XF	Unc	BU
2008 Proof	10,000	Value: 22.50				

KM# 1111b 20 PENCE
0.9167 Gold, 21.4 mm. **Ruler:** Elizabeth II **Obv:** Head in tiara right **Rev:** Section of Royal Arms - lion's tails **Shape:** 7-sided

Date	Mintage	F	VF	XF	Unc	BU
2008 Proof	—	Value: 700				

KM# 1111c 20 PENCE
Platinum APW, 21.4 mm. **Ruler:** Elizabeth II **Obv:** Head in tiara right **Rev:** Section of Royal Arms - lion's tails **Shape:** 7-sided

Date	Mintage	F	VF	XF	Unc	BU
2008 Proof	—	Value: 1,200				

KM# 1122 20 PENCE
5.0000 g., Copper-Nickel, 21.4 mm. **Ruler:** Elizabeth II **Obv:** Head right. Obverse of KM#990 **Rev:** Royal Arms part. Reverse of KM#1111 **Note:** Mule.

Date	Mintage	F	VF	XF	Unc	BU
ND(2008)	—	20.00	30.00	40.00	—	—

KM# 1111a.1 20 PENCE
5.0000 g., 0.9250 Silver partially gilt 0.1487 oz. ASW, 21.4 mm. **Ruler:** Elizabeth II **Obv:** Head with tiara right **Rev:** Section of Royal Arms - lion's tails

Date	Mintage	F	VF	XF	Unc	BU
2012 Proof	—	Value: 35.00				

KM# 991   50 PENCE
8.0000 g., Copper-Nickel, 27.3 mm. **Ruler:** Elizabeth II **Obv:** Head with tiara right **Rev:** Britannia seated right with shield, spear and lion **Shape:** 7-sided

Date	Mintage	F	VF	XF	Unc	BU
2001	84,998,500	—	—	1.00	3.50	4.00
2001 Proof	45,617	Value: 4.00				
2002	23,907,500	—	—	1.00	3.50	4.00
2002 Proof	60,770	Value: 4.00				
2003	23,583,000	—	—	1.00	3.50	4.00
2003 Proof	43,513	Value: 4.00				
2004	35,315,500	—	—	1.00	3.50	4.00
2004 Proof	35,020	Value: 4.00				
2005	25,363,500	—	—	1.00	3.50	4.00
2005 Proof	40,563	Value: 4.00				
2006	24,567,000	—	—	1.00	3.50	4.00
2006 Proof	37,689	Value: 4.00				
2007	11,200,000	—	—	1.00	3.50	4.00
2007 Proof	38,215	Value: 4.00				
2008	3,500,000	—	—	1.50	5.00	6.00

KM# 991b   50 PENCE
0.9167 Gold, 27.3 mm. **Ruler:** Elizabeth II **Obv:** Head with tiara right **Rev:** Britannia seated right with shield, spear and lion **Shape:** 7-sided

Date	Mintage	F	VF	XF	Unc	BU
2002 Proof	—	Value: 700				
2008 Proof	—	Value: 650				

KM# 1036   50 PENCE
8.0000 g., Copper-Nickel, 27.3 mm. **Ruler:** Elizabeth II **Subject:** Woman's Social and Political Union, 100th Anniversary **Obv:** Head with tiara right **Rev:** Standing suffragette chained to railings and holding banner **Edge:** Plain **Shape:** 7-sided

Date	Mintage	F	VF	XF	Unc	BU
2003	3,124,030	—	—	1.00	3.50	4.00
2003 Proof	35,513	Value: 9.50				

KM# 1036a   50 PENCE
8.0000 g., 0.9250 Silver 0.2379 oz. ASW, 27.3 mm. **Ruler:** Elizabeth II **Subject:** Woman's Social and Political Union, 100th Anniversary **Obv:** Head with tiara right **Rev:** Standing suffragette chained to railings and holding banner **Edge:** Plain **Shape:** 7-sided

Date	Mintage	F	VF	XF	Unc	BU
2003 Proof	6,267	Value: 45.00				

Note: Also exists as a Piefort, P40.

KM# 1036b   50 PENCE
15.5000 g., 0.9166 Gold 0.4568 oz. AGW, 27.3 mm. **Ruler:** Elizabeth II **Subject:** Woman's Social and Political Union, 100th Anniversary **Obv:** Head with tiara right **Rev:** Standing suffragette chained to railings and holding banner **Edge:** Plain **Shape:** 7-sided

Date	Mintage	F	VF	XF	Unc	BU
2003 Proof	942	Value: 750				

KM# 1047   50 PENCE
8.0000 g., Copper-Nickel, 27.3 mm. **Ruler:** Elizabeth II **Subject:** Roger Bannister, 50th Anniversary of the four minute mile **Obv:** Head with tiara right **Rev:** Running legs, stop watch and value **Edge:** Plain

Date	Mintage	F	VF	XF	Unc	BU
2004	9,032,500	—	—	1.50	5.00	6.00
2004 Proof	35,020	Value: 7.50				

KM# 1047a   50 PENCE
8.0000 g., 0.9250 Silver 0.2379 oz. ASW, 27.3 mm. **Ruler:** Elizabeth II **Subject:** Roger Bannister, 50th Anniversary four minute mile **Obv:** Head with tiara right **Rev:** Running legs, stop watch and value **Shape:** 7-sided

Date	Mintage	F	VF	XF	Unc	BU
2004 Proof	4,924	Value: 50.00				

Note: Also exists as a Piedfort, P43.

KM# 1050   50 PENCE
8.0000 g., Copper-Nickel, 27.3 mm. **Ruler:** Elizabeth II **Subject:** Samuel Johnson's Dictonary of the English Language, 250th Anniversary **Obv:** Head with tiara right **Rev:** Dictonary entries for Fifty and Pence **Edge:** Plain **Shape:** 7-sided

Date	Mintage	F	VF	XF	Unc	BU
2005	17,649,000	—	—	1.00	3.50	4.00
2005 Proof	40,563	Value: 6.00				

KM# 1050a   50 PENCE
8.0000 g., 0.9250 Silver 0.2379 oz. ASW, 27.3 mm. **Ruler:** Elizabeth II **Subject:** Samuel Johnson's Dictonary of the English Language, 250th Anniversary **Obv:** Head with tiara right **Rev:** Dictonary entries for Fifty and Pence **Edge:** Plain **Shape:** 7-sided

Date	Mintage	F	VF	XF	Unc	BU
2005 Proof	4,029	Value: 45.00				

Note: Also exists as a Piedfort, P48.

KM# 1050b   50 PENCE
15.5000 g., 0.9167 Gold 0.4568 oz. AGW, 27.3 mm. **Ruler:** Elizabeth II **Subject:** Samuel Johnson's Dictonary of the English Language, 250th Anniversary **Obv:** Head with tiara right **Rev:** Dictonary entries for Fifty and Pence **Edge:** Plain **Shape:** 7-sided

Date	Mintage	F	VF	XF	Unc	BU
2005 Proof	1,000	Value: 750				

KM# 1057   50 PENCE
8.0000 g., Copper-Nickel, 27.3 mm. **Ruler:** Elizabeth II **Subject:** Victoria Cross, 150th Anniversary **Obv:** Head with tiara right **Rev:** Victoria Cross Medal, obverse and reverse views **Edge:** Plain **Shape:** 7-sided

Date	Mintage	F	VF	XF	Unc	BU
2006	12,087,000	—	—	1.50	5.00	6.00
2006 Proof	Est. 50,000	Value: 7.50				
2007 Proof	—	Value: 7.50				

KM# 1057a   50 PENCE
8.0000 g., 0.9250 Silver 0.2379 oz. ASW **Ruler:** Elizabeth II **Subject:** Victoria Cross, 150th Anniversary **Obv:** Head with tiara right **Rev:** Victoria Cross Medal, obverse and reverse views

Date	Mintage	F	VF	XF	Unc	BU
2006 Proof	7,500	Value: 40.00				

Note: Also exists as a Piedfort, P53.

KM# 1058a   50 PENCE
8.0000 g., 0.9250 Silver 0.2379 oz. ASW, 27.3 mm. **Ruler:** Elizabeth II **Subject:** Victoria Cross, 150th Anniversary **Obv:** Head with tiara right **Rev:** Heroic Act scene of a soldier carring a wounded comrade with outline of the Victoria Cross in the background **Shape:** 7-sided

Date	Mintage	F	VF	XF	Unc	BU
2006 Proof	—	Value: 40.00				

Note: Also exists as a Piedfort, P-54.

KM# 1058   50 PENCE
8.0000 g., Copper-Nickel, 27.3 mm. **Ruler:** Elizabeth II **Subject:** Victoria Cross, 150th Anniversary **Obv:** Head with tiara right **Rev:** Heroic Act scene of a soldier carring a wounded comrade with outline of the Victoria Cross in the background **Edge:** Plain **Shape:** 7-sided

Date	Mintage	F	VF	XF	Unc	BU
2006	10,000,500	—	—	1.50	5.00	6.00
2006 Proof	Est. 50,000	Value: 7.50				

KM# 1073   50 PENCE
8.0000 g., Copper-Nickel, 27.3 mm. **Ruler:** Elizabeth II **Subject:** Scouting Movement, 100th Anniversary **Obv:** Head with tiara right **Rev:** Fleur-de-lis emblem superimposed on globe **Edge:** Plain **Shape:** Seven sided

Date	Mintage	F	VF	XF	Unc	BU
2007	7,710,750	—	—	1.50	5.00	6.00
2007 Proof	Est. 50,000	Value: 7.50				

KM# 1073a   50 PENCE
8.0000 g., 0.9250 Silver 0.2379 oz. ASW, 27.3 mm. **Ruler:** Elizabeth II **Subject:** Scouting Movement, 100th Anniversary **Obv:** Head with tiara right **Rev:** Fleur-de-lis emblem superimposed on globe **Edge:** Plain **Shape:** 7-sided

Date	Mintage	F	VF	XF	Unc	BU
2007 Proof	10,895	Value: 60.00				

Note: Also exists as a Piedfort, P-59.

KM# 1073b   50 PENCE
15.5000 g., 0.9166 Gold 0.4568 oz. AGW, 27.3 mm. **Ruler:** Elizabeth II **Subject:** Scouting Movement, 100th Anniversary **Obv:** Head with tiara right **Rev:** Fleur-de-lis emblem superimposed on globe **Edge:** Plain **Shape:** 7-sided

Date	Mintage	F	VF	XF	Unc	BU
2007 Proof	1,250	Value: 775				

KM# 1112   50 PENCE
8.0000 g., Copper-Nickel, 27.3 mm. **Ruler:** Elizabeth II **Obv:** Head with tiara right **Rev:** Section of the Royal Arms - bottom center **Shape:** 7-sided

Date	Mintage	F	VF	XF	Unc	BU
2008	22,747,000	—	—	1.00	3.50	4.00
2008 Proof	36,333	Value: 7.00				
2009 In sets only		—	—	1.00	3.50	4.00
2009 Proof	40,000	Value: 7.00				
2010 In sets only		—	—	1.00	3.50	4.00
2010 Proof	40,000	Value: 7.00				
2011 In sets only		—	—	1.00	3.50	4.00
2011 Proof	—	Value: 7.00				
2012		—	—	1.00	3.50	4.00
2012 Proof	—	Value: 7.00				

KM# 1112a   50 PENCE
8.0000 g., 0.9250 Silver 0.2379 oz. ASW, 27.3 mm. **Ruler:** Elizabeth II **Obv:** Head in tiara right **Rev:** Section of Royal Arms - bottom center **Shape:** 7-sided

Date	Mintage	F	VF	XF	Unc	BU
2008 Proof	—	Value: 50.00				

Note: Also exists as a Piedfort, P-97.

Date	Mintage	F	VF	XF	Unc	BU
2009 Proof	—	Value: 50.00				
2010 Proof	—	Value: 50.00				
2011 Proof	—	Value: 50.00				

Note: Also exists as a Piedfort, P-82.

KM# 1112b   50 PENCE
15.5000 g., 0.9167 Gold 0.4568 oz. AGW, 27.3 mm. **Ruler:** Elizabeth II **Obv:** Head in tiara right **Rev:** Section of Royal Arms - bottom center **Shape:** 7-sided

Date	Mintage	F	VF	XF	Unc	BU
2008 Proof	—	Value: 825				
2009 Proof	—	Value: 825				

KM# 1112c   50 PENCE
Platinum APW, 27.3 mm. **Ruler:** Elizabeth II **Obv:** Head in tiara right **Rev:** Section of Royal Arms - bottom center **Shape:** 7-sided

Date	Mintage	F	VF	XF	Unc	BU
2008 Proof	—	Value: 1,350				

KM# 1150   50 PENCE
8.0000 g., Copper-Nickel, 27.3 mm. **Ruler:** Elizabeth II **Subject:** London Olympics, 2012 - Athletics **Obv:** Head with tiara right

Rev: Youth's drawing of kid going over vault **Edge:** Plain **Shape:** 7-sided

Date	Mintage	F	VF	XF	Unc	BU
2009	—	—	—	1.00	3.50	4.00
2011	900,000	—	—	—	2.50	3.50

KM# 1114   50 PENCE
8.0000 g., Copper-Nickel, 27.3 mm. **Ruler:** Elizabeth II **Subject:** Royal Botanical Gardens at Kew, 250th Anniversary **Obv:** Head with tiara right **Rev:** Pagoda and vine, 1759-2009 **Edge:** Plain **Shape:** 7-sided

Date	Mintage	F	VF	XF	Unc	BU
2009	10,000	—	—	1.50	6.00	5.00
2009 Proof	—	Value: 7.50				

KM# 1114a   50 PENCE
8.0000 g., 0.9250 Silver 0.2379 oz. ASW, 27.3 mm. **Ruler:** Elizabeth II **Subject:** Royal Botanical Gardens at Kew, 250th Anniversary **Obv:** Head right **Rev:** Pagoda and vine, 1759 2009 **Edge:** Plain **Shape:** 7-sided

Date	Mintage	F	VF	XF	Unc	BU
2009 Proof	7,500	Value: 50.00				

Note: Also exists as a Piedfort, P98

KM# 1114b   50 PENCE
15.5000 g., 0.9160 Gold 0.4565 oz. AGW, 27.3 mm. **Ruler:** Elizabeth II **Subject:** Royal Botanical Gardens at Kew, 250th Anniversary **Obv:** Head right **Rev:** Pagoda and vine, 1759 2009 **Edge:** Plain **Shape:** 7-sided

Date	Mintage	F	VF	XF	Unc	BU
2009 Proof	1,000	Value: 750				

KM# 1150a   50 PENCE
8.0000 g., 0.9250 Silver 0.2379 oz. ASW, 27.3 mm. **Ruler:** Elizabeth II **Subject:** London Olympics, 2012 **Obv:** Head with tiara right **Rev:** Youth drawing of high jumper

Date	Mintage	F	VF	XF	Unc	BU
2009 Proof	—	Value: 50.00				

KM# 1165   50 PENCE
8.0000 g., Copper-Nickel, 27.3 mm. **Ruler:** Elizabeth II **Subject:** Girl Guides, 100th Anniversary **Obv:** Head with tiara right **Rev:** Circle of six trifoils **Edge:** Plain **Shape:** 7-sided

Date	Mintage	F	VF	XF	Unc	BU
2010	510,090	—	—	1.50	4.00	5.00
2010 Proof	—	Value: 10.00				

KM# 1165a   50 PENCE
8.0000 g., 0.9250 Silver 0.2379 oz. ASW, 27.3 mm. **Ruler:** Elizabeth II **Subject:** Girl Guides, 100th Anniversary **Obv:** Head with tiara right **Rev:** Circle of six trifoils **Edge:** Plain **Shape:** 7-sided

Date	Mintage	F	VF	XF	Unc	BU
2010 Proof	—	Value: 50.00				

Note: Also exists as a Piedfort, P99

KM# 1166   50 PENCE
8.0000 g., Copper-Nickel, 27.3 mm. **Ruler:** Elizabeth II **Subject:** 2012 London Olympics - Aquatics **Obv:** Head with tiara right **Edge:** Plain **Shape:** 7-sided

Date	Mintage	F	VF	XF	Unc	BU
2011	1,000,000	—	—	1.50	5.00	6.00

KM# 1167   50 PENCE
8.0000 g., Copper-Nickel, 27.3 mm. **Ruler:** Elizabeth II **Subject:** 2012 London Paralympics - Archery **Obv:** Head with tiara right **Edge:** Plain **Shape:** 7-sided

Date	Mintage	F	VF	XF	Unc	BU
2011	800,000	—	—	1.50	5.00	6.00

KM# 1168   50 PENCE
8.0000 g., Copper-Nickel, 27.3 mm. **Ruler:** Elizabeth II **Subject:** 2012 London Olympics - Canoeing **Obv:** Head with tiara right **Edge:** Plain **Shape:** 7-sided

Date	Mintage	F	VF	XF	Unc	BU
2011	800,000	—	—	1.50	5.00	6.00

KM# 1169   50 PENCE
8.0000 g., Copper-Nickel, 27.3 mm. **Ruler:** Elizabeth II **Subject:** 2012 London Olympics - Cycling **Obv:** Head with tiara right **Rev:** Cycle racing in a Velodrome **Edge:** Plain **Shape:** 7-sided

Date	Mintage	F	VF	XF	Unc	BU
2011	400,000	—	—	1.50	5.00	6.00

KM# 1170   50 PENCE
8.0000 g., Copper-Nickel, 27.3 mm. **Ruler:** Elizabeth II **Subject:** 2012 London Olympics - Gymnastics **Obv:** Head with tiara right **Edge:** Plain **Shape:** 7-sided

Date	Mintage	F	VF	XF	Unc	BU
2011	900,000	—	—	1.50	5.00	6.00

KM# 1171   50 PENCE
8.0000 g., Copper-Nickel, 27.3 mm. **Ruler:** Elizabeth II **Subject:** 2012 London Olympics - Hockey **Obv:** Head with tiara right **Edge:** Plain **Shape:** 7-sided

Date	Mintage	F	VF	XF	Unc	BU
2011	1,000,000	—	—	1.50	5.00	6.00

KM# 1172   50 PENCE
8.0000 g., Copper-Nickel, 27.3 mm. **Ruler:** Elizabeth II **Subject:** 2012 London Olympics - Rowing **Obv:** Head with tiara right **Edge:** Plain **Shape:** 7-sided

Date	Mintage	F	VF	XF	Unc	BU
2011	700,000	—	—	1.50	5.00	6.00

KM# 1173   50 PENCE
8.0000 g., Copper-Nickel, 27.3 mm. **Ruler:** Elizabeth II **Subject:** 2012 London Olympics - Triathlon **Obv:** Head with tiara right **Edge:** Plain **Shape:** 7-sided

Date	Mintage	F	VF	XF	Unc	BU
2011	1,000,000	—	—	—	—	6.00

KM# 1174   50 PENCE
8.0000 g., Copper-Nickel, 27.3 mm. **Ruler:** Elizabeth II **Subject:** 2012 London Olympics - Badminton **Obv:** Head with tiara right **Edge:** Plain **Shape:** 7-sided

Date	Mintage	F	VF	XF	Unc	BU
2011	900,000	—	—	1.50	5.00	6.00

KM# 1175   50 PENCE
8.0000 g., Copper-Nickel, 27.3 mm. **Ruler:** Elizabeth II **Subject:** 2012 London Olympics - Boxing **Obv:** Head with tiara right **Edge:** Plain **Shape:** 7-sided

Date	Mintage	F	VF	XF	Unc	BU
2011	800,000	—	—	1.50	5.00	6.00

KM# 1176   50 PENCE
8.0000 g., Copper-Nickel, 27.3 mm. **Ruler:** Elizabeth II **Subject:** 2012 London Olympics - Equestrian **Obv:** Head with tiara right **Edge:** Plain **Shape:** 7-sided

Date	Mintage	F	VF	XF	Unc	BU
2011	—	—	—	—	—	6.00

KM# 1177   50 PENCE
8.0000 g., Copper-Nickel, 27.3 mm. **Ruler:** Elizabeth II **Subject:** 2012 London Olympics - Modern Pentathlon **Obv:** Head with tiara right **Edge:** Plain **Shape:** 7-sided

Date	Mintage	F	VF	XF	Unc	BU
2011	—	—	—	1.50	5.00	6.00

KM# 1179   50 PENCE
8.0000 g., Copper-Nickel, 27.3 mm. **Ruler:** Elizabeth II **Subject:** 2012 London Olympics - Shooting **Obv:** Head with tiara right **Edge:** Plain **Shape:** 7-sided

Date	Mintage	F	VF	XF	Unc	BU
2011	—	—	—	1.50	5.00	6.00

KM# 1180   50 PENCE
8.0000 g., Copper-Nickel, 27.3 mm. **Ruler:** Elizabeth II **Subject:** 2012 London Paralympics - Table Tennis **Obv:** Head with tiara right **Edge:** Plain **Shape:** 7-sided

Date	Mintage	F	VF	XF	Unc	BU
2011	1,000,000	—	—	1.50	5.00	6.00

KM# 1181   50 PENCE
8.0000 g., Copper-Nickel, 27.3 mm. **Ruler:** Elizabeth II **Subject:** 2012 London Olympics - Volleyball **Shape:** 7-sided

Date	Mintage	F	VF	XF	Unc	BU
2011	1,000,000	—	—	1.50	5.00	6.00

KM# 1182 50 PENCE
8.0000 g., Copper-Nickel, 27.3 mm. **Ruler:** Elizabeth II **Subject:** 2012 London Olympics - Canoeing **Shape:** 7-sided

Date	Mintage	F	VF	XF	Unc	BU
2011	800,000	—	—	1.50	5.00	6.00

KM# 1183 50 PENCE
8.0000 g., Copper-Nickel, 27.3 mm. **Ruler:** Elizabeth II **Subject:** 2012 London Paralympics - Goalball **Obv:** Head with tiara right **Edge:** Plain **Shape:** 7-sided

Date	Mintage	F	VF	XF	Unc	BU
2011	900,000	—	—	1.50	5.00	6.00

KM# 1185 50 PENCE
8.0000 g., Copper-Nickel, 27.3 mm. **Ruler:** Elizabeth II **Subject:** 2012 London Olympics - Taekwondo **Obv:** Head with tiara right **Edge:** Plain **Shape:** 7-sided

Date	Mintage	F	VF	XF	Unc	BU
2011	—	—	—	1.50	5.00	6.00

KM# 1186 50 PENCE
8.0000 g., Copper-Nickel, 27.3 mm. **Ruler:** Elizabeth II **Subject:** 2012 London Olympics - Weightlifting **Obv:** Head with tiara right **Edge:** Plain **Shape:** 7-sided

Date	Mintage	F	VF	XF	Unc	BU
2011	—	—	—	1.50	5.00	6.00

KM# 1187 50 PENCE
8.0000 g., Copper-Nickel, 27.3 mm. **Ruler:** Elizabeth II **Subject:** 2012 London Paralympics - Wheelchair Rugby **Obv:** Head with tiara right **Edge:** Plain **Shape:** 7-sided

Date	Mintage	F	VF	XF	Unc	BU
2011	—	—	—	1.50	5.00	6.00

KM# 1188 50 PENCE
8.0000 g., Copper-Nickel, 27.3 mm. **Ruler:** Elizabeth II **Subject:** 2012 Summer Olympics - Wrestling **Obv:** Head with tiara right **Edge:** Plain **Shape:** 7-sided

Date	Mintage	F	VF	XF	Unc	BU
2011	—	—	—	1.50	5.00	6.00

KM# 1189 50 PENCE
8.0000 g., Copper-Nickel, 27.3 mm. **Ruler:** Elizabeth II **Subject:** 2012 London Paralympics - Boccia **Obv:** Head with tiara right **Edge:** Plain **Shape:** 7-sided

Date	Mintage	F	VF	XF	Unc	BU
2011	900,000	—	—	1.50	5.00	6.00

KM# 1190 50 PENCE
8.0000 g., Copper-Nickel, 27.3 mm. **Ruler:** Elizabeth II **Subject:** 2012 London Olympics - Basketball **Obv:** Head with tiara right **Edge:** Plain **Shape:** 7-sided

Date	Mintage	F	VF	XF	Unc	BU
2011	—	—	—	1.50	5.00	6.00

KM# 1191 50 PENCE
8.0000 g., Copper-Nickel, 27.3 mm. **Ruler:** Elizabeth II **Subject:** 2012 London Olympics - Fencing **Obv:** Head with tiara right **Edge:** Plain **Shape:** 7-sided

Date	Mintage	F	VF	XF	Unc	BU
2011	1,000,000	—	—	1.50	5.00	6.00

KM# 1192 50 PENCE
8.0000 g., Copper-Nickel, 27.3 mm. **Ruler:** Elizabeth II **Subject:** 2012 London Olympics - Handball **Obv:** Head with tiara right **Edge:** Plain **Shape:** 7-sided

Date	Mintage	F	VF	XF	Unc	BU
2011	—	—	—	1.50	5.00	6.00

KM# 1193 50 PENCE
8.0000 g., Copper-Nickel, 27.3 mm. **Ruler:** Elizabeth II **Subject:** 2012 London Olympics - Football (Soccer) **Obv:** Head with tiara right **Edge:** Plain **Shape:** 7-sided

Date	Mintage	F	VF	XF	Unc	BU
2011	—	—	—	1.50	5.00	6.00

KM# 1194 50 PENCE
8.0000 g., Copper-Nickel, 27.3 mm. **Ruler:** Elizabeth II **Subject:** 2012 London Olympics - Tennis **Obv:** Head with tiara right **Edge:** Plain **Shape:** 7-sided

Date	Mintage	F	VF	XF	Unc	BU
2011	—	—	—	1.50	5.00	6.00

KM# 1195 50 PENCE
8.0000 g., Copper-Nickel, 27.3 mm. **Ruler:** Elizabeth II **Subject:** London Olympics - Sailing **Obv:** Head with tiara right **Edge:** Plain **Shape:** 7-sided

Date	Mintage	F	VF	XF	Unc	BU
2011	—	—	—	1.00	5.00	6.00

KM# 1196 50 PENCE
8.0000 g., Copper-Nickel, 27.3 mm. **Ruler:** Elizabeth II **Subject:** World Wildlife Fund, 50th Anniversary **Obv:** Head with tiara right **Rev:** Panda in center of animal shaped blocks **Edge:** Plain **Shape:** 7-sided

Date	Mintage	F	VF	XF	Unc	BU
2011	Est. 40,000	—	—	1.50	5.00	6.00
2011 Proof	—	Value: 8.50				

KM# 1196a 50 PENCE
8.0000 g., 0.9250 Silver 0.2379 oz. ASW, 27.3 mm. **Ruler:** Elizabeth II **Subject:** World Wildlife Fund, 50th Anniversary **Obv:** Head with tiara right **Rev:** Panda at center, animal shapes as blocks **Edge:** Plain **Shape:** 7-sided

Date	Mintage	F	VF	XF	Unc	BU
2011 Proof	—	Value: 50.00				

Note: Also exists as a Piedfort, P86

KM# 1184 50 PENCE
8.0000 g., Copper-Nickel, 24.3 mm. **Ruler:** Elizabeth II **Subject:** 2012 London Olympics - Judo **Obv:** Head with tiara right **Edge:** Plain **Shape:** 7-sided

Date	Mintage	F	VF	XF	Unc	BU
2011	—	—	—	1.50	5.00	6.00

KM# 1112a.1 50 PENCE
8.0000 g., 0.9250 Silver partially gilt 0.2379 oz. ASW, 27.3 mm. **Ruler:** Elizabeth II **Obv:** Head with tiara right **Rev:** Section of Royal Arms - bottom center

Date	Mintage	F	VF	XF	Unc	BU
2012 Proof	—	Value: 50.00				

KM# 1178 50 PENCE
8.0000 g., Copper-Nickel, 27.3 mm. **Ruler:** Elizabeth II **Subject:** 2012 London Olympics - Sailing **Obv:** Head with tiara right **Edge:** Plain **Shape:** 7-sided

Date	Mintage	F	VF	XF	Unc	BU
2012	—	—	—	1.50	5.00	6.00

KM# 1013 POUND
9.5000 g., Nickel-Brass, 22.5 mm. **Ruler:** Elizabeth II **Subject:** Northern Ireland **Obv:** Head with tiara right **Rev:** Celtic cross with a pimpernel flower at the center **Edge:** Reeded and lettered **Edge Lettering:** DECUS ET TUTAMEN

Date	Mintage	F	VF	XF	Unc	BU
2001	63,968,065	—	—	3.00	6.00	7.50
2001 Proof	45,617	Value: 7.50				

KM# 1013a POUND
9.5000 g., 0.9250 Silver 0.2825 oz. ASW, 22.5 mm. **Ruler:** Elizabeth II **Subject:** Northern Ireland **Obv:** Head with tiara right **Rev:** Celtic cross with a pimpernel flower in the center **Edge:** Reeded and lettered **Edge Lettering:** DECUS ET TUTAMEN

Date	Mintage	F	VF	XF	Unc	BU
2001 Proof	25,000	Value: 45.00				

Note: Also exists as a Piedfort, P101

KM# 1030   POUND
9.5000 g., Nickel-Brass, 22.5 mm. **Subject:** England **Obv:** Head with tiara right **Rev:** Three lions passant left **Edge:** Reeded and lettered **Edge Lettering:** DECUS ET TUTAMEN

Date	Mintage	F	VF	XF	Unc	BU
2002	77,818,000	—	—	3.00	6.00	7.00
2002 Proof	60,770	Value: 7.50				

KM# 1030a   POUND
9.5000 g., 0.9250 Silver 0.2825 oz. ASW, 22.5 mm. **Subject:** England **Obv:** Head with tiara right **Rev:** Three lions passant left **Edge:** Reeded and lettered **Edge Lettering:** DECUS ET TUTAMEN

Date	Mintage	F	VF	XF	Unc	BU
2002 Proof	—	Value: 45.00				

Note: Also exists as a Piedfort, P102

KM# 1030b   POUND
0.9167 Gold, 22.5 mm. **Subject:** England **Obv:** Head with tiara right **Rev:** Three lions left passant left **Edge:** Reeded and lettered **Edge Lettering:** DECUS ET TUTAMEN

Date	Mintage	F	VF	XF	Unc	BU
2002 Proof	—	Value: 850				

KM# 993   POUND
9.5000 g., Nickel-Brass, 22.5 mm. **Subject:** United Kingdom **Obv:** Head with tiara right **Rev:** Royal Arms with supporters **Edge:** Reeded and lettered **Edge Lettering:** DECUS ET TUTAMEN

Date	Mintage	F	VF	XF	Unc	BU
2003	61,596,500	—	—	3.00	6.00	7.50
2003 Proof	43,513	Value: 7.50				

KM# 1048   POUND
9.5000 g., Nickel-Brass, 22.5 mm. **Obv:** Head with tiara right **Rev:** Forth Rail Bridge in Scotland **Edge:** Reeded and ornamented

Date	Mintage	F	VF	XF	Unc	BU
2004	39,162,000	—	—	3.50	7.50	9.00
2004 Proof	35,020	Value: 9.00				

KM# 1048a   POUND
9.5000 g., 0.9250 Silver 0.2825 oz. ASW, 22.5 mm. **Obv:** Head with tiara right **Rev:** Forth Railway Bridge in Scotland **Edge:** Ornamented and reeded

Date	Mintage	F	VF	XF	Unc	BU
2004 Proof	Est. 20,000	Value: 45.00				

Note: Also exists as a Piedfort, P44

KM# 1048b   POUND
19.6190 g., 0.9166 Gold 0.5781 oz. AGW, 22.5 mm. **Obv:** Head with tiara right **Rev:** Forth Railway Bridge in Scotland **Edge:** Reeded and ornamented

Date	Mintage	F	VF	XF	Unc	BU
2004 Proof	Est. 1,500	Value: 1,100				

KM# 1051   POUND
9.5000 g., Nickel-Brass, 22.5 mm. **Obv:** Head with tiara right **Rev:** Menai Bridge to the Isle of Anglesey

Date	Mintage	F	VF	XF	Unc	BU
2005	99,429,500	—	—	3.00	6.00	7.50
2005 Proof	40,563	Value: 10.00				

KM# 1051a   POUND
9.5000 g., 0.9250 Silver 0.2825 oz. ASW, 22.5 mm. **Obv:** Head with tiara right **Rev:** Menai Bridge to the Isle of Anglesey **Edge:** Reeded and lettered **Edge Lettering:** PLEIDOL WYF I'M GWLAD

Date	Mintage	F	VF	XF	Unc	BU
2005 Proof	Est. 15,000	Value: 45.00				

Note: Also exists as a Piedfort, P50

KM# 1051b   POUND
19.6190 g., 0.9167 Gold 0.5782 oz. AGW, 22.5 mm. **Obv:** Head with tiara right **Rev:** Menai Bridge to the Isle of Anglesey **Edge:** Reeded and lettered **Edge Lettering:** PLEIDOL WYF I'M GWLAD

Date	Mintage	F	VF	XF	Unc	BU
2005 Proof	Est. 1,500	Value: 850				

KM# 1051a.2   POUND
9.5000 g., 0.9250 Silver 0.2825 oz. ASW, 22.5 mm. **Obv:** Elizabeth II **Rev:** Menai Bridge to the Isle of Anglesey **Edge:** Reeded and ornamented

Date	Mintage	F	VF	XF	Unc	BU
2005 Proof	Est. 20,000	Value: 45.00				

KM# 1051b.2   POUND
19.6190 g., 0.9166 Gold 0.5781 oz. AGW, 22.5 mm. **Obv:** Head with tiara right **Rev:** Menai Bridge to the Isle of Anglesey **Edge:** Reeded and ornamented

Date	Mintage	F	VF	XF	Unc	BU
2005 Proof	Est. 1,500	Value: 850				

KM# 1059   POUND
9.6000 g., Nickel-Brass, 22.5 mm. **Obv:** Head with tiara right **Rev:** Egyptian Arch Railway Bridge at Newry **Edge:** Reeded and lettered

Date	Mintage	F	VF	XF	Unc	BU
2006	38,938,000	—	—	4.00	8.00	9.00
2006 Proof	37,689	Value: 10.00				
2007 Proof	—	Value: 10.00				

KM# 1059a   POUND
9.5000 g., 0.9250 Silver 0.2825 oz. ASW, 22.5 mm. **Ruler:** Elizabeth II **Obv:** Head with tiara right **Rev:** Egyptian Arch Railway Bridge at Newry **Edge:** Reeded and lettered **Edge Lettering:** DECUS ET TUTAMEN

Date	Mintage	F	VF	XF	Unc	BU
2006 Proof	Est. 20,000	Value: 50.00				

Note: Also exists as a Piedfort, P55

KM# 1059a.2   POUND
9.5000 g., 0.9250 Silver 0.2825 oz. ASW, 22.5 mm. **Ruler:** Elizabeth II **Obv:** Head with tiara right **Rev:** Egyptian Arch Railway Bridge at Newry **Edge:** Reeded and ornamented

Date	Mintage	F	VF	XF	Unc	BU
2006 Proof	Est. 20,000	Value: 45.00				

KM# 1059b   POUND
19.6190 g., 0.9167 Gold 0.5782 oz. AGW, 22.5 mm. **Ruler:** Elizabeth II **Obv:** Head with tiara right **Rev:** Egyptian Arch Railway Bridge at Newry **Edge:** Reeded and lettered **Edge Lettering:** DECUS ET TUTAMEN

Date	Mintage	F	VF	XF	Unc	BU
2006 Proof	—	Value: 875				

KM# 1059b.2   POUND
19.6190 g., 0.9166 Gold 0.5781 oz. AGW, 22.5 mm. **Ruler:** Elizabeth II **Obv:** Head with tiara right **Rev:** Egyptian Arch Railway Bridge at Newry **Edge:** Reeded and ornamented

Date	Mintage	F	VF	XF	Unc	BU
2006 Proof	Est. 1,500	Value: 1,100				

KM# 1074   POUND
9.5000 g., Nickel-Brass, 22.5 mm. **Ruler:** Elizabeth II **Obv:** Head with tiara right **Rev:** Millennium Bridge at Gateshead **Edge:** Reeded and ornamented

Date	Mintage	F	VF	XF	Unc	BU
2007	26,180,160	—	—	4.00	8.00	9.00
2007 Proof	38,215	Value: 10.00				

KM# 1074a   POUND
9.5000 g., 0.9250 Silver 0.2825 oz. ASW, 22.5 mm. **Ruler:** Elizabeth II **Obv:** head with tiara right **Rev:** Millennium Bridge at Gateshead **Edge:** Reeded and ornamented

Date	Mintage	F	VF	XF	Unc	BU
2007 Proof	Est. 20,000	Value: 45.00				

Note: Also exists as a Piedfort, P60

KM# 1074b   POUND
19.6190 g., 0.9166 Gold 0.5781 oz. AGW, 22.5 mm. **Ruler:** Elizabeth II **Obv:** Head with tiara right **Rev:** Millennium Bridge at Gateshead **Edge:** Reeded and ornamented

Date	Mintage	F	VF	XF	Unc	BU
2007 Proof	Est. 1,500	Value: 850				

KM# 993a   POUND
9.5000 g., 0.9250 Silver 0.2825 oz. ASW, 22.5 mm. **Ruler:** Elizabeth II **Subject:** United Kingdom **Obv:** Head with tiara right **Rev:** Royal Arms with supporters **Edge:** Reeded and lettered **Edge Lettering:** DECUS ET TUTAMEN

Date	Mintage	F	VF	XF	Unc	BU
2003 Proof	15,830	Value: 45.00				

Note: Also exists as a Piedfort, P41

KM# 1113   POUND
9.5000 g., Nickel-Brass, 22.5 mm. **Ruler:** Elizabeth II **Obv:** Head with tiara right **Rev:** Shield of the Royal Arms **Edge:** Reeded and lettered **Edge Lettering:** DECUS ET TUTAMEN

Date	Mintage	F	VF	XF	Unc	BU
2008	43,827,300	—	—	3.00	7.50	6.00
2008 Proof	36,333	Value: 7.50				
2009	27,625,600	—	—	4.00	9.00	8.00
2009 Proof	40,000	Value: 9.00				
2010	38,505,000	—	—	3.00	7.50	6.00
2010 Proof	40,000	Value: 7.50				
2011	—	—	—	3.00	7.50	6.00
2011 Proof	—	Value: 7.50				
2012	—	—	—	3.00	7.50	6.00
2012 Proof	—	Value: 7.50				

KM# 1113a   POUND
9.5000 g., 0.9250 Silver 0.2825 oz. ASW, 22.5 mm. **Ruler:** Elizabeth II **Obv:** Head in tiara right **Rev:** Shield of the Royal Arms

Date	Mintage	F	VF	XF	Unc	BU
2008 Proof	5,000	Value: 50.00				

Note: Also exists as a Piedfort, P103

Date	Mintage	F	VF	XF	Unc	BU
2009	50,000	—	—	—	—	50.00
2009 Proof	20,000	Value: 60.00				
2010	50,000	—	—	—	—	50.00
2010 Proof	20,000	Value: 60.00				

KM# 1113b   POUND
16.6190 g., 0.9167 Gold 0.4898 oz. AGW, 22.5 mm. **Ruler:** Elizabeth II **Obv:** Head in tiara right **Rev:** Shield of the Royal Arms

Date	Mintage	F	VF	XF	Unc	BU
2008 Proof	860	Value: 1,100				
2009 Proof	1,000	Value: 1,050				

KM# 993b   POUND
19.6000 g., 0.9167 Gold 0.5776 oz. AGW, 22.5 mm. **Ruler:** Elizabeth II **Subject:** United Kingdom **Obv:** Head with tiara right **Rev:** Royal Arms with supporters **Edge:** Reeded and lettered **Edge Lettering:** DECUS ET TUTAMEN

Date	Mintage	F	VF	XF	Unc	BU
2008 Proof	Est. 2,008	Value: 1,100				

KM# 1113c   POUND
Platinum APW, 22.5 mm. **Ruler:** Elizabeth II **Obv:** Head in tiara right **Rev:** Shield of the Royal Arms

Date	Mintage	F	VF	XF	Unc	BU
2008 Proof	—	Value: 1,650				

KM# 1158   POUND
9.5000 g., Nickel-Brass, 22.5 mm. **Ruler:** Elizabeth II **Obv:** Head with tiara right **Rev:** City of London arms, three smaller arms below **Edge:** Reeded and lettered **Edge Lettering:** DOMINE DIRIGE NOS

Date	Mintage	F	VF	XF	Unc	BU
2010	—	—	—	3.00	6.00	7.50
2010 Proof	—	Value: 10.00				

KM# 1158a   POUND
9.5000 g., 0.9250 Silver 0.2825 oz. ASW, 22.5 mm. **Ruler:** Elizabeth II **Obv:** Head with tiara right **Rev:** City of London arms, three smaller arms below

Date	Mintage	F	VF	XF	Unc	BU
2010 Proof	20,000	Value: 60.00				

Note: Also exists as a Piedfort, P75

KM# 1158b   POUND
19.6190 g., 0.9167 Gold 0.5782 oz. AGW, 22.5 mm. **Ruler:** Elizabeth II **Obv:** Head with tiara right **Rev:** City of London arms, three smaller arms below

Date	Mintage	F	VF	XF	Unc	BU
2010 Proof	2,500	Value: 1,100				

KM# 1159   POUND
9.5000 g., Nickel-Brass, 22.5 mm. **Ruler:** Elizabeth II **Obv:** Head with tiara right **Rev:** City of Belfast arms, three smaller arms below **Edge:** Reeded and lettered **Edge Lettering:** PRO TANTO QUID RETRIBUAMUS

Date	Mintage	F	VF	XF	Unc	BU
2010	—	—	—	3.00	6.00	7.50
2010 Proof	—	Value: 10.00				

KM# 1159a POUND
9.5000 g., 0.9250 Silver 0.2825 oz. ASW, 22.5 mm. **Ruler:** Elizabeth II **Obv:** Head with tiara right **Rev:** City of Belfast arms, three smaller arms below

Date	Mintage	F	VF	XF	Unc	BU
2010 Proof	20,000	Value: 60.00				

Note: Also exists as a Piedfort, P76

KM# 1159b POUND
19.6190 g., 0.9167 Gold 0.5782 oz. AGW, 22.5 mm. **Ruler:** Elizabeth II **Obv:** Head with tiara right **Rev:** City of Belfast arms, three smaller arms below

Date	Mintage	F	VF	XF	Unc	BU
2010 Proof	2,500	Value: 1,100				

KM# 1197 POUND
9.5000 g., Nickel-Brass, 22.5 mm. **Ruler:** Elizabeth II **Obv:** Head with tiara right **Rev:** Edinburgh city arms, three smaller arms below **Edge:** Reeded and lettered **Edge Lettering:** NISI DOMINUS FRUSTRA

Date	Mintage	F	VF	XF	Unc	BU
2011	—	—	—	3.00	6.00	7.50
2011 Proof	—	Value: 10.00				

KM# 1197a POUND
9.5000 g., 0.9250 Silver 0.2825 oz. ASW, 22.5 mm. **Ruler:** Elizabeth II **Obv:** Head with tiara right **Rev:** Edinburgh City arms, three smaller arms below

Date	Mintage	F	VF	XF	Unc	BU
2011 Proof	—	Value: 45.00				

Note: Also exists as a Piedfort, P83

KM# 1198 POUND
9.5000 g., Nickel-Brass, 22.5 mm. **Ruler:** Elizabeth II **Obv:** Head with tiara right **Rev:** Cardiff city arms, three smaller arms below **Edge:** Reeded and lettered **Edge Lettering:** DDRAIG GOCH DDYRY CYCHWYN

Date	Mintage	F	VF	XF	Unc	BU
2011	—	—	—	3.00	6.00	7.50
2011 Proof	—	Value: 10.00				

KM# 1198a POUND
9.5000 g., 0.9250 Silver 0.2825 oz. ASW, 22.5 mm. **Ruler:** Elizabeth II **Obv:** Head with tiara right **Rev:** Cardiff city arms, three smaller arms below

Date	Mintage	F	VF	XF	Unc	BU
2011 Proof	—	Value: 45.00				

Note: Also exists as a Piedfort, P84

KM# 1113a.1 POUND
9.5000 g., 0.9250 Silver partially gilt 0.2825 oz. ASW, 22.5 mm. **Ruler:** Elizabeth II **Obv:** Head with tiara right **Rev:** Shield of the Royal Arms

Date	Mintage	F	VF	XF	Unc	BU
2012 Proof	—	Value: 60.00				

KM# 994 2 POUNDS
12.0000 g., Bi-Metallic Copper-Nickel center in Nickel-Brass ring, 28.4 mm. **Ruler:** Elizabeth II **Subject:** Technology **Obv:** Head with tiara right **Rev:** Symbolic depiction in concentric circles of technological development from the Iron Age to the Internet **Edge Lettering:** STANDING ON THE SHOULDERS OF GIANTS

Date	Mintage	F	VF	XF	Unc	BU
2001	34,984,750	—	—	5.00	9.50	12.00
2001 Proof	—	Value: 12.00				
2002	13,024,750	—	—	5.00	9.50	12.00
2002 Proof	—	Value: 12.00				
2003	17,531,250	—	—	5.00	9.50	12.00
2003 Proof	43,513	Value: 12.00				
2004	11,981,500	—	—	5.00	9.50	12.00
2004 Proof	35,020	Value: 12.00				
2005	3,837,250	—	—	5.00	9.50	12.00
2005 Proof	40,563	Value: 12.00				
2006	16,715,000	—	—	5.00	9.50	12.00
2006 Proof	—	Value: 12.00				

Date	Mintage	F	VF	XF	Unc	BU
2007	10,270,000	—	—	5.00	9.50	12.00
2007 Proof	—	Value: 12.00				
2008	30,107,000	—	—	5.00	9.50	12.00
2008 Proof	—	Value: 12.00				
2009	8,775,000	—	—	5.00	9.50	12.00
2009 Proof	—	Value: 12.00				
2010	2,015,000	—	—	5.00	9.50	12.00
2010 Proof	—	Value: 12.00				
2011	—	—	—	5.00	9.50	12.00
2011 Proof	—	Value: 12.00				
2012	—	—	—	5.00	9.50	12.00
2012 Proof	—	Value: 12.00				

KM# 1014 2 POUNDS
11.9700 g., Bi-Metallic Copper-Nickel center in Nickel-Brass ring, 28.35 mm. **Ruler:** Elizabeth II **Subject:** First Transatlantic Radio Transmission **Obv:** Head with tiara right within circle **Rev:** Symbolic design **Edge:** Reeded and inscribed **Edge Lettering:** WIRELESS BRIDGES THE ATLANTIC... MARCONI... 1901

Date	Mintage	F	VF	XF	Unc	BU
2001	4,558,000	—	—	5.00	9.50	12.00
2001 Proof	—	Value: 12.00				

KM# 1014a 2 POUNDS
12.0000 g., 0.9250 Silver with gilt ring 0.3569 oz. ASW, 28.4 mm. **Ruler:** Elizabeth II **Subject:** First Transatlantic Radio Transmission **Obv:** Head with tiara right within circle **Rev:** Symbolic design **Edge Lettering:** WIRELESS BRIDGES THE ATLANTIC...MARCONI 1901...

Date	Mintage	F	VF	XF	Unc	BU
2001 Proof	11,488	Value: 45.00				

Note: Also exists as a Piefort, P106

KM# 1014b 2 POUNDS
15.9700 g., 0.9166 Gold Yellow gold plated Red Gold center in Red Gold ring 0.4706 oz. AGW, 28.4 mm. **Ruler:** Elizabeth II **Subject:** First Transatlantic Radio Transmission **Obv:** Head with tiara right **Rev:** Symbolic design

Date	Mintage	F	VF	XF	Unc	BU
2001 Proof	1,658	Value: 875				

KM# 994c 2 POUNDS
15.9800 g., 0.9167 Gold 0.4710 oz. AGW, 28.35 mm. **Ruler:** Elizabeth II **Subject:** Technology **Obv:** Head with tiara right **Rev:** Symbolic depiction in concentric circles of technological development from the Iron Age to the Internet

Date	Mintage	F	VF	XF	Unc	BU
2002 Proof	—	Value: 875				

KM# 1031 2 POUNDS
12.0000 g., Bi-Metallic Copper-Nickel center in Nickel-Brass ring, 28.4 mm. **Ruler:** Elizabeth II **Subject:** 17th Commonwealth Games - Manchester, England **Obv:** Head with tiara right **Rev:** Runner breaking ribbon at finish line, national flag of England in circle behind athlete **Edge:** Reeded and lettered **Edge Lettering:** SPIRIT OF FRIENDSHIP MANCHESTER 2002

Date	Mintage	F	VF	XF	Unc	BU
2002	650,500	—	—	6.00	12.00	15.00
2002 Proof	—	Value: 15.00				

KM# 1031a 2 POUNDS
12.0000 g., 0.9250 Silver Silver center in Gold plated ring 0.3569 oz. ASW, 28.4 mm. **Ruler:** Elizabeth II **Subject:** Commonwealth Games - England **Obv:** Head with tiara right **Rev:** Runner breaking ribbon at finish line **Edge:** Reeded and lettered

Date	Mintage	F	VF	XF	Unc	BU
2002 Proof	10,000	Value: 45.00				

Note: Also exists as a Piefort, P107

KM# 1031b 2 POUNDS
15.9800 g., 0.9160 Gold Yellow gold center in Red Gold ring 0.4706 oz. AGW, 28.4 mm. **Ruler:** Elizabeth II **Subject:** Commonwealth Games - England **Obv:** Head with tiara right **Rev:** Runner breaking ribbon at finish line **Edge:** Reeded and lettered

Date	Mintage	F	VF	XF	Unc	BU
2002 Proof	500	Value: 750				

KM# 1032 2 POUNDS
12.0000 g., Bi-Metallic Copper-Nickel center in Nickel-Brass ring, 28.4 mm. **Ruler:** Elizabeth II **Subject:** 17th Commonwealth Games - Manchester, England **Obv:** Head with tiara right **Rev:** Runner breaking ribbon at finish line, national flag of Scotland in circle behind athlete **Edge:** Reeded and lettered

Date	Mintage	F	VF	XF	Unc	BU
2002	771,750	—	—	6.00	12.00	15.00
2002 Proof	—	Value: 15.00				

KM# 1032a 2 POUNDS
12.0000 g., 0.9250 Silver Silver center with Gold plated ring 0.3569 oz. ASW, 28.4 mm. **Ruler:** Elizabeth II **Subject:** Commonwealth Games - Scotland **Obv:** Head with tiara right **Rev:** Runner breaking ribbon at finish line **Edge:** Reeded and lettered

Date	Mintage	F	VF	XF	Unc	BU
2002 Proof	10,000	Value: 35.00				

Note: Also exists as a Piefort, P108

KM# 1032b 2 POUNDS
15.9800 g., 0.9160 Gold Yellow gold center in Red Gold ring 0.4706 oz. AGW, 28.4 mm. **Ruler:** Elizabeth II **Subject:** Commonwealth Games - Scotland **Obv:** Head with tiara right **Rev:** Runner breaking ribbon at finish line **Edge:** Reeded and lettered

Date	Mintage	F	VF	XF	Unc	BU
2002 Proof	500	Value: 875				

KM# 1033 2 POUNDS
12.0000 g., Bi-Metallic Copper-Nickel center in Nickel-Brass ring, 28.4 mm. **Ruler:** Elizabeth II **Subject:** 17th Commonwealth Games - Manchester, England **Obv:** Head with tiara right **Rev:** Runner breaking ribbon at finish line, national flag of Wales in circle behind athlete **Edge:** Reeded and lettered **Edge Lettering:** SPIRIT OF FRIENDSHIP MANCHESTER 2002

Date	Mintage	F	VF	XF	Unc	BU
2002	588,500	—	—	6.00	12.00	15.00
2002 Proof	—	Value: 15.00				

KM# 1033a 2 POUNDS
12.0000 g., 0.9250 Silver Silver center in Gold plated ring 0.3569 oz. ASW, 28.4 mm. **Ruler:** Elizabeth II **Subject:** Commonwealth Games - Wales **Obv:** Head with tiara right **Rev:** Runner breaking ribbon at finish line **Edge:** Reeded and lettered

Date	Mintage	F	VF	XF	Unc	BU
2002 Proof	10,000	Value: 35.00				

Note: Also exists as a Piefort, P109

KM# 1033b 2 POUNDS
15.9800 g., 0.9160 Gold Yellow Gold center in Red Gold ring 0.4706 oz. AGW, 28.4 mm. **Ruler:** Elizabeth II **Subject:** Commonwealth Games - Wales **Obv:** Head with tiara right **Rev:** Runner breaking ribbon at finish line **Edge:** Reeded and lettered

Date	Mintage	F	VF	XF	Unc	BU
2002 Proof	500	Value: 875				

KM# 1034 2 POUNDS
12.0000 g., Bi-Metallic Copper-Nickel center in Nickel-Brass ring, 28.4 mm. **Ruler:** Elizabeth II **Subject:** 17th Commonwealth Games - Manchester, England **Obv:** Head with tiara right **Rev:** Runner breaking ribbon at finish line, national flag of Northern Ireland in circle behind athlete **Edge:** Reeded and lettered **Edge Lettering:** SPIRIT OF FRIENDSHIP MANCHESTER 2002

Date	Mintage	F	VF	XF	Unc	BU
2002	485,500	—	—	6.00	12.00	15.00
2002 Proof	—	Value: 15.00				

KM# 1034a   2 POUNDS
12.0000 g., 0.9250 Silver Silver center in Gold plated ring 0.3569 oz. ASW, 28.4 mm. **Ruler:** Elizabeth II **Subject:** Commonwealth Games - Northern Ireland **Obv:** Head with tiara right **Rev:** Runner breaking ribbon at finish line **Edge:** Reeded and lettered

Date	Mintage	F	VF	XF	Unc	BU
2002 Proof	10,000			Value: 35.00		

Note: Also exists as a Piefort, P110

KM# 1034b   2 POUNDS
15.9800 g., 0.9160 Gold Yellow Gold center in Red Gold ring 0.4706 oz. AGW, 28.4 mm. **Ruler:** Elizabeth II **Subject:** Commonwealth Games - Northern Ireland **Obv:** Head with tiara right **Rev:** Runner breaking ribbon at finish line **Edge:** Reeded and lettered

Date	Mintage	F	VF	XF	Unc	BU
2002 Proof	500			Value: 875		

KM# 1037   2 POUNDS
12.0000 g., Bi-Metallic Copper-Nickel center in Nickel-Brass ring, 28.4 mm. **Ruler:** Elizabeth II **Subject:** 50th Anniversary of the Discovery of DNA **Obv:** Head with tiara right **Rev:** DNA Double Helix **Edge:** Reeded and inscribed **Edge Lettering:** DEOXYRIBONUCLEIC ACID

Date	Mintage	F	VF	XF	Unc	BU
ND(2003)	4,299,000	—	—	6.00	12.00	15.00
ND(2003) Proof	43,513			Value: 15.00		

KM# 1037a   2 POUNDS
12.0000 g., 0.9250 Silver Silver center in Gold plated ring 0.3569 oz. ASW, 28.4 mm. **Ruler:** Elizabeth II **Obv:** Head with tiara right **Rev:** DNA Double Helix **Edge:** Reeded and lettered

Date	Mintage	F	VF	XF	Unc	BU
ND(2003) Proof	11,204			Value: 35.00		

Note: Also exists as a Piefort, P42

KM# 1037b   2 POUNDS
15.9800 g., 0.9167 Gold Yellow gold center in Red gold ring 0.4710 oz. AGW, 28.4 mm. **Ruler:** Elizabeth II **Obv:** Head with tiara right **Rev:** DNA Double Helix **Edge:** Reeded and lettered

Date	Mintage	F	VF	XF	Unc	BU
ND2003 Proof	1,500			Value: 875		

KM# 1049   2 POUNDS
12.0000 g., Bi-Metallic Nickel-Brass center in Copper-Nickel ring, 28.4 mm. **Ruler:** Elizabeth II **Subject:** Richard Trevithick, Inventor of the First Steam Locomotive **Obv:** Head with tiara right **Rev:** First steam locomotive **Rev. Legend:** 2004 R. TREVITHICK 1804 INVENTION-INDUSTRY-PROGRESS **Edge:** Incuse railway line motif

Date	Mintage	F	VF	XF	Unc	BU
2004	5,004,500	—	—	6.00	12.00	15.00
2004 Proof	35,020			Value: 15.00		

KM# 1049a   2 POUNDS
12.0000 g., 0.9250 Silver Silver center in Gold plated ring 0.3569 oz. ASW, 28.4 mm. **Ruler:** Elizabeth II **Obv:** Head with tiara right **Rev:** First steam locomotive **Rev. Legend:** 2004 R. TREVITHICK 1804 INVENTION-INDUSTRY-PROGRESS **Edge:** Incuse railway line motif

Date	Mintage	F	VF	XF	Unc	BU
2004	1,923	—	—	—	—	50.00

Note: Also exists as a Piefort, P45

Date	Mintage	F	VF	XF	Unc	BU
2004 Proof	19,233			Value: 35.00		

KM# 1049b   2 POUNDS
15.9800 g., 0.9166 Gold Yellow Gold center in Red Gold ring 0.4709 oz. AGW, 28.4 mm. **Ruler:** Elizabeth II **Obv:** Head with tiara right **Rev:** First steam locomotive **Rev. Legend:** 2004 R. TREVITHICK 1804 INVENTION-INDUSTRY-PROGRESS **Edge:** Incuse railway line motif

Date	Mintage	F	VF	XF	Unc	BU
2004 Proof	1,500			Value: 875		

KM# 1052   2 POUNDS
12.0000 g., Bi-Metallic Nickel-Brass center in Copper-Nickel ring, 28.4 mm. **Ruler:** Elizabeth II **Subject:** 400th Anniversary - The Gunpowder Plot **Obv:** Head with tiara right **Rev:** Circular design of Royal scepters, swords and crosiers **Edge:** Reeded and lettered **Edge Lettering:** REMEMBER REMEMBER THE FIFTH OF NOVEMBER

Date	Mintage	F	VF	XF	Unc	BU
ND (2005)	5,140,500	—	—	6.00	12.00	15.00
ND(2005) Proof	40,563			Value: 15.00		

Note: Also exists as a Piefort, P46

KM# 1056   2 POUNDS
Bi-Metallic Nickel-Brass center in Copper-Nickel ring, 28.4 mm. **Ruler:** Elizabeth II **Subject:** 60th Anniversary of the End of WW II **Obv:** Head with tiara right **Rev:** St. Paul's Cathedral amid search light beams **Edge:** Reeded and lettered **Edge Lettering:** IN VICTORY MAGNANIMITY IN PEACE GOODWILL

Date	Mintage	F	VF	XF	Unc	BU
ND (2005)	10,191,000	—	—	6.00	12.00	15.00

KM# 1056a   2 POUNDS
12.0000 g., 0.9250 Silver Silver center in Gold-plated ring 0.3569 oz. ASW, 28.4 mm. **Ruler:** Elizabeth II **Subject:** 60th Anniversary of the End of WWII **Obv:** Crowned head right **Rev:** St. Paul's Cathedral amid search light beams **Edge:** Reeded and lettered **Edge Lettering:** IN VICTORY MAGNANIMITY IN PEACE GOODWILL

Date	Mintage	F	VF	XF	Unc	BU
ND(2005) Proof	21,734			Value: 35.00		

Note: Also exists as a Piefort, P49

KM# 1056b   2 POUNDS
15.9700 g., 0.9167 Gold 0.4707 oz. AGW, 28.4 mm. **Ruler:** Elizabeth II **Subject:** 60th Anniversary of the End of WWII **Obv:** Crowned head right **Rev:** St. Paul's Cathedral amid search light beams **Edge:** Reeded and lettered **Edge Lettering:** IN VICTORY MAGNANIMITY IN PEACE GOODWILL

Date	Mintage	F	VF	XF	Unc	BU
ND(2005) Proof	2,924			Value: 875		

KM# 994a   2 POUNDS
12.0000 g., 0.9250 Silver 0.3569 oz. ASW, 28.35 mm. **Ruler:** Elizabeth II **Subject:** Technology **Obv:** Head with tiara right **Rev:** Symbolic depiction in concentric circles of technological development from the Iron Age to the Internet **Note:** Gold plated silver ring, silver center.

Date	Mintage	F	VF	XF	Unc	BU
2006 Proof	—			Value: 45.00		

KM# 1060   2 POUNDS
12.0000 g., Bi-Metallic Copper-Nickel center in Nickel-Brass ring, 28.4 mm. **Ruler:** Elizabeth II **Subject:** 200th Birthday of Engineer Isambard Kingdom Brunel **Obv:** Head with tiara right **Rev:** Isambard Brunel **Edge Lettering:** 1806-1859 ISAMBARD KINGDOM BRUNEL ENGINEER

Date	Mintage	F	VF	XF	Unc	BU
2006	7,925,250	—	—	—	16.00	20.00
2006 Proof	Est. 50,000			Value: 20.00		

KM# 1061   2 POUNDS
12.0000 g., Bi-Metallic Copper-Nickel center in Nickel-Brass ring, 28.4 mm. **Ruler:** Elizabeth II **Subject:** Engineering Achievements of Isambard Kingdom Brunel **Obv:** Head with tiara right **Rev:** Paddington Station structural supports **Edge Lettering:** SO MANY IRONS IN THE FIRE

Date	Mintage	F	VF	XF	Unc	BU
2006	7,452,250	—	—	—	16.00	20.00
2006 Proof	Est. 50,000			Value: 20.00		

KM# 1060a   2 POUNDS
12.0000 g., 0.9250 Silver with gilt ring 0.3569 oz. ASW, 28.4 mm. **Ruler:** Elizabeth II **Subject:** Brunel's 200th Birthday **Obv:** Head with tiara right **Rev:** Brunel and gears

Date	Mintage	F	VF	XF	Unc	BU
2006 Proof	—			Value: 55.00		

Note: Also exists as a Piefort, P56

KM# 1060b   2 POUNDS
15.9800 g., 0.9160 Gold Yellow Gold center in Red Gold ring 0.4706 oz. AGW, 28.4 mm. **Ruler:** Elizabeth II **Subject:** Brunel's 200th Birthday **Obv:** Head with tiara right **Rev:** Brunel and gears

Date	Mintage	F	VF	XF	Unc	BU
2006 Proof	—			Value: 875		

KM# 1061a   2 POUNDS
12.0000 g., 0.9250 Silver center in gilt ring 0.3569 oz. ASW, 28.4 mm. **Ruler:** Elizabeth II **Subject:** Brunel's engineering achievements **Obv:** Head with tiara right **Rev:** Archways

Date	Mintage	F	VF	XF	Unc	BU
2006 Proof	—			Value: 55.00		

Note: Also exists as a Piefort, P57

KM# 1061b   2 POUNDS
15.9800 g., 0.9160 Gold Yellow Gold center in Red Gold ring 0.4706 oz. AGW, 28.4 mm. **Ruler:** Elizabeth II **Subject:** Brunel's engineering achievements **Obv:** Head with tiara right **Rev:** Archways

Date	Mintage	F	VF	XF	Unc	BU
2006 Proof	—			Value: 875		

KM# 1075   2 POUNDS
12.0000 g., Bi-Metallic Copper-Nickel center in Brass ring, 28.4 mm. **Ruler:** Elizabeth II **Subject:** 200th Anniversary of the Abolition of the Slave Trade **Obv:** Bust right **Rev:** Chain crossing 1807 date **Edge:** Reeded and lettered **Edge Lettering:** AM I NOT A MAN AND A BROTHER

Date	Mintage	F	VF	XF	Unc	BU
2007	8,445,000	—	—	6.00	12.50	15.00
2007 Proof	Est. 50,000			Value: 15.00		

KM# 1075a   2 POUNDS
12.0000 g., 0.9250 Silver center in Gold plated ring 0.3569 oz. ASW, 28.4 mm. **Ruler:** Elizabeth II **Subject:** Abolition of the Slave Trade **Obv:** Elizabeth II right **Rev:** Zero in 1807 date as a broken chain link **Edge:** Reeded and lettered **Edge Lettering:** AM I NOT A MAN AND A BROTHER

Date	Mintage	F	VF	XF	Unc	BU
2007 Proof	7,095			Value: 55.00		

Note: Also exists as a Piefort, P61

KM# 1075b   2 POUNDS
15.9700 g., 0.9166 Gold Yellow Gold center in Red Gold ring 0.4706 oz. AGW, 28.4 mm. **Ruler:** Elizabeth II **Subject:** Abolition of the Slave Trade **Obv:** Head with tiara right **Rev:** Zero in 1807 date as a broken chain link **Edge:** Reeded and lettered **Edge Lettering:** AM I NOT A MAN AND A BROTHER

Date	Mintage	F	VF	XF	Unc	BU
2007 Proof	1,000			Value: 875		

KM# 1076   2 POUNDS
12.0000 g., Bi-Metallic Copper-Nickel center in Nickel-Brass ring, 28.4 mm. **Ruler:** Elizabeth II **Subject:** 300th Anniversary of the Act of Union of England and Scotland **Obv:** Head with tiara right **Rev:** Combination of British and Scottish arms **Edge:** Reeded and lettered **Edge Lettering:** UNITED INTO ONE KINGDOM

Date	Mintage	F	VF	XF	Unc	BU
2007	7,545,000	—	—	6.00	12.50	15.00
2007 Proof	Est. 50,000			Value: 15.00		

KM# 1076a   2 POUNDS
12.0000 g., 0.9250 Silver center in Gold Plated ring 0.3569 oz. ASW, 28.4 mm. **Ruler:** Elizabeth II **Subject:** 300th Anniv. Union of Scotland and England **Obv:** Head with tiara right **Rev:** Combined English and Scottish arms **Edge:** Reeded and lettered

Date	Mintage	F	VF	XF	Unc	BU
2007 Proof	8,310			Value: 55.00		

Note: Also exists as a Piefort, P62

KM# 1076b   2 POUNDS
15.9800 g., 0.9166 Gold Yellow Gold center in Red Gold ring 0.4709 oz. AGW, 28.4 mm. **Ruler:** Elizabeth II **Subject:** 300th Anniv. Union of Scotland and England **Obv:** Head with tiara right **Rev:** Combined English and Scottish arms **Edge:** Reeded and lettered

Date	Mintage	F	VF	XF	Unc	BU
2007 Proof	750			Value: 875		

KM# 1105   2 POUNDS
12.0000 g., Bi-Metallic Copper-nickel center in brass ring, 28.4 mm. **Ruler:** Elizabeth II **Subject:** London 1908 - Olympics **Obv:** Head with tiara right **Rev:** Sprint track **Edge:** Lettered and reeded **Edge Lettering:** THE 4TH OLYMPIAD LONDON

Date	Mintage	F	VF	XF	Unc	BU
2008	910,000	—	—	6.00	15.00	12.50
2008 Proof	—	Value: 15.00				

KM# 1106   2 POUNDS
12.0000 g., Bi-Metallic Copper-Nickel center in Brass ring, 28.4 mm. **Ruler:** Elizabeth II **Subject:** Beijing - London Olympic Flag handoff **Obv:** Head with tiara right **Rev:** London 2012 Games Flag hand off **Edge Lettering:** I CALL UPON THE YOUTH OF THE WORLD

Date	Mintage	F	VF	XF	Unc	BU
2008	918,000	—	—	—	18.00	22.00
2008 Proof	Est. 250,000	Value: 45.00				

KM# 1106a   2 POUNDS
12.0000 g., 0.9250 Silver Silver center in Gilt ring 0.3569 oz. ASW, 28.4 mm. **Ruler:** Elizabeth II **Obv:** Head with tiara right **Rev:** Handoff of the Olympic Flag

Date	Mintage	F	VF	XF	Unc	BU
2008 Proof	—	Value: 55.00				

Note: Also exists as a Piefort, P65

KM# 1106b   2 POUNDS
15.9800 g., 0.9160 Gold 0.4706 oz. AGW, 28.4 mm. **Ruler:** Elizabeth II **Subject:** Countdown to 2010 London Olympics **Obv:** Head right **Rev:** Handoff of the Olympic flag **Edge Lettering:** I CALL UPON THE YOUTH OF THE WORLD

Date	Mintage	F	VF	XF	Unc	BU
2009 Proof	3,000	Value: 875				

KM# 1115   2 POUNDS
12.0000 g., Bi-Metallic Copper-Nickel center in Nickel-Brass ring., 28.4 mm. **Ruler:** Elizabeth II **Subject:** Charles Darwin, 200th Anniversary of Birth **Obv:** Head with tiara right **Rev:** Darwin and ape heads facing **Edge Lettering:** ON THE ORIGIN OF SPECIES 1859

Date	Mintage	F	VF	XF	Unc	BU
2009	3,903,000	—	—	—	16.00	20.00
2009 Proof	—	Value: 25.00				

KM# 1115a   2 POUNDS
12.0000 g., 0.9250 Silver Silver center in Gilt ring 0.3569 oz. ASW, 28.4 mm. **Ruler:** Elizabeth II **Subject:** Charles Darwin, 200th Anniversary of Brith **Obv:** Head with tiara right **Rev:** Darwin and ape heads facing

Date	Mintage	F	VF	XF	Unc	BU
2009 Proof	—	Value: 55.00				

Note: Also exists as a Piefort, P66

KM# 1115b   2 POUNDS
15.9800 g., 0.9160 Gold Yellow Gold center in Red Gold ring 0.4706 oz. AGW, 28.4 mm. **Ruler:** Elizabeth II **Subject:** Charles Darwin, 200th Anniversary of Birth **Obv:** Head with tiara right **Rev:** Darwin and ape heads facing

Date	Mintage	F	VF	XF	Unc	BU
2009 Proof	—	Value: 875				

KM# 1116   2 POUNDS
12.0000 g., Bi-Metallic Copper-Nickel center in Nickel-Brass ring, 28.4 mm. **Ruler:** Elizabeth II **Subject:** Robert Burns, 250th Anniversary of Birth **Obv:** Head with tiara right **Rev:** Reeded and lettered **Edge Lettering:** SHOULD AULD ACQUAINTANCE BE FORGOT

Date	Mintage	F	VF	XF	Unc	BU
2009	3,253,000	—	—	—	16.00	20.00
2009 Proof	—	Value: 25.00				

KM# 1116a   2 POUNDS
12.0000 g., 0.9250 Silver Sivler center in Gilt ring 0.3569 oz. ASW, 28.4 mm. **Ruler:** Elizabeth II **Subject:** Robert Burns, 250th Anniversary of Birth **Obv:** Head with tiara right **Rev:** Text

Date	Mintage	F	VF	XF	Unc	BU
2009 Proof	—	Value: 55.00				

Note: Also exists as a Piefort, P

KM# 1116b   2 POUNDS
15.9700 g., 0.9167 Gold Yellow Gold center in Red Gold ring 0.4707 oz. AGW, 28.4 mm. **Ruler:** Elizabeth II **Subject:** Robert Burns, 250th Anniversary of Birth **Obv:** Head with tiara right **Rev:** Text

Date	Mintage	F	VF	XF	Unc	BU
2009 Proof	1,000	Value: 875				

KM# 1160   2 POUNDS
11.9700 g., Bi-Metallic Copper-Nickel center in Nickel-Brass ring, 28.35 mm. **Ruler:** Elizabeth II **Subject:** Florence Nightingale, 100th Anniversary of Death **Obv:** Head with tiara right **Rev:** Hand taking pulse **Edge Lettering:** 150 YEARS OF NURSING

Date	Mintage	F	VF	XF	Unc	BU
2010	—	—	—	6.00	12.00	15.00
2010 Proof	—	Value: 15.00				

KM# 1199   2 POUNDS
11.9700 g., Bi-Metallic Copper-Nickel center in Nickel-Brass ring, 28.4 mm. **Ruler:** Elizabeth II **Subject:** Mary Rose, 500th Anniversary **Obv:** Head with tiara right **Rev:** H.M.S. Mary Rose under sail **Edge:** Reeded and lettered **Edge Lettering:** YOUR NOBLEST SHIPPE 1511

Date	Mintage	F	VF	XF	Unc	BU
2011	—	—	—	6.00	12.00	15.00

KM# 1199a   2 POUNDS
12.0000 g., 0.9250 Silver center in Gilt ring 0.3569 oz. ASW, 28.4 mm. **Ruler:** Elizabeth II **Subject:** Mary Rose, 500th Anniversary **Obv:** Head with tiara right **Rev:** H.M.S. Mary Rose under sail

Date	Mintage	F	VF	XF	Unc	BU
2011 Proof	—	Value: 55.00				

Note: Also exists as a Piefort, P87

KM# 1199b   2 POUNDS
15.9800 g., 0.9166 Gold Yellow Gold center in Red Gold ring 0.4709 oz. AGW, 28.4 mm. **Ruler:** Elizabeth II **Subject:** Mary Rose, 500th Anniversary **Obv:** Head with tiara right **Rev:** H.M.S. Mary Rose under sail

Date	Mintage	F	VF	XF	Unc	BU
2011 Proof	—	Value: 875				

KM# 1200   2 POUNDS
11.9700 g., Bi-Metallic Copper-Nickel center in Nickel-Brass ring, 28.4 mm. **Ruler:** Elizabeth II **Subject:** King James Bible, 500th Anniversary **Obv:** Head in tiara right **Rev:** Lead type and printed page of bible text **Edge:** Reeded and lettered **Edge Lettering:** THE AUTHORIZED VERSION

Date	Mintage	F	VF	XF	Unc	BU
2011	—	—	—	6.00	12.00	15.00
2011 Proof	—	Value: 15.00				

KM# 1200a   2 POUNDS
12.0000 g., 0.9250 Silver center in Gilt ring 0.3569 oz. ASW, 28.4 mm. **Ruler:** Elizabeth II **Subject:** King James Bible, 500th Anniversary **Obv:** Head with tiara right **Rev:** Lead type and printed page

Date	Mintage	F	VF	XF	Unc	BU
2011 Proof	—	Value: 55.00				

Note: Also exists as a Piefort, P88

KM# 994a.1   2 POUNDS
12.0000 g., 0.9250 Silver partially gilt 0.3569 oz. ASW, 28.35 mm. **Ruler:** Elizabeth II **Obv:** Head with tiara right **Rev:** Symbolic depictions of technological development

Date	Mintage	F	VF	XF	Unc	BU
2012 Proof	—	Value: 50.00				

KM# 1015   5 POUNDS
28.2800 g., Copper-Nickel, 38.6 mm. **Ruler:** Elizabeth II **Subject:** Centennial of Queen Victoria's death **Obv:** Head with tiara right **Rev:** Young portrait from stamp, within industrial "V" **Edge:** Reeded

Date	Mintage	F	VF	XF	Unc	BU
2001	851,491	—	—	—	15.00	18.00
2001 Proof	—	Value: 20.00				

KM# 1015a   5 POUNDS
28.2800 g., 0.9250 Silver 0.8410 oz. ASW, 38.6 mm. **Ruler:** Elizabeth II **Subject:** Centennial of Queen Victoria **Obv:** Head with tiara right **Rev:** Queen Victoria's portrait within "V"

Date	Mintage	F	VF	XF	Unc	BU
2001 Proof	—	Value: 50.00				

KM# 1015b   5 POUNDS
39.9400 g., 0.9167 Gold 1.1771 oz. AGW **Ruler:** Elizabeth II **Subject:** Centennial of Queen Victoria **Obv:** Head with tiara right **Rev:** Queen Victoria's portrait within "V"

Date	Mintage	F	VF	XF	Unc	BU
2001 Proof	1,000	Value: 2,100				

KM# 1024   5 POUNDS
28.2800 g., Copper-Nickel, 38.6 mm. **Ruler:** Elizabeth II **Subject:** Queen's Golden Jubilee of Reign **Obv:** Crowned bust in royal garb right **Rev:** Queen on horse **Edge:** Reeded

Date	Mintage	F	VF	XF	Unc	BU
2002	3,469,243	—	—	—	15.00	18.00

Note: Mintage figure includes KM#1035

Date	Mintage	F	VF	XF	Unc	BU
2002 Proof	—	Value: 20.00				

KM# 1024a   5 POUNDS
28.2800 g., 0.9250 Silver 0.8410 oz. ASW, 38.6 mm. **Ruler:** Elizabeth II **Subject:** Queen's Golden Jubilee of Reign **Obv:** Crowned bust in royal garb right **Rev:** Queen on horse **Edge:** Reeded

Date	Mintage	F	VF	XF	Unc	BU
2002 Proof	—	Value: 50.00				

KM# 1024b 5 POUNDS
39.9400 g., 0.9167 Gold 1.1771 oz. AGW, 38.6 mm. **Ruler:**
Elizabeth II **Subject:** Queen's Golden Jubilee of Reign **Obv:**
Crowned bust in royal garb right **Rev:** Queen on horse left **Edge:**
Reeded

Date	Mintage	F	VF	XF	Unc	BU
2002 Proof	—	Value: 2,100				

KM# 1035 5 POUNDS
28.2800 g., Copper-Nickel, 38.6 mm. **Ruler:** Elizabeth II
Subject: Queen Mother **Obv:** Head with tiara right **Rev:** Queen
Mother's portrait in wreath **Edge:** Reeded

Date	Mintage	F	VF	XF	Unc	BU
ND(2002)	—	—	—	—	15.00	18.00

Note: Mintage included with KM#1024.
| ND(2002) Proof | — | Value: 20.00 | | | | |

KM# 1035a 5 POUNDS
28.2800 g., Silver, 38.6 mm. **Ruler:** Elizabeth II **Subject:** Queen
Mother **Obv:** Head with tiara right **Rev:** Queen Mother's portrait
in wreath **Edge:** Reeded

Date	Mintage	F	VF	XF	Unc	BU
ND(2002) Proof	25,000	Value: 50.00				

KM# 1035b 5 POUNDS
39.9400 g., 0.9167 Gold 1.1771 oz. AGW, 38.6 mm. **Ruler:**
Elizabeth II **Subject:** Queen Mother **Obv:** Head with tiara right
Rev: Queen Mother's portrait in wreath **Edge:** Reeded

Date	Mintage	F	VF	XF	Unc	BU
ND(2002) Proof	3,000	Value: 2,100				

KM# 1038 5 POUNDS
28.2800 g., Copper-Nickel, 38.6 mm. **Ruler:** Elizabeth II
Subject: Queen's Golden Jubilee **Obv:** Queen's stylized portrait
Rev: Childlike lettering **Edge:** Reeded

Date	Mintage	F	VF	XF	Unc	BU
2003	1,307,147	—	—	—	15.00	18.00
2003 Proof	43,513	Value: 20.00				

KM# 1038a 5 POUNDS
28.2800 g., 0.9250 Silver 0.8410 oz. ASW, 38.6 mm. **Ruler:**
Elizabeth II **Subject:** Queen's Golden Jubilee **Obv:** Stylized
Queens portrait **Rev:** Childlike lettering **Edge:** Reeded

Date	Mintage	F	VF	XF	Unc	BU
2003 Proof	28,758	Value: 50.00				

KM# 1038b 5 POUNDS
39.9400 g., 0.9166 Gold 1.1770 oz. AGW, 38.6 mm. **Ruler:**
Elizabeth II **Subject:** Queen's Golden Jubilee **Obv:** Stylized
Queens portrait **Rev:** Childlike lettering **Edge:** Reeded

Date	Mintage	F	VF	XF	Unc	BU
2003 Proof	1,896	Value: 2,100				

KM# 1055 5 POUNDS
28.2800 g., Copper-Nickel, 38.6 mm. **Ruler:** Elizabeth II
Subject: Entente Cordiale **Obv:** Head with tiara right **Rev:**
Britannia and Marianne **Edge:** Reeded

Date	Mintage	F	VF	XF	Unc	BU
2004	1,205,594	—	—	—	15.00	18.00
2004 Proof	51,527	Value: 20.00				

KM# 1055a 5 POUNDS
28.2800 g., 0.9250 Silver 0.8410 oz. ASW, 38.6 mm. **Ruler:**
Elizabeth II **Subject:** Entente Cordiale **Obv:** Head with tiara right
Rev: Britannia and Marianne **Edge:** Reeded

Date	Mintage	F	VF	XF	Unc	BU
2004 Proof	11,295	Value: 50.00				

Note: Also exists as a Piefort, P47

KM# 1055b 5 POUNDS
39.9400 g., 0.9167 Gold 1.1771 oz. AGW, 38.6 mm. **Ruler:**
Elizabeth II **Subject:** Entente Cordiale **Obv:** Head with tiara right
Rev: Britannia and Marianne **Edge:** Reeded

Date	Mintage	F	VF	XF	Unc	BU
2004 Proof	926	Value: 2,100				

KM# 1055c 5 POUNDS
94.2000 g., 0.9995 Platinum 3.0270 oz. APW, 38.6 mm. **Ruler:**
Elizabeth II **Subject:** Entente Cordiale **Obv:** Head with tiara right
Rev: Britannia and Marianne **Edge:** Reeded

Date	Mintage	F	VF	XF	Unc	BU
2004 Proof	501	Value: 5,700				

KM# 1053 5 POUNDS
28.2800 g., Copper-Nickel, 38.6 mm. **Ruler:** Elizabeth II
Subject: Battle of Trafalgar **Obv:** Head with tiara right **Obv.
Legend:** ELIZABETH • II D • G • REG • F • D **Rev:** HMS Victory
and HMS Temeraire at Trafalgar **Rev. Legend:** TRAFALGAR
Edge: Reeded

Date	Mintage	F	VF	XF	Unc	BU
2005	1,075,516	—	—	—	15.00	18.00
2005 Proof	40,563	Value: 20.00				

KM# 1053a 5 POUNDS
28.2800 g., 0.9250 Silver 0.8410 oz. ASW, 38.6 mm. **Ruler:**
Elizabeth II **Subject:** Battle of Trafalgar **Obv:** Head with tiara right
Obv. Legend: ELIZABETH • II D • G • REG • F • D **Rev:** Ships
HMS Victory and Temeraire at Trafalgar **Rev. Legend:**
TRAFALGAR **Edge:** Reeded

Date	Mintage	F	VF	XF	Unc	BU
2005 Proof	21,448	Value: 50.00				

Note: Also exists as a Piefort, P51

KM# 1053b 5 POUNDS
39.9400 g., 0.9167 Gold 1.1771 oz. AGW, 38.6 mm. **Ruler:**
Elizabeth II **Subject:** Battle of Trafalgar **Obv:** Head with tiara right
Obv. Legend: ELIZABETH • II D • G • REG • F • D **Rev:** Ships
HMS Victory and Temeraire at Trafalgar **Rev. Legend:**
TRAFALGAR **Edge:** Reeded

Date	Mintage	F	VF	XF	Unc	BU
2005 Proof	1,805	Value: 2,100				

KM# 1054 5 POUNDS
28.2800 g., Copper-Nickel, 38.6 mm. **Ruler:** Elizabeth II **Obv:**
Head with tiara right **Obv. Legend:** ELIZABETH • II D • G • REG
• F • D **Rev:** Uniformed facing 1/2 bust of Admiral Horatio Nelson
Rev. Legend: HORATIO NELSON **Edge:** Reeded

Date	Mintage	F	VF	XF	Unc	BU
2005	—	—	—	—	15.00	18.00

Note: Mintage included with KM#1053b, 2005.
| 2005 Proof | 40,563 | Value: 20.00 | | | | |

KM# 1054a 5 POUNDS
28.2800 g., 0.9250 Silver 0.8410 oz. ASW, 38.6 mm. **Ruler:**
Elizabeth II **Obv:** Queen's head with tiara right **Obv. Legend:**
ELIZABETH • II D • G • REG • F • D **Rev:** Uniformed facing 1/2
bust of Admiral Horatio Nelson **Rev. Legend:** HORATIO
NELSON

Date	Mintage	F	VF	XF	Unc	BU
2005 Proof	12,852	Value: 50.00				

Note: Also exists as a Piefort, P52

KM# 1054b 5 POUNDS
39.9400 g., 0.9167 Gold 1.1771 oz. AGW, 38.6 mm. **Ruler:**
Elizabeth II **Subject:** Battle of Trafalgar **Obv:** Queen's head with
tiara right **Obv. Legend:** ELIZABETH • II D • G • REG • F • D
Rev: Uniformed facing 1/2 bust of Admiral Horatio Nelson **Rev.
Legend:** HORATIO NELSON

Date	Mintage	F	VF	XF	Unc	BU
2005 Proof	1,700	Value: 2,100				

KM# 1062 5 POUNDS
28.2800 g., Copper-Nickel, 38.6 mm. **Ruler:** Elizabeth II **Obv:**
Head with tiara right **Rev:** Three bannered trumpets **Edge:**
Reeded

Date	Mintage	F	VF	XF	Unc	BU
2006	—	—	—	—	20.00	25.00
2006 Proof	Est. 50,000	Value: 30.00				

KM# 1062a 5 POUNDS
28.2800 g., 0.9250 Silver 0.8410 oz. ASW **Ruler:** Elizabeth II
Subject: Queen's 80th Birthday Celebration **Obv:** Queens head
right **Obv. Legend:** ELIZABETH • II D • G • REG • F • D **Rev:**
Three bannered trumpets **Rev. Legend:** VIVAT REGINA **Edge:**
Reeded

Date	Mintage	F	VF	XF	Unc	BU
2006 Proof	—	Value: 50.00				

Note: Also exists as a Piefort, P58

KM# 1062b 5 POUNDS
39.9400 g., 0.9167 Gold 1.1771 oz. AGW, 38.6 mm. **Ruler:**
Elizabeth II **Subject:** Queen's 80th Birthday Celebration **Obv:**
Queen's head with tiara right **Obv. Legend:** ELIZABETH • II D •
G • REG • F • D **Rev:** Three bannered trumpets **Rev. Legend:**
VIVAT REGINA **Edge:** Reeded

Date	Mintage	F	VF	XF	Unc	BU
2006 Proof	—	Value: 2,100				

KM# 1077 5 POUNDS
28.2800 g., Copper-Nickel, 38.6 mm. **Ruler:** Elizabeth II
Subject: Queen's 60th Wedding Anniversary **Obv:** Conjoined
busts of Queen Elizabeth II and Prince Philip **Rev:** Westminster
Abbey's North Rose Window **Edge:** Reeded

Date	Mintage	F	VF	XF	Unc	BU
2007	—	—	—	—	20.00	25.00
2007 Proof	Est. 50,000	Value: 30.00				

KM# 1077a 5 POUNDS
28.2800 g., 0.9250 Silver 0.8410 oz. ASW, 38.6 mm. **Ruler:**
Elizabeth II **Subject:** 60th Wedding Anniversary **Obv:** Conjoined
busts of Queen Elizabeth II and Prince Philip **Rev:** Westminster
Abbey's North Rose Window **Edge Lettering:** MY STRENGTH
AND STAY

Date	Mintage	F	VF	XF	Unc	BU
ND (2007) Proof	Est. 35,000	Value: 50.00				

Note: Also exists as a Piefort, P63

KM# 1077b 5 POUNDS
39.9400 g., 0.9167 Gold 1.1771 oz. AGW, 28.4 mm. **Ruler:**
Elizabeth II **Subject:** 60th Wedding Anniversary **Obv:** Conjoined

busts of Queen Elizabeth II and Prince Philip **Rev:** Westminster Abbey's North Rose Window **Edge Lettering:** MY STRENGTH AND STAY

Date	Mintage	F	VF	XF	Unc	BU
ND (2007) Proof	Est. 2,500					Value: 2,100

Note: Also exists as a Piefort, P64

KM# 1103 5 POUNDS
28.2800 g., Copper-Nickel, 38.6 mm. **Ruler:** Elizabeth II **Subject:** Charles, Prince of Wales 60th Birthday **Obv:** Head with tiara right **Rev:** Head right of Prince Charles

Date	Mintage	F	VF	XF	Unc	BU
2008	500,000	—	—	—	18.00	15.00
2008 Proof					Value: 20.00	

KM# 1104 5 POUNDS
28.2800 g., Copper-Nickel, 38.6 mm. **Ruler:** Elizabeth II **Subject:** Elizabeth I Accession 1558-2008 **Obv:** Head with tiara right **Rev:** Bust of Elizabeth I

Date	Mintage	F	VF	XF	Unc	BU
2008	500,000	—	—	—	15.00	18.00
2008 Proof					Value: 20.00	

KM# 1103a 5 POUNDS
28.2800 g., Silver, 38.6 mm. **Ruler:** Elizabeth II **Subject:** Charles, Prince of Wales 60th Birthday **Obv:** Head with tiara right **Rev:** Head right of Prince Charles

Date	Mintage	F	VF	XF	Unc	BU
2008 Proof	10,398				Value: 50.00	

Note: Exists as a Piedfort, P113.

KM# 1104a 5 POUNDS
28.2800 g., Silver, 38.6 mm. **Ruler:** Elizabeth II **Subject:** Elizabeth I Accession 1558-2008 **Obv:** Head with tiara right **Rev:** Bust of Elizabeth I

Date	Mintage	F	VF	XF	Unc	BU
2008 Proof	7,446				Value: 2,100	

Note: Exists as a Piedfort, P67

KM# 1118 5 POUNDS
28.2800 g., Copper-Nickel, 38.6 mm. **Ruler:** Elizabeth II **Obv:** Head with tiara right **Rev:** Henry VIII standing, HR flanking

Date	Mintage	F	VF	XF	Unc	BU
2009 Proof	—				Value: 40.00	

KM# 1118a 5 POUNDS
28.2800 g., 0.9250 Silver 0.8410 oz. ASW, 38.6 mm. **Ruler:** Elizabeth II **Obv:** Head with tiara right **Rev:** Henry VIII standing, HR flanking

Date	Mintage	F	VF	XF	Unc	BU
2009 Proof	20,000				Value: 50.00	

Note: Also exists as a Piedfort, P70

KM# 1121 5 POUNDS
28.2800 g., Copper-Nickel, 38.61 mm. **Ruler:** Elizabeth II **Subject:** Countdown to 2012 London Olympics **Obv:** Bust right **Rev:** Swimmer, stopwatch, 3 in center

Date	Mintage	F	VF	XF	Unc	BU
2009	500,000	—	—	—	20.00	25.00
2009 Proof					Value: 30.00	

KM# 1121a 5 POUNDS
28.2800 g., 0.9250 Silver 0.8410 oz. ASW, 38.61 mm. **Ruler:** Elizabeth II **Subject:** Countdown to the 2010 London Olympics **Obv:** Bust right **Rev:** Swimmer, stopwatch, 3 in center

Date	Mintage	F	VF	XF	Unc	BU
2009 Proof	30,000				Value: 50.00	

KM# 1121b 5 POUNDS
39.9400 g., 0.9167 Gold 1.1771 oz. AGW, 38.61 mm. **Ruler:** Elizabeth II **Subject:** Countdown to 2012 London Olympics **Rev:** 3 in large stopwatch, swimmer

Date	Mintage	F	VF	XF	Unc	BU
2009 Proof	—				Value: 2,100	

KM# 1140 5 POUNDS
28.2800 g., 0.9250 Silver 0.8410 oz. ASW, 38.6 mm. **Ruler:** Elizabeth II **Subject:** London Olympics, 2012 **Obv:** Head with tiara right **Rev:** Angel of the North, blue logo

Date	Mintage	F	VF	XF	Unc	BU
2009 Proof	95,000				Value: 50.00	

KM# 1141 5 POUNDS
28.2800 g., 0.9250 Silver 0.8410 oz. ASW, 38.6 mm. **Ruler:** Elizabeth II **Subject:** London Olympics, 2012 **Obv:** Head with tiara right **Rev:** Big Ben, blue logo

Date	Mintage	F	VF	XF	Unc	BU
2009 Proof	95,000				Value: 50.00	

KM# 1141a 5 POUNDS
28.2800 g., Copper-Nickel, 38.6 mm. **Ruler:** Elizabeth II **Subject:** London Olympics, 2012 **Obv:** Head in tiara right **Rev:** Big Ben, blue logo

Date	Mintage	F	VF	XF	Unc	BU
2009 Proof	—				Value: 30.00	

KM# 1142 5 POUNDS
28.2800 g., 0.9250 Silver 0.8410 oz. ASW, 38.6 mm. **Ruler:** Elizabeth II **Subject:** London Olympics, 2012 **Obv:** Head with tiara right **Rev:** Flying Scotsman, blue logo

Date	Mintage	F	VF	XF	Unc	BU
2009 Proof	95,000				Value: 50.00	

KM# 1143 5 POUNDS
28.2800 g., 0.9250 Silver 0.8410 oz. ASW, 38.6 mm. **Ruler:** Elizabeth II **Subject:** London Olympics, 2012 **Obv:** Head with tiara right **Rev:** Globe Theatre, blue logo

Date	Mintage	F	VF	XF	Unc	BU
2009 Proof	95,000				Value: 50.00	

KM# 1144 5 POUNDS
28.2800 g., 0.9250 Silver 0.8410 oz. ASW, 38.6 mm. **Ruler:** Elizabeth II **Subject:** London Olympics, 2012 **Obv:** Head with tiara right **Rev:** Man in leg braces, Issac Newton quote, blue logo

Date	Mintage	F	VF	XF	Unc	BU
2009 Proof	95,000				Value: 50.00	

KM# 1145 5 POUNDS
28.2800 g., 0.9250 Silver 0.8410 oz. ASW, 38.6 mm. **Ruler:** Elizabeth II **Series:** London Olympics, 2012 **Obv:** Head with tiara right **Rev:** Stonehenge, blue logo

Date	Mintage	F	VF	XF	Unc	BU
2009 Proof	95,000				Value: 50.00	

KM# 1139 5 POUNDS
28.2800 g., Copper-Nickel, 38.6 mm. **Ruler:** Elizabeth II **Obv:** Head with tiara right **Rev:** Runners and stopwatch, 2 in center

Date	Mintage	F	VF	XF	Unc	BU
2010	500,000	—	—	—	20.00	25.00
2010 Proof					Value: 30.00	

KM# 1139a 5 POUNDS
28.2800 g., 0.9250 Silver 0.8410 oz. ASW, 38.6 mm. **Ruler:** Elizabeth II **Obv:** Head with tiara right **Rev:** Runners and stopwatch, 2 in center

Date	Mintage	F	VF	XF	Unc	BU
2010 Proof	—				Value: 50.00	

KM# 1139b 5 POUNDS
39.9400 g., 0.9167 Gold 1.1771 oz. AGW, 38.61 mm. **Ruler:** Elizabeth II **Subject:** Countdown to the 2012 London Olympics **Obv:** Head with tiara right **Rev:** Runners and stopwatch, 2 in center

Date	Mintage	F	VF	XF	Unc	BU
2010 Proof	—				Value: 2,100	

KM# 1146 5 POUNDS
28.2800 g., 0.9250 Silver 0.8410 oz. ASW, 38.6 mm. **Ruler:** Elizabeth II **Subject:** London Olympics, 2012 **Obv:** Head with tiara right **Rev:** Churchill figure and quote, blue logo

Date	Mintage	F	VF	XF	Unc	BU
2010 Proof	95,000				Value: 50.00	

KM# 1146a 5 POUNDS
28.2800 g., Copper-Nickel, 38.6 mm. **Ruler:** Elizabeth II **Subject:** London Olympics, 2012 **Obv:** Head with tiara right **Rev:** Churchill figure and quote, blue logo

Date	Mintage	F	VF	XF	Unc	BU
2010 Proof	—				Value: 40.00	

KM# 1147 5 POUNDS
28.2800 g., 0.9250 Silver 0.8410 oz. ASW, 38.6 mm. **Ruler:** Elizabeth II **Subject:** London Olympics, 2012 **Obv:** Head with tiara right **Rev:** Unity, flora, blue logo

Date	Mintage	F	VF	XF	Unc	BU
2010 Proof	95,000				Value: 50.00	

KM# 1148 5 POUNDS
28.2800 g., 0.9990 Silver 0.9083 oz. ASW, 38.6 mm. **Ruler:** Elizabeth II **Subject:** London Olympics, 2012 **Obv:** Head with tiara right **Rev:** Buckingham Palace and the Mall, blue logo

Date	Mintage	F	VF	XF	Unc	BU
2010 Proof	95,000	Value: 50.00				

KM# 1148a 5 POUNDS
28.2800 g., Copper-Nickel, 38.6 mm. **Ruler:** Elizabeth II **Subject:** London Olympics, 2012 **Obv:** Head with tiara right **Rev:** Buckingham Palace and the Mall, blue logo

Date	Mintage	F	VF	XF	Unc	BU
2010 Proof	—	Value: 40.00				

KM# 1149 5 POUNDS
28.2800 g., 0.9250 Silver 0.8410 oz. ASW, 38.6 mm. **Ruler:** Elizabeth II **Subject:** London Olympics, 2010 **Obv:** Head with tiara right **Rev:** Musical instruments, blue logo

Date	Mintage	F	VF	XF	Unc	BU
2010 Proof	95,000	Value: 50.00				

KM# 1151 5 POUNDS
28.2800 g., Copper-Nickel, 38.6 mm. **Ruler:** Elizabeth II **Subject:** Restoration of the Monarchy, 1660 **Obv:** Head with tiara right

Date	Mintage	F	VF	XF	Unc	BU
2010	—	—	—	—	20.00	25.00

KM# 1151a 5 POUNDS
28.2800 g., 0.9250 Silver 0.8410 oz. ASW, 38.6 mm. **Ruler:** Elizabeth II **Subject:** Restoration of the Monarchy, 1660 **Obv:** Head with tiara right

Date	Mintage	F	VF	XF	Unc	BU
2010 Proof	—	Value: 50.00				

Note: Also exists as a Piedfort, P114

KM# 1151b 5 POUNDS
39.9400 g., 0.9167 Gold 1.1771 oz. AGW, 38.61 mm. **Ruler:** Elizabeth II **Subject:** Restoration of the Monarchy, 1660 **Obv:** Head with tiara right **Rev:** Crown above wreath

Date	Mintage	F	VF	XF	Unc	BU
2010 Proof	—	Value: 2,100				

KM# 1152 5 POUNDS
28.2800 g., 0.9250 Silver 0.8410 oz. ASW, 38.6 mm. **Ruler:** Elizabeth II **Subject:** London Olympics, 2012 **Obv:** Head with tiara right **Rev:** Giants Causeway, orange logo

Date	Mintage	F	VF	XF	Unc	BU
2010 Proof	95,000	Value: 50.00				

KM# 1153 5 POUNDS
28.2800 g., 0.9250 Silver 0.8410 oz. ASW, 38.6 mm. **Ruler:** Elizabeth II **Subject:** London Olympics, 2012 **Obv:** Head with tiara right **Rev:** Coastline, orange logo

Date	Mintage	F	VF	XF	Unc	BU
2010 Proof	95,000	Value: 50.00				

KM# 1154 5 POUNDS
28.2800 g., 0.9250 Silver 0.8410 oz. ASW, 38.6 mm. **Ruler:** Elizabeth II **Subject:** London Olympics, 2012 **Obv:** Head with tiara right **Rev:** River Thames, orange logo

Date	Mintage	F	VF	XF	Unc	BU
2010 Proof	95,000	Value: 50.00				

KM# 1155 5 POUNDS
28.2800 g., 0.9250 Silver 0.8410 oz. ASW, 38.6 mm. **Ruler:** Elizabeth II **Subject:** London Olympics, 2012 **Obv:** Head with tiara right **Rev:** British flora -oak leaves and acorn, orange logo

Date	Mintage	F	VF	XF	Unc	BU
2010 Proof	95,000	Value: 50.00				

KM# 1156 5 POUNDS
28.2800 g., 0.9250 Silver 0.8410 oz. ASW, 38.6 mm. **Ruler:** Elizabeth II **Subject:** London Olympics, 2012 **Obv:** Head with tiara right **Rev:** Owl, orange logo

Date	Mintage	F	VF	XF	Unc	BU
2010 Proof	95,000	Value: 50.00				

KM# 1157 5 POUNDS
28.2800 g., 0.9250 Silver 0.8410 oz. ASW, 38.6 mm. **Ruler:** Elizabeth II **Subject:** London Olympics, 2012 **Obv:** Head with tiara right **Rev:** Weather vane, orange logo

Date	Mintage	F	VF	XF	Unc	BU
2010 Proof	95,000	Value: 50.00				

KM# 1201 5 POUNDS
28.2800 g., Copper-Nickel, 38.6 mm. **Ruler:** Elizabeth II **Subject:** Prince Philip's 90th Birthday **Obv:** Head with tiara right **Rev:** Large head of Prince Philip in profile right

Date	Mintage	F	VF	XF	Unc	BU
2011	—	—	—	—	20.00	25.00
2011 Proof	—	Value: 30.00				

KM# 1201a 5 POUNDS
28.2800 g., 0.9250 Silver 0.8410 oz. ASW, 38.6 mm. **Ruler:** Elizabeth II **Subject:** Prince Philip, 90th Birthday

Date	Mintage	F	VF	XF	Unc	BU
2011 Proof	—	Value: 50.00				

Note: Also exists as a Piedfort, P89

KM# 1201b 5 POUNDS
39.9400 g., 0.9167 Gold 1.1771 oz. AGW, 38.61 mm. **Ruler:** Elizabeth II **Subject:** Prince Philip's 90th Birthday **Obv:** Head with tiara right **Rev:** Large head of Prince Philip in profile right

Date	Mintage	F	VF	XF	Unc	BU
2011 Proof	—	Value: 2,100				

KM# 1202 5 POUNDS
28.2800 g., Copper-Nickel, 38.6 mm. **Ruler:** Elizabeth II **Subject:** Countdown to London Olympics, 2012 **Obv:** Head with tiara right **Rev:** 1 between wheels of cyclist traveling left

Date	Mintage	F	VF	XF	Unc	BU
2011	—	—	—	—	20.00	25.00
2011 Proof	—	Value: 30.00				

KM# 1202a 5 POUNDS
28.2800 g., 0.9250 Silver 0.8410 oz. ASW, 38.6 mm. **Ruler:** Elizabeth II **Subject:** Countdown to London Olympics, 2012 **Obv:** Head with tiara right **Rev:** 1 between wheels of cyclist traveling left

Date	Mintage	F	VF	XF	Unc	BU
2011 Proof	—	Value: 50.00				

KM# 1203 5 POUNDS
28.2800 g., Copper-Nickel, 38.6 mm. **Ruler:** Elizabeth II **Subject:** Royal Wedding - William and Katherine **Rev:** Heads facing

Date	Mintage	F	VF	XF	Unc	BU
2011	—	—	—	—	20.00	25.00

KM# 1203a 5 POUNDS
28.2800 g., 0.9250 Silver 0.8410 oz. ASW, 38.6 mm. **Ruler:** Elizabeth II **Subject:** Royal Wedding - William and Catherine

Date	Mintage	F	VF	XF	Unc	BU
2011 Proof	—	Value: 50.00				

KM# 1163 25 POUNDS
8.5100 g., 0.9167 Gold 0.2508 oz. AGW, 22 mm. **Ruler:** Elizabeth II **Subject:** London Olympics, 2012 **Obv:** Head with tiara right **Rev:** Mercury and cyclists

Date	Mintage	F	VF	XF	Unc	BU
2010 Proof	20,000	Value: 800				

KM# 1164 50 POUNDS
17.0200 g., 0.9167 Gold 0.5016 oz. AGW, 27 mm. **Ruler:** Elizabeth II **Subject:** London Olympics, 2012 **Obv:** Head with tiara right **Rev:** Diana and runners

Date	Mintage	F	VF	XF	Unc	BU
2010 Proof	20,000	Value: 1,000				

KM# 1162 100 POUNDS
32.6900 g., 0.9167 Gold 0.9634 oz. AGW, 32.7 mm. **Ruler:** Elizabeth II **Subject:** London Olympics, 2012 **Obv:** Head with tiara right **Rev:** Neptune and sailing

Date	Mintage	F	VF	XF	Unc	BU
2010 Proof	7,500	Value: 1,850				

SOVEREIGN COINAGE

KM# 1117 1/4 SOVEREIGN
2.0000 g., 0.9170 Gold 0.0590 oz. AGW, 13.5 mm. **Ruler:** Elizabeth II **Obv:** Head with tiara right **Rev:** St. George slaying dragon

Date	Mintage	F	VF	XF	Unc	BU
2009	50,000	—	—	—	—	115
2009 Proof	25,000	Value: 135				
2010	250,000	—	—	—	—	115
2010 Proof	25,000	Value: 135				
2011	—	—	—	—	—	115
2011 Proof	15,000	Value: 135				

KM# 1001 1/2 SOVEREIGN
3.9900 g., 0.9170 Gold 0.1176 oz. AGW **Ruler:** Elizabeth II
Obv: Head with tiara right **Rev:** St. George slaying the dragon

Date	Mintage	F	VF	XF	Unc	BU
2001	94,763	—	—	—	—	BV
2001 Proof	10,000	BV+5%				
2002	61,347	—	—	—	—	BV
2003	47,818	—	—	—	—	BV
2003 Proof	14,750	BV+5%				
2004	34,924	—	—	—	—	BV
2006	30,299	—	—	—	—	BV
2006 Proof	8,500	BV+5%				
2007	75,000	—	—	—	—	BV
2007 Proof	7,500	BV+5%				
2008	75,000	—	—	—	—	BV
2008 Proof	7,500	BV+5%				

KM# 1025 1/2 SOVEREIGN
3.9900 g., 0.9167 Gold 0.1176 oz. AGW, 19.3 mm. **Ruler:**
Elizabeth II **Subject:** Queen Elizabeth II's Golden Jubilee **Obv:**
Head with tiara right **Rev:** Crowned arms within wreath, date
below **Edge:** Reeded

Date	Mintage	F	VF	XF	Unc	BU
2002	61,347	—	—	—	—	225
2002 Proof	10,000	Value: 250				

KM# 1064 1/2 SOVEREIGN
3.9940 g., 0.9167 Gold 0.1177 oz. AGW, 19.3 mm. **Ruler:**
Elizabeth II **Obv:** Head with tiara right **Rev:** Knight fighting dragon
with sword **Edge:** Reeded

Date	Mintage	F	VF	XF	Unc	BU
2005	30,299	—	—	—	—	BV
2005 Proof	5,011	Value: 225				

KM# 1001.1 1/2 SOVEREIGN
3.9900 g., 0.9170 Gold 0.1176 oz. AGW **Ruler:** Elizabeth II
Obv: Heas with tiara right **Rev:** St. George slaying the dragon

Date	Mintage	F	VF	XF	Unc	BU
2009	50,000	—	—	—	—	BV
2009 Proof	6,000	BV				
2010	250,000	—	—	—	—	BV
2010 Proof	7,000	BV				
2011	—	—	—	—	—	BV
2011 Proof	—	BV				

KM# 1002 SOVEREIGN
7.9881 g., 0.9170 Gold 0.2355 oz. AGW **Ruler:** Elizabeth II
Obv: Head with tiara right **Rev:** St. George slaying the dragon

Date	Mintage	F	VF	XF	Unc	BU
2001	49,462	—	—	—	—	BV
2001 Proof	15,000	Value: 425				
2002	75,264	—	—	—	—	BV
2003	43,230	—	—	—	—	BV
2003 Proof	19,750	Value: 425				
2004	30,688	—	—	—	—	BV
2006	45,542	—	—	—	—	BV
2006 Proof	16,000	Value: 425				
2007	75,000	—	—	—	—	BV
2007 Proof	12,500	Value: 425				
2008	75,000	—	—	—	—	BV
2008 Proof	12,500	Value: 425				

KM# 1026 SOVEREIGN
7.9800 g., 0.9167 Gold 0.2352 oz. AGW, 22 mm. **Ruler:**
Elizabeth II **Subject:** Queen Elizabeth II's Golden Jubilee **Obv:**
Head with tiara right **Rev:** Crowned arms within wreath, date
below **Edge:** Reeded

Date	Mintage	F	VF	XF	Unc	BU
2002	75,264	—	—	—	—	BV
2002 Proof	20,500	Value: 425				

KM# 1065 SOVEREIGN
7.9880 g., 0.9176 Gold 0.2356 oz. AGW, 22.05 mm. **Ruler:**
Elizabeth II **Obv:** Head with tiara right **Rev:** Knight fighting dragon
with sword **Edge:** Reeded

Date	Mintage	F	VF	XF	Unc	BU
2005	45,542	—	—	—	—	BV
2005 Proof	17,500	Value: 425				

KM# 1002.1 SOVEREIGN
7.9810 g., 0.9170 Gold 0.2353 oz. AGW **Ruler:** Elizabeth II
Obv: Head with tiara right **Rev:** St. George slaying the dragon

Date	Mintage	F	VF	XF	Unc	BU
2009	75,000	—	—	—	—	BV
2009 Proof	12,500	Value: 425				
2010	250,000	—	—	—	—	BV
2010 Proof	12,500	Value: 425				
2011	—	—	—	—	—	BV
2011 Proof	12,500	Value: 425				

KM# 1027 2 POUNDS
15.9700 g., 0.9167 Gold 0.4707 oz. AGW, 28.4 mm. **Ruler:**
Elizabeth II **Subject:** Queen Elizabeth II's Golden Jubilee **Obv:**
Head with tiara right **Rev:** Crowned arms within wreath, date
below **Edge:** Reeded

Date	Mintage	F	VF	XF	Unc	BU
2002 Proof	8,000	Value: 850				

KM# 1066 2 POUNDS
15.9760 g., 0.9167 Gold 0.4708 oz. AGW, 28.4 mm. **Ruler:**
Elizabeth II **Obv:** Head with tiara right **Rev:** Knight fighting dragon
with sword **Edge:** Reeded

Date	Mintage	F	VF	XF	Unc	BU
2005 Proof	5,000	Value: 850				

KM# 1072 2 POUNDS
15.9700 g., 0.9167 Gold 0.4707 oz. AGW, 28.4 mm. **Ruler:**
Elizabeth II **Obv:** Head with tiara right **Rev:** St. George slaying
the Dragon **Edge:** Reeded

Date	Mintage	F	VF	XF	Unc	BU
2006 Proof	3,500	Value: 850				
2007 Proof	2,500	Value: 875				
2008 Proof	2,500	Value: 875				

KM# 1072.1 2 POUNDS
15.9700 g., 0.9170 Gold 0.4708 oz. AGW **Ruler:** Elizabeth II
Obv: Head with tiara right **Rev:** St. George slaying the dragon

Date	Mintage	F	VF	XF	Unc	BU
2009 Proof	2,500	Value: 875				
2010 Proof	2,750	Value: 875				
2011 Proof	2,950	Value: 875				

KM# 1003 5 POUNDS
39.9400 g., 0.9170 Gold 1.1775 oz. AGW, 36 mm. **Ruler:**
Elizabeth II **Obv:** Head with tiara right **Rev:** St. George slaying
dragon **Edge:** Reeded

Date	Mintage	F	VF	XF	Unc	BU
2001 (u)	1,000	—	—	—	—	2,100
2001 Proof	1,000	Value: 2,250				
2003	812	—	—	—	—	2,100
2003 Proof	2,250	Value: 2,150				
2004	1,000	—	—	—	—	2,100
2004 Proof	1,750					
2006	1,000	—	—	—	—	2,100
2006 Proof	1,750	Value: 2,150				
2007	768	—	—	—	—	2,100
2007 Proof	1,750	Value: 2,150				
2008	750	—	—	—	—	2,100
2008 Proof	1,750	Value: 2,150				

KM# 1028 5 POUNDS
39.9400 g., 0.9167 Gold 1.1771 oz. AGW, 36 mm. **Ruler:**
Elizabeth II **Subject:** Queen Elizabeth II's Golden Jubilee **Obv:**
Head with tiara right **Rev:** Crowned arms within wreath **Edge:**
Reeded

Date	Mintage	F	VF	XF	Unc	BU
2002	1,370	—	—	—	—	2,100
2002 Proof	3,000	Value: 2,150				

KM# 1067 5 POUNDS
39.9400 g., 0.9167 Gold 1.1771 oz. AGW, 36 mm. **Ruler:**
Elizabeth II **Obv:** Head with tiara right **Rev:** Knight fighting dragon
with sword **Edge:** Reeded

Date	Mintage	F	VF	XF	Unc	BU
2005	936	—	—	—	—	2,100
2005 Proof	2,500	Value: 2,150				

KM# 1003.1 5 POUNDS
39.9400 g., 0.9167 Gold 1.1775 oz. AGW **Ruler:** Elizabeth II
Obv: Head with tiara right **Rev:** St. George slaying the dragon

Date	Mintage	F	VF	XF	Unc	BU
2009	1,000	—	—	—	—	2,100
2009 Proof	1,750	Value: 2,150				
2010	1,000	—	—	—	—	2,100
2010 Proof	2,000	Value: 2,150				
2011 Proof	—	Value: 2,150				

BULLION COINAGE

Until 1990, .917 Gold was commonly alloyed with copper by the British Royal Mint.

All proof issues have designers name as P. Nathan. The
uncirculated issues use only Nathan.

KM# 1016 20 PENCE
3.2400 g., 0.9584 Silver 0.0998 oz. ASW, 16.5 mm. **Ruler:**
Elizabeth II **Subject:** Britannia Bullion **Obv:** Head with tiara right
Rev: Una and Lion **Edge:** Reeded

Date	Mintage	F	VF	XF	Unc	BU
2001 Proof	15,000	Value: 25.00				

KM# 1079 20 PENCE
3.2400 g., 0.9584 Silver 0.0998 oz. ASW, 16.5 mm. **Ruler:**
Elizabeth II **Obv:** Head with tiara right **Rev:** Britannia standing
Edge: Reeded

Date	Mintage	F	VF	XF	Unc	BU
2002 Proof	—	Value: 25.00				
2004 Proof	—	Value: 25.00				
2006 Proof	—	Value: 25.00				

KM# 1044 20 PENCE
3.2400 g., 0.9584 Silver 0.0998 oz. ASW, 16.5 mm. **Ruler:**
Elizabeth II **Obv:** Head with tiara right **Rev:** Britannia portrait
behind wavy lines **Edge:** Reeded

Date	Mintage	F	VF	XF	Unc	BU
2003 Proof	5,848	Value: 35.00				

KM# 1085 20 PENCE
3.2400 g., 0.9584 Silver 0.0998 oz. ASW, 16.5 mm. **Ruler:**
Elizabeth II **Obv:** Head with tiara right **Rev:** Britannia seated with
shield left **Edge:** Reeded

Date	Mintage	F	VF	XF	Unc	BU
2005 Proof	3,273	Value: 25.00				

KM# 1088 20 PENCE
3.2400 g., 0.9584 Silver 0.0998 oz. ASW, 16.5 mm. **Ruler:**
Elizabeth II **Obv:** Head with tiara right **Rev:** Britannia seated with
reclining lion right **Edge:** Reeded

Date	Mintage	F	VF	XF	Unc	BU
2007 Proof	3,401	Value: 25.00				

KM# 1095 20 PENCE
3.2400 g., 0.9584 Silver 0.0998 oz. ASW, 16.5 mm. **Ruler:**
Elizabeth II **Obv:** Head with tiara right **Rev:** Britannia standing
facing left with trident, flowing garment, shield **Edge:** Reeded

Date	Mintage	F	VF	XF	Unc	BU
2008 Proof	5,000	Value: 35.00				

KM# 1123 20 PENCE
3.2400 g., 0.9580 Silver 0.0998 oz. ASW, 16.5 mm. **Ruler:**
Elizabeth II **Obv:** Head right **Rev:** Britania in chariot right

Date	Mintage	F	VF	XF	Unc	BU
2009 Proof	6,000	Value: 35.00				

KM# 1131   20 PENCE
3.2400 g., 0.9580 Silver 0.0998 oz. ASW, 16.5 mm. **Ruler:**
Elizabeth II **Obv:** Head right **Rev:** Britannia bust right

Date	Mintage	F	VF	XF	Unc	BU
2010 Proof	8,000	Value: 35.00				

KM# 1017   50 PENCE
8.1100 g., 0.9584 Silver 0.2499 oz. ASW, 27.3 mm. **Ruler:**
Elizabeth II **Subject:** Britannia Bullion **Obv:** Head with tiara right
Rev: Una and Lion **Edge:** Reeded

Date	Mintage	F	VF	XF	Unc	BU
2001 Proof	5,000	Value: 35.00				

KM# 1080   50 PENCE
8.1100 g., 0.9584 Silver 0.2499 oz. ASW, 22 mm. **Ruler:**
Elizabeth II **Obv:** Head with tiara right **Rev:** Britannia standing
Edge: Reeded

Date	Mintage	F	VF	XF	Unc	BU
2002 Proof	—	Value: 35.00				
2004 Proof	—	Value: 35.00				
2006 Proof	—	Value: 35.00				

KM# 1045   50 PENCE
8.1100 g., 0.9584 Silver 0.2499 oz. ASW, 22 mm. **Ruler:**
Elizabeth II **Obv:** Head with tiara right **Rev:** Britannia portrait
behind wavy lines **Edge:** Reeded

Date	Mintage	F	VF	XF	Unc	BU
2003 Proof	3,669	Value: 35.00				

KM# 1086   50 PENCE
8.1100 g., 0.9584 Silver 0.2499 oz. ASW, 22 mm. **Ruler:**
Elizabeth II **Obv:** Head with tiara right **Rev:** Britannia seated with
shield left **Edge:** Reeded

Date	Mintage	F	VF	XF	Unc	BU
2005 Proof	2,360	Value: 35.00				

KM# 1089   50 PENCE
8.1100 g., 0.9584 Silver 0.2499 oz. ASW, 22 mm. **Ruler:**
Elizabeth II **Obv:** Head with tiara right **Rev:** Britannia seated with
reclining lion right **Edge:** Reeded

Date	Mintage	F	VF	XF	Unc	BU
2007 Proof	2,500	Value: 35.00				

KM# 1096   50 PENCE
8.1100 g., 0.9584 Silver 0.2499 oz. ASW, 22 mm. **Ruler:**
Elizabeth II **Obv:** Head with tiara right **Rev:** Britannia standing
facing left with trident, flowing garment, shield **Edge:** Reeded

Date	Mintage	F	VF	XF	Unc	BU
2008 Proof	2,500	Value: 45.00				

KM# 1124   50 PENCE
8.1100 g., 0.9580 Silver 0.2498 oz. ASW, 22 mm. **Ruler:**
Elizabeth II **Obv:** Head right **Rev:** Britannia in chariot right

Date	Mintage	F	VF	XF	Unc	BU
2009 Proof	2,500	Value: 50.00				

KM# 1132   50 PENCE
8.1100 g., 0.9580 Silver 0.2498 oz. ASW, 22 mm. **Ruler:**
Elizabeth II **Obv:** Head right **Rev:** Britannia bust right

Date	Mintage	F	VF	XF	Unc	BU
2010 Proof	3,500	Value: 50.00				

KM# 1018   POUND
16.2200 g., 0.9584 Silver 0.4998 oz. ASW, 27 mm. **Ruler:**
Elizabeth II **Subject:** Britannia Bullion **Obv:** Head with tiara right
Rev: Una and Lion" **Edge:** Reeded

Date	Mintage	F	VF	XF	Unc	BU
2001 Proof	5,000	Value: 50.00				

KM# 1081   POUND
16.2200 g., 0.9584 Silver 0.4998 oz. ASW, 27 mm. **Ruler:**
Elizabeth II **Obv:** Head with tiara right **Rev:** Britannia standing
Edge: Reeded

Date	Mintage	F	VF	XF	Unc	BU
2002 Proof	—	Value: 50.00				
2004 Proof	—	Value: 50.00				
2006 Proof	—	Value: 50.00				

KM# 1046   POUND
16.2200 g., 0.9584 Silver 0.4998 oz. ASW, 27 mm. **Ruler:**
Elizabeth II **Obv:** Head with tiara right **Rev:** Britannia portrait
behind wavy lines **Edge:** Reeded

Date	Mintage	F	VF	XF	Unc	BU
2003 Proof	3,669	Value: 50.00				

KM# 1087   POUND
16.2200 g., 0.9584 Silver 0.4998 oz. ASW, 27 mm. **Ruler:**
Elizabeth II **Obv:** Head with tiara right **Rev:** Britannia seated with
shield left **Edge:** Reeded

Date	Mintage	F	VF	XF	Unc	BU
2005 Proof	2,360	Value: 50.00				

KM# 1090   POUND
16.2200 g., 0.9584 Silver 0.4998 oz. ASW, 27 mm. **Ruler:**
Elizabeth II **Obv:** Head with tiara right **Rev:** Britannia seated with
reclining lion right **Edge:** Reeded

Date	Mintage	F	VF	XF	Unc	BU
2007 Proof	2,500	Value: 50.00				

KM# 1097   POUND
16.2200 g., 0.9584 Silver 0.4998 oz. ASW, 27 mm. **Ruler:**
Elizabeth II **Obv:** Head with tiara right **Rev:** Britannia standing
facing left with trident, flowing garment, shield **Edge:** Reeded

Date	Mintage	F	VF	XF	Unc	BU
2008 Proof	2,500	Value: 60.00				

KM# 1125   POUND
16.2200 g., 0.9580 Silver 0.4996 oz. ASW, 27 mm. **Ruler:**
Elizabeth II **Obv:** Head right **Rev:** Britannia in chariot right

Date	Mintage	F	VF	XF	Unc	BU
2009 Proof	2,500	Value: 75.00				

KM# 1133   POUND
16.2200 g., 0.9580 Silver 0.4996 oz. ASW, 27 mm. **Ruler:**
Elizabeth II **Obv:** Head right **Rev:** Britannia bust right

Date	Mintage	F	VF	XF	Unc	BU
2010 Proof	3,500	Value: 70.00				

KM# 1019   2 POUNDS
32.4500 g., 0.9584 Silver 0.9998 oz. ASW, 40 mm. **Ruler:**
Elizabeth II **Subject:** Britannia Bullion **Obv:** Head with tiara right
Rev: Una and Lion **Edge:** Reeded

Date	Mintage	F	VF	XF	Unc	BU
2001	44,816	—	—		38.00	42.00
2001 Proof	3,047	Value: 65.00				

KM# 1029   2 POUNDS
32.5400 g., 0.9580 Silver 1.0022 oz. ASW, 40 mm. **Ruler:**
Elizabeth II **Obv:** Head with tiara right **Rev:** Standing Britannia
Edge: Reeded

Date	Mintage	F	VF	XF	Unc	BU
2002	36,543	—	—		—	38.00
2002 Proof	—	Value: 60.00				
2004	100,000	—	—		—	38.00
2004 Proof	2,174	Value: 60.00				
2006	100,000	—	—		—	38.00
2006 Proof	2,529	Value: 60.00				
2012	—	—	—		—	38.00
2012 Proof	—	Value: 60.00				

KM# 1039   2 POUNDS
32.4500 g., 0.9580 Silver 0.9994 oz. ASW, 40 mm. **Ruler:**
Elizabeth II **Subject:** Britannia Bullion **Obv:** Head with tiara right
Rev: Britannia portrait behind wavy puzzle-like lines **Edge:** Reeded

Date	Mintage	F	VF	XF	Unc	BU
2003	73,271	—	—		—	38.00
2003 Proof	2,016	Value: 65.00				

KM# 1063   2 POUNDS
32.4500 g., 0.9580 Silver 0.9994 oz. ASW, 40 mm. **Ruler:**
Elizabeth II **Obv:** Head with tiara right **Rev:** Seated Britannia
Edge: Reeded

Date	Mintage	F	VF	XF	Unc	BU
2005	100,000	—	—		—	38.00
2005 Proof	1,539	Value: 70.00				

KM# 1029a   2 POUNDS
32.4500 g., 0.9580 Silver partially gilt 0.9994 oz. ASW, 40 mm.
Ruler: Elizabeth II **Obv:** Head with tiara right **Rev:** Britannia
standing with shield, gilt **Edge:** Reeded

Date	Mintage	F	VF	XF	Unc	BU
2006 Proof	3,000	Value: 100				

KM# 1039a   2 POUNDS
32.4500 g., 0.9580 Silver partially gilt 0.9994 oz. ASW, 40 mm.
Ruler: Elizabeth II **Obv:** Head with tiara right **Rev:** Britannia head
gilt **Edge:** Reeded

Date	Mintage	F	VF	XF	Unc	BU
2006 Proof	3,000	Value: 100				

KM# 1063a   2 POUNDS
32.4500 g., 0.9580 Silver partially gilt 0.9994 oz. ASW, 40 mm.
Ruler: Elizabeth II **Obv:** Head with tiara right **Rev:** Britannia
seated, gilt **Edge:** Reeded

Date	Mintage	F	VF	XF	Unc	BU
2006 Proof	3,000	Value: 100				

KM# 1000a   2 POUNDS
32.4500 g., 0.9580 Silver partially gilt 0.9994 oz. ASW, 40 mm. **Ruler:** Elizabeth II **Obv:** Head with tiara right **Rev:** Britannia in chariot, gilt **Edge:** Reeded

Date	Mintage	F	VF	XF	Unc	BU
2006 Proof	3,000	Value: 100				

KM# 1019a   2 POUNDS
32.4500 g., 0.9580 Silver 0.9994 oz. ASW, 40 mm. **Ruler:** Elizabeth II **Subject:** Golden Silhouette Britannias **Obv:** Head with tiara right **Rev:** Gold plated Britannia and Lion **Edge:** Reeded

Date	Mintage	F	VF	XF	Unc	BU
2006 Proof	3,000	Value: 100				

KM# 1078   2 POUNDS
32.4500 g., 0.9580 Silver 0.9994 oz. ASW, 40 mm. **Ruler:** Elizabeth II **Subject:** Britannia series **Obv:** Elizabeth II **Rev:** Seated, bareheaded Britannia with a recumbent lion at her feet **Edge:** Reeded

Date	Mintage	F	VF	XF	Unc	BU
2007	100,000	—	—	—	—	40.00
2007 Proof	2,500	Value: 65.00				

KM# 1098   2 POUNDS
32.4500 g., 0.9584 Silver 0.9998 oz. ASW, 40 mm. **Ruler:** Elizabeth II **Obv:** Head with tiara right **Rev:** Britannia standing facing left with trident, flowing garment, shield **Edge:** Reeded

Date	Mintage	F	VF	XF	Unc	BU
2008	—	—	—	—	—	40.00
2008 Proof	—	Value: 80.00				

KM# 1000   2 POUNDS
32.5400 g., 0.9580 Silver 1.0022 oz. ASW, 40 mm. **Ruler:** Elizabeth II **Obv:** Head with tiara right **Rev:** Britannia in chariot **Edge:** Reeded

Date	Mintage	F	VF	XF	Unc	BU
2009	—	—	—	—	—	40.00
2009 Proof	—	Value: 55.00				

KM# 1134   2 POUNDS
32.4500 g., 0.9580 Silver 0.9994 oz. ASW, 40 mm. **Ruler:** Elizabeth II **Obv:** Head right **Rev:** Britannia bust right

Date	Mintage	F	VF	XF	Unc	BU
2010	—	—	—	—	—	38.00
2010 Proof	8,000	Value: 90.00				

KM# 1020   10 POUNDS
3.4100 g., 0.9167 Gold 0.1005 oz. AGW, 16.5 mm. **Ruler:** Elizabeth II **Subject:** Britannia Bullion **Obv:** Head with tiara right **Rev:** Stylized "Britannia and the Lion" **Edge:** Reeded

Date	Mintage	F	VF	XF	Unc	BU
2001	1,100	—	—	—	—BV+16%	
2001 Proof	1,557	Value: 200				

KM# 1008   10 POUNDS
3.4100 g., 0.9167 Gold 0.1005 oz. AGW, 16.5 mm. **Ruler:** Elizabeth II **Obv:** Head with tiara right **Rev:** Britannia standing **Edge:** Reeded

Date	Mintage	F	VF	XF	Unc	BU
2002	—	—	—	—	—BV+16%	
2002 Proof	1,500	Value: 200				
2004 Proof	929	Value: 225				
2006 Proof	700	Value: 225				

KM# 1040   10 POUNDS
3.4100 g., 0.9167 Gold 0.1005 oz. AGW, 16.5 mm. **Ruler:** Elizabeth II **Obv:** Head with tiara right **Rev:** Britannia portrait behind wavy lines **Edge:** Reeded

Date	Mintage	F	VF	XF	Unc	BU
2003	—	—	—	—	—BV+16%	—
2003 Proof	4,000	Value: 200				

KM# 1068   10 POUNDS
3.4100 g., 0.9167 Gold 0.1005 oz. AGW, 16.5 mm. **Ruler:** Elizabeth II **Obv:** Head with tiara right **Rev:** Seated Britannia **Edge:** Reeded

Date	Mintage	F	VF	XF	Unc	BU
2005 Proof	1,225	Value: 200				

KM# 1091   10 POUNDS
3.4100 g., 0.9167 Gold 0.1005 oz. AGW, 16.5 mm. **Ruler:** Elizabeth II **Obv:** Head with tiara right **Rev:** Britannia seated with reclining lion **Edge:** Reeded

Date	Mintage	F	VF	XF	Unc	BU
2007	—	—	—	—	—BV+16%	—
2007 Proof	893	Value: 225				

KM# 1091a   10 POUNDS
3.1100 g., 0.9999 Platinum 0.1000 oz. APW **Ruler:** Elizabeth II **Obv:** Head with tiara right **Rev:** Britannia seated with reclining lion right **Edge:** Reeded **Edge Lettering:** 16.5

Date	Mintage	F	VF	XF	Unc	BU
2007 Proof	691	Value: 300				

KM# 1099   10 POUNDS
3.4100 g., 0.9167 Gold 0.1005 oz. AGW, 16.5 mm. **Ruler:** Elizabeth II **Obv:** Head with tiara right **Rev:** Britannia standing facing left with trident, flowing garment, shield **Edge:** Reeded

Date	Mintage	F	VF	XF	Unc	BU
2008 Proof	—	Value: 210				

KM# 1099a   10 POUNDS
3.1100 g., 0.9999 Platinum 0.1000 oz. APW, 16.5 mm. **Ruler:** Elizabeth II **Obv:** Head with tiara right **Rev:** Britannia standing facing left with trident, flowing garment, shield **Edge:** Reeded

Date	Mintage	F	VF	XF	Unc	BU
2008 Proof	—	Value: 300				

KM# 1127   10 POUNDS
3.4100 g., 0.9160 Gold 0.1004 oz. AGW, 16.5 mm. **Ruler:** Elizabeth II **Obv:** Head right **Rev:** Britannia in chariot right

Date	Mintage	F	VF	XF	Unc	BU
2009 Proof	2,000	Value: 210				

KM# 1135   10 POUNDS
3.4100 g., 0.9160 Gold 0.1004 oz. AGW, 16.5 mm. **Ruler:** Elizabeth II **Obv:** Head right **Rev:** Britannia bust right

Date	Mintage	F	VF	XF	Unc	BU
2010 Proof	750	Value: 200				

KM# 1021   25 POUNDS
8.5100 g., 0.9167 Gold 0.2508 oz. AGW, 22 mm. **Ruler:** Elizabeth II **Subject:** Britannia Bullion **Obv:** Head with tiara right **Rev:** Stylized "Britannia and the Lion" **Edge:** Reeded

Date	Mintage	F	VF	XF	Unc	BU
2001	1,100	—	—	—	—BV+25%	
2001 Proof	1,500	Value: 450				
2006 Proof	—	Value: 450				

KM# 1009   25 POUNDS
8.5100 g., 0.9167 Gold 0.2508 oz. AGW, 22 mm. **Ruler:** Elizabeth II **Obv:** Head with tiara right **Rev:** Britannia standing **Edge:** Reeded

Date	Mintage	F	VF	XF	Unc	BU
2002 Proof	750	Value: 450				

Date	Mintage	F	VF	XF	Unc	BU
2004 Proof	750	Value: 450				
2006 Proof	1,000	Value: 450				

KM# 1041   25 POUNDS
8.5100 g., 0.9167 Gold 0.2508 oz. AGW, 22 mm. **Ruler:** Elizabeth II **Obv:** Head with tiara right **Rev:** Britannia portrait behind wavy lines **Edge:** Reeded

Date	Mintage	F	VF	XF	Unc	BU
2003 Proof	609	Value: 450				
2006 Proof	—	Value: 450				

KM# 1069   25 POUNDS
8.5100 g., 0.9167 Gold 0.2508 oz. AGW, 22 mm. **Ruler:** Elizabeth II **Obv:** Head with tiara right **Rev:** Seated Britannia **Edge:** Reeded

Date	Mintage	F	VF	XF	Unc	BU
2005 Proof	750	Value: 450				
2006	—	Value: 450				

KM# 1204   25 POUNDS
8.5100 g., 0.9167 Gold 0.2508 oz. AGW **Ruler:** Elizabeth II **Rev:** Standing Britannia in horse drawn chariot

Date	Mintage	F	VF	XF	Unc	BU
2006 Proof	—	Value: 450				
2009 Proof	—	Value: 450				

KM# 1092   25 POUNDS
8.5100 g., 0.9167 Gold 0.2508 oz. AGW, 22 mm. **Ruler:** Elizabeth II **Obv:** Head with tiara right **Rev:** Britannia seated with reclining lion right **Edge:** Reeded

Date	Mintage	F	VF	XF	Unc	BU
2007	—	—	—	—	—	—BV+25%
2007 Proof	1,000	Value: 450				

KM# 1092a   25 POUNDS
0.9999 Platinum APW, 22 mm. **Ruler:** Elizabeth II **Obv:** Head with tiara right **Rev:** Britannia seated with reclining lion right **Edge:** Reeded

Date	Mintage	F	VF	XF	Unc	BU
2007 Proof	—	Value: 650				

KM# 1100   25 POUNDS
8.5100 g., 0.9167 Gold 0.2508 oz. AGW, 22 mm. **Ruler:** Elizabeth II **Obv:** Head with tiara right **Rev:** Britannia standing facing left with trident, flowing garment, shield **Edge:** Reeded

Date	Mintage	F	VF	XF	Unc	BU
2008 Proof	1,000	Value: 450				

KM# 1100a   25 POUNDS
0.9999 Platinum APW, 22 mm. **Ruler:** Elizabeth II **Obv:** Head with tiara right **Rev:** Britannia standing facing left with trident, flowing garment, shield **Edge:** Reeded

Date	Mintage	F	VF	XF	Unc	BU
2008 Proof	—	Value: 650				

KM# 1128   25 POUNDS
8.5100 g., 0.9160 Gold 0.2506 oz. AGW, 22 mm. **Ruler:** Elizabeth II **Obv:** Head right **Rev:** Britannia in chariot right

Date	Mintage	F	VF	XF	Unc	BU
2009 Proof	2,250	Value: 450				

KM# 1136   25 POUNDS
8.5100 g., 0.9160 Gold 0.2506 oz. AGW, 22 mm. **Ruler:** Elizabeth II **Obv:** Head right **Rev:** Britannia bust right

Date	Mintage	F	VF	XF	Unc	BU
2010 Proof	3,000	Value: 450				

KM# 1022   50 POUNDS
17.0200 g., 0.9167 Gold 0.5016 oz. AGW, 27 mm. **Ruler:** Elizabeth II **Subject:** Britannia Bullion **Obv:** Head with tiara right **Rev:** Stylized "Britannia and the Lion" **Edge:** Reeded

Date	Mintage	F	VF	XF	Unc	BU
2001	600	—	—	—	—BV+25%	
2001 Proof	1,000	BV+5%				

KM# 1010 50 POUNDS
17.0300 g., 0.9167 Gold 0.5019 oz. AGW, 27 mm. **Ruler:** Elizabeth II **Obv:** Head with tiara right **Rev:** Britannia standing **Edge:** Reeded

Date	Mintage	F	VF	XF	Unc	BU
2002 Proof	1,000	BV+5%				
2004 Proof	—	BV+10%				
2006 Proof	—	BV+10%				

KM# 1042 50 POUNDS
17.0200 g., 0.9167 Gold 0.5016 oz. AGW, 27 mm. **Ruler:** Elizabeth II **Obv:** Head with tiara right **Rev:** Britannia portrait behind wavy lines **Edge:** Reeded

Date	Mintage	F	VF	XF	Unc	BU
2003	—	—	—	—	—BV+15%	—
2003 Proof	2,500	BV+5%				

KM# 1070 50 POUNDS
17.0300 g., 0.9167 Gold 0.5019 oz. AGW, 27 mm. **Ruler:** Elizabeth II **Obv:** Head with tiara right **Rev:** Seated Britannia **Edge:** Reeded

Date	Mintage	F	VF	XF	Unc	BU
2005 Proof	2,000	BV+5%				

KM# 1093 50 POUNDS
17.0250 g., 0.9167 Gold 0.5017 oz. AGW, 27 mm. **Ruler:** Elizabeth II **Obv:** Head with tiara right **Rev:** Britannia seated with reclining lion right **Edge:** Reeded

Date	Mintage	F	VF	XF	Unc	BU
2007	—	—	—	—	—BV+15%	—
2007 Proof	—	BV+10%				

KM# 1093a 50 POUNDS
0.9999 Platinum APW, 27 mm. **Ruler:** Elizabeth II **Obv:** Head with tiara right **Rev:** Britannia seated with reclining lion right **Edge:** Reeded

Date	Mintage	F	VF	XF	Unc	BU
2007 Proof	—	Value: 1,500				

KM# 1101 50 POUNDS
17.0250 g., 0.9167 Gold 0.5017 oz. AGW, 27 mm. **Ruler:** Elizabeth II **Obv:** Head with tiara right **Rev:** Britannia standing facing left with trident, flowing garment, shield **Edge:** Reeded

Date	Mintage	F	VF	XF	Unc	BU
2008 Proof	—	BV+10%				

KM# 1101a 50 POUNDS
0.9999 Platinum APW, 27 mm. **Ruler:** Elizabeth II **Obv:** Head with tiara right **Rev:** Britannia standing facing left with trident, flowing garment, shield **Edge:** Reeded

Date	Mintage	F	VF	XF	Unc	BU
2008 Proof	—	Value: 1,500				

KM# 1129 50 POUNDS
27.0000 g., 0.9160 Gold 0.7951 oz. AGW, 27 mm. **Ruler:** Elizabeth II **Obv:** Head right **Rev:** Britania in chariot right

Date	Mintage	F	VF	XF	Unc	BU
2009	—	—	—	—	—BV+15%	—
2009 Proof	1,250	BV+10%				

KM# 1137 50 POUNDS
17.0200 g., 0.9160 Gold 0.5012 oz. AGW, 27 mm. **Ruler:** Elizabeth II **Obv:** Head right **Rev:** Britannia bust right

Date	Mintage	F	VF	XF	Unc	BU
2010 Proof	1,250	BV+5%				

KM# 1023 100 POUNDS
34.0500 g., 0.9167 Gold 1.0035 oz. AGW, 32.7 mm. **Ruler:** Elizabeth II **Subject:** Britannia Bullion **Obv:** Head with tiara right **Rev:** Stylized "Britannia and the Lion" **Edge:** Reeded

Date	Mintage	F	VF	XF	Unc	BU
2001	900	—	—	—BV+15%	—	
2001 Proof	1,000	BV+5%				

KM# 1011 100 POUNDS
34.0500 g., 0.9167 Gold 1.0035 oz. AGW, 32.7 mm. **Ruler:** Elizabeth II **Obv:** Head with tiara right **Rev:** Britannia standing **Edge:** Reeded

Date	Mintage	F	VF	XF	Unc	BU
2002 Proof	1,000	BV+5%				
2004	—	—	—	—	—BV+15%	
2004 Proof	—	BV+5%				
2006 Proof	—	BV+5%				
2012 Proof	—	BV+5%				

KM# 1043 100 POUNDS
34.0500 g., 0.9167 Gold 1.0035 oz. AGW, 32.7 mm. **Ruler:** Elizabeth II **Obv:** Head with tiara right **Rev:** Britannia portrait behind wavy lines **Edge:** Reeded

Date	Mintage	F	VF	XF	Unc	BU
2003	—	—	—	—	—BV+15%	—
2003 Proof	1,500	BV+5%				

KM# 1071 100 POUNDS
34.0500 g., 0.9167 Gold 1.0035 oz. AGW, 32.7 mm. **Ruler:** Elizabeth II **Obv:** Head with tiara right **Rev:** Seated Britannia **Edge:** Reeded

Date	Mintage	F	VF	XF	Unc	BU
2005 Proof	1,500	BV+5%				

KM# 1094 100 POUNDS
34.0500 g., 0.9167 Gold 1.0035 oz. AGW, 32.7 mm. **Ruler:** Elizabeth II **Obv:** Head with tiara right **Rev:** Britannia seated with reclining lion right **Edge:** Reeded

Date	Mintage	F	VF	XF	Unc	BU
2007	—	—	—	—	—BV+15%	—
2007 Proof	—	BV+5%				

KM# 1094a 100 POUNDS
0.9999 Platinum APW, 32.7 mm. **Ruler:** Elizabeth II **Obv:** Head with tiara right **Rev:** Britannia seated with reclining lion right **Edge:** Reeded

Date	Mintage	F	VF	XF	Unc	BU
2007 Proof	—	Value: 2,900				

KM# 1102 100 POUNDS
34.0500 g., 0.9167 Gold 1.0035 oz. AGW, 32.7 mm. **Ruler:** Elizabeth II **Obv:** Head with tiara right **Rev:** Britannia standing facing left with trident, flowing garment, shield **Edge:** Reeded

Date	Mintage	F	VF	XF	Unc	BU
2008	—	—	—	—	—BV+15%	—
2008 Proof	—	BV+5%				

KM# 1102a 100 POUNDS
0.9999 Platinum APW, 32.7 mm. **Ruler:** Elizabeth II **Obv:** Head with tiara right **Rev:** Britannia standing facing left with trident, flowing garment, shield **Edge:** Reeded

Date	Mintage	F	VF	XF	Unc	BU
2008 Proof	—	Value: 2,900				

KM# 1130 100 POUNDS
32.6900 g., 0.9160 Gold 0.9627 oz. AGW, 32.6 mm. **Ruler:** Elizabeth II **Obv:** Head right **Rev:** Britania in chariot right

Date	Mintage	F	VF	XF	Unc	BU
2009	—	—	—	—	—BV+15%	—
2009 Proof	1,250	BV+5%				

KM# 1138 100 POUNDS
34.0500 g., 0.9160 Gold 1.0027 oz. AGW, 32.7 mm. **Ruler:** Elizabeth II **Obv:** Head right **Rev:** Britannia bust right

Date	Mintage	F	VF	XF	Unc	BU
2010	—	—	—	—	—BV+15%	—
2010 Proof	1,250	BV+5%				

PIEDFORT

KM#	Date	Mintage	Identification	Issue Price	Mkt Val
P40	2003	6,795	50 Pence. 0.9250 Silver. 16.0000 g. KM#1036a.	—	110
P41	2003	9,871	Pound. 0.9250 Silver. 19.0000 g. KM#993a.	—	115
P42	ND2003	8,728	2 Pounds. 0.9250 Silver. 24.0000 g. KM#1037a.	—	95.00
P43	2004	4,054	50 Pence. 0.9250 Silver. 24.0000 g. KM#1047a.	—	110
P44	2004	7,013	Pound. 0.9250 Silver. 19.0000 g. KM#1048a.	—	115
P45	2004	5,303	2 Pounds. 0.9250 Silver. 24.0000 g. KM#1049a.	—	125
P46	ND2005	4,585	2 Pounds. 0.9250 Silver. 24.0000 g. KM#1052a.	—	95.00
P47	2004	2,500	5 Pounds. 0.9250 Silver. 56.5600 g. KM#1055a.	—	150
P48	2005	3,808	50 Pence. 0.9250 Silver. 16.0000 g. KM#1050a.	—	110

KM#	Date	Mintage	Identification	Issue Price	Mkt Val
P49	ND2005	4,798	2 Pounds. 0.9250 Silver. 24.0000 g. KM#1056a.	—	95.00
P50	2005	6,007	Pound. 0.9250 Silver. 19.0000 g. KM#1051a.	—	115
P51	2005	—	5 Pounds. 0.9250 Silver. KM#1053a.	—	150
P52	2005	—	5 Pounds. 0.9250 Silver. KM#1054a.	—	150
P53	2006	3,532	50 Pence. 0.9250 Silver. 16.0000 g. KM#1057a.	—	110
P54	2006	3,415	50 Pence. 0.9250 Silver. 16.0000 g. KM#1058a.	—	110
P55	2006	7,500	Pound. 0.9250 Silver. 19.0000 g. KM#1051a.	—	125
P56	2006	3,199	2 Pounds. 0.9250 Silver. 24.0000 g. KM#1060a.	—	115
P57	2006	3,018	2 Pounds. 0.9250 Silver. 24.0000 g. KM#1061a.	—	115
P58	2006	5,000	5 Pounds. 0.9250 Silver. KM#1062a.	—	150
P59	2007	1,555	50 Pence. 0.9250 Silver. 16.0000 g. KM#1073a.	—	135
P60	2007	5,739	Pound. 0.9250 Silver. 19.0000 g. KM#1074a.	—	95.00
P61	2007	4,000	2 Pounds. 0.9250 Silver. 24.0000 g. KM#1075a.	—	115
P62	2007	3,990	2 Pounds. 0.9250 Silver. 24.0000 g. KM#1076a.	—	115
P63	2007	2,000	5 Pounds. 0.9250 Silver. 56.5600 g. KM#1077a.	—	150
P64	2007	250	5 Pounds. 0.9995 Platinum. 94.2000 g.	—	7,500
P65	2008	—	2 Pounds. 0.9250 Silver. 24.0000 g. KM#1106a.	—	115
P66	2009	3,500	2 Pounds. 0.9250 Silver. 24.0000 g. KM#1115a.	—	115
P67	2008	—	5 Pounds. 0.9250 Silver. 56.5600 g. KM#1104.	—	150
P68	2008	—	5 Pounds. 0.9250 Silver. 56.5600 g. KM#1103.	—	150
P70	2009	4,009	5 Pounds. 0.9250 Silver. 56.5600 g. KM#1118a.	—	180
P75	2010	3,000	Pound. 0.9250 Silver. 19.0000 g. KM#1158a.	—	110
P76	2010	5,000	Pound. 0.9250 Silver. 19.0000 g.	—	110
P77	2011	—	Penny. 0.9250 Silver. KM#1107a.	—	15.00
P78	2011	—	2 Pence. 0.9250 Silver. KM#1108a.	—	25.00
P79	2011	—	5 Pence. 0.9250 Silver. KM#1109a.	—	35.00
P80	2011	—	10 Pence. 0.9250 Silver. KM#1110a.	—	80.00
P81	2011	—	20 Pence. 0.9250 Silver. KM#1111a.	—	80.00
P82	2011	—	50 Pence. 0.9250 Silver. KM#1112a.	—	125
P83	2011	—	Pound. 0.9250 Silver. KM#1113a.	—	115
P84	2011	—	Pound. 0.9250 Silver. 19.0000 g. KM#1197a.	—	115
P85	2011	—	Pound. 0.9250 Silver. 19.0000 g. KM#1198a.	—	115
P86	2011	—	50 Pence. 0.9250 Silver. 24.0000 g. KM#1196a.	—	125
P87	2011	—	2 Pounds. 0.9250 Silver. 24.0000 g. KM#1199a.	—	115
P88	2011	—	2 Pounds. 0.9250 Silver. 24.0000 g. KM#1200a.	—	115
P89	2011	—	5 Pounds. 0.9250 Silver. 56.5600 g. KM#1201a.	—	150
P97	2008	—	50 Pence. Silver. KM#1112a	—	125
P98	2009	—	50 Pence. Silver. KM#1114a	—	125
P99	2010	—	50 Pence. Silver. KM#1165a	—	125
P101	2001	8,464	Pound. 0.9250 Silver. 19.0000 g. KM#1013a	—	115
P102	2002	6,599	Pound. 0.9250 Silver. 19.0000 g. KM#1030a	—	115
P103	2008	8,000	Pound. 0.9250 Silver. 19.0000 g. KM#1113a	—	125
P106	2001	6,759	2 Pounds. 0.9250 Silver. 24.0000 g. KM#1014a	—	125
P107	2002	—	2 Pounds. 0.9250 Silver. 24.0000 g. KM#1031a	—	125
P108	2002	—	2 Pounds. 0.9250 Silver. 24.0000 g. KM#1032a	—	125
P109	2002	—	2 Pounds. 0.9250 Silver. 24.0000 g. KM#1033a	—	125
P110	2002	—	2 Pounds. 0.9250 Silver. 24.0000 g. Piedfort w/color. KM#1034a	—	125
P111	2009	3,500	2 Pounds. Silver. 24.0000 g.	—	115
P113	2008	5,000	5 Pounds. Silver. 56.5600 g. KM#1103a	—	150
P114	2010	—	5 Pounds. Silver. 56.5600 g. KM#1151a	—	160

MAUNDY SETS

KM#	Date	Mintage	Identification	Issue Price	Mkt Val
MDS260	2001 (4)	1,132	KM#898-899, 901-902. Westminster Abbey	—	300
MDS261	2002 (4)	1,681	KM#898-899, 901-902. Canterbury Cathedral	—	300
MDS262	2003 (4)	1,608	KM#898-899, 901-902. Gloucester Cathedral	—	325

KM#	Date	Mintage	Identification	Issue Price	Mkt Val
MDS263	2004 (4)	1,613	KM#898-899, 901-902. Liverpool Cathedral	—	325
MDS264	2005 (4)	1,685	KM#898-899, 901-902. Wakefield Cathedral	—	325
MDS265	2006 (4)	1,811	KM#898-899, 901-902. Guilford Cathedral	—	325
MDS266	2007 (4)	1,822	KM#898-899, 901-902. Manchester Cathedral	—	325
MDS267	2008 (4)	1,833	KM#898-899, 901-902. St. Patrick's Cathedral	—	325
MDS268	2009 (4)	1,602	KM#898-899, 901-902.	—	325
MDS269	2010 (4)	1,617	KM#898-899, 901-902.	—	325
MDS270	2011 (4)	—	KM#898-899, 901-902.	—	325

MINT SETS

KM#	Date	Mintage	Identification	Issue Price	Mkt Val
MS129	2001 (9)	57,741	KM#986-991, 994, 1013-1015 B.U. set	22.50	25.00
MS130	2001 (9)	—	KM#986-991, 994, 1013-1014 Wedding Collection	27.50	25.00
MS131	2001 (9)	—	KM#986-991, 994, 1013-1014 Baby Gift Set	27.50	25.00
MS132	2002 (8)	60,539	KM#986-991, 994, 1030	22.50	20.00
MS133	2002 (8)	—	KM#986-991, 994, 1030 Wedding Collection	27.50	20.00
MS134	2002 (8)	—	KM#986-991, 994, 1030 Baby Gift Set	27.50	20.00
MSA135	2004 (10)	46,032	KM#986-991, 994, 1047-1049 BU Set	—	35.00
MSB135	2004 (10)	4,214	KM#986-991, 994, 1047-1049, 1055 Wedding Collection	—	35.00
MSC135	2004 (10)	34,371	KM#986-991, 994, 1047-1049, 1055 Baby Gift Set	—	35.00
MS135	2003 (10)	62,741	KM#986-991, 993, 994, 1036-1037 BU Set	22.50	35.00
MS136	2003 (10)	7,130	KM#986-991, 993, 994, 1036-1037 Wedding Collection	27.50	30.00
MS137	2003 (10)	43,128	KM#986-991, 993, 994, 1036-1037 Baby Gift Set	27.50	30.00
MS138	2005 (10)	51,776	KM#986-991, 994, 1050-1052	26.50	30.00
MS139	2005 (10)	29,924	KM#986-991, 994, 1050-1052 Baby Gift Set	36.50	35.00
MS140	2005 (3)	—	KM#1050-1052 New Coinage Set	16.25	17.50
MS141	2005 (2)	—	KM#1053-1054 Trafalgar Set	36.00	35.00
MS142	2006 (10)	74,231	KM#986-990, 1057-1061, BV set	30.00	60.00
MS143	2006 (10)	25,878	KM#986-990, 1057-1061 Baby Gift Set	38.50	60.00
MS144	2007 (6)	—	KM#986-991	—	10.00

PROOF SETS

KM#	Date	Mintage	Identification	Issue Price	Mkt Val
PS116	2001 (3)	1,500	KM#1001-1002, 1014a	795	525
PS117	2001 (4)	1,000	KM#1001-1003,1014a	1,645	2,250
PS118	2001 (4)	5,000	KM#1016-1019	—	175
PSA119	2001 (3)	1,500	KM#1001, 1002, 1014b	—	525
PSB119	2001 (4)	1,000	KM#1001, 1002, 1014b, 1015b	—	2,700
PS119	2001 (4)	1,000	KM#1020-1023	1,595	3,200
PS120	2002 (3)	5,000	KM#1025-1027	795	1,275
PS121	2002 (4)	3,000	KM#1025-1028	1,645	3,000
PS122	2002 (4)	3,358	KM#1031-1034; Standard Set	34.95	35.00
PS123	2002 (4)	673	KM#1031-1034; Display Set	44.95	40.00
PS124	2002 (4)	2,553	KM#1031a-1034a; Display Set	120	150
PS125	2002 (4)	315	KM#1031b-1034b; Display Set	1,675	3,000
PS126	2002 (4)	1,000	KM#1008-1011	1,600	3,200
PS127	2001 (10)	10,000	KM#986-991, 994, 1013-1015 Executive Proof Set in display case	115	80.00
PS128	2001 (10)	30,000	KM#986-991, 994, 1013-1015 Deluxe Proof Set in red leather case	72.50	80.00
PS129	2001 (10)	28,244	KM#986-991, 994, 1013-1015 Standard Proof Set in simple case	50.00	65.00
PS130	2001 (10)	1,351	KM#986-991, 994, 1013-1015 Gift Proof Set with a pack of occasion cards	65.00	65.00
PS131	2002 (9)	5,000	KM#986-991, 994, 1024, 1030 Executive Proof Set	100	60.00
PS132	2002 (9)	30,000	KM#986-991, 994, 1024, 1030 Deluxe Proof Set	70.00	55.00
PS133	2002 (9)	30,884	KM#986-991, 994, 1024, 1030 Standard Proof Set	48.00	55.00
PS134	2002 (9)	1,544	KM#986-991, 994, 1024, 1030 Gift Proof Set	62.40	55.00
PSA135	2002 (13)	—	KM#898a, 899a, 901a, 902a, 986c, 987c, 988b, 989b, 990b, 991b, 1030b, 994c, 1024b Queen Elizabeth II - Golden Jubilee 1952-2002, set is struck in gold (including Maundy set), in presentation box	—	11,250
PS135	2003 (11)	5,000	KM#986-991, 993, 994, 1036-1038 Executive Proof Set	100	85.00
PS136	2003 (11)	14,863	KM#986-991, 993, 994, 1036-1038 Deluxe Proof Set	72.00	80.00
PS137	2003 (11)	23,650	KM#986-991, 993, 994, 1036-1038 Standard Proof Set	50.00	80.00
PSA138	2003 (4)	3,669	KM#1039, 1044-1046	—	180

KM#	Date	Mintage	Identification	Issue Price	Mkt Val
PSB138	2004 (11)	4,101	KM#986-991, 994, 1047-1049, 1055 Executive Proof Set	—	80.00
PSC138	2004 (11)	12,968	KM#986-991, 994, 1047-1049, 1055 Deluxe Proof Set	—	80.00
PSD138	2004 (11)	17,951	KM#986-991, 994, 1047-1049, 1055 Standard Proof Set	—	80.00
PS138	2005 (12)	4,290	KM#986-991, 994, 1050-1054 Executive Set	146	95.00
PS139	2005 (12)	14,899	KM#986-991, 994, 1050-1054 Deluxe Proof Set	80.00	95.00
PS140	2005 (12)	21,374	KM#986-991, 994, 1050-1054, Standard Proof Set	60.00	95.00
PS141	2005 (3)	417	KM#1068-1070	850	1,350
PS142	2005 (4)	1,439	KM#1068-1070	1,895	2,850
PS143	2005 (4)	820	KM#1064-1066	820	1,100
PS144	2005 (4)	2,500	KM#1064-1067	1,925	2,600
PS145	2005 (2)	—	P39, P40	—	175
PS146	2006 (13)	5,000	KM#986-991, 994, 1057-1062 Executive Proof Set, wooden case	—	140
PS147	2006 (13)	15,000	KM#986-991, 994, 1057-1062 Deluxe Proof Set	82.50	140
PS148	2006 (13)	17,689	KM#986-991, 994, 1057-1062 Standard Proof Set	65.00	140
PS149	2006 (5)	3,000	KM#1000a, 1012a, 1018a, 1039, 1063a	475	525
PS150	2006 (3)	1,750	KM#1001, 1002, 1072	1,015	1,150
PS151	2006 (4)	1,750	KM#1001-1003, 1072	2,091	2,650
PS152	2007 (13)	18,215	KM#986-991, 994, 1057-1062	65.00	140
PS153	2007 (4)	1,750	KM#1001-1003, 1072	—	2,850
PS154	2007 (3)	750	KM#1001-1002, 1072	—	1,200
PS155	2007 (2)	5,000	KM#1001-1002	—	550
PS156	2007 (5)	3,000	KM#P33, P35-P38	450	500
PS160	2002 (4)	—	KM#1029, 1079-1081	—	175
PS161	2003 (4)	1,250	KM#1040-1043	—	2,800
PS162	2004 (4)	—	KM#1029, 1079-1081	—	175
PS163	2004 (4)	973	KM#1008-1011	—	3,000
PS164	2005 (4)	2,360	KM#1063, 1085-1087	—	185
PS165	2006 (4)	—	KM#1029, 1079-1081	—	175
PS166	2006 (4)	—	KM#1008-1011	—	2,900
PS167	2007 (4)	—	KM#1078, 1088-1090	—	185
PS168	2007 (4)	—	KM#1091-1094	—	2,950
PS169	2007 (4)	—	KM#1091a-1094a	—	5,850
PS170	2008 (4)	—	KM#1095-1098	—	225
PS171	2008 (4)	—	KM#1099-1102	—	3,000
PS172	2008 (4)	—	KM#1099a-1102a	—	5,850

GREECE

The Hellenic (Greek) Republic is situated in southeastern Europe on the southern tip of the Balkan Peninsula. The republic includes many islands, the most important of which are Crete and the Ionian Islands. Greece (including islands) has an area of 50,944 sq. mi. (131,940 sq. km.) and a population of 10.3 million. Capital: Athens. Greece is still largely agricultural. Tobacco, cotton, fruit and wool are exported.

MONETARY SYSTEM
100 Euro Cent = 1 Euro

REPUBLIC

EURO COINAGE
European Union Issues

The Greek Euro coinage series contains the denomination in Lepta as well.

KM# 181   EURO CENT
2.2700 g., Copper Plated Steel, 16.2 mm. **Obv:** Ancient Athenian trireme **Rev:** Denomination and globe **Edge:** Plain

Date	Mintage	F	VF	XF	Unc	BU
2002	101,000,000	—	—	—	0.35	—
2002 F in star	15,000,000	—	—	—	1.25	—
2003	35,200,000	—	—	—	0.35	—
2004	50,000,000	—	—	—	0.35	—
2005	15,000,000	—	—	—	0.35	—
2006	45,000,000	—	—	—	0.35	—
2007	60,000,000	—	—	—	0.35	—
2008	24,000,000	—	—	—	0.35	—
2009	50,000,000	—	—	—	0.35	—
2010	27,000,000	—	—	—	0.35	—

Date	Mintage	F	VF	XF	Unc	BU
2011	35,000,000	—	—	—	0.35	—
2011 Proof	2,500	Value: 15.00				

KM# 182   2 EURO CENT
3.0300 g., Copper Plated Steel, 18.7 mm. **Obv:** Corvette sailing ship **Rev:** Denomination and globe **Edge:** Grooved

Date	Mintage	F	VF	XF	Unc	BU
2002	176,000,000	—	—	—	0.50	—
2002 F in star	18,000,000	—	—	—	1.00	—
2003	10,000,000	—	—	—	0.50	—
2004	25,000,000	—	—	—	0.50	—
2005	15,000,000	—	—	—	0.50	—
2006	45,000,000	—	—	—	0.50	—
2007	25,000,103	—	—	—	0.50	—
2008	68,000,000	—	—	—	0.50	—
2009	16,000,000	—	—	—	0.50	—
2010	32,000,000	—	—	—	0.50	—
2011	47,000,000	—	—	—	0.50	—
2011 Proof	2,500	Value: 15.00				

KM# 183   5 EURO CENT
3.8600 g., Copper Plated Steel, 21.2 mm. **Obv:** Freighter **Rev:** Denomination and globe **Edge:** Plain

Date	Mintage	F	VF	XF	Unc	BU
2002	211,000,000	—	—	—	1.00	—
2002 F in star	90,000,000	—	—	—	1.25	—
2003	750,000	—	—	—	1.00	—
2004	250,000	—	—	—	1.00	—
2005	1,000,000	—	—	—	1.00	—
2006	50,000,000	—	—	—	1.00	—
2007	55,005,598	—	—	—	1.00	—
2008	50,000,000	—	—	—	1.00	—
2009	38,000,000	—	—	—	1.00	—
2010	5,000,000	—	—	—	1.00	—
2011	34,000,000	—	—	—	1.00	—
2011 Proof	2,500	Value: 15.00				

KM# 184   10 EURO CENT
4.0700 g., Brass, 19.7 mm. **Obv:** Bust of Rhgas Feriaou's half right **Rev:** Denomination and map **Edge:** Reeded

Date	Mintage	F	VF	XF	Unc	BU
2002	138,000,000	—	—	—	1.25	—
2002 F in star	100,000,000	—	—	—	2.00	—
2003	600,000	—	—	—	1.25	—
2004	10,000,000	—	—	—	1.25	—
2005	25,000,000	—	—	—	1.25	—
2006	45,000,000	—	—	—	1.25	—

KM# 211   10 EURO CENT
4.0700 g., Brass, 19.25 mm. **Obv:** Bust of Rhgas Feriaou's half right **Rev:** Relief map of Western Europe, stars, lines and value **Edge:** Reeded

Date	Mintage	F	VF	XF	Unc	BU
2007	63,000,000	—	—	—	1.25	—
2008	40,000,000	—	—	—	1.25	—
2009	46,000,000	—	—	—	1.25	—
2010	5,000,000	—	—	—	1.25	—
2011	36,000,000	—	—	—	1.25	—
2011 Proof	2,500	Value: 15.00				

KM# 185   20 EURO CENT
5.7300 g., Brass, 22.25 mm. **Obv:** Bust of John Kapodistrias half right **Rev:** Denomination and map **Edge:** Notched

Date	Mintage	F	VF	XF	Unc	BU
2002	209,000,000	—	—	—	1.25	—
2002 E in star	120,000,000	—	—	—	2.25	—
2003	800,000	—	—	—	1.25	—
2004	500,000	—	—	—	1.25	—

Date	Mintage	F	VF	XF	Unc	BU
2005	1,000,000	—	—	—	1.25	—
2006	1,000,000	—	—	—	1.25	—

KM# 212 20 EURO CENT
5.7300 g., Brass, 22.1 mm. **Obv:** Bust of John Kapodistrias' half right **Rev:** Relief map of Western Europe, stars, lines and value **Edge:** Notched

Date	Mintage	F	VF	XF	Unc	BU
2007	1,000,000	—	—	—	1.25	—
2008	20,000,000	—	—	—	1.25	—
2009	24,000,000	—	—	—	1.25	—
2010	12,000,000	—	—	—	1.25	—
2011	965,000	—	—	—	1.25	—
2011 Proof	2,500	Value: 20.00				

KM# 186 50 EURO CENT
7.8100 g., Brass, 24.2 mm. **Obv:** Bust of El. Venizelos half left **Rev:** Denomination and map **Edge:** Reeded

Date	Mintage	F	VF	XF	Unc	BU
2002	93,000,000	—	—	—	1.50	—
2002 F in star	70,000,000	—	—	—	2.50	—
2003	700,000	—	—	—	1.50	—
2004	500,000	—	—	—	1.50	—
2005	1,000,000	—	—	—	1.50	—
2006	1,000,000	—	—	—	1.50	—

KM# 213 50 EURO CENT
7.8100 g., Brass, 24.2 mm. **Obv:** Bust of El. Venizelos half left **Rev:** Relief map of Western Europe, stars, lines and value **Edge:** Reeded

Date	Mintage	F	VF	XF	Unc	BU
2007	1,000,000	—	—	—	1.00	1.50
2008	10,000,000	—	—	—	1.00	1.50
2009	7,000,000	—	—	—	1.00	1.50
2010	6,000,000	—	—	—	1.00	1.50
2011	7,000,000	—	—	—	1.00	1.50
2011 Proof	2,500	Value: 25.00				

KM# 187 EURO
7.5000 g., Bi-Metallic Copper-Nickel center in Nickel-Brass ring, 23.25 mm. **Obv:** Ancient Athenian coin design **Rev:** Denomination and map **Edge:** Segmented reeding

Date	Mintage	F	VF	XF	Unc	BU
2002	61,500,000	—	—	—	4.00	—
2002 S in star	50,000,000	—	—	—	6.00	—
2003	11,000,000	—	—	—	7.50	—
2004	10,000,000	—	—	—	5.00	—
2005	10,000,000	—	—	—	5.00	—
2006	10,000,000	—	—	—	5.00	—

KM# 214 EURO
7.5000 g., Bi-Metallic Copper-Nickel center in Nickel-Brass ring, 23.25 mm. **Obv:** Ancient Athenian coin design **Rev:** Relief map of Western Europe, stars, lines and value **Edge:** Segmented reeding

Date	Mintage	F	VF	XF	Unc	BU
2007	24,000,000	—	—	—	3.00	4.00
2008	4,000,000	—	—	—	3.00	4.00
2009	18,000,000	—	—	—	3.00	4.00
2010	11,000,000	—	—	—	3.00	4.00
2011	965,000	—	—	—	3.00	4.00
2011 Proof	2,500	Value: 40.00				

KM# 188 2 EURO
8.5000 g., Bi-Metallic Nickel-Brass center in Copper-Nickel ring, 25.75 mm. **Obv:** Europa seated on a bull **Rev:** Denomination and map **Edge:** Reeded with Greek legend and stars

Date	Mintage	F	VF	XF	Unc	BU
2002	75,400,000	—	—	—	4.00	—
2002 S in star	70,000,000	—	—	—	6.50	—
2003	550,000	—	—	—	20.00	—
2004 In sets only	30,000	—	—	—	50.00	—
2005	1,000,000	—	—	—	4.00	—
2006	1,000,000	—	—	—	4.00	—

KM# 209 2 EURO
8.5000 g., Bi-Metallic Nickel-Brass center in Copper-Nickel ring., 25.75 mm. **Subject:** 2004 Olympics **Obv:** Discus thrower **Rev:** Denomination and map **Edge:** Reeded with Greek legend and stars

Date	Mintage	F	VF	XF	Unc	BU
2004	49,500,000	—	—	—	4.00	6.00
2004 Prooflike	500,000	—	—	—	—	15.00

KM# 215 2 EURO
8.5000 g., Bi-Metallic Nickel-Brass center in Copper-Nickel ring, 25.75 mm. **Obv:** Europa seated on a bull **Rev:** Relief map of Western Europe, stars, lines and value **Edge:** Reeded with Greek legend and stars

Date	Mintage	F	VF	XF	Unc	BU
2007 In sets only	15,000	—	—	—	—	25.00
2008	2,000,000	—	—	—	3.00	10.00
2009	982,000	—	—	—	3.00	5.00
2010	2,000,000	—	—	—	3.00	5.00
2011	—	—	—	—	3.00	5.00
2011 Proof	—	Value: 50.00				

KM# 216 2 EURO
8.5000 g., Bi-Metallic Nickel-Brass center in Copper-Nickel ring, 25.75 mm. **Subject:** 50th Anniversary - Treaty of Rome **Obv:** Open treaty book **Rev:** Large value at left, modified outline of Europe at right **Edge:** Reeded with Greek legend and stars

Date	Mintage	F	VF	XF	Unc	BU
2007	4,000,000	—	—	—	—	9.00

KM# 227 2 EURO
8.5000 g., Bi-Metallic Nickel-Brass center in Copper-Nickel ring, 25.75 mm. **Subject:** European Monetary Union, 10th Anniversary **Obv:** Stick figure and Euro symbol **Rev:** Reeded with Greek legend and stars

Date	Mintage	F	VF	XF	Unc	BU
2009	4,000,000	—	—	—	—	7.00

KM# 236 2 EURO
8.5000 g., Bi-Metallic Nickel-Brass center in Copper-Nickel ring, 25.75 mm. **Subject:** Battle of Marathon, 2500th Anniversary **Rev:** Ancient Greek Warrior holding javelin running **Edge:** Reeded with Greek legend and stars

Date	Mintage	F	VF	XF	Unc	BU
2010	3,500,000	—	—	—	—	9.00

KM# 239 2 EURO
8.5000 g., Bi-Metallic Nickel-Brass center in Copper-Nickel ring, 25.75 mm. **Subject:** Special Olympics - Athens

Date	Mintage	F	VF	XF	Unc	BU
2011	1,000,000	—	—	—	6.00	7.50

KM# 245 2 EURO
8.5000 g., Bi-Metallic Nickel-Brass center in Copper-Nickel ring, 25.75 mm. **Subject:** Euro coinage, 10th Anniversary **Obv:** Euro symbol on globe at center, child-like rendering around

Date	Mintage	F	VF	XF	Unc	BU
2012	1,000,000	—	—	—	6.00	8.00
2012 Special Unc.		—	—	—	—	15.00

KM# 190 10 EURO
34.0000 g., 0.9250 Silver 1.0111 oz. ASW, 40 mm. **Subject:** Olympics **Obv:** Olympic rings in wreath above value within circle of stars **Rev:** Ancient and modern runners **Edge:** Plain **Note:** Olympics

Date	Mintage	F	VF	XF	Unc	BU
ND (2003) Proof	68,000	Value: 60.00				

KM# 191 10 EURO
34.0000 g., 0.9250 Silver 1.0111 oz. ASW, 40 mm. **Subject:** Olympics **Obv:** Olympic rings in wreath above value within circle of stars **Rev:** Ancient and modern discus throwers **Edge:** Plain

Date	Mintage	F	VF	XF	Unc	BU
ND(2003) Proof	68,000	Value: 60.00				

KM# 193 10 EURO
34.0000 g., 0.9250 Silver 1.0111 oz. ASW, 40 mm. **Subject:** Olympics **Obv:** Olympic rings in wreath above value within circle of stars **Rev:** Ancient and modern javelin throwers **Edge:** Plain

Date	Mintage	F	VF	XF	Unc	BU
ND(2003) Proof	68,000	Value: 60.00				

KM# 194 10 EURO
34.0000 g., 0.9250 Silver 1.0111 oz. ASW, 40 mm. **Subject:** Olympics **Obv:** Olympic rings in wreath above value within circle of stars **Rev:** Ancient and modern long jumpers **Edge:** Plain

Date	Mintage	F	VF	XF	Unc	BU
ND(2003) Proof	68,000	Value: 60.00				

KM# 196 10 EURO
34.0000 g., 0.9250 Silver 1.0111 oz. ASW, 40 mm. **Subject:** Olympics **Obv:** Olympic rings in wreath above value within circle of stars **Rev:** Ancient and modern relay runners **Edge:** Plain

Date	Mintage	F	VF	XF	Unc	BU
ND(2003) Proof	68,000	Value: 60.00				

KM# 197 10 EURO
34.0000 g., 0.9250 Silver 1.0111 oz. ASW, 40 mm. **Subject:** Olympics **Obv:** Olympic rings in wreath above value within circle of stars **Rev:** Ancient and modern horsemen **Edge:** Plain

Date	Mintage	F	VF	XF	Unc	BU
ND(2003) Proof	68,000	Value: 60.00				

KM# 199 10 EURO
34.0000 g., 0.9250 Silver 1.0111 oz. ASW, 40 mm. **Subject:** Olympics **Obv:** Olympic rings in wreath above value within circle of stars **Rev:** Modern ribbon dancer and two ancient female acrobats **Edge:** Plain

Date	Mintage	F	VF	XF	Unc	BU
ND(2003) Proof	68,000	Value: 60.00				

KM# 200 10 EURO
34.0000 g., 0.9250 Silver 1.0111 oz. ASW, 40 mm. **Subject:** Olympics **Obv:** Olympic rings in wreath above value within a circle of stars **Rev:** Ancient and modern female swimmers **Edge:** Plain

Date	Mintage	F	VF	XF	Unc	BU
ND(2003) Proof	68,000	Value: 60.00				

KM# 208 10 EURO
9.7500 g., 0.9250 Silver 0.2899 oz. ASW, 28.25 mm. **Subject:** Greek Presidency of E. U. **Obv:** National arms in wreath above value **Rev:** Stylized document design **Edge:** Notched

Date	Mintage	F	VF	XF	Unc	BU
2003 Proof	50,000	Value: 80.00				

KM# 202 10 EURO
34.0000 g., 0.9250 Silver 1.0111 oz. ASW, 40 mm. **Subject:** Olympics **Obv:** Olympic rings in wreath above value within circle of stars **Rev:** Ancient and modern weight lifters **Edge:** Plain

Date	Mintage	F	VF	XF	Unc	BU
ND(2004) Proof	68,000	Value: 60.00				

KM# 203 10 EURO
34.0000 g., 0.9250 Silver 1.0111 oz. ASW, 40 mm. **Subject:** Olympics **Obv:** Olympic rings in wreath above value within circle of stars **Rev:** Ancient and modern wrestlers **Edge:** Plain

Date	Mintage	F	VF	XF	Unc	BU
ND(2004) Proof	68,000	Value: 60.00				

KM# 205   10 EURO
34.0000 g., 0.9250 Silver 1.0111 oz. ASW, 40 mm. **Subject:** Olympics **Obv:** Olympic rings in wreath above value within circle of stars **Rev:** Ancient and modern handball players **Edge:** Plain

Date	Mintage	F	VF	XF	Unc	BU
ND(2004) Proof	68,000	Value: 60.00				

KM# 206   10 EURO
34.0000 g., 0.9250 Silver 1.0111 oz. ASW, 40 mm. **Subject:** Olympics **Obv:** Olympic rings in wreath above value within circle of stars **Rev:** Ancient and modern soccer players **Edge:** Plain

Date	Mintage	F	VF	XF	Unc	BU
ND(2004) Proof	68,000	Value: 60.00				

KM# 230   10 EURO
34.0000 g., 0.9250 Silver 1.0111 oz. ASW **Obv:** Wreath **Rev:** Torch runner and map of Australia

Date	Mintage	F	VF	XF	Unc	BU
2004 Proof	10,000	Value: 110				

KM# 231   10 EURO
34.0000 g., 0.9250 Silver 1.0111 oz. ASW **Rev:** Torch runner and map of Asia

Date	Mintage	F	VF	XF	Unc	BU
2004 Proof	10,000	Value: 110				

KM# 232   10 EURO
34.0000 g., 0.9250 Silver 1.0111 oz. ASW **Rev:** Torch runner and map of Africa

Date	Mintage	F	VF	XF	Unc	BU
2004 Proof	10,000	Value: 110				

KM# 233   10 EURO
34.0000 g., 0.9250 Silver 1.0111 oz. ASW **Rev:** Torch runner and map of North and South America

Date	Mintage	F	VF	XF	Unc	BU
2004 Proof	10,000	Value: 110				

KM# 217   10 EURO
9.7500 g., 0.9250 Silver 0.2899 oz. ASW **Subject:** Olympic National Park **Obv:** National arms above stylized flowers **Rev:** Four Titans above flowers in camp

Date	Mintage	F	VF	XF	Unc	BU
2005 Proof	25,000	Value: 45.00				

KM# 218   10 EURO
9.7500 g., 0.9250 Silver 0.2899 oz. ASW, 28.25 mm. **Subject:** PATRA - European Capitol of Culture - Achaia **Obv:** National arms at upper right, stylized bridge below **Rev:** PATRA logo **Edge:** Plain

Date	Mintage	F	VF	XF	Unc	BU
2006 Proof	—	Value: 50.00				

KM# 219   10 EURO
34.0000 g., 0.9250 Silver 1.0111 oz. ASW, 40.00 mm. **Obv:** National arms above stylized flowers **Rev:** Outline of Greece at left, statue of Zeus, flowers at right **Edge:** Plain

Date	Mintage	F	VF	XF	Unc	BU
2006 Proof	5,000	Value: 55.00				

KM# 220   10 EURO
34.0000 g., 0.9250 Silver 1.0111 oz. ASW, 40.00 mm. **Subject:** National Parks - Mount Olympus - International Biosphere Reserve **Obv:** National arms above stylized flowers **Rev:** Archaeological outline of Dion City above landscape **Edge:** Plain

Date	Mintage	F	VF	XF	Unc	BU
2006 Proof	5,000	Value: 55.00				

KM# 221   10 EURO
34.0000 g., 0.9250 Silver 1.0111 oz. ASW, 40.00 mm. **Subject:** National Parks - Arkoudorema River in Southern Pindos - Valia Kalda **Obv:** National arms on stylized tree **Rev:** Outlined map at upper left, bird perched on stalk, flowers at center right **Edge:** Plain

Date	Mintage	F	VF	XF	Unc	BU
2007 Proof	5,000	Value: 60.00				

KM# 222   10 EURO
34.0000 g., 0.9250 Silver 1.0111 oz. ASW, 40.00 mm. **Subject:** National Parks - Valia Kalda - Southern Pindos **Obv:** National arms on stylized tree **Rev:** Tree line **Edge:** Plain

Date	Mintage	F	VF	XF	Unc	BU
2007 Proof	5,000	Value: 60.00				

KM# 223   10 EURO
9.7500 g., 0.9250 Silver 0.2899 oz. ASW, 28.25 mm. **Subject:** 30th Anniversary Death of Maria Callas, Operatic Soprano **Obv:** National arms above denomination, facsimile signature below, music scores in background **Rev:** Bust of Maria Callas right **Edge:** Plain **Shape:** Spanish Flower

Date	Mintage	F	VF	XF	Unc	BU
2007 Proof	5,000	Value: 50.00				

KM# 224   10 EURO
9.7500 g., 0.9250 Silver 0.2899 oz. ASW, 28.25 mm. **Subject:** 50th Anniversary death of Nikos Kazantzakis, Author **Obv:** National arms above denomination, facsimile signature below **Rev:** Head of N. Kazantzakis facing 3/4 left **Edge:** Plain **Shape:** Spanish Flower

Date	Mintage	F	VF	XF	Unc	BU
2007 Proof	5,000	Value: 50.00				

KM# 225   10 EURO
9.7500 g., 0.9250 Silver 0.2899 oz. ASW, 28.25 mm. **Subject:** Acropolis Museum **Obv:** Panoramic view of the Acropolis **Rev:** Pediment sculpture

Date	Mintage	F	VF	XF	Unc	BU
2008	10,000	—	—	—	—	50.00

KM# 226   10 EURO
9.7500 g., 0.9250 Silver 0.2899 oz. ASW **Subject:** Yannis Ritsas

Date	Mintage	F	VF	XF	Unc	BU
2009 Proof	—	Value: 50.00				

KM# 228   10 EURO
9.7500 g., 0.9250 Silver 0.2899 oz. ASW, 28.25 mm. **Subject:** International Year of Astronomy

Date	Mintage	F	VF	XF	Unc	BU
2009 Proof	—	Value: 45.00				

KM# 237   10 EURO
34.0000 g., 0.9250 Silver 1.0111 oz. ASW, 40 mm. **Subject:** Sofia Vempo, 100th Anniversary of Birth **Obv:** Sofia Vempo portrait **Rev:** Stave, national emblem and value **Shape:** Spanish flower

Date	Mintage	F	VF	XF	Unc	BU
2010 Proof	5,000	Value: 65.00				

KM# 238   10 EURO
9.7500 g., 0.9250 Silver 0.2899 oz. ASW, 28.25 mm. **Subject:** International Year of Biodiversity **Obv:** Various species of Biodiversity **Rev:** Nature's species, national emblem and value **Shape:** Spanish flower

Date	Mintage	F	VF	XF	Unc	BU
2010 Proof	5,000	Value: 50.00				

KM# 240   10 EURO
9.7500 g., 0.9250 Silver 0.2899 oz. ASW, 28.25 mm. **Subject:** XIII Special Olympics, Special Olympics Founder Declaration **Obv:** Declaration over the Acropolis of Athens, Radiant Sun **Rev:** Special Olympics emblem, National arms below value **Shape:** 5 double edge notches

Date	Mintage	F	VF	XF	Unc	BU
2011 Proof, In sets only	7,500	Value: 40.00				

KM# 241   10 EURO
9.7500 g., 0.9250 Silver 0.2899 oz. ASW, 28.25 mm. **Subject:** XIII Special Olympics, Athletes in Union **Obv:** Stylized athletes around a radiant sun and olive branch **Rev:** Panathenaikon Stadium below the National Arms and value **Shape:** 5 double edge notches

Date	Mintage	F	VF	XF	Unc	BU
2011	—	—	—	—	—	—
2011 Proof, in sets only	7,500	Value: 40.00				

KM# 242   10 EURO
34.1000 g., 0.9250 Silver 1.0141 oz. ASW, 40 mm. **Subject:** Special Olympics, Highlight **Obv:** Highlight from an event during the games **Rev:** Stylized elements from the XIII Special Olympics emblem in Athens, National Arms, value below

Date	Mintage	F	VF	XF	Unc	BU
2011 Proof	2,000	Value: 130				

KM# 243   10 EURO
34.1000 g., 0.9250 Silver 1.0141 oz. ASW, 40 mm. **Subject:** Special Olympics, Torch-bearer **Obv:** Torch-bearer **Rev:** Stylized elements from the XIII Special Olympics emblem in Athens, National Arms, value below

Date	Mintage	F	VF	XF	Unc	BU
2011 Proof	2,000	Value: 130				

KM# 210   20 EURO
24.0000 g., 0.9250 Silver 0.7137 oz. ASW, 37 mm. **Subject:** Bank of Greece 75th Anniversary **Obv:** Value **Rev:** Flag

Date	Mintage	F	VF	XF	Unc	BU
2003 Proof	15,000	Value: 1,100				

KM# 192   100 EURO
10.0000 g., 0.9999 Gold 0.3215 oz. AGW, 25 mm. **Subject:** Olympics **Obv:** Olympic rings in wreath above value within circle of stars **Rev:** Knossos Palace **Edge:** Plain

Date	Mintage	F	VF	XF	Unc	BU
ND(2003) Proof	28,000	Value: 580				

KM# 195   100 EURO
10.0000 g., 0.9999 Gold 0.3215 oz. AGW, 25 mm. **Subject:** Olympics **Obv:** Olympic rings in wreath above value within circle of stars **Rev:** Krypte archway **Edge:** Plain

Date	Mintage	F	VF	XF	Unc	BU
ND(2003) Proof	28,000	Value: 580				

KM# 198   100 EURO
10.0000 g., 0.9999 Gold 0.3215 oz. AGW, 25 mm. **Subject:** Olympics **Obv:** Olympic rings in wreath above value within circle of stars **Rev:** Panathenean Stadium **Edge:** Plain

Date	Mintage	F	VF	XF	Unc	BU
ND(2003) Proof	28,000	Value: 580				

KM# 201   100 EURO
10.0000 g., 0.9999 Gold 0.3215 oz. AGW, 25 mm. **Subject:** Olympics **Obv:** Olympic rings in wreath above value within circle of stars **Rev:** Zappeion Mansion **Edge:** Plain

Date	Mintage	F	VF	XF	Unc	BU
ND(2003) Proof	28,000	Value: 580				

KM# 204   100 EURO
10.0000 g., 0.9999 Gold 0.3215 oz. AGW, 25 mm. **Subject:** Olympics **Obv:** Olympic rings in wreath above value within circle of stars **Rev:** Acropolis **Edge:** Plain

Date	Mintage	F	VF	XF	Unc	BU
ND(2004) Proof	28,000	Value: 580				

KM# 207   100 EURO
10.0000 g., 0.9999 Gold 0.3215 oz. AGW, 25 mm. **Subject:** Olympics **Obv:** Olympic rings in wreath above value within circle of stars **Rev:** Academy of Athens **Edge:** Plain

Date	Mintage	F	VF	XF	Unc	BU
ND(2004) Proof	28,000	Value: 580				

KM# 234   100 EURO
10.0000 g., 0.9990 Gold 0.3212 oz. AGW **Rev:** Classical female handing torch to kneeling runner

Date	Mintage	F	VF	XF	Unc	BU
2004 Proof	10,000	Value: 580				

KM# 235   100 EURO
10.0000 g., 0.9990 Gold 0.3212 oz. AGW **Rev:** Torch runner and flag

Date	Mintage	F	VF	XF	Unc	BU
2004 Proof	10,000	Value: 580				

KM# 244   100 EURO
7.9881 g., 0.9166 Gold 0.2354 oz. AGW, 22.1 mm. **Subject:** Special Olympics' Athletes in Union **Obv:** Stylized Athletes around a radiant sun and olive branch **Rev:** Panathenaikon Stadium below the National Arms and value

Date	Mintage	F	VF	XF	Unc	BU
2011 Proof	1,000	Value: 1,300				

KM# 229   200 EURO
31.1050 g., 0.9990 Gold 0.9990 oz. AGW, 37 mm. **Subject:** Bank of Greece, 75th Anniversary

Date	Mintage	F	VF	XF	Unc	BU
2003 Proof	1,000	Value: 7,000				

MINT SETS

KM#	Date	Mintage	Identification	Issue Price	Mkt Val
MS6	2002 (8)	50,000	KM#181-188	—	30.00
MS7	2002F (8)	5,000	KM#181-188 Issued by Ministry of Finance	—	300
MS8	2003 (8)	—	KM#181-188	—	40.00
MS9	2003 (9)	—	KM#181-188, 208	—	80.00
MS11	2004 (8)	20,000	KM#181-188 2004 Discobole commemorating Olympic Games in Athens	—	65.00
MS12	2005 (8)	25,000	KM#181-188	—	35.00
MS13	2005 (9)	25,000	KM#181-188, 220 Mount Olympus as a National Park	—	70.00
MS14	2006 (9)	25,000	KM#181-188 (2005), 220 Aegina - Korinth set	28.00	70.00
MS15	2006 (9)	25,000	KM#181-188, 218 Patras - Cultural Capital of Europe	50.00	70.00
MS16	2007 (8)	15,000	KM#181-183, 211-215 Ancient Coins of the Aegean Sea	—	50.00
MS17	2007 (9)	15,000	KM#181-183, 211-215, 224 Nikos Kazantzakis	50.00	75.00
MS18	2007 (9)	15,000	KM#181-183, 211-215, 223 Maria Callas	50.00	95.00
MS19	2008 (8)	15,000	KM#181-183, 211-215	28.00	40.00
MS20	2008 (9)	10,000	KM#181-183, 211-215, 225	45.00	55.00
MS21	2009 (8)	7,500	KM#181-183, 211-215	28.00	45.00
MS22	2009 (9)	5,000	KM#181-183, 211-215, 226	45.00	55.00
MS23	2009 (9)	5,000	KM#181-183, 211-215, 228	45.00	55.00
MS24	2010 (8)	7,500	KM#181-183, 211-215	28.00	30.00
MS25	2010 (8)	7,500	KM#181-183, 211-214, 236	28.00	30.00
MS26	2010 (9)	5,000	KM#181-183, 211-215, 237 Sofia Vempo 100th Anniversary of Birth	45.00	70.00
MS27	2010 (9)	5,000	KM#181-183, 211-215, 238 International Year of Biodiversity	45.00	70.00
MS28	2011 (8)	15,000	KM#181-183, 211-215	28.00	40.00
MS29	2011 (9)	5,000	KM#181-183, 211-215, 239	28.00	45.00
MS30	2011 (9)	7,500	KM#181-183, 211-215, 240 Special Olympics - Declaration	45.00	70.00
MS31	2011 (9)	7,500	KM#181-183, 211-215, 241 Special Olympics - Unity	45.00	70.00

PROOF SETS

KM#	Date	Mintage	Identification	Issue Price	Mkt Val
PS6	2011 (8)	2,500	KM#181-183, 211-215	115	300

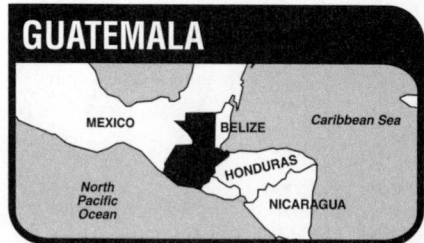

GUATEMALA

The Republic of Guatemala, the northernmost of the five Central American republics, has an area of 42,042 sq. mi. (108,890 sq. km.) and a population of 10.7 million. Capital: Guatemala City. The economy of Guatemala is heavily dependent on agriculture, however, the country is rich in nickel resources which are being developed. Coffee, cotton and bananas are exported.

Guatemala, once the site of an ancient Mayan civilization, was conquered by Pedro de Alvarado, the resourceful lieutenant of Cortes who undertook the conquest from Mexico. Cruel but strategically skillful, he progressed rapidly along the Pacific coastal lowlands to the highland plain of Quetzaltenango where the decisive battle for Guatemala was fought. After routing the Indian forces, he established the city of Guatemala in 1524. The Spanish Captaincy-General of Guatemala included all Central America but Panama. Guatemala declared its independence of Spain in 1821 and was absorbed into the Mexican empire of Augustin Iturbide (1822-23). From 1823 to 1839 Guatemala was a constituent state of the Central American Republic. Upon dissolution of that confederation, Guatemala proclaimed itself an independent republic. Like El Salvador, Guatemala suffered from internal strife between right-wing, US-backed military government and leftist indigenous peoples from ca. 1954 to ca. 1997.

MINT MARKS
(L) – London, Royal Mint

REPUBLIC

REFORM COINAGE

100 Centavos = 1 Quetzal

KM# 282   CENTAVO (Un)

0.8000 g., Aluminum, 19 mm.   **Subject:** Fray Bartolome de las Casas **Obv:** National arms **Rev:** Bust left **Edge:** Plain **Note:** 7-sided interior field

Date	Mintage	F	VF	XF	Unc	BU
2007	—	—	—	0.15	0.25	0.50

KM# 276.6   5 CENTAVOS

1.6000 g., Copper-Nickel, 16 mm.   **Obv:** National arms, smaller sized emblem, no dots by date **Obv. Legend:** REPUBLICA DE GUATEMALA 1997 **Rev:** Kapok tree center, value at right, ground below **Edge:** Reeded **Note:** Varieties exist.

Date	Mintage	F	VF	XF	Unc	BU
2006	—	—	—	0.15	0.30	0.50
2008	—	—	—	0.15	0.30	0.50
2009	—	—	—	0.15	0.30	0.50
2010	—	—	—	0.15	0.30	0.50

KM# 277.6   10 CENTAVOS

3.2000 g., Copper-Nickel, 21 mm.   **Obv:** National arms, small letters in legend **Obv. Legend:** REPUBLICA DE GUATEMALA **Rev:** Monolith **Note:** Varieties exist.

Date	Mintage	F	VF	XF	Unc	BU
2006	—	—	0.15	0.25	0.75	1.00
2008	—	—	0.15	0.25	0.75	1.00
2009	—	—	0.15	0.25	0.75	1.00

KM# 283   50 CENTAVOS

5.5000 g., Nickel-Brass, 26.5 mm.   **Obv:** National arms **Rev:** Whitenun orchid (lycaste skinneri var. alba orchidaceae) **Edge:** Reeded

Date	Mintage	F	VF	XF	Unc	BU
2001	—	—	—	0.50	1.25	1.75
2007	—	—	—	0.50	1.25	1.75

KM# 284   QUETZAL

11.0000 g., Nickel-Brass, 29 mm.   **Obv:** National arms **Rev:** PAZ above stylized dove **Edge:** Reeded

Date	Mintage	F	VF	XF	Unc	BU
2001 Small letters	—	—	—	1.00	2.50	3.00
2006	—	—	—	1.00	2.50	3.00
2008	—	—	—	1.00	2.50	3.00

KM# 287   QUETZAL

31.1035 g., 0.9999 Silver 0.9999 oz. ASW, 30 mm.   **Subject:** Canonization of Brother Pedro Betancourt **Obv:** National arms **Rev:** Standing monk **Edge:** Plain

Date	Mintage	F	VF	XF	Unc	BU
ND(2002) Proof	6,000	Value: 60.00				

KM# 288   QUETZAL

31.1035 g., 0.9990 Silver 0.9990 oz. ASW   **Subject:** Discovery of the Americas **Obv:** Shields around inner circle holding arms with date below **Rev:** Nature with fish in canoe

Date	Mintage	F	VF	XF	Unc	BU
2002 Proof	—	Value: 65.00				

KM# 289   QUETZAL

27.0000 g., 0.9250 Silver 0.8029 oz. ASW, 40 mm.   **Obv:** Arms at center surrounded by odler arms **Rev:** Ancient temple

Date	Mintage	F	VF	XF	Unc	BU
2005 Proof	—	Value: 60.00				

KM# 290   QUETZAL

27.0000 g., 0.9250 Silver 0.8029 oz. ASW, 40 mm.   **Obv:** Arms surrounded by older arms **Rev:** Female dancer and figures

Date	Mintage	F	VF	XF	Unc	BU
2007 Proof	—	Value: 60.00				

KM# 291   QUETZAL

27.0000 g., 0.9250 Silver 0.8029 oz. ASW, 40 mm.   **Subject:** Ibero-American series

Date	Mintage	F	VF	XF	Unc	BU
2010 Proof	—	Value: 60.00				

GUERNSEY

The Bailiwick of Guernsey, a British crown dependency located in the English Channel 30 miles (48 km.) west of Normandy, France, has an area of 30 sq. mi. (194 sq. km.)(including the isles of Alderney, Jethou, Herm, Brechou, and Sark), and a population of 54,000. Capital: St. Peter Port. Agriculture and cattle breeding are the main occupations.

Guernsey is administered by its own laws and customs. Unless the island is mentioned specifically, acts passed by the British Parliament are not applicable to Guernsey. During World War II, German troops occupied the island from June 30, 1940 till May 9,1945.

RULER
British

MONETARY SYSTEM
100 Pence = 1 Pound

BRITISH DEPENDENCY

DECIMAL COINAGE

KM# 89   PENNY

3.5300 g., Copper Plated Steel, 20.3 mm.   **Ruler:** Elizabeth II **Obv:** Head with tiara right **Rev:** Edible crab **Edge:** Plain

Date	Mintage	F	VF	XF	Unc	BU
2003	1,302,600	—	—	—	0.35	1.00
2006	1,731,000	—	—	—	0.35	0.75

KM# 96   2 PENCE

7.1200 g., Copper Plated Steel, 25.9 mm.   **Ruler:** Elizabeth II **Obv:** Head with tiara, shield at left **Rev:** Guernsey cows **Edge:** Plain

Date	Mintage	F	VF	XF	Unc	BU
2003	662,600	—	—	—	0.50	1.00
2006	1,322,000	—	—	—	0.50	1.00
2011	—	—	—	—	0.50	1.00
2012	—	—	—	—	0.50	1.00

KM# 97   5 PENCE

3.2500 g., Copper-Nickel, 18 mm.   **Ruler:** Elizabeth II **Obv:** Head with tiara right **Rev:** Sailboat **Edge:** Reeded

Date	Mintage	F	VF	XF	Unc	BU
2003	292,600	—	—	—	0.45	0.65
2006	1,217,000	—	—	—	0.45	0.65
2010	—	—	—	—	0.45	0.65
2012	—	—	—	—	0.45	0.65

KM# 149   10 PENCE

6.5000 g., Copper-Nickel, 24.5 mm.   **Ruler:** Elizabeth II **Obv:** Crowned head right **Rev:** Tomato plant **Edge:** Reeded

Date	Mintage	F	VF	XF	Unc	BU
2003	32,600	—	—	—	0.60	0.85
2006	26,000	—	—	—	0.60	0.85

KM# 90   20 PENCE

5.1000 g., Copper-Nickel, 21.4 mm.   **Ruler:** Elizabeth II **Obv:** Head with tiara right, small arms at left **Rev:** Island map within cogwheel **Shape:** 7-sided

Date	Mintage	F	VF	XF	Unc	BU
2003	732,600	—	—	—	0.90	1.25
2006	16,250	—	—	—	0.90	1.25
2009	—	—	—	—	0.90	1.25

KM# 145   50 PENCE

8.0000 g., Copper-Nickel, 27.3 mm.   **Ruler:** Elizabeth II **Subject:** Coronation Jubilee **Obv:** Head with tiara right **Rev:** Queen on horseback **Edge:** Plain **Shape:** 7-sided

Date	Mintage	F	VF	XF	Unc	BU
2003	—	—	—	—	1.50	2.50

KM# 145a   50 PENCE

8.1000 g., 0.9250 Silver 0.2409 oz. ASW, 27.3 mm.   **Ruler:** Elizabeth II **Subject:** Coronation Jubilee **Obv:** Head with tiara right **Rev:** Queen on horseback **Edge:** Plain **Shape:** 7-sided

Date	Mintage	F	VF	XF	Unc	BU
2003 Proof	—	Value: 25.00				

KM# 146   50 PENCE

8.0000 g., Copper-Nickel, 27.3 mm.   **Ruler:** Elizabeth II **Subject:** Coronation Jubilee **Obv:** Head with tiara right **Rev:** Queen on throne **Edge:** Plain **Shape:** 7-sided

Date	Mintage	F	VF	XF	Unc	BU
2003	—	—	—	—	1.50	2.50

KM# 146a   50 PENCE

8.1000 g., 0.9250 Silver 0.2409 oz. ASW, 27.3 mm.   **Ruler:** Elizabeth II **Subject:** Coronation Jubilee **Obv:** Head with tiara right **Rev:** Queen on throne **Edge:** Plain **Shape:** 7-sided

Date	Mintage	F	VF	XF	Unc	BU
2003 Proof	—	Value: 25.00				

KM# 147   50 PENCE

8.0000 g., Copper-Nickel, 27.3 mm.   **Ruler:** Elizabeth II **Subject:** Coronation Jubilee **Obv:** Head with tiara right **Rev:** Crown **Edge:** Plain **Shape:** 7-sided

Date	Mintage	F	VF	XF	Unc	BU
2003	—	—	—	—	1.50	2.50

KM# 147a   50 PENCE

8.1000 g., 0.9250 Silver 0.2409 oz. ASW, 27.3 mm.   **Ruler:** Elizabeth II **Subject:** Coronation Jubilee **Obv:** Head with tiara right **Rev:** Crown **Edge:** Plain **Shape:** 7-sided

Date	Mintage	F	VF	XF	Unc	BU
2003 Proof	—	Value: 25.00				

KM# 148   50 PENCE
8.0000 g., Copper-Nickel, 27.3 mm. **Ruler:** Elizabeth II **Subject:** Coronation Jubilee **Obv:** Head with tiara right **Rev:** Crowned ERII monogram **Edge:** Plain **Shape:** 7-sided

Date	Mintage	F	VF	XF	Unc	BU
2003	—	—	—	—	1.50	2.50

KM# 148a   50 PENCE
8.1000 g., 0.9250 Silver 0.2409 oz. ASW, 27.3 mm. **Ruler:** Elizabeth II **Subject:** Coronation Jubilee **Obv:** Head with tiara right **Rev:** Crowned ERII monogram **Edge:** Plain **Shape:** 7-sided

Date	Mintage	F	VF	XF	Unc	BU
2003 Proof	—	Value: 25.00				

KM# 156   50 PENCE
8.0000 g., Copper-Nickel, 27.3 mm. **Ruler:** Elizabeth II **Obv:** Head with tiara right **Rev:** Crossed flowers **Edge:** Plain **Shape:** 7-sided

Date	Mintage	F	VF	XF	Unc	BU
2003	—	—	—	—	1.75	2.75
2006	19,000	—	—	—	1.75	2.75
2008	—	—	—	—	1.75	2.75

KM# 110   POUND
9.5000 g., Nickel-Brass, 22.5 mm. **Ruler:** Elizabeth II **Subject:** Circulation Type **Obv:** Head with tiara right **Rev:** Denomination **Edge:** Reeded

Date	Mintage	F	VF	XF	Unc	BU
2001	175,000	—	—	—	2.50	3.50
2003	46,600	—	—	—	2.50	3.50
2006	11,000	—	—	—	2.50	3.50

KM# 111   POUND
9.5000 g., 0.9250 Silver 0.2825 oz. ASW, 22.5 mm. **Subject:** Queen's 75th Birthday **Obv:** Head with tiara right **Rev:** Queen's portrait in wreath **Edge:** Reeded

Date	Mintage	F	VF	XF	Unc	BU
2001 Proof	50,000	Value: 28.00				

KM# 142   POUND
30.9300 g., 0.9250 Silver 0.9198 oz. ASW, 38.6 mm. **Ruler:** Elizabeth II **Obv:** Head with tiara right **Rev:** 1/2-bust of William, Duke of Normandy holding sword at left **Edge:** Reeded

Date	Mintage	F	VF	XF	Unc	BU
2002	—	—	—	—	40.00	50.00

KM# 83   2 POUNDS
12.0000 g., Bi-Metallic Copper-Nickel center in Nickel-Brass ring, 28.35 mm. **Ruler:** Elizabeth II **Obv:** Head with tiara right **Rev:** Latent image arms on cross **Edge:** BAILIWICK OF GUERNSEY

Date	Mintage	F	VF	XF	Unc	BU
2003	19,600	—	—	—	8.50	10.00
2006	9,500	—	—	—	8.50	10.00

KM# 106   5 POUNDS
28.2800 g., Copper-Nickel, 38.6 mm. **Ruler:** Elizabeth II **Subject:** Queen Victoria Centennial **Obv:** Head with tiara right **Rev:** Bust of Queen Victoria left **Edge:** Reeded

Date	Mintage	F	VF	XF	Unc	BU
2001	12,754	—	—	—	7.50	8.50
2001 Proof	30,000	Value: 20.00				

KM# 106a   5 POUNDS
28.2800 g., 0.9250 Silver 0.8410 oz. ASW, 38.6 mm. **Ruler:** Elizabeth II **Subject:** Queen Victoria 1837-1901 **Obv:** Head with tiara right **Rev:** Bust of Queen Victoria left **Edge:** Reeded

Date	Mintage	F	VF	XF	Unc	BU
2001 Proof	10,000	Value: 50.00				

KM# 108   5 POUNDS
28.2800 g., Copper-Nickel, 38.6 mm. **Ruler:** Elizabeth II **Subject:** Queen Elizabeth's 75th Birthday **Obv:** Head with tiara right **Rev:** Queen's portrait in wreath **Edge:** Reeded

Date	Mintage	F	VF	XF	Unc	BU
2001	14,000	—	—	—	6.00	7.00

KM# 108a   5 POUNDS
28.2800 g., 0.9250 Silver 0.8410 oz. ASW, 38.6 mm. **Ruler:** Elizabeth II **Subject:** Queen's 75th Birthday **Obv:** Head with tiara right **Rev:** Queen's portrait in wreath **Edge:** Reeded

Date	Mintage	F	VF	XF	Unc	BU
2001 Proof	20,000	Value: 55.00				

KM# 114   5 POUNDS
28.2800 g., Copper-Nickel, 38.6 mm. **Ruler:** Elizabeth II **Subject:** 19th Century Monarchy **Obv:** Head with tiara right **Rev:** Four portraits **Edge:** Reeded

Date	Mintage	F	VF	XF	Unc	BU
2001	5,700	—	—	—	11.50	12.50

KM# 114a   5 POUNDS
28.2800 g., 0.9250 Silver 0.8410 oz. ASW, 38.6 mm. **Ruler:** Elizabeth II **Obv:** Head with tiara right **Rev:** Four portraits **Edge:** Reeded

Date	Mintage	F	VF	XF	Unc	BU
2001 Proof	10,000	Value: 55.00				

KM# 115   5 POUNDS
1.1300 g., 0.9170 Gold 0.0333 oz. AGW, 13.9 mm. **Ruler:** Elizabeth II **Subject:** 19th Century Monarchy **Obv:** Head with tiara right **Rev:** Four portraits **Edge:** Reeded

Date	Mintage	F	VF	XF	Unc	BU
2001 Proof	—	Value: 75.00				

KM# 117   5 POUNDS
1.1300 g., 0.9170 Gold 0.0333 oz. AGW, 13.9 mm. **Ruler:** Elizabeth II **Subject:** Queen Victoria 1837-1901 **Obv:** Head with tiara right **Rev:** Queen Victoria's portrait **Edge:** Reeded

Date	Mintage	F	VF	XF	Unc	BU
2001 Proof	300	Value: 75.00				

KM# 118   5 POUNDS
1.1300 g., 0.9170 Gold 0.0333 oz. AGW, 13.9 mm. **Ruler:** Elizabeth II **Subject:** Queen's 75th Birthday **Obv:** Head with tiara right **Rev:** Queen's portrait in wreath **Edge:** Reeded

Date	Mintage	F	VF	XF	Unc	BU
2001 Proof	250	Value: 75.00				

KM# 114b   5 POUNDS
39.9400 g., 0.9166 Gold 1.1770 oz. AGW, 38.6 mm. **Ruler:** Elizabeth II **Subject:** 19th Century Monarchy **Obv:** Head with tiara right **Rev:** Four royal portraits **Edge:** Reeded

Date	Mintage	F	VF	XF	Unc	BU
2001 Proof	200	Value: 2,150				

KM# 119   5 POUNDS
27.7100 g., Copper-Nickel, 38.6 mm. **Ruler:** Elizabeth II **Subject:** The Golden Jubilee **Obv:** Head with tiara right **Rev:** The queen in her coach **Edge:** Reeded

Date	Mintage	F	VF	XF	Unc	BU
2002	9,250	—	—	—	16.50	18.00

KM# 119a   5 POUNDS
28.2800 g., Base Metal Gilt Gold plated copper-nickel, 38.6 mm. **Ruler:** Elizabeth II **Subject:** Golden Jubilee **Obv:** Head with tiara right **Rev:** Queen in coach **Edge:** Reeded

Date	Mintage	F	VF	XF	Unc	BU
2002	50,000	—	—	—	15.00	16.50

KM# 119b   5 POUNDS
28.2800 g., 0.9250 Silver 0.8410 oz. ASW, 38.6 mm. **Ruler:** Elizabeth II **Subject:** Queen's Golden Jubilee **Obv:** Head with tiara right **Rev:** Queen in her coach **Edge:** Reeded **Note:** Prev. KM#119a.

Date	Mintage	F	VF	XF	Unc	BU
2002 Proof	20,000	Value: 50.00				

KM# 119c   5 POUNDS
39.9400 g., 0.9166 Gold 1.1770 oz. AGW, 38.6 mm. **Ruler:** Elizabeth II **Subject:** Golden Jubilee **Obv:** Head with tiara right **Rev:** Queen in coach **Edge:** Reeded

Date	Mintage	F	VF	XF	Unc	BU
2002 Proof	250	Value: 2,100				

KM# 121   5 POUNDS
27.7100 g., Copper-Nickel, 38.6 mm. **Ruler:** Elizabeth II **Subject:** Queen's Golden Jubilee **Obv:** Head with tiara right **Rev:** Trooping the Colors scene **Edge:** Reeded

Date	Mintage	F	VF	XF	Unc	BU
2002	2,000	—	—	—	17.50	20.00

KM# 121a   5 POUNDS
28.2800 g., 0.9250 Silver 0.8410 oz. ASW, 38.6 mm. **Ruler:** Elizabeth II **Subject:** Queen's Golden Jubilee **Obv:** Head with tiara right **Rev:** Trooping the Colors scene **Edge:** Reeded

Date	Mintage	F	VF	XF	Unc	BU
2002 Proof	20,000	Value: 50.00				

KM# 121b   5 POUNDS
39.9400 g., 0.9166 Gold 1.1770 oz. AGW, 38.6 mm. **Ruler:** Elizabeth II **Subject:** Golden Jubilee **Obv:** Head with tiara right **Rev:** Trooping the Colors scene **Edge:** Reeded

Date	Mintage	F	VF	XF	Unc	BU
2002 Proof	250	Value: 2,100				

KM# 122   5 POUNDS
28.2800 g., Copper-Nickel, 38.6 mm. **Ruler:** Elizabeth II **Subject:** Princess Diana **Obv:** Head with tiara right **Rev:** World and children behind cameo portrait of Diana **Edge:** Reeded

Date	Mintage	F	VF	XF	Unc	BU
2002	4,231	—	—	—	13.50	15.00

KM# 122a   5 POUNDS
28.2800 g., 0.9250 Silver 0.8410 oz. ASW **Ruler:** Elizabeth II
Subject: Princess Diana **Obv:** Head with tiara right **Rev:** World
and children behind Diana's cameo portrait **Edge:** Reeded

Date	Mintage	F	VF	XF	Unc	BU
2002 Proof	20,000	Value: 45.00				

KM# 122b   5 POUNDS
39.9400 g., 0.9167 Gold 1.1771 oz. AGW, 1.1771 mm. **Ruler:**
Elizabeth II **Subject:** Princess Diana **Obv:** Head with tiara right
Rev: World and children behind Diana's cameo portrait **Edge:**
Reeded

Date	Mintage	F	VF	XF	Unc	BU
2002 Proof	100	Value: 2,200				

KM# 124   5 POUNDS
28.2800 g., Copper-Nickel, 38.6 mm. **Ruler:** Elizabeth II
Subject: 18th Century British Monarchy **Obv:** Head with tiara
right **Rev:** Five royal portraits **Edge:** Reeded

Date	Mintage	F	VF	XF	Unc	BU
2002	1,300	—	—	—	15.00	16.50

KM# 124a   5 POUNDS
28.2800 g., 0.9250 Silver 0.8410 oz. ASW, 38.6 mm. **Ruler:**
Elizabeth II **Subject:** 18th Century British Monarchy **Obv:** Head
with tiara right **Rev:** Five royal portraits **Edge:** Reeded

Date	Mintage	F	VF	XF	Unc	BU
2002 Proof	10,000	Value: 50.00				

KM# 124b   5 POUNDS
39.9400 g., 0.9166 Gold 1.1770 oz. AGW, 38.6 mm. **Ruler:**
Elizabeth II **Subject:** 18th Century British Monarchy **Obv:** Head
with tiara right **Rev:** Five royal portraits **Edge:** Reeded

Date	Mintage	F	VF	XF	Unc	BU
2002 Proof	200	Value: 2,100				

KM# 125   5 POUNDS
1.1300 g., 0.9166 Gold 0.0333 oz. AGW, 13.9 mm. **Ruler:**
Elizabeth II **Subject:** 18th Century British Monarchy **Obv:** Head
with tiara right **Rev:** Five royal portraits **Edge:** Reeded **Note:**
Prev. KM#124b.

Date	Mintage	F	VF	XF	Unc	BU
2002 Proof	55	Value: 85.00				

KM# 127   5 POUNDS
28.2800 g., Copper-Nickel, 38.6 mm. **Ruler:** Elizabeth II
Subject: Queen Mother **Obv:** Head with tiara right **Rev:** The late
Queen Mother's portrait **Edge:** Reeded

Date	Mintage	F	VF	XF	Unc	BU
2002	1,750	—	—	—	15.00	16.50
2002 Proof	1,680	Value: 20.00				

KM# 127a   5 POUNDS
28.2800 g., 0.9250 Silver 0.8410 oz. ASW, 38.6 mm. **Ruler:**
Elizabeth II **Subject:** Queen Mother **Obv:** Head with tiara right
Rev: The late Queen Mother's portrait **Edge:** Reeded

Date	Mintage	F	VF	XF	Unc	BU
2002 Proof	15,000	Value: 50.00				

KM# 127b   5 POUNDS
39.9400 g., 0.9166 Gold 1.1770 oz. AGW, 38.6 mm. **Ruler:**
Elizabeth II **Subject:** Queen Mother **Obv:** Head with tiara right
Rev: Queen Mother's portrait **Edge:** Reeded

Date	Mintage	F	VF	XF	Unc	BU
2002 Proof	250	Value: 2,100				

KM# 128   5 POUNDS
1.1300 g., 0.9166 Gold 0.0333 oz. AGW, 13.9 mm. **Ruler:**
Elizabeth II **Subject:** Queen Mother **Obv:** Head with tiara right
Rev: The late Queen Mother's portrait **Edge:** Reeded

Date	Mintage	F	VF	XF	Unc	BU
2002 Proof	—	Value: 75.00				

KM# 129   5 POUNDS
28.2800 g., Copper-Nickel, 38.6 mm. **Ruler:** Elizabeth II
Subject: The Duke of Wellington **Obv:** Head with tiara right **Rev:**
Portrait with mounted dragoons in background **Edge:** Reeded

Date	Mintage	F	VF	XF	Unc	BU
2002	675	—	—	—	22.50	25.00

KM# 129a   5 POUNDS
28.2800 g., 0.9250 Silver 0.8410 oz. ASW, 38.6 mm. **Ruler:**
Elizabeth II **Subject:** The Duke of Wellington **Obv:** Head with
tiara right **Rev:** Portrait with multicolor mounted dragoons in
background **Edge:** Reeded

Date	Mintage	F	VF	XF	Unc	BU
2002 Proof	15,000	Value: 50.00				

KM# 129b   5 POUNDS
39.9400 g., 0.9166 Gold 1.1770 oz. AGW, 38.6 mm. **Ruler:**
Elizabeth II **Subject:** Duke of Wellington **Obv:** Head with tiara
right **Rev:** Wellington's portrait with multicolor cavalry scene
Edge: Reeded

Date	Mintage	F	VF	XF	Unc	BU
2002 Proof	200	Value: 2,100				

KM# 130   5 POUNDS
1.1300 g., 0.9166 Gold 0.0333 oz. AGW, 13.9 mm. **Ruler:**
Elizabeth II **Subject:** The Duke of Wellington **Obv:** Head with
tiara right **Rev:** Portrait with mounted dragoons in background
Edge: Reeded

Date	Mintage	F	VF	XF	Unc	BU
2002 Proof	—	Value: 75.00				

KM# 143   5 POUNDS
28.2800 g., Copper-Nickel, 38.6 mm. **Ruler:** Elizabeth II **Obv:**
Head with tiara right **Rev:** Prince William wearing sweater **Edge:**
Reeded

Date	Mintage	F	VF	XF	Unc	BU
2003	3,700	—	—	—	17.50	20.00

KM# 143a   5 POUNDS
28.2800 g., 0.9250 Silver 0.8410 oz. ASW, 38.6 mm. **Ruler:**
Elizabeth II **Obv:** Head with tiara right **Rev:** Prince William
wearing sweater **Edge:** Reeded

Date	Mintage	F	VF	XF	Unc	BU
2003 Proof	5,000	Value: 50.00				

KM# 143b   5 POUNDS
39.9400 g., 0.9166 Gold 1.1770 oz. AGW, 38.6 mm. **Ruler:**
Elizabeth II **Obv:** Head with tiara right **Rev:** Prince William
wearing sweater **Edge:** Reeded

Date	Mintage	F	VF	XF	Unc	BU
2003 Proof	200	Value: 2,100				

KM# 158   5 POUNDS
28.2800 g., Copper-Nickel, 38.7 mm. **Ruler:** Elizabeth II
Subject: Golden Hind **Obv:** Head with tiara right **Rev:** The
Golden Hind ship **Edge:** Reeded

Date	Mintage	F	VF	XF	Unc	BU
2003	300	—	—	—	25.00	

KM# 159   5 POUNDS
Copper-Nickel **Ruler:** Elizabeth II **Subject:** 17th Century
Monarchs **Obv:** Head with tiara right

Date	Mintage	F	VF	XF	Unc	BU
2003	500	—	—	—	22.50	

KM# 160   5 POUNDS
Copper-Nickel **Ruler:** Elizabeth II **Subject:** Royal Navy - H.
Nelson **Obv:** Head with tiara right

Date	Mintage	F	VF	XF	Unc	BU
2003	550	—	—	—	22.50	

KM# 175   5 POUNDS
28.3200 g., Nickel-Brass, 38 mm. **Ruler:** Elizabeth II **Subject:**
History of the Royal Navy **Rev:** Two naval vessels and Horatio
Nelson, flag in color

Date	Mintage	F	VF	XF	Unc	BU
2003 Proof	—	Value: 40.00				

KM# 176   5 POUNDS
28.3200 g., Silver, 38 mm. **Ruler:** Elizabeth II **Subject:** History
of the Royal Navy **Rev:** HMS Invincible, flag in color

Date	Mintage	F	VF	XF	Unc	BU
2004 Proof	—	Value: 50.00				

KM# 161   5 POUNDS
Copper-Nickel **Ruler:** Elizabeth II **Subject:** 16th Century
Monarchs **Obv:** Head with tiara right

Date	Mintage	F	VF	XF	Unc	BU
2004	500	—	—	—	—	22.50

KM# 162   5 POUNDS
Copper-Nickel **Ruler:** Elizabeth II **Subject:** Mallard Locomotive
Obv: Head with tiara right

Date	Mintage	F	VF	XF	Unc	BU
2004	2,193	—	—	—	—	17.50

KM# 163   5 POUNDS
Copper-Nickel **Ruler:** Elizabeth II **Subject:** City of Truro Train
Obv: Head with tiara right

Date	Mintage	F	VF	XF	Unc	BU
2004	500	—	—	—	—	22.50

KM# 164   5 POUNDS
Copper-Nickel **Ruler:** Elizabeth II **Subject:** The Boat Train **Obv:**
Head with tiara right

Date	Mintage	F	VF	XF	Unc	BU
2004	250	—	—	—	—	25.00

KM# 165   5 POUNDS
Copper-Nickel **Ruler:** Elizabeth II **Subject:** Train Spotter **Obv:**
Head with tiara right

Date	Mintage	F	VF	XF	Unc	BU
2004	300	—	—	—	—	25.00

KM# 166   5 POUNDS
Copper-Nickel **Ruler:** Elizabeth II **Subject:** Royal Navy - Henry
VIII **Obv:** Head with tiara right

Date	Mintage	F	VF	XF	Unc	BU
2004	300	—	—	—	—	25.00

KM# 167   5 POUNDS
Copper-Nickel **Ruler:** Elizabeth II **Subject:** Royal Navy -
Invincible **Obv:** Head with tiara right

Date	Mintage	F	VF	XF	Unc	BU
2004	300	—	—	—	—	25.00

KM# 150   5 POUNDS
28.2800 g., Copper-Nickel, 38.6 mm. **Ruler:** Elizabeth II
Subject: D-Day **Obv:** Head with tiara right **Rev:** British troops
storming ashore **Edge:** Reeded

Date	Mintage	F	VF	XF	Unc	BU
2004	65,611	—	—	—	15.00	16.50

KM# 154 5 POUNDS
28.2800 g., 0.9250 Silver 0.8410 oz. ASW, 38.6 mm. **Ruler:** Elizabeth II **Subject:** D-Day **Obv:** Head with tiara right **Rev:** British soldier advancing to left **Edge:** Reeded

Date	Mintage	F	VF	XF	Unc	BU
2004 Proof	10,000	Value: 85.00				

KM# 154a 5 POUNDS
39.9400 g., 0.9167 Gold 1.1771 oz. AGW, 38.6 mm. **Ruler:** Elizabeth II **Subject:** D-Day **Obv:** Head with tiara right **Rev:** British soldier advancing to left **Edge:** Reeded

Date	Mintage	F	VF	XF	Unc	BU
2004 Proof	500	Value: 2,100				

KM# 155 5 POUNDS
28.2800 g., Copper-Nickel, 38.6 mm. **Ruler:** Elizabeth II **Subject:** 150th Anniversary of the Crimean War **Obv:** Head with tiara right **Rev:** Sgt. Luke O'Connor , first army Victoria Cross winner, above Battle of Alma scene with multicolor flag **Edge:** Reeded

Date	Mintage	F	VF	XF	Unc	BU
2004 plain	—	—	—	—	25.00	27.50
2004 partial color	1,060	—	—	—	25.00	27.50

KM# 155a 5 POUNDS
28.2800 g., 0.9250 Silver 0.8410 oz. ASW, 38.6 mm. **Ruler:** Elizabeth II **Obv:** Head with tiara right **Rev:** Sgt. Luke O'Conner, first army Victoria Cross winner, above Battle of Alma scene with multicolor flag **Edge:** Reeded

Date	Mintage	F	VF	XF	Unc	BU
2004 Proof	10,000	Value: 85.00				

KM# 155b 5 POUNDS
39.9400 g., 0.9166 Gold 1.1770 oz. AGW, 38.6 mm. **Ruler:** Elizabeth II **Obv:** Head with tiara right **Rev:** Sgt. Luke O'Connor, first army Victoria Cross winner, above Battle of Alma scene with multicolor flag **Edge:** Reeded

Date	Mintage	F	VF	XF	Unc	BU
2004 Proof	500	Value: 2,100				

KM# 168a 5 POUNDS
28.2800 g., 0.9250 Silver 0.8410 oz. ASW, 38.6 mm. **Ruler:** Elizabeth II **Subject:** End of WWII **Obv:** Head with tiara right **Rev:** Churchill and George VI **Edge:** Reeded

Date	Mintage	F	VF	XF	Unc	BU
2005 Proof	5,000	Value: 85.00				

KM# 168b 5 POUNDS
39.9400 g., 0.9167 Gold 1.1771 oz. AGW, 38.6 mm. **Ruler:** Elizabeth II **Subject:** End of WWII **Obv:** Head with tiara right **Rev:** Churchill and George VI **Edge:** Reeded

Date	Mintage	F	VF	XF	Unc	BU
2005 Proof	150	Value: 2,150				

KM# 169a 5 POUNDS
39.9400 g., 0.9167 Gold 1.1771 oz. AGW, 38.6 mm. **Ruler:** Elizabeth II **Subject:** WWII Liberation **Obv:** Head with tiara right **Rev:** Soldiers and waving crowd **Edge:** Reeded

Date	Mintage	F	VF	XF	Unc	BU
2005 Proof	150	Value: 2,150				

KM# 170 5 POUNDS
28.2800 g., 0.9250 Silver 0.8410 oz. ASW, 38.6 mm. **Ruler:** Elizabeth II **Subject:** Queen's 80th Birthday **Obv:** Head with tiara right - gilt **Obv. Legend:** ELIZABETH II BAILIWICK OF GUERNSEY **Rev:** Bust at left looking upwards, tower and florals at upper right

Date	Mintage	F	VF	XF	Unc	BU
2006 Proof	—	Value: 45.00				

KM# 173 5 POUNDS
28.2800 g., 0.9250 Silver 0.8410 oz. ASW **Ruler:** Elizabeth II **Subject:** FIFA - XVIII World Football Championship - Germany 2006 **Rev:** Wembley Stadium

Date	Mintage	F	VF	XF	Unc	BU
2006 Proof	50,000	Value: 65.00				

KM# 179 5 POUNDS
28.2800 g., Copper-Nickel, 38.61 mm. **Ruler:** Elizabeth II **Subject:** Battle of Britain **Obv:** Head with tiara right **Rev:** Spitfires in color

Date	Mintage	F	VF	XF	Unc	BU
2010 Proof	—	Value: 40.00				

KM# 116 10 POUNDS
141.7500 g., 0.9990 Silver 4.5526 oz. ASW, 65 mm. **Ruler:** Elizabeth II **Subject:** 19th Century Monarchy **Obv:** Head with tiara right **Rev:** Four portraits **Edge:** Reeded

Date	Mintage	F	VF	XF	Unc	BU
2001 Proof	950	Value: 225				

KM# 126 10 POUNDS
155.5175 g., 0.9990 Silver 4.9948 oz. ASW, 65 mm. **Ruler:** Elizabeth II **Subject:** British Monarchy 18th Century **Obv:** Head with tiara right **Rev:** Five royal portraits **Edge:** Reeded

Date	Mintage	F	VF	XF	Unc	BU
2002 Proof	950	Value: 225				

KM# 151 10 POUNDS
155.5170 g., 0.9250 Silver 4.6248 oz. ASW, 65 mm. **Ruler:**

Elizabeth II **Subject:** D-Day **Obv:** Head with tiara right **Rev:** British troops storming ashore **Edge:** Reeded

Date	Mintage	F	VF	XF	Unc	BU
2004 Proof	1,944	Value: 400				

KM# 107 25 POUNDS
7.8100 g., 0.9170 Gold 0.2302 oz. AGW, 22 mm. **Ruler:** Elizabeth II **Subject:** Queen Victoria Centennial **Obv:** Head with tiara right **Rev:** Queen Victoria's portrait **Edge:** Reeded

Date	Mintage	F	VF	XF	Unc	BU
2001 Proof	2,500	Value: 445				

KM# 112 25 POUNDS
7.8100 g., 0.9170 Gold 0.2302 oz. AGW, 22 mm. **Ruler:** Elizabeth II **Subject:** Queen's 75th Birthday **Obv:** Head with tiara right **Rev:** Queen's portrait in wreath **Edge:** Reeded

Date	Mintage	F	VF	XF	Unc	BU
2001 Proof	5,000	Value: 425				

KM# 123 25 POUNDS
7.9800 g., 0.9167 Gold 0.2352 oz. AGW, 22.05 mm. **Ruler:** Elizabeth II **Subject:** Princess Diana **Obv:** Head with tiara right **Rev:** Diana's cameo portrait in wreath **Edge:** Reeded

Date	Mintage	F	VF	XF	Unc	BU
2002 Proof	2,500	Value: 450				

KM# 131 25 POUNDS
7.8100 g., 0.9166 Gold 0.2301 oz. AGW, 22 mm. **Ruler:** Elizabeth II **Subject:** The Duke of Wellington **Obv:** Head with tiara right **Rev:** Portrait with mounted dragoons in the background **Edge:** Reeded

Date	Mintage	F	VF	XF	Unc	BU
2002 Proof	2,500	Value: 425				

KM# 139 25 POUNDS
7.9800 g., 0.9166 Gold 0.2352 oz. AGW, 22 mm. **Ruler:** Elizabeth II **Subject:** Golden Jubilee **Obv:** Head with tiara right **Rev:** Queen in coach **Edge:** Reeded

Date	Mintage	F	VF	XF	Unc	BU
2002 Proof	5,000	Value: 445				

KM# 140 25 POUNDS
7.9800 g., 0.9166 Gold 0.2352 oz. AGW, 22 mm. **Ruler:** Elizabeth II **Subject:** Queen Mother **Obv:** Head with tiara right **Rev:** Queen Mother's portrait **Edge:** Reeded

Date	Mintage	F	VF	XF	Unc	BU
2002 Proof	2,500	Value: 445				

KM# 141 25 POUNDS
7.9800 g., 0.9166 Gold 0.2352 oz. AGW, 22 mm. **Ruler:** Elizabeth II **Subject:** Golden Jubilee **Obv:** Head with tiara right **Rev:** Trooping the Colors scene **Edge:** Reeded

Date	Mintage	F	VF	XF	Unc	BU
2003 Proof	5,000	Value: 445				

KM# 172 25 POUNDS
7.9800 g., 0.9166 Gold 0.2352 oz. AGW **Ruler:** Elizabeth II **Obv:** Head with tiara right **Rev:** Bust of Prince William facing **Edge:** Reeded

Date	Mintage	F	VF	XF	Unc	BU
2003 Proof	—	Value: 425				

KM# 152 25 POUNDS
7.9800 g., 0.9167 Gold 0.2352 oz. AGW, 22 mm. **Ruler:** Elizabeth II **Subject:** D-Day **Obv:** Head with tiara right **Rev:** Advancing British soldier **Edge:** Reeded

Date	Mintage	F	VF	XF	Unc	BU
2004 Proof	500	Value: 475				

KM# 174 25 POUNDS
7.9800 g., 0.9166 Gold 0.2352 oz. AGW **Ruler:** Elizabeth II **Subject:** FIFA - XVIII World Football Championship - Germany 2006 **Rev:** Wembley Stadium

Date	Mintage	F	VF	XF	Unc	BU
2006 Proof	2,500	Value: 445				

KM# 144 50 POUNDS
1000.0000 g., 0.9250 Silver 29.738 oz. ASW, 100 mm. **Ruler:** Elizabeth II **Obv:** Head with tiara right **Rev:** Prince William wearing sweater **Edge:** Reeded

Date	Mintage	F	VF	XF	Unc	BU
2003 Proof	500	Value: 1,250				

KM# 177 50 POUNDS
1000.0000 g., 0.9160 Silver 29.448 oz. ASW, 100 mm. **Ruler:** Elizabeth II **Subject:** Coronation, 50th Anniversary **Rev:** Buckingham Palace

Date	Mintage	F	VF	XF	Unc	BU
2003 Proof	Est. 999	Value: 1,100				

KM# 153 50 POUNDS
1000.0000 g., 0.9250 Silver 29.738 oz. ASW, 100 mm. **Ruler:** Elizabeth II **Subject:** D-Day **Obv:** Head with tiara right **Rev:** British troops storming ashore **Edge:** Reeded

Date	Mintage	F	VF	XF	Unc	BU
2004 Proof	600	Value: 1,300				

KM# 178 50 POUNDS
7.9800 g., 0.9160 Gold 0.2350 oz. AGW, 22.05 mm. **Ruler:** Elizabeth II **Subject:** Battle of Britain, 1940 **Rev:** Pilots scrambling to planes, some in the sky **Edge:** Reeded

Date	Mintage	F	VF	XF	Unc	BU
2008 Proof	—	Value: 475				

PIEDFORT

KM#	Date	Mintage	Identification	Mkt Val
P3	2002	100	5 Pounds. 0.9166 Gold. 79.8900 g. 38.6 mm. Queen's portrait. Queen in coach. Reeded edge.	4,250

MINT SETS

KM#	Date	Mintage	Identification	Issue Price	Mkt Val
MS10	2003 (8)	—	KM#83, 89-90, 96-97, 110, 148-49	—	22.50
MS11	2004 (1)	—	Guernsey KM#155, Alderney KM#43, Jersey KM#126, 150th Anniversary of the Crimean War	—	80.00

GUINEA

The Republic of Guinea, situated on the Atlantic Coast of Africa between Sierra Leone and Guinea-Bissau, has an area of 94,964 sq. mi. (245,860 sq. km.) and a population of 6.4 million. Capital: Conakry. Although Guinea contains one-third of the world's reserves of bauxite and significant deposits of iron ore, gold and diamonds, the economy is still dependent on agriculture, aluminum, bananas, copra and coffee are exported.

The coast of Guinea was known to Portuguese navigators of the 15th century but was seldom visited by European traders of the 16th-18th centuries because of its dangerous coastal waters. French penetration of the area began in the mid-19th century with the entering into of protectorate treaties with several of the coastal chiefs. After a long struggle with Guinea's native leader Samory Toure, France secured the area and until 1890 administered it as a part of Senegal. In 1895 the colony (Guinee Francais) became an autonomous part of the federation of French West Africa. The inhabitants were extended French citizenship in 1946 when the colony became an overseas territory of the French Union. Guinea became an independent republic on Oct. 2, 1958, when it declined to enter the new French Community.

MONETARY SYSTEM
100 Centimes = 1 Franc

REPUBLIC
REFORM COINAGE

KM# 65 2000 FRANCS
22.2000 g., 0.9000 Silver 0.6423 oz. ASW, 37 mm. **Obv:** National Arms **Rev:** Map and female figure

Date	Mintage	F	VF	XF	Unc	BU
2002 Proof	500	Value: 120				

GUYANA

The Cooperative Republic of Guyana, is situated on the northeast coast of South America, has an area of 83,000 sq. mi. (214,970 sq. km.) and a population of 729,000. Capital: Georgetown. The economy is basically agrarian. Sugar, rice and bauxite are exported.

The original area of Essequibo and Demerary, which included present-day Suriname, French Guiana, and parts of Brazil and Venezuela was sighted by Columbus in 1498. Guyana became a republic on Feb. 23, 1970. It is a member of the Commonwealth of Nations. The president is the Chief of State. The prime minister is the Head of Government. Guyana is a member of the Caribbean Community and Common Market (CARICOM).

REPUBLIC
DECIMAL COINAGE

KM# 50 DOLLAR
2.4000 g., Copper Plated Steel, 17 mm. **Obv:** Helmeted and supported arms **Rev:** Hand gathering rice **Edge:** Reeded

Date	Mintage	F	VF	XF	Unc	BU
2001	—	—	—	0.30	0.50	0.65
2002	—	—	—	0.30	0.50	0.65

Date	Mintage	F	VF	XF	Unc	BU
2005	—	—	—	0.30	0.50	0.65
2008	—	—	—	0.30	0.50	0.65

KM# 51 5 DOLLARS
3.7800 g., Copper Plated Steel, 20.5 mm. **Obv:** Helmeted and supported arms **Rev:** Sugar cane **Edge:** Reeded

Date	Mintage	F	VF	XF	Unc	BU
2002	—	—	—	0.35	0.75	1.00
2005	—	—	—	0.35	0.75	1.00
2008	—	—	—	0.35	0.75	1.00
2009	—	—	—	0.35	0.75	1.00

KM# 52 10 DOLLARS
5.0000 g., Nickel Plated Steel, 23 mm. **Obv:** Helmeted and supported arms **Rev:** Gold mining scene **Edge:** Reeded **Shape:** 7-sided **Note:** Slightly different die for each date.

Date	Mintage	F	VF	XF	Unc	BU
2007	—	—	—	0.75	1.25	1.50
2009	—	—	—	0.75	1.25	1.50

KM# 54 1000 DOLLARS
28.2800 g., 0.9250 Silver partially gilt 0.8410 oz. ASW, 38.6 mm. **Subject:** Bank of Guyana, 40th Anniversary **Obv:** Arms **Rev:** Bank building, partially gilt

Date	Mintage	F	VF	XF	Unc	BU
2005 Proof	1,000	Value: 85.00				

KM# 54a 1000 DOLLARS
28.2800 g., Copper-Nickel, 38.61 mm. **Subject:** Central Bank, 40th Anniversary **Obv:** Supported arms **Rev:** Building

Date	Mintage	F	VF	XF	Unc	BU
2005	—	—	—	—	—	50.00

KM# 55 2000 DOLLARS
28.2800 g., 0.9250 Silver 0.8410 oz. ASW, 38.61 mm. **Obv:** National Arms **Rev:** National soccer stadium

Date	Mintage	F	VF	XF	Unc	BU
2007 Proof	Est. 4,000	Value: 90.00				

KM# 56 2000 DOLLARS
25.0000 g., Copper-Nickel, 39 mm. **Obv:** National Arms **Rev:** Face design

Date	Mintage	F	VF	XF	Unc	BU
2008	—	—	—	—	—	75.00

HAITI

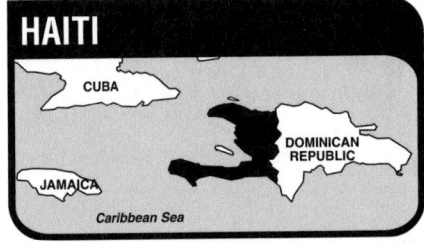

The Republic of Haiti, which occupies the western one-third of the island of Hispaniola in the Caribbean Sea between Puerto Rico and Cuba, has an area of 10,714 sq. mi. (27,750 sq. km.) and a population of 6.5 million. Capital: Port-au-Prince. The economy is based on agriculture; but light manufacturing and tourism are increasingly important. Coffee, bauxite, sugar, essential oils and handicrafts are exported.

The French language is used on Haitian coins although it is spoken by only about 10% of the populace. A form of Creole is the language of the Haitians.

MINT MARKS
A - Paris
(a) - Paris, privy marks only
R - Rome

MONETARY SYSTEM
100 Centimes = 1 Gourde

REPUBLIC
DECIMAL COINAGE

KM# 155 GOURDE
6.3000 g., Brass Plated Steel, 23 mm. **Obv:** Citadelle de Roi Christophe **Shape:** 7-sided

Date	Mintage	F	VF	XF	Unc	BU
2003	—	—	—	—	1.75	2.00
2009	—	—	—	—	1.75	2.00

KM# 156 5 GOURDES
9.2000 g., Brass Plated Steel, 28 mm. **Obv:** Four portraits in circle of Haitian statesmen top: Gen. Tonsaint Louverture, Left: Henri Christophe, Right: Jean Jacques Dessalines, Bottom: Alexandre Petion, date below **Rev:** National arms **Shape:** 7-sided

Date	Mintage	F	VF	XF	Unc	BU
2007	—	—	—	—	2.75	3.00

HONDURAS

The Republic of Honduras, situated in Central America alongside El Salvador, between Nicaragua and Guatemala, has an area of 43,277 sq. mi. (112,090 sq. km.) and a population of 5.6 million. Capital: Tegucigalpa. Agriculture, mining (gold and silver), and logging are the major economic activities, with increasing tourism and emerging petroleum resource discoveries. Precious metals, bananas, timber and coffee are exported.

From 1933 to 1940 General Tiburcio Carias Andino was dictator president of the Republic. Since 1990 democratic practices have become more consistent.

MINT MARKS
T.G. - Yoro
T.L. – Comayagua

MONETARY SYSTEM
100 Centavos = 1 Lempira

REPUBLIC
REFORM COINAGE

KM# 72.4 5 CENTAVOS
3.2000 g., Brass, 21 mm. **Obv:** National arms **Rev:** Value in circle within sprays **Edge:** Plain

Date	Mintage	F	VF	XF	Unc	BU
2002	—	—	—	0.10	0.25	0.35
2003	—	—	—	0.10	0.25	0.35
2005	—	—	—	0.10	0.25	0.35
2006	—	—	—	0.10	0.25	0.35
2007	—	—	—	0.10	0.25	0.35

KM# 76.3 10 CENTAVOS
6.0000 g., Brass, 26 mm. **Obv:** National arms, without clouds behind pyramid **Rev:** Denomination within circle, wreath surrounds **Edge:** Plain

Date	Mintage	F	VF	XF	Unc	BU
2002	—	—	0.10	0.20	0.45	0.65
2003	—	—	0.10	0.20	0.45	0.65
2005	—	—	0.10	0.20	0.45	0.65
2006	—	—	0.10	0.20	0.45	0.65

KM# 76.4 10 CENTAVOS
6.0000 g., Brass, 26 mm. **Obv:** National arms, slightly larger legend, large date **Rev:** Value in circle within wreath **Edge:** Plain

Date	Mintage	F	VF	XF	Unc	BU
2006	—	—	—	0.15	0.35	0.45
2007	—	—	—	0.15	0.35	0.45

KM# 83.2a 20 CENTAVOS
2.0000 g., Nickel Plated Steel, 18 mm. **Obv:** National arms, without clouds **Rev:** Chief Lempira head left within circle **Edge:** Reeded

Date	Mintage	F	VF	XF	Unc	BU
2007	—	—	—	0.20	0.60	1.00
2010	—	—	—	0.20	0.60	1.00

KM# 84a.2 50 CENTAVOS
5.0000 g., Nickel Plated Steel, 24 mm. **Obv:** National arms above date **Rev:** Chief Lempira head left within circle **Edge:** Reeded

Date	Mintage	F	VF	XF	Unc	BU
2005	—	—	0.15	0.35	0.90	1.25

KM# 91 10 LEMPIRAS
27.0000 g., 0.9250 Silver 0.8029 oz. ASW, 40 mm. **Obv:** State arms **Rev:** Bust of Jose Trinidad Cabanas Fiallos, president 1852-1855

Date	Mintage	F	VF	XF	Unc	BU
2005 Proof	Est. 500	Value: 120				

HONG KONG

Hong Kong, a former British colony, reverted to control of the People's Republic of China on July 1, 1997 as a Special Administrative Region. It is situated at the mouth of the Canton or Pearl River 90 miles (145 km.) southeast of Canton, has an area of 403 sq. mi. (1,040 sq. km.) and an estimated population of 6.3 million. Capital: Victoria. The free port of Hong Kong, the commercial center of the Far East, is a trans-shipment point for goods destined for China and the countries of the Pacific Rim. Light manufacturing and tourism are important components of the economy.

SPECIAL ADMINISTRATION REGION (S.A.R.)

DECIMAL COINAGE

KM# 80 50 DOLLARS
35.4300 g., 0.9250 Silver Gold plated center 1.0536 oz. ASW, 40 mm. **Series:** Five Blessings **Obv:** Bauhinia flower **Rev:** Jade Ju-I

Date	Mintage	F	VF	XF	Unc	BU
2002 Proof	60,000	Value: 85.00				

KM# 81 50 DOLLARS
35.4300 g., 0.9250 Silver Gold plated center 1.0536 oz. ASW, 40 mm. **Series:** Five Blessings **Obv:** Bauhinia flower **Rev:** Fish

Date	Mintage	F	VF	XF	Unc	BU
2002 Proof	60,000	Value: 85.00				

KM# 82 50 DOLLARS
35.2500 g., 0.9250 Silver Gold plated center 1.0483 oz. ASW, 40 mm. **Series:** Five Blessings **Obv:** Bauhinia flower **Rev:** Horses

Date	Mintage	F	VF	XF	Unc	BU
2002 Proof	60,000	Value: 85.00				

KM# 83 50 DOLLARS
35.3400 g., 0.9250 Silver Gold plated center 1.0509 oz. ASW, 40 mm. **Series:** Five Blessings **Obv:** Bauhinia flower **Rev:** Peony flower

Date	Mintage	F	VF	XF	Unc	BU
2002 Proof	60,000	Value: 85.00				

KM# 84 50 DOLLARS
35.1400 g., 0.9250 Silver Gold plated center 1.0450 oz. ASW, 40 mm. **Series:** Five Blessings **Obv:** Bauhinia flower **Rev:** Windmills

Date	Mintage	F	VF	XF	Unc	BU
2002 Proof	60,000	Value: 85.00				

PROOF SETS

KM#	Date	Mintage	Identification	Issue Price	Mkt Val
PS8	2002 (5)	60,000	KM#80-84 plus 7.8g, .9999, AGW .2508, 25mm gold medal	370	800

HUNGARY

Hungary, located in central Europe, has an area of 35,929 sq. mi. (93,030 sq. km.) and a population of 10.7 million. Capital: Budapest. The economy is based on agriculture, bauxite and a rapidly expanding industrial sector. Machinery, chemicals, iron and steel, and fruits and vegetables are exported.

MINT MARKS
BP - Budapest

MONETARY SYSTEM

Commencing 1946
100 Filler = 1 Forint

SECOND REPUBLIC
1989-present

DECIMAL COINAGE

KM# 692 FORINT
2.0500 g., Nickel-Brass, 16.5 mm. **Obv:** Crowned shield **Rev:** Denomination

Date	Mintage	F	VF	XF	Unc	BU
2001BP	—	—	—	—	0.10	0.25
2001BP Proof	3,000	Value: 3.75				
2002BP	—	—	—	—	0.10	0.25
2002BP Proof	3,000	Value: 3.75				
2003BP	—	—	—	—	0.10	0.25
2003BP Proof	7,000	Value: 3.50				
2004BP	—	—	—	—	0.10	0.25
2004BP Proof	7,000	Value: 3.50				
2005BP	—	—	—	—	0.10	0.25
2005BP Proof	—	Value: 3.50				
2006BP	—	—	—	—	0.10	0.25
2006BP Proof	—	Value: 3.50				
2007BP	—	—	—	—	0.10	0.25
2007BP Proof	—	Value: 3.50				
2008BP Proof	—	Value: 3.50				

KM# 693 2 FORINT
3.1000 g., Copper-Nickel, 19.2 mm. **Obv:** Native flower: Colchicum Hungaricum **Rev:** Denomination **Edge:** Reeded

Date	Mintage	F	VF	XF	Unc	BU
2001BP	—	—	—	—	0.20	0.35
2001BP Proof	3,000	Value: 4.25				

Date	Mintage	F	VF	XF	Unc	BU
2002BP	—	—	—	—	0.20	0.35
2002BP Proof	3,000	Value: 4.25				
2003BP	—	—	—	—	0.20	0.35
2003BP Proof	7,000	Value: 4.00				
2004BP	—	—	—	—	0.20	0.35
2004BP Proof	7,000	Value: 4.00				
2005BP	—	—	—	—	0.20	0.35
2005BP Proof	—	Value: 4.00				
2006BP	—	—	—	—	0.20	0.35
2006BP Proof	—	Value: 4.00				
2007	—	—	—	—	0.20	0.35
2007 Proof	—	Value: 4.00				
2008 Proof	—	Value: 4.00				

KM# 694 5 FORINT
4.2000 g., Nickel-Brass, 21.2 mm. **Obv:** Great White Egret **Rev:** Denomination

Date	Mintage	F	VF	XF	Unc	BU
2001BP	—	—	—	—	1.00	1.50
2001BP Proof	3,000	Value: 5.00				
2002BP	—	—	—	—	1.00	1.50
2002BP Proof	3,000	Value: 5.00				
2003BP	—	—	—	—	1.00	1.50
2003BP Proof	7,000	Value: 4.50				
2004BP	—	—	—	—	1.00	1.50
2004BP Proof	7,000	Value: 4.50				
2005BP	—	—	—	—	1.00	1.50
2005BP Proof	—	Value: 4.50				
2006BP	—	—	—	—	1.00	1.50
2006BP Proof	—	Value: 4.50				
2007BP	—	—	—	—	1.00	1.50
2007BP Proof	—	Value: 4.50				
2008BP	—	—	—	—	1.00	1.50
2008BP Proof	—	Value: 4.50				
2009BP	—	—	—	—	1.00	1.50
2010BP	—	—	—	—	1.00	1.50
2011BP	—	—	—	—	1.00	1.50

KM# 847 5 FORINT
4.2000 g., Nickel-Brass, 21.2 mm. **Obv:** Great White Egret **Obv. Legend:** MAGYARORSZAG **Rev:** Denomination

Date	Mintage	F	VF	XF	Unc	BU
2012BP	—	—	—	—	1.00	1.50

KM# 695 10 FORINT
6.1000 g., Copper-Nickel, 24.8 mm. **Obv:** Crowned shield **Rev:** Denomination **Edge:** Segmented reeding

Date	Mintage	F	VF	XF	Unc	BU
2001BP	—	—	—	—	1.00	2.50
2001BP Proof	3,000	Value: 5.50				
2002BP	—	—	—	—	1.00	2.50
2002BP Proof	3,000	Value: 5.50				
2003BP	—	—	—	—	1.00	2.50
2003BP Proof	7,000	Value: 5.00				
2004BP	—	—	—	—	1.00	2.50
2004BP Proof	7,000	Value: 5.00				
2005BP	—	—	—	—	1.00	2.50
2005BP Proof	—	Value: 5.00				
2006BP	—	—	—	—	1.00	2.50
2006BP Proof	—	Value: 5.00				
2007	—	—	—	—	1.00	2.50
2007 Proof	—	Value: 5.00				
2008	—	—	—	—	1.00	2.50
2008 Proof	—	Value: 5.00				
2009	—	—	—	—	1.00	2.50
2010	—	—	—	—	1.00	2.50
2011	—	—	—	—	1.00	2.50

KM# 779 10 FORINT
6.1000 g., Copper-Nickel, 24.8 mm. **Obv:** Attila Jozsef **Rev:** Value **Edge:** Segmented reeding

Date	Mintage	F	VF	XF	Unc	BU
2005BP	20,000	—	—	—	2.50	3.00
2005BP Proof	7,000	Value: 3.50				

KM# 848 10 FORINT
6.1000 g., Copper-Nickel, 24.8 mm. **Obv:** Crowned shield **Obv. Legend:** MAGYARORSZAG **Rev:** Denomination **Edge:** Segmented reeding

Date	Mintage	F	VF	XF	Unc	BU
2012BP	—	—	—	—	1.00	2.50

KM# 696 20 FORINT
6.9000 g., Nickel-Brass, 26.3 mm. **Obv:** Hungarian Iris **Rev:** Denomination **Edge:** Reeded

Date	Mintage	F	VF	XF	Unc	BU
2001BP	—	—	—	—	1.50	2.00
2001BP Proof	3,000	Value: 4.50				
2002BP	—	—	—	—	1.50	2.00
2002BP Proof	3,000	Value: 4.50				
2003BP	—	—	—	—	1.50	2.00
2003BP Proof	7,000	Value: 4.00				
2004BP	—	—	—	—	1.50	2.00
2004BP Proof	7,000	Value: 4.00				
2005BP	—	—	—	—	1.50	2.00
2005BP Proof	—	Value: 4.00				
2006BP	—	—	—	—	1.50	2.00
2006BP Proof	—	Value: 4.00				
2007BP	—	—	—	—	1.50	2.00
2007BP Proof	—	Value: 4.00				
2008BP	—	—	—	—	1.50	2.00
2008BP Proof	—	Value: 4.00				
2009BP	—	—	—	—	1.50	2.00
2010BP	—	—	—	—	1.50	2.00
2011BP	—	—	—	—	1.50	2.00

KM# 768 20 FORINT
6.9000 g., Nickel-Brass, 26.3 mm. **Obv:** Ferenc Deak **Rev:** Denomination **Edge:** Reeded

Date	Mintage	F	VF	XF	Unc	BU
2003BP	993,000	—	—	—	1.50	2.00
2003BP Proof	7,000	Value: 4.00				

KM# 849 20 FORINT
6.9000 g., Nickel-Brass, 26.3 mm. **Obv:** Hungarian Iris **Obv. Legend:** MAGYARORSZAG **Rev:** Denomination **Edge:** Reeded

Date	Mintage	F	VF	XF	Unc	BU
2012BP	—	—	—	—	1.50	2.50

KM# 697 50 FORINT
7.6000 g., Copper-Nickel, 27.5 mm. **Obv:** Saker falcon **Rev:** Denomination

Date	Mintage	F	VF	XF	Unc	BU
2001BP	—	—	—	—	3.00	4.00
2001BP Proof	3,000	Value: 6.00				
2002BP	—	—	—	—	3.00	3.50
2002BP Proof	3,000	Value: 5.50				
2003BP	—	—	—	—	3.00	3.50
2003BP Proof	7,000	Value: 5.00				
2004BP	—	—	—	—	3.00	3.50
2004BP Proof	7,000	Value: 5.00				
2005BP	—	—	—	—	3.00	3.50
2005BP Proof	—	Value: 5.00				
2006BP	—	—	—	—	3.00	3.50
2006BP Proof	—	Value: 5.00				
2007BP	—	—	—	—	3.00	3.50
2007BP Proof	—	Value: 5.00				
2008BP	—	—	—	—	3.00	3.50
2008BP Proof	—	Value: 5.00				
2009BP	—	—	—	—	3.00	3.50

Date	Mintage	F	VF	XF	Unc	BU
2010BP	—	—	—	—	3.00	3.50
2011BP	—	—	—	—	3.00	3.50

KM# 773 50 FORINT
7.7000 g., Copper-Nickel, 27.5 mm. **Obv:** National arms above Euro Union star circle **Rev:** Denomination **Edge:** Plain

Date	Mintage	F	VF	XF	Unc	BU
2004BP	993,000	—	—	—	3.00	3.50
2004BP Proof	7,000	Value: 6.00				

KM# 780 50 FORINT
7.7000 g., Copper-Nickel, 27.4 mm. **Subject:** International Childrens Safety Service **Obv:** Stylized crying child **Rev:** Denomination **Edge:** Plain

Date	Mintage	F	VF	XF	Unc	BU
2005BP	2,000,000	—	—	—	3.00	3.50

KM# 788 50 FORINT
7.7000 g., Copper-Nickel, 27.4 mm. **Obv:** Hungarian Red Cross 125th Anniversary seal above date and country name **Rev:** Value **Edge:** Plain

Date	Mintage	F	VF	XF	Unc	BU
2006BP	2,000,000	—	—	—	3.00	3.50

KM# 789 50 FORINT
7.7000 g., Copper-Nickel, 27.4 mm. **Subject:** 1956 Revolution **Obv:** Holed flag with Parliament building in background **Rev:** Value **Edge:** Plain

Date	Mintage	F	VF	XF	Unc	BU
2006BP	2,000,000	—	—	—	3.00	3.50

KM# 805 50 FORINT
7.7000 g., Copper-Nickel, 27.4 mm. **Subject:** Celebrating 50 years of the Treaty of Rome **Obv:** Book logo **Rev:** Value

Date	Mintage	F	VF	XF	Unc	BU
2007	2,000,000	—	—	—	1.50	2.00
2007 Proof	5,000	Value: 3.50				

KM# 850 50 FORINT
7.6000 g., Copper-Nickel, 27.5 mm. **Obv:** Saker falcon **Obv. Legend:** MAGYARORSZAG **Rev:** Denomination

Date	Mintage	F	VF	XF	Unc	BU
2012BP	—	—	—	—	3.00	3.50

KM# 760   100 FORINT
8.0000 g., Bi-Metallic Brass Plated Steel center in Stainless Steel ring, 23.8 mm. **Subject:** Lajos Kossuth **Obv:** Head right within circle **Rev:** Denomination within circle **Edge:** Reeded

Date	Mintage	F	VF	XF	Unc	BU
2002BP	997,000	—	—	—	2.00	2.50
2002BP Proof	3,000	Value: 5.00				

KM# 851   100 FORINT
8.0000 g., Bi-Metallic Brass Plated Steel center in Stainless Steel ring, 23.6 mm. **Obv:** Crowned shield **Obv. Legend:** MAGYARORZAG **Rev:** Denomination

Date	Mintage	F	VF	XF	Unc	BU
2012BP	—	—	—	—	3.50	5.00

KM# 844   100 FORINT
10.0000 g., Copper-Nickel, 30 mm. **Subject:** Hungarian Scout Association, 100th Anniversary **Obv:** Hungarian Scout emblem at right **Rev:** Scout in uniform blowing bugle towards left **Shape:** 12-sided

Date	Mintage	F	VF	XF	Unc	BU
2012BP	5,000	—	—	—	—	20.00
2012BP Proof	10,000	Value: 25.00				

KM# 721   100 FORINT (Szaz)
8.0000 g., Bi-Metallic Brass Plated Steel center in Stainless Steel ring, 23.8 mm. **Obv:** Crowned shield **Rev:** Denomination **Edge:** Reeded

Date	Mintage	F	VF	XF	Unc	BU
2001BP	—	—	—	—	3.50	5.00
2001BP Proof	3,000	Value: 8.00				
2002BP	—	—	—	—	3.50	5.00
2002BP Proof	3,000	Value: 8.00				
2003BP	—	—	—	—	3.50	5.00
2003BP Proof	7,000	Value: 7.50				
2004BP	—	—	—	—	3.50	5.00
2004BP Proof	7,000	Value: 7.50				
2005BP	—	Value: 7.50				
2005BP Proof	—	Value: 7.50				
2006BP	—	—	—	—	3.50	5.00
2006BP Proof	—	Value: 7.50				
2007BP	—	—	—	—	3.50	5.00
2007BP Proof	—	Value: 7.50				
2008BP	—	—	—	—	3.50	5.00
2008BP Proof	—	Value: 7.50				
2009BP	—	—	—	—	3.50	5.00
2010BP	—	—	—	—	3.50	5.00
2011BP	—	—	—	—	3.50	5.00

KM# 754   200 FORINT
9.4000 g., Brass, 29.2 mm. **Subject:** Childrens Literature: Ludas Matyi **Obv:** Denomination **Rev:** Man holding a goose **Edge:** Plain

Date	Mintage	F	VF	XF	Unc	BU
2001BP	12,000	—	—	—	7.50	9.50
2001BP Proof	5,000	Value: 15.00				

KM# 755   200 FORINT
Brass, 29.2 mm. **Subject:** Childrens Literature: Janos Vitez **Obv:** Denomination **Rev:** Soldier riding a flying bird **Edge:** Plain

---

Date	Mintage	F	VF	XF	Unc	BU
2001BP	12,000	—	—	—	7.50	9.50
2001BP Proof	5,000	Value: 15.00				

KM# 756   200 FORINT
Brass, 29.2 mm. **Subject:** Childrens Literature: Toldi **Obv:** Denomination **Rev:** Knight kicking a boat off the shore **Edge:** Plain

Date	Mintage	F	VF	XF	Unc	BU
2001BP	12,000	—	—	—	7.50	9.50
2001BP Proof	5,000	Value: 15.00				

KM# 757   200 FORINT
Brass, 29.2 mm. **Subject:** Childrens Literature: A Pal Utcai Fiuk **Obv:** Denomination **Rev:** Two men and cordwood **Edge:** Plain

Date	Mintage	F	VF	XF	Unc	BU
2001	12,000	—	—	—	7.50	9.50
2001 Proof	5,000	Value: 15.00				

KM# 826   200 FORINT
9.0000 g., Bi-Metallic Copper-Nickel center in Nickel-Brass ring, 28.3 mm. **Obv:** Suspension Bridge over the Danube **Rev:** Value **Edge:** Segmented reeding

Date	Mintage	F	VF	XF	Unc	BU
2009BP	—	—	—	—	4.00	5.00
2010BP	—	—	—	—	4.00	5.00
2011BP	—	—	—	—	4.00	5.00

KM# 852   200 FORINT
9.0000 g., Bi-Metallic Copper-Nickel center in Nickel-Brass ring, 28.3 mm. **Obv:** Suspension Bridge over the Danube **Obv. Legend:** MAGYARORSZAG **Rev:** Denomination **Edge:** Segmented reeding

Date	Mintage	F	VF	XF	Unc	BU
2012BP	—	—	—	—	4.00	5.00

KM# 764   500 FORINT
13.9000 g., Copper-Nickel **Subject:** Farkas Kempelen's Chess Machine **Obv:** Denomination, letters A-H and numbers 1-8 repeated along edges **Rev:** Robotic human form chess playing machine built in 1769 **Edge:** Plain **Shape:** Square, 28.43 x 28.43 mm

Date	Mintage	F	VF	XF	Unc	BU
2002BP	5,000	—	—	—	15.00	18.00
2002BP Proof	5,000	Value: 25.00				

Date	Mintage	F	VF	XF	Unc	BU
2001BP	12,000	—	—	—	7.50	9.50
2001BP Proof	5,000	Value: 15.00				

KM# 765   500 FORINT
13.8000 g., Copper-Nickel **Subject:** Rubik's Cube **Obv:** Inscription on Rubik's Cube design **Rev:** Rubik's Cube with inscription **Edge:** Plain **Shape:** Square, 28.43 x 28.43 mm

Date	Mintage	F	VF	XF	Unc	BU
2002BP	5,000	—	—	—	18.00	22.00
2002BP Proof	5,000	Value: 32.00				

KM# 781   500 FORINT
14.0000 g., Copper-Nickel **Obv:** Old wheel **Rev:** First Hungarian Post Office motor vehicle **Edge:** Plain **Shape:** Square **Note:** 28.43 x 28.43mm

Date	Mintage	F	VF	XF	Unc	BU
2005BP	5,000	—	—	—	17.00	22.00
2005BP Proof	10,000	Value: 32.00				

KM# 766   1000 FORINT
19.5000 g., Bronze Hollow coin unscrews to open **Obv:** Denomination and satellite dish **Rev:** Mercury

Date	Mintage	F	VF	XF	Unc	BU
2002BP	15,000	—	—	—	15.00	16.50

KM# 787   1000 FORINT
13.8100 g., Copper-Nickel, 28.3 mm. **Obv:** Value and partial front view of antique automobile **Rev:** Model T Ford **Edge:** Plain **Shape:** Square

Date	Mintage	F	VF	XF	Unc	BU
2006BP	10,000	—	—	—	17.00	20.00
2006BP Proof	10,000	Value: 27.00				

KM# 797   1000 FORINT
14.0000 g., Copper-Nickel, 28.43 x 28.43 mm. **Subject:** 125th Anniversary - Birth of János Adorján **Obv:** Early two cylinder

aircraft motor with propeller **Obv. Legend:** MAGYAR / KOZTARSASAG **Rev:** Early monoplane **Rev. Legend:** ADORJAN JANOS / AZ ELSO SIKERES MAGYAR / REPULOGEP TERVEZOJE **Edge:** Plain **Shape:** Square

Date	Mintage	F	VF	XF	Unc	BU
2007BP	10,000	—	—	—	20.00	17.00
2007BP Proof	10,000	Value: 27.00				

KM# 809   1000 FORINT
14.0000 g., Copper-Nickel, 28.43 x 28.43 mm. **Subject:** Telephone Herald **Edge:** Plain **Shape:** Square

Date	Mintage	F	VF	XF	Unc	BU
2008	10,000	—	—	—	20.00	17.00
2008 Proof	15,000	Value: 27.00				

KM# 813   1000 FORINT
14.0000 g., Copper-Nickel, 28.4 x 28.4 mm. **Subject:** Donat Banki, 150th Anniversary of Birth **Obv:** Denomination view of crossflow turbine **Rev:** Portrait facing in suit **Shape:** Square

Date	Mintage	F	VF	XF	Unc	BU
2009BP	10,000	—	—	—	16.00	18.00
2009BP Proof	10,000	Value: 25.00				

KM# 818   1000 FORINT
14.0000 g., Copper-Nickel, 28.4 x 28.4 mm. **Subject:** Laszlo Jozsef Biro, Inventor of the ball point pen **Obv:** Ball point pen schematic **Rev:** Bust facing **Shape:** Square

Date	Mintage	F	VF	XF	Unc	BU
2010BP	10,000	—	—	—	18.00	16.00
2010BP Proof	10,000	Value: 25.00				

KM# 829   1000 FORINT
14.0000 g., Copper-Nickel, 28.43x28.43 mm. **Subject:** Anyos Jedlik, principals of the dynamo, 1861 **Obv:** Dynamo **Rev:** Jedlik portrait

Date	Mintage	F	VF	XF	Unc	BU
2011BP	10,000	—	—	—	—	15.00
2011BP Proof	10,000	Value: 20.00				

KM# 840   1000 FORINT
14.0000 g., Copper-Nickel, 28.43x28.43 mm. **Subject:** Masat-1 satellite launch **Obv:** Land-based antenna **Rev:** Satellite above Eastern Europe map, Hungary highlighted

Date	Mintage	F	VF	XF	Unc	BU
2012BP	5,000	—	—	—	—	25.00
2012BP Proof	5,000	Value: 25.00				

KM# 752   3000 FORINT
31.4600 g., 0.9250 Silver 0.9356 oz. ASW, 38.5 mm. **Subject:** Hungarian Silver Coinage Millennium **Obv:** Denomination in ornamental frame **Rev:** Thaler design circa 1500 portraying Ladislaus I (1077-95) with the title of saint **Edge:** Reeding over "1001-2001" **Edge Lettering:** BP • NX • KB • HX • GY • F • AF • MM • C +

Date	Mintage	F	VF	XF	Unc	BU
2001BP	5,000	—	—	—	40.00	45.00
2001BP Proof	5,000	Value: 50.00				

KM# 759   3000 FORINT
31.8000 g., 0.9250 Silver 0.9457 oz. ASW, 38.7 mm. **Subject:** Centennial of First Hungarian Film "The Dance" **Obv:** Denomination **Rev:** Two dancers on film **Edge:** Reeded

Date	Mintage	F	VF	XF	Unc	BU
2001BP	3,500	—	—	—	42.00	47.50
2001BP Proof	3,500	Value: 55.00				

KM# 761   3000 FORINT
31.3300 g., 0.9250 Silver 0.9317 oz. ASW, 38.6 mm. **Subject:** Hortobagy National Park **Obv:** Landscape, denomination **Rev:** Hungarian Grey Longhorn bull **Edge:** Reeded

Date	Mintage	F	VF	XF	Unc	BU
2002BP	5,000	—	—	—	37.50	50.00
2002BP Proof	5,000	Value: 65.00				

KM# 767   3000 FORINT
31.4600 g., 0.9250 Silver 0.9356 oz. ASW **Subject:** 100th Anniversary - Birth of Kovacs Margit (1902-1977) **Obv:** Denomination **Rev:** The "Trumpet of Judgement Day"

Date	Mintage	F	VF	XF	Unc	BU
2002	4,000	—	—	—	40.00	45.00
2002 Proof	4,000	Value: 55.00				

KM# 762   3000 FORINT
31.4600 g., 0.9250 Silver 0.9356 oz. ASW, 38.5 mm. **Subject:** 200th Anniversary - National Library **Obv:** Small coat of arms in ornate frame **Rev:** Interior view of library **Edge:** Reeded

Date	Mintage	F	VF	XF	Unc	BU
2002BP	3,000	—	—	—	40.00	45.00
2002BP Proof	3,000	Value: 50.00				

KM# 763   3000 FORINT
31.4600 g., 0.9250 Silver 0.9356 oz. ASW, 38.5 mm. **Subject:** Janos Bolyai's publication of his "Appendix" **Obv:** Circular graph **Rev:** Signature above 7-line inscription, name and dates **Edge:** Reeded

Date	Mintage	F	VF	XF	Unc	BU
2002BP	3,000	—	—	—	40.00	45.00
2002BP Proof	3,000	Value: 50.00				

KM# 817   3000 FORINT
10.0000 g., 0.9250 Silver 0.2974 oz. ASW **Subject:** Ferenc Kazinczy, 250th Anniversary of Birth **Obv:** Quill pen and rolled document **Rev:** Bust facing

Date	Mintage	F	VF	XF	Unc	BU
2009	5,000	—	—	—	17.00	20.00
2009 Proof	5,000	Value: 30.00				

KM# 828 3000 FORINT
10.0000 g., 0.9250 Silver 0.2974 oz. ASW, 30 mm. **Subject:**
Hungary's EU Council Presidency, 2011 **Obv:** Crowned shield
within grometric design **Rev:** Skyline view below EU star circle

Date	Mintage	F	VF	XF	Unc	BU
2011BP	3,000	—	—	—	—	30.00
2011BP Proof	5,000	Value: 45.00				

KM# 842 3000 FORINT
24.0000 g., 0.9250 Silver 0.7137 oz. ASW, 30 mm. **Subject:**
XXX Summer Olympics, London **Obv:** Two kyack paddles **Rev:**
Three kyackers advancing right

Date	Mintage	F	VF	XF	Unc	BU
2012BP	3,000	—	—	—	—	45.00
2012BP Proof	5,000	Value: 50.00				

KM# 845 3000 FORINT
10.0000 g., 0.9250 Silver 0.2974 oz. ASW, 30x25 mm. **Subject:**
Albert Szent-Gyorgyi, Nobel prize winner **Obv:** Tomato and sliced
tomatto, value at upper right **Rev:** Szent-Gyorgyi bust at left
Shape: Horizontal oval

Date	Mintage	F	VF	XF	Unc	BU
2012BP	2,000	—	—	—	—	45.00
2012BP Proof	5,000	Value: 50.00				

KM# 846 3000 FORINT
20.0000 g., 0.9250 Silver 0.5948 oz. ASW, 34 mm. **Subject:**
Sandor Popovics, 100th Anniversary of Birth **Obv:** Architectural
statuary group **Rev:** Popovics bust

Date	Mintage	F	VF	XF	Unc	BU
2012BP	2,000	—	—	—	—	45.00
2012BP Proof	4,000	Value: 50.00				

KM# 837 3000 FORINT
20.0000 g., 0.9250 Gold 0.5948 oz. AGW, 34 mm. **Subject:**
Imre Madach's The Tragedy of Man, 150th Anniversary **Obv:**
Bust at left, large value **Rev:** Two figures standing on hilltop,
guardian in background

Date	Mintage	F	VF	XF	Unc	BU
2012BP	2,000	—	—	—	—	45.00
2012BP Proof	4,000	Value: 50.00				

KM# 751 4000 FORINT
31.4600 g., 0.9250 Silver 0.9356 oz. ASW, 26.4 x 39.6 mm.
Subject: Godollo Artist Colony Centennial **Obv:** Denomination
Rev: "Sisters" stained glass window design **Edge:** Plain **Shape:**
Vertical rectangle

Date	Mintage	F	VF	XF	Unc	BU
2001BP	4,000	—	—	—	40.00	45.00
2001BP Proof	4,000	Value: 50.00				

KM# 769 5000 FORINT
31.4600 g., 0.9250 Silver 0.9356 oz. ASW, 38.6 mm. **Subject:**
Budapest Philharmonic Orchestra **Obv:** Crowned arms in wreath
Rev: Four coin-like portraits of Erkel, Dohnanyi, Bartók and
Kodaly **Edge:** Reeded

Date	Mintage	F	VF	XF	Unc	BU
2003BP	4,000	—	—	—	37.50	42.50
2003BP Proof	4,000	Value: 50.00				

KM# 770 5000 FORINT
31.4600 g., 0.9250 Silver 0.9356 oz. ASW, 38.6 mm. **Subject:**
Janos Neumann, 100th Anniversary of Birth **Obv:** Denomination
and binary number date **Rev:** Portrait and building **Edge:** Reeded

Date	Mintage	F	VF	XF	Unc	BU
2003BP	3,000	—	—	—	40.00	45.00
2003BP Proof	3,000	Value: 55.00				

KM# 771 5000 FORINT
31.4600 g., 0.9250 Silver 0.9356 oz. ASW, 38.6 mm. **Subject:**
Rakoczi's War of Liberation **Obv:** Transylvanian ducat design
above country name, value and date **Rev:** Kuruc cavalryman with
sword and trumpet **Edge:** Reeded

Date	Mintage	F	VF	XF	Unc	BU
2003BP	3,000	—	—	—	45.00	50.00
2003BP Proof	3,000	Value: 60.00				

KM# 772 5000 FORINT
31.4600 g., 0.9250 Silver 0.9356 oz. ASW, 38.6 mm. **Subject:**
World Heritage in Hungary - Holloko **Obv:** Holloko castle ruins
above country name, value and date **Rev:** Village view behind
woman in folk costume **Edge:** Reeded

Date	Mintage	F	VF	XF	Unc	BU
2003BP	5,000	—	—	—	42.50	45.00
2003BP Proof	5,000	Value: 50.00				

KM# 774 5000 FORINT
31.4600 g., 0.9250 Silver 0.9356 oz. ASW, 38.6 mm. **Obv:**
Value **Rev:** Two Olympic boxers **Edge:** Reeded

Date	Mintage	F	VF	XF	Unc	BU
2004BP	3,000	—	—	—	45.00	47.50
2004BP Proof	9,000	Value: 50.00				

KM# 775 5000 FORINT
31.4600 g., 0.9250 Silver 0.9356 oz. ASW, 38.6 mm. **Obv:**
"Solomon Tower" above value **Rev:** Visegrad Castle with the
Solomon Tower **Edge:** Reeded

Date	Mintage	F	VF	XF	Unc	BU
2004BP	4,000	—	—	—	45.00	50.00
2004BP Proof	4,000	Value: 55.00				

KM# 776 5000 FORINT
31.4600 g., 0.9250 Silver 0.9356 oz. ASW, 38.6 mm. **Obv:**
Value and country name above Euro Union stars **Rev:** Mythical
stag seen through an ornate window **Edge:** Reeded

Date	Mintage	F	VF	XF	Unc	BU
2004BP Proof	10,000	Value: 50.00				

KM# 778 5000 FORINT
31.4600 g., 0.9250 Silver 0.9356 oz. ASW, 38.6 mm. **Subject:**
Ancient Christian Necropolis at Pecs **Obv:** Value and ancient
artifact **Rev:** Interior view of tomb **Edge:** Reeded

Date	Mintage	F	VF	XF	Unc	BU
2004BP	5,000	—	—	—	40.00	45.00
2004BP Proof	5,000	Value: 50.00				

KM# 782 5000 FORINT
31.4600 g., 0.9250 Silver 0.9356 oz. ASW, 38.6 mm. **Obv:** Bat
flying above value **Rev:** Interior cave view **Edge:** Reeded

Date	Mintage	F	VF	XF	Unc	BU
2005BP	5,000	—	—	—	45.00	50.00
2005BP Proof	5,000	Value: 55.00				

KM# 783 5000 FORINT
31.4600 g., 0.9250 Silver 0.9356 oz. ASW, 38.6 mm. **Obv:**
Hungarian National Bank building **Rev:** Ignac Alpar and life dates
Edge: Reeded

Date	Mintage	F	VF	XF	Unc	BU
ND (2005)BP	3,000	—	—	—	45.00	50.00
ND (2005)BP Proof	3,000	Value: 55.00				

KM# 784   5000 FORINT
31.4600 g., 0.9250 Silver 0.9356 oz. ASW, 38.6 mm. **Obv:**
Knight on horse with lance **Rev:** Diosgyor Castle **Edge:** Reeded

Date	Mintage	F	VF	XF	Unc	BU
2005BP	4,000	—	—	—	45.00	50.00
2005BP Proof	4,000	Value: 55.00				

KM# 785   5000 FORINT
31.4600 g., 0.9250 Silver 0.9356 oz. ASW, 38.6 mm. **Obv:**
Large building above value **Rev:** Karoli Gaspar Reformed
(Calvinist) University seal **Edge:** Reeded

Date	Mintage	F	VF	XF	Unc	BU
2005BP	3,000	—	—	—	45.00	50.00
2005BP Proof	3,000	Value: 55.00				

KM# 786   5000 FORINT
31.4600 g., 0.9250 Silver 0.9356 oz. ASW, 38.6 mm. **Obv:** Coin
design of a Transylvanian KM-10 thaler reverse dated 1605 **Rev:**
Stephan Bocskai (1557-1606) **Edge:** Reeded

Date	Mintage	F	VF	XF	Unc	BU
2005BP	3,000	—	—	—	45.00	50.00
2005BP Proof	3,000	Value: 55.00				

KM# 790   5000 FORINT
31.4600 g., 0.9250 Silver 0.9356 oz. ASW, 38.61 mm. **Series:**
Masterpieces of Ecclesiastical Architecture **Obv:** View of interior
of dome **Obv. Legend:** MAGYAR KÖZTÁRSASÁG **Rev:** Basilica
facade **Rev. Legend:** ESZTERGOMI BAZILIKA

Date	Mintage	F	VF	XF	Unc	BU
2006BP	2,500	—	—	—	50.00	55.00
2006BP Proof	3,500	Value: 60.00				

KM# 791   5000 FORINT
31.4600 g., 0.9250 Silver 0.9356 oz. ASW, 38.61 mm. **Subject:**
125th Anniversary - Birth of Béla Bartók **Obv:** Transylvanian
woodcarving **Obv. Legend:** MAGYAR KÖZTÁRSASÁG **Rev:**
Bust of Bartók right, Euro star behind **Rev:** Bust of Bartók right,
Euro star behind **Edge:** Reeded and lettered
Edge Lettering: Bartók Béla repeated three times

Date	Mintage	F	VF	XF	Unc	BU
2006BP Proof	25,000	Value: 45.00				

KM# 792   5000 FORINT
31.4600 g., 0.9250 Silver 0.9356 oz. ASW, 38.61 mm. **Series:**
Heritage Sites **Obv:** Great White Egret in flight **Obv. Legend:**
MAGYAR - KÖZTÁRSASÁG **Rev:** Landscape, Schneeberg
Mountain above Esterházy palace facade

Date	Mintage	F	VF	XF	Unc	BU
2006BP	5,000	—	—	—	42.50	47.50
2006BP Proof	5,000	Value: 50.00				

KM# 793   5000 FORINT
31.4600 g., 0.9250 Silver 0.9356 oz. ASW, 38.61 mm. **Series:**
Hungarian Castles **Subject:** Hungarian Castles **Obv:** Portrait of
Ilona Zrinyi **Obv. Legend:** MAGYAR KÖZTÁRSASÁG **Rev:**
Munkács Castle

Date	Mintage	F	VF	XF	Unc	BU
2006BP	4,000	—	—	—	42.50	47.50
2006BP Proof	4,000	Value: 50.00				

KM# 794   5000 FORINT
31.4600 g., 0.9250 Silver 0.9356 oz. ASW, 38.61 mm. **Subject:**
500th Anniversary - Victory in Nándorfehévár **Obv:** Decorative
sword hilt **Obv. Legend:** MAGYAR KÖZTÁRSASÁG **Rev:** János
Hunyadi in armor at left, John Capistrano in monk's garb at right
Rev. Inscription: NÁNDORFEHÉRVÁRI / DIADAL

Date	Mintage	F	VF	XF	Unc	BU
2006BP	2,500	—	—	—	45.00	50.00
2006BP Proof	3,500	Value: 55.00				

KM# 795   5000 FORINT
31.4600 g., 0.9250 Silver 0.9356 oz. ASW, 38.61 mm. **Subject:**
50th Anniversary - Hungarian Revolution **Obv:** 1956 repeated in
stone blocks at right **Obv. Legend:** MAGYAR KÖZTÁRSASÁG
Rev: 1956 repeated in stone blocks at left, freedom fighter's flag
at center **Rev. Legend:** MAGYAR FORRADALOM ÉS
SZABADSÁGHARC

Date	Mintage	F	VF	XF	Unc	BU
2006BP	5,000	—	—	—	42.50	47.50
2006BP Proof	5,000	Value: 50.00				

KM# 798   5000 FORINT
31.4600 g., 0.9250 Silver 0.9356 oz. ASW, 38.61 mm. **Series:**
Hungarian Castles **Obv:** Walled tower **Obv. Inscription:**
MAGYAR / KÖZTÁRSASÁG **Rev:** Gyula castle **Rev.
Inscription:** GYULAI / VÁR

Date	Mintage	F	VF	XF	Unc	BU
2007BP	4,000	—	—	—	50.00	55.00
2007BP Proof	4,000	Value: 60.00				

KM# 799   5000 FORINT
31.4600 g., 0.9250 Silver 0.9356 oz. ASW, 38.61 mm. **Subject:**
200th Anniversary - Birth of Count Lajos Batthyány **Obv:** Seal
dated 1848 with crowned arms above Batthyány's autograph
Obv. Legend: MAGYAR KÖZTÁRSASÁG **Rev:** 1/2 length figure
of Batthyány facing **Rev. Legend:** BATTHYÁNY LAJOS

Date	Mintage	F	VF	XF	Unc	BU
2007BP Proof	20,000	Value: 45.00				

KM# 800   5000 FORINT
31.4600 g., 0.9250 Silver 0.9356 oz. ASW, 38.61 mm. **Subject:**
125th Anniversary - Birth of Zoltán Kodály **Obv:** Gramophone
Obv. Legend: MAGYAR KÖZTÁRSASÁG **Rev:** Bust of Kodály
facing 3/4 right

Date	Mintage	F	VF	XF	Unc	BU
2007BP	4,000	—	—	—	42.50	47.50
2007BP Proof	6,000	Value: 50.00				

KM# 802   5000 FORINT
31.4600 g., 0.9250 Silver 0.9356 oz. ASW, 38.61 mm. **Subject:**
8ooth Anniversary - Birth of St. Elizabeth **Obv:** Stylized image of
St. Elizabeth feeding the hungry **Obv. Inscription:** Magyar /
Köztársság **Rev:** 3/4 length figure of St. Elizabeth seated facing
holding roses and bread rolls in her lap

Date	Mintage	F	VF	XF	Unc	BU
2007BP	4,000	—	—	—	52.50	55.00
2007BP Proof	4,000	Value: 60.00				

KM# 804   5000 FORINT
31.4600 g., 0.9250 Silver 0.9356 oz. ASW, 38.61 mm. **Subject:**
Great Reformed Church - Debrecen **Obv:** Church interior **Obv.
Legend:** MAGYAR KOZTARSASAG **Rev:** Church facade **Rev.
Legend:** DEBRECENI REFORMATUS NAGYTEMPLOM **Edge:**
Plain **Shape:** 12-sided

Date	Mintage	F	VF	XF	Unc	BU
2007BP	4,000	—	—	—	42.50	47.50
2007BP Proof	6,000	Value: 50.00				

KM# 811   5000 FORINT
31.4600 g., 0.9250 Silver 0.9356 oz. ASW, 38.6 mm. **Subject:**
Europa heritage site Tokaj Wine Region **Obv:** Value within grape
wreath **Rev:** Tokaj Hill and TV tower **Edge:** Reeded

Date	Mintage	F	VF	XF	Unc	BU
2008BP	5,000	—	—	—	—	48.00
2008BP Proof	15,000	Value: 55.00				

KM# 806   5000 FORINT
31.4600 g., 0.9250 Silver 0.9356 oz. ASW, 38.61 mm. **Obv:**
Grape wreath rim with denomination, legend & mintmark inside
Rev: Tokaj hill, TV tower, grapefield with a village & church **Edge:**
Milled

Date	Mintage	F	VF	XF	Unc	BU
2008	5,000	—	—	—	—	48.00
2008 Proof	15,000	Value: 55.00				

KM# 807   5000 FORINT
31.4600 g., 0.9250 Silver 0.9356 oz. ASW, 38.61 mm. **Subject:**

Castle of the Siklós **Obv:** Castle, tower, Franciscan monastery
& church **Rev:** Castle of the Siklós

Date	Mintage	F	VF	XF	Unc	BU
2008	4,000	—	—	—	—	45.00
2008 Proof	6,000	Value: 50.00				

KM# 808   5000 FORINT
31.4600 g., 0.9250 Silver 0.9356 oz. ASW, 38.61 mm. **Subject:**
29th Summer Olympics **Obv:** Coat of arms over water **Rev:** Water
polo player **Edge:** Milled

Date	Mintage	F	VF	XF	Unc	BU
2008	4,000	—	—	—	—	40.00
2008 Proof	14,000	Value: 45.00				

KM# 810   5000 FORINT
31.4600 g., 0.9250 Silver 0.9356 oz. ASW, 38.61 mm. **Subject:**
Centenery birth of Ede Teller **Obv:** Diagram of Deuterium-tritium
fusion reaction **Rev:** Portrait Ede Teller

Date	Mintage	F	VF	XF	Unc	BU
2008	4,000	—	—	—	—	45.00
2008 Proof	6,000	Value: 50.00				

KM# 812   5000 FORINT
31.4600 g., 0.9250 Silver 0.9356 oz. ASW **Subject:** Miklós
Badnóti, 100th Anniversary of Birth **Obv:** Value **Rev:** Bust in suit
facing

Date	Mintage	F	VF	XF	Unc	BU
2009	4,000	—	—	—	—	50.00
2009 Proof	4,000	Value: 55.00				

KM# 814   5000 FORINT
31.4600 g., 0.9250 Silver 0.9356 oz. ASW, 38.6 mm. **Subject:**
Dohany Street Synagogue, 150th Anniversary **Obv:** Stained
glass window **Rev:** Synagogue facade **Shape:** 12-sided

Date	Mintage	F	VF	XF	Unc	BU
2009BP	4,000	—	—	—	—	45.00
2009BP Proof	4,000	Value: 65.00				

KM# 815   5000 FORINT
31.4600 g., 0.9250 Silver 0.9356 oz. ASW, 38.61 mm. **Subject:**
Budapest - World Heritage Site **Obv:** Street scene **Rev:**
Panoramic view of Danube and Parliament

Date	Mintage	F	VF	XF	Unc	BU
2009	5,000	—	—	—	—	50.00
2009 Proof	5,000	Value: 55.00				

KM# 827   5000 FORINT
31.4600 g., 0.9250 Silver 0.9356 oz. ASW, 38.6 mm. **Subject:**
John Calvin, 500th Anniversary

Date	Mintage	F	VF	XF	Unc	BU
2009BP Proof	—	Value: 55.00				

KM# 819   5000 FORINT
31.4600 g., 0.9250 Silver 0.9356 oz. ASW, 38.61 mm. **Subject:**
Kosztolanyi Dezso, 125th Anniversary of Birth **Obv:** Architectural
element of stone **Rev:** Portrait

Date	Mintage	F	VF	XF	Unc	BU
2010BP	3,000	—	—	—	40.00	45.00
2010BP Proof	5,000	Value: 50.00				

KM# 820   5000 FORINT
31.4600 g., 0.9250 Silver 0.9356 oz. ASW, 39.6x26.4 mm.
Subject: Orseg National Park **Obv:** Butterfly **Rev:** Traditional
rural buildings **Shape:** Rectangle

Date	Mintage	F	VF	XF	Unc	BU
2010BP	3,000	—	—	—	40.00	45.00
2010BP Proof	5,000	Value: 50.00				

KM# 821   5000 FORINT
31.4600 g., 0.9250 Silver 0.9356 oz. ASW, 38.61 mm. **Subject:**
European Watersports Championships **Obv:** Value and waves
Rev: Swimmer with butterfly stroke

Date	Mintage	F	VF	XF	Unc	BU
2010BP	4,000	—	—	—	40.00	45.00
2010BP Proof	6,000	Value: 50.00				

KM# 822   5000 FORINT
0.5000 g., 0.9990 Gold 0.0161 oz. AGW, 11 mm. **Subject:**
Ferenc Erkel - 200th Anniversary of Birth **Obv:** Denomination
Rev: Large bust facing

Date	Mintage	F	VF	XF	Unc	BU
2010BP Proof	10,000	Value: 50.00				

KM# 823 5000 FORINT
31.4600 g., 0.9250 Silver 0.9356 oz. ASW, 38.61 mm. **Subject:**
Ferenc Erkel, 200th Anniversary of Birth **Obv:** House **Rev:** Bust
facing, signature below

Date	Mintage	F	VF	XF	Unc	BU
2010BP Proof	5,000	Value: 55.00				

KM# 830 5000 FORINT
31.4600 g., 0.9250 Silver 0.9356 oz. ASW, 38.61 mm. **Subject:**
Busojaras Carnival in Mohacs **Obv:** Standing figure in carnival
costume **Rev:** Horned demon face

Date	Mintage	F	VF	XF	Unc	BU
2011BP	3,000	—	—	—	—	45.00
2011BP Proof	5,000	Value: 55.00				

KM# 831 5000 FORINT
31.4600 g., 0.9250 Silver 0.9356 oz. ASW, 38.61 mm. **Subject:**
Arpad Toth, 125th Anniversary of Birth **Obv:** Handwritten poem
at center **Rev:** Toth bust

Date	Mintage	F	VF	XF	Unc	BU
2011BP	2,000	—	—	—	—	45.00
2011BP Proof	4,000	Value: 50.00				

KM# 832 5000 FORINT
31.4600 g., 0.9250 Silver 0.9356 oz. ASW, 39.6x26.4 mm.
Subject: Duna-Drava National Park **Obv:** Riverside scene **Rev:**
Bird in flight

Date	Mintage	F	VF	XF	Unc	BU
2011BP	3,000	—	—	—	—	45.00
2011BP Proof	5,000	Value: 50.00				

KM# 833 5000 FORINT
31.4600 g., 0.9250 Silver 0.9356 oz. ASW, 38.61 mm. **Subject:**
Deak-Ter Evangelistic Church, Budapest **Obv:** Altar detail **Rev:**
Church exterior **Shape:** Scalloped

Date	Mintage	F	VF	XF	Unc	BU
2011BP	3,000	—	—	—	—	45.00
2011BP Proof	5,000	Value: 50.00				

KM# 834 5000 FORINT
31.4600 g., 0.9250 Silver 0.9356 oz. ASW, 38.61 mm. **Subject:**
Istvan Bibo, 100 Anniversary of Birth **Obv:** Value and legend **Rev:**
Bibo seated, writing at table

Date	Mintage	F	VF	XF	Unc	BU
2011BP Proof	6,000	Value: 55.00				

KM# 835 5000 FORINT
0.5000 g., 0.9990 Gold 0.0161 oz. AGW, 11 mm. **Subject:**
Adam Clark, 200th Anniversary of Birth **Obv:** Large value **Rev:**
Large portrait

Date	Mintage	F	VF	XF	Unc	BU
2011BP Prooflike	10,000	—	—	—	—	75.00

KM# 843 5000 FORINT
0.5000 g., 0.9990 Gold 0.0161 oz. AGW, 11 mm. **Subject:** XXX
Summer Olympics, London **Obv:** Paddle in water **Rev:** Canoeist
advancing front

Date	Mintage	F	VF	XF	Unc	BU
2012BP Prooflike	10,000	—	—	—	—	75.00

KM# 838 5000 FORINT
31.4600 g., 0.9250 Silver 0.9356 oz. ASW, 38.61 mm. **Subject:**
Jozef Remenyi, 125th Anniversary of Birth **Obv:** Kneeling nude
female with vase on shoulder **Rev:** Remenyi profile left

Date	Mintage	F	VF	XF	Unc	BU
2012BP Proof	6,000	Value: 50.00				

KM# 839 5000 FORINT
31.4600 g., 0.9250 Silver 0.9356 oz. ASW, 38.61 mm. **Subject:**
Istvan Orkeny, 100th Anniversary of Birth **Obv:** Text forming
rectangle at center **Rev:** Large portrait

Date	Mintage	F	VF	XF	Unc	BU
2012BP	2,000	—	—	—	—	45.00
2012BP Proof	4,000	Value: 50.00				

KM# 841 10000 FORINT (Tizezer)
3.4910 g., 0.9860 Gold 0.1107 oz. AGW, 20 mm. **Subject:**
Charles I florin **Obv:** Old coin: Fleur-dis-lis at center **Rev:** Old
coin: St. John standing

Date	Mintage	F	VF	XF	Unc	BU
2012BP Proof	5,000	Value: 250				

Note: A piefort of this type exists with edge lettering

KM# 753 20000 FORINT
6.9820 g., 0.9860 Gold 0.2213 oz. AGW, 22 mm. **Subject:**
Hungarian Coinage Millennium **Obv:** Denomination **Rev:**
Hammered coinage minting scene above old coin design **Edge:**
Plain

Date	Mintage	F	VF	XF	Unc	BU
2001BP Proof	3,000	Value: 425				

KM# 777 50000 FORINT
13.9640 g., 0.9860 Gold 0.4426 oz. AGW, 25 mm. **Obv:** Value
and country name above Euro Union stars **Rev:** Mythical stag
seen through ornate window **Edge:** Reeded

Date	Mintage	F	VF	XF	Unc	BU
2004BP Proof	7,000	Value: 800				

KM# 803 50000 FORINT
10.0000 g., 0.9860 Gold 0.3170 oz. AGW, 25 mm. **Subject:**
550th Anniversary - Enthronement of Matthias Hunyadi **Obv:**
Raven holding a ring in its beak **Rev:** Portrait of Mátyás Hunyadi
based on a marble relief **Edge:** Smooth

Date	Mintage	F	VF	XF	Unc	BU
2008 Proof	5,000	Value: 575				

KM# 816 50000 FORINT
10.0000 g., 0.9860 Gold 0.3170 oz. AGW, 25 mm. **Subject:**
Ferenc Kazinczy, 250th Anniversary of Birth **Obv:** Value and
classical facade **Rev:** Bust at left

Date	Mintage	F	VF	XF	Unc	BU
2009 Proof	5,000	Value: 575				

KM# 825 50000 FORINT
6.9820 g., 0.9860 Gold 0.2213 oz. AGW, 22 mm. **Subject:** St.
Stephen and St. Emeric **Obv:** Medieval document **Rev:** St.
Stephen and prince standing

Date	Mintage	F	VF	XF	Unc	BU
2010BP Proof	5,000	Value: 425				

KM# 836 50000 FORINT
6.9820 g., 0.9860 Gold 0.2213 oz. AGW, 22 mm. **Subject:**
Franz Liszt, 200th Anniversary of Birth **Obv:** Open piano case
above musical score **Rev:** Bust right **Edge:** Plain

Date	Mintage	F	VF	XF	Unc	BU
2011BP Proof	5,000	Value: 450				

Note: A piefort exists wiht edge lettering

KM# 758 100000 FORINT
31.1040 g., 0.9860 Gold 0.9860 oz. AGW, 37 mm. **Subject:**
Saint Stephen **Obv:** Angels crowning coat of arms **Rev:** King
seated on throne **Edge:** Reeded

Date	Mintage	F	VF	XF	Unc	BU
2001BP Proof	3,000	Value: 1,750				

KM# 796 100000 FORINT
20.9460 g., 0.9860 Gold 0.6640 oz. AGW, 38.61 mm. **Subject:**
50th Anniversary - Hungarian Revolution **Obv:** 1956 repeated in
cut out stone **Rev:** 1956 repeated in cut out stone with two
freedom fighter's flags

Date	Mintage	F	VF	XF	Unc	BU
2006BP Proof	5,000	Value: 1,200				

KM# 824 500,000 FORINT
62.8380 g., 0.9860 Gold 1.9919 oz. AGW, 46 mm. **Subject:** St.

Stephan and St. Emeric **Obv:** Medieval document **Rev:** King and prince standing **Note:** 18 Ducats

Date	Mintage	F	VF	XF	Unc	BU
2010BP Proof	500	Value: 3,750				

PIEDFORTS

KM#	Date	Mintage	Identification	Mkt Val
P27	2011BP	1,500	50000 Forint. 0.9860 Gold. 13.9640 g. 22 mm. Lettered edge. KM#836.	500
P28	2012BP	1,500	10000 Forint. 0.9860 Gold. 13.9640 g. 20 mm. Lettered edge. KM#341	900

MINT SETS

KM#	Date	Mintage	Identification	Issue Price	Mkt Val
MS32	2001 (7)	—	KM#692-697, 721	—	16.50
MS33	2002 (8)	—	KM#692, 693, 694, 695, 696, 697, 721, 760	—	18.00
MS34	2003 (8)	—	KM#692, 693, 694, 695, 696, 697, 721, 768	—	17.50
MS35	2004 (8)	—	KM#692, 693, 694, 695, 696, 697, 721, 773	—	19.00
MS36	2005 (8)	—	KM#692-697, 721, 779 Magyarorszag Penzemei	—	20.00
MS37	2006 (7)	—	KM#692-697, 721, plus silver 1946 KM532	—	17.50

PROOF SETS

KM#	Date	Mintage	Identification	Issue Price	Mkt Val
PS26	2001 (7)	—	KM#692-697, 721	35.00	37.50
PS27	2002 (8)	—	KM#692-697, 721, 760	—	42.50
PS28	2003 (8)	—	KM#692-697, 721, 768	—	40.00
PS29	2004 (8)	—	KM#692-697, 721, 773	—	40.00
PS30	2005 (8)	7,000	KM#692-697, 721, 779	—	37.50
PS31	2006 (7)	—	KM#692-697, 721	—	35.00
PS32	2007 (8)	—	KM#692-697, 721, 805	—	40.00
PS33	2008 (7)	—	KM#692-697, 721	—	35.00

ICELAND

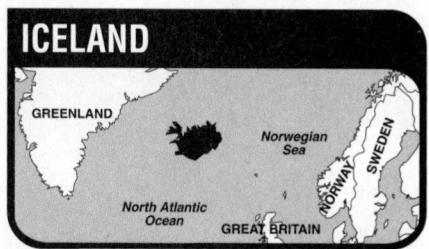

Iceland, an island of recent volcanic origin in the North Atlantic east of Greenland and immediately south of the Arctic Circle, has an area of 39,768 sq. mi. (103,000 sq. km.) and a population of just over 300,000. Capital: Reykjavik. Fishing is the chief industry and accounts for a little less than 60 percent of the exports.

REPUBLIC

REFORM COINAGE

100 Old Kronur = 1 New Krona

KM# 27a KRONA
4.0000 g., Nickel Plated Steel, 21.5 mm. **Obv:** Giant facing **Rev:** Cod **Edge:** Reeded

Date	Mintage	F	VF	XF	Unc	BU
2003	5,144,000	—	—	—	0.85	1.70
2005	5,000,000	—	—	—	0.85	1.70
2006	10,000,000	—	—	—	0.85	1.70
2007	10,000,000	—	—	—	0.85	1.70
2011	—	—	—	—	0.85	1.70

KM# 28a 5 KRONUR
5.6000 g., Nickel Plated Steel, 24.5 mm. **Obv:** Quartered design of Eagle, dragon, bull and giant **Rev:** Two dolphins leaping left **Edge:** Reeded

Date	Mintage	F	VF	XF	Unc	BU
2005	2,000,000	—	—	—	2.25	3.25
2007	10,000,000	—	—	—	2.25	3.25
2008	—	—	—	—	2.25	3.25

KM# 29.1a 10 KRONUR
7.0000 g., Nickel Plated Steel, 27.5 mm. **Obv:** Quartered design of Eagle, dragon, bull and giant **Rev:** Four capelins left **Edge:** Reeded

Date	Mintage	F	VF	XF	Unc	BU
2004	2,000,000	—	—	—	1.85	2.75
2005	4,505,000	—	—	—	1.85	2.75
2006	7,800,000	—	—	—	1.85	2.75
2008	—	—	—	—	1.85	2.75

KM# 31 50 KRONUR
8.2500 g., Nickel-Brass, 23 mm. **Obv:** Quartered design of eagle, dragon, bull and giant **Rev:** Crab **Edge:** Reeded

Date	Mintage	F	VF	XF	Unc	BU
2001	2,000,000	—	—	—	4.25	5.00
2005	2,000,000	—	—	—	4.25	5.00

KM# 35 100 KRONUR
8.5000 g., Nickel-Brass, 25.5 mm. **Obv:** Quartered design of Eagle, dragon, bull and giant **Rev:** Lumpfish left **Edge:** Reeded

Date	Mintage	F	VF	XF	Unc	BU
2001	2,140,000	—	—	—	6.50	7.75
2004	2,400,000	—	—	—	6.50	7.75
2006	2,000,000	—	—	—	6.50	7.75
2007	3,000,000	—	—	—	6.50	7.75
2011	—	—	—	—	6.50	7.75

INDIA - REPUBLIC

The Republic of India, a subcontinent jutting southward from the mainland of Asia, has an area of 1,269,346 sq. mi. (3,287,590 sq. km.) and a population of over 900 million, second only to that of the People's Republic of China. Capital: New Delhi. India's economy is based on agriculture and industrial activity. Engineering goods, cotton apparel and fabrics, handicrafts, tea, iron and steel are exported.

The Republic of India is a member of the Common-wealth of Nations. The president is the Chief of State. The prime minister is the Head of Government.

MINT MARKS
(Mint marks usually appear directly below the date.)
B - Mumbai (Bombay), proof issues only
(B) - Mumbai (Bombay), diamond
(C) - Calcutta, no mint mark
(H) - Hyderabad, star (1963--)
M - Mumbai (Bombay), proof only after 1996
(N) - Noida, dot
(T) - Taegu (Korea), star below first or last date digit

REPUBLIC

DECIMAL COINAGE

KM# 54 25 PAISE
2.8200 g., Stainless Steel, 19 mm. **Obv:** Small Lion capitol of Ashoka Pillar above value **Rev:** Rhinoceros left **Edge:** Plain **Note:** Varieties of date size exist.

Date	Mintage	F	VF	XF	Unc	BU
2001(B)	—	—	0.10	0.20	1.00	—
2001(C)	—	—	0.10	0.20	1.00	—
2001(H)	—	—	0.15	0.25	1.00	—
2002(B)	—	—	0.15	0.25	1.00	—
2002(C)	—	—	0.15	0.25	1.00	—
2002(H)	—	—	0.25	0.40	1.00	—

KM# 69 50 PAISE
3.8000 g., Stainless Steel, 22 mm. **Subject:** Parliament Building in New Delhi **Obv:** Denomination **Rev:** Building

Date	Mintage	F	VF	XF	Unc	BU
2001(B)	—	—	0.15	0.25	0.50	—
2001(C)	—	—	0.15	0.25	0.50	—
2001(H)	—	—	0.20	0.40	0.75	—
2001(N)	—	—	0.15	0.25	0.50	—
2002(B)	—	—	0.15	0.25	0.50	—
2002(C)	—	—	0.15	0.25	0.50	—
2002(H)	—	—	0.15	0.25	0.50	—
2002(N)	—	—	0.15	0.25	0.50	—
2003(B)	—	—	0.15	0.25	0.50	—
2003(N)	—	—	0.15	0.25	0.50	—
2003(C)	—	—	0.15	0.25	0.50	—
2007(C)	—	—	0.15	0.25	0.50	—
2007(N)	—	—	0.15	0.25	0.50	—

KM# 374 50 PAISE
Stainless Steel, 23 mm. **Obv:** Lion capitol of Ashoka Pillar **Rev:** Clenched fist and value

Date	Mintage	F	VF	XF	Unc	BU
2008(C)	—	—	—	—	0.50	0.75
2008(Hy)	—	—	—	—	0.50	0.75
2008(M)	—	—	—	—	0.50	0.75
2008(N)	—	—	—	—	0.50	0.75

KM# 398 50 PAISE
Stainless Steel, 19 mm. **Obv:** Lion capitol of Ashoka Pillar **Rev:** Value flanked by flora **Edge:** Reeded

Date	Mintage	F	VF	XF	Unc	BU
2011(M)	—	—	—	—	0.50	0.75
2012(H)	—	—	—	—	0.50	0.75

KM# 92.2 RUPEE
4.9000 g., Stainless Steel, 25 mm. **Obv:** Lion capitol of Ashoka Pillar **Rev:** Denomination and date, grain ears flank **Edge:** Plain **Note:** Mint mark varieties exist.

Date	Mintage	F	VF	XF	Unc	BU
2001(B)	—	—	0.20	0.40	0.70	—
2001(C)	—	—	0.20	0.40	0.70	—
2001(K)	—	—	0.20	0.40	0.70	—
2001(N)	—	—	0.20	0.40	0.70	—
2001(H)	—	—	0.20	0.40	0.70	—

Note: Small and large mint mark exist, doubled left or right of wheat stalks

Date	Mintage	F	VF	XF	Unc	BU
2002(B)	—	—	0.20	0.40	0.70	—
2002(N)	—	—	0.20	0.40	0.70	—
2002(C)	—	—	0.20	0.40	0.70	—
2002(H)	—	—	0.20	0.40	0.70	—
2003(B)	—	—	0.20	0.40	0.70	—
2003(C)	—	—	0.20	0.40	0.70	—
2003(H)	—	—	0.20	0.40	0.70	—
2004(B)	—	—	0.20	0.40	0.70	—
2004(C)	—	—	0.20	0.40	0.70	—
2004(H)	—	—	0.20	0.40	0.70	—
2004(N)	—	—	0.20	0.40	0.70	—

KM# 313 RUPEE
4.9500 g., Stainless Steel, 25 mm. **Subject:** 100th Anniversary - Birth of Jaya Prakash Narayan **Obv:** Lion capitol of Ashoka Pillar **Rev:** Bust of Jaya Prakash Narayan slightly left **Edge:** Plain

Date	Mintage	F	VF	XF	Unc	BU
2002(B)	—	—	0.45	0.75	1.00	—
2002(B) Proof	—	Value: 3.00				
2002(C)	—	—	0.45	0.75	1.00	—
2002(H)	—	—	0.45	0.75	1.00	—

KM# 314 RUPEE
4.9500 g., Stainless Steel, 25 mm. **Subject:** Maharana Pratap
Obv: Lion capitol of Ashoka Pillar **Rev:** Bust left in national
costume **Edge:** Plain

Date	Mintage	F	VF	XF	Unc	BU
2003(B)	—	—	0.45	0.75	1.00	—
2003(B) Proof	—	Value: 2.50				
2003(H)	—	—	0.45	0.75	1.00	—

KM# 316 RUPEE
4.8500 g., Stainless Steel, 25 mm. **Obv:** Lion capitol of Ashoka
Pillar **Rev:** 3/4 length military figure Veer Durgadass with spear
left **Edge:** Plain

Date	Mintage	F	VF	XF	Unc	BU
2003(B)	—	—	0.50	0.80	1.25	—
2003(B) Proof	—	Value: 2.50				
2003(H)	—	—	0.50	0.80	1.25	—

KM# 321 RUPEE
5.0000 g., Stainless Steel, 24.9 mm. **Subject:** 150th
Anniversary of the Indian Postal Service **Obv:** Lion capitol of
Ashoka Pillar above value **Rev:** Partial postage stamp design
Edge: Grooved

Date	Mintage	F	VF	XF	Unc	BU
2004(C)	—	—	—	—	2.00	—
2004(C) Proof	—	Value: 3.50				

KM# 322 RUPEE
4.9500 g., Stainless Steel, 24.8 mm. **Obv:** Lion capitol of Ashoka
Pillar at left, value at right **Rev:** Cross dividing four dots **Edge:**
Plain

Date	Mintage	F	VF	XF	Unc	BU
2005(C)	—	—	—	—	2.00	—
2005(H)	—	—	—	—	0.20	—
2007(H)	—	—	—	—	2.00	—

KM# 331 RUPEE
4.9000 g., Stainless Steel, 25 mm. **Subject:** Bharata Natyam
Dance Expressions **Obv:** Lion capitol of Ashoka Pillar **Rev:**
Gesture of hand with thumb up **Edge:** Plain

Date	Mintage	F	VF	XF	Unc	BU
2007(C)	—	—	—	0.40	1.00	—
2007(H)	—	—	—	0.40	1.00	—
2007(N)	—	—	—	0.40	1.00	—
2008(B)	—	—	—	0.40	1.00	—
2008(C)	—	—	—	0.40	1.00	—
2008(Hy)	—	—	—	0.40	1.00	—
2008(N)	—	—	—	0.40	1.00	—
2008(M)	—	—	—	0.40	1.00	—
2009(B)	—	—	—	0.40	1.00	—

Date	Mintage	F	VF	XF	Unc	BU
2009(C)	—	—	—	—	1.00	—
2009(Hy)	—	—	—	—	1.00	—
2009(M)	—	—	—	—	1.00	—
2009(N)	—	—	—	—	1.00	—

KM# 385 RUPEE
4.9500 g., Stainless Steel, 24.8 mm. **Subject:** Reserve Bank of
India, 75th Anniversary **Obv:** Lion capitol of Ashoka Pillar above
value **Rev:** Lion advancing left, palm tree in background

Date	Mintage	F	VF	XF	Unc	BU
2010	—	—	—	—	—	1.00

KM# 394 RUPEE
4.9500 g., Stainless Steel, 22 mm. **Obv:** Lion capitol of Ashoka
Pillar **Rev:** New Rupee symbol above value

Date	Mintage	F	VF	XF	Unc	BU
2011	—	—	—	—	1.00	—

KM# 121.5 2 RUPEES
6.0600 g., Copper-Nickel, 26 mm. **Subject:** National Integration
Obv: Type C Lion capitol of Ashoka Pillar **Rev:** Flag on map
Edge: Plain **Note:** 11-sided

Date	Mintage	F	VF	XF	Unc	BU
2001(B)	—	—	0.40	0.70	1.50	—
2001(C)	—	—	0.40	0.70	1.50	—
2001(H)	—	—	0.40	0.70	1.50	—
2002(B)	—	—	0.40	0.70	1.50	—
2002(C)	—	—	0.40	0.70	1.50	—
2002(H)	—	—	0.40	0.70	1.50	—
2002(N)	—	—	0.40	0.70	1.50	—
2003(B)	—	—	—	0.70	1.50	—
2003(C)	—	—	—	0.70	1.50	—
2003(H)	—	—	—	0.70	1.50	—
2004(B)	—	—	—	0.70	1.50	—
2004(C)	—	—	—	0.70	1.50	—
2004(H)	—	—	—	0.70	1.50	—

KM# 121.3 2 RUPEES
6.0000 g., Copper-Nickel, 26 mm. **Subject:** National Integration
Obv: Type A Lion capitol of Ashoka Pillar **Rev:** Flag on map
Edge: Plain **Shape:** 11-sided **Note:** Reduced size, non magnetic.

Date	Mintage	F	VF	XF	Unc	BU
2001(B)	—	—	0.40	0.70	1.50	—
2001(C)	—	—	0.40	0.70	1.50	—
2002(C)	—	—	0.40	0.70	1.50	—
2003(C)	—	—	0.40	0.70	1.50	—
2003(H)	—	—	0.40	0.70	1.50	—

KM# 303 2 RUPEES
6.2400 g., Copper-Nickel, 25.7 mm. **Subject:** 100th Anniversary
- Birth of Dr. Syama P. Mookerjee **Obv:** Type B Lion capitol of
Ashoka Pillar above denomination **Rev:** Bust of Dr.
Mookerjeeright **Edge:** Plain

Date	Mintage	F	VF	XF	Unc	BU
2001(B)	—	—	1.25	2.00	3.00	—
2001(C)	—	—	1.25	2.00	3.00	—
2001(C) Proof	—	Value: 7.50				
2001	—	—	1.25	2.00	3.00	—
2001(N)	—	—	1.25	2.00	3.00	—

KM# 305 2 RUPEES
6.1000 g., Copper-Nickel, 25.7 mm. **Subject:** Sant Tukaram
Obv: Lion capitol of Ashoka Pillar above value **Rev:** Seated
musician **Shape:** Eleven sided

Date	Mintage	F	VF	XF	Unc	BU
2002(B)	—	—	—	1.25	2.00	—
2002(C)	—	—	—	1.25	2.00	—
2002(C)	—	Value: 5.00				

KM# 307 2 RUPEES
6.0500 g., Copper-Nickel **Subject:** 150th Anniversary - Indian
Railways **Obv:** Lion capitol of Ashoka Pillar above value **Rev:**
Cartoon elephant holding railroad lantern **Edge:** Plain **Shape:**
11-sided

Date	Mintage	F	VF	XF	Unc	BU
2003(B)	—	—	—	1.25	2.00	—
2003(C)	—	—	—	1.25	2.00	—
2003(C) Proof	—	Value: 5.00				
2003(H)	—	—	—	1.75	2.00	—

KM# 334 2 RUPEES
6.0000 g., Copper-Nickel, 26 mm. **Subject:** 150th Anniversary
- Telecommunications **Obv:** Lion capitol of Ashoka Pillar **Rev:**
Cartoon bird standing holding cell phone **Edge:** Plain **Shape:** 11-
sided

Date	Mintage	F	VF	XF	Unc	BU
2004(B)	—	—	—	—	2.00	—
2004(B) Proof	—	Value: 5.00				

KM# 326 2 RUPEES
5.8000 g., Stainless Steel **Obv:** Lion capitol of Ashoka Pillar at
left and value at right **Rev:** Cross with U-shaped arms and dots
Edge: Plain **Note:** Size varies 26.75 - 27.07 mm

Date	Mintage	F	VF	XF	Unc	BU
2005(B)	—	—	—	0.50	1.35	—
2005(C)	—	—	—	0.50	1.35	—
2005(H)	—	—	—	0.50	1.35	—
2005(N)	—	—	—	0.50	1.35	—
2006(B) small date	—	—	—	0.40	1.00	—
2006(B) large date	—	—	—	0.40	1.00	—
2006(B)	—	—	—	0.40	1.00	—
2006(N)	—	—	—	0.40	1.00	—
2007(B)	—	—	—	0.40	1.00	—
2007(H)	—	—	—	0.40	1.00	—

KM# 350 2 RUPEES
6.0000 g., Stainless Steel, 26.9 mm. **Subject:** 75th Anniversary

Indian Air Force **Obv:** Lion capitol of Ashoka Pillar at left and value at right **Rev:** Planes in flight **Edge:** Plain **Shape:** 11-sided

Date	Mintage	F	VF	XF	Unc	BU
2007(C)	—	—	—	2.00	3.00	—
2007(C) Proof	—	Value: 5.00				

KM# 327 2 RUPEES
5.8000 g., Stainless Steel, 27 mm. **Obv:** Lion capitol of Ashoka Pillar at center **Obv. Inscription:** INDIA in Hindi and English **Rev:** Hasta Mudra - hand gesture from the dance Bharata Natyam **Edge:** Plain

Date	Mintage	F	VF	XF	Unc	BU
2007(B)	—	—	—	0.50	1.25	—

Note: Mintmark position varies 1 or 2 mm below date.

2007(C)	—	—	—	0.50	1.25	—
2007(H)	—	—	—	—	1.25	—
2008(B)	—	—	—	—	1.25	—
2008(C)	—	—	—	—	1.25	—
2008(H)	—	—	—	—	1.25	—
2008(N)	—	—	—	—	1.25	—
2009(B)	—	—	—	—	1.25	—
2009(C)	—	—	—	—	1.25	—
2009(H)	—	—	—	—	1.25	—
2009(N)	—	—	—	—	1.25	—
2010(B)	—	—	—	—	1.25	—

KM# 375 2 RUPEES
Stainless Steel, 27 mm. **Subject:** Natya Mudra **Obv:** Lion capitol of Ashoka Pillar **Rev:** Value

Date	Mintage	F	VF	XF	Unc	BU
2008(C)	—	—	—	—	2.00	—
2008(Hy)	—	—	—	—	2.00	—
2008(M)	—	—	—	—	2.00	—
2008(N)	—	—	—	—	2.00	—
2009(C)	—	—	—	—	2.00	—
2009(Hy)	—	—	—	—	2.00	—
2009(M)	—	—	—	—	2.00	—
2009(N)	—	—	—	—	2.00	—

KM# 368 2 RUPEES
5.8000 g., Stainless Steel, 27 mm. **Subject:** Louis Braile, 200th Anniversary of Birth **Obv:** Lion capitol of Ashoka Pillar **Rev:** fFacing portrait above Braile text

Date	Mintage	F	VF	XF	Unc	BU
2008(Hy) In sets only	—	—	—	—	—	1.25
2009(C)	—	—	—	—	0.50	1.25
2009(B)	—	—	—	—	0.50	1.25
2009(H)	—	—	—	—	0.50	1.25
2009(Hy)	—	—	—	—	0.50	1.25

KM# 386 2 RUPEES
5.8000 g., Stainless Steel, 27 mm. **Subject:** Reserve Bank of India, 75th Anniversary **Obv:** Lion capitol of Ashoka Pillar **Rev:** Lion advancing left, palm tree in background

Date	Mintage	F	VF	XF	Unc	BU
2010	—	—	—	—	—	2.00

KM# 395 2 RUPEES
5.8000 g., Stainless Steel, 25 mm. **Obv:** Lion capitol of Ashoka Pillar **Rev:** New Rupee symbol above value **Edge:** Reeded

Date	Mintage	F	VF	XF	Unc	BU
2011	—	—	—	—	2.00	—

KM# 154.2 5 RUPEES
8.9100 g., Copper-Nickel, 23 mm. **Obv:** Lion capitol of Ashoka Pillar **Rev:** Denomination flanked by flowers **Edge:** Reeded

Date	Mintage	F	VF	XF	Unc	BU
2001(C)	—	—	8.00	10.00	15.00	—
2002(C)	—	—	8.00	10.00	15.00	—
2003(C)	—	—	8.00	10.00	15.00	—

KM# 154.4 5 RUPEES
Copper-Nickel, 23 mm. **Obv:** Lion capitol of Ashoka Pillar as seen on 2 Rupees, KM#121.5 **Rev:** Denomination flanked by flowers

Date	Mintage	F	VF	XF	Unc	BU
2001(B)	—	—	0.40	0.70	1.50	—
2002(B)	—	—	0.40	0.70	1.50	—
2003(B)	—	—	0.40	0.70	1.50	—
2004(B)	—	—	0.40	0.70	1.50	—

KM# 154.1 5 RUPEES
9.3000 g., Copper-Nickel, 23.4 mm. **Obv:** Lion capitol of Ashoka Pillar **Rev:** Denomination flanked by flowers **Edge:** Security **Note:** (C) - Calcutta mint has issued 2 distinctly different security edge varieties every year 1992-2003 with large dots and thick center line, w/small dots and narrow center line.

Date	Mintage	F	VF	XF	Unc	BU
2001(B)	—	—	0.40	0.70	1.50	—
2001(C) Plain 1	—	—	0.40	0.70	1.50	—
2001(C) Serif 1	—	—	1.50	3.00	5.00	—
2001(H)	—	—	0.40	0.90	2.25	—
2002(C)	—	—	0.40	0.70	1.50	—
2002(N)	—	—	0.40	0.70	1.50	—
2003(C)	—	—	0.40	0.70	1.50	—

KM# 304 5 RUPEES
9.0700 g., Copper-Nickel, 23.19 mm. **Subject:** 2600th Anniversary Birth of Bhagwan Mahavir **Obv:** Lion capitol of Ashoka Pillar above denomination **Rev:** Swastika above hand in irregular frame **Edge:** Security

Date	Mintage	F	VF	XF	Unc	BU
2001(B)	—	—	1.00	2.00	3.00	5.00
2001(B) Proof	—	Value: 6.50				
2001(N)	—	—	1.00	2.00	3.00	5.00

KM# 308 5 RUPEES
8.9200 g., Copper-Nickel, 23.1 mm. **Subject:** Dadabhai Naroji **Obv:** Lion capitol of Ashoka Pillar above value **Rev:** Bust of Naroji 3/4 right **Edge:** Security

Date	Mintage	F	VF	XF	Unc	BU
ND(2003)(B)	—	—	—	1.75	3.00	5.00
ND(2003)(C)	—	—	—	1.75	3.00	5.00
ND(2003)(H)	—	—	—	1.75	3.00	5.00

KM# 317.1 5 RUPEES
8.8000 g., Copper-Nickel, 23.1 mm. **Obv:** Lion capitol of Ashoka Pillar **Rev:** K. Kamaraj bust 3/4 left, dates below **Edge:** Security

Date	Mintage	F	VF	XF	Unc	BU
ND(2003)(B)	—	—	1.00	1.75	3.00	5.00
ND(2003)(B) Proof	—	Value: 7.50				
ND(2003)(H)	—	—	1.25	2.00	3.50	5.50
ND(2003)(C)	—	—	1.00	1.75	3.00	5.00

KM# 317.2 5 RUPEES
8.8000 g., Copper-Nickel, 23.1 mm. **Obv:** Lion capitol of Ashoka Pillar **Rev:** K. Kamaraj 3/4 left, dates below **Edge:** Reeded

Date	Mintage	F	VF	XF	Unc	BU
ND (2003)(H)	—	—	5.00	7.00	11.00	—

KM# 329 5 RUPEES
9.0700 g., Bi-Metallic Brass center in Copper-Nickel ring, 23.25 mm. **Obv:** Lion capitol of Ashoka Pillar, value below **Rev:** Shastri bust 3/4 left **Rev. Legend:** LALBAHADUR SHASTRI BIRTH CENTENARY **Edge:** Security

Date	Mintage	F	VF	XF	Unc	BU
ND(2004)	—	—	—	—	3.50	5.00

KM# 336 5 RUPEES
9.0000 g., Stainless Steel, 23 mm. **Subject:** 100th Anniversary Birth of Lal Bahadur Shastri **Obv:** Lion capitol of Ashoka Pillar **Rev:** Shastri bust 3/4 right **Edge:** Security

Date	Mintage	F	VF	XF	Unc	BU
ND(2004)(C)	—	—	—	—	3.50	5.00
ND(2004)(C) Proof	—	Value: 8.00				

KM# 325 5 RUPEES
8.8500 g., Copper-Nickel, 23 mm. **Subject:** 75th Anniversary Dandi March **Obv:** Lion capitol of Ashoka Pillar **Rev:** Ghandi leading marchers **Edge:** Security type

Date	Mintage	F	VF	XF	Unc	BU
ND(2005)(B)	—	—	—	—	3.00	5.00
ND(2005)(B) Proof	—	Value: 7.50				

KM# 365a 5 RUPEES
6.0300 g., Stainless Steel, 23 mm. **Subject:** Dandi March

Date	Mintage	F	VF	XF	Unc	BU
ND(2005)(B)	—	—	—	—	4.00	5.00

KM# 324 5 RUPEES
8.8500 g., Copper-Nickel, 23 mm. **Obv:** Lion capitol of Ashoka Pillar **Rev:** Mahatma Basaveshwara bust 3/4 left **Edge:** Security

Date	Mintage	F	VF	XF	Unc	BU
ND(2006)(B)	—	—	0.40	1.00	3.00	5.00
ND(2006)(B) Proof	—	Value: 6.00				

KM# 324a 5 RUPEES
6.0000 g., Stainless Steel **Subject:** Mahatma Basveshwara

Date	Mintage	F	VF	XF	Unc	BU
ND(2006)(B)	—	—	—	—	—	2.50

KM# 354 5 RUPEES
6.0300 g., Stainless Steel, 22.8 mm. **Subject:** O.N.G.C., 50th Anniversary **Obv:** Lion capitol of Ashoka Pillar, value below

Date	Mintage	F	VF	XF	Unc	BU
ND(2006)(C)	—			—	4.00	5.00
ND(2006)(H)	—			—	4.00	5.00

KM# 355   5 RUPEES

9.5000 g., Copper-Nickel, 23.1 mm.   **Subject:** Jagathguru Sree Narayana Guruden **Obv:** Lion capitol of Ashoka Pillar **Rev:** Bust facing

Date	Mintage	F	VF	XF	Unc	BU
ND(2006)(B)	—			—	3.00	5.00

KM# 355a   5 RUPEES

6.0300 g., Stainless Steel, 22.9 mm.   **Subject:** Jagadguru Shree Narayan Guru

Date	Mintage	F	VF	XF	Unc	BU
ND(2006)(B)	—			—	4.00	5.00

KM# 357   5 RUPEES

6.0300 g., Copper-Nickel, 22.9 mm.   **Subject:** State Bank of India, 200th Anniversary **Obv:** Lion capitol of Ashoka Pillar, value below **Edge:** Reeded

Date	Mintage	F	VF	XF	Unc	BU
ND(2006)(C)	—			—	4.00	5.00
ND(2006)(H)	—			—	4.00	5.00

KM# 330   5 RUPEES

6.0300 g., Stainless Steel, 23 mm.   **Subject:** Information Technology **Obv:** Lion capitol of Ashoka Pillar **Rev:** Waves below value **Edge:** Security

Date	Mintage	F	VF	XF	Unc	BU
2007(B)	—	—	—	—	4.00	5.00
2007(C)	—	—	—	—	4.00	5.00
2007(H)	—	—	—	—	4.00	5.00
2007(N)	—	—	—	—	4.00	5.00
2008(B)	—	—	—	—	4.00	5.00
2008(H)	—	—	—	—	4.00	5.00
2008(K)	—	—	—	—	4.00	5.00
2008(N)	—	—	—	—	4.00	5.00

KM# 328   5 RUPEES

9.5000 g., Copper-Nickel, 23.10 mm.   **Subject:** 150th Anniversary Birth of L. B. G. Tilak **Obv:** Lion capitol of Ashoka Pillar **Rev:** Bust of Tilak facing slightly right **Edge:** Security

Date	Mintage	F	VF	XF	Unc	BU
2007(B)	—	—	—	—	3.50	5.00

KM# 356   5 RUPEES

6.0300 g., Copper-Nickel, 22.9 mm.   **Subject:** Tilakji **Note:** Withdrawn.

Date	Mintage	F	VF	XF	Unc	BU
2007(N)	—	—	—	—	10.00	15.00

KM# 359   5 RUPEES

6.0300 g., Stainless Steel, 22.9 mm.   **Subject:** First War of Independence **Obv:** Lion capitol of Ashoka Pillar, value below

Date	Mintage	F	VF	XF	Unc	BU
ND(2007)(B)	—			—	4.00	5.00

KM# 360   5 RUPEES

6.0300 g., Stainless Steel, 23 mm.   **Rev:** Ghandi seated facing

Date	Mintage	F	VF	XF	Unc	BU
2007	—			—	4.00	5.00

KM# 390   5 RUPEES

6.0300 g., Stainless Steel, 22.9 mm.   **Obv:** Lion capitol of Ashoka Pillar **Rev:** Cross

Date	Mintage	F	VF	XF	Unc	BU
2007	—			—	4.00	5.00

KM# 328a   5 RUPEES

6.0300 g., Stainless Steel, 22.9 mm.   **Subject:** 150th Anniversary Birth of L. B. G. Tilak **Obv:** Lion capitol of Ashoka Pillar **Rev:** Bust of Tilak facing slightly right

Date	Mintage	F	VF	XF	Unc	BU
2008	—			—	4.00	5.00

KM# 336a   5 RUPEES

6.0300 g., Stainless Steel, 22.9 mm.   **Subject:** Lal Bahadur Shastri **Obv:** Lion capitol of Ashoka Pillar

Date	Mintage	F	VF	XF	Unc	BU
ND(2004)(C)	—			—	4.00	5.00
ND(2004)(H)	—			—	4.00	5.00

KM# 365   5 RUPEES

6.0300 g., Nickel-Bronze, 23 mm.   **Subject:** St. Alphonsa, 100th Anniversary **Obv:** Lion capitol of Ashoka Pillar **Rev:** Bust facing in habit

Date	Mintage	F	VF	XF	Unc	BU
2009(B)	—			—	4.00	5.00

KM# 367   5 RUPEES

6.0300 g., Nickel-Bronze, 23 mm.   **Subject:** C. N. Annadurai, 100th Anniversary of Birth **Obv:** Lion capitol of Ashoka Pillar **Rev:** Portrait, signature below

Date	Mintage	F	VF	XF	Unc	BU
2009(B)	—			—	4.00	5.00

KM# 373   5 RUPEES

6.0000 g., Nickel-Brass, 23 mm.   **Obv:** Lion capitol of Ashoka Pillar **Rev:** Value flanked by flowers

Date	Mintage	F	VF	XF	Unc	BU
2009(C)	—	—	—	—	3.50	5.00
2009(M)	—	—	—	—	3.50	5.00
2009(Hy)	—	—	—	—	3.50	5.00

KM# 376   5 RUPEES

6.0300 g., Nickel-Brass, 22.9 mm.   **Subject:** 60th Anniversary of Commonwealth **Obv:** Lion capitol of Ashoka Pillar **Rev:** Building

Date	Mintage	F	VF	XF	Unc	BU
2009	—			—	4.00	5.00

KM# 384   5 RUPEES

6.0300 g., Stainless Steel, 22.9 mm.   **Obv:** Lion capitol of Ashoka Pillar **Rev:** Perarignar head right

Date	Mintage	F	VF	XF	Unc	BU
2009	—			—	4.00	5.00

KM# 392   5 RUPEES

6.0300 g., Stainless Steel, 22.9 mm.   **Subject:** Dr. Rajendra Prasad **Obv:** Lion capitol of Ashoka Pillar

Date	Mintage	F	VF	XF	Unc	BU
2009	—			—	4.00	5.00

KM# 377   5 RUPEES

6.0000 g., Nickel-Brass, 23 mm.   **Obv:** Lion capitol of Ashoka Pillar **Rev:** C. Subramaniam facing **Edge:** Reeded

Date	Mintage	F	VF	XF	Unc	BU
2010	—			—	4.00	5.00

KM# 381   5 RUPEES

6.0300 g., Nickel-Brass, 22.9 mm.   **Subject:** Mother Theresa, 100th Anniversary of Birth **Obv:** Lion capitol of Ashoka Pillar **Rev:** Bust facing

Date	Mintage	F	VF	XF	Unc	BU
2010	—			—	3.50	5.00

KM# 387   5 RUPEES

6.0300 g., Stainless Steel, 22.9 mm.   **Subject:** Reserve Bank of India, 75th Anniversary **Obv:** Lion capitol of Ashoka Pillar **Rev:** Lion advancing left, palm tree in background

Date	Mintage	F	VF	XF	Unc	BU
2010	—			—	4.00	5.00

KM# 378   5 RUPEES

6.0000 g., Nickel-Brass, 23 mm.   **Subject:** Brihadeeswarar Temple, 1000th Anniversary **Obv:** Lion capitol of Ashoka Pillar **Rev:** Statue of King Raja Rajan I before temple **Edge:** Reeded

Date	Mintage	F	VF	XF	Unc	BU
2011	—			—	4.00	5.00

KM# 379 5 RUPEES
6.0000 g., Nickel-Brass, 23 mm. **Subject:** Income Tax, 150th Anniversary **Obv:** Lion capitol of Ashoka Pillar **Rev:** Chanakya portrait at right **Edge:** Reeded

Date	Mintage	F	VF	XF	Unc	BU
2011	—	—	—	—	4.00	5.00

KM# 393 5 RUPEES
6.0000 g., Nickel-Brass, 23 mm. **Subject:** Rabindranath Tagore, 150th Anniversary of Birth **Obv:** Lion capitol of Ashoka Pillar **Rev:** Bust facing **Edge:** Reeded

Date	Mintage	F	VF	XF	Unc	BU
2011	—	—	—	—	4.00	5.00

KM# 397 5 RUPEES
Nickel-Brass, 23 mm. **Subject:** Civil Aviation, 100th Anniversary **Obv:** Lion capitol of Ashoka Pillar **Rev:** Aircraft

Date	Mintage	F	VF	XF	Unc	BU
2011(B)	—	—	—	—	4.00	5.00

KM# 399 5 RUPEES
Nickel-Brass, 23 mm. **Obv:** Lion capitol of Ashoka Pillar **Rev:** New rupee value flanked by flora **Edge:** Reeded

Date	Mintage	F	VF	XF	Unc	BU
2011(B)	—	—	—	—	4.00	5.00
2011(C)	—	—	—	—	4.00	5.00
2011(H)	—	—	—	—	4.00	5.00
2011(N)	—	—	—	—	4.00	5.00

KM# 396 5 RUPEES
Nickel-Brass, 23 mm. **Subject:** Indian Council of Medical Research, 100th Anniversary **Obv:** Lion capitol of Ashoka Pillar **Rev:** Logo

Date	Mintage	F	VF	XF	Unc	BU
2012	—	—	—	—	4.00	5.00

KM# 309 10 RUPEES
12.5000 g., Copper-Nickel, 31 mm. **Subject:** 100th Anniversary Birth of Dr. Syama P. Mookerjee **Obv:** Lion capitol of Ashoka Pillar **Rev:** Bust of Dr. Mookerjee 1/2 right **Edge:** Reeded

Date	Mintage	F	VF	XF	Unc	BU
2001(C)	—	—	—	—	9.00	10.00
2001(C) Proof	—	Value: 15.00				

KM# 344 10 RUPEES
12.5000 g., Copper-Nickel, 31 mm. **Subject:** 100th Anniversary Birth of Jaya Prakash Narayan **Obv:** Lion capitol of Ashoka Pillar **Rev:** Bust of Jaya Prakash Narayan slightly left **Edge:** Reeded

Date	Mintage	F	VF	XF	Unc	BU
2002(B)	—	—	—	—	9.00	10.00
2002(B) Proof	—	Value: 15.00				

KM# 347 10 RUPEES
12.5000 g., Copper-Nickel, 31 mm. **Subject:** Sant Tukaram **Obv:** Lion capitol of Ashoka Pillar **Edge:** Reeded

Date	Mintage	F	VF	XF	Unc	BU
2002(C)	—	—	—	—	9.00	10.00
2002(C) Proof	—	Value: 15.00				

KM# 319 10 RUPEES
12.5000 g., Copper-Nickel, 31 mm. **Obv:** Lion capitol of Ashoka Pillar **Rev:** Bust of Maharana Pratap left

Date	Mintage	F	VF	XF	Unc	BU
2003(B)	—	—	—	—	9.00	10.00
2003(B) Proof	—	Value: 15.00				

KM# 332 10 RUPEES
12.5000 g., Copper-Nickel, 31 mm. **Obv:** Lion capitol of Ashoka Pillar **Rev:** 3/4 length military figure Veer Durgadass with spear left **Edge:** Reeded

Date	Mintage	F	VF	XF	Unc	BU
2003(B)	—	—	—	—	9.00	10.00
2003(B) Proof	—	Value: 15.00				

KM# 353 10 RUPEES
7.7000 g., Bi-Metallic Copper-Nickel center in Brass ring, 27 mm. **Subject:** Unity in Diversity **Obv:** Asoka Pillar **Rev:** Four heads sharing a common body

Date	Mintage	F	VF	XF	Unc	BU
2005(N)	—	—	—	—	8.00	10.00
2006(N)	—	—	—	—	1.50	2.50
2007(N)	—	—	—	—	1.50	2.50

KM# 371 10 RUPEES
7.7000 g., Bi-Metallic Copper-Nickel center in Brass ring, 27 mm. **Subject:** Tercentenary of Gurta-Gaddi of Shri Guru Granth Sahibji **Obv:** Lion capitol of Ashoka Pillar and value

Date	Mintage	F	VF	XF	Unc	BU
2008(Hy) In sets only	—	—	—	—	—	10.00
2008(M) In sets only	—	—	—	—	—	10.00

KM# 363 10 RUPEES
7.7000 g., Bi-Metallic Copper-Nickel center in Brass ring, 27 mm. **Subject:** Connectivity and Information Technology **Obv:** Lion capitol of Ashoka Pillar **Rev:** Large 10, wide rays above

Date	Mintage	F	VF	XF	Unc	BU
2008(N)	—	—	—	—	4.00	6.00
2009(N)	—	—	—	—	4.00	6.00
2010(N)	—	—	—	—	4.00	6.00

KM# 372 10 RUPEES
7.7000 g., Bi-Metallic Copper-Nickel center in Brass ring, 27 mm. **Subject:** Dr. Homi Bhabha - 100th Anniversary of Birth **Obv:** Lion capitol of Ashoka Pillar and value **Rev:** Portrait

Date	Mintage	F	VF	XF	Unc	BU
2009M	—	—	—	—	9.00	10.00

KM# 388 10 RUPEES
Bi-Metallic Copper-Nickel center in Brass ring, 27 mm. **Subject:** Reserve Bank of India, 75th Anniversary **Obv:** Lion capitol of Ashoka Pillar **Rev:** Lion advancing left, palm tree in background

Date	Mintage	F	VF	XF	Unc	BU
2010	—	—	—	—	9.00	10.00

KM# 400 10 RUPEES
Bi-Metallic Copper-Nickel center in Aluminum-Bronze ring, 27 mm. **Obv:** Lion capitol of Ashoka Pillar **Rev:** New rupee symbol above value

Date	Mintage	F	VF	XF	Unc	BU
2011(B)	—	—	—	—	9.00	10.00
2011(C)	—	—	—	—	9.00	10.00
2011(N)	—	—	—	—	9.00	10.00

KM# 310 50 RUPEES
30.0000 g., Copper-Nickel, 39 mm. **Subject:** 100th Anniversary Birth of Dr. Syama P. Mookerjee **Obv:** Lion capitol of Ashoka Pillar **Rev:** Bust of Dr. Mookerjee 1/2 right **Edge:** Reeded

Date	Mintage	F	VF	XF	Unc	BU
2001(C)	—	—	—	—	17.00	20.00
2001(C) Proof	—	Value: 30.00				

KM# 348 50 RUPEES
30.0000 g., Copper-Nickel, 39 mm. **Subject:** Sant Tukaram **Obv:** Lion capitol of Ashoka Pillar **Edge:** Reeded

Date	Mintage	F	VF	XF	Unc	BU
2002(C)	—	—	—	—	15.00	17.00
2002(C) Proof	—	Value: 35.00				

KM# 389 75 RUPEES
35.0000 g., 0.5000 Silver 0.5626 oz. ASW, 42 mm. **Subject:** Reserve Bank of India, 75th Anniversary **Obv:** Lion capitol of Ashoka Pillar **Rev:** Lion advancing left, palm tree in background

Date	Mintage	F	VF	XF	Unc	BU
2010(B)	—	—	—	—	50.00	55.00
2010B Proof	—	Value: 85.00				
2010(C)	—	—	—	—	50.00	55.00
2010(N)	—	—	—	—	50.00	55.00

KM# 311 100 RUPEES
35.0000 g., 0.5000 Silver 0.5626 oz. ASW, 44 mm. **Subject:** 10th Anniversary Dr, Syama P. Mookerjee **Obv:** Lion capitol of Ashoka Pillar **Rev:** Bust of Dr. Mookerjee 1/2 right **Edge:** Reeded

Date	Mintage	F	VF	XF	Unc	BU
2001(C)	—	—	—	—	60.00	65.00
2001(C) Proof	—	Value: 100				

KM# 312 100 RUPEES
35.0000 g., 0.5000 Silver 0.5626 oz. ASW, 44 mm. **Subject:** 2600th Anniversary Birth of Bhagwan Mahavir **Obv:** Lion capitol of Ashoka Pillar **Rev:** Swastika above hand in irregular frame **Edge:** Reeded

Date	Mintage	F	VF	XF	Unc	BU
2001(B)	—	—	—	—	60.00	65.00
2001(B) Proof	—	Value: 100				

KM# 345 100 RUPEES
35.0000 g., 0.5000 Silver 0.5626 oz. ASW, 44 mm. **Subject:** 100th Anniversary Birth of Jaya Prakash Narayan **Obv:** Lion capitol of Ashoka Pillar **Rev:** Bust of Jaya Prakash Narayan slightly left **Edge:** Reeded

Date	Mintage	F	VF	XF	Unc	BU
2002(B)	—	—	—	—	65.00	60.00
2002(B) Proof	—	Value: 100				

KM# 349 100 RUPEES
35.0000 g., 0.5000 Silver 0.5626 oz. ASW, 44 mm. **Subject:** Sant Tukaram **Obv:** Lion capitol of Ashoka Pillar **Edge:** Reeded

Date	Mintage	F	VF	XF	Unc	BU
2002(C)	—	—	—	—	65.00	60.00
2002(C) Proof	—	Value: 100				

KM# 340 100 RUPEES
35.0000 g., 0.5000 Silver 0.5626 oz. ASW, 44 mm. **Subject:** 150th Anniversary Indian Railways **Obv:** Lion capitol of Ashoka Pillar **Rev:** Cartoon elephant holding railroad lantern **Edge:** Reeded

Date	Mintage	F	VF	XF	Unc	BU
2003(C)	—	—	—	—	65.00	60.00
2003(C) Proof	—	Value: 100				

KM# 318 100 RUPEES
35.0000 g., 0.5000 Silver 0.5626 oz. ASW, 44 mm. **Obv:** Lion capitol of Ashoka Pillar **Rev:** K. Kamaraj above life dates **Edge:** Reeded

Date	Mintage	F	VF	XF	Unc	BU
ND(2003)(B)	—	—	—	—	65.00	60.00
ND(2003)(B) Proof	—	Value: 100				

KM# 320 100 RUPEES
35.0000 g., 0.5000 Silver 0.5626 oz. ASW, 44 mm. **Obv:** Lion capitol of Ashoka Pillar **Rev:** Bust of Maharana Pratap left **Edge:** Reeded

Date	Mintage	F	VF	XF	Unc	BU
2003(B)	—	—	—	—	65.00	60.00
2003(B) Proof	—	Value: 100				

KM# 333 100 RUPEES
35.0000 g., 0.5000 Silver 0.5626 oz. ASW, 44 mm. **Obv:** Lion capitol of Ashoka Pillar **Rev:** 3/4 length military figure Veer Durgadass with spear left **Edge:** Reeded

Date	Mintage	F	VF	XF	Unc	BU
2003(B)	—	—	—	—	65.00	60.00
2003(B) Proof	—	Value: 100				

KM# 335   100 RUPEES
35.0000 g., 0.5000 Silver 0.5626 oz. ASW, 44 mm. **Subject:**
150th Anniversary Telecommunications **Obv:** Lion capitol of
Ashoka Pillar **Rev:** Cartoon bird standing holding cell phone
Edge: Reeded

Date	Mintage	F	VF	XF	Unc	BU
2004(B)	—	—	—	—	65.00	60.00
2004(B) Proof	—	Value: 100				

KM# 337   100 RUPEES
35.0000 g., 0.5000 Silver 0.5626 oz. ASW, 44 mm. **Subject:**
100th Anniversary Birth of Lal Bahadur Shasti **Obv:** Lion capitol
of Ashoka Pillar **Rev:** Bust of Lal Bahadur Shastri 3/4 left **Edge:**
Reeded

Date	Mintage	F	VF	XF	Unc	BU
ND(2004)(C)	—	—	—	—	65.00	60.00
ND(2004)(C) Proof	—	Value: 100				

KM# 343   100 RUPEES
35.0000 g., 0.5000 Silver 0.5626 oz. ASW, 44 mm. **Subject:**
150th Anniversary Indian Postal Service **Obv:** Lion capitol of
Ashoka Pillar **Rev:** Perforation corner of a postage stamp **Edge:**
Reeded

Date	Mintage	F	VF	XF	Unc	BU
2004	—	—	—	—	65.00	60.00
2004 Proof	—	Value: 100				

KM# 338   100 RUPEES
35.0000 g., 0.5000 Silver 0.5626 oz. ASW, 44 mm. **Subject:**
75th Anniversary Dandi March **Obv:** Lion capitol of Ashoka Pillar
Rev: Ghandi leading marchers **Edge:** Reeded

Date	Mintage	F	VF	XF	Unc	BU
ND(2005)(B)	—	—	—	—	65.00	60.00
ND(2005)(B) Proof	—	Value: 100				

KM# 339   100 RUPEES
35.0000 g., 0.5000 Silver 0.5626 oz. ASW, 44 mm. **Obv:** Lion
capitol of Ashoka Pillar **Rev:** Bust of Mahatma Basaveshwara
slightly left **Edge:** Reeded

Date	Mintage	F	VF	XF	Unc	BU
ND(2006)B	—	—	—	—	65.00	60.00
ND(2006)B Proof	—	Value: 100				

KM# 351   100 RUPEES
35.0000 g., 0.5000 Silver 0.5626 oz. ASW, 44 mm. **Subject:**
75th Anniversary Indian Air Force **Obv:** Lion capitol of Ashoka
Pillar **Edge:** Reeded

Date	Mintage	F	VF	XF	Unc	BU
2007(C)	—	—	—	—	65.00	60.00
2007(C) Proof	—	Value: 100				

KM# 369   100 RUPEES
35.0000 g., 0.5000 Silver 0.5626 oz. ASW, 44 mm. **Subject:**
Louis Braile, 200th Anniversary of Birth **Obv:** Lion capitol of
Ashoka Pillar

Date	Mintage	F	VF	XF	Unc	BU
2009	—	—	—	—	60.00	65.00

KM# 383   100 RUPEES
35.0000 g., 0.5000 Silver 0.5626 oz. ASW, 44 mm. **Subject:**
Homi Bhamba **Obv:** Lion capitol of Ashoka Pillar

Date	Mintage	F	VF	XF	Unc	BU
2009	—	—	—	—	60.00	65.00
2009	—	Value: 100				

KM# 382   100 RUPEES
35.0000 g., 0.5000 Silver 0.5626 oz. ASW, 44 mm. **Subject:**
Mother Theresa, 100th Anniversary of birth **Obv:** Lion capitol of
Ashoka Pillar **Rev:** Bust facing

Date	Mintage	F	VF	XF	Unc	BU
2010	—	—	—	—	60.00	65.00
2010 Proof	—	Value: 100				

KM# 380   150 RUPEES
Silver **Subject:** Income Tax, 150th Anniversary **Obv:** Lion capitol
of Ashoka Pillar **Rev:** Chanakya portrait at right

Date	Mintage	F	VF	XF	Unc	BU
2011	—	—	—	—	—	70.00

PROOF SETS

KM#	Date	Mintage	Identification	Issue Price	Mkt Val
PS56	2001 (4)	—	KM#303, 309, 310, 311	—	125
PS57	2001 (2)	—	KM#304, 312	—	80.00
PS58	2002B (3)	—	KM#313, 344, 345	—	90.00
PS59	2002(C) (4)	—	KM#346-349	—	130
PS60	2003 (3)	—	KM#314, 319, 320	—	90.00
PS61	2003B (3)	—	KM#316, 332, 333	—	90.00
PS62	2003(C) (2)	—	KM#307, 340	—	80.00
PS63	ND(2003) (2)	—	KM#317.1,318	—	80.00
PS64	2004 (2)	—	KM#321, 343	—	75.00
PS65	2004B (2)	—	KM#334, 335	—	80.00
PS66	2004(C) (2)	—	KM#336, 337	—	80.00
PS67	2005B (2)	—	KM#325, 338	—	80.00
PS68	2006B (2)	—	KM#324, 339	—	80.00
PS69	2007 (2)	—	KM#350, 351	—	80.00

INDONESIA

   The Republic of Indonesia, the world's largest archipelago,
extends for more than 3,000 miles (4,827 km.) along the equator
from the mainland of southeast Asia to Australia. The 17,508
islands comprising the archipelago have a combined area of
788,425 sq. mi. (1,919,440 sq. km.) and a population of 205 million, including East Timor. On August 30, 1999, the Timorese
majority voted for independence. The Inter FET (International
Forces for East Timor) is now in charge of controlling the chaotic
situation. Capitol: Jakarta. Petroleum, timber, rubber, and coffee
are exported.
   Modern coinage issued by the Republic of Indonesia
includes separate series for West Irian and for the Riau Archipelago, an area of small islands between Singapore and
Sumatra.

MONETARY SYSTEM
100 Sen = 1 Rupiah

REPUBLIC

STANDARD COINAGE

KM# 60   50 RUPIAH
1.3500 g., Aluminum, 19.95 mm. **Obv:** National emblem **Rev:**
Black-naped Oriole **Edge:** Plain

Date	Mintage	F	VF	XF	Unc	BU
2001	—	—	—	—	0.30	1.00
2002	—	—	—	—	0.30	1.00

KM# 61   100 RUPIAH
1.7900 g., Aluminum, 23 mm. **Obv:** National emblem **Rev:** Palm
Cockatoo **Edge:** Plain

Date	Mintage	F	VF	XF	Unc	BU
2001	—	—	—	—	0.75	1.25
2002	—	—	—	—	0.75	1.25
2003	—	—	—	—	0.75	1.25
2004	—	—	—	—	0.75	1.25
2005	—	—	—	—	0.75	1.25
2008	—	—	—	—	0.75	1.25

KM# 66   200 RUPIAH
2.4000 g., Aluminum, 25 mm. **Obv:** National arms **Rev:** Balinese
starling bird above value **Edge:** Plain

Date	Mintage	F	VF	XF	Unc	BU
2003	—	—	—	—	1.00	1.50
2008	—	—	—	—	1.00	1.50

KM# 59   500 RUPIAH
5.3500 g., Aluminum-Bronze, 24 mm. **Obv:** National emblem
Rev: Jasmine above denomination

Date	Mintage	F	VF	XF	Unc	BU
2001	—	—	—	—	1.75	2.25
2002	—	—	—	—	1.75	2.25
2003	—	—	—	—	1.75	2.25

KM# 67 500 RUPIAH
3.0500 g., Aluminum, 27.2 mm. **Obv:** National arms **Rev:** Jasmine flower above value **Edge:** Segmented reeding

Date	Mintage	F	VF	XF	Unc	BU
2003	—	—	—	—	2.00	2.50
2008	—	—	—	—	2.00	2.50

KM# 70 1000 RUPIAH
4.5400 g., Nickel Plated Steel, 24.15 mm. **Obv:** National arms above value **Rev:** Angklung - a traditional bamboo musical instrument; West Java Provincial's Governor office in Bandung in background **Rev. Legend:** ANGKLUNG / date

Date	Mintage	F	VF	XF	Unc	BU
2010	—	—	—	—	0.75	1.00

KM# 64 25000 RUPIAH
28.2800 g., 0.9250 Silver 0.8410 oz. ASW, 38.6 mm. **Subject:** Centennial of Sukarno's Birth **Obv:** National arms **Rev:** Uniformed bust of Sukarno **Edge:** Reeded

Date	Mintage	F	VF	XF	Unc	BU
2001 Proof	500	Value: 120				

KM# 68 25000 RUPIAH
28.2800 g., 0.9250 Silver 0.8410 oz. ASW, 38.61 mm. **Subject:** Mohammas Hatta, vice-president (1945-1956) **Obv:** National Arms **Rev:** Bust facing

Date	Mintage	F	VF	XF	Unc	BU
2002 Proof	2,000	Value: 120				

KM# 65 500,000 RUPIAH
15.0000 g., 0.9990 Gold 0.4818 oz. AGW, 28.2 mm. **Subject:** Centennial of Sukarno's Birth **Obv:** National arms **Rev:** Head left **Edge:** Reeded

Date	Mintage	F	VF	XF	Unc	BU
2001 Proof	500	Value: 1,050				

KM# 69 500,000 RUPIAH
15.0000 g., 0.9990 Gold 0.4818 oz. AGW, 28.2 mm. **Subject:** Mohammad Hatta, vice-president (1945-1956) **Obv:** National Arms **Rev:** Bust facing

Date	Mintage	F	VF	XF	Unc	BU
2002 Proof	2,000	Value: 850				

IRAN

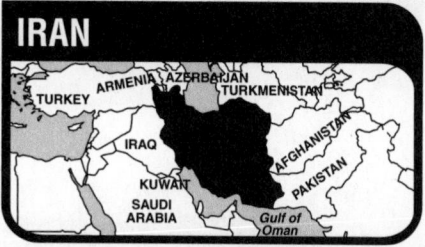

The Islamic Republic of Iran, located between the Caspian Sea and the Persian Gulf in southwestern Asia, has an area of 636,296 sq. mi. (1,648,000 sq. km.) and a population of 59.7 million. Capital: Tehran. Although predominantly an agricultural state, Iran depends heavily on oil for foreign exchange. Crude oil, carpets and agricultural products are exported.

In 1931 the Kingdom of Persia became known as the Kingdom of Iran. In 1979 the monarchy was toppled and an Islamic Republic proclaimed.

TITLES

دار الخلافة

Dar al-Khilafat

RULERS
Islamic Republic, SH1358-/1979-AD

MINT NAME

طهران

Tehran

تفليس

Tiflis

MINT MARKS
H - Heaton (Birmingham)
L - Leningrad (St. Petersburg)

COIN DATING
Iranian coins were dated according to the Moslem lunar calendar until March 21, 1925 (AD), when dating was switched to a new calendar based on the solar year, indicated by the notation SH. The monarchial calendar system was adopted in 1976 = MS2535 and was abandoned in 1978 = MS2537. The previously used solar year calendar was restored at that time.

MONETARY SYSTEM
20 Shahis = 1 Rial (100 Dinars)

ISLAMIC REPUBLIC
MILLED COINAGE

KM# 1260 50 RIALS
Copper-Nickel, 26 mm. **Subject:** Shrine of Hazrat Masumah **Obv:** Value and date **Rev:** Shrine within beaded circle **Edge:** Reeded

Date	Mintage	F	VF	XF	Unc	BU
SH1380 (2001)	—	—	2.50	3.50	5.00	—
SH1382 (2003)	—	—	2.50	3.50	5.00	—

KM# 1266 50 RIALS
3.5100 g., Aluminum-Bronze, 20.1 mm. **Obv:** Value and date **Rev:** Hazrat Masumah Shrine **Edge:** Reeded **Mint:** Tehran

Date	Mintage	F	VF	XF	Unc	BU
SH1382(2003)	—	—	—	—	50.00	—
SH1383(2004)	—	—	—	—	2.50	—
SH1384(2005)	—	—	—	—	2.50	—
SH1385(2006)	—	—	—	—	2.50	—

KM# 1261.2 100 RIALS
Copper-Nickel, 29 mm. **Obv:** Value and date **Rev:** Shrine within designed border **Note:** Thick denomination and numerals

Date	Mintage	F	VF	XF	Unc	BU
SH1380 (2001)	—	—	—	—	6.50	—
SH1382 (2003)	—	—	—	—	6.50	—

KM# 1267 100 RIALS
4.6200 g., Aluminum-Bronze, 22.9 mm. **Obv:** Value, date divides wreath below **Rev:** Imam Reza Shrine **Edge:** Reeded **Mint:** Tehran

Date	Mintage	F	VF	XF	Unc	BU
SH1382(2003)	—	—	—	—	50.00	—
SH1383(2004)	—	—	—	—	3.50	—
SH1384(2005)	—	—	—	—	3.50	—
SH1385(2006)	—	—	—	—	3.50	—

KM# 1262 250 RIALS
10.7000 g., Bi-Metallic Copper-Nickel center in Brass ring, 28.3 mm. **Obv:** Value within circle, inscription and date divide wreath **Rev:** Stylized flower within circle and wreath

Date	Mintage	F	VF	XF	Unc	BU
SH1381 (2002)	—	—	—	—	7.50	—
SH1382 (2003)	—	—	—	—	7.50	—

KM# 1268 250 RIALS
5.5000 g., Copper-Nickel, 24.6 mm. **Obv:** Value, date below divides sprays **Rev:** Stylized flower within sprays **Edge:** Plain **Mint:** Tehran

Date	Mintage	F	VF	XF	Unc	BU
SH1382(2003)	—	—	—	—	50.00	—
SH1383(2004)	—	—	—	—	4.50	—
SH1384(2005)	—	—	—	—	4.50	—
SH1385(2006)	—	—	—	—	4.50	—

KM# 1268a 250 RIALS
Aluminum-Bronze **Obv:** Value, date below divides sprays **Rev:** Stylized flower within sprays **Mint:** Tehran

Date	Mintage	F	VF	XF	Unc	BU
SH1386(2007)	—	—	—	—	4.50	—

KM# 1269 500 RIALS
8.9100 g., Bi-Metallic Aluminum-Bronze center in Copper-Nickel ring, 27.1 mm. **Obv:** Value **Rev:** Bird and flowers **Edge:** Reeded **Mint:** Tehran

IRAN (continued)

Date	Mintage	F	VF	XF	Unc	BU
SH1382(2003)	—	—	—	—	50.00	—
SH1383(2004)	—	—	—	—	6.00	—
SH1384(2005)	—	—	—	—	6.00	—
SH1385(2006)	—	—	—	—	6.00	—

KM# 1269a   500 RIALS
Aluminum-Bronze **Obv:** Value in ornamental circle **Rev:** Bird and flowers **Mint:** Tehran

Date	Mintage	F	VF	XF	Unc	BU
SH1386(2007)	—	—	—	—	6.00	—

REFORM COINAGE

KM# 1270   250 RIALS
2.8000 g., Copper-Nickel, 18.5 mm. **Rev:** Feyziyeh School

Date	Mintage	F	VF	XF	Unc	BU
AH1387 (2008)	—	—	—	—	—	5.00
SH1388 (2009)	—	—	—	—	—	5.00

KM# 1271   500 RIALS
3.9000 g., Copper-Nickel, 20.6 mm. **Rev:** Saadi Tomb

Date	Mintage	F	VF	XF	Unc	BU
SH1388 (2009)	—	—	—	—	—	6.00

KM# 1272   1000 RIALS
5.8000 g., Copper-Nickel, 23.7 mm. **Rev:** Khajou Bridge in Isfahan

Date	Mintage	F	VF	XF	Unc	BU
SH1388 (2009)	—	—	—	—	—	12.00

KM# 1274   1000 RIALS
5.8000 g., Copper-Nickel, 23.7 mm. **Rev:** Ali in star

Date	Mintage	F	VF	XF	Unc	BU
SH1389(2010)	—	—	—	—	—	12.00

KM# 1275   1000 RIALS
5.8000 g., Copper-Nickel, 23.7 mm. **Rev:** Kaaba Cubus

Date	Mintage	F	VF	XF	Unc	BU
SH1389(2010)	—	—	—	—	—	12.00

KM# 1276   2000 RIALS
Copper-Nickel **Subject:** Central Bank of the Islamic Republic of Iran, 50th Anniversary

Date	Mintage	F	VF	XF	Unc	BU
SH1389(2010)	—	—	—	—	—	25.00

KM# 1277   5000 RIALS
Copper-Nickel

Date	Mintage	F	VF	XF	Unc	BU
SH1389(2010)	—	—	—	—	—	—

BULLION COINAGE

Issued by the National Bank of Iran

KM# 1250.2   1/2 AZADI
4.0680 g., 0.9000 Gold 0.1177 oz. AGW **Obv:** Legend larger **Obv. Legend:** "Spring of Freedom"

Date	Mintage	F	VF	XF	Unc	BU
SH1381 (2002)	—	—	—	—	215	—
SH1383 (2004)	—	—	—	—	215	—

IRAQ

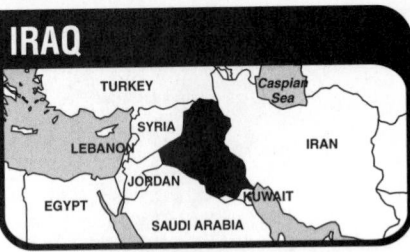

The Republic of Iraq, historically known as Mesopotamia, is located in the Near East and is bordered by Kuwait, Iran, Turkey, Syria, Jordan and Saudi Arabia. It has an area of 167,925 sq. mi. (434,920 sq. km.) and a population of 19 million. Capital: Baghdad. The economy of Iraq is based on agriculture and petroleum. Crude oil accounted for 94 percent of the exports before the war with Iran began in 1980.

Mesopotamia was the site of a number of flourishing civilizations of antiquity - Sumeria, Assyria, Babylonia, Parthia, Persia and the Biblical cities of Ur, Ninevehand and Babylon. Desired because of its favored location, which embraced the fertile alluvial plains of the Tigris and Euphrates Rivers, Mesopotamia - 'land between the rivers'- was conquered by Cyrus the Great of Persia, Alexander of Macedonia and by Arabs who made the legendary city of Baghdad the capital of the ruling caliphate. Suleiman the Magnificent conquered Mesopotamia for Turkey in1534, and it formed part of the Ottoman Empire until 1623, and from 1638 to 1917. Great Britain, given a League of Nations mandate over the territory in 1920, recognized Iraq as a kingdom in 1922. Iraq became an independent constitutional monarchy presided over by the Hashemite family, direct descendants of the prophet Mohammed, in 1932. In 1958, the army-led revolution of July 14 overthrew the monarchy and proclaimed a republic.

MONETARY SYSTEM

فَلْسًا   فَلْس   فُلوسَ   فَلْسٌ

Falus, Fulus   Fals, Fils   Falsan

50 Fils = 1 Dirham
200 Fils = 1 Riyal
1000 Fils = 1 Dinar (Pound)

REPUBLIC
DECIMAL COINAGE

KM# 175   25 DINARS
2.5000 g., Copper Plated Steel, 17.4 mm. **Obv:** Value **Rev:** Map **Edge:** Plain

Date	Mintage	F	VF	XF	Unc	BU
AH1425-2004	—	—	—	0.30	0.75	1.00

KM# 176   50 DINARS
4.3400 g., Brass Plated Steel, 22 mm. **Obv:** Value and legend **Rev:** Map **Edge:** Plain

Date	Mintage	F	VF	XF	Unc	BU
AH1425-2004	—	—	—	0.50	1.20	1.60

KM# 177   100 DINARS
4.3000 g., Stainless Steel, 22 mm. **Obv:** Value **Rev:** Map **Edge:** Reeded

Date	Mintage	F	VF	XF	Unc	BU
AH1425-2004	—	—	—	0.80	2.00	2.50

IRELAND REPUBLIC

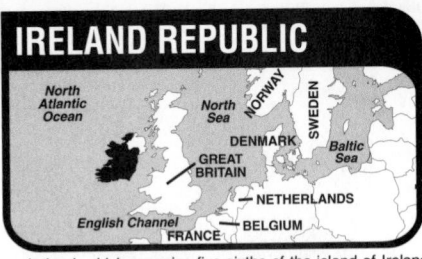

Ireland, which occupies five-sixths of the island of Ireland located in the Atlantic Ocean west of Great Britain, has an area of 27,136 sq. mi. (70,280 sq. km.) and a population of 4.3 million. Capital: Dublin. Agriculture and dairy farming are the principal industries. Meat, livestock, dairy products and textiles are exported.

REPUBLIC
EURO COINAGE
European Union Issues

KM# 32   EURO CENT
2.2700 g., Copper Plated Steel, 16.25 mm. **Obv:** Harp **Rev:** Denomination and globe **Edge:** Plain

Date	Mintage	F	VF	XF	Unc	BU
2002	404,339,788	—	—	—	0.35	—
2003	67,902,182	—	—	—	0.35	—
2004	174,833,634	—	—	—	0.35	—
2005	126,964,391	—	—	—	0.35	—
2006	105,413,273	—	—	—	0.35	—
2006 Proof	5,000	Value: 15.00				
2007	18,515,843	—	—	—	0.35	—
2007 Proof	10,000	Value: 12.00				
2008	59,002,134	—	—	—	0.35	—
2009	42,109,347	—	—	—	0.35	—
2009 Proof	5,000	Value: 12.00				
2010	4,946,711	—	—	—	0.35	—
2010 Proof	5,000	Value: 12.00				
2011	—	—	—	—	0.35	—
2011 Proof	5,000	Value: 12.00				
2012	—	—	—	—	0.35	—

KM# 33   2 EURO CENT
3.0000 g., Copper Plated Steel, 18.75 mm. **Obv:** Harp **Rev:** Denomination and globe **Edge:** Plain with groove

Date	Mintage	F	VF	XF	Unc	BU
2002	354,643,386	—	—	—	0.50	—
2003	177,290,034	—	—	—	0.50	—
2004	143,004,694	—	—	—	0.50	—
2005	72,544,884	—	—	—	0.50	—
2006	26,568,597	—	—	—	0.50	—
2006 Proof	5,000	Value: 15.00				
2007	84,291,248	—	—	—	0.50	—
2007 Proof	10,000	Value: 12.00				
2008	42,116,152	—	—	—	0.50	—
2009	7,284,499	—	—	—	0.50	—
2009 Proof	5,000	Value: 12.00				
2010	3,496,511	—	—	—	0.50	—
2010 Proof	5,000	Value: 12.00				
2011	—	—	—	—	0.50	—
2011 Proof	5,000	Value: 12.00				
2012	—	—	—	—	0.50	—

KM# 34   5 EURO CENT
4.0000 g., Copper Plated Steel, 19.60 mm. **Obv:** Harp **Rev:** Denomination and globe **Edge:** Plain

Date	Mintage	F	VF	XF	Unc	BU
2002	456,270,848	—	—	—	0.75	—
2003	48,352,370	—	—	—	0.75	—
2004	80,354,322	—	—	—	0.75	—
2005	56,454,380	—	—	—	0.75	—
2006	88,003,370	—	—	—	0.75	—
2006 Proof	5,000	Value: 18.00				

Date	Mintage	F	VF	XF	Unc	BU
2007	36,225,742	—	—	—	0.75	—
2007 Proof	10,000	Value: 15.00				
2008	61,844,008	—	—	—	0.75	—
2009	10,333,341	—	—	—	0.75	—
2009 Proof	5,000	Value: 15.00				
2010	1,023,881	—	—	—	0.75	—
2010 Proof	5,000	Value: 15.00				
2011	—	—	—	—	0.75	—
2011 Proof	5,000	Value: 15.00				
2012	—	—	—	—	0.75	—

KM# 35   10 EURO CENT
4.0700 g., Brass, 19.75 mm. **Obv:** Harp **Rev:** Denomination and map **Edge:** Reeded

Date	Mintage	F	VF	XF	Unc	BU
2002	275,913,000	—	—	—	1.00	—
2003	133,815,907	—	—	—	1.00	—
2004	36,732,778	—	—	—	1.00	—
2005	4,652,786	—	—	—	1.00	—
2006	9,208,411	—	—	—	1.00	—
2006 Proof	5,000	Value: 18.00				

KM# 47   10 EURO CENT
4.0700 g., Brass, 19.75 mm. **Obv:** Harp **Rev:** Relief map of Western Europe, stars, lines and value **Edge:** Reeded

Date	Mintage	F	VF	XF	Unc	BU
2007	54,434,307	—	—	—	1.00	—
2007 Proof	10,000	Value: 15.00				
2008	53,997,990	—	—	—	1.00	—
2009	10,850,328	—	—	—	1.00	—
2009 Proof	5,000	Value: 15.00				
2010	1,078,313	—	—	—	1.00	—
2010 Proof	5,000	Value: 15.00				
2011	—	—	—	—	1.00	—
2011 Proof	5,000	Value: 15.00				
2012	—	—	—	—	1.00	—

KM# 36   20 EURO CENT
5.7300 g., Brass, 22.25 mm. **Obv:** Harp **Rev:** Denomination and map **Edge:** Notched

Date	Mintage	F	VF	XF	Unc	BU
2002	234,575,562	—	—	—	1.25	—
2003	57,142,221	—	—	—	1.25	—
2004	32,421,447	—	—	—	1.25	—
2005	40,439,062	—	—	—	1.25	—
2006	10,357,229	—	—	—	1.25	—
2006 Proof	5,000	Value: 20.00				

KM# 48   20 EURO CENT
5.7300 g., Brass, 22.25 mm. **Obv:** Harp **Rev:** Relief map of Western Europe, stars, lines and value **Edge:** Notched

Date	Mintage	F	VF	XF	Unc	BU
2007	12,953,789	—	—	—	1.25	—
2007 Proof	10,000	Value: 18.00				
2008	45,990,533	—	—	—	1.25	—
2009	4,279,307	—	—	—	1.25	—
2009 Proof	5,000	Value: 18.00				
2010	1,027,059	—	—	—	1.25	—
2010 Proof	5,000	Value: 18.00				
2011	—	—	—	—	1.25	—
2011 Proof	5,000	Value: 18.00				
2012	—	—	—	—	1.25	—

KM# 37   50 EURO CENT
7.8100 g., Brass, 24.25 mm. **Obv:** Harp **Rev:** Denomination and map **Edge:** Reeded

Date	Mintage	F	VF	XF	Unc	BU
2002	144,144,592	—	—	—	1.50	—
2003	11,811,926	—	—	—	1.50	—
2004	6,748,912	—	—	—	1.50	—
2005	17,253,568	—	—	—	1.50	—
2006	966,138	—	—	—	1.50	—
2006 Proof	5,000					

KM# 49   50 EURO CENT
7.8100 g., Brass, 24.25 mm. **Obv:** Harp **Rev:** Relief map of Western Europe, stars, lines and value **Edge:** Reeded

Date	Mintage	F	VF	XF	Unc	BU
2007	4,991,002	—	—	—	1.50	—
2007 Proof	10,000	Value: 20.00				
2008	1,122,371	—	—	—	1.50	—
2009	1,876,011	—	—	—	1.50	—
2009 Proof	5,000	Value: 20.00				
2010	1,173,242	—	—	—	1.50	—
2010 Proof	5,000	Value: 20.00				
2011	—	—	—	—	1.50	—
2011 Proof	5,000	Value: 20.00				
2012	—	—	—	—	1.50	—

KM# 38   EURO
7.5000 g., Bi-Metallic Copper-Nickel center in Brass ring, 23.25 mm. **Obv:** Harp **Rev:** Denomination and map **Edge:** Reeded and plain sections

Date	Mintage	F	VF	XF	Unc	BU
2002	135,139,737	—	—	—	2.75	—
2003	2,520,000	—	—	—	2.75	—
2004	1,632,990	—	—	—	2.75	—
2005	6,769,777	—	—	—	2.75	—
2006	4,023,722	—	—	—	2.75	—
2006 Proof	5,000	Value: 25.00				

KM# 50   EURO
7.5000 g., Bi-Metallic Copper-Nickel center in Brass ring, 23.25 mm. **Obv:** Harp **Rev:** Relief map of Western Europe, stars, lines and value **Edge:** Reeded and plain sections

Date	Mintage	F	VF	XF	Unc	BU
2007	1,850,049	—	—	—	2.75	—
2007 Proof	10,000	Value: 22.00				
2008	2,609,757	—	—	—	2.75	—
2009	3,314,828	—	—	—	2.75	—
2009 Proof	5,000	Value: 22.00				
2010	1,082,716	—	—	—	2.75	—
2010 Proof	5,000	Value: 22.00				
2011	—	—	—	—	2.75	—
2011 Proof	5,000	Value: 22.00				
2012	—	—	—	—	2.75	—

KM# 39   2 EURO
8.5200 g., Bi-Metallic Nickel-Brass center in Copper-Nickel ring, 25.7 mm. **Obv:** Harp **Rev:** Denomination and map **Edge:** Reeded with 2's and stars

Date	Mintage	F	VF	XF	Unc	BU
2002	90,548,166	—	—	—	4.00	—
2003	2,631,076	—	—	—	4.00	—
2004	3,738,186	—	—	—	4.00	—
2005	11,982,981	—	—	—	4.00	—
2006	3,860,519	—	—	—	4.00	—
2006 Proof	5,000	Value: 28.00				

KM# 51   2 EURO
8.5200 g., Bi-Metallic Nickel-Brass center in Copper-Nickel ring, 25.7 mm. **Obv:** Harp **Rev:** Relief map of Western Europe, stars, lines and value **Edge:** Reeded with 2's and stars

Date	Mintage	F	VF	XF	Unc	BU
2007	7,595,260	—	—	—	4.00	—
2007 Proof	10,000	Value: 25.00				
2008	5,792,003	—	—	—	4.00	—
2009	30,063	—	—	—	4.00	—
2009 Proof	5,000	Value: 25.00				
2010	1,448,746	—	—	—	4.00	—
2010 Proof	5,000	Value: 25.00				
2011	—	—	—	—	4.00	—
2011 Proof	5,000	Value: 25.00				
2012	—	—	—	—	4.00	—

KM# 53   2 EURO
8.4500 g., Bi-Metallic Nickel-Brass center in Copper-Nickel ring, 25.72 mm. **Subject:** 50th Anniversary Treaty of Rome **Obv:** Open treaty book **Rev:** Large value at left, modified outline of Europe at right **Edge:** Reeded with stars and 2's

Date	Mintage	F	VF	XF	Unc	BU
2007	4,605,112	—	—	—	5.00	10.00
2007 Special Unc.	35,000	—	—	—	—	20.00
2007 Proof	10,000	Value: 25.00				

KM# 62   2 EURO
8.5200 g., Bi-Metallic Nickel-Brass center in Copper-Nickel ring, 25.72 mm. **Subject:** EMU, 10th Anniversary

Date	Mintage	F	VF	XF	Unc	BU
2009	5,000,000	—	—	—	8.00	10.00
2009 Proof	7,000	Value: 115				

KM# 71   2 EURO
8.5000 g., Bi-Metallic Nickel-Brass center in Copper-Nickel ring, 25.75 mm. **Subject:** Euro Coinage, 10th Anniversary **Obv:** Euro symbol on globe at center, child-like rendering around

Date	Mintage	F	VF	XF	Unc	BU
2012	3,000,000	—	—	—	6.00	8.00
2012 Proof		Value: 25.00				

KM# 40   5 EURO
14.1900 g., Copper-Nickel, 28.4 mm. **Subject:** Special Olympics **Obv:** Harp **Rev:** Multicolor games logo **Edge:** Reeded

Date	Mintage	F	VF	XF	Unc	BU
2003	35,000	—	—	—	15.00	18.00
2003 Proof	25,000	Value: 25.00				

KM# 56   5 EURO
8.5200 g., 0.9250 Silver 0.2534 oz. ASW, 28 mm. **Subject:** International Polar Year **Obv:** Harp within wreath **Rev:** Ernest Shackleton, Tom Crean and The Endurance in distance **Edge:** Reeded

Date	Mintage	F	VF	XF	Unc	BU
2008 Proof	5,000	Value: 90.00				

KM# 41   10 EURO
28.2800 g., 0.9250 Silver 0.8410 oz. ASW, 38.61 mm. **Subject:** Special Olympics **Obv:** Gold highlighted harp, 2003, Eire **Rev:** Gold highlighted games logo **Edge:** Reeded

Date	Mintage	F	VF	XF	Unc	BU
2003 Proof	30,000	Value: 50.00				

KM# 42   10 EURO
28.2800 g., 0.9250 Silver 0.8410 oz. ASW, 38.61 mm. **Subject:** EU Presidency **Obv:** 2004, Eire, Harp **Rev:** Stylized Celtic swan **Edge:** Reeded

Date	Mintage	F	VF	XF	Unc	BU
2004 Proof	50,000	Value: 45.00				

KM# 44   10 EURO
28.2800 g., 0.9250 Silver 0.8410 oz. ASW, 38.6 mm. **Subject:** Sir William R. Hamilton **Obv:** Eire, 2005, Harp **Rev:** Triangle in circle of Greek letters used as math symbols **Edge:** Reeded

Date	Mintage	F	VF	XF	Unc	BU
2005 Proof	30,000	Value: 55.00				

KM# 45   10 EURO
28.2800 g., 0.9250 Silver 0.8410 oz. ASW, 38.61 mm. **Subject:**

Samuel Beckett 1906-1989 **Obv:** 2006, Eire, Harp **Rev:** Face, value and play scene **Edge:** Reeded

Date	Mintage	F	VF	XF	Unc	BU
2006 Proof	35,000	Value: 50.00				

KM# 58   10 EURO
28.2800 g., 0.9250 Silver 0.8410 oz. ASW, 38.6 mm. **Subject:** European Culture - Ireland **Obv:** Irish Harp **Rev:** Celtic design

Date	Mintage	F	VF	XF	Unc	BU
2007 Proof	35,000	Value: 55.00				

KM# 54   10 EURO
28.2800 g., 0.9250 Silver 0.8410 oz. ASW, 38.61 mm. **Subject:** Skellig Michael Island **Rev:** Birds and 12 stars above island **Rev. Legend:** SCEILIG MHICHIL

Date	Mintage	F	VF	XF	Unc	BU
2008 Proof	25,000	Value: 65.00				

KM# 60   10 EURO
28.2800 g., 0.9250 Silver 0.8410 oz. ASW, 38.61 mm. **Subject:** First currency, 80th Anniversary **Obv:** Irish harp **Rev:** Ploughman design

Date	Mintage	F	VF	XF	Unc	BU
2009 Proof	15,000	Value: 55.00				

KM# 65   10 EURO
28.2800 g., 0.9250 Silver 0.8410 oz. ASW, 38.61 mm. **Subject:** The President's Award - Gaisce

Date	Mintage	F	VF	XF	Unc	BU
2010 Proof	8,000	Value: 60.00				

KM# 67   10 EURO
28.2800 g., 0.9250 Silver 0.8410 oz. ASW, 38.61 mm. **Subject:** St. Brendan the Navigator **Rev:** Medieval ship

Date	Mintage	F	VF	XF	Unc	BU
2011 Proof	15,000	Value: 60.00				

KM# 70   10 EURO
28.2800 g., 0.9250 Silver 0.8410 oz. ASW, 38.61 mm. **Subject:** Jack B. Yates

Date	Mintage	F	VF	XF	Unc	BU
2012 Proof	—	Value: 60.00				

KM# 52   15 EURO
28.2800 g., 0.9250 Silver 0.8410 oz. ASW, 37 mm. **Obv:** Stylized clover with date and harp **Rev:** Ivan Mestroviae's Seated Woman with Harp design **Edge:** Plain **Note:** Illustration reduced.

Date	Mintage	F	VF	XF	Unc	BU
2007 Proof	10,000	Value: 85.00				

Note: 8,000 were sold in a single coin case. 1,000 were sold in a two coin set with the corresponding Croatian coin, as an Ireland set. An additional 1,000 were sold with the corresponding Croatian coin as a Croatia set. coins in both sets were the same but the packaging was different.

KM# 63   15 EURO
28.2800 g., 0.9250 Silver 0.8410 oz. ASW, 38.61 mm. **Subject:** Gaelic Athletics, 125 years

Date	Mintage	F	VF	XF	Unc	BU
2009 Proof	10,000	Value: 75.00				

KM# 64   15 EURO
28.2800 g., 0.9250 Silver 0.8410 oz. ASW, 38.61 mm. **Rev:** Foal and mare

Date	Mintage	F	VF	XF	Unc	BU
2010 Proof	15,000	Value: 75.00				

KM# 68   15 EURO
28.2800 g., 0.9250 Silver 0.8410 oz. ASW, 38.61 mm. **Rev:** Salmon

Date	Mintage	F	VF	XF	Unc	BU
2011 Proof	—	Value: 75.00				

KM# 46   20 EURO
1.2400 g., 0.9990 Gold 0.0398 oz. AGW, 14 mm. **Subject:** Samuel Beckett 1906-1989 **Obv:** 2006, Eire, Harp **Rev:** Face, value and play scene **Edge:** Reeded

Date	Mintage	F	VF	XF	Unc	BU
2006 Proof	20,000	Value: 85.00				

KM# 59   20 EURO
1.2440 g., 0.9990 Gold 0.0400 oz. AGW, 14 mm. **Subject:** European Culture - Ireland **Obv:** Map **Rev:** Celtic design

Date	Mintage	F	VF	XF	Unc	BU
2007 Proof	25,000	Value: 95.00				

KM# 55   20 EURO
1.2440 g., 0.9990 Gold 0.0400 oz. AGW, 14 mm. **Subject:** Skellig Michael Island **Rev:** Birds and 12 stars above island **Rev. Legend:** SCEILIG MHICHIL

Date	Mintage	F	VF	XF	Unc	BU
2008 Proof	15,000	Value: 100				

KM# 61   20 EURO
1.2440 g., 0.9990 Gold 0.0400 oz. AGW, 14 mm. **Subject:** First currency, 80th Anniversary

Date	Mintage	F	VF	XF	Unc	BU
2009 Proof	15,000	Value: 90.00				

KM# 66   20 EURO
1.2400 g., 0.9990 Gold 0.0398 oz. AGW, 14 mm. **Subject:** The President's Award - Gaisce

Date	Mintage	F	VF	XF	Unc	BU
2010 Proof	6,000	Value: 90.00				

KM# 69   20 EURO
0.5000 g., 0.9990 Gold 0.0161 oz. AGW, 11 mm. **Rev:** Celtic Cross

Date	Mintage	F	VF	XF	Unc	BU
2011 Proof	12,000	Value: 50.00				

KM# 57   100 EURO
15.5500 g., 0.9990 Gold 0.4994 oz. AGW, 28 mm. **Subject:** International Polar Year **Obv:** Harp within wreath **Rev:** Ernest Shackleton, Tom Crean and The Endurance in distance **Edge:** Reeded

Date	Mintage	F	VF	XF	Unc	BU
2008 Proof	2,000	Value: 950				

MINT SETS

KM#	Date	Mintage	Identification	Issue Price	Mkt Val
MS10	2002 (8)	20,000	KM#32-39	16.00	200
MS11	2003 (8)	30,000	KM#32-39	20.00	65.00
MS12	2003 (9)	35,000	KM#32-40 Special Olympics	25.00	90.00
MS13	2004 (8)	40,000	KM#32-39	25.00	45.00
MS14	2005 (8)	50,000	KM#32-39 Heywood Gardens	29.00	40.00
MS15	2006 (8)	40,000	KM#32-39 Glenveagh National Park and Castle	26.00	40.00
MS16	2006 (8)	—	KM#32-39 Boy Baby Set	35.00	42.50
MS17	2006 (8)	—	KM#32-39 Girl Baby Set	35.00	42.50
MS18	2007 (8)	20,000	KM#32-34, 47-51 Aran Islands	29.00	30.00
MS19	2007 (8)	—	KM#32-34, 47-51 Boy Baby Set	—	30.00
MS20	2007 (8)	—	KM#32-34, 47-51 Girl Baby Set	—	30.00
MS21	2007 (9)	20,000	KM#32-34, 47-51, 53	—	30.00
MS22	2008 (8)	30,000	KM#32-34, 47-51 Newgrange	—	30.00
MS23	2008 (8)	—	KM#32-34, 47-51 Boy Baby Set	—	30.00
MS24	2008 (8)	—	KM#32-34, 47-51 Girl Baby Set	—	30.00
MS25	2009 (8)	25,000	KM#32-34, 47-51 GAA 125th Anniversary	—	30.00
MS26	2009 (8)	—	KM#32-34, 47-51 Boy Baby Set	—	30.00
MS27	2009 (8)	—	KM#32-34, 47-51 Girl Baby Set	—	30.00
MS28	2010 (8)	20,000	KM#32-34, 47-51 Horse	45.00	45.00
MS29	2010 (8)	—	KM#32-34, 47-51 Baby Set	45.00	45.00
MS30	2011 (8)	20,000	KM#32-34, 47-51	—	45.00
MS31	2012 (8)	—	KM#32-34, 47-51	—	45.00

PROOF SETS

KM#	Date	Mintage	Identification	Issue Price	Mkt Val
PS6	2006 (8)	5,000	KM#32-39	125	165
PS7	2006 (2)	—	KM#45, 46	—	135
PS8	2007 (9)	10,000	KM#32-34, 47-51, 53	—	165
PS9	2007 (2)	—	KM#58-59	—	150
PS10	2008 (2)	—	KM#54-55	—	165
PS11	2008 (2)	—	KM#56-57	—	950
PS12	2009 (9)	—	KM#32-34, 47-51, 58 GAA 125th Anniversary	—	200
PS13	2009 (8)	5,000	KM#32-34, 47-51, 61.	—	225
PS14	2009 (2)	5,000	KM#60, 61. Ploughman Bank Note	—	160
PS15	2010 (2)	—	KM#65-66	—	150
PS16	2010 (8)	5,000	KM#32-34, 47-51	—	200
PS17	2011 (8)	5,000	KM#32-34, 47-51	—	200

ISLE OF MAN

The Isle of Man, a dependency of the British Crown located in the Irish Sea equidistant from Ireland, Scotland and England, has an area of 227 sq. mi. (588 sq. km.) and a population of 68,000. Capital: Douglas. Agriculture, dairy farming, fishing and tourism are the chief industries.

MINT MARK
PM - Pobjoy Mint

BRITISH DEPENDENCY

DECIMAL COINAGE
100 Pence = 1 Pound

KM# 1036   PENNY
3.5600 g., Copper Plated Steel, 20.32 mm.   **Ruler:** Elizabeth II **Obv:** Head with tiara right with small triskeles dividing legend **Rev:** Ruins **Edge:** Plain

Date	Mintage	F	VF	XF	Unc	BU
2001PM AA	—	—	—	—	0.25	0.45
2001PM AC	—	—	—	—	0.25	0.45
2002PM AA	—	—	—	—	0.25	0.45
2002PM AE	—	—	—	—	0.25	0.45
2003PM AA	—	—	—	—	0.25	0.45
2003PM AE	—	—	—	—	0.25	0.45

KM# 1253   PENNY
3.5600 g., Copper Plated Steel, 20.3 mm.   **Ruler:** Elizabeth II **Obv:** Head with tiara right **Rev:** Santon War Memorial

Date	Mintage	F	VF	XF	Unc	BU
2004PM AA	—	—	—	—	0.25	0.45
2004PM AB	—	—	—	—	0.25	0.45
2005PM AA	—	—	—	—	0.25	0.45
2005PM AB	—	—	—	—	0.25	0.45
2006PM AA	—	—	—	—	0.25	0.45
2006PM AB	—	—	—	—	0.25	0.45
2007PM AA	—	—	—	—	0.25	0.45
2007PM AB	—	—	—	—	0.25	0.45
2007PM BA	—	—	—	—	0.25	0.45
2008PM AA	—	—	—	—	0.25	0.45
2009PM AA	—	—	—	—	0.25	0.45
2010PM AA	—	—	—	—	0.25	0.45
2011PM AA	—	—	—	—	0.25	0.45

KM# 1037   2 PENCE
7.1200 g., Copper Plated Steel, 25.9 mm.   **Ruler:** Elizabeth II **Obv:** Head with tiara right **Rev:** Sailboat **Edge:** Plain

Date	Mintage	F	VF	XF	Unc	BU
2001PM AA	—	—	—	—	0.40	0.60
2001PM AB	—	—	—	—	0.40	0.60
2001PM AC	—	—	—	—	0.40	0.60
2002PM AA	—	—	—	—	0.40	0.60
2002PM AB	—	—	—	—	0.40	0.60
2002PM AC	—	—	—	—	0.40	0.60
2002PM AF	—	—	—	—	0.40	0.60
2003PM AA	—	—	—	—	0.40	0.60
2003PM AF	—	—	—	—	0.40	0.60

KM# 1254   2 PENCE
7.1200 g., Copper Plated Steel, 25.9 mm.   **Ruler:** Elizabeth II **Obv:** Head with tiara right **Rev:** Albert Tower

Date	Mintage	F	VF	XF	Unc	BU
2004PM AA	—	—	—	—	0.40	0.60
2004PM AB	—	—	—	—	0.40	0.60
2005PM AA	—	—	—	—	0.40	0.60
2005PM AB	—	—	—	—	0.40	0.60
2006PM AA	—	—	—	—	0.40	0.60
2006PM AB	—	—	—	—	0.40	0.60
2007PM AA	—	—	—	—	0.40	0.60
2007PM AB	—	—	—	—	0.40	0.60
2007PM BA	—	—	—	—	0.40	0.60
2008PM AA	—	—	—	—	0.40	0.60
2009PM AA	—	—	—	—	0.40	0.60
2010PM AA	—	—	—	—	0.40	0.60
2011PM AA	—	—	—	—	0.40	0.60

KM# 1038   5 PENCE
3.2500 g., Copper-Nickel, 18 mm.   **Ruler:** Elizabeth II **Obv:** Head with tiara right **Rev:** Gaut's Cross **Edge:** Reeded

Date	Mintage	F	VF	XF	Unc	BU
2001PM AA	—	—	—	—	0.75	1.00
2002PM AA	—	—	—	—	0.75	1.00
2002PM AC	—	—	—	—	0.75	1.00
2002PM AD	—	—	—	—	0.75	1.00
2002PM AE	—	—	—	—	0.75	1.00
2003PM AA	—	—	—	—	0.75	1.00
2003PM AB	—	—	—	—	0.75	1.00
2003PM AD	—	—	—	—	0.75	1.00

KM# 1255   5 PENCE
3.2500 g., Copper-Nickel, 18 mm.   **Ruler:** Elizabeth II **Obv:** Head with tiara right **Rev:** Tower of Refuge **Edge:** Reeded

Date	Mintage	F	VF	XF	Unc	BU
2004PM AA	—	—	—	—	0.75	1.00
2004PM AB	—	—	—	—	0.75	1.00
2005PM AA	—	—	—	—	0.75	1.00
2005PM AB	—	—	—	—	0.75	1.00
2006PM AA	—	—	—	—	0.75	1.00
2006PM AB	—	—	—	—	0.75	1.00
2007PM AA	—	—	—	—	0.75	1.00
2007PM AB	—	—	—	—	0.75	1.00
2008PM AA	—	—	—	—	0.75	1.00
2009PM AA	—	—	—	—	0.75	1.00
2010PM AA	—	—	—	—	0.75	1.00
2011PM AA	—	—	—	—	0.75	1.00

KM# 1039   10 PENCE
6.5000 g., Copper-Nickel, 24.5 mm.   **Ruler:** Elizabeth II **Obv:** Head with tiara right **Rev:** Cathedral **Edge:** Reeded

Date	Mintage	F	VF	XF	Unc	BU
2001PM AA	—	—	—	—	1.00	1.50
2002PM AA	—	—	—	—	1.00	1.50
2003PM AA	—	—	—	—	1.00	1.50

KM# 1256   10 PENCE
6.5000 g., Copper-Nickel, 24.5 mm.   **Ruler:** Elizabeth II **Obv:** Head with tiara right **Rev:** Chicken Rock Lighthouse **Edge:** Reeded

Date	Mintage	F	VF	XF	Unc	BU
2004PM AA	—	—	—	—	1.00	1.50
2004PM AB	—	—	—	—	1.00	1.50
2005PM AA	—	—	—	—	1.00	1.50
2005PM AB	—	—	—	—	1.00	1.50
2006PM AA	—	—	—	—	1.00	1.50
2006PM AB	—	—	—	—	1.00	1.50
2007PM AA	—	—	—	—	1.00	1.50
2007PM AB	—	—	—	—	1.00	1.50
2008PM AA	—	—	—	—	1.00	1.50
2009PM AA	—	—	—	—	1.00	1.50
2010PM AA	—	—	—	—	1.00	1.50
2011PM AA	—	—	—	—	1.00	1.50

KM# 1040   20 PENCE
5.0000 g., Copper-Nickel, 35 mm.   **Ruler:** Elizabeth II **Subject:** Rushen Abbey **Obv:** Head with tiara right **Rev:** Monk writing **Edge:** Plain **Shape:** 7-sided

Date	Mintage	F	VF	XF	Unc	BU
2001PM AA	—	—	—	—	1.50	2.00
2001PM AB	—	—	—	—	1.50	2.00
2002PM AA	—	—	—	—	1.50	2.00
2002PM AB	—	—	—	—	1.50	2.00
2002PM AC	—	—	—	—	1.50	2.00
2003PM AA	—	—	—	—	1.50	2.00
2003PM BA	—	—	—	—	1.50	2.00

KM# 1257   20 PENCE
5.0000 g., Copper-Nickel, 21.5 mm.   **Ruler:** Elizabeth II **Obv:** Head with tiara right **Rev:** Castle Rushen Clock **Edge:** Plain **Shape:** 7-sided

Date	Mintage	F	VF	XF	Unc	BU
2004PM AA	—	—	—	—	1.50	2.00
2004PM AB	—	—	—	—	1.50	2.00
2005PM AA	—	—	—	—	1.50	2.00
2005PM AB	—	—	—	—	1.50	2.00
2006PM AA	—	—	—	—	1.50	2.00

Date	Mintage	F	VF	XF	Unc	BU
2006PM AB	—	—	—	—	1.50	2.00
2007PM AB	—	—	—	—	1.50	2.00
2007PM AB	—	—	—	—	1.50	2.00
2008PM AA	—	—	—	—	1.50	2.00
2009PM AA	—	—	—	—	1.50	2.00
2010PM AA	—	—	—	—	1.50	2.00
2011PM AA	—	—	—	—	1.50	2.00

KM# 1041   50 PENCE
8.0000 g., Copper-Nickel, 27.3 mm. **Ruler:** Elizabeth II **Obv:** Head with tiara right **Rev:** Stylized crucifix **Edge:** Plain **Shape:** 7-sided

Date	Mintage	F	VF	XF	Unc	BU
2001PM AA	—	—	—	—	2.25	2.75
2002PM AA	—	—	—	—	2.25	2.75
2003PM AA	—	—	—	—	2.25	2.75

KM# 1105   50 PENCE
8.0000 g., Copper-Nickel, 27.3 mm. **Ruler:** Elizabeth II **Subject:** Christmas **Obv:** Head with tiara right **Rev:** Postman and children **Edge:** Plain **Shape:** 7-sided

Date	Mintage	F	VF	XF	Unc	BU
2001PM BB	30,000	—	—	—	4.50	6.00

KM# 1105a   50 PENCE
8.0000 g., 0.9250 Silver 0.2379 oz. ASW, 27.3 mm. **Ruler:** Elizabeth II **Obv:** Head with tiara right **Rev:** Postman and children **Edge:** Plain **Shape:** 7-sided

Date	Mintage	F	VF	XF	Unc	BU
2001PM Proof	5,000	Value: 35.00				

KM# 1105b   50 PENCE
8.0000 g., 0.9167 Gold 0.2358 oz. AGW, 27.3 mm. **Ruler:** Elizabeth II **Obv:** Head with tiara right **Rev:** Postman and children **Edge:** Plain **Shape:** 7-sided

Date	Mintage	F	VF	XF	Unc	BU
2001PM Proof	250	Value: 425				

KM# 1160   50 PENCE
8.0000 g., Copper-Nickel, 27.3 mm. **Ruler:** Elizabeth II **Subject:** Christmas **Obv:** Head with tiara right **Rev:** Scrooge in bed **Edge:** Plain **Shape:** 7-sided

Date	Mintage	F	VF	XF	Unc	BU
2002BB PM	30,000	—	—	—	4.50	6.00

KM# 1160a   50 PENCE
8.0000 g., 0.9250 Silver 0.2379 oz. ASW, 27.3 mm. **Ruler:** Elizabeth II **Subject:** Christmas **Obv:** Head with tiara right **Rev:** Scrooge in bed **Edge:** Plain **Shape:** 7-sided

Date	Mintage	F	VF	XF	Unc	BU
2002PM Proof	5,000	Value: 35.00				

KM# 1160b   50 PENCE
8.0000 g., 0.9167 Gold 0.2358 oz. AGW, 27.3 mm. **Ruler:** Elizabeth II **Subject:** Christmas **Obv:** Head with tiara right **Rev:** Scrooge in bed **Edge:** Plain **Shape:** 7-sided

Date	Mintage	F	VF	XF	Unc	BU
2002PM Proof	250	Value: 425				

KM# 1183   50 PENCE
8.0000 g., Copper-Nickel, 27.3 mm. **Ruler:** Elizabeth II **Obv:** Head with tiara right **Rev:** "The Snowman and James" **Edge:** Plain **Shape:** 7-sided

Date	Mintage	F	VF	XF	Unc	BU
2003PM BB	10,000	—	—	—	6.50	8.00
2008PM	—	—	—	—	6.50	8.00

KM# 1183a   50 PENCE
8.0000 g., 0.9250 Silver 0.2379 oz. ASW, 27.3 mm. **Ruler:** Elizabeth II **Subject:** Elizabeth II **Obv:** Head with tiara right **Rev:** "The Snowman and James" **Edge:** Plain **Shape:** 7-sided

Date	Mintage	F	VF	XF	Unc	BU
2003PM Proof	3,000	Value: 35.00				

KM# 1183b   50 PENCE
8.0000 g., 0.9167 Gold 0.2358 oz. AGW, 27.3 mm. **Ruler:** Elizabeth II **Obv:** Head with tiara right **Rev:** "The Snowman and James" **Edge:** Plain **Shape:** 7-sided

Date	Mintage	F	VF	XF	Unc	BU
2003PM Proof	100	Value: 425				

KM# 1258   50 PENCE
8.0000 g., Copper-Nickel, 21.5 mm. **Ruler:** Elizabeth II **Obv:** Head with tiara right **Rev:** Milner's Tower **Edge:** Plain **Shape:** 7-sided

Date	Mintage	F	VF	XF	Unc	BU
2004PM AA	—	—	—	—	2.25	2.75
2004PM AB	—	—	—	—	2.25	2.75
2005PM AA	—	—	—	—	2.25	2.75
2005PM AB	—	—	—	—	2.25	2.75
2006PM AA	—	—	—	—	2.25	2.75
2006PM AB	—	—	—	—	2.25	2.75
2007PM AA	—	—	—	—	2.25	2.75
2007PM AB	—	—	—	—	2.25	2.75
2008PM AA	—	—	—	—	2.25	2.75
2009PM AA	—	—	—	—	2.25	2.75
2010PM AA	—	—	—	—	2.25	2.75
2011PM AA	—	—	—	—	2.25	2.75

KM# 1293   50 PENCE
Copper-Nickel **Ruler:** Elizabeth II **Obv:** Queen's new portrait **Rev:** Tourist Trophy Races

Date	Mintage	F	VF	XF	Unc	BU
2004PM AA	—	—	—	—	6.00	7.00
2007PM AA	—	—	—	—	6.00	7.00

KM# 1262   50 PENCE
8.0000 g., Copper-Nickel, 27.3 mm. **Ruler:** Elizabeth II **Subject:** Christmas **Obv:** Head with tiara right **Rev:** Laxey Wheel **Edge:** Plain **Shape:** 7-sided

Date	Mintage	F	VF	XF	Unc	BU
2004PM AA	—	—	—	—	6.00	7.00
2004PM BA	30,000	—	—	—	6.00	7.00

KM# 1262a   50 PENCE
9.1852 g., 0.9250 Silver 0.2732 oz. ASW, 27.3 mm. **Ruler:** Elizabeth II **Subject:** Christmas **Obv:** Head with tiara right **Rev:** Laxey Wheel **Edge:** Plain **Shape:** 7-sided

Date	Mintage	F	VF	XF	Unc	BU
2004PM Proof	5,000	Value: 35.00				

KM# 1262b   50 PENCE
15.4074 g., 0.9167 Gold 0.4541 oz. AGW, 27.3 mm. **Ruler:** Elizabeth II **Subject:** Christmas **Obv:** Head with tiara right **Rev:** Laxey Wheel **Edge:** Plain **Shape:** 7-sided

Date	Mintage	F	VF	XF	Unc	BU
2004PM Proof	250	Value: 800				

KM# 1294   50 PENCE
Copper-Nickel, 27.3 mm. **Ruler:** Elizabeth II **Obv:** Queen's new portrait **Rev:** Partridge in a pear tree **Shape:** 7-sided

Date	Mintage	F	VF	XF	Unc	BU
2005	—	—	—	—	6.50	8.00

KM# 1320.1   50 PENCE
8.0000 g., Copper-Nickel, 27.3 mm. **Ruler:** Elizabeth II **Series:** 12 Days of Christmas **Obv:** Head with tiara right **Obv. Legend:** ISLE OF MAN - ELIZABETH II **Rev:** Partridge in a Pear Tree **Rev. Legend:** CHRISTMAS **Edge:** Plain **Shape:** 7-sided

Date	Mintage	F	VF	XF	Unc	BU
2005PM AA	30,000	—	—	—	—	16.00

KM# 1320.2   50 PENCE
8.0000 g., Copper-Nickel, 27.3 mm. **Ruler:** Elizabeth II **Series:** 12 Days of Christmas **Obv:** Head with tiara right **Obv. Legend:** ISLE OF MAN - ELIZABETH II **Rev:** Partidge in a Pear Tree multicolor **Rev. Legend:** CHRISTMAS **Edge:** Plain **Shape:** 7-sided

Date	Mintage	F	VF	XF	Unc	BU
2005PM	Inc. above	—	—	—	—	20.00

KM# 1320.1a   50 PENCE
9.1825 g., 0.9250 Silver 0.2731 oz. ASW, 27.3 mm. **Ruler:** Elizabeth II **Series:** 12 Days of Christmas **Obv:** Head with tiara right **Obv. Legend:** ISLE OF MAN - ELIZABETH II **Rev:** Partridge in a Pear Tree **Rev. Legend:** CHRISTMAS **Edge:** Plain **Shape:** 7-sided

Date	Mintage	F	VF	XF	Unc	BU
2005PM Proof	—	Value: 35.00				

KM# 1320.2a   50 PENCE
8.0000 g., 0.9250 Silver 0.2379 oz. ASW, 27.3 mm. **Ruler:** Elizabeth II **Series:** 12 Days of Christmas **Obv:** Head with tiara right **Obv. Legend:** ISLE OF MAN - ELIZABETH II **Rev:** Partridge in a Pear Tree multicolor **Rev. Legend:** CHRISTMAS **Edge:** Plain **Shape:** 7-sided

Date	Mintage	F	VF	XF	Unc	BU
2005PM Proof	—	Value: 35.00				

KM# 1320b   50 PENCE
0.9167 Gold, 27.3 mm. **Ruler:** Elizabeth II **Series:** 12 Days of Christmas **Obv:** Head with tiara right **Obv. Legend:** ISLE OF MAN - ELIZABETH II **Rev:** Partridge in a Pear Tree **Rev. Legend:** CHRISTMAS **Edge:** Plain **Shape:** 7-sided

Date	Mintage	F	VF	XF	Unc	BU
2005PM Proof	—	Value: 800				

KM# 1321.1   50 PENCE
8.0000 g., Copper-Nickel, 27.3 mm. **Ruler:** Elizabeth II **Series:** 12 Days of Christmas **Obv:** Head with tiara right **Obv. Legend:** ISLE OF MAN - ELIZABETH II **Rev:** Two Turtle Doves **Rev. Legend:** CHRISTMAS **Edge:** Plain **Shape:** 7-sided

Date	Mintage	F	VF	XF	Unc	BU
2006PM AA	—	—	—	—	6.00	7.00

KM# 1321.2   50 PENCE
8.0000 g., Copper-Nickel, 27.3 mm. **Ruler:** Elizabeth II **Series:** 12 Days of Christmas **Obv:** Head with tiara right **Obv. Legend:** ISLE OF MAN - ELIZABETH II **Rev:** 2 Turtle Doves multicolor **Rev. Legend:** CHRISTMAS **Edge:** Plain **Shape:** 7-sided

Date	Mintage	F	VF	XF	Unc	BU
2006PM	—	—	—	—	8.00	10.00

KM# 1321.1a   50 PENCE
0.9250 Silver, 27.3 mm. **Ruler:** Elizabeth II **Series:** 12 Days of Christmas **Obv:** Head with tiara right **Obv. Legend:** ISLE OF MAN - ELIZABETH II **Rev:** Two Turtle Doves **Rev. Legend:** CHRISTMAS **Edge:** Plain **Shape:** 7-sided

Date	Mintage	F	VF	XF	Unc	BU
2006PM Proof	—	Value: 35.00				

KM# 1321.2a   50 PENCE
0.9250 Silver, 27.3 mm. **Ruler:** Elizabeth II **Series:** 12 Days of Christmas **Obv:** Head with tiara right **Obv. Legend:** ISLE OF MAN - ELIZABETH II **Rev:** 2 Turtle Doves multicolor **Rev. Legend:** CHRISTMAS **Edge:** Plain **Shape:** 7-sided

Date	Mintage	F	VF	XF	Unc	BU
2006PM Proof	—	Value: 40.00				

KM# 1321b   50 PENCE
0.9167 Gold, 27.3 mm. **Ruler:** Elizabeth II **Series:** 12 Days of Christmas **Obv:** Head with tiara right **Obv. Legend:** ISLE OF MAN - ELIZABETH II **Rev:** 2 Turtle Doves **Rev. Legend:** CHRISTMAS **Edge:** Plain **Shape:** 7-sided

Date	Mintage	F	VF	XF	Unc	BU
2006PM Proof	—	Value: 800				

KM# 1322.1   50 PENCE
8.0000 g., Copper-Nickel, 27.3 mm. **Ruler:** Elizabeth II **Series:** 12 Days of Christmas **Obv:** Head with tiara right **Obv. Legend:**

ISLE OF MAN - ELIZABETH II **Rev:** 3 French Hens **Rev. Legend:** CHRISTMAS **Edge:** Plain **Shape:** 7-sided

Date	Mintage	F	VF	XF	Unc	BU
2007PM AA	—			—	6.00	7.00

KM# 1322.2 50 PENCE
8.0000 g., Copper-Nickel, 27.3 mm. **Ruler:** Elizabeth II **Series:** 12 Days of Christmas **Obv:** Head with tiara right **Obv. Legend:** ISLE OF MAN - ELIZABETH II **Rev:** 3 French Hens multicolor **Rev. Legend:** CHRISTMAS **Edge:** Plain **Shape:** 7-sided

Date	Mintage	F	VF	XF	Unc	BU
2007PM	—			—	8.00	10.00

KM# 1322.1a 50 PENCE
0.9250 Silver, 27.3 mm. **Ruler:** Elizabeth II **Series:** 12 Days of Christmas **Obv:** Head with tiara right **Obv. Legend:** ISLE OF MAN - ELIZABETH II **Rev:** 3 French Hens **Rev. Legend:** CHRISTMAS **Edge:** Plain **Shape:** 7-sided

Date	Mintage	F	VF	XF	Unc	BU
2007PM Proof	—	Value: 35.00				

KM# 1322.2a 50 PENCE
0.9250 Silver, 27.3 mm. **Ruler:** Elizabeth II **Series:** 12 Days of Christmas **Obv:** Head with tiara right **Obv. Legend:** ISLE OF MAN - ELIZABETH II **Rev:** 3 French Hens multicolor **Rev. Legend:** CHRISTMAS **Edge:** Plain **Shape:** 7-sided

Date	Mintage	F	VF	XF	Unc	BU
2007PM Proof	—	Value: 40.00				

KM# 1322b 50 PENCE
0.9167 Gold, 27.3 mm. **Ruler:** Elizabeth II **Series:** 12 Days of Christmas **Obv:** Head with tiara right **Obv. Legend:** ISLE OF MAN - ELIZABETH II **Rev:** 3 French Hens **Rev. Legend:** CHRISTMAS **Edge:** Plain **Shape:** 7-sided

Date	Mintage	F	VF	XF	Unc	BU
2007PM Proof	250	Value: 800				

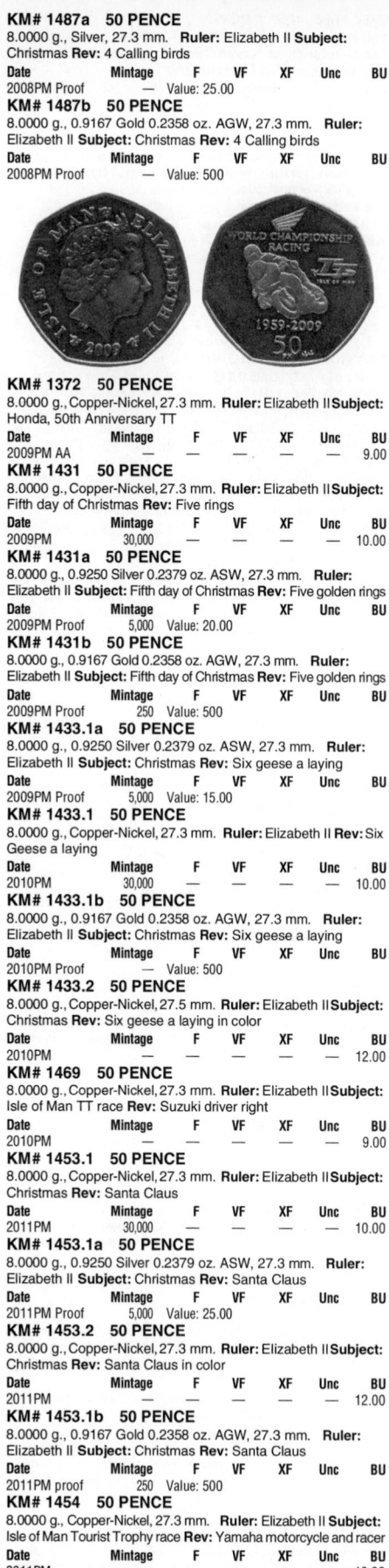

KM# 1425 50 PENCE
8.0000 g., Copper-Nickel, 27.3 mm. **Ruler:** Elizabeth II **Subject:** TT Centennial **Obv:** Head with tiara right **Rev:** Two motorcyclists within wreath

Date	Mintage	F	VF	XF	Unc	BU
2007PM	—			—	8.00	10.00

KM# 1393.1 50 PENCE
8.0000 g., Copper-Nickel, 27.3 mm. **Ruler:** Elizabeth II **Subject:** Christmas **Rev:** Snowman **Shape:** 7-sided

Date	Mintage	F	VF	XF	Unc	BU
2008PM	—			—	10.00	12.00

KM# 1393.2 50 PENCE
8.0000 g., Copper-Nickel, 27.3 mm. **Ruler:** Elizabeth II **Subject:** Christmas **Rev:** Snowman, multicolored **Shape:** 7-sided

Date	Mintage	F	VF	XF	Unc	BU
2008PM	—			—	10.00	12.00

KM# 1487 50 PENCE
8.0000 g., Copper-Nickel, 27.3 mm. **Ruler:** Elizabeth II **Subject:** Christmas **Rev:** 4 Calling Birds

Date	Mintage	F	VF	XF	Unc	BU
2008PM	—			—	—	9.00

KM# 1487a 50 PENCE
8.0000 g., Silver, 27.3 mm. **Ruler:** Elizabeth II **Subject:** Christmas **Rev:** 4 Calling birds

Date	Mintage	F	VF	XF	Unc	BU
2008PM Proof	—	Value: 25.00				

KM# 1487b 50 PENCE
8.0000 g., 0.9167 Gold 0.2358 oz. AGW, 27.3 mm. **Ruler:** Elizabeth II **Subject:** Christmas **Rev:** 4 Calling birds

Date	Mintage	F	VF	XF	Unc	BU
2008PM Proof	—	Value: 500				

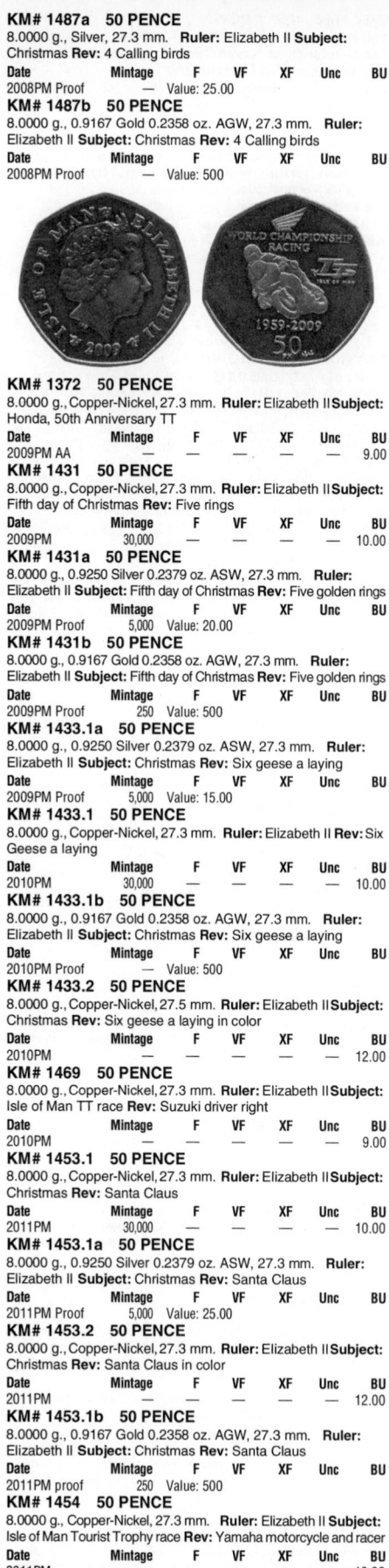

KM# 1372 50 PENCE
8.0000 g., Copper-Nickel, 27.3 mm. **Ruler:** Elizabeth II **Subject:** Honda, 50th Anniversary TT

Date	Mintage	F	VF	XF	Unc	BU
2009PM AA	—			—	—	9.00

KM# 1431 50 PENCE
8.0000 g., Copper-Nickel, 27.3 mm. **Ruler:** Elizabeth II **Subject:** Fifth day of Christmas **Rev:** Five rings

Date	Mintage	F	VF	XF	Unc	BU
2009PM	30,000			—	—	10.00

KM# 1431a 50 PENCE
8.0000 g., 0.9250 Silver 0.2379 oz. ASW, 27.3 mm. **Ruler:** Elizabeth II **Subject:** Fifth day of Christmas **Rev:** Five golden rings

Date	Mintage	F	VF	XF	Unc	BU
2009PM Proof	5,000	Value: 20.00				

KM# 1431b 50 PENCE
8.0000 g., 0.9167 Gold 0.2358 oz. AGW, 27.3 mm. **Ruler:** Elizabeth II **Subject:** Fifth day of Christmas **Rev:** Five golden rings

Date	Mintage	F	VF	XF	Unc	BU
2009PM Proof	250	Value: 500				

KM# 1433.1a 50 PENCE
8.0000 g., 0.9250 Silver 0.2379 oz. ASW, 27.3 mm. **Ruler:** Elizabeth II **Subject:** Christmas **Rev:** Six geese a laying

Date	Mintage	F	VF	XF	Unc	BU
2009PM Proof	5,000	Value: 15.00				

KM# 1433.1 50 PENCE
8.0000 g., Copper-Nickel, 27.3 mm. **Ruler:** Elizabeth II **Rev:** Six Geese a laying

Date	Mintage	F	VF	XF	Unc	BU
2010PM	30,000			—	—	10.00

KM# 1433.1b 50 PENCE
8.0000 g., 0.9167 Gold 0.2358 oz. AGW, 27.3 mm. **Ruler:** Elizabeth II **Subject:** Christmas **Rev:** Six geese a laying

Date	Mintage	F	VF	XF	Unc	BU
2010PM Proof	—	Value: 500				

KM# 1433.2 50 PENCE
8.0000 g., Copper-Nickel, 27.5 mm. **Ruler:** Elizabeth II **Subject:** Christmas **Rev:** Six geese a laying in color

Date	Mintage	F	VF	XF	Unc	BU
2010PM	—			—	—	12.00

KM# 1469 50 PENCE
8.0000 g., Copper-Nickel, 27.3 mm. **Ruler:** Elizabeth II **Subject:** Isle of Man TT race **Rev:** Suzuki driver right

Date	Mintage	F	VF	XF	Unc	BU
2010PM	—			—	—	9.00

KM# 1453.1 50 PENCE
8.0000 g., Copper-Nickel, 27.3 mm. **Ruler:** Elizabeth II **Subject:** Christmas **Rev:** Santa Claus

Date	Mintage	F	VF	XF	Unc	BU
2011PM	30,000			—	—	10.00

KM# 1453.1a 50 PENCE
8.0000 g., 0.9250 Silver 0.2379 oz. ASW, 27.3 mm. **Ruler:** Elizabeth II **Subject:** Christmas **Rev:** Santa Claus

Date	Mintage	F	VF	XF	Unc	BU
2011PM Proof	5,000	Value: 25.00				

KM# 1453.2 50 PENCE
8.0000 g., Copper-Nickel, 27.3 mm. **Ruler:** Elizabeth II **Subject:** Christmas **Rev:** Santa Claus in color

Date	Mintage	F	VF	XF	Unc	BU
2011PM	—			—	—	12.00

KM# 1453.1b 50 PENCE
8.0000 g., 0.9167 Gold 0.2358 oz. AGW, 27.3 mm. **Ruler:** Elizabeth II **Subject:** Christmas **Rev:** Santa Claus

Date	Mintage	F	VF	XF	Unc	BU
2011PM proof	250	Value: 500				

KM# 1454 50 PENCE
8.0000 g., Copper-Nickel, 27.3 mm. **Ruler:** Elizabeth II **Subject:** Isle of Man Tourist Trophy race **Rev:** Yamaha motorcycle and racer

Date	Mintage	F	VF	XF	Unc	BU
2011PM	—			—	—	10.00

KM# 1454a 50 PENCE
8.0000 g., 0.9250 Silver 0.2379 oz. ASW, 27.3 mm. **Ruler:** Elizabeth II **Subject:** Isle of Man Tourist Trophy race **Rev:** Yamaha motorcycle and racer

Date	Mintage	F	VF	XF	Unc	BU
2011PM Proof	5,000	Value: 25.00				

KM# 1128 60 PENCE
Bi-Metallic Bronze finished base metal with a silver finished rotator on reverse., 38.6 mm. **Ruler:** Elizabeth II **Subject:** Euro Currency Converter **Obv:** Head with tiara right **Rev:** Rotating map with cut out arrow revealing the Euro equivalent of the country's currency to which the arrow is pointed **Edge:** Reeded

Date	Mintage	F	VF	XF	Unc	BU
2002	15,000			—	20.00	22.50

KM# 1042 POUND
9.5000 g., Brass, 22.5 mm. **Ruler:** Elizabeth II **Subject:** Millennium Bells **Obv:** Head with tiara right **Rev:** Triskeles and three bells **Edge:** Reeded and plain sections

Date	Mintage	F	VF	XF	Unc	BU
2001PM AA	—			—	4.00	5.00
2002PM AA	—			—	4.00	5.00
2003PM AA	—			—	4.00	5.00
2003PM BA	—			—	4.00	5.00

KM# 1259 POUND
9.5000 g., Nickel-Brass, 22.5 mm. **Ruler:** Elizabeth II **Obv:** Head with tiara right **Rev:** St. John's Chapel **Edge:** Reeded and Plain Sections

Date	Mintage	F	VF	XF	Unc	BU
2004PM	—			—	4.00	5.00
2004PM AA	—			—	4.00	5.00
2004PM AB	—			—	4.00	5.00
2004PM AC	—			—	4.00	5.00
2005PM AA	—			—	4.00	5.00
2005PM AB	—			—	4.00	5.00
2006PM AA	—			—	4.00	5.00
2006PM AB	—			—	4.00	5.00
2007PM AA	—			—	4.00	5.00
2007PM BA	—			—	4.00	5.00
2007PM AB	—			—	4.00	5.00
2008PM AA	—			—	4.00	5.00
2008PM BA	—			—	4.00	5.00
2009PM AA	—			—	4.00	5.00
2010PM AA	—			—	4.00	5.00
2011PM AA	—			—	4.00	5.00

KM# 1043 2 POUNDS
12.0000 g., Bi-Metallic Copper-Nickel center in Brass ring, 28.4 mm. **Ruler:** Elizabeth II **Subject:** Thorwald's Cross **Obv:** Head with tiara right within beaded circle **Rev:** Ancient drawing within circle **Edge:** Reeded

Date	Mintage	F	VF	XF	Unc	BU
2001PM AA	—			—	6.50	7.50
2002PM AA	—			—	6.50	7.50
2003PM AA	—			—	6.50	7.50
2003PM AB	—			—	6.50	7.50

KM# 1260   2 POUNDS
12.0000 g., Bi-Metallic Copper-Nickel center in Nickel-Brass ring, 28.4 mm.   **Ruler:** Elizabeth II **Obv:** Head with tiara right **Rev:** Round Tower of Peel Castle **Edge:** Reeded

Date	Mintage	F	VF	XF	Unc	BU
2004PM AA	—	—	—	—	6.50	7.50
2005PM AA	—	—	—	—	6.50	7.50
2006PM AA	—	—	—	—	6.50	7.50
2007PM AA	—	—	—	—	6.50	7.50
2007PM AB	—	—	—	—	6.50	7.50
2008PM AA	—	—	—	—	6.50	7.50
2009PM AA	—	—	—	—	6.50	7.50
2010PM AA	—	—	—	—	6.50	7.50
2011PM AA	—	—	—	—	6.50	7.50

KM# 1476   2 POUNDS
12.0000 g., Bi-Metallic Copper-Nickel center in Brass ring, 28.4 mm.   **Ruler:** Elizabeth II **Obv:** Head with tiara right **Rev:** Furry mascot and games logo

Date	Mintage	F	VF	XF	Unc	BU
2011PM	—	—	—	—	6.00	7.50

KM# 1044   5 POUNDS
20.1000 g., Virenium, 36.5 mm.   **Ruler:** Elizabeth II **Subject:** St. Patrick's Hymn **Obv:** Head with tiara right **Rev:** Stylized cross design **Edge:** Segmented reeding

Date	Mintage	F	VF	XF	Unc	BU
2001PM AA	—	—	—	—	15.00	16.50
2002PM AA	—	—	—	—	15.00	16.50
2003PM AA	—	—	—	—	15.00	16.50

KM# 1261   5 POUNDS
20.1000 g., Virenium, 36 mm.   **Ruler:** Elizabeth II **Obv:** Head with tiara right **Rev:** Laxey Wheel **Edge:** Reeded

Date	Mintage	F	VF	XF	Unc	BU
2004PM AA	—	—	—	—	15.00	16.50
2005PM AA	—	—	—	—	15.00	16.50
2006PM AA	—	—	—	—	15.00	16.50
2007PM AA	—	—	—	—	15.00	16.50
2007PM AB	—	—	—	—	15.00	16.50

CROWN SERIES

KM# 1472   1/64 CROWN
0.4860 g., 0.9999 Gold 0.0156 oz. AGW   **Ruler:** Elizabeth II **Obv:** Bust in tiara right **Rev:** Buckingham Palace

Date	Mintage	F	VF	XF	Unc	BU
2010PM Proof	—	Value: 50.00				

KM# 1129   1/32 CROWN
1.0000 g., 0.9720 Gold 0.0312 oz. AGW, 9.8 mm.   **Ruler:** Elizabeth II **Subject:** Queen's Golden Jubilee **Obv:** Head with tiara right **Rev:** Seated crowned Queen holding sceptre at her coronation **Edge:** Plain

Date	Mintage	F	VF	XF	Unc	BU
2002 Prooflike	—	—	—	—	—	57.50

KM# 1058   1/25 CROWN
1.2440 g., 0.9999 Gold 0.0400 oz. AGW, 13.92 mm.   **Ruler:** Elizabeth II **Subject:** Year of the Snake **Obv:** Bust with tiara right **Rev:** Snake **Edge:** Reeded

Date	Mintage	F	VF	XF	Unc	BU
2001 Proof	20,000	Value: 75.00				

KM# 1067   1/25 CROWN
1.2440 g., 0.9999 Gold 0.0400 oz. AGW, 13.9 mm.   **Ruler:** Elizabeth II **Subject:** Somali Kittens **Obv:** Head with tiara right **Rev:** Two kittens **Edge:** Reeded

Date	Mintage	F	VF	XF	Unc	BU
2001	—	—	—	—	—	72.50
2001 Proof	1,000	Value: 75.00				

KM# 1067a   1/25 CROWN
1.2441 g., 0.9995 Platinum 0.0400 oz. APW, 13.9 mm.   **Ruler:** Elizabeth II **Subject:** Somali Kittens **Obv:** Head with tiara right **Rev:** Two kittens **Edge:** Reeded

Date	Mintage	F	VF	XF	Unc	BU
2001	—	—	—	—	—	80.00

KM# 1086   1/25 CROWN
1.2441 g., 0.9999 Gold 0.0400 oz. AGW, 13.9 mm.   **Ruler:** Elizabeth II **Subject:** Harry Potter **Obv:** Bust with tiara right **Rev:** Boy with magic wand **Edge:** Reeded

Date	Mintage	F	VF	XF	Unc	BU
2001 Proof	10,000	Value: 75.00				

KM# 1088   1/25 CROWN
1.2441 g., 0.9999 Gold 0.0400 oz. AGW, 13.9 mm.   **Ruler:** Elizabeth II **Series:** Harry Potter **Subject:** Journey to Hogwarts School **Obv:** Bust with tiara right **Rev:** Boat full of children going to Hogwarts School **Edge:** Reeded

Date	Mintage	F	VF	XF	Unc	BU
2001 Proof	10,000	Value: 75.00				

KM# 1090   1/25 CROWN
1.2441 g., 0.9999 Gold 0.0400 oz. AGW, 13.9 mm.   **Ruler:** Elizabeth II **Series:** Harry Potter **Subject:** First Quidditch Match **Obv:** Bust with tiara right **Rev:** Harry flying a broom **Edge:** Reeded

Date	Mintage	F	VF	XF	Unc	BU
2001 Proof	10,000	Value: 75.00				

KM# 1092   1/25 CROWN
1.2441 g., 0.9999 Gold 0.0400 oz. AGW, 13.9 mm.   **Ruler:** Elizabeth II **Series:** Harry Potter **Subject:** Birth of Norbert **Obv:** Bust with tiara right **Edge:** Reeded

Date	Mintage	F	VF	XF	Unc	BU
2001 Proof	10,000	Value: 75.00				

KM# 1094   1/25 CROWN
1.2441 g., 0.9999 Gold 0.0400 oz. AGW, 13.9 mm.   **Ruler:** Elizabeth II **Series:** Harry Potter **Subject:** School **Obv:** Bust with tiara right **Rev:** Harry in Potions class **Edge:** Reeded

Date	Mintage	F	VF	XF	Unc	BU
2001 Proof	10,000	Value: 75.00				

KM# 1096   1/25 CROWN
1.2441 g., 0.9999 Gold 0.0400 oz. AGW, 13.9 mm.   **Ruler:** Elizabeth II **Series:** Harry Potter **Subject:** Keys **Obv:** Bust with tiara right **Rev:** Harry chasing the golden snitch **Edge:** Reeded

Date	Mintage	F	VF	XF	Unc	BU
2001 Proof	10,000	Value: 75.00				

KM# 1098   1/25 CROWN
1.2441 g., 0.9999 Gold 0.0400 oz. AGW, 13.9 mm.   **Ruler:** Elizabeth II **Subject:** Year of the Horse **Obv:** Bust with tiara right **Rev:** Two horses **Edge:** Reeded

Date	Mintage	F	VF	XF	Unc	BU
2002 Proof	20,000	Value: 75.00				

KM# 1107   1/25 CROWN
1.2440 g., 0.9990 Gold 0.0400 oz. AGW, 13.92 mm.   **Ruler:** Elizabeth II **Subject:** Bengal Cat **Obv:** Head with tiara right **Rev:** Cat and kitten **Edge:** Reeded

Date	Mintage	F	VF	XF	Unc	BU
2002	—	—	—	—	—	65.00
2002 Proof	1,000	Value: 75.00				

KM# 1107a   1/25 CROWN
1.2440 g., 0.9990 Platinum 0.0400 oz. APW, 13.92 mm.   **Ruler:** Elizabeth II **Subject:** Bengal Cat **Obv:** Head with tiara right **Rev:** Cat and kitten **Edge:** Reeded

Date	Mintage	F	VF	XF	Unc	BU
2002 Proof	—	Value: 85.00				

KM# 1145   1/25 CROWN
1.2440 g., 0.9999 Gold 0.0400 oz. AGW, 13.92 mm.   **Ruler:** Elizabeth II **Subject:** Harry Potter Series **Obv:** Bust with tiara right **Rev:** Harry and friends making Polyjuice potion **Edge:** Reeded

Date	Mintage	F	VF	XF	Unc	BU
2002PM Proof	10,000	Value: 75.00				

KM# 1143   1/25 CROWN
1.2440 g., 0.9999 Gold 0.0400 oz. AGW, 13.92 mm.   **Ruler:** Elizabeth II **Subject:** Harry Potter **Obv:** Bust with tiara right **Rev:** Tom Riddle twirling Harry's magic wand **Edge:** Reeded

Date	Mintage	F	VF	XF	Unc	BU
2002PM Proof	10,000	Value: 75.00				

KM# 1147   1/25 CROWN
1.2440 g., 0.9999 Gold 0.0400 oz. AGW   **Ruler:** Elizabeth II **Subject:** Harry Potter **Obv:** Bust with tiara right **Rev:** Harry arrives at the Burrow in a flying car **Edge:** Reeded

Date	Mintage	F	VF	XF	Unc	BU
2002PM Proof	10,000	Value: 75.00				

KM# 1149   1/25 CROWN
1.2440 g., 0.9999 Gold 0.0400 oz. AGW, 13.92 mm.   **Ruler:** Elizabeth II **Subject:** Harry Potter Series **Obv:** Bust with tiara right **Rev:** Harry retrieves Gryffindor sword from snake **Edge:** Reeded

Date	Mintage	F	VF	XF	Unc	BU
2002PM Proof	10,000	Value: 75.00				

KM# 1151   1/25 CROWN
1.2240 g., 0.9999 Gold 0.0393 oz. AGW, 13.92 mm.   **Ruler:** Elizabeth II **Series:** Harry Potter **Obv:** Bust with tiara right **Rev:** Harry and Ron encounter the spider Aragog **Edge:** Reeded

Date	Mintage	F	VF	XF	Unc	BU
2002PM Proof	10,000	Value: 75.00				

KM# 1153   1/25 CROWN
1.2440 g., 0.9999 Gold 0.0400 oz. AGW, 13.92 mm.   **Ruler:** Elizabeth II **Series:** Harry Potter **Obv:** Bust with tiara right **Rev:** Harry in hospital **Edge:** Reeded

Date	Mintage	F	VF	XF	Unc	BU
2002PM Proof	10,000	Value: 75.00				

KM# 1186   1/25 CROWN
1.2440 g., 0.9999 Gold 0.0400 oz. AGW, 13.9 mm.   **Ruler:** Elizabeth II **Subject:** Lord of the Rings **Obv:** Bust with tiara right **Rev:** Frodo Baggins with short sword **Edge:** Reeded

Date	Mintage	F	VF	XF	Unc	BU
2003PM Proof	6,000	Value: 75.00				

KM# 1161   1/25 CROWN
1.2440 g., 0.9999 Gold 0.0400 oz. AGW, 13.92 mm.   **Ruler:** Elizabeth II **Subject:** Cat **Obv:** Head with tiara right **Rev:** Two Balinese kittens **Edge:** Reeded

Date	Mintage	F	VF	XF	Unc	BU
2003PM	—	—	—	—	—	65.00
2003PM Proof	—	Value: 75.00				

KM# 1161a   1/25 CROWN
1.2440 g., 0.9995 Platinum 0.0400 oz. APW, 13.92 mm.   **Ruler:** Elizabeth II **Subject:** Cat **Obv:** Head with tiara right **Rev:** Two Balinese kittens **Edge:** Reeded

Date	Mintage	F	VF	XF	Unc	BU
2003PM Proof	—	Value: 85.00				

KM# 1167   1/25 CROWN
1.2441 g., 0.9999 Gold 0.0400 oz. AGW, 13.9 mm.   **Ruler:** Elizabeth II **Subject:** Year of the Goat **Obv:** Head with tiara right **Rev:** Three goats **Edge:** Reeded

Date	Mintage	F	VF	XF	Unc	BU
2003PM Proof	20,000	Value: 75.00				

KM# 1203   1/25 CROWN
1.2440 g., 0.9999 Gold 0.0400 oz. AGW, 14 mm.   **Ruler:** Elizabeth II **Obv:** Bust with tiara right **Rev:** Harry Potter and patron fighting off a spectre **Edge:** Reeded

Date	Mintage	F	VF	XF	Unc	BU
2004PM Proof	2,500	Value: 75.00				

KM# 1205   1/25 CROWN
1.2440 g., 0.9999 Gold 0.0400 oz. AGW, 14 mm.   **Ruler:** Elizabeth II **Obv:** Bust with tiara right **Rev:** Harry Potter in the shrieking shack **Edge:** Reeded

Date	Mintage	F	VF	XF	Unc	BU
2004PM Proof	2,500	Value: 75.00				

KM# 1207   1/25 CROWN
1.2440 g., 0.9999 Gold 0.0400 oz. AGW, 14 mm.   **Ruler:** Elizabeth II **Obv:** Bust with tiara right **Rev:** Harry Potter and Professor Dumbledore **Edge:** Reeded

Date	Mintage	F	VF	XF	Unc	BU
2004PM Proof	2,500	Value: 75.00				

KM# 1209   1/25 CROWN
1.2440 g., 0.9999 Gold 0.0400 oz. AGW, 14 mm.   **Ruler:** Elizabeth II **Obv:** Bust with tiara right **Rev:** Sirius Black on flying griffin **Edge:** Reeded

Date	Mintage	F	VF	XF	Unc	BU
2004PM Proof	2,500	Value: 75.00				

KM# 1211   1/25 CROWN
1.2440 g., 0.9999 Gold 0.0400 oz. AGW, 14 mm.   **Ruler:** Elizabeth II **Obv:** Head with tiara right **Rev:** Three Olympic Swimmers **Edge:** Reeded

Date	Mintage	F	VF	XF	Unc	BU
2004PM Proof	5,000	Value: 75.00				

KM# 1213   1/25 CROWN
1.2440 g., 0.9999 Gold 0.0400 oz. AGW, 14 mm.   **Ruler:** Elizabeth II **Obv:** Head with tiara right **Rev:** Three Olympic Cyclists **Edge:** Reeded

Date	Mintage	F	VF	XF	Unc	BU
2004PM Proof	5,000	Value: 75.00				

KM# 1215   1/25 CROWN
1.2440 g., 0.9999 Gold 0.0400 oz. AGW, 14 mm.   **Ruler:** Elizabeth II **Obv:** Head with tiara right **Rev:** Three Olympic Runners **Edge:** Reeded

Date	Mintage	F	VF	XF	Unc	BU
2004PM Proof	5,000	Value: 75.00				

KM# 1217   1/25 CROWN
1.2440 g., 0.9999 Gold 0.0400 oz. AGW, 14 mm.   **Ruler:** Elizabeth II **Obv:** Head with tiara right **Rev:** Three Olympic Sail Boarders **Edge:** Reeded

Date	Mintage	F	VF	XF	Unc	BU
2004PM Proof	5,000	Value: 75.00				

KM# 1240   1/25 CROWN
1.2440 g., 0.9999 Gold 0.0400 oz. AGW, 14 mm.   **Ruler:** Elizabeth II **Obv:** Head with tiara right **Rev:** Monkey **Edge:** Reeded

Date	Mintage	F	VF	XF	Unc	BU
2004PM Proof	20,000	Value: 75.00				

KM# 1247   1/25 CROWN
1.2440 g., 0.9999 Gold 0.0400 oz. AGW, 14 mm.   **Ruler:** Elizabeth II **Obv:** Head with tiara right **Rev:** Two Tonkinese cats **Edge:** Reeded

Date	Mintage	F	VF	XF	Unc	BU
2004PM	—	—	—	—	—	65.00
2004PM Proof	1,000	Value: 75.00				

KM# 1269   1/25 CROWN
1.2440 g., 0.9999 Gold 0.0400 oz. AGW, 13.92 mm.   **Ruler:** Elizabeth II **Obv:** Bust with tiara right **Rev:** Himalayan cat and two kittens **Edge:** Reeded

Date	Mintage	F	VF	XF	Unc	BU
2005PM Proof	—	Value: 75.00				

KM# 1269a 1/25 CROWN
1.2440 g., 0.9950 Platinum 0.0398 oz. APW, 13.92 mm. Ruler: Elizabeth II Obv: Bust with tiara right Rev: Himalayan cat and two kittens Edge: Reeded

Date	Mintage	F	VF	XF	Unc	BU
2005PM Proof	— Value: 85.00					

KM# 1340 1/25 CROWN
1.2441 g., 0.9999 Gold 0.0400 oz. AGW Ruler: Elizabeth II Obv: Bust with tiara right Rev: Three Exotic Shorthair cats sitting facing Edge: Reeded

Date	Mintage	F	VF	XF	Unc	BU
2006PM	—	—	—	—	—	72.50

KM# 1343 1/25 CROWN
1.2441 g., 0.9999 Gold 0.0400 oz. AGW Ruler: Elizabeth II Obv: Bust with tiara right Obv. Legend: ELIZABETH II - ISLE OF MAN Rev: Ragdoll cat with two kittens sitting facing Edge: Reeded

Date	Mintage	F	VF	XF	Unc	BU
2007PM	—	—	—	—	—	72.00

KM# 1349 1/25 CROWN
1.2440 g., 0.9999 Gold 0.0400 oz. AGW Ruler: Elizabeth II Subject: The Tale of Peter Rabbit Obv: Bust with tiara right Obv. Legend: ELIZABETH II - ISLE OF MAN Rev: Peter walking with friends Edge: Reeded

Date	Mintage	F	VF	XF	Unc	BU
2007PM	—	—	—	—	—	72.50

KM# 1308 1/25 CROWN
1.2441 g., 0.9999 Gold 0.0400 oz. AGW Ruler: Elizabeth II Subject: 100th Anniversary of Scouting Obv: Bust with tiara right Obv. Legend: ELIZABETH II - ISLE OF MAN Rev: 3/4 length figure of Robert Baden-Powell standing facing 3/4 left, Fleur-de-lys below, images of scouting at left and right Rev. Legend: CENTENARY OF SCOUTING Edge: Reeded

Date	Mintage	F	VF	XF	Unc	BU
2007PM Proof	— Value: 75.00					

KM# 1314 1/25 CROWN
1.2400 g., 0.9999 Gold 0.0399 oz. AGW, 13.92 mm. Ruler: Elizabeth II Obv: Bust with tiara right Obv. Legend: ELIZABETH II - ISLE OF MAN Rev: Two swans facing Edge: Reeded

Date	Mintage	F	VF	XF	Unc	BU
2007 Proof	10,000 Value: 75.00					

KM# 1383 1/25 CROWN
1.2400 g., 0.9999 Gold 0.0399 oz. AGW, 13.92 mm. Ruler: Elizabeth II Obv: Bust right Rev: Chinchilla cat and kitten

Date	Mintage	F	VF	XF	Unc	BU
2009	—	—	—	—	—	72.50
2009 Proof	1,000 Value: 75.00					

KM# 1387 1/25 CROWN
1.2400 g., 0.9950 Platinum 0.0397 oz. APW, 13.92 mm. Ruler: Elizabeth II Obv: Bust right Rev: Chinchilla cat and kitten

Date	Mintage	F	VF	XF	Unc	BU
2009	—	—	—	—	—	85.00

KM# 1473 1/25 CROWN
1.2400 g., 0.9999 Gold 0.0398 oz. AGW Ruler: Elizabeth II Subject: George F. Handel, 325th Anniversary of Birth Obv: Bust in tiara right Rev: Handel bust, music score in background

Date	Mintage	F	VF	XF	Unc	BU
2010PM Proof	— Value: 100					

KM# 1435 1/25 CROWN
1.2400 g., 0.9999 Gold 0.0398 oz. AGW, 13.92 mm. Ruler: Elizabeth II Subject: Turkish Angora cat

Date	Mintage	F	VF	XF	Unc	BU
2011PM	—	—	—	—	—	100
2011PM Proof	1,000 Value: 115					

KM# 1059 1/10 CROWN
3.1100 g., 0.9999 Gold 0.1000 oz. AGW, 17.95 mm. Ruler: Elizabeth II Subject: Year of the Snake Obv: Bust with tiara right Rev: Snake Edge: Reeded

Date	Mintage	F	VF	XF	Unc	BU
2001 Proof	15,000 Value: 180					

KM# 1068 1/10 CROWN
3.1100 g., 0.9999 Gold 0.1000 oz. AGW, 18 mm. Ruler: Elizabeth II Obv: Head with tiara right Rev: Somali kittens Edge: Reeded

Date	Mintage	F	VF	XF	Unc	BU
2001	—	—	—	—	—	175
2001 Proof	1,000 Value: 180					

KM# 1068a 1/10 CROWN
3.1100 g., 0.9995 Platinum 0.0999 oz. APW, 18 mm. Ruler: Elizabeth II Obv: Head with tiara right Rev: Somali kittens Edge: Reeded

Date	Mintage	F	VF	XF	Unc	BU
2001 Proof	— Value: 200					

KM# 1328 1/10 CROWN
3.1100 g., 0.9990 Gold 0.0999 oz. AGW Ruler: Elizabeth II Subject: Harry Potter Obv: Bust right Rev: Boy with magic wand Edge: Reeded

Date	Mintage	F	VF	XF	Unc	BU
2001 Proof	7,500 Value: 180					

KM# 1329 1/10 CROWN
3.1100 g., 0.9990 Gold 0.0999 oz. AGW Ruler: Elizabeth II Subject: Harry Potter - Journey to Hogwarts Obv: Bust right Rev: Boat full of children going to Hogwarts School Edge: Reeded

Date	Mintage	F	VF	XF	Unc	BU
2001 Proof	7,500 Value: 180					

KM# 1330 1/10 CROWN
3.1100 g., 0.9990 Gold 0.0999 oz. AGW Ruler: Elizabeth II Subject: Harry Potter Obv: Bust right Rev: Harry flying on a broomstick Edge: Reeded

Date	Mintage	F	VF	XF	Unc	BU
2001 Proof	7,500 Value: 180					

KM# 1331 1/10 CROWN
3.1100 g., 0.9990 Gold 0.0999 oz. AGW Ruler: Elizabeth II Subject: Harry Potter Obv: Bust right Rev: Birth of Norbert the dragon Edge: Reeded

Date	Mintage	F	VF	XF	Unc	BU
2001 Proof	7,500 Value: 180					

KM# 1332 1/10 CROWN
3.1100 g., 0.9990 Gold 0.0999 oz. AGW Ruler: Elizabeth II Subject: Harry Potter Obv: Bust right Rev: Harry in Potions class Edge: Reeded

Date	Mintage	F	VF	XF	Unc	BU
2001 Proof	7,500 Value: 180					

KM# 1333 1/10 CROWN
3.1100 g., 0.9990 Gold 0.0999 oz. AGW Ruler: Elizabeth II Subject: Harry Potter Obv: Bust right Rev: Harry chasing a snitch Edge: Reeded

Date	Mintage	F	VF	XF	Unc	BU
2001 Proof	7,500 Value: 180					

KM# 1099 1/10 CROWN
3.1100 g., 0.9999 Gold 0.1000 oz. AGW, 17.95 mm. Ruler: Elizabeth II Subject: Year of the Horse Obv: Bust with tiara right Rev: Two horses Edge: Reeded

Date	Mintage	F	VF	XF	Unc	BU
2002 Proof	15,000 Value: 180					

KM# 1155 1/10 CROWN
3.1100 g., 0.9990 Gold 0.0999 oz. AGW, 17.95 mm. Ruler: Elizabeth II Subject: Queen's Golden Jubilee Obv: Queen's portrait Rev: Queen on horse Edge: Reeded

Date	Mintage	F	VF	XF	Unc	BU
2002PM Proof	500 Value: 180					

KM# 1108 1/10 CROWN
3.1100 g., 0.9990 Gold 0.0999 oz. AGW, 17.95 mm. Ruler: Elizabeth II Subject: Bengal Cat Obv: Head with tiara right Rev: Cat and kitten Edge: Reeded

Date	Mintage	VG	F	VF	XF	Unc
2002	—					175
2002 Proof	— Value: 180					

KM# 1108a 1/10 CROWN
3.1100 g., 0.9990 Platinum 0.0999 oz. APW, 17.95 mm. Ruler: Elizabeth II Subject: Bengal Cat Obv: Head with tiara right Rev: Cat and kitten Edge: Reeded

Date	Mintage	F	VF	XF	Unc	BU
2002	—	—	—	—	—	190

KM# 1162 1/10 CROWN
3.1100 g., 0.9999 Gold 0.1000 oz. AGW, 17.95 mm. Ruler: Elizabeth II Subject: Cat Obv: Head with tiara right Rev: Two Balinese kittens Edge: Reeded

Date	Mintage	F	VF	XF	Unc	BU
2003PM	—	—	—	—	—	175
2003PM Proof	— Value: 180					

KM# 1162a 1/10 CROWN
3.1100 g., 0.9995 Platinum 0.0999 oz. APW, 17.95 mm. Ruler: Elizabeth II Subject: Cat Obv: Head with tiara right Rev: Two Balinese kittens Edge: Reeded

Date	Mintage	F	VF	XF	Unc	BU
2003PM	—	—	—	—	—	190

KM# 1168 1/10 CROWN
3.1100 g., 0.9999 Gold 0.1000 oz. AGW, 17.95 mm. Ruler: Elizabeth II Subject: Year of the Goat Obv: Bust with tiara right Rev: Three goats Edge: Reeded

Date	Mintage	F	VF	XF	Unc	BU
2003PM Proof	— Value: 180					

KM# 1187 1/10 CROWN
3.1100 g., 0.9999 Gold 0.1000 oz. AGW, 18 mm. Ruler: Elizabeth II Subject: Lord of the Rings Obv: Bust with tiara right Rev: Aragorn with broad sword Edge: Reeded

Date	Mintage	F	VF	XF	Unc	BU
2003PM Proof	4,500 Value: 180					

KM# 1241 1/10 CROWN
3.1100 g., 0.9999 Gold 0.1000 oz. AGW, 18 mm. Ruler: Elizabeth II Obv: Head with tiara right Rev: Monkey Edge: Reeded

Date	Mintage	F	VF	XF	Unc	BU
2004PM Proof	15,000 Value: 180					

KM# 1248 1/10 CROWN
3.1100 g., 0.9999 Gold 0.1000 oz. AGW, 18 mm. Ruler: Elizabeth II Obv: Head with tiara right Rev: Two Tonkinese cats Edge: Reeded

Date	Mintage	F	VF	XF	Unc	BU
2004PM	—	—	—	—	—	150
2004PM Proof	1,000 Value: 180					

KM# 1270 1/10 CROWN
3.1100 g., 0.9999 Gold 0.1000 oz. AGW, 18 mm. Ruler: Elizabeth II Obv: Bust with tiara right Rev: Himalayan cat and two kittens Edge: Reeded

Date	Mintage	F	VF	XF	Unc	BU
2005PM Proof	— Value: 180					

KM# 1270a 1/10 CROWN
3.1100 g., 0.9950 Platinum 0.0995 oz. APW, 18 mm. Ruler: Elizabeth II Obv: Queen Elizabeth II Rev: Himalayan cat and two kittens Edge: Reeded

Date	Mintage	F	VF	XF	Unc	BU
2005PM Proof	— Value: 200					

KM# 1341 1/10 CROWN
3.1100 g., 0.9999 Gold 0.1000 oz. AGW Ruler: Elizabeth II Obv: Bust with tiara right Rev: Three Exotic Shorthair cats sitting facing Edge: Reeded

Date	Mintage	F	VF	XF	Unc	BU
2006PM	—	—	—	—	—	175

KM# 1350 1/10 CROWN
3.1100 g., 0.9999 Gold 0.1000 oz. AGW Ruler: Elizabeth II Subject: The Tale of Peter Rabbit Obv: Bust with tiara right Obv. Legend: ELIZABETH II - ISLE OF MAN Rev: Peter walking with friends Edge: Reeded

Date	Mintage	F	VF	XF	Unc	BU
2007PM	—	—	—	—	—	175

KM# 1344 1/10 CROWN
3.1100 g., 0.9999 Gold 0.1000 oz. AGW Ruler: Elizabeth II Obv: Bust with tiara right Obv. Legend: ELIZABETH II - ISLE OF MAN Rev: Ragdoll cat with two kittens sitting facing Edge: Reeded

Date	Mintage	F	VF	XF	Unc	BU
2007PM	—	—	—	—	—	175

KM# 1382 1/10 CROWN
3.1100 g., 0.9999 Gold 0.1000 oz. AGW, 17.95 mm. Ruler: Elizabeth II Obv: Bust right Rev: Chinchilla cat and kitten

Date	Mintage	F	VF	XF	Unc	BU
2009	—	—	—	—	—	175
2009 Proof	1,000 Value: 180					

KM# 1386 1/10 CROWN
3.1100 g., 0.9950 Platinum 0.0995 oz. APW, 17.95 mm. Ruler: Elizabeth II Obv: Bust right Rev: Chinchilla cat and kitten

Date	Mintage	F	VF	XF	Unc	BU
2009	—	—	—	—	—	190

KM# 1436 1/10 CROWN
3.1100 g., 0.9999 Gold 0.1000 oz. AGW, 17.95 mm. Ruler: Elizabeth II Subject: Turkish Angora Cat

Date	Mintage	F	VF	XF	Unc	BU
2011PM	—	—	—	—	—	225
2011PM Proof	1,000 Value: 240					

KM# 1060 1/5 CROWN
6.2200 g., 0.9999 Gold 0.1999 oz. AGW, 22 mm. Ruler: Elizabeth II Subject: Year of the Snake Obv: Bust with tiara right Rev: Snake Edge: Reeded

Date	Mintage	F	VF	XF	Unc	BU
2001 Proof	12,000 Value: 355					

KM# 1069 1/5 CROWN
6.2200 g., 0.9999 Gold 0.1999 oz. AGW, 22 mm. Ruler: Elizabeth II Obv: Head with tiara right Rev: Two Somali kittens Edge: Reeded

Date	Mintage	F	VF	XF	Unc	BU
2001	—	—	—	—	—	300
2001 Proof	1,000 Value: 355					

KM# 1069a 1/5 CROWN
6.2200 g., 0.9995 Platinum 0.1999 oz. APW, 22 mm. Ruler: Elizabeth II Obv: Head with tiara right Rev: Somali kittens Edge: Reeded

Date	Mintage	F	VF	XF	Unc	BU
2001	—	—	—	—	—	400

KM# 1074 1/5 CROWN
6.2200 g., 0.9999 Gold 0.1999 oz. AGW, 22 mm. Ruler: Elizabeth II Subject: Queen Mother Obv: Head with tiara right Rev: 1948 Silver wedding anniversary Edge: Reeded

Date	Mintage	F	VF	XF	Unc	BU
2001 Proof	5,000 Value: 355					

KM# 1075 1/5 CROWN
6.2200 g., 0.9999 Gold 0.1999 oz. AGW, 22 mm. Ruler: Elizabeth II Subject: Queen Mother Obv: Head with tiara right Rev: 1948 holding baby Prince Charles Edge: Reeded

Date	Mintage	F	VF	XF	Unc	BU
2001 Proof	5,000 Value: 300					

KM# 1078 1/5 CROWN
6.2200 g., 0.9999 Gold 0.1999 oz. AGW, 22 mm. Ruler: Elizabeth II Subject: Martin Frobisher Obv: Head with tiara right Rev: Portrait, ship and map Edge: Reeded

Date	Mintage	F	VF	XF	Unc	BU
2001 Proof	5,000 Value: 355					

KM# 1079 1/5 CROWN
6.2200 g., 0.9999 Gold 0.1999 oz. AGW, 22 mm. Ruler: Elizabeth II Subject: Ronald Amundsen Obv: Head with tiara right Rev: Portrait, ship and dirigible Edge: Reeded

Date	Mintage	F	VF	XF	Unc	BU
2001 Proof	5,000 Value: 355					

KM# 1082 1/5 CROWN
6.2200 g., 0.9999 Gold 0.1999 oz. AGW, 22 mm. Ruler: Elizabeth II Subject: Queen's 75th Birthday Obv: Head with tiara right Rev: Flower bouquet with a tiny diamond mounted on the bow of the ribbon Edge: Reeded

Date	Mintage	F	VF	XF	Unc	BU
2001 Proof	2,000 Value: 355					

KM# 1339 1/5 CROWN
6.1500 g., 0.9990 Gold 0.1975 oz. AGW, 21.78 mm. Ruler:

Elizabeth II **Subject:** Harry Potter **Obv:** Bust right **Rev:** Harry chasing a jeweled snitch **Edge:** Reeded

Date	Mintage	F	VF	XF	Unc	BU
2001 Proof	5,000	Value: 355				

KM# 1334   1/5 CROWN
6.1500 g., 0.9990 Gold 0.1975 oz. AGW, 21.78 mm. **Ruler:** Elizabeth II **Subject:** Harry Potter **Obv:** Bust right **Rev:** Harry with magic wand **Edge:** Reeded

Date	Mintage	F	VF	XF	Unc	BU
2001 Proof	5,000	Value: 355				

KM# 1335   1/5 CROWN
6.1500 g., 0.9990 Gold 0.1975 oz. AGW, 21.78 mm. **Ruler:** Elizabeth II **Subject:** Harry Potter - Journey to Hogwarts School **Obv:** Bust right **Rev:** Boat full of children going to Hogwarts School **Edge:** Reeded

Date	Mintage	F	VF	XF	Unc	BU
2001 Proof	5,000	Value: 355				

KM# 1336   1/5 CROWN
6.1500 g., 0.9990 Gold 0.1975 oz. AGW, 21.78 mm. **Ruler:** Elizabeth II **Subject:** Harry Potter - First Quidditch Match **Obv:** Bust right **Rev:** Harry flying a broom in a quidditch match **Edge:** Reeded

Date	Mintage	F	VF	XF	Unc	BU
2001 Proof	5,000	Value: 355				

KM# 1337   1/5 CROWN
6.1500 g., 0.9990 Gold 0.1975 oz. AGW, 21.78 mm. **Ruler:** Elizabeth II **Subject:** Harry Potter **Obv:** Bust right **Rev:** Birth of Norbert, the dragon **Edge:** Reeded

Date	Mintage	F	VF	XF	Unc	BU
2001 Proof	5,000	Value: 355				

KM# 1338   1/5 CROWN
6.1500 g., 0.9990 Gold 0.1975 oz. AGW, 21.78 mm. **Ruler:** Elizabeth II **Subject:** Harry Potter **Obv:** Bust right **Rev:** Harry in Potions class **Edge:** Reeded

Date	Mintage	F	VF	XF	Unc	BU
2001 Proof	5,000	Value: 355				

KM# 1156   1/5 CROWN
6.2200 g., 0.9990 Gold 0.1998 oz. AGW, 22 mm. **Ruler:** Elizabeth II **Subject:** Queen's Golden Jubilee **Obv:** Queen's portrait **Rev:** Queen on horse **Edge:** Reeded

Date	Mintage	F	VF	XF	Unc	BU
2002PM Proof	500	Value: 355				

KM# 1117   1/5 CROWN
6.2200 g., 0.9990 Gold 0.1998 oz. AGW, 22 mm. **Ruler:** Elizabeth II **Subject:** Queen Mother's Love of Horses **Obv:** Bust with tiara right **Rev:** Queen Mother and horse **Edge:** Reeded

Date	Mintage	F	VF	XF	Unc	BU
2002 Proof	5,000	Value: 355				

KM# 1109   1/5 CROWN
6.2200 g., 0.9990 Gold 0.1998 oz. AGW, 22 mm. **Ruler:** Elizabeth II **Subject:** Bengal Cat **Obv:** Head with tiara right **Rev:** Cat and kitten **Edge:** Reeded

Date	Mintage	VG	F	VF	XF	Unc
2002	—	—	—	—	—	
2002 Proof	1,000	Value: 355				

KM# 1109a   1/5 CROWN
6.2200 g., 0.9990 Platinum 0.1998 oz. APW, 22 mm. **Ruler:** Elizabeth II **Subject:** Bengal Cat **Obv:** Head with tiara right **Rev:** Cat and kitten **Edge:** Reeded

Date	Mintage	F	VF	XF	Unc	BU
2002	—	—	—	—	—	400

KM# 1100   1/5 CROWN
6.2200 g., 0.9999 Gold 0.1999 oz. AGW, 22 mm. **Ruler:** Elizabeth II **Subject:** Year of the Horse **Obv:** Bust with tiara right **Rev:** Two horses **Edge:** Reeded

Date	Mintage	F	VF	XF	Unc	BU
2002 Proof	12,000	Value: 355				

KM# 1113   1/5 CROWN
6.2200 g., 0.9990 Gold 0.1998 oz. AGW, 22 mm. **Ruler:** Elizabeth II **Subject:** Olympics - Salt Lake City **Obv:** Bust with tiara right **Rev:** Skier, torch and flag **Edge:** Reeded

Date	Mintage	F	VF	XF	Unc	BU
2002 Proof	5,000	Value: 355				

KM# 1114   1/5 CROWN
6.2200 g., 0.9990 Gold 0.1998 oz. AGW **Ruler:** Elizabeth II **Subject:** Olympics - Salt Lake City **Obv:** Bust with tiara right **Rev:** Bobsled, torch and stadium **Edge:** Reeded

Date	Mintage	F	VF	XF	Unc	BU
2002 Proof	5,000	Value: 355				

KM# 1120   1/5 CROWN
6.2200 g., 0.9990 Gold 0.1998 oz. AGW, 22 mm. **Ruler:** Elizabeth II **Subject:** World Cup 2002 Japan - Korea **Obv:** Bust with tiara right **Rev:** Player running right **Edge:** Reeded

Date	Mintage	F	VF	XF	Unc	BU
2002 Proof	5,000	Value: 355				

KM# 1122   1/5 CROWN
6.2200 g., 0.9990 Gold 0.1998 oz. AGW, 22 mm. **Ruler:** Elizabeth II **Subject:** World Cup 2002 Japan - Korea **Obv:** Bust with tiara right **Rev:** Player kicking to right **Edge:** Reeded

Date	Mintage	F	VF	XF	Unc	BU
2002 Proof	5,000	Value: 355				

KM# 1124   1/5 CROWN
6.2200 g., 0.9990 Gold 0.1998 oz. AGW, 22 mm. **Ruler:** Elizabeth II **Subject:** World Cup 2002 Japan - Korea **Obv:** Head with tiara right **Rev:** Player kicking to left **Edge:** Reeded

Date	Mintage	F	VF	XF	Unc	BU
2002 Proof	5,000	Value: 355				

KM# 1126   1/5 CROWN
6.2200 g., 0.9990 Gold 0.1998 oz. AGW, 22 mm. **Ruler:** Elizabeth II **Subject:** World Cup 2002 Japan - Korea **Obv:** Head with tiara right **Rev:** Player running to left **Edge:** Reeded

Date	Mintage	F	VF	XF	Unc	BU
2002 Proof	5,000	Value: 355				

KM# 1130   1/5 CROWN
6.2200 g., 0.3750 Gold 0.0750 oz. AGW, 22 mm. **Ruler:** Elizabeth II **Subject:** Elizabeth II's Golden Jubilee **Obv:** Bust with tiara right **Rev:** Seated crowned Queen holding scepter at her coronation **Edge:** Reeded

Date	Mintage	F	VF	XF	Unc	BU
2002 Proof	2,002	Value: 140				

KM# 1132   1/5 CROWN
6.2200 g., 0.3750 Gold 0.0750 oz. AGW, 22 mm. **Ruler:** Elizabeth II **Subject:** Elizabeth II's Golden Jubilee **Obv:** Bust with tiara right **Rev:** Queen on horse **Edge:** Reeded

Date	Mintage	F	VF	XF	Unc	BU
2002 Proof	2,002	Value: 140				

KM# 1134   1/5 CROWN
6.2200 g., 0.3750 Gold 0.0750 oz. AGW, 22 mm. **Ruler:** Elizabeth II **Subject:** Elizabeth II's Golden Jubilee **Obv:** Head with tiara right **Rev:** Queen with dog **Edge:** Reeded

Date	Mintage	F	VF	XF	Unc	BU
2002 Proof	2,002	Value: 140				

KM# 1136   1/5 CROWN
6.2200 g., 0.3750 Gold 0.0750 oz. AGW, 22 mm. **Ruler:** Elizabeth II **Subject:** Elizabeth II's Golden Jubilee **Obv:** Bust with tiara right **Rev:** Queen at war memorial **Edge:** Reeded

Date	Mintage	F	VF	XF	Unc	BU
2002 Proof	2,002	Value: 140				

KM# 1138   1/5 CROWN
6.2200 g., 0.9990 Gold 0.1998 oz. AGW, 22 mm. **Ruler:** Elizabeth II **Subject:** Queen Mother **Obv:** Bust with tiara right **Rev:** Queen Mother and Castle May **Edge:** Reeded

Date	Mintage	F	VF	XF	Unc	BU
2002 Proof	5,000	Value: 355				

KM# 1140   1/5 CROWN
6.2200 g., 0.9999 Gold 0.1999 oz. AGW, 22 mm. **Ruler:** Elizabeth II **Subject:** Princess Diana **Obv:** Bust with tiara right **Rev:** Diana's portrait **Edge:** Reeded

Date	Mintage	F	VF	XF	Unc	BU
2002 Proof	5,000	Value: 355				

KM# 1163   1/5 CROWN
6.2200 g., 0.9999 Gold 0.1999 oz. AGW, 22 mm. **Ruler:** Elizabeth II **Subject:** Cat **Obv:** Head with tiara right **Rev:** Two Balinese kittens **Edge:** Reeded

Date	Mintage	F	VF	XF	Unc	BU
2003PM	—	—	—	—	—	300
2003PM Proof	—	Value: 355				

KM# 1163a   1/5 CROWN
6.2200 g., 0.9995 Platinum 0.1999 oz. APW, 22 mm. **Ruler:** Elizabeth II **Subject:** Cat **Obv:** Head with tiara right **Rev:** Two Balinese kittens **Edge:** Reeded

Date	Mintage	F	VF	XF	Unc	BU
2003PM	—	—	—	—	—	385

KM# 1169   1/5 CROWN
6.2200 g., 0.9999 Gold 0.1999 oz. AGW, 22 mm. **Ruler:** Elizabeth II **Subject:** Year of the Goat **Obv:** Bust with tiara right **Rev:** Three goats **Edge:** Reeded

Date	Mintage	F	VF	XF	Unc	BU
2003PM Proof	—	Value: 355				

KM# 1175   1/5 CROWN
6.2200 g., 0.9999 Gold 0.1999 oz. AGW, 22 mm. **Ruler:** Elizabeth II **Subject:** Olympics **Obv:** Bust with tiara right **Rev:** Swimmers **Edge:** Reeded

Date	Mintage	F	VF	XF	Unc	BU
2003PM Proof	5,000	Value: 355				

KM# 1177   1/5 CROWN
6.2200 g., 0.9999 Gold 0.1999 oz. AGW, 22 mm. **Ruler:** Elizabeth II **Subject:** Olympics **Obv:** Bust with tiara right **Rev:** Runners **Edge:** Reeded

Date	Mintage	F	VF	XF	Unc	BU
2003PM Proof	5,000	Value: 355				

KM# 1179   1/5 CROWN
6.2200 g., 0.9999 Gold 0.1999 oz. AGW, 22 mm. **Ruler:** Elizabeth II **Subject:** Olympics **Obv:** Bust with tiara right **Rev:** Bicyclists **Edge:** Reeded

Date	Mintage	F	VF	XF	Unc	BU
2003PM Proof	5,000	Value: 355				

KM# 1181   1/5 CROWN
6.2200 g., 0.9999 Gold 0.1999 oz. AGW, 22 mm. **Ruler:** Elizabeth II **Subject:** Olympics **Obv:** Head with tiara right **Rev:** Sail Boarders **Edge:** Reeded

Date	Mintage	F	VF	XF	Unc	BU
2003PM Proof	—	Value: 355				

KM# 1188   1/5 CROWN
6.2200 g., 0.9999 Gold 0.1999 oz. AGW, 22 mm. **Ruler:** Elizabeth II **Subject:** Lord of the Rings **Obv:** Bust with tiara right **Rev:** Legolas with bow and arrow **Edge:** Reeded

Date	Mintage	F	VF	XF	Unc	BU
2003PM Proof	3,500	Value: 355				

KM# 1223   1/5 CROWN
6.2200 g., 0.9999 Gold 0.1999 oz. AGW, 22 mm. **Ruler:** Elizabeth II **Obv:** Bust with tiara right **Rev:** D-Day Invasion Plan Map **Edge:** Reeded

Date	Mintage	F	VF	XF	Unc	BU
2004PM Proof	5,000	Value: 355				

KM# 1225   1/5 CROWN
6.2200 g., 0.9999 Gold 0.1999 oz. AGW, 22 mm. **Ruler:** Elizabeth II **Obv:** Bust with tiara right **Rev:** Victoria Cross and battle scene **Edge:** Reeded

Date	Mintage	F	VF	XF	Unc	BU
2004PM Proof	5,000	Value: 355				

KM# 1227   1/5 CROWN
6.2200 g., 0.9999 Gold 0.1999 oz. AGW, 22 mm. **Ruler:** Elizabeth II **Obv:** Bust with tiara right **Rev:** Silver Star and battle scene **Edge:** Reeded

Date	Mintage	F	VF	XF	Unc	BU
2004PM Proof	5,000	Value: 355				

KM# 1229   1/5 CROWN
6.2200 g., 0.9999 Gold 0.1999 oz. AGW, 22 mm. **Ruler:** Elizabeth II **Obv:** Bust with tiara right **Rev:** George Cross and rescue scene **Edge:** Reeded

Date	Mintage	F	VF	XF	Unc	BU
2004PM Proof	5,000	Value: 355				

KM# 1231   1/5 CROWN
6.2200 g., 0.9999 Gold 0.1999 oz. AGW, 22 mm. **Ruler:** Elizabeth II **Obv:** Bust with tiara right **Rev:** White Rose of Finland Medal and battle scene **Edge:** Reeded

Date	Mintage	F	VF	XF	Unc	BU
2004PM Proof	5,000	Value: 355				

KM# 1233   1/5 CROWN
6.2200 g., 0.9999 Gold 0.1999 oz. AGW, 22 mm. **Ruler:** Elizabeth II **Obv:** Bust with tiara right **Rev:** The Norwegian War Medal and naval battle scene **Edge:** Reeded

Date	Mintage	F	VF	XF	Unc	BU
2004PM Proof	5,000	Value: 355				

KM# 1235   1/5 CROWN
6.2200 g., 0.9999 Gold 0.1999 oz. AGW, 22 mm. **Ruler:** Elizabeth II **Obv:** Bust with tiara right **Rev:** French Croix de Guerre and Partisan battle scene **Edge:** Reeded

Date	Mintage	F	VF	XF	Unc	BU
2004PM Proof	5,000	Value: 355				

KM# 1249.1   1/5 CROWN
6.2200 g., 0.9999 Gold 0.1999 oz. AGW, 22 mm. **Ruler:** Elizabeth II **Obv:** Head with tiara right **Rev:** Two Tonkinese cats **Edge:** Reeded

Date	Mintage	F	VF	XF	Unc	BU
2004PM	—	—	—	—	—	350
2004PM Proof	1,000	Value: 355				

KM# 1249.2   1/5 CROWN
6.2200 g., 0.9999 Gold 0.1999 oz. AGW, 22 mm. **Ruler:** Elizabeth II **Obv:** Head with tiara right **Rev:** Two multicolor Tonkinese cats **Edge:** Reeded

Date	Mintage	F	VF	XF	Unc	BU
2004PM Proof	—	Value: 355				

KM# 1198   1/5 CROWN
6.2200 g., 0.9990 Palladium 0.1998 oz., 22 mm. **Ruler:** Elizabeth II **Subject:** Palladium Bicentennial **Obv:** Head with tiara right **Rev:** Athena **Edge:** Reeded

Date	Mintage	F	VF	XF	Unc	BU
2004PM Proof	999	Value: 150				

KM# 1271   1/5 CROWN
6.2200 g., 0.9999 Gold 0.1999 oz. AGW, 22 mm. **Ruler:** Elizabeth II **Obv:** Bust with tiara right **Rev:** Himalayan cat and two kittens **Edge:** Reeded

Date	Mintage	F	VF	XF	Unc	BU
2005PM Proof	—	Value: 355				

KM# 1271a   1/5 CROWN
6.2200 g., 0.9950 Platinum 0.1990 oz. APW, 22 mm. **Ruler:** Elizabeth II **Obv:** Bust with tiara right **Rev:** Himalayan cat and two kittens **Edge:** Reeded

Date	Mintage	F	VF	XF	Unc	BU
2005PM Proof	—	Value: 390				

KM# 1295   1/5 CROWN
6.2200 g., 0.9999 Gold 0.1999 oz. AGW, 22 mm. **Ruler:** Elizabeth II **Subject:** Battles that Changed the World **Obv:** Elizabeth II **Rev:** Trojan War scene **Edge:** Reeded

Date	Mintage	F	VF	XF	Unc	BU
2006PM Proof	5,000	Value: 355				

KM# 1297   1/5 CROWN
6.2200 g., 0.9999 Gold 0.1999 oz. AGW, 22 mm. **Ruler:** Elizabeth II **Subject:** Battles that Changed the World **Obv:** Elizabeth II **Rev:** Battle of Arbela scene **Edge:** Reeded

Date	Mintage	F	VF	XF	Unc	BU
2006PM Proof	5,000	Value: 355				

KM# 1299   1/5 CROWN
6.2200 g., 0.9999 Gold 0.1999 oz. AGW, 22 mm. **Ruler:** Elizabeth II **Subject:** Battles that Changed the World **Obv:** Elizabeth II **Rev:** Battle of Thapsus scene **Edge:** Reeded

Date	Mintage	F	VF	XF	Unc	BU
2006PM Proof	5,000	Value: 355				

KM# 1301   1/5 CROWN
6.2200 g., 0.9999 Gold 0.1999 oz. AGW, 22 mm. **Ruler:** Elizabeth II **Subject:** Battles that Changed the World **Obv:** Elizabeth II **Rev:** Battle of Cologne scene **Edge:** Reeded

Date	Mintage	F	VF	XF	Unc	BU
2006PM Proof	5,000	Value: 355				

KM# 1303   1/5 CROWN
6.2200 g., 0.9999 Gold 0.1999 oz. AGW, 22 mm. **Ruler:** Elizabeth II **Subject:** Battles that Changed the World **Obv:** Elizabeth II **Rev:** Siege of Valencia scene **Edge:** Reeded

Date	Mintage	F	VF	XF	Unc	BU
2006PM Proof	5,000	Value: 355				

KM# 1305   1/5 CROWN
6.2200 g., 0.9999 Gold 0.1999 oz. AGW, 22 mm. **Ruler:** Elizabeth II **Subject:** Battles that Changed the World **Obv:** Elizabeth II **Rev:** Battle of Agincourt scene **Edge:** Reeded

Date	Mintage	F	VF	XF	Unc	BU
2006PM Proof	5,000	Value: 355				

KM# 1342   1/5 CROWN
6.2200 g., 0.9999 Gold 0.1999 oz. AGW **Ruler:** Elizabeth II **Obv:** Bust with tiara right **Rev:** Three Exotic Shorthair cats sitting facing **Edge:** Reeded

Date	Mintage	F	VF	XF	Unc	BU
2006PM	—	—	—	—	—	350

KM# 1345   1/5 CROWN
6.2200 g., 0.9999 Gold 0.1999 oz. AGW **Ruler:** Elizabeth II **Obv:** Bust with tiara right **Obv. Legend:** ELIZABETH II - ISLE OF MAN **Rev:** Ragdoll cat with two kittens sitting facing **Edge:** Reeded

Date	Mintage	F	VF	XF	Unc	BU
2007PM	—	—	—	—	—	350

KM# 1351.1   1/5 CROWN
6.2200 g., 0.9999 Gold 0.1999 oz. AGW **Ruler:** Elizabeth II **Subject:** The Tale of Peter Rabbit **Obv:** Bust with tiara right **Obv. Legend:** ELIZABETH II - ISLE OF MAN **Rev:** Peter walking with friends **Edge:** Reeded

Date	Mintage	F	VF	XF	Unc	BU
2007PM	—	—	—	—	—	350

KM# 1351.2   1/5 CROWN
6.2200 g., 0.9999 Gold 0.1999 oz. AGW **Ruler:** Elizabeth II **Subject:** The Tale of Peter Rabbit **Obv:** Bust with tiara right **Obv. Legend:** ELIZABETH II - ISLE OF MAN **Rev:** Peter walking with friends **Edge:** Reeded

Date	Mintage	F	VF	XF	Unc	BU
2007PM	—	—	—	—	—	350

KM# 1309   1/5 CROWN
6.2200 g., 0.9999 Gold 0.1999 oz. AGW **Ruler:** Elizabeth II **Subject:** 100th Anniversary of Scouting **Obv:** Bust with tiara right **Obv. Legend:** ELIZABETH II - ISLE OF MAN **Rev:** 3/4 length figure of Robert Baden-Powell standing facing 3/4 left, Fleur-de-lys below, images of scouting at left and right **Rev. Legend:** CENTENARY OF SCOUTING **Edge:** Reeded

Date	Mintage	F	VF	XF	Unc	BU
2007 Proof	—	Value: 355				

KM# 1352   1/5 CROWN
6.2200 g., 0.9999 Gold 0.1999 oz. AGW, 22 mm. **Ruler:** Elizabeth II **Subject:** Prince Charles 60th Birthday **Obv:** Bust with tiara right **Obv. Legend:** ELIZABETH II - ISLE OF MAN **Rev:** Heads of Charles, Princes William and Henry right **Edge:** Reeded

Date	Mintage	F	VF	XF	Unc	BU
2008PM Proof	5,000	Value: 355				

KM# 1375   1/5 CROWN
6.2200 g., 0.9999 Gold 0.1999 oz. AGW, 22 mm. **Ruler:** Elizabeth II **Subject:** Terra Cotta Army **Obv:** Bust right **Rev:** Making of the Soldier

Date	Mintage	F	VF	XF	Unc	BU
2009 Proof	5,000	Value: 355				

KM# 1377   1/5 CROWN
6.2200 g., 0.9999 Gold 0.1999 oz. AGW, 22 mm. **Ruler:** Elizabeth II **Subject:** Terra Cotta Army **Obv:** Bust right **Rev:** Making of the Horse

Date	Mintage	F	VF	XF	Unc	BU
2009 Proof	5,000	Value: 355				

KM# 1381   1/5 CROWN
6.2200 g., 0.9999 Gold 0.1999 oz. AGW **Ruler:** Elizabeth II **Obv:** Bust right **Rev:** Chinchilla cat and kitten

Date	Mintage	F	VF	XF	Unc	BU
2009	—	—	—	—	—	300
2009 Proof	1,000	Value: 355				

KM# 1437   1/5 CROWN
6.2200 g., 0.9999 Gold 0.1999 oz. AGW, 22 mm. **Ruler:** Elizabeth II **Subject:** Turkish Angora Cat

Date	Mintage	F	VF	XF	Unc	BU
2011PM	—	—	—	—	—	400
2011PM Proof	—	Value: 425				

KM# 1385   1/4 CROWN
6.2200 g., 0.9950 Platinum 0.1990 oz. APW, 22 mm. **Ruler:** Elizabeth II **Series:** Bust right **Obv:** Chinchilla cat and kitten

Date	Mintage	F	VF	XF	Unc	BU
2009	—	—	—	—	—	385

KM# 1061   1/2 CROWN
15.5517 g., 0.9999 Gold 0.4999 oz. AGW, 30 mm. **Ruler:** Elizabeth II **Subject:** Year of the Snake **Obv:** Bust with tiara right **Rev:** Snake **Edge:** Reeded

Date	Mintage	F	VF	XF	Unc	BU
2001 Proof	6,000	Value: 875				

KM# 1070   1/2 CROWN
15.5517 g., 0.9999 Gold 0.4999 oz. AGW, 30 mm. **Ruler:** Elizabeth II **Obv:** Head with tiara right **Rev:** Two Somali kittens **Edge:** Reeded

Date	Mintage	F	VF	XF	Unc	BU
2001	—	—	—	—	—	870
2001 Proof	1,000	Value: 875				

KM# 1071   1/2 CROWN
15.5517 g., 0.9995 Platinum 0.4997 oz. APW, 27 mm. **Ruler:** Elizabeth II **Obv:** Head with tiara right **Rev:** Two Somali kittens **Edge:** Reeded

Date	Mintage	F	VF	XF	Unc	BU
2001	—	—	—	—	—	950

KM# 1157   1/2 CROWN
15.5510 g., 0.9990 Gold 0.4995 oz. AGW, 30 mm. **Ruler:** Elizabeth II **Subject:** Queen's Golden Jubilee **Obv:** Queen's portrait **Rev:** Queen on horse **Edge:** Reeded

Date	Mintage	F	VF	XF	Unc	BU
2002PM Proof	500	Value: 875				

KM# 1101   1/2 CROWN
15.5500 g., 0.9999 Gold 0.4999 oz. AGW, 30 mm. **Ruler:** Elizabeth II **Subject:** Year of the Horse **Obv:** Bust with tiara right **Rev:** Two horses **Edge:** Reeded

Date	Mintage	F	VF	XF	Unc	BU
2002 Proof	6,000	Value: 875				

KM# 1110   1/2 CROWN
15.5510 g., 0.9990 Gold 0.4995 oz. AGW, 30 mm. **Ruler:** Elizabeth II **Subject:** Bengal Cat **Obv:** Head with tiara right **Rev:** Cat and kitten **Edge:** Reeded

Date	Mintage	VG	F	VF	XF	Unc
2002	—	—	—	—	—	—
2002 Proof	1,000	Value: 875				

KM# 1110a   1/2 CROWN
6.2200 g., 0.9990 Platinum 0.1998 oz. APW, 30 mm. **Ruler:** Elizabeth II **Subject:** Bengal Cat **Obv:** Head with tiara right **Rev:** Cat and kitten **Edge:** Reeded

Date	Mintage	F	VF	XF	Unc	BU
2002	—	—	—	—	—	390

KM# 1164   1/2 CROWN
15.5510 g., 0.9999 Gold 0.4999 oz. AGW, 30 mm. **Ruler:** Elizabeth II **Subject:** Cat **Obv:** Head with tiara right **Rev:** Two Balinese kittens **Edge:** Reeded

Date	Mintage	F	VF	XF	Unc	BU
2003PM	—	—	—	—	—	870
2003PM Proof	—	Value: 875				

KM# 1164a   1/2 CROWN
15.5510 g., 0.9995 Platinum 0.4997 oz. APW, 30 mm. **Ruler:** Elizabeth II **Subject:** Cat **Obv:** Head with tiara right **Rev:** Two Balinese kittens **Edge:** Reeded

Date	Mintage	F	VF	XF	Unc	BU
2003PM	—	—	—	—	—	950

KM# 1170   1/2 CROWN
15.5500 g., 0.9999 Gold 0.4999 oz. AGW, 30 mm. **Ruler:** Elizabeth II **Subject:** Year of the Goat **Obv:** Bust with tiara right **Rev:** Three goats **Edge:** Reeded

Date	Mintage	F	VF	XF	Unc	BU
2003PM Proof	—	Value: 875				

KM# 1189   1/2 CROWN
15.5510 g., 0.9999 Gold 0.4999 oz. AGW, 30 mm. **Ruler:** Elizabeth II **Subject:** Lord of the Rings **Obv:** Bust with tiara right **Rev:** Gimli with two battle axes **Edge:** Reeded

Date	Mintage	F	VF	XF	Unc	BU
2003PM Proof	1,000	Value: 875				

KM# 1243   1/2 CROWN
15.5520 g., 0.9999 Gold 0.4999 oz. AGW, 30 mm. **Ruler:** Elizabeth II **Obv:** Head with tiara right **Rev:** Monkey **Edge:** Reeded

Date	Mintage	F	VF	XF	Unc	BU
2004PM Proof	6,000	Value: 875				

KM# 1250   1/2 CROWN
15.5520 g., 0.9999 Gold 0.4999 oz. AGW, 30 mm. **Ruler:** Elizabeth II **Obv:** Head with tiara right **Rev:** Two Tonkinese cats **Edge:** Reeded

Date	Mintage	F	VF	XF	Unc	BU
2004PM	—	—	—	—	—	855
2004PM Proof	1,000	Value: 875				

KM# 1199   1/2 CROWN
15.5500 g., 0.9990 Bi-Metallic .999 Palladium 6.3g center in .9999 Gold 9.25 g ring 0.4994 oz., 30 mm. **Ruler:** Elizabeth II **Subject:** Palladium Bicentennial **Obv:** Bust with tiara right **Rev:** Athena **Edge:** Reeded

Date	Mintage	F	VF	XF	Unc	BU
2004PM Proof	500	Value: 1,050				

KM# 1272   1/2 CROWN
15.5510 g., 0.9999 Gold 0.4999 oz. AGW, 27 mm. **Ruler:** Elizabeth II **Obv:** Bust with tiara right **Rev:** Himalayan cat and two kittens **Edge:** Reeded

Date	Mintage	F	VF	XF	Unc	BU
2005PM Proof	—	Value: 875				

KM# 1272a   1/2 CROWN
15.5510 g., 0.9950 Platinum 0.4975 oz. APW, 27 mm. **Ruler:** Elizabeth II **Obv:** Bust with tiara right **Rev:** Himalayan cat and two kittens **Edge:** Reeded

Date	Mintage	F	VF	XF	Unc	BU
2005PM	—	—	—	—	—	950
2005PM Proof	—	Value: 960				

KM# 1346   1/2 CROWN
15.5500 g., 0.9999 Gold 0.4999 oz. AGW **Ruler:** Elizabeth II **Obv:** Bust with tiara right **Obv. Legend:** ELIZABETH II - ISLE OF MAN **Rev:** Ragdoll cat with two kittens sitting facing **Edge:** Reeded

Date	Mintage	F	VF	XF	Unc	BU
2007PM	—	—	—	—	—	870

KM# 1396   1/2 CROWN
6.2200 g., 0.9999 Gold 0.1999 oz. AGW, 30x20 mm. **Ruler:** Elizabeth II **Rev:** Tut's golden mask

Date	Mintage	F	VF	XF	Unc	BU
2008PM	—	—	—	—	—	355

KM# 1399   1/2 CROWN
6.2200 g., 0.9999 Gold 0.1999 oz. AGW **Ruler:** Elizabeth II **Obv:** Bust with tiara right in Egyptian motif **Rev:** Statue standing **Shape:** Triangle

Date	Mintage	F	VF	XF	Unc	BU
2008PM Proof	—	Value: 350				

KM# 1400   1/2 CROWN
6.2200 g., 0.9999 Gold 0.1999 oz. AGW **Ruler:** Elizabeth II **Obv:** Bust with tiara right in Egyptian motif **Rev:** Statue standing, vile of sand above **Shape:** Triangle

Date	Mintage	F	VF	XF	Unc	BU
2008PM Proof	—	Value: 355				

KM# 1380   1/2 CROWN
15.5500 g., 0.9999 Gold 0.4999 oz. AGW, 30 mm. **Ruler:** Elizabeth II **Obv:** Bust right **Rev:** Chinchilla cat and kitten

Date	Mintage	F	VF	XF	Unc	BU
2009	—	—	—	—	—	870
2009 Proof	1,000	Value: 875				

KM# 1384   1/2 CROWN
15.5500 g., 0.9950 Platinum 0.4974 oz. APW, 27 mm. **Ruler:** Elizabeth II **Obv:** Bust right **Rev:** Chinchilla cat and kitten

Date	Mintage	F	VF	XF	Unc	BU
2009	—	—	—	—	—	950

KM# 1474   1/2 CROWN
Titanium **Ruler:** Elizabeth II **Subject:** George F. Handel, 325th Anniversary of Birth **Obv:** Bust in tiara right **Rev:** Fireworks above river barges **Note:** Blue in color.

Date	Mintage	F	VF	XF	Unc	BU
2010PM Proof	—	Value: 125				

KM# 1438   1/2 CROWN
15.5500 g., 0.9999 Gold 0.4999 oz. AGW, 30 mm. **Ruler:** Elizabeth II **Subject:** Turkish Angora Cat

Date	Mintage	F	VF	XF	Unc	BU
2011PM	—	—	—	—	—	950
2011PM Proof	1,000	Value: 975				

KM# 1447   1/2 CROWN
12.0000 g., 0.9990 Silver 0.3854 oz. ASW, 38.6 mm. **Ruler:** Elizabeth II **Subject:** Olympics, London **Rev:** Horse jumper

Date	Mintage	F	VF	XF	Unc	BU
2012PM Proof	10,000	Value: 25.00				

KM# 1448   1/2 CROWN
12.0000 g., 0.9990 Silver 0.3854 oz. ASW, 38.6 mm. **Ruler:** Elizabeth II **Subject:** Olympics, London **Rev:** Track Cyclist, road cyclist in background

Date	Mintage	F	VF	XF	Unc	BU
2012PM Proof	10,000	Value: 25.00				

KM# 1449   1/2 CROWN
12.0000 g., 0.9990 Silver 0.3854 oz. ASW, 38.6 mm. **Ruler:** Elizabeth II **Subject:** Olympics, London **Rev:** Swimmer, two divers in background

Date	Mintage	F	VF	XF	Unc	BU
2012PM Proof	10,000	Value: 25.00				

KM# 1450   1/2 CROWN
12.0000 g., 0.9990 Silver 0.3854 oz. ASW, 38.6 mm. **Ruler:** Elizabeth II **Subject:** Olympics, London **Rev:** Canoeist, two rowers in background

Date	Mintage	F	VF	XF	Unc	BU
2012PM Proof	10,000	Value: 25.00				

KM# 1451   1/2 CROWN
12.0000 g., 0.9990 Silver 0.3854 oz. ASW, 38.6 mm. **Ruler:** Elizabeth II **Subject:** Olympics, London **Rev:** Judo players, two boxers in background

Date	Mintage	F	VF	XF	Unc	BU
2012PM Proof	10,000	Value: 25.00				

KM# 1452   1/2 CROWN
12.0000 g., 0.9990 Silver 0.3854 oz. ASW, 38.6 mm. **Ruler:** Elizabeth II **Subject:** Olympics, London **Rev:** Table tennis, Lawn tennis in background

Date	Mintage	F	VF	XF	Unc	BU
2012PM Proof	10,000	Value: 25.00				

KM# 1457   1/2 CROWN
12.0000 g., 0.9990 Silver 0.3854 oz. ASW, 38.6 mm. **Ruler:** Elizabeth II **Subject:** European Football Championships 2012 **Rev:** Player heading a football, Statue of Liberty in Lviv and Neptune's fountain in Gdansk

Date	Mintage	F	VF	XF	Unc	BU
2012PM Proof	10,000	Value: 25.00				

KM# 1458   1/2 CROWN
12.0000 g., 0.9990 Silver 0.3854 oz. ASW, 38.6 mm. **Ruler:** Elizabeth II **Subject:** European Football Championships 2012 **Rev:** Player passing the ball, Motherland statue in Kiev and King Sigismund's statue in Warsaw in background

Date	Mintage	F	VF	XF	Unc	BU
2012PM Proof	10,000	Value: 25.00				

KM# 1459   1/2 CROWN
12.0000 g., 0.9990 Silver 0.3854 oz. ASW, 38.6 mm. **Ruler:** Elizabeth II **Subject:** European Football Championships 2012 **Rev:** Footballer shooting, Cathedral of the Transfiguration in Donetsk and the Raclawice Panorama in Wroclaw in background

Date	Mintage	F	VF	XF	Unc	BU
2012PM Proof	10,000	Value: 25.00				

KM# 1460   1/2 CROWN
12.0000 g., 0.9990 Silver 0.3854 oz. ASW, 38.6 mm. **Ruler:** Elizabeth II **Subject:** European Football Championships 2012 **Rev:** Two footballers tackling, Cathedral of the Annunciation in Kharkiv and the Cathedral in Poznan in background

Date	Mintage	F	VF	XF	Unc	BU
2012PM Proof	10,000	Value: 25.00				

KM# 1073   CROWN
31.1035 g., 0.9999 Gold 0.9999 oz. AGW, 32.7 mm. **Ruler:** Elizabeth II **Subject:** Somali Kittens **Obv:** Bust with tiara right **Rev:** Two kittens **Edge:** Reeded

Date	Mintage	F	VF	XF	Unc	BU
2001	—	—	—	—	—	1,500
2001 Proof	1,000	Value: 1,550				

KM# 1076   CROWN
28.2800 g., Copper-Nickel, 38.6 mm. **Ruler:** Elizabeth II **Subject:** Queen Mother **Obv:** Bust with tiara right **Rev:** 1948 Silver wedding anniversary **Edge:** Reeded

Date	Mintage	F	VF	XF	Unc	BU
2001	—	—	—	—	10.00	12.00

KM# 1076a   CROWN
28.2800 g., 0.9250 Silver 0.8410 oz. ASW, 38.6 mm. **Ruler:** Elizabeth II **Subject:** Queen Mother **Obv:** Bust with tiara right **Rev:** 1948 Silver wedding anniversary **Edge:** Reeded

Date	Mintage	F	VF	XF	Unc	BU
2001 Proof	10,000	Value: 47.50				

KM# 1077   CROWN
Copper-Nickel, 38.6 mm. **Ruler:** Elizabeth II **Subject:** Queen Mother **Obv:** Bust with tiara right **Rev:** 1948 holding baby Prince Charles **Edge:** Reeded

Date	Mintage	F	VF	XF	Unc	BU
2001	—	—	—	—	10.00	12.00

KM# 1077a   CROWN
28.2800 g., 0.9250 Silver 0.8410 oz. ASW, 38.6 mm. **Ruler:** Elizabeth II **Subject:** Queen Mother **Obv:** Head with tiara right **Rev:** 1948 holding baby Prince Charles **Edge:** Reeded

Date	Mintage	F	VF	XF	Unc	BU
2001 Proof	10,000	Value: 47.50				

KM# 1080   CROWN
Copper-Nickel, 38.6 mm. **Ruler:** Elizabeth II **Subject:** Martin Frobisher **Obv:** Bust with tiara right **Rev:** Bust at left, ship at right and map below **Edge:** Reeded

Date	Mintage	F	VF	XF	Unc	BU
2001	—	—	—	—	10.00	12.00

KM# 1080a   CROWN
28.2800 g., 0.9250 Silver 0.8410 oz. ASW, 38.6 mm. **Ruler:** Elizabeth II **Subject:** Martin Frobisher **Obv:** Bust of Queen Elizabeth II right **Edge:** Reeded

Date	Mintage	F	VF	XF	Unc	BU
2001 Proof	10,000	Value: 47.50				

KM# 1081   CROWN
Copper-Nickel, 38.6 mm. **Ruler:** Elizabeth II **Subject:** Roald Amundsen **Obv:** Bust with tiara right **Rev:** Bust at right, ship at center, dirigible above at left **Edge:** Reeded

Date	Mintage	F	VF	XF	Unc	BU
2001	—	—	—	—	10.00	12.00

KM# 1081a   CROWN
28.2800 g., 0.9250 Silver 0.8410 oz. ASW, 38.6 mm. **Ruler:** Elizabeth II **Subject:** Roald Amundsen **Obv:** Bust with tiara right **Rev:** Bust at right, ship at center, dirigible at upper left **Edge:** Reeded

Date	Mintage	F	VF	XF	Unc	BU
2001 Proof	10,000	Value: 47.50				

KM# 1085   CROWN
28.2800 g., Copper-Nickel, 38.6 mm. **Ruler:** Elizabeth II **Subject:** Joey Dunlop (1952-2000) **Obv:** Bust with tiara right **Rev:** Motorcycle racer **Edge:** Reeded

Date	Mintage	F	VF	XF	Unc	BU
2001 Black finish	—	—	—	—	10.00	12.00

KM# 1085a   CROWN
28.2800 g., 0.9250 Silver 0.8410 oz. ASW, 38.6 mm. **Ruler:** Elizabeth II **Subject:** Joey Dunlop (1952-2000) **Obv:** Bust with tiara right **Rev:** Motorcycle racer **Edge:** Reeded

Date	Mintage	F	VF	XF	Unc	BU
2001 Proof	10,000	Value: 47.50				

KM# 1083   CROWN
28.2800 g., Copper-Nickel, 38.6 mm. **Ruler:** Elizabeth II **Subject:** Queen's 75th Birthday **Obv:** Bust with tiara right **Rev:** Flower bouquet **Edge:** Reeded

Date	Mintage	F	VF	XF	Unc	BU
2001	—	—	—	—	14.00	16.00

KM# 1083a   CROWN
28.2800 g., 0.9250 Silver 0.8410 oz. ASW, 38.6 mm. **Ruler:** Elizabeth II **Subject:** Queen's 75th Birthday **Obv:** Bust with tiara right **Rev:** Flower bouquet **Edge:** Reeded

Date	Mintage	F	VF	XF	Unc	BU
2001 Proof	10,000	Value: 50.00				

KM# 1087   CROWN
28.2800 g., Copper-Nickel, 38.6 mm. **Ruler:** Elizabeth II **Series:** Harry Potter **Obv:** Bust with tiara right **Rev:** Harry with magic wand **Edge:** Reeded

Date	Mintage	F	VF	XF	Unc	BU
2001	—	—	—	—	10.00	12.00

KM# 1087a   CROWN
28.2800 g., 0.9250 Silver 0.8410 oz. ASW, 38.6 mm. **Ruler:** Elizabeth II **Series:** Harry Potter **Obv:** Bust with tiara right **Rev:** Harry with magic wand **Edge:** Reeded

Date	Mintage	F	VF	XF	Unc	BU
2001 Proof	15,000	Value: 47.50				

KM# 1089 CROWN
28.2800 g., Copper-Nickel, 38.6 mm. **Ruler:** Elizabeth II **Series:** Harry Potter **Subject:** Journey to Hogwart's **Obv:** Bust with tiara right **Rev:** Boat full of children going to Hogwart's **Edge:** Reeded

Date	Mintage	F	VF	XF	Unc	BU
2001	—	—	—	—	10.00	12.00

KM# 1089a CROWN
28.2800 g., 0.9250 Silver 0.8410 oz. ASW, 38.6 mm. **Ruler:** Elizabeth II **Series:** Harry Potter **Obv:** Bust with tiara right **Rev:** Boat full of children going to Hogwart's **Edge:** Reeded

Date	Mintage	F	VF	XF	Unc	BU
2001 Proof	15,000	Value: 47.50				

KM# 1091 CROWN
Copper-Nickel **Ruler:** Elizabeth II **Series:** Harry Potter **Subject:** First Quidditch Match **Obv:** Bust with tiara right **Rev:** Harry flying his Nimbus 2000

Date	Mintage	F	VF	XF	Unc	BU
2001	—	—	—	—	10.00	12.00

KM# 1091a CROWN
28.2800 g., 0.9250 Silver 0.8410 oz. ASW **Ruler:** Elizabeth II **Series:** Harry Potter **Subject:** First Quidditch Match **Obv:** Bust with tiara right **Rev:** Harry flying his Nimbus 2000

Date	Mintage	F	VF	XF	Unc	BU
2001 Proof	15,000	Value: 47.50				

KM# 1093 CROWN
Copper-Nickel **Ruler:** Elizabeth II **Series:** Harry Potter **Subject:** Birth of Norbert **Obv:** Bust with tiara right **Rev:** Hagrid and children watching Norbert hatch

Date	Mintage	F	VF	XF	Unc	BU
2001	—	—	—	—	10.00	14.00

KM# 1093a CROWN
28.2800 g., 0.9250 Silver 0.8410 oz. ASW **Ruler:** Elizabeth II **Series:** Harry Potter **Subject:** Birth of Norbert **Obv:** Bust with tiara right **Rev:** Hagrid and children watching Norbert hatch

Date	Mintage	F	VF	XF	Unc	BU
2001 Proof	15,000	Value: 47.50				

KM# 1095 CROWN
Copper-Nickel **Ruler:** Elizabeth II **Series:** Harry Potter **Subject:** School **Obv:** Bust with tiara right **Rev:** Harry in Potions class

Date	Mintage	F	VF	XF	Unc	BU
2001	—	—	—	—	10.00	12.00

KM# 1095a CROWN
28.2800 g., 0.9250 Silver 0.8410 oz. ASW **Ruler:** Elizabeth II **Series:** Harry Potter **Subject:** School **Obv:** Bust with tiara right **Rev:** Harry in Potions class

Date	Mintage	F	VF	XF	Unc	BU
2001 Proof	15,000	Value: 47.50				

KM# 1097 CROWN
Copper-Nickel, 38.72 mm. **Ruler:** Elizabeth II **Series:** Harry Potter **Obv:** Bust with tiara right **Rev:** Harry catching the golden snitch **Edge:** Reeded

Date	Mintage	F	VF	XF	Unc	BU
2001	—	—	—	—	10.00	12.00

KM# 1097a CROWN
28.2800 g., 0.9250 Silver 0.8410 oz. ASW, 38.71 mm. **Ruler:** Elizabeth II **Series:** Harry Potter **Obv:** Bust with tiara right **Rev:** Harry catching the golden snitch **Edge:** Reeded

Date	Mintage	F	VF	XF	Unc	BU
2001 Proof	15,000	Value: 47.50				

KM# 1062 CROWN
28.2800 g., Copper-Nickel, 38.6 mm. **Ruler:** Elizabeth II **Subject:** Year of the Snake **Obv:** Bust with tiara right **Rev:** Snake **Edge:** Reeded

Date	Mintage	F	VF	XF	Unc	BU
2001	—	—	—	—	10.00	15.00

KM# 1062a CROWN
28.2800 g., 0.9250 Silver 0.8410 oz. ASW, 38.6 mm. **Ruler:** Elizabeth II **Subject:** Year of the Snake **Obv:** Head with tiara right **Rev:** Snake **Edge:** Reeded

Date	Mintage	F	VF	XF	Unc	BU
2001 Proof	30,000	Value: 47.50				

KM# 1063 CROWN
31.1035 g., 0.9999 Gold 0.9999 oz. AGW, 32.7 mm. **Ruler:** Elizabeth II **Subject:** Year of the Snake **Obv:** Bust with tiara right **Rev:** Snake **Edge:** Reeded

Date	Mintage	F	VF	XF	Unc	BU
2001	—	—	—	—	—	1,700
2001 Proof	2,000	Value: 1,725				

KM# 1072 CROWN
28.2800 g., Copper-Nickel, 38.6 mm. **Ruler:** Elizabeth II **Subject:** Somali Kittens **Obv:** Bust with tiara right **Rev:** Two kittens **Edge:** Reeded

Date	Mintage	F	VF	XF	Unc	BU
2001	—	—	—	—	11.00	15.00

KM# 1072a CROWN
31.1035 g., 0.9990 Silver 0.9990 oz. ASW, 38.6 mm. **Ruler:** Elizabeth II **Subject:** Somali Kittens **Obv:** Bust with tiara right **Rev:** Two kittens **Edge:** Reeded

Date	Mintage	F	VF	XF	Unc	BU
2001 Proof	50,000	Value: 47.50				

KM# 1102 CROWN
28.2800 g., Copper-Nickel, 38.6 mm. **Ruler:** Elizabeth II **Subject:** Year of the Horse **Obv:** Bust with tiara right **Rev:** Two horses **Edge:** Reeded

Date	Mintage	F	VF	XF	Unc	BU
2002	—	—	—	—	12.00	15.00

KM# 1102a CROWN
28.2800 g., 0.9250 Silver 0.8410 oz. ASW, 38.6 mm. **Ruler:** Elizabeth II **Subject:** Year of the Horse **Obv:** Bust with tiara right **Rev:** Two horses **Edge:** Reeded

Date	Mintage	F	VF	XF	Unc	BU
2002 Proof	30,000	Value: 47.50				

KM# 1103 CROWN
31.1000 g., 0.9999 Gold 0.9997 oz. AGW **Ruler:** Elizabeth II **Subject:** Year of the Horse **Obv:** Bust with tiara right

Date	Mintage	F	VF	XF	Unc	BU
2002 Proof	2,000	Value: 1,500				

KM# 1111 CROWN
28.2800 g., Copper-Nickel, 38.6 mm. **Ruler:** Elizabeth II **Subject:** Bengal Cat **Obv:** Bust with tiara right **Rev:** Cat and kitten **Edge:** Reeded

Date	Mintage	F	VF	XF	Unc	BU
2002	—	—	—	—	12.50	14.00

KM# 1111a CROWN
31.1035 g., 0.9990 Silver 0.9990 oz. ASW, 38.6 mm. **Ruler:** Elizabeth II **Subject:** Bengal Cat **Obv:** Bust with tiara right **Rev:** Cat and kitten **Edge:** Reeded

Date	Mintage	F	VF	XF	Unc	BU
2002 Proof	10,000	Value: 47.50				

KM# 1112 CROWN
31.1035 g., 0.9990 Gold 0.9990 oz. AGW, 33 mm. **Ruler:** Elizabeth II **Subject:** Bengal Cat **Obv:** Bust with tiara right **Rev:** Cat and kitten **Edge:** Reeded

Date	Mintage	F	VF	XF	Unc	BU
2002	—	—	—	—	—	1,550
2002 Proof	1,000	Value: 1,600				

KM# 1115 CROWN
28.2800 g., Copper-Nickel, 38.6 mm. **Ruler:** Elizabeth II **Subject:** Olympics - Salt Lake City **Obv:** Bust with tiara right **Rev:** Skier, torch and flag **Edge:** Reeded

Date	Mintage	F	VF	XF	Unc	BU
2002	—	—	—	—	10.00	12.00

KM# 1115a CROWN
28.2800 g., 0.9250 Silver 0.8410 oz. ASW, 38.6 mm. **Ruler:** Elizabeth II **Subject:** Olympics - Salt Lake City **Obv:** Bust with tiara right **Rev:** Skier, torch and flag **Edge:** Reeded

Date	Mintage	F	VF	XF	Unc	BU
2002 Proof	10,000	Value: 47.50				

KM# 1116 CROWN
28.2800 g., Copper-Nickel, 38.6 mm. **Ruler:** Elizabeth II **Subject:** Olympics - Salt Lake City **Obv:** Bust with tiara right **Rev:** Bobsled, torch and stadium **Edge:** Reeded

Date	Mintage	F	VF	XF	Unc	BU
2002	—	—	—	—	10.00	12.00

KM# 1116a CROWN
28.2800 g., 0.9250 Silver 0.8410 oz. ASW, 38.6 mm. **Ruler:** Elizabeth II **Subject:** Olympics - Salt Lake City **Obv:** Bust with tiara right **Rev:** Bobsled, torch and stadium **Edge:** Reeded

Date	Mintage	F	VF	XF	Unc	BU
2002 Proof	10,000	Value: 47.50				

KM# 1118 CROWN
28.2800 g., Copper-Nickel, 38.6 mm. **Ruler:** Elizabeth II

Subject: Queen Mother's Love of Horses **Obv:** Bust with tiara right **Rev:** Queen Mother and horse **Edge:** Reeded

Date	Mintage	F	VF	XF	Unc	BU
2002	—				10.00	12.00

KM# 1118a   CROWN
28.2800 g., Silver, 38.6 mm. **Ruler:** Elizabeth II **Subject:** Queen Mother's Love of Horses **Obv:** Bust with tiara right **Rev:** Queen Mother and horse **Edge:** Reeded

Date	Mintage	F	VF	XF	Unc	BU
2002 Proof	10,000	Value: 47.50				

KM# 1119   CROWN
35.0000 g., 0.7500 Gold 0.8439 oz. AGW, 38.6 mm. **Ruler:** Elizabeth II **Subject:** Golden Jubilee **Obv:** Bust with tiara right **Rev:** Queen Elizabeth II's young laureate bust right **Edge:** Reeded **Note:** Red Gold center in a White Gold inner ring within a Yellow Gold outer ring.

Date	Mintage	F	VF	XF	Unc	BU
2002 Proof	999	Value: 1,450				

KM# 1121   CROWN
28.2800 g., Copper-Nickel, 38.6 mm. **Ruler:** Elizabeth II **Subject:** World Cup 2002 Japan - Korea **Obv:** Bust with tiara right **Rev:** Player running right **Edge:** Reeded

Date	Mintage	F	VF	XF	Unc	BU
2002	—				10.00	12.00

KM# 1121a   CROWN
28.2800 g., 0.9250 Silver 0.8410 oz. ASW, 38.6 mm. **Ruler:** Elizabeth II **Subject:** World Cup 2002 Japan - Korea **Obv:** Bust with tiara right **Rev:** Player running right **Edge:** Reeded

Date	Mintage	F	VF	XF	Unc	BU
2002 Proof	10,000	Value: 47.50				

KM# 1123   CROWN
28.2800 g., Copper-Nickel, 38.6 mm. **Ruler:** Elizabeth II **Subject:** World Cup 2002 Japan - Korea **Obv:** Bust with tiara right **Rev:** Player kicking to right **Edge:** Reeded

Date	Mintage	F	VF	XF	Unc	BU
2002	—				10.00	12.00

KM# 1123a   CROWN
28.2800 g., 0.9250 Silver 0.8410 oz. ASW, 38.6 mm. **Ruler:** Elizabeth II **Subject:** World Cup 2002 Japan - Korea **Obv:** Bust with tiara right **Rev:** Player kicking to right **Edge:** Reeded

Date	Mintage	F	VF	XF	Unc	BU
2002 Proof	10,000	Value: 47.50				

KM# 1125   CROWN
28.2800 g., Copper-Nickel, 38.6 mm. **Ruler:** Elizabeth II **Subject:** World Cup 2002 Japan - Korea **Obv:** Bust with tiara right **Rev:** Player kicking to left **Edge:** Reeded

Date	Mintage	F	VF	XF	Unc	BU
2002	—				10.00	12.00

KM# 1125a   CROWN
28.2800 g., 0.9250 Silver 0.8410 oz. ASW, 38.6 mm. **Ruler:** Elizabeth II **Subject:** World Cup 2002 Japan - Korea **Obv:** Bust with tiara right **Rev:** Player kicking to left **Edge:** Reeded

Date	Mintage	F	VF	XF	Unc	BU
2002 Proof	10,000	Value: 47.50				

KM# 1127   CROWN
28.2800 g., Copper-Nickel, 38.6 mm. **Ruler:** Elizabeth II **Subject:** World Cup 2002 Japan - Korea **Obv:** Bust with tiara right **Rev:** Player running to left **Edge:** Reeded

Date	Mintage	F	VF	XF	Unc	BU
2002	—				10.00	12.00

KM# 1127a   CROWN
28.2800 g., 0.9250 Silver 0.8410 oz. ASW, 38.6 mm. **Ruler:** Elizabeth II **Subject:** World Cup 2002 Japan - Korea **Obv:** Bust with tiara right **Rev:** Player running to left **Edge:** Reeded

Date	Mintage	F	VF	XF	Unc	BU
2002 Proof	10,000	Value: 47.50				

KM# 1131   CROWN
28.2800 g., Copper-Nickel, 38.6 mm. **Ruler:** Elizabeth II **Subject:** Queen Elizabeth II's Golden Jubilee **Obv:** Bust with tiara right **Rev:** Seated crowned Queen holding scepter at her coronation **Edge:** Reeded

Date	Mintage	F	VF	XF	Unc	BU
2002	—				10.00	12.00

KM# 1131a   CROWN
28.2800 g., Gold Color Base Metal, 38.6 mm. **Ruler:** Elizabeth II **Subject:** Queen Elizabeth II's Golden Jubilee **Obv:** Bust with tiara right **Rev:** Seated crowned Queen holding scepter at her coronation **Edge:** Reeded

Date	Mintage	F	VF	XF	Unc	BU
2002	15,000				10.00	12.00

KM# 1131b   CROWN
28.2800 g., 0.9250 Gold Clad Silver 0.8410 oz., 38.6 mm. **Ruler:** Elizabeth II **Subject:** Queen Elizabeth II's Golden Jubilee **Obv:** Bust with tiara right **Rev:** Seated crowned Queen holding scepter at her coronation **Edge:** Reeded

Date	Mintage	F	VF	XF	Unc	BU
2002 Proof	10,000	Value: 47.50				

KM# 1133   CROWN
28.2800 g., Copper-Nickel, 38.6 mm. **Ruler:** Elizabeth II **Subject:** Queen Elizabeth II's Golden Jubilee **Obv:** Bust with tiara right **Rev:** Queen on horse **Edge:** Reeded

Date	Mintage	F	VF	XF	Unc	BU
2002	—				10.00	12.00

KM# 1133a   CROWN
28.2800 g., Gold Color Base Metal, 38.6 mm. **Ruler:** Elizabeth II **Subject:** Queen Elizabeth II's Golden Jubilee **Obv:** Bust with tiara right **Rev:** Queen on horse **Edge:** Reeded

Date	Mintage	F	VF	XF	Unc	BU
2002	15,000				10.00	12.00

KM# 1133b   CROWN
28.2800 g., 0.9250 Gold Clad Silver 0.8410 oz., 38.6 mm. **Ruler:** Elizabeth II **Subject:** Queen Elizabeth II's Golden Jubilee **Obv:** Bust with tiara right **Rev:** Queen on horse half left **Edge:** Reeded

Date	Mintage	F	VF	XF	Unc	BU
2002 Proof	10,000	Value: 47.50				

KM# 1135   CROWN
28.2800 g., Copper-Nickel, 38.6 mm. **Ruler:** Elizabeth II **Subject:** Queen Elizabeth II's Golden Jubilee **Obv:** Bust with tiara right **Rev:** Queen with her pet Corgi **Edge:** Reeded

Date	Mintage	F	VF	XF	Unc	BU
2002	—				10.00	12.00

KM# 1135a   CROWN
28.2800 g., Gold Color Base Metal, 38.6 mm. **Ruler:** Elizabeth II **Subject:** Queen Elizabeth II's Golden Jubilee **Obv:** Bust with tiara right **Rev:** Seated Queen with her pet Corgi **Edge:** Reeded

Date	Mintage	F	VF	XF	Unc	BU
2002	15,000				10.00	12.00

KM# 1135b   CROWN
28.2800 g., 0.9250 Gold Clad Silver 0.8410 oz., 38.6 mm. **Ruler:** Elizabeth II **Subject:** Queen Elizabeth II's Golden Jubilee **Obv:** Bust with tiara right **Rev:** Queen with her pet Corgi **Edge:** Reeded

Date	Mintage	F	VF	XF	Unc	BU
2002 Proof	10,000	Value: 47.50				

KM# 1137   CROWN
28.2800 g., Copper-Nickel, 38.6 mm. **Ruler:** Elizabeth II **Subject:** Queen Elizabeth II's Golden Jubilee **Obv:** Bust with tiara right **Rev:** Queen at war memorial **Edge:** Reeded

Date	Mintage	F	VF	XF	Unc	BU
2002	—				10.00	12.00

KM# 1137a   CROWN
28.2800 g., Gold Color Base Metal, 38.6 mm. **Ruler:** Elizabeth II **Subject:** Queen Elizabeth II's Golden Jubilee **Obv:** Bust with tiara right **Rev:** Queen at war memorial **Edge:** Reeded

Date	Mintage	F	VF	XF	Unc	BU
2002	15,000				10.00	12.00

KM# 1137b   CROWN
28.2800 g., Gold Clad Silver, 38.6 mm. **Ruler:** Elizabeth II **Subject:** Queen Elizabeth II's Golden Jubilee **Obv:** Bust with tiara right **Rev:** Queen at war memorial **Edge:** Reeded

Date	Mintage	F	VF	XF	Unc	BU
2002 Proof	10,000	Value: 47.50				

KM# 1139   CROWN
Copper-Nickel dark patina, 38.6 mm. **Ruler:** Elizabeth II **Subject:** Queen Mother **Obv:** Bust with tiara right **Rev:** Queen Mother and Castle May **Edge:** Reeded

Date	Mintage	F	VF	XF	Unc	BU
2002	—				10.00	12.00

KM# 1139a   CROWN
28.2800 g., 0.9250 Silver 0.8410 oz. ASW, 38.6 mm. **Ruler:** Elizabeth II **Obv:** Head with tiara right with blackened legends **Rev:** Queen Mother standing at left in front of Castle May with blackened legends

Date	Mintage	F	VF	XF	Unc	BU
2002 Proof	10,000	Value: 47.50				

KM# 1141   CROWN
28.2800 g., Copper-Nickel, 38.6 mm. **Ruler:** Elizabeth II **Subject:** Princess Diana **Obv:** Bust with tiara right **Rev:** Diana's bust facing **Edge:** Reeded

Date	Mintage	F	VF	XF	Unc	BU
2002	—				10.00	12.00

KM# 1141a   CROWN
28.2800 g., 0.9250 Silver 0.8410 oz. ASW, 38.6 mm. **Ruler:** Elizabeth II **Subject:** Princess Diana **Obv:** Bust with tiara right **Rev:** Diana facing **Edge:** Reeded

Date	Mintage	F	VF	XF	Unc	BU
2002 Proof	10,000	Value: 47.50				

KM# 1144 CROWN
28.2800 g., Copper-Nickel, 38.6 mm. **Ruler:** Elizabeth II **Series:** Harry Potter **Obv:** Bust with tiara right **Rev:** Tom Riddle twirling Harry's magic wand **Edge:** Reeded

Date	Mintage	F	VF	XF	Unc	BU
2002PM	—	—	—	—	10.00	12.00

KM# 1144a CROWN
28.2800 g., 0.9250 Silver 0.8410 oz. ASW, 28.6 mm. **Ruler:** Elizabeth II **Series:** Harry Potter **Obv:** Bust with tiara right **Rev:** Tom Riddle twirling Harry's magic wand **Edge:** Reeded

Date	Mintage	F	VF	XF	Unc	BU
2002PM Proof	15,000	Value: 50.00				

KM# 1146 CROWN
28.2800 g., Copper-Nickel, 38.6 mm. **Ruler:** Elizabeth II **Series:** Harry Potter **Obv:** Bust with tiara right **Rev:** Harry and friends making Polyjuice potion **Edge:** Reeded

Date	Mintage	F	VF	XF	Unc	BU
2002PM	—	—	—	—	10.00	12.00

KM# 1146a CROWN
28.2800 g., 0.9250 Silver 0.8410 oz. ASW, 38.6 mm. **Ruler:** Elizabeth II **Series:** Harry Potter **Obv:** Bust with tiara right **Rev:** Harry Potter and friends making Polyjuice potion **Edge:** Reeded

Date	Mintage	F	VF	XF	Unc	BU
2002PM Proof	15,000	Value: 50.00				

KM# 1148 CROWN
28.2800 g., Copper-Nickel, 38.6 mm. **Ruler:** Elizabeth II **Series:** Harry Potter **Obv:** Bust with tiara right **Rev:** Harry arrives at the Burrow in a flying car **Edge:** Reeded

Date	Mintage	F	VF	XF	Unc	BU
2002PM	—	—	—	—	10.00	12.00

KM# 1148a CROWN
28.2800 g., 0.9250 Silver 0.8410 oz. ASW, 38.6 mm. **Ruler:** Elizabeth II **Series:** Harry Potter **Obv:** Bust with tiara right **Rev:** Harry arrives at the Burrow in a flying car **Edge:** Reeded

Date	Mintage	F	VF	XF	Unc	BU
2002PM Proof	15,000	Value: 50.00				

KM# 1150 CROWN
28.2800 g., Copper-Nickel, 38.6 mm. **Ruler:** Elizabeth II **Series:** Harry Potter **Obv:** Bust with tiara right **Rev:** Harry retrieves Gryffindor sword from sorting hat **Edge:** Reeded

Date	Mintage	F	VF	XF	Unc	BU
2002PM	—	—	—	—	10.00	12.00

KM# 1150a CROWN
28.2800 g., 0.9250 Silver 0.8410 oz. ASW, 38.6 mm. **Ruler:** Elizabeth II **Series:** Harry Potter **Obv:** Bust with tiara right **Rev:** Harry retrieves Gryffindor sword from sorting hat **Edge:** Reeded

Date	Mintage	F	VF	XF	Unc	BU
2002PM Proof	15,000	Value: 50.00				

KM# 1152 CROWN
28.2800 g., Copper-Nickel, 38.6 mm. **Ruler:** Elizabeth II **Series:**
Harry Potter **Obv:** Bust with tiara right **Rev:** Harry and Ron encounter the spider Aragog **Edge:** Reeded

Date	Mintage	F	VF	XF	Unc	BU
2002PM	—	—	—	—	10.00	12.00

KM# 1152a CROWN
28.2800 g., 0.9250 Silver 0.8410 oz. ASW, 38.6 mm. **Ruler:** Elizabeth II **Series:** Harry Potter **Obv:** Bust with tiara right **Rev:** Harry and Ron encounter the spider Aragog **Edge:** Reeded

Date	Mintage	F	VF	XF	Unc	BU
2002PM Proof	15,000	Value: 50.00				

KM# 1154 CROWN
28.2800 g., Copper-Nickel, 38.6 mm. **Ruler:** Elizabeth II **Series:** Harry Potter **Obv:** Bust with tiara right **Rev:** Harry in hospital with Dobby **Edge:** Reeded

Date	Mintage	F	VF	XF	Unc	BU
2002PM	—	—	—	—	10.00	12.00

KM# 1154a CROWN
28.2800 g., 0.9250 Silver 0.8410 oz. ASW, 38.6 mm. **Ruler:** Elizabeth II **Series:** Harry Potter **Obv:** Bust with tiara right **Rev:** Harry in hospital with Dobby **Edge:** Reeded

Date	Mintage	F	VF	XF	Unc	BU
2002PM Proof	15,000	Value: 50.00				

KM# 1185 CROWN
28.2800 g., Copper-Nickel, 38.6 mm. **Ruler:** Elizabeth II **Obv:** Bust with tiara right **Rev:** Lord of the Rings characters

Edge: Reeded

Date	Mintage	F	VF	XF	Unc	BU
2003PM	100,000	—	—	—	12.50	14.50

KM# 1185a CROWN
28.2800 g., 0.9250 Silver 0.8410 oz. ASW, 38.6 mm. **Ruler:** Elizabeth II **Obv:** Bust with tiara right **Rev:** Lord of the Rings characters **Edge:** Reeded

Date	Mintage	F	VF	XF	Unc	BU
2003PM Proof	10,000	Value: 50.00				

KM# 1190 CROWN
31.1035 g., 0.9999 Gold 0.9999 oz. AGW, 32.7 mm. **Ruler:** Elizabeth II **Subject:** Lord of the Rings **Obv:** Bust with tiara right **Rev:** Man on horse **Edge:** Reeded

Date	Mintage	F	VF	XF	Unc	BU
2003PM Proof	1,000	Value: 1,550				

KM# 1191 CROWN
28.2800 g., 0.9250 Silver 0.8410 oz. ASW, 38.6 mm. **Ruler:** Elizabeth II **Subject:** Lord of the Rings **Obv:** Bust with tiara right **Rev:** Man with short sword **Edge:** Reeded

Date	Mintage	F	VF	XF	Unc	BU
2003PM Proof	5,000	Value: 47.50				

KM# 1192 CROWN
28.2800 g., 0.9250 Silver 0.8410 oz. ASW, 38.6 mm. **Ruler:** Elizabeth II **Subject:** Lord of the Rings **Obv:** Bust with tiara right **Rev:** Aragorn with broadsword **Edge:** Reeded

Date	Mintage	F	VF	XF	Unc	BU
2003PM Proof	5,000	Value: 47.50				

KM# 1193 CROWN
28.2800 g., 0.9250 Silver 0.8410 oz. ASW, 38.6 mm. **Ruler:** Elizabeth II **Subject:** Lord of the Rings **Obv:** Bust with tiara right **Rev:** Legolas **Edge:** Reeded

Date	Mintage	F	VF	XF	Unc	BU
2003PM Proof	5,000	Value: 47.50				

KM# 1194 CROWN
28.2800 g., 0.9250 Silver 0.8410 oz. ASW, 38.6 mm. **Ruler:** Elizabeth II **Subject:** Lord of the Rings **Obv:** Bust with tiara right **Rev:** Gimli with two battle axes **Edge:** Reeded

Date	Mintage	F	VF	XF	Unc	BU
2003PM Proof	5,000	Value: 47.50				

KM# 1195 CROWN
28.2800 g., 0.9250 Silver 0.8410 oz. ASW, 38.6 mm. **Ruler:** Elizabeth II **Subject:** Lord of the Rings **Obv:** Bust with tiara right **Rev:** Man on horse **Edge:** Reeded

Date	Mintage	F	VF	XF	Unc	BU
2003PM Proof	5,000	Value: 47.50				

KM# 1165 CROWN
28.2800 g., Copper-Nickel, 38.6 mm. **Ruler:** Elizabeth II **Subject:** Cat **Obv:** Bust with tiara right **Rev:** Two Balinese kittens **Edge:** Reeded

Date	Mintage	F	VF	XF	Unc	BU
2003PM	—	—	—	—	12.00	14.00

KM# 1165a CROWN
31.1035 g., 0.9990 Silver 0.9990 oz. ASW, 38.6 mm. **Ruler:** Elizabeth II **Subject:** Cat **Obv:** Head with tiara right **Rev:** Two Balinese kittens **Edge:** Reeded

Date	Mintage	F	VF	XF	Unc	BU
2003PM Proof	50,000	Value: 47.50				

KM# 1166 CROWN
31.1035 g., 0.9999 Gold 0.9999 oz. AGW, 32.7 mm. **Ruler:** Elizabeth II **Subject:** Cat **Obv:** Head with tiara right **Rev:** Two Balinese kittens **Edge:** Reeded

Date	Mintage	F	VF	XF	Unc	BU
2003PM	—	—	—	—	—	1,700
2003PM Proof	—	Value: 1,725				

KM# 1171 CROWN
28.2800 g., Copper-Nickel, 38.6 mm. **Ruler:** Elizabeth II **Subject:** Year of the Goat **Obv:** Bust with tiara right **Rev:** Three goats **Edge:** Reeded

Date	Mintage	F	VF	XF	Unc	BU
2003PM	—	—	—	—	12.00	14.00

KM# 1171a CROWN
28.2800 g., 0.9250 Silver 0.8410 oz. ASW, 38.6 mm. **Ruler:** Elizabeth II **Subject:** Year of the Goat **Obv:** Bust with tiara right **Rev:** Three goats **Edge:** Reeded

Date	Mintage	F	VF	XF	Unc	BU
2003PM Proof	30,000	Value: 47.50				

KM# 1172 CROWN
31.1035 g., 0.9999 Gold 0.9999 oz. AGW, 32.7 mm. **Ruler:** Elizabeth II **Subject:** Year of the Goat **Obv:** Bust with tiara right **Rev:** Three goats **Edge:** Reeded

Date	Mintage	F	VF	XF	Unc	BU
2003PM Proof	2,000	Value: 1,725				

KM# 1174 CROWN
28.5300 g., Copper-Nickel, 38.6 mm. **Ruler:** Elizabeth II **Obv:** Bust with tiara right **Rev:** The Star of India sailing ship **Edge:** Reeded

Date	Mintage	F	VF	XF	Unc	BU
2003PM	—	—	—	—	10.00	12.00

KM# 1176 CROWN
28.2800 g., Copper-Nickel, 38.6 mm. **Ruler:** Elizabeth II **Subject:** Olympics **Obv:** Bust with tiara right **Rev:** Swimmers **Edge:** Reeded

Date	Mintage	F	VF	XF	Unc	BU
2003PM	—	—	—	—	10.00	12.00

KM# 1176a CROWN
28.2800 g., 0.9250 Silver 0.8410 oz. ASW, 38.6 mm. **Ruler:** Elizabeth II **Subject:** Olympics **Obv:** Bust with tiara right **Rev:** Swimmers **Edge:** Reeded

Date	Mintage	F	VF	XF	Unc	BU
2003PM Proof	10,000	Value: 47.50				

KM# 1178 CROWN
28.2800 g., Copper-Nickel, 38.6 mm. **Ruler:** Elizabeth II **Subject:** Olympics **Obv:** Bust with tiara right **Rev:** Runners **Edge:** Reeded

Date	Mintage	F	VF	XF	Unc	BU
2003PM	—	—	—	—	10.00	12.00

KM# 1178a CROWN
28.2800 g., 0.9250 Silver 0.8410 oz. ASW, 38.6 mm. **Ruler:** Elizabeth II **Subject:** Olympics **Obv:** Bust with tiara right **Rev:** Runners **Edge:** Reeded

Date	Mintage	F	VF	XF	Unc	BU
2003PM Proof	10,000			Value: 47.50		

KM# 1180 CROWN
28.2800 g., Copper-Nickel, 38.6 mm. **Ruler:** Elizabeth II **Subject:** Olympics **Obv:** Bust with tiara right **Rev:** Bicyclists **Edge:** Reeded

Date	Mintage	F	VF	XF	Unc	BU
2003PM	—	—	—	—	10.00	12.00

KM# 1180a CROWN
28.2800 g., 0.9250 Silver 0.8410 oz. ASW, 38.6 mm. **Ruler:** Elizabeth II **Subject:** Olympics **Obv:** Bust with tiara right **Rev:** Bicyclists **Edge:** Reeded

Date	Mintage	F	VF	XF	Unc	BU
2003PM Proof	10,000			Value: 47.50		

KM# 1182 CROWN
28.2800 g., Copper-Nickel, 38.6 mm. **Ruler:** Elizabeth II **Subject:** Olympics **Obv:** Bust with tiara right **Rev:** Sail Boarders **Edge:** Reeded

Date	Mintage	F	VF	XF	Unc	BU
2003PM	—	—	—	—	10.00	12.00

KM# 1182a CROWN
28.2800 g., 0.9250 Silver 0.8410 oz. ASW, 38.6 mm. **Ruler:** Elizabeth II **Subject:** Olympics **Obv:** Bust with tiara right **Rev:** Sail Boarders **Edge:** Reeded

Date	Mintage	F	VF	XF	Unc	BU
2003PM Proof	10,000			Value: 47.50		

KM# 1196 CROWN
28.4400 g., Copper-Nickel, 38.6 mm. **Ruler:** Elizabeth II **Obv:** Bust with tiara right **Rev:** Four pre-1918 airplanes **Edge:** Reeded

Date	Mintage	F	VF	XF	Unc	BU
2003PM	—	—	—	—	10.00	12.00

KM# 1197 CROWN
28.4400 g., Copper-Nickel, 38.6 mm. **Obv:** Bust with tiara right **Rev:** Propeller plain, Zeppelin and two jet airliners **Edge:** Reeded

Date	Mintage	F	VF	XF	Unc	BU
2003PM	—	—	—	—	10.00	12.00

KM# 1201 CROWN
28.2800 g., Copper-Nickel, 38.6 mm. **Ruler:** Elizabeth II **Obv:** Bust with tiara right **Rev:** European Union map within hand held rope circle **Edge:** Reeded

Date	Mintage	F	VF	XF	Unc	BU
2004PM	—	—	—	—	10.00	12.00

KM# 1201a CROWN
28.2800 g., 0.9250 Silver 0.8410 oz. ASW, 38.6 mm. **Ruler:** Elizabeth II **Obv:** Bust with tiara right **Rev:** European Union map within a hand held rope circle **Edge:** Reeded

Date	Mintage	F	VF	XF	Unc	BU
2004PM Proof	10,000			Value: 50.00		

KM# 1202 CROWN
28.2800 g., Copper-Nickel, 38.6 mm. **Ruler:** Elizabeth II **Obv:** Bust with tiara right **Rev:** Harry Potter and patron fighting off a Deventer **Edge:** Reeded

Date	Mintage	F	VF	XF	Unc	BU
2004PM	—	—	—	—	15.00	17.00

KM# 1202a CROWN
28.2800 g., 0.9250 Silver 0.8410 oz. ASW, 38.6 mm. **Ruler:** Elizabeth II **Obv:** Bust with tiara right **Rev:** Harry Potter and patron fighting off a Deventer **Edge:** Reeded

Date	Mintage	F	VF	XF	Unc	BU
2004PM Proof	10,000			Value: 50.00		

KM# 1204 CROWN
28.2800 g., Copper-Nickel, 38.6 mm. **Ruler:** Elizabeth II **Obv:** Bust with tiara right **Rev:** Harry Potter in the shrieking shed **Edge:** Reeded

Date	Mintage	F	VF	XF	Unc	BU
2004PM	—	—	—	—	15.00	17.00

KM# 1204a CROWN
28.2800 g., 0.9250 Silver 0.8410 oz. ASW, 38.6 mm. **Ruler:** Elizabeth II **Obv:** Bust with tiara right **Rev:** Harry Potter in the shrieking shack **Edge:** Reeded

Date	Mintage	F	VF	XF	Unc	BU
2004PM Proof	10,000			Value: 50.00		

KM# 1206 CROWN
28.2800 g., Copper-Nickel, 38.6 mm. **Ruler:** Elizabeth II **Obv:** Bust with tiara right **Rev:** Harry Potter and Professor Dumbledore **Edge:** Reeded

Date	Mintage	F	VF	XF	Unc	BU
2004PM	—	—	—	—	15.00	17.00

KM# 1206a CROWN
28.2800 g., 0.9250 Silver 0.8410 oz. ASW, 38.6 mm. **Ruler:** Elizabeth II **Obv:** Bust with tiara right **Rev:** Harry Potter and Professor Dumbledore **Edge:** Reeded

Date	Mintage	F	VF	XF	Unc	BU
2004PM Proof	10,000			Value: 50.00		

KM# 1208 CROWN
28.2800 g., Copper-Nickel, 38.6 mm. **Ruler:** Elizabeth II **Obv:** Bust with tiara right **Rev:** Sirius Black on flying griffin **Edge:** Reeded

Date	Mintage	F	VF	XF	Unc	BU
2004PM	—	—	—	—	15.00	17.00

KM# 1208a CROWN
28.2800 g., 0.9250 Silver 0.8410 oz. ASW, 38.6 mm. **Ruler:** Elizabeth II **Obv:** Bust with tiara right **Rev:** Sirius Black on flying griffin **Edge:** Reeded

Date	Mintage	F	VF	XF	Unc	BU
2004PM Proof	10,000			Value: 50.00		

KM# 1210 CROWN
28.2800 g., Copper-Nickel, 38.6 mm. **Ruler:** Elizabeth II **Obv:** Bust with tiara right **Rev:** Three Olympic Swimmers **Edge:** Reeded

Date	Mintage	F	VF	XF	Unc	BU
2004PM	—	—	—	—	10.00	12.00

KM# 1210a CROWN
28.2800 g., 0.9250 Silver 0.8410 oz. ASW, 38.6 mm. **Ruler:** Elizabeth II **Obv:** Bust with tiara right **Rev:** Three Olympic Swimmers **Edge:** Reeded

Date	Mintage	F	VF	XF	Unc	BU
2004PM Proof	10,000			Value: 50.00		

KM# 1212 CROWN
28.2800 g., Copper-Nickel, 38.6 mm. **Ruler:** Elizabeth II **Obv:** Bust with tiara right **Rev:** Three Olympic Cyclists **Edge:** Reeded

Date	Mintage	F	VF	XF	Unc	BU
2004PM	—	—	—	—	10.00	12.00

KM# 1212a CROWN
28.2800 g., 0.9250 Silver 0.8410 oz. ASW, 38.6 mm. **Ruler:** Elizabeth II **Obv:** Bust with tiara right **Rev:** Three Olympic Cyclists **Edge:** Reeded

Date	Mintage	F	VF	XF	Unc	BU
2004PM Proof	10,000			Value: 50.00		

KM# 1214 CROWN
28.2800 g., Copper-Nickel, 38.6 mm. **Ruler:** Elizabeth II **Obv:** Bust with tiara right **Rev:** Three Olympic Runners **Edge:** Reeded

Date	Mintage	F	VF	XF	Unc	BU
2004PM	—	—	—	—	10.00	12.00

KM# 1214a CROWN
28.2800 g., 0.9250 Silver 0.8410 oz. ASW, 38.6 mm. **Ruler:** Elizabeth II **Obv:** Bust with tiara right **Rev:** Three Olympic Runners **Edge:** Reeded

Date	Mintage	F	VF	XF	Unc	BU
2004PM Proof	10,000			Value: 50.00		

KM# 1216 CROWN
28.2800 g., Copper-Nickel, 38.6 mm. **Ruler:** Elizabeth II **Obv:** Bust with tiara right **Rev:** Three Olympic Sail Boarders **Edge:** Reeded

Date	Mintage	F	VF	XF	Unc	BU
2004PM	—	—	—	—	10.00	12.00

KM# 1216a CROWN
28.2800 g., 0.9250 Silver 0.8410 oz. ASW, 38.6 mm. **Ruler:** Elizabeth II **Obv:** Bust with tiara right **Rev:** Three Olympic Sail Boarders **Edge:** Reeded

Date	Mintage	F	VF	XF	Unc	BU
2004PM Proof	10,000			Value: 50.00		

KM# 1218 CROWN
28.2800 g., Copper-Nickel, 38.6 mm. **Ruler:** Elizabeth II **Obv:** Bust with tiara right **Rev:** Ocean Liner Queen Mary 2 **Edge:** Reeded

Date	Mintage	F	VF	XF	Unc	BU
2004PM	—	—	—	—	15.00	17.00

KM# 1220 CROWN
28.2800 g., Copper-Nickel, 38.6 mm. **Ruler:** Elizabeth II **Obv:** Bust with tiara right **Rev:** Lt. Quillan portrait above Battle of Trafalgar scene **Edge:** Reeded

Date	Mintage	F	VF	XF	Unc	BU
2004PM	—	—	—	—	15.00	17.00

KM# 1220a CROWN
28.2800 g., 0.9250 Silver 0.8410 oz. ASW, 38.6 mm. **Ruler:** Elizabeth II **Obv:** Bust with tiara right **Rev:** Lt. Quillan portrait above Battle of Trafalgar scene **Edge:** Reeded

Date	Mintage	F	VF	XF	Unc	BU
2004PM Proof	10,000			Value: 50.00		

KM# 1221 CROWN
28.2800 g., Copper-Nickel, 38.6 mm. **Ruler:** Elizabeth II **Obv:** Bust with tiara right **Rev:** Napoleon and Nelson portraits above Battle of Trafalgar scene **Edge:** Reeded

Date	Mintage	F	VF	XF	Unc	BU
2004PM	—	—	—	—	15.00	17.00

KM# 1221a CROWN
28.2800 g., 0.9990 Silver 0.9083 oz. ASW, 38.6 mm. **Ruler:** Elizabeth II **Obv:** Bust with tiara right **Rev:** Napoleon and Nelson portraits above Battle of Trafalgar scene **Edge:** Reeded

Date	Mintage	F	VF	XF	Unc	BU
2004PM Proof	10,000			Value: 50.00		

KM# 1222 CROWN
28.2800 g., Copper-Nickel, 38.6 mm. **Ruler:** Elizabeth II **Obv:** Bust with tiara right **Rev:** D-Day Invasion Plan Map **Edge:** Reeded

Date	Mintage	F	VF	XF	Unc	BU
2004PM	—	—	—	—	15.00	17.00

KM# 1222a CROWN
28.2800 g., 0.9250 Silver 0.8410 oz. ASW, 38.6 mm. **Ruler:** Elizabeth II **Obv:** Bust with tiara right **Rev:** D-Day Invasion Plan Map **Edge:** Reeded

Date	Mintage	F	VF	XF	Unc	BU
2004PM Proof	10,000			Value: 50.00		

KM# 1224 CROWN
28.2800 g., Copper-Nickel, 38.6 mm. **Ruler:** Elizabeth II **Obv:** Bust with tiara right **Rev:** Victoria Cross and battle scene **Edge:** Reeded

Date	Mintage	F	VF	XF	Unc	BU
2004PM	—	—	—	—	15.00	17.00

KM# 1224a CROWN
28.2800 g., 0.8410 oz. ASW, 38.6 mm. **Ruler:** Elizabeth II **Obv:** Bust with tiara right **Rev:** Victoria Cross and battle scene **Edge:** Reeded

Date	Mintage	F	VF	XF	Unc	BU
2004PM Proof	10,000	Value: 50.00				

KM# 1226 CROWN
28.2800 g., Copper-Nickel, 38.6 mm. **Ruler:** Elizabeth II **Obv:** Bust with tiara right **Rev:** Silver Star and battle scene **Edge:** Reeded

Date	Mintage	F	VF	XF	Unc	BU
2004PM	—	—	—	—	15.00	17.00

KM# 1226a CROWN
28.2800 g., 0.9250 Silver 0.8410 oz. ASW, 38.6 mm. **Ruler:** Elizabeth II **Obv:** Bust with tiara right **Rev:** Silver Star and battle scene **Edge:** Reeded

Date	Mintage	F	VF	XF	Unc	BU
2004PM Proof	10,000	Value: 50.00				

KM# 1228 CROWN
28.2800 g., Copper-Nickel, 38.6 mm. **Ruler:** Elizabeth II **Obv:** Bust with tiara right **Rev:** George Cross and rescue scene **Edge:** Reeded

Date	Mintage	F	VF	XF	Unc	BU
2004PM	—	—	—	—	15.00	17.00

KM# 1228a CROWN
28.2800 g., 0.9250 Silver 0.8410 oz. ASW, 38.6 mm. **Ruler:** Elizabeth II **Obv:** Bust with tiara right **Rev:** George Cross and rescue scene **Edge:** Reeded

Date	Mintage	F	VF	XF	Unc	BU
2004PM Proof	10,000	Value: 50.00				

KM# 1230 CROWN
28.2800 g., Copper-Nickel, 38.6 mm. **Ruler:** Elizabeth II **Obv:** Bust with tiara right **Rev:** White Rose of Finland Medal and battle scene **Edge:** Reeded

Date	Mintage	F	VF	XF	Unc	BU
2004PM	—	—	—	—	15.00	17.00

KM# 1230a CROWN
28.2800 g., 0.9250 Silver 0.8410 oz. ASW, 38.6 mm. **Ruler:** Elizabeth II **Obv:** Bust with tiara right **Rev:** White Rose of Finland Medal and battle scene **Edge:** Reeded

Date	Mintage	F	VF	XF	Unc	BU
2004PM Proof	10,000	Value: 50.00				

KM# 1232 CROWN
28.2800 g., Copper-Nickel, 38.6 mm. **Ruler:** Elizabeth II **Obv:** Bust with tiara right **Rev:** The Norwegian War Medal and naval battle scene **Edge:** Reeded

Date	Mintage	F	VF	XF	Unc	BU
2004PM	—	—	—	—	15.00	17.00

KM# 1232a CROWN
28.2800 g., 0.9250 Silver 0.8410 oz. ASW, 38.6 mm. **Ruler:** Elizabeth II **Obv:** Bust with tiara right **Rev:** The Norwegian War Medal and a naval battle scene **Edge:** Reeded

Date	Mintage	F	VF	XF	Unc	BU
2004PM Proof	10,000	Value: 50.00				

KM# 1234 CROWN
28.2800 g., Copper-Nickel, 38.6 mm. **Ruler:** Elizabeth II **Obv:** Bust with tiara right **Rev:** French Croix de Guerre and partisan battle scene **Edge:** Reeded

Date	Mintage	F	VF	XF	Unc	BU
2004PM	—	—	—	—	15.00	17.00

KM# 1234a CROWN
28.2800 g., 0.9250 Silver 0.8410 oz. ASW, 38.6 mm. **Ruler:** Elizabeth II **Obv:** Bust with tiara right **Rev:** French Croix de Guerre and partisan battle scene **Edge:** Reeded

Date	Mintage	F	VF	XF	Unc	BU
2004PM Proof	10,000	Value: 50.00				

KM# 1236 CROWN
28.2800 g., Copper-Nickel, 38.6 mm. **Ruler:** Elizabeth II **Obv:** Bust with tiara right **Rev:** Multicolor cartoon soccer player **Edge:** Reeded

Date	Mintage	F	VF	XF	Unc	BU
2004PM	—	—	—	—	10.00	12.00

KM# 1236a CROWN
28.2800 g., 0.9250 Silver 0.8410 oz. ASW, 38.6 mm. **Ruler:** Elizabeth II **Obv:** Bust with tiara right **Rev:** Multicolor cartoon soccer player **Edge:** Reeded

Date	Mintage	F	VF	XF	Unc	BU
2004PM Proof	7,500	Value: 50.00				

KM# 1237 CROWN
28.2800 g., Copper-Nickel, 38.6 mm. **Ruler:** Elizabeth II **Obv:** Bust with tiara right **Rev:** Soccer ball in flight **Edge:** Reeded

Date	Mintage	F	VF	XF	Unc	BU
2004PM	—	—	—	—	10.00	12.00

KM# 1237a CROWN
28.2800 g., 0.9250 Silver 0.8410 oz. ASW, 38.6 mm. **Ruler:** Elizabeth II **Obv:** Bust with tiara right **Rev:** Soccer ball in flight **Edge:** Reeded

Date	Mintage	F	VF	XF	Unc	BU
2004PM Proof	7,500	Value: 50.00				

KM# 1238 CROWN
28.2800 g., Copper-Nickel, 38.6 mm. **Ruler:** Elizabeth II **Obv:** Bust with tiara right **Rev:** Gibbon monkey **Edge:** Reeded

Date	Mintage	F	VF	XF	Unc	BU
2004PM	—	—	—	—	10.00	15.00

KM# 1238a CROWN
28.2800 g., 0.9250 Silver 0.8410 oz. ASW, 38.6 mm. **Ruler:** Elizabeth II **Obv:** Bust with tiara right **Rev:** Monkey **Edge:** Reeded

Date	Mintage	F	VF	XF	Unc	BU
2004PM Proof	30,000	Value: 50.00				

KM# 1239 CROWN
31.1035 g., 0.9999 Gold 0.9999 oz. AGW, 32.7 mm. **Ruler:** Elizabeth II **Obv:** Bust with tiara right **Rev:** Monkey **Edge:** Reeded

Date	Mintage	F	VF	XF	Unc	BU
2004PM Proof	2,000	Value: 1,725				

KM# 1242 CROWN
6.2200 g., 0.9999 Gold 0.1999 oz. AGW, 22 mm. **Ruler:** Elizabeth II **Obv:** Bust with tiara right **Rev:** Monkey **Edge:** Reeded

Date	Mintage	F	VF	XF	Unc	BU
2004PM Proof	12,000	Value: 300				

KM# 1245 CROWN
28.2800 g., Copper-Nickel, 38.6 mm. **Ruler:** Elizabeth II **Subject:** Lord of the Rings **Obv:** Bust with tiara right **Rev:** Nine characters **Edge:** Reeded

Date	Mintage	F	VF	XF	Unc	BU
2004PM	100,000	—	—	—	15.00	17.00

KM# 1245a CROWN
28.2800 g., 0.9250 Silver 0.8410 oz. ASW, 38.6 mm. **Ruler:** Elizabeth II **Subject:** Lord of the Rings **Obv:** Bust with tiara right **Rev:** Nine characters **Edge:** Reeded

Date	Mintage	F	VF	XF	Unc	BU
2004PM Proof	10,000	Value: 50.00				

KM# 1246.1 CROWN
28.2800 g., Copper-Nickel, 38.6 mm. **Ruler:** Elizabeth II **Obv:** Head with tiara right **Rev:** Pair of Tonkinese cats **Edge:** Reeded

Date	Mintage	F	VF	XF	Unc	BU
2004PM	—	—	—	—	14.00	16.00

KM# 1246a.1 CROWN
31.1035 g., 0.9990 Silver 0.9990 oz. ASW, 38.6 mm. **Ruler:** Elizabeth II **Obv:** Head with tiara right **Rev:** Two Tonkinese cats **Edge:** Reeded

Date	Mintage	F	VF	XF	Unc	BU
2004PM Proof	50,000	Value: 50.00				

KM# 1246a.2 CROWN
31.1035 g., 0.9990 Silver 0.9990 oz. ASW, 38.6 mm. **Ruler:** Elizabeth II **Obv:** Head with tiara right **Rev:** Two multicolor Tonkinese cats **Edge:** Reeded

Date	Mintage	F	VF	XF	Unc	BU
2004PM Proof	—	Value: 55.00				

KM# 1251 CROWN
31.1035 g., 0.9999 Gold 0.9999 oz. AGW, 32.7 mm. **Ruler:** Elizabeth II **Obv:** Head with tiara right **Rev:** Two Tonkinese cats **Edge:** Reeded

Date	Mintage	F	VF	XF	Unc	BU
2004PM	—	—	—	—	—	1,700
2004PM Proof	1,000	Value: 1,725				

KM# 1246.2 CROWN
28.2800 g., Copper-Nickel **Ruler:** Elizabeth II **Obv:** Head with tiara right **Rev:** Two multicolor Tonkinese cats **Edge:** Reeded

Date	Mintage	F	VF	XF	Unc	BU
2004PM	—	—	—	—	14.00	16.00

KM# 1266 CROWN
28.3300 g., Copper-Nickel, 38.7 mm. **Ruler:** Elizabeth II **Obv:** Bust with tiara right **Rev:** Himalayan cat with two kittens **Edge:** Reeded

Date	Mintage	F	VF	XF	Unc	BU
2005PM	—	—	—	—	12.00	14.00

KM# 1266a CROWN
31.1030 g., 0.9990 Silver 0.9989 oz. ASW, 38.6 mm. **Ruler:** Elizabeth II **Obv:** Bust with tiara right **Rev:** Himalayan cat and two kittens **Edge:** Reeded

Date	Mintage	F	VF	XF	Unc	BU
2005PM Proof	50,000	Value: 50.00				

KM# 1268 CROWN
31.1030 g., 0.9999 Gold 0.9998 oz. AGW, 32.7 mm. **Ruler:** Elizabeth II **Obv:** Bust with tiara right **Rev:** Himalayan cat and two kittens **Edge:** Reeded

Date	Mintage	F	VF	XF	Unc	BU
2005PM Proof	—	Value: 1,725				

KM# 1273 CROWN
28.2800 g., Copper-Nickel, 38.6 mm. **Ruler:** Elizabeth II **Obv:** Bust with tiara right **Rev:** Harry Potter and the Hungarian Horn Tail, Tri-Wizard Tournament feat **Edge:** Reeded

Date	Mintage	F	VF	XF	Unc	BU
2005PM	—	—	—	—	15.00	17.00

KM# 1274 CROWN
28.2800 g., Copper-Nickel, 38.6 mm. **Ruler:** Elizabeth II **Subject:** 60th Anniversary - End of WW II **Obv:** Bust with tiara right **Rev:** Sir Winston Churchill

Date	Mintage	F	VF	XF	Unc	BU
2005	—	—	—	—	10.00	12.00

KM# 1275 CROWN
28.2800 g., Copper-Nickel, 38.6 mm. **Ruler:** Elizabeth II **Subject:** 400th Anniversary - Gunpowder plot **Obv:** Bust with tiara right **Rev:** Tower of London, Beefeaters

Date	Mintage	F	VF	XF	Unc	BU
2005	—	—	—	—	10.00	12.00

KM# 1276 CROWN
28.2800 g., Copper-Nickel, 38.6 mm. **Ruler:** Elizabeth II **Obv:**
Bust with tiara right **Rev:** Harry Potter and Tri-Wizard Tournament
feat - Underwater retrieval

Date	Mintage	F	VF	XF	Unc	BU
2005	—	—	—	—	10.00	12.00

KM# 1277 CROWN
28.2800 g., Copper-Nickel, 38.6 mm. **Ruler:** Elizabeth II **Obv:**
Bust with tiara right **Rev:** Harry Potter and pensive

Date	Mintage	F	VF	XF	Unc	BU
2005	—	—	—	—	10.00	12.00

KM# 1278 CROWN
28.2800 g., Copper-Nickel, 38.6 mm. **Ruler:** Elizabeth II **Obv:**
Bust with tiara right **Rev:** Harry Potter and portkey

Date	Mintage	F	VF	XF	Unc	BU
2005	—	—	—	—	10.00	12.00

KM# 1291 CROWN
28.2800 g., Copper-Nickel, 38.6 mm. **Ruler:** Elizabeth II
Subject: Trafalgar - 200th Anniversary **Obv:** Bust with tiara right
Rev: Nelson at Battle of Copenhagen

Date	Mintage	F	VF	XF	Unc	BU
2005	—	—	—	—	10.00	12.00

KM# 1279 CROWN
28.2800 g., Copper-Nickel, 38.6 mm. **Ruler:** Elizabeth II
Subject: The Battle of Cape St. Vincent **Obv:** Bust with tiara right
Rev: Naval battle scene

Date	Mintage	F	VF	XF	Unc	BU
2005	—	—	—	—	10.00	12.00

KM# 1280 CROWN
28.2800 g., Copper-Nickel, 38.6 mm. **Ruler:** Elizabeth II
Subject: Nelson Funeral Procession **Obv:** Bust with tiara right
Rev: Thames and Greenwich view

Date	Mintage	F	VF	XF	Unc	BU
2005	—	—	—	—	10.00	12.00

KM# 1281 CROWN
Copper-Nickel **Ruler:** Elizabeth II **Subject:** Battle of the Nile
Obv: Bust with tiara right **Rev:** Naval battle

Date	Mintage	F	VF	XF	Unc	BU
2005	—	—	—	—	10.00	12.00

KM# 1282 CROWN
28.2800 g., Copper-Nickel, 38.6 mm. **Ruler:** Elizabeth II
Subject: Norway Independence **Obv:** Bust with tiara right **Rev:**
Three swords

Date	Mintage	F	VF	XF	Unc	BU
2005	—	—	—	—	10.00	12.00

KM# 1283 CROWN
28.2800 g., Copper-Nickel, 38.6 mm. **Ruler:** Elizabeth II
Subject: Nelson - Trafalgar 300th Anniversary **Rev:** Nelson
portrait

Date	Mintage	F	VF	XF	Unc	BU
2005	—	—	—	—	10.00	12.00

KM# 1284 CROWN
28.2800 g., Copper-Nickel, 38.6 mm. **Ruler:** Elizabeth II
Subject: Battle of Trafalgar **Rev:** Naval battle scene

Date	Mintage	F	VF	XF	Unc	BU
2005	—	—	—	—	10.00	12.00

KM# 1285 CROWN
28.2800 g., Copper-Nickel, 38.6 mm. **Ruler:** Elizabeth II
Subject: Steam Packet - King Orry III **Obv:** Bust with tiara right
Rev: Ship view

Date	Mintage	F	VF	XF	Unc	BU
2005	—	—	—	—	10.00	12.00

KM# 1286 CROWN
28.2800 g., Copper-Nickel, 38.6 mm. **Ruler:** Elizabeth II
Subject: Isle of Man Steam Packet Company - 175th Anniversary
Obv: Bust with tiara right **Rev:** Modern and early ferry

Date	Mintage	F	VF	XF	Unc	BU
2005	—	—	—	—	10.00	12.00

KM# 1287 CROWN
28.2800 g., Copper-Nickel, 38.6 mm. **Ruler:** Elizabeth II **Rev:**
Motorcycle right

Date	Mintage	F	VF	XF	Unc	BU
2005	—	—	—	—	10.00	12.00

KM# 1288 CROWN
28.2800 g., Copper-Nickel, 38.6 mm. **Ruler:** Elizabeth II **Rev:**
Motorcycle forward

Date	Mintage	F	VF	XF	Unc	BU
2005	—	—	—	—	10.00	12.00

KM# 1289 CROWN
28.2800 g., Copper-Nickel, 38.6 mm. **Ruler:** Elizabeth II
Subject: Ugly Duckling story **Obv:** Bust with tiara right **Rev:** Farm
animals

Date	Mintage	F	VF	XF	Unc	BU
2005	—	—	—	—	12.00	14.00

KM# 1428 CROWN
28.2800 g., Copper-Nickel, 38.6 mm. **Ruler:** Elizabeth II
Subject: Traflagar, 200th Anniversary **Rev:** Quillian portrait
above naval battle scene

Date	Mintage	F	VF	XF	Unc	BU
2005PM	—	—	—	—	10.00	12.00

KM# 1429 CROWN
28.2800 g., Copper-Nickel, 38.6 mm. **Ruler:** Elizabeth II
Subject: Trafalgar, 200th Anniversary **Rev:** Napoleon and
Nelson portraits above Naval battle scene

Date	Mintage	F	VF	XF	Unc	BU
2005PM	—	—	—	—	10.00	12.00

KM# 1323.1 CROWN
28.2800 g., Copper-Nickel, 38.60 mm. **Ruler:** Elizabeth II
Subject: Hans Christian Anderson's Fairy Tales **Obv:** Bust with
tiarra right **Obv. Legend:** ELIZABETH II - ISLE OF MAN **Rev:**
Three bears startling Goldilocks in bed **Rev. Legend:** Goldilocks
and the Three Bears **Edge:** Reeded

Date	Mintage	F	VF	XF	Unc	BU
2006PM	—	—	—	—	—	35.00

KM# 1296 CROWN
28.2800 g., Copper-Nickel, 38.6 mm. **Ruler:** Elizabeth II
Subject: Battles that Changed the World **Obv:** Elizabeth II **Rev:** Trojan War scene **Edge:** Reeded

Date	Mintage	F	VF	XF	Unc	BU
2006PM	—	—	—	—	10.00	12.00

KM# 1296a CROWN
28.2800 g., 0.9250 Silver 0.8410 oz. ASW, 38.6 mm. **Ruler:** Elizabeth II **Subject:** Battles that Changed the World **Obv:** Elizabeth II **Rev:** Trojan War scene **Edge:** Reeded

Date	Mintage	F	VF	XF	Unc	BU
2006PM Proof	10,000	Value: 47.50				

KM# 1298 CROWN
28.2800 g., Copper-Nickel, 38.6 mm. **Ruler:** Elizabeth II
Subject: Battles that Changed the World **Obv:** Elizabeth II **Rev:** Battle of Arbela scene **Edge:** Reeded

Date	Mintage	F	VF	XF	Unc	BU
2006PM	—	—	—	—	10.00	12.00

KM# 1298a CROWN
28.2800 g., 0.9250 Silver 0.8410 oz. ASW, 38.6 mm. **Ruler:** Elizabeth II **Subject:** Battles that Changed the World **Obv:** Elizabeth II **Rev:** Battle of Arbela scene **Edge:** Reeded

Date	Mintage	F	VF	XF	Unc	BU
2006PM Proof	10,000	Value: 47.50				

KM# 1300 CROWN
28.2800 g., Copper-Nickel, 38.6 mm. **Ruler:** Elizabeth II
Subject: Battles that Changed the World **Obv:** Elizabeth II **Rev:** Battle of Thapsus scene **Edge:** Reeded

Date	Mintage	F	VF	XF	Unc	BU
2006PM	—	—	—	—	10.00	12.00

KM# 1300a CROWN
28.2800 g., 0.9250 Silver 0.8410 oz. ASW, 38.6 mm. **Ruler:** Elizabeth II **Subject:** Battles that Changed the World **Obv:** Elizabeth II **Rev:** Battle of Thapsus scene **Edge:** Reeded

Date	Mintage	F	VF	XF	Unc	BU
2006PM Proof	10,000	Value: 47.50				

KM# 1302 CROWN
28.2800 g., Copper-Nickel, 38.6 mm. **Ruler:** Elizabeth II
Subject: Battles that Changed the World **Obv:** Elizabeth II **Rev:** Battle of Cologne scene **Edge:** Reeded

Date	Mintage	F	VF	XF	Unc	BU
2006PM	—	—	—	—	10.00	12.00

KM# 1302a CROWN
28.2800 g., 0.9250 Silver 0.8410 oz. ASW, 38.6 mm. **Ruler:** Elizabeth II **Subject:** Battles that Changed the World **Obv:** Elizabeth II **Rev:** Battle of Cologne scene **Edge:** Reeded

Date	Mintage	F	VF	XF	Unc	BU
2006PM Proof	10,000	Value: 47.50				

KM# 1304 CROWN
28.2800 g., Copper-Nickel, 38.6 mm. **Ruler:** Elizabeth II
Subject: Battles that Changed the World **Obv:** Elizabeth II **Rev:** Siege of Valencia scene **Edge:** Reeded

Date	Mintage	F	VF	XF	Unc	BU
2006PM	—	—	—	—	10.00	12.00

KM# 1304a CROWN
28.2800 g., 0.9250 Silver 0.8410 oz. ASW, 38.6 mm. **Ruler:** Elizabeth II **Subject:** Battles that Changed the World **Obv:** Elizabeth II **Rev:** Siege of Valencia scene **Edge:** Reeded

Date	Mintage	F	VF	XF	Unc	BU
2006PM Proof	10,000	Value: 47.50				

KM# 1306 CROWN
28.2800 g., Copper-Nickel, 38.6 mm. **Ruler:** Elizabeth II
Subject: Battles that Changed the World **Obv:** Elizabeth II **Rev:** Battle of Agincourt scene **Edge:** Reeded

Date	Mintage	F	VF	XF	Unc	BU
2006PM	—	—	—	—	10.00	12.00

KM# 1306a CROWN
28.2800 g., 0.9250 Silver 0.8410 oz. ASW, 38.6 mm. **Ruler:** Elizabeth II **Subject:** Battles that Changed the World **Obv:** Elizabeth II **Rev:** Battle of Agincourt scene **Edge:** Reeded

Date	Mintage	F	VF	XF	Unc	BU
2006PM Proof	10,000	Value: 47.50				

KM# 1323.2 CROWN
28.2800 g., Copper-Nickel, 38.60 mm. **Ruler:** Elizabeth II
Subject: Hans Christian Anderson's Fairy Tales **Obv:** Bust with tiara right **Obv. Legend:** ELIZABETH II - ISLE OF MAN **Rev:** Three bears startling Goldilocks in bed multicolor **Rev. Legend:** Goldilocks and the Three Bears **Edge:** Reeded

Date	Mintage	F	VF	XF	Unc	BU
2006PM	—	—	—	—	—	40.00

KM# 1323.1a CROWN
28.2800 g., 0.9250 Silver 0.8410 oz. ASW, 38.60 mm. **Ruler:** Elizabeth II **Subject:** Hans Christian Anderson's Fairy Tales **Obv:** Bust with tiara right **Obv. Legend:** ELIZABETH II - ISLE OF MAN **Rev:** Three bears startling Goldilocks in bed **Rev. Legend:** Goldilocks and the Three Bears **Edge:** Reeded

Date	Mintage	F	VF	XF	Unc	BU
2006PM Proof	—	Value: 80.00				

KM# 1323.2a CROWN
28.2800 g., 0.9250 Silver 0.8410 oz. ASW, 38.60 mm. **Ruler:** Elizabeth II **Subject:** Hans Christian Anderson's Fairy Tales **Obv:** Bust with tiara right **Obv. Legend:** ELIZABETH II - ISLE OF MAN **Rev:** Three bears startling Goldilocks in bed multicolor **Rev. Legend:** Goldilocks and the Three Bears **Edge:** Reeded

Date	Mintage	F	VF	XF	Unc	BU
2006PM Proof	—	Value: 100				

KM# 1290a CROWN
28.2800 g., Copper-Nickel, 38.6 mm. **Ruler:** Elizabeth II **Obv:** Bust with tiara right **Rev:** Three Exotic Shorthair cats sitting facing **Edge:** Reeded

Date	Mintage	F	VF	XF	Unc	BU
2006PM	—	—	—	—	12.00	14.00

KM# 1290b CROWN
28.2800 g., 0.9250 Silver 0.8410 oz. ASW, 38.6 mm. **Ruler:** Elizabeth II **Obv:** Bust with tiara right **Rev:** Three Exotic Shorthair cats sitting facing **Edge:** Reeded

Date	Mintage	F	VF	XF	Unc	BU
2006PM	—	—	—	—	30.00	32.50

KM# 1290c CROWN
31.1030 g., 0.9999 Gold 0.9998 oz. AGW **Ruler:** Elizabeth II
Obv: Bust with tiara right **Rev:** Three Exotic Shorthair cats sitting facing, multicolor **Edge:** Reeded

Date	Mintage	F	VF	XF	Unc	BU
2006PM	—	—	—	—	—	1,725

KM# 1423.1 CROWN
28.2800 g., Copper-Nickel, 38.6 mm. **Ruler:** Elizabeth II
Subject: Concord, 30th Anniversary of transatlantic service **Obv:** Bust with tiara right **Rev:** Concord in flight, buildings below

Date	Mintage	F	VF	XF	Unc	BU
2006PM Proof	—	Value: 30.00				

KM# 1423.2 CROWN
28.2800 g., Copper-Nickel, 38.6 mm. **Ruler:** Elizabeth II
Subject: Concorde, 30th Anniversary of transatlantic service **Obv:** Bust with tiara right **Rev:** Concorde in flight, multicolor

Date	Mintage	F	VF	XF	Unc	BU
2006PM Proof	—	Value: 50.00				

KM# 1347 CROWN
31.1030 g., 0.9999 Gold 0.9998 oz. AGW **Ruler:** Elizabeth II
Obv: Bust with tiara right **Obv. Legend:** ELIZABETH II - ISLE OF MAN **Rev:** Ragdoll cat with two kittens sitting facing **Edge:** Reeded

Date	Mintage	F	VF	XF	Unc	BU
2007PM	—	—	—	—	—	1,725

KM# 1348.1 CROWN
Copper-Nickel **Ruler:** Elizabeth II **Subject:** The Tale of Peter Rabbit **Obv:** Bust with tiara right **Obv. Legend:** ELIZABETH II - ISLE OF MAN **Rev:** Peter walking with friends **Edge:** Reeded

Date	Mintage	F	VF	XF	Unc	BU
2007PM	—	—	—	—	—	30.00

KM# 1348.2 CROWN
Copper-Nickel **Ruler:** Elizabeth II **Subject:** The Tale of Peter Rabbit **Obv:** Bust with tiara right **Obv. Legend:** ELIZABETH II - ISLE OF MAN **Rev:** Peter walking with friends, multicolor **Edge:** Reeded

Date	Mintage	F	VF	XF	Unc	BU
2007PM	—	—	—	—	—	35.00

KM# 1348.1a CROWN
0.9250 Silver **Ruler:** Elizabeth II **Subject:** The Tale of Peter Rabbit **Obv:** Bust with tiara right **Obv. Legend:** ELIZABETH II - ISLE OF MAN **Rev:** Peter walking with friends **Edge:** Reeded

Date	Mintage	F	VF	XF	Unc	BU
2007PM Proof	—	Value: 50.00				

KM# 1348.2a CROWN
0.9250 Silver **Ruler:** Elizabeth II **Subject:** The Tale of Peter Rabbit **Obv:** Bust with tiara right **Obv. Legend:** ELIZABETH II - ISLE OF MAN **Rev:** Peter walking with friends, multicolor **Edge:** Reeded

Date	Mintage	F	VF	XF	Unc	BU
2007PM Proof	—	Value: 75.00				

KM# 1310 CROWN
28.2800 g., Copper-Nickel, 38.6 mm. **Ruler:** Elizabeth II **Subject:** 100th Anniversary of Scouting **Obv:** Bust with tiara right **Obv. Legend:** ELIZABETH II - ISLE OF MAN **Rev:** 3/4 length figure of Robert Baden-Powell standing facing 3/4 left, Fleur-de-lys below, images of scouting at left and right **Rev. Legend:** CENTENARY OF SCOUTING **Edge:** Reeded

Date	Mintage	F	VF	XF	Unc	BU
2007	—	—	—	—	17.00	20.00

KM# 1311 CROWN
28.2800 g., 0.9167 Silver 0.8334 oz. ASW **Ruler:** Elizabeth II **Subject:** 100th Anniversary of Scouting **Obv:** Bust with tiara right **Obv. Legend:** ELIZABETH II - ISLE OF MAN **Rev:** 3/4 length figure of Robert Baden-Powell standing facing 3/4 left, Fleur-de-lys below, images of scouting at left and right **Rev. Legend:** CENTENARY OF SCOUTING **Edge:** Reeded

Date	Mintage	F	VF	XF	Unc	BU
2007 Proof	—	Value: 50.00				

KM# 1312 CROWN
0.7500 Gold Yellow, white and red Gold **Ruler:** Elizabeth II **Subject:** Diamond Wedding Anniversary **Obv:** Bust with tiara right **Obv. Legend:** ELIZABETH II - ISLE OF MAN **Rev:** Crowned pair of doves surrounded by a leek, thistle, rose and shamrock **Edge:** Reeded

Date	Mintage	F	VF	XF	Unc	BU
2007 Proof	—	Value: 2,000				

KM# 1313 CROWN
28.2800 g., Copper-Nickel, 38.60 mm. **Ruler:** Elizabeth II **Obv:** Bust with tiara right **Obv. Legend:** ELIZABETH II - ISLE OF MAN **Rev:** Two swans facing **Edge:** Reeded

Date	Mintage	F	VF	XF	Unc	BU
2007	—	—	—	—	15.00	18.00

KM# 1315 CROWN
28.2800 g., 0.9167 Silver 0.8334 oz. ASW, 38.60 mm. **Ruler:** Elizabeth II **Obv:** Bust with tiara right **Obv. Legend:** ELIZABETH II - ISLE OF MAN **Rev:** Two swans facing **Edge:** Reeded

Date	Mintage	F	VF	XF	Unc	BU
2007 Proof	10,000	Value: 50.00				

KM# 1316 CROWN
28.2800 g., Copper-Nickel, 38.6 mm. **Ruler:** Elizabeth II **Subject:** Diamond Wedding Anniversary **Obv:** Conjoined busts with Philip right **Obv. Legend:** ELIZABETH II - ISLE OF MAN **Rev:** Bridal bouquet of white orchids **Rev. Legend:** Diamond Wedding of H.M. Queen Elizabeth II & H.R.H. Prince Philip **Edge:** Reeded

Date	Mintage	F	VF	XF	Unc	BU
2007	—	—	—	—	15.00	18.00

KM# 1316a CROWN
28.2800 g., 0.9167 Silver 0.8334 oz. ASW **Ruler:** Elizabeth II **Subject:** Diamond Wedding Anniversary **Obv:** Conjoined busts with Philip right **Obv. Legend:** ELIZABETH II - ISLE OF MAN **Rev:** Bridal bouquet of white orchids **Rev. Legend:** Diamond Wedding of H.M. Queen Elizabeth II & H.R.H. Prince Philip **Edge:** Reeded

Date	Mintage	F	VF	XF	Unc	BU
2007 Proof	—	Value: 50.00				

KM# 1317 CROWN
28.2800 g., Copper-Nickel **Ruler:** Elizabeth II **Subject:** Diamond Wedding Anniversary **Obv:** Conjoined busts with Philip right **Obv. Legend:** ELIZABETH II - ISLE OF MAN **Rev:** Westminster Abbey **Rev. Legend:** Diamond Wedding of H.M. Queen Elizabeth II & H.R.H. Prince Philip **Edge:** Reeded

Date	Mintage	F	VF	XF	Unc	BU
2007	—	—	—	—	15.00	18.00

KM# 1317a CROWN
28.2800 g., 0.9167 Silver 0.8334 oz. ASW **Ruler:** Elizabeth II **Subject:** Diamond Wedding Anniversary **Obv:** Conjoined busts with Philip right **Obv. Legend:** ELIZABETH II - ISLE OF MAN **Rev:** Westminster Abbey **Rev. Legend:** Diamond Wedding of H.M. Queen Elizabeth II & H.R.H. Prince Philip **Edge:** Reeded

Date	Mintage	F	VF	XF	Unc	BU
2007 Proof	—	Value: 50.00				

KM# 1318 CROWN
28.2800 g., Copper-Nickel, 38.6 mm. **Ruler:** Elizabeth II **Subject:** Diamond Wedding Anniversary **Obv:** Conjoined busts with Philip right **Obv. Legend:** ELIZABETH II - ISLE OF MAN **Rev:** Royal Family of five standing facing **Rev. Legend:** Diamond Wedding of H.M. Queen Elizabeth II & H.R.H. Prince Philip **Edge:** Reeded

Date	Mintage	F	VF	XF	Unc	BU
2007	—	—	—	—	15.00	18.00

KM# 1318a CROWN
28.2800 g., 0.9167 Silver 0.8334 oz. ASW, 38.6 mm. **Ruler:** Elizabeth II **Subject:** Diamond Wedding Anniversary **Obv:** Conjoined busts with Philip right **Obv. Legend:** ELIZABETH II - ISLE OF MAN **Rev:** Royal Family of five standing facing **Rev. Legend:** Diamond Wedding of H.M. Queen Elizabeth II & H.R.H. Prince Philip **Edge:** Reeded

Date	Mintage	F	VF	XF	Unc	BU
2007 Proof	—	Value: 50.00				

KM# 1319 CROWN
28.2800 g., Copper-Nickel, 38.6 mm. **Ruler:** Elizabeth II **Subject:** Diamond Wedding Anniversary **Obv:** Conjoined busts with Philip right **Obv. Legend:** ELIZABETH II - ISLE OF MAN **Rev:** Bride and groom standing facing **Rev. Legend:** Diamond Wedding of H.M. Queen Elizabeth II & H.R.H. Prince Philip **Edge:** Reeded

Date	Mintage	F	VF	XF	Unc	BU
2007	—	—	—	—	15.00	18.00

KM# 1319a CROWN
28.2800 g., 0.9167 Silver 0.8334 oz. ASW, 38.6 mm. **Ruler:** Elizabeth II **Subject:** Diamond Wedding Anniversary **Obv:** Conjoined busts with Philip right **Obv. Legend:** ELIZABETH II - ISLE OF MAN **Rev:** Bride and groom standing facing **Rev. Legend:** Diamond Wedding of H.M. Queen Elizabeth II & H.R.H. Prince Philip **Edge:** Reeded

Date	Mintage	F	VF	XF	Unc	BU
2007 Proof	—	Value: 50.00				

KM# 1325.1 CROWN
28.2800 g., Copper-Nickel, 38.60 mm. **Ruler:** Elizabeth II **Subject:** Hans Christian Anderson's Fairy Tales **Obv:** Bust with tiara right **Obv. Legend:** ELIZABETH II - ISLE OF MAN **Rev:** Wolf at right trying to blow pig's house down, two pigs fleeing above in background **Rev. Legend:** Three Little Pigs **Edge:** Reeded

Date	Mintage	F	VF	XF	Unc	BU
2007PM	—	—	—	—	—	35.00

KM# 1325.2 CROWN
28.2800 g., Copper-Nickel, 38.60 mm. **Ruler:** Elizabeth II **Subject:** Hans Christian Anderson's Fairy Tales **Obv:** Bust with tiara right **Obv. Legend:** ELIZABETH II - ISLE OF MAN **Rev:** Wolf at right trying to blow pig's house down, two pigs fleeing above in backgound multicolor **Rev. Legend:** Three Little Pigs **Edge:** Reeded

Date	Mintage	F	VF	XF	Unc	BU
2007PM	—	—	—	—	—	40.00

KM# 1325.1a CROWN
28.2800 g., 0.9250 Silver 0.8410 oz. ASW, 38.60 mm. **Ruler:** Elizabeth II **Subject:** Hans Christian Anderson's Fairy Tales **Obv:** Bust with tiara right **Obv. Legend:** ELIZABETH II - ISLE OF MAN **Rev:** Wolf at right trying to blow pig's house down, two pigs fleeing above in background **Rev. Legend:** Three Little Pigs **Edge:** Reeded

Date	Mintage	F	VF	XF	Unc	BU
2007PM Proof	—	Value: 50.00				

KM# 1325.2a CROWN
28.2800 g., 0.9250 Silver 0.8410 oz. ASW, 38.60 mm. **Ruler:** Elizabeth II **Subject:** Hans Christian Anderson's Fairy Tales **Obv:** Bust with tiara right **Obv. Legend:** ELIZABETH II - ISLE OF MAN **Rev:** Wolf at right trying to blow pig's house down, two pigs fleeing above in background multicolor **Rev. Legend:** Three Little Pigs **Edge:** Reeded

Date	Mintage	F	VF	XF	Unc	BU
2007PM Proof	—	Value: 75.00				

KM# 1307.1 CROWN
28.2800 g., Copper-Nickel, 38.6 mm. **Ruler:** Elizabeth II **Rev:** Ragdoll cat and kittens

Date	Mintage	F	VF	XF	Unc	BU
2007	—	—	—	—	15.00	18.00

KM# 1307.2 CROWN
28.2800 g., Copper-Nickel, 38.6 mm. **Ruler:** Elizabeth II **Rev:** Three cats, multicolor

Date	Mintage	F	VF	XF	Unc	BU
2007PM	—	—	—	—	—	25.00

KM# 1324.1 CROWN
28.2800 g., Copper-Nickel, 38.60 mm. **Ruler:** Elizabeth II **Subject:** Hans Christian Anderson's Fairy Tales **Obv:** Bust with tiara right **Obv. Legend:** ELIZABETH II - ISLE OF MAN **Rev:** Prince awakening Sleeping Beauty, castle in background **Rev. Legend:** Sleeping Beauty **Edge:** Reeded

Date	Mintage	F	VF	XF	Unc	BU
2007PM	—	—	—	—	—	25.00

KM# 1324.1a CROWN
28.2800 g., 0.9250 Silver 0.8410 oz. ASW, 38.60 mm. **Ruler:** Elizabeth II **Subject:** Hans Christian Anderson's Fairy Tales **Obv:** Bust with tiara right **Obv. Legend:** ELIZABETH II - ISLE OF MAN **Rev:** Prince wakening Sleeping Beauty, castle in background **Rev. Legend:** Sleeping Beauty **Edge:** Reeded

Date	Mintage	F	VF	XF	Unc	BU
2007PM Proof	—	Value: 50.00				

KM# 1324.2 CROWN
28.2800 g., Copper-Nickel, 38.60 mm. **Ruler:** Elizabeth II **Subject:** Hans Christian Anderson's Fairy Tales **Obv:** Bust with tiara right **Obv. Legend:** ELIZABET II - ISLE OF MAN **Rev:** Prince awakening Sleeping Beauty, castle in background multicolor **Rev. Legend:** Sleeping Beauty **Edge:** Reeded

Date	Mintage	F	VF	XF	Unc	BU
2007PM	—	—	—	—	—	25.00

KM# 1324.2a CROWN
28.2800 g., 0.9250 Silver 0.8410 oz. ASW, 38.60 mm. **Ruler:** Elizabeth II **Subject:** Hans Christian Anderson's Fairy Tales **Obv:** Bust with tiara right **Obv. Legend:** ELIZABETH II - ISLE OF MAN **Rev:** Prince awakening Sleeping Beauty, castle in background multicolor **Rev. Legend:** Sleeping Beauty **Edge:** Reeded

Date	Mintage	F	VF	XF	Unc	BU
2007PM Proof	—	Value: 50.00				

KM# 1418 CROWN
28.2800 g., Copper-Nickel, 38.6 mm. **Ruler:** Elizabeth II **Subject:** TT Centennial **Obv:** Bust with tiara right **Rev:** Motorcyclist left

Date	Mintage	F	VF	XF	Unc	BU
2007PM	—	—	—	—	15.00	17.00

KM# 1419 CROWN
28.2800 g., Copper-Nickel, 38.6 mm. **Ruler:** Elizabeth II **Subject:** TT Centennial **Obv:** Bust with tiara right **Rev:** Motorcyclists Dunlop

Date	Mintage	F	VF	XF	Unc	BU
2007PM	—	—	—	—	15.00	17.00

KM# 1420 CROWN
28.2800 g., Copper-Nickel, 38.6 mm. **Ruler:** Elizabeth II **Subject:** TT Centennial **Obv:** Bust with tiara right **Rev:** Motorcyclists Woods

Date	Mintage	F	VF	XF	Unc	BU
2007PM	—	—	—	—	15.00	17.00

KM# 1421 CROWN
28.2800 g., Copper-Nickel, 38.6 mm. **Ruler:** Elizabeth II **Subject:** TT Centennial **Obv:** Bust with tiara right **Rev:** Motorcyclists Haliwood

Date	Mintage	F	VF	XF	Unc	BU
2007PM	—	—	—	—	15.00	17.00

KM# 1422 CROWN
28.2800 g., Copper-Nickel, 38.6 mm. **Ruler:** Elizabeth II
Subject: TT Centennial **Obv:** Bust with tiara right **Rev:** Motorcyclists Colier

Date	Mintage	F	VF	XF	Unc	BU
2007PM	—	—	—	—	15.00	17.00

KM# 1394 CROWN
28.2800 g., Copper-Nickel, 38.6 mm. **Ruler:** Elizabeth II **Rev:** Snowman and James

Date	Mintage	F	VF	XF	Unc	BU
2008PM AA	—	—	—	—	—	20.00

KM# 1397 CROWN
0.9250 Silver, 56.2x40 mm. **Ruler:** Elizabeth II **Obv:** Bust with tiara right within Egyptian motif **Rev:** Seated figure and attendant **Shape:** Triangle

Date	Mintage	F	VF	XF	Unc	BU
2008PM Proof	2,500	Value: 75.00				

KM# 1398 CROWN
0.9250 Silver, 56.2x40 mm. **Ruler:** Elizabeth II **Obv:** Bust right in Tiaria within Egyptian motif **Rev:** Statue standing **Shape:** Triangle

Date	Mintage	F	VF	XF	Unc	BU
2008PM Proof	2,500	Value: 75.00				

KM# 1401 CROWN
28.2800 g., 0.9250 Silver 0.8410 oz. ASW, 38.6 mm. **Ruler:** Elizabeth II **Obv:** Bust with tiara right, multicolor band around **Rev:** Seated figures, multicolor band

Date	Mintage	F	VF	XF	Unc	BU
2008PM Proof	—	Value: 65.00				

KM# 1403 CROWN
28.2800 g., Copper-Nickel, 38.6 mm. **Ruler:** Elizabeth II
Subject: Bejing Olympics **Obv:** Bust with tiara right **Rev:** Torch runner and Great Wall of China

Date	Mintage	F	VF	XF	Unc	BU
2008PM Proof	—	Value: 25.00				

KM# 1404 CROWN
28.2800 g., Copper-Nickel, 38.6 mm. **Ruler:** Elizabeth II **Obv:** Bust wiht tiara right **Rev:** Paddington Bear

Date	Mintage	F	VF	XF	Unc	BU
2008PM Proof	—	Value: 25.00				

KM# 1405 CROWN
31.1030 g., 0.9990 Silver 0.9989 oz. ASW, 56.2x40.7 mm. **Ruler:** Elizabeth II **Obv:** Bust with tiara right **Rev:** Three figures standing, vile of sand above **Shape:** Triangle

Date	Mintage	F	VF	XF	Unc	BU
2008PM Proof	3,000	Value: 75.00				

KM# 1353 CROWN
28.2800 g., Copper-Nickel, 38.6 mm. **Ruler:** Elizabeth II
Subject: Prince Charles 60th Birthday **Obv:** Bust with tiara right **Obv. Legend:** ELIZABETH II - ISLE OF MAN **Rev:** Heads of Charles, Princes William and Henry right **Edge:** Reeded

Date	Mintage	F	VF	XF	Unc	BU
2008PM					10.00	12.00

KM# 1353a CROWN
28.2800 g., 0.9250 Silver 0.8410 oz. ASW, 38.6 mm. **Ruler:** Elizabeth II **Subject:** Prince Charles 60th Birthday **Obv:** Bust with tiara right **Obv. Legend:** ELIZABETH II - ISLE OF MAN **Rev:** Heads of Charles, Princes William and Henry right **Edge:** Reeded

Date	Mintage	F	VF	XF	Unc	BU
2008PM Proof	10,000	Value: 50.00				

KM# 1424 CROWN
28.2800 g., Copper-Nickel, 38.6 mm. **Ruler:** Elizabeth II **Obv:** Bust with tiara right **Rev:** Two cats seated

Date	Mintage	F	VF	XF	Unc	BU
2008PM	—	—	—	—	15.00	17.00

KM# 1424a CROWN
31.1050 g., 0.9990 Silver 0.9990 oz. ASW, 38.6 mm. **Ruler:** Elizabeth II **Obv:** Bust with tiara right **Rev:** Two cats seated

Date	Mintage	F	VF	XF	Unc	BU
2008PM Proof	—	Value: 50.00				

KM# 1373 CROWN
28.2800 g., Copper-Nickel, 38.6 mm. **Ruler:** Elizabeth II **Rev:** Berlin Wall and Brandenburg Gate statue group

Date	Mintage	F	VF	XF	Unc	BU
2009	—	—	—	—	15.00	18.00

KM# 1373a CROWN
28.2800 g., 0.9250 Silver 0.8410 oz. ASW, 38.6 mm. **Ruler:** Elizabeth II **Rev:** Berlin Wall and Brandenberg Gate

Date	Mintage	F	VF	XF	Unc	BU
2009 Proof	10,000	Value: 40.00				

KM# 1374 CROWN
28.2800 g., Copper-Nickel, 38.6 mm. **Ruler:** Elizabeth II
Subject: Terra Cotta Army **Obv:** Bust right **Rev:** Making of the Soldier

Date	Mintage	F	VF	XF	Unc	BU
2009	—	—	—	—	12.00	15.00

KM# 1374a CROWN
28.2800 g., 0.9250 Silver 0.8410 oz. ASW, 38.6 mm. **Ruler:** Elizabeth II **Subject:** Terra Cotta Army **Obv:** Bust right **Rev:** Making of the Soldier

Date	Mintage	F	VF	XF	Unc	BU
2009 Proof	10,000	Value: 40.00				

KM# 1376 CROWN
28.2800 g., 0.9250 Copper-Nickel 0.8410 oz., 38.6 mm. **Ruler:**
Elizabeth II **Subject:** Terra Cotta Army **Obv:** Bust right **Rev:**
Making of the Horse

Date	Mintage	F	VF	XF	Unc	BU
2009	—	—	—	—	12.00	15.00

KM# 1376a CROWN
28.2800 g., 0.9250 Silver 0.8410 oz. ASW, 38.6 mm. **Ruler:**
Elizabeth II **Subject:** Terra Cotta Army **Obv:** Bust right **Rev:**
Making of the Horse

Date	Mintage	F	VF	XF	Unc	BU
2009 Proof	10,000	Value: 40.00				

KM# 1379 CROWN
31.1050 g., 0.9999 Gold 0.9999 oz. AGW, 32.7 mm. **Ruler:**
Elizabeth II **Obv:** Bust right **Rev:** Chinchilla cat and kitten

Date	Mintage	F	VF	XF	Unc	BU
2009	—	—	—	—	—	1,700
2009 Proof	1,000	Value: 1,725				

KM# 1388 CROWN
31.1050 g., 0.9999 Gold 0.9999 oz. AGW, 45x31.1 mm. **Ruler:**
Elizabeth II **Subject:** Howard Carter, 70th Anniversary of Death
Obv: Bust right **Rev:** Pharoah and Anubis carving, encased with
sand **Shape:** Triangle

Date	Mintage	F	VF	XF	Unc	BU
2009 Proof	250	Value: 1,725				

KM# 1389 CROWN
31.1030 g., 0.9990 Silver 0.9989 oz. ASW, 56.2x40.7 mm.
Ruler: Elizabeth II **Subject:** Howard Carter, 70th Anniversary of
death **Obv:** Bust right **Rev:** Pharoah and Anubis, encased with
sand **Shape:** Triangle

Date	Mintage	F	VF	XF	Unc	BU
2009 Proof	3,000	Value: 125				

KM# 1391 CROWN
28.2800 g., Copper-Nickel, 38.6 mm. **Ruler:** Elizabeth II **Obv:**
Bust right **Rev:** Henry VIII and portraits of wives

Date	Mintage	F	VF	XF	Unc	BU
2009	—	—	—	—	15.00	18.00

KM# 1391a CROWN
28.2800 g., 0.9250 Silver 0.8410 oz. ASW, 38.6 mm. **Ruler:**
Elizabeth II **Obv:** Bust right **Rev:** Henry VIII

Date	Mintage	F	VF	XF	Unc	BU
2009 Proof	10,000	Value: 40.00				

KM# 1392 CROWN
28.2800 g., Copper-Nickel, 38.6 mm. **Ruler:** Elizabeth II
Subject: FIFA World Cup - South Africa **Obv:** Bust right **Rev:**
Two soccer players

Date	Mintage	F	VF	XF	Unc	BU
2009	—	—	—	—	15.00	18.00

KM# 1392a CROWN
28.2800 g., 0.9250 Silver 0.8410 oz. ASW, 38.6 mm. **Ruler:**
Elizabeth II **Subject:** FIFA World Cup - South Africa **Obv:** Bust
right

Date	Mintage	F	VF	XF	Unc	BU
2009 Proof	10,000	Value: 40.00				

KM# 1378.1 CROWN
28.2800 g., Copper-Nickel, 38.6 mm. **Ruler:** Elizabeth II **Obv:**
Bust right **Rev:** Chinchilla cat and kitten

Date	Mintage	F	VF	XF	Unc	BU
2009	—	—	—	—	15.00	18.00

KM# 1378.1a CROWN
31.1050 g., 0.9990 Silver 0.9990 oz. ASW, 38.6 mm. **Ruler:**
Elizabeth II **Obv:** Bust with tiara right **Rev:** Two cats

Date	Mintage	F	VF	XF	Unc	BU
2009PM Proof	—	Value: 50.00				

KM# 1378.2 CROWN
28.2800 g., Copper-Nickel, 38.6 mm. **Ruler:** Elizabeth II **Obv:**
Bust right **Rev:** Multicolor chinchilla cat and kitten

Date	Mintage	F	VF	XF	Unc	BU
2009	—	—	—	—	—	25.00

KM# 1378.2a CROWN
31.1050 g., 0.9990 Silver 0.9990 oz. ASW, 38.6 mm. **Ruler:**
Elizabeth II **Obv:** Bust with tiara right **Rev:** Two cats, multicolor

Date	Mintage	F	VF	XF	Unc	BU
2009PM Proof	—	Value: 50.00				

KM# 1390.1 CROWN
28.2800 g., Copper-Nickel, 38.6 mm. **Ruler:** Elizabeth II
Subject: Concorde test flight, 40th Anniversary **Obv:** Bust right
Rev: Concorde and five world landmarks

Date	Mintage	F	VF	XF	Unc	BU
2009	—	—	—	—	15.00	18.00

KM# 1390.1a CROWN
28.2800 g., 0.9250 Silver 0.8410 oz. ASW, 38.6 mm. **Ruler:**
Elizabeth II **Subject:** Corcorde test flight, 40th Anniversary **Obv:**
Bust right **Rev:** Concorde and five world landmarks

Date	Mintage	F	VF	XF	Unc	BU
2009 Proof	10,000	Value: 40.00				

KM# 1390.2 CROWN
28.2800 g., Copper-Nickel, 38.6 mm. **Ruler:** Elizabeth II
Subject: 40th Anniversary of test flight **Rev:** Concorde in color

Date	Mintage	F	VF	XF	Unc	BU
2009PM	—	—	—	—	—	25.00

KM# 1406 CROWN
28.2800 g., Copper-Nickel, 38.6 mm. **Ruler:** Elizabeth II **Series:**
London Olympics 2012 **Obv:** Bust wiht tiara right **Rev:** Three
cyclists before Buckingham Palace

Date	Mintage	F	VF	XF	Unc	BU
2009PM Proof	—	Value: 25.00				

KM# 1406a CROWN
28.2800 g., 0.9250 Silver 0.8410 oz. ASW, 38.6 mm. **Ruler:**
Elizabeth II **Series:** Olympics, London **Rev:** Three cyclists
speeding past Buckingham Palace

Date	Mintage	F	VF	XF	Unc	BU
2009PM Proof	10,000	Value: 50.00				

KM# 1407 CROWN
28.2800 g., Copper-Nickel, 38.6 mm. **Ruler:** Elizabeth II
Subject: London Olympics, 2012 **Obv:** Bust with tiara right **Rev:**
Rowers before Big Ben and Parliament

Date	Mintage	F	VF	XF	Unc	BU
2009PM Proof	—	Value: 25.00				

KM# 1407a CROWN
28.2800 g., 0.9250 Silver 0.8410 oz. ASW, 38.6 mm. **Ruler:**
Elizabeth II **Subject:** Olympics, London **Rev:** Skull of 4 rowers
on Thames

Date	Mintage	F	VF	XF	Unc	BU
2009PM Proof	10,000	Value: 50.00				

KM# 1408 CROWN
28.2800 g., Copper-Nickel, 38.6 mm. **Ruler:** Elizabeth II
Subject: London Olympics, 2012 **Obv:** Bust with tiara right **Rev:**
Swimmer before Tower of London

Date	Mintage	F	VF	XF	Unc	BU
2009PM Proof	—	Value: 25.00				

KM# 1408a CROWN
28.2800 g., 0.9250 Silver 0.8410 oz. ASW, 38.6 mm. **Ruler:**
Elizabeth II **Subject:** Olympics, London **Rev:** Swimmer in the
Thames, Tower of London in background

Date	Mintage	F	VF	XF	Unc	BU
2009PM Proof	10,000	Value: 50.00				

KM# 1409 CROWN
28.2800 g., Copper-Nickel, 38.6 mm. **Ruler:** Elizabeth II
Subject: London Olympics, 2012 **Obv:** Bust with tiara right **Rev:**
Two runners before St. Paul's Cathedral

Date	Mintage	F	VF	XF	Unc	BU
2009PM Proof	—	Value: 25.00				

KM# 1409a CROWN
28.2800 g., 0.9250 Silver 0.8410 oz. ASW, 38.6 mm. **Ruler:**
Elizabeth II **Subject:** Olympics, London **Rev:** Two female
runners by St. Paul's Cathedral

Date	Mintage	F	VF	XF	Unc	BU
2009PM Proof	10,000	Value: 50.00				

KM# 1410 CROWN
28.2800 g., Copper-Nickel, 38.6 mm. **Ruler:** Elizabeth II
Subject: London Olympics, 2012 **Obv:** Bust with tiara right **Rev:**
Two sailboats before Tower Bridge

Date	Mintage	F	VF	XF	Unc	BU
2009PM Proof	—	Value: 25.00				

KM# 1410a CROWN
28.2800 g., 0.9250 Silver 0.8410 oz. ASW, 38.6 mm. **Ruler:**
Elizabeth II **Subject:** Olympics, London **Rev:** Sailing on the
Thames, Tower Bridge in background

Date	Mintage	F	VF	XF	Unc	BU
2009PM Proof	10,000	Value: 50.00				

KM# 1411 CROWN
28.2800 g., Copper-Nickel, 38.6 mm. **Ruler:** Elizabeth II
Subject: London Olympics, 2012 **Obv:** Bust with tiara right **Rev:**
Two boxers before London Wheel and skyline

Date	Mintage	F	VF	XF	Unc	BU
2009PM Proof	—	Value: 25.00				

KM# 1411a CROWN
28.2800 g., 0.9250 Silver 0.8410 oz. ASW, 38.6 mm. **Ruler:** Elizabeth II **Subject:** Olympics, London **Rev:** Boxers with London architecture in background

Date	Mintage	F	VF	XF	Unc	BU
2009PM Proof	10,000		Value: 50.00			

KM# 1412 CROWN
28.2800 g., Copper-Nickel, 38.6 mm. **Ruler:** Elizabeth II **Subject:** Vancouver Olympics, 2010 **Obv:** Bust with tiara right **Rev:** Torch at center of four sports, hockey, sled, figure skating and bobsled

Date	Mintage	F	VF	XF	Unc	BU
2009PM Proof			Value: 25.00			

KM# 1413 CROWN
28.2800 g., Copper-Nickel, 38.6 mm. **Ruler:** Elizabeth II **Subject:** Vancouver Olympics, 2010 **Obv:** Bust with tiara right **Rev:** Torch at center of four sports, ski jump, snoboardiong, biathlon and Salom

Date	Mintage	F	VF	XF	Unc	BU
2009PM Proof			Value: 25.00			

KM# 1414 CROWN
28.2800 g., Copper-Nickel, 38.6 mm. **Ruler:** Elizabeth II **Subject:** Bee Gee's 50th Anniversary **Obv:** Bust with tiara right **Rev:** Band name at center

Date	Mintage	F	VF	XF	Unc	BU
2009PM Proof			Value: 25.00			

KM# 1415 CROWN
28.2800 g., Copper-Nickel, 38.6 mm. **Ruler:** Elizabeth II **Subject:** First man on the Moon, 40th Anniversary **Obv:** Bust with tiara right **Rev:** Man in space suit with American Flag on moon

Date	Mintage	F	VF	XF	Unc	BU
2009PM Proof			Value: 25.00			

KM# 1465 CROWN
31.1030 g., 0.9999 Gold with sand insert 0.9998 oz. AGW, 45x32.1 mm. **Ruler:** Elizabeth II **Subject:** Howard Carter, 70th Anniversary of Death **Shape:** Triangle

Date	Mintage	F	VF	XF	Unc	BU
2009PM Proof	250		Value: 1,850			

KM# 1417 CROWN
0.9990 Silver **Ruler:** Elizabeth II **Obv:** Bust with tiara right within ornimentation **Rev:** Kubla Kahn standing **Shape:** Vertical rectangle

Date	Mintage	F	VF	XF	Unc	BU
2010PM Proof			Value: 50.00			

KM# 1426 CROWN
28.2800 g., Copper-Nickel, 38.6 mm. **Ruler:** Elizabeth II **Obv:** Bust with tiara right **Rev:** Abyssinian Cat standing right over kitten **Edge:** Reeded

Date	Mintage	F	VF	XF	Unc	BU
2010PM				—	15.00	17.00

KM# 1426a CROWN
31.1050 g., 0.9990 Silver 0.9990 oz. ASW, 38.6 mm. **Ruler:** Elizabeth II **Obv:** Bust with tiara right **Rev:** Cat standing right

Date	Mintage	F	VF	XF	Unc	BU
2010PM Proof			Value: 50.00			

KM# 1471 CROWN
28.2800 g., Copper-Nickel, 38.6 mm. **Ruler:** Elizabeth II **Obv:** Bust in tiara right **Rev:** Buckingham Palace

Date	Mintage	F	VF	XF	Unc	BU
2010PM		—	—	—	—	10.00

KM# 1471a CROWN
28.2800 g., 0.9250 Silver 0.8410 oz. ASW, 38.6 mm. **Ruler:** Elizabeth II **Obv:** Bust in tiara right **Rev:** Buckingham Palace

Date	Mintage	F	VF	XF	Unc	BU
2010PM			Value: 50.00			
2010PM			Value: 55.00			

Note: Script WK privy mark for engagement

KM# 1439 CROWN
31.1050 g., 0.9999 Gold 0.9999 oz. AGW, 32.7 mm. **Ruler:** Elizabeth II **Subject:** Turkish Angora Cat

Date	Mintage	F	VF	XF	Unc	BU
2011PM		—	—	—	—	1,850
2011PM Proof	1,000		Value: 1,875			

KM# 1440 CROWN
28.2800 g., Copper-Nickel, 38.6 mm. **Ruler:** Elizabeth II **Subject:** Turkish Angora Cat

Date	Mintage	F	VF	XF	Unc	BU
2011PM		—	—	—	—	10.00

KM# 1440a.1 CROWN
31.1050 g., 0.9990 Silver 0.9990 oz. ASW, 38.6 mm. **Ruler:** Elizabeth II **Subject:** Turkish Angora Cat

Date	Mintage	F	VF	XF	Unc	BU
2011PM Proof	10,000		Value: 50.00			

KM# 1440a.2 CROWN
31.1050 g., 0.9990 Silver 0.9990 oz. ASW, 38.6 mm. **Ruler:** Elizabeth II **Rev:** Two cats in color

Date	Mintage	F	VF	XF	Unc	BU
2011PM		—	—	—	—	55.00

KM# 1455 CROWN
28.2800 g., Copper-Nickel, 38.6 mm. **Ruler:** Elizabeth II **Subject:** Isle of Man Tourist Trophy race **Rev:** Two racers and outline map of the Isle of Man

Date	Mintage	F	VF	XF	Unc	BU
2011PM		—	—	—	—	10.00

KM# 1455a CROWN
28.2800 g., 0.9250 Silver 0.8410 oz. ASW, 38.6 mm. **Ruler:** Elizabeth II **Subject:** Isle of Man Tourist Trophy race **Rev:** Two racers and map of the Isle of Man

Date	Mintage	F	VF	XF	Unc	BU
2011PM Proof	10,000		Value: 50.00			

KM# 1456 CROWN
31.1030 g., 0.9999 Gold 0.9998 oz. AGW, 32.7 mm. **Ruler:** Elizabeth II **Subject:** Donatello's Chellini Madonna **Rev:** Mary and child in very high relief

Date	Mintage	F	VF	XF	Unc	BU
2011PM Proof	999		Value: 1,850			

KM# 1477 CROWN
28.2800 g., Copper-Nickel, 38.6 mm. **Ruler:** Elizabeth II **Rev:** Busts right of Elizabeth II and Prince Philip, flags flanking, royal shield below

Date	Mintage	F	VF	XF	Unc	BU
2011PM		—	—	—	—	10.00

KM# 1477a CROWN
28.2800 g., 0.9250 Silver 0.8410 oz. ASW, 38.6 mm. **Ruler:** Elizabeth II **Rev:** Busts right of Elizabeth II and Prince Philip, flags flanking, royal shield below

Date	Mintage	F	VF	XF	Unc	BU
2011PM Proof	10,000		Value: 50.00			

KM# 1478 CROWN
28.2800 g., Copper-Nickel, 38.6 mm. **Ruler:** Elizabeth II **Subject:** Royal Wedding **Rev:** Busts left of Catherine Middleton in large hat and Prince William

Date	Mintage	F	VF	XF	Unc	BU
2011PM		—	—	—	—	10.00

KM# 1478a CROWN
28.2800 g., 0.9250 Silver 0.8410 oz. ASW, 38.6 mm. **Ruler:** Elizabeth II **Subject:** Royal Wedding **Rev:** Busts left of Catherine Middleton in large hat and Prince William

Date	Mintage	F	VF	XF	Unc	BU
2011PM Proof	10,000		Value: 50.00			

KM# 1485 CROWN
28.2800 g., Copper-Nickel, 38.6 mm. **Ruler:** Elizabeth II **Subject:** Year of the Rabbit **Rev:** Image of Beatrix Potter's Peter Rabbit

Date	Mintage	F	VF	XF	Unc	BU
2011PM		—	—	—	—	10.00

KM# 1485a CROWN
28.2800 g., 0.9250 Silver 0.8410 oz. ASW, 38.6 mm. **Ruler:** Elizabeth II **Subject:** Year of the Rabbit **Rev:** Beatrix Potter's Peter Rabbit

Date	Mintage	F	VF	XF	Unc	BU
2011PM Proof	10,000		Value: 50.00			

KM# 1442 CROWN
28.2800 g., Copper-Nickel, 38.6 mm. **Ruler:** Elizabeth II **Subject:** Olympics, London **Rev:** Track cyclist

Date	Mintage	F	VF	XF	Unc	BU
2012PM		—	—	—	—	10.00

KM# 1441 CROWN
28.2800 g., Copper-Nickel, 38.6 mm. **Ruler:** Elizabeth II **Subject:** Olympics, London **Rev:** Horse Jumping

Date	Mintage	F	VF	XF	Unc	BU
2012PM		—	—	—	—	10.00

KM# 1441a CROWN
28.2800 g., 0.9250 Silver 0.8410 oz. ASW, 38.6 mm. **Ruler:** Elizabeth II **Subject:** Olympics, London **Rev:** Horse jumping

Date	Mintage	F	VF	XF	Unc	BU
2012PM Proof	10,000		Value: 50.00			

KM# 1442a CROWN
28.2800 g., 0.9250 Silver 0.8410 oz. ASW, 38.6 mm. **Ruler:** Elizabeth II **Subject:** Olympics, London **Rev:** Track Cyclist

Date	Mintage	F	VF	XF	Unc	BU
2012PM Proof	10,000		Value: 50.00			

KM# 1443 CROWN
28.2800 g., Copper-Nickel, 38.6 mm. **Ruler:** Elizabeth II **Subject:** Olympics, London **Rev:** Swimmer with divers in background

Date	Mintage	F	VF	XF	Unc	BU
2012PM		—	—	—	—	10.00

KM# 1443a CROWN
28.2800 g., 0.9250 Silver 0.8410 oz. ASW, 38.6 mm. **Ruler:** Elizabeth II **Subject:** Olympics, London **Rev:** Swimmer, divers in background

Date	Mintage	F	VF	XF	Unc	BU
2012PM Proof	10,000		Value: 50.00			

KM# 1444 CROWN
28.2800 g., Copper-Nickel, 38.6 mm. **Ruler:** Elizabeth II **Subject:** Olympics, London **Rev:** Canoeist, two rowers in background

Date	Mintage	F	VF	XF	Unc	BU
2012PM		—	—	—	—	10.00

KM# 1444a CROWN
28.2800 g., 0.9250 Silver 0.8410 oz. ASW, 38.6 mm. **Ruler:** Elizabeth II **Subject:** Olympics, London **Rev:** Canoeist, two rowers in background

Date	Mintage	F	VF	XF	Unc	BU
2012PM Proof	10,000		Value: 50.00			

KM# 1445 CROWN
28.2800 g., Copper-Nickel, 38.6 mm. **Ruler:** Elizabeth II **Subject:** Olympics, London **Rev:** Judo players, two boxers in background

Date	Mintage	F	VF	XF	Unc	BU
2012PM		—	—	—	—	10.00

KM# 1445a CROWN
28.2800 g., 0.9250 Silver 0.8410 oz. ASW, 38.6 mm. **Ruler:** Elizabeth II **Subject:** Olympics, London **Rev:** Judo players, two boxers in background

Date	Mintage	F	VF	XF	Unc	BU
2012PM Proof	10,000		Value: 50.00			

KM# 1446 CROWN
28.2800 g., Copper-Nickel, 38.6 mm. **Ruler:** Elizabeth II **Subject:** Olympics, London **Rev:** Table tennis players, Lawn Tennis players in background

Date	Mintage	F	VF	XF	Unc	BU
2012PM		—	—	—	—	10.00

KM# 1446a CROWN
28.2800 g., 0.9250 Silver 0.8410 oz. ASW, 38.6 mm. **Ruler:** Elizabeth II **Subject:** Olympics, London **Rev:** Table tennis players, Lawn tennis players in background

Date	Mintage	F	VF	XF	Unc	BU
2012PM Proof	10,000		Value: 50.00			

KM# 1461 CROWN
28.2800 g., Copper-Nickel, 38.6 mm. **Ruler:** Elizabeth II

Subject: European Football Championships 2012 **Obv:** Player heading a football, Sitting Statue of Liberty in Lviv and Neptune's fountain in Gdansk in background

Date	Mintage	F	VF	XF	Unc	BU
2012PM	—	—	—	—	—	10.00

KM# 1461a   CROWN
28.2800 g., 0.9250 Silver 0.8410 oz. ASW, 38.6 mm.   **Ruler:** Elizabeth II **Subject:** European Football Championships 2012 **Rev:** Footballer heading ball, Sitting Statue of Liberty in Lviv and Neptune's fountain in Gdansk in background

Date	Mintage	F	VF	XF	Unc	BU
2012PM Proof	10,000	Value: 50.00				

KM# 1462   CROWN
28.2800 g., Copper-Nickel, 38.6 mm.   **Ruler:** Elizabeth II **Subject:** European Football Championships 2012 **Rev:** Player passing ball, Motherland Statue in Kiev and King Sigismund's statue in Warsaw

Date	Mintage	F	VF	XF	Unc	BU
2012PM	—	—	—	—	—	10.00

KM# 1462a   CROWN
28.2800 g., 0.9250 Silver 0.8410 oz. ASW, 38.6 mm.   **Ruler:** Elizabeth II **Subject:** European Football Championships 2012 **Rev:** Player passing the ball, Motherland Statue in Kiev and King Sigismund's statue in Warsaw in background

Date	Mintage	F	VF	XF	Unc	BU
2012PM Proof	10,000	Value: 50.00				

KM# 1463   CROWN
28.2800 g., Copper-Nickel, 38.6 mm.   **Ruler:** Elizabeth II **Subject:** European Football Championships 2012 **Rev:** Footballer shooting, Cathedral of the Transfiguration in Donetsk and the Raclawice Panorama in Wroclaw in background

Date	Mintage	F	VF	XF	Unc	BU
2012PM	—	—	—	—	—	10.00

KM# 1463a   CROWN
28.2800 g., 0.9250 Silver 0.8410 oz. ASW, 38.6 mm.   **Ruler:** Elizabeth II **Subject:** European Football Championships 2012 **Rev:** Footballer shooting, Cathedral of the Transfiguration in Donetsk and the Raclawice Panorama in Wroclaw in background

Date	Mintage	F	VF	XF	Unc	BU
2012PM Proof	10,000	Value: 50.00				

KM# 1464   CROWN
28.2800 g., Copper-Nickel, 38.6 mm.   **Ruler:** Elizabeth II **Subject:** European Football Championships 2012 **Rev:** Two footballers tackling, Cathedral of the Annunciation in Kharkiv and the Cathedral in Poznan in background

Date	Mintage	F	VF	XF	Unc	BU
2012PM	—	—	—	—	—	10.00

KM# 1464a   CROWN
28.2800 g., 0.9250 Silver 0.8410 oz. ASW, 38.6 mm.   **Ruler:** Elizabeth II **Subject:** European Football Championships 2012 **Rev:** Two footballers tackling, Catheral of the annunciation in Kharkiv and the Cathedral in Poznan in background

Date	Mintage	F	VF	XF	Unc	BU
2012PM Proof	10,000	Value: 50.00				

KM# 1480   CROWN
28.2800 g., Copper-Nickel, 38.6 mm.   **Ruler:** Elizabeth II **Obv:** Conjoined busts right **Rev:** Elizabeth II at coronation with scepter, orb and state crown

Date	Mintage	F	VF	XF	Unc	BU
2012PM	—	—	—	—	—	10.00

KM# 1480a   CROWN
28.2800 g., 0.9250 Silver 0.8410 oz. ASW, 38.6 mm.   **Ruler:** Elizabeth II **Obv:** Conjoined busts right **Rev:** Elizabeth II at coronation with sceptre, orb and state crown

Date	Mintage	F	VF	XF	Unc	BU
2012PM Proof	10,000	Value: 50.00				

KM# 1481   CROWN
28.2800 g., Copper-Nickel, 38.6 mm.   **Ruler:** Elizabeth II **Obv:** Conjoined busts right **Rev:** Elizabeth, the Queen Mother

Date	Mintage	F	VF	XF	Unc	BU
2012PM	—	—	—	—	—	10.00

KM# 1481a   CROWN
28.2800 g., 0.9250 Silver 0.8410 oz. ASW, 38.6 mm.   **Ruler:** Elizabeth II **Obv:** Conjoined busts right **Rev:** Elizabeth, the Queen Mother

Date	Mintage	F	VF	XF	Unc	BU
2012PM Proof	10,000	Value: 50.00				

KM# 1482   CROWN
28.2800 g., Copper-Nickel, 38.6 mm.   **Ruler:** Elizabeth II **Obv:** Conjoined busts right **Rev:** Passengers boarding Titanic

Date	Mintage	F	VF	XF	Unc	BU
2012PM	—	—	—	—	—	10.00

KM# 1482a   CROWN
28.2800 g., 0.9250 Silver 0.8410 oz. ASW, 38.6 mm.   **Ruler:** Elizabeth II **Obv:** Conjoined busts right **Rev:** Passengers boarding Titanic

Date	Mintage	F	VF	XF	Unc	BU
2012PM Proof	10,000	Value: 55.00				

KM# 1483   CROWN
28.2800 g., Copper-Nickel, 38.6 mm.   **Ruler:** Elizabeth II **Obv:** Conjoined busts right **Rev:** Titanic sailing into icefield

Date	Mintage	F	VF	XF	Unc	BU
2012PM	—	—	—	—	—	10.00

KM# 1483a   CROWN
28.2800 g., 0.9250 Silver 0.8410 oz. ASW, 38.6 mm.   **Ruler:** Elizabeth II **Obv:** Conjoined busts right **Rev:** Titanic sailing into icefield

Date	Mintage	F	VF	XF	Unc	BU
2012PM Proof	10,000	Value: 50.00				

KM# 1200   2 CROWNS
62.2000 g., 0.9990 Palladium 1.9977 oz., 40 mm.   **Ruler:** Elizabeth II **Subject:** Discovery of Palladium **Obv:** Bust with tiara right **Rev:** Pallas Athena left **Edge:** Reeded

Date	Mintage	F	VF	XF	Unc	BU
2004PM Proof	300	Value: 1,500				

KM# 1402   2 CROWNS
0.9250 Silver, 40 mm.   **Ruler:** Elizabeth II **Obv:** Bust with tiara right **Rev:** Seven Wonders of the World, multicolor central item

Date	Mintage	F	VF	XF	Unc	BU
2008PM Proof	—	Value: 100				

KM# 1064   5 CROWN
155.5175 g., 0.9999 Gold 4.9993 oz. AGW, 65 mm.   **Ruler:** Elizabeth II **Subject:** Year of the Snake **Obv:** Bust with tiara right **Rev:** Snake **Edge:** Reeded

Date	Mintage	F	VF	XF	Unc	BU
2001 Proof	250	Value: 8,500				

KM# 1104   5 CROWN
155.5100 g., 0.9999 Gold 4.9991 oz. AGW, 65 mm.   **Ruler:** Elizabeth II **Subject:** Year of the Horse **Obv:** Bust with tiara right **Rev:** Two horses **Edge:** Reeded

Date	Mintage	F	VF	XF	Unc	BU
2002 Proof	250	Value: 8,500				

KM# 1173   5 CROWN
155.5100 g., 0.9999 Gold 4.9991 oz. AGW, 65 mm.   **Ruler:** Elizabeth II **Subject:** Year of the Goat **Obv:** Bust with tiara right **Rev:** Three goats **Edge:** Reeded

Date	Mintage	F	VF	XF	Unc	BU
2003PM Proof	250	Value: 8,500				

KM# 1244   5 CROWN
155.5175 g., 0.9999 Gold 4.9993 oz. AGW, 65 mm.   **Ruler:** Elizabeth II **Obv:** Bust with tiara right **Rev:** Monkey **Edge:** Reeded

Date	Mintage	F	VF	XF	Unc	BU
2004PM Proof	250	Value: 8,500				

KM# 1219   64 CROWNS
2000.0000 g., 0.9990 Silver 64.234 oz. ASW, 140 mm.   **Ruler:** Elizabeth II **Obv:** Bust with tiara right **Rev:** Ocean Liner Queen Mary 2 **Edge:** Reeded

Date	Mintage	F	VF	XF	Unc	BU
2004PM Proof	500	Value: 2,250				

KM# 1142   100 CROWNS
3000.0000 g., 0.9999 Silver 96.438 oz. ASW, 130 mm.   **Ruler:** Elizabeth II **Subject:** Queen's Golden Jubilee **Obv:** Bust with tiara right **Rev:** Queen on horse **Edge:** Reeded **Note:** Illustration reduced.

Date	Mintage	F	VF	XF	Unc	BU
2002 Proof	500	Value: 3,250				

KM# 1184   130 CROWNS
4000.0000 g., 0.9990 Silver 128.46 oz. ASW, 130 mm.   **Ruler:** Elizabeth II **Obv:** Bust with tiara right **Rev:** Gold clad cameo portrait of Elizabeth I with a .035ct ruby inset on her forehead all within a circle of portraits **Edge:** Reeded

Date	Mintage	F	VF	XF	Unc	BU
2003PM Proof	500	Value: 4,500				

SILVER BULLION COINAGE
Angel Series

KM# 1475   ANGEL
31.1050 g., 0.9990 Silver 0.9990 oz. ASW   **Ruler:** Elizabeth II **Subject:** 15th Anniversary of the Angel **Obv:** Bust in tiara right **Rev:** St. Michael slaying dragon

Date	Mintage	F	VF	XF	Unc	BU
2010PM Proof	—	Value: 50.00				
Note: Privy mark: 15

Nobel Series

KM# 1484   NOBLE
31.1050 g., 0.9999 Silver 0.9999 oz. ASW, 38.6 mm.   **Ruler:** Elizabeth II **Obv:** Bust with tiara right **Rev:** Viking ship

Date	Mintage	F	VF	XF	Unc	BU
2011PM Prooflike	—	—	—	—	—	50.00

GOLD BULLION COINAGE
Angel Issues

KM# 1479   1/64 ANGEL
0.4860 g., 0.9999 Gold 0.0156 oz. AGW **Ruler:** Elizabeth II **Rev:** St. Michael slaying dragon

Date	Mintage	F	VF	XF	Unc	BU
2011PM Proof	—	Value: 50.00				

Note: Privy mark: Wedding bells and date

KM# 1106   1/20 ANGEL
1.5552 g., 0.9999 Gold 0.0500 oz. AGW, 18 mm. **Ruler:** Elizabeth II **Obv:** Bust with tiara right **Rev:** St. Michael slaying dragon, three crown privy mark at right **Edge:** Reeded

Date	Mintage	F	VF	XF	Unc	BU
2001 (3c) Proof	1,000	Value: 95.00				
2002 Proof	—	Value: 95.00				

Note: With candy cane privy mark

KM# 393   1/20 ANGEL
1.5551 g., 0.9999 Gold 0.0500 oz. AGW, 18 mm. **Ruler:** Elizabeth II **Obv:** Crowned bust right **Rev:** Archangel Michael slaying dragon right

Date	Mintage	F	VF	XF	Unc	BU
2001	—	—	—	—	—	90.00
2001 Proof	—	Value: 90.00				
2001 Proof	—	Value: 95.00				

Note: Privy mark: 3 Kings

2002	—	—	—	—	—	90.00
2002 Proof	—	Value: 90.00				
2002 Proof	—	Value: 95.00				

Note: Privy mark: Candy cane

2003	—	—	—	—	—	90.00
2003 Proof	—	Value: 90.00				
2003 Proof	—	Value: 95.00				

Note: Privy mark: Candy

2004	—	—	—	—	—	90.00
2004 Proof	—	Value: 90.00				
2004 Proof	—	Value: 95.00				

Note: Privy mark: Partridge in a Pear Tree

2005	—	—	—	—	—	90.00
2005 Proof	—	Value: 90.00				
2005 Proof	—	Value: 95.00				

Note: Privy mark: 2 Turtle doves

2006	—	—	—	—	—	90.00
2006 Proof	—	Value: 90.00				
2006 Proof	—	Value: 95.00				

Note: Privy mark: 3 French hens

2007	—	—	—	—	—	90.00
2007 Proof	—	Value: 90.00				
2007 Proof	—	Value: 95.00				

Note: Privy mark: 4 Calling birds

KM# 1252   1/20 ANGEL
1.5550 g., 0.9999 Gold 0.0500 oz. AGW, 18 mm. **Ruler:** Elizabeth II **Obv:** Bust with tiara right **Rev:** St. Michael and Christmas privy mark **Edge:** Reeded

Date	Mintage	F	VF	XF	Unc	BU
2004PM Proof	1,000	Value: 95.00				

KM# 1430   1/20 ANGEL
1.5500 g., 0.9999 Gold 0.0498 oz. AGW, 18 mm. **Ruler:** Elizabeth II **Rev:** St. Michael slaying the dragon

Date	Mintage	F	VF	XF	Unc	BU
2009PM Six Geese a laying privy mark Proof	1,000	Value: 125				
2010PM Seven swans a swimming privy mark Proof	1,000	Value: 125				
2011PM Eight maids a milking privy mark Proof	1,000	Value: 125				

KM# 394   1/10 ANGEL
3.1103 g., 0.9999 Gold 0.1000 oz. AGW, 23 mm. **Ruler:** Elizabeth II **Obv:** Crowned bust right **Rev:** Archangel Michael

Date	Mintage	F	VF	XF	Unc	BU
2001	—	—	—	—	—	175
2001 Proof	—	Value: 180				
2002	—	—	—	—	—	175
2002 Proof	—	Value: 180				
2003	—	—	—	—	—	175

Date	Mintage	F	VF	XF	Unc	BU
2003 Proof	—	Value: 180				
2004	—	—	—	—	—	175
2004 Proof	—	Value: 180				
2005	—	—	—	—	—	175
2005 Proof	—	Value: 180				

KM# 395   1/4 ANGEL
7.7758 g., 0.9999 Gold 0.2500 oz. AGW **Ruler:** Elizabeth II **Obv:** Crowned bust right **Rev:** Archangel Michael slaying dragon

Date	Mintage	F	VF	XF	Unc	BU
2001	—	—	—	—	—	450
2001 Proof	—	Value: 455				
2002	—	—	—	—	—	450
2002 Proof	—	Value: 455				
2003	—	—	—	—	—	450
2003 Proof	—	Value: 455				
2004	—	—	—	—	—	450
2004 Proof	—	Value: 455				
2005	—	—	—	—	—	450
2005 Proof	—	Value: 455				

KM# 397   ANGEL
31.1035 g., 0.9999 Gold 0.9999 oz. AGW **Ruler:** Elizabeth II **Obv:** Crowned bust right **Rev:** Archangel Michael slaying dragon right

Date	Mintage	F	VF	XF	Unc	BU
2001	—	—	—	—	—	1,700
2001 Proof	—	Value: 1,725				
2002	—	—	—	—	—	1,700
2002 Proof	—	Value: 1,725				
2003	—	—	—	—	—	1,700
2003 Proof	—	Value: 1,725				
2004	—	—	—	—	—	1,700
2004 Proof	—	Value: 1,725				
2005	—	—	—	—	—	1,700
2005 Proof	—	Value: 1,725				
2006	—	—	—	—	—	1,700
2006 Proof	500	Value: 1,725				
2007	—	—	—	—	—	1,700
2007 Proof	—	Value: 1,725				

KM# 397.1   ANGEL
31.1035 g., 0.9990 Gold 0.9999 oz. AGW **Ruler:** Elizabeth II **Obv:** Crowned bust right **Rev:** Archangel Michael slaying dragon right

Date	Mintage	F	VF	XF	Unc	BU
2006 Proof, High Relief	Est. 1,000	Value: 1,725				
2007 Proof, High Relief	Est. 1,000	Value: 1,725				

KM# 1466   ANGEL
31.1050 g., 0.9999 Gold 0.9999 oz. AGW, 33 mm. **Ruler:** Elizabeth II **Obv:** Bust in tiara right **Rev:** St. Michael slaying dragon

Date	Mintage	F	VF	XF	Unc	BU
2008PM	—	—	—	—	—	1,850
2008PM Proof	—	Value: 1,875				

KM# 1467   ANGEL
31.1050 g., 0.9999 Gold 0.9999 oz. AGW, 33 mm. **Ruler:** Elizabeth II **Obv:** Bust with tiara right **Rev:** St. Michael lunging right with spear

Date	Mintage	F	VF	XF	Unc	BU
2009PM Proof	—	Value: 1,875				

KM# 1468   ANGEL
31.1050 g., 0.9999 Gold 0.9999 oz. AGW, 33 mm. **Ruler:** Elizabeth II **Obv:** Bust with tiara right **Rev:** Dragon receiving spear wound

Date	Mintage	F	VF	XF	Unc	BU
2009PM Proof	—	Value: 1,875				

BI-METALLIC BULLION COINAGE

KM# 1486   NOBLE
39.1000 g., Bi-Metallic 31.105 .999 Gold center in 9.39 .999 Silver ring, 36.7 mm. **Ruler:** Elizabeth II **Rev:** Viking ship, 15 in left field

Date	Mintage	F	VF	XF	Unc	BU
2009PM Proof	3,000	Value: 1,900				

MINT SETS

KM#	Date	Mintage	Identification	Issue Price	Mkt Val
MS30	2001 (8)	—	KM#1036-1043	—	22.50
MS31	2001 (9)	—	KM#1036-1044	—	40.00
MS32	2002 (8)	—	KM#1036-1043	—	22.50
MS33	2002 (9)	—	KM#1036-1044	—	40.00
MS34	2003 (8)	—	KM#1036-1043	—	22.50
MS35	2003 (9)	—	KM#1036-1044	—	40.00
MS36	2004 (8)	—	KM#1253-1260	—	25.00
MS37	2004 (9)	—	KM#1253-1261	—	40.00
MS38	2005 (8)	—	KM#1253-1260	—	22.50
MS39	2005 (9)	—	KM#1253-1261	—	40.00
MS40	2006 (8)	—	MS#1253-1260	35.00	25.00
MS41	2006 (9)	—	KM1253-1261	42.50	40.00
MS42	2007 (8)	—	KM1253-1260	35.00	22.50
MS43	2007 (9)	—	KM1253-1261	42.50	40.00

PROOF SETS

KM#	Date	Mintage	Identification	Issue Price	Mkt Val
PS59	2001 (5)	1,000	KM#1067-1070, 1073	—	3,100
PS60	2003 (3)	—	KM#1186, 1187, 1188	—	650
PS61	2003 (5)	—	KM#1186, 1187, 1188, 1189, 1190 w/gold ring	—	3,100
PS62	2003 (5)	—	KM#1191-1195 w/gold-plated silver ring	—	245
PS63	2004 (5)	1,000	KM#1247, 1248, 1249.1, 1250, 1251	—	3,250

ISRAEL

The state of Israel, a Middle Eastern republic at the eastern end of the Mediterranean Sea, bounded by Lebanon on the north, Syria on the northeast, Jordan on the east, and Egypt on the southwest, has an area of 9,000sq. mi. (20,770 sq. km.) and a population of 6 million. Capital: Jerusalem. Finished diamonds, chemicals, citrus, textiles, minerals, electronic and transportation equipment are exported.

HEBREW COIN DATING
Modern Israel's coins carry Hebrew dating formed from a combination of the 22 consonant letters of the Hebrew alphabet and read from right to left. The Jewish calendar dates back more than 5700 years; but five millenniums are assumed in the dating of coins (until 1981). Thus, the year 5735 (1975AD) appears as 735, with the first two characters from the right indicating the number of years in hundreds; tav (400), plus shin (300). The next is lamedh (30), followed by a separation mark which has the appearance of double quotation marks, then heh (5).

The Star of David is not a mintmark. It appears only on some coins sold by the Israel Government Coins and Medals Corporation Ltd., which is owned by the Israel government, and is a division of the Prime Minister's office and sole distributor to collectors. The Star of David was first used in 1971 on the science coin to signify that it was minted in Jerusalem, but was later used by different mint facilities.

AD Date		Jewish Era
2001	התשס"א	5761

2002	התשס"ב	5762
2003	התשס"ג	5763
2004	התשס"ד	5764
2005	התשס"ה	5765
2006	התשס"ו	5766
2007	התשס"ז	5767
2008	התשס"ח	5768
2009	התשס"ט	5769
2010	התש"ע	5770

MINT MARKS

מ

(m) - Mem

(o) - Ottawa

(s) - San Francisco

None – Jerusalem

REPUBLIC

REFORM COINAGE

100 Agorot = 1 New Sheqel
1,000 Sheqalim = 1 New Sheqel

September 4, 1985

KM# 157   5 AGOROT
3.0000 g., Aluminum-Bronze, 19.5 mm. **Obv:** Ancient coin **Rev:** Value within lined square **Edge:** Plain

Date	Mintage	F	VF	XF	Unc	BU
JE5761 (2001)(dj)	6,144,000	—	—	—	0.15	—
JE5762 (2002)(dj)	6,144,000	—	—	—	0.15	—
JE5764 (2004)		—	—	—	0.15	—
JE5765 (2005)		—	—	—	0.15	—
JE5766 (2006)		—	—	—	0.15	—
JE5767 (2007)		—	—	—	0.15	—

KM# 172   5 AGOROT
3.0000 g., Aluminum-Bronze, 19.5 mm. **Subject:** Hanukka **Obv:** Ancient coin **Rev:** Value within lined square **Note:** JE5754-5768 coins contain the Star of David mint mark; the JE5747-5753 coins do not.

Date	Mintage	F	VF	XF	Unc	BU
JE5761 (2001)(u)	4,000	—	—	—	2.50	—
Note: In sets only						
JE5762 (2002)(u)	4,000	—	—	—	2.50	—
Note: In sets only						
JE5763 (2003)(u)	3,000	—	—	—	3.00	—
Note: In sets only						
JE5764 (2004)(u)	3,000	—	—	—	3.00	—
Note: In sets only						
JE5765 (2005)(u)	2,500	—	—	—	3.00	—
Note: In sets only						
JE5766 (2006)(u)	3,000	—	—	—	3.00	—
Note: In sets only						
JE5767 (2007)(u)	3,000	—	—	—	3.00	—
Note: In sets only						
JE5768 (2008)(u)	3,000	—	—	—	3.00	—
Note: In sets only						

KM# 158   10 AGOROT
4.0000 g., Aluminum-Bronze, 22 mm. **Obv:** Menorah **Rev:** Value within lined square **Edge:** Plain

Date	Mintage	F	VF	XF	Unc	BU
JE5761 (2001)(dj)	46,140,000	—	—	—	0.20	—
Note: Sides of central part of zero are rounded.						
JE5761 (2001)(so)	32,256,000	—	—	—	0.20	—
Note: Sides of central part of zero are straight.						
JE5762 (2002)(w)	4,608,000	—	—	—	0.20	—
JE5763 (2003)(dj)	22,980,000	—	—	—	0.20	—
JE5764 (2004)		—	—	—	0.20	—
JE5765 (2005)		—	—	—	0.20	—
JE5766 (2006)		—	—	—	0.20	—
JE5767 (2007)		—	—	—	0.20	—
JE5768 (2008)(dj)		—	—	—	0.20	—
JE5769 (2009)(dj)		—	—	—	0.20	—
JE5770 (2010)		—	—	—	0.20	—
JE5771 (2011)		—	—	—	0.20	—
JE5772 (2012)		—	—	—	0.20	—

KM# 173   10 AGOROT
4.0000 g., Aluminum-Bronze, 22 mm. **Subject:** Hanukka **Obv:** Menorah **Rev:** Value within lined square **Edge:** Plain **Note:** JE5754-5770 have the Star of David mint mark, JE5747-5753 coins do not.

Date	Mintage	F	VF	XF	Unc	BU
JE5761 (2001)(u)	4,000	—	—	—	3.00	—
Note: In sets only						
JE5762 (2002)(u)	4,000	—	—	—	3.00	—
Note: In sets only						
JE5763 (2003)(u)	3,000	—	—	—	3.00	—
Note: In sets only						
JE5764 (2004)(u)	3,000	—	—	—	3.00	—
Note: In sets only						
JE5765 (2005)(u)	2,500	—	—	—	3.00	—
Note: In sets only						
JE5766 (2006)(u)	3,000	—	—	—	3.00	—
Note: In sets only						
JE5767 (2007)(u)	3,000	—	—	—	3.00	—
Note: In sets only						
JE5768 (2008)(u)	3,000	—	—	—	3.00	—
Note: In sets only						
JE5769 (2009)(u)	1,800	—	—	—	3.50	—
Note: In sets only						
JE5770 (2010)(u)	1,800	—	—	—	3.50	—
Note: In sets only						

KM# 174   1/2 NEW SHEQEL
6.5000 g., Aluminum-Bronze, 26 mm. **Subject:** Hanukka **Obv:** Value **Rev:** Lyre **Note:** Coins dated JE5754-5770 have the Star of David mint mark; the coins dated JE5747-5753 do not.

Date	Mintage	F	VF	XF	Unc	BU
JE5761 (2001)(u)	4,000	—	—	—	3.50	—
Note: In sets only						
JE5762 (2002)(u)	4,000	—	—	—	3.50	—
Note: In sets only						
JE5763 (2003)(u)	3,000	—	—	—	3.50	—
Note: In sets only						
JE5764 (2004)(u)	3,000	—	—	—	3.50	—
Note: In sets only						
JE5765 (2005)(u)	2,500	—	—	—	3.50	—
Note: In sets only						
JE5766 (2006)(u)	3,000	—	—	—	3.50	—
Note: In sets only						
JE5767 (2007)(u)	3,000	—	—	—	3.50	—
Note: In sets only						
JE5768 (2008)(u)	3,000	—	—	—	3.50	—
Note: In sets only						
JE5769 (2009)(u)	1,800	—	—	—	3.50	—
Note: In sets only						
JE5770 (2010)(u)	1,800	—	—	—	3.50	—
Note: In sets only						

KM# 354   1/2 NEW SHEQEL
6.5000 g., Aluminum-Bronze, 26 mm. **Subject:** Hanukka **Obv:** Denomination **Rev:** Curacao Hanukka lamp **Edge:** Plain **Shape:** 12-sided **Note:** Struck for sets only

Date	Mintage	F	VF	XF	Unc	BU
JE5761 (2001)(u)	4,000	—	—	—	11.00	—

KM# 159   1/2 NEW SHEQEL
6.5000 g., Aluminum-Bronze, 26 mm. **Obv:** Value **Rev:** Lyre **Edge:** Plain

Date	Mintage	F	VF	XF	Unc	BU
JE5762 (2002)(so)	2,880,000	—	—	—	0.75	—
JE5762 (2002)(v)	5,760,000	—	—	—	0.75	—
Note: Length of fraction line is 4 or 4.5 mm. but which mint produced which coin is not known.						
JE5763 (2003)		—	—	—	0.75	—
JE5764 (2004)(so)	2,640,000	—	—	—	0.75	—
JE5765 (2005)		—	—	—	0.75	—
JE5766 (2006)		—	—	—	0.75	—
JE5767 (2007)		—	—	—	0.75	—
JE5768 (2008)(dj)		—	—	—	0.75	—
JE5769 (2009)		—	—	—	0.60	—
JE5770 (2010)		—	—	—	0.60	—
JE5771 (2011)		—	—	—	0.60	—

KM# 355   1/2 NEW SHEQEL
6.5000 g., Aluminum-Bronze, 26 mm. **Obv:** Value **Rev:** Yemenite Hanukka Lamp **Edge:** Twelve plain sections **Note:** Struck for sets only

Date	Mintage	F	VF	XF	Unc	BU
JE5762 (2002)(u)	4,000	—	—	—	11.00	—

KM# 389   1/2 NEW SHEQEL
6.5000 g., Aluminum-Bronze, 26 mm. **Obv:** Value **Rev:** Polish Hanukka Lamp **Edge:** Plain **Shape:** 12-sided **Note:** Struck for sets only

Date	Mintage	F	VF	XF	Unc	BU
JE5763 (2003)(u)	3,000	—	—	—	12.00	—
Note: Even though not a proof, the coin has a mem						

KM# 390   1/2 NEW SHEQEL
6.5000 g., Aluminum-Bronze, 26 mm. **Obv:** Value **Rev:** Iraqi Hanukka Lamp **Edge:** Plain **Shape:** 12-sided **Note:** Struck for sets only

Date	Mintage	F	VF	XF	Unc	BU
JE5764 (2004)(u)	3,000	—	—	—	12.00	—

KM# 391   1/2 NEW SHEQEL
6.5000 g., Aluminum-Bronze, 26 mm. **Obv:** Value **Rev:** Syrian Hanukka Lamp **Edge:** Plain **Shape:** 12-sided **Note:** Struck for sets only

Date	Mintage	F	VF	XF	Unc	BU
JE5765 (2005)(u)	2,500	—	—	—	12.00	—

KM# 415   1/2 NEW SHEQEL
6.5000 g., Aluminum-Bronze, 26 mm. **Obv:** Value and mini-Hanukka Lamp **Rev:** Dutch Hanukka Lamp **Edge:** Plain **Shape:** 12-sided **Note:** Struck for sets only

Date	Mintage	F	VF	XF	Unc	BU
JE5766 (2006)(u)	3,000	—	—	—	12.00	—

KM# 422   1/2 NEW SHEQEL
6.5000 g., Aluminum-Bronze, 26 mm. **Obv:** Value and mini-Hanukka Lamp **Rev:** Corfu (Greek) Hanukka Lamp **Edge:** Plain **Shape:** 12-sided **Note:** Struck for sets only

Date	Mintage	F	VF	XF	Unc	BU
JE5767 (2007)(u)	3,000	—	—	—	12.00	—

KM# 434   1/2 NEW SHEQEL
6.5000 g., Aluminum-Bronze, 26 mm. **Subject:** Hanukka **Obv:** Value, date, inscriptions and menorah **Rev:** Egyptian Hanukka lamp **Shape:** 12-sided **Note:** Struck for sets only

Date	Mintage	F	VF	XF	Unc	BU
JE5768 (2008)(u)	3,000	—	—	—	12.00	—

KM# 466   1/2 NEW SHEQEL
6.5000 g., Aluminum-Bronze, 26 mm. **Subject:** Hanukka **Obv:** Value, date, inscriptions and menorah **Rev:** Algerian Hanukka Lamp **Edge:** Plain **Shape:** 12-sided **Note:** Struck for sets only

Date	Mintage	F	VF	XF	Unc	BU
JE5770 (2010)(u)	1,800	—	—	—	12.00	—
JE5770 (2010)(u)	1,800	—	—	—	12.00	—

KM# 436   1/2 NEW SHEQEL
6.5000 g., Aluminum-Bronze, 26 mm. **Subject:** Hanukka **Obv:** Value, date, inscriptions and menorah **Rev:** Prague Hanukka Lamp **Shape:** 12-sided **Note:** Struck for sets only

Date	Mintage	F	VF	XF	Unc	BU
JE5769 (2009)(u)	1,800	—	—	—	12.00	—

KM# 160a   NEW SHEQEL
3.4500 g., Nickel Plated Steel, 17.97 mm. **Obv:** Value **Rev:** Lily, state emblem and ancient Hebrew inscription **Edge:** Plain

Date	Mintage	F	VF	XF	Unc	BU
JE5761 (2001)(h)	9,648,000	—	—	—	1.00	—
JE5762 (2002)(h)	18,816,000	—	—	—	1.00	—
JE5763 (2003)(v)	10,198,500	—	—	—	1.00	—

Date	Mintage	F	VF	XF	Unc	BU
JE5765 (2005)	—	—	—	—	1.00	—
JE5766 (2006)	—	—	—	—	1.00	—

Note: Coin alignment error exists. Value: $100 in Unc, $50 in XF.

Date	Mintage	F	VF	XF	Unc	BU
JE5767 (2007)	—	—	—	—	1.00	—
JE5769 (2009)	—	—	—	—	1.00	—
JE5771 (2011)	—	—	—	—	0.75	—

KM# 344 NEW SHEQEL
14.4000 g., 0.9250 Silver 0.4282 oz. ASW, 30 mm. **Series:** Independence Day **Subject:** Education **Obv:** Denomination **Rev:** Pomegranate full of symbols - Hebrew 'ABC-123', etc. **Edge:** Plain

Date	Mintage	F	VF	XF	Unc	BU
JE5761-2001(u) Prooflike	1,653	—	—	—	—	35.00

KM# 351 NEW SHEQEL
14.4000 g., 0.9250 Silver 0.4282 oz. ASW, 30 mm. **Series:** Art and Culture in Israel **Subject:** Music **Obv:** National arms and denomination **Rev:** Musical instruments **Edge:** Plain

Date	Mintage	F	VF	XF	Unc	BU
JE5761-2001(u) Prooflike	1,182	—	—	—	—	35.00

KM# 163b NEW SHEQEL
3.5000 g., Nickel Bonded Steel, 18 mm. **Subject:** Hanukka **Obv:** Value, small menorah, country name in Hebrew, English and Arabic and inscription "HANUKKA" in Hebrew and English **Rev:** Lily, state emblem, ancient Hebrew inscription and Star of David mintmark **Edge Lettering:** Plain

Date	Mintage	F	VF	XF	Unc	BU
JE5761 (2001)(u)	4,000	—	—	—	4.00	—
Note: In sets only						
JE5762 (2002)(u)	4,000	—	—	—	4.00	—
Note: In sets only						
JE5763 (2003)(u)	3,000	—	—	—	4.00	—
Note: In sets only						
JE5764 (2004)(u)	3,000	—	—	—	4.00	—
Note: In sets only						
JE5765 (2005)(u)	2,500	—	—	—	4.00	—
Note: In sets only						
JE5766 (2006)(u)	3,000	—	—	—	4.00	—
Note: In sets only						
JE5767 (2007)(u)	3,000	—	—	—	4.00	—
Note: In sets only						
JE5769 (2009)(u)	1,800	—	—	—	4.00	—
JE5770 (2010)(u)	1,800	—	—	—	4.00	—

KM# 163 NEW SHEQEL
4.0000 g., Copper-Nickel, 18 mm. **Subject:** Hanukka **Obv:** Value **Rev:** Lily, state emblem and ancient Hebrew inscription. **Note:** Coins dated JE5754-5769 have the Star of David mint mark; the JE5746-5753 coins do not.

Date	Mintage	F	VF	XF	Unc	BU
JE5761 (2001)(u)	4,000	—	—	—	4.00	—
Note: In sets only						
JE5770 (2010)	1,800	—	—	—	4.00	—
JE5762 (2002)(u)	4,000	—	—	—	4.00	—
Note: In sets only						
JE5763 (2003)(u)	3,000	—	—	—	4.00	—
Note: In sets only						
JE5764 (2004)(u)	3,000	—	—	—	4.00	—
Note: In sets only						
JE5765 (2005)(u)	2,500	—	—	—	4.00	—
Note: In sets only						
JE5766 (2006)(u)	3,000	—	—	—	4.00	—
Note: In sets only						
JE5767 (2007)(u)	3,000	—	—	—	4.00	—
Note: In sets only						
JE5769 (2009)(u)	1,800	—	—	—	4.00	—
Note: In sets only						
JE5770 (2010)(u)	—	—	—	—	4.00	—
Note: In sets only						

KM# 356 NEW SHEQEL
14.4000 g., 0.9250 Silver 0.4282 oz. ASW, 30 mm. **Series:** Independence Day **Subject:** Volunteering **Obv:** Denomination **Rev:** Heart in hands **Edge:** Plain

Date	Mintage	F	VF	XF	Unc	BU
JE5762-2002(o) Prooflike	1,364	—	—	—	—	30.00

KM# 359 NEW SHEQEL
14.4000 g., 0.9250 Silver 0.4282 oz. ASW, 30 mm. **Series:** Biblical Art **Subject:** Tower of Babel **Obv:** National arms in spiral inscription **Rev:** Tower of Hebrew verses **Edge:** Plain

Date	Mintage	F	VF	XF	Unc	BU
JE5762 (2002)(o) Prooflike	1,312	—	—	—	—	45.00

KM# 371 NEW SHEQEL
14.4000 g., 0.9250 Silver 0.4282 oz. ASW, 30 mm. **Series:** Independence Day **Subject:** Space Exploration **Obv:** "Ofeq" satellite in orbit **Rev:** "Shavit" rocket **Edge Lettering:** Hebrew: "In memory of Ilan Ramon and his colleagues in the Columbia"

Date	Mintage	F	VF	XF	Unc	BU
JE5763-2003(v) Prooflike	1,233	—	—	—	—	40.00

KM# 374 NEW SHEQEL
14.4000 g., 0.9250 Silver 0.4282 oz. ASW, 30 mm. **Series:** Biblical Art **Subject:** Jacob and Rachel **Obv:** Value **Rev:** Jacob and Rachel floating in air **Edge:** Plain

Date	Mintage	F	VF	XF	Unc	BU
JE5763-2003(u) Prooflike	1,661	—	—	—	—	42.00

KM# 380 NEW SHEQEL
14.4000 g., 0.9250 Silver 0.4282 oz. ASW, 30 mm. **Series:** Independence Day **Subject:** Children of Israel **Obv:** Value **Rev:** Parent and child **Edge:** Plain

Date	Mintage	F	VF	XF	Unc	BU
JE5764-2004(u) Prooflike	1,446	—	—	—	—	35.00

KM# 383 NEW SHEQEL
14.4000 g., 0.9250 Silver 0.4282 oz. ASW, 30 mm. **Subject:** 2004 Summer Olympics **Obv:** Four windsurfers, value and national arms **Rev:** Eight windsurfers **Edge:** Plain

Date	Mintage	F	VF	XF	Unc	BU
JE5764-2004(v) Prooflike	2,800	—	—	—	—	35.00

KM# 386 NEW SHEQEL
14.4000 g., 0.9250 Silver 0.4282 oz. ASW, 30 mm. **Series:** Biblical Art **Subject:** Burning Bush **Obv:** Burning twig and value **Rev:** Burning Bush **Edge:** Plain

Date	Mintage	F	VF	XF	Unc	BU
JE5764-2004(v)	1,274	—	—	—	—	55.00

KM# 405.1 NEW SHEQEL
1.2440 g., 0.9990 Gold 0.0400 oz. AGW, 13.92 mm. **Series:** Biblical Art **Subject:** Jacob and Rachel **Obv:** Value **Rev:** Jacob and Rachel floating in air **Edge:** Reeded

Date	Mintage	F	VF	XF	Unc	BU
JE5764 (2004)(u) Proof	6,057	Value: 100				

KM# 405.2 NEW SHEQEL
1.2440 g., 0.9990 Gold 0.0400 oz. AGW, 13.92 mm. **Series:** Biblical Art **Subject:** Jacob and Rachel **Obv:** Value **Rev:** Jacob and Rachel floating in air. Arabic legend Israel is mispelled **Edge:** Reeded

Date	Mintage	F	VF	XF	Unc	BU
JE5764 (2004)(u) Proof	682	Value: 150				

KM# 406 NEW SHEQEL
14.4000 g., 0.9250 Silver 0.4282 oz. ASW, 30 mm. **Subject:** FIFA 2006 World Cup **Obv:** Value and soccer ball **Rev:** Map and soccer ball **Edge:** Plain

Date	Mintage	F	VF	XF	Unc	BU
JE5764-2004(u) Prooflike	Est. 2,800	—	—	—	—	40.00

Note: Issued in 2006

KM# 377 NEW SHEQEL
14.4000 g., 0.9250 Silver 0.4282 oz. ASW, 30 mm. **Series:** Art and Culture in Israel **Subject:** Architecture and design **Obv:** Value **Rev:** Architecture and design **Edge:** Plain **Note:** With enamel.

Date	Mintage	F	VF	XF	Unc	BU
JE5764-2004(u)	930	—	—	—	—	35.00

KM# 412 NEW SHEQEL
14.4000 g., 0.9250 Silver 0.4282 oz. ASW, 30 mm. **Series:** Art and Culture in Israel **Subject:** Naomi Shemer **Obv:** Value **Rev:** Portrait of Naomi Shemer **Edge:** Plain

Date	Mintage	F	VF	XF	Unc	BU
JE5765-2005(u) Prooflike	1,100	—	—	—	—	35.00

KM# 396 NEW SHEQEL
14.4000 g., 0.9250 Silver 0.4282 oz. ASW, 30 mm. **Subject:** Einstein's Relativity Theory **Obv:** Concentric circles above equation **Rev:** Value above signature

Date	Mintage	F	VF	XF	Unc	BU
JE5765-2005(v) Prooflike	Est. 1,100	—	—	—	—	48.00

KM# 399 NEW SHEQEL
14.4000 g., 0.9250 Silver 0.4282 oz. ASW, 30 mm. **Series:** Biblical Art **Subject:** Moses and the Ten Commandments **Obv:** Ten Commandments and value **Rev:** Moses and the Ten Commandments

Date	Mintage	F	VF	XF	Unc	BU
JE5765-2005(u) Prooflike	1,400	—	—	—	—	45.00

KM# 402 NEW SHEQEL
14.4000 g., 0.9250 Silver 0.4282 oz. ASW, 30 mm. **Series:** Independence day **Subject:** Israel 57th Anniversary The Golden Years **Obv:** Value and olive branch **Rev:** Twisted olive tree

Date	Mintage	F	VF	XF	Unc	BU
JE5765-2005(u) Prooflike	Est. 1,100	—	—	—	—	35.00

KM# 409   NEW SHEQEL
14.4000 g., 0.9250 Silver 0.4282 oz. ASW, 30 mm. **Series:**
Biblical Art **Subject:** Abraham and the Three Angels **Obv:** Value
and stars **Rev:** Abraham and the three angels **Edge:** Reeded

Date	Mintage	F	VF	XF	Unc	BU
JE5766-2006(ig)	1,075	—	—	—	—	50.00

KM# 416   NEW SHEQEL
14.4000 g., 0.9250 Silver 0.4282 oz. ASW, 30 mm. **Series:**
Independence Day **Subject:** Higher Education in Israel **Obv:**
Value and design **Rev:** Symbols of Science, Humanities,
Technology and Mathematics **Edge:** Plain

Date	Mintage	F	VF	XF	Unc	BU
JE5766-2006(ig)	737	—	—	—	—	45.00

KM# 419   NEW SHEQEL
14.4000 g., 0.9250 Silver 0.4282 oz. ASW, 30 mm. **Series:**
UNESCO World Heritage Sites in Israel **Subject:** White City of
Tel Aviv **Obv:** Value and Bauhaus building **Rev:** Fall of Bauhaus
style building and UNESCO symbol **Edge:** Plain

Date	Mintage	F	VF	XF	Unc	BU
JE5766-2006(ig) Prooflike	Est. 1,200	—	—	—	—	50.00

KM# 423   NEW SHEQEL
14.4000 g., 0.9250 Silver 0.4282 oz. ASW, 30 mm. **Series:**
Independence Day **Subject:** Performing Arts in Israel **Obv:**
Value, state emblem and inscriptions **Rev:** Stylized actor, dancer
and musician and inscription in Hebrew, English and Arabic,
Performing Arts in Israel **Edge:** Plain

Date	Mintage	F	VF	XF	Unc	BU
JE5767-2007(ig) Prooflike	Est. 1,200	—	—	—	—	50.00

KM# 426   NEW SHEQEL
14.4000 g., 0.9250 Silver 0.4282 oz. ASW, 30 mm. **Subject:**
2008 Olympics - Judo **Obv:** Value, state emblem, judo belt and
inscriptions **Rev:** 2 judo athletes and inscriptions in Hebrew,
English and Arabic **Edge:** Plain

Date	Mintage	F	VF	XF	Unc	BU
JE5767-2007(u) Prooflike	1,160	—	—	—	—	50.00

KM# 429   NEW SHEQEL
14.4000 g., 0.9250 Silver 0.4282 oz. ASW, 30 mm. **Series:**
Biblical Art **Subject:** Isaiah, Wolf with the Lamb **Obv:** Value, state
emblem and inscriptions in Hebrew, English and Arabic **Obv.
Inscription:** And the Wolf shall dwell with the Lamb **Rev:** Wolf
and lamb lying together under a tree **Edge:** Plain

Date	Mintage	F	VF	XF	Unc	BU
JE5767-2007(v) Prooflike	Est. 1,800	—	—	—	—	55.00

KM# 437   NEW SHEQEL
1.2440 g., 0.9990 Gold 0.0400 oz. AGW, 13.92 mm. **Series:**
Biblical Art **Subject:** Abraham and the Angels **Obv:** Value, state
emblem and Moses in Hebrew, English and Arabic **Rev:** Abraham
greeting three angels **Edge:** Reeded

Date	Mintage	F	VF	XF	Unc	BU
JE5767-2007(v) Proof	1,500	Value: 120				

KM# 438   NEW SHEQEL
1.2440 g., 0.9990 Gold 0.0400 oz. AGW, 13.92 mm. **Series:**
Biblical Art **Subject:** Moses and the Ten Commandments **Obv:**
Value, state emblem and Moses in Hebrew **Rev:** Moses holding
the Ten Commandments **Edge:** Reeded

Date	Mintage	F	VF	XF	Unc	BU
JE5767-2007 Proof	2,467	Value: 120				

KM# 163a   NEW SHEQEL
4.0000 g., Copper-Nickel, 18 mm. **Subject:** Hanukka **Obv:**
Value, small menorah, country name in Hebrew, English and
Arabic and inscription "HANUKKA" in Hebrew and English **Rev:**
Lily, state emblem, ancient Hebrew inscription and Star of David
mintmark **Note:** Non-magnetic.

Date	Mintage	F	VF	XF	Unc	BU
JE5768 (2008)(u)	3,000	—	—	—	4.00	

Note: In sets only.

KM# 439   NEW SHEQEL
14.4000 g., 0.9250 Silver 0.4282 oz. ASW, 30 mm. **Series:**
Israeli Nobel Prize Laureates **Subject:** Shmuel Yosef Agnon
Obv: Value, state emblem, outline of Agnon **Rev:** Portrait of
Agnon **Edge:** Plain

Date	Mintage	F	VF	XF	Unc	BU
JE5768-2008(ig) Prooflike	666	—	—	—	—	60.00

KM# 440   NEW SHEQEL
1.2440 g., 0.9990 Gold 0.0400 oz. AGW, 13.92 mm. **Series:**
Biblical Art **Subject:** Isaiah, Wolf with the Lamb **Obv:** Value, state
emblem, and inscriptions **Rev:** Wolf and lamb lying under tree
Edge: Reeded

Date	Mintage	F	VF	XF	Unc	BU
JE5768-2008(v) Proof	Est. 5,000	Value: 120				

KM# 441   NEW SHEQEL
14.4000 g., 0.9250 Silver 0.4282 oz. ASW, 30 mm. **Series:**
Independence Day **Subject:** Israel's Sixtieth Anniversary **Obv:**
Value, state emblem and inscriptions including "Independence
Day" **Rev:** "60" the zero is shaped like a pomegranite and a dove

Date	Mintage	F	VF	XF	Unc	BU
JE5768-2008(v) Prooflike	1,800	—	—	—	—	60.00

KM# 442   NEW SHEQEL
14.4000 g., 0.9250 Silver 0.4282 oz. ASW, 30 mm. **Subject:**
Israel Defense Forces Reserves **Obv:** Triangle, state emblem
and inscription **Rev:** Teddy bear pendant over soldier's ID tag

Date	Mintage	F	VF	XF	Unc	BU
JE5768-2008(ig) Prooflike	Est. 1,200	—	—	—	—	60.00

KM# 443   NEW SHEQEL
1.2440 g., 0.9990 Gold 0.0400 oz. AGW, 13.92 mm. **Series:**
Biblical Art **Subject:** Parting of the Red Sea **Obv:** Value, state
emblem and inscriptions **Rev:** Israelites passing through the Red
Sea **Edge:** Reeded

Date	Mintage	F	VF	XF	Unc	BU
JE5769-2008(v) Proof	Est. 5,000	Value: 120				

KM# 444   NEW SHEQEL
14.4000 g., 0.9250 Silver 0.4282 oz. ASW, 30 mm. **Series:** Biblical
Art **Subject:** Parting of the Red Sea **Obv:** Value, state emblem and
inscriptions **Rev:** Israelites passing through the Red Sea

Date	Mintage	F	VF	XF	Unc	BU
JE5769-2008(v) Prooflike	Est. 1,800	—	—	—	—	60.00

KM# 453   NEW SHEQEL
14.4000 g., 0.9250 Silver 0.4282 oz. ASW, 30 mm. **Series:**
UNESCO World Heritage Sites in Israel **Subject:** Masada **Obv:**
Value, state emblem, image of Masada **Rev:** View of Masada,
UNESCO emblem, World Heritage Site emblem **Edge:** Plain

Date	Mintage	F	VF	XF	Unc	BU
JE5769 (2009)(u) Prooflike	Est. 1,800	—	—	—	—	60.00

KM# 456   NEW SHEQEL
14.4000 g., 0.9250 Silver 0.4282 oz. ASW, 30 mm. **Series:**
Independence Day **Subject:** Israel's Sixty-first Anniversary Birds
of Israel **Obv:** Value, state emblem, finch **Rev:** Three birds,
hoopoe, warbler and finch **Edge:** Plain

Date	Mintage	F	VF	XF	Unc	BU
JE5769 (2009)(u) Prooflike	1,800	—	—	—	—	60.00

KM# 459   NEW SHEQEL
14.4000 g., 0.9250 Silver 0.4282 oz. ASW, 30 mm. **Subject:**
2010 FIFA World Cup South Africa **Obv:** Soccer Player, ball,
outline of globe, value, state emblem **Rev:** Soccer ball with design
Edge: Plain

Date	Mintage	F	VF	XF	Unc	BU
JE5769 (2009)(u) Prooflike	Est. 1,800	—	—	—	—	60.00

KM# 462 NEW SHEQEL
1.2440 g., 0.9990 Gold 0.0400 oz. AGW, 13.92 mm. **Series:** Biblical Art **Subject:** Samson and the Lion **Obv:** Small stylized palm tree, value, state emblem **Rev:** Stylized Samson wrestling a lion and small stylized palm tree **Edge:** Reeded

Date	Mintage	F	VF	XF	Unc	BU
JE5769 (2009)(u) Proof	Est. 5,000				Value: 120	

KM# 463 NEW SHEQEL
14.4000 g., 0.9250 Silver 0.4282 oz. ASW, 30 mm. **Series:** Biblical Art **Subject:** Samson and the Lion **Obv:** Small stylized palm tree, value, state emblem **Rev:** Stylized Samson wrestling a lion and small stylized palm tree **Edge:** Plain

Date	Mintage	F	VF	XF	Unc	BU
JE5769 (2009)(u) Prooflike	Est. 1,800	—	—	—	—	60.00

KM# 468 NEW SHEQEL
14.4000 g., 0.9250 Silver 0.4282 oz. ASW, 30 mm. **Series:** UNESCO World Heritage Sites in Israel **Subject:** Old Akko (Acre) **Obv:** Fortress of Akko as seen agains backdrop of Mediterranean Sea, state emblem, value UNESCO logo **Rev:** Ancient fortress walls, Khan-el-Undan caravanseraie and its clock tower, underground Crussader Knights' hall, White Mosque and other buildings **Edge:** Plain

Date	Mintage	F	VF	XF	Unc	BU
JE5770 (2010)(h) Prooflike	Est. 1,800	—	—	—	—	60.00

KM# 471 NEW SHEQEL
14.4000 g., 0.9250 Silver 0.4282 oz. ASW, 30 mm. **Series:** Independence Day **Subject:** Israeli National Trail 62nd Anniversary **Obv:** Trail forming stylized 62, state emblem **Rev:** Map of Isreal highlighting trail, boot, flowers **Edge:** Plain

Date	Mintage	F	VF	XF	Unc	BU
JE5770-2010(h) Prooflike	Est. 1,800	—	—	—	—	60.00

KM# 474 NEW SHEQEL
1.2440 g., 0.9990 Gold 0.0400 oz. AGW, 13.92 mm. **Series:** Biblical Art **Subject:** Jonah in the Whale **Obv:** Small image of Jonah, value, state emblem **Rev:** Stylized Jonah in belly of whale **Edge:** Reeded

Date	Mintage	F	VF	XF	Unc	BU
JE5770-2010(v) Proof	Est. 5,000				Value: 125	

KM# 475 NEW SHEQEL
14.4000 g., 0.9250 Silver 0.4282 oz. ASW, 30 mm. **Series:** Biblical Art **Subject:** Jonah in the Whale **Obv:** Small image of Jonah, value, state emblem **Rev:** Stylized Jonah in belly of whale **Edge:** Plain

Date	Mintage	F	VF	XF	Unc	BU
JE5770-2010(v) Prooflike	Est. 1,800	—	—	—	—	65.00

KM# 478 NEW SHEQEL
14.4000 g., 0.9250 Silver 0.4282 oz. ASW, 30 mm. **Series:** Israeli Nobel Prize Laureates **Subject:** Menachem Begin **Obv:** Menachem Begin, Jimmy Carter Anwar Sadat in triple handshake on White House lawn **Rev:** Portrait of Begin **Edge:** Plain

Date	Mintage	F	VF	XF	Unc	BU
JE5771-2010(u) Prooflike	Est. 2,800	—	—	—	—	65.00

KM# 481 NEW SHEQEL
14.4000 g., 0.9250 Silver 0.4282 oz. ASW, 30 mm. **Series:** Independence Day **Subject:** Israel's sixty-third anniversary, Dead Sea **Obv:** Image of Dead Sea region, ibex and legend "DEAD SEA" in Hebrew, English and Arabic **Rev:** Value, mirror image of value, state emblem, dates, country name in Hebrew, English and Arabic and legend "INDEPENDENCE DAY" in Hebrew and English

Date	Mintage	F	VF	XF	Unc	BU
JE5771-2011(u) Prooflike	Est. 1,800				Value: 80.00	

KM# 484 NEW SHEQEL
14.4000 g., 0.9250 Silver 0.4282 oz. ASW, 30 mm. **Subject:** 2012 London Olympics, Gymnastics **Obv:** Stlyized gymnast holding a ribbon in the shape of the Star of David and legends "THE OLYMPIC DELEGATION OF ISRAEL 2012" and "gymnastics" in Hebrew, English and Arabic **Rev:** Ribbon representation of Israeli flag, statem emblem, value, dates, country name in Hebrew, English and Arabic and inscription

Date	Mintage	F	VF	XF	Unc	BU
JE5771-2011(u) Prooflike	Est. 2,800				Value: 80.00	

KM# 487 NEW SHEQEL
14.4000 g., 0.9250 Silver 0.4282 oz. ASW, 30 mm. **Series:** Biblical Art **Subject:** Elijah in the Whirlwind **Obv:** State emblem, dates, country name in Hebrew, English and Arabic and inscription "ELIJAH WENT UP BY A WHIRLWIND INTO HEAVEN" in Hebrew, English and Arabic **Rev:** Stylized Elijah ascending to heaven in a horse-drawn chariot of fire in a whilrwind with Elisha below

Date	Mintage	F	VF	XF	Unc	BU
JE5771-2011 Prooflike	Est. 1,800				Value: 80.00	

KM# 488 NEW SHEQEL
1.2440 g., 0.9990 Gold 0.0400 oz. AGW, 13.92 mm. **Series:** Biblical Art **Subject:** Elijah in the Whirlwind

Date	Mintage	F	VF	XF	Unc	BU
JE5771-2011(v) Proof	5,000				Value: 125	

KM# 352 2 NEW SHEQALIM
28.8000 g., 0.9250 Silver 0.8565 oz. ASW, 38.7 mm. **Series:** Art and Culture in Israel **Subject:** Music **Obv:** National arms and denomination **Rev:** Musical instruments **Edge:** Reeded

Date	Mintage	F	VF	XF	Unc	BU
JE5761-2001(u) Proof	1,747				Value: 55.00	

KM# 349 2 NEW SHEQALIM
28.8000 g., 0.9250 Silver 0.8565 oz. ASW, 38.7 mm. **Series:** Wildlife **Subject:** Wild goat and acacia tree **Obv:** Acacia tree **Rev:** Ibex **Edge:** Reeded

Date	Mintage	F	VF	XF	Unc	BU
JE5761-2000(u) Proof	2,000				Value: 60.00	

KM# 345 2 NEW SHEQALIM
28.8000 g., 0.9250 Silver 0.8565 oz. ASW, 38.7 mm. **Series:** Independence Day **Subject:** Education **Obv:** Denomination **Rev:** Pomegranate full of symbols **Edge:** Reeded

Date	Mintage	F	VF	XF	Unc	BU
JE5761-2001(u) Proof	1,847				Value: 50.00	

KM# 357 2 NEW SHEQALIM
28.8000 g., 0.9250 Silver 0.8565 oz. ASW, 38.7 mm. **Series:** Independence Day **Subject:** Volunteering **Obv:** Denomination **Rev:** Heart in hands **Edge:** Reeded

Date	Mintage	F	VF	XF	Unc	BU
JE5762-2002(o) Proof	1,426				Value: 48.00	

KM# 360 2 NEW SHEQALIM
28.8000 g., 0.9250 Silver 0.8565 oz. ASW, 38.7 mm. **Series:** Biblical Art **Subject:** Tower of Babel **Obv:** National arms in spiral inscription **Rev:** Tower of Hebrew verses **Edge:** Reeded

Date	Mintage	F	VF	XF	Unc	BU
JE5762-2002(o) Proof	1,295				Value: 100	

KM# 372   2 NEW SHEQALIM

28.8000 g., 0.9250 Silver 0.8565 oz. ASW, 38.7 mm. **Subject:** Space Exploration **Obv:** "Amos" satellite in orbit **Rev:** "Shavit" rocket **Edge Lettering:** Hebrew: "In memory of Ilan Ramon and his colleagues in the Columbia"

Date	Mintage	F	VF	XF	Unc	BU
JE5763-2003(v) Proof	1,249	Value: 60.00				

KM# 375   2 NEW SHEQALIM

28.8000 g., 0.9250 Silver 0.8565 oz. ASW, 38.7 mm. **Series:** Biblical Art **Subject:** Jacob and Rachel **Obv:** Value **Rev:** Figures floating in air above flower and sheep **Edge:** Reeded

Date	Mintage	F	VF	XF	Unc	BU
JE5763-2003(u) Proof	1,377	Value: 80.00				

KM# 378   2 NEW SHEQALIM

28.8000 g., 0.9250 Silver 0.8565 oz. ASW, 38.7 mm. **Series:** Art and Culture in Israel **Subject:** Architecture and design **Obv:** Value and enameled shapes **Rev:** Architectural design **Edge:** Reeded

Date	Mintage	F	VF	XF	Unc	BU
JE5764-2004(u) Proof	1,084	Value: 60.00				

KM# 381   2 NEW SHEQALIM

28.8000 g., 0.9250 Silver 0.8565 oz. ASW, 38.7 mm. **Series:** Independence Day **Subject:** Children of Israel **Obv:** Value and stylized human shapes **Rev:** Stylized parent and child **Edge:** Reeded

Date	Mintage	F	VF	XF	Unc	BU
JE5764-2004(u) Proof	1,182	Value: 50.00				

KM# 384   2 NEW SHEQALIM

28.8000 g., 0.9250 Silver 0.8565 oz. ASW, 38.7 mm. **Subject:** 2004 Summer Olympics **Obv:** Four windsurfers, value and national arms **Rev:** Eight windsurfers **Edge:** Reeded

Date	Mintage	F	VF	XF	Unc	BU
JE5764-2004(v) Proof	2,800	Value: 55.00				

KM# 387   2 NEW SHEQALIM

28.8000 g., 0.9250 Silver 0.8565 oz. ASW, 38.7 mm. **Series:** Biblical Art **Subject:** Burning Bush **Obv:** Burning twig and value **Rev:** Burning Bush **Edge:** Reeded

Date	Mintage	F	VF	XF	Unc	BU
JE5764-2004(v) Proof	1,354	Value: 90.00				

KM# 407   2 NEW SHEQALIM

28.8000 g., 0.9250 Silver 0.8565 oz. ASW, 38.7 mm. **Subject:** FIFA 2006 World Cup **Obv:** Value and soccer ball **Rev:** Map and soccer ball **Edge:** Reeded

Date	Mintage	F	VF	XF	Unc	BU
JE5764-2004(u) Proof	Est. 5,000	Value: 60.00				

Note: Issued in 2006

KM# 413   2 NEW SHEQALIM

28.8000 g., 0.9250 Silver 0.8565 oz. ASW, 38.7 mm. **Series:** Art and Culture in Israel **Subject:** Noami Shemer **Obv:** Value **Rev:** Portrait of Naomi Shemer **Edge:** Reeded

Date	Mintage	F	VF	XF	Unc	BU
JE5765-2005(u) Proof	1,100	Value: 60.00				

KM# 397   2 NEW SHEQALIM

28.8000 g., 0.9250 Silver 0.8565 oz. ASW, 38.7 mm. **Subject:** Einstein's Relativity Theory **Obv:** Concentric circles above equation **Rev:** Value above signature

Date	Mintage	F	VF	XF	Unc	BU
JE5765-2005(v) Proof	1,600	Value: 80.00				

KM# 400   2 NEW SHEQALIM

28.8000 g., 0.9250 Silver 0.8565 oz. ASW, 38.7 mm. **Series:** Biblical Art **Subject:** Moses and the Ten Commandments **Obv:** Ten Commandments and value **Rev:** Moses and Ten Commandments

Date	Mintage	F	VF	XF	Unc	BU
JE5765-2005(u) Proof	1,400	Value: 100				

KM# 403   2 NEW SHEQALIM

28.8000 g., 0.9250 Silver 0.8565 oz. ASW, 38.7 mm. **Series:** Independence Day **Subject:** Israel 57th Anniversary - The Golden Years **Obv:** Value and olive branch **Rev:** Twisted olive tree **Edge:** Reeded

Date	Mintage	F	VF	XF	Unc	BU
JE5765-2005(u) Proof	1,100	Value: 50.00				

KM# 417   2 NEW SHEQALIM

28.8000 g., 0.9250 Silver 0.8565 oz. ASW, 38.7 mm. **Series:** Independence Day **Subject:** Higher Education in Israel **Obv:** Value and design **Rev:** Symbols of Science, Humanities, Technology and Mathematics **Edge:** Reeded

Date	Mintage	F	VF	XF	Unc	BU
JE5766-2006(ig) Proof	846	Value: 60.00				

KM# 410   2 NEW SHEQALIM

28.8000 g., 0.9250 Silver 0.8565 oz. ASW, 38.7 mm. **Series:** Biblical Art **Subject:** Abraham and the Three Angels **Obv:** Value and stars **Rev:** Abraham and the three angels **Edge:** Reeded

Date	Mintage	F	VF	XF	Unc	BU
JE5766-2006(ig) Proof	967	Value: 95.00				

KM# 420   2 NEW SHEQALIM

28.8000 g., 0.9250 Silver 0.8565 oz. ASW, 38.7 mm. **Series:** UNESCO World Heritage Site in Israel **Subject:** White City of Tel Aviv **Obv:** Value and Bauhaus building **Rev:** Fall of Bauhaus building and UNESCO symbol **Edge:** Reeded

Date	Mintage	F	VF	XF	Unc	BU
JE5766-2006(ig) Proof	Est. 1,200	Value: 75.00				

KM# 424   2 NEW SHEQALIM

28.8000 g., 0.9250 Silver 0.8565 oz. ASW, 38.7 mm. **Series:** Independence Day **Subject:** Performing Arts in Israel **Obv:** Value, state emblem and inscriptions **Rev:** Stylized actor, dancer and musician and inscription in Hebrew, English and Arabiv **Edge:** Reeded

Date	Mintage	F	VF	XF	Unc	BU
JE5767-2007(ig) Proof	Est. 1,200	Value: 75.00				

KM# 427   2 NEW SHEQALIM

28.8000 g., 0.9250 Silver 0.8565 oz. ASW, 38.7 mm. **Subject:** 2008 Olympics - Judo **Obv:** Value, state emblem, judo belt and inscriptions **Rev:** 2 judo athletes and inscriptions **Edge:** Reeded

Date	Mintage	F	VF	XF	Unc	BU
JE5767-2007(u)	5,211	Value: 75.00				
Proof						

KM# 430   2 NEW SHEQALIM

28.8000 g., 0.9250 Silver 0.8565 oz. ASW, 38.7 mm. **Series:** Biblical Art **Subject:** Isaiah, Wolf with the Lamb **Obv:** Value, state emblem and inscriptions in Hebrew, English and Arabic **Obv. Inscription:** And the Wolf shall dwell with the Lamb **Rev:** Wolf and lamb lying together under a tree **Edge:** Reeded

Date	Mintage	F	VF	XF	Unc	BU
JE5767-2007(v)	Est. 2,800	Value: 90.00				
Proof						

KM# 432   2 NEW SHEQALIM

5.7000 g., Nickel Plated Steel, 21.6 mm. **Subject:** Hanukka **Obv:** Value, date, inscriptions and menorah **Rev:** Double cornucopiae (horns of plenty) draped in ribbons and filled with fruit and grain including a pomegranate **Edge:** Plain with 4 notches

Date	Mintage	F	VF	XF	Unc	BU
JE5768 (2008)(u)	3,000	—	—	—	5.00	—
Note: In sets only						
JE5769 (2009)(u)	1,800	—	—	—	5.00	—
Note: In sets only						
JE5770 (2010)(u)	1,800	—	—	—	5.00	—
Note: In sets only						

KM# 433   2 NEW SHEQALIM

5.7000 g., Nickel Plated Steel, 21.6 mm. **Obv:** Value, date and inscriptions **Rev:** Double cornucopiae (horns of plenty) draped in ribbons and filled with fruit and grain including a pomegranate **Edge:** Plain with 4 notches

Date	Mintage	F	VF	XF	Unc	BU
JE5768 (2008)(u)	Est. 26,000,000	—	—	—	1.00	—
JE5769 (2009)(u)		—	—	—	1.00	—
JE5770 (2010)		—	—	—	1.00	—

KM# 445   2 NEW SHEQALIM

28.8000 g., 0.9250 Silver 0.8565 oz. ASW, 38.7 mm. **Series:** Israeli Nobel Prize Laureates **Subject:** Shmuel Yosef Agnon **Obv:** Value, state emblem and outline of Agnon **Rev:** Portrait of Agnon **Edge:** Reeded

Date	Mintage	F	VF	XF	Unc	BU
JE5768-2008(ig)	666	Value: 90.00				
Proof						

KM# 446   2 NEW SHEQALIM

28.8000 g., 0.9250 Silver 0.8565 oz. ASW, 38.7 mm. **Series:** Independence Day **Subject:** Israel's 60th Anniversary **Obv:** Value, state emblem and inscription "Independence Day" **Rev:** "60" the zero is shaped like a pomegranate and a dove

Date	Mintage	F	VF	XF	Unc	BU
JE5768-2008(v)	1,800	Value: 110				
Proof						

KM# 447   2 NEW SHEQALIM

28.8000 g., 0.9250 Silver 0.8565 oz. ASW, 38.7 mm. **Subject:** Israel Defense Forces Reserves **Obv:** Triangle, state emblem and inscription **Rev:** Teddy bear pendant over a soldier's ID tag

Date	Mintage	F	VF	XF	Unc	BU
JE5768-2008(ig)	Est. 1,200	Value: 95.00				
Proof						

KM# 448   2 NEW SHEQALIM

28.8000 g., 0.9250 Silver 0.8565 oz. ASW, 38.7 mm. **Series:** Biblical Art **Subject:** Parting of the Red Sea **Obv:** Value, state emblem and inscriptions **Rev:** Israelites passing through the Red Sea **Edge:** Reeded

Date	Mintage	F	VF	XF	Unc	BU
JE5769-2008(v)	1,800	Value: 95.00				
Proof						

KM# 454   2 NEW SHEQALIM

28.8000 g., 0.9250 Silver 0.8565 oz. ASW, 38.7 mm. **Series:** UNESCO World Heritage Sites in Israel **Subject:** Masada **Obv:** Value, state emblem, image of Masada **Rev:** View of Masada, UNESCO emblem, World Heritage Site emblem **Edge:** Reeded

Date	Mintage	F	VF	XF	Unc	BU
JE5769 (2009)(u)	Est. 1,800	Value: 90.00				
Proof						

KM# 457   2 NEW SHEQALIM

28.8000 g., 0.9250 Silver 0.8565 oz. ASW, 38.7 mm. **Series:** Independence Day **Subject:** Israel's Sixty-first Anniversary Birds of Israel **Obv:** Value, state emblem, hoopoe **Rev:** Three birds, hoopoe, warbler and finch **Edge:** Reeded

Date	Mintage	F	VF	XF	Unc	BU
JE5769 (2009)(u)	Est. 2,800	Value: 100				
Proof						

KM# 460   2 NEW SHEQALIM

28.8000 g., 0.9250 Silver 0.8565 oz. ASW, 38.7 mm. **Subject:** 2010 FIFA World Cup South Africa **Obv:** Soccer Player, ball, outline of globe **Rev:** Soccer player with design **Edge:** Reeded

Date	Mintage	F	VF	XF	Unc	BU
JE5769 (2009)(u)	Est. 5,000	Value: 90.00				
Proof						

KM# 464   2 NEW SHEQALIM

28.8000 g., 0.9250 Silver 0.8565 oz. ASW, 38.7 mm. **Series:** Biblical Art **Subject:** Samson and the Lion **Obv:** Small stylized palm tree, value, state emblem **Rev:** Stylized Samson wrestling with a lion and small stylized palm tree **Edge:** Reeded

Date	Mintage	F	VF	XF	Unc	BU
JE5769 (2009)(u)	Est. 2,800	Value: 90.00				
Proof						

KM# 469   2 NEW SHEQALIM

28.8000 g., 0.9250 Silver 0.8565 oz. ASW, 38.7 mm. **Series:** UNESCO World Heritage Sites in Israel **Subject:** Old Akko (Acre) **Obv:** Fortress of Akko as seen against backdrop of Mediterranean Sea, state emblem, value **Rev:** Ancient fortress walls, Khan-el-Umdan caravanseraie and its clock tower, underground Crusader Knights' Hall, White Mosque and other buildings **Edge:** Reeded

Date	Mintage	F	VF	XF	Unc	BU
JE5770 (2010)(h)	Est. 2,800	Value: 90.00				
Proof						

KM# 472   2 NEW SHEQALIM

28.8000 g., 0.9250 Silver 0.8565 oz. ASW, 38.7 mm. **Series:** Independence Day **Subject:** Israel National Trail **Obv:** Trail forming stylized 62, state emblem **Rev:** Map of Israel highlighting national trail, boot, flowers **Edge:** Reeded

Date	Mintage	F	VF	XF	Unc	BU
JE5770-2010(h)	Est. 1,800	Value: 90.00				
Proof						

KM# 476   2 NEW SHEQALIM

28.8000 g., 0.9250 Silver 0.8565 oz. ASW, 38.7 mm. **Series:** Biblical Art **Subject:** Jonah in the Whale **Obv:** Small image of Jonah, value, state emblem **Rev:** Stylized Jonah in belly of whale **Edge:** Reeded

Date	Mintage	F	VF	XF	Unc	BU
JE5770-2010(v)	Est. 2,800	Value: 95.00				
Proof						

KM# 479 2 NEW SHEQALIM

28.8000 g., 0.9250 Silver 0.8565 oz. ASW, 38.7 mm. **Series:** Israeli Nobel Pize Laureates **Subject:** Menachem Begin **Obv:** Menachem Begin, Jimmy Carter and Anwar Sadat in triple handshake on White House lawn, state emblem **Rev:** Portrait of Menachem Begin **Edge:** Reeded

Date	Mintage	F	VF	XF	Unc	BU
JE5771-2010(u) Proof	Est. 2,800			Value: 95.00		

KM# 482 2 NEW SHEQALIM

28.8000 g., 0.9250 Silver 0.8565 oz. ASW, 38.7 mm. **Series:** Independence Day **Subject:** Israel's sixty-third anniversary, Dead Sea **Obv:** Image of Dead Sea region, ibex and legend "DEAD SEA" in Hebrew, English and Arabic **Rev:** Value, mirror image of value, state emblem, dates, country name in Hebrew, English and Arabic and legend "INDEPENDENCE DAY" in Hebrew and English **Edge:** Reeded

Date	Mintage	F	VF	XF	Unc	BU
JE5771-2011 Proof	Est. 5,000			Value: 120		

KM# 485 2 NEW SHEQALIM

8.8000 g., 0.9250 Silver 0.2617 oz. ASW, 38.7 mm. **Subject:** 2012 London Olympics, Gymnastics **Obv:** Stylized gymnast holding a ribbon in the shape of the Star of David and legends "THE OLYMPIC DELEGATION OF ISRAEL 2012" and "gymnastics" in Hebrew, English and Arabic **Rev:** Ribbon representation of Israeli flag, state emblem, value, dates, country name in Hebrew, English and Arabic and inscription **Edge:** Reeded

Date	Mintage	F	VF	XF	Unc	BU
JE5771-2011(u) Proof	Est. 555			Value: 1,200		

KM# 489 2 NEW SHEQALIM

28.8000 g., 0.9250 Silver 0.8565 oz. ASW, 38.7 mm. **Series:** Biblical Art **Subject:** Elijah caught up in the firestorm **Obv:** State emblem, dates, country name in Herew, English and Arabic and inscription "ELIJAH WENT UP BY A WHIRLWIND INTO HEAVEN" in Hebrew, English and Arabic **Rev:** Stylized Elijah ascending to heaven in a horse-drawn chariot of fire in a whirlwind with Elisha below **Edge:** Reeded

Date	Mintage	F	VF	XF	Unc	BU
JE5771-2011(v) Proof	Est. 2,800			Value: 120		

KM# 207 5 NEW SHEQALIM

8.2000 g., Copper-Nickel, 24 mm. **Obv:** Value **Rev:** Ancient column capitol **Edge:** Plain **Shape:** 12-sided

---

Date	Mintage	F	VF	XF	Unc	BU
JE5762 (2002)(wg)	4,464,000	—	—	—	3.75	—

Note: The JE5762 coins are practically round.

Date	Mintage	F	VF	XF	Unc	BU
JE5765 (2005)	—	—	—	—	3.00	—
JE5766 (2006)	—	—	—	—	3.00	—
JE5768 (2008)	—	—	—	—	3.00	—
JE5769 (2009)	—	—	—	—	3.00	—
JE5771 (2011)	—	—	—	—	3.00	—

KM# 217 5 NEW SHEQALIM

8.2000 g., Copper-Nickel, 24 mm. **Obv:** Value, small menorah and inscription Hanukka **Rev:** Ancient column capitol **Edge:** Plain **Shape:** 12-sided **Note:** Coins dated JE5754-5770 have the Star of David mint mark; the JE5751-5753 coins do not.

Date	Mintage	F	VF	XF	Unc	BU
JE5762 (2002)(u)	4,000	—	—	—	7.00	—
Note: In sets only						
JE5763 (2003)(u)	3,000	—	—	—	8.00	—
Note: In sets only						
JE5764 (2004)(u)	3,000	—	—	—	8.00	—
Note: In sets only						
JE5765 (2005)(u)	2,500	—	—	—	8.00	—
Note: In sets only						
JE5766 (2006)(u)	3,000	—	—	—	8.00	—
Note: In sets only						
JE5767 (2007)(u)	3,000	—	—	—	8.00	—
Note: In sets only						
JE5768 (2008)(u)	3,000	—	—	—	8.00	—
Note: In sets only						
JE5769 (2009)(u)	1,800	—	—	—	8.00	—
JE5770 (2010)	1,800	—	—	—	8.00	—
JE5770 (2010)(u)	1,800	—	—	—	8.00	—

KM# 408 5 NEW SHEQALIM

7.7770 g., 0.9990 Gold 0.2498 oz. AGW, 27 mm. **Subject:** FIFA 2006 World Cup **Obv:** Value and soccer ball **Rev:** Map and soccer ball **Edge:** Reeded **Note:** Issued in 2006

Date	Mintage	F	VF	XF	Unc	BU
JE5764-2004(u) Proof	Est. 655			Value: 525		

KM# 461 5 NEW SHEQALIM

7.7700 g., 0.9990 Gold 0.2496 oz. AGW, 27 mm. **Subject:** 2010 FIFA World Cup South Africa **Obv:** Soccer Player, ball, outline of globe **Rev:** Soccer ball with design **Edge:** Reeded

Date	Mintage	F	VF	XF	Unc	BU
JE5769 (2009)(u) Proof	Est. 888			Value: 500		

KM# 315 10 NEW SHEQALIM

7.0000 g., Bi-Metallic Aureate bonded Bronze center in Nickel bonded Steel ring, 23 mm. **Obv:** Value, text and menorah within circle and vertical lines **Rev:** Palm tree and baskets within half beaded circle **Edge:** Reeded

Date	Mintage	F	VF	XF	Unc	BU
JE5761 (2001)(u)	4,000	—	—	—	9.00	—
Note: In sets only						
JE5762 (2002)(u)	4,000	—	—	—	9.00	—
Note: In sets only						
JE5763 (2003)(u)	3,000	—	—	—	10.00	—
Note: In sets only						
JE5764 (2004)(u)	3,000	—	—	—	10.00	—
Note: In sets only						
JE5765 (2005)(u)	2,500	—	—	—	10.00	—
Note: In sets only						
JE5766 (2006)(u)	3,000	—	—	—	10.00	—
Note: In sets only						
JE5767 (2007)(u)	3,000	—	—	—	10.00	—
Note: In sets only						
JE5768 (2008)(u)	3,000	—	—	—	10.00	—

Date	Mintage	F	VF	XF	Unc	BU
JE5769 (2009)(u)	1,800	—	—	—	10.00	—
Note: In sets only						
JE5770 (2010)(u)	1,800	—	—	—	10.00	—
Note: In sets only						

KM# 346 10 NEW SHEQALIM

16.9600 g., 0.9170 Gold 0.5000 oz. AGW, 30 mm. **Series:** Independence Day **Subject:** Education **Obv:** Value **Rev:** Pomegranate full of symbols - Hebrew for 'ABC - 123', etc. **Edge:** Reeded

Date	Mintage	F	VF	XF	Unc	BU
JE5761-2001(u) Proof	660			Value: 1,050		

KM# 353 10 NEW SHEQALIM

16.9600 g., 0.9170 Gold 0.5000 oz. AGW, 30 mm. **Series:** Art and Culture of Israel **Subject:** Music **Obv:** National arms and value **Rev:** Musical instruments **Edge:** Reeded

Date	Mintage	F	VF	XF	Unc	BU
JE5761-2001(u) Proof	766			Value: 1,000		

KM# 358 10 NEW SHEQALIM

16.9600 g., 0.9166 Gold 0.4998 oz. AGW, 30 mm. **Series:** Independence Day **Subject:** Volunteering **Obv:** Value **Rev:** Heart in hands **Edge:** Reeded

Date	Mintage	F	VF	XF	Unc	BU
JE5762-2002(o) Proof	617			Value: 1,050		

KM# 361 10 NEW SHEQALIM

16.9600 g., 0.9170 Gold 0.5000 oz. AGW, 30 mm. **Series:** Biblical Art **Subject:** Tower of Babel **Obv:** National arms in spiral inscription **Rev:** Tower of Hebrew verses **Edge:** Reeded

Date	Mintage	F	VF	XF	Unc	BU
JE5762-2002(o) Proof	750			Value: 1,100		

KM# 270 10 NEW SHEQALIM

7.0000 g., Bi-Metallic Aureate Bonded Bronze center in Nickel Bonded Steel ring, 23 mm. **Obv:** Value, vertical lines and text within circle **Rev:** Palm tree and baskets within half beaded circle **Edge:** Reeded

Date	Mintage	F	VF	XF	Unc	BU
JE5762 (2002)(h)	4,749,000	—	—	—	5.00	—
JE5765 (2005)	—	—	—	—	5.00	—

Note: Coin alignment error exists. Value: $200 in Unc, $100 in XF.

Date	Mintage	F	VF	XF	Unc	BU
JE5766 (2006)	—	—	—	—	5.00	—
JE5769 (2009)	—	—	—	—	5.00	—
JE5770 (2010)	—	—	—	—	5.00	—
JE5771 (2011)	—	—	—	—	5.00	—

KM# 373 10 NEW SHEQALIM

16.9600 g., 0.9170 Gold 0.5000 oz. AGW, 30 mm. **Subject:** Space Exploration **Obv:** "Eros" satellite in orbit **Rev:** "Shavit" rocket **Edge Lettering:** Hebrew: In memory of Ilan Ramon and his colleagues in the Columbia"

Date	Mintage	F	VF	XF	Unc	BU
JE5763-2003(v) Proof	573			Value: 1,050		

KM# 376 10 NEW SHEQALIM

16.9600 g., 0.9170 Gold 0.5000 oz. AGW, 30 mm. **Series:** Biblical Art **Subject:** Jacob and Rachel **Obv:** Value **Rev:** Jacob and Rachel floating in air above tree and sheep **Edge:** Reeded

Date	Mintage	F	VF	XF	Unc	BU
JE5763-2003(u) Proof	686			Value: 1,100		

KM# 379 10 NEW SHEQALIM

16.9600 g., 0.9170 Gold 0.5000 oz. AGW, 30 mm. **Series:** Art and Culture in Israel **Subject:** Architecture and Design **Obv:** Value **Rev:** Architectural design **Edge:** Reeded

Date	Mintage	F	VF	XF	Unc	BU
JE5764-2004(u) Proof	555			Value: 1,100		

KM# 382 10 NEW SHEQALIM
16.9600 g., 0.9170 Gold 0.5000 oz. AGW, 30 mm. **Series:** Independence Day **Subject:** Children of Israel **Obv:** Value **Rev:** Stylized parent and child **Edge:** Reeded

Date	Mintage	F	VF	XF	Unc	BU
JE5764-2004(u) Proof	539			Value: 1,100		

KM# 385 10 NEW SHEQALIM
16.9600 g., 0.9170 Gold 0.5000 oz. AGW, 30 mm. **Subject:** 2004 Summer Olympics **Obv:** Four windsurfers, value and national arms **Rev:** Eight windsurfers **Edge:** Reeded

Date	Mintage	F	VF	XF	Unc	BU
JE5764-2004(v) Proof	540			Value: 1,100		

KM# 388 10 NEW SHEQALIM
16.9600 g., 0.9170 Gold 0.5000 oz. AGW, 30 mm. **Series:** Biblical Art **Subject:** Burning Bush **Obv:** Burning twig and value **Rev:** Burning Bush **Edge:** Reeded

Date	Mintage	F	VF	XF	Unc	BU
JE5764-2004(v) Proof	555			Value: 1,100		

KM# 398 10 NEW SHEQALIM
16.9600 g., 0.9166 Gold 0.4998 oz. AGW, 30 mm. **Subject:** Einstein's Relativity Theory **Obv:** Concentric circles above equation **Rev:** Value above signature **Edge:** Reeded

Date	Mintage	F	VF	XF	Unc	BU
JE5765-2005(v) Proof	555			Value: 1,100		

KM# 401 10 NEW SHEQALIM
16.9600 g., 0.9166 Gold 0.4998 oz. AGW, 30 mm. **Series:** Biblical Art **Subject:** Moses and the Ten Commandments **Obv:** The Ten Commandments and value **Rev:** Moses and Ten Commandments **Edge:** Reeded

Date	Mintage	F	VF	XF	Unc	BU
JE5765-2005(u) Proof	555			Value: 1,100		

KM# 404 10 NEW SHEQALIM
16.9600 g., 0.9166 Gold 0.4998 oz. AGW, 30 mm. **Series:** Independence Day **Subject:** Israel 57th Anniversary - Golden years **Obv:** Value and olive branch **Rev:** Twisted olive tree **Edge:** Reeded

Date	Mintage	F	VF	XF	Unc	BU
JE5765-2005(u) Proof	485			Value: 1,100		

KM# 414 10 NEW SHEQALIM
16.9600 g., 0.9170 Gold 0.5000 oz. AGW, 30 mm. **Series:** Art and culture in Israel **Subject:** Naomi Shemer **Obv:** Value **Rev:** Portrait of Naomi Shemer **Edge:** Reeded

Date	Mintage	F	VF	XF	Unc	BU
JE5765-2005(u) Proof	455			Value: 1,100		

KM# 418 10 NEW SHEQALIM
16.9600 g., 0.9170 Gold 0.5000 oz. AGW, 30 mm. **Series:** Independence Day **Subject:** Higher Education in Israel **Obv:** Value and design **Rev:** Symbols of Science, Humanities, Technology and Mathematics **Edge:** Reeded

Date	Mintage	F	VF	XF	Unc	BU
JE5766-2006(ig) Proof	444			Value: 950		

KM# 411 10 NEW SHEQALIM
16.9600 g., 0.9170 Gold 0.5000 oz. AGW, 30 mm. **Series:** Biblical Art **Subject:** Abraham and the Three Angels **Obv:** Value and stars **Rev:** Abraham and the three angels **Edge:** Reeded

Date	Mintage	F	VF	XF	Unc	BU
JE5766-2006(ig) Proof	555			Value: 950		

KM# 421 10 NEW SHEQALIM
16.9600 g., 0.9170 Gold 0.5000 oz. AGW, 30 mm. **Series:** UNESCO World Heritage Sites in Israel **Subject:** White City of Tel Aviv **Obv:** Value and Bauhaus building **Rev:** Face of Bauhaus building and UNESCO symbol **Edge:** Reeded

Date	Mintage	F	VF	XF	Unc	BU
JE5766-2006(ig) Proof	Est. 555			Value: 1,100		

KM# 425 10 NEW SHEQALIM
16.9600 g., 0.9170 Gold 0.5000 oz. AGW, 30 mm. **Series:** Independence Day **Subject:** Performing Arts in Israel **Obv:** Value, state emblem and inscriptions **Rev:** Stylized actor, dancer and musician and inscription in Hebrew, English and Arabic, "Performing Arts in Israel" **Edge:** Reeded

Date	Mintage	F	VF	XF	Unc	BU
JE5767-2007(ig) Proof	Est. 444			Value: 1,150		

KM# 428 10 NEW SHEQALIM
16.9600 g., 0.9170 Gold 0.5000 oz. AGW, 30 mm. **Subject:** 2008 Olympics - Judo **Obv:** Value, state emblem, judo belt and inscriptions **Rev:** 2 judo athletes and inscriptions in Hebrew, English and Arabic **Edge:** Reeded

Date	Mintage	F	VF	XF	Unc	BU
JE5767 (2007)(u) Proof	548			Value: 1,150		

KM# 431 10 NEW SHEQALIM
16.9600 g., 0.9170 Gold 0.5000 oz. AGW, 30 mm. **Series:** Biblical Art **Subject:** Isaiah, Wolf with the Lamb **Obv:** Value, state emblem and inscriptions in Hebrew, English and Arabic. **Obv. Inscription:** And the Wolf shall dwell with the Lamb **Rev:** Wolf and lamb lying together under a tree **Edge:** Reeded

Date	Mintage	F	VF	XF	Unc	BU
JE5767-2007(v) Proof	555			Value: 1,100		

KM# 452 10 NEW SHEQALIM
16.9600 g., 0.9170 Gold 0.5000 oz. AGW, 30 mm. **Series:** Biblical Art **Subject:** Parting of the Red Sea **Obv:** Value, state emblem and inscriptions **Rev:** Israelites passing through the Red Sea **Edge:** Reeded

Date	Mintage	F	VF	XF	Unc	BU
JE5769-2008(v) Proof	Est. 555			Value: 1,100		

KM# 449 10 NEW SHEQALIM
16.9600 g., 0.9170 Gold 0.5000 oz. AGW, 30 mm. **Series:** Israeli Nobel Prize Laureates **Subject:** Shmuel Yosef Agnon **Obv:** Value, state emblem and outline of Agnon **Rev:** Portrait of Agnon **Edge:** Reeded

Date	Mintage	F	VF	XF	Unc	BU
JE5768-2008(ig)	322			Value: 1,100		

KM# 450 10 NEW SHEQALIM
16.9600 g., 0.9170 Gold 0.5000 oz. AGW, 30 mm. **Series:** Independence Day **Subject:** Israel's 60th Anniversary **Obv:** Value, state emblem and inscription "Independence Day" **Rev:** "60" the zero is shaped like a pomegranite and a dove **Edge:** Reeded

Date	Mintage	F	VF	XF	Unc	BU
JE5768-2008(v) Proof	444			Value: 1,100		

KM# 451 10 NEW SHEQALIM
16.9600 g., 0.9170 Gold 0.5000 oz. AGW, 30 mm. **Subject:** Israel Defense Force Reserves **Obv:** Value over a triangle, state emblem and inscriptions **Rev:** Teddy bear pendant over a soldier's ID tag **Edge:** Reeded

Date	Mintage	F	VF	XF	Unc	BU
JE5768-2008 Proof	Est. 444			Value: 1,100		

KM# 455 10 NEW SHEQALIM
16.9600 g., 0.9170 Gold 0.5000 oz. AGW, 30 mm. **Series:** UNESCO World Heritage Sites in Israel **Subject:** Masada **Obv:** Value, state emblem, image of Masada **Rev:** View of Masada, UNESCO emblem, World Heritage Site Emblem **Edge:** Reeded

Date	Mintage	F	VF	XF	Unc	BU
JE5679 (2009)(u) Proof	Est. 555			Value: 1,100		

KM# 458 10 NEW SHEQALIM
16.9600 g., 0.9170 Gold 0.5000 oz. AGW, 30 mm. **Series:** Independence Day **Subject:** Israel's Sixty-first Anniversary Birds of Israel **Obv:** Value, state emblem, warbler **Rev:** Three birds, hoopoe, warbler and finch **Edge:** Reeded

Date	Mintage	F	VF	XF	Unc	BU
JE5769 (2009)(u) Proof	Est. 650			Value: 1,150		

KM# 465 10 NEW SHEQALIM
16.9600 g., 0.9170 Gold 0.5000 oz. AGW, 30 mm. **Series:** Biblical Art **Subject:** Samson and the Lion **Obv:** Small stylized palm tree, value, state emblem **Rev:** Stylized Samson wrestling a lion, stylized palm tree **Edge:** Reeded

Date	Mintage	F	VF	XF	Unc	BU
JE5769 (2009)(u) Proof	Est. 555			Value: 1,100		

KM# 470   10 NEW SHEQALIM

16.9600 g., 0.9170 Gold 0.5000 oz. AGW, 30 mm. **Series:** UNESCO World Heritage Sites in Israel **Subject:** Old Akko (Acre) **Obv:** Fortress of Akko as seen against backdrop of Mediterranean Sea, state emblem, value **Rev:** Ancient fortress walls, Khan-el-Umdan caravanseraie and its clock tower, underground Crusader Knights' hall, White Mosque and other buildings **Edge:** Reeded

Date	Mintage	F	VF	XF	Unc	BU
JE5770 (2010)(h)	Est. 555	Value: 1,100				
Proof						

KM# 473   10 NEW SHEQALIM

16.9500 g., 0.9170 Gold 0.4997 oz. AGW, 30 mm. **Series:** Independence Day **Subject:** Israel National Trail **Obv:** Trail forming stylized 62, state emblem **Rev:** Map of Israel highlighting trail, boot, flowers **Edge:** Reeded

Date	Mintage	F	VF	XF	Unc	BU
JE5770-2010(h)	Est. 555	Value: 1,100				
Proof						

KM# 477   10 NEW SHEQALIM

16.9600 g., 0.9170 Gold 0.5000 oz. AGW, 30 mm. **Series:** Biblical Art **Subject:** Jonah in the Whale **Obv:** Small image of Jonah, value, state emblem **Rev:** Stylized Jonah in belly of whale **Edge:** Reeded

Date	Mintage	F	VF	XF	Unc	BU
JE5770-2010	Est. 555	Value: 1,100				
Proof						

KM# 480   10 NEW SHEQALIM

16.9600 g., 0.9170 Gold 0.5000 oz. AGW, 30 mm. **Series:** Israeli Nobel Prize Laureates **Subject:** Menachem Begin **Obv:** Menachem Begin, Jimmy Carter adn Anwar Sadat in triple handshake on White House lawn, state emblem **Rev:** Portrait of Menachem Begin **Edge:** Reeded

Date	Mintage	F	VF	XF	Unc	BU
JE5771-2010(u)	Est. 888	Value: 1,100				
Proof						

KM# 483   10 NEW SHEQALIM

16.9600 g., 0.9170 Gold 0.5000 oz. AGW, 30 mm. **Series:** Independence Day **Subject:** Israel's sixty-third anniversary, Dead Sea **Obv:** Image of Dead Sea region, ibex and legend "DEAD SEA" in Hebrew, English and Arabic **Rev:** Western wall of the Temple, dates and legends "JERUSALEM" in Hebrew, English and Arabic and "1 OZ FINE GOLD .999" in English and Hebrew

Date	Mintage	F	VF	XF	Unc	BU
JE5771-2011(u)	Est. 555	Value: 1,200				
Proof						

KM# 486   10 NEW SHEQALIM

16.9600 g., 0.9170 Gold 0.5000 oz. AGW, 30 mm. **Subject:** 2012 London Olympics, Gymnastics **Obv:** Stylized gymnast holding a ribbon in the shape of the Star of David and legends "THE OLYMPIC DELEGATION OF ISRAEL 2012" and "gymnastics" in Hebrew, English and Arabic **Rev:** Ribbon represenatation of Israeli flag, state emblem, value, dates, country name in Hebrew, English and Arabic and inscription **Edge:** Reeded

Date	Mintage	F	VF	XF	Unc	BU
JE5771-2011(u)	Est. 555	Value: 1,200				
Proof						

KM# 490   10 NEW SHEQALIM

16.9600 g., 0.9170 Gold 0.5000 oz. AGW, 30 mm. **Series:** Biblical Art **Subject:** Elijah in the Whirlwind **Obv:** State emblem, dates, country name in Hebrew, English and Arabic and inscription "ELIJAH WENT UP BY A WHIRLWIND INTO HEAVEN" in Hebrew, English and Arabic **Rev:** Stylized Elijah ascending to heaven in a horse-drawn chariot of fire in a whirlwind with Elisha below **Edge:** Reeded

Date	Mintage	F	VF	XF	Unc	BU
JE5771-2011	Est. 555	Value: 1,200				
Proof						

BULLION COINAGE

KM# 467   20 NEW SHEQALIM

31.1000 g., 0.9990 Gold 0.9988 oz. AGW, 32 mm. **Subject:** Tower of David **Obv:** State emblem above lion of Megiddo and country name in Hebrew, English and Arabic **Rev:** Tower of David near the Jaffa Gate in Jerusalem **Edge:** Plain

Date	Mintage	F	VF	XF	Unc	BU
JE5770 (2010)(u)	Est. 3,600	—	—	—	—	BV+20%

KM# 491   20 NEW SHEQALIM

31.1000 g., 0.9990 Gold 0.9988 oz. AGW, 32 mm. **Subject:** Western Wall of the Temple **Obv:** State emblem above lion of Megiddo **Rev:** Sestern wall of the Temple, dates and legends "JERUSALEM" in Hebrew, English and Arabic and "1 OZ FINE GOLD .9999" in English and Hebrew

Date	Mintage	F	VF	XF	Unc	BU
JE5771 (2011)(u)	Est. 3,600	—	—	—	—	BV+20%

MINT SETS

KM#	Date	Mintage	Identification	Issue Price	Mkt Val
MS86	JE5761 (2001) (7)	4,000	KM#163b, 172-174, 217, 315, 354 (plastic case) 350th Anniversary of the Jewish Community of Curacao	24.00	37.00
MS88	JE5762 (2002) (7)	4,000	KM#163b, 172-174, 217, 315, 355 (plastic case) Yemenite Jewry (issued 2001)	27.00	40.00
MS89	JE5761-5762 (2001-2002) (9)	3,000	KM#157, 158, 160a (JE5761), 157-159, 160a, 207, 270 (JE5762) plus Twin Towers medal (folder) Israel - New York	—	30.00
MS91	JE5763 (2003) (7)	3,000	KM#163b, 172-174, 217, 315, 389 (plastic case) The March of the Living into Poland (issued 2002)	30.00	42.00
MS93	JE5764 (2004) (7)	3,000	KM#163b, 172-174, 217, 315, 390 (plastic case) Iraqi Jewry (issued 2003)	—	40.00
MS94	JE5761-5763 (2001-2003) (6)	3,000	KM#157-159, 160a, 207, 270 (various dates) (folder) Bank of Israel Jubilee; (given or sold to Bank of Israel employees and VIP guests, not to the general public; issued 2004)	—	45.00
MS96	JE5765 (2005) (7)	2,500	KM#163b, 172-174, 217, 315, 391 (plastic case) Syrian Jewry (issued 2004)	—	42.00
MS97	JE5764-5765 (2004-2005) (6)	3,000	KM#158, 159 (JE5764), 157, 160a, 207, 270 (JE5765) (folder) Israel Today	37.00	35.00
MS98	JE5766 (2006) (7)	2,700	KM#163b, 172-174, 217, 315, 415 (folder) Dutch Jewry (issued 2005)	45.00	45.00
MS99	JE5766 (2006) (7)	300	KM#163b, 172-174, 217, 315, 415 (plastic case) Dutch Jewry (issued 2005)	—	45.00
MS100	JE5766 (2006) (6)	2,000	KM#157-159, 160a, 207, 270 (folder) To the North With Love	37.00	35.00
MS103	JE5767-5768 (2007-2008) (8)	1,000	KM#157-159, 160a (JE5767), 158, 159, 207, 433 (JE5768) (folder) The Negev Shall Blossom	37.00	46.00
MS101	JE5767 (2007) (7)	3,000	KM#163b, 172-174, 217, 315, 422 (folder) Greek Jewry (issued 2006)	43.00	42.00
MS102	JE5768 (2008) (8)	3,000	KM#163a, 172-174, 217, 315, 432, 434 (folder) Egyptian Jewry (issued 2007)	43.00	45.00
MS104	JE5769 (2009) (7)	1,800	KM#163b, 173, 174, 217, 315, 432, 436 (folder) Glorious Prague (issued 2008)	43.00	45.00
MS105	JE5770 (2010) (7)	1,800	KM#163b, 173, 174, 217, 315, 432, 466 (folder) Jews of Algeria	43.00	45.00
MS107	JE5769-5770 (2009-10) (6)	—	KM#160a, 207, 433 (JE5769), 158, 159, 270 (JE5770) (folder) 2010 coin set, Type II	29.95	30.00
MS108	JE5770-5771 (2010-2011) (5)	—	KM#433 (JE5770), 158, 159, 160a, 207, 270 (JE5771) The Western Wall, 2011 Uncirculated Coin Set	36.00	36.00

ITALY

The Italian Republic, a 700-mile-long peninsula extending into the heart of the Mediterranean Sea, has an area of 116,304 sq. mi. (301,230 sq. km.) and a population of 60 million. Capital: Rome. The economy centers around agriculture, manufacturing, forestry and fishing. Machinery, textiles, clothing and motor vehicles are exported.

MINT
R - Rome

REPUBLIC
DECIMAL COINAGE

KM# 91 LIRA
0.6200 g., Aluminum, 17 mm. **Obv:** Balance scales **Rev:** Cornucopia, value and date **Note:** The 1968-1969 and 1982-2001 dates were issued in sets only.

Date	Mintage	F	VF	XF	Unc	BU
2001R	100,000	—	—	—	20.00	—
2001R Proof	10,000	Value: 40.00				

KM# 219 LIRA
11.0000 g., 0.8350 Silver 0.2953 oz. ASW, 29 mm. **Subject:** History of the Lira - Lira of 1946 (KM#87) **Obv:** Head with laureate left within circle **Rev:** Apple on branch within circle flanked by sprigs **Edge:** Reeded **Note:** This is a Lira Series reproducing an old coin design in the center of each coin.

Date	Mintage	F	VF	XF	Unc	BU
2001R	50,000	—	—	—	70.00	—
2001R Proof	6,100	Value: 220				

KM# 220 LIRA
6.0000 g., 0.8350 Silver 0.1611 oz. ASW, 24 mm. **Subject:** History of the Lira - Lira of 1951 (KM#91) **Obv:** Balance scale within circle **Rev:** Value and cornucopia within circle **Edge:** Reeded **Note:** This is a Lira Series reproducing an old coin design in the center of each coin.

Date	Mintage	F	VF	XF	Unc	BU
2001R	50,000	—	—	—	70.00	—
2001R Proof	6,100	Value: 220				

KM# 87a LIRA
8.0000 g., 0.9000 Gold 0.2315 oz. AGW, 21.6 mm. **Obv:** Ceres **Rev:** Orange on branch **Edge:** Plain **Note:** Official Restrike

Date	Mintage	F	VF	XF	Unc	BU
1946 (2006)R Proof	1,999	Value: 450				

KM# 91a LIRA
4.0000 g., 0.9000 Gold 0.1157 oz. AGW, 17.2 mm. **Obv:** Balance scale **Rev:** Cornucopia, date and value **Edge:** Plain **Note:** Official Restrike

Date	Mintage	F	VF	XF	Unc	BU
1951 (2006)R Proof	1,999	Value: 250				

KM# 94 2 LIRE
0.8000 g., Aluminum, 18 mm. **Obv:** Honey bee **Rev:** Olive branch and value **Edge:** Reeded **Note:** The 1968-1969 and 1982-2001 dates were issued in sets only.

Date	Mintage	F	VF	XF	Unc	BU
2001R	100,000	—	—	—	18.00	—
2001R Proof	10,000	Value: 40.00				

KM# 88a 2 LIRE
11.0000 g., 0.9000 Gold 0.3183 oz. AGW, 24.1 mm. **Obv:** Farmer plowing field **Rev:** Wheat ear **Edge:** Plain **Note:** Official Restrike

Date	Mintage	F	VF	XF	Unc	BU
1946 (2006)R Proof	1,999	Value: 700				

KM# 94a 2 LIRE
5.0000 g., 0.9000 Gold 0.1447 oz. AGW, 18.3 mm. **Obv:** Honey bee **Rev:** Olive branch **Edge:** Reeded **Note:** Official Restrike

Date	Mintage	F	VF	XF	Unc	BU
1953 (2006)R Proof	1,999	Value: 350				

KM# 92 5 LIRE
1.0350 g., Aluminum, 20.12 mm. **Obv:** Rudder **Rev:** Dolphin and value **Edge:** Plain

Date	Mintage	F	VF	XF	Unc	BU
2001R	100,000	—	—	—	12.00	—
2001R Proof	10,000	Value: 20.00				

KM# 89a 5 LIRE
16.0000 g., 0.9000 Gold 0.4630 oz. AGW, 26.7 mm. **Obv:** Italia with torch **Rev:** Bunch of grapes **Edge:** Reeded **Note:** Official Restrike

Date	Mintage	F	VF	XF	Unc	BU
1946 (2006)R Proof	1,999	Value: 1,000				

KM# 92a 5 LIRE
6.0000 g., 0.9000 Gold 0.1736 oz. AGW, 20.2 mm. **Obv:** Rudder **Rev:** Dolphin and value **Edge:** Plain **Note:** Official Restrike

Date	Mintage	F	VF	XF	Unc	BU
1951 (2006)R Proof	1,999	Value: 450				

KM# 93 10 LIRE
1.6000 g., Aluminum, 23.25 mm. **Obv:** Plow **Rev:** Value within wheat ears **Edge:** Plain

Date	Mintage	F	VF	XF	Unc	BU
2001R	100,000	—	—	—	12.00	—
2001R Proof	10,000	Value: 35.00				

KM# 90a 10 LIRE
19.0000 g., 0.9000 Gold 0.5498 oz. AGW, 29 mm. **Obv:** Pegasus **Rev:** Olive branch **Edge:** Lettered **Edge Lettering:** REPVBBLICA ITALIANA **Note:** Official Restrike

Date	Mintage	F	VF	XF	Unc	BU
1946 (2006)R Proof	1,999	Value: 1,150				

KM# 93a 10 LIRE
10.0000 g., 0.9000 Gold 0.2893 oz. AGW, 23.3 mm. **Obv:** Plow **Rev:** Value within wheat ears **Edge:** Plain **Note:** Official Restrike

Date	Mintage	F	VF	XF	Unc	BU
1951 (2006)R Proof	1,999	Value: 650				

KM# 97.2 20 LIRE
3.6000 g., Aluminum-Bronze, 21.25 mm. **Obv:** Wheat sprigs within head left **Rev:** Oak leaves divide value and date **Edge:** Plain

Date	Mintage	F	VF	XF	Unc	BU
2001R	100,000	—	—	—	12.00	—
2001R Proof	10,000	Value: 35.00				

KM# 97.1a 20 LIRE
8.0000 g., 0.9000 Gold 0.2315 oz. AGW, 21.3 mm. **Obv:** Head laureate left **Rev:** Oak leaves divides date and value **Edge:** Reeded **Note:** Official Restrike

Date	Mintage	F	VF	XF	Unc	BU
1957 (2006)R Proof	1,999	Value: 550				

KM# 183 50 LIRE
4.5000 g., Copper-Nickel, 19 mm. **Obv:** Turreted head left **Rev:** Large value within wreath of produce

Date	Mintage	F	VF	XF	Unc	BU
2001R	100,000	—	—	—	10.00	—
2001R Proof	10,000	Value: 18.00				

KM# 95.1a 50 LIRE
14.0000 g., 0.9000 Gold 0.4051 oz. AGW, 24.8 mm. **Obv:** Italia **Rev:** Vulcan **Edge:** Reeded **Note:** Official Restrike

Date	Mintage	F	VF	XF	Unc	BU
1954 (2006)R Proof	1,999	Value: 850				

KM# 183a 50 LIRE
9.0000 g., 0.9000 Gold 0.2604 oz. AGW, 19.2 mm. **Obv:** Roma **Rev:** Value within wreath **Edge:** Plain **Note:** Official Restrike

Date	Mintage	F	VF	XF	Unc	BU
1996 (2006)R Proof	1,999	Value: 550				

KM# 159 100 LIRE
4.5000 g., Copper-Nickel, 22 mm. **Obv:** Turreted head left **Rev:** Large value within circle flanked by sprigs **Edge:** Segmented reeding

Date	Mintage	F	VF	XF	Unc	BU
2001R	100,000	—	—	—	12.00	—
2001R Proof	10,000	Value: 35.00				

KM# 96.1a 100 LIRE
18.0000 g., 0.9000 Gold 0.5208 oz. AGW, 27.8 mm. **Obv:** Ancient athlete **Rev:** Minerva standing **Edge:** Reeded **Note:** Official Restrike

Date	Mintage	F	VF	XF	Unc	BU
1955 (2006)R Proof	1,999	Value: 1,100				

KM# 159a 100 LIRE
9.0000 g., 0.9000 Gold 0.2604 oz. AGW, 22 mm. **Obv:** Turreted head left **Rev:** Large value within circle flanked by sprigs **Edge:** Segmented reeding **Note:** Official Restrike

Date	Mintage	F	VF	XF	Unc	BU
1993 (2006)R Proof	1,999	Value: 550				

KM# 105 200 LIRE
5.0000 g., Aluminum-Bronze, 24 mm. **Obv:** Head right **Rev:** Value within gear **Edge:** Reeded

Date	Mintage	F	VF	XF	Unc	BU
2001R	100,000	—	—	—	18.00	—
2001R Proof	10,000	Value: 40.00				

KM# 105a 200 LIRE
11.0000 g., 0.9000 Gold 0.3183 oz. AGW, 24 mm. **Obv:** Head right **Rev:** Value within gear **Edge:** Reeded **Note:** Official Restrike

Date	Mintage	F	VF	XF	Unc	BU
1977 (2006)R Proof	1,999	Value: 700				

KM# 98 500 LIRE
11.0000 g., 0.8350 Silver 0.2953 oz. ASW, 29.3 mm. **Obv:**

Columbus' ships **Rev:** Bust left within wreath **Edge:** Dates in raised lettering

Date	Mintage	F	VF	XF	Unc	BU
2001R	100,000	—	—	—	45.00	—
2001R Proof	10,000	Value: 215				

KM# 111 500 LIRE
6.8000 g., Bi-Metallic Aluminum-Bronze center in Stainless Steel ring, 25.8 mm. **Obv:** Head left within circle **Rev:** Plaza within circle flanked by sprigs **Edge:** Segmented reeding

Date	Mintage	F	VF	XF	Unc	BU
2001R	100,000	—	—	—	12.00	—
2001R Proof	10,000	Value: 35.00				

KM# 98a 500 LIRE
18.0000 g., 0.9000 Gold 0.5208 oz. AGW, 29 mm. **Obv:** Columbus' ships **Rev:** Bust left within wreath **Edge:** Lettered **Edge Lettering:** REPVBBLICA ITALIANA *** 1958*** **Note:** Official Restrike

Date	Mintage	F	VF	XF	Unc	BU
1958 (2006)R Proof	1,999	Value: 1,100				

KM# 99a 500 LIRE
18.0000 g., 0.9000 Gold 0.5208 oz. AGW, 29 mm. **Obv:** Seated Italia **Rev:** Lady **Edge:** Lettered **Edge Lettering:** "1 CENTENARIO VNITA'D'ITALIA * 1861-1961*" **Note:** Official Restrike

Date	Mintage	F	VF	XF	Unc	BU
1961 (2006)R Proof	1,999	Value: 1,100				

KM# 100a 500 LIRE
18.0000 g., 0.9000 Gold 0.5208 oz. AGW, 29 mm. **Obv:** Dante **Rev:** Hell **Edge:** Lettered **Edge Lettering:** "7 CENTENARIO DELLA NASCITA DI DANTE" **Note:** Official Restrike

Date	Mintage	F	VF	XF	Unc	BU
1965 (2006)R Proof	1,999	Value: 1,100				

KM# 111a 500 LIRE
14.0000 g., Bi-Metallic .750 Gold center in .900 Gold ring, 25.8 mm. **Obv:** Head left within circle **Rev:** Plaza within circle flanked by sprigs **Edge:** Segmented reeding **Note:** Official Restrike

Date	Mintage	F	VF	XF	Unc	BU
1982 (2006)R Proof	1,999	Value: 325				

KM# 194 1000 LIRE
Bi-Metallic Copper-Nickel center in Aluminum-Bronze ring, 27 mm. **Subject:** European Union **Obv:** Head left within circle **Rev:** Corrected map with United Germany within globe design

Date	Mintage	F	VF	XF	Unc	BU
2001R	100,000	—	—	—	10.00	—
2001R Proof	10,000	Value: 35.00				

KM# 236 1000 LIRE
14.6000 g., 0.8350 Silver 0.3919 oz. ASW, 31.4 mm. **Obv:** Giuseppe Verdi **Rev:** Building

Date	Mintage	F	VF	XF	Unc	BU
2001R	115,000	—	—	—	50.00	—
2001R Proof	10,000	Value: 100				

KM# 190a 1000 LIRE
17.0000 g., 0.9000 Gold 0.4919 oz. AGW, 27 mm. **Obv:** Roma **Rev:** European map **Edge:** Segmented reeding **Note:** Official Restrike

Date	Mintage	F	VF	XF	Unc	BU
1997 (2006)R Proof	1,999	Value: 900				

KM# 101a 1000 LIRE
24.0000 g., 0.9000 Gold 0.6944 oz. AGW, 31.2 mm. **Obv:** Concordia **Rev:** Geometric shape above value **Edge Lettering:** REPVBBLICA ITALIANA **Note:** Official restrike.

Date	Mintage	F	VF	XF	Unc	BU
1970 (2006)R Proof	1,999	Value: 1,350				

KM# 234 50000 LIRE
7.5000 g., 0.9000 Gold 0.2170 oz. AGW, 20 mm. **Subject:** 250th Anniversary - Palace of Caserta **Obv:** Front view of palace **Rev:** Fountain, date and denomination

Date	Mintage	F	VF	XF	Unc	BU
2001R Proof	6,200	Value: 475				

KM# 233 100000 LIRE
15.0000 g., 0.9000 Gold 0.4340 oz. AGW, 25 mm. **Subject:** 700th Anniversary - Pulpit at the Church of St. Andrea a Pistoia **Obv:** Full pulpit **Rev:** Enlarged detail of the pulpit

Date	Mintage	F	VF	XF	Unc	BU
2001R Proof	4,500	Value: 900				

EURO COINAGE
European Union Issues

KM# 210 EURO CENT
2.3000 g., Copper Plated Steel, 16.3 mm. **Obv:** Castle del Monte **Rev:** Value and globe **Edge:** Plain

Date	Mintage	F	VF	XF	Unc	BU
2002R	1,348,899,500	—	—	—	0.25	—
2003R	9,629,000	—	—	—	0.35	—
2003R Proof	12,000	Value: 10.00				
2004R	100,000,000	—	—	—	0.25	—
2004R Proof	12,000	Value: 7.00				
2005R	180,000,000	—	—	—	0.35	—
2005R Proof	12,000	Value: 5.00				
2006R	159,000,000	—	—	—	0.25	—
2006R Proof	12,000	Value: 5.00				
2007R	215,000,000	—	—	—	0.25	—
2007R Proof	12,000	Value: 5.00				
2008R	180,000,000	—	—	—	0.25	—
2008R Proof	5,000	Value: 5.00				
2009R	174,951,500	—	—	—	0.25	—
2009R Proof	5,500	Value: 5.00				
2010R	42,000,000	—	—	—	0.25	—
2010R Proof	5,000	Value: 5.00				
2011R	134,000,000	—	—	—	0.25	—
2011R Proof	5,000	Value: 5.00				

KM# 211 2 EURO CENT
3.0300 g., Copper Plated Steel, 18.7 mm. **Obv:** Observation tower in Turin **Rev:** Value and globe **Edge:** Plain

Date	Mintage	F	VF	XF	Unc	BU
2002R	1,099,166,250	—	—	—	0.25	—
2003R	21,817,000	—	—	—	0.25	—
2003R Proof	12,000	Value: 10.00				
2004R	120,000,000	—	—	—	0.25	—
2004R Proof	12,000	Value: 7.00				
2005R	120,000,000	—	—	—	0.25	—
2005R Proof	12,000	Value: 5.00				
2006R	196,000,000	—	—	—	0.25	—
2006R Proof	12,000	Value: 5.00				
2007R	140,000,000	—	—	—	0.25	—
2007R Proof	12,000	Value: 5.00				
2008R	135,000,000	—	—	—	0.25	—
2008R Proof	5,000	Value: 5.00				
2009R	184,951,500	—	—	—	0.25	—
2009R Proof	5,500	Value: 5.00				
2010R	115,000,000	—	—	—	0.25	—
2010R Proof	5,000	Value: 5.00				
2011R	109,000,000	—	—	—	0.25	—
2011R Proof	5,000	Value: 5.00				

KM# 212 5 EURO CENT
3.9500 g., Copper Plated Steel, 19.64 mm. **Obv:** Colosseum **Rev:** Value and globe **Edge:** Plain

Date	Mintage	F	VF	XF	Unc	BU
2002R	1,341,742,204	—	—	—	0.25	—
2003R	1,960,000	—	—	—	10.00	—
2003R Proof	12,000	Value: 20.00				
2004R	10,000,000	—	—	—	0.25	—
2004R Proof	12,000	Value: 8.00				
2005R	70,000,000	—	—	—	0.25	—
2005R Proof	12,000	Value: 6.00				
2006R	119,000,000	—	—	—	0.25	—
2006R Proof	12,000	Value: 6.00				
2007R	85,000,000	—	—	—	0.25	—
2007R Proof	12,000	Value: 6.00				
2008R	90,000,000	—	—	—	0.25	—
2008R Proof	5,000	Value: 6.00				
2009R	84,955,000	—	—	—	0.25	—
2009R Proof	5,500	Value: 6.00				
2010R	32,000,000	—	—	—	0.25	—
2010R Proof	5,000	Value: 6.00				
2011R	37,000,000	—	—	—	0.25	—
2011R Proof	5,000	Value: 6.00				

KM# 213 10 EURO CENT
4.1000 g., Brass, 19.8 mm. **Obv:** Venus by Botticelli **Rev:** Value and map **Edge:** Reeded

Date	Mintage	F	VF	XF	Unc	BU
2002R	1,142,383,000	—	—	—	0.25	—
2003R	29,976,000	—	—	—	0.50	—
2003R Proof	12,000	Value: 15.00				
2004R	5,000,000	—	—	—	10.00	—
2004R Proof	12,000	Value: 10.00				
2005R	100,000,000	—	—	—	0.50	—
2005R Proof	12,000	Value: 7.00				
2006R	180,000,000	—	—	—	0.50	—
2006R Proof	12,000	Value: 7.00				
2007R	105,000,000	—	—	—	0.50	—
2007R Proof	12,000	Value: 7.00				

KM# 247 10 EURO CENT
4.0700 g., Brass, 19.7 mm. **Obv:** Venus by Botticelli **Rev:** Relief Map of Western Europe, stars, lines and value **Edge:** Reeded

Date	Mintage	F	VF	XF	Unc	BU
2008R	104,955,000	—	—	—	0.25	0.35
2008R Proof	5,000	Value: 7.00				
2009R	105,951,500	—	—	—	0.25	0.35
2009R Proof	5,500	Value: 7.00				
2010R	57,000,000	—	—	—	0.25	0.35
2010R Proof	5,000	Value: 7.00				
2011R	76,000,000	—	—	—	0.25	0.35
2011R Proof	5,000	Value: 7.00				
2012R	—	—	—	—	0.25	0.35
2012R Proof	—	Value: 7.00				

KM# 214 20 EURO CENT
5.7300 g., Brass, 22.1 mm. **Obv:** Futuristic sculpture by Boccioni **Rev:** Value and map **Edge:** Notched

Date	Mintage	F	VF	XF	Unc	BU
2002R	1,411,836,000	—	—	—	0.30	—
2003R	26,155,000	—	—	—	0.30	—
2003R Proof	12,000	Value: 16.00				
2004R	5,000,000	—	—	—	0.50	—
2004R Proof	12,000	Value: 14.00				
2005R	5,000,000	—	—	—	5.00	—
2005R Proof	12,000	Value: 8.00				
2006R	5,000,000	—	—	—	5.00	—
2006R Proof	12,000	Value: 8.00				
2007R	5,000,000	—	—	—	0.50	—
2007R Proof	12,000	Value: 8.00				

KM# 248 20 EURO CENT
5.7300 g., Brass, 22.1 mm. **Obv:** Futuristic sculpture **Rev:** Relief map of Western Europe, stars, lines and value **Edge:** Reeded

Date	Mintage	F	VF	XF	Unc	BU
2008R	4,955,000	—	—	—	1.00	1.25
2008R Proof	5,000	Value: 8.00				
2009R	59,951,500	—	—	—	1.00	1.25
2009R Proof	5,500	Value: 8.00				
2010R	23,000,000	—	—	—	1.00	1.25
2010R Proof	5,000	Value: 8.00				
2011R	67,000,000	—	—	—	1.00	1.25
2011R Proof	5,000	Value: 8.00				
2012R	—	—	—	—	1.00	1.25
2012R Proof	—	Value: 8.00				

KM# 215 50 EURO CENT
7.8100 g., Brass, 24.2 mm. **Obv:** Sculpture of Marcus Aurelius on horseback **Rev:** Value and map **Edge:** Reeded

Date	Mintage	F	VF	XF	Unc	BU
2002R	1,136,718,000	—	—	—	0.80	—
2003R	44,825,000	—	—	—	1.00	—

Date	Mintage	F	VF	XF	Unc	BU
2003R Proof	12,000	Value: 18.00				
2004R	5,000,000	—	—	—	—	4.00
2004R Proof	12,000	Value: 16.00				
2005R	5,000,000	—	—	—	—	1.00
2005R Proof	12,000	Value: 10.00				
2006R	5,000,000	—	—	—	—	1.00
2006R Proof	12,000	Value: 10.00				
2007R	5,000,000	—	—	—	—	1.00
2007R Proof	12,000	Value: 10.00				

KM# 249   50 EURO CENT
7.8100 g., Brass, 24.2 mm. **Obv:** Sculpture of Marcus Aurelius on horseback **Rev:** Relief map of Western Europe, stars, lines and value **Edge:** Reeded

Date	Mintage	F	VF	XF	Unc	BU
2008R	4,955,000	—	—	—	1.25	1.50
2008R Proof	5,000	Value: 10.00				
2009R	2,451,500	—	—	—	1.25	1.50
2009R Proof	5,500	Value: 10.00				
2010R	9,000,000	—	—	—	1.25	1.50
2010R Proof	5,000	Value: 10.00				
2011R	5,000,000	—	—	—	1.25	1.50
2011R Proof	5,000	Value: 10.00				
2012R	—	—	—	—	1.25	1.50
2012R Proof	—	Value: 10.00				

KM# 216   EURO
7.5000 g., Bi-Metallic Copper-Nickel center in Nickel-Brass ring, 23.2 mm. **Obv:** Male figure drawing by Leonardo da Vinci within circle of stars **Rev:** Value and map within circle **Edge:** Reeded and plain sections

Date	Mintage	F	VF	XF	Unc	BU
2002R	966,025,300	—	—	—	1.60	—
2003R	66,474,000	—	—	—	2.00	—
2003R Proof	12,000	Value: 20.00				
2004R	5,000,000	—	—	—	5.00	—
2004R Proof	12,000	Value: 18.00				
2005R	5,000,000	—	—	—	5.00	—
2005R Proof	12,000	Value: 15.00				
2006R	108,000,000	—	—	—	2.00	—
2006R Proof	12,000	Value: 15.00				
2007R	135,000,000	—	—	—	2.00	—
2007R Proof	12,000	Value: 15.00				

KM# 250   EURO
7.5000 g., Bi-Metallic Copper-Nickel center in Nickel-Brass ring, 23.2 mm. **Obv:** Male figure drawing by Leonardo da Vinci **Rev:** Relief map of Western Europe, stars, lines and value **Edge:** Reeded and plain sections

Date	Mintage	F	VF	XF	Unc	BU
2008R	134,955,000	—	—	—	2.50	2.75
2008R Proof	5,000	Value: 15.00				
2009R	144,951,500	—	—	—	2.50	2.75
2009R Proof	5,500	Value: 15.00				
2010R	50,000,000	—	—	—	2.50	2.75
2010R Proof	5,000	Value: 15.00				
2011R	88,000,000	—	—	—	2.50	2.75
2011R Proof	5,000	Value: 15.00				
2012R	—	—	—	—	2.50	2.75
2012R Proof	—	Value: 15.00				

KM# 217   2 EURO
8.5000 g., Bi-Metallic Nickel-Brass center in Copper-Nickel ring, 25.75 mm. **Obv:** Bust of Dante Aligheri left **Rev:** Value and map within circle **Edge:** Reeded **Edge Lettering:** 2's and stars

Date	Mintage	F	VF	XF	Unc	BU
2002R	463,702,000	—	—	—	4.00	—
2003R	36,160,000	—	—	—	4.00	—
2003R Proof	12,000	Value: 25.00				
2004R	7,000,000	—	—	—	6.00	—
2004R Proof	12,000	Value: 22.00				
2005R	62,000,000	—	—	—	4.00	—
2005R Proof	12,000	Value: 20.00				

Date	Mintage	F	VF	XF	Unc	BU
2006R	10,000,000	—	—	—	4.00	—
2006R Proof	12,000	Value: 20.00				
2007R	5,000,000	—	—	—	5.00	—
2007R Proof	12,000	Value: 20.00				

KM# 237   2 EURO
8.5000 g., Bi-Metallic Nickel-Brass center in Copper-Nickel ring, 25.75 mm. **Obv:** World Food Program globe within circle **Rev:** Value and map within circle **Edge:** Reeded and lettered **Edge Lettering:** 2's and stars

Date	Mintage	F	VF	XF	Unc	BU
2004R	16,000,000	—	—	—	5.00	6.00

KM# 245   2 EURO
8.5000 g., Bi-Metallic Nickel-Brass center in Copper-Nickel ring, 25.75 mm. **Subject:** European Constitution **Obv:** Europa holding an open book while sitting on a bull within circle **Rev:** Value and map within circle **Edge:** Reeding over stars and 2's

Date	Mintage	F	VF	XF	Unc	BU
2005R	18,000,000	—	—	—	4.00	5.00

KM# 246   2 EURO
8.5000 g., Bi-Metallic Nickel-Brass center in Copper-Nickel ring, 25.75 mm. **Subject:** Torino Winter Olympics **Obv:** Skier and other designs within circle **Rev:** Value and map within circle **Edge:** Reeded with stars and 2's

Date	Mintage	F	VF	XF	Unc	BU
2006R	40,000,000	—	—	—	4.00	5.00

KM# 280   2 EURO
8.5000 g., Bi-Metallic Nickel-Brass center in Copper-Nickel ring, 25.75 mm. **Subject:** Turin Olympics **Obv:** Skier and town view **Rev:** Value and map within circle

Date	Mintage	F	VF	XF	Unc	BU
2006R	40,000,000	Value: 5.00				

KM# 311   2 EURO
8.5000 g., Bi-Metallic Nickel-Brass center in Copper-Nickel ring, 25.75 mm. **Subject:** Treaty of Rome, 50th Anniversary **Obv:** Open treaty

Date	Mintage	F	VF	XF	Unc	BU
2007R	5,000,000	—	—	—	4.00	5.00

KM# 251   2 EURO
8.5000 g., Bi-Metallic Nickel-Brass center in Copper-Nickel ring, 25.75 mm. **Obv:** Bust of Dante Aligheri **Rev:** Relief map of Western Europe, stars, lines and value **Edge:** Reeded **Edge Lettering:** 2's and stars

Date	Mintage	F	VF	XF	Unc	BU
2008R	2,455,000	—	—	—	4.00	5.00
2008R Proof	5,000	Value: 10.00				
2009R	1,951,500	—	—	—	4.00	5.00
2009R Proof	5,500	Value: 10.00				
2010R	6,000,000	—	—	—	4.00	5.00
2010R Proof	5,000	Value: 10.00				
2011R	20,000,000	—	—	—	4.00	5.00
2011R Proof	5,000	Value: 10.00				
2012R	—	—	—	—	4.00	5.00
2012R Proof	—	Value: 10.00				

KM# 301   2 EURO
8.5000 g., Bi-Metallic Nickel-Brass center in Copper-Nickel ring, 25.75 mm. **Subject:** Declaration of Rights **Obv:** Nude male and female figures

Date	Mintage	F	VF	XF	Unc	BU
2008R	5,000,000	—	—	—	5.00	6.00

KM# 310   2 EURO
8.5000 g., Bi-Metallic Nickel-Brass center in Copper-Nickel ring, 25.75 mm. **Subject:** Louis Braille **Obv:** Hand reading book in braille font

Date	Mintage	F	VF	XF	Unc	BU
2009R	2,000,000	—	—	—	5.00	6.00

KM# 312   2 EURO
8.5000 g., Bi-Metallic Nickel-Brass center in Copper-Nickel ring, 25.75 mm. **Subject:** European Monetrary Union, 10th Anniversary **Obv:** Stick figure and Euro symbol

Date	Mintage	F	VF	XF	Unc	BU
2009R	2,000,000	—	—	—	4.00	5.00
2009R Proof	5,500	Value: 25.00				

KM# 328   2 EURO
8.5000 g., Bi-Metallic Nickel-Brass center in Copper-Nickel ring., 25.75 mm. **Subject:** Camillo Benso Count of Cavour **Obv:** Bust 3/4 right

Date	Mintage	F	VF	XF	Unc	BU
2010R	4,000,000	—	—	—	5.00	6.00
2010R Special Unc.	16,000	—	—	—	—	8.00
2010R Proof	5,000	Value: 25.00				

KM# 338   2 EURO
8.5000 g., Bi-Metallic Nickel-Brass center in Copper-Nickel ring, 25.75 mm. **Subject:** Italian Unification, 150th Anniversary **Obv:** Three banners

Date	Mintage	F	VF	XF	Unc	BU
2011R	10,000,000	—	—	—	6.00	7.50
2011R Special Unc.	20,000	—	—	—	—	15.00
2011R Proof	5,000	Value: 25.00				

KM# 350   2 EURO
8.5000 g., Bi-Metallic Nickel-Brass center in Copper-Nickel ring, 25.75 mm. **Subject:** Eurocoinage, 10th Anniversary **Obv:** Euro symbol on globe at center, child-like drawings around

Date	Mintage	F	VF	XF	Unc	BU
2012R	15,000,000	—	—	—	5.00	6.00

KM# 355   2 EURO
8.5000 g., Bi-Metallic Nickel-Brass plated Nickel center in Copper-Nickel ring, 25.75 mm. **Obv:** Giovanni Pascoli bust

Date	Mintage	F	VF	XF	Unc	BU
2012R	—	—	—	—	5.00	6.00

KM# 302   5 EURO
18.0000 g., 0.9250 Silver 0.5353 oz. ASW, 32 mm. **Subject:** Antonia Meucci - 200th Birthday

Date	Mintage	F	VF	XF	Unc	BU
2003R		—	—	—	—	62.00

KM# 252   5 EURO
18.0000 g., 0.9250 Silver 0.5353 oz. ASW, 32 mm. **Subject:** People in Europe

Date	Mintage	F	VF	XF	Unc	BU
2003R	25,000	Value: 40.00				
2003R Proof	8,000	Value: 65.00				

KM# 253   5 EURO
18.0000 g., 0.9250 Silver 0.5353 oz. ASW, 32 mm. **Subject:** Work in Europe

Date	Mintage	F	VF	XF	Unc	BU
2003R	50,000	—	—	—	35.00	40.00
2003R Proof	12,000	Value: 65.00				

KM# 238   5 EURO
18.0000 g., 0.9250 Silver 0.5353 oz. ASW, 32 mm. **Subject:** World Cup Soccer - Germany 2006 **Obv:** Santa Croce Square in Florence **Rev:** Soccer ball and world globe design

Date	Mintage	F	VF	XF	Unc	BU
2004R Proof	35,000	Value: 100				

KM# 239   5 EURO
18.0000 g., 0.9250 Silver 0.5353 oz. ASW, 32 mm. **Subject:** Madam Butterfly **Obv:** La Scala Opera House, where Madam Butterfly was first performed there in 1904 **Rev:** Geisha

Date	Mintage	F	VF	XF	Unc	BU
2004R	30,000	—	—	—	35.00	40.00
2004R Proof	12,000	Value: 60.00				

KM# 254   5 EURO
18.0000 g., 0.9250 Silver 0.5353 oz. ASW, 32 mm. **Subject:** 50th Anniversary of Italian Television

Date	Mintage	F	VF	XF	Unc	BU
2004R	40,000	—	—	—	35.00	40.00
2004R Proof	15,000	Value: 65.00				

KM# 255   5 EURO
18.0000 g., 0.9250 Silver 0.5353 oz. ASW, 32 mm. **Subject:** 85th Birthday of Federico Fellini

Date	Mintage	F	VF	XF	Unc	BU
2005R	35,000	—	—	—	30.00	35.00
2005R Proof	22,000	Value: 60.00				

KM# 256   5 EURO
18.0000 g., 0.9250 Silver 0.5353 oz. ASW, 32 mm. **Subject:** 2006 Olympic Winter Games Torino Ski Jump

Date	Mintage	F	VF	XF	Unc	BU
2005R	35,000	—	—	—	30.00	35.00
2005R Proof	40,000	Value: 60.00				

KM# 257   5 EURO
18.0000 g., 0.9250 Silver 0.5353 oz. ASW, 32 mm. **Subject:** 2006 Olympic Winter Games Cross Country Skiing

Date	Mintage	F	VF	XF	Unc	BU
2005R	35,000	—	—	—	30.00	35.00
2005R Proof	40,000	Value: 50.00				

KM# 266   5 EURO
18.0000 g., 0.9250 Silver 0.5353 oz. ASW, 32 mm. **Subject:** 2006 Olympic Games Torino Figure Skating

Date	Mintage	F	VF	XF	Unc	BU
2005	40,000	—	—	—	30.00	35.00
2005 Proof		Value: 50.00				

KM# 282   5 EURO
18.0000 g., 0.9250 Silver 0.5353 oz. ASW, 32 mm. **Subject:** FIFA World Cup

Date	Mintage	F	VF	XF	Unc	BU
2006R	—	—	—	—	60.00	62.00
2006R Proof	—	Value: 65.00				

KM# 294   5 EURO
18.0000 g., 0.9250 Silver 0.5353 oz. ASW, 32 mm. **Subject:** Arturo Toscani - 50th Aniversary Death

Date	Mintage	F	VF	XF	Unc	BU
2007R	—	—	—	—	60.00	62.00

KM# 291   5 EURO
18.0000 g., 0.9250 Silver 0.5353 oz. ASW, 32 mm. **Subject:** Kyoto Agreement - 5th Anniversary **Obv:** Allegorical representation of nature rebelling against pollution **Rev:** Allegorical representation of clear air with a spiral of vital energy

Date	Mintage	F	VF	XF	Unc	BU
2007R Special Unc	20,000	—	—	—	50.00	55.00
2007R Proof	7,000	Value: 100				

KM# 292   5 EURO
18.0000 g., 0.9250 Silver 0.5353 oz. ASW, 32 mm. **Subject:** Giuseppe Garibaldi - 200th Anniversary Birth **Obv:** Portrait facing **Rev:** Harbor Lympia in Nice

Date	Mintage	F	VF	XF	Unc	BU
2007R Special Unc.	8,000	—	—	—	35.00	40.00

KM# 293   5 EURO
18.0000 g., 0.9250 Silver 0.5353 oz. ASW, 32 mm. **Subject:** Aitero Spinelini 100th Birthday **Obv:** Bust 3/4 facing **Rev:** Representation of Ventotene island and Parliament hemicycle

Date	Mintage	F	VF	XF	Unc	BU
2007R Special Unc.	7,000	—	—	—	35.00	40.00

KM# 323   5 EURO
18.0000 g., 0.9250 Silver 0.5353 oz. ASW, 32 mm. **Subject:** Arturo Toscanini. 50th Death Anniversary **Obv:** Profile left **Rev:** Hand with baton, and musical instruments

Date	Mintage	F	VF	XF	Unc	BU
2007R Special Unc.	7,000	—	—	—	35.00	40.00

KM# 281   5 EURO
18.0000 g., 0.9250 Silver 0.5353 oz. ASW, 32 mm. **Subject:** Italian Republic - 60th Anniversary

Date	Mintage	F	VF	XF	Unc	BU
2008R	—	—	—	—	60.00	62.00
2008R Proof	—	Value: 65.00				

KM# 303   5 EURO
18.0000 g., 0.9250 Silver 0.5353 oz. ASW, 32 mm. **Subject:** Anna Magnani - 100th Birthday

Date	Mintage	F	VF	XF	Unc	BU
2008R	—	—	—	—	60.00	62.00

KM# 304   5 EURO
18.0000 g., 0.9250 Silver 0.5353 oz. ASW, 32 mm. **Subject:** Italian Constitution - 60th Anniversary

Date	Mintage	F	VF	XF	Unc	BU
2008	—	—	—	—	45.00	48.00

KM# 325   5 EURO
18.0000 g., 0.9250 Silver 0.5353 oz. ASW, 32 mm. **Series:** IFAD, 30th Anniversary

Date	Mintage	F	VF	XF	Unc	BU
2008R	—	—	—	—	62.00	65.00
2008R Proof	5,000	Value: 75.00				

KM# 326   5 EURO
18.0000 g., 0.9250 Silver 0.5353 oz. ASW, 32 mm. **Subject:** Antonio Meucci **Obv:** Bust 3/4 facing right

Date	Mintage	F	VF	XF	Unc	BU
2008R Proof	—	Value: 45.00				

KM# 313   5 EURO
18.0000 g., 0.9250 Silver 0.5353 oz. ASW, 32 mm. **Subject:** Giro d'Italy - Cycling Race Centennial **Obv:** Two cyclists **Rev:** Bicycle and map of Italy

Date	Mintage	F	VF	XF	Unc	BU
2009R Special Unc.	14,000	—	—	—	45.00	50.00

KM# 314   5 EURO
18.0000 g., 0.9250 Silver 0.5353 oz. ASW, 32 mm. **Subject:** World Aquatics Championships **Obv:** River God reclining **Rev:** Two swimmers

Date	Mintage	F	VF	XF	Unc	BU
2009R	5,500	—	—	—	45.00	50.00

KM# 315   5 EURO
18.0000 g., 0.9250 Silver 0.5353 oz. ASW, 32 mm. **Subject:** Herculaneum Discovery, 300th Anniversary **Obv:** Four dogs nipping at horse **Rev:** Marble relief of nymph drawing water with a horn

Date	Mintage	F	VF	XF	Unc	BU
2009R Special Unc.	9,000	—	—	—	45.00	50.00

KM# 327   5 EURO
18.0000 g., 0.9250 Silver 0.5353 oz. ASW, 32 mm. **Subject:** FINA, 13th Anniversary **Obv:** Sculpture Allegory of the Tiber River **Rev:** Swimmer Mosaics decorating the Foro Italico

Date	Mintage	F	VF	XF	Unc	BU
2009R Special Unc.	21,000	—	—	—	35.00	40.00
2009R Proof	5,500	Value: 65.00				

KM# 329   5 EURO
18.0000 g., 0.9250 Silver 0.5353 oz. ASW, 32 mm. **Subject:** Alfa Romeo 100th Anniversary **Obv:** Two Automobiles: 24HP in back, new Giulietta in front **Rev:** Company logo

Date	Mintage	F	VF	XF	Unc	BU
2010R Special Unc.	17,000	—	—	—	35.00	40.00
2010R Proof	5,500	Value: 60.00				

KM# 330   5 EURO
18.0000 g., 0.9250 Silver 0.5353 oz. ASW, 32 mm. **Subject:** Confindustria 100th Anniversary **Obv:** Female head left, mechanical gears within spiral at right **Rev:** Linear eagle and 100 logo

Date	Mintage	F	VF	XF	Unc	BU
2010R Special Unc.	7,500	—	—	—	35.00	37.00

KM# 331   5 EURO
18.0000 g., 0.9250 Silver 0.5353 oz. ASW, 32 mm. **Subject:** Santa Chiara in Naples **Obv:** Church facade **Rev:** Cloister interior

Date	Mintage	F	VF	XF	Unc	BU
2010R Proof	7,500	Value: 65.00				

KM# 341   5 EURO
18.0000 g., 0.9250 Silver 0.5353 oz. ASW, 32 mm. **Subject:** Italian unification, 150th Anniversary

Date	Mintage	F	VF	XF	Unc	BU
2011R Proof	—	Value: 50.00				

KM# 343 5 EURO
18.0000 g., 0.9250 Silver 0.5353 oz. ASW, 32 mm. **Subject:**
Italian Council of State, 180th Anniversary

Date	Mintage	F	VF	XF	Unc	BU
2011R Proof	7,000	Value: 50.00				

KM# 344 5 EURO
18.0000 g., 0.9250 Silver 0.5353 oz. ASW, 32 mm. **Subject:**
Historical Building of the Italian Mint, 100th Anniversary

Date	Mintage	F	VF	XF	Unc	BU
2011R Proof	7,000	Value: 50.00				

KM# 345 5 EURO
18.0000 g., 0.9250 Silver 0.5353 oz. ASW, 32 mm. **Subject:**
Art in Italy - Anagini

Date	Mintage	F	VF	XF	Unc	BU
2011R Proof	7,000	Value: 50.00				

KM# 353 5 EURO
18.0000 g., 0.9250 Silver 0.5353 oz. ASW, 32 mm. **Subject:**
Italian Monetary Unification, 150th Anniversary **Obv:** Italia head
in vertical oval **Rev:** Alegory and fruits

Date	Mintage	F	VF	XF	Unc	BU
2012R Proof	—	Value: 50.00				

KM# 258 10 EURO
22.0000 g., 0.9250 Silver 0.6542 oz. ASW, 34 mm. **Subject:**
People In Europe

Date	Mintage	F	VF	XF	Unc	BU
2003	25,000	—	—	—	70.00	75.00
2003R Proof	8,000	Value: 120				

KM# 259 10 EURO
22.0000 g., 0.9250 Silver 0.6542 oz. ASW, 34 mm. **Subject:**
Italian Presidency of E.U.

Date	Mintage	F	VF	XF	Unc	BU
2003R	40,000	—	—	—	45.00	50.00
2003R Proof	8,000	Value: 120				

KM# 240 10 EURO
22.0000 g., 0.9250 Silver 0.6542 oz. ASW, 34 mm. **Subject:**
City of Genoa **Obv:** Sculpture and art works **Rev:** Tower and
harbor map

Date	Mintage	F	VF	XF	Unc	BU
2004R	20,000	—	—	—	55.00	60.00
2004R Proof	10,500	Value: 70.00				

KM# 241 10 EURO
22.0000 g., 0.9250 Silver 0.6542 oz. ASW, 34 mm. **Subject:**
Giacomo Puccini **Obv:** Puccini wearing hat **Rev:** Stage, music
and quill

Date	Mintage	F	VF	XF	Unc	BU
2004R	13,500	—	—	—	70.00	75.00
2004R Proof	8,000	Value: 100				

KM# 260 10 EURO
22.0000 g., 0.9250 Silver 0.6542 oz. ASW, 34 mm. **Subject:**
2006 Olympic Winter Games Torino Alpine Skiing

Date	Mintage	F	VF	XF	Unc	BU
2005R Proof	40,000	Value: 85.00				

KM# 261 10 EURO
22.0000 g., 0.9250 Silver 0.6542 oz. ASW, 34 mm. **Subject:**
2006 Olympic Winter Games Torino Ice Hockey

Date	Mintage	F	VF	XF	Unc	BU
2005R Proof	35,000	Value: 85.00				

KM# 262 10 EURO
22.0000 g., 0.9250 Silver 0.6542 oz. ASW, 34 mm. **Subject:**
2006 Olympic Winter Games Torino Speed Skating

Date	Mintage	F	VF	XF	Unc	BU
2005R Proof	35,000	Value: 85.00				

KM# 268 10 EURO
22.0000 g., 0.9250 Silver 0.6542 oz. ASW, 34 mm. **Subject:**
60th Anniversary UN "ONU"

Date	Mintage	F	VF	XF	Unc	BU
2005	25,000	—	—	—	50.00	55.00

KM# 271 10 EURO
22.0000 g., 0.9250 Silver 0.6542 oz. ASW, 34 mm. **Subject:**
Peace and Freedom In Europe

Date	Mintage	F	VF	XF	Unc	BU
2005 Proof	22,000	Value: 60.00				

KM# 283 10 EURO
22.0000 g., 0.9250 Silver 0.6542 oz. ASW, 34 mm. **Subject:**
FIFA World Cup - Germany

Date	Mintage	F	VF	XF	Unc	BU
2006R Proof	20,000	Value: 75.00				

KM# 284 10 EURO
22.0000 g., 0.9250 Silver 0.6542 oz. ASW **Subject:** Andre
Martenga - 500th Anniversary

Date	Mintage	F	VF	XF	Unc	BU
2006R Proof	8,000	Value: 75.00				

KM# 285 10 EURO
22.0000 g., 0.9250 Silver 0.6542 oz. ASW, 34 mm. **Subject:**
Leonardo da Vinci

Date	Mintage	F	VF	XF	Unc	BU
2006R Proof	25,000	Value: 75.00				

KM# 286 10 EURO
22.0000 g., 0.9250 Silver 0.6542 oz. ASW, 34 mm. **Subject:**
UNICEF 60th Anniversary

Date	Mintage	F	VF	XF	Unc	BU
2006R Proof	15,000	Value: 75.00				

KM# 295 10 EURO
22.0000 g., 0.9250 Silver 0.6542 oz. ASW, 34 mm. **Subject:**
Treaty of Rome, 50th Anniversary

Date	Mintage	F	VF	XF	Unc	BU
2007R Proof	20,504	Value: 75.00				

KM# 296 10 EURO
22.0000 g., 0.9250 Silver 0.6542 oz. ASW, 34 mm. **Subject:**
Antonia Canova - 250th Anniversary Birth **Obv:** Portrait facing
Rev: Sculpture Eros and Psyche

Date	Mintage	F	VF	XF	Unc	BU
2007R Proof	8,000	Value: 65.00				

KM# 297 10 EURO
22.0000 g., 0.9250 Silver 0.6542 oz. ASW, 34 mm. **Subject:**
Mint of Rome's School of Medallic Art - 100th Anniversary **Obv:**
Sculptor designing medal, from a medal by Giuseppe Romagnoli
Rev: School logo

Date	Mintage	F	VF	XF	Unc	BU
2007R Proof	8,000	Value: 65.00				

KM# 324 10 EURO
22.0000 g., 0.9250 Silver 0.6542 oz. ASW, 34 mm. **Subject:**
Treaty of Rome, 50th Anniversary **Obv:** Pavement pattern from
Capitol Square in Rome **Rev:** Steps leading up to Capitol

Date	Mintage	F	VF	XF	Unc	BU
2007R Proof	22,000	Value: 65.00				

KM# 305 10 EURO
22.0000 g., 0.9250 Silver 0.6542 oz. ASW, 34 mm. **Subject:**
Andrea Palladio - 500th Birthday

Date	Mintage	F	VF	XF	Unc	BU
2008 Proof	16,000	Value: 75.00				

KM# 306 10 EURO
22.0000 g., 0.9250 Silver 0.6542 oz. ASW, 34 mm. **Subject:**
University of Perugia - 700th Anniversary

Date	Mintage	F	VF	XF	Unc	BU
2008 Proof	9,000	Value: 75.00				

KM# 316 10 EURO
22.0000 g., 0.9250 Silver 0.6542 oz. ASW, 34 mm. **Subject:**
International Year of Astronomy **Obv:** Head right, astrolabe at
left **Rev:** Galilei's telescope, details of an astrolabe and sky

Date	Mintage	F	VF	XF	Unc	BU
2009R Proof	9,000	Value: 75.00				

KM# 317 10 EURO
22.0000 g., 0.9250 Silver 0.6542 oz. ASW, 34 mm. **Subject:**
Guglielmo Maroni's Nobel Prize in Physics **Obv:** Bust and yacht
Elettra **Rev:** Radio receiver and antenna and radio waves

Date	Mintage	F	VF	XF	Unc	BU
2009R Proof	18,000	Value: 75.00				

KM# 318 10 EURO
22.0000 g., 0.9250 Silver 0.6542 oz. ASW, 34 mm. **Subject:**
Annibale Carracci, 400th Anniversary **Obv:** 1/2 length figure
standing **Rev:** Historical cart

Date	Mintage	F	VF	XF	Unc	BU
2009R Proof	9,000	Value: 75.00				

KM# 319 10 EURO
22.0000 g., 0.9250 Silver 0.6542 oz. ASW, 34 mm. **Subject:**
Futurist movement, 100th Anniversary **Obv:** Building design **Rev:**
Round sculpture

Date	Mintage	F	VF	XF	Unc	BU
2009R Proof	9,000	Value: 75.00				

KM# 337 10 EURO
22.0000 g., 0.9250 Silver 0.6542 oz. ASW, 34 mm. **Subject:**
L'Aquila Earthquake, reconstruction

Date	Mintage	F	VF	XF	Unc	BU
2009R Proof	—	Value: 75.00				

KM# 332 10 EURO
22.0000 g., 0.9250 Silver 0.6542 oz. ASW, 34 mm. **Subject:**
Caravaggio 400th Death Anniversary **Obv:** Bust 3/4 facing left,
basket of fruit below **Rev:** Medussa head painting detail

Date	Mintage	F	VF	XF	Unc	BU
2010R Proof	7,500	Value: 70.00				

KM# 333 10 EURO
22.0000 g., 0.9250 Silver 0.6542 oz. ASW, 34 mm. **Subject:**
Giorgione, 500th Death Anniverdary **Obv:** Bust 3/4 left **Rev:**
Detail from the painting "La Tempesta"

Date	Mintage	F	VF	XF	Unc	BU
2010R Proof	7,500	Value: 70.00				

KM# 334 10 EURO
22.0000 g., 0.9250 Silver 0.6542 oz. ASW, 34 mm. **Subject:**
Arts of Italy, Aquileia **Obv:** Basilica and architechtural floorplan
Rev: Interpertation from the "Tabula Peuntigeriana"

Date	Mintage	F	VF	XF	Unc	BU
2010R Proof	7,500	Value: 70.00				

KM# 342 10 EURO
22.0000 g., 0.9250 Silver 0.6542 oz. ASW, 34 mm. **Subject:**
Giorgio Vasari, 500th Anniversary of Birth

Date	Mintage	F	VF	XF	Unc	BU
2011R Proof	7,000	Value: 70.00				

KM# 339 10 EURO
22.0000 g., 0.9250 Silver 0.6542 oz. ASW, 34 mm. **Subject:**
Amerigo Vespucci

Date	Mintage	F	VF	XF	Unc	BU
2011R Proof	7,000	Value: 70.00				

KM# 340 10 EURO
22.0000 g., 0.9250 Silver 0.6542 oz. ASW, 34 mm. **Subject:**
Alcide de Gasperi, 130th Anniversary of Birth

Date	Mintage	F	VF	XF	Unc	BU
2011R Proof	7,000	Value: 70.00				

KM# 346 10 EURO
22.0000 g., 0.9250 Silver 0.6542 oz. ASW, 34 mm. **Subject:**
Art in Italy - Torino

Date	Mintage	F	VF	XF	Unc	BU
2011R Proof	7,000	Value: 70.00				

KM# 349 10 EURO
22.0000 g., 0.9250 Silver 0.6542 oz. ASW **Subject:** Bari **Obv:**
St. Nicolas Church **Shape:** 34

Date	Mintage	F	VF	XF	Unc	BU
2011R Proof	7,000	Value: 70.00				

KM# 354 10 EURO
22.0000 g., 0.9250 Silver 0.6542 oz. ASW, 34 mm. **Subject:**
Francesco Guardi, 300th anniversary of Birth **Obv:** Venice from
the lagoon **Rev:** Guardi bust

Date	Mintage	F	VF	XF	Unc	BU
2012R Proof	—	Value: 70.00				

KM# 263 20 EURO
6.4500 g., 0.9000 Gold 0.1866 oz. AGW, 21 mm. **Subject:** Arts
in Europe - Italy

Date	Mintage	F	VF	XF	Unc	BU
2003R Proof	6,000	Value: 395				

KM# 242 20 EURO
6.4500 g., 0.9000 Gold 0.1866 oz. AGW, 21 mm. **Obv:** Arts In
Europe: Belgium **Rev:** Flying bird obscuring a man's face

Date	Mintage	F	VF	XF	Unc	BU
2004R Proof	6,000	Value: 385				

KM# 243 20 EURO
6.4500 g., 0.9000 Gold 0.1866 oz. AGW, 21 mm. **Subject:**
World Cup Soccer - Germany 2006 **Obv:** Mascot **Rev:** Soccer
ball and world globe

Date	Mintage	F	VF	XF	Unc	BU
2004R Proof	7,500	Value: 395				

KM# 265 20 EURO
6.4500 g., 0.9000 Gold 0.1866 oz. AGW, 21 mm. **Subject:** 2006
Olympic Winter Games Torino Porte Palatine Gate

Date	Mintage	F	VF	XF	Unc	BU
2005R Proof	10,000	Value: 375				

KM# 267 20 EURO
6.4500 g., 0.9000 Gold 0.1866 oz. AGW, 21 mm. **Subject:** 2006
Olympic Games Torino Madama Palace

Date	Mintage	F	VF	XF	Unc	BU
2005R Proof	10,000	Value: 375				

KM# 269 20 EURO
6.4500 g., 0.9000 Gold 0.1866 oz. AGW, 21 mm. **Subject:** 2006
Olympic Games Torino Stupinigi Palace

Date	Mintage	F	VF	XF	Unc	BU
2005R Proof	10,000	Value: 375				

KM# 272 20 EURO
6.4500 g., 0.9000 Gold 0.1866 oz. AGW, 21 mm. **Subject:** Art
In Europe - Finland **Obv:** Sailing ship

Date	Mintage	F	VF	XF	Unc	BU
2005R Proof	5,000	Value: 400				

KM# 287 20 EURO
6.4500 g., 0.9000 Gold 0.1866 oz. AGW, 21 mm. **Subject:** FIFA
World Cup

Date	Mintage	F	VF	XF	Unc	BU
2006R Proof	4,350	Value: 450				

KM# 288 20 EURO
6.4500 g., 0.9000 Gold 0.1866 oz. AGW, 21 mm. **Subject:**
European Arts - Germany

Date	Mintage	F	VF	XF	Unc	BU
2006R Proof	3,100	Value: 450				

KM# 298 20 EURO
6.4500 g., 0.9000 Gold 0.1866 oz. AGW, 21 mm. **Subject:**
Treaty of Rome - 50th Anniversary **Obv:** Pavement pattern in
Capital Square in Rome **Rev:** Steps leading to Capital Building

Date	Mintage	F	VF	XF	Unc	BU
2007R Proof	4,000	Value: 450				

KM# 299 20 EURO
6.4500 g., 0.9000 Gold 0.1866 oz. AGW, 21 mm. **Subject:**
European Art - Ireland **Obv:** Sailing ship **Rev:** Tara Brooch

Date	Mintage	F	VF	XF	Unc	BU
2007R Proof	3,500	Value: 450				

KM# 307 20 EURO
6.4500 g., 0.9000 Gold 0.1866 oz. AGW, 21 mm. **Subject:**
Andrea Palladio - 500th Birthday **Obv:** Head left **Rev:** Building
façade and floorplans

Date	Mintage	F	VF	XF	Unc	BU
2008R Proof	5,500	Value: 450				

KM# 308 20 EURO
6.4500 g., 0.9000 Gold 0.1866 oz. AGW, 21 mm. **Subject:** Arts
in Europe - Netherlands **Obv:** Sailing ship

Date	Mintage	F	VF	XF	Unc	BU
2008R Proof	2,011	Value: 450				

KM# 320 20 EURO
6.4500 g., 0.9000 Gold 0.1866 oz. AGW, 21 mm. **Subject:**
Guglielmo Marconi, 100th Anniversary of Nobel in Physics **Obv:**
Bust and yacht Elettra **Rev:** Radio receiver with antenna and
radio waves

Date	Mintage	F	VF	XF	Unc	BU
2009R Proof	5,000	Value: 390				

KM# 321 20 EURO
6.4500 g., 0.9000 Gold 0.1866 oz. AGW, 21 mm. **Subject:** Arts
in Europe - Great Britain **Obv:** Sailing ship **Rev:** Venus by Edward
B. Jones

Date	Mintage	F	VF	XF	Unc	BU
2009R Proof	3,000	Value: 400				

KM# 335 20 EURO
6.4500 g., 0.9000 Gold 0.1866 oz. AGW, 21 mm. **Subject:** Arts
of Europe - Sweden **Obv:** Sailing ship **Rev:** Viking Helmet

Date	Mintage	F	VF	XF	Unc	BU
2010R Proof	2,000	Value: 400				

KM# 347 20 EURO
6.4500 g., 0.9000 Gold 0.1866 oz. AGW, 21 mm. **Subject:** Flora
in art

Date	Mintage	F	VF	XF	Unc	BU
2011R Proof	1,500	Value: 400				

KM# 352 20 EURO
6.4510 g., 0.9000 Gold 0.1867 oz. AGW, 21 mm. **Subject:**
Fauna in Art - Middle ages **Obv:** Face at center of triskles **Rev:**
Two peacocks face-to-face

Date	Mintage	F	VF	XF	Unc	BU
2012R Proof	—	Value: 375				

KM# 264 50 EURO
16.1300 g., 0.9000 Gold 0.4667 oz. AGW, 28 mm. **Subject:**
Arts in Europe - Austria

Date	Mintage	F	VF	XF	Unc	BU
2003R Proof	6,000	Value: 850				

KM# 244 50 EURO
16.1300 g., 0.9000 Gold 0.4667 oz. AGW, 28 mm. **Obv:** Arts In
Europe: Denmark **Rev:** Angel carrying away two children

Date	Mintage	F	VF	XF	Unc	BU
2004R Proof	6,000	Value: 850				

KM# 270 50 EURO
16.1300 g., 0.9000 Gold 0.4667 oz. AGW, 28 mm. **Subject:**
2006 Olympic Games Torino Emanuele Filiberto

Date	Mintage	F	VF	XF	Unc	BU
2005R Proof	6,000	Value: 825				

KM# 273 50 EURO
16.1300 g., 0.9000 Gold 0.4667 oz. AGW, 28 mm. **Subject:** Art
In Europe - France

Date	Mintage	F	VF	XF	Unc	BU
2005R Proof	5,000	Value: 850				

KM# 274 50 EURO
16.1300 g., 0.9000 Gold 0.4667 oz. AGW, 28 mm. **Subject:**
2006 Olympic Games Torino Olympic Torch

Date	Mintage	F	VF	XF	Unc	BU
2006R Proof	5,000	Value: 850				

KM# 289 50 EURO
16.1300 g., 0.9000 Gold 0.4667 oz. AGW, 28 mm. **Subject:**
European Arts - Greece

Date	Mintage	F	VF	XF	Unc	BU
2006R Proof	1,792	Value: 900				

KM# 300 50 EURO
16.1300 g., 0.9000 Gold 0.4667 oz. AGW, 28 mm. **Subject:**
European Art - Norway **Obv:** Sailing ship **Rev:** Painting "The
Scream" by Edvard Munch

Date	Mintage	F	VF	XF	Unc	BU
2007R Proof	2,000	Value: 900				

KM# 309 50 EURO
16.1300 g., 0.9000 Gold 0.4667 oz. AGW, 28 mm. **Subject:**
Arts in Europe - Portugal

Date	Mintage	F	VF	XF	Unc	BU
2008R Proof	2,000	Value: 900				

KM# 322 50 EURO
16.1300 g., 0.9000 Gold 0.1774 oz. AGW, 28 mm. **Subject:** Arts
in Europe - Spain **Obv:** Sailing ship **Rev:** Sagrada Familia of
Antoni Gaudí

Date	Mintage	F	VF	XF	Unc	BU
2009R Proof	2,000	Value: 900				

KM# 336 50 EURO
16.1300 g., 0.9000 Gold 0.4667 oz. AGW, 28 mm. **Subject:** Arts of Europe - Hungary **Obv:** Sailing ship **Rev:** Detail of painting "Rozsi Szinyei Merse" by Pal Szinyel Merse

Date	Mintage	F	VF	XF	Unc	BU
2010R Proof	1,500	Value: 900				

KM# 348 50 EURO
16.1300 g., 0.9000 Gold 0.4667 oz. AGW, 28 mm. **Subject:** Flora in art

Date	Mintage	F	VF	XF	Unc	BU
2011R Proof	1,000	Value: 850				

KM# 351 50 EURO
16.1290 g., 0.9000 Gold 0.4667 oz. AGW, 28 mm. **Subject:** Flora in Art - Middle ages **Obv:** Stylized animal's head facing **Rev:** Statue of lions confronted

Date	Mintage	F	VF	XF	Unc	BU
2012R Proof	—	Value: 850				

MINT SETS

KM#	Date	Mintage	Identification	Issue Price	Mkt Val
MS39	2001 (12)	125,200	KM#91-94, 97.2, 98, 105, 111, 159, 183, 194, 236	—	235
MS40	2002 (8)	50,000	KM#210-217	—	22.00
MS41	2003 (8)	50,000	KM#210-217	—	30.00
MS42	2003 (9)	50,000	KM#210-217, 253	—	70.00
MS43	2004 (8)	40,000	KM#210-217	—	35.00
MS44	2004 (9)	40,000	KM#210-217, 254	—	75.00
MS45	2005 (8)	35,000	KM#210-217	—	35.00
MS46	2005 (9)	35,000	KM#210-217, 255	—	75.00
MS47	2006 (8)	25,000	KM#210-217	—	30.00
MS48	2007 (8)	20,000	KM#210-217	—	30.00
MS49	2008 (8)	20,000	KM#210-216, 301	—	45.00
MS50	2008 (9)	5,000	KM#210-217, 281	—	125

PROOF SETS

KM#	Date	Mintage	Identification	Issue Price	Mkt Val
PS25	2001 (12)	10,000	KM#91-94, 97.2, 98, 105, 111, 159, 183, 194, 236	—	650
PS26	2003 (9)	12,000	KM#210-217, 253	—	200
PS27	2004 (9)	15,000	KM#210-217, 254	—	170
PS28	2005 (9)	12,000	KM#210-217, 255	—	140
PS29	2006 (9)	10,000	KM#210-217	—	80.00
PS30	2007 (8)	7,000	KM#210-217	—	80.00
PS31	2008 (9)	5,000	KM#210-212, 247-251, 325	—	145
PS32	2009 (10)	5,500	KM#210-212, 247-251, 312, 327	—	165
PS33	2010 (10)	5,000	KM#210-212, 247-251, 328, 329	—	165
PS34	2011 (10)	5,000	KM#210-212, 247-251, 338, 341	—	165

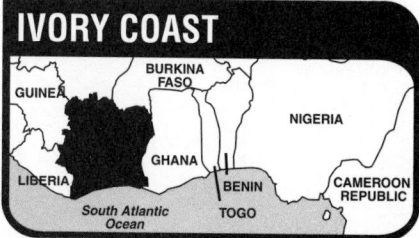

IVORY COAST

The Republic of the Ivory Coast, (Cote d'Ivoire), a former French Overseas territory located on the south side of the African bulge between Liberia and Ghana, has an area of 124,504 sq. mi. (322,463 sq. km.) and a population of 11.8 million. Capital: Yamoussoukro. The predominantly agricultural economy is one of Africa's most prosperous. Coffee, tropical woods, cocoa, and bananas are exported.

REPUBLIC

DECIMAL COINAGE

KM# 6 1000 FRANCS
25.0000 g., 0.9250 Silver 0.7435 oz. ASW, 38.6 mm. **Obv:** National arms **Rev:** Mamouth and embedded tooth fragment

Date	Mintage	F	VF	XF	Unc	BU
2010 Proof	2,500	Value: 75.00				

KM# 8 1000 FRANCS
25.0000 g., 0.9250 Silver 0.7435 oz. ASW, 38.61 mm. **Obv:** National arms **Rev:** Map of Africa with montage of animals, blue field

Date	Mintage	F	VF	XF	Unc	BU
2010 Proof	2,500	Value: 75.00				

KM# 7 1500 FRANCS
273.0000 g., 0.9250 Silver 8.1185 oz. ASW, 50 mm. **Subject:** Qibia Compass **Obv:** National arms **Rev:** Legend and design around center disc for compass spoon

Date	Mintage	F	VF	XF	Unc	BU
2010 Antique patina	—				500	

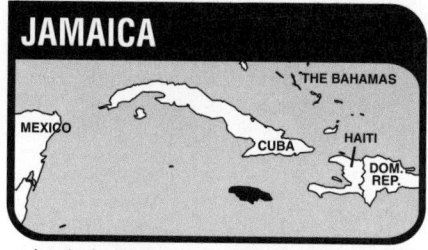

JAMAICA

Jamaica is situated in the Caribbean Sea 90 miles south of Cuba, has an area of 4,244 sq. mi. (10,990 sq. km.) and a population of 2.1 million. Capital: Kingston. The economy is founded chiefly on mining, tourism and agriculture. Aluminum, bauxite, sugar, rum and molasses are exported.

Jamaica is a member of the Commonwealth of Nations. Elizabeth II is the Head of State, as Queen of Jamaica.

MONETARY SYSTEM
100 Cents = 1 Dollar

COMMONWEALTH

DECIMAL COINAGE

KM# 64 CENT
1.2200 g., Aluminum, 21.08 mm. **Ruler:** Elizabeth II **Series:** F.A.O. **Obv:** National arms **Obv. Legend:** JAMAICA **Rev:** Ackee fruit above value **Edge:** Plain **Shape:** 12-sided

Date	Mintage	F	VF	XF	Unc	BU
2002	—			0.25	0.50	0.75
2002 Proof	500	Value: 1.00				

KM# 146.2 10 CENTS
2.4000 g., Copper Plated Steel, 17 mm. **Ruler:** Elizabeth II **Series:** National Heroes **Subject:** Paul Bogle **Obv:** National arms **Obv. Legend:** JAMAICA **Rev:** Bust facing **Edge:** Plain **Note:** Reduced size.

Date	Mintage	F	VF	XF	Unc	BU
2002	—			0.25	0.50	0.75
2002 Proof	500	Value: 2.00				
2003	—			0.25	0.50	0.75
2008	—			0.25	0.50	0.75

KM# 167 25 CENTS
3.6000 g., Copper Plated Steel, 20 mm. **Ruler:** Elizabeth II **Series:** National Heroes **Subject:** Marcus Garvey **Obv:** National arms **Obv. Legend:** JAMAICA **Rev:** Head 1/4 right **Edge:** Plain

Date	Mintage	F	VF	XF	Unc	BU
2002	—			0.25	0.50	0.75
2002 Proof	500	Value: 3.00				
2003	—			0.25	0.50	0.75

KM# 164 DOLLAR
2.9100 g., Nickel Plated Steel, 18.5 mm. **Ruler:** Elizabeth II **Series:** National Heroes **Subject:** Sir Alexander Bustamante **Obv:** National arms **Obv. Legend:** JAMAICA **Rev:** Bust facing **Edge:** Plain **Shape:** 7-sided

Date	Mintage	F	VF	XF	Unc	BU
2002	—			0.40	1.00	1.50
2002 Proof	500	Value: 4.00				
2003	—			0.40	1.00	1.50
2005	—			0.40	1.00	1.50
2006	—			0.40	1.00	1.50

KM# 189 DOLLAR
2.9000 g., Nickel Plated Steel, 18.5 mm. **Ruler:** Elizabeth II **Rev:** Sir Alexander Bustamante

Date	Mintage	F	VF	XF	Unc	BU
2008	—			—	1.00	1.50
2009	—			—	1.00	1.50

KM# 163 5 DOLLARS
4.3000 g., Nickel Plated Steel, 21.5 mm. **Ruler:** Elizabeth II **Series:** National Heroes **Subject:** Norman Manley **Obv:** National arms **Obv. Legend:** JAMAICA **Rev:** Head left **Edge:** Reeded

Date	Mintage	F	VF	XF	Unc	BU
2002	—			1.50	2.50	3.50
2002 Proof	500	Value: 5.00				
2006	—			1.50	2.50	3.50

KM# 197 10 DOLLARS
28.2800 g., 0.9250 Silver 0.8410 oz. ASW, 38.61 mm. **Ruler:** Elizabeth II **Subject:** UNICEF, 55th Anniversary

Date	Mintage	F	VF	XF	Unc	BU
2001 Proof	Est. 500	Value: 125				

KM# 181 10 DOLLARS
5.9400 g., Nickel Plated Steel **Ruler:** Elizabeth II **Series:** National Heroes **Subject:** George William Gordon **Obv:** National arms **Obv. Legend:** JAMAICA / TEN DOLLARS - (date) **Rev:** Bust facing **Edge:** Plain **Shape:** Scalloped **Note:** Diameter varies: 24-24.6.

Date	Mintage	F	VF	XF	Unc	BU
2002	—	—	—	1.50	3.00	4.00
2002 Proof	500	Value: 9.00				
2005	—	—	—	1.50	3.00	4.00

KM# 190 10 DOLLARS
6.0000 g., Nickel Plated Steel, 24.5 mm. **Ruler:** Elizabeth II **Obv:** Arms **Obv. Legend:** JAMAICA / TEN DOLLARS (date) **Rev:** George William Gordon

Date	Mintage	F	VF	XF	Unc	BU
2008	—	—	—	—	6.00	7.50
2009	—	—	—	—	6.00	7.50

KM# 182 20 DOLLARS
7.8000 g., Bi-Metallic Copper-Nickel center in Nickel-Brass ring, 23 mm. **Ruler:** Elizabeth II **Series:** National Heroes **Subject:** Marcus Garvey **Obv:** Value above national arms within circle **Obv. Legend:** JAMAICA **Rev:** Head 1/4 right within circle **Edge:** Segmented reeding

Date	Mintage	F	VF	XF	Unc	BU
2001	—	—	—	1.50	3.00	4.00
2002	—	—	—	1.50	3.00	4.00
2002 Proof	500	Value: 15.00				

KM# 186 25 DOLLARS
28.2800 g., 0.9250 Silver 0.8410 oz. ASW, 38.6 mm. **Ruler:** Elizabeth II **Subject:** UNICEF **Obv:** Arms with supporters **Rev:** Two boys above "Pals" **Edge:** Reeded

Date	Mintage	F	VF	XF	Unc	BU
2001 Proof	—	Value: 65.00				

KM# 185 25 DOLLARS
28.2800 g., 0.9250 Silver 0.8410 oz. ASW, 38.6 mm. **Ruler:** Elizabeth II **Subject:** IAAF World Junior Championships **Obv:** Arms with supporters and value **Rev:** Female runner **Edge:** Reeded

Date	Mintage	F	VF	XF	Unc	BU
2002 Proof	5,500	Value: 70.00				

KM# 184 50 DOLLARS
28.4500 g., 0.9250 Silver 0.8461 oz. ASW, 38.6 mm. **Ruler:** Elizabeth II **Subject:** Millennium **Obv:** Arms with supporters **Rev:** Family within radiant sun **Edge:** Reeded

Date	Mintage	F	VF	XF	Unc	BU
ND(2002) Proof	5,000	Value: 60.00				

PROOF SETS

KM#	Date	Mintage	Identification	Issue Price	Mkt Val
PS33	2002 (8)	500	KM#64, 146.2, 163, 164, 167, 181, 182, 185	99.00	105

JAPAN

Japan, a constitutional monarchy situated off the east coast of Asia, has an area of 145,809 sq. mi. (377,835 sq. km.) and a population of 123.2 million. Capital: Tokyo. Japan, one of the major industrial nations of the world, exports machinery, motor vehicles, electronics and chemicals.

Japanese coinage of concern to this catalog includes those issued for the Ryukyu Islands (also called Liuchu), a chain of islands extending southwest from Japan toward Taiwan (Formosa), before the Japanese government converted the islands into a prefecture under the name Okinawa. Many of the provinces of Japan issued their own definitive coinage under the Shogunate.

RULERS

Emperors

Akihito (Heisei), 1989-

平 成

Years 1 –

NOTE: The personal name of the emperor is followed by the name that he chose for his regnal era.

MONETARY UNITS

Yen 　円 or 圓 or 圓

EMPIRE
REFORM COINAGE

Y# 95.2 YEN
1.0000 g., Aluminum, 20 mm. **Ruler:** Akihito **Obv:** Sprouting branch divides authority and value **Rev:** Value within circles above date **Edge:** Plain

Date	Mintage	F	VF	XF	Unc	BU
Yr.13(2001)	7,786,000	—	—	0.70	1.25	1.50
Yr.13(2001) Proof	238,000	Value: 3.00				
Yr.14(2002)	9,425,000	—	0.70	1.25	—	1.50
Yr.14(2002) Proof	242,000	Value: 5.00				
Yr.15(2003)	117,131,000	—	—	—	—	0.50
Yr.15(2003) Proof	275,000	Value: 3.00				
Yr.16(2004)	52,623,000	—	—	—	—	0.50
Yr.16(2004) Proof	280,000	Value: 3.00				
Yr.17(2005)	29,761,000	—	—	—	—	0.50
Yr.17(2005) Proof	258,000	Value: 3.00				
Yr.18(2006)	129,347,000	—	—	—	—	0.25
Yr.18(2006) Proof	247,000	Value: 3.00				
Yr.19(2007)	223,702,200	—	—	—	—	0.25
Yr.19(2007) Proof	201,800	Value: 3.00				
Yr.20(2008)	134,642,800	—	—	—	—	0.25
Yr.20(2008) Proof	168,200	Value: 3.00				
Yr.21(2009)	47,925,000	—	—	—	—	0.25
Yr.21(2009) Proof	78,000	Value: 3.00				
Yr.22(2010)	Est. 7,775,000	—	—	—	—	0.25
Yr.22(2010) Proof	—	Value: 3.00				
Yr.23(2011)	—	—	—	—	—	0.25
Yr.23(2011) Proof	—	Value: 3.00				
Yr.24 (2012)	—	—	—	—	—	0.25
Yr.24 (2012) Proof	—	Value: 3.00				

Y# 96.2 5 YEN
3.7500 g., Brass, 22 mm. **Ruler:** Akihito **Obv:** Hole in center flanked by a seed leaf with authority on top and date below **Rev:** Gear design around center hole with bending rice stalk above value in horizontal lines below

Date	Mintage	F	VF	XF	Unc	BU
Yr.13(2001)	77,787,000	—	—	—	—	0.35
Yr.13(2001) Proof	238,000	Value: 1.75				
Yr.14(2002)	143,420,000	—	—	—	—	0.35
Yr.14(2002) Proof	242,000	Value: 1.75				
Yr.15(2003)	102,031,000	—	—	—	—	0.35
Yr.15(2003) Proof	275,000	Value: 1.75				
Yr.16(2004)	70,623,000	—	—	—	—	0.35
Yr.16(2004) Proof	280,000	Value: 1.75				
Yr.17(2005)	15,761,000	—	—	0.50	0.75	1.00
Yr.17(2005) Proof	258,000	Value: 3.00				
Yr.18(2006)	9,347,000	—	—	0.75	1.25	1.50
Yr.18(2006) Proof	247,000	Value: 4.00				
Yr.19(2007)	9,702,200	—	—	—	1.25	1.50
Yr.19(2007) Proof	201,800	Value: 4.00				
Yr.20(2008)	9,642,800	—	—	0.75	1.25	1.50
Yr.20(2008) Proof	168,200	Value: 4.00				
Yr.21(2009)	3,925,000	—	—	0.50	1.25	1.50
Yr.21(2009) Proof	78,000	Value: 4.00				
Yr.22(2010)	Est. 380,000	—	—	1.25	1.75	2.00
Yr.22(2010) Proof	—	Value: 4.00				
Yr.23(2011)	—	—	—	1.25	1.75	2.00
Yr.23(2011) Proof	—	Value: 4.00				
Yr.24 (2012)	—	—	—	1.25	1.75	2.00
Yr.24 (2012) Proof	—	Value: 4.00				

Y# 97.2 10 YEN
4.5000 g., Bronze, 23.5 mm. **Ruler:** Akihito **Obv:** Temple divides authority and value **Rev:** Value within wreath

Date	Mintage	F	VF	XF	Unc	BU
Yr.13(2001)	541,786,000	—	—	—	—	0.45
Yr.13(2001) Proof	238,000	Value: 1.75				
Yr.14(2002)	455,425,000	—	—	—	—	0.45
Yr.14(2002) Proof	242,000	Value: 1.75				
Yr.15(2003)	551,131,000	—	—	—	—	0.45
Yr.15(2003) Proof	275,000	Value: 1.75				
Yr.16(2004)	592,623,000	—	—	—	—	0.45
Yr.16(2004) Proof	280,000	Value: 1.75				
Yr.17(2005)	503,761,000	—	—	—	—	0.45
Yr.17(2005) Proof	258,000	Value: 1.75				
Yr.18(2006)	440,347,000	—	—	—	—	0.45
Yr.18(2006) Proof	247,000	Value: 1.75				
Yr.19(2007)	388,702,200	—	—	—	—	0.45
Yr.19(2007) Proof	201,800	Value: 1.75				
Yr.20(2008)	362,642,800	—	—	—	—	0.45
Yr.20(2008) Proof	168,200	Value: 1.75				
Yr.21(2009)	337,925,000	—	—	—	—	0.45
Yr.21(2009) Proof	78,000	Value: 1.75				
Yr.22(2010)	Est. 328,775,000	—	—	—	—	0.45
Yr.22(2010) Proof	—	Value: 1.75				
Yr.23(2011)	—	—	—	—	—	0.45
Yr.23(2011) Proof	—	Value: 1.75				
Yr.24(2012)	—	—	—	—	—	0.45
Yr.24(2012) Proof	—	Value: 1.75				

Y# 101.2 50 YEN
4.0000 g., Copper-Nickel, 21 mm. **Ruler:** Akihito **Obv:** Center hole flanked by chrysanthemums, authority at top and value below **Rev:** Value above hole in center **Edge:** Reeded

Date	Mintage	F	VF	XF	Unc	BU
Yr.13(2001)	7,786,000	—	—	—	—	3.00
Yr.13(2001) Proof	238,000	Value: 4.00				
Yr.14(2002)	11,425,000	—	—	—	—	3.00
Yr.14(2002) Proof	242,000	Value: 7.00				
Yr.15(2003)	10,131,000	—	—	—	—	3.00
Yr.15(2003) Proof	275,000	Value: 7.00				
Yr.16(2004)	9,623,000	—	—	—	—	3.00
Yr.16(2004) Proof	280,000	Value: 7.00				

Date	Mintage	F	VF	XF	Unc	BU
Yr.17(2005)	9,761,000	—	—	—	—	3.00
Yr.17(2005) Proof	258,000	Value: 7.00				
Yr.18(2006)	10,347,000	—	—	—	—	3.00
Yr.18(2006) Proof	247,000	Value: 7.00				
Yr.19(2007)	9,702,200	—	—	—	—	3.00
Yr.19(2007) Proof	201,800	Value: 7.00				
Yr.20(2008)	8,642,800	—	—	—	—	3.00
Yr.20(2008) Proof	168,200	Value: 7.00				
Yr.21(2009)	8,793,000	—	—	—	—	4.00
Yr.21(2009) Proof	78,000	Value: 7.00				
Yr.22(2010)	Est. 380,000	—	—	—	—	7.00
Yr.22(2010) Proof	—	Value: 7.00				
Yr.23(2011)	—	—	—	—	—	4.00
Yr.23(2011) Proof	—	Value: 7.00				
Yr.24(2012)	—	—	—	—	—	4.00
Yr.24(2012) Proof	—	Value: 7.00				

Y# 98.2 100 YEN
4.8000 g., Copper-Nickel, 22.6 mm. **Ruler:** Akihito **Obv:** Cherry blossoms **Rev:** Large numeral 100, date in western numerals **Edge:** Reeded

Date	Mintage	F	VF	XF	Unc	BU
Yr.13(2001)	7,786,000	—	—	—	—	7.50
Yr.13(2001) Proof	238,000	Value: 10.00				
Yr.14(2002)	10,425,000	—	—	—	—	5.00
Yr.14(2002) Proof	242,000	Value: 8.00				
Yr.15(2003)	98,131,000	—	—	—	—	2.50
Yr.15(2003) Proof	275,000	Value: 5.00				
Yr.16(2004)	204,623,000	—	—	—	—	2.50
Yr.16(2004) Proof	280,000	Value: 5.00				
Yr.17(2005)	299,761,000	—	—	—	—	2.50
Yr.17(2005) Proof	258,000	Value: 5.00				
Yr.18(2006)	216,347,000	—	—	—	—	2.00
Yr.18(2006) Proof	247,000	Value: 5.00				
Yr.19(2007)	129,702,200	—	—	—	—	2.00
Yr.19(2007) Proof	201,800	Value: 5.00				
Yr.20(2008)	93,642,800	—	—	—	—	2.00
Yr.20(2008) Proof	168,200	Value: 5.00				
Yr.21(2009)	114,925,000	—	—	—	—	2.00
Yr.21(2009) Proof	78,000	Value: 5.00				
Yr.22(2010)	Est. 67,775,000	—	—	—	—	2.00
Yr.22(2010) Proof	—	Value: 5.00				
Yr.23(2011)	—	—	—	—	—	2.00
Yr.23(2011) Proof	—	Value: 5.00				
Yr.24(2012)	—	—	—	—	—	2.00
Yr.24(2012) Proof	—	Value: 5.00				

Y# 125 500 YEN
7.0000 g., Nickel-Brass, 26.5 mm. **Ruler:** Akihito **Obv:** Pawlownia flower and highlighted legends **Rev:** Value with latent zeros **Edge:** Slanted reeding

Date	Mintage	F	VF	XF	Unc	BU
Yr.13(2001)	607,813,000	—	—	—	—	9.00
Yr.13(2001) Proof	238,000	Value: 15.00				
Yr.14(2002)	504,419,000	—	—	—	—	9.00
Yr.14(2002) Proof	242,000	Value: 15.00				
Yr.15(2003)	438,130,000	—	—	—	—	9.00
Yr.15(2003) Proof	275,000	Value: 15.00				
Yr.16(2004)	356,623,000	—	—	—	—	9.00
Yr.16(2004) Proof	280,000	Value: 15.00				
Yr.17(2005)	334,762,000	—	—	—	—	9.00
Yr.17(2005) Proof	258,000	Value: 15.00				
Yr.18(2006)	381,346,000	—	—	—	—	9.00
Yr.18(2006) Proof	247,000	Value: 15.00				
Yr.19(2007)	401,701,200	—	—	—	—	9.00
Yr.19(2007) Proof	201,800	Value: 15.00				
Yr.20(2008)	432,642,800	—	—	—	—	9.00
Yr.20(2008) Proof	168,200	Value: 15.00				
Yr.21(2009)	342,925,000	—	—	—	—	9.00
Yr.21(2009) Proof	78,000	Value: 15.00				
Yr.22(2010)	Est. 406,775,000	—	—	—	—	9.00
Yr.22(2010) Proof	—	Value: 15.00				
Yr.23(2011)	—	—	—	—	—	9.00
Yr.23(2011) Proof	—	Value: 15.00				
Yr.24(2012)	—	—	—	—	—	9.00
Yr.24(2012) Proof	—	Value: 15.00				

Y# 126 500 YEN
7.0000 g., Copper-Nickel-Zinc, 26.5 mm. **Ruler:** Akihito **Subject:** World Cup Soccer - Europe & Africa **Obv:** Four players and map background **Rev:** Games logo within shooting star wreath **Edge:** Reeded

Date	Mintage	VG	F	VF	XF	BU
Yr.14(2002)	10,000,000	—	—	—	—	10.00

Y# 127 500 YEN
7.0000 g., Copper-Nickel-Zinc, 26.5 mm. **Ruler:** Akihito **Subject:** World Cup Soccer - Asia & Oceania **Obv:** Three players and map background **Rev:** Games logo within shooting star wreath **Edge:** Reeded

Date	Mintage	VG	F	VF	XF	BU
Yr. 14(2002)	10,000,000	—	—	—	—	10.00

Y# 128 500 YEN
7.0000 g., Copper-Nickel-Zinc, 26.5 mm. **Ruler:** Akihito **Subject:** World Cup Soccer - North & South America **Obv:** Four players and map background **Rev:** Games logo **Edge:** Reeded

Date	Mintage	VG	F	VF	XF	BU
Yr. 14 (2002)	10,000,000	—	—	—	—	10.00

Y# 133 500 YEN
7.0000 g., Copper-Nickel-Zinc, 26.5 mm. **Ruler:** Akihito **Subject:** Expo 2005 - Aichi, Japan **Obv:** Pacific map an globe **Rev:** Circular Expo logo

Date	Mintage	VG	F	VF	XF	BU
Yr. 17(2005)	8,241,000	—	—	—	—	10.00

Y# 134 500 YEN
15.6000 g., 0.9990 Silver 0.5010 oz. ASW, 28 mm. **Ruler:** Akihito **Subject:** Chubu International Airport **Obv:** Aircraft wing in flight over airport **Rev:** Aircraft silhouettes over maps

Date	Mintage	F	VF	XF	Unc	BU
Yr. 17(2005) Proof	50,000	Value: 85.00				

Y# 137 500 YEN
7.0000 g., Copper-Nickel-Zinc, 26.5 mm. **Ruler:** Akihito **Subject:** 50th Anniversary of Japanese Antarctic Research **Obv:** Ship and two dogs **Rev:** Map of Antarctica **Edge:** Helical ridges

Date	Mintage	F	VF	XF	Unc	BU
Yr.19(2007)	6,600,000	—	—	—	—	12.00

Y# 139 500 YEN
7.0000 g., Copper-Nickel-Zinc, 26.5 mm. **Ruler:** Akihito **Subject:** Centenary of Japanese immigration to Brazil/Japan-Brazil year of exchange **Obv:** Ship **Rev:** Crossed sprigs of cherry and coffee **Note:** Prev. #Y143.

Date	Mintage	F	VF	XF	Unc	BU
Yr. 20 (2008)	4,800,000	—	—	—	—	15.00

Y# 145 500 YEN
7.1000 g., Bi-Metallic Copper-Nickel center in Nickel-Brass ring, 26.5 mm. **Ruler:** Akihito **Subject:** Shimane Prefecture **Obv:** Bell shaped bronze vessel, artifact from Kamoiwakura **Rev:** Cash coin

Date	Mintage	F	VF	XF	Unc	BU
Yr.20(2008)	1,940,000	—	—	—	15.00	17.50
Yr.20(2008)	30,000	Value: 50.00				

Y# 141 500 YEN
7.1000 g., Bi-Metallic Copper-Nickel center in Nickel-Brass ring, 26.5 mm. **Ruler:** Akihito **Subject:** Hokkaido Prefecture **Obv:** Lake Toya and the former Hokkaido Government Building

Date	Mintage	F	VF	XF	Unc	BU
Yr.20(2008)	2,070,000	—	—	—	15.00	17.50
Yr.20(2008)	30,000	Value: 50.00				

Y# 143 500 YEN
7.1000 g., Bi-Metallic Copper-Nickel center in Nickel-Brass ring, 26.5 mm. **Ruler:** Akihito **Subject:** Kyoto Prefecture **Obv:** Scene from an antique illustrated version of the Tale of Genji **Rev:** Cash coin

Date	Mintage	F	VF	XF	Unc	BU
Yr.20(2008)	2,020,000	—	—	—	15.00	17.50
Yr20(2008)	30,000	Value: 50.00				

Y# 151 500 YEN
7.0000 g., Copper-Nickel-Zinc, 26.5 mm. **Ruler:** Akihito **Subject:** Japanese - Brazil Imigration Centennial **Obv:** Commemorative statue in Santos Port **Note:** Recalled

Date	Mintage	F	VF	XF	Unc	BU
yr.20(2008)	4,800,000	—	—	—	—	15.00

Y# 147 500 YEN
7.1000 g., Bi-Metallic Copper-Nickel center in Nickel-Brass ring, 26.5 mm. **Ruler:** Akihito **Subject:** Nagano Prefecture **Obv:** Zenkoji Temple and ox

Date	Mintage	F	VF	XF	Unc	BU
Yr.21(2009)	1,800,000	—	—	—	15.00	17.50
Yr.21(2009) Proof	30,000	Value: 50.00				

Y# 149 500 YEN
7.1000 g., Bi-Metallic Copper-Nickel center in Nickel-Brass ring, 26.5 mm. **Ruler:** Akihito **Subject:** Niigata Prefecture **Obv:** Two Japanese crested ibises and rice terrace

Date	Mintage	F	VF	XF	Unc	BU
Yr.21(2009)	1,810,000	—	—	—	15.00	17.50
Yr.21(2009) Proof	30,000	Value: 50.00				

Y# 153   500 YEN
7.1000 g., Bi-Metallic Copper-Nickel center in Nickel-Brass ring,
26.5 mm.   **Ruler:** Akihito **Subject:** Ibaraki Prefecture **Obv:**
Kairakuen Garden and plum tree **Rev:** Cast Japanese coin

Date	Mintage	F	VF	XF	Unc	BU
Yr.21(2009)	1,840,000	—	—	—	15.00	17.50
Yr.21(2009) Proof	30,000	Value: 50.00				

Y# 155   500 YEN
7.1000 g., Bi-Metallic Copper-Nickel center in Nickel-Brass ring,
26.5 mm.   **Ruler:** Akihito **Subject:** Nara Prefecture **Obv:**
Kentoshi-sen -Ship of the Japanese envoy to China in Tang
Dynasty **Rev:** Cast Japanese coin

Date	Mintage	F	VF	XF	Unc	BU
Yr.21(2009)	1,770,000	—	—	—	15.00	17.50
Yr.21(2009) Proof	30,000	Value: 50.00				

Y# 157   500 YEN
7.0000 g., Nickel-Brass, 26.5 mm.   **Ruler:** Akihito **Subject:** 20th
Anniversary of Emperor's Enthronement **Obv:** Imperial
chrysthantem crest **Rev:** Chrysthantem blosums

Date	Mintage	F	VF	XF	Unc	BU
Yr.21(2009)	9,950,000	—	—	—	—	12.50
Yr.21(2009) Proof	50,000	Value: 30.00				

Y# 159   500 YEN
7.1000 g., Bi-Metallic Copper-Nickel center in Nickel-Brass ring,
26.5 mm.   **Ruler:** Akihito **Subject:** Local Autonomy
commemorative - Kochi Prefecture **Obv:** SAKAMOTO Ryoma
Rev: Legend for 47 prefectures coin program, and ancient coin
design reading "local autonomy"

Date	Mintage	F	VF	XF	Unc	BU
Yr.22(2010)	1,930,000	—	—	—	15.00	17.50
Yr.22(2010) Proof	30,000	Value: 50.00				

Y# 161   500 YEN
7.1000 g., Bi-Metallic Copper-Nickel center in Nickel-Brass ring,
26.5 mm.   **Ruler:** Akihito **Subject:** Local Autonomy
commemorative - Gifu Prefecture **Obv:** Shirakawa village and
Chinese milk vetch **Rev:** Legend for 47 prefectures coin program,
and ancient coin design reading "local autonomy"

Date	Mintage	F	VF	XF	Unc	BU
Yr.22(2010)	1,830,000	—	—	—	15.00	17.50
Yr.22(2010) Proof	30,000	Value: 50.00				

Y# 163   500 YEN
7.1000 g., Bi-Metallic Copper-Nickel center in Nickel-Brass ring,
26.5 mm.   **Ruler:** Akihito **Subject:** Local Autonomy
commemorative - Fukui Prefecture **Obv:** Fukuiraptor
(foreground) and Fukuisaurus **Rev:** Legend for 47 prefectures
coin program, and ancient coin design reading "local autonomy"

Date	Mintage	F	VF	XF	Unc	BU
Yr.22(2010)	1,830,000	—	—	—	15.00	17.50
Yr.22(2010) Proof	30,000	Value: 50.00				

Y# 165   500 YEN
7.1000 g., Bi-Metallic Copper-Nickel center in Nickel-Brass ring,
26.5 mm.   **Ruler:** Akihito **Subject:** Local Autonomy
commemorative - Aichi **Obv:** Prefectural capitol building and
rabbit-ear iris **Rev:** Legend for 47 prefectures coin program, and
ancient coin design reading "local autonomy"

Date	Mintage	F	VF	XF	Unc	BU
Yr.22 (2010)	1,950,000	—	—	—	15.00	17.50
Yr.22 (2010) Proof	30,000	Value: 50.00				

Y# 167   500 YEN
7.1000 g., Bi-Metallic Copper-Nickel center in Nickel-Brass ring,
26.5 mm.   **Ruler:** Akihito **Subject:** Local Autonomy
commemorative - Aomori **Obv:** Jomon period structure and
figurines **Rev:** Legend for 47 prefectures coin program and
ancient coin design reading "local autonomy"

Date	Mintage	F	VF	XF	Unc	BU
Yr.22 (2010)	1,900,000	—	—	—	15.00	17.50
Yr.22 (2010) Proof	30,000	Value: 50.00				

Y# 169   500 YEN
7.1000 g., Bi-Metallic Copper-Nickel center in Nickel-Brass ring,
26.5 mm.   **Ruler:** Akihito **Subject:** Local Autonomy
commemorative - Saga **Obv:** OKUMA Shigenobu and Saga
Nishiki fabric **Rev:** Legend for 47 prefectures coin program, and
ancient coin design reading "local autonomy"

Date	Mintage	F	VF	XF	Unc	BU
Yr.22 (2010)	1,910,000	—	—	—	15.00	17.50
Yr.22 (2010) Proof	30,000	Value: 50.00				

Y# 171   500 YEN
7.1000 g., Bi-Metallic Copper-Nickel center in Nickel-Brass ring,
26.5 mm.   **Ruler:** Akihito **Subject:** Local Autonomy
commemorative - Toyama **Obv:** Owara Kaze-no-bon Festival
dancers **Rev:** Legend for 47 prefectures coin program and
ancient coin design reading "local autonomy"

Date	Mintage	F	VF	XF	Unc	BU
Yr. 23 (2011)	—	—	—	—	15.00	17.50
Yr. 23 (2011) Proof	Est. 30,000	Value: 50.00				

Y# 173   500 YEN
7.1000 g., Bi-Metallic Copper-Nickel center in Nickel-Brass ring,
26.5 mm.   **Ruler:** Akihito **Subject:** Local Autonomy
commemorative - Tottori **Obv:** Nageiredo Hall at Mitokusan
Sanbutsuji Temple **Rev:** Legend for 47 prefectures coin program
and ancient coin design reading "local autonomy"

Date	Mintage	F	VF	XF	Unc	BU
Yr. 23 (2011)	—	—	—	—	15.00	17.50
Yr. 23 (2011) Proof	Est. 30,000	Value: 50.00				

Y# 175   500 YEN
7.1000 g., Bi-Metallic Copper-Nickel center in Nickel-Brass ring,
26.5 mm.   **Ruler:** Akihito **Subject:** Local Autonomy
commemorative - Kumamoto **Obv:** Kumamoto Castle **Rev:**
Legend for 47 prefectures con program and ancient coin design
reading "local autonomy"

Date	Mintage	F	VF	XF	Unc	BU
Yr. 23 (2011)	—	—	—	—	15.00	17.50
Yr. 23 (2011) Proof	Est. 30,000	Value: 50.00				

Y# 177   500 YEN
7.1000 g., Bi-Metallic Copper-Nickel center in Nickel-Brass ring,
26.5 mm.   **Ruler:** Akihito **Subject:** Shiga Prefecture

Date	Mintage	F	VF	XF	Unc	BU
Yr. 23 (2011)	—	—	—	—	15.00	17.50
Yr. 23 (2011) Proof	Est. 30,000	Value: 50.00				

Y# 179   500 YEN
7.1000 g., Bi-Metallic Copper-Nickel center in Nickel-Brass ring,
26.5 mm.   **Ruler:** Akihito **Subject:** Iwate Prefecture

Date	Mintage	F	VF	XF	Unc	BU
Yr. 23 (2011)	—	—	—	—	15.00	17.50
Yr. 23 (2011) Proof	Est. 30,000	Value: 50.00				

Y# 181   500 YEN
7.1000 g., Bi-Metallic Copper-Nickel center in Nickel-Brass ring,
26.5 mm.   **Ruler:** Akihito **Subject:** Akita Prefecture

Date	Mintage	F	VF	XF	Unc	BU
Yr. 24 (2012)	—	—	—	—	15.00	17.50
Yr. 24 (2012) Proof	Est. 30,000	Value: 50.00				

Y# 183   500 YEN
7.1000 g., Bi-Metallic Copper-Nickel center in Nickel-Brass ring,
26.5 mm.   **Ruler:** Akihito **Subject:** Okinawa **Rev:** Naha Giant
Tug-of-war and Eisa folk dance

Date	Mintage	F	VF	XF	Unc	BU
Yr.24(2012)	—	—	—	—	15.00	17.50
Yr.24(2012) Proof	—	Value: 50.00				

Y# 185   500 YEN
7.1000 g., Bi-Metallic Copper-Nickel center in Nickel-Brass ring,
26.5 mm.   **Ruler:** Akihito **Subject:** Kanagawa **Rev:** Great
Buddah of Kamakura

Date	Mintage	F	VF	XF	Unc	BU
Yr.24(2012)	—	—	—	—	15.00	17.50
Yr.24(2012) Proof	Est. 30,000	Value: 50.00				

Y# 187   500 YEN
7.1000 g., Bi-Metallic Copper-Nickel center in Nickel-Brass ring,
26.5 mm.   **Ruler:** Akihito **Subject:** Miyazaki **Rev:** Miyazaki
Prefectural Government Building

Date	Mintage	F	VF	XF	Unc	BU
Yr.24(2012)	—	—	—	—	15.00	17.50
Yr.24(2012) Proof	Est. 30,000	Value: 50.00				

Y# 129   1000 YEN
31.1000 g., 0.9990 Silver 0.9988 oz. ASW, 40 mm.   **Ruler:**
Akihito **Subject:** World Cup Soccer **Obv:** Trophy within flower
sprigs **Rev:** Games logo flanked by players **Edge:** Reeded

Date	Mintage	F	VF	XF	Unc	BU
Yr. 14 (2002) Proof	100,000	Value: 200				

Y# 132   1000 YEN
31.1000 g., 0.9990 Silver 0.9988 oz. ASW, 40 mm.   **Ruler:**
Akihito **Subject:** 50th Anniversary of the reversion of the Amami
Islands **Obv:** Lily and bird in multicolor enamel **Rev:** Map of the
Amami-shoto

Date	Mintage	F	VF	XF	Unc	BU
Yr. 15 (2003) Proof	50,000	Value: 220				

Y# 131   1000 YEN
31.1000 g., 0.9990 Silver 0.9988 oz. ASW, 40 mm. **Ruler:** Akihito **Subject:** 5th Winter Asian Games, Aomori **Obv:** Skier and skater **Rev:** Three red apples and multicolor games logo

Date	Mintage	VG	F	VF	XF	BU
Yr.15 (2003) Proof	50,000				Value: 625	

Y# 135   1000 YEN
31.1000 g., 0.9990 Silver 0.9988 oz. ASW, 40 mm. **Ruler:** Akihito **Subject:** Expo 2005 **Obv:** Blue and white enamel Pacific map in wreath **Rev:** Expo logo

Date	Mintage	F	VF	XF	Unc	BU
Yr. 16(2004) Proof	70,000				Value: 165	

Y# 138   1000 YEN
31.1000 g., 1.0000 Silver 0.9998 oz. ASW, 40 mm. **Ruler:** Akihito **Subject:** 50th Anniversary of Japan's Entry into the United Nations **Obv:** Globe and plum blossom wreath (enameled blue, pink and green) **Rev:** UN emblem

Date	Mintage	F	VF	XF	Unc	BU
Yr.18(2006) Proof	70,000				Value: 165	

Y# 140   1000 YEN
31.1000 g., 0.9990 Silver 0.9988 oz. ASW, 40 mm. **Ruler:** Akihito **Obv:** Dual multicolor rainbows **Obv. Inscription:** SKILLS / 2007 **Rev:** Mount Fuji **Rev. Legend:** International Skills Festival for All, Japan **Edge:** Helical ridges **Note:** Prev. #Y142.

Date	Mintage	F	VF	XF	Unc	BU
Yr.19(2007) Proof	80,000				Value: 75.00	

Y# 142   1000 YEN
31.1000 g., 0.9990 Silver 0.9988 oz. ASW, 40 mm. **Ruler:** Akihito **Subject:** Hokkaido Prefecture **Obv:** Lake Toya and two multicolor red-crowned cranes in flight **Rev:** Cherry blossoms and crescent

Date	Mintage	F	VF	XF	Unc	BU
Yr.20(2008) Proof	100,000				Value: 135	

Y# 144   1000 YEN
31.1000 g., 0.9990 Silver 0.9988 oz. ASW, 40 mm. **Ruler:** Akihito **Subject:** Kyoto Prefecture **Obv:** Multicolor scene from an antique illustrated version of the Tale of Genji **Rev:** Cherry blossoms and crescent

Date	Mintage	F	VF	XF	Unc	BU
Yr.20(2008) Proof	100,000				Value: 120	

Y# 146   1000 YEN
31.1000 g., 0.9990 Silver 0.9988 oz. ASW, 40 mm. **Ruler:** Akihito **Subject:** Shimane Prefecture **Obv:** Multicolor peony flowers and Otoriosame chogin coin **Rev:** Cherry blossoms and crescent

Date	Mintage	F	VF	XF	Unc	BU
Yr.20(2008) Proof	100,000				Value: 115	

Y# 154   1000 YEN
31.1000 g., 0.9990 Silver 0.9988 oz. ASW **Ruler:** Akihito **Subject:** Ibaraki Prefecture **Obv:** Multicolor H-II launch vehicle and Mt. Tsukuba **Rev:** Snow crystal, moon and cherry blossom

Date	Mintage	F	VF	XF	Unc	BU
Yr.21(2008) Proof	100,000				Value: 100	

Y# 156   1000 YEN
31.1000 g., 0.9990 Silver 0.9988 oz. ASW **Ruler:** Akihito **Subject:** Nara Prefecture **Obv:** Daigokuden Audience Hall in multicolor, cherry blossoms and Kemari (ancient ball players) **Rev:** Snow crystal, moon and cherry blossoms

Date	Mintage	F	VF	XF	Unc	BU
Yr.21(2008) Proof	100,000				Value: 115	

Y# 148   1000 YEN
31.1000 g., 0.9990 Silver 0.9988 oz. ASW, 40 mm. **Ruler:** Akihito **Subject:** Nagano Prefecture **Obv:** Multicolor Japan Alps and Kamikochi

Date	Mintage	F	VF	XF	Unc	BU
Yr.21(2009) Proof	100,000				Value: 115	

Y# 150   1000 YEN
31.1000 g., 0.9990 Silver 0.9988 oz. ASW, 40 mm. **Ruler:** Akihito **Subject:** Niigata Prefecture **Obv:** Two Japanese crested ibis and Sado Island

Date	Mintage	F	VF	XF	Unc	BU
Yr.21(2009) Proof	100,000				Value: 100	

Y# 160   1000 YEN
31.1000 g., 0.9990 Silver 0.9988 oz. ASW, 40 mm. **Ruler:** Akihito **Subject:** Local Autonomy commemorative - Kochi Prefecture **Obv:** SAKAMOTO Ryoma and Katsurahama Beach **Rev:** Snowflakes, cherry blossoms, and crescent moon with legend **Rev. Legend:** Local Autonomy 60 Years

Date	Mintage	F	VF	XF	Unc	BU
Yr.22(2010) Proof; colorized	100,000				Value: 130	

Y# 162   1000 YEN
31.1000 g., 0.9990 Silver 0.9988 oz. ASW, 40 mm. **Ruler:** Akihito **Subject:** Local Autonomy commemorative - Gifu Prefecture **Obv:** Cormorant fishing on the Nagara River **Rev:** Snowflakes, cherry blossoms, and crescent moon with legend **Rev. Legend:** Local Autonomy 60 Years

Date	Mintage	F	VF	XF	Unc	BU
Yr.22(2010) Proof; colorized	100,000				Value: 130	

Y# 164   1000 YEN
31.1000 g., 0.9990 Silver 0.9988 oz. ASW, 40 mm. **Ruler:** Akihito **Subject:** Local Autonomy commemorative - Fukui Prefecture **Obv:** Fukuiraptor and Tojinbo Cliffs **Rev:** Snowflakes, cherry blossoms, and crescent moon with legend **Rev. Legend:** Local Autonomy 60 Years

Date	Mintage	F	VF	XF	Unc	BU
Yr.22(2010) Proof; colorized	100,000				Value: 130	

Y# 166   1000 YEN
31.1000 g., 1.0000 Silver 0.9998 oz. ASW, 40 mm. **Ruler:** Akihito **Subject:** Local Autonomy commemorative - Aichi **Obv:** Golden dolphin, rabbit-ear iris and the Atsumi Peninsula **Rev:** Snowflakes, cherry blossoms and crescent moon with legend reading "local autonomy 60 years"

Date	Mintage	F	VF	XF	Unc	BU
Yr.22 (2010) Proof	100,000				Value: 130	

Y# 168   1000 YEN
31.1000 g., 1.0000 Silver 0.9998 oz. ASW, 40 mm. **Ruler:** Akihito **Subject:** Local Autonomy commemorative - Aomori **Obv:** Traditional parade floats and apples **Rev:** Snowflakes, cherry blossoms and crescent moon with legend reading "local autonomy 60 years"

Date	Mintage	F	VF	XF	Unc	BU
Yr.22 (2010) Proof	100,000				Value: 130	

Y# 170   1000 YEN
31.1000 g., 1.0000 Silver 0.9998 oz. ASW, 40 mm. **Ruler:** Akihito **Subject:** Local Autonomy commemorative - Saga **Obv:** OKUMA Shigenobu and Imari - Arita ware **Rev:** Snowflakes, cherry blossoms and crescent moon with legend reading "local autonomy 60 years"

Date	Mintage	F	VF	XF	Unc	BU
Yr.22 (2010) Proof	100,000				Value: 130	

Y# 172 1000 YEN
31.1050 g., 1.0000 Silver 1.0000 oz. ASW, 40 mm. **Ruler:**
Akihito **Subject:** Local Autonomy commemorative - Toyama
Obv: Tateyama mountain range rising from the sea **Rev:**
Snowflakes, cherry blossoms and crescent moon with legend
reading "local autonomy 60 years" **Edge:** Reeded

Date	Mintage	F	VF	XF	Unc	BU
Yr. 23 (2011) Proof	100,000	Value: 130				

Y# 174 1000 YEN
31.1000 g., 1.0000 Silver 0.9998 oz. ASW, 40 mm. **Ruler:**
Akihito **Subject:** Local Autonomy commemorative - Tottori **Obv:**
Tottori Sand Dunes and San'in Kaigan Coast **Rev:** Snowflakes,
cherry blossoms and crescent moon with legend reading "local
autonomy 60 years" **Edge:** Reeded

Date	Mintage	F	VF	XF	Unc	BU
Yr. 23 (2011) Proof	100,000	Value: 130				

Y# 176 1000 YEN
31.1000 g., 1.0000 Silver 0.9998 oz. ASW, 40 mm. **Ruler:**
Akihito **Subject:** Local Autonomy commemorative - Kumamoto
Obv: Mount Aso **Rev:** Snowflakes, cherry blossoms and crescent
moon with legend reading "local autonomy 60 years" **Edge:**
Reeded

Date	Mintage	F	VF	XF	Unc	BU
Yr. 23 (2011) Proof	100,000	Value: 130				

Y# 178 1000 YEN
31.1050 g., 0.9990 Silver 0.9990 oz. ASW, 40 mm. **Ruler:**
Akihito **Subject:** Shiga Prefecture **Rev:** Lake Biwa, family of little
grebe birds and Ukimido temple **Edge:** Reeded

Date	Mintage	F	VF	XF	Unc	BU
Yr. 23 (2011) Proof	100,000	Value: 115				

Y# 180 1000 YEN
31.1050 g., 0.9990 Silver 0.9990 oz. ASW, 40 mm. **Ruler:**
Akihito **Subject:** Iwate Prefecture **Rev:** Konjiko-do, the golden
hall of Chuson-ji Temple, lotus and Pure Land Garden of Motsu-
ji temple **Edge:** Reeded

Date	Mintage	F	VF	XF	Unc	BU
Yr. 23 (2011) Proof	100,000	Value: 110				

Y# 182 1000 YEN
31.1050 g., 0.9990 Silver 0.9990 oz. ASW, 40 mm. **Ruler:**
Akihito **Subject:** Akita Prefecture **Rev:** Nobu Shirase, Antartic
explorer, Namahage folk ritual **Edge:** Reeded

Date	Mintage	F	VF	XF	Unc	BU
Yr. 24 (2012) Proof	10,000	Value: 110				

Y# 184 1000 YEN
31.1000 g., 0.9990 Silver 0.9988 oz. ASW, 40 mm. **Ruler:**
Akihito **Subject:** Okinawa **Rev:** State Hall in Suri and Kumidori
dancer

Date	Mintage	F	VF	XF	Unc	BU
Yr.24(2012) Proof	100,000	Value: 100				

Y# 186 1000 YEN
31.1000 g., 0.9990 Silver 0.9988 oz. ASW, 40 mm. **Ruler:**
Akihito **Subject:** Kanagawa **Rev:** Tsurugaoka Hachimangu
Shrine and horseback archery - Yabusame

Date	Mintage	F	VF	XF	Unc	BU
Yr.24(2012) Proof	—	Value: 100				

KM# 188 1000 YEN
31.1000 g., 0.9990 Silver 0.9988 oz. ASW, 40 mm. **Ruler:**
Akihito **Subject:** Miyazaki **Rev:** Miyazaki Prefectural
Government Building and Takachiho Yokagura dancer

Date	Mintage	F	VF	XF	Unc	BU
Yr.24(2012) Proof	—	Value: 100				

Y# 130 10000 YEN
15.6000 g., 0.9990 Gold 0.5010 oz. AGW, 26 mm. **Ruler:** Akihito
Subject: World Cup Soccer **Obv:** Two soccer players **Rev:**
Games logo **Edge:** Reeded

Date	Mintage	F	VF	XF	Unc	BU
Yr.14(2002) Proof	100,000	Value: 1,000				

Y# 136 10000 YEN
15.6000 g., 0.9990 Gold 0.5010 oz. AGW, 26 mm. **Ruler:** Akihito
Subject: Expo 2005 **Obv:** Two owls on globe **Rev:** Expo logo

Date	Mintage	F	VF	XF	Unc	BU
Yr. 16(2004) Proof	70,000	Value: 1,000				

Y# 158 10000 YEN
20.0000 g., 0.9990 Gold 0.6423 oz. AGW, 28 mm. **Ruler:** Akihito
Subject: 20th Anniversary of Emperor's enthronment **Obv:**
Imperial christaniumn crest **Rev:** Phoenix, an auspicious cloud,
Niju-bashi bridge

Date	Mintage	F	VF	XF	Unc	BU
Yr.21(2009) Proof	130,000	Value: 1,200				

MINT SETS

KM#	Date	Mintage	Identification	Issue Price	Mkt Val
MS125	2001 (6)	8,000	Y#95.2-98.2, 101.2, 125 Mint exhibition in Fukuoka	16.00	30.00
MS126	2001 (6)	85,000	Y#95.2-98.2, 101.2, 125 Osaka cherry blossoms box	17.00	30.00
MS127	2001 (6)	10,000	Y#95.2-98.2, 101.2, 125 Hiroshima cherry blossoms box	17.00	33.00
MS128	2001 (6)	10,000	Y#95.2-98.2, 101.2, 125 12th Tokyo International Coin Convention	17.00	30.00
MS129	2001 (6)	5,000	Y#95.2-98.2, 101.2, 125 Beautiful Future Exposition	17.00	30.00
MS130	2001 (6)	8,000	Y#95.2-98.2, 101.2, 125 Kagoshima Coin and Stamp Show	17.00	30.00
MS131	2001 (6)	5,000	Y#95.2-98.2, 101.2, 125 Tokyo Mint Fair	17.00	33.00
MS132	2001 (6)	5,000	Y#95.2-98.2, 101.2, 125 Yamaguchi Exposition	17.00	40.00
MS133	2001 (6)	193,600	Y#95.2-98.2, 101.2, 125 21st Century Commemorative Respect for the Aged	17.00	27.00
MS134	2001 (6)	190,300	Y#95.2-98.2, 101.2, 125 Ryukyu World Cultural Sites	17.00	27.00
MS135	2001 (6)	8,300	Y#95.2-98.2, 101.2, 125 "Anniversary" folder	18.00	33.00
MS136	2001 (1)	4,000	Y#125 Mint Visit Commemorative	8.00	10.00
MS137	2001 (6)	224,000	Y#95.2-98.2, 101.2, 125 Mint Bureau Box	15.00	27.00
MS138	2001 (6)	7,300	Y#95.2-98.2, 101.2, 125 "Japan Coins"	17.00	30.00
MS139	2001 (2)	5,000	Y#96.2, 125 "Japan Coins" (short set)	8.50	13.00
MS140	2001 (6)	128,700	Y#95.2-98.2, 101.2, 125 World Intangible Heritage - Nogaku	17.00	27.00
MS141	2002 (1)	3,000	Y#125 Mint Visit Commemorative	7.50	10.00
MS142	2002 (2)	7,000	Y#95.2-98.2, 102.2, 125 "Anniversary" folder	18.00	27.00
MS143	2002 (2)	4,000	Y#96.2, 125. "Japan Coins" (short set)	8.50	13.00
MS144	2002 (6)	6,000	Y#95.2-98.2, 101.2, 125 "Japan Coins"	17.00	23.00
MS145	2002 (6)	4,000	Y#95.2-98.2, 101.2, 125 Mint exhibition in Takamatsu	16.00	33.00
MS146	2002 (6)	80,000	Y#95.2-98.2, 101.2, 125 Osaka cherry blossoms	16.00	20.00
MS147	2002 (6)	10,000	Y#95.2-98.2, 101.2, 125 Hiroshima cherry blossoms	16.00	23.00
MS148	2002 (6)	10,000	Y#95.2-98.2, 101.2, 125 13th Tokyo Int'l Coin Convention	16.00	20.00
MS149	2002 (6)	6,000	Y#95.2-98.2, 101.2, 125 Mint exhibition in Sendai	16.00	23.00
MS150	2002 (6)	194,000	Y#95.2-98.2, 101.2, 125 Respect for the Aged	19.00	20.00
MS151	2002 (6)	6,000	Y#95.2-98.2, 101.2, 125 Matsuyama Coin and Stamp Show	16.00	23.00
MS152	2002 (6)	3,000	Y395.2-98.2, 101.2, 125 Tokyo Mint Fair	16.00	120
MS153	2002 (6)	2,000	Y#95.2-98.2, 101.2, 125 Birthday folder (with sound recording function)	25.00	40.00
MS154	2002 (6)	214,800	Y395.2-98.2, 101.2, 125 Mint Bureau box	15.00	20.00
MSA141	2002 (3)	50,000	Y#126-128 World Cup soccer	26.00	35.00
MS155	2003 (6)	8,000	Y#95.2-98.2, 101.2, 125 "Japan Coins"	17.00	20.00
MS156	2003 (6)	7,000	Y#95.2-98.2, 101.2, 125 "Anniversary" folder	18.00	20.00
MS157	2003 (6)	3,000	Y#95.2-98.2, 101.2, 125 "Anniversary" folder (with sound recording function)	25.00	27.00
MS158	2003 (6)	6,000	Y#95.2-98.2, 101.2, 125 Mint exhibition in Okayama	16.00	30.00
MS159	2003 (6)	80,000	Y#95.2-98.2, 101.2, 125 Osaka cherry blossoms	16.00	20.00
MS160	2003 (6)	10,000	Y#95.2-98.2, 101.2, 125 Hiroshima cherry blossoms	16.00	20.00
MS161	2003 (6)	10,000	Y#95.2-98.2, 101.2, 125 14th Tokyo Int'l Coin Convention	16.00	20.00
MS162	2003 (6)	6,000	Y#95.2-98.2, 101.2, 125 First Osaka Coin Show	16.00	20.00
MS163	2003 (6)	235,000	Y#95.2-98.2, 101.2, 125 Birth of Astro Boy	19.00	20.00

KM#	Date	Mintage Identification	Issue Price	Mkt Val
MS164	2003 (6)	130,000 Y#95.2-98.2, 101.2, 125 Respect for the Aged	19.00	17.00
MS165	2003 (6)	5,000 Y#95.2-98.2, 101.2, 125 Tokyo Mint Fair - Mint Collection in Omote-sando	17.00	30.00
MS166	2003 (6)	5,000 Y#95.2-98.2, 101.2, 125 Mint exhibition in Sapporo	17.00	27.00
MS167	2003 (6)	5,000 Y#95.2-98.2, 101.2, 125 Yonago Coin and Stamp Show	17.00	23.00
MS168	2003 (6)	205,000 Y#95.2-98.2, 101.2, 125 Mint Bureau box	17.00	16.00
MS169	2003 (6)	100,000 Y#95.2-98.2, 101.2, 125 2003 Central League Champions - Hanshin Tigers	22.00	27.00
MS170	2003 (6)	100,000 Y#95.2-98.2, 101.2, 125 2003 Pacific league Champions - Fukuoka Daiei Hawks	22.00	16.00
MS171	2003 (6)	5,000 Y#95.2-98.2, 101.2, 126 400th Anniversary of the Establishment of Government in Edo	22.00	200
MS172	2004 (6)	8,000 Y#95.2-98.2, 101.2, 125 "Japan Coin Set"	19.00	20.00
MS173	2004 (6)	5,000 Y#95.2-98.2, 101.2, 125 "Anniversary" folder	20.00	22.00
MS174	2004 (6)	5,000 Y#95.2-98.2, 101.2, 125 Anniversary folder (with sound recording function)	28.50	27.00
MS175	2004 (6)	4,000 Y#95.2-98.2, 101.2, 125 Mint exhibition in Fukui	18.00	53.00
MS176	2004 (6)	70,000 Y#95.2-98.2, 101.2, 125 Osaka cherry blossoms	18.00	20.00
MS177	2004 (6)	10,000 Y#95.2-98.2, 101.2, 125 Hiroshima cherry blossoms	18.00	20.00
MS178	2004 (6)	10,000 Y#95.2-98.2, 101.2, 125 15th Tokyo Int'l Coin Convention	18.00	20.00
MS179	2004 (6)	6,000 Y#95.2-98.2, 101.2, 125 Second Osaka Coin Show	18.00	20.00
MS180	2004 (6)	100,000 Y#95.2-98.2, 101.2, 125 World Intangible Heritage series: Bunraku puppets	19.00	20.00
MS181	2004 (6)	122,500 Y#95.2-98.2, 101.2, 125 Respect for the Aged	20.00	20.00
MS182	2004 (6)	5,000 Y#95.2-98.2, 101.2, 125 Mint exhibition in Tosu	18.00	23.00
MS183	2004 (6)	189,000 Y#95.2-98.2, 101.2, 125 Mint Bureau box	16.00	17.00
MS184	2004 (6)	5,000 Y#95.2-98.2, 101.2, 125 Gifu Coin and Stamp Show	17.00	23.00
MS185	2004 (6)	226,000 Y#95.2-98.2, 101.2, 125 30th Birthday of Hello Kitty (cartoon character)	22.00	23.00
MS186	2004 (6)	5,000 Y#95.2-98.2, 101.2, 125 Tokyo Mint Fair - 40th Anniversary - Issue of Commemorative Coins	17.00	33.00
MS187	2004 (6)	44,000 Y#95.2-98.2, 101.2, 125 2004 Central League Champions - Chunichi Dragons	21.00	17.00
MS188	2004 (6)	38,500 Y#95.2-98.2, 101.2, 125 2004 Pacific League Champions - Seibu Lions	21.00	17.00
MS189	2005 (6)	200,000 Y#95.2-98.2, 101.2, 133 Expo 2005, Aichi	22.00	23.00
MS190	2005 (6)	8,000 Y#95.2-98.2, 101.2, 125 "Japan Coin Set"	17.00	16.00
MS191	2005 (6)	5,000 Y#95.2-98.2, 101.2, 125 "Anniversary" folder	19.00	20.00
MS192	2005 (6)	2,000 Y#95.2-98.2, 101.2, 125 Anniversary folder (with sound recording function)	27.50	27.00
MS193	2005 (6)	5,000 Y#95.2-98.2, 101.2, 125 Mint exhibition in Shizuoka	17.00	33.00
MS194	2005 (6)	60,000 Y#95.2-98.2, 101.2, 125 Osaka cherry blossoms	17.00	23.00
MS195	2005 (6)	10,000 Y#95.2-98.2, 101.2, 125 Hiroshima Flower Tour	17.00	20.00
MS196	2005 (6)	10,000 Y#95.2-98.2, 101.2, 125 16th Tokyo International Coin Convention	17.00	20.00
MS197	2005 (6)	5,000 Y#95.2-98.2, 101.2, 125 Third Osaka Coin Show	17.00	20.00
MS198	2005 (6)	126,500 Y#95.2-98.2, 101.2, 125 World Cultural Heritage Series: Kii Hills Sacred Places and Pilgrimage Trails	18.00	20.00
MS199	2005 (6)	104,500 Y#95.2-98.2, 101.2, 125 Respect for the Aged	19.00	20.00
MS200	2005 (6)	5,000 Y#95.2-98.2, 101.2, 125 Mint Exhibition in Morioka	18.00	23.00
MS201	2005 (6)	5,000 Y#95.2-98.2, 101.2, 125 Koriyama Coin and Stamp Show	17.00	23.00
MS202	2005 (6)	182,000 Y#95.2-98.2, 101.2, 125 35th Anniversary of Doraemon (cartoon character)	17.00	30.00
MS203	2005 (6)	141,000 Y#95.2-98.2, 101.2, 125 Mint Bureau Box	16.00	18.00
MS204	2005 (6)	75,800 Y#95.2-98.2, 101.2, 125 World Natural Heritage	18.00	20.00
MS205	2005 (6)	5,000 Y#95.2-98.2, 101.2, 125 Mint Bureau Tokyo Fair / 50th Anniversary of One-Yen Aluminum Coin	17.00	40.00
MS206	2005 (6)	83,600 Y#95.2-98.2, 101.2, 125 2005 Central League Champions - Hanshin Tigers	21.00	20.00
MS207	2005 (6)	56,600 Y#95.2-98.2, 101.2, 125 2005 Pacific League Champions - Chiba Lotte Marines	21.00	20.00
MSA189	2005 (6)	1,000 Y#95.2-98.2, 101.2, 125 34th International Coin Convention, Basel	—	—
MS208	2006 (6)	5,000 Y#95.2-98.2, 101.2, 125 Mint exhibition in Oita	17.00	17.50
MS209	2006 (6)	9,000 Y#95.2-98.2, 101.2, 125 "Japan Coin Set"	18.00	18.00
MS210	2006 (6)	5,000 Y#95.2-98.2, 101.2, 125 "Anniversary" Folder	19.00	20.00
MS211	2006 (6)	189,400 Y#95.2-98.2, 101.2, 125 Mint Bureau box	16.00	17.00
MS212	2006 (6)	66,000 Y#95.2-98.2, 101.2, 125 World Intangible Heritage Series: Kabuki Theater	18.00	18.00
MS213	2006 (6)	60,000 Y#95.2-98.2, 101.2, 125 Osaka Cherry Blossoms	17.00	17.50
MS214	2006 (6)	8,000 Y#95.2-98.2, 101.2, 125 Hiroshima Flower Tour	17.00	17.50
MS215	2006 (6)	8,000 Y#95.2-98.2, 101.2, 125 17th Tokyo International Coin Convention	18.00	18.50
MS216	2006 (6)	85,500 Y#95.2-98.2, 101.2, 125 Respect for the Aged	19.00	20.00
MS217	2006 (6)	4,000 Y#95.2-98.2, 101.2, 125 Third Osaka Coin Show	17.00	18.50
MS218	2006 (6)	4,000 Y#95.2-98.2, 101.2, 125 Mint Exhibition in Kofu	17.00	17.50
MS219	2006 (6)	105,200 Y#95.2-98.2, 101.2, 125 80th Anniversary of Pooh-Bear	22.00	22.50
MS220	2006 (6)	3,500 Y#95.2-98.2, 101.2, 125 Nagasaki Coin and Stamp Show	17.00	17.50
MS221	2006 (6)	4,000 Y#95.2-98.2, 101.2, 125 Mint Bureau Tokyo Fair/"The Dawn of Modern Japan"	17.00	50.00
MS222	2006 (6)	49,600 Y#95.2-98.2, 101.2, 125 2006 Central League Champions - Chunichi Dragons	21.00	27.00
MS223	2006 (6)	56,600 Y#95.2-98.2, 101.2, 125 2006 Pacific League Champions - Japan Hamfighters	21.00	27.00
MS224	2007 (6)	180,000 Y#95.2-98.2, 101.2, 137 50th Anniversary of Japanese Antarctic Research	23.00	30.00
MS225	2007 (6)	4,000 Y#95.2-98.2, 101.2, 125 Mint exhibition in Tsukuba	17.00	18.00
MS226	2007 (6)	8,000 Y#95.2-98.2, 101.2, 125 "Japan Coin Set"	18.00	20.00
MS227	2007 (6)	5,700 Y#95.2-98.2, 101.2, 125 "Anniversary" folder	19.00	20.00
MS228	2007 (6)	150,000 Y#95.2-98.2, 101.2, 125 Mint Bureau box	16.00	18.00
MS229	2007 (6)	82,200 Y#95.2-98.2, 101.2, 125 "Gongitsune" 75th Anniversary of Publication	22.00	25.00
MS230	2007 (6)	7,000 Y#95.2-98.2, 101.2, 125 Hiroshima Flower Tour	18.00	—
MS231	2007 (6)	60,000 Y#95.2-98.2, 101.2, 125 Osaka cherry blossoms	17.00	18.00
MS232	2007 (6)	6,000 Y#95.2-98.2, 101.2, 125 18th Tokyo International Coin Convention	17.00	18.00
MS233	2007 (6)	4,000 Y#95.2-98.2, 101.2, 125 Fifth Osaka Coin Show	17.00	18.00
MS234	2007 (6)	76,500 Y#95.2-98.2, 101.2, 125 Rose of Versailles, Lady Oscar	22.00	25.00
MS235	2007 (6)	2,720 Y#95.2-98.2, 101.2, 125 Mint exhibition in Matsue	17.00	18.00
MS236	2007 (6)	4,000 Y#95.2-98.2, 101.2, 125 Nagoya Coin and Stamp Show	17.00	18.00
MS237	2007 (6)	69,000 Y#95.2-98.2, 101.2, 125 Respect for the Aged	19.00	20.00
MS238	2007 (6)	4,000 Y#95.2-98.2, 101.2, 125 Mint Bureau Tokyo Fair/50th anniversary of introduction of the 100-yen coin	17.00	18.00
MS239	2007 (6)	45,200 Y#95.2-98.2, 101.2, 125 2007 Central League Champions - Yomiuri Giants	21.00	22.00
MS240	2007 (6)	36,500 Y#95.2-98.2, 101.2, 125 2007 Pacific League Champions - Japan Hamfighters	21.00	22.00
MS241	2007 (6)	74,500 Y#95.2-98.2, 101.2, 125 World Cultural Heritage Series: Iwami Silver Mines Ruins and Cultural Landscape	18.00	20.00
MS242	2008 (6)	4,000 Y#95.2-98.2, 101.2, 125, Mint exhibition in Miyazaki	18.00	20.00
MS243	2008 (6)	15,100 Y#95.2-98.2, 101.2, 125, "Japan Coin Set"	19.00	20.00
MS244	2008 (6)	7,500 Y#95.2-98.2, 101.2, 125, "Anniversary" folder	20.00	20.00
MS245	2008 (6)	154,022 Y#95.2-98.2, 101.2, 125, Mint Bureau Box	17.00	20.00
MS246	2008 (6)	4,500 Y#95.2-98.2, 101.2, 125, Hiroshima Flower Tour	18.00	20.00
MS247	2008 (6)	60,000 Y#95.2-98.2, 101.2, 125, Osaka cherry blossoms	18.00	20.00
MS248	2008 (6)	5,500 Y#95.2-98.2, 101.2, 125, 19th Tokyo International Coin Convention	18.00	20.00
MS249	2008 (6)	4,000 Y#25.2-98.2, 101.2, 125, G8 Finance Ministers' meeting, Osaka	18.00	18.00
MS250	2008 (6)	3,500 Y#95.2-98.2, 101.2, 125, Sixth Osaka Coin Show.	18.00	20.00
MS251	2008 (6)	4,000 Y#95.2-98.2, 101.2, 125, Kobe Coin and Stamp Exposition.	18.00	18.00
MS252	2008 (6)	142,000 Y#95.2-98.2, 101.2, 125, Japan-Brazil Year of Exchange and Centenary of Japanese Immigration to Brazil	24.00	25.00
MS253	2008 (6)	100,000 Y#95.2-98.2, 101.2, 125, Children's song coin set, Red Dragonfly.	23.00	25.00
MS254	2008 (6)	4,000 Y#95.2-98.2, 101.2, 125 Mint Bureau Tokyo Fair/"Japan's Attractions"	20.00	—
MS255	2009 (6)	4,000 Y#95.2-Y98.2, 101.2, 125 32nd World Money Festival, Nagoya	20.00	—
MS256	2009 (6)	— Y95.2-Y98.2, 101.2, 125 Japan Coin Set	21.00	—
MS257	2009 (6)	— Y95.2-Y98.2, 101.2, 125 Anniversary folder	22.00	—
MS258	2009 (6)	4,500 Y95.2-Y98.2, 101.2, 125 Hiroshima Flower Tour	20.00	—
MS259	2009 (6)	60,000 Y95.2-Y98.2, 101.2, 125 Osaka cherry blossoms	20.00	—
MS260	2009 (6)	5,500 Y95.2-Y98.2, 101.2, 125 20th Toyko International Coin Convention	20.00	—
MS261	2009 (6)	150,000 Y95.2-Y98.2, 101.2, 125 Mint Bureau box	19.00	—
MS262	2009 (6)	3,500 Y95.2-Y98.2, 101.2, 125 Mint exhibition in Niigata	20.00	—
MS263	2009 (6)	4,000 Y95.2-Y98.2, 101.2, 125 Seventh Osaka Coin Show	20.00	—
MS264	2009 (6)	5,000 Y95.2-Y98.2, 101.2, 125 Aqua Metropolis Osaka 2009	20.00	—
MS265	2009 (6)	3,500 Y95.2-Y98.2, 101.2, 125 Yamagata Coin and Stamp Exibition	20.00	—
MS266	2009 (6)	7,413 Y95.2-Y98.2, 101.2, 125 2009 Niigata Sports Festival	19.00	—
MS267	2009 (6)	70,000 Y95.2-Y98.2, 101.2, 125 Music box set, "My Home Town"	25.00	—
MS268	2009 (6)	4,000 Y95.2-Y98.2, 101.2, 125 Mint Future Fair, "Hallmark" case	20.00	—
MS270	2010 (6)	6,000 Y#95.2-98.2, 101.2, 125 33rd World Money Festival	20.00	—
MS276	2010 (6)	6,000 Y95.2-98.2, 101.2, 125 21st Tokyo International Coin Convention	—	20.00
MS269	2010 (6)	— Y95.2-98.2, 101.2, 125 "Mint Set 2010"	—	—
MS271	2010 (6)	— Y95.2-98.2, 101.2, 125 "Japan Coin Set"	—	21.00
MS272	2010 (6)	— Y95.2-98.2, 101.2, 125 "Anniversary" folder	—	22.00
MS273	2010 (6)	6,000 Y95.2-98.2, 101.2, 125 Toshima Monozukuri set	20.00	—
MS274	2010 (6)	5,000 Y95.2-98.2, 101.2, 125 Hiroshima Flower Tour	20.00	—
MS275	2010 (6)	60,000 Y95.2-98.2, 101.2, 125 Osaka cherry blossoms	—	20.00
MS277	2010 (6)	4,000 Y95.2-98.2, 101.2, 125 Mint Exhibition in Gifu	—	20.00
MS278	2010 (6)	5,500 Y95.2-98.2, 101.2, 125 Eighth Osaka Coin Show	—	20.00
MS279	2010 (6)	4,000 Y95.2-98.2, 101.2, 125 Kumamoto Coin and Stamp Exhibition	—	20.00

KM#	Date	Mintage	Identification	Issue Price	Mkt Val
MS280	2010 (6)	50,000	Y95.2-98.2, 101.2, 125 Intangible Cultural Heritage (2009 enrollments)	—	22.00
MS281	2010 (6)	7,000	Y95.2-98.2, 101.2, 125 2010 Chiba Sports Festival	20.00	—
MS282	2010 (6)	60,000	Y95.2-98.2, 101.2, 125 Music box set, "Snow"	26.00	—

PIEFORT PROOF SETS (PPS)

KM#	Date	Mintage	Identification	Issue Price	Mkt Val
PS85	2010 (6)	20,000	Y95.2-98.2, 101.2, 125 120 years of Japan-Turkey Amity (with 50 lira Turkish coin on same subject included)	144	—

PROOF SETS

KM#	Date	Mintage	Identification	Issue Price	Mkt Val
PS32	2001 (6)	138,000	Y#95.2-98.2, 101.2, 125 Mint Bureau Box	62.50	47.00
PS33	2001 (6)	100,000	Y#95.2-98.2, 101.2, 125 Old Type Coin Series (Trade dollar medallet)	62.50	53.00
PS38	2002 (2)	50,000	Y#129, 130 World Cup	385	550
PS34	2002 (6)	144,000	Y#95.2-98.2, 101.2, 125 Mint Bureau box	62.50	53.00
PS35	2002 (6)	3,000	Y#95.2-98.2, 101.2, 125 15th Anniversary of Proof Sets	62.50	100
PS36	2002 (6)	95,000	Y#95.2-98.2, 101.2, 125 Techno medal set	62.50	53.00
PS39	2003 (6)	98,400	Y#95.2-98.2, 101.2, 125 Mint Bureau box, with date plaquette	67.50	53.00
PS40	2003 (6)	90,000	Y#95.2-98.2, 101.2, 125 Astro Boy	115	100
PS41	2003 (6)	5,000	Y#95.2-98.2, 101.2, 125 Tokyo Mint Fair - Mint Collection in Omote-Sando	67.50	100
PS42	2003 (6)	70,000	Y#95.2-98.2, 101.2, 125 Mickey Mouse	125	120
PS43	2003 (6)	5,000	Y#95.2-98.2, 101.2, 125 400th Anniversary - Establishment of Government in Edo	67.50	165
PS50	2004 (2)	35,000	Y#135-136 Expo 2005, Aichi	425	500
PS44	2004 (6)	94,900	Y#95.2-98.2, 101.2, 125 Mint Bureau box with date plaquette	71.00	60.00
PS45	2004 (6)	13,100	Y#95.2-98.2, 101.2, 125 Mint Bureau box without date plaquette	70.00	100
PS46	2004 (6)	60,000	Y#95.2-98.2, 101.2, 125 70h Anniversary - Pro Baseball	120	145
PS47	2004 (6)	60,000	Y#95.2-98.2, 101.2, 125 Techno Medal Series 2	71.00	60.00
PS48	2004 (6)	50,000	Y#95.2-98.2, 101.2, 125 30th Birthday of Hello Kitty (cartoon character)	120	150
PS49	2004 (6)	5,000	Y#95.2-98.2, 101.2, 125 Tokyo Mint Fair - 40th Anniversary - Issue of Commemorative Coins	71.00	100
PSA40	2003 (6)	6,600	Y#95.2-98.2, 101.2, 125 Mint Bureau Box without Date Plaquette	66.00	100
PS51	2005 (6)	76,700	Y#95.2-98.2, 101.2, 125 Mint Bureau Box with date plaquette	71.00	65.00
PS52	2005 (6)	10,000	Y#95.2-98.2, 101.2, 125 Mint Bureau Box without date plaquette	70.00	100
PS53	2005 (6)	60,000	Y#95.2-98.2, 101.2, 125 35th Anniversary of Doraemon (cartoon character)	125	170
PS54	2005 (6)	34,000	Y#95.2-98.2, 101.2, 125 50th Anniversary of One-Yen Aluminum Coin	125	170
PS55	2005 (6)	30,000	Y#95.2-98.2, 101.2, 125 50th Anniversary of the Pencil Rocket	125	100
PS56	2005 (6)	47,300	Y#95.2-98.2, 101.2, 125 Techno Medal Series #3	71.00	65.00
PS62	2006 (6)	4,000	Y#95.2-98.2, 101.2, 125 Mint Bureau Tokyo Fair/"The Dawn of Modern Japan"	71.00	150
PS57	2006 (6)	63,420	Y#95.2-98.2, 101.2, 125 Mint Bureau box with date plaquette	71.00	65.00
PS58	2006 (6)	8,700	Y#95.2-98.2, 101.2, 125 Mint Bureau Box without date plaquette	70.00	65.00
PS59	2006 (6)	35,000	Y#95.2-98.2, 101.2, 125 120th Anniversary of Cherry Blossom Viewing at the Mint	125	125
PS60	2006 (6)	46,000	Y#95.2-98.2, 101.2, 125 Australia-Japan Year of Exchange; includes Australian 1oz Silver coin KM#838	128	145

KM#	Date	Mintage	Identification	Issue Price	Mkt Val
PS61	2006 (6)	49,900	Y#95.2-98.2, 101.2, 125 50th Anniversary of Debut of Ishihara Yujiro (film actor)	125	120
PS63	2007 (6)	40,000	Y#95.2-98.2, 101.2, 125 20-yen Gold Coin Memorial	125	150
PS64	2007 (6)	53,200	Y#95.2-98.2, 101.2, 125 Mint Bureau box, with date plaquette	71.00	75.00
PS65	2007 (6)	7,000	Y#95.2-98.2, 101.2, 125 Mint Bureau box, without date plaquette	70.00	75.00
PS66	2007 (6)	35,000	Y#95.2-98.2, 101.2, 125 60th Anniversary of Resumption of Cherry Blossom Viewing (at the Mint)	125	125
PS67	2007 (6)	40,100	Y#95.2-98.2, 101.2, 125 Sakamoto Ryohma (pre-Meiji loyalist, assassinated 1867)	125	125
PS68	2007 (6)	33,500	Y#95.2-98.2, 101.2, 125 11th IAAF World Championships in Athletics, Osaka (plus silver medal)	125	125
PS69	2007 (6)	3,000	Y#95.2-98.2, 101.2, 125 Mint Bureau Tokyo Fair/50th anniversary of introduction of the 100-yen coin	71.00	75.00
PS70	2007 (6)	30,000	Y#95.2-98.2, 101.2, 125 Japan-New Zealand Friendship (with NZ KM#232 coin)	125	125
PSA39	2007 (6)	7,000	Y#95.2-98.2, 101.2, 125 Mint Bureau box, without date plaquette	66.00	100
PS71	2008 (6)	55,200	Y95.2-95.2, 101.2, 125 Mint Bureau box with date plaquette	75.00	75.00
PS72	2008 (6)	6,000	Y95.2-98.2, 101.2, 125 Mint Bureau box without date plaquette	73.50	75.00
PS73	2008 (6)	27,000	Y95.2-98.2, 101.2, 125 Cherry blossom viewing (at the mint)	130	130
PS74	2008 (6)	44,000	Y95.2-Y98.2, 101.2, 125 150th Anniversary of Japanese-French relations (with French 1.5 euro coin KM1550.)	130	130
PS75	2008 (6)	33,000	Y95.2-98.2, 101.2, 125 1300th Anniversary of the Wado Kaichin coin (with a silver replica)	100	100
PS76	2008 (6)	3,000	Y95.2-Y98.2, 101.2, 125 Mint Bureau Tokyo Fair - Japan Attractions	79.00	75.00
PS77	2009 (6)	60,000	Y95.2-Y98.2, 101.2, 125 Mint Bureau box with date plaquette	79.00	—
PS78	2009 (6)	5,600	Y95.2-Y98.2, 101.2, 125 Mint Bureau box without date plaquette	77.50	—
PS79	2009 (6)	25,000	Y95.2-Y98.2, 101.2, 125 Cherry blossom viewing (at the mint)	136	—
PS80	2009 (6)	25,000	Y95.2-Y98.2, 101.2, 125 80 years of Japan/Canada Amity (with $5 Canadian coin KM#1036 included)	136	—
PS81	2009 (6)	30,000	Y95.2-Y98.2, 101.2, 125 400 years of Japan/Dutch Commerce (with Dutch 5 coin, KM287 included)	136	—
PS82	2009 (6)	3,000	Y95.2-98.2, 101.2, 125 Mint Bureau Tokyo Fair/"Hallmark 80 years"	83.00	—
PS83	2010 (6)	—	Y95.2-98.2, 101.2, 125 Mint Bureau box, with date plaquette	—	—
PS84	2010 (6)	20,000	Y95.2-98.2, 101.2, 125 Cherry blossom viewing (at the Mint)	144	—
PS86	2010 (6)	20,000	Y95.2-98.2, 101.2, 125 Techno set, with medal included showing iridescent features (new mint technology)	111	—
PS87	2010 (6)	20,000	Y95.2-98.2, 101.2, 125 "A Dog of Flanders" set, with Belgian 20 KM#305 proof coin included	144	—

JERSEY

The Bailiwick of Jersey, a British Crown dependency located in the English Channel 12 miles (19 km.) west of Normandy, France, has an area of 45 sq. mi. (117 sq. km.) and a population of 74,000. Capital: St. Helier. The economy is based on agriculture and cattle breeding – the importation of cattle is prohibited to protect the purity of the island's world-famous strain of milk cows.

The island together with the Bailiwick of Guernsey, is the only part of the Dutchy of Normady belonging to the British Crown, has been a possession of Britain since the Norman conquest of 1066. Jersey is administered by its own laws and customs. Unless the island is mentioned specifically, acts passed by the British Parliament are not applicable to Jersey. During WW II, German troops occupied the island from 1940 to 1945.

RULER
British

BRITISH DEPENDENCY

DECIMAL COINAGE
100 New Pence = 1 Pound

KM# 103 PENNY
3.5600 g., Copper Plated Steel, 20.3 mm. **Ruler:** Elizabeth II **Obv:** Crowned head right **Rev:** Le Hoeq Watchtower, St. Clement **Edge:** Plain

Date	Mintage	F	VF	XF	Unc	BU
2002	1,520,000	—	—	0.15	0.65	—
2003	1,575,000	—	—	0.15	0.65	—
2005	—	—	—	0.15	0.65	—
2006	585,000	—	—	0.15	0.65	—
2008	4,800,000	—	—	0.15	0.65	—

KM# 104 2 PENCE
7.1200 g., Copper Plated Steel, 25.91 mm. **Ruler:** Elizabeth II **Obv:** Head with tiara right **Rev:** L'Hermitage, St. Helier **Edge:** Plain

Date	Mintage	F	VF	XF	Unc	BU
2002	1,259,000	—	—	0.20	0.65	—
2003	10,000	—	—	0.20	0.65	—
2005	400,000	—	—	0.20	0.65	—
2006	1,200,000	—	—	0.20	0.65	—
2008	2,459,000	—	—	0.20	0.65	—

KM# 105 5 PENCE
3.2500 g., Copper-Nickel, 18 mm. **Ruler:** Elizabeth II **Obv:** Head with tiara right **Rev:** Seymour Tower, Grouville, L'Avathigon **Edge:** Reeded

Date	Mintage	F	VF	XF	Unc	BU
2002	1,200,000	—	—	0.20	0.65	—
2003	1,005,000	—	—	0.20	0.65	—
2006	1,200,000	—	—	0.20	0.65	—
2008	3,600,000	—	—	0.20	0.65	—

KM# 106 10 PENCE
6.5000 g., Copper-Nickel, 24.5 mm. **Ruler:** Elizabeth II **Obv:** Head with tiara right **Rev:** La Hougne Bie, Faldouet, St. Martin

Date	Mintage	F	VF	XF	Unc	BU
2002	500,000	—	—	—	1.25	1.50
2003	10,000	—	—	—	1.25	1.50
2005	—	—	—	—	1.25	1.50

Date	Mintage	F	VF	XF	Unc	BU
2006	—	—	—	—	1.25	1.50
2007	630,000	—	—	—	1.25	1.50
2010	—	—	—	—	1.25	1.50

KM# 107 20 PENCE
5.0000 g., Copper-Nickel, 21.4 mm. **Ruler:** Elizabeth II **Obv:** Head with tiara right

Date	Mintage	F	VF	XF	Unc	BU
2002	975,500	—	—	—	1.00	1.25
2003	10,000	—	—	—	1.00	1.25
2005	500,000	—	—	—	1.00	1.25
2006	500,000	—	—	—	1.00	1.25
2007	780,000	—	—	—	1.00	1.25
2009	1,500,000	—	—	—	1.00	1.25

KM# 108 50 PENCE
8.0000 g., Copper-Nickel, 27.3 mm. **Ruler:** Elizabeth II **Obv:** Crowned bust right **Rev:** Gothic gate arch **Edge:** Plain

Date	Mintage	F	VF	XF	Unc	BU
2003	10,000	—	—	1.00	2.50	3.00
2005	200,000	—	—	1.00	2.50	3.00
2006	300,000	—	—	1.00	2.50	3.00
2009	480,000	—	—	1.00	2.50	3.00

KM# 123a 50 PENCE
8.0000 g., 0.9250 Silver 0.2379 oz. ASW, 27.3 mm. **Ruler:** Elizabeth II **Subject:** Coronation, 50th Anniversary **Obv:** Crowned head right **Rev:** Archbishop crowning Queen **Edge:** Plain **Shape:** 7-sided

Date	Mintage	F	VF	XF	Unc	BU
2003 Proof	15,000	Value: 25.00				

KM# 123 50 PENCE
8.0000 g., Copper-Nickel, 27.3 mm. **Ruler:** Elizabeth II **Subject:** Coronation, 50th Anniversary **Obv:** Crowned head right **Rev:** Archbishop crowning Queen **Edge:** Plain **Shape:** 7-sided

Date	Mintage	F	VF	XF	Unc	BU
2003	10,000	—	—	—	2.50	3.00

KM# 148 50 PENCE
8.0000 g., Copper-Nickel, 27.3 mm. **Ruler:** Elizabeth II **Subject:** Coronation, 50th Anniversary **Rev:** Regalia in quatrilobe **Shape:** 7-sided

Date	Mintage	F	VF	XF	Unc	BU
2003	—	—	—	—	2.50	3.50

KM# 148a 50 PENCE
8.0000 g., 0.9250 Silver 0.2379 oz. ASW, 27.3 mm. **Ruler:** Elizabeth II **Subject:** Coronation, 50th Anniversary **Rev:** Regalia in quatrilobe **Shape:** 7-sided

Date	Mintage	F	VF	XF	Unc	BU
2003 Proof	15,000	Value: 25.00				

KM# 149 50 PENCE
8.0000 g., Copper-Nickel, 27.3 mm. **Ruler:** Elizabeth II **Subject:** Coronation, 50th Anniversary **Rev:** Queen facing, seated on throne **Shape:** 7-sided

Date	Mintage	F	VF	XF	Unc	BU
2003	10,000	—	—	—	2.50	3.50

KM# 149a 50 PENCE
8.0000 g., 0.9250 Silver 0.2379 oz. ASW, 27.3 mm. **Ruler:** Elizabeth II **Subject:** Coronation, 50th Anniversary **Rev:** Queen facing, seated on throne **Shape:** 7-sided

Date	Mintage	F	VF	XF	Unc	BU
2003 Proof	15,000	Value: 25.00				

KM# 150 50 PENCE
8.0000 g., Copper-Nickel, 27.3 mm. **Ruler:** Elizabeth II **Subject:** Coronation, 50th Anniversary **Rev:** Crown, scepter and shield **Shape:** 7-sided

Date	Mintage	F	VF	XF	Unc	BU
2003	10,000	—	—	—	2.50	3.50

KM# 150a 50 PENCE
8.0000 g., 0.9250 Silver 0.2379 oz. ASW, 27.3 mm. **Ruler:** Elizabeth II **Subject:** Coronation, 50th Anniversary **Rev:** Crown, sceptre and shield **Shape:** 7-sided

Date	Mintage	F	VF	XF	Unc	BU
2003 Proof	15,000	Value: 25.00				

KM# 101 POUND
9.5000 g., Nickel-Brass, 22.5 mm. **Ruler:** Elizabeth II **Obv:** Head with tiara right **Rev:** Schooner, Resolute **Edge Lettering:** CAESAREA INSULA

Date	Mintage	F	VF	XF	Unc	BU
2003	10,000	—	—	—	4.00	4.50
2005	200,000	—	—	—	4.00	4.50
2006	93,000	—	—	—	4.00	4.50

KM# 160 POUND
1.2400 g., 0.9990 Gold 0.0398 oz. AGW, 13.92 mm. **Ruler:** Elizabeth II **Subject:** Trafalgar, 200th Anniversary

Date	Mintage	F	VF	XF	Unc	BU
2005 Proof	—	Value: 100				

KM# 173 POUND
1.2400 g., 0.9990 Gold 0.0398 oz. AGW, 13.92 mm. **Ruler:** Elizabeth II **Subject:** Princess Diana

Date	Mintage	F	VF	XF	Unc	BU
2007 Proof	—	Value: 100				

KM# 102 2 POUNDS
12.0000 g., Bi-Metallic Copper-Nickel center in Nickel-Brass ring, 28.4 mm. **Ruler:** Elizabeth II **Obv:** Head with tiara right **Rev:** Latent image value within circle of assorted shields **Edge Lettering:** CAESAREA INSULA

Date	Mintage	F	VF	XF	Unc	BU
2003	10,000	—	—	—	10.00	12.00
2006	3,500	—	—	—	10.00	12.00

KM# 111 5 POUNDS
28.2800 g., Copper-Nickel, 38.6 mm. **Ruler:** Elizabeth II **Subject:** Princess Diana **Obv:** Crowned head right **Rev:** Diana's cameo above people **Edge:** Reeded

Date	Mintage	F	VF	XF	Unc	BU
2002	—	—	—	—	13.50	15.00

KM# 111a 5 POUNDS
28.2800 g., 0.9250 Silver 0.8410 oz. ASW, 38.6 mm. **Ruler:** Elizabeth II **Subject:** Princess Diana **Obv:** Crowned head right **Rev:** Diana's cameo above people **Edge:** Reeded

Date	Mintage	F	VF	XF	Unc	BU
2002 Proof	20,000	Value: 45.00				

KM# 111b 5 POUNDS
39.9400 g., 0.9167 Gold 1.1771 oz. AGW, 38.6 mm. **Ruler:** Elizabeth II **Subject:** Princess Diana **Obv:** Crowned head right **Rev:** Diana's cameo above people **Edge:** Reeded

Date	Mintage	F	VF	XF	Unc	BU
2002 Proof	100	Value: 2,150				

KM# 113 5 POUNDS
28.2800 g., Copper-Nickel, 38.6 mm. **Ruler:** Elizabeth II **Subject:** Queen Mother **Obv:** Crowned head right **Rev:** Queen Mother's bust right (circa 1918) **Rev. Legend:** HER MAJESTY QUEEN ELIZABETH THE QUEEN MOTHER **Edge:** Reeded

Date	Mintage	F	VF	XF	Unc	BU
2002	—	—	—	—	13.50	15.00

KM# 113a 5 POUNDS
28.2800 g., 0.9250 Silver 0.8410 oz. ASW, 38.6 mm. **Ruler:** Elizabeth II **Subject:** Queen Mother **Obv:** Crowned head right **Rev:** Queen Mother's bust right, (circa 1918) **Rev. Legend:** HER MAJESTY QUEEN ELIZABETH THE QUEEN MOTHER **Edge:** Reeded

Date	Mintage	F	VF	XF	Unc	BU
2002 Proof	15,000	Value: 50.00				

KM# 113b 5 POUNDS
39.9400 g., 0.9166 Gold 1.1770 oz. AGW, 38.6 mm. **Ruler:** Elizabeth II **Subject:** Queen Mother **Obv:** Crowned head right **Rev:** Queen Mother's bust right, (circa 1918) **Rev. Legend:** HER MAJESTY QUEEN ELIZABETH THE QUEEN MOTHER **Edge:** Reeded

Date	Mintage	F	VF	XF	Unc	BU
2002 Proof	250	Value: 2,100				

KM# 115 5 POUNDS
28.2800 g., Copper-Nickel, 38.6 mm. **Ruler:** Elizabeth II **Subject:** Golden Jubilee **Obv:** Crowned head right **Rev:** Abbey procession scene **Edge:** Reeded

Date	Mintage	F	VF	XF	Unc	BU
2002	—	—	—	—	13.50	15.00

KM# 115a 5 POUNDS
28.2800 g., 0.9250 Silver 0.8410 oz. ASW, 38.6 mm. **Ruler:** Elizabeth II **Subject:** Golden Jubilee **Obv:** Crowned head right **Rev:** Abbey procession scene **Edge:** Reeded

Date	Mintage	F	VF	XF	Unc	BU
2002 Proof	20,000	Value: 50.00				

KM# 115b 5 POUNDS
39.9400 g., 0.9166 Gold 1.1770 oz. AGW, 38.6 mm. **Ruler:** Elizabeth II **Subject:** Golden Jubilee **Obv:** Crowned head right **Rev:** Abbey procession scene **Edge:** Reeded

Date	Mintage	F	VF	XF	Unc	BU
2002 Proof	100	Value: 2,150				

KM# 117 5 POUNDS
28.2800 g., Copper-Nickel, 38.6 mm. **Ruler:** Elizabeth II **Subject:** Duke of Wellington **Obv:** Crowned head right **Rev:** Wellington's portrait with multicolor infantry scene **Edge:** Reeded

Date	Mintage	F	VF	XF	Unc	BU
2002	—	—	—	—	13.50	15.00

KM# 117a 5 POUNDS
28.2800 g., 0.9250 Silver 0.8410 oz. ASW, 38.6 mm. **Ruler:** Elizabeth II **Subject:** Duke of Wellington **Obv:** Crowned head right **Rev:** Wellington's portrait with multicolor infantry scene **Edge:** Reeded

Date	Mintage	F	VF	XF	Unc	BU
2002 Proof	15,000	Value: 50.00				

KM# 117b 5 POUNDS
39.9400 g., 0.9166 Gold 1.1770 oz. AGW, 38.6 mm. **Ruler:** Elizabeth II **Subject:** Duke of Wellington **Obv:** Crowned head right **Rev:** Wellington's portrait with multicolor infantry scene **Edge:** Reeded

Date	Mintage	F	VF	XF	Unc	BU
2002 Proof	200	Value: 2,100				

KM# 119 5 POUNDS
28.2800 g., Copper-Nickel, 38.6 mm. **Ruler:** Elizabeth II **Subject:** Golden Jubilee **Obv:** Crowned head right **Rev:** Honor guard and memorial **Edge:** Reeded

Date	Mintage	F	VF	XF	Unc	BU
2003	—	—	—	—	13.50	15.00

KM# 119a 5 POUNDS
28.2800 g., 0.9250 Silver 0.8410 oz. ASW, 38.6 mm. **Ruler:** Elizabeth II **Subject:** Golden Jubilee **Obv:** Crowned head right **Rev:** Honor guard and monument **Edge:** Reeded

Date	Mintage	F	VF	XF	Unc	BU
2003 Proof	20,000	Value: 50.00				

KM# 119b 5 POUNDS
39.9400 g., 0.9166 Gold 1.1770 oz. AGW, 38.6 mm. **Ruler:** Elizabeth II **Subject:** Golden Jubilee **Obv:** Crowned head right **Rev:** Honor guard and monument **Edge:** Reeded

Date	Mintage	F	VF	XF	Unc	BU
2003 Proof	250	Value: 2,100				

KM# 121 5 POUNDS
28.2800 g., Copper-Nickel, 38.6 mm. **Ruler:** Elizabeth II **Obv:** Crowned head right **Rev:** Bust of Prince William facing and crowned arms with supporters **Edge:** Reeded

Date	Mintage	F	VF	XF	Unc	BU
2003	—	—	—	—	16.50	18.00

KM# 121a 5 POUNDS
28.2800 g., 0.9250 Silver 0.8410 oz. ASW, 38.6 mm. **Ruler:**
Elizabeth II **Obv:** Crowned head right **Rev:** Bust of Prince William
facing and crowned arms with supporters **Edge:** Reeded

Date	Mintage	F	VF	XF	Unc	BU
2003 Proof	5,000	Value: 47.50				

KM# 121b 5 POUNDS
39.9400 g., 0.9166 Gold 1.1770 oz. AGW, 38.6 mm. **Ruler:**
Elizabeth II **Obv:** Crowned head right **Rev:** Bust of Prince William
facing and crowned arms with supporters **Edge:** Reeded

Date	Mintage	F	VF	XF	Unc	BU
2003 Proof	200	Value: 2,100				

KM# 130 5 POUNDS
28.2800 g., 0.9250 Silver 0.8410 oz. ASW, 38.6 mm. **Ruler:**
Elizabeth II **Subject:** Drake **Obv:** Crowned head right **Rev:** Naval
leader Sir Francis Drake

Date	Mintage	F	VF	XF	Unc	BU
2003 Proof	—	Value: 75.00				

KM# 131 5 POUNDS
28.2800 g., 0.9250 Silver 0.8410 oz. ASW, 38.6 mm. **Ruler:**
Elizabeth II **Subject:** Sovereign Of The Seas **Obv:** Crowned
head right **Rev:** The Sovereign of the Seas ship

Date	Mintage	F	VF	XF	Unc	BU
2003 Proof	—	Value: 75.00				

KM# 132 5 POUNDS
28.2800 g., 0.9250 Silver 0.8410 oz. ASW, 38.6 mm. **Ruler:**
Elizabeth II **Subject:** John Fisher **Obv:** Crowned head right **Rev:**
WWI Naval leader Sir John Fisher

Date	Mintage	F	VF	XF	Unc	BU
2003 Proof	—	Value: 75.00				

KM# 133 5 POUNDS
28.2800 g., 0.9250 Silver 0.8410 oz. ASW, 38.6 mm. **Ruler:**
Elizabeth II **Subject:** HMS Victory **Obv:** Crowned head right **Rev:**
Nelson's flag ship HMS Victory, multicolor flag at top

Date	Mintage	F	VF	XF	Unc	BU
2004 Proof	—	Value: 75.00				

KM# 134 5 POUNDS
28.2800 g., 0.9250 Silver 0.8410 oz. ASW, 38.6 mm. **Ruler:**
Elizabeth II **Subject:** Cunningham **Obv:** Crowned head right
Rev: WWII Admiral Andrew B. Cunningham

Date	Mintage	F	VF	XF	Unc	BU
2003 Proof	—	Value: 75.00				

KM# 135 5 POUNDS
28.2800 g., 0.9250 Silver 0.8410 oz. ASW, 38.6 mm. **Ruler:**
Elizabeth II **Subject:** Conqueror **Obv:** Crowned head right **Rev:**
Submarine HMS Conqueror

Date	Mintage	F	VF	XF	Unc	BU
2003 Proof	—	Value: 75.00				

KM# 144 5 POUNDS
28.2800 g., Copper-Nickel, 38.6 mm. **Ruler:** Elizabeth II
Subject: Royal Navy

Date	Mintage	F	VF	XF	Unc	BU
2003	—	—	—	—	—	15.00

KM# 144a 5 POUNDS
28.2800 g., 0.9250 Silver 0.8410 oz. ASW, 38.61 mm. **Ruler:**
Elizabeth II **Subject:** History of the Royal Navy **Obv:** Head left
with tiarra **Obv. Legend:** ELIZABETH II BALIWICK - OF JERSEY
Rev: Five heads of King Alfred the Great, Sir Francis Drake,
Admirals Horatio Nelson, John Fisher and John Woodward at
five ships, colored flag at top **Edge:** Reeded

Date	Mintage	F	VF	XF	Unc	BU
2003 Proof	—	Value: 75.00				

KM# 139 5 POUNDS
28.2800 g., 0.9250 Silver 0.8410 oz. ASW, 38.6 mm. **Ruler:**
Elizabeth II **Subject:** Driver and Fireman **Obv:** Crowned head
right **Rev:** Familiar image from the Golden Age of Steam: the
driver and fireman

Date	Mintage	F	VF	XF	Unc	BU
2004 Proof	—	Value: 75.00				

KM# 124 5 POUNDS
28.2800 g., Copper-Nickel, 38.6 mm. **Ruler:** Elizabeth II **Obv:**
Crowned head right **Rev:** British Horsa gliders in flight **Edge:**
Reeded **Note:** D-Day

Date	Mintage	F	VF	XF	Unc	BU
2004	—	—	—	—	15.00	17.00

KM# 124a 5 POUNDS
28.2800 g., 0.9250 Silver 0.8410 oz. ASW, 38.6 mm. **Ruler:**
Elizabeth II **Obv:** Crowned head right **Rev:** British Horsa gliders
in flight

Date	Mintage	F	VF	XF	Unc	BU
2004 Proof	10,000	Value: 85.00				

KM# 124b 5 POUNDS
39.9400 g., 0.9167 Gold 1.1771 oz. AGW, 38.6 mm. **Ruler:**
Elizabeth II **Obv:** Crowned head right **Rev:** British Horsa gliders
in flight

Date	Mintage	F	VF	XF	Unc	BU
2004 Proof	500	Value: 2,100				

KM# 126 5 POUNDS
28.2800 g., Copper-Nickel, 38.6 mm. **Ruler:** Elizabeth II
Subject: 150th Anniversary of the Crimean War **Obv:** Crowned
head right **Rev:** Charge of the Light Brigade scene with one blue
uniform behind the Earl of Cardigan **Edge:** Reeded

Date	Mintage	F	VF	XF	Unc	BU
2004 plain	—	—	—	—	25.00	27.50

KM# 126a 5 POUNDS
28.2800 g., 0.9250 Silver 0.8410 oz. ASW, 38.6 mm. **Ruler:**
Elizabeth II **Obv:** Crowned head right **Rev:** Charge of the Light
Brigade scene with one blue uniform behind the Earl of Cardigan
Edge: Reeded

Date	Mintage	F	VF	XF	Unc	BU
2004 Proof	10,000	Value: 85.00				

KM# 126b 5 POUNDS
39.9400 g., 0.9166 Gold 1.1770 oz. AGW, 38.6 mm. **Ruler:**
Elizabeth II **Obv:** Crowned head right **Rev:** Charge of the Light
Brigade scene with one blue uniform behind the Earl of Cardigan
Edge: Reeded

Date	Mintage	F	VF	XF	Unc	BU
2004 Proof	500	Value: 2,100				

KM# 136 5 POUNDS
28.2800 g., 0.9250 Silver 0.8410 oz. ASW, 38.6 mm. **Ruler:**
Elizabeth II **Subject:** Coronation **Obv:** Crowned head right **Rev:**
The Pacific Class Coronation

Date	Mintage	F	VF	XF	Unc	BU
2004 Proof	—	Value: 75.00				

KM# 137 5 POUNDS
28.2800 g., 0.9250 Silver 0.8410 oz. ASW, 38.6 mm. **Ruler:**
Elizabeth II **Subject:** Flying Scotsman **Obv:** Crowned head right
Rev: Famous Flying Scotsman Locomotive, designed by Sir Nigel
Gresley

Date	Mintage	F	VF	XF	Unc	BU
2004 Proof	—	Value: 75.00				

KM# 138 5 POUNDS
28.2800 g., 0.9250 Silver 0.8410 oz. ASW, 38.6 mm. **Ruler:**
Elizabeth II **Subject:** Golden Arrow **Obv:** Crowned head right
Rev: The Golden Arrow, which ran from London to Dover en route
to Paris

Date	Mintage	F	VF	XF	Unc	BU
2004 Proof	—	Value: 75.00				

KM# 140 5 POUNDS
28.2800 g., 0.9250 Silver 0.8410 oz. ASW, 38.6 mm. **Ruler:**
Elizabeth II **Subject:** Tunnel **Obv:** Crowned head right **Rev:**
Familiar image from the Golden Age of Steam: A locomotive
steaming out of a tunnel

Date	Mintage	F	VF	XF	Unc	BU
2004	—	Value: 75.00				

KM# 141 5 POUNDS
28.2800 g., 0.9250 Silver 0.8410 oz. ASW, 38.6 mm. **Ruler:**
Elizabeth II **Subject:** Evening Star **Obv:** Crowned head right
Rev: The Evening Star - representing the last British Rail Steam
Locomotive

Date	Mintage	F	VF	XF	Unc	BU
2004 Proof	—	Value: 75.00				

KM# 127 5 POUNDS
Copper-Nickel **Ruler:** Elizabeth II **Subject:** Battle of Trafalgar
Obv: Crowned head right

Date	Mintage	F	VF	XF	Unc	BU
2005	—	—	—	—	7.50	10.00

KM# 127a 5 POUNDS
28.2800 g., 0.9250 Silver 0.8410 oz. ASW, 38.6 mm. **Ruler:**
Elizabeth II **Subject:** Nelson Trafalger **Obv:** Crowned head right
Rev: 200th Anniversary of the Battle of Trafalgar, image of Nelson
with a gilded ship in the background

Date	Mintage	F	VF	XF	Unc	BU
2005 Proof	—	Value: 75.00				

KM# 128 5 POUNDS
Copper-Nickel **Ruler:** Elizabeth II **Subject:** 60th Anniversary -
End of WW II **Obv:** Crowned head right **Rev:** Big Ben Tower

Date	Mintage	F	VF	XF	Unc	BU
2005	—	—	—	—	7.50	10.00

KM# 128a 5 POUNDS
28.2800 g., 0.9250 Silver 0.8410 oz. ASW, 38.6 mm. **Ruler:**
Elizabeth II **Subject:** WWII Liberation **Obv:** Crowned head right
Rev: Big Ben Tower **Edge:** Reeded

Date	Mintage	F	VF	XF	Unc	BU
2005 Proof	5,000	Value: 85.00				

KM# 128b 5 POUNDS
39.9400 g., 0.9167 Gold 1.1771 oz. AGW, 38.6 mm. **Ruler:**
Elizabeth II **Subject:** WWII Liberation **Obv:** Crowned head right
Rev: Big Ben Tower **Edge:** Reeded

Date	Mintage	F	VF	XF	Unc	BU
2005 Proof	150	Value: 2,150				

KM# 129 5 POUNDS
Copper-Nickel **Ruler:** Elizabeth II **Subject:** WW II Liberation
Obv: Crowned head right **Rev:** Returning evacuees **Edge:**
Reeded

Date	Mintage	F	VF	XF	Unc	BU
2005	—	—	—	—	7.50	10.00

KM# 129a 5 POUNDS
39.9400 g., 0.9167 Gold 1.1771 oz. AGW, 38.6 mm. **Ruler:**
Elizabeth II **Subject:** WWII Liberation **Obv:** Crowned head right
Rev: Returning evacuees **Edge:** Reeded

Date	Mintage	F	VF	XF	Unc	BU
2005 Proof	150	Value: 2,150				

KM# 164 5 POUNDS
28.2800 g., 0.9250 Silver 0.8410 oz. ASW, 38.61 mm. **Ruler:**
Elizabeth II **Subject:** Charles Robert Darwin

Date	Mintage	F	VF	XF	Unc	BU
2005 Proof	Est. 25,000	Value: 60.00				

KM# 142 5 POUNDS

28.2800 g., 0.9250 Silver 0.8410 oz. ASW, 38.6 mm. **Ruler:** Elizabeth II **Subject:** Queen's 80th Birthday **Obv:** Head with tiara right - gilt **Obv. Legend:** ELIZABETH II BAILIWICK - OF JERSEY **Rev:** Queen horseback facing

Date	Mintage	F	VF	XF	Unc	BU
2006 Proof	—	Value: 45.00				

KM# 142a 5 POUNDS

28.2800 g., 0.9250 Silver partially gilt 0.8410 oz. ASW, 38.6 mm. **Ruler:** Elizabeth II **Subject:** Elizabeth II's 80th Birthday **Obv:** Head with tiara right **Obv. Legend:** ELIZABETH II BAILIWICK - OF JERSEY **Rev:** Queen on horseback **Edge:** Reeded

Date	Mintage	F	VF	XF	Unc	BU
2006 Proof	—	Value: 45.00				

KM# 145 5 POUNDS

28.2800 g., Copper-Nickel, 38.61 mm. **Ruler:** Elizabeth II **Subject:** Elizabeth II's 80th Birthday **Rev:** Bobby Moore and Wembley's Royal Box

Date	Mintage	F	VF	XF	Unc	BU
2006	—	—	—	—	—	15.00

KM# 145a 5 POUNDS

28.2800 g., 0.9250 Silver 0.8410 oz. ASW, 38.61 mm. **Ruler:** Elizabeth II **Subject:** Elizabeth II, 80th Birthday **Rev:** Bobby Moor and Wembley's Royal Box

Date	Mintage	F	VF	XF	Unc	BU
2006 Proof	—	Value: 60.00				

KM# 163 5 POUNDS

28.2800 g., 0.9250 Silver 0.8410 oz. ASW **Ruler:** Elizabeth II **Subject:** Sir Winston Churchill

Date	Mintage	F	VF	XF	Unc	BU
2006 Proof	Est. 25,000	Value: 60.00				

KM# 165 5 POUNDS

28.2800 g., 0.9250 Silver 0.8410 oz. ASW, 38.61 mm. **Ruler:** Elizabeth II **Subject:** Robert (Bobby) Moore, soccer player

Date	Mintage	F	VF	XF	Unc	BU
2006 Proof	Est. 25,000	Value: 60.00				

KM# 166 5 POUNDS

28.2800 g., 0.9250 Silver 0.8410 oz. ASW, 38.61 mm. **Ruler:** Elizabeth II **Subject:** Florence Nightingale

Date	Mintage	F	VF	XF	Unc	BU
2006 Proof	25,000	Value: 60.00				

KM# 167 5 POUNDS

28.2800 g., Copper-Nickel, 38.61 mm. **Ruler:** Elizabeth II **Subject:** Guy Penrose Gibson, Victoria Cross

Date	Mintage	F	VF	XF	Unc	BU
2006	—	—	—	—	—	15.00

KM# 167a 5 POUNDS

28.2800 g., 0.9250 Silver 0.8410 oz. ASW, 38.61 mm. **Ruler:** Elizabeth II **Subject:** Guy Penrose Gibson, Victoria Cross

Date	Mintage	F	VF	XF	Unc	BU
2006 Proof	Est. 30,000	Value: 50.00				

KM# 168 5 POUNDS

28.2800 g., 0.9250 Silver 0.8410 oz. ASW, 38.61 mm. **Ruler:** Elizabeth II **Subject:** Nicholson

Date	Mintage	F	VF	XF	Unc	BU
2006 Proof	—	Value: 50.00				

KM# 169 5 POUNDS

28.2800 g., 0.9250 Silver 0.8410 oz. ASW, 38.61 mm. **Ruler:** Elizabeth II **Subject:** Hook, Char and Bro

Date	Mintage	F	VF	XF	Unc	BU
2006 Proof	—	Value: 50.00				

KM# 170 5 POUNDS

28.2800 g., 0.9250 Silver 0.8410 oz. ASW, 38.61 mm. **Ruler:** Elizabeth II **Subject:** First Lanc Fusiliers

Date	Mintage	F	VF	XF	Unc	BU
2006 Proof	—	Value: 50.00				

KM# 171 5 POUNDS

28.2800 g., 0.9250 Silver 0.8410 oz. ASW, 38.61 mm. **Ruler:** Elizabeth II **Subject:** Noel Godfrey Chavasse

Date	Mintage	F	VF	XF	Unc	BU
2006 Proof	—	Value: 50.00				

KM# 172 5 POUNDS

28.2800 g., 0.9250 Silver 0.8410 oz. ASW, 38.61 mm. **Ruler:** Elizabeth II **Subject:** David MacKay

Date	Mintage	F	VF	XF	Unc	BU
2006 Proof	—	Value: 50.00				

KM# 174 5 POUNDS

28.2800 g., 0.9250 Silver 0.8410 oz. ASW, 38.61 mm. **Ruler:** Elizabeth II **Subject:** Elizabeth, the Queen Mother

Date	Mintage	F	VF	XF	Unc	BU
2007 Proof	Est. 2,500	Value: 60.00				

KM# 175 5 POUNDS

28.2800 g., 0.9250 Silver 0.8410 oz. ASW, 38.61 mm. **Ruler:** Elizabeth II **Subject:** Henry VIII

Date	Mintage	F	VF	XF	Unc	BU
2007 Proof	Est. 25,000	Value: 60.00				

KM# 176 5 POUNDS

28.2800 g., 0.9250 Silver 0.8410 oz. ASW, 38.61 mm. **Ruler:** Elizabeth II **Subject:** Diana, Princess of Wales

Date	Mintage	F	VF	XF	Unc	BU
2007 Proof	Est. 25,000	Value: 60.00				

KM# 177 5 POUNDS

28.2800 g., 0.9250 Silver 0.8410 oz. ASW, 38.61 mm. **Ruler:** Elizabeth II **Subject:** Christopher Wren

Date	Mintage	F	VF	XF	Unc	BU
2007 Proof	Est. 25,000	Value: 60.00				

KM# 178 5 POUNDS

28.2800 g., Copper-Nickel, 38.61 mm. **Ruler:** Elizabeth II **Subject:** Elizabeth II and Prince Philip, 60th Wedding Anniversary **Rev:** Elizabeth and Philip, 1947

Date	Mintage	F	VF	XF	Unc	BU
2007	—	—	—	—	—	15.00

KM# 178a 5 POUNDS

28.2800 g., 0.9250 Silver 0.8410 oz. ASW, 38.61 mm. **Ruler:** Elizabeth II **Subject:** Elizabeth II and Prince Philip, 60th Wedding Anniversary **Rev:** Elizabeth and Philip, 1947

Date	Mintage	F	VF	XF	Unc	BU
2007 Proof	—	Value: 60.00				

KM# 179 5 POUNDS

28.2800 g., Copper-Nickel, 38.61 mm. **Ruler:** Elizabeth II **Subject:** Elizabeth II and Prince Philip, 60th Wedding Anniversary **Rev:** Westminster Abbey

Date	Mintage	F	VF	XF	Unc	BU
2007	—	—	—	—	—	15.00

KM# 179a 5 POUNDS

28.2800 g., Silver, 38.61 mm. **Ruler:** Elizabeth II **Subject:** Elizabeth II and Prince Philip, 60th Wedding Anniversary **Rev:** Westminster Abbey

Date	Mintage	F	VF	XF	Unc	BU
2007 Proof	—	Value: 60.00				

KM# 180 5 POUNDS

28.2800 g., 0.9250 Copper-Nickel 0.8410 oz., 38.61 mm. **Ruler:** Elizabeth II **Subject:** Elizabeth II and Prince Philip, 60th Wedding Anniversary **Rev:** Wedding cake

Date	Mintage	F	VF	XF	Unc	BU
2007	—	—	—	—	—	15.00

KM# 180a 5 POUNDS

28.2800 g., 0.9250 Silver 0.8410 oz. ASW, 38.61 mm. **Ruler:** Elizabeth II **Subject:** Elizabeth II and Prince Philip, 60th Wedding Anniversary **Rev:** Wedding cake

Date	Mintage	F	VF	XF	Unc	BU
2007 Proof	—	Value: 60.00				

KM# 181 5 POUNDS

28.2800 g., Copper-Nickel, 38.61 mm. **Ruler:** Elizabeth II **Subject:** Elizabeth II and Prince Philip, 60th Wedding Anniversary **Rev:** Elizabeth and Prince Philip, 2007

Date	Mintage	F	VF	XF	Unc	BU
2007	—	—	—	—	—	15.00

KM# 181a 5 POUNDS

28.2800 g., 0.9250 Silver 0.8410 oz. ASW, 38.61 mm. **Ruler:** Elizabeth II **Subject:** Elizabeth II and Prince Philip, 60th Wedding Anniversary **Rev:** Elizabeth and Philip, 2007

Date	Mintage	F	VF	XF	Unc	BU
2007 Proof	—	Value: 60.00				

KM# 182 5 POUNDS

28.2800 g., Copper-Nickel, 38.61 mm. **Ruler:** Elizabeth II **Subject:** Royal Air Force **Rev:** Barnes Wallis, Roy Chadwick, Guy Penrose Gibson

Date	Mintage	F	VF	XF	Unc	BU
2008	—	—	—	—	—	15.00

KM# 182a 5 POUNDS

26.0000 g., Brass, 38.61 mm. **Ruler:** Elizabeth II **Subject:** Royal Air Force **Rev:** Barnes Wallis, Roy Chadwick, Guy Penrose Gibson

Date	Mintage	F	VF	XF	Unc	BU
2008 Proof	Est. 25,000	Value: 30.00				

KM# 182b 5 POUNDS

28.2800 g., 0.9250 Silver 0.8410 oz. ASW, 38.61 mm. **Ruler:** Elizabeth II **Subject:** Royal Air Force **Rev:** Barnes Wallis, Roy Chadwick, Guy Penrose Gibson

Date	Mintage	F	VF	XF	Unc	BU
2008 Proof	Est. 25,000	Value: 60.00				

KM# 183 5 POUNDS

28.2800 g., Copper-Nickel, 38.61 mm. **Ruler:** Elizabeth II **Subject:** Royal Air Force **Rev:** Reginald Joseph Mitchell, Spitfire

Date	Mintage	F	VF	XF	Unc	BU
2008	—	—	—	—	—	15.00

KM# 183a 5 POUNDS

28.2800 g., 0.9250 Silver 0.8410 oz. ASW, 38.61 mm. **Ruler:** Elizabeth II **Subject:** Royal Air Force **Rev:** Reginald Joseph Mitchell, Spitfire

Date	Mintage	F	VF	XF	Unc	BU
2008 Proof	—	Value: 60.00				

KM# 184 5 POUNDS

28.2800 g., Copper-Nickel, 38.61 mm. **Ruler:** Elizabeth II **Subject:** Royal Air Force **Rev:** Battle of Britain

Date	Mintage	F	VF	XF	Unc	BU
2008	—	—	—	—	—	15.00

KM# 185 5 POUNDS

28.2800 g., Copper-Nickel, 38.61 mm. **Ruler:** Elizabeth II **Subject:** Royal Air Force **Rev:** Frank Whittle

Date	Mintage	F	VF	XF	Unc	BU
2008	—	—	—	—	—	15.00

KM# 186 5 POUNDS

28.2800 g., Copper-Nickel, 38.61 mm. **Ruler:** Elizabeth II **Subject:** Royal Air Force **Rev:** Hugh Trenchard, founder of the British Air Force

Date	Mintage	F	VF	XF	Unc	BU
2008	—	—	—	—	—	15.00

KM# 186a 5 POUNDS

28.2800 g., 0.9250 Silver 0.8410 oz. ASW, 38.61 mm. **Ruler:** Elizabeth II **Subject:** Royal Air Force **Rev:** Hugh Trenchard, founder of the British Air Force

Date	Mintage	F	VF	XF	Unc	BU
2008 Proof	—	Value: 60.00				

KM# 187 5 POUNDS

28.2800 g., Copper-Nickel, 38.61 mm. **Ruler:** Elizabeth II **Subject:** British Air Force

Date	Mintage	F	VF	XF	Unc	BU
2008	—	—	—	—	—	15.00

KM# 188 5 POUNDS

28.2800 g., Copper-Nickel, 38.61 mm. **Ruler:** Elizabeth II **Subject:** Royal Air Force

Date	Mintage	F	VF	XF	Unc	BU
2008	—	—	—	—	—	15.00

KM# 189 5 POUNDS

28.2800 g., Copper-Nickel, 38.61 mm. **Ruler:** Elizabeth II **Subject:** Royal Air Force

Date	Mintage	F	VF	XF	Unc	BU
2008	—	—	—	—	—	15.00

KM# 190 5 POUNDS

28.2800 g., Copper-Nickel, 38.61 mm. **Ruler:** Elizabeth II **Subject:** Royal Air Force

Date	Mintage	F	VF	XF	Unc	BU
2008	—	—	—	—	—	15.00

KM# 191 5 POUNDS

28.2800 g., Copper-Nickel, 38.61 mm. **Ruler:** Elizabeth II **Subject:** Royal Air Force

Date	Mintage	F	VF	XF	Unc	BU
2008	—	—	—	—	—	15.00

KM# 193.1 5 POUNDS

Copper-Nickel, 38.61 mm. **Ruler:** Elizabeth II **Subject:** End of World War I **Obv:** Head in tiara right **Rev:** Sundial motif **Shape:** 8

Date	Mintage	F	VF	XF	Unc	BU
2008	—	—	—	—	—	18.00

KM# 193.2 5 POUNDS

Copper-Nickel, 38.61 mm. **Ruler:** Elizabeth II **Subject:** End of World War I **Obv:** Head in tiara right **Rev:** Sundial motif in color **Shape:** Number 8

Date	Mintage	F	VF	XF	Unc	BU
2008	—	—	—	—	—	25.00

KM# 193a 5 POUNDS

28.0000 g., 0.9250 Silver 0.8327 oz. ASW, 38.61 mm. **Ruler:** Elizabeth II **Subject:** End of World War I **Obv:** Head with tiara right **Rev:** Sundial motif **Shape:** Number 8

Date	Mintage	F	VF	XF	Unc	BU
2008 Proof	9,500	Value: 60.00				

KM# 193b 5 POUNDS

28.0000 g., 0.9160 Gold 0.8246 oz. AGW, 38.61 mm. **Ruler:** Elizabeth II **Subject:** End of World War I **Obv:** Head with tiara right **Rev:** Sundial motif **Shape:** Numeral 8

Date	Mintage	F	VF	XF	Unc	BU
2008 Proof	Est. 450	Value: 1,500				

KM# 194 5 POUNDS

Silver **Ruler:** Elizabeth II **Rev:** St. George slaying the dragon

Date	Mintage	F	VF	XF	Unc	BU
2008	—	—	—	—	—	—

KM# 146 5 POUNDS

28.2800 g., 0.9250 Silver 0.8410 oz. ASW, 38.6 mm. **Ruler:** Elizabeth II **Subject:** Battle of Agincourt, 1415 **Obv:** Head right **Rev:** Archers and horsemen

Date	Mintage	F	VF	XF	Unc	BU
2009 Proof	2,500	Value: 55.00				

KM# 147 5 POUNDS

155.5000 g., 0.9250 Silver partially gilt 4.6243 oz. ASW, 65 mm. **Ruler:** Elizabeth II **Obv:** Head right **Rev:** St. George slaying dragon, partially gilt

Date	Mintage	F	VF	XF	Unc	BU
2009 Proof	450	Value: 350				

KM# 195 5 POUNDS

28.2800 g., Copper-Nickel, 38.61 mm. **Ruler:** Elizabeth II **Subject:** Henry VIII, 500th Anniversary of reign

Date	Mintage	F	VF	XF	Unc	BU
2009	—	—	—	—	—	15.00

KM# 195a 5 POUNDS

28.2800 g., 0.9250 Silver 0.8410 oz. ASW, 38.61 mm. **Ruler:** Elizabeth II **Subject:** Henry VIII, 500th Anniversary of reign

Date	Mintage	F	VF	XF	Unc	BU
2009 Proof	—	Value: 60.00				

KM# 195b   5 POUNDS
39.9400 g., 0.9160 Gold 1.1762 oz. AGW, 38.91 mm. **Ruler:** Elizabeth II **Subject:** Henry VIII, 500th Anniversary of reign

Date	Mintage	F	VF	XF	Unc	BU
2009 Proof	—	Value: 2,150				

KM# 197   5 POUNDS
28.2800 g., 0.9250 Silver 0.8410 oz. ASW, 38.61 mm. **Ruler:** Elizabeth II **Subject:** British Battles - Agincourt

Date	Mintage	F	VF	XF	Unc	BU
2009 Proof	25,000	Value: 60.00				

KM# 198   5 POUNDS
28.2800 g., 0.9250 Silver 0.8410 oz. ASW, 38.61 mm. **Ruler:** Elizabeth II **Subject:** British Battles - Somme

Date	Mintage	F	VF	XF	Unc	BU
2009 Proof	Est. 25,000	Value: 60.00				

KM# 199   5 POUNDS
28.2800 g., 0.9250 Silver 0.8410 oz. ASW, 38.61 mm. **Ruler:** Elizabeth II **Subject:** British Battles - Normandie

Date	Mintage	F	VF	XF	Unc	BU
2009 Proof	Est. 25,000	Value: 60.00				

KM# 200   5 POUNDS
28.2800 g., 0.9250 Silver 0.8410 oz. ASW, 38.61 mm. **Ruler:** Elizabeth II **Subject:** British Battles - El Alamein

Date	Mintage	F	VF	XF	Unc	BU
2009 Proof	Est. 25,000	Value: 60.00				

KM# 201   5 POUNDS
28.2800 g., 0.9250 Silver 0.8410 oz. ASW, 38.61 mm. **Ruler:** Elizabeth II **Subject:** British Battles - Hastings

Date	Mintage	F	VF	XF	Unc	BU
2009 Proof	Est. 25,000	Value: 60.00				

KM# 202   5 POUNDS
28.2800 g., 0.9250 Silver 0.8410 oz. ASW, 38.61 mm. **Ruler:** Elizabeth II **Subject:** British Battles - Bosworth

Date	Mintage	F	VF	XF	Unc	BU
2009 Proof	Est. 25,000	Value: 60.00				

KM# 203   5 POUNDS
28.2800 g., 0.9250 Silver 0.8410 oz. ASW, 38.61 mm. **Ruler:** Elizabeth II **Subject:** British Battles - Naseby

Date	Mintage	F	VF	XF	Unc	BU
2009 Proof	Est. 25,000	Value: 60.00				

KM# 204   5 POUNDS
28.2800 g., 0.9250 Silver 0.8410 oz. ASW, 38.61 mm. **Ruler:** Elizabeth II **Subject:** British Battles - Culloden

Date	Mintage	F	VF	XF	Unc	BU
2009 Proof	Est. 25,000	Value: 60.00				

KM# 205   5 POUNDS
28.2800 g., 0.9250 Silver 0.8410 oz. ASW, 38.61 mm. **Ruler:** Elizabeth II **Subject:** British Battles - Waterloo

Date	Mintage	F	VF	XF	Unc	BU
2009 Proof	Est. 25,000	Value: 60.00				

KM# 206   5 POUNDS
28.2800 g., 0.9250 Silver 0.8410 oz. ASW, 38.61 mm. **Ruler:** Elizabeth II **Subject:** British Battles - Alma

Date	Mintage	F	VF	XF	Unc	BU
2009 Proof	Est. 25,000	Value: 60.00				

KM# 207   5 POUNDS
28.2800 g., 0.9250 Silver 0.8410 oz. ASW, 38.61 mm. **Ruler:** Elizabeth II **Subject:** British Battles - Rorkes Drift

Date	Mintage	F	VF	XF	Unc	BU
2009 Proof	Est. 25,000	Value: 60.00				

KM# 208   5 POUNDS
28.2800 g., 0.9250 Silver 0.8410 oz. ASW, 38.61 mm. **Ruler:** Elizabeth II **Subject:** British Battles - Mafeking

Date	Mintage	F	VF	XF	Unc	BU
2009 Proof	Est. 25,000	Value: 60.00				

KM# 211a   5 POUNDS
28.2800 g., 0.9250 Silver 0.8410 oz. ASW, 38.61 mm. **Ruler:** Elizabeth II **Subject:** James Cook

Date	Mintage	F	VF	XF	Unc	BU
2009 Proof	—	Value: 60.00				

KM# 212   5 POUNDS
28.2800 g., Copper-Nickel, 38.61 mm. **Ruler:** Elizabeth II **Subject:** Robert F. Scott

Date	Mintage	F	VF	XF	Unc	BU
2009	—	—	—	—	—	15.00

KM# 211   5 POUNDS
28.2800 g., Copper-Nickel, 38.61 mm. **Ruler:** Elizabeth II **Subject:** James Cook

Date	Mintage	F	VF	XF	Unc	BU
2009	—	—	—	—	—	15.00

KM# 212a   5 POUNDS
28.2800 g., 0.9250 Silver 0.8410 oz. ASW, 38.61 mm. **Ruler:** Elizabeth II **Subject:** Robert F. Scott

Date	Mintage	F	VF	XF	Unc	BU
2009 Proof	—	Value: 60.00				

KM# 213   5 POUNDS
28.2800 g., Copper-Nickel, 38.61 mm. **Ruler:** Elizabeth II **Subject:** Naval Airforce

Date	Mintage	F	VF	XF	Unc	BU
2009	—	—	—	—	—	15.00

KM# 213a   5 POUNDS
28.2800 g., 0.9250 Silver 0.8410 oz. ASW, 38.61 mm. **Ruler:** Elizabeth II **Subject:** Naval Airforce

Date	Mintage	F	VF	XF	Unc	BU
2009 Proof	—	Value: 60.00				

KM# 214   5 POUNDS
28.2800 g., Copper-Nickel, 38.61 mm. **Ruler:** Elizabeth II **Subject:** Falkland War

Date	Mintage	F	VF	XF	Unc	BU
2009	—	—	—	—	—	15.00

KM# 214a   5 POUNDS
28.2800 g., 0.9250 Copper-Nickel 0.8410 oz., 38.61 mm. **Ruler:** Elizabeth II **Subject:** Falkland War

Date	Mintage	F	VF	XF	Unc	BU
2009 Proof	—	Value: 60.00				

KM# 215   5 POUNDS
28.2800 g., Copper-Nickel, 38.61 mm. **Ruler:** Elizabeth II **Subject:** H.M.S. Ark Royal

Date	Mintage	F	VF	XF	Unc	BU
2009	—	—	—	—	—	15.00

KM# 216   5 POUNDS
28.2800 g., 0.9250 Silver 0.8410 oz. ASW, 38.61 mm. **Ruler:** Elizabeth II **Subject:** H.M.S. Ark Royal

Date	Mintage	F	VF	XF	Unc	BU
2009 Proof	—	Value: 60.00				

KM# 217   5 POUNDS
28.2800 g., 0.9250 Silver 0.8410 oz. ASW, 38.6 mm. **Ruler:** Elizabeth II **Obv:** Head with tiara right **Rev:** Katherine Middleton and Prince WIlliam facing

Date	Mintage	F	VF	XF	Unc	BU
2011 Proof	—	Value: 85.00				

KM# 143   10 POUNDS
155.5000 g., 0.9250 Silver partially gilt 4.6243 oz. ASW, 65 mm. **Ruler:** Elizabeth II **Subject:** 50th Anniversary of Coronation **Obv:** Queens silver portrait on gold plated fields **Rev:** Crown and scepter above arms, gold plated

Date	Mintage	F	VF	XF	Unc	BU
2003	2,000	—	—	—	135	150

KM# 154   10 POUNDS
155.5000 g., 0.9160 Gold 4.5793 oz. AGW, 65 mm. **Ruler:** Elizabeth II **Subject:** Crimean War, 150th anniversary **Rev:** Light Brigade, Earl of Cardigan

Date	Mintage	F	VF	XF	Unc	BU
2004 Proof	—	Value: 8,500				

KM# 159   10 POUNDS
155.5000 g., 0.9250 Silver 4.6243 oz. ASW, 65 mm. **Ruler:** Elizabeth II **Subject:** End of World War II, 60th Anniversary **Rev:** Parlament buildings

Date	Mintage	F	VF	XF	Unc	BU
2005 Proof	—	Value: 200				

KM# 161   10 POUNDS
155.5000 g., 0.9160 Gold 4.5793 oz. AGW, 65 mm. **Ruler:** Elizabeth II **Subject:** Trafalgar, 200th Anniversary

Date	Mintage	F	VF	XF	Unc	BU
2005 Proof	—	Value: 8,500				

KM# 192   10 POUNDS
155.5000 g., 0.9250 Silver 4.6243 oz. ASW, 65 mm. **Ruler:** Elizabeth II **Subject:** Royal Air Force **Rev:** Reginald Joseph Mitchell, founder of the Royal Air Force

Date	Mintage	F	VF	XF	Unc	BU
2008 Proof	Est. 1,943	Value: 200				

KM# 112   25 POUNDS
7.9800 g., 0.9167 Gold 0.2352 oz. AGW, 22.05 mm. **Ruler:** Elizabeth II **Subject:** Princess Diana **Obv:** Crowned head right **Rev:** Diana's portrait **Edge:** Reeded

Date	Mintage	F	VF	XF	Unc	BU
2002 Proof	2,500	Value: 425				

KM# 114   25 POUNDS
7.9800 g., 0.9166 Gold 0.2352 oz. AGW, 22 mm. **Ruler:** Elizabeth II **Subject:** Queen Mother **Obv:** Crowned head right **Rev:** Queen Mother's portrait circa 1918 **Edge:** Reeded

Date	Mintage	F	VF	XF	Unc	BU
2002 Proof	2,500	Value: 425				

KM# 116   25 POUNDS
7.9800 g., 0.9166 Gold 0.2352 oz. AGW, 22 mm. **Ruler:** Elizabeth II **Subject:** Golden Jubilee **Obv:** Crowned head right **Rev:** Abbey procession scene **Edge:** Reeded

Date	Mintage	F	VF	XF	Unc	BU
2002 Proof	2,500	Value: 425				

KM# 118   25 POUNDS
7.9800 g., 0.9166 Gold 0.2352 oz. AGW, 22 mm. **Ruler:** Elizabeth II **Subject:** Duke of Wellington **Obv:** Crowned head right **Rev:** Wellington's portrait with infantry scene **Edge:** Reeded

Date	Mintage	F	VF	XF	Unc	BU
2002 Proof	2,500	Value: 425				

KM# 151   25 POUNDS
7.9800 g., 0.9160 Gold 0.2350 oz. AGW, 22.05 mm. **Ruler:** Elizabeth II **Rev:** Multipe portraits of Alfred, Drake, Nelson, Fisher and Woodward and the Mary Rose, Visctory, Warspite, Ark Royal and Conqueror

Date	Mintage	F	VF	XF	Unc	BU
2003 Proof	—	Value: 425				

KM# 120   25 POUNDS
7.9800 g., 0.9166 Gold 0.2352 oz. AGW, 22 mm. **Ruler:** Elizabeth II **Subject:** Golden Jubilee **Obv:** Crowned head right **Rev:** Honor guard and monument **Edge:** Reeded

Date	Mintage	F	VF	XF	Unc	BU
2003 Proof	5,000	Value: 425				

KM# 155   25 POUNDS
7.9800 g., 0.9160 Gold 0.2350 oz. AGW, 22.05 mm. **Ruler:** Elizabeth II **Subject:** Crimean War, 150th anniversary **Rev:** Light Brigade, Earl of Cardigan

Date	Mintage	F	VF	XF	Unc	BU
2004 Proof	—	Value: 425				

KM# 125   25 POUNDS
7.9800 g., 0.9167 Gold 0.2352 oz. AGW, 22 mm. **Ruler:** Elizabeth II **Subject:** D-Day **Obv:** Crowned head right **Rev:** British Horsa gliders in flight **Edge:** Reeded

Date	Mintage	F	VF	XF	Unc	BU
2004 Proof	500	Value: 425				

KM# 152   25 POUNDS
7.9800 g., 0.9160 Gold 0.2350 oz. AGW, 22.05 mm. **Ruler:** Elizabeth II **Rev:** Locomotive 6220 Coronation, and LMSR Pacific

Date	Mintage	F	VF	XF	Unc	BU
2004 Proof	Est. 2,500	Value: 425				

KM# 153   25 POUNDS
7.9800 g., 0.9160 Gold 0.2350 oz. AGW, 22.05 mm. **Ruler:** Elizabeth II **Rev:** British Railway's locomotive 92229 Evening Star

Date	Mintage	F	VF	XF	Unc	BU
2004 Proof	Est. 2,500	Value: 425				

KM# 156   25 POUNDS
7.9800 g., 0.9160 Gold 0.2350 oz. AGW, 22.05 mm. **Ruler:** Elizabeth II **Subject:** Royal Navy **Rev:** H.M.S. Vicotry

Date	Mintage	F	VF	XF	Unc	BU
2004 Proof	—	Value: 425				

KM# 157   25 POUNDS
7.9800 g., 0.9160 Gold 0.2350 oz. AGW, 22.05 mm. **Ruler:** Elizabeth II **Subject:** Royal Navy **Rev:** Admiral Andrew B. Cunningham

Date	Mintage	F	VF	XF	Unc	BU
2004 Proof	—	Value: 425				

KM# 158   25 POUNDS
7.9800 g., 0.9160 Gold 0.2350 oz. AGW, 22.05 mm. **Ruler:** Elizabeth II **Subject:** Royal Navy **Rev:** Submarine H.M.S. Conqueror

Date	Mintage	F	VF	XF	Unc	BU
2004 Proof	—	Value: 425				

KM# 162   25 POUNDS
7.9800 g., 0.9160 Gold 0.2350 oz. AGW, 22.05 mm. **Ruler:** Elizabeth II **Subject:** Trafalgar, 200th Anniversary

Date	Mintage	F	VF	XF	Unc	BU
2005 Proof	—	Value: 425				

KM# 196   25 POUNDS
7.9800 g., 0.9160 Gold 0.2350 oz. AGW, 22.05 mm. **Ruler:** Elizabeth II **Subject:** Henry VIII, 500th Anniversary of reign

Date	Mintage	F	VF	XF	Unc	BU
2009 Proof	Est. 995	Value: 425				

KM# 209   25 POUNDS
7.9800 g., 0.9160 Gold 0.2350 oz. AGW, 22.05 mm. **Ruler:** Elizabeth II **Subject:** British Battles - Agincourt

Date	Mintage	F	VF	XF	Unc	BU
2009 Proof	Est. 995	Value: 425				

KM# 210   25 POUNDS
7.9800 g., 0.9160 Gold 0.2350 oz. AGW, 22.05 mm. **Ruler:** Elizabeth II **Subject:** British Battles - Somme

Date	Mintage	F	VF	XF	Unc	BU
2009 Proof	Est. 995	Value: 425				

KM# 122   50 POUNDS
1000.0000 g., 0.9250 Silver 29.738 oz. ASW, 100 mm. **Ruler:** Elizabeth II **Obv:** Crowned head right **Rev:** Bust facing and crowned arms with supporters **Edge:** Reeded

Date	Mintage	F	VF	XF	Unc	BU
2003 Proof	500	Value: 1,150				

PIEDFORT

KM#	Date	Mintage	Identification	Mkt Val
P3	2002	100	5 Pounds. 0.9166 Gold. 56.5600 g. 38.6 mm. Queen's portrait. Abbey procession scene. Reeded edge. Underweight piefort	1,900

MINT SETS

KM#	Date	Mintage	Identification	Issue Price	Mkt Val
MS7	2004 (1)	—	Jersey KM#126, Guernsey KM#155, Alderney KM#43, 150th Anniversary of the Crimean War	—	100

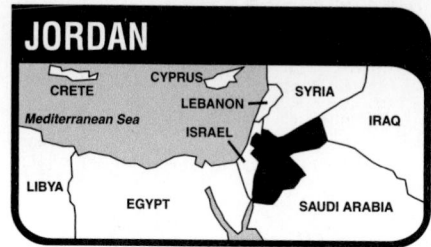

JORDAN

The Hashemite Kingdom of Jordan, a constitutional monarchy in southwest Asia, has an area of 37,738 sq. mi.(91,880 sq. km.) and a population of 3.5 million. Capital: Amman. Agriculture and tourism comprise Jordan's economic base. Chief exports are phosphates, tomatoes and oranges.

RULER
Abdullah Ibn Al-Hussein, 1999-

MONETARY SYSTEM
100 Piastres = 1 Dinar

KINGDOM

DECIMAL COINAGE

KM# 78.2   QIRSH (Piastre)
5.4700 g., Copper Plated Steel, 24.9 mm. **Ruler:** Abdullah **Obv:** King Abdullah II **Rev:** Islamic date left, Christian date right **Edge:** Plain

Date	Mintage	F	VF	XF	Unc	BU
2009	—	—	—	—	7.50	10.00

KM# 78.1   QIRSH (Piastre)
5.4700 g., Copper Plated Steel, 25 mm. **Ruler:** Abdullah II **Obv:** King Abdullah II **Rev:** Christian date left, Islamic date right **Edge:** Plain

Date	Mintage	F	VF	XF	Unc	BU
AH1430-2009	—	—	—	—	1.00	1.50
AH1432-2011	—	—	—	—	1.00	1.50

KM# 73   5 PIASTRES
5.0000 g., Nickel Plated Steel, 25.8 mm. **Ruler:** Abdullah II **Obv:** Bust right **Rev:** Value to left within lines below date with written value at lower right **Edge:** Milled

Date	Mintage	F	VF	XF	Unc	BU
AH1427-2006	—	—	—	—	1.50	2.00
AH1429-2008	—	—	—	—	1.50	2.00
AH1430-2009	—	—	—	—	1.50	2.00

KM# 74   10 PIASTRES
8.0000 g., Nickel Plated Steel, 28 mm. **Ruler:** Abdullah II **Obv:** Bust right **Rev:** Value at left within lines below date with written value at lower right **Edge:** Milled

Date	Mintage	F	VF	XF	Unc	BU
AH1425-2004	—	—	—	—	1.75	3.50
AH1427-2006	—	—	—	—	1.75	3.50
AH1429-2008	—	—	—	—	1.75	3.50
AH1430-2009	—	—	—	—	1.75	3.50

KM# 83   1/4 DINAR
7.4000 g., Nickel-Brass, 26.5 mm. **Ruler:** Abdullah II **Obv:** Bust right **Edge:** Plain **Shape:** 7-sided

Date	Mintage	F	VF	XF	Unc	BU
AH1425-2004	—	—	—	—	2.00	3.00
AH1427-2006	—	—	—	—	2.00	3.00
AH1429-2008	—	—	—	—	2.00	3.00
AH1430-2009	—	—	—	—	2.00	3.00

KM# 79   1/2 DINAR
9.6700 g., Bi-Metallic Copper-Nickel center in Brass ring, 29 mm. **Ruler:** Abdullah II **Obv:** Bust right within circle **Rev:** Value in center of circled wreath **Edge:** Plain **Shape:** 7-sided

Date	Mintage	F	VF	XF	Unc	BU
AH1427-2006	—	—	—	—	3.00	4.00
AH1429-2008	—	—	—	—	3.00	4.00
AH1430-2009	—	—	—	—	3.00	4.00

KM# 75   3 DINARS
28.5000 g., Brass, 40 mm. **Ruler:** Abdullah II **Subject:** Amman: Arabic Culture Capital **Obv:** Bust right **Rev:** Building **Edge:** Milled

Date	Mintage	F	VF	XF	Unc	BU
AH1423//2002	2,000	—	—	—	120	—

Note: Only 500 sold to collectors. Rest were taken by Amman municipality as official gifts

KM# 86   5 DINARS
120.0000 g., Bronze, 60 mm. **Ruler:** Abdullah **Subject:** Selection of Petra as one of the new Seven Wonders of the World **Obv:** King Abdullah II and Queen Rania **Rev:** Petra **Edge:** Milled

Date	Mintage	F	VF	XF	Unc	BU
AH1428-2008 Proof	500	Value: 160				

KM# 84   10 DINARS
120.0000 g., 0.9990 Silver 3.8541 oz. ASW, 60 mm. **Ruler:** Abdullah **Subject:** 60th Anniversary of Jordan's Independence **Obv:** King Abdullah I and Independence speech **Rev:** The National Assembly building **Edge:** Milled

Date	Mintage	F	VF	XF	Unc	BU
2006 Proof	250	Value: 250				

Note: Issued primarily for use as official state gifts

KM# 88   10 DINARS
31.1050 g., 0.9990 Silver 0.9990 oz. ASW, 40 mm. **Ruler:** Abdullah II **Subject:** Accession, 10th Anniversary **Obv:** Bust facing **Rev:** Crowned and mantled shield

Date	Mintage	F	VF	XF	Unc	BU
2009 Proof	2,250	Value: 150				

KM# 87   20 DINARS
120.0000 g., 0.9990 Silver 3.8541 oz. ASW, 60 mm. **Ruler:** Abdullah **Subject:** Selection of Petra as one of the new Seven Wonders of the World **Obv:** King Abdullah II and Queen Rania **Rev:** Petra **Edge:** Milled

Date	Mintage	F	VF	XF	Unc	BU
AH1428-2008 Proof	500	Value: 260				

KM# 89   50 DINARS
16.9600 g., 0.9990 Gold 0.5447 oz. AGW, 30 mm. **Ruler:** Abdullah II **Subject:** Accession, 10th Anniversary **Obv:** Bust **Rev:** Arms

Date	Mintage	F	VF	XF	Unc	BU
2009 Proof	1,750	Value: 975				

KM# 85   60 DINARS
72.7500 g., 0.9170 Gold 2.1447 oz. AGW, 40 mm. **Ruler:** Abdullah **Subject:** 60th Anniversary of Jordan's Independence **Obv:** King Abdullah II **Rev:** Treasury in Petra **Edge:** Milled

Date	Mintage	F	VF	XF	Unc	BU
2006 Proof	250	Value: 3,750				

Note: Issued primarily for use as official state gifts

MINT SETS

KM#	Date	Mintage	Identification	Issue Price	Mkt Val
MS4	2000-2004 (5)	—	KM#73-74, 78.1, 79, 83, mixed dates	—	20.00

PROOF SETS

KM#	Date	Mintage	Identification	Issue Price	Mkt Val
PS14	2006 (2)	250	KM#84-85	—	3,500
PS15	2008 (2)	—	KM#86-87	—	425

KAZAKHSTAN

The Republic of Kazakhstan (formerly Kazakhstan S.S.R.) is bordered to the west by the Caspian Sea and Russia, to the north by Russia, in the east by the Peoples Republic of China and in the south by Uzbekistan and Kirghizia. It has an area of 1,049,155 sq. mi. (2,717,300 sq. km.) and a population of 16.7 million. Capital: Astana. Rich in mineral resources including coal, tungsten, copper, lead, zinc and manganese with huge oil and natural gas reserves. Agriculture is very important, (it previously represented 20 percent of the total arable acreage of the combined U.S.S.R.) Non-ferrous metallurgy, heavy engineering and chemical industries are leaders in its economy.

MONETARY SYSTEM
100 Tyin = 1 Tenge

REPUBLIC

DECIMAL COINAGE

KM# 23   TENGE
1.6000 g., Brass, 15 mm. **Obv:** National emblem **Rev:** Value flanked by designs **Edge:** Plain

Date	Mintage	F	VF	XF	Unc	BU
2002	—	—	—	—	0.50	0.85
2004	—	—	—	—	0.50	0.85
2005	—	—	—	—	0.50	0.85
2011	—	—	—	—	0.50	0.85

KM# 64   2 TENGE
1.8200 g., Brass, 16 mm. **Obv:** National emblem **Rev:** Value flanked by designs **Edge:** Plain

Date	Mintage	F	VF	XF	Unc	BU
2005	—	—	—	—	0.65	1.20
2006	—	—	—	—	0.65	1.20

KM# 24   5 TENGE
2.2000 g., Brass, 17.3 mm. **Obv:** National emblem **Rev:** Value flanked by designs

Date	Mintage	F	VF	XF	Unc	BU
2002	—	—	—	—	0.50	0.85
2004	—	—	—	—	0.50	0.85
2005	—	—	—	—	0.50	0.85
2006	—	—	—	—	0.50	0.85
2010	—	—	—	—	0.50	0.85
2011	—	—	—	—	0.50	0.85

KM# 25   10 TENGE
2.8000 g., Brass, 19.6 mm. **Obv:** National emblem **Rev:** Value above design

Date	Mintage	F	VF	XF	Unc	BU
2002	—	—	—	—	0.75	1.25
2004	—	—	—	—	0.75	1.25
2005	—	—	—	—	0.75	1.25
2006	—	—	—	—	0.75	1.25
2010	—	—	—	—	0.75	1.25
2011	—	—	—	—	0.75	1.25

KM# 26   20 TENGE
2.8600 g., Copper-Nickel, 18.3 mm. **Obv:** National emblem **Rev:** Value above design **Edge:** Segmented reeding **Edge Lettering:** * CTO TENGE * Y 3 TENGE

Date	Mintage	F	VF	XF	Unc	BU
2002	—	—	—	—	1.00	1.75
2004	—	—	—	—	1.00	1.75
2006	—	—	—	—	1.00	1.75
2010	—	—	—	—	1.00	1.75
2011	—	—	—	—	1.00	1.75

KM# 40   50 TENGE
11.5000 g., Copper-Nickel, 31 mm. **Obv:** Eagle superimposed on ornate 10 **Edge:** Reeded and plain sections

Date	Mintage	F	VF	XF	Unc	BU
2001	—	—	—	—	4.00	6.50

KM# 41   50 TENGE
11.2000 g., Copper-Nickel, 31.1 mm. **Subject:** Gabiden Mustafin **Obv:** National emblem above value **Rev:** Bust 1/4 left **Edge:** Segmented reeding

Date	Mintage	F	VF	XF	Unc	BU
ND(2002)	—	—	—	—	4.00	6.50

KM# 69   50 TENGE
Copper-Nickel, 31 mm. **Subject:** Gabit Mosrepov **Obv:** Symbol and value **Rev:** Bust facing

Date	Mintage	F	VF	XF	Unc	BU
2002	—	—	—	—	4.00	6.50

KM# 27   50 TENGE
4.7000 g., Copper-Nickel, 23.1 mm. **Obv:** National emblem **Rev:** Value above design

Date	Mintage	F	VF	XF	Unc	BU
2002	—	—	—	—	2.00	3.50

KM# 70   50 TENGE
Copper-Nickel, 31 mm. **Subject:** 200th Anniversary of Makhambet Utemisov **Obv:** Symbol and value

Date	Mintage	F	VF	XF	Unc	BU
2003	—	—	—	—	4.00	6.50

KM# 54   50 TENGE
11.5000 g., Copper-Nickel, 31.1 mm. **Obv:** National emblem above value **Rev:** Painter Abylichan Kasteev (1904-1973) **Edge:** Reeded and plain sections

Date	Mintage	F	VF	XF	Unc	BU
2004	—	—	—	—	4.00	6.50

KM# 65   50 TENGE
11.5000 g., Copper-Nickel, 31.1 mm. **Subject:** Alken Margulan **Obv:** National emblem above value **Rev:** Bust facing **Edge:** Segmented reeding

Date	Mintage	F	VF	XF	Unc	BU
2004	—	—	—	—	4.00	6.50

KM# 58   50 TENGE
11.5000 g., Copper-Nickel, 31.1 mm. **Subject:** 10th Anniversary of the Constitution **Obv:** National emblem above value **Rev:** National emblem within circle above book **Edge:** Segmented reeding

Date	Mintage	F	VF	XF	Unc	BU
2005	—	—	—	—	4.00	6.50

KM# 71   50 TENGE
10.9500 g., Copper-Nickel, 31 mm. **Subject:** 60 Years Victory WWII **Obv:** Symbol and value

Date	Mintage	F	VF	XF	Unc	BU
2005	—	—	—	—	4.00	6.50

KM# 79   50 TENGE
11.2200 g., Copper-Nickel, 31 mm. **Subject:** 20th Anniversary **Obv:** National arms above value **Rev:** Happy woman **Edge:** Segmented reeding

Date	Mintage	F	VF	XF	Unc	BU
ND (2006)	—	—	—	—	4.00	6.50

KM# 73   50 TENGE
11.3700 g., Copper-Nickel, 31 mm. **Obv:** Human figure and solar system **Rev:** Astronaut and solar system **Edge:** Segmented reeding

Date	Mintage	F	VF	XF	Unc	BU
2006	50,000	—	—	—	4.00	6.00

KM# 74 50 TENGE
11.3700 g., Copper-Nickel, 31 mm. **Obv:** National arms on tapestry **Rev:** Woman with baby in cradle **Edge:** Segmented reeding

Date	Mintage	F	VF	XF	Unc	BU
2006	—				4.00	6.00

KM# 75 50 TENGE
11.3700 g., Copper-Nickel, 31 mm. **Obv:** National arms **Rev:** Altai Snowcock **Edge:** Segmented reeding

Date	Mintage	F	VF	XF	Unc	BU
2006	50,000				4.00	9.00

KM# 77 50 TENGE
11.3700 g., Copper-Nickel, 31 mm. **Obv:** National arms **Rev:** Altyn Kyran Order Breast Star **Edge:** Segmented reeding

Date	Mintage	F	VF	XF	Unc	BU
2006	50,000				4.00	6.00

KM# 78 50 TENGE
11.3700 g., Copper-Nickel, 31 mm. **Obv:** National arms **Rev:** Zhubanov bust and music score **Edge:** Segmented reeding

Date	Mintage	F	VF	XF	Unc	BU
2006	50,000				4.00	6.00

KM# 80 50 TENGE
10.8900 g., Copper-Nickel, 31.10 mm. **Subject:** 50th Anniversary Launch of Sputnik I **Obv:** Stylized view of solar system **Obv. Legend:** REPUBLIC OF KAZAKHSTAN **Rev:** Sputnik I in space, earth in background **Rev. Legend:** THE FIRST SPACE SATELLITE OF THE EARTH **Edge:** Segmented reeding

Date	Mintage	F	VF	XF	Unc	BU
ND(2007)	—				4.00	6.00

KM# 81 50 TENGE
11.1100 g., Copper-Nickel, 31 mm. **Obv:** National arms, value below **Obv. Legend:** КАЗАКСТАН.... **Rev:** Eurasian Spoonbill standing left **Rev. Legend:** ... • PLATALEA LEUCORODIA **Edge:** Segmented reeding

Date	Mintage	F	VF	XF	Unc	BU
2007	—				4.00	7.50

KM# 164 50 TENGE
11.3700 g., Copper-Nickel, 31 mm. **Obv:** National arms on tapestry **Rev:** Child and two men

Date	Mintage	F	VF	XF	Unc	BU
2007	—				4.00	6.00

KM# 165 50 TENGE
11.3700 g., Copper-Nickel, 31 mm. **Obv:** National arms above value **Rev:** Otan badge

Date	Mintage	F	VF	XF	Unc	BU
2007	—				4.00	6.00

KM# 86 50 TENGE
Copper-Nickel, 31 mm. **Obv:** National Arms

Date	Mintage	F	VF	XF	Unc	BU
2008 Prooflike	—					12.00

KM# 169 50 TENGE
11.3700 g., Copper-Nickel, 31 mm. **Obv:** National arms on tapersry background **Rev:** Two horsemen

Date	Mintage	F	VF	XF	Unc	BU
2008	—				4.00	6.00

KM# 170 50 TENGE
11.3700 g., Copper-Nickel, 31 mm. **Obv:** National arms above vlaue **Rev:** Dank Order Star

Date	Mintage	F	VF	XF	Unc	BU
2008	—				4.00	6.00

KM# 171 50 TENGE
11.3700 g., Copper-Nickel, 31 mm. **Obv:** National arms **Rev:** Aibyn Order Star

Date	Mintage	F	VF	XF	Unc	BU
2008	—				4.00	6.00

KM# 172 50 TENGE
11.3700 g., Copper-Nickel, 31 mm. **Subject:** Astana capital, 10th Anniversary **Obv:** National arms **Rev:** Architecture

Date	Mintage	F	VF	XF	Unc	BU
2008	—				4.00	6.00

KM# 201 50 TENGE
11.3700 g., Copper-Nickel, 31 mm. **Obv:** National emblem **Rev:** Building views

Date	Mintage	F	VF	XF	Unc	BU
2008	50,000					7.50

KM# 202 50 TENGE
11.3700 g., Copper-Nickel, 31 mm. **Rev:** Spaceship

Date	Mintage	F	VF	XF	Unc	BU
2008 Proof	50,000					7.50

KM# 132 50 TENGE
Copper-Nickel, 31 mm. **Subject:** Betashar **Obv:** Arms **Rev:** Two figures standing

Date	Mintage	F	VF	XF	Unc	BU
2009	50,000					10.00

KM# 135 50 TENGE
0.5000 g., 0.9990 Gold 0.0161 oz. AGW, 11 mm. **Obv:** Value **Rev:** Cat head sculpture

Date	Mintage	F	VF	XF	Unc	BU
2009 Proof	14,000					50.00

KM# 140   50 TENGE
Copper-Nickel, 31 mm. **Obv:** Arms **Rev:** Parassat medal insignia

Date	Mintage	F	VF	XF	Unc	BU
2009	50,000	—				10.00

KM# 141   50 TENGE
Copper-Nickel **Obv:** Arms **Rev:** Porcupine advancing right
Shape: 31

Date	Mintage	F	VF	XF	Unc	BU
2009	50,000	—				15.00

KM# 144   50 TENGE
Copper-Nickel, 31 mm. **Obv:** Man standing in solar system **Rev:** Apollo-Soyoz space craft

Date	Mintage	F	VF	XF	Unc	BU
2009	50,000	—				10.00

KM# 145   50 TENGE
Copper-Nickel, 31 mm. **Obv:** Arms **Rev:** Star of the Order of Dostyk

Date	Mintage	F	VF	XF	Unc	BU
2009	50,000	—				10.00

KM# 146   50 TENGE
Copper-Nickel, 31 mm. **Subject:** T. Bassenov, 100th Anniversary of Birth **Obv:** Arms **Rev:** Bust at right, architectural column

Date	Mintage	F	VF	XF	Unc	BU
2009	50,000	—				10.00

KM# 152   50 TENGE
0.5000 g., 0.9990 Gold 0.0161 oz. AGW, 11 mm. **Subject:** Ahalavlinky Treasure **Obv:** Value **Rev:** Historical jewlery design

Date	Mintage	F	VF	XF	Unc	BU
2009 Proof	14,000	Value: 45.00				

KM# 174   50 TENGE
Copper-Nickel, 31 mm. **Subject:** Moon Exploration, 40th Anniversary **Obv:** Figure standing within solar system design **Rev:** Lunar Rover vehicle

Date	Mintage	F	VF	XF	Unc	BU
2010	—					5.00

KM# 175   50 TENGE
Copper-Nickel, 31 mm. **Subject:** Great Victory, 65th Anniversary **Obv:** National Emblem, value below **Rev:** Order star, 1945 above

Date	Mintage	F	VF	XF	Unc	BU
2010	—					5.00

KM# 39   100 TENGE
6.2300 g., Bi-Metallic Copper-Nickel center in Brass ring, 24.4 mm. **Obv:** National emblem **Rev:** Value within lined circle flanked by designs **Edge:** Reeding over incuse value

Date	Mintage	F	VF	XF	Unc	BU
2002	—				3.50	5.50
2004	—				3.50	5.50
2005	—				3.50	5.50
2006	—				3.50	5.50
2007	—				3.50	5.50

KM# 49   100 TENGE
6.4000 g., Bi-Metallic Copper-Nickel center in Brass ring, 24.5 mm. **Obv:** Stylized chicken **Rev:** Value within lined circle flanked by designs **Edge:** Reeded and lettered

Date	Mintage	F	VF	XF	Unc	BU
2003	100,000	—	—		4.00	6.50

KM# 50   100 TENGE
6.4000 g., Bi-Metallic Copper-Nickel center in Brass ring, 24.5 mm. **Obv:** Stylized panther **Rev:** Value within lined circle flanked by designs **Edge:** Reeded and lettered

Date	Mintage	F	VF	XF	Unc	BU
2003	100,000	—			4.00	6.50

KM# 51   100 TENGE
6.4000 g., Bi-Metallic Copper-Nickel center in Brass ring, 24.5 mm. **Obv:** Stylized wolf's head **Rev:** Value within lined circle flanked by designs **Edge:** Reeded and lettered

Date	Mintage	F	VF	XF	Unc	BU
2003	100,000	—			4.00	6.50

KM# 52   100 TENGE
6.4000 g., Bi-Metallic Copper-Nickel center in Brass ring, 24.5 mm. **Obv:** Stylized sheep's head **Rev:** Value within lined circle flanked by designs **Edge:** Reeded and lettered

Date	Mintage	F	VF	XF	Unc	BU
2003	100,000	—			4.00	6.50

KM# 116   100 TENGE
31.1000 g., 0.9250 Silver 0.9249 oz. ASW, 37 mm. **Subject:** Olympics **Obv:** Arms and stylized stadium **Rev:** Two cyclists

Date	Mintage	F	VF	XF	Unc	BU
2004 Proof	—	Value: 55.00				

KM# 119   100 TENGE
31.1000 g., 0.9250 Silver 0.9249 oz. ASW, 37 mm. **Subject:** FIFA World Cup, Germany **Obv:** Arms and stylized stadium **Rev:** Two soccer players and large ball

Date	Mintage	F	VF	XF	Unc	BU
2004 Proof	—	Value: 55.00				

KM# 120   100 TENGE
1.2400 g., 0.9990 Gold 0.0398 oz. AGW, 13.92 mm. **Subject:** King Kroisos **Obv:** Arms **Rev:** Head left, coin, temple

Date	Mintage	F	VF	XF	Unc	BU
2004 Proof	—	Value: 85.00				

KM# 121   100 TENGE
1.2400 g., 0.9990 Gold 0.0398 oz. AGW, 13.92 mm. **Subject:** King Midas **Rev:** King Midas reclining on bench

Date	Mintage	F	VF	XF	Unc	BU
2004 Proof	—	Value: 85.00				

KM# 122   100 TENGE
1.2400 g., 0.9990 Gold 0.0398 oz. AGW, 13.92 mm. **Subject:** Ancient Turkestan **Obv:** Arms **Rev:** Camel caravan and building

Date	Mintage	F	VF	XF	Unc	BU
2004 Proof	—	Value: 85.00				

KM# 188   100 TENGE
1.2400 g., 0.9990 Gold 0.0398 oz. AGW, 13.92 mm. **Rev:** Marco Polo

Date	Mintage	F	VF	XF	Unc	BU
2004 Proof	15,000	Value: 100				

KM# 57   100 TENGE
6.4000 g., Bi-Metallic Copper-Nickel center in Brass ring,
24.5 mm. **Subject:** 60th Anniversary of the UN **Obv:** UN logo
as part of the number 60 **Rev:** Value within lined circle flanked
by designs **Edge:** Reeded and lettered

Date	Mintage	F	VF	XF	Unc	BU
2005	—	—	—	—	5.00	7.50

KM# 191   100 TENGE
31.1050 g., 0.9250 Silver 0.9250 oz. ASW, 38.61 mm. **Subject:**
Torino Winter Olympics **Rev:** Three stone cross-country skiers

Date	Mintage	F	VF	XF	Unc	BU
2005 Proof	10,000	Value: 60.00				

KM# 95   100 TENGE
31.1050 g., 0.9250 Silver 0.9250 oz. ASW, 38.61 mm. **Subject:**
Baiturrahman Mosque **Rev:** Mosque and reflecting pool

Date	Mintage	F	VF	XF	Unc	BU
2006 (2008) Proof	6,000	Value: 80.00				

KM# 98   100 TENGE
31.1050 g., 0.9250 Silver 0.9250 oz. ASW, 38.61 mm. **Subject:**
Zahir Mosque **Rev:** Mosque

Date	Mintage	F	VF	XF	Unc	BU
2006 Proof	6,000	Value: 80.00				

KM# 195   100 TENGE
31.1050 g., 0.9250 Silver 0.9250 oz. ASW, 38.61 mm. **Subject:**
Olympics 2008 **Obv:** National emblem in stadium **Rev:** Boxers

Date	Mintage	F	VF	XF	Unc	BU
2006 Proof	4,000	Value: 75.00				

KM# 200   100 TENGE
1.2400 g., 0.9990 Gold 0.0398 oz. AGW, 13.92 mm. **Obv:**
National emblem **Rev:** Decoration

Date	Mintage	F	VF	XF	Unc	BU
2006 Proof	18,000	Value: 100				

KM# 166   100 TENGE
31.1000 g., 0.9250 Silver 0.9249 oz. ASW, 37 mm. **Subject:**
Olympics - Pentathlon **Obv:** National arms and stylized stadium
Rev: Five sports

Date	Mintage	F	VF	XF	Unc	BU
2007 Proof	—	Value: 55.00				

KM# 96   100 TENGE
31.1050 g., 0.9250 Silver 0.9250 oz. ASW, 38.61 mm. **Subject:**
Faisal Mosque, Islamabad **Rev:** Mosque

Date	Mintage	F	VF	XF	Unc	BU
2006 (2008) Proof	6,000	Value: 80.00				

KM# 97   100 TENGE
31.1050 g., 0.9250 Silver 0.9250 oz. ASW, 38.61 mm. **Subject:**
Hodja Akhmed Yassavi Mausoleum Turkestan **Rev:** Mausoleum

Date	Mintage	F	VF	XF	Unc	BU
2006 (2008) Proof	6,000	Value: 80.00				

KM# 110   100 TENGE
31.1050 g., 0.9250 Silver 0.9250 oz. ASW, 38.61 mm. **Subject:**
Chingis Khan **Rev:** Khan on horseback facing

Date	Mintage	F	VF	XF	Unc	BU
2008 Proof	13,000	Value: 65.00				

KM# 125   100 TENGE
31.1050 g., 0.9250 Silver 0.9250 oz. ASW, 38.61 mm. **Subject:**
Attila the Hun **Rev:** Medallic Profile right

Date	Mintage	F	VF	XF	Unc	BU
2009 Proof	13,000	Value: 75.00				

KM# 126   100 TENGE
31.1050 g., 0.9250 Silver 0.9250 oz. ASW, 38.61 mm. **Subject:**
2010 Olympics **Rev:** Ski jumper over Vancouver skyline

Date	Mintage	F	VF	XF	Unc	BU
2009 Proof	12,000	Value: 55.00				

KM# 134   100 TENGE
31.1000 g., 0.9990 Silver partially gilt 0.9988 oz. ASW **Subject:**
Caracal **Obv:** Arms **Rev:** Caracal cat head facing, partially gilt

Date	Mintage	F	VF	XF	Unc	BU
2009 Proof	13,000	Value: 55.00				

KM# 136   100 TENGE
1.2400 g., 0.9990 Gold 0.0398 oz. AGW, 13.92 mm. **Obv:** Value
Rev: Cat head sculpture

Date	Mintage	F	VF	XF	Unc	BU
2009 Proof	9,500	—	—	—	—	—

KM# 147   100 TENGE
31.1000 g., 0.9250 Silver 0.9249 oz. ASW, 38.6 mm. **Obv:** Arms
Rev: Tiger advancing right

Date	Mintage	F	VF	XF	Unc	BU
2009 Proof	13,000	Value: 65.00				

KM# 151   100 TENGE
31.1000 g., 0.9990 Silver 0.9988 oz. ASW, 38.61 mm. **Subject:**
World Cup, South Africa **Obv:** Arms and stadium **Rev:** Soccer
Player, gilt ball

Date	Mintage	F	VF	XF	Unc	BU
2009 Proof	—	Value: 50.00				

KM# 153   100 TENGE
1.2400 g., 0.9990 Gold 0.0398 oz. AGW, 13.92 mm. **Subject:**
Zhalavlinky Treasure **Obv:** Arms **Rev:** Historic jewelery design

Date	Mintage	F	VF	XF	Unc	BU
2009 Proof	9,500			Value: 85.00		

KM# 176   100 TENGE
31.1000 g., 0.9250 Silver 0.9249 oz. ASW, 38.61 mm. **Obv:**
State Emblem, gilt horsemen at right **Rev:** Queen Tomris

Date	Mintage	F	VF	XF	Unc	BU
2010 Proof	—			Value: 70.00		

KM# 66   500 TENGE
24.0000 g., 0.9250 Silver 0.7137 oz. ASW, 37 mm. **Obv:** Man
seated under tree playing stringed instrument **Rev:** Stringed
instrument, musical notes

Date	Mintage	F	VF	XF	Unc	BU
2001 Proof	—			Value: 50.00		

KM# 37   500 TENGE
23.9000 g., 0.9250 Silver 0.7107 oz. ASW, 37 mm. **Subject:**
Wildlife **Obv:** Value **Rev:** Female Saiga with two calves **Edge:**
Plain

Date	Mintage	F	VF	XF	Unc	BU
2001 Proof	3,000			Value: 90.00		

KM# 38   500 TENGE
23.8100 g., 0.9250 Silver 0.7081 oz. ASW, 36.9 mm. **Subject:**
10 Years of Independence **Obv:** Monument and flag **Rev:**
National emblem within design above value **Edge:** Plain

Date	Mintage	F	VF	XF	Unc	BU
2001 Proof	3,000			Value: 125		

KM# 55   500 TENGE
24.0000 g., 0.9250 Silver 0.7137 oz. ASW, 37 mm. **Obv:** Value
Rev: Altai Mountain petroglyph **Edge:** Plain

Date	Mintage	F	VF	XF	Unc	BU
2001 Proof	3,000			Value: 175		

KM# 112   500 TENGE
24.0000 g., 0.9250 Silver 0.7137 oz. ASW **Subject:** Applied art,
stringed instrument **Obv:** Man seated under tree **Rev:** Stringed
instrument and notes

Date	Mintage	F	VF	XF	Unc	BU
2001 Proof	—			Value: 42.00		

KM# 42   500 TENGE
23.9000 g., 0.9250 Silver 0.7107 oz. ASW, 37 mm. **Subject:**
Music **Obv:** Musician and value divided by tree **Rev:** Musical
instruments **Edge:** Plain

Date	Mintage	F	VF	XF	Unc	BU
2002 Proof	—			Value: 165		

KM# 43   500 TENGE
23.9000 g., 0.9250 Silver 0.7107 oz. ASW, 37 mm. **Subject:**
Prehistoric Art **Obv:** Value **Rev:** Prehistoric cave art **Edge:** Plain

Date	Mintage	F	VF	XF	Unc	BU
2002 Proof	3,000			Value: 140		

KM# 44   500 TENGE
23.9000 g., 0.9250 Silver 0.7107 oz. ASW, 37 mm. **Subject:**
Bighorn Sheep **Obv:** Value **Rev:** Kazakhstan Argali Ram **Edge:**
Plain

Date	Mintage	F	VF	XF	Unc	BU
2002 Proof	3,000			Value: 120		

KM# 113   500 TENGE
24.0000 g., 0.9250 Silver 0.7137 oz. ASW, 37 mm. **Subject:**
Petroglyph **Obv:** Value on traditional weave pattern **Rev:** Horse
petroglyph

Date	Mintage	F	VF	XF	Unc	BU
2002 Proof	—			Value: 60.00		

KM# 183   500 TENGE
24.0000 g., 0.9250 Silver 0.7137 oz. ASW, 36. mm. **Obv:** Large
value within brick arch design **Rev:** Byzantine church and floor plan

Date	Mintage	F	VF	XF	Unc	BU
2002 Proof	3,000			Value: 75.00		

KM# 53   500 TENGE
24.0000 g., 0.9250 Silver 0.7137 oz. ASW, 37 mm. **Obv:** Value
Rev: Great Bustard bird standing on ground **Edge:** Plain

Date	Mintage	F	VF	XF	Unc	BU
2003 Proof	3,000			Value: 75.00		

KM# 56   500 TENGE
24.0000 g., 0.9250 Silver 0.7137 oz. ASW, 37 mm. **Subject:**
Applied Arts **Obv:** Folk Dancer **Rev:** Cultural artifacts **Edge:** Plain

Date	Mintage	F	VF	XF	Unc	BU
2003 Proof	3,000			Value: 80.00		

KM# 184   500 TENGE
24.0000 g., 0.9250 Silver 0.7137 oz. ASW **Rev:** Warriors in a cave

Date	Mintage	F	VF	XF	Unc	BU
2003 Proof	3,000			Value: 75.00		

KM# 185   500 TENGE
24.0000 g., 0.9250 Silver 0.7137 oz. ASW, 36 mm. **Obv:**
Intricate tile design **Rev:** View of Kecensci Mausoleum

Date	Mintage	F	VF	XF	Unc	BU
2003 Proof	3,000			Value: 75.00		

KM# 59   500 TENGE
31.1000 g., 0.9250 Bi-Metallic Blackend silver center in proof
silver ring 0.9249 oz., 38.6 mm. **Subject:** "Denga" **Obv:** Black
square holed coin design above value **Rev:** Black square holed
coin design and metal content statement **Edge:** Reeded

Date	Mintage	F	VF	XF	Unc	BU
2004 Proof	5,000			Value: 90.00		

KM# 117   500 TENGE
31.1000 g., 0.9250 Silver partially gilt 0.9249 oz. ASW, 38.6 mm.
Obv: Three riders **Rev:** Golden deer ornament **Shape:** 12-sided

Date	Mintage	F	VF	XF	Unc	BU
2004 Proof	—			Value: 100		

KM# 186   500 TENGE
24.0000 g., 0.9250 Silver 0.7137 oz. ASW. **Rev:** Saker Falcon

Date	Mintage	F	VF	XF	Unc	BU
2004 Proof	3,000	Value: 75.00				

KM# 187   500 TENGE
24.0000 g., 0.9250 Silver 0.7137 oz. ASW, 37 mm. **Rev:** Cave painting of a Shaman in Tamgaly

Date	Mintage	F	VF	XF	Unc	BU
2004 Proof	3,000	Value: 75.00				

KM# 189   500 TENGE
24.0000 g., 0.9250 Silver 0.7137 oz. ASW, 36 mm. **Obv:** Tree of Life **Rev:** Three stone figures

Date	Mintage	F	VF	XF	Unc	BU
2004 Proof	3,000	Value: 75.00				

KM# 190   500 TENGE
24.0000 g., 0.9250 Silver 0.7137 oz. ASW, 36 mm. **Obv:** Woman in national costume playing the zither **Rev:** Zither and musical notes

Date	Mintage	F	VF	XF	Unc	BU
2004 Proof	3,000	Value: 75.00				

KM# 60   500 TENGE
24.0000 g., 0.9250 Silver 0.7137 oz. ASW, 37 mm. **Obv:** Value **Rev:** Prehistoric art horseman **Edge:** Plain

Date	Mintage	F	VF	XF	Unc	BU
2005 Proof	3,000	Value: 70.00				

KM# 61   500 TENGE
24.0000 g., 0.9250 Silver 0.7137 oz. ASW, 37 mm. **Obv:** Value **Rev:** Two Goitered Gazelles **Edge:** Plain

Date	Mintage	F	VF	XF	Unc	BU
2005 Proof	3,000	Value: 70.00				

KM# 62   500 TENGE
31.1000 g., 0.9250 Silver 0.9249 oz. ASW, 38.6 mm. **Obv:** Horse race and value **Rev:** Gold plated tiger **Edge:** Plain **Shape:** 12-sided

Date	Mintage	F	VF	XF	Unc	BU
2005 Proof	5,000	Value: 120				

KM# 63   500 TENGE
31.1000 g., 0.9250 Bi-Metallic Blackened Silver center in proof Silver ring 0.9249 oz., 38.6 mm. **Subject:** "Drakhma" coin **Obv:** Old coin design **Rev:** Old coin design **Edge:** Reeded

Date	Mintage	F	VF	XF	Unc	BU
2005 Proof	5,000	Value: 65.00				

KM# 72   500 TENGE
31.1000 g., 0.9250 Silver 0.9249 oz. ASW, 38.6 mm. **Obv:** Horse race and value **Rev:** Gold plated rider **Edge:** Plain

Date	Mintage	F	VF	XF	Unc	BU
2005 Proof	5,000	Value: 100				

KM# 124   500 TENGE
24.0000 g., 0.9250 Silver 0.7137 oz. ASW, 37 mm. **Subject:** Zhoshi Khan Mausoleum **Rev:** 3/4 view of building facade

Date	Mintage	F	VF	XF	Unc	BU
2005 Proof	—	Value: 50.00				

KM# 192   500 TENGE
24.0000 g., 0.9250 Silver 0.7137 oz. ASW, 36 mm. **Obv:** Man seated with stringed musical instrument **Rev:** two string musical instruments, musical notes at right

Date	Mintage	F	VF	XF	Unc	BU
2005 Proof	3,000	Value: 75.00				

KM# 193   500 TENGE
7.7800 g., 0.9990 Gold 0.2499 oz. AGW, 25 mm. **Obv:** State shield **Rev:** head of a dhole

Date	Mintage	F	VF	XF	Unc	BU
2005 Proof	—	Value: 750				

KM# 162   500 TENGE
0.9990 Gold **Obv:** Archway **Rev:** Al-Baram Mosque in Mecca

Date	Mintage	F	VF	XF	Unc	BU
2006 Proof	—	Value: 500				

KM# 163   500 TENGE
0.9990 Gold **Obv:** Archway **Rev:** Al-Nabawi Mosque in Medina

Date	Mintage	F	VF	XF	Unc	BU
2006 Proof	—	—				

KM# 76   500 TENGE
31.1000 g., 0.9250 Silver 0.9249 oz. ASW **Series:** Flora **Rev:** Tulopa Regeli in multicolor

Date	Mintage	F	VF	XF	Unc	BU
2006 Proof	—	Value: 150				

KM# 83   500 TENGE
24.0000 g., 0.9250 Silver 0.7137 oz. ASW, 38.7 mm. **Obv:** Value at center **Rev:** Tetraogallus Altalcus, Altai Snowcock

Date	Mintage	F	VF	XF	Unc	BU
2006 Proof	3,000	Value: 100				

KM# 84   500 TENGE
31.1000 g., 0.9250 Bi-Metallic Blackened Silver center in proof Silver ring. 0.9249 oz., 38.6 mm. **Subject:** "Dirkhem" coin **Obv:** Old coin design **Rev:** Old coin design **Edge:** Reeded

Date	Mintage	F	VF	XF	Unc	BU
2006 Proof	5,000	Value: 65.00				

KM# 194   500 TENGE
24.0000 g., 0.9250 Silver 0.7137 oz. ASW **Rev:** Triumph cars

Date	Mintage	F	VF	XF	Unc	BU
2006 Proof	3,000	Value: 75.00				

KM# 196   500 TENGE
31.1050 g., 0.9250 Silver 0.9250 oz. ASW, 38.61 mm. **Obv:** National emblem **Rev:** Figure seated at loom

Date	Mintage	F	VF	XF	Unc	BU
2006 Proof	4,000	Value: 75.00				

KM# 197   500 TENGE
31.1050 g., 0.9250 Silver 0.9250 oz. ASW, 38.61 mm. **Obv:** State emblem **Rev:** Central Mosque in Almati

Date	Mintage	F	VF	XF	Unc	BU
2006 Proof	4,000	Value: 75.00				

KM# 198   500 TENGE
31.1050 g., 0.9250 Silver 0.9250 oz. ASW, 38.61 mm. **Rev:** female with apples, a drawing by Sidorkin

Date	Mintage	F	VF	XF	Unc	BU
2006 Proof	4,000	Value: 75.00				

KM# 199   500 TENGE
41.0000 g., Bi-Metallic Silver and Tantalum, 38.61 mm. **Obv:** Figure standing within solar system **Rev:** Spaceman and orbits of planets

Date	Mintage	F	VF	XF	Unc	BU
2006 Proof	4,000	Value: 135				

KM# 168   500 TENGE
7.7700 g., 0.9990 Gold 0.2496 oz. AGW, 25 mm. **Obv:** Arms **Rev:** Lynx, crystal eyes **Rev. Legend:** FELIS LYNX

Date	Mintage	F	VF	XF	Unc	BU
2007 Proof	—	Value: 475				

KM# 82   500 TENGE
41.4000 g., Bi-Metallic Sterling Silver ring., 38.61 mm. **Subject:** 50th Anniversary Launch of Sputnik I **Obv:** Stylized view of our solar system, multicolor **Obv. Legend:** REPUBLIC OF KAZAKHSTAN **Rev:** Sputnik I in space, earth in background, multicolor **Rev. Legend:** THE FIRST SPACE SATELLITE OF THE EARTH **Edge:** Reeded

Date	Mintage	F	VF	XF	Unc	BU
ND(2007) Proof	4,000	Value: 100				

KM# 85   500 TENGE
31.1000 g., 0.9250 Bi-Metallic Blackened Silver center in proof Silver ring. 0.9249 oz., 38.6 mm.   **Subject:** "Otyrar" coin **Obv:** Old coin design **Rev:** Old coin design **Edge:** Reeded

Date	Mintage	F	VF	XF	Unc	BU
2007 Proof	4,000	Value: 75.00				

KM# 87   500 TENGE
24.0000 g., 0.9250 Silver 0.7137 oz. ASW, 38.6 mm.   **Obv:** Value **Rev:** Terekin Valley - noble deer petraglyph

Date	Mintage	F	VF	XF	Unc	BU
2007 Proof	3,000	Value: 90.00				

KM# 88   500 TENGE
31.1000 g., 0.9250 Silver 0.9249 oz. ASW **Subject:** Movement series - myth **Obv:** Value within square **Rev:** Design

Date	Mintage	F	VF	XF	Unc	BU
2007 Proof	4,000	Value: 80.00				

KM# 89   500 TENGE
31.1000 g., 0.9250 Silver 0.9249 oz. ASW, 38.6 mm.   **Subject:** Gold of the Romans **Obv:** Four horseman **Rev:** Gilt Roman seal ring **Shape:** 12-sided

Date	Mintage	F	VF	XF	Unc	BU
2007 Proof	5,000	Value: 100				

KM# 90   500 TENGE
31.1000 g., 0.9250 Silver 0.9249 oz. ASW, 38.6 mm.   **Obv:** State emblem **Rev:** Church

Date	Mintage	F	VF	XF	Unc	BU
2007 Proof	4,000	Value: 75.00				

KM# 91   500 TENGE
31.1000 g., 0.9250 Silver 0.9249 oz. ASW, 38.6 mm.   **Obv:** State emblem **Rev:** Traditional family

Date	Mintage	F	VF	XF	Unc	BU
2007 Proof	4,000	Value: 70.00				

KM# 92   500 TENGE
31.1000 g., 0.9250 Silver 0.9249 oz. ASW, 38.6 mm.   **Obv:** Leaves **Rev:** Tree growth rings, multicolor seeds

Date	Mintage	F	VF	XF	Unc	BU
2007 Proof	4,000	Value: 75.00				

KM# 93   500 TENGE
24.0000 g., 0.9250 Silver 0.7137 oz. ASW, 38.6 mm.   **Subject:** Spoon billed duck **Obv:** Value **Rev:** Duck in reeds

Date	Mintage	F	VF	XF	Unc	BU
2007 Proof	3,000	Value: 85.00				

KM# 167   500 TENGE
7.7800 g., 0.9990 Gold 0.2499 oz. AGW, 25 mm.   **Subject:** Olympics, high jump **Obv:** Arms and stylized stadium **Rev:** Female high jump

Date	Mintage	F	VF	XF	Unc	BU
2007 Proof	—	Value: 460				

KM# 94   500 TENGE
31.1050 g., 0.9250 Silver 0.9250 oz. ASW, 38.6 mm.   **Subject:** National currency, 15th Anniversary **Obv:** Three coin designs

Date	Mintage	F	VF	XF	Unc	BU
2008 Proof	5,000	Value: 75.00				

KM# 99   500 TENGE
31.1050 g., 0.9250 Silver 0.9250 oz. ASW, 38.61 mm.   **Subject:** Eurasic Capitals - Astana **Rev:** Skyline montage

Date	Mintage	F	VF	XF	Unc	BU
2008 Proof	5,000	Value: 75.00				

KM# 100   500 TENGE
24.0000 g., 0.9250 Silver 0.7137 oz. ASW, 38.61 mm.   **Subject:** Tien Shan - Brown Bear **Rev:** Bear seated

Date	Mintage	F	VF	XF	Unc	BU
2008 Proof	3,000	Value: 85.00				

KM# 101   500 TENGE
31.1050 g., 0.9250 Silver 0.9250 oz. ASW, 38.61 mm.   **Subject:** Nomad Gold **Rev:** Diadem fragment **Shape:** 12-sided

Date	Mintage	F	VF	XF	Unc	BU
2008 Proof	5,000	Value: 115				

KM# 102   500 TENGE
31.1050 g., 0.9250 Silver 0.9250 oz. ASW, 38.61 mm.   **Subject:** Kalmykov **Rev:** Fantasy scene

Date	Mintage	F	VF	XF	Unc	BU
2008 Proof	4,000	Value: 80.00				

KM# 103   500 TENGE
31.1050 g., 0.9250 Silver 0.9250 oz. ASW, 38.61 mm.   **Subject:** Kyz Kuu **Rev:** Two horseback riders

Date	Mintage	F	VF	XF	Unc	BU
2008 Proof	4,000	Value: 80.00				

KM# 104   500 TENGE
31.1050 g., 0.9250 Silver 0.9250 oz. ASW, 38.61 mm. **Subject:**
Linum Olgae **Rev:** Flowers

Date	Mintage	F	VF	XF	Unc	BU
2008 Proof	4,000	Value: 100				

KM# 105   500 TENGE
31.1050 g., 0.9250 Silver 0.9250 oz. ASW, 38.61 mm. **Subject:**
National Currency, 15th Anniversary **Rev:** Coin and bank note
montage

Date	Mintage	F	VF	XF	Unc	BU
2008 Proof	5,000	Value: 75.00				

KM# 106   500 TENGE
24.0000 g., 0.9250 Silver 0.7137 oz. ASW, 38.6x28.8 mm.
Subject: Papilio Alexanor **Rev:** Two butterflies **Shape:** oval

Date	Mintage	F	VF	XF	Unc	BU
2008 Proof	4,000	Value: 115				

KM# 107   500 TENGE
31.1050 g., 0.9250 Silver 0.9250 oz. ASW, 38.61 mm. **Subject:**
Saraichik Coin **Rev:** Coin of the 14th Century

Date	Mintage	F	VF	XF	Unc	BU
2008 Proof	5,000	Value: 75.00				

KM# 108   500 TENGE
41.4000 g., Bi-Metallic Silver and Titanium, 38.61 mm. **Subject:**
Vostok **Rev:** Space ship

Date	Mintage	F	VF	XF	Unc	BU
2008 Proof	4,000	Value: 110				

KM# 109   500 TENGE
31.1050 g., 0.9250 Silver 0.9250 oz. ASW, 38.61 mm. **Subject:**
Zharkent Mosque **Rev:** Mosque

Date	Mintage	F	VF	XF	Unc	BU
2008 Proof	400	Value: 75.00				

KM# 118   500 TENGE
24.0000 g., 0.9250 Silver 0.7137 oz. ASW, 37 mm. **Subject:**
Kazakhstan Railroads, 100th Anniversary **Obv:** Arms **Rev:** Modern
train and Steam locomotive, country route map in background

Date	Mintage	F	VF	XF	Unc	BU
2008 Proof	—	Value: 55.00				

KM# 131   500 TENGE
31.1050 g., 0.9250 Silver 0.9250 oz. ASW, 38.61 mm. **Subject:**
Almaty Aport **Rev:** Apple tree branch and flower

Date	Mintage	F	VF	XF	Unc	BU
2009 Proof	4,000	Value: 80.00				

KM# 149   500 TENGE
31.1050 g., 0.9250 Silver 0.9250 oz. ASW, 38.61 mm. **Subject:**
Balkhash Tiger **Rev:** Tiger on the hunt

Date	Mintage	F	VF	XF	Unc	BU
2009 Proof	5,000	Value: 75.00				

KM# 133   500 TENGE
31.1050 g., 0.9990 Silver 0.9990 oz. ASW, 38.61 mm. **Subject:**
Betashar **Rev:** Two figures standing

Date	Mintage	F	VF	XF	Unc	BU
2009 Proof	4,000	Value: 75.00				

KM# 139   500 TENGE
31.1050 g., 0.9250 Silver 0.9250 oz. ASW, 38.6 mm. **Subject:**
Nur-Astana Mosque **Rev:** Mosque

Date	Mintage	F	VF	XF	Unc	BU
2009 Proof	4,000	Value: 75.00				

KM# 142   500 TENGE
24.0000 g., 0.9250 Silver 0.7137 oz. ASW, 38.61 mm. **Rev:**
Porcupine left with quills raised

Date	Mintage	F	VF	XF	Unc	BU
2009 Proof	3,000	Value: 90.00				

KM# 143   500 TENGE
31.1050 g., 0.9990 Silver 0.9990 oz. ASW, 38.61 mm. **Rev:** Satir
head facing **Shape:** 12-sided

Date	Mintage	F	VF	XF	Unc	BU
2009 Proof	5,000	Value: 100				

KM# 130   500 TENGE
41.1000 g., Bi-Metallic Silver and Titanium, 38.61 mm. **Subject:**
Apollo - Soyoz Missions **Rev:** Spacecraft docked in orbit above
the earth

Date	Mintage	F	VF	XF	Unc	BU
2009 Proof	4,000	Value: 115				

KM# 137   500 TENGE
31.1050 g., 0.9250 Silver 0.9250 oz. ASW, 38.61 mm. **Subject:**
Coin of Almaty **Rev:** 13th Century coin

Date	Mintage	F	VF	XF	Unc	BU
2009 Proof	4,000	Value: 100				

KM# 127   500 TENGE
7.7800 g., 0.9990 Gold 0.2499 oz. AGW, 25 mm. **Subject:**
Olympics - Biathlon **Obv:** Arms and stylized stadium **Rev:**
Biathlon, 2 cross country skiers and shooter

Date	Mintage	F	VF	XF	Unc	BU
2009 Proof	5,000	Value: 445				

KM# 128   500 TENGE
31.1000 g., 0.9990 Gold 0.9988 oz. AGW, 38.6 mm. **Subject:**
Almaty Aport **Obv:** Value and leaves **Rev:** Apples and flower

Date	Mintage	F	VF	XF	Unc	BU
2009 Proof	4,000	Value: 65.00				

KM# 129   500 TENGE
31.1000 g., 0.9250 Silver 0.9249 oz. ASW, 36.6 mm. **Subject:**
Alpamys Batyr **Obv:** Arms **Rev:** Historical figure

Date	Mintage	F	VF	XF	Unc	BU
2009 Proof	5,000	Value: 55.00				

KM# 138   500 TENGE
24.0000 g., 0.9250 Silver 0.7137 oz. ASW, 28.61x28.81 mm.
Subject: Flamingo **Obv:** Partial butterfly **Rev:** Pair of flamingos
standing in holographic water **Shape:** Vertical oval

Date	Mintage	F	VF	XF	Unc	BU
2009 Proof	4,000	Value: 80.00				

KM# 148   500 TENGE
7.7800 g., 0.9990 Gold 0.2499 oz. AGW, 21.87 mm. **Rev:** Tiger
walking right

Date	Mintage	F	VF	XF	Unc	BU
2009 Proof	3,000	Value: 450				

KM# 150   500 TENGE
7.7800 g., 0.9990 Gold 0.2499 oz. AGW, 25 mm. **Subject:**
Uncia **Obv:** Arms **Rev:** Snow Leopard head left

Date	Mintage	F	VF	XF	Unc	BU
2009 Proof	5,000	Value: 445				

KM# 179   500 TENGE
31.1000 g., 0.9250 Silver 0.9249 oz. ASW **Obv:** Three horsemen
Rev: Buckle, gilt pair of seated raindeer **Shape:** 12-sided

Date	Mintage	F	VF	XF	Unc	BU
2010 Proof	5,000	Value: 85.00				

KM# 177   500 TENGE
31.1000 g., 0.9250 Silver 0.9249 oz. ASW **Obv:** Outline of three
pelicans **Rev:** Pelecanus Crispus, pelican standing

Date	Mintage	F	VF	XF	Unc	BU
2010 Proof	5,000	Value: 75.00				

KM# 178   500 TENGE
31.1000 g., 0.9250 Silver 0.9249 oz. ASW, 38.6 mm. **Subject:**
Otau Koteru **Obv:** National Emblem **Rev:** Horseman and large
ceremonial umbrella

Date	Mintage	F	VF	XF	Unc	BU
2010 Proof	5,000	Value: 90.00				

KM# 180   500 TENGE
31.1000 g., 0.9250 Silver 0.9249 oz. ASW **Subject:** Flora **Rev:**
Papaver Pavoninum in color

Date	Mintage	F	VF	XF	Unc	BU
2010 Proof	4,000	Value: 90.00				

KM# 181   500 TENGE
3.1100 g., 0.9990 Gold 0.0999 oz. AGW, 16 mm. **Obv:** Archway
Rev: Dome of the Rock, Jerusalem

Date	Mintage	F	VF	XF	Unc	BU
2010 Proof	—	Value: 200				

KM# 182   500 TENGE
31.1000 g., 0.9250 Silver 0.9249 oz. ASW **Rev:** Musical instrument

Date	Mintage	F	VF	XF	Unc	BU
2010 Proof	—	Value: 75.00				

KM# 68   1000 TENGE
7.7800 g., 0.9990 Gold 0.2499 oz. AGW, 20 mm. **Obv:** Two
winged ibexes **Rev:** Ancient warrior **Edge:** Reeded

Date	Mintage	F	VF	XF	Unc	BU
2001 Proof	—	Value: 445				

KM# 114   1000 TENGE
67.2500 g., 0.9250 Silver 1.9999 oz. ASW, 50 mm. **Subject:**
National Currency, 10th Anniversary **Obv:** Flag, multicolor **Rev:**
Coin and bank note designs

Date	Mintage	F	VF	XF	Unc	BU
2003 Proof	—	Value: 150				

KM# 115   1000 TENGE
67.2500 g., 0.9250 Silver 1.9999 oz. ASW, 50 mm. **Subject:**
National Currency, 10th Anniversary **Obv:** Arms, gilt and blue
enamel **Rev:** Coin montage

Date	Mintage	F	VF	XF	Unc	BU
2003 Proof	—	Value: 170				

KM# 67   5000 TENGE
1000.0000 g., 0.9250 Silver 29.738 oz. ASW, 100 mm. **Subject:**
10th Anniversary of Independence **Obv:** National arms above
value **Rev:** Monument statue

Date	Mintage	F	VF	XF	Unc	BU
2001 Proof	—	Value: 1,150				

KM# 173   5000 TENGE
1000.0000 g., 0.9250 Silver 29.738 oz. ASW, 100 mm. **Subject:**

Astana capitol, 10th anniversary **Obv:** National arms **Rev:** Architectural elements

Date	Mintage	F	VF	XF	Unc	BU
2008 Proof	—	Value: 1,250				

BULLION COINAGE

KM# 161 TENGE
31.1050 g., 0.9990 Silver 0.9990 oz. ASW, 38.61 mm. **Obv:** Arms **Rev:** Snow Leopard standing right on rock

Date	Mintage	F	VF	XF	Unc	BU
2009	—	—	—	—	—	65.00

KM# 160 2 TENGE
64.2100 g., 0.9990 Silver 2.0622 oz. ASW, 50 mm. **Obv:** Arms **Rev:** Snow Leopard standing right on rock

Date	Mintage	F	VF	XF	Unc	BU
2009	—	—	—	—	—	125

KM# 159 5 TENGE
155.0000 g., 0.9990 Silver 4.9782 oz. ASW, 65 mm. **Obv:** Arms **Rev:** Snow Leopard standing right on rock

Date	Mintage	F	VF	XF	Unc	BU
2009	—	—	—	—	—	250

KM# 157 10 TENGE
3.1100 g., 0.9990 Gold 0.0999 oz. AGW **Obv:** Arms **Rev:** Snow Leopard standing right on rock

Date	Mintage	F	VF	XF	Unc	BU
2009	—	—	—	—	—	225

KM# 158 10 TENGE
311.0500 g., 0.9990 Silver 9.9901 oz. ASW **Obv:** Arms **Rev:** Snow Leopard standing right on rock

Date	Mintage	F	VF	XF	Unc	BU
2009	—	—	—	—	—	550

KM# 156 20 TENGE
7.7800 g., 0.9990 Gold 0.2499 oz. AGW **Obv:** Arms **Rev:** Snow Leopard standing right on rock

Date	Mintage	F	VF	XF	Unc	BU
2009	—	—	—	—	—	450

KM# 155 50 TENGE
15.5500 g., 0.9990 Gold 0.4994 oz. AGW, 25 mm. **Obv:** Arms **Rev:** Snow Leopard standing right on rock

Date	Mintage	F	VF	XF	Unc	BU
2009	—	—	—	—	—	900

KM# 154 100 TENGE
31.1050 g., 0.9990 Gold 0.9990 oz. AGW, 32 mm. **Obv:** Arms **Rev:** Snow Leopard standing right on rock

Date	Mintage	F	VF	XF	Unc	BU
2009	—	—	—	—	—	1,750

KENYA

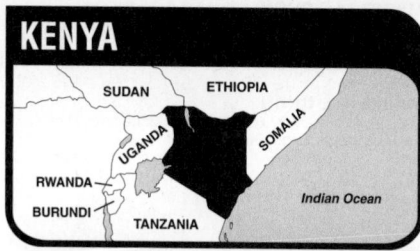

The Republic of Kenya, located on the east coast of Central Africa, has an area of 224,961 sq. mi (582,650 sq. km.) and a population of 20.1 million. Capital: Nairobi. The predominantly agricultural country exports coffee, tea and petroleum products.

Independence was attained on Dec. 12, 1963. Kenya became a republic in 1964. It is a member of the Commonwealth of Nations. The president is Chief of State and Head of Government.

MONETARY SYSTEM
100 Cents = 1 Shilling

REPUBLIC
STANDARD COINAGE

KM# 39 5 CENTS
Copper Clad Steel **Subject:** First President **Obv:** National arms **Rev:** Bust of Mzee Jomo Kenyatta left **Note:** Initially a planned issue, abandoned prior to release for circulation.

Date	Mintage	F	VF	XF	Unc	BU
2005	—	—	—	—	—	—

KM# 40 10 CENTS
Copper Clad Steel **Subject:** First President **Obv:** National arms **Rev:** Bust of Mzee Jomo Kenyatta left **Note:** Initially a planned issue, abandoned prior to release for circulation.

Date	Mintage	F	VF	XF	Unc	BU
2005	—	—	—	—	—	—

KM# 41 50 CENTS
4.5000 g., Nickel Plated Steel, 21.9 mm. **Subject:** First President **Obv:** National arms, value **Rev:** Bust of Mwee Jomo Kenyatta left

Date	Mintage	F	VF	XF	Unc	BU
2005	—	—	—	—	0.60	0.80
2009	—	—	—	—	0.60	0.80

KM# 34 SHILLING
5.4600 g., Nickel Plated Steel, 23.9 mm. **Subject:** First President **Obv:** Value above national arms **Rev:** Bust of President Mzee Jomo Kenyata left **Edge:** Segmented reeding

Date	Mintage	F	VF	XF	Unc	BU
2005	—	—	—	—	0.80	1.20
2009	—	—	—	—	0.80	1.20
2010	—	—	—	—	0.80	1.20

KM# 37 5 SHILLINGS
3.7500 g., Bi-Metallic Aluminum-Bronze center in Copper-Nickel ring, 19.5 mm. **Subject:** First President **Obv:** Value above national arms **Obv. Legend:** REPUBLIC OF KENYA **Rev:** Bust of President Mzee Jomo Kenyatta left **Edge:** Reeded

Date	Mintage	F	VF	XF	Unc	BU
2005	—	—	—	0.60	1.50	2.00
2009	—	—	—	0.60	1.50	2.00

KM# 35 10 SHILLINGS
5.0000 g., Bi-Metallic Copper-Nickel center in Aluminum-Bronze ring, 23 mm. **Subject:** First President **Obv:** Value above national arms **Obv. Legend:** REPUBLIC OF KENYA **Rev:** Bust of Mzee Jomo Kenyatta left **Edge:** Reeded

Date	Mintage	F	VF	XF	Unc	BU
2005	—	—	—	0.90	2.25	3.00
2009	—	—	—	0.90	2.25	3.00

KM# 36 20 SHILLINGS
9.0000 g., Bi-Metallic Aluminum-Bronze center in Copper-Nickel ring, 26 mm. **Subject:** First President **Obv:** Large value above national arms **Obv. Legend:** REPUBLIC OF KENYA **Rev:** Bust of President Mzee Jomo Kenyatta left **Edge:** Segmented reeding

Date	Mintage	F	VF	XF	Unc	BU
2005	—	—	—	1.20	3.00	4.00
2009	—	—	—	1.20	3.00	4.00

KM# 33 40 SHILLINGS
11.0000 g., Bi-Metallic Copper-Nickel center in Nickel-Brass ring, 27.5 mm. **Obv:** Bust of H. E. Mwai Kibaki facing **Rev:** National arms, value below **Edge:** Reeded and lettered **Edge Lettering:** 40 YEARS OF INDEPENDENCE **Note:** Issued December 11, 2003.

Date	Mintage	F	VF	XF	Unc	BU
ND(2003)	—	—	—	—	6.00	7.50

KM# 38 1000 SHILLINGS
31.1030 g., 0.9250 Silver 0.9249 oz. ASW, 38.61 mm. **Subject:** 40th Anniversary Independence **Obv:** National arms **Rev:** Bust of President H. E. Mwai Kibaki facing

Date	Mintage	F	VF	XF	Unc	BU
ND(2003) Proof	—	Value: 65.00				

KM# 43 5000 SHILLINGS
39.9400 g., 0.9160 Gold 1.1762 oz. AGW, 27.5 mm. **Obv:** Mwai Emilio Stanley Kibaki, president **Rev:** Arms with supporters

Date	Mintage	F	VF	XF	Unc	BU
2003 Proof	—	Value: 2,200				

KIRIBATI

The Republic of Kiribati (formerly the Gilbert Islands), consists of 30 coral atolls and islands spread over more than one million sq. mi. (2,590,000 sq. km.) of the southwest Pacific Ocean, has an area of 332 sq. mi. (717 sq. km.) and a population of 64,200. Capital: Bairiki, on Tarawa. In addition to the Gilbert Islands proper, Kiribati includes Ocean Island, the Central and Southern Line Islands, and the Phoenix Islands, though possession of Canton and Enderbury of the Phoenix Islands is disputed with the United States. Most families engage in subsistence fishing. Copra and phosphates are exported, mostly to Australia and New Zealand.

Kiribati is a member of the Commonwealth of Nations. The President is the Head of State and Head of Government.

MONETARY SYSTEM
100 Cents = 1 Dollar

REPUBLIC
DECIMAL COINAGE

KM# 40 5 CENTS
4.2400 g., Brass, 22.9 mm. **Obv:** National arms **Rev:** Gorilla **Edge:** Reeded

Date	Mintage	F	VF	XF	Unc	BU
2003	—	—	—	—	1.00	1.50

KM# 52 200 DOLLARS
31.1000 g., 0.9990 Gold 0.9988 oz. AGW, 36 mm. **Obv:** Shield **Rev:** The Holy Family - Joseph, Mary and Jesus

Date	Mintage	F	VF	XF	Unc	BU
2005 Proof	—	Value: 1,800				

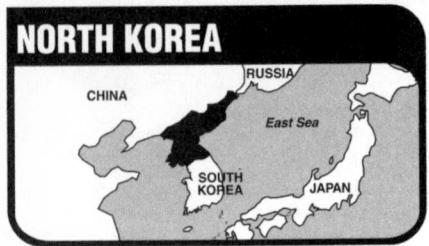

NORTH KOREA

The Democratic Peoples Republic of Korea, situated in northeastern Asia on the northern half of the Korean peninsula between the Peoples Republic of China and the Republic of Korea, has an area of 46,540 sq. mi. (120,540 sq. km.) and a population of 20 million. Capital: Pyongyang. The economy is based on heavy industry and agriculture. Metals, minerals and farm produce are exported.

MONETARY SYSTEM
100 Chon = 1 Won

MINT
Pyongyang

DATING
In the year 2001 the North Korean adopted the "Juche" dating system which is based on the birth year of Kim II Sung, founder of North Korea. He was born in 1911. "Quel" refers to month and "Quil" refers to day. 9 Quel 3 Quil refers to September 3rd. The western dates on these coins follow the "Juche" date in parenthesis.

PEOPLES REPUBLIC
DECIMAL COINAGE

KM# 183 1/2 CHON
2.1600 g., Aluminum, 27.02 mm. **Obv:** State arms **Rev:** Horse **Edge:** Plain

Date	Mintage	F	VF	XF	Unc	BU
2002	—	—	—	—	1.25	1.50

KM# 184 1/2 CHON
2.1600 g., Aluminum, 27.02 mm. **Obv:** State arms **Rev:** Orangutan **Edge:** Plain

Date	Mintage	F	VF	XF	Unc	BU
2002	—	—	—	—	1.25	1.50

KM# 185 1/2 CHON
2.1600 g., Aluminum, 27.02 mm. **Obv:** State arms **Rev:** Leopard **Edge:** Plain

Date	Mintage	F	VF	XF	Unc	BU
2002	—	—	—	—	1.25	1.50

KM# 186 1/2 CHON
2.1600 g., Aluminum, 27.02 mm. **Obv:** State arms **Rev:** Two giraffes **Edge:** Plain

Date	Mintage	F	VF	XF	Unc	BU
2002	—	—	—	—	1.25	1.50

KM# 187 1/2 CHON
2.1600 g., Aluminum, 27.02 mm. **Obv:** State arms **Rev:** Helmeted guineafowl **Edge:** Plain

Date	Mintage	F	VF	XF	Unc	BU
2002	—	—	—	—	1.25	1.50

KM# 188 1/2 CHON
2.1600 g., Aluminum, 27.02 mm. **Obv:** State arms **Rev:** Mamushi pit viper **Edge:** Plain

Date	Mintage	F	VF	XF	Unc	BU
2002	—	—	—	—	1.25	1.50

KM# 189 1/2 CHON
2.1600 g., Aluminum, 27.02 mm. **Obv:** State arms **Rev:** Bighorn sheep **Edge:** Plain

Date	Mintage	F	VF	XF	Unc	BU
2002	—	—	—	—	1.25	1.50

KM# 190 1/2 CHON
2.1600 g., Aluminum, 27.02 mm. **Obv:** State arms **Rev:** Hippopotamus **Edge:** Plain

Date	Mintage	F	VF	XF	Unc	BU
2002	—	—	—	—	1.25	1.50

KM# 191 1/2 CHON
2.1600 g., Aluminum, 27.02 mm. **Subject:** FAO **Obv:** State arms **Rev:** Ancient ship **Edge:** Plain

Date	Mintage	F	VF	XF	Unc	BU
2002	—	—	—	—	1.25	1.50

KM# 192 1/2 CHON
2.1600 g., Aluminum, 27.02 mm. **Subject:** FAO **Obv:** State arms **Rev:** Archaic ship **Edge:** Plain

Date	Mintage	F	VF	XF	Unc	BU
2002	—	—	—	—	1.25	1.50

KM# 193 1/2 CHON
2.1600 g., Aluminum, 27.02 mm. **Subject:** FAO **Obv:** State arms **Rev:** Modern train **Edge:** Plain

Date	Mintage	F	VF	XF	Unc	BU
2002	—	—	—	—	1.25	1.50

KM# 194 1/2 CHON
2.1600 g., Aluminum, 27.02 mm. **Subject:** FAO **Obv:** State arms **Rev:** Jet airliner **Edge:** Plain

Date	Mintage	F	VF	XF	Unc	BU
2002	—	—	—	—	1.25	1.50

KM# 195 CHON
4.6300 g., Brass, 21.7 mm. **Subject:** FAO **Obv:** State arms **Rev:** Antique steam locomotive **Edge:** Plain

Date	Mintage	F	VF	XF	Unc	BU
2002	—	—	—	—	1.50	1.75

KM# 196 CHON
4.6300 g., Brass, 21.7 mm. **Subject:** FAO **Obv:** State arms **Rev:** Antique automobile **Edge:** Plain

Date	Mintage	F	VF	XF	Unc	BU
2002	—	—	—	—	1.50	1.75

KM# 197 2 CHON
6.0400 g., Copper-Nickel, 24.2 mm. **Subject:** FAO **Obv:** State arms **Rev:** Antique touring car **Edge:** Plain

Date	Mintage	F	VF	XF	Unc	BU
2002	—	—	—	—	2.00	2.50

KM# 499 50 CHON
Aluminum, 27 mm. **Rev:** Two bicyclists

Date	Mintage	F	VF	XF	Unc	BU
2001 Proof, rare	—					

KM# 162.2 WON
7.0000 g., Aluminum, 40 mm. **Obv:** State arms, date above value **Rev:** Radiant Korean map and landmarks **Edge:** Plain

Date	Mintage	F	VF	XF	Unc	BU
2001 Proof	—	Value: 15.00				

KM# 351 WON
7.0000 g., Aluminum, 40 mm. **Obv:** State arms, date and value below **Rev:** North Korean Arch of Triumph **Edge:** Plain

Date	Mintage	F	VF	XF	Unc	BU
2001 Proof	—	Value: 12.00				

KM# 352 WON
28.6000 g., Brass, 40.1 mm. **Obv:** State arms, value below **Rev:** North Korean Arch of Triumph **Edge:** Plain

Date	Mintage	F	VF	XF	Unc	BU
2001 Proof	—	Value: 15.00				

KM# 353 WON
6.4500 g., Aluminum, 40 mm. **Obv:** State arms, value below **Rev:** N. Korean landmarks and tourists above ship **Edge:** Plain

Date	Mintage	F	VF	XF	Unc	BU
2001 Proof	—	Value: 12.00				

KM# 354 WON
27.6300 g., Brass, 40 mm. **Obv:** State arms, date and value below **Rev:** N. Korean landmarks and tourists above ship **Edge:** Plain

Date	Mintage	F	VF	XF	Unc	BU
2001 Proof	—	Value: 15.00				

KM# 355 WON
6.7500 g., Aluminum, 40 mm. **Obv:** State arms, value below **Rev:** Temple of Heaven above Hong Kong city view below **Edge:** Plain

Date	Mintage	F	VF	XF	Unc	BU
ND Proof	—	Value: 12.00				

KM# 356 WON
28.1000 g., Brass, 40 mm. **Obv:** State arms, date and value below **Rev:** Temple of Heaven above, Hong Kong city view below **Edge:** Plain

Date	Mintage	F	VF	XF	Unc	BU
2001 Proof	—	Value: 15.00				

KM# 294a WON
6.7500 g., Aluminum, 40 mm. **Obv:** State arms **Rev:** Antique ceramics **Edge:** Plain

Date	Mintage	F	VF	XF	Unc	BU
2001 Proof	—	Value: 15.00				

KM# 358 WON
6.7500 g., Aluminum, 40 mm. **Obv:** State arms **Rev:** Old fort **Edge:** Plain

Date	Mintage	F	VF	XF	Unc	BU
2001 Proof	—	Value: 12.00				

KM# 358a WON
28.1000 g., Brass, 40 mm. **Obv:** State arms **Rev:** Old fort **Edge:** Plain

Date	Mintage	F	VF	XF	Unc	BU
2001 Proof	—	Value: 15.00				

KM# 359 WON
7.0000 g., Aluminum, 40.1 mm. **Obv:** State arms **Rev:** Old couple above dates1945-2000 **Edge:** Plain

Date	Mintage	F	VF	XF	Unc	BU
2001 Proof	—	Value: 12.00				

KM# 359a WON
27.8000 g., Brass, 40.1 mm. **Obv:** State arms **Rev:** Old couple above dates 1945-2000 **Edge:** Plain

Date	Mintage	F	VF	XF	Unc	BU
2001 Proof	—	Value: 15.00				

KM# 360 WON
27.8000 g., Brass, 40.1 mm. **Obv:** State arms **Rev:** Blue Dragon **Edge:** Plain

Date	Mintage	F	VF	XF	Unc	BU
2001 Proof	—	Value: 20.00				

KM# 361 WON
7.0000 g., Aluminum, 40.1 mm. **Obv:** State arms **Rev:** Head of Deng Zio Ping 3/4 left, 1904-1997 flanking, sprigs below **Edge:** Plain

Date	Mintage	F	VF	XF	Unc	BU
2001 Proof	—	Value: 12.00				

KM# 361a WON
27.8000 g., Brass, 40.1 mm. **Obv:** State arms **Rev:** Head 3/4 left divides dates(1904-1997) flanked by sprigs **Edge:** Plain

Date	Mintage	F	VF	XF	Unc	BU
2001 Proof	—	Value: 15.00				

KM# 362 WON
7.0000 g., Aluminum, 40.1 mm. **Obv:** State arms **Rev:** Children flying a kite **Edge:** Plain

Date	Mintage	F	VF	XF	Unc	BU
2001 Proof	—	Value: 15.00				

KM# 362a WON
27.8000 g., Brass, 40.1 mm. **Obv:** State arms **Rev:** Children flying a kite **Edge:** Plain

Date	Mintage	F	VF	XF	Unc	BU
2001 Proof	—	Value: 17.50				

KM# 363 WON
7.0000 g., Aluminum, 40.1 mm. **Obv:** State arms **Rev:** Children on seesaw **Edge:** Plain

Date	Mintage	F	VF	XF	Unc	BU
2001 Proof	—	Value: 15.00				

KM# 363a WON
27.8000 g., Brass, 40.1 mm. **Obv:** State arms **Rev:** Children on seesaw **Edge:** Plain

Date	Mintage	F	VF	XF	Unc	BU
2001 Proof	—	Value: 17.50				

KM# 364 WON
7.0000 g., Aluminum, 40.1 mm. **Obv:** State arms **Rev:** Children wrestling **Edge:** Plain

Date	Mintage	F	VF	XF	Unc	BU
2001 Proof	—	Value: 15.00				

KM# 364a WON
27.8000 g., Brass, 40.1 mm. **Obv:** State arms **Rev:** Children wrestling **Edge:** Plain

Date	Mintage	F	VF	XF	Unc	BU
2001 Proof	—	Value: 17.50				

KM# 365 WON
7.0000 g., Aluminum, 40.1 mm. **Obv:** State arms **Rev:** Girl on swing **Edge:** Plain

Date	Mintage	F	VF	XF	Unc	BU
2001 Proof	—	Value: 15.00				

KM# 365a WON
27.8000 g., Brass, 40.1 mm. **Obv:** State arms **Rev:** Girl on swing **Edge:** Plain

Date	Mintage	F	VF	XF	Unc	BU
2001 Proof	—	Value: 17.50				

KM# 366 WON
7.0000 g., Aluminum, 40.1 mm. **Obv:** State arms **Rev:** Girls jumping rope **Edge:** Plain

Date	Mintage	F	VF	XF	Unc	BU
2001 Proof	—	Value: 15.00				

KM# 366a WON
27.8000 g., Brass, 40.1 mm. **Obv:** State arms **Rev:** Girls jumping rope **Edge:** Plain

Date	Mintage	F	VF	XF	Unc	BU
2001 Proof	—	Value: 17.50				

KM# 367 WON
8.7000 g., Aluminum, 40.4 mm. **Obv:** State arms **Rev:** "Kumdang-2 Injection" in center square on leaves **Edge:** Plain

Date	Mintage	F	VF	XF	Unc	BU
2001 Proof	—	Value: 15.00				

KM# 367a WON
26.5400 g., Brass, 40.2 mm. **Obv:** State arms **Rev:** "Kumdang-2 Injection" in center square on leaves **Edge:** Plain

Date	Mintage	F	VF	XF	Unc	BU
2001 Proof	—	Value: 17.50				

KM# 368 WON
27.6100 g., Brass, 40.2 mm. **Obv:** State arms **Rev:** Bust of Kim Il-Sung, 1912-1994 flanking, sprigs below **Edge:** Plain

Date	Mintage	F	VF	XF	Unc	BU
JU90-2001 Proof	—	Value: 17.50				

KM# 369 WON
6.5500 g., Aluminum, 40.4 mm. **Obv:** State arms **Rev:** Train at left, couple below jet plane at right **Edge:** Plain

Date	Mintage	F	VF	XF	Unc	BU
2001 Proof	—	Value: 15.00				

KM# 370 WON
27.5600 g., Brass, 40.1 mm. **Obv:** State arms **Rev:** Train at left, couple below jet plane at right **Edge:** Plain

Date	Mintage	F	VF	XF	Unc	BU
2001 Proof	—	Value: 17.50				

KM# 371 WON
5.0500 g., Aluminum, 35 mm. **Obv:** State arms **Rev:** Hong Kong city view **Edge:** Plain

Date	Mintage	F	VF	XF	Unc	BU
2001 Proof	—	Value: 10.00				

KM# 372 WON
6.4000 g., Aluminum, 40 mm. **Obv:** State arms **Rev:** Bust with beard facing flanked by text **Edge:** Plain

Date	Mintage	F	VF	XF	Unc	BU
2001 Proof	—	Value: 12.00				

KM# 372a WON
27.7000 g., Brass, 40 mm. **Obv:** State arms **Rev:** Bust with beard facing flanked by text **Edge:** Plain

Date	Mintage	F	VF	XF	Unc	BU
2001 Proof	—	Value: 15.00				

KM# 373 WON
6.9000 g., Aluminum, 40 mm. **Subject:** 1996 Olympics **Obv:** State arms **Rev:** Two green gymnasts and multicolor flame **Edge:** Plain

Date	Mintage	F	VF	XF	Unc	BU
2001 Proof	—	Value: 15.00				

KM# 374 WON
7.0000 g., Aluminum, 40 mm. **Obv:** State arms **Rev:** Taedong Gatehouse **Edge:** Plain

Date	Mintage	F	VF	XF	Unc	BU
2001 Proof	—	Value: 15.00				

KM# 375 WON
8.5000 g., Aluminum, 40.2 mm. **Obv:** State arms **Rev:** Logo above Baektn Mountain volcano crater **Edge:** Plain

Date	Mintage	F	VF	XF	Unc	BU
JU90-2001 Proof	—	Value: 10.00				

KM# 238a   WON
7.1400 g., Aluminum, 40.1 mm.   **Obv:** State arms **Rev:** Tiger and cub **Edge:** Plain

Date	Mintage	F	VF	XF	Unc	BU
2001 Proof	—	Value: 17.00				

KM# 376   WON
7.1000 g., Aluminum, 40.1 mm.   **Subject:** 1996 Olympics **Obv:** State arms **Rev:** Horse jumping **Edge:** Plain

Date	Mintage	F	VF	XF	Unc	BU
2001 Proof	—	Value: 15.00				

KM# 377   WON
7.0000 g., Aluminum, 40.1 mm.   **Subject:** 1996 Olympics **Obv:** State arms **Rev:** Four runners **Edge:** Plain

Date	Mintage	F	VF	XF	Unc	BU
2001 Proof	—	Value: 15.00				

KM# 378   WON
6.8400 g., Aluminum, 40.1 mm.   **Obv:** State arms **Rev:** Monument flanked by multicolor flags and flowers **Edge:** Plain

Date	Mintage	F	VF	XF	Unc	BU
2001 Proof	—	Value: 12.00				

KM# 379   WON
6.6000 g., Aluminum, 40.1 mm.   **Obv:** State arms **Rev:** Olympic diver **Edge:** Plain

Date	Mintage	F	VF	XF	Unc	BU
2001 Proof	—	Value: 15.00				

KM# 380   WON
6.9100 g., Aluminum, 40.1 mm.   **Obv:** State arms **Rev:** Olympic handball player **Edge:** Plain

Date	Mintage	F	VF	XF	Unc	BU
2001 Proof	—	Value: 15.00				

KM# 381   WON
7.1100 g., Aluminum, 40.2 mm.   **Obv:** State arms **Rev:** Olympic high bar gymnast **Edge:** Plain

Date	Mintage	F	VF	XF	Unc	BU
2001 Proof	—	Value: 15.00				

KM# 381a   WON
28.8200 g., Brass, 40.1 mm.   **Obv:** State arms **Rev:** Olympic high bar gymnast **Edge:** Plain

Date	Mintage	F	VF	XF	Unc	BU
2001 Proof	—	Value: 17.50				

KM# 382   WON
6.5000 g., Aluminum, 40.1 mm.   **Obv:** State arms **Rev:** Olympic archer **Edge:** Plain

Date	Mintage	F	VF	XF	Unc	BU
2001 Proof	—	Value: 15.00				

KM# 382a   WON
27.4100 g., Brass, 40.2 mm.   **Obv:** State arms **Rev:** Olympic archer **Edge:** Plain

Date	Mintage	F	VF	XF	Unc	BU
2001 Proof	—	Value: 17.50				

KM# 383   WON
7.1000 g., Aluminum, 40.1 mm.   **Obv:** State arms **Rev:** Olympic hurdler **Edge:** Plain

Date	Mintage	F	VF	XF	Unc	BU
2001 Proof	—	Value: 15.00				

KM# 383a   WON
28.0000 g., Brass, 40.1 mm.   **Obv:** State arms **Rev:** Olympic hurdler **Edge:** Plain

Date	Mintage	F	VF	XF	Unc	BU
2001 Proof	—	Value: 17.50				

KM# 384   WON
7.1500 g., Aluminum, 40.1 mm.   **Obv:** State arms **Rev:** Kim Il Sung's birthplace side view **Edge:** Plain

Date	Mintage	F	VF	XF	Unc	BU
JU90-2001 Proof	—	Value: 15.00				

KM# 385   WON
7.0000 g., Aluminum, 40.1 mm.   **Obv:** State arms **Rev:** Mt. Kumgang Fairy playing flute **Edge:** Plain

Date	Mintage	F	VF	XF	Unc	BU
2001 Proof	—	Value: 12.00				

KM# 385a   WON
28.1600 g., Brass, 40.2 mm.   **Obv:** State arms **Rev:** Mt. Kumgang Fairy playing flute **Edge:** Plain

Date	Mintage	F	VF	XF	Unc	BU
2001 Proof	—	Value: 15.00				

KM# 452   WON
27.4400 g., Brass, 40 mm.   **Obv:** State arms **Rev:** Early sailing ship **Rev. Legend:** • HISTORY OF SEAFARING • MERCHANTMAN - THE DPR KOREA . KORYO PERIOD . 918-1392 **Edge:** Plain

Date	Mintage	F	VF	XF	Unc	BU
2001 Proof	—	Value: 9.00				

KM# 505   WON
28.0000 g., Brass   **Obv:** National arms **Rev:** Rainbow lori

Date	Mintage	F	VF	XF	Unc	BU
2001 Proof	—	Value: 8.50				

KM# 157   WON
6.6700 g., Aluminum, 40 mm.   **Subject:** Seafaring Ships **Obv:** State arms **Rev:** Cruise ship below stylized head left profile **Edge:** Plain

Date	Mintage	F	VF	XF	Unc	BU
JU90-2001 Proof	—	Value: 10.00				

KM# 157a   WON
29.0500 g., Brass, 40.2 mm.   **Obv:** State arms **Rev:** Cruise ship below stylized head profile left **Edge:** Plain

Date	Mintage	F	VF	XF	Unc	BU
2001 Proof	—	Value: 17.50				

KM# 458   WON
5.0000 g., Aluminum, 35 mm.   **Obv:** National arms, Country name **Rev:** Krugenstern

Date	Mintage	F	VF	XF	Unc	BU
2001 Proof	—	Value: 7.00				

KM# 158   WON
17.0000 g., Copper-Nickel, 35 mm.   **Subject:** First Nobel Prize Winner in Literature - Sully Prudhomme **Obv:** State arms **Rev:** Half length seated bust left flanked by shelves and books **Edge:** Plain

Date	Mintage	F	VF	XF	Unc	BU
ND(2001) Proof	2,000	Value: 100				

KM# 158a WON
5.0000 g., Aluminum, 35 mm. **Subject:** Nobel prize in literature, Sully Prudhomme

Date	Mintage	F	VF	XF	Unc	BU
2001 Proof			Value: 6.00			

KM# 158b WON
16.2000 g., Brass, 35 mm. **Subject:** First Nobel Prize Winner in Literature - Sully Prudhomme **Obv:** State arms **Rev:** Half length seated bust left flanked by shelves and books **Edge:** Plain

Date	Mintage	F	VF	XF	Unc	BU
ND(2001) Proof			Value: 10.00			

KM# 159 WON
17.0000 g., Copper-Nickel, 35 mm. **Subject:** First Nobel Prize Winner in Physics - Wilhelm C. Roentgen **Obv:** State arms **Rev:** Bust 3/4 right at left with same person seated in lab at right **Edge:** Plain

Date	Mintage	F	VF	XF	Unc	BU
ND(2001) Proof	2,000	Value: 100				

KM# 159a WON
5.0000 g., Aluminum, 35 mm. **Subject:** Nobel in Physics, Wilhelm C. Rontgen

Date	Mintage	F	VF	XF	Unc	BU
2001 Proof			Value: 6.00			

KM# 159b WON
16.2000 g., Brass, 35 mm. **Subject:** First Nobel Prize in Physics - Wiliam C. Rontgen **Obv:** State arms **Rev:** Bust 3/4 right at left with same person seated in lab at right **Edge:** Plain

Date	Mintage	F	VF	XF	Unc	BU
ND(2001) Proof			Value: 10.00			

KM# 160 WON
16.2000 g., Brass, 35 mm. **Subject:** Nipponia Nippon **Obv:** State arms **Rev:** Two nest building Japanese ibis **Edge:** Plain

Date	Mintage	F	VF	XF	Unc	BU
JU90-2001 Proof			Value: 15.00			

KM# 160a WON
17.0000 g., Copper-Nickel, 35 mm. **Subject:** Wildlife **Obv:** State arms **Rev:** Two nesting Japanese Ibis birds **Edge:** Plain

Date	Mintage	F	VF	XF	Unc	BU
JU2001 Proof	200	Value: 100				

KM# 160b WON
5.3500 g., Aluminum, 35.1 mm. **Obv:** State arms **Rev:** Two nest building Japanese Ibis birds **Edge:** Plain

Date	Mintage	F	VF	XF	Unc	BU
JU90-2001 Proof			Value: 15.00			

KM# 202 WON
17.0000 g., Copper-Nickel, 35 mm. **Subject:** School Ships **Obv:** State arms **Rev:** SS Krusenstern **Edge:** Plain

Date	Mintage	F	VF	XF	Unc	BU
ND(2001) Proof	200	Value: 100				

KM# 204 WON
17.0000 g., Copper-Nickel, 35 mm. **Subject:** Wildlife **Obv:** State arms **Rev:** Two standing Japanese Ibis birds **Edge:** Plain

Date	Mintage	F	VF	XF	Unc	BU
JU90-2001 Proof	100	Value: 150				

KM# 207 WON
17.0000 g., Copper-Nickel, 35 mm. **Subject:** Wildlife **Obv:** State arms **Rev:** Two Korean Longtail Gorals **Edge:** Plain

Date	Mintage	F	VF	XF	Unc	BU
JU90-2001 Proof	200	Value: 100				

KM# 207a WON
16.0500 g., Brass, 35 mm. **Obv:** State arms **Rev:** Two Longtail Gorals **Edge:** Plain

Date	Mintage	F	VF	XF	Unc	BU
JU90-2001 Proof			Value: 12.50			

KM# 207b WON
5.3500 g., Aluminum, 35.1 mm. **Obv:** State arms **Rev:** Two Longtail Gorals **Edge:** Plain

Date	Mintage	F	VF	XF	Unc	BU
JU90-2001 Proof			Value: 10.00			

KM# 209 WON
17.0000 g., Copper-Nickel, 35 mm. **Subject:** First Nobel Prize Winner in Medicine - Emil A. von Behring **Obv:** State arms **Rev:** Lab beaker divides half length figures facing each other **Edge:** Plain

Date	Mintage	F	VF	XF	Unc	BU
ND(2001) Proof	2,000	Value: 100				

KM# 209b WON
16.0000 g., Brass, 35 mm. **Subject:** Nobel prize in Medicine, Emil von Behring

Date	Mintage	F	VF	XF	Unc	BU
2001 Proof			Value: 7.00			

KM# 209a WON
5.0000 g., Aluminum, 35 mm. **Subject:** Nobel prize in Medicine, Emil von Behring

Date	Mintage	F	VF	XF	Unc	BU
2001 Proof			Value: 6.00			

KM# 210 WON
17.0000 g., Copper-Nickel, 35 mm. **Subject:** First Nobel Prize Winner in Peace - Henri Dunant **Obv:** State arms **Rev:** Bust facing at left, war wounded at right **Edge:** Plain

Date	Mintage	F	VF	XF	Unc	BU
ND(2001) Proof	2,000	Value: 100				

KM# 210a WON
5.0000 g., Aluminum, 35 mm. **Subject:** Nobel Peace Prize, Jean H. Dunant

Date	Mintage	F	VF	XF	Unc	BU
2001 Proof			Value: 6.00			

KM# 210b WON
5.0000 g., Aluminum, 35 mm. **Subject:** Nobel Peace prize, Jean H. Dunant

Date	Mintage	F	VF	XF	Unc	BU
2001 Proof			Value: 7.00			

KM# 211 WON
17.0000 g., Copper-Nickel, 35 mm. **Subject:** First Nobel Prize Winner in Chemistry - Jacobus Van't Hoff **Obv:** State arms **Rev:** Standing figures in lab scene **Edge:** Plain

Date	Mintage	F	VF	XF	Unc	BU
ND(2001) Proof	2,000	Value: 100				

KM# 211a WON
5.0000 g., Aluminum, 35 mm. **Subject:** Nobel in Chemistry, Jacob van't Hoff

Date	Mintage	F	VF	XF	Unc	BU
2001 Proof			Value: 6.00			

KM# 211b WON
16.0000 g., Brass, 35 mm. **Subject:** Nobel prize in Chemistry, Jabob van't Hoff

Date	Mintage	F	VF	XF	Unc	BU
2001 Proof			Value: 7.00			

KM# 212 WON
17.0000 g., Copper-Nickel, 35 mm. **Subject:** First Nobel Prize Winner in Peace - Frederic Passy **Obv:** State arms **Rev:** Head left at right with allegorical scene at left **Edge:** Plain

Date	Mintage	F	VF	XF	Unc	BU
ND(2001) Proof	2,000	Value: 100				

KM# 212a WON
5.0000 g., Aluminum, 35 mm. **Subject:** Nobel Peace Prize, Frederic Passy

Date	Mintage	F	VF	XF	Unc	BU
2001 Proof			Value: 6.00			

KM# 212b WON
16.0000 g., Brass, 35 mm. **Subject:** Nobel Peace Prize, Frederic Passy

Date	Mintage	F	VF	XF	Unc	BU
2001 Proof			Value: 7.00			

KM# 232 WON
28.1100 g., Brass, 40 mm. **Obv:** State arms **Rev:** White-bellied woodpecker **Edge:** Plain

Date	Mintage	F	VF	XF	Unc	BU
2001 Proof			Value: 27.50			

KM# 233 WON
28.1100 g., Brass, 40 mm. **Obv:** State arms **Rev:** Black grouse **Edge:** Plain

Date	Mintage	F	VF	XF	Unc	BU
2001 Proof			Value: 27.50			

KM# 234 WON
28.1100 g., Brass, 40 mm. **Obv:** State arms **Rev:** Sand grouse
Edge: Plain

Date	Mintage	F	VF	XF	Unc	BU
2001 Proof	—	Value: 27.50				

KM# 235 WON
28.1100 g., Brass, 40 mm. **Obv:** State arms **Rev:** Fairy Pitta bird **Edge:** Plain

Date	Mintage	F	VF	XF	Unc	BU
2001 Proof	—	Value: 27.50				

KM# 236 WON
28.1100 g., Brass, 40 mm. **Obv:** State arms **Rev:** Mythical "Hyonmu" **Edge:** Plain

Date	Mintage	F	VF	XF	Unc	BU
2001 Proof	—	Value: 27.50				

KM# 236a WON
7.0000 g., Aluminum, 40 mm. **Obv:** State arms **Rev:** "Hyonmu" **Edge:** Plain

Date	Mintage	F	VF	XF	Unc	BU
2001 Proof	—	Value: 17.50				

KM# 237 WON
28.1100 g., Brass, 40 mm. **Obv:** State arms **Rev:** Blue Dragon
Edge: Plain

Date	Mintage	F	VF	XF	Unc	BU
2001 Proof	—	Value: 27.50				

KM# 238 WON
28.1100 g., Brass, 40 mm. **Obv:** State arms **Rev:** Two tigers
Edge: Plain

Date	Mintage	F	VF	XF	Unc	BU
2001 Proof	—	Value: 27.50				

KM# 239 WON
28.1100 g., Brass, 40 mm. **Obv:** State arms **Rev:** Brontosaurus
Edge: Plain

Date	Mintage	F	VF	XF	Unc	BU
2001 Proof	—	Value: 27.50				

KM# 247 WON
26.9500 g., Brass, 40 mm. **Obv:** State arms **Rev:** Soldier watching an air raid on a Yalu River bridge **Edge:** Plain

Date	Mintage	F	VF	XF	Unc	BU
2001 Proof	—	Value: 20.00				

KM# 248 WON
7.0000 g., Aluminum, 40 mm. **Obv:** State arms **Rev:** Multicolor rabbit and hearts **Edge:** Plain **Note:** Year of the Rabbit

Date	Mintage	F	VF	XF	Unc	BU
2001 Proof	—	Value: 20.00				

KM# 290 WON
28.2000 g., Brass, 40.1 mm. **Obv:** State arms **Rev:** Bust of Kim Johg-Il facing above flower sprigs **Edge:** Plain

Date	Mintage	F	VF	XF	Unc	BU
JU90-2001 Proof	—	Value: 20.00				

KM# 291 WON
28.2000 g., Brass, 40.1 mm. **Obv:** State arms **Rev:** Bust of Kim Jung-Suk facing, 1917-1949 flanking, flower sprigs below **Edge:** Plain

Date	Mintage	F	VF	XF	Unc	BU
JU90-2001 Proof	—	Value: 20.00				

KM# 293 WON
28.2000 g., Brass, 40.2 mm. **Obv:** State arms **Rev:** Olympic runners **Edge:** Crude reeding

Date	Mintage	F	VF	XF	Unc	BU
2001 Proof	—	Value: 20.00				

KM# 294 WON
28.2000 g., Brass, 40.2 mm. **Obv:** State arms **Rev:** Antique porcelain objects **Edge:** Plain

Date	Mintage	F	VF	XF	Unc	BU
2001 Proof	—	Value: 20.00				

KM# 310 WON
Aluminum **Obv:** State arms **Rev:** Tomb of King Tongmyong

Date	Mintage	F	VF	XF	Unc	BU
2001 Proof	—	Value: 12.00				

KM# 458a WON
16.0000 g., Brass, 35 mm. **Subject:** Tall ships **Obv:** Arms **Rev:** Krugenstern

Date	Mintage	F	VF	XF	Unc	BU
2001 Proof	—	Value: 8.00				

KM# 459 WON
Brass, 35 mm. **Subject:** Return of Hong Kong **Obv:** Arms **Rev:** Architecture

Date	Mintage	F	VF	XF	Unc	BU
2001 Proof	—	Value: 6.50				

KM# 460 WON
Brass, 35 mm. **Subject:** Return of Hong Kong **Obv:** Skyline **Rev:** Dragon boat

Date	Mintage	F	VF	XF	Unc	BU
2001 Proof	—	Value: 12.00				

KM# 461 WON
6.0000 g., Aluminum, 38 mm. **Obv:** National arms, Central Bank name **Rev:** Speed skater

Date	Mintage	F	VF	XF	Unc	BU
2001 Proof	—	—	—	—	—	—

KM# 461a WON
25.0000 g., Brass **Subject:** 2002 Olympics **Obv:** Arms **Rev:** Speedskater

Date	Mintage	F	VF	XF	Unc	BU
2001 Proof	—	Value: 10.00				

KM# 462 WON
Aluminum, 40 mm. **Subject:** Tae Kwon do **Obv:** Arms **Rev:** Two sportsmen

Date	Mintage	F	VF	XF	Unc	BU
2001 Proof	—	Value: 8.00				

KM# 462a WON
28.0000 g., Brass, 40 mm. **Obv:** National arms, Country name **Rev:** Two Taekwondo players

Date	Mintage	F	VF	XF	Unc	BU
2001 Proof	—	Value: 7.00				

KM# 463 WON
Aluminum, 40 mm. **Obv:** Arms **Rev:** Multicolor flowers

Date	Mintage	F	VF	XF	Unc	BU
2001 Proof	—	Value: 8.00				

KM# 464 WON
Aluminum, 40 mm. **Obv:** Arms **Rev:** Woodpecker on branch (Dryocopus Javensis)

Date	Mintage	F	VF	XF	Unc	BU
2001 Proof	—	Value: 8.00				

KM# 465 WON
Aluminum, 35 mm. **Obv:** Arms **Rev:** Zhou Enlai portrait facing

Date	Mintage	F	VF	XF	Unc	BU
2001 Proof	—	Value: 8.00				

KM# 466 WON
Aluminum, 40 mm. **Obv:** Arms **Rev:** Buddha seated, facing

Date	Mintage	F	VF	XF	Unc	BU
2001 Proof	—	Value: 7.00				

KM# 467 WON
Brass **Obv:** Arms **Rev:** Buddha seated, facing

Date	Mintage	F	VF	XF	Unc	BU
2001 Proof	—	Value: 10.00				

KM# 468 WON
Brass **Obv:** Arms **Rev:** Couple embracing, 1945-2000

Date	Mintage	F	VF	XF	Unc	BU
ND(2001) Proof	—	Value: 10.00				

KM# 504 WON
7.0000 g., Aluminum, 40 mm. **Obv:** National arms **Rev:** Rainbow lori in color

Date	Mintage	F	VF	XF	Unc	BU
2001 Proof	—	Value: 8.50				

KM# 506 WON
7.0000 g., Aluminum **Rev:** Mandarian Ducks in color

Date	Mintage	F	VF	XF	Unc	BU
2001	—	Value: 8.50				

KM# 507 WON
Brass **Rev:** Mandarin Ducks

Date	Mintage	F	VF	XF	Unc	BU
2001 Proof	—	Value: 9.00				

KM# 535 WON
7.0000 g., Aluminum, 40 mm. **Obv:** National arms **Rev:** Power in teh frowing area of Kaeseong in color

Date	Mintage	F	VF	XF	Unc	BU
2001 Proof	—	—	—	—	—	—

KM# 539 WON
7.0000 g., Aluminum, 40 mm. **Obv:** National arms **Rev:** Panda seated in color, eating

Date	Mintage	F	VF	XF	Unc	BU
2001 Proof	—	Value: 7.50				

KM# 541 WON
7.0000 g., Aluminum, 40 mm. **Obv:** National arms **Rev:** Two pandas in color

Date	Mintage	F	VF	XF	Unc	BU
2001 Proof	—	Value: 7.50				

KM# 542 WON
28.0000 g., Brass **Obv:** National arms, name of the Central Bank **Rev:** Two pandas

Date	Mintage	F	VF	XF	Unc	BU
2001 Proof	—	Value: 8.00				

KM# 548 WON
7.0000 g., Aluminum, 40 mm. **Obv:** National arms, name of the Central Bank **Rev:** Rainbow lori in color

Date	Mintage	F	VF	XF	Unc	BU
2001 Proof	—	Value: 7.50				

KM# 549 WON
7.0000 g., Aluminum, 40 mm. **Obv:** National arms, name of the Central Bank **Rev:** Manderin duck in color

Date	Mintage	F	VF	XF	Unc	BU
2001 Proof	—	Value: 7.50				

KM# 556 WON
Brass **Rev:** Show jumper

Date	Mintage	F	VF	XF	Unc	BU
2001 Proof	—	Value: 8.00				

KM# 557 WON
7.0000 g., Aluminum, 40 mm. **Obv:** National arms, name of the Central Bank **Rev:** Rythem dancers and logo in color

Date	Mintage	F	VF	XF	Unc	BU
2001 Proof	—	Value: 7.50				

KM# 558 WON
7.0000 g., Aluminum, 40 mm. **Obv:** National arms, name of the Central Bank **Rev:** Chinese Peony

Date	Mintage	F	VF	XF	Unc	BU
2001 Proof	—	Value: 7.50				

KM# 559 WON
7.0000 g., Aluminum, 40 mm. **Obv:** National arms, name of the Central Bank **Rev:** Panda seated in color eating

Date	Mintage	F	VF	XF	Unc	BU
2001 Proof	—	Value: 7.50				

KM# 560 WON
Brass, 28 mm. **Obv:** National arms, name of the Central Bank **Rev:** Panda seated eating

Date	Mintage	F	VF	XF	Unc	BU
2001 Proof	—	Value: 8.00				

KM# 561 WON
28.0000 g., Brass, 40 mm. **Obv:** National arms, name of the Central Bank **Rev:** Soldiers attack bridge over the Yalu river at Dandong (1951)

Date	Mintage	F	VF	XF	Unc	BU
2001 Proof	—	Value: 7.50				

KM# 562 WON
28.0000 g., Brass, 40 mm. **Obv:** National arms **Rev:** Soldiers attack bridge over the Yalu river at Dandong (1951)

Date	Mintage	F	VF	XF	Unc	BU
2001 Proof	—	Value: 7.50				

KM# 563 WON
28.0000 g., Brass, 40 mm. **Obv:** National arms, name of the Central Bank **Rev:** Tower of Friendship in Pyeongyang with North Korean and P.R.C. flags

Date	Mintage	F	VF	XF	Unc	BU
2001 Proof	—	Value: 8.00				

KM# 568 WON
7.0000 g., Aluminum, 40 mm. **Obv:** National arms **Rev:** Rocket and satelite

Date	Mintage	F	VF	XF	Unc	BU
2001 Proof	—	Value: 6.50				

KM# 568a WON
28.0000 g., Brass, 40 mm. **Obv:** National arms **Rev:** Rocket and satellite

Date	Mintage	F	VF	XF	Unc	BU
2001	—	Value: 7.50				

KM# 572 WON
28.0000 g., Brass, 40 mm. **Obv:** National arms, country name **Rev:** Dragon rising

Date	Mintage	F	VF	XF	Unc	BU
2001 Proof	—	Value: 7.50				

KM# 573 WON
28.0000 g., Brass, 40 mm. **Obv:** National arms, name of the Central Bank **Rev:** Dragon rising

Date	Mintage	F	VF	XF	Unc	BU
2001 Proof	—	Value: 7.50				

KM# 574 WON
Brass **Obv:** National arms, country name **Rev:** Two girls on the seasaw

Date	Mintage	F	VF	XF	Unc	BU
2001 Proof	—	Value: 7.50				

KM# 575 WON
Brass **Obv:** National arms, Central Bank name **Rev:** Two girls on the seasaw

Date	Mintage	F	VF	XF	Unc	BU
2001 Proof	—	Value: 7.50				

KM# 576 WON
Brass **Obv:** National arms, country name **Rev:** Korean struggle

Date	Mintage	F	VF	XF	Unc	BU
2001 Proof	—	Value: 7.50				

KM# 577 WON
Brass **Obv:** National arms, Central Bank name **Rev:** Korean struggle

Date	Mintage	F	VF	XF	Unc	BU
2001 Proof	—	Value: 7.50				

KM# 578 WON
Brass **Obv:** National arms, country name **Rev:** Child on swing

Date	Mintage	F	VF	XF	Unc	BU
2001 Proof	—	Value: 7.50				

KM# 579 WON
Brass **Obv:** National arms, Central Bank name **Rev:** Child on swing

Date	Mintage	F	VF	XF	Unc	BU
2001 Proof	—	Value: 7.50				

KM# 580 WON
Brass **Obv:** National arms, country name **Rev:** Children skipping

Date	Mintage	F	VF	XF	Unc	BU
2001 Proof	—	Value: 7.50				

KM# 581 WON
28.0000 g., Brass, 40 mm. **Obv:** National arms, Central Bank name **Rev:** Children skipping

Date	Mintage	F	VF	XF	Unc	BU
2001 Proof	—	Value: 7.50				

KM# 608 WON
7.0000 g., Aluminum, 40 mm. **Obv:** National arms, Central Bank name **Rev:** Rabbit in color

Date	Mintage	F	VF	XF	Unc	BU
2001 Proof	—	Value: 7.50				

KM# 609 WON
28.0000 g., Brass, 40 mm. **Obv:** National arms, country name **Rev:** Rabbit

Date	Mintage	F	VF	XF	Unc	BU
2001 Proof	—	Value: 7.50				

KM# 616 WON
7.0000 g., Aluminum, 40 mm. **Obv:** National arms, Central Bank name **Rev:** White bellied woodpecker

Date	Mintage	F	VF	XF	Unc	BU
2001 Proof	—	Value: 6.00				

KM# 617 WON
7.0000 g., Aluminum, 40 mm. **Obv:** National arms, Country name **Rev:** Black grouse

Date	Mintage	F	VF	XF	Unc	BU
2001 Proof	—	Value: 6.00				

KM# 618 WON
7.0000 g., Aluminum, 40 mm. **Obv:** National arms, Country name **Rev:** Sand grouse

Date	Mintage	F	VF	XF	Unc	BU
2001 Proof	—	Value: 6.00				

KM# 619 WON
7.0000 g., Aluminum, 40 mm. **Obv:** National arms, Country name **Rev:** Indian Pitta bird

Date	Mintage	F	VF	XF	Unc	BU
2001 Proof	—	Value: 6.00				

KM# 636 WON
28.0000 g., Brass, 40 mm. **Obv:** National arms, Country name **Rev:** Two siberian tigers

Date	Mintage	F	VF	XF	Unc	BU
2001 Proof	—	Value: 7.00				

KM# 641 WON
7.0000 g., Aluminum, 40 mm. **Obv:** National arms, Country name **Rev:** Gojumong, first king

Date	Mintage	F	VF	XF	Unc	BU
2001 Proof	—	Value: 6.00				

KM# 642 WON
28.0000 g., Brass, 40 mm. **Obv:** National arms, Country name **Rev:** Gojumong, 1st king

Date	Mintage	F	VF	XF	Unc	BU
2001 Proof	—	Value: 7.00				

KM# 643 WON
28.0000 g., Brass, 40 mm. **Obv:** National arms, Central Bank name **Rev:** Gojumong, 1st king

Date	Mintage	F	VF	XF	Unc	BU
2001 Proof	—	Value: 7.00				

KM# 644 WON
7.0000 g., Aluminum, 40 mm. **Obv:** National arms, Country name **Rev:** Buddha figure as Myogilsand as rock relief in inner diamond mountain

Date	Mintage	F	VF	XF	Unc	BU
2001 Proof	—	Value: 6.00				

KM# 645 WON
28.0000 g., Brass, 40 mm. **Obv:** National arms, Country name **Rev:** Buddha figure Myogilsang as rock relief in inner diamond mountain

Date	Mintage	F	VF	XF	Unc	BU
2001 Proof	—	Value: 7.00				

KM# 646 WON
Aluminum **Obv:** Dragon and country name **Rev:** King Gojoseon

Date	Mintage	F	VF	XF	Unc	BU
2001 Proof	—	Value: 6.00				

KM# 647 WON
28.0000 g., Brass, 40 mm. **Obv:** Dragon and country name **Rev:** King Gojoseon

Date	Mintage	F	VF	XF	Unc	BU
2001 Proof	—	Value: 7.00				

KM# 648 WON
28.0000 g., Brass, 40 mm. **Obv:** Dragon, Central Bank name **Rev:** King Gojoseon

Date	Mintage	F	VF	XF	Unc	BU
2001 Proof	—	Value: 7.00				

KM# 663 WON
7.0000 g., Aluminum, 40 mm. **Obv:** National arms, Central Bank name **Rev:** Map of Korea in circle

Date	Mintage	F	VF	XF	Unc	BU
2001 Proof	—	Value: 6.00				

KM# 664 WON
28.0000 g., Brass, 40 mm. **Obv:** National arms, Country name **Rev:** Map of Korea in circle

Date	Mintage	F	VF	XF	Unc	BU
2001 Proof	—	Value: 7.00				

KM# 666 WON
28.0000 g., Brass, 40 mm. **Obv:** National arms, Country name **Rev:** First married couple to see again after the 1945 seperation

Date	Mintage	F	VF	XF	Unc	BU
2001 Proof	—	Value: 7.00				

KM# 670 WON
28.0000 g., Brass, 40 mm. **Obv:** National arms, Central Bank name **Rev:** Kim Jeongil and Kim Daejung embrace

Date	Mintage	F	VF	XF	Unc	BU
2001 Proof	—	Value: 7.00				

KM# 671 WON
28.0000 g., Brass, 40 mm. **Obv:** National arms, Central bank name **Rev:** Picture pose of Kim Jeongil and Kim Daejung

Date	Mintage	F	VF	XF	Unc	BU
2001 Proof	—	Value: 7.00				

KM# 672 WON
28.0000 g., Brass, 40 mm. **Obv:** National arms, Central Bank name **Rev:** Kim Jeongil and Kim Daejung sign joint agreement

Date	Mintage	F	VF	XF	Unc	BU
2001 Proof	—	Value: 7.00				

KM# 674 WON
28.0000 g., Brass, 40 mm. **Subject:** Sydney Olympics, 2000 **Obv:** National arms, Country name **Rev:** Archer

Date	Mintage	F	VF	XF	Unc	BU
2001 Proof	—	Value: 7.00				

KM# 675 WON
28.0000 g., Brass, 40 mm. **Obv:** National arms, Country name **Rev:** Handball player

Date	Mintage	F	VF	XF	Unc	BU
2001 Proof	—	Value: 7.00				

KM# 676 WON
7.0000 g., Aluminum, 40 mm. **Obv:** National arms, Country name **Rev:** Korean ringer

Date	Mintage	F	VF	XF	Unc	BU
2001 Proof	—	Value: 6.00				

KM# 677 WON
28.0000 g., Brass, 40 mm. **Subject:** Sydney Olympics **Obv:** National arms, Country name **Rev:** Korean ringer

Date	Mintage	F	VF	XF	Unc	BU
2001 Proof	—	Value: 7.00				

KM# 691 WON
28.0000 g., Brass, 40 mm. **Subject:** Kim Ilseong's 90th birthday
Obv: National arms, Central Bank name **Rev:** Kim Ilseong

Date	Mintage	F	VF	XF	Unc	BU
2001 Proof	—	Value: 7.00				

KM# 692 WON
28.0000 g., Brass, 40 mm. **Obv:** National arms, Central Bank name **Rev:** Kim Jeongil

Date	Mintage	F	VF	XF	Unc	BU
2001 Proof	—	Value: 7.00				

KM# 693 WON
28.0000 g., Brass, 40 mm. **Obv:** National arms, Central Bank name **Rev:** Kim Jeongsuk

Date	Mintage	F	VF	XF	Unc	BU
2001 Proof	—	Value: 7.00				

KM# 698 WON
7.0000 g., Aluminum, 40 mm. **Obv:** National arms, Country name **Rev:** House where Kim Ilseong was born

Date	Mintage	F	VF	XF	Unc	BU
2001 Proof	—	Value: 6.00				

KM# 699 WON
28.0000 g., Brass, 40 mm. **Obv:** National arms, Country name **Rev:** House were Kim Ilseong was born

Date	Mintage	F	VF	XF	Unc	BU
2001 Proof	—	Value: 7.00				

KM# 700 WON
28.0000 g., Brass, 40 mm. **Obv:** National arms, Central Bank name **Rev:** House where Kim Ilseong was born

Date	Mintage	F	VF	XF	Unc	BU
2001 Proof	—	Value: 7.00				

KM# 701 WON
28.0000 g., Brass, 40 mm. **Obv:** National arms **Rev:** Mountain hut

Date	Mintage	F	VF	XF	Unc	BU
2001 Proof	—	—	—	—	—	—

KM# 702 WON
7.0000 g., Aluminum, 40 mm. **Obv:** National arms **Rev:** House where Kim Jeongsuk was born

Date	Mintage	F	VF	XF	Unc	BU
2001 Proof	—	—	—	—	—	—

KM# 703 WON
28.0000 g., Brass, 40 mm. **Obv:** National arms **Rev:** House where Kim Jeongsuk was born

Date	Mintage	F	VF	XF	Unc	BU
2001 Proof	—	—	—	—	—	—

KM# 706 WON
7.0000 g., Aluminum, 40 mm. **Obv:** National arms, Country name **Rev:** East gate of Pyeongyang

Date	Mintage	F	VF	XF	Unc	BU
2001 Proof	—	Value: 6.00				

KM# 707 WON
28.0000 g., Brass, 40 mm. **Obv:** National arms, Country name **Rev:** East gate of Pyeongyang

Date	Mintage	F	VF	XF	Unc	BU
2001 Proof	—	Value: 7.00				

KM# 708 WON
28.0000 g., Brass, 40 mm. **Obv:** National arms, Central Bank name **Rev:** East gate of Pyeongyang

Date	Mintage	F	VF	XF	Unc	BU
2001 Proof	—	Value: 7.00				

KM# 709 WON
7.0000 g., Aluminum, 40 mm. **Obv:** National arms, Country name **Rev:** North gate of Pyeongyang reconstructed

Date	Mintage	F	VF	XF	Unc	BU
2001 Proof	—	Value: 6.00				

KM# 710 WON
28.0000 g., Brass, 40 mm. **Obv:** National arms, Country name **Rev:** North gate of Pyeongyang reconstructed

Date	Mintage	F	VF	XF	Unc	BU
2001 Proof	—	Value: 7.00				

KM# 711 WON
28.0000 g., Brass, 40 mm. **Obv:** National arms, Central Bank name **Rev:** North gate of Pyeongyang reconstructed

Date	Mintage	F	VF	XF	Unc	BU
2001 Proof	—	Value: 7.00				

KM# 712 WON
28.0000 g., Brass, 40 mm. **Obv:** National arms, Country name with date **Rev:** Celadon pottery

Date	Mintage	F	VF	XF	Unc	BU
2001 Proof	—	Value: 7.00				

KM# 713 WON
28.0000 g., Brass, 40 mm. **Obv:** National arms, Country name **Rev:** Celadon pottery

Date	Mintage	F	VF	XF	Unc	BU
2001 Proof	—	Value: 7.00				

KM# 714 WON
28.0000 g., Brass, 40 mm. **Obv:** National arms, Central bank name **Rev:** Celadon pottery

Date	Mintage	F	VF	XF	Unc	BU
2001 Proof	—	Value: 7.00				

KM# 719 WON
28.0000 g., Brass, 40 mm. **Obv:** National arms, Central Bank name **Rev:** Ginsing plant

Date	Mintage	F	VF	XF	Unc	BU
2001 Proof	—	Value: 7.00				

KM# 721 WON
7.0000 g., Aluminum, 40 mm. **Obv:** National arms, Central Bank name **Rev:** Fairwell to the steam railway, 1945 and again in 2001

Date	Mintage	F	VF	XF	Unc	BU
2001 Proof	—	Value: 6.00				

KM# 722 WON
28.0000 g., Brass, 40 mm. **Obv:** National arms, Central Bank name **Rev:** Fairwell to the steam train, 1945, and then again, 2001

Date	Mintage	F	VF	XF	Unc	BU
2001 Proof	—	Value: 7.00				

KM# 724 WON
7.0000 g., Aluminum, 40 mm. **Obv:** National arms. Central Bank name **Rev:** Married couple in front of Pyongyang attractions with national flag and ferryboat

Date	Mintage	F	VF	XF	Unc	BU
2001 Proof	—	Value: 6.00				

KM# 725 WON
28.0000 g., Brass, 40 mm. **Obv:** National arms, Country name **Rev:** Married couple in front of Pyongyang attractions with national flag and ferryboat

Date	Mintage	F	VF	XF	Unc	BU
2001 Proof	—	Value: 7.00				

KM# 726 WON
7.0000 g., Aluminum, 40 mm. **Obv:** National arms, Central Bank name **Rev:** Ferryboat from Koreans in Japan on the route from Niigata to Wonsan

Date	Mintage	F	VF	XF	Unc	BU
2001 Proof	—	Value: 6.00				

KM# 727 WON
28.0000 g., Brass, 40 mm. **Obv:** National arms, Central Bank name **Rev:** Ferryboat from Koreans in Japan on the route from Niigata to Wonsan

Date	Mintage	F	VF	XF	Unc	BU
2001 Proof	—	Value: 7.00				

KM# 728 WON
7.0000 g., Aluminum, 40 mm. **Obv:** National arms, Country name **Rev:** Arch of Triumph on Moranbong in Pyeongyang

Date	Mintage	F	VF	XF	Unc	BU
2001 Proof	—	Value: 6.00				

KM# 729 WON
28.0000 g., Brass, 40 mm. **Obv:** National arms, Central Bank name **Rev:** Arch of Triumph on Moranbong in Pyeongyang

Date	Mintage	F	VF	XF	Unc	BU
2001 Proof	—	Value: 7.00				

KM# 730 WON
7.0000 g., Aluminum, 40 mm. **Obv:** National arms, Central Bank name **Rev:** Chonji crater on the Paektusan

Date	Mintage	F	VF	XF	Unc	BU
2001 Proof	—	Value: 6.00				

KM# 731 WON
28.0000 g., Brass, 40 mm. **Obv:** National arms, Central Bank name **Rev:** Chonji crater on the Paektusan

Date	Mintage	F	VF	XF	Unc	BU
2001 Proof	—	Value: 7.00				

KM# 746 WON
28.0000 g., Brass, 40 mm. **Obv:** National arms **Rev:** Kim Jeongill in Pudong industrial area of Shanghai

Date	Mintage	F	VF	XF	Unc	BU
2001 Proof	—	—	—	—	—	—

KM# 718 WON
Aluminum, 40 mm. **Obv:** National arms, Central Bank name **Rev:** Ginsing plant

Date	Mintage	F	VF	XF	Unc	BU
2001 Proof	—	Value: 7.00				

KM# 749 WON
28.0000 g., Brass, 40 mm. **Obv:** National arms, Central Bank name **Rev:** Deng Xiaoping between peonies

Date	Mintage	F	VF	XF	Unc	BU
2001 Proof	—	Value: 7.00				

KM# 750 WON
17.0000 g., Copper-Nickel, 35 mm. **Obv:** National arms **Rev:** Orca before tourist boat

Date	Mintage	F	VF	XF	Unc	BU
2001 Proof	—	Value: 14.00				

KM# 751 WON
5.0000 g., Aluminum, 35 mm. **Obv:** National arms, Central Bank name **Rev:** Orca before tourist boat

Date	Mintage	F	VF	XF	Unc	BU
2001 Proof	—	Value: 6.00				

KM# 751a WON
16.0000 g., Brass, 35 mm. **Obv:** National arms, Central Bank name **Rev:** Orca before tourist boat

Date	Mintage	F	VF	XF	Unc	BU
2001 Proof	—	Value: 7.00				

KM# 752 WON
17.0000 g., Copper-Nickel, 35 mm. **Obv:** National arms, Country name **Rev:** Humpback whale

Date	Mintage	F	VF	XF	Unc	BU
2001 Proof	—	Value: 14.00				

KM# 753 WON
5.0000 g., Aluminum, 35 mm. **Obv:** National arms, Central Bank name **Rev:** Humpback whale

Date	Mintage	F	VF	XF	Unc	BU
2001 Proof	—	Value: 6.00				

KM# 753a WON
16.0000 g., Brass, 35 mm. **Obv:** National arms, Central Bank name **Rev:** Humpback whale

Date	Mintage	F	VF	XF	Unc	BU
2001 Proof	—	Value: 7.00				

KM# 754 WON
17.0000 g., Copper-Nickel, 35 mm. **Obv:** National arms, Country name **Rev:** Sperm whale

Date	Mintage	F	VF	XF	Unc	BU
2001 Proof	—	Value: 14.00				

KM# 755 WON
5.0000 g., Aluminum, 35 mm. **Obv:** National arms, Central Bank name **Rev:** Sperm whale

Date	Mintage	F	VF	XF	Unc	BU
2001 Proof	—	Value: 6.00				

KM# 755a WON
16.0000 g., Brass, 35 mm. **Obv:** National arms, Central Bank name **Rev:** Sperm whale

Date	Mintage	F	VF	XF	Unc	BU
2001 Proof	—	Value: 7.00				

KM# 756 WON
17.0000 g., Copper-Nickel, 35 mm. **Obv:** National arms, Country name **Rev:** Pilot whale

Date	Mintage	F	VF	XF	Unc	BU
2001 Proof	—	Value: 14.00				

KM# 757 WON
5.0000 g., Aluminum, 35 mm. **Obv:** National arms, Central Bank name **Rev:** Pilot whale

Date	Mintage	F	VF	XF	Unc	BU
2001 Proof	—	Value: 6.00				

KM# 757a WON
16.0000 g., Brass, 35 mm. **Obv:** National arms, Central Bank name **Rev:** Pilot whale

Date	Mintage	F	VF	XF	Unc	BU
2001 Proof	—	Value: 7.00				

KM# 758 WON
17.0000 g., Copper-Nickel, 35 mm. **Obv:** National arms, Country name **Rev:** Northern Right Whale

Date	Mintage	F	VF	XF	Unc	BU
2001 Proof	—	Value: 14.00				

KM# 759 WON
5.0000 g., Aluminum, 35 mm. **Obv:** National arms, Central Bank name **Rev:** Northern Right Whale

Date	Mintage	F	VF	XF	Unc	BU
2001 Proof	—	Value: 14.00				

KM# 759a WON
16.0000 g., Brass, 35 mm. **Obv:** National arms, Central Bank name **Rev:** Northern Right Whale

Date	Mintage	F	VF	XF	Unc	BU
2001 Proof	—	Value: 10.00				

KM# 760 WON
17.0000 g., Copper-Nickel, 35 mm. **Obv:** National arms, Country name **Rev:** Blue whale

Date	Mintage	F	VF	XF	Unc	BU
2001 Proof	—	Value: 14.00				

KM# 761 WON
5.0000 g., Aluminum, 35 mm. **Obv:** National arms, Central Bank name **Rev:** Blue Whale

Date	Mintage	F	VF	XF	Unc	BU
2001 Proof	—	Value: 6.00				

KM# 761a WON
16.0000 g., Brass, 35 mm. **Obv:** National arms, Central Bank name **Rev:** Blue whale

Date	Mintage	F	VF	XF	Unc	BU
2001 Proof	—	Value: 7.00				

KM# 762 WON
17.0000 g., Copper-Nickel, 35 mm. **Obv:** National arms, Country name **Rev:** Bowhead whale

Date	Mintage	F	VF	XF	Unc	BU
2001 Proof	—	Value: 14.00				

KM# 763 WON
5.0000 g., Aluminum, 35 mm. **Obv:** National arms, Central Bank name **Rev:** Bowhead whale

Date	Mintage	F	VF	XF	Unc	BU
2001 Proof	—	Value: 6.00				

KM# 763a WON
16.0000 g., Brass, 35 mm. **Obv:** National arms, Central Bank name **Rev:** Bowhead whale

Date	Mintage	F	VF	XF	Unc	BU
2001 Proof	—	Value: 7.00				

KM# 764 WON
17.0000 g., Copper-Nickel, 35 mm. **Obv:** National arms, Country name **Rev:** Killer whale off the coast

Date	Mintage	F	VF	XF	Unc	BU
2001 Proof	—	Value: 14.00				

KM# 765 WON
5.0000 g., Aluminum, 35 mm. **Obv:** Naitonal arms, Central Bank name **Rev:** Killer whale off the coast

Date	Mintage	F	VF	XF	Unc	BU
2001 Proof	—	Value: 6.00				

KM# 765a WON
16.0000 g., Brass, 35 mm. **Obv:** National arms, Central Bank name **Rev:** Killer whale off the coast

Date	Mintage	F	VF	XF	Unc	BU
2001 Proof	—	Value: 7.00				

KM# 766 WON
15.0000 g., 0.9990 Silver 0.4818 oz. ASW, 35 mm. **Obv:** National arms, Country name **Rev:** Northern Right Whale

Date	Mintage	F	VF	XF	Unc	BU
2001 Proof	—	Value: 35.00				

KM# 767   WON
5.0000 g., Aluminum, 35 mm. **Obv:** National arms, Country name **Rev:** Chinese dragon boat

Date	Mintage	F	VF	XF	Unc	BU
2001 Proof	—	Value: 6.00				

KM# 767a   WON
Brass, 35 mm. **Obv:** National arms, Country name **Rev:** Chinese dragon boat

Date	Mintage	F	VF	XF	Unc	BU
2001 Proof	—	Value: 7.00				

KM# 769   WON
16.0000 g., Brass, 35 mm. **Obv:** East gate of Pyeongyang **Rev:** Krusenstern

Date	Mintage	F	VF	XF	Unc	BU
2001 Proof	—	Value: 7.00				

KM# 771   WON
6.0000 g., Aluminum, 38 mm. **Obv:** National arms, Central Bank name **Rev:** White-tailed sea eagle

Date	Mintage	F	VF	XF	Unc	BU
2001 Proof	—	Value: 8.00				

KM# 771a   WON
25.0000 g., Brass, 38 mm. **Obv:** National arms, Central Bank name **Rev:** White-tailed sea eagle

Date	Mintage	F	VF	XF	Unc	BU
2001 Proof	—	—	—	—	—	—

KM# 772   WON
7.0000 g., Aluminum, 40 mm. **Obv:** National arms, Country name **Rev:** Taekwondo kicker

Date	Mintage	F	VF	XF	Unc	BU
2001 Proof	—	Value: 6.00				

KM# 772a   WON
28.0000 g., Brass, 40 mm. **Obv:** National arms, Country name **Rev:** Taekwondo kicker

Date	Mintage	F	VF	XF	Unc	BU
2001 Proof	—	Value: 7.00				

KM# 773   WON
7.0000 g., Aluminum, 40 mm. **Obv:** National arms, Country name **Rev:** Taekwondo kicker

Date	Mintage	F	VF	XF	Unc	BU
2001 Proof	—					

KM# 774   WON
Aluminum, 40 mm. **Obv:** National arms, Central Bank name **Rev:** Two taekwondo players

Date	Mintage	F	VF	XF	Unc	BU
2001 Proof	—	Value: 6.00				

KM# 470   WON
Brass, 35 mm. **Subject:** 2004 Olympics **Obv:** Arms **Rev:** Three Karate Sportsmen

Date	Mintage	F	VF	XF	Unc	BU
2002 Proof	—	Value: 6.50				

KM# 471   WON
Brass **Obv:** Arms **Rev:** Bridge

Date	Mintage	F	VF	XF	Unc	BU
2002 (91) Proof	—	Value: 7.50				

KM# 305   WON
7.0000 g., Aluminum, 40 mm. **Obv:** Arms **Rev:** Tomb of King Kong Min

Date	Mintage	F	VF	XF	Unc	BU
2002 Proof	—	Value: 7.50				

KM# 474   WON
Brass **Obv:** Arms **Rev:** Family about to hug

Date	Mintage	F	VF	XF	Unc	BU
2002 Proof	—	Value: 10.00				

KM# 475   WON
Brass, 40 mm. **Obv:** Arms **Rev:** Three people in group hug

Date	Mintage	F	VF	XF	Unc	BU
2002 Proof	—	Value: 10.00				

KM# 476   WON
Brass **Obv:** Arms **Rev:** Four dragons around map of North Korea

Date	Mintage	F	VF	XF	Unc	BU
2002 Proof	—	Value: 10.00				

KM# 305a   WON
28.2000 g., Brass, 40.2 mm. **Obv:** State arms **Rev:** Tomb of King Kong Min **Edge:** Plain

Date	Mintage	F	VF	XF	Unc	BU
JU91-2002 Proof	—	Value: 20.00				

KM# 306   WON
7.1000 g., Aluminum, 40 mm. **Obv:** State arms **Rev:** Two horses within circle of Asian zodiac animals **Edge:** Plain **Note:** Prev. KM#398.

Date	Mintage	F	VF	XF	Unc	BU
2002 Proof	—	Value: 20.00				

KM# 306a   WON
28.2000 g., Brass, 40.2 mm. **Obv:** State arms **Rev:** Two horses within circle of Asian zodiac animals **Edge:** Plain

Date	Mintage	F	VF	XF	Unc	BU
2002 Proof	—	Value: 20.00				

KM# 308   WON
6.9000 g., Aluminum, 40 mm. **Obv:** State arms **Rev:** Arirang dancer with cranes flying above **Edge:** Plain **Note:** Prev. KM#390.

Date	Mintage	F	VF	XF	Unc	BU
JU91-(2002) Proof	—	Value: 15.00				

KM# 308a   WON
28.2000 g., Brass, 40.2 mm. **Subject:** Arirang **Obv:** State arms **Rev:** Performers and flying cranes **Edge:** Plain

Date	Mintage	F	VF	XF	Unc	BU
JU91-(2002) Proof	—	Value: 20.00				

KM# 313   WON
6.7000 g., Aluminum, 40 mm. **Obv:** State arms **Rev:** Arirang dancer **Edge:** Plain **Note:** Prev. KM#389.

Date	Mintage	F	VF	XF	Unc	BU
JU91-(2002) Proof	—	Value: 15.00				

KM# 313a   WON
28.2000 g., Brass, 40.2 mm. **Subject:** Arirang **Obv:** State arms **Rev:** Dancer with upheld arms **Edge:** Plain

Date	Mintage	F	VF	XF	Unc	BU
JU91-(2002) Proof	—	Value: 20.00				

KM# 388   WON
7.1000 g., Aluminum, 40 mm. **Obv:** State arms **Rev:** Arirang dancer Silhouette **Edge:** Plain

Date	Mintage	F	VF	XF	Unc	BU
2002 Proof	—	Value: 15.00				

KM# 391   WON
7.1000 g., Aluminum, 40 mm. **Obv:** State arms **Rev:** Arirang ribbon dancer **Edge:** Plain

Date	Mintage	F	VF	XF	Unc	BU
JU91-2002 Proof	—	Value: 15.00				

KM# 392   WON
7.0000 g., Aluminum, 40 mm. **Obv:** State arms **Rev:** May Day Stadium **Edge:** Plain

Date	Mintage	F	VF	XF	Unc	BU
JU91-2002 Proof	—	Value: 12.00				

KM# 392a   WON
28.5000 g., Brass, 40.1 mm. **Obv:** State arms **Rev:** May Day Stadium **Edge:** Plain

Date	Mintage	F	VF	XF	Unc	BU
JU91-2002 Proof	—	Value: 15.00				

KM# 393   WON
7.1000 g., Aluminum, 40 mm. **Obv:** State arms **Rev:** Woman floating above stadium **Edge:** Plain

Date	Mintage	F	VF	XF	Unc	BU
JU91-2002 Proof	—	Value: 15.00				

KM# 393a   WON
28.2000 g., Brass, 40 mm. **Obv:** State arms **Rev:** Woman floating above stadium **Edge:** Plain

Date	Mintage	F	VF	XF	Unc	BU
JU91-2002 Proof	—	Value: 17.50				

KM# 394   WON
27.5000 g., Brass, 40 mm. **Obv:** State arms **Rev:** Ribbon dancer with Korea shaped ribbon **Edge:** Plain

Date	Mintage	F	VF	XF	Unc	BU
JU91-2002 Proof	—	Value: 17.50				

KM# 395 WON
27.5000 g., Brass, 40 mm. **Obv:** State arms **Rev:** Dancer in the shape of Korea **Edge:** Plain

Date	Mintage	F	VF	XF	Unc	BU
JU91-2002 Proof	—	Value: 17.50				

KM# 396 WON
7.0000 g., Aluminum, 40 mm. **Obv:** State arms **Rev:** Bust with hat facing divides dates(1337-1392) above building foundation **Edge:** Plain

Date	Mintage	F	VF	XF	Unc	BU
JU91-2002 Proof	—	Value: 15.00				

KM# 397 WON
7.0000 g., Aluminum, 40 mm. **Obv:** State arms **Rev:** Victorious athletes hugging **Edge:** Plain

Date	Mintage	F	VF	XF	Unc	BU
JU91-(2002) Proof	—	Value: 10.00				

KM# 397a WON
28.2400 g., Brass, 40 mm. **Obv:** State arms **Rev:** Victorious athletes hugging **Edge:** Plain

Date	Mintage	F	VF	XF	Unc	BU
JU91-(2002) Proof	—	Value: 12.50				

KM# 399 WON
4.8600 g., Aluminum, 35 mm. **Obv:** State arms **Rev:** Cantering horse **Edge:** Plain

Date	Mintage	F	VF	XF	Unc	BU
JU91-(2002) Proof	—	Value: 15.00				

KM# 399a WON
16.9300 g., Brass, 35 mm. **Obv:** State arms **Rev:** Cantering horse **Edge:** Plain

Date	Mintage	F	VF	XF	Unc	BU
JU91-(2002) Proof	—	Value: 15.00				

KM# 400 WON
5.1000 g., Aluminum, 35 mm. **Obv:** State arms **Rev:** Two wrestlers **Edge:** Plain

Date	Mintage	F	VF	XF	Unc	BU
JU91-(2002) Proof	—	Value: 12.50				

KM# 400a WON
16.5000 g., Brass, 35 mm. **Obv:** State arms **Rev:** Two wrestlers **Edge:** Plain

Date	Mintage	F	VF	XF	Unc	BU
JU91-(2002) Proof	—	Value: 15.00				

KM# 310a WON
28.2000 g., Brass, 40.2 mm. **Obv:** State arms **Rev:** Tomb of King Tongmyong **Edge:** Plain

Date	Mintage	F	VF	XF	Unc	BU
JU91-2002 Proof	—	Value: 15.00				

KM# 786 WON
5.0000 g., Aluminum, 35 mm. **Subject:** Year of the Horse **Obv:** National arms, Country name **Rev:** Horse head

Date	Mintage	F	VF	XF	Unc	BU
2002 Proof	—	Value: 6.00				

KM# 786a WON
16.0000 g., Brass, 35 mm. **Obv:** National arms, Country name **Rev:** Horse head

Date	Mintage	F	VF	XF	Unc	BU
2002 Proof	—	Value: 7.00				

KM# 794 WON
7.0000 g., Aluminum, 40 mm. **Obv:** National arms **Rev:** Reconstruction of the Mausoleums for King Dangun

Date	Mintage	F	VF	XF	Unc	BU
2002 Proof	—	Value: 6.00				

KM# 795 WON
28.0000 g., Brass, 40 mm. **Obv:** Naitonal arms, Country name **Rev:** Reconstruction of the mausoleum for King Dangun

Date	Mintage	F	VF	XF	Unc	BU
2002 Proof	—	Value: 7.00				

KM# 796 WON
7.0000 g., Aluminum, 40 mm. **Obv:** National arms **Rev:** Dongmyeong, 1st King of Goguryeo

Date	Mintage	F	VF	XF	Unc	BU
2002 Proof	—	Value: 6.00				

KM# 797 WON
28.0000 g., Brass, 40 mm. **Obv:** National arms **Rev:** Dongmyeong, 1st King of Goguryeo

Date	Mintage	F	VF	XF	Unc	BU
2002 Proof	—	Value: 7.00				

KM# 798 WON
7.0000 g., Aluminum, 40 mm. **Obv:** National arms, Central Bank name **Rev:** Wanggeon, 1st King of Goryeo dynasty

Date	Mintage	F	VF	XF	Unc	BU
2002 Proof	—	Value: 6.00				

KM# 799 WON
28.0000 g., Brass, 40 mm. **Obv:** National arms, Central Bank name **Rev:** Wanggeon, 1st King of Goryeo dynasty

Date	Mintage	F	VF	XF	Unc	BU
2002 Proof	—	Value: 7.00				

KM# 800 WON
7.0000 g., Aluminum, 40 mm. **Obv:** National arms **Rev:** Jeon Bongjun

Date	Mintage	F	VF	XF	Unc	BU
2002 Proof	—	Value: 6.00				

KM# 801 WON
28.0000 g., Brass, 40 mm. **Obv:** National arms, Central Bank name **Rev:** Jeon Bongjun

Date	Mintage	F	VF	XF	Unc	BU
2002 Proof	—	Value: 7.00				

KM# 821 WON
7.0000 g., Aluminum, 40 mm. **Obv:** National arms **Rev:** Prince Hodong and Princess Nakrang on horseback

Date	Mintage	F	VF	XF	Unc	BU
2002 Proof	—	Value: 6.00				

KM# 821a WON
28.0000 g., Brass, 40 mm. **Obv:** National arms **Rev:** Prince Hodong and Princess Nakrang on horseback

Date	Mintage	F	VF	XF	Unc	BU
2002 Proof	—	Value: 7.00				

KM# 822 WON
7.0000 g., Aluminum, 40 mm. **Obv:** National arms **Rev:** Half-length figures of Prince Hodong and Princess Nakrang

Date	Mintage	F	VF	XF	Unc	BU
2002 Proof	—	Value: 6.00				

KM# 822a WON
28.0000 g., Brass, 40 mm. **Obv:** National arms **Rev:** Half-length figures of Prince Hodong and Princess Nakrang

Date	Mintage	F	VF	XF	Unc	BU
2002 Proof	—	Value: 8.00				

KM# 836 WON
4.0000 g., Aluminum, 35 mm. **Obv:** National arms, Central Bank and Country name **Rev:** Ariang inscription

Date	Mintage	F	VF	XF	Unc	BU
2002 Proof	Est. 1,000	Value: 6.00				

KM# 837 WON
4.0000 g., Aluminum, 35 mm. **Obv:** National arms, Central Bank and Country name **Rev:** Three soldiers

Date	Mintage	F	VF	XF	Unc	BU
2002 Proof	—	Value: 7.00				

KM# 838 WON
4.0000 g., Aluminum, 35 mm. **Obv:** Naitonal arms, Central Bank and Country name **Rev:** Princess fairy paying flute

Date	Mintage	F	VF	XF	Unc	BU
2002 Proof	—	Value: 7.00				

KM# 839 WON
4.0000 g., Aluminum, 35 mm. **Obv:** National arms, Central Bank and Country name **Rev:** Bronze statue

Date	Mintage	F	VF	XF	Unc	BU
2002 Proof	—	Value: 6.00				

KM# 840 WON
4.0000 g., Aluminum, 35 mm. **Obv:** National arms, Central Bank and Country name **Rev:** Women in the worship of the Sun

Date	Mintage	F	VF	XF	Unc	BU
2002	—	Value: 6.00				

KM# 841 WON
4.0000 g., Aluminum, 35 mm. **Obv:** National arms, Central Bank and Country name **Rev:** Three principals of unification

Date	Mintage	F	VF	XF	Unc	BU
2002 Proof	—	Value: 6.00				

KM# 842 WON
4.0000 g., Aluminum, 35 mm. **Obv:** National arms, Central Bank and Country name **Rev:** Dancing children

Date	Mintage	F	VF	XF	Unc	BU
2002 Proof	—	Value: 6.00				

KM# 843 WON
31.1050 g., 0.9990 Gold 0.9990 oz. AGW, 35 mm. **Obv:** National arms, Central Bank and Country name **Rev:** Arirang inscription

Date	Mintage	F	VF	XF	Unc	BU
2002 Proof	—	Value: 1,600				

KM# 882 WON
Copper-Nickel, 38 mm. **Obv:** National arms, Central Bank name **Rev:** World cup tophy, player and Brandenburg gate

Date	Mintage	F	VF	XF	Unc	BU
2002 Proof	—	Value: 14.00				

KM# 882b WON
25.0000 g., Brass, 38 mm. **Obv:** National arms, Central Bank name **Rev:** World cup, player and Brandenberg Gate

Date	Mintage	F	VF	XF	Unc	BU
2002 Proof	—	Value: 7.00				

KM# 882a WON
6.0000 g., Aluminum, 38 mm. **Obv:** National arms, Central Bank name **Rev:** World cup, player and Brandenburg Gate

Date	Mintage	F	VF	XF	Unc	BU
2002 Proof	—	Value: 6.00				

KM# 264 WON
7.0000 g., Aluminum, 40 mm. **Obv:** National arms **Rev:** Sheep in center of Asian Zodiac animals

Date	Mintage	F	VF	XF	Unc	BU
2003 Proof	—	Value: 6.00				

KM# 264a WON
28.4700 g., Brass, 40 mm. **Obv:** State arms **Rev:** Sheep within circle of Asian Zodiac animals **Edge:** Plain

Date	Mintage	F	VF	XF	Unc	BU
2003 Proof	—	Value: 22.00				

KM# 319   WON
9.6200 g., Aluminum, 40 mm. **Obv:** State arms **Rev:** Helmeted head with two antenna-like horns on the helmet **Edge:** Plain

Date	Mintage	F	VF	XF	Unc	BU
JU92-2003 Proof	—	Value: 15.00				

KM# 319a   WON
28.2000 g., Brass, 40.2 mm. **Obv:** State arms **Rev:** Helmeted head with two antenna-like horns on helmet **Edge:** Plain

Date	Mintage	F	VF	XF	Unc	BU
JU92-2003 Proof	—	Value: 17.50				

KM# 323   WON
6.9400 g., Aluminum, 40 mm. **Obv:** State arms **Rev:** Turtle shaped armoured ship of 1592 **Edge:** Plain

Date	Mintage	F	VF	XF	Unc	BU
JU92-2003 Proof	—	Value: 15.00				

KM# 323a   WON
28.1000 g., Brass, 40.2 mm. **Obv:** State arms **Rev:** Turtle-shaped armoured ship of 1592 **Edge:** Plain

Date	Mintage	F	VF	XF	Unc	BU
JU92-2003 Proof	—	Value: 20.00				

KM# 403   WON
7.0000 g., Aluminum, 40 mm. **Obv:** National arms, Central Bank name **Rev:** Kang Kam-cheo bust facing

Date	Mintage	F	VF	XF	Unc	BU
2003 Proof	—	Value: 7.00				

KM# 403a   WON
22.1000 g., Brass, 40 mm. **Obv:** State arms **Rev:** Kang Kam-cheo bust facing **Edge:** Plain

Date	Mintage	F	VF	XF	Unc	BU
JU92-2003 Proof	—	Value: 17.50				

KM# 404   WON
9.6300 g., Aluminum, 40 mm. **Obv:** State arms **Rev:** Armored bust wearing a horned helmet **Edge:** Plain

Date	Mintage	F	VF	XF	Unc	BU
JU92-2003 Proof	—	Value: 15.00				

KM# 404a   WON
22.2500 g., Brass, 40 mm. **Obv:** State arms **Rev:** Armored bust wearing a horned helmet **Edge:** Plain

Date	Mintage	F	VF	XF	Unc	BU
JU92-2003 Proof	—	Value: 17.50				

KM# 405   WON
7.0000 g., Aluminum, 40 mm. **Obv:** State arms **Rev:** Ram within circle of Asian Zodiac animals **Edge:** Plain

Date	Mintage	F	VF	XF	Unc	BU
2003 Proof	—	Value: 15.00				

KM# 405a   WON
28.4400 g., Brass, 40 mm. **Obv:** State arms **Rev:** Ram within circle of Asian Zodiac animals **Edge:** Plain

Date	Mintage	F	VF	XF	Unc	BU
2003 Proof	—	Value: 17.50				

KM# 406   WON
10.1500 g., Aluminum, 40 mm. **Obv:** State arms **Rev:** Children kicking a shuttlecock **Edge:** Plain

Date	Mintage	F	VF	XF	Unc	BU
JU92-2003 Proof	—	Value: 15.00				

KM# 406a   WON
24.6300 g., Brass, 40 mm. **Obv:** State arms **Rev:** Children kicking a shuttlecock **Edge:** Plain

Date	Mintage	F	VF	XF	Unc	BU
JU92-2003 Proof	—	Value: 17.50				

KM# 407a   WON
23.1000 g., Brass, 40 mm. **Obv:** State arms **Rev:** Children playing jacks **Edge:** Plain

Date	Mintage	F	VF	XF	Unc	BU
JU92-2003 Proof	—	Value: 17.50				

KM# 408a   WON
24.5600 g., Brass, 40 mm. **Obv:** State arms **Rev:** Children spinning tops **Edge:** Plain

Date	Mintage	F	VF	XF	Unc	BU
JU92-2003 Proof	—	Value: 17.50				

KM# 410a   WON
24.6400 g., Brass, 40 mm. **Obv:** State arms **Rev:** Large dome building **Edge:** Plain

Date	Mintage	F	VF	XF	Unc	BU
JU92-2003 Proof	—	Value: 17.50				

KM# 904   WON
31.1050 g., 0.9990 Silver 0.9990 oz. ASW, 40 mm. **Subject:** Athens olympics **Obv:** National arms, Central Bank name **Rev:** Wrestlers

Date	Mintage	F	VF	XF	Unc	BU
2003 Proof	Est. 1,000	Value: 45.00				

KM# 918   WON
25.0000 g., Brass, 38 mm. **Obv:** National arms, Central Bank name **Rev:** Steamship Princess Charlotte of Prussia

Date	Mintage	F	VF	XF	Unc	BU
2003 Proof	Est. 500	Value: 45.00				

KM# 919   WON
25.0000 g., Brass, 35 mm. **Obv:** National arms, Central Bank name **Rev:** Ship Queen Maria

Date	Mintage	F	VF	XF	Unc	BU
2003 Proof	—	Value: 45.00				

KM# 920   WON
25.0000 g., Brass, 38 mm. **Obv:** National arms **Rev:** Trans-atlantic sail steamship Helena Sloman

Date	Mintage	F	VF	XF	Unc	BU
2003 Proof	—	Value: 45.00				

KM# 924   WON
25.0000 g., Brass, 38 mm. **Obv:** National arms, Central Bank name **Rev:** Alder, 1835 steam locomotive

Date	Mintage	F	VF	XF	Unc	BU
2003 Proof	Est. 500	Value: 45.00				

KM# 925   WON
25.0000 g., Silver, 38 mm. **Obv:** National arms, Central Bank name **Rev:** Saxonia, 1838 steam locomotive

Date	Mintage	F	VF	XF	Unc	BU
2003 Proof	—	Value: 45.00				

KM# 926   WON
25.0000 g., Brass, 38 mm. **Obv:** National arms, Central Bank name **Rev:** Rheingold, 1928 Steam locomotive

Date	Mintage	F	VF	XF	Unc	BU
2003 Proof	—	Value: 45.00				

KM# 930   WON
25.0000 g., Brass, 38 mm. **Obv:** National arms, Central Bank name **Rev:** Gorch Fock 1 sailing ship

Date	Mintage	F	VF	XF	Unc	BU
2003 Proof	—	Value: 45.00				

KM# 265   WON
17.7000 g., Brass, 23.2 x 40.1 mm. **Obv:** State arms **Rev:** White-tufted-ear Marmoset **Edge:** Plain

Date	Mintage	F	VF	XF	Unc	BU
2004	—	Value: 27.50				

KM# 266   WON
17.7000 g., Brass, 23.2 x 40.1 mm. **Obv:** State arms **Rev:** Cercopjthecus Mitis monkey **Edge:** Plain

Date	Mintage	F	VF	XF	Unc	BU
2004 Proof	—	Value: 27.50				

KM# 267   WON
17.7000 g., Brass, 23.2 x 40.1 mm. **Obv:** State arms **Rev:** Two
Saguinus Midas monkeys **Edge:** Plain

Date	Mintage	F	VF	XF	Unc	BU
2004 Proof	—	Value: 27.50				

KM# 330   WON
9.9200 g., Aluminum, 45 mm. **Obv:** State arms **Rev:** Mountain
cabin **Edge:** Plain **Note:** Prev. KM#411.

Date	Mintage	F	VF	XF	Unc	BU
JU93-2004 Proof	—	Value: 15.00				

KM# 330a   WON
26.4500 g., Brass, 45 mm. **Obv:** State arms **Rev:** Mountain
cabin **Edge:** Plain

Date	Mintage	F	VF	XF	Unc	BU
JU93-2004 Proof	—	Value: 20.00				

KM# 331   WON
10.0000 g., Aluminum, 45 mm. **Obv:** State arms **Rev:** Kim Il
Sung's birthplace, front view **Edge:** Plain **Note:** Prev. KM#412.

Date	Mintage	F	VF	XF	Unc	BU
JU93-2004 Proof	—	Value: 15.00				

KM# 331a   WON
26.4500 g., Brass, 45 mm. **Obv:** State arms **Rev:** Sung's birth
place, front view **Edge:** Plain

Date	Mintage	F	VF	XF	Unc	BU
JU93-2004 Proof	—	Value: 20.00				

KM# 332   WON
10.0000 g., Aluminum, 45 mm. **Obv:** State arms **Rev:** Kim Il
Sung's birthplace, side view **Edge:** Plain **Note:** Prev. KM#413.

Date	Mintage	F	VF	XF	Unc	BU
JU93-2004 Proof	—	Value: 15.00				

KM# 332a   WON
26.4500 g., Brass, 45 mm. **Obv:** State arms **Rev:** Sung's
birthplace, side view **Edge:** Plain

Date	Mintage	F	VF	XF	Unc	BU
JU93-2004 Proof	—	Value: 20.00				

KM# 333   WON
10.0000 g., Aluminum, 45 mm. **Obv:** Naitonal arms, Central
Bank name **Rev:** Kim Jeongsuk

Date	Mintage	F	VF	XF	Unc	BU
2004 Proof	—	Value: 8.00				

KM# 333a   WON
26.4500 g., Brass, 45 mm. **Obv:** State arms **Rev:** Kim Jung
Sook facing **Edge:** Plain

Date	Mintage	F	VF	XF	Unc	BU
JU93-2004 Proof	—	Value: 22.50				

KM# 334   WON
10.0000 g., Aluminum, 45 mm. **Obv:** National arms, Central
Bank name **Rev:** Kim Jeong-il bust facing

Date	Mintage	F	VF	XF	Unc	BU
2004 Proof	—	Value: 8.00				

KM# 334a   WON
26.4500 g., Brass, 45 mm. **Obv:** State arms **Rev:** Kim Jong-il
bust facing **Edge:** Plain

Date	Mintage	F	VF	XF	Unc	BU
JU93-2004 Proof	—	Value: 22.50				

KM# 335   WON
10.0000 g., Aluminum, 45 mm. **Obv:** National arms, Central
Bank name **Rev:** Kim Il-seong bust facing

Date	Mintage	F	VF	XF	Unc	BU
2004 Proof	—	Value: 8.00				

KM# 335a   WON
26.4500 g., Brass, 45 mm. **Obv:** State arms **Rev:** Kim Il-seong
bust facing **Edge:** Plain

Date	Mintage	F	VF	XF	Unc	BU
JU93-2004 Proof	—	Value: 22.50				

KM# 336   WON
10.1000 g., Aluminum, 45 mm. **Obv:** State arms **Rev:** Kim Il-
sung flower, orchid **Edge:** Plain **Note:** Prev. KM#414.

Date	Mintage	F	VF	XF	Unc	BU
JU93-2004 Proof	—	Value: 15.00				

KM# 336a   WON
26.4500 g., Brass, 45 mm. **Obv:** State arms **Rev:** Kim Il-sung
flower, orchid **Edge:** Plain

Date	Mintage	F	VF	XF	Unc	BU
JU93-2004 Proof	—	Value: 20.00				

KM# 337   WON
10.1000 g., Aluminum, 45 mm. **Obv:** State arms **Rev:** Kim Jong-
Il flower, peony **Edge:** Plain **Note:** Prev. KM#415.

Date	Mintage	F	VF	XF	Unc	BU
JU93-2004 Proof	—	Value: 15.00				

KM# 337a   WON
26.4500 g., Brass, 45 mm. **Obv:** State arms **Rev:** Kim Jong-Il
flower, peony **Edge:** Plain

Date	Mintage	F	VF	XF	Unc	BU
JU93-2004 Proof	—	Value: 20.00				

KM# 338   WON
9.9300 g., Aluminum, 45 mm. **Obv:** State arms **Rev:** Jin Dal
Lae flower, Rose of Sharon **Edge:** Plain **Note:** Prev. KM#416.

Date	Mintage	F	VF	XF	Unc	BU
JU93-2004 Proof	—	Value: 15.00				

KM# 338a   WON
26.4500 g., Brass, 45 mm. **Obv:** State arms **Rev:** Rose of
Sharon flowers **Edge:** Plain

Date	Mintage	F	VF	XF	Unc	BU
JU93-2004 Proof	—	Value: 20.00				

KM# 410   WON
20.0000 g., Aluminum, 40 mm. **Obv:** National arms, Central
bank name **Rev:** Sports hall in Pyeongyang

Date	Mintage	F	VF	XF	Unc	BU
2004 Proof	—	Value: 16.00				

KM# 939   WON
7.0000 g., Aluminum, 40 mm. **Obv:** National arms, Central Bank
arms **Rev:** Monkey in the center of the Zodiac

Date	Mintage	F	VF	XF	Unc	BU
2004 Proof	—	Value: 10.00				

KM# 939a   WON
28.0000 g., Brass, 35 mm. **Obv:** National arms, Central Bank
name **Rev:** Monkey in center of Zodiac

Date	Mintage	F	VF	XF	Unc	BU
2004 Proof	—	Value: 30.00				

KM# 994   WON
25.0000 g., Brass, 38 mm. **Obv:** National arms, Central Bank
name **Rev:** Statsraad Lehmkuhl sailing ship

Date	Mintage	F	VF	XF	Unc	BU
2004 Proof	—	Value: 45.00				

KM# 995   WON
25.0000 g., Brass, 38 mm. **Obv:** Naitonal arms, Central Bank
name **Rev:** Henry Hudson's Halve Maen

Date	Mintage	F	VF	XF	Unc	BU
2004 Proof	—	Value: 45.00				

KM# 1016 WON
7.0000 g., Aluminum, 40 mm. **Obv:** National arms, Central Bank name **Rev:** Rooster within Zodiac circle

Date	Mintage	F	VF	XF	Unc	BU
2005 Proof	—	Value: 17.50				

KM# 1016a WON
28.0000 g., Brass, 40 mm. **Obv:** National arms, Central Bank name **Rev:** Rooster in Zodiac circle

Date	Mintage	F	VF	XF	Unc	BU
2005 Proof	—	Value: 20.00				

KM# 1019 WON
28.0000 g., 0.9990 Brass 0.8993 oz., 40 mm. **Obv:** National arms, Central Bank name **Rev:** Timber and tap in color

Date	Mintage	F	VF	XF	Unc	BU
2005 Proof	—	—	—	—	—	30.00

KM# 1020 WON
7.0000 g., Aluminum, 40 mm. **Obv:** National arms, Central Bank name **Rev:** Hae Mosu in the sky with the five dragons

Date	Mintage	F	VF	XF	Unc	BU
2005 Proof	—	Value: 17.50				

KM# 1020a WON
28.0000 g., Brass, 40 mm. **Obv:** National arms, Central Bank name **Rev:** Hae Mosu in flight with the five dragons

Date	Mintage	F	VF	XF	Unc	BU
2005 Proof	—	Value: 20.00				

KM# 1024 WON
7.0000 g., Aluminum, 40 mm. **Obv:** National arms, Central Bank name **Rev:** Admiral Yi Sunsin and turtle boat

Date	Mintage	F	VF	XF	Unc	BU
2005 Proof	—	Value: 10.00				

KM# 1024a WON
28.0000 g., Brass, 40 mm. **Obv:** National arms, Central Bank name **Rev:** Admiral Yi Sunsin and turtle boat

Date	Mintage	F	VF	XF	Unc	BU
2005 Proof	—	Value: 15.00				

KM# 1025 WON
7.0000 g., Aluminum, 40 mm. **Obv:** National arms, Central Bank name **Rev:** General Hong Beomdo

Date	Mintage	F	VF	XF	Unc	BU
2005 Proof	—	Value: 14.00				

KM# 1025a WON
28.0000 g., Brass, 40 mm. **Obv:** National arms, Central Bank name **Rev:** General Hong Beomdo

Date	Mintage	F	VF	XF	Unc	BU
2005 Proof	—	Value: 20.00				

KM# 1034 WON
25.0000 g., Brass, 40 mm. **Obv:** National arms, Central Bank name **Rev:** Rally in front of the monument ot the three principals of reunification

Date	Mintage	F	VF	XF	Unc	BU
2005 Proof	—	Value: 20.00				

KM# 1035 WON
28.0000 g., Brass, 40 mm. **Obv:** National arms, Central Bank name **Rev:** Demonstration on the crater lake

Date	Mintage	F	VF	XF	Unc	BU
2005 Proof	—	Value: 20.00				

KM# 1036 WON
28.0000 g., Brass, 40 mm. **Obv:** National arms, Central Bank name **Rev:** Three drum dance

Date	Mintage	F	VF	XF	Unc	BU
2005 Proof	—	Value: 20.00				

KM# 1040 WON
28.0000 g., Brass, 40 mm. **Obv:** National arms, Central Bank name **Rev:** Map of Korea, pair of peace doves, rainbow

Date	Mintage	F	VF	XF	Unc	BU
2005 Proof	—	Value: 10.00				

KM# 1043 WON
28.0000 g., Brass **Obv:** National arms, Central Bank name **Rev:** Tomb of the Unknown Soldier in Moscow, Russian legend **Edge Lettering:** 40

Date	Mintage	F	VF	XF	Unc	BU
2005 Proof	—	Value: 14.00				

KM# 1044 WON
28.0000 g., Brass, 40 mm. **Obv:** National arms, Central Bank name **Rev:** Memorial to mothers in St. Petersburg, Russian legend

Date	Mintage	F	VF	XF	Unc	BU
2005 Proof	—	Value: 14.00				

KM# 1074 WON
6.0000 g., Aluminum, 38 mm. **Subject:** Torino Winter Olympics, 2006 **Obv:** National arms, Central Bank name **Rev:** Bobsled

Date	Mintage	F	VF	XF	Unc	BU
2005 Proof	—	Value: 12.00				

KM# 1074a WON
25.0000 g., Brass, 38 mm. **Subject:** Torino Winter Olympics, 2006 **Obv:** National arms, Central Bank name **Rev:** Bobsled

Date	Mintage	F	VF	XF	Unc	BU
2005 Proof	—	Value: 30.00				

KM# 1088 WON
28.0000 g., Brass, 40 mm. **Obv:** National arms, Central Bank name **Rev:** Dog in color

Date	Mintage	F	VF	XF	Unc	BU
2006 Proof	—	Value: 30.00				

KM# 1089 WON
7.0000 g., Aluminum, 40 mm. **Obv:** National arms, Central Bank name **Rev:** Ryuhwa, Mother of King Dongmyeong

Date	Mintage	F	VF	XF	Unc	BU
2006 Proof	—	Value: 10.00				

KM# 1089a WON
28.0000 g., Brass, 40 mm. **Obv:** National arms, Central Bank name **Rev:** Ryuhwa, Mother of King Dongmyeong

Date	Mintage	F	VF	XF	Unc	BU
2006 Proof	—	Value: 14.00				

KM# 1109 WON
28.0000 g., Brass, 40 mm. **Obv:** National arms, Central Bank name **Rev:** Pig in color

Date	Mintage	F	VF	XF	Unc	BU
2007 Proof	—	Value: 30.00				

KM# 483 WON
Copper-Nickel **Subject:** Uzgn Monument **Obv:** Arms **Rev:** Map and building

Date	Mintage	F	VF	XF	Unc	BU
2008 Proof	—	Value: 15.00				

KM# 781 2 WON
7.0000 g., 0.9990 Silver 0.2248 oz. ASW, 30 mm. **Obv:** National arms, Central Bank name **Rev:** Panda in color

Date	Mintage	F	VF	XF	Unc	BU
2001 Proof	Est. 5,000	Value: 30.00				

KM# 892 2 WON
7.0000 g., 0.9990 Silver 0.2248 oz. ASW, 30 mm. **Obv:** National arms, Central Bank name **Rev:** Two panda in color

Date	Mintage	F	VF	XF	Unc	BU
2002 Proof	Est. 5,000	Value: 30.00				

KM# 249 2 WON
7.0000 g., 0.9990 Silver 0.2248 oz. ASW, 30 mm. **Obv:** State arms **Rev:** Two multicolor pandas **Edge:** Plain

Date	Mintage	F	VF	XF	Unc	BU
2003 Proof	—	Value: 30.00				

KM# 933 2 WON
7.0000 g., 0.9990 Silver 0.2248 oz. ASW, 30 mm. **Obv:** National arms, Central Bank name **Rev:** High speed train in Aichi

Date	Mintage	F	VF	XF	Unc	BU
2003 Proof	—	Value: 30.00				

KM# 934 2 WON
7.0000 g., 0.9990 Silver 0.2248 oz. ASW, 30 mm. **Obv:** National Arms, Central Bank name **Rev:** Two soccer players in color

Date	Mintage	F	VF	XF	Unc	BU
2003 Proof	—	Value: 30.00				

KM# 417 2 WON
24.6600 g., Brass, 31.6x45.75 mm. **Obv:** State arms **Rev:** Half length uniformed figure standing in land rover saluting below dates 1904-2004 **Edge:** Plain **Shape:** Rectangle

Date	Mintage	F	VF	XF	Unc	BU
ND(2004) Proof	—	Value: 25.00				

KM# 969 2 WON
25.0000 g., Brass, 40 mm. **Obv:** Dokdo, rocky islands, Central Bank name **Rev:** Map of the Island group

Date	Mintage	F	VF	XF	Unc	BU
2004 Proof	—	Value: 25.00				

KM# 970 2 WON
25.0000 g., Brass, 40 mm. **Obv:** Dokdo, rocky islands, Central Bank name **Rev:** Fisher Ahn Yongbok

Date	Mintage	F	VF	XF	Unc	BU
2004 Proof	—	Value: 25.00				

KM# 971 2 WON
25.0000 g., Brass, 40 mm. **Obv:** Dokdo, rocky islands, Central Bank name **Rev:** Seodo, western island

Date	Mintage	F	VF	XF	Unc	BU
2004 Proof	2,004	Value: 25.00				

KM# 972 2 WON
25.0000 g., Brass, 40 mm. **Obv:** Dokdo, rocky islands, Central Bank name **Rev:** Eastern island, Dongdo

Date	Mintage	F	VF	XF	Unc	BU
2004 Proof	—	Value: 25.00				

KM# 973 2 WON
25.0000 g., Brass, 40 mm. **Obv:** Dokdo, rocky islands, Central Bank name **Rev:** Three brother islands

Date	Mintage	F	VF	XF	Unc	BU
2004 Proof	—	Value: 25.00				

KM# 974 2 WON
25.0000 g., Brass, 40 mm. **Obv:** Dokdo, rocky islands, Central Bank name **Rev:** Chicken island

Date	Mintage	F	VF	XF	Unc	BU
2004 Proof	—	Value: 25.00				

KM# 975 2 WON
25.0000 g., Brass, 40 mm. **Obv:** Dokdo, rocky islands, Central Bank name **Rev:** Candle island

Date	Mintage	F	VF	XF	Unc	BU
2004 Proof	—	Value: 25.00				

KM# 976 2 WON
25.0000 g., Brass, 40 mm. **Obv:** Dokdo, rocky islands, Central Bank name **Rev:** Dome island

Date	Mintage	F	VF	XF	Unc	BU
2004 Proof	—	Value: 25.00				

KM# 1008 2 WON
7.0000 g., 0.9990 Silver 0.2248 oz. ASW, 30 mm. **Obv:** National arms, Central Bank name **Rev:** Three pandas in color

Date	Mintage	F	VF	XF	Unc	BU
2004 Proof	Est. 5,000	Value: 30.00				

KM# 1078 2 WON
7.0000 g., Silver, 30 mm. **Obv:** National arms, Central Bank name **Rev:** Panda in color

Date	Mintage	F	VF	XF	Unc	BU
2005 Proof	Est. 5,000	Value: 30.00				

KM# 1079 2 WON
7.0000 g., 0.9990 Silver partially gilt 0.2248 oz. ASW, 30 mm. **Subject:** Battle of Trafalgar, 200th Anniversary **Obv:** National arms, Central Bank name **Rev:** Horatio Nelson and the H.M.S. Victory, partially gilt

Date	Mintage	F	VF	XF	Unc	BU
2005 Proof	Est. 5,000	Value: 30.00				

KM# 1101 2 WON
7.0000 g., 0.9990 Silver 0.2248 oz. ASW, 30 mm. **Obv:** National arms, Central Bank name **Rev:** Two pandas in color

Date	Mintage	F	VF	XF	Unc	BU
2006 Proof	Est. 5,000	Value: 30.00				

KM# 1124 2 WON
7.0000 g., 0.9990 Silver 0.2248 oz. ASW, 30 mm. **Obv:** National arms, Central Bank name **Rev:** Panda in color

Date	Mintage	F	VF	XF	Unc	BU
2007 Proof	Est. 5,000	Value: 30.00				

KM# 339 3 WON
12.5500 g., Aluminum, 50.1 mm. **Obv:** Korean map **Rev:** Huh Jun Chosun doctor at left, books at right **Edge:** Plain

Date	Mintage	F	VF	XF	Unc	BU
JU93-2004 Proof	—	Value: 20.00				

KM# 339a 3 WON
40.5300 g., Brass, 50.2 mm. **Obv:** Korean map **Rev:** Huh Jun Chosun doctor at left, books at right **Edge:** Plain

Date	Mintage	F	VF	XF	Unc	BU
JU93-2004 Proof	—	Value: 25.00				

KM# 203   5 WON
15.0000 g., 0.9990 Silver 0.4818 oz. ASW, 35 mm. **Subject:**
School Ships **Obv:** State arms **Rev:** SS Krusenstern **Edge:** Plain

Date	Mintage	F	VF	XF	Unc	BU
ND(2001) Proof	500	Value: 75.00				

KM# 205   5 WON
15.0000 g., 0.9990 Silver 0.4818 oz. ASW, 35 mm. **Subject:**
Wildlife **Obv:** State arms **Rev:** Two standing Japanese Ibis birds
Edge: Plain

Date	Mintage	F	VF	XF	Unc	BU
JU90-2001 Proof	100	Value: 200				

KM# 206   5 WON
15.0000 g., 0.9990 Silver 0.4818 oz. ASW, 35 mm. **Subject:**
Wildlife **Obv:** State arms **Rev:** Two nesting Japanese Ibis birds
Edge: Plain

Date	Mintage	F	VF	XF	Unc	BU
JU90-2001 Proof	3,000	Value: 50.00				

KM# 208   5 WON
15.0000 g., 0.9990 Silver 0.4818 oz. ASW, 35 mm. **Subject:** Wildlife
Obv: State arms **Rev:** Two Korean Longtail Gorals **Edge:** Plain

Date	Mintage	F	VF	XF	Unc	BU
JU90-2001 Proof	3,000	Value: 50.00				

KM# 219   5 WON
14.9600 g., 0.9990 Silver 0.4805 oz. ASW, 35 mm. **Obv:** State
arms **Rev:** Dragon ship **Edge:** Plain

Date	Mintage	F	VF	XF	Unc	BU
2001 Proof	5,000	Value: 35.00				

KM# 226   5 WON
20.0000 g., 0.9990 Silver 0.6423 oz. ASW, 33.8 mm. **Subject:**
Olympics **Obv:** State arms **Rev:** Hurdler **Edge:** Reeded

Date	Mintage	F	VF	XF	Unc	BU
2001 Proof	—	Value: 35.00				

KM# 240   5 WON
14.9400 g., 0.9990 Silver 0.4798 oz. ASW, 35 mm. **Obv:** State
arms **Rev:** "Orca" (Killer Whale) **Edge:** Plain

Date	Mintage	F	VF	XF	Unc	BU
2001 Proof	—	Value: 60.00				

KM# 241   5 WON
14.9200 g., 0.9990 Silver 0.4792 oz. ASW, 35 mm. **Obv:** State
arms **Rev:** Orca and Eco-Tourists in boat **Edge:** Plain

Date	Mintage	F	VF	XF	Unc	BU
2001 Proof	—	Value: 60.00				

KM# 242   5 WON
14.8700 g., 0.9990 Silver 0.4776 oz. ASW, 35 mm. **Obv:** State
arms **Rev:** "Pottwal" (Sperm Whale) **Edge:** Plain

Date	Mintage	F	VF	XF	Unc	BU
2001 Proof	—	Value: 60.00				

KM# 243   5 WON
14.9500 g., 0.9990 Silver 0.4802 oz. ASW, 35 mm. **Obv:** State
arms **Rev:** "Buckelwal" (Humpback Whale) **Edge:** Plain

Date	Mintage	F	VF	XF	Unc	BU
2001 Proof	—	Value: 60.00				

KM# 244   5 WON
14.9300 g., 0.9990 Silver 0.4795 oz. ASW, 35 mm. **Obv:** State
arms **Rev:** "Groenlandwal" (Greenland Right Whale) **Edge:** Plain

Date	Mintage	F	VF	XF	Unc	BU
2001 Proof	—	Value: 60.00				

KM# 245   5 WON
14.9500 g., 0.9990 Silver 0.4802 oz. ASW, 35 mm. **Obv:** State
arms **Rev:** "Blauwal" (Blue Whale) **Edge:** Plain

Date	Mintage	F	VF	XF	Unc	BU
2001 Proof	—	Value: 60.00				

KM# 246   5 WON
14.9600 g., 0.9990 Silver 0.4805 oz. ASW, 35 mm. **Obv:** State
arms **Rev:** "Grindwal" (Pilot Whale) **Edge:** Plain

Date	Mintage	F	VF	XF	Unc	BU
2001 Proof	—	Value: 60.00				

KM# 250   5 WON
14.9600 g., 0.9990 Silver 0.4805 oz. ASW, 35 mm. **Subject:**
Return of Hong Kong to China **Obv:** State arms **Rev:** City view
Edge: Plain

Date	Mintage	F	VF	XF	Unc	BU
2001 Proof	—	Value: 20.00				

KM# 694   5 WON
27.0000 g., 0.9990 Silver 0.8672 oz. ASW, 40 mm. **Obv:**
National arms, Country name **Rev:** Kim Ilseong

Date	Mintage	F	VF	XF	Unc	BU
2001 Proof	—	Value: 70.00				

KM# 695   5 WON
Silver, 40 mm. **Obv:** National arms, Country name **Rev:** Kim
Jeongil

Date	Mintage	F	VF	XF	Unc	BU
2001 Proof	—	Value: 75.00				

KM# 696   5 WON
27.0000 g., 0.9990 Silver 0.8672 oz. ASW, 40 mm. **Obv:**
National arms, Central Bank name **Rev:** Kim Jeongsuk

Date	Mintage	F	VF	XF	Unc	BU
2001 Proof	—	Value: 75.00				

KM# 747   5 WON
27.0000 g., Silver, 40 mm. **Obv:** National arms, Country name
Rev: Confucius

Date	Mintage	F	VF	XF	Unc	BU
2001 Proof	—	Value: 135				

KM# 770   5 WON
15.0000 g., 0.9990 Silver 0.4818 oz. ASW, 35 mm. **Obv:**
National arms, Central Bank name **Rev:** Krusenstern

Date	Mintage	F	VF	XF	Unc	BU
2001 Proof	—	Value: 32.00				

KM# 782   5 WON
15.0000 g., Silver, 35 mm. **Obv:** National arms, Central Bank
name **Rev:** Two pandas

Date	Mintage	F	VF	XF	Unc	BU
2001 Proof	Est. 5,000	Value: 32.00				

KM# 783   5 WON
15.0000 g., 0.9990 Silver 0.4818 oz. ASW, 35 mm. **Obv:**
National arms, Central Bank name **Rev:** Titanic

Date	Mintage	F	VF	XF	Unc	BU
2001 Proof	Est. 5,000	Value: 32.00				

KM# 784   5 WON
Silver **Obv:** National arms, Central Bank name **Rev:** Five masted
ship, Royal Clipper

Date	Mintage	F	VF	XF	Unc	BU
2001 Proof	—	Value: 32.00				

KM# 785   5 WON
15.0000 g., 0.9990 Silver 0.4818 oz. ASW, 35 mm. **Subject:**
2002 Soccer - Korea and Japan **Obv:** National arms, Central
Bank name **Rev:** Player and stadium

Date	Mintage	F	VF	XF	Unc	BU
2001 Proof	Est. 5,000	Value: 32.00				

KM# 251   5 WON
14.9000 g., 0.9990 Silver 0.4785 oz. ASW, 35 mm. **Subject:**
Year of the Horse **Obv:** State arms **Rev:** Cantering horse **Edge:**
Plain

Date	Mintage	F	VF	XF	Unc	BU
2002 Proof	—	Value: 30.00				

KM# 252   5 WON
14.9200 g., 0.9990 Silver 0.4792 oz. ASW, 35 mm. **Subject:**
Korean Games **Obv:** State arms **Rev:** Two wrestlers **Edge:** Plain

Date	Mintage	F	VF	XF	Unc	BU
JU91-2002 Proof	—	Value: 20.00				

KM# 303   5 WON
15.0000 g., 0.9990 Silver 0.4818 oz. ASW, 35 mm. **Obv:** State
arms **Rev:** Janggo dancer **Edge:** Segmented reeding

Date	Mintage	F	VF	XF	Unc	BU
JU91-2002 Proof	—	Value: 30.00				

KM# 304   5 WON
15.0000 g., 0.9990 Silver 0.4818 oz. ASW, 35 mm. **Obv:** State arms **Rev:** Armored Knight **Edge:** Segmented reeding

Date	Mintage	F	VF	XF	Unc	BU
JU91-2002 Proof	—	Value: 30.00				

KM# 790   5 WON
15.0000 g., 0.9990 Silver 0.4818 oz. ASW **Obv:** National arms, Country name **Rev:** Horse head **Shape:** 35

Date	Mintage	F	VF	XF	Unc	BU
2002 Proof	—	Value: 35.00				

KM# 877   5 WON
15.0000 g., 0.9990 Silver 0.4818 oz. ASW, 35 mm. **Obv:** National arms, Central Bank name **Rev:** Map of Korea

Date	Mintage	F	VF	XF	Unc	BU
2002 Proof	—	Value: 45.00				

KM# 878   5 WON
15.0000 g., 0.9990 Silver 0.4818 oz. ASW, 35 mm. **Obv:** National arms, Central Bank name **Rev:** Traditional Korean wedding

Date	Mintage	F	VF	XF	Unc	BU
2002 Proof	—	Value: 35.00				

KM# 879   5 WON
15.0000 g., 0.9990 Silver 0.4818 oz. ASW, 35 mm. **Obv:** National arms, Central Bank name **Rev:** Trasitional wedding procession

Date	Mintage	F	VF	XF	Unc	BU
2002 Proof	—	Value: 35.00				

KM# 893   5 WON
20.0000 g., 0.9990 Silver 0.6423 oz. ASW, 38 mm. **Obv:** Naitonal arms, Central Bank name **Rev:** Asian wild ox

Date	Mintage	F	VF	XF	Unc	BU
2002 Proof	—	Value: 60.00				

KM# 894   5 WON
20.0000 g., 0.9990 Silver 0.6423 oz. ASW, 38 mm. **Obv:** National arms, Central Bank name **Rev:** Two scocer players with flag

Date	Mintage	F	VF	XF	Unc	BU
2002 Proof	Est. 5,000	Value: 35.00				

KM# 895   5 WON
20.0000 g., 0.9990 Silver 0.6423 oz. ASW, 38 mm. **Obv:** National arms, Central Bank name **Rev:** Celebrating player in Yokohama stadium

Date	Mintage	F	VF	XF	Unc	BU
2002 Proof	—	Value: 60.00				

KM# 327   5 WON
20.0000 g., 0.9990 Silver 0.6423 oz. ASW, 35 mm. **Obv:** State arms **Rev:** "Turtle Boat" of 1592 **Edge:** Segmented reeding

Date	Mintage	F	VF	XF	Unc	BU
JU92-2003 Proof	—	Value: 35.00				

KM# 328   5 WON
20.0000 g., 0.9990 Silver 0.6423 oz. ASW, 35 mm. **Obv:** State arms **Rev:** Olympic fencers **Edge:** Segmented reeding

Date	Mintage	F	VF	XF	Unc	BU
JU92-2003 Proof	—	Value: 35.00				

KM# 329   5 WON
20.0000 g., 0.9990 Silver 0.6423 oz. ASW, 35 mm. **Obv:** State arms **Rev:** Three wild horses **Edge:** Segmented reeding

Date	Mintage	F	VF	XF	Unc	BU
JU92-2003 Proof	—	Value: 35.00				

KM# 900   5 WON
20.0000 g., 0.9990 Silver 0.6423 oz. ASW, 35 mm. **Obv:** National arms, Central Bank name **Rev:** Swan

Date	Mintage	F	VF	XF	Unc	BU
2003 Proof	Est. 1,000	Value: 45.00				

KM# 901   5 WON
20.0000 g., 0.9990 Silver 0.6423 oz. ASW, 35 mm. **Obv:** National arms, Central Bank name **Rev:** Pelican

Date	Mintage	F	VF	XF	Unc	BU
2003 Proof	—	Value: 45.00				

KM# 902   5 WON
20.0000 g., 0.9990 Silver 0.6423 oz. ASW, 35 mm. **Obv:** National arms, **Rev:** Stone eagle

Date	Mintage	F	VF	XF	Unc	BU
2003 Proof	—	Value: 45.00				

KM# 903   5 WON
31.1050 g., 0.9990 Silver 0.9990 oz. ASW, 40 mm. **Obv:** National arms, Central Bank name **Rev:** Chinese pangolin and young

Date	Mintage	F	VF	XF	Unc	BU
2003 Proof	Est. 1,000	Value: 60.00				

KM# 935   5 WON
15.0000 g., 0.9990 Silver 0.4818 oz. ASW, 30 mm. **Subject:** Franz Schubert, 175th anniversary of death **Obv:** National arms, Central Bank name **Rev:** Franz Schubert

Date	Mintage	F	VF	XF	Unc	BU
2003 Proof	—	Value: 45.00				

KM# 936   5 WON
20.0000 g., 0.9990 Silver 0.6423 oz. ASW, 38 mm. **Obv:** National arms, Central Bank name **Rev:** Horatio Nelson and H.M.S. Victory

Date	Mintage	F	VF	XF	Unc	BU
2003 Proof	—	Value: 45.00				

KM# 937   5 WON
20.0000 g., 0.9990 Silver 0.6423 oz. ASW, 38 mm. **Obv:** National arms, Central Bank name **Rev:** Leopard

Date	Mintage	F	VF	XF	Unc	BU
2003 Proof	Est. 5,000	Value: 40.00				

KM# 1009   5 WON
15.0000 g., 0.9990 Silver 0.4818 oz. ASW, 35 mm. **Obv:** National arms, Central Bank name **Rev:** Red deer in forest glade in color

Date	Mintage	F	VF	XF	Unc	BU
2004 Proof	—	Value: 60.00				

KM# 1010   5 WON
15.0000 g., 0.9990 Silver 0.4818 oz. ASW, 35 mm. **Obv:** National arms, Central Bank name **Rev:** Kingfisher in color

Date	Mintage	F	VF	XF	Unc	BU
2004 Proof	—	Value: 60.00				

KM# 1011   5 WON
31.1050 g., 0.9990 Silver 0.9990 oz. ASW, 35 mm. **Obv:** National arms, Central Bank name **Rev:** Bewick's swan in flight in color

Date	Mintage	F	VF	XF	Unc	BU
2004 Proof	—	Value: 60.00				

KM# 1012   5 WON
15.0000 g., 0.9990 Silver 0.4818 oz. ASW, 35 mm. **Obv:** National arms, Central Bank name **Rev:** Two blue whales and iceberg in color

Date	Mintage	F	VF	XF	Unc	BU
2004 Proof	—	Value: 60.00				

KM# 1013   5 WON
15.0000 g., 0.9990 Silver 0.4818 oz. ASW, 35 mm. **Obv:** National arms, Central Bank name **Rev:** Lion in color

Date	Mintage	F	VF	XF	Unc	BU
2004 Proof	—	Value: 60.00				

KM# 1014   5 WON
20.0000 g., 0.9990 Silver 0.6423 oz. ASW, 38 mm. **Obv:** National arms, Central Bank name **Rev:** Leopard

Date	Mintage	F	VF	XF	Unc	BU
2004 Proof	—	Value: 45.00				

KM# 1015   5 WON
1.1500 g., Aluminum, 21 mm. **Obv:** National arms, Central Bank name **Rev:** Large numeral 5

Date	Mintage	F	VF	XF	Unc	BU
2005	—	—	—	—	3.00	5.00

KM# 1080   5 WON
15.0000 g., 0.9990 Silver 0.4818 oz. ASW, 35 mm. **Subject:** Tschaikowsky, 165 Birthday **Obv:** National arms, Central Bank name **Rev:** Peter Tschaikowsky

Date	Mintage	F	VF	XF	Unc	BU
2005 Proof	—	Value: 45.00				

KM# 1081   5 WON
15.0000 g., 0.9990 Silver 0.4818 oz. ASW, 35 mm. **Obv:** National arms, Central Bank name **Rev:** Squirrel in color

Date	Mintage	F	VF	XF	Unc	BU
2005 Proof	—	Value: 30.00				

KM# 1082   5 WON
15.0000 g., 0.9990 Silver 0.4818 oz. ASW, 35 mm. **Obv:** National arms, Central Bank name **Rev:** Firefox in color

Date	Mintage	F	VF	XF	Unc	BU
2005 Proof	—	Value: 30.00				

KM# 1083   5 WON
20.0000 g., 0.9990 Silver 0.6423 oz. ASW, 38 mm. **Obv:** National arms, Central Bank name **Rev:** Saiga antelope

Date	Mintage	F	VF	XF	Unc	BU
2005 Proof	—	Value: 45.00				

KM# 1084   5 WON
20.0000 g., 0.9990 Silver 0.6423 oz. ASW, 38 mm. **Obv:** National arms, Central Bank name **Rev:** Malayian Tapir and young

Date	Mintage	F	VF	XF	Unc	BU
2005 Proof	Est. 5,000	Value: 45.00				

KM# 1085   5 WON
20.0000 g., 0.9990 Silver 0.6423 oz. ASW, 38 mm. **Obv:** National arms, Central Bank name **Rev:** Sedov sailing ship

Date	Mintage	F	VF	XF	Unc	BU
2005 Proof	Est. 5,000	Value: 45.00				

KM# 1102   5 WON
15.0000 g., 0.9990 Silver 0.4818 oz. ASW, 35 mm. **Obv:** National arms, Central Bank name **Rev:** Orca whale in color

Date	Mintage	F	VF	XF	Unc	BU
2006 Proof	—	Value: 60.00				

KM# 1103   5 WON
15.0000 g., 0.9990 Silver 0.4818 oz. ASW, 35 mm. **Obv:** National arms, Central Bank name **Rev:** javanese flying frog in color

Date	Mintage	F	VF	XF	Unc	BU
2006 Proof	—	Value: 60.00				

KM# 1104   5 WON
15.0000 g., 0.9990 Silver 0.4818 oz. ASW, 35 mm. **Obv:** National arms, Central Bank name **Rev:** Hymalayian Pheasant in color

Date	Mintage	F	VF	XF	Unc	BU
2006 Proof	—	Value: 60.00				

KM# 1105   5 WON
15.0000 g., 0.9990 Silver 0.4818 oz. ASW, 35 mm. **Obv:** National arms, Central Bank name **Rev:** Karl Marx bust left

Date	Mintage	F	VF	XF	Unc	BU
2006 Proof	—	Value: 45.00				

KM# 1106   5 WON
20.0000 g., 0.9990 Silver 0.6423 oz. ASW, 38 mm. **Obv:** National arms, Central Bank name **Rev:** Mir sailing ship

Date	Mintage	F	VF	XF	Unc	BU
2006 Proof	Est. 5,000	Value: 45.00				

KM# 1107   5 WON
20.0000 g., 0.9990 Silver 0.6423 oz. ASW, 38 mm. **Subject:** Bejing Summer Olympics, 2008 **Obv:** National arms, Central Bank name **Rev:** Handball player making shot

Date	Mintage	F	VF	XF	Unc	BU
2006 Proof	Est. 5,000	Value: 35.00				

KM# 1108   5 WON
20.0000 g., 0.9990 Silver 0.6423 oz. ASW, 38 mm. **Subject:** Bejing Summer Olympics, 2008 **Obv:** National arms, Central Bank name **Rev:** Archer before target

Date	Mintage	F	VF	XF	Unc	BU
2006 Proof	Est. 5,000	Value: 35.00				

KM# 1125   5 WON
15.0000 g., 0.9990 Silver 0.4818 oz. ASW, 35 mm. **Obv:** National arms, Central Bank name **Rev:** Japanese snow money in color

Date	Mintage	F	VF	XF	Unc	BU
2007 Proof	—	Value: 60.00				

KM# 1126   5 WON
20.0000 g., 0.9990 Silver 0.6423 oz. ASW, 38 mm. **Obv:** National arms, Central Bank name **Rev:** Siberian musk deer

Date	Mintage	F	VF	XF	Unc	BU
2007 Proof	Est. 5,000	Value: 60.00				

KM# 1127   5 WON
20.0000 g., 0.9990 Silver 0.6423 oz. ASW, 38 mm. **Obv:** National arms, Central Bank name **Rev:** Ming treasure ship

Date	Mintage	F	VF	XF	Unc	BU
2007 Proof	Est. 5,000	Value: 45.00				

KM# 220   7 WON
20.0000 g., 0.9990 Silver 0.6423 oz. ASW, 38 mm. **Subject:** 2002 Olympics **Obv:** State arms **Rev:** Two speed skaters **Edge:** Plain

Date	Mintage	F	VF	XF	Unc	BU
2001 Proof	10,000	Value: 40.00				

KM# 221   7 WON
20.0000 g., 0.9990 Silver 0.6423 oz. ASW, 38 mm. **Subject:** Endangered Wildlife **Obv:** State arms **Rev:** White-tailed sea Eagle **Edge:** Plain

Date	Mintage	F	VF	XF	Unc	BU
2001 Proof	10,000	Value: 35.00				

KM# 881   7 WON
20.0000 g., 0.9990 Silver 0.6423 oz. ASW **Obv:** Naitonal arms, Central Bank name **Rev:** Taekwondo **Shape:** 38

Date	Mintage	F	VF	XF	Unc	BU
2002 Proof	—	Value: 35.00				

KM# 883   7 WON
20.0000 g., 0.9990 Silver 0.6423 oz. ASW, 38 mm. **Obv:** National arms, Central Bank name **Rev:** World Cup, player and Brandenburg Gate

Date	Mintage	F	VF	XF	Unc	BU
2002 Proof	—	Value: 30.00				

KM# 921   7 WON
20.0000 g., 0.9990 Silver 0.6423 oz. ASW, 38 mm. **Obv:** National arms, Central Bank name **Rev:** Steamer Princess Charlotte of Prussia

Date	Mintage	F	VF	XF	Unc	BU
2003 Proof	Est. 500	Value: 70.00				

KM# 922   7 WON
20.0000 g., 0.9990 Silver 0.6423 oz. ASW, 35 mm. **Obv:** National arms, Central Bank name **Rev:** Steamship Queen Maria

Date	Mintage	F	VF	XF	Unc	BU
2003 Proof	—	Value: 75.00				

KM# 923   7 WON
20.0000 g., 0.9990 Silver 0.6423 oz. ASW, 38 mm. **Obv:** National arms, Central Bank name **Rev:** Transatlantic sail steamship Helena Sloman

Date	Mintage	F	VF	XF	Unc	BU
2003 Proof	Est. 500	Value: 75.00				

KM# 927   7 WON
20.0000 g., 0.9990 Silver 0.6423 oz. ASW, 38 mm. **Obv:** National arms, Central Bank name **Rev:** Adler, 1835 steam locomotive

Date	Mintage	F	VF	XF	Unc	BU
2003 Proof	—	Value: 60.00				

KM# 928   7 WON
20.0000 g., 0.9990 Silver 0.6423 oz. ASW, 38 mm. **Obv:** National arms, Central Bank name **Rev:** Saxonia, 1838 steam locomotive

Date	Mintage	F	VF	XF	Unc	BU
2003 Proof	—	Value: 60.00				

KM# 929   7 WON
20.0000 g., 0.9990 Silver 0.6423 oz. ASW, 38 mm. **Obv:** National arms, Central Bank name **Rev:** Rheingold, 1928 steam locomotive

Date	Mintage	F	VF	XF	Unc	BU
2003 Proof	—	Value: 60.00				

KM# 931   7 WON
20.0000 g., 0.9990 Silver 0.6423 oz. ASW, 38 mm. **Obv:** National arms, Central Bank name **Rev:** Gorch Fock I, sailing ship

Date	Mintage	F	VF	XF	Unc	BU
2003 Proof	—	Value: 60.00				

KM# 932   7 WON
20.0000 g., 0.9990 Silver 0.6423 oz. ASW, 38 mm. **Obv:** National arms, Central Bank name **Rev:** Skier

Date	Mintage	F	VF	XF	Unc	BU
2003 Proof	Est. 5,000	Value: 40.00				

KM# 477   7 WON
20.0000 g., Bi-Metallic Silver center in Brass ring. **Obv:** Arms **Rev:** Stadium along river

Date	Mintage	F	VF	XF	Unc	BU
2004 Proof	—	Value: 55.00				

KM# 945   7 WON
20.0000 g., Silver, 23x40 mm. **Obv:** East gate of Pyeongyang **Rev:** Mormoset **Shape:** Rectangle

Date	Mintage	F	VF	XF	Unc	BU
2004 Proof	—	Value: 35.00				

KM# 946   7 WON
20.0000 g., 0.9990 Silver 0.6423 oz. ASW, 23x40 mm. **Obv:** East gate of Pyeongyang **Rev:** Blue monkey **Shape:** Rectangle

Date	Mintage	F	VF	XF	Unc	BU
2004 Proof	—	Value: 35.00				

KM# 947   7 WON
20.0000 g., Silver, 23x40 mm. **Obv:** East gate of Pyeongyang **Rev:** Monkies **Shape:** Rectangle

Date	Mintage	F	VF	XF	Unc	BU
2004 Proof	—	Value: 35.00				

KM# 996   7 WON
20.0000 g., 0.9990 Silver 0.6423 oz. ASW, 38 mm. **Obv:** National arms, Central Bank name **Rev:** Statsraad Lehmkuhl sailing ship

Date	Mintage	F	VF	XF	Unc	BU
2004 Proof	Est. 3,000	Value: 60.00				

KM# 997   7 WON
20.0000 g., 0.9990 Silver 0.6423 oz. ASW, 38 mm. **Obv:** National arms, Central Bank name **Rev:** Henry Hudson's Halve Maen

Date	Mintage	F	VF	XF	Unc	BU
2004 Proof	Est. 3,000	Value: 60.00				

KM# 998   7 WON
20.0000 g., 0.9990 Silver 0.6423 oz. ASW, 38 mm. **Subject:** 1980 Lake PLacid Olympics **Obv:** National arms, Central Bank name **Rev:** Speed skater

Date	Mintage	F	VF	XF	Unc	BU
2004 Proof	Est. 5,000	Value: 35.00				

KM# 1071   7 WON
20.0000 g., 0.9990 Silver 0.6423 oz. ASW, 38 mm. **Subject:** Squaw Valley 1960 Winter Olympics **Obv:** National arms, Central Bank name **Rev:** Ice Dancing

Date	Mintage	F	VF	XF	Unc	BU
2005 Proof	Est. 5,000	Value: 45.00				

KM# 1072   7 WON
20.0000 g., 0.9990 Silver 0.6423 oz. ASW, 38 mm. **Subject:** Calgary Winter Olympics, 1988 **Obv:** National arms, Central Bank name

Date	Mintage	F	VF	XF	Unc	BU
2005 Proof	Est. 5,000	Value: 45.00				

KM# 1073   7 WON
20.0000 g., 0.9990 Silver 0.6423 oz. ASW, 38 mm. **Subject:** Nagano Winter Olympics, 1998 **Obv:** National arms, Central Bank name **Rev:** Snowboarder

Date	Mintage	F	VF	XF	Unc	BU
2005 Proof	—	Value: 45.00				

KM# 1075   7 WON
20.0000 g., 0.9990 Silver 0.6423 oz. ASW, 38 mm. **Subject:** Torino Winter Olympics, 2006 **Obv:** National arms, Central Bank name **Rev:** bobsled

Date	Mintage	F	VF	XF	Unc	BU
2005 Proof	—	Value: 45.00				

KM# 1076   7 WON
20.0000 g., 0.9990 Silver 0.6423 oz. ASW, 38 mm. **Obv:** National arms, Central Bank name **Rev:** Black faced spoonbill

Date	Mintage	F	VF	XF	Unc	BU
2005 Proof	Est. 5,000	Value: 60.00				

KM# 1077   7 WON
20.0000 g., 0.9990 Silver 0.6423 oz. ASW, 38 mm. **Obv:** National arms, Central Bank name **Rev:** Flying dog

Date	Mintage	F	VF	XF	Unc	BU
2005 Proof	Est. 5,000	Value: 60.00				

KM# 292   10 WON
31.0000 g., 0.9990 Silver 0.9956 oz. ASW, 40.2 mm. **Obv:** State arms **Rev:** Kim Il-Seung bust facing, 1912-1994 flanking, sprigs below **Edge:** Plain

Date	Mintage	F	VF	XF	Unc	BU
JU90-2001 Proof	—	Value: 45.00				

KM# 295   10 WON
31.0000 g., 0.9990 Silver 0.9956 oz. ASW, 40.2 mm. **Obv:** State arms **Rev:** Mountain cabin **Edge:** Plain

Date	Mintage	F	VF	XF	Unc	BU
JU90-2001 Proof	—	Value: 45.00				

KM# 296   10 WON
31.0000 g., 0.9990 Silver 0.9956 oz. ASW, 40.2 mm. **Obv:** State arms **Rev:** "KUMDANG - 2 INJECTION" in center of leaves **Edge:** Plain

Date	Mintage	F	VF	XF	Unc	BU
2001 Proof	—	Value: 50.00				

KM# 297   10 WON
31.0000 g., 0.9990 Silver 0.9956 oz. ASW, 40.2 mm. **Obv:** State arms **Rev:** Train scene and a couple below a jet liner **Rev. Legend:** ...1945 - 2001... **Edge:** Plain

Date	Mintage	F	VF	XF	Unc	BU
ND(2001) Proof	—	Value: 45.00				

KM# 298   10 WON
31.0000 g., 0.9990 Silver 0.9956 oz. ASW, 40.2 mm. **Obv:** State arms **Rev:** Cruise ship below stylized head left profile **Edge:** Plain

Date	Mintage	F	VF	XF	Unc	BU
JU90-2001 Proof	—	Value: 50.00				

KM# 299   10 WON
31.0000 g., 0.9990 Silver 0.9956 oz. ASW, 40.2 mm. **Obv:** State arms **Rev:** Old fortress **Edge:** Plain

Date	Mintage	F	VF	XF	Unc	BU
JU90-2001 Proof	—	Value: 47.50				

KM# 300   10 WON
31.0000 g., 0.9990 Silver 0.9956 oz. ASW, 40.2 mm. **Obv:** State arms **Rev:** Landmarks, flag and tourist couple above cruise ship **Edge:** Plain

Date	Mintage	F	VF	XF	Unc	BU
JU90-2001 Proof	—	Value: 45.00				

KM# 301   10 WON
31.0000 g., 0.9990 Silver 0.9956 oz. ASW, 40.2 mm. **Obv:** State arms **Rev:** 2 facing half length men shaking hands **Edge:** Plain

Date	Mintage	F	VF	XF	Unc	BU
JU90-2001 Proof	—	Value: 45.00				

KM# 302   10 WON
31.0000 g., 0.9990 Silver 0.9956 oz. ASW, 40.1 mm. **Obv:** State arms **Rev:** Great East Gate **Edge:** Plain

Date	Mintage	F	VF	XF	Unc	BU
JU90-2001 Proof	—	Value: 47.50				

KM# 357   10 WON
31.0000 g., 0.9990 Silver 0.9956 oz. ASW, 40.2 mm. **Obv:** State arms **Rev:** Antique ceramic items **Edge:** Plain

Date	Mintage	F	VF	XF	Unc	BU
2001 Proof	—	Value: 45.00				

KM# 386   10 WON
30.7600 g., 0.9990 Silver 0.9879 oz. ASW, 40.1 mm. **Obv:** State arms **Rev:** Kim Jung Sook facing flanked by dates (1917-1949) above flower sprigs **Edge:** Plain

Date	Mintage	F	VF	XF	Unc	BU
JU90-2001 Proof	—	Value: 47.50				

KM# 387   10 WON
30.7600 g., 0.9990 Silver 0.9879 oz. ASW, 40.1 mm. **Obv:** State arms **Rev:** Kim Jung-Il bust facing, sprigs below **Edge:** Plain

Date	Mintage	F	VF	XF	Unc	BU
JU90-2001 Proof	—	Value: 47.50				

KM# 152   10 WON
31.0000 g., 0.9990 Silver 0.9956 oz. ASW, 39.8 mm. **Subject:** Asian Money Fair **Obv:** State arms **Rev:** Two snakes **Edge:** Reeded and plain sections

Date	Mintage	F	VF	XF	Unc	BU
2001 Proof	—	Value: 60.00				

KM# 153   10 WON
31.0000 g., 0.9990 Silver 0.9956 oz. ASW, 39.8 mm. **Subject:** Tortoise-Serpent **Obv:** State arms **Rev:** Mythical creature **Edge:** Reeded and plain sections

Date	Mintage	F	VF	XF	Unc	BU
2001 Proof	—	Value: 55.00				

KM# 227   10 WON
31.0600 g., 0.9250 Silver 0.9237 oz. ASW, 39.9 mm. **Subject:** General Ri Sun Sin **Obv:** State arms **Rev:** Helmeted head 1/4 left **Edge:** Reeded

Date	Mintage	F	VF	XF	Unc	BU
2001 Proof	—	Value: 47.50				

KM# 253   10 WON
31.1100 g., 0.9990 Silver 0.9992 oz. ASW, 40.2 mm. **Obv:** State

arms **Rev:** Deng Xio Ping head 3/4 left, 1904-1997 flanking, sprigs below **Edge:** Plain

Date	Mintage	F	VF	XF	Unc	BU
2001	—	Value: 45.00				

KM# 697   10 WON
27.0000 g., 0.9990 Silver 0.8672 oz. ASW, 40 mm. **Obv:** National arms, value in English **Rev:** Kim Jeongsuk

Date	Mintage	F	VF	XF	Unc	BU
2001 Proof	—	Value: 60.00				

KM# 704   10 WON
31.1050 g., Silver, 40 mm. **Obv:** National arms, Country name **Rev:** House where Kim Ilseong was born

Date	Mintage	F	VF	XF	Unc	BU
2001 Proof	—	—	—	—	—	—

KM# 705   10 WON
31.1050 g., 0.9990 Silver 0.9990 oz. ASW, 40 mm. **Obv:** National arms, Country name **Rev:** House where Kim Jeongsuk was born

Date	Mintage	F	VF	XF	Unc	BU
2001 Proof	—	—	—	—	—	—

KM# 732   10 WON
7.0000 g., Aluminum, 40 mm. **Obv:** East gate of Pyeongyang **Rev:** Married couple before flag and ferryboat

Date	Mintage	F	VF	XF	Unc	BU
2001 Proof	—	—	—	—	—	—

KM# 733   10 WON
7.0000 g., Aluminum, 40 mm. **Obv:** East gate of Pyeongyang **Rev:** Ferryboat between Korea and Japan

Date	Mintage	F	VF	XF	Unc	BU
2001 Proof	—	—	—	—	—	—

KM# 734   10 WON
7.0000 g., Aluminum, 40 mm. **Obv:** East gate of Pyeongyang **Rev:** Triumphial arch of Moranbong in Pyeongyang

Date	Mintage	F	VF	XF	Unc	BU
2001 Proof	—	—	—	—	—	—

KM# 735   10 WON
Aluminum, 40 mm. **Obv:** East gate of Pyeongyang **Rev:** Chonji crater in Paektusan

Date	Mintage	F	VF	XF	Unc	BU
2001 Proof	—	—	—	—	—	—

KM# 740   10 WON
Silver, 40 mm. **Obv:** National arms, Country name **Rev:** Triumphial arch of Moranbong in Pyeongyang

Date	Mintage	F	VF	XF	Unc	BU
2001 Proof	—	—	—	—	—	—

KM# 741   10 WON
Silver, 40 mm. **Obv:** National arms, Country name **Rev:** Chonji crater in Paektusan

Date	Mintage	F	VF	XF	Unc	BU
2001 Proof	—	—	—	—	—	—

KM# 775   10 WON
7.0000 g., Aluminum, 40 mm. **Obv:** East gate in Pyeongyang **Rev:** Taekwondo player

Date	Mintage	F	VF	XF	Unc	BU
2001 Proof	—	Value: 6.00				

KM# 776   10 WON
7.0000 g., Aluminum, 40 mm. **Obv:** National arms, Country name **Rev:** Two taekwondo players

Date	Mintage	F	VF	XF	Unc	BU
2001 Proof	—	Value: 6.00				
2007 Proof	—	Value: 6.00				

KM# 779   10 WON
31.1050 g., 0.9990 Silver 0.9990 oz. ASW, 40 mm. **Obv:** National arms, Central Bank name **Rev:** Taewankdo kicker

Date	Mintage	F	VF	XF	Unc	BU
2001 Proof	—	Value: 60.00				

KM# 780   10 WON
31.1050 g., 0.9990 Silver 0.9990 oz. ASW, 40 mm. **Obv:** National arms, Central Bank name **Rev:** Two taekwondo players

Date	Mintage	F	VF	XF	Unc	BU
2001 Proof	—	Value: 60.00				

KM# 401   10 WON
31.0000 g., 0.9990 Silver 0.9956 oz. ASW, 40.1 mm. **Obv:** State arms **Rev:** Arirang dancer **Edge:** Plain

Date	Mintage	F	VF	XF	Unc	BU
JU91-2002 Proof	—	Value: 45.00				

KM# 402   10 WON
31.0000 g., 0.9990 Silver 0.9956 oz. ASW, 40.1 mm. **Obv:** State arms **Rev:** Arirang ribbon dancer **Edge:** Plain

Date	Mintage	F	VF	XF	Unc	BU
JU91-2002 Proof	—	Value: 45.00				

KM# 307   10 WON
31.0000 g., 0.9990 Silver 0.9956 oz. ASW, 40.1 mm. **Obv:** State arms **Rev:** Two horses within a circle of Asian Zodiac animals **Edge:** Plain

Date	Mintage	F	VF	XF	Unc	BU
2002 Proof	—	Value: 45.00				

KM# 309   10 WON
31.0000 g., 0.9990 Silver 0.9956 oz. ASW, 40.2 mm. **Subject:** Arirang **Obv:** State arms **Rev:** Performers and flying cranes **Edge:** Plain

Date	Mintage	F	VF	XF	Unc	BU
JU91-2002 Proof	—	Value: 45.00				

KM# 311   10 WON
31.0000 g., 0.9990 Silver 0.9956 oz. ASW, 40.2 mm. **Obv:** State arms **Rev:** Tomb of King Tongmyong **Edge:** Plain

Date	Mintage	F	VF	XF	Unc	BU
JU91-2002 Proof	—	Value: 45.00				

KM# 312   10 WON
31.0000 g., 0.9990 Silver 0.9956 oz. ASW, 40.2 mm. **Obv:** State arms **Rev:** Tomb of King Kong Min **Edge:** Plain

Date	Mintage	F	VF	XF	Unc	BU
JU91-2002 Proof	—	Value: 45.00				

KM# 314   10 WON
31.0000 g., 0.9990 Silver 0.9956 oz. ASW, 40.2 mm. **Subject:** Arirang **Obv:** State arms **Rev:** Stylized dancer **Edge:** Plain

Date	Mintage	F	VF	XF	Unc	BU
2002 Proof	—	Value: 45.00				

KM# 315   10 WON
31.0000 g., 0.9990 Silver 0.9956 oz. ASW, 40.2 mm. **Obv:** State arms **Rev:** Korean map shaped dancer **Edge:** Plain

Date	Mintage	F	VF	XF	Unc	BU
JU91-2002 Proof	—	Value: 47.50				

KM# 316   10 WON
31.0000 g., 0.9990 Silver 0.9956 oz. ASW, 40.2 mm. **Obv:** State arms **Rev:** Korean map shaped ribbon dancer **Edge:** Plain

Date	Mintage	F	VF	XF	Unc	BU
JU91-2002 Proof	—	Value: 47.50				

KM# 317   10 WON
31.0000 g., 0.9990 Silver 0.9956 oz. ASW, 40.2 mm. **Obv:** State arms **Rev:** Victorious athletes hugging **Edge:** Plain

Date	Mintage	F	VF	XF	Unc	BU
JU91-2002 Proof	—	Value: 45.00				

KM# 318   10 WON
31.0000 g., 0.9990 Silver 0.9956 oz. ASW, 40.2 mm. **Obv:** State arms **Rev:** Woman floating above arena **Edge:** Plain

Date	Mintage	F	VF	XF	Unc	BU
JU91-2002 Proof	—	Value: 45.00				

KM# 254   10 WON
30.7700 g., 0.9990 Silver 0.9882 oz. ASW, 40.15 mm. **Obv:** State arms **Rev:** Tangun bust facing and his tomb **Edge:** Plain

Date	Mintage	F	VF	XF	Unc	BU
JU91-2002 Proof	—	Value: 42.50				

KM# 255   10 WON
30.9400 g., 0.9990 Silver 0.9937 oz. ASW, 40.2 mm. **Subject:** Jongmongju and Sonjukgyo **Obv:** State arms **Rev:** Head with hat facing above building foundation **Edge:** Plain

Date	Mintage	F	VF	XF	Unc	BU
JU91-2002 Proof	—	Value: 42.50				

KM# 231   10 WON
31.0000 g., 0.9990 Silver 0.9956 oz. ASW, 39.9 mm. **Subject:** Kim III Sung **Obv:** State arms **Rev:** Bust facing **Edge:** Segmented reeding

Date	Mintage	F	VF	XF	Unc	BU
JU91-2002 Proof	—	Value: 50.00				

KM# 812   10 WON
31.1050 g., 0.9990 Silver 0.9990 oz. ASW, 40 mm. **Obv:** National arms, Central Bank name **Rev:** Dongmyeong, 1st King of Goguryeo

Date	Mintage	F	VF	XF	Unc	BU
2002 Proof	—	Value: 60.00				

KM# 813   10 WON
31.1050 g., 0.9990 Silver 0.9990 oz. ASW, 40 mm. **Obv:** National arms, Central Bank name **Rev:** Wanggeon, 1st King of Goryeo dynasty

Date	Mintage	F	VF	XF	Unc	BU
2002 Proof	—	Value: 60.00				

KM# 814   10 WON
31.1050 g., 0.9990 Silver 0.9990 oz. ASW, 40 mm. **Obv:** National arms, Central Bank name **Rev:** Jeon Bongjun

Date	Mintage	F	VF	XF	Unc	BU
2002 Proof	—	Value: 60.00				

KM# 823   10 WON
31.1050 g., 0.9990 Silver 0.9990 oz. ASW, 40 mm. **Obv:** National arms **Rev:** Prince Hodong and Princess Nakrang on horseback

Date	Mintage	F	VF	XF	Unc	BU
2002 Proof	—	Value: 60.00				

KM# 824   10 WON
31.1050 g., 0.9990 Silver 0.9990 oz. ASW, 40 mm. **Obv:** National arms **Rev:** Half-length figures of Prince Hodong and Princess Nakrang

Date	Mintage	F	VF	XF	Unc	BU
2002 Proof	—	Value: 60.00				

KM# 827   10 WON
7.0000 g., Aluminum, 40 mm. **Obv:** East gate of Pyeongyang **Rev:** Reconstruction of the Mausoleum of King Dongmyeong

Date	Mintage	F	VF	XF	Unc	BU
2002 Proof	—	Value: 7.00				

KM# 828   10 WON
7.0000 g., Aluminum, 40 mm. **Obv:** East gate in Pyeongyang **Rev:** Mausoleum for Gongmin

Date	Mintage	F	VF	XF	Unc	BU
2002 Proof	—	Value: 7.00				

KM# 829   10 WON
7.0000 g., Aluminum, 40 mm. **Obv:** East gate in Pyeongyang **Rev:** Stadium

Date	Mintage	F	VF	XF	Unc	BU
2002 Proof	—	Value: 7.00				

KM# 860   10 WON
7.0000 g., Aluminum, 40 mm. **Obv:** East gate of Pyeongyang **Rev:** The family

Date	Mintage	F	VF	XF	Unc	BU
2002 Proof	—	Value: 7.00				

KM# 861   10 WON
7.0000 g., Aluminum, 40 mm. **Obv:** East gate of Pyeongyang **Rev:** Map of Korea with the four cardinal compass points

Date	Mintage	F	VF	XF	Unc	BU
2002 Proof	—	Value: 7.00				

KM# 862   10 WON
7.0000 g., Aluminum, 40 mm. **Obv:** East gate of Pyeongyang **Rev:** Ryhmathic dancing and map of Korea

Date	Mintage	F	VF	XF	Unc	BU
2002 Proof	—	Value: 7.00				

KM# 863   10 WON
7.0000 g., Aluminum, 40 mm. **Obv:** East gate of Pyeongyang **Rev:** Drum dancer in form of the map of Korea

Date	Mintage	F	VF	XF	Unc	BU
2002 Proof	—	Value: 7.00				

KM# 864   10 WON
7.0000 g., Aluminum, 40 mm. **Obv:** East gate of Pyeongyang **Rev:** Victory celebration of Korean Teammates

Date	Mintage	F	VF	XF	Unc	BU
2002 Proof	—	Value: 7.00				

KM# 865   10 WON
28.0000 g., Brass, 40 mm. **Obv:** East gate of Pyeongyang **Rev:** Family

Date	Mintage	F	VF	XF	Unc	BU
2002 Proof	—	Value: 7.00				

KM# 870   10 WON
31.1050 g., 0.9990 Silver 0.9990 oz. ASW, 40 mm. **Obv:** National arms, Central Bank name **Rev:** Family

Date	Mintage	F	VF	XF	Unc	BU
2002 Proof	—	Value: 60.00				

KM# 871   10 WON
31.1050 g., 0.9990 Silver 0.9990 oz. ASW, 40 mm. **Obv:** National arms, Central Bank name **Rev:** Map of Korea with the four cardinal points

Date	Mintage	F	VF	XF	Unc	BU
2002 Proof	—	Value: 60.00				

KM# 833   10 WON
31.1050 g., 0.9990 Silver 0.9990 oz. ASW, 40 mm. **Obv:** National arms, Central Bank name **Rev:** Stadium

Date	Mintage	F	VF	XF	Unc	BU
2002 Proof	—	Value: 60.00				

KM# 884   10 WON
31.1050 g., 0.9990 Silver 0.9990 oz. ASW, 40 mm. **Subject:** Final issue of the German Mark **Obv:** National arms, Central Bank name **Rev:** Mark coin and Brandenburg Gate in color

Date	Mintage	F	VF	XF	Unc	BU
2002 Proof	Est. 2,001	Value: 85.00				

KM# 885   10 WON
31.1050 g., 0.9990 Silver 0.9990 oz. ASW, 40 mm. **Subject:** Final issue of the Belgian franc **Obv:** National arms, Central Bank name **Rev:** Franc and Axon in Brussels

Date	Mintage	F	VF	XF	Unc	BU
2002 Proof	Est. 2,001	Value: 85.00				

KM# 886   10 WON
31.1050 g., 0.9990 Silver 0.9990 oz. ASW, 40 mm. **Subject:** Final issue of the Greek Drachma **Obv:** National arms, Central Bank name **Rev:** Drachma and Acropolis in color

Date	Mintage	F	VF	XF	Unc	BU
2002 Proof	Est. 2,001	Value: 85.00				

KM# 887   10 WON
31.1050 g., 0.9990 Silver 0.9990 oz. ASW, 40 mm. **Subject:** Final issue of the Austrian schilling **Obv:** National arms, Central bank name **Rev:** Schilling and St. Stephen's in Vienna in color

Date	Mintage	F	VF	XF	Unc	BU
2002 Proof	Est. 2,001	Value: 85.00				

KM# 888   10 WON
31.1050 g., 0.9990 Silver 0.9990 oz. ASW, 40 mm. **Subject:** Final issue of the Netherland Gulden **Obv:** National arms, Central Bank name **Rev:** Gulden and Windmill in color

Date	Mintage	F	VF	XF	Unc	BU
2002 Proof	Est. 2,001	Value: 85.00				

KM# 889   10 WON
31.1050 g., 0.9990 Silver 0.9990 oz. ASW, 40 mm. **Subject:** Final issue of the San Marino Lira **Obv:** National arms, Central Bank name **Rev:** Lira and Mount Titano in color

Date	Mintage	F	VF	XF	Unc	BU
2002 Proof	Est. 2,001	Value: 85.00				

KM# 890   10 WON
31.1050 g., 0.9990 Silver 0.9990 oz. ASW, 40 mm. **Subject:** Final Vatican Lira **Obv:** National arms, Central Bank name **Rev:** Lira coin and St. Peter's in color

Date	Mintage	F	VF	XF	Unc	BU
2002 Proof	Est. 2,001	Value: 85.00				

KM# 409   10 WON
30.9400 g., 0.9990 Silver 0.9937 oz. ASW, 40 mm. **Obv:** State arms **Rev:** Children spinning tops **Edge:** Plain

Date	Mintage	F	VF	XF	Unc	BU
JU92-2003 Proof	—	Value: 45.00				

KM# 320   10 WON
31.0000 g., 0.9990 Silver 0.9956 oz. ASW, 40.2 mm. **Obv:** State arms **Rev:** Helmeted head with two antenna-like horns on helmet **Edge:** Plain

Date	Mintage	F	VF	XF	Unc	BU
JU92-2003 Proof	—	Value: 47.50				

KM# 321   10 WON
31.0000 g., 0.9990 Silver 0.9956 oz. ASW, 40.2 mm. **Obv:** State arms **Rev:** Helmeted head with horns **Edge:** Plain

Date	Mintage	F	VF	XF	Unc	BU
JU92-2003 Proof	—	Value: 47.50				

KM# 322   10 WON
31.0000 g., 0.9990 Silver 0.9956 oz. ASW, 40.2 mm. **Obv:** State arms **Rev:** Armored bust of Kang Kam-cheon facing (948-1031) wearing winged helmet **Edge:** Plain

Date	Mintage	F	VF	XF	Unc	BU
JU92-2003 Proof	—	Value: 47.50				

KM# 324   10 WON
31.0000 g., 0.9990 Silver 0.9956 oz. ASW, 40.2 mm. **Obv:** State arms **Rev:** Turtle-shaped armored ship of 1592 **Edge:** Plain

Date	Mintage	F	VF	XF	Unc	BU
JU92-2003 Proof	—	Value: 45.00				

KM# 325   10 WON
31.0000 g., 0.9990 Silver 0.9956 oz. ASW, 40.2 mm. **Obv:** State arms **Rev:** Children playing jacks **Edge:** Plain

Date	Mintage	F	VF	XF	Unc	BU
JU92-2003 Proof	—	Value: 45.00				

KM# 326   10 WON
31.0000 g., 0.9990 Silver 0.9956 oz. ASW, 40.2 mm. **Obv:** State arms **Rev:** Children kicking a shuttlecock **Edge:** Plain

Date	Mintage	F	VF	XF	Unc	BU
JU92-2003 Proof	—	Value: 45.00				

KM# 453   10 WON
31.0000 g., 0.9990 Silver 0.9956 oz. ASW **Subject:** FIFA World Championship - Germany 2006 **Obv:** National arms **Rev:** Two hands holding up cup in rays at lower right, two small players at left. **Rev. Legend:** WORLD CUP **Rev. Inscription:** FIFA

Date	Mintage	F	VF	XF	Unc	BU
JU92-2003 Proof	—	Value: 60.00				

KM# 896   10 WON
7.0000 g., Aluminum, 40 mm. **Obv:** East gate of Pyeongand **Rev:** Sheep in center of Zodac

Date	Mintage	F	VF	XF	Unc	BU
2003 Proof	—	Value: 7.00				

KM# 898   10 WON
31.1050 g., 0.9990 Silver 0.9990 oz. ASW, 40 mm. **Obv:** Naitonal arms **Rev:** Sheep at center of Zodiac

Date	Mintage	F	VF	XF	Unc	BU
2003 Proof	—	Value: 60.00				

KM# 905   10 WON
31.1050 g., 0.9990 Silver 0.9990 oz. ASW, 40 mm. **Obv:** National arms, Central Bank name **Rev:** Highway and vehicles, train

Date	Mintage	F	VF	XF	Unc	BU
2003 Proof	Est. 1,000	Value: 70.00				

KM# 906   10 WON
7.0000 g., Aluminum, 40 mm. **Obv:** East gate of Pyeongyang **Rev:** Eulji Mundeok

Date	Mintage	F	VF	XF	Unc	BU
2003 Proof	—	Value: 7.00				

KM# 907   10 WON
7.0000 g., Aluminum, 40 mm. **Obv:** East gate of Pyrongyang **Rev:** Yeon Gaesomun

Date	Mintage	F	VF	XF	Unc	BU
2003 Proof	—	Value: 7.00				

KM# 908   10 WON
7.0000 g., Aluminum, 40 mm. **Obv:** East gate of Pyeongyang **Rev:** Gang Gaesomun

Date	Mintage	F	VF	XF	Unc	BU
2003 Proof	—	Value: 7.00				

KM# 911   10 WON
28.0000 g., Brass, 40 mm. **Obv:** East gate of Pyeongyang **Rev:** Gang Camchan

Date	Mintage	F	VF	XF	Unc	BU
2003 Proof	—	Value: 7.00				

KM# 915   10 WON
7.0000 g., Aluminum, 40 mm. **Obv:** East gate of Pyeongyang **Rev:** Turtle boat

Date	Mintage	F	VF	XF	Unc	BU
2003 Proof	—	Value: 7.00				

KM# 342   10 WON
31.0000 g., 0.9990 Silver 0.9956 oz. ASW, 40 mm. **Obv:** State arms **Rev:** Domed building **Edge:** Plain

Date	Mintage	F	VF	XF	Unc	BU
JU93-2004 Proof	—	Value: 47.50				

KM# 343   10 WON
31.0000 g., 0.9990 Silver 0.9956 oz. ASW, 40 mm. **Obv:** State arms **Rev:** Pigeon on branch **Edge:** Segmented reeding

Date	Mintage	F	VF	XF	Unc	BU
JU93-2004 Proof	—	Value: 45.00				

KM# 344   10 WON
31.0000 g., 0.9990 Silver 0.9956 oz. ASW, 40 mm. **Obv:** State arms **Rev:** Two Leiothrix birds **Edge:** Segmented reeding

Date	Mintage	F	VF	XF	Unc	BU
JU93-2004 Proof	—	Value: 45.00				

KM# 345   10 WON
31.0000 g., 0.9990 Silver 0.9956 oz. ASW, 40 mm. **Obv:** State arms **Rev:** Two cranes standing in water **Edge:** Segmented reeding

Date	Mintage	F	VF	XF	Unc	BU
JU93-2004 Proof	—	Value: 47.50				

KM# 346   10 WON
31.0000 g., 0.9990 Silver 0.9956 oz. ASW, 40 mm. **Obv:** State arms **Rev:** Curlew bird **Edge:** Segmented reeding

Date	Mintage	F	VF	XF	Unc	BU
JU93-2004 Proof	—	Value: 45.00				

KM# 347   10 WON
31.0000 g., 0.9990 Silver 0.9956 oz. ASW, 40 mm. **Obv:** State arms **Rev:** Goshawk on branch **Edge:** Segmented reeding

Date	Mintage	F	VF	XF	Unc	BU
JU93-2004 Proof	—	Value: 45.00				

KM# 418   10 WON
31.0000 g., 0.9990 Silver 0.9956 oz. ASW, 39.7 mm. **Obv:** State arms **Rev:** Ibis standing in water **Edge:** Segmented reeding

Date	Mintage	F	VF	XF	Unc	BU
JU93-2004 Proof	—	Value: 50.00				

KM# 938   10 WON
31.1050 g., 0.9990 Silver 0.9990 oz. ASW, 40 mm. **Obv:** National arms, Central Bank name **Rev:** Monkey King Sun Wukong from Journey to the West

Date	Mintage	F	VF	XF	Unc	BU
2004 Proof	—	Value: 70.00				

KM# 940   10 WON
31.1050 g., 0.9990 Silver 0.9990 oz. ASW, 40 mm. **Obv:** National arms, Central Bank name **Rev:** Monkey in center of Zodiac

Date	Mintage	F	VF	XF	Unc	BU
2004 Proof	—	Value: 60.00				

KM# 948   10 WON
Silver, 32x46 mm. **Subject:** Deng Xiaoping, 100th Birth Anniversary **Obv:** National arms **Rev:** Deng Xiaoping saluting **Shape:** Vertical rectangle

Date	Mintage	F	VF	XF	Unc	BU
2004 Proof	—	Value: 60.00				

KM# 951   10 WON
31.1050 g., 0.9990 Silver 0.9990 oz. ASW, 40 mm. **Obv:** Naitonal arms, Central Bank name **Rev:** Broad throaded bird

Date	Mintage	F	VF	XF	Unc	BU
2004 Proof	—	Value: 45.00				

KM# 952   10 WON
31.1050 g., 0.9990 Silver 0.9990 oz. ASW, 40 mm. **Obv:** Naitonal arms, Central Bank name **Rev:** Imperial eagle

Date	Mintage	F	VF	XF	Unc	BU
2004 Proof	—	Value: 45.00				

KM# 953   10 WON
31.1050 g., 0.9990 Silver 0.9990 oz. ASW, 40 mm. **Obv:** National arms, Central Bank name **Rev:** Bittern

Date	Mintage	F	VF	XF	Unc	BU
2004 Proof	—	Value: 45.00				

KM# 954   10 WON
31.1050 g., 0.9990 Silver 0.9990 oz. ASW, 40 mm. **Obv:** National arms, Central Bank name **Rev:** Pheasant

Date	Mintage	F	VF	XF	Unc	BU
2004 Proof	—	Value: 45.00				

KM# 999   10 WON
31.1050 g., 0.9990 Silver 0.9990 oz. ASW, 40 mm. **Obv:** National arms, Central Bank name **Rev:** Tallinn castle in color, Estonian Krone

Date	Mintage	F	VF	XF	Unc	BU
2004 Proof				Value: 85.00		

KM# 1000   10 WON
31.1050 g., 0.9990 Silver 0.9990 oz. ASW, 40 mm. **Obv:** National arms, Central Bank name **Rev:** Malta's lira and Fort St. Angelo in color

Date	Mintage	F	VF	XF	Unc	BU
2004 Proof	Est. 2,004			Value: 85.00		

KM# 1001   10 WON
31.1050 g., 0.9990 Silver 0.9990 oz. ASW, 40 mm. **Obv:** National arms, Central Bank name **Rev:** Polish zloty and Danzig Grain Tower in color

Date	Mintage	F	VF	XF	Unc	BU
2004 Proof				Value: 85.00		

KM# 1002   10 WON
31.1050 g., 0.9990 Silver 0.9990 oz. ASW, 40 mm. **Obv:** National arms, Central Bank name **Rev:** Slovakian Korun and Bratislava castle in color

Date	Mintage	F	VF	XF	Unc	BU
2004 Proof	Est. 2,004			Value: 85.00		

KM# 1003   10 WON
31.1050 g., 0.9990 Silver 0.9990 oz. ASW, 40 mm. **Obv:** National arms, Central Bank name **Rev:** Czech Korun and Prague castle in color

Date	Mintage	F	VF	XF	Unc	BU
2004 Proof	Est. 2,004			Value: 85.00		

KM# 1004   10 WON
31.1050 g., 0.9990 Silver 0.9990 oz. ASW, 40 mm. **Obv:** National arms, Central Bank name **Rev:** Hungarian Forint and St. Stephan statue in Budapest castle in color

Date	Mintage	F	VF	XF	Unc	BU
2004 Proof	Est. 2,004			Value: 85.00		

KM# 1005   10 WON
31.1050 g., 0.9990 Silver 0.9990 oz. ASW, 40 mm. **Obv:** National arms, Central Bank name **Rev:** Cypriot Pound and Temple of Apollo

Date	Mintage	F	VF	XF	Unc	BU
2004 Proof	Est. 2,004			Value: 85.00		

KM# 1006   10 WON
31.1050 g., 0.9990 Silver 0.9990 oz. ASW, 40 mm. **Subject:** Athens olympics **Obv:** National arms, Central Bank name **Rev:** Discus thrower in color

Date	Mintage	F	VF	XF	Unc	BU
2004 Proof				Value: 115		

KM# 1007   10 WON
31.1050 g., 0.9990 Silver 0.9990 oz. ASW, 40 mm. **Obv:** National arms, Central Bank name **Rev:** Gorch Fock II sailing ship in color

Date	Mintage	F	VF	XF	Unc	BU
2004 Proof	Est. 2,004			Value: 115		

KM# 420   10 WON
30.9100 g., 0.9990 Silver 0.9927 oz. ASW, 40 mm. **Subject:** End of WWII 60th Anniversary **Obv:** State arms **Rev:** Multicolor radiant map, doves, rainbow and inscription **Edge:** Plain

Date	Mintage	F	VF	XF	Unc	BU
JU94-2005 Proof				Value: 45.00		

KM# 425   10 WON
1.6700 g., Aluminum, 23 mm. **Obv:** State arms **Rev:** Value

Date	Mintage	F	VF	XF	Unc	BU
JU94(2005)	—	—	—	—	1.00	1.25

KM# 1017   10 WON
31.1050 g., 0.9990 Silver 0.9990 oz. ASW, 40 mm. **Obv:** National arms, Central Bank name **Rev:** Rooster within Zodiac circle

Date	Mintage	F	VF	XF	Unc	BU
2005 Proof				Value: 50.00		

KM# 1021   10 WON
7.0000 g., Aluminum, 40 mm. **Obv:** East gate in Pyeongyang **Rev:** Hae Mosu in flight with the five dragons

Date	Mintage	F	VF	XF	Unc	BU
2005 Proof				Value: 20.00		

KM# 1023   10 WON
31.1050 g., 0.9990 Silver 0.9990 oz. ASW, 40 mm. **Obv:** National arms, Central Bank name **Rev:** Hae Mosu in flight with the five dragons

Date	Mintage	F	VF	XF	Unc	BU
2005 Proof				Value: 50.00		

KM# 1026   10 WON
7.0000 g., Aluminum, 40 mm. **Obv:** East gate of Pyeongyang **Rev:** Admiral Yi Sunsin and turtle boat

Date	Mintage	F	VF	XF	Unc	BU
2005 Proof				Value: 20.00		

KM# 1027   10 WON
7.0000 g., Aluminum, 40 mm. **Obv:** East gate of Pyeongyang **Rev:** General Hong Beomdo

Date	Mintage	F	VF	XF	Unc	BU
2005 Proof				Value: 20.00		

KM# 1030   10 WON
31.1050 g., 0.9990 Silver 0.9990 oz. ASW, 40 mm. **Obv:** National arms, Central Bank name **Rev:** Admiral Yi Sunsin and turtle boat

Date	Mintage	F	VF	XF	Unc	BU
2005 Proof				Value: 50.00		

KM# 1031   10 WON
31.1050 g., 0.9990 Silver 0.9990 oz. ASW, 40 mm. **Obv:** National arms, Central Bank name **Rev:** General Hong Beomdo

Date	Mintage	F	VF	XF	Unc	BU
2005	—	—	—	—	—	—

KM# 1037   10 WON
31.1050 g., 0.9990 Silver 0.9990 oz. ASW, 40 mm. **Obv:** National arms, Central Bank name **Rev:** March before the monument of the three principals of reunification

Date	Mintage	F	VF	XF	Unc	BU
2005 Proof				Value: 50.00		

KM# 1038   10 WON
31.1050 g., 0.9990 Silver 0.9990 oz. ASW, 40 mm. **Obv:** National arms, Central Bank name **Rev:** Demonstrations before crater lake

Date	Mintage	F	VF	XF	Unc	BU
2005 Proof				Value: 50.00		

KM# 1039   10 WON
31.1050 g., 0.9990 Silver 0.9990 oz. ASW, 40 mm. **Obv:** National arms, Central Bank name **Rev:** Three drum dance

Date	Mintage	F	VF	XF	Unc	BU
2005 Proof				Value: 50.00		

KM# 1045   10 WON
31.1050 g., 0.9990 Silver 0.9990 oz. ASW, 40 mm. **Obv:** National arms, Central Bank name **Rev:** Tomb of the unknown solder in Moscow

Date	Mintage	F	VF	XF	Unc	BU
2005 Proof				Value: 85.00		

KM# 1046   10 WON
31.1050 g., 0.9990 Silver 0.9990 oz. ASW, 40 mm. **Obv:** National arms, Central Bank name **Rev:** Monument to mothers in St. Petersburg, Russian legend

Date	Mintage	F	VF	XF	Unc	BU
2005 Proof				Value: 85.00		

KM# 1090   10 WON
7.0000 g., Aluminum, 40 mm. **Obv:** East gate of Pyeongyang **Rev:** Ryuhwa, mother of King Dongmyeong

Date	Mintage	F	VF	XF	Unc	BU
2006 Proof				Value: 15.00		

KM# 1091   10 WON
31.1050 g., 0.9990 Silver 0.9990 oz. ASW, 40 mm. **Obv:** National arms, Central Bank name **Rev:** Ryuhwa, mother of King Dongmyeong

Date	Mintage	F	VF	XF	Unc	BU
2006 proof				Value: 50.00		

KM# 496   10 WON
7.0000 g., Aluminum, 40 mm. **Rev:** Eastern City Gate in Pyeongyang

Date	Mintage	F	VF	XF	Unc	BU
2007 Proof				Value: 7.50		

KM# 501   10 WON
7.0000 g., Aluminum, 40 mm. **Obv:** Eastern city gate in Pyeongyang **Rev:** Brontosaurus

Date	Mintage	F	VF	XF	Unc	BU
2007 Proof				Value: 6.50		

KM# 508   10 WON
7.0000 g., Aluminum, 40 mm. **Obv:** Eastern gate in Pyeongyang **Rev:** Rainbow lori in color

Date	Mintage	F	VF	XF	Unc	BU
2007 Proof				Value: 8.50		

KM# 509   10 WON
7.0000 g., Aluminum **Obv:** Eastern Gate in Pyeongyang **Rev:** Manderian Duck in color

Date	Mintage	F	VF	XF	Unc	BU
2007 Proof				Value: 8.50		

KM# 514   10 WON
7.0000 g., Aluminum, 40 mm. **Obv:** East gate in Pyeoongyang **Rev:** Sports gym and emblem in color

Date	Mintage	F	VF	XF	Unc	BU
2007 Proof				Value: 8.50		

KM# 536   10 WON
7.0000 g., Aluminum, 40 mm. **Obv:** Eastern gate in Pyeongyang **Rev:** Growth in the Kaeseong area

Date	Mintage	F	VF	XF	Unc	BU
2007 Proof				Value: 7.50		

KM# 538   10 WON
7.0000 g., Silver, 40 mm. **Obv:** Eastern gate in Pyeongyang **Rev:** Chinese Peony

Date	Mintage
	Value: 7.50

KM# 540   10 WON
7.0000 g., Aluminum, 40 mm. **Obv:** Eastern gate of Pyeongyang **Rev:** Panda seated eating

Date	Mintage	F	VF	XF	Unc	BU
2007 Proof				Value: 7.50		

KM# 543   10 WON
7.0000 g., Aluminum, 40 mm. **Obv:** Eastern gate in Pyeongyang **Rev:** Two pandas

Date	Mintage	F	VF	XF	Unc	BU
2007 Proof				Value: 7.50		

KM# 569   10 WON
7.0000 g., Aluminum, 40 mm. **Obv:** Eastern gate in Pyeongyang **Rev:** Rocket and satellite

Date	Mintage	F	VF	XF	Unc	BU
2007 Proof				Value: 6.50		

KM# 582   10 WON
7.0000 g., Aluminum, 40 mm. **Obv:** Eastern gate in Pyeongyang **Rev:** Dragon rising

Date	Mintage	F	VF	XF	Unc	BU
2007 Proof				Value: 6.00		

KM# 583   10 WON
7.0000 g., Aluminum, 40 mm. **Obv:** Eastern gate in Pyeongyang **Rev:** Two girls on seasaw

Date	Mintage	F	VF	XF	Unc	BU
2007 Proof				Value: 6.00		

KM# 584   10 WON
Aluminum **Obv:** Eastern gate in Pyeongyang **Rev:** Korean struggle

Date	Mintage	F	VF	XF	Unc	BU
2007 Proof				Value: 6.00		

KM# 585   10 WON
Aluminum **Obv:** Eastern gate in Pyeongyang **Rev:** Girl on swing

Date	Mintage	F	VF	XF	Unc	BU
2007 Proof				Value: 6.00		

KM# 586   10 WON
7.0000 g., Aluminum, 40 mm. **Obv:** Eastern gate in Pyeongyang **Rev:** Girls skipping

Date	Mintage	F	VF	XF	Unc	BU
2007 Proof				Value: 6.00		

KM# 610   10 WON
7.0000 g., Aluminum, 40 mm. **Obv:** Eastern gate in Pyeongyang **Rev:** Rabbit

Date	Mintage	F	VF	XF	Unc	BU
2007 Proof				Value: 7.50		

KM# 620   10 WON
7.0000 g., Aluminum, 40 mm. **Obv:** Eastern gate in Pyeongyang **Rev:** White bellied woodpecker

Date	Mintage	F	VF	XF	Unc	BU
2007 Proof				Value: 6.00		

KM# 621   10 WON
7.0000 g., Aluminum, 40 mm. **Obv:** Eastern gate in Pyeongyang **Rev:** Black grouse

Date	Mintage	F	VF	XF	Unc	BU
2007 Proof				Value: 6.00		

KM# 622   10 WON
7.0000 g., Aluminum, 40 mm. **Obv:** Eastern gate in Pyeongyang **Rev:** Sand Grouse

Date	Mintage	F	VF	XF	Unc	BU
2007 Proof				Value: 6.00		

KM# 623   10 WON
7.0000 g., Aluminum, 40 mm. **Obv:** Eastern gate in Pyeongyang **Rev:** Indian Pitta bird

Date	Mintage	F	VF	XF	Unc	BU
2007 Proof				Value: 6.00		

KM# 632   10 WON
7.0000 g., Aluminum, 40 mm. **Obv:** Eastern gate in Pyeongyang **Rev:** Blue dragon right

Date	Mintage	F	VF	XF	Unc	BU
2007 Proof	—	—	—	—	—	—

KM# 637   10 WON
7.0000 g., Aluminum, 40 mm. **Obv:** Eastern gate in Pyeongyang **Rev:** Two siberian tigers

Date	Mintage	F	VF	XF	Unc	BU
2007 Proof				Value: 6.00		

KM# 649   10 WON
Aluminum, 40 mm. **Obv:** Eastern gate in Pyeongyang **Rev:** King Goguryeo

Date	Mintage	F	VF	XF	Unc	BU
2007 Proof						

KM# 650   10 WON
Aluminum, 40 mm. **Obv:** Eastern gate in Pyeongyang **Rev:** Buddha figure

Date	Mintage	F	VF	XF	Unc	BU
2007 Proof	—	—	—	—	—	—

KM# 651   10 WON
Aluminum, 40 mm. **Obv:** Eastern gate in Pyeongyang **Rev:** King Gojoseon

Date	Mintage	F	VF	XF	Unc	BU
2007 Proof				Value: 6.00		

KM# 667   10 WON
7.0000 g., Aluminum, 40 mm. **Obv:** Eastern gate in Pyeongyang
Rev: First married couple to see again since the 1945 division

Date	Mintage	F	VF	XF	Unc	BU
2007 Proof	—	—	—	—	—	—

KM# 715   10 WON
7.0000 g., Aluminum, 40 mm. **Obv:** East gate of Pyeongyang
Rev: Celadon pottery

Date	Mintage	F	VF	XF	Unc	BU
2007 Proof	—	Value: 6.00				

KM# 802   10 WON
7.0000 g., Aluminum, 40 mm. **Obv:** East gate in Pyeongyang
Rev: Reconstruction of the mausoleum for King Dangun

Date	Mintage	F	VF	XF	Unc	BU
2007 Proof	—	Value: 10.00				

KM# 803   10 WON
7.0000 g., Aluminum, 40 mm. **Obv:** East gatet in Pyeongyang
Rev: Dongmyeong, 1st King of Goguryeb

Date	Mintage	F	VF	XF	Unc	BU
2007 Proof	—	Value: 10.00				

KM# 804   10 WON
7.0000 g., Aluminum, 40 mm. **Obv:** East gate in Pyeongyang
Rev: Wanggeon, 1st king of Goryeo dynasty

Date	Mintage	F	VF	XF	Unc	BU
2007 Proof	—	Value: 10.00				

KM# 805   10 WON
7.0000 g., Aluminum, 40 mm. **Obv:** East gate in Pyeongyang
Rev: Jeong Mongju

Date	Mintage	F	VF	XF	Unc	BU
2007 Proof	—	Value: 10.00				

KM# 806   10 WON
7.0000 g., Aluminum, 40 mm. **Obv:** East gate in Pyeongyang
Rev: Jeon Bongjun

Date	Mintage	F	VF	XF	Unc	BU
2007 Proof	—	Value: 10.00				

KM# 850   10 WON
7.0000 g., Aluminum, 40 mm. **Obv:** East gate of Pyeongyang
Rev: Dancer

Date	Mintage	F	VF	XF	Unc	BU
2007 Proof	—	Value: 6.00				

KM# 851   10 WON
7.0000 g., Aluminum, 40 mm. **Obv:** East gate of Pyeongyang
Rev: Dancer

Date	Mintage	F	VF	XF	Unc	BU
2007 Proof	—	Value: 7.00				

KM# 852   10 WON
7.0000 g., Aluminum, 40 mm. **Obv:** National arms, Central Bank name **Rev:** Female in national costume

Date	Mintage	F	VF	XF	Unc	BU
2007 Proof	—	Value: 7.00				

KM# 853   10 WON
7.0000 g., Aluminum, 40 mm. **Obv:** National arms, Central Bank name **Rev:** Crane dancer

Date	Mintage	F	VF	XF	Unc	BU
2007 Proof	—	Value: 7.00				

KM# 854   10 WON
7.0000 g., Aluminum, 40 mm. **Obv:** National arms, Central Bank name **Rev:** Fairy princess

Date	Mintage	F	VF	XF	Unc	BU
2007 Proof	—	Value: 7.00				

KM# 880   10 WON
6.0000 g., 0.9990 Aluminum 0.1927 oz., 38 mm. **Obv:** East gate of Pyeongyang **Rev:** Taekwando

Date	Mintage	F	VF	XF	Unc	BU
2007 Proof	—	Value: 6.00				

KM# 736   20 WON
28.0000 g., Brass, 40 mm. **Obv:** East gate of Pyeongyang **Rev:** Married couple before Korean flag and ferryboat

Date	Mintage	F	VF	XF	Unc	BU
2001 Proof	—	—	—	—	—	—

KM# 737   20 WON
28.0000 g., Brass, 40 mm. **Obv:** East gate of Pyeongyang **Rev:** Ferryboat between Korea and Japan

Date	Mintage	F	VF	XF	Unc	BU
2001 Proof	—	Value: 7.00				

KM# 738   20 WON
28.0000 g., Brass, 40 mm. **Obv:** East gate in Pyeongyang **Rev:** Triumphial arch of Moranbong in Pyeongyang

Date	Mintage	F	VF	XF	Unc	BU
2001 Proof	—	—	—	—	—	—

KM# 739   20 WON
28.0000 g., Brass, 40 mm. **Obv:** East gate in Pyeongyang **Rev:** Chonji crater in Paektusan

Date	Mintage	F	VF	XF	Unc	BU
2001 Proof	—	—	—	—	—	—

KM# 768   20 WON
16.0000 g., Brass, 35 mm. **Obv:** East gate of Pyeongyang **Rev:** Chinese Dragon boat

Date	Mintage	F	VF	XF	Unc	BU
2001 Proof	—	Value: 7.00				

KM# 777   20 WON
28.0000 g., Brass, 40 mm. **Obv:** East gate of Pyeongyang **Rev:** Taekwondo kicker

Date	Mintage	F	VF	XF	Unc	BU
2001 Proof	—	Value: 7.00				

KM# 778   20 WON
28.0000 g., Brass, 40 mm. **Obv:** East gate of Pyeongyang **Rev:** Two taekwondo players

Date	Mintage	F	VF	XF	Unc	BU
2001 Proof	—	Value: 7.00				

KM# 787   20 WON
16.0000 g., Brass, 35 mm. **Obv:** East gate of Pyeongyang **Rev:** Horse head

Date	Mintage	F	VF	XF	Unc	BU
2002 Proof	—	Value: 7.00				

KM# 788   20 WON
16.0000 g., Brass, 35 mm. **Obv:** East gate of Pyeongyang **Rev:** Horse right

Date	Mintage	F	VF	XF	Unc	BU
2002 Proof	—	—	—	—	—	—

KM# 789   20 WON
28.0000 g., Brass, 40 mm. **Obv:** East gate of Pyeongyang **Rev:** Two horses

Date	Mintage	F	VF	XF	Unc	BU
2002 Proof	—	Value: 7.00				

KM# 809   20 WON
28.0000 g., Brass, 40 mm. **Obv:** East gate of Pyeongyang **Rev:** Wanggeon, 1st King of Goryeo dynasty

Date	Mintage	F	VF	XF	Unc	BU
2002 Proof	—	Value: 7.00				

KM# 810   20 WON
28.0000 g., Brass, 40 mm. **Obv:** East gate of Pyeongyang **Rev:** Jeong Mongju

Date	Mintage	F	VF	XF	Unc	BU
2002 Proof	—	Value: 7.00				

KM# 830   20 WON
28.0000 g., Brass, 40 mm. **Obv:** East gate of Pyeongyang **Rev:** Resconstruction of the Mausoleums of King Dongmyeong

Date	Mintage	F	VF	XF	Unc	BU
2002 Proof	—	Value: 7.00				

KM# 831   20 WON
28.0000 g., Brass, 40 mm. **Obv:** East gate of Pyeongyang **Rev:** Mausoleum of King Gongmin

Date	Mintage	F	VF	XF	Unc	BU
2002 Proof	—	Value: 7.00				

KM# 832   20 WON
28.0000 g., Brass, 40 mm. **Obv:** East gate of Pyeongyang **Rev:** Stadium

Date	Mintage	F	VF	XF	Unc	BU
2002 Proof	—	Value: 7.00				

KM# 866   20 WON
28.0000 g., Brass, 40 mm. **Obv:** East gate of Pyeongyang **Rev:** Map of Korea with the four cardinal directions

Date	Mintage	F	VF	XF	Unc	BU
2002 Proof	—	Value: 7.00				

KM# 867   20 WON
28.0000 g., Brass, 40 mm. **Obv:** East gate of Pyeongyang **Rev:** Rythem dancers and map of Korea

Date	Mintage	F	VF	XF	Unc	BU
2002 Proof	—	Value: 7.00				

KM# 897   20 WON
28.0000 g., Brass, 40 mm. **Obv:** East gate of Pyeongyang **Rev:** Sheep in center of Zodiac

Date	Mintage	F	VF	XF	Unc	BU
2003 Proof	—	Value: 7.00				

KM# 909   20 WON
28.0000 g., Brass, 40 mm. **Obv:** East gate of Pyeongyang **Rev:** Eulji Mundeok

Date	Mintage	F	VF	XF	Unc	BU
2003 Proof	—	Value: 7.00				

KM# 910   20 WON
28.0000 g., Brass, 40 mm. **Obv:** East gate in Pyeongyang **Rev:** Yeon Gaesomun

Date	Mintage	F	VF	XF	Unc	BU
2003 Proof	—	Value: 7.00				

KM# 916   20 WON
28.0000 g., Brass, 40 mm. **Obv:** East gate of Pyeongyang **Rev:** Turtle boat

Date	Mintage	F	VF	XF	Unc	BU
2003 Proof	—	Value: 7.00				

KM# 256   20 WON
42.0600 g., 0.9990 Silver 1.3509 oz. ASW, 45.1 mm. **Obv:** State arms **Rev:** Rose of sharon flower **Edge:** Plain

Date	Mintage	F	VF	XF	Unc	BU
JU93-2004 Proof	—	Value: 65.00				

KM# 257   20 WON
42.2160 g., 0.9990 Silver 1.3559 oz. ASW, 45.1 mm. **Obv:** State arms **Rev:** Kim Jong-Il, Peony flower **Edge:** Plain

Date	Mintage	F	VF	XF	Unc	BU
JU93-2004 Proof	—	Value: 65.00				

KM# 258   20 WON
41.9200 g., 0.9990 Silver 1.3464 oz. ASW, 45.1 mm. **Obv:** State arms **Rev:** Kim Il-seung, Orchid flowers **Edge:** Plain

Date	Mintage	F	VF	XF	Unc	BU
JU93-2004 Proof	—	Value: 65.00				

KM# 259   20 WON
42.0000 g., 0.9990 Silver 1.3489 oz. ASW, 45.1 mm. **Obv:** State arms **Rev:** Kim Il Sung's birth place, side view **Edge:** Plain

Date	Mintage	F	VF	XF	Unc	BU
JU93-2004 Proof	—	Value: 65.00				

KM# 260   20 WON
41.6200 g., 0.9990 Silver 1.3367 oz. ASW, 45.1 mm. **Obv:** State arms **Rev:** Mountain cabin **Edge:** Plain

Date	Mintage	F	VF	XF	Unc	BU
JU93-2004 Proof	—	Value: 65.00				

KM# 261   20 WON
41.9100 g., 0.9990 Silver 1.3460 oz. ASW, 45.1 mm. **Obv:** State arms **Rev:** Kim Il Sung's birth place, front view **Edge:** Plain

Date	Mintage	F	VF	XF	Unc	BU
JU93-2004 Proof	—	Value: 65.00				

KM# 340   20 WON
31.0000 g., 0.9990 Silver 0.9956 oz. ASW, 39.8 mm. **Obv:** State arms **Rev:** Kim Jong-Il and Vladimir Putin clasping hands **Edge:** Segmented reeding

Date	Mintage	F	VF	XF	Unc	BU
2004 Proof	—	Value: 50.00				

KM# 341   20 WON
31.0000 g., 0.9990 Silver 0.9956 oz. ASW, 39.8 mm. **Obv:** State arms **Rev:** Bust facing **Edge:** Segmented reeding

Date	Mintage	F	VF	XF	Unc	BU
2004 Proof	—	Value: 50.00				

KM# 419   20 WON
31.0000 g., 0.9990 Silver 0.9956 oz. ASW, 39.75 mm. **Subject:** Historic Pyongyang Meeting **Obv:** State arms **Rev:** Kim Jong-Il and Kim Dae-Jung clasping hands, English legend **Edge:** Segmented reeding

Date	Mintage	F	VF	XF	Unc	BU
2004 Proof	—	Value: 50.00				

KM# 942   20 WON
19.0000 g., Copper, 23x40 mm. **Obv:** East gate of Pyeongyang **Rev:** Marmoset **Shape:** Rectangle

Date	Mintage	F	VF	XF	Unc	BU
2004 Proof	—	Value: 8.00				

KM# 943   20 WON
19.0000 g., Copper, 23x40 mm. **Obv:** East gate of Pyeongyang **Rev:** Blue monkey

Date	Mintage	F	VF	XF	Unc	BU
2004 Proof	—	Value: 8.00				

KM# 944   20 WON
19.0000 g., Copper, 23x40 mm. **Obv:** East gate of Pyeongyang **Rev:** two monkies

Date	Mintage	F	VF	XF	Unc	BU
2004 Proof	—	Value: 8.00				

KM# 949   20 WON
Brass, 40 mm. **Obv:** East gate of Pyeongyang **Rev:** Sports hall in Pyeongyang

Date	Mintage	F	VF	XF	Unc	BU
2004 Proof	—	Value: 14.00				

KM# 955   20 WON
42.2160 g., 0.9990 Silver 1.3559 oz. ASW, 45 mm. **Obv:** National arms, Central Bank name **Rev:** Kim Ilseong

Date	Mintage	F	VF	XF	Unc	BU
2004 Proof	—	Value: 70.00				

KM# 956   20 WON
42.2160 g., 0.9990 Silver 1.3559 oz. ASW, 45 mm. **Obv:** National arms, Central Bank name **Rev:** Kim Jeongil

Date	Mintage	F	VF	XF	Unc	BU
2004 Proof	—	Value: 70.00				

KM# 957   20 WON
42.2160 g., 0.9990 Silver 1.3559 oz. ASW, 45 mm. **Obv:** Naitonal arms, Central Bank name **Rev:** Kim Jeongsuk

Date	Mintage	F	VF	XF	Unc	BU
2004 Proof	—	Value: 70.00				

KM# 966   20 WON
31.1050 g., 0.9990 Silver 0.9990 oz. ASW, 40 mm. **Obv:** National arms, Central Bank name **Rev:** Kim Jeongil and Hu Jintao

Date	Mintage	F	VF	XF	Unc	BU
2004 Proof	—	Value: 60.00				

KM# 977   20 WON
31.1050 g., 0.9990 Silver 0.9990 oz. ASW, 40 mm. **Obv:** Dokdo, rocky islands, Central Bank name **Rev:** Map of the island group

Date	Mintage	F	VF	XF	Unc	BU
2004 Proof	—	Value: 70.00				

KM# 978   20 WON
31.1050 g., 0.9990 Silver 0.9990 oz. ASW, 40 mm. **Obv:** Dokdo, rocky islands, Central Bank name **Rev:** Fisher Ahn Yongbok

Date	Mintage	F	VF	XF	Unc	BU
2004 Proof	—	Value: 70.00				

KM# 979   20 WON
31.1050 g., 0.9990 Silver 0.9990 oz. ASW, 40 mm. **Obv:** Dokdo, rocky islands, Central Bank name **Rev:** West island

Date	Mintage	F	VF	XF	Unc	BU
2004 Proof	—	Value: 70.00				

KM# 980   20 WON
31.1050 g., 0.9990 Silver 0.9990 oz. ASW, 40 mm. **Obv:** Dokdo, rocky islands, Central Bank name **Rev:** East island

Date	Mintage	F	VF	XF	Unc	BU
2004 Proof	—	Value: 70.00				

KM# 981   20 WON
31.1050 g., 0.9990 Silver 0.9990 oz. ASW, 40 mm. **Obv:** Dokdo, rocky islands, Central Bank name **Rev:** Three brother island

Date	Mintage	F	VF	XF	Unc	BU
2004 Proof	—	Value: 70.00				

KM# 982   20 WON
31.1050 g., 0.9990 Silver 0.9990 oz. ASW, 40 mm. **Obv:** Dokdo, rocky islands, Central Bank name **Rev:** Chicken island

Date	Mintage	F	VF	XF	Unc	BU
2004 Proof	—	Value: 70.00				

KM# 983   20 WON
31.1050 g., 0.9990 Silver 0.9990 oz. ASW, 40 mm. **Obv:** Dokdo, rocky islands, Central Bank name **Rev:** Candle island

Date	Mintage	F	VF	XF	Unc	BU
2004 Proof	—	Value: 70.00				

KM# 984   20 WON
31.1050 g., 0.9990 Silver 0.9990 oz. ASW, 40 mm. **Obv:** Dokdo, rocky islands, Central Bank name **Rev:** Dome island

Date	Mintage	F	VF	XF	Unc	BU
2004 Proof	—	Value: 70.00				

KM# 478   20 WON
27.3000 g., Brass, 40 mm. **Obv:** Temple **Rev:** Multicolor rooster right

Date	Mintage	F	VF	XF	Unc	BU
2005 Proof	—	Value: 10.00				

KM# 479   20 WON
31.1050 g., 0.9990 Silver 0.9990 oz. ASW **Obv:** Arms **Rev:** A puppy, dog's head facing

Date	Mintage	F	VF	XF	Unc	BU
2005 Proof	—	Value: 45.00				

KM# 1022   20 WON
28.0000 g., Brass, 40 mm. **Obv:** East gate of Pyeongyang **Rev:** Hae Mosu in flight with the five dragons

Date	Mintage	F	VF	XF	Unc	BU
2005 Proof	—	Value: 20.00				

KM# 1028   20 WON
28.0000 g., Brass, 40 mm. **Obv:** East gate of Pyeongyang **Rev:** Admiral Yi Sunsin and turtle boat

Date	Mintage	F	VF	XF	Unc	BU
2005 Proof	—	Value: 12.50				

KM# 1029   20 WON
28.0000 g., Brass, 40 mm. **Obv:** East gate of Pyeongyong **Rev:** General Hong Beomdo

Date	Mintage	F	VF	XF	Unc	BU
2005 Proof	—	Value: 12.50				

KM# 1041   20 WON
28.0000 g., Brass, 40 mm. **Obv:** East gate of Pyeongyang **Rev:** Map of Korea, pair of peace doves, rainbow

Date	Mintage	F	VF	XF	Unc	BU
2005 Proof	—	Value: 12.50				

KM# 1049   20 WON
31.1050 g., 0.9990 Silver 0.9990 oz. ASW, 40 mm. **Obv:** National arms, Central Bank name **Rev:** Dongmyeong, 1st king of Goguryeo

Date	Mintage	F	VF	XF	Unc	BU
2005 Proof	—	Value: 65.00				

KM# 1050   20 WON
31.1050 g., 0.9990 Silver 0.9990 oz. ASW, 40 mm. **Obv:** National arms, Central Bank name **Rev:** Blue dragon, Cheongryong, of the East

Date	Mintage	F	VF	XF	Unc	BU
2005 Proof	—	Value: 45.00				

KM# 1051   20 WON
31.1050 g., 0.9990 Silver 0.9990 oz. ASW, 40 mm. **Obv:** National arms, Central Bank name **Rev:** Red bird, Jujak, of the South

Date	Mintage	F	VF	XF	Unc	BU
2005 Proof	—	Value: 45.00				

KM# 1052   20 WON
31.1050 g., 0.9990 Silver 0.9990 oz. ASW, 40 mm. **Obv:** National arms, Central Bank name **Rev:** White tiger, Baekho, of the West

Date	Mintage	F	VF	XF	Unc	BU
2005 Proof	—	Value: 45.00				

KM# 1053   20 WON
31.1050 g., 0.9990 Silver 0.9990 oz. ASW, 40 mm. **Obv:** National arms, Central Bank name **Rev:** Black snake, Hyeonmu, of the North

Date	Mintage	F	VF	XF	Unc	BU
2005 Proof	—	Value: 45.00				

KM# 1054   20 WON
31.1050 g., 0.9990 Silver 0.9990 oz. ASW, 40 mm. **Obv:** National arms, Central Bank name **Rev:** Horse and rider

Date	Mintage	F	VF	XF	Unc	BU
2005 Proof	—	Value: 45.00				

KM# 1055   20 WON
31.1050 g., 0.9990 Silver 0.9990 oz. ASW, 40 mm. **Obv:** National arms, Central Bank name **Rev:** Horse drummers

Date	Mintage	F	VF	XF	Unc	BU
2005 Proof	—	Value: 45.00				

KM# 1056   20 WON
31.1050 g., 0.9990 Silver 0.9990 oz. ASW, 40 mm. **Obv:** National arms, Central Bank name **Rev:** Bugler to horse

Date	Mintage	F	VF	XF	Unc	BU
2005 Proof	—	Value: 45.00				

KM# 1057   20 WON
31.1050 g., 0.9990 Silver 0.9990 oz. ASW, 40 mm. **Obv:** National arms, Central Bank name **Rev:** Horseback hunter

Date	Mintage	F	VF	XF	Unc	BU
2005 Proof	—	Value: 45.00				

KM# 1058   20 WON
31.1050 g., 0.9990 Silver 0.9990 oz. ASW, 40 mm. **Obv:** National arms, Central Bank name **Rev:** Crane and bamboo image by Yi Kyeongyun

Date	Mintage	F	VF	XF	Unc	BU
2005 Proof	—	Value: 65.00				

KM# 1059   20 WON
31.1050 g., 0.9990 Silver 0.9990 oz. ASW, 40 mm. **Obv:** National arms, Central Bank name **Rev:** Ibis, image by Kim Sik

Date	Mintage	F	VF	XF	Unc	BU
2005 Proof	—	Value: 65.00				

KM# 1060   20 WON
31.1050 g., 0.9990 Silver 0.9990 oz. ASW, 40 mm. **Obv:** National arms, Central Bank name **Rev:** Pheasant by Jang Seungeop

Date	Mintage	F	VF	XF	Unc	BU
2005 Proof	—	Value: 65.00				

KM# 1061   20 WON
31.1050 g., 0.9990 Silver 0.9990 oz. ASW, 40 mm. **Obv:** National arms, Central Bank name **Rev:** Fairy princess of the diamond mountain

Date	Mintage	F	VF	XF	Unc	BU
2005 Proof	—	Value: 65.00				

KM# 1062   20 WON
31.1050 g., 0.9990 Silver 0.9990 oz. ASW, 40 mm. **Obv:** National arms, Central Bank name **Rev:** Big stone in the diamond mountain

Date	Mintage	F	VF	XF	Unc	BU
2005 Proof	—	Value: 65.00				

KM# 1063   20 WON
31.1050 g., 0.9990 Silver 0.9990 oz. ASW, 40 mm. **Obv:** National arms, Central Bank name **Rev:** Two rabbits

Date	Mintage	F	VF	XF	Unc	BU
2005 Proof	Est. 2,000	Value: 45.00				

KM# 1064   20 WON
31.1050 g., 0.9990 Silver 0.9990 oz. ASW, 40 mm. **Obv:** National arms, Central Bank name **Rev:** Cat

Date	Mintage	F	VF	XF	Unc	BU
2005 Proof	Est. 2,000	Value: 45.00				

KM# 1065   20 WON
31.1050 g., 0.9990 Silver 0.9990 oz. ASW, 40 mm. **Subject:** North-South Railway connection **Obv:** National arms, Central Bank name **Rev:** Map of Korea and railway line

Date	Mintage	F	VF	XF	Unc	BU
2005 Proof	—	Value: 65.00				

KM# 1066   20 WON
31.1050 g., 0.9990 Silver 0.9990 oz. ASW, 40 mm. **Obv:** National arms, Central Bank name **Rev:** FIFA World Cup trophy

Date	Mintage	F	VF	XF	Unc	BU
2005 Proof	—	Value: 45.00				

KM# 480   20 WON
23.7000 g., Brass, 40 mm. **Obv:** Temple **Rev:** Multicolor German shepard

Date	Mintage	F	VF	XF	Unc	BU
2006 Proof	—	Value: 10.00				

KM# 481   20 WON
Brass **Obv:** Arms **Rev:** Bejeweled female head

Date	Mintage	F	VF	XF	Unc	BU
2006 Proof	—	Value: 10.00				

KM# 482   20 WON
27.3000 g., Brass, 40 mm. **Obv:** Temple **Rev:** Multicolor pig and pigletts

Date	Mintage	F	VF	XF	Unc	BU
2007 Proof	—	Value: 10.00				

KM# 497 20 WON
28.0000 g., Brass, 40 mm. **Rev:** Eastern city gate of Pyeongyang

Date	Mintage	F	VF	XF	Unc	BU
2007 Proof	—	Value: 8.50				

KM# 502 20 WON
28.0000 g., Brass, 40 mm. **Obv:** Eastern city gate of Pyeongyang **Rev:** Brontosaurus

Date	Mintage	F	VF	XF	Unc	BU
2007 Proof	—	Value: 8.50				

KM# 570 20 WON
28.0000 g., Brass, 40 mm. **Obv:** Eastern gate in Pyeongyang **Rev:** Rocket and satellite

Date	Mintage	F	VF	XF	Unc	BU
2007 Proof	—	Value: 7.50				

KM# 587 20 WON
28.0000 g., Brass, 40 mm. **Obv:** Eastern gate in Pyeongyang **Rev:** Dragon rising

Date	Mintage	F	VF	XF	Unc	BU
2007 Proof	—	Value: 7.50				

KM# 588 20 WON
28.0000 g., Brass, 40 mm. **Obv:** Eastern gate in Pyeongyang **Rev:** Two girls on seasaw

Date	Mintage	F	VF	XF	Unc	BU
2007 Proof	—	Value: 7.50				

KM# 589 20 WON
28.0000 g., Brass, 40 mm. **Obv:** Eastern gate in Pyeongyang **Rev:** Korean struggle

Date	Mintage	F	VF	XF	Unc	BU
2007 Proof	—	Value: 7.50				

KM# 590 20 WON
28.0000 g., Brass, 40 mm. **Obv:** Eastern gate in Pyeongyang **Rev:** Girl on swing

Date	Mintage	F	VF	XF	Unc	BU
2007 Proof	—	Value: 7.50				

KM# 591 20 WON
28.0000 g., Brass, 40 mm. **Obv:** Eastern gate in Pyeongyang **Rev:** Children Skipping

Date	Mintage	F	VF	XF	Unc	BU
2007 Proof	—	Value: 7.50				

KM# 624 20 WON
28.0000 g., Brass, 40 mm. **Obv:** Eastern gate in Pyeongyang **Rev:** White bellied woodpecker

Date	Mintage	F	VF	XF	Unc	BU
2007 Proof	—	Value: 7.00				

KM# 625 20 WON
28.0000 g., Brass, 40 mm. **Obv:** Eastern gate in Pyeongyang **Rev:** Black grouse

Date	Mintage	F	VF	XF	Unc	BU
2007 Proof	—	Value: 7.00				

KM# 626 20 WON
28.0000 g., Brass, 40 mm. **Obv:** Eastern gate in Pyeongyang **Rev:** Sand Grouse

Date	Mintage	F	VF	XF	Unc	BU
2007 Proof	—	Value: 7.00				

KM# 627 20 WON
28.0000 g., Brass, 40 mm. **Obv:** Eastern gate in Pyeongyang **Rev:** Indian Pitta bird

Date	Mintage	F	VF	XF	Unc	BU
2007 Proof	—	Value: 7.00				

KM# 633 20 WON
28.0000 g., Brass, 40 mm. **Obv:** Eastern gate in Pyeongyang **Rev:** Blue dragon right

Date	Mintage	F	VF	XF	Unc	BU
2007 Proof	—	Value: 7.00				

KM# 638 20 WON
28.0000 g., Brass, 40 mm. **Obv:** Eastern gate in Pyeongyang **Rev:** Two siberian tigers

Date	Mintage	F	VF	XF	Unc	BU
2007 Proof	—	Value: 7.00				

KM# 652 20 WON
28.0000 g., Brass, 40 mm. **Obv:** Eastern gate in Pyeongyang **Rev:** Dongmyeong, King of Goguryeo

Date	Mintage	F	VF	XF	Unc	BU
2007 Proof	—	Value: 7.00				

KM# 653 20 WON
28.0000 g., Brass, 40 mm. **Obv:** Eastern gate in Pyeongyang **Rev:** Buddha figure

Date	Mintage	F	VF	XF	Unc	BU
2007 Proof	—	Value: 7.00				

KM# 654 20 WON
28.0000 g., Brass, 40 mm. **Obv:** Eastern gate in Pyeongyang **Rev:** Dangun, King of Gojoseon

Date	Mintage	F	VF	XF	Unc	BU
2007 Proof	—	Value: 7.00				

KM# 668 20 WON
28.0000 g., Brass, 40 mm. **Obv:** Eastern gate in Pyeongyang **Rev:** First married couple to meet again after the 1945 division

Date	Mintage	F	VF	XF	Unc	BU
2007 Proof	—	Value: 7.00				

KM# 690 20 WON
28.0000 g., Brass, 40 mm. **Obv:** East gate of Pyeongyang **Rev:** Hyonmu

Date	Mintage	F	VF	XF	Unc	BU
2007 Proof	—	Value: 7.00				

KM# 716 20 WON
28.0000 g., Brass, 40 mm. **Obv:** East gate of Pyeongyang **Rev:** Celadon pottery

Date	Mintage	F	VF	XF	Unc	BU
2007 Proof	—	Value: 7.00				

KM# 807 20 WON
28.0000 g., Brass, 40 mm. **Obv:** East gate in Pyeongyang **Rev:** Reconstruction of the mausoleum of King Dangun

Date	Mintage	F	VF	XF	Unc	BU
2007 Proof	—	Value: 7.00				

KM# 808 20 WON
28.0000 g., Brass, 40 mm. **Obv:** East gate of Pyeongyang **Rev:** Dongmyeong, 1st King of Goguryeo

Date	Mintage	F	VF	XF	Unc	BU
2007 Proof	—	Value: 7.00				

KM# 811 20 WON
28.0000 g., Brass, 40 mm. **Obv:** East gate of Pyeongyang **Rev:** Jeon Bongjun

Date	Mintage	F	VF	XF	Unc	BU
2007 Proof	—	Value: 7.00				

KM# 855 20 WON
28.0000 g., Brass, 40 mm. **Obv:** East gate of Pyeongyang **Rev:** Dancer

Date	Mintage	F	VF	XF	Unc	BU
2007 Proof	—	Value: 7.00				

KM# 856 20 WON
28.0000 g., Brass, 40 mm. **Obv:** East gate of Pyeongyang **Rev:** Dancer

Date	Mintage	F	VF	XF	Unc	BU
2007 Proof	—	Value: 7.00				

KM# 857 20 WON
28.0000 g., Brass, 40 mm. **Obv:** East gate of Pyeongyang **Rev:** Woman in national costume

Date	Mintage	F	VF	XF	Unc	BU
2007 Proof	—	Value: 7.00				

KM# 858 20 WON
28.0000 g., Brass, 40 mm. **Obv:** East gate of Pyeongyang **Rev:** Crane dancer

Date	Mintage	F	VF	XF	Unc	BU
2007 Proof	—	Value: 7.00				

KM# 859 20 WON
28.0000 g., Brass, 40 mm. **Obv:** East gate of Pyeongyang **Rev:** Fairy princess

Date	Mintage	F	VF	XF	Unc	BU
2007 Proof	—	Value: 7.00				

KM# 868 20 WON
28.0000 g., Brass, 40 mm. **Obv:** East gate of Pyeongyang **Rev:** Drum dancers in shape of Korean map

Date	Mintage	F	VF	XF	Unc	BU
2007 Proof	—	Value: 7.00				

KM# 869 20 WON
28.0000 g., Brass, 40 mm. **Obv:** East gate of Pyeongyang **Rev:** Korean team victory celebration

Date	Mintage	F	VF	XF	Unc	BU
2007 Proof	—	Value: 7.00				

KM# 1128 20 WON
28.0000 g., Brass, 40 mm. **Obv:** National arms, Central Bank name **Rev:** Hoopoe

Date	Mintage	F	VF	XF	Unc	BU
2007 Proof	Est. 2,000	Value: 17.50				

KM# 1129 20 WON
28.0000 g., Brass, 40 mm. **Obv:** National arms, Central Bank name **Rev:** Ural owl

Date	Mintage	F	VF	XF	Unc	BU
2007 Proof	Est. 2,000	Value: 17.50				

KM# 1130 20 WON
28.0000 g., Brass, 40 mm. **Obv:** National arms, Central Bank name **Rev:** Eagle

Date	Mintage	F	VF	XF	Unc	BU
2007 Proof	Est. 2,000	Value: 17.50				

KM# 1131 20 WON
28.0000 g., Brass, 40 mm. **Obv:** National arms, Central Bank name **Rev:** White rhino

Date	Mintage	F	VF	XF	Unc	BU
2007 Proof	Est. 2,000	Value: 17.50				

KM# 1132 20 WON
28.0000 g., Brass, 40 mm. **Obv:** National arms, Central Bank name **Rev:** African elephant family

Date	Mintage	F	VF	XF	Unc	BU
2007 Proof	Est. 2,000	Value: 17.50				

KM# 1133 20 WON
28.0000 g., Brass, 40 mm. **Obv:** National arms, Central Bank name **Rev:** Lion family

Date	Mintage	F	VF	XF	Unc	BU
2007 Proof	Est. 2,000	Value: 17.50				

KM# 1134 20 WON
28.0000 g., Brass, 40 mm. **Obv:** National arms, Central Bank name **Rev:** Cape Buffalo

Date	Mintage	F	VF	XF	Unc	BU
2007 Proof	Est. 2,000	Value: 17.50				

KM# 1135 20 WON
28.0000 g., Brass **Obv:** National arms, Central Bank name **Rev:** Marine turtle

Date	Mintage	F	VF	XF	Unc	BU
2007 Proof	Est. 2,000	Value: 17.50				

KM# 1136 20 WON
28.0000 g., Brass, 40 mm. **Obv:** National arms, Central Bank name **Rev:** Penguin

Date	Mintage	F	VF	XF	Unc	BU
2007 Proof	Est. 2,000	Value: 17.50				

KM# 1137 20 WON
28.0000 g., Brass, 40 mm. **Obv:** National arms, Central Bank name **Rev:** Emu

Date	Mintage	F	VF	XF	Unc	BU
2007 Proof	—	Value: 17.50				

KM# 1138 20 WON
28.0000 g., Brass, 40 mm. **Obv:** National arms, Central Bank name **Rev:** Eagle owl

Date	Mintage	F	VF	XF	Unc	BU
2007 Proof	Est. 2,000	Value: 17.50				

KM# 1139 20 WON
28.0000 g., Brass, 40 mm. **Obv:** National arms, Central Bank name **Rev:** Lemur

Date	Mintage	F	VF	XF	Unc	BU
2007 Proof	Est. 2,000	Value: 17.50				

KM# 1140 20 WON
28.0000 g., Brass, 40 mm. **Obv:** National arms, Central Bank name **Rev:** Lion

Date	Mintage	F	VF	XF	Unc	BU
2007 Proof	Est. 2,000	Value: 17.50				

KM# 1141 20 WON
28.0000 g., Brass, 40 mm. **Obv:** National arms, Central Bank name **Rev:** Two Arfican elephants

Date	Mintage	F	VF	XF	Unc	BU
2007 Proof	Est. 2,000	Value: 17.50				

KM# 484 20 WON
27.3000 g., Brass, 40 mm. **Obv:** Temple **Rev:** Multicolor goat left

Date	Mintage	F	VF	XF	Unc	BU
2008 Proof	—	Value: 10.00				

KM# 485 20 WON
27.3000 g., Brass, 40 mm. **Obv:** Temple **Rev:** Multicolor snake and flowers

Date	Mintage	F	VF	XF	Unc	BU
2008 Proof	—	Value: 10.00				

KM# 486 20 WON
27.3000 g., Brass, 40 mm. **Obv:** Temple **Rev:** Multicolor, two rabbits

Date	Mintage	F	VF	XF	Unc	BU
2008 Proof	—	Value: 10.00				

KM# 487 20 WON
27.3000 g., Brass, 40 mm. **Obv:** Temple **Rev:** Multicolor two white rats

Date	Mintage	F	VF	XF	Unc	BU
2008 Proof	—	Value: 10.00				

KM# 488 20 WON
27.3000 g., Brass, 40 mm. **Obv:** Temple **Rev:** Multicolor monkey seated on branch

Date	Mintage	F	VF	XF	Unc	BU
2008 Proof	—	Value: 10.00				

KM# 489 20 WON
27.3000 g., Brass, 40 mm. **Obv:** Temple **Rev:** Multicolor tiger

Date	Mintage	F	VF	XF	Unc	BU
2008 Proof	—	Value: 10.00				

KM# 490 20 WON
27.3000 g., Brass, 40 mm. **Obv:** Temple **Rev:** Multicolor horse prancing right

Date	Mintage	F	VF	XF	Unc	BU
2008 Proof	—	Value: 10.00				

KM# 491 20 WON
27.3000 g., Brass, 40 mm. **Obv:** Temple **Rev:** Multicolor two oxen

Date	Mintage	F	VF	XF	Unc	BU
2009 Proof	—	Value: 10.00				

KM# 495 20 WON
Aluminum, 45 mm. **Obv:** Raised Pagoda in ornamental loop **Rev:** Tiger with color inlay **Edge:** Plain

Date	Mintage	F	VF	XF	Unc	BU
2010	—	—	—	—	—	20.00

KM# 891   50 WON
155.0000 g., 999.0000 Silver 4978.1 oz. ASW, 65 mm.   **Obv:**
National arms, Central Bank name **Rev:** Orca whale

Date	Mintage	F	VF	XF	Unc	BU
2002 Proof	Est. 500	Value: 400				

KM# 815   50 WON
1.2400 g., 0.9990 Gold 0.0398 oz. AGW, 14 mm.   **Obv:** Naitonal
arms, Central Bank name **Rev:** Wanggeon, 1st King of Goryeo
Dynasty

Date	Mintage	F	VF	XF	Unc	BU
2003 Proof	Est. 20,000	Value: 90.00				

KM# 262   50 WON
70.0000 g., 0.9990 Silver 2.2482 oz. ASW, 50 mm.   **Obv:** Korean
map **Rev:** Huh Jun Chosun doctor at left, books at right **Edge:**
Plain

Date	Mintage	F	VF	XF	Unc	BU
JU93-2004 Proof	—	Value: 100				

KM# 426   50 WON
2.0100 g., Aluminum, 25 mm.   **Obv:** State arms **Rev:** Value

Date	Mintage	F	VF	XF	Unc	BU
JU94-2005	—	—	—	—	1.20	1.50

KM# 427   100 WON
2.2700 g., Aluminum, 27 mm.   **Obv:** State arms **Rev:** Value

Date	Mintage	F	VF	XF	Unc	BU
JU94-2005	—	—	—	—	1.35	1.75

KM# 445   200 WON
5.1900 g., 0.9990 Silver 0.1667 oz. ASW, 30.00 mm.   **Series:**
Endangered Wildlife **Obv:** Fortress Gate **Rev:** Polar Bear
standing facing **Rev. Legend:** URSUS MARITIMUS **Edge:** Plain

Date	Mintage	F	VF	XF	Unc	BU
2007 Proof	5,000	Value: 550				

KM# 1110   200 WON
25.0000 g., Brass, 38 mm.   **Subject:** Railways in Russia, 170th
Anniversary **Obv:** East gate of Pyeongyang **Rev:** Steam train

Date	Mintage	F	VF	XF	Unc	BU
2007 Proof	Est. 200	Value: 70.00				

KM# 1111   200 WON
25.0000 g., Brass, 35 mm.   **Obv:** East gate of Pyeongyang **Rev:**
Constantine Eduardovic and Sputnik

Date	Mintage	F	VF	XF	Unc	BU
2007 Proof	—	Value: 25.00				

KM# 1086   250 WON
26.9600 g., 0.9000 Silver 0.7801 oz. ASW   **Obv:** Old coins and
Central Bank name

Date	Mintage	F	VF	XF	Unc	BU
2005	Est. 1,000	—	—	—	—	25.00

KM# 835   400 WON
20.0000 g., 0.9990 Gold 0.6423 oz. AGW, 35 mm.   **Obv:**
National arms, Central Bank name **Rev:** Korean folk games,
wrestling

Date	Mintage	F	VF	XF	Unc	BU
2002 Proof	—	Value: 1,200				

KM# 441   500 WON
12.0000 g., 0.9990 Silver 0.3854 oz. ASW, 38.00 mm.   **Subject:**
170th Anniversary First Public Railway St. Petersburg - Zarskoje
Selo **Obv:** Fortress Gate **Rev:** First train arriving **Edge:** Plain

Date	Mintage	F	VF	XF	Unc	BU
ND(2007) Proof	5,000	Value: 70.00				

KM# 447   500 WON
12.0000 g., 0.9990 Silver 0.3854 oz. ASW, 38.00 mm.   **Subject:**
150th Anniversay Birth of Ziolkowski and 50th Anniversary
Launch of Sputnik I **Obv:** Fortress Gate **Rev:** Bust of Ziolkowski
facing 3/4 right at lower left, Sputnik circling earth at upper right
Edge: Plain

Date	Mintage	F	VF	XF	Unc	BU
ND(2007) Proof	5,000	Value: 65.00				

KM# 1112   500 WON
12.0000 g., Silver, 38 mm.   **Obv:** East gate of Pyeongyong **Rev:**
Great Wall and Temple of Heaven in Bejing

Date	Mintage	F	VF	XF	Unc	BU
2007 Proof	Est. 5,000	Value: 35.00				

KM# 1113   500 WON
12.0000 g., 0.9990 Silver 0.3854 oz. ASW, 38 mm.   **Subject:**
Bejing Olympics, 2008 **Obv:** East gate of Pyeongyong **Rev:**
Fencing

Date	Mintage	F	VF	XF	Unc	BU
2007 Proof	—	Value: 35.00				

KM# 1114   500 WON
12.0000 g., 0.9990 Silver 0.3854 oz. ASW, 38 mm.   **Subject:**
Bejing Olympics, 2008 **Obv:** East gate of Pyeongyong **Rev:**
Boxing

Date	Mintage	F	VF	XF	Unc	BU
2007 Proof	—	Value: 35.00				

KM# 1115   500 WON
12.0000 g., 0.9990 Silver 0.3854 oz. ASW, 38 mm.   **Subject:**
Bejing Olympics, 2008 **Obv:** East gate of Pyeongyong **Rev:**
Swimming

Date	Mintage	F	VF	XF	Unc	BU
2007 Proof	Est. 5,000	Value: 35.00				

KM# 1116   500 WON
12.0000 g., 0.9990 Silver 0.3854 oz. ASW, 38 mm.   **Subject:**
Bejing Olympics, 2008 **Obv:** East gate of Pyeongyong **Rev:**
Weightlifting

Date	Mintage	F	VF	XF	Unc	BU
2007 Proof	Est. 5,000	Value: 35.00				

KM# 1117   500 WON
12.0000 g., 0.9990 Silver 0.3854 oz. ASW, 38 mm.   **Subject:**
Bejing Olympics, 2008 **Obv:** East gate of Pyeongyong **Rev:**
Baseball

Date	Mintage	F	VF	XF	Unc	BU
2007 Proof	Est. 5,000	Value: 35.00				

KM# 1118   500 WON
12.0000 g., 0.9990 Silver 0.3854 oz. ASW, 38 mm.   **Subject:**
Bejing Olympics, 2008 **Obv:** East gate of Pyeongyong **Rev:**
Wrestlers

Date	Mintage	F	VF	XF	Unc	BU
2007 Proof	—	Value: 35.00				

KM# 1119   500 WON
12.0000 g., 0.9990 Silver 0.3854 oz. ASW, 38 mm.   **Subject:**
Bejing Olympics, 2008 **Obv:** East gate of Pyeongyong **Rev:**
Gymnast

Date	Mintage	F	VF	XF	Unc	BU
2007 Proof	—	Value: 35.00				

KM# 1120   500 WON
12.0000 g., 0.9990 Silver 0.3854 oz. ASW, 28 mm.   **Subject:**
Bejing Olympics, 2008 **Obv:** East gate of Pyeongyong **Rev:**
Kayakers

Date	Mintage	F	VF	XF	Unc	BU
2007 Proof	Est. 5,000	Value: 35.00				

KM# 1121   500 WON
12.0000 g., 0.9990 Silver 0.3854 oz. ASW, 38 mm.   **Subject:**
Bejing Olympics, 2008 **Obv:** East gate of Pyeongyong **Rev:**
Hurdler

Date	Mintage	F	VF	XF	Unc	BU
2007 Proof	Est. 5,000	Value: 35.00				

KM# 1122   500 WON
12.0000 g., 0.9990 Silver 0.3854 oz. ASW, 38 mm.   **Subject:**
Bejing Olympics, 2008 **Obv:** East gate of Pyeongyong **Rev:**
Taekwondo

Date	Mintage	F	VF	XF	Unc	BU
2007 Proof	Est. 5,000	Value: 35.00				

KM# 1123   500 WON
12.0000 g., 0.9990 Silver 0.3854 oz. ASW, 38 mm.   **Subject:**
Bejing Olympics, 2008 **Obv:** East gate of Pyeongyong **Rev:**
Olympic Sport

Date	Mintage	F	VF	XF	Unc	BU
2007 Proof	—	Value: 35.00				

KM# 443   500 WON
12.0000 g., 0.9990 Silver 0.3854 oz. ASW, 38.00 mm.   **Subject:**
Lunar Year of the Rat **Obv:** Fortress Gate **Rev:** Two rats within
circle of Lunar figures **Edge:** Plain

Date	Mintage	F	VF	XF	Unc	BU
2008	—	—	—	—	—	50.00
2008 Proof	5,000	Value: 70.00				

KM# 1178   500 WON
12.0000 g., 0.9990 Silver 0.3854 oz. ASW, 38 mm.   **Subject:**
Bejing Summer Olympics, 2008 **Obv:** East gate of Pyeongyang
Rev: Great Wall, Temple of Heaven and Soccer player

Date	Mintage	F	VF	XF	Unc	BU
2008 Proof	Est. 5,000	Value: 35.00				

KM# 1179   500 WON
12.0000 g., 0.9990 Silver 0.3854 oz. ASW, 38 mm.   **Subject:**
Bejing Summer Olympics, 2008 **Obv:** East gate of Pyeongyang
Rev: Hockey player

Date	Mintage	F	VF	XF	Unc	BU
2008 Proof	Est. 5,000	Value: 35.00				

KM# 1180   500 WON
12.0000 g., 0.9990 Silver 0.3854 oz. ASW, 38 mm.   **Subject:**
Bejing Summer Olympics, 2008 **Obv:** East gate of Pyeongyang
Rev: Basketball player

Date	Mintage	F	VF	XF	Unc	BU
2008 Proof	Est. 5,000	Value: 35.00				

KM# 1181   500 WON
12.0000 g., 0.9990 Silver 0.3854 oz. ASW, 38 mm.   **Subject:**
Bejing Summer Olympics, 2008 **Obv:** East gate of Pyeongyang
Rev: Archer

Date	Mintage	F	VF	XF	Unc	BU
2008 Proof	Est. 5,000	Value: 35.00				

KM# 1182   500 WON
12.0000 g., 0.9990 Silver 0.3854 oz. ASW, 38 mm.   **Subject:**
Bejing Summer Olympics, 2008 **Obv:** East gate of Pyeongyang
Rev: Volleyball

Date	Mintage	F	VF	XF	Unc	BU
2008 Proof	Est. 5,000	Value: 35.00				

KM# 1183   500 WON
12.0000 g., 0.9990 Silver 0.3854 oz. ASW, 38 mm.   **Subject:**
Bejing Summer Olympics, 2008 **Obv:** East gate of Pyeongyang
Rev: Table tennis

Date	Mintage	F	VF	XF	Unc	BU
2008 Proof	Est. 5,000	Value: 35.00				

KM# 1184   500 WON
12.0000 g., 0.9990 Silver 0.3854 oz. ASW, 38 mm.   **Subject:**
Bejing Summer Olympics, 2008 **Obv:** East gate of Pyeongyang
Rev: Rowers

Date	Mintage	F	VF	XF	Unc	BU
2008 Proof	Est. 5,000	Value: 35.00				

KM# 717   700 WON
31.1050 g., 0.9990 Gold 0.9990 oz. AGW   **Obv:** National arms
Rev: Caledon pottery

Date	Mintage	F	VF	XF	Unc	BU
2001 Proof	—	Value: 1,750				

KM# 720   700 WON
31.1050 g., 0.9990 Gold 0.9990 oz. AGW, 40 mm.   **Obv:**
National arms, Central Bank name **Rev:** Ginsing plant

Date	Mintage	F	VF	XF	Unc	BU
2001 Proof	—	Value: 1,750				

KM# 723   700 WON
31.1050 g., 0.9990 Gold 0.9990 oz. AGW, 40 mm.   **Obv:**
National arms **Rev:** End of the steam train in 1945 and again in
2001

Date	Mintage	F	VF	XF	Unc	BU
2001 Proof	—	Value: 1,750				

KM# 742   700 WON
31.1050 g., 0.9990 Gold 0.9990 oz. AGW, 40 mm.   **Obv:**
National arms, Central Bank name **Rev:** Ferryboat, married
couple and flag

Date	Mintage	F	VF	XF	Unc	BU
2001 Proof	—	Value: 1,750				

KM# 743   700 WON
31.1050 g., 0.9999 Gold 0.9999 oz. AGW, 40 mm.   **Obv:**
National arms, Central Bank name **Rev:** Ferryboat between
Korea and Japan

Date	Mintage	F	VF	XF	Unc	BU
2001 Proof	—	Value: 1,750				

KM# 744   700 WON
31.1050 g., 0.9990 Gold 0.9990 oz. AGW, 40 mm.   **Obv:**
National arms, Central Bank name **Rev:** Triumphial arch of
Moranbong in Pyeongyang

Date	Mintage	F	VF	XF	Unc	BU
2001 Proof	—	Value: 1,750				

KM# 745   700 WON
31.1050 g., 0.9990 Gold 0.9990 oz. AGW, 40 mm.   **Obv:**
National arms, Central Bank name **Rev:** Chonji crater in
Paektusan

Date	Mintage	F	VF	XF	Unc	BU
2001 Proof	—	Value: 1,750				

KM# 748   700 WON
31.1050 g., 0.9990 Gold 0.9990 oz. AGW, 40 mm.   **Obv:**
National arms, Central Bank name **Rev:** Kim Jeongil and Jiang
Zemin clasping hands

Date	Mintage	F	VF	XF	Unc	BU
2001 Proof	—	Value: 1,750				

KM# 503   700 WON
31.1050 g., 0.9990 Gold 0.9990 oz. AGW, 40 mm.   **Obv:**
National arms **Rev:** Brontosaurus

Date	Mintage	F	VF	XF	Unc	BU
2002 Proof	—	Value: 1,750				

KM# 537   700 WON
31.1050 g., 0.9990 Gold 0.9990 oz. AGW   **Obv:** National arms
Rev: Zhou Enlai, president of the P.R.C.

Date	Mintage	F	VF	XF	Unc	BU
2002 Proof	—	Value: 1,750				

KM# 612 700 WON
31.1050 g., 0.9990 Gold 0.9990 oz. AGW **Obv:** National arms **Rev:** Chinese Junk at sail

Date	Mintage	F	VF	XF	Unc	BU
2002 Proof	—	Value: 1,750				

KM# 634 700 WON
31.1050 g., 0.9990 Gold 0.9990 oz. AGW **Obv:** National arms, Central Bank name **Rev:** Blue dragon right

Date	Mintage	F	VF	XF	Unc	BU
2002 Proof	—	Value: 1,750				

KM# 640 700 WON
31.1050 g., 0.9990 Gold 0.9990 oz. AGW **Obv:** National arms, Country name **Rev:** Two siberian tigers

Date	Mintage	F	VF	XF	Unc	BU
2002 Proof	—	Value: 1,750				

KM# 655 700 WON
31.1050 g., 0.9990 Gold 0.9990 oz. AGW, 40 mm. **Obv:** National arms, Central Bank name **Rev:** Dongmyeong, King of Goguryeo

Date	Mintage	F	VF	XF	Unc	BU
2002 Proof	—	Value: 1,750				

KM# 656 700 WON
31.1050 g., 0.9990 Gold 0.9990 oz. AGW, 40 mm. **Obv:** National arms, Central Bank name **Rev:** Buddha figure

Date	Mintage	F	VF	XF	Unc	BU
2002 Proof	—	Value: 1,750				

KM# 657 700 WON
31.1050 g., 0.9990 Gold 0.9990 oz. AGW, 40 mm. **Obv:** National arms, Central Bank name **Rev:** Dangun, King of Gojoseon

Date	Mintage	F	VF	XF	Unc	BU
2002 Proof	—	Value: 1,750				

KM# 791 700 WON
31.1050 g., 0.9990 Gold 0.9990 oz. AGW, 35 mm. **Obv:** National arms **Rev:** Horse head

Date	Mintage	F	VF	XF	Unc	BU
2002 Proof	—	Value: 1,750				

KM# 792 700 WON
31.1050 g., 0.9990 Gold 0.9990 oz. AGW, 35 mm. **Obv:** National arms **Rev:** Horse to the right

Date	Mintage	F	VF	XF	Unc	BU
2002 Proof	—	Value: 1,750				

KM# 793 700 WON
31.1050 g., 0.9990 Gold 0.9990 oz. AGW, 35 mm. **Obv:** National arms **Rev:** Two horses in center of the Zodiac

Date	Mintage	F	VF	XF	Unc	BU
2002 Proof	—	Value: 1,750				

KM# 816 700 WON
31.1050 g., 0.9990 Gold 0.9990 oz. AGW, 40 mm. **Obv:** National arms, Central Bank name **Rev:** Reconstruction of the Mousoleum for King Dangun

Date	Mintage	F	VF	XF	Unc	BU
2002 Proof	—	Value: 1,750				

KM# 817 700 WON
31.1050 g., 0.9990 Gold 0.9990 oz. AGW, 40 mm. **Obv:** National arms, Central Bank name **Rev:** Dongmyeong, 1st King of Goguryeo

Date	Mintage	F	VF	XF	Unc	BU
2002 Proof	—	Value: 1,750				

KM# 818 700 WON
31.1050 g., 0.9990 Gold 0.9990 oz. AGW, 40 mm. **Obv:** National arms, Central Bank name **Rev:** Wanggeon, 1st King of Boryeo Dynasty

Date	Mintage	F	VF	XF	Unc	BU
2002 Proof	—	Value: 1,750				

KM# 819 700 WON
31.1050 g., 0.9990 Gold 0.9990 oz. AGW, 40 mm. **Obv:** National arms, Central Bank name **Rev:** Jeong Mongju

Date	Mintage	F	VF	XF	Unc	BU
2002 Proof	—	Value: 1,750				

KM# 820 700 WON
31.1050 g., 0.9990 Gold 0.9990 oz. AGW, 40 mm. **Obv:** National arms, Central Bank name **Rev:** Jeon Bongjun

Date	Mintage	F	VF	XF	Unc	BU
2002 Proof	—	Value: 1,750				

KM# 825 700 WON
31.1050 g., 0.9990 Gold 0.9990 oz. AGW, 40 mm. **Obv:** National arms **Rev:** Prince Hodong and Princess Nakrang on horseback

Date	Mintage	F	VF	XF	Unc	BU
2002 Proof	—	Value: 1,750				

KM# 826 700 WON
31.1050 g., 0.9990 Gold 0.9990 oz. AGW, 40 mm. **Obv:** National arms **Rev:** Half-length figures of Prince Hodong and Princess Nakrang

Date	Mintage	F	VF	XF	Unc	BU
2002 Proof	—	Value: 1,750				

KM# 834 700 WON
31.1050 g., 0.9990 Gold 0.9990 oz. AGW, 35 mm. **Obv:** National Arms, Central Bank name **Rev:** Bust of Kim Ilseong

Date	Mintage	F	VF	XF	Unc	BU
2002 Proof	—	Value: 1,750				

KM# 844 700 WON
31.1050 g., 0.9990 Gold 0.9990 oz. AGW, 35 mm. **Obv:** National arms, Central Bank and Country name **Rev:** The soldiers

Date	Mintage	F	VF	XF	Unc	BU

KM# 845 700 WON
31.1050 g., 0.9990 Gold 0.9990 oz. AGW, 35 mm. **Obv:** National arms, Central Bank and Country name **Rev:** Fairy princess

Date	Mintage	F	VF	XF	Unc	BU
2002 Proof	—	Value: 1,750				

KM# 846 700 WON
31.1050 g., 0.9990 Gold 0.9990 oz. AGW, 35 mm. **Obv:** National arms, Central Bank and Country name **Rev:** Bronze statue

Date	Mintage	F	VF	XF	Unc	BU
2002 Proof	—	Value: 1,750				

KM# 847 700 WON
31.1050 g., 0.9990 Gold 0.9990 oz. AGW, 35 mm. **Obv:** National arms, Central Bank and Country name **Rev:** Female worshipers of the sun

Date	Mintage	F	VF	XF	Unc	BU
2002 Proof	—	Value: 1,750				

KM# 848 700 WON
31.1050 g., 0.9990 Gold 0.9990 oz. AGW, 35 mm. **Obv:** National arms, Central Bank and Country name **Rev:** Trhee prinicpals of re-unification

Date	Mintage	F	VF	XF	Unc	BU
2002 Proof	—	Value: 1,750				

KM# 849 700 WON
31.1050 g., 0.9990 Gold 0.9990 oz. AGW, 35 mm. **Obv:** National arms, Central Bank and Country name **Rev:** Dancing children

Date	Mintage	F	VF	XF	Unc	BU
2002 Proof	—	Value: 1,750				

KM# 872 700 WON
31.1050 g., 0.9990 Gold 0.9990 oz. AGW, 40 mm. **Obv:** National arms, Central bank name **Rev:** Family

Date	Mintage	F	VF	XF	Unc	BU
2002 Proof	—	Value: 1,750				

KM# 873 700 WON
31.1050 g., 0.9990 Gold 0.9990 oz. AGW, 40 mm. **Obv:** National arms, Central Bank name **Rev:** Map of Korea with four cardinal compass points

Date	Mintage	F	VF	XF	Unc	BU
2002 Proof	—	Value: 1,750				

KM# 874 700 WON
31.1050 g., 0.9990 Gold 0.9990 oz. AGW, 40 mm. **Obv:** Naitonal arms, Central Bank name **Rev:** Rythem dancer and map of Korea

Date	Mintage	F	VF	XF	Unc	BU
2002 Proof	—	Value: 1,750				

KM# 875 700 WON
31.1050 g., 0.9990 Gold 0.9990 oz. AGW, 40 mm. **Obv:** National arms, Central Bank name **Rev:** Drum dancers and map of Korea

Date	Mintage	F	VF	XF	Unc	BU
2002 Proof	—	Value: 1,750				

KM# 876 700 WON
31.1050 g., 0.9990 Gold 0.9990 oz. AGW, 40 mm. **Obv:** National arms, Central Bank name **Rev:** Korean team victory celebration

Date	Mintage	F	VF	XF	Unc	BU
2002 Proof	—	Value: 1,750				

KM# 899 700 WON
31.1050 g., 0.9990 Gold 0.9990 oz. AGW, 40 mm. **Obv:** East gate of Pyeongyang **Rev:** Sheep at center of Zodiac

Date	Mintage	F	VF	XF	Unc	BU
2003 Proof	—	Value: 1,750				

KM# 912 700 WON
31.1050 g., 0.9990 Gold 0.9990 oz. AGW, 40 mm. **Obv:** National arms, Central Bank name **Rev:** Eulji Mundeok

Date	Mintage	F	VF	XF	Unc	BU
2003 Proof	—	Value: 1,750				

KM# 913 700 WON
31.1050 g., 0.9990 Gold 0.9990 oz. AGW, 40 mm. **Obv:** National arms, Central Bank name **Rev:** Yeon Gaesomun

Date	Mintage	F	VF	XF	Unc	BU
2003 Proof	—	Value: 1,750				

KM# 914 700 WON
31.1050 g., 0.9990 Gold 0.9990 oz. AGW, 40 mm. **Obv:** National arms, Central Bank name **Rev:** Gang Camchan

Date	Mintage	F	VF	XF	Unc	BU
2003 Proof	—	Value: 1,750				

KM# 917 700 WON
31.1050 g., 0.9990 Gold 0.9990 oz. AGW, 40 mm. **Obv:** National arms, Central Bank name **Rev:** Turtle boat

Date	Mintage	F	VF	XF	Unc	BU
2003 Proof	—	Value: 1,750				

KM# 941 700 WON
31.1050 g., 0.9990 Gold 0.9990 oz. AGW, 40 mm. **Obv:** Naitonal arms, Central Bank name **Rev:** Monkey at center of Zodiac

Date	Mintage	F	VF	XF	Unc	BU
2004 Proof	—	Value: 1,800				

KM# 1018 700 WON
31.1050 g., 0.9990 Gold 0.9990 oz. AGW, 40 mm. **Obv:** National arms, Central Bank name **Rev:** Rooster within Zodiac circle

Date	Mintage	F	VF	XF	Unc	BU
2005 Proof	—	Value: 1,800				

KM# 1032 700 WON
31.1050 g., 0.9990 Gold 0.9990 oz. AGW, 40 mm. **Obv:** National arms, Central Bank name **Rev:** Admiral Yi Sunsin and turtle boat

Date	Mintage	F	VF	XF	Unc	BU
2005 Proof	—	Value: 1,800				

KM# 1033 700 WON
31.1050 g., 0.9990 Gold 0.9990 oz. AGW, 40 mm. **Obv:** National arms, Central Bank name **Rev:** General Hong Beomdo

Date	Mintage	F	VF	XF	Unc	BU
2005 Proof	—	Value: 1,800				

KM# 1042 700 WON
31.1050 g., 0.9990 Gold 0.9990 oz. AGW, 40 mm. **Obv:** National arms, Central Bank name **Rev:** Map of Korea, two peace doves, rainbow

Date	Mintage	F	VF	XF	Unc	BU
2005 Proof	—	Value: 1,800				

KM# 1047 700 WON
31.1050 g., 0.9990 Gold 0.9990 oz. AGW, 40 mm. **Obv:** National arms, Central Bank name **Rev:** Tomb of the unknown soldier in Moscow, Russian legend

Date	Mintage	F	VF	XF	Unc	BU
2005 Proof	—	Value: 1,800				

KM# 1048 700 WON
31.1050 g., 0.9990 Gold 0.9990 oz. AGW, 40 mm. **Obv:** National arms, Central Bank name **Rev:** Memorial to mothers in St. Petersburg

Date	Mintage	F	VF	XF	Unc	BU
2005 Proof	—	Value: 1,800				

KM# 428 700 WON
15.5500 g., 0.9990 Silver 0.4994 oz. ASW, 30.00 mm. **Series:** European Union Euro Commemoratives **Obv:** National arms **Rev:** Schleswig-Holstein City gate in relief in tiger's-eye **Edge:** Plain

Date	Mintage	F	VF	XF	Unc	BU
2006 Proof	3,000	Value: 70.00				

KM# 429 700 WON
15.5500 g., 0.9990 Silver 0.4994 oz. ASW, 30.00 mm. **Series:** European Union Euro Commemoratives **Obv:** National arms **Rev:** Vatican in relief in tiger's-eye **Edge:** Plain

Date	Mintage	F	VF	XF	Unc	BU
2006 Proof	3,000	Value: 70.00				

KM# 430 700 WON
15.5500 g., 0.9990 Silver 0.4994 oz. ASW, 30.00 mm. **Series:** European Union Euro Commemoratives **Obv:** National arms **Rev:** Male Olympic statue - discus - Athens in relief in tiger's-eye **Edge:** Plain

Date	Mintage	F	VF	XF	Unc	BU
2006 Proof	3,000	Value: 70.00				

KM# 431 700 WON
15.5500 g., 0.9990 Silver 0.4994 oz. ASW, 30.00 mm. **Series:** European Union Euro Commemoratives **Obv:** National arms **Rev:** 50th Anniversary Austrian States Treaty in relief in tiger's-eye **Edge:** Plain

Date	Mintage	F	VF	XF	Unc	BU
2006 Proof	3,000	Value: 70.00				

KM# 432 700 WON
15.5500 g., 0.9990 Silver 0.4994 oz. ASW, 30.00 mm. **Series:** European Union Euro Commemoratives **Obv:** National arms **Rev:** Don Quixote in relief in tiger's-eye **Edge:** Plain

Date	Mintage	F	VF	XF	Unc	BU
2006 Proof	3,000	Value: 70.00				

KM# 433   700 WON
15.5500 g., 0.9990 Silver 0.4994 oz. ASW, 30.00 mm. **Series:** European Union Euro Commemoratives **Obv:** National arms **Rev:** Head of Henri, Grand Duke of Luxembourg at left facing right, crowned H at right in relief in tiger's-eye **Edge:** Plain

Date	Mintage	F	VF	XF	Unc	BU
2006 Proof	3,000	Value: 70.00				

KM# 434   700 WON
15.5500 g., 0.9990 Silver 0.4994 oz. ASW, 30 mm. **Series:** European Union Euro Commemoratives **Obv:** National arms **Rev:** Italian FAO logo in relief in tiger's-eye **Edge:** Plain

Date	Mintage	F	VF	XF	Unc	BU
2006 Proof	3,000	Value: 70.00				

KM# 435   700 WON
15.5500 g., 0.9990 Silver 0.4994 oz. ASW, 30 mm. **Series:** European Union Euro Commemoratives **Obv:** National arms **Rev:** Finland - stylized flower in relief in tiger's-eye **Edge:** Plain

Date	Mintage	F	VF	XF	Unc	BU
2006 Proof	3,000	Value: 70.00				

KM# 436   700 WON
15.5500 g., 0.9990 Silver 0.4994 oz. ASW, 30 mm. **Series:** European Union Euro Commemoratives **Obv:** National arms **Rev:** Conjoined heads of Grand Duke Henri of Luxembourg and King Albert of Belgium left in relief in tiger's-eye **Edge:** Plain

Date	Mintage	F	VF	XF	Unc	BU
2006 Proof	3,000	Value: 70.00				

KM# 437   700 WON
15.5500 g., 0.9990 Silver 0.4994 oz. ASW, 30 mm. **Series:** European Union Euro Commemoratives **Obv:** National arms **Rev:** San Marino - bust of Bartolomeo Borghesi slightly right in relief in tiger's-eye **Edge:** Plain

Date	Mintage	F	VF	XF	Unc	BU
2006 Proof	3,000	Value: 70.00				

KM# 438   700 WON
15.5500 g., 0.9990 Silver tigereye colored center 0.4994 oz. ASW, 30 mm. **Series:** European Union Euro Commemoratives **Obv:** National arms **Rev:** Vatican - World Youth Day in Cologne **Edge:** Plain

Date	Mintage	F	VF	XF	Unc	BU
2006 Proof	3,000	Value: 70.00				

KM# 439   700 WON
15.5500 g., 0.9990 Silver 0.4994 oz. ASW, 30 mm. **Series:** European Union Euro Commemoratives **Obv:** National arms **Rev:** San Marino - Year of Physics design in relief in tiger's-eye **Edge:** Plain

Date	Mintage	F	VF	XF	Unc	BU
2006 Proof	3,000	Value: 70.00				

KM# 958   1000 WON
42.2160 g., 0.9990 Gold 1.3559 oz. AGW, 45 mm. **Obv:** National arms, Central Bank name **Rev:** Kim Ilseong

Date	Mintage	F	VF	XF	Unc	BU
2004 Proof	—	Value: 2,450				

KM# 959   1000 WON
42.2160 g., 0.9990 Gold 1.3559 oz. AGW, 45 mm. **Obv:** National arms, Central Bank name **Rev:** Kim Jeongil

Date	Mintage	F	VF	XF	Unc	BU
2004 Proof	—	Value: 2,450				

KM# 960   1000 WON
42.2160 g., 0.9990 Gold 1.3559 oz. AGW, 45 mm. **Obv:** National arms, Central Bank name **Rev:** Kim Jeongsuk

Date	Mintage	F	VF	XF	Unc	BU
2004 Proof	—	Value: 2,450				

KM# 961   1000 WON
42.2160 g., 0.9990 Gold 1.3559 oz. AGW, 45 mm. **Obv:** National arms, Central Bank name **Rev:** Kim Ilseong's birthplace

Date	Mintage	F	VF	XF	Unc	BU
2004 Proof	—	Value: 2,450				

KM# 962   1000 WON
42.2160 g., 0.9990 Gold 1.3559 oz. AGW, 45 mm. **Obv:** National arms, Central Bank name **Rev:** Mountain cottage of Kim Jeongil

Date	Mintage	F	VF	XF	Unc	BU
2004 Proof	—	Value: 2,450				

KM# 963   1000 WON
42.2160 g., 0.9990 Gold 1.3559 oz. AGW, 45 mm. **Obv:** National arms, Central Bank name **Rev:** House where Kim Jeongsuk was born

Date	Mintage	F	VF	XF	Unc	BU
2004 Proof	—	Value: 2,450				

KM# 1097   1000 WON
20.0000 g., 0.9990 Silver 0.6423 oz. ASW, 38 mm. **Subject:** Lake Placid Winter Olympics, 1936 **Obv:** National arms, Central Bank name **Rev:** Bobsled

Date	Mintage	F	VF	XF	Unc	BU
2006 Proof	Est. 5,000	Value: 45.00				

KM# 1098   1000 WON
20.0000 g., 0.9990 Silver 0.6423 oz. ASW, 38 mm. **Subject:** Sarajevo Winter Olympics, 1984 **Obv:** National arms, Central Bank name **Rev:** Ice Hockey player

Date	Mintage	F	VF	XF	Unc	BU
2006 Proof	Est. 5,000	Value: 45.00				

KM# 1099   1000 WON
20.0000 g., 0.9990 Silver 0.6423 oz. ASW, 38 mm. **Obv:** National arms, Central Bank name **Rev:** Soccer player and Brazil flag and map

Date	Mintage	F	VF	XF	Unc	BU
2006 Proof	Est. 5,000	Value: 45.00				

KM# 1100   1000 WON
20.0000 g., 0.9990 Silver 0.6423 oz. ASW, 38 mm. **Subject:** Bejing Summer Olympics, 2008 **Obv:** National arms, Central Bank name **Rev:** Gymnast on pommel horse

Date	Mintage	F	VF	XF	Unc	BU
2006 Proof	—	Value: 35.00				

KM# 440   1000 WON
20.0000 g., 0.9990 Silver 0.6423 oz. ASW, 38 mm. **Obv:** National arms **Rev:** Arctic animals with map of North Pole in background **Rev. Legend:** INTERNATIONAL POLAR YEAR / ARCTIC ANIMALS **Edge:** Plain

Date	Mintage	F	VF	XF	Unc	BU
ND(2007) Proof	—	Value: 85.00				

KM# 446   1000 WON
20.0000 g., 0.9990 Silver 0.6423 oz. ASW, 38 mm. **Series:** Endangered Wildlife **Obv:** Fortress Gate **Rev:** Polar Bear standing facing **Rev. Legend:** URSUS MAITIMUS **Edge:** Plain

Date	Mintage	F	VF	XF	Unc	BU
2007 Proof	5,000	Value: 70.00				

KM# 1186   1000 WON
20.0000 g., 0.9990 Silver 0.6423 oz. ASW, 38 mm. **Subject:** Vancouver Winter Olympics, 2010 **Obv:** East gate of Pyeongyang **Rev:** Nordic Combine and triumphial arch

Date	Mintage	F	VF	XF	Unc	BU
2008 Proof	—	Value: 45.00				

KM# 1187   1000 WON
20.0000 g., 0.9990 Silver 0.6423 oz. ASW, 38 mm. **Subject:** Wold Cup Soccer, South Africa, 2010 **Obv:** East gate of Pyeongyang **Rev:** Soccer foul play

Date	Mintage	F	VF	XF	Unc	BU
2008 Proof	Est. 5,000	Value: 35.00				

KM# 993   1500 WON
70.0000 g., 0.9990 Gold 2.2482 oz. AGW, 50 mm. **Obv:** Map of Korea, Central Bank name **Rev:** Court physician Heo Jun

Date	Mintage	F	VF	XF	Unc	BU
2004 Proof	—	Value: 4,000				

KM# 1067   1500 WON
31.1050 g., 0.9990 Silver 0.9990 oz. ASW, 40 mm. **Obv:** Trumpeter, Central Bank name **Rev:** Triumphial arch in Pyeongyang

Date	Mintage	F	VF	XF	Unc	BU
2005 Proof	—	Value: 115				

KM# 1069   1500 WON
31.1050 g., 0.9990 Silver 0.9990 oz. ASW, 40 mm. **Subject:** Worker's Party, 60th Anniversary **Obv:** National arms, Central Bank name **Rev:** Party emblem

Date	Mintage	F	VF	XF	Unc	BU
2005 Proof	—	Value: 115				

KM# 1070   1500 WON
31.1050 g., 0.9990 Gold 0.9990 oz. AGW, 40 mm. **Subject:** Worker's Party,60th Anniversary **Obv:** National arms, Central Bank name **Rev:** Party emblem

Date	Mintage	F	VF	XF	Unc	BU
2005 Proof	—	Value: 1,800				

KM# 1092   1500 WON
31.1050 g., 0.9990 Silver 0.9990 oz. ASW, 40 mm. **Obv:** National arms, Central Bank name **Rev:** Two dogs

Date	Mintage	F	VF	XF	Unc	BU
2006 Proof	Est. 2,000	Value: 60.00				

KM# 1093   1500 WON
31.1050 g., 0.9990 Silver 0.9990 oz. ASW, 40 mm. **Obv:** National arms, Central Bank name **Rev:** Bronze staue of flying horse

Date	Mintage	F	VF	XF	Unc	BU
2006 Proof	—	Value: 115				

KM# 1094   1500 WON
31.1050 g., 0.9990 Silver 0.9990 oz. ASW, 40 mm. **Obv:** National arms, Central Bank name **Rev:** Triumphial arch

Date	Mintage	F	VF	XF	Unc	BU
2006 Proof	—	Value: 115				

KM# 1142   1500 WON
31.1050 g., 0.9990 Silver 0.9990 oz. ASW, 40 mm. **Obv:** National arms, Central Bank name **Rev:** Hoopoe

Date	Mintage	F	VF	XF	Unc	BU
2007 Proof	Est. 500	Value: 60.00				

KM# 1143   1500 WON
31.1050 g., 0.9990 Silver 0.9990 oz. ASW, 40 mm. **Obv:** National arms, Central Bank name **Rev:** Ural owl

Date	Mintage	F	VF	XF	Unc	BU
2007 Proof	Est. 500	Value: 100				

KM# 1144   1500 WON
31.1050 g., 0.9990 Silver 0.9990 oz. ASW, 40 mm. **Obv:** National arms, Central Bank name **Rev:** Eagle

Date	Mintage	F	VF	XF	Unc	BU
2007 Proof	—	Value: 60.00				

KM# 1145   1500 WON
31.1050 g., 0.9990 Silver 0.9990 oz. ASW, 40 mm. **Obv:** National arms, Central Bank name **Rev:** White Rhino

Date	Mintage	F	VF	XF	Unc	BU
2007 Proof	Est. 500	Value: 60.00				

KM# 1146   1500 WON
31.1050 g., 0.9990 Silver 0.9990 oz. ASW, 40 mm. **Obv:** National arms, Central Bank name **Rev:** African elephant family

Date	Mintage	F	VF	XF	Unc	BU
2007 Proof	Est. 500	Value: 60.00				

KM# 1147   1500 WON
31.1050 g., 0.9990 Silver 0.9990 oz. ASW, 40 mm. **Obv:** National arms, Central Bank name **Rev:** Lion family

Date	Mintage	F	VF	XF	Unc	BU
2007 Proof	Est. 500	Value: 60.00				

KM# 1148   1500 WON
31.1050 g., 0.9990 Silver 0.9990 oz. ASW, 40 mm. **Obv:** National arms, Central Bank name **Rev:** Cape buffalo

Date	Mintage	F	VF	XF	Unc	BU
2007 Proof	Est. 500	Value: 60.00				

KM# 1149   1500 WON
31.1050 g., 0.9990 Silver 0.9990 oz. ASW, 40 mm. **Obv:** National arms, Central Bank name **Rev:** Marine turtle

Date	Mintage	F	VF	XF	Unc	BU
2007 Proof	Est. 500	Value: 60.00				

KM# 1150   1500 WON
31.1050 g., 0.9990 Silver 0.9990 oz. ASW, 40 mm. **Obv:** National arms, Central Bank name **Rev:** Penguin

Date	Mintage	F	VF	XF	Unc	BU
2007 Proof	Est. 500	Value: 60.00				

KM# 1151   1500 WON
31.1050 g., 0.9990 Silver 0.9990 oz. ASW, 40 mm. **Obv:** National arms, Central Bank name **Rev:** Emu

Date	Mintage	F	VF	XF	Unc	BU
2007 Proof	Est. 500	Value: 60.00				

KM# 1152   1500 WON
31.1050 g., 0.9990 Silver 0.9990 oz. ASW, 40 mm. **Obv:** National arms, Central Bank name **Rev:** Eagle owl

Date	Mintage	F	VF	XF	Unc	BU
2007 Proof	Est. 500	Value: 60.00				

KM# 1153   1500 WON
31.1050 g., 0.9990 Silver 0.9990 oz. ASW, 40 mm. **Obv:** National arms, Central Bank name **Rev:** Lemur

Date	Mintage	F	VF	XF	Unc	BU
2007 Proof	Est. 500	Value: 60.00				

KM# 1154   1500 WON
31.1050 g., 0.9990 Silver 0.9990 oz. ASW, 40 mm. **Obv:** National arms, Central Bank name **Rev:** Lion

Date	Mintage	F	VF	XF	Unc	BU
2007 Proof	Est. 500	Value: 60.00				

KM# 1155   1500 WON
31.1050 g., 0.9990 Silver 0.9990 oz. ASW, 40 mm. **Obv:** National arms, Central Bank name **Rev:** Two African elephants

Date	Mintage	F	VF	XF	Unc	BU
2007 Proof	Est. 500	Value: 60.00				

KM# 1176   1500 WON
31.1050 g., 0.9990 Silver 0.9990 oz. ASW, 40 mm. **Subject:** Nationhood, 60th Anniversary **Obv:** National arms, Central Bank name **Rev:** National flag, star above

Date	Mintage	F	VF	XF	Unc	BU
2008 Proof	—	Value: 115				

KM# 1185   1500 WON
31.1050 g., 0.9990 Silver 0.9990 oz. ASW, 40 mm. **Subject:** Bejing Summer Olympics, 2008 **Obv:** East gate of Pyeongyang **Rev:** Ancient ring gymnast

Date	Mintage	F	VF	XF	Unc	BU
2008 Proof	Est. 5,000	Value: 60.00				

KM# 950   2000 WON
31.1050 g., 0.9990 Bi-Metallic Gold center in Silver ring 0.9990 oz., 40 mm. **Obv:** National arms, Central Bank name **Rev:** Sports hall in Pyeongyang

Date	Mintage	F	VF	XF	Unc	BU
2004 Proof	—	Value: 2,200				

KM# 964   2000 WON
31.1050 g., 0.9990 Gold 0.9990 oz. AGW, 35 mm. **Subject:** 10th Anniversary of the takeover **Obv:** National arms, Central Bank name **Rev:** Kim Jeongil

Date	Mintage	F	VF	XF	Unc	BU
2004 Proof	—	Value: 2,100				

KM# 965   2000 WON
31.1050 g., 0.9990 Gold 0.9990 oz. AGW, 35 mm. **Obv:**
National arms, Central Bank name **Rev:** Kim Jeongil and Kim
Daejung

Date	Mintage	F	VF	XF	Unc	BU
2004 Proof	—	Value: 2,000				

KM# 967   2000 WON
31.1050 g., 0.9990 Gold 0.9990 oz. AGW, 35 mm. **Obv:**
National arms, Central Bank name **Rev:** Kim Jeongil and Hu
Jintao

Date	Mintage	F	VF	XF	Unc	BU
2004 Proof	—	Value: 2,000				

KM# 968   2000 WON
31.1050 g., 0.9990 Gold 0.9990 oz. AGW, 35 mm. **Obv:**
National arms, Central Bank name **Rev:** Kim Jeongil and Vladimir
Putin

Date	Mintage	F	VF	XF	Unc	BU
2004 Proof	—	Value: 2,100				

KM# 985   2000 WON
31.1050 g., 0.9990 Gold 0.9990 oz. AGW, 40 mm. **Obv:** Dokdo,
rocky islands, Central Bank name **Rev:** Island group map

Date	Mintage	F	VF	XF	Unc	BU
2004 Proof	—	Value: 2,000				

KM# 986   2000 WON
31.1050 g., 0.9990 Gold 0.9990 oz. AGW, 40 mm. **Obv:** Dokdo,
rocky islands, Central Bank name **Rev:** Fisher Ahn Yongbok

Date	Mintage	F	VF	XF	Unc	BU
2004 Proof	—	Value: 2,100				

KM# 987   2000 WON
31.1050 g., 0.9990 Gold 0.9990 oz. AGW, 40 mm. **Obv:** Dokdo,
rocky islands, Central Bank name **Rev:** West Island

Date	Mintage	F	VF	XF	Unc	BU
2004 Proof	—	Value: 2,100				

KM# 988   2000 WON
31.1050 g., 0.9990 Gold 0.9990 oz. AGW, 40 mm. **Obv:** Dokdo,
rocky islands, Central Bank name **Rev:** East island

Date	Mintage	F	VF	XF	Unc	BU
2004 Proof	—	Value: 2,100				

KM# 989   2000 WON
31.1050 g., 0.9990 Gold 0.9990 oz. AGW, 40 mm. **Obv:** Dokdo,
rocky islands, Central Bank name **Rev:** Three brothers islands

Date	Mintage	F	VF	XF	Unc	BU
2004 Proof	—	Value: 2,100				

KM# 990   2000 WON
31.1050 g., 0.9990 Gold 0.9990 oz. AGW, 40 mm. **Obv:** Dokdo,
rocky islands, Central Bank name **Rev:** Chicken island

Date	Mintage	F	VF	XF	Unc	BU
2004 Proof	—	Value: 2,100				

KM# 991   2000 WON
31.1050 g., 0.9990 Gold 0.9990 oz. AGW, 40 mm. **Obv:** Dokdo,
rocky islands, Central Bank name **Rev:** Candle island

Date	Mintage	F	VF	XF	Unc	BU
2004 Proof	—	Value: 2,100				

KM# 1087   2500 WON
33.3300 g., 0.9000 Gold 0.9644 oz. AGW **Obv:** Old coins and
Central Bank name

Date	Mintage	F	VF	XF	Unc	BU
2005	Est. 200	—	—	—	—	2,050

KM# 442   15000 WON
7.7800 g., 0.9990 Gold 0.2499 oz. AGW, 26 mm. **Subject:** 170th
Anniversary First Public Railway St. Petersburg - Zarskoje Selo
Obv: Fortress Gate **Rev:** First train arriving **Edge:** Plain

Date	Mintage	F	VF	XF	Unc	BU
ND(2007) Proof	2,000	Value: 450				

KM# 448   15000 WON
7.7800 g., 0.9990 Gold 0.2499 oz. AGW, 26 mm. **Subject:** 150th
Anniversary Birth of Ziolkowski and 50th Anniversary Launch of
Sputnik I **Obv:** Fortress Gate **Rev:** Bust of Ziolkowski facing 3/4
right at lower left, Sputnik circling earth at top right **Edge:** Plain

Date	Mintage	F	VF	XF	Unc	BU
ND(2007) Proof	2,000	Value: 550				

KM# 444   15000 WON
7.7800 g., 0.9990 Gold 0.2499 oz. AGW, 26 mm. **Subject:**
Lunar Year of the Rat **Obv:** Fortress Gate **Rev:** Two rats within
circle of Lunar figures **Edge:** Plain

Date	Mintage	F	VF	XF	Unc	BU
2008 Proof	2,000	Value: 550				

KM# 1068   60000 WON
31.1050 g., 0.9990 Gold 0.9990 oz. AGW, 35 mm. **Obv:**
Trumpeter, Central Bank name **Rev:** Triumphia arch in
Pyeongyang

Date	Mintage	F	VF	XF	Unc	BU
2005 Proof	—	Value: 1,800				

KM# 1095   60000 WON
31.1050 g., 0.9990 Gold 0.9990 oz. AGW, 35 mm. **Obv:**
National arms, Central Bank name **Rev:** Bronze statue of flying
horse

Date	Mintage	F	VF	XF	Unc	BU
2006 Proof	—	Value: 2,100				

KM# 1096   60000 WON
31.1050 g., 0.9990 Gold 0.9990 oz. AGW, 35 mm. **Obv:**
National arms, Central Bank name **Rev:** Triumphial arch

Date	Mintage	F	VF	XF	Unc	BU
2006 Proof	—	Value: 2,100				

KM# 1156   60000 WON
31.1050 g., 0.9990 Gold 0.9990 oz. AGW, 35 mm. **Obv:**
National arms, Central Bank name **Rev:** Hoopoe

Date	Mintage	F	VF	XF	Unc	BU
2007 Proof	Est. 500	Value: 2,100				

KM# 1157   60000 WON
31.1050 g., 0.9990 Gold 0.9990 oz. AGW, 35 mm. **Obv:**
National arms, Central Bank name **Rev:** Ural owl

Date	Mintage	F	VF	XF	Unc	BU
2007 Proof	—	Value: 2,100				

KM# 1158   60000 WON
31.1050 g., 0.9990 Gold 0.9990 oz. AGW, 35 mm. **Obv:**
National arms, Central Bank name **Rev:** Eagle

Date	Mintage	F	VF	XF	Unc	BU
2007 Proof	Est. 500	Value: 2,100				

KM# 1159   60000 WON
31.1050 g., 0.9990 Gold 0.9990 oz. AGW, 35 mm. **Obv:**
National arms, Central Bank name **Rev:** White rhino

Date	Mintage	F	VF	XF	Unc	BU
2007 Proof	Est. 500	Value: 2,100				

KM# 1160   60000 WON
31.1050 g., 0.9990 Gold 0.9990 oz. AGW, 35 mm. **Obv:**
National arms, Central Bank name **Rev:** African elephant family

Date	Mintage	F	VF	XF	Unc	BU
2007 Proof	Est. 500	Value: 2,100				

KM# 1161   60000 WON
31.1050 g., 0.9990 Gold 0.9990 oz. AGW, 35 mm. **Obv:**
National arms, Central Bank name **Rev:** Lion family

Date	Mintage	F	VF	XF	Unc	BU
2007 Proof	Est. 500	Value: 2,100				

KM# 1162   60000 WON
31.1050 g., 0.9990 Gold 0.9990 oz. AGW, 35 mm. **Obv:**
National arms, Central Bank name **Rev:** Cape buffalo

Date	Mintage	F	VF	XF	Unc	BU
2007 Proof	Est. 500	Value: 2,100				

KM# 1163   60000 WON
31.1050 g., 0.9990 Gold 0.9990 oz. AGW, 35 mm. **Obv:**
National arms, Central Bank name **Rev:** Marine turtle

Date	Mintage	F	VF	XF	Unc	BU
2007 Proof	Est. 500	Value: 2,100				

KM# 1164   60000 WON
31.1050 g., 0.9990 Gold 0.9990 oz. AGW, 35 mm. **Obv:**
National arms, Central Bank name **Rev:** Penguin

Date	Mintage	F	VF	XF	Unc	BU
2007 Proof	Est. 500	Value: 2,100				

KM# 1165   60000 WON
31.1050 g., 0.9990 Gold 0.9990 oz. AGW, 35 mm. **Obv:**
National arms, Central Bank name **Rev:** Emu

Date	Mintage	F	VF	XF	Unc	BU
2007 Proof	Est. 500	Value: 2,100				

KM# 1166   60000 WON
31.1050 g., 0.9990 Gold 0.9990 oz. AGW, 35 mm. **Obv:**
National arms, Central Bank name **Rev:** Eagle owl

Date	Mintage	F	VF	XF	Unc	BU
2007 Proof	Est. 500	Value: 2,100				

KM# 1167   60000 WON
31.1050 g., 0.9990 Gold 0.9990 oz. AGW, 35 mm. **Obv:**
National arms, Central Bank name **Rev:** Lemur

Date	Mintage	F	VF	XF	Unc	BU
2007 Proof	Est. 500	Value: 2,100				

KM# 1168   60000 WON
31.1050 g., 0.9990 Gold 0.9990 oz. AGW, 35 mm. **Obv:**
National arms, Central Bank name **Rev:** Lion

Date	Mintage	F	VF	XF	Unc	BU
2007 Proof	Est. 500	Value: 2,100				

KM# 1169   60000 WON
31.1050 g., 0.9990 Gold 0.9990 oz. AGW, 35 mm. **Obv:**
National arms, Central Bank name **Rev:** Two African elephants

Date	Mintage	F	VF	XF	Unc	BU
2007 Proof	—	Value: 2,100				

KM# 1177   60000 WON
31.1050 g., 0.9990 Gold 0.9990 oz. AGW, 35 mm. **Subject:**
Nationhood, 60th Anniversary **Obv:** National arms, Central Bank
name **Rev:** National flag, star above

Date	Mintage	F	VF	XF	Unc	BU
2008 Proof	—	Value: 2,100				

REFORM COINAGE
100 (Old) Won = 1 (new) Won

KM# 1170   CHON
Aluminum, 18 mm. **Obv:** National arms, Central Bank name

Date	Mintage	F	VF	XF	Unc	BU
2008	—	—	—	—	3.00	5.00

KM# 1171   5 CHON
Aluminum, 19 mm. **Obv:** National arms, Central Bank name
Rev: Magnolia

Date	Mintage	F	VF	XF	Unc	BU
2008	—	—	—	—	3.00	5.00

KM# 1172   10 CHON
1.0000 g., Aluminum, 20 mm. **Obv:** National arms, Central
Bank name **Rev:** Rhododendron

Date	Mintage	F	VF	XF	Unc	BU
2002	—	—	—	—	1.00	1.75

KM# 1173   50 CHON
1.5000 g., Aluminum, 22 mm. **Obv:** National arms, Central Bank
name **Rev:** Begonia

Date	Mintage	F	VF	XF	Unc	BU
2002	—	—	—	—	1.00	2.00

KM# 1174   WON
1.8000 g., Aluminum, 24 mm. **Obv:** National arms, Central Bank
name **Rev:** Beognia

Date	Mintage	F	VF	XF	Unc	BU
2002	—	—	—	—	1.50	2.50

KM# 1188   2 WON
7.0000 g., 0.9990 Silver 0.2248 oz. ASW, 30 mm. **Obv:** National
arms, Central Bank name **Rev:** Panda in color

Date	Mintage	F	VF	XF	Unc	BU
2008 Proof	Est. 5,000	Value: 30.00				

KM# 1217   2 WON
7.0000 g., 0.9990 Silver 0.2248 oz. ASW, 30 mm. **Obv:** National
arms, Central Bank name **Rev:** Panda in color

Date	Mintage	F	VF	XF	Unc	BU
2009 Proof	Est. 5,000	Value: 30.00				

KM# 1220   2 WON
7.0000 g., 0.9990 Silver 0.2248 oz. ASW, 30 mm. **Obv:** National
arms, Central Bank name **Rev:** Corwn gate of the Dresden
Zwingers

Date	Mintage	F	VF	XF	Unc	BU
2009 Proof	—	Value: 30.00				

KM# 1221   2 WON
7.0000 g., 0.9990 Silver 0.2248 oz. ASW, 30 mm. **Obv:** National
arms, Central Bank name **Rev:** Acropolis in Athens

Date	Mintage	F	VF	XF	Unc	BU
2009 Proof	—	Value: 30.00				

KM# 1222   2 WON
7.0000 g., 0.9990 Silver 0.2248 oz. ASW, 30 mm. **Obv:** National
arms, Central Bank name **Rev:** Sydney Opera House

Date	Mintage	F	VF	XF	Unc	BU
2009 Proof	—	Value: 30.00				

KM# 1223   2 WON
7.0000 g., 0.9990 Silver 0.2248 oz. ASW, 30 mm. **Obv:** National
arms, Central Bank name **Rev:** Angkor Wat temple complex

Date	Mintage	F	VF	XF	Unc	BU
2009 Proof	—	Value: 30.00				

KM# 1224   2 WON
7.0000 g., 0.9990 Silver 0.2248 oz. ASW, 30 mm. **Obv:** National
arms, Central Bank name **Rev:** Minakshi and Sundareshwara
temples in Madurai

Date	Mintage	F	VF	XF	Unc	BU
2009 Proof	—	Value: 30.00				

KM# 1225   2 WON
7.0000 g., 0.9990 Silver 0.2248 oz. ASW, 30 mm. **Obv:** National
arms, Central Bank name **Rev:** Kremlin in Moscow

Date	Mintage	F	VF	XF	Unc	BU
2009 Proof	—	Value: 30.00				

KM# 1226   2 WON
7.0000 g., 0.9990 Silver 0.2248 oz. ASW, 30 mm. **Obv:** National
arms, Central Bank name **Rev:** Abu Simbel

Date	Mintage	F	VF	XF	Unc	BU
2009 Proof	—	Value: 30.00				

KM# 1227   2 WON
7.0000 g., 0.9990 Silver 0.2248 oz. ASW, 30 mm. **Obv:** National
arms, Central Bank name **Rev:** Eiffel Tower in Paris

Date	Mintage	F	VF	XF	Unc	BU
2009 Proof	—	Value: 30.00				

KM# 1228   2 WON
7.0000 g., 0.9990 Silver 0.2248 oz. ASW, 30 mm. **Obv:** National
arms, Central Bank name **Rev:** Dalai Lama's Palace in Lhasa

Date	Mintage	F	VF	XF	Unc	BU
2009 Proof	—	Value: 30.00				

KM# 1229   2 WON
7.0000 g., 0.9990 Silver 0.2248 oz. ASW, 30 mm. **Obv:** National
arms, Central Bank name **Rev:** Terracotta warriors of King Qin
Shihuangdi in China

Date	Mintage	F	VF	XF	Unc	BU
2009 Proof	—	Value: 30.00				

KM# 1230   2 WON
7.0000 g., 0.9990 Silver 0.2248 oz. ASW, 30 mm. **Obv:** National
arms, Central Bank name **Rev:** Palace at Versailles

Date	Mintage	F	VF	XF	Unc	BU
2009 Proof	—	Value: 30.00				

KM# 1231   2 WON
7.0000 g., 0.9990 Silver 0.2248 oz. ASW, 30 mm. **Obv:** National arms, Central Bank name **Rev:** Aachen Cathedral

Date	Mintage	F	VF	XF	Unc	BU
2010 Proof	—	Value: 30.00				

KM# 1232   2 WON
7.0000 g., 0.9990 Silver 0.2248 oz. ASW, 30 mm. **Obv:** National arms, Central Bank name **Rev:** Leaning Tower of Pisa

Date	Mintage	F	VF	XF	Unc	BU
2010 Proof	—	Value: 30.00				

KM# 1233   2 WON
7.0000 g., 0.9990 Silver 0.2248 oz. ASW, 30 mm. **Obv:** National arms, Central Bank name **Rev:** Chapel in Luzern

Date	Mintage	F	VF	XF	Unc	BU
2010 Proof	—	Value: 30.00				

KM# 1272   2 WON
7.0000 g., 0.9990 Silver 0.2248 oz. ASW, 30 mm. **Obv:** National arms, Central Bank name **Rev:** Three pandas in color

Date	Mintage	F	VF	XF	Unc	BU
2010 Proof	Est. 5,000	Value: 30.00				

KM# 1276   2 WON
7.0000 g., 0.9990 Silver 0.2248 oz. ASW, 30 mm. **Obv:** National arms, Central Bank name **Rev:** Great Mosque of Cordoba

Date	Mintage	F	VF	XF	Unc	BU
2010 Proof	—	Value: 30.00				

KM# 1277   2 WON
7.0000 g., 0.9990 Silver 0.2248 oz. ASW, 30 mm. **Obv:** National arms, Central Bank name **Rev:** Cathedral of Santiago de Compostela

Date	Mintage	F	VF	XF	Unc	BU
2010 Proof	—	Value: 30.00				

KM# 1278   2 WON
7.0000 g., 0.9990 Silver 0.2248 oz. ASW, 30 mm. **Obv:** National arms, Central Bank name **Rev:** Timbuktu

Date	Mintage	F	VF	XF	Unc	BU
2010 Proof	—	Value: 30.00				

KM# 1279   2 WON
7.0000 g., 0.9990 Silver 0.2248 oz. ASW, 30 mm. **Obv:** National arms, Central Bank name **Rev:** London's Big Ben clock tower

Date	Mintage	F	VF	XF	Unc	BU
2010 Proof	—	Value: 30.00				

KM# 1280   2 WON
7.0000 g., 0.9990 Silver 0.2248 oz. ASW, 30 mm. **Obv:** National arms, Central Bank name **Rev:** Prague castle

Date	Mintage	F	VF	XF	Unc	BU
2010 Proof	—	Value: 30.00				

KM# 1281   2 WON
7.0000 g., 0.9990 Silver 0.2248 oz. ASW, 30 mm. **Obv:** National arms, Central Bank name **Rev:** Teoihuacan pyramid

Date	Mintage	F	VF	XF	Unc	BU
2010 Proof	—	Value: 30.00				

KM# 1282   2 WON
7.0000 g., 0.9990 Silver 0.2248 oz. ASW, 30 mm. **Obv:** National arms, Central Bank name **Rev:** Forbidden city

Date	Mintage	F	VF	XF	Unc	BU
2010 Proof	—	Value: 30.00				

KM# 1189   5 WON
20.0000 g., 0.9990 Silver 0.6423 oz. ASW, 38 mm. **Obv:** National arms, Central Bank name **Rev:** Sailing ship Grand Duchess Elizabeth

Date	Mintage	F	VF	XF	Unc	BU
2008 Proof	Est. 5,000	Value: 45.00				

KM# 1191   5 WON
20.0000 g., 0.9990 Silver 0.6423 oz. ASW, 38 mm. **Obv:** National arms, Central Bank name **Rev:** Four-masted schooner Elizabeth Bandi and three-masted bark Seute Deern

Date	Mintage	F	VF	XF	Unc	BU
2008 Proof	Est. 5,000	Value: 45.00				

KM# 1219   5 WON
20.0000 g., 0.9990 Silver 0.6423 oz. ASW, 38 mm. **Obv:** National arms, Central Bank name **Rev:** U.S.C.G. Barque Eagle

Date	Mintage	F	VF	XF	Unc	BU
2008 Proof	—	Value: 45.00				

KM# 1190   5 WON
20.0000 g., 0.9990 Silver 0.6423 oz. ASW, 38 mm. **Obv:** National arms, Central Bank name **Rev:** Three-masted sailing ship Passat

Date	Mintage	F	VF	XF	Unc	BU
2009 Proof	Est. 5,000	Value: 45.00				

KM# 1192   5 WON
20.0000 g., 0.9990 Silver 0.6423 oz. ASW, 38 mm. **Obv:** National arms, Central Bank name **Rev:** Sail training ship Deutschland

Date	Mintage	F	VF	XF	Unc	BU
2009 Proof	Est. 5,000	Value: 45.00				

KM# 1193   5 WON
20.0000 g., 0.9990 Silver 0.6423 oz. ASW, 38 mm. **Obv:** National arms, Central Bank name **Rev:** Three-masted sailing ship Gorch Fock II

Date	Mintage	F	VF	XF	Unc	BU
2009 Proof	Est. 5,000	Value: 45.00				

KM# 1218   5 WON
20.0000 g., 0.9990 Silver 0.6423 oz. ASW, 38 mm. **Obv:** National arms, Central Bank name **Rev:** Sailing ship Dar Mlodziezy

Date	Mintage	F	VF	XF	Unc	BU
2009 Proof	—	Value: 45.00				

KM# 1273   5 WON
20.0000 g., 0.9990 Silver 0.6423 oz. ASW, 38 mm. **Obv:** National arms, Central Bank name **Rev:** Philippine hood eagle

Date	Mintage	F	VF	XF	Unc	BU
2010 Proof	—	Value: 60.00				

KM# 1274   5 WON
20.0000 g., 0.9990 Silver 0.6423 oz. ASW, 38 mm. **Obv:** National arms, Central Bank name **Rev:** Tibetian ox

Date	Mintage	F	VF	XF	Unc	BU
2010 Proof	—	Value: 60.00				

KM# 1194   10 WON
1.0000 g., 0.9160 Gold 0.0294 oz. AGW, 16 mm. **Obv:** National arms, Central Bank name **Rev:** Rickmer Rickmers

Date	Mintage	F	VF	XF	Unc	BU
2008	7,500	—	—	—	—	75.00

KM# 1195   10 WON
1.0000 g., 0.9160 Gold 0.0294 oz. AGW, 16 mm. **Obv:** National arms, Central Bank name **Rev:** Prussen

Date	Mintage	F	VF	XF	Unc	BU
2008	Est. 7,500	—	—	—	—	75.00

KM# 1196.1   10 WON
1.0000 g., 0.9160 Gold 0.0294 oz. AGW, 16 mm. **Obv:** National arms, Central Bank name **Rev:** Alexander von Humboldt **Rev: Legend:** ...Humoldt **Note:** Error spelling of ship's name

Date	Mintage	F	VF	XF	Unc	BU
2008	401	—	—	—	—	90.00

KM# 1196.2   10 WON
1.0000 g., 0.9160 Gold 0.0294 oz. AGW, 16 mm. **Obv:** National arms, Central Bank name **Rev:** Alexander von Humbolt **Rev: Legend:** ...Humboldt **Note:** Ship's name corrected.

Date	Mintage	F	VF	XF	Unc	BU
2008	7,100	—	—	—	—	75.00

KM# 1197   10 WON
1.0000 g., 0.9160 Gold 0.0294 oz. AGW, 16 mm. **Obv:** National arms, Central Bank name **Rev:** Grand Duchess Elizabeth

Date	Mintage	F	VF	XF	Unc	BU
2008	Est. 7,500	—	—	—	—	75.00

KM# 1198   10 WON
1.0000 g., 0.9160 Gold 0.0294 oz. AGW, 16 mm. **Obv:** National arms, Central Bank name **Rev:** Three masted training ship Passat

Date	Mintage	F	VF	XF	Unc	BU
2008	7,500	—	—	—	—	75.00

KM# 1199   10 WON
1.0000 g., 0.9160 Gold 0.0294 oz. AGW, 16 mm. **Obv:** National arms, Central Bank name **Rev:** Four-masted schoner Elizabeth Bandi and three-masted bark Seute Deern

Date	Mintage	F	VF	XF	Unc	BU
2008 Proof	—	—	—	—	—	75.00

KM# 1200   10 WON
1.0000 g., 0.9160 Gold 0.0294 oz. AGW, 16 mm. **Obv:** National arms, Central Bank name **Rev:** Sail training ship Deutschland

Date	Mintage	F	VF	XF	Unc	BU
2008	Est. 7,500	—	—	—	—	75.00

KM# 1201   10 WON
1.0000 g., 0.9160 Gold 0.0294 oz. AGW, 16 mm. **Obv:** National arms, Central Bank name **Rev:** Three-masted barque Gorch Fock II

Date	Mintage	F	VF	XF	Unc	BU
2008	Est. 7,500	—	—	—	—	75.00

KM# 1235   10 WON
0.5000 g., 0.9990 Gold 0.0161 oz. AGW, 11 mm. **Obv:** National arms, Central Bank name **Rev:** Alhambra in Granada

Date	Mintage	F	VF	XF	Unc	BU
2009 Proof	—	Value: 35.00				

KM# 1234   10 WON
0.5000 g., 0.9990 Gold 0.0161 oz. AGW, 11 mm. **Obv:** National arms, Central Bank name **Rev:** Cathedral of the Holy Family in Barcelona

Date	Mintage	F	VF	XF	Unc	BU
2009 Proof	—	Value: 35.00				

KM# 1236   10 WON
1.0000 g., 0.9990 Gold 0.0321 oz. AGW, 14 mm. **Obv:** National arms, Central Bank name **Rev:** Crown tower in Dresden Zwigers

Date	Mintage	F	VF	XF	Unc	BU
2009 Proof	—	Value: 70.00				

KM# 1237   10 WON
1.0000 g., 0.9990 Gold 0.0321 oz. AGW, 14 mm. **Obv:** National arms, Central Bank name **Rev:** Acropolis in Athens

Date	Mintage	F	VF	XF	Unc	BU
2009 Proof	—	Value: 70.00				

KM# 1238   10 WON
1.0000 g., 0.9990 Silver 0.0321 oz. ASW, 14 mm. **Obv:** National arms, Central Bank name **Rev:** Sydney Opera House

Date	Mintage	F	VF	XF	Unc	BU
2009 Proof	—	Value: 70.00				

KM# 1239   10 WON
1.0000 g., 0.9990 Gold 0.0321 oz. AGW, 14 mm. **Obv:** National arms, Central Bank name **Rev:** Angkor Wat temple complex

Date	Mintage	F	VF	XF	Unc	BU
2009 Proof	—	Value: 70.00				

KM# 1240   10 WON
1.0000 g., 0.9990 Gold 0.0321 oz. AGW, 14 mm. **Obv:** National arms, Central Bank name **Rev:** Minaksji and Sundareshwara Temples in Maduari

Date	Mintage	F	VF	XF	Unc	BU
2009 Proof	—	Value: 70.00				

KM# 1241   10 WON
1.0000 g., 0.9990 Gold 0.0321 oz. AGW, 14 mm. **Obv:** National arms, Central Bank name **Rev:** Kremlin in Moscow

Date	Mintage	F	VF	XF	Unc	BU
2009 Proof	—	Value: 70.00				

KM# 1242   10 WON
1.0000 g., 0.9990 Gold 0.0321 oz. AGW, 14 mm. **Obv:** National arms, Central Bank name **Rev:** Abu Simbel

Date	Mintage	F	VF	XF	Unc	BU
2009 Proof	—	Value: 70.00				

KM# 1243   10 WON
1.0000 g., 0.9990 Gold 0.0321 oz. AGW, 14 mm. **Obv:** National arms, Central Bank name **Rev:** Eiffel Tower in Paris

Date	Mintage	F	VF	XF	Unc	BU
2009 Proof	—	Value: 70.00				

KM# 1244   10 WON
1.0000 g., 0.9990 Gold 0.0321 oz. AGW, 14 mm. **Obv:** National arms, Central Bank name **Rev:** Dali Lama's Palace in Lhasa

Date	Mintage	F	VF	XF	Unc	BU
2009 Proof	—	Value: 70.00				

KM# 1245   10 WON
1.0000 g., 0.9990 Gold 0.0321 oz. AGW, 14 mm. **Obv:** National arms, Central Bank name **Rev:** Terra Cotta Warriors

Date	Mintage	F	VF	XF	Unc	BU
2009 Proof	—	Value: 70.00				

KM# 1246   10 WON
1.0000 g., 0.9990 Gold 0.0321 oz. AGW, 14 mm. **Obv:** National arms, Central Bank name **Rev:** Palace in Versalles

Date	Mintage	F	VF	XF	Unc	BU
2009 Proof	—	Value: 70.00				

KM# 1247   10 WON
1.0000 g., 0.9990 Gold 0.0321 oz. AGW, 14 mm. **Obv:** National arms, Central Bank name **Rev:** Aachen Cathedral

Date	Mintage	F	VF	XF	Unc	BU
2009 Proof	—	Value: 70.00				

KM# 1248   10 WON
1.0000 g., 0.9990 Gold 0.0321 oz. AGW, 14 mm. **Obv:** National arms, Central Bank name **Rev:** Leaning tower of Pisa

Date	Mintage	F	VF	XF	Unc	BU
2009 Proof	—	Value: 70.00				

KM# 1249   10 WON
1.0000 g., 0.9990 Gold 0.0321 oz. AGW, 14 mm. **Obv:** National arms, Central Bank name **Rev:** Chapel in Luzern

Date	Mintage	F	VF	XF	Unc	BU
2009 Proof	—	Value: 70.00				

KM# 1262   10 WON
Brass, 40 mm. **Obv:** National arms, Central Bank name **Rev:** South tower in Kaeseong

Date	Mintage	F	VF	XF	Unc	BU
2010 Proof	—	Value: 7.00				

KM# 1263   10 WON
Brass, 40 mm. **Obv:** National arms, Central Bank name **Rev:** Mausoleum of King Wanggeon

Date	Mintage	F	VF	XF	Unc	BU
2010 Proof	—	Value: 7.00				

KM# 1264   10 WON
Brass, 40 mm. **Obv:** National arms, Central Bank name **Rev:** Birthplace of Pyochung

Date	Mintage	F	VF	XF	Unc	BU
2010 Proof	—	Value: 7.00				

KM# 1265   10 WON
Brass, 40 mm. **Obv:** National arms, Central Bank name **Rev:** Stone pagoda of Hyunhwa in Seongkyunkwan

Date	Mintage	F	VF	XF	Unc	BU
2010 Proof	—	Value: 7.00				

KM# 1266   10 WON
Brass, 40 mm. **Obv:** National arms, Central Bank name **Rev:** Seongkyunkwan

Date	Mintage	F	VF	XF	Unc	BU
2010 Proof	—	Value: 7.00				

KM# 1267   10 WON
Brass, 40 mm. **Obv:** National arms, Central Bank name **Rev:**

Anhwa Temple

Date	Mintage	F	VF	XF	Unc	BU
2010 Proof	—	Value: 7.00				

KM# 1268 10 WON
Brass, 40 mm. **Obv:** National arms, Central Bank name **Rev:** Nahanjun in Anhwa Temple

Date	Mintage	F	VF	XF	Unc	BU
2010 Proof	—	Value: 7.00				

KM# 1269 10 WON
Brass, 40 mm. **Obv:** National arms, Central Bank name **Rev:** Turned wheel in Yungtong Temple

Date	Mintage	F	VF	XF	Unc	BU
2010 Proof	—	Value: 7.00				

KM# 1270 10 WON
Brass, 40 mm. **Obv:** National arms, Central Bank name **Rev:** Shrine in Sungyang Sowon

Date	Mintage	F	VF	XF	Unc	BU
2010 Proof	—	Value: 7.00				

KM# 1271 10 WON
Brass, 40 mm. **Obv:** National arms, Central Bank name **Rev:** Waterfall in Pakyeon

Date	Mintage	F	VF	XF	Unc	BU
2010 Proof	—	Value: 7.00				

KM# 1275 10 WON
0.5000 g., 0.9990 Gold 0.0161 oz. AGW, 11 mm. **Obv:** National arms, Central Bank name **Rev:** Ernesto "Che" Guevara

Date	Mintage	F	VF	XF	Unc	BU
2010 Proof	—	Value: 50.00				

KM# 1283 10 WON
1.0000 g., 0.9990 Gold 0.0321 oz. AGW, 14 mm. **Obv:** National arms, Central Bank name **Rev:** Grand Mosque in Cordoba

Date	Mintage	F	VF	XF	Unc	BU
2010 Proof	—	Value: 70.00				

KM# 1284 10 WON
1.0000 g., 0.9990 Gold 0.0321 oz. AGW, 14 mm. **Obv:** National arms, Central Bank name **Rev:** Cathedral of Santiago de Compostela

Date	Mintage	F	VF	XF	Unc	BU
2010 Proof	—	Value: 70.00				

KM# 1285 10 WON
1.0000 g., 0.9990 Gold 0.0321 oz. AGW, 14 mm. **Obv:** National arms, Central Bank name **Rev:** Timbuktu

Date	Mintage	F	VF	XF	Unc	BU
2010 Proof	—	Value: 70.00				

KM# 1286 10 WON
1.0000 g., 0.9990 Silver 0.0321 oz. ASW, 14 mm. **Obv:** National arms, Central Bank name **Rev:** London's Big Ben tower

Date	Mintage	F	VF	XF	Unc	BU
2010 Proof	—	Value: 70.00				

KM# 1287 10 WON
1.0000 g., 0.9990 Gold 0.0321 oz. AGW, 14 mm. **Obv:** National arms, Central Bank name **Rev:** Prague castle

Date	Mintage	F	VF	XF	Unc	BU
2010 Proof	—	Value: 70.00				

KM# 1288 10 WON
1.0000 g., 0.9990 Gold 0.0321 oz. AGW, 14 mm. **Obv:** National arms, Central Bank name **Rev:** Teotihuacan pyramid

Date	Mintage	F	VF	XF	Unc	BU
2010 Proof	—	Value: 70.00				

KM# 1289 10 WON
1.0000 g., 0.9990 Silver 0.0321 oz. ASW, 14 mm. **Obv:** National arms, Central Bank name **Rev:** Forbidden City

Date	Mintage	F	VF	XF	Unc	BU
2010 Proof	—	Value: 70.00				

KM# 1175 20 WON
28.0000 g., Brass, 40 mm. **Obv:** East gate of Pyeongyang **Rev:** Dragon in color

Date	Mintage	F	VF	XF	Unc	BU
2008 Proof	—	Value: 7.50				

KM# 1202 20 WON
Brass, 30 mm. **Obv:** East gate of Pyeongyang **Rev:** Rat in color

Date	Mintage	F	VF	XF	Unc	BU
2009 Proof	—	Value: 6.00				

KM# 1203 20 WON
Brass, 30 mm. **Obv:** East gate of Pyeongyang **Rev:** Ox in color

Date	Mintage	F	VF	XF	Unc	BU
2009 Proof	—	Value: 6.00				

KM# 1204 20 WON
Brass, 30 mm. **Obv:** East gate of Pyeongyang **Rev:** Tiger in color

Date	Mintage	F	VF	XF	Unc	BU
2009 Proof	—	Value: 6.00				

KM# 1205 20 WON
Brass, 30 mm. **Obv:** East gate of Pyeongyang **Rev:** Rabbit in color

Date	Mintage	F	VF	XF	Unc	BU
2009 Proof	—	Value: 6.00				

KM# 1206 20 WON
Brass, 30 mm. **Obv:** East gate of Pyeongyang **Rev:** Dragon in color

Date	Mintage	F	VF	XF	Unc	BU
2009 Proof	—	Value: 6.00				

KM# 1207 20 WON
Brass, 30 mm. **Obv:** East gate of Pyeongyang **Rev:** Snake in color

Date	Mintage	F	VF	XF	Unc	BU
2009 Proof	—	Value: 6.00				

KM# 1208 20 WON
Brass, 30 mm. **Obv:** East gate of Pyeongyang **Rev:** Horse in color

Date	Mintage	F	VF	XF	Unc	BU
2009 Proof	—	Value: 6.00				

KM# 1209 20 WON
Brass, 30 mm. **Obv:** East gate of Pyeongyang **Rev:** Goat in color

Date	Mintage	F	VF	XF	Unc	BU
2009 Proof	—	Value: 6.00				

KM# 1210 20 WON
Brass, 30 mm. **Obv:** East gate of Pyeongyang **Rev:** Monkey in color

Date	Mintage	F	VF	XF	Unc	BU
2009 Proof	—	Value: 6.00				

KM# 1211 20 WON
Brass, 30 mm. **Obv:** East gate of Pyeongyang **Rev:** Rooster in color

Date	Mintage	F	VF	XF	Unc	BU
2009 Proof	—	Value: 6.00				

KM# 1212 20 WON
Brass, 30 mm. **Obv:** East gate of Pyeongyang **Rev:** Dog in color

Date	Mintage	F	VF	XF	Unc	BU
2009 Proof	—	Value: 6.00				

KM# 1213 20 WON
Brass, 30 mm. **Obv:** East gate of Pyeongyang **Rev:** Pin in color

Date	Mintage	F	VF	XF	Unc	BU
2009 Proof	—	Value: 6.00				

KM# 492 20 WON
Aluminum, 45 mm. **Obv:** Raised Pagoda in ornamental loop **Rev:** Hippopotamus with color inlay **Rev. Legend:** Hippopotamus amphibius **Edge:** Plain

Date	Mintage	F	VF	XF	Unc	BU
2010	—	—	—	—	—	20.00

KM# 493 20 WON
Aluminum, 45 mm. **Obv:** Raised Pagoda with ornamental loop **Rev:** Rabbit with color inlay **Edge:** Plain

Date	Mintage	F	VF	XF	Unc	BU
2010	—	—	—	—	—	20.00

KM# 494 20 WON
Aluminum, 45 mm. **Obv:** Raised Pagoda in ornamental loop **Rev:** Deer with color inlay **Edge:** Plain

Date	Mintage	F	VF	XF	Unc	BU
2010	—	—	—	—	—	20.00

KM# 1250 20 WON
Brass, 45 mm. **Obv:** East gate in Pyeongyang **Rev:** Rat in center of Zodiac

Date	Mintage	F	VF	XF	Unc	BU
2010 Proof	—	—	—	—	—	7.00

KM# 1251 20 WON
Brass, 45 mm. **Obv:** East gate in Pyeongyang **Rev:** Buffalo at center of Zodiac

Date	Mintage	F	VF	XF	Unc	BU
2010 Proof	—	Value: 7.00				

KM# 1252 20 WON
Brass, 45 mm. **Obv:** East gate in Pyeongyang **Rev:** Tiger at center of Zodiac

Date	Mintage	F	VF	XF	Unc	BU
2010 Proof	—	Value: 7.00				

KM# 1253 20 WON
Brass, 45 mm. **Obv:** East gate in Pyeongyang **Rev:** Rabbit in center of Zodiac

Date	Mintage	F	VF	XF	Unc	BU
2010 Proof	—	Value: 7.00				

KM# 1254 20 WON
Brass, 45 mm. **Obv:** East gate in Pyeongyang **Rev:** Dragon at center of Zodiac

Date	Mintage	F	VF	XF	Unc	BU
2010 Proof	—	Value: 7.00				

KM# 1255 20 WON
Brass, 45 mm. **Obv:** East gate in Pyeongyang **Rev:** Snake in center of Zodiac

Date	Mintage	F	VF	XF	Unc	BU
2010 Proof	—	Value: 7.00				

KM# 1256 20 WON
Brass, 45 mm. **Obv:** East gate in Pyeongyang **Rev:** Horse in center of Zodiac

Date	Mintage	F	VF	XF	Unc	BU
2010 Proof	—	Value: 7.00				

KM# 1257 20 WON
Brass, 45 mm. **Obv:** East gate in Pyeongyang **Rev:** Goat in center of Zodiac

Date	Mintage	F	VF	XF	Unc	BU
2010 Proof	—	Value: 7.00				

KM# 1258 20 WON
Brass, 45 mm. **Obv:** East gate in Pyeongyang **Rev:** Monkey in center of Zodiac

Date	Mintage	F	VF	XF	Unc	BU
2010 Proof	—	Value: 7.00				

KM# 1259 20 WON
Brass, 45 mm. **Obv:** East gate in Pyeongyang **Rev:** Rooster in center of Zodiac

Date	Mintage	F	VF	XF	Unc	BU
2010 Proof	—	Value: 7.00				

KM# 1260 20 WON
Brass, 45 mm. **Obv:** East gate in Pyeongyang **Rev:** Dog in center of Zodiac

Date	Mintage	F	VF	XF	Unc	BU
2010 Proof	—	Value: 7.00				

KM# 1261 20 WON
Brass, 45 mm. **Obv:** East gate in Pyeongyang **Rev:** Pig in center of Zodiac

Date	Mintage	F	VF	XF	Unc	BU
2010 Proof	—	Value: 7.00				

KM# 1214 350 WON
6.2000 g., 0.9990 Silver 0.1991 oz. ASW, 35 mm. **Obv:** East gate of Pyeongyang **Rev:** Chinese Junk, Marco Polo

Date	Mintage	F	VF	XF	Unc	BU
2009 Proof	Est. 5,000	Value: 25.00				

KM# 1215 350 WON
6.2000 g., 0.9990 Silver 0.1991 oz. ASW, 35 mm. **Obv:** East gate of Pyeongyang **Rev:** Viking ship and map of the Atlantic, Leif Eriksson

Date	Mintage	F	VF	XF	Unc	BU
2009 Proof	Est. 5,000	Value: 25.00				

KM# 1216 1000 WON
20.0000 g., 0.9990 Silver 0.6423 oz. ASW, 38 mm. **Subject:** World Cup Soccer, South Africa, 2010 **Obv:** East gate of Pyeongyang **Rev:** Two soccer players

Date	Mintage	F	VF	XF	Unc	BU
2009 Proof	Est. 10,000	Value: 35.00				

SOUTH KOREA

The Republic of Korea, situated in northeastern Asia on the southern half of the Korean peninsula between North Korea and the Korean Strait, has an area of 38,025 sq. mi. (98,480 sq. km.) and a population of 42.5 million. Capital: Seoul. The economy is based on agriculture and light and medium industry. Some of the world's largest oil tankers are built here. Automobiles, plywood, electronics, and textile products are exported.

NOTE: For earlier coinage see Korea.

MINT

KOMSCO - Korea Minting and Security Printing Corporation

REPUBLIC

REFORM COINAGE

10 Hwan = 1 Won

KM# 31   WON

0.7290 g., Aluminum, 17.2 mm. **Obv:** Rose of Sharon **Rev:** Value and date

Date	Mintage	F	VF	XF	Unc	BU
2001	130,000	—	—	—	0.15	0.25
2002	122,000	—	—	—	0.15	0.25
2003	20,000	—	—	—	0.15	0.25
2004	25,500	—	—	—	0.15	0.25
2005	38,000	—	—	—	0.15	0.25
2006	53,000	—	—	—	0.15	0.25
2007	53,000	—	—	—	0.15	0.25
2010	—	—	—	—	0.15	0.25
2011	—	—	—	—	0.15	0.25

KM# 32   5 WON

2.9500 g., Brass, 20.4 mm. **Obv:** Iron-clad turtle boat **Rev:** Value and date **Edge:** Plain

Date	Mintage	F	VF	XF	Unc	BU
2001	130,000	—	—	0.10	0.20	0.30
2002	120,000	—	—	0.10	0.20	0.30
2003	20,000	—	—	0.10	0.20	0.30
2004	25,500	—	—	0.10	0.20	0.30
2005	38,000	—	—	0.10	0.20	0.30
2006	53,000	—	—	0.10	0.20	0.30
2007	53,000	—	—	0.10	0.20	0.30
2008	—	—	—	0.10	0.20	0.30
2009	—	—	—	0.10	0.20	0.30
2010	—	—	—	0.10	0.20	0.30
2011	—	—	—	0.10	0.20	0.30

KM# 33.2   10 WON

4.0600 g., Brass **Obv:** Pagoda at Pul Guk Temple **Rev:** Thicker value below date

Date	Mintage	F	VF	XF	Unc	BU
2001	345,000,000	—	—	—	0.35	0.50
2002	100,000,000	—	—	—	0.35	0.50
2003	128,000,000	—	—	—	0.35	0.50
2004	135,000,000	—	—	—	0.35	0.50
2005	250,000,000	—	—	—	0.35	0.50

KM# 33.2a   10 WON

1.2200 g., Aluminum-Bronze, 18 mm. **Obv:** Pagoda at Pul Guk Temple **Rev:** Value below date

Date	Mintage	F	VF	XF	Unc	BU
2006	109,200,000	—	—	—	0.10	0.35
2007	—	—	—	—	0.10	0.35

Date	Mintage	F	VF	XF	Unc	BU
2008	—	—	—	—	0.10	0.35
2009	—	—	—	—	0.10	0.35

KM# 103   10 WON

1.2200 g., Copper Clad Aluminum, 18 mm. **Obv:** Pagoda at Pul Guk Temple **Rev:** Value below date **Edge:** Plain **Mint:** KOMSCO **Note:** Prev. KM #106.

Date	Mintage	F	VF	XF	Unc	BU
2006	40,800,000	—	—	0.10	0.20	0.25
2007	210,000,000	—	—	0.10	0.20	0.25
2008	—	—	—	0.10	0.20	0.25
2009	—	—	—	0.10	0.20	0.25
2010	—	—	—	0.10	0.20	0.25
2011	—	—	—	0.10	0.20	0.25

KM# 34   50 WON

4.1600 g., Copper-Nickel-Zinc, 21.6 mm. **Series:** F.A.O. **Obv:** Text below sagging oat sprig **Rev:** Value and date **Edge:** Reeded **Note:** Die varieties exist.

Date	Mintage	F	VF	XF	Unc	BU
2001	102,000,000	—	—	0.10	0.35	1.00
2002	100,000,000	—	—	0.10	0.35	0.50
2003	169,000,000	—	—	0.10	0.35	0.50
2004	100,000,000	—	—	0.10	0.45	1.00
2005	90,000,000	—	—	0.10	0.35	0.50
2006	120,000,000	—	—	0.10	0.35	0.50
2007	50,000,000	—	—	0.10	0.35	0.50
2008	—	—	—	0.10	0.35	0.50
2009	—	—	—	0.10	0.35	0.50
2010	—	—	—	0.10	0.35	0.50
2011	—	—	—	0.10	0.35	0.50

KM# 35.2   100 WON

5.4200 g., Copper-Nickel, 24 mm. **Obv:** Admiral Yi-Sun-Sin, large bust with hat facing **Rev:** Value and date **Edge:** Reeded

Date	Mintage	F	VF	XF	Unc	BU
2001	470,000,000	—	0.25	0.50	1.00	3.00
2002	490,000,000	—	0.15	0.25	0.55	1.00
2003	415,000,000	—	0.15	0.25	0.55	1.00
2004	250,000,000	—	0.15	0.25	0.55	1.00
2005	205,000,000	—	0.15	0.25	0.55	1.00
2006	310,000,000	—	0.15	0.25	0.55	0.75
2007	240,000,000	—	0.15	0.25	0.55	0.75
2008	—	—	0.15	0.25	0.55	0.75
2009	—	—	0.15	0.25	0.55	0.75
2010	—	—	0.15	0.25	0.55	0.75
2011	—	—	0.15	0.25	0.55	0.75

KM# 27   500 WON

7.7000 g., Copper-Nickel, 26.5 mm. **Obv:** Manchurian crane **Rev:** Value and date **Edge:** Reeded

Date	Mintage	F	VF	XF	Unc	BU
2001	113,000,000	—	—	1.00	2.50	5.00
2002	110,000,000	—	—	1.00	2.50	5.00
2003	122,000,000	—	—	1.00	2.50	5.00
2004	45,000,000	—	—	1.00	2.50	5.00
2005	105,000,000	—	—	1.00	2.50	5.00
2006	170,000,000	—	—	1.00	2.50	5.00
2007	70,000,000	—	—	1.00	2.50	5.00
2008	—	—	—	1.00	2.50	5.00
2009	—	—	—	1.00	2.50	5.00
2010	—	—	—	1.00	2.50	5.00
2011	—	—	—	1.00	2.50	5.00

KM# 89   1000 WON

12.0000 g., Brass, 32 mm. **Series:** World Cup Soccer **Obv:** FIFA World Cup logo **Rev:** Mascot soccer player **Edge:** Reeded **Mint:** Seoul

Date	Mintage	F	VF	XF	Unc	BU
2001	102,000	—	—	—	10.00	12.00

KM# 112   1000 WON

12.0000 g., Aluminum-Bronze, 32 mm. **Rev:** Soccer player **Mint:** KOMSCO

Date	Mintage	F	VF	XF	Unc	BU
2002	102,002	—	—	—	—	12.50

KM# 127   1000 WON

10.1000 g., Tri-Metallic Copper center in Copper-Nickel inner ring in Copper-Nickel-Zinc outer ring, 28.2 mm. **Subject:** Expo 2012 **Obv:** Mascots Yeony and Suny **Rev:** Expo logo **Mint:** KOMSCO

Date	Mintage	F	VF	XF	Unc	BU
2012	137,512	—	—	—	—	20.00

KM# 115   2000 WON

26.0000 g., Copper, 40 mm. **Subject:** 14th Asian Games, Busan **Rev:** Bird sanctuary **Mint:** KOMSCO

Date	Mintage	F	VF	XF	Unc	BU
2002 Proof	—	Value: 20.00				

KM# 116   2000 WON

26.0000 g., Copper-Nickel, 40 mm. **Rev:** Torch and sport images **Mint:** KOMSCO

Date	Mintage	F	VF	XF	Unc	BU
2002 Proof	—	Value: 30.00				

KM# 124   5000 WON

15.5000 g., 0.9990 Silver 0.4978 oz. ASW, 32 mm. **Subject:** Expo 2012 **Obv:** Korean Pavilion with latent image **Rev:** Expo logo in color **Mint:** KOMSCO

Date	Mintage	F	VF	XF	Unc	BU
2012 Proof	20,000	Value: 45.00				

KM# 125   5000 WON

15.5000 g., 0.9990 Silver 0.4978 oz. ASW, 32 mm. **Subject:** Expo 2012 **Obv:** Theme Pavilion and latent image **Rev:** Expo logo in color **Mint:** KOMSCO

Date	Mintage	F	VF	XF	Unc	BU
2012 Proof	20,000	Value: 40.00				

KM# 90   10000 WON

31.1035 g., 0.9990 Silver 0.9990 oz. ASW, 35 mm. **Series:** World Cup Soccer **Subject:** Gwangju Stadium **Obv:** Multicolor soccer logo **Rev:** Player heading the ball **Edge:** Reeded **Mint:** Seoul

Date	Mintage	F	VF	XF	Unc	BU
2001 Proof	37,000	Value: 50.00				

KM# 91 10000 WON
31.1035 g., 0.9990 Silver 0.9990 oz. ASW, 35 mm. **Series:** World Sup Soccer **Subject:** Busan Stadium **Obv:** Multicolor soccer logo **Rev:** Player kicking the ball **Edge:** Reeded **Mint:** Seoul

Date	Mintage	F	VF	XF	Unc	BU
2001 Proof	37,000	Value: 50.00				

KM# 92 10000 WON
31.1035 g., 0.9990 Silver 0.9990 oz. ASW, 35 mm. **Series:** World Cup Soccer **Subject:** Daegu Stadium **Obv:** Multicolor soccer logo **Rev:** Player controlling the ball **Edge:** Reeded **Mint:** Seoul

Date	Mintage	F	VF	XF	Unc	BU
2001 Proof	37,000	Value: 50.00				

KM# 93 10000 WON
31.1035 g., 0.9990 Silver 0.9990 oz. ASW, 35 mm. **Series:** World Cup Soccer **Subject:** Suwon Stadium **Obv:** Multicolor soccer logo **Rev:** Player kicking the ball **Edge:** Reeded **Mint:** Seoul

Date	Mintage	F	VF	XF	Unc	BU
2001 Proof	37,000	Value: 50.00				

KM# 98 10000 WON
31.1035 g., 0.9990 Silver 0.9990 oz. ASW, 35 mm. **Obv:** Multicolor FIFA World Cup logo **Rev:** Player "Heading" ball **Edge:** Reeded **Mint:** Seoul

Date	Mintage	F	VF	XF	Unc	BU
2002 Proof	—	Value: 50.00				

KM# 99 10000 WON
31.1035 g., 0.9990 Silver 0.9990 oz. ASW, 35 mm. **Obv:** Multicolor FIFA World Cup logo **Rev:** Goalie catching ball **Edge:** Reeded **Mint:** Seoul

Date	Mintage	F	VF	XF	Unc	BU
2002 Proof	—	Value: 50.00				

KM# 100 10000 WON
31.1035 g., 0.9990 Silver 0.9990 oz. ASW, 35 mm. **Obv:** Multicolor FIFA World Cup logo **Rev:** Player's leg kicking ball **Edge:** Reeded **Mint:** Seoul

Date	Mintage	F	VF	XF	Unc	BU
2002 Proof	—	Value: 50.00				

KM# 101 10000 WON
31.1035 g., 0.9990 Silver 0.9990 oz. ASW, 35 mm. **Obv:** Multicolor FIFA World Cup logo **Rev:** Two players' legs and ball **Edge:** Reeded **Mint:** Seoul

Date	Mintage	F	VF	XF	Unc	BU
2002 Proof	—	Value: 50.00				

KM# 118 10000 WON
Silver, 38.61 mm. **Subject:** 14th Asian Games, Busan **Obv:** Multicolor games logo **Rev:** Two dancers **Mint:** KOMSCO

Date	Mintage	F	VF	XF	Unc	BU
2002 Proof	—	Value: 90.00				

KM# 117 10000 WON
31.1050 g., 0.9990 Silver 0.9990 oz. ASW, 40 mm. **Rev:** Stadium, mascot at top **Mint:** KOMSCO

Date	Mintage	F	VF	XF	Unc	BU
2005 Proof	—	Value: 90.00				

KM# 126 10000 WON
31.1050 g., 0.9990 Silver 0.9990 oz. ASW, 40 mm. **Subject:** Expo 2012 **Obv:** Exposition's Sky Tower and sea image **Rev:** Expo logo in color **Mint:** KOMSCO

Date	Mintage	F	VF	XF	Unc	BU
2012 Proof	20,000	Value: 60.00				

KM# 128 15000 WON
7.7700 g., 0.9990 Gold 0.2496 oz. AGW, 22 mm. **Subject:** Expo 2012 **Obv:** The Big-O maine stage **Rev:** Expo logo **Mint:** KOMSCO

Date	Mintage	F	VF	XF	Unc	BU
2012 Proof	10,000	Value: 500				

KM# 94 20000 WON
15.5518 g., 0.9990 Gold 0.4995 oz. AGW, 28 mm. **Series:** World Cup Soccer **Obv:** Soccer logo **Rev:** World Cup soccer trophy **Edge:** Reeded **Mint:** Seoul

Date	Mintage	F	VF	XF	Unc	BU
2001 Proof	20,000	Value: 900				

KM# 113 20000 WON
15.5500 g., 0.9990 Gold 0.4994 oz. AGW, 28 mm. **Rev:** World Cup venues on map **Mint:** KOMSCO

Date	Mintage	F	VF	XF	Unc	BU
2002 Proof	19,502	Value: 925				

KM# 119 20000 WON
15.5500 g., 0.9990 Gold 0.4994 oz. AGW **Subject:** 14th Asian Games, Busan **Obv:** Games logo **Rev:** Crown **Mint:** KOMSCO

Date	Mintage	F	VF	XF	Unc	BU
2002 Proof	—	Value: 925				

KM# 102 20000 WON
20.7000 g., 0.9990 Silver 0.6648 oz. ASW **Subject:** 60th Anniversary of Independence **Obv:** Adult hand reaching out towards child's hand **Mint:** KOMSCO **Note:** Prev. KM #103.

Date	Mintage	F	VF	XF	Unc	BU
2005 Proof	10,000	Value: 65.00				

KM# 97 20000 WON
20.7000 g., Silver, 35 mm. **Obv:** Blue circle with APEC, 2005 Korea at bottom at upper center, Vista Pacific Economic Cooperation and value below **Rev:** APEC on World map at upper center, building below with Korean words below it

Date	Mintage	F	VF	XF	Unc	BU
2005 Proof	10,000	Value: 65.00				

KM# 104 20000 WON
19.0000 g., 0.9990 Silver 0.6102 oz. ASW **Subject:** 560th Year of Hangeul - Alphabet characters **Obv:** Early alphabet characters **Legend:** THE BANK OF KOREA **Rev:** Modern alphabet characters **Shape:** Round with square center hole **Mint:** KOMSCO

Date	Mintage	F	VF	XF	Unc	BU
2006 Proof	—	Value: 75.00				

KM# 105 20000 WON
19.0000 g., 0.9990 Silver 0.6102 oz. ASW, 33.00 mm. **Series:** Traditional Folk Dance **Subject:** Talchum - Mask Dances **Obv:** Mask at center surrounded by 6 other masks **Obv. Legend:** THE BANK OF KOREA **Rev:** Mask dancer at left center **Edge:** Plain **Shape:** 12-sided **Mint:** KOMSCO **Note:** Prev. KM #102.

Date	Mintage	F	VF	XF	Unc	BU
2007 Proof	50,000	Value: 75.00				

KM# 106 20000 WON
19.0000 g., 0.9990 Silver 0.6102 oz. ASW, 33 mm. **Subject:** Mask dance **Rev:** Ganggangsullae ("Circle dance") **Shape:** 12-sided **Mint:** KOMSCO

Date	Mintage	F	VF	XF	Unc	BU
2008 Proof	50,000	Value: 75.00				

KM# 108 20000 WON
19.0000 g., 0.9000 Silver 0.5498 oz. ASW, 33 mm. **Subject:** Mask dance **Rev:** Youngsan Juldarigi (Tug of War) **Mint:** KOMSCO

Date	Mintage	F	VF	XF	Unc	BU
2009 Proof	50,000	Value: 75.00				

KM# 109 20000 WON
19.0000 g., 0.9990 Silver 0.6102 oz. ASW, 33 mm. **Subject:** Traditional Folk Games - Yeongsan Juldarigi (Tug of war) **Mint:** KOMSCO

Date	Mintage	F	VF	XF	Unc	BU
2009 Proof	50,000	Value: 55.00				

KM# 129 20000 WON
15.5500 g., 0.9990 Gold 0.4994 oz. AGW, 28 mm. **Subject:** Expo 2012 **Obv:** International Pavilion **Rev:** Expo logo **Mint:** KOMSCO

Date	Mintage	F	VF	XF	Unc	BU
2012 Proof	6,000	Value: 950				

KM# 95 30000 WON
31.1035 g., 0.9990 Gold 0.9990 oz. AGW, 35 mm. **Series:** World Cup Soccer **Obv:** Soccer logo **Rev:** Nude soccer player flanked by other players **Edge:** Reeded **Mint:** Seoul

Date	Mintage	F	VF	XF	Unc	BU
2001 Proof	12,000	Value: 1,775				

KM# 114 30000 WON
31.1050 g., 0.9990 Gold 0.9990 oz. AGW, 35 mm. **Obv:** World Cup soccer trophy **Rev:** Stadium, fireworks, soccer ball **Mint:** KOMSCO

Date	Mintage	F	VF	XF	Unc	BU
2002 Proof	12,002	Value: 1,800				

KM# 120 30000 WON
31.1050 g., 0.9990 Gold 0.9990 oz. AGW, 35 mm. **Subject:** 14th Asian Games, Busan **Obv:** Games logo **Rev:** Many hands reaching upwards **Mint:** KOMSCO

Date	Mintage	F	VF	XF	Unc	BU
2002 Proof	—	Value: 1,850				

KM# 107 30000 WON
Silver **Subject:** Flag, 60th Anniversary **Obv:** Flag **Rev:** Multicolor 60 logo **Mint:** KOMSCO

Date	Mintage	F	VF	XF	Unc	BU
2008 Proof	—	Value: 75.00				

KM# 110 30000 WON
19.0000 g., 0.9990 Silver 0.6102 oz. ASW, 33 mm. **Subject:** UNESCO World Heritage Site - Jongmyo Shrine **Obv:** Main Hall of the Jongmyo Shrine **Rev:** Scene of the Royal Ancestral Ritual in the shrine **Edge:** Reeded **Mint:** KOMSCO

Date	Mintage	F	VF	XF	Unc	BU
2010 Proof	50,000	Value: 60.00				

KM# 111 30000 WON
19.0000 g., 0.9990 Silver 0.6102 oz. ASW, 33 mm. **Subject:** G-20 Summit in Seoul **Obv:** Gwang-Hwa-Mun restored on Independence Day **Rev:** Multicolor lantern in national colors **Edge:** Reeded **Mint:** KOMSCO

Date	Mintage	F	VF	XF	Unc	BU
2010 Proof	50,000	Value: 55.00				

KM# 121 50000 WON
19.0000 g., 0.9990 Silver 0.6102 oz. ASW, 33 mm. **Subject:** Jeju Volcanic Island and Lava Tubes - UNESCO World Heritage Site **Obv:** Volcano Crater **Rev:** Lava tubes **Mint:** KOMSCO

Date	Mintage	F	VF	XF	Unc	BU
2011 Proof	30,000	Value: 55.00				

KM# 122 50000 WON
19.0000 g., 0.9990 Silver 0.6102 oz. ASW, 33 mm. **Subject:** International Association of Athletics Federations Championships **Obv:** High Jumping athlete **Rev:** Athlete running thru finish line tape in color **Mint:** KOMSCO

Date	Mintage	F	VF	XF	Unc	BU
2011 Proof	30,000	Value: 100				

KM# 123 50000 WON
19.0000 g., 0.9990 Silver 0.6102 oz. ASW, 33 mm. **Subject:** Nuclear Security Summit **Obv:** Five hands raising up globe **Rev:** Summit logo in color **Mint:** KOMSCO

Date	Mintage	F	VF	XF	Unc	BU
2012 Proof	20,000	Value: 40.00				

KM# 130 50000 WON
19.0000 g., 0.9990 Silver 0.6102 oz. ASW, 33 mm. **Subject:** UNESCO World Heritage Site - Seokguram Grotto and Bulguksa Temple **Mint:** KOMSCO

Date	Mintage	F	VF	XF	Unc	BU
2012 Proof	—	Value: 50.00				

MINT SETS

KM#	Date	Mintage Identification	Issue Price	Mkt Val
MS8	2001 (7)	— KM#27, 31, 32, 33.2, 34, 35.2, 89	10.00	22.50

PROOF SETS

KM#	Date	Mintage Identification	Issue Price	Mkt Val
PS10	2001 (6)	2,002 KM#90-95	—	2,500

KUWAIT

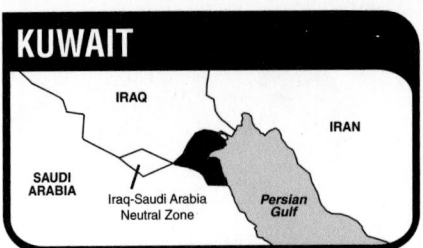

The State of Kuwait, a constitutional monarchy located on the Arabian Peninsula at the northwestern corner of the Persian Gulf, has an area of 6,880 sq. mi. (17,820 sq. km.) and a population of 1.7 million. Capital: Kuwait. Petroleum, the basis of the economy, provides 95 percent of the exports.

RULERS

Al Sabah Dynasty
Jabir Ibn Ahmad, 1977-2006
Sabah Al Ahmad Al Sabah, 2006-

MONETARY SYSTEM
1000 Fils = 1 Dinar

SOVEREIGN EMIRATE
MODERN COINAGE

KM# 9a FILS
2.4100 g., 0.9250 Silver 0.0717 oz. ASW, 17 mm. **Ruler:** Jabir Ibn Ahmad **Obv:** Value within circle **Rev:** Ship with sails

Date	Mintage	F	VF	XF	Unc	BU
AH1429-2008 Proof	—	Value: 65.00				

KM# 9c FILS
2.4100 g., 0.9250 Silver Gilt 0.0717 oz. ASW, 17 mm. **Obv:** Value within circle **Rev:** Dhow, dates below

Date	Mintage	F	VF	XF	Unc	BU
AH1429-2008 Proof	—	Value: 75.00				

KM# 10 5 FILS
2.5000 g., Nickel-Brass, 19.5 mm. **Ruler:** Jabir Ibn Ahmad **Obv:** Value within circle **Rev:** Dhow, dates below

Date	Mintage	F	VF	XF	Unc	BU
AH1422-2001	—	—	0.10	0.20	0.40	—
AH1424-2003	—	—	0.10	0.20	0.40	—
AH1426-2005	—	—	0.10	0.20	0.40	—
AH1427-2006	—	—	0.10	0.20	0.40	—
AH1427-2007	—	—	0.10	0.20	0.40	—
AH1428-2008	—	—	0.10	0.20	0.40	—
AH1429-2008	—	—	0.10	0.20	0.40	—
AH1430-2009	—	—	0.10	0.20	0.40	—
AH1431-2010	—	—	0.10	0.20	0.40	—

KM# 10a 5 FILS
3.0100 g., 0.9250 Silver 0.0895 oz. ASW, 19.5 mm. **Ruler:** Jabir Ibn Ahmad **Obv:** Value within circle **Rev:** Ship with sails

Date	Mintage	F	VF	XF	Unc	BU
AH1429-2008 Proof	—	Value: 70.00				

KM# 10c 5 FILS
3.0100 g., 0.9250 Silver Gilt 0.0895 oz. ASW, 19.5 mm. **Obv:** Value in circle **Rev:** Dhow, dates below

Date	Mintage	F	VF	XF	Unc	BU
AH1429-2008 Proof	—	Value: 80.00				

KM# 11 10 FILS
3.7500 g., Nickel-Brass, 21 mm. **Ruler:** Jabir Ibn Ahmad **Obv:** Value within circle **Rev:** Dhow, dates below

Date	Mintage	F	VF	XF	Unc	BU
AH1422-2001	—	—	—	0.25	0.75	—
AH1424-2003	—	—	—	0.25	0.75	—
AH1426-2005	—	—	—	0.25	0.75	—
AH1427-2006	—	—	—	0.25	0.75	—
AH1428-2007	—	—	—	0.25	0.75	—
AH1429-2008	—	—	—	0.25	0.75	—
AH1430-2009	—	—	—	0.25	0.75	—
AH1431-2010	—	—	—	0.25	0.75	—

KM# 11a 10 FILS
4.3500 g., 0.9250 Silver 0.1294 oz. ASW, 21 mm. **Ruler:** Jabir Ibn Ahmad **Obv:** Value within circle **Rev:** Ship with sails

Date	Mintage	F	VF	XF	Unc	BU
AH1429-2008 Proof	—	Value: 75.00				

KM# 11c 10 FILS
4.3500 g., 0.9250 Silver Gilt 0.1294 oz. ASW, 21 mm. **Obv:** Value within circle **Rev:** Dhow, dates below

Date	Mintage	F	VF	XF	Unc	BU
AH1429-2008 Proof	—	Value: 85.00				

KM# 12c 20 FILS
Stainless Steel, 20 mm. **Ruler:** Jabir Ibn Ahmad **Obv:** Value **Rev:** Dhow, dates below

Date	Mintage	F	VF	XF	Unc	BU
AH1422-2001	—	—	0.20	0.35	1.00	—
AH1424-2003	—	—	0.20	0.35	1.00	—
AH1426-2005	—	—	0.20	0.35	1.00	—

KM# 12 20 FILS
3.0000 g., Copper-Nickel, 20 mm. **Ruler:** Jabir Ibn Ahmad **Obv:** Value within circle **Rev:** Dhow, dates below **Edge:** Reeded **Note:** Varieties exist.

Date	Mintage	F	VF	XF	Unc	BU
AH1424-2003	—	—	0.20	0.45	2.00	—
AH1426-2005	—	—	0.20	0.45	2.00	—
AH1427-2006	—	—	0.20	0.45	2.00	—
AH1428-2007	—	—	0.20	0.45	2.00	—
AH1429-2008	—	—	0.20	0.45	2.00	—
AH1430-2009	—	—	0.20	0.45	2.00	—

KM# 12a 20 FILS
3.3700 g., 0.9250 Silver 0.1002 oz. ASW, 20 mm. **Ruler:** Jabir Ibn Ahmad **Obv:** Value within circle **Rev:** Dhow, dates below

Date	Mintage	F	VF	XF	Unc	BU
AH1429-2008 Proof	—	Value: 80.00				

KM# 12d 20 FILS
3.3700 g., 0.9250 Silver Gilt 0.1002 oz. ASW, 20 mm. **Obv:** Value within cricle **Rev:** Dhow, dates below

Date	Mintage	F	VF	XF	Unc	BU
1429-2008 Proof	—	Value: 90.00				

KM# 13 50 FILS
4.5000 g., Copper-Nickel, 23 mm. **Ruler:** Jabir Ibn Ahmad **Obv:** Value within circle **Rev:** Dhow, dates below **Edge:** Reeded

Date	Mintage	F	VF	XF	Unc	BU
AH1422-2001	—	—	0.25	0.35	1.25	—
AH1424-2003	—	—	0.25	0.35	1.00	—
AH1426-2005	—	—	0.25	0.35	1.00	—
AH1427-2006	—	—	0.25	0.35	1.00	—
AH1428-2007	—	—	0.25	0.35	1.00	—
AH1429-2008	—	—	0.25	0.35	1.00	—
AH1430-2009	—	—	0.25	0.35	1.00	—
AH1431-2010	—	—	0.25	0.35	1.00	—

KM# 13a 50 FILS
5.0700 g., 0.9250 Silver 0.1508 oz. ASW, 23 mm. **Ruler:** Jabir Ibn Ahmad **Obv:** Value within circle **Rev:** Ship with sails

Date	Mintage	F	VF	XF	Unc	BU
AH1429-2008 Proof	—	Value: 85.00				

KM# 13c 50 FILS
5.0700 g., 0.9250 Silver Gilt 0.1508 oz. ASW, 23 mm. **Obv:** Value within circle **Rev:** Dhow, dates below

Date	Mintage	F	VF	XF	Unc	BU
1429-2008 Proof	—	Value: 100				

KM# 14 100 FILS
6.5000 g., Copper-Nickel, 26 mm. **Ruler:** Jabir Ibn Ahmad **Obv:** Value within circle **Rev:** Dhow, dates below **Edge:** Reeded

Date	Mintage	F	VF	XF	Unc	BU
AH1424-2003	—	—	0.50	0.75	1.50	—
AH1426-2005	—	—	0.50	0.75	1.50	—
AH1427-2006	—	—	0.50	0.75	1.50	—
AH1428-2007	—	—	0.50	0.75	1.50	—
AH1429-2008	—	—	0.50	0.75	1.50	—
AH1430-2009	—	—	0.50	0.75	1.50	—

KM# 14a 100 FILS

7.3400 g., 0.9250 Silver 0.2183 oz. ASW, 26 mm. **Ruler:** Jabir Ibn Ahmad **Obv:** Value within circle **Rev:** Ship with sails

Date	Mintage	F	VF	XF	Unc	BU
AH1429-2008 Proof	—	Value: 90.00				

KM# 14c 100 FILS

7.3400 g., 0.9250 Silver Gilt 0.2183 oz. ASW, 26 mm. **Obv:** Value within circle **Rev:** Dhow, dates below

Date	Mintage	F	VF	XF	Unc	BU
1429-2008 Proof	—	Value: 110				

PROOF SETS

KM#	Date	Mintage	Identification	Issue Price	Mkt Val
PS5	2008 (6)	—	KM#9a-14a	—	475
PS6	2008 (6)	—	KM#9c-11c, 12d, 13c-14c	—	500

KYRGYZSTAN

The Kyrgyz Republic, (formerly Kirghiz S.S.R., a Union Republic of the U.S.S.R.), is an independent state since Aug. 31, 1991, a member of the United Nations and of the C.I.S. It was the last state of the Union Republics to declare its sovereignty. Capital: Bishkek (formerly Frunze).

MONETARY SYSTEM
100 Tiyin = 1 Som

REPUBLIC

STANDARD COINAGE

KM# 11 TIYIN

1.0000 g., Aluminum-Bronze, 13.98 mm. **Obv:** National arms **Rev:** Flower at left of value **Edge:** Reeded **Note:** Prev. KM #8.

Date	Mintage	F	VF	XF	Unc	BU
2008 In sets only	95,000	—	—	—	0.65	1.00

KM# 12 10 TIYIN

1.3000 g., Brass Plated Steel, 15 mm. **Obv:** National arms **Rev:** Flower at left of value **Edge:** Plain **Note:** Prev. KM #9.

Date	Mintage	F	VF	XF	Unc	BU
2008	—	—	—	—	0.85	1.50

KM# 13 50 TIYIN

1.8000 g., Brass Plated Steel, 17 mm. **Obv:** National arms **Rev:** Flower at left of value **Edge:** Plain **Note:** Prev. KM #10.

Date	Mintage	F	VF	XF	Unc	BU
2008	—	—	—	—	1.25	2.00

KM# 19 SOM

12.0000 g., Copper-Nickel, 30 mm. **Series:** Great Silk Road

---

Subject: Tashrabat **Obv:** Arms **Rev:** Fortress

Date	Mintage	F	VF	XF	Unc	BU
2008 Prooflike	5,000	—	—	—	10.00	15.00

KM# 14 SOM

2.5000 g., Nickel Plated Steel, 19 mm. **Obv:** National arms **Rev:** Symbol at left of denomination **Edge:** Reeded **Note:** Prev. KM#11.

Date	Mintage	F	VF	XF	Unc	BU
2008	—	—	—	—	1.50	2.25

KM# 20 SOM

28.2800 g., Copper-Nickel, 30 mm. **Series:** Great Silk Road **Subject:** Uzgen architecture complex

Date	Mintage	F	VF	XF	Unc	BU
2008 Prooflike	5,000	—	—	—	10.00	15.00

KM# 21 SOM

12.0000 g., Copper-Nickel, 30 mm. **Subject:** Uzgen Architectural Complex **Obv:** Arms **Rev:** Tower and building - map above

Date	Mintage	F	VF	XF	Unc	BU
2008 Prooflike	5,000	—	—	—	10.00	15.00

KM# 35 SOM

12.0000 g., Copper-Nickel, 30 mm. **Series:** Great Silk Road **Subject:** Burana Tower **Rev:** Tower and map

Date	Mintage	F	VF	XF	Unc	BU
2008 Prooflike	5,000	—	—	—	10.00	15.00

KM# 31 SOM

12.0000 g., Copper-Nickel, 30 mm. **Series:** Great Silk Road **Subject:** Suilaman Mountain

Date	Mintage	F	VF	XF	Unc	BU
2009 Prooflike	5,000	—	—	—	10.00	15.00

KM# 33 SOM

12.0000 g., Copper-Nickel, 30 mm. **Series:** Great Silk Road **Subject:** Lake Issykkul

Date	Mintage	F	VF	XF	Unc	BU
2009 Prooflike	5,000	—	—	—	10.00	15.00

KM# 45 SOM

12.0000 g., Copper-Nickel, 30 mm. **Subject:** Pobeda Peak **Obv:** National arms above stylized peaks **Rev:** Mountian range

Date	Mintage	F	VF	XF	Unc	BU
2011	5,000	—	—	—	—	25.00

KM# 47 SOM

12.0000 g., Copper-Nickel, 30 mm. **Obv:** National arms **Rev:** Khan-Tengri Peak

Date	Mintage	F	VF	XF	Unc	BU
2011	5,000	—	—	—	—	25.00

KM# 15 3 SOM

3.2000 g., Nickel Plated Steel, 21 mm. **Obv:** National arms **Rev:** Symbol above right of denomination **Edge:** Reeded **Note:** Prev. KM #12.

Date	Mintage	F	VF	XF	Unc	BU
2008	—	—	—	—	1.25	2.00

KM# 16 5 SOM

4.2000 g., Nickel Plated Steel, 23 mm. **Obv:** National arms **Rev:** Symbol at right of value **Edge:** Reeded **Note:** Prev. KM #13.

Date	Mintage	F	VF	XF	Unc	BU
2008	—	—	—	—	1.50	2.50

KM# 4 10 SOM

28.2800 g., 0.9250 Silver 0.8410 oz. ASW, 38.6 mm. **Subject:** Tenth Anniversary of Republic **Obv:** National arms within circle **Rev:** Value and Khan Tengri mountain **Edge:** Reeded **Note:** Prev. KM #3.

Date	Mintage	F	VF	XF	Unc	BU
2001 Proof	1,000	Value: 175				

KM# 5 10 SOM

28.2800 g., 0.9250 Silver 0.8410 oz. ASW, 38.6 mm. **Subject:** International Year of the mountains **Obv:** National arms **Rev:** Edelweiss flower and mountain **Edge:** Reeded **Note:** Prev. KM #4.

Date	Mintage	F	VF	XF	Unc	BU
2002 Proof	1,000	Value: 125				

KM# 6   10 SOM
28.2800 g., 0.9250 Silver 0.8410 oz. ASW, 38.6 mm. **Subject:**
International Year of the Mountains **Obv:** National arms **Rev:** Argali
Ram head and mountain **Edge:** Reeded **Note:** Prev. KM #5.

Date	Mintage	F	VF	XF	Unc	BU
2002 Proof	1,000	Value: 125				

KM# 36   10 SOM
28.2800 g., 0.9250 Silver partially gilt 0.8410 oz. ASW, 38.6 mm.
Subject: Som, 10th Anniversary **Obv:** National arms **Rev:** Som
coin designs, some gilt

Date	Mintage	F	VF	XF	Unc	BU
2003 Proof	—	Value: 150				

KM# 7   10 SOM
28.2800 g., 0.9250 Silver partially gilt 0.8410 oz. ASW, 38.6 mm.
Subject: Genesis of the Kyrgyz Statehood **Obv:** Arms **Rev:**
Classical designs

Date	Mintage	F	VF	XF	Unc	BU
2003 Proof	1,000	Value: 250				

KM# 8   10 SOM
28.2800 g., 0.9250 Silver 0.8410 oz. ASW, 38.6 mm. **Subject:**
60 Years of Great Victory **Rev:** Figure of a mother, eternal light,
Victory Memorial complex **Note:** Prev. KM #6.

Date	Mintage	F	VF	XF	Unc	BU
2005 Proof	1,000	Value: 110				

KM# 9   10 SOM
28.2800 g., 0.8250 Silver partially gilt 0.7501 oz. ASW, 38.6 mm.
Series: Great Silk Road **Subject:** Tashrabat **Note:** Prev. KM #7.

Date	Mintage	F	VF	XF	Unc	BU
2005 Proof	1,500	Value: 100				

KM# 10   10 SOM
28.2800 g., 0.9250 Silver 0.8410 oz. ASW, 38.6 mm. **Subject:**
Shanghai Cooperation **Obv:** Arms **Rev:** Multicolor logo of the
Shanghai Cooperation Organization

Date	Mintage	F	VF	XF	Unc	BU
2007 Proof	1,000	Value: 180				

KM# 22   10 SOM
28.2800 g., 0.9250 Silver partially gilt 0.8410 oz. ASW, 38.6 mm.
Series: Great Silk Road **Subject:** Uzgen Architectural Complex

Date	Mintage	F	VF	XF	Unc	BU
2007 Proof	1,500	Value: 120				

KM# 18   10 SOM
28.2800 g., 0.9250 Silver partially gilt 0.8410 oz. ASW, 38.6 mm.
Series: Great Silk Road **Subject:** Burana Tower **Rev:** Buildings
with partial gilting

Date	Mintage	F	VF	XF	Unc	BU
2008 Proof	1,500	Value: 110				

KM# 23   10 SOM
28.2800 g., 0.9250 Silver 0.8410 oz. ASW, 38.6 mm. **Series:**
Capitals of the Eurasia Economic Community **Subject:** City of
Bishkek **Obv:** National emblem **Rev:** Horseman statue,
multicolor logo

Date	Mintage	F	VF	XF	Unc	BU
2008 Proof	2,500	Value: 90.00				

KM# 24   10 SOM
28.2800 g., 0.9250 Silver 0.8410 oz. ASW, 38.6 mm. **Rev:**
Chynqyz Aytmatov

Date	Mintage	F	VF	XF	Unc	BU
2009 Proof	2,000	Value: 75.00				

KM# 25   10 SOM
28.2800 g., 0.9250 Silver 0.8410 oz. ASW, 38.6 mm. **Series:**
Chinqiz Aitmatov's work's **Rev:** Jamila

Date	Mintage	F	VF	XF	Unc	BU
2009 Proof	3,000	Value: 75.00				

KM# 26   10 SOM
28.2800 g., 0.9250 Silver 0.8410 oz. ASW, 38.6 mm. **Series:**
Chingiz Aitmatov's works **Rev:** Duishen

Date	Mintage	F	VF	XF	Unc	BU
2009 Proof	3,000	Value: 75.00				

KM# 27 10 SOM
28.2800 g., 0.9250 Silver 0.8410 oz. ASW, 38.6 mm. **Series:** Chinqiz Aitmatov's works **Rev:** Mother field

Date	Mintage	F	VF	XF	Unc	BU
2009 Proof	3,000	Value: 75.00				

KM# 28 10 SOM
28.2800 g., 0.9250 Silver 0.8410 oz. ASW, 38.5 mm. **Series:** Chinqiz Aitmatov's works **Rev:** Farewell, Gulsary!

Date	Mintage	F	VF	XF	Unc	BU
2009 Proof	3,000	Value: 75.00				

KM# 29 10 SOM
28.2800 g., 0.9250 Silver 0.8410 oz. ASW, 38.5 mm. **Series:** Chinqiz Aitmatov's works **Rev:** The white ship

Date	Mintage	F	VF	XF	Unc	BU
2009 Proof	3,000	Value: 75.00				

KM# 32 10 SOM
28.2800 g., 0.9250 Silver Partially gilt 0.8410 oz. ASW, 38.6 mm. **Series:** Great Silk Road **Subject:** Suliman Mountain

Date	Mintage	F	VF	XF	Unc	BU
2009 Proof	1,500	Value: 110				

KM# 34 10 SOM
28.2800 g., 0.9250 Silver partially gilt 0.8410 oz. ASW, 38.6 mm. **Series:** Great Silk Road **Subject:** Lake Issykkul

Date	Mintage	F	VF	XF	Unc	BU
2009 Proof	1,500	Value: 110				

KM# 38 10 SOM
31.1000 g., 0.9250 Silver 0.9249 oz. ASW, 38.6 mm. **Obv:** National arms at top of repeating motif **Rev:** Eagle in flight right, multicolor logo below

Date	Mintage	F	VF	XF	Unc	BU
2009 Proof	3,000	Value: 90.00				

KM# 41 10 SOM
31.1000 g., 0.9250 Silver 0.9249 oz. ASW, 38.6 mm. **Obv:** National emblem and linear design **Rev:** Two people riding deer, as in a cave painting; multicolor logo below

Date	Mintage	F	VF	XF	Unc	BU
2009 Proof	3,000	Value: 95.00				

KM# 43 10 SOM
5.4000 g., Nickel Plated Steel, 24.5 mm. **Obv:** National Arms **Rev:** Symbol above value

Date	Mintage	F	VF	XF	Unc	BU
2009	—	—	—	—	4.50	6.00

KM# 39 10 SOM
31.1000 g., 0.9250 Silver 0.9249 oz. ASW, 38.6 mm. **Obv:** National Arms, multicolor design **Rev:** Frame construction of a Yurta

Date	Mintage	F	VF	XF	Unc	BU
2010 Proof	3,000	Value: 75.00				

KM# 40 10 SOM
31.1000 g., 0.9250 Silver 0.9249 oz. ASW, 38.6 mm. **Subject:** EurAsEC 10th Anniversary **Obv:** National arms and globe **Rev:** Five world sites, multicolor logo at center

Date	Mintage	F	VF	XF	Unc	BU
2010 Proof	2,000	Value: 75.00				

KM# 44 10 SOM
28.2800 g., Silver partially gilt, 38.6 mm. **Obv:** National arms **Rev:** Colored flag above map with Manas on horseback right **Edge:** Reeded

Date	Mintage	F	VF	XF	Unc	BU
2011 Proof	Est. 2,000	Value: 75.00				

KM# 46 10 SOM
28.2800 g., 0.9250 Silver 0.8410 oz. ASW, 38.6 mm. **Subject:** Pobeda Peak **Obv:** National arms above stylized mountains **Rev:** Mountian range **Edge:** Reeded

Date	Mintage	F	VF	XF	Unc	BU
2011 Proof	3,000	Value: 75.00				

KM# 48 10 SOM
31.1000 g., 0.9250 Silver partially gilt 0.9249 oz. ASW, 38.6 mm. **Subject:** Great Silk Road **Obv:** National arms above caravan riding right **Rev:** Skyline views and Silk Road map of Eurasia **Edge:** Reeded

Date	Mintage	F	VF	XF	Unc	BU
2011 Proof	Est. 2,000	Value: 75.00				

KM# 49 10 SOM
33.9400 g., 0.9250 Silver 1.0093 oz. ASW, 39 mm. **Subject:** World of our Children **Obv:** National arms and six flowers **Rev:** Child's drawing in color of sun, girl and medow **Edge:** Reeded

Date	Mintage	F	VF	XF	Unc	BU
2011 Proof	Est. 3,000	Value: 75.00				

KM# 37 100 SOM
6.2200 g., 0.9990 Gold 0.1998 oz. AGW, 22 mm. **Rev:** Two horsemen

Date	Mintage	F	VF	XF	Unc	BU
2008 Proof	—	Value: 350				

KM# 42 100 SOM
31.1000 g., 0.9250 Silver 0.9249 oz. ASW, 38.61 mm. **Rev:** Panthera Tigris, gilt tiger

Date	Mintage	F	VF	XF	Unc	BU
2009 Proof	13,000	Value: 100				

MINT SETS

KM#	Date	Mintage	Identification	Issue Price	Mkt Val
MS1	2008 (6)	—	KM#11-16	—	30.00

LAO

The Lao Peoples Democratic Republic, located on the Indo-Chinese Peninsula between the Socialist Republic of Vietnam and the Kingdom of Thailand, has an area of 91,428 sq. mi. (236,800 km.) and a population of 3.6 million. Capital Vientiane. Agriculture employs 95 per cent of the people. Tin, lumber and coffee are exported.

MONETARY SYSTEM
100 Att = 1 Kip

PEOPLES DEMOCRATIC REPUBLIC

STANDARD COINAGE

KM# 151 500 KIP
0.5000 g., 0.9990 Gold 0.0161 oz. AGW, 11 mm. **Rev:** Lion's head

Date	Mintage	F	VF	XF	Unc	BU
2009 Proof	—	Value: 50.00				

KM# 152 500 KIP
0.5000 g., 0.9990 Gold 0.0161 oz. AGW, 11 mm. **Subject:** Year of the Tiger **Rev:** Tiger

Date	Mintage	F	VF	XF	Unc	BU
2010 Proof	Est. 5,000	Value: 50.00				

KM# 85 1000 KIP
31.5000 g., 0.9990 Silver 1.0117 oz. ASW, 38.5 mm. **Subject:** Olympics **Obv:** State emblem **Rev:** Freestyle skier **Edge:** Reeded

Date	Mintage	F	VF	XF	Unc	BU
2001 Proof	—	Value: 50.00				

KM# 96 1000 KIP
31.4500 g., 0.9990 Silver 1.0101 oz. ASW, 38.5 mm. **Obv:** State emblem **Rev:** Soccer player **Edge:** Reeded

Date	Mintage	F	VF	XF	Unc	BU
2001 Proof	—	Value: 50.00				

KM# 122 1000 KIP
1.2400 g., 0.9990 Gold 0.0398 oz. AGW, 13.92 mm. **Rev:** Tiger head

Date	Mintage	F	VF	XF	Unc	BU
2003 Proof	Est. 15,000	Value: 90.00				

KM# 126 1000 KIP
Silver **Subject:** Beijing olympics, 2008 **Rev:** Torch relay between Parthenon in Athens and Temple of Heaven in Beijing

Date	Mintage	F	VF	XF	Unc	BU
2004	—	Value: 30.00				

KM# 136 1000 KIP
1.2400 g., 0.9990 Gold 0.0398 oz. AGW, 13.92 mm. **Rev:** Wat Phu Champasak

Date	Mintage	F	VF	XF	Unc	BU
2005 Proof	—	Value: 90.00				

KM# 150 1000 KIP
Silver **Rev:** Map of the railroad from Zining to Lhasa

Date	Mintage	F	VF	XF	Unc	BU
2008 Proof	—	Value: 75.00				

KM# 104 1000 KIP
36.4700 g., 0.9250 Silver 1.0846 oz. ASW, 38.6 mm. **Subject:** Terra Cotta Warriors **Obv:** Arms **Rev:** Gilt warrior standing, background warriors face right **Note:** Central gilt warrior is detachable and stands upright.

Date	Mintage	F	VF	XF	Unc	BU
2009 Proof	5,000	Value: 100				

KM# 105 1000 KIP
36.4700 g., 0.9250 Silver 1.0846 oz. ASW, 38.61 mm. **Subject:** Terra Cotta Warrior **Obv:** Arms **Rev:** Gilt standing warrior, warriors in background facing **Note:** Central gilt warrior is detachable and stands upright.

Date	Mintage	F	VF	XF	Unc	BU
2009 Proof	5,000	Value: 100				

KM# 106 1000 KIP
36.4700 g., 0.9250 Silver 1.0846 oz. ASW, 38.6 mm. **Subject:** Terra Cotta Warrior **Obv:** Arms **Rev:** Archer kneeling **Note:** Central gilt warrior is detachable and stands upright.

Date	Mintage	F	VF	XF	Unc	BU
2009 Proof	1,000	Value: 100				

KM# 107 1000 KIP
36.4700 g., 0.9250 Silver 1.0846 oz. ASW **Subject:** Terra Cotta Warrior **Obv:** Arms **Rev:** Gilt horse **Note:** Central gilt warrior is detachable and stands upright.

Date	Mintage	F	VF	XF	Unc	BU
2009 Proof	1,000	Value: 100				

KM# 153 1000 KIP
28.2800 g., 0.9250 Silver 0.8410 oz. ASW, 38.61 mm. **Subject:** World Cup 2010 in South Africa **Rev:** Sculpture of soccer players

Date	Mintage	F	VF	XF	Unc	BU
2010 Proof	—	Value: 60.00				

KM# 119 5000 KIP
0.3000 g., 0.9990 Gold 0.0096 oz. AGW, 7 mm. **Rev:** Cichlasoma fish

Date	Mintage	F	VF	XF	Unc	BU
2003	—	—	—	—	—	50.00

KM# 124 5000 KIP
0.3000 g., 0.9990 Gold 0.0096 oz. AGW, 7 mm. **Rev:** Rhino

Date	Mintage	F	VF	XF	Unc	BU
2004	—	—	—	—	—	50.00

KM# 127 5000 KIP
37.0000 g., Gold Plated Bronze, 45 mm. **Rev:** Majextic rooster as a laser engraving

Date	Mintage	F	VF	XF	Unc	BU
2005	Est. 28,000	—	—	—	—	35.00

KM# 129 5000 KIP
0.3000 g., 0.9990 Gold 0.0096 oz. AGW, 7 mm. **Rev:** Majestic rooster in pose

Date	Mintage	F	VF	XF	Unc	BU
2005 Proof	—	Value: 50.00				

KM# 139 5000 KIP
0.3000 g., 0.9990 Gold 0.0096 oz. AGW, 7 mm. **Subject:** Year of the Dog **Rev:** Dog with kinegram background

Date	Mintage	F	VF	XF	Unc	BU
2006	—	—	—	—	—	50.00

KM# 113 10000 KIP
1.2400 g., 0.9990 Gold 0.0398 oz. AGW, 13.92 mm. **Rev:** Two redshank dress apes

Date	Mintage	F	VF	XF	Unc	BU
2001 Proof	—	Value: 90.00				

KM# 114 10000 KIP
1.2400 g., 0.9990 Gold 0.0398 oz. AGW, 13.92 mm. **Rev:** Horse drawing in color by Xu Beihong

Date	Mintage	F	VF	XF	Unc	BU
2002	—	—	—	—	—	90.00

KM# 120 10000 KIP
1.2400 g., 0.9990 Gold 0.0398 oz. AGW, 13.92 mm. **Rev:** Cichlasoma fish

Date	Mintage	F	VF	XF	Unc	BU
2003	—	—	—	—	—	90.00

KM# 125 10000 KIP
1.2400 g., 0.9990 Gold 0.0398 oz. AGW, 13.92 mm. **Rev:** Black crested gibbon

Date	Mintage	F	VF	XF	Unc	BU
2004	—	—	—	—	—	90.00

KM# 130 10000 KIP
1.2400 g., 0.9990 Gold 0.0398 oz. AGW, 13.92 mm. **Obv:** National Arms **Rev:** Majestic rooster right

Date	Mintage	F	VF	XF	Unc	BU
2005	—	—	—	—	—	75.00

KM# 133 10000 KIP
1.2400 g., 0.9990 Gold 0.0398 oz. AGW, 13.92 mm. **Obv:** National arms **Rev:** Mazu seated, waves in background

Date	Mintage	F	VF	XF	Unc	BU
2005	Est. 6,888	Value: 90.00				

KM# 140 10000 KIP
1.2400 g., 0.9990 Gold 0.0398 oz. AGW, 13.92 mm. **Subject:** Year of the Dog **Rev:** Don seated

Date	Mintage	F	VF	XF	Unc	BU
2006	—	—	—	—	—	90.00

KM# 142 10000 KIP
1.2400 g., 0.9990 Gold 0.0398 oz. AGW, 13.92 mm. **Rev:** Mazu standing

Date	Mintage	F	VF	XF	Unc	BU
2006	—	—	—	—	—	90.00

KM# 146 10000 KIP
1.2400 g., 0.9990 Gold 0.0398 oz. AGW **Rev:** Buddha in meditation **Shape:** 13.92

Date	Mintage	F	VF	XF	Unc	BU
2006	Est. 6,888	—	—	—	—	90.00

KM# 149 10000 KIP
1.2400 g., 0.9990 Gold 0.0398 oz. AGW, 13.92 mm. **Subject:** Year of the Pig **Obv:** National arms **Rev:** Pig

Date	Mintage	F	VF	XF	Unc	BU
2007	—	—	—	—	—	90.00

KM# 154 10000 KIP
1.0000 g., 0.9990 Gold 0.0321 oz. AGW, 13.92 mm. **Subject:** World Cup Soccer, South Africa **Rev:** Sculpture of soccer players

Date	Mintage	F	VF	XF	Unc	BU
2010 Proof	—	Value: 90.00				

KM# 86 15000 KIP
20.0000 g., 0.9250 Silver 0.5948 oz. ASW, 38.7 mm. **Subject:** Year of the Horse **Obv:** State emblem **Rev:** Multicolor horse **Edge:** Reeded

Date	Mintage	F	VF	XF	Unc	BU
2002 Proof	9,500	Value: 50.00				

KM# 87 15000 KIP
20.0000 g., 0.9250 Silver 0.5948 oz. ASW, 38.7 mm. **Subject:** Year of the Horse **Obv:** State emblem **Rev:** Horse with multicolor holographic background **Edge:** Reeded

Date	Mintage	F	VF	XF	Unc	BU
2002 Proof	9,500	Value: 55.00				

KM# 116 15000 KIP
20.0000 g., 0.9250 Silver 0.5948 oz. ASW **Obv:** National arms **Rev:** Shoulder-spot cichlid in color

Date	Mintage	F	VF	XF	Unc	BU
2003 Proof	Est. 2,300	Value: 60.00				

KM# 117 15000 KIP
20.0000 g., 0.9250 Silver 0.5948 oz. ASW, 38 mm. **Rev:** Chilasoma flower horn fish swimming left

Date	Mintage	F	VF	XF	Unc	BU
2003 Proof	—	Value: 60.00				

KM# 118 15000 KIP
20.0000 g., 0.9250 Silver 0.5948 oz. ASW, 38 mm. **Rev:** Fish in color kinegram

Date	Mintage	F	VF	XF	Unc	BU
2003 Proof	—	Value: 60.00				

KM# 123 15000 KIP
20.0000 g., 0.9990 Silver 0.6423 oz. ASW **Rev:** Black crested gibbon

Date	Mintage	F	VF	XF	Unc	BU
2004 Proof	Est. 3,800	Value: 60.00				

KM# 94 15000 KIP
20.0000 g., 0.9990 Silver 0.6423 oz. ASW, 38.7 mm. **Obv:** State emblem **Rev:** Multicolor Golden Monkey **Edge:** Reeded

Date	Mintage	F	VF	XF	Unc	BU
2004 Proof	2,300	Value: 55.00				

KM# 128 15000 KIP
20.0000 g., 0.9990 Silver 0.6423 oz. ASW **Rev:** Majestic Rooster with kinegram background

Date	Mintage	F	VF	XF	Unc	BU
2005 Proof	Est. 3,800	Value: 60.00				

KM# 132 15000 KIP
20.0000 g., 0.9250 Silver 0.5948 oz. ASW, 38 mm. **Obv:** National arms **Rev:** Mazu seated, waves in background

Date	Mintage	F	VF	XF	Unc	BU
2005 Proof	Est. 6,888	Value: 60.00				

KM# 98 15000 KIP
Silver, 38.7 mm. **Issuer:** Bank of Lao PDR **Obv:** National arms **Obv. Legend:** THE LAO PEOPLE'S DEMOCRATIC REPUBLIC **Rev:** Statue of Mazu with stylized Phoenix at left and right **Rev. Legend:** GODDESS OF THE SEA **Edge:** Reeded

Date	Mintage	F	VF	XF	Unc	BU
2006 Proof	6,888	Value: 65.00				

KM# 137 15000 KIP
20.0000 g., 0.9990 Silver 0.6423 oz. ASW, 38 mm. **Subject:** Year of the Dog **Rev:** Three dogs

Date	Mintage	F	VF	XF	Unc	BU
2006 Proof	—	Value: 60.00				

KM# 138 15000 KIP
Silver **Subject:** Year of the Dog **Rev:** Dog with kinegram background

Date	Mintage	F	VF	XF	Unc	BU
2006 Proof	—	Value: 60.00				

KM# 145 15000 KIP
20.0000 g., 0.9250 Silver 0.5948 oz. ASW, 38 mm. **Rev:** Buddha head facing

Date	Mintage	F	VF	XF	Unc	BU
2006 Proof	Est. 6,888	Value: 60.00				

KM# 148 15000 KIP
20.0000 g., 0.9990 Silver 0.6423 oz. ASW, 38 mm. **Subject:** Year of the Pig **Obv:** National arms **Rev:** Pig with kinegram background

Date	Mintage	F	VF	XF	Unc	BU
2007 Proof	—	Value: 60.00				

KM# 115 50000 KIP
7.7800 g., 0.9990 Gold 0.2499 oz. AGW, 22 mm. **Obv:** National arms **Rev:** Horse advancing right

Date	Mintage	F	VF	XF	Unc	BU
2002	—	—	—	—	—	475

KM# 88 60000 KIP
155.5175 g., 0.9250 Silver 4.6248 oz. ASW, 65 mm. **Subject:** Year of the Horse **Obv:** State emblem **Rev:** Multicolor horse **Edge:** Reeded

Date	Mintage	F	VF	XF	Unc	BU
2002 Proof	1,000	Value: 225				

KM# 89 100000 KIP
15.5518 g., 0.9999 Gold 0.4999 oz. AGW, 27 mm. **Subject:** Year of the Horse **Obv:** State emblem **Rev:** Horse **Edge:** Reeded

Date	Mintage	F	VF	XF	Unc	BU
2002	2,000	Value: 925				

KM# 121 100000 KIP
15.5500 g., 0.9990 Gold 0.4994 oz. AGW, 27 mm. **Rev:** Cichlasoma fish left

Date	Mintage	F	VF	XF	Unc	BU
2003 Proof	Est. 888	Value: 950				

KM# 95 100000 KIP
15.5518 g., 0.9990 Gold 0.4995 oz. AGW, 27 mm. **Obv:** State emblem **Rev:** Black Gibbon on holographic background **Edge:** Reeded

Date	Mintage	F	VF	XF	Unc	BU
2004 Proof	888	Value: 950				

KM# 131 100000 KIP
15.5500 g., 0.9990 Gold 0.4994 oz. AGW, 27 mm. **Rev:** Majestic rooster right , kinegram background

Date	Mintage	F	VF	XF	Unc	BU
2005 Proof	Est. 888	Value: 950				

KM# 134 100000 KIP
15.5500 g., 0.9990 Gold 0.4994 oz. AGW **Rev:** Mazu seated, waves in background

Date	Mintage	F	VF	XF	Unc	BU
2005 Proof	Est. 688	Value: 950				

KM# 141 100000 KIP
15.5500 g., 0.9990 Gold 0.4994 oz. AGW **Subject:** Year of the Dog

Date	Mintage	F	VF	XF	Unc	BU
2006 Proof	Est. 888	Value: 950				

KM# 143 100000 KIP
15.5500 g., 0.9990 Gold 0.4994 oz. AGW, 27 mm. **Rev:** Mazu half lenght left

Date	Mintage	F	VF	XF	Unc	BU
2006 Proof	Est. 688	Value: 950				

KM# 147 100000 KIP
15.5500 g., 0.9990 Gold 0.4994 oz. AGW, 27 mm. **Rev:** Buddha in meditation

Date	Mintage	F	VF	XF	Unc	BU
2006 Proof	Est. 688	Value: 950				

KM# 103 100000 KIP
7.7750 g., 0.9990 Gold 0.2497 oz. AGW, 27 mm. **Subject:** President Print Souphanouvong, 100th Anniversary of Birth **Obv:** Bust facing **Rev:** Presidential Palace

Date	Mintage	F	VF	XF	Unc	BU
ND (2009) Proof	1,000	Value: 450				

KM# 102 100000 KIP
38.5000 g., 0.9250 Silver 1.1449 oz. ASW, 36.5 mm. **Subject:** President Print Souphanouvong, 100th Anniversary of Birth **Obv:** Bust facing **Rev:** Presidential Palace

Date	Mintage	F	VF	XF	Unc	BU
ND (2009) Proof	1,000	Value: 100				

KM# 90 1000000 KIP
155.5175 g., 0.9999 Gold 4.9993 oz. AGW, 55 mm. **Subject:** Year of the Horse **Obv:** State emblem **Rev:** Horse with multicolor holographic background **Edge:** Reeded

Date	Mintage	F	VF	XF	Unc	BU
2002 Proof	500	Value: 9,000				

KM# 135 1000000 KIP
155.5000 g., 0.9990 Gold 4.9942 oz. AGW **Rev:** Mazu seated, waves in background

Date	Mintage	F	VF	XF	Unc	BU
2005 Proof	99	Value: 9,500				

KM# 99 1000000 KIP
155.5150 g., 0.9999 Gold 4.9992 oz. AGW, 55.0 mm. **Issuer:** Bank of Lao PDR **Obv:** National arms **Obv. Legend:** THE LAO PEOPLE'S DEMOCRATIC REPUBLIC **Rev:** Multi-latent color bust of Lord Buddha "Fo Guang Pu Zhao" facing with diamond insert in forehead **Edge:** Reeded

Date	Mintage	F	VF	XF	Unc	BU
2006 Proof	99	Value: 9,750				

KM# 144 1000000 KIP
155.5000 g., 0.9990 Gold 4.9942 oz. AGW **Rev:** Mazu standing

Date	Mintage	F	VF	XF	Unc	BU
2006 Proof	Est. 99	Value: 9,500				

PROOF SETS

KM#	Date	Mintage	Identification	Issue Price	Mkt Val
PS7	2000-2001 (3)	3,500	KM#74-76	138	200
PS8	2000-2001 (3)	500	KM#74-76	214	300
PS9	2000-2001 (2)	800	KM#78, 83	—	1,100

LATVIA

The Republic of Latvia, the central Baltic state in east Europe, has an area of 24,749 sq. mi. (43,601 sq. km.) and a population of *2.6 million. Capital: Riga. Livestock raising and manufacturing are the chief industries. Butter, bacon, fertilizers and telephone equipment are exported.

MONETARY SYSTEM
100 Santimu = 1 Lats

MODERN REPUBLIC
STANDARD COINAGE

KM# 15 SANTIMS
1.6000 g., Copper Clad Steel, 15.65 mm. **Obv:** National arms **Rev:** Value flanked by diamonds below lined arch **Edge:** Plain

Date	Mintage	F	VF	XF	Unc	BU
2003	30,000,000	—	—	0.10	0.30	0.40
2005	20,000,000	—	—	0.10	0.30	0.40
2007	25,000,000	—	—	0.10	0.30	0.40
2008	75,000,000	—	—	0.10	0.30	0.40

KM# 21 2 SANTIMI
1.9000 g., Copper Clad Steel, 17 mm. **Obv:** National arms **Rev:** Lined arch above value flanked by diamonds **Edge:** Plain

Date	Mintage	F	VF	XF	Unc	BU
2006	18,000,000	—	—	0.20	0.45	0.60
2007	30,000,000	—	—	0.20	0.45	0.60
2009	50,000,000	—	—	0.20	0.45	0.60

KM# 16 5 SANTIMI
2.5000 g., Nickel-Brass, 18.5 mm. **Obv:** National arms **Obv. Legend:** LATVIJAS REPUBLIKA **Rev:** Lined arch above value flanked by diamonds **Edge:** Plain

Date	Mintage	F	VF	XF	Unc	BU
2006	8,000,000	—	—	0.30	0.75	1.00
2007	15,000,000	—	—	0.30	0.75	1.00
2009	10,000,000	—	—	0.30	0.75	1.00

KM# 17 10 SANTIMU
3.2500 g., Nickel-Brass, 19.9 mm. **Obv:** National arms **Rev:** Lined arch above value flanked by diamonds **Edge:** Plain

Date	Mintage	F	VF	XF	Unc	BU
2008	15,000,000	—	—	0.50	1.00	1.50

KM# 22.1 20 SANTIMU
4.0000 g., Nickel-Brass, 21.5 mm. **Obv:** National arms **Rev:** Lined arch above value flanked by diamonds **Edge:** Plain **Note:** 1.5mm thick.

Date	Mintage	F	VF	XF	Unc	BU
2007	7,000,000	—	—	0.50	1.00	2.00
2009	10,000,000	—	—	0.50	1.00	2.00

KM# 13 50 SANTIMU
3.5000 g., Copper-Nickel, 18.8 mm. **Obv:** National arms **Rev:** Triple sprig above value **Edge:** Reeded

Date	Mintage	F	VF	XF	Unc	BU
2007	4,000,000	—	—	2.00	3.00	4.00
2009	5,000,000	—	—	2.00	3.00	4.00

KM# 70 100 SANTIMU
31.4700 g., 0.9250 Silver 0.9359 oz. ASW, 38.6 mm. **Obv:** Baron von Muenchausen with chain of birds around a dog with a lantern hanging from its tail. **Rev:** Baron von Muenchausen and dog hunting a circle of animals **Edge Lettering:** LATVIJAS BANKA LATVIJAS REPUBLIKA

Date	Mintage	F	VF	XF	Unc	BU
2005 Proof	Est. 5,000	Value: 65.00				

KM# 49 LATS
31.4700 g., 0.9250 Silver 0.9359 oz. ASW, 38.6 mm. **Subject:** Hanseatic City of Cesis **Obv:** City arms **Rev:** Sailing ship above, inverted walled city view below **Edge Lettering:** LATVIJAS REPUBLIKA • LATVIJAS BANKA

Date	Mintage	F	VF	XF	Unc	BU
2001 Proof	Est. 15,000	Value: 70.00				

KM# 50 LATS
31.4700 g., 0.9250 Silver 0.9359 oz. ASW **Series:** Ice Hockey **Obv:** Arms with supporters **Rev:** Hockey player

Date	Mintage	F	VF	XF	Unc	BU
2001 Proof	Est. 15,000	Value: 90.00				

KM# 51 LATS
31.4700 g., 0.9250 Silver 0.9359 oz. ASW, 38.6 mm. **Subject:** Heaven **Obv:** Stylized design **Rev:** Stylized woman holding sun **Edge:** Plain

Date	Mintage	F	VF	XF	Unc	BU
2001 Proof	Est. 5,000	Value: 55.00				

KM# 54 LATS
4.8000 g., Copper-Nickel, 21.75 mm. **Obv:** Arms with supporters **Rev:** Nesting stork above value **Edge Lettering:** LATVIJAS BANKA • LATVIJAS BANKA

Date	Mintage	F	VF	XF	Unc	BU
2001	250,000	—	—	7.00	12.00	15.00

KM# 55 LATS
31.4700 g., 0.9250 Silver 0.9359 oz. ASW, 38.6 mm. **Subject:** National Library **Obv:** Country name and diamonds pattern **Rev:** Library building sketch and diamonds design **Edge Lettering:** GAISMU SAUCA • GAISMA AUSA

Date	Mintage	F	VF	XF	Unc	BU
2002 Proof	Est. 5,000			Value: 80.00		

KM# 56 LATS
15.0000 g., 0.9250 Silver with gilt obverse 0.4461 oz. ASW, 28 mm. **Subject:** Coin of Fortune **Obv:** Totally gold plated sun above country name **Rev:** Waning moon, date and value **Edge:** Plain

Date	Mintage	F	VF	XF	Unc	BU
2002 Proof	Est. 5,000			Value: 250		

KM# 52 LATS
31.4700 g., 0.9250 Silver 0.9359 oz. ASW, 38.6 mm. **Subject:** Destiny **Obv:** Stylized design **Rev:** Apple tree and landscape **Edge:** Plain

Date	Mintage	F	VF	XF	Unc	BU
2002 Proof	Est. 5,000			Value: 85.00		

KM# 53 LATS
31.4700 g., 0.9250 Silver 0.9359 oz. ASW, 38.6 mm. **Subject:** Hanseatic City of Kuldiga **Obv:** City arms **Rev:** City view and ships **Edge:** Lettered

Date	Mintage	F	VF	XF	Unc	BU
2002 Proof	Est. 15,000			Value: 80.00		

KM# 57 LATS
31.4700 g., 0.9250 Silver 0.9359 oz. ASW, 38.6 mm. **Subject:** Olympics 2004 **Obv:** Arms with supporters **Rev:** Ancient wrestlers **Edge Lettering:** LATVIJAS BANKA • LATVIJAS BANKA

Date	Mintage	F	VF	XF	Unc	BU
2002 Proof	Est. 26,000			Value: 70.00		

KM# 60 LATS
31.4700 g., 0.9250 Silver 0.9359 oz. ASW, 38.6 mm. **Subject:** Courland **Obv:** Crowned arms above partially built ship **Rev:** Hemp weighing scene with Iron foundry and brick wall in background **Edge Lettering:** LATVIJAS REPUBLIKA • LATVIJAS BANKA

Date	Mintage	F	VF	XF	Unc	BU
2003 Proof	Est. 5,000			Value: 70.00		

KM# 71 LATS
31.4700 g., 0.9250 Silver 0.9359 oz. ASW, 38.6 mm. **Subject:** Vidzeme **Obv:** Crowned arms above horse drawn wagon **Rev:** Two men sawing wood **Edge Lettering:** LATVIJAS BANKA • LATVIJAS REPUBLIKA

Date	Mintage	F	VF	XF	Unc	BU
ND (2003) Proof	—			Value: 55.00		
2004 Proof	Est. 5,000			Value: 55.00		

KM# 72 LATS
31.4700 g., 0.9250 Silver 0.9359 oz. ASW, 38.6 mm. **Subject:** Latgale **Obv:** Madonna and Child above landscape **Rev:** Man sowing seeds and an angel **Edge Lettering:** LATVIJAS BANKA • LATVIJAS REPUBLIKA

Date	Mintage	F	VF	XF	Unc	BU
ND (2003) Proof	—			Value: 55.00		
2004 Proof	Est. 5,000			Value: 55.00		

KM# 75 LATS
31.4700 g., 0.9250 Silver 0.9359 oz. ASW, 38.61 mm. **Subject:** Hanseatic City of Valmiera **Obv:** Coat of arms **Rev:** St. Simanis Church with VALMIERA and reflection of sailing ship **Edge:** LATVIJAS REPUBLIKA • LATVIJAS BANKA

Date	Mintage	F	VF	XF	Unc	BU
2003 Proof	Est. 15,000			Value: 55.00		

KM# 58 LATS
4.8000 g., Copper-Nickel, 21.75 mm. **Obv:** Arms with supporters **Rev:** Ant above value **Edge Lettering:** LATVIJAS BANKA • LATVIJAS BANKA

Date	Mintage	F	VF	XF	Unc	BU
2003	250,000	—	—	5.00	6.50	8.00

KM# 64 LATS
31.4700 g., 0.9250 Silver 0.9359 oz. ASW, 38.6 mm. **Subject:** Latvian European Union Membership **Obv:** Arms with supporters **Rev:** P.S. LATVIJA-ES 2004 above value **Edge Lettering:** LATVIJAS BANKA • LATVIJAS BANKA

Date	Mintage	F	VF	XF	Unc	BU
2004 Proof	Est. 15,000			Value: 65.00		

KM# 61 LATS

4.8000 g., Copper-Nickel, 21.75 mm. **Obv:** Arms with supporters **Rev:** Spriditis with shovel above value **Edge Lettering:** LATVIJAS BANKA • LATVIJAS BANKA

Date	Mintage	F	VF	XF	Unc	BU
2004	500,000	—	—	3.00	4.00	6.00

KM# 62 LATS

17.1500 g., Bi-Metallic Dark Blue Niobium 7.15g center in .900 Silver 10g ring, 34 mm. **Subject:** Coin of Time **Obv:** Heraldic Rose **Rev:** Clock dial in center, rings of hours, minutes, months and days around **Edge:** Plain

Date	Mintage	F	VF	XF	Unc	BU
2004	Est. 5,000	—	—	—	75.00	85.00

KM# 63 LATS

31.4700 g., 0.9250 Silver 0.9359 oz. ASW, 38.6 mm. **Obv:** Arms with supporters **Rev:** World Cup Soccer player **Edge Lettering:** LATVIJA three times

Date	Mintage	F	VF	XF	Unc	BU
2004 Proof	Est. 50,000	Value: 70.00				

KM# 67 LATS

4.8000 g., Copper-Nickel, 21.75 mm. **Obv:** National arms **Obv. Legend:** LATVIJAS REPUBLIKA **Rev:** Mushroom above value **Edge Lettering:** LATVIJAS BANKA • LATVIJAS BANKA

Date	Mintage	F	VF	XF	Unc	BU
2004	500,000	—	—	3.00	4.00	5.00

KM# 68 LATS

31.4700 g., 0.9250 Silver 0.9359 oz. ASW, 38.6 mm. **Subject:** Janis Plieksans "Rainis" **Obv:** Mountains and value **Rev:** Laser picture of Rainis the mountain climbing poet, dramatist and patriot. **Edge Lettering:** LATVIJAS BANKA • LATVIJAS REPUBLIKA

Date	Mintage	F	VF	XF	Unc	BU
2005 Proof	Est. 5,000	Value: 45.00				

KM# 69 LATS

31.4700 g., 0.9250 Silver 0.9359 oz. ASW, 38.6 mm. **Obv:** National arms **Rev:** Bobsled **Edge Lettering:** LATVIJA (three times)

Date	Mintage	F	VF	XF	Unc	BU
2005 Proof	Est. 15,000	Value: 45.00				

KM# 65 LATS

4.8000 g., Copper-Nickel, 21.75 mm. **Obv:** Arms with supporters **Rev:** Weathercock (from the spire of Riga's St. Peter Church) above value **Edge Lettering:** LATVIJAS BANKA • LATVIJAS BANKA

Date	Mintage	F	VF	XF	Unc	BU
2005	500,000	—	—	3.00	6.00	7.00

KM# 76 LATS

31.4700 g., 0.9250 Silver 0.9359 oz. ASW, 38.61 mm. **Subject:** Ice Hockey World Championship **Obv:** Large coat of arms, date below **Rev:** Two hockey players viewed from above, RIGA 2006 on either side with hockey puck in center **Edge Lettering:** LATVIJA (three times)

Date	Mintage	F	VF	XF	Unc	BU
2005 Proof	Est. 5,000	Value: 55.00				

KM# 77 LATS

31.4700 g., 0.9250 Silver 0.9359 oz. ASW, 38.61 mm. **Subject:** Hanseatic City of Koknese **Obv:** Coat of arms **Rev:** Koknese castle on top with moon and sun on sides, reflection of Hanseatic Castle and ship on bottom **Edge Lettering:** LATVIJAS REPUBLIKA • LATVIJAS BANKA

Date	Mintage	F	VF	XF	Unc	BU
2005 Proof	Est. 15,000	Value: 45.00				

KM# 81 LATS

1.2442 g., 0.9999 Gold 0.0400 oz. AGW, 13.92 mm. **Subject:** Art Nouveau **Obv:** Ribbon design **Obv. Legend:** RIGAS / LATVIJAS REPUBLIKA **Rev:** Stone face **Edge:** Reeded

Date	Mintage	F	VF	XF	Unc	BU
2005 Proof	Est. 20,000	Value: 80.00				

KM# 66 LATS

4.8000 g., Copper-Nickel, 21.75 mm. **Obv:** National arms **Obv. Legend:** LATVIJAS REPUBLIKA **Rev:** Pretzel above value **Edge Lettering:** LATVIJAS BANKA • LATVIJAS BANKA

Date	Mintage	F	VF	XF	Unc	BU
2005	500,000	—	—	3.00	4.00	6.00

KM# 73 LATS

4.8000 g., Copper-Nickel, 21.75 mm. **Subject:** Summer Solstice **Obv:** National arms **Rev:** Head wearing Ligo wreath above value **Edge Lettering:** LATVIJAS BANKA • LATVIJAS BANKA

Date	Mintage	F	VF	XF	Unc	BU
2006	500,000	—	—	3.00	4.00	6.00

KM# 74 LATS

4.8000 g., Copper-Nickel, 21.75 mm. **Obv:** National arms **Rev:** Pine cone above value **Edge Lettering:** LATVIJAS BANKA • LATVIJAS BANKA

Date	Mintage	F	VF	XF	Unc	BU
2006	1,000,000	—	—	3.00	5.00	6.00

KM# 78 LATS

31.4700 g., 0.9250 Silver 0.9359 oz. ASW, 38.61 mm. **Subject:** The Barricades of January 1991 **Obv:** Stylized bonfire flames **Obv. Legend:** janvāris 1991 **Rev:** Latvian mythological hero with raised sword against the background of concrete block barricades, rising sun behind **Edge Lettering:** LATVIJAS BANKA (twice)

Date	Mintage	F	VF	XF	Unc	BU
2006 Proof	Est. 5,000	Value: 55.00				

KM# 79 LATS

31.4700 g., 0.9250 Silver 0.9359 oz. ASW, 38.61 mm. **Subject:** Krisjanis Barons **Obv:** Starry sky on left with value on right side **Rev:** Portrait of Barons on right side and starry sky on left **Edge Lettering:** LATVIJAS BANKA • LATVIJAS REPUBLIKA

Date	Mintage	F	VF	XF	Unc	BU
2006 Proof	Est. 5,000	Value: 55.00				

KM# 80 LATS

31.4700 g., 0.9250 Silver 0.9359 oz. ASW, 38.61 mm. **Subject:** Krishjanis Valdemars **Obv:** Seagul flying above water on left, value on right **Rev:** Portrait of Valdemars on right with sea on left **Edge Lettering:** LATVIJAS BANKA • LATVIJAS REPUBLIKA

Date	Mintage	F	VF	XF	Unc	BU
2006 Proof	Est. 5,000	Value: 55.00				

KM# 82 LATS

31.4700 g., 0.9250 Silver 0.9359 oz. ASW, 38.61 mm. **Subject:** Fight for Freedom **Obv:** Outline of Latvia with three stars above **Obv. Inscription:** LATVIJAS REPUBLIKA **Rev:** Two crossed swords outlined against the sun **Rev. Inscription:** NO ZOBENA SAULE LECA **Edge:** Plain

Date	Mintage	F	VF	XF	Unc	BU
2006 Proof	Est. 5,000	Value: 55.00				

KM# 83 LATS

31.4700 g., 0.9250 Silver 0.9359 oz. ASW, 38.61 mm. **Subject:** Hanseatic City of Straupe **Obv:** Coat of arms, date and value below **Obv. Inscription:** ROOP / 1 LATS **Rev:** Lielstraupe castle church top, reflection of Hanseatic ship with trees on both sides on bottom **Edge Lettering:** LATVIJAS REPUBLIKA • LATVIJAS BANKA

Date	Mintage	F	VF	XF	Unc	BU
2006 Proof	Est. 15,000	Value: 55.00				

KM# 84 LATS

27.0000 g., 0.9990 Silver 0.8672 oz. ASW, 38.61 mm. **Subject:** Coin of Digits **Obv:** Arabic O in center of haptagon against an oriental background **Rev:** Roman I in center of heptagon **Shape:** 7-sided

Date	Mintage	F	VF	XF	Unc	BU
2006 Proof	2,007	Value: 400				

KM# 12 LATS

4.8000 g., Copper-Nickel, 21.75 mm. **Obv:** Arms with supporters **Rev:** Salmon above value **Edge Lettering:** LATVIJAS BANKA • LATVIJAS BANKA

Date	Mintage	F	VF	XF	Unc	BU
2007	7,000,000	—	—	2.00	4.00	7.00
2008	25,000,000	—	—	2.00	4.00	7.00

KM# 85 LATS
4.8000 g., Copper-Nickel, 21.75 mm. **Obv:** National arms **Obv.**
Legend: LATVIJAS REPUBLIKA **Rev:** Snowman **Edge**
Lettering: LATVIJAS BANKA • LATVIJAS BANKA

Date	Mintage	F	VF	XF	Unc	BU
2007	1,000,000	—	—	3.00	4.00	6.00

KM# 86 LATS
4.8000 g., Copper-Nickel, 21.75 mm. **Obv:** National arms **Obv.**
Legend: LATVIJAS REPUBLIKA **Rev:** Medieval owl figurine
Edge Lettering: LATVIJAS BANKA • LATVIJAS BANKA

Date	Mintage	F	VF	XF	Unc	BU
2007	1,000,000	—	—	2.00	4.00	6.00

KM# 87 LATS
31.4700 g., 0.9250 Silver 0.9359 oz. ASW, 38.6 mm. **Subject:**
Foreign Rulers **Obv:** Fragment of a large coat of arms **Rev:** Large
coat of arms broken into fragments **Edge:** Plain

Date	Mintage	F	VF	XF	Unc	BU
2007 Proof	—				Value: 65.00	

KM# 88 LATS
31.4700 g., 0.9250 Silver 0.9359 oz. ASW, 38.6 mm. **Subject:**
Rebirth of the State **Obv:** Large coat of arms **Rev:** Sun with its
rays forming the red-white-red flag of the Republic **Edge:** Plain

Date	Mintage	F	VF	XF	Unc	BU
2007 Proof	Est. 5,000				Value: 65.00	

KM# 89 LATS
31.4700 g., 0.9250 Silver 0.9359 oz. ASW, 38.6 mm. **Subject:**
Sigulda **Obv:** Horse and sword within pendant **Rev:** Gauja Valley
with the Turaida Castle and Sigulda Castle **Edge Lettering:**
LATVIJAS REPUBLIKA • LATVIJAS BANKA

Date	Mintage	F	VF	XF	Unc	BU
2007 Proof	Est. 5,000				Value: 65.00	

KM# 90 LATS
17.1500 g., Bi-Metallic Dark Purple, 34 mm. **Subject:** Coin of
Time II **Obv:** Heraldic rose at center **Rev:** Outer ring signs of the
zodiac, inner circle different evolutionary stages of the plant world
Edge: Plain

Date	Mintage	F	VF	XF	Unc	BU
2007	7,000	—	—	—	75.00	85.00

KM# 91 LATS
1.2442 g., 0.9990 Gold 0.0400 oz. AGW, 13.92 mm. **Obv:** Small
coat of arms **Rev:** Logo of the publishing house Zelta abele **Edge:**
Reeded

Date	Mintage	F	VF	XF	Unc	BU
2007 Proof	Est. 15,000				Value: 75.00	

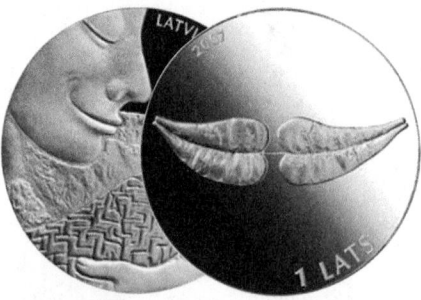

KM# 97 LATS
31.4700 g., 0.9250 Silver 0.9359 oz. ASW, 38.6 mm. **Subject:**
Coin of life **Obv:** Mother holding gilt wrapped child **Rev:** Golden
heart-shaped leaves **Edge:** Plain

Date	Mintage	F	VF	XF	Unc	BU
2007 Proof	5,000				Value: 80.00	

KM# 98 LATS
22.0000 g., 0.9250 Silver 0.6542 oz. ASW, 35 mm. **Subject:**
Lucky Coin **Obv:** Cat perched on rooftop peak **Rev:** Chimney-
sweep with ladder and rope coil with bruch and weight. **Edge**
Lettering: LATVIJAS BANKA • LATVIJAS BANKA

Date	Mintage	F	VF	XF	Unc	BU
2008 Proof	5,000				Value: 55.00	

KM# 99 LATS
31.4700 g., 0.9250 Silver 0.9359 oz. ASW, 38.6 mm. **Subject:**
90th Anniversary of Statehood **Obv:** First Arms of the Republic
Rev: Two children holding multicolor flag **Edge Lettering:**
LATVIJAS BANKA (twice)

Date	Mintage	F	VF	XF	Unc	BU
2008 Proof	5,000				Value: 80.00	

KM# 92 LATS
4.8000 g., Copper-Nickel, 21.75 mm. **Obv:** National arms **Obv.**
Legend: LATVIJAS REPUBLIKA **Rev:** Water Lily **Edge**
Lettering: LATVIJAS BANKA • LATVIJAS BANKA

Date	Mintage	F	VF	XF	Unc	BU
2008	1,000,000	—	—	3.00	4.00	6.00

KM# 93 LATS
12.4000 g., Copper-Nickel, 30 mm. **Obv:** Woman walking
holding flowers **Rev:** Man walking holding wreath **Edge**
Lettering: DZIESMAI SODIEN LIELA DIENA

Date	Mintage	F	VF	XF	Unc	BU
2008	30,000	—	—	—	7.00	9.00

KM# 93a LATS
31.4700 g., 0.9250 Silver 0.9359 oz. ASW, 38.61 mm. **Obv:**
Woman walking holding flowers **Rev:** Man walking holding wreath
Edge Lettering: DZIESMAI SODIEN LIELA DIENA

Date	Mintage	F	VF	XF	Unc	BU
2008 Proof	10,000				Value: 65.00	

KM# 94 LATS
31.4700 g., 0.9250 Silver 0.9359 oz. ASW **Subject:** Hanseatic
City of Limbazi **Obv:** Hanseatic city seal with coat of arms **Rev:**
Limbazi Castle ruins and St. Johns Church with reflection of
Hanseatic Ship on lower half **Edge Lettering:** LATVIJAS
REPUBLIKA • LATVIJAS BANKA **Shape:** 38.61

Date	Mintage	F	VF	XF	Unc	BU
2008 Proof	15,000				Value: 65.00	

KM# 95 LATS
31.4700 g., 0.9250 Silver 0.9359 oz. ASW, 38.6 mm. **Subject:**
Basketball **Obv:** Three stars and stylized basket ball design **Rev:**
Two basketball players and a jump shot **Edge Lettering:**
LATVIJAS BANKA • LATVIJAS REPUBLIKA

Date	Mintage	F	VF	XF	Unc	BU
2008 Proof	5,000				Value: 55.00	

KM# 107 LATS
4.8000 g., Copper-Nickel, 21.75 mm. **Obv:** National arms **Rev:** Chimney sweep standing with brush and ladder **Edge Lettering:** LATVIJAS BANKA • LATVIJAS BANKA

Date	Mintage	F	VF	XF	Unc	BU
2008	1,000,000	—	—	—	4.00	6.00

KM# 101 LATS
4.8000 g., Copper-Nickel, 21.75 mm. **Obv:** National Arms **Rev:** Namejs ring **Edge Lettering:** LATVIJAS BANKA • LATVIJAS BANKA

Date	Mintage	F	VF	XF	Unc	BU
2009	1,000,000	—	—	2.00	4.00	6.00

KM# 100 LATS
20.0000 g., 0.9250 Silver 0.5948 oz. ASW, 34 mm. **Subject:** Children's drawing contest - My Dream Coin **Obv:** State Arms **Rev:** Piglet right **Edge Lettering:** LATVIJAS BANKA • LATVIJAS BANKA

Date	Mintage	F	VF	XF	Unc	BU
2009 Proof	5,000	Value: 60.00				

KM# 102 LATS
31.4700 g., 0.9250 Silver 0.9359 oz. ASW, 38.6 mm. **Subject:** Time of the Land-Surveyors, Novel's 130th Anniversary **Obv:** Brali Kaudzites standing **Rev:** Six figures form novel, forming spokes of wheel **Edge Lettering:** LATVIJAS REPUBLICA • LATVIJAS BANKA

Date	Mintage	F	VF	XF	Unc	BU
2009 Proof	7,000	Value: 55.00				

KM# 103 LATS
31.4700 g., 0.9250 Silver 0.9359 oz. ASW, 38.6 mm. **Subject:** University of Latvia **Obv:** Oak tree within wreath, partially minted photo image **Rev:** Owl standing on open book, University building in background **Edge Lettering:** VIVAT • CRESCAT • FLOREAT

Date	Mintage	F	VF	XF	Unc	BU
2009 Proof	7,000	Value: 55.00				

KM# 104 LATS
26.0000 g., 0.9250 Silver 0.7732 oz. ASW, 32x32 mm. **Subject:** Coin of Water **Obv:** Water droplets **Rev:** Snowflake crystal **Edge:** Plain **Shape:** Square

Date	Mintage	F	VF	XF	Unc	BU
2009 Proof	7,000	Value: 65.00				

KM# 105 LATS
22.0000 g., 0.9250 Silver 0.6542 oz. ASW, 35 mm. **Subject:** Christmas Tree, 500th Anniversary **Obv:** Three children in folktale costumes **Rev:** Man walking with cut tree in moonlight, squirrel jumping from tree **Edge Lettering:** LATVIJAS BANKA • LATVIJAS REPUBLIKA

Date	Mintage	F	VF	XF	Unc	BU
2009 Proof	20,000	Value: 60.00				

KM# 106 LATS
4.8000 g., Copper-Nickel, 21.75 mm. **Obv:** National Arms **Rev:** Christmas tree, heart as ornament **Edge Lettering:** LATVIJAS BANKA • LATVIJAS BANKA

Date	Mintage	F	VF	XF	Unc	BU
2009	1,000,000	—	—	—	4.00	6.00

KM# 108 LATS
4.8000 g., Copper-Nickel, 21.75 mm. **Obv:** National arms **Rev:** Toad **Edge Lettering:** LATVIJAS BANKA • LATVIJAS BANKA

Date	Mintage	F	VF	XF	Unc	BU
2010	1,000,000	—	—	—	4.00	5.00

KM# 109 LATS
20.7000 g., 0.9250 Silver with amber insert 0.6156 oz. ASW, 35 mm. **Subject:** Amber Coin **Obv:** Amber stone on seashore **Rev:** Eye with amber as pupil **Edge:** Plain

Date	Mintage	F	VF	XF	Unc	BU
2010 Proof	7,000	Value: 60.00				

KM# 110 LATS
12.4000 g., Copper-Nickel, 30 mm. **Subject:** The Latvian ABC Book **Obv:** Cock **Rev:** Teacher with students **Edge Lettering:** LATVIJAS BANKA • LATVIJAS REPUBLIKA

Date	Mintage	F	VF	XF	Unc	BU
2010	10,000	—	—	—	—	10.00

KM# 111 LATS
31.4700 g., 0.9250 Silver 0.9359 oz. ASW, 38.61 mm. **Subject:** Latvian ABC Book **Obv:** Cock **Rev:** Teacher and students **Edge Lettering:** LATVIJAS BANKA • LATVIJAS REPUBLIKA

Date	Mintage	F	VF	XF	Unc	BU
2010 Proof	5,000	Value: 65.00				

KM# 112 LATS
31.4700 g., 0.9250 Silver 0.9359 oz. ASW, 38.61 mm. **Subject:** Duke Jacob, 400th Anniversary of birth **Obv:** Bust right, value at bottom **Rev:** Arms **Edge Lettering:** LATVIJAS REPUBLIKA • LATVIJAS BANKA

Date	Mintage	F	VF	XF	Unc	BU
2010 Proof	5,000	Value: 65.00				

KM# 113 LATS
31.4700 g., 0.9250 Silver 0.9359 oz. ASW, 38.61 mm. **Subject:** Declaration of Independence, 20th Anniversary **Obv:** Three small buds, red in color **Rev:** Elderly female with yoke of oppression **Edge Lettering:** LATVIJAS BANKA (twice)

Date	Mintage	F	VF	XF	Unc	BU
2010 Proof	7,000	Value: 65.00				

KM# 114   LATS
17.1500 g., Bi-Metallic Niobium center within 10g of .900 Silver
ring, 34 mm.   **Subject:** Coin of Time III **Obv:** Heraldic Rose **Rev:**
Forests, fields, rocks and water in center, eight lunar phases
around **Edge:** Plain

Date	Mintage	F	VF	XF	Unc	BU
2010	7,000	—	—	—	—	60.00

KM# 117   LATS
4.8000 g., Copper-Nickel, 21.75 mm.   **Obv:** National arms **Rev:**
Horseshoe with open end upwards **Edge Lettering:** LATVIJAS
BANKA • LATVIJAS BANKA

Date	Mintage	F	VF	XF	Unc	BU
2010	500,000	—	—	—	4.00	6.00

KM# 118   LATS
4.8000 g., Copper-Nickel, 21.75 mm.   **Obv:** Naitonal arms **Rev:**
Horseshoe with open end downwards **Edge Lettering:**
LATVIJAS BANKA • LATVIJAS BANKA

Date	Mintage	F	VF	XF	Unc	BU
2010	500,000	—	—	—	4.00	6.00

KM# 119   LATS
4.8000 g., Copper-Nickel, 21.75 mm.   **Obv:** National arms **Rev:**
Beer stein **Edge Lettering:** LATVIJAS BANKA • LATVIJAS
BANKA

Date	Mintage	F	VF	XF	Unc	BU
2011	1,000,000	—	—	—	4.00	6.00

KM# 120   LATS
26.0000 g., 0.9250 Silver 0.7732 oz. ASW, 32x32 mm.   **Subject:**
Aleksandris Caks **Obv:** Window, glass with imprints of lips and
leaves **Rev:** Cobble-stone paving, leave with lips imprint

Date	Mintage	F	VF	XF	Unc	BU
2011 Proof	7,000	Value: 60.00				

KM# 121   LATS
31.4700 g., 0.9250 Silver 0.9359 oz. ASW, 38.61 mm.   **Subject:**
Rundale Palace **Obv:** Arms of Earl Ernst Johann von Biron **Rev:**
Ariel view of the palace and gardens

Date	Mintage	F	VF	XF	Unc	BU
2011 Proof	5,000	Value: 60.00				

KM# 122   LATS
31.4700 g., 0.9250 Silver 0.9359 oz. ASW, 38.61 mm.   **Subject:**
Hansa Cities - Riga **Obv:** Riga arms, gothic ornaments flanking
Rev: Riga city view at top, Hanseatic ship inverted below

Date	Mintage	F	VF	XF	Unc	BU
2011 Proof	15,000	Value: 65.00				

KM# 123   LATS
22.0000 g., 0.9250 Silver 0.6542 oz. ASW, 35 mm.   **Subject:**
Riga Cathedral **Obv:** Angel at left **Rev:** Cross at left, cathedral
exterior at right

Date	Mintage	F	VF	XF	Unc	BU
2011 Proof	5,000	Value: 55.00				

KM# 124   LATS
12.5000 g., 0.9250 Silver 0.3717 oz. ASW, 28 mm.   **Subject:**
Riga coinage, 800th Anniversary **Obv:** Pfennig of Bishop Albert
(1198-1229) - Bishop in mitre **Rev:** Pfennig of Bishop Albert on
frosted surface

Date	Mintage	F	VF	XF	Unc	BU
2011 Proof	5,000	Value: 65.00				

KM# 125   LATS
22.0000 g., 0.9250 Silver 0.6542 oz. ASW, 35 mm.   **Subject:**
Railways in Latvia, 50th Anniversary **Obv:** Steam locomotive's
drive wheel **Rev:** Steam locomotive profile

Date	Mintage	F	VF	XF	Unc	BU
2011 Proof	5,000	Value: 65.00				

KM# 126   LATS
Bi-Metallic Granite center in .925 Silver ring, 35 mm.   **Subject:**
Granite Stone **Obv:** Country name at top, denomination at bottom
Rev: National folk ornamentation

Date	Mintage	F	VF	XF	Unc	BU
2011 Proof	7,000	Value: 60.00				

KM# 127   LATS
4.8000 g., Copper-Nickel, 21.75 mm.   **Obv:** National arms with
supporters **Rev:** Gingerbread heart **Edge Lettering:** LATVIJAS
BANKA • LATVIJAS BANKA

Date	Mintage	F	VF	XF	Unc	BU
2011	1,000,000	—	—	—	4.00	5.00

KM# 128   LATS
22.0000 g., 0.9250 Silver 0.6542 oz. ASW, 35 mm.   **Subject:**
Latvia's participation in the 2012 London Olympics

Date	Mintage	F	VF	XF	Unc	BU
2012 Proof	—	Value: 60.00				

KM# 129   LATS
22.0000 g., 0.9250 Silver 0.6542 oz. ASW, 35 mm.   **Subject:**
Riga Zoo, 100th Anniversary

Date	Mintage	F	VF	XF	Unc	BU
2012 Proof	5,000	Value: 60.00				

KM# 130   LATS
25.0000 g., 0.9250 Silver 0.7435 oz. ASW, 37 mm.   **Subject:**
Bank of Latvia and national currency, 90th Anniversary

Date	Mintage	F	VF	XF	Unc	BU
2012 Proof	10,000	Value: 60.00				

KM# 131   LATS
26.0000 g., 0.9250 Silver 0.7732 oz. ASW, 32x32 mm.   **Subject:**
Riga Technical University, 150th Anniversary

Date	Mintage	F	VF	XF	Unc	BU
2012 Proof	3,000	Value: 60.00				

KM# 132   LATS
22.0000 g., 0.9250 Silver 0.6542 oz. ASW, 35 mm.   **Subject:** K.
Zale

Date	Mintage	F	VF	XF	Unc	BU
2012 Proof	7,000	Value: 60.00				

KM# 133   LATS
22.0000 g., 0.9250 Silver 0.6542 oz. ASW, 35 mm.   **Subject:**
Latvian National Traditions

Date	Mintage	F	VF	XF	Unc	BU
2012 Proof	5,000	Value: 60.00				

KM# 134   LATS
22.0000 g., 0.9250 Silver 0.6542 oz. ASW, 35 mm.   **Subject:** K.
Blaumanis

Date	Mintage	F	VF	XF	Unc	BU
2012 Proof	3,000	Value: 60.00				

KM# 38   2 LATI
9.5000 g., Bi-Metallic Nickel-Brass center in Copper-Nickel ring,
26.3 mm.   **Obv:** Arms with supporters within circle **Rev:** Cow
above value within circle **Edge Lettering:** LATVIJAS BANKA

Date	Mintage	F	VF	XF	Unc	BU
2003 In sets only	30,000	—	—	—	—	12.00
2009	2,000,000	—	—	7.00	8.00	9.00

KM# 59   5 LATI
1.2442 g., 0.9999 Gold 0.0400 oz. AGW, 13.92 mm.   **Obv:** Bust
right **Rev:** Arms with supporters above value **Edge:** Reeded
Note: Remake of the popular KM-9 design

Date	Mintage	F	VF	XF	Unc	BU
2003 Proof	Est. 20,000	Value: 125				

KM# 96   20 LATI
10.0000 g., 0.9990 Gold 0.3212 oz. AGW, 22 mm.   **Obv:**
Woman's head covered with scarf **Rev:** Vessel with a milk bottle,
apple, jug of milk, bread & knife on table

Date	Mintage	F	VF	XF	Unc	BU
2008	5,000	—	—	—	—	650

LEBANON

The Lebanese Republic, situated on the eastern shore of the Mediterranean Sea between Syria and Israel, has an area of 4,015 sq. mi. (10,400 sq. km.) and a population of 3.5 million. Capital: Beirut. The economy is based on agriculture, trade and tourism. Fruit, other foodstuffs and textiles are exported.

MONETARY SYSTEM
100 Piastres = 1 Livre (Pound)

REPUBLIC

STANDARD COINAGE

KM# 40   25 LIVRES
2.8200 g., Nickel Plated Steel, 20.5 mm.   **Obv:** Large value on cedar tree **Rev:** Value within square design **Rev. Legend:** BANQUE DU LIBAN **Edge:** Plain

Date	Mintage	F	VF	XF	Unc	BU
2002(c)	—	—	—	0.30	0.80	1.20
2009(v)	—	—	—	0.30	0.80	1.20

KM# 37a   50 LIVRES
Nickel, 18.35 mm.   **Obv:** Cedar tree with Arabic value superimposed. Arabic legend above, date below. **Rev:** Value in center.

Date	Mintage	F	VF	XF	Unc	BU
2006	—	—	—	0.50	1.20	1.80

KM# 38a   100 LIVRES
4.0500 g., Stainless Steel, 22.48 mm. **Obv:** Arabic legend above large value on cedar tree **Rev:** Stylized flag above large value "100" **Rev. Legend:** BANQUE DU LIBAN **Edge:** Plain

Date	Mintage	F	VF	XF	Unc	BU
2003(c)	—	—	—	0.60	1.50	2.00

KM# 38b   100 LIVRES
4.0700 g., Copper Plated Steel, 22.49 mm. **Obv:** Arabic legend above large value on cedar tree **Rev:** Stylized flag above large value "100" **Rev. Legend:** BANQUE DU LIBAN **Edge:** Plain

Date	Mintage	F	VF	XF	Unc	BU
2006	—	—	—	0.60	1.50	2.00
2009	—	—	—	0.60	1.50	2.00

KM# 38   100 LIVRES
4.0000 g., Brass, 22.5 mm. **Obv:** Arabic legend above large value on cedar tree **Rev:** Stylized flag above large value "100" **Rev. Legend:** BANQUE DU LIBAN **Edge:** Plain

Date	Mintage	F	VF	XF	Unc	BU
2006(c)	—	—	—	0.65	1.50	2.00

KM# 36   250 LIVRES
5.0000 g., Aluminum-Bronze, 23.5 mm.   **Obv:** Arabic legend above large value on cedar tree **Rev:** Large 250 within eliptical border design **Edge:** Reeded

Date	Mintage	F	VF	XF	Unc	BU
2003(c)	—	—	—	0.75	1.85	2.50
2006(a)	—	—	—	0.75	1.85	2.50
2009(v)	—	—	—	0.75	1.85	2.50

KM# 39   500 LIVRES
6.0600 g., Nickel Plated Steel, 24.5 mm.   **Obv:** Arabic legend above large value on cedar tree **Rev:** Large value "500", thick segmented circular border **Rev. Legend:** BANQUE DU LIBAN **Edge:** Plain

Date	Mintage	F	VF	XF	Unc	BU
2003(c)	—	—	—	0.90	2.25	3.00
2006(a)	—	—	—	0.90	2.25	3.00
2009(v)	—	—	—	0.90	2.25	3.00

LESOTHO

The Kingdom of Lesotho, a constitutional monarchy located within the east-central part of the Republic of South Africa, has an area of 11,720 sq. mi. (30,350 sq. km.) and a population of 1.5 million. Capital: Maseru. The economy is based on subsistence agriculture and livestock raising. Wool, mohair, and cattle are exported.

Lesotho (formerly Basutoland) was sparsely populated until the end of the 16th century. Between the 16th and 19th centuries an influx of refugees from tribal wars led to the development of a distinct Basotho group. During the reign of tribal chief Mashoeshoe I (1823-70), a series of wars with the Orange Free State resulted in the loss of large areas of territory to South Africa. Mashoeshoe appealed to the British for help, and Basutoland was constituted a native state under British protection. In 1871 it was annexed to Cape Colony, but was restored to direct control by the Crown in 1884. From 1884 to 1959 legislative and executive authority was vested in a British High Commissioner. The constitution of 1959 recognized the expressed wish of the people for independence, which was attained on Oct. 4, 1966.

Lesotho is a member of the Commonwealth of Nations. The king is Head of State.

RULERS
Moshoeshoe II, 1966-1990
Letsie III, 1990-1995
Moshoeshoe II, 1995-

MONETARY SYSTEM
100 Licente/Lisente = 1 Maloti/Loti

KINGDOM

STANDARD COINAGE
100 Licente/Lisente = 1 Maloti/Loti

KM# 62   5 LICENTE (Lisente)
1.6400 g., Brass Plated Steel, 15 mm.   **Ruler:** Letsie III **Obv:** Arms with supporters **Rev:** Two pine trees among grass, hills and value

Date	Mintage	F	VF	XF	Unc	BU
2006	—	—	—	0.35	0.75	1.00

KM# 63   10 LICENTE (Lisente)
1.9600 g., Brass Plated Steel, 16 mm.   **Ruler:** Moshoeshoe II **Obv:** Arms with supporters **Rev:** Angora goat

Date	Mintage	F	VF	XF	Unc	BU
2010	—	—	—	1.00	1.50	

KM# 66   LOTI
3.8800 g., Nickel Plated Steel, 21 mm.   **Ruler:** Letsie III **Obv:** Native seated right **Rev:** Value at left of arms with supporters

Date	Mintage	F	VF	XF	Unc	BU
2010	—	—	—	—	1.50	2.00

KM# 59   5 MALOTI
6.3700 g., Nickel Plated Steel, 25 mm.   **Ruler:** Moshoeshoe II **Obv:** Arms with supporters **Rev:** Wheat sprigs and value

Date	Mintage	F	VF	XF	Unc	BU
2010	—	—	—	—	4.50	5.00

KM# 73   25 MALOTI
Silver   **Ruler:** Moshoeshoe II **Subject:** Central Bank, 25th Anniversary

Date	Mintage	F	VF	XF	Unc	BU
2005 Proof	—	Value: 75.00				

LIBERIA

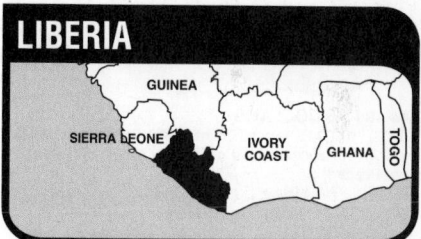

The Republic of Liberia, located on the southern side of the West African bulge between Sierra Leone and Ivory Coast, has an area of 38,250 sq. mi. (111,370 sq. km) and a population of 2.2 million. Capital: Monrovia. The major industries are agriculture, mining and lumbering. Iron ore, diamonds, rubber, coffee and coca are exported.

MINT MARKS
PM - Pobjoy Mint

MONETARY SYSTEM
100 Cents = 1 Dollar

REPUBLIC

STANDARD COINAGE
100 Cents = 1 Dollar

KM# 618   5 CENTS
5.0200 g., Copper-Nickel, 23.8 mm.   **Obv:** National arms **Rev:** Chimpanzee family **Edge:** Plain

Date	Mintage	F	VF	XF	Unc	BU
2003	—	—	—	—	1.50	2.00

KM# 651   5 DOLLARS
14.5600 g., Copper-Nickel, 38 mm. **Obv:** National arms **Rev:** Japanese "Zero" flying over Pearl Harbor **Edge:** Reeded

Date	Mintage	F	VF	XF	Unc	BU
2001	—	—	—	—	10.00	12.00

KM# 568   5 DOLLARS
14.6300 g., Copper-Nickel, 33.1 mm. **Subject:** Battle of Gettysburg **Obv:** National arms **Rev:** Cannon and crossed flags divides busts facing **Edge:** Reeded **Note:** This also exists in an obverse denominated type for $2,000. Also see KM828.

Date	Mintage	F	VF	XF	Unc	BU
2001B	—	—	—	—	12.00	14.00

KM# 494   5 DOLLARS
8.5000 g., 0.9999 Silver 0.2732 oz. ASW, 30 mm. **Subject:** Soccer **Obv:** National arms **Rev:** Soccer player divides circle **Edge:** Reeded

Date	Mintage	F	VF	XF	Unc	BU
2002 Proof	3,000	Value: 30.00				

KM# 829   5 DOLLARS
14.9400 g., Copper-Nickel, 32.9 mm. **Subject:** 12th Anniversary Columbia Space Shuttle **Obv:** National arms **Rev:** Astronaut, space shuttle **Edge:** Reeded

Date	Mintage	F	VF	XF	Unc	BU
2003	—	—	—	—	8.00	10.00

KM# 831   5 DOLLARS
15.5500 g., 0.9990 Niobium 0.4994 oz., 38 mm. **Series:** From ancient to Modern Sports **Obv:** National arms **Rev:** Discus throwers **Edge:** Plain

Date	Mintage	F	VF	XF	Unc	BU
2004	2,004	—	—	—	—	30.00

KM# 832   5 DOLLARS
15.5500 g., 0.9990 Niobium 0.4994 oz., 38 mm. **Series:** From Ancient to Modern Sports **Obv:** National arms **Rev:** Javelin throwers **Edge:** Plain

Date	Mintage	F	VF	XF	Unc	BU
2004	2,004	—	—	—	—	30.00

KM# 833   5 DOLLARS
15.5500 g., 0.9990 Niobium 0.4994 oz., 38 mm. **Series:** From ancient to Modern Sports **Obv:** National arms **Rev:** Broad jumpers **Edge:** Plain

Date	Mintage	F	VF	XF	Unc	BU
2004	2,004	—	—	—	—	30.00

KM# 834   5 DOLLARS
15.5500 g., 0.9990 Niobium 0.4994 oz., 38 mm. **Series:** From Ancient to Modern Sports **Obv:** National arms **Rev:** Runners **Edge:** Plain

Date	Mintage	F	VF	XF	Unc	BU
2004	2,004	—	—	—	—	30.00

KM# 835   5 DOLLARS
15.5500 g., 0.9990 Niobium 0.4994 oz., 38 mm. **Series:** From Ancient to Modern Sports **Obv:** National arms **Rev:** Wrestlers **Edge:** Plain

Date	Mintage	F	VF	XF	Unc	BU
2004	2,004	—	—	—	—	30.00

KM# 809   5 DOLLARS
25.9500 g., Silver, 39.97 mm. **Subject:** Papal visits to Africa **Obv:** National arms **Rev:** 1/2 length multicolor figure of Pope John Paul II at center left, outlined map of Africa at center right in background **Edge:** Reeded

Date	Mintage	F	VF	XF	Unc	BU
2005 Proof	—	Value: 35.00				

KM# 810   5 DOLLARS
25.7200 g., Silver, 39.92 mm. **Obv:** National arms **Rev:** St. Peter's square in background, multicolor bust of Pope Benedict XVI in oval frame at upper right **Edge:** Reeded

Date	Mintage	F	VF	XF	Unc	BU
2005 Proof	—	Value: 40.00				

KM# 664   5 DOLLARS
6.4000 g., Bi-Metallic Brass center in Copper-Nickel ring, 25.7 mm. **Obv:** National arms **Rev:** Pope and cathedral within circle **Edge:** Reeded

Date	Mintage	F	VF	XF	Unc	BU
2005	—	—	—	—	12.00	14.00

KM# 865   5 DOLLARS
7.7800 g., Niobium partially gilt, 35 mm. **Subject:** 10th Anniversary of the Euro - San Marino **Rev:** Castle

Date	Mintage	F	VF	XF	Unc	BU
2006 Proof	10,000	Value: 50.00				

KM# 866   5 DOLLARS
7.7800 g., Niobium partially gilt, 35 mm. **Subject:** 10th Anniversary of the Euro - Slovakia **Rev:** Bratislava Castle

Date	Mintage	F	VF	XF	Unc	BU
2006 Proof	10,000	Value: 50.00				

KM# 867   5 DOLLARS
7.7800 g., Niobium partially gilt, 35 mm. **Subject:** 10th Anniversary of the Euro - Latvia **Rev:** Old Buildings

Date	Mintage	F	VF	XF	Unc	BU
2006 Proof	10,000	Value: 50.00				

KM# 868   5 DOLLARS
7.7800 g., Niobium partially gilt, 35 mm. **Subject:** 10th Anniversary of the Euro - Monaco **Rev:** Ariel view of Principality

Date	Mintage	F	VF	XF	Unc	BU
2006 Proof	10,000	Value: 50.00				

KM# 869   5 DOLLARS
7.7800 g., Niobium partially gilt, 35 mm. **Subject:** 10th Anniversary of the Euro - Slovenia **Rev:** Hill-top buildings

Date	Mintage	F	VF	XF	Unc	BU
2006 Proof	10,000	Value: 50.00				

KM# 724   5 DOLLARS
26.3000 g., Silver Plated Bronze, 38.6 mm. **Obv:** National arms **Rev:** Multicolor Pope John Paul II with cross **Edge:** Reeded

Date	Mintage	F	VF	XF	Unc	BU
2007 Proof	—	Value: 30.00				

KM# 733   5 DOLLARS
27.0000 g., Copper-Nickel Silvered and Gilt, 38.61 mm. **Subject:** The Black Madonna of Czestochowa **Obv:** Arms **Obv. Legend:** REPUBLIC OF LIBERIA **Rev:** 1/2 length figure of Madonna facing with child

Date	Mintage	F	VF	XF	Unc	BU
2007 Proof	1,000	Value: 40.00				

KM# 958   5 DOLLARS
31.1050 g., Copper-Nickel Silver plated **Rev:** Martin van Buren multicolor applique

Date	Mintage	F	VF	XF	Unc	BU
2009	—	—	—	—	—	5.00

KM# 951   5 DOLLARS
31.1050 g., Copper-Nickel Silver plated **Rev:** George Washington multicolor applique

Date	Mintage	F	VF	XF	Unc	BU
2009	—	—	—	—	—	5.00

KM# 952   5 DOLLARS
31.1050 g., Copper-Nickel Silver plated **Rev:** John Adams multicolor applique

Date	Mintage	F	VF	XF	Unc	BU
2009	—	—	—	—	—	5.00

KM# 953   5 DOLLARS
31.1050 g., Copper-Nickel Silver plated **Rev:** Thomas Jefferson multicolor applique

Date	Mintage	F	VF	XF	Unc	BU
2009	—	—	—	—	—	5.00

KM# 954   5 DOLLARS
31.1050 g., Copper-Nickel Silver plated **Rev:** James Madison multicolor applique

Date	Mintage	F	VF	XF	Unc	BU
2009	—	—	—	—	—	5.00

KM# 955   5 DOLLARS
31.1050 g., Copper-Nickel Silver plated **Rev:** James Monroe multicolor applique

Date	Mintage	F	VF	XF	Unc	BU
2009	—	—	—	—	—	5.00

KM# 956   5 DOLLARS
31.1050 g., Copper-Nickel Silver plated **Rev:** John Quincey Adams multicolor applique

Date	Mintage	F	VF	XF	Unc	BU
2009	—	—	—	—	—	5.00

KM# 957   5 DOLLARS
31.1050 g., Copper-Nickel Silver plated **Rev:** Andrew Jackson multicolor applique

Date	Mintage	F	VF	XF	Unc	BU
2009	—	—	—	—	—	5.00

KM# 959   5 DOLLARS
31.1050 g., Copper-Nickel Silver plated **Rev:** William Henry Harrison multicolor applique

Date	Mintage	F	VF	XF	Unc	BU
2009	—	—	—	—	—	5.00

KM# 960   5 DOLLARS
31.1050 g., Copper-Nickel Silver plated **Rev:** John Tyler multicolor applique

Date	Mintage	F	VF	XF	Unc	BU
2009	—	—	—	—	—	5.00

KM# 961   5 DOLLARS
31.1050 g., Copper-Nickel Silver plated **Rev:** James K. Polk multicolor applique

Date	Mintage	F	VF	XF	Unc	BU
2009	—	—	—	—	—	5.00

KM# 962   5 DOLLARS
31.1050 g., Copper-Nickel Silver plated **Rev:** Zachary Taylor multicolor applique

Date	Mintage	F	VF	XF	Unc	BU
2009	—	—	—	—	—	5.00

KM# 963   5 DOLLARS
31.1050 g., Copper-Nickel Silver plated **Rev:** Millard Filmore multicolor applique

Date	Mintage	F	VF	XF	Unc	BU
2009	—	—	—	—	—	5.00

KM# 964   5 DOLLARS
31.1050 g., Copper-Nickel Silver plated **Rev:** Franklin Pierce multicolor applique

Date	Mintage	F	VF	XF	Unc	BU
2009	—	—	—	—	—	5.00

KM# 965   5 DOLLARS
31.1050 g., Copper-Nickel Silver plated **Rev:** James Buchanan multicolor applique

Date	Mintage	F	VF	XF	Unc	BU
2009	—	—	—	—	—	5.00

KM# 966   5 DOLLARS
31.1050 g., Copper-Nickel Silver plated **Rev:** Abraham Lincoln multicolor applique

Date	Mintage	F	VF	XF	Unc	BU
2009	—	—	—	—	—	5.00

KM# 967   5 DOLLARS
31.1050 g., Copper-Nickel Silver plated **Rev:** Andrew Johnson multicolor applique

Date	Mintage	F	VF	XF	Unc	BU
2009	—	—	—	—	—	5.00

KM# 968   5 DOLLARS
31.1050 g., Copper-Nickel Silver plated **Rev:** Ulysses S. Grant multicolor applique

Date	Mintage	F	VF	XF	Unc	BU
2009	—	—	—	—	—	5.00

KM# 969 5 DOLLARS
31.1050 g., Copper-Nickel Silver plated **Rev:** Rutherford B. Hayes multicolor applique

Date	Mintage	F	VF	XF	Unc	BU
2009	—	—	—	—	—	5.00

KM# 970 5 DOLLARS
31.1050 g., Copper-Nickel Silver plated **Rev:** James A. Garfield multicolor applique

Date	Mintage	F	VF	XF	Unc	BU
2009	—	—	—	—	—	5.00

KM# 971 5 DOLLARS
31.1050 g., Copper-Nickel Silver plated **Rev:** Chester Arthur multicolor underprint

Date	Mintage	F	VF	XF	Unc	BU
2009	—	—	—	—	—	5.00

KM# 972 5 DOLLARS
31.1050 g., Copper-Nickel Silver plated **Rev:** Grover Cleveland multicolor applique

Date	Mintage	F	VF	XF	Unc	BU
2009	—	—	—	—	—	5.00

KM# 973 5 DOLLARS
31.1050 g., Copper-Nickel Silver plated **Rev:** Benjamin Harrison multicolor applique

Date	Mintage	F	VF	XF	Unc	BU
2009	—	—	—	—	—	5.00

KM# 974 5 DOLLARS
31.1050 g., Copper-Nickel Silver plated **Rev:** William McKinley multicolor applique

Date	Mintage	F	VF	XF	Unc	BU
2009	—	—	—	—	—	5.00

KM# 975 5 DOLLARS
31.1050 g., Copper-Nickel Silver plated **Rev:** Theodore Roosevelt multicolor applique

Date	Mintage	F	VF	XF	Unc	BU
2009	—	—	—	—	—	5.00

KM# 976 5 DOLLARS
31.1050 g., Copper-Nickel Silver plated **Rev:** William Howard Taft multicolor applique

Date	Mintage	F	VF	XF	Unc	BU
2009	—	—	—	—	—	5.00

KM# 977 5 DOLLARS
31.1050 g., Copper-Nickel Silver plated **Rev:** Woodrow Wilson multicolor applique

Date	Mintage	F	VF	XF	Unc	BU
2009	—	—	—	—	—	5.00

KM# 978 5 DOLLARS
31.1050 g., Copper-Nickel Silver plated **Rev:** Warren G. Harding multicolor applique

Date	Mintage	F	VF	XF	Unc	BU
2009	—	—	—	—	—	5.00

KM# 979 5 DOLLARS
31.1050 g., Copper-Nickel Silver plated **Rev:** Calvin Collidge multicolor applique

Date	Mintage	F	VF	XF	Unc	BU
2009	—	—	—	—	—	5.00

KM# 980 5 DOLLARS
31.1050 g., Copper-Nickel Silver plated **Rev:** Herbert Hoover multicolor applique

Date	Mintage	F	VF	XF	Unc	BU
2009	—	—	—	—	—	5.00

KM# 981 5 DOLLARS
31.1050 g., Copper-Nickel Silver plated **Rev:** Franklin D. Roosevelt multicolor applique

Date	Mintage	F	VF	XF	Unc	BU
2009	—	—	—	—	—	5.00

KM# 982 5 DOLLARS
31.1050 g., Copper-Nickel Silver plated **Rev:** Harry S Truman multicolor applique

Date	Mintage	F	VF	XF	Unc	BU
2009	—	—	—	—	—	5.00

KM# 983 5 DOLLARS
31.1050 g., Copper-Nickel Silver plated **Rev:** Swight D. Eisenhower multicolor applique

Date	Mintage	F	VF	XF	Unc	BU
2009	—	—	—	—	—	5.00

KM# 984 5 DOLLARS
31.1050 g., Copper-Nickel Silver plated **Rev:** John F. Kennedy multicolor applique

Date	Mintage	F	VF	XF	Unc	BU
2009	—	—	—	—	—	5.00

KM# 985 5 DOLLARS
31.1050 g., Copper-Nickel Silver plated **Rev:** Lyndon B. Johnson multicolor applique

Date	Mintage	F	VF	XF	Unc	BU
2009	—	—	—	—	—	5.00

KM# 986 5 DOLLARS
31.1050 g., Copper-Nickel Silver plated **Rev:** Richard M. Nixon multicolor applique

Date	Mintage	F	VF	XF	Unc	BU
2009	—	—	—	—	—	5.00

KM# 987 5 DOLLARS
31.1050 g., Copper-Nickel Silver plated **Rev:** Gerald R. Ford multicolor applique

Date	Mintage	F	VF	XF	Unc	BU
2009	—	—	—	—	—	5.00

KM# 988 5 DOLLARS
31.1050 g., Copper-Nickel Silver plated **Rev:** Jimmy Carter multicolor applique

Date	Mintage	F	VF	XF	Unc	BU
2009	—	—	—	—	—	5.00

KM# 989 5 DOLLARS
31.1050 g., Copper-Nickel Silver plated **Rev:** Ronald Reagan multicolor applique

Date	Mintage	F	VF	XF	Unc	BU
2009	—	—	—	—	—	5.00

KM# 990 5 DOLLARS
31.1050 g., Copper-Nickel Silver plated **Rev:** George H. W. Bush multicolor applique

Date	Mintage	F	VF	XF	Unc	BU
2009	—	—	—	—	—	5.00

KM# 991 5 DOLLARS
31.1050 g., Copper-Nickel Silver plated **Rev:** Bill Clinton multicolor applique

Date	Mintage	F	VF	XF	Unc	BU
2009	—	—	—	—	—	5.00

KM# 992 5 DOLLARS
31.1050 g., Copper-Nickel Silver plated **Rev:** George W. Bush multicolor applique

Date	Mintage	F	VF	XF	Unc	BU
2009	—	—	—	—	—	5.00

KM# 993 5 DOLLARS
31.1050 g., Copper-Nickel Silver palted **Rev:** Barack Obama multicolor applique

Date	Mintage	F	VF	XF	Unc	BU
2009	—	—	—	—	—	5.00

KM# 513 10 DOLLARS
28.5000 g., Copper-Nickel, 38.6 mm. **Series:** Moments of Freedom **Subject:** Hungarian Revolution of 1848 **Obv:** National arms **Rev:** Multicolor heroic scene **Edge:** Reeded

Date	Mintage	F	VF	XF	Unc	BU
2001 Proof	9,999	Value: 12.00				

KM# 491 10 DOLLARS
25.2500 g., 0.9250 Silver 0.7509 oz. ASW, 36.8 mm. **Subject:** Illusion **Obv:** National arms **Rev:** Stylized head with glasses facing **Edge:** Plain **Shape:** 10-sided

Date	Mintage	F	VF	XF	Unc	BU
2001 Proof	5,000	Value: 37.50				

KM# 777 10 DOLLARS
14.5500 g., Copper-Nickel, 32 mm. **Subject:** 43rd President of USA **Obv:** National arms **Obv. Legend:** REPUBLIC OF LIBERIA **Rev:** George W. Bush, flag in background

Date	Mintage	F	VF	XF	Unc	BU
2001 Proof	—	Value: 12.00				

KM# 822 10 DOLLARS
1.2400 g., Gold, 13.68 mm. **Obv:** National arms **Rev:** Bust of Marlene Dietrich facing **Edge:** Reeded

Date	Mintage	F	VF	XF	Unc	BU
2001 Proof	—	Value: 75.00				

KM# 493 10 DOLLARS
770.0000 g., Copper, 100 mm. **Subject:** Wreck of the Princess Louisa **Obv:** National arms **Rev:** Sailing ship **Edge:** Reeded **Note:** Illustration reduced. With an encased glass shard recovered from the wreck site of the Princess Louisa.

Date	Mintage	F	VF	XF	Unc	BU
2001	2,000	—	—	—	225	—

KM# 510 10 DOLLARS
33.2400 g., Copper Gilt, 40.1 mm. **Obv:** National arms **Rev:** Multicolor holographic bald eagle **Edge:** Reeded

Date	Mintage	F	VF	XF	Unc	BU
2001	20,000	—	—	—	—	35.00

KM# 537 10 DOLLARS
28.5000 g., Copper-Nickel, 38.6 mm. **Subject:** Moments of Freedom **Obv:** National arms **Rev:** Multicolor Buddha, spelled "Budha" on the coin **Edge:** Reeded

Date	Mintage	F	VF	XF	Unc	BU
2001 Proof	9,999	Value: 12.00				

KM# 538 10 DOLLARS
28.5000 g., Copper-Nickel, 38.6 mm. **Subject:** Moments of Freedom **Obv:** National arms **Rev:** Multicolor Battle of Marathon scene **Edge:** Reeded

Date	Mintage	F	VF	XF	Unc	BU
2001 Proof	9,999	Value: 12.00				

KM# 539   10 DOLLARS
28.5000 g., Copper-Nickel, 38.6 mm. **Series:** Moments of Freedom **Obv:** National arms **Rev:** Multicolor founding of Liberia design **Edge:** Reeded

Date	Mintage	F	VF	XF	Unc	BU
2001 Proof	9,999	Value: 12.00				

KM# 540   10 DOLLARS
28.5000 g., Copper-Nickel, 38.6 mm. **Series:** Moments of Freedom **Obv:** National arms **Rev:** Multicolor portrait of Constantine I **Edge:** Reeded

Date	Mintage	F	VF	XF	Unc	BU
2001 Proof	9,999	Value: 12.00				

KM# 541   10 DOLLARS
28.5000 g., Copper-Nickel, 38.6 mm. **Series:** Moments of Freedom **Obv:** National arms **Rev:** Multicolor William Tell statue **Edge:** Reeded

Date	Mintage	F	VF	XF	Unc	BU
2001 Proof	9,999	Value: 12.00				

KM# 542   10 DOLLARS
28.5000 g., Copper-Nickel, 38.6 mm. **Series:** Moments of Freedom **Obv:** National arms **Rev:** Multicolor bust facing **Edge:** Reeded

Date	Mintage	F	VF	XF	Unc	BU
2001 Proof	9,999	Value: 12.00				

KM# 543   10 DOLLARS
28.5000 g., Copper-Nickel, 38.6 mm. **Series:** Moments of Freedom **Obv:** National arms **Rev:** Multicolor head with headdress and battle scene **Edge:** Reeded

Date	Mintage	F	VF	XF	Unc	BU
2001 Proof	9,999	Value: 12.00				

KM# 544   10 DOLLARS
28.5000 g., Copper-Nickel, 38.6 mm. **Series:** Moments of Freedom **Obv:** National arms **Rev:** Multicolor Brandenburg Gate scene **Edge:** Reeded

Date	Mintage	F	VF	XF	Unc	BU
2001 Proof	9,999	Value: 12.00				

KM# 545   10 DOLLARS
28.5000 g., Copper-Nickel, 38.6 mm. **Series:** Moments of Freedom **Obv:** National arms **Rev:** Multicolor half length figure facing **Edge:** Reeded

Date	Mintage	F	VF	XF	Unc	BU
2001 Proof	9,999	Value: 12.00				

KM# 546   10 DOLLARS
28.5000 g., Copper-Nickel, 38.6 mm. **Series:** Moments of Freedom **Obv:** National arms **Rev:** Multicolor Sitting Bull portrait **Edge:** Reeded

Date	Mintage	F	VF	XF	Unc	BU
2001 Proof	9,999	Value: 12.00				

KM# 547   10 DOLLARS
28.5000 g., Copper-Nickel, 38.6 mm. **Series:** Moments of Freedom **Obv:** National arms **Rev:** Multicolor Declaration of Independence scene **Edge:** Reeded

Date	Mintage	F	VF	XF	Unc	BU
2001 Proof	9,999	Value: 12.00				

KM# 548   10 DOLLARS
28.5000 g., Copper-Nickel, 38.6 mm. **Series:** Moments of Freedom **Obv:** National arms **Rev:** Multicolor allegorical woman **Edge:** Reeded

Date	Mintage	F	VF	XF	Unc	BU
2001 Proof	9,999	Value: 12.00				

KM# 549   10 DOLLARS
28.5000 g., Copper-Nickel, 38.6 mm. **Series:** Moments of Freedom **Obv:** National arms **Rev:** Multicolor bust of Gandhi looking down **Edge:** Reeded

Date	Mintage	F	VF	XF	Unc	BU
2001 Proof	9,999	Value: 12.00				

KM# 550   10 DOLLARS
28.5000 g., Copper-Nickel, 38.6 mm. **Series:** Moments of Freedom **Obv:** National arms **Rev:** Multicolor picture of a soldier at the moment he is shot in battle **Edge:** Reeded

Date	Mintage	F	VF	XF	Unc	BU
2001 Proof	9,999	Value: 12.00				

KM# 551   10 DOLLARS
28.5000 g., Copper-Nickel, 38.6 mm. **Series:** Moments of Freedom **Obv:** National arms **Rev:** Multicolor inmates behind wire fence scene **Edge:** Reeded

Date	Mintage	F	VF	XF	Unc	BU
2001 Proof	9,999	Value: 12.00				

KM# 552   10 DOLLARS
28.5000 g., Copper-Nickel, 38.6 mm. **Series:** Moments of Freedom **Obv:** National arms **Rev:** Multicolor Iwo Jima flag raising scene **Edge:** Reeded

Date	Mintage	F	VF	XF	Unc	BU
2001 Proof	9,999	Value: 12.00				

KM# 553   10 DOLLARS
28.5000 g., Copper-Nickel, 38.6 mm. **Series:** Moments of Freedom **Obv:** National arms **Rev:** Multicolor UN logo and dove **Edge:** Reeded

Date	Mintage	F	VF	XF	Unc	BU
2001 Proof	9,999	Value: 12.00				

KM# 554   10 DOLLARS
28.5000 g., Copper-Nickel, 38.6 mm. **Series:** Moments of Freedom **Obv:** National arms **Rev:** Multicolor Solzhenitsyn portrait **Edge:** Reeded

Date	Mintage	F	VF	XF	Unc	BU
2001 Proof	9,999	Value: 12.00				

KM# 555   10 DOLLARS
28.5000 g., Copper-Nickel, 38.6 mm. **Series:** Moments of Freedom **Obv:** National arms **Rev:** Multicolor Spartacus and troops **Edge:** Reeded

Date	Mintage	F	VF	XF	Unc	BU
2001 Proof	9,999	Value: 12.00				

KM# 556   10 DOLLARS
28.5000 g., Copper-Nickel, 38.6 mm. **Series:** Moments of Freedom **Obv:** National arms **Rev:** Multicolor Soviet tank in Prague **Edge:** Reeded

Date	Mintage	F	VF	XF	Unc	BU
2001 Proof	9,999	Value: 12.00				

KM# 557   10 DOLLARS
28.5000 g., Copper-Nickel, 38.6 mm. **Series:** Moments of Freedom **Obv:** National arms **Rev:** Multicolor Bastille scene **Edge:** Reeded

Date	Mintage	F	VF	XF	Unc	BU
2001 Proof	9,999	Value: 12.00				

KM# 558   10 DOLLARS
28.5000 g., Copper-Nickel, 38.6 mm. **Series:** Moments of Freedom **Obv:** National arms **Rev:** Multicolor Nelson Mandela and fist **Edge:** Reeded

Date	Mintage	F	VF	XF	Unc	BU
2001 Proof	9,999	Value: 12.00				

KM# 559   10 DOLLARS
28.5000 g., Copper-Nickel, 38.6 mm. **Series:** Moments of Freedom **Obv:** National arms **Rev:** Multicolor circuit board and world globe **Edge:** Reeded

Date	Mintage	F	VF	XF	Unc	BU
2001 Proof	9,999	Value: 12.00				

KM# 994   10 DOLLARS
0.9990 Gold, 12 mm. **Obv:** National Arms **Rev:** Franklin, Jefferson, Adams and Declaration of Independence

Date	Mintage	F	VF	XF	Unc	BU
2001 Proof	—	Value: 70.00				

KM# 654   10 DOLLARS
15.3300 g., Copper-Nickel, 33.2 mm. **Obv:** National arms **Rev:** "GEORGE W. BUSH..." No value at bottom **Edge:** Reeded

Date	Mintage	F	VF	XF	Unc	BU
2002	—	—	—	—	—	10.00

KM# 705   10 DOLLARS
31.1035 g., 0.9990 Silver 0.9990 oz. ASW, 38.6 mm. **Subject:** 2002 World Football Championship - Japan - South Korea **Obv:** National arms **Rev:** Pagoda superimposed on a soccer ball, legend around **Edge:** Reeded

Date	Mintage	F	VF	XF	Unc	BU
2002 Proof	—	Value: 45.00				

KM# 806   10 DOLLARS
14.3000 g., Copper-Nickel, 33.11 mm. **Obv:** National arms **Rev:**
Bust of President Bush facing at left, soldier standing at right
facing, flag in background **Rev. Legend:** America's Fight For
Freedom **Edge:** Reeded

Date	Mintage	F	VF	XF	Unc	BU
2002	—	—	—	—	10.00	12.00

KM# 807   10 DOLLARS
26.3000 g., Copper-Nickel, 40.36 mm. **Subject:** America's First
Ladies **Obv:** National arms **Rev:** Bust of Jacqueline Kennedy
facing, small oval portrait of President John F. Kennedy at right
Edge: Reeded

Date	Mintage	F	VF	XF	Unc	BU
2003 Proof	—	Value: 15.00				

KM# 824   10 DOLLARS
14.6000 g., Copper-Nickel, 33 mm. **Subject:** Abraham Lincoln
Obv: National arms **Rev:** Bust facing at left, Lincoln Memorial in
background **Edge:** Reeded

Date	Mintage	F	VF	XF	Unc	BU
2003 Proof	20,000	Value: 12.00				

KM# 708   10 DOLLARS
25.1000 g., 0.9250 Silver 0.7464 oz. ASW, 38.6 mm. **Obv:**
National arms **Rev:** Clipper ship "Flying Cloud" **Edge:** Reeded

Date	Mintage	F	VF	XF	Unc	BU
2003 Proof	—	Value: 35.00				

KM# 602   10 DOLLARS
25.0000 g., 0.9250 Silver 0.7435 oz. ASW, 38.6 mm. **Obv:**
National arms **Rev:** Icarus and Daedalus in flight **Edge:** Reeded

Date	Mintage	F	VF	XF	Unc	BU
2003 Proof	—	Value: 35.00				

KM# 603   10 DOLLARS
25.0000 g., 0.9250 Silver 0.7435 oz. ASW, 38.6 mm. **Obv:**
National arms **Rev:** First parachute **Edge:** Reeded

Date	Mintage	F	VF	XF	Unc	BU
2003 Proof	—	Value: 35.00				

KM# 604   10 DOLLARS
25.0000 g., 0.9250 Silver 0.7435 oz. ASW, 38.6 mm. **Obv:**
National arms **Rev:** Montgolfier ballon **Edge:** Reeded

Date	Mintage	F	VF	XF	Unc	BU
2003 Proof	—	Value: 35.00				

KM# 605   10 DOLLARS
25.0000 g., 0.9250 Silver 0.7435 oz. ASW, 38.6 mm. **Obv:**
National arms **Rev:** Otto v. Lillenthal **Edge:** Reeded

Date	Mintage	F	VF	XF	Unc	BU
2003 Proof	—	Value: 35.00				

KM# 606   10 DOLLARS
25.0000 g., 0.9250 Silver 0.7435 oz. ASW, 38.6 mm. **Obv:**
National arms **Rev:** Wright Brothers **Edge:** Reeded

Date	Mintage	F	VF	XF	Unc	BU
2003 Proof	—	Value: 35.00				

KM# 607   10 DOLLARS
25.0000 g., 0.9250 Silver 0.7435 oz. ASW, 38.6 mm. **Obv:**
National arms **Rev:** Mach 1- Bell X **Edge:** Reeded

Date	Mintage	F	VF	XF	Unc	BU
2003 Proof	—	Value: 35.00				

KM# 608   10 DOLLARS
25.0000 g., 0.9250 Silver 0.7435 oz. ASW, 38.6 mm. **Obv:**
National arms **Rev:** The Concorde **Edge:** Reeded

Date	Mintage	F	VF	XF	Unc	BU
2003 Proof	—	Value: 35.00				

KM# 823   10 DOLLARS
1.2300 g., Gold, 13.88 mm. **Subject:** 2006 World Football
championship Germany **Obv:** National arms **Rev:** Football at
lower left, stadium at center **Rev. Legend:** DEUTSCHLAND 2006
Edge: Reeded

Date	Mintage	F	VF	XF	Unc	BU
2004 Proof	—	Value: 75.00				

KM# 611   10 DOLLARS
62.2070 g., 0.9990 Silver 1.9979 oz. ASW, 50 mm. **Obv:**
National arms left of window design with Tiffany Glass inlay **Rev:**
Window design with Tiffany Glass inlay **Edge:** Plain

Date	Mintage	F	VF	XF	Unc	BU
2004	999	—	—	—	—	200

KM# 740   10 DOLLARS
20.0000 g., 0.9990 Silver partially gilt 0.6423 oz. ASW,
38.00 mm. **Series:** Endangered Wildlife **Obv:** National arms

Obv. Legend: REPUBLIC OF LIBERIA **Rev:** Gilt Siberian Tiger
with diamonds inset in eyes **Rev. Legend:** RUSSIA **Edge:** Plain

Date	Mintage	F	VF	XF	Unc	BU
2004 Proof	5,000	Value: 175				

KM# 741   10 DOLLARS
20.0000 g., 0.9990 Silver partially gilt 0.6423 oz. ASW,
38.00 mm. **Series:** Endangered Wildlife **Obv:** National arms
Obv. Legend: REPUBLIC OF LIBERIA **Rev:** Two gilt Hyacinth
Macaws perched on branch with diamond insets in eyes **Rev.
Legend:** BRAZIL **Edge:** Plain

Date	Mintage	F	VF	XF	Unc	BU
2004 Proof	5,000	Value: 175				

KM# 742   10 DOLLARS
20.0000 g., 0.9990 Silver partially gilt 0.6423 oz. ASW,
38.00 mm. **Series:** Endangered Wildlife **Obv:** National arms
Obv. Legend: REPUBLIC OF LIBERIA **Rev:** Gilt young Giant
Panda seated eating bamboo shoots **Rev. Legend:** CHINA
Edge: Plain

Date	Mintage	F	VF	XF	Unc	BU
2004 Proof	5,000	Value: 175				

KM# 743   10 DOLLARS
20.0000 g., 0.9990 Silver partially gilt 0.6423 oz. ASW,
38.00 mm. **Subject:** Endangered Wildlife **Obv:** National arms
Obv. Legend: REPUBLIC OF LIBERIA **Rev:** Two gilt Bald
Eagles. one perched at left, one alighting at center right **Rev.
Legend:** USA **Edge:** Plain

Date	Mintage	F	VF	XF	Unc	BU
2004 Proof	5,000	Value: 175				

KM# 744   10 DOLLARS
20.0000 g., 0.9990 Silver partially gilt 0.6423 oz. ASW, 38 mm.
Series: Endangered Wildlife **Obv:** National arms **Obv. Legend:**
REPUBLIC OF LIBERIA **Rev:** Gilt Puma standing with diamonds
inset in eyes **Rev. Legend:** MEXICO **Edge:** Plain

Date	Mintage	F	VF	XF	Unc	BU
2004 Proof	5,000	Value: 175				

KM# 745   10 DOLLARS
20.0000 g., 0.9990 Silver partially gilt 0.6423 oz. ASW, 38 mm.
Series: Endangered Wildlife **Obv:** National arms **Obv. Legend:**
REPUBLIC OF LIBERIA **Rev:** Gilt Red-ruffed Lemur on branch
with diamonds inset in eyes **Rev. Legend:** MADAGASCAR
Edge: Plain

Date	Mintage	F	VF	XF	Unc	BU
2004 Proof	5,000	Value: 175				

KM# 746   10 DOLLARS
20.0000 g., 0.9990 Silver partially gilt 0.6423 oz. ASW, 38 mm.
Series: Endangered Wildlife **Obv:** National arms **Obv. Legend:**
REPUBLIC OF LIBERIA **Rev:** Two gilt Andean Condors, one
lifting off at center, one perched at right **Rev. Legend:** CHILE
Edge: Plain

Date	Mintage	F	VF	XF	Unc	BU
2004 Proof	5,000	Value: 175				

KM# 747   10 DOLLARS
20.0000 g., 0.9990 Silver partially gilt 0.6423 oz. ASW, 38 mm.
Series: Endangered Wildlife **Obv:** National arms **Obv. Legend:**
REPUBLIC OF LIBERIA **Rev:** Two gilt Yellow-eyed Penguins
standing facing with diamonds inset in eyes **Rev. Legend:** NEW
ZEALAND **Edge:** Plain

Date	Mintage	F	VF	XF	Unc	BU
2004 Proof	5,000	Value: 175				

KM# 748   10 DOLLARS
20.0000 g., 0.9990 Silver partially gilt 0.6423 oz. ASW, 38 mm.
Series: Endangered Wildlife **Obv:** National arms **Obv. Legend:**
REPUBLIC OF LIBERIA **Rev:** Gilt African lion standing facing
with diamonds inset in eyes **Rev. Legend:** SOUTH AFRICA
Edge: Plain

Date	Mintage	F	VF	XF	Unc	BU
2004 Proof	5,000	Value: 175				

KM# 749   10 DOLLARS
20.0000 g., 0.9990 Silver partially gilt 0.6423 oz. ASW, 38 mm.
Series: Endangered Wildlife **Obv:** National arms **Obv. Legend:**
REPUBLIC OF LIBERIA **Rev:** Two gilt perched Kookaburras with
diamonds inset in eyes **Rev. Legend:** AUSTRALIA **Edge:** Plain

Date	Mintage	F	VF	XF	Unc	BU
2004 Proof	5,000	Value: 175				

KM# 750   10 DOLLARS
20.0000 g., 0.9990 Silver partially gilt 0.6423 oz. ASW, 38 mm.
Series: Endangered Wildlife **Obv:** National arms **Obv. Legend:**
REPUBLIC OF LIBERIA **Rev:** Gilt Polar Bear standing facing
with diamonds inset in eyes **Rev. Legend:** CANADA **Edge:** Plain

Date	Mintage	F	VF	XF	Unc	BU
2004 Proof	5,000	Value: 175				

KM# 751   10 DOLLARS
20.0000 g., 0.9990 Silver partially gilt 0.6423 oz. ASW   **Series:**
Endangered Wildlife **Obv:** National arms **Obv. Legend:**
REPUBLIC OF LIBERIA **Rev:** Gilt perched Blakiston's Fish-owl
with diamonds inset in eyes **Rev. Legend:** JAPAN

Date	Mintage	F	VF	XF	Unc	BU
2004 Proof	5,000	Value: 175				

KM# 808   10 DOLLARS
14.5800 g., Copper-Nickel, 32.98 mm. **Obv:** National arms **Rev:**
Bust of President Ronald Reagon facing, flag in background
Edge: Reeded

Date	Mintage	F	VF	XF	Unc	BU
2004	—	—	—	—	8.00	10.00

KM# 830   10 DOLLARS
15.6200 g., Copper-Nickel, 33.3 mm. **Obv:** National arms **Rev:**
Flag at left, bust of 43rd President George W. Bush facing at right
Edge: Reeded

Date	Mintage	F	VF	XF	Unc	BU
2004	—	—	—	—	10.00	12.00

KM# 738   10 DOLLARS
27.1900 g., Copper-Nickel, 43 mm. **Subject:** Death of Pope
John-Paul II **Edge:** Reeded

Date	Mintage	F	VF	XF	Unc	BU
2005	—	—	—	—	12.00	14.00

KM# 739.1   10 DOLLARS
25.0000 g., 0.9250 Silver 0.7435 oz. ASW   **Subject:** Death of
Pope John-Paul II **Rev:** Silhouette of John-Paul gilt, backgound
in Ruthenium

Date	Mintage	F	VF	XF	Unc	BU
2005	7,500	—	—	—	—	60.00

KM# 739.2   10 DOLLARS
25.0000 g., 0.9250 Silver 0.7435 oz. ASW   **Subject:** Death of
Pope John-Paul II **Rev:** Silhouette of John-Paul gilt, blackened
background

Date	Mintage	F	VF	XF	Unc	BU
2005	7,500	—	—	—	—	47.50

KM# 752   10 DOLLARS
20.0000 g., 0.9990 Silver partially gilt 0.6423 oz. ASW, 38 mm.
Series: Endangered Wildlife **Obv:** National arms **Obv. Legend:**
REPUBLIC OF LIBERIA **Rev:** Gilt Koala perched on branch with
diamonds inset in eyes **Rev. Legend:** AUSTRALIA **Edge:** Plain

Date	Mintage	F	VF	XF	Unc	BU
2005 Proof	5,000	Value: 150				

KM# 753   10 DOLLARS
20.0000 g., 0.9990 Silver partially gilt 0.6423 oz. ASW, 38 mm.
Series: Endangered Wildlife **Obv:** National arms **Obv. Legend:**
REPUBLIC OF LIBERIA **Rev:** Two perched gilt Yellow-eared
Conures with diamonds inset in eyes **Rev. Legend:** COLOMBIA
Edge: Plain

Date	Mintage	F	VF	XF	Unc	BU
2005 Proof	5,000	Value: 150				

KM# 754   10 DOLLARS
20.0000 g., 0.9990 Silver partially gilt 0.6423 oz. ASW, 38 mm.
Series: Endangered Wildlife **Obv:** National arms **Obv. Legend:**
REPUBLIC OF LIBERIA **Rev:** Gilt Iberian Lynx standing facing
with diamonds inset in eyes **Rev. Legend:** SPAIN **Edge:** Plain

Date	Mintage	F	VF	XF	Unc	BU
2005 Proof	5,000	Value: 150				

KM# 755   10 DOLLARS
20.0000 g., 0.9990 Silver partially gilt 0.6423 oz. ASW, 38 mm.
Series: Endangered Wildlife **Obv:** National arms **Obv. Legend:**
REPUBLIC OF LIBERIA **Rev:** Two perched gilt Yellow-crested
Cockatoos **Rev. Legend:** INDONESIA **Edge:** Plain

Date	Mintage	F	VF	XF	Unc	BU
2005 Proof	5,000	Value: 150				

KM# 756   10 DOLLARS
20.0000 g., 0.9990 Silver partially gilt 0.6423 oz. ASW, 38 mm.
Series: Endangered Wildlife **Obv:** National arms **Obv. Legend:**
REPUBLIC OF LIBERIA **Rev:** Gilt Jaguar resting on branch with
diamonds inset in eyes **Rev. Legend:** BELIZE **Edge:** Plain

Date	Mintage	F	VF	XF	Unc	BU
2005 Proof	5,000	Value: 150				

KM# 757   10 DOLLARS
20.0000 g., 0.9990 Silver partially gilt 0.6423 oz. ASW, 38 mm.
Series: Endangered Wildlife **Obv:** National arms **Obv. Legend:**
REPUBLIC OF LIBERIA **Rev:** Two perched gilt Plate-billed
Mountain Toucans with diamonds inset in eyes **Rev. Legend:**
ECUADOR **Edge:** Plain

Date	Mintage	F	VF	XF	Unc	BU
2005 Proof	5,000	Value: 150				

KM# 758   10 DOLLARS
20.0000 g., 0.9990 Silver partially gilt 0.6423 oz. ASW, 38 mm.
Series: Endangered Wildlife **Obv:** National arms **Obv. Legend:**
REPUBLIC OF LIBERIA **Rev:** Gilt Red Panda resting facing with
diamonds inset in eyes **Rev. Legend:** INDIA **Edge:** Plain

Date	Mintage	F	VF	XF	Unc	BU
2005 Proof	5,000	Value: 150				

KM# 759   10 DOLLARS
20.0000 g., 0.9990 Silver partially gilt 0.6423 oz. ASW, 38 mm.
Series: Endangered Wildlife **Obv:** National arms **Obv. Legend:**
REPUBLIC OF LIBERIA **Rev:** Two perched gilt Resplendent
Quetzals with diamonds inset in eyes **Rev. Legend:**
GUATEMALA **Edge:** Plain

Date	Mintage	F	VF	XF	Unc	BU
2005 Proof	5,000	Value: 150				

KM# 760   10 DOLLARS
20.0000 g., 0.9990 Silver partially gilt 0.6423 oz. ASW, 38 mm.
Series: Endangered Wildlife **Obv:** National arms **Obv. Legend:**
REPUBLIC OF LIBERIA **Rev:** Gilt Snow Leopard standing left
looking back with diamonds inset in eyes **Rev. Legend:** NEPAL
Edge: Plain

Date	Mintage	F	VF	XF	Unc	BU
2005 Proof	5,000	Value: 150				

KM# 761   10 DOLLARS
20.0000 g., 0.9990 Silver partially gilt 0.6423 oz. ASW, 38 mm.
Series: Endangered Wildlife **Obv:** National arms **Obv. Legend:**
REPUBLIC OF LIBERIA **Rev:** Gilt Fossa standing right on branch
facing with diamonds inset in eyes **Rev. Legend:** MADAGASCAR
Edge: Plain

Date	Mintage	F	VF	XF	Unc	BU
2005 Proof	5,000	Value: 150				

KM# 762   10 DOLLARS
20.0000 g., 0.9990 Silver partially gilt 0.6423 oz. ASW, 38 mm.
Series: Endangered Wildlife **Obv:** National arms **Obv. Legend:**
REPUBLIC OF LIBERIA **Rev:** Two gilt Chilean Flamingos
standing left with diamonds inset in eyes **Rev. Legend:**
ARGENTINA **Edge:** Plain

Date	Mintage	F	VF	XF	Unc	BU
2005 Proof	5,000	Value: 150				

KM# 763   10 DOLLARS
20.0000 g., 0.9990 Silver partially gilt 0.6423 oz. ASW, 38 mm.
Series: Endangered Wildlife **Obv:** National arms **Obv. Legend:**
REPUBLIC OF LIBERIA **Rev:** Two gilt White-winged ducks, one
standing, one swimming right with diamonds inset in eyes **Rev.
Legend:** THAILAND **Edge:** Plain

Date	Mintage	F	VF	XF	Unc	BU
2005 Proof	5,000	Value: 150				

KM# 860   10 DOLLARS
25.0000 g., 0.9250 Silver 0.7435 oz. ASW, 38.6 mm. **Subject:**
Poison frogs **Rev:** Green Frog, multicolor

Date	Mintage	F	VF	XF	Unc	BU
2005 Proof	2,500	Value: 50.00				

KM# 861   10 DOLLARS
25.0000 g., 0.9250 Silver 0.7435 oz. ASW, 38.6 mm. **Subject:**
Poison frogs **Rev:** Red frog, multicolor

Date	Mintage	F	VF	XF	Unc	BU
2005 Proof	2,500	Value: 50.00				

KM# 862   10 DOLLARS
25.0000 g., 0.9250 Silver 0.7435 oz. ASW, 38.6 mm. **Subject:**
Poison frogs **Rev:** Blue frog, multicolor

Date	Mintage	F	VF	XF	Unc	BU
2005 Proof	2,500	Value: 50.00				

KM# 864   10 DOLLARS
0.5000 g., 0.5850 Gold 0.0094 oz. AGW, 11 mm. **Subject:** 25th
Anniversary of the Krugerrand **Obv:** Shield **Rev:** Paul Krueger
bust left

Date	Mintage	F	VF	XF	Unc	BU
2005 Proof	—	Value: 35.00				

KM# 996   10 DOLLARS
62.2000 g., 0.9990 Silver 1.9977 oz. ASW, 50 mm. **Subject:**
Romanesque Architecture **Rev:** Facade, Tiffany Glass insert

Date	Mintage	F	VF	XF	Unc	BU
2005 Antique finish	999	—	—	—	100	—

KM# 843   10 DOLLARS
0.7300 g., 0.9990 Gold 0.0234 oz. AGW, 11 mm. **Obv:** Arms
Rev: John F. Kennedy head left

Date	Mintage	F	VF	XF	Unc	BU
2006 Proof	20,000	Value: 60.00				

KM# 764   10 DOLLARS
20.0000 g., 0.9990 Silver partially gilt 0.6423 oz. ASW, 38 mm.
Series: Endangered Wildlife **Obv:** National arms **Obv. Legend:**
REPUBLIC OF LIBERIA **Rev:** Gilt Crested Genet on branch
facing with diamonds inset in eyes **Rev. Legend:** CAMEROON
Edge: Plain

Date	Mintage	F	VF	XF	Unc	BU
2006 Proof	5,000	Value: 150				

KM# 765   10 DOLLARS
20.0000 g., 0.9990 Silver partially gilt 0.6423 oz. ASW, 38 mm.
Series: Endangered Wildlife **Obv:** National arms **Obv. Legend:**
REPUBLIC OF LIBERIA **Rev:** Two gilt Dalmatian Pelicans, one
swimming, one standing with diamonds inset in eyes **Rev.
Legend:** MONTENEGRO **Edge:** Plain

Date	Mintage	F	VF	XF	Unc	BU
2006 Proof	5,000	Value: 150				

KM# 766   10 DOLLARS
20.0000 g., 0.9990 Silver partially gilt 0.6423 oz. ASW, 38 mm.
Series: Endangered Wildlife **Obv:** National arms **Obv. Legend:**
REPUBLIC OF LIBERIA **Rev:** Gilt Hairy-bared Dwarf Lemue
standing on branch with diamonds inset in eyes **Rev. Legend:**
MADAGASCAR **Edge:** Plain

Date	Mintage	F	VF	XF	Unc	BU
2006 Proof	5,000	Value: 150				

KM# 767   10 DOLLARS
20.0000 g., 0.9990 Silver partially gilt 0.6423 oz. ASW, 38 mm.
Series: Endangered Wildlife **Obv:** National arms **Obv. Legend:**
REPUBLIC OF LIBERIA **Rev:** Two gilt Visayan Tarictics perched
on branches with diamonds inset in eyes **Rev. Legend:**
Philippines **Edge:** Plain

Date	Mintage	F	VF	XF	Unc	BU
2006 Proof	5,000	Value: 150				

KM# 768   10 DOLLARS
20.0000 g., 0.9990 Silver partially gilt 0.6423 oz. ASW, 38 mm.
Series: Endangered Wildlife **Obv:** National arms **Obv. Legend:**
REPUBLIC OF LIBERIA **Rev:** Two gilt Ethiopian Wolves, one
seated, one laying with diamonds inset in eyes **Rev. Legend:**
ETHIOPIA **Edge:** Plain

Date	Mintage	F	VF	XF	Unc	BU
2006 Proof	5,000	Value: 150				

KM# 769   10 DOLLARS
20.0000 g., 0.9990 Silver partially gilt 0.6423 oz. ASW, 38 mm.
Series: Endangered Wildlife **Obv:** National arms **Obv. Legend:**
REPUBLIC OF LIBERIA **Rev:** Two gilt Kakapos perched on a
branch with diamonds inset in eyes **Rev. Legend:** NEW
ZEALAND **Edge:** Plain

Date	Mintage	F	VF	XF	Unc	BU
2006 Proof	5,000	Value: 150				

KM# 770 10 DOLLARS
20.0000 g., 0.9990 Silver partially gilt 0.6423 oz. ASW, 38 mm.
Series: Endangered Wildlife **Obv:** National arms **Obv. Legend:**
REPUBLIC OF LIBERIA **Rev:** Gilt Spectacled Bear standing with
diamonds inset in eyes **Rev. Legend:** BOLIVIA **Edge:** Plain

Date	Mintage	F	VF	XF	Unc	BU
2006 Proof	5,000	Value: 150				

KM# 771 10 DOLLARS
20.0000 g., 0.9990 Silver partially gilt 0.6423 oz. ASW, 38 mm.
Series: Endangered Wildlife **Obv:** National arms **Obv. Legend:**
REPUBLIC OF LIBERIA **Rev:** Two gilt Mauritius Kestrels perched
on branch with diamonds inset in eyes **Rev. Legend:**
MAURITIUS **Edge:** Plain

Date	Mintage	F	VF	XF	Unc	BU
2006 Proof	5,000	Value: 150				

KM# 772 10 DOLLARS
20.0000 g., 0.9990 Silver Partially gilt 0.6423 oz. ASW, 38 mm.
Series: Endangered Wildlife **Obv:** National arms **Obv. Legend:**
REPUBLIC OF LIBERIA **Rev:** Two gilt Mhorr Gazelles, one
standing, one resting with diamonds inset in eyes **Rev. Legend:**
MALI **Edge:** Plain

Date	Mintage	F	VF	XF	Unc	BU
2006 Proof	5,000	Value: 150				

KM# 773 10 DOLLARS
20.0000 g., 0.9990 Silver partially gilt 0.6423 oz. ASW, 38 mm.
Series: Endangered Wildlife **Obv:** National arms **Obv. Legend:**
REPUBLIC OF LIBERIA **Rev:** Two gilt Blue Lorikeets perched
on branches with diamonds inset in eyes **Rev. Legend:** FRENCH
POLYNESIA **Edge:** Plain

Date	Mintage	F	VF	XF	Unc	BU
2006 Proof	5,000	Value: 150				

KM# 774 10 DOLLARS
20.0000 g., 0.9990 Silver partially gilt 0.6423 oz. ASW, 38 mm.
Series: Endangered Wildlife **Obv:** National arms **Obv. Legend:**
REPUBLIC OF LIBERIA **Rev:** Gilt resting Arabian Leopard with
diamonds inset in eyes **Rev. Legend:** SAUDI ARABIA **Edge:** Plain

Date	Mintage	F	VF	XF	Unc	BU
2006 Proof	5,000	Value: 150				

KM# 775 10 DOLLARS
20.0000 g., 0.9990 Silver partially gilt 0.6423 oz. ASW, 38 mm.
Series: Endangered Wildlife **Obv:** National arms **Obv. Legend:**
REPUBLIC OF LIBERIA **Rev:** Two gilt Hawaiian Geese standing
with diamonds inset in eyes **Rev. Legend:** USA **Edge:** Plain

Date	Mintage	F	VF	XF	Unc	BU
2006 Proof	5,000	Value: 150				

KM# 827 10 DOLLARS
14.6000 g., Copper-Nickel, 33 mm. **Subject:** Abraham Lincoln
Obv: National arms **Rev:** Bust facing 3/4 right **Edge:** Reeded

Date	Mintage	F	VF	XF	Unc	BU
2006 Proof	50,000	Value: 10.00				

KM# 725 10 DOLLARS
3.1100 g., 0.9990 Gold 0.0999 oz. AGW, 16 mm. **Obv:** National
arms **Rev:** Leopard head **Edge:** Reeded

Date	Mintage	F	VF	XF	Unc	BU
2007 Proof	120	Value: 200				

KM# 734 10 DOLLARS
25.0000 g., 0.9250 Silver 0.7435 oz. ASW, 38.61 mm. **Subject:**
The Black Madonna of Czestochowa **Obv:** Arms **Obv. Legend:**
REPUBLIC OF LIBERIA **Rev:** 1/2 length figure of Madonna facing
with child

Date	Mintage	F	VF	XF	Unc	BU
2007 Proof	1,000	Value: 70.00				

KM# 643 20 DOLLARS
15.5500 g., 0.9990 Silver 0.4994 oz. ASW, 30.4 mm. **Obv:** St.
Peter's Basilica **Rev:** Bust of Pope facing **Edge:** Reeded

Date	Mintage	F	VF	XF	Unc	BU
2001S Proof	—	Value: 28.00				

KM# 650 20 DOLLARS
19.9100 g., 0.9990 Silver 0.6395 oz. ASW, 40 mm. **Obv:**
National arms **Rev:** Bust of Charles Lindbergh facing and Spirit
of St. Louis in background **Edge:** Reeded

Date	Mintage	F	VF	XF	Unc	BU
2001 Proof	—	Value: 40.00				

KM# 715 20 DOLLARS
20.0000 g., 0.9990 Silver 0.6423 oz. ASW, 40.3 mm. **Series:**
American History **Obv:** National arms **Rev:** First Continental
Congress in prayer **Edge:** Reeded

Date	Mintage	F	VF	XF	Unc	BU
2001 Proof	20,000	Value: 32.00				

KM# 716 20 DOLLARS
20.0000 g., 0.9990 Silver 0.6423 oz. ASW, 40.3 mm. **Series:**
American History **Obv:** National arms **Rev:** U.S. Constitution
Ratification, text in stars of folded flag **Edge:** Reeded

Date	Mintage	F	VF	XF	Unc	BU
2001 Proof	20,000	Value: 32.00				

KM# 717 20 DOLLARS
20.0000 g., 0.9990 Silver 0.6423 oz. ASW, 40.3 mm. **Series:**
American History **Obv:** National arms **Rev:** Washington's
Inauguration scene **Edge:** Reeded

Date	Mintage	F	VF	XF	Unc	BU
2001 Proof	20,000	Value: 32.00				

KM# 718 20 DOLLARS
20.0000 g., 0.9990 Silver 0.6423 oz. ASW, 40.3 mm. **Series:**
American History **Obv:** National arms **Rev:** Appomattox
Courthouse surrender scene with Lee and Grant **Edge:** Reeded

Date	Mintage	F	VF	XF	Unc	BU
2001 Proof	20,000	Value: 32.00				

KM# 514 20 DOLLARS
31.1035 g., 0.9990 Silver 0.9990 oz. ASW, 38.2 mm. **Subject:**
Bush-Cheney Inauguration **Obv:** White House **Rev:** Conjoined
busts right **Edge:** Reeded

Date	Mintage	F	VF	XF	Unc	BU
2001 Proof	—	Value: 45.00				

KM# 616 20 DOLLARS
31.2000 g., 0.9990 Silver gilt 1.0021 oz. ASW, 38.7 mm. **Obv:**
National arms **Rev:** Diamond studded scorpion (Scorpio) **Edge:**
Reeded

Date	Mintage	F	VF	XF	Unc	BU
2002 Proof	—	Value: 60.00				

KM# 617 20 DOLLARS
31.2000 g., 0.9990 Silver gilt 1.0021 oz. ASW, 38.7 mm. **Obv:**
National arms **Rev:** Diamond studded archer (Sagittarius) **Edge:**
Reeded

Date	Mintage	F	VF	XF	Unc	BU
2002 Proof	—	Value: 60.00				

KM# 825 20 DOLLARS
20.0000 g., Silver, 40 mm. **Series:** America's First Ladies
Subject: Mary Todd Lincoln **Obv:** National arms **Rev:** Bust facing
slightly left at center left, oval portrait of Abraham Lincoln at right
Edge: Reeded

Date	Mintage	F	VF	XF	Unc	BU
2003 Proof	20,000	Value: 32.50				

KM# 826 20 DOLLARS
20.0000 g., Silver, 40 mm. **Series:** History of America **Subject:**
Emancipation Proclamation **Obv:** National arms **Rev:** Lincoln
seated with seven politicians gathered **Edge:** Reeded

Date	Mintage	F	VF	XF	Unc	BU
2004 Proof	20,000	Value: 37.50				

KM# 634 25 DOLLARS
0.7300 g., 0.9990 Gold 0.0234 oz. AGW, 11.1 mm. **Obv:**
National arms **Rev:** Joan of Arc **Edge:** Reeded

Date	Mintage	F	VF	XF	Unc	BU
2001 Proof	—	Value: 60.00				

KM# 666 25 DOLLARS
1.5200 g., Gold, 13.68 mm. **Subject:** Abraham Lincoln **Obv:**
National arms **Rev:** Statue of Lincoln seated **Edge:** Reeded

Date	Mintage	F	VF	XF	Unc	BU
2001 Proof	—	Value: 90.00				

KM# 719 20 DOLLARS
20.0000 g., 0.9990 Silver 0.6423 oz. ASW, 40.3 mm. **Series:**
American History **Obv:** National arms **Rev:** Prohibition, hatchet,
barrels and bottles destruction **Edge:** Reeded

Date	Mintage	F	VF	XF	Unc	BU
2001 Proof	20,000	Value: 32.00				

KM# 720 20 DOLLARS
20.0000 g., 0.9990 Silver 0.6423 oz. ASW, 40.3 mm. **Series:**
American History **Obv:** National arms **Rev:** Cuban Missile Crisis,
Castro, Khrushchev, Kennedy, missiles and map **Edge:** Reeded

Date	Mintage	F	VF	XF	Unc	BU
2001 Proof	20,000	Value: 32.00				

KM# 721 20 DOLLARS
20.0000 g., 0.9990 Silver 0.6423 oz. ASW, 40.3 mm. **Series:**
American History **Obv:** National arms **Rev:** First Man on Moon,
Armstrong and Lander **Edge:** Reeded

Date	Mintage	F	VF	XF	Unc	BU
2001 Proof	20,000	Value: 32.00				

KM# 722 20 DOLLARS
20.0000 g., 0.9990 Silver 0.6423 oz. ASW, 40.3 mm. **Series:**
American History **Obv:** National arms **Rev:** Desert Storm, soldier,
helicopter, rocket launcher etc. **Edge:** Reeded

Date	Mintage	F	VF	XF	Unc	BU
2001 Proof	20,000	Value: 32.00				

KM# 667   25 DOLLARS
0.7300 g., 0.9990 Gold 0.0234 oz. AGW, 11 mm. **Obv:** National arms **Rev:** Mount Rushmore **Edge:** Reeded

Date	Mintage	F	VF	XF	Unc	BU
2001 Proof	20,000				Value: 65.00	

KM# 995   25 DOLLARS
0.7300 g., 0.9990 Gold 0.0234 oz. AGW, 11 mm. **Obv:** National Arms **Rev:** Martin Luther King and Washington Monument

Date	Mintage	F	VF	XF	Unc	BU
2001 Proof	—				Value: 70.00	

KM# 669   25 DOLLARS
0.7300 g., 0.9990 Gold 0.0234 oz. AGW, 11 mm. **Subject:** Abraham Lincoln **Obv:** National arms **Rev:** Bust facing at right, Lincoln Memorial in background **Edge:** Reeded

Date	Mintage	F	VF	XF	Unc	BU
2002 Proof	20,000				Value: 65.00	

KM# 730   25 DOLLARS
0.0234 oz. 0.9990 Gold 0.0008 oz. AGW **Obv:** Shield **Rev:** Map of Germany and stars

Date	Mintage	F	VF	XF	Unc	BU
2003B Proof	—				Value: 35.00	

KM# 804   25 DOLLARS
1.2500 g., 0.9990 Gold 0.0401 oz. AGW, 14.5 x 9 mm. **Subject:** R. M. S. Titanic - Expedition 2000 **Obv:** National arms **Obv. Legend:** REPUBLIC OF LIBERIA **Rev:** Titanic with small piece of recovered coal embedded in hull. **Edge:** Reeded **Shape:** Oval

Date	Mintage	F	VF	XF	Unc	BU
2005 Proof	—				Value: 80.00	

KM# 731   50 DOLLARS
222.0800 g., 0.9990 Silver 7.1326 oz. ASW, 80.04 mm. **Subject:** Japanese Attack on Pearl Harbor **Obv:** National arms **Obv. Legend:** REPUBLIC OF LIBERIA **Rev:** USA flag hologram at upper left, bust of Franklin D. Roosevelt facing above Japanese aircraft attacking ship in harbor **Rev. Legend:** REMEMBERING PEARL HARBOR - DECEMBER 7, 1941

Date	Mintage	F	VF	XF	Unc	BU
2001 Proof	—				Value: 275	

KM# 495   50 DOLLARS
907.0000 g., 0.9990 Silver 29.130 oz. ASW, 100 mm. **Subject:** Wreck of the Princess Louisa **Obv:** National arms and value **Rev:** Ship under sail **Edge:** Reeded **Note:** Each coin has a cob coin recovered from the wreck site encased in a hole with clear resin. Illustration reduced.

Date	Mintage	F	VF	XF	Unc	BU
2001	500	—	—	—	1,150	—

KM# 776   50 DOLLARS
93.3000 g., 0.9990 Silver partially gilt 2.9965 oz. ASW, 65.00 mm. **Series:** Endangered Wildlife **Obv:** National arms **Obv. Legend:** REPUBLIC OF LIBERIA **Rev:** Two gilt Cheetahs, one sitting, one resting with diamonds inset in eyes **Rev. Legend:** TANZANIA **Edge:** Plain

Date	Mintage	F	VF	XF	Unc	BU
2005 Proof	999				Value: 450	

KM# 726   50 DOLLARS
62.2070 g., 0.9990 Silver 1.9979 oz. ASW, 50 mm. **Obv:** National arms **Rev:** Leopard lying across a map of Africa **Edge:** Reeded

Date	Mintage	F	VF	XF	Unc	BU
2007 Proof	500				Value: 100	

KM# 844   100 DOLLARS
1000.0000 g., 0.9990 Silver 32.117 oz. ASW **Subject:** Tanks of World War II - T-34

Date	Mintage	F	VF	XF	Unc	BU
2008 Proof	1,000				Value: 1,500	

KM# 845   100 DOLLARS
1000.0000 g., 0.9990 Silver 32.117 oz. ASW **Subject:** Tanks of World War II - VI-Tiger

Date	Mintage	F	VF	XF	Unc	BU
2008 Proof	1,000				Value: 1,500	

KM# 846   100 DOLLARS
1000.0000 g., 0.9990 Silver 32.117 oz. ASW, 120 mm. **Obv:** Arms **Rev:** St. Paul standing, events of his life around

Date	Mintage	F	VF	XF	Unc	BU
2008 Proof	1,000				Value: 2,000	

KM# 727   2500 DOLLARS
155.5175 g., 0.9990 Gold 4.9948 oz. AGW, 60 mm. **Obv:** National arms **Rev:** Leopard lying across a map of Africa **Edge:** Reeded

Date	Mintage	F	VF	XF	Unc	BU
2007 Proof	48				Value: 9,250	

PATTERNS
Including off metal strikes

KM#	Date	Mintage	Identification	Mkt Val
Pn58	2001	—	10 Dollars. Copper-Nickel. 29.2500 g. 38.2 mm. National arms. "9-11" Flag raising scene. Plain edge.	125
Pn59	2001	—	20 Dollars. Silver Plated Base Metal. 5.3100 g. 20 mm. National arms. "9-11" Flag raising scene. Plain edge.	75.00
Pn60	2001	—	100 Dollars. Base Metal Gilt. 3.4200 g. 16 mm. National arms. "9-11" Flag raising scene. Plain edge.	50.00

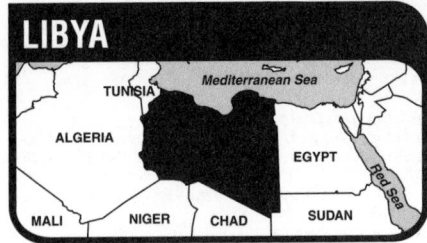

LIBYA

The Socialist People's Libyan Arab Jamahariya, located on the north-central coast of Africa between Tunisia and Egypt, has an area of 679,358 sq. mi. (1,759,540 sq. km.) and a population of 3.9 million. Capital: Tripoli. Crude oil, which accounts for 90 per cent of the export earnings, is the mainstay of the economy.

TITLES

المملكة الليبية

al-Mamlaka(t) al-Libiya(t)

الجمهورية الليبية

al-Jomhuriya(t) al-Arabiya(t) al-Libiya(t)

MONETARY SYSTEM
10 Milliemes = 1 Piastre
100 Piastres = 1 Pound

GREAT SOCIALIST PEOPLE'S LIBYAN ARAB JAMAHIRIYA

STANDARD COINAGE
1000 Dirhams = 1 Dinar

KM# 28   50 DIRHAMS
6.2500 g., Copper-Nickel, 25 mm. **Obv:** Armored equestrian **Rev:** Value at center **Shape:** Scalloped

Date	Mintage	F	VF	XF	Unc	BU
MD1377-2009	—	—	—	2.50	6.00	—

KM# 29   100 DIRHAMS
Copper-Nickel, 27 mm. **Obv:** Armored Equestrian **Rev:** Value at center

Date	Mintage	F	VF	XF	Unc	BU
MD1377-2009	—	—	—	4.50	9.00	—

KM# 26   1/4 DINAR
11.1500 g., Nickel-Brass, 28 mm. **Obv:** Libyan knight on horse with gun 1/2 left surrounded by name of Libyan Arab Jamahiriya, ornamental legend with date **Rev:** Value in Arabic script above wheat ears in ornamented frame **Edge:** Ten alternating reeded and plain flat sections **Shape:** 10-sided

Date	Mintage	F	VF	XF	Unc	BU
MD1369	—	—	—	5.00	8.00	10.00

Note: Restruck in 2001-2002

KM# 30   1/4 DINAR
11.5000 g., Nickel-Brass, 28 mm. **Obv:** Armored horseman **Rev:** Value at center **Shape:** 10-sided

Date	Mintage	F	VF	XF	Unc	BU
MD1377-2009	—	—	—	9.00	12.50	—

KM# 27   1/2 DINAR
11.5000 g., Bi-Metallic Aluminumn bronze center in Copper-Nickel ring., 30 mm. **Obv:** Man on horse with gun 1/2 left, ornamental legend with date **Rev:** Value in Arabic script above wheat ears in ornamented frame **Edge:** Reeded

Date	Mintage	F	VF	XF	Unc	BU
MD1372	—	—	—	—	10.00	12.00

KM# 31 1/2 DINAR
11.5000 g., Bi-Metallic Aluminum-Bronze center in Copper-Nickel ring, 30 mm. **Obv:** Armored horseman **Rev:** Value at center **Edge:** Reeded

Date	Mintage	F	VF	XF	Unc	BU
MD1377-2009	—				12.50	15.00

LIECHTENSTEIN

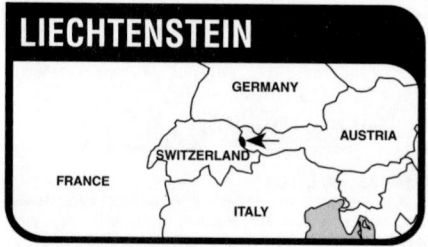

The Principality of Liechtenstein, located in central Europe on the east bank of the Rhine between Austria and Switzerland, has an area of 62 sq. mi. (160 sq. km.) and a population of 27,200. Capital: Vaduz. The economy is based on agriculture and light manufacturing. Canned goods, textiles, ceramics and precision instruments are exported.

RULERS
Prince Hans Adam II, 1990-

MINT MARKS
B - Bern

PRINCIPALITY

REFORM COINAGE
100 Rappen = 1 Frank

Y# 24 10 FRANKEN
29.9500 g., 0.9000 Silver 0.8666 oz. ASW, 37.3 mm. **Ruler:** Prince Hans Adam II **Subject:** 200 Years of Sovereignty **Obv:** Vertical inscription between crowned arms and value **Rev:** Johann I (1760-1836) **Edge:** Reeded

Date	Mintage	F	VF	XF	Unc	BU
ND (2006)B Proof	—	Value: 55.00				

Y# 25 50 FRANKEN
8.8800 g., 0.9990 Gold 0.2852 oz. AGW. **Ruler:** Prince Hans Adam II **Subject:** 200th Anniversary of Sovereignty

Date	Mintage	F	VF	XF	Unc	BU
ND (2006)B Proof	—	Value: 525				

LITHUANIA

The Republic of Lithuania, southernmost of the Baltic states in east Europe, has an area of 25,174 sq. mi.(65,201 sq. km.) and a population of *3.6 million. Capital: Vilnius. The economy is based on livestock raising and manufacturing. Hogs, cattle, hides and electric motors are exported.

Lithuania declared its independence March 11, 1990 and it was recognized by the United States on Sept. 2, 1991, followed by the Soviet government in Moscow on Sept. 6. They were seated in the UN General Assembly on Sept. 17, 1991.

MODERN REPUBLIC

REFORM COINAGE
100 Centas = 1 Litas

KM# 106 10 CENTU
2.6000 g., Nickel-Brass, 17 mm. **Obv:** National arms **Rev:** Value **Edge:** Reeded

Date	Mintage	F	VF	XF	Unc	BU
2003 In sets only	—					0.60
2003 Proof	10,000	Value: 5.00				
2006	—					0.40
2006 Proof	2,000	Value: 45.00				
2007	—					0.40
2008	—					0.40
2008 Prooflike	200					5.00
2009	—					0.40
2009 Prooflike	500					20.00
2010	—					0.40
2011 In sets only	—					0.75
2012 In sets only	4,000					0.75

KM# 107 20 CENTU
4.8000 g., Nickel-Brass, 20.5 mm. **Obv:** National arms **Rev:** Value **Edge:** Reeded

Date	Mintage	F	VF	XF	Unc	BU
2003 In sets only	—					1.50
2003 Proof	10,000	Value: 2.00				
2007	—	—	—	—		1.00
2008	—	—	—	—		1.00
2008 Prooflike	200	—	—	—		5.00
2009	—	—	—	—		1.00
2009 Prooflike	500	—	—	—		3.00
2010	—	—	—	—		1.00
2011 In sets only	—	—	—	—		2.00
2012 In sets only	4,000	—	—	—		2.00

KM# 108 50 CENTU
6.0000 g., Nickel-Brass, 23 mm. **Obv:** National arms **Rev:** Value within designed circle **Edge:** Reeded

Date	Mintage	F	VF	XF	Unc	BU
2003 In sets only	—					4.00
2003 Proof	10,000	Value: 2.00				
2008	—	—	—	—	0.50	1.50
2008 Prooflike	200	—	—	—	—	30.00
2009 In sets only	5,000	—	—	—	—	10.00
2009 Prooflike	500	—	—	—	—	4.00
2010 In sets only	3,500	—	—	—	—	10.00
2011 In sets only	—	—	—	—	—	4.00
2012 In sets only	4,000	—	—	—	—	4.00

KM# 111 LITAS
6.2500 g., Copper-Nickel, 22.3 mm. **Obv:** National arms **Rev:** Value within circle above lined designs **Edge:** Reeded

Date	Mintage	F	VF	XF	Unc	BU
2001	—	—	—	—	1.50	2.00
2002	—	—	—	—	1.50	2.00
2003 In sets only	—	—	—	—	—	5.00
2003 Proof	10,000	Value: 8.00				
2008	—	—	—	—	1.50	2.00
2008 Prooflike	200	—	—	—	—	10.00
2009	—	—	—	—	1.50	2.00
2009 Prooflike	500	—	—	—	—	4.00
2010	—	—	—	—	1.50	2.00
2011 In sets only	—	—	—	—	—	3.00
2012 In sets only	4,000	—	—	—	—	3.00

KM# 137 LITAS
6.1500 g., Copper-Nickel, 22.2 mm. **Subject:** 425th Anniversary - University of Vilnius **Obv:** Knight on horse within rope wreath **Rev:** Building within court yard **Edge:** Segmented reeding

Date	Mintage	F	VF	XF	Unc	BU
2004	200,000	—	—	—	2.00	4.00

KM# 142 LITAS
6.4100 g., Copper-Nickel, 22.35 mm. **Obv:** Knight on horse within circle **Rev:** Palace **Edge:** Segmented reeding

Date	Mintage	F	VF	XF	Unc	BU
2005	1,000,000	—	—	—	1.75	2.50

KM# 162 LITAS
6.2500 g., Copper-Nickel, 22.3 mm. **Subject:** Vilnius - European Culture Capital **Obv:** National Arms **Rev:** Female figure standing at easel

Date	Mintage	F	VF	XF	Unc	BU
2009	1,000,000	—	—	—	1.50	2.50

KM# 172 LITAS
6.2500 g., Copper-Nickel, 22.2 mm. **Subject:** Battle of Grunwald, 600th Anniversary **Obv:** National arms **Rev:** Long spears attacking each other

Date	Mintage	F	VF	XF	Unc	BU
2010	—	—	—	—	1.75	2.50

KM# 177 LITAS
6.2500 g., Copper-Nickel, 22.3 mm. **Subject:** Basketball **Obv:** National arms **Rev:** Basketball

Date	Mintage	F	VF	XF	Unc	BU
2011	1,000,000	—	—	—	3.00	7.00

KM# 112   2 LITAI

7.5000 g., Bi-Metallic Copper-Nickel center in Aluminum-Bronze ring, 25 mm.   **Obv:** National arms within circle **Rev:** Value within circle **Edge:** Segmented reeding

Date	Mintage	F	VF	XF	Unc	BU
2001	—	—	—	—	3.00	5.00
2002	—	—	—	—	3.00	5.00
2003 In sets only	—	—	—	—	—	6.00
2003 Proof	10,000	Value: 3.50				
2008	—	—	—	—	2.25	3.00
2008 Prooflike	200	—	—	—	—	30.00
2009	—	—	—	—	3.00	5.00
2009 Prooflike	500	—	—	—	—	25.00
2010	—	—	—	—	3.00	5.00
2011 In sets only	—	—	—	—	—	5.00
2012 In sets only	4,000	—	—	—	—	5.00

KM# 132   5 LITAI

28.2800 g., 0.9250 Silver 0.8410 oz. ASW, 38.6 mm.   **Series:** Endangered Wildlife **Obv:** Knight on horse **Rev:** Barn owl in flight **Edge Lettering:** LIETUVOS BANKAS

Date	Mintage	F	VF	XF	Unc	BU
2002 Proof	3,000	Value: 150				

KM# 113   5 LITAI

10.2600 g., Bi-Metallic Aluminum-Bronze center in Copper-Nickel ring, 27.5 mm.   **Obv:** National arms within circle **Rev:** Value within circle **Edge Lettering:** PENKI LITAI

Date	Mintage	F	VF	XF	Unc	BU
2003 In sets only	—	—	—	—	—	14.00
2003 Proof	10,000	Value: 15.00				
2008 In sets only	3,800	—	—	—	—	15.00
2008 Prooflike	200	—	—	—	—	30.00
2009	—	—	—	—	5.00	7.50
2009 Prooflike	500	—	—	—	—	20.00
2010 In sets only	3,500	—	—	—	—	15.00
2011 In sets only	—	—	—	—	—	10.00
2012 In sets only	4,000	—	—	—	—	10.00

KM# 131   10 LITU

13.1500 g., Copper-Nickel, 28.7 mm.   **Obv:** Knight on horse on shield within aerial harbor view **Rev:** Shield within city view **Edge Lettering:** KLAIPEDAI - 75 (twice)

Date	Mintage	F	VF	XF	Unc	BU
2002 Proof	5,000	Value: 25.00				

KM# 157   10 LITU

1.2440 g., 0.9990 Gold 0.0400 oz. AGW, 13.9 mm.   **Obv:** Town gate **Rev:** Mathematical arc **Rev. Legend:** Sectio Aurea

Date	Mintage	F	VF	XF	Unc	BU
2007 Proof	7,000	Value: 120				

KM# 160   10 LITU

1.2400 g., 0.9990 Gold 0.0398 oz. AGW, 13.92 mm.   **Obv:** Castle gate **Rev:** Geometric design

Date	Mintage	F	VF	XF	Unc	BU
2007LMK Proof	7,000	Value: 120				

KM# 169   10 LITU

11.4000 g., 0.9250 Silver 0.3390 oz. ASW, 28.7 mm.   **Subject:** Lithuanian Culture - Music **Obv:** Vilnus **Rev:** Two chello and musical notations

Date	Mintage	F	VF	XF	Unc	BU
2010 Proof	10,000	Value: 45.00				

KM# 175   10 LITU

12.4400 g., 0.9250 Silver 0.3699 oz. ASW, 28.7 mm.   **Subject:** Lithuanian Culture - Theatre **Obv:** State emblem **Rev:** Theatre motif **Edge Lettering:** LIETUVOS KULTURA * TEATRAS (twice)

Date	Mintage	F	VF	XF	Unc	BU
2011 Proof	10,000	Value: 35.00				

KM# 129   50 LITU

28.2800 g., 0.9250 Silver 0.8410 oz. ASW, 38.61 mm.   **Subject:** Motiejus Valancius' 200th Birthday **Obv:** Knight on horse within shield above church and landscape **Rev:** Bust facing **Edge Lettering:** LIETUVISKAS ZODIS RASTAS IR TIKEJMAS TAUTOS GYVASTIS

Date	Mintage	F	VF	XF	Unc	BU
2001 Proof	2,000	Value: 200				

KM# 130   50 LITU

28.2800 g., 0.9250 Silver 0.8410 oz. ASW, 38.61 mm.   **Subject:** Jonas Basanavicius (1851-1927) **Obv:** Knight on horse **Rev:** Jonas Basanavicius **Edge Lettering:** KAD AUSRAI AUSTANT PRAVISTU IR LIETUVOS DVASIA

Date	Mintage	F	VF	XF	Unc	BU
2001 Proof	2,000	Value: 200				

KM# 133   50 LITU

28.2800 g., 0.9250 Silver 0.8410 oz. ASW, 38.61 mm.   **Series:** Historical Architecture **Obv:** Republic of Lithuania coat of arms **Rev:** Trakai Island Castle **Edge Lettering:** ISTORIJOS IR ARCHITEKTUROS PAMINKLAI

Date	Mintage	F	VF	XF	Unc	BU
2002 Proof	1,500	Value: 100				

KM# 134   50 LITU

28.2800 g., 0.9250 Silver 0.8410 oz. ASW, 38.6 mm.   **Obv:** Knight on horse above value **Rev:** Vilnus Cathedral **Edge Lettering:** ISTORIJOS IR ARCHITEKTUROS PAMINKLAI

Date	Mintage	F	VF	XF	Unc	BU
2003 Proof	1,500	Value: 200				

KM# 135   50 LITU

28.2800 g., 0.9250 Silver 0.8410 oz. ASW, 38.6 mm.   **Subject:** Olympics **Obv:** Knight on horse above value **Rev:** Stylized cyclists **Edge Lettering:** XXVIII OLIMPIADOS ZAIDYNEMS

Date	Mintage	F	VF	XF	Unc	BU
2003 Proof	2,000	Value: 140				

KM# 138   50 LITU

28.2800 g., 0.9250 Silver 0.8410 oz. ASW, 38.6 mm.   **Series:** Historical Architecture **Subject:** 425th Anniversary - University of Vilnius **Obv:** Knight on horse **Rev:** Old university buildings **Edge:** Lettered **Edge Lettering:** ISTORIJOS IR ARCHITEKTUROS PAMINKLAI

Date	Mintage	F	VF	XF	Unc	BU
2004 Proof	2,000	Value: 120				

KM# 139 50 LITU
28.2800 g., 0.9250 Silver 0.8410 oz. ASW, 38.6 mm. **Obv:**
Knight on horse **Rev:** Pazaislis Monastery **Edge:** Lettered **Edge
Lettering:** ISTORIJOS IR ARCHITEKTUROS PAMINKLAI

Date	Mintage	F	VF	XF	Unc	BU
2004 Proof	1,500	Value: 140				

KM# 140 50 LITU
28.2800 g., 0.9250 Silver 0.8410 oz. ASW, 38.6 mm. **Subject:**
First Lithuanian Statute of 1529 **Obv:** Knight on horse **Rev:**
Seated and kneeling figures **Edge:** Lettered **Edge Lettering:**
"BUKIME TEISES VERGAI, KAD GALETUME NAUDOTIS
LAISVEMIS"

Date	Mintage	F	VF	XF	Unc	BU
2004 Proof	1,000	Value: 200				

KM# 141 50 LITU
28.2800 g., 0.9250 Silver 0.8410 oz. ASW, 38.6 mm. **Subject:**
Curonian Spit **Obv:** Knight on horse **Rev:** Shifting sand dunes
design **Edge:** Ornamented pattern from Neringa emblem

Date	Mintage	F	VF	XF	Unc	BU
2004 Proof	2,000	Value: 170				

KM# 143 50 LITU
28.2800 g., 0.9250 Silver 0.8410 oz. ASW, 38.61 mm. **Series:**
Historical Architecture **Obv:** Denar coin with Knight on horse **Rev:**
Kernavé hill fort **Edge Lettering:** ISTORIJOS IR
ARCHITEKTUROS PAMINKLAI

Date	Mintage	F	VF	XF	Unc	BU
2005 Proof	2,000	Value: 140				

KM# 147 50 LITU
28.2800 g., 0.9250 Silver 0.8410 oz. ASW, 38.6 mm. **Subject:**
1905 Lithuanian Congress **Obv:** Knight on horse **Rev:** Legend
and inscription **Edge:** Ornamented

Date	Mintage	F	VF	XF	Unc	BU
2005 Proof	1,500	Value: 220				

KM# 144 50 LITU
28.2800 g., 0.9250 Silver 0.8410 oz. ASW, 38.6 mm. **Subject:**
150th Anniversary - National Museum **Obv:** Trio of ancient
Lithuanian coins **Rev:** Man blowing horn **Edge Lettering:** PRO
PUBLICO BONO

Date	Mintage	F	VF	XF	Unc	BU
2005 Proof	1,500	Value: 325				

KM# 145 50 LITU
28.2800 g., 0.9250 Silver 0.8410 oz. ASW, 38.6 mm. **Subject:**
Knight on horse and cross **Rev:** Cardinal Vincentas Sladkevicius
Edge Lettering: LET OUR LIFE BE BUILT ON GOODNESS
AND HOPE

Date	Mintage	F	VF	XF	Unc	BU
2005 Proof	2,000	Value: 90.00				

KM# 148 50 LITU
28.2800 g., 0.9250 Silver 0.8410 oz. ASW, 38.6 mm. **Obv:**
National arms on forest background **Rev:** Lynx prowling **Edge:**
Stylized lynx paw prints

Date	Mintage	F	VF	XF	Unc	BU
2006 Proof	3,000	Value: 175				

KM# 149 50 LITU
28.2800 g., 0.9250 Silver 0.8410 oz. ASW, 38.6 mm. **Obv:**
National arms against castle wall background **Rev:** Medininkai
Castle **Edge Lettering:** ISTORIJOS IR ARCHITEKTUROS
PAMINKLAI

Date	Mintage	F	VF	XF	Unc	BU
2006 Proof	2,500	Value: 200				

KM# 151 50 LITU
28.2800 g., 0.9250 Silver 0.8410 oz. ASW, 38.61 mm. **Subject:**
1831 Uprising **Obv:** Small national arms above battle scene **Obv.
Legend:** LIETUVA **Rev:** Bust of Pliaterytė facing **Rev. Legend:**
EMILIJA PLIATERYTĖ **Edge Lettering:** 1831 * SUKILIMAS

Date	Mintage	F	VF	XF	Unc	BU
2006 Proof	2,500	Value: 200				

KM# 152 50 LITU
28.2800 g., 0.9250 Silver 0.8410 oz. ASW, 38.6 mm. **Subject:**
XXIX Olympics 2008 - Beijing **Obv:** National arms **Obv. Legend:**
LIETUVA **Rev:** Stylized swimmer right **Rev. Legend:** PEKINAS

Date	Mintage	F	VF	XF	Unc	BU
2007 Proof	5,000	Value: 150				

KM# 161 50 LITU
28.2800 g., 0.9250 Silver 0.8410 oz. ASW, 38.6 mm. **Subject:**
Panemune Castle **Obv:** Shield and fortress detail **Rev:** Castle
towers

Date	Mintage	F	VF	XF	Unc	BU
2007LMK Proof	5,000	Value: 100				

KM# 153   50 LITU
28.2800 g., 0.9250 Silver 0.8410 oz. ASW, 38.6 mm. **Series:** European Cultural Heritage **Obv:** National arms surrounded by seven archaic crosses **Obv. Legend:** LIETUVA **Rev:** Circular latent image surrounded by seven archaic crosses

Date	Mintage	F	VF	XF	Unc	BU
2008 Proof	10,000	Value: 75.00				

KM# 155   50 LITU
28.2800 g., 0.9250 Silver 0.8410 oz. ASW, 38.6 mm. **Obv:** National arms **Obv. Legend:** LIETUVA **Rev:** Partial castle wall, towers **Rev. Legend:** KAUNO PILIS

Date	Mintage	F	VF	XF	Unc	BU
2008 Proof	10,000	Value: 95.00				

KM# 154   50 LITU
28.2800 g., 0.9250 Silver 0.8410 oz. ASW, 38.6 mm. **Subject:** 550th Anniversary Birth of St. Casimer **Obv:** National arms on shield **Obv. Legend:** LIETUVA **Rev:** St. Casimer standing holding flowers **Rev. Legend:** SV. KAZIMIERAS

Date	Mintage	F	VF	XF	Unc	BU
2008 Proof	5,000	Value: 200				

KM# 159   50 LITU
28.2800 g., 0.9250 Silver 0.8410 oz. ASW, 38.6 mm. **Subject:** Lithuania Nature **Obv:** National Arms **Rev:** Bee

Date	Mintage	F	VF	XF	Unc	BU
2008 Proof	10,000	Value: 170				

KM# 163   50 LITU
28.2800 g., 0.9250 Silver 0.8410 oz. ASW, 38.6 mm. **Subject:** Vilnius - European Culture Capital **Obv:** National Arms **Rev:** Female figure standing at easel

Date	Mintage	F	VF	XF	Unc	BU
2009 Proof	10,000	Value: 190				

KM# 164   50 LITU
28.2800 g., 0.9250 Silver 0.8410 oz. ASW, 38.6 mm. **Subject:** Tytuvenai **Obv:** National Arms in Shield **Rev:** Tytuvenai Church facade at left

Date	Mintage	F	VF	XF	Unc	BU
2009 Proof	10,000	Value: 200				

KM# 165   50 LITU
28.2800 g., 0.9250 Silver 0.8410 oz. ASW, 38.6 mm. **Subject:** Nature, Naktiziede **Obv:** Knight on horseback left **Rev:** Flowers

Date	Mintage	F	VF	XF	Unc	BU
2009LMK Proof	—	Value: 150				

KM# 170   50 LITU
28.2800 g., 0.9250 Silver 0.8410 oz. ASW, 38.61 mm. **Subject:** Biržai Castle **Obv:** Viltus in shield **Rev:** Castle view and ariel plan

Date	Mintage	F	VF	XF	Unc	BU
2010 Proof	10,000	Value: 95.00				

KM# 171   50 LITU
28.2800 g., 0.9250 Silver 0.8410 oz. ASW, 38.61 mm. **Obv:** Vilnus **Rev:** Misgurnus Fossilis - European Weather Loach **Edge Lettering:** LIETUVOS GAMTA

Date	Mintage	F	VF	XF	Unc	BU
2010 Proof	10,000	Value: 75.00				

KM# 176   50 LITU
3.1000 g., 0.9990 Gold 0.0996 oz. AGW, 16.25 mm. **Subject:** Basketball **Obv:** State emblem **Rev:** Basketball

Date	Mintage	F	VF	XF	Unc	BU
2011 Proof	5,000	Value: 650				

KM# 174   50 LITU
28.2800 g., 0.9250 Silver 0.8410 oz. ASW, 38.61 mm. **Subject:** Gabriele Petkevicaite-Bite, 150th Anniversary of Birth **Obv:** State emblem **Rev:** Portrait **Edge Lettering:** AD ASTRA (repeated 3 times)

Date	Mintage	F	VF	XF	Unc	BU
2011 Proof	10,000	Value: 60.00				

KM# 158   100 LITU
7.7800 g., 0.9990 Gold 0.2499 oz. AGW, 22.3 mm. **Subject:** Use of the Name Lithuania Millenium **Obv:** Linear National Arms **Rev:** Circular Legend

Date	Mintage	F	VF	XF	Unc	BU
2007 Proof	5,000	Value: 450				

KM# 156   100 LITU
7.7800 g., 0.9999 Gold 0.2501 oz. AGW, 22.3 mm. **Subject:** Millennium of name "Lithuania" **Obv:** Stylized national arms **Obv. Legend:** LIETUVA **Rev:** Partial parchment **Rev. Legend:** LIETUVOS DIDZIOJI KUNIGAIKSTYSTS

Date	Mintage	F	VF	XF	Unc	BU
2008 Proof	10,000	Value: 450				

KM# 166 100 LITU
7.7800 g., 0.9990 Gold 0.2499 oz. AGW, 22.3 mm. **Subject:** 1000th Anniversary of Name Lithuania **Obv:** Linear knight **Rev:** Timeline

Date	Mintage	F	VF	XF	Unc	BU
2009LMK Proof	10,000	Value: 450				

KM# 136 200 LITU
15.0000 g., Bi-Metallic .900 Gold 7.9g. center in a .925 Silver 7.1g. ring, 27 mm. **Subject:** 750th Anniversary - King Mindaugas **Obv:** Knight on horse **Obv. Legend:** LIETUVA **Rev:** Seated King **Rev. Legend:** MINDAUGO KARUNAVIMAS **Edge Lettering:** LIETUVOS KARALYSTE 1253

Date	Mintage	F	VF	XF	Unc	BU
2003 Proof	2,000	Value: 1,250				

KM# 146 500 LITU
31.1000 g., 0.9999 Gold 0.9997 oz. AGW, 32.5 mm. **Obv:** Knight on horse **Rev:** Palace **Edge:** Plain

Date	Mintage	F	VF	XF	Unc	BU
2005 Proof	1,000	Value: 1,800				

KM# 173 500 LITU
31.1000 g., 0.9990 Gold 0.9988 oz. AGW, 32.5 mm. **Subject:** Battle of Grunwald **Obv:** Shield around seated king **Rev:** Knights on horseback, warriors on foot

Date	Mintage	F	VF	XF	Unc	BU
2010 Proof	1,000	Value: 1,950				

MINT SETS

KM#	Date	Mintage	Identification	Issue Price	Mkt Val
MS4	2003 (6)	10,000	KM#106-108, 111-113	7.50	35.00
MS5	2008 (9)	4,000	KM#85-87, 106-108, 111-113 KM#85-87 are dated 1991.	30.00	30.00
MS6	2009 (9)	—	KM#85-87, 106-108, 111-113	—	30.00
MS7	2010 (6)	—	KM#106-108, 111-113 plus medal	—	14.00
MS8	2011 (6)	—	KM#106-108, 111-113 plus medal	—	14.00

LUXEMBOURG

The Grand Duchy of Luxembourg is located in western Europe between Belgium, Germany and France, has an area of 1,103 sq. mi. (2,586 sq. km.) and a population of 377,100. Capital: Luxembourg. The economy is based on steel.

RULER
Henri, 2000-

MINT MARKS
A - Paris
(b) - Brussels, privy marks only
H – Gunzburg
(n) – lion - Namur
(u) - Utrecht, privy marks only

GRAND DUCHY
EURO COINAGE
European Economic Community Issues

KM# 75 EURO CENT
2.3000 g., Copper Plated Steel, 16.25 mm. **Ruler:** Henri **Obv:** Head right **Rev:** Value and globe **Edge:** Plain

Date	Mintage	F	VF	XF	Unc	BU
2002(u)	34,557,500	—	—	—	0.35	0.50
2002(u) Proof	1,500	Value: 3.00				
2003(u)	1,500,000	—	—	—	0.50	0.75
2003(u) Proof	1,500	Value: 3.00				
2004(u)	21,001,000	—	—	—	0.35	0.50
2004(u) Proof	1,500	Value: 3.00				
2005(u)	7,000,000	—	—	—	0.35	0.50
2005(u) Proof	1,500	Value: 3.00				
2006(u)	4,000,000	—	—	—	0.35	0.50
2006(u) Proof	2,000	Value: 4.00				
2007(a)	6,000,000	—	—	—	0.35	0.50
2007(a) Proof	2,500	Value: 4.00				
2008(a)	10,000,000	—	—	—	0.35	0.50
2008(a) Proof	2,500	Value: 4.00				
2009(u)	4,000,000	—	—	—	0.35	0.50
2009(u) Proof	2,500	Value: 4.00				
2010(u)	6,000,000	—	—	—	0.35	0.50
2010(u) Proof	1,500	Value: 4.00				
2011(u)	—	—	—	—	0.35	0.50
2011(u) Proof	1,500	Value: 4.00				
2012(u)	—	—	—	—	0.35	0.50
2012(u) Proof	—	Value: 4.00				

KM# 76 2 EURO CENT
3.0600 g., Copper Plated Steel, 18.75 mm. **Ruler:** Henri **Obv:** Head right **Rev:** Value and globe **Edge:** Grooved

Date	Mintage	F	VF	XF	Unc	BU
2002(u)	35,917,500	—	—	—	0.50	0.75
2002(u) Proof	1,500	Value: 5.00				
2003(u)	1,500,000	—	—	—	0.65	0.85
2003(u) Proof	1,500	Value: 5.00				
2004(u)	20,001,000	—	—	—	0.50	0.75
2004(u) Proof	1,500	Value: 5.00				
2005(u)	13,000,000	—	—	—	0.50	0.75
2005(u) Proof	1,500	Value: 5.00				
2006(u)	4,000,000	—	—	—	0.50	0.75
2006(u) Proof	2,000	Value: 6.00				
2007(a)	8,000,000	—	—	—	0.50	0.75
2007(a) Proof	2,500	Value: 6.00				
2008(a)	12,000,000	—	—	—	0.50	0.75
2008(a) Proof	2,500	Value: 6.00				
2009(u)	3,000,000	—	—	—	0.50	0.75
2009(u) Proof	2,500	Value: 6.00				
2010(u)	8,000,000	—	—	—	0.50	0.75
2010(u) Proof	1,500	Value: 6.00				
2011(u)	—	—	—	—	0.50	0.75
2011(u) Proof	1,500	Value: 6.00				
2012(u)	—	—	—	—	0.50	0.75
2012(u) Proof	—	Value: 6.00				

KM# 77 5 EURO CENT
3.9200 g., Copper Plated Steel, 21.25 mm. **Ruler:** Henri **Obv:** Head right **Rev:** Value and globe **Edge:** Plain

Date	Mintage	F	VF	XF	Unc	BU
2002(u)	28,917,500	—	—	—	0.75	1.00
2002(u) Proof	1,500	Value: 7.00				
2003(u)	4,500,000	—	—	—	1.00	1.25
2003(u) Proof	1,500	Value: 7.00				
2004(u)	16,001,000	—	—	—	0.75	1.00
2004(u) Proof	1,500	Value: 7.00				
2005(u)	6,000,000	—	—	—	0.75	1.00
2005(u) Proof	1,500	Value: 7.00				
2006(u)	5,000,000	—	—	—	0.75	1.00
2006(u) Proof	2,000	Value: 8.00				
2007(a)	5,000,000	—	—	—	0.75	1.00
2007(a) Proof	2,500	Value: 9.00				
2008(a)	9,000,000	—	—	—	0.75	1.00
2008(a) Proof	2,500	Value: 9.00				
2009(u)	6,000,000	—	—	—	0.75	1.00
2009(u) Proof	2,500	Value: 9.00				
2010(u)	6,000,000	—	—	—	0.75	1.00
2010(u) Proof	1,500	Value: 9.00				
2011(u)	—	—	—	—	0.75	1.00
2011(u) Proof	1,500	Value: 9.00				
2012(u)	—	—	—	—	0.75	1.00
2012(u) Proof	—	Value: 9.00				

KM# 78 10 EURO CENT
4.1000 g., Brass, 19.75 mm. **Ruler:** Henri **Obv:** Grand Duke's portrait **Rev:** Value and map **Edge:** Reeded

Date	Mintage	F	VF	XF	Unc	BU
2002(u)	25,117,500	—	—	—	0.75	—
2002(u) Proof	1,500	Value: 14.00				
2003(u)	1,500,000	—	—	—	1.00	—
2003(u) Proof	1,500	Value: 14.00				
2004(u)	12,001,000	—	—	—	0.75	—
2004(u) Proof	1,500	Value: 14.00				
2005(u)	2,000,000	—	—	—	0.75	—
2005(u) Proof	1,500	Value: 14.00				
2006(u)	4,000,000	—	—	—	0.75	—
2006(u) Proof	2,000	Value: 14.00				

KM# 89 10 EURO CENT
4.1000 g., Brass, 19.75 mm. **Ruler:** Henri **Obv:** Prince's portrait **Rev:** Relief map of Western Europe, stars, lines and value **Edge:** Reeded

Date	Mintage	F	VF	XF	Unc	BU
2007(a)	5,000,000	—	—	—	0.75	1.00
2007(a) Proof	2,500	Value: 14.00				
2008(a)	5,000,000	—	—	—	0.75	1.00
2008(a) Proof	2,500	Value: 14.00				
2009(u)	4,000,000	—	—	—	0.75	1.00
2009(u) Proof	2,500	Value: 14.00				
2010(u)	4,000,000	—	—	—	0.75	1.00
2010(u) Proof	1,500	Value: 14.00				
2011(u)	—	—	—	—	0.75	1.00
2011(u) Proof	1,500	Value: 14.00				
2012(u)	—	—	—	—	0.75	1.00
2012(u) Proof	—	Value: 14.00				

KM# 79 20 EURO CENT
5.7400 g., Brass, 22.25 mm. **Ruler:** Henri **Obv:** Grand Duke's portrait **Rev:** Value and map **Edge:** Notched

Date	Mintage	F	VF	XF	Unc	BU
2002(u)	25,717,500	—	—	—	1.00	—
2002(u) Proof	1,500	Value: 16.00				
2003(u)	1,500,000	—	—	—	1.25	—

Date	Mintage	F	VF	XF	Unc	BU
2003(u) Proof	1,500	Value: 16.00				
2004(u)	14,001,000	—	—	—	1.00	—
2004(u) Proof	1,500	Value: 16.00				
2005(u)	6,000,000	—	—	—	1.00	—
2005(u) Proof	1,500	Value: 16.00				
2006(u)	7,000,000	—	—	—	1.00	—
2006(u) Proof	2,000	Value: 16.00				

KM# 90 20 EURO CENT
5.7400 g., Brass, 22.25 mm. **Ruler:** Henri **Obv:** Prince's portrait **Rev:** Relief map of Western Europe, stars, lines and value **Edge:** Notched

Date	Mintage	F	VF	XF	Unc	BU
2007(a)	8,000,000	—	—	—	1.00	1.25
2007(a) Proof	2,500	Value: 16.00				
2008(a)	6,000,000	—	—	—	1.00	1.25
2008(a) Proof	2,500	Value: 16.00				
2009(u)	5,000,000	—	—	—	1.00	1.25
2009(u) Proof	2,500	Value: 16.00				
2010(u)	8,000,000	—	—	—	1.00	1.25
2010(u) Proof	1,500	Value: 16.00				
2011(u)	—	—	—	—	1.00	1.25
2011(u) Proof	1,500	Value: 16.00				
2012(u)	—	—	—	—	1.00	1.25
2012(u) Proof	—	Value: 16.00				

KM# 80 50 EURO CENT
7.8000 g., Brass, 24.25 mm. **Ruler:** Henri **Obv:** Grand Duke's portrait **Rev:** Value and map **Edge:** Reeded

Date	Mintage	F	VF	XF	Unc	BU
2002(u)	21,917,500	—	—	—	1.25	—
2002(u) Proof	1,500	Value: 18.00				
2003(u)	2,500,000	—	—	—	1.50	—
2003(u) Proof	1,500	Value: 18.00				
2004(u)	10,001,000	—	—	—	1.25	—
2004(u) Proof	1,500	Value: 18.00				
2005(u)	3,000,000	—	—	—	1.25	—
2005(u) Proof	1,500	Value: 18.00				
2006(u)	3,000,000	—	—	—	1.25	—
2006(u) Proof	2,000	Value: 18.00				

KM# 91 50 EURO CENT
7.8000 g., Brass, 24.25 mm. **Ruler:** Henri **Obv:** Prince's portrait **Rev:** Relief map of Western Europe, stars, lines and value **Edge:** Reeded

Date	Mintage	F	VF	XF	Unc	BU
2007(a)	4,000,000	—	—	—	1.25	1.50
2007(a) Proof	2,500	Value: 18.00				
2008(a)	4,000,000	—	—	—	1.25	1.50
2008(a) Proof	2,500	Value: 18.00				
2009(u)	2,000,000	—	—	—	1.25	1.50
2009(u) Proof	2,500	Value: 18.00				
2010(u)	5,000,000	—	—	—	1.25	1.50
2010(u) Proof	1,500	Value: 18.00				
2011(u)	—	—	—	—	1.25	1.50
2011(u) Proof	1,500	Value: 18.00				
2012(u)	—	—	—	—	1.25	1.50
2012(u) Proof	—	Value: 18.00				

KM# 81 EURO
7.5000 g., Bi-Metallic Copper-Nickel center in Nickel-Brass ring, 23.25 mm. **Ruler:** Henri **Obv:** Grand Duke's portrait **Rev:** Value and map within divided circle **Edge:** Segmented reeding

Date	Mintage	F	VF	XF	Unc	BU
2002(u)	21,318,525	—	—	—	2.50	—
2002(u) Proof	1,500	Value: 18.00				
2003(u)	1,500,000	—	—	—	2.75	—
2003(u) Proof	1,500	Value: 18.00				
2004(u)	9,001,000	—	—	—	2.50	—
2004(u) Proof	1,500	Value: 18.00				
2005(u)	2,000,000	—	—	—	2.50	—
2005(u) Proof	1,500	Value: 18.00				
2006(u)	1,000,000	—	—	—	2.50	—
2006(u) Proof	2,000	Value: 18.00				

KM# 92 EURO
7.5000 g., Bi-Metallic Copper-Nickel center in Nickel-Brass ring, 23.25 mm. **Ruler:** Henri **Obv:** Prince's portrait **Rev:** Relief map of Western Europe, stars, lines and value **Edge:** Segmented reeding

Date	Mintage	F	VF	XF	Unc	BU
2007(a)	480,000	—	—	—	2.25	2.75
2007(a) Proof	2,500	Value: 24.00				
2008(a)	480,000	—	—	—	2.25	2.75
2008(a) Proof	2,500	Value: 24.00				
2009(u)	240,000	—	—	—	2.25	2.75
2009(u) Proof	2,500	Value: 24.00				
2010(u)	1,000,000	—	—	—	2.25	2.75
2010(u) Proof	1,500	Value: 24.00				
2011(u)	—	—	—	—	2.25	2.75
2011(u) Proof	1,500	Value: 24.00				
2012(u)	—	—	—	—	2.25	2.75
2012(u) Proof	—	Value: 24.00				

KM# 82 2 EURO
8.5000 g., Bi-Metallic Nickel-Brass center in Copper-Nickel ring, 25.75 mm. **Ruler:** Henri **Obv:** Grand Duke's portrait **Rev:** Value and map within divided circle **Edge:** Reeded with 2's and stars

Date	Mintage	F	VF	XF	Unc	BU
2002(u)	18,517,500	—	—	—	3.75	—
2002(u) Proof	1,500	Value: 28.00				
2003(u)	3,500,000	—	—	—	4.50	—
2003(u) Proof	1,500	Value: 28.00				
2004(u)	7,553,200	—	—	—	4.00	—
2004(u) Proof	1,500	Value: 28.00				
2005(u)	3,500,000	—	—	—	4.00	—
2005(u) Proof	1,500	Value: 28.00				
2006(u)	2,000,000	—	—	—	4.00	—
2006(u) Proof	2,000	Value: 28.00				

KM# 85 2 EURO
8.5000 g., Bi-Metallic Nickel-Brass center in Copper-Nickel ring, 25.75 mm. **Ruler:** Henri **Obv:** Head right and crowned monogram within 1/2 star circle **Rev:** Value and map within divided circle **Edge:** Reeded with 2's and stars

Date	Mintage	F	VF	XF	Unc	BU
2004(u)	2,447,800	—	—	—	7.00	9.00
2004(u) Special Unc.	10,000	—	—	—	—	50.00
2004(u) Proof	4,000	Value: 50.00				

KM# 87 2 EURO
8.5000 g., Bi-Metallic Nickel-Brass center in Copper-Nickel ring, 25.75 mm. **Ruler:** Henri **Obv:** Conjoined heads right within circle

Rev: Value and map within divided circle **Edge:** Reeded with 2's and stars

Date	Mintage	F	VF	XF	Unc	BU
2005	2,720,000	—	—	—	7.00	9.00
2005 Special Unc.	10,000	—	—	—	—	75.00
2005 Proof	4,000	Value: 50.00				

KM# 88 2 EURO
8.5000 g., Bi-Metallic Nickel-Brass center in Copper-Nickel ring, 25.75 mm. **Ruler:** Henri **Obv:** Conjoined heads right within circle and star border **Rev:** Value and map within divided circle **Edge:** Reeded with 2's and stars

Date	Mintage	F	VF	XF	Unc	BU
2006	1,030,000	—	—	—	7.00	9.00
2006 Special Unc.	15,000	—	—	—	—	32.00
2006 Proof	4,500	Value: 50.00				

KM# 93 2 EURO
8.5000 g., Bi-Metallic Nickel-Brass center in Copper-Nickel ring, 25.75 mm. **Ruler:** Henri **Obv:** Prince's portrait **Rev:** Relief map of Western Europe, stars, lines and value **Edge:** Reeded with 2's and stars

Date	Mintage	F	VF	XF	Unc	BU
2007(a)	4,000,000	—	—	—	4.00	5.00
2007(a) Proof	2,500	Value: 28.00				
2008(a)	6,000,000	—	—	—	4.00	5.00
2008(a) Proof	2,500	Value: 28.00				
2009(u)	240,000	—	—	—	6.00	7.50
2009(u) Proof	2,500	Value: 30.00				
2010(u)	3,500,000	—	—	—	4.00	5.00
2010(u) Proof	1,500	Value: 30.00				
2011(u)	—	—	—	—	4.00	5.00
2011(u) Proof	1,500	Value: 30.00				
2012(u)	—	—	—	—	4.00	5.00
2012(u) Proof	—	Value: 30.00				

KM# 94 2 EURO
8.5000 g., Bi-Metallic Nickel-Brass center in Copper-Nickel ring, 25.75 mm. **Ruler:** Henri **Subject:** 50th Anniversary Treaty of Rome **Obv:** Open treaty book with latent image on left hand page **Obv. Legend:** LËTZEBUERG **Rev:** Large value at left, modified outline of Europe at right **Edge:** Reeded with 2's and stars

Date	Mintage	F	VF	XF	Unc	BU
2007(a)	2,026,000	—	—	—	6.50	9.00
2007(a) Special Unc.	15,000	—	—	—	—	25.00
2007(a) Proof	5,000	Value: 30.00				

KM# 95 2 EURO
8.5000 g., Bi-Metallic Nickel-Brass center in Copper-Nickel ring, 25.75 mm. **Ruler:** Henri **Obv:** Palace in background at left, head 3/4 left at right **Obv. Legend:** LETZEBUERG **Rev:** Large value at left, modified outline of Europe at right **Edge:** Reeded with 2's and stars

Date	Mintage	F	VF	XF	Unc	BU
2007(a)	1,011,000	—	—	—	6.50	9.00
2007(a) Special Unc.	15,000	—	—	—	—	25.00
2007(a) Proof	5,000	Value: 40.00				

KM# 96   2 EURO
8.5000 g., Bi-Metallic Nickel-Brass center in Copper-Nickel ring, 25.75 mm.   **Ruler:** Henri **Obv:** Head at left, Chateau de Berg at right **Obv. Legend:** LETZEBUERG **Rev:** Large value at left, modified outline of Europe at right **Edge:** Reeded with 2's and stars

Date	Mintage	F	VF	XF	Unc	BU
2008(a)	1,000,000	—	—	4.00	5.00	6.25
2008(a) Proof	5,000	Value: 15.00				
2008(a) Special Unc.	15,000	—	—	—	—	30.00

KM# 106   2 EURO
8.5000 g., Bi-Metallic Nickel-Brass center in Copper-Nickel ring, 25.75 mm.   **Ruler:** Henri **Subject:** 90th Anniversary of Grand Duchess Charlotte **Obv:** Conjoined busts of Charlotte and Henri **Edge:** Reeded with 2's and stars

Date	Mintage	F	VF	XF	Unc	BU
2009	822,500	—	—	—	7.00	9.00
2009 Special Unc.	10,000	—	—	—	—	30.00
2009 Proof	2,500	Value: 15.00				

KM# 107   2 EURO
8.5000 g., Bi-Metallic Nickel-Brass center in Copper-Nickel ring, 25.75 mm.   **Ruler:** Henri **Subject:** European Monetary Union - 10th Anniversary **Obv:** Alternating stick figure with Euro emblem design or Head of Grand-Duke **Edge:** Reeded with 2's and stars

Date	Mintage	F	VF	XF	Unc	BU
2009	812,500	—	—	—	5.00	6.00
2009 Special Unc.	10,000	—	—	—	—	30.00
2009 Proof	2,500	Value: 15.00				

KM# 115   2 EURO
8.5000 g., Bi-Metallic Nickel-Brass center in Copper-Nickel ring, 25.75 mm.   **Ruler:** Henri **Obv:** Henry head facing, crowned shield **Rev:** Large value at left, modified outline mape of Europe at right **Edge:** Reeded with 2's and stars

Date	Mintage	F	VF	XF	Unc	BU
2010(a)	500,000	—	—	—	6.50	9.00
2010(a) Special Unc.	7,500	—	—	—	—	30.00
2010(a) Proof	1,500	Value: 20.00				

KM# 116   2 EURO
8.5000 g., Bi-Metallic Nickel-Brass center in Copper-Nickel ring, 25.75 mm.   **Ruler:** Henri **Subject:** Jean of Luxembourg - Nassau, 50th Anniversary of his appointment as Grand Duke **Obv:** Conjoined head left of Charlotte, Jean and Henri **Edge:** Reeded with 2's and stars

Date	Mintage	F	VF	XF	Unc	BU
2011	707,500	—	—	—	7.00	9.00
2011 Special Unc.	7,500	—	—	—	—	30.00
2011 Proof	1,500	Value: 15.00				

KM# 119   2 EURO
8.5000 g., Bi-Metallic Nickel-Brass center in Copper-Nickel ring, 25.75 mm.   **Ruler:** Henri **Subject:** Euro coinage, 10th Anniversary **Obv:** Euro symbol on globe, child-like rendering around

Date	Mintage	F	VF	XF	Unc	BU
2012	1,400,000	—	—	—	6.00	8.00

KM# 84   5 EURO
6.2200 g., 0.9990 Gold 0.1998 oz. AGW, 20 mm.   **Ruler:** Henri **Subject:** European Central Bank **Obv:** Grand Duke Henri **Rev:** Building

Date	Mintage	F	VF	XF	Unc	BU
2003(u) Proof	20,000	Value: 300				

KM# 108   5 EURO
16.6000 g., Bi-Metallic Niobium center in .925 Silver ring, 34 mm.   **Ruler:** Henri **Subject:** Vianden Castle **Obv:** Head right **Rev:** Castle view

Date	Mintage	F	VF	XF	Unc	BU
2009	7,500	—	—	—	—	150

KM# 109   5 EURO
Bi-Metallic Nordic Gold center in .925 Silver ring, 34 mm.   **Ruler:** Henri **Subject:** Common Kestrel **Obv:** Head right **Rev:** Bird

Date	Mintage	F	VF	XF	Unc	BU
2009 Proof	3,000	Value: 60.00				

KM# 111   5 EURO
16.6000 g., Bi-Metallic Niobium center in .925 Silver ring, 34 mm.   **Ruler:** Henri **Subject:** Chateau d'Esch-Sur-Sûre **Obv:** Head right **Rev:** Chateau view

Date	Mintage	F	VF	XF	Unc	BU
2010 Prooflike	3,000	—	—	—	—	100

KM# 112   5 EURO
Bi-Metallic Nordic Gold center in .925 Silver ring, 34 mm.   **Ruler:** Henri **Subject:** Flora and Fauna - Arnica Montana **Obv:** Head right **Rev:** Flowers

Date	Mintage	F	VF	XF	Unc	BU
2010 Proof	3,000	Value: 50.00				

KM# 117   5 EURO
16.6000 g., Bi-Metallic Niobium center in .925 Silver ring, 34 mm.   **Ruler:** Henri **Subject:** Mersch Castle **Obv:** Head right **Rev:** Castle vie

Date	Mintage	F	VF	XF	Unc	BU
2011 Prooflike	3,000	—	—	—	—	100

KM# 113   700 EURO CENTS
20.0000 g., 0.9250 Silver 0.5948 oz. ASW, 34 mm.   **Ruler:** Henri **Subject:** 700th Anniversary - Marriage of John of Luxembourg

Date	Mintage	F	VF	XF	Unc	BU
2010 Proof	3,000	Value: 75.00				

KM# 97   10 EURO
3.1100 g., 0.9990 Gold 0.0999 oz. AGW, 25.71 mm.   **Ruler:** Henri **Subject:** Culture **Obv:** Head right **Rev:** Hellenic sculpture head

Date	Mintage	F	VF	XF	Unc	BU
2004 Proof	5,000	Value: 175				

KM# 99   10 EURO
8.0000 g., Bi-Metallic Titanium center in .925 Silver ring, 26 mm.   **Ruler:** Henri **Subject:** State Bank 150th Anniversary **Obv:** Head right **Rev:** Bank Plaza

Date	Mintage	F	VF	XF	Unc	BU
2006	7,500	—	—	—	—	150

KM# 101   10 EURO
3.1100 g., 0.9990 Gold 0.0999 oz. AGW, 16 mm.   **Ruler:** Henri **Obv:** Head right **Rev:** Wild pig of Titelberg

Date	Mintage	F	VF	XF	Unc	BU
2006 Proof	5,000	Value: 200				

KM# 104   10 EURO
10.3700 g., 0.9990 Gold 0.3331 oz. AGW, 23 mm.   **Ruler:** Henri **Subject:** Banque Central - 10th Anniversary **Obv:** Head right **Rev:** Old and new bank buildings

Date	Mintage	F	VF	XF	Unc	BU
2008 Proof	1,250	Value: 600				

KM# 110   10 EURO
3.1100 g., 0.9990 Gold 0.0999 oz. AGW, 16 mm.   **Ruler:** Henri **Subject:** Deer of Orval's Refuge **Obv:** Head right **Rev:** Stag seated, flower in background

Date	Mintage	F	VF	XF	Unc	BU
2009 Proof	3,000	Value: 200				

KM# 114   10 EURO
13.5000 g., Bi-Metallic Titanium center in .925 Silver ring, 34 mm.   **Ruler:** Henri **Subject:** Schengen Accord, 25th Anniversary **Obv:** Head right **Rev:** Building

Date	Mintage	F	VF	XF	Unc	BU
2010 Prooflike	3,000	—	—	—	—	125

KM# 118   10 EURO
16.1500 g., Bi-Metallic Nordic Gold center in .925 Silver ring, 34 mm.   **Ruler:** Henri **Subject:** Flora and Fauna - Otter

Date	Mintage	F	VF	XF	Unc	BU
2011 Proof	3,000	Value: 50.00				

KM# 102   20 EURO
13.5000 g., Bi-Metallic Titanium center in .925 Silver ring, 34 mm.   **Ruler:** Henri **Obv:** Three heads facing **Rev:** Council D'Etat building

Date	Mintage	F	VF	XF	Unc	BU
2006	4,000	—	—	—	—	120

KM# 83   25 EURO
22.8500 g., 0.9250 Silver 0.6795 oz. ASW, 37 mm.   **Ruler:** Henri **Subject:** European Court System **Obv:** Grand Duke Henri **Rev:** Sword scale on law book

Date	Mintage	F	VF	XF	Unc	BU
2002(u) Proof	20,000	Value: 100				

KM# 86   25 EURO
22.8500 g., 0.9250 Silver 0.6795 oz. ASW, 37 mm.   **Ruler:** Henri **Subject:** European Parliament **Obv:** Grand Duke Henri **Rev:** Parliament

Date	Mintage	F	VF	XF	Unc	BU
2004(u) Proof	20,000	Value: 100				

KM# 98   25 EURO
22.8000 g., 0.9250 Silver 0.6780 oz. ASW, 37 mm.   **Ruler:** Henri **Subject:** EU Presidency **Obv:** Head right **Rev:** Conseil de l'Union building in Brussels

Date	Mintage	F	VF	XF	Unc	BU
2005 Proof	10,000	Value: 100				

KM# 100   25 EURO
22.8000 g., 0.9250 Silver 0.6780 oz. ASW, 37 mm.   **Ruler:** Henri **Obv:** Head right **Rev:** European Commission building "Berlaymont" in Brussels

Date	Mintage	F	VF	XF	Unc	BU
2006 Proof	5,000	Value: 110				

KM# 103   25 EURO
22.8500 g., 0.9250 Silver 0.6795 oz. ASW, 37 mm.   **Ruler:** Henri **Subject:** European Court of Auditors 30th Anniversary

Date	Mintage	F	VF	XF	Unc	BU
2007 Proof	3,000	Value: 80.00				

KM# 105   25 EURO
22.8500 g., 0.9250 Silver 0.6795 oz. ASW, 37 mm.   **Ruler:** Henri **Subject:** European Investment Bank

Date	Mintage	F	VF	XF	Unc	BU
2008 Proof	4,000	Value: 275				

MINT SETS

KM#	Date	Mintage	Identification	Issue Price	Mkt Val
MS7	2002 (8)	35,000	KM#75-82	—	20.00
MS8	2002 (8)	—	KM#75-82	—	20.00
MS9	2003 (8)	50,000	KM#75-82, Adolph Brucke	—	30.00
MS10	2003 (8)	3,500	KM#75-82 plus stamps	—	75.00
MS11	2004 (8)	40,000	KM#75-82	—	50.00
MS12	2004 (8)	6,400	KM#75-82 plus stamps	—	50.00
MS13	2004 (8)	500	KM#75-82, Grand Duke	—	—
MS14	2004 (8)	500	KM#75-82, Ducal Palace	—	—
MS15	2005 (9)	20,000	KM#75-82, 87	40.00	65.00
MS16	2005 (8)	6,500	KM#75-82 plus stamps	—	55.00
MS17	2005 (8)	2,000	KM#75-82, Women and Myth, signed by Gastauer	—	75.00
MS18	2006 (9)	15,000	KM#75-82, 88	40.00	65.00
MS19	2006 (8)	2,000	KM#75-82 plus stamps	—	75.00
MS20	2007 (9)	11,000	KM#75-78, 89-93, 94	37.50	50.00
MS21	2008 (9)	10,000	KM#75-77, 89-93, 96	37.50	40.00
MS22	2009 (9)	10,000	KM#75-77, 89-93, 106	37.50	40.00
MS23	2010 (9)	7,500	KM#75-77, 89-93, 115	37.50	40.00
MS24	2011 (9)	7,500	KM#75-77, 89-93, 116	37.50	40.00

PROOF SETS

KM#	Date	Mintage	Identification	Issue Price	Mkt Val
PS2	2002 (8)	1,500	KM#75-82	100	300
PS3	2003 (8)	1,500	KM#75-82	100	300
PS4	2004 (9)	1,500	KM#75-82, 85	105	300
PS5	2005 (9)	1,500	KM#75-82, 87	105	250
PS6	2006 (9)	2,000	KM#75-82, 88	120	200
PS7	2007 (10)	2,500	KM#75-77, 89-95	125	200
PS8	2008 (9)	2,500	KM#75-77, 89-93, 96	125	250
PS9	2004-08 (6)	2,500	KM#85, 87, 88, 94, 95, 96	105	200
PS10	2009 (10)	2,000	KM#75-77, 89-93, 106, 107	125	250
PS11	2010 (9)	2,500	KM#75-77, 89-93, 115	125	250
PS12	2011 (9)	1,500	KM#75-77, 89-93, 116	125	200

MACAU

The Province of Macao, a Portuguese overseas province located in the South China Sea 40 miles southwest of Hong Kong, consists of the peninsula of Macao and the islands of Taipa and Coloane. It has an area of 6.2 sq. mi. (16 sq. km.) and a population of 500,000. Capital: Macao. Macao's economy is based on light industry, commerce, tourism, fishing, and gold trading - Macao is one of the entirely free markets for gold in the world. Cement, textiles, fireworks, vegetable oils, and metal products are exported.

In 1987, Portugal and China agreed that Macao would become a Chinese Territory in 1999. In December of 1999, Macao became a special administrative zone of China.

MINT MARKS
(p) - Pobjoy Mint
(s) - Singapore Mint

Pobjoy Mint   Singapore Mint

MONETARY SYSTEM
100 Avos = 1 Pataca

SPECIAL ADMINISTRATIVE REGION (S.A.R.)

STANDARD COINAGE
100 Avos = 1 Pataca

KM# 70   10 AVOS
1.3800 g., Brass, 17 mm.   **Obv:** MACAU written at center with date below **Rev:** Crowned lion dance scene above value flanked by mint marks

Date	Mintage	F	VF	XF	Unc	BU
2005	—	—	—	—	0.75	1.25
2007	—	—	—	—	0.75	1.25

KM# 72   50 AVOS
4.5900 g., Brass, 23 mm.   **Obv:** MACAU written across center of globe with date below **Rev:** The dragon dance led by a man

Date	Mintage	F	VF	XF	Unc	BU
2003	—	—	—	—	1.50	2.50
2005	—	—	—	—	1.50	2.50

KM# 57   PATACA
9.1800 g., Copper-Nickel, 25.98 mm.   **Obv:** MACAU written across center of globe with date below **Rev:** Guia Fortress and Chapel of Our Lady of Guia **Edge:** Reeded

Date	Mintage	F	VF	XF	Unc	BU
2003	—	—	—	0.60	1.50	2.00
2005	—	—	—	0.60	1.50	2.00
2007	—	—	—	—	1.50	2.00

KM# 56   5 PATACAS
10.1000 g., Copper-Nickel   **Obv:** MACAU written across center of globe with date below **Rev:** Chinese junk, ruins of St. Paul's Cathedral in background **Edge:** Plain **Shape:** 12-sided

Date	Mintage	F	VF	XF	Unc	BU
2003	—	—	—	—	6.50	10.00
2005	—	—	—	—	6.50	10.00
2007	—	—	—	—	6.50	10.00

KM# 153   10 PATACAS
0.3000 g., 0.9990 Gold 0.0096 oz. AGW, 7 mm.   **Obv:** A Ma statue **Rev:** Lotus flower

Date	Mintage	F	VF	XF	Unc	BU
2009 Proof	Est. 5,000	Value: 25.00				

KM# 142   20 PATACAS
31.1050 g., 0.9990 Silver 0.9990 oz. ASW, 40.7 mm.   **Subject:** Year of the Rat **Obv:** A Ma Temple **Rev:** Rat, multicolor flowers at right

Date	Mintage	F	VF	XF	Unc	BU
2008 Proof	6,000	Value: 130				

KM# 145   20 PATACAS
31.1050 g., 0.9990 Silver 0.9990 oz. ASW, 40.7 mm.   **Subject:** Year of the Ox **Obv:** Moorish Barracks **Rev:** Ox, multicolor flowers at right

Date	Mintage	F	VF	XF	Unc	BU
2009 Proof	—	Value: 60.00				

KM# 151   20 PATACAS
31.1050 g., 0.9990 Silver 0.9990 oz. ASW, 40.7 mm.   **Obv:** A Ma statue **Rev:** Lotus flower

Date	Mintage	F	VF	XF	Unc	BU
2009 Proof	Est. 5,600	Value: 75.00				

KM# 156   20 PATACAS
31.1050 g., 0.9990 Silver 0.9990 oz. ASW, 40.7 mm.   **Subject:** Year of the Tiger **Rev:** Tiger in color

Date	Mintage	F	VF	XF	Unc	BU
2010 Proof	Est. 6,000	Value: 75.00				

KM# 159   20 PATACAS
31.1050 g., 0.9990 Silver 0.9990 oz. ASW, 40.7 mm.   **Obv:** Rabbit in color **Rev:** Dom Pedro V theater

Date	Mintage	F	VF	XF	Unc	BU
2011 Proof	Est. 6,000	Value: 75.00				

KM# 162   20 PATACAS
28.2800 g., 0.9250 Silver 0.8410 oz. ASW, 40.7 mm.   **Subject:** Year of the Dragon **Obv:** Dragon in color

Date	Mintage	F	VF	XF	Unc	BU
2012 Proof	—	Value: 150				

KM# 128   50 PATACAS
28.2800 g., 0.9250 Silver partially gilt 0.8410 oz. ASW   **Subject:** 1st World Championship Grand Prix **Rev:** Two race cars - gilt

Date	Mintage	F	VF	XF	Unc	BU
2003 Proof	5,000	Value: 75.00				

KM# 154   50 PATACAS
1.2400 g., 0.9990 Gold 0.0398 oz. AGW, 13.92 mm.   **Obv:** A Ma statue **Rev:** Lotus flower

Date	Mintage	F	VF	XF	Unc	BU
2009 Proof	Est. 5,000	Value: 90.00				

KM# 102   100 PATACAS
28.2800 g., 0.9250 Silver 0.8410 oz. ASW   **Subject:** Year of the Snake **Obv:** Church façade **Rev:** Snake

Date	Mintage	F	VF	XF	Unc	BU
2001 Proof	4,000	Value: 55.00				

KM# 107   100 PATACAS
28.2800 g., 0.9250 Silver 0.8410 oz. ASW, 38.6 mm.   **Subject:** Year of the Horse **Obv:** Church façade flanked by stars **Rev:** Horse above value **Edge:** Reeded

Date	Mintage	F	VF	XF	Unc	BU
2002 Proof	4,000	Value: 45.00				

KM# 122   100 PATACAS
28.2800 g., 0.9250 Silver 0.8410 oz. ASW   **Subject:** 5th Anniversary Return of Macao to China

Date	Mintage	F	VF	XF	Unc	BU
2004 Proof	10,000	Value: 60.00				

KM# 130   100 PATACAS
28.2800 g., 0.9250 Silver 0.8410 oz. ASW   **Series:** Lunar **Subject:** Year of the Monkey

Date	Mintage	F	VF	XF	Unc	BU
2004	1,000	—	—	—	—	60.00
2004 Proof	4,000	Value: 75.00				

KM# 134   100 PATACAS
28.2800 g., 0.9250 Silver 0.8410 oz. ASW   **Series:** Lunar **Subject:** Year of the Rooster **Rev:** Stylized rooster walking left

Date	Mintage	F	VF	XF	Unc	BU
2005 Proof	—	Value: 90.00				

KM# 137   100 PATACAS
28.2800 g., 0.9250 Silver 0.8410 oz. ASW   **Subject:** IV East Asian Games - FRIENDSHIP

Date	Mintage	F	VF	XF	Unc	BU
2005 Proof	6,000	Value: 75.00				

KM# 139   100 PATACAS
28.2800 g., 0.9250 Silver 0.8410 oz. ASW   **Series:** Lunar **Subject:** Year of the Dog **Rev:** Stylized dog standing left

Date	Mintage	F	VF	XF	Unc	BU
2006 Proof	—	Value: 90.00				

KM# 148   100 PATACAS
31.1050 g., 0.9250 Silver 0.9250 oz. ASW, 40 mm.   **Subject:** Year of the Pig **Rev:** Pig in color

Date	Mintage	F	VF	XF	Unc	BU
2007 Proof	Est. 15,000	Value: 90.00				

KM# 143   100 PATACAS
155.5000 g., 0.9990 Silver 4.9942 oz. ASW, 65 mm.   **Subject:** Year of the Rat **Obv:** A Ma Temple **Rev:** Rat, multicolor flowers at right **Note:** Illustration reduced.

Date	Mintage	F	VF	XF	Unc	BU
2008 Proof	500	Value: 250				

KM# 146   100 PATACAS
155.5000 g., 0.9990 Silver 4.9942 oz. ASW, 65 mm.   **Subject:** Year of the Ox **Obv:** Moorish Barracks **Rev:** Ox, multicolor flowers at right **Note:** Illustration reduced.

Date	Mintage	F	VF	XF	Unc	BU
2009 Proof	500	Value: 250				

KM# 152   100 PATACAS
155.5000 g., 0.9990 Silver 4.9942 oz. ASW, 65 mm.   **Obv:** A Ma statue **Rev:** Lotus flower

Date	Mintage	F	VF	XF	Unc	BU
2009 Proof	Est. 1,000	Value: 275				

KM# 157   100 PATACAS
155.5000 g., 0.9990 Silver 4.9942 oz. ASW, 65 mm.   **Subject:** Year of the Tiger **Rev:** Tiger in color

Date	Mintage	F	VF	XF	Unc	BU
2010 Proof	Est. 500	Value: 450				

KM# 160   100 PATACAS
155.5000 g., 0.9990 Silver 4.9942 oz. ASW, 65 mm.   **Subject:** Year of the Rabbit **Obv:** Rabbit in color **Rev:** Dom Pedro V theater

Date	Mintage	F	VF	XF	Unc	BU
2011 Proof	500	Value: 400				

KM# 163   100 PATACAS
155.5000 g., 0.9990 Silver 4.9942 oz. ASW, 65 mm. **Subject:**
Year of the Dragon **Obv:** Dragon in color

Date	Mintage	F	VF	XF	Unc	BU
2012 Proof	—	Value: 750				

KM# 123   200 PATACAS
28.2800 g., 0.9250 Silver partially gilt. 0.8410 oz. ASW **Subject:**
5th Anniversary Return of Macao to China

Date	Mintage	F	VF	XF	Unc	BU
2004 Proof	10,000	Value: 75.00				

KM# 138   200 PATACAS
28.2800 g., 0.9250 Silver partially gilt 0.8410 oz. ASW **Subject:**
IV East Asian Games **Rev:** U-N-I-T-Y in blocks at left - bottom.
logo at upper right

Date	Mintage	F	VF	XF	Unc	BU
2005 Proof	6,000	Value: 120				

KM# 103   250 PATACAS
3.9900 g., 0.9167 Gold 0.1176 oz. AGW **Subject:** Year of the
Snake **Obv:** Church façade **Rev:** Snake

Date	Mintage	F	VF	XF	Unc	BU
2001 Proof	2,500	Value: 240				

KM# 108   250 PATACAS
3.9900 g., 0.9167 Gold 0.1176 oz. AGW, 19.3 mm. **Subject:**
Year of the Horse **Obv:** Church of St. Paul façade **Rev:** Horse
above value **Edge:** Reeded

Date	Mintage	F	VF	XF	Unc	BU
2002 Proof	2,500	Value: 240				

KM# 119   250 PATACAS
3.9900 g., 0.9167 Gold 0.1176 oz. AGW, 19.3 mm. **Subject:**
Year of the Goat **Obv:** Church façade **Rev:** Goat above value
Edge: Reeded

Date	Mintage	F	VF	XF	Unc	BU
2003 Proof	2,500	Value: 240				

KM# 131   250 PATACAS
3.9900 g., 0.9167 Gold 0.1176 oz. AGW **Series:** Lunar **Subject:**
Year of the Monkey

Date	Mintage	F	VF	XF	Unc	BU
2004 Proof	2,500	Value: 280				

KM# 135   250 PATACAS
2.8300 g., 0.9990 Gold 0.0909 oz. AGW **Series:** Lunar **Subject:**
Year of the Rooster **Rev:** Stylized rooster walking left

Date	Mintage	F	VF	XF	Unc	BU
2005 Proof	—	Value: 280				

KM# 140   250 PATACAS
3.1100 g., 0.9990 Gold 0.0999 oz. AGW **Series:** Lunar **Subject:**
Year of the Dog **Rev:** Stylized dog standing left - multicolor

Date	Mintage	F	VF	XF	Unc	BU
2006 Proof	—	Value: 280				

KM# 149   250 PATACAS
3.1100 g., 0.9990 Gold 0.0999 oz. AGW, 18 mm. **Subject:** Year
of the Pig **Rev:** Pig in color

Date	Mintage	F	VF	XF	Unc	BU
2007 Proof	Est. 7,000	Value: 220				

KM# 144   250 PATACAS
7.7900 g., 0.9990 Gold 0.2502 oz. AGW **Subject:** Year of the
Rat **Obv:** Temple **Rev:** Rat and multicolor flowers at right

Date	Mintage	F	VF	XF	Unc	BU
2008 Proof	—	Value: 525				

KM# 147   250 PATACAS
7.7700 g., 0.9990 Gold 0.2496 oz. AGW **Subject:** Year of the
Ox **Obv:** Moorish Barracks **Rev:** Ox, multicolor flowers at right

Date	Mintage	F	VF	XF	Unc	BU
2009 Proof	—	Value: 550				

KM# 155   250 PATACAS
7.7800 g., 0.9990 Gold 0.2499 oz. AGW, 22 mm. **Obv:** A Ma
statue **Rev:** Lotus flower

Date	Mintage	F	VF	XF	Unc	BU
2009 Proof	Est. 1,600	Value: 550				

KM# 158   250 PATACAS
7.7800 g., 0.9990 Gold 0.2499 oz. AGW, 22 mm. **Subject:** Year
of the Tiger **Rev:** Tiger in color

Date	Mintage	F	VF	XF	Unc	BU
2010 Proof	Est. 3,000	Value: 700				

KM# 161   250 PATACAS
7.7800 g., 0.9990 Gold 0.2499 oz. AGW, 22 mm. **Subject:** Year
of the Rabbit **Obv:** Rabbit in color **Rev:** Dom Pedro V theater

Date	Mintage	F	VF	XF	Unc	BU
2011(s) Proof	Est. 3,000	Value: 700				

KM# 104   500 PATACAS
7.9900 g., 0.9167 Gold 0.2355 oz. AGW **Subject:** Year of the
Snake **Obv:** Church façade **Rev:** Snake

Date	Mintage	F	VF	XF	Unc	BU
2001 Proof	2,500	Value: 550				

KM# 109   500 PATACAS
7.9800 g., 0.9167 Gold 0.2352 oz. AGW, 22.05 mm. **Subject:**
Year of the Horse **Obv:** Church façade **Rev:** Horse above value
Edge: Reeded

Date	Mintage	F	VF	XF	Unc	BU
2002 Proof	2,500	Value: 550				

KM# 120   500 PATACAS
7.9800 g., 0.9167 Gold 0.2352 oz. AGW, 22 mm. **Subject:** Year
of the Goat **Obv:** Church façade **Rev:** Goat above value **Edge:**
Reeded

Date	Mintage	F	VF	XF	Unc	BU
2003 Proof	2,500	Value: 550				

KM# 129   500 PATACAS
7.9600 g., 0.9167 Gold 0.2346 oz. AGW **Subject:** 1st World
Championship Grand Prix **Rev:** Two race cars

Date	Mintage	F	VF	XF	Unc	BU
2003 Proof	2,000	Value: 550				

KM# 124   500 PATACAS
62.2060 g., 0.9990 Silver partially gilt 1.9979 oz. ASW **Subject:**
5th Anniversary Return of Macao to China

Date	Mintage	F	VF	XF	Unc	BU
2004 Proof	1,000	Value: 120				

KM# 132   500 PATACAS
7.9800 g., 0.9167 Gold 0.2352 oz. AGW **Series:** Lunar **Subject:**
Year of the Monkey

Date	Mintage	F	VF	XF	Unc	BU
2004 Proof	2,500	Value: 525				

KM# 136   500 PATACAS
7.9600 g., 0.9990 Gold 0.2557 oz. AGW **Series:** Lunar **Subject:**
Year of the Rooster **Rev:** Stylized rooster walking left

Date	Mintage	F	VF	XF	Unc	BU
2005 Proof	—	Value: 550				

KM# 141   500 PATACAS
7.9600 g., 0.9990 Gold 0.2557 oz. AGW **Series:** Lunar **Subject:**
Year of the Dog **Rev:** Stylized dog standing left

Date	Mintage	F	VF	XF	Unc	BU
2006 Proof	—	Value: 550				

KM# 150   500 PATACAS
7.9600 g., 0.9990 Gold 0.2557 oz. AGW, 22 mm. **Subject:** Year
of the Pig **Rev:** Pig in color

Date	Mintage	F	VF	XF	Unc	BU
2007 Proof	Est. 4,000	Value: 600				

KM# 164   500 PATACAS
7.7800 g., 0.9990 Gold 0.2499 oz. AGW, 22 mm. **Subject:** Year
of the Dragon **Obv:** Dragon in color

Date	Mintage	F	VF	XF	Unc	BU
2012 Proof	—	Value: 950				

KM# 105   1000 PATACAS
16.9760 g., 0.9167 Gold 0.5003 oz. AGW **Subject:** Year of the
Snake **Obv:** Church façade flanked by stars **Rev:** Snake

Date	Mintage	F	VF	XF	Unc	BU
2001 Proof	4,000	Value: 1,000				

KM# 110   1000 PATACAS
15.9700 g., 0.9167 Gold 0.4707 oz. AGW, 28.4 mm. **Subject:**
Year of the Horse **Obv:** Church façade **Rev:** Horse above value
Edge: Reeded

Date	Mintage	F	VF	XF	Unc	BU
2002 Proof	4,000	Value: 1,000				

KM# 118   1000 PATACAS
28.2800 g., 0.9250 Silver 0.8410 oz. ASW, 38.6 mm. **Subject:**
Year of the Goat **Obv:** Church façade **Rev:** Goat above value
Edge: Reeded

Date	Mintage	F	VF	XF	Unc	BU
2003 Proof	4,000	Value: 45.00				

KM# 121   1000 PATACAS
15.9760 g., 0.9170 Gold 0.4710 oz. AGW **Subject:** Year of the
Goat **Obv:** Church façade flanked by stars **Rev:** Goat above value
Edge: Reeded

Date	Mintage	F	VF	XF	Unc	BU
2003 Proof	4,000	Value: 1,000				

KM# 125   1000 PATACAS
155.5150 g., 0.9990 Silver 4.9947 oz. ASW **Subject:** 5th
Anniversary Return of Macao to China

Date	Mintage	F	VF	XF	Unc	BU
2004 Proof	3,000	Value: 310				

KM# 133   1000 PATACAS
15.9800 g., 0.9167 Gold 0.4710 oz. AGW **Series:** Lunar
Subject: Year of the Monkey

Date	Mintage	F	VF	XF	Unc	BU
2004	500		—	—	950	—
2004 Proof	4,000	Value: 1,000				

KM# 126   2000 PATACAS
155.5150 g., 0.9990 Silver partially gilt 4.9947 oz. ASW **Subject:**
5th Anniversary Return of Macao to China

Date	Mintage	F	VF	XF	Unc	BU
2004 Proof	1,500	Value: 300				

PROOF SETS

KM#	Date	Mintage	Identification	Issue Price	Mkt Val
PS16	2001 (3)	2,500	KM#103-105	849	1,800
PS17	2002 (3)	4,000	KM#108-110	849	1,800
PS18	2003 (3)	2,500	KM#119-121	849	1,800
PS19	2004 (4)	—	KM#130-133	—	2,000
PS20	2005 (3)	—	KM#134-136	—	925
PS21	2006 (3)	—	KM#139-141	—	925
PS22	2007 (3)	—	KM#148-150	—	925
PS23	2008 (3)	—	KM#142-144	—	925
PS24	2009 (3)	—	KM#145-147	—	875
PS25	2010 (3)	—	KM#156-158	—	1,225
PS26	2011 (3)	—	KM#159-161	—	1,175
PS27	2012 (3)	—	KM#162-164	—	1,850

MACEDONIA

The Republic of Macedonia is land-locked, and is bordered
in the north by Yugoslavia, to the east by Bulgaria, in the south
by Greece and to the west by Albania and has an area of 9,781
sq. mi. (25,713 sq. km.) and a population at the 1991 census was
2,038,847, of which the predominating ethnic groups were Mace-
donians. The capital is Skopje.

On Nov. 20, 1991 parliament promulgated a new constitution, and declared its independence on Nov.20, 1992, but failed
to secure EC and US recognition owing to Greek objections to
use of the name *Macedonia*. On Dec. 11, 1992, the UN Security
Council authorized the expedition of a small peacekeeping force
to prevent hostilities spreading into Macedonia.

There is a 120-member single-chamber National Assembly.

REPUBLIC
STANDARD COINAGE

KM# 2   DENAR
5.1500 g., Brass, 23.7 mm. **Obv:** Macedonian sheepdog **Obv.
Legend:** РЕПУБЛИКА МАКЕДОНИЈА **Rev:** Radiant value
Edge: Plain

Date	Mintage	F	VF	XF	Unc	BU
2001	12,874,000	—	0.20	0.35	1.50	4.00
2006	—	—	—	—	1.25	3.75
2008	—	—	—	—	1.25	3.75

KM# 3   2 DENARI
5.1500 g., Brass, 23.7 mm. **Obv:** Trout above water **Obv.
Legend:** РЕПУБЛИКА МАКЕДОНИЈА **Rev:** Radiant value
Edge: Plain

Date	Mintage	F	VF	XF	Unc	BU
2001	11,672,000	—	—	0.50	1.25	3.00
2006	—	—	—	0.50	1.00	2.50
2008	—	—	—	—	1.00	2.50

KM# 4   5 DENARI
7.2500 g., Brass, 27.5 mm. **Obv:** European lynx **Obv. Legend:** РЕПУБЛИКА МАКЕДОНИЈА **Rev:** Radiant value **Edge:** Plain

Date	Mintage	F	VF	XF	Unc	BU
2001	6,921,000	—	0.35	0.75	1.75	3.50
2006	—	—	—	—	1.50	3.00
2008	—	—	—	—	1.50	3.00

KM# 13   10 DENARI
10.0000 g., 0.9160 Gold 0.2945 oz. AGW, 27 mm. **Subject:** 10th Anniversary of Independence **Obv:** Value in circle within radiant map **Rev:** Grape vine

Date	Mintage	F	VF	XF	Unc	BU
2001	1,000	—	—	—	550	575

KM# 31   10 DENARI
6.6000 g., Copper-Nickel-Zinc, 24.5 mm. **Obv:** Peacock **Rev:** Value within rays

Date	Mintage	F	VF	XF	Unc	BU
2008	—	—	—	—	—	2.00

KM# 32   50 DENARI
7.7000 g., Brass, 26.5 mm. **Obv:** Classical female bust right **Rev:** Value within rays

Date	Mintage	F	VF	XF	Unc	BU
2008	—	—	—	—	—	2.00

KM# 22   60 DENARI
6.0000 g., 0.9160 Gold 0.1767 oz. AGW, 23.8 mm. **Subject:** 100th Anniversary - Statehood **Obv:** Monument above value within circle **Rev:** Djorce Petrov

Date	Mintage	F	VF	XF	Unc	BU
2003	500	—	—	—	375	400

KM# 23   60 DENARI
6.0000 g., 0.9160 Gold 0.1767 oz. AGW, 23.8 mm. **Subject:** 100th Anniversary - Statehood **Obv:** Monument above value within circle **Rev:** Krste Petkov-Misirkov

Date	Mintage	F	VF	XF	Unc	BU
2003	500	—	—	—	375	400

KM# 24   60 DENARI
6.0000 g., 0.9160 Gold 0.1767 oz. AGW, 23.8 mm. **Subject:** 100th Anniversary - Statehood **Obv:** Monument above value within circle **Rev:** Metodije Andonov

Date	Mintage	F	VF	XF	Unc	BU
2003	500	—	—	—	375	400

KM# 25   60 DENARI
6.0000 g., 0.9160 Gold 0.1767 oz. AGW, 23.8 mm. **Subject:** 100th Anniversary - Statehood **Obv:** Monument above value within circle **Rev:** Mihailo Apostolski

Date	Mintage	F	VF	XF	Unc	BU
2003	500	—	—	—	375	400

KM# 26   60 DENARI
6.0000 g., 0.9160 Gold 0.1767 oz. AGW, 23.8 mm. **Subject:** 100th Anniversary - Statehood **Obv:** Monument above value within circle **Rev:** Blaze Koneski

Date	Mintage	F	VF	XF	Unc	BU
2003	500	—	—	—	375	400

KM# 21   60 DENARI
8.0000 g., 0.9160 Gold 0.2356 oz. AGW, 23.8 mm. **Subject:** 50th Anniversary of separation from Greece **Obv:** The Monifest **Rev:** Monastery

Date	Mintage	F	VF	XF	Unc	BU
2004	500	—	—	—	425	450

KM# 14   100 DENARI
6.0000 g., 0.9160 Gold 0.1767 oz. AGW, 23.8 mm. **Subject:** 100th Anniversary of Statehood **Obv:** Monument above value within circle **Rev:** Cherry tree cannon divides circle

Date	Mintage	F	VF	XF	Unc	BU
2003 Proof	500	Value: 400				

KM# 15   100 DENARI
6.0000 g., 0.9160 Gold 0.1767 oz. AGW, 23.8 mm. **Subject:** 100th Anniversary of Statehood - Goce Delcev **Obv:** Monument above value within circle **Rev:** Bust facing within circle

Date	Mintage	F	VF	XF	Unc	BU
2003 Proof	500	Value: 400				

KM# 16   100 DENARI
6.0000 g., 0.9160 Gold 0.1767 oz. AGW, 23.8 mm. **Subject:** 100th Anniversary of Statehood - Pitu Guli **Obv:** Monument above value within circle **Rev:** Head with hat facing within circle

Date	Mintage	F	VF	XF	Unc	BU
2003 Proof	500	Value: 400				

KM# 17   100 DENARI
6.0000 g., 0.9160 Gold 0.1767 oz. AGW, 23.8 mm. **Subject:** 100th Anniversary of Statehood - Jane Sandanski **Obv:** Monument above value within circle **Rev:** Head facing within circle

Date	Mintage	F	VF	XF	Unc	BU
2003 Proof	500	Value: 400				

KM# 18   100 DENARI
6.0000 g., 0.9160 Gold 0.1767 oz. AGW, 23.8 mm. **Subject:** 100th Anniversary of Statehood - Dame Gruev **Obv:** Monument above value within circle **Rev:** Bust left within circle

Date	Mintage	F	VF	XF	Unc	BU
2003 Proof	500	Value: 400				

KM# 19   100 DENARI
6.0000 g., 0.9160 Gold 0.1767 oz. AGW, 23.8 mm. **Subject:** 100th Anniversary of Statehood - Nikola Karev **Obv:** Monument above value within circle **Rev:** Bust right within circle

Date	Mintage	F	VF	XF	Unc	BU
2003 Proof	500	Value: 400				

KM# 28   100 DENARI
6.0000 g., 0.9160 Gold 0.1767 oz. AGW **Subject:** 100th Anniversary of Statehood - Djorce Petrov **Obv:** Monument **Rev:** Bust facing

Date	Mintage	F	VF	XF	Unc	BU
2003 Proof	500	Value: 400				

KM# 29   100 DENARI
6.0000 g., 0.9160 Gold 0.1767 oz. AGW **Subject:** 100th Anniversary of Statehood - Krste Petkov-Misirkov **Obv:** Monument **Rev:** Bust facing

Date	Mintage	F	VF	XF	Unc	BU
2003 Proof	500	Value: 400				

KM# 30   100 DENARI
6.0000 g., 0.9160 Gold 0.1767 oz. AGW **Subject:** 100th Anniversary of statehood - Metodije Adamov-Cengo **Obv:** Monument **Rev:** Bust facing

Date	Mintage	F	VF	XF	Unc	BU
2003 Proof	500	Value: 400				

KM# 33   100 DENARI
6.0000 g., 0.9160 Gold 0.1767 oz. AGW, 23.8 mm. **Subject:** 100th Anniversary of Statehood - Mihailo Apostolski **Obv:** Monument **Rev:** Bust facing in field cap

Date	Mintage	F	VF	XF	Unc	BU
2003 Proof	500	Value: 400				

KM# 34   100 DENARI
6.0000 g., 0.9160 Gold 0.1767 oz. AGW, 23.8 mm. **Subject:** 100th Anniversary of Statehood - Blaze Koneski **Obv:** Monument **Rev:** Bust facing, wearing glasses

Date	Mintage	F	VF	XF	Unc	BU
2003 Proof	500	Value: 400				

PATTERNS

KM#	Date	Mintage	Identification	Mkt Val
Pn1	2003	50	100 Denari. 0.9250 Silver. 7.0000 g. KM#14	150
Pn2	2003	50	100 Denari. 0.9260 Silver. 7.0000 g. KM#15.	150
Pn3	2003	50	100 Denari. 0.9250 Silver. 7.0000 g. KM#16.	150
Pn4	2003	50	100 Denari. 0.9250 Silver. 7.0000 g. KM#17.	150
Pn5	2003	50	100 Denari. 0.9250 Silver. 7.0000 g. KM#18.	150
Pn6	2003	50	100 Denari. 0.9250 Silver. 7.0000 g. KM#19.	150
Pn7	2003	50	100 Denari. 0.9250 Silver. 7.0000 g.	150
Pn8	2003	50	100 Denari. 0.9250 Silver. 7.0000 g. KM#29.	150
Pn9	2003	50	100 Denari. 0.9250 Silver. 7.0000 g. KM#30.	150
Pn10	2003	50	100 Denari. 0.9250 Silver. 7.0000 g. KM#33.	150

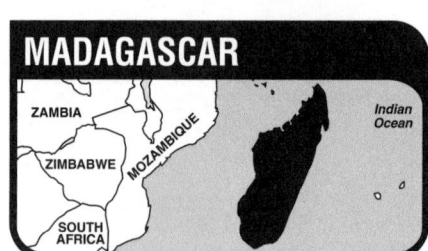

MADAGASCAR

The Republic of Madagascar, an independent member of the French Community located in the Indian Ocean 250 miles (402 km.) off the southeast coast of Africa, has an area of 226,656 sq. mi. (587,040 sq. km.) and a population of 10 million. Capital: Antananarivo. The economy is primarily agricultural; large bauxite deposits are being developed. Coffee, vanilla, graphite, and rice are exported.

MONETARY SYSTEM
100 Centimes = 1 Franc

MINT MARKS
(a) - Paris, privy marks only
SA - Pretoria

MALAGASY REPUBLIC

STANDARD COINAGE
Madagasikara Republic 1 Ariary = 100 Iraimbilanja

KM# 8 FRANC
2.4000 g., Stainless Steel **Obv:** Poinsettia **Rev:** Value within horns of ox head above sprigs

Date	Mintage	F	VF	XF	Unc	BU
2002(a)	—	0.15	0.20	0.40	1.45	—

REPUBLIC
Madagasikara Republic
STANDARD COINAGE
Madagasikara Republic 1 Ariary = 100 Iraimbilanja

KM# 28 10 FRANCS (2 Ariary)
4.3400 g., Bronze (Red To Yellow), 21.9 mm. **Obv:** Monkey **Obv. Legend:** BANKY FOIBEN'I MADAGASIKARA **Rev:** Value within steer horns flanked by sprigs **Edge:** Plain

Date	Mintage	F	VF	XF	Unc	BU
2003	—	—	—	1.00	2.50	3.50

KM# 29 ARIARY
4.9300 g., Stainless Steel, 22 mm. **Obv:** Flower **Obv. Legend:** BANKY FOIBEN'I MADAGASIKARA **Rev:** Value within steer horns above sprigs **Edge:** Plain

Date	Mintage	F	VF	XF	Unc	BU
2004(a)	—	—	—	0.90	2.25	3.00

KM# 30 2 ARIARY
3.2300 g., Copper Plated Steel, 21 mm. **Obv:** Plant **Obv. Legend:** BANKY FOIBEN'I MADAGASIKARA **Rev:** Value within steer horns flanked by sprigs **Edge:** Reeded

Date	Mintage	F	VF	XF	Unc	BU
2003	—	—	—	0.90	2.25	3.00

KM# 25.2 50 ARIARY
10.1500 g., Stainless Steel, 30 mm. **Obv:** Star above value within sprays **Rev:** Avenue of the Baobabs **Rev. Inscription:** Motto C **Edge:** Plain **Shape:** 11-sided

Date	Mintage	F	VF	XF	Unc	BU
2005	—	—	—	2.40	6.00	—

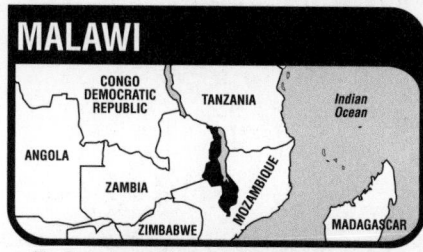

MALAWI

The Republic of Malawi (formerly Nyasaland), located in southeastern Africa to the west of Lake Malawi (Nyasa), has an area of 45,745 sq. mi. (118,480 sq. km.) and a population of 7 million. Capital: Lilongwe. The economy is predominantly agricultural. Tobacco, tea, peanuts and cotton are exported.

REPUBLIC
DECIMAL COINAGE
100 Tambala = 1 Kwacha

KM# 33a TAMBALA
Copper Plated Steel, 17.3 mm. **Obv:** Arms with supporters **Rev:** 2 Talapia fish **Edge:** Plain

Date	Mintage	F	VF	XF	Unc	BU
2003	—	—	—	—	1.00	1.50

KM# 34a 2 TAMBALA
Copper Plated Steel, 20.3 mm. **Obv:** Arms with supporters **Rev:** Paradise whydah bird divides date and value, designer's initials "P.V." **Edge:** Plain

Date	Mintage	F	VF	XF	Unc	BU
2003	—	—	—	—	1.00	1.50

KM# 32.2 5 TAMBALA
Nickel Plated Steel, 19.35 mm. **Obv:** Arms with supporters **Rev:** Purple heron, value, designer's initials "P.V."

Date	Mintage	F	VF	XF	Unc	BU
2003	—	—	—	—	2.50	3.00

KM# 162 5 TAMBALA
28.2800 g., 0.9250 Silver 0.8410 oz. ASW, 38.61 mm. **Subject:** Journey through Africe **Obv:** National arms **Rev:** Saraha lizard

Date	Mintage	F	VF	XF	Unc	BU
2006 Proof	Est. 15,000	Value: 60.00				

KM# 27 10 TAMBALA
5.6200 g., Nickel Plated Steel, 23.6 mm. **Obv:** Bust right **Rev:** Bundled corn cobs divide date and value

Date	Mintage	F	VF	XF	Unc	BU
2003	—	—	—	—	2.25	3.00

KM# 29 20 TAMBALA
7.5200 g., Nickel Clad Steel, 26.5 mm. **Obv:** Bust right **Rev:** Elephants

Date	Mintage	F	VF	XF	Unc	BU
2003	—	—	—	—	3.75	4.50

KM# 30 50 TAMBALA
4.4000 g., Brass Plated Steel, 22 mm. **Obv:** Bust right **Rev:** Arms with supporters **Shape:** 7-sided

Date	Mintage	F	VF	XF	Unc	BU
2003	—	—	—	—	4.50	5.00

KM# 66 50 TAMBALA
4.4000 g., Brass Plated Steel, 22 mm. **Obv:** State arms and supporters with country name below **Rev:** Zebras with date above and value below **Shape:** 7-sided

Date	Mintage	F	VF	XF	Unc	BU
2004	—	—	—	—	4.50	5.00

KM# 28 KWACHA
9.0000 g., Brass Plated Steel, 26 mm. **Obv:** Bust right **Rev:** Fish eagle

Date	Mintage	F	VF	XF	Unc	BU
2003	—	—	—	—	7.00	10.00

KM# 65 KWACHA
Brass Plated Steel, 26 mm. **Obv:** State arms, country name **Rev:** Fish eagle, date

Date	Mintage	F	VF	XF	Unc	BU
2004	—	—	—	—	2.50	3.50

KM# 201 KWACHA
31.1050 g., 0.9990 Silver 0.9990 oz. ASW, 47x27 mm. **Rev:** Impalla

Date	Mintage	F	VF	XF	Unc	BU
2009 Proof	100	—	—	—	—	—

Note: Individually numbered

KM# 202 KWACHA
0.6200 g., 0.9990 Gold 0.0199 oz. AGW, 11 mm. **Rev:** Impalla

Date	Mintage	F	VF	XF	Unc	BU
2009 Proof	100	Value: 50.00				

KM# 203 KWACHA
3.1100 g., 0.9990 Gold 0.0999 oz. AGW, 18 mm. **Rev:** Impalla

Date	Mintage	F	VF	XF	Unc	BU
2009 Proof	100	Value: 250				

KM# 204 KWACHA
7.7800 g., 0.9990 Gold 0.2499 oz. AGW, 25 mm. **Rev:** Impalla

Date	Mintage	F	VF	XF	Unc	BU
2009 Proof	100	Value: 550				

KM# 205 KWACHA
15.5500 g., Gold, 30 mm. **Rev:** Impalla

Date	Mintage	F	VF	XF	Unc	BU
2009 Proof	100	Value: 1,150				

KM# 59 5 KWACHA
Brass, 45x27.5 mm. **Obv:** National arms, date and value **Rev:** USS Coral Sea aircraft carrier **Edge:** Plain

Date	Mintage	F	VF	XF	Unc	BU
2005 Proof	—	Value: 22.50				

KM# 62   5 KWACHA
Brass, 45x27.5 mm. **Obv:** National arms,date and value **Rev:**
Ship USSR Molotov **Edge:** Plain

Date	Mintage	F	VF	XF	Unc	BU
2005 Proof	—	Value: 22.50				

KM# 63   5 KWACHA
Brass, 45x27.5 mm. **Obv:** National arms,date and value **Rev:**
Ship USS Missouri **Edge:** Plain

Date	Mintage	F	VF	XF	Unc	BU
2005 Proof	—	Value: 22.50				

KM# 64   5 KWACHA
Brass, 45x27.5 mm. **Obv:** National arms,date and value **Rev:**
Ship HMS Hood **Edge:** Plain

Date	Mintage	F	VF	XF	Unc	BU
2005 Proof	—	Value: 22.50				

KM# 98   5 KWACHA
29.1000 g., Copper-Nickel, 38.7 mm. **Obv:** Arms **Rev:** Pope
John Paul II holding child

Date	Mintage	F	VF	XF	Unc	BU
2005 Proof	—	Value: 25.00				

KM# 44   5 KWACHA
22.0000 g., Silver Plated Copper-Nickel, 40 mm. **Subject:** Asian
Zodiac Animals **Obv:** Queen Elizabeth II above Zambian arms
Rev: Multicolor stylized rat **Edge:** Reeded

Date	Mintage	F	VF	XF	Unc	BU
2005 Prooflike	835	—	—	—	—	17.50

KM# 45   5 KWACHA
22.0000 g., Silver Plated Copper-Nickel, 40 mm. **Subject:** Asian
Zodiac Animals **Obv:** Queen Elizabeth II above Zambian arms
Rev: Multicolor stylized ox **Edge:** Reeded

Date	Mintage	F	VF	XF	Unc	BU
2005 Prooflike	835	—	—	—	—	17.50

KM# 46   5 KWACHA
22.0000 g., Silver Plated Copper-Nickel, 40 mm. **Subject:** Asian
Zodiac Animals **Obv:** Queen Elizabeth II above Zambian arms
Rev: Multicolor stylized tiger **Edge:** Reeded

Date	Mintage	F	VF	XF	Unc	BU
2005 Prooflike	835	—	—	—	—	17.50

KM# 47   5 KWACHA
22.0000 g., Silver Plated Copper-Nickel, 40 mm. **Subject:** Asian
Zodiac Animals **Obv:** Queen Elizabeth II above Zambian arms
Rev: Multicolor stylized rabbit **Edge:** Reeded

Date	Mintage	F	VF	XF	Unc	BU
2005 Prooflike	835	—	—	—	—	17.50

KM# 48   5 KWACHA
22.0000 g., Silver Plated Copper-Nickel, 40 mm. **Subject:** Asian
Zodiac Animals **Obv:** Queen Elizabeth II above Zambian arms
Rev: Multicolor stylized dragon **Edge:** Reeded

Date	Mintage	F	VF	XF	Unc	BU
2005 Prooflike	835	—	—	—	—	17.50

KM# 49   5 KWACHA
22.0000 g., Silver Plated Copper-Nickel, 40 mm. **Subject:** Asian
Zodiac Animals **Obv:** Queen Elizabeth II above Zambian arms
Rev: Multicolor stylized snake **Edge:** Reeded

Date	Mintage	F	VF	XF	Unc	BU
2005 Prooflike	835	—	—	—	—	17.50

KM# 50   5 KWACHA
22.0000 g., Silver Plated Copper-Nickel, 40 mm. **Subject:** Asian
Zodiac Animals **Obv:** Queen Elizabeth II above Zambian arms
Rev: Multicolor stylized horse **Edge:** Reeded

Date	Mintage	F	VF	XF	Unc	BU
2005 Prooflike	835	—	—	—	—	17.50

KM# 51   5 KWACHA
22.0000 g., Silver Plated Copper-Nickel, 40 mm. **Subject:** Asian
Zodiac Animals **Obv:** Queen Elizabeth II above Zambian arms
Rev: Multicolor stylized goat **Edge:** Reeded

Date	Mintage	F	VF	XF	Unc	BU
2005 Prooflike	835	—	—	—	—	17.50

KM# 52   5 KWACHA
22.0000 g., Silver Plated Copper-Nickel, 40 mm. **Subject:** Asian
Zodiac Animals **Obv:** Queen Elizabeth II above Zambian arms
Rev: Multicolor stylized monkey **Edge:** Reeded

Date	Mintage	F	VF	XF	Unc	BU
2005 Proolike	835	—	—	—	—	17.50

KM# 53   5 KWACHA
22.0000 g., Silver Plated Copper-Nickel, 40 mm. **Subject:** Asian
Zodiac Animals **Obv:** Queen Elizabeth II above Zambian arms
Rev: Multicolor stylized rooster **Edge:** Reeded

Date	Mintage	F	VF	XF	Unc	BU
2005 Prooflike	835	—	—	—	—	17.50

KM# 54   5 KWACHA
22.0000 g., Silver Plated Copper-Nickel, 40 mm. **Subject:** Asian
Zodiac Animals **Obv:** Queen Elizabeth II above Zambian arms
Rev: Multicolor stylized dog **Edge:** Reeded

Date	Mintage	F	VF	XF	Unc	BU
2005 Prooflike	835	—	—	—	—	17.50

KM# 55   5 KWACHA
22.0000 g., Silver Plated Copper-Nickel, 40 mm. **Subject:** Asian
Zodiac Animals **Obv:** Queen Elizabeth II above Zambian arms
Rev: Multicolor stylized pig **Edge:** Reeded

Date	Mintage	F	VF	XF	Unc	BU
2005 Prooflike	835	—	—	—	—	17.50

KM# 57   5 KWACHA
10.2500 g., Bi-Metallic Copper-Nickel ring and Nickel-Brass
center, 27 mm. **Obv:** State arms and supporters with country
name below **Obv. Legend:** MALAWI **Rev:** Fisherman at work
with date above and value below **Edge:** Reeded

Date	Mintage	F	VF	XF	Unc	BU
2006	—	—	—	—	3.50	5.00

KM# 159   5 KWACHA
28.2800 g., 0.9250 Silver 0.8410 oz. ASW, 38.61 mm. **Subject:**
Journey through Africa **Obv:** National arms **Rev:** Lion

Date	Mintage	F	VF	XF	Unc	BU
2006 Proof	Est. 15,000	Value: 60.00				

KM# 160   5 KWACHA
28.2800 g., 0.9250 Silver 0.8410 oz. ASW, 38.61 mm. **Subject:**
Journey through Africa **Obv:** National arms **Rev:** African elephant

Date	Mintage	F	VF	XF	Unc	BU
2006 Proof	Est. 15,000	Value: 60.00				

KM# 161   5 KWACHA
28.2800 g., 0.9250 Silver 0.8410 oz. ASW, 38.61 mm. **Subject:**
Journey through Africa **Obv:** National Arms **Rev:** Lake Malawi

Date	Mintage	F	VF	XF	Unc	BU
2006 Proof	Est. 15,000	Value: 60.00				

KM# 163   5 KWACHA
28.2800 g., 0.9250 Silver 0.8410 oz. ASW, 38.61 mm. **Subject:**
Journey through Arfica **Obv:** National arms **Rev:** Mt. Kilimanjaro

Date	Mintage	F	VF	XF	Unc	BU
2006 Proof	Est. 15,000	Value: 60.00				

KM# 164   5 KWACHA
28.2800 g., 0.9250 Silver 0.8410 oz. ASW, 38.61 mm. **Subject:**
Journey through Africa **Obv:** National arms **Rev:** Tribal life

Date	Mintage	F	VF	XF	Unc	BU
2006 Proof	Est. 15,000	Value: 60.00				

KM# 165   5 KWACHA
28.2800 g., 0.9250 Silver 0.8410 oz. ASW, 38.61 mm. **Rev:**
Safari in color

Date	Mintage	F	VF	XF	Unc	BU
2006 Proof	Est. 15,000	Value: 60.00				

KM# 166   5 KWACHA
31.1050 g., 0.9250 Silver 0.9250 oz. ASW, 38.61 mm. **Rev:**
Victoria Falls in color

Date	Mintage	F	VF	XF	Unc	BU
2006 Proof	Est. 15,000	Value: 60.00				

KM# 167   5 KWACHA
28.2800 g., 0.9250 Silver 0.8410 oz. ASW, 38.61 mm. **Rev:**
Table top mountain in Cape town

Date	Mintage	F	VF	XF	Unc	BU
2006 Proof	Est. 15,000	Value: 60.00				

KM# 168   5 KWACHA
28.2800 g., 0.9250 Silver 0.8410 oz. ASW, 38.61 mm. **Rev:** Nile
in color

Date	Mintage	F	VF	XF	Unc	BU
2006 Proof	Est. 15,000	Value: 60.00				

KM# 169   5 KWACHA
28.2800 g., 0.9250 Silver 0.8410 oz. ASW, 38.61 mm. **Rev:**
Pyramids in color

Date	Mintage	F	VF	XF	Unc	BU
2006 Proof	Est. 15,000	Value: 60.00				

KM# 170   5 KWACHA
28.2800 g., 0.9250 Silver 0.8410 oz. ASW, 38.61 mm. **Rev:**
Great Sphinx in color

Date	Mintage	F	VF	XF	Unc	BU
2006 Proof	Est. 15,000	Value: 60.00				

KM# 196   5 KWACHA
27.0000 g., Copper-Nickel, 40 mm. **Subject:** 2000th
Anniversary of the ambush in the forest against the legions of
Varus **Rev:** Centopah of Marcus Caelius and the 18th Legion

Date	Mintage	F	VF	XF	Unc	BU
2009	Est. 5,000	—	—	—	—	20.00

KM# 197   5 KWACHA
20.0000 g., Silver Plated Copper, 40 mm. **Rev:** Battleship
Bismarck in color

Date	Mintage	F	VF	XF	Unc	BU
2009	Est. 5,000	—	—	—	—	30.00

KM# 198   5 KWACHA
20.0000 g., Silver Plated Copper, 40 mm. **Rev:** Ship Tirpitz in
color

Date	Mintage	F	VF	XF	Unc	BU
2009	Est. 5,000	—	—	—	—	30.00

KM# 199   5 KWACHA
20.0000 g., Silver Plated Copper, 40 mm. **Rev:** Ship Gneisenau
in color

Date	Mintage	F	VF	XF	Unc	BU
2009	Est. 5,000	—	—	—	—	30.00

KM# 200   5 KWACHA
20.0000 g., Silver Plated Copper, 40 mm. **Rev:** Ship
Scharnhorst in color

Date	Mintage	F	VF	XF	Unc	BU
2009	Est. 5,000	—	—	—	—	30.00

KM# 195 5 KWACHA
27.0000 g., Copper-Nickel, 40 mm. **Subject:** 2000th Anniversary of the ambush in the forest against the legions of Varus **Rev:** Arminius

Date	Mintage	F	VF	XF	Unc	BU
2009	Est. 5,000	—	—	—	—	20.00

KM# 39 10 KWACHA
29.1000 g., Copper-Nickel, 38.7 mm. **Subject:** Soccer World Championship **Obv:** Arms with supporters **Rev:** Soccer players **Edge:** Reeded

Date	Mintage	F	VF	XF	Unc	BU
2002 Proof	— Value: 50.00					

KM# 117 10 KWACHA
Silver **Rev:** U.S.S. Nimitz

Date	Mintage	F	VF	XF	Unc	BU
2002 Proof	— Value: 40.00					

KM# 80 10 KWACHA
24.0000 g., 0.9990 Silver 0.7708 oz. ASW, 38.5 mm. **Obv:** Arms **Rev:** Pope John Paul II in mitre and vestments

Date	Mintage	F	VF	XF	Unc	BU
2003 Proof	— Value: 30.00					

KM# 42 10 KWACHA
19.7400 g., 0.9990 Silver 0.6340 oz. ASW, 29.9 mm. **Subject:** XXVII Olympic Games - Athens 2004 **Obv:** Arms with supporters divides date **Obv. Legend:** REPUBLIC OF MALAWI **Rev:** Two rowers within circle flanked by sprigs **Edge:** Reeded

Date	Mintage	F	VF	XF	Unc	BU
2003 Proof	— Value: 40.00					

KM# 102 10 KWACHA
19.3000 g., Silver, 38 mm. **Subject:** Antelopes of Africa **Obv:** National arms **Rev:** Eland

Date	Mintage	F	VF	XF	Unc	BU
2003 Proof	— Value: 25.00					

KM# 103 10 KWACHA
19.3000 g., Silver, 38 mm. **Subject:** Antelopes of Africa **Obv:** National Arms **Rev:** Nyala

Date	Mintage	F	VF	XF	Unc	BU
2003 Proof	— Value: 25.00					

KM# 104 10 KWACHA
19.3000 g., Silver, 38 mm. **Subject:** Antelopes of Africa **Obv:** National Arms **Rev:** Springbok

Date	Mintage	F	VF	XF	Unc	BU
2003 Proof	— Value: 25.00					

KM# 105 10 KWACHA
19.3000 g., Silver, 38 mm. **Subject:** Antelopes of Africa **Obv:** National Arms **Rev:** Kudu

Date	Mintage	F	VF	XF	Unc	BU
2003 Proof	— Value: 25.00					

KM# 106 10 KWACHA
19.3000 g., Silver, 38 mm. **Subject:** Antelopes of Africa **Obv:** National Arms **Rev:** Sable pair

Date	Mintage	F	VF	XF	Unc	BU
2003 Proof	— Value: 25.00					

KM# 107 10 KWACHA
Bronze gilt **Obv:** National Arms **Rev:** John Paul II in mitre and vestments

Date	Mintage	F	VF	XF	Unc	BU
2003 Proof	— Value: 7.50					

KM# 118 10 KWACHA
Silver **Subject:** Elizabeth, the Queen Mother, First anniversary of death

Date	Mintage	F	VF	XF	Unc	BU
2003 Proof	— Value: 30.00					

KM# 119 10 KWACHA
0.9250 Silver, 38.6 mm. **Rev:** Trans-Siberian Railway

Date	Mintage	F	VF	XF	Unc	BU
2003 Proof	— Value: 45.00					

KM# 120 10 KWACHA
Silver **Subject:** Los Angeles Olympics, 1984 **Rev:** Ribbon dancer

Date	Mintage	F	VF	XF	Unc	BU
2003 Proof	— Value: 45.00					

KM# 61 10 KWACHA
29.1500 g., Copper-Nickel silver plated, 38.7 mm. **Subject:** Endangered Wildlife **Obv:** National arms **Rev:** Multicolor Leopard with cub **Edge:** Reeded

Date	Mintage	F	VF	XF	Unc	BU
2004 Proof	— Value: 17.00					

KM# 86 10 KWACHA
29.1500 g., Copper-Nickel silver plated, 38.7 mm. **Subject:** Endangered Wildlife **Obv:** National arms **Rev:** Multicolor Lion and cub **Edge:** Reeded

Date	Mintage	F	VF	XF	Unc	BU
2004 Proof	— Value: 17.00					

KM# 60 10 KWACHA
29.1500 g., Copper-Nickel silver plated, 38.7 mm. **Subject:** Endangered Wildlife **Obv:** National arms **Rev:** Multicolor Zebra and colt **Edge:** Reeded

Date	Mintage	F	VF	XF	Unc	BU
2004 Proof	— Value: 17.00					

KM# 84 10 KWACHA
29.1400 g., Copper-Nickel, 38.7 mm. **Obv:** National arms **Rev:** Multicolor elephant and calf **Edge:** Reeded

Date	Mintage	F	VF	XF	Unc	BU
2004 Proof	— Value: 17.00					

KM# 89 10 KWACHA
29.1500 g., Copper-Nickel silver plated, 38.7 mm. **Obv:** National arms **Rev:** Multicolor Deer and fawn **Edge:** Reeded

Date	Mintage	F	VF	XF	Unc	BU
2004 Proof	— Value: 17.00					

KM# 90 10 KWACHA
29.1500 g., Copper-Nickel silver plated, 38.7 mm. **Obv:** National arms **Rev:** Multicolor Giraffe and her calf **Edge:** Reeded

Date	Mintage	F	VF	XF	Unc	BU
2004 Proof	— Value: 17.00					

KM# 81 10 KWACHA
Copper-Nickel silver plated **Obv:** Arms **Rev:** Chevrotain advancing left

Date	Mintage	F	VF	XF	Unc	BU
2005 Proof	— Value: 17.00					

KM# 82 10 KWACHA
Copper-Nickel silver plated **Obv:** Arms **Rev:** Lemur on branch

Date	Mintage	F	VF	XF	Unc	BU
2005 Proof	— Value: 17.00					

KM# 83 10 KWACHA
Copper-Nickel silver plated **Obv:** Arms **Rev:** Pigmy Hippo

Date	Mintage	F	VF	XF	Unc	BU
2005 Proof	— Value: 17.00					

KM# 88 10 KWACHA
Copper-Nickel **Obv:** Arms **Rev:** Oryx in photo insert

Date	Mintage	F	VF	XF	Unc	BU
2005	—	—	—	—	—	20.00

KM# 71 10 KWACHA
23.5000 g., Silver Plated Copper-Nickel, 39 mm. **Subject:** Endangered wildlife **Obv:** National arms **Rev:** Tree pangolin (Manis Tricuspis)

Date	Mintage	F	VF	XF	Unc	BU
2005 Proof	— Value: 17.00					

KM# 87 10 KWACHA
Copper-Nickel **Obv:** Arms **Rev:** Monkeys in photo insert

Date	Mintage	F	VF	XF	Unc	BU
2005 Proof	— Value: 17.50					

KM# 130 10 KWACHA
24.5000 g., Silver Plated Brass, 38.6 mm. **Obv:** State shield **Rev:** Crocodile

Date	Mintage	F	VF	XF	Unc	BU
2005 Proof	Est. 1,000 Value: 15.00					

KM# 131 10 KWACHA
24.5000 g., Silver Plated Brass, 38.6 mm. **Rev:** Pygmy Chimpanzie

Date	Mintage	F	VF	XF	Unc	BU
2005 Proof	— Value: 15.00					

KM# 132 10 KWACHA
Silver Plated Brass, 38.6 mm. **Rev:** Corner

Date	Mintage	F	VF	XF	Unc	BU
2005 Proof	1,000 Value: 15.00					

KM# 58 10 KWACHA
15.1000 g., Bi-Metallic Copper-Nickel center with Nickel-Brass ring, 28 mm. **Obv:** State arms and supporters with country name below **Obv. Legend:** MALAWI **Rev:** Farm worker harvesting **Edge:** Coarse reeding

Date	Mintage	F	VF	XF	Unc	BU
2006	—	—	—	—	4.50	6.00

KM# 157 10 KWACHA
Silver Plated **Subject:** World Cup Soccer 2006 **Obv:** National arms **Rev:** Soccer player in the stadium

Date	Mintage	F	VF	XF	Unc	BU
2006 Proof	— Value: 15.00					

KM# 158 10 KWACHA
28.2800 g., 0.9250 Silver 0.8410 oz. ASW, 38.6 mm. **Subject:** Elizabeth II, 80th Birthday **Obv:** National arms **Rev:** Elizabeth II

Date	Mintage	F	VF	XF	Unc	BU
2006 Proof	— Value: 37.50					

KM# 99 10 KWACHA
0.9990 Silver, 20x40 mm. **Obv:** Arms **Rev:** deRutter painting of ships

Date	Mintage	F	VF	XF	Unc	BU
2007 Proof	— Value: 45.00					

KM# 100   10 KWACHA
Silver, 38.6 mm. **Obv:** Arms **Rev:** Puccini colorized

Date	Mintage	F	VF	XF	Unc	BU
2007 Proof	—	Value: 40.00				

KM# 185   10 KWACHA
Silver Plated Copper-Nickel, 45x30 mm. **Obv:** State arms **Rev:** Treaty of Rome anniversary in color

Date	Mintage	F	VF	XF	Unc	BU
2007 Proof	—	Value: 15.00				

KM# 186   10 KWACHA
Silver Plated Copper-Nickel, 45x30 mm. **Rev:** Mother Theresa in color

Date	Mintage	F	VF	XF	Unc	BU
2007 Proof	—	Value: 15.00				

KM# 187   10 KWACHA
Silver Plated Copper-Nickel, 45x30 mm. **Rev:** Verdespaleis Centennial

Date	Mintage	F	VF	XF	Unc	BU
2007 Proof	—	Value: 15.00				

KM# 188   10 KWACHA
Silver Plated Copper-Nickel, 45x30 mm. **Rev:** Ship painting of Michiel de Ruyter

Date	Mintage	F	VF	XF	Unc	BU
2007 Proof	—	Value: 15.00				

KM# 189   10 KWACHA
Silver Plated Copper-Nickel, 45x30 mm. **Rev:** Tulips in color

Date	Mintage	F	VF	XF	Unc	BU
2007 Proof	—	Value: 15.00				

KM# 190   10 KWACHA
Silver Plated Copper-Nickel **Rev:** 60th Anniversary, treaty of Rome, color

Date	Mintage	F	VF	XF	Unc	BU
2007 Proof	—	Value: 15.00				

KM# 191   10 KWACHA
Silver Plated Copper-Nickel **Rev:** Love and Psyche, in color

Date	Mintage	F	VF	XF	Unc	BU
2007 Proof	—	Value: 15.00				

KM# 192   10 KWACHA
Silver Plated Copper-Nickel **Rev:** Giuseppe Garibaldi in color

Date	Mintage	F	VF	XF	Unc	BU
2007 Proof	—	Value: 15.00				

KM# 110   10 KWACHA
62.2000 g., 0.9990 Silver 1.9977 oz. ASW, 42x42 mm. **Rev:** Lion with two crystal eyes

Date	Mintage	F	VF	XF	Unc	BU
2009 Proof	2,500	Value: 135				

KM# 91   10 KWACHA
23.5000 g., Silver Plated Copper-Nickel, 39 mm. **Subject:** Endangered Frogs - Blue Poison Arrowfrog **Rev:** Multicolor blue frog right

Date	Mintage	F	VF	XF	Unc	BU
2010 Proof	—	Value: 24.00				

KM# 92   10 KWACHA
23.5000 g., Silver Plated Copper-Nickel, 39 mm. **Subject:** Endangered Frogs - Dyeing Poison Arrow frog **Rev:** Multicolor blue frog left

Date	Mintage	F	VF	XF	Unc	BU
2010 Proof	—	Value: 24.00				

KM# 93   10 KWACHA
23.5000 g., Silver Plated Copper-Nickel, 39 mm. **Subject:** Endangered Frogs - Darwin Frog **Rev:** Multicolor green frog right

Date	Mintage	F	VF	XF	Unc	BU
2010 Proof	—	Value: 24.00				

KM# 94   10 KWACHA
23.5000 g., Silver Plated Copper-Nickel, 39 mm. **Subject:** Endangered Frogs - Panamanian Spotted frog **Rev:** Multicolor orange and black frog

Date	Mintage	F	VF	XF	Unc	BU
2010 Proof	—	Value: 24.00				

KM# 95   10 KWACHA
23.5000 g., Silver Plated Copper-Nickel, 39 mm. **Subject:** Endangered Frogs - Purple frog **Rev:** Multicolor purple frog left

Date	Mintage	F	VF	XF	Unc	BU
2010 Proof	—	Value: 24.00				

KM# 96   10 KWACHA
23.5000 g., Silver Plated Copper-Nickel, 39 mm. **Subject:** Endangered Frogs - Carnileri Harlequin **Rev:** Multicolor red frog left

Date	Mintage	F	VF	XF	Unc	BU
2010 Proof	—	Value: 24.00				

KM# 97   10 KWACHA
23.5000 g., Silver Plated Copper-Nickel, 39 mm. **Subject:** Endangered Frogs - Tree frog **Rev:** Multicolor tree frog

Date	Mintage	F	VF	XF	Unc	BU
2010 Proof	—	Value: 24.00				

KM# 184   15 KWACHA
20.0000 g., 0.9990 Silver 0.6423 oz. ASW, 38 mm. **Rev:** Brandenburg gate in color, map of Germany

Date	Mintage	F	VF	XF	Unc	BU
2006 Proof	Est. 1,000	Value: 90.00				

KM# 56   20 KWACHA
31.1000 g., 0.9990 Silver 0.9988 oz. ASW, 38.6 mm. **Series:** The Big Five **Obv:** National arms **Rev:** Two water buffalo on green malachite center insert **Edge:** Plain

Date	Mintage	F	VF	XF	Unc	BU
2004 Proof	3,000	Value: 55.00				

KM# 67   20 KWACHA
31.1000 g., 0.9990 Silver 0.9988 oz. ASW, 38.6 mm. **Series:** The Big Five **Obv:** National arms **Rev:** Elephant family on Haematite (blood stone) center insert **Edge:** Plain

Date	Mintage	F	VF	XF	Unc	BU
2004 Proof	3,000	Value: 55.00				

KM# 68   20 KWACHA
31.1000 g., 0.9990 Silver 0.9988 oz. ASW, 38.6 mm. **Series:** The Big Five **Obv:** National arms **Rev:** Leopard family on hawk or falcon-eye center insert **Edge:** Plain

Date	Mintage	F	VF	XF	Unc	BU
2004 Proof	3,000	Value: 55.00				

KM# 69   20 KWACHA
31.1000 g., 0.9990 Silver 0.9988 oz. ASW, 38.6 mm. **Series:** The Big Five **Obv:** National arms **Rev:** Lion family on tiger-eye center insert **Edge:** Plain

Date	Mintage	F	VF	XF	Unc	BU
2004 Proof	3,000	Value: 55.00				

KM# 70   20 KWACHA
31.1000 g., 0.9990 Silver 0.9988 oz. ASW, 38.6 mm. **Series:** The Big Five **Obv:** National arms **Rev:** Rhinoceros family on heliotrope center insert **Edge:** Plain

Date	Mintage	F	VF	XF	Unc	BU
2004 Proof	3,000	Value: 55.00				

KM# 133   20 KWACHA
Acrylic, 65 mm. **Subject:** Year of the Dog

Date	Mintage	F	VF	XF	Unc	BU
2006	Est. 2,000	—	—	—	—	75.00

KM# 134   20 KWACHA
31.1050 g., 0.9990 Silver 0.9990 oz. ASW, 31x25 mm. **Subject:** Year of the Rat **Obv:** Temple of Heaven

Date	Mintage	F	VF	XF	Unc	BU
2006 Proof	Est. 2,000	Value: 75.00				

KM# 135   20 KWACHA
31.1050 g., 0.9990 Silver 0.9990 oz. ASW, 31x25 mm. **Subject:** Year of the Ox **Obv:** Temple of Heaven

Date	Mintage	F	VF	XF	Unc	BU
2006 Proof	Est. 2,000	Value: 75.00				

KM# 136   20 KWACHA
31.1050 g., 0.9990 Silver 0.9990 oz. ASW, 31x25 mm. **Subject:** Year of the Tiger **Obv:** Temple of Heaven

Date	Mintage	F	VF	XF	Unc	BU
2006 Proof	Est. 2,000	Value: 75.00				

KM# 137   20 KWACHA
31.1050 g., 0.9990 Silver 0.9990 oz. ASW, 31x25 mm. **Subject:** Year of the Hare **Obv:** Temple of Heaven

Date	Mintage	F	VF	XF	Unc	BU
2006 Proof	Est. 2,000	Value: 75.00				

KM# 138   20 KWACHA
31.1050 g., 0.9990 Silver 0.9990 oz. ASW, 31x25 mm. **Subject:** Year of the dragon **Obv:** Temple of Heaven

Date	Mintage	F	VF	XF	Unc	BU
2006 Proof	Est. 2,000	Value: 75.00				

KM# 139   20 KWACHA
31.1050 g., 0.9990 Silver 0.9990 oz. ASW, 31x25 mm. **Subject:** Year of the Snake **Obv:** Temple of Heaven

Date	Mintage	F	VF	XF	Unc	BU
2006 Proof	Est. 2,000	Value: 75.00				

KM# 140   20 KWACHA
31.1050 g., 0.9990 Silver 0.9990 oz. ASW, 31x25 mm. **Subject:** Year of the Horse **Obv:** Temple of Heaven

Date	Mintage	F	VF	XF	Unc	BU
2006 Proof	Est. 2,000	Value: 75.00				

KM# 141   20 KWACHA
31.1050 g., 0.9990 Silver 0.9990 oz. ASW, 31x25 mm. **Subject:** Year of the goat **Obv:** Temple of Heaven

Date	Mintage	F	VF	XF	Unc	BU
2006 Proof	Est. 2,000	Value: 75.00				

KM# 142   20 KWACHA
31.1050 g., 0.9990 Silver 0.9990 oz. ASW, 31x25 mm. **Subject:** Year of the monkey **Obv:** Temple of Heaven

Date	Mintage	F	VF	XF	Unc	BU
2006 Proof	Est. 2,000	Value: 75.00				

KM# 143   20 KWACHA
31.1050 g., 0.9990 Silver 0.9990 oz. ASW, 31x25 mm. **Subject:** Year of the Rooster **Obv:** Temple of Heaven

Date	Mintage	F	VF	XF	Unc	BU
2006 Proof	Est. 2,000	Value: 75.00				

KM# 144   20 KWACHA
31.1050 g., 0.9990 Silver 0.9990 oz. ASW, 31x25 mm. **Subject:** Year of the Dog **Obv:** Temple of Heaven

Date	Mintage	F	VF	XF	Unc	BU
2006 Proof	Est. 2,000	Value: 75.00				

KM# 145   20 KWACHA
31.1050 g., 0.9990 Silver 0.9990 oz. ASW, 31x25 mm. **Subject:** Year of the pig **Obv:** Temple of Heaven

Date	Mintage	F	VF	XF	Unc	BU
2006 Proof	Est. 2,000	Value: 75.00				

KM# 147   20 KWACHA
31.1050 g., 0.9990 Silver 0.9990 oz. ASW **Rev:** Sitting panda, city view of Moscow and flag in color

Date	Mintage	F	VF	XF	Unc	BU
2006 Proof	Est. 5,000	Value: 60.00				

KM# 148   20 KWACHA
31.1050 g., 0.9990 Silver 0.9990 oz. ASW **Rev:** Sitting panda, city view of Osaka and flag in color

Date	Mintage	F	VF	XF	Unc	BU
2006 Proof	Est. 5,000	Value: 60.00				

KM# 149   20 KWACHA
31.1050 g., 0.9990 Silver 0.9990 oz. ASW **Rev:** Sitting panda, city view of Paris and flag in color

Date	Mintage	F	VF	XF	Unc	BU
2006 Proof	Est. 5,000	Value: 60.00				

KM# 150   20 KWACHA
31.1050 g., 0.9990 Silver 0.9990 oz. ASW **Rev:** Sitting panda, city view of Mexico City and flag in color

Date	Mintage	F	VF	XF	Unc	BU
2006 Proof	Est. 5,000	Value: 60.00				

KM# 151   20 KWACHA
31.1050 g., 0.9990 Silver 0.9990 oz. ASW **Rev:** Sitting panda, city view of Madrid and flag in color

Date	Mintage	F	VF	XF	Unc	BU
2006 Proof	Est. 5,000	Value: 60.00				

KM# 152   20 KWACHA
31.1050 g., 0.9990 Silver 0.9990 oz. ASW **Rev:** Panda on rock, city view of Pyeongyang and flag in color

Date	Mintage	F	VF	XF	Unc	BU
2006 Proof	5,000	Value: 60.00				

KM# 153   20 KWACHA
31.1050 g., 0.9990 Silver 0.9990 oz. ASW

Date	Mintage	F	VF	XF	Unc	BU
2006 Proof	Est. 5,000	Value: 60.00				

KM# 154   20 KWACHA
31.1050 g., 0.9990 Silver 0.9990 oz. ASW **Rev:** Panda on rock, city view of Berlin and flag in color

Date	Mintage	F	VF	XF	Unc	BU
2006 Proof	Est. 3,000	Value: 60.00				

KM# 155   20 KWACHA
31.1050 g., 0.9990 Silver 0.9990 oz. ASW **Rev:** Panda on rock, city view of London and flag in color

Date	Mintage	F	VF	XF	Unc	BU
2006 Proof	5,000	Value: 60.00				

KM# 156   20 KWACHA
31.1050 g., 0.9990 Silver 0.9990 oz. ASW **Rev:** Panda on rock, city view of Hong Kong and flag in color

Date	Mintage	F	VF	XF	Unc	BU
2006 Proof	Est. 5,000	Value: 60.00				

KM# 74 20 KWACHA
0.5000 g., 0.9990 Gold 0.0161 oz. AGW **Subject:** Springbnok, 40 years, first design

Date	Mintage	F	VF	XF	Unc	BU
2007 Proof	—	Value: 70.00				

KM# 75 20 KWACHA
0.5000 g., 0.9990 Gold 0.0161 oz. AGW **Subject:** Springbok, 40th Anniversary, second desgin

Date	Mintage	F	VF	XF	Unc	BU
2007 Proof	—	Value: 70.00				

KM# 76 20 KWACHA
0.5000 g., 0.9990 Gold 0.0161 oz. AGW **Subject:** Springbok, 40th Anniversary, third design

Date	Mintage	F	VF	XF	Unc	BU
2007 Proof	—	Value: 70.00				

KM# 111 20 KWACHA
28.2800 g., 0.9250 Silver 0.8410 oz. ASW, 38.61 mm. **Subject:** Biosphere Reserves **Obv:** National Arms **Rev:** Goat on hillside, multicolor flower

Date	Mintage	F	VF	XF	Unc	BU
2010 Proof	8,000	Value: 60.00				

KM# 77 40 KWACHA
1.0000 g., 0.9990 Gold 0.0321 oz. AGW **Rev:** Springbok

Date	Mintage	F	VF	XF	Unc	BU
2008 Proof	—	Value: 100				

KM# 78 40 KWACHA
1.0000 g., 0.9990 Palladium 0.0321 oz. **Rev:** Springbok

Date	Mintage	F	VF	XF	Unc	BU
2008 Proof	—	Value: 75.00				

KM# 79 40 KWACHA
1.0000 g., 0.9990 Platinum 0.0321 oz. APW **Rev:** Springbok

Date	Mintage	F	VF	XF	Unc	BU
2008 Proof	—	Value: 125				

KM# 43 50 KWACHA
141.2100 g., Bronze with Gold Plated center and Silver Plated ring, 65 mm. **Subject:** Republic of China **Obv:** Large building above value within circle **Rev:** Conjoined busts facing within circle **Edge:** Reeded **Note:** Illustration reduced.

Date	Mintage	F	VF	XF	Unc	BU
2004 Proof	1,000	Value: 85.00				

KM# 108 50 KWACHA
Silver **Obv:** National Arms **Rev:** Soccer ball in flight from Germany to South Africa

Date	Mintage	F	VF	XF	Unc	BU
2006 Proof	—	Value: 45.00				

KM# 109 50 KWACHA
Silver **Obv:** National Arms **Rev:** Two female hurdlers

Date	Mintage	F	VF	XF	Unc	BU
2008 Proof	—	Value: 45.00				

KM# 193 50 KWACHA
27.0000 g., Silver Plated Brass with sterling silver inlay, 38.6 mm. **Rev:** Springbock

Date	Mintage	F	VF	XF	Unc	BU
2008	Est. 4,444	—	—	—	—	70.00

KM# 194 50 KWACHA
1.0000 g., 0.9990 Silver 0.0321 oz. ASW, 8.5x15 mm. **Rev:** Springbock

Date	Mintage	F	VF	XF	Unc	BU
2008 Proof	Est. 5,000	Value: 14.00				

KM# 85 50 KWACHA
62.2100 g., 0.9990 Silver 1.9980 oz. ASW, 42x42 mm. **Obv:** Arms **Rev:** White lion with crystal inserts in eyes **Shape:** Square

Date	Mintage	F	VF	XF	Unc	BU
2009 Proof	2,500	Value: 175				

KM# 146 75 KWACHA
4.0000 g., 0.9990 Gold 0.1285 oz. AGW, 20 mm. **Obv:** Temple of Mazu **Rev:** Mazu, goddess of protection

Date	Mintage	F	VF	XF	Unc	BU
2006 Proof	Est. 3,000	Value: 275				

KM# 171 100 KWACHA
Gold **Subject:** 2008 Bejing Olympics **Rev:** Two hurdlers

Date	Mintage	F	VF	XF	Unc	BU
2006 Proof	—	—	—	—	—	—

PATTERNS
Including off metal strikes

KM#	Date	Mintage	Identification	Mkt Val
Pn2	2002	—	10 Kwacha. Copper-Nickel. 29.0200 g. 38.7 mm. National arms. Alexander the Great. Reeded edge.	—
Pn3	2002	—	10 Kwacha. Copper-Nickel. 29.0200 g. 38.7 mm. National arms. Olympic torch under two world globes. Reeded edge.	—
Pn4	2002	—	10 Kwacha. Copper-Nickel. 29.0200 g. 38.7 mm. National arms. "MILLENNIUM" above Mona Lisa like portrait. Reeded edge.	—
Pn5	2003	—	10 Kwacha. Silver Plated. 29.4500 g. 38.7 mm. National arms. Trans-Siberian Express train. Reeded edge.	—
Pn6	2003	—	10 Kwacha. Silver Plated. 29.4500 g. 38.7 mm. National arms. Blesbok antelope. Reeded edge.	—
Pn7	2003	—	10 Kwacha. Copper-Nickel. 29.0200 g. 38.7 mm. National arms. Eland antelope. Reeded edge.	—
Pn8	2003	—	10 Kwacha. Copper-Nickel. 29.0200 g. 38.7 mm. National arms. Kudu antelope. Reeded edge.	—
Pn9	2003	—	10 Kwacha. Silver Plated. 29.4500 g. 38 mm. Nyala antelope.	—
Pn15	ND (2004)	—	10 Kwacha. Silver Plated. 29.2200 g. 38.7 mm. National arms. Multicolor pair of birds with chick. Reeded edge.	15.00

The independent limited constitutional monarchy of Malaysia, which occupies the southern part of the Malay Peninsula in Southeast Asia and the northern part of the island of Borneo, has an area of 127,316 sq. mi. (329,750 sq. km.) and a population of 15.4 million. Capital: Kuala Lumpur. The economy is based on agriculture, mining and forestry. Rubber, tin, timber and palm oil are exported.

Malaysia came into being on Sept. 16, 1963, as a federation of Malaya (Johore, Kelantan, Kedah, Perlis, Trengganu, Negri-Sembilan, Pahang, Perak, Selangor, Penang, Malacca), Singapore, Sabah (British North Borneo) and Sarawak. Following two serious racial riots involving Malays and Chinese, Singapore withdrew from the federation on Aug. 9, 1965. Malaysia is a member of the Commonwealth of Nations.

MINT MARK
FM - Franklin Mint, U.S.A.

CONSTITUTIONAL MONARCHY

STANDARD COINAGE
100 Sen = 1 Ringgit (Dollar)

KM# 49 SEN
1.8000 g., Bronze Clad Steel, 17.66 mm. **Obv:** Value divides date below flower blossom **Obv. Legend:** BANK NEGARA MALAYSIA **Rev:** Drum **Edge:** Plain

Date	Mintage	F	VF	XF	Unc	BU
2001	213,645,000	—	—	—	0.15	0.25
2002	185,220,000	—	—	—	0.15	0.25
2003	235,350,000	—	—	—	0.15	0.25
2004	227,700,000	—	—	—	0.15	0.25
2005	437,400,000	—	—	—	0.15	0.25
2006	328,050,000	—	—	—	0.15	0.25
2007		—	—	—	0.15	0.25

KM# 50 5 SEN
1.4000 g., Copper-Nickel, 16.25 mm. **Obv:** Value divides date below flower blossom **Obv. Legend:** BANK NEGARA MALAYSIA **Rev:** Top with string **Edge:** Reeded

Date	Mintage	F	VF	XF	Unc	BU
2001	94,617,472	—	—	—	0.15	0.25
2002	85,316,000	—	—	—	0.15	0.25
2003	75,690,000	—	—	—	0.15	0.25
2004	11,520,000	—	—	—	0.15	0.25
2005	119,520,000	—	—	—	0.15	0.25
2006	87,120,000	—	—	—	0.15	0.25
2007	97,200,338	—	—	—	0.15	0.25
2008	91,440,000	—	—	—	0.15	0.25
2009	125,172,842	—	—	—	0.15	0.25
2010		—	—	—	0.15	0.25
2011		—	—	—	0.15	0.25

KM# 201 5 SEN
1.7200 g., Stainless Steel, 17.78 mm. **Obv:** Flower, date and value **Obv. Legend:** BANK NEGARA MALAYSIA **Rev:** Geometric pattern

Date	Mintage	F	VF	XF	Unc	BU
2011		—	—	—	0.15	0.25
2012		—	—	—	0.15	0.25

KM# 51 10 SEN
2.8200 g., Copper-Nickel, 19.4 mm. **Obv:** Value divides date below flower blossom **Obv. Legend:** BANK NEGARA MALAYSIA **Rev:** Ceremonial table **Edge:** Reeded

Date	Mintage	F	VF	XF	Unc	BU
2001	313,422,000	—	—	—	0.25	0.40
2002	290,451,948	—	—	—	0.25	0.40
2003	8,640,000	—	—	—	0.25	0.40
2004	170,640,000	—	—	—	0.25	0.40
2005	316,800,000	—	—	—	0.25	0.40
2006	304,560,000	—	—	—	0.25	0.40
2007	237,967,970	—	—	—	0.25	0.40
2008	241,560,000	—	—	—	0.25	0.40
2009	336,150,800	—	—	—	0.25	0.40
2010	—	—	—	—	0.25	0.40
2011	—	—	—	—	0.25	0.40

KM# 202 10 SEN
2.9800 g., Stainless Steel, 18.8 mm. **Obv:** Flower, date and value **Obv. Legend:** BANK NEGARA MALAYSIA **Rev:** Star-like geometric pattern **Edge:** Reeded

Date	Mintage	F	VF	XF	Unc	BU
2011	—	—	—	—	0.25	0.40
2012	—	—	—	—	0.25	0.40

KM# 52 20 SEN
5.6600 g., Copper-Nickel, 23.6 mm. **Obv:** Value divides date below flower blossom **Obv. Legend:** BANK NEGARA MALAYSIA **Rev:** Basket with food and utensils **Edge:** Reeded

Date	Mintage	F	VF	XF	Unc	BU
2001	278,802,000	—	—	—	0.35	0.50
2002	131,279,881	—	—	—	0.35	0.50
2003	—	—	—	—	0.35	0.50
2004	96,840,000	—	—	—	0.35	0.50
2005	209,700,000	—	—	—	0.35	0.50
2006	155,880,000	—	—	—	0.35	0.50
2007	212,897,236	—	—	—	0.35	0.50
2008	19,764,000	—	—	—	0.35	0.50
2009	—	—	—	—	0.35	0.50
2010	—	—	—	—	0.35	0.50
2011	—	—	—	—	0.35	0.50

KM# 203 20 SEN
4.1800 g., Nickel-Brass, 20.6 mm. **Obv:** Flower, date and value **Obv. Legend:** BANK NEGARA MALAYSIA **Rev:** flowers on patterned background

Date	Mintage	F	VF	XF	Unc	BU
2011	—	—	—	—	0.35	0.50
2012	—	—	—	—	0.35	0.50

KM# 77 25 SEN
9.1400 g., Brass, 30 mm. **Series:** Endangered Species **Obv:** Logo left, value right **Rev:** Sumatran Rhinoceros **Edge:** Reeded

Date	Mintage	F	VF	XF	Unc	BU
2003	100,000	—	—	—	—	5.00

KM# 78 25 SEN
9.1400 g., Brass, 30 mm. **Series:** Endangered Species **Obv:** Logo left, value right **Rev:** Elephant **Edge:** Reeded

Date	Mintage	F	VF	XF	Unc	BU
2003	100,000	—	—	—	—	8.00

KM# 79 25 SEN
9.1400 g., Brass, 30 mm. **Series:** Endangered Species **Obv:** Logo left, value right **Rev:** Orangutan **Edge:** Reeded

Date	Mintage	F	VF	XF	Unc	BU
2003	100,000	—	—	—	—	5.00

KM# 80 25 SEN
9.1400 g., Brass, 30 mm. **Series:** Endangered Species **Obv:** Logo left, value right **Rev:** Sumatran Tiger **Edge:** Reeded

Date	Mintage	F	VF	XF	Unc	BU
2003	100,000	—	—	—	—	5.00

KM# 81 25 SEN
9.1400 g., Brass, 30 mm. **Series:** Endangered Species **Obv:** Logo left, value right **Rev:** Slow Loris on branch **Edge:** Reeded

Date	Mintage	F	VF	XF	Unc	BU
2003	100,000	—	—	—	—	5.00

KM# 82 25 SEN
9.1400 g., Brass, 30 mm. **Series:** Endangered Species **Obv:** Logo left, value right **Rev:** Barking Deer **Edge:** Reeded

Date	Mintage	F	VF	XF	Unc	BU
2003	100,000	—	—	—	—	5.00

KM# 83 25 SEN
9.1400 g., Brass, 30 mm. **Series:** Endangered Species **Obv:** Logo left, value right **Rev:** Malayan Tapir **Edge:** Reeded

Date	Mintage	F	VF	XF	Unc	BU
2003	100,000	—	—	—	—	5.00

KM# 84 25 SEN
9.1400 g., Brass, 30 mm. **Series:** Endangered Species **Obv:** Logo left, value right **Rev:** Serow **Edge:** Reeded

Date	Mintage	F	VF	XF	Unc	BU
2003	100,000	—	—	—	—	5.00

KM# 85 25 SEN
9.1400 g., Brass, 30 mm. **Series:** Endangered Species **Obv:** Logo left, value right **Rev:** Sambar Deer **Edge:** Reeded

Date	Mintage	F	VF	XF	Unc	BU
2003	100,000	—	—	—	—	5.00

KM# 86 25 SEN
9.1400 g., Brass, 30 mm. **Series:** Endangered Species **Obv:** Logo left, value right **Rev:** Seated Proboscis Monkey flanked by sprigs **Edge:** Reeded

Date	Mintage	F	VF	XF	Unc	BU
2003	100,000	—	—	—	—	5.00

KM# 87 25 SEN
9.1400 g., Brass, 30 mm. **Series:** Endangered Species **Obv:** Logo left, value right **Rev:** Gaur **Edge:** Reeded

Date	Mintage	F	VF	XF	Unc	BU
2003	100,000	—	—	—	—	5.00

KM# 88 25 SEN
9.1400 g., Brass, 30 mm. **Series:** Endangered Species **Obv:** Logo left, value right **Rev:** Clouded Leopard **Edge:** Reeded

Date	Mintage	F	VF	XF	Unc	BU
2003	100,000	—	—	—	—	5.00

KM# 89 25 SEN
9.1400 g., Brass, 30 mm. **Series:** Endangered Species **Obv:** Logo left, value right **Obv. Legend:** BANK NEGARA MALAYSIA - SIRI HAIWAN TERANCAM **Rev:** Straw-headed Bulbul bird (Barau-Barau) **Edge:** Reeded

Date	Mintage	F	VF	XF	Unc	BU
2005	40,000	—	—	—	—	5.00

KM# 90 25 SEN
9.1400 g., Brass, 30 mm. **Series:** Endangered Species **Obv:** Logo left, value right **Obv. Legend:** BANK NEGARA MALAYSIA - SIRI HAIWAN TERANCAM **Rev:** Great Argus Pheasant (Kuang Raya) **Edge:** Reeded

Date	Mintage	F	VF	XF	Unc	BU
2005	40,000	—	—	—	—	5.00

KM# 91 25 SEN
9.1400 g., Brass, 30 mm. **Series:** Endangered Species **Obv:** Logo left, value right **Obv. Legend:** BANK NEGARA MALAYSIA - SIRI HAIWAN TERANCAM **Rev:** White-collared Kingfisher (Pekaka Sungai) **Edge:** Reeded

Date	Mintage	F	VF	XF	Unc	BU
2005	40,000	—	—	—	—	5.00

KM# 92 25 SEN
9.1400 g., Brass, 30 mm. **Series:** Endangered Species **Obv:** Logo left, value right **Obv. Legend:** BANK NEGARA MALAYSIA - SIRI HAIWAN TERANCAM **Rev:** White-bellied Sea Eagle (Lang Siput) perched on branch **Edge:** Reeded

Date	Mintage	F	VF	XF	Unc	BU
2005	40,000	—	—	—	—	5.00

KM# 93 25 SEN
9.1600 g., Brass, 30 mm. **Series:** Endangered Species **Obv:** Logo left, value right **Obv. Legend:** BANK NEGARA MALAYSIA - SIRI HAIWAN TERANCAM **Rev:** Asian Fairy Bluebird (Dendang Gajah) **Edge:** Reeded

Date	Mintage	F	VF	XF	Unc	BU
2005	40,000	—	—	—	—	5.00

KM# 94 25 SEN
9.1600 g., Brass, 30 mm. **Series:** Endangered Species **Obv:** Logo left, value right **Obv. Legend:** BANK NEGARA MALAYSIA - SIRI HAIWAN TERANCAM **Rev:** Rhinoceros Hornbill bird (Enggang Badak) **Edge:** Reeded

Date	Mintage	F	VF	XF	Unc	BU
2005	40,000	—	—	—	—	5.00

KM# 95 25 SEN
9.1600 g., Brass, 30 mm. **Series:** Endangered Species **Obv:** Logo left, value right **Obv. Legend:** BANK NEGARA MALAYSIA - SIRI HAIWAN TERANCAM **Rev:** Nicobar Pigeon (Merpati Emas) **Edge:** Reeded

Date	Mintage	F	VF	XF	Unc	BU
2005	40,000	—	—	—	—	5.00

KM# 96 25 SEN
9.1600 g., Brass, 30 mm. **Series:** Endangered Species **Obv:** Logo left, value right **Obv. Legend:** BANK NEGARA MALAYSIA - SIRI HAIWAN TERANCAM **Rev:** Two Crested Wood Partridges (Siul Berjambul) **Edge:** Reeded

Date	Mintage	F	VF	XF	Unc	BU
2005	40,000	—	—	—	—	5.00

KM# 97 25 SEN
9.1600 g., Brass, 30 mm. **Series:** Endangered Species **Obv:** Logo left, value right **Obv. Legend:** BANK NEGARA MALAYSIA - SIRI HAIWAN TERANCAM **Rev:** Black and Red Broadbill bird (Takau Rakit) **Edge:** Reeded

Date	Mintage	F	VF	XF	Unc	BU
2005	40,000	—	—	—	—	5.00

KM# 98 25 SEN
9.1600 g., Brass, 30 mm. **Series:** Endangered Species **Obv:** Logo left, value right **Obv. Legend:** BANK NEGARA MALAYSIA - SIRI HAIWAN TERANCAM **Rev:** Green Imperial Pigeon (Pergam Besar) on branch **Edge:** Reeded

Date	Mintage	F	VF	XF	Unc	BU
2005	40,000	—	—	—	—	5.00

KM# 99 25 SEN
9.1600 g., Brass, 30 mm. **Series:** Endangered Species **Obv:** Logo left, value right **Obv. Legend:** BANK NEGARA MALAYSIA - SIRI HAIWAN TERANCAM **Rev:** Great Egret (Bangau Besar) **Edge:** Reeded

Date	Mintage	F	VF	XF	Unc	BU
2005	40,000	—	—	—	—	5.00

KM# 100 25 SEN
9.1600 g., Brass, 30 mm. **Series:** Endangered Species **Obv:** Logo left, value right **Obv. Legend:** BANK NEGARA MALAYSIA - SIRI HAIWAN TERANCAM **Rev:** Brown Shrike (Tirjup Tanah) on branch **Edge:** Reeded

Date	Mintage	F	VF	XF	Unc	BU
2005	40,000	—	—	—	—	5.00

KM# 104 25 SEN
Brass, 34 mm. **Series:** Endangered Species **Obv:** Logo and value **Obv. Legend:** BANK NEGARA MALAYSIA - SIRI HAIWAN TERANCAM **Rev:** Hawksbill turtle (Penyu Karah)

Date	Mintage	F	VF	XF	Unc	BU
2006	40,000	—	—	—	—	5.00

KM# 103 25 SEN
Brass, 34 mm. **Series:** Endangered Species **Obv:** Logo and value **Obv. Legend:** BANK NEGARA MALAYSIA - SIRI HAIWAN TERANCAM **Rev:** Green turtle (Penyu Agar)

Date	Mintage	F	VF	XF	Unc	BU
2006	40,000	—	—	—	—	5.00

KM# 102 25 SEN
Brass, 34 mm. **Series:** Endangered Species **Obv:** Logo and value **Obv. Legend:** BANK NEGARA MALAYSIA - SIRI HAIWAN TERANCAM **Rev:** Leatherback turtle (Penyu Belimbing)

Date	Mintage	F	VF	XF	Unc	BU
2006	40,000	—	—	—	—	5.00

KM# 101   25 SEN

Brass, 34 mm. **Series:** Endangered Species **Obv:** Logo and value **Obv. Legend:** BANK NEGARA MALAYSIA - SIRI HAIWAN TERANCAM **Rev:** Olive Ridley Turtle (Pengu Lipas)

Date	Mintage	F	VF	XF	Unc	BU
2006	40,000	—	—	—	—	5.00

KM# 105   25 SEN

15.5000 g., Brass, 34 mm. **Series:** Endangered Species **Obv:** Logo and value **Obv. Legend:** BANK NEGARA MALAYSIA - SIRI HAIWAN TERANCAM **Rev:** Dugong **Edge:** Reeded

Date	Mintage	F	VF	XF	Unc	BU
2006	40,000	—	—	—	—	8.00

KM# 106   25 SEN

15.5000 g., Brass, 34 mm. **Series:** Endangered Species **Obv:** Logo and value **Obv. Legend:** BANK NEGARA MALAYSIA - SIRI HAIWAN TERANCAM **Rev:** Whale Shark (Jerung Paus) **Edge:** Reeded

Date	Mintage	F	VF	XF	Unc	BU
2006	40,000	—	—	—	—	5.00

KM# 107   25 SEN

15.5000 g., Brass, 34 mm. **Series:** Endangered Species **Obv:** Logo and value **Obv. Legend:** BANK NEGARA MALAYSIA - SIRI HAIWAN TERANCAM **Rev:** Irraddy Dolphin (Lumba-Lumba Empesut) **Edge:** Reeded

Date	Mintage	F	VF	XF	Unc	BU
2006	40,000	—	—	—	—	5.00

KM# 108   25 SEN

15.5000 g., Brass, 34 mm. **Series:** Endangered Species **Obv:** Logo and value **Obv. Legend:** BANK NEGARA MALAYSIA - SIRI HAIWAN TERANCAM **Rev:** Bottlenose Dolphin (Lumba Lumba) **Edge:** Reeded

Date	Mintage	F	VF	XF	Unc	BU
2006	40,000	—	—	—	—	5.00

KM# 109   25 SEN

15.5000 g., Brass, 34 mm. **Series:** Endangered Species **Obv:** Logo and value **Obv. Legend:** BANK NEGARA MALAYSIA - SIRI HAIWAN TERANCAM **Rev:** Siamese Crocodile (Buaya Siam) **Edge:** Reeded

Date	Mintage	F	VF	XF	Unc	BU
2006	40,000	—	—	—	—	5.00

KM# 110   25 SEN

15.5000 g., Brass, 34 mm. **Series:** Endangered Species **Obv:** Logo and value **Obv. Legend:** BANK NEGARA MALAYSIA - SIRI HAIWAN TERANCAM **Rev:** Indopacific Crocodile (Buaya Tembaga) **Edge:** Reeded

Date	Mintage	F	VF	XF	Unc	BU
2006	40,000	—	—	—	—	5.00

KM# 111   25 SEN

15.5000 g., Brass, 34 mm. **Series:** Endangered Species **Obv:** Logo and value **Obv. Legend:** BANK NEGARA MALAYSIA - SIRI HAIWAN TERANCAM **Rev:** Malayan Gharial (Buaya Julong) **Edge:** Reeded

Date	Mintage	F	VF	XF	Unc	BU
2006	40,000	—	—	—	—	5.00

KM# 112   25 SEN

15.5000 g., Brass, 34 mm. **Series:** Endangered Species **Obv:** Logo and value **Obv. Legend:** BANK NEGARA MALAYSIA - SIRI HAIWAN TERANCAM **Rev:** Painted Terrapin turtle (Tuntung Laut) **Edge:** Reeded

Date	Mintage	F	VF	XF	Unc	BU
2006	40,000	—	—	—	—	5.00

KM# 53   50 SEN

9.3300 g., Copper-Nickel, 27.75 mm. **Obv:** Value divides date below flower blossom **Obv. Legend:** BANK NEGARA MALAYSIA **Rev:** Ceremonial kite **Edge Lettering:** BANK NEGARA MALAYSIA (twice)

Date	Mintage	F	VF	XF	Unc	BU
2001	67,371,000	—	—	—	0.65	0.85
2002	61,928,000	—	—	—	0.65	0.85
2003	32,580,000	—	—	—	0.65	0.85
2004	37,890,000	—	—	—	0.65	0.85
2005	691,680,006	—	—	—	0.65	0.85
2006	19,480,000	—	—	—	0.65	0.85
2007	—	—	—	—	0.65	0.85
2008	61,380,000	—	—	—	0.65	0.85
2009	94,691,783	—	—	—	0.65	0.85
2010	—	—	—	—	0.65	0.85
2011	—	—	—	—	0.65	0.85

KM# 204   50 SEN

5.6600 g., Nickel-Brass Plated Copper, 22.65 mm. **Obv:** Flower, date and value **Obv. Legend:** BANK NEGARA MALAYSIA **Rev:** Vine on patterned circle **Edge:** Notched

Date	Mintage	F	VF	XF	Unc	BU
2011	—	—	—	—	0.65	0.85
2012	—	—	—	—	0.65	0.85

KM# 71   RINGGIT

16.8000 g., Copper-Nickel, 33.7 mm. **Subject:** XXI SEA Games **Obv:** Games logo **Rev:** Cartoon mascot **Edge:** Reeded

Date	Mintage	F	VF	XF	Unc	BU
2001	200,000	—	—	—	5.00	6.00

KM# 165   RINGGIT

10.4000 g., Copper Plated Zinc, 26 mm. **Subject:** 10th Men's Hockey World Cup **Obv:** Logo **Obv. Legend:** BANK NEGARA MALAYSIA **Rev:** 2 stylized players **Rev. Legend:** KEJOHANAN HOKI LELAKI PIALA DUNIA **Edge:** Reeded

Date	Mintage	F	VF	XF	Unc	BU
2002	100,000	—	—	—	—	12.00

KM# 168   RINGGIT

Brass **Subject:** 45th National Day **Obv:** Buildings, tower, metro liner **Obv. Legend:** BANK NEGARA MALAYSIA **Rev:** Stylized waving flag **Rev. Legend:** 45 TAHUN MERDEKA

Date	Mintage	F	VF	XF	Unc	BU
2002	10,000	—	—	—	—	10.00

KM# 74   RINGGIT

16.8000 g., Copper-Nickel, 33.7 mm. **Subject:** Coronation of Agong XII **Obv:** Head with headdress facing **Rev:** Arms with supporters within sprigs **Edge:** Reeded **Note:** Prev. KM#72.

Date	Mintage	F	VF	XF	Unc	BU
ND(2002)	100,000	—	—	—	6.00	7.00

KM# 171   RINGGIT

Brass **Subject:** XIII NAM Summit **Obv:** Modern building, plaza **Obv. Legend:** MALAYSIA - BANK NEGARA MALAYSIA **Rev:** Stylized dove in rays **Rev. Legend:** XIII CONFERENCE OF HEADS OF STATE OR GOVERNMENT OF THE NON-ALIGNED MOVEMENT

Date	Mintage	F	VF	XF	Unc	BU
2003 Proof	9,400	Value: 10.00				

KM# 174   RINGGIT

Brass **Subject:** LIMA - 7th Bi-annual Langkawi Island Trade Fair **Obv:** Jet fighter plane above naval missile corvette **Obv. Legend:** BANK NEGARA MALAYSIA **Rev:** Logo **Rev. Legend:** LANGKAWI INTERNATIONAL MARITIME & AEROSPACE

Date	Mintage	F	VF	XF	Unc	BU
2003	25,000	—	—	—	—	10.00

KM# 177   RINGGIT

Brass **Subject:** 10th Session Islamic Summit Conference **Obv:** Circular Arabic text **Obv. Legend:** BANK NEGARA MALAYSIA **Rev:** Symmetrical design **Rev. Legend:** PERSIDANGAN KETUA-KETUA NEGARASLAM

Date	Mintage	F	VF	XF	Unc	BU
2003	25,000	—	—	—	—	10.00

KM# 200   RINGGIT

8.1500 g., Bi-Metallic Copper-Nickel center in Nickel-Brass ring, 26.5 mm. **Subject:** 46th Anniversary of Independence **Rev:** Group of four people

Date	Mintage	F	VF	XF	Unc	BU
2003	—	—	—	—	—	6.00

KM# 114   RINGGIT

Copper-Nickel **Subject:** Century of Tunku Abdul Rahman **Obv:** National arms **Obv. Legend:** BANK NEGARA MALAYSIA - BAPA KEMERDEKAAN **Rev:** 3/4 length figure of Tunku Abdul Rahman left with right hand raised **Rev. Legend:** Y. T. M. TUNKU ABDUL RAHMAN PUTRA AL-HAJ

Date	Mintage	F	VF	XF	Unc	BU
2005	25,000	—	—	—	—	10.00

KM# 132   RINGGIT

Brass **Subject:** 30th Annual Meeting Islamic Development Bank **Obv:** Circular Arabic text **Obv. Legend:** BANK NEGARA MALYSIA - MESYUARAT TAHUNAN BANK PEMBANCUNAN ISLAM KE - 30 **Rev:** Logo

Date	Mintage	F	VF	XF	Unc	BU
2005	20,000	—	—	—	—	10.00

KM# 135   RINGGIT

Copper-Nickel **Subject:** 11th ASEAN Summit **Obv:** Twin towers center right **Obv. Legend:** BANK NEGARA MALAYSIA - SIDANG KEMUNCAK ASEAN KE-11 **Rev:** Logo

Date	Mintage	F	VF	XF	Unc	BU
2005	20,000	—	—	—	—	8.00

KM# 138   RINGGIT

Bi-Metallic **Subject:** Songket - The Regal Heritage **Obv:** Stylized flower - Bunga Ketola **Obv. Legend:** BANK NEGARA MALAYSIA **Rev:** Floral pattern below inscription

Date	Mintage	F	VF	XF	Unc	BU
2005	20,000	—	—	—	—	8.00

KM# 141   RINGGIT

Brass **Subject:** 50th Anniversary Mara Technology University **Obv:** Large "50" with horizontal lines in background **Obv. Legend:** BANK NEGARA MALAYSIA - JUBLI EMAS UITM **Rev:** Logo **Rev. Legend:** Universiti Teknologi Mara

Date	Mintage	F	VF	XF	Unc	BU
ND(2006)	12,050	—	—	—	—	8.00

KM# 144 RINGGIT
Brass **Subject:** 50th Anniversary P. Felda **Obv:** 1/2 length figure of Felda 3/4 right **Obv. Legend:** BANK NEGARA MALYSIA **Rev:** Two opposed hands holding symbol **Rev. Legend:** MENEMPA KEJAYAAN

Date	Mintage	F	VF	XF	Unc	BU
2006	10,000	—	—	—	—	8.00

KM# 147 RINGGIT
Brass **Subject:** 9th Malaysian Plan **Obv:** Bust 3/4 right **Obv. Legend:** BANK NEGARA MALAYSIA - CEMERLANG GEMILANG TERBILANg **Rev:** Globe logo **Rev. Legend:** RANCANGAN MALAYSIA KE SEMBILAN

Date	Mintage	F	VF	XF	Unc	BU
2006	10,000	—	—	—	—	8.00

KM# 162 RINGGIT
Brass **Subject:** 200th Anniversary Malaysian Police Force **Obv:** Police badge **Obv. Legend:** BANK NEGARA MALAYSIA **Rev:** Two hands clasped in sprays

Date	Mintage	F	VF	XF	Unc	BU
2007	20,000	—	—	—	—	7.00

KM# 182 RINGGIT
8.8000 g., Aluminum-Bronze, 30 mm. **Subject:** Installation of Agong XIII **Obv:** National arms within wreath **Rev:** Facing portrait

Date	Mintage	F	VF	XF	Unc	BU
2007	10,000	—	—	—	—	7.00
2007 Proof	600	—	—	—	—	—

KM# 185 RINGGIT
8.8000 g., Aluminum-Bronze, 30 mm. **Subject:** Independence, 50th Anniversary **Obv:** National Arms **Rev:** 50 above city skyline

Date	Mintage	F	VF	XF	Unc	BU
2007	10,000	—	—	—	—	7.00
2007 Proof	2,000	—	—	—	—	—

KM# 188 RINGGIT
8.8000 g., Aluminum-Bronze, 30 mm. **Subject:** Royal Malaysian Air Force, 50th Anniversary **Obv:** Air Force insignia **Rev:** Old and modern plane

Date	Mintage	F	VF	XF	Unc	BU
2008	10,000	—	—	—	—	7.00
2008 Proof	350	—	—	—	—	—

KM# 191 RINGGIT
8.8000 g., Aluminum-Bronze, 30 mm. **Subject:** St. John's Ambulance, 100th Anniversary **Obv:** St. John's insignia in wreath above valve **Rev:** Cliernt being loaded into ambulance

Date	Mintage	F	VF	XF	Unc	BU
2008	10,000	—	—	—	—	7.00
2008 Proof	350	—	—	—	—	—

KM# 155 RINGGIT
8.8000 g., Brass, 30 mm. **Subject:** Bank Negara Malaysia, 50th Anniversary **Obv:** Bank logo **Rev:** 14-pointed star

Date	Mintage	F	VF	XF	Unc	BU
2009	13,700	—	—	—	—	7.00
2009 Proof	3,300	—	—	—	—	—

KM# 159 RINGGIT
8.0000 g., Brass, 30 mm. **Subject:** Parliament, 50th Anniversary **Obv:** National Arms and 2 maces **Rev:** Parliament Building

Date	Mintage	F	VF	XF	Unc	BU
2009	10,000	—	—	—	—	7.00
2009 Proof	450	—	—	—	—	—

KM# 194 RINGGIT
8.8000 g., Aluminum-Bronze, 30 mm. **Subject:** International Year of Astronomy **Obv:** Adult and Child looking to the heavens **Rev:** Langkawi National Observatory

Date	Mintage	F	VF	XF	Unc	BU
2009	10,000	—	—	—	—	6.00
2009 Proof	350	—	—	—	—	—

KM# 197 RINGGIT
8.8000 g., Aluminum-Bronze, 30 mm. **Subject:** Royal Malaysian Navy, 75th Anniversary **Obv:** Submarine **Rev:** Navy insignia

Date	Mintage	F	VF	XF	Unc	BU
2009	10,000	—	—	—	—	6.00
2009 Proof	450	—	—	—	—	—

KM# 72 10 RINGGIT
21.7000 g., 0.9250 Silver 0.6453 oz. ASW, 35.7 mm. **Subject:** XXI SEA Games **Obv:** Games logo **Rev:** Cartoon mascot **Edge:** Reeded

Date	Mintage	F	VF	XF	Unc	BU
2001 Proof	3,000	Value: 70.00				

KM# 75 10 RINGGIT
21.7000 g., 0.9250 Silver 0.6453 oz. ASW, 35.7 mm. **Subject:** Coronation of Agong XII **Obv:** Head with headdress facing **Rev:** Arms with supporters within sprigs **Edge:** Reeded

Date	Mintage	F	VF	XF	Unc	BU
ND(2002) Proof	10,000	Value: 120				

KM# 166 10 RINGGIT
16.8000 g., 0.9250 Silver 0.4996 oz. ASW, 32 mm. **Subject:** 10th Men's Hockey World Cup **Obv:** Official logo of the World Cup games **Obv. Legend:** BANK NEGARA MALAYSIA **Rev:** 2 stylized players in front of the Kuala Lumpur skyline **Rev. Legend:** KEJOHANAN HOKI LELAKI PIALA

Date	Mintage	F	VF	XF	Unc	BU
2002 Proof	3,000	Value: 160				

KM# 169 10 RINGGIT
0.9250 Silver **Subject:** 45th National Day **Obv:** Buildings, tower, metro liner **Obv. Legend:** BANK NEGARA MALAYSIA **Rev:** Stylized waving flag **Rev. Legend:** 45 TAHUN MERDEKA

Date	Mintage	F	VF	XF	Unc	BU
2002 Proof	1,800	Value: 120				

KM# 172 10 RINGGIT
0.9250 Silver **Subject:** XIII NAM Summit **Obv:** Modern building, plaza **Obv. Legend:** MALAYSIA - BANK NEGARA MALAYSIA **Rev:** Stylized dove in rays **Rev. Legend:** XIII CONFERENCE OF HEADS OF STATE OR GOVERNMENT OF THE NON-ALIGNED MOVEMENT

Date	Mintage	F	VF	XF	Unc	BU
2003 Proof	2,400	Value: 120				

KM# 175 10 RINGGIT
0.9250 Silver **Subject:** LIMA - 7th bi-annual Langkawi Island Trade Fair **Obv:** Jet fighter plane above naval missile corvette **Obv. Legend:** BANK NEGARA MALAYSIA **Rev. Legend:** LANGKAWI INTERNATIONAL MARITIME & SPACE

Date	Mintage	F	VF	XF	Unc	BU
2003 Proof	—	Value: 120				

KM# 178 10 RINGGIT
0.9250 Silver **Subject:** 10th Session Islamic Summit Conference **Obv:** Circular Arabic Text **Obv. Legend:** BANK NEGARA MALAYSIA **Rev:** Symmetrical pattern **Rev. Legend:** PERSIDANGAN KETUA - KETUA NEGARA ISLAM

Date	Mintage	F	VF	XF	Unc	BU
2003 Proof	300	Value: 120				

KM# 115 10 RINGGIT
0.9250 Silver **Subject:** Century of Tunku Abdul Rahman **Obv:** National arms **Obv. Legend:** BANK NEGARA MALAYSIA - BAPA KEMERDEKAAN **Rev:** 3/4 length figure of Tunku Abdul Rahman left with right hand raised **Rev. Legend:** Y. T. M. TUNKU ABDUL RAHMAN PUTRA AL-HAJ

Date	Mintage	F	VF	XF	Unc	BU
2005 Proof	200	Value: 120				

KM# 136 10 RINGGIT
21.7000 g., Silver, 35.7 mm. **Subject:** 11th ASEAN Summit **Obv:** Twin towers center right **Obv. Legend:** BANK NEGARA MALAYSIA - SIDANG KEMUNCAK ASEAN KE-11 **Rev:** Logo

Date	Mintage	F	VF	XF	Unc	BU
2005 Proof	250	Value: 120				

KM# 139 10 RINGGIT
21.7000 g., Silver, 35.7 mm. **Subject:** Songket - The Regal Heritage **Obv:** Uniform pattern - Bunga Bintang **Obv. Legend:** BANK NEGARA MALAYSIA **Rev:** Floral pattern below inscription

Date	Mintage	F	VF	XF	Unc	BU
2005 Proof	250	Value: 120				

KM# 142 10 RINGGIT
21.7000 g., Silver, 35.7 mm. **Subject:** 50th Anniversary Mara Technology Universit **Obv:** Large "50" with horizontal lines in background **Obv. Legend:** BANK NEGARA MALAYSIA - JUBLI EMAS UITM **Rev:** Logo **Rev. Legend:** Universiti Teknologi Mara

Date	Mintage	F	VF	XF	Unc	BU
ND(2006) Proof	500	Value: 110				

KM# 145 10 RINGGIT
31.1100 g., Silver, 40 mm. **Subject:** 50th Anniversary P. Felda **Obv:** Outlined map of South East Asia above logo **Obv. Legend:** BANK NEGARA MALAYSIA **Rev:** Monument at left, Felda with 4 others at right **Rev. Legend:** MENEMPA KEJAYAAN

Date	Mintage	F	VF	XF	Unc	BU
2006 Proof	300	Value: 110				

KM# 148 10 RINGGIT
21.0000 g., Silver, 35.7 mm. **Subject:** 9th Malaysian Plan **Obv:** Bust 3/4 right **Obv. Legend:** BANK NEGARA MALAYSIA - CEMERLANG GEMILANG TERBILANG **Rev:** Globe logo **Rev. Legend:** RANCANGAN MALAYSIA KE SEMBILAN

Date	Mintage	F	VF	XF	Unc	BU
2006 Proof	300	Value: 110				

KM# 163 10 RINGGIT
21.0000 g., Silver, 35.70 mm. **Subject:** 200th Anniversary Malaysian Police Force **Obv:** Police badge **Obv. Legend:** BANK NEGARA MALAYSIA **Rev:** Two hands clasped in sprays

Date	Mintage	F	VF	XF	Unc	BU
2007 Proof	500	Value: 110				

KM# 183 10 RINGGIT
21.0000 g., 0.9250 Silver 0.6245 oz. ASW, 35.7 mm. **Subject:** Installation of Agong XIII **Obv:** National arms in wreath **Rev:** Portrait facing

Date	Mintage	F	VF	XF	Unc	BU
2007 Proof	200	Value: 100				

KM# 186 10 RINGGIT
21.0000 g., 0.9250 Silver 0.6245 oz. ASW, 35.7 mm. **Subject:** Independence, 50th Anniversary **Obv:** National Arms **Rev:** 50 above city skyline

Date	Mintage	F	VF	XF	Unc	BU
2007 Proof	200	Value: 100				

KM# 189 10 RINGGIT
21.0000 g., 0.9250 Silver 0.6245 oz. ASW, 35.7 mm. **Subject:** Royal Malaysian Air Force, 50th Anniversary **Obv:** Air Force insignia **Rev:** Old and new plane

Date	Mintage	F	VF	XF	Unc	BU
2008 Proof	350	Value: 100				

KM# 192 10 RINGGIT
21.0000 g., 0.9250 Silver 0.6245 oz. ASW, 35.7 mm. **Subject:** St. John's Ambulance **Obv:** St. John's emblem in wreath above vlaue **Rev:** Client being loaded into ambulance

Date	Mintage	F	VF	XF	Unc	BU
2008 Proof	350	Value: 100				

KM# 156 10 RINGGIT
21.0000 g., 0.9250 Silver 0.6245 oz. ASW, 35.7 mm. **Subject:** Bank Negara Malaysia, 50th Anniversary **Obv:** Bank logo **Rev:** 14-pointed star

Date	Mintage	F	VF	XF	Unc	BU
2009 Proof	400	Value: 100				

KM# 160 10 RINGGIT
21.0000 g., 0.9250 Silver 0.6245 oz. ASW, 35.7 mm. **Subject:** Parliament, 50th Anniversary **Obv:** National Arms and 2 maces **Rev:** Parliament Building

Date	Mintage	F	VF	XF	Unc	BU
2009 Proof	300	Value: 120				

KM# 195 10 RINGGIT
21.0000 g., 0.9250 Silver 0.6245 oz. ASW, 35.7 mm. **Subject:** International Year of Astronomy **Obv:** Adult and child looking to the heavens **Rev:** Langkawi Naitonal Observatory

Date	Mintage	F	VF	XF	Unc	BU
2009 Proof	350	Value: 120				

KM# 198 10 RINGGIT
21.0000 g., 0.9250 Silver 0.6245 oz. ASW, 35.7 mm. **Subject:** Royal Malaysian navy, 75th Anniversary **Obv:** Submarine **Rev:** Navy insignia

Date	Mintage	F	VF	XF	Unc	BU
2009 Proof	300	Value: 120				

KM# 133 20 RINGGIT
31.1000 g., Silver, 40 mm. **Subject:** 30th Annual Meeting Islamic Development Bank **Obv:** Mosque **Obv. Legend:** BANK NEGARA MALAYSIA **Rev:** Logo

Date	Mintage	F	VF	XF	Unc	BU
2005 Proof	1,000	Value: 100				

KM# 157 50 RINGGIT
10.0700 g., 0.9990 Gold 0.3234 oz. AGW, 25 mm. **Subject:** Bank Negara Malaysia, 50th Anniversary **Obv:** Bank logo **Rev:** 14-pointed star

Date	Mintage	F	VF	XF	Unc	BU
2009 Proof	300	Value: 1,000				

KM# 73 100 RINGGIT
8.6000 g., 0.9160 Gold 0.2533 oz. AGW, 22 mm. **Subject:** XXI SEA Games **Obv:** Games logo **Rev:** Cartoon mascot **Edge:** Reeded

Date	Mintage	F	VF	XF	Unc	BU
2001 Proof	500	Value: 800				

KM# 76 100 RINGGIT
8.6000 g., 0.9160 Gold 0.2533 oz. AGW, 22 mm. **Subject:** Coronation of Agong XII **Obv:** Head with headdress facing **Rev:** Arms with supporters within sprigs **Edge:** Reeded

Date	Mintage	F	VF	XF	Unc	BU
ND(2002) Proof	—	Value: 900				

KM# 167 100 RINGGIT
9.0000 g., 0.9000 Gold 0.2604 oz. AGW, 22 mm. **Subject:** 10th Men's Hockey World Cup **Obv:** Official logo **Obv. Legend:** BANK NEGARA MALAYSIA **Rev:** 2 stylized players in front of Kuala Lumpur skyline **Rev. Legend:** KEJOHANAN HOKI LELAKI PIALA

Date	Mintage	F	VF	XF	Unc	BU
2002 Proof	1,000	Value: 700				

KM# 170 100 RINGGIT
8.6000 g., 0.9999 Gold 0.2765 oz. AGW **Subject:** 45th National Day **Obv:** Buildings, tower, metro liner **Obv. Legend:** BANK NEGARA MALAYSIA **Rev:** Stylized waving flag **Rev. Legend:** 45 TAHUN MERDEKA

Date	Mintage	F	VF	XF	Unc	BU
2002 Proof	300	Value: 900				

KM# 173 100 RINGGIT
8.6000 g., 0.9999 Gold 0.2765 oz. AGW, 22 mm. **Subject:** XIII NAM Summit **Obv:** Modern building, plaza **Obv. Legend:** MALAYSIA - BANK NEGARA MALAYSIA **Rev:** Stylized dove in rays **Rev. Legend:** XIII CONFERENCE OF HEADS OF STATE OR GOVERNMENT OF THE NON-ALIGNED MOVEMENT

Date	Mintage	F	VF	XF	Unc	BU
2003 Proof	300	Value: 900				

KM# 176 100 RINGGIT
8.6000 g., 0.9999 Gold 0.2765 oz. AGW, 22 mm. **Subject:** LIMA - 7th bi-annual Langkawi Island Trade Fair **Obv:** Jet fighter plane above naval missile corvette **Obv. Legend:** BANK NEGARA MALAYSIA **Rev:** Logo **Rev. Legend:** LANGKAWI INTERNATIONAL MARITIME & AEROSPACE

Date	Mintage	F	VF	XF	Unc	BU
2003 Proof	50	Value: 1,400				

KM# 179 100 RINGGIT
8.6000 g., 0.9999 Gold 0.2765 oz. AGW, 22 mm. **Obv:** Circular Arabic text **Obv. Legend:** BANK NEGARA MALAYSIA **Rev:** Symmetrical design **Rev. Legend:** PERSIDANGAN KETUA - KETUA NEGARA ISLAM

Date	Mintage	F	VF	XF	Unc	BU
2003 Proof	200	Value: 900				

KM# 116 100 RINGGIT
0.9999 Gold **Subject:** Century of Tunku Abdul Rahman **Obv:** National arms **Obv. Legend:** BANK NEGARA MALAYSIA - BAPA KEMERDEKAAN **Rev:** 3/4 length figure of Tunku Abdul Rahman left with right hand raised **Rev. Legend:** Y. T. M. TUNKU ABDUL RAHMAN PUTRA AL-HAJ

Date	Mintage	F	VF	XF	Unc	BU
2005 Proof	100	Value: 900				

KM# 137 100 RINGGIT
8.6000 g., Gold, 22 mm. **Subject:** 11th ASEAN Summit **Obv:** Twin towers center right **Obv. Legend:** BANK NEGARA MALAYSIA - SIDANG KEMUNCAK ASEAN KE-11 **Rev:** Logo

Date	Mintage	F	VF	XF	Unc	BU
2005 Proof	200	Value: 900				

KM# 140 100 RINGGIT
8.6000 g., Gold, 22 mm. **Subject:** Songket - The Regal Heritage **Obv:** Uniform pattern - Tampur Kesemak **Obv. Legend:** BANK NEGARA MALAYSIA **Rev:** Floral pattern below inscription

Date	Mintage	F	VF	XF	Unc	BU
2005 Proof	150	Value: 900				

KM# 143 100 RINGGIT
8.6000 g., Gold, 22 mm. **Subject:** 50th Anniversary Mara Technology University **Obv:** Large "50" with horizontal lines in background **Obv. Legend:** BANK NEGARA MALAYSIA - JUBLI EMAS UITM **Rev:** Logo **Rev. Legend:** Universiti Teknologi Mara

Date	Mintage	F	VF	XF	Unc	BU
ND(2006) Proof	300	Value: 900				

KM# 146 100 RINGGIT
9.0000 g., Gold, 22 mm. **Subject:** 50th Anniversary P. Felda **Obv:** 1/2 length figure of Felda 3/4 right **Obv. Legend:** BANK NEGARA MALAYSIA **Rev:** Stylized palm tree at left, rubber tree trunk at right **Rev. Legend:** MENEMPA KEJAYAAN

Date	Mintage	F	VF	XF	Unc	BU
2006 Proof	200	Value: 900				

KM# 149 100 RINGGIT
7.9600 g., Gold, 22 mm. **Subject:** 9th Malaysian Plan **Obv:** Bust 3/4 right **Obv. Legend:** BANK NEGARA MALAYSIA - CEMERLANG GEMILANG TERBILANG **Rev:** Globe logo **Rev. Legend:** RANCANGAN MALAYSIA KE SEMBILAN

Date	Mintage	F	VF	XF	Unc	BU
2006 Proof	500	Value: 900				

KM# 164 100 RINGGIT
7.9600 g., Gold, 22 mm. **Subject:** 200th Anniversary Malaysian Police Force **Obv:** Police badge **Obv. Legend:** BANK NEGARA MALAYSIA **Rev:** Two hands clasped in sprays

Date	Mintage	F	VF	XF	Unc	BU
2007 Proof	500	Value: 900				

KM# 184 100 RINGGIT
7.9600 g., 0.9999 Gold 0.2559 oz. AGW, 22 mm. **Subject:** Installation of the King **Obv:** National Arms within wreath **Rev:** Facing portrait

Date	Mintage	F	VF	XF	Unc	BU
2007 Proof	100	Value: 900				

KM# 187 100 RINGGIT
7.9600 g., 0.9999 Gold 0.2559 oz. AGW, 22 mm. **Subject:** Independence, 50th Anniversary **Obv:** National Arms **Rev:** 50 above city skyline

Date	Mintage	F	VF	XF	Unc	BU
2007 Proof	100	Value: 900				

KM# 190 100 RINGGIT
7.9600 g., 0.9999 Gold 0.2559 oz. AGW, 22 mm. **Subject:** Royal Malaysian Air Force, 50th Anniversary **Obv:** Royal Airforce insignia **Rev:** Old and new plane

Date	Mintage	F	VF	XF	Unc	BU
2008 Proof	100	Value: 900				

KM# 193 100 RINGGIT
7.9600 g., 0.9999 Gold 0.2559 oz. AGW, 22 mm. **Subject:** St. John's Ambulance, 100th Anniversary **Obv:** St. John's insignia in wreath above value **Rev:** Client being loaded into ambulance

Date	Mintage	F	VF	XF	Unc	BU
2008 Proof	100	Value: 900				

KM# 158 100 RINGGIT
7.9600 g., 0.9990 Gold 0.2557 oz. AGW, 22 mm. **Subject:** Bank Negara Malaysia, 50th Anniversary **Obv:** Bank logo **Rev:** 14-pointed star

Date	Mintage	F	VF	XF	Unc	BU
2009 Proof	300	Value: 1,000				

KM# 180 100 RINGGIT
7.9600 g., 0.9999 Gold 0.2559 oz. AGW, 22 mm. **Subject:** Parliament, 50th Anniversary **Obv:** National arms above mace and sceptre **Rev:** Parliament buildings, sunburst

Date	Mintage	F	VF	XF	Unc	BU
2009 Proof	100	Value: 800				

KM# 196 100 RINGGIT
7.9600 g., 0.9999 Gold 0.2559 oz. AGW, 22 mm. **Subject:** International Year of Astronomy **Obv:** Adult and child looking to the ehavens **Rev:** Langkawi National Observatory

Date	Mintage	F	VF	XF	Unc	BU
2009 Proof	100	Value: 900				

KM# 199 100 RINGGIT
7.9600 g., 0.9999 Gold 0.2559 oz. AGW, 22 mm. **Subject:** Royal Malaysian Navy, 75th Anniversary **Obv:** Submarine **Rev:** Navy insignia

Date	Mintage	F	VF	XF	Unc	BU
2009 Proof	100	Value: 900				

PROOF SETS

KM#	Date	Mintage	Identification	Issue Price	Mkt Val
PS19	2003 (2)	300	KM#171, 172	—	150
PS20	2003 (3)	300	KM#171-173	—	1,200
PS21	2003 (2)	300	KM#174, 175	—	200
PS22	2003 (3)	100	KM#174-176	—	1,800
PS23	2003 (2)	500	KM#177, 178	—	150
PS24	2003 (3)	250	KM#177-179	—	1,100
PS25	2005 (2)	300	KM#114, 115	—	150
PS26	2005 (3)	100	KM#114-116	—	1,400
PS27	2005 (2)	1,000	KM#132, 133	—	150
PS28	2005 (3)	500	KM#132-134	—	1,200
PS29	2005 (2)	200	KM#135, 136	—	150
PS30	2005 (3)	150	KM#135-137	—	1,200
PS31	2006 (2)	150	KM#138, 139	—	150
PS32	2005 (3)	150	KM#138-140	—	1,200
PS33	2006 (2)	300	KM#141, 142	—	150
PS34	2006 (3)	300	KM#141-143	—	1,200
PS35	2006 (2)	500	KM#144, 145	—	150
PS36	2006 (3)	500	KM#144-146	—	1,100
PS37	2006 (2)	300	KM#147, 148	—	150
PS38	2006 (3)	500	KM#147-149	—	950
PS39	2007 (2)	200	KM#162, 163	—	150
PS40	2007 (3)	200	KM#162-164	—	950

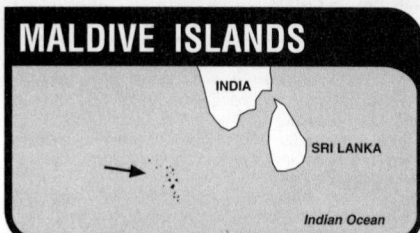

MALDIVE ISLANDS

The Republic of Maldives, an archipelago of 2,000 coral islets in the northern Indian Ocean 417 miles (671 km.) west of Ceylon, has an area of 116 sq. mi. (298 sq. km.) and a population of 189,000. Capital: Male. Fishing employs 95% of the male work force. Dried fish, copra and coir yarn are exported.

The Maldive Islands were visited by Arab traders and converted to Islam in 1153. After being harassed in the 16th and 17th centuries by Mopla pirates of the Malabar coast and Portuguese raiders, the Maldivians voluntarily placed themselves under the suzerainty of Ceylon. In 1887 the islands became an internally self-governing British protectorate and a nominal dependency of Ceylon. Traditionally a sultanate, the Maldives became a republic in 1953 but restored the sultanate in 1954. The Sultanate of the Maldive Islands attained complete internal and external autonomy on July 26, 1965, and on Nov. 11, 1968, again became a republic. The Maldives is a member of the Commonwealth of Nations.

MONETARY SYSTEM
100 Lari = 1 Rupee (Rufiyaa)

2ND REPUBLIC
STANDARD COINAGE
100 Laari = 1 Rufiyaa

KM# 68 LAARI
0.4700 g., Aluminum, 18.2 mm. **Obv:** Value **Rev:** Palm tree within circle **Edge:** Plain

Date	Mintage	F	VF	XF	Unc	BU
AH1423-2002	—	—	—	0.10	0.15	0.20

KM# 70 10 LAARI
1.9500 g., Aluminum, 23 mm. **Obv:** Value **Rev:** Maldivian sailing ship - Odi **Shape:** Scalloped

Date	Mintage	F	VF	XF	Unc	BU
AH1422-2001	—	—	—	0.10	0.20	0.30

KM# 73b RUFIYAA
6.5400 g., Nickel Plated Steel, 25.8 mm. **Obv:** Value **Obv. Legend:** REPUBLIC OF MALDIVES **Rev:** National arms **Edge:** Reeded

Date	Mintage	F	VF	XF	Unc	BU
AH1428-2007	—	—	—	0.50	2.00	3.00

KM# 88 2 RUFIYAA
11.7000 g., Brass, 25.47 mm. **Obv:** Value **Rev:** Pacific triton sea shell **Edge:** Reeded and lettered **Edge Lettering:** REPUBLIC OF MALDIVES

Date	Mintage	F	VF	XF	Unc	BU
AH1428-2007	—	—	—	2.25	5.50	7.50

MALTA

The Republic of Malta, an independent parliamentary democracy, is situated in the Mediterranean Sea between Sicily and North Africa. With the islands of Gozo and Comino, Malta has an area of 124 sq. mi. (320 sq. km.) and a population of 386,000. Capital: Valletta. Malta has no proven mineral resources, an agriculture insufficient to its needs, and a small, but expanding, manufacturing facility. Clothing, textile yarns and fabrics, and knitted wear are exported.

For more than 3,500 years Malta was ruled, in succession by Phoenicians, Carthaginians, Romans, Arabs, Normans, the Knights of Malta, France and Britain. Napoleon seized Malta by treachery in 1798. The French were ousted by a Maltese insurrection assisted by Britain, and in 1814 Malta, of its own free will, became a part of the British Empire. Malta obtained full independence in Sept., 1964; electing to remain within the Commonwealth with the British monarch as the nominal head of state.

Malta became a republic on Dec. 13, 1974, but remained a member of the Commonwealth of Nations. The president is Chief of State. The prime minister is the Head of Government.

RULER
British, until 1964

REPUBLIC
DECIMAL COINAGE
10 Mils = 1 Cent; 100 Cents = 1 Pound

KM# 5 2 MILS
0.9500 g., Aluminum, 20.3 mm. **Obv:** Maltese cross **Rev:** Value within 3/4 wreath **Shape:** Scalloped

Date	Mintage	F	VF	XF	Unc	BU
2005 In sets only	—	—	—	—	—	4.00
2006 In sets only	—	—	—	—	—	4.00
2007 In sets only	—	—	—	—	—	4.00

REFORM COINAGE
1982 - Present

10 Mils = 1 Cent; 100 Cents = 1 Lira = (Pound)

KM# 93 CENT
2.8100 g., Nickel-Brass, 18.51 mm. **Obv:** Crowned shield within sprigs **Rev:** Common Weasel (ballottra) below value **Edge:** Plain

Date	Mintage	F	VF	XF	Unc	BU
2001	—	—	0.40	0.50	1.00	—
2002 In sets only	—	—	—	—	1.00	—
2004	—	—	0.40	0.50	0.75	—
2005 In sets only	—	—	—	—	1.00	—
2006 In sets only	—	—	—	—	1.00	—
2007 In sets only	—	—	—	—	1.00	—

KM# 94 2 CENTS
2.2600 g., Copper-Nickel, 17.78 mm. **Obv:** Crowned shield within sprigs **Rev:** Zebbuga branch and value **Edge:** Reeded

Date	Mintage	F	VF	XF	Unc	BU
2002	—	—	0.75	1.00	1.25	—
2004	—	—	0.75	1.00	1.25	—
2005	—	—	—	—	1.25	—
2006 In sets only	—	—	—	—	1.25	—
2007 In sets only	—	—	—	—	1.25	—

KM# 95 5 CENTS
3.5100 g., Copper-Nickel, 19.78 mm. **Obv:** Crowned shield within sprigs **Rev:** Freshwater Crab (il-Qobru) and value **Edge:** Reeded

Date	Mintage	F	VF	XF	Unc	BU
2001	—	—	0.75	1.00	1.25	2.00
2005 In sets only	—	—	—	—	—	2.00
2006 In sets only	—	—	—	—	—	2.00
2007 In sets only	—	—	—	—	—	2.00

KM# 96 10 CENTS
5.0100 g., Copper-Nickel, 21.78 mm. **Obv:** Crowned shield within sprigs **Rev:** Lampuka and value **Edge:** Reeded

Date	Mintage	F	VF	XF	Unc	BU
2005	—	—	1.25	1.50	2.00	—
2006 In sets only	—	—	—	—	2.00	—
2007 In sets only	—	—	—	—	2.00	—

KM# 97 25 CENTS
6.1900 g., Copper-Nickel, 24.95 mm. **Obv:** Crowned shield within sprigs **Rev:** Ghirlanda flower and value

Date	Mintage	F	VF	XF	Unc	BU
2001	—	—	2.25	2.50	3.00	—
2005	—	—	2.25	2.50	3.00	—
2006 In sets only	—	—	—	—	3.00	—
2007 In sets only	—	—	—	—	3.00	—

KM# 98 50 CENTS
8.0000 g., Copper-Nickel, 27 mm. **Obv:** Crowned shield within sprigs **Rev:** Tulliera plant and value **Edge Lettering:** BANK CENTRALI TA' MALTA

Date	Mintage	F	VF	XF	Unc	BU
2001	—	—	2.50	5.00	10.00	—
2005 In sets only	—	—	—	—	10.00	—
2006 In sets only	—	—	—	—	10.00	—
2007 In sets only	—	—	—	—	10.00	—

KM# 99 LIRA
13.0000 g., Nickel, 29.82 mm. **Obv:** Crowned shield within sprigs **Rev:** Merill bird and value **Edge Lettering:** BANK CENTRALI TA' MALTA

Date	Mintage	F	VF	XF	Unc	BU
2005	—	—	—	4.50	6.50	12.00
2006 In sets only	—	—	—	—	—	12.00
2007 In sets only	—	—	—	—	—	12.00

KM# 117 5 LIRI
28.2800 g., 0.9250 Silver 0.8410 oz. ASW, 38.6 mm. **Obv:** Crowned shield within sprigs **Rev:** Enrico Mizzi right **Edge:** Reeded

Date	Mintage	F	VF	XF	Unc	BU
2001 Proof	2,000	Value: 80.00				

KM# 118 5 LIRI
28.2800 g., 0.9250 Silver 0.8410 oz. ASW, 38.6 mm. **Obv:** Crowned shield within sprigs **Rev:** Nicolo Isouard left **Edge:** Reeded

Date	Mintage	F	VF	XF	Unc	BU
2002 Proof	2,000	Value: 80.00				

KM# 120 5 LIRI
28.2800 g., 0.9250 Silver 0.8410 oz. ASW, 38.6 mm. **Obv:** Crowned shield within sprigs **Rev:** Sir Adriano Dingli as Grand Commander of the St. Michael and George Order **Edge:** Reeded

Date	Mintage	F	VF	XF	Unc	BU
2003 Proof	2,000	Value: 80.00				

KM# 121 5 LIRI
28.2800 g., 0.9250 Silver 0.8410 oz. ASW, 38.6 mm. **Obv:** Crowned shield within sprigs **Rev:** Painter Giuseppe Cali with palette **Edge:** Reeded

Date	Mintage	F	VF	XF	Unc	BU
2004 Proof	2,000	Value: 120				

KM# 138 5 LIRI
Silver, 39 mm. **Subject:** Zammit **Edge:** Reeded

Date	Mintage	F	VF	XF	Unc	BU
2006 Proof	—	Value: 25.00				

KM# 123 5 LIRI
28.2800 g., 0.9250 Silver 0.8410 oz. ASW, 38.61 mm. **Subject:** 450th Anniversary of Jean de la Valette appointed Grand master **Rev:** de la Vallete standing facing left, city of Valletta map at lower left

Date	Mintage	F	VF	XF	Unc	BU
ND(2007) Proof	25,000	Value: 75.00				

KM# 119 10 LIRI
1.2400 g., 0.9990 Gold 0.0398 oz. AGW, 13.92 mm. **Obv:** Crowned shield within sprigs **Rev:** Xprunara sailboat **Edge:** Reeded

Date	Mintage	F	VF	XF	Unc	BU
2002 Prooflike	Est. 25,000	—	—	—	—	130

KM# 122 25 LIRI
3.9940 g., 0.9167 Gold 0.1177 oz. AGW, 19.3 mm. **Subject:** Accession to the European Union **Obv:** Crowned shield within sprigs **Rev:** Maltese flag under European Union star circle **Edge:** Reeded

Date	Mintage	F	VF	XF	Unc	BU
2004 Proof	6,000	Value: 290				

KM# 124 25 LIRI
6.5000 g., 0.9200 Gold 0.1923 oz. AGW, 21 mm. **Subject:** 450th Anniversary Jean de la Valette Appointed as Grand Master **Rev:** de la Valette standing facing left, city of Valletta map at lower left

Date	Mintage	F	VF	XF	Unc	BU
ND(2007) Proof	2,500	Value: 375				

EURO COINAGE

KM# 125 EURO CENT
2.3000 g., Copper Plated Steel, 16.25 mm. **Obv:** Doorway **Rev:** Denomination and globe **Edge:** Plain

Date	Mintage	F	VF	XF	Unc	BU
2008	—	—	—	—	—	1.00
2009 In sets only	40,000	—	—	—	—	1.50
2010 In sets only	30,000	—	—	—	—	1.50
2011 In sets only	50,000	—	—	—	—	1.50

KM# 126 2 EURO CENT
3.0600 g., Copper Plated Steel, 18.75 mm. **Obv:** Doorway **Rev:** Denomination and globe **Edge:** Grooved

Date	Mintage	F	VF	XF	Unc	BU
2008	—	—	—	—	—	0.70
2009 In sets only	40,000	—	—	—	—	2.00
2010 In sets only	30,000	—	—	—	—	2.00
2011 In sets only	50,000	—	—	—	—	2.00

KM# 127 5 EURO CENT
3.9200 g., Copper Plated Steel, 21.25 mm. **Obv:** Doorway **Rev:** Denomination and globe

Date	Mintage	F	VF	XF	Unc	BU
2008	—	—	—	—	—	0.70
2009 In sets only	40,000	—	—	—	—	2.50
2010 In sets only	30,000	—	—	—	—	2.50
2011 In sets only	50,000	—	—	—	—	2.50

KM# 128 10 EURO CENT
4.1000 g., Brass, 19.75 mm. **Obv:** Crowned shield within wreath **Rev:** Value and relief map of Europe **Edge:** Notched

Date	Mintage	F	VF	XF	Unc	BU
2008	—	—	—	—	—	1.00
2009 In sets only	40,000	—	—	—	—	3.00
2010 In sets only	30,000	—	—	—	—	3.00
2011 In sets only	50,000	—	—	—	—	3.00

KM# 129 20 EURO CENT
5.7500 g., Brass, 22.25 mm. **Obv:** Crowned shield within wreath **Rev:** Denomination and Map of Western Europe **Edge:** Notched

Date	Mintage	F	VF	XF	Unc	BU
2008	—	—	—	—	—	1.50
2009 In sets only	40,000	—	—	—	—	4.00
2010 In sets only	30,000	—	—	—	—	4.00
2011 In sets only	50,000	—	—	—	—	4.00

KM# 130 50 EURO CENT
7.8000 g., Brass, 24.25 mm. **Obv:** Crowned shield within wreath **Rev:** Relief map of Western Europe **Edge:** Reeded

Date	Mintage	F	VF	XF	Unc	BU
2008	—	—	—	—	—	2.00
2009 In sets only	40,000	—	—	—	—	5.00
2010 In sets only	30,000	—	—	—	—	5.00
2011 In sets only	50,000	—	—	—	—	5.00

KM# 131 EURO
7.5000 g., Bi-Metallic Copper-Nickel center in Nickel-Brass ring, 23.25 mm. **Obv:** Maltese Cross **Rev:** Value and relief map of Europe **Edge:** Segmented reeding

Date	Mintage	F	VF	XF	Unc	BU
2008	—	—	—	—	—	4.00
2009 In sets only	—	—	—	—	—	5.00
2010 In sets only	—	—	—	—	—	5.00
2011 In sets only	—	—	—	—	—	5.00

KM# 132 2 EURO
8.5000 g., Bi-Metallic Nickel-Brass center in Copper-Nickel ring, 25.75 mm. **Obv:** Maltese Cross **Rev:** Value and Relief Map of Western Europe **Edge:** Reeded with 2s and Maltese Crosses

Date	Mintage	F	VF	XF	Unc	BU
2008	—	—	—	—	—	6.00
2009 In sets only	—	—	—	—	—	8.00
2010 In sets only	—	—	—	—	—	8.00
2011 In sets only	—	—	—	—	—	8.00

KM# 134 2 EURO
8.5000 g., Bi-Metallic Nickel-Brass center in Copper-Nickel ring, 25.75 mm. **Subject:** E.M.U., 10th Anniversary **Obv:** Stick figure and large E symbol **Rev:** Value and relief map of Western Europe **Edge:** Segmented reeding

Date	Mintage	F	VF	XF	Unc	BU
2009	7,000,000	—	—	—	—	6.00

KM# 144 2 EURO
8.5000 g., Bi-Metallic Nickel-Brass center in Copper-Nickel ring, 25.75 mm. **Subject:** First Elected Representatives of 1849

Date	Mintage	F	VF	XF	Unc	BU
2011	375,000	—	—	—	6.00	8.00
2011 Special Unc.	50,000	—	—	—	—	15.00
2011 Proof	5,000	Value: 25.00				

KM# 139 2 EURO
8.5000 g., Bi-Metallic Nickel-Brass center in Copper-Nickel ring, 25.75 mm. **Subject:** Euro Coinage, 10th Anniversary **Obv:** Euro symbol on globe, child-like rendering around

Date	Mintage	F	VF	XF	Unc	BU
2012	7,000,000	—	—	—	6.00	8.00
2012 Proof	—	Value: 25.00				

KM# 136 10 EURO
28.2800 g., 0.9250 Silver 0.8410 oz. ASW, 38.6 mm. **Subject:** Auberge de Castille **Rev:** Building tower

Date	Mintage	F	VF	XF	Unc	BU
2008 Proof	18,000	Value: 60.00				

KM# 133 10 EURO
28.2800 g., 0.9250 Silver 0.8410 oz. ASW, 38.6 mm. **Rev:** La Castellania, Merchant's Street, Valletta

Date	Mintage	F	VF	XF	Unc	BU
2009 Proof	15,000	Value: 60.00				

KM# 140 10 EURO
28.2800 g., 0.9250 Silver 0.8410 oz. ASW, 38.61 mm. **Subject:** Valetta - Auberge d'Italie **Obv:** Crowned shield **Rev:** Archetectural detail

Date	Mintage	F	VF	XF	Unc	BU
2010 Proof	12,500	Value: 65.00				

KM# 142 10 EURO
28.2800 g., 0.9250 Silver 0.8410 oz. ASW, 38.61 mm. **Subject:** Phoenicians in Malta **Obv:** Crowned shield **Rev:** Ancient Phoenician boat

Date	Mintage	F	VF	XF	Unc	BU
2011 Proof	10,000	Value: 75.00				

KM# 137 50 EURO
6.5000 g., 0.9160 Gold 0.1914 oz. AGW, 21 mm. **Subject:** Auberge de Castille **Rev:** Building tower

Date	Mintage	F	VF	XF	Unc	BU
2008 Proof	3,000	Value: 350				

KM# 135 50 EURO
6.5000 g., 0.9160 Gold 0.1914 oz. AGW, 21 mm. **Rev:** La Castellania, Merchant's Street, Valletta

Date	Mintage	F	VF	XF	Unc	BU
2009 Proof	3,000	Value: 350				

KM# 141 50 EURO
6.5000 g., 0.9160 Gold 0.1914 oz. AGW, 21 mm. **Subject:** Valetta - Auberge d'Italie **Obv:** Crowned shield **Rev:** Archetectural detail

Date	Mintage	F	VF	XF	Unc	BU
2010 Proof	3,000	Value: 400				

KM# 143 50 EURO
6.5000 g., 0.9160 Gold 0.1914 oz. AGW, 21 mm. **Subject:** Phoenicians in Malta **Obv:** Crowned shield **Rev:** Ancient Phoenician boat

Date	Mintage	F	VF	XF	Unc	BU
2011 Proof	2,000	Value: 375				

MINT SETS

KM#	Date	Mintage	Identification	Issue Price	Mkt Val
MS26	2005 (8)	—	KM#5, 93-99	—	35.00
MS27	2006 (8)	—	KM#5, 93-99	—	37.50
MS28	2007 (8)	—	KM#5, 93-99	—	45.00
MS29	2008 (8)	40,000	KM#125-132, wooden box	—	70.00
MS30	2008 (8)	30,000	KM#125-132, Malta Post and Lombard Bank card	—	45.00

PROOF SETS

KM#	Date	Mintage	Identification	Issue Price	Mkt Val
PS12	2008 (9)	40,000	KM#125-132, plus ingot	—	80.00

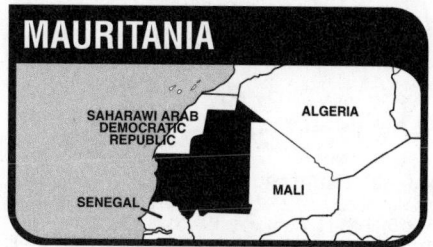

MAURITANIA

SAHARAWI ARAB DEMOCRATIC REPUBLIC
ALGERIA
SENEGAL
MALI

The Islamic Republic of Mauritania, located in northwest Africa bounded by Western Sahara, Mali, Algeria, Senegal and the Atlantic Ocean, has an area of 397,955 sq. mi.(1,030,700 sq. km.) and a population of 1.9 million. Capital: Nouakchott. The economy centers on herding, agriculture, fishing and mining. Iron ore, copper concentrates and fish products are exported.

On June 28, 1973, in a move designed to emphasize its non-alignment with France, Mauritania converted its currency from the old French-supported C.F.A. franc unit to a new unit called the Ouguiya.

MONETARY SYSTEM
5 Khoums = 1 Ouguiya

REPUBLIC
STANDARD COINAGE

KM# 6 OUGUIYA
3.6000 g., Copper-Nickel-Aluminum, 21 mm. **Obv:** National emblem divides date above value **Obv. Legend:** BANQUE CENTRALE DE MAURITANIE **Rev:** Star and crescent divide sprigs with legend below value, all within circle **Edge:** Reeded

Date	Mintage	F	VF	XF	Unc	BU
AH1423//2003	—	—	—	0.50	1.25	2.00

KM# 3 5 OUGUIYA
5.8800 g., Copper-Nickel-Aluminum, 25 mm. **Obv:** National emblem divides date above value **Obv. Legend:** BANQUE CENTRALE DE MAURITANIE **Rev:** Star and crescent divide sprigs below value within circle **Edge:** Plain

Date	Mintage	F	VF	XF	Unc	BU
AH1423//2003	—	—	—	1.75	3.50	5.00
AH1425//2004	—	—	—	1.75	3.50	5.00

KM# 3a 5 OUGUIYA
6.0000 g., Copper Plated Steel, 25 mm. **Obv:** National emblem divides date above value **Obv. Legend:** BANQUE CENTRALE DE MAURITANIE **Rev:** Star and crescent divides sprigs below value within circle **Edge:** Plain

Date	Mintage	F	VF	XF	Unc	BU
AH1425//2004	—	—	—	1.00	2.00	3.00
AH1426//2005	—	—	—	1.00	2.00	3.00
AH1430//2009	—	—	—	1.00	2.00	3.00

KM# 4 10 OUGUIYA
6.0000 g., Copper-Nickel, 25 mm. **Obv:** National emblem divides date above value **Obv. Legend:** BANQUE CENTRALE DE MAURITANIE **Rev:** Crescent and star divide sprigs below value within circle **Edge:** Reeded

Date	Mintage	F	VF	XF	Unc	BU
AH1423//2003	—	—	—	2.00	4.00	5.50
AH1425//2004	—	—	—	2.00	4.00	5.50

KM# 4a 10 OUGUIYA
5.8000 g., Nickel Plated Steel, 24.5 mm. **Obv:** National emblem divides date above value **Obv. Legend:** BANQUE CENTRALE DE MAURITANIE **Rev:** Crescent and star divides sprigs within value within circle **Edge:** Reeded

Date	Mintage	F	VF	XF	Unc	BU
AH1425//2004	—	—	—	1.25	3.00	4.50
AH1426//2005	—	—	—	1.25	3.00	4.50

KM# 5 20 OUGUIYA
8.0000 g., Copper-Nickel, 28 mm. **Obv:** National emblem divides date above value **Obv. Legend:** BANQUE CENTRALE DE MAURITANIE **Rev:** Star and crescent divide sprigs below value within circle **Edge:** Reeded

Date	Mintage	F	VF	XF	Unc	BU
AH1423//2003	—	—	—	3.00	6.00	8.00
AH1425//2004	—	—	—	3.00	6.00	8.00

KM# 5a 20 OUGUIYA
7.8000 g., Nickel Plated Steel, 28 mm. **Obv:** National emblem divides date above value **Obv. Legend:** BANQUE CENTRALE DE MAURITANIE **Rev:** Star and crescent divide sprigs below value within circle **Edge:** Reeded

Date	Mintage	F	VF	XF	Unc	BU
AH1425//2004	—	—	—	2.00	4.00	6.00
AH1426//2005	—	—	—	2.00	4.00	6.00
AH1430//2009	—	—	—	2.00	4.00	6.00

KM# 8 20 OUGUIYA
Bi-Metallic Copper-Nickel center in Brass ring **Obv:** Value within wreath **Rev:** National arms above value

Date	Mintage	F	VF	XF	Unc	BU
2009	—	—	—	—	6.00	7.50
2010	—	—	—	—	6.00	7.50

KM# 9 50 OUGUIYA
Bi-Metallic Nickel-Brass center in Copper-Nickel ring **Obv:** Value above wreath **Rev:** National arms above value

Date	Mintage	F	VF	XF	Unc	BU
2010	—	—	—	—	5.00	7.50

MAURITIUS

The Republic of Mauritius, is located in the Indian Ocean 500 miles (805 km.) east of Madagascar, has an area of 790 sq. mi. (1,860 sq. km.) and a population of 1 million. Capital: Port Louis. Sugar provides 90 percent of the export revenue.

Mauritius became independent on March 12, 1968. It is a member of the Commonwealth of Nations.

MONETARY SYSTEM
100 Cents = 1 Rupee

REPUBLIC

STANDARD COINAGE

KM# 52 5 CENTS
3.0000 g., Copper Plated Steel **Obv:** Value within beaded circle **Rev:** Bust of Sir Seewoosagur Ramgoolam 3/4 right

Date	Mintage	F	VF	XF	Unc	BU
2003	—	—	—	0.10	0.35	0.50
2004	—	—	—	0.10	0.35	0.50
2005	—	—	—	0.10	0.35	0.50
2007	—	—	—	0.10	0.35	0.50
2010	—	—	—	0.10	0.35	0.50

KM# 53 20 CENTS
3.0000 g., Nickel Plated Steel, 19 mm. **Obv:** Value within beaded circle **Rev:** Bust of Sir Seewoosagur Ramgoolam 3/4 right

Date	Mintage	F	VF	XF	Unc	BU
2001	—	—	—	0.20	0.50	0.75
2003	—	—	—	0.20	0.50	0.75
2004	—	—	—	0.20	0.50	0.75
2005	—	—	—	0.20	0.50	0.75
2007	—	—	—	0.20	0.50	0.75
2010	—	—	—	0.20	0.50	0.75

KM# 54 1/2 RUPEE
5.9000 g., Nickel Plated Steel, 23.6 mm. **Obv:** Stag left **Rev:** Bust of Sir Seewoosagur Ramgoolam 3/4 right

Date	Mintage	F	VF	XF	Unc	BU
2002	—	—	—	0.60	1.50	2.00
2003	—	—	—	0.60	1.50	2.00
2004	—	—	—	0.60	1.50	2.00
2005	—	—	—	0.60	1.50	2.00
2007	—	—	—	0.60	1.50	2.00
2009	—	—	—	0.60	1.50	2.00
2010	—	—	—	0.60	1.50	2.00

KM# 55 RUPEE
7.5000 g., Copper-Nickel, 26.6 mm. **Obv:** Shield divides date above value **Rev:** Bust of Sir Seewoosagur Ramgoolam 3/4 right **Edge:** Reeded

Date	Mintage	F	VF	XF	Unc	BU
2002	—	—	—	0.65	1.65	2.75
2004	—	—	—	0.65	1.65	2.75
2005	—	—	—	0.65	1.65	2.75
2007	—	—	—	0.65	1.65	2.75
2008	—	—	—	0.65	1.65	2.75
2009	—	—	—	0.65	1.65	2.75
2010	—	—	—	0.65	1.65	2.75

KM# 56 5 RUPEES
12.4000 g., Copper-Nickel, 31 mm. **Obv:** Value within palm trees **Rev:** Bust of Sir Seewoosagur Ramgoolam 3/4 right

Date	Mintage	F	VF	XF	Unc	BU
2009	—	—	—	—	3.00	5.00
2010	—	—	—	—	3.00	5.00

KM# 66 20 RUPEES
10.1000 g., Bi-Metallic Copper-Nickel center in Aluminum-Bronze ring, 27.96 mm. **Obv:** Modern tower **Rev:** Bust of Sir Seewoosagur Ramgoolam KT 3/4 right **Edge:** Reeded

Date	Mintage	F	VF	XF	Unc	BU
2007	—	—	—	2.00	5.00	7.00

KM# 65 100 RUPEES
36.5700 g., 0.9250 Silver 1.0875 oz. ASW, 43.9 mm. **Obv:** National arms, date below **Obv. Legend:** MAURITIUS ONE HUNDRED RUPEES **Rev:** Bust of Gandhi 3/4 right **Rev. Legend:** MAHATMA GANDHI CENTENARY OF ARRIVAL IN MAURITIUS **Edge:** Reeded

Date	Mintage	F	VF	XF	Unc	BU
2001 Proof	—	Value: 125				

KM# 67 1500 RUPEES
7.7800 g., 0.9990 Platinum 0.2499 oz. APW, 25 mm. **Subject:** Sir Seewoosagur Ramgoolan **Obv:** Portrait **Rev:** State House **Edge:** Plain

Date	Mintage	F	VF	XF	Unc	BU
2009 Proof	—	Value: 500				

MEXICO

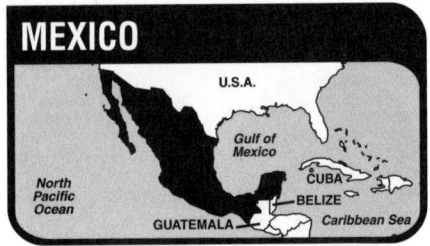

The United Mexican States, located immediately south of the United States has an area of 759,529 sq. mi. (1,967,183 sq. km.) and an estimated population of 100 million. Capital: Mexico City. The economy is based on agriculture, manufacturing and mining. Oil, cotton, silver, coffee, and shrimp are exported.

UNITED STATES
REFORM COINAGE
1 New Peso = 1000 Old Pesos; 100 centavos = 1 New Peso; 100 Centavos = 1 Peso

KM# 546 5 CENTAVOS
1.5800 g., Stainless Steel, 15.5 mm. **Obv:** National arms **Rev:** Large value **Edge:** Plain

Date	Mintage	F	VF	XF	Unc	BU
2001Mo	34,811,000	—	—	0.15	0.20	0.50
2002Mo	14,901,000	—	—	0.20	0.75	1.00

KM# 547 10 CENTAVOS
2.0800 g., Stainless Steel, 17 mm. **Obv:** National arms, eagle left **Rev:** Large value

Date	Mintage	F	VF	XF	Unc	BU
2001Mo	618,061,000	—	—	0.20	0.25	0.30
2002Mo	463,968,000	—	—	0.20	0.25	0.30
2003Mo	378,938,000	—	—	0.20	0.25	0.30
2004Mo	393,705,000	—	—	0.20	0.25	0.30
2005Mo	488,594,000	—	—	0.20	0.25	0.30
2006Mo	473,261,000	—	—	0.20	0.25	0.30
2007Mo	498,735,000	—	—	0.20	0.25	0.30
2008Mo	433,951,000	—	—	0.20	0.25	0.30

KM# 934 10 CENTAVOS
1.7500 g., Stainless Steel, 14 mm. **Obv:** National arms **Rev:** Large value **Edge:** Grooved

Date	Mintage	F	VF	XF	Unc	BU
2009Mo	90,968,000	—	—	—	0.10	0.25
2010Mo	—	—	—	—	0.10	0.25
2011Mo	—	—	—	—	0.10	0.25

KM# 548 20 CENTAVOS
3.0400 g., Aluminum-Bronze, 19.5 mm. **Obv:** National arms, eagle left **Rev:** Value and date within 3/4 wreath **Shape:** 12-sided

Date	Mintage	F	VF	XF	Unc	BU
2001Mo	234,360,000	—	—	0.25	0.35	0.40
2002Mo	229,256,000	—	—	0.25	0.35	0.40
2003Mo	149,518,000	—	—	0.25	0.35	0.40
2004Mo	174,351,000	—	—	0.25	0.35	0.40
2005Mo	204,426,000	—	—	0.25	0.35	0.40
2006Mo	234,263,000	—	—	0.25	0.35	0.40
2007Mo	234,301,000	—	—	0.25	0.35	0.40
2008Mo	214,313,000	—	—	0.25	0.35	0.40
2009Mo	41,167,000	—	—	0.25	0.35	0.40

KM# 935   20 CENTAVOS

2.2580 g., Stainless Steel, 15.3 mm. **Obv:** National arms **Rev:** Value and date within wreath **Edge:** Segmented reeding

Date	Mintage	F	VF	XF	Unc	BU
2009Mo	—	—	—	—	0.25	0.35
2010Mo	—	—	—	—	0.25	0.35
2011Mo	—	—	—	—	0.25	0.35

KM# 549   50 CENTAVOS

4.3900 g., Aluminum-Bronze, 22 mm. **Obv:** National arms, eagle left **Rev:** Value and date within 1/2 designed wreath **Shape:** 12-sided

Date	Mintage	F	VF	XF	Unc	BU
2001Mo	199,006,000	—	—	0.45	0.75	1.00
2002Mo	94,552,000	—	—	0.45	0.75	1.00
2003Mo	124,522,000	—	—	0.45	0.75	1.00
2004Mo	154,434,000	—	—	0.45	0.75	1.00
2005Mo	179,296,000	—	—	0.45	0.75	1.00
2006Mo	234,142,000	—	—	0.45	0.75	1.00
2007Mo	253,634,000	—	—	0.45	0.75	1.00
2008Mo	249,279,000	—	—	0.45	0.75	1.00
2009Mo	90,602,000	—	—	0.45	0.75	1.00

KM# 936   50 CENTAVOS

3.1030 g., Stainless Steel, 17 mm. **Obv:** National arms **Rev:** Value and date within wreath **Edge:** Reeded

Date	Mintage	F	VF	XF	Unc	BU
2009Mo	—	—	—	—	0.75	1.00
2010Mo	—	—	—	—	0.75	1.00
2011Mo	—	—	—	—	0.75	1.00

KM# 603   PESO

3.9500 g., Bi-Metallic Aluminum-Bronze center in Stainless Steel ring, 21 mm. **Obv:** National arms, eagle left within circle **Rev:** Value and date within circle **Note:** Similar to KM#550 but without N.

Date	Mintage	F	VF	XF	Unc	BU
2001Mo	208,576,000	—	—	—	1.25	2.75
2002Mo	119,514,000	—	—	—	1.25	2.75
2003Mo	169,320,000	—	—	—	1.25	2.75
2004Mo	208,611,000	—	—	—	1.25	2.75
2005Mo	253,923,000	—	—	—	1.25	2.75
2006Mo	289,834,000	—	—	—	1.25	2.75
2007Mo	368,408,000	—	—	—	1.25	2.75
2008Mo	363,878,000	—	—	—	1.25	2.75
2009Mo	239,229,000	—	—	—	1.25	2.75
2010Mo	209,313,000	—	—	—	0.75	1.25
2011Mo	—	—	—	—	0.75	1.00

KM# 604   2 PESOS

5.1900 g., Bi-Metallic Aluminum-Bronze center in Stainless Steel ring, 23 mm. **Obv:** National arms, eagle left within circle **Rev:** Value and date within center circle of assorted emblems **Note:** Similar to KM#551, but denomination without N.

Date	Mintage	F	VF	XF	Unc	BU
2001Mo	74,563,000	—	—	—	2.35	4.00
2002Mo	74,547,000	—	—	—	2.35	4.00
2003Mo	39,814,000	—	—	—	2.35	4.00
2004Mo	89,496,000	—	—	—	2.35	4.00
2005Mo	94,532,000	—	—	—	2.35	4.00
2006Mo	144,123,000	—	—	—	2.35	4.00
2007Mo	129,422,000	—	—	—	2.35	4.00
2008Mo	134,235,000	—	—	—	2.35	4.00
2009Mo	64,650,000	—	—	—	2.35	4.00

Date	Mintage	F	VF	XF	Unc	BU
2010Mo	34,878,000	—	—	—	1.00	1.50
2011Mo	—	—	—	—	1.00	1.50

KM# 651   5 PESOS

31.1710 g., 0.9990 Silver 1.0011 oz. ASW, 40 mm. **Series:** Endangered Wildlife **Obv:** National arms in center of past and present arms **Rev:** Manatee, value and date **Edge:** Reeded

Date	Mintage	F	VF	XF	Unc	BU
2001Mo	30,000	—	—	—	40.00	50.00

KM# 653   5 PESOS

31.1710 g., 0.9990 Silver 1.0011 oz. ASW, 40 mm. **Series:** Endangered Wildlife **Subject:** Aguila Arpia **Obv:** National arms in center of past and present arms **Rev:** Crowned Harpy Eagle perched on branch, value and date

Date	Mintage	F	VF	XF	Unc	BU
2001Mo	30,000	—	—	—	40.00	50.00

KM# 654   5 PESOS

31.1710 g., 0.9990 Silver 1.0011 oz. ASW, 40 mm. **Series:** Endangered Wildlife **Subject:** Oso Negro **Obv:** National arms in center of past and present arms **Rev:** Black bear, value and date

Date	Mintage	F	VF	XF	Unc	BU
2001Mo	30,000	—	—	—	40.00	50.00

KM# 658   5 PESOS

31.1710 g., 0.9990 Silver 1.0011 oz. ASW, 40 mm. **Series:** Endangered Wildlife **Obv:** National arms in center of past and present arms **Rev:** Jaguar, value and date

Date	Mintage	F	VF	XF	Unc	BU
2001Mo	30,000	—	—	—	40.00	50.00

KM# 659   5 PESOS

31.1710 g., 0.9990 Silver 1.0011 oz. ASW, 40 mm. **Series:** Endangered Wildlife **Obv:** National arms in center of past and present arms **Rev:** Prairie dog, value and date

Date	Mintage	F	VF	XF	Unc	BU
2001Mo	30,000	—	—	—	40.00	50.00

KM# 660   5 PESOS

31.1710 g., 0.9990 Silver 1.0011 oz. ASW, 40 mm. **Series:** Endangered Wildlife **Obv:** National arms in center of past and present arms **Rev:** Volcano rabbit, value and date

Date	Mintage	F	VF	XF	Unc	BU
2001Mo	30,000	—	—	—	40.00	50.00

KM# 605   5 PESOS

7.0700 g., Bi-Metallic Aluminum-Bronze center in Stainless Steel ring, 25.5 mm. **Obv:** National arms, eagle left within circle **Rev:** Value within circle **Note:** Similar to KM#552 but denomination without N.

Date	Mintage	F	VF	XF	Unc	BU
2001Mo	79,169,000	—	—	2.00	3.50	8.00
2002Mo	34,754,000	—	—	2.00	3.50	6.00
2003Mo	54,676,000	—	—	2.00	3.50	6.00
2004Mo	89,518,000	—	—	2.00	3.50	6.00
2005Mo	94,482,000	—	—	2.00	3.50	6.00
2006Mo	89,447,000	—	—	2.00	3.50	6.00
2007Mo	123,382,000	—	—	2.00	3.50	6.00
2008Mo	9,939,000	—	—	2.50	4.00	6.00
2009Mo	9,898,000	—	—	2.50	4.00	6.00
2010Mo	6,929,000	—	—	2.50	3.00	3.50
2011Mo	—	—	—	1.00	2.00	2.50

KM# 678   5 PESOS

27.0000 g., 0.9250 Silver 0.8029 oz. ASW, 40 mm. **Subject:** Ibero-America: Acapulco Galleon **Obv:** National arms in center of past and present arms **Rev:** Spanish galleon with Pacific Ocean background and trading scene in foreground **Edge:** Reeded

Date	Mintage	F	VF	XF	Unc	BU
2003Mo Proof	5,000	Value: 90.00				

KM# 765   5 PESOS

31.1035 g., 0.9250 Silver 0.9250 oz. ASW, 40 mm. **Subject:** Palacio de Bellas Artes **Obv:** Mexican Eagle and Snake **Rev:** Palace of Fine Arts **Edge:** Reeded

Date	Mintage	F	VF	XF	Unc	BU
2005Mo Proof	—	Value: 90.00				

KM# 769   5 PESOS

15.5518 g., 0.9990 Silver 0.4995 oz. ASW, 33 mm. **Subject:** Monetary Reform of 1905 **Obv:** Mexican Eagle and Snake **Rev:** Cap and rays coin design

Date	Mintage	F	VF	XF	Unc	BU
2005Mo Proof	1,505	Value: 45.00				

KM# 770   5 PESOS

31.1035 g., 0.9990 Silver 0.9990 oz. ASW, 40 mm. **Subject:** World Cup Soccer **Obv:** Mexican Eagle and Snake **Rev:** Mayan Pelota player and soccer ball

Date	Mintage	F	VF	XF	Unc	BU
2006Mo Proof	40,000	Value: 65.00				

KM# 805   5 PESOS

31.1050 g., 0.9250 Silver 0.9250 oz. ASW **Obv:** Eagle on cactus **Rev:** Mayan ball game

Date	Mintage	F	VF	XF	Unc	BU
2006Mo Proof	—	Value: 75.00				

KM# 894   5 PESOS

7.0700 g., Bi-Metallic Aluminum-bronze center in stainless steel ring, 25.5 mm. **Series:** Mexican Independence, 200th Anniversary **Subject:** Ignacio Rayon **Obv:** National Arms - Eagle left **Rev:** Ignacio Rayon bust left

Date	Mintage	F	VF	XF	Unc	BU
2008Mo	9,934,397	—	—	0.75	1.50	—
2008Mo Prooflike	4,267	—	—	—	—	7.50

KM# 895   5 PESOS

7.0700 g., Bi-Metallic Aluminum-bronze center in stainless steel ring, 25.5 mm. **Series:** Mexican Revolution 100th Anniversary **Subject:** Alvaro Obregon **Obv:** National Arms - Eagle left **Rev:** Alvaro Obregon bust 3/4 facing left

Date	Mintage	F	VF	XF	Unc	BU
2008Mo	9,948,722	—	—	0.75	1.50	—
2008Mo Prooflike	4,727	—	—	—	—	7.50

KM# 896   5 PESOS

7.0700 g., Bi-Metallic Aluminum-bronze center in stainless steel ring, 25.5 mm. **Series:** Mexican Independence 200th Anniversary **Subject:** Carlos Maria de Bustamante **Obv:** National Arms - Eagle left **Rev:** Carlos Maria de Bustamante bust left

Date	Mintage	F	VF	XF	Unc	BU
2008Mo	9,941,302	—	—	0.75	1.50	—
2008Mo Prooflike	4,852	—	—	—	—	7.50

KM# 897   5 PESOS

7.0700 g., Bi-Metallic Aluminum-bronze center in stainless steel ring, 25.5 mm. **Series:** Mexican Revolution 100th Anniversary **Subject:** Jose Vasconcelos **Obv:** National Arms - Eagle left **Rev:** Jose Vasconcelos bust left

Date	Mintage	F	VF	XF	Unc	BU
2008Mo	9,939,839	—	—	0.75	1.50	—
2008Mo Prooflike	4,767	—	—	—	—	7.50

KM# 898   5 PESOS

7.0700 g., Bi-Metallic Aluminum-bronze center in stainless steel ring, 25.5 mm. **Series:** Mexican Independence 200th Anniversary **Subject:** Francisco Xavier Mina **Obv:** National Arms - Eagle left **Rev:** Francisco Mina bust 3/4 facing left

Date	Mintage	F	VF	XF	Unc	BU
2008Mo	9,914,938	—	—	0.75	1.50	—
2008Mo Prooflike	4,523	—	—	—	—	7.50

KM# 899 5 PESOS
7.0700 g., Bi-Metallic Aluminum-bronze center in stainless steel ring, 25.5 mm. **Series:** Mexican Revolution 100th Anniversary **Subject:** Francisco Villa **Obv:** National Arms - Eagle left **Rev:** Francisco Villa on horseback left

Date	Mintage	F	VF	XF	Unc	BU
2008Mo	9,917,084	—	—	0.75	1.50	—
2008Mo Prooflike	4,866	—	—	—	—	7.50

KM# 900 5 PESOS
7.0700 g., Bi-Metallic Aluminum-Bronze center in Stainless Steel ring, 25.5 mm. **Series:** Mexican Independence 200th Anniversary **Subject:** Francisco Primode Verdad y Ramos **Obv:** National Arms - Eagle left **Rev:** Francisco Primode Verdad y Ramos bust right

Date	Mintage	F	VF	XF	Unc	BU
2008Mo	9,937,000	—	—	0.75	1.50	—
2008Mo Prooflike	3,279	—	—	—	—	7.50

KM# 901 5 PESOS
7.0700 g., Bi-Metallic Aluminum-Bronze center in Stainless Steel ring, 25.5 mm. **Series:** Mexican Revolution 100th Anniversary **Subject:** Heriberto Jara **Obv:** National Arms - Eagle left **Rev:** Heriberto Jara bust 3/4 left

Date	Mintage	F	VF	XF	Unc	BU
2008Mo	9,936,333	—	—	0.75	1.50	—
2008Mo Prooflike	4,870	—	—	—	—	7.50

KM# 902 5 PESOS
7.0700 g., Bi-Metallic Aluminum-Bronze center in Stainless Steel ring, 25.5 mm. **Series:** Mexican Independence 200th Anniversary **Subject:** Mariano Matamoros **Obv:** National Arms - Eagle left **Rev:** Mariano Matamoros bust 3/4 facing right

Date	Mintage	F	VF	XF	Unc	BU
2008Mo	9,947,802	—	—	0.75	1.50	—
2008Mo Prooflike	4,820	—	—	—	—	7.50

KM# 903 5 PESOS
7.0700 g., Bi-Metallic Aluminum-Bronze center Stainless Steel ring, 25.5 mm. **Series:** Mexican Revolution 100th Anniversary **Subject:** Ricardo Magon **Obv:** National Arms - Eagle left **Rev:** Ricardo Magon bust right

Date	Mintage	F	VF	XF	Unc	BU
2008Mo	9,940,278	—	—	0.75	1.50	—
2008Mo Prooflike	4,690	—	—	—	—	7.50

KM# 904 5 PESOS
7.0700 g., Bi-Metallic Aluminum-Bronze center in Stainless Steel ring, 25.5 mm. **Series:** Mexican Independence 200th Anniversary **Subject:** Miguel Remos Arizpe **Obv:** National Arms - Eagle left **Rev:** Miguel Arizpe bust right

Date	Mintage	F	VF	XF	Unc	BU
2008Mo	9,927,433	—	—	0.75	1.50	—
2008Mo Prooflike	4,863	—	—	—	—	7.50

KM# 905 5 PESOS
7.0700 g., Bi-Metallic Aluminum-Bronze center in Stainless Steel ring, 25.5 mm. **Series:** Mexican Revolution 100th Anniversary **Subject:** Francisco Mugica **Obv:** National arms, eagle left **Rev:** Francisco Mugica bust 3/4 facing left

Date	Mintage	F	VF	XF	Unc	BU
2008Mo	9,926,537	—	—	0.75	1.50	—
2008Mo Prooflike	4,588	—	—	—	—	7.50

KM# 906 5 PESOS
7.0700 g., Bi-Metallic Aluminum-Bronze center in Stainless Steel ring, 25.5 mm. **Series:** Mexican Independence 200th Anniversary **Subject:** Hermenegildo Galeana **Obv:** National Arms, eagle left **Rev:** Hermenegildo Galeana bust 3/4 facing left

Date	Mintage	F	VF	XF	Unc	BU
2008Mo	9,935,901	—	—	0.75	1.50	—
2008Mo Prooflike	4,966	—	—	—	—	7.50

KM# 907 5 PESOS
7.0700 g., Bi-Metallic Aluminum-Bronze center in Stainless Steel ring, 25.5 mm. **Series:** Mexican Revolution, 100th Anniversary **Subject:** Filomeno Mata **Obv:** National arms, eagle left **Rev:** Filomeno Mata bust facing.

Date	Mintage	F	VF	XF	Unc	BU
2009Mo	9,935,689	—	—	0.75	1.50	—
2009Mo Prooflike	4,920	—	—	—	—	7.50

KM# 908 5 PESOS
7.0700 g., Bi-Metallic Aluminum-Bronze cetner in Stainless Steel ring, 25.5 mm. **Series:** Mexican Independence 200th Anniversary **Subject:** Jose Maria Cos **Obv:** National arms, eagle left. **Rev:** Jose Maria Cos bust right

Date	Mintage	F	VF	XF	Unc	BU
2009Mo	9,935,040	—	—	0.75	1.50	—
2009Mo Prooflike	4,950	—	—	—	—	7.50

KM# 909 5 PESOS
7.0700 g., Bi-Metallic Aluminum-Bronze center in Stainless Steel ring, 25.5 mm. **Series:** Mexican Revolution 100th Anniversary **Subject:** Carmen Serdan **Obv:** National Amrs, Eagle left **Rev:** Carmen Serdan bust facing

Date	Mintage	F	VF	XF	Unc	BU
2009Mo	7,160,841	—	—	0.75	1.50	—
2009Mo Prooflike	4,787	—	—	—	—	7.50

KM# 910 5 PESOS
7.0700 g., Bi-Metallic Aluminum-Bronze center in Stainless Steel ring, 25.5 mm. **Series:** Mexican Independence, 200th Anniversary **Subject:** Pedro Moreno **Obv:** National arms, eagle left **Rev:** Pedro Moreno bust 3/4 right

Date	Mintage	F	VF	XF	Unc	BU
2009Mo	6,942,480	—	—	0.75	1.50	—
2009Mo Prooflike	4,940	—	—	—	—	7.50

KM# 911 5 PESOS
7.0700 g., Bi-Metallic Aluminum-Bronze center in Stainless Steel ring, 25.5 mm. **Series:** Mexican Revolution 100th Anniversary **Subject:** Andres Molina Enriquez **Obv:** National arms, eagle left **Rev:** Andres Enriquez, bust 3/4 right

Date	Mintage	F	VF	XF	Unc	BU
2009Mo	6,942,763	—	—	0.75	1.50	—
2009Mo Prooflike	4,666	—	—	—	—	7.50

KM# 912 5 PESOS
7.0700 g., Bi-Metallic Aluminum-Bronze center in Stainless Steel ring, 25.5 mm. **Series:** Mexican Independence, 200th Anniversary **Subject:** Agustin de Iturbide **Obv:** National arms, eagle left **Rev:** Agustin de Iturbide bust left

Date	Mintage	F	VF	XF	Unc	BU
2009Mo	6,944,222	—	—	0.75	1.50	—
2009Mo Prooflike	4,838	—	—	—	—	7.50

KM# 913 5 PESOS
7.0700 g., Bi-Metallic Aluminumn-Bronze center in Stainless Steel ring, 25.5 mm. **Series:** Mexican Revolution 100th Anniversary **Subject:** Luis Cabrera **Obv:** National Arms, eagle left **Rev:** Luis Cabrera bust 3/4 facing front

Date	Mintage	F	VF	XF	Unc	BU
2009Mo	6,902,593	—	—	0.75	1.50	—
2009Mo Prooflike	4,656	—	—	—	—	7.50

KM# 914 5 PESOS
7.0700 g., Bi-Metallic Aluminum-Bronze center Stainless Steel ring, 25.5 mm. **Series:** Mexican Independence, 200th Anniversary **Subject:** Nicolas Bravo **Obv:** National Arms, Eagle left **Rev:** Nicolas Bravo bust 3/4 facing left

Date	Mintage	F	VF	XF	Unc	BU
2009Mo	6,960,174	—	—	0.75	0.50	—
2009Mo Prooflike	4,780	—	—	—	—	7.50

KM# 915 5 PESOS
7.0700 g., Bi-Metallic Aluminum-bronze center in Stainless steel ring, 25.5 mm. **Series:** Mexican Revolution 100th Anniversary **Subject:** Eulalio Gutierrez **Obv:** National Arms, eagle left **Rev:** Eulalio Gutierrez bust 3/4 right

Date	Mintage	F	VF	XF	Unc	BU
2009Mo	6,908,760	—	—	0.75	1.50	—
2009Mo Prooflike	4,862	—	—	—	—	7.50

KM# 916 5 PESOS
7.0700 g., Bi-Metallic Aluminum-Bronze center in Stainless Steel ring, 25.5 mm. **Series:** Mexican Independence 200th Anniversary **Subject:** Servando de Mier **Obv:** National Arms, eagle left **Rev:** Servando de Mier bust left

Date	Mintage	F	VF	XF	Unc	BU
2009Mo	6,937,421	—	—	0.75	1.50	—
2009Mo Prooflike	4,675	—	—	—	—	7.50

KM# 917 5 PESOS
7.0700 g., Bi-Metallic Aluminum-Bronze center in Stainless Steel ring, 25.5 mm. **Series:** Mexican Revolution 100th Anniversary **Subject:** Otilio Montano **Obv:** National Arms, eagle left **Rev:** Otilio Montano bust left

Date	Mintage	F	VF	XF	Unc	BU
2009Mo	6,890,052	—	—	0.75	1.50	—
2009Mo Prooflike	4,923	—	—	—	—	7.50

KM# 918 5 PESOS
7.0700 g., Bi-Metallic Aluminum-Bronze center in Stainless Steel ring, 25.5 mm. **Series:** Mexican Revolution 100th Anniversary **Subject:** Belisario Dominquez **Obv:** National Arms, eagle left **Rev:** Belisario Dominquez bust 3/4 left

Date	Mintage	F	VF	XF	Unc	BU
2009Mo	6,926,606	—	—	0.75	1.50	—
2009Mo Prooflike	4,773	—	—	—	—	7.50

KM# 919 5 PESOS
7.0700 g., Bi-Metallic Aluminum-Bronze center in Stainless Steel ring, 25.5 mm. **Series:** Mexican Independence 200th Anniversary **Subject:** Leona Vicario **Obv:** National Arms, eagle left **Rev:** Leona Vicario bust left

Date	Mintage	F	VF	XF	Unc	BU
2009Mo	6,937,872	—	—	0.75	1.50	—
2009Mo Prooflike	4,730	—	—	—	—	7.50

KM# 920 5 PESOS
7.0700 g., Bi-Metallic Aluminumn-Bronze center in Stainless Steel ring, 25.5 mm. **Series:** Mexican Independence 200th Anniversary **Subject:** Miguel Hidalgo y Costilla **Obv:** National Arms, eagle left **Rev:** Hildalgo bust

Date	Mintage	F	VF	XF	Unc	BU
2010Mo	6,932,486	—	—	0.75	1.50	—
2010Mo Prooflike	4,763	—	—	—	—	7.50

KM# 922   5 PESOS
7.0700 g., Bi-Metallic Aluminum-Bronze center in Stainless Steel ring, 25.5 mm.   **Series:** Mexican Revolution 100th Anniversary **Subject:** Francisco I. Madero **Rev:** Francisco I. Madero head facing 1/4 left

Date	Mintage	F	VF	XF	Unc	BU
2010Mo	6,930,998	—	—	0.75	1.50	—
2010Mo Prooflike	4,750	—	—	—	—	7.50

KM# 923   5 PESOS
7.0700 g., Bi-Metallic Aluminum-Bronze center in Stainless Steel ring, 25.5 mm.   **Series:** Mexican Independence 200th Anniversary **Subject:** Jose Maria Morelos y Pavon **Rev:** Jose Maria Morelos y Pavon head facing 1/2 right

Date	Mintage	F	VF	XF	Unc	BU
2010Mo	6,927,961	—	—	0.75	1.50	—
2010Mo Prooflike	4,725	—	—	—	—	7.50

KM# 924   5 PESOS
7.0700 g., Bi-Metallic Aluminum-Bronze center in Stainless Steel ring, 25.5 mm.   **Series:** Mexican Revolution 100th Anniversary **Subject:** Emiliano Zapata **Rev:** Emiliano Zapata head 1/4 facing left

Date	Mintage	F	VF	XF	Unc	BU
2010Mo	6,921,306	—	—	0.75	1.50	—
2010Mo Prooflike	4,810	—	—	—	—	7.50

KM# 925   5 PESOS
7.0700 g., Bi-Metallic Aluminum-Bronze center in Stainless Steel ring, 25.5 mm.   **Series:** Mexican Independence 200th Anniversary **Subject:** Vicente Guerrero **Rev:** Vicente Guerrero head facing 1/4 left

Date	Mintage	F	VF	XF	Unc	BU
2010Mo	6,929,709	—	—	0.75	1.50	—
2010Mo Prooflike	4,716	—	—	—	—	7.50

KM# 926   5 PESOS
7.0700 g., Bi-Metallic Aluminum-Bronze center in Stainless Steel ring, 25.5 mm.   **Series:** Mexican Revolution 100th Anniversary **Subject:** Venustiano Carranza **Rev:** Venustiano Carranza head 1/4 facing left

Date	Mintage	F	VF	XF	Unc	BU
2010Mo	6,936,993	—	—	0.75	1.50	—
2010Mo Prooflike	4,837	—	—	—	—	7.50

KM# 927   5 PESOS
7.0700 g., Bi-Metallic Aluminum-Bronze center in Stainless Steel ring, 25.5 mm.   **Series:** Mexican Independence 200th Anniversary **Subject:** Ignacio Allende **Rev:** Ignacio Allende head facing 1/2 left

Date	Mintage	F	VF	XF	Unc	BU
2010Mo	6,939,957	—	—	0.75	1.50	—
2010Mo Prooflike	4,752	—	—	—	—	7.50

KM# 928   5 PESOS
7.0700 g., Bi-Metallic Aluminum-Bronze center in Stainless Steel ring, 25.5 mm.   **Series:** Mexican Revolution 100th Anniversary **Subject:** La Soldadera **Rev:** Female soldier's head facing 1/4 left

Date	Mintage	F	VF	XF	Unc	BU
2010Mo	6,936,336	—	—	0.75	1.50	—
2010Mo Prooflike	4,730	—	—	—	—	7.50

KM# 929   5 PESOS
7.0700 g., Bi-Metallic Aluminum-Bronze center in Stainless Steel ring, 25.5 mm.   **Series:** Mexican Indpendence 200th Anniversary **Subject:** Guadalupe Victoria **Rev:** Guadalupe Victoria head 1/4 facing left

Date	Mintage	F	VF	XF	Unc	BU
2010Mo	6,935,638	—	—	0.75	1.50	—
2010Mo Prooflike	4,767	—	—	—	—	7.50

KM# 930   5 PESOS
7.0700 g., Bi-Metallic Aluminum-Bronze center in Stainless Steel ring, 25.5 mm.   **Series:** Mexican Revolution 100th Anniversary **Subject:** Jose Mario Pino Suarez **Rev:** Jose Mario Pino Suarez head

Date	Mintage	F	VF	XF	Unc	BU
2010Mo	6,930,255	—	—	0.75	1.50	—
2010Mo Prooflike	4,752	—	—	—	—	7.50

KM# 931   5 PESOS
7.0700 g., Bi-Metallic Aluminum-Bronze center in Stainless Steel ring, 25.5 mm.   **Series:** Mexican Independence 200th Anniversary **Subject:** Josefa Ortiz de Dominguez **Rev:** Josefa Ortiz de Dominguez head right

Date	Mintage	F	VF	XF	Unc	BU
2010Mo	6,936,400	—	—	0.75	1.50	—
2010Mo Prooflike	4,743	—	—	—	—	7.50

KM# 636   10 PESOS
10.3300 g., Bi-Metallic Copper-Nickel-Zinc center in Aluminum-Bronze ring, 28 mm.   **Series:** Millennium **Obv:** National arms **Obv. Legend:** ESTADOS UNIDOS MEXICANOS **Rev:** Aztec carving **Edge Lettering:** ANO (year) repeated 3 times

Date	Mintage	F	VF	XF	Unc	BU
2001Mo	44,768,000	—	—	3.00	4.00	8.00

KM# 616   10 PESOS
10.3300 g., Bi-Metallic Copper-Nickel-Zinc center in Aluminum-Bronze ring, 28 mm.   **Obv:** National arms **Obv. Legend:** ESTADOS UNIDOS MEXICANOS **Rev:** Aztec design

Date	Mintage	F	VF	XF	Unc	BU
2002Mo	44,721,000	—	—	2.50	4.00	8.00
2004Mo	74,739,000	—	—	2.50	4.00	8.00
2005Mo	64,616,000	—	—	2.50	4.00	8.00
2006Mo	84,575,000	—	—	2.50	4.00	8.00
2007Mo	89,678,000	—	—	2.50	4.00	8.00
2008Mo	64,744,000	—	—	2.50	4.00	8.00
2009Mo	54,812,000	—	—	2.00	3.00	6.00
2010Mo	54,822,000	—	—	2.00	3.00	6.00
2011Mo		—	—		2.00	3.50

KM# 679   10 PESOS
31.1040 g., 0.9990 Silver 0.9990 oz. ASW, 39.9 mm.   **Series:** First **Subject:** 180th Anniversary of Federation **Obv:** National arms **Obv. Legend:** ESTADOS UNIDOS MEXICANOS **Rev:** State Arms **Rev. Legend:** ESTADO DE ZACATECAS **Edge:** Reeded

Date	Mintage	F	VF	XF	Unc	BU
2003Mo Proof	10,000	Value: 70.00				

KM# 680   10 PESOS
31.1040 g., 0.9990 Silver 0.9990 oz. ASW, 39.9 mm.   **Series:** First **Subject:** 180th Anniversary of Federation **Obv:** National arms **Obv. Legend:** ESTADOS UNIDOS MEXICANOS **Rev:** State arms **Rev. Legend:** ESTADO DE YUCATÁN **Edge:** Reeded

Date	Mintage	F	VF	XF	Unc	BU
2003Mo Proof	10,000	Value: 70.00				

KM# 681   10 PESOS
31.1040 g., 0.9990 Silver 0.9990 oz. ASW, 39.9 mm.   **Series:** First **Subject:** 180th Anniversary of Federation **Obv:** National arms **Obv. Legend:** ESTADOS UNIDOS MEXICANOS **Rev:** State arms **Rev. Legend:** ESTADO DE VERACRUZ-LLAVE **Edge:** Reeded

Date	Mintage	F	VF	XF	Unc	BU
2003Mo Proof	10,000	Value: 70.00				

KM# 682   10 PESOS
31.1040 g., 0.9990 Silver 0.9990 oz. ASW, 39.9 mm.   **Series:** First **Subject:** 180th Anniversary of Frederation **Obv:** National arms **Obv. Legend:** ESTADOS UNIDOS MEXICANOS **Rev:** State arms **Rev. Legend:** ESTADO DE TLAXCALA **Edge:** Reeded

Date	Mintage	F	VF	XF	Unc	BU
2003Mo Proof	10,000	Value: 70.00				

KM# 683   10 PESOS
31.1040 g., 0.9990 Silver 0.9990 oz. ASW, 39.9 mm.   **Series:** First **Subject:** 180th Anniversary of Federation **Obv:** National arms **Obv. Legend:** ESTADOS UNIDOS MEXICANOS **Rev:** State arms **Rev. Legend:** ESTADO DE TAMAULIPAS **Edge:** Reeded

Date	Mintage	F	VF	XF	Unc	BU
2004Mo Proof	10,000	Value: 70.00				

KM# 684   10 PESOS
31.1040 g., 0.9990 Silver 0.9990 oz. ASW, 39.9 mm.   **Series:** First **Subject:** 180th Anniversary of Federation **Obv:** National arms **Obv. Legend:** ESTADOS UNIDOS DE MEXICANOS **Rev:** State arms **Rev. Legend:** ESTADO DE TABASCO **Edge:** Reeded

Date	Mintage	F	VF	XF	Unc	BU
2004Mo Proof	10,000	Value: 70.00				

KM# 685   10 PESOS
31.1040 g., 0.9990 Silver 0.9990 oz. ASW, 39.9 mm.   **Series:** First **Subject:** 180th Anniversary of Federation **Obv:** National arms **Obv. Legend:** ESTADOS UNIDOS MEXICANOS **Rev:** State arms **Rev. Legend:** ESTADO DE SONORA **Edge:** Reeded **Note:** Mexican States: Sonora

Date	Mintage	F	VF	XF	Unc	BU
2004Mo Proof	10,000	Value: 70.00				

KM# 686   10 PESOS
31.1040 g., 0.9990 Silver 0.9990 oz. ASW, 39.9 mm.   **Series:** First **Subject:** 180th Anniversary of Federation **Obv:** National arms **Obv. Legend:** ESTADOS UNIDOS DE MEXICANOS **Rev:** State arms **Rev. Legend:** ESTADO DE SINALOA **Edge:** Reeded **Note:** Mexican States: Sinaloa

Date	Mintage	F	VF	XF	Unc	BU
2004Mo Proof	10,000	Value: 70.00				

KM# 687   10 PESOS
31.1040 g., 0.9990 Silver 0.9990 oz. ASW, 39.9 mm.   **Series:** First **Subject:** 180th Anniversary of Federation **Obv:** National arms **Obv. Legend:** ESTADOS UNIDOS MEXICANOS **Rev:** State arms **Rev. Legend:** ESTADO DE SAN LUIS POTOSÍ **Edge:** Reeded

Date	Mintage	F	VF	XF	Unc	BU
2004Mo Proof	10,000	Value: 70.00				

KM# 735   10 PESOS
31.1040 g., 0.9990 Silver 0.9990 oz. ASW, 39.9 mm.   **Series:** First **Subject:** 180th Anniversary of Federation **Obv:** National arms **Obv. Legend:** ESTADOS UNIDOS MEXICANOS **Rev:** State arms **Rev. Legend:** ESTADO DE QUINTANA ROO

Date	Mintage	F	VF	XF	Unc	BU
2004 Proof	10,000	Value: 70.00				

KM# 733 10 PESOS
31.1040 g., 0.9990 Silver 0.9990 oz. ASW, 39.9 mm. **Series:** First **Subject:** 180th Anniversary of Federation **Obv:** National arms **Obv. Legend:** ESTADOS UNIDOS MEXICANOS **Rev:** State arms **Rev. Legend:** ESTADO DE QUERÉTARO ARTEAGA **Edge:** Reeded

Date	Mintage	F	VF	XF	Unc	BU
2004 Proof	10,000	Value: 70.00				

KM# 737 10 PESOS
31.1040 g., 0.9990 Silver 0.9990 oz. ASW, 39.9 mm. **Series:** First **Subject:** 180th Anniversary of Federation **Obv:** National arms **Obv. Legend:** ESTADOS UNIDOS MEXICANOS **Rev:** State arms **Rev. Legend:** ESTADO DE PUEBLA **Edge:** Reeded

Date	Mintage	F	VF	XF	Unc	BU
2004Mo Proof	10,000	Value: 70.00				

KM# 739 10 PESOS
31.1040 g., 0.9990 Bi-Metallic 0.9990 oz., 39.9 mm. **Series:** First **Subject:** 180th Anniversary of Federation **Obv:** National arms **Obv. Legend:** ESTADOS UNIDOS MEXICANOS **Rev:** State arms **Rev. Legend:** ESTADO DE OAXACA **Edge:** Reeded

Date	Mintage	F	VF	XF	Unc	BU
2004Mo Proof	10,000	Value: 70.00				

KM# 741 10 PESOS
31.1040 g., 0.9990 Silver 0.9990 oz. ASW, 39.9 mm. **Series:** First **Subject:** 180th Anniversary of Federation **Obv:** National arms **Obv. Legend:** ESTADOS UNIDOS MEXICANOS **Rev:** State arms **Rev. Legend:** ESTADO DE NUEVO LEÓN **Edge:** Reeded

Date	Mintage	F	VF	XF	Unc	BU
2004Mo Proof	10,000	Value: 70.00				

KM# 743 10 PESOS
31.1040 g., 0.9990 Silver 0.9990 oz. ASW, 39.9 mm. **Series:** First **Subject:** 180th Anniversary of Federation **Obv:** National arms **Obv. Legend:** ESTADOS UNIDOS MEXICANOS **Rev:** State arms **Rev. Legend:** ESTADO DE NAYARIT **Edge:** Reeded

Date	Mintage	F	VF	XF	Unc	BU
2004Mo Proof	10,000	Value: 70.00				

KM# 745 10 PESOS
31.1040 g., 0.9990 Silver 0.9990 oz. ASW, 39.9 mm. **Series:** First **Subject:** 180th Anniversary of Federation **Obv:** National arms **Obv. Legend:** ESTADOS UNIDOS MEXICANOS **Rev:** State arms **Rev. Legend:** ESTADO DE MORELOS **Edge:** Reeded

Date	Mintage	F	VF	XF	Unc	BU
2004Mo Proof	10,000	Value: 70.00				

KM# 796 10 PESOS
31.1040 g., 0.9990 Silver 0.9990 oz. ASW, 39.9 mm. **Series:** First **Subject:** 180th Anniversary of Federation **Obv:** National arms **Obv. Legend:** ESTADOS UNIDOS MEXICANOS **Rev:** State arms **Rev. Legend:** ESTADO DE MICHOACÁN DE OCAMPO **Edge:** Reeded

Date	Mintage	F	VF	XF	Unc	BU
2004Mo Proof	10,000	Value: 70.00				

KM# 747 10 PESOS
31.1040 g., 0.9990 Silver 0.9990 oz. ASW, 39.9 mm. **Series:** First **Subject:** 180th Anniversary of Federation **Obv:** National arms **Obv. Legend:** ESTADOS UNIDOS MEXICANOS **Rev:** State arms **Rev. Legend:** ESTADO DE MÉXICO **Edge:** Reeded

Date	Mintage	F	VF	XF	Unc	BU
2004Mo Proof	10,000	Value: 70.00				

KM# 749 10 PESOS
31.1040 g., 0.9990 Silver 0.9990 oz. ASW, 39.9 mm. **Series:** First **Subject:** 180th Anniversary of Federation **Obv:** National arms **Obv. Legend:** ESTADOS UNIDOS MEXICANOS **Rev:** State arms **Rev. Legend:** ESTADO DE JALISCO **Edge:** Reeded

Date	Mintage	F	VF	XF	Unc	BU
2004Mo Proof	10,000	Value: 70.00				

KM# 766 10 PESOS
31.1035 g., 0.9990 Silver 0.9990 oz. ASW, 40 mm. **Subject:** Cervantes Festival **Obv:** Mexican Eagle and Snake **Rev:** Don Quixote **Edge:** Reeded

Date	Mintage	F	VF	XF	Unc	BU
2005Mo Proof	1,205	Value: 75.00				

KM# 768 10 PESOS
31.1035 g., 0.9990 Silver 0.9990 oz. ASW, 40 mm. **Subject:** 470th Anniversary - Mexico City Mint **Obv:** Mexican Eagle and Snake **Rev:** Antique coin press

Date	Mintage	F	VF	XF	Unc	BU
2005Mo Proof	2,005	Value: 65.00				

KM# 711 10 PESOS
31.1040 g., 0.9990 Silver 0.9990 oz. ASW, 39.9 mm. **Series:** First **Subject:** 180th Anniversary of Federation **Obv:** National arms **Obv. Legend:** ESTADOS UNIDOS MEXICANOS **Rev:** State arms **Rev. Legend:** ESTADO DE HIDALGO **Edge:** Reeded

Date	Mintage	F	VF	XF	Unc	BU
2005Mo Proof	10,000	Value: 70.00				

KM# 710 10 PESOS
31.1040 g., 0.9990 Silver 0.9990 oz. ASW, 39.9 mm. **Series:** First **Subject:** 180th Anniversary of Federation **Obv:** National arms **Obv. Legend:** ESTADOS UNIDOS MEXICANOS **Rev:** State arms **Rev. Legend:** ESTADO DE GUERRERO **Edge:** Reeded

Date	Mintage	F	VF	XF	Unc	BU
2005Mo Proof	10,000	Value: 70.00				

KM# 709 10 PESOS
31.1040 g., 0.9990 Silver 0.9990 oz. ASW, 39.9 mm. **Series:** First **Subject:** 180th Anniversary of Federation **Obv:** National arms **Obv. Legend:** ESTADOS UNIDOS MEXICANOS **Rev:** State arms **Rev. Legend:** ESTADO DE GUANAJUATO **Edge:** Reeded

Date	Mintage	F	VF	XF	Unc	BU
2005Mo Proof	10,000	Value: 70.00				

KM# 708 10 PESOS
31.1040 g., 0.9990 Silver 0.9990 oz. ASW, 39.9 mm. **Series:** First **Subject:** 180th Anniversary of Federation **Obv:** National arms **Obv. Legend:** ESTADOS UNIDOS MEXICANOS **Rev:** State arms **Rev. Legend:** ESTADO DE DURANGO **Edge:** Reeded

Date	Mintage	F	VF	XF	Unc	BU
2005Mo Proof	10,000	Value: 70.00				

KM# 707 10 PESOS
31.1040 g., 0.9990 Silver 0.9990 oz. ASW, 39.9 mm. **Series:** First **Subject:** 180th Anniversary of Federation **Obv:** National arms **Obv. Legend:** ESTADOS UNIDOS MEXICANOS **Rev:** Federal District arms **Rev. Legend:** DISTRITO FEDERAL **Edge:** Reeded

Date	Mintage	F	VF	XF	Unc	BU
2005Mo Proof	10,000	Value: 70.00				

KM# 753 10 PESOS
31.1040 g., 0.9990 Silver 0.9990 oz. ASW, 39.9 mm. **Series:** First **Subject:** 180th Anniversary of Federation **Obv:** National arms **Obv. Legend:** ESTADOS UNIDOS MEXICANOS **Rev:** State arms **Rev. Legend:** ESTADO DE CHIHUAHUA **Edge:** Reeded

Date	Mintage	F	VF	XF	Unc	BU
2005Mo Proof	10,000	Value: 70.00				

KM# 706 10 PESOS
31.1040 g., 0.9990 Silver 0.9990 oz. ASW, 39.9 mm. **Series:** First **Subject:** 180th Anniversary of Federation **Obv:** National arms **Obv. Legend:** ESTADOS UNIDOS MEXICANOS **Rev:** State arms **Rev. Legend:** ESTADO DE CHIAPAS **Edge:** Reeded

Date	Mintage	F	VF	XF	Unc	BU
2005Mo Proof	10,000	Value: 70.00				

KM# 728 10 PESOS
31.1040 g., 0.9990 Silver 0.9990 oz. ASW, 39.9 mm. **Series:** First **Subject:** 180th Anniversary of Federation **Obv:** National arms **Obv. Legend:** ESTADOS UNIDOS MEXICANOS **Rev:** State arms **Rev. Legend:** ESTADO DE COLIMA **Edge:** Reeded

Date	Mintage	F	VF	XF	Unc	BU
2005Mo Proof	10,000	Value: 70.00				

KM# 751 10 PESOS
31.1040 g., 0.9990 Silver 0.9990 oz. ASW, 39.9 mm. **Series:** First **Subject:** 180th Anniversary of Federation **Obv:** National arms **Obv. Legend:** ESTADOS UNIDOS MEXICANOS **Rev:** State arms **Rev. Legend:** ESTADO DE COAHUILA DE ZARAGOZA **Edge:** Reeded

Date	Mintage	F	VF	XF	Unc	BU
2005Mo Proof	10,000	Value: 70.00				

KM# 726 10 PESOS
31.1040 g., 0.9990 Silver 0.9990 oz. ASW, 39.9 mm. **Series:** First **Subject:** 180th Anniversary of Federation **Obv:** National arms **Obv. Legend:** ESTADOS UNIDOS MEXICANOS **Rev:** State arms **Rev. Legend:** ESTADO DE CAMPECHE **Edge:** Reeded

Date	Mintage	F	VF	XF	Unc	BU
2005Mo Proof	10,000	Value: 70.00				

KM# 724 10 PESOS
31.1040 g., 0.9990 Silver 0.9990 oz. ASW, 39.9 mm. **Series:** First **Subject:** 180th Anniversary of Federation **Obv:** National arms **Obv. Legend:** ESTADOS UNIDOS MEXICANOS **Rev:** State arms **Rev. Legend:** ESTADO DE BAJA CALIFORNIA SUR **Edge:** Reeded

Date	Mintage	F	VF	XF	Unc	BU
2005Mo Proof	10,000	Value: 70.00				

KM# 722 10 PESOS
31.1040 g., 0.9990 Silver 0.9990 oz. ASW, 39.9 mm. **Series:** First **Subject:** 180th Anniversary of Federation **Obv:** National arms **Obv. Legend:** ESTADOS UNIDOS MEXICANOS **Rev:** State arms **Rev. Legend:** ESTADO DE BAJA CALIFORNIA **Edge:** Reeded

Date	Mintage	F	VF	XF	Unc	BU
2005Mo Proof	10,000	Value: 70.00				

KM# 720 10 PESOS
31.1040 g., 0.9990 Silver 0.9990 oz. ASW, 39.9 mm. **Series:**
First **Subject:** 180th Anniversary of Federation **Obv:** National
arms **Obv. Legend:** ESTADOS UNIDOS MEXICANOS **Rev:**
State arms **Rev. Legend:** ESTADO DE AGUASCALIENTES
Edge: Reeded

Date	Mintage	F	VF	XF	Unc	BU
2005Mo Proof	10,000	Value: 70.00				

KM# 718 10 PESOS
31.1040 g., 0.9990 Silver 0.9990 oz. ASW, 40 mm. **Series:**
Second **Obv:** National arms **Obv. Legend:** ESTADOS UNIDOS
MEXICANOS **Rev:** Facade of the San Marcos garden above
sculpture of national emblem at left, San Antonio Temple at right
Rev. Legend: AGUASCALIENTES **Edge:** Reeded

Date	Mintage	F	VF	XF	Unc	BU
2005Mo Proof	6,000	Value: 65.00				

KM# 757 10 PESOS
31.1040 g., 0.9990 Silver 0.9990 oz. ASW, 40 mm. **Series:**
Second **Obv:** National arms **Obv. Legend:** ESTADOS UNIDOS
MEXICANOS **Rev:** Rams head, mountain outline in background
Rev. Legend: BAJA CALIFORNIA - GOBIERNO DEL ESTADO
Edge: Reeded

Date	Mintage	F	VF	XF	Unc	BU
2005Mo Proof	6,000	Value: 65.00				

KM# 755 10 PESOS
31.1040 g., 0.9990 Silver 0.9990 oz. ASW, 40 mm. **Obv:**
National arms **Rev:** Baja California del Norte arms

Date	Mintage	F	VF	XF	Unc	BU
2005Mo Proof	—	Value: 75.00				

KM# 763 10 PESOS
31.1040 g., 0.9990 Silver 0.9990 oz. ASW, 40 mm. **Obv:**
National arms **Rev:** Benito Juarez **Edge:** Reeded

Date	Mintage	F	VF	XF	Unc	BU
2006Mo Proof	—	Value: 75.00				

KM# 761 10 PESOS
31.1040 g., 0.9990 Silver 0.9990 oz. ASW, 40 mm. **Series:**
Second **Obv:** National arms **Obv. Legend:** ESTADOS UNIDOS
MEXICANOS **Rev:** Outlined map of peninsula at center, cave
painting of deer behind, cactus at right **Rev. Legend:** ESTADO
DE BAJA CALIFORNIA SUR **Edge:** Reeded

Date	Mintage	F	VF	XF	Unc	BU
2006Mo Proof	6,000	Value: 65.00				

KM# 759 10 PESOS
31.1040 g., 0.9990 Silver 0.9990 oz. ASW, 40 mm. **Series:**
Second **Obv:** National arms **Obv. Legend:** ESTADOS UNIDOS
MEXICANOS **Rev:** Jade mask - Calakmul, Campeche **Rev.
Legend:** ESTADO DE CAMPECHE **Edge:** Reeded

Date	Mintage	F	VF	XF	Unc	BU
2006Mo Proof	6,000	Value: 65.00				

KM# 780 10 PESOS
31.1040 g., 0.9990 Silver 0.9990 oz. ASW, 40 mm. **Series:**
Second **Obv:** National arms **Obv. Legend:** ESTADOS UNIDOS
MEXICANOS **Rev:** Outlined map with turtle, mine cart above
grapes at center, Friendship dam above Christ of the Nodas at
left, chimneys above crucibles and bell tower of Santiago's
cathedral at right **Rev. Inscription:** COAHUILA DE ZARAGOZA
Edge: Reeded

Date	Mintage	F	VF	XF	Unc	BU
2006Mo Proof	6,000	Value: 65.00				

KM# 776 10 PESOS
31.1040 g., 0.9990 Silver 0.9990 oz. ASW, 40 mm. **Series:**
Second **Obv:** National arms **Obv. Legend:** ESTADOS UNIDOS
MEXICANOS **Rev:** State arms at lower center, Nevado de Colima
and Volcan de Fuego volcanos in background **Rev. Legend:**
Colima **Rev. Inscription:** GENEROSO **Edge:** Reeded

Date	Mintage	F	VF	XF	Unc	BU
2006Mo Proof	6,000	Value: 65.00				

KM# 772 10 PESOS
31.1040 g., 0.9990 Silver 0.9990 oz. ASW, 40 mm. **Series:**
Second **Obv:** National arms **Obv. Legend:** ESTADOS UNIDOS
MEXICANOS **Rev:** Head of Pakal, ancient Mayan king, Palenque
Rev. Legend: ESTADO DE CHIAPAS - CABEZA MAYA DEL
REY PAKAL, PALENQUE **Edge:** Reeded

Date	Mintage	F	VF	XF	Unc	BU
2006Mo Proof	6,000	Value: 65.00				

KM# 774 10 PESOS
31.1040 g., 0.9990 Silver 0.9990 oz. ASW, 40 mm. **Series:**
Second **Obv:** National arms **Obv. Legend:** ESTADOS UNIDOS
MEXICANOS **Rev:** Angel of Liberty **Rev. Legend:** MÉXICO -
ANGEL DE LA LIBERTAD, CHIHUAHUA **Edge:** Reeded

Date	Mintage	F	VF	XF	Unc	BU
2006Mo Proof	6,000	Value: 65.00				

KM# 778 10 PESOS
31.1040 g., 0.9990 Silver 0.9990 oz. ASW, 40 mm. **Series:**
Second **Obv:** National arms **Obv. Legend:** ESTADOS UNIDOS
MEXICANOS **Rev:** National Palace **Rev. Legend:** DISTRITO
FEDERAL - ANTIGUO AYUNTAMIENTO **Edge:** Reeded

Date	Mintage	F	VF	XF	Unc	BU
2006Mo Proof	6,000	Value: 65.00				

KM# 786 10 PESOS
31.1040 g., 0.9990 Silver 0.9990 oz. ASW, 40 mm. **Series:**
Second **Obv:** National arms **Obv. Legend:** ESTADOS UNIDOS
MEXICANOS **Rev:** Tree **Rev. Legend:** PRIMERA RESERVA
NACIONAL FORESTAL - DURANGO **Edge:** Reeded

Date	Mintage	F	VF	XF	Unc	BU
2006Mo Proof	6,000	Value: 65.00				

KM# 788 10 PESOS
31.1040 g., 0.9990 Silver 0.9990 oz. ASW, 40 mm. **Series:**
Second **Obv:** National arms **Obv. Legend:** ESTADOS UNIDOS
MEXICANOS **Rev:** State arms at center, statue of Miguel Hidalgo
at left, monument to Pípila at lower right **Rev. Inscription:**
Guanajuato **Edge:** Reeded

Date	Mintage	F	VF	XF	Unc	BU
2006Mo Proof	6,000	Value: 65.00				

KM# 790 10 PESOS
31.1040 g., 0.9990 Silver 0.9990 oz. ASW, 40 mm. **Series:**
Second **Obv:** National arms **Obv. Legend:** ESTADOS UNIDOS
MEXICANOS **Rev:** Stylized portrait of Vicente Guerrero at left,
church of Taxco at upper center, Acapulco's la Quebrada with
diver above Christmas Eve flower and mask **Rev. Legend:**
GUERRERO **Edge:** Reeded

Date	Mintage	F	VF	XF	Unc	BU
2006Mo Proof	6,000	Value: 65.00				

KM# 792 10 PESOS
31.1040 g., 0.9990 Silver 0.9990 oz. ASW, 40 mm. **Series:**
Second **Obv:** National arms **Obv. Legend:** ESTADOS UNIDOS
MEXICANOS **Rev:** Monument of Pachuca Hidalgo **Rev.
Inscription:** *RELOJ / MONUMENTAL / DE / PACHUCA /
HIDALGO - La / Bella / Airosa* **Edge:** Reeded

Date	Mintage	F	VF	XF	Unc	BU
2006Mo Proof	6,000	Value: 65.00				

KM# 794 10 PESOS
31.1040 g., 0.9990 Silver 0.9990 oz. ASW, 40 mm. **Series:**
Second **Obv:** National arms **Obv. Legend:** ESTADOS UNIDOS
MEXICANOS **Rev:** Hospicio Cabañas orphanage **Rev. Legend:**
ESTADO DE JALISCCO **Edge:** Reeded

Date	Mintage	F	VF	XF	Unc	BU
2006Mo Proof	6,000	Value: 65.00				

KM# 830 10 PESOS
31.1040 g., 0.9990 Silver 0.9990 oz. ASW, 40 mm. **Series:**
Second **Obv:** National arms **Obv. Legend:** ESTADOS UNIDOS
MEXICANOS **Rev:** Pyramid of the Loona (Moon) **Rev. Legend:**
ESTADO DE MÉXICO **Edge:** Reeded

Date	Mintage	F	VF	XF	Unc	BU
2006Mo Proof	6,000	Value: 65.00				

KM# 831 10 PESOS
31.1040 g., 0.9990 Silver 0.9990 oz. ASW, 40 mm. **Series:**
Second **Obv:** National arms **Obv. Legend:** ESTADOS UNIDOS
MEXICANOS **Rev:** Four Monarch butterflies **Rev. Legend:**
ESTADO DE MICHOACÁN **Edge:** Reeded

Date	Mintage	F	VF	XF	Unc	BU
2006Mo Proof	6,000	Value: 65.00				

KM# 832 10 PESOS
31.1040 g., 0.9990 Silver 0.9990 oz. ASW, 40 mm. **Series:**
Second **Obv:** National arms **Obv. Legend:** ESTADOS UNIDOS
MEXICANOS **Rev:** 1/2 length figure of Chinelo (local dancer) at
right, Palacio de Cortes in background **Rev. Inscription:**
ESTADO DE / MORELOS **Edge:** Reeded

Date	Mintage	F	VF	XF	Unc	BU
2006Mo Proof	6,000	Value: 65.00				

KM# 833 10 PESOS
31.1040 g., 0.9990 Silver 0.9990 oz. ASW, 40 mm. **Series:**
Second **Obv:** National arms **Obv. Legend:** ESTADOS UNIDOS
MEXICANOS **Rev:** Isle de Mexcaltitlán **Rev. Legend:** ESTADO
DE NAYARIT **Edge:** Reeded

Date	Mintage	F	VF	XF	Unc	BU
2007Mo Proof	6,000	Value: 65.00				

KM# 834 10 PESOS
31.1040 g., 0.9990 Silver 0.9990 oz. ASW, 40 mm. **Series:**
Second **Obv:** National arms **Obv. Legend:** ESTADOS UNIDOS
MEXICANOS **Rev:** Old foundry in Pargue Fundidora (public park)
at right, Cerro de la Silla (Saddle Hill) in background **Rev.
Legend:** ESTADO DE NUEVO LEÓN **Edge:** Reeded

Date	Mintage	F	VF	XF	Unc	BU
2007Mo Proof	6,000	Value: 65.00				

KM# 835 10 PESOS
31.1040 g., 0.9990 Silver 0.9990 oz. ASW, 40 mm. **Series:**
Second **Obv:** National arms **Obv. Legend:** ESTADOS UNIDOS
MEXICANOS **Rev:** Teatro Macedonio Alcala (theater) **Rev.
Legend:** OAXACA **Edge:** Reeded

Date	Mintage	F	VF	XF	Unc	BU
2007Mo Proof	6,000	Value: 65.00				

KM# 836 10 PESOS
31.1040 g., 0.9990 Silver 0.9990 oz. ASW, 40 mm. **Series:**
Second **Obv:** National arms **Obv. Legend:** ESTADOS UNIDOS
MEXICANOS **Rev:** Talavera porcelain dish **Rev. Legend:**
ESTADO DE PUEBLA **Edge:** Reeded

Date	Mintage	F	VF	XF	Unc	BU
2007Mo Proof	6,000	Value: 65.00				

KM# 837 10 PESOS
31.1040 g., 0.9990 Silver 0.9990 oz. ASW, 40 mm. **Series:**
Second **Obv:** National arms **Obv. Legend:** ESTADOS UNIDOS
MEXICANOS **Rev:** Mask at left, rays above state arms at center,
Mayan ruins at right **Rev. Legend:** QUINTANA ROO **Edge:**
Reeded

Date	Mintage	F	VF	XF	Unc	BU
2007Mo Proof	6,000	Value: 65.00				

KM# 838 10 PESOS
31.1040 g., 0.9990 Silver 0.9990 oz. ASW, 40 mm. **Series:**
Second **Obv:** National arms **Obv. Legend:** ESTADOS UNIDOS
MEXICANOS **Rev:** Acqueduct of Querétaro at left, church of
Santa Rosa de Viterbo at right **Rev. Legend:** ESTADO DE
QUERÉTARO ARTEAGA **Edge:** Reeded

Date	Mintage	F	VF	XF	Unc	BU
2007Mo Proof	6,000	Value: 65.00				

KM# 839 10 PESOS
31.1040 g., Silver, 40 mm. **Series:** Second **Obv:** National arms
Obv. Legend: ESTADOS UNIDOS MEXICANOS **Rev:** Facade
of Caja Real **Rev. Legend:** • SAN LUIS POTOSÍ • **Edge:** Reeded

Date	Mintage	F	VF	XF	Unc	BU
2007Mo Proof	6,000	Value: 65.00				

KM# 840 10 PESOS
31.1040 g., 0.9990 Silver 0.9990 oz. ASW, 40 mm. **Series:**
Second **Obv:** National arms **Obv. Legend:** ESTADOS UNIDOS
MEXICANOS **Rev:** Shield on pile of cactus fruits **Rev. Legend:**
ESTADO DE SINALOA - LUGAR DE PITAHAYAS **Edge:** Reeded

Date	Mintage	F	VF	XF	Unc	BU
2007Mo Proof	6,000	Value: 65.00				

KM# 841 10 PESOS
31.1040 g., 0.9990 Silver 0.9990 oz. ASW, 40 mm. **Series:**
Second **Obv:** National arms **Obv. Legend:** ESTADOS UNIDOS
MEXICANOS **Rev:** Local in Dance of the Deer at left, cactus at
right, mountains in background **Rev. Legend:** ESTADO DE
SONORA **Edge:** Reeded

Date	Mintage	F	VF	XF	Unc	BU
2007Mo Proof	6,000	Value: 65.00				

KM# 842 10 PESOS
31.1040 g., 0.9990 Silver 0.9990 oz. ASW, 40 mm. **Series:**
Second **Obv:** National arms **Obv. Legend:** ESTADOS UNIDOS
MEXICANOS **Rev:** Fuente de los Pescadores (fisherman
fountain) at lower left, giant head from the Olmec-pre-Hispanic
culture at right, Planetario Tabasco in background **Rev. Legend:**
TABASCO **Edge:** Reeded

Date	Mintage	F	VF	XF	Unc	BU
2007Mo Proof	6,000	Value: 65.00				

KM# 843 10 PESOS
31.1040 g., 0.9990 Silver 0.9990 oz. ASW, 40 mm. **Series:**
Second **Obv:** National arms **Obv. Legend:** ESTADOS UNIDOS
MEXICANOS **Rev:** Ridge - Cerro Del Bernal, Gonzáles **Rev.
Legend:** TAMAULIPAS **Edge:** Reeded

Date	Mintage	F	VF	XF	Unc	BU
2007Mo Proof	6,000	Value: 65.00				

KM# 844 10 PESOS
31.1040 g., 0.9990 Silver 0.9990 oz. ASW, 40 mm. **Series:**
Second **Obv:** National arms **Obv. Legend:** ESTADOS UNIDOS
MEXICANOS **Rev:** Basilica de Ocotlán at left, state arms above
Capilla Abierta, Plaza de Toros Ranchero Aguilar below,
Exconvento de San Francisco at right **Rev. Legend:** ESTADO
DE TLAXCALA **Edge:** Reeded

Date	Mintage	F	VF	XF	Unc	BU
2007Mo Proof	6,000	Value: 65.00				

KM# 845 10 PESOS
31.1040 g., 0.9990 Silver 0.9990 oz. ASW, 40 mm. **Series:**
Second **Obv:** National arms **Obv. Legend:** ESTADOS UNIDOS
MEXICANOS **Rev:** Pyramid of El Tajín **Rev. Legend:** •
VERACRUZ • - • DE IGNACIO DE LA LLAVE • **Edge:** Reeded

Date	Mintage	F	VF	XF	Unc	BU
2007Mo Proof	6,000	Value: 65.00				

KM# 846 10 PESOS
31.1030 g., 0.9990 Silver 0.9989 oz. ASW, 40 mm. **Series:**
Second **Obv:** National arms **Obv. Legend:** ESTADOS UNIDOS
MEXICANOS **Rev:** Stylized pyramid of Chichén-Itzá **Rev.
Legend:** Castillo de Chichén Itzá **Rev. Inscription:** YUCATÁN
Edge: Reeded

Date	Mintage	F	VF	XF	Unc	BU
2007Mo Proof	6,000	Value: 65.00				

KM# 847 10 PESOS
31.1040 g., 0.9990 Silver 0.9990 oz. ASW, 40 mm. **Series:**
Second **Obv:** National arms **Obv. Legend:** ESTADOS UNIDOS
MEXICANOS **Rev:** Cable car above Monumento al Minero at left,
Cathedral de Zacatecas at center right **Rev. Legend:** Zacatecas
Edge: Reeded

Date	Mintage	F	VF	XF	Unc	BU
2007Mo Proof	6,000	Value: 65.00				

KM# 637 20 PESOS
Bi-Metallic Copper-Nickel center within Brass ring, 32 mm.
Subject: Xiuhtecuhtli **Obv:** National arms, eagle left within circle
Rev: Aztec with torch within spiked circle

Date	Mintage	F	VF	XF	Unc	BU
2001Mo	2,478,000	—	—	2.50	16.00	18.00

KM# 638 20 PESOS
Bi-Metallic Copper-Nickel center within Brass ring, 32 mm.
Subject: Octavio Paz **Obv:** National arms, eagle left within circle
Rev: Head 1/4 right within circle

Date	Mintage	F	VF	XF	Unc	BU
2001Mo	2,515,000	—	2.50	3.50	16.00	18.50

KM# 704 20 PESOS
62.4000 g., 0.9990 Silver 2.0041 oz. ASW, 48.1 mm. **Subject:**
400th Anniversary of Don Quijote de la Manchia **Obv:** National
arms **Rev:** Skeletal figure horseback with spear galloping right
Edge: Plain

Date	Mintage	F	VF	XF	Unc	BU
ND(2005)Mo Proof	10,000	Value: 85.00				

KM# 767 20 PESOS
62.4000 g., 0.9990 Silver 2.0041 oz. ASW, 48 mm. **Subject:**
80th Anniversary - Bank of Mexico **Obv:** National arms **Rev:** 100
Peso banknote design of 1925

Date	Mintage	F	VF	XF	Unc	BU
2005Mo	—	—	—	—	—	80.00
2005Mo Proof	3,005	Value: 90.00				

KM# 688 100 PESOS
33.9400 g., Bi-Metallic .925 Silver 16.812g center in Aluminum-
Bronze ring, 39.04 mm. **Series:** First **Subject:** 180th
Anniversary of Federation **Obv:** National arms **Obv. Legend:**
ESTADOS UNIDOS MEXICANOS **Rev:** State arms **Rev.**
Legend: ESTADO DE ZACATECAS **Edge:** Segmented reeding

Date	Mintage	F	VF	XF	Unc	BU
2003Mo	244,900	—	—	—	40.00	50.00

KM# 696 100 PESOS
29.1690 g., Bi-Metallic .999 Gold 17.154g center in .999 Silver
12.015g ring, 34.5 mm. **Series:** First **Subject:** 180th Anniversary
of Federation **Obv:** National arms **Obv. Legend:** ESTADOS
UNIDOS MEXICANOS **Rev:** State arms **Rev. Legend:** ESTADO
DE ZACATECAS **Edge:** Segmented reeding

Date	Mintage	F	VF	XF	Unc	BU
2003Mo Proof	1,000	Value: 1,200				

KM# 689 100 PESOS
33.9400 g., Bi-Metallic .925 Silver 16.812g center in Aluminum-
Bronze ring, 39.04 mm. **Series:** First **Subject:** 180th
Anniversary of Federation **Obv:** National arms **Obv. Legend:**
ESTADOS UNIDOS MEXICANOS **Rev:** State arms **Rev.**
Legend: ESTADO DE YUCATÁN **Edge:** Segmented reeding

Date	Mintage	F	VF	XF	Unc	BU
2003Mo	235,763	—	—	—	40.00	50.00

KM# 697 100 PESOS
29.1690 g., Bi-Metallic .999 Gold 17.154g center in .999 Silver
12.015g ring, 34.5 mm. **Series:** First **Subject:** 180th Anniversary
of Federation **Obv:** National arms **Obv. Legend:** ESTADOS
UNIDOS MEXICANOS **Rev:** State arms **Rev. Legend:** ESTADO
DE YUCATÁN **Edge:** Segmented reeding

Date	Mintage	F	VF	XF	Unc	BU
2003Mo Proof	1,000	Value: 1,200				

KM# 690 100 PESOS
33.9400 g., Bi-Metallic .925 Silver 16.812g center in Aluminum-
Bronze ring, 39.04 mm. **Series:** First **Subject:** 180th Anniversary
of Federation **Obv:** National arms **Obv. Legend:** ESTADOS
UNIDOS MEXICANOS **Rev:** State arms **Rev. Legend:** ESTADO
DE VERACRUZ-LLAVE **Edge:** Segmented reeding

Date	Mintage	F	VF	XF	Unc	BU
2003Mo	248,810	—	—	—	40.00	50.00

KM# 698 100 PESOS
29.1690 g., Bi-Metallic .999 Gold 17.154g center in .999 Silver
12.015g ring, 34.5 mm. **Series:** First **Subject:** 180th Anniversary
of Federation **Obv:** National arms **Obv. Legend:** ESTADOS
UNIDOS MEXICANOS **Rev:** State arms **Rev. Legend:** ESTADO
DE VERACRUZ-LLAVE **Edge:** Segmented reeding

Date	Mintage	F	VF	XF	Unc	BU
2003Mo Proof	1,000	Value: 1,200				

KM# 691 100 PESOS
33.9400 g., Bi-Metallic .925 Silver 16.812g center in Aluminum-
Bronze ring, 39.9 mm. **Series:** First **Subject:** 180th Anniversary
of Federation **Obv:** National arms **Obv. Legend:** ESTADOS
UNIDOS MEXICANOS **Rev:** State arms **Rev. Legend:** ESTADO
DE TLAXCALA **Edge:** Segmented reeding

Date	Mintage	F	VF	XF	Unc	BU
2003Mo	248,976	—	—	—	35.00	40.00

KM# 699 100 PESOS
29.1690 g., Bi-Metallic .999 Gold 17.154g center in .999 Silver
12.015g ring, 34.5 mm. **Series:** First **Subject:** 180th Anniversary
of Federation **Obv:** National arms **Obv. Legend:** ESTADOS
UNIDOS MEXICANOS **Rev:** State arms **Rev. Legend:** ESTADO
DE TLAXCALA **Edge:** Segmented reeding

Date	Mintage	F	VF	XF	Unc	BU
2003Mo Proof	1,000	Value: 1,200				

KM# 692 100 PESOS
33.9400 g., Bi-Metallic .925 Silver 16.812g center in Aluminum-
Bronze ring, 39.04 mm. **Series:** First **Subject:** 180th Anniversary
of Federation **Obv:** National arms **Obv. Legend:** ESTADOS
UNIDOS MEXICANOS **Rev:** State arms **Rev. Legend:** ESTADO
DE TAMAULIPAS **Edge:** Segmented reeding

Date	Mintage	F	VF	XF	Unc	BU
2004Mo	249,398	—	—	—	35.00	40.00

KM# 700 100 PESOS
29.1690 g., Bi-Metallic .999 Gold 17.154g center in .999 Silver
12.015g ring, 34.5 mm. **Series:** First **Subject:** 180th Anniversary
of Federation **Obv:** National arms **Obv. Legend:** ESTADOS
UNIDOS MEXICANOS **Rev:** State arms **Rev. Legend:** ESTADO
DE TAMAULIPAS **Edge:** Segmented reeding

Date	Mintage	F	VF	XF	Unc	BU
2004Mo Proof	1,000	Value: 1,200				

KM# 693 100 PESOS
33.9400 g., Bi-Metallic .925 Silver 16.812g center in Aluminum-
Bronze ring, 39.04 mm. **Series:** First **Subject:** 180th
Anniversary of Federation **Obv:** National arms **Obv. Legend:**
ESTADOS UNIDOS MEXICANOS **Rev:** State arms **Rev.**
Legend: ESTADO DE TABASCO **Edge:** Segmented reeding

Date	Mintage	F	VF	XF	Unc	BU
2004Mo	249,318	—	—	—	35.00	40.00

KM# 701 100 PESOS
29.1690 g., Bi-Metallic .999 Gold 17.154g center in .999 Silver
12.015g ring, 34.5 mm. **Series:** First **Subject:** 180th Anniversary
of Federation **Obv:** National arms **Obv. Legend:** ESTADOS
UNIDOS MEXICANOS **Rev:** State arms **Rev. Legend:** ESTADO
DE TABASCO **Edge:** Segmented reeding

Date	Mintage	F	VF	XF	Unc	BU
2004Mo Proof	1,000	Value: 1,200				

KM# 694 100 PESOS
33.9400 g., Bi-Metallic .925 Silver 16.812g center in Aluminum-
Bronze ring, 39.04 mm. **Series:** First **Subject:** 180th
Anniversary of Federation **Obv:** National arms **Obv. Legend:**
ESTADOS UNIDOS MEXICANOS **Rev:** State arms **Rev.**
Legend: ESTADO DE SONORA **Edge:** Segmented reeding

Date	Mintage	F	VF	XF	Unc	BU
2004Mo	249,300	—	—	—	35.00	40.00

KM# 702 100 PESOS
29.1690 g., Bi-Metallic .999 Gold 17.154g center in .999 Silver
12.015g ring, 34.5 mm. **Series:** First **Subject:** 180th Anniversary
of Federation **Obv:** National arms **Obv. Legend:** ESTADOS
UNIDOS MEXICANOS **Rev:** State arms **Rev. Legend:** ESTADO
DE SONORA **Edge:** Segmented reeding

Date	Mintage	F	VF	XF	Unc	BU
2004Mo Proof	1,000	Value: 1,200				

KM# 695 100 PESOS
33.9400 g., Bi-Metallic .925 Silver 16.812g center in Aluminum-
Bronze ring, 39.04 mm. **Series:** First **Subject:** 180th
Anniversary of Federation **Obv:** National arms **Obv. Legend:**
ESTADOS UNIDOS MEXICANOS **Rev:** State arms **Rev.**
Legend: ESTADO DE SINALOA **Edge:** Segmented reeding

Date	Mintage	F	VF	XF	Unc	BU
2004Mo	244,722	—	—	—	35.00	40.00

KM# 703 100 PESOS
29.1690 g., Bi-Metallic .999 Gold 17.154g center in .999 Silver
12.015g ring, 34.5 mm. **Series:** First **Subject:** 180th Anniversary
of Federation **Obv:** National arms **Obv. Legend:** ESTADOS
UNIDOS MEXICANOS **Rev:** State arms **Rev. Legend:** ESTADO
DE SINALOA **Edge:** Segmented reeding

Date	Mintage	F	VF	XF	Unc	BU
2004Mo Proof	1,000	Value: 1,200				

KM# 803 100 PESOS
33.9400 g., Bi-Metallic .925 Silver 16.812g center in Aluminum-

Bronze ring, 39.04 mm. **Series:** First **Subject:** 180th Anniversary of Federation **Obv:** National arms **Obv. Legend:** ESTADOS UNIDOS MEXICANOS **Rev:** State arms **Rev. Legend:** ESTADO DE SAN LUIS POTOSÍ **Edge:** Segmented reeding

Date	Mintage	F	VF	XF	Unc	BU
2004Mo	249,662	—	—	—	35.00	40.00

KM# 806   100 PESOS
29.1690 g., Bi-Metallic .999 Gold 17.154g center in .999 silver 12.015 ring, 34.5 mm. **Series:** First **Subject:** 180th Anniversary of Federation **Obv:** National arms **Obv. Legend:** ESTADOS UNIDOS MEXICANOS **Rev:** State arms **Rev. Legend:** ESTADO DE SAN LUIS POTOSÍ **Edge:** Segmented reeding

Date	Mintage	F	VF	XF	Unc	BU
2004Mo Proof	1,000	Value: 1,200				

KM# 736   100 PESOS
33.9400 g., Bi-Metallic .925 Silver 16.812g center in Aluminum-Bronze ring, 39.04 mm. **Series:** First **Subject:** 180th Anniversary of Federation **Obv:** National arms **Obv. Legend:** ESTADOS UNIDOS MEXICANOS **Rev:** State arms **Rev. Legend:** ESTADO DE QUINTANA ROO **Edge:** Segmented reeding

Date	Mintage	F	VF	XF	Unc	BU
2004Mo	249,134	—	—	—	35.00	40.00

KM# 807   100 PESOS
29.1690 g., Bi-Metallic .999 Gold 17.154g center in .999 Silver 12.015g ring, 34.5 mm. **Series:** First **Subject:** 180th Anniversary of Federation **Obv:** National arms **Obv. Legend:** ESTADOS UNIDOS MEXICANOS **Rev:** State arms **Rev. Legend:** ESTADO DE QUINTANA ROO **Edge:** Segmented reeding

Date	Mintage	F	VF	XF	Unc	BU
2004Mo Proof	1,000	Value: 1,200				

KM# 734   100 PESOS
33.9400 g., Bi-Metallic .925 Silver 16.812g center in Aluminum-Bronze ring, 39.04 mm. **Series:** First **Subject:** 180th Anniversary of Federation **Obv:** National arms **Obv. Legend:** ESTADOS UNIDOS MEXICANOS **Rev:** State arms **Rev. Legend:** ESTADO DE QUERÉTARO ARTEAGA **Edge:** Segmented reeding

Date	Mintage	F	VF	XF	Unc	BU
2004Mo	249,263	—	—	—	35.00	40.00

KM# 808   100 PESOS
29.1690 g., Bi-Metallic .999 Gold 17.154g center in .999 Silver 12.015g ring, 34.5 mm. **Series:** First **Subject:** 180th Anniversary of Federation **Obv:** National arms **Obv. Legend:** ESTADOS UNIDOS MEXICANOS **Rev:** State arms **Rev. Legend:** ESTADO DE QUERÉTARO ARTEAGA **Edge:** Segmented reeding

Date	Mintage	F	VF	XF	Unc	BU
2004Mo Proof	1,000	Value: 1,200				

KM# 738   100 PESOS
33.9400 g., Bi-Metallic .925 Silver 16.812g center in Aluminum-Bronze ring, 39.04 mm. **Series:** First **Subject:** 180th Anniversary of Federation **Obv:** National arms **Obv. Legend:** ESTADOS UNIDOS MEXICANOS **Rev:** State arms **Rev. Legend:** ESTADO DE PUEBLA **Edge:** Segmented reeding

Date	Mintage	F	VF	XF	Unc	BU
2004Mo	248,850	—	—	—	35.00	40.00

KM# 809   100 PESOS
Bi-Metallic .999 Gold 17.154g center in .999 Silver 12.015g ring, 34.5 mm. **Series:** First **Subject:** 180th Anniversary of Federation **Obv:** National arms **Obv. Legend:** ESTADOS UNIDOS MEXICANOS **Rev:** State arms **Rev. Legend:** ESTADO DE PUEBLA **Edge:** Segmented reeding

Date	Mintage	F	VF	XF	Unc	BU
2004Mo Proof	1,000	Value: 1,200				

KM# 740   100 PESOS
33.9400 g., Bi-Metallic .925 Silver 16.812g center in Aluminum-Bronze ring, 39.04 mm. **Series:** First **Subject:** 180th Anniversary of Federation **Obv:** National arms **Obv. Legend:** ESTADOS UNIDOS MEXICANOS **Rev:** State arms **Rev. Legend:** ESTADO DE OAXACA **Edge:** Segmented reeding

Date	Mintage	F	VF	XF	Unc	BU
2004Mo	249,589	—	—	—	35.00	40.00

KM# 810   100 PESOS
29.1690 g., Bi-Metallic .999 Gold 17.154g center in .999 Silver 12.015g ring, 34.5 mm. **Series:** First **Subject:** 180th Anniversary of Federation **Obv:** National arms **Obv. Legend:** ESTADOS UNIDOS MEXICANOS **Rev:** State arms **Rev. Legend:** ESTADO DE OAXACA **Edge:** Segmented reeding

Date	Mintage	F	VF	XF	Unc	BU
2004Mo Proof	1,000	Value: 1,200				

KM# 742   100 PESOS
33.9400 g., Bi-Metallic .925 Silver 16.812g center in Aluminum-Bronze ring, 39.04 mm. **Series:** First **Subject:** 180th Anniversary of Federation **Obv:** National arms **Obv. Legend:** ESTADOS UNIDOS MEXICANOS **Rev:** State arms **Rev. Legend:** ESTADO DE NUEVO LEÓN **Edge:** Segmented reeding

Date	Mintage	F	VF	XF	Unc	BU
2004Mo	249,199	—	—	—	35.00	40.00

KM# 811   100 PESOS
29.1690 g., Bi-Metallic .999 Gold 17.154g center in .999 Silver 12.015g ring, 34.5 mm. **Series:** First **Subject:** 180th Anniversary of Federation **Obv:** National arms **Obv. Legend:** ESTADOS UNIDOS MEXICANOS **Rev:** State arms **Rev. Legend:** ESTADO DE NUEVO LEÓN **Edge:** Segmented reeding

Date	Mintage	F	VF	XF	Unc	BU
2004Mo Proof	1,000	Value: 1,200				

KM# 744   100 PESOS
33.9400 g., Bi-Metallic .925 Silver 16.812g center in Aluminum-Bronze ring, 39.04 mm. **Series:** First **Subject:** 180th Anniversary of Federation **Obv:** National arms **Obv. Legend:** ESTADOS UNIDOS MEXICANOS **Rev:** State arms **Rev. Legend:** ESTADO DE NAYARIT **Edge:** Segmented reeding

Date	Mintage	F	VF	XF	Unc	BU
2004Mo	248,305	—	—	—	35.00	40.00

KM# 812   100 PESOS
29.1690 g., Bi-Metallic .999 Gold 17.154g center in .999 Silver 12.015g ring, 34.5 mm. **Series:** First **Subject:** 180th Anniversary of Federation **Obv:** National arms **Obv. Legend:** ESTADOS UNIDOS MEXICANOS **Rev:** State arms **Rev. Legend:** ESTADO DE NAYARIT **Edge:** Segmented reeding

Date	Mintage	F	VF	XF	Unc	BU
2004Mo Proof	1,000	Value: 1,200				

KM# 746   100 PESOS
33.9400 g., Bi-Metallic .925 Silver 16.812g center in Aluminum-Bronze ring, 39.04 mm. **Series:** First **Subject:** 180th Anniversary of Federation **Obv:** National arms **Obv. Legend:** ESTADOS UNIDOS MEXICANOS **Rev:** State arms **Rev. Legend:** ESTADO DE MORELOS **Edge:** Segmented reeding

Date	Mintage	F	VF	XF	Unc	BU
2004Mo	249,260	—	—	—	35.00	40.00

KM# 813   100 PESOS
29.1690 g., Bi-Metallic .999 Gold 17.154g center in .999 Silver 12.015g ring, 34.5 mm. **Series:** First **Subject:** 180th Anniversary of Federation **Obv:** National arms **Obv. Legend:** ESTADOS UNIDOS MEXICANOS **Rev:** State arms **Rev. Legend:** ESTADO DE MORELOS **Edge:** Segmented reeding

Date	Mintage	F	VF	XF	Unc	BU
2004Mo Proof	1,000	Value: 1,200				

KM# 804   100 PESOS
33.9400 g., Bi-Metallic .925 Silver 16.812g center in Aluminum-Bronze ring, 39.04 mm. **Series:** First **Subject:** 180th Anniversary of Federation **Obv:** National arms **Obv. Legend:** ESTADOS UNIDOS MEXICANOS **Rev:** State arms **Rev. Legend:** ESTADO DE MICHOACÁN DE OCAMPO **Edge:** Segmented reeding

Date	Mintage	F	VF	XF	Unc	BU
2004Mo	249,492	—	—	—	35.00	40.00

KM# 814   100 PESOS
29.1690 g., Bi-Metallic .999 Gold 17.154g center in .999 12.015g ring, 34.5 mm. **Series:** First **Subject:** 180th Anniversary of Federation **Obv:** National arms **Obv. Legend:** ESTADOS UNIDOS MEXICANOS **Rev:** State arms **Rev. Legend:** ESTADO DE MICHOACÁN DE OCAMPO **Edge:** Segmented reeding

Date	Mintage	F	VF	XF	Unc	BU
2004Mo Proof	1,000	Value: 1,200				

KM# 748   100 PESOS
33.9400 g., Bi-Metallic .925 Silver 16.812g center in Aluminum-Bronze ring, 39.04 mm. **Series:** First **Subject:** 180th Anniversary of Federation **Obv:** National arms **Obv. Legend:** ESTADOS UNIDOS MEXICANOS **Rev:** State arms **Rev. Legend:** ESTADO DE MÉXICO **Edge:** Segmented reeding

Date	Mintage	F	VF	XF	Unc	BU
2004Mo	249,800	—	—	—	35.00	40.00

KM# 815   100 PESOS
29.1690 g., Bi-Metallic .999 Gold 17.154 center in .999 Silver 12.015 ring, 34.5 mm. **Series:** First **Subject:** 180th Anniversary of Federation **Obv:** National arms **Obv. Legend:** ESTADOS UNIDOS MEXICANOS **Rev:** State arms **Rev. Legend:** ESTADO DE MÉXICO **Edge:** Segmented reeding

Date	Mintage	F	VF	XF	Unc	BU
2004Mo Proof	1,000	Value: 1,200				

KM# 750   100 PESOS
33.9400 g., Bi-Metallic .925 Silver 16.812g center in Aluminum-Bronze ring, 39.04 mm. **Series:** First **Subject:** 180th Anniversary of Federation **Obv:** National arms **Obv. Legend:** ESTADOS UNIDOS MEXICANOS **Rev:** State arms **Rev. Legend:** ESTADO DE JALISCO **Edge:** Segmented reeding

Date	Mintage	F	VF	XF	Unc	BU
2004Mo	249,115	—	—	—	35.00	40.00

KM# 816   100 PESOS
29.1690 g., Bi-Metallic .999 Gold 17.154g center in .999 Silver 12.015g ring, 34.5 mm. **Series:** First **Subject:** 180th Anniversary of Federation **Obv:** National arms **Obv. Legend:** ESTADOS UNIDOS MEXICANOS **Rev:** State arms **Rev. Legend:** ESTADO DE JALISCO **Edge:** Segmented reeding

Date	Mintage	F	VF	XF	Unc	BU
2004Mo Proof	1,000	Value: 1,200				

KM# 705   100 PESOS
33.7400 g., Bi-Metallic .925 16.812g Silver center in Aluminum-

Bronze ring, 39 mm. **Subject:** 400th Anniversary of Don Quijote de la Manchia **Obv:** National arms **Obv. Legend:** ESTADOS UNIDOS MEXICANOS **Rev:** Skeletal figure on horseback with spear galloping right **Edge:** Segmented reeding

Date	Mintage	F	VF	XF	Unc	BU
2005Mo	726,833	—	—	—	25.00	32.00
2005Mo Proof	3,761	Value: 75.00				

KM# 730   100 PESOS
33.8250 g., Bi-Metallic .925 Silver 16.812g center in Aluminum-Bronze ring, 39.9 mm. **Subject:** Monetary Reform Centennial **Obv:** National arms **Rev:** Radiant Liberty Cap divides date above value within circle **Edge:** Segmented reeding

Date	Mintage	F	VF	XF	Unc	BU
2005Mo	49,716	—	—	—	40.00	45.00
2005Mo Proof	—	Value: 75.00				

KM# 731   100 PESOS
33.8250 g., Bi-Metallic .925 Silver 16.812g center in Aluminum-Bronze ring, 39.9 mm. **Subject:** Mexico City Mint's 470th Anniversary **Obv:** National arms **Rev:** Screw press, value and date within circle **Edge:** Segmented reeding

Date	Mintage	F	VF	XF	Unc	BU
2005Mo	49,895	—	—	—	40.00	45.00
2005Mo Proof	—	Value: 95.00				

KM# 732   100 PESOS
33.8250 g., Bi-Metallic .925 Silver 16.812g center in Aluminum-Bronze ring, 39.9 mm. **Subject:** Bank of Mexico's 80th Anniversary **Obv:** National arms **Rev:** Back design of the 1925 hundred peso note **Edge:** Segmented reeding

Date	Mintage	F	VF	XF	Unc	BU
2005Mo	49,712	—	—	—	40.00	45.00
2005Mo Proof	—	Value: 95.00				

KM# 717   100 PESOS
33.9400 g., Bi-Metallic .925 Silver 16.812g center in Brass ring, 39.04 mm. **Series:** First **Subject:** 180th Anniversary of Federation **Obv:** National arms **Obv. Legend:** ESTADOS UNIDOS MEXICANOS **Rev:** State arms **Rev. Legend:** ESTADO DE HIDALGO **Edge:** Segmented reeding

Date	Mintage	F	VF	XF	Unc	BU
2005Mo	249,820	—	—	—	35.00	40.00

KM# 817   100 PESOS
29.1690 g., Bi-Metallic .999 Gold 17.154g center in .999 Silver 12.015g ring, 34.5 mm. **Series:** First **Subject:** 180th Anniversary of Federation **Obv:** National arms **Obv. Legend:** ESTADOS UNIDOS MEXICANOS **Rev:** State arms **Rev. Legend:** ESTADO DE HIDALGO **Edge:** Segmented reeding

Date	Mintage	F	VF	XF	Unc	BU
2005Mo Proof	1,000	Value: 1,200				

KM# 716   100 PESOS
33.9400 g., Bi-Metallic .925 Silver 16.812g center in Brass ring, 39.04 mm. **Series:** First **Subject:** 180th Anniversary of Federation **Obv:** National arms **Obv. Legend:** ESTADOS UNIDOS MEXICANOS **Rev:** State arms **Rev. Legend:** ESTADO DE GUERRERO **Edge:** Segmented reeding

Date	Mintage	F	VF	XF	Unc	BU
2005Mo	248,850	—	—	—	35.00	40.00

KM# 818   100 PESOS
29.1690 g., Bi-Metallic .999 Gold 17.154g center in .999 Silver 12.015 ring, 34.5 mm. **Series:** First **Subject:** 180th Anniversary of Federation **Obv:** National arms **Obv. Legend:** ESTADOS UNIDOS MEXICANOS **Rev:** State arms **Rev. Legend:** ESTADO DE GUERRERO **Edge:** Segmented reeding

Date	Mintage	F	VF	XF	Unc	BU
2005Mo Proof	1,000	Value: 1,200				

KM# 715   100 PESOS
33.9400 g., Bi-Metallic .925 Silver 16.812g center in Brass ring, 39.04 mm. **Series:** First **Subject:** 180th Anniversary of Federation **Obv:** National arms **Obv. Legend:** ESTADOS UNIDOS MEXICANOS **Rev:** State arms **Rev. Legend:** ESTADO DE GUANAJUATO **Edge:** Segmented reeding

Date	Mintage	F	VF	XF	Unc	BU
2005Mo	249,489	—	—	—	35.00	40.00

KM# 819   100 PESOS
29.1690 g., Bi-Metallic .999 Gold 17.154g center in .999 Silver 12.015g ring, 34.5 mm. **Series:** First **Subject:** 180th Anniversary of Federation **Obv:** National arms **Obv. Legend:** ESTADOS UNIDOS MEXICANOS **Rev:** State arms **Rev. Legend:** ESTADO DE GUANAJUATO **Edge:** Segmented reeding

Date	Mintage	F	VF	XF	Unc	BU
2005Mo Proof	1,000	Value: 1,200				

KM# 714   100 PESOS
33.9400 g., Bi-Metallic .925 Silver 16.812g center in Brass ring, 39.04 mm. **Series:** First **Subject:** 180th Anniversary of Federation **Obv:** National arms **Obv. Legend:** ESTADOS UNIDOS MEXICANOS **Rev:** State arms **Rev. Legend:** ESTADO DE DURANGO **Edge:** Segmented reeding

Date	Mintage	F	VF	XF	Unc	BU
2005Mo	249,774	—	—	—	35.00	40.00

KM# 820   100 PESOS
29.1690 g., Bi-Metallic .999 Gold 17.154g center in .999 silver 12.015g ring, 34.5 mm. **Series:** First **Subject:** 180th Anniversary of Federation **Obv:** National arms **Obv. Legend:** ESTADOS UNIDOS MEXICANOS **Rev:** State arms **Rev. Legend:** ESTADO DE DURANGO **Edge:** Segmented reeding

Date	Mintage	F	VF	XF	Unc	BU
2005Mo Proof	1,000	Value: 1,200				

KM# 713   100 PESOS
33.9400 g., Bi-Metallic .925 Silver 16.812g center in Brass ring, 39.04 mm. **Series:** First **Subject:** 180th Anniversary of Federation **Obv:** National arms **Obv. Legend:** ESTADOS UNIDOS MEXICANOS **Rev:** Federal District arms **Rev. Legend:** DISTRITO FEDERAL **Edge:** Segmented reeding

Date	Mintage	F	VF	XF	Unc	BU
2005Mo	249,461	—	—	—	35.00	40.00

KM# 821   100 PESOS
29.1690 g., Bi-Metallic .999 Gold 17.154g center in .999 Silver 12.015g ring, 34.5 mm. **Series:** First **Subject:** 180th Anniversary of Federation **Obv:** National arms **Obv. Legend:** ESTADOS UNIDOS MEXICANOS **Rev:** Federal District arms **Rev. Legend:** DISTRITO FEDERAL **Edge:** Segmented reeding

Date	Mintage	F	VF	XF	Unc	BU
2005Mo Proof	1,000	Value: 1,200				

KM# 754   100 PESOS
33.9400 g., Bi-Metallic .925 Silver 16.812g center in Aluminum-

Bronze ring, 39.04 mm. **Series:** First **Subject:** 180th Anniversary of Federation **Obv:** National arms **Obv. Legend:** ESTADO DE CHIHUAHUA **Rev:** State arms **Rev. Legend:** ESTADO DE CHIHUAHUA **Edge:** Segmented reeding

Date	Mintage	F	VF	XF	Unc	BU
2005Mo	249,102	—	—	—	35.00	40.00

KM# 822   100 PESOS
29.1690 g., Bi-Metallic .999 Gold 17.154g center in .999 Silver 12.015g ring, 34.5 mm. **Series:** First **Subject:** 180th Anniversary of Federation **Obv:** National arms **Obv. Legend:** ESTADOS UNIDOS MEXICANOS **Rev:** State arms **Rev. Legend:** ESTADO DE CHIHUAHUA **Edge:** Segmented reeding

Date	Mintage	F	VF	XF	Unc	BU
2005Mo Proof	1,000	Value: 1,200				

KM# 712   100 PESOS
33.9400 g., Bi-Metallic .925 Silver 16.812g center in Brass ring, 39.04 mm. **Series:** First **Subject:** 180th Anniversary of Federation **Obv:** National arms **Obv. Legend:** ESTADOS UNIDOS MEXICANOS **Rev:** State arms **Rev. Legend:** ESTADO DE CHIAPAS **Edge:** Segmented reeding

Date	Mintage	F	VF	XF	Unc	BU
2005Mo	249,417	—	—	—	35.00	40.00

KM# 823   100 PESOS
29.1690 g., Bi-Metallic .999 Gold 17.154g center in .999 Silver 12.015g ring, 34.5 mm. **Series:** First **Subject:** 180th Anniversary of Federation **Obv:** National arms **Obv. Legend:** ESTADOS UNIDOS MEXICANOS **Rev:** State arms **Rev. Legend:** ESTADO DE CHIAPAS **Edge:** Segmented reeding

Date	Mintage	F	VF	XF	Unc	BU
2005Mo Proof	1,000	Value: 1,200				

KM# 729   100 PESOS
33.8250 g., Bi-Metallic .925 Silver 16.812g center in Aluminum-Bronze ring, 39.04 mm. **Series:** First **Subject:** 180th Anniversary of Federation **Obv:** National arms **Obv. Legend:** ESTADOS UNIDOS MEXICANOS **Rev:** State arms **Rev. Legend:** ESTADO DE COLIMA **Edge:** Segmented reeding

Date	Mintage	F	VF	XF	Unc	BU
2005Mo	248,850	—	—	—	35.00	40.00

KM# 824   100 PESOS
29.1690 g., Bi-Metallic .999 Gold 17.154g center in .999 Silver 12.015g ring, 34.5 mm. **Series:** First **Subject:** 180th Anniversary of Federation **Obv:** National arms **Obv. Legend:** ESTADOS UNIDOS MEXICANOS **Rev:** State arms **Rev. Legend:** ESTADO DE COLIMA **Edge:** Segmented reeding

Date	Mintage	F	VF	XF	Unc	BU
2005Mo Proof	1,000	Value: 1,200				

KM# 752   100 PESOS
33.9400 g., Bi-Metallic .925 Silver 16.812g center in Aluminum-Bronze ring, 39.04 mm. **Series:** First **Subject:** 180th Anniversary of Federation **Obv:** National arms **Obv. Legend:** ESTADOS UNIDOS MEXICANOS **Rev:** State arms **Rev. Legend:** ESTADO DE COAHUILA DE ZARAGOZA **Edge:** Segmented reeding

Date	Mintage	F	VF	XF	Unc	BU
2005Mo	247,991	—	—	—	35.00	40.00

KM# 825   100 PESOS
29.1690 g., Bi-Metallic .999 Gold 17.154g center in .999 Silver 12.015g ring, 34.5 mm. **Series:** First **Subject:** 180th Anniversary of Federation **Obv:** National arms **Obv. Legend:** ESTADOS UNIDOS MEXICANOS **Rev:** State arms **Rev. Legend:** ESTADO DE COAHUILA DE ZARAGOZA **Edge:** Segmented reeding

Date	Mintage	F	VF	XF	Unc	BU
2005Mo Proof	1,000	Value: 1,200				

KM# 727   100 PESOS
33.9400 g., Bi-Metallic .925 Silver 16.812g center in Aluminum-Bronze ring, 39.04 mm.   **Series:** First **Subject:** 180th Anniversary of Federation **Obv:** National arms **Obv. Legend:** ESTADOS UNIDOS MEXICANOS **Rev:** State arms **Rev. Legend:** ESTADO DE CAMPECHE **Edge:** Segmented reeding

Date	Mintage	F	VF	XF	Unc	BU
2005Mo	249,040	—	—	—	35.00	40.00

KM# 826   100 PESOS
29.1690 g., Bi-Metallic .999 Gold 17.154g center in .999 Silver 12.015g ring, 34.5 mm.   **Series:** First **Subject:** 180th Anniversary of Federation **Obv:** National arms **Obv. Legend:** ESTADOS UNIDOS MEXICANOS **Rev:** State arms **Rev. Legend:** ESTADO DE CAMPECHE **Edge:** Segmented reeding

Date	Mintage	F	VF	XF	Unc	BU
2005Mo Proof	1,000	Value: 1,200				

KM# 725   100 PESOS
33.9400 g., Bi-Metallic .925 Silver 16.812g center in Aluminum-Bronze ring, 39.04 mm.   **Series:** First **Subject:** 180th Anniversary of Federation **Obv:** National arms **Obv. Legend:** ESTADOS UNIDOS MEXICANOS **Rev:** State arms **Rev. Legend:** ESTADO DE BAJA CALIFORNIA SUR **Edge:** Segmented reeding

Date	Mintage	F	VF	XF	Unc	BU
2005Mo	249,585	—	—	—	35.00	40.00

KM# 827   100 PESOS
29.1690 g., Bi-Metallic .999 Gold 17.154g center in .999 Silver 12.015g ring, 34.5 mm.   **Series:** First **Subject:** 180th Anniversary of Federation **Obv:** National arms **Obv. Legend:** ESTADOS UNIDOS MEXICANOS **Rev:** State arms **Rev. Legend:** ESTADO DE BAJA CALIFORNIA SUR **Edge:** Segmented reeding

Date	Mintage	F	VF	XF	Unc	BU
2005Mo Proof	1,000	Value: 1,200				

KM# 723   100 PESOS
33.9400 g., Bi-Metallic .925 Silver 16.812g center in Aluminum-Bronze ring, 39.04 mm.   **Series:** First **Subject:** 180th Anniversary of Federation **Obv:** National arms **Obv. Legend:** ESTADOS UNIDOS MEXICANOS **Rev:** State arms **Rev. Legend:** ESTADO DE BAJA CALIFORNIA **Edge:** Segmented reeding

Date	Mintage	F	VF	XF	Unc	BU
2005Mo	249,263	—	—	—	35.00	40.00

KM# 828   100 PESOS
29.1690 g., Bi-Metallic .999 Gold 17.154g center in .999 Silver 12.015g ring, 34.5 mm.   **Series:** First **Subject:** 180th Anniversary of Federation **Obv:** National arms **Obv. Legend:** ESTADOS UNIDOS MEXICANOS **Rev:** State arms **Rev. Legend:** ESTADO DE BAJA CALIFORNIA **Edge:** Segmented reeding

Date	Mintage	F	VF	XF	Unc	BU
2005Mo Proof	1,000	Value: 1,200				

KM# 721   100 PESOS
33.9400 g., Bi-Metallic .925 Silver 16.812g center in Aluminum-Bronze ring, 39.04 mm.   **Series:** First **Subject:** 180th Anniversary of Federation **Obv:** National arms **Obv. Legend:** ESTADOS UNIDOS MEXICANOS **Rev:** Estados de Aguascalientes state arms **Rev. Legend:** ESTADO DE AGUASCALIENTES **Edge:** Segmented reeding

Date	Mintage	F	VF	XF	Unc	BU
2005Mo	248,410	—	—	—	35.00	40.00

KM# 829   100 PESOS
29.1690 g., Bi-Metallic .999 Gold 17.154g center in .999 Silver 12.015g ring, 34.5 mm.   **Series:** First **Subject:** 180th Anniversary of Federation **Obv:** National arms **Obv. Legend:** ESTADOS UNIDOS MEXICANOS **Rev:** State arms **Rev. Legend:** ESTADO DE AGUASCALIENTES **Edge:** Segmented reeding

Date	Mintage	F	VF	XF	Unc	BU
2005Mo Proof	1,000	Value: 1,200				

KM# 719   100 PESOS
33.8250 g., Bi-Metallic .925 Silver 16.812g center in Aluminum-Bronze ring, 39.04 mm.   **Series:** Second **Obv:** National arms **Obv. Legend:** ESTADOS UNIDOS MEXICANOS **Rev:** Facade of the San Marcos garden above sculpture of national emblem at left, San Antonio Temple at right **Rev. Legend:** AGUASCALIENTES **Edge:** Segmented reeding

Date	Mintage	F	VF	XF	Unc	BU
2005Mo	149,705	—	—	—	25.00	30.00

KM# 862   100 PESOS
29.1690 g., Bi-Metallic .999 Gold 17.154g center in .999 Silver 12.015g ring, 34.5 mm.   **Series:** Second **Obv:** National arms **Obv. Legend:** ESTADOS UNIDOS MEXICANOS **Rev:** Facade of the San Marcos garden above sculpture of national emblem at left, San Antonio temple at right **Rev. Legend:** AGUASCALIENTES **Edge:** Segmented reeding

Date	Mintage	F	VF	XF	Unc	BU
2005Mo Proof	600	Value: 1,200				

KM# 758   100 PESOS
33.9400 g., Bi-Metallic .925 Silver 16.812g center in Aluminum-Bronze ring, 39.04 mm.   **Series:** Second **Obv:** National arms **Obv. Legend:** ESTADOS UNIDOS MEXICANOS **Rev:** Ram's head and value within circle **Rev. Legend:** BAJA CALIFORNIA - GOBIERNO DEL ESTADO **Edge:** Segmented reeding

Date	Mintage	F	VF	XF	Unc	BU
2005Mo	149,771	—	—	—	25.00	30.00

KM# 863   100 PESOS
29.1690 g., Bi-Metallic .999 Gold 17.154g center in .999 Silver 12.015g ring, 34.5 mm.   **Series:** Second **Obv:** National arms **Obv. Legend:** ESTTADOS UNIDOS MEXICANOS **Rev:** Ram's head, mountain outline in background **Rev. Legend:** BAJA CALIFORNIA - GOBIERNO DEL ESTADO **Edge:** Segmented reeding

Date	Mintage	F	VF	XF	Unc	BU
2005Mo Proof	600	Value: 1,200				

KM# 762   100 PESOS
33.9400 g., Bi-Metallic .925 Silver 16.812g center in Aluminum-Bronze ring, 39.04 mm.   **Series:** Second **Obv:** National arms **Obv. Legend:** ESTADOS UNIDOS MEXICANOS **Rev:** Outlined map of peninsula at center, cave painting of deer behind, cactus at right **Rev. Legend:** ESTADO DE BAJA CALIFORNIA SUR **Edge:** Segmented reeding

Date	Mintage	F	VF	XF	Unc	BU
2005Mo	149,152	—	—	—	25.00	30.00

KM# 764   100 PESOS
33.7000 g., Bi-Metallic .925 Silver 16.812g center in Aluminum-Bronze ring   **Subject:** 200th Anniversary Birth of Benito Juarez Garcia **Obv:** National arms **Rev:** Bust 1/4 left within circle

Date	Mintage	F	VF	XF	Unc	BU
2006Mo	49,913	—	—	—	40.00	45.00

KM# 864   100 PESOS
29.1690 g., Bi-Metallic .999 Gold 17.154g center in .999 Silver 12.015g ring, 34.5 mm.   **Series:** Second **Obv:** National arms **Obv. Legend:** ESTADOS UNIDOS MEXICANOS **Rev:** Outlined map of peninsula at center, cave painting of deer behind, cactus at right **Rev. Legend:** ESTADO DE BAJA CALIFORNIA SUR **Edge:** Segmented reeding

Date	Mintage	F	VF	XF	Unc	BU
2006Mo Proof	600	Value: 1,200				

KM# 760   100 PESOS
33.9400 g., Bi-Metallic .925 Silver 16.812g center in Aluminum-Bronze ring, 39.04 mm.   **Series:** Second **Subject:** Estado de Campeche **Obv:** National arms **Obv. Legend:** ESTADOS UNIDOS MEXICANOS **Rev:** Jade mask - Calakmul, Campeche **Rev. Legend:** ESTADO DE CAMPECHE **Edge:** Segmented reeding

Date	Mintage	F	VF	XF	Unc	BU
2006Mo	149,803	—	—	—	25.00	30.00

KM# 865   100 PESOS
29.1690 g., Bi-Metallic .999 Gold 17.154g center in .999 Silver 12.015g ring, 34.5 mm.   **Series:** Second **Obv:** National arms **Obv. Legend:** ESTADOS UNIDOS MEXICANOS **Rev:** Jade mask - Calakmul, Campeche **Rev. Legend:** ESTADO DE CAMPECHE **Edge:** Segmented reeding

Date	Mintage	F	VF	XF	Unc	BU
2006Mo Proof	600	Value: 1,200				

KM# 781   100 PESOS
33.7000 g., Bi-Metallic .925 Silver 16.812g center in Aluminum-Bronze ring, 39.04 mm.   **Series:** Second **Obv:** National arms **Obv. Legend:** ESTADOS UNIDOS MEXICANOS **Rev:** Outlined map with turtle, mine cart above grapes at center, Friendship Dam above Christ of the Nodas at left, chimneys above crucibles and bell tower of Santiago's cathedral at right **Rev. Legend:** COAHUILA DE ZARAGOZA **Edge:** Segmented reeding

Date	Mintage	F	VF	XF	Unc	BU
2006Mo	149,560	—	—	—	25.00	30.00

KM# 866   100 PESOS
29.1690 g., Bi-Metallic .999 Gold 17.154g center in .999 Silver 12.015g ring, 34.5 mm.   **Series:** Second **Obv:** National arms **Obv. Legend:** ESTADOS UNIDOS MEXICANOS **Rev:** Outlined map with turtle, mine cart above grapes at center, Friendship dam above Christ of the Nodas at left, chimneys above crucibles and bell tower of Santiago's cathedral at right **Rev. Inscription:** COAHUILA DE ZARAGOZA **Edge:** Segmented reeding

Date	Mintage	F	VF	XF	Unc	BU
2006Mo Proof	600	Value: 1,200				

KM# 777   100 PESOS
33.9400 g., Bi-Metallic .925 Silver 16.812g center in Aluminum-Bronze ring, 39.04 mm.   **Series:** Second **Obv:** National arms **Obv. Legend:** ESTADOS UNIDOS MEXICANOS **Rev:** State arms at lower center, Nevado de Colima and Volcan de Fuego volcanos in background **Rev. Legend:** Colima **Rev. Inscription:** GENEROSO **Edge:** Segmented reeding

Date	Mintage	F	VF	XF	Unc	BU
2006Mo	149,041	—	—	—	25.00	30.00

KM# 867   100 PESOS
29.1690 g., Bi-Metallic .999 Gold 17.154g center in .999 Silver 12.015g ring, 34.5 mm.   **Series:** Second **Obv:** National arms **Obv. Legend:** ESTADOS UNIDOS MEXICANOS **Rev:** State arms at lower center, Nevado de Colima and Volcan de Fuego volcanos in background **Rev. Legend:** Colima **Rev. Inscription:** GENEROSO **Edge:** Segmented reeding

Date	Mintage	F	VF	XF	Unc	BU
2006Mo Proof	600	Value: 1,200				

KM# 773 100 PESOS

33.9400 g., Bi-Metallic .925 Silver 16.812g center in Aluminum-Bronze ring, 39.04 mm. **Series:** Second **Obv:** National arms **Obv. Legend:** ESTADOS UNIDOS MEXICANOS **Rev:** Head of Pakal, ancient Mayan king, Palenque **Rev. Legend:** ESTADO DE CHIAPAS - CABEZA MAYA DEL REY PAKAL, PALENQUE **Edge:** Segmented reeding

Date	Mintage	F	VF	XF	Unc	BU
2006Mo	149,491	—	—	—	25.00	30.00

KM# 868 100 PESOS

29.1690 g., Bi-Metallic .999 Gold 17.154g center in .999 Silver 12.015g ring, 34.5 mm. **Series:** Second **Obv:** National arms **Obv. Legend:** ESTADOS UNIDOS MEXICANOS **Rev:** Head of Pakal, ancient Mayan king, Palenque **Rev. Legend:** ESTADO DE CHIAPAS - CABEZA MAYA DEL REY PAKAL, PALENQUE **Edge:** Segmented reeding

Date	Mintage	F	VF	XF	Unc	BU
2006Mo Proof	600	Value: 1,200				

KM# 775 100 PESOS

33.9400 g., Bi-Metallic .925 Silver 16.812g center in Aluminum-Bronze ring, 39.04 mm. **Series:** Second **Obv:** National arms **Obv. Legend:** ESTADOS UNIDOS MEXICANOS **Rev:** Angel of Liberty **Rev. Legend:** MÉXICO - ANGEL DE LA LIBERTAD, CHIHUAHUA **Edge:** Segmented reeding

Date	Mintage	F	VF	XF	Unc	BU
2006Mo	149,557	—	—	—	25.00	30.00

KM# 869 100 PESOS

29.1690 g., Bi-Metallic .999 Gold 17.154g center in .999 Silver 12.015g ring, 34.5 mm. **Series:** Second **Obv:** National arms **Obv. Legend:** ESTADOS UNIDOS MEXICANOS **Rev:** Angel of Liberty **Rev. Legend:** MÉXICO - ANGEL DE LA LIBERTAD, CHIHUAHUA **Edge:** Segmented reeding

Date	Mintage	F	VF	XF	Unc	BU
2006Mo Proof	600	Value: 1,200				

KM# 779 100 PESOS

33.9400 g., Bi-Metallic .925 Silver 16.812g center in Aluminum-Bronze ring, 39.04 mm. **Series:** Second **Obv:** National arms **Obv. Legend:** ESTADOS UNIDOS MEXICANOS **Rev:** National Palace **Rev. Legend:** DISTRITO FEDERAL - ANTIGUO AYUNTAMIENTO **Edge:** Segmented reeding

Date	Mintage	F	VF	XF	Unc	BU
2006Mo	149,525	—	—	—	25.00	30.00

KM# 870 100 PESOS

29.1690 g., Bi-Metallic .999 Gold 17.154g center in .999 Silver 12.015g ring, 34.5 mm. **Series:** Second **Obv:** National arms **Obv. Legend:** ESTADOS UNIDOS MEXICANOS **Rev:** National palace **Rev. Legend:** DISTRITO FEDERAL - ANTIGUO AYUNTAMIENTO **Edge:** Segmented reeding

Date	Mintage	F	VF	XF	Unc	BU
2006Mo Proof	600	Value: 1,200				

KM# 787 100 PESOS

33.9400 g., Bi-Metallic .925 Silver 16.812g center in Brass ring, 39.04 mm. **Series:** Second **Obv:** National arms **Obv. Legend:** ESTADOS UNIDOS MEXICANOS **Rev:** Tree **Rev. Legend:** PRIMERA RESERVA NACIONAL FORESTAL - DURANGO **Edge:** Segmented reeding

Date	Mintage	F	VF	XF	Unc	BU
2006Mo	149,034	—	—	—	25.00	30.00

KM# 871 100 PESOS

29.1690 g., Bi-Metallic .999 Gold 17.154g center in .999 Silver 12.015g ring, 34.5 mm. **Series:** Second **Obv:** National arms **Obv. Legend:** ESYADOS UNIDOS MEXICANOS **Rev:** Tree **Rev. Legend:** PRIMERA RESERVA NACIONAL RORESTAL - DURANGO **Edge:** Segmented reeding

Date	Mintage	F	VF	XF	Unc	BU
2006Mo Proof	600	Value: 1,200				

KM# 789 100 PESOS

33.9400 g., Bi-Metallic .925 Silver 16.812g center in Brass ring, 39.04 mm. **Series:** Second **Obv:** National arms **Obv. Legend:** ESTADOS UNIDOS MEXICANOS **Rev:** State arms at center, statue of Miguel Hidalgo at left, monument to Pipla at lower right **Rev. Inscription:** Guanajuato **Edge:** Segmented reeding

Date	Mintage	F	VF	XF	Unc	BU
2006Mo	149,921	—	—	—	25.00	30.00

KM# 872 100 PESOS

29.1690 g., Bi-Metallic .999 Gold 17.154g center in .999 Silver 12.015g ring, 34.50 mm. **Series:** Second **Obv:** National arms **Obv. Legend:** ESTADOS UNIDOS MEXICANOS **Rev:** State arms at lower center, statue of Miguel Hidalgo at left, monument to Pipila at lower right **Rev. Inscription:** Guanajauto **Edge:** Segmented reeding

Date	Mintage	F	VF	XF	Unc	BU
2006Mo Proof	600	Value: 1,200				

KM# 791 100 PESOS

33.9400 g., Bi-Metallic .925 Silver 16.812g center in Brass ring, 39.04 mm. **Series:** Second **Obv:** National arms **Obv. Legend:** ESTADOS UNIDOS MEXICANOS **Rev:** Stylized portrait of Vicente Guerrero at left, church of Taxco at upper center, Acapulco's la Quebrada with diver above Christmas Eve flower and mask **Rev. Legend:** GUERRERO **Edge:** Segmented reeding

Date	Mintage	F	VF	XF	Unc	BU
2006Mo	149,675	—	—	—	25.00	30.00

KM# 873 100 PESOS

29.1690 g., Bi-Metallic .999 Gold 17.154g center in .999 Silver 12.015g ring, 34.5 mm. **Series:** Second **Obv:** National arms **Obv. Legend:** ESTADOS UNIDOS MEXICANOS **Rev:** Stylized portrait of Vicente Guerrero at left, church of Taxco at upper center, Acapulco's la Quebrada with diver over Christmas Eve flower and mask **Rev. Legend:** GUERRERO **Edge:** Segmented reeding

Date	Mintage	F	VF	XF	Unc	BU
2006Mo Proof	600	Value: 1,200				

KM# 793 100 PESOS

33.9400 g., Bi-Metallic .925 Silver 16.812g center in Aluminum-Bronze ring, 39.04 mm. **Series:** Second **Obv:** National arms **Obv. Legend:** ESTADOS UNIDOS MEXICANOS **Rev:** Monument of Pachuca Hidalgo **Rev. Inscription:** RELOJ / MONUMENTAL / DE / PACHUCA / HIDALGO - La / Bella / Airosa **Edge:** Segmented reeding

Date	Mintage	F	VF	XF	Unc	BU
2006Mo	149,273	—	—	—	25.00	30.00

KM# 874 100 PESOS

29.1690 g., Bi-Metallic .999 Gold 17.154g center in .999 Silver 12.015g ring, 34.5 mm. **Series:** Second **Obv:** National arms **Obv. Legend:** ESTADOS UNIDOS MEXICANOS **Rev:** Monument of Pachuca Hidalgo **Rev. Inscription:** RELOJ / MONUMENTAL / DE / PACHUCA / HIDALGO **Edge:** Segmented reeding

Date	Mintage	F	VF	XF	Unc	BU
2006Mo Proof	600	Value: 1,200				

KM# 795 100 PESOS

33.9400 g., Bi-Metallic .925 Silver 16.812g center in Brass ring, 39.04 mm. **Series:** Second **Obv:** National arms **Rev:** Hospicio Cabañas orphanage **Rev. Legend:** ESTADO DE JALISCO **Edge:** Segmented reeding

Date	Mintage	F	VF	XF	Unc	BU
2006Mo	149,750	—	—	—	25.00	30.00

KM# 875 100 PESOS

29.1690 g., Bi-Metallic .999 Gold 17.154g center in .999 Silver 12.015g ring, 34.5 mm. **Series:** Second **Obv:** National arms **Obv. Legend:** ESTADOS UNIDOS MEXICANOS **Rev:** Hospicio Cabañas orphanage **Rev. Legend:** ESTADO DE JALISCO **Edge:** Segmented reeding

Date	Mintage	F	VF	XF	Unc	BU
2006Mo Proof	600	Value: 1,200				

KM# 802 100 PESOS

33.9400 g., Bi-Metallic .925 Silver 16.812g center in Aluminum-Bronze ring, 39.04 mm. **Series:** Second **Obv:** National arms **Obv. Legend:** ESTADOS UNIDOS MEXICANOS **Rev:** Pyramid de la Loona (moon) **Rev. Legend:** ESTADO DE MÉXICO **Edge:** Segmented reeding

Date	Mintage	F	VF	XF	Unc	BU
2006Mo	149,377	—	—	—	25.00	30.00

KM# 876 100 PESOS

29.1690 g., Bi-Metallic .999 Gold 17.154g center in .999 Silver 12.015g ring, 34.5 mm. **Series:** Second **Obv:** National arms **Obv. Legend:** ESTADOS UNIDOS MEXICANOS **Rev:** Pyramid de la Looona (moon) **Rev. Legend:** ESTADO DE MÉXICO **Edge:** Segmented reeding

Date	Mintage	F	VF	XF	Unc	BU
2006Mo Proof	600	Value: 1,200				

KM# 785 100 PESOS

33.9400 g., Bi-Metallic .925 Silver 16.812g center in Aluminum-Bronze ring, 39.04 mm. **Series:** Second **Obv:** National arms **Obv. Legend:** ESTADOS UNIDOS MEXICANOS **Rev:** Four Monarch butterflies **Rev. Legend:** ESTADO DE MICHOACÁN **Edge:** Segmented reeding

Date	Mintage	F	VF	XF	Unc	BU
2006Mo	149,730	—	—	—	25.00	30.00

KM# 877 100 PESOS

29.1690 g., Bi-Metallic .999 Gold 17.154g center in .999 Silver 12.015g ring, 34.5 mm. **Series:** Second **Obv:** National arms **Obv. Legend:** ESTADOS UNIDOS MEXICANOS **Rev:** Four Monarch butterflies **Rev. Legend:** ESTADO DE MICHOACÁN **Edge:** Segmented reeding

Date	Mintage	F	VF	XF	Unc	BU
2006Mo Proof	600	Value: 1,200				

KM# 800 100 PESOS

33.9400 g., Bi-Metallic .925 Silver 16.812g center in Aluminum-Bronze ring, 39.04 mm. **Series:** Second **Obv:** National arms **Obv. Legend:** ESTADOS UNIDOS MEXICANOS **Rev:** 1/2 length figure of Chinelo (local dancer) at right, Palacio de Cortes in background **Rev. Inscription:** ESTADO DE / MORELOS **Edge:** Segmented reeding

Date	Mintage	F	VF	XF	Unc	BU
2006Mo	149,648	—	—	—	25.00	30.00

KM# 878 100 PESOS

29.1690 g., Bi-Metallic .999 Gold 17.154g center in .999 Silver 12.015g ring, 34.5 mm. **Series:** Second **Obv:** National arms **Obv. Legend:** ESTADOS UNIDOS MEXICANOS **Rev:** 1/2 length figure of Chinelo (local dancer) at right, Palacio de Cortes in background **Rev. Inscription:** ESTADO DE / MORELOS **Edge:** Segmented reeding

Date	Mintage	F	VF	XF	Unc	BU
2006Mo Proof	600	Value: 1,200				

KM# 798 100 PESOS

33.9400 g., 33.8250 Bi-Metallic .925 Silver 16.812g center in

Aluminum-Bronze ring 36.908 oz., 39.04 mm. **Series:** Second **Obv:** National arms **Obv. Legend:** ESTADOS UNIDOS MEXICANOS **Rev:** Isle de Mexcaltitlán **Rev. Legend:** ESTADO DE NAYARIT **Edge:** Segmented reeding

Date	Mintage	F	VF	XF	Unc	BU
2007Mo	149,560	—	—	—	25.00	30.00

KM# 879 100 PESOS
29.1690 g., Bi-Metallic .999 Gold 17.154g center in .999 12.015g ring, 34.5 mm. **Series:** Second **Obv:** National arms **Obv. Legend:** ESTADOS UNIDOS MEXICANOS **Rev:** Isle de Mexcaltitlán **Rev. Legend:** ESTADO DE NAYARIT **Edge:** Segmented reeding

Date	Mintage	F	VF	XF	Unc	BU
2007Mo Proof	600	Value: 1,200				

KM# 848 100 PESOS
33.9400 g., Bi-Metallic .925 Silver 20.1753 center in Aluminum-Bronze ring, 39.04 mm. **Series:** Second **Obv:** National arms **Obv. Legend:** ESTADOS UNIDOS MEXICANOS **Rev:** Old foundry in Parque Fundidora (public park) at right, Cerro de la Silla (Saddle Hill) in background **Rev. Legend:** ESTADO DE NUEVO LÉON **Edge:** Segmented reeding

Date	Mintage	F	VF	XF	Unc	BU
2007Mo	149,425	—	—	—	25.00	30.00

KM# 880 100 PESOS
29.1690 g., Bi-Metallic .999 Gold 17.154g center in .999 Silver 12.015g ring, 34.5 mm. **Series:** Second **Obv:** National arms **Obv. Legend:** ESTADOS UNIDOS MEXICANOS **Rev:** Old foundry in Parque Fundidora (public park) at right, Cerro de la Silla (Saddle hill) in background **Rev. Legend:** ESTADO DE NUEVO LÉON **Edge:** Segmented reeding

Date	Mintage	F	VF	XF	Unc	BU
2007Mo Proof	600	Value: 1,200				

KM# 849 100 PESOS
33.9400 g., Bi-Metallic .925 Silver 20.1753g center in Aluminum-Bronze ring, 39.04 mm. **Series:** Second **Obv:** National arms **Obv. Legend:** ESTADOS UNIDOS MEXICANOS **Rev:** Teatro Macedonio Alcala (theater) **Rev. Legend:** OAXACA **Edge:** Segmented reeding

Date	Mintage	F	VF	XF	Unc	BU
2007Mo	149,892	—	—	—	25.00	30.00

KM# 881 100 PESOS
29.1690 g., Bi-Metallic .999 Gold 17.154g center in .999 Silver 12.015g ring, 34.50 mm. **Series:** Second **Obv:** National arms **Obv. Legend:** ESTADOS UNIDOS MEXICANOS **Rev:** Teatro Macedonio Alcala (theater) **Rev. Legend:** OAXACA **Edge:** Segmented reeding

Date	Mintage	F	VF	XF	Unc	BU
2007Mo Proof	600	Value: 1,200				

KM# 850 100 PESOS
33.9400 g., Bi-Metallic .925 Silver 20.1753g center in Aluminum-Bronze ring, 39.04 mm. **Series:** Second **Obv:** National arms **Obv. Legend:** ESTADOS UNIDOS MEXICANOS **Rev:** Talavera porcelain dish **Rev. Legend:** ESTADO DE PUEBLA **Edge:** Segmented reeding

Date	Mintage	F	VF	XF	Unc	BU
2007Mo	149,474	—	—	—	25.00	30.00

KM# 882 100 PESOS
29.1690 g., Bi-Metallic .999 Gold 17.154g center in .999 Silver 12.015g ring, 34.5 mm. **Series:** Second **Obv:** National arms **Obv. Legend:** ESTADOS UNIDOS MEXICANOS **Rev:** Talavera porcelain dish **Rev. Legend:** ESTADO DE PUEBLA **Edge:** Segmented reeding

Date	Mintage	F	VF	XF	Unc	BU
2007Mo Proof	600	Value: 1,200				

KM# 851 100 PESOS
33.9400 g., Bi-Metallic .925 Silver 20.1753g center in Aluminum-Bronze ring, 39.04 mm. **Series:** Second **Obv:** National arms **Obv. Legend:** ESTADOS UNIDOS MEXICANOS **Rev:** Mask at left, rays above state arms at center **Rev. Legend:** QUINTANA ROO **Edge:** Segmented reeding

Date	Mintage	F	VF	XF	Unc	BU
2007Mo	149,582	—	—	—	25.00	30.00

KM# 883 100 PESOS
29.1690 g., Bi-Metallic .999 Gold 17.154g center in .999 Silver 12.015g ring, 34.5 mm. **Series:** Second **Obv:** National arms **Obv. Legend:** ESTADOS UNIDOS MEXICANOS **Rev:** Mask at left, rays above state arms at center, Mayan ruins at right **Rev. Legend:** QUINTANA ROO **Edge:** Segmented reeding

Date	Mintage	F	VF	XF	Unc	BU
2007Mo Proof	600	Value: 1,200				

KM# 852 100 PESOS
33.9400 g., Bi-Metallic .925 Silver 20.1753 center in Aluminum-Bronze ring, 39.04 mm. **Series:** Second **Obv:** National arms **Obv. Legend:** ESTADOS UNIDOS MEXICANOS **Rev:** Aqueduct of Querétaro at left, church of Santa Rosa de Verbero at right **Rev. Legend:** ESTADO DE QUERÉTARO ARTEAGA **Edge:** Segmented reeding

Date	Mintage	F	VF	XF	Unc	BU
2007Mo	149,127	—	—	—	25.00	30.00

KM# 884 100 PESOS
29.1690 g., Bi-Metallic .999 Gold 17.154g center in .999 Silver 12.015g ring, 34.5 mm. **Series:** Second **Obv:** National arms **Obv. Legend:** ESTADOS UNIDOS MEXICANOS **Rev:** Aqueduct of Querétaro at left, church of Santa Rosa de Verbero at right **Rev. Legend:** ESTADO DE QUERÉTARO ARTEAGA **Edge:** Segmented reeding

Date	Mintage	F	VF	XF	Unc	BU
2007Mo Proof	600	Value: 1,200				

KM# 853 100 PESOS
33.9400 g., Bi-Metallic .925 Silver 20.1753g center in Aluminum-Bronze ring, 39.04 mm. **Series:** Second **Obv:** National arms **Obv. Legend:** ESTADOS UNIDOS MEXICANOS **Rev:** Facade of Caja Real **Rev. Legend:** • SAN LUIS POTOSÍ • **Edge:** Segmented reeding

Date	Mintage	F	VF	XF	Unc	BU
2007Mo	148,750	—	—	—	25.00	30.00

KM# 885 100 PESOS
29.1690 g., Bi-Metallic .999 Gold 17.154g center in .999 Silver 12.015 ring, 34.5 mm. **Series:** Second **Obv:** National arms **Obv. Legend:** ESTADOS UNIDOS MEXICANOS **Rev:** Facade of Caja Real **Rev. Legend:** • SAN LUIS POTOSÍ • **Edge:** Segmented reeding

Date	Mintage	F	VF	XF	Unc	BU
2007Mo Proof	600	Value: 1,200				

KM# 854 100 PESOS
33.9400 g., Bi-Metallic .925 Silver 20.1753g center in Aluminum-Bronze ring, 39.04 mm. **Series:** Second **Obv:** National arms **Obv. Legend:** ESTADOS UNIDOS MEXICANOS **Rev:** Shield on pile of cactus fruits **Rev. Legend:** ESTADO DE SINALOA - LUGAR DE PITAHAYAS **Edge:** Segmented reeding

Date	Mintage	F	VF	XF	Unc	BU
2007Mo	149,032	—	—	—	25.00	30.00

KM# 886 100 PESOS
29.1690 g., Bi-Metallic .999 Gold 17.154 center in .999 Silver 12.015g ring, 34.5 mm. **Series:** Second **Obv:** National arms **Obv. Legend:** ESTADOS UNIDOS MEXICANOS **Rev:** Shield on pile of cactus fruits **Rev. Legend:** ESTADO DE SINALOA - LUGAR DE PITAHAYES **Edge:** Segmented reeding

Date	Mintage	F	VF	XF	Unc	BU
2007Mo Proof	600	Value: 1,200				

KM# 855 100 PESOS
33.9400 g., Bi-Metallic .925 Silver 20.1753 center in Aluminum-Bronze ring, 39.04 mm. **Series:** Second **Obv:** National arms **Obv. Legend:** ESTADOS UNIDOS MEXICANOS **Rev:** Local in Dance of the Deer at left, cactus at right, mountains in background **Rev. Legend:** ESTADO DE SONORA **Edge:** Segmented reeding

Date	Mintage	F	VF	XF	Unc	BU
2007Mo	149,891	—	—	—	25.00	30.00

KM# 887 100 PESOS
29.1690 g., Bi-Metallic .999 Gold 17.154g center in .999 Silver 12.015g ring, 34.5 mm. **Series:** Second **Obv:** National arms **Obv. Legend:** ESTADOS UNIDOS MEXICANOS **Rev:** Local in Dance of the Deer at left, cactus at right, mountains in background **Rev. Legend:** ESTADO DE SONORA **Edge:** Segmented reeding

Date	Mintage	F	VF	XF	Unc	BU
2007Mo Proof	600	Value: 1,200				

KM# 856 100 PESOS
33.9400 g., Bi-Metallic .925 Silver 20.1753 center in Aluminum-Bronze ring, 39.04 mm. **Series:** Second **Obv:** National arms **Obv. Legend:** ESTADOS UNIDOS MEXICANOS **Rev:** Fuente de los Pescadores (fisherman fountain) at lower left, giant head from the Olmec-pre-Hispanic culture at right, Planetario Tabasco in background **Rev. Legend:** TABASCO **Edge:** Segmented reeding

Date	Mintage	F	VF	XF	Unc	BU
2007Mo	149,715	—	—	—	25.00	30.00

KM# 888 100 PESOS
29.1690 g., Bi-Metallic .999 Gold 17.154g center in .999 Silver 12.015g ring, 34.5 mm. **Series:** Second **Obv:** National arms **Obv. Legend:** ESTADOS UNIDOS MEXICANOS **Rev:** Fuente de los Pescadores (fisherman fountain) at lower left, giant head from the Olmec-pre-Hispanic culture at right, Planetario Tabasco in background **Rev. Legend:** TABASCO **Edge:** Segmented reeding

Date	Mintage	F	VF	XF	Unc	BU
2007Mo Proof	600	Value: 1,200				

KM# 857 100 PESOS
33.9400 g., Bi-Metallic .925 Silver 20.1753g center in Aluminum-Bronze ring, 39.04 mm. **Series:** Second **Obv:** National arms **Obv. Legend:** ESTADOS UNIDOS MEXICANOS **Rev:** Ridge - Cerro Del Bernal, Gonzáles **Rev. Legend:** TAMAULIPAS **Edge:** Segmented reeding

Date	Mintage	F	VF	XF	Unc	BU
2007Mo	149,776	—	—	—	25.00	30.00

KM# 889 100 PESOS
29.1690 g., Bi-Metallic .999 Gold 17.154g center in .999 Silver 12.015g ring, 34.5 mm. **Series:** Second **Obv:** National arms **Obv. Legend:** ESTADOS DE MEXICANOS **Rev:** Ridge - Cerro Del Bernal, Gonzáles **Rev. Legend:** TAMAULIPAS **Edge:** Segmented reeding

Date	Mintage	F	VF	XF	Unc	BU
2007Mo Proof	600	Value: 1,200				

KM# 858 100 PESOS
33.9400 g., Bi-Metallic .925 Silver 20.1753g center in Aluminum-Bronze ring, 39.04 mm. **Series:** Second **Obv:** National arms **Obv. Legend:** ESTADOS UNIDOS MEXICANOS **Rev:** Basilica de Ocotlán at left, state arms above Capilla Abierta, Plaza de Toros Ranchero Aguilar below, Exconvento de San Francisco at right **Rev. Legend:** ESTADO DE TLAXCALA **Edge:** Segmented reeding

Date	Mintage	F	VF	XF	Unc	BU
2007Mo	149,465	—	—	—	25.00	30.00

KM# 890 100 PESOS
29.1690 g., Bi-Metallic .999 Gold 17.154g center in .999 Silver 12.015g ring, 34.5 mm. **Series:** Second **Obv:** National arms **Obv. Legend:** ESTADOS UNIDOS MEXICANOS **Rev:** Basilica de Ocotlán at left, state arms above Capilla Abierta, Plaza de Toros Ranchero Aguilar below, Exconvento de San Francisco at right **Rev. Legend:** ESTADO DE TLAXCALA **Edge:** Segmented reeding

Date	Mintage	F	VF	XF	Unc	BU
2007Mo Proof	600	Value: 1,200				

KM# 859 100 PESOS
33.9400 g., Bi-Metallic .912 Silver 20.1753g center in Aluminum-Bronze ring, 39.04 mm. **Series:** Second **Obv:** National arms **Obv. Legend:** ESTADOS UNIDOS MEXICANOS **Rev:** Pyramid of El Tajín **Rev. Legend:** • VERACRUZ • - • DE IGNACIO DE LA LLAVE • **Edge:** Segmented reeding

Date	Mintage	F	VF	XF	Unc	BU
2007Mo	149,703	—	—	—	25.00	30.00

KM# 891 100 PESOS
29.1690 g., Bi-Metallic .999 Gold 17.154g center in .999 Silver 12.015g ring, 34.5 mm. **Series:** Second **Obv:** National arms **Obv. Legend:** ESTADOS UNIDOS MEXICANOS **Rev:** Pyramid of El Tajin **Rev. Legend:** • VERACRUZ • - • DE IGNACIO DE LA LLAVE • **Edge:** Segmented reeding

Date	Mintage	F	VF	XF	Unc	BU
2007Mo Proof	600	Value: 1,200				

KM# 860 100 PESOS
33.9400 g., Bi-Metallic .925 Silver 20.1753 center in Aluminum-Bronze ring, 39.04 mm. **Series:** Second **Obv:** National arms **Obv. Legend:** ESTADOS UNIDOS MEXICANOS **Rev:** Stylized pyramid of Chichén Itzá **Rev. Legend:** Castillo de Chichén Itzá **Edge:** Segmented reeding

Date	Mintage	F	VF	XF	Unc	BU
2007Mo	149,579	—	—	—	25.00	30.00

KM# 892 100 PESOS
29.1690 g., Bi-Metallic .999 Gold 17.154g center in .999 Silver 12.015g ring, 34.5 mm. **Series:** Second **Obv:** National arms **Obv. Legend:** ESTADOS UNIDOS MEXICANOS **Rev:** Stylized pyramid of Chichén-Itzá **Rev. Inscription:** YUCATÁN **Edge:** Segmented reeding

Date	Mintage	F	VF	XF	Unc	BU
2007Mo Proof	600	Value: 1,200				

KM# 861 100 PESOS
33.9400 g., Bi-Metallic .925 Silver 20.1753g center in Aluminum-Bronze ring, 39.04 mm. **Series:** Second **Obv:** National arms **Obv. Legend:** ESTADOS UNIDOS MEXICANOS **Rev:** Cable car above Monumento al Minero at left, Cathedral of Zacatecas at center right **Rev. Legend:** ZACATECAS **Edge:** Segmented reeding

Date	Mintage	F	VF	XF	Unc	BU
2007Mo	148,833	—	—	—	25.00	30.00

KM# 893 100 PESOS
29.1690 g., Bi-Metallic .999 Gold 17.154g center in .999 Silver 12.015g ring, 34.5 mm. **Series:** Second **Obv:** National arms **Obv. Legend:** ESTADOS UNIDOS MEXICANOS **Rev:** Cable car above Monumento al Minero at left, Cathedral of Zacatecas at center right **Rev. Legend:** Zacatecas **Edge:** Segmented reeding

Date	Mintage	F	VF	XF	Unc	BU
2007Mo Proof	600	Value: 1,200				

KM# 932 200 PESOS
41.6666 g., 0.9000 Gold 1.2056 oz. AGW, 37 mm. **Subject:** Independence 200th Anniversary **Obv:** National Arms **Rev:** Winged Victory

Date	Mintage	F	VF	XF	Unc	BU
2010Mo	50,000	—	—	—	—	2,800
2010Mo Proof	4,998	Value: 2,500				

KM# 771 50000 PESOS
7.7700 g., 0.9990 Gold 0.2496 oz. AGW, 23 mm. **Subject:** World Cup Soccer **Obv:** Mexican Eagle and Snake **Rev:** Kneeling Mayan Pelota player and soccer ball

Date	Mintage	F	VF	XF	Unc	BU
2006Mo Proof	9,505	Value: 600				

SILVER BULLION COINAGE
Libertad Series

KM# 921 100 PESOS
1000.0000 g., 0.9990 Silver 32.117 oz. ASW **Obv:** National arms in center of past and present arms **Rev:** Aztec Calendar **Edge:** Plain

Date	Mintage	F	VF	XF	Unc	BU
2010Mo Prooflike	1,500	—	—	—	—	2,000

KM# 609 1/20 ONZA (1/20 Troy Ounce of Silver)
1.5551 g., 0.9990 Silver 0.0499 oz. ASW **Obv:** National arms, eagle left **Rev:** Winged Victory

Date	Mintage	F	VF	XF	Unc	BU
2001Mo	4,500	—	—	—	—	25.00
2001Mo Proof	1,500	Value: 30.00				
2002Mo	50,000	—	—	—	—	16.00
2002Mo Proof	2,800	Value: 25.00				
2003Mo	30,000	—	—	—	—	16.00
2003Mo Proof	4,400	Value: 25.00				
2004Mo	30,000	—	—	—	—	16.00
2004Mo Proof	2,700	Value: 25.00				
2005Mo	15,000	—	—	—	—	16.00
2005Mo Proof	2,600	Value: 25.00				
2006Mo	20,000	—	—	—	—	16.00
2006Mo Proof	3,300	Value: 25.00				
2007Mo	3,500	—	—	—	—	16.00
2007Mo Proof	4,000	Value: 25.00				
2008Mo	7,000	—	—	—	—	16.00
2008Mo Proof	3,300	Value: 25.00				
2009Mo	10,000	—	—	—	—	16.00
2009Mo Proof	5,000	Value: 25.00				
2010Mo	12,000	—	—	—	—	16.00
2010Mo Proof	10,000	Value: 25.00				
2011Mo	—	—	—	—	—	16.00
2011Mo Proof	—	Value: 25.00				

KM# 610 1/10 ONZA (1/10 Troy Ounce of Silver)
3.1103 g., 0.9990 Silver 0.0999 oz. ASW **Obv:** National arms, eagle left **Rev:** Winged Victory

Date	Mintage	F	VF	XF	Unc	BU
2001Mo	25,000	—	—	—	—	27.50
2001Mo Proof	1,500	Value: 36.00				
2002Mo	35,000	—	—	—	—	20.00
2002Mo Proof	2,800	Value: 30.00				
2003Mo	20,000	—	—	—	—	20.00
2003Mo Proof	4,900	Value: 30.00				
2004Mo	15,000	—	—	—	—	20.00
2004Mo Proof	2,500	Value: 30.00				
2005Mo	9,277	—	—	—	—	20.00
2005Mo Proof	3,000	Value: 27.50				
2006Mo	15,000	—	—	—	—	20.00
2006Mo Proof	3,000	Value: 27.50				
2007Mo	3,500	—	—	—	—	20.00
2007Mo Proof	4,000	Value: 27.50				
2008Mo	10,000	—	—	—	—	20.00
2008Mo Proof	5,000	Value: 27.50				
2009Mo	10,000	—	—	—	—	20.00
2009Mo Proof	5,000	Value: 27.50				
2010Mo	12,000	—	—	—	—	20.00
2010Mo Proof	10,000	Value: 27.50				
2011Mo	—	—	—	—	—	20.00
2011Mo Proof	—	Value: 27.50				

KM# 611 1/4 ONZA (1/4 Troy Ounce of Silver)
7.7758 g., 0.9990 Silver 0.2497 oz. ASW **Obv:** National arms, eagle left **Rev:** Winged Victory

Date	Mintage	F	VF	XF	Unc	BU
2001Mo	25,000	—	—	—	—	36.00
2001Mo Proof	1,000	Value: 44.00				
2002Mo	35,000	—	—	—	—	27.50
2002Mo Proof	2,800	Value: 40.00				
2003Mo	22,000	—	—	—	—	27.50
2003Mo Proof	3,900	Value: 40.00				
2004Mo	15,000	—	—	—	—	27.50
2004Mo Proof	2,500	Value: 40.00				
2005Mo	15,000	—	—	—	—	27.50
2005Mo Proof	2,400	Value: 37.00				
2006Mo	15,000	—	—	—	—	25.00
2006Mo Proof	2,900	Value: 37.00				
2007Mo	3,500	—	—	—	—	25.00
2007Mo Proof	3,000	Value: 37.00				
2008Mo	9,000	—	—	—	—	25.00
2008Mo Proof	2,800	Value: 37.00				
2009Mo	10,000	—	—	—	—	25.00
2009Mo Proof	3,000	Value: 37.00				
2010Mo	20,000	—	—	—	—	25.00
2010Mo Proof	5,000	Value: 37.00				
2011Mo	—	—	—	—	—	25.00
2011Mo Proof	—	Value: 37.00				

KM# 612 1/2 ONZA (1/2 Troy Ounce of Silver)
15.5517 g., 0.9990 Silver 0.4995 oz. ASW **Obv:** National arms, eagle left **Rev:** Winged Victory

Date	Mintage	F	VF	XF	Unc	BU
2001Mo	20,000	—	—	—	—	45.00
2001Mo Proof	1,000	Value: 60.00				
2002Mo	35,000	—	—	—	—	37.00
2002Mo Proof	2,800	Value: 50.00				
2003Mo	28,000	—	—	—	—	37.00
2003Mo Proof	3,400	Value: 50.00				
2004Mo	20,000	—	—	—	—	37.00
2004Mo Proof	2,500	Value: 50.00				
2005Mo	10,000	—	—	—	—	37.00
2005Mo Proof	2,800	Value: 44.00				
2006Mo	15,000	—	—	—	—	37.00
2006Mo Proof	2,900	Value: 44.00				
2007Mo	3,500	—	—	—	—	37.00
2007Mo Proof	1,500	Value: 44.00				
2008Mo	9,000	—	—	—	—	37.00
2008Mo Proof	2,500	Value: 44.00				
2009Mo	10,000	—	—	—	—	37.00
2009Mo Proof	3,000	Value: 44.00				
2010Mo	20,000	—	—	—	—	37.00
2010Mo Proof	5,000	Value: 44.00				
2011Mo	—	—	—	—	—	37.00
2011Mo Proof	—	Value: 44.00				

KM# 639 ONZA (Troy Ounce of Silver)
31.1000 g., 0.9990 Silver 0.9988 oz. ASW **Subject:** Libertad **Obv:** National arms, eagle left within center of past and present arms **Rev:** Winged Victory **Edge:** Reeded

Date	Mintage	F	VF	XF	Unc	BU
2001Mo	725,000	—	—	—	—	60.00
2001Mo Proof	2,000	Value: 140				
2002Mo	854,000	—	—	—	—	55.00
2002Mo Proof	3,800	Value: 150				
2003Mo	805,000	—	—	—	—	55.00
2003Mo Proof	5,400	Value: 130				
2004Mo	450,000	—	—	—	—	75.00
2004Mo Proof	3,000	Value: 130				
2005Mo	698,281	—	—	—	—	90.00
2005Mo Proof	3,300	Value: 150				
2006Mo	300,000	—	—	—	—	55.00
2006Mo Proof	4,000	Value: 140				
2007Mo	200,000	—	—	—	—	95.00
2007Mo Proof	5,800	Value: 150				
2008Mo	950,000	—	—	—	—	65.00
2008Mo Proof	11,000	Value: 150				
2009Mo	1,650,000	—	—	—	—	75.00
2009Mo Proof	10,000	Value: 150				
2010Mo	1,000,000	—	—	—	—	75.00
2010Mo Proof	10,000	Value: 140				
2011Mo	—	—	—	—	—	75.00
2011Mo Proof	—	Value: 140				

KM# 614 2 ONZAS (2 Troy Ounces of Silver)
62.2070 g., 0.9990 Silver 1.9979 oz. ASW, 48 mm. **Subject:** Libertad **Obv:** National arms, eagle left within center of past and present arms **Rev:** Winged Victory **Edge:** Reeded

Date	Mintage	F	VF	XF	Unc	BU
2001Mo	6,700	—	—	—	—	120
2001Mo Proof	500	Value: 300				
2002Mo	8,700	—	—	—	—	110
2002Mo Proof	1,000	Value: 225				
2003Mo	9,500	—	—	—	—	110
2003Mo Proof	800	Value: 225				
2004Mo	8,000	—	—	—	—	100
2004Mo Proof	1,000	Value: 175				
2005Mo	3,549	—	—	—	—	100
2005Mo Proof	600	Value: 500				
2006Mo	5,800	—	—	—	—	100
2006Mo Proof	1,100	Value: 175				
2007Mo	8,000	—	—	—	—	100
2007Mo Proof	500	Value: 250				
2008Mo	17,000	—	—	—	—	110
2008Mo Proof	1,000	Value: 170				
2009Mo	46,000	—	—	—	—	110
2009Mo Proof	6,200	Value: 150				
2010Mo	14,000	—	—	—	—	110
2010Mo Proof	1,300	Value: 190				
2011Mo	—	—	—	—	—	110
2011Mo Proof	—	Value: 190				

KM# 615 5 ONZAS (5 Troy Ounces of Silver)
155.5175 g., 0.9990 Silver 4.9948 oz. ASW, 65 mm. **Subject:**
Libertad **Obv:** National arms, eagle left within center of past and
present arms **Rev:** Winged Victory **Edge:** Reeded **Note:**
Illustration reduced.

Date	Mintage	F	VF	XF	Unc	BU
2001Mo	4,000	—	—	—	—	190
2001Mo Proof	600	Value: 325				
2002Mo	5,200	—	—	—	—	190
2002Mo Proof	1,000	Value: 325				
2003Mo	6,000	—	—	—	—	180
2003Mo Proof	1,500	Value: 250				
2004Mo	3,923	—	—	—	—	180
2004Mo Proof	800	Value: 225				
2005Mo	2,401	—	—	—	—	205
2005Mo Proof	1,000	Value: 225				
2006Mo	3,000	—	—	—	—	180
2006Mo Proof	700	Value: 265				
2007Mo	3,000	—	—	—	—	180
2007Mo Proof	500	Value: 205				
2008Mo	9,000	—	—	—	—	205
2008Mo Proof	900	Value: 270				
2009Mo	21,000	—	—	—	—	225
2009Mo Proof	5,000	Value: 270				
2010Mo	9,500	—	—	—	—	250
2010Mo Proof	2,000	Value: 270				

KM# 677 KILO (32.15 Troy Ounces of Silver)
999.9775 g., 0.9990 Silver 32.116 oz. ASW, 110 mm. **Subject:**
Collector Bullion **Obv:** National arms in center of past and present
arms **Rev:** Winged Victory **Edge:** Reeded

Date	Mintage	F	VF	XF	Unc	BU
2001Mo Prooflike	—	—	—	—	—	2,200
2002Mo Prooflike	1,820	—	—	—	—	1,750
2003Mo Prooflike	1,514	—	—	—	—	1,650
2004Mo Prooflike	1,501	—	—	—	—	1,800
2005Mo Prooflike	500	—	—	—	—	1,750
2006Mo Prooflike	874	—	—	—	—	1,650
2007Mo Prooflike	700	—	—	—	—	1,650
2008Mo	2,003	—	—	—	—	1,400
2008Mo Prooflike	1,700	—	—	—	—	1,650
2009Mo	4,000	—	—	—	—	—
2009Mo Prooflike	1,700	—	—	—	—	1,650
2010Mo	4,000	—	—	—	—	1,400
2010Mo Prooflike	1,500	—	—	—	—	1,650

GOLD BULLION COINAGE

KM# 671 1/20 ONZA (1/20 Ounce of Pure Gold)
1.5551 g., 0.9990 Gold 0.0499 oz. AGW, 13 mm. **Obv:** National
arms, eagle left **Rev:** Winged Victory **Edge:** Reeded **Note:**
Design similar to KM#609. Value estimates do not include the
high taxes and surcharges added to the issue prices by the
Mexican Government.

Date	Mintage	F	VF	XF	Unc	BU
2002Mo	5,000	—	—	—	—	BV+30%
2003Mo	800	—	—	—	—	BV+32%
2004Mo	4,000	—	—	—	—	BV+30%
2005Mo	3,200	—	—	—	—	BV+30%
2005Mo Proof	400	BV+35%				
2006Mo	3,000	—	—	—	—	BV+30%
2006Mo Proof	520	BV+35%				
2007Mo	1,200	—	—	—	—	BV+30%
2007Mo Proof	500	BV+35%				
2008Mo	800	—	—	—	—	BV+30%
2008Mo Proof	500	BV+35%				
2009Mo	2,000	—	—	—	—	BV+30%
2009Mo Proof	600	BV+35%				

Date	Mintage	F	VF	XF	Unc	BU
2010Mo	1,500	—	—	—	—	BV+35%
2010Mo Proof	600	BV+35%				

KM# 672 1/10 ONZA (1/10 Ounce of Pure Gold)
3.1103 g., 0.9990 Gold 0.0999 oz. AGW, 16 mm. **Obv:** National
arms, eagle left **Rev:** Winged Victory **Note:**
Design similar to KM#610. Value estimates do not include the
high taxes and surcharges added to the issue prices by the
Mexican Government.

Date	Mintage	F	VF	XF	Unc	BU
2002Mo	5,000	—	—	—	—	BV+20%
2003Mo	300	—	—	—	—	BV+22%
2004Mo	2,000	—	—	—	—	BV+20%
2005Mo	500	—	—	—	—	BV+20%
2005Mo Proof	400	BV+22%				
2006Mo	2,500	—	—	—	—	BV+20%
2006Mo Proof	520	BV+22%				
2007Mo	1,200	—	—	—	—	BV+20%
2007Mo Proof	500	BV+22%				
2008Mo	2,500	—	—	—	—	BV+20%
2008Mo Proof	500	BV+22%				
2009Mo	9,000	—	—	—	—	BV+20%
2009Mo Proof	600	BV+22%				
2010Mo	4,500	—	—	—	—	BV+20%
2010Mo Proof	600	BV+22%				

KM# 673 1/4 ONZA (1/4 Ounce of Pure Gold)
7.7758 g., 0.9990 Gold 0.2497 oz. AGW, 23 mm. **Obv:** National
arms, eagle left **Rev:** Winged Victory **Edge:** Reeded **Note:**
Design similar to KM#611. Value estimates do not include the
high taxes and surcharges added to the issue prices by the
Mexican Government.

Date	Mintage	F	VF	XF	Unc	BU
2002Mo	5,000	—	—	—	—	BV+12%
2003Mo	300	—	—	—	—	BV+14%
2004Mo	1,500	—	—	—	—	BV+12%
2004Mo Proof	1,000	BV+15%				
2005Mo	500	—	—	—	—	BV+14%
2005Mo Proof	2,600	BV+15%				
2006Mo	1,500	—	—	—	—	BV+12%
2006Mo Proof	2,120	BV+15%				
2007Mo	500	—	—	—	—	BV+14%
2007Mo Proof	1,500	BV+15%				
2008Mo	800	—	—	—	—	BV+14%
2008Mo Proof	800	BV+15%				
2009Mo	3,000	—	—	—	—	BV+12%
2009Mo Proof	1,700	BV+15%				
2010Mo	1,500	—	—	—	—	BV+12%
2010Mo Proof	1,000	BV+15%				

KM# 674 1/2 ONZA (1/2 Ounce of Pure Gold)
15.5517 g., 0.9990 Gold 0.4995 oz. AGW, 29 mm. **Obv:**
National arms, eagle left **Rev:** Winged Victory **Edge:** Reeded
Note: Design similar to KM#612. Value estimates do not include
the high taxes and surcharges added to the issue prices by the
Mexican Government.

Date	Mintage	F	VF	XF	Unc	BU
2002Mo	5,000	—	—	—	—	BV+8%
2003Mo	300	—	—	—	—	BV+10%
2004Mo	500	—	—	—	—	BV+8%
2005Mo	500	—	—	—	—	BV+10%
2005Mo Proof	400	BV+12%				
2006Mo	500	—	—	—	—	BV+10%
2006Mo Proof	520	BV+12%				
2007Mo	500	—	—	—	—	BV+10%
2007Mo Proof	500	BV+12%				
2008Mo	300	—	—	—	—	BV+10%
2008Mo Proof	500	BV+12%				
2009Mo	3,000	—	—	—	—	BV+8%
2009Mo Proof	600	BV+12%				
2010Mo	1,500	—	—	—	—	BV+8%
2010Mo Proof	600	BV+12%				

KM# 675 ONZA (Ounce of Pure Gold)
31.1035 g., 0.9990 Gold 0.9990 oz. AGW, 34.5 mm. **Obv:**
National arms, eagle left **Rev:** Winged Victory **Edge:** Reeded
Note: Design similar to KM#639. Value estimates do not include
the high taxes and surcharges added to the issue prices by the
Mexican Government.

Date	Mintage	F	VF	XF	Unc	BU
2002Mo	15,000	—	—	—	—	BV+3%
2003Mo	500	—	—	—	—	BV+4%
2004Mo	3,000	—	—	—	—	BV+3%
2005Mo	3,000	—	—	—	—	BV+3%
2005Mo Proof	250	BV+5%				
2006Mo	4,000	—	—	—	—	BV+3%
2006Mo Proof	520	BV+5%				
2007Mo	2,500	—	—	—	—	BV+3%
2007Mo Proof	500	BV+5%				
2008Mo	800	—	—	—	—	BV+3%
2008Mo Proof	500	BV+5%				
2009Mo	6,200	—	—	—	—	BV+3%
2009Mo Proof	600	BV+5%				
2010Mo	4,000	—	—	—	—	BV+3%
2010Mo Proof	6,000	BV+5%				

BANK SETS

Hard Case Sets unless otherwise noted.

KM#	Date	Mintage	Identification	Issue Price	Mkt Val
BS38	2001 (10)	—	KM#546-549, 603-605, 636-638 Set in folder	—	65.00
BS39	2002 (8)	—	KM#546-549, 603-605, 616 Set in folder	—	30.00
BS40	2003 (6)	—	KM#547-549, 603-605 Set in folder	—	30.00

MOLDOVA

The Republic of Moldova (formerly the Moldavian S.S.R.) is
bordered in the north, east and south by the Ukraine and on the
west by Romania. It has an area of 13,000 sq.mi. (33,700 sq.km.)
and a population of 4.4 million. The capital is Chisinau. Agricultural products are mainly cereals, grapes, tobacco, sugar
beets and fruits. Food processing, clothing, building materials
and agricultural machinery manufacturing dominate industry.

MONETARY SYSTEM
100 Bani = 1 Leu

REPUBLIC
DECIMAL COINAGE

KM# 1 BAN
0.6700 g., Aluminum, 14.5 mm. **Obv:** National arms **Rev:** Value
divides date above monogram **Edge:** Plain

Date	Mintage	F	VF	XF	Unc	BU
2004	—	—	—	—	0.25	0.50
2006	—	—	—	—	0.25	0.50

KM# 2 5 BANI
0.7500 g., Aluminum, 16 mm. **Obv:** National arms **Rev:**
Monogram divides sprigs below value and date **Edge:** Plain

Date	Mintage	F	VF	XF	Unc	BU
2001	—	—	—	0.15	0.35	0.50
2002	—	—	—	0.15	0.35	0.50
2003	—	—	—	0.15	0.35	0.50
2004	—	—	—	0.15	0.35	0.50
2005	—	—	—	0.15	0.35	0.50
2006	—	—	—	0.15	0.35	0.50
2008	—	—	—	0.15	0.35	0.50
2010	—	—	—	0.15	0.35	0.50

KM# 7 10 BANI
0.8500 g., Aluminum, 16.6 mm. **Obv:** National arms **Rev:** Value,
date and monogram **Edge:** Plain

Date	Mintage	F	VF	XF	Unc	BU
2001	—	—	—	—	0.40	0.60
2002	—	—	—	—	0.40	0.60
2003	—	—	—	—	0.40	0.60
2004	—	—	—	—	0.40	0.60
2005	—	—	—	—	0.40	0.60
2006	—	—	—	—	0.40	0.60
2008	—	—	—	—	0.40	0.60
2010	—	—	—	—	0.40	0.60
2011	—	—	—	—	0.40	0.60

KM# 3 25 BANI
0.9500 g., Aluminum, 17.5 mm. **Obv:** National arms **Rev:**
Monogram divides sprigs below value and date **Edge:** Plain

Date	Mintage	F	VF	XF	Unc	BU
2001	—	—	—	0.20	0.50	0.75
2002	—	—	—	0.20	0.50	0.75
2003	—	—	—	0.20	0.50	0.75
2004	—	—	—	0.20	0.50	0.75
2005	—	—	—	0.20	0.50	0.75
2006	—	—	—	0.20	0.50	0.75
2008	—	—	—	0.20	0.50	0.75

Date	Mintage	F	VF	XF	Unc	BU
2010	—	—	—	—	0.20	0.50	0.75
2011	—	—	—	—	0.20	0.50	0.75

KM# 10   50 BANI
3.1000 g., Brass Clad Steel, 19 mm. **Obv:** National arms **Rev:** Value and date within grapevine **Edge:** Reeded

Date	Mintage	F	VF	XF	Unc	BU
2003	—	—	—	—	1.50	2.00
2005	—	—	—	—	1.50	2.00
2008	—	—	—	—	1.50	2.00

KM# 12   10 LEI
13.5000 g., 0.9250 Silver 0.4015 oz. ASW, 24.5 mm. **Obv:** National arms above value **Rev:** European wildcat within circle **Edge:** Plain

Date	Mintage	F	VF	XF	Unc	BU
2001 Proof	1,000	Value: 65.00				

KM# 13   10 LEI
13.5000 g., 0.9250 Silver 0.4015 oz. ASW, 24.5 mm. **Obv:** National arms above value **Rev:** Green Woodpecker on tree within circle **Edge:** Plain

Date	Mintage	F	VF	XF	Unc	BU
2001 Proof	1,000	Value: 60.00				

KM# 19   10 LEI
13.4500 g., 0.9250 Silver 0.4000 oz. ASW, 24.5 mm. **Obv:** National arms above value **Rev:** European Mink within circle **Edge:** Plain

Date	Mintage	F	VF	XF	Unc	BU
2003 Proof	500	Value: 65.00				

KM# 20   10 LEI
13.4500 g., 0.9250 Silver 0.4000 oz. ASW, 24.5 mm. **Obv:** National arms above value **Rev:** Black Storks within circle **Edge:** Plain

Date	Mintage	F	VF	XF	Unc	BU
2003 Proof	500	Value: 65.00				

KM# 25   10 LEI
25.0000 g., Nickel Plated Brass, 30 mm. **Subject:** Wine Holiday **Obv:** National arms above value **Rev:** Wine grapes, goblet and flask **Edge:** Plain

Date	Mintage	F	VF	XF	Unc	BU
2003 Proof	—	Value: 12.50				

KM# 22   10 LEI
13.5000 g., 0.9250 Silver 0.4015 oz. ASW, 24.5 mm. **Obv:** National arms above value **Rev:** Pine Marten within circle **Edge:** Plain

Date	Mintage	F	VF	XF	Unc	BU
2004 Proof	500	Value: 65.00				

KM# 29   10 LEI
25.0000 g., Nickel Plated Brass, 30 mm. **Subject:** European Women's Chess Championship **Obv:** Arms, date at top, value at bottom **Obv. Legend:** REPUBLICA - 2005 - MOLDOVA **Rev:** 2 chess figures on board at left, map at right **Rev. Inscription:** 2005 CHISINAU **Edge:** Plain

Date	Mintage	F	VF	XF	Unc	BU
2005 Proof	—	Value: 12.50				

KM# 30   10 LEI
13.5000 g., 0.9250 Silver 0.4015 oz. ASW, 24.5 mm. **Obv:** Arms, value below **Obv. Legend:** REPUBLICA MOLDOVA **Rev:** Imperial eagle on branch, legend follows the coin circumference **Edge:** Plain

Date	Mintage	F	VF	XF	Unc	BU
2005 Proof	500	Value: 65.00				

KM# 33   10 LEI
13.5000 g., 0.9250 Silver 0.4015 oz. ASW, 24.5 mm. **Obv:** Arms, value below **Obv. Legend:** REPUBLICA - 2006 - MOLDOVA **Rev:** Bird in grass, legend around circumference using Latin name **Edge:** Plain

Date	Mintage	F	VF	XF	Unc	BU
2006 Proof	500	Value: 65.00				

KM# 38   10 LEI
13.5000 g., 0.9250 Silver 0.4015 oz. ASW, 24.5 mm. **Rev:** Common ground squirrel

Date	Mintage	F	VF	XF	Unc	BU
2006 Proof	500	Value: 65.00				

KM# 43   10 LEI
13.5000 g., 0.9250 Silver 0.4015 oz. ASW, 24.5 mm. **Rev:** White water lilly

Date	Mintage	F	VF	XF	Unc	BU
2008 Proof	500	Value: 60.00				

KM# 47   20 LEI
13.5000 g., 0.9250 Silver 0.4015 oz. ASW, 22 mm. **Subject:** Assumption of the Virgin Mary

Date	Mintage	F	VF	XF	Unc	BU
2009 Proof	1,000	Value: 40.00				

KM# 36   50 LEI
16.5000 g., 0.9250 Silver 0.4907 oz. ASW, 30 mm. **Subject:** Vazile Alecsandri, 180th Anniversary **Obv:** Arms **Rev:** Bust and landscape

Date	Mintage	F	VF	XF	Unc	BU
2001 Proof	1,000	Value: 40.00				

KM# 17   50 LEI
16.5000 g., 0.9250 Silver 0.4907 oz. ASW, 30 mm. **Obv:** National arms above value **Rev:** Constantin Brancusi and building **Edge:** Plain

Date	Mintage	F	VF	XF	Unc	BU
2001 Proof	1,000	Value: 65.00				

KM# 18   50 LEI
16.5000 g., 0.9250 Silver 0.4907 oz. ASW, 30 mm. **Obv:** National arms above value **Rev:** Vasile Alecsandri with book and landscape **Edge:** Plain

Date	Mintage	F	VF	XF	Unc	BU
2001 Proof	1,000	Value: 65.00				

KM# 21   50 LEI
16.5000 g., 0.9250 Silver 0.4907 oz. ASW, 29.8 mm. **Subject:** Effigy of Dimitrie Cantemir **Obv:** National arms above value **Rev:** Bust facing flanked by dates and scroll **Edge:** Plain

Date	Mintage	F	VF	XF	Unc	BU
2003 Proof	500	Value: 165				

KM# 14   50 LEI
16.5500 g., 0.9250 Silver 0.4922 oz. ASW, 29.9 mm. **Subject:** Effigy of Miron Costin **Obv:** National arms above value **Rev:** Bust with hat 1/4 right flanked by dates and books **Edge:** Plain

Date	Mintage	F	VF	XF	Unc	BU
2003 Proof	500	Value: 165				

KM# 23   50 LEI
16.5000 g., 0.9250 Silver 0.4907 oz. ASW, 30 mm. **Obv:** National arms above value **Rev:** Bust of Bishop facing holding scepter **Edge:** Plain

Date	Mintage	F	VF	XF	Unc	BU
2004 Proof	500	Value: 90.00				

KM# 31   50 LEI
16.5000 g., 0.9250 Silver 0.4907 oz. ASW, 30 mm. **Subject:** 415th Anniversary - Birth of Grigore Ureche **Obv:** Arms, date divides legend at top, value below **Obv. Legend:** REPUBLICA MOLDOVA **Rev:** Bust faces right, scroll with feather pen at right, inscription on scroll **Rev. Legend:** GRIGORE URECHE **Rev. Inscription:** Letopisetul Tarii Moldovei **Edge:** Plain

Date	Mintage	F	VF	XF	Unc	BU
2005 Proof	—	Value: 120				

KM# 34   50 LEI
16.5000 g., 0.9250 Silver 0.4907 oz. ASW, 30 mm. **Subject:** 200th Anniversary - Birth of Alexandru Donici **Obv:** Arms, date divides legend, value below **Obv. Legend:** REPUBLICA MOLDOVA **Rev:** Bust of Donici facing, life dates on ribbon below **Rev. Legend:** ALEXANDRU DONICI

Date	Mintage	F	VF	XF	Unc	BU
2006 Proof	—	Value: 120				

KM# 40   50 LEI
16.5000 g., 0.9250 Silver 0.4907 oz. ASW, 30 mm. **Subject:** Metropolitian Varilaam **Rev:** Bust 3/4 right

Date	Mintage	F	VF	XF	Unc	BU
2007 Proof	500	Value: 120				

KM# 41   50 LEI
16.5000 g., 0.9250 Silver 0.4907 oz. ASW, 30 mm. **Subject:** Pottery Tradition **Rev:** Hand modeling clay vessel on pottery wheel

Date	Mintage	F	VF	XF	Unc	BU
2007 Proof	500	Value: 60.00				

KM# 44   50 LEI
16.5000 g., 0.9250 Silver 0.4907 oz. ASW, 30 mm. **Subject:** Oak tree in Stefan **Rev:** Oak tree

Date	Mintage	F	VF	XF	Unc	BU
2008 Proof	500	Value: 75.00				

KM# 45 50 LEI
16.5000 g., 0.9250 Silver 0.4907 oz. ASW, 30 mm. **Subject:**
Cooper Trade **Rev:** Barrell maker

Date	Mintage	F	VF	XF	Unc	BU
2008 Proof	500	Value: 55.00				

KM# 48 50 LEI
16.5000 g., 0.9250 Silver 0.4907 oz. ASW, 30 mm. **Subject:**
Geodezic arc of Struve **Rev:** Map

Date	Mintage	F	VF	XF	Unc	BU
2009 Proof	500	Value: 75.00				

KM# 49 50 LEI
16.5000 g., 0.9250 Silver 0.4907 oz. ASW, 30 mm. **Subject:**
Rule of Vasile Lupu **Rev:** Open book and coat-of-arms

Date	Mintage	F	VF	XF	Unc	BU
2009 Proof	500	Value: 75.00				

KM# 50 50 LEI
16.5000 g., 0.9250 Silver 0.4907 oz. ASW, 30 mm. **Subject:**
Traditional weaving **Rev:** Woman seated at weaving frame

Date	Mintage	F	VF	XF	Unc	BU
2009 Proof	500	Value: 70.00				

KM# 53 50 LEI
16.5000 g., 0.9990 Silver 0.5299 oz. ASW, 30 mm. **Subject:**
Traditional Musical Instruments **Obv:** National arms **Rev:** Violinh,
bagpipem, pan pike and flute

Date	Mintage	F	VF	XF	Unc	BU
2010 Proof	500	Value: 35.00				

KM# 54 50 LEI
16.5000 g., 0.9990 Silver 0.5299 oz. ASW, 30 mm. **Obv:**
National arms **Rev:** Archeological complex of Old Orhei

Date	Mintage	F	VF	XF	Unc	BU
2010 Proof	500	Value: 45.00				

KM# 55 50 LEI
13.0000 g., 0.9990 Silver 0.4175 oz. ASW, 28 mm. **Subject:**
Maria Cebotari, 100th Anniversary of Birth **Obv:** National arms
Rev: Cebotari bust left

Date	Mintage	F	VF	XF	Unc	BU
2010 Proof	500	Value: 45.00				

KM# 56 50 LEI
13.0000 g., 0.9990 Silver 0.4175 oz. ASW, 28 mm. **Subject:**
Doina and Ion Aldea-Teodorovici **Obv:** National arms **Rev:**
Conjoined busts right

Date	Mintage	F	VF	XF	Unc	BU
2010 Proof	500	Value: 45.00				

KM# 58 50 LEI
16.5000 g., 0.9990 Silver 0.5299 oz. ASW, 30 mm. **Subject:**
Moldovan Football, 100th Anniversary **Obv:** National Arms **Rev:**
Soccer player

Date	Mintage	F	VF	XF	Unc	BU
2010 Proof	300	Value: 45.00				

KM# 59 50 LEI
16.5000 g., 0.9990 Silver 0.5299 oz. ASW, 30 mm. **Subject:**
Annunciation Church in Chisinau, 200th Anniversary **Obv:**
National Arms **Rev:** Church façade

Date	Mintage	F	VF	XF	Unc	BU
2010 Proof	500	Value: 45.00				

KM# 60 50 LEI
13.0000 g., 0.9990 Silver 0.4175 oz. ASW, 28 mm. **Subject:**
Grigore Vieru **Obv:** National Arms **Rev:** Profile bust right

Date	Mintage	F	VF	XF	Unc	BU
2010 Proof	500	Value: 45.00				

KM# 65 50 LEI
13.0000 g., 0.9990 Silver 0.4175 oz. ASW, 28 mm. **Subject:**
Bogdan Petriceicu Hasdeu **Obv:** National arms **Rev:** Bust **Edge:**
Reeded

Date	Mintage	F	VF	XF	Unc	BU
2011 Proof	500	Value: 50.00				

KM# 67 50 LEI
13.0000 g., 0.9990 Silver 0.4175 oz. ASW, 28 mm. **Subject:**
Alexandru Bernardazzi, 180th Anniversary of Birth **Obv:** National
arms **Rev:** Portrait **Edge:** Reeded

Date	Mintage	F	VF	XF	Unc	BU
2011 Proof	500	Value: 50.00				

KM# 68 50 LEI
16.5000 g., 0.9990 Silver 0.5299 oz. ASW, 30 mm. **Obv:**
National arms **Rev:** Spoonbill standing left, oval background
Edge: Reeded

Date	Mintage	F	VF	XF	Unc	BU
2011 Proof	500	Value: 50.00				

KM# 69 50 LEI
16.5000 g., 0.9990 Silver 0.5299 oz. ASW, 30 mm. **Subject:**
Holiday Traditions **Obv:** National arms **Rev:** Carolers **Edge:**
Reeded

Date	Mintage	F	VF	XF	Unc	BU
2011 Proof	1,000	Value: 50.00				

KM# 16 100 LEI
31.1000 g., 0.9250 Silver 0.9249 oz. ASW, 37 mm. **Subject:**
10th Anniversary of Independence **Obv:** National arms above
value **Rev:** Arch monument within circle above value and sprigs
Edge: Plain

Date	Mintage	F	VF	XF	Unc	BU
2001 Proof	1,000	Value: 220				

KM# 26 100 LEI
7.8000 g., 0.9999 Gold 0.2507 oz. AGW, 24 mm. **Obv:** National
arms above value **Rev:** King Stephan the Great (1456-1504)
Edge: Plain

Date	Mintage	F	VF	XF	Unc	BU
2004 Proof	—	Value: 400				

KM# 32 100 LEI
31.1000 g., 0.9250 Silver 0.9249 oz. ASW, 37 mm. **Subject:**
Burebista - King of Dacians **Obv:** Arms, date divides legend at
top, value below **Obv. Legend:** REPUBLICA MOLDOVA **Rev:**
Bust of Burebista at left, battle scene of Geto-Dacians with
Romans at right **Rev. Legend:** BUREBISTA REGELE DACILOR
Edge: Plain

Date	Mintage	F	VF	XF	Unc	BU
2005 Proof	500	Value: 300				

KM# 35 100 LEI
31.1000 g., 0.9250 Silver 0.9249 oz. ASW, 37 mm. **Subject:**
15th Anniversary - Independence Proclamation of the Republic
of Moldova **Obv:** Arms, date divides legend above, value below
Obv. Legend: REPUBLICA MOLDOVA **Rev:** Map of Moldova
within stars in inner circle, legend around **Rev. Legend:**
PROCLAMAREA INDEPENDENTEI / 1991-2006 **Edge:** Plain

Date	Mintage	F	VF	XF	Unc	BU
2006 Proof	500	Value: 500				

KM# 37 100 LEI
31.1050 g., 0.9250 Silver 0.9250 oz. ASW, 37 mm. **Subject:**
National Bank, 15th Anniversary **Obv:** Arms **Rev:** Bank building
and coins

Date	Mintage	F	VF	XF	Unc	BU
2006 Proof	500	Value: 140				

KM# 39 100 LEI
31.1050 g., 0.9990 Silver 0.9990 oz. ASW, 37 mm. **Subject:**
National Bank, 15th Anniversary **Rev:** Bank building

Date	Mintage	F	VF	XF	Unc	BU
2006 Proof	500	Value: 140				

KM# 42 100 LEI
31.1050 g., 0.9250 Silver 0.9250 oz. ASW, 37 mm. **Subject:**
Petru Rares **Rev:** Bust 3/4 right

Date	Mintage	F	VF	XF	Unc	BU
2007 Proof	500	Value: 450				

KM# 46 100 LEI
31.1000 g., 0.9250 Silver 0.9249 oz. ASW, 37 mm. **Subject:**
Antioh Cantemir **Rev:** Half-length figure standing 3/4 left

Date	Mintage	F	VF	XF	Unc	BU
2008 Proof	1,000	Value: 100				

KM# 52 100 LEI
15.5000 g., 0.9990 Gold 0.4978 oz. AGW, 28 mm. **Subject:**
Dimitrie Cantemir **Obv:** National Arms **Rev:** Cantemir seated at
desk

Date	Mintage	F	VF	XF	Unc	BU
2008 Proof	300	Value: 950				

KM# 51 100 LEI
22.5000 g., 0.9250 Silver 0.6691 oz. ASW, 34 mm. **Subject:**
Moldovan Chronicals, 15-18 Centuries **Rev:** Man seated writing

Date	Mintage	F	VF	XF	Unc	BU
2009 Proof	1,000	Value: 90.00				

KM# 57 100 LEI
15.5000 g., 0.9990 Gold 0.4978 oz. AGW, 28 mm. **Subject:**
Doina and Ion Aldea-Teodorovici **Obv:** National arms **Rev:**
Conjoined busts right

Date	Mintage	F	VF	XF	Unc	BU
2010 Proof	300	Value: 950				

KM# 61   100 LEI
15.5000 g., 0.9990 Gold 0.4978 oz. AGW, 28 mm. **Subject:** Grigore Vieru **Obv:** National Arms **Rev:** Profile bust left

Date	Mintage	F	VF	XF	Unc	BU
2010 Proof	300	Value: 950				

KM# 62   100 LEI
31.1000 g., 0.9990 Silver 0.9988 oz. ASW, 37 mm. **Subject:** National Bank of Moldova, 20th Anniversary **Obv:** National arms **Rev:** National Bank logo **Edge:** Reeded

Date	Mintage	F	VF	XF	Unc	BU
2011 Proof	500	Value: 75.00				

KM# 63   100 LEI
31.1000 g., 0.9990 Silver 0.9988 oz. ASW, 37 mm. **Subject:** Independence, 20th Anniversary **Obv:** National arms **Rev:** Father and son holding Moldovian flag **Edge:** Reeded

Date	Mintage	F	VF	XF	Unc	BU
2011 Proof	1,000	Value: 75.00				

KM# 64   100 LEI
31.1000 g., 0.9990 Silver 0.9988 oz. ASW, 37 mm. **Subject:** Chisinau, 575th Anniversary of Founding of the City **Obv:** National arms **Rev:** Mazarachi Hill **Edge:** Reeded

Date	Mintage	F	VF	XF	Unc	BU
2011 Proof	1,000	Value: 75.00				

KM# 66   100 LEI
7.8000 g., 0.9990 Gold 0.2505 oz. AGW, 24 mm. **Subject:** Bogdan Petriceicu Hasdeu **Obv:** National arms **Rev:** Bust **Edge:** Reeded

Date	Mintage	F	VF	XF	Unc	BU
2011 Proof	300	Value: 475				

MONACO

The Principality of Monaco, located on the Mediterranean coast nine miles from Nice, has an area of 0.58 sq. mi. (1.9 sq. km.) and a population of 26,000. Capital: Monaco-Ville. The economy is based on tourism and the manufacture of cosmetics, gourmet foods and highly specialized electronics. Monaco also derives its revenue from a tobacco monopoly and the sale of postage stamps for philatelic purpose. Gambling in Monte Carlo accounts for only a small fraction of the country's revenue.

RULERS
Rainier III, 1949-2005
Albert II, 2005-

MINT PRIVY MARKS
(a) - Paris (privy marks only)
    Horseshoe - 2001 and 2002
    Heart – 2002-2003
    French Horn with starfish in water – 2003-
(p) - Thunderbolt - Poissy

MONETARY SYSTEM
100 Euro Cents = 1 Euro

PRINCIPALITY
EURO COINAGE

KM# 167   EURO CENT
2.3000 g., Copper Plated Steel, 16.25 mm. **Ruler:** Rainier III **Obv:** Crowned arms **Rev:** Value and globe **Edge:** Plain

Date	Mintage	F	VF	XF	Unc	BU
2001(a)	327,200	—	—	—	20.00	35.00
2001(a) Proof	3,500	Value: 75.00				
2002(a) In sets only	40,000	—	—	—	—	75.00
2003(a)	—	—	—	—	—	10.00
2004(a) Proof	14,999	Value: 25.00				
2005(a) Proof	35,000	Value: 50.00				

KM# 188   EURO CENT
2.3000 g., Copper Plated Steel, 16.25 mm. **Ruler:** Albert II **Obv:** Crowned arms within circle of stars **Rev:** Value and globe

Date	Mintage	F	VF	XF	Unc	BU
2006 Proof	11,180	Value: 30.00				
2007	—	—	—	—	—	30.00
2009 In sets only	8,020	—	—	—	—	30.00

KM# 168   2 EURO CENT
3.0600 g., Copper Plated Steel, 18.75 mm. **Ruler:** Rainier III **Obv:** Crowned arms **Rev:** Value and globe **Edge:** Grooved

Date	Mintage	F	VF	XF	Unc	BU
2001(a)	393,400	—	—	—	15.00	30.00
2001(a) Proof	3,500	Value: 85.00				
2002(a) In sets only	40,000	—	—	—	—	85.00
2003(a)	—	—	—	—	—	10.00
2004(a) Proof	14,999	Value: 35.00				
2005(a) Proof	35,000	Value: 50.00				

KM# 189   2 EURO CENT
3.0600 g., Copper Plated Steel, 18.75 mm. **Ruler:** Albert II **Obv:** Crowned arms within circle of stars **Rev:** Value and globe **Edge:** Grooved

Date	Mintage	F	VF	XF	Unc	BU
2006 Proof	11,260	Value: 25.00				
2007	—	—	—	—	—	25.00
2009 In sets only	8,020	—	—	—	—	25.00

KM# 169   5 EURO CENT
3.9200 g., Copper Plated Steel, 21.25 mm. **Ruler:** Rainier III **Obv:** Crowned arms **Rev:** Value and globe **Edge:** Plain

Date	Mintage	F	VF	XF	Unc	BU
2001(a)	320,000	—	—	—	20.00	35.00
2001(a) Proof	3,500	Value: 95.00				
2002(a) In sets only	40,000	—	—	—	—	85.00
2003(a)	—	—	—	—	—	15.00
2004(a) Proof	14,999	Value: 45.00				
2005(a) Proof	35,000	Value: 55.00				

KM# 190   5 EURO CENT
3.9200 g., Copper Plated Steel, 21.25 mm. **Ruler:** Albert II **Obv:** Crowned arms within circle of stars **Rev:** Value and globe

Date	Mintage	F	VF	XF	Unc	BU
2006 Proof	11,180	Value: 30.00				
2007	—	—	—	—	—	30.00
2009 In sets only	8,020	—	—	—	—	30.00
2011 In sets only	7,000	—	—	—	—	30.00

KM# 170   10 EURO CENT
4.1000 g., Brass, 19.75 mm. **Ruler:** Rainier III **Obv:** Knight on horse **Rev:** Value and map **Edge:** Reeded

Date	Mintage	F	VF	XF	Unc	BU
2001(a)	320,000	—	—	—	15.00	25.00
2001(a) Proof	3,500	Value: 110				
2002(a)	407,200	—	—	—	8.00	12.00
2003(a)	100,800	—	—	—	12.00	16.00
2004(a) Proof	14,999	Value: 50.00				

KM# 181   10 EURO CENT
4.1000 g., Brass, 19.75 mm. **Ruler:** Albert II **Obv:** Crowned AA monogram **Rev:** Relief map of Western Europe, stars, lines and value **Edge:** Reeded

Date	Mintage	F	VF	XF	Unc	BU
2006(a) Proof	11,180	Value: 50.00				

KM# 191   10 EURO CENT
4.1000 g., Brass, 19.75 mm. **Ruler:** Albert II **Obv:** Crowned AA monogram **Rev:** Relief map of western Europe, stars, lines and value **Edge:** Reeded

Date	Mintage	F	VF	XF	Unc	BU
2007(a)	—	—	—	—	—	30.00
2009(a) In sets only	8,020	—	—	—	—	30.00
2011(a) In sets only	7,000	—	—	—	—	30.00

KM# 171   20 EURO CENT
5.7400 g., Brass, 22.25 mm. **Ruler:** Rainier III **Obv:** Knight on horse **Rev:** Value and map **Edge:** Notched

Date	Mintage	F	VF	XF	Unc	BU
2001(a)	386,400	—	—	—	15.00	20.00
2001(a) Proof	3,500	Value: 120				
2002(a)	376,000	—	—	—	12.00	16.00
2003(a)	100,000	—	—	—	12.00	16.00
2004(a) Proof	14,999	Value: 60.00				

KM# 182   20 EURO CENT
5.7400 g., Brass, 22.25 mm. **Ruler:** Albert II **Obv:** Crowned AA monogram **Rev:** Relief map of Western Europe, stars, lines and value **Edge:** Notched

Date	Mintage	F	VF	XF	Unc	BU
2006(a) Proof	11,180	Value: 60.00				

KM# 192   20 EURO CENT
5.7400 g., Brass, 22.25 mm. **Ruler:** Albert II **Obv:** Crowned AA monogram **Rev:** Relief map of western Europe, stars, lines and value **Edge:** Notched

Date	Mintage	F	VF	XF	Unc	BU
2007(a)	—	—	—	—	—	30.00
2009(a) In sets only	8,020	—	—	—	—	30.00
2011(a) In sets only	7,000	—	—	—	—	30.00

KM# 172   50 EURO CENT
7.8000 g., Brass, 24.25 mm. **Ruler:** Rainier III **Obv:** Knight on horse **Rev:** Value and map **Edge:** Reeded

Date	Mintage	F	VF	XF	Unc	BU
2001 (a)	320,000	—	—	—	15.00	30.00
2001 (a) Proof	3,500	Value: 130				
2002 (a)	364,000	—	—	—	8.00	12.00
2003 (a)	100,000	—	—	—	12.00	16.00
2004 (a) Proof	14,999	Value: 65.00				

KM# 183   50 EURO CENT
7.8000 g., Brass, 24.25 mm. **Ruler:** Albert II **Obv:** Crowned AA monogram **Rev:** Relief map of Western Europe, stars, lines and value **Edge:** Reeded

Date	Mintage	F	VF	XF	Unc	BU
2006(a) Proof	11,180	Value: 65.00				

KM# 193   50 EURO CENT
7.8000 g., Brass, 24.25 mm. **Ruler:** Albert II **Obv:** Crowned AA monogram **Rev:** Relief map of western Europe, stars, lines and values **Edge:** Reeded

Date	Mintage	F	VF	XF	Unc	BU
2007(a)	—	—	—	—	—	30.00
2009(a) In sets only	8,020	—	—	—	—	30.00
2011(a) In sets only	7,000	—	—	—	—	30.00

KM# 173   EURO
7.5000 g., Bi-Metallic Copper-Nickel center in Nickel-Brass ring, 23.25 mm. **Ruler:** Rainier III **Obv:** Conjoined heads of Prince Ranier and Crown Prince Albert right within circle **Rev:** Value and map **Edge:** Segmented reeding

Date	Mintage	F	VF	XF	Unc	BU
2001(a)	991,100	—	—	—	10.00	12.00
2001(a) Proof	3,500	Value: 145				
2002(a)	512,500	—	—	—	11.00	14.00
2003(a)	135,000	—	—	—	13.50	18.50
2004(a) Proof	14,999	Value: 75.00				

KM# 184   EURO
7.5000 g., Bi-Metallic Copper-Nickel center in Nickel-Brass ring, 23.25 mm.   **Ruler:** Albert II **Obv:** Head right of Prince Albert **Rev:** Relief map of Western Europe, stars, lines and value **Edge:** Segmented reeding

Date	Mintage	F	VF	XF	Unc	BU
2006(a) Proof	11,180	Value: 75.00				

KM# 194   EURO
7.5000 g., Bi-Metallic Copper-Nickel center in Nickel-Brass ring, 23.25 mm.   **Ruler:** Albert II **Obv:** Head right **Rev:** Relief map of western Europe, stars, lines and value **Edge:** Segmented reeding

Date	Mintage	F	VF	XF	Unc	BU
2007(a)	100,000	—	—	—	—	18.00
2009(a) In sets only	8,020	—	—	—	—	30.00
2011(a) In sets only	7,000	—	—	—	—	30.00

KM# 174   2 EURO
8.5000 g., Bi-Metallic Nickel-Brass center in Copper-Nickel ring, 25.75 mm.   **Ruler:** Rainier III **Obv:** Head right within circle flanked by stars **Rev:** Value and map **Edge:** Reeded with 2s and stars

Date	Mintage	F	VF	XF	Unc	BU
2001(a)	919,800	—	—	—	14.00	25.00
2001(a) Proof	3,500	Value: 165				
2002(a)	496,000	—	—	—	15.00	18.00
2003(a)	228,000	—	—	—	17.50	22.50
2004(a) Proof	14,999	Value: 100				

KM# 185   2 EURO
8.5000 g., Bi-Metallic Nickel-Brass center in Copper-Nickel ring, 25.75 mm.   **Ruler:** Albert II **Obv:** Prince Albert's head right **Rev:** Relief map of Western Europe, stars, lines and value **Edge:** Reeded with 2's and stars

Date	Mintage	F	VF	XF	Unc	BU
2006(a) Proof	11,180	Value: 130				

KM# 186   2 EURO
8.5000 g., Bi-Metallic Nickel-Brass center in Copper-Nickel ring., 25.75 mm.   **Ruler:** Albert II **Subject:** Princess Grace, 25th Anniversary of Death **Obv:** Head of Princess Grace left **Rev:** Relief map of Western Europe, stars, lines and value **Edge:** Reeded with 2s and stars

Date	Mintage	F	VF	XF	Unc	BU
2007(a)	20,000	—	—	—	850	1,250

KM# 195   2 EURO
8.5000 g., Bi-Metallic Nickel-Brass center in Copper-Nickel ring, 25.75 mm.   **Ruler:** Albert II **Obv:** Head right **Rev:** Relief map of western Europe, stars, lines and values **Edge:** Reeded with 2's and stars

Date	Mintage	F	VF	XF	Unc	BU
2007(a)	—	—	—	—	65.00	
2009(a)	250,000	—	—	—	35.00	
2009(a) In sets only	8,000	—	—	—	—	150
2010(a) Proof	25,000	Value: 300				
2011(a)	1,039,052	—	—	—	35.00	150

KM# 196   2 EURO
8.5000 g., Bi-Metallic Nickel-Brass center in Copper-Nickel ring, 25.75 mm.   **Ruler:** Albert II **Subject:** Royal Wedding of Prince Albert II and Princess Charlène **Obv:** Conjoined heads left

Date	Mintage	F	VF	XF	Unc	BU
2011A	147,877	—	—	—	—	75.00

KM# 180   5 EURO
12.0000 g., 0.9000 Silver 0.3472 oz. ASW, 29 mm.   **Ruler:** Rainier III **Obv:** Bust right **Rev:** Saint standing

Date	Mintage	F	VF	XF	Unc	BU
2004 (a) Proof	14,999	Value: 150				

KM# 197   5 EURO
12.0000 g., 0.9000 Silver 0.3472 oz. ASW, 29 mm.   **Ruler:** Albert II **Subject:** Prince Albert II, 50th Birthday **Obv:** Bust right **Rev:** Crowned and mantled arms

Date	Mintage	F	VF	XF	Unc	BU
2008(a) Prooflike	9,000	—	—	—	—	185

KM# 178   10 EURO
25.0000 g., 0.9250 Silver 0.7435 oz. ASW, 37 mm.   **Ruler:** Rainier III **Obv:** Conjoined busts of Prince Ranier and Crown Prince Albert right **Rev:** Arms

Date	Mintage	F	VF	XF	Unc	BU
2003(a) Proof	4,000	Value: 465				

KM# 187   10 EURO
3.2200 g., 0.9000 Gold 0.0932 oz. AGW   **Ruler:** Albert II **Subject:** Death of Rainier III **Obv:** Principality arms **Rev:** Head of Rainier III right

Date	Mintage	F	VF	XF	Unc	BU
2005(a) Proof	3,313	Value: 550				

KM# 177   20 EURO
18.0000 g., 0.9250 Gold 0.5353 oz. AGW, 32 mm.   **Ruler:** Rainier III **Obv:** Bust right **Rev:** Arms

Date	Mintage	F	VF	XF	Unc	BU
2002(a) Proof	10,000	Value: 1,100				

KM# 198   20 EURO
6.4500 g., 0.9000 Gold 0.1866 oz. AGW, 21 mm.   **Ruler:** Albert II **Subject:** Prince Albert II, 50th Birthday **Obv:** Bust right **Rev:** Crowned and mantled arms

Date	Mintage	F	VF	XF	Unc	BU
2008(a) Proof	3,000	Value: 600				

KM# 179   100 EURO
29.0000 g., 0.9000 Gold 0.8391 oz. AGW **Ruler:** Rainier III **Obv:** Bust right **Rev:** Knight on horse

Date	Mintage	F	VF	XF	Unc	BU
2003(a) Proof	1,000	Value: 3,250				

MINT SETS

KM#	Date	Mintage	Identification	Issue Price	Mkt Val
MS1	2001 (8)	20,000	KM#167-174, exercise caution, privately packaged and deceptively false sets exist	35.00	225
MS2	2002 (8)	40,000	KM#167-174, exercise caution, privately packaged and deceptively false sets exist	35.00	325
MS3	2009 (8)	8,000	KM#188-195	—	600

PROOF SETS

KM#	Date	Mintage	Identification	Issue Price	Mkt Val
PS1	2001 (8)	3,500	KM#167-174	—	1,000
PS2	2004 (9)	14,999	KM#167-174, 180	—	700
PS3	2005 (3)	35,000	KM#167-169	—	160
PS4	2006 (8)	11,180	KM#181-185, 188-190	—	475

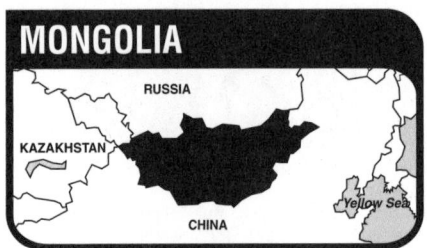

MONGOLIA

Mongolia, (formerly the Mongolian Peoples Republic) a landlocked country in central Asia between Russia and the People's Republic of China, has an area of 604,250 sq. mi. (1,565,000 sq. km.) and a population of 2.26 million. Capital: Ulaan Baator. Animal herds and flocks are the chief economic asset. Wool, cattle, butter, meat and hides are exported.

For earlier issues see Russia - Tannu Tuva.

MONETARY SYSTEM
100 Mongo = 1 Tugrik

STATE

DECIMAL COINAGE

KM# 302   100 TUGRIK
Silver   **Subject:** XXVI Summer Olympics, Atlanta **Obv:** Arms **Rev:** 1904 St. Louis World's Fair Program Cover

Date	Mintage	F	VF	XF	Unc	BU
2002 Proof	—	Value: 25.00				

KM# 254   100 TUGRIK
25.0000 g., 0.9250 Silver 0.7435 oz. ASW **Obv:** Arms **Rev:** Yin-Yang symbol

Date	Mintage	F	VF	XF	Unc	BU
2007 Proof	—	Value: 30.00				

KM# 306   100 TUGRIK
26.0000 g., 0.9250 Silver 0.7732 oz. ASW, 38.5 mm.   **Subject:** Wonders of the World **Obv:** National emblem **Rev:** Rome's Colosseum

Date	Mintage	F	VF	XF	Unc	BU
2008 Prooflike	—	—	—	—	—	35.00

KM# 307   100 TUGRIK
26.4000 g., 0.9250 Silver 0.7851 oz. ASW, 38.5 mm.   **Subject:** Wonders of the World **Obv:** National Emblem **Rev:** Chichen Itza pyramid

Date	Mintage	F	VF	XF	Unc	BU
2008 Prooflike	—	—	—	—	—	35.00

KM# 308   100 TUGRIK
25.0000 g., 0.9250 Silver 0.7435 oz. ASW **Obv:** National emblem **Rev:** Treasury at Petra

Date	Mintage	F	VF	XF	Unc	BU
2008 Proof	—	Value: 75.00				

KM# 282   250 TUGRIK
15.5000 g., 0.9250 Silver 0.4609 oz. ASW, 33 mm.   **Subject:** Zodiac - Capricorn **Rev:** Seated goat left, partially gilt

Date	Mintage	F	VF	XF	Unc	BU
2007	7,000	—	—	—	—	25.00

KM# 283   250 TUGRIK
15.5000 g., 0.9250 Silver 0.4609 oz. ASW, 33 mm.   **Subject:** Zodiac - Aquarius **Rev:** Man pouring water, partially gilt

Date	Mintage	F	VF	XF	Unc	BU
2007	7,000	—	—	—	—	25.00

KM# 284   250 TUGRIK
15.5000 g., 0.9250 Silver 0.4609 oz. ASW, 33 mm.   **Subject:** Zodiac - Piceis **Rev:** Two fish partially gilt

Date	Mintage	F	VF	XF	Unc	BU
2007	7,000	—	—	—	—	25.00

KM# 285   250 TUGRIK
15.5000 g., 0.9250 Silver 0.4609 oz. ASW, 33 mm. **Subject:** Zodiac - Aries **Rev:** Ram seated partially gilt

Date	Mintage	F	VF	XF	Unc	BU
2007	7,000	—	—	—	—	25.00

KM# 286   250 TUGRIK
15.5000 g., 0.9250 Silver 0.4609 oz. ASW, 33 mm. **Subject:** Zodiac - Taurus **Rev:** Bull, partially gilt

Date	Mintage	F	VF	XF	Unc	BU
2007	7,000	—	—	—	—	25.00

KM# 287   250 TUGRIK
15.5000 g., 0.9250 Silver 0.4609 oz. ASW, 33 mm. **Subject:** Zodiac - Gemini **Rev:** Twins, partially gilt

Date	Mintage	F	VF	XF	Unc	BU
2007	7,000	—	—	—	—	25.00

KM# 288   250 TUGRIK
15.5000 g., 0.9250 Silver 0.4609 oz. ASW, 33 mm. **Subject:** Zodiac - Cancer **Rev:** Crab - partially gilt

Date	Mintage	F	VF	XF	Unc	BU
2007	7,000	—	—	—	—	25.00

KM# 289   250 TUGRIK
15.5000 g., 0.9250 Silver 0.4609 oz. ASW, 33 mm. **Subject:** Zodiac - Leo **Rev:** Lion walking left, partially gilt

Date	Mintage	F	VF	XF	Unc	BU
2007	7,000	—	—	—	—	25.00

KM# 290   250 TUGRIK
15.5000 g., 0.9250 Silver 0.4609 oz. ASW, 33 mm. **Subject:** Zodiac - Virgo **Rev:** Female, partially gilt

Date	Mintage	F	VF	XF	Unc	BU
2007	7,000	—	—	—	—	25.00

KM# 291   250 TUGRIK
15.5000 g., 0.9250 Silver 0.4609 oz. ASW, 33 mm. **Subject:** Zodiac - Libra **Rev:** Scales, partially gilt

Date	Mintage	F	VF	XF	Unc	BU
2007	7,000	—	—	—	—	25.00

KM# 292   250 TUGRIK
15.5000 g., 0.9250 Silver 0.4609 oz. ASW, 33 mm. **Subject:** Zodiac - Scorpio **Rev:** Scorpion, partially gilt

Date	Mintage	F	VF	XF	Unc	BU
2007	7,000	—	—	—	—	25.00

KM# 293   250 TUGRIK
15.5000 g., 0.9250 Silver 0.4609 oz. ASW, 33 mm. **Subject:** Zodiac - Sagittarius **Rev:** Centar, partailly gilt

Date	Mintage	F	VF	XF	Unc	BU
2007	7,000	—	—	—	—	25.00

KM# 300   250 TUGRIK
15.5000 g., 0.9990 Silver 0.4978 oz. ASW, 33 mm. **Subject:** Moscow Waterworks **Rev:** Building in multicolor, aqueduct in background

Date	Mintage	F	VF	XF	Unc	BU
2007	1,000	—	—	—	—	45.00

KM# 301   250 TUGRIK
15.5000 g., 0.9990 Silver 0.4978 oz. ASW, 33 mm. **Subject:** Moscow Metro **Rev:** Subway train, multicolor

Date	Mintage	F	VF	XF	Unc	BU
2007	1,000	—	—	—	—	45.00

KM# 270   250 TUGRIK
15.5500 g., 0.9250 Silver 0.4624 oz. ASW, 37 mm. **Subject:** Baby Boy **Obv:** Arms **Rev:** Baby seated on flower, multicolor **Shape:** Heart

Date	Mintage	F	VF	XF	Unc	BU
2008 Proof	2,500	Value: 40.00				

KM# 271   250 TUGRIK
15.5500 g., 0.9250 Silver 0.4624 oz. ASW, 37 mm. **Subject:** Baby Girl **Obv:** Arms **Rev:** Baby Girl on flower **Shape:** Heart

Date	Mintage	F	VF	XF	Unc	BU
2008 Proof	2,500	Value: 40.00				

KM# 189   500 TUGRIK
25.0000 g., 0.9250 Silver 0.7435 oz. ASW, 38.7 mm. **Obv:** National emblem above value **Rev:** Protoceratops Andrewsi **Edge:** Reeded

Date	Mintage	F	VF	XF	Unc	BU
2001 Proof	2,500	Value: 45.00				

KM# 190   500 TUGRIK
25.0000 g., 0.9250 Silver 0.7435 oz. ASW **Obv:** National emblem above value **Rev:** Velociraptor Mongoliensis

Date	Mintage	F	VF	XF	Unc	BU
2001 Proof	2,500	Value: 45.00				

KM# 191   500 TUGRIK
25.0000 g., 0.9250 Silver 0.7435 oz. ASW **Series:** Olympics **Obv:** National emblem above value **Rev:** Speed skater

Date	Mintage	F	VF	XF	Unc	BU
2001 Proof	15,000	Value: 35.00				

KM# 192   500 TUGRIK
25.0000 g., 0.9250 Silver 0.7435 oz. ASW **Series:** Olympics **Obv:** National emblem above value **Rev:** Cross-country skiers

Date	Mintage	F	VF	XF	Unc	BU
2001 Proof	20,000	Value: 32.00				

KM# 195   500 TUGRIK
Copper-Nickel, 22.1 mm. **Subject:** Sukhe-Bataar **Obv:** National emblem and value **Rev:** Crowned head facing **Edge:** Plain

Date	Mintage	F	VF	XF	Unc	BU
2001	—	—	—	—	2.50	3.00

KM# 238   500 TUGRIK
20.0000 g., 0.9250 Silver 0.5948 oz. ASW **Subject:** Gobi Desert Brown Bear **Obv:** Arms **Rev:** Bear standing on rock in stream

Date	Mintage	F	VF	XF	Unc	BU
2001 Proof	—	Value: 28.00				

KM# 239   500 TUGRIK
31.1050 g., 0.9990 Silver 0.9990 oz. ASW, 38.5 mm. **Subject:** Year of the Snake **Rev:** Snake

Date	Mintage	F	VF	XF	Unc	BU
2001 Proof	—	Value: 65.00				

KM# 239a   500 TUGRIK
31.1050 g., 0.9990 Silver partially gilt 0.9990 oz. ASW **Subject:** Year of the Snake **Obv:** Arms **Rev:** Snake, gilt

Date	Mintage	F	VF	XF	Unc	BU
2001 Proof	—	Value: 75.00				

KM# 241   500 TUGRIK
31.1050 g., 0.9990 Silver 0.9990 oz. ASW, 38.5 mm. **Subject:** Year of the Horse **Obv:** Arms **Rev:** Horse

Date	Mintage	F	VF	XF	Unc	BU
2002 Proof	—	Value: 65.00				

KM# 241a   500 TUGRIK
31.1050 g., 0.9990 Silver partially gilt 0.9990 oz. ASW, 38.5 mm. **Subject:** Year of the Horse **Rev:** Horse, gilt

Date	Mintage	F	VF	XF	Unc	BU
2002 Proof	—	Value: 75.00				

KM# 200   500 TUGRIK
25.5700 g., 0.9250 Silver 0.7604 oz. ASW, 38.5 mm. **Subject:** Marco Polo, Homeward **Obv:** National emblem above value **Rev:** Five-masted sailing junk **Edge:** Reeded

Date	Mintage	F	VF	XF	Unc	BU
2003 Proof	5,000	Value: 45.00				

KM# 205 500 TUGRIK
25.0000 g., 0.9250 Silver 0.7435 oz. ASW, 38.6 mm. **Obv:**
National emblem above value **Rev:** Medallion divides busts
Edge: Reeded

Date	Mintage	F	VF	XF	Unc	BU
2003 Proof	5,000	Value: 65.00				

KM# 206 500 TUGRIK
1.2440 g., 0.9999 Gold 0.0400 oz. AGW, 13.92 mm. **Obv:**
National emblem above value **Rev:** Five masted sailing junk
Edge: Reeded

Date	Mintage	F	VF	XF	Unc	BU
2003 Proof	25,000	Value: 75.00				

KM# 207 500 TUGRIK
1.2440 g., 0.9999 Gold 0.0400 oz. AGW, 13.92 mm. **Obv:**
National emblem above value **Rev:** Medallion divides busts
Edge: Reeded

Date	Mintage	F	VF	XF	Unc	BU
2003 Proof	25,000	Value: 80.00				

KM# 204 500 TUGRIK
25.0000 g., 0.9250 Silver 0.7435 oz. ASW, 38 mm. **Obv:**
National emblem above value **Rev:** Wolf within full moon **Edge:**
Reeded

Date	Mintage	F	VF	XF	Unc	BU
2003 Proof	10,000	Value: 60.00				

KM# 229 500 TUGRIK
31.1050 g., 0.9990 Silver 0.9990 oz. ASW **Obv:** Arms above
legend **Rev:** Ram standing left

Date	Mintage	F	VF	XF	Unc	BU
2003	—	—	—	—	—	65.00

KM# 229a 500 TUGRIK
31.1050 g., 0.9990 Silver partialy gilt 0.9990 oz. ASW, 38.5 mm.
Subject: Year of the Ram **Obv:** Arms **Rev:** Ram standing left, gilt

Date	Mintage	F	VF	XF	Unc	BU
2003 Proof	—	Value: 75.00				

KM# 208 500 TUGRIK
25.0000 g., 0.9250 Silver 0.7435 oz. ASW, 38 mm. **Obv:**
National emblem above value **Rev:** Holographic Osprey catching
fish **Edge:** Reeded

Date	Mintage	F	VF	XF	Unc	BU
2004 Proof	5,000	Value: 50.00				

KM# 218 500 TUGRIK
31.2400 g., 0.9990 Silver 1.0033 oz. ASW, 38.59 mm. **Series:**
Chinese Lunar **Subject:** Year of the Monkey **Obv:** National
emblem **Rev:** Monkey seated on branch - gilt, border of
scampering monkeys **Edge:** Reeded

Date	Mintage	F	VF	XF	Unc	BU
ND(2004) Proof	20,000	Value: 45.00				

KM# 219 500 TUGRIK
1.2400 g., 0.9999 Gold 0.0399 oz. AGW **Series:** Chinese Lunar
Subject: Year of the Monkey **Obv:** National emblem **Rev:**
Monkey seated on branch

Date	Mintage	F	VF	XF	Unc	BU
ND(2004) Proof	—	Value: 65.00				

KM# 244 500 TUGRIK
31.1050 g., 0.9990 Silver 0.9990 oz. ASW, 38.5 mm. **Subject:**
Year of the Monkey **Obv:** Arms **Rev:** Monkey

Date	Mintage	F	VF	XF	Unc	BU
2004 Proof	—	Value: 65.00				

KM# 244a 500 TUGRIK
31.1050 g., 0.9990 Silver partially gilt 0.9990 oz. ASW, 38.5 mm.
Subject: Year of the Monkey **Obv:** Arms **Rev:** Monkey, gilt

Date	Mintage	F	VF	XF	Unc	BU
2004 Proof	—	Value: 75.00				

KM# 209 500 TUGRIK
24.9300 g., 0.9250 Bi-Metallic with .925 Silver oval in center
0.7414 oz., 30 mm. **Obv:** National emblem above value, niobium
leopard in oval center **Rev:** Snow Leopard **Edge:** Reeded **Shape:**
Oval

Date	Mintage	F	VF	XF	Unc	BU
2005 Proof	5,000	Value: 90.00				

KM# 210 500 TUGRIK
31.1035 g., 0.9990 Silver 0.9990 oz. ASW, 35x35 mm. **Obv:**
Bronze plated horse and rider on antiqued silver with national
emblem and value **Rev:** Bronze plated horse and rider on
antiqued silver above date **Edge:** Reeded **Shape:** Square

Date	Mintage	F	VF	XF	Unc	BU
2005	2,500	—	—	—	70.00	75.00

KM# 210a 500 TUGRIK
31.1035 g., 0.9990 Silver 0.9990 oz. ASW, 35x35 mm. **Obv:**
Gold plated horse and rider with national emblem and value **Rev:**
Gold plated horse and rider above date **Edge:** Reeded

Date	Mintage	F	VF	XF	Unc	BU
2005 Proof	2,500	Value: 85.00				

KM# 304 500 TUGRIK
31.1000 g., 0.9990 Silver 0.9988 oz. ASW **Obv:** National
emblem **Rev:** Sumo Wrestler Yokozuna Ounomatsu in color

Date	Mintage	F	VF	XF	Unc	BU
2005 Proof	—	Value: 125				

KM# 246 500 TUGRIK
31.1050 g., 0.9990 Silver 0.9990 oz. ASW, 38.5 mm. **Subject:**
Year of the Rooster **Obv:** Arms **Rev:** Rooster standing right

Date	Mintage	F	VF	XF	Unc	BU
2005 Proof	—	Value: 70.00				

KM# 246a 500 TUGRIK
31.1050 g., 0.9990 Silver 0.9990 oz. ASW, 38.5 mm. **Subject:**
Year of the Rooster **Obv:** Arms **Rev:** Rooster, gilt

Date	Mintage	F	VF	XF	Unc	BU
2005 Proof	—	Value: 80.00				

KM# 230 500 TUGRIK
25.0000 g., 0.9250 Silver 0.7435 oz. ASW **Rev:** Swan with
crystal insert

Date	Mintage	F	VF	XF	Unc	BU
2006 Proof	—	Value: 135				

KM# 231 500 TUGRIK
25.0000 g., 0.9250 Silver 0.7435 oz. ASW **Rev:** Gobi bear head
with crystal inserts

Date	Mintage	F	VF	XF	Unc	BU
2006 Proof	—	Value: 165				

KM# 248 500 TUGRIK
25.0000 g., 0.9250 Silver 0.7435 oz. ASW **Subject:** Long Eared
Jerboa **Obv:** Arms **Rev:** Long eared jerboa, crystal eyes **Shape:**
38.6

Date	Mintage	F	VF	XF	Unc	BU
2006 Proof	2,500	Value: 145				

KM# 249 500 TUGRIK
25.0000 g., 0.9250 Silver 0.7435 oz. ASW, 38.6 mm. **Obv:** Arms
Rev: Scorpion, crystal tail point

Date	Mintage	F	VF	XF	Unc	BU
2006 Proof	2,500	Value: 185				

KM# 250 500 TUGRIK
25.0000 g., 0.9250 Silver 0.7435 oz. ASW, 38.6 mm. **Rev:** Tiger,
head facing, crystal eyes

Date	Mintage	F	VF	XF	Unc	BU
2006 Proof	2,500	Value: 150				

KM# 251 500 TUGRIK
31.1050 g., 0.9990 Silver 0.9990 oz. ASW, 38.5 mm. **Subject:**
Year of the Dog **Obv:** Arms **Rev:** Dog standing

Date	Mintage	F	VF	XF	Unc	BU
2006 Proof	—	Value: 60.00				

KM# 251a 500 TUGRIK
31.1050 g., 0.9990 Silver 0.9990 oz. ASW, 38.5 mm. **Subject:**
Year of the Dog **Obv:** Arms **Rev:** Dog standing, gilt

Date	Mintage	F	VF	XF	Unc	BU
2006 Proof	—	Value: 70.00				

KM# 260 500 TUGRIK
25.0000 g., 0.9250 Silver 0.7435 oz. ASW, 38.6 mm. **Subject:**
Great Mongolian State, 800th Anniversary **Obv:** Arms **Rev:**
Chinggis Khan and black pennant

Date	Mintage	F	VF	XF	Unc	BU
2006 Proof	2,500	Value: 75.00				

KM# 261 500 TUGRIK
25.0000 g., 0.9250 Silver 0.7435 oz. ASW, 38.61 mm. **Subject:**
Great Mongolian State, 800th Anniversary **Obv:** Arms **Rev:** Nine
white pennants

Date	Mintage	F	VF	XF	Unc	BU
2006 Proof	2,500	Value: 75.00				

KM# 212 500 TUGRIK
31.1050 g., 0.9990 Silver 0.9990 oz. ASW, 38 mm. **Obv:** Arms
and value **Rev:** Wolverine head facing with diamonds in eyes
Rev. Inscription: WILDLIFE PROTECTION GULO GULO

Date	Mintage	F	VF	XF	Unc	BU
2007	—	—	—	—	—	160

KM# 265 500 TUGRIK
31.1050 g., 0.9990 Silver 0.9990 oz. ASW, 38.61 mm. **Subject:**
Society Space exploration **Obv:** Arms **Rev:** Sputnik, rocket, three
figures

Date	Mintage	F	VF	XF	Unc	BU
2007 Proof	1,000	Value: 75.00				

KM# 266 500 TUGRIK
31.1050 g., 0.9990 Silver 0.9990 oz. ASW, 38.61 mm. **Subject:**
Soviet Space Exploration **Rev:** Laika, first dog in space

Date	Mintage	F	VF	XF	Unc	BU
2007 Proof	500	Value: 85.00				

KM# 267 500 TUGRIK
31.1050 g., 0.9990 Silver 0.9990 oz. ASW, 38.61 mm. **Subject:**
Soviet Space Exploration **Obv:** Arms **Rev:** Sputnik

Date	Mintage	F	VF	XF	Unc	BU
2007 Proof	500	Value: 85.00				

KM# 268 500 TUGRIK
31.1050 g., 0.9990 Silver 0.9990 oz. ASW, 38.61 mm. **Subject:**
Soviet Space Exploration **Obv:** Arms **Rev:** Yuri Gagarian

Date	Mintage	F	VF	XF	Unc	BU
2007 Proof	500	Value: 85.00				

KM# 269 500 TUGRIK
31.1050 g., 0.9990 Silver 0.9990 oz. ASW, 38.61 mm. **Subject:**
Soviet Space Exploration **Obv:** Arms **Rev:** Mir space station

Date	Mintage	F	VF	XF	Unc	BU
2007 Proof	1,000	Value: 85.00				

KM# 222 500 TUGRIK
25.0000 g., 0.9250 Silver 0.7435 oz. ASW, 38.61 mm. **Subject:**
Wonders of the World **Obv:** Arms **Rev:** Multicolor Chichen Itza

Date	Mintage	F	VF	XF	Unc	BU
2008	2,500	—	—	—	—	75.00

KM# 223 500 TUGRIK
25.0000 g., 0.9250 Silver 0.7435 oz. ASW, 38.6 mm. **Subject:**
Wonders of the World **Obv:** Arms **Rev:** Multicolor Treasury at
Petra

Date	Mintage	F	VF	XF	Unc	BU
2008	2,500	—	—	—	—	75.00

KM# 224 500 TUGRIK
25.0000 g., 0.9250 Silver 0.7435 oz. ASW, 38.61 mm. **Subject:**
Wonders of the World **Obv:** Arms **Rev:** Multicolor Taj Mahal

Date	Mintage	F	VF	XF	Unc	BU
2008	2,500	—	—	—	—	75.00

KM# 225 500 TUGRIK
25.0000 g., 0.9250 Silver 0.7435 oz. ASW, 38.61 mm. **Subject:**
Wonders of the World **Obv:** Arms **Rev:** Multicolor Machu Picchu

Date	Mintage	F	VF	XF	Unc	BU
2008	2,500	—	—	—	—	75.00

KM# 226 500 TUGRIK
25.0000 g., 0.9250 Silver 0.7435 oz. ASW, 38.61 mm. **Subject:**
Wonders of the World **Obv:** Arms **Rev:** Multicolor Great Wall of
China

Date	Mintage	F	VF	XF	Unc	BU
2008	2,500	—	—	—	—	75.00

KM# 227 500 TUGRIK
25.0000 g., 0.9250 Silver 0.7435 oz. ASW, 38.61 mm. **Subject:**
Wonders of the World **Obv:** Arms **Rev:** Multicolor Colosseum in
Rome

Date	Mintage	F	VF	XF	Unc	BU
2008	2,500	—	—	—	—	75.00

KM# 228 500 TUGRIK
25.0000 g., 0.9250 Silver 0.7435 oz. ASW, 38.61 mm. **Subject:**
Wonders of the World **Obv:** Arms **Rev:** Multicolor Christ the
Redeemer statue in Rio

Date	Mintage	F	VF	XF	Unc	BU
2008	2,500	—	—	—	—	75.00

KM# 213 500 TUGRIK
31.1000 g., 0.9990 Silver 0.9988 oz. ASW, 39mm. **Subject:**
Year of the Rat **Obv:** National emblem, value below **Rev:** Three
rats in grass **Edge:** Reeded

Date	Mintage	F	VF	XF	Unc	BU
2008	20,000	—	—	—	—	45.00

KM# 213a 500 TUGRIK
31.1000 g., 0.9990 Silver 0.9988 oz. ASW, 39.0 mm. **Subject:**
Year of the Rat **Obv:** National emblem, value below **Rev:** Three
gilt rats in grass **Edge:** Reeded

Date	Mintage	F	VF	XF	Unc	BU
2008 Proof	5,000	Value: 50.00				

KM# 255 500 TUGRIK
25.0000 g., 0.9250 Silver 0.7435 oz. ASW, 38.6 mm. **Subject:**
Frederic Chopin **Obv:** Arms **Rev:** Bust right, color keyboard
vertical in center

Date	Mintage	F	VF	XF	Unc	BU
2008 Proof	1,000	Value: 90.00				

KM# 256 500 TUGRIK
31.1050 g., 0.9990 Silver 0.9990 oz. ASW, 38.6 mm. **Subject:**
Year of the Rat **Obv:** Arms **Rev:** Two mice

Date	Mintage	F	VF	XF	Unc	BU
2008 Proof	—	Value: 55.00				

KM# 256a 500 TUGRIK
31.1050 g., 0.9990 Silver partially gilt 0.9990 oz. ASW, 38.6 mm.
Subject: Year of the Rat **Obv:** Arms **Rev:** Two mice, gilt

Date	Mintage	F	VF	XF	Unc	BU
2008 Proof	—	Value: 65.00				

KM# 272 500 TUGRIK
25.0000 g., 0.9250 Silver 0.7435 oz. ASW, 38.6 mm. **Series:**
Mongolian Olympians, Baatarjav **Obv:** Arms

Date	Mintage	F	VF	XF	Unc	BU
2008 Proof	2,500	Value: 55.00				

KM# 273   500 TUGRIK
25.0000 g., 0.9250 Silver 0.7435 oz. ASW, 38.61 mm. **Subject:** Mongolian Olympians - Badar-Uugan

Date	Mintage	F	VF	XF	Unc	BU
2008 Proof	2,500	Value: 55.00				

KM# 274   500 TUGRIK
25.0000 g., 0.9990 Silver 0.8029 oz. ASW, 38.61 mm. **Subject:** Mongolian Olympians - Serdamba

Date	Mintage	F	VF	XF	Unc	BU
2008 Proof	2,500	Value: 55.00				

KM# 275   500 TUGRIK
25.0000 g., 0.9250 Silver 0.7435 oz. ASW, 38.61 mm. **Subject:** Mongolian Olympians - Tuvshinbayar

Date	Mintage	F	VF	XF	Unc	BU
2008 Proof	2,500	Value: 55.00				

KM# 276   500 TUGRIK
25.0000 g., 0.9250 Silver 0.7435 oz. ASW, 38.61 mm. **Subject:** Mongolian Olympians - Gundegmaa

Date	Mintage	F	VF	XF	Unc	BU
2008 Proof	2,500	Value: 55.00				

KM# 279   500 TUGRIK
0.5000 g., 0.9990 Gold 0.0161 oz. AGW, 11 mm. **Subject:** Mongolian Olympic Sports - Archery

Date	Mintage	F	VF	XF	Unc	BU
2008 Proof	15,000	—	—	—	—	50.00

KM# 280   500 TUGRIK
25.0000 g., 0.9250 Silver 0.7435 oz. ASW, 38.61 mm. **Obv:** Arms **Rev:** Two snow leopards, multicolor

Date	Mintage	F	VF	XF	Unc	BU
2008 Proof	2,500	Value: 65.00				

KM# 281   500 TUGRIK
25.0000 g., 0.9250 Silver 0.7435 oz. ASW, 38.61 mm. **Obv:** Arms **Rev:** The Almas, multicolor changing insert

Date	Mintage	F	VF	XF	Unc	BU
2008 Proof	2,500	Value: 55.00				

KM# 305   500 TUGRIK
25.0000 g., 0.9250 Silver 0.7435 oz. ASW, 38.61 mm. **Subject:** Frederic Chopin **Obv:** National emblem **Rev:** Piano keys in color, bust at right

Date	Mintage	F	VF	XF	Unc	BU
2008 Proof	—	Value: 75.00				

KM# 312   500 TUGRIK
31.1050 g., 0.9990 Silver 0.9990 oz. ASW, 38.61 mm. **Subject:** Year of the Rat **Rev:** Mouse in multicolor

Date	Mintage	F	VF	XF	Unc	BU
2008 Proof	—	Value: 65.00				

KM# 258   500 TUGRIK
31.1050 g., 0.9990 Silver 0.9990 oz. ASW, 38.6 mm. **Subject:** Year of the Ox **Obv:** Arms **Rev:** Ox

Date	Mintage	F	VF	XF	Unc	BU
2009 Proof	—	Value: 60.00				

KM# 258a   500 TUGRIK
31.1050 g., 0.9990 Silver partially gilt 0.9990 oz. ASW, 38.6 mm. **Subject:** Year of the Ox **Obv:** Arms **Rev:** Ox, gilt

Date	Mintage	F	VF	XF	Unc	BU
2009 Proof	—	Value: 70.00				

KM# 309   500 TUGRIK
31.1000 g., 0.9250 Silver 0.9249 oz. ASW, 38.6 mm. **Subject:** Endangered Wildlife **Obv:** National Emblem **Rev:** Owl's head facing (Strix Uralensis) crystal insert eyes

Date	Mintage	F	VF	XF	Unc	BU
2011 Antique finish	2,500	—	—	—	—	150

KM# 310   500 TUGRIK
0.5000 g., 0.9990 Gold 0.0161 oz. AGW, 11 mm. **Subject:** Endangered Wildlife **Obv:** National emblem **Rev:** Ural Owl (Strix Uralersis) standing left

Date	Mintage	F	VF	XF	Unc	BU
2011 Proof	15,000	—	—	—	—	75.00

KM# 199   1000 TUGRIK
31.1100 g., 0.9250 Silver 0.9252 oz. ASW, 38.6 mm. **Obv:** National emblem above value **Obv. Inscription:** Denomination spelled "TOGROG" **Rev:** Head facing **Edge:** Reeded

Date	Mintage	F	VF	XF	Unc	BU
2002	17,000	—	—	—	42.00	45.00

KM# 303   1000 TUGRIK
Copper-Nickel, 38 mm. **Obv:** National emblem **Rev:** Two soccer players

Date	Mintage	F	VF	XF	Unc	BU
2003 Prooflike	2,000	—	—	—	—	10.00

KM# 233   1000 TUGRIK
Gold **Rev:** Snow leopard

Date	Mintage	F	VF	XF	Unc	BU
2005 Proof	—	Value: 95.00				

KM# 253   1000 TUGRIK
1.2400 g., 0.9990 Gold 0.0398 oz. AGW **Subject:** Mozart **Obv:** Arms **Rev:** Portrait and profile heads above building

Date	Mintage	F	VF	XF	Unc	BU
2006 Proof	—	Value: 80.00				

KM# 262   1000 TUGRIK
1.2400 g., 0.9990 Gold 0.0398 oz. AGW, 13.92 mm. **Obv:** Arms **Rev:** Scorpion

Date	Mintage	F	VF	XF	Unc	BU
2006 Proof	25,000	Value: 95.00				

KM# 263   1000 TUGRIK
1.2400 g., 0.9990 Silver 0.0398 oz. ASW, 13.9 mm. **Obv:** Arms **Rev:** Long-eared Jerboa

Date	Mintage	F	VF	XF	Unc	BU
2006 Proof	—	Value: 95.00				

KM# 264   1000 TUGRIK
1.2400 g., 0.9990 Gold 0.0398 oz. AGW, 13.9 mm. **Obv:** Arms **Rev:** Gobi Bear

Date	Mintage	F	VF	XF	Unc	BU
2006 Proof	25,000	Value: 95.00				

KM# 294   1000 TUGRIK
62.2000 g., 0.9990 Silver 1.9977 oz. ASW, 50 mm. **Rev:** Tsarina Catherina multicolor

Date	Mintage	F	VF	XF	Unc	BU
2007 Proof	500	Value: 145				

KM# 295   1000 TUGRIK
62.2000 g., 0.9990 Silver 1.9977 oz. ASW, 50 mm. **Rev:** Tsar Nicholas I, multicolor

Date	Mintage	F	VF	XF	Unc	BU
2007 Proof	500	Value: 145				

KM# 296   1000 TUGRIK
62.2000 g., 0.9990 Silver 1.9977 oz. ASW, 50 mm. **Rev:** Tsar Nicholas II

Date	Mintage	F	VF	XF	Unc	BU
2007 Proof	500	Value: 145				

KM# 297 1000 TUGRIK
62.2000 g., 0.9990 Silver 1.9977 oz. ASW, 50 mm. **Rev:** Tsar
Ivan IV, multicolor

Date	Mintage	F	VF	XF	Unc	BU
2007 Proof	500	Value: 145				

KM# 298 1000 TUGRIK
62.2000 g., 0.9990 Silver 1.9977 oz. ASW, 50 mm. **Rev:** Tsar
Peter I, multicolor

Date	Mintage	F	VF	XF	Unc	BU
2007 Proof	500	Value: 145				

KM# 299 1000 TUGRIK
62.2000 g., 0.9990 Silver 1.9977 oz. ASW, 50 mm. **Rev:** Tsar
Yuri

Date	Mintage	F	VF	XF	Unc	BU
2007 Proof	500	Value: 145				

KM# 214 1000 TUGRIK
1.2400 g., 0.9990 Gold 0.0398 oz. AGW, 14.0 mm. **Subject:**
Year of the Rat **Obv:** National emblem, value below **Edge:**
Reeded

Date	Mintage	F	VF	XF	Unc	BU
2008 Proof	10,000	Value: 75.00				

KM# 277 1000 TUGRIK
1.2400 g., 0.9990 Gold 0.0398 oz. AGW, 13.92 mm. **Subject:**
Mongolian Olympic Sports - Boxing **Rev:** Two fighters in the ring

Date	Mintage	F	VF	XF	Unc	BU
2008 Proof	15,000	Value: 85.00				

KM# 278 1000 TUGRIK
1.2400 g., 0.9990 Gold 0.0398 oz. AGW, 13.92 mm. **Subject:**
Mongolian Olympic Sports - Judo **Rev:** Judo athlete getting fliped

Date	Mintage	F	VF	XF	Unc	BU
2008 Proof	15,000	Value: 85.00				

KM# 311 1000 TUGRIK
1.2400 g., 0.9990 Gold 0.0398 oz. AGW, 13.92 mm. **Subject:**
Frederic Chopin **Obv:** National Emblem **Rev:** Piano keyboard
vertical at left, bust at right

Date	Mintage	F	VF	XF	Unc	BU
2011 Proof	—	Value: 100				

KM# 240 2500 TUGRIK
7.7700 g., 0.9990 Gold 0.2496 oz. AGW **Subject:** Year of the
Snake **Obv:** Arms **Rev:** Snake

Date	Mintage	F	VF	XF	Unc	BU
2001 Proof	2,000	Value: 500				

KM# 242 2500 TUGRIK
7.7000 g., 0.9990 Gold 0.2473 oz. AGW **Subject:** Year of the
Horse **Obv:** Arms **Rev:** Year of the Horse

Date	Mintage	F	VF	XF	Unc	BU
2002 Proof	—	Value: 500				

KM# 243 2500 TUGRIK
155.5000 g., 0.9990 Silver partially gilt 4.9942 oz. ASW, 65 mm.
Subject: Year of the Ram **Obv:** Arms **Rev:** Ram standing left, gilt

Date	Mintage	F	VF	XF	Unc	BU
2003 Proof	4,000	Value: 325				

KM# 245 2500 TUGRIK
155.5000 g., 0.9990 Silver partially gilt 4.9942 oz. ASW, 65 mm.
Subject: Year of the Monkey **Obv:** Arms **Rev:** Monkey, gilt

Date	Mintage	F	VF	XF	Unc	BU
2004 Proof	4,000	Value: 325				

KM# 220 2500 TUGRIK
7.7800 g., 0.9999 Gold 0.2501 oz. AGW **Series:** Chinese Lunar
Subject: Year of the Monkey **Obv:** National emblem **Rev:**
Monkey seated on branch **Edge:** Reeded

Date	Mintage	F	VF	XF	Unc	BU
ND(2004) Proof	2,000	Value: 525				

KM# 247 2500 TUGRIK
155.5000 g., 0.9990 Silver partially gilt 4.9942 oz. ASW, 65 mm.
Subject: Year of the Rooster **Obv:** Arms **Rev:** Rooster, gilt

Date	Mintage	F	VF	XF	Unc	BU
2005 Proof	4,000	Value: 325				

KM# 252 2500 TUGRIK
155.5000 g., 0.9990 Silver partially gilt 4.9942 oz. ASW, 65 mm.
Subject: Year of the Dog **Obv:** Arms **Rev:** Dog standing, gilt

Date	Mintage	F	VF	XF	Unc	BU
2006 Proof	—	Value: 325				

KM# 257 2500 TUGRIK
155.5000 g., 0.9990 Silver partially gilt 4.9942 oz. ASW, 65 mm.
Subject: Year of the Rat **Obv:** Arms **Rev:** Two mice, gilt

Date	Mintage	F	VF	XF	Unc	BU
2008 Proof	—	Value: 325				

KM# 259 2500 TUGRIK
155.5000 g., 0.9990 Silver partially gilt 4.9942 oz. ASW, 65 mm.
Subject: Year of the Ox **Obv:** Arms **Rev:** Ox, gilt

Date	Mintage	F	VF	XF	Unc	BU
2009 Proof	—	Value: 325				

KM# 198 5000 TUGRIK
155.5000 g., 0.9990 Silver 4.9942 oz. ASW, 40x90 mm.
Subject: Year of the Horse **Obv:** National emblem above value
to left of Palace Museum **Rev:** Five multicolor running horses
Edge: Plain **Note:** Round-cornered rectangle. Photo reduced.

Date	Mintage	F	VF	XF	Unc	BU
2002 Proof	—	Value: 225				

KM# 232 5000 TUGRIK
155.5000 g., 0.9990 Silver 4.9942 oz. ASW, 40x90 mm. **Rev:**
Three sumo wrestlers, multicolor **Shape:** Rectangle **Note:**
Illustration reduced.

Date	Mintage	F	VF	XF	Unc	BU
2005 Proof	—	Value: 300				

KM# 221 100000 TUGRIK
3000.0000 g., 0.9990 Silver 96.351 oz. ASW **Series:** Chinese
Lunar **Subject:** Year of the Monkey **Obv:** National emblem **Rev:**
Monkey seated on branch

Date	Mintage	F	VF	XF	Unc	BU
ND(2004) Proof	—	Value: 3,750				

KM# 215 100000 TUGRIK
3000.0000 g., 0.9990 Silver 96.351 oz. ASW, 130.0 mm.
Subject: Year of the Rat **Obv:** National emblem, value below
Rev: Three rats in grass **Edge:** Reeded **Note:** Serial number on
edge.

Date	Mintage	F	VF	XF	Unc	BU
2008 Proof	500	Value: 3,750				

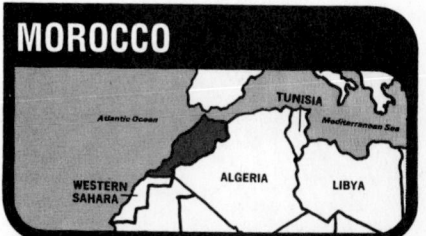

The Kingdom of Morocco, situated on the northwest corner
of Africa, has an area of 432,620 sq. mi. (710,850 sq. km.) and
a population of 36 million. Capital: Rabat. The economy is essentially agricultural. Phosphates, fresh and preserved vegetables,
canned fish, and raw materials are exported.

KINGDOM
1956-

Mohammed VI
AH1420/1999AD

REFORM COINAGE
100 Santimat = 1 Dirham

Y# 112 5 SANTIMAT
2.0000 g., Aluminum-Bronze, 17.5 mm. **Obv:** Crowned arms
with supporters **Rev:** Value, flower and dates **Edge:** Plain

Date	Mintage	F	VF	XF	Unc	BU
AH1423-2002	—	—	—	—	0.50	1.00

Y# 114 10 SANTIMAT
3.0000 g., Aluminum-Bronze, 20 mm. **Obv:** Crowned arms with
supporters **Rev:** Value, design of "sport and solidarity" **Edge:**
Reeded

Date	Mintage	F	VF	XF	Unc	BU
AH1423-2002	—	—	—	—	1.00	2.00

Y# 136 10 SANTIMAT
3.0000 g., Brass Plated Steel, 20 mm.

Date	Mintage	F	VF	XF	Unc	BU
AH1432-2011	—	—	—	—	1.00	2.00

Y# 115 20 SANTIMAT
4.0000 g., Aluminum-Bronze, 23 mm. **Obv:** Crowned arms with
supporters **Rev:** Value, design of "tourist and craftsmen trade"
Edge: Reeded

Date	Mintage	F	VF	XF	Unc	BU
AH1423-2002	—	—	—	—	1.50	3.00

Y# 137 20 SANTIMAT
4.0000 g., Brass Plated Steel, 23 mm. **Edge:** Reeded

Date	Mintage	F	VF	XF	Unc	BU
AH1432-2011	—	—	—	—	1.50	3.00

Y# 116 1/2 DIRHAM
4.0000 g., Copper-Nickel, 21 mm. **Obv:** Crowned arms with

supporters **Rev:** Value, design theme "telecommunications and new technologies" **Edge:** Reeded

Date	Mintage	F	VF	XF	Unc	BU
AH1423-2002	—	—	—	—	2.00	3.00

Y# 138 1/2 DIRHAM
4.0000 g., Nickel Plated Steel, 21 mm. **Obv:** Crowned national arms with supporters **Rev:** Two fish and large value **Edge:** Reeded

Date	Mintage	F	VF	XF	Unc	BU
AH1432-2011	—	—	—	—	3.00	5.00

Y# 117 DIRHAM
6.0000 g., Copper-Nickel, 24 mm. **Obv:** Head 3/4 left **Rev:** Crowned arms with supporters above value **Edge:** Reeded

Date	Mintage	F	VF	XF	Unc	BU
AH1423-2002	—	—	—	—	3.00	5.00

Y# 139 DIRHAM
6.0000 g., Nickel Plated Steel, 24 mm. **Obv:** Head left **Rev:** Crowned national arms with supporters, value below **Edge:** Reeded

Date	Mintage	F	VF	XF	Unc	BU
AH1432-2011	—	—	—	—	3.50	5.00

Y# 140 5 DIRHAMS
7.5000 g., Bi-Metallic Nordic Gold center in Copper-Nickel ring, 25 mm. **Obv:** Head left **Rev:** Mosque **Edge:** Segmented reeding

Date	Mintage	F	VF	XF	Unc	BU
AH1432-2011	—	—	—	—	6.00	9.00

Y# 118 2 DIRHAMS
7.0000 g., Copper-Nickel, 26 mm. **Obv:** Head 3/4 left within octagon shape **Rev:** Crowned arms with supporters above value within octagon shape **Edge:** Reeded

Date	Mintage	F	VF	XF	Unc	BU
AH1423-2002	—	—	—	—	4.00	6.00

Y# 109 5 DIRHAMS
7.5000 g., Bi-Metallic Nickel-Brass center in Copper-Nickel ring, 25 mm. **Obv:** Head 3/4 left **Rev:** Crowned arms with supporters above value **Edge:** Segmented reeding

Date	Mintage	F	VF	XF	Unc	BU
AH1423-2002	—	—	—	—	6.00	9.00

Y# 110 10 DIRHAMS
9.0000 g., Bi-Metallic Copper-Nickel center in Brass ring, 26.9 mm. **Obv:** Head 3/4 left **Rev:** Crowned arms with supporters above value **Edge:** Reeded

Date	Mintage	F	VF	XF	Unc	BU
AH1423-2002	—	—	—	—	10.00	15.00

Y# 141 10 DIRHAMS
9.0000 g., Bi-Metallic Copper-Nickel center in Nordic Gold ring, 27 mm. **Obv:** Head left **Rev:** Building and palm tree at left, large value at right

Date	Mintage	F	VF	XF	Unc	BU
AH1432-2011	—	—	—	—	10.00	15.00

Y# 107 250 DIRHAMS
25.0000 g., 0.9250 Silver 0.7435 oz. ASW, 37 mm. **Subject:** Inauguration of Mohammed VI 2nd Anniversary **Obv:** Head 3/4 left **Rev:** Crowned arms with supporters above value **Edge:** Reeded

Date	Mintage	F	VF	XF	Unc	BU
AH1422-2001	—	—	—	—	55.00	70.00

Y# 95 250 DIRHAMS
25.0000 g., 0.9250 Silver 0.7435 oz. ASW, 37 mm. **Subject:** World Children's Day **Obv:** Head 3/4 left **Rev:** Children standing on open book within globe **Edge:** Reeded

Date	Mintage	F	VF	XF	Unc	BU
AH1422-2001	—	—	—	—	55.00	70.00
AH1422-2001 Proof	—	Value: 90.00				

Y# 95a 250 DIRHAMS
25.0000 g., 0.9999 Gold 0.8037 oz. AGW, 37 mm. **Subject:** World Children's Day **Obv:** Head 3/4 left **Rev:** Two children standing on an open book within globe **Edge:** Reeded **Note:** Prev. Y#95.

Date	Mintage	F	VF	XF	Unc	BU
AH1422-2001 Proof	2,800	Value: 1,450				

Y# 108 250 DIRHAMS
25.0000 g., 0.9250 Silver 0.7435 oz. ASW, 37 mm. **Subject:** Mohammed VI's Inauguration 3rd Anniversary **Obv:** Head 3/4 left **Rev:** Crowned arms with supporters above value **Edge:** Reeded **Note:** Slightly different legend of Y-107

Date	Mintage	F	VF	XF	Unc	BU
AH1423-2002	—	—	—	—	55.00	70.00
AH1423-2002 Proof	—	Value: 90.00				

Y# 113 250 DIRHAMS
25.0000 g., 0.9250 Silver 0.7435 oz. ASW, 37 mm. **Subject:** Marriage of King Mohammed VI, July 12, 2002 **Obv:** Head 3/4 left **Rev:** Crown above radiant flowers **Edge:** Reeded

Date	Mintage	F	VF	XF	Unc	BU
ND (2002) Proof	—	Value: 90.00				

Y# 119 250 DIRHAMS
25.0000 g., 0.9250 Silver 0.7435 oz. ASW, 37 mm. **Subject:** Birth of Crown Prince Moulay Al Hassan **Obv:** Head 3/4 left **Rev:** Crowned arms with supporters above value

Date	Mintage	F	VF	XF	Unc	BU
ND(2003) Proof	—	Value: 90.00				

Y# 120 250 DIRHAMS
25.0000 g., 0.9250 Silver 0.7435 oz. ASW, 37 mm. **Subject:** 50th Anniversary - Kingdom **Obv:** Conjoined heads right **Rev:** Crowned arms with supporters above value

Date	Mintage	F	VF	XF	Unc	BU
AH1424-2003	—	—	—	—	55.00	70.00
AH1424-2003 Proof	—	Value: 90.00				

Y# 111 250 DIRHAMS
25.0000 g., 0.9250 Silver 0.7435 oz. ASW, 37 mm. **Subject:** Mohammed VI's Inauguration 4th Anniversary **Obv:** Head 3/4 left **Rev:** Crowned arms with supporters above value **Edge:** Reeded **Note:** Virtually identical to Y-107 and Y-108.

Date	Mintage	F	VF	XF	Unc	BU
AH1424-2003	—	—	—	—	55.00	70.00

Y# 122 250 DIRHAMS
25.0000 g., 0.9250 Silver 0.7435 oz. ASW, 37 mm. **Subject:** 5th Anniversary of Mohammed VI's Reign **Obv:** Head 3/4 left, national arms **Rev:** Crowned arms with supporters above value **Edge:** Reeded **Note:** Vitually identical to Y-107, 108 and 111.

Date	Mintage	F	VF	XF	Unc	BU
AH1425-2004	—	—	—	—	55.00	70.00

Y# 121 250 DIRHAMS
25.0000 g., 0.9250 Silver 0.7435 oz. ASW, 37 mm. **Subject:** Year of Handicapped Persons **Obv:** Head 3/4 left **Rev:** Stylized figures

Date	Mintage	F	VF	XF	Unc	BU
AH1425-2004	—	—	—	—	55.00	70.00

Y# 123 250 DIRHAMS
25.0000 g., 0.9250 Silver 0.7435 oz. ASW, 37 mm. **Subject:** 30th Anniversary - Green March **Obv:** Head 3/4 left **Rev:** Men marching left with flags aloft

Date	Mintage	F	VF	XF	Unc	BU
AH1426-2005	—	—	—	—	55.00	70.00

Y# 124 250 DIRHAMS
25.0000 g., 0.9250 Silver 0.7435 oz. ASW, 37 mm. **Subject:** 6th Anniversary of Mohammed VI's Reign **Obv:** Head 3/4 left **Rev:** Crowned arms with supporters above value **Edge:** Reeded **Note:** Virtually identical to Y-107, 108, 111 and 122

Date	Mintage	F	VF	XF	Unc	BU
AH1426-2005	—	—	—	—	55.00	70.00

Y# 125 250 DIRHAMS
25.0000 g., 0.9250 Silver 0.7435 oz. ASW, 37 mm. **Subject:** 6th Anniversary of Mohammed VI's Reign **Obv:** Head 3/4 left **Rev:** Crowned arms with supporters above value **Edge:** Reeded **Note:** Virtually identical to Y-107, 108, 111 and 122

Date	Mintage	F	VF	XF	Unc	BU
AH1427-2006	—	—	—	—	55.00	70.00

Y# 126 250 DIRHAMS
25.0000 g., 0.9250 Silver 0.7435 oz. ASW, 37 mm. **Subject:** 8th Anniversary of Mohammed VI's reign **Obv:** Head 3/4 left **Rev:** Corwned arms with supporters, value below **Edge:** Reeded

Date	Mintage	F	VF	XF	Unc	BU
AH1428/2007	—	—	—	—	55.00	70.00

Y# 127 250 DIRHAMS
25.0000 g., 0.9250 Silver 0.7435 oz. ASW, 37 mm. **Subject:**

9th Anniversary of Mohammed VI's reign **Obv:** Head 3/4 left **Rev:** Crowned arms with supporters above value **Edge:** Reeded

Date	Mintage	F	VF	XF	Unc	BU
AH1429-2008 Proof	1,000	Value: 70.00				

Y# 128   250 DIRHAMS
25.0000 g., 0.9250 Silver 0.7435 oz. ASW, 37 mm. **Subject:** 12 Centuries of Monarchy

Date	Mintage	F	VF	XF	Unc	BU
AH1429-2008 Proof	5,000	Value: 70.00				

Y# 133   250 DIRHAMS
6.4500 g., 0.9000 Gold 0.1866 oz. AGW, 21 mm. **Subject:** 12 Centuries of Monarchy

Date	Mintage	F	VF	XF	Unc	BU
AH1429-2008	3,000	Value: 350				

Y# 129   250 DIRHAMS
25.0000 g., 0.9250 Silver 0.7435 oz. ASW, 37 mm. **Subject:** 10th Anniversary of Mohammed VI's reign **Obv:** Head 3/4 left **Rev:** Crowned arms with supporters above value **Edge:** Reeded

Date	Mintage	F	VF	XF	Unc	BU
AH1430-2009 Proof	1,500	Value: 70.00				

Y# 130   250 DIRHAMS
25.0000 g., 0.9250 Silver 0.7435 oz. ASW, 37 mm. **Subject:** Bank al Maghrib, 50th Anniversary **Obv:** Head 3/4 left

Date	Mintage	F	VF	XF	Unc	BU
AH1430-2009 Proof	—	Value: 70.00				

Y# 131   250 DIRHAMS
25.0000 g., 0.9250 Silver 0.7435 oz. ASW, 37 mm. **Subject:**

11th Anniversary of Mohammed VI's reign **Obv:** Head 3/4 left **Rev:** Crowned arms with supporters above value **Edge:** Reeded

Date	Mintage	F	VF	XF	Unc	BU
AH1431-2010 Proof	1,500	Value: 70.00				

Y# 132   250 DIRHAMS
25.0000 g., 0.9250 Silver 0.7435 oz. ASW, 37 mm. **Subject:** Green March, 35th Anniversary **Edge:** Reeded

Date	Mintage	F	VF	XF	Unc	BU
AH1431-2010 Proof	1,000	Value: 70.00				

Y# 135   500 DIRHAMS
Bi-Metallic **Obv:** Head left **Rev:** Building

Date	Mintage	F	VF	XF	Unc	BU
AH1430-2009 Proof	—					

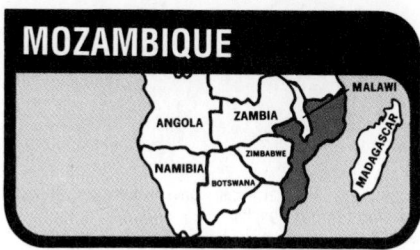

MOZAMBIQUE

The Republic of Mozambique, a former overseas province of Portugal, stretches for 1,430 miles (2,301 km.) along the southeast coast of Africa, has an area of 302,330 sq. mi. (801,590 sq. km.) and a population of 14.1 million, 99 % of whom are native Africans of the Bantu tribes. Capital: Maputo. Agriculture is the chief industry. Cashew nuts, cotton, sugar, copra and tea are exported.

Mozambique became a member of the Commonwealth of Nations in November 1995. The President is Head of State; the Prime Minister is Head of Government.

REPUBLIC

REFORM COINAGE
100 Centavos = 1 Metical; 1994

KM# 130   1000 METICAIS
25.7100 g., 0.9800 Silver 0.8100 oz. ASW, 38.5 mm. **Subject:** Pedro De Covilha, 1498 **Obv:** National arms within circle **Rev:** Sailing ship within circle **Edge:** Reeded

Date	Mintage	F	VF	XF	Unc	BU
2003 Proof	—	Value: 45.00				

KM# 131   10000 METICAIS
8.0400 g., Bi-Metallic Stainless Steel center in Brass ring, 26.6 mm. **Obv:** National arms within circle **Rev:** Rhino within circle **Edge:** Segmented reeding

Date	Mintage	F	VF	XF	Unc	BU
2003	—	3.50	5.00	7.50	12.00	

REFORM COINAGE
(New) Metical = 1,000 Meticals; 2005

KM# 132   CENTAVO
2.0000 g., Copper Plated Steel, 15 mm. **Obv:** Bank logo, date **Obv. Legend:** BANCO DE MOÇAMBIQUE **Rev:** Rhinoceros standing left, value **Edge:** Plain

Date	Mintage	F	VF	XF	Unc	BU
2006	—	—	—	—	0.15	0.25

KM# 133   5 CENTAVOS
2.3000 g., Copper Plated Steel, 19 mm. **Obv:** Bank logo, date **Obv. Legend:** BANCO DE MOÇAMBIQUE **Rev:** Cheetah standing left, value **Edge:** Reeded

Date	Mintage	F	VF	XF	Unc	BU
2006	—	—	—	0.10	0.25	0.35

KM# 134   10 CENTAVOS
3.0600 g., Brass Plated Steel, 17 mm. **Obv:** Bank logo, date **Obv. Legend:** BANCO DE MOÇAMBIQUE **Rev:** Farmer cultivating with tractor, value **Edge:** Reeded

Date	Mintage	F	VF	XF	Unc	BU
2006	—	—	—	0.15	0.35	0.50

KM# 135   20 CENTAVOS
4.1000 g., Brass Plated Steel, 20 mm. **Obv:** Bank logo, date **Obv. Legend:** BANCO DE MOÇAMBIQUE **Rev:** Cotton plant, value **Edge:** Reeded

Date	Mintage	F	VF	XF	Unc	BU
2006	—	—	—	0.20	0.50	0.75

KM# 136   50 CENTAVOS
5.7400 g., Brass Plated Steel, 23 mm. **Obv:** Bank logo, date **Obv. Legend:** BANCO DE MOÇAMBIQUE **Rev:** Giant Kingfisher perched on branch, value **Edge:** Reeded

Date	Mintage	F	VF	XF	Unc	BU
2006	—	—	—	0.50	1.25	1.75

KM# 137   METICAL
5.3000 g., Nickel Plated Steel, 21 mm. **Obv:** Bank logo, date **Obv. Legend:** BANCO DE MOÇAMBIQUE **Rev:** Young woman seated left writing, value **Edge:** Plain **Shape:** 7-sided

Date	Mintage	F	VF	XF	Unc	BU
2006	—	—	—	0.45	1.10	1.50

KM# 138   2 METICAIS
6.0000 g., Nickel Plated Steel, 24 mm. **Obv:** Bank logo, date **Obv. Legend:** BANCO DE MOÇAMBIQUE **Rev:** Coelacanth fish, value **Edge:** Segmented reeding

Date	Mintage	F	VF	XF	Unc	BU
2006	—	—	—	0.75	1.80	2.50

KM# 139   5 METICAIS
6.5000 g., Nickel Plated Steel, 27 mm.   **Obv:** Bank logo, date
Obv. Legend: BANCO DE MOÇAMBIQUE **Rev:** Timbila (similar
to a xylophone), value **Edge:** Reeded

Date	Mintage	F	VF	XF	Unc	BU
2006	—	—	—	1.20	3.00	4.00

KM# 140   10 METICAIS
7.5000 g., Bi-Metallic Nickel Clad Steel center in Brass ring.,
25 mm.   **Obv:** Bank logo **Obv. Legend:** BANCO • DE •
MOCAMBIQUE **Rev:** Modern bank building, value below **Edge:**
Reeded

Date	Mintage	F	VF	XF	Unc	BU
2006	—	—	—	1.50	3.75	5.00

NAGORNO-KARABAKH

Nagorno-Karabakh, an ethnically Armenian enclave inside
Azerbaijan (pop., 1991 est.: 193,000), SW region. It occupies an
area of 1,700 sq mi (4,400 square km) on the NE flank of the Karabakh Mountain Range, with the capital city of Stepanakert.

Russia annexed the area from Persia in 1813, and in 1923
it was established as an autonomous province of the Azerbaijan
S.S.R. In 1988 the region's ethnic Armenian majority demonstrated against Azerbaijani rule, and in 1991, after the breakup of
the U.S.S.R. brought independence to Armenia and Azerbaijan,
war broke out between the two ethnic groups. On January 8, 1992
the leaders of Nagorno-Karabakh declared independence as the
Republic of Mountainous Karabakh (RMK). Since 1994, following
a cease-fire, ethnic Armenians have held Karabakh, though officially it remains part of Azerbaijan. Karabakh remains sovereign,
but the political and military condition is volatile and tensions frequently flare into skirmishes.

Its marvelous nature and geographic situation, have all facil-
itated Karabakh to be a center of science, poetry and, especially,
of the musical culture of Azerbaijan.

MONETARY SYSTEM
100 Luma = 1 Dram

REPUBLIC
STANDARD COINAGE

KM# 6   50 LUMA
0.9500 g., Aluminum, 19.8 mm.   **Obv:** National arms **Rev:** Horse
cantering left **Edge:** Plain

Date	Mintage	F	VF	XF	Unc	BU
2004	—	—	—	—	1.00	1.25

KM# 7   50 LUMA
0.9500 g., Aluminum, 19.8 mm.   **Obv:** National arms **Rev:**
Gazelle **Edge:** Plain

Date	Mintage	F	VF	XF	Unc	BU
2004	—	—	—	—	1.00	1.25

KM# 8   DRAM
1.1300 g., Aluminum, 21.7 mm.   **Obv:** National arms **Rev:**
Pheasant **Edge:** Plain

Date	Mintage	F	VF	XF	Unc	BU
2004	—	—	—	—	1.00	1.25

KM# 9   DRAM
1.1200 g., Aluminum, 21.7 mm.   **Obv:** National arms **Rev:** 1/2-
length Saint facing **Edge:** Plain

Date	Mintage	F	VF	XF	Unc	BU
2004	—	—	—	—	1.25	1.50

KM# 10   DRAM
1.1300 g., Aluminum, 21.7 mm.   **Obv:** National arms **Rev:**
Cheetah facing **Edge:** Plain

Date	Mintage	F	VF	XF	Unc	BU
2004	—	—	—	—	1.00	1.25

KM# 11   5 DRAMS
4.4000 g., Brass, 21.8 mm.   **Obv:** National arms **Rev:** Church
Edge: Plain

Date	Mintage	F	VF	XF	Unc	BU
2004	—	—	—	—	1.25	1.50

KM# 12   5 DRAMS
4.5000 g., Brass, 21.8 mm.   **Obv:** National arms **Rev:** Monument
faces **Edge:** Plain

Date	Mintage	F	VF	XF	Unc	BU
2004	—	—	—	—	1.00	1.25

KM# 23   1000 DRAMS
31.4300 g., 0.9990 Silver 1.0094 oz. ASW, 38.9 mm.   **Obv:**
National arms **Rev:** Archer **Edge:** Plain

Date	Mintage	F	VF	XF	Unc	BU
2003 Proof	—	Value: 75.00				

KM# 24   1000 DRAMS
31.3300 g., 0.9990 Silver 1.0062 oz. ASW, 38.39 mm.   **Series:**
Armenian architectural sculpture **Obv:** National arms **Rev:**
Church of the Holy Cross at Aghthamar, Turkey **Edge:** Plain

Date	Mintage	F	VF	XF	Unc	BU
2003 Proof	—	Value: 75.00				

KM# 25   1000 DRAMS
31.3000 g., 0.9990 Silver 1.0053 oz. ASW, 38.92 mm.   **Obv:**
National arms **Rev:** Bust of Kevork Chavoush 3/4 left **Edge:** Plain

Date	Mintage	F	VF	XF	Unc	BU
2004 Proof	—	Value: 75.00				

KM# 19   1000 DRAMS
31.3700 g., 0.9990 Silver 1.0075 oz. ASW, 38.9 mm.   **Obv:**
National arms **Rev:** Leopard head facing **Edge:** Plain

Date	Mintage	F	VF	XF	Unc	BU
2004 Proof	—	Value: 65.00				

KM# 19a   1000 DRAMS
31.3700 g., 0.9990 Silver Gilt 1.0075 oz. ASW, 38.9 mm.   **Obv:**
National arms **Rev:** Leopard head facing **Edge:** Plain

Date	Mintage	F	VF	XF	Unc	BU
2004 Proof	—	Value: 75.00				

KM# 20   1000 DRAMS
31.3700 g., 0.9990 Silver 1.0075 oz. ASW, 38.9 mm.   **Obv:**
National arms **Rev:** Standing Brown Bear **Edge:** Plain

Date	Mintage	F	VF	XF	Unc	BU
2004 Proof	—	Value: 75.00				

KM# 20a   1000 DRAMS
31.3700 g., 0.9990 Silver Gilt 1.0075 oz. ASW, 38.9 mm.   **Obv:**
National arms **Rev:** Standing Brown Bear **Edge:** Plain

Date	Mintage	F	VF	XF	Unc	BU
2004 Proof	—	Value: 85.00				

KM# 21 1000 DRAMS
31.3700 g., 0.9990 Silver 1.0075 oz. ASW, 38.9 mm. **Obv:** National arms **Rev:** Eagle head within circle **Edge:** Plain

Date	Mintage	F	VF	XF	Unc	BU
2004 Proof	—	Value: 75.00				

KM# 21a 1000 DRAMS
31.3700 g., 0.9990 Silver Gilt 1.0075 oz. ASW, 38.9 mm. **Obv:** National arms **Rev:** Eagle head within circle **Edge:** Plain

Date	Mintage	F	VF	XF	Unc	BU
2004 Proof	—	Value: 85.00				

KM# 22 1000 DRAMS
31.1200 g., 0.9990 Silver 0.9995 oz. ASW, 38.9 mm. **Obv:** National arms **Rev:** 1918 Genocide Victims Monument **Edge:** Plain

Date	Mintage	F	VF	XF	Unc	BU
2004 Proof	—	Value: 65.00				

NAMIBIA

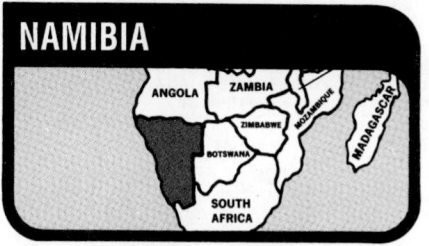

The Republic of Namibia, once the German colonial territory of German South West Africa, and later South West Africa, is situated on the Atlantic coast of southern Africa, bounded on the north by Angola, on the east by Botswana, and on the south by South Africa. It has an area of 318,261 sq. mi. (824,290 sq. km.) and a population of *1.4 million. Capital: Windhoek. Diamonds, copper, lead, zinc, and cattle are exported.

On June 17, 1985 the Transitional Government of National Unity was installed. Negotiations were held in 1988 between Angola, Cuba, and South Africa reaching a peaceful settlement on Aug. 5, 1988. By April 1989 Cuban troops were to withdraw from Angola and South African troops from Namibia. The Transitional Government resigned on Feb. 28, 1988 for the upcoming elections of the constituent assembly in Nov. 1989. Independence was finally achieved on March 12, 1990 within the Commonwealth of Nations. The President is the Head of State; the Prime Minister is Head of Government.

MONETARY SYSTEM
100 Cents = 1 Namibia Dollar

REPUBLIC
1990 - present
DECIMAL COINAGE

KM# 1 5 CENTS
2.2000 g., Nickel Plated Steel, 17 mm. **Obv:** National arms **Rev:** Value left, aloe plant within 3/4 sun design

Date	Mintage	F	VF	XF	Unc	BU
2002	—	—	—	0.20	0.50	0.75
2007	—	—	—	0.20	0.50	0.75
2009	—	—	—	0.20	0.50	0.75

KM# 2 10 CENTS
3.4000 g., Nickel Plated Steel, 21.5 mm. **Obv:** National arms **Rev:** Camelthorn tree right, partial sun design left, value below

Date	Mintage	F	VF	XF	Unc	BU
2002	—	—	—	0.35	1.00	1.25
2009	—	—	—	0.35	1.00	1.25

KM# 3 50 CENTS
4.4300 g., Nickel Plated Steel, 24 mm. **Obv:** National arms **Rev:** Quiver tree right, partial sun design upper left, value below

Date	Mintage	F	VF	XF	Unc	BU
2008	—	—	—	—	1.75	2.00

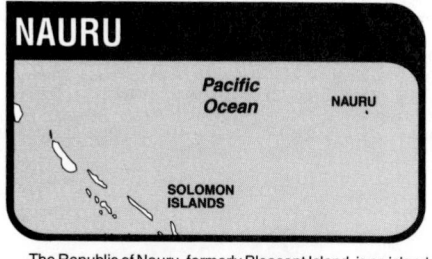

KM# 4 DOLLAR
5.0000 g., Brass, 22.4 mm. **Obv:** National arms **Rev:** Value divides Bateleur eagle at right, partial sun design at left

Date	Mintage	F	VF	XF	Unc	BU
2002	—	—	—	1.25	3.50	6.00
2006	—	—	—	1.25	3.50	6.00
2008	—	—	—	1.25	3.50	6.00
2010	—	—	—	1.25	3.50	6.00

KM# 21 10 DOLLARS
Bi-Metallic Aluminum-Bronze center in Copper-Nickel ring, 30 mm. **Subject:** Bank of Namibia, 20th Anniversary **Obv:** National arms **Rev:** Dr. Sam Nujoma bust facing **Edge:** Segmented reeding

Date	Mintage	F	VF	XF	Unc	BU
2010	—	—	—	—	—	7.50

NAURU

The Republic of Nauru, formerly Pleasant Island, is an island republic in the western Pacific Ocean west of the Gilbert Islands. It has an area of 8-1/2 sq. mi. and a population of 7,254. It is known for its phosphate deposits. Nauru is a special member of the Commonwealth of Nations.

RULER
British, until 1968

MONETARY SYSTEM
100 Cents = 1 (Australian) Dollar

REPUBLIC
DECIMAL COINAGE

KM# 45 DOLLAR
Silver, 39 mm. **Subject:** Elizabeth II and Prince Philip, 60th Wedding Anniversary **Obv:** National arms **Rev:** Wedding portraits

Date	Mintage	F	VF	XF	Unc	BU
2007 Proof	—	Value: 40.00				

KM# 38 DOLLAR
27.0000 g., Silver Plated Copper, 38.6 mm. **Subject:** Guardian Angel **Obv:** Arms **Rev:** Angel standing, swarovski crystals in hair

Date	Mintage	F	VF	XF	Unc	BU
2009 Proof	10,000	Value: 35.00				

KM# 44 DOLLAR
27.0000 g., Silver Plated Copper, 38.61 mm. **Subject:** Guardian Angel

Date	Mintage	F	VF	XF	Unc	BU
2009 Proof	10,000	Value: 50.00				

KM# 47 DOLLAR
Silver, 39 mm. **Subject:** WWII AZNAC troops **Obv:** Head in tiaria right, National arms at right **Rev:** Flag and Bugler

Date	Mintage	F	VF	XF	Unc	BU
2011 Proof	—	Value: 40.00				

KM# 46 5 DOLLARS
Silver, 39 mm. **Subject:** Elizabeth II and Prince Philip, 60th Wedding anniversary **Obv:** National arms **Rev:** Engagement photo

Date	Mintage	F	VF	XF	Unc	BU
2007 Proof	—	Value: 40.00				

KM# 36 5 DOLLARS
0.5000 g., 0.9990 Gold 0.0161 oz. AGW, 11 mm. **Subject:** Kaiser Wilhelm **Obv:** Arms **Rev:** Bust right

Date	Mintage	F	VF	XF	Unc	BU
2008 Proof	—	Value: 65.00				

KM# 37 5 DOLLARS
0.5000 g., 0.9990 Gold 0.0161 oz. AGW, 11 mm. **Subject:** Christmas **Obv:** Arms **Rev:** Bells ringing

Date	Mintage	F	VF	XF	Unc	BU
2008 Proof	—	Value: 65.00				

KM# 39 5 DOLLARS
0.5000 g., 0.9990 Gold 0.0161 oz. AGW **Issuer:** 11 **Subject:** Christmas **Obv:** Arms **Rev:** Teddy bear seated

Date	Mintage	F	VF	XF	Unc	BU
2009 Proof	—	Value: 55.00				

KM# 18   10 DOLLARS
31.1000 g., 0.9990 Silver 0.9988 oz. ASW   **Subject:** Discontinuation of the German Mark **Obv:** National arms **Obv. Legend:** BANK OF NAURU

Date	Mintage	F	VF	XF	Unc	BU
2001 Proof	—	Value: 95.00				

KM# 13   10 DOLLARS
31.2500 g., 0.9990 Silver 71.5 x 72 1.0037 oz. ASW, 72 mm. **Subject:** First Euro Coinage **Obv:** National arms, matte finish **Rev:** Denomination, inscription and partially gold-plated 1 Euro reverse coin design, Proof finish **Edge:** Plain **Shape:** Like a map

Date	Mintage	F	VF	XF	Unc	BU
2002 Proof	—	Value: 95.00				

KM# 15   10 DOLLARS
31.1000 g., 0.9990 Silver 0.9988 oz. ASW, 40 mm. **Series:** Save the Whales **Obv:** National arms **Obv. Legend:** BANK OF NAURU **Rev:** Blue Whale on mother-of-pearl insert **Edge:** Plain

Date	Mintage	F	VF	XF	Unc	BU
2002 Proof	2,000	Value: 85.00				

KM# 14   10 DOLLARS
34.6000 g., 0.9250 Silver with gold plated or gold attachment 1.0289 oz. ASW, 38.5 mm. **Subject:** Brandenburg Gate **Obv:** National arms **Rev:** Brandenburg Gate **Edge:** Plain **Note:** Gold color 1mm thick

Date	Mintage	F	VF	XF	Unc	BU
2002 Proof/Matte	—	Value: 150				

KM# 19   10 DOLLARS
31.1000 g., 0.9990 Silver 0.9988 oz. ASW   **Subject:** European Union - Mark and Euro **Obv:** National arms **Obv. Legend:** BANK OF NAURU

Date	Mintage	F	VF	XF	Unc	BU
2003 Proof	5,000	Value: 75.00				

KM# 20   10 DOLLARS
1.2400 g., 0.9990 Gold 0.0398 oz. AGW, 13.92 mm. **Subject:** First Anniversary of the Euro **Obv:** National arms **Obv. Legend:** BANK OF NAURU **Rev:** Euro symbol **Edge:** Reeded

Date	Mintage	F	VF	XF	Unc	BU
2003 Proof	—	Value: 75.00				

KM# 21   10 DOLLARS
1.2400 g., 0.9990 Gold 0.0398 oz. AGW   **Subject:** Treasure of Priamos in Troja **Obv:** National arms **Obv. Legend:** BANK OF NAURU

Date	Mintage	F	VF	XF	Unc	BU
2003 Proof	—	Value: 85.00				

KM# 22   10 DOLLARS
1.2400 g., 0.9990 Gold 0.0398 oz. AGW   **Subject:** Treasure of Nibelungen **Obv:** National arms **Obv. Legend:** BANK OF NAURU

Date	Mintage	F	VF	XF	Unc	BU
2003 Proof	—	Value: 85.00				

KM# 23   10 DOLLARS
30.9500 g., Silver With removable gold or gilt 2.6g Reichstag building attachment with 2004/ NAURU 0077 on reverse **Subject:** European Monuments **Obv:** National arms **Obv.**

Legend: BANK OF NAURU **Rev. Legend:** GERMANY - DEUTSCHER REICHSTAG **Edge:** Plain

Date	Mintage	F	VF	XF	Unc	BU
2003 Proof/Matte	—	Value: 150				

KM# 24   10 DOLLARS
Silver With removable gold or gilt attachment **Series:** European Monuments **Subject:** Palazzo Pubblico in San Marino **Obv:** National arms **Obv. Legend:** BANK OF NAURU **Edge:** Plain

Date	Mintage	F	VF	XF	Unc	BU
2005 Proof/Matte	—	Value: 150				

KM# 25   10 DOLLARS
1.2400 g., 0.9990 Gold 0.0398 oz. AGW   **Subject:** East Gothic stylized eagle broach from Domagnano, Italy in National Museum in Nuremburg **Obv:** National arms **Obv. Legend:** BANK OF NAURU

Date	Mintage	F	VF	XF	Unc	BU
2005 Proof	25,000	Value: 85.00				

KM# 35   10 DOLLARS
31.1050 g., 0.9990 Silver 0.9990 oz. ASW   **Subject:** German Railways, 150th Anniversary **Obv:** National Arms **Rev:** Baureihi "01"

Date	Mintage	F	VF	XF	Unc	BU
2005 Proof	—	Value: 60.00				

KM# 40   10 DOLLARS
1.2400 g., 0.9990 Gold 0.0398 oz. AGW, 13.92 mm. **Obv:** National Arms **Rev:** Ludwig Erhard

Date	Mintage	F	VF	XF	Unc	BU
2005 Proof	—	Value: 85.00				

KM# 26   10 DOLLARS
1.2400 g., 0.9990 Gold 0.0398 oz. AGW   **Subject:** Angela Dorothea Merkel, Chancellor of Germany **Obv:** National arms **Obv. Legend:** BANK OF NAURU

Date	Mintage	F	VF	XF	Unc	BU
2005 Proof	—	Value: 85.00				

KM# 41   10 DOLLARS
31.1000 g., 0.9990 Silver 0.9988 oz. ASW, 38.61 mm. **Rev:** Tower Bridge, gilt

Date	Mintage	F	VF	XF	Unc	BU
2005	2,000	Value: 200				

KM# 43   10 DOLLARS
31.1050 g., 0.9990 Silver 0.9990 oz. ASW, 38.6 mm. **Rev:** St. Stephens Church, Vienna partially gilt

Date	Mintage	F	VF	XF	Unc	BU
2005 Proof	2,000	Value: 50.00				

KM# 27   10 DOLLARS
1.2400 g., 0.9990 Gold 0.0398 oz. AGW   **Subject:** Konrad Adenauer at 1949 demonstration **Obv:** National arms **Obv. Legend:** BANK OF NAURU

Date	Mintage	F	VF	XF	Unc	BU
2006 Proof	15,000	Value: 85.00				

KM# 28   10 DOLLARS
1.2400 g., 0.9990 Gold 0.0398 oz. AGW   **Subject:** Volkswagen **Obv:** National arms **Obv. Legend:** BANK OF NAURU

Date	Mintage	F	VF	XF	Unc	BU
2006 Proof	—	Value: 85.00				

KM# 29   10 DOLLARS
1.2400 g., 0.9990 Gold 0.0398 oz. AGW   **Subject:** Conrad Schumann in Berlin 1961 **Obv:** National arms **Obv. Legend:** BANK OF NAURU

Date	Mintage	F	VF	XF	Unc	BU
2006 Proof	—	Value: 85.00				

KM# 30   10 DOLLARS
1.2400 g., 0.9990 Gold 0.0398 oz. AGW   **Subject:** Olympic Stadium in Munich 1972 **Obv:** National arms **Obv. Legend:** BANK OF NAURU

Date	Mintage	F	VF	XF	Unc	BU
2006 Proof	—	Value: 85.00				

KM# 31   10 DOLLARS
1.2400 g., 0.9990 Gold 0.0398 oz. AGW   **Subject:** Independent Activists 1980 **Obv:** National arms **Obv. Legend:** BANK OF NAURU

Date	Mintage	F	VF	XF	Unc	BU
2006 Proof	—	Value: 85.00				

KM# 32 10 DOLLARS

1.2400 g., 0.9990 Gold 0.0398 oz. AGW **Subject:** Brandenburg Gate in Berlin 1990 **Obv. Legend:** BANK OF NAURU

Date	Mintage	F	VF	XF	Unc	BU
2006 Proof	—	Value: 85.00				

KM# 33 10 DOLLARS

1.2400 g., 0.9990 Gold 0.0398 oz. AGW **Subject:** European Union 2002 **Obv:** National arms **Obv. Legend:** BANK OF NAURU

Date	Mintage	F	VF	XF	Unc	BU
2006 Proof	—	Value: 85.00				

KM# 34 10 DOLLARS

1.2400 g., 0.9990 Gold 0.0398 oz. AGW **Subject:** Johannes Rau, German President, 1999-2004 **Obv:** National arms **Obv. Legend:** BANK OF NAURU

Date	Mintage	F	VF	XF	Unc	BU
2006 Proof	—	Value: 85.00				

KM# 42 10 DOLLARS

31.1000 g., 0.9990 Silver 0.9988 oz. ASW, 38.61 mm. **Rev:** Tower of Pisa, gilt

Date	Mintage	F	VF	XF	Unc	BU
2006 Proof	2,000	Value: 200				

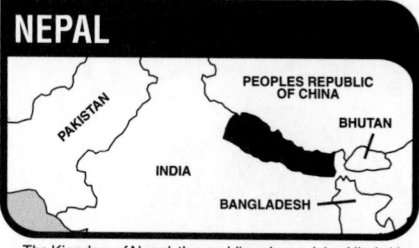

NEPAL

The Kingdom of Nepal, the world's only surviving Hindu kingdom, is a landlocked country occupying the southern slopes of the Himalayas. It has an area of 56,136 sq. mi. (140,800 sq. km.) and a population of 18 million. Capital: Kathmandu. Nepal has deposits of coal, copper, iron and cobalt, but they are largely unexploited. Agriculture is the principal economic activity. Rice, timber and jute are exported, with tourism being the other major foreign exchange earner.

On June 2, 2001 tragedy struck the royal family when Crown Prince Dipendra used an assault rifle to kill his father, mother and other members of the royal family as the result of a dispute over his current lady friend. He died 48 hours later, as King, from self inflicted gunshot wounds. Gyanendra began his second reign as King (his first was a short time as a toddler, 1950-51).

DATING

Bikram Samvat Era (VS)

From 1888AD most copper coins were dated in the Bikram Samvat (VS) era. To convert take VS date - 57 =AD date. Coins with this era have VS before the year in the listing. Tthis era is used for all coins struck in Nepal since 1911AD.

RULER

SHAH DYNASTY

क्षानेन दक्षीर विक्रम

Gyanendra Bir Bikram
VS2058-/2001-AD

NUMERALS

Nepal has used more variations of numerals on their coins than any other nation. The most common are illustrated in the numeral chart in the introduction. The chart below illustrates some variations encompassing the last four centuries.

1	2	3	4	5	6	7	8	9	0
۹	2	3	४	५	६	७	८	९	०

NUMERICS

One एक

Two दूइ

Ten	दसा
Twenty-five	पचीसा
Fifty	पचासा
Hundred	सय

DENOMINATIONS

Rupee रुपैयाँ

Legend on reverse

श्री श्री श्री गोरपनाथ
Shri Shri Shri Gorakhanatha in 8 petals

KINGDOM
Shah Dynasty

Gyanendra Bir Bikram
VS2058-2064 / 2001- 2007AD

DECIMAL COINAGE
100 Paisa = 1 Rupee

KM# 1173 10 PAISA

Aluminum, 17 mm. **Obv:** Royal crown **Edge:** Plain

Date	Mintage	F	VF	XF	Unc	BU
VS2058 (2001)	—	—	—	—	1.00	1.50

KM# 1148 25 PAISA

Aluminum, 20 mm. **Obv:** Royal crown **Edge:** Plain

Date	Mintage	F	VF	XF	Unc	BU
VS2058 (2001)	—	—	—	—	0.50	0.75
VS2059 (2002)	—	—	—	—	0.50	0.75
VS2060 (2003)	—	—	—	—	0.50	0.75

KM# 1149 50 PAISA

Aluminum, 22.5 mm. **Obv:** Royal crown **Rev:** Swayambhunath **Edge:** Plain

Date	Mintage	F	VF	XF	Unc	BU
VS2058 (2001)	—	—	—	—	0.50	0.75
VS2059 (2002)	—	—	—	—	0.50	0.75

KM# 1179 50 PAISA

1.4100 g., Aluminum, 22.5 mm. **Obv:** Crown above crossed flags **Rev:** Swayambhunath **Edge:** Plain

Date	Mintage	F	VF	XF	Unc	BU
VS2060 (2003)	—	—	—	—	0.40	0.50
VS2061 (2004)	—	—	—	—	0.40	0.50

KM# 1150.1 RUPEE

Brass Plated Steel **Rev:** Large (8.5mm) temple, medium '1' (4.5mm) **Edge:** Reeded **Note:** Non-magnetic.

Date	Mintage	F	VF	XF	Unc	BU
VS2058 (2001)	—	—	—	—	1.00	1.50

KM# 1150.2 RUPEE

Brass Plated Steel **Obv:** Traditional design **Rev:** Small (7mm high) temple, small (4mm) "1" **Edge:** Plain **Note:** Magnetic.

Date	Mintage	F	VF	XF	Unc	BU
VS2058 (2001)	—	—	—	—	1.00	1.50
VS2059 (2002)	—	—	—	—	1.00	1.50
VS2060 (2003)	—	—	—	—	1.00	1.50

KM# 1150.3 RUPEE

3.9600 g., Brass, 20 mm. **Obv:** Traditional design **Rev:** Small (6.5mm high) temple, small (4mm) "1" **Edge:** Plain

Date	Mintage	F	VF	XF	Unc	BU
VS2058 (2001)	—	—	—	—	0.50	0.75

KM# 1150.4 RUPEE

3.9600 g., Brass Plated Steel, 20 mm. **Obv:** Traditional design **Rev:** Small (7mm high) temple, large (4.5mm) "1" **Note:** Magnetic.

Date	Mintage	F	VF	XF	Unc	BU
VS2059 (2002)	—	—	—	—	1.00	1.50
VS2060 (2003)	—	—	—	—	1.00	1.50

KM# 1180 RUPEE

3.9600 g., Brass Plated Steel, 20 mm. **Obv:** Traditional design **Rev:** Wagheshwari Temple **Edge:** Plain **Note:** "1" in denomination of a different style.

Date	Mintage	F	VF	XF	Unc	BU
VS2061 (2004)	—	—	—	—	0.75	1.00

KM# 1181 RUPEE

3.9400 g., Brass Plated Steel, 19.95 mm. **Obv:** Traditional design **Rev:** Sri Talbarahi Temple with outline mountain scene behind **Edge:** Plain

Date	Mintage	F	VF	XF	Unc	BU
VS2062(2005)	—	—	—	0.50	1.20	1.60

KM# 1170 2 RUPEES

4.9400 g., Brass, 25 mm. **Obv:** Traditional square design **Rev:** People with flag celebrating 50 Years of Democracy **Edge:** Plain

Date	Mintage	F	VF	XF	Unc	BU
VS2058(2001)	—	—	—	—	0.50	0.75

KM# 1151.2 2 RUPEES

Brass, 25 mm. **Obv:** Traditional design **Rev:** Three domed building **Edge:** Plain

Date	Mintage	F	VF	XF	Unc	BU
VS2058 (2001)	—	—	—	—	1.50	2.00
VS2059 (2002)	—	—	—	—	1.50	2.00
VS2060 (2003)	—	—	—	—	1.50	2.00

KM# 1151.1 2 RUPEES

5.0700 g., Brass Plated Steel, 25 mm. **Obv:** Traditional design **Rev:** Three domed building **Edge:** Plain **Note:** Edge varieties exist. Prev. KM#1151. Magnetic.

Date	Mintage	F	VF	XF	Unc	BU
VS2060 (2003)	—	—	—	—	1.50	2.00

KM# 1151.1a 2 RUPEES

6.7000 g., Silver, 25 mm. **Obv:** Traditional design **Rev:** Three domed building **Edge:** Plain

Date	Mintage	F	VF	XF	Unc	BU
VS2060(2003)	—	—	—	—	100	—

KM# 1159 25 RUPEE

8.3600 g., Copper-Nickel, 29.1 mm. **Obv:** Crowned bust right **Rev:** Traditional design **Edge:** Plain

Date	Mintage	F	VF	XF	Unc	BU
VS2058 (2001)	—	—	—	—	4.00	5.00
VS2059 (2002)	—	—	—	—	4.00	5.00

KM# 1164   25 RUPEE
8.6000 g., Copper-Nickel, 29.1 mm. **Subject:** Silver Jubilee **Obv:** Traditional design **Rev:** Stylized face design **Edge:** Plain

Date	Mintage	F	VF	XF	Unc	BU
VS2060 (2003)	—	—	—	—	4.00	5.00

KM# 1183   25 RUPEE
8.5500 g., Copper-Nickel, 29.1 mm. **Subject:** World Hindu Federation **Obv:** Traditional design **Edge:** Plain

Date	Mintage	F	VF	XF	Unc	BU
VS2062 (2005)	—	—	—	—	4.00	5.00

KM# 1160   50 RUPEE
20.1000 g., Brass, 37.7 mm. **Subject:** 50th Anniversary of Scouting in Nepal **Obv:** Traditional design **Rev:** Scouting emblem within beaded wreath **Edge:** Plain

Date	Mintage	F	VF	XF	Unc	BU
VS2058 (2001)	—	—	—	—	9.00	10.00

KM# 1182   50 RUPEE
8.6000 g., Copper-Nickel, 29 mm. **Subject:** Golden Jubilee of Supreme Court **Obv:** Traditional design **Rev:** Supreme Court building **Edge:** Plain

Date	Mintage	F	VF	XF	Unc	BU
VS2063 (2006)	—	—	—	—	6.00	9.00

KM# 1157   100 RUPEE
20.0000 g., Brass, 38.7 mm. **Subject:** Buddha **Obv:** Traditional design **Rev:** Seated Buddha teaching five seated monks **Edge:** Reeded

Date	Mintage	F	VF	XF	Unc	BU
VS2058 (2001)	30,000	—	—	—	10.00	12.00

KM# 1161   200 RUPEE
18.1000 g., 0.5000 Silver 0.2910 oz. ASW, 29.6 mm. **Subject:** 50th Anniversary of the Nepal Chamber of Commerce **Obv:** Traditional design **Rev:** Swastika within rotary gear **Edge:** Plain

Date	Mintage	F	VF	XF	Unc	BU
VS2059 (2002)	—	—	—	—	20.00	25.00

KM# 1162   200 RUPEE
18.1000 g., 0.5000 Silver 0.2910 oz. ASW, 29.6 mm. **Subject:** 50th Anniversary of Civil Service **Obv:** Traditional design **Rev:** Crown above flags and value **Edge:** Plain

Date	Mintage	F	VF	XF	Unc	BU
VS2059 (2002)	—	—	—	—	20.00	25.00

KM# 1171   250 RUPEE
18.0000 g., 0.5000 Silver 0.2893 oz. ASW, 29 mm. **Subject:** 2600th Anniversary of Bhagawan Mahavir **Obv:** Traditional design **Rev:** Haloed head above value **Edge:** Plain

Date	Mintage	F	VF	XF	Unc	BU
VS2058 (2001)	—	—	—	—	25.00	30.00

KM# 1176   250 RUPEE
17.8300 g., 0.5000 Silver 0.2866 oz. ASW, 31.6 mm. **Subject:** Marwadi, non-profit making organization **Obv:** Traditional design **Rev:** Swastika within circle **Edge:** Reeded

Date	Mintage	F	VF	XF	Unc	BU
VS2060 (2003)	—	—	—	—	25.00	30.00

KM# 1184   250 RUPEE
18.0000 g., Silver, 32 mm. **Subject:** 400th Anniversary of Guru Granth Sahib **Obv:** Traditional design **Rev:** Holy Book of Sikhs **Edge:** Reeded

Date	Mintage	F	VF	XF	Unc	BU
VS2061 (2004)	—	—	—	—	25.00	30.00

KM# 1174   300 RUPEE
22.5000 g., 0.5000 Silver 0.3617 oz. ASW, 31.8 mm. **Subject:** Economic Growth Through Export **Obv:** Traditional design **Rev:** Two joined hands in front of globe **Edge:** Reeded

Date	Mintage	F	VF	XF	Unc	BU
VS2060 (2003)	—	—	—	—	22.00	28.00

KM# 1177   500 RUPEE
23.0000 g., 0.9000 Silver 0.6655 oz. ASW, 31.7 mm. **Subject:** Management Education 50th Anniversary **Obv:** Traditional design **Rev:** Six point star outline **Edge:** Reeded

Date	Mintage	F	VF	XF	Unc	BU
VS2060 (2003)	—	—	—	—	30.00	35.00

KM# 1163   500 RUPEE
23.3400 g., 0.9000 Silver 0.6753 oz. ASW, 32 mm. **Subject:**

50th Anniversary of the Conquest of Mt. Everest **Obv:** Traditional design **Rev:** Mountain and map above value **Edge:** Reeded

Date	Mintage	F	VF	XF	Unc	BU
VS2060 (2003)	—	—	—	—	30.00	35.00

KM# 1185   500 RUPEE
20.1000 g., Silver, 32 mm. **Subject:** 50th Anniversary of Nepal-United Nations **Obv:** Traditional design **Rev:** Head of the late King Mahendra Bir Birkam **Edge:** Reeded

Date	Mintage	F	VF	XF	Unc	BU
VS2062	—	—	—	—	25.00	30.00

KM# 1175   1000 RUPEE
35.0000 g., Silver, 40 mm. **Subject:** 100 Years - Rotary Club **Edge:** Reeded

Date	Mintage	F	VF	XF	Unc	BU
VS2062 (2005)	—	—	—	—	45.00	50.00

KM# 1178   1000 RUPEE
35.2000 g., 0.5000 Silver 0.5658 oz. ASW, 40 mm. **Subject:** Rastriya Bank 50th Anniversary **Obv:** Traditional square design **Rev:** Bank seal above value **Edge:** Reeded

Date	Mintage	F	VF	XF	Unc	BU
VS2062 (2005)	—	—	—	—	27.00	32.00

KM# 1158   1500 RUPEE
20.0000 g., 0.9250 Silver 0.5948 oz. ASW, 38.7 mm. **Subject:** Buddha **Obv:** Traditional design **Rev:** Seated Buddha teaching five seated monks **Edge:** Reeded

Date	Mintage	F	VF	XF	Unc	BU
VS2058 (2001) Proof	15,000	Value: 35.00				

KM# 1172   2000 RUPEE
31.2000 g., 0.7200 Silver 0.7222 oz. ASW, 40 mm. **Subject:** Gyanendra's Accession to the Throne **Obv:** Crowned bust right **Rev:** Upright sword above value in circular design **Edge:** Reeded

Date	Mintage	F	VF	XF	Unc	BU
VS2058 (2001)	—	—	—	—	40.00	45.00

KM# 1201   2000 RUPEE
31.1050 g., 0.9990 Silver 0.9990 oz. ASW, 40 mm. **Subject:** Conquest of Mt. Everest 50th Anniversary **Rev:** Sir Edmond Hillary and Tenzing Norgay at Summit

Date	Mintage	F	VF	XF	Unc	BU
VS2060 (2003) Proof	8,000	Value: 80.00				

KM# 1191   2000 RUPEE
31.2000 g., 0.9250 Silver 0.9278 oz. ASW, 38.61 mm. **Subject:** 2006 FIFA World Cup - Germany **Obv:** Traditional design

Date	Mintage	F	VF	XF	Unc	BU
VS2063 (2006) (2006)	—	—	—	—	45.00	50.00

ASARFI GOLD COINAGE
(Asarphi)

Fractional designations are approximate for this series. Actual Gold Weight (AGW) is used to identify each type.

KM# 1200 ASARPHI
7.7700 g., 0.9999 Gold 0.2498 oz. AGW, 22 mm. **Subject:** Conquest of Mt. Everest **Rev:** Sir Edward Hillary and Tenzing Norgay at Summit

Date	Mintage	F	VF	XF	Unc	BU
VS2060 (2003)	2,000	—	—	—	800	—

KM# 1153 0.3G ASARPHI
0.3000 g., 0.9999 Gold 0.0096 oz. AGW, 7 mm. **Subject:** Buddha **Obv:** Traditional design **Rev:** Seated Buddha **Edge:** Plain

Date	Mintage	VG	F	VF	XF	BU
VS2058 (2001)	30,000	—	—	—	—	25.00

KM# 1154 1/25-OZ. ASARFI
1.2441 g., 0.9999 Gold 0.0400 oz. AGW, 13.92 mm. **Subject:** Buddha **Obv:** Traditional design **Rev:** Seated Buddha **Edge:** Reeded

Date	Mintage	VG	F	VF	XF	BU
VS2058 (2001)	25,000	—	—	—	—	75.00

KM# 1155 1/10-OZ. ASARFI
3.1104 g., 0.9999 Gold 0.1000 oz. AGW, 17.95 mm. **Subject:** Buddha **Obv:** Traditional design **Rev:** Seated Buddha **Edge:** Reeded

Date	Mintage	VG	F	VF	XF	BU
VS2058 (2001)	15,000	—	—	—	—	185

KM# 1156 1/2-OZ. ASARFI
15.5518 g., 0.9999 Gold 0.4999 oz. AGW, 27 mm. **Subject:** Buddha **Obv:** Traditional design **Rev:** Seated Buddha **Edge:** Reeded

Date	Mintage	VG	F	VF	XF	BU
VS2058 (2001) Proof	2,500	Value: 900				

SECULAR STATE

Gyanendra Bir Bikram
VS2058-2064 / 2001- 2007AD

DECIMAL COINAGE
100 Paisa = 1 Rupee

KM# 1186 25 RUPEE
8.5000 g., Copper-Nickel, 29 mm. **Subject:** 125th Anniversary - First Nepal Postal Stamp Issue **Obv:** Features image of legendary 1 Anna stamp **Rev:** Traditional mailman on the reverse

Date	Mintage	F	VF	XF	Unc	BU
VS2063 (2006)	—	—	—	—	7.00	9.00
VS2064 (2006)	—	—	—	—	7.00	9.00

DEMOCRATIC REPUBLIC

DECIMAL COINAGE
100 Paisa = 1 Rupee

KM# 1204 RUPEE
Brass Plated Steel, 19 mm. **Obv:** Mt. Everest within square **Rev:** Map of Nepal

Date	Mintage	F	VF	XF	Unc	BU
VS2064	—	—	—	—	2.00	3.50

KM# 1188 2 RUPEES
5.0000 g., Brass Plated Steel, 24.93 mm. **Obv:** Farmer plowing with water buffalos **Rev:** Mount Everest **Edge:** Plain

Date	Mintage	F	VF	XF	Unc	BU
VS2063(2006)	—	—	—	1.50	2.75	3.50

KM# 1189 50 RUPEE
8.6000 g., Copper-Nickel, 29 mm. **Subject:** 250th Anniversary Hindu festival "Kimari Jatra" **Obv:** Kumari Temple at Durbar Square in Kathmandu **Rev:** Bust of Goddess Kumari facing **Edge:** Plain

Date	Mintage	F	VF	XF	Unc	BU
VS2064 (2006)	—	—	—	—	8.00	10.00

KM# 1190 500 RUPEE
14.1900 g., 0.5000 Silver 0.2281 oz. ASW, 32 mm. **Subject:** 250th Anniversary Hindu festival "Kimari Jatra" **Obv:** Kumari Temple at Durbar Square in Kathmandu **Rev:** Bust of Goddess Kumari facing **Edge:** Reeded

Date	Mintage	F	VF	XF	Unc	BU
VS2064 (2007)	—	—	—	—	25.00	30.00

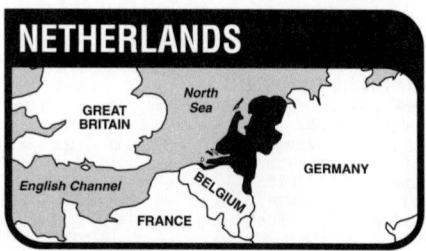

NETHERLANDS

The Kingdom of the Netherlands, a country of Western Europe fronting on the North Sea and bordered by Belgium and Germany, has an area of 15,770 sq. mi. (41,500 sq. km.) and a population of 16.4 million. Capital: Amsterdam, but the seat of government is at The Hague. The economy is based on dairy farming and a variety of industrial activities. Chemicals, yarns and fabrics, and meat products are exported.

NOTE: Excepting the World War II issues struck at U.S. mints, all of the modern coins were struck at the Utrecht Mint (or at the annex in the Birmingham Mint, 1980-2000) and bear the caduceus mint mark of that facility. They also bear the mint-masters' marks.

The BES-islands (Bonaire, St. Eustatius and Saba) have been added to the Netherlands as special municipalities on Oct. 10, 2010. On these islands the U.S. dollar has been the official currency.

RULERS
KINGDOM OF THE NETHERLANDS
Beatrix, 1980—

MINT PRIVY MARKS
Utrecht

Date	Privy Mark
1806-present	Caduceus

MINTMASTERS' PRIVY MARKS
Utrecht Mint

Date	Privy Mark
2001	Wine tendril w/grapes
2002	Wine tendril w/grapes and star
2003	Sails of a clipper

NOTE: A star adjoining the privy mark indicates that the piece was struck at the beginning of the term of office of a successor. (The star was used only if the successor had not chosen his own mark yet.)

NOTE: Since October 1999, the Dutch Mint has taken the title of Royal Dutch Mint.

MONETARY SYSTEM
Until January 29, 2002
100 Cents = 1 Gulden
Since January 1, 2002
100 Euro Cents = 1 Euro

KINGDOM
DECIMAL COINAGE

KM# 202 5 CENTS
3.5000 g., Bronze, 21 mm. **Ruler:** Beatrix **Obv:** Head left with vertical inscription **Rev:** Value within vertical lines **Edge:** Plain

Date	Mintage	F	VF	XF	Unc	BU
2001	15,815,000	—	—	—	—	0.70
2001 Proof	17,000	Value: 4.00				

KM# 203 10 CENTS
1.5000 g., Nickel, 15 mm. **Ruler:** Beatrix **Obv:** Head left with vertical inscription **Rev:** Value and vertical lines **Edge:** Reeded

Date	Mintage	F	VF	XF	Unc	BU
2001	25,600,000	—	—	—	0.45	0.75
2001 Proof	17,000	Value: 4.00				

KM# 204 25 CENTS
3.0000 g., Nickel, 19 mm. **Ruler:** Beatrix **Obv:** Head left with vertical inscription **Obv. Inscription:** Beatrix/Konincin Der/Nederlanden **Rev:** Value within vertical and horizontal lines **Edge:** Reeded

Date	Mintage	F	VF	XF	Unc	BU
2001	11,515,000	—	—	—	0.30	1.00
2001 Proof	17,000	Value: 6.00				

KM# 205 GULDEN
6.0000 g., Nickel, 25 mm. **Ruler:** Beatrix **Obv:** Head left with vertical inscription **Rev:** Value within vertical and horizontal lines **Edge Lettering:** GOD * ZIJ * MET * ONS *

Date	Mintage	F	VF	XF	Unc	BU
2001	6,414,500	—	—	—	—	1.25
2001 Proof	17,000	Value: 7.50				

KM# 233 GULDEN
6.0000 g., Nickel, 25 mm. **Ruler:** Beatrix **Obv:** Head left within inscription **Rev:** Child art design **Edge Lettering:** GOD * ZIJ * MET * ONS *

Date	Mintage	F	VF	XF	Unc	BU
2001	16,009,000	—	—	—	—	4.00
2001 Prooflike	32,000	—	—	—	—	6.00

KM# 233a GULDEN
7.1000 g., 0.9250 Silver 0.2111 oz. ASW, 25 mm. **Ruler:** Beatrix **Obv:** Head left within inscription **Rev:** Child art design **Edge Lettering:** GOD * ZIJ * MET * ONS *

Date	Mintage	F	VF	XF	Unc	BU
2001 Prooflike	360	—	—	—	—	2,400

Note: Given as gifts to workers at the mint

KM# 233b GULDEN
13.2000 g., 0.9990 Gold 0.4239 oz. AGW, 25 mm. **Ruler:** Beatrix **Obv:** Head left within inscription **Rev:** Child art design **Note:** 98 of 100 pieces melted down, with 2 known in museum collections.

Date	Mintage	F	VF	XF	Unc	BU
2001 Prooflike; Rare	100	—	—	—	—	—

KM# 205a GULDEN
7.1000 g., 0.9250 Silver 0.2111 oz. ASW **Ruler:** Beatrix **Obv:** Head left with vertical inscription **Rev:** Value within vertical and horizontal lines **Edge Lettering:** GOD*ZIJ*MET*OMS*

Date	Mintage	F	VF	XF	Unc	BU
2001 Prooflike	200,000	—	—	—	—	15.00

KM# 205b GULDEN
13.2000 g., 0.9990 Gold 0.4239 oz. AGW **Ruler:** Beatrix **Obv:** Head left with vertical inscription **Rev:** Value within vertical and horizontal lines **Edge Lettering:** GOD*ZIJ*MET*ONS* **Note:** Prev. KM#205a.

Date	Mintage	F	VF	XF	Unc	BU
2001 Prooflike	25,500	—	—	—	—	625

Note: Mintage includes KM#205c.

KM# 205c GULDEN
13.2000 g., 0.9990 Gold 0.4239 oz. AGW **Ruler:** Beatrix **Obv:** Head left with vertical inscription **Rev:** Value within vertical and horizontal lines **Edge:** Plain, missing lettering

Date	Mintage	F	VF	XF	Unc	BU
2001 Prooflike	Est. 500	—	—	—	—	1,000

KM# 206 2-1/2 GULDEN
10.0000 g., Nickel, 29 mm. **Ruler:** Beatrix **Obv:** Head left with vertical inscription **Rev:** Value within horizontal, vertical and diagonal lines **Edge Lettering:** GOD * ZIJ * MET * ONS *

Date	Mintage	F	VF	XF	Unc	BU
2001	315,000	—	—	—	6.00	10.00
2001 Proof	17,000	Value: 16.00				

KM# 210 5 GULDEN
9.2500 g., Bronze Clad Nickel, 23.5 mm. **Ruler:** Beatrix **Obv:** Head left with vertical inscription **Rev:** Value within horizontal, vertical and diagonal lines **Edge:** GOD * ZIJ * MET * ONS *

Date	Mintage	F	VF	XF	Unc	BU
2001	115,000	—	—	—	6.00	10.00
2001 Proof	17,000	Value: 15.50				

EURO COINAGE
European Union Issues

KM# 234 EURO CENT
2.3000 g., Copper Plated Steel, 16.2 mm. **Ruler:** Beatrix **Obv:** Head left among stars **Rev:** Value and globe **Edge:** Plain

Date	Mintage	F	VF	XF	Unc	BU
2001	179,800,000	—	—	—	0.35	0.50
2001 Proof	16,500	—	—	—	—	—
2002	600,000	—	—	—	3.00	1.25
2002 Proof	16,500	Value: 5.00				
2003	5,866,000	—	—	—	0.50	0.75
2003 Proof	13,000	Value: 4.00				
2004	11,396,000	—	—	—	0.50	0.75
2004 Proof	5,000	Value: 4.00				
2005	545,000	—	—	—	1.50	2.00
2005 Proof	5,000	Value: 4.00				
2006	378,000	—	—	—	1.50	2.00
2006 Proof	3,500	Value: 4.00				
2007	332,000	—	—	—	1.50	2.00
2007 Proof	10,000	Value: 3.50				
2008	413,000	—	—	—	1.50	2.00
2008 Proof	10,000	Value: 3.50				
2009	335,000	—	—	—	1.50	2.00
2009 Proof	75,000	Value: 3.50				
2010	235,000	—	—	—	1.50	2.00
2010 Proof	5,000	Value: 3.50				
2011	—	—	—	—	1.50	2.00
2011 Proof	5,000	Value: 3.50				
2012	—	—	—	—	1.50	2.00
2012 Proof	—	Value: 3.50				

KM# 235 2 EURO CENT
3.0600 g., Copper Plated Steel, 18.7 mm. **Ruler:** Beatrix **Obv:** Head left among stars **Rev:** Value and globe **Edge:** Grooved

Date	Mintage	F	VF	XF	Unc	BU
2001	142,100,000	—	—	—	0.50	0.75
2001 Proof	16,500	—	—	—	—	—
2002	52,224,000	—	—	—	0.75	1.00
2002 Proof	16,500	—	—	—	—	—
2003	150,750,000	—	—	—	0.50	0.75
2003 Proof	13,000	—	—	—	—	—
2004	115,622,000	—	—	—	0.50	0.75
2004 Proof	5,000	Value: 4.00				
2005	595,000	—	—	—	1.50	2.00
2005 Proof	5,000	Value: 4.00				
2006	378,000	—	—	—	1.50	2.00
2006 Proof	3,500	Value: 4.00				
2007	338,000	—	—	—	1.50	2.00
2007 Proof	10,000	Value: 3.50				
2008	413,000	—	—	—	1.50	2.00
2008 Proof	10,000	Value: 3.50				
2009	335,000	—	—	—	1.50	2.00
2009 Proof	75,000	Value: 3.50				
2010	235,000	—	—	—	1.50	2.00
2010 Proof	5,000	Value: 3.50				
2011	—	—	—	—	1.50	2.00
2011 Proof	5,000	Value: 3.50				
2012	—	—	—	—	1.50	2.00
2012 Proof	—	Value: 3.50				

KM# 236 5 EURO CENT
3.9200 g., Copper Plated Steel, 21.25 mm. **Ruler:** Beatrix **Obv:** Head left among stars **Rev:** Value and globe **Edge:** Plain

Date	Mintage	F	VF	XF	Unc	BU
2001	206,400,000	—	—	—	0.50	0.75
2001 Proof	16,500	—	—	—	—	—
2002	700,000	—	—	—	1.75	3.50
2002 Proof	16,500	—	—	—	—	—
2003	874,000	—	—	—	1.50	5.00
2003 Proof	13,000	—	—	—	—	—
2004	306,000	—	—	—	2.00	2.50
2004 Proof	5,000	Value: 4.00				
2005	80,605,000	—	—	—	1.00	1.25
2005 Proof	5,000	Value: 4.00				
2006	60,318,000	—	—	—	1.00	1.25
2006 Proof	3,500	Value: 4.00				
2007	75,764,000	—	—	—	1.00	1.25
2007 Proof	10,000	Value: 3.50				
2008	50,413,000	—	—	—	1.00	1.25
2008 Proof	10,000	Value: 3.50				
2009	70,335,000	—	—	—	1.00	1.25
2009 Proof	75,000	Value: 3.50				
2010	70,235,000	—	—	—	1.00	1.25
2010 Proof	5,000	Value: 3.50				
2011	40,100,000	—	—	—	1.00	1.25
2011 Proof	5,000	Value: 3.50				
2012	—	—	—	—	1.00	1.25
2012 Proof	—	Value: 3.50				

KM# 237 10 EURO CENT
4.1000 g., Brass, 19.7 mm. **Ruler:** Beatrix **Obv:** Head left among stars **Rev:** Value and map

Date	Mintage	F	VF	XF	Unc	BU
2001	194,200,000	—	—	—	0.75	1.00
2001 Proof	16,500	—	—	—	—	—
2002	600,000	—	—	—	1.50	5.00
2002 Proof	16,500	—	—	—	—	—
2003	818,000	—	—	—	1.50	2.00
2003 Proof	13,000	—	—	—	—	—
2004	262,000	—	—	—	2.00	2.50
2004 Proof	5,000	Value: 6.00				
2005	510,000	—	—	—	1.75	2.00
2005 Proof	5,000	Value: 6.00				
2006	393,000	—	—	—	1.75	2.50
2006 Proof	3,500	Value: 6.00				

KM# 268 10 EURO CENT
4.1000 g., Brass, 19.7 mm. **Ruler:** Beatrix **Obv:** Head of Queen Beatrix left **Rev:** Relief map of Western Europe, stars, lines and value

Date	Mintage	F	VF	XF	Unc	BU
2007	292,000	—	—	—	1.75	2.50
2007 Proof	10,000	Value: 5.00				
2008	363,000	—	—	—	1.75	2.75
2008 Proof	10,000	Value: 5.00				
2009	285,000	—	—	—	1.75	2.50
2009 Proof	7,500	Value: 5.00				
2010	202,000	—	—	—	1.75	2.50
2010 Proof	5,000	Value: 5.00				
2011	—	—	—	—	1.75	2.50
2011 Proof	5,000	Value: 5.00				
2012	—	—	—	—	1.75	2.50
2012 Proof	—	Value: 5.00				

KM# 238 20 EURO CENT
5.7400 g., Brass, 22.2 mm. **Ruler:** Beatrix **Obv:** Head left among stars **Rev:** Value and map **Edge:** Notched

Date	Mintage	F	VF	XF	Unc	BU
2001	92,300,000	—	—	—	1.00	1.25
2001 Proof	16,500	—	—	—	—	—
2002	50,691,000	—	—	—	1.00	1.25
2002 Proof	16,500	—	—	—	—	—
2003	57,821,000	—	—	—	1.00	1.25
2003 Proof	13,000	—	—	—	—	—
2004	20,430,000	—	—	—	1.00	1.50
2004 Proof	5,000	Value: 8.00				
2005	510,000	—	—	—	2.00	3.00
2005 Proof	5,000	Value: 8.00				
2006	393,000	—	—	—	2.00	3.00
2006 Proof	3,500	Value: 8.00				

KM# 269 20 EURO CENT
5.7000 g., Brass, 22.2 mm. **Ruler:** Beatrix **Obv:** Head of Queen Beatrix left **Rev:** Relief map of Western Europe, stars, lines and value **Edge:** Notched

Date	Mintage	F	VF	XF	Unc	BU
2007	510,000	—	—	—	2.00	3.00
2007 Proof	10,000	Value: 7.00				
2008	293,000	—	—	—	2.50	3.00
2008 Proof	10,000	Value: 7.00				
2009	363,000	—	—	—	2.00	3.00
2009 Proof	7,500	Value: 7.00				
2010	285,000	—	—	—	2.50	3.00
2010 Proof	5,000	Value: 7.00				
2011	202,000	—	—	—	2.50	3.00
2011 Proof	5,000	Value: 7.00				
2012	—	—	—	—	2.50	3.00
2012 Proof	—	Value: 7.00				

KM# 239 50 EURO CENT
7.8000 g., Brass, 24.2 mm. **Ruler:** Beatrix **Obv:** Head left among stars **Rev:** Value and map **Edge:** Notched

Date	Mintage	F	VF	XF	Unc	BU
2001	87,000,000	—	—	—	1.25	1.50
2001 Proof	16,500	—	—	—	—	—
2002	80,160,000	—	—	—	1.25	1.50
2002 Proof	16,500	—	—	—	—	—
2003	810,000	—	—	—	2.00	2.50
2003 Proof	13,000	—	—	—	—	—
2004	269,000	—	—	—	2.25	3.00
2004 Proof	5,000	Value: 10.00				

Date	Mintage	F	VF	XF	Unc	BU
2005	510,000	—	—	—	2.00	2.50
2005 Proof	5,964	Value: 10.00				
2006	363,000	—	—	—	2.00	2.50
2006 Proof	3,500	Value: 10.00				

KM# 270 50 EURO CENT
7.8000 g., Brass, 24.2 mm. **Ruler:** Beatrix **Obv:** Head of Quen Beatrix left **Rev:** Relief map of Western Europe, stars, lines and value **Edge:** Notched

Date	Mintage	F	VF	XF	Unc	BU
2007	293,000	—	—	—	2.00	2.75
2007 Proof	10,000	Value: 9.00				
2008	263,000	—	—	—	2.00	2.75
2008 Proof	10,000	Value: 9.00				
2009	285,000	—	—	—	2.00	2.75
2009 Proof	7,500	Value: 9.00				
2010	202,000	—	—	—	2.00	2.75
2010 Proof	5,000	Value: 9.00				
2011	—	—	—	—	2.00	2.75
2011 Proof	5,000	Value: 9.00				
2012	—	—	—	—	2.00	2.75
2012 Proof	—	Value: 9.00				

KM# 240 EURO
7.5000 g., Bi-Metallic Copper-Nickel center in Brass ring, 23.2 mm. **Ruler:** Beatrix **Obv:** Half head left within 1/2 circle and star border, name within vertical lines **Rev:** Value and map within circle **Edge:** Segmented reeding

Date	Mintage	F	VF	XF	Unc	BU
2001	67,200,000	—	—	—	2.50	3.00
2001 Proof	16,500	—	—	—	—	—
2002	22,560,000	—	—	—	2.50	3.00
2002 Proof	16,500	—	—	—	—	—
2003	950,000	—	—	—	3.50	4.00
2003 Proof	13,000	—	—	—	—	—
2004	235,000	—	—	—	5.00	6.00
2004 Proof	5,000	Value: 15.00				
2005	332,000	—	—	—	4.00	5.00
2005 Proof	5,964	Value: 15.00				
2006	393,000	—	—	—	4.00	5.00
2006 Proof	3,500	Value: 15.00				

KM# 271 EURO
7.5000 g., Bi-Metallic Copper-Nickel center in Nickel-Brass ring, 23.25 mm. **Ruler:** Beatrix **Obv:** Queen's profile left **Rev:** Relief map of Western Europe, stars, lines and value **Edge:** Segmented reeding

Date	Mintage	F	VF	XF	Unc	BU
2007	224,000	—	—	—	3.50	4.00
2007 Proof	10,000	Value: 14.50				
2008	288,000	—	—	—	3.50	4.00
2008 Proof	10,000	Value: 14.50				
2009	185,000	—	—	—	3.50	4.00
2009 Proof	7,500	Value: 14.50				
2010	166,000	—	—	—	3.50	4.00
2010 Proof	5,000	Value: 14.50				
2011	—	—	—	—	3.50	4.00
2011 Proof	5,000	Value: 14.50				
2012	—	—	—	—	3.50	4.00
2012 Proof	—	Value: 14.50				

KM# 241 2 EURO
8.5000 g., Bi-Metallic Nickel-Brass center in Copper-Nickel ring, 25.75 mm. **Ruler:** Beatrix **Obv:** Profile left within 1/2 circle and star border, name within vertical lines **Rev:** Value and map within circle **Edge Lettering:** GOD * ZIJ * MET * ONS *

Date	Mintage	F	VF	XF	Unc	BU
2001	116,400,000	—	—	—	4.00	4.50
2001 Proof	16,500	—	—	—	—	—
2002	36,432,000	—	—	—	4.50	12.00
2002 Proof	16,500	—	—	—	—	—
2003	749,000	—	—	—	5.50	8.00
2003 Proof	13,000	—	—	—	—	—
2004	245,000	—	—	—	7.00	12.00
2004 Proof	5,000	Value: 18.00				
2005	332,000	—	—	—	6.00	8.00
2005 Proof	5,964	Value: 18.00				
2006	341,000	—	—	—	6.00	10.00
2006 Proof	3,500	Value: 18.00				

KM# 272 2 EURO
8.5000 g., Bi-Metallic Nickel-Brass center in Copper-Nickel ring, 25.75 mm. **Ruler:** Beatrix **Obv:** Queen's profile left **Rev:** Relief map of Western Europe, stars, lines and value **Edge Lettering:** GOD * ZIJ * MET * ONS *

Date	Mintage	F	VF	XF	Unc	BU
2007	345,000	—	—	—	6.00	8.00
2007 Proof	10,000	Value: 17.50				
2008	288,000	—	—	—	6.00	8.00
2008 Proof	10,000	Value: 17.50				
2009	225,000	—	—	—	6.00	8.00
2009 Proof	7,500	Value: 17.50				
2010	166,000	—	—	—	6.00	8.00
2010 Proof	5,000	Value: 17.50				
2011	—	—	—	—	6.00	8.00
2011 Proof	5,000	Value: 17.50				
2012	—	—	—	—	6.00	8.00
2012 Proof	—	Value: 17.50				

KM# 273 2 EURO
8.5000 g., Bi-Metallic Nickel-Brass center in Copper-Nickel ring, 25.75 mm. **Ruler:** Beatrix **Subject:** 50th Anniversary Treaty of Rome **Obv:** Open treaty book **Rev:** Large value at left, modified outline of Europe at right **Edge Lettering:** GOD * ZU * MET * ONS * **Note:** 15,000 BU coins are in a Benelux set

Date	Mintage	F	VF	XF	Unc	BU
2007	6,333,000	—	—	—	6.00	15.00
2007 Proof	10,000	Value: 22.00				

KM# 281 2 EURO
8.5000 g., Bi-Metallic Nickel-Brass center in Copper-Nickel ring, 25.75 mm. **Ruler:** Beatrix **Subject:** European Monetary Union, 10th Anniversary **Rev:** Stick figure and euro symbol **Edge Lettering:** *GOD *ZIJ *MET *ONS

Date	Mintage	F	VF	XF	Unc	BU
2009	5,300,000	—	—	—	4.50	15.00
2009 Proof from set	7,500	Value: 60.00				
2009 Proof in box	2,000	Value: 160				

KM# 298 2 EURO
8.5000 g., Bi-Metallic Nickel-Brass center in Copper-Nickel ring, 25.75 mm. **Ruler:** Beatrix **Obv:** Beatrix at left, Erasmus writing at right

Date	Mintage	F	VF	XF	Unc	BU
2011	4,003,000	—	—	—	4.50	30.00
2011 Proof from set	5,000	Value: 50.00				
2011 Proof in box	2,000	Value: 140				

KM# 308 2 EURO
Bi-Metallic Nickel-Brass center in Copper-Nickel ring, 25.75 mm. **Ruler:** Beatrix **Subject:** 10 years of euro-coins **Obv:** Euro symbol on globe, child-like images around

Date	Mintage	F	VF	XF	Unc	BU
2012	3,500,000	—	—	—	4.50	—
2012 Proof	—	Value: 25.00				
2012 Special Unc.	15,000	—	—	—	—	15.00

KM# 245 5 EURO
11.9000 g., 0.9250 Silver 0.3539 oz. ASW, 29 mm. **Ruler:** Beatrix **Subject:** Vincent Van Gogh **Obv:** Head facing **Rev:** Tilted head facing **Edge Lettering:** GOD * ZIJ * MET * ONS *

Date	Mintage	F	VF	XF	Unc	BU
ND(2003)	1,000,000	—	—	—	BV	15.00
ND(2003) Prooflike	100,000	—	—	—	—	30.00

KM# 252 5 EURO
11.9000 g., 0.9250 Silver 0.3539 oz. ASW **Ruler:** Beatrix **Subject:** New EEC member countries **Obv:** Head left **Rev:** Names of old and new member countries **Edge Lettering:** GOD * ZIJ * MET * ONS *

Date	Mintage	F	VF	XF	Unc	BU
2004	600,000	—	—	—	BV	17.50
2004 Proof	55,000	Value: 90.00				

KM# 253 5 EURO
11.9000 g., 0.9250 Silver 0.3539 oz. ASW **Ruler:** Beatrix **Subject:** 50th Anniversary - End of colonization of Netherlands Antilles **Obv:** Head left **Rev:** Fruit and date within beaded circle **Edge Lettering:** GOD * ZIJ * MET * ONS *

Date	Mintage	F	VF	XF	Unc	BU
2004	650,000	—	—	—	BV	17.50
2004 Proof	26,900	Value: 45.00				

KM# 254 5 EURO
11.9100 g., 0.9250 Silver 0.3542 oz. ASW, 29 mm. **Ruler:** Beatrix **Subject:** 60th Anniversary of Liberation **Obv:** Queen's image **Rev:** Value and dots **Edge Lettering:** GOD * ZIJ * MET * ONS *

Date	Mintage	F	VF	XF	Unc	BU
2005	630,000	—	—	—	BV	17.50
2005 Proof	40,000	Value: 40.00				

KM# 255 5 EURO
11.9000 g., 0.9250 Silver 0.3539 oz. ASW, 29 mm. **Ruler:** Beatrix **Obv:** Queen's silhouette centered on a world globe **Rev:** Value above Australia on a world globe **Edge Lettering:** GOD * ZIJ * MET * ONS *

Date	Mintage	F	VF	XF	Unc	BU
2006	500,000	—	—	—	BV	17.50
2006 Proof	22,500	Value: 45.00				

KM# 266   5 EURO
11.9000 g., 0.9250 Silver 0.3539 oz. ASW, 28.9 mm.   **Ruler:** Beatrix **Obv:** Queen Beatrix **Rev:** Rembrandt **Edge Lettering:** GOD * Z IJ * MET * ONS *

Date	Mintage	F	VF	XF	Unc	BU
ND(2006)	655,000	—	—	—	BV	17.50
ND(2006) Proof	35,000	Value: 35.00				

KM# 267   5 EURO
11.9000 g., 0.9250 Silver 0.3539 oz. ASW, 29 mm.   **Ruler:** Beatrix **Subject:** Tax Service, 200th Anniversary **Obv:** Queen's portrait **Rev:** Circles with dates 1806-2006 **Edge Lettering:** GOD * ZIJ * MET * ONS *

Date	Mintage	F	VF	XF	Unc	BU
2006	359,189	—	—	—	BV	17.50
2006 Prooflike	40,000	—	—	—	—	25.00
2006 Proof	15,000	Value: 60.00				

KM# 277   5 EURO
11.9000 g., 0.9250 Silver 0.3539 oz. ASW, 29 mm.   **Ruler:** Beatrix **Subject:** Admiral M.A. de Ruyter, 400th Anniversary of Birth **Obv:** Queen's head 1/4 left **Rev:** deRuyter's head 1/4 right **Edge Lettering:** GOD * ZIJ * MET * ONS *

Date	Mintage	F	VF	XF	Unc	BU
2007	520,500	—	—	—	BV	17.50
2007 Proof	17,500	Value: 40.00				

KM# 279   5 EURO
15.5000 g., 0.9250 Silver 0.4609 oz. ASW, 33 mm.   **Ruler:** Beatrix **Subject:** Architecture **Obv:** Portrait facing in names of famous architects **Rev:** Books around map of the Netherlands **Edge Lettering:** GOD * ZIJ * MET * ONS *

Date	Mintage	F	VF	XF	Unc	BU
2008 Proof	24,505	Value: 40.00				

KM# 279a   5 EURO
10.5000 g., Silver Plated Copper, 29 mm.   **Ruler:** Beatrix **Subject:** Architecture **Obv:** Portrait facing in names of famous Architects **Rev:** Architecture books around map of the Netherlands

Date	Mintage	F	VF	XF	Unc	BU
2008	350,000	—	—	—	10.00	15.00

KM# 282   5 EURO
15.5000 g., 0.9250 Silver 0.4609 oz. ASW, 33 mm.   **Ruler:** Beatrix **Subject:** Manhattan 400th Anniversary **Obv:** Bottom tip of Manhattan Island today **Rev:** Bottom tip of Manhattan Island in 1609 **Edge Lettering:** GOD * ZIJ * MET * ONS *

Date	Mintage	F	VF	XF	Unc	BU
2009 Proof	20,000	Value: 55.00				

KM# 282a   5 EURO
10.5000 g., Silver Plated Copper, 29 mm.   **Ruler:** Beatrix **Subject:** Manhattan 400th Anniversary **Obv:** Tip of Manhattan Island today **Rev:** Tip of Manhattan Island in 1609

Date	Mintage	F	VF	XF	Unc	BU
2009	303,209	—	—	—	10.00	15.00

KM# 287   5 EURO
15.5000 g., 0.9250 Silver 0.4609 oz. ASW, 33 mm.   **Ruler:** Beatrix **Subject:** Netherlands-Japanese Friendship **Obv:** Guilder design of 1982 with Queen **Rev:** Value and date **Edge Lettering:** GOD * ZIJ * MET * ONS *

Date	Mintage	F	VF	XF	Unc	BU
2009 Proof	45,000	Value: 40.00				

KM# 287a   5 EURO
10.5000 g., Silver Plated Copper, 29 mm.   **Ruler:** Beatrix **Subject:** Netherlands-Japanese Friendship **Obv:** Guilder design of 1982 with Queen **Rev:** Value and date

Date	Mintage	F	VF	XF	Unc	BU
2009	343,859	—	—	—	8.00	10.00

KM# 294   5 EURO
11.9000 g., 0.9250 Silver 0.3539 oz. ASW, 33 mm.   **Ruler:** Beatrix **Subject:** Max Havelaar, 150th Anniversary **Obv:** Queen **Rev:** Ink pen, words in spiral, figures walking around edge **Edge Lettering:** GOD * ZIJ * MET * ONS *

Date	Mintage	F	VF	XF	Unc	BU
2010 Proof	15,000	Value: 50.00				

KM# 294a   5 EURO
10.5000 g., Silver Plated Copper, 29 mm.   **Ruler:** Beatrix **Subject:** Max Havelaar, 150th Anniversary of Birth **Obv:** Queen **Rev:** Ink pen, words in spiral, figures walking around edge **Edge Lettering:** GOD * ZIJ * MET * ONS *

Date	Mintage	F	VF	XF	Unc	BU
2010	275,010	—	—	—	9.00	12.00

KM# 296   5 EURO
15.5000 g., 0.9250 Silver 0.4609 oz. ASW, 33 mm.   **Ruler:** Beatrix **Subject:** Waterland **Obv:** Queen's bust facing, and reflected in water **Rev:** Map of the Netherlands, partly below sea level

Date	Mintage	F	VF	XF	Unc	BU
2010	17,500	Value: 45.00				

KM# 296a   5 EURO
10.5000 g., Silver Plated Copper, 29 mm.   **Ruler:** Beatrix **Subject:** Waterland **Obv:** Queens bust facing and reflected in water **Rev:** Map of the Netherlands, partily below sea level

Date	Mintage	F	VF	XF	Unc	BU
2010	227,500	—	—	—	—	10.00

KM# 302a   5 EURO
10.5000 g., Silver Plated Copper, 29 mm.   **Ruler:** Beatrix **Subject:** Anniversary 100 year Mintbuilding **Obv:** Bust facing **Rev:** Screw press and a QR-code which is to scan with a **Edge Lettering:** GOD * ZIJ * MET * ONS *

Date	Mintage	F	VF	XF	Unc	BU
2011	71,618	—	—	—	—	15.00

KM# 304a   5 EURO
Silver Plated Copper, 29 mm.   **Ruler:** Beatrix **Subject:** Painting **Obv:** Queen looking at city view painting **Rev:** Window **Edge Lettering:** GOD * ZIJ * MET * ONS *

Date	Mintage	F	VF	XF	Unc	BU
2011	250,000	—	—	—	—	12.00

KM# 299   5 EURO
15.5000 g., 0.9250 Silver 0.4609 oz. ASW, 33 mm.   **Ruler:** Beatrix **Subject:** World Wildlife Fund, 50th Anniversary **Obv:** Profile left at center of tree leaves **Rev:** Value at center of root system **Edge Lettering:** GOD * ZIJ * MET * ONS *

Date	Mintage	F	VF	XF	Unc	BU
2011 Proof	17,500	Value: 40.00				

KM# 301   5 EURO
10.5000 g., Silver Plated Copper, 29 mm.   **Ruler:** Beatrix **Subject:** World Wildlife Fund, 50th Anniversary **Obv:** Profile head at center of tree leaves **Rev:** Value at center of root system **Edge Lettering:** GOD * ZIJ * MET * ONS *

Date	Mintage	F	VF	XF	Unc	BU
2011 Proof	250,000	Value: 10.00				

KM# 302   5 EURO
15.5000 g., 0.9250 Silver 0.4609 oz. ASW, 33 mm.   **Ruler:** Beatrix **Subject:** Anniversary 100 year Mintbuilding **Obv:** Bust facing **Rev:** Screw press and a QR-code which is to scan with a mobile telephone **Edge Lettering:** GOD * ZIJ * MET * ONS *

Date	Mintage	F	VF	XF	Unc	BU
2011 Proof	17,500	Value: 40.00				

KM# 304   5 EURO
15.5000 g., 0.9250 Silver 0.4609 oz. ASW, 33 mm.   **Ruler:** Beatrix **Subject:** Painting **Obv:** Queen looking at city view painting **Rev:** Window **Edge Lettering:** GOD * ZIJ * MET * ONS *

Date	Mintage	F	VF	XF	Unc	BU
2011	250,000	—	—	—	—	30.00
2011 Proof	12,500	Value: 40.00				

KM# 309   5 EURO
15.5000 g., 0.9250 Silver 0.4609 oz. ASW, 33 mm.   **Ruler:** Beatrix **Subject:** 400 years of diplomatic relations Netherlands-Turkey **Edge Lettering:** GOD * ZIJ * MET * ONS *

Date	Mintage	F	VF	XF	Unc	BU
2012 Proof						

KM# 309a   5 EURO
10.5000 g., Silver Plated Copper, 29 mm.   **Ruler:** Beatrix **Subject:** 400 years of diplomatic relations Netherlands-Turkey **Edge Lettering:** GOD * ZIJ * MET * ONS *

Date	Mintage	F	VF	XF	Unc	BU
2012						

KM# 243   10 EURO
17.8000 g., 0.9250 Silver 0.5293 oz. ASW, 33 mm.   **Ruler:** Beatrix **Subject:** Wedding of Willem-Alexander and Maxima **Obv:** Queen's head left **Rev:** Conjoined busts left **Edge Lettering:** GOD * ZIJ * MET * ONS *

Date	Mintage	F	VF	XF	Unc	BU
2002	990,800	—	—	—	BV	40.00
2002 Proof	80,000	Value: 55.00				

KM# 244   10 EURO
6.7200 g., 0.9000 Gold 0.1944 oz. AGW, 22.5 mm.   **Ruler:** Beatrix **Subject:** Crown Prince's Wedding **Obv:** Head left **Rev:** Two facing silhouettes **Edge:** Reeded

Date	Mintage	F	VF	XF	Unc	BU
2002 Prooflike	33,000	—	—	—	—	400

KM# 246   10 EURO
6.7200 g., 0.9000 Gold 0.1944 oz. AGW, 22.5 mm.   **Ruler:** Beatrix **Subject:** Vincent Van Gogh **Obv:** Head facing **Rev:** Tilted head facing **Edge:** Reeded

Date	Mintage	F	VF	XF	Unc	BU
ND(2003) Prooflike	20,000	—	—	—	—	400

KM# 248 10 EURO
17.8000 g., 0.9250 Silver 0.5293 oz. ASW, 33 mm. **Ruler:** Beatrix **Obv:** Head left **Rev:** Multi-views of Prince Willem-Alexander, Princess Catherina-Amalia and Princess Maxima **Edge Lettering:** GOD * ZIJ * MET * ONS *

Date	Mintage	F	VF	XF	Unc	BU
2004	1,000,000	—	—	—	BV	25.00
2004 Proof	50,000	Value: 40.00				

KM# 247 10 EURO
6.7200 g., 0.9000 Gold 0.1944 oz. AGW, 22.5 mm. **Ruler:** Beatrix **Subject:** New EEC members **Obv:** Head left **Rev:** Value and legend **Edge:** Reeded

Date	Mintage	F	VF	XF	Unc	BU
2004 Proof	6,000	Value: 700				

KM# 251 10 EURO
6.7200 g., 0.9000 Gold 0.1944 oz. AGW, 22.5 mm. **Ruler:** Beatrix **Subject:** 50 Years of Domestic Autonomy, 1954-2004 (for Netherlands Antilles) **Obv:** Small head left **Rev:** Fruit and date within beaded circle **Edge:** Reeded

Date	Mintage	F	VF	XF	Unc	BU
2004 Proof	3,800	Value: 600				

KM# 261 10 EURO
17.8000 g., 0.9250 Silver 0.5293 oz. ASW, 33 mm. **Ruler:** Beatrix **Subject:** Silver Jubilee of Reign **Obv:** Queen's photo **Rev:** Queen taking oath photo **Edge Lettering:** GOD * ZIJ * MET * ONS *

Date	Mintage	F	VF	XF	Unc	BU
2005	1,000,000	—	—	—	BV	25.00
2005 Proof	59,754	Value: 40.00				

KM# 264 10 EURO
6.7200 g., 0.9000 Gold 0.1944 oz. AGW, 22.5 mm. **Ruler:** Beatrix **Subject:** 60th Anniversary of Liberation **Obv:** Queen and dots **Rev:** Value and dots **Edge:** Reeded

Date	Mintage	F	VF	XF	Unc	BU
2005 Proof	6,000	Value: 600				

KM# 289 10 EURO
6.7200 g., 0.9000 Gold 0.1944 oz. AGW, 22.5 mm. **Ruler:** Beatrix **Series:** Tax Services, 200th Anniversary **Obv:** Queen's portrait **Rev:** Florin of 1807 **Edge:** Reeded

Date	Mintage	F	VF	XF	Unc	BU
2006 Proof	5,500	Value: 600				

KM# 290 10 EURO
6.7200 g., 0.9000 Gold 0.1944 oz. AGW, 22.5 mm. **Ruler:** Beatrix **Subject:** Netherlands-Australian Friendship, 400th Anniversary **Obv:** Queens portrait within lines of a globe **Rev:** Australia, value and dates **Edge:** Reeded

Date	Mintage	F	VF	XF	Unc	BU
2006 Proof	3,500	Value: 800				

KM# 291 10 EURO
6.7200 g., 0.9000 Gold 0.1944 oz. AGW, 22.5 mm. **Ruler:** Beatrix **Subject:** Rembrant, 400th Anniversary of Birth **Obv:** Queen's portrait **Rev:** Self-portrait **Edge:** Reeded

Date	Mintage	F	VF	XF	Unc	BU
2006 Proof	8,500	Value: 400				

KM# 278 10 EURO
6.7200 g., 0.9000 Gold 0.1944 oz. AGW, 22.5 mm. **Ruler:** Beatrix **Subject:** Admiral M.A. de Ruyter, 400th Birthday **Obv:** Head 1/4 left **Rev:** Head 1/4 right **Edge:** Reeded

Date	Mintage	F	VF	XF	Unc	BU
2007 Proof	7,000	Value: 400				

KM# 280 10 EURO
6.7200 g., 0.9000 Gold 0.1944 oz. AGW, 22.5 mm. **Ruler:** Beatrix **Subject:** Architecture **Obv:** Portrait facing in names of famous architects **Rev:** Architecture books around map of the Netherlands **Edge:** Reeded

Date	Mintage	F	VF	XF	Unc	BU
2008 Proof	8,000	Value: 400				

KM# 283 10 EURO
6.7200 g., 0.9000 Gold 0.1944 oz. AGW, 22.5 mm. **Ruler:** Beatrix **Subject:** Dutch settlement of Manhattan, NY 400th Anniversary **Obv:** Bottom tip of Manhattan Island today **Rev:** Bottom tip of Manhattan Island in 1609 **Edge:** Reeded

Date	Mintage	F	VF	XF	Unc	BU
2009 Proof	6,500	Value: 400				

KM# 288 10 EURO
6.7200 g., 0.9000 Gold 0.1944 oz. AGW, 22.5 mm. **Ruler:** Beatrix **Subject:** Netherlands-Japanese Friendship **Obv:** Guilder design of 1982 with Queen **Rev:** Value and date **Edge:** Reeded

Date	Mintage	F	VF	XF	Unc	BU
2009 Proof	5,418	Value: 400				

KM# 295 10 EURO
6.7200 g., 0.9000 Gold 0.1944 oz. AGW, 22.5 mm. **Ruler:** Beatrix **Subject:** Max Havelaar, 150th Anniversary of Birth **Rev:** Ink pen, words in spiral, firgures walking around edge **Edge:** Reeded

Date	Mintage	F	VF	XF	Unc	BU
2010 Proof	4,699	Value: 400				

KM# 297 10 EURO
6.7200 g., 0.9000 Gold 0.1944 oz. AGW, 22.5 mm. **Ruler:** Beatrix **Subject:** Waterland **Obv:** Bust of Queen facing and reflected in water **Rev:** Map of the Netherlands, partly under sea level

Date	Mintage	F	VF	XF	Unc	BU
2010 Proof	4,500	Value: 400				

KM# 300 10 EURO
6.7200 g., 0.9000 Gold 0.1944 oz. AGW, 22.5 mm. **Ruler:** Beatrix **Subject:** World Wildlife Fund, 50th Anniversary **Obv:** Profile left at center of tree leaves **Rev:** Value at center of root system **Edge:** Reeded

Date	Mintage	F	VF	XF	Unc	BU
2011 Proof	4,000	Value: 400				

KM# 303 10 EURO
6.7500 g., 0.9000 Gold 0.1953 oz. AGW, 22.5 mm. **Ruler:** Beatrix **Obv:** Head facing **Rev:** Screw press and a QR-code which is to scan with a mobile telephone **Edge:** Reeded

Date	Mintage	F	VF	XF	Unc	BU
2011 Proof	4,000	Value: 400				

KM# 305 10 EURO
6.7200 g., 0.9000 Gold 0.1944 oz. AGW, 22.5 mm. **Ruler:** Beatrix **Subject:** Painting **Obv:** Queen looking at city view painting **Rev:** Window **Edge:** Reeded

Date	Mintage	F	VF	XF	Unc	BU
2011 Proof	3,500	Value: 400				

KM# 310 10 EURO
6.7200 g., 0.9000 Gold 0.1944 oz. AGW, 22.5 mm. **Ruler:** Beatrix **Subject:** 400 years of diplomatic relations Netherlands-Turkey **Edge:** Reeded

Date	Mintage	F	VF	XF	Unc	BU
2012 Proof	—	Value: 400				

KM# 249 20 EURO
8.5000 g., 0.9000 Gold 0.2459 oz. AGW, 25 mm. **Ruler:** Beatrix **Subject:** Birth of Crown-Princess - Catharina-Amalia - July 12, 2003 **Obv:** Bust left **Rev:** Holographic images: left, Princess Maxima; front, Princess Catharina-Amalia; right, Prince Willem-Alexander **Edge:** Reeded

Date	Mintage	F	VF	XF	Unc	BU
2004 Proof	5,345	Value: 530				

KM# 262 20 EURO
8.5000 g., 0.9000 Gold 0.2459 oz. AGW, 25 mm. **Ruler:** Beatrix **Subject:** Silver Jubilee of Reign **Obv:** Queen's photo **Rev:** Queen taking oath photo **Edge:** Reeded

Date	Mintage	F	VF	XF	Unc	BU
2005 Proof	5,001	Value: 530				

KM# 250 50 EURO
13.4400 g., 0.9000 Gold 0.3889 oz. AGW, 27 mm. **Ruler:** Beatrix **Subject:** Birth of Crown-Princess - Catharina-Amalia - July 12, 2003 **Obv:** Bust left **Rev:** Holographic images: left, Princess Maxima; front, Princess Catharina-Amalia; right, Prince Willem-Alexander **Edge:** Reeded

Date	Mintage	F	VF	XF	Unc	BU
2004 Proof	3,500	Value: 775				

KM# 263 50 EURO
13.4400 g., 0.9000 Gold 0.3889 oz. AGW, 27 mm. **Ruler:** Beatrix **Subject:** Silver Jubilee of Reign **Obv:** Queen's photo **Rev:** Queen taking oath photo **Edge:** Reeded

Date	Mintage	F	VF	XF	Unc	BU
2005 Proof	3,500	Value: 775				

TRADE COINAGE

KM# 190.2 DUCAT
3.4940 g., 0.9830 Gold 0.1104 oz. AGW **Ruler:** Beatrix **Obv:** Knight divides date with larger letters in legend **Rev:** Inscription within decorated square

Date	Mintage	F	VF	XF	Unc	BU
2001 Proof	7,500	Value: 250				
2002 Proof	3,400	Value: 250				
2003 Proof	3,800	Value: 250				
2004 Proof	2,120	Value: 450				
2005 Proof	2,243	Value: 200				
2006 Proof	2,097	Value: 300				
2007 Proof	2,250	Value: 250				
2008 Proof	3,260	Value: 250				
2009 Proof	2,750	Value: 250				
2010 Proof	1,870	Value: 250				
2011 Proof	—	Value: 250				
2012 Proof						

KM# 211 2 DUCAT
6.9880 g., 0.9830 Gold 0.2208 oz. AGW, 26 mm. **Ruler:** Beatrix **Obv:** Knight divides date within beaded circle **Rev:** Inscription within decorated square

Date	Mintage	F	VF	XF	Unc	BU
2002 Proof	6,650	Value: 475				
2003 Proof	4,500	Value: 475				
2004 Proof	2,015	Value: 475				
2005 Proof	3,500	Value: 475				
2006 Proof	1,800	Value: 550				
2007 Proof	2,000	Value: 475				
2008 Proof	2,100	Value: 475				
2009 Proof	2,000	Value: 475				
2010 Proof	2,000	Value: 475				
2011 Proof	1,640	Value: 500				
2012 Proof	—	—	—	—	—	—

SILVER BULLION COINAGE

KM# 311 DUCAT
28.2500 g., 0.8750 Silver 0.7947 oz. ASW, 40 mm. **Ruler:** Beatrix **Subject:** Utrecht **Obv:** Crowned shield **Rev:** Stadtholder Willem III with shield of Utrecht **Edge:** Reeded

Date	Mintage	F	VF	XF	Unc	BU
2012 Proof	—	Value: 60.00				

KM# 312 DUCAT
28.2500 g., 0.8750 Silver 0.7947 oz. ASW, 40 mm. **Ruler:** Beatrix **Subject:** Friesland **Obv:** Crowned shield **Rev:** Willem Lodewijk van Nassau - Dillenbrug with shield of Friesland **Edge:** Reeded

Date	Mintage	F	VF	XF	Unc	BU
2012 Proof	—	Value: 60.00				

KM# 242 SILVER DUCAT
28.2500 g., 0.8730 Silver 0.7929 oz. ASW, 40 mm. **Ruler:** Beatrix **Obv:** Crowned shield **Rev:** Armored knight with sword divides date and circle, shield in front **Edge:** Reeded **Note:** Utrecht coin design circa 1659 based on KM#48.

Date	Mintage	F	VF	XF	Unc	BU
2001 Proof	9,000	Value: 40.00				

KM# 256 SILVER DUCAT
28.2500 g., 0.8730 Silver 0.7929 oz. ASW, 40 mm. **Ruler:** Beatrix **Obv:** Crowned shield **Rev:** Armored knight with Gelderland arms **Edge:** Reeded

Date	Mintage	F	VF	XF	Unc	BU
2002 Proof	9,400	Value: 40.00				

KM# 257 SILVER DUCAT
28.2500 g., 0.8730 Silver 0.7929 oz. ASW, 40 mm. **Ruler:**
Beatrix **Obv:** Crowned shield **Rev:** Armored knight with sword
holding arms of Holland **Edge:** Reeded

Date	Mintage	F	VF	XF	Unc	BU
2003 Proof	4,100	Value: 50.00				

KM# 258 SILVER DUCAT
28.2500 g., 0.8730 Silver 0.7929 oz. ASW, 40 mm. **Ruler:**
Beatrix **Obv:** Crowned shield **Rev:** Armored knight holding sword
with Zeeland arms **Edge:** Reeded

Date	Mintage	F	VF	XF	Unc	BU
2004 Proof	4,109	Value: 50.00				

KM# 259 SILVER DUCAT
28.2500 g., 0.8730 Silver 0.7929 oz. ASW, 40 mm. **Ruler:**
Beatrix **Obv:** Crowned shield **Rev:** Armored knight holding sword
with Friesland arms **Edge:** Reeded

Date	Mintage	F	VF	XF	Unc	BU
2005 Proof	4,000	Value: 50.00				

KM# 260 SILVER DUCAT
28.2500 g., 0.8730 Silver 0.7929 oz. ASW, 40 mm. **Ruler:**
Beatrix **Obv:** Crowned shield **Rev:** Armored knight holding sword
with Groningen arms **Edge:** Reeded

Date	Mintage	F	VF	XF	Unc	BU
2006 Proof	4,000	Value: 50.00				

KM# 275 SILVER DUCAT
28.2500 g., 0.8730 Silver 0.7929 oz. ASW, 40 mm. **Ruler:**
Beatrix **Obv:** Crowned shield **Rev:** Armored knight holding sword
with Overyssel arms **Edge:** Reeded

Date	Mintage	F	VF	XF	Unc	BU
2007 Proof	3,500	Value: 45.00				

KM# 292 SILVER DUCAT
28.2500 g., 0.8730 Silver 0.7929 oz. ASW, 40 mm. **Ruler:**

Beatrix **Subject:** Northern Brabant **Obv:** Crowned shield **Rev:**
John I, Count of Brabant standing with shield **Edge:** Reeded

Date	Mintage	F	VF	XF	Unc	BU
2008 Proof	3,000	Value: 50.00				

KM# 284 SILVER DUCAT
28.2500 g., 0.8730 Silver 0.7929 oz. ASW, 40 mm. **Ruler:**
Beatrix **Rev:** Jan I standing with sword and Gelderland arms

Date	Mintage	F	VF	XF	Unc	BU
2009 Proof	3,000	Value: 50.00				

KM# 293 SILVER DUCAT
28.2500 g., 0.8730 Silver 0.7929 oz. ASW, 40 mm. **Ruler:**
Beatrix **Subject:** Limburg **Obv:** Crowned shield **Rev:** Philip II of
Montmorency, Count of Horne, standing **Edge:** Reeded

Date	Mintage	F	VF	XF	Unc	BU
2009 Proof	3,500	Value: 50.00				

KM# 285 SILVER DUCAT
28.2500 g., 0.8750 Silver 0.7947 oz. ASW, 40 mm. **Ruler:**
Beatrix **Obv:** William of Orange standing with Zuid-Holland arms
Edge: Reeded

Date	Mintage	F	VF	XF	Unc	BU
2010 Proof	2,850	Value: 50.00				

KM# 286 SILVER DUCAT
28.2500 g., 0.8750 Silver 0.7947 oz. ASW, 40 mm. **Ruler:**
Beatrix **Obv:** Frederik Hendrik standing with Gelderland arms
Edge: Reeded

Date	Mintage	F	VF	XF	Unc	BU
2010 Proof	3,100	Value: 50.00				

KM# 306 SILVER DUCAT
28.2500 g., 0.8730 Silver 0.7929 oz. ASW, 40 mm. **Ruler:**
Beatrix **Obv:** Crowned shield **Rev:** Floris V **Edge:** Reeded

Date	Mintage	F	VF	XF	Unc	BU
2011 Proof	—	Value: 50.00				

KM# 307 SILVER DUCAT
28.2500 g., 0.8750 Silver 0.7947 oz. ASW, 40 mm. **Ruler:**
Beatrix **Subject:** Zeeland **Obv:** Crowned shield **Rev:** Michiel de
Ruyter with shield of Zeeland **Edge:** Reeded

Date	Mintage	F	VF	XF	Unc	BU
2011 Proof	—	Value: 50.00				

PATTERNS
Including off metal strikes

KM#	Date	Mintage	Identification	Mkt Val
Pn164	2001	—	Gulden. Nickel. Medal rotation	—
Pn165	2001	—	2 Euro Cent. Nickel.	100
Pn166	2001	—	Euro. Brass. KM240	150

MINT SETS

KM#	Date	Mintage	Identification	Issue Price	Mkt Val
MS4	2001 (6)	85,000	KM#202-206, 210	12.00	25.00
MS5	2001 (8)	68,000	KM#234-241 Charity set, Disabled Sports	15.00	15.00
MS6	2002 (8)	105,000	KM#234-241 Charity set, Blind Escort Dogs Fund	15.00	30.00
MS7	2002 (8)	59,500	KM#234-241 Last FDC set	15.00	30.00
MS8	2002 (8)	25,000	KM#234-241 plus bear medal Baby set	15.50	30.00
MS9	2002 (8)	10,000	KM#234-241 plus medal Wedding Set	15.50	35.00
MS10	2002 (8)	3,500	KM#234-241 plus medal Queen Beatrix set	20.00	110
MS11	2002 (8)	2,002	KM#234-241 plus medal 10th Day of the Mint	22.00	150
MS12	2002 (8)	10,000	KM#234-241 plus medal VOC set I	22.00	30.00
MS13	2002 (8)	10,000	KM#234-241 plus medal VOC set II	22.00	30.00
MS14	2002 (9)	10,000	KM#234-241 plus medal VOC set III	22.00	30.00
MS15	2002 (8)	10,000	KM#234-241 plus medal VOC set IV	22.00	30.00
MS16	2002 (8)	3,000	KM#234-241 plus medal BVC	30.00	40.00
MS17A	2002 (8)	2,500	KM#234-241 VVV - Irisgiftset	20.00	40.00
MS17	2002 (1)	9,200	KM#243 plus stamp	30.00	55.00
MS18	2002 (8)	1,000	KM#234-241 plus medal Theo Peters (Christmas)	99.00	60.00
MS19	2003 (8)	75,000	KM#234-241 Charity set, Epilepsy fund	15.50	25.00
MS20	2003 (8)	15,000	KM#234-241 Information set Denmark	20.00	40.00
MS21	2003 (9)	10,000	KM#234-241 VVV - Irisgiftset	15.50	25.00
MS22	2003 (8)	10,000	KM#234-241 plus medal VOC set V	22.00	25.00
MS23	2003 (8)	10,000	KM#234-241 plus medal VOC set VI	42.00	45.00
MS24	2003 (7)	2,003	KM#234-241 plus medal Day of the Mint	25.00	100
MS25	2003 (8)	1,000	KM#234-241 plus bi-color medal Theo Peters Jubilee set	—	25.00
MS26	2003 (7)	100	KM#234-241 plus silver medal Theo Peters Jubilee set	70.00	50.00
MS27	2003 (8)	25	KM#234-241 plus golden medal Theo Peters Jubilee set	400	250
MS28	2003 (8)	25,000	KM#234-241 plus bear medal Baby set	20.00	25.00
MS29	2003 (8)	15,000	KM#234-241 plus medal Wedding set	20.00	25.00
MS30	2003 (8)	1,000	KM#234-241 Theo Peters Christmas set + bi-colour medal	—	25.00
MS31	2003 (8)	150	KM#234-241 plus silver medal Theo Peters Christmas set	70.00	50.00
MS32	2003 (8)	50	KM#234-241 plus golden medal Theo Peters Christmas set	400	275
MS33	2003 (8)	3,500	KM#234-241 plus medal Mintmasters I	20.00	60.00
MS34	2003 (8)	1,000	KM#234-241 World Money Fair	20.00	100
MS35	2003 (8)	15,000	KM#234-241 Farewell to Wim Duisenberg	—	35.00
MS36	2003 (8)	20,000	KM#234-241 plus silver medal Royal Birth of Princess Catharina-Amalia	22.00	25.00
MS37	2003 (16)	10,000	KM#234-241 and Luxembourg KM#75-81, 40 Benelux Set	40.00	45.00

KM#	Date	Mintage	Identification	Issue Price	Mkt Val
MS38	2003 (40)	10,000	KM#224-231 plus Germany KM#207-214 plus Spain KM#1040-1047 plus Belgium KM#224-231 and Austria KM#3082-3089 Charles V Set	85.00	85.00
MS39	2004 (8)	3,500	KM#234-241 plus medal Mintmasters II	20.00	60.00
MS40	2004 (8)	10,000	KM#234-241 Wedding set plus medal	18.00	30.00
MS41	2004 (9)	20,000	KM#234-241 Baby set plus bear medal	20.00	30.00
MS42	2004 (8)	1,000	KM#234-241 Basel World Money Fair	20.00	110
MS43	2004 (24)	35,000	KM#234-241 and Luxembourg KM#75-81 plus Belgium KM#224-231 Benelux set with silver medal	60.00	60.00
MS44	2004 (10)	10,000	KM#234-241 Queen Juliana set plus silver guilder, KM#184 and 30mm silver medal	25.00	30.00
MS45	2004 (9)	1,500	KM#234-241 Theo Peters Christmas set plus bi-color medal	30.00	30.00
MS46	2004 (8)	3,500	KM#234-241 VVV - Iris gift set	20.00	30.00
MS47	2004 (9)	150	KM#234-241 Theo Peters Christmas set plus silver medal	100	100
MS48	2004 (9)	50	KM#234-241 Theo Peters Christmas set plus golden medal	500	500
MS49	2004 (8)	50,000	KM#234-241 Fire - Burn Centre Charity set	18.00	30.00
MS50	2004 (9)	—	KM#234-241 Day of the Mint plus medal	25.00	150
MS51	2005 (9)	3,500	KM#234-241 Mintmasters III plus medal	20.00	60.00
MS52	2005 (9)	—	KM#234-241 Day of the Mint plus medal	25.00	150
MS53	2005 (9)	10,000	KM#234-241 Wedding set plus medal	18.00	27.50
MS54	2005 (9)	20,000	KM#234-241 Baby set plus bear medal	20.00	27.50
MS55	2005 (9)	20,000	KM#234-241 Nijntje set (Dick Bruna) plus medal	18.00	27.50
MS56	2005 (8)	55,000	KM#234-241 Charity set: Princess Beatrix Fonds	18.00	25.00
MS57	2005 (24)	20,000	KM#234-241, Belgium 224-231, Luxembourg 75-81 Benelux set: Belgium, Netherlands plus Luxembourg with silver medal	60.00	60.00
MS58	2005 (8)	1,000	KM#234-241 World Money Fair, Basel	25.00	110
MS59	2005 (8)	15,000	KM#234-241 60th Anniversary Liberation plus Canadian 25 cent	35.00	35.00
MS60	2005 (9)	1,000	KM#234-241 Theo Peters Christmas set plus bi-color medal	30.00	30.00
MS61	2005 (9)	100	KM#234-241 Theo Peters Christmas set plus silver medal	120	80.00
MS62	2005 (9)	25	KM#234-241 Theo Peters Christmas set plus golden medal	550	300
MS63	2006 (10)	3,500	KM#234-241 Mintmasters IV plus medal	20.00	40.00
MS64	2006 (10)	4,000	KM#234-241 5 sets plus a Rembrandt silver medal and 1 set with a Rembrandt 5 Euro coin (6x8)	250	210
MS65	2006 (10)	500	KM#234-241 5 sets with Rembrandt silver medal and one set with Rembrandt 10 euro coin (6x8)	900	900
MS66	2006 (8)	45,000	KM#234-241 Charity set: Kika	18.00	30.00
MS67	2006 (9)	2,750	KM#231-241 Baby set boy plus bear medal	20.00	30.00
MS68	2006 (9)	100	KM#234-241 Baby set boy plus silver medal	—	95.00
MS69	2006 (8)	25	KM#234-241 Baby set boy plus gold medal	—	500
MS70	2006 (9)	2,750	KM#234-241 Baby set girl plus bear medal	20.00	30.00
MS71	2006 (8)	100	KM#234-241 Baby set girl plus silver medal	—	95.00
MS72	2006 (9)	25	KM#234-241 Baby set girl, plus gold medal	—	500
MS73	2006 (9)	15,000	KM#234-241 Benelux set: Belgium, 224-231, Luxembourg 75-81 plus Netherlands	65.00	65.00
MS74	2006 (9)	1,050	KM#234-241 Wedding set plus medal	22.00	30.00
MS75	2006 (8)	1,500	KM#234-241 Royal Dutch Mint Christmas set	30.00	30.00
MS76	2006 (9)	600	KM#234-241 Theo Peters Christmas set plus bi-color medal	35.00	40.00
MS77	2006 (9)	100	KM#234-241 Christmas set plus silver medal	150	100
MS78	2006 (9)	25	KM#234-241 Christmas set plus golden medal	650	400
MS79	2006 (8)	1,000	KM#234-241 Berlin Coin Fair	25.00	45.00
MS80	2006 (9)	—	KM#234-241 Day of the Mint set plus medal	25.00	120
MS81	2006 (8)	10,000	KM#234-241 200 Years of Coins in Kingdom of Holland	25.00	30.00
MS82	2007 (9)	3,500	KM#234-236, 268-272 Mintmasters V plus medal	20.00	40.00
MS83	2007 (9)	100	KM#234-236, 268-272 Mintmasters V plus silver medal	—	500
MS84	2007 (9)	3,500	KM#234-236, 268-272 Michiel de Ruyter sets, 1 plus silver medal and 1 set with Ruyter's 5 euro coin	—	250
MS85	2007 (8)	500	KM#234-236, 268-272 Michiel de Ruyter sets, 1 set with silver medal and 1 set with Ruyter's 10 euro coin	900	900
MS86	2007 (8)	40,000	KM#234-236, 268-272 National set	18.00	27.50
MS87	2007 (9)	3,000	KM#234-236, 268-272 Baby set boy plus bear medal	20.00	27.50
MS88	2007 (9)	100	KM#234-236, 268-272 Baby set boy plus silver medal	—	95.00
MS89	2007 (9)	3,000	KM#234-236, 268-272 Baby set girl plus bear medal	20.00	27.50
MS90	2007 (9)	100	KM#234-236, 268-272 Baby set girl plus silver medal	—	95.00
MS92	2007 (9)	1,050	KM#234-236, 268-272 Wedding set plus medal	22.00	27.50
MS93	2007 (9)	1,000	KM#234-236, 268-272 Christmas set plus bi-color medal	35.00	40.00
MS94	2007 (9)	100	KM#234-236, 268-272 Christmas set plus silver medal	150	150
MS95	2007 (9)	25	KM#234-236, 268-272 Christmas set plus golden medal	650	650
MS96	2007 (8)	1,000	KM#234-236, 268-272 Berlin Coin Fair	25.00	75.00
MS97	2007 (9)	—	KM#234-236, 268-272 Day of the Mint plus medal	25.00	100
MS98	2007 (8)	5,000	KM#234-236, 268-272 200 Years of Royal Predicate	25.00	28.00
MS109	2001 (6)	120,000	KM#202-206, 210 Introduction Euro-coins, no medal	15.00	25.00
MS112	2001 (6)	1,000	KM#202-206, 210 BOLEGO-VOK	—	60.00
MS113	2001 (6)	1,000	KM#202-206, 210 De Akerendam II, with a silver 2 stuiver coin from the wreck	125	145
MS114	2001 (6)	1,000	KM#202-206, 210 United Seven Provinces Groningen	40.00	40.00
MS115	2001 (6)	1,000	KM#202-206, 210 United Seven Provinces Utrecht	40.00	40.00
MS116	2001 (6)	21,000	KM#202-206, 210 Baby set + bear medal	15.50	25.00
MS117	2001 (6)	1,015	KM#202-206, 210 Onderlinge "s-Grdevenhage"	—	70.00
MS121	2001 (8)	68,000	KM#234-241 Charity set, disabled sport	15.00	17.00
MS122	2002 (8)	105,000	KM#234-241 Charity set, blind escort dogs fund	15.00	30.00
MS123	2002 (8)	59,500	KM#234-241 Last FDS-set	15.00	30.00
MS124	2002 (8)	25,000	KM#234-241 Baby set + bear medal	15.50	30.00
MS125	2002 (8)	10,000	KM#234-241 Wedding-set + medal	15.50	35.00
MS126	2002 (8)	3,500	KM#234-241 Queen Beatrix + medal	20.00	110
MS127	2002 (8)	2,002	KM#234-241 10th day of the Mint + medal	22.00	175
MS128	2002 (8)	10,000	KM#234-241 VOC set I + medal	22.00	35.00
MS129	2002 (8)	10,000	KM#234-241 VOC set II + medal	22.00	30.00
MS130	2002 (8)	10,000	KM#234-241 VOC set III + medal	22.00	30.00
MS131	2002 (8)	10,000	KM#234-241 VOC set IV + medal	22.00	30.00
MS132	2002 (8)	3,000	KM#234-241 BVC + medal	30.00	40.00
MS133	2002 (8)	9,200	KM#234-241 10 Euro + poststamp	30.00	30.00
MS134	2002 (8)	2,500	KM#234-241 VVV-Iris gift set	20.00	40.00
MS135	2002 (8)	1,000	KM#234-241 Theo Peters (Christmas) + medal	99.00	90.00
MS136	2003 (8)	75,000	KM#234-241 Charity set, epilepsy fund	15.50	25.00
MS137	2003 (8)	15,000	KM#234-241 Information set Denmark	20.00	40.00
MS138	2003 (8)	10,000	KM#234-241 VVV-Iris gift set	20.00	25.00
MS139	2003 (8)	10,000	KM#234-241 VOC set V + medal	22.00	25.00
MS140	2003 (8)	10,000	KM#234-241 VOC set VI + medal	42.00	45.00
MS141	2003 (8)	2,003	KM#234-241 Day of the mint + medal	25.00	140
MS142	2003 (8)	1,000	KM#234-241 Theo Peters jubilee set + bi-colour medal	—	30.00
MS143	2003 (8)	100	KM#234-241 Theo Peters jubilee set + silver medal	70.00	70.00
MS144	2003 (8)	25	KM#234-241 Theo Peters jubilee set + golden medal	400	410
MS145	2003 (8)	25,000	KM#234-241 Baby set + bear medal	20.00	25.00
MS146	2003 (8)	15,000	KM#234-241 Wedding-set + medal	20.00	25.00
MS147	2003 (8)	1,000	KM#234-241 Theo Peters Christmas set + bi-colour medal	—	30.00
MS148	2003 (8)	150	KM#234-241 Theo Peters Christmas set + silver medal	70.00	70.00
MS149	2003 (8)	50	KM#234-241 Theo Peters Christmas set + golden medal	400	1,000
MS150	2003 (8)	3,500	KM#234-241 Mint masters I + medal	20.00	60.00
MS151	2003 (8)	1,000	KM#234-241 World Money Fair Basel	20.00	130
MS152	2003 (8)	15,000	KM#234-241 Information set Hungary	20.00	40.00
MS153	2003 (8)	20,000	KM#234-241 Royal birthset of Princess Catharina-Amalia December 7 + silver medal	22.00	25.00
MS154	2003 (8)	10,000	KM#234-241 Benelux set, with Belgium (8) KM#224-231 and Luxembourg (8) KM#75-81	40.00	45.00
MS155	2003 (8)	10,000	KM#234-241 Charles V set + medal, with Germany (8) KM#207-214, Spain (8) KM#1040-1047, Belgium (8) KM#224-231, and Austria (8) KM#3082-3089	85.00	85.00
MS156	2004 (8)	3,500	KM#234-241 Mintmasters II + medal	20.00	60.00
MS157	2004 (8)	10,000	KM#234-241 Wedding-set + medal	18.00	30.00
MS158	2004 (8)	20,000	KM#234-241 Baby set + bear medal	20.00	30.00
MS159	2004 (8)	1,000	KM#234-241 World Money Fair Basel	20.00	110
MS160	2004 (8)	35,000	KM#234-241 Benelux: Belgium, Netherlands + Luxembourg. With silver medal	60.00	60.00
MS161	2004 (8)	10,000	KM#234-241 Queen Juliana-set + silver guilder KM#184 and 30mm silver medal	25.00	30.00
MS162	2004 (8)	1,500	KM#234-241 Theo Peters Christmas set + bi-colour medal	30.00	30.00
MS163	2004 (8)	3,500	KME234-241 VVV-Iris gift set	30.00	25.00
MS164	2004 (8)	150	KM#234-241 Theo Peters Christmas set + silver medal	100	100
MS165	2004 (8)	50	KM#234-241 Theo Peters Christmas set + golden medal	500	500
MS166	2004 (8)	50,000	KM#234-241 Charity set, Fire-burn Centre	18.00	30.00
MS167	2004 (8)	2,004	KM#234-241 Day of the Mint + medal	25.00	150
MS168	2005 (8)	3,500	KM#234-241 Mintmasters III + medal	20.00	60.00
MS169	2005 (8)	2,005	KM#234-241 Day of the Mint + medal	25.00	150
MS170	2005 (8)	10,000	KM#234-241 Wedding-set + medal	18.00	27.50
MS171	2005 (8)	20,000	KM#234-241 Baby set + bear medal	20.00	27.50
MS172	2005 (8)	20,000	KM#234-241 Nijntje-set (Dick Bruna) + medal	18.00	27.50
MS173	2005 (8)	55,000	KM#234-241 Charity set: Princess Beatrix Fonds	18.00	27.50
MS174	2005 (8)	20,000	KM#234-241 Benelux: Belgium, Netherlands + Luxembourg. With silver medal	60.00	60.00
MS175	2005 (8)	1,000	KM#234-241 World Money Fair Basel	25.00	110
MS176	2005 (8)	15,000	KM#234-241 60th Anniversary Liberation + Canadian 25 ct	35.00	35.00
MS177	2005 (8)	1,000	KM#234-241 Theo Peters Christmas set + bi-colour medal	30.00	30.00
MS178	2005 (8)	100	KM#234-241 Theo Peters Christmas set + silver medal	120	120
MS179	2005 (8)	25	KM#234-241 Theo Peters Christmas set + golden medal	550	550
MS180	2006 (8)	3,500	KM#234-241 Mintmasters IV + medal	20.00	40.00
MS181	2006 (8)	4,000	KM#234-241 5 sets with a Rembrandt silver medal and one set with the Rembrandt 5 euro coin	250	250

KM#	Date	Mintage	Identification	Issue Price	Mkt Val
MS182	2006 (8)	500	KM#234-241 5 sets with a Rembrandt silver medal and one set with the Rembrandt 10 euro coin	900	900
MS183	2006 (8)	45,000	KM#234-241 Charity set: (Kika)	18.00	30.00
MS184	2006 (8)	2,750	KM#234-241 Baby set boy + bear medal	20.00	30.00
MS185	2006 (8)	100	KM#234-241 Baby set boy + silver medal	—	95.00
MS186	2006 (8)	25	KM#234-241 Baby set boy + gold medal	—	500
MS187	2006 (8)	2,750	KM#234-241 Baby set girl + bear medal	20.00	30.00
MS188	2006 (8)	100	KM#234-241 Baby set girl + silver medal	—	95.00
MS189	2006 (8)	25	KM#234-241 Baby set girl + gold medal	—	500
MS190	2006 (8)	15,000	KM#234-241 Benelux: Belgium, Netherlands + Luxembourg. With silver medal	65.00	65.00
MS192	2006 (8)	1,050	KM#234-241 Wedding-set + medal	22.00	30.00
MS193	2006 (8)	1,500	KM#234-241 Christmas set Royal Dutch Mint	30.00	30.00
MS194	2006 (8)	600	KM#234-241 Theo Peters Christmas set + bi-colour medal	35.00	40.00
MS195	2006 (8)	100	KM#234-241 Christmas set + silver medal	150	150
MS196	2006 (8)	25	KM#234-241 Christmas set + golden medal	650	650
MS197	2006 (8)	1,000	KM#234-241 Berlin Coin Fair	25.00	45.00
MS198	2006 (8)	2,006	KM#234-241 Day of the Mint + medal	25.00	120
MS199	2006 (8)	10,000	KM#234-241 200 years coins in Kingdom Holland	25.00	30.00
MS200	2007 (8)	3,500	KM#234-236, 268-272 Mintmasters V + medal	20.00	40.00
MS201	2007 (8)	100	KM#234-236, 268-272 Mintmasters V + silver medal	—	600
MS202	2007 (8)	3,500	KM#234-236, 268-272 5 sets Michiel de Ruyter + silver medal and one set with the Michiel de Ruyter 5 euro coin BU	250	250
MS203	2007 (8)	500	KM#234-236, 268-272 5 sets Michiel de Ruyter + silver medal and one set with the Michiel de Ruyter 10 euro coin	900	900
MS204	2007 (8)	40,000	KM#234-236, 268-272 Charity set	18.00	27.50
MS205	2007 (8)	3,000	KM#234-236, 268-272 Baby set boy + bear medal	20.00	27.50
MS206	2007 (8)	100	KM#234-236, 268-272 Baby set boy + silver medal	—	95.00
MS207	2007 (8)	3,000	KM#234-236, 268-272 Baby set girl + bear medal	20.00	27.50
MS208	2007 (8)	100	KM#234-236, 268-272 Baby set girl + silver medal	—	95.00
MS209	2007 (8)	15,000	KM#234-236, 268-272 Benelux: Belgium, Netherlands + Luxembourg. With silver medal + 3x 2 Euro Rome Treaty	75.00	75.00
MS210	2007 (8)	1,050	KM#234-236, 268-272 Wedding-set + medal	22.00	27.50
MS211	2007 (8)	1,000	KM#234-236, 268-272 Christmas set + bi-colour medal	35.00	40.00
MS212	2007 (8)	100	KM#234-236, 268-272 Christmas set + silver medal	150	150
MS213	2007 (8)	25	KM#234-236, 268-272 Christmas set + golden medal	650	650
MS214	2007 (8)	500	KM#234-236, 268-272 Berlin Coin Fair	25.00	90.00
MS215	2007 (8)	2,007	KM#234-236, 268-272 Day of the Mint + medal	25.00	100
MS216	2007 (8)	5,000	KM#234-236, 268-272 200 years of Royal predicate	25.00	28.00
MS217	2008 (8)	3,500	KM#234-236, 268-272 Mintmasters VI + medal	20.00	40.00
MS218	2008 (8)	100	KM#234-236, 268-272 Mintmasters VI + silver medal	20.00	500
MS219	2008 (8)	40,000	KM#234-236, 268-272 National set	20.00	27.50
MS220	2008 (8)	2,500	KM#234-236, 268-272 Baby set boy + bear medal	25.00	27.50
MS221	2008 (8)	100	KM#234-236, 268-272 Baby set boy + silver medal	65.00	65.00
MS222	2008 (8)	2,500	KM#234-236, 268-272 Baby set girl + bear medal	25.00	27.50
MS223	2008 (8)	100	KM#234-236, 268-272 Baby set girl + silver medal	65.00	65.00
MS224	2008 (8)	12,500	KM#234-236, 268-272 Benelux: Belgium, Netherlands + Luxembourg. With silver medal	75.00	75.00
MS225	2008 (8)	1,250	KM#234-236, 268-272 Wedding-set + medal	22.00	27.50
MS226	2008 (8)	500	KM#234-236, 268-272 Christmas set + bi-colour medal	35.00	40.00
MS227	2008 (8)	50	KM#234-236, 268-272 Christmas set + silver medal	130	135
MS228	2008 (8)	25	KM#234-236, 268-272 Christmas set + golden medal	850	850
MS229	2008 (8)	500	KM#234-236, 268-272 Berlin Coin Fair	25.00	75.00
MS230	2008 (8)	2,008	KM#234-236, 268-272 Day of the Mint + medal	25.00	80.00
MS231	2008 (8)	5,000	KM#234-236, 268-272 150 year Queen Emma + silver medal	32.00	35.00
MS232	2008 (8)	500	KM#234-236, 268-272 Theo Peters Jubilation set + bi-colour medal	35.00	40.00
MS233	2008 (8)	50	KM#234-236, 268-272 Theo Peters Jubilation set + silver medal	130	135
MS234	2008 (8)	25	KM#234-236, 268-272 Theo Peters Jubilation set + golden medal	850	850
MS235	2008 (8)	500	KM#234-236, 268-272 5 sets "2 centuries Amsterdam capitol of the Netherlands" + gold plated silver medals and one set with the golden Arctecture 10 euro coin	900	850

PROOF SETS

KM#	Date	Mintage	Identification	Issue Price	Mkt Val
PS54	2001 (6)	17,000	KM#202-206, 210 Booklet 5 Guilder	50.00	45.00
PS55	2001 (2)	500	KM#190.2, 242 Gold and Silver Ducat	50.00	220
PS56	2002 (2)	—	KM#190.2, 211 Golden Ducats	—	650
PS58	2003 (2)	—	KM#190.2, 211 Golden ducats in wooden box	230	650
PS59	2003 (8)	2,000	KM#234-241 Frigate "The Netherland" and silver medal and numbered ingot	85.00	125
PS63	2001 (7)	17,000	KM#202-207, 210 Booklet 5 guilder	50.00	110
PS64	2001 (2)	500	KM#190.2, 242 Gold + silver ducat	—	220
PS65	2002 (2)	—	KM#190.2, 211 Golden ducats	—	650
PS66	2002 (3)	—	KM#190.2, 211, 256 Golden ducats + silver ducat	—	665
PS67	2003 (2)	—	KM#190.2, 211 Golden ducats in wooden box	230	650
PS68	2004 (8)	5,000	KM#234-241 Proofset in wooden box	60.00	90.00
PS69	2005 (8)	5,000	KM#234-241 Proofset in wooden box	60.00	90.00
PS70	2005 (2)	2,500	KM#254, 264 60 years of freedom	—	550
PS71	2006 (8)	3,500	KM#234-241, Proofset in wooden box	—	90.00
PS72	2006 (1)	—	5 Euro KM#255, Australian $5	90.00	110
PS73	2006 (1)	—	5 Euro KM#255, 10 Euro, Australian $5 and $10	—	650
PS74	2007 (9)	10,000	KM#234-236, 268-272, 273	—	90.00
PS75	2008 (8)	10,000	KM#234-236, 268-272	—	65.00
PS76	2003 (8)	2,000	KM#234-241 Frigateship "The Netherland" + silver medal and numbered ingot. "Mintmaster Set" in wooden box	125	125
PS77	2004 (8)	1,000	KM#234-241 Value transport over sea during the eighty year of war + silver medal and numbered ingot. "Mintmaster Set" in wooden box	125	125
PS78	2005 (8)	1,000	KM#234-241 Value transport over sea 1650-1750 + silver medal and numbered ingot. "Mintmaster Set" in wooden box	125	125
PS79	2006 (8)	1,500	KM#234-241 Plus silver medal and numbered ingot. "Mintmaster Set" in wooden box	125	125
PS80	2009 (1)	2,000	KM281 EMU	25.00	150
PS81	2009 (9)	7,500	KM234-236, 268-272, 281	—	70.00
PS82	2010 (8)	5,000	KM234-236, 268-272	—	60.00
PS83	2011 (1)	1,500	KM298 Erasmus	30.00	140
PS84	2011 (9)	5,000	KM234-236, 268-272, 298	—	100
PS85	2009 (9)	7,500	KM234-236, 268-272, 281	—	65.00
PS86	2010 (8)	5,000	KM234-236, 268-272	—	60.00
PS87	2011 (9)	5,000	KM234-236, 268-272, 298	—	90.00
PS88	2004 (8)	10,000	KM#234-241	—	70.00
PS89	2005 (8)	10,000	KM#234-241	—	70.00

PROOF-LIKE SETS (PL)

KM#	Date	Mintage	Identification	Issue Price	Mkt Val
PL3	2001 (8)	16,500	KM#234-241	50.00	40.00
PL4	2002 (2)	—	KM#243, 244 Wedding set (10 Euro in silver and gold) in plastic box	145	400
PL5	2002 (2)	—	KM#243, 244 Wedding set in wooden box	145	400
PL6	2002 (8)	15,500	KM#234-241	50.00	40.00
PL7	2003 (8)	10,000	KM#234-241	50.00	40.00
PL12	2001 (8)	16,500	KM#234-241	50.00	40.00
PL13	2002 (2)	—	KM#243-244 Wedding set (10 Euro silver and gold) in plastic box	145	400
PL14	2002 (2)	—	KM#243-244 Wedding set in wooden box	145	400
PL15	2002 (8)	16,500	KM#234-241	50.00	40.00
PL16	2003 (8)	16,500	KM#234-241	50.00	40.00

SELECT SETS (FLEUR DE COIN)

KM#	Date	Mintage	Identification	Issue Price	Mkt Val
SS90	2001 (6)	120,000	KM#202-206, 210 Introduction to Euro Coins	15.00	25.00
SS91	2001 (6)	3,400	KM#202-206, 210 Queen Julianna Medal	17.50	30.00
SS92	2001 (6)	100	KM#202-206, 210 Queen Julianna Medal; some coins dated 2000 in error	17.50	150
SS93	2001 (6)	1,000	KM#202-206, 210 BOLEGO - VOK	—	120
SS94	2001 (6)	1,000	KM#202-206, 210, 2 Stuiver coin from the wreck of the De Akerendam II	125	120
SS95	2001 (6)	1,000	KM#202-206, 210 United Provinces, Groningen Medal	40.00	20.00
SS96	2001 (6)	21,000	KM#202-206, 210 Baby set plus bear medal	15.50	25.00
SS97	2001 (6)	1,015	KM#202-206, 210 Onderlinge "'s-Gravenhage"	70.00	250

SPECIMEN FDC SETS (FLEUR DE COIN)

KM#	Date	Mintage	Identification	Issue Price	Mkt Val
SS95A	2001 (6)	1,000	KM202-206, 210 United Provinces, Utrecht Medal	40.00	40.00

The Netherlands Antilles, comprises two groups of islands in the West Indies: Aruba (until 1986), Bonaire and Curacao and their dependencies near the Venezuelan coast and St. Eustatius, Saba, and the southern part of St. Martin (*St. Maarten*) southeast of Puerto Rico. The island group has an area of 371 sq. mi. (960 sq. km.) and a population of 225,000. Capital: Willemstad. Chief industries are the refining of crude oil and tourism. Petroleum products and phosphates are exported.

RULERS
Beatrix, 1980-

MINT MARKS
Y – York Mint

Utrecht Mint
(privy marks only)

Date	Privy Mark
2001	Wine tendril with grapes
2002	Wine tendril with grapes and star
2003	Sails of a clipper

MONETARY SYSTEM
100 Cents = 1 Gulden

DUTCH ADMINISTRATION

DECIMAL COINAGE

KM# 32 CENT
0.7000 g., Aluminum, 14 mm. **Ruler:** Beatrix **Obv:** Orange blossom within circle **Rev:** Value within circle of geometric designed border **Edge:** Reeded

Date	Mintage	F	VF	XF	Unc	BU
2001(u)	12,806,500	—	—	0.10	0.20	0.50

Date	Mintage	F	VF	XF	Unc	BU
2002(u) In sets only	6,000	—	—	—	—	1.50
2003(u)	19,604,000	—	—	0.10	0.20	0.50
2004(u) In sets only	7,100	—	—	—	0.60	1.50
2005(u)	—	—	—	0.10	0.60	1.50
2006(u)	—	—	—	0.10	0.60	1.50
2007(u)	—	—	—	0.10	0.60	1.50
2008(u)	—	—	—	0.10	0.60	1.50
2009(u)	—	—	—	0.10	0.60	1.50
2010(u)	—	—	—	0.10	0.60	1.50
2011(u)	—	—	—	0.10	0.60	1.50

KM# 33 5 CENTS
1.1600 g., Aluminum, 16 mm. **Ruler:** Beatrix **Obv:** Orange blossom within circle **Rev:** Value within circle, geometric designed border **Edge:** Reeded

Date	Mintage	F	VF	XF	Unc	BU
2001	2,006,500	—	—	0.20	0.60	1.25
2002 In sets only	6,000	—	—	—	—	2.50
2003	3,104,000	—	—	0.30	0.60	1.25
2004	2,402,100	—	—	0.30	0.50	1.25
2005	—	—	—	0.30	0.50	1.50
2006	—	—	—	0.30	0.50	1.50
2007	—	—	—	0.30	0.50	1.50
2008	—	—	—	0.30	0.50	1.50
2009	—	—	—	0.30	0.50	1.50
2010	—	—	—	0.30	0.50	1.50
2011	—	—	—	0.30	0.50	1.50

KM# 34 10 CENTS
3.0000 g., Nickel Bonded Steel, 18 mm. **Ruler:** Beatrix **Obv:** Orange blossom within circle **Rev:** Value within circle, geometric designed border **Edge:** Reeded

Date	Mintage	F	VF	XF	Unc	BU
2001 In sets only	11,500	—	—	—	—	3.00
2002 In sets only	6,000	—	—	—	—	3.00
2003	2,104,000	—	—	0.50	1.00	1.75
2004	2,202,100	—	—	0.50	1.00	1.75
2005	—	—	—	0.50	1.00	1.75
2006	—	—	—	0.50	1.00	1.75
2007	—	—	—	0.50	1.00	1.75
2008	—	—	—	0.50	1.00	1.75
2009	—	—	—	0.50	1.00	1.75
2010	—	—	—	0.50	1.00	1.75
2011	—	—	—	—	—	2.00

KM# 35 25 CENTS
3.5000 g., Nickel Bonded Steel, 20.2 mm. **Ruler:** Beatrix **Obv:** Orange blossom within circle **Rev:** Value within circle, geometric designed border **Edge:** Reeded

Date	Mintage	F	VF	XF	Unc	BU
2001 In sets only	11,500	—	—	—	—	3.00
2002 In sets only	6,000	—	—	—	—	3.00
2003	1,404,000	—	—	0.50	1.25	1.50
2004	1,502,100	—	—	0.50	1.25	1.50
2005	—	—	—	0.50	1.25	1.50
2006	—	—	—	0.50	1.25	1.50
2007	—	—	—	0.50	1.25	1.50
2008	—	—	—	0.50	1.25	1.50
2009	—	—	—	0.50	1.25	1.50
2010	—	—	—	0.50	1.25	1.50
2011	—	—	—	—	—	2.00

KM# 36 50 CENTS
5.0000 g., Aureate Steel, 24 mm. **Ruler:** Beatrix **Obv:** Orange blossom within circle, designed border **Rev:** Value within circle of pearls and shell border **Edge:** Plain **Shape:** 4-sided

Date	Mintage	F	VF	XF	Unc	BU
2001 In sets only	11,500	—	—	—	—	4.00

Date	Mintage	F	VF	XF	Unc	BU
2002 In sets only	6,000	—	—	—	—	6.00
2003 In sets only	9,000	—	—	—	—	4.00
2004 In sets only	7,100	—	—	—	—	4.00
2005	—	—	—	0.75	3.00	4.00
2006	—	—	—	0.75	3.00	4.00
2007	—	—	—	0.75	3.00	4.00
2008	—	—	—	0.75	3.00	4.00
2009	—	—	—	0.75	3.00	4.00
2010	—	—	—	0.75	3.00	4.00
2011	—	—	—	—	—	5.00

KM# 37 GULDEN
6.0000 g., Aureate Steel, 24 mm. **Ruler:** Beatrix **Obv:** Head left **Rev:** Crowned shield divides value above date and ribbon **Edge Lettering:** GOD * ZIJ * MET * ONS *

Date	Mintage	F	VF	XF	Unc	BU
2001 In sets only	11,500	—	—	—	—	4.00
2002 In sets only	6,000	—	—	—	—	6.00
2003	504,000	—	—	0.75	3.00	6.00
2004 In sets only	7,100	—	—	—	—	6.00
2005	—	—	—	0.75	3.00	5.00
2006	—	—	—	0.75	3.00	5.00
2007	—	—	—	0.75	3.00	5.00
2008	—	—	—	0.75	3.00	5.00
2009	—	—	—	0.75	3.00	5.00
2010	—	—	—	0.75	3.00	5.00
2011	—	—	—	—	—	7.00

KM# 38 2-1/2 GULDEN
9.0000 g., Aureate Steel, 28 mm. **Ruler:** Beatrix **Obv:** Head left **Rev:** Crowned shield divides value above date and ribbon **Edge Lettering:** GOD * ZIJ * MET * ONS *

Date	Mintage	F	VF	XF	Unc	BU
2001 In sets only	11,500	—	—	—	—	6.00
2002 In sets only	6,000	—	—	—	—	8.00
2003 In sets only	9,000	—	—	—	—	6.00
2004 In sets only	7,100	—	—	—	—	6.00
2005	—	—	—	1.00	5.00	6.00
2006	—	—	—	1.00	5.00	6.00
2007	—	—	—	1.00	5.00	6.00
2008	—	—	—	1.00	5.00	6.00
2009	—	—	—	1.00	5.00	6.00
2010	—	—	—	1.00	5.00	6.00
2011	—	—	—	—	—	10.00

KM# 43 5 GULDEN
14.0000 g., Aureate Bonded Steel, 26 mm. **Ruler:** Beatrix **Obv:** Head left **Rev:** Crowned shield divides value above date and ribbon **Edge Lettering:** GOD * ZIJ * MET * ONS *

Date	Mintage	F	VF	XF	Unc	BU
2001 In sets only	9,500	—	—	—	—	7.50
2002 In sets only	6,000	—	—	—	—	7.50
2003 In sets only	7,000	—	—	—	—	7.50
2004	102,100	—	—	2.00	5.00	8.00
2005	—	—	—	2.00	5.00	8.00
2006	—	—	—	2.00	5.00	8.00
2007	—	—	—	2.00	5.00	8.00
2008	—	—	—	2.00	5.00	8.00
2009	—	—	—	2.00	5.00	8.00
2010	—	—	—	2.00	5.00	8.00
2011	—	—	—	—	—	10.00

KM# 74 5 GULDEN
11.9000 g., 0.9250 Silver 0.3539 oz. ASW, 29 mm. **Ruler:** Beatrix **Subject:** 50th Anniversary - Charter for the Kingdom of Netherlands including Aruba as third party **Obv:** Head left **Rev:** Triangular design with hands writing signatures around value **Edge Lettering:** GOD * ZIJ * MET * ONS *

Date	Mintage	F	VF	XF	Unc	BU
2004(u) Proof	4,000	Value: 35.00				

KM# 74.1 5 GULDEN
11.0000 g., Aureate Bonded Steel, 26 mm. **Ruler:** Beatrix **Subject:** 50th Anniversary - End To Dutch Colonial Rule **Obv:** Head left **Rev:** Triangular signatures around value **Edge Lettering:** GOD * ZIJ * MET * ONS *

Date	Mintage	F	VF	XF	Unc	BU
2004	10,000	—	—	7.00	15.00	20.00

KM# 76 5 GULDEN
11.9000 g., 0.9250 Silver 0.3539 oz. ASW, 29 mm. **Ruler:** Beatrix **Subject:** Queen's Silver Jubilee **Obv:** Head left **Rev:** Child art and value **Edge Lettering:** GOD * ZIJ * MET * ONS *

Date	Mintage	F	VF	XF	Unc	BU
2005(u) Proof	4,000	Value: 35.00				

KM# 76.1 5 GULDEN
11.0000 g., Aureate Bonded Steel, 26 mm. **Ruler:** Beatrix **Subject:** Queen's Silver Jubilee **Obv:** Head left **Rev:** Child art and value **Edge Lettering:** GOD * ZIJ * MET * ONS *

Date	Mintage	F	VF	XF	Unc	BU
2005	10,000	—	—	7.00	15.00	20.00

KM# 80 5 GULDEN
11.9000 g., 0.9250 Silver 0.3539 oz. ASW, 29 mm. **Ruler:** Beatrix **Subject:** 50 Years Brishopric Willemstad **Obv:** Logo Brishopric **Rev:** Cathedral **Edge Lettering:** GOD * ZIJ * MET * ONS *

Date	Mintage	F	VF	XF	Unc	BU
2008 Proof	—	Value: 35.00				

KM# 79 5 GULDEN
11.9000 g., 0.9250 Silver 0.3539 oz. ASW, 29 mm. **Ruler:** Beatrix **Obv:** Antoine Maduro **Rev:** Crowned shield divides value **Edge Lettering:** GOD * ZIJ * MET * ONS *

Date	Mintage	F	VF	XF	Unc	BU
2009 Proof	1,250	Value: 35.00				

KM# 49 10 GULDEN
31.1035 g., 0.9250 Silver 0.9250 oz. ASW, 40 mm. **Ruler:** Beatrix **Subject:** Gold Trade Coins: Sulla Aureus **Obv:** Crowned shield divides value above date and ribbon **Rev:** Bust facing with two gold coins at lower left **Edge:** Plain

Date	Mintage	F	VF	XF	Unc	BU
2001(u) Proof	589	Value: 80.00				

KM# 50 10 GULDEN
31.1035 g., 0.9250 Silver 0.9250 oz. ASW, 40 mm. **Ruler:** Beatrix **Subject:** Gold Trade Coins: Constantin I Solidus **Obv:** Crowned shield divides value above date and ribbon **Rev:** Bust facing with two gold coins at lower right **Edge:** Plain

Date	Mintage	F	VF	XF	Unc	BU
2001(u) Proof	578	Value: 80.00				

KM# 51 10 GULDEN
31.1035 g., 0.9250 Silver 0.9250 oz. ASW, 40 mm. **Ruler:**
Beatrix **Subject:** Gold Trade Coins: Clovis I Tremissis fiorino
d'oro **Obv:** Crowned shield divides value above date and ribbon
Rev: Bust facing with two gold coins **Edge:** Plain

Date	Mintage	F	VF	XF	Unc	BU
2001(u) Proof	566	Value: 80.00				

KM# 52 10 GULDEN
31.1035 g., 0.9250 Silver 0.9250 oz. ASW, 40 mm. **Ruler:**
Beatrix **Subject:** Gold Trade Coins: Cosimo de'Medici Fiorino
d'oro **Obv:** Crowned shield divides value above date and ribbon
Rev: Bust facing with two gold coins **Edge:** Plain

Date	Mintage	F	VF	XF	Unc	BU
2001(u) Proof	575	Value: 80.00				

KM# 53 10 GULDEN
31.1035 g., 0.9250 Silver 0.9250 oz. ASW, 40 mm. **Ruler:**
Beatrix **Subject:** Gold Trade Coins: Dandolo Ducato d'Oro **Obv:**
Crowned shield divides value above date and ribbon **Rev:** Bust
facing with two gold coins **Edge:** Plain

Date	Mintage	F	VF	XF	Unc	BU
2001(u) Proof	490	Value: 80.00				

KM# 54 10 GULDEN
31.1035 g., 0.9250 Silver 0.9250 oz. ASW, 40 mm. **Ruler:**
Beatrix **Subject:** Gold Trade Coins: Philips IV Ecu d'or la chaise
Obv: Crowned shield divides value above date and ribbon **Rev:**
Bust facing with two gold coins **Edge:** Plain

Date	Mintage	F	VF	XF	Unc	BU
2001(u) Proof	460	Value: 80.00				

KM# 55 10 GULDEN
31.1035 g., 0.9250 Silver 0.9250 oz. ASW, 40 mm. **Ruler:**
Beatrix **Subject:** Gold Trade Coins: Edward III Nobel **Obv:**
Crowned shield divides value above date and ribbon **Rev:**
Crowned bust facing with two gold coins **Edge:** Plain

Date	Mintage	F	VF	XF	Unc	BU
2001(u) Proof	575	Value: 80.00				

KM# 56 10 GULDEN
31.1035 g., 0.9250 Silver 0.9250 oz. ASW, 40 mm. **Ruler:**
Beatrix **Subject:** Gold Trade Coins: Carolus IV Rhine Gold
Guilder **Obv:** Crowned shield divides value above date and ribbon
Rev: Bust facing with two gold coins **Edge:** Plain

Date	Mintage	F	VF	XF	Unc	BU
2001(u) Proof	430	Value: 80.00				

KM# 57 10 GULDEN
31.1035 g., 0.9250 Silver 0.9250 oz. ASW, 40 mm. **Ruler:**
Beatrix **Subject:** Gold Trade Coins: John II Franc d'or a cheval
Obv: Crowned shield divides value above date and ribbon **Rev:**
Bust facing with two gold coins **Edge:** Plain

Date	Mintage	F	VF	XF	Unc	BU
2001(u) Proof	464	Value: 80.00				

KM# 58 10 GULDEN
31.1035 g., 0.9250 Silver 0.9250 oz. ASW, 40 mm. **Ruler:**
Beatrix **Subject:** Gold Trade Coins: Philip the Good Adriesguilder
Obv: Crowned shield divides value above date and ribbon
Rev: Bust facing with two gold coins **Edge:** Plain

Date	Mintage	F	VF	XF	Unc	BU
2001(u) Proof	250	Value: 120				

KM# 59 10 GULDEN
31.1035 g., 0.9250 Silver 0.9250 oz. ASW, 40 mm. **Ruler:**
Beatrix **Subject:** Gold Trade Coins: Louis XI Ecu d'or au soleil
Obv: Crowned shield divides value above date and ribbon **Rev:**
Bust facing with two gold coins **Edge:** Plain

Date	Mintage	F	VF	XF	Unc	BU
2001(u) Proof	450	Value: 80.00				

KM# 60 10 GULDEN
31.1035 g., 0.9250 Silver 0.9250 oz. ASW, 40 mm. **Ruler:**
Beatrix **Subject:** Gold Trade Coins: Elisabeth I Sovereign **Obv:**
Crowned shield divides value above date and ribbon **Rev:** Bust
facing with two gold coins **Edge:** Plain

Date	Mintage	F	VF	XF	Unc	BU
2001(u) Proof	450	Value: 80.00				

KM# 61 10 GULDEN
31.1035 g., 0.9250 Silver 0.9250 oz. ASW, 40 mm. **Ruler:**
Beatrix **Subject:** Gold Trade Coins: Carolus V Carolus Guilder
Obv: Crowned shield divides value above date and ribbon **Rev:**
Bust facing with two gold coins **Edge:** Plain

Date	Mintage	F	VF	XF	Unc	BU
2001(u) Proof	440	Value: 80.00				

KM# 62 10 GULDEN
31.1035 g., 0.9250 Silver 0.9250 oz. ASW, 40 mm. **Ruler:**
Beatrix **Subject:** Gold Trade Coins: Philips II Real **Obv:** Crowned
shield divides value above date and ribbon **Rev:** Bust facing with
two gold coins **Edge:** Plain

Date	Mintage	F	VF	XF	Unc	BU
2001(u) Proof	440	Value: 80.00				

KM# 63 10 GULDEN
31.1035 g., 0.9250 Silver 0.9250 oz. ASW, 40 mm. **Ruler:**
Beatrix **Subject:** Gold Trade Coins: Maurits Ducat **Obv:** Crowned
shield divides value above date and ribbon **Rev:** Bust facing with
two gold coins **Edge:** Plain

Date	Mintage	F	VF	XF	Unc	BU
2001(u) Proof	443	Value: 80.00				

KM# 64 10 GULDEN
31.1035 g., 0.9250 Silver 0.9250 oz. ASW, 40 mm. **Ruler:**
Beatrix **Subject:** Gold Trade Coins: Isabella and Albrecht Double
Albertin **Obv:** Crowned shield divides value above date and
ribbon **Rev:** Conjoined busts facing with two gold coins **Edge:**
Plain

Date	Mintage	F	VF	XF	Unc	BU
2001(u) Proof	490	Value: 80.00				

KM# 65 10 GULDEN
31.1035 g., 0.9250 Silver 0.9250 oz. ASW, 40 mm. **Ruler:**
Beatrix **Subject:** Gold Trade Coins: William III Golden Rider **Obv:**
Crowned shield divides value above date and ribbon **Rev:** Bust
facing with two gold coins **Edge:** Plain

Date	Mintage	F	VF	XF	Unc	BU
2001(u) Proof	440	Value: 80.00				

KM# 66 10 GULDEN
31.1035 g., 0.9250 Silver 0.9250 oz. ASW, 40 mm. **Ruler:**
Beatrix **Subject:** Gold Trade Coins: Louis XIII Louis d'or **Obv:**
Crowned shield divides value above date and ribbon **Rev:** Bust
facing with two gold coins **Edge:** Plain

Date	Mintage	F	VF	XF	Unc	BU
2001(u) Proof	440	Value: 80.00				

KM# 67 10 GULDEN
31.1035 g., 0.9250 Silver 0.9250 oz. ASW, 40 mm. **Ruler:**
Beatrix **Subject:** Gold Trade Coins: Catharina the Great Rubel
Obv: Crowned shield divides value above date and ribbon **Rev:**
Crowned laureate bust facing with two gold coins **Edge:** Plain

Date	Mintage	F	VF	XF	Unc	BU
2001(u) Proof	560	Value: 100				

KM# 68 10 GULDEN
31.1035 g., 0.9250 Silver 0.9250 oz. ASW, 40 mm. **Ruler:**
Beatrix **Subject:** Gold Trade Coins: Maria Theresia Double
Sovereign **Obv:** Crowned shield divides value above date and
ribbon **Rev:** Bust facing with two gold coins **Edge:** Plain

Date	Mintage	F	VF	XF	Unc	BU
2001(u) Proof	440	Value: 80.00				

KM# 69 10 GULDEN
31.1035 g., 0.9250 Silver 0.9250 oz. ASW, 40 mm. **Ruler:**
Beatrix **Subject:** Gold Trade Coins: Napolean Bonaparte 20
Franc **Obv:** Crowned shield divides value above date and ribbon
Rev: Bust facing with two gold coins **Edge:** Plain

Date	Mintage	F	VF	XF	Unc	BU
2001(u) Proof	555	Value: 80.00				

KM# 70 10 GULDEN
31.1035 g., 0.9250 Silver 0.9250 oz. ASW, 40 mm. **Ruler:**
Beatrix **Series:** Gold Trade Coins: Wilhelmina Golden 10 Guilder
Obv: Crowned shield divides value above date and ribbon **Rev:**
Bust facing with two gold coins **Edge:** Plain

Date	Mintage	F	VF	XF	Unc	BU
2001(u) Proof	440	Value: 80.00				

KM# 71 10 GULDEN
31.1035 g., 0.9250 Silver 0.9250 oz. ASW, 40 mm. **Ruler:**
Beatrix **Subject:** Gold Trade Coins: George III Sovereign **Obv:**
Crowned shield divides value above date and ribbon **Rev:** Bust
facing with two gold coins **Edge:** Plain

Date	Mintage	F	VF	XF	Unc	BU
2001(u) Proof	440	Value: 80.00				

KM# 72 10 GULDEN
31.1035 g., 0.9250 Silver 0.9250 oz. ASW, 40 mm. **Ruler:**
Beatrix **Subject:** Gold Trade Coins: Albert I Belgium 20 Franc
Obv: Crowned shield divides value above date and ribbon **Rev:**
Bust facing with two gold coins **Edge:** Plain

Date	Mintage	F	VF	XF	Unc	BU
2001(u) Proof	490	Value: 80.00				

KM# 84 10 GULDEN
17.0000 g., 0.9250 Silver 0.5055 oz. ASW, 33 mm. **Ruler:**
Beatrix **Subject:** Mariage of Willem-Alexander and Maxima **Obv:**
Queen's head left **Rev:** Conjoined busts left **Edge Lettering:**
GOD * ZIJ * MET * ONS *

Date	Mintage	F	VF	XF	Unc	BU
2002(u) Proof	1,500	Value: 45.00				

KM# 75 10 GULDEN
6.7200 g., 0.9000 Gold 0.1944 oz. AGW **Ruler:** Beatrix **Subject:**
50th Anniversary - End to Dutch Colonial Rule **Obv:** Head left
Rev: Triangular signatures around value **Edge:** Reeded

Date	Mintage	F	VF	XF	Unc	BU
2004 Proof	1,000	Value: 400				

KM# 77 10 GULDEN
6.7200 g., 0.9000 Gold 0.1944 oz. AGW, 22.5 mm. **Ruler:**
Beatrix **Subject:** Queen's Silver Jubilee **Obv:** Head left **Rev:**
Child art and value **Edge:** Reeded

Date	Mintage	F	VF	XF	Unc	BU
2005(u) Proof	1,500	Value: 400				

KM# 78 10 GULDEN
1.2442 g., 0.9990 Gold 0.0400 oz. AGW, 13.92 mm. **Ruler:**
Beatrix **Subject:** Year of the dolphin **Obv:** Head left **Obv.
Legend:** BEATRIX KONINGIN DER NEDERLANDEN **Rev:**
Stylized outlines of birds above dolphins at sunset **Rev. Legend:**
NEDERLANDSE ANTILLEN - JAAR VAN DE DOLFIJN **Edge:**
Reeded

Date	Mintage	F	VF	XF	Unc	BU
2007(u) Proof	5,000	Value: 100				

KM# 81 10 GULDEN
17.0000 g., 0.9250 Silver 0.5055 oz. ASW, 33 mm. **Ruler:**
Beatrix **Subject:** Farewell to the Netherlands Antilles **Obv:**
Autonomy monument with five birds **Rev:** Crowned shield divided
value **Edge Lettering:** GOD * ZIJ * MET * ONS *

Date	Mintage	F	VF	XF	Unc	BU
2010(u) Proof	5,000	Value: 45.00				

KM# 82 25 GULDEN
25.0000 g., 0.9250 Silver 0.7435 oz. ASW, 38 mm. **Ruler:**
Beatrix **Obv:** 175 year Bank of the Netherlands Antilles **Rev:**
Sailing ship

Date	Mintage	F	VF	XF	Unc	BU
2003 Prooflike	1,500	—	—	—	—	50.00

KM# 83 25 GULDEN
25.0000 g., 0.9250 Silver 0.7435 oz. ASW, 38 mm. **Ruler:**
Beatrix **Obv:** 50 years of monument care **Rev:** Folker FXVIII plane
over route map **Edge Lettering:** GOD * ZIJ * MET * ONS *

Date	Mintage	F	VF	XF	Unc	BU
2004 Proof	5,000	Value: 45.00				

MINT SETS

KM#	Date	Mintage	Identification	Issue Price	Mkt Val
MS22	2001 (8)	6,500	KM#32-38, 43	15.00	30.00
MS23	2002 (8)	6,000	KM#32-38, 43	15.00	40.00
MS24	2003 (8)	4,000	KM#32-38, 43	15.00	30.00
MS25	2004 (8)	2,100	KM#32-38, 43	15.00	30.00
MS26	2005 (8)	3,500	KM#32-38, 43	17.00	25.00
MS27	2006 (8)	2,000	KM#32-38, 43	20.00	25.00
MS28	2007 (8)	2,000	KM#32-38, 43	20.00	25.00
MS29	2008 (8)	2,000	KM#32-38, 43	21.00	25.00
MS30	2009 (8)	2,000	KM#32-38, 43	27.00	27.00
MS31	2010 (8)	2,000	KM#32-38, 43	28.00	28.00
MS32	2011 (8)	2,000	KM#32-38, 43	28.00	30.00

NEW CALEDONIA

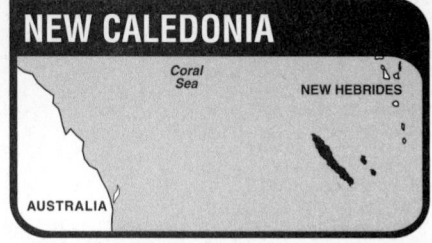

The French Associated State of New Caledonia is a group of about 25 islands in the South Pacific. They are situated about 750 miles (1,207 km.) east of Australia. The territory, which includes the dependencies of Isle des Pins, Loyalty Islands, Isle Huon, Isles Belep, Isles Chesterfield, Isle Walpole, Wallis and Futuna Islands and has a total land area of 7,358 sq. mi.(19,060 sq. km.) and a population of *156,000. Capital: Noumea. The islands are rich in minerals; New Caledonia has some of the world's largest known deposit of nickel. Nickel, nickel castings, coffee and copra are exported.

MINT MARK
Paris, privy marks only

MONETARY SYSTEM
100 Centimes = 1 Franc

FRENCH ASSOCIATED STATE

DECIMAL COINAGE

KM# 10   FRANC
1.3000 g., Aluminum, 23 mm. **Obv:** Seated figure holding torch, legend added **Obv. Legend:** I. E. O. M. **Rev:** Kagu bird within sprigs below value

Date	Mintage	F	VF	XF	Unc	BU
2001(a)	100,000	—	—	0.15	0.50	1.25
2002(a)	1,200,000	—	—	0.15	0.50	1.25
2003(a)	2,000,000	—	—	0.15	0.50	1.25
2004(a)	1,200,000	—	—	0.15	0.50	1.25
2005(a)	700,000	—	—	0.15	0.50	1.25
2006(a)	1,600,000	—	—	0.15	0.50	1.25
2007(a)	2,000,000	—	—	0.15	0.50	1.25
2008(a)	2,800,000	—	—	0.15	0.50	1.25
2009(a)	—	—	—	0.15	0.50	1.25
2010(a)	—	—	—	0.15	0.50	1.25
2011(a)	—	—	—	0.15	0.50	1.25

KM# 14   2 FRANCS
2.2000 g., Aluminum, 27 mm. **Obv:** Seated figure holding torch, legend added **Obv. Legend:** I. E. O. M. **Rev:** Kagu bird and value within sprigs

Date	Mintage	F	VF	XF	Unc	BU
2001(a)	800,000	—	—	0.25	0.75	1.50
2002(a)	1,200,000	—	—	0.25	0.75	1.50
2003(a)	2,400,000	—	—	0.20	0.65	1.50
2004(a)	200,000	—	—	0.20	0.65	1.50
2005(a)	530,000	—	—	0.20	0.65	1.50
2006(a)	1,200,000	—	—	0.20	0.65	1.50
2007(a)	600,000	—	—	0.20	0.65	1.50
2008(a)	2,400,000	—	—	0.20	0.65	1.50
2009(a)	—	—	—	0.20	0.65	1.50
2011(a)	—	—	—	0.20	0.65	1.50

KM# 16   5 FRANCS
3.7500 g., Aluminum, 31 mm. **Obv:** Seated figure holding torch,

---

legend added **Obv. Legend:** I. E. O. M. **Rev:** Kagu bird and value within sprigs

Date	Mintage	F	VF	XF	Unc	BU
2001(a)	600,000	—	—	0.50	1.00	2.00
2002(a)	480,000	—	—	0.50	1.00	2.00
2003(a)	700,000	—	—	0.40	1.00	2.00
2004(a)	1,000,000	—	—	0.40	1.00	2.00
2005(a)	360,000	—	—	0.40	1.00	2.00
2006(a)	480,000	—	—	0.40	1.00	2.00
2007(a)	960,000	—	—	0.40	1.00	2.00
2008(a)	1,700,000	—	—	0.40	1.00	2.00
2009(a)	—	—	—	0.40	1.00	2.00
2010(a)	—	—	—	0.40	1.00	2.00
2011(a)	—	—	—	0.40	1.00	2.00

KM# 11   10 FRANCS
6.0000 g., Nickel, 24 mm. **Obv:** Liberty head left **Obv. Legend:** I. E. O. M. **Rev:** Sailboat above value

Date	Mintage	F	VF	XF	Unc	BU
2001(a)	100,000	—	—	0.65	1.25	2.75
2002(a)	200,000	—	—	0.65	1.25	2.75
2003(a)	800,000	—	—	0.65	1.25	2.75
2004(a)	600,000	—	—	0.65	1.25	2.75
2005(a)	64,000	—	—	0.65	1.25	2.75

KM# 11a   10 FRANCS
6.0000 g., Copper-Nickel, 24 mm. **Obv:** Liberty head left **Rev:** Sailboat above value **Edge:** Reeded

Date	Mintage	F	VF	XF	Unc	BU
2006(a)	60,000	—	—	0.65	1.25	2.75
2007(a)	1,000,000	—	—	0.65	1.25	2.75
2008(a)	1,200,000	—	—	0.65	1.25	2.75
2009(a)	—	—	—	0.65	1.25	2.75
2010(a)	—	—	—	0.65	1.25	2.75
2011(a)	—	—	—	0.65	1.25	2.75

KM# 12   20 FRANCS
10.0000 g., Nickel, 28.5 mm. **Obv:** Liberty head left **Obv. Legend:** I. O. E. M. **Rev:** Three ox heads above value

Date	Mintage	F	VF	XF	Unc	BU
2001(a)	150,000	—	—	1.00	1.75	3.25
2002(a)	250,000	—	—	1.00	1.75	3.25
2003(a)	250,000	—	—	1.00	1.75	3.25
2004(a)	500,000	—	—	1.00	1.75	3.25
2005(a)	300,000	—	—	1.00	1.75	3.25

KM# 12a   20 FRANCS
10.0000 g., Copper-Nickel, 28.5 mm. **Obv:** Liberty head left **Rev:** Three ox heads above value **Edge:** Reeded

Date	Mintage	F	VF	XF	Unc	BU
2006(a)	300,000	—	—	1.00	1.75	3.25
2007(a)	800,000	—	—	1.25	1.75	3.25
2008(a)	800,000	—	—	1.25	1.75	3.25
2009(a)	—	—	—	1.25	1.75	3.25
2010(a)	—	—	—	1.25	1.75	3.25
2011(a)	—	—	—	1.25	1.75	3.25

KM# 13   50 FRANCS
15.0000 g., Nickel, 33 mm. **Obv:** Liberty head left **Obv. Legend:** I. E. O. M. **Rev:** Hut above value in center of palm and pine trees

Date	Mintage	F	VF	XF	Unc	BU
2001(a)	100,000	—	—	1.25	2.00	4.00
2002(a)	—	—	—	1.25	2.00	4.00
2003(a)	75,000	—	—	1.25	2.00	4.00
2004(a)	150,000	—	—	1.25	2.00	4.00
2005(a)	54,000	—	—	1.25	2.00	4.00

KM# 13a   50 FRANCS
15.0000 g., Copper-Nickel **Obv:** Liberty head left **Rev:** Hut in center of palm and pine trees, value below **Edge:** Reeded

Date	Mintage	F	VF	XF	Unc	BU
2006(a)	75,000	—	—	1.25	2.00	4.00
2007(a)	225,000	—	—	1.25	2.00	4.00
2008(a)	375,000	—	—	1.25	2.00	4.00
2009(a)	—	—	—	1.25	2.00	4.00

KM# 15   100 FRANCS
10.0000 g., Nickel-Bronze, 30 mm. **Obv:** Liberty head left **Rev:** Hut above value in center of palm and pine trees

Date	Mintage	F	VF	XF	Unc	BU
2001(a)	100,000	—	—	1.50	3.00	5.00
2002(a)	620,000	—	—	1.50	3.00	6.00
2003(a)	500,000	—	—	1.50	3.00	5.00
2004(a)	500,000	—	—	1.50	3.00	5.00
2005(a)	180,000	—	—	1.50	3.00	5.00

KM# 15a   100 FRANCS
10.0000 g., Aluminum-Bronze, 30 mm. **Obv:** Liberty head left **Rev:** Hut above value in center of palm and pine trees **Edge:** Reeded

Date	Mintage	F	VF	XF	Unc	BU
2006(a)	300,000	—	—	1.50	3.00	5.00
2007(a)	800,000	—	—	1.50	3.00	5.00
2008(a)	1,100,000	—	—	1.50	3.00	5.00
2009(a)	—	—	—	1.50	3.00	5.00
2010(a)	—	—	—	1.50	3.00	5.00

MINT SETS

KM#	Date	Mintage	Identification	Issue Price	Mkt Val
MS1	2001 (7)	3,000	KM#10-16	—	25.00
MS2	2002 (7)	5,000	KM#10-16	—	25.00
MS3	2004 (7)	3,000	KM#10-16	—	25.00

NEW ZEALAND

New Zealand, a parliamentary state located in the Southwest Pacific 1,250 miles (2,011 km.) east of Australia, has an area of 103,883 sq. mi. (268,680 sq. km.) and a population of *3.4 million. Capital: Wellington. Wool, meat, dairy products and some manufactured items are exported.

Decimal Currency was introduced in 1967 with special sets commemorating the last issues of pound sterling (1965) and the first of the decimal issues. Since then dollars and sets of coins have been issued nearly every year.

New Zealand is a founding member of the Commonwealth of Nations. Elizabeth II is the Head of State as the Queen of New Zealand; the Prime Minister is the Head of Government.

RULER
British

STATE
1907 - present

DECIMAL COINAGE
100 Cents = 1 Dollar

(c) Royal Australian Mint, Canberra

(l) Royal Mint, Llantrisant

(o) Royal Canadian Mint, Ottawa or Winnipeg

(m) B.H. Mayer, Germany

(n) Norwegian Mint, Kongsberg

(p) South African Mint, Pretoria

(v) Valcambi SA, Switzerland

(w) Perth Mint, Western Australia

KM# 116   5 CENTS

2.8300 g., Copper-Nickel, 19.43 mm.   **Ruler:** Elizabeth II **Obv:** Head with tiara right **Rev:** Value below tuatara **Edge:** Reeded **Note:** Many recalled and melted in 2006.

Date	Mintage	F	VF	XF	Unc	BU
2001(I)	20,000,000	—	—	0.10	0.50	1.00
2001(c) In sets only	2,910	—	—	—	4.00	5.00
2001(c) Proof	1,364	Value: 3.00				
2002(I)	40,500,000	—	—	0.10	0.50	1.00
2002(c) In sets only	3,000	—	—	—	5.00	6.00
2002(c) Proof	1,500	Value: 3.00				
2003(I)	30,000,000	—	—	—	0.50	1.00
2003(c) In sets only	1,496	—	—	—	5.00	6.00
2003 Proof	3,000	Value: 3.00				
2004(I)	15,000,000	—	—	—	2.00	3.00

Note: All but 48,000 melted. Many of these survivors have recently come onto the NZ market in bulk.

2004(c) In sets only	2,800	—	—	—	20.00	30.00
2004(c) Proof	1,750	Value: 3.00				
2005(c) In sets only	3,000	—	—	—	8.00	12.00
2005(c) Proof	2,250	Value: 3.00				
2006(c) In sets only	—	—	—	—	8.00	12.00
2006(c) Proof	—	Value: 3.00				

KM# 117   10 CENTS

5.6600 g., Copper-Nickel, 23.62 mm.   **Ruler:** Elizabeth II **Obv:** Head with tiara right **Rev:** Value above koruru **Edge:** Reeded **Note:** Many recalled and melted in 2006.

Date	Mintage	F	VF	XF	Unc	BU
2001(I)	10,000,000	—	—	0.10	0.30	0.50
2001(c) In sets only	2,910	—	—	—	6.00	8.00
2001(c) Proof	1,364	Value: 4.00				
2002(I)	10,000,000	—	—	0.10	0.30	0.50
2002(c) In sets only	3,000	—	—	—	3.00	5.00
2002(c) Proof	1,500	Value: 4.00				
2003(I)	13,000,000	—	—	0.10	0.30	0.50
2003(c) In sets only	3,000	—	—	—	5.00	8.00
2003(I) Proof	1,496	Value: 4.00				
2004(I)	6,500,000	—	—	—	0.30	0.50
2004(c) In sets only	—	—	—	—	5.00	8.00
2004(c) Proof	1,750	Value: 4.00				
2005	2,000,000	—	—	—	30.00	40.00

Note: All but 28,000 melted.

2005(c) In sets only	3,000	—	—	—	20.00	30.00
2005(c) Proof	2,250	Value: 4.00				
2006(c) In sets only	3,000	—	—	—	10.00	15.00
2006(c) Proof	2,100	Value: 4.00				

KM# 117a   10 CENTS

3.3100 g., Copper Plated Steel, 20.5 mm.   **Ruler:** Elizabeth II **Obv:** Head with tiara right **Rev:** Value above koruru **Edge:** Plain

Date	Mintage	F	VF	XF	Unc	BU
2006(o)	140,200,000	—	—	—	0.20	0.40
2007(o)	15,000,000	—	—	—	—	—
2007(c) In sets only	5,000	—	—	—	—	5.00
2007(c) Proof	3,500	Value: 4.00				
2008(I) In sets only	4,000	—	—	—	—	5.00
2008(I) Proof	3,000	Value: 4.00				
2009(o)	30,000,000	—	—	—	0.20	0.40
2009(w) In sets only	2,000	—	—	—	—	5.00
2009(w) Proof	1,500	Value: 4.00				
2010 In sets only	2,000	—	—	—	—	5.00
2010 Proof	—	Value: 4.00				
2011(o)	10,400,000	—	—	—	2.00	0.40
2011(o) Proof	—	Value: 4.00				
2012(u)	—	—	—	—	2.00	0.40
2012(u) Proof	—	Value: 4.00				

KM# 234   10 CENTS

3.3100 g., Copper Plated Steel, 20.5 mm.   **Ruler:** Elizabeth II **Obv:** Head with tiara right **Rev:** Tuatara right **Edge:** Plain

Date	Mintage	F	VF	XF	Unc	BU
2007(c) In sets only	15,000	—	—	—	0.50	5.00

KM# 118   20 CENTS

11.3100 g., Copper-Nickel, 28.58 mm.   **Ruler:** Elizabeth II **Obv:** Head with tiara right **Rev:** Value below Pukaki **Edge:** Reeded **Note:** Many recalled and melted in 2006.

Date	Mintage	F	VF	XF	Unc	BU
2001(c) In sets only	2,910	—	—	—	—	4.00
2001(c) Proof	1,364	Value: 10.00				
2002(I)	7,000,000	—	—	—	0.50	—
2002(c) In sets only	3,000	—	—	—	—	5.00
2002(c) Proof	1,500	Value: 10.00				
2003(c) In sets only	3,000	—	—	—	—	4.00
2003(c) Proof	3,000	Value: 10.00				
2004(I)	8,500,000	—	—	—	0.50	—
2004(c) In sets only	2,800	—	—	—	—	5.00
2004(c) Proof	1,750	Value: 10.00				
2005(I)	4,000,000	—	—	—	—	15.00

Note: All but 178,000 melted.

2005(c) In sets only	3,000	—	—	—	—	5.00
2005(c) Proof	2,250	Value: 10.00				
2006(c) In sets only	3,000	—	—	—	—	5.00
2006(c) Proof	2,100	Value: 10.00				

KM# 118a   20 CENTS

4.0000 g., Nickel Plated Steel, 21.75 mm.   **Ruler:** Elizabeth II **Obv:** Head with tiara right **Rev:** Value below Pukaki **Shape:** Scalloped

Date	Mintage	F	VF	XF	Unc	BU
2006(o)	116,600,000	—	—	—	0.40	0.65
2007(c) In sets only	5,000	—	—	—	—	7.00
2007(c) Proof	4,000	Value: 8.00				
2008(o)	80,000,000	—	—	—	0.40	0.65
2008(I) In sets only	4,000	—	—	—	—	7.00
2008(I) Proof	3,000	Value: 8.00				
2009(w) In sets only	2,000	—	—	—	—	7.00
2009(w) Proof	1,500	Value: 8.00				
2010 In sets only	2,000	—	—	—	—	7.00
2010 Proof	—	Value: 8.00				
2011(o) In sets only	2,000	—	—	—	—	7.00
2011(o) Proof	—	Value: 8.00				
2012(u)	—	—	—	—	—	7.00
2012(u) Proof	—	Value: 8.00				

KM# 119   50 CENTS

13.6100 g., Copper-Nickel, 31.75 mm.   **Ruler:** Elizabeth II **Obv:** Head with tiara right **Rev:** H.M.S. Endeavour and value **Edge:** Segmented reeding **Note:** Many recalled and melted in 2006.

Date	Mintage	F	VF	XF	Unc	BU
2001(I)	5,000,000	—	—	—	1.00	—
2001(c) In sets only	2,910	—	—	—	—	4.00
2001(c) Proof	1,364	Value: 5.00				
2002(I)	3,000,000	—	—	0.50	1.00	—
2002(c) In sets only	3,000	—	—	—	—	4.00

Date	Mintage	F	VF	XF	Unc	BU
2002(c) Proof	1,500	Value: 5.00				
2003(I)	2,500,000	—	—	0.50	1.00	—
2003(c) In sets only	3,000	—	—	—	—	4.00
2003(c) Proof	1,496	Value: 5.00				
2004(I)	2,000,000	—	—	—	1.00	—
2004(c) In sets only	2,800	—	—	—	—	4.00
2004(c) Proof	1,750	Value: 5.00				
2005(I)	1,000,000	—	—	—	7.50	—

Note: All but 503,800 melted.

2005(c) In sets only	3,000	—	—	—	—	4.00
2005(c) Proof	2,250	Value: 5.00				
2006(c) In sets only	3,000	—	—	—	—	4.00
2006(c) Proof	2,100	Value: 5.00				

KM# 135   50 CENTS

13.6100 g., Copper-Nickel, 31.75 mm.   **Ruler:** Elizabeth II **Subject:** Lord of the Rings **Obv:** Head with tiara right **Rev:** Frodo's head facing to left of vine and value **Edge:** Reeded

Date	Mintage	F	VF	XF	Unc	BU
2003(I)	41,221	—	—	—	—	15.00

KM# 136   50 CENTS

13.6100 g., Copper-Nickel, 31.75 mm.   **Ruler:** Elizabeth II **Subject:** Lord of the Rings **Obv:** Head with tiara right **Rev:** Head of Gandalf with hat facing and value **Edge:** Reeded

Date	Mintage	F	VF	XF	Unc	BU
2003(I)	41,221	—	—	—	—	15.00

KM# 137   50 CENTS

13.6100 g., Copper-Nickel, 31.75 mm.   **Ruler:** Elizabeth II **Subject:** Lord of the Rings **Obv:** Head with tiara right **Rev:** Head of Aragorn facing and value **Edge:** Reeded

Date	Mintage	F	VF	XF	Unc	BU
2003(I)	41,221	—	—	—	—	15.00

KM# 138   50 CENTS

13.6100 g., Copper-Nickel, 31.75 mm.   **Ruler:** Elizabeth II **Subject:** Lord of the Rings **Obv:** Head with tiara right **Rev:** Head of Gollum facing and value **Edge:** Reeded

Date	Mintage	F	VF	XF	Unc	BU
2003(I)	38,400	—	—	—	—	15.00

KM# 139 50 CENTS

13.6100 g., Copper-Nickel, 31.75 mm. **Ruler:** Elizabeth II **Subject:** Lord of the Rings **Obv:** Head with tiara right **Rev:** Saruman, value **Edge:** Reeded

Date	Mintage	F	VF	XF	Unc	BU
2003(l)	38,400	—	—	—	—	15.00

KM# 140 50 CENTS

13.6100 g., Copper-Nickel, 31.75 mm. **Ruler:** Elizabeth II **Subject:** Lord of the Rings **Obv:** Head with tiara right **Rev:** Head of Sauron left and value **Edge:** Reeded

Date	Mintage	F	VF	XF	Unc	BU
2003(l)	38,400	—	—	—	—	15.00

KM# 235 50 CENTS

13.6100 g., Copper-Nickel, 31.75 mm. **Ruler:** Elizabeth II **Subject:** Lord of the Rings **Obv:** Head with tiara right **Rev:** Boromir

Date	Mintage	F	VF	XF	Unc	BU
2003(l)	6,889	—	—	—	—	18.00

KM# 236 50 CENTS

13.6100 g., Copper-Nickel, 31.75 mm. **Ruler:** Elizabeth II **Subject:** Lord of the Rings **Obv:** Head with tiara right **Rev:** Gimli

Date	Mintage	F	VF	XF	Unc	BU
2003(l)	6,889	—	—	—	—	18.00

KM# 237 50 CENTS

13.6100 g., Copper-Nickel, 31.75 mm. **Ruler:** Elizabeth II **Subject:** Lord of the Rings **Obv:** Head with tiara right **Rev:** Legolas

Date	Mintage	F	VF	XF	Unc	BU
2003(l)	6,889	—	—	—	—	18.00

KM# 238 50 CENTS

13.6100 g., Copper-Nickel, 31.75 mm. **Ruler:** Elizabeth II **Subject:** Lord of the Rings **Obv:** Head with tiara right **Rev:** Merry

Date	Mintage	F	VF	XF	Unc	BU
2003(l)	6,889	—	—	—	—	18.00

KM# 239 50 CENTS

13.6100 g., Copper-Nickel, 31.75 mm. **Ruler:** Elizabeth II **Subject:** Lord of the Rings **Obv:** Head with tiara right **Rev:** Pippin

Date	Mintage	F	VF	XF	Unc	BU
2003(l)	6,889	—	—	—	—	18.00

KM# 240 50 CENTS

13.6100 g., Copper-Nickel, 31.75 mm. **Ruler:** Elizabeth II **Subject:** Lord of the Rings **Obv:** Head with tiara right **Rev:** Sam

Date	Mintage	F	VF	XF	Unc	BU
2003(l)	6,889	—	—	—	—	18.00

KM# 241 50 CENTS

13.6100 g., Copper-Nickel, 31.75 mm. **Ruler:** Elizabeth II **Subject:** Lord of the Rings **Obv:** Head with tiara right **Rev:** Arwen

Date	Mintage	F	VF	XF	Unc	BU
2003(l)	4,068	—	—	—	—	20.00

KM# 242 50 CENTS

13.6100 g., Copper-Nickel, 31.75 mm. **Ruler:** Elizabeth II **Subject:** Lord of the Rings **Obv:** Head with tiara right **Rev:** Elrond

Date	Mintage	F	VF	XF	Unc	BU
2003(l)	4,068	—	—	—	—	20.00

KM# 243 50 CENTS

13.6100 g., Copper-Nickel, 31.75 mm. **Ruler:** Elizabeth II **Subject:** Lord of the Rings **Obv:** Head with tiara right **Rev:** Eowyn

Date	Mintage	F	VF	XF	Unc	BU
2003(l)	4,068	—	—	—	—	20.00

KM# 244 50 CENTS

13.6100 g., Copper-Nickel, 31.75 mm. **Ruler:** Elizabeth II **Subject:** Lord of the Rings **Obv:** Head with tiara right **Rev:** Galadriel

Date	Mintage	F	VF	XF	Unc	BU
2003(l)	4,068	—	—	—	—	20.00

KM# 245 50 CENTS

13.6100 g., Copper-Nickel, 31.75 mm. **Ruler:** Elizabeth II **Subject:** Lord of the Rings **Obv:** Head with tiara right **Rev:** An Orc

Date	Mintage	F	VF	XF	Unc	BU
2003(l)	4,068	—	—	—	—	20.00

KM# 246 50 CENTS

13.6100 g., Copper-Nickel, 31.75 mm. **Ruler:** Elizabeth II **Subject:** Lord of the Rings **Obv:** Head with tiara right **Rev:** Treebeard

Date	Mintage	F	VF	XF	Unc	BU
2003(l)	4,068	—	—	—	—	20.00

KM# 119a 50 CENTS

5.0000 g., Nickel Plated Steel, 24.75 mm. **Ruler:** Elizabeth II **Obv:** Head with tiara right **Rev:** Ship, H.M.S. Endeavour

Date	Mintage	F	VF	XF	Unc	BU
2006(o)	70,200,000	—	—	—	0.75	1.00
2007(c) In sets only	5,000	—	—	—	—	8.00
2007(c) Proof	3,500	Value: 10.00				
2008(l) In sets only	4,000	—	—	—	—	8.00
2008(l) Proof	3,000	Value: 10.00				
2009(o)	20,000,000	—	—	—	0.75	1.00
2009(w) In sets only	2,000	—	—	—	—	8.00
2009(w) Proof	1,500	Value: 10.00				
2010 In sets only	2,000	—	—	—	—	8.00
2010 Proof	—	Value: 10.00				
2011(o) In sets only	2,000	—	—	—	—	8.00
2011(o) Proof	—	Value: 10.00				
2012(u)	—	—	—	—	—	8.00
2012(u) Proof	—	Value: 10.00				

KM# 279 50 CENTS

Aluminum-Bronze, 38.74 mm. **Ruler:** Elizabeth II **Subject:** Narnia **Obv:** Head with tiara right **Rev:** Peter

Date	Mintage	F	VF	XF	Unc	BU
2006(c)	20,000	—	—	—	—	6.00

KM# 280 50 CENTS

Aluminum-Bronze, 38.74 mm. **Ruler:** Elizabeth II **Subject:** Narnia **Obv:** Head with tiara right **Rev:** Susan

Date	Mintage	F	VF	XF	Unc	BU
2006(c)	20,000	—	—	—	—	6.00

KM# 281 50 CENTS

Aluminum-Bronze, 38.74 mm. **Ruler:** Elizabeth II **Subject:** Narnia **Obv:** Head with tiara right **Rev:** Edmund

Date	Mintage	F	VF	XF	Unc	BU
2006(c)	20,000	—	—	—	—	6.00

KM# 282 50 CENTS

Aluminum-Bronze, 38.74 mm. **Ruler:** Elizabeth II **Subject:** Narnia **Obv:** Head with tiara right **Rev:** Lucy

Date	Mintage	F	VF	XF	Unc	BU
2006(c)	20,000	—	—	—	—	6.00

KM# 283 50 CENTS

Aluminum-Bronze, 38.74 mm. **Ruler:** Elizabeth II **Subject:** Narnia **Obv:** Head with tiara right **Rev:** Mr. Tumnus

Date	Mintage	F	VF	XF	Unc	BU
2006(c)	20,000	—	—	—	—	6.00

KM# 284 50 CENTS

Aluminum-Bronze, 38.74 mm. **Ruler:** Elizabeth II **Subject:** Narnia **Obv:** Head with tiara right **Rev:** Ginarrbrik

Date	Mintage	F	VF	XF	Unc	BU
2006(c)	20,000	—	—	—	—	6.00

KM# 120 DOLLAR

8.0000 g., Aluminum-Bronze, 23 mm. **Ruler:** Elizabeth II **Obv:** Head with tiara right **Rev:** Kiwi bird within sprigs, value below **Edge:** Segmented reeding

Date	Mintage	F	VF	XF	Unc	BU
2001(c) In sets only	2,910	—	—	—	—	4.00
2001(c) Proof	1,364	Value: 5.00				
2002(l)	8,000,000	—	—	—	1.00	2.50
2002(c) In sets only	4,000	—	—	—	—	4.00
2002(c) Proof	1,500	Value: 5.00				
2003(l)	4,000,000	—	—	—	1.00	2.50
2003(c) In sets only	5,000	—	—	—	—	4.00
2003(c) Proof	1,750	Value: 5.00				
2004(l)	2,700,000	—	—	—	1.00	2.50
2004(c) In sets only	3,500	—	—	—	—	4.00
2004(c) Proof	2,250	Value: 5.00				
2005(l)	2,000,000	—	—	—	1.00	2.50
2005(c) In sets only	4,000	—	—	—	—	4.00
2005(c) Proof	2,250	Value: 5.00				
2006(c) In sets only	3,000	—	—	—	—	4.00
2006(c) Proof	2,100	Value: 5.00				
2007(c)	5,000	—	—	—	—	4.00
2007(c) Proof	3,500	Value: 5.00				
2008(l)	6,000,000	—	—	—	1.00	2.50
2008(l) In sets only	4,000	—	—	—	—	4.00
2008(l) Proof	3,000	Value: 5.00				
2009(w) In sets only	2,000	—	—	—	—	4.00
2009(w) Proof	1,500	Value: 5.00				
2010 In sets only	2,000	—	—	—	—	4.00
2010 Proof	—	Value: 5.00				
2011(o) In sets only	2,000	—	—	—	—	4.00
2011(o) Proof	—	Value: 5.00				
2012(u)	—	—	—	—	—	4.00
2012(u) Proof	—	Value: 5.00				

KM# 141 DOLLAR

28.2800 g., Aluminum-Bronze, 38.61 mm. **Ruler:** Elizabeth II **Subject:** Lord of the Rings **Obv:** Head with tiara right **Rev:** Inscribed ring around value **Edge:** Reeded

Date	Mintage	F	VF	XF	Unc	BU
2003(l)	30,081	—	—	—	—	15.00

Note: Mintage includes 10,454 in sets.

KM# 141a DOLLAR

28.2800 g., 0.9250 Silver 0.8410 oz. ASW, 38.61 mm. **Ruler:** Elizabeth II **Obv:** Head with tiara right **Rev:** Gold-plated ring and edge **Edge:** Reeded

Date	Mintage	F	VF	XF	Unc	BU
2003(l) Proof	39,244	Value: 70.00				

KM# 142 DOLLAR

28.2800 g., Aluminum-Bronze, 38.61 mm. **Ruler:** Elizabeth II **Subject:** Lord of the Rings **Obv:** Head with tiara right **Rev:** Head of Frodo looking down above inscription **Edge:** Reeded

Date	Mintage	F	VF	XF	Unc	BU
2003(l)	10,454	—	—	—	—	10.00

KM# 143 DOLLAR

28.2800 g., Aluminum-Bronze, 38.61 mm. **Ruler:** Elizabeth II

Subject: Lord of the Rings **Obv:** Head with tiara right **Rev:** View of Sauron, value **Edge:** Reeded

Date	Mintage	F	VF	XF	Unc	BU
2003(I)	10,454	—	—	—	—	10.00

KM# 247   DOLLAR
28.2800 g., 0.9250 Silver 0.8410 oz. ASW, 38.61 mm. **Ruler:** Elizabeth II **Subject:** Lord of the Rings **Obv:** Head with tiara right **Rev:** Aragorn's Coronation

Date	Mintage	F	VF	XF	Unc	BU
2003(I) Proof	3,057	Value: 70.00				

KM# 248   DOLLAR
28.2800 g., 0.9250 Silver 0.8410 oz. ASW, 38.61 mm. **Ruler:** Elizabeth II **Subject:** Lord of the Rings **Obv:** Head with tiara right **Rev:** King Theoden

Date	Mintage	F	VF	XF	Unc	BU
2003(I) Proof	2,022	Value: 70.00				

KM# 249   DOLLAR
28.2800 g., 0.9250 Silver 0.8410 oz. ASW, 38.61 mm. **Ruler:** Elizabeth II **Subject:** Lord of the Rings **Obv:** Head with tiara right **Rev:** Flight to the Ford

Date	Mintage	F	VF	XF	Unc	BU
2003(I) Proof	2,020	Value: 70.00				

KM# 250   DOLLAR
28.2800 g., 0.9250 Silver 0.8410 oz. ASW, 38.61 mm. **Ruler:** Elizabeth II **Subject:** Lord of the Rings **Obv:** Head with tiara right **Rev:** Mirror of Galadriel

Date	Mintage	F	VF	XF	Unc	BU
2003(I) Proof	2,036	Value: 70.00				

KM# 251   DOLLAR
28.2800 g., 0.9250 Silver 0.8410 oz. ASW, 38.61 mm. **Ruler:** Elizabeth II **Subject:** Lord of the Rings **Obv:** Head with tiara right **Rev:** Frodo offering ring to Nazgul

Date	Mintage	F	VF	XF	Unc	BU
2003(I) Proof	1,784	Value: 70.00				

KM# 252   DOLLAR
28.2800 g., 0.9250 Silver 0.8410 oz. ASW, 38.61 mm. **Ruler:** Elizabeth II **Subject:** Lord of the Rings **Obv:** Head with tiara right **Rev:** Bridge of Kazad-Dum

Date	Mintage	F	VF	XF	Unc	BU
2003(I) Proof	952	Value: 70.00				

KM# 253   DOLLAR
28.2800 g., 0.9250 Silver 0.8410 oz. ASW, 38.61 mm. **Ruler:** Elizabeth II **Subject:** Lord of the Rings **Obv:** Head with tiara right **Rev:** Shelob's Lair

Date	Mintage	F	VF	XF	Unc	BU
2003(I) Proof	917	Value: 70.00				

KM# 254   DOLLAR
28.2800 g., 0.9250 Silver 0.8410 oz. ASW, 38.61 mm. **Ruler:** Elizabeth II **Subject:** Lord of the Rings **Obv:** Head with tiara right **Rev:** Taming of Smeagol

Date	Mintage	F	VF	XF	Unc	BU
2003(I) Proof	1,017	Value: 70.00				

KM# 255   DOLLAR
28.2800 g., 0.9250 Silver 0.8410 oz. ASW, 38.61 mm. **Ruler:** Elizabeth II **Subject:** Lord of the Rings **Obv:** Head with tiara right **Rev:** Dark Lord's Tower and the Eye

Date	Mintage	F	VF	XF	Unc	BU
2003(I) Proof	1,002	Value: 70.00				

KM# 256   DOLLAR
28.2800 g., 0.9250 Silver 0.8410 oz. ASW, 38.61 mm. **Ruler:** Elizabeth II **Subject:** Lord of the Rings **Obv:** Head with tiara right **Rev:** Knife in the Dark

Date	Mintage	F	VF	XF	Unc	BU
2003(I) Proof	967	Value: 70.00				

KM# 257   DOLLAR
28.2800 g., 0.9250 Silver 0.8410 oz. ASW, 38.61 mm. **Ruler:** Elizabeth II **Subject:** Lord of the Rings **Obv:** Head with tiara right **Rev:** Gandalf and Saruman

Date	Mintage	F	VF	XF	Unc	BU
2003(I) Proof	867	Value: 70.00				

KM# 258   DOLLAR
28.2800 g., 0.9250 Silver 0.8410 oz. ASW, 38.61 mm. **Ruler:** Elizabeth II **Subject:** Lord of the Rings **Obv:** Head with tiara right **Rev:** Council of Elrond

Date	Mintage	F	VF	XF	Unc	BU
2003(I) Proof	1,204	Value: 70.00				

KM# 259 DOLLAR

28.2800 g., 0.9250 Silver 0.8410 oz. ASW, 38.61 mm. **Ruler:** Elizabeth II **Subject:** Lord of the Rings **Obv:** Head with tiara right **Rev:** Helm's Deep

Date	Mintage	F	VF	XF	Unc	BU
2003(I) Proof	967	Value: 70.00				

KM# 260 DOLLAR

28.2800 g., 0.9250 Silver 0.8410 oz. ASW, 38.61 mm. **Ruler:** Elizabeth II **Subject:** Lord of the Rings **Obv:** Head with tiara right **Rev:** Frodo & Co. at Mt. Doom

Date	Mintage	F	VF	XF	Unc	BU
2003(I) Proof	917	Value: 70.00				

KM# 261 DOLLAR

28.2800 g., 0.9250 Silver 0.8410 oz. ASW, 38.61 mm. **Ruler:** Elizabeth II **Subject:** Lord of the Rings **Obv:** Head with tiara right **Rev:** Departure of Boromir

Date	Mintage	F	VF	XF	Unc	BU
2003(I) Proof	917	Value: 70.00				

KM# 262 DOLLAR

28.2800 g., 0.9250 Silver 0.8410 oz. ASW, 38.61 mm. **Ruler:** Elizabeth II **Subject:** Lord of the Rings **Obv:** Head with tiara right **Rev:** Meeting of Treebeard

Date	Mintage	F	VF	XF	Unc	BU
2003(I) Proof	867	Value: 70.00				

KM# 263 DOLLAR

28.2800 g., 0.9250 Silver 0.8410 oz. ASW, 38.61 mm. **Ruler:** Elizabeth II **Subject:** Lord of the Rings **Obv:** Head with tiara right **Rev:** Battle of Minas Tirith / Pelenor Fields

Date	Mintage	F	VF	XF	Unc	BU
2003(I) Proof	867	Value: 70.00				

KM# 264 DOLLAR

28.2800 g., 0.9250 Silver 0.8410 oz. ASW, 38.61 mm. **Ruler:** Elizabeth II **Subject:** Lord of the Rings **Obv:** Head with tiara right **Rev:** Gandalf Reappears

Date	Mintage	F	VF	XF	Unc	BU
2003(I) Proof	967	Value: 70.00				

KM# 265 DOLLAR

28.2800 g., 0.9250 Silver 0.8410 oz. ASW, 38.61 mm. **Ruler:** Elizabeth II **Subject:** Lord of the Rings **Obv:** Head with tiara right **Rev:** Army of the Dead

Date	Mintage	F	VF	XF	Unc	BU
2003(I) Proof	917	Value: 70.00				

KM# 266 DOLLAR

28.2800 g., 0.9250 Silver 0.8410 oz. ASW, 38.61 mm. **Ruler:** Elizabeth II **Subject:** Lord of the Rings **Obv:** Head with tiara right **Rev:** Travel to the Undying Lands

Date	Mintage	F	VF	XF	Unc	BU
2003(I) Proof	867	Value: 70.00				

KM# 267 DOLLAR

28.2800 g., 0.9250 Silver 0.8410 oz. ASW, 38.61 mm. **Ruler:** Elizabeth II **Subject:** Lord of the Rings **Obv:** Head with tiara right **Rev:** Great River

Date	Mintage	F	VF	XF	Unc	BU
2003(I) Proof	867	Value: 70.00				

KM# 268 DOLLAR

28.2800 g., 0.9250 Silver 0.8410 oz. ASW, 38.61 mm. **Ruler:** Elizabeth II **Subject:** Lord of the Rings **Obv:** Head with tiara right **Rev:** Death of the Witch King

Date	Mintage	F	VF	XF	Unc	BU
2003(I) Proof	867	Value: 70.00				

KM# 269 DOLLAR

28.2800 g., 0.9250 Silver 0.8410 oz. ASW, 38.61 mm. **Ruler:** Elizabeth II **Subject:** Lord of the Rings **Obv:** Head with tiara right **Rev:** March of the Oliphants

Date	Mintage	F	VF	XF	Unc	BU
2003(I) Proof	867	Value: 70.00				

KM# 152 DOLLAR

31.1350 g., 0.9990 Silver 1.0000 oz. ASW, 40 mm. **Ruler:** Elizabeth II **Obv:** Crowned head right **Rev:** Little spotted kiwi **Edge:** Reeded

Date	Mintage	F	VF	XF	Unc	BU
2004(c)	2,500	—	—	—	—	45.00
2004(c) Proof	2,000	Value: 50.00				

Note: Includes 500 struck in 2008 for sets.

KM# 157 DOLLAR

Aluminum-Bronze, 38.74 mm. **Ruler:** Elizabeth II **Subject:** ANZAC **Obv:** Crowned head right **Rev:** Soldiers from Chun uk Bair battle with rifles and bayonets **Edge:** Reeded

Date	Mintage	F	VF	XF	Unc	BU
2005 Proof	15,000	Value: 25.00				

KM# 153   DOLLAR
31.6350 g., 0.9990 Silver 1.0160 oz. ASW, 40.6 mm.   **Ruler:** Elizabeth II **Obv:** Crowned head right **Rev:** Rowi Kiwi **Edge:** Reeded

Date	Mintage	F	VF	XF	Unc	BU
2005(w)	10,000	—	—	—	—	45.00
2005(w)	4,000	Value: 60.00				

KM# 153a   DOLLAR
31.6350 g., 0.9990 Silver 1.0160 oz. ASW, 38.74 mm.   **Ruler:** Elizabeth II **Rev:** Kiwi

Date	Mintage	F	VF	XF	Unc	BU
2005(w) Proof	2,700	Value: 80.00				

Note: Mintage includes 500 struck in 2008 for sets.

Date	Mintage	F	VF	XF	Unc	BU
2005(w) Proof	5,000	Value: 50.00				

Note: Each has different packaging.

KM# 154   DOLLAR
31.1350 g., 0.9990 Silver 1.0000 oz. ASW, 40 mm.   **Ruler:** Elizabeth II **Subject:** ANZAC **Obv:** Crowned head right **Rev:** Soldiers seated, multicolor flag in background **Edge:** Reeded

Date	Mintage	F	VF	XF	Unc	BU
2005 P Proof	15,000	Value: 110				

KM# 156   DOLLAR
28.2800 g., Aluminum-Bronze, 38.61 mm.   **Ruler:** Elizabeth II **Subject:** Lions Rugby Tour **Obv:** Crowned head right **Rev:** Rugby player, Lions crest and New Zealand map

Date	Mintage	F	VF	XF	Unc	BU
2005(l)	15,000	—	—	—	—	20.00

KM# 156a   DOLLAR
28.2800 g., 0.9250 Silver 0.8410 oz. ASW, 38.61 mm.   **Ruler:** Elizabeth II **Series:** Rugby player, Lions crest & New Zealand map **Subject:** Lions Rugby Tour **Obv:** Crowned head right **Edge:** Reeded

Date	Mintage	F	VF	XF	Unc	BU
2005(l) Proof	5,000	Value: 50.00				

KM# 159   DOLLAR
20.0000 g., Aluminum-Bronze, 38.74 mm.   **Ruler:** Elizabeth II **Subject:** King Kong **Obv:** Crowned head right **Rev:** King Kong **Edge:** Reeded

Date	Mintage	F	VF	XF	Unc	BU
2005(w)	7,000	—	—	—	—	20.00

KM# 160   DOLLAR
20.0000 g., Aluminum-Bronze, 38.74 mm.   **Ruler:** Elizabeth II **Subject:** King Kong **Obv:** Crowned head right **Rev:** Multicolored King Kong **Edge:** Reeded

Date	Mintage	F	VF	XF	Unc	BU
2005(w)	4,000	—	—	—	—	35.00

KM# 161   DOLLAR
20.0000 g., Aluminum-Bronze, 38.74 mm.   **Ruler:** Elizabeth II **Subject:** King Kong **Obv:** Crowned head right **Rev:** Carl Denham and camera in multicolor **Edge:** Reeded

Date	Mintage	F	VF	XF	Unc	BU
2005	4,000	—	—	—	—	35.00

KM# 162   DOLLAR
20.0000 g., Aluminum-Bronze, 38.74 mm.   **Ruler:** Elizabeth II **Subject:** King Kong **Obv:** Crowned head right **Rev:** Ann Darrow and Jack Driscoll multicolored **Edge:** Reeded

Date	Mintage	F	VF	XF	Unc	BU
2005	4,000	—	—	—	—	35.00

KM# 164   DOLLAR
31.1350 g., 0.9990 Silver partially gold plated 1.0000 oz. ASW, 40.6 mm.   **Ruler:** Elizabeth II **Obv:** Crowned head right **Rev:** King Kong partially gold plated

Date	Mintage	F	VF	XF	Unc	BU
2005(w) Proof	3,000	Value: 70.00				

KM# 276   DOLLAR
20.0000 g., Aluminum-Bronze, 38.74 mm.   **Ruler:** Elizabeth II **Subject:** Emblem **Obv:** Head with tiara right **Rev:** Rowi and chick inside patterned ring

Date	Mintage	F	VF	XF	Unc	BU
2005(w)	20,000	—	—	—	—	25.00

KM# 158   DOLLAR
28.2800 g., 0.9990 Silver 0.9083 oz. ASW, 38.61 mm.   **Ruler:** Elizabeth II **Subject:** FIFA **Obv:** Crowned head right **Rev:** Soccer player, silver fern and map

Date	Mintage	F	VF	XF	Unc	BU
2006(v) Proof	7,500	Value: 50.00				

KM# 285   DOLLAR
31.1000 g., 0.9990 Silver with gold highlights 0.9988 oz. ASW, 40 mm.   **Ruler:** Elizabeth II **Subject:** Narnia **Obv:** Head with tiara right **Rev:** White Witch

Date	Mintage	F	VF	XF	Unc	BU
2006(c) Proof	2,000	Value: 70.00				

KM# 286   DOLLAR
20.0000 g., Aluminum-Bronze, 38.74 mm.   **Ruler:** Elizabeth II **Subject:** Narnia **Obv:** Head with tiara right **Rev:** Asian, lion standing right

Date	Mintage	F	VF	XF	Unc	BU
2006(c)	8,000	—	—	—	—	20.00

KM# 287   DOLLAR
31.1350 g., 0.9990 Silver With Gold highlights 1.0000 oz. ASW, 40 mm.   **Ruler:** Elizabeth II **Subject:** Narnia **Obv:** Head with tiara right **Rev:** Asian

Date	Mintage	F	VF	XF	Unc	BU
2006(c) Proof	4,320	Value: 70.00				

KM# 288   DOLLAR
31.1350 g., 0.9990 Silver 1.0000 oz. ASW, 40 mm.   **Ruler:** Elizabeth II **Subject:** Narnia **Obv:** Head with tiara right **Rev:** Wardrobe from the Lion, Witch and Wardrobe series

Date	Mintage	F	VF	XF	Unc	BU
2006(c) Proof	1,000	Value: 70.00				

KM# 289   DOLLAR
20.0000 g., Aluminum-Bronze, 38.74 mm.   **Ruler:** Elizabeth II **Subject:** Queen's 80th birthday **Obv:** Head with tiara right **Rev:** Heraldic arms

Date	Mintage	F	VF	XF	Unc	BU
2006	2,000	—	—	—	—	30.00

KM# 290   DOLLAR
31.1350 g., 0.9990 Silver 1.0000 oz. ASW, 38.74 mm.   **Ruler:** Elizabeth II **Subject:** Queen's 80th birthday **Obv:** Head with tiara right **Rev:** Heraldic arms

Date	Mintage	F	VF	XF	Unc	BU
2006 Proof	1,500	—	—	—	—	

KM# 291   DOLLAR
31.1350 g., 0.9990 Silver 1.0000 oz. ASW, 40 mm.   **Ruler:** Elizabeth II **Obv:** Head with tiara right **Rev:** North Island Brown Kiwi **Edge:** Reeded

Date	Mintage	F	VF	XF	Unc	BU
2006(w)	3,000	—	—	—	—	50.00

KM# 291a   DOLLAR
31.1350 g., 0.9990 Silver 1.0000 oz. ASW, 40 mm.   **Ruler:** Elizabeth II **Obv:** Head with tiara right **Rev:** North Island Brown Kiwi **Edge:** Reeded

Date	Mintage	F	VF	XF	Unc	BU
2006(w) Proof	2,000	Value: 80.00				

Note: Mintage includes 500 struck in 2008 for sets.

KM# 293   DOLLAR
20.0000 g., Aluminum-Bronze, 38.74 mm.   **Ruler:** Elizabeth II **Subject:** NZ Gold Rushes - West Coast **Obv:** Head with tiara right **Rev:** 1860s miners

Date	Mintage	F	VF	XF	Unc	BU
2006(w)	1,500	—	—	—	—	30.00

KM# 294   DOLLAR
31.1350 g., 0.9990 Silver with gold highlights 1.0000 oz. ASW, 40.60 mm.   **Ruler:** Elizabeth II **Subject:** NZ Gold Rushes - Thames/Coromandel **Obv:** Head with tiara right **Rev:** Gold panning

Date	Mintage	F	VF	XF	Unc	BU
2006(w) Proof	3,000	Value: 90.00				

KM# 232   DOLLAR
31.1350 g., 0.9990 Silver 1.0000 oz. ASW, 40 mm.   **Ruler:** Elizabeth II **Subject:** Aoraki - Mount Cook, Japanese Friendship **Obv:** Head with tiara right **Obv. Legend:** NEW ZEALAND - ELIZABETH II **Rev:** Flowers in bloom, Mount Cook in background multicolor **Note:** Also released in a Japanese proof set.

Date	Mintage	F	VF	XF	Unc	BU
2007(j) Proof	70,000	Value: 90.00				

KM# 296   DOLLAR
1.2440 g., 0.9990 Gold 0.0400 oz. AGW, 13.92 mm.   **Ruler:** Elizabeth II **Subject:** 50th anniversary of Scott Base **Obv:** Head with tiara right **Rev:** Scott Base, Antarctica and International Polar Year logo

Date	Mintage	F	VF	XF	Unc	BU
2007(m) Proof	10,000	Value: 100				

KM# 297   DOLLAR
31.1350 g., 0.9990 Silver 1.0000 oz. ASW, 40 mm.   **Ruler:** Elizabeth II **Subject:** 50th anniversary of Scott Base **Obv:** Head with tiara right **Rev:** Scott Base, Antarctica and International Polar Year logo

Date	Mintage	F	VF	XF	Unc	BU
2007(m) Proof	10,000	Value: 80.00				

KM# 298   DOLLAR
28.2800 g., 0.9250 Silver 0.8410 oz. ASW, 38.61 mm.   **Ruler:** Elizabeth II **Subject:** Scouting centenary **Obv:** Head with tiara right

Date	Mintage	F	VF	XF	Unc	BU
2007(l) Proof	1,500	Value: 80.00				

KM# 299   DOLLAR
28.2800 g., Copper-Nickel, 38.61 mm.   **Ruler:** Elizabeth II **Subject:** Scouting centenary **Obv:** Head with tiara right

Date	Mintage	F	VF	XF	Unc	BU
2007(l)	1,900	—	—	—	—	50.00

KM# 300 DOLLAR
31.1350 g., 0.9990 Silver 1.0000 oz. ASW, 40 mm. **Ruler:** Elizabeth II **Obv:** Head with tiara right **Rev:** Great Spotted Kiwi **Edge:** Reeded

Date	Mintage	F	VF	XF	Unc	BU
2007(m)	4,000	—	—	—	—	50.00

KM# 300a DOLLAR
31.1350 g., 0.9990 Silver 1.0000 oz. ASW, 40 mm. **Ruler:** Elizabeth II **Obv:** Head with tiara right **Rev:** Great Spotted Kiwi **Edge:** Reeded

Date	Mintage	F	VF	XF	Unc	BU
2007(m) Proof	3,000	Value: 100				

Note: Mintage includes 500 struck in 2008 for sets.

KM# 302 DOLLAR
31.1350 g., Copper-Nickel, 40 mm. **Ruler:** Elizabeth II **Subject:** Elizabeth & Philip Diamond Wedding **Obv:** Head with tiara right **Rev:** Royal crests **Edge:** Reeded

Date	Mintage	F	VF	XF	Unc	BU
2007(m)	1,600	—	—	—	—	30.00

KM# 302a DOLLAR
31.1050 g., 0.9990 Silver 0.9990 oz. ASW, 40 mm. **Ruler:** Elizabeth II **Subject:** Elizabeth & Philip Diamond Wedding **Obv:** Head with tiara right **Rev:** Royal crests **Edge:** Reeded

Date	Mintage	F	VF	XF	Unc	BU
2007(m) Proof	1,500	Value: 80.00				

KM# 321 DOLLAR
30.8000 g., Brass, 30 mm. **Ruler:** Elizabeth II **Rev:** Sir Edmond Hillary with Mt. Everest **Edge:** Reeded **Note:** Sold in a PNC cover only

Date	Mintage	F	VF	XF	Unc	BU
2008(w)	4,000	—	—	—	—	20.00

KM# 309 DOLLAR
31.1350 g., 0.9990 Silver 1.0000 oz. ASW, 40 mm. **Ruler:** Elizabeth II **Obv:** Head with tiara right **Rev:** Haast Tokoeka Kiwi

Date	Mintage	F	VF	XF	Unc	BU
2008(w)	8,000	—	—	—	—	60.00

KM# 309a DOLLAR
31.1350 g., 0.9990 Silver 1.0000 oz. ASW, 40 mm. **Ruler:** Elizabeth II **Obv:** Head with tiara right **Rev:** Haast Tokoeka Kiwi

Date	Mintage	F	VF	XF	Unc	BU
2008(w) Proof	5,000	Value: 85.00				

Note: Includes 500 for 2004-2008 sets.

KM# 311 DOLLAR
31.1350 g., 0.9990 Silver 1.0000 oz. ASW, 40.6 mm. **Ruler:** Elizabeth II **Subject:** Sir Edmund Hillary **Obv:** Head with tiara right **Rev:** Hillary with Mt. Everest in background

Date	Mintage	F	VF	XF	Unc	BU
2008(w) Proof	10,000	Value: 90.00				

KM# 322 DOLLAR
31.1350 g., 0.9990 Silver 1.0000 oz. ASW, 40 mm. **Ruler:** Elizabeth II **Subject:** Icons of New Zealand **Rev:** Kiwi with map of New Zealand **Edge:** Reeded

Date	Mintage	F	VF	XF	Unc	BU
2009(m)	10,000	—	—	—	—	50.00
2009(m) Proof	7,500	Value: 80.00				

KM# 323 DOLLAR
31.1350 g., 0.9990 Silver 1.0000 oz. ASW, 40 mm. **Ruler:** Elizabeth II **Obv:** Bust right **Rev:** Southern Right Whale **Edge:** Reeded

Date	Mintage	F	VF	XF	Unc	BU
2009(m) Prooflike	11,500	—	—	—	—	70.00

KM# 324 DOLLAR
31.1350 g., 0.9990 Silver 1.0000 oz. ASW, 40 mm. **Ruler:** Elizabeth II **Rev:** Haast's Eagle

Date	Mintage	F	VF	XF	Unc	BU
2009(m) Prooflike	11,500	—	—	—	—	80.00

KM# 325 DOLLAR
31.1350 g., 0.9990 Silver 1.0000 oz. ASW, 40 mm. **Ruler:** Elizabeth II **Rev:** Giant Moa

Date	Mintage	F	VF	XF	Unc	BU
2009(m) Prooflike	1,500	—	—	—	—	80.00

KM# 326 DOLLAR
31.1350 g., 0.9990 Silver 1.0000 oz. ASW, 40 mm. **Ruler:** Elizabeth II **Rev:** Colossal squid **Edge:** Reeded

Date	Mintage	F	VF	XF	Unc	BU
2009(m) Prooflike	1,500	—	—	—	—	80.00

KM# 327 DOLLAR
31.1350 g., 0.9990 Silver 1.0000 oz. ASW, 40 mm. **Ruler:** Elizabeth II **Rev:** Giant Weta **Edge:** Reeded

Date	Mintage	F	VF	XF	Unc	BU
2009(m) Prooflike	1,500	—	—	—	—	80.00

KM# 328 DOLLAR
26.4500 g., Copper-Nickel, 39.19 mm. **Ruler:** Elizabeth II **Subject:** Reserve Bank of New Zealand, 75th Anniversary **Rev:** Tui and Kowhai as on 1940-65 bronze penny

Date	Mintage	F	VF	XF	Unc	BU
2009(o)	2,000	—	—	—	—	30.00

KM# 331 DOLLAR
31.1050 g., 0.9990 Silver 0.9990 oz. ASW, 40 mm. **Ruler:** Elizabeth II **Subject:** Icons of New Zealand **Rev:** Kiwi and Southern Cross **Edge:** Reeded

Date	Mintage	F	VF	XF	Unc	BU
2010(m)	Est. 12,500	—	—	—	—	60.00
2010(m) Proof	Est. 8,500	Value: 90.00				

KM# 333 DOLLAR
31.1050 g., 0.9990 Silver 0.9990 oz. ASW, 40 mm. **Ruler:** Elizabeth II **Subject:** 2010 FIFA World Cup **Rev:** Soccer player with stylized NS koru **Edge:** Reeded

Date	Mintage	F	VF	XF	Unc	BU
2010	10,000	—	—	—	—	100

Note: Mintage includes 1500 in NZ Post packaging.

KM# 335 DOLLAR
31.1050 g., 0.9990 Silver 0.9990 oz. ASW, 40 mm. **Ruler:** Elizabeth II **Obv:** Head in tiara right **Rev:** Kiwi and fern

Date	Mintage	F	VF	XF	Unc	BU
2011 Proof	7,000	Value: 75.00				

KM# 121 2 DOLLARS
10.0000 g., Aluminum-Bronze, 26.5 mm. **Ruler:** Elizabeth II **Obv:** Head with tiara right **Rev:** White heron (kotuku) above value **Edge:** Reeded with groove

Date	Mintage	F	VF	XF	Unc	BU
2001(l)	3,000,000	—	—	—	2.50	5.00
2001(c) In sets only	2,910	—	—	—	—	6.00
2001(c) Proof	2,000	Value: 7.50				
2002(l)	6,000,000	—	—	—	2.50	5.00
2002(c) In sets only	3,000	—	—	—	—	6.00
2002(c) Proof	2,000	Value: 7.50				
2003(l)	6,000,000	—	—	—	2.50	5.00
2003(c) In sets only	3,000	—	—	—	—	6.00
2003(c) Proof	3,000	Value: 7.50				
2004(c) In sets only	2,800	—	—	—	—	5.00
2004 Proof	3,500	Value: 7.50				
2005(l)	5,000,000	—	—	—	2.50	5.00
2005(c) In sets only	3,000	—	—	—	—	6.00
2005(c) Proof	3,000	Value: 7.50				
2006(c) In sets only	3,000	—	—	—	—	6.00
2006(c) Proof	2,100	Value: 7.50				
2007(c)	5,000	—	—	—	—	6.00
2007(c) Proof	4,000	Value: 7.50				
2008(l) In sets only	4,000	—	—	—	—	6.00
2008(l) Proof	3,000	Value: 7.50				
2009(w) In sets only	2,000	—	—	—	—	6.00
2009(w) Proof	1,500	Value: 7.50				
2010 In sets only	2,000	—	—	—	—	6.00
2010 Proof	—	Value: 7.50				
2011(o)	8,000,000	—	—	—	2.50	5.00
2011(o) Proof	—	Value: 7.50				
2012(u)	—	—	—	—	—	6.00
2012(u) Proof	—	Value: 7.50				

KM# 128 5 DOLLARS
28.2800 g., Copper-Nickel, 38.6 mm. **Ruler:** Elizabeth II **Subject:** Kereru Bird **Obv:** Head with tiara right **Rev:** Wood Pigeon on branch **Edge:** Reeded

Date	Mintage	F	VF	XF	Unc	BU
2001(l)	1,500	—	—	—	25.00	—

KM# 128a 5 DOLLARS
28.2800 g., 0.9990 Silver 0.9083 oz. ASW **Ruler:** Elizabeth II **Obv:** Head with tiara right **Rev:** Pigeon on branch

Date	Mintage	F	VF	XF	Unc	BU
2001 Proof	1,000	Value: 80.00				

KM# 149 5 DOLLARS
28.2800 g., 0.9250 Silver 0.8410 oz. ASW, 38.6 mm. **Ruler:** Elizabeth II **Subject:** Royal Visit (canceled after coin issue) **Obv:** Head with tiara right **Rev:** Queen with flowers and two girls **Edge:** Reeded

Date	Mintage	F	VF	XF	Unc	BU
2001 Proof	2,000	Value: 100				

Note: 200 issued in stamp cover

KM# 131 5 DOLLARS
28.2800 g., Copper-Nickel, 38.6 mm. **Ruler:** Elizabeth II **Subject:** Architectural Heritage **Obv:** Head with tiara right **Rev:** Auckland Sky Tower **Edge:** Reeded

Date	Mintage	F	VF	XF	Unc	BU
2002(l)	3,000	—	—	—	12.50	—

Note: 500 pieces were housed in a stamp cover

KM# 131a 5 DOLLARS
28.2800 g., 0.9250 Silver 0.8410 oz. ASW, 38.6 mm. **Ruler:** Elizabeth II **Subject:** Architectural Heritage **Obv:** Head with tiara right **Rev:** Auckland Sky Tower **Edge:** Reeded

Date	Mintage	F	VF	XF	Unc	BU
2002(l)	2,000	Value: 40.00				

Note: 500 pieces were housed in a stamp cover

KM# 145 5 DOLLARS
27.2200 g., Copper-Nickel, 38.74 mm. **Ruler:** Elizabeth II **Obv:** Head with tiara right **Rev:** Hector's Dolphins jumping out of the water **Edge:** Reeded

Date	Mintage	F	VF	XF	Unc	BU
2002(c)	4,000	—	—	—	35.00	—

Note: 500 pieces were housed in a stamp covers

KM# 145a 5 DOLLARS
27.2220 g., 0.9990 Silver 0.8743 oz. ASW **Ruler:** Elizabeth II **Obv:** Head with tiara right **Rev:** Two Hector's Dolphins jumping out of the water **Edge:** Reeded

Date	Mintage	F	VF	XF	Unc	BU
2002(c)	Est. 2,000	—	—	—	—	100

Note: 500 in stamp covers

KM# 151 5 DOLLARS
28.2800 g., 0.9250 Silver Gilt 0.8410 oz. ASW, 38.61 mm. **Ruler:** Elizabeth II **Subject:** Queen's Jubilee **Obv:** Gilt head with tiara right **Rev:** Scepter with "Great Star of Africa' at left of vertical band with crowns and shields **Edge:** Reeded

Date	Mintage	F	VF	XF	Unc	BU
2002(l) Proof	25,000	Value: 80.00				

Note: 100 pieces were housed in a stamp cover, value $85

KM# 272a 5 DOLLARS
28.2800 g., 0.9250 Silver 0.8410 oz. ASW, 38.61 mm. **Ruler:** Elizabeth II **Subject:** America's Cup **Obv:** Head with tiara right **Rev:** Yachts

Date	Mintage	F	VF	XF	Unc	BU
2002(l) Proof	4,000	Value: 50.00				

Note: Includes 500 in stamp cover, value $50.

KM# 272   5 DOLLARS
28.2800 g., Copper-Nickel, 38.61 mm. **Ruler:** Elizabeth II
Subject: America's cup

Date	Mintage	F	VF	XF	Unc	BU
2002(l)	6,000	—	—	—	—	20.00

KM# 132   5 DOLLARS
26.7000 g., Copper-Nickel, 38.6 mm. **Ruler:** Elizabeth II **Obv:**
Head with tiara right **Rev:** Giant Kokopu fish divides circle **Edge:**
Reeded

Date	Mintage	F	VF	XF	Unc	BU
2003(c)	2,400	—	—	—	14.00	27.50

Note: Includes 400 issued in a stamp cover.

KM# 132a   5 DOLLARS
28.2800 g., 0.9990 Silver Gold plated 0.9083 oz. ASW, 38.6 mm.
Ruler: Elizabeth II **Obv:** Head with tiara right **Rev:** Giant Kokopu
fish **Edge:** Reeded

Date	Mintage	F	VF	XF	Unc	BU
2003(c) Proof	1,700	Value: 75.00				

Note: Includes 200 issued in a stamp cover

KM# 133   5 DOLLARS
26.7200 g., Copper-Nickel, 38.6 mm. **Ruler:** Elizabeth II
Subject: Chatham Island Taiko **Obv:** Head with tiara right **Rev:**
Magenta Petrel **Edge:** Reeded

Date	Mintage	F	VF	XF	Unc	BU
2004(2003)	1,350	—	—	—	—	35.00

KM# 147   5 DOLLARS
28.2300 g., 0.9250 Silver 0.8395 oz. ASW, 38.6 mm. **Ruler:**
Elizabeth II **Subject:** 50th Anniversary of Coronation **Obv:** Gold
plated crowned head right **Rev:** Crown above fern and flowers
Edge: Reeded

Date	Mintage	F	VF	XF	Unc	BU
2003 Proof	25,000	Value: 80.00				

Note: Includes 100 issued in a stamp cover

KM# 133a   5 DOLLARS
28.2800 g., 0.9990 Silver 0.9083 oz. ASW, 38.74 mm. **Ruler:**
Elizabeth II **Obv:** Head with tiara right **Rev:** Chatham Island Taiko

Date	Mintage	F	VF	XF	Unc	BU
2004 Proof	1,300	Value: 60.00				

KM# 146   5 DOLLARS
27.2200 g., Copper-Nickel, 38.74 mm. **Ruler:** Elizabeth II **Obv:**
Head with tiara right **Rev:** Fiordland Crested Penguin **Edge:**
Reeded

Date	Mintage	F	VF	XF	Unc	BU
2005(2004)	4,000	—	—	—	25.00	30.00

KM# 146a   5 DOLLARS
27.2200 g., 0.9990 Silver 0.8742 oz. ASW, 38.74 mm. **Ruler:**
Elizabeth II **Obv:** Head with tiara right **Rev:** Fiordland Crested
Penguin **Edge:** Reeded

Date	Mintage	F	VF	XF	Unc	BU
2005	3,500	—	—	—	—	50.00

KM# 148   5 DOLLARS
27.2200 g., Copper-Nickel, 38.74 mm. **Ruler:** Elizabeth II **Obv:**
Head with tiara right **Rev:** Falcon on tree stump **Edge:** Reeded

Date	Mintage	F	VF	XF	Unc	BU
2006	4,000	—	—	—	25.00	30.00

KM# 148a   5 DOLLARS
28.2800 g., 0.9990 Silver 0.9083 oz. ASW, 38.74 mm. **Ruler:**
Elizabeth II **Obv:** Head with tiara right **Rev:** New Zealand Falcon
on tree stump **Edge:** Reeded

Date	Mintage	F	VF	XF	Unc	BU
2006 Proof	2,500	Value: 50.00				

KM# 150   5 DOLLARS
27.2200 g., Copper-Nickel, 38.74 mm. **Ruler:** Elizabeth II
Subject: Tuatara **Obv:** Head with tiara right **Rev:** Tuatara
(Sphenodon punctatus), a lizard-like reptile **Edge:** Reeded

Date	Mintage	F	VF	XF	Unc	BU
2007(c)	3,000	—	—	—	25.00	30.00

KM# 150a   5 DOLLARS
28.2800 g., 0.9990 Silver 0.9083 oz. ASW, 38.74 mm. **Ruler:**
Elizabeth II **Subject:** Tuatara **Obv:** Head with tiara right **Rev:**
Tuatara right **Edge:** Reeded

Date	Mintage	F	VF	XF	Unc	BU
2007(c) Proof	4,000	Value: 80.00				

KM# 233   5 DOLLARS
28.2800 g., 0.9990 Silver 0.9083 oz. ASW, 38.6 mm. **Ruler:**
Elizabeth II **Subject:** Hamilton's frog **Obv:** Head with tiara right
Obv. Legend: NEW ZEALAND - ELIZABETH II **Rev:** Frog
perched on branch at left center

Date	Mintage	F	VF	XF	Unc	BU
2008	4,000	—	—	—	35.00	40.00

KM# 233a   5 DOLLARS
28.2800 g., 0.9990 Silver 0.9083 oz. ASW, 38.61 mm. **Ruler:**
Elizabeth II **Rev:** Hamilton's frog **Edge:** Reeded

Date	Mintage	F	VF	XF	Unc	BU
2008(l) Proof	4,000	Value: 90.00				

Note: Mintage includes 1500 struck in 2009

KM# 329   5 DOLLARS
22.0000 g., Copper-Nickel, 38.60 mm. **Ruler:** Elizabeth II **Rev:**
Kakapo **Edge:** Reeded

Date	Mintage	F	VF	XF	Unc	BU
2009(w)	2,000	—	—	—	25.00	30.00

KM# 329a   5 DOLLARS
31.1350 g., 0.9990 Silver 1.0000 oz. ASW, 38.61 mm. **Ruler:**
Elizabeth II **Rev:** Kakapo

Date	Mintage	F	VF	XF	Unc	BU
2009(w) Proof	4,000	Value: 90.00				

KM# 334   5 DOLLARS
31.1000 g., Copper-Nickel, 38.7 mm. **Ruler:** Elizabeth II **Series:**
Maui's Dolphin, subspecies of the Hector Dolphin **Rev:** Dolphin
jumping right **Edge:** Reeded

Date	Mintage	F	VF	XF	Unc	BU
2010	2,000	—	—	—	—	35.00

KM# 129   10 DOLLARS
3.8879 g., 0.9990 Gold 0.1249 oz. AGW, 18 mm. **Ruler:**
Elizabeth II **Obv:** Head with tiara right **Rev:** Salvage ship above
value **Edge:** Reeded

Date	Mintage	F	VF	XF	Unc	BU
2001 Proof	600	Value: 275				

KM# 130   10 DOLLARS
7.7759 g., 0.9990 Gold 0.2497 oz. AGW, 22 mm. **Ruler:**
Elizabeth II **Obv:** Head with tiara right **Rev:** Ship above value
Edge: Reeded

Date	Mintage	F	VF	XF	Unc	BU
2001 Proof	600	Value: 525				

KM# 273   10 DOLLARS
Nickel-Brass gold plated, 28.4 mm. **Ruler:** Elizabeth II **Subject:**
America's Cup **Obv:** Head with tiara right **Rev:** Map, cup and
yachts

Date	Mintage	F	VF	XF	Unc	BU
2002(l)	5,000	—	—	—	—	45.00

KM# 274   10 DOLLARS
15.5520 g., 0.9990 Gold 0.4995 oz. AGW, 28.4 mm. **Ruler:**
Elizabeth II **Subject:** America's Cup **Obv:** Head with tiara right
Rev: Map, cup and yachts

Date	Mintage	F	VF	XF	Unc	BU
2002(l) Proof	900	Value: 950				

KM# 144   10 DOLLARS
39.9400 g., 0.9170 Gold 1.1775 oz. AGW, 38.61 mm. **Ruler:**

Elizabeth II **Subject:** Lord of the Rings **Obv:** Head with tiara right **Rev:** The One Ring **Edge:** Reeded

Date	Mintage	F	VF	XF	Unc	BU
2003(I) Proof	1,198	Value: 2,150				

KM# 270 10 DOLLARS
39.9400 g., 0.9170 Gold 1.1775 oz. AGW, 38.61 mm. **Ruler:** Elizabeth II **Subject:** Lord of the Rings **Obv:** Head with tiara right **Rev:** Frodo **Edge:** Reeded

Date	Mintage	F	VF	XF	Unc	BU
2003(I) Proof	142	Value: 2,150				

KM# 271 10 DOLLARS
39.9400 g., 0.9170 Gold 1.1775 oz. AGW, 38.61 mm. **Ruler:** Elizabeth II **Subject:** Lord of the Rings **Obv:** Head with tiara right **Rev:** Sauron **Edge:** Reeded

Date	Mintage	F	VF	XF	Unc	BU
2003(I) Proof	142	Value: 2,150				

KM# 275 10 DOLLARS
38.5000 g., 0.9170 Gold 1.1350 oz. AGW, 38.61 mm. **Ruler:** Elizabeth II **Subject:** Pukaki **Obv:** Head with tiara right **Rev:** Statue of Pukaki **Edge:** Reeded

Date	Mintage	F	VF	XF	Unc	BU
2004(I) Proof	300	Value: 3,500				
2004(I) NW RB Proof	2	—	—	—	—	—

Note: Initials added for presention to Ngati Whakaue (Maori tribe) and the Reserve Bank.

KM# 165 10 DOLLARS
7.9880 g., 0.9170 Gold 0.2355 oz. AGW, 22.05 mm. **Ruler:** Elizabeth II **Subject:** Lions Rugby Tour **Obv:** Crowned head right **Edge:** Reeded

Date	Mintage	F	VF	XF	Unc	BU
2005(I) Proof	1,000	Value: 475				

KM# 155 10 DOLLARS
7.7500 g., 0.9990 Gold 0.2489 oz. AGW, 17.53 mm. **Ruler:** Elizabeth II **Subject:** ANZAC **Obv:** Crowned head right **Rev:** New Zealand soldier playing bugle in front of War Memorial **Edge:** Reeded

Date	Mintage	F	VF	XF	Unc	BU
2005	1,000	—	—	—	—	475

KM# 295 10 DOLLARS
31.1350 g., 0.9990 Gold 1.0000 oz. AGW, 34 mm. **Ruler:** Elizabeth II **Subject:** Narnia **Obv:** Head with tiara right **Rev:** Asian

Date	Mintage	F	VF	XF	Unc	BU
2006 Proof	365	Value: 1,850				

KM# 307 10 DOLLARS
7.7770 g., 0.9990 Gold 0.2498 oz. AGW, 20 mm. **Ruler:** Elizabeth II **Subject:** Queen's 80th birthday **Obv:** Head with tiara right **Rev:** Heraldic arms

Date	Mintage	F	VF	XF	Unc	BU
2006 Proof	500	Value: 475				

KM# 308 10 DOLLARS
15.5540 g., 0.9990 Gold 0.4996 oz. AGW, 25.10 mm. **Ruler:** Elizabeth II **Subject:** Gold Rushes - Otago **Obv:** Head with tiara right **Rev:** Picks, shovels and nuggets

Date	Mintage	F	VF	XF	Unc	BU
2006(w) Proof	500	Value: 950				

KM# 304 10 DOLLARS
7.7750 g., 0.9990 Gold 0.2497 oz. AGW, 26 mm. **Ruler:** Elizabeth II **Subject:** Elizabeth & Philip Diamond Wedding Anniversary **Obv:** Head with tiara right **Rev:** Royal crests

Date	Mintage	F	VF	XF	Unc	BU
2007(m) Proof	300	Value: 500				

KM# 305 10 DOLLARS
31.1350 g., 0.9170 Gold 0.9179 oz. AGW, 38.61 mm. **Ruler:** Elizabeth II **Subject:** Scouting centenary **Obv:** Head with tiara right

Date	Mintage	F	VF	XF	Unc	BU
2007(I) Proof	150	Value: 1,850				

KM# 306 10 DOLLARS
7.7855 g., 0.9990 Gold 0.2500 oz. AGW, 20.6 mm. **Ruler:** Elizabeth II **Subject:** Sir Edmund Hilary **Obv:** Head with tiara right **Rev:** Ed Hilary with Mt. Everest in background

Date	Mintage	F	VF	XF	Unc	BU
2008(w) Proof	1,953	Value: 525				

KM# 330 10 DOLLARS
7.7750 g., 0.9990 Gold 0.2497 oz. AGW, 26 mm. **Ruler:** Elizabeth II **Subject:** Icons of New Zealand **Rev:** Kiwi and map of New Zealand **Edge:** Reeded

Date	Mintage	F	VF	XF	Unc	BU
2009(m) Proof	1,500	Value: 575				

KM# 332 10 DOLLARS
7.7750 g., 0.9990 Gold 0.2497 oz. AGW, 26. mm. **Ruler:** Elizabeth II **Subject:** Icons of New Zealand **Rev:** Kiwi and Southern Cross **Edge:** Reeded

Date	Mintage	F	VF	XF	Unc	BU
2010(m) Proof	1,800	Value: 575				

MINT SETS

KM#	Date	Mintage	Identification	Issue Price	Mkt Val
MS50	2001 (7)	2,910	KM#116-121, 128	18.50	70.00
MS51	2002 (7)	3,000	KM#116-121, 145. Hector's dolphin.	18.00	60.00
MS52	2003 (7)	3,000	KM#116-121, 132. Giant Kokopu.	18.00	75.00
MS53	2003 (6)	34,332	KM#135-140. Lord of the Rings, Light vs. Dark set.	19.95	100
MS54	2003 (9)	2,821	KM#135-137; 235-240. Fellowship of the Ring.	—	175
MS55	2003 (18)	4,068	KM#135-140; 235-246. Lord of the Rings. Character collection.	—	325
MS56	2003 (3)	10,454	KM#141, 142, 143. Lord of the Rings. Battle for the Ring set.	29.95	35.00
MS57	2004 (7)	2,800	KM#116-121, 133. Taiko.	33.00	150
MS58	2005 (7)	3,000	KM#116-121; 146. Crested Penguin.	33.00	120
MS59	2006 (7)	3,000	KM#116-121; 148. Falcon.	33.00	110
MS60	2003-5-6 (7)	5,000	Mixed Set for Change over to smaller size coins. KM#116 (2003); 117-119 (2005); KM#117a-119a (2006).	7.50	70.00
MS61	2007 (6)	5,000	KM#117a-119a; 120-121; 150. Tuatara.	33.00	60.00
MS62	2008 (6)	4,000	KM#117a-119a; 120-121; 233. Hamilton's frog.	37.50	70.00
MS63	2009 (6)	2,000	KM#117a-119a; 120-121; 329. Kakapo.	—	60.00
MS64	2009 (5)	1,500	KM#323-327. Giants of New Zealand.	—	400

PROOF SETS

KM#	Date	Mintage	Identification	Issue Price	Mkt Val
PS45	2001 (7)	1,366	KM#116-121, 128a	49.25	125
PS46	2001 (2)	600	KM#129-130	400	575
PS47	2001 (7)	1,500	KM#116-121, 128a	60.00	125
PS48	2003 (1)	810	KM#141a and 5 others.	—	350
PS49	2003	—	Five coins as per PS48, less 141a	—	—
PS50	2003 (3)	133	KM#144; 270; 271. Lord of the Rings. Gold set.	—	5,750
PS51	2003 (2)	9	KM#270; 271. Lord of the Rings.	—	4,000
PS52	2003 (7)	1,496	KM#116-121, 132a.	60.00	125
PS53	2004 (7)	1,750	KM#116-121, 133. Chatham Islands Taiko	—	200
PS54	2005 (7)	2,250	KM#116-121; 146a. Crested Penguin.	88.00	120
PS55	2006 (7)	2,100	KM#116-121; 148a. Falcon.	90.00	125
PS56	2006 (3)	1,000	KM#285; 287; 288.	—	225
PS57	2007 (6)	3,500	KM#117a-119a; 120-121; 150a. Tuatara.	88.00	120
PS58	2007 (7)	69,000	KM#232, NZ Aoraki dollar and Japan 95.2; 96.2; 97.2; 98.2; 101.2; 125.	115	125
PS59	2008 (6)	3,000	KM#117a-119a; 120-121; 233a. Hamilton's frog.	94.00	125
PS60	2004-08 (5)	500	KM#152; 153a; 291a; 300a; 309a. Kiwi.	375	450
PS61	2009 (6)	1,500	KM#117a-119a; 120-121; 329a. Kakapo.	—	125

NICARAGUA

The Republic of Nicaragua, situated in Central America between Honduras and Costa Rica, has an area of 50,193 sq. mi. (129,494 sq. km.) and a population of *3.7 million. Capital: Managua. Agriculture, mining (gold and silver) and hardwood logging are the principal industries. Cotton, meat, coffee and sugar are exported.

MONETARY SYSTEM
100 Centavos = 1 Cordoba

REPUBLIC
DECIMAL COINAGE

KM# 97 5 CENTAVOS
3.0000 g., Copper Plated Steel, 18.5 mm. **Obv:** National arms **Rev:** Value within circle **Edge:** Plain

Date	Mintage	F	VF	XF	Unc	BU
2002	—	—	—	—	0.25	0.50

KM# 98 10 CENTAVOS
4.0000 g., Brass Plated Steel, 20.5 mm. **Obv:** National arms **Rev:** Value within circle **Edge:** Reeded and plain sections

Date	Mintage	F	VF	XF	Unc	BU
2002	—	—	—	—	0.45	0.85

KM# 105 10 CENTAVOS
Aluminum, 20.5 mm. **Obv:** National arms **Rev:** Value at center

Date	Mintage	F	VF	XF	Unc	BU
2007	—	—	—	—	0.45	0.85

KM# 99 25 CENTAVOS
5.0000 g., Brass Plated Steel, 23.25 mm. **Obv:** National arms **Rev:** Value within circle **Edge:** Segmented reeding

Date	Mintage	F	VF	XF	Unc	BU
2002	—	—	—	—	0.65	1.25
2003	—	—	—	—	0.65	1.25
2007	—	—	—	—	0.65	1.25

KM# 104 25 CENTAVOS
Brass **Obv:** Arms **Rev:** Value at center **Rev. Legend:** EN DIOS CONFIAMOS

Date	Mintage	F	VF	XF	Unc	BU
2007	—	—	—	—	1.50	2.50

KM# 89 CORDOBA
6.2000 g., Nickel Clad Steel, 25 mm. **Obv:** National emblem **Rev:** Value above sprigs within circle **Edge:** Reeded

Date	Mintage	F	VF	XF	Unc	BU
2002	—	—	—	—	2.50	3.00

KM# 101 CORDOBA
6.2500 g., Nickel Clad Steel, 25 mm. **Obv:** National arms **Rev:** Large value "1" **Rev. Legend:** EN DIOS CONFIAMOS **Edge:** Reeded

Date	Mintage	F	VF	XF	Unc	BU
2002	—	—	0.35	0.90	2.25	3.00
2007	—	—	0.35	0.90	2.25	3.00
2008	—	—	0.35	0.90	2.25	3.00
2009	—	—	0.35	0.90	2.25	3.00
2010	—	—	0.35	0.90	2.25	3.00

KM# 100 10 CORDOBAS
27.1200 g., 0.9250 Silver 0.8065 oz. ASW, 40 mm. **Subject:**

Ibero-America **Obv:** National arms in circle of arms **Rev:** Sail boat **Edge:** Reeded

Date	Mintage	F	VF	XF	Unc	BU
2002 Proof	—	Value: 50.00				

KM# 102   10 CORDOBAS
8.4700 g., Brass Plated Steel, 26.5 mm. **Obv:** National arms **Rev:** Value at upper left, circular latent image BCN below, statue of Andrés Castro at right **Edge Lettering:** B C N repeated 4 times

Date	Mintage	F	VF	XF	Unc	BU
2007	—	—	—	—	—	4.00

NIGERIA

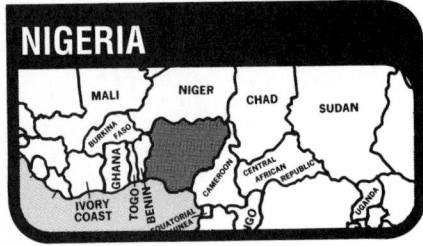

The Federal Republic of Nigeria, situated on the Atlantic coast of West Africa has an area of 356,669 sq. mi. (923,770 sq. km.). Nigeria is a member of the Commonwealth of Nations. The President is the Head of State and the Head of Government.

FEDERAL REPUBLIC

DECIMAL COINAGE
100 Kobo = 1 Naira

KM# 17   KOBO
4.6700 g., Brass, 23.2 mm. **Obv:** Arms with supporters **Rev:** Monkey musicians below value **Edge:** Reeded

Date	Mintage	F	VF	XF	Unc	BU
2003	—	—	—	—	15.00	20.00

KM# 13.3   50 KOBO
3.5000 g., Nickel Clad Steel, 19.44 mm. **Obv:** Arms with supporters **Obv. Legend:** FEDERAL REPUBLIC of NIGERIA **Rev:** Value at left, corn cob and stalk at right **Edge:** Plain **Note:** Reduced size.

Date	Mintage	F	VF	XF	Unc	BU
2006	—	—	—	—	1.00	1.35

KM# 18   NAIRA
5.4300 g., Bi-Metallic Brass center in Stainless Steel ring, 21.48 mm. **Obv:** National arms **Obv. Legend:** FEDERAL REPUBLIC of NIGERIA **Rev:** Small bust of Herbert Macaulay above value **Edge:** Plain

Date	Mintage	F	VF	XF	Unc	BU
2006	—	—	—	—	2.00	3.00

KM# 19   2 NAIRA
7.4800 g., Bi-Metallic Stainless Steel center in Copper-Brass ring, 25.99 mm. **Obv:** National arms **Obv. Legend:** FEDERAL REPUBLIC OF NIGERIA **Rev:** Large value, National Assembly in background **Edge:** Coarse reeding

Date	Mintage	F	VF	XF	Unc	BU
2006	—	—	—	—	3.00	4.00

NIUE

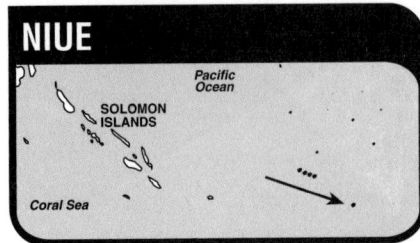

Niue, or Savage Island, a dependent state of New Zealand is located in the Pacific Ocean east of Tonga and southeast of Samoa. The size is 100 sq. mi. (260 sq. km.) with a population of *2,000. Chief village and port is Alofi. Bananas and copra are exported.

MINT MARK
PM - Pobjoy Mint

NEW ZEALAND
DEPENDENT STATE

DECIMAL COINAGE

KM# 193   5 CENTS
4.3000 g., Copper Plated Bronze, 19 mm. **Ruler:** Elizabeth II **Obv:** Head right **Rev:** Two whales

Date	Mintage	F	VF	XF	Unc	BU
2009	—	—	—	—	1.00	2.00
2010	—	—	—	—	1.00	2.00

KM# 194   10 CENTS
5.8000 g., Copper Plated Bronze, 22 mm. **Ruler:** Elizabeth II **Obv:** Head right **Rev:** Coconut crab **Edge:** Reeded

Date	Mintage	F	VF	XF	Unc	BU
2009	—	—	—	—	1.50	2.00
2010	—	—	—	—	1.50	2.00

KM# 195   20 CENTS
7.3000 g., Nickel Plated Bronze, 25 mm. **Ruler:** Elizabeth II **Obv:** Head right **Rev:** Two scuba divers and coral

Date	Mintage	F	VF	XF	Unc	BU
2009	—	—	—	—	2.00	4.00
2010	—	—	—	—	2.00	4.00

KM# 606   50 CENTS
15.5500 g., 0.9990 Silver 0.4994 oz. ASW, 35 mm. **Ruler:** Elizabeth II **Subject:** Olympics **Rev:** Boxers, ancient and modern

Date	Mintage	F	VF	XF	Unc	BU
2004-2008 Proof	—	Value: 40.00				

KM# 607   50 CENTS
15.5000 g., 0.9990 Silver 0.4978 oz. ASW, 35 mm. **Ruler:** Elizabeth II **Subject:** Olympics **Rev:** Long Jumpers - ancient and modern

Date	Mintage	F	VF	XF	Unc	BU
2004-2008 Proof	—	Value: 40.00				

KM# 608   50 CENTS
15.5000 g., 0.9990 Silver 0.4978 oz. ASW, 35 mm. **Ruler:** Elizabeth II **Subject:** Olympics **Rev:** Shot Put, ancient and modern

Date	Mintage	F	VF	XF	Unc	BU
2004-2008 Proof	—	Value: 40.00				

KM# 609   50 CENTS
15.5000 g., 0.9990 Silver 0.4978 oz. ASW, 35 mm. **Ruler:** Elizabeth II **Subject:** Olympics **Rev:** Archer, ancient and modern

Date	Mintage	F	VF	XF	Unc	BU
2004-2008 Proof	—	Value: 40.00				

KM# 610   50 CENTS
15.5000 g., 0.9990 Silver 0.4978 oz. ASW, 35 mm. **Ruler:**

Elizabeth II **Subject:** Olympics **Rev:** Equestrian - ancient and modern views

Date	Mintage	F	VF	XF	Unc	BU
2004-2008 Proof	—				Value: 40.00	

KM# 611   50 CENTS
15.5000 g., 0.9990 Silver 0.4978 oz. ASW, 35 mm. **Ruler:** Elizabeth II **Subject:** Olympics **Rev:** Discus - ancient and modern views

Date	Mintage	F	VF	XF	Unc	BU
2004-2008 Proof	—				Value: 40.00	

KM# 612   50 CENTS
15.5000 g., 0.9990 Silver 0.4978 oz. ASW, 35 mm. **Ruler:** Elizabeth II **Subject:** Olympics **Rev:** Track - ancient and modern views

Date	Mintage	F	VF	XF	Unc	BU
2004-2008 Proof	—				Value: 40.00	

KM# 613   50 CENTS
15.5000 g., 0.9990 Silver 0.4978 oz. ASW, 35 mm. **Ruler:** Elizabeth II **Subject:** Olympics **Rev:** Wrestlers - ancient and modern views

Date	Mintage	F	VF	XF	Unc	BU
2004-2008 Proof	—				Value: 40.00	

KM# 614   50 CENTS
15.5000 g., 0.9990 Silver 0.4978 oz. ASW, 35 mm. **Ruler:** Elizabeth II **Subject:** Olympics **Rev:** Javlin thrower - ancient and modern views

Date	Mintage	F	VF	XF	Unc	BU
2004-2008 Proof	—				Value: 40.00	

KM# 615   50 CENTS
15.5000 g., 0.9990 Silver 0.4978 oz. ASW, 35 mm. **Ruler:** Elizabeth II **Subject:** Olympics **Rev:** Soccer - ancient and modern view

Date	Mintage	F	VF	XF	Unc	BU
2004-2008 Proof	—				Value: 40.00	

KM# 616   50 CENTS
15.5000 g., 0.9990 Silver 0.4978 oz. ASW, 35 mm. **Ruler:** Elizabeth II **Subject:** Olympics **Rev:** Field Hockey - ancient and modern views

Date	Mintage	F	VF	XF	Unc	BU
2004-2008 Proof	—				Value: 40.00	

KM# 263   50 CENTS
15.5500 g., 0.9990 Silver 0.4994 oz. ASW, 35 mm. **Ruler:** Elizabeth II **Series:** Year of the Rooster **Rev:** Multicolor rooster standing right, sunrise

Date	Mintage	F	VF	XF	Unc	BU
2005	—				Value: 30.00	

KM# 292   50 CENTS
15.5500 g., 0.9990 Silver 0.4994 oz. ASW, 35 mm. **Ruler:** Elizabeth II **Subject:** Year of the Dog **Rev:** Multicolor dog

Date	Mintage	F	VF	XF	Unc	BU
2005 Proof	—				Value: 35.00	

KM# 189   50 CENTS
15.5000 g., 0.9990 Silver 0.4978 oz. ASW, 28 mm. **Ruler:** Elizabeth II **Subject:** Year of the Pig **Obv:** Head right **Rev:** Multicolor pig

Date	Mintage	F	VF	XF	Unc	BU
2007 Proof	—				Value: 50.00	

KM# 196   50 CENTS
9.3000 g., Nickel Plated Bronze, 28 mm. **Ruler:** Elizabeth II **Obv:** Head right **Rev:** Outrigger canoe **Edge:** Segmented reeding

Date	Mintage	F	VF	XF	Unc	BU
2009	—	—	—	—	5.00	7.50
2010	—	—	—	—	5.00	7.50

KM# 786   2012 CENTS
31.1000 g., 0.9990 Silver 0.9988 oz. ASW, 30.5x5.5 mm. **Ruler:** Elizabeth II **Obv:** Queen's head at left, Titanic sailing left **Rev:** Ship's bell and other items **Shape:** oval

Date	Mintage	F	VF	XF	Unc	BU
2012 Proof	Est. 200				Value: 100	

KM# 786a   2012 CENTS
31.1000 g., 0.9990 Silver 0.9988 oz. ASW, 31.5x5.5 mm. **Ruler:** Elizabeth II **Obv:** Queen's head at left, Titanic sailing left, sky in color **Rev:** Ship's bell and other items **Shape:** oval

Date	Mintage	F	VF	XF	Unc	BU
2012 Proof	Est. 200				Value: 100	

KM# 462   1/33 DOLLAR
42.5000 g., 0.9990 Silver 1.3650 oz. ASW, 41.7x40 mm. **Ruler:** Elizabeth II **Rev:** Sistine Chapel Corner featuring Haman's punishment

Date	Mintage	F	VF	XF	Unc	BU
2010 Proof	500				Value: 75.00	

KM# 463   1/33 DOLLAR
42.5000 g., 0.9990 Silver 1.3650 oz. ASW, 41.7x40 mm. **Ruler:** Elizabeth II **Rev:** Sistine Chapel Arch featuring the Prophet Jonah

Date	Mintage	F	VF	XF	Unc	BU
2010 Proof	500				Value: 75.00	

KM# 464   1/33 DOLLAR
42.5000 g., 0.9990 Silver 1.3650 oz. ASW, 41.7x40 mm. **Ruler:** Elizabeth II **Rev:** Sistine Chapel Corner Spandrel featuring the Brazen Serpent

Date	Mintage	F	VF	XF	Unc	BU
2010 Proof	500				Value: 75.00	

KM# 465   1/33 DOLLAR
26.8000 g., 0.9990 Silver 0.8607 oz. ASW, 29x36.1 mm. **Ruler:** Elizabeth II **Rev:** Sistine Chapel Arch featuring the Prophet Jeremiah

Date	Mintage	F	VF	XF	Unc	BU
2010 Proof	500				Value: 60.00	

KM# 466   1/33 DOLLAR
26.8000 g., 0.9990 Silver 0.8607 oz. ASW, 29x36.1 mm. **Ruler:** Elizabeth II **Rev:** Sistine Chapel Arch with Salmon

Date	Mintage	F	VF	XF	Unc	BU
2010 Proof	500				Value: 60.00	

KM# 467   1/33 DOLLAR
26.8000 g., 0.9990 Silver 0.8607 oz. ASW, 29x36.1 mm. **Ruler:** Elizabeth II **Rev:** Sistine Chapel Arch with Persian Sibyl

Date	Mintage	F	VF	XF	Unc	BU
2010 Proof	500				Value: 60.00	

KM# 468   1/33 DOLLAR
21.0000 g., 0.9990 Silver 0.6745 oz. ASW, 23x36.1 mm. **Ruler:** Elizabeth II **Rev:** Sistine Chapel Arch with Roboam

Date	Mintage	F	VF	XF	Unc	BU
2010 Proof	500				Value: 45.00	

KM# 469   1/33 DOLLAR
26.8000 g., 0.9990 Silver 0.8607 oz. ASW, 29x36.1 mm. **Ruler:** Elizabeth II **Rev:** Sistine Chapel Arch with Prophet Ezekiel

Date	Mintage	F	VF	XF	Unc	BU
2010 Proof	500				Value: 60.00	

KM# 470   1/33 DOLLAR
26.8000 g., 0.9990 Silver 0.8607 oz. ASW, 29x36.1 mm. **Ruler:** Elizabeth II **Rev:** Sistine Chapel Arch with Ozias

Date	Mintage	F	VF	XF	Unc	BU
2010 Proof	500				Value: 60.00	

KM# 471   1/33 DOLLAR
21.0000 g., 0.9990 Silver 0.6745 oz. ASW, 23x36.1 mm. **Ruler:** Elizabeth II **Rev:** Sistine Chapel Arch with Erythraean Sibyl

Date	Mintage	F	VF	XF	Unc	BU
2010 Proof	500				Value: 45.00	

KM# 472 1/33 DOLLAR
26.8000 g., 0.9990 Silver 0.8607 oz. ASW, 29x36.1 mm. **Ruler:**
Elizabeth II **Rev:** Sistine Chapel Arch with Zorobabel

Date	Mintage	F	VF	XF	Unc	BU
2010 Proof	500	Value: 55.00				

KM# 473 1/33 DOLLAR
21.0000 g., 0.9990 Silver 0.6745 oz. ASW, 23x36.1 mm. **Ruler:**
Elizabeth II **Rev:** Sistine Chapel Arch with Prophet Joel

Date	Mintage	F	VF	XF	Unc	BU
2010 Proof	500	Value: 45.00				

KM# 474 1/33 DOLLAR
35.5000 g., 0.9990 Silver 1.1402 oz. ASW, 29x47.8 mm. **Ruler:**
Elizabeth II **Rev:** Sistine Chapel vault depicting Genesis creation
story of Separation of Light from Darkness

Date	Mintage	F	VF	XF	Unc	BU
2010 Proof	500	Value: 75.00				

KM# 475 1/33 DOLLAR
35.5000 g., 0.9990 Silver 1.1402 oz. ASW, 29x47.8 mm. **Ruler:**
Elizabeth II **Rev:** Sistine Chapel vault depecting Genesis story
of Creation of Sun and Moon

Date	Mintage	F	VF	XF	Unc	BU
2010 Proof	500	Value: 75.00				

KM# 476 1/33 DOLLAR
35.5000 g., 0.9990 Silver 1.1402 oz. ASW, 29x47.8 mm. **Ruler:**
Elizabeth II **Rev:** Sistine Chapel vault depicting Genesis creation
story of the Separation of Land and Water

Date	Mintage	F	VF	XF	Unc	BU
2010 Proof	500	Value: 75.00				

KM# 477 1/33 DOLLAR
28.0000 g., 0.9990 Silver 0.8993 oz. ASW, 23x47.8 mm. **Ruler:**
Elizabeth II **Rev:** Sistine Chapel vault depicting Genesis story of
the Creation of Adam

Date	Mintage	F	VF	XF	Unc	BU
2010 Proof	500	Value: 60.00				

KM# 478 1/33 DOLLAR
35.5000 g., 0.9990 Silver 1.1402 oz. ASW, 29x47.8 mm. **Ruler:**
Elizabeth II **Rev:** Sistine Chapel vault depicting the story of the
Creation of Eve

Date	Mintage	F	VF	XF	Unc	BU
2010 Proof	500	Value: 75.00				

KM# 479 1/33 DOLLAR
28.0000 g., 0.9990 Silver 0.8993 oz. ASW, 23x47.8 mm. **Ruler:**
Elizabeth II **Rev:** Sistine Chapel vault depicting the Genesis story
of Original Sin

Date	Mintage	F	VF	XF	Unc	BU
2010 Proof	500	Value: 60.00				

KM# 480 1/33 DOLLAR
35.5000 g., 0.9990 Silver 1.1402 oz. ASW, 29x47.7 mm. **Ruler:**
Elizabeth II **Rev:** Sistine Chapel vault depicting the Genesis story
of the Sacrifice of Noah

Date	Mintage	F	VF	XF	Unc	BU
2010 Proof	500	Value: 75.00				

KM# 481 1/33 DOLLAR
28.0000 g., 0.9990 Silver 0.8993 oz. ASW, 23x47.8 mm. **Ruler:**
Elizabeth II **Rev:** Sistine Chapel vault depicting the Genesis story
of the Flood

Date	Mintage	F	VF	XF	Unc	BU
2010 Proof	500	Value: 60.00				

KM# 482 1/33 DOLLAR
35.5000 g., 0.9990 Silver 1.1402 oz. ASW, 29x47.8 mm. **Ruler:**
Elizabeth II **Rev:** Sistine Chapel vault depicting the Genesis story
of the Drunkenness of Noah

Date	Mintage	F	VF	XF	Unc	BU
2010 Proof	500	Value: 75.00				

KM# 483 1/33 DOLLAR
26.8000 g., 0.9990 Silver 0.8607 oz. ASW, 29x36.1 mm. **Ruler:**
Elizabeth II **Rev:** Sistine Chapel Arch depicting the Libyan Sibyl

Date	Mintage	F	VF	XF	Unc	BU
2010 Proof	500	Value: 60.00				

KM# 484 1/33 DOLLAR
26.8000 g., 0.9990 Silver 0.8607 oz. ASW, 29x36.1 mm. **Ruler:**
Elizabeth II **Rev:** Sistine Chapel Arch depicting Jesse

Date	Mintage	F	VF	XF	Unc	BU
2010 Proof	500	Value: 60.00				

KM# 485 1/33 DOLLAR
26.8000 g., 0.9990 Silver 0.8607 oz. ASW, 29x36.1 mm. **Ruler:**
Elizabeth II **Rev:** Sistine Chapel Arch depicting the Prophet Daniel

Date	Mintage	F	VF	XF	Unc	BU
2010 Proof	500	Value: 60.00				

KM# 486 1/33 DOLLAR
21.0000 g., 0.9990 Silver 0.6745 oz. ASW, 23x36.1 mm. **Ruler:**
Elizabeth II **Rev:** Sistine Chapel Arch depicting Asa

Date	Mintage	F	VF	XF	Unc	BU
2010 Proof	500	Value: 45.00				

KM# 487 1/33 DOLLAR
26.8000 g., 0.9990 Silver 0.8607 oz. ASW, 29x36.1 mm. **Ruler:**
Elizabeth II **Rev:** Sistine Chapel Arch depicting the Cumaean
Sibyl

Date	Mintage	F	VF	XF	Unc	BU
2010 Proof	500	Value: 60.00				

KM# 488 1/33 DOLLAR
21.0000 g., 0.9990 Silver 0.6745 oz. ASW, 23x36.1 mm. **Ruler:**
Elizabeth II **Rev:** Sistine Chapel Arch depicting Ezekias

Date	Mintage	F	VF	XF	Unc	BU
2010 Proof	500	Value: 45.00				

KM# 489 1/33 DOLLAR
26.8000 g., 0.9990 Silver 0.8607 oz. ASW, 29x.36.1 mm. **Ruler:**
Elizabeth II **Rev:** Sistine Chapel Arch depicting the Prophet Isiah

Date	Mintage	F	VF	XF	Unc	BU
2010 Proof	500	Value: 60.00				

KM# 490 1/33 DOLLAR
26.8000 g., 0.9990 Silver 0.8607 oz. ASW, 29x36.1 mm. **Ruler:**
Elizabeth II **Rev:** Sistine Chapel Arch depicting Josias

Date	Mintage	F	VF	XF	Unc	BU
2010 Proof	500	Value: 60.00				

KM# 491 1/33 DOLLAR
21.0000 g., 0.9990 Silver 0.6745 oz. ASW, 23x36.1 mm. **Ruler:**
Elizabeth II **Rev:** Sistine Chapel Arch depicting the Delphic Sibyl

Date	Mintage	F	VF	XF	Unc	BU
2010 Proof	500	Value: 45.00				

KM# 492 1/33 DOLLAR
42.5000 g., 0.9990 Silver 1.3650 oz. ASW, 41.7x40 mm. **Ruler:**
Elizabeth II **Rev:** Sistine Chapel corner spandrel depicting David
& Goliath

Date	Mintage	F	VF	XF	Unc	BU
2010 Proof	500	Value: 75.00				

KM# 493 1/33 DOLLAR
42.5000 g., 0.9990 Silver 1.3650 oz. ASW, 41.7x40 mm. **Ruler:**
Elizabeth II **Rev:** Sistine Chapel Arch vault depicting the Prophet
Zechariah

Date	Mintage	F	VF	XF	Unc	BU
2010 Proof	500	Value: 75.00				

KM# 494 1/33 DOLLAR
42.5000 g., 0.9990 Silver 1.3650 oz. ASW, 41.7x40 mm. **Ruler:**
Elizabeth II **Rev:** Sistine Chapel corner spandrel depicting Judith
& Holofornes

Date	Mintage	F	VF	XF	Unc	BU
2010 Proof	500	Value: 75.00				

KM# 526 1/24 DOLLAR
42.5000 g., 0.9990 Silver 1.3650 oz. ASW, 41.7x40 mm. **Ruler:**
Elizabeth II **Obv:** Head with tiara right **Rev:** Partial DaVinci
drawing

Date	Mintage	F	VF	XF	Unc	BU
2011 Proof	500	Value: 75.00				

KM# 527 1/24 DOLLAR
42.5000 g., 0.9990 Silver 1.3650 oz. ASW, 41.7x40 mm. **Ruler:**
Elizabeth II **Obv:** Head with tiara right **Rev:** Partial DaVinci
drawing

Date	Mintage	F	VF	XF	Unc	BU
2011 Proof	500	Value: 75.00				

KM# 528 1/24 DOLLAR
42.5000 g., 0.9990 Silver 1.3650 oz. ASW, 41.7x40 mm. **Ruler:**
Elizabeth II **Obv:** Head with tiara right **Rev:** Partial DaVinci
drawing

Date	Mintage	F	VF	XF	Unc	BU
2011 Proof	500	Value: 75.00				

KM# 529 1/24 DOLLAR
42.5000 g., 0.9990 Silver 1.3650 oz. ASW, 41.7x40 mm. **Ruler:**
Elizabeth II **Obv:** Head with tiara right **Rev:** Partial DaVinci
drawing

Date	Mintage	F	VF	XF	Unc	BU
2011 Proof	500	Value: 75.00				

KM# 530 1/24 DOLLAR
42.5000 g., 0.9990 Silver 1.3650 oz. ASW, 41.7x40 mm. **Ruler:**
Elizabeth II **Obv:** Head with tiara right **Rev:** Partial DaVinci
drawing

Date	Mintage	F	VF	XF	Unc	BU
2011 Proof	500	Value: 75.00				

KM# 531 1/24 DOLLAR
42.5000 g., 0.9990 Silver 1.3650 oz. ASW, 41.7x40 mm. **Ruler:**
Elizabeth II **Obv:** Head with tiara right **Rev:** Partial DaVinci
drawing

Date	Mintage	F	VF	XF	Unc	BU
2011 Proof	500	Value: 75.00				

KM# 534 1/24 DOLLAR
42.5000 g., 0.9990 Silver 1.3650 oz. ASW, 41.7x40 mm. **Ruler:**
Elizabeth II **Obv:** Head with tiara right **Rev:** Partial DaVinci
drawing

Date	Mintage	F	VF	XF	Unc	BU
2011 Proof	500	Value: 75.00				

KM# 532 1/24 DOLLAR
42.5000 g., 0.9990 Silver 1.3650 oz. ASW, 41.7x40 mm. **Ruler:**
Elizabeth II **Obv:** Head with tiara right **Rev:** Partial DaVinci
drawing

Date	Mintage	F	VF	XF	Unc	BU
2011 Proof	500	Value: 75.00				

KM# 533 1/24 DOLLAR
42.5000 g., 0.9990 Silver 1.3650 oz. ASW **Ruler:** Elizabeth II
Obv: Head in tiara right **Rev:** Partial DaVinci drawing

Date	Mintage	F	VF	XF	Unc	BU
2011 Proof	500	Value: 75.00				

KM# 535 1/24 DOLLAR
42.5000 g., 0.9990 Silver 1.3650 oz. ASW, 41.7x40 mm. **Ruler:**
Elizabeth II **Obv:** Head with tiara right **Rev:** Partial DaVinci
drawing

Date	Mintage	F	VF	XF	Unc	BU
2011 Proof	500	Value: 75.00				

KM# 536 1/24 DOLLAR
42.5000 g., 0.9990 Silver 1.3650 oz. ASW, 41.7x40 mm. **Ruler:**
Elizabeth II **Obv:** Head in tiara right **Rev:** Partial DaVinci drawing

Date	Mintage	F	VF	XF	Unc	BU
2011 Proof	500	Value: 75.00				

KM# 537 1/24 DOLLAR
42.5000 g., 0.9990 Silver 1.3650 oz. ASW, 41.7x40 mm. **Ruler:**
Elizabeth II **Obv:** Head with tiara right **Rev:** Partial DaVinci
drawing

Date	Mintage	F	VF	XF	Unc	BU
2011 Proof	500	Value: 75.00				

KM# 538 1/24 DOLLAR
42.5000 g., 0.9990 Silver 1.3650 oz. ASW, 41.7x40 mm. **Ruler:**
Elizabeth II **Obv:** Head with tiara right **Rev:** Partial DaVinci
drawing

Date	Mintage	F	VF	XF	Unc	BU
2011 Proof	500	Value: 75.00				

KM# 539 1/24 DOLLAR
42.5000 g., 0.9990 Silver 1.3650 oz. ASW, 41.7x40 mm. **Ruler:**
Elizabeth II **Obv:** Head with tiara right **Rev:** Partial DaVinci
drawing

Date	Mintage	F	VF	XF	Unc	BU
2011 Proof	500	Value: 75.00				

KM# 540 1/24 DOLLAR
42.5000 g., 0.9990 Silver 1.3650 oz. ASW, 41.7x40 mm. **Ruler:**
Elizabeth II **Obv:** Head with tiara right **Rev:** Partial DaVinci
drawing

Date	Mintage	F	VF	XF	Unc	BU
2011 Proof	500	Value: 75.00				

KM# 541 1/24 DOLLAR
42.5000 g., 0.9990 Silver 1.3650 oz. ASW, 41.7x40 mm. **Ruler:**
Elizabeth II **Obv:** Head with tiara right **Rev:** Partial DaVinci
drawing

Date	Mintage	F	VF	XF	Unc	BU
2011 Proof	500	Value: 75.00				

KM# 542 1/24 DOLLAR
42.5000 g., 0.9990 Silver 1.3650 oz. ASW, 41.7x40 mm. **Ruler:**
Elizabeth II **Obv:** Head with tiara right **Rev:** Partial DaVinci
drawing

Date	Mintage	F	VF	XF	Unc	BU
2011 Proof	500	Value: 75.00				

KM# 543 1/24 DOLLAR
42.5000 g., 0.9990 Silver 1.3650 oz. ASW, 41.7x40 mm. **Ruler:**
Elizabeth II **Obv:** Head with tiara right **Rev:** Partial DaVinci
drawing

Date	Mintage	F	VF	XF	Unc	BU
2011 Proof	500	Value: 75.00				

KM# 544 1/24 DOLLAR
42.5000 g., 0.9990 Silver 1.3650 oz. ASW, 41.7x40 mm. **Ruler:**
Elizabeth II **Obv:** Head with tiara right **Rev:** Partial DaVinci
drawing

Date	Mintage	F	VF	XF	Unc	BU
2011 Proof	500	Value: 75.00				

KM# 545 1/24 DOLLAR
42.5000 g., 0.9990 Silver 1.3650 oz. ASW, 41.7x40 mm. **Ruler:**
Elizabeth II **Obv:** Head with tiara right **Rev:** Partial DaVinci
drawing

Date	Mintage	F	VF	XF	Unc	BU
2011 Proof	500	Value: 75.00				

KM# 546 1/24 DOLLAR
42.5000 g., 0.9990 Silver 1.3650 oz. ASW, 41.7x40 mm. **Ruler:**
Elizabeth II **Obv:** Head with tiara right **Rev:** Partial DaVinci
drawing

Date	Mintage	F	VF	XF	Unc	BU
2011 Proof	500	Value: 75.00				

KM# 547 1/24 DOLLAR
42.5000 g., 0.9990 Silver 1.3650 oz. ASW, 41.7x40 mm. **Ruler:**
Elizabeth II **Obv:** Head with tiara right **Rev:** Partial DaVinci
drawing

Date	Mintage	F	VF	XF	Unc	BU
2011 Proof	500	Value: 75.00				

KM# 548 1/24 DOLLAR
42.5000 g., 0.9990 Silver 1.3650 oz. ASW, 41.7x40 mm. **Ruler:**
Elizabeth II **Obv:** Head with tiara right **Rev:** Partial DaVinci
drawing

Date	Mintage	F	VF	XF	Unc	BU
2011 Proof	500	Value: 75.00				

KM# 549 1/24 DOLLAR
42.5000 g., 0.9990 Silver 1.3650 oz. ASW, 41.7x40 mm. **Ruler:**
Elizabeth II **Obv:** Head with tiara right **Rev:** Partial DaVinci
drawing

Date	Mintage	F	VF	XF	Unc	BU
2011 Proof	500	Value: 75.00				

KM# 624 1/14 DOLLAR
15.0000 g., 0.9990 Silver 0.4818 oz. ASW, 29x48 mm. **Ruler:**
Elizabeth II **Obv:** Head with tiara right **Rev:** Two scenes from the
Passion of Christ **Shape:** Vertical rectangle

Date	Mintage	F	VF	XF	Unc	BU
2001 Proof	250	Value: 45.00				

KM# 625 1/14 DOLLAR
15.0000 g., 0.9990 Silver 0.4818 oz. ASW, 29x48 mm. **Ruler:**
Elizabeth II **Obv:** Head with tiara right **Rev:** Two scenes from the
Passion of Christ **Shape:** Vertical rectangle

Date	Mintage	F	VF	XF	Unc	BU
2011 Proof	250	Value: 45.00				

KM# 626 1/14 DOLLAR
15.0000 g., 0.9990 Silver 0.4818 oz. ASW, 29x48 mm. **Ruler:**
Elizabeth II **Obv:** Head in tiara right **Rev:** Two scenes from the
Passion of Christ **Shape:** Vertical rectangle

Date	Mintage	F	VF	XF	Unc	BU
2011 Proof	250	Value: 45.00				

KM# 627 1/14 DOLLAR
15.0000 g., 0.9990 Silver 0.4818 oz. ASW, 36x48 mm. **Ruler:**
Elizabeth II **Obv:** Head in tiara right **Rev:** The Cruxifixion of Christ
Shape: Vertical rectangle

Date	Mintage	F	VF	XF	Unc	BU
2011 Proof	250	Value: 50.00				

KM# 628 1/14 DOLLAR
15.0000 g., 0.9990 Silver 0.4818 oz. ASW, 29x48 mm. **Ruler:**
Elizabeth II **Obv:** Head with tiara right **Rev:** Two scenes form the
Passion of Christ **Shape:** Vertical rectangle

Date	Mintage	F	VF	XF	Unc	BU
2011 Proof	250	Value: 45.00				

KM# 629 1/14 DOLLAR
15.0000 g., 0.9990 Silver 0.4818 oz. ASW, 29x48 mm. **Ruler:**
Elizabeth II **Obv:** Head with tiara right **Rev:** Two scenes from the
Passion of Christ **Shape:** Vertical rectangle

Date	Mintage	F	VF	XF	Unc	BU
2011 Proof	250	Value: 40.00				

KM# 630 1/14 DOLLAR
15.0000 g., 0.9990 Silver 0.4818 oz. ASW, 29x48 mm. **Ruler:**
Elizabeth II **Obv:** Head with tiara right **Rev:** Two scenes from the
Passion of Christ **Shape:** Vertical rectangle

Date	Mintage	F	VF	XF	Unc	BU
2011 Proof	250	Value: 45.00				

KM# 631 1/14 DOLLAR
15.0000 g., 0.9990 Silver 0.4818 oz. ASW, 29x48 mm. **Ruler:**
Elizabeth II **Obv:** Head with tiara right **Rev:** Two scenes from the
Passion of Christ **Shape:** Vertical rectangle

Date	Mintage	F	VF	XF	Unc	BU
2011 Proof	250	Value: 45.00				

KM# 632 1/14 DOLLAR
15.0000 g., 0.9990 Silver 0.4818 oz. ASW, 29x48 mm. **Ruler:**
Elizabeth II **Obv:** Head with tiara right **Rev:** Two scenes from the
Passion of Christ **Shape:** Vertical rectangle

Date	Mintage	F	VF	XF	Unc	BU
2011 Proof	250	Value: 45.00				

KM# 633 1/14 DOLLAR
15.0000 g., 0.9990 Silver 0.4818 oz. ASW, 29x48 mm. **Ruler:**
Elizabeth II **Obv:** Head with tiara right **Rev:** Two scenes from the
Passion of Christ **Shape:** Vertical rectangle

Date	Mintage	F	VF	XF	Unc	BU
2011 Proof	250	Value: 45.00				

KM# 634 1/14 DOLLAR
15.0000 g., 0.9990 Silver 0.4818 oz. ASW, 36x48 mm. **Ruler:**
Elizabeth II **Obv:** Head with tiara right **Rev:** Two scenes from the
Passion of Christ **Shape:** Vertical rectangle

Date	Mintage	F	VF	XF	Unc	BU
2011 Proof	250	Value: 50.00				

KM# 635 1/14 DOLLAR
15.0000 g., 0.9990 Silver 0.4818 oz. ASW, 29x48 mm. **Ruler:**
Elizabeth II **Obv:** Head with tiara right **Rev:** Two scenes from the
Passion of Christ **Shape:** Vertical rectangle

Date	Mintage	F	VF	XF	Unc	BU
2011 Proof	250	Value: 45.00				

KM# 636 1/14 DOLLAR
15.0000 g., 0.9990 Silver 0.4818 oz. ASW, 29x48 mm. **Ruler:**
Elizabeth II **Obv:** Head with tiara right **Rev:** Two scenes from the
Passion of Christ **Shape:** Vertical rectangle

Date	Mintage	F	VF	XF	Unc	BU
2011 Proof	250	Value: 45.00				

KM# 637 1/14 DOLLAR
15.0000 g., 0.9990 Silver 0.4818 oz. ASW, 29x48 mm. **Ruler:**
Elizabeth II **Obv:** Head with tiara right **Rev:** Two scenes from the
Passion of Christ **Shape:** Vertical rectangle

Date	Mintage	F	VF	XF	Unc	BU
2011 Proof	250	Value: 45.00				

KM# 574 1/9 DOLLAR
25.4000 g., 0.9990 Silver 0.8158 oz. ASW, 24x41 mm. **Ruler:**
Elizabeth II **Subject:** Fragment of Villa of Mysteries fresco
Shape: Vertical rectangle

Date	Mintage	F	VF	XF	Unc	BU
2011 Proof	250	Value: 60.00				

KM# 575 1/9 DOLLAR
25.4000 g., 0.9990 Silver 0.8158 oz. ASW, 24x41 mm. **Ruler:**
Elizabeth II **Subject:** Villa of Mysteries Fresco

Date	Mintage	F	VF	XF	Unc	BU
2011 Proof	250	Value: 60.00				

KM# 576 1/9 DOLLAR
33.8000 g., 0.9990 Silver 1.0856 oz. ASW, 32x41 mm. **Ruler:**
Elizabeth II **Subject:** Villa of Mysteries fresco

Date	Mintage	F	VF	XF	Unc	BU
2011 Proof	250	Value: 60.00				

KM# 577 1/9 DOLLAR
33.8000 g., 0.9990 Silver 1.0856 oz. ASW, 32.41 mm. **Ruler:**
Elizabeth II **Subject:** Villa of Mysteries fresco

Date	Mintage	F	VF	XF	Unc	BU
2011 Proof	250	Value: 60.00				

KM# 578 1/9 DOLLAR
50.7000 g., 0.9990 Silver 1.6283 oz. ASW, 48x41 mm. **Ruler:**
Elizabeth II **Subject:** Villa of Mysteries fresco

Date	Mintage	F	VF	XF	Unc	BU
2011 Proof	250	Value: 85.00				

KM# 579 1/9 DOLLAR
50.7000 g., 0.9990 Silver 1.6283 oz. ASW, 48x41 mm. **Ruler:**
Elizabeth II **Subject:** Villa of Mysteries fresco

Date	Mintage	F	VF	XF	Unc	BU
2011 Proof	250	Value: 85.00				

KM# 580 1/9 DOLLAR
33.8000 g., 0.9990 Silver 1.0856 oz. ASW, 32x41 mm. **Ruler:**
Elizabeth II **Subject:** Villa of Mysteries fresco

Date	Mintage	F	VF	XF	Unc	BU
2011 Proof	250	Value: 60.00				

KM# 581 1/9 DOLLAR
50.7000 g., 0.9990 Silver 1.6283 oz. ASW, 48x41 mm. **Ruler:**
Elizabeth II **Subject:** Villa of Mysteries fresco

Date	Mintage	F	VF	XF	Unc	BU
2011 Proof	250	Value: 85.00				

KM# 582 1/9 DOLLAR
50.7000 g., 0.9990 Silver 1.6283 oz. ASW, 48x41 mm. **Ruler:**
Elizabeth II **Subject:** Villa of Mysteries fresco

Date	Mintage	F	VF	XF	Unc	BU
2011 Proof	250	Value: 85.00				

KM# 123 DOLLAR
28.2800 g., Copper-Nickel, 38.6 mm. **Ruler:** Elizabeth II
Subject: Snoopy as an Ace **Obv:** Crowned head right **Rev:**
Snoopy flying his dog house **Edge:** Reeded

Date	Mintage	F	VF	XF	Unc	BU
2001	100,000	—	—	—	3.00	4.50

KM# 128 DOLLAR
28.2800 g., Copper-Nickel, 38.6 mm. **Ruler:** Elizabeth II **Series:**
Pokemon **Obv:** Crowned shield within sprigs **Rev:** Bulbasaur
Edge: Reeded

Date	Mintage	F	VF	XF	Unc	BU
2001	100,000	—	—	—	12.00	14.00

KM# 129 DOLLAR
7.7700 g., 0.9990 Silver 0.2496 oz. ASW, 22 mm. **Ruler:**
Elizabeth II **Series:** Pokemon **Obv:** Crowned shield within sprigs
Rev: Bulbasaur **Edge:** Reeded

Date	Mintage	F	VF	XF	Unc	BU
2001 Proof	20,000	Value: 18.00				

KM# 131 DOLLAR
28.2800 g., Copper-Nickel, 38.6 mm. **Ruler:** Elizabeth II **Series:**
Pokemon **Obv:** Crowned shield within sprigs **Rev:** Charmander
Edge: Reeded

Date	Mintage	F	VF	XF	Unc	BU
2001	100,000	—	—	—	12.00	14.00

KM# 132 DOLLAR
7.7700 g., 0.9990 Silver 0.2496 oz. ASW, 22 mm. **Ruler:**
Elizabeth II **Series:** Pokemon **Obv:** Crowned shield within sprigs
Rev: Charmander **Edge:** Reeded

Date	Mintage	F	VF	XF	Unc	BU
2001 Proof	20,000	Value: 18.00				

KM# 134 DOLLAR
28.2800 g., Copper-Nickel, 38.6 mm. **Ruler:** Elizabeth II **Series:**
Pokemon **Obv:** Crowned shield within sprigs **Rev:** Meowth **Edge:**
Reeded

Date	Mintage	F	VF	XF	Unc	BU
2001	100,000	—	—	—	12.00	14.00

KM# 135 DOLLAR
7.7700 g., 0.9990 Silver 0.2496 oz. ASW, 22 mm. **Ruler:**
Elizabeth II **Series:** Pokemon **Obv:** Crowned shield within sprigs
Rev: Meowth **Edge:** Reeded

Date	Mintage	F	VF	XF	Unc	BU
2001 Proof	20,000	Value: 18.00				

KM# 137 DOLLAR
28.2800 g., Copper-Nickel, 38.6 mm. **Ruler:** Elizabeth II **Series:**
Pokemon **Obv:** Crowned shield within sprigs **Rev:** Pikachu **Edge:**
Reeded

Date	Mintage	F	VF	XF	Unc	BU
2001	100,000	—	—	—	12.00	14.00

KM# 138 DOLLAR
7.7700 g., 0.9990 Silver 0.2496 oz. ASW, 22 mm. **Ruler:**
Elizabeth II **Series:** Pokemon **Obv:** Crowned shield within sprigs
Rev: Pikachu **Edge:** Reeded

Date	Mintage	F	VF	XF	Unc	BU
2001 Proof	20,000	Value: 18.00				

KM# 140 DOLLAR
28.2800 g., Copper-Nickel, 38.6 mm. **Ruler:** Elizabeth II **Series:**
Pokemon **Obv:** Crowned shield within sprigs **Rev:** Squirtle **Edge:**
Reeded

Date	Mintage	F	VF	XF	Unc	BU
2001	100,000	—	—	—	12.00	14.00

KM# 141 DOLLAR
7.7700 g., 0.9990 Silver 0.2496 oz. ASW, 22 mm. **Ruler:**
Elizabeth II **Series:** Pokemon **Obv:** Crowned shield within sprigs
Rev: Squirtle **Edge:** Reeded

Date	Mintage	F	VF	XF	Unc	BU
2001 Proof	20,000	Value: 18.00				

KM# 146 DOLLAR
28.2800 g., Copper-Nickel, 38.6 mm. **Ruler:** Elizabeth II
Subject: Pokemon Series **Obv:** Crowned shield within sprigs
Rev: Pikachu **Edge:** Reeded

Date	Mintage	F	VF	XF	Unc	BU
2002PM	100,000	—	—	—	3.00	4.50

KM# 151 DOLLAR
28.2800 g., Copper-Nickel, 38.6 mm. **Ruler:** Elizabeth II
Subject: Pokemon Series **Obv:** Crowned shield within sprigs
Rev: Pichu **Edge:** Reeded

Date	Mintage	F	VF	XF	Unc	BU
2002PM	100,000	—	—	—	3.00	4.50

KM# 156   DOLLAR
28.2800 g., Copper-Nickel, 38.6 mm. **Ruler:** Elizabeth II
Subject: Pokemon Series **Obv:** Crowned shield within sprigs
Rev: Mewtwo **Edge:** Reeded

Date	Mintage	F	VF	XF	Unc	BU
2002PM	100,000	—	—	—	3.00	4.50

KM# 161   DOLLAR
28.2800 g., Copper-Nickel, 38.6 mm. **Ruler:** Elizabeth II
Subject: Pokemon Series **Obv:** Crowned shield within sprigs
Rev: Entei **Edge:** Reeded

Date	Mintage	F	VF	XF	Unc	BU
2002PM	100,000	—	—	—	3.00	4.50

KM# 166   DOLLAR
28.2800 g., Copper-Nickel, 38.6 mm. **Ruler:** Elizabeth II
Subject: Pokemon Series **Obv:** Crowned shield within sprigs
Rev: Celebi **Edge:** Reeded

Date	Mintage	F	VF	XF	Unc	BU
2002PM	100,000	—	—	—	3.00	4.50

KM# 186   DOLLAR
31.1050 g., 0.9990 Silver 0.9990 oz. ASW **Ruler:** Elizabeth II
Subject: Marshalls of China's Army, 50th Anniversary **Obv:** Head
right **Rev:** Multicolor scene of military men

Date	Mintage	F	VF	XF	Unc	BU
2005	1,000	—	—	—	—	70.00

KM# 187   DOLLAR
31.1050 g., 0.9990 Silver 0.9990 oz. ASW **Ruler:** Elizabeth II
Subject: World War II, 60th Anniversary **Obv:** Bust right **Rev:**
Multicolor badge

Date	Mintage	F	VF	XF	Unc	BU
2005	1,000	—	—	—	—	70.00

KM# 188   DOLLAR
31.1050 g., 0.9990 Silver 0.9990 oz. ASW **Ruler:** Elizabeth II
Series: Bust right **Obv:** Multicolor image of two astronauts, rocket
and map of China

Date	Mintage	F	VF	XF	Unc	BU
2005 Proof	—	Value: 75.00				

KM# 293   DOLLAR
31.1050 g., 0.9990 Silver 0.9990 oz. ASW, 45 mm. **Ruler:**
Elizabeth II **Subject:** Year of the Dog **Rev:** Multicolor dog

Date	Mintage	F	VF	XF	Unc	BU
2005 Proof	—	Value: 60.00				

KM# 264   DOLLAR
31.1000 g., 0.9990 Silver 0.9988 oz. ASW, 45 mm. **Ruler:**
Elizabeth II **Subject:** Year of the Rooster **Rev:** Multicolor rooster
standing right, sunrise

Date	Mintage	F	VF	XF	Unc	BU
2005 Proof	—	Value: 55.00				

KM# 262   DOLLAR
Bronze partially silvered, 38.61 mm. **Ruler:** Elizabeth II **Subject:**
Thomas Alva Edison **Rev:** Lightbulb

Date	Mintage	F	VF	XF	Unc	BU
2005	—	—	—	—	—	30.00

KM# 262a   DOLLAR
31.1050 g., 0.9990 Silver partially gilt 0.9990 oz. ASW **Ruler:**
Elizabeth II **Subject:** Thomas Alva Edison **Rev:** Lightbulb,
partailly gilt

Date	Mintage	F	VF	XF	Unc	BU
2005 Proof	Est. 2,500	Value: 100				

KM# 275   DOLLAR
31.1050 g., 0.9990 Silver 0.9990 oz. ASW **Ruler:** Elizabeth II
Subject: 60th Anniversary, China

Date	Mintage	F	VF	XF	Unc	BU
2005 Proof	Est. 1,000	Value: 120				

KM# 276   DOLLAR
31.1050 g., 0.9990 Silver 0.9990 oz. ASW **Ruler:** Elizabeth II
Subject: Mao Zedong and the Red Army in Bejing

Date	Mintage	F	VF	XF	Unc	BU
2005 Proof	—	Value: 100				

KM# 277   DOLLAR
31.1050 g., 0.9990 Silver 0.9990 oz. ASW **Ruler:**
Elizabeth II **Subject:** Chinese space acheivements **Rev:**
Multicolor rocket, flag, map

Date	Mintage	F	VF	XF	Unc	BU
2005 Proof	Est. 5,000	Value: 75.00				

KM# 300   DOLLAR
31.1050 g., 0.9990 Silver 0.9990 oz. ASW, 45 mm. **Ruler:**
Elizabeth II **Subject:** Dogs of the World **Rev:** Multicolor Bichon
standing before the Louvre

Date	Mintage	F	VF	XF	Unc	BU
2006 Proof	Est. 3,000	Value: 60.00				

KM# 301   DOLLAR
31.1050 g., 0.9990 Silver 0.9990 oz. ASW, 45 mm. **Ruler:**
Elizabeth II **Subject:** Dogs of the World **Rev:** Multicolor Welsh
Corgi before Buckingham Palace

Date	Mintage	F	VF	XF	Unc	BU
2006 Proof	Est. 3,000	Value: 60.00				

KM# 302   DOLLAR
31.1050 g., 0.9990 Silver 0.9990 oz. ASW, 45 mm. **Ruler:**
Elizabeth II **Subject:** Dogs of the World **Rev:** Poodle before the
Palace at Versailles

Date	Mintage	F	VF	XF	Unc	BU
2006 Proof	Est. 3,000	Value: 60.00				

KM# 303   DOLLAR
31.1050 g., 0.9990 Silver 0.9990 oz. ASW, 45 mm. **Ruler:**
Elizabeth II **Subject:** Dogs of the World **Rev:** Bare dog before
the Potala Plast

Date	Mintage	F	VF	XF	Unc	BU
2006 Proof	Est. 3,000	Value: 60.00				

KM# 304   DOLLAR
31.1050 g., 0.9990 Silver 0.9990 oz. ASW, 45 mm. **Ruler:**
Elizabeth II **Subject:** Dogs of the World **Rev:** Pekineese before
the Palastmuseum

Date	Mintage	F	VF	XF	Unc	BU
2006 Proof	Est. 3,000	Value: 60.00				

KM# 305   DOLLAR
31.1050 g., 0.9990 Silver 0.9990 oz. ASW, 45 mm. **Ruler:**
Elizabeth II **Subject:** Dogs of the World **Rev:** Malteser before the
Schonbrunn

Date	Mintage	F	VF	XF	Unc	BU
2006 Proof	Est. 3,000	Value: 60.00				

KM# 306   DOLLAR
31.1050 g., 0.9990 Silver 0.9990 oz. ASW, 45 mm. **Ruler:**
Elizabeth II **Subject:** Dogs of the World **Rev:** Japanese Chin
before Emeror's palace in Kyoto

Date	Mintage	F	VF	XF	Unc	BU
2006 Proof	Est. 3,000	Value: 60.00				

KM# 307   DOLLAR
31.1050 g., 0.9990 Silver 0.9990 oz. ASW, 45 mm. **Ruler:**
Elizabeth II **Subject:** Dogs of the World **Rev:** King Charles
Spaniel before Westminster Abbey

Date	Mintage	F	VF	XF	Unc	BU
2006 Proof	Est. 3,000	Value: 60.00				

KM# 308   DOLLAR
31.1050 g., 0.9990 Silver 0.9990 oz. ASW, 45 mm. **Ruler:**
Elizabeth II **Subject:** Dogs of the World **Rev:** Butterfly dog before
the Kings Palace in Madrid

Date	Mintage	F	VF	XF	Unc	BU
2006 Proof	Est. 3,000	Value: 60.00				

KM# 309   DOLLAR
31.1050 g., 0.9990 Silver 0.9990 oz. ASW, 45 mm. **Ruler:**
Elizabeth II **Subject:** Olympics **Rev:** Discus thrower

Date	Mintage	F	VF	XF	Unc	BU
ND Proof	Est. 2,008	Value: 70.00				

KM# 310   DOLLAR
31.1050 g., 0.9990 Silver 0.9990 oz. ASW, 45 mm. **Ruler:**
Elizabeth II **Subject:** Olympics **Rev:** Sprinter

Date	Mintage	F	VF	XF	Unc	BU
ND Proof	Est. 2,008	Value: 70.00				

KM# 311   DOLLAR
31.1050 g., 0.9990 Silver 0.9990 oz. ASW, 45 mm. **Ruler:**
Elizabeth II **Subject:** Olympics **Rev:** Long Jump

Date	Mintage	F	VF	XF	Unc	BU
ND Proof	Est. 2,008	Value: 70.00				

KM# 312   DOLLAR
31.1050 g., 0.9990 Silver 0.9990 oz. ASW, 45 mm. **Ruler:**
Elizabeth II **Subject:** Olympics **Rev:** Javelin Thrower

Date	Mintage	F	VF	XF	Unc	BU
ND Proof	Est. 2,008	Value: 70.00				

KM# 313   DOLLAR
31.1050 g., 0.9990 Silver 0.9990 oz. ASW, 45 mm. **Ruler:**
Elizabeth II **Subject:** Olympics **Rev:** Weightlifter

Date	Mintage	F	VF	XF	Unc	BU
ND Proof	Est. 2,008	Value: 70.00				

KM# 314   DOLLAR
31.1050 g., 0.9990 Silver 0.9990 oz. ASW, 45 mm. **Ruler:**
Elizabeth II **Subject:** Olympics **Rev:** Hammer Throw

Date	Mintage	F	VF	XF	Unc	BU
ND Proof	Est. 2,008	Value: 70.00				

KM# 315   DOLLAR
31.1050 g., 0.9990 Silver 0.9990 oz. ASW, 45 mm. **Ruler:**
Elizabeth II **Subject:** Olympics **Rev:** Archery

Date	Mintage	F	VF	XF	Unc	BU
ND Proof	Est. 2,008	Value: 70.00				

KM# 316   DOLLAR
31.1050 g., 0.9990 Silver 0.9990 oz. ASW, 45 mm. **Ruler:**
Elizabeth II **Subject:** Olympics **Rev:** Lacrosse player

Date	Mintage	F	VF	XF	Unc	BU
ND Proof	Est. 2,008	Value: 70.00				

KM# 317   DOLLAR
31.1050 g., 0.9990 Silver 0.9990 oz. ASW, 45 mm. **Ruler:**
Elizabeth II **Subject:** Olympics **Rev:** Soccer player

Date	Mintage	F	VF	XF	Unc	BU
ND Proof	Est. 2,008	Value: 70.00				

KM# 318   DOLLAR
31.1050 g., 0.9990 Silver 0.9990 oz. ASW, 45 mm. **Ruler:**
Elizabeth II **Subject:** Olympics **Rev:** Boxer

Date	Mintage	F	VF	XF	Unc	BU
ND Proof	Est. 2,008	Value: 70.00				

KM# 319   DOLLAR
31.1050 g., 0.9990 Silver 0.9990 oz. ASW, 45 mm. **Ruler:**
Elizabeth II **Subject:** Olympics **Rev:** Equestrian

Date	Mintage	F	VF	XF	Unc	BU
ND Proof	Est. 2,008	Value: 70.00				

KM# 320   DOLLAR
31.1050 g., 0.9990 Silver 0.9990 oz. ASW, 45 mm. **Ruler:**
Elizabeth II **Subject:** Olympics **Rev:** Wrestler

Date	Mintage	F	VF	XF	Unc	BU
ND Proof	Est. 2,008	Value: 70.00				

KM# 321   DOLLAR
31.1050 g., 0.9990 Silver 0.9990 oz. ASW, 35x46 mm. **Ruler:**
Elizabeth II **Subject:** Life of Christ **Rev:** Radiant Mary **Shape:**
Vertical rectangle

Date	Mintage	F	VF	XF	Unc	BU
2006 Proof	Est. 1,000	Value: 100				

KM# 322   DOLLAR
31.1050 g., 0.9990 Silver 0.9990 oz. ASW, 35x46 mm. **Ruler:**
Elizabeth II **Subject:** Life of Christ **Rev:** Mary and Child (1483)
Shape: Vertical rectangle

Date	Mintage	F	VF	XF	Unc	BU
2006 Proof	Est. 1,000	Value: 100				

KM# 323   DOLLAR
31.1050 g., 0.9990 Silver 0.9990 oz. ASW, 35x46 mm. **Ruler:**
Elizabeth II **Subject:** Life of Christ **Rev:** Christ in the Jrodan
(1478) **Shape:** Vertical rectangle

Date	Mintage	F	VF	XF	Unc	BU
2006 Proof	Est. 1,000	Value: 100				

KM# 324   DOLLAR
31.1050 g., 0.9990 Silver 0.9990 oz. ASW, 35x46 mm. **Ruler:** Elizabeth II **Subject:** Life of Christ **Rev:** Jesus Christ (1481) **Shape:** Vertical rectangle

Date	Mintage	F	VF	XF	Unc	BU
2006 Proof	Est. 1,000	Value: 100				

KM# 325   DOLLAR
31.1050 g., 0.9990 Silver 0.9990 oz. ASW, 35x46 mm. **Ruler:** Elizabeth II **Subject:** Life of Christ **Rev:** betrayal of Judas (1303) **Shape:** Vertical rectangle

Date	Mintage	F	VF	XF	Unc	BU
2006 Proof	Est. 1,000	Value: 100				

KM# 326   DOLLAR
31.1050 g., 0.9990 Silver 0.9990 oz. ASW, 35x46 mm. **Ruler:** Elizabeth II **Subject:** Life of Christ **Rev:** Stations of the Cross (1517) **Shape:** Vertical rectangle

Date	Mintage	F	VF	XF	Unc	BU
2006 Proof	Est. 1,000	Value: 100				

KM# 327   DOLLAR
31.1050 g., 0.9990 Silver 0.9990 oz. ASW, 35x46 mm. **Ruler:** Elizabeth II **Subject:** Life of Christ **Rev:** Jesus on the Cross (1558) **Shape:** Vertical rectangle

Date	Mintage	F	VF	XF	Unc	BU
2006 Proof	Est. 1,000	Value: 100				

KM# 329   DOLLAR
31.1050 g., 0.9990 Silver 0.9990 oz. ASW, 35x45 mm. **Ruler:** Elizabeth II **Subject:** Life of Christ **Rev:** Heaven **Shape:** Vertical rectangle

Date	Mintage	F	VF	XF	Unc	BU
2006 Proof	Est. 1,000	Value: 100				

KM# 328   DOLLAR
31.1050 g., 0.9990 Silver 0.9990 oz. ASW, 35x46 mm. **Ruler:** Elizabeth II **Subject:** Life of Christ **Rev:** Ascension (1520) **Shape:** Vertical rectangle

Date	Mintage	F	VF	XF	Unc	BU
2006 Proof	Est. 1,000	Value: 100				

KM# 176   DOLLAR
28.2800 g., 0.9250 Silver 0.8410 oz. ASW **Ruler:** Elizabeth II **Obv:** Tiarra head of Elizabeth II right at left, multicolor Van Gogh's painting "Starry Night" with 3 zircon crystals as stars at center right. **Obv. Inscription:** ELIZABETH II - NIUE ISLAND **Rev:** Van Gogh's painting "Vase with Twelve Sunflowers" at left, self portrait of artist with brush at upper right **Rev. Inscription:** VAN GOGH / Vincent **Edge:** Plain **Shape:** Rectangular, 39.94 x 27.97 mm

Date	Mintage	F	VF	XF	Unc	BU
2007 Proof	10,000	Value: 85.00				

KM# 331   DOLLAR
28.2800 g., 0.9250 Silver 0.8410 oz. ASW **Ruler:** Elizabeth II **Subject:** Year of the Pig

Date	Mintage	F	VF	XF	Unc	BU
2007 Proof	Est. 5,000	Value: 55.00				

KM# 332   DOLLAR
28.2800 g., 0.9250 Silver 0.8410 oz. ASW **Ruler:** Elizabeth II **Subject:** Year of the Pig **Rev:** Three little pigs dancing, brick house, wolf

Date	Mintage	F	VF	XF	Unc	BU
2007	—	—	—	—	—	55.00

KM# 334   DOLLAR
28.2800 g., 0.9250 Silver 0.8410 oz. ASW, 38.61 mm. **Ruler:** Elizabeth II **Rev:** Female advancing left with long dress **Rev. Legend:** Change Flies to the Moon

Date	Mintage	F	VF	XF	Unc	BU
2007	Est. 5,000	—	—	—	—	55.00

KM# 335   DOLLAR
28.2800 g., 0.9250 Silver 0.8410 oz. ASW, 38.61 mm. **Ruler:** Elizabeth II **Rev:** Man weiding axe against tree **Rev. Legend:** Wu Gang cuts the sweet-scented osmanthus tree

Date	Mintage	F	VF	XF	Unc	BU
2007	Est. 5,000	—	—	—	—	55.00

KM# 336   DOLLAR
28.2800 g., 0.9250 Silver 0.8410 oz. ASW, 38.61 mm. **Ruler:** Elizabeth II **Rev:** Group visiting palace **Rev. Legend:** Emperor Mint of Tang Dynasty visit the Moon Palace at Night

Date	Mintage	F	VF	XF	Unc	BU
2007	Est. 5,000	—	—	—	—	55.00

KM# 337   DOLLAR
28.2800 g., 0.9250 Silver 0.8410 oz. ASW, 38.61 mm. **Ruler:** Elizabeth II **Rev:** Rabbit with mortar and pestile in house yard **Rev. Legend:** The jade rabbit pounds the medicine of immortality

Date	Mintage	F	VF	XF	Unc	BU
2007 Proof	Est. 5,000	—	—	—	—	55.00

KM# 212   DOLLAR
Silver **Ruler:** Elizabeth II **Rev:** Ox seated multicolor lotus flower

Date	Mintage	F	VF	XF	Unc	BU
2008 Antique finish	—	—	—	—	—	55.00

KM# 192   DOLLAR
31.1050 g., 0.9990 Silver 0.9990 oz. ASW **Ruler:** Elizabeth II **Subject:** Year of the Ox **Obv:** Head right **Rev:** Multicolor ox

Date	Mintage	F	VF	XF	Unc	BU
2008//2009 Proof	10,000	Value: 75.00				

KM# 201   DOLLAR
28.2800 g., 0.9250 Silver 0.8410 oz. ASW, 38.61 mm. **Ruler:** Elizabeth II **Subject:** Amber Road **Obv:** Roman cart and map, Elizabeth II head at lower left **Rev:** Church, goblet, ancient coin, amber insert **Rev. Legend:** ELBLAG SZLAK BURSZTYNOWY

Date	Mintage	F	VF	XF	Unc	BU
2008 Antique finish	10,000	—	—	—	—	80.00

KM# 202   DOLLAR
28.2800 g., 0.9250 Silver 0.8410 oz. ASW, 38.61 mm. **Ruler:** Elizabeth II **Subject:** Amber Road **Obv:** Roman cart, map, Elizabeth II head at lower left **Rev:** Antonius Pius coins, Nepture statue, mine shaft, amber insert **Rev. Legend:** GDANSK SZLAK BURSZTYNOWY

Date	Mintage	F	VF	XF	Unc	BU
2008 Antique finish	10,000	—	—	—	—	80.00

KM# 203   DOLLAR
28.2800 g., 0.9250 Silver 0.8410 oz. ASW, 38.61 mm. **Ruler:** Elizabeth II **Subject:** Amber Road **Obv:** Roman cart, map, Elizabeth II head at lower left **Rev:** Building, statue, amber insert **Rev. Legend:** WROCLAW SZLAK BURSZTYNOWY

Date	Mintage	F	VF	XF	Unc	BU
2008 Antique finish	10,000	—	—	—	—	140

KM# 204   DOLLAR
28.2800 g., 0.9990 Silver 0.9083 oz. ASW, 38.61 mm. **Ruler:** Elizabeth II **Subject:** Amber Road **Rev:** Castle, sword, amber insert **Rev. Legend:** SZLAK BURSZTYNOWY KALININGRAD

Date	Mintage	F	VF	XF	Unc	BU
2008 Antique finish	10,000	—	—	—	—	125

KM# 211   DOLLAR
28.2800 g., 0.9250 Silver 0.8410 oz. ASW, 28x40 mm. **Ruler:** Elizabeth II **Obv:** Head of Elizabeth II at lower left, Portrait of Lautrec at top right **Rev:** Toulouse-Lautrec and can-can girl

Date	Mintage	F	VF	XF	Unc	BU
2008 Proof	15,000	Value: 75.00				

KM# 338   DOLLAR
31.1050 g., 0.9990 Silver 0.9990 oz. ASW, 45 mm. **Ruler:** Elizabeth II **Subject:** Year of the Rat **Rev:** Rat in field, sun rays above

Date	Mintage	F	VF	XF	Unc	BU
2008	Est. 8,000	—	—	—	—	65.00

KM# 339   DOLLAR
31.1050 g., 0.9990 Silver 0.9990 oz. ASW, 45 mm. **Ruler:** Elizabeth II **Subject:** Year of the Rat **Rev:** Rat left before house

Date	Mintage	F	VF	XF	Unc	BU
2008	Est. 8,000	—	—	—	—	65.00

KM# 340   DOLLAR
31.1050 g., 0.9990 Silver 0.9990 oz. ASW, 45 mm. **Ruler:** Elizabeth II **Subject:** Year of the Rat **Rev:** Rat standing on hind legs sniffing flora

Date	Mintage	F	VF	XF	Unc	BU
2008	Est. 8,000	—	—	—	—	70.00

KM# 341   DOLLAR
, 45 mm. **Ruler:** Elizabeth II **Rev:** Multicolor Happy mouse

Date	Mintage	F	VF	XF	Unc	BU
2008 Proof	—	Value: 60.00				

KM# 342   DOLLAR
31.1050 g., 0.9990 Silver 0.9990 oz. ASW, 45 mm. **Ruler:** Elizabeth II **Rev:** Multicolor wealthy rat

Date	Mintage	F	VF	XF	Unc	BU
2008 Proof	—	Value: 60.00				

KM# 343 DOLLAR
31.1050 g., 0.9990 Silver 0.9990 oz. ASW, 45 mm. **Ruler:**
Elizabeth II **Rev:** Multicolor happy rat

Date	Mintage	F	VF	XF	Unc	BU
2008 Proof	—	Value: 60.00				

KM# 344 DOLLAR
31.1050 g., 0.9990 Silver 0.9990 oz. ASW, 45 mm. **Ruler:**
Elizabeth II **Rev:** Multicolor successful rat

Date	Mintage	F	VF	XF	Unc	BU
2008 Proof	—	Value: 60.00				

KM# 345 DOLLAR
31.1050 g., 0.9990 Silver 0.9990 oz. ASW, 45 mm. **Ruler:**
Elizabeth II **Rev:** Multicolor rat holding charm

Date	Mintage	F	VF	XF	Unc	BU
2008 Proof	Est. 10,000	Value: 60.00				

KM# 346 DOLLAR
3.1100 g., 0.9990 Gold 0.0999 oz. AGW, 18 mm. **Ruler:**
Elizabeth II **Rev:** Rat in garden

Date	Mintage	F	VF	XF	Unc	BU
2008 Proof	Est. 10,000	Value: 185				

KM# 347 DOLLAR
28.2800 g., 0.9250 Silver 0.8410 oz. ASW, 38.61 mm. **Ruler:**
Elizabeth II **Rev:** Rat standing infront of multicolor cut cheese
wheel

Date	Mintage	F	VF	XF	Unc	BU
2008 Proof	Est. 10,000	Value: 50.00				

KM# 348 DOLLAR
28.2800 g., 0.9250 Silver 0.8410 oz. ASW, 38.61 mm. **Ruler:**
Elizabeth II **Rev:** Multicolor dancing mice in garland

Date	Mintage	F	VF	XF	Unc	BU
2008 Proof	—	Value: 50.00				

KM# 197 DOLLAR
17.3000 g., Aluminum-Brass, 32 mm. **Ruler:** Elizabeth II **Obv:**
Head right **Rev:** Swordfish **Edge:** Reeded

Date	Mintage	F	VF	XF	Unc	BU
2009	—	—	—	—	7.50	12.50

KM# 231 DOLLAR
31.1030 g., 0.9990 Silver 0.9989 oz. ASW, 38.6 mm. **Ruler:**
Elizabeth II **Subject:** Year of the Tiger **Rev:** Tiger cub in basket
playing with ball

Date	Mintage	F	VF	XF	Unc	BU
2009 Proof	6,000	Value: 80.00				

KM# 232 DOLLAR
31.1030 g., 0.9990 Silver 0.9989 oz. ASW, 38.6 mm. **Ruler:**
Elizabeth II **Subject:** Year of the Tiger **Rev:** Tiger advancing left

Date	Mintage	F	VF	XF	Unc	BU
2009 Proof	6,000	Value: 80.00				

KM# 551 DOLLAR
28.2800 g., 0.9250 Silver 0.8410 oz. ASW, 38.61 mm. **Ruler:**
Elizabeth II **Subject:** Father Frost **Rev:** Father and Mrs. Frost
standing, multicolor

Date	Mintage	F	VF	XF	Unc	BU
2009 Proof	Est. 6,000	Value: 65.00				

KM# 198 DOLLAR
17.3000 g., Copper Plated Bronze, 32 mm. **Ruler:** Elizabeth II
Obv: Head right **Rev:** Taro leaves **Edge:** Reeded

Date	Mintage	F	VF	XF	Unc	BU
2010	—	—	—	—	7.50	12.50

KM# 234 DOLLAR
28.2800 g., 0.9250 Silver 0.8410 oz. ASW, 40x40 mm. **Ruler:**
Elizabeth II **Obv:** Head right, footprints in field **Rev:** Antilocapra
Americana, two antelope running right **Shape:** Square

Date	Mintage	F	VF	XF	Unc	BU
2010 Proof	9,000	Value: 80.00				

KM# 235 DOLLAR
28.2800 g., 0.9250 Silver 0.8410 oz. ASW, 38.6 mm. **Ruler:**
Elizabeth II **Obv:** Head right **Rev:** Lycaena Virgavreae multicolor
butterfly

Date	Mintage	F	VF	XF	Unc	BU
2010 Proof	8,000	Value: 80.00				

KM# 236 DOLLAR
14.1400 g., 0.9250 Silver 0.4205 oz. ASW, 25x28 mm. **Ruler:**
Elizabeth II **Obv:** Head right on musical score **Rev:** Chopin bust
at left, score **Shape:** Square

Date	Mintage	F	VF	XF	Unc	BU
2010 Proof	6,000	Value: 80.00				

KM# 238 DOLLAR
28.2800 g., 0.9250 Silver 0.8410 oz. ASW, 36.81 mm. **Ruler:**
Elizabeth II **Subject:** Fire **Obv:** Head right, images of early man
Rev: Volcano and men around fire in multicolor

Date	Mintage	F	VF	XF	Unc	BU
2010 Proof	6,000	Value: 100				

KM# 239 DOLLAR
28.2800 g., 0.9250 Silver 0.8410 oz. ASW, 40x28 mm. **Ruler:**
Elizabeth II **Obv:** Head right, aircraft propeller, wing schematic
Rev: Greek warrior shield and multicolor Icarus in flight **Shape:**
Rectangle

Date	Mintage	F	VF	XF	Unc	BU
2010 Proof	6,000	Value: 100				

KM# 240 DOLLAR
28.2800 g., 0.9250 Silver 0.8410 oz. ASW, 28x40 mm. **Ruler:**
Elizabeth II **Obv:** Head right, propeller, wing schematic **Rev:**
Montgolfier brothers and balloon **Shape:** Rectangle

Date	Mintage	F	VF	XF	Unc	BU
2010 Proof	6,000	Value: 75.00				

KM# 241 DOLLAR
28.2800 g., 0.9250 Silver 0.8410 oz. ASW, 40x28 mm. **Ruler:**
Elizabeth II **Obv:** Head right, Monet painting **Rev:** Claude Monet
portrait and painting **Shape:** Verticle rectangle

Date	Mintage	F	VF	XF	Unc	BU
2010 Proof	15,000	Value: 85.00				

KM# 242 DOLLAR
28.2800 g., 0.9250 Silver 0.8410 oz. ASW, 38.61 mm. **Ruler:**
Elizabeth II **Obv:** Elizabeth II head at top left, building **Rev:**
Napoleon at left, troops in color at right

Date	Mintage	F	VF	XF	Unc	BU
2010 Proof	10,000	Value: 90.00				

KM# 243 DOLLAR
28.2800 g., 0.9250 Silver 0.8410 oz. ASW, 38.6 mm. **Ruler:**
Elizabeth II **Subject:** 65th Anniversary - End of World War II **Obv:**
Head right at top, three Soviet medals below **Rev:** Soviet flat,
rose and eternal light

Date	Mintage	F	VF	XF	Unc	BU
2010 Proof	7,000	Value: 95.00				

KM# 244 DOLLAR
28.2800 g., 0.9250 Silver 0.8410 oz. ASW, 38.6 mm. **Ruler:**
Elizabeth II **Obv:** Head at left, ship, coins, artifacts **Rev:** Stupsk

Date	Mintage	F	VF	XF	Unc	BU
2010 Proof	8,000	Value: 90.00				

KM# 251 DOLLAR
31.1050 g., 0.9990 Silver 0.9990 oz. ASW, 38.6 mm. **Ruler:**
Elizabeth II **Subject:** Peanuts 60th Anniversary **Rev:** Snoopy as
conductor with flowers, Woodstock with red ribbon

Date	Mintage	F	VF	XF	Unc	BU
2010 Prooflike	3,000	—	—	—	—	80.00

KM# 365 DOLLAR
28.2800 g., 0.9250 Silver 0.8410 oz. ASW, 38.61 mm. **Ruler:**
Elizabeth II **Subject:** WWII, 65th Anniversary **Obv:** Elizabeth II
head, WWI medal and two stars below **Rev:** Russian flag and
medal ribbon

Date	Mintage	F	VF	XF	Unc	BU
2010 Proof	7,000	Value: 60.00				

KM# 366 DOLLAR
28.2800 g., 0.9250 Silver 0.8410 oz. ASW, 38.61 mm. **Ruler:**
Elizabeth II **Obv:** Englarged butterfly wing **Rev:** Butterfly -
Parnassius Apollo

Date	Mintage	F	VF	XF	Unc	BU
2010 Proof	8,000	Value: 60.00				

KM# 367 DOLLAR
28.2800 g., 0.9250 Silver 0.8410 oz. ASW, 38.61 mm. **Ruler:** Elizabeth II **Subject:** Amber Route - Stare Hradisko **Rev:** Amber insert, old celtic style coin

Date	Mintage	F	VF	XF	Unc	BU
2010 Antique finish	10,000	—	—	—	—	55.00

KM# 369 DOLLAR
14.1400 g., 0.9250 Silver 0.4205 oz. ASW, 32 mm. **Ruler:** Elizabeth II **Subject:** Cartoon Characters - Mis Uszatek **Obv:** Elizabeth II head left, movie film **Rev:** Image of rabbits and bear

Date	Mintage	F	VF	XF	Unc	BU
2010 Proof	8,000	Value: 40.00				

KM# 370 DOLLAR
28.2800 g., 0.9250 Silver 0.8410 oz. ASW **Ruler:** Elizabeth II **Obv:** Elizabeth II head right, Cupid **Rev:** Romeo and Juliet about to kiss

Date	Mintage	F	VF	XF	Unc	BU
2010 Proof	9,000	Value: 60.00				

KM# 392 DOLLAR
14.1400 g., 0.9250 Silver 0.4205 oz. ASW, 32 mm. **Ruler:** Elizabeth II **Subject:** Cartoon Characters - Wolf and the HareH **Rev:** Wolf and hare characters in multicolor

Date	Mintage	F	VF	XF	Unc	BU
2010 Proof	8,000	Value: 45.00				

KM# 393 DOLLAR
28.2800 g., 0.9250 Silver 0.8410 oz. ASW, 40x28 mm. **Ruler:** Elizabeth II **Obv:** Queen's head at top left, three airplane views **Rev:** Otto Lilienthal and the glider **Shape:** Rectangle

Date	Mintage	F	VF	XF	Unc	BU
2010 Proof	6,000	Value: 70.00				

KM# 394 DOLLAR
28.2800 g., 0.9250 Silver 0.8410 oz. ASW, 38.8 mm. **Ruler:** Elizabeth II **Obv:** Queen's head right within star pattern **Rev:** Two portraits of Sitting Bull in multicolor

Date	Mintage	F	VF	XF	Unc	BU
2010 Proof	6,000	Value: 75.00				

KM# 395 DOLLAR
28.2800 g., 0.9250 Silver 0.8410 oz. ASW, 40x40 mm. **Ruler:** Elizabeth II **Obv:** Head in tiara right within diamond, footprints in background **Rev:** Platypus (Ornithorhynchus anatinus) **Shape:** Square

Date	Mintage	F	VF	XF	Unc	BU
2010 Proof	9,000	Value: 65.00				

KM# 396 DOLLAR
28.2800 g., 0.9250 Silver with amber insert 0.8410 oz. ASW, 38.61 mm. **Ruler:** Elizabeth II **Subject:** Amber Route - Carnuntum **Rev:** Arches, ancient coin and statue

Date	Mintage	F	VF	XF	Unc	BU
2010 Antique patina	10,000	Value: 60.00				

KM# 398 DOLLAR
28.2800 g., 0.9250 Silver with amber insert 0.8410 oz. ASW,

38.61 mm. **Ruler:** Elizabeth II **Subject:** Amber Route - Szombathely **Rev:** Cathedral, ancient coin

Date	Mintage	F	VF	XF	Unc	BU
2010 Antique patina	10,000	Value: 60.00				

KM# 400 DOLLAR
28.2800 g., 0.9250 Silver 0.8410 oz. ASW, 27x45 mm. **Ruler:** Elizabeth II **Subject:** Milan Cathedral **Obv:** Cathedral's flying buttresses, stained glass colored inset **Rev:** Front facade of cathedral, stained glass colored inset **Shape:** Vertical oval

Date	Mintage	F	VF	XF	Unc	BU
2010 Proof	5,000	Value: 70.00				

KM# 401 DOLLAR
28.2800 g., 0.9250 Silver 0.8410 oz. ASW, 27x45 mm. **Ruler:** Elizabeth II **Subject:** Cologne Cathedral **Obv:** Cathedral side exterior, stained glass colored inset **Rev:** Cathedral floor plan and facade, stained glass colored inset **Shape:** Vertical oval

Date	Mintage	F	VF	XF	Unc	BU
2010 Proof	5,000	Value: 70.00				

KM# 402 DOLLAR
28.2800 g., 0.9250 Silver 0.8410 oz. ASW, 27x45 mm. **Ruler:** Elizabeth II **Subject:** Notre Dame Cathedral **Obv:** Cathedral side view, stained glass colored inset **Rev:** Linear cathedral interior view, cathedral facade, stained glass colored inset **Shape:** Vertical oval

Date	Mintage	F	VF	XF	Unc	BU
2010 Proof	5,000	Value: 70.00				

KM# 403 DOLLAR
28.2800 g., 0.9250 Silver 0.8410 oz. ASW, 28x40 mm. **Ruler:**

Elizabeth II **Subject:** Alfons Mucha, 150th Anniversary of Birth
Obv: Standing Female in multicolor **Rev:** Female portrait and
Mucha portrait in multicolor **Shape:** Vertical Rectangle

Date	Mintage	F	VF	XF	Unc	BU
2010 Proof	5,000	Value: 80.00				

KM# 404   DOLLAR
28.2800 g., 0.9250 Silver 0.8410 oz. ASW, 28x40 mm.   **Ruler:**
Elizabeth II **Subject:** Carl Brullov **Obv:** Female on horseback in
color **Rev:** Two females with grape wreath above, Brullov portrait,
Three nuns singing below; all in color **Shape:** Vertical Rectangle

Date	Mintage	F	VF	XF	Unc	BU
2010 Proof	5,000	Value: 75.00				

KM# 406   DOLLAR
28.2800 g., 0.9250 Silver 0.8410 oz. ASW, 40x40 mm.   **Ruler:**
Elizabeth II **Obv:** Head with tiara right, in diamond, footprints in
background **Rev:** Venus Flytrap in color **Shape:** Square

Date	Mintage	F	VF	XF	Unc	BU
2010 Proof	9,000	Value: 70.00				

KM# 407   DOLLAR
28.2800 g., 0.9250 Silver 0.8410 oz. ASW, 41 mm.   **Ruler:**
Elizabeth II **Subject:** Good Luck **Obv:** Head with tiara right,
horseshoes below **Rev:** horshoes and clover

Date	Mintage	F	VF	XF	Unc	BU
2010 Proof	10,000	Value: 70.00				

KM# 412   DOLLAR
28.2800 g., 0.9250 Silver 0.8410 oz. ASW, 38.61 mm.   **Ruler:**
Elizabeth II **Subject:** Siberia **Obv:** Head with tiara right **Rev:**
Khanty-Mansiysk

Date	Mintage	F	VF	XF	Unc	BU
2010 Proof-like	4,000	—	—	—	—	60.00

KM# 413   DOLLAR
28.2800 g., 0.9250 Silver 0.8410 oz. ASW, 38.61 mm.   **Ruler:**
Elizabeth II **Subject:** Siberia **Obv:** Head with tiara right **Rev:** Uray

Date	Mintage	F	VF	XF	Unc	BU
2010 Proof-like	4,000	—	—	—	—	60.00

KM# 414   DOLLAR
28.2800 g., 0.9250 Silver 0.8410 oz. ASW, 38.61 mm.   **Ruler:**
Elizabeth II **Subject:** Siberia **Obv:** Head with tiara right **Rev:**
Surgut

Date	Mintage	F	VF	XF	Unc	BU
2010 Proof-like	4,000	—	—	—	—	60.00

KM# 415   DOLLAR
28.2800 g., 0.9250 Silver 0.8410 oz. ASW, 38.61 mm.   **Ruler:**
Elizabeth II **Subject:** Siberia **Obv:** Head with tiara right **Rev:**
Nizhnevartovsk

Date	Mintage	F	VF	XF	Unc	BU
2010 Proof-like	4,000	—	—	—	—	60.00

KM# 417   DOLLAR
28.2800 g., 0.9250 Silver 0.8410 oz. ASW, 38.61 mm.   **Ruler:**
Elizabeth II **Subject:** Famous Love Stories - Samson and Dalilah
Obv: Head with tiara right, Cupid below **Rev:** Portraits of Samson
and Dalilah

Date	Mintage	F	VF	XF	Unc	BU
2010 Proof	9,000	Value: 70.00				

KM# 418   DOLLAR
31.1000 g., 0.9990 Silver 0.9988 oz. ASW, 40 mm.   **Ruler:**
Elizabeth II **Subject:** Jaroslawl, 100th Anniversary **Obv:** Head
with tiara right **Rev:** Banner in color

Date	Mintage	F	VF	XF	Unc	BU
2010 Proof	2,000	Value: 75.00				

KM# 419   DOLLAR
31.1000 g., 0.9990 Silver 0.9988 oz. ASW, 40 mm.   **Ruler:**
Elizabeth II **Subject:** Jaroslawl, 1000th Anniversary **Obv:** Head
with tiara right **Rev:** Three church towers in color

Date	Mintage	F	VF	XF	Unc	BU
2010 Proof	9,000	Value: 75.00				

KM# 420   DOLLAR
31.1000 g., 0.9990 Silver 0.9988 oz. ASW, 40 mm.   **Ruler:**
Elizabeth II **Subject:** Jaroslawl, 1000th Anniversary **Obv:** Head
in tiara right **Rev:** Town square in color

Date	Mintage	F	VF	XF	Unc	BU
2010 Proof	9,000	Value: 75.00				

KM# 421 DOLLAR
28.2800 g., 0.9250 Silver 0.8410 oz. ASW, 36.81 mm. **Ruler:** Elizabeth II **Subject:** Cultural Achievements **Obv:** Head with tiara at center **Rev:** Bow and arrows, Bow and firestarting kit

Date	Mintage	F	VF	XF	Unc	BU
2010 Proof	6,000	Value: 80.00				

KM# 422 DOLLAR
28.2800 g., 0.9250 Silver 0.8410 oz. ASW, 44 mm. **Ruler:** Elizabeth II **Subject:** Christmas star **Obv:** Head with tiara right, snowflakes around **Rev:** Children before christmas tree in color **Shape:** 7-pointed star

Date	Mintage	F	VF	XF	Unc	BU
2010 Proof	15,000	Value: 95.00				

KM# 426 DOLLAR
28.2800 g., 0.9250 Silver 0.8410 oz. ASW, 41 mm. **Ruler:** Elizabeth II **Subject:** Four Leaf Clover **Obv:** Head with titara right, clovers **Rev:** four clovers and ripple background

Date	Mintage	F	VF	XF	Unc	BU
2010 Proof	10,000	Value: 70.00				

KM# 427 DOLLAR
28.2800 g., 0.9250 Silver 0.8410 oz. ASW, 38.61 mm. **Ruler:** Elizabeth II **Subject:** Veliky Novgorod **Obv:** Head with tiara right, montage of ship and coins at right **Rev:** Market scene, Church; city arms below

Date	Mintage	F	VF	XF	Unc	BU
2010 Proof	8,000	Value: 75.00				

KM# 428 DOLLAR
28.2800 g., 0.9250 Silver 0.8410 oz. ASW, 38.61 mm. **Ruler:** Elizabeth II **Subject:** Year of the Rabbit **Obv:** Head with tiara right **Rev:** Rabbit seated in field

Date	Mintage	F	VF	XF	Unc	BU
2010 Proof	3,000	Value: 75.00				

KM# 429 DOLLAR
28.2800 g., 0.9250 Silver 0.8410 oz. ASW, 38.61 mm. **Ruler:** Elizabeth II **Subject:** Year of the Rabbit **Obv:** Head with tiara right **Rev:** Two rabbits holding heart at center

Date	Mintage	F	VF	XF	Unc	BU
2010 Proof	3,000	Value: 75.00				

KM# 432 DOLLAR
28.2800 g., 0.9250 Silver 0.8410 oz. ASW, 40x28 mm. **Ruler:** Elizabeth II **Subject:** Francisco Goya **Obv:** Head with tiara right at left, painting of man and woman at right **Rev:** Goya and Clothed female reclining **Shape:** Rectangle

Date	Mintage	F	VF	XF	Unc	BU
2010 Proof	10,000	Value: 80.00				

KM# 433 DOLLAR
28.2800 g., 0.9250 Silver 0.8410 oz. ASW, 38.61 mm. **Ruler:** Elizabeth II **Subject:** Peter the Great **Obv:** Head with tiara right above ship and city view **Rev:** Half-length figure holding coins, map in background

Date	Mintage	F	VF	XF	Unc	BU
2010 Proof	4,000	Value: 75.00				

KM# 434 DOLLAR
28.2800 g., 0.9250 Silver 0.8410 oz. ASW, 38.61 mm. **Ruler:** Elizabeth II **Subject:** Sea of Love **Obv:** Head in tiara right above sunset at sea with heart at center **Rev:** Two white doves in flight over sea, within heart

Date	Mintage	F	VF	XF	Unc	BU
2010 Proof	7,000	Value: 70.00				

KM# 435 DOLLAR
15.5500 g., 0.9250 Silver 0.4624 oz. ASW, 35 mm. **Ruler:** Elizabeth II **Subject:** Prehistoric art - Chauvet cave **Rev:** Two figures of cats

Date	Mintage	F	VF	XF	Unc	BU
2010 Proof	1,000	Value: 65.00				

KM# 436 DOLLAR
15.5500 g., 0.9250 Silver 0.4624 oz. ASW, 35 mm. **Ruler:** Elizabeth II **Subject:** Prehistoric art - Altamira cave **Rev:** Bison artwork

Date	Mintage	F	VF	XF	Unc	BU
2010 Proof	1,000	Value: 65.00				

KM# 437 DOLLAR
15.5500 g., 0.9250 Silver 0.4624 oz. ASW, 35 mm. **Ruler:** Elizabeth II **Subject:** Prehistoric art - Lascaux cave **Rev:** Horse art

Date	Mintage	F	VF	XF	Unc	BU
2010 Proof	1,000	Value: 65.00				

KM# 438 DOLLAR
15.5500 g., 0.9250 Silver 0.4624 oz. ASW, 35 mm. **Ruler:** Elizabeth II **Subject:** Prehistoric art - Jabbaren cave **Rev:** Male figure with bow

Date	Mintage	F	VF	XF	Unc	BU
2010 Proof	1,000	Value: 65.00				

KM# 439 DOLLAR
15.5500 g., 0.9250 Silver 0.4624 oz. ASW, 35 mm. **Ruler:** Elizabeth II **Subject:** Prehistoric art - Tadrart cave **Rev:** Elephant art

Date	Mintage	F	VF	XF	Unc	BU
2010 Proof	1,000	Value: 65.00				

KM# 440 DOLLAR
28.2800 g., Copper-Nickel, 38.61 mm. **Ruler:** Elizabeth II **Subject:** Lifetime of Service **Obv:** Head in tiara right **Rev:** Conjoined busts of Elizabeth II and Prince Philip

Date	Mintage	F	VF	XF	Unc	BU
2010	—	—	—	—	—	20.00

KM# 440a DOLLAR
28.2800 g., 0.9250 Silver 0.8410 oz. ASW, 38.61 mm. **Ruler:**
Elizabeth II **Subject:** Lifetime of Service **Obv:** Head with tiara
right **Rev:** Conjoined busts of Elizabeth II and Prince Philip

Date	Mintage	F	VF	XF	Unc	BU
2010 Proof	19,500	Value: 50.00				

KM# 441 DOLLAR
31.1000 g., 0.9990 Silver 0.9988 oz. ASW, 38.61 mm. **Ruler:**
Elizabeth II **Subject:** Slovic mythology - Perun **Rev:** Two
warriors, tree in background

Date	Mintage	F	VF	XF	Unc	BU
2010 Proof	1,000	Value: 65.00				

KM# 454 DOLLAR
Silver **Ruler:** Elizabeth II **Subject:** Polish Stadiums **Rev:** Michail
Ktzov stadium

Date	Mintage	F	VF	XF	Unc	BU
2010 Proof	—	Value: 55.00				

KM# 455 DOLLAR
Silver **Ruler:** Elizabeth II **Subject:** Polish Stadiums **Rev:**
Gdansk

Date	Mintage	F	VF	XF	Unc	BU
2010 Proof	—	Value: 55.00				

KM# 456 DOLLAR
31.1030 g., 0.9990 Silver 0.9989 oz. ASW, 40 mm. **Ruler:**
Elizabeth II **Subject:** Giah Thong - safe conduct pass **Obv:** Head
with tiara right **Rev:** Two soldiers below Viet Nam flag

Date	Mintage	F	VF	XF	Unc	BU
2010 Prooflike	—	—	—	—	—	50.00

KM# 495 DOLLAR
28.2800 g., 0.9250 Silver 0.8410 oz. ASW, 38.61 mm. **Ruler:**
Elizabeth II **Subject:** Zodiac Mucha Paintings **Rev:** Aries

Date	Mintage	F	VF	XF	Unc	BU
2010 Proof	10,000	Value: 55.00				

KM# 496 DOLLAR
28.2800 g., 0.9250 Silver 0.8410 oz. ASW, 38.61 mm. **Ruler:**
Elizabeth II **Subject:** Zodiac Mucha Paintings **Rev:** Taurus

Date	Mintage	F	VF	XF	Unc	BU
2010 Proof	10,000	Value: 55.00				

KM# 497 DOLLAR
28.2800 g., 0.9250 Silver 0.8410 oz. ASW, 38.61 mm. **Ruler:**
Elizabeth II **Subject:** Zodiac Mucha Paintings **Rev:** Gemini

Date	Mintage	F	VF	XF	Unc	BU
2010 Proof	10,000	Value: 55.00				

KM# 498 DOLLAR
28.2800 g., 0.9250 Silver 0.8410 oz. ASW, 38.61 mm. **Ruler:**
Elizabeth II **Subject:** Zodiac Mucha Paintings **Rev:** Cancer

Date	Mintage	F	VF	XF	Unc	BU
2010 Proof	10,000	Value: 55.00				

KM# 499 DOLLAR
28.2800 g., 0.9250 Silver 0.8410 oz. ASW **Ruler:** Elizabeth II
Subject: Zodiac Mucha Paintings **Rev:** Leo

Date	Mintage	F	VF	XF	Unc	BU
2010 Proof	10,000	Value: 55.00				

KM# 500 DOLLAR
28.2500 g., 0.9250 Silver 0.8401 oz. ASW, 38.61 mm. **Ruler:**
Elizabeth II **Subject:** Zodiac Mucha Paintings **Rev:** Virgo

Date	Mintage	F	VF	XF	Unc	BU
2010 Proof	10,000	Value: 55.00				

KM# 501 DOLLAR
28.2800 g., 0.9250 Silver 0.8410 oz. ASW, 38.61 mm. **Ruler:**
Elizabeth II **Subject:** Zodiac Mucha Paintings **Rev:** Libra

Date	Mintage	F	VF	XF	Unc	BU
2010 Proof	10,000	Value: 55.00				

KM# 502 DOLLAR
28.2800 g., 0.9250 Silver 0.8410 oz. ASW, 38.61 mm. **Ruler:**
Elizabeth II **Subject:** Zodiac Mucha Paintings **Rev:** Scorpio

Date	Mintage	F	VF	XF	Unc	BU
2010 Proof	10,000	Value: 55.00				

KM# 503 DOLLAR
28.2800 g., 0.9250 Silver 0.8410 oz. ASW, 38.61 mm. **Ruler:**
Elizabeth II **Subject:** Zodiac Mucha Paintings **Rev:** Sagittarius

Date	Mintage	F	VF	XF	Unc	BU
2010 Proof	10,000	Value: 55.00				

KM# 557 DOLLAR
28.2800 g., 0.9250 Silver 0.8410 oz. ASW, 30x50 mm. **Ruler:**
Elizabeth II **Subject:** Westminister Abbey **Obv:** Head with tiara
at left, interior view of end windows **Rev:** Exterior view with rose
window detail **Shape:** vertical oval

Date	Mintage	F	VF	XF	Unc	BU
2010 Proof	5,000	Value: 100				

KM# 558 DOLLAR
28.2800 g., 0.9250 Silver 0.8410 oz. ASW, 30x50 mm. **Ruler:** Elizabeth II **Subject:** Stephansdom, Wein **Obv:** Head in tiara at left, view of organ screena dn statue detail **Rev:** Exterior rendering and detail **Shape:** Vertical oval

Date	Mintage	F	VF	XF	Unc	BU
2010 Proof	5,000	Value: 100				

KM# 504 DOLLAR
28.2800 g., 0.9250 Silver 0.8410 oz. ASW, 38.61 mm. **Ruler:** Elizabeth II **Subject:** Zodiac Mucha Paintings **Rev:** Capricorn

Date	Mintage	F	VF	XF	Unc	BU
2011 Proof	10,000	Value: 55.00				

KM# 505 DOLLAR
28.2800 g., 0.9250 Silver 0.8410 oz. ASW, 38.61 mm. **Ruler:** Elizabeth II **Subject:** Zodiac Mucha Painting **Rev:** Aquarius

Date	Mintage	F	VF	XF	Unc	BU
2011 Proof	10,000	Value: 55.00				

KM# 506 DOLLAR
28.2800 g., 0.9250 Silver 0.8410 oz. ASW, 38.61 mm. **Ruler:** Elizabeth II **Subject:** Zodiac Mucha Paintings **Rev:** Pisces

Date	Mintage	F	VF	XF	Unc	BU
2011 Proof	10,000	Value: 55.00				

KM# 508 DOLLAR
Silver **Ruler:** Elizabeth II **Subject:** Russian Cartoons

Date	Mintage	F	VF	XF	Unc	BU
2011 Proof	—	Value: 60.00				

KM# 509 DOLLAR
Silver **Ruler:** Elizabeth II **Subject:** Russian Cartoons

Date	Mintage	F	VF	XF	Unc	BU
2011 Proof	—	Value: 60.00				

KM# 510 DOLLAR
28.2800 g., 0.9250 Silver 0.8410 oz. ASW, 55.6x41.6 mm. **Ruler:** Elizabeth II **Subject:** Year of the Rabbit **Rev:** Rabbit in the snow **Shape:** Horizontal oval

Date	Mintage	F	VF	XF	Unc	BU
2011 Proof	5,000	Value: 55.00				

KM# 514 DOLLAR
31.1050 g., Silver Plated Copper-Nickel, 40 mm. **Ruler:** Elizabeth II **Subject:** Royal Engagement **Obv:** Head with tiara right **Rev:** Prince William and Catherine Middleton facing

Date	Mintage	F	VF	XF	Unc	BU
2011 Proof	10,000	Value: 25.00				

KM# 515 DOLLAR
31.1000 g., Silver Plated Copper, 40 mm. **Ruler:** Elizabeth II **Subject:** Diana - A wife, Princess, Mother, Legend

Date	Mintage	F	VF	XF	Unc	BU
2011 Proof	10,000	Value: 20.00				

KM# 516 DOLLAR
31.1000 g., Silver Plated Copper, 40 mm. **Ruler:** Elizabeth II **Subject:** Diana - Wedding to Charles

Date	Mintage	F	VF	XF	Unc	BU
2011 Proof	10,000	Value: 20.00				

KM# 517 DOLLAR
31.1000 g., Silver Plated Copper, 40 mm. **Ruler:** Elizabeth II **Subject:** Diana - Engaement to Prince Charles

Date	Mintage	F	VF	XF	Unc	BU
2011 Proof	10,000	Value: 20.00				

KM# 518 DOLLAR
31.1000 g., Silver Plated Copper, 40 mm. **Ruler:** Elizabeth II **Subject:** Diana - Quote

Date	Mintage	F	VF	XF	Unc	BU
2011 Proof	10,000	Value: 20.00				

KM# 519 DOLLAR
31.1000 g., Silver Plated Copper, 40 mm. **Ruler:** Elizabeth II **Subject:** Diana - Mother Teresa

Date	Mintage	F	VF	XF	Unc	BU
2011 Proof	10,000	Value: 20.00				

KM# 520 DOLLAR
31.1000 g., Silver Plated Copper, 40 mm. **Ruler:** Elizabeth II **Subject:** Diana - We will always remember

Date	Mintage	F	VF	XF	Unc	BU
2011 Proof	10,000	Value: 20.00				

KM# 554 DOLLAR
28.2800 g., 0.9250 Silver 0.8410 oz. ASW, 41 mm. **Ruler:** Elizabeth II **Obv:** Head with tiara right, three elephants and hologram **Rev:** Hologram elephant and two elephants under tree

Date	Mintage	F	VF	XF	Unc	BU
2011 Proof	Est. 10,000	Value: 75.00				

KM# 555 DOLLAR
28.2800 g., 0.9250 Silver 0.8410 oz. ASW, 38.61 mm. **Ruler:** Elizabeth II **Subject:** Hanseatic Towns - Szezecin **Obv:** Head with tiara right at left, map and ship **Rev:** Churches and ship at dock, town shield

Date	Mintage	F	VF	XF	Unc	BU
2011 Proof	Est. 3,000	Value: 75.00				

KM# 556 DOLLAR
28.2800 g., 0.9250 Silver 0.8410 oz. ASW, 38.61 mm. **Ruler:** Elizabeth II **Subject:** Yunona and Avos **Obv:** Head with tiara right, ornate frame in background **Rev:** Couple facing, seascape in background

Date	Mintage	F	VF	XF	Unc	BU
2011 Proof	Est. 5,000	Value: 75.00				

KM# 559 DOLLAR
28.2800 g., 0.9250 Silver 0.8410 oz. ASW, 38.61 mm. **Ruler:** Elizabeth II **Subject:** Russian municipalities - Krasnoyarsk **Obv:** Head with tiara right **Rev:** Town view

Date	Mintage	F	VF	XF	Unc	BU
2011 Proof	2,000	Value: 75.00				

KM# 560 DOLLAR
28.2800 g., 0.9250 Silver 0.8410 oz. ASW, 38.61 mm. **Ruler:** Elizabeth II **Subject:** Russian municipalities - Norilsk **Obv:** Head with tiara right **Rev:** Town view, shield above

Date	Mintage	F	VF	XF	Unc	BU
2011 Proof	2,000	Value: 75.00				

KM# 561 DOLLAR
28.2800 g., 0.9250 Silver 0.8410 oz. ASW, 38.61 mm. **Ruler:** Elizabeth II **Subject:** Russian municipalities - Belgorod **Obv:** Head with tiara right **Rev:** Statue at center, shield at left, tower at right

Date	Mintage	F	VF	XF	Unc	BU
2011 Proof	2,000	Value: 75.00				

KM# 562 DOLLAR
28.2800 g., 0.9250 Silver 0.8410 oz. ASW, 30x50 mm. **Ruler:** Elizabeth II **Subject:** Russian municipalities - Irkutsk **Obv:** Head with tiara right **Rev:** Town view **Shape:** Vertical oval

Date	Mintage	F	VF	XF	Unc	BU
2011 Proof	2,000	Value: 75.00				

Rhacophorus reinwardti

KM# 571 DOLLAR
28.2800 g., 0.9250 Silver 0.8410 oz. ASW, 40x40 mm. **Ruler:** Elizabeth II **Obv:** Head with diadem right, tracks in background **Rev:** Flying frog, Rhacophorus reinwardti **Shape:** Square

Date	Mintage	F	VF	XF	Unc	BU
2011 Proof	5,000	Value: 75.00				

KM# 583 DOLLAR
14.1400 g., 0.9250 Silver 0.4205 oz. ASW, 32 mm. **Ruler:**
Elizabeth II **Subject:** Russian comics - Bolek i Lolek **Rev:** Two
western children on horseback

Date	Mintage	F	VF	XF	Unc	BU
2011 Proof	Est. 4,000	Value: 55.00				

KM# 585 DOLLAR
28.2800 g., 0.9250 Silver 0.8410 oz. ASW, 40x28 mm. **Ruler:**
Elizabeth II **Obv:** Head with tiara right, five girls in painting **Rev:**
Diego Velazquez and painting of female nude

Date	Mintage	F	VF	XF	Unc	BU
2011 Proof	Est. 5,000	Value: 85.00				

KM# 586 DOLLAR
28.2800 g., 0.9250 Silver 0.8410 oz. ASW, 38.61 mm. **Ruler:**
Elizabeth II **Subject:** Amber Route - Aquileia **Rev:** Statue of
Romulus and Remus and wolf, amber insert

Date	Mintage	F	VF	XF	Unc	BU
2011 Antique finish	Est. 10,000	—	—	—	—	75.00

KM# 617 DOLLAR
28.2800 g., 0.9250 Silver 0.8410 oz. ASW, 38.61 mm. **Ruler:**
Elizabeth II **Obv:** Bust with tiara right before sailing ship in ornate
frame **Rev:** Yunona and Avos facing each other in color, ship
below

Date	Mintage	F	VF	XF	Unc	BU
2011 Proof	Est. 5,000	Value: 75.00				

KM# 618 DOLLAR
28.2800 g., 0.9250 Silver 0.8410 oz. ASW, 38.61 mm. **Ruler:**
Elizabeth II **Obv:** Head with tiara at left, map and sailing ship at
right, HANSA on ribbon above **Rev:** Town view of the port of
Szczecin

Date	Mintage	F	VF	XF	Unc	BU
2011 Proof	Est. 3,000	Value: 75.00				

KM# 619 DOLLAR
28.2800 g., 0.9250 Silver 0.8410 oz. ASW, 41 mm. **Ruler:**
Elizabeth II **Obv:** Head in tiara at left, elephant in designs **Rev:**
Two elephants at tree, elephant in hologram

Date	Mintage	F	VF	XF	Unc	BU
2011 Proof	Est. 10,000	Value: 75.00				

KM# 621 DOLLAR
16.8100 g., 0.9250 Silver 0.4999 oz. ASW, 36.81 mm. **Ruler:**
Elizabeth II **Obv:** Head with tiara right **Rev:** Chinese dragon
prancing right with ball

Date	Mintage	F	VF	XF	Unc	BU
2011 Proof	Est. 6,000	Value: 75.00				

KM# 622 DOLLAR
16.8100 g., 0.9250 Silver 0.4999 oz. ASW, 36.81 mm. **Ruler:**
Elizabeth II **Obv:** Head with tiara right **Rev:** Child's fantasy
dragon, knight and castle

Date	Mintage	F	VF	XF	Unc	BU
2011 Proof	Est. 6,000	Value: 75.00				

KM# 641 DOLLAR
28.2800 g., 0.9250 Silver 0.8410 oz. ASW, 40x28 mm. **Ruler:**
Elizabeth II **Obv:** Portrait at left, paining **Rev:** Portrait at left,
painting **Shape:** Horizontal rectangle

Date	Mintage	F	VF	XF	Unc	BU
2011 Proof	5,000	Value: 100				

KM# 647 DOLLAR
31.1050 g., 0.9990 Silver 0.9990 oz. ASW, 38.61 mm. **Ruler:**
Elizabeth II **Subject:** First European to cross the Simpson Desert
Obv: Head with tiara right **Rev:** Simpson Desert and Ted Colson
in 3-D color **Edge:** Reeded

Date	Mintage	F	VF	XF	Unc	BU
2011 Proof	2,000	Value: 75.00				

KM# 652 DOLLAR
28.2800 g., 0.9250 Silver 0.8410 oz. ASW, 38.61 mm. **Ruler:**
Elizabeth II **Subject:** Papilio Machaon **Obv:** Head in tiara right,
butterfly wing in background **Rev:** Butterfly in color

Date	Mintage	F	VF	XF	Unc	BU
2011 Proof	Est. 5,000	Value: 65.00				

KM# 653 DOLLAR
Silver Plated Copper, 40 mm. **Ruler:** Elizabeth II **Subject:** Star
Wars - Obi-Wan Kenobi

Date	Mintage	F	VF	XF	Unc	BU
2011	Est. 50,000	—	—	—	—	25.00

KM# 654 DOLLAR
Silver Plated Copper, 40 mm. **Ruler:** Elizabeth II **Subject:** Star Wars - Yoda

Date	Mintage	F	VF	XF	Unc	BU
2011	Est. 50,000	—	—	—	—	25.00

KM# 655 DOLLAR
Silver Plated Copper, 40 mm. **Ruler:** Elizabeth II **Subject:** Star Wars - Princess Leia

Date	Mintage	F	VF	XF	Unc	BU
2011	Est. 50,000	—	—	—	—	25.00

KM# 656 DOLLAR
Silver Plated Copper, 40 mm. **Ruler:** Elizabeth II **Subject:** Star Wars - Luke Skywalker

Date	Mintage	F	VF	XF	Unc	BU
2011	Est. 50,000	—	—	—	—	25.00

KM# 657 DOLLAR
Silver Plated Copper, 40 mm. **Ruler:** Elizabeth II **Subject:** Star Wars - C3PO

Date	Mintage	F	VF	XF	Unc	BU
2011	Est. 50,000	—	—	—	—	25.00

KM# 658 DOLLAR
Silver Plated Copper, 40 mm. **Ruler:** Elizabeth II **Subject:** Star Wars - R2-D2

Date	Mintage	F	VF	XF	Unc	BU
2011	Est. 50,000	—	—	—	—	25.00

KM# 659 DOLLAR
Silver Plated Copper, 40 mm. **Ruler:** Elizabeth II **Subject:** Star Wars - Darth Vader

Date	Mintage	F	VF	XF	Unc	BU
2011	Est. 50,000	—	—	—	—	25.00

KM# 660 DOLLAR
Silver Plated Copper, 40 mm. **Ruler:** Elizabeth II **Subject:** Star Wars - Emperor Palpatine

Date	Mintage	F	VF	XF	Unc	BU
2011	Est. 50,000	—	—	—	—	25.00

KM# 661 DOLLAR
Silver Plated Copper, 40 mm. **Ruler:** Elizabeth II **Subject:** Star Wars - Han Solo

Date	Mintage	F	VF	XF	Unc	BU
2011	Est. 50,000	—	—	—	—	25.00

KM# 662 DOLLAR
Silver Plated Copper, 40 mm. **Ruler:** Elizabeth II **Subject:** Star Wars - Chewbacca

Date	Mintage	F	VF	XF	Unc	BU
2011	Est. 50,000	—	—	—	—	25.00

KM# 674 DOLLAR
28.2800 g., 0.9250 Silver 0.8410 oz. ASW, 40x28 mm. **Ruler:** Elizabeth II **Rev:** Orville and Wilbur Wright **Shape:** Rectangle

Date	Mintage	F	VF	XF	Unc	BU
2011 Proof	Est. 6,000	Value: 75.00				

KM# 688 DOLLAR
16.8100 g., 0.9250 Silver gilt 0.4999 oz. ASW, 38.61 mm. **Ruler:** Elizabeth II **Subject:** Amber Route **Rev:** Map of European cities

Date	Mintage	F	VF	XF	Unc	BU
2011 Proof	Est. 15,000	Value: 85.00				

KM# 690 DOLLAR
28.2800 g., 0.9250 Silver 0.8410 oz. ASW, 40.7 mm. **Ruler:** Elizabeth II **Subject:** Lucky-coin - Ladybug **Obv:** Head with tiara right, ladybug and flowers **Rev:** Ladybug and flowers

Date	Mintage	F	VF	XF	Unc	BU
2011 Proof	Est. 10,000	Value: 80.00				

KM# 703 DOLLAR
10.0000 g., 0.9250 Silver 0.2974 oz. ASW, 13x30 mm. **Ruler:**
Elizabeth II **Rev:** Amber insert in gilt floral motif **Shape:** Vertical
rectangle

Date	Mintage	F	VF	XF	Unc	BU
2011	Est. 12,000	—	—	—	—	50.00

KM# 704 DOLLAR
28.2800 g., 0.9250 Silver 0.8410 oz. ASW, 30x50 mm. **Ruler:**
Elizabeth II **Subject:** Barcerlona Cathedral **Obv:** Cross and
interior cathedral view **Rev:** Exterior cathedral view **Shape:** Oval

Date	Mintage	F	VF	XF	Unc	BU
2011 Proof	5,000	Value: 100				

KM# 705 DOLLAR
28.2800 g., 0.9250 Silver 0.8410 oz. ASW, 30x50 mm. **Ruler:**
Elizabeth II **Subject:** Prague's St. Wenceslas Cathedral **Obv:**
Cathedral window at top, side exterior view below **Rev:** Cathedral
window and ceiling motif **Shape:** Vertical Oval

Date	Mintage	F	VF	XF	Unc	BU
2011 Proof	5,000	Value: 100				

KM# 706 DOLLAR
28.2800 g., 0.9250 Silver 0.8410 oz. ASW, 30x50 mm. **Ruler:**
Elizabeth II **Subject:** Cracow's St. Mary Cathedral **Obv:**
Cathedral window and sculpture scene **Rev:** Cathedral Window,
exterior view and ceiling rendering **Shape:** Vertical oval

Date	Mintage	F	VF	XF	Unc	BU
2011 Proof	1,500	Value: 100				

KM# 707 DOLLAR
28.2800 g., 0.9250 Silver 0.8410 oz. ASW, 35x45 mm. **Ruler:**
Elizabeth II **Subject:** Love Love Love **Obv:** Queens head within
open egg design **Rev:** Two cherubs and heart **Shape:** Vertical oval

Date	Mintage	F	VF	XF	Unc	BU
2011 Proof	7,000	Value: 100				

KM# 709 DOLLAR
16.8100 g., 0.9250 Silver 0.4999 oz. ASW, 38.61 mm. **Ruler:**
Elizabeth II **Obv:** Ancient horsecart **Obv. Legend:** SZLAK
BURSZTYNOWY **Rev:** Neptune statue, ancient coin, mine
building, amber insert **Rev. Legend:** GDANSK

Date	Mintage	F	VF	XF	Unc	BU
2011 Proof	Est. 12,000	Value: 100				

KM# 711 DOLLAR
14.1400 g., 0.9250 Silver 0.4205 oz. ASW, 32 mm. **Ruler:**
Elizabeth II **Subject:** Russian Cartoon - Reksio **Rev:** Dog, cat
and rooster in color

Date	Mintage	F	VF	XF	Unc	BU
2011 Proof	Est. 6,000	Value: 100				

KM# 741 DOLLAR
28.2800 g., 0.9250 Silver 0.8410 oz. ASW **Ruler:** Elizabeth II
Obv: Head crowned at top, key **Rev:** Cat walking through open
door **Shape:** Irregular

Date	Mintage	F	VF	XF	Unc	BU
2011 Proof	7,000	Value: 75.00				

KM# 789 DOLLAR
16.8100 g., 0.9250 Silver 0.4999 oz. ASW, 38.61 mm. **Ruler:**
Elizabeth II **Subject:** Szlak Bursztynowey - Gdansk **Rev:** Mine
buildings, amber, coins and Neptune statue

Date	Mintage	F	VF	XF	Unc	BU
2011	Est. 12,000	—	—	—	—	75.00

KM# 735 DOLLAR
28.2800 g., 0.9250 Silver 0.8410 oz. ASW, 38.61 mm. **Ruler:**
Elizabeth II **Subject:** Hannibal Barkas **Obv:** Two elephant heads
facing each other **Rev:** Hannibal's head left above three war
elephants

Date	Mintage	F	VF	XF	Unc	BU
2012 Proof	Est. 5,000	Value: 100				

KM# 644 DOLLAR
28.2800 g., 0.9250 Silver 0.8410 oz. ASW, 35.1x45.1 mm.
Ruler: Elizabeth II **Subject:** Year of the Dragon **Obv:** Head with
crown right **Rev:** Multicolor dragon **Shape:** Vertical oval

Date	Mintage	F	VF	XF	Unc	BU
2012 Proof	5,000	Value: 100				

KM# 645 DOLLAR
28.2800 g., 0.9250 Silver 0.8410 oz. ASW, 35.1x45.1 mm.
Ruler: Elizabeth II **Subject:** Year of the Dragon **Obv:** Head with
crown right **Rev:** Multicolor juvenile dragon **Shape:** Vertical oval

Date	Mintage	F	VF	XF	Unc	BU
2012 Proof	5,000	Value: 100				

KM# 646 DOLLAR
28.2800 g., 0.9250 Silver 0.8410 oz. ASW, 45.1x35.1 mm.
Ruler: Elizabeth II **Subject:** Year of the Dragon **Obv:** Head with

crown right **Rev:** Multicolor Love dragon forming heart **Shape:** Horizontal oval

Date	Mintage	F	VF	XF	Unc	BU
2012 Proof	5,000	Value: 100				

KM# 687   DOLLAR
31.1050 g., 0.9250 Silver 0.9250 oz. ASW, 39 mm. **Ruler:** Elizabeth II **Rev:** Crowned fantasy fish **Shape:** 12-sided

Date	Mintage	F	VF	XF	Unc	BU
2012 Proof	2,000	Value: 80.00				

KM# 725   DOLLAR
Nickel Plated Copper, 40.7 mm. **Ruler:** Elizabeth II **Subject:** Star Wars - Tuskin Raider

Date	Mintage	F	VF	XF	Unc	BU
2012	50,000	—	—	—	—	25.00

KM# 726   DOLLAR
Nickel Plated Copper, 40.7 mm. **Ruler:** Elizabeth II **Subject:** Star Wars - Ewok Wicket

Date	Mintage	F	VF	XF	Unc	BU
2012	50,000	—	—	—	—	25.00

KM# 727   DOLLAR
Silver, 40.7 mm. **Ruler:** Elizabeth II **Subject:** Star Wars - Nien Nunb

Date	Mintage	F	VF	XF	Unc	BU
2012	50,000	—	—	—	—	25.00

KM# 728   DOLLAR
Nickel Plated Copper, 40.7 mm. **Ruler:** Elizabeth II **Subject:** Star Wars - Lando Calrissan

Date	Mintage	F	VF	XF	Unc	BU
2012	50,000	—	—	—	—	25.00

KM# 729   DOLLAR
Nickel Plated Copper, 40.7 mm. **Ruler:** Elizabeth II **Subject:** Star Wars - Grant Moff Tarkin

Date	Mintage	F	VF	XF	Unc	BU
2012	50,000	—	—	—	—	25.00

KM# 730   DOLLAR
Nickel Plated Copper, 40.7 mm. **Ruler:** Elizabeth II **Subject:** Star Wars - Storm Trooper

Date	Mintage	F	VF	XF	Unc	BU
2012	50,000	—	—	—	—	25.00

KM# 731   DOLLAR
Nickel Plated Copper, 40.7 mm. **Ruler:** Elizabeth II **Subject:** Star Wars - Jabba the Huntt

Date	Mintage	F	VF	XF	Unc	BU
2012	50,000	—	—	—	—	25.00

KM# 732   DOLLAR
Nickel Plated Copper, 40.7 mm. **Ruler:** Elizabeth II **Subject:** Star Wars - Admiral Ackbar

Date	Mintage	F	VF	XF	Unc	BU
2012	50,000	—	—	—	—	25.00

KM# 733   DOLLAR
Nickel Plated Copper, 40.7 mm. **Ruler:** Elizabeth II **Subject:** Star Wars - Jawa

Date	Mintage	F	VF	XF	Unc	BU
2012	50,000	—	—	—	—	25.00

KM# 734   DOLLAR
Nickel Plated Copper, 40.7 mm. **Ruler:** Elizabeth II **Subject:** Star Wars - Roba Fett

Date	Mintage	F	VF	XF	Unc	BU
2012	50,000	—	—	—	—	25.00

KM# 739   DOLLAR
15.5500 g., 0.9990 Silver 0.4994 oz. ASW, 36 mm. **Ruler:** Elizabeth II **Subject:** Viet Nam War, 50th Anniversary of Australia's involvement **Rev:** Two soldiers on patrol, on close, helicopter above

Date	Mintage	F	VF	XF	Unc	BU
2012 Proof	2,500	Value: 50.00				

KM# 757   DOLLAR
25.0000 g., 0.9250 Silver 0.7435 oz. ASW, 40 mm. **Ruler:** Elizabeth II **Subject:** Battle for Australia - Bombing of Darwin **Rev:** Soldier with machine gun post and Japanese plane in sky, ship in distance

Date	Mintage	F	VF	XF	Unc	BU
2012 Proof	Est. 1,942	Value: 75.00				

KM# 758   DOLLAR
25.0000 g., 0.9250 Silver 0.7435 oz. ASW, 40 mm. **Ruler:** Elizabeth II **Subject:** Battle for Australia - Sydney Harbor **Rev:** Sub, ship and pontoon plane with Sydney Harbor bridge

Date	Mintage	F	VF	XF	Unc	BU
2012 Proof	Est. 1,942	Value: 100				

KM# 759 DOLLAR
25.0000 g., 0.9250 Silver 0.7435 oz. ASW, 40 mm. **Ruler:**
Elizabeth II **Subject:** Battle for Australia - Kokoda Track **Rev:**
Two injured soldiers being protected by third

Date	Mintage	F	VF	XF	Unc	BU
2012 Proof	Est. 1,942	Value: 100				

KM# 760 DOLLAR
25.0000 g., 0.9250 Silver 0.7435 oz. ASW, 40 mm. **Ruler:**
Elizabeth II **Subject:** Battle for Australia - Coral Sea **Rev:** Battle
ship and planes

Date	Mintage	F	VF	XF	Unc	BU
2012 Proof	Est. 1,942	Value: 100				

KM# 761 DOLLAR
25.0000 g., 0.9250 Silver 0.7435 oz. ASW, 40 mm. **Ruler:**
Elizabeth II **Subject:** First car to cross Australia - The Brush **Obv:**
Head with crown right **Rev:** Early automobile, color landscape
below

Date	Mintage	F	VF	XF	Unc	BU
2012 Proof	Est. 2,500	Value: 100				

KM# 763 DOLLAR
28.2800 g., 0.9250 Silver 0.8410 oz. ASW, 30x50 mm. **Ruler:**
Elizabeth II **Rev:** Fisherman and nice trout **Rev. Legend:**
BEGINNER'S LUCK **Shape:** Vertical oval

Date	Mintage	F	VF	XF	Unc	BU
2012 Proof	Est. 7,000	Value: 100				

KM# 764 DOLLAR
28.2800 g., 0.9250 Silver 0.8410 oz. ASW, 28x40 mm. **Ruler:**
Elizabeth II **Subject:** Ksenia of Petersburg **Rev:** Female saint
with cane, church at lower left **Shape:** Vertical rectangle

Date	Mintage	F	VF	XF	Unc	BU
2012 Proof	Est. 7,000	Value: 100				

KM# 765 DOLLAR
28.2800 g., 0.9250 Silver 0.8410 oz. ASW, 38.61 mm. **Ruler:**
Elizabeth II **Subject:** Russian Cities - Kuzbas **Rev:** Statue of
Worker, gear in background

Date	Mintage	F	VF	XF	Unc	BU
2012 Proof	Est. 4,000	Value: 100				

KM# 766 DOLLAR
28.2800 g., 0.9250 Silver 0.8410 oz. ASW, 38.61 mm. **Ruler:**
Elizabeth II **Subject:** Russian Cities - Novosibirsk **Rev:** Church
tower, bridge in distance

Date	Mintage	F	VF	XF	Unc	BU
2012 Proof	Est. 2,000	Value: 100				

KM# 767 DOLLAR
28.2800 g., 0.9250 Silver 0.8410 oz. ASW, 38.61 mm. **Ruler:**
Elizabeth II **Subject:** Stars Flight **Rev:** International Space
Station and Russian stamp

Date	Mintage	F	VF	XF	Unc	BU
2012 Proof	Est. 5,000	Value: 100				

KM# 768 DOLLAR
28.2800 g., 0.9250 Silver 0.8410 oz. ASW, 38.61 mm. **Ruler:**
Elizabeth II **Subject:** War of 1812 - Artillery **Rev:** Solder standing
beside canon

Date	Mintage	F	VF	XF	Unc	BU
2012 Proof	Est. 5,000	Value: 100				

KM# 769 DOLLAR
28.2800 g., 0.9250 Silver 0.8410 oz. ASW, 38.61 mm. **Ruler:**
Elizabeth II **Subject:** War of 1812 - Cavalry **Rev:** Horseman with
sword

Date	Mintage	F	VF	XF	Unc	BU
2012 Proof	Est. 5,000	Value: 100				

KM# 770 DOLLAR
28.2800 g., 0.9250 Silver 0.8410 oz. ASW, 38.61 mm. **Ruler:**
Elizabeth II **Subject:** War of 1812 - Infantry **Rev:** Soldier with rifle

Date	Mintage	F	VF	XF	Unc	BU
2012 Proof	Est. 5,000	Value: 1,000				

KM# 771 DOLLAR
28.2800 g., 0.9250 Silver 0.8410 oz. ASW, 38.61 mm. **Ruler:**
Elizabeth II **Subject:** War of 1812 - Generals

Date	Mintage	F	VF	XF	Unc	BU
2012 Proof	Est. 5,000	Value: 100				

KM# 772 DOLLAR
27.5000 g., Silver Plated Copper-Nickel, 40 mm. **Ruler:**
Elizabeth II **Subject:** Benedict XVI's visit to Brazil, 5th
Anniversary **Rev:** Statue of Nossa Senhora, image of Benedict

Date	Mintage	F	VF	XF	Unc	BU
2012 Proof	Est. 1,000	Value: 25.00				

KM# 773 DOLLAR
16.8100 g., 0.9250 Silver 0.4999 oz. ASW, 38.61 mm. **Ruler:**
Elizabeth II **Subject:** Stare Hradisko **Obv:** Queen's head at left,
two horse cart at right **Rev:** Celtic coin image and art, amber insert

Date	Mintage	F	VF	XF	Unc	BU
2012	Est. 12,000	Value: 50.00				

KM# 775 DOLLAR
16.8100 g., 0.9250 Silver 0.4999 oz. ASW, 29x39 mm. **Ruler:**
Elizabeth II **Subject:** Imperial Faberge Eggs - Coronation egg
Rev: Egg and state coach

Date	Mintage	F	VF	XF	Unc	BU
2012 Proof	Est. 9,999	Value: 75.00				

KM# 779 DOLLAR
16.8100 g., 0.9250 Silver 0.4999 oz. ASW, 38.61 mm. **Ruler:**
Elizabeth II **Subject:** Silk Route - Wroclaw **Obv:** Queen's head
at left, two horse cart at right **Rev:** Old building at left, statue at right

Date	Mintage	F	VF	XF	Unc	BU
2012 Proof	Est. 12,000	Value: 75.00				

KM# 781 DOLLAR
28.2800 g., 0.9250 Silver 0.8410 oz. ASW, 38.61 mm. **Ruler:**
Elizabeth II **Subject:** March 8th, International Woman's Day **Obv:**
Head with tiara right **Rev:** Flowers, date in Russian

Date	Mintage	F	VF	XF	Unc	BU
2012 Proof	Est. 2,000	Value: 75.00				

KM# 787 DOLLAR
0.3000 g., 0.9990 Gold 0.0096 oz. AGW, 11 mm. **Ruler:**
Elizabeth II **Obv:** Head with tiara right **Rev:** Princess Grace of
Monaco (Grace Kelly) head left

Date	Mintage	F	VF	XF	Unc	BU
2012 Proof	Est. 5,000	Value: 75.00				

KM# 790 DOLLAR
28.2800 g., 0.9250 Silver 0.8410 oz. ASW, 28x40 mm. **Ruler:**
Elizabeth II **Subject:** Art of Hunting, Fox Hunt **Obv:** Pointer, left
Rev: Fox, hounds and riders **Shape:** Vertical rectangle

Date	Mintage	F	VF	XF	Unc	BU
2012 Proof	4,000	Value: 100				

KM# 792 DOLLAR
14.1400 g., 0.9250 Silver 0.4205 oz. ASW, 49.9x32.8x9.15 mm.
Ruler: Elizabeth II **Subject:** Swallow's Nest **Obv:** Island view
Rev: Castle atop cliff **Shape:** Irregular

Date	Mintage	F	VF	XF	Unc	BU
2012 Proof	Est. 3,000	Value: 100				

KM# 794 DOLLAR
16.8100 g., 0.9250 Silver 0.4999 oz. ASW, 38.61 mm. **Ruler:**
Elizabeth II **Subject:** Szlak Bursztynowy - Szombathely **Rev:** Old
coin, building, amber insert

Date	Mintage	F	VF	XF	Unc	BU
2012 Proof	Est. 12,000	Value: 75.00				

KM# 800 DOLLAR
28.2800 g., 0.9250 Silver 0.8410 oz. ASW, 38.61 mm. **Ruler:**
Elizabeth II **Rev:** Goliath Birdwing butterfly **Rev. Legend:**
ORNITHOPTERA GOLIATH

Date	Mintage	F	VF	XF	Unc	BU
2012 Proof	Est. 8,000	Value: 100				

KM# 804 DOLLAR
14.1400 g., 0.9250 Silver 0.4205 oz. ASW, 37x30 mm. **Ruler:** Elizabeth II **Subject:** Me **Obv:** Queen's head with tiara right, four baloon hearts **Rev:** Bird facing left **Shape:** Irregular

Date	Mintage	F	VF	XF	Unc	BU
2012 Proof	Est. 10,000	Value: 75.00				

KM# 805 DOLLAR
14.1400 g., 0.9250 Silver 0.4205 oz. ASW, 37x30 mm. **Ruler:** Elizabeth II **Subject:** You **Obv:** Queen's head in tiara at right, three heart baloons **Rev:** Bird facing right **Shape:** Irregular

Date	Mintage	F	VF	XF	Unc	BU
2012 Proof	Est. 10,000	Value: 75.00				

KM# 265 2 DOLLARS
62.2100 g., 0.9990 Silver 1.9980 oz. ASW, 55 mm. **Ruler:** Elizabeth II **Subject:** Year of the Rooster **Rev:** Multicolor rooster standing right, sunrise

Date	Mintage	F	VF	XF	Unc	BU
2005 Proof	—	Value: 85.00				

KM# 294 2 DOLLARS
62.2000 g., 0.9990 Silver 1.9977 oz. ASW, 55 mm. **Ruler:** Elizabeth II **Subject:** Year of the Dog **Rev:** Multicolor dog

Date	Mintage	F	VF	XF	Unc	BU
2005 Proof	—	Value: 95.00				

KM# 269 2 DOLLARS
1.2400 g., 0.9990 Gold 0.0398 oz. AGW, 14 mm. **Ruler:** Elizabeth II **Subject:** Year of the Rooster

Date	Mintage	F	VF	XF	Unc	BU
2005 Proof	—	Value: 80.00				

KM# 270 2 DOLLARS
1.5600 g., 0.9990 Gold 0.0501 oz. AGW, 18 mm. **Ruler:** Elizabeth II **Subject:** Year of the Rooster

Date	Mintage	F	VF	XF	Unc	BU
2005 Proof	—	Value: 110				

KM# 271 2 DOLLARS
3.1100 g., 0.9990 Gold 0.0999 oz. AGW, 18 mm. **Ruler:** Elizabeth II **Subject:** Year of the Rooster

Date	Mintage	F	VF	XF	Unc	BU
2005 Proof	—	Value: 185				

KM# 278 2 DOLLARS
3.1100 g., 0.9990 Gold 0.0999 oz. AGW, 18 mm. **Ruler:** Elizabeth II **Subject:** Chinese space acheivements **Rev:** Multicolor rocket, flag, map

Date	Mintage	F	VF	XF	Unc	BU
2005 Proof	Est. 3,000	Value: 195				

KM# 279 2 DOLLARS
31.1050 g., 0.9990 Silver 0.9990 oz. ASW, 35x46 mm. **Ruler:** Elizabeth II **Subject:** Impressionist paintings **Rev:** Multicolor painting of a bridge **Shape:** Vertical rectangle

Date	Mintage	F	VF	XF	Unc	BU
2005 Proof	Est. 2,005	Value: 65.00				

KM# 280 2 DOLLARS
31.1050 g., 0.9990 Silver 0.9990 oz. ASW, 35x46 mm. **Ruler:** Elizabeth II **Subject:** Impressionist paintings **Rev:** Multicolor painting of a female **Shape:** Vertical rectangle

Date	Mintage	F	VF	XF	Unc	BU
2005 Proof	Est. 2,005	Value: 65.00				

KM# 281 2 DOLLARS
31.1050 g., 0.9990 Silver 0.9990 oz. ASW, 35x46 mm. **Ruler:** Elizabeth II **Subject:** Impressionists paintings **Rev:** Multicolor painting of a village **Shape:** Vertical rectangle

Date	Mintage	F	VF	XF	Unc	BU
2005 Proof	Est. 2,005	Value: 65.00				

KM# 282 2 DOLLARS
31.1050 g., 0.9990 Silver 0.9990 oz. ASW, 35x46 mm. **Ruler:** Elizabeth II **Subject:** Impressionists paintings **Rev:** Multicolor painting of a seaside **Shape:** Vertical rectangle

Date	Mintage	F	VF	XF	Unc	BU
2005 Proof	Est. 2,005	Value: 65.00				

KM# 283 2 DOLLARS
31.1050 g., 0.9990 Silver 0.9990 oz. ASW, 35x46 mm. **Ruler:** Elizabeth II **Subject:** Impressionists paintings **Rev:** Multicolor painting of Paris **Shape:** Vertical rectangle

Date	Mintage	F	VF	XF	Unc	BU
2005 Proof	Est. 2,005	Value: 65.00				

KM# 284 2 DOLLARS
31.1050 g., 0.9990 Silver 0.9990 oz. ASW, 35x46 mm. **Ruler:** Elizabeth II **Subject:** Impressionists paintings **Rev:** Multicolor painting of female **Shape:** Vertical rectangle

Date	Mintage	F	VF	XF	Unc	BU
2005 Proof	Est. 2,005	Value: 65.00				

KM# 285 2 DOLLARS
31.1050 g., 0.9990 Silver 0.9990 oz. ASW, 35x46 mm. **Ruler:** Elizabeth II **Subject:** Impressionists paintings **Rev:** Multicolor painting of dancers **Shape:** Vertical rectangle

Date	Mintage	F	VF	XF	Unc	BU
2005 Proof	Est. 2,005	Value: 65.00				

KM# 286 2 DOLLARS
31.1050 g., 0.9990 Silver 0.9990 oz. ASW, 35x46 mm. **Ruler:** Elizabeth II **Subject:** Impressionists paintings **Rev:** Multicolor painting of Fifer **Shape:** Vertical rectangle

Date	Mintage	F	VF	XF	Unc	BU
2005 Proof	Est. 2,005	Value: 65.00				

KM# 287 2 DOLLARS
31.1050 g., 0.9990 Silver 0.9990 oz. ASW, 35x46 mm. **Ruler:** Elizabeth II **Subject:** Impressionists paintings **Rev:** Multicolor painting of boats **Shape:** Vertical rectangle

Date	Mintage	F	VF	XF	Unc	BU
2005 Proof	Est. 2,005	Value: 65.00				

KM# 288 2 DOLLARS
31.1050 g., 0.9990 Silver 0.9990 oz. ASW, 35x46 mm. **Ruler:** Elizabeth II **Subject:** Impressionists paintings **Obv:** Multicolor painting of Paris scene **Shape:** Vertical rectangle

Date	Mintage	F	VF	XF	Unc	BU
2005 Proof	Est. 2,005	Value: 65.00				

KM# 289 2 DOLLARS
31.1050 g., 0.9990 Silver 0.9990 oz. ASW, 35x46 mm. **Ruler:** Elizabeth II **Subject:** Impressionists paintings **Rev:** Multicolor painting of a maiden **Shape:** Vertical rectangle

Date	Mintage	F	VF	XF	Unc	BU
2005 Proof	Est. 2,005	Value: 65.00				

KM# 290 2 DOLLARS
31.1050 g., 0.9990 Silver 0.9990 oz. ASW, 35x46 mm. **Ruler:** Elizabeth II **Subject:** Impressionis paintings **Rev:** Multicolor painting of an artist **Shape:** Vertical rectangle

Date	Mintage	F	VF	XF	Unc	BU
2005 Proof	Est. 2,005	Value: 65.00				

KM# 291 2 DOLLARS
31.1050 g., 0.9990 Silver 0.9990 oz. ASW, 35x46 mm. **Ruler:** Elizabeth II **Subject:** Impressionists paintings **Rev:** Multicolor painting of Canada **Shape:** Vertical rectangle

Date	Mintage	F	VF	XF	Unc	BU
2005 Proof	Est. 2,005	Value: 65.00				

KM# 298 2 DOLLARS
1.5600 g., 0.9990 Gold 0.0501 oz. AGW, 16 mm. **Ruler:** Elizabeth II **Subject:** Year of the Dog **Rev:** Multicolor dog

Date	Mintage	F	VF	XF	Unc	BU
2005 Proof	—	Value: 95.00				

KM# 299 2 DOLLARS
3.1100 g., 0.9990 Gold 0.0999 oz. AGW, 18 mm. **Ruler:** Elizabeth II **Subject:** Year of the Dog **Rev:** Multicolor dog

Date	Mintage	F	VF	XF	Unc	BU
2005 Proof	—	Value: 185				

KM# 330 2 DOLLARS
62.2000 g., 0.9990 Silver 1.9977 oz. ASW, 30x70 mm. **Ruler:** Elizabeth II **Subject:** Life of Christ **Rev:** Last Supper (1495) **Shape:** Vertical rectangle

Date	Mintage	F	VF	XF	Unc	BU
2006 Proof	Est. 1,000	Value: 175				

KM# 190 2 DOLLARS
1.5000 g., 0.9990 Gold 0.0482 oz. AGW **Ruler:** Elizabeth II **Subject:** Year of the Pig **Obv:** Head right **Rev:** Multicolor pig

Date	Mintage	F	VF	XF	Unc	BU
2007 Proof	—	Value: 95.00				

KM# 205 2 DOLLARS
31.1050 g., 0.9990 Silver 0.9990 oz. ASW, 40.7 mm. **Ruler:** Elizabeth II **Subject:** Peoples Republic of China, 60th Anniversary **Rev:** Dragon and scenes of China in multicolor

Date	Mintage	F	VF	XF	Unc	BU
2008 Proof	6,888	Value: 150				

KM# 214 2 DOLLARS
62.2100 g., 0.9990 Silver 1.9980 oz. ASW, 63x27 mm. **Ruler:** Elizabeth II **Subject:** Feng Shui **Rev:** Multicolor blossoming peonies **Shape:** Vertical rectangle

Date	Mintage	F	VF	XF	Unc	BU
2009 Prooflike	16,888	—	—	—	—	200

KM# 185 2 DOLLARS
31.1050 g., 0.9990 Silver Partially gilt 0.9990 oz. ASW, 40 mm. **Ruler:** Elizabeth II **Subject:** Year of the Ox **Rev:** Gilt ox advancing left

Date	Mintage	F	VF	XF	Unc	BU
2009 Proof	20,000	Value: 185				

KM# 199 2 DOLLARS
25.0000 g., 0.9250 Silver 0.7435 oz. ASW, 38.6 mm. **Ruler:** Elizabeth II **Rev:** Two spinner dolphins leaping, swarovski crystal chip in eye

Date	Mintage	F	VF	XF	Unc	BU
2009 Proof	2,500	Value: 50.00				

KM# 200 2 DOLLARS
0.5000 g., 0.9990 Gold 0.0161 oz. AGW, 11 mm. **Ruler:** Elizabeth II **Rev:** Two spinner dolphins leaping out of the water

Date	Mintage	F	VF	XF	Unc	BU
2009 Proof	10,000	Value: 50.00				

KM# 209 2 DOLLARS
1.0000 g., 0.9000 Gold 0.0289 oz. AGW **Ruler:** Elizabeth II **Subject:** Frederic Chopin **Obv:** Elizabeth II head right **Rev:** Chopin bust and autograph

Date	Mintage	F	VF	XF	Unc	BU
2009 Proof	10,000	Value: 100				

KM# 210 2 DOLLARS
31.1050 g., 0.9990 Silver 0.9990 oz. ASW, 40.7 mm. **Ruler:** Elizabeth II **Obv:** Head right **Rev:** Two black swans, multicolor

Date	Mintage	F	VF	XF	Unc	BU
2009 Proof	10,000	Value: 80.00				

KM# 215   2 DOLLARS
31.1050 g., 0.9990 Silver 0.9990 oz. ASW, 40 mm. **Ruler:**
Elizabeth II **Subject:** Russian Ballet **Rev:** Anna Pavlova in
multicolor

Date	Mintage	F	VF	XF	Unc	BU
2009 Prooflike	5,000	—	—	—	—	120

KM# 216   2 DOLLARS
31.1030 g., 0.9990 Silver 0.9989 oz. ASW, 40.7 mm. **Ruler:**
Elizabeth II **Subject:** Russian Ballet **Rev:** Matilda Kshesinskaya
in multicolor

Date	Mintage	F	VF	XF	Unc	BU
2009 Prooflike	10,000	—	—	—	—	100

KM# 217   2 DOLLARS
31.1050 g., 0.9990 Silver 0.9990 oz. ASW, 40.7 mm. **Ruler:**
Elizabeth II **Subject:** Russian Ballet **Rev:** Sergey Lefar in
multicolor

Date	Mintage	F	VF	XF	Unc	BU
2009 Prooflike	10,000	—	—	—	—	100

KM# 218   2 DOLLARS
31.1050 g., 0.9990 Silver 0.9990 oz. ASW, 40.7 mm. **Ruler:**
Elizabeth II **Subject:** Russian Ballet **Rev:** Sergi Daighilev in
multicolor

Date	Mintage	F	VF	XF	Unc	BU
2009 Prooflike	10,000	—	—	—	—	100

KM# 219   2 DOLLARS
31.1030 g., 0.9990 Silver 0.9989 oz. ASW, 40.7 mm. **Ruler:**
Elizabeth II **Subject:** Russian Ballet **Rev:** Vaslav Fomich Nijinsky

Date	Mintage	F	VF	XF	Unc	BU
2009 Prooflike	10,000	—	—	—	—	100

KM# 220   2 DOLLARS
31.1050 g., 0.9990 Silver 0.9990 oz. ASW, 40.7 mm. **Ruler:**
Elizabeth II **Subject:** Panagyurishte Treasure **Rev:** Vessel in the
shape of a female head right

Date	Mintage	F	VF	XF	Unc	BU
2009	5,000	—	—	—	—	120

KM# 221   2 DOLLARS
31.1050 g., 0.9990 Silver 0.9990 oz. ASW, 40.7 mm. **Ruler:**
Elizabeth II **Subject:** Panagyurishte Treasure **Rev:** Vessel in
shape of female head left

Date	Mintage	F	VF	XF	Unc	BU
2009	5,000	—	—	—	—	120

KM# 222   2 DOLLARS
31.1050 g., 0.9990 Silver 0.9990 oz. ASW, 40.7 mm. **Ruler:**
Elizabeth II **Subject:** Panagyurishte Treasure **Rev:** Vessel in
shape of ram's head

Date	Mintage	F	VF	XF	Unc	BU
2009	5,000	—	—	—	—	120

KM# 223   2 DOLLARS
31.1050 g., 0.9990 Silver 0.9990 oz. ASW, 40 mm. **Ruler:**
Elizabeth II **Subject:** Peoples Republic of China, 60th
Anniversary **Rev:** Multicolor background, astronaut, olympic
flame and dragon motifs

Date	Mintage	F	VF	XF	Unc	BU
2009 Prooflike	6,888	—	—	—	—	95.00

KM# 224   2 DOLLARS
31.1050 g., 0.9990 Silver 0.9990 oz. ASW, 40.7 mm. **Ruler:**
Elizabeth II **Series:** Soviet Automobiles **Rev:** GAZ 12 ZIM in
multicolor

Date	Mintage	F	VF	XF	Unc	BU
2009 Prooflike	15,000	—	—	—	—	80.00

KM# 225   2 DOLLARS
31.1050 g., 0.9990 Silver 0.9990 oz. ASW, 40.7 mm. **Ruler:**
Elizabeth II **Subject:** Soviet Automobiles **Rev:** GAZ M290
Pobeda in multicolor

Date	Mintage	F	VF	XF	Unc	BU
2009 Prooflike	15,000	—	—	—	—	80.00

KM# 226   2 DOLLARS
31.1050 g., 0.9990 Silver 0.9990 oz. ASW, 40.7 mm. **Ruler:**
Elizabeth II **Subject:** Soviet Automobiles **Rev:** GAZ M21 Volga

Date	Mintage	F	VF	XF	Unc	BU
2009 Prooflike	15,000	—	—	—	—	80.00

KM# 227   2 DOLLARS
31.1050 g., 0.9990 Silver 0.9990 oz. ASW, 40.7 mm. **Ruler:**
Elizabeth II **Subject:** Soviet Automobiles **Rev:** Moskvich 400

Date	Mintage	F	VF	XF	Unc	BU
2009 Prooflike	15,000	—	—	—	—	80.00

KM# 229   2 DOLLARS
31.1050 g., 0.9990 Silver partially gilt 0.9990 oz. ASW, 40 mm.
Ruler: Elizabeth II **Subject:** Year of the Ox **Rev:** Ox, partially gilt

Date	Mintage	F	VF	XF	Unc	BU
2009 Proof	2,000	Value: 100				

KM# 350   2 DOLLARS
25.0000 g., 0.9990 Silver 0.8029 oz. ASW, 38.61 mm. **Ruler:**
Elizabeth II **Rev:** Partridge in a pair tree

Date	Mintage	F	VF	XF	Unc	BU
2009	1,500	Value: 70.00				

KM# 351   2 DOLLARS
25.0000 g., 0.9990 Silver 0.8029 oz. ASW, 38.61 mm. **Ruler:**
Elizabeth II **Rev:** Two turtle doves

Date	Mintage	F	VF	XF	Unc	BU
2009 Proof	1,500	Value: 70.00				

KM# 352   2 DOLLARS
25.0000 g., 0.9990 Silver 0.8029 oz. ASW, 38.61 mm. **Ruler:**
Elizabeth II **Rev:** Three French hens

Date	Mintage	F	VF	XF	Unc	BU
2009 Proof	1,500	Value: 70.00				

KM# 353   2 DOLLARS
25.0000 g., 0.9990 Silver 0.8029 oz. ASW, 38.61 mm. **Ruler:**
Elizabeth II **Rev:** Four Colly Birds

Date	Mintage	F	VF	XF	Unc	BU
2009 Proof	1,500	Value: 70.00				

KM# 354   2 DOLLARS
25.0000 g., 0.9990 Silver 0.8029 oz. ASW, 38.61 mm. **Ruler:**
Elizabeth II **Rev:** Five golden rings

Date	Mintage	F	VF	XF	Unc	BU
2009 Proof	1,500	Value: 70.00				

KM# 355   2 DOLLARS
25.0000 g., 0.9990 Silver 0.8029 oz. ASW, 38.61 mm. **Ruler:**
Elizabeth II **Rev:** Six Geese a-laying

Date	Mintage	F	VF	XF	Unc	BU
2009 Proof	1,500	Value: 70.00				

KM# 356   2 DOLLARS
25.0000 g., 0.9990 Silver 0.8029 oz. ASW, 38.61 mm. **Ruler:**
Elizabeth II **Rev:** Seven swans a-swimming

Date	Mintage	F	VF	XF	Unc	BU
2009 Proof	1,500	Value: 70.00				

KM# 357   2 DOLLARS
25.0000 g., 0.9990 Silver 0.8029 oz. ASW, 38.61 mm. **Ruler:**
Elizabeth II **Rev:** Eight maids a-milking

Date	Mintage	F	VF	XF	Unc	BU
2009 Proof	1,500	Value: 70.00				

KM# 358   2 DOLLARS
25.0000 g., 0.9990 Silver 0.8029 oz. ASW, 38.61 mm. **Ruler:**
Elizabeth II **Rev:** Nine ladies dancing

Date	Mintage	F	VF	XF	Unc	BU
2009 Proof	1,500	Value: 70.00				

KM# 359   2 DOLLARS
25.0000 g., 0.9990 Silver 0.8029 oz. ASW, 38.61 mm. **Ruler:**
Elizabeth II **Rev:** Ten Lords a-leaping

Date	Mintage	F	VF	XF	Unc	BU
2009 Proof	1,500	Value: 70.00				

KM# 360   2 DOLLARS
25.0000 g., 0.9990 Silver 0.8029 oz. ASW, 38.61 mm. **Ruler:**
Elizabeth II **Rev:** Eleven Pipers Piping

Date	Mintage	F	VF	XF	Unc	BU
2009 Proof	1,500	Value: 70.00				

KM# 361   2 DOLLARS
25.0000 g., 0.9990 Silver 0.8029 oz. ASW, 38.61 mm. **Ruler:**
Elizabeth II **Rev:** Twelve drummers drumming

Date	Mintage	F	VF	XF	Unc	BU
2009 Proof	1,500	Value: 70.00				

KM# 362   2 DOLLARS
62.2000 g., 0.9990 Silver 1.9977 oz. ASW, 63x27 mm. **Ruler:**
Elizabeth II **Rev:** Flowers **Shape:** Vertical rectangle

Date	Mintage	F	VF	XF	Unc	BU
2009 Proof	16,888	Value: 110				

KM# 363 2 DOLLARS
1.0000 g., 0.9990 Gold 0.0321 oz. AGW, 12 mm. **Ruler:**
Elizabeth II **Rev:** Chopin bust

Date	Mintage	F	VF	XF	Unc	BU
2009 Proof	10,000				Value: 80.00	

KM# 552 2 DOLLARS
Silver **Ruler:** Elizabeth II **Subject:** Russian Cartoons

Date	Mintage	F	VF	XF	Unc	BU
2009 Proof	—				Value: 65.00	

KM# 553 2 DOLLARS
Silver **Ruler:** Elizabeth II **Subject:** Russian Cartoons

Date	Mintage	F	VF	XF	Unc	BU
2009 Proof	—				Value: 65.00	

KM# 206 2 DOLLARS
31.1050 g., 0.9990 Silver 0.9990 oz. ASW, 40.7 mm. **Ruler:**
Elizabeth II **Rev:** Two white swans, red heart in background

Date	Mintage	F	VF	XF	Unc	BU
2010 Proof	20,000				Value: 65.00	

KM# 213 2 DOLLARS
56.6000 g., 0.9250 Silver 1.6832 oz. ASW, 55.6x41.6 mm.
Ruler: Elizabeth II **Subject:** Coronation Egg **Obv:** Open egg -
Queen Elizabeth head right **Rev:** Faberge Egg and coach **Shape:**
Vertical oval

Date	Mintage	F	VF	XF	Unc	BU
2010	5,000	—	—	—	—	100

KM# 228 2 DOLLARS
31.1050 g., 0.9990 Silver 0.9990 oz. ASW, 40 mm. **Ruler:**
Elizabeth II **Subject:** Gai Thong Hanh, Safe Conduct Pass **Rev:**
Viet Nam flag and soldiers, partially gilt

Date	Mintage	F	VF	XF	Unc	BU
2010 Proof	5,000				Value: 140	

KM# 233 2 DOLLARS
62.2100 g., 0.9990 Silver partially gilt 1.9980 oz. ASW, 40 mm.
Ruler: Elizabeth II **Subject:** Year of the Tiger **Rev:** Tiger partially
gilt

Date	Mintage	F	VF	XF	Unc	BU
2010 Proof	20,000				Value: 120	

KM# 237 2 DOLLARS
1.0000 g., 0.9000 Gold 0.0289 oz. AGW, 12 mm. **Ruler:**
Elizabeth II **Obv:** Head right **Rev:** Copernicus bust 3/4 left

Date	Mintage	F	VF	XF	Unc	BU
2010 Proof	5,000				Value: 75.00	

KM# 245 2 DOLLARS
31.1030 g., 0.9990 Silver 0.9989 oz. ASW, 40.7 mm. **Ruler:**
Elizabeth II **Subject:** Famous express trains - Trans Siberian
Express **Rev:** Steam train traveling left, multicolor

Date	Mintage	F	VF	XF	Unc	BU
2010 Proof	15,000				Value: 80.00	

KM# 246 2 DOLLARS
31.1030 g., 0.9990 Silver 0.9989 oz. ASW, 40.7 mm. **Ruler:**
Elizabeth II **Subject:** Famous express trains **Rev:** British
Railways Flying Scotsman locomotive right, multicolor

Date	Mintage	F	VF	XF	Unc	BU
2010 Proof	15,000				Value: 80.00	

KM# 247 2 DOLLARS
31.1030 g., 0.9990 Silver 0.9989 oz. ASW, 40.7 mm. **Ruler:**
Elizabeth II **Subject:** Famous express trains - Orient Express
Rev: Steam train right, multicolor

Date	Mintage	F	VF	XF	Unc	BU
2010 Proof	15,000				Value: 80.00	

KM# 248 2 DOLLARS
31.1030 g., 0.9990 Silver 0.9989 oz. ASW, 40.7 mm. **Ruler:**
Elizabeth II **Subject:** Famous Express trains - 20th Century
Limited **Rev:** Streamlined steam train left, multicolored

Date	Mintage	F	VF	XF	Unc	BU
2010 Proof	15,000				Value: 80.00	

KM# 249 2 DOLLARS
31.1050 g., 0.9990 Silver 0.9990 oz. ASW, 40.7 mm. **Ruler:**
Elizabeth II **Subject:** Love is precious **Rev:** Two white swans and
red floral heart

Date	Mintage	F	VF	XF	Unc	BU
2010 Proof	20,000				Value: 90.00	

KM# 252 2 DOLLARS
31.1050 g., 0.9990 Silver 0.9990 oz. ASW, 38.6 mm. **Ruler:**
Elizabeth II **Subject:** Peanuts 60th Anniversary **Rev:** Charlie
Brown with Snoopy and birthday cake

Date	Mintage	F	VF	XF	Unc	BU
2010 Prooflike	3,000	—	—	—	—	80.00

KM# 253 2 DOLLARS
31.1050 g., 0.9990 Silver 0.9990 oz. ASW, 38.6 mm. **Ruler:**
Elizabeth II **Subject:** Peanuts 60th Anniversary **Rev:** Schroeder
and Lucy by piano

Date	Mintage	F	VF	XF	Unc	BU
2010 Prooflike	3,000	—	—	—	—	80.00

KM# 371 2 DOLLARS
56.5600 g., 0.9250 Silver 1.6820 oz. ASW, 55.6x41.6 mm.
Ruler: Elizabeth II **Subject:** Faberge egg - Lily of the Valley **Obv:**
Elizabeth II head right, open egg **Rev:** Egg on stand **Shape:**
Vertical oval

Date	Mintage	F	VF	XF	Unc	BU
2010 Proof	7,000				Value: 100	

KM# 373   2 DOLLARS
31.1050 g., 0.9990 Silver 0.9990 oz. ASW, 37.1x31.9 mm.
Ruler: Elizabeth II **Subject:** Kiki Lala **Shape:** Heart with ribbon

Date	Mintage	F	VF	XF	Unc	BU
2010 Proof	Est. 3,000	Value: 60.00				

KM# 374   2 DOLLARS
31.1050 g., 0.9990 Silver 0.9990 oz. ASW, 37.1x31.9 mm.
Ruler: Elizabeth II **Subject:** My Melo **Shape:** Heart with ribbon

Date	Mintage	F	VF	XF	Unc	BU
2010 Proof	Est. 3,000	Value: 60.00				

KM# 381   2 DOLLARS
31.1050 g., 0.9990 Silver 0.9990 oz. ASW, 40.2 mm. **Ruler:**
Elizabeth II **Subject:** Russian Musicians **Rev:** Viktor Tsoy at
lower right in multicolor

Date	Mintage	F	VF	XF	Unc	BU
2010 Proof	2,000	Value: 65.00				

KM# 382   2 DOLLARS
31.1050 g., 0.9990 Silver 0.9990 oz. ASW, 40.2 mm. **Ruler:**
Elizabeth II **Subject:** Russian Musicians **Rev:** Vladimir Vysotsky
at lower right in multicolor

Date	Mintage	F	VF	XF	Unc	BU
2010 Proof	2,000	Value: 65.00				

KM# 383   2 DOLLARS
31.1050 g., 0.9990 Silver 0.9990 oz. ASW **Ruler:** Elizabeth II
Rev: Portrait in multicolor

Date	Mintage	F	VF	XF	Unc	BU
2010 Proof	Est. 2,000	Value: 65.00				

KM# 384   2 DOLLARS
31.1050 g., 0.9990 Silver 0.9990 oz. ASW, 38.61 mm. **Ruler:**
Elizabeth II **Subject:** Miffy with friends

Date	Mintage	F	VF	XF	Unc	BU
2010 Proof	Est. 3,000	Value: 60.00				

KM# 385   2 DOLLARS
31.1050 g., 0.9990 Silver 0.9990 oz. ASW, 38.61 mm. **Ruler:**
Elizabeth II **Subject:** Miffy on turtle

Date	Mintage	F	VF	XF	Unc	BU
2010 Proof	Est. 3,000	Value: 60.00				

KM# 386   2 DOLLARS
31.1050 g., 0.9990 Silver 0.9990 oz. ASW, 38.61 mm. **Ruler:**
Elizabeth II **Subject:** Miffy celebration

Date	Mintage	F	VF	XF	Unc	BU
2010 Proof	Est. 3,000	Value: 60.00				

KM# 390   2 DOLLARS
31.1030 g., 0.9990 Silver 0.9989 oz. ASW, 40.7 mm. **Ruler:**
Elizabeth II **Subject:** Yamal **Rev:** Child wearing fur coat in
multicolor

Date	Mintage	F	VF	XF	Unc	BU
2010 Proof	5,000	Value: 55.00				

KM# 391   2 DOLLARS
31.1030 g., 0.9990 Silver 0.9989 oz. ASW, 40.7 mm. **Ruler:**
Elizabeth II **Subject:** Yamal **Rev:** Gas and Oil exploration in
multicolor

Date	Mintage	F	VF	XF	Unc	BU
2010 Proof	5,000	Value: 55.00				

KM# 408   2 DOLLARS
31.1030 g., 0.9990 Silver 0.9989 oz. ASW, 40.7 mm. **Ruler:**
Elizabeth II **Series:** Russian Transport **Obv:** Head with tiara right
Rev: Bus in multicolor

Date	Mintage	F	VF	XF	Unc	BU
2010 Proof	15,000	Value: 60.00				

KM# 409   2 DOLLARS
31.1030 g., 0.9990 Silver 0.9989 oz. ASW, 40.7 mm. **Ruler:**
Elizabeth II **Subject:** Russian Transport **Obv:** Head with tiara
right **Rev:** Trolley Bus in multicolor

Date	Mintage	F	VF	XF	Unc	BU
2010 Proof	15,000	Value: 60.00				

KM# 410   2 DOLLARS
31.1030 g., 0.9990 Silver 0.9989 oz. ASW, 40.7 mm. **Ruler:**
Elizabeth II **Subject:** Russian Transport **Obv:** Head with tiara
right **Rev:** Metro in color

Date	Mintage	F	VF	XF	Unc	BU
2010 Proof	15,000	Value: 60.00				

KM# 411   2 DOLLARS
31.1030 g., 0.9990 Silver 0.9989 oz. ASW, 40.7 mm. **Ruler:**
Elizabeth II **Subject:** Russian Transport **Obv:** Head with tiara
right **Rev:** Tram in color

Date	Mintage	F	VF	XF	Unc	BU
2010 Proof	15,000	Value: 60.00				

KM# 416   2 DOLLARS
28.2800 g., 0.9250 Silver 0.8410 oz. ASW, 38.61 mm. **Ruler:**
Elizabeth II **Obv:** Head with tiara right **Rev:** Kirovo Chepetsk

Date	Mintage	F	VF	XF	Unc	BU
2010 Proof	2,000	Value: 70.00				

KM# 424   2 DOLLARS
56.5600 g., 0.9250 Silver 1.6820 oz. ASW, 41.6x55.6 mm.
Ruler: Elizabeth II **Subject:** Faberge Imperial Eggs - Clover Leaf
Obv: Head with tiara right above opened egg **Rev:** Egg on stand
in color **Shape:** Vertical oval

Date	Mintage	F	VF	XF	Unc	BU
2010 Proof	7,000	Value: 125				

KM# 431   2 DOLLARS
1.0000 g., 0.9000 Silver 0.0289 oz. ASW, 12 mm. **Ruler:**
Elizabeth II **Subject:** Tadeusz Kosciuszko **Obv:** Head with tiara
right **Rev:** Head left, signature below

Date	Mintage	F	VF	XF	Unc	BU
2010 Proof	5,000	Value: 50.00				

KM# 442   2 DOLLARS
25.0000 g., 0.9250 Silver 0.7435 oz. ASW, 38.61 mm. **Ruler:**
Elizabeth II **Subject:** Twelve days of Christmas **Rev:** Partidge in
a pear tree

Date	Mintage	F	VF	XF	Unc	BU
2010 Proof	1,500	Value: 60.00				

KM# 443   2 DOLLARS
25.0000 g., 0.9250 Silver 0.7435 oz. ASW, 38.61 mm. **Ruler:**
Elizabeth II **Subject:** Twelve days of Christmas **Rev:** Turtle dove

Date	Mintage	F	VF	XF	Unc	BU
2010 Proof	1,500	Value: 60.00				

KM# 444   2 DOLLARS
25.0000 g., 0.9250 Silver 0.7435 oz. ASW, 38.61 mm. **Ruler:**
Elizabeth II **Subject:** Twelve days of Christmas **Rev:** French hen

Date	Mintage	F	VF	XF	Unc	BU
2010 Proof	1,500	Value: 60.00				

KM# 445   2 DOLLARS
25.0000 g., 0.9250 Silver 0.7435 oz. ASW **Ruler:** Elizabeth II
Subject: Twelve days of Christmas **Rev:** Calling bird

Date	Mintage	F	VF	XF	Unc	BU
2010 Proof	1,500	Value: 60.00				

KM# 446   2 DOLLARS
25.0000 g., 0.9250 Silver 0.7435 oz. ASW, 38.61 mm. **Ruler:**
Elizabeth II **Subject:** Twelve days of Christmas **Rev:** Golden
rings

Date	Mintage	F	VF	XF	Unc	BU
2010 Proof	1,500	Value: 60.00				

KM# 447   2 DOLLARS
25.0000 g., 0.9250 Silver 0.7435 oz. ASW, 38.61 mm. **Ruler:**
Elizabeth II **Subject:** Twelve days of Christmas **Rev:** Geese a
laying

Date	Mintage	F	VF	XF	Unc	BU
2010 Proof	1,500	Value: 60.00				

KM# 448   2 DOLLARS
25.0000 g., 0.9250 Silver 0.7435 oz. ASW, 38.61 mm. **Ruler:**
Elizabeth II **Subject:** Twelve days of Christmas **Rev:** Swans a
swimming

Date	Mintage	F	VF	XF	Unc	BU
2010 Proof	1,500	Value: 60.00				

KM# 449   2 DOLLARS
25.0000 g., 0.9250 Silver 0.7435 oz. ASW, 38.61 mm. **Ruler:**
Elizabeth II **Subject:** Twelve days of Christmas **Rev:** Maids a
milking

Date	Mintage	F	VF	XF	Unc	BU
2010 Proof	1,500	Value: 60.00				

KM# 450   2 DOLLARS
25.0000 g., 0.9250 Silver 0.7435 oz. ASW, 38.61 mm. **Ruler:**
Elizabeth II **Subject:** Twelve days of Christmas **Rev:** Ladies
dancing

Date	Mintage	F	VF	XF	Unc	BU
2010 Proof	1,500	Value: 60.00				

KM# 451   2 DOLLARS
25.0000 g., 0.9250 Silver 0.7435 oz. ASW, 38.61 mm. **Ruler:**
Elizabeth II **Subject:** Twelve days of Christmas **Rev:** Lords a
leaping

Date	Mintage	F	VF	XF	Unc	BU
2010 Proof	1,500	Value: 60.00				

KM# 452   2 DOLLARS
25.0000 g., 0.9250 Silver 0.7435 oz. ASW, 38.61 mm. **Ruler:**
Elizabeth II **Subject:** Twelve days of Christmas **Rev:** Pipers
piping

Date	Mintage	F	VF	XF	Unc	BU
2010 Proof	1,500	Value: 60.00				

KM# 453   2 DOLLARS
25.0000 g., 0.9250 Silver 0.7435 oz. ASW, 38.61 mm. **Ruler:**
Elizabeth II **Subject:** Twelve days of Christmas **Rev:** Drummers
drumming

Date	Mintage	F	VF	XF	Unc	BU
2010 Proof	1,500	Value: 60.00				

KM# 457   2 DOLLARS
31.1030 g., 0.9990 Silver 0.9989 oz. ASW, 38.61 mm. **Ruler:**
Elizabeth II **Subject:** Bulgarian theme roses - Survachka **Rev:**
Figure-8 floral arrangement

Date	Mintage	F	VF	XF	Unc	BU
2010 Proof	3,000	Value: 55.00				

KM# 458   2 DOLLARS
31.1030 g., 0.9990 Silver 0.9989 oz. ASW, 38.61 mm. **Ruler:**
Elizabeth II **Subject:** Bulgarian rose **Rev:** Top view into colored
pink rose, gilt border

Date	Mintage	F	VF	XF	Unc	BU
2010	6,000	Value: 50.00				

KM# 459   2 DOLLARS
31.1030 g., 0.9990 Silver 0.9989 oz. ASW, 38.61 mm. **Ruler:**
Elizabeth II **Subject:** Bulgarian rose theme - Martenitsa **Rev:**
tassle like device

Date	Mintage	F	VF	XF	Unc	BU
2010 Proof	3,000	Value: 55.00				

KM# 460   2 DOLLARS
31.1030 g., 0.9990 Silver 0.9989 oz. ASW, 38.61 mm. **Ruler:**
Elizabeth II **Rev:** Saint Peter icon

Date	Mintage	F	VF	XF	Unc	BU
2010 Proof	2,000	Value: 60.00				

KM# 461   2 DOLLARS
31.1030 g., 0.9990 Silver 0.9989 oz. ASW, 38.61 mm. **Ruler:**
Elizabeth II **Rev:** Saint Paul icon

Date	Mintage	F	VF	XF	Unc	BU
2010 Proof	2,000	Value: 60.00				

KM# 550   2 DOLLARS
Silver, 40 mm. **Ruler:** Elizabeth II **Subject:** Korean War, 60th
Anniversary **Rev:** Soldier in multicolor

Date	Mintage	F	VF	XF	Unc	BU
2010 Proof	2,000	Value: 70.00				

KM# 372   2 DOLLARS
31.1050 g., 0.9990 Silver 0.9990 oz. ASW, 37.1x31.9 mm.
Ruler: Elizabeth II **Subject:** Hello Kitty **Shape:** Heart with ribbon

Date	Mintage	F	VF	XF	Unc	BU
2010 Proof	Est. 3,000	Value: 50.00				

KM# 507   2 DOLLARS
31.1000 g., 0.9990 Silver 0.9988 oz. ASW, 40.7 mm. **Ruler:**
Elizabeth II **Subject:** Love is precious **Rev:** Two pink flamingos
within heart

Date	Mintage	F	VF	XF	Unc	BU
2011 Proof	20,000	Value: 50.00				

KM# 521   2 DOLLARS
31.1000 g., 0.9990 Silver 0.9988 oz. ASW **Ruler:** Elizabeth II
Subject: The Evangelists - St. Mathew and angel **Rev:** Icon in
color

Date	Mintage	F	VF	XF	Unc	BU
2011 Proof	2,000	Value: 60.00				

KM# 522   2 DOLLARS
31.1000 g., 0.9990 Silver 0.9988 oz. ASW **Ruler:** Elizabeth II
Subject: The Evangelists - St Mark with lion **Rev:** Icon in color

Date	Mintage	F	VF	XF	Unc	BU
2011 Proof	2,000	Value: 60.00				

KM# 523   2 DOLLARS
31.1000 g., 0.9990 Silver 0.9988 oz. ASW **Ruler:** Elizabeth II
Subject: The Evangelists - Luke and oxen **Rev:** Icon in color

Date	Mintage	F	VF	XF	Unc	BU
2011 Proof	2,000	Value: 60.00				

KM# 524   2 DOLLARS
31.1000 g., 0.9990 Silver 0.9988 oz. ASW **Ruler:** Elizabeth II
Subject: The Evangelists - John and eagle **Rev:** Icon in color

Date	Mintage	F	VF	XF	Unc	BU
2011 Proof	2,000	Value: 60.00				

KM# 525   2 DOLLARS
31.1000 g., 0.9990 Silver 0.9988 oz. ASW **Ruler:** Elizabeth II
Subject: Eternal Love **Rev:** Two white doves within flora and
scrolls

Date	Mintage	F	VF	XF	Unc	BU
2011 Proof	5,000	Value: 50.00				

KM# 563   2 DOLLARS
31.1050 g., 0.9990 Silver 0.9990 oz. ASW **Ruler:** Elizabeth II
Subject: Pirates of the Caribbean - Blackbeard **Obv:** Head with
crown right **Rev:** Blackbeard in multicolor

Date	Mintage	F	VF	XF	Unc	BU
2011 Proof	2,000	Value: 75.00				

KM# 564   2 DOLLARS
31.1050 g., 0.9990 Silver 0.9990 oz. ASW **Ruler:** Elizabeth II
Series: Pirates of the Caribbean - Bartholomew Roberts **Obv:**
Head with crown right **Rev:** Bartholomew Roberts in multicolor

Date	Mintage	F	VF	XF	Unc	BU
2011 Proof	2,000	Value: 75.00				

KM# 565   2 DOLLARS
31.1050 g., 0.9990 Silver 0.9990 oz. ASW **Ruler:** Elizabeth II
Subject: Pirates of the Caribbean - Henry Avery **Obv:** Head with
crown right **Rev:** Henry Avery in multicolor

Date	Mintage	F	VF	XF	Unc	BU
2011 Proof	2,000	Value: 75.00				

KM# 566   2 DOLLARS
3.1050 g., 0.9990 Silver 0.0997 oz. ASW **Ruler:** Elizabeth II
Subject: Pirates of the Caribbean - Calico Jack **Obv:** Head with
crown right **Rev:** Calico Jack and two ladies in multicolor

Date	Mintage	F	VF	XF	Unc	BU
2011 Proof	2,000	Value: 75.00				

KM# 567   2 DOLLARS
31.1050 g., 0.9990 Silver 0.9990 oz. ASW **Ruler:** Elizabeth II
Subject: Legends of the Air **Obv:** Head with crown right **Rev:** B-
2 Spirit Stealth Bomber in color

Date	Mintage	F	VF	XF	Unc	BU
2011 Proof	2,000	Value: 75.00				

KM# 568   2 DOLLARS
31.1050 g., 0.9990 Silver 0.9990 oz. ASW **Ruler:** Elizabeth II

Subject: Legends of the Air **Obv:** Head with crown right **Rev:** F-
16 Fighting Falcon

Date	Mintage	F	VF	XF	Unc	BU
2011 Proof	2,000	Value: 75.00				

KM# 569   2 DOLLARS
31.1050 g., 0.9990 Silver 0.9990 oz. ASW **Ruler:** Elizabeth II
Subject: Legends of the Air **Obv:** Head with crown right **Rev:**
AH-64D Apache Longbow in color

Date	Mintage	F	VF	XF	Unc	BU
2011 Proof	2,000	Value: 75.00				

KM# 570   2 DOLLARS
31.1050 g., 0.9990 Silver 0.9990 oz. ASW **Ruler:** Elizabeth II
Subject: Legends of the Air **Obv:** Head with crown right **Rev:** B-
52 Stratofortress Bomber

Date	Mintage	F	VF	XF	Unc	BU
2011 Proof	2,000	Value: 75.00				

KM# 573   2 DOLLARS
31.1050 g., 0.9990 Silver 0.9990 oz. ASW, 38.61 mm. **Ruler:**
Elizabeth II **Subject:** First crossing of the Simpson Desert, 75th
Anniversary **Obv:** Head with crown right **Rev:** Ted Colson in color

Date	Mintage	F	VF	XF	Unc	BU
2011 Proof	2,000	Value: 75.00				

KM# 589   2 DOLLARS
31.1030 g., 0.9990 Silver 0.9989 oz. ASW, 33x55 mm. **Ruler:**
Elizabeth II **Subject:** Kagaya Art Zodiac - Leo

Date	Mintage	F	VF	XF	Unc	BU
2011 Proof	8,000	Value: 75.00				

KM# 590   2 DOLLARS
31.1030 g., 0.9990 Silver 0.9989 oz. ASW, 33x55 mm. **Ruler:**
Elizabeth II **Subject:** Kagaya Art Zodiac - Virgo

Date	Mintage	F	VF	XF	Unc	BU
2011 Proof	8,000	Value: 75.00				

KM# 591   2 DOLLARS
31.1030 g., 0.9990 Silver 0.9989 oz. ASW, 33x55 mm. **Ruler:**
Elizabeth II **Subject:** Kagaya Art Zodiac - Libra **Shape:** Vertical
rectangle

Date	Mintage	F	VF	XF	Unc	BU
2011 Proof	8,000	Value: 75.00				

KM# 592   2 DOLLARS
31.1030 g., 0.9990 Silver 0.9989 oz. ASW, 33x55 mm. **Ruler:**
Elizabeth II **Subject:** Kagaya Art Zodiac - Scorpio **Shape:**
Vertical rectangle

Date	Mintage	F	VF	XF	Unc	BU
2011 Proof	8,000	Value: 75.00				

KM# 593   2 DOLLARS
31.1030 g., 0.9990 Silver 0.9989 oz. ASW, 33x55 mm. **Ruler:**
Elizabeth II **Subject:** Kagaya Art Zodiac - Sagittarius **Shape:**
Vertical rectangle

Date	Mintage	F	VF	XF	Unc	BU
2011 Proof	8,000	Value: 75.00				

KM# 601   2 DOLLARS
31.1030 g., 0.9990 Silver 0.9989 oz. ASW, 40.7 mm. **Ruler:**
Elizabeth II **Subject:** Love Forever **Obv:** Head with crown right
Rev: Two doves in flight, two golden rings, word Forever in many
languages in background

Date	Mintage	F	VF	XF	Unc	BU
2011 Proof	20,000	Value: 65.00				

KM# 602   2 DOLLARS
31.1030 g., 0.9990 Silver 0.9989 oz. ASW, 40.7 mm. **Ruler:**
Elizabeth II **Subject:** Supersonic Transport - TU-144 **Rev:** Plane
color image

Date	Mintage	F	VF	XF	Unc	BU
2011 Proof	8,000	Value: 65.00				

KM# 603   2 DOLLARS
31.1030 g., 0.9990 Silver 0.9989 oz. ASW, 40.7 mm. **Ruler:**
Elizabeth II **Subject:** Supersonic Transport - Concorde **Rev:**
Plane color image

Date	Mintage	F	VF	XF	Unc	BU
2011 Proof	8,000	Value: 65.00				

KM# 639   2 DOLLARS
31.1350 g., 0.9990 Silver 1.0000 oz. ASW, 27x47 mm. **Ruler:**
Elizabeth II **Subject:** Orthodox shrines, Holy Trinity **Obv:** Head
with crown right **Rev:** Five saints seated around table, partially
gilt and colored **Edge:** Plain **Shape:** Vertical rectangle, convex

Date	Mintage	F	VF	XF	Unc	BU
2011 Proof	Est. 3,000	Value: 100				

KM# 640   2 DOLLARS

31.1350 g., 0.9990 Silver 1.0000 oz. ASW, 27x47 mm.   **Ruler:**
Elizabeth II **Subject:** Orthodox Shrines, Christ Pantokrator **Obv:**
Head with crown right **Rev:** Christ facing holding gospels, partially
gilt and colored **Edge:** Plain **Shape:** Vertical rectangle, convex

Date	Mintage	F	VF	XF	Unc	BU
2011 Proof	3,000	Value: 100				

KM# 642   2 DOLLARS

31.1050 g., 0.9990 Silver 0.9990 oz. ASW, 55x33 mm.   **Ruler:**
Elizabeth II **Obv:** Head with crown right **Rev:** First man in space,
multicolor **Shape:** rectangle

Date	Mintage	F	VF	XF	Unc	BU
2011 Proof	5,000					100

KM# 643   2 DOLLARS

31.1050 g., 0.9990 Silver 0.9990 oz. ASW, 55x33 mm.   **Ruler:**
Elizabeth II **Obv:** Head with crown right **Rev:** First space walk

Date	Mintage	F	VF	XF	Unc	BU
2011 Proof	5,000	Value: 100				

KM# 663   2 DOLLARS

31.1050 g., 0.9990 Silver 0.9990 oz. ASW, 40 mm.   **Ruler:**
Elizabeth II **Subject:** Star Wars - C3PO and R2D2

Date	Mintage	F	VF	XF	Unc	BU
2011 Prooflike	Est. 7,500	—	—	—	—	120

KM# 664   2 DOLLARS

31.1050 g., 0.9990 Silver 0.9990 oz. ASW, 40 mm.   **Ruler:**
Elizabeth II **Subject:** Star Wars - Darth Vader

Date	Mintage	F	VF	XF	Unc	BU
2011 Prooflike	Est. 7,500	—	—	—	—	120

KM# 665   2 DOLLARS

31.1050 g., 0.9990 Silver 0.9990 oz. ASW, 40 mm.   **Ruler:**
Elizabeth II **Subject:** Star Wars - Emperor Palpatine

Date	Mintage	F	VF	XF	Unc	BU
2011 Prooflike	Est. 7,500	—	—	—	—	120

KM# 666   2 DOLLARS

31.1050 g., 0.9990 Silver 0.9990 oz. ASW, 40 mm.   **Ruler:**
Elizabeth II **Subject:** Star Wars - Death Star

Date	Mintage	F	VF	XF	Unc	BU
2011 Prooflike	Est. 7,500	—	—	—	—	120

KM# 667   2 DOLLARS

31.1050 g., 0.9990 Silver 0.9990 oz. ASW, 40 mm.   **Ruler:**
Elizabeth II **Subject:** Star Wars - Han Solo and Chewbacca

Date	Mintage	F	VF	XF	Unc	BU
2011 Prooflike	Est. 7,500	—	—	—	—	120

KM# 668   2 DOLLARS

31.1050 g., 0.9990 Silver 0.9990 oz. ASW, 40 mm.   **Ruler:**
Elizabeth II **Subject:** Star Wars - Luke Skywalker and Princess
Leia

Date	Mintage	F	VF	XF	Unc	BU
2011 Prooflike	Est. 7,500	—	—	—	—	120

KM# 669   2 DOLLARS

31.1050 g., 0.9990 Silver 0.9990 oz. ASW, 40 mm.   **Ruler:**
Elizabeth II **Series:** Star Wars - Storm Trooper

Date	Mintage	F	VF	XF	Unc	BU
2011 Prooflike	Est. 7,500	—	—	—	—	120

KM# 670   2 DOLLARS

31.1050 g., 0.9990 Silver 0.9990 oz. ASW, 40 mm.   **Ruler:**
Elizabeth II **Subject:** Star Wars - Obi-Wan Kenobi and Yoda

Date	Mintage	F	VF	XF	Unc	BU
2011 Prooflike	Est. 7,500	—	—	—	—	120

KM# 671   2 DOLLARS

31.1050 g., 0.9990 Silver 0.9990 oz. ASW, 40 mm.   **Ruler:**
Elizabeth II **Subject:** Anne Geddes - Boy

Date	Mintage	F	VF	XF	Unc	BU
2011 Prooflike	3,000	—	—	—	—	100

KM# 672   2 DOLLARS

31.1050 g., 0.9990 Silver 0.9990 oz. ASW, 40 mm.   **Ruler:**
Elizabeth II **Subject:** Anne Geddes - Girl

Date	Mintage	F	VF	XF	Unc	BU
2011 Prooflike	3,000	—	—	—	—	100

KM# 673   2 DOLLARS

15.5500 g., 0.9250 Silver 0.4624 oz. ASW, 35 mm.   **Ruler:**
Elizabeth II **Rev:** Mexican redknee tarantula in color

Date	Mintage	F	VF	XF	Unc	BU
2011	1,250	—	—	—	—	125

KM# 692   2 DOLLARS

31.1050 g., 0.9990 Silver 0.9990 oz. ASW, 38.61 mm.   **Ruler:**
Elizabeth II **Obv:** Head with crown right **Rev:** Virgin Mary with
arms outstretched in color **Edge:** Reeded

Date	Mintage	F	VF	XF	Unc	BU
2011 Proof	3,000	Value: 100				

KM# 736   2 DOLLARS

56.5600 g., 0.9250 Silver 1.6820 oz. ASW, 41.6x55.6 mm.
Ruler: Elizabeth II **Subject:** Imperial Faberge Egg - Pansy Egg

Obv: Head right in filigree, open egg below **Rev:** Pansy flowers around closed egg **Shape:** Vertical oval

Date	Mintage	F	VF	XF	Unc	BU
2011 Proof	7,000	Value: 200				

KM# 802   2 DOLLARS
31.1000 g., 0.9990 Silver 0.9988 oz. ASW, 40.7 mm. **Ruler:** Elizabeth II **Rev:** School children playing with globe

Date	Mintage	F	VF	XF	Unc	BU
2011 Proof	Est. 6,000	Value: 100				

KM# 594   2 DOLLARS
31.1030 g., 0.9990 Silver 0.9989 oz. ASW, 33x55 mm. **Ruler:** Elizabeth II **Subject:** Kagaya Art Zodiac - Capricorn **Shape:** Vertical rectangle

Date	Mintage	F	VF	XF	Unc	BU
2012 Proof	8,000	Value: 75.00				

KM# 595   2 DOLLARS
31.1030 g., 0.9990 Silver 0.9989 oz. ASW, 33x55 mm. **Ruler:** Elizabeth II **Subject:** Kagaya Art Zodiac - Aquarius **Shape:** Vertical rectangle

Date	Mintage	F	VF	XF	Unc	BU
2012 Proof	8,000	Value: 75.00				

KM# 596   2 DOLLARS
31.1030 g., 0.9990 Silver 0.9989 oz. ASW, 33x55 mm. **Ruler:** Elizabeth II **Subject:** Kagaya Art Zodiac - Pisces **Shape:** Vertical rectangle

Date	Mintage	F	VF	XF	Unc	BU
2012 Proof	8,000	Value: 75.00				

KM# 597   2 DOLLARS
31.1030 g., 0.9990 Silver 0.9989 oz. ASW, 33x55 mm. **Ruler:** Elizabeth II **Subject:** Kagaya Art Zodiac - Aries **Shape:** Vertical rectangle

Date	Mintage	F	VF	XF	Unc	BU
2012 Proof	8,000	Value: 75.00				

KM# 598   2 DOLLARS
31.1030 g., 0.9990 Silver 0.9989 oz. ASW, 33x55 mm. **Ruler:** Elizabeth II **Subject:** Kagaya Art Zodiac - Taurus **Shape:** Vertical rectangle

Date	Mintage	F	VF	XF	Unc	BU
2012 Proof	8,000	Value: 75.00				

KM# 599   2 DOLLARS
31.1030 g., 0.9990 Silver 0.9989 oz. ASW, 33x55 mm. **Ruler:** Elizabeth II **Subject:** Kagaya Art Zodiac - Gemini **Shape:** Vertical rectangle

Date	Mintage	F	VF	XF	Unc	BU
2012 Proof	8,000	Value: 75.00				

KM# 600   2 DOLLARS
31.1030 g., 0.9990 Silver 0.9989 oz. ASW, 33x55 mm. **Ruler:** Elizabeth II **Subject:** Kagaya Art Zodiac - Cancer **Shape:** Vertical rectangle

Date	Mintage	F	VF	XF	Unc	BU
2012 Proof	8,000	Value: 75.00				

KM# 638   2 DOLLARS
31.1050 g., 0.9990 Silver 0.9990 oz. ASW, 40.7 mm. **Ruler:** Elizabeth II **Obv:** Head with crown right **Rev:** H.M.S. Titanic sailing right within compass points

Date	Mintage	F	VF	XF	Unc	BU
2012 Proof	2,229	Value: 80.00				

KM# 675   2 DOLLARS
28.2800 g., Copper-Nickel, 38.61 mm. **Ruler:** Elizabeth II **Rev:** Crowned state flowers **Edge:** Reeded

Date	Mintage	F	VF	XF	Unc	BU
2012	—	—	—	—	—	25.00

KM# 675a   2 DOLLARS
28.2800 g., 0.9250 Silver 0.8410 oz. ASW, 38.61 mm. **Ruler:** Elizabeth II **Rev:** Crowned state flowers

Date	Mintage	F	VF	XF	Unc	BU
2012 Proof	19,500	Value: 80.00				

KM# 676   2 DOLLARS
31.1050 g., 0.9990 Silver 0.9990 oz. ASW, 40.7 mm. **Ruler:** Elizabeth II **Rev:** Florida alligator, gilt **Edge:** Reeded

Date	Mintage	F	VF	XF	Unc	BU
2012 Proof	2,500	Value: 80.00				

KM# 677   2 DOLLARS
31.1050 g., 0.9990 Silver 0.9990 oz. ASW, 40.7 mm. **Ruler:** Elizabeth II **Subject:** Year of the Dragon **Rev:** Dragon

Date	Mintage	F	VF	XF	Unc	BU
2012 Proof	2,500	Value: 80.00				

KM# 691   2 DOLLARS
31.1050 g., 0.9990 Silver 0.9990 oz. ASW, 27x47 mm. **Ruler:** Elizabeth II **Subject:** Orthodox Shrines **Rev:** Faith, Hope and Charity and their mother, Sofia **Edge:** Plain

Date	Mintage	F	VF	XF	Unc	BU
2012 Proof	3,000	Value: 100				

KM# 693   2 DOLLARS
31.1050 g., 0.9990 Silver partially gilt 0.9990 oz. ASW, 38.61 mm. **Ruler:** Elizabeth II **Rev:** Feng Shui - two Koi Carp gilt

Date	Mintage	F	VF	XF	Unc	BU
2012 Proof	10,000	Value: 100				

KM# 694   2 DOLLARS
31.1050 g., 0.9990 Silver 0.9990 oz. ASW **Ruler:** Elizabeth II **Subject:** Nickelodeon's Sponge Bob **Rev:** Sponge Bob **Shape:** Square

Date	Mintage	F	VF	XF	Unc	BU
2012 Proof	100,000	Value: 60.00				

KM# 695   2 DOLLARS
31.1050 g., 0.9990 Silver 0.9990 oz. ASW **Ruler:** Elizabeth II
Subject: Nickelodeon's Sponge Bob **Rev:** Patrick Star **Shape:**
Square

Date	Mintage	F	VF	XF	Unc	BU
2012 Proof	100,000				Value: 60.00	

KM# 696   2 DOLLARS
31.1050 g., 0.9990 Silver 0.9990 oz. ASW **Ruler:** Elizabeth II
Subject: Nickelodeon's Sponge Bob **Rev:** Sandy Cheeks
Shape: Square

Date	Mintage	F	VF	XF	Unc	BU
2012 Proof	100,000				Value: 60.00	

KM# 697   2 DOLLARS
31.1050 g., 0.9990 Silver 0.9990 oz. ASW **Ruler:** Elizabeth II
Subject: Nickelodeon's Sponge Bob **Rev:** Gary (snail) **Shape:**
Square

Date	Mintage	F	VF	XF	Unc	BU
2012 Proof	100,000				Value: 60.00	

KM# 712   2 DOLLARS
31.1050 g., 0.9990 Silver 0.9990 oz. ASW, 40.7 mm. **Ruler:**
Elizabeth II **Rev:** Dragon

Date	Mintage	F	VF	XF	Unc	BU
2012 Proof	50,000				Value: 50.00	

KM# 717   2 DOLLARS
31.1050 g., 0.9999 Silver 0.9999 oz. ASW, 40.7 mm. **Ruler:**
Elizabeth II **Subject:** Star Wars - Droin

Date	Mintage	F	VF	XF	Unc	BU
2012 Prooflike	10,000	—	—	—	—	125

KM# 718   2 DOLLARS
31.1050 g., 0.9990 Silver 0.9990 oz. ASW, 40.7 mm. **Ruler:**
Elizabeth II **Subject:** Star Wars - Darth Maul

Date	Mintage	F	VF	XF	Unc	BU
2012 Prooflike	10,000	—	—	—	—	125

KM# 719   2 DOLLARS
31.1050 g., 0.9990 Silver 0.9990 oz. ASW, 40.7 mm. **Ruler:**
Elizabeth II **Subject:** Star Wars - young Obi Wan Kenobi

Date	Mintage	F	VF	XF	Unc	BU
2012 Prooflike	10,000	—	—	—	—	125

KM# 720   2 DOLLARS
31.1050 g., 0.9990 Silver 0.9990 oz. ASW, 40.7 mm. **Ruler:**
Elizabeth II **Subject:** Star Wars - Mace Windu

Date	Mintage	F	VF	XF	Unc	BU
2012 Prooflike	10,000	—	—	—	—	125

KM# 721   2 DOLLARS
31.1050 g., 0.9990 Silver 0.9990 oz. ASW, 40.7 mm. **Ruler:**
Elizabeth II **Subject:** Star Wars - Yoda

Date	Mintage	F	VF	XF	Unc	BU
2012 Prooflike	10,000	—	—	—	—	125

KM# 722   2 DOLLARS
31.1050 g., 0.9990 Silver 0.9990 oz. ASW, 40.7 mm. **Ruler:**
Elizabeth II **Subject:** Star Wars - Queen Amiidala

Date	Mintage	F	VF	XF	Unc	BU
2012 Prooflike	10,000	—	—	—	—	125

KM# 723   2 DOLLARS
31.1050 g., 0.9990 Silver 0.9990 oz. ASW, 40.7 mm. **Ruler:**
Elizabeth II **Subject:** Star Wars - Qui Con

Date	Mintage	F	VF	XF	Unc	BU
2012 Prooflike	10,000	—	—	—	—	125

KM# 724   2 DOLLARS
31.1050 g., 0.9990 Silver 0.9990 oz. ASW, 40.7 mm. **Ruler:**
Elizabeth II **Subject:** Star Wars - young Annikan

Date	Mintage	F	VF	XF	Unc	BU
2012 Prooflike	10,000	—	—	—	—	125

KM# 743   2 DOLLARS
15.5500 g., 0.9990 Silver 0.4994 oz. ASW, 33 mm. **Ruler:**
Elizabeth II **Subject:** Year of the Dragon **Rev:** Dragon with pearl
in color

Date	Mintage	F	VF	XF	Unc	BU
2012 Proof	8,000				Value: 50.00	

KM# 744   2 DOLLARS
31.1050 g., 0.9990 Silver 0.9990 oz. ASW, 45x31 mm. **Ruler:**
Elizabeth II **Subject:** Year of the Dragon, Lucky Red dragon **Rev:**
Red dragon lying down with rays in backgorund **Shape:**
Horizontal oval

Date	Mintage	F	VF	XF	Unc	BU
2012 Proof	4,000				Value: 100	

KM# 745   2 DOLLARS
31.1050 g., 0.9990 Silver 0.9990 oz. ASW, 45x31 mm. **Ruler:**
Elizabeth II **Subject:** Year of the Dragon - Lucky Blue Dragon
Rev: Blue dragon lying down, rays in background **Shape:**
Horizontal oval

Date	Mintage	F	VF	XF	Unc	BU
2012 Proof	8,000				Value: 100	

KM# 746   2 DOLLARS
31.1050 g., 0.9990 Silver 0.9990 oz. ASW, 40.7 mm. **Ruler:**
Elizabeth II **Subject:** Year of the Dragon - Lunar Fan Dragon
Rev: Dragon seated left, colored lunar hand fan in background

Date	Mintage	F	VF	XF	Unc	BU
2012 Proof	4,000				Value: 100	

KM# 756   2 DOLLARS
56.5600 g., 0.9250 Silver 1.6820 oz. ASW, 41.6x55.6 mm.
Ruler: Elizabeth II **Subject:** Imperial Faberge Eggs - Bay Tree
Rev: Bay tree **Shape:** Vertical oval

Date	Mintage	F	VF	XF	Unc	BU
2012 Proof	Est. 7,000				Value: 100	

KM# 762   2 DOLLARS
39.6000 g., 0.9250 Silver 1.1776 oz. ASW, 48.61 mm. **Ruler:**
Elizabeth II **Subject:** Love Notes **Rev:** Cupid writing on central
tablet

Date	Mintage	F	VF	XF	Unc	BU
2012 Proof	Est. 3,000	Value: 100				

KM# 782   2 DOLLARS
31.1050 g., 0.9990 Silver 0.9990 oz. ASW, 40.7 mm. **Ruler:**
Elizabeth II **Subject:** WWII Nose Art - Yellow Rose

Date	Mintage	F	VF	XF	Unc	BU
2012	Est. 3,000	—	—	—	—	75.00

KM# 783   2 DOLLARS
31.1050 g., 0.9990 Silver 0.9990 oz. ASW, 40.7 mm. **Ruler:**
Elizabeth II **Subject:** WWII Nose Art - Briefing Time

Date	Mintage	F	VF	XF	Unc	BU
2012	Est. 3,000	—	—	—	—	75.00

KM# 784   2 DOLLARS
31.1050 g., 0.9990 Silver 0.9990 oz. ASW, 40.7 mm. **Ruler:**
Elizabeth II **Subject:** WWII Nose Art - Memphis Belle

Date	Mintage	F	VF	XF	Unc	BU
2012	Est. 3,000	—	—	—	—	75.00

KM# 795   2 DOLLARS
10.0000 g., 0.9250 Silver 0.2974 oz. ASW, 32 mm. **Ruler:**
Elizabeth II **Subject:** Four seasons, central device **Rev:** Flowers,
leaves and crystal

Date	Mintage	F	VF	XF	Unc	BU
2012 Proof	Est. 9,999	Value: 75.00				

KM# 796   2 DOLLARS
12.0000 g., 0.9250 Silver 0.3569 oz. ASW, 35x35 mm. **Ruler:**
Elizabeth II **Subject:** Four seasons - Spring **Rev:** Springtime flora
and crystal **Shape:** Irregular

Date	Mintage	F	VF	XF	Unc	BU
2012 Proof	Est. 9,999	Value: 75.00				

KM# 797   2 DOLLARS
12.0000 g., 0.9250 Silver 0.3569 oz. ASW, 35x35 mm. **Ruler:**
Elizabeth II **Subject:** Four seasons - Summer **Rev:** Summer flora
and crystal **Shape:** Irregular

Date	Mintage	F	VF	XF	Unc	BU
2012 Proof	Est. 9,999	Value: 75.00				

KM# 798   2 DOLLARS
12.0000 g., 0.9250 Silver 0.3569 oz. ASW, 35x35 mm. **Ruler:**
Elizabeth II **Subject:** Four seasons - Autumn **Rev:** Autumn
foilage and crystal **Shape:** Irregular

Date	Mintage	F	VF	XF	Unc	BU
2012 Proof	Est. 9,999	Value: 75.00				

KM# 799   2 DOLLARS
12.0000 g., 0.9250 Silver 0.3569 oz. ASW, 35x35 mm. **Ruler:**
Elizabeth II **Subject:** Four seasons - Winter **Rev:** Winter foilage
and crystal **Shape:** Irregular

Date	Mintage	F	VF	XF	Unc	BU
2012 Proof	Est. 9,999	Value: 75.00				

KM# 803   2 DOLLARS
0.9990 Silver, 40.7 mm. **Ruler:** Elizabeth II **Rev:** Great White
Shark

Date	Mintage	F	VF	XF	Unc	BU
2012 Proof	5,000	Value: 100				

KM# 785   3 DOLLARS
33.3000 g., 0.9250 Silver 0.9903 oz. ASW, 38.61 mm. **Ruler:**
Elizabeth II **Subject:** Polish Radio, station 3 **Obv:** Head with tiara
right **Rev:** Radio microphone and sound arcs

Date	Mintage	F	VF	XF	Unc	BU
2012 Proof	Est. 3,333	Value: 75.00				

KM# 295   5 DOLLARS
155.5000 g., 0.9990 Silver 4.9942 oz. ASW, 70 mm. **Ruler:**
Elizabeth II **Subject:** Year of the Dog **Rev:** Multicolor dog

Date	Mintage	F	VF	XF	Unc	BU
2005 Proof	—	Value: 200				

KM# 266   5 DOLLARS
155.5000 g., 0.9990 Silver 4.9942 oz. ASW, 70 mm. **Ruler:**
Elizabeth II **Subject:** Year of the Rooster **Rev:** Multicolor rooster
standing right, sunrise

Date	Mintage	F	VF	XF	Unc	BU
2005 Proof	—	Value: 200				

KM# 272   5 DOLLARS
6.2200 g., 0.9990 Gold 0.1998 oz. AGW, 25 mm. **Ruler:**
Elizabeth II **Subject:** Year of the Rooster

Date	Mintage	F	VF	XF	Unc	BU
2005 Proof	—	Value: 375				

KM# 273   5 DOLLARS
15.5500 g., 0.9990 Gold 0.4994 oz. AGW, 33 mm. **Ruler:**
Elizabeth II **Subject:** Year of the Rooster

Date	Mintage	F	VF	XF	Unc	BU
2005 Proof	—	Value: 900				

KM# 333   5 DOLLARS
15.5000 g., 0.9170 Gold 0.4570 oz. AGW, 27 mm. **Ruler:**
Elizabeth II **Subject:** Amber Road - Gdansk **Rev:** Nepture statue,
castle, amber insert

Date	Mintage	F	VF	XF	Unc	BU
2007	—	—	—	—	—	825

KM# 191   5 DOLLARS
15.5000 g., 0.9000 Gold 0.4485 oz. AGW, 27 mm. **Ruler:**
Elizabeth II **Subject:** Amber road **Obv:** Bust and Roman cart
Rev: Kaliningrad Castle, Roman coin, Amber insert

Date	Mintage	F	VF	XF	Unc	BU
2008 Proof	2,000	Value: 800				

KM# 230   5 DOLLARS
62.2100 g., 0.9990 Silver 1.9980 oz. ASW, 50x32 mm. **Ruler:**
Elizabeth II **Subject:** Battleship: Tripitz **Shape:** Rectangle

Date	Mintage	F	VF	XF	Unc	BU
2009	1,000	—	—	—	—	150

KM# 349   5 DOLLARS
15.5000 g., 0.9000 Gold 0.4485 oz. AGW, 27 mm. **Ruler:**
Elizabeth II **Subject:** Amber Road - Elblag **Rev:** Amber insert

Date	Mintage	F	VF	XF	Unc	BU
2009 Proof	—	Value: 800				

KM# 364 5 DOLLARS
77.7000 g., 0.9990 Silver 2.4955 oz. ASW, 50x32 mm. **Ruler:** Elizabeth II **Rev:** Battleship Tirpitz sailing left **Shape:** Wavy rectangle

Date	Mintage	F	VF	XF	Unc	BU
2009 Proof	1,000	Value: 125				

KM# 250 5 DOLLARS
0.5000 g., 0.9990 Gold 0.0161 oz. AGW, 11 mm. **Ruler:** Elizabeth II **Rev:** Ned Kelly

Date	Mintage	F	VF	XF	Unc	BU
2010 Proof	—	Value: 65.00				

KM# 368 5 DOLLARS
15.5000 g., 0.9000 Gold 0.4485 oz. AGW, 27 mm. **Ruler:** Elizabeth II **Subject:** Amber road - Stare Hradisko **Rev:** Amber insert

Date	Mintage	F	VF	XF	Unc	BU
2010	2,000	—	—	—	—	800

KM# 376 5 DOLLARS
2.5000 g., 0.9990 Gold 0.0803 oz. AGW, 14x26.7 mm. **Ruler:** Elizabeth II **Subject:** Kitty **Shape:** Vertical rectangle

Date	Mintage	F	VF	XF	Unc	BU
2010 Proof	Est. 2,000	Value: 175				

KM# 377 5 DOLLARS
2.5000 g., 0.9990 Gold 0.0803 oz. AGW, 14x26.7 mm. **Ruler:** Elizabeth II **Subject:** Kiki Lala **Shape:** Vertical rectangle

Date	Mintage	F	VF	XF	Unc	BU
2010 Proof	Est. 2,000	Value: 175				

KM# 378 5 DOLLARS
2.5000 g., 0.9990 Gold 0.0803 oz. AGW, 14x26.7 mm. **Ruler:** Elizabeth II **Subject:** My Melo **Shape:** Vertical rectangle

Date	Mintage	F	VF	XF	Unc	BU
2010 Proof	Est. 2,000	Value: 175				

KM# 397 5 DOLLARS
15.5000 g., 0.9000 Gold 0.4485 oz. AGW, 27 mm. **Ruler:** Elizabeth II **Subject:** Amber Road - Carnuntum **Rev:** Arches, ancient coin, statue

Date	Mintage	F	VF	XF	Unc	BU
2010	2,000	Value: 800				

KM# 399 5 DOLLARS
15.5000 g., 0.9000 Gold 0.4485 oz. AGW, 27 mm. **Ruler:** Elizabeth II **Subject:** Amber Route - Szombathely **Rev:** Cathedral, ancient coin

Date	Mintage	F	VF	XF	Unc	BU
2010 Matte finish	2,000	Value: 800				

KM# 423 5 DOLLARS
15.5000 g., 0.9000 Gold 0.4485 oz. AGW, 27 mm. **Ruler:** Elizabeth II **Subject:** Christmas Star **Obv:** Head with tiara right, snowflakes around **Rev:** Three children and christmas tree, crystal insets

Date	Mintage	F	VF	XF	Unc	BU
2010 Proof	2,000	Value: 800				

KM# 430 5 DOLLARS
15.5000 g., 0.9000 Gold 0.4485 oz. AGW, 27 mm. **Ruler:** Elizabeth II **Obv:** Head with tiara right, wing enlargment as background **Rev:** Butterfly - Lycaena Virgaureae

Date	Mintage	F	VF	XF	Unc	BU
2010 Proof	1,000	Value: 825				

KM# 513 5 DOLLARS
50.0000 g., 0.9990 Silver 1.6059 oz. ASW, 35.2x35.2 mm. **Ruler:** Elizabeth II **Subject:** The three kings of 1936 **Obv:** Head with tiara right **Rev:** Busts left of George V, Edward VIII and George VI

Date	Mintage	F	VF	XF	Unc	BU
2011 Proof	2,500	Value: 100				

KM# 587 5 DOLLARS
27.0000 g., 0.9000 Gold 0.7812 oz. AGW, 27 mm. **Ruler:** Elizabeth II **Subject:** Amber Route - Aquileia **Rev:** Rhomulus and Remus suckling at she-wolf, amber insert

Date	Mintage	F	VF	XF	Unc	BU
2011	Est. 2,000	—	—	—	—	1,400

KM# 620 5 DOLLARS
1.0000 g., 0.9990 Gold 0.0321 oz. AGW, 12x8 mm. **Ruler:** Elizabeth II **Obv:** Head with crown right **Rev:** Baby tiger, diamond chip and paw print **Shape:** Rectangle

Date	Mintage	F	VF	XF	Unc	BU
2011 Proof	Est. 5,000	Value: 100				

KM# 623 5 DOLLARS
8.6000 g., 0.9000 Gold 0.2488 oz. AGW, 22 mm. **Ruler:** Elizabeth II **Obv:** Head with tiara right **Rev:** Dragon rearing upwards, paw to mouth

Date	Mintage	F	VF	XF	Unc	BU
2011 Proof	Est. 1,000	—	—	—	—	475

KM# 651 5 DOLLARS
25.0000 g., 0.9990 Silver 0.8029 oz. ASW, 40.6 mm. **Ruler:** Elizabeth II **Obv:** Head with tiara right **Rev:** Tasmanian tiger in lenticular 3-D **Edge:** Reeded

Date	Mintage	F	VF	XF	Unc	BU
2011 Proof	3,000	Value: 75.00				

KM# 689 5 DOLLARS
6.0000 g., 0.9990 Gold 0.1927 oz. AGW, 21 mm. **Ruler:** Elizabeth II **Subject:** Amber Route **Rev:** Map of European cities

Date	Mintage	F	VF	XF	Unc	BU
2011 Proof	999	Value: 400				

KM# 710 5 DOLLARS
6.0000 g., 0.9999 Gold 0.1929 oz. AGW, 21 mm. **Ruler:** Elizabeth II **Obv:** Ancient horsecart **Obv. Legend:** SZLAK BURSZTYNOWY **Rev:** Nepture statue, coin, mine building, amber insert **Rev. Legend:** Gdansk

Date	Mintage	F	VF	XF	Unc	BU
2011 Proof	999	Value: 375				

KM# 678 5 DOLLARS
40.0000 g., 0.9990 Silver 1.2847 oz. ASW, 29x47 mm. **Ruler:** Elizabeth II **Subject:** Year of the Dragon

Date	Mintage	F	VF	XF	Unc	BU
2012 Proof	—	Value: 100				

KM# 679 5 DOLLARS
40.0000 g., 0.9990 Silver 1.2847 oz. ASW, 29x47 mm. **Ruler:** Elizabeth II **Subject:** Year of the Dragon

Date	Mintage	F	VF	XF	Unc	BU
2012 Proof	—	Value: 100				

KM# 680 5 DOLLARS
40.0000 g., 0.9990 Silver 1.2847 oz. ASW, 29x47 mm. **Ruler:** Elizabeth II **Subject:** Year of the Dragon

Date	Mintage	F	VF	XF	Unc	BU
2012 Proof	—	Value: 100				

KM# 681 5 DOLLARS
40.0000 g., 0.9990 Silver 1.2847 oz. ASW, 29x47 mm. **Ruler:** Elizabeth II **Subject:** Year of the Dragon

Date	Mintage	F	VF	XF	Unc	BU
2012 Proof	—	Value: 100				

KM# 682 5 DOLLARS
40.0000 g., 0.9990 Silver 1.2847 oz. ASW, 29x47 mm. **Ruler:** Elizabeth II **Subject:** Year of the Dragon

Date	Mintage	F	VF	XF	Unc	BU
2012 Proof	—	Value: 100				

KM# 683 5 DOLLARS
40.0000 g., 0.9990 Silver 1.2847 oz. ASW, 29x47 mm. **Ruler:** Elizabeth II **Subject:** Year of the Dragon

Date	Mintage	F	VF	XF	Unc	BU
2012 Proof	—	Value: 100				

KM# 684 5 DOLLARS
40.0000 g., 0.9990 Silver 1.2847 oz. ASW, 29x47 mm. **Ruler:** Elizabeth II **Subject:** Year of the Dragon

Date	Mintage	F	VF	XF	Unc	BU
2012 Proof	—	Value: 100				

KM# 685 5 DOLLARS
40.0000 g., 0.9990 Silver 1.2847 oz. ASW, 29x47 mm. **Ruler:** Elizabeth II **Subject:** Year of the Dragon

Date	Mintage	F	VF	XF	Unc	BU
2012 Proof	—	Value: 100				

KM# 686 5 DOLLARS
40.0000 g., 0.9990 Silver 1.2847 oz. ASW, 29x47 mm. **Ruler:** Elizabeth II **Subject:** Year of the Dragon

Date	Mintage	F	VF	XF	Unc	BU
2012 Proof	—	Value: 100				

KM# 698 5 DOLLARS
0.5000 g., 0.9990 Gold 0.0161 oz. AGW, 11 mm. **Ruler:** Elizabeth II **Rev:** Ned Kelly standing, name vertacally at left **Edge:** Reeded

Date	Mintage	F	VF	XF	Unc	BU
2012 Proof	5,000	Value: 75.00				

KM# 716 5 DOLLARS
1.2400 g., 0.9999 Gold 0.0399 oz. AGW, 13.92 mm. **Ruler:** Elizabeth II **Rev:** Dragon

Date	Mintage	F	VF	XF	Unc	BU
2012 Proof	5,000	Value: 125				

KM# 738 5 DOLLARS
155.5500 g., 0.9990 Silver 4.9958 oz. ASW, 65 mm. **Ruler:** Elizabeth II **Subject:** Vietnam War, 50th Anniversary of Australia's involvement **Rev:** Two soldiers with rifles on patrol, helicopter above

Date	Mintage	F	VF	XF	Unc	BU
2012 Proof	400	Value: 250				

KM# 748 5 DOLLARS
100.0000 g., 0.9990 Silver 3.2117 oz. ASW, 52.5x118 mm. **Ruler:** Elizabeth II **Subject:** DaVinci's Last Supper **Rev:** Bartholomew **Shape:** Vertical rectangle

Date	Mintage	F	VF	XF	Unc	BU
2012 Proof	750	Value: 150				

KM# 749 5 DOLLARS
100.0000 g., 0.9990 Silver 3.2117 oz. ASW, 52.5x118 mm. **Ruler:** Elizabeth II **Subject:** DaVinci's Last Supper **Rev:** James Minor and Andrew **Shape:** Vertical rectangle

Date	Mintage	F	VF	XF	Unc	BU
2012 Proof	750	Value: 150				

KM# 750 5 DOLLARS
100.0000 g., 0.9990 Silver 3.2117 oz. ASW, 52.5x118 mm. **Ruler:** Elizabeth II **Subject:** DaVinci's Last Supper **Rev:** Judas Iscariot, Peter and John **Shape:** Vertical rectangle

Date	Mintage	F	VF	XF	Unc	BU
2012 Proof	750	Value: 150				

KM# 751 5 DOLLARS
100.0000 g., 0.9990 Silver 3.2117 oz. ASW, 52.5x118 mm. **Ruler:** Elizabeth II **Subject:** DaVinci's Last Supper **Rev:** Jesus **Shape:** Vertical rectangle

Date	Mintage	F	VF	XF	Unc	BU
2012 Proof	750	Value: 150				

KM# 752 5 DOLLARS
100.0000 g., 0.9990 Silver 3.2117 oz. ASW, 52.5x118 mm. **Ruler:** Elizabeth II **Subject:** DaVinci's Last Supper **Rev:** Thomas, James the Greater, Philip **Shape:** Vertical rectangle

Date	Mintage	F	VF	XF	Unc	BU
2012 Proof	750	Value: 150				

KM# 753 5 DOLLARS
100.0000 g., 0.9990 Silver 3.2117 oz. ASW, 52.5x118 mm. **Ruler:** Elizabeth II **Subject:** DaVinci's Last Supper **Rev:** Matthew **Shape:** Vertical rectangle

Date	Mintage	F	VF	XF	Unc	BU
2012 Proof	750	Value: 150				

KM# 754 5 DOLLARS
100.0000 g., 0.9990 Silver 3.2117 oz. ASW, 52.5x118 mm. **Ruler:** Elizabeth II **Subject:** DaVinci's Last Supper **Rev:** Jude Thaddeus and Simon the Zealot **Shape:** Vertical rectangle

Date	Mintage	F	VF	XF	Unc	BU
2012 Proof	750	Value: 150				

KM# 774   5 DOLLARS
6.0000 g., 0.9999 Gold 0.1929 oz. AGW, 21 mm.   **Ruler:** Elizabeth II **Subject:** Stare Hradisko **Obv:** Queen's head at left, two horse cart at right **Rev:** Centic coin design and art

Date	Mintage	F	VF	XF	Unc	BU
2012 Proof	999	Value: 400				

KM# 776   5 DOLLARS
6.0000 g., 0.9000 Gold 0.1736 oz. AGW, 16.7x22.3 mm.   **Ruler:** Elizabeth II **Subject:** Imperial Faberge Eggs - Coronation egg **Rev:** Egg and state coach

Date	Mintage	F	VF	XF	Unc	BU
2012 Proof	Est. 777	Value: 375				

KM# 780   5 DOLLARS
6.0000 g., 0.9999 Gold 0.1929 oz. AGW, 21 mm.   **Ruler:** Elizabeth II **Subject:** Silk Route - Wroclaw **Obv:** Queen's head at left, two horse cart at right **Rev:** Old building at left, statue at right

Date	Mintage	F	VF	XF	Unc	BU
2012 Proof	Est. 999	Value: 400				

KM# 801   5 DOLLARS
6.0000 g., 0.9990 Gold 0.1927 oz. AGW, 21 mm.   **Ruler:** Elizabeth II **Subject:** Szlak Bursztynowy - Szombathely **Rev:** Building, old coins and amber insert

Date	Mintage	F	VF	XF	Unc	BU
2012 Proof	Est. 999	Value: 400				

KM# 296   15 DOLLARS
500.0000 g., 0.9990 Silver 16.058 oz. ASW, 100 mm.   **Ruler:** Elizabeth II **Subject:** Year of the Dog **Rev:** Multicolor dog

Date	Mintage	F	VF	XF	Unc	BU
2005 Proof	—	Value: 600				

KM# 124   10 DOLLARS
28.2800 g., 0.9250 Silver 0.8410 oz. ASW, 38.6 mm.   **Ruler:** Elizabeth II **Subject:** Snoopy as an Ace **Obv:** Crowned head right **Rev:** Snoopy flying his dog house **Edge:** Reeded

Date	Mintage	F	VF	XF	Unc	BU
2001 Proof	10,000	Value: 35.00				

KM# 130   10 DOLLARS
28.2800 g., 0.9250 Silver 0.8410 oz. ASW, 38.6 mm.   **Ruler:** Elizabeth II **Series:** Pokeman **Obv:** Crowned shield within sprigs **Rev:** Bulbasaur **Edge:** Reeded

Date	Mintage	F	VF	XF	Unc	BU
2001 Proof	10,000	Value: 35.00				

KM# 133   10 DOLLARS
28.2800 g., 0.9250 Silver 0.8410 oz. ASW, 38.6 mm.   **Ruler:** Elizabeth II **Series:** Pokeman **Obv:** Crowned shield within sprigs **Rev:** Charmander **Edge:** Reeded

Date	Mintage	F	VF	XF	Unc	BU
2001 Proof	10,000	Value: 35.00				

KM# 136   10 DOLLARS
28.2800 g., 0.9250 Silver 0.8410 oz. ASW, 38.6 mm.   **Ruler:** Elizabeth II **Series:** Pokeman **Obv:** Crowned shield within sprigs **Rev:** Meowth **Edge:** Reeded

Date	Mintage	F	VF	XF	Unc	BU
2001 Proof	10,000	Value: 35.00				

KM# 139   10 DOLLARS
28.2800 g., 0.9250 Silver 0.8410 oz. ASW, 38.6 mm.   **Ruler:** Elizabeth II **Series:** Pokeman **Obv:** Crowned shield within sprigs **Rev:** Pikachu **Edge:** Reeded

Date	Mintage	F	VF	XF	Unc	BU
2001 Proof	10,000	Value: 35.00				

KM# 142   10 DOLLARS
28.2800 g., 0.9250 Silver 0.8410 oz. ASW, 38.6 mm.   **Ruler:** Elizabeth II **Series:** Pokeman **Obv:** Crowned shield within sprigs **Rev:** Squirtle **Edge:** Reeded

Date	Mintage	F	VF	XF	Unc	BU
2001 Proof	10,000	Value: 35.00				

KM# 147   10 DOLLARS
28.2800 g., 0.9250 Silver 0.8410 oz. ASW, 38.6 mm.   **Ruler:** Elizabeth II **Subject:** Pokémon Series **Obv:** Crowned shield within sprigs **Rev:** Pikachu **Edge:** Reeded

Date	Mintage	F	VF	XF	Unc	BU
2002PM Proof	10,000	Value: 35.00				

KM# 152   10 DOLLARS
28.2800 g., 0.9250 Silver 0.8410 oz. ASW, 38.6 mm.   **Ruler:** Elizabeth II **Subject:** Pokémon Series **Obv:** Crowned shield within sprigs **Rev:** Pichu **Edge:** Reeded

Date	Mintage	F	VF	XF	Unc	BU
2002PM Proof	10,000	Value: 35.00				

KM# 157   10 DOLLARS
28.2800 g., 0.9250 Silver 0.8410 oz. ASW, 38.6 mm.   **Ruler:** Elizabeth II **Subject:** Pokémon Series **Obv:** Crowned shield within sprigs **Rev:** Mewtwo **Edge:** Reeded

Date	Mintage	F	VF	XF	Unc	BU
2002PM Proof	10,000	Value: 35.00				

KM# 162   10 DOLLARS
28.2800 g., 0.9250 Silver 0.8410 oz. ASW, 38.6 mm.   **Ruler:** Elizabeth II **Subject:** Pokémon Series **Obv:** Crowned shield within sprigs **Rev:** Entei **Edge:** Reeded

Date	Mintage	F	VF	XF	Unc	BU
2002PM Proof	10,000	Value: 35.00				

KM# 167   10 DOLLARS
28.2800 g., 0.9250 Silver 0.8410 oz. ASW, 38.6 mm.   **Ruler:** Elizabeth II **Subject:** Pokémon Series **Obv:** Crowned shield within sprigs **Rev:** Celebi **Edge:** Reeded

Date	Mintage	F	VF	XF	Unc	BU
2002PM Proof	10,000	Value: 35.00				

KM# 274   10 DOLLARS
31.1050 g., 0.9990 Gold 0.9990 oz. AGW, 38.6 mm.   **Ruler:** Elizabeth II **Subject:** Year of the Rooster

Date	Mintage	F	VF	XF	Unc	BU
2005 Proof	—	Value: 1,800				

KM# 254   10 DOLLARS
155.5000 g., 0.9990 Silver 4.9942 oz. ASW, 65 mm.   **Ruler:** Elizabeth II **Subject:** Peanuts 60th Anniversary **Rev:** Peanut character heads around a central Snoopy

Date	Mintage	F	VF	XF	Unc	BU
2010 Prooflike	1,000	—	—	—	—	225

KM# 375   10 DOLLARS
100.0000 g., 0.9990 Silver 3.2117 oz. ASW, 64x54.2 mm.   **Ruler:** Elizabeth II **Subject:** Kitty and friends **Shape:** Heart

Date	Mintage	F	VF	XF	Unc	BU
2010 Proof	Est. 1,000	Value: 150				

KM# 387   10 DOLLARS
155.5000 g., 0.9990 Silver 4.9942 oz. ASW, 65 mm.   **Ruler:** Elizabeth II **Subject:** Miffy with cake

Date	Mintage	F	VF	XF	Unc	BU
2010 Proof	Est. 1,500	Value: 200				

KM# 125   20 DOLLARS
1.2400 g., 0.9999 Gold 0.0399 oz. AGW, 13.9 mm.   **Ruler:** Elizabeth II **Subject:** Snoopy as an Ace **Obv:** Crowned head right **Rev:** Snoopy flying his dog house **Edge:** Reeded

Date	Mintage	F	VF	XF	Unc	BU
2001 Proof	10,000	Value: 85.00				

KM# 148   20 DOLLARS
1.2400 g., 0.9999 Gold 0.0399 oz. AGW, 13.92 mm.   **Ruler:** Elizabeth II **Subject:** Pokémon Series **Obv:** Crowned shield within sprigs **Rev:** Pikachu **Edge:** Reeded

Date	Mintage	F	VF	XF	Unc	BU
2002PM Proof	10,000	Value: 80.00				

KM# 153   20 DOLLARS
1.2400 g., 0.9999 Gold 0.0399 oz. AGW, 13.9 mm.   **Ruler:** Elizabeth II **Subject:** Pokémon Series **Obv:** Crowned shield within sprigs **Rev:** Pichu **Edge:** Reeded

Date	Mintage	F	VF	XF	Unc	BU
2002PM Proof	10,000	Value: 80.00				

KM# 158   20 DOLLARS
1.2400 g., 0.9999 Gold 0.0399 oz. AGW, 13.92 mm.   **Ruler:** Elizabeth II **Subject:** Pokémon Series **Obv:** Crowned shield within sprigs **Rev:** Mewtwo **Edge:** Reeded

Date	Mintage	F	VF	XF	Unc	BU
2002PM Proof	10,000	Value: 80.00				

KM# 163   20 DOLLARS
1.2400 g., 0.9999 Gold 0.0399 oz. AGW, 13.9 mm.   **Ruler:** Elizabeth II **Subject:** Pokémon Series **Obv:** Crowned shield within sprigs **Rev:** Entei **Edge:** Reeded

Date	Mintage	F	VF	XF	Unc	BU
2002PM Proof	10,000	Value: 80.00				

KM# 168   20 DOLLARS
1.2400 g., 0.9999 Gold 0.0399 oz. AGW, 13.9 mm.   **Ruler:** Elizabeth II **Subject:** Pokémon Series **Obv:** Crowned shield within sprigs **Rev:** Celebi **Edge:** Reeded

Date	Mintage	F	VF	XF	Unc	BU
2002PM Proof	10,000	Value: 80.00				

KM# 379   20 DOLLARS
0.9170 Gold, 13.9x16.7 mm.   **Ruler:** Elizabeth II **Subject:** Hello Kitty **Shape:** Face **Note:** Center part to KM#380.

Date	Mintage	F	VF	XF	Unc	BU
2010 Proof	Est. 1,000	Value: 450				

KM# 255 25 DOLLARS
15.5500 g., 0.9990 Gold 0.4994 oz. AGW, 22 mm. **Ruler:**
Elizabeth II **Subject:** Peanuts 60th Anniversary **Rev:** Snoopy
dancing, Charlie Brown's zig-zag shirt pattern in background

Date	Mintage	F	VF	XF	Unc	BU
2010 Prooflike	1,000	—	—	—	—	900

KM# 388 25 DOLLARS
7.7700 g., 0.9990 Gold 0.2496 oz. AGW, 22 mm. **Ruler:**
Elizabeth II **Subject:** Miffy with key

Date	Mintage	F	VF	XF	Unc	BU
2010 Proof	1,000	Value: 450				

KM# 715 25 DOLLARS
7.7800 g., 0.9999 Gold 0.2501 oz. AGW, 22 mm. **Ruler:**
Elizabeth II **Rev:** Dragon

Date	Mintage	F	VF	XF	Unc	BU
2012 Proof	2,000	Value: 465				

KM# 268 30 DOLLARS
1000.0000 g., 0.9990 Silver 32.117 oz. ASW, 120 mm. **Ruler:**
Elizabeth II **Subject:** Year of the Rooster **Rev:** Multicolor rooster
standing right, sunrise

Date	Mintage	F	VF	XF	Unc	BU
2005 Proof	—	Value: 1,250				

KM# 297 30 DOLLARS
1000.0000 g., 0.9990 Silver 32.117 oz. ASW, 120 mm. **Ruler:**
Elizabeth II **Subject:** Year of the Dog **Rev:** Multicolor dog

Date	Mintage	F	VF	XF	Unc	BU
2005 Proof	—	Value: 1,250				

KM# 380 30 DOLLARS
0.9170 Gold, 30 mm. **Ruler:** Elizabeth II **Subject:** Bears **Note:**
Outer ring for KM#379

Date	Mintage	F	VF	XF	Unc	BU
2010 Proof	Est. 1,000	Value: 600				

KM# 742 30 DOLLARS
1000.0000 g., 0.9990 Silver 32.117 oz. ASW, 100 mm. **Ruler:**
Elizabeth II **Subject:** Year of the Dragon **Rev:** Dragon with pearl
in color

Date	Mintage	F	VF	XF	Unc	BU
2012 Proof	250	Value: 1,200				

KM# 788 30 DOLLARS
1000.0000 g., 0.9990 Silver 32.117 oz. ASW, 100 mm. **Ruler:**
Elizabeth II **Subject:** Russian municipalities - Belgorod **Obv:**
Head with crown right **Rev:** Statue, shield and building

Date	Mintage	F	VF	XF	Unc	BU
2012 Proof	—	Value: 1,300				

KM# 126 50 DOLLARS
3.1100 g., 0.9999 Gold 0.1000 oz. AGW, 17.9 mm. **Ruler:**
Elizabeth II **Subject:** Snoopy as an Ace **Obv:** Crowned head right
Rev: Snoopy flying his dog house **Edge:** Reeded

Date	Mintage	F	VF	XF	Unc	BU
2001 Proof	7,500	Value: 185				

KM# 149 50 DOLLARS
3.1100 g., 0.9999 Gold 0.1000 oz. AGW, 17.9 mm. **Ruler:**
Elizabeth II **Subject:** Pokémon Series **Obv:** Crowned shield
within sprigs **Rev:** Pikachu **Edge:** Reeded

Date	Mintage	F	VF	XF	Unc	BU
2002PM Proof	7,500	Value: 185				

KM# 154 50 DOLLARS
3.1100 g., 0.9999 Gold 0.1000 oz. AGW, 17.9 mm. **Ruler:**
Elizabeth II **Subject:** Pokémon Series **Obv:** Crowned shield
within sprigs **Rev:** Pichu **Edge:** Reeded

Date	Mintage	F	VF	XF	Unc	BU
2002PM Proof	7,500	Value: 185				

KM# 159 50 DOLLARS
3.1100 g., 0.9999 Gold 0.1000 oz. AGW, 17.9 mm. **Ruler:**
Elizabeth II **Subject:** Pokémon Series **Obv:** Crowned shield
within sprigs **Rev:** Mewtwo **Edge:** Reeded

Date	Mintage	F	VF	XF	Unc	BU
2002PM Proof	7,500	Value: 185				

KM# 164 50 DOLLARS
3.1100 g., 0.9999 Gold 0.1000 oz. AGW, 17.9 mm. **Ruler:**
Elizabeth II **Subject:** Pokémon Series **Obv:** Crowned shield
within sprigs **Rev:** Entei **Edge:** Reeded

Date	Mintage	F	VF	XF	Unc	BU
2002PM Proof	7,500	Value: 185				

KM# 169 50 DOLLARS
3.1100 g., 0.9999 Gold 0.1000 oz. AGW, 17.9 mm. **Ruler:**
Elizabeth II **Subject:** Pokémon Series **Obv:** Crowned shield
within sprigs **Rev:** Celebi **Edge:** Reeded

Date	Mintage	F	VF	XF	Unc	BU
2002PM Proof	7,500	Value: 185				

KM# 256 50 DOLLARS
15.5500 g., 0.9990 Gold 0.4994 oz. AGW, 30 mm. **Ruler:**
Elizabeth II **Subject:** Peanuts 60th Anniversary **Rev:** Snoopy as
a king

Date	Mintage	F	VF	XF	Unc	BU
2010 Prooflike	1,000	—	—	—	—	900

KM# 389 50 DOLLARS
15.5500 g., 0.9990 Gold 0.4994 oz. AGW, 30 mm. **Ruler:**
Elizabeth II **Subject:** Miffy in flowers

Date	Mintage	F	VF	XF	Unc	BU
2010 Proof	Est. 1,000	Value: 900				

KM# 584 50 DOLLARS
250.0000 g., 0.9990 Silver 8.0293 oz. ASW, 67.35x90 mm.
Ruler: Elizabeth II **Subject:** Russian Royal Family **Obv:** Nicholas
II and family standing as Saints in the Othodox Church, head with
tiara right below **Rev:** Oval portrait images of the Imperial family
Shape: Vertical Oval

Date	Mintage	F	VF	XF	Unc	BU
2011 Proof	400	Value: 400				

KM# 702 50 DOLLARS
62.2000 g., 0.9999 Gold 1.9995 oz. AGW **Ruler:** Elizabeth II
Rev: John Wycliff and Jan Hus

Date	Mintage	F	VF	XF	Unc	BU
2011 Proof	Est. 1,000	Value: 3,700				

KM# 714 50 DOLLARS
31.1050 g., 0.9999 Gold 0.9999 oz. AGW, 32 mm. **Ruler:**
Elizabeth II **Rev:** Dragon

Date	Mintage	F	VF	XF	Unc	BU
2012 Proof	2,000	Value: 1,850				

KM# 777 50 DOLLARS
31.1000 g., 0.9999 Gold 0.9997 oz. AGW, 29.2x39 mm. **Ruler:**
Elizabeth II **Subject:** Imperial Faberge Eggs - Corconation Egg
Rev: Egg and state coach

Date	Mintage	F	VF	XF	Unc	BU
2012 Proof	Est. 333	Value: 1,850				

KM# 778 50 DOLLARS
250.0000 g., 0.9990 Silver 8.0293 oz. ASW, 67.35x90 mm.
Ruler: Elizabeth II **Subject:** Imperial Faberge Eggs - Coronation
Egg **Rev:** Egg and state coach

Date	Mintage	F	VF	XF	Unc	BU
2012 Proof	Est. 333	Value: 350				

KM# 791 50 DOLLARS
250.0000 g., 0.9990 Silver 8.0293 oz. ASW, 67.35x90 mm.
Ruler: Elizabeth II **Subject:** Great Ukrainian Hetmans **Obv:**
Seven shields around central head of Queen Elizabeth **Rev:**
Seven busts around central shield **Shape:** Vertical oval

Date	Mintage	F	VF	XF	Unc	BU
2012 Proof	400	Value: 400				

KM# 793 50 DOLLARS
250.0000 g., 0.9250 Silver 7.4345 oz. ASW, 67.35x90 mm.
Ruler: Elizabeth II **Subject:** Royal Hunting **Obv:** Saint on
horseback **Rev:** Horseman with falcon **Shape:** Vertical oval

Date	Mintage	F	VF	XF	Unc	BU
2012 Proof	Est. 400	Value: 400				

KM# 127 100 DOLLARS
6.2200 g., 0.9999 Gold 0.1999 oz. AGW, 22 mm. **Ruler:**
Elizabeth II **Subject:** Snoopy as an Ace **Obv:** Crowned head right
Rev: Snoopy flying his dog house **Edge:** Reeded

Date	Mintage	F	VF	XF	Unc	BU
2001 Proof	5,000	Value: 400				

KM# 150 100 DOLLARS
6.2200 g., 0.9999 Gold 0.1999 oz. AGW, 22 mm. **Ruler:**
Elizabeth II **Subject:** Pokémon Series **Obv:** Crowned shield
within sprigs **Rev:** Pikachu **Edge:** Reeded

Date	Mintage	F	VF	XF	Unc	BU
2002PM Proof	5,000	Value: 400				

KM# 155 100 DOLLARS
6.2200 g., 0.9999 Gold 0.1999 oz. AGW, 22 mm. **Ruler:**
Elizabeth II **Subject:** Pokémon Series **Obv:** Crowned shield
within sprigs **Rev:** Pichu **Edge:** Reeded

Date	Mintage	F	VF	XF	Unc	BU
2002PM Proof	5,000	Value: 400				

KM# 160   100 DOLLARS
6.2200 g., 0.9999 Gold 0.1999 oz. AGW, 22 mm. **Ruler:**
Elizabeth II **Subject:** Pokémon Series **Obv:** Crowned shield
within sprigs **Rev:** Mewtwo **Edge:** Reeded

Date	Mintage	F	VF	XF	Unc	BU
2002PM Proof	5,000	Value: 400				

KM# 165   100 DOLLARS
6.2200 g., 0.9999 Gold 0.1999 oz. AGW, 22 mm. **Ruler:**
Elizabeth II **Subject:** Pokémon Series **Obv:** Crowned shield
within sprigs **Rev:** Entei **Edge:** Reeded

Date	Mintage	F	VF	XF	Unc	BU
2002PM Proof	5,000	Value: 400				

KM# 170   100 DOLLARS
6.2200 g., 0.9999 Gold 0.1999 oz. AGW, 22 mm. **Ruler:**
Elizabeth II **Subject:** Pokémon Series **Obv:** Crowned shield
within sprigs **Rev:** Celebi **Edge:** reeded

Date	Mintage	F	VF	XF	Unc	BU
2002PM Proof	5,000	Value: 400				

KM# 425   100 DOLLARS
93.3000 g., 0.9000 Gold 2.6996 oz. AGW, 41.6x55.6 mm.
Ruler: Elizabeth II **Subject:** Imperial Faberge Egg - Coronation
Egg **Obv:** Head with tiara right above opened egg **Rev:**
Coronation egg and coach **Shape:** Vertical oval

Date	Mintage	F	VF	XF	Unc	BU
2010 Proof	222	Value: 4,850				

KM# 511   100 DOLLARS
31.1030 g., 0.9990 Gold 0.9989 oz. AGW, 38.61 mm. **Ruler:**
Elizabeth II **Obv:** Head with tiara right **Rev:** Tasmanian tiger in
color

Date	Mintage	F	VF	XF	Unc	BU
2011 Proof	200	Value: 1,850				

KM# 572   100 DOLLARS
93.3000 g., 0.9000 Gold 2.6996 oz. AGW, 41.6x55.6 mm.
Ruler: Elizabeth II **Subject:** Imperial Faberge Egg **Obv:** Head
with tiara right, open egg below **Rev:** Clover leaf floral egg on
stand **Shape:** Vertical oval

Date	Mintage	F	VF	XF	Unc	BU
2011 Proof	222	Value: 4,850				

KM# 648   100 DOLLARS
93.3000 g., 0.9000 Gold 2.6996 oz. AGW, 41.6x55.6 mm.
Ruler: Elizabeth II **Subject:** Imperial Easter Egg - Lilly **Obv:** Head
with tiara right, open egg below **Rev:** Egg on stand, lillys around

Date	Mintage	F	VF	XF	Unc	BU
2011 Proof	Est. 222	Value: 4,500				

KM# 650   100 DOLLARS
50.0000 g., 0.9990 Silver partially gilt 1.6059 oz. ASW, 35.2 x
35.2 mm. **Ruler:** Elizabeth II **Obv:** Head with tiara right **Rev:**
Three Kings of 1936 - George V, Edward VIII, George VI
selectively gilt **Edge:** Reeded **Shape:** Square

Date	Mintage	F	VF	XF	Unc	BU
2011 Proof	1,500	Value: 160				

KM# 701   100 DOLLARS
139.5000 g., 0.9999 Gold 4.4844 oz. AGW, 50 mm. **Ruler:**
Elizabeth II **Subject:** General Perina, Battle of Britain pilot **Rev:**
Perina as pilot

Date	Mintage	F	VF	XF	Unc	BU
2011 Proof	400	Value: 8,000				

KM# 747   100 DOLLARS
400.0000 g., 0.9997 Silver gilt 12.855 oz. ASW, 90 mm. **Ruler:**
Elizabeth II **Subject:** Szlak Bursztynowy **Obv:** Queen's head at
left, Roman horse cart at right **Rev:** Map of central Europe, amber
insert

Date	Mintage	F	VF	XF	Unc	BU
2011 Proof	245	Value: 500				

KM# 737   100 DOLLARS
31.1050 g., 0.9990 Gold 0.9990 oz. AGW, 38.61 mm. **Ruler:**
Elizabeth II **Rev:** Tasmanian Wedge-Tailed Eagle **Edge:** Reeded
and numbered

Date	Mintage	F	VF	XF	Unc	BU
2012 Proof	150	Value: 1,750				

KM# 755   100 DOLLARS
93.3000 g., 0.9000 Gold 2.6996 oz. AGW, 41.6x55.6 mm.
Ruler: Elizabeth II **Subject:** Imperial Faberge Eggs - Duchess
of Marlborough **Rev:** Serpent at bottom stem of egg **Shape:**
Vertical oval

Date	Mintage	F	VF	XF	Unc	BU
2012 Proof	222	Value: 5,000				

KM# 512   200 DOLLARS
62.2000 g., 0.9990 Gold 1.9977 oz. AGW, 35.2x35.2 mm.
Ruler: Elizabeth II **Subject:** Three kings of 1935 **Obv:** Head with
tiara right **Rev:** Head left of George V, Edward VIII and George VI

Date	Mintage	F	VF	XF	Unc	BU
2011 Proof	250	Value: 3,650				

KM# 649   200 DOLLARS
62.2100 g., 0.9990 Gold 1.9980 oz. AGW, 35.2x35.2 mm.
Ruler: Elizabeth II **Obv:** Head with tiara right **Rev:** Three kings
of 1936 - George V, Edward VIII, George VI in 3-D **Edge:** Reeded
Shape: Square

Date	Mintage	F	VF	XF	Unc	BU
2011 Proof	75	Value: 3,800				

KM# 713   200 DOLLARS
155.5500 g., 0.9999 Gold 5.0003 oz. AGW **Ruler:** Elizabeth II
Rev: Dragon

Date	Mintage	F	VF	XF	Unc	BU
2012 Proof	100	Value: 9,000				

	ELIZABETH II NIUE
	1 kg 999
	✦
	2012

KM# 740   200 DOLLARS
1000.0000 g., 0.9990 Silver 32.117 oz. ASW, 118.2x52.7 mm.
Ruler: Elizabeth II **Obv:** Head with crown at left **Rev:** Two
dragons flanking center ball **Shape:** Horizontal rectangle

Date	Mintage	F	VF	XF	Unc	BU
2012 Proof	1,800	Value: 1,250				

KM# 700   250 DOLLARS
348.5000 g., 0.9999 Gold 11.202 oz. AGW, 65 mm. **Ruler:**
Elizabeth II **Rev:** Jan Amos Komensky seated at desk with globe

Date	Mintage	F	VF	XF	Unc	BU
2011 Proof	Est. 250	Value: 20,000				

KM# 405   3000 DOLLARS
500.0000 g., 0.9999 Gold 16.073 oz. AGW, 67.35x90 mm.
Ruler: Elizabeth II **Subject:** Russian Royal Family **Obv:** Seven
figures as Orthodox Saints, Elizabeth head with tiara below **Rev:**
Oval portaits of Nicholas II and his family **Shape:** Vertical Oval

Date	Mintage	F	VF	XF	Unc	BU
2010 Proof	23	Value: 28,500				

KM# 588   3000 DOLLARS
500.0000 g., 0.9999 Gold 16.073 oz. AGW, 67.35x90 mm.
Ruler: Elizabeth II **Subject:** Royal Hunting **Obv:** Russian saint
on horseback, head with tiara right below, multicolor **Rev:**
Russian figure on horseback with falcon, multicolor

Date	Mintage	F	VF	XF	Unc	BU
2011 Proof	40	Value: 28,500				

KM# 699 10000 DOLLARS
1000.0000 g., 0.9999 Gold 32.146 oz. AGW, 85 mm. **Ruler:** Elizabeth II **Rev:** Good Queen Ann seated on throne

Date	Mintage	F	VF	XF	Unc	BU
2011 Proof	Est. 150	Value: 57,500				

KM# 708 10000 DOLLARS
1000.0000 g., 0.9999 Gold 32.146 oz. AGW, 90 mm. **Ruler:** Elizabeth II **Obv:** Ancient horsecart **Obv. Legend:** SZLAK BURSZTYNOWY **Rev:** European map with cities, amber insert

Date	Mintage	F	VF	XF	Unc	BU
2011	Est. 12	Value: 57,500				

MINT SETS

KM#	Date	Mintage	Identification	Issue Price	Mkt Val
MS1	2009 (5)	20,000	KM#193-197	—	30.00
MS2	2010 (5)	10,000	KM#193-196, 198	—	30.00

NORWAY

The Kingdom of Norway (*Norge, Noreg*), a constitutional monarchy located in northwestern Europe, has an area of 150,000sq. mi. (324,220 sq. km.), including the island territories of Spitzbergen (Svalbard) and Jan Mayen, and a population of *4.2 million. Capital: Oslo (Christiania). The diversified economic base of Norway includes shipping, fishing, forestry, agriculture, and manufacturing. Nonferrous metals, paper and paperboard, paper pulp, iron, steel and oil are exported.

RULER
Harald V, 1991-

MINT MARK
(h) - Crossed hammers – Kongsberg

MONETARY SYSTEM
100 Ore = 1 Krone

KINGDOM
DECIMAL COINAGE

KM# 460 50 ORE
3.6000 g., Bronze, 18.5 mm. **Ruler:** Harald V **Obv:** Crown **Rev:** Stylized animal and value **Edge:** Plain

Date	Mintage	VG	F	VF	XF	BU
2001 without star	16,848,250	—	—	—		0.40
2001 with star	13,291,750	—	—	—	1.00	2.00
2001 Proof	Est. 11,000	Value: 10.00				
2002	28,293,000	—	—	—		0.40
2002 Proof	Est. 11,000	Value: 10.00				
2003	15,533,000	—	—	—		0.40
2003 Proof	10,800	Value: 10.00				
2004	14,807,000	—	—	—		0.40
2004 Proof	8,550	Value: 10.00				
2005	4,963,000	—	—	—		0.40
2005 Proof	8,550	Value: 10.00				
2006	30,227,000	—	—	—		0.40
2006 Proof	8,550	Value: 10.00				
2007	20,117,000	—	—	—		0.40
2007 Proof	6,582	Value: 10.00				
2008	19,391,000	—	—	—		0.40
2008 Proof	7,091	Value: 10.00				
2009	9,903,000	—	—	—		0.40
2009 Proof	6,310	Value: 10.00				
2010	14,982,000	—	—	—		0.40
2010 Proof	5,119	Value: 10.00				
2011 11 in date reversed	Est. 8,000,000	—	—	—		0.40
2011 11 in date corrected	Est. 2,000,000	—	—	—		0.40
2011 Proof	Est. 7,500	Value: 10.00				

KM# 462 KRONE
4.3500 g., Copper-Nickel, 21 mm. **Ruler:** Harald V **Obv:** Crowned monograms form cross within circle with center hole **Rev:** Bird on vine above center hole date and value below

Date	Mintage	VG	F	VF	XF	BU
2001 without star	43,128,650	—	—	—		0.65
2001 with star	7,355,350	—	—	—	1.25	2.50
2001 Proof	Est. 11,000	Value: 10.00				
2002	21,313,000	—	—	—		0.65
2002 Proof	Est. 11,000	Value: 10.00				
2003	24,093,000	—	—	—		0.65
2003 Proof	10,800	Value: 10.00				
2004	25,151,000	—	—	—		0.65
2004 Proof	8,550	Value: 10.00				
2005	25,648,000	—	—	—		0.65
2005 Proof	8,550	Value: 10.00				
2006	63,129,000	—	—	—		0.65
2006 Proof	8,550	Value: 10.00				
2007	47,108,000	—	—	—		0.65
2007 Proof	6,582	Value: 10.00				
2008	46,047,000	—	—	—		0.65
2008 Proof	7,091	Value: 10.00				
2009	50,055,000	—	—	—		0.65
2009 Proof	6,310	Value: 10.00				
2010	40,015,000	—	—	—		0.65
2010 Proof	5,119	Value: 10.00				
2011		—	—	—		0.50
2011 Proof	Est. 7,500	Value: 10.00				

KM# 463 5 KRONER
7.8500 g., Copper-Nickel, 26 mm. **Ruler:** Harald V **Subject:** Order of St. Olaf **Obv:** Hole at center of order chain **Rev:** Center hole divides sprigs, value above and date below **Edge:** Reeded

Date	Mintage	VG	F	VF	XF	BU
2001	480,000	—	—	—		2.00
2001 Proof	Est. 11,000	Value: 12.50				
2002	3,622,000	—	—	—		1.50
2002 Proof	Est. 11,000	Value: 12.50				
2003	827,000	—	—	—		1.50
2003 Proof	10,800	Value: 12.50				
2004	503,000	—	—	—		1.50
2004 Proof	8,550	Value: 12.50				
2005	503,000	—	—	—		2.00
2005 Proof	8,550	Value: 12.50				
2006	509,000	—	—	—		1.50
2006 Proof	8,500	Value: 12.50				
2007	9,152,000	—	—	—		1.50
2007 Proof	6,582	Value: 12.50				
2008	5,502,000	—	—	—		1.50
2008 Proof	7,091	Value: 12.50				
2009	10,020,000	—	—	—		1.50
2009 Proof	6,310	Value: 12.50				

KM# 457 10 KRONER
6.8000 g., Nickel-Brass, 24 mm. **Ruler:** Harald V **Obv:** Head right **Rev:** Stylized church rooftop, value and date **Edge:** Segmented reeding

Date	Mintage	VG	F	VF	XF	BU
2001 without star	9,854,000	—	—	—		3.50
2001 with star	10,000	—	—	—		50.00
2001 Proof	Est. 11,000	Value: 10.00				
2002	1,123,000	—	—	—		3.50
2002 Proof	Est. 11,000	Value: 10.00				
2003	957,000	—	—	—		3.50
2003 Proof	10,800	Value: 10.00				
2004	503,000	—	—	—		4.50
2004 Proof	8,550	Value: 10.00				
2005	466,000	—	—	—		4.50
2005 Proof	10,555	Value: 10.00				
2006	497,000	—	—	—		3.50
2006 Proof	8,550	Value: 10.00				
2007	474,000	—	—	—		3.50
2007 Proof	6,582	Value: 10.00				
2008	565,000	—	—	—		3.50
2009	475,000	—	—	—		3.50
2009 Proof	6,310	Value: 10.00				
2010		—	—	—		3.50
2010 Proof	—	Value: 10.00				

KM# 482 10 KRONER
6.8000 g., Nickel-Brass, 24 mm. **Ruler:** Harald V **Subject:** Henrik Vergeland **Obv:** Head right **Rev:** Spectacles and vertical signature

Date	Mintage	F	VF	XF	Unc	BU
2008	4,628,000	—	—	—		3.50
2008 Proof	7,091	Value: 10.00				

KM# 483 10 KRONER
6.8000 g., Nickel-Brass, 24 mm. **Ruler:** Harald V **Subject:** Ole Bull 100th Anniversary of Birth **Obv:** Head right **Rev:** Bust and music score **Edge:** Segmented reeding

Date	Mintage	F	VF	XF	Unc	BU
2010	955,000	—	—	—		3.00
2010 Proof	5,119	Value: 10.00				

KM# 484 10 KRONER
6.8000 g., Nickel-Brass, 24 mm. **Ruler:** Harald V **Subject:** Norway's first University, 200th Anniversary **Obv:** Head right **Rev:** Column

Date	Mintage	F	VF	XF	Unc	BU
2011		—	—	—		3.00
2011 Proof	7,500	Value: 10.00				

KM# 453 20 KRONER
9.9000 g., Nickel-Brass, 27.5 mm. **Ruler:** Harald V **Obv:** Head right **Rev:** Value above 1/2 ancient boat

Date	Mintage	VG	F	VF	XF	BU
2001	4,194,000	—	—	—	—	5.00
2001 with star	10,000	—	—	—	—	2.00
2001 Proof	—	Value: 25.00				
2002	18,218,000	—	—	—	—	5.00
2003	30,061,000	—	—	—	—	5.00
2003 Proof	11,100	Value: 25.00				
2005	553,000	—	—	—	—	5.00
2005 Proof	8,800	Value: 25.00				
2007	493,000	—	—	—	—	5.00
2007 Proof	7,091	Value: 25.00				
2008	481,000	—	—	—	—	5.00
2008 Proof	6,310	Value: 25.00				
2009	473,000	—	—	—	—	5.00
2009 Proof	7,500	Value: 25.00				
2010	—	—	—	—	—	5.00
2010 Proof	—	Value: 25.00				

KM# 471 20 KRONER
9.9000 g., Nickel-Brass, 27.5 mm. **Ruler:** Harald V **Subject:** Niels Henrik Abel **Obv:** Head right **Rev:** Pair of glasses, dates and value within mathematical graphs **Edge:** Plain

Date	Mintage	F	VF	XF	Unc	BU
2002	2,230,000	—	—	—	5.50	12.00
2002 Proof	Est. 11,000	Value: 25.00				

KM# 478 20 KRONER
9.9000 g., Nickel-Brass, 27.5 mm. **Ruler:** Harald V **Subject:** First Norwegian Railroad **Obv:** Head right **Rev:** Railroad track switch and value **Edge:** Plain

Date	Mintage	F	VF	XF	Unc	BU
2004	499,000	—	—	—	5.50	20.00
2004 Proof	8,550	Value: 25.00				

KM# 479 20 KRONER
9.9000 g., Nickel-Brass, 27.5 mm. **Ruler:** Harald V **Obv:** Head right **Rev:** Henrik Ibsen caricature walking left, signature **Edge:** Plain

Date	Mintage	F	VF	XF	Unc	BU
2006	10,000	—	—	—	5.50	12.00
2006 Proof	—	Value: 10.00				

KM# 469 100 KRONER
33.6000 g., 0.9250 Silver 0.9992 oz. ASW, 39 mm. **Ruler:** Harald V **Subject:** Nobel Peace Prize Centennial **Obv:** Rampant crowned lion left holding axe **Rev:** Head left **Edge:** Plain

Date	Mintage	F	VF	XF	Unc	BU
2001 Proof	Est. 50,000	Value: 125				

KM# 472 100 KRONER
33.8000 g., 0.9250 Silver 1.0052 oz. ASW, 39 mm. **Ruler:** Harald V **Subject:** 1905 Independence from Sweden **Obv:** Three kings **Rev:** Farm field **Edge:** Plain

Date	Mintage	F	VF	XF	Unc	BU
2003 Proof	65,000	Value: 70.00				

KM# 474 100 KRONER
33.8000 g., 0.9250 Silver 1.0052 oz. ASW, 39 mm. **Ruler:** Harald V **Subject:** 1905 Liberation **Obv:** Three kings **Rev:** Off shore ocean oil well **Edge:** Plain

Date	Mintage	F	VF	XF	Unc	BU
2004 Proof	65,000	Value: 70.00				

KM# 476 100 KRONER
33.8000 g., 0.9250 Silver 1.0052 oz. ASW, 39 mm. **Ruler:** Harald V **Obv:** Three kings **Rev:** Circuit board **Edge:** Plain

Date	Mintage	F	VF	XF	Unc	BU
2005 Proof	72,000	Value: 70.00				

KM# 480 200 KRONER
16.8500 g., 0.9250 Silver 0.5011 oz. ASW, 32 mm. **Ruler:** Harald V **Subject:** Henrik Wergeland, 200th Birth Anniversary **Obv:** Head right **Rev:** Spectacles and signature

Date	Mintage	F	VF	XF	Unc	BU
2008 Proof	40,000	Value: 100				

KM# 481 200 KRONER
16.8500 g., 0.9250 Silver 0.5011 oz. ASW, 32 mm. **Ruler:** Harald V **Subject:** Knut Hamsun 150th Birth Anniversary **Obv:** Crowned shield **Rev:** Streppled portrait, novel text and signature

Date	Mintage	F	VF	XF	Unc	BU
2009 Proof	40,000	Value: 100				

KM# 485 200 KRONER
16.8500 g., 0.9250 Silver 0.5011 oz. ASW, 32 mm. **Ruler:** Harald V **Subject:** World Ski Championships, 2011 **Obv:** Head right **Rev:** Different types of skiers

Date	Mintage	F	VF	XF	Unc	BU
2011 Proof	40,000	Value: 100				

KM# 486 200 KRONER
16.8500 g., 0.9250 Silver 0.5011 oz. ASW, 32 mm. **Ruler:** Harald V **Obv:** Head right **Rev:** Various Athletics, Javelin, track, skating, snowboarding, table tennis.

Date	Mintage	F	VF	XF	Unc	BU
2011 Proof	40,000	Value: 100				

KM# 470 1500 KRONER
16.9600 g., 0.9170 Gold 0.5000 oz. AGW, 27 mm. **Ruler:** Harald V **Subject:** Nobel Peace Prize Centennial **Obv:** Head right **Rev:** Reverse design of the prize medal **Edge:** Plain

Date	Mintage	VG	F	VF	XF	BU
ND(2001) Matte Proof	7,500	Value: 1,100				

KM# 473 1500 KRONER
16.9600 g., 0.9170 Gold 0.5000 oz. AGW, 27 mm. **Ruler:** Harald V **Subject:** 1905 Liberation **Obv:** Three kings **Rev:** Various leaf types **Edge:** Plain

Date	Mintage	F	VF	XF	Unc	BU
2003 Proof	10,000	Value: 1,000				

KM# 475 1500 KRONER
16.9600 g., 0.9170 Gold 0.5000 oz. AGW, 27 mm. **Ruler:** Harald V **Subject:** 1905 Liberation **Obv:** Three kings **Rev:** Liquid drops on hard surface **Edge:** Plain

Date	Mintage	F	VF	XF	Unc	BU
2004 Proof	10,000	Value: 1,000				

KM# 477 1500 KRONER
16.9600 g., 0.9170 Gold 0.5000 oz. AGW, 27 mm. **Ruler:** Harald V **Obv:** Three kings **Rev:** Binary language **Edge:** Plain

Date	Mintage	F	VF	XF	Unc	BU
2005 Proof	10,000	Value: 1,000				

MINT SETS

KM#	Date	Mintage	Identification	Issue Price	Mkt Val
MS59	2001 (5)	17,000	KM453, 457, 460, 462, 463. Uncirculated set, souvenir version, Norwegian text	20.00	30.00
MS60	2001 (5)	30,000	KM453, 457, 460, 462, 463. Children's (Baby) set.	18.00	30.00
MS61	2001 (5)	2,000	KM453, 457, 460, 462, 463 plus medal.	27.00	27.00
MS62	2001 (5)	—	KM453, 457, 460, 462, 463. Uncirculated set, classic version (hard plastic case)	—	30.00
MS63	2002 (5)	55,000	KM453, 457, 460, 462, 463. Uncirculated set, classic version (hard plastic case)	—	32.00
MS64	2003 (5)	55,000	KM453, 457, 460, 462, 463. Uncirculated set, classic version (hard plastic case)	—	32.00
MS65	2004 (5)	35,000	KM#457, 460, 462, 463, 478. Uncirculated set, classic version (hard plastic case)	—	25.00
MS66	2005 (5)	32,000	KM453, 457, 460, 462, 463. Uncirculated set, classic version (hard plastic case)	—	25.00

PROOF SETS

KM#	Date	Mintage	Identification	Issue Price	Mkt Val
PS13	2002 (5)	10,000	KM#457, 460, 462, 463, 471, Classic proof set	—	75.00
PS14	2003 (5)	10,000	KM453, 457, 460, 462, 463, Classic proof set	—	95.00
PS15	2004 (5)	7,800	KM#457, 460, 462, 463, 478, Classic proof set	—	100
PS16	2005 (5)	7,800	KM453, 457, 460, 462, 463, Classic proof set	—	95.00

OMAN

The Sultanate of Oman (formerly Muscat and Oman), an independent monarchy located in the southeastern part of the Arabian Peninsula, has an area of 82,030 sq. mi. (212,460 sq. km.) and a population of *1.3 million. Capital: Muscat. The economy is based on agriculture, herding and petroleum. Petroleum products, dates, fish and hides are exported.

RULER:
Qaboos ibn al-Sa'id, AH1390-/1970AD-

SULTANATE

REFORM COINAGE
1000 Baisa = 1 Omani Rial

KM# 150 5 BAISA
2.6500 g., Bronze Clad Steel, 19 mm. **Ruler:** Qabus bin Sa'id AH1390-/1970AD- **Obv:** National arms **Rev:** Value and dates

Date	Mintage	F	VF	XF	Unc	BU
AH1429-2008	—	—	—	0.20	0.50	0.75

KM# 151 10 BAISA
4.0400 g., Bronze Clad Steel, 22.5 mm. **Ruler:** Qabus bin Sa'id AH1390-/1970AD- **Obv:** National arms **Rev:** Value with both dates

Date	Mintage	F	VF	XF	Unc	BU
AH1429-2008	—	—	—	0.30	0.75	1.00

KM# 152a   25 BAISA
2.6300 g., Nickel Clad Steel, 17.95 mm.   **Ruler:** Qabus bin Sa'id AH1390-/1970AD-   **Obv:** National arms   **Rev:** Value with both dates   **Edge:** Reeded

Date	Mintage	F	VF	XF	Unc	BU
AH1427-2007	—	—	—	0.35	0.90	1.25
AH1428-2008	—	—	—	0.35	0.90	1.25
AH1429-2009	—	—	—	0.35	0.90	1.25
AH1430-2010	—	—	—	0.35	0.90	1.25

KM# 152   25 BAISA
3.0300 g., Copper-Nickel, 18 mm.   **Ruler:** Qabus bin Sa'id AH1390-/1970AD-   **Obv:** National arms   **Rev:** Value and both dates   **Edge:** Plain

Date	Mintage	F	VF	XF	Unc	BU
AH1428-2008	—	—	0.15	0.35	0.90	1.25
AH1429-2009	—	—	0.15	0.35	0.90	1.25

KM# 153a   50 BAISA
5.5700 g., Nickel Clad Steel, 24 mm.   **Ruler:** Qabus bin Sa'id AH1390-/1970AD-   **Obv:** National arms   **Rev:** Value with both dates   **Edge:** Reeded

Date	Mintage	F	VF	XF	Unc	BU
AH1427-2007	—	—	—	0.60	1.50	2.00
AH1428-2008	—	—	—	0.60	1.50	2.00
AH1429-2009	—	—	—	0.60	1.50	2.00
AH1430-2010	—	—	—	0.60	1.50	2.00

KM# 153   50 BAISA
6.4000 g., Copper-Nickel, 24 mm.   **Ruler:** Qabus bin Sa'id AH1390-/1970AD-   **Obv:** National arms   **Rev:** Value with both dates   **Edge:** Reeded

Date	Mintage	F	VF	XF	Unc	BU
AH1429-2008	—	—	0.25	0.60	1.50	2.00

KM# 154   OMANI RIAL
28.2800 g., 0.9250 Silver 0.8410 oz. ASW, 38.6 mm.   **Ruler:** Qabus bin Sa'id AH1390-/1970AD-   **Subject:** 31st National Day and Environment Year   **Obv:** National arms   **Rev:** Multicolor map design   **Edge:** Reeded

Date	Mintage	F	VF	XF	Unc	BU
2001	500	—	—	—	90.00	—
2001 Proof	105	Value: 150				

KM# 154a   OMANI RIAL
37.8000 g., 0.9160 Gold 1.1132 oz. AGW, 38.6 mm.   **Ruler:** Qabus bin Sa'id AH1390-/1970AD-   **Subject:** 31st National Day and Environment Year   **Obv:** National arms   **Rev:** Multicolor map design   **Edge:** Reeded

Date	Mintage	F	VF	XF	Unc	BU
2001	350	—	—	—	1,700	—
2001 Proof	105	Value: 1,850				

KM# 156   OMANI RIAL
28.2800 g., 0.9250 Silver 0.8410 oz. ASW, 38.7 mm.   **Ruler:** Qabus bin Sa'id AH1390-/1970AD-   **Series:** Environment Collection   **Obv:** National arms   **Rev:** Hoopoe bird standing right multicolor

Date	Mintage	F	VF	XF	Unc	BU
2002 Proof	1,000	Value: 75.00				

KM# 157   OMANI RIAL
28.2800 g., 0.9250 Silver 0.8410 oz. ASW, 38.7 mm.   **Ruler:** Qabus bin Sa'id AH1390-/1970AD-   **Series:** Environment Collection   **Obv:** National arms   **Rev:** Dolphin right multicolor

Date	Mintage	F	VF	XF	Unc	BU
2002 Proof	1,000	Value: 75.00				

KM# 158   OMANI RIAL
28.2800 g., 0.9250 Silver 0.8410 oz. ASW, 38.7 mm.   **Ruler:** Qabus bin Sa'id AH1390-/1970AD-   **Series:** Environment Collection   **Obv:** National arms   **Rev:** Turtle left multicolor

Date	Mintage	F	VF	XF	Unc	BU
2002 Proof	1,000	Value: 75.00				

KM# 159   OMANI RIAL
28.2800 g., 0.9250 Silver 0.8410 oz. ASW, 38.7 mm.   **Ruler:** Qabus bin Sa'id AH1390-/1970AD-   **Series:** Environment Collection   **Obv:** National arms   **Rev:** Flower multicolor

Date	Mintage	F	VF	XF	Unc	BU
2002 Proof	1,000	Value: 75.00				

KM# 160   OMANI RIAL
28.2800 g., 0.9250 Silver 0.8410 oz. ASW, 38.7 mm.   **Ruler:** Qabus bin Sa'id AH1390-/1970AD-   **Series:** Environment Collection   **Obv:** National arms   **Rev:** Ibex standing left multicolor

Date	Mintage	F	VF	XF	Unc	BU
2002 Proof	1,000	Value: 75.00				

KM# 161   OMANI RIAL
28.2800 g., 0.9250 Silver 0.8410 oz. ASW, 38.7 mm.   **Ruler:** Qabus bin Sa'id AH1390-/1970AD-   **Series:** Environment Collection   **Obv:** National arms   **Rev:** Butterfly multicolor

Date	Mintage	F	VF	XF	Unc	BU
2002 Proof	1,000	Value: 75.00				

KM# 162   OMANI RIAL
28.2800 g., 0.9250 Silver 0.8410 oz. ASW, 38.7 mm.   **Ruler:** Qabus bin Sa'id AH1390-/1970AD-   **Subject:** Population Census - December, 2003

Date	Mintage	F	VF	XF	Unc	BU
2003 Rare	—	—	—	—	—	—

KM# 155   OMANI RIAL
28.2800 g., 0.9250 Silver 0.8410 oz. ASW, 38.6 mm.   **Ruler:** Qabus bin Sa'id AH1390-/1970AD-   **Subject:** The Sindibad Voyage, 1980/1981   **Obv:** National arms   **Rev:** Sailing ship below map within circle   **Edge:** Reeded

Date	Mintage	F	VF	XF	Unc	BU
2003 Proof	—	Value: 65.00				

KM# 163   OMANI RIAL
28.2800 g., 0.9250 Silver 0.8410 oz. ASW, 38.7 mm.   **Ruler:** Qabus bin Sa'id AH1390-/1970AD- **Subject:** 35th National Day **Obv:** Oman Map

Date	Mintage	F	VF	XF	Unc	BU
AH1427-2005	—	—	—	—	100	120

KM# 164   OMANI RIAL
28.2800 g., 0.9250 Silver 0.8410 oz. ASW, 38.7 mm.   **Ruler:** Qabus bin Sa'id AH1390-/1970AD- **Subject:** 40th Anniversary of First Oil Export from Oman

Date	Mintage	F	VF	XF	Unc	BU
2007	—	—	—	—	90.00	100

KM# 165   OMANI RIAL
28.2800 g., 0.9250 Silver 0.8410 oz. ASW, 38.7 mm.   **Ruler:** Qabus bin Sa'id AH1390-/1970AD- **Subject:** 29th GCC Summit held in Muscat in December 2008

Date	Mintage	F	VF	XF	Unc	BU
2008	—	—	—	—	100	120

KM# 166   OMANI RIAL
28.2800 g., 0.9250 Silver 0.8410 oz. ASW, 38.7 mm.   **Ruler:** Qabus bin Sa'id AH1390-/1970AD- **Subject:** 19th Arabian Gulf Cup

Date	Mintage	F	VF	XF	Unc	BU
2008	—	—	—	—	250	—

PAKISTAN

The Islamic Republic of Pakistan, located on the Indian sub-continent between India and Afghanistan, has an area of 310,404 sq. mi. (803,940 sq. km.) and a population of 130 million. Capital: Islamabad. Pakistan is mainly an agricultural land although the industrial base is expanding rapidly. Yarn, textiles, cotton, rice, medical instruments, sports equipment and leather are exported.

TITLE

پاکستان

Pakistan

ISLAMIC REPUBLIC
DECIMAL COINAGE

100 Paisa = 1 Rupee

KM# 62   RUPEE
4.0000 g., Bronze, 20 mm.   **Obv:** Head of Jinnah facing left **Rev:** Mosque above value **Edge:** Reeded

Date	Mintage	F	VF	XF	Unc	BU
2001	146,996,000	0.20	0.25	0.35	0.65	0.75
2002	192,252,000	0.20	0.25	0.35	0.65	0.75
2003	217,996,000	0.20	0.25	0.35	0.65	0.75
2004	162,210,000	0.20	0.25	0.35	0.65	0.75
2005	202,330,000	0.20	0.25	0.35	0.65	0.75
2006	113,135,000	0.20	0.25	0.35	0.65	0.75

KM# 67   RUPEE
1.7500 g., Aluminum, 20 mm.   **Obv:** Head left **Rev:** Mosque

Date	Mintage	F	VF	XF	Unc	BU
2007	201,670,000	—	—	—	—	2.00
2008	97,953,000	—	—	—	—	2.00
2009	80,280,000	—	—	—	—	2.00
2010	100,000,000	—	—	—	—	2.00
2011	—	—	—	—	—	2.00
2012	—	—	—	—	—	2.00

KM# 64   2 RUPEES
5.0000 g., Nickel-Brass, 22.5 mm.   **Obv:** Crescent, star and date above sprigs **Rev:** Value below mosque and clouds **Edge:** Reeded

Date	Mintage	F	VF	XF	Unc	BU
2001	85,444,000	0.20	0.30	0.45	0.85	1.00
2002	148,940,000	0.20	0.30	0.45	0.85	1.00
2003	125,220,000	0.20	0.30	0.45	0.85	1.00
2004	105,148,000	0.20	0.30	0.45	0.85	1.00
2005	98,912,000	0.20	0.30	0.45	0.85	1.00
2006	34,432,000	0.20	0.30	0.45	0.85	1.00

KM# 68   2 RUPEES
Aluminum   **Obv:** Star and crescent, wheat ears below **Rev:** Mosque

Date	Mintage	F	VF	XF	Unc	BU
2007	100,848,000	—	—	—	—	2.00
2008	—	—	—	—	—	2.00
2009	100,000,000	—	—	—	—	2.00
2010	5,337,000	—	—	—	—	2.00
2011	—	—	—	—	—	2.00

KM# 65   5 RUPEES
6.5000 g., Copper-Nickel, 24 mm.   **Obv:** Cresent, star and date above sprays **Rev:** Value within star design and sprigs **Edge:** Reeded

Date	Mintage	F	VF	XF	Unc	BU
2002	35,668,000	0.50	1.00	1.50	3.00	3.25
2003	138,566,000	0.50	1.00	1.50	3.00	3.25
2004	224,228,000	0.50	—	1.50	3.00	3.25
2005	148,248,000	0.50	—	—	3.00	3.25
2006	177,222,000	—	—	—	3.00	3.25

KM# 66   10 RUPEES
7.5000 g., Copper-Nickel, 27.5 mm.   **Obv:** Cresent, star and date above sprays **Rev:** Flowers and inscription **Rev. Inscription:** Year of Fatima Jinnah **Edge:** Reeded

Date	Mintage	F	VF	XF	Unc	BU
2003	200,000	—	—	4.00	6.50	7.50

KM# 69   10 RUPEES
8.2500 g., Copper-Nickel, 27.5 mm.   **Subject:** Benazir Bhutto **Obv:** Star and crescent, wheat wreath below **Rev:** Bust facing, Urdu script legend above

Date	Mintage	F	VF	XF	Unc	BU
2007	—	—	—	—	—	5.00
2008	300,000	—	—	—	—	5.00

KM# 70   10 RUPEES
8.2500 g., Copper-Nickel, 27.5 mm.   **Subject:** Pakistan - China Friendship, 60 years of Peoples' Republic of China **Obv:** Crescent and star **Rev:** Pakistan and Chinese flags, clasped hands below

Date	Mintage	F	VF	XF	Unc	BU
2009	100,000	—	—	—	4.50	6.50

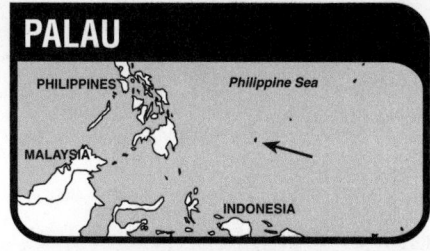

PALAU

The Republic of Palau, a group of about 100 islands and islets, is generally considered a part of the Caroline Islands. It is located about 1,000 miles southeast of Manila and about the same distance southwest of Saipan and has an area of 179 sq. mi. and a population of 12,116. Capital: Koror.

REPUBLIC

MILLED COINAGE

KM# 86   DOLLAR
1.2441 g., 0.9999 Gold 0.0400 oz. AGW, 13.94 mm. **Subject:** Marine Life Protection **Obv:** Prone Mermaid **Rev:** Two fish

Date	Mintage	F	VF	XF	Unc	BU
2001 Proof	—	Value: 65.00				

KM# 87   DOLLAR
1.2441 g., 0.9999 Gold 0.0400 oz. AGW, 13.94 mm. **Subject:** Marine Life Protection **Obv:** Seated Mermaid with raised arm above value **Rev:** Two glittering fish

Date	Mintage	F	VF	XF	Unc	BU
2001 Proof	—	Value: 65.00				

KM# 88   DOLLAR
1.2441 g., 0.9999 Gold 0.0400 oz. AGW, 13.94 mm. **Subject:** Marine Life Protection **Obv:** Figurehead Mermaid and value **Rev:** Moorish Idol fish

Date	Mintage	F	VF	XF	Unc	BU
2001 Proof	—	Value: 65.00				

KM# 89   DOLLAR
1.2441 g., 0.9999 Gold 0.0400 oz. AGW, 13.94 mm. **Subject:** Marine Life Protection **Obv:** Figurehead Mermaid and value **Rev:** Moorish Idol fish

Date	Mintage	F	VF	XF	Unc	BU
2001 Proof	—	Value: 65.00				

KM# 60   DOLLAR
26.8000 g., Copper-Nickel, 37.2 mm. **Subject:** Marine Life Protection **Obv:** Seated Mermaid with raised arm above value **Rev:** Two glittering fish **Edge:** Reeded

Date	Mintage	F	VF	XF	Unc	BU
2001 Proof	—	Value: 30.00				

KM# 61   DOLLAR
26.8000 g., Copper-Nickel, 37.2 mm. **Subject:** Marine Life Protection **Obv:** Prone Mermaid above value **Rev:** Two glittering fish **Edge:** Reeded

Date	Mintage	F	VF	XF	Unc	BU
2001 Proof	—	Value: 32.50				

KM# 62   DOLLAR
26.8000 g., Copper-Nickel, 37.2 mm. **Subject:** Marine Life Protection **Obv:** Figurehead mermaid and value **Rev:** Moorish-Idol fish **Edge:** Reeded

Date	Mintage	F	VF	XF	Unc	BU
2001 Proof	—	Value: 30.00				

KM# 52   DOLLAR
26.8600 g., Copper-Nickel, 37.3 mm. **Subject:** Marine Life Protection **Obv:** Mermaid figurehead and value **Rev:** Multicolor jellyfish **Edge:** Reeded

Date	Mintage	F	VF	XF	Unc	BU
2001 Proof	—	Value: 30.00				

KM# 253   DOLLAR
1.2500 g., 0.9990 Gold 0.0401 oz. AGW, 13.9 mm. **Obv:** Mermaid body-surfing wave **Rev:** Blue angelfish

Date	Mintage	F	VF	XF	Unc	BU
2001 Proof	—	Value: 65.00				

KM# 254   DOLLAR
1.2400 g., 0.9990 Gold 0.0398 oz. AGW, 13.9 mm. **Obv:** Large breasted mermaid on beach **Rev:** Emperor Angelfish

Date	Mintage	F	VF	XF	Unc	BU
2001 Proof	—	Value: 65.00				

KM# 287   DOLLAR
35.0000 g., Copper-Nickel, 50 mm. **Obv:** National Arms **Rev:** Cut card corners, Queens of Hearts, Clubs

Date	Mintage	F	VF	XF	Unc	BU
ND (2001)	—	—	—	—	—	25.00
Antique finish						

KM# 288   DOLLAR
35.0000 g., Copper-Nickel, 50 mm. **Obv:** National arms **Rev:** Cut card corner, Queen of Spades, diamonds

Date	Mintage	F	VF	XF	Unc	BU
ND (2001)	—	—	—	—	—	25.00
Antique finish						

KM# 56   DOLLAR
26.8000 g., Copper-Nickel, 37.2 mm. **Subject:** Marine Life Protection **Obv:** Mermaid figurehead and value **Rev:** Multicolor fish scene **Edge:** Reeded

Date	Mintage	F	VF	XF	Unc	BU
2002 Proof	—	Value: 32.50				

KM# 57   DOLLAR
26.8000 g., Copper-Nickel, 37.2 mm.   **Subject:** Marine Life Protection **Obv:** Mermaid figurehead on approaching ship **Rev:** Multicolor reflective fish scene under an acrylic layer **Edge:** Reeded

Date	Mintage	F	VF	XF	Unc	BU
2002 Proof	—	Value: 37.50				

KM# 63   DOLLAR
26.8000 g., Copper-Nickel, 37.2 mm.   **Subject:** Marine Life Protection **Obv:** Figurehead mermaid and value **Rev:** Blue Tang Fish **Edge:** Reeded

Date	Mintage	F	VF	XF	Unc	BU
2002 Proof	—	Value: 37.50				

KM# 64   DOLLAR
26.8000 g., Copper-Nickel, 37.2 mm.   **Subject:** Marine Life Protection **Obv:** Figurehead mermaid and value **Rev:** Multicolor whales **Edge:** Reeded

Date	Mintage	F	VF	XF	Unc	BU
2002 Proof	—	Value: 37.50				

KM# 65   DOLLAR
26.8000 g., Copper-Nickel, 37.2 mm.   **Subject:** Marine Life Protection **Obv:** Mermaid washing hair and value **Rev:** Multicolor jellyfish **Edge:** Reeded

Date	Mintage	F	VF	XF	Unc	BU
2002 Proof	—	Value: 37.50				

KM# 90   DOLLAR
1.2441 g., 0.9999 Gold 0.0400 oz. AGW, 13.94 mm.   **Subject:** Marine Life Protection **Obv:** Figurehead Mermaid and value **Rev:** Multicolor whales

Date	Mintage	F	VF	XF	Unc	BU
2002 Proof	—	Value: 65.00				

KM# 91   DOLLAR
1.2441 g., 0.9999 Gold 0.0400 oz. AGW, 13.94 mm.   **Subject:** Marine Life Protection **Obv:** Figurehead Mermaid and value **Rev:** Pufferfish

Date	Mintage	F	VF	XF	Unc	BU
2002 Proof	—	Value: 65.00				

KM# 92   DOLLAR
1.2441 g., 0.9999 Gold 0.0400 oz. AGW, 13.94 mm.   **Subject:** Marine Life Protection **Obv:** Seated Mermaid with both arms raised and value **Rev:** Jellyfish

Date	Mintage	F	VF	XF	Unc	BU
2002 Proof	—	Value: 65.00				

KM# 93   DOLLAR
1.2441 g., 0.9999 Gold 0.0400 oz. AGW, 13.94 mm.   **Subject:** Marine Life Protection **Obv:** Figurehead Mermaid and value **Rev:** Blue Tang Fish

Date	Mintage	F	VF	XF	Unc	BU
2002 Proof	—	Value: 65.00				

KM# 94   DOLLAR
1.2441 g., 0.9999 Gold 0.0400 oz. AGW, 13.94 mm.   **Subject:** Marine Life Protection **Obv:** Figurehead mermaid and value **Rev:** Lionfish

Date	Mintage	F	VF	XF	Unc	BU
2002 Proof	—	Value: 65.00				

KM# 95   DOLLAR
1.2441 g., 0.9999 Gold 0.0400 oz. AGW, 13.94 mm.   **Subject:** Marine Life Protection **Obv:** Mermaid riding dolphin and value **Rev:** Starfish

Date	Mintage	F	VF	XF	Unc	BU
2003 Proof	—	Value: 65.00				

KM# 96   DOLLAR
1.2441 g., 0.9999 Gold 0.0400 oz. AGW, 13.94 mm.   **Subject:** Marine Life Protection **Obv:** Seated Mermaid on shell and value **Rev:** Multicolor Orca **Edge:** Reeded   Proof

Date	Mintage	F	VF	XF	Unc	BU
2003 Proof	—	Value: 65.00				

KM# 97   DOLLAR
1.2441 g., 0.9999 Gold 0.0400 oz. AGW, 13.94 mm.   **Subject:** Marine Life Protection **Obv:** Mermaid under radiant sun and value **Rev:** Crab

Date	Mintage	F	VF	XF	Unc	BU
2003 Proof	—	Value: 65.00				

KM# 98   DOLLAR
1.2441 g., 0.9999 Gold 0.0400 oz. AGW, 13.94 mm.   **Subject:** Marine Life Protection **Obv:** Mermaid riding turtle and value **Rev:** Two glittering fish

Date	Mintage	F	VF	XF	Unc	BU
2003 Proof	—	Value: 65.00				

KM# 66   DOLLAR
26.8000 g., Copper-Nickel, 37.2 mm.   **Subject:** Marine Life Protection **Obv:** Mermaid under sun and value **Rev:** Orange crab **Edge:** Reeded

Date	Mintage	F	VF	XF	Unc	BU
2003 Proof	—	Value: 37.50				

KM# 67   DOLLAR
26.8000 g., Copper-Nickel, 37.2 mm.   **Subject:** Marine Life Protection **Obv:** Mermaid riding turtle and value **Rev:** Two glittering fish **Edge:** Reeded

Date	Mintage	F	VF	XF	Unc	BU
2003 Proof	—	Value: 37.50				

KM# 68   DOLLAR
26.8000 g., Copper-Nickel, 37.2 mm.   **Subject:** Marine Life Protection **Obv:** Seated Mermaid on shell and value **Rev:** Multicolor Orca **Edge:** Reeded

Date	Mintage	F	VF	XF	Unc	BU
2003 Proof	—	Value: 37.50				

KM# 69 DOLLAR
26.8000 g., Copper-Nickel, 37.2 mm. **Subject:** Marine Life Protection **Obv:** Mermaid playing shell guitar and value **Rev:** Green fish **Edge:** Reeded

Date	Mintage	F	VF	XF	Unc	BU
2003 Proof	—			Value: 37.50		

KM# 256 DOLLAR
Copper-Nickel, 38.6 mm. **Obv:** Mermaid on dolphin **Rev:** Red starfish - multicolor

Date	Mintage	F	VF	XF	Unc	BU
2003	—	—	—	—	—	25.00

KM# 70 DOLLAR
26.8000 g., Copper-Nickel, 37.2 mm. **Subject:** Marine Life Protection **Obv:** Seated Mermaid on rock and value **Rev:** School of blue fish **Edge:** Reeded

Date	Mintage	F	VF	XF	Unc	BU
2004 Proof	—			Value: 37.50		

KM# 71 DOLLAR
26.8000 g., Copper-Nickel, 37.2 mm. **Subject:** Marine Life Protection **Obv:** Side view of Mermaid facing right and value **Rev:** Clownfish **Edge:** Reeded

Date	Mintage	F	VF	XF	Unc	BU
2004 Proof	—			Value: 37.50		

KM# 72 DOLLAR
26.8000 g., Copper-Nickel, 37.2 mm. **Subject:** Marine Life Protection **Obv:** Mermaid flanked by dolphins **Rev:** Multicolor dolphin head **Edge:** Reeded

Date	Mintage	F	VF	XF	Unc	BU
2004 Proof	—			Value: 37.50		

KM# 123 DOLLAR
Copper-Nickel, 37.2 mm. **Subject:** Marine Life Protection **Obv:** Mermaid seated inside a giant conch shell **Rev:** Puffer fish **Edge:** Reeded

Date	Mintage	F	VF	XF	Unc	BU
2004 Proof	—			Value: 35.00		

KM# 124 DOLLAR
Copper-Nickel, 37.2 mm. **Subject:** Marine Life Protection **Obv:** Seated Mermaid **Rev:** Sea turtle **Edge:** Reeded

Date	Mintage	F	VF	XF	Unc	BU
2004 Proof	—			Value: 50.00		

KM# 99 DOLLAR
1.2441 g., 0.9999 Gold 0.0400 oz. AGW, 13.94 mm. **Subject:** Marine Life Protection **Obv:** Mermaid under radiant sun and value **Rev:** Clownfish

Date	Mintage	F	VF	XF	Unc	BU
2004 Proof	—			Value: 65.00		

KM# 100 DOLLAR
1.2441 g., 0.9999 Gold 0.0400 oz. AGW, 13.94 mm. **Subject:** Marine Life Protection **Obv:** Mermaid flanked by dolphins **Rev:** Multicolor dolphin head

Date	Mintage	F	VF	XF	Unc	BU
2004 Proof	—			Value: 65.00		

KM# 101 DOLLAR
1.2441 g., 0.9999 Gold 0.0400 oz. AGW, 13.94 mm. **Subject:** Marine Life Protection **Obv:** Mermaid sitting in a shell listening to a conch shell **Rev:** Sea Horse

Date	Mintage	F	VF	XF	Unc	BU
2005 Proof	—			Value: 65.00		

KM# 139 DOLLAR
26.8000 g., Copper-Nickel, 37.2 mm. **Subject:** Marine Life - Protection **Obv:** Mermaid fixing hair, dolphin jumping **Rev:** School of fish

Date	Mintage	F	VF	XF	Unc	BU
2005	—	—	—	—	—	37.50

KM# 140 DOLLAR
26.8000 g., Copper-Nickel, 37.2 mm. **Subject:** Marine Life - Protection **Obv:** Mermaid seated in shell, listening to shell **Rev:** Multicolor sea horse

Date	Mintage	F	VF	XF	Unc	BU
2005	—	—	—	—	—	37.50

KM# 141 DOLLAR
26.8000 g., Copper-Nickel **Subject:** Marine Life - Protection **Obv:** Mermaid and dolphin **Rev:** Multicolor fish scene

Date	Mintage	F	VF	XF	Unc	BU
2005	—	—	—	—	—	37.50

KM# 255 DOLLAR
Copper-Nickel, 38.6 mm. **Obv:** Mermaid seated on rock **Rev:** Stingray - multicolor

Date	Mintage	F	VF	XF	Unc	BU
2005	—	—	—	—	—	37.00

KM# 125   DOLLAR
Copper-Nickel, 37.2 mm. **Subject:** Marine Life Protection **Obv:**
Mermaid with head tilted back **Rev:** Barracuda

Date	Mintage	F	VF	XF	Unc	BU
2006 Proof	—				Value: 37.50	

KM# 126   DOLLAR
Copper-Nickel, 37.2 mm. **Subject:** Marine Life Protection **Obv:**
Two mermaids **Rev:** Parrot fish

Date	Mintage	F	VF	XF	Unc	BU
2006 Proof	—				Value: 50.00	

KM# 127   DOLLAR
Copper-Nickel, 37.2 mm. **Subject:** Marine Life Protection **Obv:**
Mermaid swimming downward **Rev:** Hog Fish **Edge:** Reeded

Date	Mintage	F	VF	XF	Unc	BU
2006 Proof	—				Value: 32.50	

KM# 128   DOLLAR
Copper-Nickel, 37.2 mm. **Subject:** Marine Life Protection **Obv:**
Seated mermaid with bird perched on outstretched hand **Rev:**
Mahi Mahi **Edge:** Reeded

Date	Mintage	F	VF	XF	Unc	BU
2006 Proof	—				Value: 47.50	

KM# 129   DOLLAR
Copper-Nickel, 37.2 mm. **Subject:** Marine Life Protection **Obv:**
Mermaid, sailing ship and sun **Rev:** Box Fish **Edge:** Reeded

Date	Mintage	F	VF	XF	Unc	BU
2006 Proof	—				Value: 45.00	

KM# 142   DOLLAR
20.0000 g., 0.9990 Silver 0.6423 oz. ASW **Obv:** Arms **Rev:**
Snowflake with blue crystal **Shape:** 38.6

Date	Mintage	F	VF	XF	Unc	BU
2006 Proof	2,500				Value: 65.00	

KM# 334   DOLLAR
27.0000 g., Copper-Nickel, 38.61 mm. **Rev:** Eclectus Parrot
head right

Date	Mintage	F	VF	XF	Unc	BU
2006 Proof	Est. 5,000				Value: 20.00	

KM# 335   DOLLAR
27.0000 g., Copper-Nickel, 38.61 mm. **Rev:** Fruit dove head right

Date	Mintage	F	VF	XF	Unc	BU
2006 Proof	Est. 5,000				Value: 20.00	

KM# 336   DOLLAR
27.0000 g., Copper-Nickel, 38.61 mm. **Rev:** Rainbow lorikeet
head left

Date	Mintage	F	VF	XF	Unc	BU
	Est. 5,000				Value: 20.00	

KM# 257   DOLLAR
25.0000 g., 0.9250 Silver 0.7435 oz. ASW, 38.6 mm. **Obv:** Arms
Rev: White pearl in shell **Shape:** Heart

Date	Mintage	F	VF	XF	Unc	BU
2006 Proof	500				Value: 125	

KM# 322   DOLLAR
0.5000 g., 0.9990 Gold 0.0161 oz. AGW, 11.8 mm. **Obv:**
National arms **Rev:** Elephant shrew

Date	Mintage	F	VF	XF	Unc	BU
2006 Proof	—				Value: 90.00	

KM# 323   DOLLAR
0.5000 g., 0.9990 Gold 0.0161 oz. AGW, 11.8 mm. **Obv:**
National arms **Rev:** Rhino beetle

Date	Mintage	F	VF	XF	Unc	BU
2006 Proof	—				Value: 90.00	

KM# 324   DOLLAR
0.5000 g., 0.9990 Gold 0.0161 oz. AGW, 11.8 mm. **Obv:**
National arms **Rev:** Buffalo Weaver

Date	Mintage	F	VF	XF	Unc	BU
2006 Proof	—				Value: 90.00	

KM# 325   DOLLAR
0.5000 g., 0.9990 Gold 0.0161 oz. AGW, 11.8 mm. **Obv:**
National arms **Rev:** Ant lion

Date	Mintage	F	VF	XF	Unc	BU
2006 Proof	—				Value: 90.00	

KM# 326   DOLLAR
0.5000 g., 0.9990 Gold 0.0161 oz. AGW, 11.8 mm. **Obv:**
National arms **Rev:** Leopard tortoise

Date	Mintage	F	VF	XF	Unc	BU
2006 Proof	—				Value: 90.00	

KM# 144   DOLLAR
27.0000 g., 0.9250 Silver 0.8029 oz. ASW **Obv:** Shield **Rev:**
Multicolor John Paul II waving

Date	Mintage	F	VF	XF	Unc	BU
2007 Proof	—				Value: 45.00	

KM# 145   DOLLAR
1.2440 g., 0.9990 Gold 0.0400 oz. AGW, 13.92 mm. **Subject:**
Marine Life - Protection **Obv:** Neptune and mermaid seated on
rocks **Rev:** Tropical fish

Date	Mintage	F	VF	XF	Unc	BU
2007 Proof	—				Value: 75.00	

KM# 150   DOLLAR
25.0000 g., 0.9250 Silver 0.7435 oz. ASW **Subject:** Pacific
Wildlife **Obv:** Shield **Rev:** Multicolor seahorse

Date	Mintage	F	VF	XF	Unc	BU
2007 Proof	—				Value: 70.00	

KM# 116   DOLLAR
25.7300 g., Silver Plated Bronze, 38.6 mm. **Obv:** National arms
Rev: Multicolor Pope John Paul II with cross **Edge:** Reeded

Date	Mintage	F	VF	XF	Unc	BU
2007 Proof	—				Value: 37.50	

KM# 118 DOLLAR
27.0000 g., Copper-Nickel, 38.61 mm. **Series:** Marine Life
Protection **Obv:** Neptune reclining with trident, mermaid at his
side **Obv. Legend:** REPUBLIC OF PALAU **Rev:** Multicolor
Doctor Fish

Date	Mintage	F	VF	XF	Unc	BU
2007 Proof	5,000	Value: 35.00				

KM# 121 DOLLAR
27.0000 g., Copper-Nickel, 38.61 mm. **Obv:** Shield with
Neptune holding trident, mermaid reclining at his side,
RAINBOW'S / END below **Obv. Legend:** REPUBLIC OF PALAU
Rev: Red racing car 3/4 left **Rev. Legend:** FERRARI - 60 YEARS
ANNIVERSARY

Date	Mintage	F	VF	XF	Unc	BU
ND(2007) Proof	5,000	Value: 35.00				

KM# 120 DOLLAR
0.5000 g., 0.9990 Gold 0.0161 oz. AGW, 11.0 mm. **Obv:** Shield
with Neptune holding trident, mermaid reclining at his side,
RAINBOW'S / END below **Obv. Legend:** REPUBLIC OF PALAU
Shape: 4-leaf clover **Note:** Uniface

Date	Mintage	F	VF	XF	Unc	BU
2007 Proof	25,000	Value: 50.00				

KM# 258 DOLLAR
25.0000 g., 0.9990 Silver 0.8029 oz. ASW **Subject:** Pacific
Wildlife **Rev:** Seahorse - prism

Date	Mintage	F	VF	XF	Unc	BU
2007 Proof	—	Value: 50.00				

KM# 337 DOLLAR
0.5000 g., 0.9990 Gold 0.0161 oz. AGW, 11 mm. **Subject:**
Christopher Columbus, 500th Anniversary **Rev:** Columbus'
flagship, Santa Maria

Date	Mintage	F	VF	XF	Unc	BU
2007 Proof	—	Value: 75.00				

KM# 338 DOLLAR
1.2400 g., 0.9990 Gold 0.0398 oz. AGW, 13.92 mm. **Subject:**
Easter, 2007 **Rev:** Christ's resurection

Date	Mintage	F	VF	XF	Unc	BU
2007 Proof	Est. 15,000	Value: 100				

KM# 339 DOLLAR
0.5000 g., 0.9990 Gold 0.0161 oz. AGW, 11 mm. **Subject:**
Deutsche Bundesbank, 50th anniversary **Rev:** Pile of coins

Date	Mintage	F	VF	XF	Unc	BU
2007 Proof	—	Value: 75.00				

KM# 154 DOLLAR
26.8000 g., Copper-Nickel silver plated, 38.61 mm. **Subject:**
150th Anniversary of the Appriations **Obv:** Shield **Rev:** Statue of
Our Lady of Lourdes and holy water vile

Date	Mintage	F	VF	XF	Unc	BU
2008 Proof	—	Value: 22.50				

KM# 155 DOLLAR
26.8000 g., Copper-Nickel, 37.2 mm. **Subject:** Dealer Button
Obv: Shield **Rev:** Vegas Chips and cards, Ace of Clubs corner cut

Date	Mintage	F	VF	XF	Unc	BU
2008	—	—	—	—	—	25.00

KM# 156 DOLLAR
26.8000 g., Copper-Nickel, 37.2 mm. **Subject:** Dealer Buttons
Obv: Shield **Rev:** Vegas Chips and cards, Ace of Diamonds
corner cut

Date	Mintage	F	VF	XF	Unc	BU
2008	—	—	—	—	—	25.00

KM# 157 DOLLAR
26.8000 g., Copper-Nickel, 37.2 mm. **Subject:** Dear Buttons
Obv: Shield **Rev:** Vegas Chips and cards, Ace of Heats corner cut

Date	Mintage	F	VF	XF	Unc	BU
2008	—	—	—	—	—	25.00

KM# 158 DOLLAR
26.8000 g., Copper-Nickel, 37.2 mm. **Obv:** Shield **Rev:** Vegas
chips and cards, Ace of Spades corner cut

Date	Mintage	F	VF	XF	Unc	BU
2008	—	—	—	—	—	25.00

KM# 159 DOLLAR
1.2400 g., 0.9990 Gold 0.0398 oz. AGW, 13.9 mm. **Subject:**
St. Francis of Assisi **Obv:** Shield **Rev:** Bust facing

Date	Mintage	F	VF	XF	Unc	BU
2008 Proof	—	Value: 75.00				

KM# 160 DOLLAR
1.2440 g., 0.9900 Gold 0.0396 oz. AGW, 13.9 mm. **Subject:**
St, Francis of Assisi **Obv:** Shield **Rev:** Multicolor bust facing

Date	Mintage	F	VF	XF	Unc	BU
2008	—	—	—	—	—	80.00

KM# 161 DOLLAR
0.5000 g., 0.9990 Gold 0.0161 oz. AGW, 11 mm. **Obv:** Shield
Rev: Multicolor poppy **Shape:** Irregular

Date	Mintage	F	VF	XF	Unc	BU
2008	—	—	—	—	—	60.00

KM# 162 DOLLAR
0.5000 g., 0.9990 Gold 0.0161 oz. AGW, 11 mm. **Subject:**
Everlasting love **Obv:** Shield **Rev:** Heart **Shape:** Heart

Date	Mintage	F	VF	XF	Unc	BU
2008	—	—	—	—	—	60.00

KM# 163 DOLLAR
1.2440 g., 0.9990 Gold 0.0400 oz. AGW **Subject:** Marine Life-
Protection **Obv:** Neptune and mermaid seated on rock **Rev:** Grey
reef shark

Date	Mintage	F	VF	XF	Unc	BU
2008 Proof	1,500	Value: 85.00				

KM# 164 DOLLAR
26.8000 g., Copper-Nickel, 37.2 mm. **Subject:** Endangered
Wildlife **Obv:** Shield **Rev:** Multicolor Tiger shark

Date	Mintage	F	VF	XF	Unc	BU
2008	—	—	—	—	—	35.00

KM# 165   DOLLAR
26.8000 g., Copper-Nickel, 37.2 mm. **Subject:** Endangered
Wildlife **Obv:** Shield **Rev:** Multicolor Hawksbill turtle

Date	Mintage	F	VF	XF	Unc	BU
2008	—				—	37.50

KM# 166   DOLLAR
26.8000 g., Copper-Nickel, 37.2 mm. **Subject:** Endangered
Wildlife **Obv:** Shield **Rev:** Multicolored Regal angelfish swimming
right

Date	Mintage	F	VF	XF	Unc	BU
2008 Proof	—	Value: 37.50				

KM# 167   DOLLAR
26.8000 g., Copper-Nickel, 37.2 mm. **Subject:** Endangered
Wildlife **Obv:** Shield **Rev:** Multicolor Spiny lobster

Date	Mintage	F	VF	XF	Unc	BU
2008 Proof	—	Value: 30.00				

KM# 259   DOLLAR
0.5000 g., 0.9990 Gold 0.0161 oz. AGW, 11 mm. **Subject:**
Sitting bull **Obv:** Shield **Rev:** Portrait facing

Date	Mintage	F	VF	XF	Unc	BU
2008 Proof	—	Value: 60.00				

KM# 177   DOLLAR
1.2440 g., 0.9990 Gold 0.0400 oz. AGW, 13.9 mm. **Obv:** Shield
Rev: Madonna and child

Date	Mintage	F	VF	XF	Unc	BU
ND(2009) Proof	25,000	Value: 80.00				

KM# 178   DOLLAR
1.2440 g., 0.9990 Gold 0.0400 oz. AGW, 13.9 mm. **Subject:**
FIAA World Cup - South Africa **Obv:** Shield **Rev:** Soccer ball,
South African flag and Water Buffalo

Date	Mintage	F	VF	XF	Unc	BU
2009 Proof	—	Value: 75.00				

KM# 222   DOLLAR
27.0000 g., Silver Plated Copper, 38.6 mm. **Rev:** Lighthouse of
Alexandria, multicolor

Date	Mintage	F	VF	XF	Unc	BU
2009 Prooflike	5,000	—	—	—	—	20.00

KM# 223   DOLLAR
27.0000 g., Silver Plated Copper, 38.6 mm. **Rev:** Zeus statue,
multicolor

Date	Mintage	F	VF	XF	Unc	BU
2009 Prooflike	—	—	—	—	—	20.00

KM# 224   DOLLAR
27.0000 g., Silver Plated Copper, 38.6 mm. **Rev:** Hanging
Garden of Babylon, multicolor

Date	Mintage	F	VF	XF	Unc	BU
2009 Prooflike	5,000	—	—	—	—	20.00

KM# 225   DOLLAR
27.0000 g., Silver Plated Copper, 38.6 mm. **Rev:** Mausoleum,
multicolor

Date	Mintage	F	VF	XF	Unc	BU
2009 Prooflike	5,000	—	—	—	—	20.00

KM# 226   DOLLAR
27.0000 g., Silver Plated Copper, 38.6 mm. **Rev:** Pyramids,
multicolor

Date	Mintage	F	VF	XF	Unc	BU
2009 Prooflike	5,000	—	—	—	—	20.00

KM# 227   DOLLAR
27.0000 g., Silver Plated Copper, 38.6 mm. **Rev:** Artemis
temple, multicolor

Date	Mintage	F	VF	XF	Unc	BU
2009 Prooflike	5,000	—	—	—	—	20.00

KM# 228   DOLLAR
27.0000 g., Silver Plated Copper, 38.6 mm. **Rev:** Colosus of
Rhodes, multicolor

Date	Mintage	F	VF	XF	Unc	BU
2009 Prooflike	5,000	—	—	—	—	20.00

KM# 229   DOLLAR
27.0000 g., Silver Plated Copper, 38.6 mm. **Subject:** Ducati -
Casey Stoner **Rev:** Motorcycle left, multicolor

Date	Mintage	F	VF	XF	Unc	BU
2009 Prooflike	2,008	—	—	—	—	25.00

KM# 230 DOLLAR
27.0000 g., Silver Plated Copper, 38.6 mm. **Subject:** Ducati - Troy Bayliss **Rev:** Motorcycle, multicolor

Date	Mintage	F	VF	XF	Unc	BU
2009 Prooflike	2,008	—	—	—	—	25.00

KM# 233 DOLLAR
27.0000 g., Copper-Nickel, 38.6 mm. **Subject:** Marine Life Protection **Obv:** Neptune standing, two mermaids below **Rev:** Lionfish, multicolor

Date	Mintage	F	VF	XF	Unc	BU
2009 Prooflike	5,000	—	—	—	—	25.00

KM# 234 DOLLAR
1.0000 g., 0.9990 Gold 0.0321 oz. AGW, 13.9 mm. **Subject:** Marine Life Protection **Rev:** Lionfish

Date	Mintage	F	VF	XF	Unc	BU
2009 Proof	25,000	Value: 65.00				

KM# 235 DOLLAR
0.5000 g., 0.9990 Gold 0.0161 oz. AGW, 11.8 mm. **Subject:** Augustus Aureus **Rev:** Head laureate right

Date	Mintage	F	VF	XF	Unc	BU
MMIX (2009)	15,000	—	—	—	—	40.00

KM# 236 DOLLAR
0.5000 g., 0.9990 Gold 0.0161 oz. AGW, 11.8 mm. **Subject:** Germanicus Dupondius **Rev:** General in quadriga right

Date	Mintage	F	VF	XF	Unc	BU
MMIX (2009)	15,000	—	—	—	—	40.00

KM# 237 DOLLAR
0.5000 g., 0.9990 Gold 0.0161 oz. AGW, 11.8 mm. **Subject:** Julius Caesar Denarius **Rev:** Head laureate right

Date	Mintage	F	VF	XF	Unc	BU
MMIX (2009)	15,000	—	—	—	—	40.00

KM# 238 DOLLAR
0.5000 g., 0.9990 Gold 0.0161 oz. AGW, 11.8 mm. **Subject:** Brutus Denarius **Rev:** Cap flanked by two daggers

Date	Mintage	F	VF	XF	Unc	BU
MMIX (2009)	15,000	—	—	—	—	40.00

KM# 239 DOLLAR
1.2400 g., 0.9990 Gold 0.0398 oz. AGW, 13.9 mm. **Subject:** Salesian Order, 150th Anniversary **Rev:** Don Bosco facing

Date	Mintage	F	VF	XF	Unc	BU
2009 Proof	15,000	Value: 65.00				

KM# 240 DOLLAR
0.5000 g., 0.9990 Gold 0.0161 oz. AGW, 11 mm. **Rev:** Pebbled **Shape:** 5-pointed star

Date	Mintage	F	VF	XF	Unc	BU
ND (2009)	25,000	—	—	—	—	40.00

KM# 241 DOLLAR
1.2400 g., 0.9990 Gold 0.0398 oz. AGW, 13.9 mm. **Subject:** Fontana de Trevi **Rev:** Trevi fountain and building facade

Date	Mintage	F	VF	XF	Unc	BU
2009 Proof	15,000	—	—	—	—	65.00

KM# 244 DOLLAR
0.5000 g., 0.9990 Gold 0.0161 oz. AGW, 11.8 mm. **Subject:** First didrachm **Rev:** Twins sucking at she-wolf

Date	Mintage	F	VF	XF	Unc	BU
MMIX (2009)	15,000	—	—	—	—	40.00

KM# 245 DOLLAR
0.5000 g., 0.9990 Gold 0.0161 oz. AGW, 11.8 mm. **Subject:** Claudius aureus **Rev:** Head laureate right

Date	Mintage	F	VF	XF	Unc	BU
MMIX (2009)	15,000	—	—	—	—	40.00

KM# 246 DOLLAR
0.5000 g., 0.9990 Gold 0.0161 oz. AGW, 11.8 mm. **Subject:** Tiberius aureus **Rev:** Head laureate right

Date	Mintage	F	VF	XF	Unc	BU
MMIX (2009)	15,000	—	—	—	—	40.00

KM# 247 DOLLAR
0.5000 g., 0.9990 Gold 0.0161 oz. AGW, 11.8 mm. **Subject:** Caligula aureus **Rev:** Head laureate right

Date	Mintage	F	VF	XF	Unc	BU
MMIX (2009)	15,000	—	—	—	—	40.00

KM# 260 DOLLAR
Silver Plated Copper, 30x30 mm. **Subject:** 2000th Anniversary Teutobury Forest Battle **Obv:** Shield **Rev:** Warrior in forest battle, multicolor **Shape:** Square

Date	Mintage	F	VF	XF	Unc	BU
MMIX (2009) Proof	2,500	Value: 30.00				

KM# 261 DOLLAR
25.0000 g., 0.9990 Silver 0.8029 oz. ASW, 38.6 mm. **Subject:** Pacific Wildlife **Obv:** Arms **Rev:** Barn Swallow - prism

Date	Mintage	F	VF	XF	Unc	BU
2009 Proof	2,500	Value: 50.00				

KM# 262 DOLLAR
25.0000 g., 0.9990 Silver 0.8029 oz. ASW, 38.6 mm. **Subject:** Pacific Wildlife **Obv:** Arms **Rev:** Gecko on rock - prism

Date	Mintage	F	VF	XF	Unc	BU
2009 Proof	2,500	Value: 50.00				

KM# 263 DOLLAR
0.5000 g., 0.9990 Gold 0.0161 oz. AGW, 11 mm. **Rev:** 4-leaf clover, green

Date	Mintage	F	VF	XF	Unc	BU
2009		—	—	—	—	65.00

KM# 269 DOLLAR
Copper-Nickel, 37.2 mm. **Subject:** Protect Wildlife - Angelfish **Rev:** Angelfish - Prisim

Date	Mintage	F	VF	XF	Unc	BU
2009		—	—	—	—	35.00

KM# 270 DOLLAR
Copper-Nickel, 37.2 mm. **Subject:** Apostles - Peter **Rev:** Multicolor icon image

Date	Mintage	F	VF	XF	Unc	BU
2009 Proof	1,000	Value: 25.00				

KM# 271 DOLLAR
Copper-Nickel, 37.2 mm. **Subject:** Apostles - James Minor **Rev:**
Multicolor icon image

Date	Mintage	F	VF	XF	Unc	BU
2009 Proof	1,000	Value: 25.00				

KM# 272 DOLLAR
Copper-Nickel, 37.2 mm. **Subject:** Apostles - John **Rev:**
Multicolor icon image

Date	Mintage	F	VF	XF	Unc	BU
2009 Proof	1,000	Value: 25.00				

KM# 273 DOLLAR
Copper-Nickel, 37.2 mm. **Subject:** Apostle - Simon **Rev:**
Multicolor icon image

Date	Mintage	F	VF	XF	Unc	BU
2009 Proof	1,000	Value: 25.00				

KM# 274 DOLLAR
Copper-Nickel, 37.2 mm. **Subject:** Apostles - Matthaeus **Rev:**
Multicolor icon image

Date	Mintage	F	VF	XF	Unc	BU
2009 Proof	1,000	Value: 25.00				

KM# 275 DOLLAR
Copper-Nickel, 37.2 mm. **Subject:** Apostles - Thomas **Rev:**
Multicolor icon image

Date	Mintage	F	VF	XF	Unc	BU
2009 Proof	1,000	Value: 25.00				

KM# 276 DOLLAR
Copper-Nickel, 37.2 mm. **Subject:** Apostles - Judas Thaddaeus
Rev: Multicolor icon image

Date	Mintage	F	VF	XF	Unc	BU
2009 Proof	1,000	Value: 25.00				

KM# 277 DOLLAR
Copper-Nickel, 37.2 mm. **Subject:** Apostles - Bartholomew **Rev:**
Multicolor icon image

Date	Mintage	F	VF	XF	Unc	BU
2009 Proof	1,000	Value: 25.00				

KM# 278 DOLLAR
Copper-Nickel, 37.2 mm. **Subject:** Apostles - Philip **Rev:**
Multicolor icon image

Date	Mintage	F	VF	XF	Unc	BU
2009 Proof	1,000	Value: 25.00				

KM# 279 DOLLAR
Copper-Nickel, 37.2 mm. **Subject:** Apostles - John Major **Rev:**
Multicolor icon image

Date	Mintage	F	VF	XF	Unc	BU
2009 Proof	1,000	Value: 25.00				

KM# 280 DOLLAR
Copper-Nickel, 37.2 mm. **Subject:** Apostles - Andrew **Rev:**
Multicolor icon image

Date	Mintage	F	VF	XF	Unc	BU
2009 Proof	1,000	Value: 25.00				

KM# 281 DOLLAR
Copper-Nickel, 37.2 mm. **Subject:** Apostles - Judas Iscariot
Rev: Multicolor icon image

Date	Mintage	F	VF	XF	Unc	BU
2009 Proof	1,000	Value: 25.00				

KM# 282 DOLLAR
26.8000 g., Copper-Nickel, 37.2 mm. **Subject:** Endangered
Wildlife - Orange Lined Tigerfish **Rev:** Multicolor fish left

Date	Mintage	F	VF	XF	Unc	BU
2009 Proof	—	Value: 37.50				

KM# 283 DOLLAR
26.8000 g., Copper-Nickel, 37.2 mm. **Subject:** Endangered
Wildlife - Blue Grilled Angelfish **Rev:** Multicolor fish

Date	Mintage	F	VF	XF	Unc	BU
2009 Proof	—	Value: 37.50				

KM# 284 DOLLAR
26.8000 g., Copper-Nickel, 37.2 mm. **Subject:** Endangered Wildlife - Green Turtle **Rev:** Multicolor turtle

Date	Mintage	F	VF	XF	Unc	BU
2009 Proof	—	Value: 37.50				

KM# 285 DOLLAR
26.8000 g., Copper-Nickel, 37.2 mm. **Subject:** Endangered Wildlife - Sailfin Tang fish **Rev:** Multicolor fish right

Date	Mintage	F	VF	XF	Unc	BU
2009 Proof	—	Value: 37.50				

KM# 286 DOLLAR
26.8000 g., Copper-Nickel, 37.2 mm. **Subject:** Endangered Wildlife - Clown Trigger fish **Rev:** Multicolor fish left

Date	Mintage	F	VF	XF	Unc	BU
2009 Proof	—	Value: 37.50				

KM# 321 DOLLAR
0.5000 g., 0.9990 Gold 0.0161 oz. AGW, 11.8 mm. **Obv:** National arms **Rev:** Pamir, sail training vessel

Date	Mintage	F	VF	XF	Unc	BU
2009 Proof	25,000	Value: 90.00				

KM# 266 DOLLAR
25.0000 g., 0.9250 Silver 0.7435 oz. ASW, 30x30 mm. **Subject:** Battle of Grimwald **Rev:** Vyautas and Jagiello busts **Shape:** Square

Date	Mintage	F	VF	XF	Unc	BU
2010 Proof	—	Value: 50.00				

KM# 267 DOLLAR
25.0000 g., 0.9990 Silver 0.8029 oz. ASW, 30x30 mm. **Subject:** Battle of Grunwald **Rev:** Warrior on horseback in color **Shape:** Square

Date	Mintage	F	VF	XF	Unc	BU
2010 Proof	2,500	Value: 55.00				

KM# 268 DOLLAR
25.0000 g., 0.9990 Silver 0.8029 oz. ASW, 30x30 mm. **Subject:** Battle of Grunwald **Rev:** Knight kneeling in color **Shape:** Square

Date	Mintage	F	VF	XF	Unc	BU
2010 Proof	2,500	Value: 55.00				

KM# 303 DOLLAR
0.5000 g., 0.9990 Gold 0.0161 oz. AGW, 11mm mm. **Obv:** National arms **Rev:** Teddy bear **Shape:** Irregular

Date	Mintage	F	VF	XF	Unc	BU
ND(2010)	25,000	—	—	—	—	75.00

KM# 307 DOLLAR
35.0000 g., Copper-Nickel, 50 mm. **Subject:** Hold Cards **Obv:** National arms **Rev:** King of Hearts and Clubs

Date	Mintage	F	VF	XF	Unc	BU
2010 Antique patina	5,000	—	—	—	—	40.00

KM# 308 DOLLAR
35.0000 g., Copper-Nickel, 50 mm. **Subject:** Hold Cards **Obv:** National arms **Rev:** King of Spades and Diamonds

Date	Mintage	F	VF	XF	Unc	BU
2010 Antique patina	5,000	—	—	—	—	40.00

KM# 309 DOLLAR
0.5000 g., 0.9999 Gold 0.0161 oz. AGW, 11.8 mm. **Obv:** National arms **Rev:** Nero coin

Date	Mintage	F	VF	XF	Unc	BU
2010	15,000	—	—	—	—	60.00

KM# 310 DOLLAR
0.5000 g., 0.9999 Gold 0.0161 oz. AGW, 11.8 mm. **Obv:** National arms **Rev:** Vespasian coin

Date	Mintage	F	VF	XF	Unc	BU
2010	15,000	—	—	—	—	60.00

KM# 311 DOLLAR
0.5000 g., 0.9990 Silver 0.0161 oz. ASW, 11.8 mm. **Obv:** National arms **Rev:** Titus coin

Date	Mintage	F	VF	XF	Unc	BU
2010	15,000	—	—	—	—	60.00

KM# 312 DOLLAR
0.5000 g., 0.9999 Gold 0.0161 oz. AGW, 11.8 mm. **Obv:** National arms **Rev:** Domitian coin

Date	Mintage	F	VF	XF	Unc	BU
2010	15,000	—	—	—	—	60.00

KM# 313 DOLLAR
27.0000 g., Silver Plated Copper, 38.61 mm. **Obv:** Mermaid **Rev:** Hammerhead shark color image

Date	Mintage	F	VF	XF	Unc	BU
2010 Prooflike	5,000	—	—	—	—	25.00

KM# 315   DOLLAR
1.0000 g., 0.9999 Gold 0.0321 oz. AGW, 13.92 mm. **Obv:**
Mermaid **Rev:** Hammerhead sharks

Date	Mintage	F	VF	XF	Unc	BU
2010 Proof	25,000	Value: 100				

KM# 316   DOLLAR
27.0000 g., Silver Plated Copper, 35x35 mm. **Obv:** National
arms **Rev:** Fernando Alonso and racecar in color

Date	Mintage	F	VF	XF	Unc	BU
2010 Prooflike	5,000	—	—	—	—	50.00

KM# 317   DOLLAR
0.5000 g., 0.9999 Gold 0.0161 oz. AGW, 11 mm. **Obv:** National
arms **Rev:** Angel **Shape:** Irregular

Date	Mintage	F	VF	XF	Unc	BU
ND(2010)	15,000	—	—	—	—	50.00

KM# 327   DOLLAR
0.5000 g., 0.9990 Gold 0.0161 oz. AGW, 11.8 mm. **Obv:**
National arms **Rev:** Romulus & Remus

Date	Mintage	F	VF	XF	Unc	BU
2010 Proof	15,000	Value: 50.00				

KM# 130   2 DOLLARS
10.0000 g., 0.9990 Silver 0.3212 oz. ASW, 30.0 mm. **Obv:**
Shield with Neptune holding trident, mermaid reclining at his side
Obv. Legend: REPUBLIC OF PALAU **Rev:** Red racing car 3/4
right **Rev. Legend:** FERRARI - 60 YEARS ANNIVERSARY

Date	Mintage	F	VF	XF	Unc	BU
ND(2007) Proof	2,500	Value: 55.00				

KM# 131   2 DOLLARS
10.0000 g., 0.9990 Silver 0.3212 oz. ASW, 30.0 mm. **Obv:**
Shield with Neptune holding trident, mermaid reclining at his side
Obv. Legend: REPUBLIC OF PALAU **Rev:** Red racing car 3/4
right **Rev. Legend:** FERRARI - 60 YEARS ANNIVERSARY

Date	Mintage	F	VF	XF	Unc	BU
ND(2007) Proof	2,500	Value: 55.00				

KM# 132   2 DOLLARS
10.0000 g., 0.9990 Silver 0.3212 oz. ASW, 30.00 mm. **Obv:**
Shield with Neptune holding trident, mermaid reclining at his side
Obv. Legend: REPUBLIC OF PALAU **Rev:** Red racing car front
view **Rev. Legend:** FERRARI - 60 YEARS ANNIVERSARY

Date	Mintage	F	VF	XF	Unc	BU
ND(2007) Proof	2,500	Value: 55.00				

KM# 133   2 DOLLARS
10.0000 g., 0.9990 Silver 0.3212 oz. ASW, 30.0 mm. **Obv:**
Shield with Neptune holding trident, mermaid reclining at his side
Obv. Legend: REPUBLIC OF PALAU **Rev:** Looking down on
red racing car approaching in turn **Rev. Legend:** FERRARI - 60
YEARS ANNIVERSARY

Date	Mintage	F	VF	XF	Unc	BU
ND(2007) Proof	2,500	Value: 55.00				

KM# 134   2 DOLLARS
10.0000 g., 0.9990 Silver 0.3212 oz. ASW, 30.0 mm. **Obv:**
Shield with Neptune holding trident, reclining mermaid at his side
Obv. Legend: REPUBLIC OF PALAU **Rev:** Front view of red
racing car **Rev. Legend:** FERRARI - 60 YEARS ANNIVERSARY

Date	Mintage	F	VF	XF	Unc	BU
ND(2007) Proof	2,500	Value: 55.00				

KM# 135   2 DOLLARS
10.0000 g., 0.9990 Silver 0.3212 oz. ASW, 30.0 mm. **Obv:**
Shield with Neptune holding trident, mermaid reclining at his side
Obv. Legend: REPUBLIC OF PALAU **Rev:** Red racing car
approaching 3/4 right **Rev. Legend:** FERRARI - 60 YEARS
ANNIVERSARY

Date	Mintage	F	VF	XF	Unc	BU
ND(2007) Proof	2,500	Value: 100				

KM# 319   2 DOLLARS
15.5000 g., 0.9250 Silver 0.4609 oz. ASW, 35 mm. **Subject:**
World of Insects **Obv:** National arms **Rev:** Large color dragon fly
- Blue Eye Hawker

Date	Mintage	F	VF	XF	Unc	BU
2010 Proof	1,000	Value: 50.00				

KM# 53   5 DOLLARS
25.0000 g., 0.9000 Silver 0.7234 oz. ASW, 37.2 mm. **Series:**
Marine Life Protection **Obv:** Neptune **Rev:** Multicolor jellyfish
Edge: Reeded

Date	Mintage	F	VF	XF	Unc	BU
2001 Proof	—	Value: 75.00				

KM# 75   5 DOLLARS
25.0000 g., 0.9000 Silver 0.7234 oz. ASW, 37.2 mm. **Subject:**
Marine Life Protection **Obv:** Neptune behind Polynesian ship and
value **Rev:** Moorish-Idol fish **Edge:** Reeded

Date	Mintage	F	VF	XF	Unc	BU
2001 Proof	—	Value: 75.00				

KM# 76   5 DOLLARS
Silver, 37.2 mm. **Subject:** Marine Life Protection **Obv:** Neptune
riding seahorse and value **Rev:** Fish **Edge:** Reeded

Date	Mintage	F	VF	XF	Unc	BU
2001 Proof	—	Value: 75.00				

KM# 115   5 DOLLARS
25.0000 g., 0.9000 Silver 0.7234 oz. ASW, 37.2 mm. **Subject:**
Marine Life Protection **Obv:** Neptune waist deep in water above
value with mermaid to the left and behind **Rev:** Multicolor
iridescent fish scene **Edge:** Reeded

Date	Mintage	F	VF	XF	Unc	BU
2001 Proof	—	Value: 70.00				

KM# 331   5 DOLLARS
25.0000 g., 0.9000 Silver 0.7234 oz. ASW, 38.61 mm. **Rev:**
Angelfish

Date	Mintage	F	VF	XF	Unc	BU
2001 Proof	Est. 3,000	Value: 50.00				

KM# 332   5 DOLLARS
25.0000 g., 0.9000 Silver 0.7234 oz. ASW, 38.61 mm. **Rev:**
Blowfish

Date	Mintage	F	VF	XF	Unc	BU
2002 Proof	Est. 3,000	Value: 55.00				

KM# 77   5 DOLLARS
25.0000 g., 0.9000 Silver 0.7234 oz. ASW, 37.2 mm. **Subject:**
Marine Life Protection **Obv:** Neptune in shell boat **Rev:** Blue Tang
Fish **Edge:** Reeded

Date	Mintage	F	VF	XF	Unc	BU
2002 Proof	—	Value: 75.00				

KM# 78   5 DOLLARS
25.0000 g., 0.9000 Silver 0.7234 oz. ASW, 37.2 mm. **Subject:**
Marine Life Protection **Obv:** Neptune in sea chariot **Rev:**
Multicolor whales **Edge:** Reeded

Date	Mintage	F	VF	XF	Unc	BU
2002 Proof	—	Value: 75.00				

KM# 79   5 DOLLARS
25.0000 g., 0.9000 Silver 0.7234 oz. ASW, 37.2 mm. **Subject:**
Marine Life Protection **Obv:** Zeus and value **Rev:** Multicolor puffer
fish **Edge:** Reeded

Date	Mintage	F	VF	XF	Unc	BU
2002 Proof	—	Value: 75.00				

KM# 80   5 DOLLARS
25.0000 g., 0.9000 Silver 0.7234 oz. ASW, 37.2 mm. **Subject:**
Marine Life Protection **Obv:** Neptune standing behind Polynesian
ship **Rev:** Multicolor Jellyfish **Edge:** Reeded

Date	Mintage	F	VF	XF	Unc	BU
2002 Proof	—	Value: 70.00				

KM# 102 5 DOLLARS
25.0000 g., 0.9000 Silver 0.7234 oz. ASW, 32 mm. **Subject:**
Marine Life Protection **Obv:** Neptune in sea chariot with two
merhorses **Rev:** Two multicolor reflective fish

Date	Mintage	F	VF	XF	Unc	BU
2002 Proof	—	Value: 60.00				

KM# 103 5 DOLLARS
25.0000 g., 0.9000 Silver 0.7234 oz. ASW, 32 mm. **Subject:**
Marine Life Protection **Obv:** Neptune standing in waves **Rev:**
Multicolor starfish

Date	Mintage	F	VF	XF	Unc	BU
2003 Proof	—	Value: 60.00				

KM# 104 5 DOLLARS
25.0000 g., 0.9000 Silver 0.7234 oz. ASW, 32 mm. **Subject:**
Marine Life Protection **Obv:** Neptune standing in sea chariot **Rev:**
Two multicolor reflective fish

Date	Mintage	F	VF	XF	Unc	BU
2003 Proof	—	Value: 60.00				

KM# 105 5 DOLLARS
25.0000 g., 0.9000 Silver 0.7234 oz. ASW, 32 mm. **Subject:**
Marine Life Protection **Rev:** Multicolor Orca

Date	Mintage	F	VF	XF	Unc	BU
2003 Proof	—	Value: 60.00				

KM# 106 5 DOLLARS
25.0000 g., 0.9000 Silver 0.7234 oz. ASW, 32 mm. **Subject:**
Marine Life Protection **Obv:** Neptune in sea chariot **Rev:**
Multicolor Napoleon Fish

Date	Mintage	F	VF	XF	Unc	BU
2003 Proof	—	Value: 60.00				

KM# 333 5 DOLLARS
25.0000 g., 0.9000 Silver 0.7234 oz. ASW, 38.61 mm. **Rev:** Crab

Date	Mintage	F	VF	XF	Unc	BU
2003 Proof	Est. 3,000	Value: 55.00				

KM# 107 5 DOLLARS
25.0000 g., 0.9000 Silver 0.7234 oz. ASW, 32 mm. **Subject:**
Marine Life Protection **Obv:** Neptune seated behind mermaid
Rev: Multicolor school of sweetlips fish

Date	Mintage	F	VF	XF	Unc	BU
2004 Proof	—	Value: 60.00				

KM# 108 5 DOLLARS
25.0000 g., 0.9000 Silver 0.7234 oz. ASW, 32 mm. **Subject:**
Marine Life Protection **Obv:** Standing Neptune and ship **Rev:**
Multicolor Porcupine fish

Date	Mintage	F	VF	XF	Unc	BU
2004 Proof	—	Value: 75.00				

KM# 109 5 DOLLARS
25.0000 g., 0.9000 Silver 0.7234 oz. ASW, 32 mm. **Subject:**
Marine Life Protection **Obv:** Neptune in sea chariot **Rev:**
Multicolor Loggerhead turtle

Date	Mintage	F	VF	XF	Unc	BU
2004 Proof	—	Value: 75.00				

KM# 110 5 DOLLARS
25.0000 g., 0.9000 Silver 0.7234 oz. ASW, 32 mm. **Subject:**
Marine Life Protection **Obv:** Neptune and merhorse **Rev:**
Multicolor dolphin head

Date	Mintage	F	VF	XF	Unc	BU
2004 Proof	—	Value: 75.00				

KM# 81 5 DOLLARS
25.0000 g., 0.9000 Silver 0.7234 oz. ASW, 37.2 mm. **Subject:**
Marine Life Protection **Obv:** Neptune with treasure chest **Rev:**
Clownfish **Edge:** Reeded

Date	Mintage	F	VF	XF	Unc	BU
2004 Proof	—	Value: 75.00				

KM# 111 5 DOLLARS
25.0000 g., 0.9000 Silver 0.7234 oz. ASW, 32 mm. **Subject:**
Marine Life Protection **Obv:** Neptune flanked by mermaids **Rev:**
Multicolor sea horse

Date	Mintage	F	VF	XF	Unc	BU
2005 Proof	—	Value: 75.00				

KM# 113 5 DOLLARS
25.0000 g., 0.9000 Silver 0.7234 oz. ASW, 32 mm. **Subject:**
Marine Life Protection **Obv:** Neptune flanked by mermaids **Rev:**
Multicolor fish with ring-like stripes **Edge:** Reeded

Date	Mintage	F	VF	XF	Unc	BU
2005 Proof	—	Value: 75.00				

KM# 114 5 DOLLARS
25.0000 g., 0.9000 Silver 0.7234 oz. ASW, 32 mm. **Subject:**
Marine Life Protection **Obv:** Neptune in shell boat talking to a
dolphin **Rev:** Multicolor reef fish scene **Edge:** Reeded

Date	Mintage	F	VF	XF	Unc	BU
2006 Proof	—	Value: 75.00				

KM# 143 5 DOLLARS
25.0000 g., 0.9250 Silver with meteorite insert. 0.7435 oz. ASW
Subject: Nantan Meteorite fall, May 1516 **Obv:** Shield **Rev:**
Farmer and oxen plowing field, meteorite insert

Date	Mintage	F	VF	XF	Unc	BU
2006 Proof	2,500	Value: 100				

KM# 185 5 DOLLARS
24.8500 g., 0.9990 Silver 0.7981 oz. ASW, 38.6 mm. **Rev:** Black
pearl oyster

Date	Mintage	F	VF	XF	Unc	BU
2006 Proof	2,500	Value: 300				

KM# 186   5 DOLLARS
25.0000 g., 0.9990 Silver 0.8029 oz. ASW, 38.61 mm. **Subject:**
Pacific Wildlife **Rev:** Rainbow Lorikeet head left

Date	Mintage	F	VF	XF	Unc	BU
2006 Proof	5,000	Value: 55.00				

KM# 187   5 DOLLARS
25.0000 g., 0.9990 Silver 0.8029 oz. ASW, 38.61 mm. **Subject:**
Pacific Wildlife **Rev:** Eclectus Parrot head right

Date	Mintage	F	VF	XF	Unc	BU
2006 Proof	5,000	Value: 55.00				

KM# 188   5 DOLLARS
25.0000 g., 0.9990 Silver 0.8029 oz. ASW, 38.61 mm. **Subject:**
Pacific Wildlife **Rev:** Fruit dove head right

Date	Mintage	F	VF	XF	Unc	BU
2006 Proof	5,000	Value: 55.00				

KM# 189   5 DOLLARS
31.1050 g., 0.9990 Silver 0.9990 oz. ASW, 38.61 mm. **Subject:**
One ounce of luck **Rev:** Four-leaf clover

Date	Mintage	F	VF	XF	Unc	BU
2006 Proof	5,000	Value: 65.00				

KM# 190   5 DOLLARS
25.0000 g., 0.9250 Silver 0.7435 oz. ASW, 38.61 mm. **Subject:**
Dream Island **Rev:** Pacific island scene - beach, boat and sunset

Date	Mintage	F	VF	XF	Unc	BU
2006 Proof	5,000	Value: 50.00				

KM# 151   5 DOLLARS
25.0000 g., 0.9250 Silver 0.7435 oz. ASW, 38.6 mm. **Subject:**
Pacific Wildlife **Obv:** Shield **Rev:** Multicolor nautilus shell

Date	Mintage	F	VF	XF	Unc	BU
2007 Proof	—	Value: 70.00				

KM# 152   5 DOLLARS
25.0000 g., 0.9250 Silver 0.7435 oz. ASW **Subject:** Pacific
Wildlife **Obv:** Shield **Rev:** Multicolor starfish

Date	Mintage	F	VF	XF	Unc	BU
2007 Proof	—	Value: 70.00				

KM# 153   5 DOLLARS
25.0000 g., 0.9250 Silver 0.7435 oz. ASW **Subject:** Good
heavens! **Obv:** Multicolor devil and angel child **Shape:** Heart

Date	Mintage	F	VF	XF	Unc	BU
2007 Proof	2,500	Value: 65.00				

KM# 138   5 DOLLARS
24.7000 g., Silver, 38.6 mm. **Series:** Marine Life Protection **Obv:**
National arms with Neptune and mermaid **Rev:** Pearl in oyster
shell - multicolor **Edge:** Reeded

Date	Mintage	F	VF	XF	Unc	BU
2007 Proof	2,500	Value: 185				

KM# 119   5 DOLLARS
25.0000 g., 0.9000 Silver 0.7234 oz. ASW, 38.61 mm. **Series:**
Marine Life Protection **Obv:** Neptune reclining with trident,
mermaid at his side **Obv. Legend:** REPUBLIC OF PALAU **Rev:**
Multicolor Doctor Fish

Date	Mintage	F	VF	XF	Unc	BU
2007 Proof	1,500	Value: 120				

KM# 122   5 DOLLARS
25.0000 g., 0.5000 Silver 0.4019 oz. ASW, 38.61 mm. **Obv:**
Shield with Neptune holding trident, mermaid reclining at his side,
RAINBOW'S / End below **Obv. Legend:** REPUBLIC OF PALAU
Rev: Red racing car 3/4 right **Rev. Legend:** FERRARI - 60
YEARS ANNIVERSARY

Date	Mintage	F	VF	XF	Unc	BU
ND(2007) Proof	2,500	Value: 75.00				

KM# 136   5 DOLLARS
25.0000 g., 0.9250 Silver 0.7435 oz. ASW, 38.61 mm. **Series:**
Pacific Wildlife **Obv:** National arms **Obv. Legend:** REPUBLIC
OF PALAU **Rev:** Saltwater Crocodile with green crystal eye

Date	Mintage	F	VF	XF	Unc	BU
2007 Proof	2,500	Value: 75.00				

KM# 137   5 DOLLARS
24.7000 g., 0.9250 Silver 0.7345 oz. ASW, 38.5 mm. **Obv:**
Outrigger canoe above shield **Obv. Legend:** REPUBLIC OF
PALAU **Rev:** Pearl in colorized shell **Rev. Legend:** MARINE LIFE
PROTECTION / Pearl of the sea **Edge:** Reeded

Date	Mintage	F	VF	XF	Unc	BU
2008 Proof	2,500	Value: 125				

KM# 168   5 DOLLARS
25.0000 g., 0.9250 Silver 0.7435 oz. ASW, 30x45 mm. **Obv:**
Shield **Rev:** Don Quiote in armor **Shape:** Vertical oval

Date	Mintage	F	VF	XF	Unc	BU
2008 Proof	—	Value: 70.00				

KM# 169   5 DOLLARS
25.0000 g., 0.9250 Silver 0.7435 oz. ASW **Subject:** Pacific
Wildlife **Obv:** Shield **Rev:** Multicolor hologram, blue butterfly
(Papilio Pericles) **Shape:** 37.2

Date	Mintage	F	VF	XF	Unc	BU
2008 Proof	2,500	Value: 60.00				

KM# 170   5 DOLLARS
25.0000 g., 0.9250 Silver 0.7435 oz. ASW, 37.2 mm. **Subject:** Pacific Wildlife **Obv:** Shield **Rev:** Multicolor sulphur butterfly (Hebomoia Leucippe)

Date	Mintage	F	VF	XF	Unc	BU
2008 Proof	2,500	Value: 60.00				

KM# 171   5 DOLLARS
25.0000 g., 0.9250 Silver 0.7435 oz. ASW, 37.2 mm. **Subject:** Pacific Wildlife **Obv:** Shield **Rev:** Multicolor hologram, butterfly

Date	Mintage	F	VF	XF	Unc	BU
2008 Proof	2,500	Value: 60.00				

KM# 172   5 DOLLARS
25.0000 g., 0.9250 Silver 0.7435 oz. ASW, 38.6 mm. **Subject:** Telescope, 400th Anniversary **Obv:** Shield **Rev:** Hans Lippersheg, lens insert

Date	Mintage	F	VF	XF	Unc	BU
2008 Matte finish	1,608	—	—	—	—	70.00

KM# 173   5 DOLLARS
25.0000 g., 0.9250 Silver 0.7435 oz. ASW, 38.6 mm. **Subject:** Telescope, 400th Anniversary **Obv:** Shield **Rev:** The Hubble Telescope, lens insert

Date	Mintage	F	VF	XF	Unc	BU
2008 Matte finish	1,608	—	—	—	—	70.00

KM# 174   5 DOLLARS
Copper-Nickel, 38.6 mm. **Subject:** Endangered Wildlife **Obv:** Shield **Rev:** Multicolor yellow fish

Date	Mintage	F	VF	XF	Unc	BU
2008 Proof	—	—	—	—	—	25.00

KM# 175   5 DOLLARS
25.0000 g., 0.9250 Silver 0.7435 oz. ASW, 38.6 mm. **Subject:** Everything for you **Obv:** Shield **Rev:** Multicolor, outstretched hand, ribbon above **Shape:** Heart

Date	Mintage	F	VF	XF	Unc	BU
2008 Proof	2,500	Value: 100				

KM# 192   5 DOLLARS
25.0000 g., 0.9250 Silver partially gilt 0.7435 oz. ASW, 30x45 mm. **Subject:** Illusion Autum Leaves **Rev:** Gilt leaf **Shape:** Oval

Date	Mintage	F	VF	XF	Unc	BU
2008 Proof	2,500	Value: 75.00				

KM# 179   5 DOLLARS
25.0000 g., 0.9250 Silver 0.7435 oz. ASW, 38.61 mm. **Subject:** Scent of Paradise **Obv:** Shield **Rev:** Multicolor open coconut, scented

Date	Mintage	F	VF	XF	Unc	BU
2009	2,500	—	—	—	—	65.00

KM# 180   5 DOLLARS
25.0000 g., 0.9250 Silver 0.7435 oz. ASW, 38.5 mm. **Subject:** Jewels of the Sea **Obv:** Shield **Rev:** Multicolor blue oyster with inset pearl

Date	Mintage	F	VF	XF	Unc	BU
2009 Proof	2,500	Value: 150				

KM# 181   5 DOLLARS
25.0000 g., 0.9250 Silver 0.7435 oz. ASW, 38.5 mm. **Subject:** Louis Braile, 200th Anniversary of Birth **Obv:** Shield **Rev:** Portrait of Braile

Date	Mintage	F	VF	XF	Unc	BU
2009 Matte finish	2,500	—	—	—	—	45.00

KM# 182   5 DOLLARS
25.0000 g., 0.9250 Silver 0.7435 oz. ASW **Subject:** Missing you **Obv:** Shield **Rev:** Two angels, multicolor, crystal insert **Shape:** Heart

Date	Mintage	F	VF	XF	Unc	BU
2009 Proof	2,500	Value: 55.00				

KM# 196   5 DOLLARS
25.0000 g., 0.9250 Silver 0.7435 oz. ASW, 38.61 mm. **Subject:** Pacific Wildlife **Rev:** Angelfish

Date	Mintage	F	VF	XF	Unc	BU
2009 Proof	2,500	Value: 60.00				

KM# 197   5 DOLLARS
25.0000 g., 0.9250 Silver 0.7435 oz. ASW, 38.61 mm. **Subject:** Pacific Wildlife **Rev:** Barn Swallow

Date	Mintage	F	VF	XF	Unc	BU
2009 Proof	2,500	Value: 60.00				

KM# 198   5 DOLLARS
25.0000 g., 0.9250 Silver 0.7435 oz. ASW, 38.61 mm. **Subject:** Pacific Wildlife **Rev:** Gecko

Date	Mintage	F	VF	XF	Unc	BU
2009 Proof	2,500	Value: 60.00				

KM# 199   5 DOLLARS
25.0000 g., 0.9250 Silver 0.7435 oz. ASW, 38.61 mm. **Subject:** Exceptional Animals **Rev:** Bird of Paradise

Date	Mintage	F	VF	XF	Unc	BU
2009 Proof	2,500	Value: 55.00				

KM# 200   5 DOLLARS
25.0000 g., 0.9250 Silver 0.7435 oz. ASW, 38.61 mm. **Subject:** Exceptional Animals **Rev:** Peacock

Date	Mintage	F	VF	XF	Unc	BU
2009 Proof	2,500	Value: 55.00				

KM# 201   5 DOLLARS
25.0000 g., 0.9250 Silver 0.7435 oz. ASW, 38.61 mm. **Subject:** Marine Life Protection **Rev:** Lionfish

Date	Mintage	F	VF	XF	Unc	BU
2009 Proof	1,500	Value: 65.00				

KM# 202   5 DOLLARS
25.0000 g., 0.9990 Silver 0.8029 oz. ASW, 38.61 mm. **Subject:** Fall of the Berlin Wall **Rev:** Brandenberg Gate, half with and half without wall

Date	Mintage	F	VF	XF	Unc	BU
2009 Proof	2,009	Value: 110				

KM# 203   5 DOLLARS
20.0000 g., 0.9250 Silver 0.5948 oz. ASW, 38.61 mm. **Rev:** Sail training vessel Pamir

Date	Mintage	F	VF	XF	Unc	BU
2009 Proof	2,500	Value: 50.00				

KM# 204   5 DOLLARS
25.0000 g., 0.9250 Silver 0.7435 oz. ASW, 38.61 mm. **Subject:** Wonders of the Ancient World **Rev:** Lighthouse at Alexandria

Date	Mintage	F	VF	XF	Unc	BU
2009 Proof	2,500	Value: 65.00				

KM# 205   5 DOLLARS
25.0000 g., 0.9250 Silver 0.7435 oz. ASW **Subject:** Wonders of the Ancient World **Rev:** Statue of Zeus

Date	Mintage	F	VF	XF	Unc	BU
2009 Proof	2,500	Value: 65.00				

KM# 206   5 DOLLARS
25.0000 g., 0.9250 Silver 0.7435 oz. ASW, 38.61 mm. **Subject:** Wonders of the Ancient World **Rev:** Hanging Gardens of Babylon

Date	Mintage	F	VF	XF	Unc	BU
2009 Proof	2,500	Value: 65.00				

KM# 207   5 DOLLARS
25.0000 g., 0.9250 Silver 0.7435 oz. ASW, 38.61 mm. **Subject:** Wonders of the Ancient World **Rev:** Mausoleum of Halicarnassus

Date	Mintage	F	VF	XF	Unc	BU
2009 Proof	2,500	Value: 65.00				

KM# 208   5 DOLLARS
25.0000 g., 0.9250 Silver 0.7435 oz. ASW, 38.61 mm. **Subject:** Wonders of the Ancient World **Rev:** Pyramids of Giza

Date	Mintage	F	VF	XF	Unc	BU
2009 Proof	2,500	Value: 65.00				

KM# 209   5 DOLLARS
25.0000 g., 0.9250 Silver 0.7435 oz. ASW, 38.61 mm. **Subject:** Wonders of the Ancient World **Rev:** Temple of Artemis

Date	Mintage	F	VF	XF	Unc	BU
2009 Proof	2,500	Value: 65.00				

KM# 210   5 DOLLARS
25.0000 g., 0.9250 Silver 0.7435 oz. ASW, 38.61 mm. **Subject:** Wonders of the Ancient World **Rev:** Colossus of Rhodes

Date	Mintage	F	VF	XF	Unc	BU
2009 Proof	2,500	Value: 65.00				

KM# 211   5 DOLLARS
25.0000 g., 0.9250 Silver 0.7435 oz. ASW, 38.6 mm. **Subject:** Flora and Mountains of the Alps **Rev:** Zugspitze and blue flower

Date	Mintage	F	VF	XF	Unc	BU
2009 Proof	2,500	Value: 65.00				

KM# 212   5 DOLLARS
25.0000 g., 0.9250 Silver 0.7435 oz. ASW, 38.61 mm. **Subject:** Flora and Mountains of the Alps **Rev:** Grossglockner and white flower

Date	Mintage	F	VF	XF	Unc	BU
2009 Proof	2,500	Value: 65.00				

KM# 213   5 DOLLARS
25.0000 g., 0.9250 Silver 0.7435 oz. ASW, 38.61 mm. **Subject:** Flora and Mountains of the Alps **Rev:** Matterhorn and pink flower

Date	Mintage	F	VF	XF	Unc	BU
2009 Proof	2,500	Value: 65.00				

KM# 214   5 DOLLARS
25.0000 g., 0.9250 Silver 0.7435 oz. ASW, 38.61 mm. **Subject:** Flora and Mountains of the Alps **Rev:** Dachstein and purple flower

Date	Mintage	F	VF	XF	Unc	BU
2009 Proof	2,500	Value: 65.00				

KM# 215   5 DOLLARS
25.0000 g., 0.9250 Silver 0.7435 oz. ASW, 38.61 mm. **Subject:** Flora and Mountains of the Alps **Rev:** Mont Blanc and orange flower

Date	Mintage	F	VF	XF	Unc	BU
2009 Proof	2,500	Value: 65.00				

KM# 216   5 DOLLARS
25.0000 g., 0.9250 Silver 0.7435 oz. ASW, 38.61 mm. **Subject:** Flora and Mountains of the Alps **Rev:** Watzmann and purple flower

Date	Mintage	F	VF	XF	Unc	BU
2009 Proof	2,500	Value: 65.00				

KM# 217   5 DOLLARS
25.0000 g., 0.9250 Silver 0.7435 oz. ASW, 38.61 mm. **Subject:** Flora and Mountains of the Alps **Rev:** Oetscher and yellow flower

Date	Mintage	F	VF	XF	Unc	BU
2009 Proof	2,500	Value: 65.00				

KM# 218   5 DOLLARS
25.0000 g., 0.9250 Silver 0.7435 oz. ASW, 38.61 mm. **Subject:** Flora and Mountains of the Alps **Rev:** Piz Buin and pink flower

Date	Mintage	F	VF	XF	Unc	BU
2009 Proof	2,500	Value: 65.00				

KM# 242   5 DOLLARS
20.0000 g., 0.9250 Silver 0.5948 oz. ASW, 38.6 mm. **Subject:** Finnish icebreaker Tarmo **Rev:** Ship left in ice pack

Date	Mintage	F	VF	XF	Unc	BU
2009 Proof	2,500	Value: 40.00				

KM# 264   5 DOLLARS
25.0000 g., 0.9250 Silver 0.7435 oz. ASW, 38.61 mm. **Subject:** Treasures of the World - Emeralds **Rev:** Mule mine cart and emerald insert

Date	Mintage	F	VF	XF	Unc	BU
2009 Antique	2,000	Value: 85.00				

KM# 265   5 DOLLARS
25.0000 g., 0.9250 Silver 0.7435 oz. ASW, 38.6 mm. **Obv:** Arms **Rev:** Our Lady of the Gate of Dawn, partially gilt

Date	Mintage	F	VF	XF	Unc	BU
2009 Proof	1,000	Value: 75.00				

KM# 248   5 DOLLARS
25.0000 g., 0.9250 Silver 0.7435 oz. ASW, 38.6 mm. **Subject:** Marine Life Protection **Rev:** Blue freshwater pearl set within multicolor shell

Date	Mintage	F	VF	XF	Unc	BU
2010 Proof	2,500	Value: 75.00				

KM# 249   5 DOLLARS
25.0000 g., 0.9250 Silver 0.7435 oz. ASW, 38.6 mm. **Subject:** Scent of Paradise - Sea breeze fragrance **Rev:** Female surfboarder in multicolor wave

Date	Mintage	F	VF	XF	Unc	BU
2010	2,500	—	—	—	—	60.00

KM# 289   5 DOLLARS
25.0000 g., 0.9250 Silver 0.7435 oz. ASW, 38.61 mm. **Obv:** National arms **Rev:** St. Basil's Cathedral in color

Date	Mintage	F	VF	XF	Unc	BU
2010 Proof	2,500	Value: 60.00				

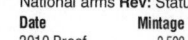

KM# 290   5 DOLLARS
25.0000 g., 0.9250 Silver 0.7435 oz. ASW, 38.61 mm. **Obv:** National arms **Rev:** Statue of Liberty in color

Date	Mintage	F	VF	XF	Unc	BU
2010 Proof	2,500	Value: 60.00				

KM# 291   5 DOLLARS
25.0000 g., 0.9250 Silver 0.7435 oz. ASW, 38.61 mm. **Obv:**
National arms **Rev:** Kiyomizu Temple in color

Date	Mintage	F	VF	XF	Unc	BU
2010 Proof	2,500	Value: 60.00				

KM# 295   5 DOLLARS
25.0000 g., 0.9250 Silver 0.7435 oz. ASW, 38.61 mm. **Obv:**
National arms **Rev:** Mt. Elbrus and Rhododendron in color

Date	Mintage	F	VF	XF	Unc	BU
2010 Proof	2,500	Value: 60.00				

KM# 299   5 DOLLARS
25.0000 g., 0.9250 Silver 0.7435 oz. ASW, 38.61 mm. **Obv:**
National arms **Rev:** Mt. Vinson and Colobanthus quitensis in color

Date	Mintage	F	VF	XF	Unc	BU
2010 Proof	2,500	Value: 60.00				

KM# 292   5 DOLLARS
25.0000 g., 0.9250 Silver 0.7435 oz. ASW, 38.61 mm. **Obv:**
National arms **Rev:** Neuschwanstein Castle in color

Date	Mintage	F	VF	XF	Unc	BU
2010 Proof	2,500	Value: 60.00				

KM# 296   5 DOLLARS
25.0000 g., 0.9250 Silver 0.7435 oz. ASW, 38.61 mm. **Obv:**
National arms **Rev:** Carstensz Pyramid and Orchidacae in color

Date	Mintage	F	VF	XF	Unc	BU
2010 Proof	2,500	Value: 60.00				

KM# 300   5 DOLLARS
25.0000 g., 0.9250 Silver 0.7435 oz. ASW, 38.61 mm. **Obv:**
National arms **Rev:** Mt. Elger and Arnica montana in color

Date	Mintage	F	VF	XF	Unc	BU
2010 Proof	2,500	Value: 60.00				

KM# 293   5 DOLLARS
25.0000 g., 0.9250 Silver 0.7435 oz. ASW, 38.61 mm. **Obv:**
National arms **Rev:** Mt. Everest and Meconopsis betonicifolia in
color

Date	Mintage	F	VF	XF	Unc	BU
2010 Proof	250	Value: 60.00				

KM# 297   5 DOLLARS
25.0000 g., 0.9250 Silver 0.7435 oz. ASW, 38.61 mm. **Obv:**
National arms **Rev:** Mount McKinley and Anaphalis margaritacea
in color

Date	Mintage	F	VF	XF	Unc	BU
2010 Proof	2,500	Value: 60.00				

KM# 301   5 DOLLARS
25.0000 g., 0.9250 Silver 0.7435 oz. ASW, 38.61 mm. **Obv:**
National arms **Rev:** Ayers Rock and Calytrix longiflora in color

Date	Mintage	F	VF	XF	Unc	BU
2010 Proof	2,500	Value: 60.00				

KM# 294   5 DOLLARS
25.0000 g., 0.9250 Silver 0.7435 oz. ASW, 38.61 mm. **Obv:**
National arms **Rev:** Mt. Kilimanjaro and Protea kilimandscharica
in color

Date	Mintage	F	VF	XF	Unc	BU
2010 Proof	2,500	Value: 60.00				

KM# 302   5 DOLLARS
25.0000 g., 0.9250 Silver 0.7435 oz. ASW, 38.61 mm. **Obv:**
National arms **Rev:** Mt. Alpspitze and Campanula alpina in color

Date	Mintage	F	VF	XF	Unc	BU
2010 Proof	2,500	Value: 60.00				

KM# 298   5 DOLLARS
25.0000 g., 0.9250 Silver 0.7435 oz. ASW, 38.61 mm. **Obv:**
National arms **Rev:** Mt. Aconcagua and Aechmea distichantha
in color

Date	Mintage	F	VF	XF	Unc	BU
2010 Proof	2,500	Value: 60.00				

KM# 306 5 DOLLARS
25.0000 g., 0.9250 Silver 0.7435 oz. ASW, 38.61 mm. **Obv:** Naitonal arms **Rev:** Christmas star above winter home scene in color

Date	Mintage	F	VF	XF	Unc	BU
2010 Proof	2,500	Value: 60.00				

KM# 314 5 DOLLARS
25.0000 g., 0.9250 Silver 0.7435 oz. ASW, 38.61 mm. **Obv:** National arms **Rev:** Hammerhead shark in color image

Date	Mintage	F	VF	XF	Unc	BU
2010 Proof	1,500	Value: 60.00				

KM# 191 10 DOLLARS
62.2050 g., 0.9990 Silver 1.9979 oz. ASW, 50 mm. **Subject:** Tiffany Art **Rev:** Renaissance doorway

Date	Mintage	F	VF	XF	Unc	BU
2007 Matte Proof	999	Value: 500				

KM# 193 10 DOLLARS
62.2100 g., 0.9990 Silver 1.9980 oz. ASW, 50 mm. **Subject:** Tiffany Art **Rev:** Mannerism, staircase design

Date	Mintage	F	VF	XF	Unc	BU
2008 Matte Proof	999	Value: 450				

KM# 194 10 DOLLARS
62.2100 g., 0.9990 Silver 1.9980 oz. ASW, 42x42 mm. **Subject:** WWII Battleships **Rev:** Japan's Yamato

Date	Mintage	F	VF	XF	Unc	BU
2008 Proof	1,000	Value: 300				

KM# 195 10 DOLLARS
62.2100 g., 0.9990 Silver 1.9980 oz. ASW, 42x42 mm. **Subject:** WWII Battleships **Rev:** USS Missouri, gilt eagle above

Date	Mintage	F	VF	XF	Unc	BU
2008 Proof	1,000	Value: 175				

KM# 184 10 DOLLARS
62.2500 g., 0.9990 Silver 1.9993 oz. ASW, 42x42 mm. **Subject:** WWII Battleships **Obv:** Shield **Rev:** Bismarck, gilt Iron Cross above **Shape:** Square

Date	Mintage	F	VF	XF	Unc	BU
2009 Proof		Value: 165				

KM# 219 10 DOLLARS
62.2100 g., 0.9990 Silver 1.9980 oz. ASW, 50 mm. **Subject:** Tiffany Art **Rev:** Baroque facade

Date	Mintage	F	VF	XF	Unc	BU
2009 Matte Proof	—	Value: 400				

KM# 220 10 DOLLARS
62.2100 g., 0.9990 Silver 1.9980 oz. ASW, 50 mm. **Rev:** Amber insert

Date	Mintage	F	VF	XF	Unc	BU
2009 Matte Proof	2,500	Value: 275				

KM# 221 10 DOLLARS
62.2100 g., 0.9990 Silver 1.9980 oz. ASW, 42x42 mm. **Subject:** WWII Battleship **Rev:** Britains's HMS Prince of Wales, gilt Union Jack above

Date	Mintage	F	VF	XF	Unc	BU
2009 Proof	1,000	Value: 145				

KM# 250   10 DOLLARS
62.2000 g., 0.9990 Silver 1.9977 oz. ASW, 42x42 mm. **Subject:**
Russian Battleship Marat **Rev:** Battleship sailing left

Date	Mintage	F	VF	XF	Unc	BU
2010 Proof	1,000	Value: 80.00				

KM# 252   10 DOLLARS
64.2100 g., 0.9990 Silver 2.0622 oz. ASW, 50 mm. **Subject:**
Tiffany Art - Rococo **Obv:** Arms at lower right, glass insert **Rev:**
Cherus at left, glass insert

Date	Mintage	F	VF	XF	Unc	BU
2010 Antique	999	—	—	—	—	325

KM# 304   10 DOLLARS
62.2100 g., 0.9250 Silver 1.8500 oz. ASW, 42x42 mm. **Obv:**
National arms **Rev:** French Battleship Richelieu, gilt flag at top
Shape: Square

Date	Mintage	F	VF	XF	Unc	BU
2010 Proof	1,000	Value: 100				

KM# 320   10 DOLLARS
62.2000 g., 0.9250 Silver 1.8497 oz. ASW, 55 mm. **Subject:**
Sagrada Familia **Obv:** National arms **Rev:** Scenes from the Birth
of Jesus, insert

Date	Mintage	F	VF	XF	Unc	BU
2010 Proof	2,500	Value: 115				

KM# 318   10 DOLLARS
62.2100 g., 0.9990 Silver 1.9980 oz. ASW, 50 mm. **Subject:**
Tiffany Glass **Obv:** National arms **Rev:** Theater box froms, red
glass insert

Date	Mintage	F	VF	XF	Unc	BU
2011 Antique patina	999	—	—	—	—	100

KM# 176   20 DOLLARS
164.0000 g., 0.9990 Silver 5.2672 oz. ASW, 63 mm. **Obv:** Auto
steering wheel **Rev:** Side sillouette of Corvette 206

Date	Mintage	F	VF	XF	Unc	BU
2008 Proof	—	Value: 200				

KM# 183   500 DOLLARS
77.7000 g., 0.9990 Gold 2.4955 oz. AGW, 42x42 mm. **Obv:**
Shield **Rev:** Battleship Bismark

Date	Mintage	F	VF	XF	Unc	BU
2009 Proof	77	Value: 4,000				

KM# 243   500 DOLLARS
77.7500 g., 0.9990 Gold 2.4971 oz. AGW, 42x42 mm. **Subject:**
H.M.S. Prince of Wales **Rev:** Battleship right, Royal Navy flag
above

Date	Mintage	F	VF	XF	Unc	BU
2009 Proof	77	Value: 4,000				

KM# 251   500 DOLLARS
77.7500 g., 0.9990 Gold 2.4971 oz. AGW, 42x42 mm. **Subject:**
Battleship Marat **Rev:** Battleship sailing left

Date	Mintage	F	VF	XF	Unc	BU
2010 Proof	77	Value: 4,000				

KM# 305   500 DOLLARS
77.7500 g., 0.9999 Gold 2.4994 oz. AGW, 42x42 mm. **Obv:**
National arms **Rev:** French battleship Richelieu **Shape:** Square

Date	Mintage	F	VF	XF	Unc	BU
2010 Proof	77	Value: 4,250				

PROOF SETS

KM#	Date	Mintage	Identification	Issue Price	Mkt Val
PS4	2007 (6)	2,500	KM#130-135	—	375

PANAMA

The Republic of Panama, a Central American country situated between Costa Rica and Colombia, has an area of 29,762
sq. mi. (78,200 sq. km.) and a population of *2.4 million. Capital:
Panama City. The Panama Canal is the country's biggest asset;
servicing world related transit trade and international commerce.
Bananas, refined petroleum, sugar and shrimp are exported.

MONETARY SYSTEM
100 Centesimos = 1 Balboa

REPUBLIC

DECIMAL COINAGE

KM# 125   CENTESIMO
2.4400 g., Copper Plated Zinc, 18.96 mm. **Obv:** Written value

Obv. Legend: REPUBLICA DE PANAMA Rev: Native Urraca bust left Edge: Plain

Date	Mintage	F	VF	XF	Unc	BU
2001(c)	160,000,000	—	—	—	0.50	1.00
2008(c)		—	—	—	0.50	1.00

KM# 133   5 CENTESIMOS

5.0000 g., Copper-Nickel, 21.15 mm. Subject: Sara Sotillo Obv: National coat of arms Obv. Legend: REPUBLICA DE PANAMA Rev: Head of Sotillo 3/4 right Edge: Plain

Date	Mintage	F	VF	XF	Unc	BU
2001(c)	8,000,000	—	—	—	0.30	1.00
2008(c)		—	—	—	0.30	1.00

KM# 127   1/10 BALBOA

2.2680 g., Copper-Nickel Clad Copper, 17.91 mm. Obv: National coat of arms Obv. Legend: REPUBLICA DE PANAMA Rev: Armored bust of Balboa left Edge: Reeded

Date	Mintage	F	VF	XF	Unc	BU
2001(c)	15,000,000	—	—	0.50	0.75	1.00
2008(c)	28,000,000	—	—	0.50	0.75	1.00

KM# 135   25 CENTESIMOS

5.6700 g., Copper-Nickel Clad Copper, 24.26 mm. Obv: National coat of arms Obv. Legend: REPUBLICA DE PANAMA Rev: Tower and Spanish ruins Edge: Reeded Note: Released in 2004

Date	Mintage	F	VF	XF	Unc	BU
2003(c)	6,000,000	—	—	0.50	2.00	3.00
2003(c) Proof	2,000	Value: 25.00				

KM# 136   25 CENTESIMOS

5.6700 g., Copper-Nickel Clad Copper, 24.26 mm. Obv: National coat of arms Obv. Legend: REPUBLICA DE PANAMA Rev: King's Bridge Rev. Legend: Puente Del Rey Edge: Reeded

Date	Mintage	F	VF	XF	Unc	BU
2005(c)	3,000,000	—	—	—	1.00	1.50
2005(c) Proof	2,000	Value: 12.00				

KM# 128   1/4 BALBOA

5.6700 g., Copper-Nickel Clad Copper, 24.26 mm. Obv: National coat of arms Obv. Legend: REPUBLICA DE PANAMA Rev: Armored bust of Balboa left Edge: Reeded

Date	Mintage	F	VF	XF	Unc	BU
2001(c)	12,000,000	—	—	0.35	0.75	2.00
2006(c)		—	—	0.35	0.75	2.00
2008(c)		—	—	0.35	0.75	2.00

KM# 137   1/4 BALBOA

5.6700 g., Copper-Nickel Clad Copper, 24.26 mm. Subject: Breast Cancer Awareness Obv: National coat of arms Obv. Legend: REPUBLICA DE PANAMA Rev: Ribbon Rev. Legend: Protegete Mujer Edge: Reeded

Date	Mintage	F	VF	XF	Unc	BU
2008(c)	14,000,000	—	—	—	1.00	2.00

Note: Also available in a laminated Breast Cancer Awareness pink bookmark

KM# 137a   1/4 BALBOA

5.6700 g., Copper-Nickel Clad Copper, 24.26 mm. Subject: Breast Cancer Awareness Obv: National coat of arms Obv. Legend: REPUBLICA DE PANAMA Rev: Pink Ribbon Rev. Legend: Protegete Mujer Edge: Reeded

Date	Mintage	F	VF	XF	Unc	BU
2008(c) Proof, pink colored ribbon	2,500	Value: 75.00				

Note: Pink ribbon proof issued in red plush case with black cardboard sleeve with printed pink ribbon

KM# 138   1/4 BALBOA

5.6700 g., Copper-Nickel Clad Copper, 24.26 mm. Subject: 50th Anniversary of the Children's Hospital Obv: National coat of arms Obv. Legend: REPUBLICA DE PANAMA Rev: Children's Hospital Edge: Reeded

Date	Mintage	F	VF	XF	Unc	BU
2008	6,000,000	—	—	—	2.00	3.00

KM# 138a   1/4 BALBOA

5.6700 g., Copper-Nickel Clad Copper, 24.26 mm. Subject: 50th Anniversary of the Children's Hospital Obv: National coat of arms Obv. Legend: REPUBLICA DE PANAMA Rev: Children's Hospital Edge: Reeded

Date	Mintage	F	VF	XF	Unc	BU
2008(c) Proof	1,000	Value: 30.00				

KM# 139   50 CENTESIMOS

11.3400 g., Copper-Nickel Clad Copper, 30.6 mm. Subject: Centenary of the National Bank of Panama Obv: National coat of arms Obv. Legend: REPUBLICA DE PANAMA Rev: BNP Building - Banco Nacional de Panama Rev. Legend: BANCO NACIONAL DE PANAMA CENTENARIO Edge: Reeded

Date	Mintage	F	VF	XF	Unc	BU
2009(c)	4,000,000	—	—	—	2.00	3.00

KM# 139a   50 CENTESIMOS

11.3400 g., Copper-Nickel Clad Copper, 30.6 mm. Subject: Centenary - National Bank of Panama Obv: National coat of arms Obv. Legend: REPUBLICA DE PANAMA Rev: BNP building - 1904-2004 Rev. Legend: BANCO NACIONAL DE PANAMA CENTENARIO Edge: Reeded

Date	Mintage	F	VF	XF	Unc	BU
2009(c) Proof	2,000	Value: 40.00				

KM# 129   1/2 BALBOA

11.3400 g., Copper-Nickel Clad Copper, 30.61 mm. Obv: National coat of arms Obv. Legend: REPUBLICA DE PANAMA Rev: Armored bust of Balboa left Edge: Reeded

Date	Mintage	F	VF	XF	Unc	BU
2001(c)	600,000	—	—	1.00	2.25	4.00
2008(c)	5,800,000	—	—	0.75	1.25	2.00

KM# 140   1/2 BALBOA

11.3400 g., Copper-Nickel Clad Copper, 30.6 mm. Subject: Convent of the Conception Obv: National arms Rev: Building ruins Edge: Reeded

Date	Mintage	F	VF	XF	Unc	BU
2010(c)	3,000,000	—	—	—	2.00	3.00

KM# 142   1/2 BALBOA

11.3400 g., Copper-Nickel Clad Copper, 50.61 mm. Obv: National arms Obv. Legend: REPUBLICA DE PANAMA/MEDIO BALBOA Rev: Crowned Hapsburg shield Rev. Legend: MONEDA DE 1580 / PANAMA VIEJO

Date	Mintage	F	VF	XF	Unc	BU
2011	3,000,000	—	—	—	4.00	5.00

KM# 134   BALBOA

22.6800 g., Copper-Nickel Clad Copper, 38.1 mm. Obv: Bust of President Mireya Moscoso left, flanked by dates of her presidency Rev: Flag and canal scene Edge: Reeded

Date	Mintage	F	VF	XF	Unc	BU
2004(c)	348,000	—	—	2.00	6.00	15.00
2004(c) Proof	2,000	Value: 62.00				

KM# 141   BALBOA

7.2000 g., Bi-Metallic Brass center in Nickel ring, both plated on Stainless Steel core, 26.5 mm. Obv: National arms Obv. Legend: REPUBLICA DE PANAMA / date Rev: Balboa left Rev. Legend: VASCO NUNEZ DE BALBOA / UN BALBOA Edge Lettering: PANAMA (reeding) 1 BALBOA (reeding)

Date	Mintage	F	VF	XF	Unc	BU
2011		—	—	—	3.00	6.00

PAPUA NEW GUINEA

The Independent State of Papua New Guinea occupies the eastern half of the island of New Guinea. It lies north of Australia near the equator and borders on West Irian. The country, which includes nearby Bismark archipelago, Buka and Bougainville, has an area of 178,260 sq. mi. (461,690 sq. km.) and a population of 3.7 million that is divided into more than 1,000 separate tribes, speaking more than 700 mutually unintelligible languages. Capital: Port Moresby. The economy is agricultural, and exports copra, rubber, cocoa, coffee, tea, gold and copper

Papua New Guinea is a member of the Commonwealth of Nations. Elizabeth II is Head of State, as Queen of Papua New Guinea.

CONSTITUTIONAL MONARCHY
Commonwealth of Nations

STANDARD COINAGE

KM# 1 TOEA
2.0000 g., Bronze, 17.65 mm. **Obv:** National emblem **Rev:** Butterfly and value **Edge:** Plain

Date	Mintage	F	VF	XF	Unc	BU
2001	—	—	—	0.25	1.00	10.00
2002	—	—	—	0.15	1.00	10.00
2004	—	—	—	0.10	1.00	10.00

KM# 2 2 TOEA
4.1000 g., Bronze, 21.6 mm. **Obv:** National emblem **Rev:** Lion fish **Edge:** Plain

Date	Mintage	F	VF	XF	Unc	BU
2001	—	—	—	0.30	0.75	12.00
2002	—	—	—	0.25	0.60	12.00
2004	—	—	—	0.15	0.45	12.00

KM# 3a 5 TOEA
2.5500 g., Nickel Plated Steel, 19.53 mm. **Obv:** National emblem **Rev:** Plateless turtle **Edge:** Reeded

Date	Mintage	F	VF	XF	Unc	BU
2002	—	—	—	0.50	1.25	2.50
2005	—	—	—	0.40	1.00	2.00
2010	—	—	—	0.40	1.00	2.00

KM# 4 10 TOEA
5.6500 g., Copper-Nickel, 23.72 mm. **Obv:** National emblem **Rev:** Cuscus and value **Edge:** Reeded

Date	Mintage	F	VF	XF	Unc	BU
2001	—	Value: 2.50				

KM# 4a 10 TOEA
5.1600 g., Nickel Plated Steel, 23.72 mm. **Obv:** National emblem **Rev:** Cuscus and value **Edge:** Reeded

Date	Mintage	F	VF	XF	Unc	BU
2002	—	—	—	0.80	2.00	3.00
2004	—	—	—	0.80	2.00	3.00
2005	—	—	—	6.00	1.50	3.00
2006	—	—	—	0.60	1.50	2.50
2009	—	—	—	0.60	1.50	2.50

KM# 5a 20 TOEA
10.1300 g., Nickel Plated Steel, 28.65 mm. **Obv:** National emblem **Rev:** Bennett's Cassoway and value **Edge:** Reeded

Date	Mintage	F	VF	XF	Unc	BU
2004	—	—	—	0.80	2.00	3.00
2005	—	—	—	0.80	2.00	3.00
2006	—	—	—	0.60	1.50	2.50
2009	—	—	—	0.60	1.50	2.50

KM# 53 50 TOEA
12.1000 g., Nickel Plated Steel, 30 mm. **Subject:** St. John's Ambulance, 50th Anniversary **Obv:** National emblem **Rev:** Ambulance corps logo **Shape:** 7-sided

Date	Mintage	F	VF	XF	Unc	BU
2007	—	—	—	—	4.00	5.00

KM# 54 50 TOEA
12.1000 g., Nickel Plated Steel, 30 mm. **Subject:** Bank of Papua New Guinea, 35th Anniversary **Obv:** National emblem **Rev:** Bank logo in colored central applique

Date	Mintage	F	VF	XF	Unc	BU
2008	—	—	—	—	4.00	5.00

KM# 6a KINA
14.6100 g., Nickel Plated Steel, 33.28 mm. **Obv:** Native design **Rev:** Two Salt Water Crocodiles **Edge:** Reeded

Date	Mintage	F	VF	XF	Unc	BU
2002	—	—	—	1.60	4.00	5.00
2004	—	—	—	1.40	3.50	4.50

KM# 6b KINA
11.1300 g., Nickel Plated Steel, 30 mm. **Obv:** Native design **Rev:** Two Salt Water Crocodiles **Edge:** Reeded

Date	Mintage	F	VF	XF	Unc	BU
2005	—	—	—	1.20	3.00	4.00
2010	—	—	—	1.20	3.00	4.00

KM# 51 2 KINA
12.2000 g., Bi-Metallic Aluminum-Bronze center in Copper-Nickel ring, 33.3 mm. **Subject:** Bank of Papua New Guinea, 35th Anniversary **Obv:** Bird of Pariaise **Rev:** Bank logo **Edge:** Reeded

Date	Mintage	F	VF	XF	Unc	BU
2008	—	—	—	—	—	5.00

PARAGUAY

The Republic of Paraguay, a landlocked country in the heart of South America surrounded by Argentina, Bolivia and Brazil, has an area of 157,048 sq. mi. (406,750 sq. km.) and a population of *4.5 million, 95 percent of whom are of mixed Spanish and Indian descent. Capital: Asuncion. The country is predominantly agrarian, with no important mineral deposits or oil reserves. Meat, timber, hides, oilseeds, tobacco and cotton account for 70 percent of Paraguay's export revenue.

During the Triple Alliance War (1864-1870) in which Paraguay faced Argentina, Brazil and Uruguay, Asuncion's ladies gathered in an Assembly on Feb. 24, 1867 and decided to give up their jewelry in order to help the national defense. The President of the Republic, Francisco Solano Lopez accepted the offering and ordered one twentieth of it be used to mint the first Paraguayan gold coins according to the Decree of the 11th of Sept.1867.

Two dies were made, one by Bouvet, and another by an American, Leonard Charles, while only the die made by Bouvet was eventually used.

MINT MARK
HF – LeLocle (Swiss)

REPUBLIC
REFORM COINAGE
100 Centimos = 1 Guarani

KM# 197 GUARANI
27.0000 g., 0.9250 Silver 0.8029 oz. ASW, 39.7 mm. **Subject:** 50th Anniversary of the Central Bank **Obv:** Naval gunship **Obv. Legend:** REPUBLICA DEL PARAGUAY **Obv. Inscription:** CAÑONERO PARAGUAY **Rev:** Bank building within circle **Rev. Legend:** BANCO CENTRAL DEL PARAGUAY **Edge:** Reeded

Date	Mintage	F	VF	XF	Unc	BU
2002 Proof	3,000		Value: 75.00			

KM# 199 GUARANI
26.8600 g., 0.9250 Silver 0.7988 oz. ASW, 40.03 mm. **Series:** 5th Ibero-America **Subject:** Encounter of the Two Worlds **Obv:** National arms in center with ten national arms in outer circle **Obv. Legend:** REPUBLICA DEL PARAGUAY **Rev:** Native in canoe with outline of South America in background at left, early sailing ship at lower right. **Rev. Legend:** ENCUENTRO DE DOS MUNDOS **Edge:** Reeded

Date	Mintage	F	VF	XF	Unc	BU
2002 Proof			Value: 60.00			

KM# 200 GUARANI
27.0000 g., 0.9250 Silver 0.8029 oz. ASW **Subject:** 60th Anniversary of Currency Reform **Obv:** National arms **Obv. Legend:** REPUBLICA DEL PARAGUAY **Rev:** Outline map of Paraguay **Edge:** Reeded

Date	Mintage	F	VF	XF	Unc	BU
2003 Proof			Value: 80.00			

KM# 201 GUARANI
26.9000 g., 0.9250 Silver 0.8000 oz. ASW, 40.04 mm. **Subject:** FIFA - XVIII World Football Championship - Germany 2006 **Obv:** National arms **Obv. Legend:** REPUBLICA DEL PARAGUAY **Rev:** Two opponents after ball **Rev. Legend:** COPA MUNDIAL DE LA FIFA - ALEMANIA **Edge:** Reeded

Date	Mintage	F	VF	XF	Unc	BU
2003 Proof	50,000		Value: 50.00			

KM# 202 GUARANI
27.0000 g., 0.9250 Silver 0.8029 oz. ASW **Subject:** FIFA - XVIII World Football Championship - Germany 2006 **Obv:** National arms **Obv. Legend:** REPUBLICA DEL PARAGUAY **Rev:** Ball in goal **Edge:** Reeded

Date	Mintage	F	VF	XF	Unc	BU
2004 Proof	50,000		Value: 50.00			

KM# 204 GUARANI
27.0000 g., 0.9250 Silver 0.8029 oz. ASW **Series:** 6th Ibero-America **Subject:** Encounter of the Two Worlds **Obv:** National arms in center with ten national arms in outer circle **Obv. Legend:** REPUBLICA DEL PARAGUAY **Rev:** Church of the Most Holy, Trinidad in Yaguarón **Rev. Legend:** ENCUENTRO DE DOS MUNDOS - IGLESIA DE LA SANTISIMA TRINIDAD **Edge:** Reeded

Date	Mintage	F	VF	XF	Unc	BU
2005 Proof			Value: 65.00			

KM# 191a 50 GUARANIES
Brass Plated Steel **Obv:** Uniformed bust facing **Rev:** Value above river dam **Note:** Magnetic

Date	Mintage	F	VF	XF	Unc	BU
2005	10,000,000	—	—	—	0.75	1.00

KM# 191b 50 GUARANIES
1.0100 g., Aluminum, 18.98 mm. **Obv:** Bust of Major General J.F. Estigarribia facing **Obv. Legend:** REPUBLICA DEL PARAGUAY **Rev:** Acaray River Dam **Rev. Inscription:** REPRESA ACARAY **Edge:** Plain **Note:** Reduced size

Date	Mintage	F	VF	XF	Unc	BU
2006	25,000,000	—	—	—	1.00	2.00
2008		—	—	—	1.00	2.00
2011		—	—	—	1.00	2.00

KM# 177a 100 GUARANIES
5.4500 g., Brass Plated Steel **Obv:** Bust of General Jose E. Dias facing **Obv. Legend:** REPUBLICA DEL PARAGUAY **Rev:** Ruins of Humaita **Rev. Inscription:** RUINAS DE HUMAITA 1865/70 **Note:** Reduced weight and thickness.

Date	Mintage	F	VF	XF	Unc	BU
2004	15,000,000	—	—	—	1.50	2.00
2005	10,000,000	—	—	—	1.50	2.00

KM# 177b 100 GUARANIES
3.6600 g., Nickel-Steel, 20.94 mm. **Obv:** Bust of General Jose E. Dias facing **Obv. Legend:** REPUBLICA DEL PARAGUAY **Rev:** Ruins of Humaita **Rev. Inscription:** RUINAS DE HUMAITA 1865/70 **Edge:** Plain

Date	Mintage	F	VF	XF	Unc	BU
2006	30,000,000	—	—	—	1.50	2.00
2007	25,000,000	—	—	—	1.50	2.00
2008		—	—	—	1.50	2.00
2011		—	—	—	1.50	2.00

KM# 195 500 GUARANIES
7.8200 g., Brass Plated Steel **Obv:** Head of General Bernardino Caballero facing **Obv. Legend:** REPUBLICA DEL PARAGUAY **Rev:** Bank above value within circle **Rev. Legend:** BANCO CENTRAL DEL PARAGUAY

Date	Mintage	F	VF	XF	Unc	BU
2002	15,000,000	—	—	—	2.50	3.00
2005	5,000,000	—	—	—	2.50	3.00

KM# 195a 500 GUARANIES
4.8000 g., Nickel-Steel, 23 mm. **Obv:** Head of General Bernardino Caballero facing **Obv. Legend:** REPUBLICA DEL PARAGUAY **Rev:** Bank above value in circle **Rev. Legend:** BANCO CENTRAL DEL PARAGUAY **Edge:** Plain

Date	Mintage	F	VF	XF	Unc	BU
2006	12,000,000	—	—	—	2.00	2.50
2007	25,000,000	—	—	—	2.00	2.50
2008		—	—	—	2.00	2.50

KM# 198 MIL (1000) GUARANIES
6.0700 g., Nickel-Steel, 25 mm. **Obv:** Bust of Major General Francisco Solano Lopez facing **Obv. Legend:** REPUBLICA DEL PARAGUAY **Rev:** National Heroes Pantheon **Rev. Legend:** BANCO CENTRAL DEL PARAGUAY **Rev. Inscription:** PANTEON NACIONAL / DE LOS HEROES **Edge:** Plain

Date	Mintage	F	VF	XF	Unc	BU
2006	25,000,000	—	—	—	3.00	4.00
2007	35,000,000	—	—	—	3.00	4.00
2008		—	—	—	3.00	4.00

KM# 203 1500 GUARANIES
6.7000 g., 0.9990 Gold 0.2152 oz. AGW **Subject:** XVIII World Football Championship - Germany 2006 **Obv:** National arms **Obv. Legend:** REPUBLICA DEL PARAGUAY **Rev:** Ball in goal

Date	Mintage	F	VF	XF	Unc	BU
2004 Proof	25,000		Value: 450			

The Republic of Peru, located on the Pacific coast of South America, has an area of 496,225 sq. mi. (1,285,220sq. km.) and a population of *21.4 million. Capital: Lima. The diversified economy includes mining, fishing and agriculture. Fishmeal, copper, sugar, zinc and iron ore are exported.

MINT MARKS
L, LIMAE (monogram), Lima (monogram), LIMA = Lima

REPUBLIC

REFORM COINAGE
1/M Intis = 1 Nuevo Sol; 100 (New) Centimos = 1 Nuevo Sol

KM# 303.4 CENTIMO
1.8800 g., Brass, 15.9 mm. **Obv:** National arms, accent mark above "u" **Rev:** Without Braille dots, no Chavez **Edge:** Plain **Note:** LIMA monogram is mint mark.

Date	Mintage	F	VF	XF	Unc	BU
2001LIMA	—	—	—	—	0.25	0.40
2002LIMA	—	—	—	—	0.25	0.40
2004LIMA	—	—	—	—	0.25	0.40
2005LIMA	22,750,000	—	—	—	0.25	0.40
2006LIMA	19,750,000	—	—	—	0.25	0.40

KM# 303.4a CENTIMO
0.8200 g., Aluminum, 16 mm. **Obv:** National arms **Rev:** Value flanked by designs **Edge:** Plain **Note:** LIMA monogram is mint mark.

Date	Mintage	F	VF	XF	Unc	BU
2005LIMA	Inc. above	—	—	—	0.25	0.40
2006LIMA	19,200,000	—	—	—	0.50	0.75
2007LIMA	48,800,000	—	—	—	0.25	0.30
2008LIMA	63,800,000	—	—	—	0.25	0.30
2009LIMA	62,000,000	—	—	—	0.25	0.30
2010LIMA	73,000,000	—	—	—	0.25	0.30

KM# 304.4 5 CENTIMOS
2.6900 g., Brass, 18 mm. **Obv:** National arms, accent above "u" **Rev:** Value flanked by designs. Without Braille dots, with accent above "e" **Edge:** Plain **Note:** LIMA monogram is mint mark.

Date	Mintage	F	VF	XF	Unc	BU
2001LIMA	—	—	—	—	0.35	0.50
2002LIMA	—	—	—	—	0.35	0.50
2005LIMA	8,950,000	—	—	—	0.35	0.50
2006LIMA	11,400,000	—	—	—	0.35	0.50
2007LIMA	12,800,000	—	—	—	0.35	0.50

KM# 304.4a 5 CENTIMOS
1.0200 g., Aluminum, 18 mm. **Obv:** National arms **Rev:** Value flanked by native designs **Edge:** Plain **Note:** LIMA monogram is mint mark.

Date	Mintage	F	VF	XF	Unc	BU
2007LIMA	12,400,000	—	—	—	0.35	0.50
2008LIMA	11,600,000	—	—	—	0.30	0.40
2009LIMA	20,000,000	—	—	—	0.30	0.40
2010LIMA	24,000,000	—	—	—	0.30	0.40
2011LIMA	—	—	—	—	0.30	0.40

KM# 305.4 10 CENTIMOS
3.5000 g., Brass, 20.5 mm. **Obv:** National arms, accent above "u" **Rev:** Without braille dots, accent above "e" **Edge:** Plain **Note:** LIMA monogram is mint mark.

Date	Mintage	F	VF	XF	Unc	BU
2001LIMA	—	—	—	—	0.65	0.85
2002LIMA	—	—	—	—	0.65	0.85
2003LIMA	—	—	—	—	0.65	0.85
2004LIMA	—	—	—	—	0.65	0.85
2005LIMA	39,500,000	—	—	—	0.40	0.50
2006LIMA	54,200,000	—	—	—	0.40	0.50
2007LIMA	64,800,000	—	—	—	0.40	0.50
2008LIMA	79,400,000	—	—	—	0.40	0.50
2009LIMA	63,000,000	—	—	—	0.40	0.50
2010LIMA	82,000,000	—	—	—	0.40	0.50
2011LIMA	—	—	—	—	0.40	0.50
2012LIMA	—	—	—	—	0.40	0.50

KM# 306.4 20 CENTIMOS
4.4000 g., Brass, 23 mm. **Obv:** National arms, accent above "u" **Rev:** Without braille dots, accent above "e" **Edge:** Plain **Note:** LIMA monogram is mint mark.

Date	Mintage	F	VF	XF	Unc	BU
2001LIMA	—	—	—	—	0.85	1.20
2002LIMA	—	—	—	—	0.85	1.20
2004LIMA	—	—	—	—	0.85	1.20
2006LIMA	3,700,000	—	—	—	0.75	1.00
2007LIMA	18,000,000	—	—	—	0.50	0.75
2008LIMA	24,300,000	—	—	—	0.50	0.75
2009LIMA	15,500,000	—	—	—	0.50	0.75
2010LIMA	25,000,000	—	—	—	0.50	0.75
2011LIMA	—	—	—	—	0.50	0.75

KM# 307.4 50 CENTIMOS
5.4500 g., Copper-Nickel-Zinc, 22 mm. **Obv:** National arms, accent above "u" **Rev:** Without braille, accent above "e" **Edge:** Reeded **Note:** LIMA monogram is mint mark.

Date	Mintage	F	VF	XF	Unc	BU
2001LIMA	—	—	—	—	1.00	1.75
2002LIMA	—	—	—	—	1.50	1.75
2003LIMA	—	—	—	—	1.50	1.75
2004LIMA	—	—	—	—	1.50	1.75
2005LIMA	14,600,000	—	—	—	0.75	1.00
2006LIMA	—	—	—	—	0.75	1.00
2007LIMA	—	—	—	—	0.75	1.00
2008LIMA	—	—	—	—	0.75	1.00
2009LIMA	26,700,000	—	—	—	0.75	1.00
2010LIMA	5,180,000	—	—	—	0.75	1.00
2011LIMA	—	—	—	—	0.75	1.00

KM# 345 SOL
7.3000 g., Copper-Nickel, 25.5 mm. **Obv:** National arms **Rev:** Chullpas de Sillustan ruins

Date	Mintage	F	VF	XF	Unc	BU
2011	10,000,000	—	—	—	2.50	3.00

KM# 308.4 NUEVO SOL
7.3200 g., Copper-Nickel-Zinc, 25.5 mm. **Obv:** National arms, accent above "u" **Rev:** Without braille, accent above "e" **Edge:** Reeded **Note:** LIMA monogram is mint mark.

Date	Mintage	F	VF	XF	Unc	BU
2001LIMA	—	—	—	—	2.50	3.00
2002LIMA	—	—	—	—	2.50	3.00
2003LIMA	—	—	—	—	2.50	3.00
2004LIMA	—	—	—	—	2.50	3.00
2005LIMA	14,600,000	—	—	—	1.25	1.50
2006LIMA	19,700,000	—	—	—	1.25	1.50
2007LIMA	36,700,000	—	—	—	1.25	1.50
2008LIMA	42,800,000	—	—	—	1.25	1.50
2009LIMA	34,330,000	—	—	—	1.25	1.50
2010LIMA	—	—	—	—	1.25	1.50
2011LIMA	—	—	—	—	1.25	1.50

KM# 329 NUEVO SOL
33.6250 g., 0.9250 Silver 0.9999 oz. ASW, 37 mm. **Subject:** 450th Anniversary - San Marcos University **Obv:** National arms **Rev:** University seal and building **Edge:** Reeded **Note:** LIMA monogram is mint mark.

Date	Mintage	F	VF	XF	Unc	BU
2001 Proof	—	Value: 60.00				

KM# 330 NUEVO SOL
33.6250 g., 0.9999 oz. ASW, 37 mm. **Subject:** 50th Anniversary - Numismatic Society of Peru **Obv:** National arms **Rev:** Stylized design within circle **Edge:** Reeded **Note:** LIMA monogram is mint mark.

Date	Mintage	F	VF	XF	Unc	BU
2001 Proof	—	Value: 50.00				

KM# 331 NUEVO SOL
33.6250 g., 0.9250 Silver 0.9999 oz. ASW, 37 mm. **Subject:** 200th Anniversary - von Humboldt's visit to Peru **Obv:** National arms **Rev:** Seated figure 1/4 left **Edge:** Reeded **Note:** LIMA monogram is mint mark.

Date	Mintage	F	VF	XF	Unc	BU
2002 Proof	Est. 1,000	Value: 65.00				

KM# 334 NUEVO SOL
27.0800 g., 0.9250 Silver 0.8053 oz. ASW, 40 mm. **Series:** Fifth Ibero-America **Obv:** National arms in center with ten national arms in outer circle **Obv. Legend:** BANCO CENTRAL DE RESERVA DEL PERÚ **Rev:** Ceramic - Indians in reed boats **Rev. Legend:** PERÚ **Edge:** Reeded

Date	Mintage	F	VF	XF	Unc	BU
2002 Proof	Est. 17,000	Value: 65.00				

KM# 332 NUEVO SOL
33.6250 g., 0.9250 Silver 0.9999 oz. ASW, 37 mm. **Subject:** 125th Anniversary of the Inmaculate Jesuitas - Lima College **Obv:** National arms **Rev:** Statue and 3/4 crowned shield **Edge:** Reeded **Note:** LIMA monogram is mint mark.

Date	Mintage	F	VF	XF	Unc	BU
2003 Proof	Est. 1,000	Value: 65.00				

KM# 333 NUEVO SOL
33.6250 g., 0.9250 Silver 0.9999 oz. ASW, 37 mm. **Subject:** 180th Anniversary of Peru's Congress **Obv:** National arms **Rev:** Statue in front of building **Edge:** Reeded **Note:** LIMA monogram is mint mark.

Date	Mintage	F	VF	XF	Unc	BU
2003	Est. 1,000	—	—	—	—	65.00

KM# 335 NUEVO SOL
27.0000 g., 0.9250 Silver 0.8029 oz. ASW, 40 mm. **Subject:** FIFA World Cup Soccer **Obv:** Arms within wreath **Rev:** Action scene beneath globe **Edge:** Reeded

Date	Mintage	F	VF	XF	Unc	BU
2004 Proof	Est. 50,000	Value: 60.00				

KM# 339 NUEVO SOL
27.0000 g., 0.9250 Silver 0.8029 oz. ASW, 40 mm. **Series:** 6th Ibero-America **Subject:** Lost city of the Incas **Obv:** National arms in center with ten national arms in outer ring **Obv. Legend:** BANCO CENTRAL DE RESERVA DEL PERÚ **Rev:** Village ruins **Rev. Legend:** MACHU PICCHU . PERÚ **Edge:** Reeded

Date	Mintage	F	VF	XF	Unc	BU
2005 Proof	Est. 17,000	Value: 60.00				

KM# 356 NUEVO SOL
33.6250 g., 0.9250 Silver 0.9999 oz. ASW, 37 mm. **Subject:** Lima Regatta Club, 130th Anniversary

Date	Mintage	F	VF	XF	Unc	BU
2005	Est. 1,000	—	—	—	—	55.00

KM# 357 NUEVO SOL
27.0000 g., 0.9250 Silver 0.8029 oz. ASW, 40 mm. **Subject:** Volleyball **Rev:** Two volleyball players and net

Date	Mintage	F	VF	XF	Unc	BU
2007	Est. 14,000	—	—	—	—	55.00

KM# 358 NUEVO SOL
33.6250 g., 0.9250 Silver 0.9999 oz. ASW, 37 mm. **Subject:** Lima-Huancayo Railway, 100th Anniversary **Rev:** Deisel and Steam trains in valley

Date	Mintage	F	VF	XF	Unc	BU
2008	Est. 1,000	—	—	—	—	55.00

KM# 359 NUEVO SOL
27.0000 g., 0.9250 Silver 0.8029 oz. ASW, 40 mm. **Subject:** Historical coins of Peru

Date	Mintage	F	VF	XF	Unc	BU
2010	—	—	—	—	—	55.00

KM# 340 NUEVO SOL
7.3200 g., Copper-Nickel-Zinc, 25.5 mm. **Series:** Wealth and pride of Peru **Obv:** National arms **Rev:** Tumi de oro **Edge:** Reeded

Date	Mintage	F	VF	XF	Unc	BU
2010Lima	10,000,000	—	—	—	2.50	3.00

KM# 341 NUEVO SOL
7.3200 g., Copper-Nickel-Zinc, 25.5 mm. **Series:** Wealth and pride of Peru **Obv:** National arms **Rev:** Sarcophagus of Karajia

Date	Mintage	F	VF	XF	Unc	BU
2010Lima	10,000,000	—	—	—	2.50	3.00

KM# 342 NUEVO SOL
7.3200 g., Copper-Nickel-Zinc, 25.5 mm. **Obv:** National Arms **Rev:** Estela de Ramondi

Date	Mintage	F	VF	XF	Unc	BU
2010LIMA	10,000,000	—	—	—	2.50	3.00

KM# 346 NUEVO SOL
7.3200 g., Copper-Nickel-Zinc, 25.5 mm. **Rev:** Monastery of Santa Catalina and plaza

Date	Mintage	F	VF	XF	Unc	BU
2011	10,000,000	—	—	—	2.50	3.00

KM# 313 2 NUEVOS SOLES
5.6200 g., Bi-Metallic Nickel-Brass center in Stainless Steel ring, 22.2 mm. **Obv:** National arms within circle **Rev:** Stylized bird in flight to left of value within circle **Edge:** Plain **Note:** LIMA monogram is mint mark.

Date	Mintage	F	VF	XF	Unc	BU
2002LIMA	—	—	—	—	4.50	5.00
2003LIMA	—	—	—	—	4.50	5.00
2004LIMA	—	—	—	—	4.50	5.00
2005LIMA	56,226,509	—	—	—	2.00	2.50
2006LIMA	5,100,000	—	—	—	2.00	2.50
2007LIMA	7,000,000	—	—	—	2.00	2.50
2008LIMA	5,800,000	—	—	—	2.00	2.50
2009LIMA	7,000,000	—	—	—	2.00	2.50

KM# 343 2 NUEVOS SOLES
5.6200 g., Bi-Metallic Brass center in Stainless Steel ring, 22.38 mm. **Obv:** National Arms **Rev:** Hummingbird from the Inca Lines, large value at right

Date	Mintage	F	VF	XF	Unc	BU
2010LIMA	6,235,000	—	—	—	2.50	3.00
2011LIMA	—	—	—	—	2.50	3.00

KM# 316 5 NUEVOS SOLES
6.6700 g., Bi-Metallic Nickel-Brass center in Stainless Steel ring, 24.32 mm. **Obv:** National arms within circle **Rev:** Stylized bird in flight to left of value within circle **Edge:** Reeded **Note:** LIMA monogram is mint mark.

Date	Mintage	F	VF	XF	Unc	BU
2001LIMA	—	—	—	—	6.50	7.00
2002LIMA	—	—	—	—	6.50	7.00
2004LIMA	—	—	—	—	6.50	7.00
2005LIMA	6,000,000	—	—	—	4.00	5.00
2006LIMA	5,500,000	—	—	—	4.00	5.00
2007LIMA	6,400,000	—	—	—	4.00	5.00
2008LIMA	9,900,000	—	—	—	4.00	5.00
2009Lima	10,000,000	—	—	—		

KM# 344 5 NUEVOS SOLES
6.6700 g., Bi-Metallic Brass center in Stainless Steel ring, 24.38 mm. **Obv:** National Arms **Rev:** Frigate bird from the Nasca lines, large value at right

Date	Mintage	F	VF	XF	Unc	BU
2010LIMA	6,000,000	—	—	—	5.00	6.00
2011LIMA	—	—	—	—	5.00	6.00

PHILIPPINES

The Republic of the Philippines, an archipelago in the western Pacific 500 miles (805 km.) from the southeast coast of Asia, has an area of 115,830 sq. mi. (300,000 sq. km.) and a population of *64.9 million. Capital: Manila. The economy of the 7,000-island group is based on agriculture, forestry and fishing. Timber, coconut products, sugar and hemp are exported.

MINT MARKS
BSP - Bangko Sentral Pilipinas
M, MA - Manila

REPUBLIC

REFORM COINAGE
100 Sentimos = 1 Piso

KM# 273 SENTIMO
2.0000 g., Copper Plated Steel, 15.5 mm. **Obv:** Value and date **Rev:** Central bank seal within circle and gear design, 1993 (date Central Bank was established) below **Rev. Legend:** BANGKO SENTRAL NG PILIPINAS - 1993

Date	Mintage	F	VF	XF	Unc	BU
2001	—	—	—	—	0.10	0.15
2002	—	—	—	—	0.10	0.15
2004	—	—	—	—	0.10	0.15
2005	—	—	—	—	0.10	0.15
2006	—	—	—	—	0.10	0.15
2007	—	—	—	—	0.10	0.15
2008	—	—	—	—	0.10	0.15
2009	—	—	—	—	0.10	0.15

KM# 268 5 SENTIMOS
1.9000 g., Copper Plated Steel, 15.5 mm. **Obv:** Numeral value around center hole **Rev:** Hole in center with date, bank and name around border, 1993 (date Central Bank was established) below **Rev. Legend:** BANGKO CENTRAL NG PILIPINAS - 1993 **Edge:** Plain

Date	Mintage	F	VF	XF	Unc	BU
2001	—	—	—	0.10	0.20	0.25
2002	—	—	—	0.10	0.20	0.25
2003	—	—	—	0.10	0.20	0.25
2004	—	—	—	0.10	0.50	1.00
2005	—	—	—	0.10	0.20	0.25
2006	—	—	—	0.10	0.20	0.25
2007	—	—	—	0.10	0.20	0.25
2008	—	—	—	0.10	0.20	0.25
2009	—	—	—	0.10	0.20	0.25
2011	—	—	—	0.10	0.20	0.25

KM# 270.1 10 SENTIMOS
2.5000 g., Copper Plated Steel, 17 mm. **Obv:** Value and date

Rev: Central Bank seal within circle and gear design, 1993 (date Central Bank was established) below **Rev. Legend:** BANGKO SENTRAL NG PILIPINAS - 1993 **Edge:** Reeded

Date	Mintage	F	VF	XF	Unc	BU
2001	—	—	—	0.10	0.30	0.40
2002	—	—	—	0.10	0.30	0.40
2004	—	—	—	0.75	1.50	2.50
2005	—	—	—	0.10	0.30	0.40

KM# 270.2 10 SENTIMOS
2.5000 g., Copper Plated Steel, 17 mm. **Obv:** Value high on coin, different font, date **Rev:** Central Bank seal within circle and gear design **Rev. Legend:** BANGKO SENTRAL NG PILIPINAS - 1993 **Edge:** Reeded

Date	Mintage	F	VF	XF	Unc	BU
2006	—	—	—	0.10	0.30	0.40
2007	—	—	—	0.10	0.30	0.40
2008	—	—	—	0.10	0.30	0.40
2009	—	—	—	0.10	0.30	0.40
2011	—	—	—	0.10	0.30	0.40

KM# 271 25 SENTIMOS
3.8000 g., Brass, 20 mm. **Obv:** Value and date **Rev:** Central Bank seal within circle and gear design, 1993 (date Central Bank was established) below **Rev. Legend:** BANGKO SENTRAL NG PILIPINAS - 1993 **Edge:** Plain

Date	Mintage	F	VF	XF	Unc	BU
2001	—	—	0.10	0.25	0.60	0.80
2002	—	—	0.10	0.25	0.60	0.80
2003	—	—	0.10	0.25	0.60	0.80

KM# 271a 25 SENTIMOS
3.6000 g., Brass Plated Steel, 20 mm. **Obv:** Value and date **Rev:** Central Bank seal within circle and gear design **Rev. Legend:** BANGKO SENTRAL NG PILIPINAS - 1993 **Edge:** Plain

Date	Mintage	F	VF	XF	Unc	BU
2004	—	—	—	0.25	2.00	2.50
2005	—	—	—	0.25	1.00	1.25
2006	—	—	—	0.25	1.00	1.25
2007	—	—	—	0.25	1.00	1.25
2008	—	—	—	0.25	0.50	1.00
2009	—	—	—	0.25	0.50	1.00
2010	—	—	—	0.25	0.50	1.00
2011	—	—	—	0.25	0.50	1.00

KM# 269 PISO
6.1000 g., Copper-Nickel, 24 mm. **Obv:** Head of Jose Rizal right, value and date **Rev:** Bank seal within circle and gear design, 1993 (date Central Bank was established) below **Rev. Legend:** BANGKO SENTRAL NG PILIPINAS - 1993 **Edge:** Reeded

Date	Mintage	F	VF	XF	Unc	BU
2001	—	—	0.25	0.50	1.25	1.75
2002	—	—	0.25	0.50	1.25	1.75
2003 Non Magnetic	—	—	—	—	—	10.00

KM# 269a PISO
5.4000 g., Nickel Plated Steel, 24 mm. **Obv:** Head of Jose Rizal right, value and date **Rev:** Bank seal within circle and gear design **Rev. Legend:** BANGKO SENTRAL NG PILIPINAS - 1993 **Edge:** Reeded

Date	Mintage	F	VF	XF	Unc	BU
2003	—	—	—	1.00	2.00	3.00
2004	—	—	—	0.45	5.00	7.00
2005	—	—	—	0.45	1.10	1.50
2006	—	—	—	0.45	1.10	1.50
2007	—	—	—	0.45	1.10	1.50
2008	—	—	—	0.45	1.10	1.50
2009	—	—	—	0.45	1.10	1.50
2010	—	—	—	0.45	1.10	1.50
2011	—	—	—	0.45	1.10	1.50

KM# 272 5 PISO
7.7000 g., Nickel-Brass, 27 mm. **Obv:** Head of Emilio Aguinaldo right, value and date within scalloped border **Rev:** Central Bank seal within circle and gear design within scalloped border, 1993 (date Central Bank was established) below **Rev. Legend:** BANGKO SENTRAL NG PILIPINAS - 1993 **Edge:** Plain

Date	Mintage	F	VF	XF	Unc	BU
2001BSP	—	—	1.00	2.00	3.00	4.50
2002	—	—	0.35	0.70	1.75	3.00
2003	—	—	0.35	0.70	1.75	3.00
2004	—	—	0.50	1.00	5.00	6.00
2005	—	—	0.35	0.70	1.75	4.00
2006	—	—	0.35	0.70	1.75	3.00
2007	—	—	0.35	0.70	1.75	3.00
2008	—	—	0.35	0.70	1.75	3.00
2009	—	—	0.35	0.70	1.75	3.00
2010	—	—	0.35	0.70	1.75	3.00

KM# 278 10 PISO
8.7000 g., Bi-Metallic Aluminum-Bronze center in Copper-Nickel ring, 26.5 mm. **Obv:** Conjoined heads right within circle **Rev:** Bank seal within circle and gear design, 1993 (date Central Bank was established) below **Rev. Legend:** BANGKO SENTRAL NG PILIPINAS - 1993 **Edge:** Segmented reeding

Date	Mintage	F	VF	XF	Unc	BU
2001	—	—	0.70	1.40	3.50	5.50
2002	—	—	0.60	1.20	2.00	3.00
2003	—	—	0.60	1.20	3.00	4.00
2004	—	—	0.80	2.00	5.00	8.00
2005	—	—	0.75	1.50	3.75	5.00
2006	—	—	0.60	1.20	3.00	4.00
2007	—	—	0.75	1.50	3.75	5.00
2008	—	—	0.75	1.50	3.75	5.00
2009	—	—	0.75	1.50	3.75	5.00
2010	—	—	0.75	1.50	3.75	5.00

MINT SETS

KM#	Date	Mintage	Identification	Issue Price	Mkt Val
MS39	2005 (7)	—	KM#268-273, 278 plus medal	10.00	15.00
MS40	2006 (7)	—	KM#268-273, 278	10.00	12.50

PITCAIRN ISLANDS

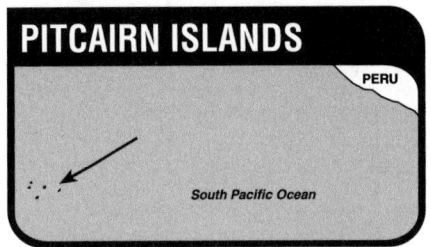

South Pacific Ocean

A small volcanic island, along with the uninhabited islands of Oeno, Henderson, and Ducie, constitute the British Colony of Pitcairn Islands. The main island has an area of about 2 sq. mi. (5 sq. km.) and a population of *68. It is located 1350 miles southeast of Tahiti. The islanders subsist on fishing, garden produce and crops. The sale of postage stamps and carved curios to passing ships brings cash income.

New Zealand currency has been used since July 10, 1967.

BRITISH COLONY
REGULAR COINAGE

KM# 54 5 CENTS
3.4000 g., Copper Plated Bronze, 19 mm. **Ruler:** Elizabeth II **Obv:** Head right **Rev:** Anchor from the H.M.A.V. Bounty

Date	Mintage	F	VF	XF	Unc	BU
2009	20,000	—	—	—	—	2.00
2010	20,000	—	—	—	—	2.00

KM# 55 10 CENTS
4.6000 g., Copper Plated Bronze, 22 mm. **Ruler:** Elizabeth II **Obv:** Head right **Rev:** Bell from H.M.A.V. Bounty **Edge:** Reeded

Date	Mintage	F	VF	XF	Unc	BU
2009	20,000	—	—	—	—	3.00
2010	20,000	—	—	—	—	3.00

KM# 56 20 CENTS
6.5000 g., Nickel Plated Bronze, 25 mm. **Ruler:** Elizabeth II **Obv:** Head right **Rev:** Bible from H.M.A.V. Bounty

Date	Mintage	F	VF	XF	Unc	BU
2009	20,000	—	—	—	—	5.00
2010	20,000	—	—	—	—	5.00

KM# 57 50 CENTS
8.0000 g., Copper-Nickel **Ruler:** Elizabeth II **Obv:** Head right **Rev:** Pitcairn Longboat

Date	Mintage	F	VF	XF	Unc	BU
2009	—	—	—	—	—	8.00
2010	—	—	—	—	—	8.00

KM# 14 DOLLAR
Copper-Nickel, 38.8 mm. **Ruler:** Elizabeth II **Obv:** Bust facing right **Rev:** Queen Mum, Elizabeth II and Margaret facing **Rev. Legend:** 80th Birthday of H.M. Queen Elizabeth II

Date	Mintage	F	VF	XF	Unc	BU
2006	—	—	—	—	10.00	12.00

KM# 58 DOLLAR
16.3000 g., Aluminum-Brass, 32 mm. **Ruler:** Elizabeth II **Obv:** Head right **Rev:** Cannon from H.A.M.V. Bounty **Edge:** Reeded

Date	Mintage	F	VF	XF	Unc	BU
2009	20,000	—	—	—	—	12.00
2010	20,000	—	—	—	—	12.00

KM# 45 2 DOLLARS
31.1050 g., 0.9990 Silver 0.9990 oz. ASW, 40.7 mm. **Ruler:** Elizabeth II **Subject:** Year of the Rat **Rev:** Multicolor rat seated right

Date	Mintage	F	VF	XF	Unc	BU
2008 Prooflike	30,000	—	—	—	—	65.00

KM# 46 2 DOLLARS
31.1050 g., 0.9990 Silver 0.9990 oz. ASW, 40.7 mm. **Ruler:** Elizabeth II **Rev:** Multicolor HMAV Bounty under full sail right

Date	Mintage	F	VF	XF	Unc	BU
2008 Prooflike	5,000	—	—	—	—	75.00

KM# 47 2 DOLLARS
31.1050 g., 0.9990 Silver Partially gilt 0.9990 oz. ASW, 40.7 mm. **Ruler:** Elizabeth II **Rev:** HMAV Bounty under full sail right

Date	Mintage	F	VF	XF	Unc	BU
2008 Proof	1,500	Value: 85.00				

KM# 59 2 DOLLARS
19.5000 g., Aluminum-Brass, 35 mm. **Ruler:** Elizabeth II **Obv:** Head right **Rev:** Helm (wheel) from H.M.A.V. Bounty **Edge:** Segmented reeding

Date	Mintage	F	VF	XF	Unc	BU
2009	20,000	—	—	—	—	15.00

KM# 51 2 DOLLARS
31.1050 g., 0.9990 Silver partially gilt 0.9990 oz. ASW, 40.7 mm. **Ruler:** Elizabeth II **Rev:** Captain William Bligh partially gilt

Date	Mintage	F	VF	XF	Unc	BU
2009 Proof	1,500	Value: 100				

KM# 67 2 DOLLARS
31.1050 g., Silver partially gilt, 40.7 mm. **Ruler:** Elizabeth II **Rev:** Ox striding right, gilt

Date	Mintage	F	VF	XF	Unc	BU
2009 Proof	15,000	Value: 80.00				

KM# 68 2 DOLLARS
31.1050 g., 0.9990 Silver 0.9990 oz. ASW, 40.7 mm. **Ruler:** Elizabeth II **Rev:** Ox striding right, color

Date	Mintage	F	VF	XF	Unc	BU
2009 Proof	15,000	Value: 80.00				

KM# 60 2 DOLLARS
Brass, 36 mm. **Ruler:** Elizabeth II **Rev:** H.M.A.V. Bounty at sail **Edge:** Segmented reeding

Date	Mintage	F	VF	XF	Unc	BU
2010	20,000	—	—	—	—	15.00

KM# 61 2 DOLLARS
15.5000 g., 0.9250 Silver 0.4609 oz. ASW, 35 mm. **Ruler:** Elizabeth II **Subject:** Deep sea fish **Rev:** Black sea devil (Melanocetus Johnsonii) in color

Date	Mintage	F	VF	XF	Unc	BU
2010 Proof	1,000	Value: 75.00				

KM# 62 2 DOLLARS
15.5500 g., 0.9250 Silver 0.4624 oz. ASW, 35 mm. **Ruler:** Elizabeth II **Subject:** Deep sea fish **Rev:** White spotted jellyfish in color

Date	Mintage	F	VF	XF	Unc	BU
2010 Proof	—	Value: 75.00				

KM# 63 2 DOLLARS
15.5500 g., 0.9250 Silver 0.4624 oz. ASW, 35 mm. **Ruler:** Elizabeth II **Subject:** Deep sea fish **Rev:** Laternfish (Mychtophios) in color

Date	Mintage	F	VF	XF	Unc	BU
2010 Proof	1,000	Value: 75.00				

KM# 65 2 DOLLARS
31.1050 g., 0.9990 Silver partially gilt 0.9990 oz. ASW, 40.7 mm. **Ruler:** Elizabeth II **Rev:** H.M.A.V. Bounty at sail, gilt

Date	Mintage	F	VF	XF	Unc	BU
2010 Proof	3,000	Value: 125				

KM# 66 2 DOLLARS
31.1050 g., 0.9990 Silver partially gilt 0.9990 oz. ASW, 40.7 mm. **Ruler:** Elizabeth II **Rev:** Fletcher Christian facing, partially gilt

Date	Mintage	F	VF	XF	Unc	BU
2010 Proof	3,000	Value: 125				

KM# 64 2 DOLLARS
31.1050 g., 0.9990 Silver 0.9990 oz. ASW, 40.7 mm. **Ruler:** Elizabeth II **Subject:** Alice in Wonderland **Rev:** March Hare within backward clock face

Date	Mintage	F	VF	XF	Unc	BU
2011 Proof	15,000	Value: 85.00				

KM# 69 2 DOLLARS
31.1050 g., 0.9990 Silver 0.9990 oz. ASW, 40.7 mm. **Ruler:** Elizabeth II **Rev:** Rabbit in snow, multicolor

Date	Mintage	F	VF	XF	Unc	BU
2011 Proof	15,000	Value: 125				

KM# 12 5 DOLLARS
31.1000 g., 0.9990 Silver with Mother-of-Pearl inset 0.9988 oz. ASW, 40 mm. **Ruler:** Elizabeth II **Series:** Save the Whales **Obv:** Crowned bust right **Obv. Legend:** ELIZABETH II • PITCAIRN ISLANDS **Rev:** Humpback Whale and date on mother-of-pearl inset **Edge:** Plain

Date	Mintage	F	VF	XF	Unc	BU
2002 Proof	2,000	Value: 85.00				

KM# 50   5 DOLLARS
1.2700 g., 0.9999 Gold 0.0408 oz. AGW, 13.92 mm.   **Ruler:**
Elizabeth II **Obv:** Crowned bust right **Obv. Legend:** Elizabeth II
Pitcairn Islands **Rev:** Bounty Bible and ship

Date	Mintage	F	VF	XF	Unc	BU
2005 Proof	—	Value: 75.00				

KM# 48   10 DOLLARS
1.2440 g., 0.9999 Gold 0.0400 oz. AGW, 14 mm.   **Ruler:**
Elizabeth II **Rev:** HMAV Bounty under full sail right

Date	Mintage	F	VF	XF	Unc	BU
2008 Proof	10,000	Value: 165				

KM# 49   25 DOLLARS
7.7700 g., 0.9990 Gold 0.2496 oz. AGW, 22 mm.   **Ruler:**
Elizabeth II **Rev:** HMAV Bounty under full sail right

Date	Mintage	F	VF	XF	Unc	BU
2008 Proof	1,500	Value: 775				

MINT SETS

KM#	Date	Mintage	Identification	Issue Price	Mkt Val
MS1	2009 (6)	20,000	KM#54; 55; 56; 57; 58; 59	—	45.00
MS2	2010 (6)	20,000	KM#54; 55; 56; 57; 58; 60	—	45.00

POLAND

The Republic of Poland, located in central Europe, has an
area of 120,725 sq. mi. (312,680 sq. km.) and a population of
*38.2 million. Capital: Warszawa (Warsaw). The economy is
essentially agricultural, but industrial activity provides the products for foreign trade. Machinery, coal, coke, iron, steel and transport equipment are exported.

MINT MARKS
MV, MW, MW-monogram - Warsaw Mint, 1965-
CHI - Valcambi, Switzerland
Other letters appearing with date denote the Mintmaster at
the time the coin was struck.

REPUBLIC
Democratic

REFORM COINAGE
100 Old Zlotych = 1 Grosz; 10,000 Old Zlotych = 1 Zloty

Y# 276   GROSZ
1.6400 g., Brass, 15.5 mm. **Obv:** National arms **Obv. Legend:**
RZECZPOSPOLITA POLSKA **Rev:** Drooping oak leaf over value
Edge: Reeded

Date	Mintage	F	VF	XF	Unc	BU
2001MW	210,000,020	—	—	—	0.10	0.20
2002MW	240,000,000	—	—	—	0.10	0.20
2003MW	250,000,000	—	—	—	0.10	0.20
2004MW	300,000,000	—	—	—	0.10	0.20
2005MW	375,000,000	—	—	—	0.10	0.20
2006MW	184,000,000	—	—	—	0.10	0.20
2007MW	330,000,000	—	—	—	0.10	0.20
2008MW	—	—	—	—	0.10	0.20
2009MW	—	—	—	—	0.10	0.20
2010MW	—	—	—	—	0.10	0.20
2011MW	—	—	—	—	0.10	0.20
2012MW	—	—	—	—	0.10	0.20

Y# 277   2 GROSZE
2.1300 g., Brass, 17.5 mm. **Obv:** National arms **Obv. Legend:**
RZECZPOSPOLITA POLSKA **Rev:** Drooping oak leaves above
value **Edge:** Plain

Date	Mintage	F	VF	XF	Unc	BU
2001MW	86,100,000	—	—	—	0.15	0.25
2002MW	83,910,000	—	—	—	0.15	0.25
2003MW	80,000,000	—	—	—	0.15	0.25

Date	Mintage	F	VF	XF	Unc	BU
2004MW	100,000,000	—	—	—	0.15	0.25
2005MW	163,003,250	—	—	—	0.15	0.25
2006MW	105,000,000	—	—	—	0.15	0.25
2007MW	160,000,000	—	—	—	0.15	0.25
2008MW	—	—	—	—	0.15	0.25
2009MW	—	—	—	—	0.15	0.25
2010MW	—	—	—	—	0.15	0.25
2011MW	—	—	—	—	0.15	0.25

Y# 278   5 GROSZY
2.5900 g., Brass, 19.5 mm. **Obv:** National arms **Obv. Legend:**
RZECZPOSPOLITA POLSKA **Rev:** Value at upper left of oak
leaves **Edge:** Segmented reeding

Date	Mintage	F	VF	XF	Unc	BU
2001MW	67,368,000	—	—	—	0.25	0.45
2002MW	67,200,000	—	—	—	0.25	0.45
2003MW	48,000,000	—	—	—	0.25	0.45
2004MW	62,500,000	—	—	—	0.25	0.45
2005MW	113,000,000	—	—	—	0.25	0.45
2006MW	54,000,000	—	—	—	0.25	0.45
2007MW	116,000,000	—	—	—	0.25	0.45
2008MW	—	—	—	—	0.25	0.45
2009MW	—	—	—	—	0.25	0.45
2010MW	—	—	—	—	0.25	0.45
2011MW	—	—	—	—	0.25	0.45

Y# 279   10 GROSZY
2.5500 g., Copper-Nickel, 16.5 mm.   **Obv:** National arms **Obv.
Legend:** RZECZPOSPOLITA POLSKA **Rev:** Value within wreath

Date	Mintage	F	VF	XF	Unc	BU
2001MW	62,820,000	—	—	—	0.40	0.60
2002MW	10,500,000	—	—	—	0.40	0.60
2003MW	31,500,000	—	—	—	0.40	0.60
2004MW	70,500,000	—	—	—	0.40	0.60
2005MW	94,000,000	—	—	—	0.40	0.60
2006MW	40,000,000	—	—	—	0.40	0.60
2007MW	100,000,000	—	—	—	0.40	0.60
2008MW	—	—	—	—	0.40	0.60
2009MW	—	—	—	—	0.40	0.60
2010MW	—	—	—	—	0.40	0.60
2011MW	—	—	—	—	0.40	0.60
2012MW	—	—	—	—	0.40	0.60

Y# 280   20 GROSZY
3.2200 g., Copper-Nickel, 18.5 mm.   **Obv:** National arms **Obv.
Legend:** RZECZPOSPOLITA POLSKA **Rev:** Value within artistic
design **Edge:** Reeded

Date	Mintage	F	VF	XF	Unc	BU
2001MW	41,980,001	—	—	—	0.65	0.85
2002MW	10,500,000	—	—	—	0.65	0.85
2003MW	20,400,000	—	—	—	0.65	0.85
2004MW	40,000,025	—	—	—	0.65	0.85
2005MW	37,000,000	—	—	—	0.65	0.85
2006MW	35,000,000	—	—	—	0.65	0.85
2007MW	68,000,000	—	—	—	0.65	0.85
2008MW	—	—	—	—	0.65	0.85
2009MW	—	—	—	—	0.65	0.85
2010MW	—	—	—	—	0.65	0.85
2011MW	—	—	—	—	0.65	0.85

Y# 281   50 GROSZY
3.9400 g., Copper-Nickel, 20.5 mm.   **Obv:** National arms **Obv.
Legend:** RZECZPOSPOLITA POLSKA **Rev:** Value to right of
sprig **Edge:** Reeded

Date	Mintage	F	VF	XF	Unc	BU
2008MW	—	—	—	—	1.00	1.25
2009MW	—	—	—	—	1.00	1.25
2010MW	—	—	—	—	1.00	1.25
2011MW	—	—	—	—	1.00	1.25

Y# 282   ZLOTY
5.0300 g., Copper-Nickel, 23 mm.   **Obv:** National arms **Obv.
Legend:** RZECZPOSPOLITA POLSKA **Rev:** Value within wreath
Edge: Segmented reeding

Date	Mintage	F	VF	XF	Unc	BU
2008MW	—	—	—	—	1.75	2.00
2009MW	—	—	—	—	1.75	2.00
2010MW	—	—	—	—	1.75	2.00
2011MW	—	—	—	—	1.75	2.00

Y# 408   2 ZLOTE
8.1500 g., Brass, 27 mm.   **Subject:** Wieliczka Salt Mine **Obv:**
Crowned eagle with wings open **Rev:** Ancient salt miners

Date	Mintage	F	VF	XF	Unc	BU
2001	500,000	—	—	3.50	7.00	12.00

Y# 410   2 ZLOTE
8.1500 g., Brass, 27 mm.   **Subject:** Amber Route **Obv:** Crowned
eagle with wings open **Rev:** Ancient Roman coin and map with
route marked in stars

Date	Mintage	F	VF	XF	Unc	BU
2001	500,000	—	—	3.50	7.00	12.00

Y# 412   2 ZLOTE
8.1500 g., Brass, 27 mm.   **Subject:** 15 Years of the Constitutional
Court **Obv:** Crowned eagle with wings open **Rev:** Crowned eagle
head and scale **Edge:** * NBP * eight times

Date	Mintage	F	VF	XF	Unc	BU
2001MW	500,000	—	—	—	3.00	5.00

Y# 414   2 ZLOTE
8.1500 g., Brass, 27 mm.   **Obv:** Crowned eagle with wings open
Rev: Butterfly **Edge:** * NBP * eight times

Date	Mintage	F	VF	XF	Unc	BU
2001MW	600,000	—	—	4.00	8.00	15.00

Y# 418   2 ZLOTE
8.1500 g., Brass, 27 mm.   **Subject:** Cardinal Stefan Wyszynski
Obv: Crowned eagle with wings open **Rev:** Bust left wearing
mitre **Edge:** "NBP" eight times

Date	Mintage	F	VF	XF	Unc	BU
2001MW	1,200,000	—	—	—	3.00	5.00

Y# 421   2 ZLOTE
8.1500 g., Brass, 27 mm.   **Subject:** Michal Siedlecki **Obv:**
Crowned eagle with wings open **Rev:** Bust left and art work **Edge:**
NBP eight times

Date	Mintage	F	VF	XF	Unc	BU
2001MW	600,000	—	—	—	3.00	5.00

Y# 422   2 ZLOTE
8.1500 g., Brass, 27 mm.   **Subject:** Koledicy **Obv:** Crowned
eagle with wings open **Rev:** Christmas celebration scene

Date	Mintage	F	VF	XF	Unc	BU
2001MW	600,000	—	—	—	3.00	5.00

Y# 423   2 ZLOTE
8.1500 g., Brass, 27 mm.   **Subject:** Jan III Sobieski **Obv:**
Crowned eagle with wings open **Rev:** Bust facing **Edge
Lettering:** * NBP * eight times

Date	Mintage	F	VF	XF	Unc	BU
2001MW	500,000	—	—	3.50	7.00	12.00

Y# 426   2 ZLOTE
8.1500 g., Brass, 27 mm.   **Subject:** Henryk Wieniawski **Obv:**
Crowned eagle with wings open **Rev:** Bust left and violin **Edge
Lettering:** * NBP * eight times

Date	Mintage	F	VF	XF	Unc	BU
2001MW	600,000	—	—	—	3.00	5.00

Y# 427   2 ZLOTE
8.1500 g., Brass, 27 mm.   **Obv:** Crowned eagle with wings open
Rev: European Pond Turtles **Edge Lettering:** * NBP * eight times

Date	Mintage	F	VF	XF	Unc	BU
2002MW	750,000	—	—	3.50	7.00	12.00

Y# 431   2 ZLOTE
8.1500 g., Brass, 27 mm.   **Subject:** Bronislaw Malinowski **Obv:**
Crowned eagle with wings open **Rev:** Bust facing and Trobriand
Islanders **Edge Lettering:** * NBP * eight times

Date	Mintage	F	VF	XF	Unc	BU
2002MW	680,000	—	—	—	3.50	5.50

Y# 433   2 ZLOTE
8.1500 g., Brass, 27 mm.   **Subject:** World Cup Soccer **Obv:**
National arms **Rev:** Soccer players **Edge Lettering:** * NBP * eight
times

Date	Mintage	F	VF	XF	Unc	BU
2002MW	1,000,000	—	—	—	3.00	5.00

Y# 439   2 ZLOTE
8.1000 g., Brass, 26.8 mm.   **Subject:** August II (1697-1706,
1709-1733) **Obv:** National arms **Rev:** Head facing **Edge
Lettering:** * NBP * eight times

Date	Mintage	F	VF	XF	Unc	BU
2002MW	620,000	—	—	—	4.00	7.00

Y# 440   2 ZLOTE
8.1500 g., Brass, 27 mm.   **Subject:** Gen. Wladyslaw Anders
Obv: Crowned eagle with wings open **Rev:** Uniformed bust facing
and cross **Edge Lettering:** * NBP * eight times

Date	Mintage	F	VF	XF	Unc	BU
2002MW	680,000	—	—	—	3.00	5.00

Y# 443   2 ZLOTE
8.1500 g., Brass, 27 mm.   **Subject:** Malbork Castle **Obv:**
Crowned eagle with wings open **Rev:** Castle **Edge Lettering:** *
NBP * eight times

Date	Mintage	F	VF	XF	Unc	BU
2002MW	680,000	—	—	—	3.00	5.00

Y# 444   2 ZLOTE
8.1500 g., Brass, 27 mm.   **Subject:** Jan Matejko **Obv:**
Denomination, crowned eagle and artist's palette **Rev:** Jester
behind portrait **Edge Lettering:** * NBP * eight times

Date	Mintage	F	VF	XF	Unc	BU
2002MW	700,000	—	—	—	3.00	5.00

Y# 445   2 ZLOTE
8.1500 g., Brass, 27 mm.   **Subject:** Eels **Obv:** Crowned eagle
with wings open **Rev:** Two European eels **Edge Lettering:** * NBP
* eight times

Date	Mintage	F	VF	XF	Unc	BU
2003MW	450,000	—	—	6.00	12.00	20.00

Y# 446   2 ZLOTE
7.7500 g., Brass, 27 mm.   **Subject:** Children **Obv:** Children and
square design above crowned eagle, date and value **Rev:**
Children on square design **Edge Lettering:** * NBP * eight times
Note: Center hole.

Date	Mintage	F	VF	XF	Unc	BU
2003MW	2,500,000	—	—	—	4.50	6.50

Y# 447   2 ZLOTE
8.1500 g., Brass, 27 mm.   **Subject:** City of Poznan (Posen) **Obv:**
Crowned eagle with wings open **Rev:** Clock face and tower
flanked by goat heads **Edge Lettering:** * NBP * eight times

Date	Mintage	F	VF	XF	Unc	BU
2003MW	600,000	—	—	—	5.00	8.00

Y# 451   2 ZLOTE
8.1500 g., Brass, 27 mm. **Subject:** Easter Monday Festival **Obv:** Crowned eagle with wings open **Rev:** Festival scene **Edge Lettering:** * NBP * eight times

Date	Mintage	F	VF	XF	Unc	BU
2003MW	600,000	—	—	—	4.00	7.00

Y# 477   2 ZLOTE
8.1500 g., Brass, 27 mm. **Obv:** Crowned eagle with wings open and artist's palette **Rev:** Self portrait of Jacek Malczewski **Edge Lettering:** * NBP * eight times

Date	Mintage	F	VF	XF	Unc	BU
2003MW	600,000	—	—	—	3.50	5.50

Y# 486   2 ZLOTE
8.1500 g., Brass, 27 mm. **Subject:** Lubuskie District **Obv:** Crowned eagle with wings open on map **Rev:** Shield with stag left **Edge Lettering:** * NBP * eight times

Date	Mintage	F	VF	XF	Unc	BU
2004MW	820,000	—	—	—	3.00	5.00

Y# 455   2 ZLOTE
8.1500 g., Brass, 27 mm. **Subject:** Petroleum and Gas Industry 150th Anniversary **Obv:** Crowned eagle with wings open **Rev:** Portrait and refinery **Edge Lettering:** * NBP * eight times

Date	Mintage	F	VF	XF	Unc	BU
2003MW	600,000	—	—	—	3.50	5.50

Y# 479   2 ZLOTE
8.1500 g., Brass, 27 mm. **Subject:** 80th Anniversary of the Modern Zloty Currency **Obv:** Crowned eagle with wings open above value **Rev:** Bust left **Edge Lettering:** * NBP * eight times

Date	Mintage	F	VF	XF	Unc	BU
2004MW	800,000	—	—	—	3.00	5.00

Y# 487   2 ZLOTE
8.1500 g., Brass, 27 mm. **Subject:** Lodzkie District **Obv:** Crowned eagle with wings open on map **Rev:** Shield with two creatures above an eagle **Edge Lettering:** * NBP * eight times

Date	Mintage	F	VF	XF	Unc	BU
2004MW	920,000	—	—	—	3.00	5.00

Y# 456   2 ZLOTE
8.1500 g., Brass, 27 mm. **Subject:** General B. S. Maczek **Obv:** Crowned eagle with wings open **Rev:** Military uniformed portrait **Edge Lettering:** * NBP * eight times

Date	Mintage	F	VF	XF	Unc	BU
2003MW	700,000	—	—	—	3.00	5.00

Y# 481   2 ZLOTE
8.1500 g., Brass, 27 mm. **Subject:** Poland Joining the European Union **Obv:** Crowned eagle with wings open above value **Rev:** Map and stars **Edge Lettering:** * NBP * eight times

Date	Mintage	F	VF	XF	Unc	BU
2004MW	1,000,000	—	—	—	3.00	5.00

Y# 488   2 ZLOTE
8.1500 g., Brass, 27 mm. **Subject:** Malopolskie District **Obv:** Crowned eagle with wings open on map **Rev:** Shield with crowned eagle **Edge Lettering:** * NBP * eight times

Date	Mintage	F	VF	XF	Unc	BU
2004MW	920,000	—	—	—	3.00	5.00

Y# 465   2 ZLOTE
8.1500 g., Aluminum-Bronze, 27 mm. **Subject:** Pope John Paul II **Obv:** Small national arms at lower right with cross in background **Obv. Legend:** RZECZPOSPOLITA POLSKA **Rev:** Pope in prayer at left, cross in background **Edge Lettering:** * NBP * eight times

Date	Mintage	F	VF	XF	Unc	BU
2003MW	2,000,000	—	—	—	3.00	5.00

Y# 484   2 ZLOTE
8.1500 g., Brass, 27 mm. **Subject:** Dolnoslaskie (Lower Silesian) District **Obv:** Crowned eagle with wings open on map **Rev:** Silesian eagle on shield **Edge Lettering:** * NBP * eight times

Date	Mintage	F	VF	XF	Unc	BU
2004MW	700,000	—	—	—	4.00	6.00

Y# 489   2 ZLOTE
8.1500 g., Brass, 27 mm. **Subject:** Mazowieckie District **Obv:** Crowned eagle with wings open on map **Rev:** Eagle on shield **Edge Lettering:** * NBP * eight times

Date	Mintage	F	VF	XF	Unc	BU
2004MW	920,000	—	—	—	3.00	5.00

Y# 473   2 ZLOTE
8.1500 g., Brass, 27 mm. **Obv:** Crowned eagle with wings open **Rev:** Stanislaus Leszcywski **Edge Lettering:** * NBP * eight times

Date	Mintage	F	VF	XF	Unc	BU
2003MW	600,000	—	—	—	3.50	5.50

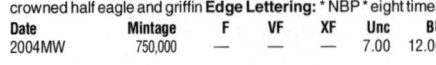

Y# 485   2 ZLOTE
8.1500 g., Brass, 27 mm. **Subject:** Kujawsko-Pomorskie District **Obv:** Crowned eagle with wings open on map **Rev:** Shield with crowned half eagle and griffin **Edge Lettering:** * NBP * eight times

Date	Mintage	F	VF	XF	Unc	BU
2004MW	750,000	—	—	—	7.00	12.00

Y# 490   2 ZLOTE
8.1500 g., Brass, 27 mm. **Subject:** Podkarpackie District **Obv:** Crowned eagle with wings open on map **Rev:** Shield with iron cross above griffin and lion **Edge Lettering:** * NBP * eight times

Date	Mintage	F	VF	XF	Unc	BU
2004MW	920,000	—	—	—	3.00	5.00

Y# 491   2 ZLOTE
8.1500 g., Brass, 27 mm.   **Subject:** Podlaskie District **Obv:** Crowned eagle with wings open on map **Rev:** Shield with Polish eagle above Lithuanian knight **Edge Lettering:** * NBP * eight times

Date	Mintage	F	VF	XF	Unc	BU
2004MW	900,000	—	—	—	3.00	5.00

Y# 501   2 ZLOTE
8.1500 g., Brass, 27 mm.   **Subject:** Polish Police 85th Anniversary **Obv:** Crowned eagle with wings open **Rev:** Police badge **Edge Lettering:** * NBP * eight times

Date	Mintage	F	VF	XF	Unc	BU
2004MW	760,000	—	—	—	3.00	5.00

Y# 516   2 ZLOTE
8.1500 g., Brass, 27 mm.   **Subject:** Olympics **Obv:** Crowned eagle with wings open **Rev:** Ancient runners **Edge Lettering:** * NBP * eight times

Date	Mintage	F	VF	XF	Unc	BU
2004MW	1,000,000	—	—	—	3.00	5.00

Y# 492   2 ZLOTE
8.1500 g., Brass, 27 mm.   **Subject:** Pomorskie District **Obv:** Crowned eagle with wings open on map **Rev:** Griffin on shield **Edge Lettering:** * NBP * eight times

Date	Mintage	F	VF	XF	Unc	BU
2004MW	900,000	—	—	—	3.00	5.00

Y# 503   2 ZLOTE
8.1500 g., Brass, 27 mm.   **Subject:** Polish Senate **Obv:** Crowned eagle with wings open **Rev:** Senate eagle and speaker's staff **Edge Lettering:** * NBP * eight times

Date	Mintage	F	VF	XF	Unc	BU
2004MW	760,000	—	—	—	3.00	5.00

Y# 607   2 ZLOTE
8.1500 g., Brass, 27 mm.   **Obv:** National arms on outlined map **Obv. Legend:** RZECZPOSPOLITA POLSKA **Rev:** Region arms **Rev. Legend:** WOJEWODZTWO - OPOLSKIE **Edge Lettering:** * NBP * eight times

Date	Mintage	F	VF	XF	Unc	BU
2004MW	900,000	—	—	—	3.00	5.00

Y# 493   2 ZLOTE
8.1500 g., Brass, 27 mm.   **Subject:** Slaskie (Silesia) District **Obv:** Crowned eagle with wings open on map **Rev:** Eagle on shield **Edge Lettering:** * NBP * eight times

Date	Mintage	F	VF	XF	Unc	BU
2004MW	960,000	—	—	—	3.00	5.00

Y# 505   2 ZLOTE
8.1500 g., Brass, 27 mm.   **Obv:** Crowned eagle with wings open **Rev:** Aleksander Czekanowski (1833-1876) **Edge Lettering:** * NBP * eight times

Date	Mintage	F	VF	XF	Unc	BU
2004MW	700,000	—	—	—	3.00	5.00

Y# 464   2 ZLOTE
8.1500 g., Brass, 27 mm.   **Obv:** Crowned eagle with wings open **Rev:** Harbor Porpoises **Edge Lettering:** * NBP * eight times

Date	Mintage	F	VF	XF	Unc	BU
2004MW	800,000	—	—	3.50	7.00	12.00

Y# 496   2 ZLOTE
8.1500 g., Brass, 27 mm.   **Subject:** Warsaw Uprising 60th Anniversary **Obv:** Crowned eagle with wings open **Rev:** Resistance symbol on brick wall **Edge Lettering:** * NBP * eight times

Date	Mintage	F	VF	XF	Unc	BU
2004MW	900,000	—	—	—	3.00	5.00

Y# 507   2 ZLOTE
8.1500 g., Brass, 27 mm.   **Obv:** National arms **Obv. Legend:** RZECZPOSPOLITA POLSKA **Rev:** Harvest fest couple in folk costume at left, large group in background at right **Rev. Legend:** DOZYNKI **Edge Lettering:** * NBP * eight times

Date	Mintage	F	VF	XF	Unc	BU
2004MW	850,000	—	—	—	3.00	5.00

Y# 512   2 ZLOTE
8.1500 g., Brass, 27 mm.   **Obv:** Crowned eagle with wings open and artist's palette **Rev:** Stanislaw Wyspianski (1869-1907) **Edge Lettering:** * NBP * eight times

Date	Mintage	F	VF	XF	Unc	BU
2004MW	900,000	—	—	—	3.00	5.00

Y# 499   2 ZLOTE
8.1500 g., Brass, 27 mm.   **Obv:** Crowned eagle with wings open **Rev:** Gen. Stanislaw F. Sosabowski **Edge Lettering:** * NBP * eight times

Date	Mintage	F	VF	XF	Unc	BU
2004MW	850,000	—	—	—	3.00	5.00

Y# 509   2 ZLOTE
8.1500 g., Brass, 27 mm.   **Subject:** Warsaw Fine Arts Academy Centennial **Obv:** Crowned eagle with wings open **Rev:** Painter's hands **Edge Lettering:** * NBP * eight times

Date	Mintage	F	VF	XF	Unc	BU
2004MW	850,000	—	—	—	3.00	5.00

Y# 514   2 ZLOTE
8.1500 g., Brass, 27 mm.   **Obv:** National arms on outlined map **Rev:** Wojewodztwo-Lubelskie arms with stag on shield **Edge Lettering:** * NBP * eight times

Date	Mintage	F	VF	XF	Unc	BU
2004MW	820,000	—	—	—	—	7.50

Y# 283 2 ZLOTE

5.2100 g., Bi-Metallic Copper-Nickel center in Aluminum-Bronze ring, 21.5 mm. **Obv:** National arms within circle **Obv. Legend:** RZECZPOSPOLITA POLSKA **Rev:** Value flanked by oak leaves **Edge:** Plain

Date	Mintage	F	VF	XF	Unc	BU
2005MW	5,000,000	—	—	—	4.00	4.50
2006MW	5,000,000	—	—	—	4.00	4.50
2007MW	20,000,000	—	—	—	4.00	4.50
2008MW	—	—	—	—	4.00	4.50
2009MW	—	—	—	—	4.00	4.50
2010MW	—	—	—	—	4.00	4.50
2011MW	—	—	—	—	4.00	4.50

Y# 520 2 ZLOTE

8.1500 g., Brass, 27 mm. **Obv:** National arms **Rev:** Owl perched on nest with owlets **Rev. Legend:** PUCHACZ - Bubo-bubo **Edge Lettering:** * NBP * eight times

Date	Mintage	F	VF	XF	Unc	BU
2005MW	990,000	—	—	—	4.00	7.00

Y# 521 2 ZLOTE

8.1500 g., Brass, 27 mm. **Obv:** Crowned eagle with wings open **Rev:** Ship within circle **Edge Lettering:** * NBP * eight times

Date	Mintage	F	VF	XF	Unc	BU
2005MW	920,000	—	—	—	3.50	5.50

Y# 522 2 ZLOTE

8.1500 g., Brass, 26.8 mm. **Subject:** Japan's Aichi Expo **Obv:** Crowned eagle with wings open **Rev:** Two cranes flying over Mt. Fuji with rising sun background **Edge Lettering:** * NBP * eight times

Date	Mintage	F	VF	XF	Unc	BU
2005MW	1,000,000	—	—	—	3.50	5.50

Y# 524 2 ZLOTE

8.1500 g., Brass, 27 mm. **Subject:** Obrony Jasnej Gory **Obv:** Crowned eagle with wings open **Rev:** Half length figure left and bombarded city scene **Edge Lettering:** * NBP * eight times

Date	Mintage	F	VF	XF	Unc	BU
2005MW	1,000,000	—	—	—	4.00	6.00

Y# 525 2 ZLOTE

8.1500 g., Brass, 27 mm. **Subject:** Pope John-Paul II **Obv:** National arms **Obv. Legend:** RZECZPOSPOLITA POLSKA **Rev:** Bust right at left, outline of St. Peter's Baslica at center right **Edge Lettering:** * NBP * eight times

Date	Mintage	F	VF	XF	Unc	BU
2005MW	4,000,000	—	—	—	4.00	6.00

Y# 527 2 ZLOTE

8.1500 g., Brass, 27 mm. **Obv:** Crowned eagle with wings open **Rev:** Bust 1/4 left with horse head and goose at left **Edge Lettering:** * NBP * eight times

Date	Mintage	F	VF	XF	Unc	BU
2005MW	850,000	—	—	—	3.00	5.00

Y# 528 2 ZLOTE

8.1500 g., Brass, 27 mm. **Obv:** Crowned eagle above wall **Rev:** Kolobrzeg Lighthouse **Edge Lettering:** * NBP * eight times

Date	Mintage	F	VF	XF	Unc	BU
2005MW	1,100,000	—	—	—	3.00	5.00

Y# 529 2 ZLOTE

8.1500 g., Brass, 27 mm. **Obv:** National arms above gateway **Rev:** Wioclawek Cathedral **Edge Lettering:** * NBP * eight times

Date	Mintage	F	VF	XF	Unc	BU
2005MW	1,100,000	—	—	—	3.00	5.00

Y# 530 2 ZLOTE

8.1500 g., Brass, 27 mm. **Obv:** National arms **Rev:** Bust of King Stanislaus Poniatowski right **Edge Lettering:** * NBP * eight times

Date	Mintage	F	VF	XF	Unc	BU
2005MW	990,000	—	—	—	3.00	5.00

Y# 541 2 ZLOTE

8.1500 g., Brass, 27 mm. **Obv:** Eagle, value, palette and paint

brushes **Rev:** Painter Tadeusz Makowski **Edge Lettering:** * NBP * eight times

Date	Mintage	F	VF	XF	Unc	BU
2005MW	900,000	—	—	—	3.00	5.00

Y# 558 2 ZLOTE

8.1500 g., Brass, 27 mm. **Subject:** 60th Anniversary of WWII **Obv:** National arms **Edge Lettering:** * NBP * eight times

Date	Mintage	F	VF	XF	Unc	BU
2005MW	1,000,000	—	—	—	3.00	5.00

Y# 560 2 ZLOTE

8.1500 g., Brass, 27 mm. **Obv:** National arms on outline map **Obv. Legend:** RZECZPOSPOLITA POLSKA **Rev:** Region arms **Rev. Legend:** WOJEWOZTWO SWIETOKRZYSKIE **Edge Lettering:** * NBP * eight times

Date	Mintage	F	VF	XF	Unc	BU
2005MW	900,000	—	—	—	3.00	5.00

Y# 562 2 ZLOTE

8.1500 g., Brass, 27 mm. **Obv:** National arms **Rev:** Region Wielkopolskie **Edge Lettering:** * NBP * eight times

Date	Mintage	F	VF	XF	Unc	BU
2005MW	940,000	—	—	—	3.00	5.00

Y# 563 2 ZLOTE

8.1500 g., Brass, 27 mm. **Obv:** National arms on outlined map **Obv. Legend:** RZECZPOSPOLITA POLSKA **Rev:** Region arms **Rev. Legend:** WOJEWODZTWO ZACHODIOPOMORSKIE **Edge Lettering:** * NBP * eight times

Date	Mintage	F	VF	XF	Unc	BU
2005	—	—	—	—	3.00	5.00

Y# 564 2 ZLOTE

8.1500 g., Brass, 27 mm. **Obv:** National arms **Rev:** City of Gniezno **Edge Lettering:** * NBP * eight times

Date	Mintage	F	VF	XF	Unc	BU
2005	1,250,000	—	—	—	3.00	5.00

Y# 565   2 ZLOTE
8.1500 g., Brass, 27 mm.   **Obv:** National arms **Rev:** Solidarity
Edge Lettering: * NBP * eight times

Date	Mintage	F	VF	XF	Unc	BU
2005MW	1,000,000	—	—	—	3.00	5.00

Y# 608   2 ZLOTE
8.1500 g., Brass, 27 mm.   **Subject:** 500th Anniversary Birth of
Nikolaja Reja **Obv:** National arms **Obv. Legend:**
RZECZPOSPOLITA POLSKA **Rev:** Bust of Reja facing 3/4 right
Edge Lettering: NBP eight times

Date	Mintage	F	VF	XF	Unc	BU
2005	850,000	—	—	—	3.00	5.00

Y# 614   2 ZLOTE
8.1500 g., Brass, 27 mm.   **Obv:** National arms on outlined map
Obv. Legend: RZECZPOSPOLITA POLSKA **Rev:** Region arms
Rev. Legend: WOJEWÓDZTWO WARMINSKO - MAZURSKIE
Edge Lettering: * NBP * eight times

Date	Mintage	F	VF	XF	Unc	BU
2005MW	900,000	—	—	—	3.00	5.00

Y# 753   2 ZLOTE
8.1500 g., Brass, 27 mm.   **Subject:** Cizsyn **Rev:** Round tower

Date	Mintage	F	VF	XF	Unc	BU
2005MW	—	—	—	—	3.00	5.00

Y# 532   2 ZLOTE
8.1500 g., Brass, 27 mm.   **Obv:** National arms **Rev:** St. John's
Night dancer **Edge Lettering:** * NBP * eight times

Date	Mintage	F	VF	XF	Unc	BU
2006MW	1,000,000	—	—	—	2.50	4.00

Y# 534   2 ZLOTE
8.1500 g., Brass, 27 mm.   **Obv:** National arms **Rev:** Alpine
Marmot standing **Edge Lettering:** * NBP * eight times

Date	Mintage	F	VF	XF	Unc	BU
2006MW	1,400,000	—	—	—	3.00	6.00

Y# 543   2 ZLOTE
8.1500 g., Brass, 27 mm.   **Obv:** Polish Eagle above castle gate
Rev: Bochnia church **Edge Lettering:** * NBP * eight times

Date	Mintage	F	VF	XF	Unc	BU
2006MW	1,100,000	—	—	—	3.00	5.00

Y# 544   2 ZLOTE
8.1500 g., Brass, 27 mm.   **Obv:** Polish Eagle above castle gate
Rev: Chelm church **Edge Lettering:** * NBP * eight times

Date	Mintage	F	VF	XF	Unc	BU
2006MW	1,100,000	—	—	—	3.00	5.00

Y# 545   2 ZLOTE
8.1500 g., Brass, 27 mm.   **Obv:** Polish Eagle above castle gate
Rev: Chelmno Palace **Edge Lettering:** * NBP * eight times

Date	Mintage	F	VF	XF	Unc	BU
2006MW	1,100,000	—	—	—	3.00	5.00

Y# 546   2 ZLOTE
8.1500 g., Brass, 27 mm.   **Obv:** Polish Eagle above castle gate
Rev: Elblag tower **Edge Lettering:** * NBP * eight times

Date	Mintage	F	VF	XF	Unc	BU
2006MW	1,100,000	—	—	—	3.00	5.00

Y# 547   2 ZLOTE
8.1500 g., Brass, 27 mm.   **Obv:** Polish Eagle above castle gate
Rev: Castle **Rev. Legend:** KOSCIOL W. HACZOWIE **Edge
Lettering:** * NBP * eight times

Date	Mintage	F	VF	XF	Unc	BU
2006MW	1,000,000	—	—	—	3.00	5.00

Y# 548   2 ZLOTE
8.1500 g., Brass, 27 mm.   **Obv:** National arms above gateway

Rev: Legnica tower and building **Edge Lettering:** * NBP * eight
times

Date	Mintage	F	VF	XF	Unc	BU
2006MW	1,100,000	—	—	—	3.00	5.00

Y# 549   2 ZLOTE
8.1500 g., Brass, 27 mm.   **Obv:** Polish Eagle above castle gate
Rev: Pszczyna palace **Edge Lettering:** * NBP * eight times

Date	Mintage	F	VF	XF	Unc	BU
2006MW	1,100,000	—	—	—	3.00	5.00

Y# 550   2 ZLOTE
8.1500 g., Brass, 27 mm.   **Obv:** Polish Eagle above castle gate
Rev: Sandomierz palace **Edge Lettering:** * NBP * eight times

Date	Mintage	F	VF	XF	Unc	BU
2006MW	1,100,000	—	—	—	3.00	5.00

Y# 566   2 ZLOTE
8.1500 g., Brass, 27 mm.   **Obv:** National arms **Rev:** City of
Jaroslaw **Edge Lettering:** * NBP * eight times

Date	Mintage	F	VF	XF	Unc	BU
2006MW	1,200,000	—	—	—	3.00	5.00

Y# 569   2 ZLOTE
8.1500 g., Brass, 27 mm.   **Obv:** National arms **Rev:** Castle Zagan
Edge Lettering: * NBP * eight times

Date	Mintage	F	VF	XF	Unc	BU
2006MW	1,100,000	—	—	—	3.00	5.00

Y# 570   2 ZLOTE
815.0000 g., Brass, 27 mm.   **Obv:** National arms above gateway
Rev: City of Nysa **Edge Lettering:** * NBP * eight times

Date	Mintage	F	VF	XF	Unc	BU
2006MW	1,100,000	—	—	—	5.00	3.00

Y# 571   2 ZLOTE
8.1500 g., Brass, 27 mm.   **Subject:** 30th Anniversary of June
1976 **Obv:** National arms **Edge Lettering:** * NBP * eight times

Date	Mintage	F	VF	XF	Unc	BU
2006MW	1,000,000	—	—	—	3.00	5.00

Y# 573   2 ZLOTE
8.1500 g., Brass, 27 mm.   **Obv:** Polish eagle above wall **Rev:**
Nowy Sacz church **Edge Lettering:** * NBP * eight times

Date	Mintage	F	VF	XF	Unc	BU
2006MW	1,100,000	—	—	—	3.00	5.00

Y# 574   2 ZLOTE
8.1500 g., Brass, 27 mm.   **Subject:** 500th Anniversary of the
Publication of the Statute by Laski **Obv:** National arms above
value **Rev:** Jan Laski and book **Edge Lettering:** * NBP * eight
times

Date	Mintage	F	VF	XF	Unc	BU
2006MW	1,000,000	—	—	—	3.00	5.00

Y# 575   2 ZLOTE
8.1500 g., Brass, 27 mm.   **Subject:** Aleksander Gierymski
(painter) **Obv:** Palette, brushes at left, national arms at right **Obv.
Legend:** RZECZPOSPOLITA POLSKA **Rev:** Bust of Gierymski
facing at left, coastline village in background **Edge Lettering:** *
NBP * eight times

Date	Mintage	F	VF	XF	Unc	BU
2006MW	1,000,000	—	—	—	3.00	5.00

Y# 576   2 ZLOTE
8.1500 g., Brass, 27 mm.   **Obv:** National arms **Rev:** Knight on
horseback **Edge Lettering:** * NBP * eight times

Date	Mintage	F	VF	XF	Unc	BU
2006MW	1,000,000	—	—	—	3.00	5.00

Y# 580   2 ZLOTE
8.1500 g., Brass, 27 mm.   **Obv:** Polish eagle above wall **Rev:**
Kalisz building **Edge Lettering:** * NBP * eight times

Date	Mintage	F	VF	XF	Unc	BU
2006MW	1,100,000	—	—	—	3.00	5.00

Y# 582   2 ZLOTE
8.1500 g., Brass, 27 mm.   **Obv:** National arms **Obv. Legend:**
RZECZPOSPOLITA POLSKA **Rev:** Queen's head left as on KM-
20, coin design from 1932 **Edge Lettering:** * NBP * eight times

Date	Mintage	F	VF	XF	Unc	BU
2006MW	1,000,000	—	—	—	3.00	5.00

Y# 605   2 ZLOTE
8.1500 g., Brass, 27 mm.   **Obv:** National arms **Obv. Legend:**
RZECZPOSPOLITA POLSKA **Rev:** Skier and marksman
standing **Rev. Legend:** XX ZIMOWE IGAZYSKA OLIMPIJSKIE
- TURYN **Edge Lettering:** * NBP * eight times

Date	Mintage	F	VF	XF	Unc	BU
2006MW	1,200,000	—	—	—	3.00	5.00

Y# 606   2 ZLOTE
8.1500 g., Brass, 27 mm.   **Obv:** National arms **Obv. Legend:**
RZECZPOSPOLITA POLSKA **Rev:** Large soccer ball with fancy
linked date 2006 **Rev. Legend:** MISTRZOSTWA SWIATA W
PItCE NOZNEJ NIEMCY - FIFA **Edge Lettering:** * NBP * eight
times

Date	Mintage	F	VF	XF	Unc	BU
2006MW	1,200,000	—	—	—	3.00	5.00

Y# 609   2 ZLOTE
8.1500 g., Brass, 27 mm.   **Subject:** 100th Anniversary - Warsaw
School of Economics **Obv:** National arms **Obv. Legend:**
RZECZPOSPOLITA POLSKA **Rev:** School facade **Rev.
Legend:** SZKOLA CLOWNA HANDLOWA W WARSZAWIE
Rev. Inscription: Large SGH **Edge Lettering:** * NBP * eight
times

Date	Mintage	F	VF	XF	Unc	BU
2006MW	1,000,000	—	—	—	3.00	5.00

Y# 591   2 ZLOTE
8.0300 g., Brass, 26.77 mm.   **Subject:** 100th Anniversary Death
of Konrad Korzeniowski **Obv:** National arms **Obv. Legend:**
RZECZPOSPOLITA POLSKA **Rev:** Head of Korzeniowski facing
slightly right at left, open book at lower center, sailing ship at right
Edge Lettering: NBP repeated

Date	Mintage	F	VF	XF	Unc	BU
2007	—	—	—	—	3.00	

Y# 577   2 ZLOTE
8.1500 g., Brass, 27 mm.   **Obv:** Crowned eagle **Rev:** Kwidzyn
Castle **Edge Lettering:** * NBP * eight times

Date	Mintage	F	VF	XF	Unc	BU
2007MW	1,000,000	—	—	—	3.00	5.00

Y# 578   2 ZLOTE
8.1500 g., Brass, 27 mm.   **Obv:** Crowned eagle **Rev:** Grey Seal
and silhouette **Edge Lettering:** * NBP * eight times

Date	Mintage	F	VF	XF	Unc	BU
2007MW	1,000,000	—	—	—	4.00	7.00

Y# 586   2 ZLOTE
8.1500 g., Brass, 27 mm.   **Subject:** 75th Anniversary Breaking
the Enigma Code **Obv:** National arms **Obv. Legend:**
RZECZPOSPOLITA POLSKA **Rev:** Enigma machine wheel
Edge Lettering: * NBP * eight times

Date	Mintage	F	VF	XF	Unc	BU
2007MW	900,000	—	—	—	3.00	5.00

Y# 590   2 ZLOTE
8.1500 g., Brass, 27 mm.   **Obv:** National arms **Obv. Legend:**
RZECZPOSPOLITA POLSKA **Rev:** Bust of Domeyko facing **Rev.
Legend:** IGNACY DOMEYKO 1802 - 1889 **Edge Lettering:** *
NBP * eight times

Date	Mintage	F	VF	XF	Unc	BU
2007MW	900,000	—	—	—	3.00	5.00

Y# 592   2 ZLOTE
8.1500 g., Brass, 27 mm.   **Subject:** History of Zloty **Obv:** Nike
at left, obverse of 5 Zlotych, Y#18, national arms below **Obv.
Legend:** RZECZPOLPOLITA POLSKA **Rev:** Spray at left of
reverse of 5 Zlotych, Y# 18 **Edge Lettering:** * NBP * eight times

Date	Mintage	F	VF	XF	Unc	BU
2007MW	900,000	—	—	—	3.00	5.00

Y# 594   2 ZLOTE
8.1500 g., Brass, 27 mm. **Subject:** 750th Anniversary
Municipality of Krakau **Obv:** National arms **Obv. Legend:**
RZECZPOSPOLITA POLSKA **Rev:** Knight standing facing with
spear and shield **Edge Lettering:** * NBP * eight times

Date	Mintage	F	VF	XF	Unc	BU
2007MW	900,000	—	—	—	3.00	5.00

Y# 610   2 ZLOTE
8.1500 g., Brass, 27 mm. **Subject:** Artic Explorers Antoni B.
Dombrowolski and Henryk Arctowski **Obv:** National arms **Obv.
Legend:** RZECZPOSPOLITA POLSKA **Rev:** Explorer's bust
facing at bottom, sailing ship in background **Edge Lettering:** *
NBP * eight times

Date	Mintage	F	VF	XF	Unc	BU
2007MW	900,000	—	—	—	3.00	5.00

Y# 611   2 ZLOTE
8.1500 g., Brass, 27 mm. **Obv:** National arms **Obv. Legend:**
RZECZPOSPOLITA POLSKA **Rev:** Ciezkozbrojny in armor,
horseback left **Rev. Legend:** RYCERZ CIEZKOZBROJNY-XV
Edge Lettering: * NBP * eight times

Date	Mintage	F	VF	XF	Unc	BU
2007MW	900,000	—	—	—	3.00	5.00

Y# 612   2 ZLOTE
8.1500 g., Brass, 27 mm. **Subject:** 70th Anniversary Death of
Szymanowski **Obv:** National arms **Obv. Legend:**
RZECZPOSPOLITA POLSKA **Rev:** Bust facing 3/4 right at left,
music score in background **Rev. Legend:** ROCZNICA URODZIN
KAROLA SYMANOWSKIEGO **Edge Lettering:** * NBP * eight
times

Date	Mintage	F	VF	XF	Unc	BU
2007MW	900,000	—	—	—	3.00	5.00

Y# 613   2 ZLOTE
8.1500 g., Brass, 27 mm. **Obv:** National arms above gateway
Obv. Legend: RZECZPOSPOLITA POLSKA **Rev:** Buildings
Rev. Legend: STARGARD - SZCZECINSKI **Edge Lettering:** *
NBP * eight times

Date	Mintage	F	VF	XF	Unc	BU
2007MW	1,000,000	—	—	—	3.00	5.00

Y# 615   2 ZLOTE
8.1500 g., Brass, 27 mm. **Obv:** National arms above gateway
Obv. Legend: RZECZPOSPOLITA POLSKA **Rev:** Building with
branches at left and right **Rev. Legend:** BRZEG **Edge Lettering:**
* NBP * eight times

Date	Mintage	F	VF	XF	Unc	BU
2007MW	1,000,000	—	—	—	3.00	5.00

Y# 616   2 ZLOTE
8.1500 g., Brass, 27 mm. **Obv:** National arms above gateway
Obv. Legend: RZECZPOSPOLITA POLSKA **Rev:** Church **Rev.
Legend:** LOMZA **Edge Lettering:** * NBP alternating normal and
inverted 4x

Date	Mintage	F	VF	XF	Unc	BU
2007MW	1,000,000	—	—	—	3.00	5.00

Y# 617   2 ZLOTE
8.1500 g., Brass, 27 mm. **Obv:** National arms above gateway
Obv. Legend: RZECZPOSPOLITA POLSKA **Rev:** Church **Rev.
Legend:** PLOCK **Edge Lettering:** * NBP * eight times

Date	Mintage	F	VF	XF	Unc	BU
2007MW	1,000,000	—	—	—	3.00	5.00

Y# 618   2 ZLOTE
8.1500 g., Brass, 27 mm. **Obv:** National arms above gateway
Obv. Legend: RZECZPOSPOLITA POLSKA **Rev:** Church **Rev.
Legend:** PRZEMYSL **Edge Lettering:** * NBP * eight times

Date	Mintage	F	VF	XF	Unc	BU
2007MW	1,000,000	—	—	—	3.00	5.00

Y# 619   2 ZLOTE
8.1500 g., Brass, 27 mm. **Obv:** National arms above gateway
Obv. Legend: RZECZPOSPOLITA POLSKA **Rev:** Towered
gateway **Rev. Legend:** RACIBÓRZ **Edge Lettering:** * NBP *
eight times

Date	Mintage	F	VF	XF	Unc	BU
2007MW	1,000,000	—	—	—	3.00	5.00

Y# 620   2 ZLOTE
8.1500 g., Brass, 27 mm. **Obv:** National arms above gateway
Obv. Legend: RZECZPOSPOLITA POLSKA **Rev:** Church **Rev.
Legend:** SLUPSK **Edge Lettering:** NBP repeated

Date	Mintage	F	VF	XF	Unc	BU
2007MW	1,000,000	—	—	—	3.00	5.00

Y# 621   2 ZLOTE
8.1500 g., Brass, 27 mm. **Obv:** National arms above gateway
Obv. Legend: RZECZPOSPOLITA POLSKA **Rev:** Church **Rev.
Legend:** SWIDNICA **Edge Lettering:** * NBP * eight times

Date	Mintage	F	VF	XF	Unc	BU
2007MW	1,000,000	—	—	—	3.00	5.00

Y# 622   2 ZLOTE
8.1500 g., Brass, 27 mm. **Obv:** National arms **Obv. Legend:**
RZECZPOSPOLITA POLSKE **Rev:** Town view **Rev. Legend:**
MIASTO SREDNIOWIECZNE - W TORUNIU **Edge Lettering:** *
NBP * eight times

Date	Mintage	F	VF	XF	Unc	BU
2007MW	900,000	—	—	—	3.00	5.00

Y# 623   2 ZLOTE
8.1500 g., Brass, 27 mm. **Obv:** National arms above gateway
Obv. Legend: RZECZPOSPOLITA POLSKA **Rev:** Church **Rev.
Legend:** GORZÓW WIELKOPOLSKI **Edge Lettering:** * NBP *
eight times

Date	Mintage	F	VF	XF	Unc	BU
2007MW	1,000,000	—	—	—	3.00	5.00

Y# 624   2 ZLOTE
8.1500 g., Brass, 27 mm. **Obv:** National arms above gateway
Obv. Legend: RZECZPOSPOLITA POLSKA **Rev:** Church at
lower right, houses to left, fortress in upper background **Rev.
Legend:** KLODZKO **Edge Lettering:** * NBP * eight times

Date	Mintage	F	VF	XF	Unc	BU
2007MW	1,000,000	—	—	—	3.00	5.00

Y# 625   2 ZLOTE
8.1500 g., Brass, 27 mm.   **Obv:** National arms above gateway
Obv. Legend: RZECZPOSPOLITA POLSKE **Rev:** Church **Rev.**
Legend: TARNOW **Edge Lettering:** * NBP * eight times

Date	Mintage	F	VF	XF	Unc	BU
2007MW	1,000,000	—	—	—	3.00	5.00

Y# 626   2 ZLOTE
8.1500 g., Brass, 27 mm.   **Subject:** Leon Wyczolkowski **Obv:**
Artist's palette, brushes at left, national arms at right **Obv.**
Legend: RZECZPOSPOLITA POLSKA **Rev:** Bust facing **Edge**
Lettering: * NBP * eight times

Date	Mintage	F	VF	XF	Unc	BU
2007MW	900,000	—	—	—	3.00	5.00

Y# 629   2 ZLOTE
8.1500 g., Brass, 27 mm.   **Subject:** 40th Anniversary "Rocznica"
March **Obv:** National arms above value **Obv. Legend:**
RZECZPOSPOLITA POLSKA **Rev:** University of Warsaw coat
of arms above political protest marchers **Edge Lettering:** * NBP
* eight times

Date	Mintage	F	VF	XF	Unc	BU
2008MW	1,400,000	—	—	0.90	2.25	3.00

Y# 630   2 ZLOTE
8.1500 g., Brass, 27 mm.   **Obv:** National arms above gateway
Obv. Legend: RZECZPOSPOLITA POLSKA **Rev:** Building **Rev.**
Legend: LOWICZ **Edge Lettering:** * NBP * eight times

Date	Mintage	F	VF	XF	Unc	BU
2008MW	1,100,000	—	—	0.90	2.25	3.00

Y# 631   2 ZLOTE
8.1500 g., Brass, 27 mm.   **Obv:** National arms above gateway
Obv. Legend: RZECZPOSPOLITA POLSKA **Rev:** Monument
Rev. Legend: KONIN **Edge Lettering:** * NBP * eight times

Date	Mintage	F	VF	XF	Unc	BU
2008MW	1,100,000	—	—	0.90	2.25	3.00

Y# 633   2 ZLOTE
8.1500 g., Brass, 27 mm.   **Subject:** 65th Anniversary Warsaw
Uprising **Obv:** National arms **Obv. Legend:** RZECZPOSPOLITA
POLSKA **Rev:** Star of David in barbed wire, female freedom
fighter at right. **Rev. Legend:** POWSTANIA W GETCIE
WARSZAWSKIM 65. ROCZNICA **Edge Lettering:** * NBP * eight
times

Date	Mintage	F	VF	XF	Unc	BU
2008MW	1,750,000	—	—	—	3.00	5.00

Y# 634   2 ZLOTE
8.1500 g., Brass, 27 mm.   **Subject:** Zbigniew Herbert **Obv:**
National arms **Obv. Legend:** RZECZPOSPOLITA POLSKA **Rev:**
Head of Herbert right **Edge Lettering:** * NBP * eight times

Date	Mintage	F	VF	XF	Unc	BU
2008MW	1,510,000	—	—	—	3.00	4.00

Y# 638   2 ZLOTE
8.1500 g., Brass, 27 mm.   **Subject:** Siberian Exiles **Obv:**
National arms **Obv. Legend:** RZECZPOSPOLITA POLSKA **Rev:**
Bleak forest **Rev. Inscription:** SYBIRACY **Edge Lettering:** *
NBP * eight times

Date	Mintage	F	VF	XF	Unc	BU
2008MW	1,500,000	—	—	—	3.00	4.00

Y# 641   2 ZLOTE
8.1500 g., Brass, 27 mm.   **Subject:** Kazimierz Dolny **Obv:**
National arms **Obv. Legend:** RZECZPOSPOLITA POLSKA **Rev:**
City view **Edge Lettering:** * NBP * eight times

Date	Mintage	F	VF	XF	Unc	BU
2008MW	1,380,000	—	—	—	3.00	4.00

Y# 627   2 ZLOTE
8.1500 g., Brass, 27 mm.   **Obv:** National arms above flags **Obv.**
Legend: RZECZPOSPOLITA POLSKA **Rev:** Peregrine Falcon
perched on branch **Rev. Legend:** SOKOL WEDROWNY - Falco
peregrinus **Edge Lettering:** * NBP * eight times

Date	Mintage	F	VF	XF	Unc	BU
2008MW	1,600,000	—	—	—	3.00	4.00

Y# 628   2 ZLOTE
8.1500 g., Brass, 27 mm.   **Obv:** National arms above gateway
Obv. Legend: RZECZPOSPOLITA POLSKA **Rev:** National arms
ar upper left, Piotrków Tribunal building at lower right **Rev.**
Legend: PIOTRKÓW - TRYBUNALSKI **Edge Lettering:** * NBP
* eight times

Date	Mintage	F	VF	XF	Unc	BU
2008MW	1,100,000	—	—	0.90	2.25	3.00

Y# 644   2 ZLOTE
8.1500 g., Brass, 27 mm.   **Subject:** 29th Olympic Games Beijing
2008 **Obv:** Eagle **Rev:** Two rowers in boat & a square **Edge**
Lettering: * NBP * eight times

Date	Mintage	F	VF	XF	Unc	BU
2008	2,000,000	—	—	—	3.00	4.00

Y# 648   2 ZLOTE
8.1500 g., Brass, 27 mm.   **Subject:** Polish Travellers & Explorers
Obv: Eagle **Rev:** Bust of Bronislaw Pilsudski **Edge Lettering:** *
NBP * eight times

Date	Mintage	F	VF	XF	Unc	BU
2008	1,100,000	—	—	—	3.00	4.00

Y# 650   2 ZLOTE
8.1500 g., Brass, 27 mm.   **Subject:** 90th Anniversary of
Regaining Freedom **Obv:** Eagle **Rev:** Order of Polonia Restituta
Edge Lettering: * NBP * eight times

Date	Mintage	F	VF	XF	Unc	BU
2008	1,200,000	—	—	—	3.00	4.00

Y# 656   2 ZLOTE
8.1500 g., Brass, 27 mm.   **Subject:** 450th Anniversary of the
Polish Post **Obv:** Eagle **Rev:** Post rider on horse **Edge:** NBP

Date	Mintage	F	VF	XF	Unc	BU
2008	1,400,000	—	—	—	3.00	4.00

Y# 659   2 ZLOTE
8.1500 g., Brass, 27 mm. **Subject:** 400th Anniversary of Polish settlement in North America **Obv:** Eagle **Rev:** Man blowing glassware **Edge Lettering:** * NBP * eight times

Date	Mintage	F	VF	XF	Unc	BU
2008	1,200,000	—	—	—	3.00	4.00

Y# 662   2 ZLOTE
8.1500 g., Brass, 27 mm. **Subject:** 90th Anniversary of the Greater Poland Uprising **Obv:** Eagle **Rev:** Bust of Igancy Jan Paderewski, soldiers at bottom **Edge Lettering:** * NBP * eight times

Date	Mintage	F	VF	XF	Unc	BU
2008	1,100,000	—	—	—	3.00	4.00

Y# 663   2 ZLOTE
8.1500 g., Brass, 27 mm. **Subject:** Belsko - Biala **Obv:** National arms above gateway **Rev:** Building

Date	Mintage	F	VF	XF	Unc	BU
2008MW	—	—	—	—	3.00	4.00

Y# 670   2 ZLOTE
8.1500 g., Brass, 27 mm. **Subject:** Polish Cavalry **Obv:** National arms above value **Rev:** Hussar Knights, XVII Century

Date	Mintage	F	VF	XF	Unc	BU
2009MW	1,400,000	—	—	—	3.00	4.00

Y# 673   2 ZLOTE
8.1500 g., Brass, 27 mm. **Subject:** Supreme Chamber of Control, 90th Anniversary **Obv:** National arms above value **Rev:** Building

Date	Mintage	F	VF	XF	Unc	BU
2009MW	1,200,000	—	—	—	3.00	4.00

Y# 675   2 ZLOTE
8.1500 g., Brass, 27 mm. **Subject:** Central Banking, 180th Anniversary **Obv:** National arms above value **Rev:** Five coins

Date	Mintage	F	VF	XF	Unc	BU
2009MW	1,300,000	—	—	—	3.00	4.00

Y# 678   2 ZLOTE
8.1500 g., Brass, 27 mm. **Subject:** Green Lizards **Obv:** National arms above value **Rev:** Two green lizards on rocks (lacerta viridis) **Rev. Legend:** JASZCZURKA

Date	Mintage	F	VF	XF	Unc	BU
2009MW	1,700,000	—	—	—	3.00	4.00

Y# 680   2 ZLOTE
8.1500 g., Brass, 27 mm. **Subject:** General Elections of 1989 **Obv:** National arms above eagle **Rev:** Election notice within wreath

Date	Mintage	F	VF	XF	Unc	BU
2009MW	1,300,000	—	—	—	3.00	4.00

Y# 684   2 ZLOTE
8.1500 g., Brass, 27 mm. **Subject:** Czeslaw Niemen **Obv:** National arms above value **Rev:** Two dimensional facing portrait

Date	Mintage	F	VF	XF	Unc	BU
2009MW	1,400,000	—	—	—	3.00	4.00

Y# 687   2 ZLOTE
8.1500 g., Brass, 27 mm. **Subject:** Poets of the Warsaw uprising, 65th Anniversary **Obv:** National arms above eagle

Date	Mintage	F	VF	XF	Unc	BU
2009MW	1,400,000	—	—	—	3.00	4.00

Y# 690   2 ZLOTE
8.1500 g., Brass, 27 mm. **Subject:** First Cadre March **Obv:** National arms above value **Rev:** Military badge

Date	Mintage	F	VF	XF	Unc	BU
2009MW	1,000,000	—	—	—	3.00	4.00

Y# 692   2 ZLOTE
8.1500 g., Brass, 27 mm. **Subject:** Liquidation of Lodz Ghetto **Obv:** National arms above value **Rev:** Silhouette of Ghetto

Date	Mintage	F	VF	XF	Unc	BU
2009MW	1,000,000	—	—	—	3.00	4.00

Y# 694   2 ZLOTE
8.1500 g., Brass, 27 mm. **Subject:** Westerplatte **Obv:** National arms above value **Rev:** Three soldiers and map

Date	Mintage	F	VF	XF	Unc	BU
2009	1,400,000	—	—	—	3.00	4.00

Y# 697   2 ZLOTE
8.1500 g., Brass, 27 mm. **Subject:** Tatar Mountain Rescue **Obv:** National arms above value **Rev:** Mountain climber

Date	Mintage	F	VF	XF	Unc	BU
2009MW	1,400,000	—	—	—	3.00	4.00

Y# 700   2 ZLOTE
8.1500 g., Brass, 27 mm. **Subject:** Fr. Jerzy Popieluszko, 25th Anniversary of Murder **Obv:** National arms above value **Rev:** Portrait and candle memorial

Date	Mintage	F	VF	XF	Unc	BU
2009MW	1,500,000	—	—	—	3.00	4.00

Y# 703   2 ZLOTE
8.1500 g., Brass, 27 mm. **Subject:** Poles saving Jews **Obv:** National arms above value **Rev:** Broken brick wall

Date	Mintage	F	VF	XF	Unc	BU
2009MW	1,400,000	—	—	—	3.00	4.00

Y# 705   2 ZLOTE
8.1500 g., Brass, 27 mm. **Subject:** Wald Strzeminski **Obv:** Artist palette and National arms **Rev:** Portrait at left

Date	Mintage	F	VF	XF	Unc	BU
2009MW	1,300,000	—	—	—	3.00	4.00

Y# 707   2 ZLOTE
8.1500 g., Brass, 27 mm. **Subject:** Polish Underground **Obv:** National arms above value **Rev:** Monogram of resistance and map of Poland

Date	Mintage	F	VF	XF	Unc	BU
2009MW	1,000,000	—	—	—	3.00	4.00

Y# 709   2 ZLOTE
8.1500 g., Brass, 27 mm.   **Subject:** Czestochowa **Rev:** Church

Date	Mintage	F	VF	XF	Unc	BU
2009MW	—	—	—	—	3.00	4.00

Y# 710   2 ZLOTE
8.1500 g., Brass, 27 mm.   **Subject:** Jedrzejow Cistercian
Monastery **Rev:** Church

Date	Mintage	F	VF	XF	Unc	BU
2009MW	—	—	—	—	3.00	4.00

Y# 711   2 ZLOTE
8.1500 g., Brass, 27 mm.   **Subject:** Trzebnica **Rev:** Building

Date	Mintage	F	VF	XF	Unc	BU
2009MW	—	—	—	—	3.00	4.00

Y# 712   2 ZLOTE
8.1500 g., Brass, 27 mm.   **Subject:** Liberation of Auschwitz **Obv:**
National arms above value **Rev:** Three prisoners and camp gate
sign

Date	Mintage	F	VF	XF	Unc	BU
2010MW	1,000,000	—	—	—	3.00	4.00

Y# 715   2 ZLOTE
8.1500 g., Brass, 27 mm.   **Subject:** Vancouver Winter Olympics
Obv: National arms above value **Rev:** Ski jump athlete

Date	Mintage	F	VF	XF	Unc	BU
2010MW	1,400,000	—	—	—	3.00	4.00

Y# 718   2 ZLOTE
8.1500 g., Brass, 27 mm.   **Subject:** Imperial Guard **Obv:**
National arms above value **Rev:** Napoleonic era mounted soldier

Date	Mintage	F	VF	XF	Unc	BU
2010MW	1,400,000	—	—	—	3.00	4.00

Y# 721   2 ZLOTE
8.1500 g., Brass, 27 mm.   **Subject:** Katyn Crime **Obv:** National
arms above value **Rev:** City name above cap

Date	Mintage	F	VF	XF	Unc	BU
2010MW	1,000,000	—	—	—	3.00	4.00

Y# 723   2 ZLOTE
8.1500 g., Brass, 27 mm.   **Obv:** National arms above value **Rev:**
Bat

Date	Mintage	F	VF	XF	Unc	BU
2010	—	—	—	—	3.00	4.00

Y# 725   2 ZLOTE
8.1500 g., Brass, 27 mm.   **Subject:** Polish Scouting Centennial

Date	Mintage	F	VF	XF	Unc	BU
2010MW	1,100,000	—	—	—	3.00	4.00

Y# 727   2 ZLOTE
8.1500 g., Brass, 27 mm.   **Subject:** Popular Music - Krzyzt of
Komeda

Date	Mintage	F	VF	XF	Unc	BU
2010MW	1,400,000	—	—	—	3.00	4.00

Y# 730   2 ZLOTE
8.1500 g., Brass, 27 mm.   **Subject:** Jan Twardowski

Date	Mintage	F	VF	XF	Unc	BU
2010MW	1,000,000	—	—	—	3.00	4.00

Y# 732   2 ZLOTE
8.1500 g., Brass, 27 mm.   **Subject:** Battles of Grunwald and
Kluszyn

Date	Mintage	F	VF	XF	Unc	BU
2010MW	1,400,000	—	—	—	3.00	4.00

Y# 735   2 ZLOTE
8.1500 g., Brass   **Subject:** Battle of Warsaw

Date	Mintage	F	VF	XF	Unc	BU
2010MW	1,200,000	—	—	—	3.00	4.00

Y# 737   2 ZLOTE
8.1500 g., Brass, 27 mm.   **Subject:** August of 1980

Date	Mintage	F	VF	XF	Unc	BU
2010MW	1,400,000	—	—	—	3.00	4.00

Y# 742   2 ZLOTE
8.1500 g., Brass, 27 mm.   **Subject:** Polish Explorers - Benedykt
Dybowski

Date	Mintage	F	VF	XF	Unc	BU
2010MW Proof	1,200,000	—	—	—	3.00	4.00

Y# 744   2 ZLOTE
8.1500 g., Brass, 27 mm.   **Subject:** Krzeszow

Date	Mintage	F	VF	XF	Unc	BU
2010MW	1,000,000	—	—	—	3.00	4.00

Y# 746   2 ZLOTE
8.1500 g., Brass, 27 mm.   **Subject:** Arthur Grottger

Date	Mintage	F	VF	XF	Unc	BU
2010MW	1,300,000	—	—	—	3.00	4.00

Y# 749   2 ZLOTE
8.1500 g., Brass, 27 mm.   **Subject:** Kalwaria Zebrzydowska
Obv: National Arms above value **Rev:** Statue of Saint, Church
in background

Date	Mintage	F	VF	XF	Unc	BU
2010MW	—	—	—	—	3.00	4.00

Y# 751   2 ZLOTE
8.1500 g., Brass, 27 mm.   **Subject:** City of Warsaw

Date	Mintage	F	VF	XF	Unc	BU
2010MW	—	—	—	—	3.00	4.00

Y# 752   2 ZLOTE
815.0000 g., Brass, 27 mm.   **Subject:** City of Trzemeszno

Date	Mintage	F	VF	XF	Unc	BU
2010	—	—	—	—	3.00	4.00

Y# 759   2 ZLOTE
8.1500 g., Brass, 27 mm.   **Subject:** Gorlice **Obv:** National Arms above value **Rev:** City view

Date	Mintage	F	VF	XF	Unc	BU
2010	1,000,000	—	—	—	3.00	4.00

Y# 760   2 ZLOTE
8.1500 g., Brass, 27 mm.   **Subject:** Miechow **Obv:** National Arms above value **Rev:** Building tower

Date	Mintage	F	VF	XF	Unc	BU
2010	1,000,000	—	—	—	3.00	4.00

Y# 761   2 ZLOTE
8.1500 g., Brass, 27 mm.   **Subject:** Katowice **Obv:** National Arms above value **Rev:** Town factory view

Date	Mintage	F	VF	XF	Unc	BU
2010	1,000,000	—	—	—	3.00	4.00

Y# 815   2 ZLOTE
8.1500 g., Brass, 27 mm.   **Subject:** Krzysztof Komeda **Rev:** Head left

Date	Mintage	F	VF	XF	Unc	BU
2010MW	—	—	—	—	3.00	4.00

Y# 762   2 ZLOTE
8.1500 g., Brass, 27 mm.   **Subject:** Borsuk **Obv:** National Arms above value **Rev:** Eurasian Badgers

Date	Mintage	F	VF	XF	Unc	BU
2011	1,500,000	—	—	—	3.00	4.00

Y# 764   2 ZLOTE
8.1500 g., Brass, 27 mm.   **Subject:** Zofia Stryjenska **Obv:** National arms, value and artist pallet with brushes **Rev:** Portrait facing

Date	Mintage	F	VF	XF	Unc	BU
2011	1,000,000	—	—	—	3.00	4.00

Y# 767   2 ZLOTE
8.1500 g., Brass, 27 mm.   **Subject:** Independent Student's Union, 30th Anniversary

Date	Mintage	F	VF	XF	Unc	BU
2011MW	800,000	—	—	—	3.00	4.00

Y# 769   2 ZLOTE
8.1500 g., Brass, 27 mm.   **Subject:** Smolensk plane crash

Date	Mintage	F	VF	XF	Unc	BU
2011MW	800,000	—	—	—	3.00	4.00

Y# 772   2 ZLOTE
8.1500 g., Brass, 27 mm.   **Subject:** Beautification of Pope John Paul II **Obv:** Eagle **Rev:** Bust within rays

Date	Mintage	F	VF	XF	Unc	BU
2011MW	1,000,000	—	—	—	3.00	4.00

Y# 777   2 ZLOTE
8.1500 g., Brass, 27 mm.   **Subject:** Poland's presidency of the Council of the European Union

Date	Mintage	F	VF	XF	Unc	BU
2011MW	800,000	—	—	—	3.00	4.00

Y# 780   2 ZLOTE
8.1500 g., Brass, 27 mm.   **Subject:** History of the Polish Cavalry - Uhlan

Date	Mintage	F	VF	XF	Unc	BU
2011MW	1,000,000	—	—	—	3.00	4.00

Y# 783   2 ZLOTE
8.1500 g., Brass, 27 mm.   **Subject:** Gdynia

Date	Mintage	F	VF	XF	Unc	BU
2011MW	800,000	—	—	—	3.00	4.00

Y# 784   2 ZLOTE
8.1500 g., Brass, 27 mm.   **Subject:** Warsaw Pilgrimage to the Marian Shrine of Jasna Gora in Czestochowa, 300th Anniversary

Date	Mintage	F	VF	XF	Unc	BU
2011MW	800,000	—	—	—	3.00	4.00

Y# 785   2 ZLOTE
8.1500 g., Brass, 27 mm.   **Subject:** Czeslaw Milosz

Date	Mintage	F	VF	XF	Unc	BU
2011MW	800,000	—	—	—	3.00	4.00

Y# 788   2 ZLOTE
8.1500 g., Brass, 27 mm.   **Subject:** Mlawa

Date	Mintage	F	VF	XF	Unc	BU
2011MW	800,000	—	—	—	3.00	4.00

Y# 789   2 ZLOTE
8.1500 g., Brass, 27 mm.   **Subject:** Ignacy Jan Paderewski

Date	Mintage	F	VF	XF	Unc	BU
2011MW	800,000	—	—	—	3.00	4.00

Y# 792   2 ZLOTE
8.1500 g., Brass, 27 mm.   **Subject:** Silesian Uprising

Date	Mintage	F	VF	XF	Unc	BU
2011MW	800,000	—	—	—	3.00	4.00

Y# 794 2 ZLOTE
8.1500 g., Brass, 27 mm. **Subject:** Poznan

Date	Mintage	F	VF	XF	Unc	BU
2011MW	800,000	—	—	—	3.00	4.00

Y# 795 2 ZLOTE
8.1500 g., Brass, 27 mm. **Subject:** Society for the Protection of the Blind, 100th Anniversary

Date	Mintage	F	VF	XF	Unc	BU
2011MW	800,000	—	—	—	3.00	4.00

Y# 797 2 ZLOTE
8.1500 g., Brass, 27 mm. **Subject:** Ferdynand Ossendowski

Date	Mintage	F	VF	XF	Unc	BU
2011MW	900,000	—	—	—	3.00	4.00

Y# 799 2 ZLOTE
8.1500 g., Brass, 27 mm. **Subject:** Polonia Warszawa football club

Date	Mintage	F	VF	XF	Unc	BU
2011MW	800,000	—	—	—	3.00	4.00

Y# 801 2 ZLOTE
8.1500 g., Brass, 27 mm. **Subject:** Jeremi Przybora and Jerzy Wasowski

Date	Mintage	F	VF	XF	Unc	BU
2011MW	800,000	—	—	—	3.00	4.00

Y# 804 2 ZLOTE
8.1500 g., Brass, 27 mm. **Subject:** Lodz **Rev:** Building and architectural detail

Date	Mintage	F	VF	XF	Unc	BU
2011MW	—	—	—	—	3.00	4.00

Y# 805 2 ZLOTE
8.1500 g., Brass, 27 mm. **Subject:** Krakow **Rev:** Church along riverfront

Date	Mintage	F	VF	XF	Unc	BU
2011MW Proof	—	—	—	—	3.00	4.00

Y# 806 2 ZLOTE
8.1500 g., Brass, 27 mm. **Subject:** Kalisz **Rev:** Chruch

Date	Mintage	F	VF	XF	Unc	BU
2011MW	—	—	—	—	3.00	4.00

Y# 809 2 ZLOTE
8.1500 g., Brass, 27 mm. **Subject:** Christmas Charity Orchestra, 20th Anniversary **Rev:** Guitar with love hearts

Date	Mintage	F	VF	XF	Unc	BU
2012MW	—	—	—	—	3.00	4.00

Y# 811 2 ZLOTE
8.1500 g., Brass, 27 mm. **Subject:** Cooperative banking in Poland, 150th Anniversary **Rev:** Stack of money adn coins, wheat ear in center

Date	Mintage	F	VF	XF	Unc	BU
2012MW	—	—	—	—	3.00	4.00

Y# 813 2 ZLOTE
8.1500 g., Silver, 27 mm. **Subject:** Ulma, Baranek and Kowalski families **Rev:** Mother holding child

Date	Mintage	F	VF	XF	Unc	BU
2012MW	—	—	—	—	3.00	4.00

Y# 284 5 ZLOTYCH
6.5400 g., Bi-Metallic Aluminum-Bronze center in Copper-Nickel ring, 24 mm. **Obv:** National arms within circle **Obv. Legend:** RZECZPOSPOLITA POLSKA **Rev:** Value within circle flanked by oak leaves

Date	Mintage	F	VF	XF	Unc	BU
2008MW	—	—	—	—	7.00	8.00
2009MW	—	—	—	—	7.00	8.00
2010MW	—	—	—	—	7.00	8.00
2011MW	—	—	—	—	7.00	8.00

Y# 800 5 ZLOTYCH
7.0700 g., 0.9250 Silver 0.2102 oz. ASW, 24 mm. **Subject:** Polonia Warszawa football club

Date	Mintage	F	VF	XF	Unc	BU
2011MW Proof	50,000	Value: 30.00				

Y# 406 10 ZLOTYCH
14.1400 g., 0.9250 Silver 0.4205 oz. ASW **Subject:** Year 2001 **Obv:** Crowned eagle with wings open **Rev:** Printed circuit board

Date	Mintage	F	VF	XF	Unc	BU
2001MW Proof	35,000	Value: 75.00				

Y# 413 10 ZLOTYCH
14.1400 g., 0.9250 Silver 0.4205 oz. ASW, 32 mm. **Subject:** 15 Years of the Constitutional Court **Obv:** Crowned eagle suspended from a judge's neck chain **Rev:** Crowned eagle head and balance scale **Edge Lettering:** TRYBUNAL KONSTYTUCYJNY W SLUZBIE PANSTWA PRAWA

Date	Mintage	F	VF	XF	Unc	BU
2001MW Proof	25,000	Value: 65.00				

Y# 419 10 ZLOTYCH
14.1400 g., 0.9250 Silver 0.4205 oz. ASW, 32 mm. **Subject:** Cardinal Stefan Wyszynski **Obv:** Crowned eagle with wings open above ribbon **Rev:** Half length figure facing with raised hands **Edge Lettering:** 100 • ROCZNIA URODZIN

Date	Mintage	F	VF	XF	Unc	BU
2001MW Proof	60,000	Value: 30.00				

Y# 425 10 ZLOTYCH
14.2100 g., 0.9250 Silver 0.4226 oz. ASW, 32 mm. **Subject:**

Jan III Sobieski **Obv:** Crowned eagle with wings open **Rev:** 3/4 armored bust facing with army in background **Edge:** Plain

Date	Mintage	F	VF	XF	Unc	BU
2001MW Proof	24,000	Value: 120				

Y# 458   10 ZLOTYCH

14.1400 g., 0.9250 Silver 0.4205 oz. ASW, 32 mm. **Obv:** Crowned eagle with wings open **Rev:** Jan Sobieski, type II **Edge:** Plain

Date	Mintage	F	VF	XF	Unc	BU
2001MW Proof	17,000	Value: 175				

Y# 459   10 ZLOTYCH

14.1400 g., 0.9250 Silver 0.4205 oz. ASW, 32 mm. **Obv:** Three violins **Rev:** Henryk Wieniawski **Edge:** Plain

Date	Mintage	F	VF	XF	Unc	BU
2001MW Proof	28,000	Value: 60.00				

Y# 460   10 ZLOTYCH

14.1400 g., 0.9250 Silver 0.4205 oz. ASW, 32 mm. **Obv:** Crowned eagle with wings open above fish **Rev:** Michal Siedlecki **Edge:** Plain

Date	Mintage	F	VF	XF	Unc	BU
2001MW Proof	26,000	Value: 60.00				

Y# 432   10 ZLOTYCH

14.1400 g., 0.9250 Silver 0.4205 oz. ASW, 32 mm. **Subject:** Bronislaw Malinowski **Obv:** Small crowned eagle with wings open to right of bust facing **Rev:** Trobriand Islands village scene **Edge Lettering:** etnolog, antropolog kultury

Date	Mintage	F	VF	XF	Unc	BU
2002MW Proof	33,500	Value: 35.00				

Y# 434   10 ZLOTYCH

14.1400 g., 0.9250 Silver 0.4205 oz. ASW, 32 mm. **Subject:** World Cup Soccer **Obv:** Crowned eagle with wings open **Rev:** Soccer player **Edge Lettering:** etnolog, antropolog kultury

Date	Mintage	F	VF	XF	Unc	BU
2002MW Proof	55,000	Value: 27.50				

Y# 435   10 ZLOTYCH

14.1400 g., 0.9250 Silver 0.4205 oz. ASW, 32 mm. **Subject:** World Cup Soccer **Obv:** Amber soccer ball inset entering goal net **Rev:** Two soccer players with amber soccer ball inset **Edge Lettering:** etnolog, antropolog kultury

Date	Mintage	F	VF	XF	Unc	BU
2002MW Proof	65,000	Value: 75.00				

Y# 437   10 ZLOTYCH

14.1400 g., 0.9250 Silver 0.4205 oz. ASW, 32 mm. **Subject:** Pope John Paul II **Obv:** Crowned eagle with wings open within two views of praying Pope **Rev:** Pope facing radiant Holy Door **Edge:** Plain

Date	Mintage	F	VF	XF	Unc	BU
2002MW Proof	80,000	Value: 45.00				

Y# 441   10 ZLOTYCH

14.2000 g., 0.9250 Silver 0.4223 oz. ASW, 32 mm. **Subject:** Gen. Wladyslaw Anders **Obv:** Crowned eagle with wings open, cross and multicolor flowers **Rev:** Uniformed bust right **Edge:** Plain

Date	Mintage	F	VF	XF	Unc	BU
2002MW Proof	40,000	Value: 120				

Y# 450   10 ZLOTYCH

14.1400 g., 0.9250 Silver 0.4205 oz. ASW, 32 mm. **Subject:** August II (1697-1706, 1709-1735) **Obv:** Crowned eagle with wings open **Rev:** Portrait and Order of the White Eagle **Edge:** Plain

Date	Mintage	F	VF	XF	Unc	BU
2002MW Proof	30,000	Value: 90.00				

Y# 453   10 ZLOTYCH

14.1400 g., 0.9250 Silver 0.4205 oz. ASW, 32 mm. **Subject:** Great Orchestra of Christmas Charity **Obv:** Large inscribed heart above crowned eagle with wings open **Rev:** Boy playing flute **Edge:** Plain

Date	Mintage	F	VF	XF	Unc	BU
2003MW Proof	47,000	Value: 45.00				

Y# 468   10 ZLOTYCH

14.1400 g., 0.9250 Silver 0.4205 oz. ASW, 32 mm. **Obv:** Tanks on battlefield **Rev:** General Maczek **Edge:** Plain

Date	Mintage	F	VF	XF	Unc	BU
2003MW Proof	44,000	Value: 35.00				

Y# 469   10 ZLOTYCH

14.1400 g., 0.9250 Silver 0.4205 oz. ASW, 32 mm. **Subject:** Gas and Oil Industry **Obv:** Crowned eagle and highway leading to city view **Rev:** Portrait and refinery **Edge:** Plain

Date	Mintage	F	VF	XF	Unc	BU
2003MW Proof	43,000	Value: 35.00				

Y# 474   10 ZLOTYCH

14.1400 g., 0.9250 Silver 0.4205 oz. ASW, 32 mm. **Obv:** Crowned eagle with wings open **Rev:** Stanislaus I and wife's portrait **Edge:** Plain

Date	Mintage	F	VF	XF	Unc	BU
2003MW Proof	45,000	Value: 35.00				

Y# 475   10 ZLOTYCH

14.1400 g., 0.9250 Silver 0.4205 oz. ASW, 32 mm. **Obv:** Crowned eagle with wings open **Rev:** Half-length figure of Stanislaus I with his wife in background **Edge:** Plain

Date	Mintage	F	VF	XF	Unc	BU
2003MW Proof	40,000	Value: 45.00				

Y# 448   10 ZLOTYCH

14.1400 g., 0.9250 Silver 0.4205 oz. ASW, 32 mm. **Subject:**

City of Poznan (Posen) **Obv:** Old coin design and arched door **Rev:** Old coin design and city view **Edge:** Plain

Date	Mintage	F	VF	XF	Unc	BU
2003MW Proof	39,000	Value: 75.00				

Y# 480   10 ZLOTYCH

14.1400 g., 0.9250 Silver 0.4205 oz. ASW, 32 mm. **Subject:** 80th Anniversary of the Modern Zloty Currency **Obv:** Man wearing glasses behind crowned eagle with wings open **Rev:** Bust left **Edge:** Plain

Date	Mintage	F	VF	XF	Unc	BU
2004MW Proof	55,000	Value: 35.00				

Y# 482   10 ZLOTYCH

14.1400 g., 0.9250 Silver 0.4205 oz. ASW, 32 mm. **Subject:** Poland Joining the European Union **Obv:** Crowned eagle in blue circle with yellow stars **Rev:** Multicolor European Union and Polish flags **Edge:** Plain

Date	Mintage	F	VF	XF	Unc	BU
2004MW Proof	78,000	Value: 65.00				

Y# 497   10 ZLOTYCH

14.1400 g., 0.9250 Silver 0.4205 oz. ASW, 32 mm. **Subject:** Warsaw Uprising 60th Anniversary **Obv:** Crowned eagle and value on resistance symbol **Rev:** Polish soldier wearing captured German helmet **Edge:** Plain

Date	Mintage	F	VF	XF	Unc	BU
2004MW Proof	92,000	Value: 30.00				

Y# 500   10 ZLOTYCH

14.1400 g., 0.9250 Silver 0.4205 oz. ASW, 32 mm. **Obv:** Polish paratrooper badge **Rev:** Gen. Sosabowski and descending paratrooper **Edge:** Plain

Date	Mintage	F	VF	XF	Unc	BU
2004MW Proof	56,000	Value: 30.00				

Y# 502   10 ZLOTYCH

14.1400 g., 0.9250 Silver 0.4205 oz. ASW, 32 mm. **Subject:** Polish Police 85th Anniversary **Obv:** Crowned eagle with wings open **Rev:** Seal partially overlapping police badge **Edge:** Plain

Date	Mintage	F	VF	XF	Unc	BU
2004MW Proof	65,000	Value: 30.00				

Y# 506   10 ZLOTYCH

14.1400 g., 0.9250 Silver 0.4205 oz. ASW, 32 mm. **Obv:** Siberian landscape above crowned eagle and value **Rev:** Aleksander Czekanowski (1833-1876) **Edge:** Plain

Date	Mintage	F	VF	XF	Unc	BU
2004MW Proof	45,000	Value: 30.00				

Y# 510   10 ZLOTYCH
14.1400 g., 0.9250 Silver 0.4205 oz. ASW, 32 mm. **Subject:** Warsaw Fine Arts Academy Centennial **Obv:** Crowned eagle with wings open within city square **Rev:** Art studio **Edge:** Plain

Date	Mintage	F	VF	XF	Unc	BU
2004MW Proof	75,000	Value: 30.00				

Y# 517   10 ZLOTYCH
14.1400 g., 0.9250 Silver 0.4205 oz. ASW, 32 mm. **Subject:** Olympics **Obv:** Crowned eagle with wings open and woman **Rev:** Fencers in front of Parthenon **Edge:** Plain

Date	Mintage	F	VF	XF	Unc	BU
2004MW Proof	70,000	Value: 30.00				

Y# 518   10 ZLOTYCH
14.1400 g., 0.9250 Silver 0.4205 oz. ASW, 32 mm. **Subject:** Olympics **Obv:** Crowned eagle with wings open within gold plated center **Rev:** Ancient athlete within gold plated circle **Edge:** Plain

Date	Mintage	F	VF	XF	Unc	BU
2004MW Proof	90,000	Value: 35.00				

Y# 523   10 ZLOTYCH
14.2300 g., 0.9250 Silver 0.4232 oz. ASW, 43.2 x 29.2 mm. **Subject:** Japan's Aichi Expo **Obv:** Monument **Rev:** Two cranes **Edge:** Plain **Shape:** Quarter of circle

Date	Mintage	F	VF	XF	Unc	BU
2005MW Proof	80,000	Value: 45.00				

Y# 526   10 ZLOTYCH
14.1400 g., 0.9250 Silver partially gilt 0.4205 oz. ASW, 32.1 mm. **Obv:** Crowned eagle with wings open above date and grasping hands **Rev:** Gold plated bust right and church **Edge:** Plain

Date	Mintage	F	VF	XF	Unc	BU
2005MW Proof	—	Value: 30.00				

Y# 537   10 ZLOTYCH
14.1400 g., 0.9250 Silver 0.4205 oz. ASW, 32 mm. **Obv:** Horse drawn carriage **Rev:** Green duck and Konstanty Ildefons Galczynski in top hat **Edge:** Plain

Date	Mintage	F	VF	XF	Unc	BU
2005MW Proof	62,000	Value: 30.00				

Y# 539   10 ZLOTYCH
14.1400 g., 0.9250 Silver 0.4205 oz. ASW, 32 mm. **Obv:** Baptismal font and Polish eagle **Rev:** Pope John Paul II and St. Peter's Basilica **Edge:** Plain

Date	Mintage	F	VF	XF	Unc	BU
2005MW Proof	170,000	Value: 32.00				

Y# 552   10 ZLOTYCH
14.1400 g., 0.9250 Silver 0.4205 oz. ASW, 32 mm. **Obv:** Crowned eagle above value **Rev:** Stanislaw August Poniatowski and shadow **Edge:** Plain

Date	Mintage	F	VF	XF	Unc	BU
2005MW Proof	60,000	Value: 35.00				

Y# 553   10 ZLOTYCH
14.1400 g., 0.9250 Silver 0.4205 oz. ASW, 32 mm. **Obv:** Crowned eagle above value **Rev:** Stanislaw August Poniatowski and crowned monogram **Edge:** Plain

Date	Mintage	F	VF	XF	Unc	BU
2005MW Proof	60,000	Value: 35.00				

Y# 554   10 ZLOTYCH
14.1400 g., 0.9250 Silver 0.4205 oz. ASW, 32 mm. **Subject:** End of WWII 60th Anniversary **Obv:** Crowned eagle above soldier silhouettes and value **Rev:** City view in ruins above bird with green sprig **Edge:** Plain

Date	Mintage	F	VF	XF	Unc	BU
2005MW Proof	70,000	Value: 40.00				

Y# 568   10 ZLOTYCH
14.1400 g., 0.9250 Silver 0.4205 oz. ASW, 32 mm. **Obv:** Sail ship and obverse design of Y-31 **Rev:** Reverse design of Y-31 on radiant design **Edge:** Lettered

Date	Mintage	F	VF	XF	Unc	BU
2005MW Proof	61,000	Value: 35.00				

Y# 596   10 ZLOTYCH
14.1800 g., 0.9250 Silver 0.4217 oz. ASW, 32 mm. **Subject:** 500th Anniversary - Birth of M. Reja **Obv:** National arms in oval, value below **Obv. Legend:** RZECZPOSPOLITA POLSKA **Rev:** Bust of Reja 3/4 right **Rev. Legend:** 500. ROCZNICA URODZIN MIKOLAJA REJA **Edge:** Plain

Date	Mintage	F	VF	XF	Unc	BU
2005MW Proof	60,000	Value: 30.00				

Y# 599   10 ZLOTYCH
14.1800 g., 0.9250 Silver 0.4217 oz. ASW, 32 mm. **Series:** History of the Zloty **Obv:** National arms at upper left, 1932 dated 10 Zlotych obverse at lower right, building facade in background **Obv. Legend:** RZECZPOSPOLITA POLSKA **Rev:** Reverse of 1932 dated coin with head of Queen Jadwiga **Rev. Legend:** DZIEJE ZLOTEGO **Edge:** Plain

Date	Mintage	F	VF	XF	Unc	BU
2006MW Proof	61,000	Value: 40.00				

Y# 556   10 ZLOTYCH
14.1400 g., 0.9250 Silver 0.4205 oz. ASW, 32 mm. **Subject:** 2006 Winter Olympics **Obv:** Small national arms at left, figure skating couple at center **Obv. Legend:** RZECZPOSPOLITA POLSKA **Rev:** Female figure skater **Rev. Legend:** XX ZIMOWE IGRZYSKA OLIMPIJSKIE **Edge:** Plain

Date	Mintage	F	VF	XF	Unc	BU
2006MW Proof	72,000	Value: 32.00				

Y# 555   10 ZLOTYCH
14.1400 g., 0.9250 Silver 0.4205 oz. ASW, 32 mm. **Subject:** 2006 Winter Olympics **Obv:** Snow boarder above crowned eagle **Rev:** Snow boarder **Edge:** Plain

Date	Mintage	F	VF	XF	Unc	BU
2006MW Proof	71,400	Value: 30.00				

Y# 598   10 ZLOTYCH
14.1500 g., 0.9250 Silver 0.4208 oz. ASW, 32 mm. **Subject:** 30th Anniversary June 1976 **Obv:** National arms divides denomination, split railroad tracks below **Obv. Legend:** RZECZPOSPOLITA POLSKA **Rev:** 3/4 length woman standing with child, outlined row of shielded forces in background **Rev. Legend:** 30. ROCZNICA - CZERWCA 1976 **Edge:** Plain

Date	Mintage	F	VF	XF	Unc	BU
2006MW Proof	56,000	Value: 32.00				

Y# 754   10 ZLOTYCH
14.1400 g., Bi-Metallic, 32 mm. **Subject:** World Cup soccer **Obv:** Eagle within net **Rev:** Player kicking ball, sun

Date	Mintage	F	VF	XF	Unc	BU
2006 Proof	—	Value: 75.00				

Y# 600   10 ZLOTYCH
14.1000 g., 0.9250 Silver 0.4193 oz. ASW, 32 mm. **Subject:** 125th Anniversary - Birth of Szymanowskiego **Obv:** Piano keys at left, national arms on music score at right **Obv. Legend:** RZECZPOSPOLITA POLSKA **Rev:** Bust of Szymanowskiego 3/4 left, music composition at back of head and over upper body, dates as hologram at left **Rev. Legend:** 125. ROCZNICA URODZIN KAROLA SZYMANOWSKIEGO **Edge:** Plain

Date	Mintage	F	VF	XF	Unc	BU
2007MW Proof	55,000	Value: 35.00				

Y# 601   10 ZLOTYCH
14.3000 g., 0.9250 Silver 0.4253 oz. ASW, 14 mm. **Subject:** Arctic Explorers **Obv:** Sailing ship at center, national arms at right with denomination below **Obv. Legend:** RZECZPOSPOLITA POLSKA **Rev:** Busts of Henryk Arctowski and Antoni Dobrowolski facing, polar outline map at lower left **Edge:** Plain

Date	Mintage	F	VF	XF	Unc	BU
2007MW Proof	60,000	Value: 35.00				

Y# 602   10 ZLOTYCH
14.0500 g., 0.9250 Silver 0.4178 oz. ASW, 31.95 x 22.39 mm.
Obv: Helmeted national arms, sword and denomination below
Obv. Legend: RZECZPOSPOLITA - POLSKA **Rev:** Chivalrous
knight on horseback jousting right **Rev. Inscription:** RYCERZ -
CIEZKOZBROJNY **Edge:** Plain **Shape:** Rectangular

Date	Mintage	F	VF	XF	Unc	BU
2007MW Proof	57,000	Value: 45.00				

Y# 585   10 ZLOTYCH
14.1400 g., 0.9250 Silver 0.4205 oz. ASW, 32 mm. **Obv:**
Mountains, Polish Eagle and value **Rev:** Ignacy Domeyko **Edge:**
Plain

Date	Mintage	F	VF	XF	Unc	BU
2007MW Proof	55,000	Value: 32.00				

Y# 587   10 ZLOTYCH
14.1400 g., 0.9250 Silver 0.4205 oz. ASW, 32 mm. **Subject:**
75th Anniversary - Breaking the Enigma Code **Obv:** Polish Eagle
on circuit board **Rev:** Segmented letters **Edge:** Lettered

Date	Mintage	F	VF	XF	Unc	BU
2007MW Proof	55,000	Value: 50.00				

Y# 589   10 ZLOTYCH
14.1400 g., 0.9250 Silver 0.4205 oz. ASW, 32 mm. **Obv:** Angel,
Polish Eagle and obverse coin design of Y-18 **Rev:** Reverse coin
design of Y-18 on wheat ears **Edge:** Plain

Date	Mintage	F	VF	XF	Unc	BU
2007MW Proof	57,000	Value: 40.00				

Y# 595   10 ZLOTYCH
14.1400 g., 0.9250 Silver 0.4205 oz. ASW, 32 mm. **Subject:**
Municipality of Krakow, 750th Anniversary **Obv:** City gate tower,
national arms at lower right **Obv. Legend:** RZECZPOSPOLITA
POLSKA **Rev:** Knight with shield standing facing

Date	Mintage	F	VF	XF	Unc	BU
2007MW Proof	58,000	Value: 50.00				

Y# 632   10 ZLOTYCH
14.1400 g., 0.9250 Silver 0.4205 oz. ASW, 32 mm. **Subject:**
40th Anniversary "Rocznica" March **Obv:** National arms at upper
right, manuscript pages fluttering at left **Obv. Legend:**
RZECZPOSPOLITA POLSKA **Rev:** Student protesters in front
of gates of Warsaw University, military police in silhouette in
foreground

Date	Mintage	F	VF	XF	Unc	BU
2008MW Proof	118,000	Value: 50.00				

Y# 635   10 ZLOTYCH
14.1400 g., 0.9250 Silver 0.4205 oz. ASW, 32 mm. **Subject:**
Zbigniew Herbert **Obv:** Bust of Herbert 3/4 right at left, national
arms at lower right **Rev:** Statue of Nike **Edge:** Plain

Date	Mintage	F	VF	XF	Unc	BU
2008MW Proof	—	Value: 40.00				

Y# 645   10 ZLOTYCH
14.4000 g., 0.9250 Silver with gilt center 0.4282 oz. ASW,
32 mm. **Subject:** The 29th Olympic Games Beijing 2008 **Obv:**
Chinese ornament & dragon **Rev:** Swimmer

Date	Mintage	F	VF	XF	Unc	BU
2008 Proof	140,000	Value: 50.00				

Y# 639   10 ZLOTYCH
14.1400 g., 0.9250 Silver 0.4205 oz. ASW, 32 mm. **Subject:**
Siberian Exiles **Obv:** Small national arms at left, human outlines
at right **Obv. Legend:** RZECZPOSPOLITA POLSKA **Rev:** Tree
lines with imbedded triangular crystal below **Rev. Inscription:**
SYBIRACY **Edge:** Plain

Date	Mintage	F	VF	XF	Unc	BU
2008MW Proof	135,000	Value: 35.00				

Y# 646   10 ZLOTYCH
14.1400 g., 0.9250 Silver 0.4205 oz. ASW, 32 mm. **Subject:**

Date	Mintage	F	VF	XF	Unc	BU
2008 Proof	150,000	Value: 30.00				

Y# 649   10 ZLOTYCH
14.1400 g., 0.9250 Silver 0.4205 oz. ASW, 32 mm. **Subject:**
Polish Travellers & Explorers **Obv:** Man & woman holding child
Rev: Bust of Bronislaw Pilsudski

Date	Mintage	F	VF	XF	Unc	BU
2008 Proof	99,000	Value: 32.00				

Y# 655   10 ZLOTYCH
14.1400 g., 0.9250 Silver 0.4205 oz. ASW, 32 mm. **Subject:**
450th Anniversary of the Polish Post **Obv:** Eagle on top right,
post stamp in center with man on horse **Rev:** Post courier

Date	Mintage	F	VF	XF	Unc	BU
2008 Proof	135,000	Value: 35.00				

Y# 658   10 ZLOTYCH
14.1400 g., 0.9250 Silver 0.4205 oz. ASW, 32 mm. **Subject:**
400th Anniversary - Polish Settlement in North America **Obv:**
Man blowing glassware left **Rev:** Man blowing glassware right

Date	Mintage	F	VF	XF	Unc	BU
2008 Proof	126,000	Value: 35.00				

Y# 661   10 ZLOTYCH
14.1400 g., 0.9250 Silver 0.4205 oz. ASW, 32 mm. **Subject:**
90th Anniversary of the Greater Poland Uprising **Obv:** Eagle at
top, Commander riding horse followed by soldiers **Rev:** Rose at
left, Bust of Igancy Jan Paderewski at right

Date	Mintage	F	VF	XF	Unc	BU
2008 Proof	107,000	Value: 40.00				

Y# 695   10 ZLOTYCH
14.1400 g., 0.9250 Silver 0.4205 oz. ASW, 32 mm. **Subject:**
70th Anniversary of the start of World War II **Obv:** Eagle and map

of Nazi and Soviet invasion **Rev:** Planes dropping bombs on Wielun

Date	Mintage	F	VF	XF	Unc	BU
2009MW Proof	100,000	Value: 45.00				

Y# 671   10 ZLOTYCH
14.4000 g., 0.9250 Silver 0.4282 oz. ASW, 22x32 mm. **Obv:** Eagle, flag and armor **Rev:** Hussar Knights, XVII Century **Shape:** Vertical rectangle

Date	Mintage	F	VF	XF	Unc	BU
2009 Proof	100,000	Value: 50.00				

Y# 688   10 ZLOTYCH
14.1400 g., 0.9250 Silver Gold plated center in silver ring 0.4205 oz. ASW, 27 mm. **Subject:** Poets of the Uprising **Obv:** National arms **Rev:** Tadeusz Gajcy portrait

Date	Mintage	F	VF	XF	Unc	BU
2009MW Proof	100,000	Value: 45.00				

Y# 674   10 ZLOTYCH
14.4000 g., 0.9250 Silver 0.4282 oz. ASW, 32 mm. **Subject:** Supreme Chamber, 90th Anniversary **Obv:** Building **Rev:** Monogram hologram

Date	Mintage	F	VF	XF	Unc	BU
2009MW Proof	100,000	Value: 55.00				

Y# 676   10 ZLOTYCH
14.4000 g., 0.9250 Silver 0.4282 oz. ASW, 32 mm. **Subject:** Central Banking, 180th Anniversary **Obv:** National arms above building **Rev:** Portrait above banknote

Date	Mintage	F	VF	XF	Unc	BU
2009MW Proof	92,000	Value: 45.00				

Y# 681   10 ZLOTYCH
14.1400 g., 0.9250 Silver 0.4205 oz. ASW, 32 mm. **Subject:** General Elections of 1989 **Obv:** Eagle **Rev:** Pope John Paul II and Solidarity banner in color

Date	Mintage	F	VF	XF	Unc	BU
2009MW Proof	100,000	Value: 35.00				

Y# 685   10 ZLOTYCH
14.1400 g., 0.9250 Silver 0.4205 oz. ASW, 29x29 mm. **Subject:** Czeslaw Niemen **Obv:** National arms and large portrait **Rev:** Female crying **Shape:** Square

Date	Mintage	F	VF	XF	Unc	BU
2009MW Proof	100,000	Value: 45.00				

Y# 686   10 ZLOTYCH
14.1400 g., 0.9250 Silver 0.4205 oz. ASW, 32 mm. **Subject:** Cezeslaw Neiman **Obv:** National arms and portrait **Rev:** Abstract painting

Date	Mintage	F	VF	XF	Unc	BU
2009MW Proof	100,000	Value: 45.00				

Y# 689   10 ZLOTYCH
14.1400 g., 0.9250 Silver with gold plated ring 0.4205 oz. ASW, 32 mm. **Subject:** Poets of the uprising **Obv:** National arms **Rev:** Krzystof Baczynski portrait facing

Date	Mintage	F	VF	XF	Unc	BU
2009MW Proof	100,000	Value: 45.00				

Y# 691   10 ZLOTYCH
14.1400 g., 0.9250 Silver 0.4205 oz. ASW, 32 mm. **Subject:** First Cadre Company March **Obv:** National arms and eagle atop stelle monument **Rev:** Troops marching, song and music

Date	Mintage	F	VF	XF	Unc	BU
2009MW Proof	50,000	Value: 50.00				

Y# 698   10 ZLOTYCH
14.1400 g., 0.9250 Silver 0.4205 oz. ASW, 32 mm. **Series:** Tatar Rescues, 100th Anniversary **Obv:** National arms and logo colorized **Rev:** Mountains and figure of Karlowicz

Date	Mintage	F	VF	XF	Unc	BU
2009MW Proof	100,000	Value: 45.00				

Y# 701   10 ZLOTYCH
14.1400 g., 0.9250 Silver 0.4205 oz. ASW, 32 mm. **Subject:** Fr. Jerzy Popielosko, 25th Anniversary of Murder **Obv:** Rose on monument **Rev:** Statue and tear drop on map of Poland

Date	Mintage	F	VF	XF	Unc	BU
2009MW Proof	100,000	Value: 45.00				

Y# 706   10 ZLOTYCH
28.2800 g., 0.9250 Silver 0.8410 oz. ASW, 40x28 mm. **Subject:** Wald Strzeminski **Obv:** Portrait and multicolor palette **Rev:** Artwork **Shape:** Rectangle

Date	Mintage	F	VF	XF	Unc	BU
2009MW Proof	100,000	Value: 45.00				

Y# 708   10 ZLOTYCH
14.1400 g., 0.9250 Silver 0.4205 oz. ASW, 32 mm. **Subject:** Polish Underground State **Obv:** National arms and monogram and cloth flag **Rev:** Figure and cloth flag

Date	Mintage	F	VF	XF	Unc	BU
2009MW Proof	50,000	Value: 55.00				

Y# 713   10 ZLOTYCH
14.1400 g., 0.9250 Silver 0.4205 oz. ASW, 32 mm. **Subject:** Auschwitz liberation **Obv:** National arms, camp sign and barbed wire fence **Rev:** Prisoner and barbed wire fence

Date	Mintage	F	VF	XF	Unc	BU
2010MW Proof	80,000	Value: 45.00				

Y# 716   10 ZLOTYCH
14.1400 g., 0.9250 Silver 0.4205 oz. ASW, 32 mm. **Subject:**
Vancouver Winter Olympics **Obv:** Speedskaters **Rev:** Biathlon

Date	Mintage	F	VF	XF	Unc	BU
2010MW Proof	80,000	Value: 45.00				

Y# 719   10 ZLOTYCH
14.1400 g., 0.9250 Silver 0.4205 oz. ASW, 32x22 mm. **Subject:**
Napoleonic Imperial Guard **Obv:** National arms and helmet **Rev:**
Mounted Napoleonic Guard member **Shape:** Vertical rectangle

Date	Mintage	F	VF	XF	Unc	BU
2010MW Proof	100,000	Value: 45.00				

Y# 722   10 ZLOTYCH
14.1400 g., 0.9250 Silver 0.4205 oz. ASW, 32 mm. **Subject:**
Katyn Crime **Obv:** National emblem and silhouette of a badge
Rev: Field of crosses

Date	Mintage	F	VF	XF	Unc	BU
2010MW Antiqued	80,000	—	—	—	50.00	—

Y# 726   10 ZLOTYCH
14.1400 g., 0.9250 Silver 0.4205 oz. ASW, 32 mm. **Subject:**
Polish Scouting Centennial

Date	Mintage	F	VF	XF	Unc	BU
2010MW Proof	90,000	Value: 30.00				

Y# 728   10 ZLOTYCH
14.1400 g., 0.9250 Silver 0.4205 oz. ASW, 32 mm. **Subject:**
Popular Music - Marke Grechuta

Date	Mintage	F	VF	XF	Unc	BU
2010MW Proof	100,000	Value: 30.00				

Y# 729   10 ZLOTYCH
14.1400 g., 0.9250 Silver 0.4205 oz. ASW, 28.2x28.2 mm.
Subject: Popular Music - Marek Grechuta **Shape:** Square

Date	Mintage	F	VF	XF	Unc	BU
2010MW Proof	100,000	Value: 35.00				

Y# 731   10 ZLOTYCH
14.1400 g., 0.9250 Silver 0.4205 oz. ASW, 32 mm. **Subject:**
Jan Twardowski

Date	Mintage	F	VF	XF	Unc	BU
2010MW Proof	80,000	Value: 35.00				

Y# 733   10 ZLOTYCH
14.1400 g., 0.9250 Silver 0.4205 oz. ASW, 40x26 mm. **Subject:**
Battles of Grunwald, Kluszyn **Shape:** Oval

Date	Mintage	F	VF	XF	Unc	BU
2010MW Proof	100,000	Value: 35.00				

Y# 736   10 ZLOTYCH
28.2800 g., 0.9250 Silver 0.8410 oz. ASW, 38.6 mm. **Subject:**
Battle of Warsaw **Rev:** Battle scene in color

Date	Mintage	F	VF	XF	Unc	BU
2010MW Proof	100,000	Value: 40.00				

Y# 738   10 ZLOTYCH
14.1400 g., 0.9250 Silver 0.4205 oz. ASW, 32 mm. **Subject:**
August of 1980, 30th Anniversary

Date	Mintage	F	VF	XF	Unc	BU
2010MW Proof	100,000	Value: 35.00				

Y# 743   10 ZLOTYCH
14.1400 g., 0.9250 Silver 0.4205 oz. ASW, 32 mm. **Subject:**
Polish Explorers - Benedykt Dybowski

Date	Mintage	F	VF	XF	Unc	BU
2010MW Proof	100,000	Value: 35.00				

Y# 745   10 ZLOTYCH
28.2800 g., 0.9250 Silver 0.8410 oz. ASW, 38.61 mm. **Subject:**
Krzeszow

Date	Mintage	F	VF	XF	Unc	BU
2010MW Proof	80,000	Value: 40.00				

Y# 747   10 ZLOTYCH
28.2800 g., 0.9250 Silver 0.8410 oz. ASW, 40x28 mm. **Subject:**
Arthur Grottger

Date	Mintage	F	VF	XF	Unc	BU
2010MW Proof	100,000	Value: 40.00				

Y# 750   10 ZLOTYCH
14.1400 g., 0.9250 Silver 0.4205 oz. ASW, 40x26 mm. **Subject:**
Battle of Grunwald **Shape:** Oval

Date	Mintage	F	VF	XF	Unc	BU
2010MW Proof	100,000	Value: 45.00				

Y# 758   10 ZLOTYCH
14.1400 g., 0.9250 Silver 0.4205 oz. ASW, 32 mm. **Subject:**
Benedykt Dybowski **Obv:** Books **Rev:** Bust facing, map in
background

Date	Mintage	F	VF	XF	Unc	BU
2010 Proof	60,000	Value: 55.00				

Y# 807   10 ZLOTYCH
14.1400 g., 0.9250 Silver 0.4205 oz. ASW, 32 mm. **Subject:**
Krzysztof Komeda **Rev:** Komeda and movie film real

Date	Mintage	F	VF	XF	Unc	BU
2010MW Proof	—	Value: 50.00				

Y# 808   10 ZLOTYCH
14.1400 g., 0.9250 Silver 0.4205 oz. ASW, 28.2x28.2 mm.
Subject: Krzysztof Komeda **Shape:** Square

Date	Mintage	F	VF	XF	Unc	BU
2010MW Proof	—	Value: 50.00				

Y# 768   10 ZLOTYCH
14.1400 g., 0.9250 Silver 0.4205 oz. ASW, 32 mm. **Subject:**
Independent Student's Union, 30th Anniversary

Date	Mintage	F	VF	XF	Unc	BU
2011MW Proof	50,000	Value: 30.00				

Y# 770   10 ZLOTYCH
14.1400 g., 0.9250 Silver 0.4205 oz. ASW, 32 mm. **Subject:**
Smolensk plane crash

Date	Mintage	F	VF	XF	Unc	BU
2011MW Proof	30,000	Value: 30.00				

Y# 778   10 ZLOTYCH
14.1400 g., 0.9250 Silver 0.4205 oz. ASW, 32 mm. **Subject:**
Poland's presidency of the Council of the European Union

Date	Mintage	F	VF	XF	Unc	BU
2011MW Proof	50,000	Value: 30.00				

Y# 781   10 ZLOTYCH
14.1400 g., Silver, 22.4x32 mm. **Subject:** 22.4x32 **Shape:**
Vertical rectangle

Date	Mintage	F	VF	XF	Unc	BU
2011MW Proof	50,000	Value: 50.00				

Y# 786   10 ZLOTYCH
14.1400 g., 0.9250 Silver 0.4205 oz. ASW, 32 mm. **Subject:**
Czeslaw Milosz

Date	Mintage	F	VF	XF	Unc	BU
2011MW Proof	50,000	Value: 30.00				

Y# 790   10 ZLOTYCH
14.1400 g., 0.9250 Silver 0.4205 oz. ASW, 32 mm. **Subject:**
Ignacy Jan Paderewski

Date	Mintage	F	VF	XF	Unc	BU
2011MW Proof	50,000	Value: 30.00				

Y# 793   10 ZLOTYCH
14.1400 g., 0.9250 Silver 0.4205 oz. ASW, 32 mm. **Subject:**
Silesian Uprising

Date	Mintage	F	VF	XF	Unc	BU
2011MW Proof	50,000	Value: 30.00				

Y# 796   10 ZLOTYCH
14.1400 g., 0.9250 Silver 0.4205 oz. ASW, 32 mm. **Subject:**
Society for the Protection of the Blind, 100th Anniversary

Date	Mintage	F	VF	XF	Unc	BU
2011MW Proof	50,000	Value: 30.00				

Y# 798   10 ZLOTYCH
14.1400 g., 0.9250 Silver 0.4205 oz. ASW, 32 mm. **Subject:**
Ferdynand Ossendowski

Date	Mintage	F	VF	XF	Unc	BU
2011MW Proof	50,000	Value: 30.00				

Y# 802   10 ZLOTYCH
14.1400 g., 0.9250 Silver 0.4205 oz. ASW, 28.2x28.2 mm.
Subject: Jeremi Przybora and Jerzy Wasowski **Shape:** Square

Date	Mintage	F	VF	XF	Unc	BU
2011MW Proof	50,000	Value: 30.00				

Y# 803   10 ZLOTYCH
14.1400 g., 0.9250 Silver 0.4205 oz. ASW, 32 mm. **Subject:**
Jeremi Przybora and Jerzy Wasowski

Date	Mintage	F	VF	XF	Unc	BU
2011MW Proof	50,000	Value: 30.00				

Y# 810   10 ZLOTYCH
14.1400 g., 0.9250 Silver 0.4205 oz. ASW, 28.7x30 mm.
Subject: Christmas Charity Orchestra, 20th Anniversary **Obv:**
Piano keyboard **Rev:** Guitar with hearts **Shape:** Heart

Date	Mintage	F	VF	XF	Unc	BU
2012MW Proof	60,000	Value: 50.00				

Y# 812   10 ZLOTYCH
14.1400 g., 0.9250 Silver 0.4205 oz. ASW, 32 mm. **Subject:**
Cooperative Banking in Poland, 150th Anniversary **Obv:** Eagle
at left, bank building at right **Rev:** Pile of coin and banknotes at
center, semi-circle of stick figures holding hands at right

Date	Mintage	F	VF	XF	Unc	BU
2012MW Proof	40,000	Value: 50.00				

Y# 409   20 ZLOTYCH
28.2800 g., 0.9250 Silver 0.8410 oz. ASW, 38.6 mm. **Subject:**
Wieliezce Salt Mine **Obv:** Crowned eagle with wings open in
center of rock **Rev:** Ancient salt miners **Edge:** Plain

Date	Mintage	F	VF	XF	Unc	BU
2001MW Proof	25,000	Value: 250				

Y# 411   20 ZLOTYCH
28.2800 g., 0.9250 Silver 0.8410 oz. ASW, 38.6 mm. **Subject:**
Amber Route **Obv:** Crowned eagle and two ancient Roman silver
cups **Rev:** Piece of amber mounted above an ancient Roman
coin design and map with the route marked with stars **Edge:** Plain

Date	Mintage	F	VF	XF	Unc	BU
2001MW Antique finish	30,000	—	—	—	750	—

Y# 415   20 ZLOTYCH
28.2800 g., 0.9250 Silver 0.8410 oz. ASW, 38.6 mm. **Obv:**
Crowned eagle with wings open flanked by flags **Rev:** European
Swallowtail Butterfly **Edge:** Plain

Date	Mintage	F	VF	XF	Unc	BU
2001MW Proof	27,000	Value: 300				

Y# 424   20 ZLOTYCH
28.7700 g., 0.9250 Silver 0.8556 oz. ASW, 38.6 mm. **Subject:**
Christmas **Obv:** Ornate city view **Rev:** Celebration scene
including an attached zirconia star **Edge:** Plain

Date	Mintage	F	VF	XF	Unc	BU
2001MW Antique patina	55,000	—	—	—	225	—

Y# 428 20 ZLOTYCH
28.2800 g., 0.9250 Silver 0.8410 oz. ASW, 38.6 mm. **Obv:**
Crowned eagle with wings open flanked by flags **Rev:** European
Pond Turtles **Edge:** Plain

Date	Mintage	F	VF	XF	Unc	BU
2002 Proof	35,000	Value: 175				

Y# 442 20 ZLOTYCH
28.0500 g., 0.9250 Silver 0.8342 oz. ASW, 39.94x27.93 mm.
Subject: Jan Matejko **Obv:** Seated figure with crowned eagle at
lower right **Rev:** Head facing with multicolor artist's palette **Edge:**
Plain **Shape:** Rectangle

Date	Mintage	F	VF	XF	Unc	BU
2002MW Proof	57,000	Value: 200				

Y# 457 20 ZLOTYCH
28.2800 g., 0.9250 Silver 0.8410 oz. ASW, 38.6 mm. **Obv:**
National arms at lower left, castle complex in background **Rev:**
Malborku castle, reddish-brown ceramic applique, **Rev. Legend:**
ZAMEK W MALBORKU **Edge:** Plain

Date	Mintage	F	VF	XF	Unc	BU
2002MW Antique patina	51,000	—	—	—	100	—

Y# 449 20 ZLOTYCH
28.4700 g., 0.9250 Silver 0.8466 oz. ASW, 38.6 mm. **Obv:**
Crowned eagle with wings open **Rev:** European Eels and world
globe **Edge:** Plain

Date	Mintage	F	VF	XF	Unc	BU
2003MW Proof	—	Value: 250				

Y# 452 20 ZLOTYCH
28.2800 g., 0.9250 Silver 0.8410 oz. ASW, 38.6 mm. **Subject:**
Easter Monday Festival **Obv:** Crowned eagle on lace curtain
above lamb and multicolor Easter eggs **Rev:** Festival scene
Edge: Plain

Date	Mintage	F	VF	XF	Unc	BU
2003MW Proof	44,000	Value: 100				

Y# 471 20 ZLOTYCH
28.2800 g., 0.9250 Silver 0.8410 oz. ASW, 40 x 40 mm. **Obv:**
Standing Pope John Paul II **Rev:** Pope"s portrait **Edge:** Plain
Shape: Square

Date	Mintage	F	VF	XF	Unc	BU
2003MW Proof	83,000	Value: 75.00				

Y# 478 20 ZLOTYCH
28.2800 g., 0.9250 Silver 0.8410 oz. ASW, 27.93x39.94 mm.
Obv: "Death" allegory closing an old man's eyes, national arms
at lower right **Rev:** Self portrait of Jacek Malczewski, palette at
lower right multicolor **Edge:** Plain **Shape:** Rectangle

Date	Mintage	F	VF	XF	Unc	BU
2003MW Proof	64,000	Value: 65.00				

Y# 498 20 ZLOTYCH
28.2800 g., 0.9250 Silver 0.8410 oz. ASW, 38.6 mm. **Subject:**
Lodz Ghetto (1940-1944) **Obv:** Silhouette on wall **Rev:** Child
with a pot **Edge:** Plain

Date	Mintage	F	VF	XF	Unc	BU
2004MW Matte	64,000	—	—	—	45.00	

Y# 504 20 ZLOTYCH
28.2800 g., 0.9250 Silver 0.8410 oz. ASW, 38.6 mm. **Subject:**
Polish Senate **Obv:** Crowned eagle above Senate chamber **Rev:**
Senate eagle and speaker's staff **Edge:** Plain

Date	Mintage	F	VF	XF	Unc	BU
2004MW Proof	67,000	Value: 75.00				

Y# 508 20 ZLOTYCH
28.2800 g., 0.9250 Silver 0.8410 oz. ASW, 38.6 mm. **Obv:**
Crowned eagle in harvest wreath **Rev:** Harvest fest parade **Edge:**
Plain

Date	Mintage	F	VF	XF	Unc	BU
2004MW Proof	74,000	Value: 45.00				

Y# 513 20 ZLOTYCH
28.2800 g., 0.9250 Silver 0.8410 oz. ASW, 40x28 mm. **Obv:**
Mother and children **Rev:** Stanislaw Wyspianski (1869-1907)
Edge: Plain

Date	Mintage	F	VF	XF	Unc	BU
2004MW Proof	80,000	Value: 55.00				

Y# 515 20 ZLOTYCH
28.2800 g., 0.9250 Silver 0.8410 oz. ASW, 38.6 mm. **Obv:**
National arms **Obv. Legend:** RZECZPOSPOLITA POLSKA **Rev:**
2 Harbor Porpoises **Rev. Legend:** MORSWIN - Phocoena
phocoena **Edge:** Plain

Date	Mintage	F	VF	XF	Unc	BU
2004MW Proof	56,000	Value: 175				

Y# 531 20 ZLOTYCH
28.8400 g., 0.9250 Silver 0.8576 oz. ASW, 38.6 mm. **Obv:**
Polish eagle above value **Rev:** Eagle Owl with nestlings **Edge:**
Plain

Date	Mintage	F	VF	XF	Unc	BU
2005MW Proof	61,000	Value: 150				

Y# 542 20 ZLOTYCH
28.2800 g., 0.9250 Silver 0.8410 oz. ASW, 28 x 40 mm. **Obv:**
Sneak thief stealing from a miser **Rev:** Painter Tadeusz Makowski
Edge: Plain **Shape:** Rectangular

Date	Mintage	F	VF	XF	Unc	BU
2005MW Proof	70,000	Value: 60.00				

Y# 597 20 ZLOTYCH
28.5000 g., 0.9250 Silver 0.8475 oz. ASW, 38.5 mm. **Subject:**
350 Years, Defence of Góry **Obv:** National arms to right of
outlined Góry **Obv. Legend:** RZECZPOSPOLITA POLSKA **Obv.
Inscription:** Tutaj zawsze / bylismy woini / JAN PAWEL II **Rev:**
1/2 length figure of man at lower right, Góry under bombardment
in background **Rev. Legend:** 350 - LECIE OBRONY JASNEJ
GÓRY **Edge:** Lettered **Edge Lettering:** CZESTOCHOWA 2005
repeated three times

Date	Mintage	F	VF	XF	Unc	BU
2005MW Proof	69,000	Value: 55.00				

Y# 604 20 ZLOTYCH
28.1400 g., Silver, 39.95x27.97 mm. **Subject:** Aleksander
Gierymski **Obv:** National arms at upper right, painting of elderly
woman carrying baskets **Rev:** Bust of Gierymski facing at center,
harbor scene at right, painter's palette at lower left multicolor
Edge: Plain **Shape:** Rectangle

Date	Mintage	F	VF	XF	Unc	BU
2006MW Proof	66,000	Value: 65.00				

Y# 535   20 ZLOTYCH
28.8400 g., 0.9250 Silver 0.8576 oz. ASW, 38.6 mm. **Obv:** Polish eagle above value **Rev:** Alpine Marmot standing **Edge:** Plain

Date	Mintage	VF	XF	Unc	BU
2006MW Proof	60,000	Value: 125			

Y# 533   20 ZLOTYCH
28.8400 g., 0.9250 Silver 0.8576 oz. ASW, 38.6 mm. **Obv:** Polish eagle above value **Rev:** Multicolor holographic spider web **Edge:** Plain

Date	Mintage	F	VF	XF	Unc	BU
2006MW Proof	65,000	Value: 115				

Y# 584   20 ZLOTYCH
28.4700 g., 0.9250 Silver 0.8466 oz. ASW, 38.6 mm. **Obv:** Polish Eagle on old wood **Rev:** Multi-color wood behind Haczowie church **Edge:** Plain

Date	Mintage	F	VF	XF	Unc	BU
2006MW Proof	—	Value: 60.00				

Y# 579   20 ZLOTYCH
28.2800 g., 0.9250 Silver 0.8410 oz. ASW, 38.6 mm. **Obv:** Crowned eagle **Rev:** Two Grey Seal females and pup with two silhouettes in background **Edge:** Plain

Date	Mintage	F	VF	XF	Unc	BU
2007MW Proof	58,000	Value: 125				

Y# 603   20 ZLOTYCH
28.2500 g., 0.9250 Silver 0.8401 oz. ASW, 38.5 mm. **Subject:** Medieval Principality of Sredniowieczne in Torin **Obv:** City arms at right, national arms below walled city gate in background **Obv. Legend:** RZECZPOSPOLITA POLSKA **Rev.** City view **Rev. Legend:** MIASTO SREDNIOWIECZNE W TORUNIU **Edge:** Plain

Date	Mintage	F	VF	XF	Unc	BU
2007MW Proof	58,000	Value: 70.00				

Y# 636   20 ZLOTYCH
28.3800 g., Silver, 38.6 mm. **Subject:** 65th Anniversary Warsaw Ghetto Uprising **Obv:** Small national arms at left, flames, shattered wall **Obv. Legend:** RZECZPOSPOLITA POLSKA **Rev:** Tree, Star of David, wall in backgound **Rev. Inscription:** 65. ROCZNICA POWSTANIA / W GETCIE WARSZAWSKIM **Edge:** Plain

Date	Mintage	F	VF	XF	Unc	BU
2008MW Proof	—	Value: 60.00				

Y# 642   20 ZLOTYCH
28.2800 g., Silver, 38.61 mm. **Subject:** Kazimierz Dolny **Obv:** Part of a wall and an eagle **Rev:** Houses and a well

Date	Mintage	F	VF	XF	Unc	BU
2008 Proof	125,000	Value: 50.00				

Y# 637   20 ZLOTYCH
28.2800 g., 0.9250 Silver 0.8410 oz. ASW, 38.61 mm. **Obv:** National arms **Obv. Legend:** RZECZPOSPOLITA POLSKA **Rev:** Peregrine Falcon by 2 chicks in nest at right **Rev. Legend:** SOKOL WEDROWNY - Falco peregrinus **Edge:** Plain

Date	Mintage	F	VF	XF	Unc	BU
2008MW Proof	107,000	Value: 80.00				

Y# 651   20 ZLOTYCH
28.2800 g., Silver, 38.61 mm. **Subject:** 90th Anniversary of Regaining Freedom **Obv:** War decoration left side, eagle top right **Rev:** 3 generals

Date	Mintage	F	VF	XF	Unc	BU
2008 Proof	110,000	Value: 55.00				

Y# 679   20 ZLOTYCH
28.2800 g., 0.9250 Silver 0.8410 oz. ASW, 38.6 mm. **Subject:** Green Lizard **Obv:** National arms above value **Rev:** Two green lizards in nature

Date	Mintage	F	VF	XF	Unc	BU
2009MW Proof	100,000	Value: 45.00				

Y# 693   20 ZLOTYCH
28.2800 g., 0.9250 Silver 0.8410 oz. ASW, 38.6 mm. **Subject:**

Liquidation of the Lotz Ghetto **Obv:** New oak sprig amongst broken bricks **Rev:** Oak tree, bare and with leaves, star of David within

Date	Mintage	F	VF	XF	Unc	BU
2009MW Antiqued	50,000	—	—	—	45.00	—

Y# 704 20 ZLOTYCH
28.2800 g., 0.9250 Silver 0.8410 oz. ASW, 38.6 mm. **Subject:** Honoring Poles who saved the Jews **Obv:** National arms above broken brick wall **Rev:** Three portraits

Date	Mintage	F	VF	XF	Unc	BU
2009MW Proof	100,000	Value: 40.00				

Y# 724 20 ZLOTYCH
28.2800 g., 0.9250 Silver 0.8410 oz. ASW, 38.61 mm. **Subject:** Horseshoe Bat

Date	Mintage	F	VF	XF	Unc	BU
2010MW Proof	100,000	Value: 37.50				

Y# 763 20 ZLOTYCH
28.8400 g., 0.9250 Silver 0.8576 oz. ASW, 38.6 mm. **Subject:** Borsuk **Obv:** National Arms above value **Rev:** Eurasian Badgers

Date	Mintage	F	VF	XF	Unc	BU
2011 Proof	80,000	Value: 60.00				

Y# 765 20 ZLOTYCH
28.2800 g., 0.9250 Silver 0.8410 oz. ASW, 40x28 mm. **Subject:** Zofia Stryjenska **Obv:** Horseback scene, National Arms at right **Rev:** Portrait with artist pallet with brushes **Shape:** Rectangle

Date	Mintage	F	VF	XF	Unc	BU
2011 Proof	50,000	Value: 55.00				

Y# 771 20 ZLOTYCH
28.2800 g., Silver, 38.61 mm. **Subject:** Smolensk plane crash

Date	Mintage	F	VF	XF	Unc	BU
2011MW Proof	—	Value: 50.00				

Y# 773 20 ZLOTYCH
14.1400 g., 0.9250 Silver 0.4205 oz. ASW, 38.61 mm. **Subject:** John Paul II Beautification **Rev:** Pope waving, earth in background in color

Date	Mintage	F	VF	XF	Unc	BU
2011MW Proof	80,000	Value: 50.00				

Y# 814 20 ZLOTYCH
28.2800 g., 0.9250 Silver 0.8410 oz. ASW, 38.61 mm. **Subject:** Ulma, Baranek and Kowalski families **Obv:** Fields and town view **Rev:** Family faces seen thru broken fenceboards

Date	Mintage	F	VF	XF	Unc	BU
2012MW	40,000	—	—	—	50.00	—
Antique patina						

Y# 682 25 ZLOTYCH
1.0000 g., 0.9000 Gold 0.0289 oz. AGW, 12 mm. **Subject:** General Elections of 1989 **Obv:** National arms above value **Rev:** Solidarity logo

Date	Mintage	F	VF	XF	Unc	BU
2009MW Proof	40,000	Value: 65.00				

Y# 740 25 ZLOTYCH
1.0000 g., 0.9000 Gold 0.0289 oz. AGW, 12 mm. **Subject:** Constitutional Tribunal

Date	Mintage	F	VF	XF	Unc	BU
2010MW Proof	10,000	Value: 75.00				

Y# 774 25 ZLOTYCH
1.0000 g., 0.9000 Gold 0.0289 oz. AGW, 12 mm. **Subject:** John Paul II Beautification

Date	Mintage	F	VF	XF	Unc	BU
2011MW Proof	10,000	Value: 75.00				

Y# 739 30 ZLOTYCH
1.7000 g., 0.9000 Gold 0.0492 oz. AGW, 16 mm. **Subject:** August of 1980

Date	Mintage	F	VF	XF	Unc	BU
2010MW Proof	50,000	Value: 100				

Y# 702 37 ZLOTYCH
1.7500 g., 0.9000 Gold 0.0506 oz. AGW, 16 mm. **Subject:** Fr.

Jorzy Popieluszko, 25th Anniversary of Murder **Obv:** National arms above large 37 **Rev:** Many hands holding crosses

Date	Mintage	F	VF	XF	Unc	BU
2009MW Proof	60,000	Value: 100				

Y# 652 50 ZLOTYCH
3.1300 g., Gold, 18 mm. **Subject:** 90th Annniversary of Regaining Freedom **Obv:** Tomb of the unknown soldier **Rev:** Mounted Commander-In-Chief Jósef Pilsudski

Date	Mintage	F	VF	XF	Unc	BU
2008 Proof	8,800	Value: 125				

Y# 416 100 ZLOTYCH
8.0000 g., 0.9000 Gold 0.2315 oz. AGW, 21 mm. **Subject:** Wladyslaw I (1320-33) **Obv:** Crowned eagle with wings open **Rev:** Crowned bust facing **Edge:** Plain

Date	Mintage	F	VF	XF	Unc	BU
2001MW Proof	2,000	Value: 875				

Y# 417 100 ZLOTYCH
8.0000 g., 0.9000 Gold 0.2315 oz. AGW, 21 mm. **Subject:** Boleslaw III (1102-1138) **Obv:** Crowned eagle with wings open **Rev:** Pointed crowned bust facing **Edge:** Plain

Date	Mintage	F	VF	XF	Unc	BU
2001MW Proof	2,000	Value: 875				

Y# 462 100 ZLOTYCH
8.0000 g., 0.9000 Gold 0.2315 oz. AGW, 21 mm. **Obv:** Crowned eagle with wings open **Rev:** Jan Sobieski III **Edge:** Plain

Date	Mintage	F	VF	XF	Unc	BU
2001MV Proof	2,200	Value: 875				

Y# 436 100 ZLOTYCH
8.0000 g., 0.9000 Gold 0.2315 oz. AGW, 21 mm. **Subject:** World Cup Soccer **Obv:** Crowned eagle with wings open and world background **Rev:** Soccer player **Edge:** Plain

Date	Mintage	F	VF	XF	Unc	BU
2002MW Proof	4,500	Value: 450				

Y# 429 100 ZLOTYCH
8.0000 g., 0.9000 Gold 0.2315 oz. AGW, 21 mm. **Obv:** Crowned eagle with wings open **Rev:** Crowned bust facing **Edge:** Plain

Date	Mintage	F	VF	XF	Unc	BU
2002MW Proof	2,400	Value: 875				

Y# 430 100 ZLOTYCH
8.0000 g., 0.9000 Gold 0.2315 oz. AGW, 21 mm. **Obv:** Crowned eagle with wings open **Rev:** Crowned bust 1/4 left **Edge:** Plain

Date	Mintage	F	VF	XF	Unc	BU
2002MW Proof	2,200	Value: 875				

Y# 454   100 ZLOTYCH
8.0000 g., 0.9000 Gold 0.2315 oz. AGW, 21 mm. **Obv:** Crowned eagle with wings open **Rev:** Uniformed bust 1/4 left **Edge:** Plain

Date	Mintage	F	VF	XF	Unc	BU
2003MW Proof	2,000	Value: 1,000				

Y# 466   100 ZLOTYCH
8.0000 g., 0.9000 Gold 0.2315 oz. AGW, 21 mm. **Subject:** 750th Anniversary - City Charter **Obv:** Door knocker and church **Rev:** Clock face and tower **Edge:** Plain

Date	Mintage	F	VF	XF	Unc	BU
2003MW Proof	2,100	Value: 750				

Y# 467   100 ZLOTYCH
8.0000 g., 0.9000 Gold 0.2315 oz. AGW, 21 mm. **Obv:** Crowned eagle with wings open **Rev:** Kazimierz IV (1447-1492) **Edge:** Plain

Date	Mintage	F	VF	XF	Unc	BU
2003MW Proof	2,300	Value: 750				

Y# 476   100 ZLOTYCH
8.0000 g., 0.9000 Gold 0.2315 oz. AGW, 21 mm. **Obv:** Crowned eagle with wings open **Rev:** Stanislaus I and eagle **Edge:** Plain

Date	Mintage	F	VF	XF	Unc	BU
2003MW Proof	2,500	Value: 750				

Y# 494   100 ZLOTYCH
8.0000 g., 0.9000 Gold 0.2315 oz. AGW, 21 mm. **Obv:** Crowned eagle with wings open **Rev:** King Przemysl II (1295-1296) **Edge:** Plain

Date	Mintage	F	VF	XF	Unc	BU
2004MW Proof	3,400	Value: 550				

Y# 495   100 ZLOTYCH
8.0000 g., 0.9000 Gold 0.2315 oz. AGW, 21 mm. **Obv:** Crowned eagle with wings open **Rev:** King Zygmunt I (1506-1548) **Edge:** Plain

Date	Mintage	F	VF	XF	Unc	BU
2004MW Proof	3,400	Value: 550				

Y# 540   100 ZLOTYCH
8.0000 g., 0.9000 Gold 0.2315 oz. AGW, 21 mm. **Obv:** St. Peters Basilica dome **Rev:** Pope John Paul II and baptismal font **Edge:** Plain

Date	Mintage	F	VF	XF	Unc	BU
2005MW Proof	18,700	Value: 450				

Y# 581   100 ZLOTYCH
8.0000 g., 0.9000 Gold 0.2315 oz. AGW, 21 mm. **Obv:** Line of soccer players on soccer ball surface with Polish eagle in one of the sections **Rev:** Two soccer players **Edge:** Plain

Date	Mintage	F	VF	XF	Unc	BU
2006MW Proof	—	Value: 450				

Y# 640   100 ZLOTYCH
8.0000 g., 0.9000 Gold 0.2315 oz. AGW, 21 mm. **Subject:** Siberian Exiles **Obv:** Small national arms at left, bleak forest at right **Obv. Legend:** RZECZPOSPOLITA POLSKA **Rev:** Grieving mother with child by tree at lower right, building in background at left **Rev. Legend:** SYBIRACY

Date	Mintage	F	VF	XF	Unc	BU
2008MW Proof	12,000	Value: 450				

Y# 657   100 ZLOTYCH
8.0000 g., 0.9000 Gold 0.2315 oz. AGW, 21 mm. **Subject:** 400th Anniversary of Polish Settlement in North America **Obv:** Eagle in center against wind rose. Outline of Europe & North America. **Rev:** Center wind rose surrounded by 4 men working

Date	Mintage	F	VF	XF	Unc	BU
2008 Proof	9,500	Value: 450				

Y# 665   100 ZLOTYCH
8.0000 g., 0.9000 Gold 0.2315 oz. AGW, 21 mm. **Subject:** Poles in the US, 400th Anniversary **Obv:** National Arms, North America and Europe map, compass **Rev:** Four glass maker views

Date	Mintage	F	VF	XF	Unc	BU
2008MW Proof	9,500	Value: 450				

Y# 699   100 ZLOTYCH
8.0000 g., 0.9000 Gold 0.2315 oz. AGW, 21 mm. **Subject:** Tatar Rescue, 100th Anniversary **Obv:** Figure of Mariusz Zaruski **Rev:** Mountains and reszue helicopter image

Date	Mintage	F	VF	XF	Unc	BU
2009MW Proof	10,000	Value: 450				

Y# 714   100 ZLOTYCH
8.0000 g., 0.9000 Gold 0.2315 oz. AGW, 21 mm. **Subject:** Auschwitz liberation **Obv:** Prisoner and railroad track entrance **Rev:** Buildings

Date	Mintage	F	VF	XF	Unc	BU
2010MW Proof	8,000	Value: 450				

Y# 741   100 ZLOTYCH
8.0000 g., 0.9000 Gold 0.2315 oz. AGW, 21 mm. **Subject:** Constitutional Tribunal

Date	Mintage	F	VF	XF	Unc	BU
2010MW Proof	5,000	Value: 450				

Y# 766   100 ZLOTYCH
8.0000 g., 0.9000 Gold 0.2315 oz. AGW, 21 mm. **Subject:** Smolensk plane crash **Rev:** President Lech Kaczynski and wife Maria

Date	Mintage	F	VF	XF	Unc	BU
2011 Proof	—	Value: 475				

Y# 775   100 ZLOTYCH
8.0000 g., 0.9000 Gold 0.2315 oz. AGW, 21 mm. **Subject:** John Paul II Beautification

Date	Mintage	F	VF	XF	Unc	BU
2011MW Proof	8,000	Value: 450				

Y# 779   100 ZLOTYCH
8.0000 g., 0.9000 Gold 0.2315 oz. AGW, 21 mm. **Subject:** Poland's presidency of the Council of the European Union

Date	Mintage	F	VF	XF	Unc	BU
2011MW Proof	4,000	Value: 450				

Y# 407   200 ZLOTYCH
Tri-Metallic Gold with Palladium center, Gold with Silver ring, Gold with Copper outer limit, 27 mm. **Subject:** Year 2001 **Obv:** Crowned eagle with wings open within a swirl **Rev:** Couple looking into the future **Edge:** Plain

Date	Mintage	F	VF	XF	Unc	BU
2001MW Proof	4,000	Value: 550				

Y# 420   200 ZLOTYCH
15.5000 g., 0.9000 Gold 0.4485 oz. AGW, 27 mm. **Subject:** Cardinal Stefan Wyszynski **Obv:** Pillar divides arms and eagle **Rev:** Bust left within arch **Edge Lettering:** 100 ROCZNIA URODZIN

Date	Mintage	F	VF	XF	Unc	BU
2001MW Proof	4,500	Value: 850				

Y# 463   200 ZLOTYCH
15.5000 g., 0.9000 Gold 0.4485 oz. AGW, 27 mm. **Obv:** Standing violinist **Rev:** Henryk Wieniawski **Edge Lettering:** XII MIEDZYNARODOWY KONKURS SKRZYPCOWY IM HENRYKA WIENIAWSKIEGO

Date	Mintage	F	VF	XF	Unc	BU
2001MW Proof	2,000	Value: 1,150				

Y# 438   200 ZLOTYCH
15.5000 g., 0.9000 Gold 0.4485 oz. AGW, 27 mm. **Subject:** Pope John Paul II **Obv:** Bust left and small eagle with wings open **Rev:** Pope facing radiant Holy Door **Edge:** Plain

Date	Mintage	F	VF	XF	Unc	BU
2002MW Proof	5,000	Value: 1,200				

Y# 470   200 ZLOTYCH
15.5000 g., 0.9000 Gold 0.4485 oz. AGW, 27 mm. **Subject:** Gas and Oil Industry **Obv:** Crowned eagle, oil wells and refinery **Rev:** Scientist at work **Edge:** Plain

Date	Mintage	F	VF	XF	Unc	BU
2003MW Proof	2,100	Value: 1,250				

Y# 472   200 ZLOTYCH
15.5000 g., 0.9000 Gold 0.4485 oz. AGW, 27 mm. **Obv:** Standing Pope John Paul II **Rev:** Seated Pope **Edge:** Plain

Date	Mintage	F	VF	XF	Unc	BU
2003MW Proof	4,900	Value: 1,300				

Y# 483   200 ZLOTYCH
15.5000 g., 0.9000 Gold 0.4485 oz. AGW, 27 mm. **Subject:** Poland Joining the European Union **Obv:** Polish euro coin design elements **Rev:** Polish euro coin design elements **Edge:** Plain

Date	Mintage	F	VF	XF	Unc	BU
2004MW Proof	4,400	Value: 850				

Y# 511   200 ZLOTYCH
15.5000 g., 0.9000 Gold 0.4485 oz. AGW, 27 mm. **Subject:** Warsaw Fine Arts Academy Centennial **Obv:** Campus view **Rev:** Statue and building **Edge:** Plain

Date	Mintage	F	VF	XF	Unc	BU
2004MW Proof	5,000	Value: 850				

Y# 519   200 ZLOTYCH
15.5000 g., 0.9000 Gold 0.4485 oz. AGW, 27 mm. **Subject:** Olympics **Obv:** Woman and crowned eagle **Rev:** Ancient runners painted on pottery **Edge:** Plain

Date	Mintage	F	VF	XF	Unc	BU
2004MW Proof	6,000	Value: 850				

Y# 538   200 ZLOTYCH
15.5000 g., 0.9000 Gold 0.4485 oz. AGW, 27 mm. **Obv:** Horse drawn carriage **Rev:** Konstanty Ildefons Galczynski in top hat **Edge:** Plain

Date	Mintage	F	VF	XF	Unc	BU
2005MW Proof	3,500	Value: 850				

Y# 536   200 ZLOTYCH
15.5000 g., 0.9000 Gold 0.4485 oz. AGW, 27 mm. **Obv:** Chopin
Rev: Nagoya Castle roof tops and Mt. Fuji **Edge:** Plain **Note:**
Aichi Expo Japan

Date	Mintage	F	VF	XF	Unc	BU
2005MW Proof	4,200	Value: 850				

Y# 672   200 ZLOTYCH
15.5000 g., 0.9000 Gold 0.4485 oz. AGW, 27 mm. **Obv:** Helmet
and breastplate **Rev:** Knight of the 15th Century

Date	Mintage	F	VF	XF	Unc	BU
2007 Proof	10,500	Value: 850				

Y# 643   200 ZLOTYCH
15.5000 g., 0.9000 Gold 0.4485 oz. AGW, 27 mm. **Subject:**
Zbigniew Herbert **Obv:** Eagle and Zbigniew Herbert **Rev:**
Mounted statue of Marcus Aurelius

Date	Mintage	F	VF	XF	Unc	BU
2008 Proof	11,200	Value: 850				

Y# 647   200 ZLOTYCH
15.5000 g., 0.9000 Gold 0.4485 oz. AGW, 27 mm. **Series:** The
29th Olympic Games Beijing 2008 **Obv:** Two kites and an eagle
Rev: Female pole vault jumper

Date	Mintage	F	VF	XF	Unc	BU
2008 Proof	—	Value: 850				

Y# 653   200 ZLOTYCH
15.5000 g., 0.9000 Gold 0.4485 oz. AGW, 27 mm. **Subject:**
90th Anniversary of Regaining Freedom **Obv:** Tomb of the
unknown soldier **Rev:** Mounted Commander-In-Chief Jozef
Pilsudski

Date	Mintage	F	VF	XF	Unc	BU
2008 Proof	10,000	Value: 850				

Y# 654   200 ZLOTYCH
15.5000 g., 0.9000 Gold 0.4485 oz. AGW, 27 mm. **Subject:** 450
years of the Polish Post **Obv:** Eagle right, bottom against post
stamp **Rev:** Horse with rider crossing bridge

Date	Mintage	F	VF	XF	Unc	BU
2008 Proof	11,000	Value: 850				

Y# 660   200 ZLOTYCH
15.5000 g., 0.9000 Gold 0.4485 oz. AGW, 27 mm. **Subject:**
90th Anniversary of the Greater Poland Uprising **Obv:** Eagle at
left, eagle at right with chain **Rev:** Charging cavalrymen and
German soldiers firing at them

Date	Mintage	F	VF	XF	Unc	BU
2008 Proof	9,400	Value: 850				

Y# 664   200 ZLOTYCH
15.5000 g., 0.9000 Gold 0.4485 oz. AGW, 27 mm. **Subject:**
Warsaw Ghetto **Obv:** Building on fire, Naitonal arms **Rev:** Face
looking out from broken brick wall

Date	Mintage	F	VF	XF	Unc	BU
2008MW Proof	12,000	Value: 850				

Y# 696   200 ZLOTYCH
15.1500 g., 0.9000 Gold 0.4384 oz. AGW, 27 mm. **Obv:** Eagle
and statue, flames in background **Rev:** Stefan Starzonski,
Warsaw Mayor; Burning of the Clock Tower

Date	Mintage	F	VF	XF	Unc	BU
2009 Proof	10,500	Value: 850				

Y# 677   200 ZLOTYCH
15.5000 g., 0.9000 Gold 0.4485 oz. AGW, 27 mm. **Subject:**
Central Banking, 180th Anniversary **Obv:** National arms above
crowned shield **Rev:** Building and portrait

Date	Mintage	F	VF	XF	Unc	BU
2009MW Proof	8,500	Value: 850				

Y# 683   200 ZLOTYCH
15.5000 g., 0.9000 Gold 0.4485 oz. AGW, 27 mm. **Subject:**
General election of 1989 **Obv:** National arms above shipyard
scene **Rev:** Lech Walesa silhouette before crowd

Date	Mintage	F	VF	XF	Unc	BU
2009MW Proof	10,000	Value: 850				

Y# 717   200 ZLOTYCH
15.5000 g., 0.9000 Gold 0.4485 oz. AGW, 27 mm. **Subject:**
Vancouver Winter Olympics **Obv:** Downhill skiing **Rev:** Cross
Country skiing

Date	Mintage	F	VF	XF	Unc	BU
2010MW Proof	8,000	Value: 850				

Y# 720   200 ZLOTYCH
15.5000 g., 0.9000 Gold 0.4485 oz. AGW, 27 mm. **Subject:**
Napoleonic Imperial Guard **Obv:** Pile of arms **Rev:** Galloping
guardsman

Date	Mintage	F	VF	XF	Unc	BU
2010MW Proof	10,500	Value: 850				

Y# 734   200 ZLOTYCH
15.5000 g., 0.9000 Gold 0.4485 oz. AGW, 27 mm. **Subject:**
Battles of Grunwald and Kluszyn

Date	Mintage	F	VF	XF	Unc	BU
2010MW Proof	10,500	Value: 850				

Y# 782   200 ZLOTYCH
15.5000 g., 0.9000 Gold 0.4485 oz. AGW, 27 mm. **Subject:**
Polish Cavalry - Uhlan **Edge Lettering:** 22.4x32

Date	Mintage	F	VF	XF	Unc	BU
2011MW Proof	5,000	Value: 850				

Y# 787   200 ZLOTYCH
15.5000 g., 0.9000 Gold 0.4485 oz. AGW, 27 mm. **Subject:**
Czeslaw Milosz

Date	Mintage	F	VF	XF	Unc	BU
2011MW Proof	4,000	Value: 850				

Y# 791   200 ZLOTYCH
15.5000 g., 0.9000 Gold 0.4485 oz. AGW, 27 mm. **Subject:**
Ignacy Jan Paderewski

Date	Mintage	F	VF	XF	Unc	BU
2011MW Proof	3,000	Value: 850				

Y# 776   1000 ZLOTYCH
93.3000 g., 0.9990 Gold 2.9965 oz. AGW, 50 mm. **Subject:**
John Paul II Beautification

Date	Mintage	F	VF	XF	Unc	BU
2011MW Proof	500	Value: 5,500				

GOLD BULLION COINAGE

Y# 292 50 ZLOTYCH
3.1000 g., 0.9999 Gold 0.0997 oz. AGW, 18 mm. **Obv:** Crowned eagle with wings open, all within circle **Rev:** Golden eagle

Date	Mintage	F	VF	XF	Unc	BU
2002	500	—	—	—	BV	220
2004	2,000	—	—	—	BV	200
2006	1,600	—	—	—	BV	200
2007	2,000	—	—	—	BV	200
2008	—	—	—	—	BV	200

Y# 293 100 ZLOTYCH
7.7800 g., 0.9999 Gold 0.2501 oz. AGW, 22 mm. **Obv:** Crowned eagle with wings open, all within circle **Rev:** Golden eagle

Date	Mintage	F	VF	XF	Unc	BU
2002	800	—	—	—	BV	475
2004	1,000	—	—	—	BV	475
2006	900	—	—	—	BV	475
2007	1,500	—	—	—	BV	475
2008	—	—	—	—	BV	475

Y# 294 200 ZLOTYCH
15.5000 g., 0.9000 Gold 0.4485 oz. AGW, 27 mm. **Obv:** Crowned eagle with wings open within beaded circle **Rev:** Golden eagle

Date	Mintage	F	VF	XF	Unc	BU
2002	1,000	—	—	—	BV	850
2004	1,000	—	—	—	BV	850
2006	900	—	—	—	BV	850
2007	1,500	—	—	—	BV	850
2008	—	—	—	—	BV	850

Y# 295 500 ZLOTYCH
31.1035 g., 0.9999 Gold 0.9999 oz. AGW, **Obv:** Crowned eagle with wings open within beaded circle **Rev:** Golden eagle

Date	Mintage	F	VF	XF	Unc	BU
2002	1,000	—	—	—	BV	1,850
2004	2,500	—	—	—	BV	1,850
2006	600	—	—	—	BV	1,850
2007	2,500	—	—	—	BV	1,850
2008	—	—	—	—	BV	1,850

MINT SETS

KM#	Date	Mintage	Identification	Issue Price	Mkt Val
MS5	2007 (11)	2,000	Y#276-284, 465, 525, mixed date set - 1995-2007	39.95	37.50

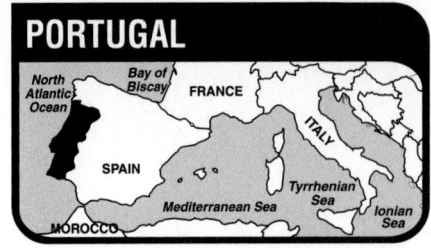

The Portuguese Republic, located in the western part of the Iberian Peninsula in southwestern Europe, has an area of 35,553 sq. mi. (92,080 sq. km.) and a population of *10.5 million. Capital: Lisbon. Portugal's economy is based on agriculture, tourism, minerals, fisheries and a rapidly expanding industrial sector. Textiles account for 33% of the exports and Portuguese wine is world famous. Portugal has become Europe's number one producer of copper and the world's largest producer of cork.

RULER
Republic, 1910 to date

MONETARY SYSTEM
100 Cents = 1 Euro

REPUBLIC

DECIMAL COINAGE

KM# 631a ESCUDO
4.6000 g., 0.9167 Gold 0.1356 oz. AGW, 16 mm. **Subject:** Last Escudo **Obv:** Design above shield with "Au" above top left corner of shield **Rev:** Flower design above value **Edge:** Plain

Date	Mintage	F	VF	XF	Unc	BU
2001INCM	50,000	—	—	—	210	225

KM# 634.1 20 ESCUDOS
6.9000 g., Copper-Nickel, 26.5 mm. **Obv:** Shield divides date with value below **Obv. Legend:** REPUBLICA PORTUGUESA **Rev:** Nautical windrose

Date	Mintage	F	VF	XF	Unc	BU
2001INCM	Est. 250,000	—	—	—	2.75	3.50

KM# 733 500 ESCUDOS
13.9600 g., 0.5000 Silver 0.2244 oz. ASW, 30.1 mm. **Subject:** Porto, European Culture Capital **Obv:** National arms and value **Rev:** Stylized design **Edge:** Reeded

Date	Mintage	F	VF	XF	Unc	BU
2001INCM	—	—	—	—	9.50	8.50
2001INCM Proof	10,000	Value: 60.00				

KM# 733a 500 ESCUDOS
Gold **Subject:** Porto, European Culture Capital **Obv:** National arms and value **Rev:** Stylized design **Edge:** Reeded

Date	Mintage	F	VF	XF	Unc	BU
2001INCM Proof	5,000	Value: 550				

KM# 734 1000 ESCUDOS
26.9500 g., 0.5000 Silver 0.4332 oz. ASW, 40 mm. **Obv:**

National arms and value **Obv. Legend:** REPUBLICA PORTUGUESA 2001 **Rev:** Soccer ball within net **Rev. Legend:** 10º Campeonato Europeu de Futebol - UEFA Euro 2004 Portugal **Edge:** Reeded

Date	Mintage	F	VF	XF	Unc	BU
2001INCM	50,000	—	—	—	17.50	18.50
2001INCM Proof	—	Value: 75.00				

EURO COINAGE
European Union Issues

KM# 740 EURO CENT
2.3000 g., Copper Plated Steel, 16.25 mm. **Obv:** Royal seal of 1134 with country name and cross **Rev:** Value and globe **Edge:** Plain

Date	Mintage	F	VF	XF	Unc	BU
2002	278,106,172	—	—	—	0.35	0.50
2002 Proof	15,000	Value: 7.00				
2003	50,000	—	—	—	0.35	0.50
2003 Proof	15,000	Value: 7.00				
2004	75,000,000	—	—	—	0.35	0.50
2004 Proof	15,000	Value: 7.00				
2005	40,000,000	—	—	—	0.35	0.50
2005 Proof	10,000	Value: 7.00				
2006	30,000,000	—	—	—	0.35	0.50
2006 Proof	3,000	Value: 7.00				
2007	105,000,000	—	—	—	0.35	0.50
2007 Proof	2,500	Value: 7.00				
2008	75,000,000	—	—	—	0.35	0.50
2008 Proof	3,500	Value: 7.00				
2009	60,000,000	—	—	—	0.35	0.50
2009 Proof	4,000	Value: 7.00				
2010	15,000,000	—	—	—	0.35	0.50
2010 Proof	4,500	Value: 7.00				
2011	20,000,000	—	—	—	0.35	0.50
2011 Proof	3,500	Value: 7.00				
2012	—	—	—	—	0.35	0.50
2012 Proof	—	Value: 7.00				

KM# 741 2 EURO CENT
3.0600 g., Copper Plated Steel, 18.75 mm. **Obv:** Royal seal of 1134 with country name and cross **Rev:** Value and globe **Edge:** Grooved

Date	Mintage	F	VF	XF	Unc	BU
2002	324,376,590	—	—	—	0.50	0.65
2002 Proof	15,000	Value: 9.00				
2003	50,000	—	—	—	—	2.50
	Note: In sets only					
2003 Proof	15,000	Value: 9.00				
	Note: In sets only					
2004	1,000,000	—	—	—	0.50	0.65
2004 Proof	15,000	Value: 9.00				
2005	10,000,000	—	—	—	0.50	0.65
2005 Proof	10,000	Value: 9.00				
2006	1,000,000	—	—	—	0.50	0.65
2006 Proof	3,000	Value: 9.00				
2007	10,000,000	—	—	—	0.50	0.65
2007 Proof	2,500	Value: 9.00				
2008	35,000,000	—	—	—	0.50	0.65
2008 Proof	3,500	Value: 9.00				
2009	45,000,000	—	—	—	0.50	0.65
2009 Proof	4,000	Value: 9.00				
2010	10,000,000	—	—	—	0.50	0.65
2010 Proof	4,500	Value: 9.00				
2011	30,000,000	—	—	—	0.50	0.65
2011 Proof	3,500	Value: 9.00				
2012	—	—	—	—	0.50	0.65
2012 Proof	—	Value: 9.00				

KM# 742 5 EURO CENT
3.9200 g., Copper Plated Steel, 21.25 mm. **Obv:** Royal seal of 1134 with country name and cross **Rev:** Value and globe **Edge:** Plain

Date	Mintage	F	VF	XF	Unc	BU
2002	234,512,047	—	—	—	0.75	1.00
2002 Proof	15,000	Value: 10.00				
2003	50,000	—	—	—	—	4.00
	Note: In sets only					

Date	Mintage	F	VF	XF	Unc	BU
2003 Proof	15,000	Value: 10.00				
Note: In sets only						
2004	40,000,000	—	—	—	0.75	1.00
2004 Proof	15,000	Value: 10.00				
2005	30,000,000	—	—	—	0.75	1.00
2005 Proof	10,000	Value: 10.00				
2006	20,000,000	—	—	—	0.75	1.00
2006 Proof	3,000	Value: 10.00				
2007	25,000,000	—	—	—	0.75	1.00
2007 Proof	2,500	Value: 10.00				
2008	25,000,000	—	—	—	0.75	1.00
2008 Proof	3,500	Value: 10.00				
2009	25,000,000	—	—	—	0.75	1.00
2009 Proof	4,000	Value: 10.00				
2010	5,000,000	—	—	—	0.75	1.00
2010 Proof	4,500	Value: 10.00				
2011	25,000,000	—	—	—	0.75	1.00
2011 Proof	3,500	Value: 10.00				
2012	—	—	—	—	0.75	1.00
2012 Proof	—	Value: 10.00				

KM# 743 10 EURO CENT
4.1000 g., Brass, 19.75 mm. **Obv:** Royal seal of 1142, country name in circular design **Rev:** Value and map **Edge:** Reeded

Date	Mintage	F	VF	XF	Unc	BU
2002	220,289,835	—	—	—	0.75	1.00
2002 Proof	15,000	Value: 12.00				
2003	6,332,000	—	—	—	1.00	1.50
2003 Proof	15,000	Value: 12.00				
Note: In sets only						
2004	1,000,000	—	—	—	1.50	2.00
2004 Proof	15,000	Value: 12.00				
2005	1,000,000	—	—	—	1.50	2.00
2005 Proof	10,000	Value: 12.00				
2006	1,000,000	—	—	—	1.50	2.00
2006 Proof	3,000	Value: 12.00				
2007	21,500	—	—	—	1.50	2.00
2007 Proof	2,500	Value: 12.00				

KM# 763 10 EURO CENT
4.1000 g., Brass, 19.75 mm. **Obv:** Royal seal of 1142, country name in circular design **Rev:** Relief map of Western Europe, stars, lines and value **Edge:** Reeded

Date	Mintage	F	VF	XF	Unc	BU
2008	1,000,000	—	—	—	1.50	2.00
2008 Proof	3,500	Value: 12.00				
2009	10,000,000	—	—	—	1.50	2.00
2009 Proof	4,000	Value: 12.00				
2010	—	—	—	—	1.50	2.00
2010 Proof	4,500	Value: 12.00				
2011	—	—	—	—	1.50	2.00
2011 Proof	3,500	Value: 12.00				
2012	—	—	—	—	1.50	2.00
2012 Proof	—	Value: 12.00				

KM# 744 20 EURO CENT
5.7400 g., Brass, 22.25 mm. **Obv:** Royal seal of 1142, country name in circular design **Rev:** Value and map **Edge:** Notched

Date	Mintage	F	VF	XF	Unc	BU
2002	147,411,038	—	—	—	1.00	1.25
2002 Proof	15,000	Value: 14.00				
2003	9,493,600	—	—	—	1.25	1.50
2003 Proof	15,000	Value: 14.00				
2004	1,000,000	—	—	—	1.50	2.00
2004 Proof	15,000	Value: 14.00				
2005	25,000,000	—	—	—	1.50	2.00
2005 Proof	10,000	Value: 14.00				
2006	20,000,000	—	—	—	1.50	2.00
2006 Proof	3,000	Value: 14.00				
2007	21,500	—	—	—	1.50	2.00
2007 Proof	2,500	Value: 14.00				

KM# 764 20 EURO CENT
5.7400 g., Brass, 22.25 mm. **Obv:** Royal seal of 1142, country name in circular design **Rev:** Relief map of Western Europe, stars, lines and value **Edge:** Notched

Date	Mintage	F	VF	XF	Unc	BU
2008	1,000,000	—	—	—	1.50	2.00
2008 Proof	3,500	Value: 14.00				
2009	20,000,000	—	—	—	1.50	2.00
2009 Proof	4,000	Value: 14.00				
2010	5,000,000	—	—	—	1.50	2.00
2010 Proof	4,500	Value: 14.00				
2011	10,000,000	—	—	—	1.50	2.00
2011 Proof	3,500	Value: 14.00				
2012	—	—	—	—	1.50	2.00
2012 Proof	—	Value: 14.00				

KM# 777 1/4 EURO
1.5600 g., 0.9990 Gold 0.0501 oz. AGW, 14 mm. **Series:** Portugal Universal **Subject:** King Alfons I, the Conqueror **Obv:** National arms, value **Obv. Legend:** REPÚBLICA PORTUGUESA **Rev:** Stylized 3/4 length armored figure standing facing **Rev. Legend:** D. AFONSO HENRIQUES **Edge:** Reeded **Note:** Each coin is numbered.

Date	Mintage	F	VF	XF	Unc	BU
2006	30,000	—	—	—	—	145

KM# 826 1/4 EURO
1.5600 g., 0.9990 Gold 0.0501 oz. AGW, 14 mm. **Subject:** Anthony of Padua

Date	Mintage	F	VF	XF	Unc	BU
2007	30,000	—	—	—	—	125

KM# 827 1/4 EURO
1.5600 g., 0.9990 Gold 0.0501 oz. AGW, 14 mm. **Subject:** King Denis

Date	Mintage	F	VF	XF	Unc	BU
2008	30,000	—	—	—	—	125

KM# 787 1/4 EURO
1.5600 g., 0.9990 Gold 0.0501 oz. AGW, 14 mm. **Subject:** Vasco da Gama

Date	Mintage	F	VF	XF	Unc	BU
2009	20,000	—	—	—	125	—

KM# 794 1/4 EURO
1.5600 g., 0.9990 Gold 0.0501 oz. AGW, 14 mm. **Subject:** Luis Vaz de Camoes

Date	Mintage	F	VF	XF	Unc	BU
2010	15,000	—	—	—	—	145

KM# 805 1/4 EURO
1.5600 g., 0.9990 Gold 0.0501 oz. AGW, 14 mm. **Subject:** Fr. António Vieira **Obv:** National arms **Rev:** Linear portrait of Vieira

Date	Mintage	F	VF	XF	Unc	BU
2011	10,000	—	—	—	—	125

KM# 807 1/4 EURO
1.5600 g., 0.9990 Gold 0.0501 oz. AGW, 14 mm. **Subject:** Spain and Portugal's accession to the European Union, 25th Anniversary

Date	Mintage	F	VF	XF	Unc	BU
2011	12,500	—	—	—	—	125

KM# 814 1/4 EURO
1.5600 g., 0.9990 Gold 0.0501 oz. AGW, 14 mm. **Subject:** Carlos Seixas, composer **Obv:** National arms **Rev:** Head facing, name at left, dates at right

Date	Mintage	F	VF	XF	Unc	BU
2012	15,000	—	—	—	—	145

KM# 745 50 EURO CENT
7.8000 g., Brass, 24.25 mm. **Obv:** Royal seal of 1142, country name in circular design **Rev:** Value and map **Edge:** Reeded

Date	Mintage	F	VF	XF	Unc	BU
2002	151,947,133	—	—	—	1.50	2.00
2002 Proof	15,000	Value: 16.00				
2003	10,353,000	—	—	—	1.50	2.00
2003 Proof	15,000	Value: 16.00				
Note: In sets only						
2004	1,000,000	—	—	—	2.50	3.00
2004 Proof	15,000	Value: 16.00				
2005	1,000,000	—	—	—	2.50	3.00
2005 Proof	10,000	Value: 16.00				
2006	1,000,000	—	—	—	2.50	3.00
2006 Proof	3,000	Value: 16.00				
2007INCM	21,500	—	—	—	2.50	3.00
2007INCM Proof	2,500	Value: 16.00				

KM# 765 50 EURO CENT
7.8000 g., Brass, 24.25 mm. **Obv:** Royal seal of 1142, country name in circular design **Rev:** Relief map of Western Europe, stars, lines and value **Edge:** Reeded

Date	Mintage	F	VF	XF	Unc	BU
2008	5,000,000	—	—	—	2.50	3.00
2008 Proof	3,500	Value: 16.00				
2009	20,000,000	—	—	—	2.50	3.00
2009 Proof	4,000	Value: 16.00				
2010	20,000,000	—	—	—	2.50	3.00
2010 Proof	4,500	Value: 16.00				
2011	—	—	—	—	2.50	3.00
2011 Proof	3,500	Value: 16.00				
2012	—	—	—	—	2.50	3.00
2012 Proof	—	Value: 16.00				

KM# 746 EURO
7.5000 g., Bi-Metallic Copper-Nickel center in Nickel-Brass ring, 23.25 mm. **Obv:** Royal seal of 1144, country name in looped design **Rev:** Value and map **Edge:** Segmented reeding

Date	Mintage	F	VF	XF	Unc	BU
2002	100,228,135	—	—	—	2.00	2.50
Note: Variety in the edge milling, 28 or 29.						
2002 Proof	15,000	Value: 18.00				
2003	16,206,875	—	—	—	2.00	2.50
2003 Proof	15,000	Value: 18.00				
2004	20,000,000	—	—	—	2.00	2.50
2004 Proof	15,000	Value: 18.00				
2005	20,000,000	—	—	—	2.00	2.50
2005 Proof	10,000	Value: 18.00				
2006	20,000,000	—	—	—	2.00	2.50
2006 Proof	3,000	Value: 18.00				
2007	4,935,400	—	—	—	2.00	2.50
2007 Proof	2,500	Value: 18.00				

KM# 766 EURO
7.5000 g., Bi-Metallic Copper-Nickel center in Nickel-Brass ring, 23.25 mm. **Obv:** Royal seal of 1144, country name in looped design **Rev:** Relief map of Western Europe, stars, lines and value **Edge:** Segmented reeding

Date	Mintage	F	VF	XF	Unc	BU
2008	5,000,000	—	—	—	2.75	3.50
2008 Proof	3,500	Value: 18.00				
2009	20,000,000	—	—	—	2.75	3.50
2009 Proof	4,000	Value: 18.00				
2010	20,000,000	—	—	—	2.75	3.50
2010 Proof	4,500	Value: 18.00				
2011	5,000,000	—	—	—	2.75	3.50
2011 Proof	3,500	Value: 18.00				
2012	—	—	—	—	2.75	3.50
2012 Proof	—	Value: 18.00				

KM# 828 1-1/2 EURO
10.0000 g., Copper-Nickel, 26.5 mm. **Subject:** Internaitonal Medical Care **Obv:** National Arms **Rev:** AMI logo

Date	Mintage	F	VF	XF	Unc	BU
2008	300,000	—	—	—	10.00	12.50

KM# 828a 1-1/2 EURO
8.0000 g., Copper-Nickel, 26.5 mm. **Subject:** International Medical Assistance **Obv:** National arms **Rev:** AMI logo

Date	Mintage	F	VF	XF	Unc	BU
2008 Special Unc.	50,000	—	—	—	20.00	25.00

KM# 828b 1-1/2 EURO
10.0000 g., 0.9250 Silver 0.2974 oz. ASW, 26.5 mm. **Subject:** International Medical Assistance **Obv:** National arms **Rev:** AMI logo

Date	Mintage	F	VF	XF	Unc	BU
2008 Proof	5,000	Value: 60.00				

KM# 788   1-1/2 EURO
10.3700 g., 0.9990 Gold 0.3331 oz. AGW, 26.5 mm. **Subject:**
Numismatics - Marabitino of Sancho II **Obv:** Cross of shields
Rev: King on horseback

Date	Mintage	F	VF	XF	Unc	BU
2009 Proof	2,500	Value: 650				

KM# 789   1-1/2 EURO
Copper-Nickel, 26.5 mm. **Obv:** Numismatics - Marabitino of
Sancho II

Date	Mintage	F	VF	XF	Unc	BU
2009 Proof	150,000	—	—	—	5.00	6.00

KM# 795   1-1/2 EURO
8.0000 g., Copper-Nickel, 26.5 mm. **Subject:** Against Famine

Date	Mintage	F	VF	XF	Unc	BU
2010	100,000	—	—	—	5.00	6.00
2010INCM Special Unc.	100,000	—	—	—	—	10.00

KM# 795a   1-1/2 EURO
10.0000 g., 0.9250 Silver 0.2974 oz. ASW, 26.5 mm. **Subject:**
Against Famine

Date	Mintage	F	VF	XF	Unc	BU
2010 Proof	5,000	Value: 55.00				

KM# 747   2 EURO
8.5000 g., Bi-Metallic Nickel-Brass center in Copper-Nickel ring,
25.75 mm. **Obv:** Royal seal of 1144, country name in looped
design **Rev:** Value and map **Edge:** Reeding over castles and
shields

Date	Mintage	F	VF	XF	Unc	BU
2002	61,930,775	—	—	—	3.50	4.00
2002 Proof	15,000	Value: 22.00				
2003	5,979,750	—	—	—	4.25	5.00
2003 Proof	15,000	Value: 22.00				
Note: In sets only						
2004	1,000,000	—	—	—	5.50	6.00
2004 Proof	15,000	Value: 22.00				
2005	1,000,000	—	—	—	5.50	6.00
2005 Proof	10,000	Value: 22.00				
2006	1,000,000	—	—	—	5.50	6.00
2006 Proof	3,000	Value: 22.00				
2007	21,500	—	—	—	5.50	6.00
2007 Proof	2,500	Value: 22.00				

KM# 771   2 EURO
8.5000 g., Bi-Metallic Nickel-Brass center in Copper-Nickel ring,
25.75 mm. **Subject:** 50th Anniversary Treaty of Rome **Obv:**
Open treaty book **Rev:** Large value at left, modified outline of
Europe at right **Edge:** Reeded and lettered

Date	Mintage	F	VF	XF	Unc	BU
2007	1,500,000	—	—	—	4.50	6.00
2007 Prooflike	15,000	—	—	—	—	12.50
2007 Proof	5,000	Value: 25.00				

KM# 772   2 EURO
8.5000 g., Bi-Metallic Nickel-Brass center in Copper-Nickel ring,
25.75 mm. **Subject:** European Union President **Obv:** Large tree,
small national arms at lower left **Obv. Inscription:** POR / TV /
GAL **Rev:** Large value at left, revised map of Europe at right
Edge: Reeded with repeated symbols

Date	Mintage	F	VF	XF	Unc	BU
2007	1,250,000	—	—	—	4.50	6.00
2007 Prooflike	15,000	—	—	—	—	12.50
2007 Proof	5,000	Value: 25.00				

KM# 767   2 EURO
8.5200 g., Bi-Metallic Nickel-Brass center in Copper-Nickel ring,
25.7 mm. **Obv:** Royal seal of 1144, country name in looped
design **Rev:** Relief map of Western Europe, stars, lines and value
Edge: Reeding over castles and shields

Date	Mintage	F	VF	XF	Unc	BU
2008 In sets only	—	—	—	—	—	6.00
2008 Proof	—	Value: 22.00				
2009 In sets only	—	—	—	—	—	6.00
2009 Proof	—	Value: 22.00				
2010	—	—	—	—	—	6.00
2010 Proof	—	Value: 22.00				
2011	—	—	—	—	—	6.00
2011 Proof	—	Value: 22.00				
2012	—	—	—	—	—	6.00
2012 Proof	—	Value: 22.00				

KM# 784   2 EURO
8.5000 g., Bi-Metallic Nickel-Brass center in Copper-Nickel ring,
25.75 mm. **Subject:** Declaration of Human Rights, 60th
Anniversary **Obv:** Seal above field

Date	Mintage	F	VF	XF	Unc	BU
2008INCM	1,000,000	—	—	—	4.00	5.00

KM# 785   2 EURO
8.5000 g., Bi-Metallic Nickel-Brass center in Copper-Nickel ring,
25.75 mm. **Subject:** European Monetary Union, 10th
Anniversary **Obv:** Stick figure and Euro symbol

Date	Mintage	F	VF	XF	Unc	BU
2009	1,250,000	—	—	6.00	12.00	—

KM# 786   2 EURO
8.5000 g., Bi-Metallic Nickel-Brass center in Copper-Nickel ring,
25.75 mm. **Subject:** Lusofonia Games **Rev:** Figure with long
flowing ribbon

Date	Mintage	F	VF	XF	Unc	BU
2009INCM	1,275,000	—	—	—	—	5.00

KM# 796   2 EURO
8.5000 g., Bi-Metallic Nickel-Brass center in Copper-Nickel ring,
25.75 mm. **Subject:** Portuguese Republic, 100th Anniversary

Date	Mintage	F	VF	XF	Unc	BU
2010INCM	—	—	—	—	6.00	7.00

KM# 804   2 EURO
8.5000 g., Bi-Metallic Nickel-Brass center in Copper-Nickel ring,
25.75 mm. **Subject:** Fernão Mendes Pinto, 500th Anniversary
of Birth **Obv:** Sailing ship right

Date	Mintage	F	VF	XF	Unc	BU
2011	500,000	—	—	—	6.00	7.00
2011 Special Unc.	12,500	—	—	—	—	9.00
2011 Proof	7,500	Value: 25.00				

KM# 812   2 EURO
8.5000 g., Bi-Metallic Nickel-Brass center in Copper-Nickel ring,
25.75 mm. **Subject:** Euro circulation, 10th Anniversary **Obv:**
Euro symbol on globe, childlike images around

Date	Mintage	F	VF	XF	Unc	BU
2012	500,000	—	—	—	6.00	7.00

Date	Mintage	F	VF	XF	Unc	BU
2012 Special Unc.	10,000	—	—	—	—	9.00
2012 Proof	10,000	Value: 25.00				

KM# 813   2 EURO
8.5000 g., Bi-Metallic Nickel-Brass center in Copper-Nickel ring,
25.75 mm. **Subject:** Guimarães, European Cultural Capital
Obv: Stylized cross and castle

Date	Mintage	F	VF	XF	Unc	BU
2012	500,000	—	—	—	6.00	7.00
2012 Special Unc.	10,000	—	—	—	—	9.00
2012 Proof	10,000	Value: 25.00				

KM# 783   2-1/2 EURO
9.8500 g., Copper-Nickel, 28 mm. **Obv:** Small national arms on
stringed instrument at right **Rev:** Fado musician at lower left
Edge: Coarse reeding

Date	Mintage	F	VF	XF	Unc	BU
2008	150,000	—	—	—	6.00	9.00

KM# 783a   2-1/2 EURO
12.0000 g., 0.9250 Silver 0.3569 oz. ASW, 28 mm. **Obv:** Small
national arms on stringed instrument at right **Rev:** Fado musician
at lower left

Date	Mintage	F	VF	XF	Unc	BU
2008 Proof	20,000	Value: 60.00				

KM# 790   2-1/2 EURO
10.0000 g., Copper-Nickel, 28 mm. **Subject:** Bejing Olympics

Date	Mintage	F	VF	XF	Unc	BU
2008	487,500	—	—	—	6.00	7.00

KM# 790a   2-1/2 EURO
12.0000 g., 0.9250 Silver 0.3569 oz. ASW, 28 mm. **Subject:**
Bejing Olympics

Date	Mintage	F	VF	XF	Unc	BU
2008 Proof	12,500	Value: 60.00				

KM# 824   2-1/2 EURO
10.0000 g., Copper-Nickel, 28 mm. **Subject:** UNESCO - World
Historic Site, Porto **Obv:** National arms **Rev:** Bridge and town
view

Date	Mintage	F	VF	XF	Unc	BU
2008	80,000	—	—	—	10.00	15.00

KM# 824a   2-1/2 EURO
12.0000 g., 0.9250 Silver 0.3569 oz. ASW, 28 mm. **Subject:**
UNESCO Historic Site - Porto **Obv:** National arms **Rev:** Bridge
and town view

Date	Mintage	F	VF	XF	Unc	BU
2008 Proof	5,000	Value: 60.00				

KM# 825   2-1/2 EURO
10.0000 g., Copper-Nickel, 28 mm. **Subject:** UNESCO Historic
Site - Wine region of Alto Douro **Obv:** National arms and river
Rev: Terraced fields

Date	Mintage	F	VF	XF	Unc	BU
2008	80000	—	—	—	10.00	12.50

KM# 825a   2-1/2 EURO
12.0000 g., 0.9250 Silver 0.3569 oz. ASW, 28 mm. **Subject:**
UNESCO historic sites - Wine region of Alto Douro **Obv:** National
arms and river **Rev:** Terraced fields

Date	Mintage	F	VF	XF	Unc	BU
2008 Proof	5,000	Value: 60.00				

KM# 792   2-1/2 EURO
Copper-Nickel, 28 mm. **Subject:** UNESCO Heritage Site -
Hieronymites Monastery **Obv:** Arched cieling design, National
arms **Rev:** Façade detail

Date	Mintage	F	VF	XF	Unc	BU
2009	150,000	—	—	—	6.00	7.00

KM# 791   2-1/2 EURO
Copper-Nickel, 28 mm. **Subject:** Portugese Literature **Obv:**
Portrait of Fernando António Nogueira de Seabra, and text **Rev:**
Stylized portrait of Luis Vaz de Camões and lines

Date	Mintage	F	VF	XF	Unc	BU
2009	150,000	—	—	—	6.00	7.00

KM# 791a   2-1/2 EURO
12.0000 g., 0.9250 Silver 0.3569 oz. ASW, 28 mm. **Subject:**
Portuguese Literature

Date	Mintage	F	VF	XF	Unc	BU
2009 Proof	14,000	Value: 60.00				

KM# 791b   2-1/2 EURO
15.5500 g., 0.9990 Gold 0.4994 oz. AGW, 28 mm. **Subject:**
Portuguese Literature

Date	Mintage	F	VF	XF	Unc	BU
2009 Proof	2,500	Value: 950				

KM# 792a   2-1/2 EURO
12.0000 g., 0.9250 Silver 0.3569 oz. ASW, 28 mm. **Subject:**
UNESCO World Heritage Site - Hieronymites Monastery **Obv:**
Arched ceiling design, National arms **Rev:** Façade detail

Date	Mintage	F	VF	XF	Unc	BU
2009 Proof	5,000	Value: 60.00				

KM# 793 2-1/2 EURO
10.0000 g., Copper-Nickel, 28 mm. **Obv:** National arms, rope splice below **Rev:** Fortification

Date	Mintage	F	VF	XF	Unc	BU
2009	150,000	—	—	—	6.00	7.00

KM# 793a 2-1/2 EURO
12.0000 g., 0.9250 Silver 0.3569 oz. ASW, 28 mm. **Subject:** UNESCO - World Heritage Site - Belém **Obv:** Naitonal arms, rope splice below **Rev:** Fortress

Date	Mintage	F	VF	XF	Unc	BU
2009 Proof	5,000	Value: 60.00				

KM# 797a 2-1/2 EURO
12.0000 g., 0.9250 Silver 0.3569 oz. ASW, 28 mm. **Subject:** FIFA Soccer - South Africa

Date	Mintage	F	VF	XF	Unc	BU
2010INCM Proof	12,500	Value: 55.00				

KM# 797 2-1/2 EURO
10.0000 g., Copper-Nickel, 28 mm. **Subject:** FIFA Soccer - South Africa

Date	Mintage	F	VF	XF	Unc	BU
2010INCM	120,000	—	—	—	6.00	7.00

KM# 798 2-1/2 EURO
10.0000 g., Copper-Nickel, 28 mm. **Subject:** Palace Square, Lisbon

Date	Mintage	F	VF	XF	Unc	BU
2010INCM	120,000	—	—	—	6.00	7.00

KM# 798a 2-1/2 EURO
12.0000 g., 0.9250 Silver 0.3569 oz. ASW, 28 mm. **Subject:** Palace Square, Lisbon

Date	Mintage	F	VF	XF	Unc	BU
2010INCM Proof	15,000	Value: 55.00				

KM# 798b 2-1/2 EURO
15.5500 g., 0.9990 Gold 0.4994 oz. AGW, 28 mm. **Subject:** Palace Square, Lisbon

Date	Mintage	F	VF	XF	Unc	BU
2010INCM Proof	2,500	Value: 950				

KM# 800 2-1/2 EURO
10.0000 g., Copper-Nickel, 28 mm. **Subject:** Torres Defence Line, 200th Anniversary

Date	Mintage	F	VF	XF	Unc	BU
2010INCM	—	—	—	—	6.00	7.00

KM# 800a 2-1/2 EURO
12.0000 g., 0.9250 Silver 0.3569 oz. ASW, 28 mm. **Subject:** Torres Defence Line, 200th Anniversary

Date	Mintage	F	VF	XF	Unc	BU
2010INCM Proof	—	Value: 55.00				

KM# 801 2-1/2 EURO
10.0000 g., Copper-Nickel, 28 mm. **Subject:** UNESCO World Cultural Heritage site - Coa Valley

Date	Mintage	F	VF	XF	Unc	BU
2010INCM	120,000	—	—	—	6.00	7.00

KM# 801a 2-1/2 EURO
12.0000 g., 0.9250 Silver 0.3569 oz. ASW, 28 mm. **Subject:** UNESCO World Cultural Heritage Site - Coa Valley

Date	Mintage	F	VF	XF	Unc	BU
2010INCM Proof	5,000					

KM# 806 2-1/2 EURO
10.0000 g., Copper-Nickel, 28 mm. **Subject:** European explorers **Obv:** National arms, tree branch and Chinese characters **Rev:** Two portraits

Date	Mintage	F	VF	XF	Unc	BU
2011	100,000	—	—	—	—	7.00

KM# 806a 2-1/2 EURO
12.0000 g., 0.9250 Silver 0.3569 oz. ASW, 28 mm. **Subject:** European explorers **Obv:** National arms, tree branch and Chinese characters **Rev:** Two portraits

Date	Mintage	F	VF	XF	Unc	BU
2011 Proof	—	Value: 55.00				

KM# 806b 2-1/2 EURO
15.5500 g., 0.9990 Gold 0.4994 oz. AGW, 28 mm. **Subject:** European explorers **Obv:** National arms, tree branch, Chinese characters **Rev:** Two portraits

Date	Mintage	F	VF	XF	Unc	BU
2011 Proof	—	Value: 950				

KM# 809 2-1/2 EURO
10.0000 g., Copper-Nickel, 28 mm. **Subject:** Army College, 100th Anniversary **Obv:** National arms and sword **Rev:** Sword and cadet cap

Date	Mintage	F	VF	XF	Unc	BU
2011	100,000	—	—	—	—	7.00

KM# 809a 2-1/2 EURO
12.0000 g., 0.9250 Silver 0.3569 oz. ASW, 28 mm. **Subject:** Army College, 100th Anniversary **Obv:** National arms and sword **Rev:** Sword and cadet cap

Date	Mintage	F	VF	XF	Unc	BU
2011 Proof	—	Value: 55.00				

KM# 810 2-1/2 EURO
10.0000 g., Copper-Nickel, 28 mm. **Subject:** Pico Island, Azores. Wine growing landscape **Obv:** National arms and tree **Rev:** Grape leaf and vine fields

Date	Mintage	F	VF	XF	Unc	BU
2011	100,000	—	—	—	—	7.00

KM# 810a 2-1/2 EURO
12.0000 g., 0.9250 Silver 0.3569 oz. ASW, 28 mm. **Subject:** Pico Island, Azores, Wine growing landscape **Obv:** National arms and tree **Rev:** Wine leaf, wine fields in background

Date	Mintage	F	VF	XF	Unc	BU
2011 Proof	3,000	Value: 55.00				

KM# 815 2-1/2 EURO
10.0000 g., Copper-Nickel, 28 mm. **Subject:** José Malhoa **Obv:** Female model at left, national arms at right **Rev:** Malhoa half-length figure with artist pallet and brushes

Date	Mintage	F	VF	XF	Unc	BU
2012	100,000	—	—	—	—	25.00

KM# 815a 2-1/2 EURO
12.0000 g., 0.9250 Silver 0.3569 oz. ASW, 28 mm. **Subject:** José Malhoa **Obv:** Female model seated at left, national arms at right **Rev:** Malhoa half-length figure standing with artist pallet and brushes

Date	Mintage	F	VF	XF	Unc	BU
2012 Proof	10,000	Value: 55.00				

KM# 815b 2-1/2 EURO
15.5500 g., 0.9990 Gold 0.4994 oz. AGW, 28 mm. **Subject:** José Malhoa **Obv:** Female model seated at left, national arms at right **Rev:** Malhoa half-length figure standing wiht artist pallet and brushes

Date	Mintage	F	VF	XF	Unc	BU
2012 Proof	1,500	Value: 950				

KM# 816 2-1/2 EURO
10.0000 g., Copper-Nickel, 28 mm. **Subject:** Portugal's participation in 2012 London Olympics **Obv:** National arms and laurel branch **Rev:** Two judo players, geometric pattern

Date	Mintage	F	VF	XF	Unc	BU
2012	300,000	—	—	—	—	10.00

KM# 816a 2-1/2 EURO
12.0000 g., 0.9250 Silver 0.3569 oz. ASW, 28 mm. **Subject:** Portugal's participation in 2012 London Olympics **Obv:** National arms and laurel branch **Rev:** Judo players, geometric pattern

Date	Mintage	F	VF	XF	Unc	BU
2012 Proof	5,000	Value: 55.00				

KM# 816b 2-1/2 EURO
Bi-Metallic 3.1 g. Gold center in 12 g. Silver ring, 28 mm. **Subject:** Portugal's participation in 2012 London Olympics **Obv:** National arms and laurel branch **Rev:** Judo players and geometric pattern

Date	Mintage	F	VF	XF	Unc	BU
2012 Proof	2,500	Value: 600				

KM# 819 2-1/2 EURO
12.0000 g., Copper-Nickel, 28 mm. **Subject:** Guimarães - UNESCO World Heritage site **Obv:** National arms and city plan **Rev:** Linear architectural representations

Date	Mintage	F	VF	XF	Unc	BU
2012	100,000	—	—	—	—	25.00

KM# 819a 2-1/2 EURO
12.0000 g., 0.9250 Silver 0.3569 oz. ASW, 28 mm. **Subject:** Guimarães - UNESCO World Heritage site **Obv:** National arms, linear city plan **Rev:** Linear architectural renderings

Date	Mintage	F	VF	XF	Unc	BU
2012 Proof	3,000	Value: 55.00				

KM# 749 5 EURO
14.0000 g., 0.5000 Silver 0.2250 oz. ASW, 30 mm. **Subject:** 150th Anniversary - First Portuguese Postage Stamp **Obv:** National arms and value within partial stamp design **Rev:** Partial postal stamp design **Edge:** Reeded

Date	Mintage	F	VF	XF	Unc	BU
2003INCM	300,000	—	—	—	12.50	30.00

KM# 749a 5 EURO
14.0000 g., 0.9250 Silver 0.4163 oz. ASW, 30 mm. **Obv:** National arms and value within partial stamp design **Rev:** Partial postal stamp design

Date	Mintage	F	VF	XF	Unc	BU
2003INCM	20,000	—	—	—	—	30.00
2003INCM Proof	20,000	Value: 55.00				

KM# 749b 5 EURO
17.5000 g., 0.9166 Gold 0.5157 oz. AGW, 30 mm. **Obv:** National arms and value within partial stamp design **Rev:** Partial postal stamp design

Date	Mintage	F	VF	XF	Unc	BU
2003INCM Proof	10,000	Value: 1,000				

KM# 754 5 EURO
14.0000 g., 0.5000 Silver 0.2250 oz. ASW, 30 mm. **Subject:** Convent of Christ **Obv:** National arms above value flanked by designs **Rev:** Ornate convent window **Edge:** Reeded

Date	Mintage	F	VF	XF	Unc	BU
2004INCM	300,000	—	—	—	30.00	32.50

KM# 754a 5 EURO
14.0000 g., 0.9250 Silver 0.4163 oz. ASW, 30 mm. **Subject:** Convent of Christ **Obv:** National arms above value flanked by designs **Rev:** Ornate convent window **Edge:** Reeded

Date	Mintage	F	VF	XF	Unc	BU
2004INCM Proof	10,000	Value: 60.00				

KM# 755 5 EURO
14.0000 g., 0.5000 Silver 0.2250 oz. ASW, 30 mm. **Subject:** Historic City of Evora **Obv:** National arms and value on city map silhouette **Rev:** Architectural highlights **Edge:** Reeded

Date	Mintage	F	VF	XF	Unc	BU
2004INCM	300,000	—	—	—	30.00	32.50

KM# 755a 5 EURO
14.0000 g., 0.9250 Silver 0.4163 oz. ASW, 30 mm. **Subject:** Historic City of Evora **Obv:** National arms and value on city map silhouette **Rev:** Architectural highlights **Edge:** Reeded

Date	Mintage	F	VF	XF	Unc	BU
2004INCM Proof	10,000	Value: 60.00				

KM# 762 5 EURO
14.0000 g., 0.5000 Silver 0.2250 oz. ASW, 30 mm. **Subject:** 800th Anniversary Birth of Pope John XXI **Obv:** National arms at lower right with archways in backgound **Obv. Legend:** REPUBLICA PORTUGUESA **Rev:** 1/2 length figure of Pope facing at right with staff dividing dates, small shield at left **Edge:** Reeded

Date	Mintage	F	VF	XF	Unc	BU
2005INCM	300,000	—	—	—	30.00	32.50

KM# 762a 5 EURO
14.0000 g., 0.9250 Silver 0.4163 oz. ASW, 30 mm. **Subject:** 800th Anniversary Birth of Pope John XXI **Obv:** National arms at lower right with archways in background **Obv. Legend:** REPUBLICA PORTUGUESA **Rev:** 1/2 length figure of Pope facing at right with staff dividing dates, small shield at left **Edge:** Reeded

Date	Mintage	F	VF	XF	Unc	BU
2005INCM Proof	15,000	Value: 65.00				

KM# 762b 5 EURO
17.5000 g., 0.9167 Gold 0.5157 oz. AGW, 30 mm. **Subject:** 800th Anniversary Birth of Pope John XXI **Obv:** National arms at lower right, archways in background **Obv. Legend:** REPUBLICA PORTUGUESA **Edge:** Reeded

Date	Mintage	F	VF	XF	Unc	BU
2005INCM Proof	7,500	Value: 1,000				

KM# 760 5 EURO
14.0000 g., 0.5000 Silver 0.2250 oz. ASW, 30 mm. **Obv:** National arms within circle **Obv. Legend:** REPUBLICA PORTUGUESA **Rev:** Angra do Heroismo - Azores Terceira, emblem above **Rev. Legend:** CENTRO HISTÓRICO DE ANGRA DO HEROISMA **Edge:** Reeded

Date	Mintage	F	VF	XF	Unc	BU
2005	300,000	—	—	—	30.00	32.50

KM# 760a 5 EURO
14.0000 g., 0.9250 Silver 0.4163 oz. ASW, 30 mm. **Obv:**
National arms within circle **Obv. Legend:** REPUBLICA
PORTUGUESA **Rev:** Angra do Heroisma - Azores Terceira,
emblem above **Rev. Legend:** CENTRO HISTÓRICO DE ANGRA
DO HEROISMA **Edge:** Reeded

Date	Mintage	F	VF	XF	Unc	BU
2005 Proof	15,000	Value: 60.00				

KM# 761 5 EURO
14.0000 g., 0.5000 Silver 0.2250 oz. ASW, 30 mm. **Obv:** Design
divides national arms and value **Obv. Legend:** REPUBLICA
PORTUGUESA **Rev:** Batalha monastery and emblem **Rev.
Legend:** MONTEIRO DA BATALHA **Edge:** Reeded

Date	Mintage	F	VF	XF	Unc	BU
2005	300,000	—	—	—	30.00	32.50

KM# 761a 5 EURO
14.0000 g., 0.9250 Silver 0.4163 oz. ASW, 30 mm. **Obv:** Design
divides national arms and value **Obv. Legend:** REPUBLICA
PORTUGUESA **Rev:** Batalha monastery and emblem **Rev.
Legend:** MONTEIRO DA BATALHA **Edge:** Reeded

Date	Mintage	F	VF	XF	Unc	BU
2005 Proof	15,000	Value: 60.00				

KM# 769 5 EURO
14.0000 g., 0.5000 Silver 0.2250 oz. ASW, 30 mm. **Subject:**
UNESCO - Cultural preservation **Obv:** National arms above value
Obv. Legend: REPUBLICA PORTUGUESA **Rev:** Outlined view
Rev. Legend: PAISAGEM CULTURAL DE SINTRA **Edge:**
Reeded

Date	Mintage	F	VF	XF	Unc	BU
2006INCM	82,000	—	—	—	30.00	32.50

KM# 769a 5 EURO
14.0000 g., 0.9250 Silver 0.4163 oz. ASW, 30 mm. **Subject:**
UNESCO - Cultural preservation **Obv:** National arms above value
Obv. Legend: REPUBLICA PORTUGUESA **Rev:** Outlined view
Rev. Legend: PAISAGEM CULTURAL DE SINTRA **Edge:**
Reeded

Date	Mintage	F	VF	XF	Unc	BU
2006INCM Proof	6,000	Value: 60.00				

KM# 779 5 EURO
14.0000 g., 0.5000 Silver 0.2250 oz. ASW **Subject:** Alcobaça
Monastery **Obv:** National arms **Obv. Legend:** REPÚBLICA
PORTUGUESA **Edge:** Reeded

Date	Mintage	F	VF	XF	Unc	BU
2006INCM	82,000	—	—	—	25.00	27.50

KM# 779a 5 EURO
14.0000 g., 0.9250 Silver 0.4163 oz. ASW **Subject:** Alcobaça
Monestary **Obv:** National arms **Obv. Legend:** REPÚBLICA
PORTUGUESA **Edge:** Reeded

Date	Mintage	F	VF	XF	Unc	BU
2006INCM Proof	6,000	Value: 60.00				

KM# 782 5 EURO
13.9500 g., 0.5000 Silver 0.2242 oz. ASW, 30 mm. **Series:**
UNESCO - World Heritage **Subject:** National Forest Reserve in
Madeira Nature Park **Obv:** National arms **Obv. Legend:**

REPÚBLICA PORTUGUESA **Rev:** Foliage with small UNESCO
World Heritage logo at lower right **Rev. Legend:** FLORESTA
LAURISSILVA DA MADEIRA **Edge:** Reeded

Date	Mintage	F	VF	XF	Unc	BU
2007INCM	75,000	—	—	—	25.00	27.50

KM# 782a 5 EURO
14.0000 g., 0.9250 Silver 0.4163 oz. ASW, 30 mm. **Series:**
UNESCO - World Heritage **Subject:** National Forest Reserve in
Madeira Nature Park **Obv:** National arms **Obv. Legend:**
REPÚBLICA PORTUGUESA **Rev:** Foliage with small UNESCO
World Heritage logo at lower right **Rev. Legend:** FLORESTA
LAURISSILVA DA MADEIRA **Edge:** Reeded

Date	Mintage	F	VF	XF	Unc	BU
2007INCM Proof	6,000	Value: 65.00				

KM# 770 5 EURO
14.0000 g., 0.5000 Silver 0.2250 oz. ASW, 30 mm. **Subject:**
World Scouting Centennial **Obv:** Portuguese Arms, World
Scouting emblem **Obv. Legend:** REPUBLICA PORTUGUESA
1907-2007 CENTENARIO DO ESCUTISMO MUNDIAL **Rev:**
Linear portrait of Lord Robert Baden-Powell **Rev. Legend:** UM
MUNDO UMA PROMESA **Edge:** Reeded

Date	Mintage	F	VF	XF	Unc	BU
ND(2007)	70,000	—	—	—	25.00	27.50

KM# 770a 5 EURO
14.0000 g., 0.9250 Silver 0.4163 oz. ASW, 30 mm. **Subject:**
World Scouting Centennial **Obv:** National arms, World Scouting
emblem **Obv. Legend:** REPUBLICA PORTUGUESA 1907 -
2007 CENTENARIO DO ESCUTISMO MUNDIAL **Rev:** Linear
portrait of Lord Robert Baden-Powell **Rev. Legend:** UM MUNDO
UMA PROMESA **Edge:** Reeded

Date	Mintage	F	VF	XF	Unc	BU
ND(2007) Proof	10,000	Value: 60.00				

KM# 781 5 EURO
14.0400 g., 0.5000 Silver 0.2257 oz. ASW, 30 mm. **Subject:**
Equal Opportunities **Obv:** Small national arms above moon
shaped arc **Obv. Legend:** República Portuguesa **Rev:** Small 3
persons logo above 12 stars along rim **Rev. Legend:** Ano
Europeu da Igualdade de Oportunidades para Todos **Edge:**
Reeded

Date	Mintage	F	VF	XF	Unc	BU
2007INCM	70,000	—	—	—	25.00	27.50

KM# 781a 5 EURO
14.0000 g., 0.9250 Silver 0.4163 oz. ASW, 30 mm. **Subject:**
Equal Opportunities **Obv:** Small national arms above moon
shaped arc **Obv. Legend:** República Portuguesa **Rev:** Small 3
persons logo above 12 stars along rim **Rev. Legend:** Ano
Europeu da Igualdade de Oportunidades para Todos **Edge:**
Reeded

Date	Mintage	F	VF	XF	Unc	BU
2007INCM Proof	7,500	Value: 65.00				

KM# 802 5 EURO
14.0000 g., Copper-Nickel, 30 mm. **Subject:** Numismatic
Treasurers - Justo of John II

Date	Mintage	F	VF	XF	Unc	BU
2010INCM	150,000	—	—	—	12.00	15.00

KM# 802a 5 EURO
15.5500 g., 0.9990 Gold 0.4994 oz. AGW, 30 mm. **Subject:**
Numismatic Treasurers - Justo of John II

Date	Mintage	F	VF	XF	Unc	BU
2010INCM Proof	2,500	Value: 950				

KM# 817 5 EURO
14.0000 g., Copper-Nickel, 30 mm. **Subject:** Numismatic
Treasurers - João V **Obv:** Bust right **Rev:** Crowned arms

Date	Mintage	F	VF	XF	Unc	BU
2012L	150,000	—	—	—	—	25.00

KM# 817a 5 EURO
15.5500 g., 0.9990 Gold 0.4994 oz. AGW, 30 mm. **Subject:**
Numismatic Treasurers - João V **Obv:** Bust right **Rev:** Crowned
shield

Date	Mintage	F	VF	XF	Unc	BU
2012 Proof	—	Value: 950				

KM# 811 7.5 EURO
18.5000 g., Copper-Nickel, 33 mm. **Subject:** Numismatic
Treasurers - Manuel I **Obv:** Short cross **Rev:** National Arms in
center of dourble ring legend

Date	Mintage	F	VF	XF	Unc	BU
2011 Proof	100,000	Value: 35.00				

KM# 811a 7.5 EURO
23.3300 g., 0.9990 Gold 0.7493 oz. AGW, 33 mm. **Subject:**
Numismatic Treasurers - Manuel I **Obv:** Short Cross **Rev:**
Crowned national shield within double ring legend

Date	Mintage	F	VF	XF	Unc	BU
2011 Proof	—	Value: 1,425				

KM# 750 8 EURO
21.1000 g., 0.5000 Silver 0.3392 oz. ASW, 36 mm. **Obv:**
National arms, value and flag-covered globe **Rev:** Flag-covered
globe and "Euro 2004" soccer games logo **Edge:** Reeded

Date	Mintage	F	VF	XF	Unc	BU
2003INCM	1,500,000	—	—	—	35.00	37.50

KM# 750a 8 EURO
31.1000 g., 0.9250 Silver 0.9249 oz. ASW, 36 mm. **Obv:**
National arms, value and flag-covered globe **Rev:** Flag-covered
globe and "Euro 2004" soccer games logo

Date	Mintage	F	VF	XF	Unc	BU
2003INCM Prooflike	30,000	—	—	—	—	100
2003INCM Proof	15,000	Value: 165				

KM# 750b 8 EURO
31.1000 g., 0.9166 Gold 0.9165 oz. AGW, 36 mm. **Obv:**
National arms, value and flag-covered globe **Rev:** Flag-covered
globe and "Euro 2004" soccer games logo

Date	Mintage	F	VF	XF	Unc	BU
2003INCM Proof	10,000	Value: 1,850				

KM# 751 8 EURO
21.1000 g., 0.5000 Silver 0.3392 oz. ASW, 36 mm. **Obv:**
National arms and value below many bubbles **Rev:** "Euro 2004"
soccer games logo below many hearts **Edge:** Reeded

Date	Mintage	F	VF	XF	Unc	BU
2003INCM	1,500,000	—	—	—	35.00	37.50

KM# 751a 8 EURO
31.1000 g., 0.9250 Silver 0.9249 oz. ASW, 36 mm. **Obv:**
National arms and value below many bubbles **Rev:** "Euro 2004"
soccer games logo below many hearts

Date	Mintage	F	VF	XF	Unc	BU
2003INCM Prooflike	—	—	—	—	—	100
2003INCM Proof	15,000	Value: 165				

KM# 751b 8 EURO
31.1000 g., 0.9166 Gold 0.9165 oz. AGW, 36 mm. **Obv:**
National arms and value below many bubbles **Rev:** "Euro 2004"
soccer games logo below many hearts

Date	Mintage	F	VF	XF	Unc	BU
2003INCM Proof	10,000	Value: 1,850				

KM# 752   8 EURO
21.1000 g., 0.5000 Silver 0.3392 oz. ASW, 36 mm. **Obv:**
National arms and value **Rev:** "Euro 2004" soccer games logo in
center with partial text background **Edge:** Reeded

Date	Mintage	F	VF	XF	Unc	BU
2003INCM	1,500,000	—	—	—	35.00	37.50

KM# 752a   8 EURO
31.1000 g., 0.9250 Silver 0.9249 oz. ASW, 36 mm. **Obv:**
National arms and value **Rev:** "Euro 2004" soccer games logo in
center with partial text background

Date	Mintage	F	VF	XF	Unc	BU
2003INCM Prooflike		—	—	—	—	100
2003INCM Proof	15,000	Value: 165				

KM# 752b   8 EURO
31.1000 g., 0.9166 Gold 0.9165 oz. AGW, 36 mm. **Obv:**
National arms and value **Rev:** "Euro 2004" soccer games logo in
center with partial text background

Date	Mintage	F	VF	XF	Unc	BU
2003INCM Proof	10,000	Value: 1,850				

KM# 753   8 EURO
21.2200 g., 0.5000 Silver 0.3411 oz. ASW, 36 mm. **Subject:**
Expansion of the European Union **Obv:** Radiant national arms
and value **Rev:** European map **Edge:** Reeded

Date	Mintage	F	VF	XF	Unc	BU
2004INCM	300,000	—	—	—	25.00	27.50

KM# 753a   8 EURO
31.1000 g., 0.9250 Silver 0.9249 oz. ASW, 36 mm. **Subject:**
Expansion of the European Union **Obv:** Radiant national arms
and value **Rev:** European map **Edge:** Reeded

Date	Mintage	F	VF	XF	Unc	BU
2004INCM Proof	35,000	Value: 60.00				

KM# 756   8 EURO
21.0000 g., 0.5000 Silver 0.3376 oz. ASW, 36 mm. **Subject:**
Euro 2004 Soccer **Obv:** National arms **Rev:** Stylized goal keeper
Edge: Reeded

Date	Mintage	F	VF	XF	Unc	BU
2004INCM	1,500,000	—	—	—	25.00	27.50

KM# 756a   8 EURO
31.1000 g., 0.9250 Silver 0.9249 oz. ASW, 36 mm. **Subject:**
Euro 2004 Soccer **Obv:** National arms **Rev:** Stylized goal keeper
Edge: Reeded

Date	Mintage	F	VF	XF	Unc	BU
2004INCM	30,000	—	—	—	—	80.00
2004INCM Proof	15,000	Value: 150				

KM# 756b   8 EURO
31.1000 g., 0.9166 Gold 0.9165 oz. AGW, 36 mm. **Subject:**
Euro 2004 Soccer **Obv:** National arms **Rev:** Stylized goal keeper
Edge: Reeded

Date	Mintage	F	VF	XF	Unc	BU
2004INCM Proof	10,000	Value: 1,850				

KM# 757   8 EURO
21.0000 g., 0.9250 Silver 0.6245 oz. ASW, 36 mm. **Subject:**
Euro 2004 Soccer **Obv:** National arms **Rev:** Face of player
making shot **Edge:** Reeded

Date	Mintage	F	VF	XF	Unc	BU
2004INCM	1,500,000	—	—	—	25.00	27.50

KM# 757a   8 EURO
31.1000 g., 0.9250 Silver 0.9249 oz. ASW, 36 mm. **Subject:**
Euro 2004 Soccer **Obv:** National arms **Rev:** Face of player
making a shot **Edge:** Reeded

Date	Mintage	F	VF	XF	Unc	BU
2004INCM	30,000	—	—	—	—	80.00
2004INCM Proof	15,000	Value: 150				

KM# 757b   8 EURO
31.1000 g., 0.9165 Gold 0.9166 oz. AGW, 36 mm. **Subject:**
Euro 2004 Soccer **Obv:** National arms **Rev:** Face of player
making a shot **Edge:** Reeded

Date	Mintage	F	VF	XF	Unc	BU
2004INCM Proof	10,000	Value: 1,850				

KM# 758   8 EURO
21.0000 g., 0.5000 Silver 0.3376 oz. ASW, 36 mm. **Subject:**
Euro 2004 Soccer **Obv:** National arms **Rev:** Symbolic explosion
of a goal **Edge:** Reeded

Date	Mintage	F	VF	XF	Unc	BU
2004INCM	1,500,000	—	—	—	25.00	27.50

KM# 758a   8 EURO
31.1000 g., 0.9250 Silver 0.9249 oz. ASW, 36 mm. **Subject:**
Euro 2004 Soccer **Obv:** National arms **Rev:** Symbolic explosion
of a goal **Edge:** Reeded

Date	Mintage	F	VF	XF	Unc	BU
2004INCM	30,000	—	—	—	—	80.00
2004INCM Proof	15,000	Value: 150				

KM# 758b   8 EURO
31.1000 g., 0.9166 Gold 0.9165 oz. AGW, 36 mm. **Subject:**
Euro 2004 Soccer **Obv:** National arms **Rev:** Symbolic explosion
of a goal **Edge:** Reeded

Date	Mintage	F	VF	XF	Unc	BU
2004INCM Proof	10,000	Value: 1,850				

KM# 773   8 EURO
21.0000 g., 0.5000 Silver 0.3376 oz. ASW, 36 mm. **Subject:**
60th Anniversary End of WW II **Obv:** Quill pens horizontal at left
center, national arms at lower righr **Obv. Inscription:**
REPÚBLICA PORTUGUESA **Rev:** Four quill pens upright,
outlined map of Europe in background **Rev. Inscription:** FIM DA
II GUERRA MUNDIAL **Edge:** Reeded

Date	Mintage	F	VF	XF	Unc	BU
2005INCM	300,000	—	—	—	30.00	32.50

KM# 773a   8 EURO
31.1000 g., 0.9250 Silver 0.9249 oz. ASW, 36 mm. **Subject:**
60th Anniversary End of WW II **Obv:** Quill pens horizontal at left
center, national arms at lower right **Obv. Inscription:**
REPÚBLICA PORTUGUESA **Rev:** Four quill pens upright,
outlined map of Europe in background **Rev. Inscription:** FIM DA
II GUERRA MUNDIAL **Edge:** Reeded

Date	Mintage	F	VF	XF	Unc	BU
2005INCM Proof	35,000	Value: 70.00				

KM# 776   8 EURO
20.8000 g., 0.5000 Silver 0.3344 oz. ASW, 36 mm. **Series:**
Famous Europeans **Subject:** Prince Henry the Navigator **Obv:**
Small national arms and shield **Obv. Legend:** REPÚBLICA
PORTUGUESA **Rev:** Tiny bust 3/4 right **Edge:** Reeded

Date	Mintage	F	VF	XF	Unc	BU
2006INCM	100,000	—	—	—	30.00	32.50

KM# 776a   8 EURO
31.1000 g., 0.9250 Silver 0.9249 oz. ASW, 36 mm. **Series:**
Famous Europeans **Subject:** Prince Henry the Navigator **Obv:**
Small national arms and shield **Obv. Legend:** REPÚBLICA
PORTUGUESA **Rev:** Tiny bust 3/4 right **Edge:** Reeded

Date	Mintage	F	VF	XF	Unc	BU
2006INCM Proof	35,000	Value: 65.00				

KM# 778   8 EURO
21.0000 g., 0.5000 Silver 0.3376 oz. ASW, 36 mm. **Subject:**
150th Anniversary Railroad Lisbon - Carregado **Obv:** National
arms on wavy flag **Obv. Legend:** REPÚBLICA PORTUGUESA
Rev: Vertical railroad track divides two shields **Rev. Legend:** 150
ANOS DA PRIMEIRA LINHA FERREA LISBOA CARREGADO
Edge: Reeded

Date	Mintage	F	VF	XF	Unc	BU
2006INCM	100,000	—	—	—	32.50	35.00

KM# 778a   8 EURO
31.1000 g., 0.9250 Silver 0.9249 oz. ASW, 36 mm. **Subject:**
150th Anniversary Railroad Lisbon - Carregado **Obv:** National
srms on wavy flag **Obv. Legend:** REPÚBLICA PORTUGUESA
Rev: Vertical railroad track divides two shields **Rev. Legend:** 150
ANOSDA PRIMEIRA LINHA FERREA LISBOA CARREGADO
Edge: Reeded

Date	Mintage	F	VF	XF	Unc	BU
2006INCM Proof	35,000	Value: 75.00				

KM# 822   8 EURO
21.0000 g., 0.5000 Silver 0.3376 oz. ASW, 36 mm. **Subject:**
Early flying inventions - the Passarola of Bartolomeu de Gusmão
Obv: Large value and small national arms **Rev:** Schematic of
flying machine

Date	Mintage	F	VF	XF	Unc	BU
2007	70,000	—	—	—	20.00	25.00

KM# 822a   8 EURO
31.1050 g., 0.9250 Silver 0.9250 oz. ASW, 36 mm. **Subject:**
Early flying inventions - the Passarola of Bartolomeu de Gusmão
Obv: Large value, small national arms **Rev:** Schematic of early
flying machine

Date	Mintage	F	VF	XF	Unc	BU
2007 Proof	25,000	Value: 65.00				

KM# 748   10 EURO
27.0000 g., 0.5000 Silver 0.4340 oz. ASW, 40 mm. **Subject:**
Nautica **Obv:** National arms within circle of assorted shields **Rev:**
Sailing ship and sextant **Edge:** Reeded

Date	Mintage	F	VF	XF	Unc	BU
2003INCM	350,000	—	—	—	22.50	25.00

KM# 748a   10 EURO
27.0000 g., 0.9250 Silver 0.8029 oz. ASW, 40 mm. **Obv:**
National arms within circle of assorted shields **Rev:** Sailing ship
and sextant **Edge:** Reeded

Date	Mintage	F	VF	XF	Unc	BU
2003INCM Proof	10,000	Value: 70.00				

KM# 759   10 EURO
27.0000 g., 0.5000 Silver 0.4340 oz. ASW, 40 mm. **Subject:**
Olympics **Obv:** National arms above stylized value **Rev:** Stylized
sail above Olympic rings **Edge:** Reeded

Date	Mintage	F	VF	XF	Unc	BU
2004INCM	350,000	—	—	—	25.00	27.50

KM# 759a   10 EURO
27.0000 g., 0.9250 Silver 0.8029 oz. ASW, 40 mm. **Subject:**
Olympics **Obv:** National arms above stylized value **Rev:** Stylized
sail above Olympic rings **Edge:** Reeded

Date	Mintage	F	VF	XF	Unc	BU
2004INCM Proof	15,000	Value: 65.00				

KM# 768   10 EURO
27.0000 g., 0.5000 Silver 0.4340 oz. ASW, 40 mm. **Subject:**
Arquitectura e Monumentos - Sé do Porto **Obv:** National arms
above value in circle of multi-national coats of arms **Rev:** Church
facade **Edge:** Reeded

Date	Mintage	F	VF	XF	Unc	BU
2005INCM		—	—	—	—	30.00
2005INCM Proof	300,000	Value: 75.00				

KM# 820   10 EURO
27.0000 g., 0.5000 Silver 0.4340 oz. ASW, 40 mm. **Subject:**
Iberoamerican series - Architecture **Rev:** Façade of the Cathedral
Sé de Porto

Date	Mintage	F	VF	XF	Unc	BU
2005	30,000	—	—	—	30.00	35.00

KM# 820a   10 EURO
27.0000 g., 0.9250 Silver 0.8029 oz. ASW, 40 mm. **Subject:**
Iberoamerican Series - Architecture **Rev:** Façade of Cathedral
of Sé do Porto

Date	Mintage	F	VF	XF	Unc	BU
2005 Proof	12,000	Value: 115				

KM# 774   10 EURO
27.0000 g., 0.5000 Silver 0.4340 oz. ASW, 40 mm. **Subject:**
XVIII World Championship Football Games - Germany 2006 **Obv:**
National arms above stadium **Obv. Legend:** REPÚBLICA
PORTUGUESA **Rev:** Circular legend above sticks representing
stadium fans **Rev. Legend:** CAMPEONATO DO MUNDO DE
FUTEBOL FIFA ALEMANHA 2006 **Edge:** Reeded

Date	Mintage	F	VF	XF	Unc	BU
2006INCM	100,000	—	—	—	37.50	40.00

KM# 774a   10 EURO
27.0000 g., 0.9250 Silver 0.8029 oz. ASW, 40 mm. **Subject:**
XVIII World Championship Football Games - Germany 2006 **Obv:**
National arms above stadium **Obv. Inscription:** REPÚBLICA
PORTUGUESA **Rev:** Circular legend above sticks representing
stadium fans **Edge:** Reeded

Date	Mintage	F	VF	XF	Unc	BU
2006INCM Proof	25,000	Value: 85.00				

KM# 775   10 EURO
27.0000 g., 0.5000 Silver 0.4340 oz. ASW, 40 mm. **Subject:**
20th Anniversary of Spain and Portugal's membership in the
European Union **Obv:** National arms **Obv. Legend:** REPÚBLICA
PORTUGUESA **Rev:** Viaduct, outlined map of Europe above
Rev. Legend: ADESÃO AS COMUNIDADES EUROPIAS **Edge:**
Reeded

Date	Mintage	F	VF	XF	Unc	BU
2006INCM	100,000	—	—	—	27.50	30.00

KM# 775a   10 EURO
27.0000 g., 0.9250 Silver 0.8029 oz. ASW, 40 mm. **Subject:**
20th Anniversary of Spain and Portugal's membership in
European Union **Obv:** National arms **Obv. Legend:** REPÚBLICA
PORTUGUESA **Rev:** Viaduct, outlined map of Europe above
Rev. Legend: ADESÃO AS COMUNIDADES EUROPIAS **Edge:**
Reeded

Date	Mintage	F	VF	XF	Unc	BU
2006INCM Proof	25,000	Value: 70.00				

KM# 821   10 EURO
27.0000 g., 0.5000 Silver 0.4340 oz. ASW, 40 mm. **Subject:**
Iberoamerican Series - Olympics **Rev:** Warrior running, two
modern runners

Date	Mintage	F	VF	XF	Unc	BU
2007	100,000	—	—	—	25.00	30.00

KM# 821a   10 EURO
27.0000 g., 0.9250 Silver 0.8029 oz. ASW, 40 mm. **Subject:**
Iberoamerican Series - Olympics **Rev:** Ancient warrior running,
two modern runners

Date	Mintage	F	VF	XF	Unc	BU
2007 Proof	12,000	Value: 115				

KM# 823   10 EURO
27.0000 g., 0.5000 Silver 0.4340 oz. ASW, 40 mm. **Subject:**
Sailing World Cup - Cascais **Obv:** National arms and stylized
sails and waves **Rev:** Stylized sails and waves

Date	Mintage	F	VF	XF	Unc	BU
2007	70,000	—	—	—	25.00	30.00

KM# 823a   10 EURO
27.0000 g., 0.9250 Silver 0.8029 oz. ASW, 40 mm. **Subject:**
World Sailing Championships - Cascais **Obv:** National arms and
stylized sails and waves **Rev:** Stylized sails and waves

Date	Mintage	F	VF	XF	Unc	BU
2007 Proof	7,500	Value: 75.00				

KM# 803   10 EURO
27.0000 g., 0.9250 Silver 0.8029 oz. ASW, 40 mm. **Subject:**
The Escudo

Date	Mintage	F	VF	XF	Unc	BU
2010INCM	100,000	—	—	—	32.50	35.00

KM# 803a   10 EURO
27.0000 g., 0.5000 Silver 0.4340 oz. ASW, 40 mm. **Subject:**
The Escudo

Date	Mintage	F	VF	XF	Unc	BU
2010INCM Proof	12,000	Value: 85.00				

KM# 808   10 EURO
27.0000 g., Copper-Nickel, 40 mm. **Subject:** Spain and
Portugal's accession to the European Union, 25th Anniversary

Date	Mintage	F	VF	XF	Unc	BU
2011	100,000	—	—	—	—	7.00

KM# 808a   10 EURO
27.0000 g., 0.9250 Silver 0.8029 oz. ASW, 40 mm. **Subject:**
Spain and Portugal's accession to the European Union, 25th
Anniversary

Date	Mintage	F	VF	XF	Unc	BU
2011 Proof	6,000	Value: 55.00				

KM# 818   10 EURO
27.0000 g., Copper-Nickel, 40 mm. **Subject:** Ibero-American
series, 20th Anniversary **Obv:** National arms in center of other
countries arms **Rev:** Stylized sails

Date	Mintage	F	VF	XF	Unc	BU
2012	100,000	—	—	—	—	25.00

KM# 818a   10 EURO
27.0000 g., 0.9250 Silver 0.8029 oz. ASW, 40 mm. **Subject:**
Ibero-American series, 20th Anniversary **Obv:** National arms at
center of other national arms **Rev:** Stylized sails

Date	Mintage	F	VF	XF	Unc	BU
2012 Proof	10,000	Value: 55.00				

MINT SETS

KM#	Date	Mintage	Identification	Issue Price	Mkt Val
MS32	2002 (8)	50,000	KM#740-747	—	50.00
MS33	2003 (8)	50,000	KM#740-747	—	50.00
MS34	2004 (8)	50,000	KM#740-747	—	45.00
MS35	2005 (8)	30,000	KM#740-747	—	45.00
MS36	2006 (8)	12,500	KM#740-747	—	45.00

PROOF SETS

KM#	Date	Mintage	Identification	Issue Price	Mkt Val
PS45	2002 (8)	15,000	KM#740-747	—	120
PS46	2003 (8)	15,000	kM#740-747	—	110
PS47	2004 (8)	15,000	KM#740-747	—	110
PS48	2005 (8)	10,000	KM#740-747	—	110
PS49	2006 (8)	3,000	KM#740-747	—	110
PS50	2007 (8)	2,500	KM#740-747	—	300
PS51	2008 (8)	3,500	KM#740-742, 763-767	—	150
PS52	2009 (8)	4,000	KM#740-742, 763-767	—	150
PS53	2010 (8)	4,500	KM#740-742, 763-767	—	100
PS54	2011 (8)	3,500	KM#740-742, 763-767	—	100

QATAR

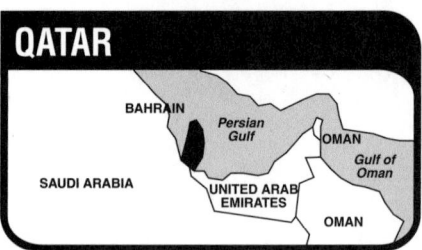

The State of Qatar, an emirate in the Persian Gulf between
Bahrain and Trucial Oman, has an area of 4,247sq. mi. (11,000
sq. km.) and a population of *469,000. Capital: Doha. Oil is the
chief industry and export.

TITLES

Daulat Qatar

RULERS
Al-Thani Dynasty
Hamad bin Khalifah, 1995-

MONETARY SYSTEM
100 Dirhem = 1 Riyal

STATE

STANDARD COINAGE

KM# 69   DIRHAM
Copper Plated Silver, 15 mm. **Ruler:** Hamad bin Khalifa **Obv:**
National Arms **Rev:** Value

Date	Mintage	F	VF	XF	Unc	BU
AH1429-2008	—					

KM# 12   5 DIRHAMS
3.7500 g., Bronze, 21.9 mm. **Ruler:** Hamad bin Khalifa **Obv:**
National arms **Rev:** Value **Edge:** Plain

Date	Mintage	F	VF	XF	Unc	BU
AH1427-2006	—	—	—	0.35	0.90	1.25

KM# 13 10 DIRHAMS
7.5000 g., Bronze, 27 mm. **Ruler:** Hamad bin Khalifa **Obv:** National arms **Rev:** Value **Edge:** Plain

Date	Mintage	F	VF	XF	Unc	BU
AH1427-2006	—	—	—	0.60	1.50	2.00

KM# 8 25 DIRHAMS
3.5000 g., Copper-Nickel, 20 mm. **Ruler:** Hamad bin Khalifa **Obv:** National arms **Rev:** Value **Rev. Legend:** STATE OF QATAR **Edge:** Reeded

Date	Mintage	F	VF	XF	Unc	BU
AH1424-2003	—	—	0.30	0.65	1.50	2.50

KM# 14 25 DIRHAMS
3.5000 g., Copper-Nickel, 20 mm. **Ruler:** Hamad bin Khalifa **Obv:** National arms **Rev:** Value **Edge:** Reeded

Date	Mintage	F	VF	XF	Unc	BU
AH1427-2006	—	—	—	0.75	1.85	2.50
AH1429-2008	—	—	—	0.75	1.85	2.50

KM# 14a 25 DIRHAMS
Nickel Plated Steel, 20 mm. **Ruler:** Hamad bin Khalifa **Obv:** National Arms **Rev:** Value

Date	Mintage	F	VF	XF	Unc	BU
AH1429-2008	—	—	—	—	1.50	3.00

KM# 9 50 DIRHAMS
6.5000 g., Copper-Nickel, 25 mm. **Ruler:** Hamad bin Khalifa **Obv:** National arms **Rev:** Value **Edge:** Reeded

Date	Mintage	F	VF	XF	Unc	BU
AH1424-2003	—	—	—	—	2.00	3.00

KM# 15 50 DIRHAMS
6.5000 g., Copper-Nickel, 25 mm. **Ruler:** Hamad bin Khalifa **Obv:** National arms **Rev:** Value **Edge:** Reeded

Date	Mintage	F	VF	XF	Unc	BU
AH1427-2006	—	—	—	0.80	2.00	2.75
AH1429-2008	—	—	—	0.80	2.00	2.75

KM# 15a 50 DIRHAMS
6.5000 g., Nickel Plated Steel, 25 mm. **Ruler:** Hamad bin Khalifa **Obv:** National Arms **Rev:** Value

Date	Mintage	F	VF	XF	Unc	BU
AH1429-2008	—	—	—	—	2.25	4.50

KM# 16 RIYAL
Aluminum-Bronze **Ruler:** Hamad bin Khalifa **Subject:** 15th Asian Games **Obv:** Arms above value **Rev:** Multicolor Fox on Bicycle, cartoon character

Date	Mintage	F	VF	XF	Unc	BU
2006	—	—	—	—	—	25.00

KM# 34 RIYAL
Aluminum-Bronze, 38.74 mm. **Ruler:** Hamad bin Khalifa **Subject:** 15th Asian Games **Obv:** Arms **Rev:** Multicolor mascot with flag

Date	Mintage	F	VF	XF	Unc	BU
2006	25,000	—	—	—	—	25.00

KM# 35 RIYAL
Aluminum-Bronze, 38.74 mm. **Ruler:** Hamad bin Khalifa **Subject:** 15th Asian Games **Obv:** Arms **Rev:** Multicolor mascot kicking soccer ball

Date	Mintage	F	VF	XF	Unc	BU
2006	25,000	—	—	—	—	25.00

KM# 36 RIYAL
Aluminum-Bronze, 38.74 mm. **Ruler:** Hamad bin Khalifa **Subject:** 15th Asian Games **Obv:** Arms **Rev:** Three multicolor torches

Date	Mintage	F	VF	XF	Unc	BU
2006	25,000	—	—	—	—	25.00

KM# 37 RIYAL
Aluminum-Bronze, 38.74 mm. **Ruler:** Hamad bin Khalifa **Subject:** 15th Asian Games **Obv:** Arms **Rev:** Two figures with linked arms

Date	Mintage	F	VF	XF	Unc	BU
2006	25,000	—	—	—	—	25.00

KM# 38 RIYAL
Aluminum-Bronze, 38.74 mm. **Ruler:** Hamad bin Khalifa **Subject:** 15th Asian Games **Obv:** Arms **Rev:** Figure with outstretched arms

Date	Mintage	F	VF	XF	Unc	BU
2006	25,000	—	—	—	—	25.00

KM# 25 10 RIYALS
31.1035 g., 0.9990 Silver 0.9990 oz. ASW, 40.5 mm. **Ruler:** Hamad bin Khalifa **Subject:** 15th Asian Games **Obv:** Arms **Rev:** Runner trailing green color

Date	Mintage	F	VF	XF	Unc	BU
2006 Proof	25,000	Value: 110				

KM# 26 10 RIYALS
31.1035 g., 0.9990 Silver 0.9990 oz. ASW, 40.5 mm. **Ruler:** Hamad bin Khalifa **Subject:** 15th Asian Games **Obv:** Arms **Rev:** Cyclist trailing red color

Date	Mintage	F	VF	XF	Unc	BU
2006 Proof	25,000	Value: 110				

KM# 27 10 RIYALS
31.1035 g., 0.9990 Silver 0.9990 oz. ASW, 40.5 mm. **Ruler:** Hamad bin Khalifa **Subject:** 15th Asian Games **Obv:** Arms **Rev:** Soccer player legs on green color

Date	Mintage	F	VF	XF	Unc	BU
2006 Proof	25,000	Value: 110				

KM# 28 10 RIYALS
31.1035 g., 0.9990 Silver 0.9990 oz. ASW, 40.5 mm. **Ruler:** Hamad bin Khalifa **Subject:** 15th Asian Games **Obv:** Arms **Rev:** Ribbon dancer trailing red color

Date	Mintage	F	VF	XF	Unc	BU
2006 Proof	25,000	Value: 110				

KM# 29 10 RIYALS
31.1035 g., 0.9990 Silver 0.9990 oz. ASW, 40.5 mm. **Ruler:** Hamad bin Khalifa **Subject:** 15th Asian Games **Obv:** Arms **Rev:** Karate contestants and dark yellow color

Date	Mintage	F	VF	XF	Unc	BU
2006 Proof	25,000	Value: 110				

KM# 30 10 RIYALS
31.1035 g., 0.9990 Silver 0.9990 oz. ASW, 40.5 mm. **Ruler:** Hamad bin Khalifa **Subject:** 15th Asian Games **Obv:** Arms **Rev:** Swimmer in aqua colored water

Date	Mintage	F	VF	XF	Unc	BU
2006 Proof	25,000	Value: 110				

KM# 31 10 RIYALS
31.1035 g., 0.9990 Silver 0.9990 oz. ASW, 40.5 mm. **Ruler:** Hamad bin Khalifa **Subject:** 15th Asian Games **Obv:** Arms **Rev:** Table tennis player and orange-brownish color

Date	Mintage	F	VF	XF	Unc	BU
2006 Proof	25,000	Value: 110				

KM# 32   10 RIYALS
31.1035 g., 0.9990 Silver 0.9990 oz. ASW, 40.5 mm. **Ruler:** Hamad bin Khalifa **Subject:** 15th Asian Games **Obv:** Arms **Rev:** Tennis player and aqua color

Date	Mintage	F	VF	XF	Unc	BU
2006 Proof	25,000	Value: 110				

KM# 33   10 RIYALS
31.1035 g., 0.9990 Silver 0.9990 oz. ASW, 40.5 mm. **Ruler:** Hamad bin Khalifa **Subject:** 15th Asian Games **Obv:** Arms **Rev:** Volleyball player trailing purple color

Date	Mintage	F	VF	XF	Unc	BU
2006 Proof	25,000	Value: 110				

KM# 40   100 RIYALS
24.0000 g., 0.9250 Silver 0.7137 oz. ASW, 37 mm. **Ruler:** Hamad bin Khalifa **Subject:** Yousif al Sharif **Obv:** Wing desing **Rev:** Male bust

Date	Mintage	F	VF	XF	Unc	BU
2002 Proof	—	—	—	—	—	—

KM# 42   100 RIYALS
100.0000 g., 0.9990 Silver 3.2117 oz. ASW, 80 mm. **Ruler:** Hamad bin Khalifa **Subject:** Doha Cultural festival

Date	Mintage	F	VF	XF	Unc	BU
2003 Proof	—	—	—	—	—	—

KM# 17   100 RIYALS
Gold   **Ruler:** Hamad bin Khalifa **Subject:** 15th Asian Games **Obv:** Arms above value **Rev:** Games mascot Fox on Bicycle cartoon character

Date	Mintage	F	VF	XF	Unc	BU
2006 Proof	Est. 10,000	Value: 550				

KM# 18   100 RIYALS
17.0000 g., 0.9200 Gold 0.5028 oz. AGW, 31 mm. **Ruler:** Hamad bin Khalifa **Obv:** Arms **Rev:** Central Bank building **Edge:** Reeded

Date	Mintage	F	VF	XF	Unc	BU
2006 Proof	300	Value: 1,500				

KM# 19   100 RIYALS
10.0000 g., 0.9999 Gold 0.3215 oz. AGW, 24.5 mm. **Ruler:** Hamad bin Khalifa **Subject:** 15th Asian Games **Obv:** Arms **Rev:** Khalifa Stadium **Edge:** Reeded

Date	Mintage	F	VF	XF	Unc	BU
2006 Proof	—	Value: 650				

KM# 20   100 RIYALS
10.0000 g., 0.9999 Gold 0.3215 oz. AGW, 24.5 mm. **Ruler:** Hamad bin Khalifa **Subject:** 15th Asian Games **Obv:** Arms **Rev:** Two oryxes head-butting **Edge:** Reeded

Date	Mintage	F	VF	XF	Unc	BU
2006 Proof	—	Value: 650				

KM# 21   100 RIYALS
10.0000 g., 0.9999 Gold 0.3215 oz. AGW, 24.5 mm. **Ruler:** Hamad bin Khalifa **Subject:** 15th Asian Games **Obv:** Arms **Rev:** Falcon bust **Edge:** Reeded

Date	Mintage	F	VF	XF	Unc	BU
2006 Proof	—	Value: 650				

KM# 22   100 RIYALS
10.0000 g., 0.9999 Gold 0.3215 oz. AGW, 24.5 mm. **Ruler:** Hamad bin Khalifa **Subject:** 15th Asian Games **Obv:** Arms **Rev:** Coffee pot **Edge:** Reeded

Date	Mintage	F	VF	XF	Unc	BU
2006 Proof	—	Value: 650				

KM# 23   100 RIYALS
10.0000 g., 0.9999 Gold 0.3215 oz. AGW, 24.5 mm. **Ruler:** Hamad bin Khalifa **Subject:** 15th Asian Games **Obv:** Arms **Rev:** Radiant sun **Edge:** Reeded

Date	Mintage	F	VF	XF	Unc	BU
2006 Proof	—	Value: 650				

KM# 76   100 RIYALS
22.2400 g., 0.9250 Silver 0.6614 oz. ASW, 37 mm. **Ruler:** Hamad bin Khalifa **Subject:** 2008 Arab States Stamp Exhibition **Obv:** National Arms **Rev:** Two profiles right

Date	Mintage	F	VF	XF	Unc	BU
2008 Proof	1,000	Value: 90.00				

KM# 77   100 RIYALS
22.2400 g., 0.9250 Silver 0.6614 oz. ASW, 37 mm. **Ruler:** Hamad bin Khalifa **Subject:** Central Municipal Council, 10th Anniversary **Obv:** National Arms in color **Rev:** Democracy House in color

Date	Mintage	F	VF	XF	Unc	BU
2009 Proof	—	—	—	—	—	—

KM# 78   100 RIYALS
Silver **Ruler:** Hamad bin Khalifa **Subject:** 10th Gulf Cooperation Council Banking Conference

Date	Mintage	F	VF	XF	Unc	BU
2011 Proof	—	Value: 60.00				

KM# 47   200 RIYALS
Gold **Ruler:** Hamad bin Khalifa **Subject:** al Wabra Wildlife Preservation, 50th Anniversary **Rev:** Blue headed macaw

Date	Mintage	F	VF	XF	Unc	BU
2003 Proof	240	—	—	—	—	—

KM# 67   200 RIYALS
0.9990 Silver, 40 mm. **Ruler:** Hamad bin Khalifa **Subject:** Doha Cultural Festival **Obv:** Wing emblem **Rev:** Four men seated under archway

Date	Mintage	F	VF	XF	Unc	BU
2004 Proof	—	—	—	—	—	—

KM# 79   200 RIYALS
Silver gilt **Ruler:** Hamad bin Khalifa **Subject:** 10th Gulf Cooperation Council Banking Conference

Date	Mintage	F	VF	XF	Unc	BU
2011 Proof	—	Value: 100				

KM# 11   250 RIYALS
Silver **Ruler:** Hamad bin Khalifa **Subject:** 4th WTO Conference **Obv:** National arms **Rev:** WTO logo, value, date, and legend in English and Islamic

Date	Mintage	F	VF	XF	Unc	BU
AH1422 (2001) Proof	1,000	Value: 650				

KM# 41   250 RIYALS
31.0000 g., 0.9990 Gold 0.9956 oz. AGW, 37 mm. **Ruler:** Hamad bin Khalifa **Subject:** Yousif al Sharif **Obv:** Wing design **Rev:** Male bust

Date	Mintage	F	VF	XF	Unc	BU
2002 Proof	—	—	—	—	—	—

KM# 55   250 RIYALS
120.0000 g., 0.9990 Silver 3.8541 oz. ASW, 60 mm. **Ruler:** Hamad bin Khalifa **Subject:** al Wabra Wildlife Preservation, 50th Anniversary **Rev:** Dama gazelle

Date	Mintage	F	VF	XF	Unc	BU
2003 Proof	1,800	—	—	—	—	—

KM# 43   250 RIYALS
100.0000 g., 0.9990 Silver partially gilt 3.2117 oz. ASW, 80 mm. **Ruler:** Hamad bin Khalifa **Subject:** Doha Cultural festival

Date	Mintage	F	VF	XF	Unc	BU
2003 Proof	1,000	—	—	—	—	—

KM# 44   250 RIYALS
120.0000 g., 0.9990 Silver 3.8541 oz. ASW, 60 mm. **Ruler:** Hamad bin Khalifa **Subject:** al Wabra Wildlife Preservation, 50th Anniversary **Rev:** Blue headed macaw in color

Date	Mintage	F	VF	XF	Unc	BU
2003 Proof	1,800	—	—	—	—	—

KM# 45   250 RIYALS
120.0000 g., 0.9990 Silver 3.8541 oz. ASW, 60 mm. **Ruler:** Hamad bin Khalifa **Subject:** al Wabra Wildlife Preservation, 50th Anniversary **Rev:** bird in color

Date	Mintage	F	VF	XF	Unc	BU
2003 Proof	1,800	—	—	—	—	—

KM# 46   250 RIYALS
120.0000 g., 0.9990 Silver 3.8541 oz. ASW, 60 mm. **Ruler:** Hamad bin Khalifa **Subject:** al Wabra Wildlife Preservation, 50th Anniversary **Rev:** Macaw in color

Date	Mintage	F	VF	XF	Unc	BU
2003 Proof	1,800	—	—	—	—	—

KM# 53   250 RIYALS
120.0000 g., 0.9990 Silver 3.8541 oz. ASW, 60 mm. **Ruler:** Hamad bin Khalifa **Subject:** al Wabra Wildlife Preservation, 50th Anniversary **Rev:** Gazelle

Date	Mintage	F	VF	XF	Unc	BU
2003 Proof	1,800	—	—	—	—	—

KM# 54   250 RIYALS
120.0000 g., 0.9990 Silver 3.8541 oz. ASW, 60 mm. **Ruler:** Hamad bin Khalifa **Subject:** al Wabra Wildlife Preservation, 50th Anniversary **Rev:** Sommering gazelle

Date	Mintage	F	VF	XF	Unc	BU
2003 Proof	1,800	—	—	—	—	—

KM# 56   250 RIYALS
120.0000 g., 0.9990 Silver 3.8541 oz. ASW, 60 mm. **Ruler:** Hamad bin Khalifa **Subject:** al Wabra Wildlife Preservation, 50th Anniversary **Rev:** Stilt gazelle

Date	Mintage	F	VF	XF	Unc	BU
2003 Proof	1,800	—	—	—	—	—

KM# 65   250 RIYALS
120.0000 g., 0.9990 Silver 3.8541 oz. ASW, 60 mm. **Ruler:** Hamad bin Khalifa **Subject:** National Council for Culture, Arts and Heritage, 5th Anniversary **Obv:** Bust 1/4 left **Rev:** Text and emblem

Date	Mintage	F	VF	XF	Unc	BU
2003 Proof	1,000	Value: 300				

KM# 70   250 RIYALS
120.0000 g., 0.9990 Silver 3.8541 oz. ASW, 60 mm. **Ruler:** Hamad bin Khalifa **Subject:** National Council for Culture, Arts and Heritage

Date	Mintage	F	VF	XF	Unc	BU
2006 Proof	—	—	—	—	—	—

KM# 39   300 RIYALS
1000.0000 g., 0.9990 Silver 32.117 oz. ASW, 100.0 mm. **Ruler:** Hamad bin Khalifa **Obv:** National arms **Obv. Legend:** STATE OF QATAR **Rev:** Sports montage around game's logo **Rev. Inscription:** 15TH ASIAN GAMES / DOHA 2006 **Edge:** Plain

Date	Mintage	F	VF	XF	Unc	BU
2006 Proof	5,000	Value: 1,250				

KM# 68   1000 RIYALS
0.9990 Gold, 40 mm. **Ruler:** Hamad bin Khalifa **Subject:** Doha Coultural Festival **Obv:** Wing design **Rev:** Four men seated under archway

Date	Mintage	F	VF	XF	Unc	BU
2004 Proof	—	—	—	—	—	—

KM# 48   2000 RIYALS
Gold **Ruler:** Hamad bin Khalifa **Subject:** al Wabra Wildlife Preservation, 50th Anniversary **Rev:** bird

Date	Mintage	F	VF	XF	Unc	BU
2003 Proof	240	—	—	—	—	—

KM# 72   2000 RIYALS
40.6400 g., 0.9250 Silver 1.2086 oz. ASW, 50 mm. **Ruler:** Hamad bin Khalifa **Subject:** National Day **Obv:** National Arms in color **Rev:** State of Qatar, National arms in color

Date	Mintage	F	VF	XF	Unc	BU
2007 Proof	500	Value: 900				

KM# 73   2000 RIYALS
40.6400 g., 0.9250 Silver 1.2086 oz. ASW, 50 mm. **Ruler:** Hamad bin Khalifa **Subject:** National Day **Obv:** National Arms in color **Rev:** Qatar Central Bank, National arms in color

Date	Mintage	F	VF	XF	Unc	BU
2007 Proof	500	Value: 900				

KM# 49   5000 RIYALS
Gold **Ruler:** Hamad bin Khalifa **Subject:** al Wabra Wildlife Preservation, 50th Anniversary **Rev:** macaw

Date	Mintage	F	VF	XF	Unc	BU
2003 Proof	240	—	—	—	—	—

KM# 57 5000 RIYALS
Gold **Ruler:** Hamad bin Khalifa **Subject:** al Wabra Wildlife Preservation, 50th Anniversary **Rev:** Gazelle

Date	Mintage	F	VF	XF	Unc	BU
2003 Proof	240	—	—	—	—	—

KM# 58 5000 RIYALS
Gold **Ruler:** Hamad bin Khalifa **Subject:** al Wabra Wildlife Preservation, 50th Anniversary **Rev:** Sommering Gazelle

Date	Mintage	F	VF	XF	Unc	BU
2003 Proof	240	—	—	—	—	—

KM# 59 5000 RIYALS
Gold **Ruler:** Hamad bin Khalifa **Subject:** al Wabra Wildlife Preservation, 50th Anniversary **Rev:** Dama Gazelle

Date	Mintage	F	VF	XF	Unc	BU
2003 Proof	240	—	—	—	—	—

KM# 60 5000 RIYALS
Gold **Ruler:** Hamad bin Khalifa **Subject:** al Wabra Wildlife Preservation, 50th Anniversary **Rev:** Stilt Gazelle

Date	Mintage	F	VF	XF	Unc	BU
2003 Proof	240	—	—	—	—	—

KM# 66 5000 RIYALS
160.0000 g., 0.9990 Gold 5.1388 oz. AGW, 60 mm. **Ruler:** Hamad bin Khalifa **Subject:** National Council for Culture, Arts and Heritage, 5th Anniversary **Obv:** Bust 1/4 left **Rev:** Text and emblem

Date	Mintage	F	VF	XF	Unc	BU
2003 Proof	500	—	—	—	—	7,750

KM# 71 5000 RIYALS
160.0000 g., 0.9990 Gold 5.1388 oz. AGW, 60 mm. **Ruler:** Hamad bin Khalifa **Subject:** National Council for Culture, Arts and Heritage

Date	Mintage	F	VF	XF	Unc	BU
2006 Proof	—	—	—	—	—	—

KM# 50 10000 RIYALS
Platinum APW **Ruler:** Hamad bin Khalifa **Subject:** al Wabra Wildlife Preservation, 50th Anniversary **Rev:** Blue headed macaw

Date	Mintage	F	VF	XF	Unc	BU
2003 Proof	120	—	—	—	—	—

KM# 51 10000 RIYALS
Platinum APW **Ruler:** Hamad bin Khalifa **Subject:** al Wabra Wildlife Preservation, 50th Anniversary **Rev:** bird

Date	Mintage	F	VF	XF	Unc	BU
2003 Proof	120	—	—	—	—	—

KM# 52 10000 RIYALS
Platinum APW **Ruler:** Hamad bin Khalifa **Subject:** al Wabra Wildlife Preservation, 50th Anniversary **Rev:** Macaw

Date	Mintage	F	VF	XF	Unc	BU
2003 Proof	120	—	—	—	—	—

KM# 61 10000 RIYALS
Platinum APW **Ruler:** Hamad bin Khalifa **Subject:** al Wabra Wildlife Preservation, 50th Anniversary **Rev:** Gazelle

Date	Mintage	F	VF	XF	Unc	BU
2003 Proof	120	—	—	—	—	—

KM# 62 10000 RIYALS
Platinum APW **Ruler:** Hamad bin Khalifa **Subject:** al Wabra Wildlife Preservation, 50th Anniversary **Rev:** Sommering gazelle

Date	Mintage	F	VF	XF	Unc	BU
2003 Proof	120	—	—	—	—	—

KM# 63 10000 RIYALS
Platinum APW **Ruler:** Hamad bin Khalifa **Subject:** al Wabra Wildlife Preservation, 50th Anniversary **Rev:** Dama gazelle

Date	Mintage	F	VF	XF	Unc	BU
2003 Proof	120	—	—	—	—	—

KM# 64 10000 RIYALS
Platinum APW **Ruler:** Hamad bin Khalifa **Subject:** al Wabra Wildlife Preservation, 50th Anniversary **Rev:** Stilt gazelle

Date	Mintage	F	VF	XF	Unc	BU
2003 Proof	120	—	—	—	—	—

KM# 24 10000 RIYALS
1000.0000 g., 0.9999 Gold 32.146 oz. AGW, 75.3 mm. **Ruler:** Hamad bin Khalifa **Subject:** 15th Asian Games **Obv:** Arms **Rev:** Radiant sun **Edge:** Reeded **Note:** Illustration reduced.

Date	Mintage	F	VF	XF	Unc	BU
2006 Proof	—	Value: 48,000				

KM# 74 10000 RIYALS
70.1600 g., 0.9160 Gold 2.0661 oz. AGW, 50 mm. **Ruler:** Hamad bin Khalifa **Subject:** National Day **Obv:** National Arms **Rev:** State of Qatar, National Arms

Date	Mintage	F	VF	XF	Unc	BU
2007 Proof	500	Value: 4,500				

KM# 75 10000 RIYALS
70.1600 g., 0.9160 Gold 2.0661 oz. AGW, 50 mm. **Ruler:** Hamad bin Khalifa **Subject:** National Day **Obv:** National Arms **Rev:** Qatar Central Bank, National Arms

Date	Mintage	F	VF	XF	Unc	BU
2007 Proof	500	Value: 4,500				

ROMANIA

Romania (formerly the Socialist Republic of Romania), a country in southeast Europe, has an area of 91,699 sq. mi. (237,500 sq. km.) and a population of 23.2 million. Capital: Bucharest. Machinery, foodstuffs, raw minerals and petroleum products are exported. Heavy industry and oil have become increasingly important to the economy since 1959. Romania joined the European Union in January 2007.

MONETARY SYSTEM
100 Bani = 1 Leu

REPUBLIC
STANDARD COINAGE

KM# 115 LEU
2.5200 g., Copper Plated Steel, 19 mm. **Obv:** Value flanked by sprigs **Rev:** Shield divides date

Date	Mintage	F	VF	XF	Unc	BU
2002 Proof	1,500	Value: 5.00				
2003 Proof	2,000	Value: 5.00				
2004 Proof	2,000	Value: 5.00				
2005	—	—	—	—	1.00	—
2005 Proof	—	Value: 6.00				
2006 Proof	1,000	Value: 6.00				

KM# 114 5 LEI
3.3000 g., Nickel Plated Steel, 21 mm. **Obv:** Value flanked by oak leaves **Rev:** Shield divides date **Edge:** Plain

Date	Mintage	F	VF	XF	Unc	BU
2002 Proof	1,500	Value: 5.00				
2003 Proof	2,000	Value: 5.00				
2004 Proof	—	Value: 5.00				
2005 Proof	—	Value: 5.00				

KM# 116 10 LEI
4.7000 g., Nickel Clad Steel, 23 mm. **Obv:** Value within sprigs **Rev:** Shield divides date **Edge:** Plain

Date	Mintage	F	VF	XF	Unc	BU
2002 Proof	1,500	Value: 6.00				
2003 Proof	2,000	Value: 6.00				

KM# 109 20 LEI
5.0000 g., Brass Clad Steel, 24 mm. **Obv:** Crowned bust of Prince Stefan Cel Mare facing, flanked by dots **Rev:** Value and date within half sprigs and dots **Edge:** Plain **Note:** Date varieties exist.

Date	Mintage	F	VF	XF	Unc	BU
2002 Proof	1,500	Value: 7.50				
2003 Proof	2,000	Value: 7.50				

KM# 159 50 LEI
15.5510 g., 0.9990 Silver 0.4995 oz. ASW, 31.1 mm. **Series:** Romanian Aviation **Obv:** AVIONUL VUIA 1 - 1906 airplane **Rev:** Traian Vuia **Edge:** Plain **Shape:** Octagonal

Date	Mintage	F	VF	XF	Unc	BU
2001 Proof	500	Value: 165				

KM# 160 50 LEI
15.5510 g., 0.9990 Silver 0.4995 oz. ASW, 31.1 mm. **Series:** Romanian Aviation **Obv:** Avionul Coanda 1910, world's first (?) jet airplane **Rev:** Portrait of Henri Coanda **Edge:** Plain **Shape:** Octagonal

Date	Mintage	F	VF	XF	Unc	BU
2001 Proof	500	Value: 165				

KM# 161 50 LEI
15.5510 g., 0.9990 Silver 0.4995 oz. ASW, 27 mm. **Series:** Romanian Aviation **Obv:** IAR CV-11 airplane **Rev:** Elie Carafoli **Edge:** Plain **Shape:** Octagonal

Date	Mintage	F	VF	XF	Unc	BU
2001 Proof	500	Value: 165				

KM# 110 50 LEI
5.9000 g., Brass Clad Steel, 26 mm. **Obv:** Bust left flanked by dots **Rev:** Sprig divides date and value **Edge:** Plain

Date	Mintage	F	VF	XF	Unc	BU
2002 Proof	1,500	Value: 8.00				
2003 Proof	2,000	Value: 8.00				

KM# 167 50 LEI
15.5510 g., 0.9990 Silver 0.4995 oz. ASW, 29.5 mm. **Subject:** National Parks: Retezat **Obv:** National arms in triangular design **Rev:** Chamois **Edge:** Plain **Shape:** Rounded triangle

Date	Mintage	F	VF	XF	Unc	BU
2002 Proof	500	Value: 200				

KM# 168 50 LEI
15.5510 g., 0.9990 Silver 0.4995 oz. ASW, 29.5 mm. **Subject:** National Parks: Pictrosul Mare **Obv:** National arms in triangular design **Rev:** Eagle **Edge:** Plain **Shape:** Rounded triangle

Date	Mintage	F	VF	XF	Unc	BU
2002 Proof	500	Value: 200				

KM# 169 50 LEI
15.5510 g., 0.9990 Silver 0.4995 oz. ASW, 29.5 mm. **Subject:** National Parks: Piatra Craiului **Obv:** National arms in triangular design **Rev:** Lynx **Edge:** Plain **Shape:** Rounded triangle

Date	Mintage	F	VF	XF	Unc	BU
2002 Proof	500	Value: 200				

KM# 186   50 LEI
15.5510 g., 0.9990 Silver 0.4995 oz. ASW, 27 mm.   **Subject:**
Birds **Obv:** Stylized water drop **Rev:** Dalmatian Pelicans within
circle **Edge:** Plain

Date	Mintage	F	VF	XF	Unc	BU
2003 Proof	500	Value: 100				

KM# 187   50 LEI
15.5510 g., 0.9990 Silver 0.4995 oz. ASW, 27 mm.   **Subject:**
Birds **Obv:** Stylized water drop **Rev:** Great Egret within circle
Edge: Plain

Date	Mintage	F	VF	XF	Unc	BU
2003 Proof	500	Value: 100				

KM# 188   50 LEI
15.5510 g., 0.9990 Silver 0.4995 oz. ASW, 27 mm.   **Subject:**
Birds **Obv:** Stylized water drop **Rev:** Common Kingfisher within
circle **Edge:** Plain

Date	Mintage	F	VF	XF	Unc	BU
2003 Proof	500	Value: 100				

KM# 111   100 LEI
8.7500 g., Nickel Plated Steel, 29 mm.   **Obv:** Bust with headdress
1/4 right **Rev:** Value within sprigs **Edge Lettering:** ROMANIA

Date	Mintage	F	VF	XF	Unc	BU
2002 Proof	1,500	Value: 8.00				
2003 Proof	2,000	Value: 8.00				
2004 Proof	2,000	Value: 8.00				
2005	—	—	—	—	2.50	—
2005 Proof	2,000	Value: 9.00				
2006 Proof	1,000	Value: 9.00				

KM# 165   100 LEI
1.2240 g., 0.9990 Gold 0.0393 oz. AGW, 13.9 mm.   **Subject:**
History of Gold - "The Apahida Eagle" **Obv:** National arms in
ornamental circle above value **Edge:** Plain

Date	Mintage	F	VF	XF	Unc	BU
2003 Proof	2,000	Value: 125				

KM# 166   100 LEI
1.2240 g., 0.9990 Gold 0.0393 oz. AGW, 14 mm.   **Subject:**
History of Gold - Engolpion **Obv:** National arms and country name
above two stylized birds and value **Rev:** Jeweled double headed
eagle pendant

Date	Mintage	F	VF	XF	Unc	BU
2004 Proof	1,000	Value: 165				

KM# 170   500 LEI
6.2200 g., 0.9990 Gold 0.1998 oz. AGW, 11.75 mm.   **Subject:**
History of Gold - Treasure of Pietroasa **Rev:** "Big Clip" of
Pietroasa

Date	Mintage	F	VF	XF	Unc	BU
	250	—	—	—	—	700

KM# 171   500 LEI
6.2200 g., 0.9990 Gold 0.1998 oz. AGW, 11.75 mm.   **Subject:**
History of Gold - Treasure of Pietroasa **Rev:** "Medium Clip" of
Pietroasa

Date	Mintage	F	VF	XF	Unc	BU
2001	250	—	—	—	—	700

KM# 172   500 LEI
6.2200 g., 0.9990 Gold 0.1998 oz. AGW, 11.75 mm.   **Subject:**
History of Gold - Treasure of Pietroasa **Rev:** 12-sided golden bowl

Date	Mintage	F	VF	XF	Unc	BU
2001	250	—	—	—	—	700

KM# 173   500 LEI
6.2200 g., 0.9990 Gold 0.1998 oz. AGW, 11.75 mm.   **Subject:**
History of Gold - Treasure of Pietroasa **Rev:** Pitcher

Date	Mintage	F	VF	XF	Unc	BU
2001	250	—	—	—	—	700

KM# 176   500 LEI
6.2200 g., 0.9990 Gold 0.1998 oz. AGW, 23.2 mm.   **Subject:**
Christian Monuments **Rev:** Mogosoaia Palace **Shape:** Square

Date	Mintage	F	VF	XF	Unc	BU
2001	250	—	—	—	—	550

KM# 145   500 LEI
3.7000 g., Aluminum, 25 mm.   **Obv:** Shield within sprigs **Rev:**
Value within 3/4 wreath **Edge:** Lettered **Edge Lettering:**
ROMANIA (three times)

Date	Mintage	F	VF	XF	Unc	BU
2001	—	—	—	0.75	2.00	—
2002 Proof	1,500	Value: 7.00				
2003 Proof	2,000	Value: 7.00				
2004 Proof	2,000	Value: 7.00				
2005	—	—	—	—	3.00	—
2005 Proof	1,000	Value: 8.00				
2006	—	—	—	—	3.00	—
2006 Proof	—	Value: 8.00				

KM# 174   500 LEI
6.2200 g., 0.9990 Gold 0.1998 oz. AGW, 23.2 mm.   **Subject:**
Christian Monuments **Rev:** Bistritz Monastery

Date	Mintage	F	VF	XF	Unc	BU
2002	250	—	—	—	—	550

KM# 175   500 LEI
6.2200 g., 0.9990 Gold 0.1998 oz. AGW, 23.2 mm.   **Subject:**
Christian Monuments **Rev:** Coltea Church

Date	Mintage	F	VF	XF	Unc	BU
2002	250	—	—	—	—	550

KM# 177   500 LEI
31.1030 g., 0.9990 Silver 0.9989 oz. ASW, 37 mm.   **Subject:**
150th Anniversary - Birth of Ciprian Porumbescu, Composer
Obv: Partial piano and violin left of National arms and value **Rev:**
Portrait and musical score **Edge:** Plain

Date	Mintage	F	VF	XF	Unc	BU
2003 Proof	500	Value: 160				

KM# 178   500 LEI
31.1030 g., 0.9990 Silver 0.9989 oz. ASW, 37 mm.   **Subject:**
500th Anniversary - Establishment of Bishopric of Ramnic **Obv:**
National arms and value above inscription **Rev:** Bishopric's coat-
of-arms **Edge:** Plain

Date	Mintage	F	VF	XF	Unc	BU
2003 Proof	500	Value: 160				

KM# 179   500 LEI
31.1030 g., 0.9990 Silver 0.9989 oz. ASW, 37 mm.   **Subject:**
Romanian Numismatic Society Centennial **Obv:** Cornucopia
pouring forth coins, value below **Rev:** Minerva and torch **Rev.
Legend:** CENTENARUL SOCIETATII NUMISMATICE
ROMANE, 1903-2003 **Edge:** Plain

Date	Mintage	F	VF	XF	Unc	BU
2003 Proof	1,000	Value: 150				

KM# 180   500 LEI
31.1030 g., 0.9990 Silver 0.9989 oz. ASW, 37 mm.   **Subject:**
140th Anniversary - University of Bucharest **Obv:** Vertical
inscription divides National arms, value and date at left. University
emblem at right **Obv. Inscription:** ROMANIA **Rev:** Cameo at
right and crowned arms at left above University Building **Rev.
Inscription:** Upper: UNIVERSITATEA DIN BUCURESTI / 140
DE ANI; Lower: INTEMEIATA LA 1864 DE / AL IOAN CUZA
Edge: Plain

Date	Mintage	F	VF	XF	Unc	BU
2004 Proof	500	Value: 180				

KM# 193   500 LEI
31.1035 g., 0.9990 Silver 0.9990 oz. ASW, 37 mm.   **Subject:**
150th Anniversary - Birth of Anghel Saligny **Obv:** Arms at left
above Cernavoda bridge, inscription, date, and value below **Obv.
Inscription:** PODUL DE LA CERNAVODA **Rev:** Bust of bridge
builder Anghel Saligny half right, life dates at right, his signature
below at left **Edge:** Plain

Date	Mintage	F	VF	XF	Unc	BU
2004 Proof	500	Value: 350				

KM# 163   500 LEI
31.1030 g., 0.9990 Silver 0.9989 oz. ASW, 37 mm.   **Subject:**
Christian Feudal Art Monuments **Obv:** National arms, date and
value at left, belfry tower of church at right **Rev:** Cotroceni
Monastery church **Edge:** Plain **Shape:** 10-sided

Date	Mintage	F	VF	XF	Unc	BU
2004 Proof	500	Value: 150				

KM# 164   500 LEI
31.1030 g., 0.9990 Silver 0.9989 oz. ASW, 37 mm.   **Subject:**
Christian Feudal Art Monuments **Obv:** National arms, bell and value
Rev: St. Trei Ierarhi church in Iasi **Edge:** Plain **Shape:** 10-sided

Date	Mintage	F	VF	XF	Unc	BU
2004 Proof	500	Value: 150				

KM# 194 500 LEI
31.1035 g., 0.9990 Silver 0.9990 oz. ASW, 37 mm. **Subject:** 125th Anniversary - National Bank **Obv:** National arms and coin design of 5 Lei dated 1880 **Rev:** Bank building **Edge:** Plain

Date	Mintage	F	VF	XF	Unc	BU
2005 Proof	—	Value: 1,000				

KM# 153 1000 LEI
2.0000 g., Aluminum, 22 mm. **Subject:** Constantin Brancoveanu **Obv:** Value above shield within lined circle **Rev:** Bust with headdress facing **Edge:** Plain with serrated sections

Date	Mintage	VG	F	VF	XF	Unc
2001	—	—	—	—	0.25	2.50
2002	—	—	—	—	0.25	2.50
2002 Proof	1,500	Value: 12.00				
2003	—	—	—	—	0.25	2.50
2003 Proof	2,000	Value: 12.00				
2004	—	—	—	—	0.25	2.50
2004 Proof	2,000	Value: 12.00				
2005	—	—	—	—	0.25	2.50
2005 Proof	—	Value: 13.00				
2006 Proof	1,000	Value: 13.00				

KM# 156 1000 LEI
15.5510 g., 0.9990 Gold 0.4995 oz. AGW, 27 mm. **Subject:** 1900th Anniversary of the First Roman-Dacian War **Obv:** Traian's column and shield **Rev:** Monument divides cameos **Edge:** Plain

Date	Mintage	VG	F	VF	XF	Unc
2001 Proof	500	Value: 950				

KM# 181 2000 LEI
25.0000 g., Bi-Metallic .999 Silver, 10g center in .999 Gold, 15g ring, 35 mm. **Subject:** Ion Heliade Radulescu (1802-1872) **Obv:** Lyre at left, national arms in divided circle design **Rev:** Ion Heliade Radulescu above signature **Edge:** Reeded

Date	Mintage	F	VF	XF	Unc	BU
2002 Proof	500	Value: 1,000				

KM# 158 5000 LEI
2.5000 g., Aluminum, 24 mm. **Obv:** Value and country name **Rev:** Sprig divides date and shield **Edge:** Plain **Shape:** 12-sided

Date	Mintage	F	VF	XF	Unc	BU
2001	—	—	—	—	0.50	—
2002	—	—	—	—	0.50	—
2002 Proof	1,500	Value: 15.00				
2003	—	—	—	—	0.25	—
2003 Proof	2,000	Value: 15.00				
2004	—	—	—	—	0.25	—
2004 Proof	2,000	Value: 16.00				
2005	—	—	—	—	0.25	—
2005 Proof	2,000	Value: 17.00				
2006 Proof	1,000	Value: 17.00				

KM# 162 5000 LEI
31.1035 g., 0.9990 Gold 0.9990 oz. AGW, 35 mm. **Subject:** Constantin Brancusi 125th Anniversary of Birth **Obv:** National arms, value and sculpture **Rev:** Bearded portrait and signature **Edge:** Plain

Date	Mintage	F	VF	XF	Unc	BU
2001 Proof	500	Value: 2,250				

KM# 183 5000 LEI
31.1030 g., 0.9990 Gold 0.9989 oz. AGW, 35 mm. **Subject:** Ion Luca Caragiale, playright (1852-1912) **Obv:** National arms, value and masks of Comedy and Tragedy **Rev:** Portrait **Edge:** Plain

Date	Mintage	F	VF	XF	Unc	BU
2002 Proof	250	Value: 2,500				

KM# 184 5000 LEI
31.1030 g., 0.9990 Gold 0.9989 oz. AGW, 35 mm. **Subject:** Bran Castle (1378-2003) **Obv:** Two coats of arms on shield above value **Rev:** Castle view **Edge:** Plain

Date	Mintage	F	VF	XF	Unc	BU
2003 Proof	250	Value: 2,000				

KM# 185 5000 LEI
31.1030 g., 0.9990 Gold 0.9989 oz. AGW, 35 mm. **Subject:** Stephen the Great **Obv:** National arms, value above coin design in wall **Rev:** Portrait of Stephen and Putna Monastery

Date	Mintage	F	VF	XF	Unc	BU
2004 Proof	250	Value: 2,000				

REFORM COINAGE - 2005
10,000 Old Leu = 1 New Leu

 (see below, KM# 189 image placement)

KM# 189 BAN
2.4000 g., Brass Plated Steel, 16.8 mm. **Subject:** Monetary Reform of 2005 **Obv:** National arms flanked by stars **Rev:** Value **Edge:** Plain

Date	Mintage	F	VF	XF	Unc	BU
2005	—	—	—	—	0.30	0.50
2005 Proof	—	Value: 2.50				
2006	—	—	—	—	0.30	0.50
2006 Proof	—	Value: 2.50				
2007	—	—	—	—	0.30	0.50
2007 Proof	—	Value: 2.50				
2008	—	—	—	—	0.30	0.50
2008 Proof	—	Value: 2.50				
2009	—	—	—	—	0.30	0.50
2009 Proof	—	Value: 2.50				
2010	—	—	—	—	0.30	0.50
2010 Proof	—	Value: 2.50				
2011	—	—	—	—	0.30	0.50
2011 Proof	—	Value: 2.50				
2012	—	—	—	—	0.30	0.50

KM# 190 5 BANI
2.8000 g., Copper Plated Steel, 18.25 mm. **Subject:** Monetary Reform of 2005 **Obv:** National arms flanked by stars **Obv. Legend:** ROMANIA **Rev:** Value **Edge:** Reeded

Date	Mintage	F	VF	XF	Unc	BU
2005	—	—	—	—	0.50	0.75
2005 Proof	—	Value: 5.00				
2006	—	—	—	—	0.50	0.75
2006 Proof	—	Value: 5.00				
2007	—	—	—	—	0.50	0.75
2007 Proof	—	Value: 5.00				
2008	—	—	—	—	0.50	0.75
2008 Proof	—	Value: 5.00				
2009	—	—	—	—	0.50	0.75
2009 Proof	—	Value: 5.00				
2010	—	—	—	—	0.50	0.75
2010 Proof	—	Value: 5.00				
2011	—	—	—	—	0.50	0.75
2011 Proof	—	Value: 5.00				
2012	—	—	—	—	0.50	0.75

KM# 191 10 BANI
4.0000 g., Nickel Plated Steel, 20.4 mm. **Subject:** Monetary Reform of 2005 **Obv:** National arms flanked by stars **Obv. Legend:** ROMANIA **Rev:** Value **Edge:** Segmented reeding

Date	Mintage	F	VF	XF	Unc	BU
2005	—	—	—	—	0.65	0.85
2005 Proof	—	Value: 7.00				
2006	—	—	—	—	0.60	0.80
2006 Proof	—	Value: 7.00				
2007	—	—	—	—	0.50	0.75
2007 Proof	—	Value: 7.00				
2008	—	—	—	—	0.50	0.70
2008 Proof	—	Value: 7.00				
2009	—	—	—	—	0.50	0.70
2009 Proof	—	Value: 7.00				
2010	—	—	—	—	0.50	0.70
2010 Proof	—	Value: 7.00				
2011	—	—	—	—	0.50	0.70
2011 Proof	—	Value: 7.00				
2012	—	—	—	—	0.50	0.70

KM# 192 50 BANI
6.1000 g., Nickel-Brass, 23.75 mm. **Subject:** Monetary Reform of 2005 **Obv:** National arms flanked by stars **Obv. Legend:** ROMANIA **Rev:** Value **Edge:** Lettered **Edge Lettering:** ROMANIA twice

Date	Mintage	F	VF	XF	Unc	BU
2005	—	—	—	—	0.85	1.00
2005 Proof	—	Value: 10.00				
2006	—	—	—	—	0.75	0.85
2006 Proof	—	Value: 10.00				
2007	—	—	—	—	0.65	0.75
2007 Proof	—	Value: 10.00				
2008	—	—	—	—	0.65	0.75
2008 Proof	—	Value: 10.00				
2009	—	—	—	—	0.65	0.75
2009 Proof	—	Value: 10.00				
2010	—	—	—	—	0.65	0.75
2010 Proof	—	Value: 10.00				
2011	—	—	—	—	0.65	0.75
2011 Proof	—	Value: 10.00				

KM# 209 LEU
23.5000 g., Copper Plated Tombac, 37 mm. **Subject:** 140th Anniversary Founding Romanian Academy **Edge:** Plain

Date	Mintage	F	VF	XF	Unc	BU
2006 Proof	35	Value: 750				

KM# 220 LEU
23.5000 g., Copper Plated Tombac, 37 mm. **Subject:** Centennial - Birth of Mircea Eliade **Obv:** Shield and value **Rev:** Portrait facing **Edge:** Reeded

Date	Mintage	F	VF	XF	Unc	BU
2007 Proof	250	Value: 150				

KM# 223 LEU
23.5000 g., Copper Plated Tombac, 37 mm. **Subject:** Dimitrie Cantemir, (Prince of Moldavia 1710-1711), Scientist **Edge:** Reeded

Date	Mintage	F	VF	XF	Unc	BU
2007 Proof	250	Value: 150				

KM# 226   LEU
23.5000 g., Copper Plated Tombac, 37 mm. **Subject:** Stephan the Great **Edge:** Reeded

Date	Mintage	F	VF	XF	Unc	BU
2007 Proof	250	Value: 150				

KM# 199   LEU
23.5000 g., Copper Plated Tombac, 37 mm. **Subject:** 130th Anniversary of Proclamation of Independence **Obv:** Shield and "The Smardan Assault" painting by Nicolae Grigoresuv **Rev:** Meeting of the Parliament

Date	Mintage	F	VF	XF	Unc	BU
2007 Proof	130	Value: 250				

KM# 258   LEU
23.5000 g., Copper Plated Tombac, 37 mm. **Subject:** Bucharest, 550th Anniversary **Obv:** Vlad Tepes **Rev:** Buildings

Date	Mintage	F	VF	XF	Unc	BU
2009 Proof	250	Value: 150				

KM# 208   5 LEI
31.1000 g., 0.9990 Silver 0.9988 oz. ASW, 37 mm. **Subject:** 100th Anniversary - Birth of Grigore Vasiliu-Birlic **Edge:** Plain

Date	Mintage	F	VF	XF	Unc	BU
2005 Proof	150	Value: 1,200				

KM# 210   5 LEI
31.1000 g., 0.9990 Silver 0.9988 oz. ASW, 37 mm. **Subject:** 140th Anniversary Founding Romanian Academy **Edge:** Plain

Date	Mintage	F	VF	XF	Unc	BU
2006 Proof	500	Value: 300				

KM# 212   5 LEI
31.1000 g., 0.9990 Silver 0.9988 oz. ASW, 37 mm. **Subject:** Christian Feudal Art - "Wooden Church from Ieud-Deal" **Obv:** Fragment of mural in Ieud Church depicting Isaac, Abraham and Jacob at top, inscription, value and date in lower half **Obv. Inscription:** ROMANIA **Rev:** Front view of Ieud Church against frosted background **Rev. Inscription:** BISERICA DE LEMN IEUD DEAL **Edge:** Plain

Date	Mintage	F	VF	XF	Unc	BU
2006 Proof	500	Value: 170				

KM# 213   5 LEI
31.1030 g., 0.9990 Silver 0.9989 oz. ASW, 37 mm. **Subject:** 150th Anniversary - Establishment of the European Commission of the Danube **Edge:** Plain

Date	Mintage	F	VF	XF	Unc	BU
2006 Proof	500	Value: 170				

KM# 216   5 LEI
31.1030 g., 0.9990 Silver 0.9989 oz. ASW, 37 mm. **Subject:** Church from Densus **Obv:** 14th century icon on which "The Holy Trinity of Densus" was painted at left, arms with value below at center, inscription at right **Obv. Inscription:** ROMANIA **Rev:** Image of Densus Church as from the altar apse, central pillar at right **Rev. Inscription:** BISERICA DE LA DENSUS **Edge:** Plain

Date	Mintage	F	VF	XF	Unc	BU
2006 Proof	500	Value: 170				

KM# 236   5 LEI
31.1050 g., 0.9990 Silver 0.9990 oz. ASW, 37 mm. **Subject:** Wooden Church of Ievd Deal **Obv:** Fragment of mural painting **Rev:** Front view of church

Date	Mintage	F	VF	XF	Unc	BU
2006 Proof	500	Value: 160				

KM# 217   5 LEI
31.1030 g., 0.9990 Silver 0.9989 oz. ASW, 37 mm. **Subject:** Sibiu - European Capital of Culture **Obv:** 2 city towers in Sibiu at left, fortress wall connecting them, Potter's Tower in background, coat of arms at right **Obv. Inscription:** ROMANIA **Rev:** City of Sibiu's logo at bottom, 2 line inscription at left, 3 line inscription at right, 4 famous edifices at center **Rev. Inscription:** SIBIU / 2007 and CAPITALA / CULTURALA / EUROPEANA **Edge:** Plain

Date	Mintage	F	VF	XF	Unc	BU
2007 Proof	500	Value: 400				

KM# 221   5 LEI
15.5500 g., 0.9990 Silver 0.4994 oz. ASW, 30 mm. **Subject:** Centennial - Birth of Mircea Eliade **Obv:** Shield and value **Rev:** Portrait facing **Edge:** Reeded

Date	Mintage	F	VF	XF	Unc	BU
2007 Proof	250	Value: 300				

KM# 224   5 LEI
15.5500 g., 0.9990 Silver 0.4994 oz. ASW, 30 mm. **Subject:** Dimitrie Cantemir, (Prince of Moldavia 1710-1711), Scientist **Edge:** Reeded

Date	Mintage	F	VF	XF	Unc	BU
2007 Proof	250	Value: 300				

KM# 227   5 LEI
15.5000 g., 0.9990 Silver 0.4978 oz. ASW, 30 mm. **Subject:** Stephan the Great **Edge:** Reeded

Date	Mintage	F	VF	XF	Unc	BU
2007 Proof	250	Value: 300				

KM# 200   5 LEI
15.5500 g., 0.9990 Silver 0.4994 oz. ASW, 30 mm. **Subject:**
130th Anniversary of Proclamation of Independence **Obv:** Shield
and "The Smardan Assault" painting by Nicolae Grigoresuv **Rev:**
Meeting of the Parliament

Date	Mintage	F	VF	XF	Unc	BU
2007 Proof	130	Value: 500				

KM# 242   5 LEI
15.5500 g., 0.9990 Silver 0.4994 oz. ASW, 30 mm. **Subject:**
Ovidivs Naso **Rev:** Half-length figure

Date	Mintage	F	VF	XF	Unc	BU
2008 Proof	500	Value: 170				

KM# 207   10 LEI
1.2240 g., 0.9990 Gold 0.0393 oz. AGW, 13.92 mm. **Subject:**
History of Gold - The Persinari Hoard **Edge:** Reeded

Date	Mintage	F	VF	XF	Unc	BU
2005 Proof	1,000	Value: 200				

KM# 203   10 LEI
1.2240 g., 0.9990 Gold 0.0393 oz. AGW, 13.92 mm. **Subject:**
Histoy of Gold - The Cuculeni Báiceni Hoard **Obv:** Romania's
Coat of Arms with denomination **Rev:** Cheekpiece of the gold
helmet in the Cucuteni-Baiceni hoard **Edge:** Reeded

Date	Mintage	F	VF	XF	Unc	BU
2006 Proof	500	Value: 250				

KM# 229   10 LEI
31.1030 g., 0.9990 Silver 0.9989 oz. ASW, 37 mm. **Subject:**
50th Anniversary - Treaty of Rome **Edge:** Reeded

Date	Mintage	F	VF	XF	Unc	BU
2007 Proof	500	Value: 400				

KM# 233   10 LEI
31.1030 g., 0.9990 Silver 0.9989 oz. ASW, 37 mm. **Subject:**
Snagov Monastery **Obv:** Shield and saints **Rev:** Monastery
Building

Date	Mintage	F	VF	XF	Unc	BU
2007 Proof	500	Value: 160				

KM# 234   10 LEI
31.1030 g., 0.9990 Silver 0.9989 oz. ASW, 37 mm. **Subject:**
Romanian Oil Industry, 150th Anniversary **Obv:** Shield,
Mehedinteanu Refinery **Rev:** Drilling well and pump jack

Date	Mintage	F	VF	XF	Unc	BU
2007 Proof	500	Value: 140				

KM# 240   10 LEI
31.1050 g., 0.9990 Silver 0.9990 oz. ASW, 37 mm. **Subject:**
Petroleum Industry, 150th Anniversary **Rev:** Oil derrick and pump

Date	Mintage	F	VF	XF	Unc	BU
2007 Proof	500	Value: 150				

KM# 241   10 LEI
31.1050 g., 0.9990 Silver 0.9990 oz. ASW, 37 mm. **Subject:**
Snagov Monastery **Rev:** Building and bust

Date	Mintage	F	VF	XF	Unc	BU
2007 Proof	500	Value: 170				

KM# 230   10 LEI
31.1000 g., 0.9990 Silver 0.9988 oz. ASW, 37 mm. **Subject:**
150th Anniversary of First Postage Stamp **Rev:** "Cap de Bour"
(bull's head) stamp **Edge:** Reeded

Date	Mintage	F	VF	XF	Unc	BU
2008 Proof	1,000	Value: 175				

KM# 231   10 LEI
31.1030 g., 0.9990 Silver 0.9989 oz. ASW, 37 mm. **Subject:**
80th Anniversary Romanian Broadcasting Co. **Obv:** Radio
Romania, years 1928 and 2008, coat of arms **Rev:** Radio set
from 30's, logo of Radio Romania, headphones **Edge:** Reeded

Date	Mintage	F	VF	XF	Unc	BU
2008 Proof	500	Value: 300				

KM# 232   10 LEI
1.2440 g., 0.9990 Gold 0.0400 oz. AGW, 13.92 mm. **Subject:**
Hoard of Hinova **Obv:** Romanian Coat of Arms, necklace parts **Rev:**
Necklace parts, four bell shaped necklace parts, muff **Edge:** Reeded

Date	Mintage	F	VF	XF	Unc	BU
2008 Proof	500	Value: 135				

KM# 243   10 LEI
31.1050 g., 0.9990 Silver 0.9990 oz. ASW, 37 mm. **Subject:**
Romanian Broadcast Company, 80th anniversary **Rev:** Radio
and headset

Date	Mintage	F	VF	XF	Unc	BU
2008 Proof	500	Value: 250				

KM# 244   10 LEI
31.1050 g., 0.9990 Silver 0.9990 oz. ASW, 37 mm. **Subject:**
Costin Kiritescu **Rev:** Bust facing

Date	Mintage	F	VF	XF	Unc	BU
2008 Proof	500	Value: 170				

KM# 245   10 LEI
31.1050 g., 0.9990 Silver 0.9990 oz. ASW, 37 mm. **Subject:**
First printed book in Walachia, 500th Anniversary **Rev:** Building
and printers at press

Date	Mintage	F	VF	XF	Unc	BU
2008 Proof	500	Value: 170				

KM# 246   10 LEI
31.1050 g., 0.9990 Silver 0.9990 oz. ASW, 37 mm. **Subject:**
Simon Barnutiu **Rev:** Bust facing

Date	Mintage	F	VF	XF	Unc	BU
2008 Proof	500	Value: 150				

KM# 247   10 LEI
31.1050 g., 0.9990 Silver 0.9990 oz. ASW, 37 mm. **Subject:**
Cozia Monastery **Rev:** Church building

Date	Mintage	F	VF	XF	Unc	BU
2008 Proof	500	Value: 165				

KM# 248   10 LEI
31.1050 g., 0.9990 Silver 0.9990 oz. ASW, 37 mm. **Subject:**
Sambata des Sus Monastery **Rev:** Church building

Date	Mintage	F	VF	XF	Unc	BU
2008 Proof	500	Value: 165				

KM# 249   10 LEI
31.1050 g., 0.9990 Silver 0.9990 oz. ASW, 37 mm. **Subject:**
Voronet Monastery **Rev:** Church building

Date	Mintage	F	VF	XF	Unc	BU
2008 Proof	500	Value: 165				

KM# 250   10 LEI
31.1050 g., 0.9990 Silver 0.9990 oz. ASW, 37 mm. **Subject:**
European Monitary Union, 10th Anniversary **Rev:** Stick figure
and Euro symbol

Date	Mintage	F	VF	XF	Unc	BU
2009 Proof	1,000	Value: 150				

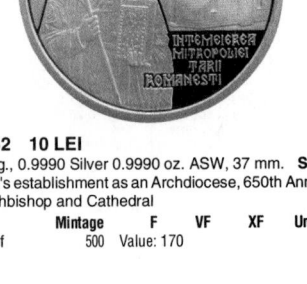

KM# 251   10 LEI
31.1050 g., 0.9990 Silver 0.9990 oz. ASW, 37 mm. **Subject:**
Alexander Macedonski **Rev:** Bust left

Date	Mintage	F	VF	XF	Unc	BU
2009 Proof	500	Value: 150				

KM# 252   10 LEI
31.1050 g., 0.9990 Silver 0.9990 oz. ASW, 37 mm. **Subject:**
Walachia's establishment as an Archdiocese, 650th Anniversary
Rev: Archbishop and Cathedral

Date	Mintage	F	VF	XF	Unc	BU
2009 Proof	500	Value: 170				

KM# 253   10 LEI
31.1050 g., 0.9990 Silver 0.9990 oz. ASW, 37 mm. **Subject:**
Statistical Office, 150th Anniversary **Rev:** Two busts and
document

Date	Mintage	F	VF	XF	Unc	BU
2009 Proof	500	Value: 150				

KM# 254   10 LEI
31.1050 g., 0.9990 Silver 0.9990 oz. ASW, 37 mm. **Subject:**
Bucharest - Giurgiv Railway, 150th Anniversary **Rev:** Steam train

Date	Mintage	F	VF	XF	Unc	BU
2009 Proof	500	Value: 170				

KM# 255   10 LEI
31.1050 g., 0.9990 Silver 0.9990 oz. ASW, 37 mm. **Subject:**
Bucharest, 550th Anniversary **Rev:** Architectural elements

Date	Mintage	F	VF	XF	Unc	BU
2009 Proof	500	Value: 160				

KM# 256   10 LEI
31.1050 g., 0.9990 Silver 0.9990 oz. ASW, 37 mm. **Subject:**
Constanta Harbor, 100th Anniversary **Rev:** Ship and buildings

Date	Mintage	F	VF	XF	Unc	BU
2009 Proof	500	Value: 160				

KM# 257   10 LEI
31.1050 g., 0.9990 Silver 0.9990 oz. ASW, 37 mm. **Subject:**
Tropaeum Traiani, 1900th Anniversary **Rev:** Ancient Roman
building, Emperor Trajan

Date	Mintage	F	VF	XF	Unc	BU
2009 Proof	500	Value: 150				

KM# 211   50 LEI
6.4500 g., 0.9000 Gold 0.1866 oz. AGW, 21 mm. **Subject:** 140th
Anniversary Founding Romanian Academy **Edge:** Plain

Date	Mintage	F	VF	XF	Unc	BU
2006 Proof	35	Value: 3,000				

KM# 198   100 LEI
1.2440 g., 0.9990 Gold 0.0400 oz. AGW, 13.93 mm. **Obv:**
National arms in wreath **Obv. Legend:** ROMANIA **Rev:** Medieval
helmet - "COIF POIANA COTOFENESTI" **Edge:** Reeded

Date	Mintage	F	VF	XF	Unc	BU
2003 Proof	—	Value: 100				

KM# 222   100 LEI
6.4500 g., 0.9000 Gold 0.1866 oz. AGW, 21 mm. **Subject:**
Centennial - Birth of Mircea Eliade **Obv:** Shield and value **Rev:**
Portrait facing **Edge:** Reeded

Date	Mintage	F	VF	XF	Unc	BU
2007 Proof	250	Value: 900				

KM# 225   100 LEI
6.4500 g., 0.9000 Gold 0.1866 oz. AGW, 21 mm. **Subject:**
Dimitrie Cantemir, (Prince of Moldavia 1710-1711), Scientist
Edge: Reeded

Date	Mintage	F	VF	XF	Unc	BU
2007 Proof	250	Value: 900				

KM# 228   100 LEI
6.4520 g., 0.9000 Gold 0.1867 oz. AGW, 21 mm. **Subject:** 550th
Anniversary - Ascension Prince Stephen the Great into Moldavia
Edge: Reeded

Date	Mintage	F	VF	XF	Unc	BU
2007 Proof	250	Value: 900				

KM# 201   100 LEI
6.4520 g., 0.9000 Gold 0.1867 oz. AGW, 21 mm. **Subject:** 130th
Anniversary of Proclamation of Independence **Obv:** Shield and
"The Smardan Assault" painting by Nicole Grigorescu **Rev:**
Meeting of the Parliament

Date	Mintage	F	VF	XF	Unc	BU
2007 Proof	130	Value: 1,500				

KM# 235   100 LEI
6.4520 g., 0.9990 Gold 0.2072 oz. AGW, 21 mm. **Subject:** Battles
of Marasti, Marasesti, Oituz 90th Anniversary **Obv:** Mausoleum of
Marasesti **Rev:** Group of soldiers at Battle of Marasti

Date	Mintage	F	VF	XF	Unc	BU
2007 Proof	250	Value: 550				

KM# 206   500 LEI
31.1000 g., 0.9990 Gold 0.9988 oz. AGW, 35 mm. **Subject:**
50th Anniversary - Death of George Enescu **Edge:** Plain

Date	Mintage	F	VF	XF	Unc	BU
2005 Proof	250	Value: 2,250				

KM# 214 500 LEI
31.1030 g., 0.9990 Gold 0.9989 oz. AGW, 35 mm. **Subject:** 350th Anniversary - Establishment of the Patriarchal Cathedral **Edge:** Plain

Date	Mintage	F	VF	XF	Unc	BU
2006 Proof	250	Value: 3,000				

KM# 204 500 LEI
31.1035 g., 0.9990 Gold 0.9990 oz. AGW, 35 mm. **Subject:** Romania's Accession to European Union, January 1 2007 **Obv:** Romania's Coat of Arms surrounded by 12 stars of European Union **Rev:** Map of the European Union including Romania **Edge:** Plain

Date	Mintage	F	VF	XF	Unc	BU
2007 Proof	250	Value: 3,000				

KM# 205 500 LEI
31.1035 g., 0.9990 Gold 0.9990 oz. AGW, 35 mm. **Subject:** Nicolae Balcescu (1819-1852) **Obv:** Romania's Coat of Arms and **Obv. Inscription:** Justice and Brotherhood **Rev:** Portrait of Nicolae Balcescu **Edge:** Plain

Date	Mintage	F	VF	XF	Unc	BU
2007 Proof	250	Value: 2,250				

MINT SETS

KM#	Date	Mintage	Identification	Issue Price	Mkt Val
MS6	2005 (4)	—	KM#189-192	—	50.00
MS4	2006 (4)	—	KM189-192, plus medal	—	75.00
MS5	2007 (4)	1,000	KM189-192, plus medal	—	60.00

PROOF SETS

KM#	Date	Mintage	Identification	Issue Price	Mkt Val
PS4	2001 (3)	500	KM#159, 160, 161	80.00	525
PS5	2002 (9)	1,500	KM#109-111, 114-116, 145, 153, 158	20.00	75.00
PS6	2003 (9)	2,000	KM#109-111, 114-116, 145, 153, 158	20.00	75.00
PS7	2003 (3)	500	KM#186, 187, 188	—	325
PSA8	2004 (5)	—	KM#111, 115, 145, 153, 158	—	50.00
PS8	2004 (2)	500	KM#163, 164	—	325
PS9	2005 (10)	—	KM#111, 115, 145, 153, 158, 189-192 plus medal	—	80.00
PS10	2006 (10)	—	KM#111, 115, 145, 153, 158, 189-192	—	80.00
PS11	2006 (3)	—	KM#209, 210, 211	—	4,050
PS12	2007 (3)	—	KM#220, 221, 222	—	1,350
PS13	2007 (3)	—	KM#223, 224, 225	—	1,350
PS14	2007 (3)	—	KM#226, 227, 228	—	1,350
PS15	2007 (5)	—	KM#189-192 plus Silver 75th Anniversary of Rodna Mountains National Park medal	—	50.00
PS17	2008 (4)	—	KM#189-192 plus silver medal Antipa Museum	—	50.00

RUSSIA

The Russia Federation, formerly the central power of the Union of Soviet Socialist Republics and now of the Commonwealth of Independent States occupies the northern part of Asia and the eastern part of Europe, has an area of 17,075,400 sq. km. Capital: Moscow. Exports include iron and steel, crude oil, timber, and nonferrous metals.

In the fall of 1991, events moved swiftly in the Soviet Union. Estonia, Latvia and Lithuania won their independence and were recognized by Moscow, Sept. 6. The Commonwealth of Independent States was formed Dec. 8, 1991 in Mensk by Belarus, Russia and Ukraine. It was expanded at a summit Dec. 21, 1991 to include 11 of the 12 remaining republics (excluding Georgia) of the old U.S.S.R.

RUSSIAN FEDERATION
Issued by the БАНК РОССИИ
(Bank of Russia)

REFORM COINAGE
January 1, 1998

1,000 Old Roubles = 1 New Rouble

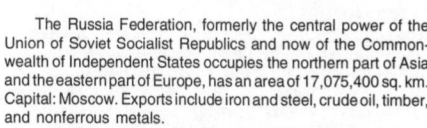

Y# 600 KOPEK
1.5000 g., Copper-Nickel Plated Steel, 15.5 mm. **Obv:** St. George **Obv. Legend:** БАНК РОССИИ **Rev:** Value above vine sprig **Edge:** Plain

Date	Mintage	F	VF	XF	Unc	BU
2001M	—	—	—	—	0.30	0.40
2001СП	—	—	—	—	0.30	0.40
2002M	—	—	—	—	0.30	0.40
2002СП	—	—	—	—	0.30	0.40
2003M	—	—	—	—	0.30	0.40
2003СП	—	—	—	—	0.30	0.40
2004M	—	—	—	—	0.30	0.40
2004СП	—	—	—	—	0.30	0.40
2005M	—	—	—	—	0.30	0.40
2005СП	—	—	—	—	0.30	0.40
2006M	—	—	—	—	0.30	0.40
2006СП	—	—	—	—	0.30	0.40
2007M	—	—	—	—	0.30	0.40
2007СП	—	—	—	—	0.30	0.40
2008M	—	—	—	—	0.30	0.40

Date	Mintage	F	VF	XF	Unc	BU
2008СП	—	—	—	—	0.30	0.40
2009M	—	—	—	—	1.00	2.00
2009СП	—	—	—	—	1.00	2.00

Y# 601 5 KOPEKS
2.6000 g., Copper-Nickel Clad Steel, 18.5 mm. **Obv:** St. George **Obv. Legend:** БАНК РОССИИ **Rev:** Value above vine sprig **Edge:** Plain

Date	Mintage	F	VF	XF	Unc	BU
2001M	—	—	—	—	0.40	0.60
2001СП	—	—	—	—	0.40	0.60
2002	—	—	80.00	95.00	120	
2002M	—	—	—	—	0.40	0.60
2002СП	—	—	—	—	0.40	0.60
2003	—	—	10.00	15.00	25.00	
2003M	—	—	—	—	0.35	0.50
2003СП	—	—	—	—	0.35	0.50
2004M	—	—	—	—	0.35	0.50
2004СП	—	—	—	—	0.35	0.50
2005M	—	—	—	—	0.35	0.50
2005СП	—	—	—	—	0.35	0.50
2006M	—	—	—	—	0.35	0.50
2006СП	—	—	—	—	0.35	0.50
2007M	—	—	—	—	0.35	0.50
2007СП	—	—	—	—	0.35	0.50
2008M	—	—	—	—	0.35	0.50
2008СП	—	—	—	—	0.35	0.50
2009M	—	—	—	—	1.00	2.00
2009СП	—	—	—	—	1.00	2.00

Y# 601a 5 KOPEKS
Brass Plated Steel **Obv:** St. George on horseback slaying dragon right **Obv. Legend:** БАНК РОССИИ **Rev:** Value above vine sprig **Edge:** Plain

Date	Mintage	F	VF	XF	Unc	BU
2006СП	—	—	—	—	300	—

Y# 602 10 KOPEKS
1.9500 g., Brass, 17.5 mm. **Obv:** St. George horseback right slaying dragon **Rev:** Value above vine sprig **Edge:** Reeded

Date	Mintage	F	VF	XF	Unc	BU
2001M	—	—	—	—	0.50	0.80
2001СП	—	—	—	—	0.50	0.80
2002M	—	—	—	—	0.50	0.80
2002СП	—	—	—	—	0.50	0.80
2003M	—	—	—	—	0.50	0.80
2003СП	—	—	—	—	0.50	0.80
2004M	—	—	—	—	0.50	0.80
2004СП	—	—	—	—	0.50	0.80
2005M	—	—	—	—	0.50	0.80
2005СП	—	—	—	—	0.50	0.80
2006M	—	—	—	—	0.50	0.80
2006СП	—	—	—	—	0.50	0.80

Y# 602a 10 KOPEKS
1.8500 g., Brass Clad Steel, 17.5 mm. **Obv:** St. George on horseback slaying dragon to right **Obv. Legend:** БАНК РОССИИ **Rev:** Denomination above vine sprig **Edge:** Plain

Date	Mintage	F	VF	XF	Unc	BU
2006M	—	—	—	—	0.50	0.80
2006СП	—	—	—	—	0.50	0.80
2007M	—	—	—	—	0.50	0.80
2007СП	—	—	—	—	0.50	0.80
2008M	—	—	—	—	0.50	0.80
2008СП	—	—	—	—	0.50	0.80
2009M	—	—	—	—	0.50	0.80
2009СП	—	—	—	—	0.50	0.80
2010M	—	—	—	—	0.50	0.80
2010СП	—	—	—	—	0.50	0.80
2011M	—	—	—	—	0.50	0.80

Date	Mintage	F	VF	XF	Unc	BU
2011СП	—	—	—	—	0.50	0.80
2012М	—	—	—	—	0.50	0.80

Y# 603   50 KOPEKS

2.9000 g., Brass, 19.5 mm. **Obv:** St. George on horseback slaying dragon right **Rev:** Value above vine sprig **Edge:** Reeded

Date	Mintage	F	VF	XF	Unc	BU
2001M Rare	—	—	—	5,000		
2002M	—	—	—	—	1.50	3.00
2002СП	—	—	—	—	1.50	3.00
2003M	—	—	—	—	0.80	1.00
2003СП	—	—	—	—	0.80	1.00
2004M	—	—	—	—	0.80	1.00
2004СП	—	—	—	—	0.80	1.00
2005M	—	—	—	—	0.80	1.00
2005СП	—	—	—	—	0.80	1.00
2006M	—	—	—	—	0.80	1.00
2006СП	—	—	—	—	0.80	1.00

Y# 603a   50 KOPEKS

2.7500 g., Brass Clad Steel, 19.5 mm. **Obv:** St. George on horseback slaying dragon right **Rev:** Value above vine sprig **Edge:** Plain

Date	Mintage	F	VF	XF	Unc	BU
2006M	—	—	—	—	0.80	1.00
2006СП	—	—	—	—	0.80	1.00
2007M	—	—	—	—	0.80	1.00
2007СП	—	—	—	—	0.80	1.00
2008M	—	—	—	—	0.80	1.00
2008СП	—	—	—	—	0.80	1.00
2009M	—	—	—	—	0.80	1.00
2009СП	—	—	—	—	0.80	1.00
2010M	—	—	—	—	0.80	1.00
2010СП	—	—	—	—	0.80	1.00
2011M	—	—	—	—	0.80	1.00
2011СП	—	—	—	—	0.80	1.00
2012M	—	—	—	—	0.80	1.00

Y# 745   ROUBLE

17.4000 g., 0.9000 Silver 0.5035 oz. ASW, 32.8 mm. **Obv:** Double-headed eagle within beaded circle **Rev:** Altai argalia sheep **Edge:** Reeded

Date	Mintage	F	VF	XF	Unc	BU
2001(sp) Proof	7,500		Value: 45.00			

Y# 746   ROUBLE

17.4000 g., 0.9000 Silver 0.5035 oz. ASW, 32.8 mm. **Obv:** Double-headed eagle within beaded circle **Rev:** Beavers **Edge:** Reeded

Date	Mintage	F	VF	XF	Unc	BU
2001(sp) Proof	7,500		Value: 45.00			

Y# 604   ROUBLE

3.2500 g., Copper-Nickel-Zinc, 20.5 mm. **Obv:** Double-headed eagle **Rev:** Value **Edge:** Reeded

Date	Mintage	F	VF	XF	Unc	BU
2001M Rare	—	—	—	—		

Y# 731   ROUBLE

3.2100 g., Copper-Nickel, 20.7 mm. **Obv:** Double-headed eagle **Rev:** Stylized design above hologram **Edge:** Reeded

Date	Mintage	F	VF	XF	Unc	BU
2001СПМД	100,000,000	—	—	—	1.50	2.00

Y# 732   ROUBLE

17.4300 g., 0.9000 Silver 0.5043 oz. ASW, 32.8 mm. **Subject:** Sturgeon **Obv:** Double-headed eagle within beaded circle **Rev:** Sakhalin sturgeon and other fish **Edge:** Reeded

Date	Mintage	F	VF	XF	Unc	BU
2001 Proof	7,500		Value: 45.00			

Y# 758   ROUBLE

17.4400 g., 0.9000 Silver 0.5046 oz. ASW, 33 mm. **Obv:** Double-headed eagle within beaded circle **Rev:** Chinese Goral **Edge:** Reeded

Date	Mintage	F	VF	XF	Unc	BU
2002(sp) Proof	10,000		Value: 30.00			

Y# 759   ROUBLE

17.4400 g., 0.9000 Silver 0.5046 oz. ASW, 33 mm. **Obv:** Double-headed eagle within beaded circle **Rev:** Sei Whale **Edge:** Reeded

Date	Mintage	F	VF	XF	Unc	BU
2002(sp) Proof	10,000		Value: 30.00			

Y# 760   ROUBLE

17.4400 g., 0.9000 Silver 0.5046 oz. ASW, 33 mm. **Subject:** Golden Eagle **Obv:** Double-headed eagle within beaded circle **Rev:** Golden Eagle with nestling **Edge:** Reeded

Date	Mintage	F	VF	XF	Unc	BU
2002(sp) Proof	10,000		Value: 30.00			

Y# 833   ROUBLE

3.2500 g., Copper-Nickel-Zinc, 20.5 mm. **Obv:** Two headed eagle, curved bank name and date below **Rev:** Value and flower **Edge:** Reeded

Date	Mintage	F	VF	XF	Unc	BU
2002(m) Mint sets only	15,000	—	—	—	—	—
2002(sp) Mint sets only	15,000	—	—	—	—	—
2003(sp)	15,000	—	—	300	400	500
2005(m)	—	—	—	—	2.00	3.00
2005(sp)	—	—	—	—	2.00	3.00
2006(m)	—	—	—	—	2.00	3.00
2006(sp)	—	—	—	—	2.00	3.00
2007(m)	—	—	—	—	2.00	3.00
2007(sp)	—	—	—	—	2.00	3.00
2008(m)	—	—	—	—	2.00	3.00
2008(sp)	—	—	—	—	2.00	3.00
2009(m)	—	—	—	—	2.00	3.00
2009(sp)	—	—	—	—	2.00	3.00

Y# A834   ROUBLE

7.7800 g., 0.9250 Silver 0.2314 oz. ASW, 0.25 mm. **Subject:** St. Petersburg **Obv:** Double-headed eagle within beaded circle **Rev:** Angel on steeple of Cathedral in fortress

Date	Mintage	F	VF	XF	Unc	BU
2002 Proof	5,000		Value: 25.00			

Y# 770   ROUBLE

8.5300 g., 0.9250 Silver 0.2537 oz. ASW, 25 mm. **Subject:** Ministry of Education **Obv:** Double-headed eagle within beaded circle **Rev:** Seedling within open book **Edge:** Reeded

Date	Mintage	F	VF	XF	Unc	BU
2002(m) Proof	3,000		Value: 50.00			

Y# 771   ROUBLE

8.5300 g., 0.9250 Silver 0.2537 oz. ASW, 25 mm. **Subject:** Ministry of Finances **Obv:** Double-headed eagle within beaded circle **Rev:** Caduceus in monogram **Edge:** Reeded

Date	Mintage	F	VF	XF	Unc	BU
2002(sp) Proof	3,000		Value: 50.00			

Y# 772 ROUBLE
8.5300 g., 0.9250 Silver 0.2537 oz. ASW, 25 mm. **Subject:** Ministry of Economic Development **Obv:** Double-headed eagle within beaded circle **Rev:** Crowned double-headed eagle with cornucopia and caduceus **Edge:** Reeded

Date	Mintage	F	VF	XF	Unc	BU
2002(sp) Proof	3,000	Value: 50.00				

Y# 773 ROUBLE
8.5300 g., 0.9250 Silver 0.2537 oz. ASW, 25 mm. **Subject:** Ministry of Foreign Affairs **Obv:** Double-headed eagle within beaded circle **Rev:** Crowned two-headed eagle above crossed sprigs **Edge:** Reeded

Date	Mintage	F	VF	XF	Unc	BU
2002(sp) Proof	3,000	Value: 50.00				

Y# 774 ROUBLE
8.5300 g., 0.9250 Silver 0.2537 oz. ASW, 25 mm. **Subject:** Ministry of Internal Affairs **Obv:** Double-headed eagle within beaded circle **Rev:** Crowned two-headed eagle with round breast **Edge:** Reeded

Date	Mintage	F	VF	XF	Unc	BU
2002(sp) Proof	3,000	Value: 50.00				

Y# 775 ROUBLE
8.5300 g., 0.9250 Silver 0.2537 oz. ASW, 25 mm. **Subject:** Ministry of Justice **Obv:** Double-headed eagle within beaded circle **Rev:** Crowned double-headed eagle with column on breast shield **Edge:** Reeded

Date	Mintage	F	VF	XF	Unc	BU
2002(sp) Proof	3,000	Value: 50.00				

Y# 776 ROUBLE
8.5300 g., 0.9250 Silver 0.2537 oz. ASW, 25 mm. **Subject:** Russian Armed Forces **Obv:** Double-headed eagle within beaded circle **Rev:** Double-headed eagle with crowned top pointed breast shield **Edge:** Reeded

Date	Mintage	F	VF	XF	Unc	BU
2002(m) Proof	3,000	Value: 50.00				

Y# 835 ROUBLE
7.7800 g., 0.9250 Silver 0.2314 oz. ASW, 25 mm. **Subject:** St. Petersburg **Obv:** Double-headed eagle within beaded circle **Rev:** Sphinx

Date	Mintage	F	VF	XF	Unc	BU
2002 Proof	5,000	Value: 25.00				

Y# 836 ROUBLE
7.7800 g., 0.9250 Silver 0.2314 oz. ASW, 25 mm. **Subject:** St. Petersburg **Obv:** Double-headed eagle within beaded circle **Rev:** Small ship

Date	Mintage	F	VF	XF	Unc	BU
2002 Proof	5,000	Value: 25.00				

Y# 837 ROUBLE
7.7800 g., 0.9250 Silver 0.2314 oz. ASW, 25 mm. **Subject:** St. Petersburg **Obv:** Double-headed eagle within beaded circle **Rev:** Lion

Date	Mintage	F	VF	XF	Unc	BU
2002 Proof	5,000	Value: 25.00				

Y# 838 ROUBLE
7.7800 g., 0.9250 Silver 0.2314 oz. ASW, 25 mm. **Subject:** St. Petersburg **Obv:** Double-headed eagle within beaded circle **Rev:** Horse sculpture

Date	Mintage	F	VF	XF	Unc	BU
2002 Proof	5,000	Value: 25.00				

Y# 839 ROUBLE
7.7800 g., 0.9250 Silver 0.2314 oz. ASW, 25 mm. **Subject:** St. Petersburg **Obv:** Double-headed eagle within beaded circle **Rev:** Griffin

Date	Mintage	F	VF	XF	Unc	BU
2002 Proof	5,000	Value: 25.00				

Y# 814 ROUBLE
17.4000 g., 0.9000 Silver 0.5035 oz. ASW, 32.8 mm. **Obv:** Double-headed eagle within beaded circle **Rev:** Arctic foxes **Edge:** Reeded

Date	Mintage	F	VF	XF	Unc	BU
2003(sp) Proof	10,000	Value: 30.00				

Y# 816 ROUBLE
17.4000 g., 0.9000 Silver 0.5035 oz. ASW, 32.8 mm. **Obv:** Double-headed eagle within beaded circle **Rev:** Pygmy Cormorant drying its wings **Edge:** Reeded

Date	Mintage	F	VF	XF	Unc	BU
2003(sp) Proof	10,000	Value: 30.00				

Y# 815 ROUBLE
17.4000 g., 0.9000 Silver 0.5035 oz. ASW, 32.8 mm. **Obv:** Double-headed eagle within beaded circle **Rev:** Chinese Softshell turtle **Edge:** Reeded

Date	Mintage	F	VF	XF	Unc	BU
2003(sp) Proof	10,000	Value: 35.00				

Y# 828 ROUBLE
17.2800 g., 0.9000 Silver 0.5000 oz. ASW, 33 mm. **Obv:** Two headed eagle within beaded circle **Rev:** Amur Forest Cat on branch **Edge:** Reeded

Date	Mintage	F	VF	XF	Unc	BU
2004(sp) Proof	10,000	Value: 30.00				

Y# 1029 ROUBLE
16.8000 g., 0.9250 Silver 0.4996 oz. ASW, 32.8 mm. **Subject:** The Great Bustard

Date	Mintage	F	VF	XF	Unc	BU
2004 Proof	—	Value: 30.00				

Y# 881 ROUBLE
17.2800 g., 0.5000 Silver 0.2778 oz. ASW, 32.8 mm. **Obv:** Double-headed eagle within beaded circle **Rev:** Rush Toad **Edge:** Reeded

Date	Mintage	F	VF	XF	Unc	BU
2004 Proof	—	Value: 45.00				

Y# 882 ROUBLE
16.8100 g., 0.4999 Silver 0.2702 oz. ASW, 32.8 mm. **Obv:** Double-headed eagle within beaded circle **Rev:** Two Marbled Murrelet sea birds **Edge:** Reeded

Date	Mintage	F	VF	XF	Unc	BU
2005 Proof	—	Value: 30.00				

Y# 883 ROUBLE
16.8100 g., 0.4999 Silver 0.2702 oz. ASW, 32.8 mm. **Obv:** Double-headed eagle within beaded circle **Rev:** Asiatic Wild Dog **Edge:** Reeded

Date	Mintage	F	VF	XF	Unc	BU
2005 Proof	—	Value: 45.00				

Y# 884 ROUBLE
16.8100 g., 0.4999 Silver 0.2702 oz. ASW, 32.8 mm. **Obv:** Double-headed eagle within beaded circle **Rev:** Volkhov Whitefish **Edge:** Reeded

Date	Mintage	F	VF	XF	Unc	BU
2005 Proof	—	Value: 30.00				

Y# 916 ROUBLE
8.5300 g., 0.9250 Silver 0.2537 oz. ASW, 25 mm. **Obv:** Double-headed eagle **Rev:** Russian Navy Emblem **Edge:** Reeded

Date	Mintage	F	VF	XF	Unc	BU
2005 Proof	10,000	Value: 25.00				

Y# 917   ROUBLE
8.5300 g., 0.9250 Silver 0.2537 oz. ASW, 25 mm. **Obv:** Double-headed eagle **Rev:** Russian Marine circa 1705 **Edge:** Reeded

Date	Mintage	F	VF	XF	Unc	BU
2005 Proof	10,000	Value: 25.00				

Y# 918   ROUBLE
8.5300 g., 0.9250 Silver 0.2537 oz. ASW, 25 mm. **Obv:** Double-headed eagle **Rev:** Russian Marine circa 2005 **Edge:** Reeded

Date	Mintage	F	VF	XF	Unc	BU
2005 Proof	10,000	Value: 25.00				

Y# 981   ROUBLE
15.5500 g., 0.9250 Silver 0.4624 oz. ASW, 33 mm. **Obv:** Double headed eagle **Rev:** Mongolian Gazelle **Edge:** Reeded

Date	Mintage	F	VF	XF	Unc	BU
2006 Proof	—	Value: 50.00				

Y# 1058   ROUBLE
33.9000 g., 0.9250 Silver 1.0081 oz. ASW, 39 mm. **Subject:** Swan Goose

Date	Mintage	F	VF	XF	Unc	BU
2006 Proof	—	Value: 40.00				

Y# 1059   ROUBLE
33.9000 g., 0.9250 Silver 1.0081 oz. ASW, 39 mm. **Subject:** Ussury Clawed Newt

Date	Mintage	F	VF	XF	Unc	BU
2006 Proof	—	Value: 40.00				

Y# 1069   ROUBLE
7.7800 g., 0.9250 Silver 0.2314 oz. ASW, 22.6 mm. **Subject:** Airborne Troops

Date	Mintage	F	VF	XF	Unc	BU
2006 Proof	—	Value: 25.00				

Y# 1070   ROUBLE
7.7800 g., 0.9250 Silver 0.2314 oz. ASW, 22.6 mm. **Subject:** Airborne Troops

Date	Mintage	F	VF	XF	Unc	BU
2006 Proof	—	Value: 25.00				

Y# 1071   ROUBLE
7.7800 g., 0.9250 Silver 0.2314 oz. ASW, 22.6 mm. **Subject:** Airborne Troops

Date	Mintage	F	VF	XF	Unc	BU
2006 Proof	—	Value: 25.00				

Y# 1072   ROUBLE
7.7800 g., 0.9250 Silver 0.2314 oz. ASW, 22.6 mm. **Subject:** Submarine Forces

Date	Mintage	F	VF	XF	Unc	BU
2006 Proof	—	Value: 25.00				

Y# 1073   ROUBLE
7.7800 g., 0.9250 Silver 0.2314 oz. ASW, 22.6 mm. **Subject:** Submarine Forces

Date	Mintage	F	VF	XF	Unc	BU
2006 Proof	—	Value: 25.00				

Y# 1074   ROUBLE
7.7800 g., Silver, 22.6 mm. **Subject:** Submarine Forces

Date	Mintage	F	VF	XF	Unc	BU
2006 Proof	—	Value: 25.00				

Y# 1075   ROUBLE
Silver **Subject:** Bogolyvbovo Township

Date	Mintage	F	VF	XF	Unc	BU
2006 Proof	—	Value: 25.00				

Y# 961   ROUBLE
15.5500 g., 0.9250 Silver 0.4624 oz. ASW, 33 mm. **Obv:** Double headed eagle **Rev:** Red banded snake **Edge:** Reeded

Date	Mintage	F	VF	XF	Unc	BU
2007 Proof	—	Value: 30.00				

Y# 962   ROUBLE
15.5500 g., 0.9250 Silver 0.4624 oz. ASW, 33 mm. **Obv:** Double headed eagle **Rev:** Pallid Harrier in flight

Date	Mintage	F	VF	XF	Unc	BU
2007 Proof	—	Value: 50.00				

Y# 1109   ROUBLE
33.9000 g., 0.9250 Silver 1.0081 oz. ASW, 39 mm. **Subject:** Ringed seal

Date	Mintage	F	VF	XF	Unc	BU
2007 Proof	—	Value: 40.00				

Y# 1110   ROUBLE
7.7800 g., 0.9250 Silver 0.2314 oz. ASW, 33 mm. **Subject:** Space Force

Date	Mintage	F	VF	XF	Unc	BU
2007 Proof	—	Value: 30.00				

Y# 1112   ROUBLE
33.9000 g., 0.9250 Silver 1.0081 oz. ASW, 3 mm. **Subject:** Space Force

Date	Mintage	F	VF	XF	Unc	BU
2007 Proof	—	Value: 30.00				

Y# 1111   ROUBLE
7.7800 g., 0.9250 Silver 0.2314 oz. ASW, 33 mm. **Subject:** Space Force

Date	Mintage	F	VF	XF	Unc	BU
2007 Proof	—	Value: 30.00				

Y# 1146   ROUBLE
16.8000 g., 0.9250 Silver 0.4996 oz. ASW **Subject:** Emperor Dragon Fly **Shape:** 33

Date	Mintage	F	VF	XF	Unc	BU
2008 Proof	—	Value: 30.00				

Y# 1151   ROUBLE
16.8000 g., 0.9250 Silver 0.4996 oz. ASW, 32.8 mm. **Subject:** City of Moscow

Date	Mintage	F	VF	XF	Unc	BU
2008 Proof	—	Value: 25.00				

Y# 833a   ROUBLE
3.0000 g., Nickel Plated Steel, 20.5 mm. **Obv:** Two headed eagle, curved bank name and date below

Date	Mintage	F	VF	XF	Unc	BU
2009ММД	—	—	—	—	0.75	1.50
2009СПМД	—	—	—	—	0.75	1.50
2010ММД	—	—	—	—	0.75	1.50
2010СПМД	—	—	—	—	2.00	3.00
2011ММД	—	—	—	—	0.75	1.50

Y# 1204   ROUBLE
16.8000 g., 0.9250 Silver 0.4996 oz. ASW, 33 mm. **Subject:** Air Force

Date	Mintage	F	VF	XF	Unc	BU
2009 Proof	—	Value: 30.00				

Y# 1205   ROUBLE
16.8000 g., 0.9250 Silver 0.4996 oz. ASW, 33 mm. **Subject:** Air Force

Date	Mintage	F	VF	XF	Unc	BU
2009 Proof	—	Value: 30.00				

Y# 1206   ROUBLE
16.8000 g., 0.9250 Silver 0.4996 oz. ASW, 33 mm. **Subject:** Air Force

Date	Mintage	F	VF	XF	Unc	BU
2009 Proof	—	Value: 30.00				

Y# 1244   ROUBLE
7.7800 g., 0.9250 Silver 0.2314 oz. ASW, 33 mm. **Subject:** Armored Forces **Rev:** Crowned eagle emblem

Date	Mintage	F	VF	XF	Unc	BU
2010 Proof	—	Value: 30.00				

Y# 1245   ROUBLE
7.7800 g., 0.9250 Silver 0.2314 oz. ASW, 33 mm. **Subject:** Armored Force **Rev:** Tank advancing left

Date	Mintage	F	VF	XF	Unc	BU
2010 Proof	—	Value: 30.00				

Y# 1246   ROUBLE
7.7800 g., 0.9250 Silver 0.2314 oz. ASW, 33 mm. **Subject:** Armored Force **Rev:** Tank advancing right

Date	Mintage	F	VF	XF	Unc	BU
2010 Proof	—	—	—	—	—	30.00

Y# 1253   ROUBLE
7.7800 g., 0.9250 Silver 0.2314 oz. ASW, 22.6 mm. **Subject:** Russian Aviation

Date	Mintage	F	VF	XF	Unc	BU
2010 Proof	—	Value: 30.00				

Y# 1254   ROUBLE
7.7800 g., 0.9250 Silver 0.2314 oz. ASW, 33 mm. **Subject:** Russian Aviation

Date	Mintage	F	VF	XF	Unc	BU
2010 Proof	—	Value: 30.00				

Y# 1302   ROUBLE
7.7800 g., 0.9250 Silver 0.2314 oz. ASW, 25 mm. **Subject:** Russian Aviation **Rev:** TU-144 flying right, color tracer

Date	Mintage	F	VF	XF	Unc	BU
2011 Proof	5,000	Value: 30.00				

Y# 1303 ROUBLE
7.7800 g., 0.9250 Silver 0.2314 oz. ASW, 25 mm. **Subject:** Russian Aviation **Rev:** U-2 biplane in flight left, color tracer

Date	Mintage	F	VF	XF	Unc	BU
2011 Proof	5,000	Value: 30.00				

Y# 1310 ROUBLE
7.7800 g., 0.9250 Silver 0.2314 oz. ASW, 25 mm. **Subject:** Strategis Missile Forces **Rev:** Emblem with crowned double ehaded eagle

Date	Mintage	F	VF	XF	Unc	BU
2011 Proof	5,000	Value: 30.00				

Y# 1311 ROUBLE
7.7800 g., 0.9250 Silver 0.2314 oz. ASW, 25 mm. **Subject:** Strategic Missile Forces **Rev:** Mobile missile system

Date	Mintage	F	VF	XF	Unc	BU
2011 Proof	5,000	Value: 30.00				

Y# 1312 ROUBLE
7.7800 g., 0.9250 Silver 0.2314 oz. ASW, 25 mm. **Subject:** Strategic Missile Forces **Rev:** Missile system against mountian background

Date	Mintage	F	VF	XF	Unc	BU
2011 Proof	5,000	Value: 30.00				

Y# 605 2 ROUBLES
5.1000 g., Copper-Nickel-Zinc, 23 mm. **Obv:** Double-headed eagle **Rev:** Value and vine sprig **Edge:** Segmented reeding

Date	Mintage	F	VF	XF	Unc	BU
2001M Rare						

Y# 730 2 ROUBLES
17.0000 g., 0.9250 Silver 0.5055 oz. ASW, 33 mm. **Subject:** V.I. Dal **Obv:** Double-headed eagle **Rev:** Portrait, book, signature, figures **Edge:** Reeded

Date	Mintage	F	VF	XF	Unc	BU
2001(m) Proof	7,500	Value: 40.00				

Y# 675 2 ROUBLES
5.1000 g., Copper-Nickel, 23 mm. **Subject:** Yuri Gagarin **Obv:** Value and date to left of vine sprig **Rev:** Uniformed bust facing **Edge:** Segmented reeding

Date	Mintage	F	VF	XF	Unc	BU
2001	—	—	100	125	175	—
2001ММД	10,000,000	—	—	—	2.00	4.00
2001СПМД	10,000,000	—	—	—	2.00	4.00

Y# 1002 2 ROUBLES
16.8100 g., 0.9250 Silver 0.4999 oz. ASW, 33 mm. **Subject:** V. I. Dal. 200th Anniversary of birth

Date	Mintage	F	VF	XF	Unc	BU
2001 Proof	—	Value: 30.00				

Y# 742 2 ROUBLES
17.0000 g., 0.9250 Silver 0.5055 oz. ASW, 33 mm. **Subject:** Zodiac Signs **Obv:** Double-headed eagle within beaded circle **Rev:** Leo **Edge:** Reeded

Date	Mintage	F	VF	XF	Unc	BU
2002(m) Proof	20,000	Value: 35.00				

Y# 834 2 ROUBLES
5.1000 g., Copper-Nickel-Zinc, 23 mm. **Obv:** Two headed eagle above curved inscription **Rev:** Value and flower **Edge:** Segmented reeding

Date	Mintage	F	VF	XF	Unc	BU
2002ММД Mint sets only	15,000	—	—	—	—	—
2002СПМД Mint sets only	15,000	—	—	—	—	—
2003ММД	15,000	—	—	300	400	500
2006ММД	—	—	—	—	4.00	5.00
2006СПМД	—	—	—	—	4.00	5.00
2007ММД	—	—	—	—	4.00	5.00
2007СПМД	—	—	—	—	4.00	5.00
2008ММД	—	—	—	—	4.00	5.00
2008СПМД	—	—	—	—	4.00	5.00
2009ММД	—	—	—	—	4.00	5.00
2009СПМД	—	—	—	—	4.00	5.00

Y# 747 2 ROUBLES
17.0000 g., 0.9250 Silver 0.5055 oz. ASW, 33 mm. **Subject:** Zodiac Signs **Obv:** Double-headed eagle within beaded circle **Rev:** Virgo and stars **Edge:** Reeded

Date	Mintage	F	VF	XF	Unc	BU
2002(m) Proof	20,000	Value: 30.00				

Y# 761 2 ROUBLES
17.0000 g., 0.9250 Silver 0.5055 oz. ASW, 33 mm. **Subject:** Zodiac Signs **Obv:** Double-headed eagle within beaded circle **Rev:** Capricorn **Edge:** Reeded

Date	Mintage	F	VF	XF	Unc	BU
2002(sp) Proof	20,000	Value: 35.00				

Y# 762 2 ROUBLES
17.0000 g., 0.9250 Silver 0.5055 oz. ASW, 33 mm. **Subject:** Zodiac Signs **Obv:** Double-headed eagle within beaded circle **Rev:** Sagittarius **Edge:** Reeded

Date	Mintage	F	VF	XF	Unc	BU
2002(sp) Proof	20,000	Value: 30.00				

Y# 766 2 ROUBLES
17.0000 g., 0.9250 Silver 0.5055 oz. ASW, 33 mm. **Subject:** Zodiac Signs **Obv:** Double-headed eagle within beaded circle **Rev:** Scorpion **Edge:** Reeded

Date	Mintage	F	VF	XF	Unc	BU
2002(m) Proof	20,000	Value: 35.00				

Y# 768 2 ROUBLES
17.0000 g., 0.9250 Silver 0.5055 oz. ASW, 33 mm. **Subject:** Zodiac Signs **Obv:** Double-headed eagle **Rev:** Balance scale **Edge:** Reeded

Date	Mintage	F	VF	XF	Unc	BU
2002(sp) Proof	20,000	Value: 30.00				

Y# 793 2 ROUBLES
17.0000 g., 0.9250 Silver 0.5055 oz. ASW, 33 mm. **Subject:** L.P. Orlova **Obv:** Double-headed eagle **Rev:** Head facing **Edge:** Reeded

Date	Mintage	F	VF	XF	Unc	BU
2002(m) Proof	10,000	Value: 25.00				

Y# 803   2 ROUBLES
17.1000 g., 0.9250 Silver 0.5085 oz. ASW, 32.8 mm. **Subject:**
Zodiac signs **Obv:** Double-headed eagle within beaded circle
Rev: Pisces **Edge:** Reeded

Date	Mintage	F	VF	XF	Unc	BU
2003(sp) Proof	20,000	Value: 35.00				

Y# 804   2 ROUBLES
17.1000 g., 0.9250 Silver 0.5085 oz. ASW, 32.8 mm. **Subject:**
Zodiac signs **Obv:** Double-headed eagle within beaded circle
Rev: Aquarius **Edge:** Reeded

Date	Mintage	F	VF	XF	Unc	BU
2003(m) Proof	20,000	Value: 35.00				

Y# 820   2 ROUBLES
17.0000 g., 0.9250 Silver 0.5055 oz. ASW, 33 mm. **Subject:**
Zodiac signs **Obv:** Double-headed eagle within beaded circle
Rev: Cancer Crayfish **Edge:** Reeded

Date	Mintage	F	VF	XF	Unc	BU
2003(sp) Proof	20,000	Value: 35.00				

Y# 840   2 ROUBLES
16.8100 g., 0.9250 Silver 0.4999 oz. ASW, 33 mm. **Rev:** Guil
Yarovsky

Date	Mintage	F	VF	XF	Unc	BU
2003(m) Proof	10,000	Value: 20.00				

Y# 841   2 ROUBLES
16.8100 g., 0.9250 Silver 0.4999 oz. ASW, 33 mm. **Rev:** Fedor
Tyutchev

Date	Mintage	F	VF	XF	Unc	BU
2003(sp) Proof	10,000	Value: 20.00				

Y# 844   2 ROUBLES
17.0000 g., 0.9250 Silver 0.5055 oz. ASW, 33 mm. **Subject:**
Zodiac Signs **Obv:** Double-headed eagle within beaded circle
Rev: Aries

Date	Mintage	F	VF	XF	Unc	BU
2003 Proof	20,000	Value: 25.00				

Y# 845   2 ROUBLES
17.0000 g., 0.9250 Silver 0.5055 oz. ASW **Subject:** Zodiac
Signs **Obv:** Double-headed eagle within beaded circle **Rev:**
Taurus

Date	Mintage	F	VF	XF	Unc	BU
2003 Proof	20,000	Value: 25.00				

Y# 846   2 ROUBLES
17.0000 g., 0.9250 Silver 0.5055 oz. ASW, 33 mm. **Subject:**
Zodiac Signs **Obv:** Double-headed eagle within beaded circle
Rev: Gemini

Date	Mintage	F	VF	XF	Unc	BU
2003 Proof	20,000	Value: 22.50				

Y# 842   2 ROUBLES
16.8100 g., 0.9250 Silver 0.4999 oz. ASW, 33 mm. **Rev:** V. P.
Tchkalov

Date	Mintage	F	VF	XF	Unc	BU
2004(m) Proof	7,000	Value: 20.00				

Y# 843   2 ROUBLES
16.8100 g., 0.9250 Silver 0.4999 oz. ASW, 33 mm. **Rev:** Mikhail
Glinka

Date	Mintage	F	VF	XF	Unc	BU
2004(m) Proof	7,000	Value: 20.00				

Y# 1021   2 ROUBLES
16.8000 g., 0.9250 Silver 0.4996 oz. ASW, 33 mm. **Subject:**
Sini Rerikh, 100th Anniversary of Birth

Date	Mintage	F	VF	XF	Unc	BU
2004 Proof	—	Value: 30.00				

Y# 897   2 ROUBLES
17.0000 g., 0.9250 Silver 0.5055 oz. ASW, 33 mm. **Obv:**
Double-headed eagle **Rev:** Gemini twins **Edge:** Reeded

Date	Mintage	F	VF	XF	Unc	BU
2005 Proof	20,000	Value: 30.00				

Y# 899   2 ROUBLES
17.0000 g., 0.9250 Silver 0.5055 oz. ASW, 33 mm. **Obv:**
Double-headed eagle **Rev:** Cancer Crayfish **Edge:** Reeded

Date	Mintage	F	VF	XF	Unc	BU
2005 Proof	20,000	Value: 30.00				

Y# 901   2 ROUBLES
17.0000 g., 0.9250 Silver 0.5055 oz. ASW, 33 mm. **Obv:**
Double-headed eagle **Rev:** Leo lion **Edge:** Reeded

Date	Mintage	F	VF	XF	Unc	BU
2005 Proof	20,000	Value: 30.00				

Y# 905   2 ROUBLES
17.0000 g., 0.9250 Silver 0.5055 oz. ASW, 33 mm. **Obv:**
Double-headed eagle **Rev:** Mikhail Sholokhov with pen in hand
Edge: Reeded

Date	Mintage	F	VF	XF	Unc	BU
2005 Proof	10,000	Value: 25.00				

Y# 909   2 ROUBLES
17.0000 g., 0.9250 Silver 0.5055 oz. ASW, 33 mm. **Obv:**

Double-headed eagle **Rev:** Peter Klodt viewing man and horse
statue **Edge:** Reeded

Date	Mintage	F	VF	XF	Unc	BU
2005 Proof	10,000	Value: 25.00				

Y# 914   2 ROUBLES
17.0000 g., 0.9250 Silver 0.5055 oz. ASW, 33 mm. **Obv:**
Double-headed eagle **Rev:** Virgo standing lady **Edge:** Reeded

Date	Mintage	F	VF	XF	Unc	BU
2005 Proof	20,000	Value: 30.00				

Y# 919   2 ROUBLES
17.0000 g., 0.9250 Silver 0.5055 oz. ASW, 33 mm. **Obv:**
Double-headed eagle **Rev:** Libra - 2 stylized birds forming a
balance scale **Edge:** Reeded

Date	Mintage	F	VF	XF	Unc	BU
2005 Proof	20,000	Value: 30.00				

Y# 921   2 ROUBLES
17.0000 g., 0.9250 Silver 0.5055 oz. ASW, 33 mm. **Obv:**
Double-headed eagle **Rev:** Scorpio scorpion **Edge:** Reeded

Date	Mintage	F	VF	XF	Unc	BU
2005 Proof	20,000	Value: 30.00				

Y# 926   2 ROUBLES
17.0000 g., 0.9250 Silver 0.5055 oz. ASW, 33 mm. **Obv:**
Double-headed eagle **Rev:** Sagittarius the archer **Edge:** Reeded

Date	Mintage	F	VF	XF	Unc	BU
2005 Proof	20,000	Value: 30.00				

Y# 928   2 ROUBLES
17.0000 g., 0.9250 Silver 0.5055 oz. ASW, 33 mm. **Obv:**
Double-headed eagle **Rev:** Capricorn as half goat and fish **Edge:**
Reeded

Date	Mintage	F	VF	XF	Unc	BU
2005 Proof	20,000	Value: 30.00				

Y# 930 2 ROUBLES
17.0000 g., 0.9250 Silver 0.5055 oz. ASW, 33 mm. **Obv:** Double-headed eagle **Rev:** Pisces as catfish and sturgeon **Edge:** Reeded

Date	Mintage	F	VF	XF	Unc	BU
2005 Proof	20,000	Value: 30.00				

Y# 932 2 ROUBLES
17.0000 g., 0.9250 Silver 0.5055 oz. ASW, 33 mm. **Obv:** Double-headed eagle **Rev:** Aries ram **Edge:** Reeded

Date	Mintage	F	VF	XF	Unc	BU
2005 Proof	20,000	Value: 30.00				

Y# 934 2 ROUBLES
17.0000 g., 0.9250 Silver 0.5055 oz. ASW, 33 mm. **Obv:** Double-headed eagle **Rev:** Taurus bull **Edge:** Reeded

Date	Mintage	F	VF	XF	Unc	BU
2005 Proof	20,000	Value: 30.00				

Y# 936 2 ROUBLES
17.0000 g., 0.9250 Silver 0.5055 oz. ASW, 33 mm. **Obv:** Double-headed eagle **Rev:** Aquarius water carrier **Edge:** Reeded

Date	Mintage	F	VF	XF	Unc	BU
2005 Proof	20,000	Value: 30.00				

Y# 1054 2 ROUBLES
16.8000 g., 0.9250 Silver 0.4996 oz. ASW, 33 mm. **Subject:** O. K. Antonov, 100th Anniversary of Birth

Date	Mintage	F	VF	XF	Unc	BU
2006 Proof	—	Value: 35.00				

Y# 1055 2 ROUBLES
16.8000 g., 0.9250 Silver 0.4996 oz. ASW, 33 mm. **Subject:** M. A. Vrubel, 150th Anniversary of Birth

Date	Mintage	F	VF	XF	Unc	BU
2006 Proof	—	Value: 35.00				

Y# 1056 2 ROUBLES
16.8000 g., 0.9250 Silver 0.4996 oz. ASW, 33 mm. **Subject:** A. A. Ivanov, 200th Anniversary of Birth

Date	Mintage	F	VF	XF	Unc	BU
2006 Proof	—	Value: 35.00				

Y# 1057 2 ROUBLES
16.8000 g., 0.9250 Silver 0.4996 oz. ASW, 33 mm. **Subject:** D. D. Shostakovich, 100th Anniversary of Birth

Date	Mintage	F	VF	XF	Unc	BU
2006 Proof	—	Value: 35.00				

Y# 967 2 ROUBLES
17.0000 g., 0.9250 Silver 0.5055 oz. ASW, 33.0 mm. **Subject:** 100th Anniversary Birth of Gerasimov **Obv:** Two-headed eagle **Rev:** Gerasimov recreating a man's face **Rev. Legend:** М. М. ГЕРАСИМОВ

Date	Mintage	F	VF	XF	Unc	BU
2007(m) Proof	10,000	Value: 35.00				

Y# 968 2 ROUBLES
17.0000 g., 0.9250 Silver 0.5055 oz. ASW, 33.0 mm. **Subject:** 150th Anniversary Birth of Tsiolkovsky **Rev:** Bust of Tsiolkovsky 3/4 right at left, scheme of two flight vehicles with earth in background at upper right **Rev. Legend:** К. Э. ЦИОЛКОВСКИЙ **Edge:** Reeded

Date	Mintage	F	VF	XF	Unc	BU
2007(m) Proof	10,000	Value: 35.00				

Y# 1104 2 ROUBLES
16.8000 g., 0.9250 Silver 0.4996 oz. ASW, 33 mm. **Subject:** S.P. Korolyov, 100th Anniversary of Birth

Date	Mintage	F	VF	XF	Unc	BU
2007 Proof	—	Value: 35.00				

Y# 1105 2 ROUBLES
16.8000 g., 0.9250 Silver 0.4996 oz. ASW, 33 mm. **Subject:** V.M. Bekhterev, 150th Anniversary of Birth

Date	Mintage	F	VF	XF	Unc	BU
2007 Proof	—	Value: 35.00				

Y# 1106 2 ROUBLES
16.8000 g., 0.9250 Silver 0.4996 oz. ASW, 33 mm. **Subject:** L. Euler, 300th Anniversary of Birth

Date	Mintage	F	VF	XF	Unc	BU
2007 Proof	—	Value: 35.00				

Y# 1107 2 ROUBLES
16.8000 g., 0.9250 Silver 0.4996 oz. ASW, 33 mm. **Subject:** V. P. Soloviev - Sedoy, 100th Anniversary of Birth

Date	Mintage	F	VF	XF	Unc	BU
2007 Proof	—	Value: 35.00				

Y# 979 2 ROUBLES
15.5500 g., 0.9250 Silver 0.4624 oz. ASW, 33 mm. **Obv:** Double headed eagle **Rev:** Black caped marmot **Edge:** Reeded

Date	Mintage	F	VF	XF	Unc	BU
2008 Proof	—	Value: 32.00				

Y# 980 2 ROUBLES
15.5500 g., 0.9250 Silver 0.4624 oz. ASW, 33 mm. **Obv:** Double headed eagle **Rev:** Shemaya fish **Edge:** Reeded

Date	Mintage	F	VF	XF	Unc	BU
2008 Proof	—	Value: 32.00				

Y# 1131 2 ROUBLES
16.8000 g., 0.9250 Silver 0.4996 oz. ASW, 33 mm. **Subject:** L. D. Landau, 100th Anniversary of Birth

Date	Mintage	F	VF	XF	Unc	BU
2008 Proof	—	Value: 35.00				

Y# 1132 2 ROUBLES
16.8000 g., 0.9250 Silver 0.4996 oz. ASW, 33 mm. **Subject:** V. P. Glushko, 100th Anniversary of Birth

Date	Mintage	F	VF	XF	Unc	BU
2008 Proof	—	Value: 35.00				

Y# 1133 2 ROUBLES
16.8000 g., 0.9250 Silver 0.4996 oz. ASW, 33 mm. **Subject:** D. F. Oistrakh, 100th Anniversary of Birth

Date	Mintage	F	VF	XF	Unc	BU
2008 Proof	—	Value: 35.00				

Y# 1134 2 ROUBLES
16.8000 g., 0.9250 Silver 0.4996 oz. ASW, 33 mm. **Subject:** I. M. Frank, 100th Anniversary of Birth

Date	Mintage	F	VF	XF	Unc	BU
2008 Proof	—	Value: 35.00				

Y# 1135 2 ROUBLES
16.8000 g., 0.9250 Silver 0.4996 oz. ASW, 33 mm. **Subject:** N. N. Nosoc, 100th Anniversary of Birth

Date	Mintage	F	VF	XF	Unc	BU
2008 Proof	—	Value: 35.00				

Y# 1136 2 ROUBLES
16.8000 g., 0.9250 Silver 0.4996 oz. ASW, 33 mm. **Subject:** V. I. Nemirovich, 100th Anniversary of Birth

Date	Mintage	F	VF	XF	Unc	BU
2008 Proof	—	Value: 35.00				

Y# 1137 2 ROUBLES
16.8000 g., 0.9250 Silver 0.4996 oz. ASW, 33 mm. **Subject:** E. V. Vuchetich, 100th Anniversary of Birth

Date	Mintage	F	VF	XF	Unc	BU
2008 Proof	—	Value: 35.00				

Y# 834a 2 ROUBLES
5.0000 g., Nickel Plated Steel, 23 mm. **Obv:** Two headed eagle, curved bank name and denomination below **Edge:** Segmented reeding

Date	Mintage	F	VF	XF	Unc	BU
2009ММД	—	—	—	—	0.50	0.75
2009СПМД	—	—	—	—	0.50	0.75
2010ММД	—	—	—	—	0.50	0.75
2010СПМД	—	—	—	—	0.50	0.75
2011ММД	—	—	—	—	0.50	0.75
2011СПМД	—	—	—	—	0.50	0.75
2012ММД	—	—	—	—	0.50	0.75
2012СПМД	—	—	—	—	0.50	0.75

Y# 1158 2 ROUBLES
16.8000 g., 0.9250 Silver 0.4996 oz. ASW **Subject:** D. I. Mendeleyev, 175th Anniversary of Birth

Date	Mintage	F	VF	XF	Unc	BU
2009 Proof	—	Value: 35.00				

Y# 1190 2 ROUBLES
16.8000 g., 0.9250 Silver 0.4996 oz. ASW, 33 mm. **Subject:** A. V. Koltsov, 200th Anniversary of Birth

Date	Mintage	F	VF	XF	Unc	BU
2009 Proof	—	Value: 35.00				

Y# 1191 2 ROUBLES
16.8000 g., 0.9250 Silver 0.4996 oz. ASW, 33 mm. **Subject:** A. N. Voronikhin, 250th Anniversary of Birth

Date	Mintage	F	VF	XF	Unc	BU
2009 Proof	—	Value: 35.00				

Y# 1192 2 ROUBLES
16.8000 g., 0.9250 Silver 0.4996 oz. ASW, 33 mm. **Subject:** G. S. Ulanova, 100th Anniversary of Birth

Date	Mintage	F	VF	XF	Unc	BU
2009 Proof	—	Value: 35.00				

Y# 1193 2 ROUBLES
16.8000 g., 0.9250 Silver 0.4996 oz. ASW, 33 mm. **Subject:** L. I. Yashin, Soccer player

Date	Mintage	F	VF	XF	Unc	BU
2009 Proof	—	Value: 45.00				

Y# 1194 2 ROUBLES
16.8000 g., 0.9250 Silver 0.4996 oz. ASW, 33 mm. **Subject:** E. I. Beskov, Soccer player

Date	Mintage	F	VF	XF	Unc	BU
2009 Proof	—	Value: 45.00				

Y# 1195 2 ROUBLES
16.8000 g., 0.9250 Silver 0.4996 oz. ASW, 33 mm. **Subject:** E. A. Stresov, Soccer player

Date	Mintage	F	VF	XF	Unc	BU
2009 Proof	—	Value: 45.00				

Y# 1196 2 ROUBLES
16.8000 g., 0.9250 Silver 0.4996 oz. ASW, 33 mm. **Subject:** V. M. Bobrov, Hockey player

Date	Mintage	F	VF	XF	Unc	BU
2009 Proof	—	Value: 45.00				

Y# 1197 2 ROUBLES
16.8000 g., 0.9250 Silver 0.4996 oz. ASW, 33 mm. **Subject:** A. N. Maltzev, Hockey player

Date	Mintage	F	VF	XF	Unc	BU
2009 Proof	—	Value: 45.00				

Y# 1198 2 ROUBLES
16.8000 g., 0.9250 Silver 0.4996 oz. ASW, 33 mm. **Subject:** V. B. Kharlamov, Hockey player

Date	Mintage	F	VF	XF	Unc	BU
2009 Proof	—	Value: 45.00				

Y# 1216 2 ROUBLES
16.8000 g., 0.9250 Silver 0.4996 oz. ASW, 33 mm. **Subject:** N. I. Pirogov, 200th Anniversary of Birth

Date	Mintage	F	VF	XF	Unc	BU
2010 Proof	—	Value: 35.00				

Y# 1217   2 ROUBLES
16.8000 g., 0.9250 Silver 0.4996 oz. ASW, 33 mm. **Subject:** I. I. Levitan, 150th Anniversary of Birth

Date	Mintage	F	VF	XF	Unc	BU
2010 Proof	—				Value: 35.00	

Y# 1218   2 ROUBLES
16.8000 g., 0.9250 Silver 0.4996 oz. ASW, 33 mm. **Subject:** G. S. Ulanova, 100th Anniversary of Birth

Date	Mintage	F	VF	XF	Unc	BU
2010 Proof	—				Value: 35.00	

Y# 1248   2 ROUBLES
16.8000 g., 0.9250 Silver 0.4996 oz. ASW, 33 mm. **Subject:** Sika Deer

Date	Mintage	F	VF	XF	Unc	BU
2010 Proof	—				Value: 32.00	

Y# 1249   2 ROUBLES
16.8000 g., 0.9250 Silver 0.4996 oz. ASW, 33 mm. **Subject:** Short tailed albatross

Date	Mintage	F	VF	XF	Unc	BU
2010 Proof	—				Value: 32.00	

Y# 1250   2 ROUBLES
16.8000 g., 0.9250 Silver 0.4996 oz. ASW, 33 mm. **Subject:** Gjursa

Date	Mintage	F	VF	XF	Unc	BU
2010 Proof	—				Value: 32.00	

Y# 1307   2 ROUBLES
20.3500 g., 0.9250 Silver 0.6052 oz. ASW, 33 mm. **Subject:** Year of Russian Culture and Language in Italy **Obv:** St. George slaying dragon **Rev:** St. Nicholas church in Bari

Date	Mintage	F	VF	XF	Unc	BU
2011 Proof	10,000				Value: 60.00	

Y# 1319   2 ROUBLES
15.5500 g., 0.9250 Silver 0.4624 oz. ASW, 33 mm. **Subject:** M.M. Botvinnik **Rev:** Chess player and board

Date	Mintage	F	VF	XF	Unc	BU
2011 Proof	3,000				Value: 30.00	

Y# 1320   2 ROUBLES
15.5500 g., 0.9250 Silver 0.4624 oz. ASW, 33 mm. **Subject:** A.I. Raykin **Rev:** Portrait left **Edge:** Reeded

Date	Mintage	F	VF	XF	Unc	BU
2011 Proof	3,000				Value: 30.00	

Y# 677   3 ROUBLES
34.8800 g., 0.9000 Silver 1.0092 oz. ASW, 39 mm. **Subject:** 225 Years - Bolshoi Theater **Obv:** Double-headed eagle **Rev:** Standing figures facing **Edge:** Reeded

Date	Mintage	F	VF	XF	Unc	BU
2001 Proof	7,500				Value: 55.00	

Y# 680   3 ROUBLES
34.8800 g., 0.9000 Silver 1.0092 oz. ASW, 39 mm. **Subject:** 40th Anniversary of Manned Space Flight - Yuri Gagarin **Obv:** Double-headed eagle **Rev:** Uniformed bust holding dove **Edge:** Reeded

Date	Mintage	F	VF	XF	Unc	BU
2001 Proof	7,500				Value: 55.00	

Y# 682   3 ROUBLES
34.8800 g., 0.9000 Silver 1.0092 oz. ASW, 39 mm. **Subject:**

Siberian Exploration **Obv:** Double-headed eagle **Rev:** Men riding horses, deer and sleds **Edge:** Reeded

Date	Mintage	F	VF	XF	Unc	BU
2001 Proof	5,000				Value: 70.00	

Y# 733   3 ROUBLES
34.8800 g., 0.9000 Silver 1.0092 oz. ASW, 39 mm. **Subject:** 200th Anniversary of Navigation School **Obv:** Double-headed eagle **Rev:** Navigational tools and building **Edge:** Reeded

Date	Mintage	F	VF	XF	Unc	BU
2001 Proof	5,000				Value: 70.00	

Y# 734   3 ROUBLES
34.8800 g., 0.9000 Silver 1.0092 oz. ASW, 39 mm. **Subject:** First Moscow Savings Bank **Obv:** Double-headed eagle **Rev:** Beehive above building within circle **Edge:** Reeded

Date	Mintage	F	VF	XF	Unc	BU
2001 Proof	17,500				Value: 45.00	

Y# 735   3 ROUBLES
34.8800 g., 0.9000 Silver 1.0092 oz. ASW, 39 mm. **Subject:** State Labor Savings Bank **Obv:** Double-headed eagle **Rev:** Dam, passbook and tractor **Edge:** Reeded

Date	Mintage	F	VF	XF	Unc	BU
2001 Proof	17,500				Value: 45.00	

Y# 736   3 ROUBLES
34.8800 g., 0.9000 Silver 1.0092 oz. ASW, 39 mm. **Subject:** Savings Bank of the Russian Federation **Obv:** Double-headed eagle **Rev:** Chevrons above building **Edge:** Reeded

Date	Mintage	F	VF	XF	Unc	BU
2001 Proof	17,500				Value: 45.00	

Y# 737   3 ROUBLES
34.8800 g., 0.9000 Silver 1.0092 oz. ASW, 39 mm.   **Subject:**
10th Anniversary - Commonwealth of Independent States **Obv:**
Double-headed eagle **Rev:** Hologram below logo **Edge:** Reeded

Date	Mintage	F	VF	XF	Unc	BU
2001 Proof	7,500	Value: 50.00				

Y# 738   3 ROUBLES
34.8800 g., 0.9000 Silver 1.0092 oz. ASW, 39 mm.   **Subject:**
Olympics **Obv:** Double-headed eagle **Rev:** Cross-country skiers
Edge: Reeded

Date	Mintage	F	VF	XF	Unc	BU
2002 Proof	25,000	Value: 50.00				

Y# 744   3 ROUBLES
34.8800 g., 0.9000 Silver 1.0092 oz. ASW, 39 mm.   **Subject:**
St. John's Nunnery, St. Petersburg **Obv:** Double-headed eagle
Rev: Nunnery and cameo **Edge:** Reeded

Date	Mintage	F	VF	XF	Unc	BU
2002 Proof	5,000	Value: 55.00				

Y# 778   3 ROUBLES
34.8800 g., 0.9000 Silver 1.0092 oz. ASW, 39 mm.   **Subject:**
Kideksha **Obv:** Double-headed eagle **Rev:** Three churches on
river bank **Edge:** Reeded

Date	Mintage	F	VF	XF	Unc	BU
2002(sp) Proof	10,000	Value: 60.00				

Y# 779   3 ROUBLES
34.8800 g., 0.9000 Silver 1.0092 oz. ASW, 39 mm.   **Subject:**
Iversky Monastery, Valdaiy **Obv:** Double-headed eagle **Rev:**
Building complex on an island in Lake Valdaiy **Edge:** Reeded

Date	Mintage	F	VF	XF	Unc	BU
2002(sp) Proof	10,000	Value: 60.00				

Y# 780   3 ROUBLES
34.8800 g., 0.9000 Silver 1.0092 oz. ASW, 39 mm.   **Subject:**
Miraculous Savior Church **Obv:** Double-headed eagle **Rev:**
Church with separate bell tower **Edge:** Reeded

Date	Mintage	F	VF	XF	Unc	BU
2002(m) Proof	5,000	Value: 55.00				

Y# 781   3 ROUBLES
34.8800 g., 0.9000 Silver 1.0092 oz. ASW, 39 mm.   **Subject:**
Works of Dionissy **Obv:** Double-headed eagle **Rev:** "The Crucifix"
Edge: Reeded

Date	Mintage	F	VF	XF	Unc	BU
2002(sp) Proof	10,000	Value: 45.00				

Y# 755   3 ROUBLES
34.8800 g., 0.9000 Silver 1.0092 oz. ASW, 39 mm.   **Subject:**
Admiral Nakhimov **Obv:** Double-headed eagle **Rev:** Monument,
Admiral with cannon and naval battle scene **Edge:** Reeded

Date	Mintage	F	VF	XF	Unc	BU
2002(sp) Proof	10,000	Value: 45.00				

Y# 787   3 ROUBLES
34.8800 g., 0.9000 Silver 1.0092 oz. ASW, 39 mm.   **Subject:**
World Cup Soccer **Obv:** Double-headed eagle **Rev:** Soccer ball
within circle of players **Edge:** Reeded

Date	Mintage	F	VF	XF	Unc	BU
2002(sp) Proof	25,000	Value: 40.00				

Y# 756   3 ROUBLES
34.8800 g., 0.9000 Silver 1.0092 oz. ASW, 39 mm.   **Subject:**
Hermitage **Obv:** Double-headed eagle **Rev:** Statues and arch
Edge: Reeded

Date	Mintage	F	VF	XF	Unc	BU
2002(sp) Proof	10,000	Value: 50.00				

Y# 885   3 ROUBLES
34.8000 g., 0.9000 Silver 1.0069 oz. ASW, 38.7 mm.   **Subject:**
City of Pskov 1100th Anniversary **Obv:** Double-headed eagle
Rev: Walled city view **Edge:** Reeded

Date	Mintage	F	VF	XF	Unc	BU
2003(sp) Proof	—	Value: 55.00				

Y# 801   3 ROUBLES
34.8000 g., 0.9000 Silver 1.0069 oz. ASW, 38.7 mm.   **Subject:**
Veborg **Obv:** Double-headed eagle **Rev:** Sailing ships and
buildings **Edge:** Reeded

Date	Mintage	F	VF	XF	Unc	BU
2003(sp) Proof	10,000	Value: 55.00				

Y# 802   3 ROUBLES
34.7500 g., 0.9000 Silver 1.0055 oz. ASW, 38.7 mm.   **Subject:**
Lunar Calendar **Obv:** National emblem **Rev:** Mountain goat in
crescent **Edge:** Reeded

Date	Mintage	F	VF	XF	Unc	BU
2003(m) Proof	15,000	Value: 50.00				

Y# 805   3 ROUBLES
34.8400 g., 0.9000 Silver 1.0081 oz. ASW, 38.8 mm.   **Subject:**
Zodiac signs **Obv:** Double-headed eagle within beaded circle
Rev: Leo **Edge:** Reeded

Date	Mintage	F	VF	XF	Unc	BU
2003(m) Proof	30,000	Value: 50.00				

Y# 806   3 ROUBLES
34.7400 g., 0.9000 Silver 1.0052 oz. ASW, 38.8 mm.   **Subject:**
St. Daniel's Monastery **Obv:** Double-headed eagle **Rev:** Statue
and monastery **Edge:** Reeded

Date	Mintage	F	VF	XF	Unc	BU
2003(m) Proof	10,000	Value: 50.00				

Y# 807   3 ROUBLES
34.7400 g., 0.9000 Silver 1.0052 oz. ASW, 38.8 mm.   **Subject:**
World Biathlon Championships **Obv:** Double-headed eagle **Rev:**
Rifleman and archer on skis **Edge:** Reeded

Date	Mintage	F	VF	XF	Unc	BU
2003(m) Proof	7,500	Value: 50.00				

Y# 808   3 ROUBLES
34.7400 g., 0.9000 Silver 1.0052 oz. ASW, 38.8 mm.   **Obv:**
Double-headed eagle **Rev:** Monastery **Edge:** Reeded

Date	Mintage	F	VF	XF	Unc	BU
2003(m) Proof	10,000	Value: 45.00				

Y# 809   3 ROUBLES
34.7400 g., 0.9000 Silver 1.0052 oz. ASW, 38.8 mm.   **Subject:**
First Kamchatka Expedition **Obv:** Double-headed eagle **Rev:**
Natives, fish and ship **Edge:** Reeded

Date	Mintage	F	VF	XF	Unc	BU
2003(sp) Proof	10,000	Value: 45.00				

Y# 810   3 ROUBLES
34.7400 g., 0.9000 Silver 1.0052 oz. ASW, 38.8 mm.   **Subject:**
Zodiac signs **Obv:** Double-headed eagle within beaded circle
Rev: Virgo **Edge:** Reeded

Date	Mintage	F	VF	XF	Unc	BU
2003(sp)	30,000	Value: 40.00				

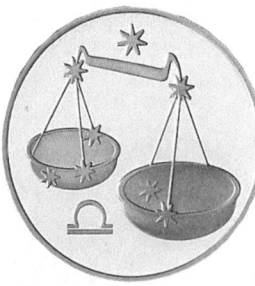

Y# 811   3 ROUBLES
34.7400 g., 0.9000 Silver 1.0052 oz. ASW, 38.8 mm.   **Subject:**
Zodiac signs **Obv:** Double-headed eagle within beaded circle
Rev: Libra **Edge:** Reeded

Date	Mintage	F	VF	XF	Unc	BU
2003(m) Proof	30,000	Value: 45.00				

Y# 812   3 ROUBLES
34.7400 g., 0.9000 Silver 1.0052 oz. ASW, 38.8 mm.   **Subject:**
Diveyevsky Monastery **Obv:** Double-headed eagle **Rev:** Cameo
above churches **Edge:** Reeded

Date	Mintage	F	VF	XF	Unc	BU
2003(sp) Proof	10,000	Value: 45.00				

Y# 813   3 ROUBLES
34.7400 g., 0.9000 Silver 1.0052 oz. ASW, 38.8 mm.   **Subject:**
Zodiac Signs **Obv:** Double-headed eagle within beaded circle
Rev: Scorpio **Edge:** Reeded

Date	Mintage	F	VF	XF	Unc	BU
2003(m) Proof	30,000	Value: 40.00				

Y# 847   3 ROUBLES
34.5600 g., 0.9000 Silver 1.0000 oz. ASW, 39 mm.   **Rev:** St.
Trinity Monastery

Date	Mintage	F	VF	XF	Unc	BU
2003(sp) Proof	10,000	Value: 45.00				

Y# 848   3 ROUBLES
34.5600 g., 0.9000 Silver 1.0000 oz. ASW, 39 mm.   **Subject:**
Zodiac Signs **Obv:** Double-headed eagle within beaded circle
Rev: Sagittarius

Date	Mintage	F	VF	XF	Unc	BU
2003(sp) Proof	30,000	Value: 40.00				

Y# 849   3 ROUBLES
34.5600 g., 0.9000 Silver 1.0000 oz. ASW, 39 mm.   **Subject:**
Zodiac Signs **Obv:** Double-headed eagle within beaded circle
Rev: Capricorn

Date	Mintage	F	VF	XF	Unc	BU
2003(m) Proof	30,000	Value: 40.00				

Y# 1012   3 ROUBLES
33.9000 g., 0.9250 Silver 1.0081 oz. ASW, 39 mm.   **Subject:**
Year of the Goat

Date	Mintage	F	VF	XF	Unc	BU
2003 Proof	—	Value: 50.00				

Y# 850   3 ROUBLES
34.5600 g., 0.9000 Silver 1.0000 oz. ASW, 39 mm.   **Subject:**
Lunar Calendar **Rev:** Monkey

Date	Mintage	F	VF	XF	Unc	BU
2004(m) Proof	15,000	Value: 45.00				

Y# 851   3 ROUBLES
34.5600 g., 0.9000 Silver 1.0000 oz. ASW, 39 mm.   **Subject:**
Zodiac Signs **Obv:** Double-headed eagle within beaded circle
Rev: Aquarius

Date	Mintage	F	VF	XF	Unc	BU
2004(sp) Proof	30,000	Value: 40.00				

Y# 852   3 ROUBLES
34.5600 g., 0.9000 Silver 1.0000 oz. ASW, 39 mm.   **Rev:** Tomsk

Date	Mintage	F	VF	XF	Unc	BU
2004(m) Proof	8,000	Value: 55.00				

Y# 853   3 ROUBLES
34.5600 g., 0.9000 Silver 1.0000 oz. ASW, 39 mm.   **Subject:**
Zodiac Signs **Obv:** Double-headed eagle within beaded circle
Rev: Pisces

Date	Mintage	F	VF	XF	Unc	BU
2004(m) Proof	30,000	Value: 40.00				

Y# 854 3 ROUBLES
34.5600 g., 0.9000 Silver 1.0000 oz. ASW, 39 mm. **Rev:** Epiphany Cathedral, Moscow

Date	Mintage	F	VF	XF	Unc	BU
2004(m) Proof	8,000	Value: 55.00				

Y# 855 3 ROUBLES
34.5600 g., 0.9000 Silver 1.0000 oz. ASW, 39 mm. **Subject:** Zodiac Signs **Obv:** Double-headed eagle within beaded circle **Rev:** Aries

Date	Mintage	F	VF	XF	Unc	BU
2004(sp) Proof	30,000	Value: 40.00				

Y# 856 3 ROUBLES
34.5600 g., 0.9000 Silver 1.0000 oz. ASW, 39 mm. **Rev:** Soccer

Date	Mintage	F	VF	XF	Unc	BU
2004(sp) Proof	10,000	Value: 40.00				

Y# 857 3 ROUBLES
34.5600 g., 0.9000 Silver 1.0000 oz. ASW, 39 mm. **Subject:** Zodiac Signs **Obv:** Double-headed eagle within beaded circle **Rev:** Taurus

Date	Mintage	F	VF	XF	Unc	BU
2004(sp) Proof	30,000	Value: 40.00				

Y# 858 3 ROUBLES
34.5600 g., 0.9000 Silver 1.0000 oz. ASW, 39 mm. **Rev:** Olympic torch

Date	Mintage	F	VF	XF	Unc	BU
2004(m) Proof	20,000	Value: 50.00				

Y# 859 3 ROUBLES
34.5600 g., 0.9000 Silver 1.0000 oz. ASW, 39 mm. **Subject:** Zodiac Signs **Obv:** Double-headed eagle within beaded circle **Rev:** Gemini

Date	Mintage	F	VF	XF	Unc	BU
2004(m) Proof	30,000	Value: 40.00				

Y# 860 3 ROUBLES
34.5600 g., 0.9000 Silver 1.0000 oz. ASW, 39 mm. **Subject:** Zodiac Signs **Obv:** Double-headed eagle within beaded circle **Rev:** Cancer

Date	Mintage	F	VF	XF	Unc	BU
2004(sp) Proof	30,000	Value: 40.00				

Y# 861 3 ROUBLES
34.5600 g., 0.9000 Silver 1.0000 oz. ASW, 39 mm. **Rev:** Church of the Sign of the Holy Mother of God

Date	Mintage	F	VF	XF	Unc	BU
2004(m) Proof	8,000	Value: 55.00				

Y# 862 3 ROUBLES
34.5600 g., 0.9000 Silver 1.0000 oz. ASW, 39 mm. **Rev:** Transfiguration icon

Date	Mintage	F	VF	XF	Unc	BU
2004(m) Proof	8,000	Value: 55.00				

Y# 863 3 ROUBLES
34.5600 g., 0.9000 Silver 1.0000 oz. ASW, 39 mm. **Rev:** Peter I's monetary reform

Date	Mintage	F	VF	XF	Unc	BU
2004(sp) Proof	8,000	Value: 75.00				

Y# 1013 3 ROUBLES
33.9000 g., 0.9250 Silver 1.0081 oz. ASW, 39 mm. **Subject:** 2nd Kamchatka Expedition, 1733-43

Date	Mintage	F	VF	XF	Unc	BU
2004 Proof	—	Value: 65.00				

Y# 1015 3 ROUBLES
33.9000 g., 0.9250 Silver 1.0081 oz. ASW, 39 mm. **Subject:** Theophanes the Greek

Date	Mintage	F	VF	XF	Unc	BU
2004 Proof	—	Value: 65.00				

Y# 1020 3 ROUBLES
33.9000 g., 0.9250 Silver 1.0081 oz. ASW, 39 mm. **Subject:** Church of the Virgin Nativity in Gordniya

Date	Mintage	F	VF	XF	Unc	BU
2004 Proof	—	Value: 65.00				

Y# 1022 3 ROUBLES
33.9000 g., 0.9250 Silver 1.0081 oz. ASW, 39 mm. **Subject:** Reindeer

Date	Mintage	F	VF	XF	Unc	BU
2004 Proof	—	Value: 70.00				

Y# 892 3 ROUBLES
33.9400 g., 0.9250 Silver 1.0093 oz. ASW, 39 mm. **Obv:** Double-headed eagle **Rev:** Rooster and crescent moon **Edge:** Reeded

Date	Mintage	F	VF	XF	Unc	BU
2005 Proof	15,000	Value: 45.00				

Y# 893 3 ROUBLES
33.9400 g., 0.9250 Silver 1.0093 oz. ASW, 39 mm. **Subject:** 60th Anniversary - Victory Over Germany **Obv:** Double-headed eagle **Rev:** Soldier and wife circa 1945 **Edge:** Reeded

Date	Mintage	F	VF	XF	Unc	BU
2005 Proof	35,000	Value: 40.00				

Y# 903 3 ROUBLES
33.9400 g., 0.9250 Silver 1.0093 oz. ASW, 39 mm. **Obv:** Double-headed eagle **Rev:** St. Nicholas Cathedral in Kaliningrad **Edge:** Reeded

Date	Mintage	F	VF	XF	Unc	BU
2005 Proof	10,000	Value: 50.00				

Y# 904 3 ROUBLES
33.9400 g., 0.9250 Silver 1.0093 oz. ASW, 39 mm. **Obv:** Double-headed eagle **Rev:** Kropotkin Metro Station in Moscow **Edge:** Reeded

Date	Mintage	F	VF	XF	Unc	BU
2005 Proof	10,000	Value: 50.00				

Y# 906 3 ROUBLES
33.9400 g., 0.9250 Silver 1.0093 oz. ASW, 39 mm. **Subject:** Helsinki Games **Obv:** Double-headed eagle **Rev:** Stylized track and field athletes **Edge:** Reeded

Date	Mintage	F	VF	XF	Unc	BU
2005 Proof	10,000	Value: 45.00				

Y# 908 3 ROUBLES
33.9400 g., 0.9250 Silver 1.0093 oz. ASW, 39 mm. **Obv:** Double-headed eagle **Rev:** Virgin Monastery in Raifa, Tatarstan **Edge:** Reeded

Date	Mintage	F	VF	XF	Unc	BU
2005 Proof	10,000	Value: 45.00				

Y# 910 3 ROUBLES
33.9400 g., 0.9250 Silver 1.0093 oz. ASW, 39 mm. **Obv:** Double-headed eagle **Rev:** Kazan Theater Building **Edge:** Reeded

Date	Mintage	F	VF	XF	Unc	BU
2005 Proof	10,000	Value: 50.00				

Y# 923 3 ROUBLES
33.9400 g., 0.9250 Silver 1.0093 oz. ASW, 39 mm. **Subject:** 625th Anniversary - Battle of Kulikovo **Obv:** Double-headed eagle **Rev:** Carved Lion and Griffin between opposing armies **Edge:** Reeded

Date	Mintage	F	VF	XF	Unc	BU
2005 Proof	10,000	Value: 50.00				

Y# 955 3 ROUBLES
33.9400 g., 0.9250 Silver 1.0093 oz. ASW, 39 mm. **Subject:** Moscow's Lomonosov University **Obv:** Two headed eagle **Rev:** Lomonosov statue before university building and Moscow skyline **Edge:** Reeded

Date	Mintage	F	VF	XF	Unc	BU
2005(m) Proof	10,000	Value: 40.00				

Y# 1038 3 ROUBLES
33.9000 g., 0.9250 Silver 1.0081 oz. ASW **Subject:** I. V. Russakov, House of Culture **Shape:** 39

Date	Mintage	F	VF	XF	Unc	BU
2005 Proof	—	Value: 60.00				

Y# 1039 3 ROUBLES
33.9000 g., 0.9250 Silver 1.0081 oz. ASW, 39 mm. **Subject:** Novosibirsk State Academic Opera & Ballet

Date	Mintage	F	VF	XF	Unc	BU
2005 Proof	—	Value: 60.00				

Y# 1040 3 ROUBLES
33.9000 g., 0.9250 Silver 1.0081 oz. ASW, 39 mm. **Subject:** Year of the Rooster

Date	Mintage	F	VF	XF	Unc	BU
2006 Proof	—	Value: 60.00				

Y# 1041 3 ROUBLES
33.9000 g., 0.9250 Silver 1.0081 oz. ASW, 39 mm. **Subject:** Parliament, 100th Anniversary

Date	Mintage	F	VF	XF	Unc	BU
2006 Proof	—	Value: 60.00				

Y# 1046 3 ROUBLES
33.9000 g., 0.9250 Silver 1.0081 oz. ASW, 39 mm. **Subject:** Tretyakov State Gallery, 150th Anniversary

Date	Mintage	F	VF	XF	Unc	BU
2006 Proof	—	Value: 60.00				

Y# 1048 3 ROUBLES
33.9000 g., 0.9250 Silver 1.0081 oz. ASW **Subject:** Russia Savings **Shape:** 39

Date	Mintage	F	VF	XF	Unc	BU
2006 Proof	—	Value: 60.00				

Y# 1052   3 ROUBLES
169.0000 g., 0.9250 Silver 5.0258 oz. ASW, 60 mm. **Subject:** State bank Building, Nizhny Novgorod

Date	Mintage	F	VF	XF	Unc	BU
2006 Proof	—				Value: 275	

Y# 1060   3 ROUBLES
33.9000 g., 0.9250 Silver 1.0081 oz. ASW, 33 mm. **Subject:** Moscow's Kremlin and Red Square

Date	Mintage	F	VF	XF	Unc	BU
2006 Proof	—				Value: 70.00	

Y# 1065   3 ROUBLES
33.9000 g., 0.9250 Silver 1.0081 oz. ASW, 39 mm. **Subject:** XX Winter Olympics, Torino

Date	Mintage	F	VF	XF	Unc	BU
2006 Proof	12,500				Value: 95.00	

Y# 1066   3 ROUBLES
33.9000 g., 0.9250 Silver 1.0081 oz. ASW, 39 mm. **Subject:** FIFA World Cup, Germany

Date	Mintage	F	VF	XF	Unc	BU
2006 Proof	—				Value: 75.00	

Y# 1079   3 ROUBLES
33.9000 g., 0.9250 Silver 1.0081 oz. ASW, 39 mm. **Subject:** Year of the Dog

Date	Mintage	F	VF	XF	Unc	BU
2006 Proof	—				Value: 60.00	

Y# 966   3 ROUBLES
33.9400 g., 0.9250 Silver 1.0093 oz. ASW, 39.0 mm. **Subject:** 250th Anniversary Academy of the Arts **Obv:** Two-headed eagle **Rev:** Relief image of Minerva group **Rev. Legend:** РОССИЙСКАЯ - АКАДЕМИЯ ХУДОЖЕСТВ **Edge:** Reeded

Date	Mintage	F	VF	XF	Unc	BU
2007(m) Proof	10,000				Value: 50.00	

Y# 1080   3 ROUBLES
33.9000 g., 0.9250 Silver 1.0081 oz. ASW, 39 mm. **Subject:** International Arctic Year

Date	Mintage	F	VF	XF	Unc	BU
2007 Proof	—				Value: 60.00	

Y# 1086   3 ROUBLES
33.9000 g., 0.9250 Silver 1.0081 oz. ASW, 39 mm. **Subject:** Academy of Arts, 250th Anniversary

Date	Mintage	F	VF	XF	Unc	BU
2007 Proof	—				Value: 60.00	

Y# 1087   3 ROUBLES
33.9000 g., 0.9250 Silver 1.0081 oz. ASW **Subject:** First Artificial Earth Satellite, 50th Anniversary

Date	Mintage	F	VF	XF	Unc	BU
2007 Proof	—				Value: 60.00	

Y# 1088   3 ROUBLES
33.9000 g., 0.9250 Silver 1.0081 oz. ASW, 39 mm. **Subject:** Andrew Rublyov

Date	Mintage	F	VF	XF	Unc	BU
2007 Proof	—				Value: 60.00	

Y# 1092   3 ROUBLES
33.9000 g., 0.9250 Silver 1.0081 oz. ASW, 39 mm. **Subject:** Bashkira, 450th Anniversary of annexation by Russia

Date	Mintage	F	VF	XF	Unc	BU
2007 Proof	—				Value: 60.00	

Y# 1100   3 ROUBLES
33.9000 g., 0.9250 Silver 1.0081 oz. ASW **Subject:** Nevyansk inclined tower, Sverdlorsk Region

Date	Mintage	F	VF	XF	Unc	BU
2007 Proof	—				Value: 60.00	

Y# 1103   3 ROUBLES
33.9000 g., 0.9250 Silver 1.0081 oz. ASW, 39 mm. **Subject:** Kazan Railway Station, Moscow

Date	Mintage	F	VF	XF	Unc	BU
2007 Proof	—				Value: 60.00	

Y# 1114   3 ROUBLES
33.9000 g., 0.9250 Silver 1.0081 oz. ASW, 39 mm. **Subject:** Year of the Rat

Date	Mintage	F	VF	XF	Unc	BU
2007 Proof	—				Value: 60.00	

Y# 1113   3 ROUBLES
33.9000 g., 0.9250 Silver 1.0081 oz. ASW, 39 mm. **Subject:** Year of the Boar

Date	Mintage	F	VF	XF	Unc	BU
2008 Proof	—				Value: 60.00	

Y# 1115   3 ROUBLES
33.9000 g., 0.9250 Silver 1.0081 oz. ASW, 39 mm. **Subject:** Russian Postage Stamp - 150th Anniversary of Introduction

Date	Mintage	F	VF	XF	Unc	BU
2008 Proof	—				Value: 60.00	

Y# 1118   3 ROUBLES
33.9000 g., 0.9250 Silver 1.0081 oz. ASW, 39 mm. **Subject:** I. M. Schenov Medical Academy, 250th Anniversary

Date	Mintage	F	VF	XF	Unc	BU
2008 Proof	—				Value: 60.00	

Y# 1119   3 ROUBLES
33.9000 g., 0.9250 Silver 1.0081 oz. ASW, 39 mm. **Subject:** Udmurtiya, 450th Anniversary of annexation into Russia

Date	Mintage	F	VF	XF	Unc	BU
2008 Proof	—				Value: 60.00	

Y# 1124   3 ROUBLES
33.9000 g., 0.9250 Silver 1.0081 oz. ASW, 39 mm. **Subject:** Cathedral of St. Demetrius, Vladimir

Date	Mintage	F	VF	XF	Unc	BU
2008 Proof	—				Value: 60.00	

Y# 1126   3 ROUBLES
33.9000 g., 0.9250 Silver 1.0081 oz. ASW, 39 mm. **Subject:** N. I. Sevastyanov, House of Trade Unions

Date	Mintage	F	VF	XF	Unc	BU
2008 Proof	—				Value: 60.00	

Y# 1127   3 ROUBLES
33.9000 g., 0.9250 Silver 1.0081 oz. ASW, 39 mm. **Subject:** Cathedral of the Nativity of our Lady, Snetogorsk

Date	Mintage	F	VF	XF	Unc	BU
2008 Proof	—				Value: 60.00	

Y# 1128   3 ROUBLES
33.9000 g., 0.9250 Silver 1.0081 oz. ASW, 39 mm. **Subject:** Assumption Church (Admiralty's)

Date	Mintage	F	VF	XF	Unc	BU
2008 Proof	—				Value: 60.00	

Y# 1129   3 ROUBLES
33.9000 g., 0.9250 Silver 1.0081 oz. ASW, 39 mm. **Subject:** St. Nicholas Cathedral, Yakutsk

Date	Mintage	F	VF	XF	Unc	BU
2008 Proof	—				Value: 60.00	

Y# 1130   3 ROUBLES
33.9000 g., 0.9250 Silver 1.0081 oz. ASW, 39 mm. **Subject:** St. Vladimir Cathedral, Zadonsk

Date	Mintage	F	VF	XF	Unc	BU
2008 Proof	—				Value: 60.00	

Y# 1138   3 ROUBLES
33.9000 g., 0.9250 Silver 1.0081 oz. ASW, 39 mm. **Subject:** European Beaver

Date	Mintage	F	VF	XF	Unc	BU
2008 Proof	—				Value: 60.00	

Y# 1147   3 ROUBLES
33.9000 g., 0.9250 Silver 1.0081 oz. ASW, 39 mm. **Subject:** Kamchatka Volcano

Date	Mintage	F	VF	XF	Unc	BU
2008 Proof	—				Value: 60.00	

Y# 1150   3 ROUBLES
33.9000 g., 0.9250 Silver 1.0081 oz. ASW, 39 mm. **Subject:** World walking Race Cup, Cheboksary

Date	Mintage	F	VF	XF	Unc	BU
2008 Proof	—				Value: 60.00	

Y# 1152   3 ROUBLES
33.9000 g., 0.9250 Silver 1.0081 oz. ASW, 39 mm. **Subject:** 29th Summer Olympics Bejing

Date	Mintage	F	VF	XF	Unc	BU
2008 Proof	—				Value: 60.00	

Y# 1180   3 ROUBLES
33.9000 g., 0.9250 Silver 1.0081 oz. ASW, 39 mm. **Subject:** St. George the Victorious

Date	Mintage	F	VF	XF	Unc	BU
2009	280,000	—	—	—	—	60.00
2010	500,000	—	—	—	—	60.00

Y# 992   3 ROUBLES
33.9000 g., 0.9250 Silver 1.0081 oz. ASW, 39 mm. **Subject:** Year of the Bull **Obv:** Double headed eagle **Rev:** Stylized bull

Date	Mintage	F	VF	XF	Unc	BU
2009 Proof	—				Value: 50.00	

Y# 1159   3 ROUBLES
33.9000 g., 0.9250 Silver 1.0081 oz. ASW, 39 mm. **Subject:** Moon research, 50th Anniversary

Date	Mintage	F	VF	XF	Unc	BU
2009 Proof	—				Value: 60.00	

Y# 1161   3 ROUBLES
33.9000 g., 0.9250 Silver 1.0081 oz. ASW, 39 mm. **Subject:** Russian Currency

Date	Mintage	F	VF	XF	Unc	BU
2009 Proof	—				Value: 60.00	

Y# 1166   3 ROUBLES
33.9000 g., 0.9250 Silver 1.0081 oz. ASW, 39 mm. **Subject:** A. P. Chekhov, 150th Anniversary of Birth

Date	Mintage	F	VF	XF	Unc	BU
2009 Proof	—				Value: 60.00	

Y# 1170   3 ROUBLES
33.9000 g., 0.9250 Silver 1.0081 oz. ASW, 39 mm. **Subject:** Kalmyk Peoples, 400th Anniversary of annexation into Russia

Date	Mintage	F	VF	XF	Unc	BU
2009 Proof	—				Value: 60.00	

Y# 1173   3 ROUBLES
33.9000 g., 0.9250 Silver 1.0081 oz. ASW, 39 mm. **Subject:** N. V. Gogol, 200th Anniversary of Birth

Date	Mintage	F	VF	XF	Unc	BU
2009 Proof	—				Value: 60.00	

Y# 1177   3 ROUBLES
33.9000 g., 0.9250 Silver 1.0081 oz. ASW, 39 mm. **Subject:** Poltava Battle, 300th Anniversary

Date	Mintage	F	VF	XF	Unc	BU
2009 Proof	—				Value: 60.00	

Y# 1182   3 ROUBLES
33.9000 g., 0.9250 Silver 1.0081 oz. ASW, 39 mm. **Subject:** Vitebsky Railway Station, St. Petersburg

Date	Mintage	F	VF	XF	Unc	BU
2009 Proof	—				Value: 60.00	

Y# 1183   3 ROUBLES
33.9000 g., 0.9250 Silver 1.0081 oz. ASW, 39 mm. **Subject:** Tula Kremlin

Date	Mintage	F	VF	XF	Unc	BU
2009 Proof	—				Value: 60.00	

Y# 1185   3 ROUBLES
33.9000 g., 0.9250 Silver 1.0081 oz. ASW, 39 mm. **Subject:** Odygitriya Church

Date	Mintage	F	VF	XF	Unc	BU
2009 Proof	—				Value: 60.00	

Y# 1188   3 ROUBLES
33.9000 g., 0.9250 Silver 1.0081 oz. ASW, 39 mm. **Subject:** Intercession Cathedral, Voronezsh

Date	Mintage	F	VF	XF	Unc	BU
2009 Proof	—				Value: 60.00	

Y# 1189   3 ROUBLES
33.9000 g., 0.9250 Silver 1.0081 oz. ASW, 39 mm. **Subject:** Tales of the Russian People

Date	Mintage	F	VF	XF	Unc	BU
2009 Proof	—				Value: 60.00	

Y# 1199   3 ROUBLES
33.9000 g., 0.9250 Silver 1.0081 oz. ASW, 39 mm. **Subject:** Velikly Novgorod

Date	Mintage	F	VF	XF	Unc	BU
2009 Proof	—				Value: 60.00	

Y# 1207   3 ROUBLES
33.9000 g., 0.9250 Silver 1.0081 oz. ASW, 39 mm. **Subject:** Fauna - Bear

Date	Mintage	F	VF	XF	Unc	BU
2009 Proof	—				Value: 60.00	

Y# 1208   3 ROUBLES
33.9000 g., 0.9250 Silver 1.0081 oz. ASW, 39 mm. **Series:** Year of the Tiger

Date	Mintage	F	VF	XF	Unc	BU
2009 Proof	—				Value: 60.00	

Y# 1214   3 ROUBLES
31.1050 g., 0.9990 Silver 0.9990 oz. ASW **Subject:** St. George the Victorious

Date	Mintage	F	VF	XF	Unc	BU
2010 Proof	—				Value: 55.00	

Y# 1219   3 ROUBLES
33.9000 g., 0.9250 Silver 1.0081 oz. ASW, 39 mm. **Subject:** Savior's Transfiguration Cathedral, Bolkhov

Date	Mintage	F	VF	XF	Unc	BU
2010 Proof	—				Value: 55.00	

Y# 1220 3 ROUBLES
33.9000 g., 0.9250 Silver 1.0081 oz. ASW, 39 mm. **Subject:** Vovnushki Battle tower

Date	Mintage	F	VF	XF	Unc	BU
2010 Proof	—	Value: 55.00				

Y# 1221 3 ROUBLES
16.8000 g., 0.9250 Silver 0.4996 oz. ASW, 33 mm. **Subject:** Holy Trinity Church, St. Petersburg

Date	Mintage	F	VF	XF	Unc	BU
2010 Proof	—	Value: 35.00				

Y# 1222 3 ROUBLES
33.9000 g., 0.9250 Silver 1.0081 oz. ASW, 39 mm. **Subject:** Round Square, Petrozavodsk

Date	Mintage	F	VF	XF	Unc	BU
2010 Proof	—	Value: 55.00				

Y# 1228 3 ROUBLES
33.9000 g., 0.9250 Silver 1.0081 oz. ASW, 39 mm. **Subject:** Bank of Russia, 150th Anniversary

Date	Mintage	F	VF	XF	Unc	BU
2010 Proof	—	Value: 55.00				

Y# 1232 3 ROUBLES
33.9000 g., 0.9250 Silver 1.0081 oz. ASW, 39 mm. **Subject:** UNESCO Heritage Site - Yaroslav

Date	Mintage	F	VF	XF	Unc	BU
2010 Proof	—	Value: 55.00				

Y# 1237 3 ROUBLES
33.9000 g., 0.9250 Silver 1.0081 oz. ASW, 39 mm. **Subject:** A. P. Chekhov, 200th Anniversary of Birth

Date	Mintage	F	VF	XF	Unc	BU
2010 Proof	—	Value: 55.00				

Y# 1241 3 ROUBLES
31.1000 g., 0.9250 Silver 0.9249 oz. ASW, 39 mm. **Subject:** Great Patriotic War, 65th Anniversary

Date	Mintage	F	VF	XF	Unc	BU
2010 Proof	—	Value: 55.00				

Y# 1242 3 ROUBLES
33.9000 g., 0.9250 Silver 1.0081 oz. ASW, 39 mm. **Subject:** Great Patriotic War, 65th Anniversary

Date	Mintage	F	VF	XF	Unc	BU
2010 Proof	—	Value: 55.00				

Y# 1243 3 ROUBLES
33.9000 g., 0.9250 Silver 1.0081 oz. ASW, 39 mm. **Subject:** Great Patriotic War, 65th Anniversary

Date	Mintage	F	VF	XF	Unc	BU
2010 Proof	—	Value: 55.00				

Y# 1247 3 ROUBLES
33.9000 g., 0.9250 Silver 1.0081 oz. ASW, 39 mm. **Subject:** Year of the Rabbit

Date	Mintage	F	VF	XF	Unc	BU
2010 Proof	—	Value: 50.00				

Y# 1251 3 ROUBLES
33.9000 g., 0.9250 Silver 1.0081 oz. ASW, 39 mm. **Subject:** EAEC, 10th Anniversary

Date	Mintage	F	VF	XF	Unc	BU
2010 Proof	—	Value: 55.00				

Y# 1252 3 ROUBLES
33.9000 g., 0.9250 Silver 1.0081 oz. ASW, 39 mm. **Subject:** EAEC, National Costumes

Date	Mintage	F	VF	XF	Unc	BU
2010 Proof	—	Value: 55.00				

Y# 1265 3 ROUBLES
31.1000 g., 0.9250 Silver 0.9249 oz. ASW **Subject:** Russian Census

Date	Mintage	F	VF	XF	Unc	BU
2010 Proof	—	Value: 55.00				

Y# 1269 3 ROUBLES
16.8000 g., 0.9250 Silver 0.4996 oz. ASW, 33 mm. **Subject:** I. K. Rodnina, Figure skater

Date	Mintage	F	VF	XF	Unc	BU
2010 Proof	—	Value: 40.00				

Y# 1270 3 ROUBLES
16.8000 g., 0.9250 Silver 0.4996 oz. ASW, 33 mm. **Subject:** A. G. Zaitsev, figure skater

Date	Mintage	F	VF	XF	Unc	BU
2010 Proof	—	Value: 40.00				

Y# 1271 3 ROUBLES
16.8000 g., 0.9250 Silver 0.4996 oz. ASW, 33 mm. **Subject:** L. A. Pakhomova, Figure skater

Date	Mintage	F	VF	XF	Unc	BU
2010 Proof	—	Value: 40.00				

Y# 1272 3 ROUBLES
16.8000 g., 0.9250 Silver 0.4996 oz. ASW, 33 mm. **Subject:** A. G. Gorshkov, Figure skater

Date	Mintage	F	VF	XF	Unc	BU
2010 Proof	—	Value: 40.00				

Y# 1273 3 ROUBLES
33.9000 g., 0.9250 Silver 1.0081 oz. ASW, 39 mm. **Subject:** 39th World Chess Olympics

Date	Mintage	F	VF	XF	Unc	BU
2010 Proof	—	Value: 55.00				

Y# 1282 3 ROUBLES
31.1050 g., 0.9990 Silver 0.9990 oz. ASW, 39 mm. **Subject:** Cathedral of the Virgin of Kazan and St. Sergiy of Radonezh, City of Kursk **Rev:** St. Sergius Kazansky Cathedral in Kursk **Edge:** Reeded

Date	Mintage	F	VF	XF	Unc	BU
2011СПМД Proof	7,500	Value: 80.00				

Y# 1285 3 ROUBLES
31.1050 g., 0.9250 Silver 0.9250 oz. ASW, 39 mm. **Rev:** Flag above five soldiers

Date	Mintage	F	VF	XF	Unc	BU
2011 Proof	3,000	Value: 75.00				

Y# 1287 3 ROUBLES
31.1050 g., 0.9990 Silver 0.9990 oz. ASW, 39 mm. **Rev:** U.A. Gagarian agains background of stars and earth in color **Edge:** Reeded

Date	Mintage	F	VF	XF	Unc	BU
2011 Proof	7,500	Value: 100				

Y# 1289 3 ROUBLES
31.1050 g., 0.9990 Silver 0.9990 oz. ASW, 39 mm. **Rev:** Female in national costume and wildlife native to Buryat flanking

Date	Mintage	F	VF	XF	Unc	BU
2011 Proof	3,000	Value: 80.00				

Y# 1293 3 ROUBLES
31.1050 g., 0.9250 Silver 0.9250 oz. ASW, 39 mm. **Subject:** 2014 Winter Olympics - Sochi - Biathlon **Rev:** Athlethe on skies with rifle, pitsunda pinecone in color at lower right

Date	Mintage	F	VF	XF	Unc	BU
2014 (2011) Proof	35,000	Value: 75.00				

Y# 1294 3 ROUBLES
31.1050 g., 0.9250 Silver 0.9250 oz. ASW, 39 mm. **Subject:** 2014 Winter Olympics - Sochi - Alpine Skiing **Rev:** Mountain skier and magnolia in color at lower right

Date	Mintage	F	VF	XF	Unc	BU
2014 (2011) Proof	35,000	Value: 90.00				

Y# 1295 3 ROUBLES
31.1050 g., 0.9250 Silver 0.9250 oz. ASW, 39 mm. **Subject:** 2014 Winter Olympics - Sochi - Figure Skater **Rev:** Figure skater and Voronov snowdrop in color at lower right

Date	Mintage	F	VF	XF	Unc	BU
2014 (2011) Proof	35,000	Value: 90.00				

Y# 1296 3 ROUBLES
31.1050 g., 0.9250 Silver 0.9250 oz. ASW, 39 mm. **Subject:** 2014 Winter Olympics - Sochi - Hockey **Rev:** Hockey player and branch of cork oak in color at lower left

Date	Mintage	F	VF	XF	Unc	BU
2014 (2011) Proof	35,000	Value: 90.00				

Y# 1315 3 ROUBLES
31.1050 g., 0.9250 Silver 0.9250 oz. ASW, 39 mm. **Rev:** Three children picking flowers and drawing

Date	Mintage	F	VF	XF	Unc	BU
2011 Proof	5,000	Value: 60.00				

Y# 1316 3 ROUBLES
31.1050 g., 0.9250 Silver 0.9250 oz. ASW, 39 mm. **Subject:** The Great Silk Way **Rev:** Camel rider against a background of desert ruins

Date	Mintage	F	VF	XF	Unc	BU
2011 Proof	5,000	Value: 60.00				

Y# 799 5 ROUBLES
6.4500 g., Copper-Nickel Clad Copper, 25 mm. **Obv:** Two headed eagle, curved bank name and denomination below **Edge:** Segmented reeding

Date	Mintage	F	VF	XF	Unc	BU
2002ММД In sets only	15,000	—	—	—	—	—
2002СПМД In sets only	15,000	—	—	—	—	—
2003ММД	15,000	—	—	150	200	250
2008ММД	—	—	—	—	3.00	4.00
2008СПМД	—	—	—	—	3.00	4.00
2009ММД	—	—	—	—	3.00	4.00
2009СПМД	—	—	—	—	4.00	5.00

Y# 829 5 ROUBLES
47.2400 g., Bi-Metallic .900 Silver 21.34g center in .900 Gold 25.9g ring, 39.5 mm. **Obv:** Double-headed eagle **Rev:** Uglich city view **Edge:** Reeded

Date	Mintage	F	VF	XF	Unc	BU
2004(sp) Proof	5,000	Value: 950				

Y# 1076 5 ROUBLES
47.2400 g., 0.9000 Silver .900 Silver 21.34g center in .900 Gold 25.9g ring 1.3669 oz. ASW, 39.5 mm. **Subject:** City of Turyev-Polsky

Date	Mintage	F	VF	XF	Unc	BU
2006 Proof	250	Value: 950				

Y# 1154 5 ROUBLES
47.2400 g., 0.9000 Silver .900 Silver 21.34g center in .900 Gold 25.9g ring 1.3669 oz. ASW, 39.5 mm. **Subject:** Pereslavl Zalessky

Date	Mintage	F	VF	XF	Unc	BU
2008 Proof	1,000	Value: 1,150				

Y# 1155 5 ROUBLES
47.2400 g., 0.9000 Silver .900 Silver 21.34g center in .900 Gold 25.9g ring 1.3669 oz. ASW, 39.5 mm. **Subject:** Alexandrov

Date	Mintage	F	VF	XF	Unc	BU
2008 Proof	—	Value: 1,150				

Y# 799a 5 ROUBLES
6.0000 g., Nickel Plated Steel, 25 mm. **Obv:** Two headed eagle, curved bank name and denomination below

Date	Mintage	F	VF	XF	Unc	BU
2009ММД	—	—	—	—	2.00	3.00
2009СПМД	—	—	—	—	2.00	3.00
2010ММД	—	—	—	—	2.00	3.00
2010СПМД	—	—	—	—	4.00	5.00
2011ММД	—	—	—	—	2.00	3.00
2011СПМД	—	—	—	—	2.00	3.00
2012ММД	—	—	—	—	2.00	3.00
2012СПМД	—	—	—	—	2.00	3.00

Y# 676 10 ROUBLES
8.2200 g., Bi-Metallic Copper-Nickel center in Brass ring, 27 mm. **Subject:** Yuri Gagarin **Obv:** Value with latent image in zero within circle and sprigs **Rev:** Helmeted bust 1/4 right **Edge:** Reeding over denomination

Date	Mintage	F	VF	XF	Unc	BU
2001ММД	10,000,000	—	—	—	4.00	5.00
2001СПМД	10,000,000	—	—	—	4.00	5.00

Y# 686 10 ROUBLES
1.6100 g., 0.9990 Gold 0.0517 oz. AGW, 12 mm. **Subject:**

Bolshoi Theater 225 Years **Obv:** Double-headed eagle within circle **Rev:** Building above number 225 **Edge:** Reeded

Date	Mintage	F	VF	XF	Unc	BU
2001 Proof	3,000	Value: 100				

Y# 739   10 ROUBLES
8.2200 g., Bi-Metallic Copper-Nickel center in Brass ring, 27 mm. **Subject:** Ancient Towns - Derbent **Obv:** Value with latent image in zero within circle and sprigs **Rev:** Shield above walled city view **Edge:** Reeding over denomination

Date	Mintage	F	VF	XF	Unc	BU
2002ММД	5,000,000	—	—	—	4.00	5.00

Y# 740   10 ROUBLES
8.2200 g., Bi-Metallic Copper-Nickel center in Brass ring, 27 mm. **Subject:** Ancient Towns - Kostroma **Obv:** Value with latent image in zero within circle and sprigs **Rev:** Cupola, shield and river view **Edge:** Reeding over denomination

Date	Mintage	F	VF	XF	Unc	BU
2002СПМД	5,000,000	—	—	—	4.00	6.00

Y# 741   10 ROUBLES
8.2200 g., Bi-Metallic Copper-Nickel center in Brass ring, 27 mm. **Subject:** Ancient Towns - Staraya Russa **Obv:** Value with latent image in zero within circle and sprigs **Rev:** Shield and cathedral **Edge:** Reeding over denomination

Date	Mintage	F	VF	XF	Unc	BU
2002СПМД	5,000,000	—	—	—	4.00	6.00

Y# 748   10 ROUBLES
8.2200 g., Bi-Metallic Copper-Nickel center in Brass ring, 27 mm. **Subject:** Ministry of Education **Obv:** Value with latent image in zero within circle and sprigs **Rev:** Seedling within open book **Edge:** Reeding over denomination

Date	Mintage	F	VF	XF	Unc	BU
2002ММД	5,000,000	—	—	—	4.00	6.00

Y# 749   10 ROUBLES
8.2200 g., Bi-Metallic Copper-Nickel center in Brass ring, 27 mm. **Subject:** Ministry of Finance **Obv:** Value with latent image in zero within circle and sprigs **Rev:** Caduceus within monogram **Edge:** Reeding over denomination

Date	Mintage	F	VF	XF	Unc	BU
2002СПМД	5,000,000	—	—	—	4.00	6.00

Y# 750   10 ROUBLES
8.2200 g., Bi-Metallic Copper-Nickel center in Brass ring, 27 mm. **Subject:** Ministry of Economic Development and Trade **Obv:** Value with latent image in zero within circle and sprigs **Rev:** Crowned double-headed eagle with cornucopia and caduceus **Edge:** Reeding over denomination

Date	Mintage	F	VF	XF	Unc	BU
2002СПМД	5,000,000	—	—	—	4.00	6.00

Y# 751   10 ROUBLES
8.2200 g., Bi-Metallic Copper-Nickel center in Brass ring, 27 mm. **Subject:** Ministry of Foreign Affairs **Obv:** Value with latent image in zero within circle and sprigs **Rev:** Crowned double-headed eagle above crossed sprigs **Edge:** Reeding over denomination

Date	Mintage	F	VF	XF	Unc	BU
2002СПМД	5,000,000	—	—	—	4.00	6.00

Y# 752   10 ROUBLES
8.2200 g., Bi-Metallic Copper-Nickel center in Brass ring, 27 mm. **Subject:** Ministry of Internal Affairs **Obv:** Value with latent image in zero within circle and sprigs **Rev:** Crowned double-headed eagle with round breast shield **Edge:** Reeding over denomination

Date	Mintage	F	VF	XF	Unc	BU
2002ММД	5,000,000	—	—	—	4.00	6.00

Y# 753   10 ROUBLES
8.2200 g., Bi-Metallic Copper-Nickel center in Brass ring, 27 mm. **Subject:** Ministry of Justice **Obv:** Value with latent image in zero within circle and sprigs **Rev:** Crowned double-headed eagle with column on breast shield **Edge:** Reeding over denomination

Date	Mintage	F	VF	XF	Unc	BU
2002СПМД	5,000,000	—	—	—	4.00	6.00

Y# 754   10 ROUBLES
8.2200 g., Bi-Metallic Copper-Nickel center in Brass ring, 27 mm. **Subject:** Russian Armed Forces **Obv:** Value with latent image in zero within circle and sprigs **Rev:** Crowned double-headed eagle with crowned pointed top shield **Edge:** Reeding over denomination

Date	Mintage	F	VF	XF	Unc	BU
2002ММД	5,000,000	—	—	—	4.00	6.00

Y# 817   10 ROUBLES
8.3400 g., Bi-Metallic Copper-Nickel center in Brass ring, 27 mm. **Obv:** Value with latent image in zero within circle and sprigs **Rev:** Murom city view and tilted oval shields within circle **Edge:** Reeded and lettered

Date	Mintage	F	VF	XF	Unc	BU
2003(sp)	5,000,000	—	—	—	4.00	6.00

Y# 800   10 ROUBLES
8.4400 g., Bi-Metallic Copper-Nickel center in Brass ring, 27.1 mm. **Subject:** Pskov **Obv:** Value with latent image in zero within circle and sprigs **Rev:** Shield above walled city **Edge:** Reeding over lettering

Date	Mintage	F	VF	XF	Unc	BU
2003СПМД	5,000,000	—	—	—	4.00	6.00

Y# 818   10 ROUBLES
8.3400 g., Bi-Metallic Copper-Nickel center in Brass ring, 27 mm. **Obv:** Value with latent image in zero within circle and sprigs **Rev:** Kasimov city view and shield within circle **Edge:** Reeded and lettered

Date	Mintage	F	VF	XF	Unc	BU
2003СПМД	5,000,000	—	—	—	4.00	6.00

Y# 819   10 ROUBLES
8.3400 g., Bi-Metallic Copper-Nickel center in Brass ring, 27 mm. **Subject:** Dorogobuzh **Obv:** Value with latent image in zero within circle and sprigs **Rev:** Monument, city view and shield within circle **Edge:** Reeded and lettered

Date	Mintage	F	VF	XF	Unc	BU
2003ММД	5,000,000	—	—	—	4.00	6.00

Y# 824   10 ROUBLES
8.4600 g., Bi-Metallic Copper-Nickel center in Brass ring, 27.1 mm. **Subject:** Town of Ryazhsk **Obv:** Value with latent image in zero within circle and sprigs **Obv. Legend:** БАНК РОССИИ **Rev:** City view and crowned shield within circle **Edge:** Reeded and lettered

Date	Mintage	F	VF	XF	Unc	BU
2004ММД	—	—	—	—	4.00	6.00

Y# 825   10 ROUBLES
8.4600 g., Bi-Metallic Copper-Nickel center in Brass ring, 27.1 mm.   **Subject:** Town of Dmitrov **Obv:** Value with latent image in zero within circle and sprigs **Obv. Legend:** БАНК РОССИИ **Rev:** City view and crowned shield within circle **Edge:** Reeded and lettered

Date	Mintage	F	VF	XF	Unc	BU
2004ММД	5,000,000	—	—	—	4.00	6.00

Y# 826   10 ROUBLES
8.4600 g., Bi-Metallic Copper-Nickel center in Brass ring, 27.1 mm.   **Subject:** Town of Kem **Obv:** Value with latent image in zero within circle and sprigs **Obv. Legend:** БАНК РОССИИ **Rev:** City view and crowned shield within circle **Edge:** Reeded and lettered

Date	Mintage	F	VF	XF	Unc	BU
2004СПМД	5,000,000	—	—	—	4.00	6.00

Y# 827   10 ROUBLES
8.4000 g., Bi-Metallic Copper-Nickel center in Brass ring, 27 mm.   **Subject:** Great Victory, 60th Anniversary **Obv:** Value with latent image in zero within circle and sprigs **Rev:** WWII eternal flame monument above date and sprig within circle **Edge:** Reeded and lettered

Date	Mintage	F	VF	XF	Unc	BU
2005ММД	30,000,000	—	—	—	4.00	6.00
2005СПМД	30,000,000	—	—	—	4.00	6.00

Y# 886   10 ROUBLES
8.2300 g., Bi-Metallic Copper-Nickel center in Brass ring, 27 mm. **Obv:** Value with latent image in zero within circle and sprigs **Rev:** Moscow coat of arms within circle **Edge:** Reeded and lettered

Date	Mintage	F	VF	XF	Unc	BU
2005ММД	10,000,000	—	—	—	4.00	6.00

Y# 887   10 ROUBLES
8.2300 g., Bi-Metallic Copper-Nickel center in Brass ring, 27 mm. **Obv:** Value with latent image in zero within circle and sprigs **Rev:** Leningrad Oblast coat of arms within circle **Edge:** Reeded and lettered

Date	Mintage	F	VF	XF	Unc	BU
2005СПМД	10,000,000	—	—	—	4.00	6.00

Y# 888   10 ROUBLES
8.2300 g., Bi-Metallic Copper-Nickel center in Brass ring, 27 mm. **Obv:** Value with latent image in zero within circle and sprigs **Rev:** Tverskaya arms within circle **Edge:** Reeded and lettered

Date	Mintage	F	VF	XF	Unc	BU
2005ММД	10,000,000	—	—	—	4.00	6.00

Y# 889   10 ROUBLES
8.2300 g., Bi-Metallic Copper-Nickel center in Brass ring, 27 mm. **Obv:** Value with latent image in zero within circle and sprigs **Rev:** Krasnodarskiy Kray coat of arms **Edge:** Reeded and lettered

Date	Mintage	F	VF	XF	Unc	BU
2005(m)	10,000,000	—	—	—	4.00	6.00

Y# 890   10 ROUBLES
8.2300 g., Bi-Metallic Copper-Nickel center in Brass ring, 27 mm. **Obv:** Value with latent image in zero within circle and sprigs **Rev:** Orlovskaya Oblast coat of arms within circle **Edge:** Reeded and lettered

Date	Mintage	F	VF	XF	Unc	BU
2005(m)	10,000,000	—	—	—	4.00	6.00

Y# 891   10 ROUBLES
8.2300 g., Bi-Metallic Copper-Nickel center in Brass ring, 27 mm. **Obv:** Value with latent image in zero within circle and sprigs **Rev:** Tatarstan Republic coat of arms within circle **Edge:** Reeded and lettered

Date	Mintage	F	VF	XF	Unc	BU
2005СПМД	10,000,000	—	—	—	4.00	6.00

Y# 943   10 ROUBLES
8.2300 g., Bi-Metallic Copper-Nickel center in Brass ring, 27.1 mm.   **Obv:** Large value **Rev:** City of Kazan and arms

Date	Mintage	F	VF	XF	Unc	BU
2005СПМД	5,000,000	—	—	—	4.00	6.00

Y# 944   10 ROUBLES
8.2300 g., Bi-Metallic Copper-Nickel center in Brass ring, 27.1 mm.   **Obv:** Large value **Rev:** City of Borovsk and arms

Date	Mintage	F	VF	XF	Unc	BU
2005СПМД	5,000,000	—	—	—	4.00	6.00

Y# 945   10 ROUBLES
8.2300 g., Bi-Metallic Copper-Nickel center in Brass ring, 27.1 mm.   **Obv:** Large value **Rev:** City of Mzensk and shield

Date	Mintage	F	VF	XF	Unc	BU
2005ММД	5,000,000	—	—	—	4.00	6.00

Y# 946   10 ROUBLES
8.2300 g., Bi-Metallic Copper-Nickel center in Brass ring, 27.1 mm.   **Obv:** Large value **Rev:** City of Kaliningrad and shield

Date	Mintage	F	VF	XF	Unc	BU
2005ММД	5,000,000	—	—	—	4.00	6.00

Y# 938   10 ROUBLES
8.2300 g., Bi-Metallic Copper-Nickel center in Brass ring, 27 mm. **Obv:** Value with latent image in zero within circle and sprigs **Rev:** Republic of Altai arms **Edge:** Lettered and reeded

Date	Mintage	F	VF	XF	Unc	BU
2006СПМД	10,000,000	—	—	—	4.00	6.00

Y# 939   10 ROUBLES
8.2300 g., Bi-Metallic Copper-Nickel center in Brass ring, 27 mm. **Obv:** Value with latent image in zero within circle and sprigs **Rev:** Chita Region arms **Edge:** Lettered and reeded

Date	Mintage	F	VF	XF	Unc	BU
2006СПМД	10,000,000	—	—	—	4.00	6.00

Y# 940   10 ROUBLES
8.2300 g., Bi-Metallic Copper-Nickel center in Brass ring, 27 mm.

Obv: Value with latent image in zero within circle and sprigs **Rev:** Primorskij Kraj Maritime Territory coat of arms **Edge:** Lettered and reeded

Date	Mintage	F	VF	XF	Unc	BU
2006ММД	10,000,000	—			4.00	6.00

Y# 941   10 ROUBLES
8.2300 g., Bi-Metallic Copper-Nickel center in Brass ring, 27 mm. **Obv:** Value with latent image in zero within circle and sprigs **Rev:** Sakha (Yakutiya) Republic coat of arms **Edge:** Lettered and reeded

Date	Mintage	F	VF	XF	Unc	BU
2006СПМД	10,000,000	—			4.00	6.00

Y# 942   10 ROUBLES
8.2300 g., Bi-Metallic Copper-Nickel center in Brass ring, 27 mm. **Obv:** Value with latent image in zero within circle and sprigs **Rev:** Sakhalinskaya Oblast coat of arms **Edge:** Lettered and reeded

Date	Mintage	F	VF	XF	Unc	BU
2006ММД	10,000,000	—			4.00	6.00

Y# 947   10 ROUBLES
8.2300 g., Bi-Metallic Copper-Nickel center in Brass ring, 27.1 mm. **Obv:** Large value **Rev:** City of Belgorod and shield

Date	Mintage	F	VF	XF	Unc	BU
2006ММД	5,000,000	—			4.00	6.00

Y# 948   10 ROUBLES
8.2300 g., Bi-Metallic Copper-Nickel center in Brass ring, 27.1 mm. **Obv:** Large value **Rev:** City of Kargopol and shield

Date	Mintage	F	VF	XF	Unc	BU
2006ММД	5,000,000	—			4.00	6.00

Y# 949   10 ROUBLES
8.2300 g., Bi-Metallic Copper-Nickel center in Brass ring, 27.1 mm. **Obv:** Large value **Rev:** City of Turzhok and shield

Date	Mintage	F	VF	XF	Unc	BU
2006СПМД	5,000,000	—			4.00	6.00

Y# 963   10 ROUBLES
8.3000 g., Bi-Metallic Copper-Nickel center in Brass ring, 27 mm. **Obv:** Value with latent image in zero within circle and sprays **Rev:** Vologda church **Edge:** Reeded and lettered **Edge Lettering:** Denomination repeated

Date	Mintage	F	VF	XF	Unc	BU
2007ММД	2,500,000	—	—		4.00	6.00
2007СПМД	2,500,000	—			4.00	6.00

Y# 964   10 ROUBLES
8.3000 g., Bi-Metallic Copper-Nickel center in Brass ring, 27 mm. **Obv:** Value with latent image in zero within circle and sprays **Rev:** Veliky Ustyug city view **Edge:** Reeded and lettered **Edge Lettering:** Denomination repeated

Date	Mintage	F	VF	XF	Unc	BU
2007ММД	2,500,000	—	—		4.00	6.00
2007СПМД	2,500,000	—			4.00	6.00

Y# 965   10 ROUBLES
8.3000 g., Bi-Metallic Copper-Nickel center in Brass ring, 27 mm. **Obv:** Value with latent image in zero within circle and sprays **Rev:** Gdov church **Edge:** Reeded and lettered **Edge Lettering:** Denomination repeated

Date	Mintage	F	VF	XF	Unc	BU
2007ММД	2,500,000	—	—		4.00	6.00
2007СПМД	2,500,000	—			4.00	6.00

Y# 970   10 ROUBLES
8.5700 g., Bi-Metallic Copper-Nickel center in Brass ring, 27.08 mm. **Obv:** Value with latent image in zero within circle and sprays **Obv. Legend:** БАНК РОССИИ **Rev:** Rostovskaya Oblast arms **Edge:** Reeded and lettered **Edge Lettering:** Denomination repeated

Date	Mintage	F	VF	XF	Unc	BU
2007СПМД	10,000,000	—			4.00	6.00

Y# 971   10 ROUBLES
8.5700 g., Bi-Metallic Copper-Nickel center in Brass ring, 27.08 mm. **Obv:** Value with latent image in zero within circle and sprays **Obv. Legend:** БАНК РОССИИ **Rev:** Khakassia Republic arms **Edge:** Reeded and lettered **Edge Lettering:** Denomination repeated

Date	Mintage	F	VF	XF	Unc	BU
2007СПМД	10,000,000	—			4.00	6.00

Y# 972   10 ROUBLES
8.5700 g., Bi-Metallic Copper-Nickel center in Brass ring, 27.08 mm. **Obv:** Value with latent image in zero within circle and sprays **Obv. Legend:** БАНК РОССИИ **Rev:** Bashkortostan Republic arms **Edge:** Reeded and lettered **Edge Lettering:** Denomination repeated

Date	Mintage	F	VF	XF	Unc	BU
2007ММД	10,000,000	—			4.00	6.00

Y# 973   10 ROUBLES
8.5700 g., Bi-Metallic Copper-Nickel center in Brass ring, 27.08 mm. **Obv:** Value with latent image in zero within circle and sprays **Obv. Legend:** БАНК РОССИИ **Rev:** Archangelskaya Oblast arms **Edge:** Reeded and lettered **Edge Lettering:** Denomination repeated

Date	Mintage	F	VF	XF	Unc	BU
2007СПМД	10,000,000	—			4.00	6.00

Y# 974   10 ROUBLES
8.5700 g., Bi-Metallic Copper-Nickel center in brass ring., 27.08 mm. **Obv:** Value with latent image in zero within circle and sprays **Obv. Legend:** БАНК РОССИИ **Rev:** Novosibirskaya Oblast arms **Edge:** Reeded and lettered **Edge Lettering:** Denomination repeated

Date	Mintage	F	VF	XF	Unc	BU
2007ММД	10,000,000	—			4.00	6.00

Y# 993   10 ROUBLES
8.2300 g., Bi-Metallic Copper-Nickel center in Brass ring **Subject:** Lipetskaya Oblast

Date	Mintage	F	VF	XF	Unc	BU
2007ММД	10,000,000	—			2.00	3.50

Y# 975   10 ROUBLES
8.2000 g., Bi-Metallic Copper-Nickel center in Brass ring, 27.1 mm. **Obv:** Value with latent image in zero within circle and sprays **Obv. Legend:** БАНК РОССИИ **Rev:** Udmurtia Republic arms **Rev. Legend:** УДМУРТСКАЯ РЕСПУБЛИКА **Edge:** Reeded and lettered **Edge Lettering:** Denomination repeated

Date	Mintage	F	VF	XF	Unc	BU
2008ММД	5,000,000	—	—	0.90	2.25	3.00
2008СПМД	5,000,000	—	—	0.90	2.25	3.00

Y# 976   10 ROUBLES
8.2800 g., Bi-Metallic Copper-Nickel center in brass ring., 27.1 mm.   **Series:** Ancient cities **Subject:** Vladimir **Obv:** Value with latent image in zero within circle and sprays **Obv. Legend:** БАНК РОССИИ **Rev:** Small shield at upper left above city view **Rev. Legend:** ВЛАДИМИР **Edge:** Reeded and lettered **Edge Lettering:** Denomination repeated

Date	Mintage	F	VF	XF	Unc	BU
2008ММД	2,500,000	—	—	0.90	2.25	3.00
2008СПМД	2,500,000	—	—	0.90	2.25	3.00

Y# 977   10 ROUBLES
8.2300 g., Bi-Metallic Copper-Nickel center in Brass ring, 27 mm. **Obv:** Value with latent image in zero within circle and sprays **Obv. Legend:** БАНК РОССИИ **Rev:** Astrakhanskaya Oblast arms **Edge:** Reeded and lettered **Edge Lettering:** Denomination repeated

Date	Mintage	F	VF	XF	Unc	BU
2008ММД	5,000,000	—	—	0.90	2.25	3.00
2008СПМД	5,000,000	—	—	0.90	2.25	3.00

Y# 978   10 ROUBLES
8.1600 g., Bi-Metallic Copper-Nickel center in brass ring, 27 mm. **Obv:** Value with latent image in zero within circle and sprays **Obv. Legend:** БАНК РОССИИ **Rev:** Sverdlovskaya Oblast arms **Edge:** Reeded and lettered **Edge Lettering:** Denomination repeated

Date	Mintage	F	VF	XF	Unc	BU
2008ММД	5,000,000	—	—	0.90	2.25	3.00
2008СПМД	5,000,000	—	—	0.90	2.25	3.00

Y# 986   10 ROUBLES
8.0800 g., Bi-Metallic Copper-Nickel center in Brass ring, 27 mm. **Rev:** Azov town view

Date	Mintage	F	VF	XF	Unc	BU
2008ММД	2,500,000	—	—	—	2.00	3.50
2008СПМД	2,500,000	—	—	—	2.00	3.50

Y# 991   10 ROUBLES
8.0800 g., Bi-Metallic Copper-Nickel center in Brass ring, 27 mm. **Rev:** Kabardino-Balkaria Republic Arms

Date	Mintage	F	VF	XF	Unc	BU
2008ММД	5,000,000	—	—	—	2.00	3.50
2008СПМД	5,000,000	—	—	—	2.00	3.50

Y# 994   10 ROUBLES
8.2300 g., Bi-Metallic Copper-Nickel center in Brass ring **Subject:** Priozersk

Date	Mintage	F	VF	XF	Unc	BU
2008ММД	2,500,000	—	—	—	2.00	3.50
2008СПМД	2,500,000	—	—	—	2.00	3.50

Y# 995   10 ROUBLES
8.2300 g., Bi-Metallic Copper-Nickel center in Brass ring **Subject:** Smolensk

Date	Mintage	F	VF	XF	Unc	BU
2008ММД	2,500,000	—	—	—	2.00	3.50
2008СПМД	2,500,000	—	—	—	2.00	3.50

Y# 998   10 ROUBLES
5.6300 g., Brass Plated Steel, 22 mm.   **Obv:** Double headed eagle **Rev:** Value

Date	Mintage	F	VF	XF	Unc	BU
2009ММД	—	—	—	—	2.50	4.00
2010ММД	—	—	—	—	2.50	4.00
2010СПМД	—	—	—	—	2.50	4.00
2011ММД	—	—	—	—	2.50	4.00
2012ММД	—	—	—	—	2.50	4.00

Y# 982   10 ROUBLES
8.0800 g., Bi-Metallic Copper-Nickel center in Brass ring, 27 mm. **Rev:** Kaluga town view

Date	Mintage	F	VF	XF	Unc	BU
2009ММД	2,500,000	—	—	—	2.00	3.50
2009СПМД	2,500,000	—	—	—	2.00	3.50

Y# 983   10 ROUBLES
8.0800 g., Bi-Metallic Copper-Nickel center in Brass ring, 27 mm. **Rev:** Vyborg town view

Date	Mintage	F	VF	XF	Unc	BU
2009ММД	2,500,000	—	—	—	2.00	3.50
2009СПМД	2,500,000	—	—	—	2.00	3.50

Y# 984   10 ROUBLES
8.0800 g., Bi-Metallic Copper-Nickel center in Brass ring, 27 mm. **Rev:** Galich town view

Date	Mintage	F	VF	XF	Unc	BU
2009ММД	2,500,000	—	—	—	2.00	3.50
2009СПМД	2,500,000	—	—	—	2.00	3.50

Y# 985   10 ROUBLES
8.0800 g., Bi-Metallic Copper-Nickel center in Brass ring, 27 mm. **Rev:** Kalmykiya Republic arms

Date	Mintage	F	VF	XF	Unc	BU
2009ММД	5,000,000	—	—	—	2.00	3.50
2009СПМД	5,000,000	—	—	—	2.00	3.50

Y# 987   10 ROUBLES
8.0800 g., Bi-Metallic Copper-Nickel center in Brass ring, 27 mm. **Rev:** Adygeya Republic arms

Date	Mintage	F	VF	XF	Unc	BU
2009ММД	5,000,000	—	—	—	2.00	3.50
2009СПМД	5,000,000	—	—	—	2.00	3.50

Y# 988   10 ROUBLES
8.0800 g., Bi-Metallic Copper-Nickel center in Brass ring, 27 mm. **Rev:** Veliky Novgorod arms

Date	Mintage	F	VF	XF	Unc	BU
2009ММД	2,500,000	—	—	—	2.00	3.50
2009СПМД	2,500,000	—	—	—	2.00	3.50

Y# 989   10 ROUBLES
8.0800 g., Bi-Metallic Copper-Nickel center in Brass ring, 27 mm. **Rev:** Jewish Autonomous Oblast Arms

Date	Mintage	F	VF	XF	Unc	BU
2009ММД	5,000,000	—	—	—	2.00	3.50
2009СПМД	5,000,000	—	—	—	2.00	3.50

Y# 996   10 ROUBLES
8.0800 g., Bi-Metallic Copper-Nickel center in Brass ring **Subject:** Komi Republic

Date	Mintage	F	VF	XF	Unc	BU
2009СПМД	10,000,000	—	—	—	2.00	3.50

Y# 997   10 ROUBLES
8.0800 g., Bi-Metallic Copper-Nickel center in Brass ring
Subject: Kirovskaya Oblast

Date	Mintage	F	VF	XF	Unc	BU
2009СПМД	10,000,000	—	—	—	2.00	3.50

Y# 1274   10 ROUBLES
8.0800 g., Bi-Metallic Copper-Nickel center in Brass ring, 27 mm.
Subject: Russian Census

Date	Mintage	F	VF	XF	Unc	BU
2010	2,300,000	—	—	—	4.00	6.00

Y# 1275   10 ROUBLES
8.0800 g., Bi-Metallic Copper-Nickel center in Brass ring, 27 mm.
Subject: Bryansk

Date	Mintage	F	VF	XF	Unc	BU
2010	10,000,000	—	—	—	4.00	6.00

Y# 1276   10 ROUBLES
8.0800 g., Bi-Metallic Copper-Nickel center in Brass ring, 27 mm.
Subject: Yurevets, Ivanovo Region

Date	Mintage	F	VF	XF	Unc	BU
2010	10,000,000	—	—	—	4.00	6.00

Y# 1277   10 ROUBLES
8.0800 g., Bi-Metallic Copper-Nickel center in Brass ring, 27 mm.
Series: Permskiy Krai

Date	Mintage	F	VF	XF	Unc	BU
2010	200,000	—	—	—	12.00	17.50

Y# 1278   10 ROUBLES
8.0800 g., Bi-Metallic Copper-Nickel center in Brass ring, 27 mm.
Subject: Nenets Autonomous Region

Date	Mintage	F	VF	XF	Unc	BU
2010	1,950,000	—	—	—	4.00	6.00

Y# 1279   10 ROUBLES
8.0800 g., Bi-Metallic Copper-Nickel center in Brass ring, 27 mm.
Subject: Chechen Republic

Date	Mintage	F	VF	XF	Unc	BU
2010	100,000	—	—	—	80.00	100

Y# 1280   10 ROUBLES
8.0800 g., Bi-Metallic Copper-Nickel center in Brass ring, 27 mm.
Subject: Yamalo-Nenetskiy Autonomous Area

Date	Mintage	F	VF	XF	Unc	BU
2010	100,000	—	—	—	20.00	27.50

Y# 1283   10 ROUBLES
8.0800 g., Bi-Metallic Copper-Nickel center in Brass ring, 27 mm.
Rev: Solikamsk town view

Date	Mintage	F	VF	XF	Unc	BU
2011ММД	—	—	—	—	2.50	4.00
2011СПМД	—	—	—	—	2.50	4.00

Y# 1284   10 ROUBLES
8.0800 g., Bi-Metallic Copper-Nickel center in Brass ring, 27 mm.
Rev: Yelets city view

Date	Mintage	F	VF	XF	Unc	BU
2011ММД	—	—	—	—	2.50	4.00
2011СПМД	—	—	—	—	2.50	4.00

Y# 1292   10 ROUBLES
8.0800 g., Bi-Metallic Copper-Nickel center in Brass ring, 27 mm.
Rev: Shield of the Republic of Buryatia

Date	Mintage	F	VF	XF	Unc	BU
2011ММД	—	—	—	—	2.50	4.00
2011СПМД	—	—	—	—	2.50	4.00

Y# 1305   10 ROUBLES
Brass Plated Steel, 22 mm. **Subject:** Belgorod **Edge:** Segmented reeding

Date	Mintage	F	VF	XF	Unc	BU
2011СПМД	10,000,000	—	—	—	2.50	4.00

Y# 1308   10 ROUBLES
Brass Plated Steel, 22 mm. **Subject:** Kursk city arms **Edge:** Segmented reeding

Date	Mintage	F	VF	XF	Unc	BU
2011СПМД	10,000,000	—	—	—	2.50	4.00

Y# 1309   10 ROUBLES
Brass Plated Steel, 22 mm. **Subject:** Orel city arms

Date	Mintage	F	VF	XF	Unc	BU
2011	10,000,000	—	—	—	2.50	4.00

Y# 1313   10 ROUBLES
8.0800 g., Bi-Metallic Copper-Nickel center in Brass ring, 27 mm.
Rev: Voronezh Region arms

Date	Mintage	F	VF	XF	Unc	BU
2011	10,000,000	—	—	—	2.50	4.00

Y# 1314   10 ROUBLES
Brass Plated Steel, 22 mm. **Rev:** Vladikavkaz city arms **Edge:** Segmented reeding

Date	Mintage	F	VF	XF	Unc	BU
2011СПМД	10,000,000	—	—	—	2.50	4.00

Y# 1318   10 ROUBLES
Brass Plated Steel, 22 mm. **Rev:** Malgobek city arms **Edge:** Segmented reeding

Date	Mintage	F	VF	XF	Unc	BU
2011СПМД	10,000,000	—	—	—	2.50	4.00

Y# 1323   10 ROUBLES
Brass Plated Steel, 22 mm. **Rev:** Rzhev city arms **Edge:** Segmented reeding

Date	Mintage	F	VF	XF	Unc	BU
2011СПМД	10,000,000	—	—	—	2.50	4.00

Y# 678   25 ROUBLES
173.2900 g., 0.9000 Silver 5.0141 oz. ASW, 60 mm. **Subject:**

Bolshoi Theater 225 Years **Obv:** Double-headed eagle **Rev:** Dancing couple scene **Edge:** Reeded **Note:** Illustration reduced.

Date	Mintage	F	VF	XF	Unc	BU
2001 Proof	2,000	Value: 285				

Y# 683   25 ROUBLES

173.2900 g., 0.9000 Silver 5.0141 oz. ASW, 60 mm. **Subject:** Siberian Exploration **Obv:** Double-headed eagle **Rev:** Standing king and river boats **Edge:** Reeded **Note:** Illustration reduced.

Date	Mintage	F	VF	XF	Unc	BU
2001 Proof	1,000	Value: 350				

Y# 794   25 ROUBLES

173.1300 g., 0.9000 Silver 5.0094 oz. ASW, 60.2 mm. **Subject:** Foundation of Russian Savings Banks **Obv:** Double-headed eagle **Rev:** Czar Nicholas I and document **Edge:** Reeded

Date	Mintage	F	VF	XF	Unc	BU
2001(m) Proof	10,500	Value: 225				

Y# 687   25 ROUBLES

3.2000 g., 0.9990 Gold 0.1028 oz. AGW, 16 mm. **Subject:** Bolshoi Theater **Obv:** Double-headed eagle **Rev:** Ballerina **Edge:** Reeded

Date	Mintage	F	VF	XF	Unc	BU
2001 Proof	2,500	Value: 200				

Y# 999   25 ROUBLES

169.0000 g., 0.9250 Silver 5.0258 oz. ASW, 60 mm. **Subject:** Bolshoi Theater, 225th Anniversary

Date	Mintage	F	VF	XF	Unc	BU
2001 Proof	—	Value: 285				

Y# 1000   25 ROUBLES

169.0000 g., 0.9250 Silver 5.0258 oz. ASW, 60 mm. **Subject:** Savings Bank

Date	Mintage	F	VF	XF	Unc	BU
2001 Proof	—	Value: 285				

Y# 1001   25 ROUBLES

169.0000 g., 0.9250 Silver 5.0258 oz. ASW, 60 mm. **Subject:** Siberia - Development and Exploration

Date	Mintage	F	VF	XF	Unc	BU
2001 Proof	—	Value: 285				

Y# 777   25 ROUBLES

173.2900 g., 0.9000 Silver 5.0141 oz. ASW, 60 mm. **Subject:** Czar Alexander I **Obv:** Double-headed eagle **Rev:** Head right and crowned double-headed eagle above document text **Edge:** Reeded **Note:** Illustration reduced.

Date	Mintage	F	VF	XF	Unc	BU
2002(m) Proof	1,500	Value: 300				

Y# 785   25 ROUBLES

173.2900 g., 0.9000 Silver 5.0141 oz. ASW, 60 mm. **Subject:** Admiral Nakhimov **Obv:** Double-headed eagle **Rev:** Admiral watching naval battle **Edge:** Reeded **Note:** Illustration reduced.

Date	Mintage	F	VF	XF	Unc	BU
2002(sp) Proof	2,000	Value: 250				

Y# 790   25 ROUBLES

173.2900 g., 0.9000 Silver 5.0141 oz. ASW, 60 mm. **Subject:** Hermitage **Obv:** Double-headed eagle **Rev:** Staircase viewed through doorway **Edge:** Reeded **Note:** Illustration reduced.

Date	Mintage	F	VF	XF	Unc	BU
2002(sp) Proof	2,000	Value: 250				

Y# 743   25 ROUBLES

3.2000 g., 0.9990 Gold 0.1028 oz. AGW, 16 mm. **Subject:** Zodiac Signs **Obv:** Double-headed eagle within beaded circle **Rev:** Leo **Edge:** Reeded

Date	Mintage	F	VF	XF	Unc	BU
2002 Proof	10,000	Value: 200				

Y# 763   25 ROUBLES

3.2000 g., 0.9990 Gold 0.1028 oz. AGW, 16 mm. **Subject:** Zodiac Signs **Obv:** Double-headed eagle within beaded circle **Rev:** Capricorn **Edge:** Reeded

Date	Mintage	F	VF	XF	Unc	BU
2002(m)	10,000	—	—	—	—	200

Y# 764   25 ROUBLES

3.2000 g., 0.9990 Gold 0.1028 oz. AGW, 16 mm. **Subject:** Zodiac Signs **Obv:** Double-headed eagle within beaded circle **Rev:** Virgo **Edge:** Reeded

Date	Mintage	F	VF	XF	Unc	BU
2002(sp)	10,000	—	—	—	—	200

Y# 765   25 ROUBLES

3.2000 g., 0.9990 Gold 0.1028 oz. AGW, 16 mm. **Subject:**

Zodiac Signs **Obv:** Double-headed eagle within beaded circle **Rev:** Sagittarius **Edge:** Reeded

Date	Mintage	F	VF	XF	Unc	BU
2002(SP)	10,000	—	—	—	—	200

Y# 767   25 ROUBLES

3.2000 g., 0.9990 Gold 0.1028 oz. AGW, 16 mm. **Subject:** Zodiac signs **Obv:** Double-headed eagle within beaded circle **Rev:** Scorpio **Edge:** Reeded

Date	Mintage	F	VF	XF	Unc	BU
2002(m)	10,000	—	—	—	—	200

Y# 769   25 ROUBLES

3.2000 g., 0.9990 Gold 0.1028 oz. AGW **Subject:** Zodiac Signs **Obv:** Double-headed eagle within beaded circle **Rev:** Libra **Edge:** Reeded

Date	Mintage	F	VF	XF	Unc	BU
2002(sp)	10,000	—	—	—	—	200

Y# 821   25 ROUBLES

3.2000 g., 0.9990 Gold 0.1028 oz. AGW, 16 mm. **Subject:** Zodiac signs **Obv:** Double-headed eagle within beaded circle **Rev:** Cancer **Edge:** Reeded

Date	Mintage	F	VF	XF	Unc	BU
2003(sp)	50,000	—	—	—	—	200

Y# 864   25 ROUBLES

172.8000 g., 0.9000 Silver 4.9999 oz. ASW, 60 mm. **Rev:** St. Sercius Monastery

Date	Mintage	F	VF	XF	Unc	BU
2003 Proof	2,000	Value: 285				

Y# 865   25 ROUBLES

172.8000 g., 0.9000 Silver 4.9999 oz. ASW, 60 mm. **Rev:** Shlisselburg

Date	Mintage	F	VF	XF	Unc	BU
2003(m) Proof	2,000	Value: 285				

Y# 866   25 ROUBLES

172.8000 g., 0.9000 Silver 4.9999 oz. ASW, 60 mm. **Rev:** Kamchatka

Date	Mintage	F	VF	XF	Unc	BU
2003	2,000	Value: 285				

Y# 1003   25 ROUBLES

169.0000 g., 0.9250 Silver 5.0258 oz. ASW, 60 mm. **Subject:** Aquarius

Date	Mintage	F	VF	XF	Unc	BU
2003 Proof	—	Value: 285				

Y# 1004   25 ROUBLES

169.0000 g., 0.9250 Silver 5.0258 oz. ASW, 60 mm. **Subject:** Pisces

Date	Mintage	F	VF	XF	Unc	BU
2003 Proof	—	Value: 285				

Y# 1005   25 ROUBLES

169.0000 g., 0.9250 Silver 5.0258 oz. ASW, 60 mm. **Subject:** Aries

Date	Mintage	F	VF	XF	Unc	BU
2003 Proof	—	Value: 285				

Y# 1006   25 ROUBLES

169.0000 g., 0.9250 Silver 5.0258 oz. ASW, 60 mm. **Subject:** Taurus

Date	Mintage	F	VF	XF	Unc	BU
2003 Proof	—	Value: 285				

Y# 830   25 ROUBLES

177.9600 g., 0.9000 Bi-Metallic .900 Silver 172.78g planchet with .900 Gold 5.18g insert 5.1492 oz., 60 mm.   **Subject:** Monetary reform of Peter the Great **Obv:** Double-headed eagle **Rev:** Gold insert replicating the obverse and reverse designs of a 1704 one rouble coin **Edge:** Reeded **Note:** Illustration reduced.

Date	Mintage	F	VF	XF	Unc	BU
2004(sp) Proof	1,000	Value: 950				

Y# 867   25 ROUBLES

172.8000 g., 0.9000 Silver 4.9999 oz. ASW, 60 mm.   **Rev:** Valaam Church

Date	Mintage	F	VF	XF	Unc	BU
2004	1,500	Value: 300				

Y# 1014   25 ROUBLES

169.0000 g., 0.9250 Silver 5.0258 oz. ASW, 60 mm.   **Subject:** 2nd Kamchatka Expedition, 1733-43

Date	Mintage	F	VF	XF	Unc	BU
2004 Proof	—	Value: 285				

Y# 1019   25 ROUBLES

169.0000 g., 0.9250 Silver 5.0258 oz. ASW, 60 mm.   **Subject:** Holy Trinity - St. Sergius Lavra in Sergiev Posad

Date	Mintage	F	VF	XF	Unc	BU
2004 Proof	—	Value: 285				

Y# 1023   25 ROUBLES

169.0000 g., 0.9250 Silver 5.0258 oz. ASW, 60 mm.   **Subject:** Reindeer

Date	Mintage	F	VF	XF	Unc	BU
2004 Proof	—	Value: 285				

Y# 898   25 ROUBLES

3.2000 g., 0.9990 Gold 0.1028 oz. AGW, 16 mm.   **Obv:** Double-headed eagle **Rev:** Gemini twins **Edge:** Reeded

Date	Mintage	F	VF	XF	Unc	BU
2005	10,000	—	—	—	—	200

Y# 900   25 ROUBLES

3.2000 g., 0.9990 Gold 0.1028 oz. AGW, 16 mm.   **Obv:** Double-headed eagle **Rev:** Cancer crawfish **Edge:** Reeded

Date	Mintage	F	VF	XF	Unc	BU
2005 Proof	10,000	Value: 200				

Y# 902   25 ROUBLES

3.2000 g., 0.9990 Gold 0.1028 oz. AGW, 16 mm.   **Obv:** Double-headed eagle **Rev:** Leo lion **Edge:** Reeded

Date	Mintage	F	VF	XF	Unc	BU
2005	10,000	—	—	—	—	200

Y# 915   25 ROUBLES

3.2000 g., 0.9990 Gold 0.1028 oz. AGW, 16 mm.   **Obv:** Double-headed eagle **Rev:** Virgos standing lady **Edge:** Reeded

Date	Mintage	F	VF	XF	Unc	BU
2005 Proof	10,000	Value: 200				

Y# 920   25 ROUBLES

3.2000 g., 0.9990 Gold 0.1028 oz. AGW, 16 mm.   **Obv:** Double-headed eagle **Rev:** Two stylized birds forming balance scale **Edge:** Reeded

Date	Mintage	F	VF	XF	Unc	BU
2005	10,000	—	—	—	—	200

Y# 922   25 ROUBLES

3.2000 g., 0.9990 Gold 0.1028 oz. AGW, 16 mm.   **Obv:** Double-headed eagle **Rev:** Scorpio scorpion **Edge:** Reeded

Date	Mintage	F	VF	XF	Unc	BU
2005	10,000	—	—	—	—	200

Y# 927   25 ROUBLES

3.2000 g., 0.9990 Gold 0.1028 oz. AGW, 16 mm.   **Obv:** Double-headed eagle **Rev:** Sagittarius the archer **Edge:** Reeded

Date	Mintage	F	VF	XF	Unc	BU
2005	10,000	—	—	—	—	200

Y# 929   25 ROUBLES

3.2000 g., 0.9990 Gold 0.1028 oz. AGW, 16 mm.   **Obv:** Double-headed eagle **Rev:** Capricorn as half goat and fish **Edge:** Reeded

Date	Mintage	F	VF	XF	Unc	BU
2005	10,000	—	—	—	—	200

Y# 931   25 ROUBLES

3.2000 g., 0.9990 Gold 0.1028 oz. AGW, 16 mm.   **Obv:** Double-headed eagle **Rev:** Pisces as catfish and sturgeon **Edge:** Reeded

Date	Mintage	F	VF	XF	Unc	BU
2005	10,000	—	—	—	—	200

Y# 933   25 ROUBLES

3.2000 g., 0.9990 Gold 0.1028 oz. AGW, 16 mm.   **Obv:** Double-headed eagle **Rev:** Aries ram **Edge:** Reeded

Date	Mintage	F	VF	XF	Unc	BU
2005	10,000	—	—	—	—	200

Y# 935   25 ROUBLES

3.2000 g., 0.9990 Gold 0.1028 oz. AGW, 16 mm.   **Obv:** Double-headed eagle **Rev:** Taurus bull **Edge:** Reeded

Date	Mintage	F	VF	XF	Unc	BU
2005	10,000	—	—	—	—	200

Y# 937   25 ROUBLES

3.2000 g., 0.9990 Gold 0.1028 oz. AGW, 16 mm.   **Obv:** Double-headed eagle **Rev:** Aquarius water carrier **Edge:** Reeded

Date	Mintage	F	VF	XF	Unc	BU
2005	10,000	—	—	—	—	200

Y# 924   25 ROUBLES

169.0000 g., 0.9250 Silver 5.0258 oz. ASW, 60 mm.   **Subject:** 625th Anniversary - Battle of Kulikovo **Obv:** Double-headed eagle **Rev:** Mounted warriors above and below crossed swords **Edge:** Reeded **Note:** Illustration reduced.

Date	Mintage	F	VF	XF	Unc	BU
2005 Proof	1,500	Value: 300				

Y# 1047   25 ROUBLES

169.0000 g., 0.9250 Silver 5.0258 oz. ASW, 60 mm.   **Subject:** Tretyakov State Galler, 150th Anniversary

Date	Mintage	F	VF	XF	Unc	BU
2006 Proof	—	Value: 285				

Y# 1050   25 ROUBLES

169.0000 g., 0.9250 Silver 5.0258 oz. ASW, 60 mm.   **Subject:** Malye Korely

Date	Mintage	F	VF	XF	Unc	BU
2006 Proof	—	Value: 285				

Y# 1051   25 ROUBLES

169.0000 g., 0.9250 Silver 5.0258 oz. ASW, 60 mm.   **Subject:** Tikhvin Monastery, Dome of the Mother of God

Date	Mintage	F	VF	XF	Unc	BU
2006 Proof	—	Value: 285				

Y# 1053   25 ROUBLES

169.0000 g., 0.9250 Silver 5.0258 oz. ASW, 60 mm.   **Subject:** Konevsky Monastery of St. Virgin's Nativity

Date	Mintage	F	VF	XF	Unc	BU
2006 Proof	—	Value: 285				

Y# 969   25 ROUBLES

169.0000 g., 0.9250 Silver 5.0258 oz. ASW, 60.00 mm.   **Obv:** Two-headed eagle **Rev:** Vyatka St. Trifon Monastery of the Assumption, Kirov **Edge:** Reeded **Note:** Illustration reduced

Date	Mintage	F	VF	XF	Unc	BU
2007(sp) Proof	2,000	Value: 285				

Y# 1083   25 ROUBLES

169.0000 g., 0.9250 Silver 5.0258 oz. ASW, 60 mm.   **Subject:** Russian Railways, 150th Anniversary

Date	Mintage	F	VF	XF	Unc	BU
2007 Proof	—	Value: 285				

Y# 1084   25 ROUBLES
169.0000 g., 0.9250 Silver 5.0258 oz. ASW, 60 mm. **Subject:**
F. A. Golovin, first Order of St. Andrew awardee

Date	Mintage	F	VF	XF	Unc	BU
2007 Proof	—				Value: 285	

Y# 1101   25 ROUBLES
169.0000 g., 0.9250 Silver 5.0258 oz. ASW, 60 mm. **Subject:**
St. Artemy Verkolsky Monastery, Arkhamgelsk

Date	Mintage	F	VF	XF	Unc	BU
2007 Proof	—				Value: 285	

Y# 1102   25 ROUBLES
169.0000 g., 0.9250 Silver 5.0258 oz. ASW, 60 mm. **Subject:**
Pskov-Pechersky Holy Monastery of the Assumption

Date	Mintage	F	VF	XF	Unc	BU
2007 Proof	—				Value: 285	

Y# 1116   25 ROUBLES
169.0000 g., 0.9250 Silver 5.0258 oz. ASW, 60 mm. **Subject:**
Goznak, 190th Anniversary

Date	Mintage	F	VF	XF	Unc	BU
2008 Proof	—				Value: 285	

Y# 1125   25 ROUBLES
169.0000 g., 0.9250 Silver 5.0258 oz. ASW, 60 mm. **Subject:**
Astrakhan Kremlin

Date	Mintage	F	VF	XF	Unc	BU
2008 Proof	—				Value: 325	

Y# 1139   25 ROUBLES
169.0000 g., 0.9250 Silver 5.0258 oz. ASW, 60 mm. **Subject:**
European Beaver

Date	Mintage	F	VF	XF	Unc	BU
2008 Proof	—				Value: 325	

Y# 1160   25 ROUBLES
168.0000 g., 0.9250 Silver 4.9960 oz. ASW, 60 mm. **Subject:**
Alexander I Monument, 175th Anniversary

Date	Mintage	F	VF	XF	Unc	BU
2009 Proof	—				Value: 285	

Y# 1178   25 ROUBLES
168.0000 g., 0.9250 Silver 4.9960 oz. ASW, 60 mm. **Subject:**
Poltava Battle, 300th Anniversary

Date	Mintage	F	VF	XF	Unc	BU
2009 Proof	—				Value: 285	

Y# 1184   25 ROUBLES
168.0000 g., 0.9250 Silver 4.9960 oz. ASW, 60 mm. **Subject:**
Arkhangelskoye Museum

Date	Mintage	F	VF	XF	Unc	BU
2009 Proof	—				Value: 285	

Y# 1186   25 ROUBLES
168.0000 g., 0.9250 Silver 4.9960 oz. ASW, 60 mm. **Subject:**
St. Trinity Monastery, Pensu Region

Date	Mintage	F	VF	XF	Unc	BU
2009 Proof	—				Value: 285	

Y# 1187   25 ROUBLES
168.0000 g., 0.9250 Silver 4.9960 oz. ASW, 60 mm. **Subject:**
St. Nikolas Monastery, Staraya Ladoga

Date	Mintage	F	VF	XF	Unc	BU
2009 Proof	—				Value: 285	

Y# 1200   25 ROUBLES
168.0000 g., 0.9250 Silver 4.9960 oz. ASW, 60 mm. **Subject:**
Velikly Novgorod

Date	Mintage	F	VF	XF	Unc	BU
2009 Proof	—				Value: 285	

Y# 1223   25 ROUBLES
168.0000 g., 0.9250 Silver 4.9960 oz. ASW, 60 mm. **Subject:**
Khmelita, Griboyedov family estate

Date	Mintage	F	VF	XF	Unc	BU
2010 Proof	—				Value: 285	

Y# 1224   25 ROUBLES
168.0000 g., 0.9250 Silver 4.9960 oz. ASW, 60 mm. **Subject:**
Kirillo Belosersk Monastery

Date	Mintage	F	VF	XF	Unc	BU
2010 Proof	—				Value: 285	

Y# 1225   25 ROUBLES
168.0000 g., 0.9250 Silver 4.9960 oz. ASW, 60 mm. **Subject:**
Alezxandro - Svirsky Monestary

Date	Mintage	F	VF	XF	Unc	BU
2010 Proof	—				Value: 285	

Y# 1226   25 ROUBLES
168.0000 g., 0.9250 Silver 4.9960 oz. ASW, 60 mm. **Subject:**
Sanaksarsky Monestary

Date	Mintage	F	VF	XF	Unc	BU
2010 Proof	—				Value: 285	

Y# 1229   25 ROUBLES
168.0000 g., 0.9250 Silver 4.9960 oz. ASW, 60 mm. **Subject:**
Bank of Russia, 150th Anniversary

Date	Mintage	F	VF	XF	Unc	BU
2010 Proof	—				Value: 285	

Y# 1233   25 ROUBLES
169.0000 g., 0.9250 Silver 5.0258 oz. ASW, 60 mm. **Subject:**
UNESCO Heritage Site - Yaroslav

Date	Mintage	F	VF	XF	Unc	BU
2010 Proof	—				Value: 285	

Y# 1304   25 ROUBLES
155.5000 g., 0.9250 Silver 4.6243 oz. ASW, 60 mm. **Subject:**
Virgin Mary Monastery, Kazan **Rev:** Icon in color and building
complex

Date	Mintage	F	VF	XF	Unc	BU
2011 Proof	2,000				Value: 250	

Y# 1298   25 ROUBLES
Copper-Nickel, 27 mm. **Subject:** 2014 Winter Olympics - Sochi
Rev: Mountain

Date	Mintage	F	VF	XF	Unc	BU
2011	10,000,000	—	—	—	—	40.00

Y# 1306   25 ROUBLES
155.5000 g., 0.9250 Silver 4.6243 oz. ASW, 60 mm. **Subject:**
Pavlovsky Palace and park **Rev:** Hilltop building, bridge in
forefront, female statues flankings **Edge:** Reeded

Date	Mintage	F	VF	XF	Unc	BU
2011 Proof	1,500				Value: 250	

Y# 1317 25 ROUBLES
155.5000 g., 0.9250 Silver 4.6243 oz. ASW, 60 mm. **Subject:** Virgin's Saint Entrance Presentation Monastery, Optin **Rev:** Monastery buildings

Date	Mintage	F	VF	XF	Unc	BU
2011 Proof	2,000	Value: 250				

Y# 1321 25 ROUBLES
155.5000 g., 0.9250 Silver 4.6243 oz. ASW, 60 mm. **Subject:** Year of Italian Culture and Language in Russia **Rev:** Town vies of Sergiev Posad and Bari, Icon at center, Russian and Italian flags below in color

Date	Mintage	F	VF	XF	Unc	BU
2011 Proof	1,000	Value: 250				

Y# 1322 25 ROUBLES
155.5000 g., 0.9250 Silver 4.6243 oz. ASW, 60 mm. **Subject:** Kazan Cathedral, St. Petersburg **Rev:** Ariel view of Cathedral and plaza **Edge:** Reeded

Date	Mintage	F	VF	XF	Unc	BU
2011 Proof	1,500	Value: 250				

Y# 679 50 ROUBLES
8.7500 g., 0.9990 Gold 0.2810 oz. AGW, 22.6 mm. **Subject:** Bolshoi Theater **Obv:** Double-headed eagle within beaded circle **Rev:** Dueling figures **Edge:** Reeded

Date	Mintage	F	VF	XF	Unc	BU
2001 Proof	2,000	Value: 475				

Y# 684 50 ROUBLES
8.7500 g., 0.9000 Gold 0.2532 oz. AGW, 22.6 mm. **Subject:** Siberian Exploration **Obv:** Double-headed eagle within beaded circle **Rev:** Head with hat 1/4 right and boat **Edge:** Reeded

Date	Mintage	F	VF	XF	Unc	BU
2001 Proof	1,500	Value: 475				

Y# 757 50 ROUBLES
8.6444 g., 0.9000 Gold 0.2501 oz. AGW, 22.6 mm. **Subject:** Olympics **Obv:** Double-headed eagle within beaded circle **Rev:** Figure skater and flying eagle **Edge:** Reeded

Date	Mintage	F	VF	XF	Unc	BU
2002 Proof	3,000	Value: 475				

Y# 782 50 ROUBLES
7.8900 g., 0.9990 Gold 0.2534 oz. AGW, 22.6 mm. **Subject:** Works of Dionissy **Obv:** Double-headed eagle within beaded circle **Rev:** Half-length figure holding child flanked by double headed eagle and church **Edge:** Reeded

Date	Mintage	F	VF	XF	Unc	BU
2002(m) Proof	1,500	Value: 475				

Y# 786 50 ROUBLES
8.7500 g., 0.9000 Gold 0.2532 oz. AGW, 22.6 mm. **Subject:** Admiral Nakhimov **Obv:** Double-headed eagle within beaded circle **Rev:** Bust facing within circle above flags and anchor **Edge:** Reeded

Date	Mintage	F	VF	XF	Unc	BU
2002(sp) Proof	1,500	Value: 475				

Y# 788 50 ROUBLES
8.7500 g., 0.9000 Gold 0.2532 oz. AGW, 22.6 mm. **Subject:** World Cup Soccer **Obv:** Double-headed eagle within beaded circle **Rev:** Stylized player kicking soccer ball **Edge:** Reeded

Date	Mintage	F	VF	XF	Unc	BU
2002(m) Proof	3,000	Value: 475				

Y# 822 50 ROUBLES
7.8900 g., 0.9990 Gold 0.2534 oz. AGW, 22.6 mm. **Subject:** Zodiac Signs **Obv:** Double-headed eagle within beaded circle **Rev:** Virgo **Edge:** Reeded

Date	Mintage	F	VF	XF	Unc	BU
2003(sp)	30,000	—	—	—	—	475

Y# 823 50 ROUBLES
7.8900 g., 0.9990 Gold 0.2534 oz. AGW, 22.6 mm. **Subject:** Zodiac signs **Obv:** Double-headed eagle within beaded circle **Rev:** Libra **Edge:** Reeded

Date	Mintage	F	VF	XF	Unc	BU
2003(m)	30,000	—	—	—	—	475

Y# 868 50 ROUBLES
8.6400 g., 0.9000 Gold 0.2500 oz. AGW, 23 mm. **Rev:** Peter I monetary reform

Date	Mintage	F	VF	XF	Unc	BU
2003(m) Proof	1,500	Value: 475				

Y# 869 50 ROUBLES
8.6400 g., 0.9000 Gold 0.2500 oz. AGW, 23 mm. **Rev:** Ski race

Date	Mintage	F	VF	XF	Unc	BU
2003(m) Proof	1,500	Value: 475				

Y# 1007 50 ROUBLES
169.0000 g., 0.9250 Silver 5.0258 oz. ASW, 60 mm. **Subject:** Leo

Date	Mintage	F	VF	XF	Unc	BU
2003 Proof	—	Value: 475				

Y# 1008 50 ROUBLES
169.0000 g., 0.9250 Silver 5.0258 oz. ASW, 60 mm. **Subject:** Leo

Date	Mintage	F	VF	XF	Unc	BU
2003 Proof	—	Value: 475				

Y# 1009 50 ROUBLES
7.7900 g., 0.9990 Gold 0.2502 oz. AGW, 22.6 mm. **Subject:** Scorpion

Date	Mintage	F	VF	XF	Unc	BU
2003 Proof	—	Value: 475				

Y# 1010 50 ROUBLES
7.7800 g., 0.9990 Gold 0.2499 oz. AGW, 22.6 mm. **Subject:** Sagatarius

Date	Mintage	F	VF	XF	Unc	BU
2003 Proof	—	Value: 475				

Y# 1011 50 ROUBLES
7.7800 g., 0.9990 Gold 0.2499 oz. AGW, 22.6 mm. **Subject:** Capricorn

Date	Mintage	F	VF	XF	Unc	BU
2003 Proof	—	Value: 475				

Y# 870 50 ROUBLES
8.6400 g., 0.9000 Gold 0.2500 oz. AGW, 23 mm. **Rev:** Soccer player

Date	Mintage	F	VF	XF	Unc	BU
2004(sp) Proof	1,000	Value: 475				

Y# 871 50 ROUBLES
8.6400 g., 0.9000 Gold 0.2500 oz. AGW, 23 mm. **Rev:** Olympic athletes

Date	Mintage	F	VF	XF	Unc	BU
2004(m) Proof	2,000	Value: 475				

Y# 872 50 ROUBLES
8.6400 g., 0.9000 Gold 0.2500 oz. AGW, 23 mm. **Rev:** Virgin of the Son Icon

Date	Mintage	F	VF	XF	Unc	BU
2004(m) Proof	1,500	Value: 475				

Y# 1016 50 ROUBLES
7.7800 g., 0.9990 Gold 0.2499 oz. AGW, 22.6 mm. **Subject:** Theophanes the Greek

Date	Mintage	F	VF	XF	Unc	BU
2004 Proof	—	Value: 475				

Y# 1025 50 ROUBLES
7.7800 g., 0.9990 Gold 0.2499 oz. AGW, 22.6 mm. **Subject:** Reindeer

Date	Mintage	F	VF	XF	Unc	BU
2004 Proof	—	Value: 475				

Y# 1030 50 ROUBLES
7.7800 g., 0.9990 Gold 0.2499 oz. AGW, 22.6 mm. **Subject:** Aquarius

Date	Mintage	F	VF	XF	Unc	BU
2004 Proof	—	Value: 475				

Y# 1031 50 ROUBLES
7.7800 g., 0.9990 Gold 0.2499 oz. AGW, 22.6 mm.

Date	Mintage	F	VF	XF	Unc	BU
2004 Proof	—	Value: 475				

Y# 1032 50 ROUBLES
7.7800 g., 0.9990 Gold 0.2499 oz. AGW, 22.6 mm. **Subject:** Aries

Date	Mintage	F	VF	XF	Unc	BU
2004 Proof	—	Value: 475				

Y# 1033 50 ROUBLES
7.7800 g., 0.9990 Gold 0.2499 oz. AGW, 22.6 mm. **Subject:** Taurus

Date	Mintage	F	VF	XF	Unc	BU
2004 Proof	—	Value: 475				

Y# 1034 50 ROUBLES
7.7800 g., 0.9990 Gold 0.2499 oz. AGW, 22.6 mm. **Subject:** Gemni

Date	Mintage	F	VF	XF	Unc	BU
2004 Proof	—	Value: 475				

Y# 1035   50 ROUBLES
7.7800 g., 0.9990 Gold 0.2499 oz. AGW, 22.6 mm. **Subject:** Cancer

Date	Mintage	F	VF	XF	Unc	BU
2004 Proof	—	Value: 475				

Y# 894   50 ROUBLES
7.8900 g., 0.9990 Gold 0.2534 oz. AGW, 22.6 mm. **Subject:** 60th Anniversary - Victory Over Germany **Obv:** Double-headed eagle **Rev:** 60th Anniversary - Victory Over Germany medal **Edge:** Reeded

Date	Mintage	F	VF	XF	Unc	BU
2005 Proof	7,000	Value: 475				

Y# 907   50 ROUBLES
7.8900 g., 0.9990 Gold 0.2534 oz. AGW, 22.6 mm. **Subject:** Helsinki Games **Obv:** Double-headed eagle **Rev:** Stylized track and field athletes **Edge:** Reeded

Date	Mintage	F	VF	XF	Unc	BU
2005 Proof	1,500	Value: 475				

Y# 911   50 ROUBLES
7.8900 g., 0.9990 Gold 0.2534 oz. AGW, 22.6 mm. **Obv:** Double-headed eagle **Rev:** Kazan University Building **Edge:** Reeded

Date	Mintage	F	VF	XF	Unc	BU
2005 Proof	1,500	Value: 475				

Y# 1049   50 ROUBLES
7.7800 g., 0.9990 Gold 0.2499 oz. AGW, 22.6 mm. **Subject:** St. George the Victorious

Date	Mintage	F	VF	XF	Unc	BU
2006 Proof	—	Value: 475				

Y# 1063   50 ROUBLES
7.7800 g., 0.9990 Gold 0.2499 oz. AGW, 22.6 mm. **Subject:** Moscow's Kremlin and Red Square

Date	Mintage	F	VF	XF	Unc	BU
2006 Proof	—	Value: 475				

Y# 1067   50 ROUBLES
7.7800 g., 0.9990 Gold 0.2499 oz. AGW, 22.6 mm. **Subject:** XX Winter Olympics, Torino

Date	Mintage	F	VF	XF	Unc	BU
2006 Proof	—	Value: 475				

Y# 1068   50 ROUBLES
7.7800 g., 0.9990 Gold 0.2499 oz. AGW, 22.6 mm. **Subject:** FIFA World Cup, Germany

Date	Mintage	F	VF	XF	Unc	BU
2006 Proof	—	Value: 475				

Y# 1090   50 ROUBLES
7.7800 g., 0.9990 Gold 0.2499 oz. AGW, 22.6 mm. **Subject:** Andrew Rublyov

Date	Mintage	F	VF	XF	Unc	BU
2007 Proof	—	Value: 475				

Y# 1094   50 ROUBLES
7.7800 g., 0.9250 Gold 0.2314 oz. AGW, 22.6 mm. **Subject:** Bashkiria, 450th Anniversary of of annexation by Russia

Date	Mintage	F	VF	XF	Unc	BU
2007 Proof	—	Value: 475				

Y# 1097   50 ROUBLES
7.7800 g., 0.9990 Gold 0.2499 oz. AGW, 22.6 mm. **Subject:** Khakassia, 300th Anniversary of of annexation by Russia

Date	Mintage	F	VF	XF	Unc	BU
2007 Proof	—	Value: 475				

Y# 1099   50 ROUBLES
7.7800 g., 0.9990 Gold 0.2499 oz. AGW, 22.6 mm. **Subject:** St. George the Victorious

Date	Mintage	F	VF	XF	Unc	BU
2007 Proof	—	Value: 475				

Y# 1121   50 ROUBLES
7.7800 g., 0.9990 Gold 0.2499 oz. AGW, 22.6 mm. **Subject:** Udmurtiya, 450th Anniversary of annexation into Russia

Date	Mintage	F	VF	XF	Unc	BU
2008 Proof	—	Value: 475				

Y# 1123   50 ROUBLES
7.7800 g., 0.9990 Gold 0.2499 oz. AGW, 22.6 mm. **Subject:** St. George the Victorious

Date	Mintage	F	VF	XF	Unc	BU
2008 Proof	—	Value: 475				

Y# 1141   50 ROUBLES
7.7800 g., 0.9990 Gold 0.2499 oz. AGW, 22.6 mm. **Subject:** European Beaver

Date	Mintage	F	VF	XF	Unc	BU
2008 Proof	—	Value: 475				

Y# 1153   50 ROUBLES
7.7800 g., 0.9990 Gold 0.2499 oz. AGW, 22.6 mm. **Subject:** 29th Summer Olympics, Bejing

Date	Mintage	F	VF	XF	Unc	BU
2008 Proof	—	Value: 475				

Y# 1168   50 ROUBLES
7.7800 g., 0.9990 Gold 0.2499 oz. AGW, 22.6 mm. **Subject:** A. P. Chekhov, 150th Anniversary of Birth

Date	Mintage	F	VF	XF	Unc	BU
2009 Proof	—	Value: 475				

Y# 1172   50 ROUBLES
7.7800 g., 0.9990 Gold 0.2499 oz. AGW, 22.6 mm. **Subject:** Kalmyk Peoples, 400th Anniversary of annexation into Russia

Date	Mintage	F	VF	XF	Unc	BU
2009 Proof	—	Value: 475				

Y# 1175   50 ROUBLES
7.7800 g., 0.9990 Gold 0.2499 oz. AGW, 22.6 mm. **Subject:** N. V. Gogol, 200th Anniversary of Birth

Date	Mintage	F	VF	XF	Unc	BU
2009 Proof	—	Value: 475				

Y# 1181   50 ROUBLES
7.7800 g., 0.9990 Gold 0.2499 oz. AGW, 22.6 mm. **Subject:** St. George the victorious

Date	Mintage	F	VF	XF	Unc	BU
2009 Proof	—	Value: 475				

Y# 1202   50 ROUBLES
7.7800 g., 0.9990 Gold 0.2499 oz. AGW, 22.6 mm. **Subject:** Velikly Novgorod

Date	Mintage	F	VF	XF	Unc	BU
2009 Proof	—	Value: 475				

Y# 1215   50 ROUBLES
7.7800 g., 0.9990 Gold 0.2499 oz. AGW, 22.6 mm. **Subject:** St. George the victorious

Date	Mintage	F	VF	XF	Unc	BU
2010 Proof	—	Value: 475				

Y# 1230   50 ROUBLES
7.7800 g., 0.9990 Gold 0.2499 oz. AGW, 22.6 mm. **Subject:** Bank of Russia, 150th Anniversary

Date	Mintage	F	VF	XF	Unc	BU
2010 Proof	—	Value: 475				

Y# 1235   50 ROUBLES
7.7800 g., 0.9990 Gold 0.2499 oz. AGW, 22.6 mm. **Subject:** UNESCO Heritage Site - Yaroslav

Date	Mintage	F	VF	XF	Unc	BU
2010 Proof	—	Value: 475				

Y# 1239   50 ROUBLES
7.7800 g., 0.9990 Gold 0.2499 oz. AGW, 22.6 mm. **Subject:** A. P. Chekhov, 200th Anniversary of birth

Date	Mintage	F	VF	XF	Unc	BU
2010 Proof	—	Value: 475				

Y# 1286   50 ROUBLES
7.7800 g., 0.9990 Gold 0.2499 oz. AGW, 22.6 mm. **Rev:** Griffin with sword and shield above garland **Edge:** Reeded

Date	Mintage	F	VF	XF	Unc	BU
2011 Proof	750	Value: 475				

Y# 1291   50 ROUBLES
7.7800 g., 0.9990 Gold 0.2499 oz. AGW, 22.6 mm. **Rev:** Emblem of the Republic of Buryatia

Date	Mintage	F	VF	XF	Unc	BU
2011 Proof	1,000	Value: 475				

Y# 1300   50 ROUBLES
7.7800 g., 0.9990 Gold 0.2499 oz. AGW, 22.6 mm. **Subject:** 2014 Winter Olympics - Sochi **Rev:** Four-man Bobsled **Edge:** Reeded

Date	Mintage	F	VF	XF	Unc	BU
2014 (2011) Proof	20,000	Value: 475				

Y# 1301   50 ROUBLES
7.7800 g., 0.9990 Gold 0.2499 oz. AGW, 22.6 mm. **Subject:** 2014 Winter Olympics - Sochi - Curling **Rev:** Skip and sweeper with stones in play

Date	Mintage	F	VF	XF	Unc	BU
2014 (2011) Proof	20,000	Value: 475				

Y# 795   100 ROUBLES
1111.1200 g., 0.9000 Silver 32.149 oz. ASW, 100 mm. **Subject:** The Bark Sedov **Obv:** Double-headed eagle **Rev:** Ship flanked by compass and cameo **Edge:** Reeded **Note:** Illustration reduced.

Date	Mintage	F	VF	XF	Unc	BU
2001(m) Proof	500	Value: 2,000				

Y# 681 100 ROUBLES
1111.1000 g., 0.9000 Silver 32.149 oz. ASW, 100 mm. **Subject:**
40th Anniversary of Manned Space Flight - Yuri Gagarin **Obv:**
Double-headed eagle **Rev:** Astronaut and rocket in space **Edge:**
Reeded **Note:** Illustration reduced.

Date	Mintage	F	VF	XF	Unc	BU
2001 Proof	750	Value: 1,800				

Y# 689 100 ROUBLES
1111.1000 g., 0.9000 Silver 32.149 oz. ASW, 100 mm. **Subject:**
Bolshoi Theater 225 Years **Obv:** Double-headed eagle **Rev:**
Casino gambling scene **Edge:** Reeded **Note:** Illustration
reduced.

Date	Mintage	F	VF	XF	Unc	BU
2001 Proof	500	Value: 1,850				

Y# 685 100 ROUBLES
17.4500 g., 0.9000 Gold 0.5049 oz. AGW, 30 mm. **Subject:**
Siberian Exploration **Obv:** Double-headed eagle within beaded
circle **Rev:** Head and silhouette left, sailboat and other designs
Edge: Reeded

Date	Mintage	F	VF	XF	Unc	BU
2001 Proof	1,000	Value: 950				

Y# 688 100 ROUBLES
15.7200 g., 0.9990 Gold 0.5049 oz. AGW, 30 mm. **Subject:**
Bolshoi Theater 225 Years **Obv:** Double-headed eagle within
beaded circle **Rev:** Three dancers with swords **Edge:** Reeded

Date	Mintage	F	VF	XF	Unc	BU
2001 Proof	1,500	Value: 950				

Y# 783 100 ROUBLES
1111.1200 g., 0.9000 Silver 32.149 oz. ASW, 100 mm. **Subject:**
Works of Dionissy **Obv:** Double-headed eagle **Rev:** St. Ferapont
Monastery in the center of a fresco covered cross **Edge:** Reeded
Note: Illustration reduced.

Date	Mintage	F	VF	XF	Unc	BU
2002(sp) Prooflike	500	—	—	—	—	1,350

Y# 789 100 ROUBLES
1111.1200 g., 0.9000 Silver 32.149 oz. ASW, 100 mm. **Subject:**
World Cup Soccer **Obv:** Double-headed eagle **Rev:** Soccer ball
design with map and players **Edge:** Reeded **Note:** Illustration
reduced.

Date	Mintage	F	VF	XF	Unc	BU
2002(sp) Proof	500	Value: 1,850				

Y# 791 100 ROUBLES
1111.1200 g., 0.9000 Silver 32.149 oz. ASW, 100 mm. **Subject:**
Hermitage **Obv:** Double-headed eagle **Rev:** Statues and arches
Edge: Reeded **Note:** Illustration reduced.

Date	Mintage	F	VF	XF	Unc	BU
2002(sp) Proof	1,000	Value: 1,500				

Y# 792 100 ROUBLES
17.4500 g., 0.9000 Gold 0.5049 oz. AGW, 30 mm. **Subject:**
Hermitage **Obv:** Double-headed eagle within beaded circle **Rev:**
Ancient battle scene sculpted on comb **Edge:** Reeded

Date	Mintage	F	VF	XF	Unc	BU
2002(sp) Proof	1,000	Value: 950				

Y# 873 100 ROUBLES
1111.1200 g., 0.9000 Silver 32.149 oz. ASW, 100 mm. **Rev:** St.
Petersburg

Date	Mintage	F	VF	XF	Unc	BU
2003(m) Proof	1,000	Value: 1,650				

Y# 874 100 ROUBLES
17.4500 g., 0.9000 Gold 0.5049 oz. AGW, 30 mm. **Rev:**
Petrozavodsk

Date	Mintage	F	VF	XF	Unc	BU
2003(m) Proof	1,000	Value: 950				

Y# 875 100 ROUBLES
17.4500 g., 0.9000 Gold 0.5049 oz. AGW, 30 mm. **Rev:**
Kamchatka

Date	Mintage	F	VF	XF	Unc	BU
2003(sp) Proof	1,500	Value: 950				

Y# 832 100 ROUBLES
17.2800 g., 0.9000 Gold 0.5000 oz. AGW, 30 mm. **Subject:** 2nd
Kamchatka Expedition **Obv:** Double-headed eagle **Rev:** Shaman
and two seated men **Edge:** Reeded

Date	Mintage	F	VF	XF	Unc	BU
2004(sp) Proof	1,500	Value: 950				

Y# 831 100 ROUBLES
1000.0000 g., 0.9000 Silver 28.934 oz. ASW, 100 mm. **Obv:**
Double-headed eagle **Rev:** Panel of icons painted by
Theophanes the Greek **Edge:** Reeded **Note:** Illustration reduced.

Date	Mintage	F	VF	XF	Unc	BU
2004(sp) Proof	500	Value: 1,850				

Y# 876 100 ROUBLES
1111.1200 g., 0.9000 Silver 32.149 oz. ASW, 100 mm. **Rev:**
Annunciation Cathedral Iconostasis

Date	Mintage	F	VF	XF	Unc	BU
2004(sp) Proof	500	Value: 2,000				

Y# 1024 100 ROUBLES
1000.0000 g., 0.9250 Silver 29.738 oz. ASW, 100 mm. **Subject:**
Reindeer

Date	Mintage	F	VF	XF	Unc	BU
2004 Proof	—	Value: 1,750				

Y# 1026 100 ROUBLES
1000.0000 g., 0.9990 Silver 32.117 oz. ASW, 100 mm. **Subject:**
Reindeer

Date	Mintage	F	VF	XF	Unc	BU
2004 Proof	—	Value: 1,750				

Y# 1036 100 ROUBLES
1046.0000 g., 0.9250 Silver 31.106 oz. ASW, 100 mm. **Subject:**
Rostov

Date	Mintage	F	VF	XF	Unc	BU
2004 Proof	—	Value: 1,750				

Y# 895   100 ROUBLES
1083.7400 g., 0.9250 Silver 32.228 oz. ASW, 100 mm. **Subject:**
60th Anniversary Victory Over Germany **Obv:** Double-headed
eagle **Rev:** Decorated locomotive returning soldiers circa 1945
Edge: Reeded **Note:** Illustration reduced.

Date	Mintage	F	VF	XF	Unc	BU
2005 Proof	2,000	Value: 1,750				

Y# 912   100 ROUBLES
1083.7400 g., 0.9250 Silver 32.228 oz. ASW, 100 mm. **Obv:**
Double-headed eagle **Rev:** Kazan city view with mausoleums
Edge: Reeded **Note:** Illustration reduced.

Date	Mintage	F	VF	XF	Unc	BU
2005 Proof	500	Value: 1,850				

Y# 925   100 ROUBLES
1083.7400 g., 0.9250 Silver 32.228 oz. ASW, 100 mm. **Subject:**
625th Anniversary - Battle of Kulikovo **Obv:** Double-headed eagle
Rev: Battle of Kulikovo beginning scene **Edge:** Reeded **Note:**
Illustration reduced.

Date	Mintage	F	VF	XF	Unc	BU
2005 Proof	500	Value: 1,850				

Y# 1078   100 ROUBLES
1046.0000 g., 0.9250 Silver 31.106 oz. ASW, 100 mm. **Subject:**
Yuryev Polsky

Date	Mintage	F	VF	XF	Unc	BU
2006	—	Value: 1,750				

Y# 1044   100 ROUBLES
1046.0000 g., 0.9250 Silver 31.106 oz. ASW, 100 mm. **Subject:**
Frigate Myr

Date	Mintage	F	VF	XF	Unc	BU
2006 Proof	—	Value: 1,350				

Y# 1061   100 ROUBLES
1046.0000 g., 0.9250 Silver 31.106 oz. ASW, 100 mm. **Subject:**
Moscow's Kremlin and Red Square

Date	Mintage	F	VF	XF	Unc	BU
2006 Proof	—	Value: 1,350				

Y# 1077   100 ROUBLES
1046.0000 g., 0.9250 Silver 31.106 oz. ASW, 100 mm. **Subject:**
Bogolyubovo Township

Date	Mintage	F	VF	XF	Unc	BU
2006 Proof	—	Value: 1,750				

Y# 1081   100 ROUBLES
1046.0000 g., 0.9250 Silver 31.106 oz. ASW, 100 mm. **Subject:**
International Artic Year

Date	Mintage	F	VF	XF	Unc	BU
2007 Proof	—	Value: 1,750				

Y# 1085   100 ROUBLES
1046.0000 g., 0.9250 Silver 31.106 oz. ASW, 100 mm. **Subject:**
Russian railways, 175th Anniversary

Date	Mintage	F	VF	XF	Unc	BU
2007 Proof	—	Value: 1,750				

Y# 1089   100 ROUBLES
1046.0000 g., 0.9250 Silver 31.106 oz. ASW, 100 mm. **Subject:**
Andrew Rublyov

Date	Mintage	F	VF	XF	Unc	BU
2007 Proof	—	Value: 1,750				

Y# 1093   100 ROUBLES
169.0000 g., 0.9250 Silver 5.0258 oz. ASW, 60 mm. **Subject:**
Bashkiria, 450th Anniversary of Annexation by Russia

Date	Mintage	F	VF	XF	Unc	BU
2007 Proof	—	Value: 285				

Y# 1096   100 ROUBLES
1046.0000 g., 0.9250 Silver 31.106 oz. ASW, 100 mm. **Subject:**
Khakassia, 300th Anniversary of Annexation by Russia

Date	Mintage	F	VF	XF	Unc	BU
2007 Proof	—	Value: 1,750				

Y# 1120   100 ROUBLES
1046.0000 g., 0.9250 Silver 31.106 oz. ASW, 100 mm. **Subject:**
Udmurtiya, 450th Anniversary of Annexation into Russia

Date	Mintage	F	VF	XF	Unc	BU
2008 Proof	—	Value: 1,750				

Y# 1140   100 ROUBLES
1046.0000 g., 0.9250 Silver 31.106 oz. ASW, 100 mm. **Subject:**
European Beaver

Date	Mintage	F	VF	XF	Unc	BU
2008 Proof	—	Value: 1,750				

Y# 1142   100 ROUBLES
15.5600 g., 0.9990 Gold 0.4997 oz. AGW **Subject:** European
Beaver

Date	Mintage	F	VF	XF	Unc	BU
2008 Proof	—	Value: 775				

Y# 1143   100 ROUBLES
1046.0000 g., 0.9250 Silver 31.106 oz. ASW, 100 mm. **Subject:**
European Beaver

Date	Mintage	F	VF	XF	Unc	BU
2008 Proof	—	Value: 1,350				

Y# 1156   100 ROUBLES
1046.0000 g., 0.9250 Silver 31.106 oz. ASW, 100 mm. **Subject:**
Pereslaval Zalessky

Date	Mintage	F	VF	XF	Unc	BU
2008 Proof	—	Value: 1,750				

Y# 1157   100 ROUBLES
1046.0000 g., 0.9990 Silver 33.594 oz. ASW, 100 mm. **Subject:**
Alexandrov

Date	Mintage	F	VF	XF	Unc	BU
2008 Proof	—	Value: 1,750				

Y# 1148   100 ROUBLES
1046.0000 g., 0.9250 Silver 31.106 oz. ASW, 100 mm. **Subject:**
Kamchatka Volcano

Date	Mintage	F	VF	XF	Unc	BU
2008 Proof	—	Value: 1,750				

Y# 1162   100 ROUBLES
168.0000 g., 0.9250 Silver 4.9960 oz. ASW, 60 mm. **Subject:**
Russian Currency

Date	Mintage	F	VF	XF	Unc	BU
2009 Proof	—	Value: 285				

Y# 1163   100 ROUBLES
168.0000 g., 0.9250 Silver 4.9960 oz. ASW, 60 mm. **Subject:**
Russian Currency

Date	Mintage	F	VF	XF	Unc	BU
2009 Proof	—	Value: 285				

Y# 1167   100 ROUBLES
168.0000 g., 0.9250 Silver 4.9960 oz. ASW, 60 mm. **Subject:**
A. P. Chekhov, 150th Anniversary of Birth

Date	Mintage	F	VF	XF	Unc	BU
2009 Proof	—	Value: 285				

Y# 1171   100 ROUBLES
1046.0000 g., 0.9990 Silver 33.594 oz. ASW, 100 mm. **Subject:**
Kalmyk Peoples, 400th Anniversary of annexation into Russia

Date	Mintage	F	VF	XF	Unc	BU
2009 Proof	—	Value: 1,750				

Y# 1174   100 ROUBLES
33.9000 g., 0.9250 Silver 1.0081 oz. ASW, 39 mm. **Subject:** N.
V. Gogol, 200th Anniversary of Birth

Date	Mintage	F	VF	XF	Unc	BU
2009 Proof	—	Value: 60.00				

Y# 1179   100 ROUBLES
1048.0000 g., 0.9250 Silver 31.165 oz. ASW, 100 mm. **Subject:**
Poltava Battle, 300th Anniversary

Date	Mintage	F	VF	XF	Unc	BU
2009 Proof	—	Value: 1,750				

Y# 1238   100 ROUBLES
1046.0000 g., 0.9250 Silver 31.106 oz. ASW, 100 mm. **Subject:**
A. P. Chekhov, 200th Anniversary of Birth

Date	Mintage	F	VF	XF	Unc	BU
2010 Proofllike	—	—	—	—	—	1,350

Y# 1290   100 ROUBLES
1000.0000 g., 0.9250 Silver 29.738 oz. ASW, 100 mm. **Rev:**
Man playing stringed instrument, others in backbround **Edge:**
Reeded

Date	Mintage	F	VF	XF	Unc	BU
2011 Proof	300	Value: 1,400				

Y# 1299 100 ROUBLES
1000.0000 g., 0.9250 Silver 29.738 oz. ASW, 100 mm. **Subject:** 2014 Winter Olympics - Sochi **Rev:** Montage of Russian winter sports

Date	Mintage	F	VF	XF	Unc	BU
2014 (2011) Proof	1,200	Value: 1,400				

Y# 877 200 ROUBLES
3342.3899 g., 0.9000 Silver 96.710 oz. ASW, 130 mm. **Rev:** Peter I monetary reform

Date	Mintage	F	VF	XF	Unc	BU
2003(sp) Proof	300	Value: 5,250				

Y# 1027 200 ROUBLES
31.1050 g., 0.9990 Gold 0.9990 oz. AGW **Subject:** Reindeer

Date	Mintage	F	VF	XF	Unc	BU
2004 Proof	500	Value: 3,250				

Y# 1042 200 ROUBLES
31.1000 g., 0.9990 Gold 0.9988 oz. AGW **Subject:** Parliament, 100th Anniversary

Date	Mintage	F	VF	XF	Unc	BU
2006 Proof	750	Value: 1,850				

Y# 1062 200 ROUBLES
3138.0000 g., 0.9250 Silver 93.318 oz. ASW, 100 mm. **Subject:** Moscow's Kremlin and Red Square

Date	Mintage	F	VF	XF	Unc	BU
2006 Proof	200	Value: 6,500				

Y# 1144 200 ROUBLES
31.1050 g., 0.9990 Gold 0.9990 oz. AGW **Subject:** European Beaver

Date	Mintage	F	VF	XF	Unc	BU
2008 Proof	500	Value: 3,250				

Y# 1169 200 ROUBLES
31.1050 g., 0.9990 Gold 0.9990 oz. AGW **Subject:** A. P. Chekhov, 150th Anniversary of Birth

Date	Mintage	F	VF	XF	Unc	BU
2009 Proof	500	Value: 1,850				

Y# 1176 200 ROUBLES
3120.0000 g., 0.9250 Silver 92.783 oz. ASW **Subject:** N. V. Gogol, 200th Anniversary of Birth **Edge:** 100

Date	Mintage	F	VF	XF	Unc	BU
2009 Proof	—	Value: 6,500				

Y# 1201 200 ROUBLES
31.1050 g., 0.9990 Gold 0.9990 oz. AGW **Subject:** Velikly Novgorod

Date	Mintage	F	VF	XF	Unc	BU
2009 Proof	200	Value: 7,500				

Y# 1209 200 ROUBLES
31.1050 g., 0.9990 Gold 0.9990 oz. AGW **Series:** Speed Skating

Date	Mintage	F	VF	XF	Unc	BU
2009 Proof	500	Value: 1,850				

Y# 1210 200 ROUBLES
31.1000 g., 0.9990 Gold 0.9988 oz. AGW **Subject:** Ski Jumping

Date	Mintage	F	VF	XF	Unc	BU
2009 Proof	500	Value: 1,850				

Y# 1211 200 ROUBLES
31.1000 g., 0.9990 Gold 0.9988 oz. AGW **Subject:** Luge

Date	Mintage	F	VF	XF	Unc	BU
2009 Proof	500	Value: 1,650				

Y# 1213 200 ROUBLES
31.1050 g., 0.9990 Gold 0.9990 oz. AGW **Subject:** Figure Skating

Date	Mintage	F	VF	XF	Unc	BU
2009 Proof	500	Value: 1,650				

Y# 1212 200 ROUBLES
31.1050 g., 0.9990 Gold 0.9990 oz. AGW **Subject:** Biathlon

Date	Mintage	F	VF	XF	Unc	BU
2009 Proof	500	Value: 1,650				

Y# 1234 200 ROUBLES
3130.0000 g., 0.9250 Silver 93.080 oz. ASW **Subject:** UNESCO Heritage Site - Yaroslav

Date	Mintage	F	VF	XF	Unc	BU
2010 Proof	200	Value: 6,000				

Y# 1240 200 ROUBLES
31.1000 g., 0.9990 Gold 0.9988 oz. AGW **Subject:** A. P. Chekhov, 200th Anniversary of Birth

Date	Mintage	F	VF	XF	Unc	BU
2010 Proof	500	Value: 1,650				

Y# 1255 200 ROUBLES
31.1000 g., 0.9990 Gold 0.9988 oz. AGW **Subject:** Hockey

Date	Mintage	F	VF	XF	Unc	BU
2010 Proof	—	Value: 1,850				

Y# 1256 200 ROUBLES
31.1000 g., 0.9990 Gold 0.9988 oz. AGW **Subject:** Ski Race

Date	Mintage	F	VF	XF	Unc	BU
2010 Proof	500	Value: 1,850				

Y# 1257 200 ROUBLES
31.1000 g., 0.9990 Gold 0.9988 oz. AGW **Subject:** Nordic Combined

Date	Mintage	F	VF	XF	Unc	BU
2010 Proof	500	Value: 1,650				

Y# 1258 200 ROUBLES
31.1000 g., 0.9990 Gold 0.9988 oz. AGW **Subject:** Freestyle Skiing

Date	Mintage	F	VF	XF	Unc	BU
2010 Proof	500	Value: 1,850				

Y# 1259 200 ROUBLES
31.1000 g., 0.9990 Gold 0.9988 oz. AGW **Subject:** Short Track Speed Skating

Date	Mintage	F	VF	XF	Unc	BU
2010 Proof	500	Value: 1,850				

Y# 1260 200 ROUBLES
31.1000 g., 0.9990 Gold 0.9988 oz. AGW **Subject:** Curling

Date	Mintage	F	VF	XF	Unc	BU
2010 Proof	500	Value: 1,850				

Y# 1261 200 ROUBLES
31.1000 g., 0.9990 Gold 0.9988 oz. AGW **Subject:** Snowboarding

Date	Mintage	F	VF	XF	Unc	BU
2010 Proof	500	Value: 1,850				

Y# 1262   200 ROUBLES
31.1000 g., 0.9990 Gold 0.9988 oz. AGW   **Subject:** Skeleton

Date	Mintage	F	VF	XF	Unc	BU
2010 Proof	500 Value: 1,850					

Y# 1263   200 ROUBLES
31.1000 g., 0.9990 Gold 0.9988 oz. AGW   **Subject:** Bobsled

Date	Mintage	F	VF	XF	Unc	BU
2010 Proof	500 Value: 1,850					

Y# 1264   200 ROUBLES
31.1000 g., 0.9990 Gold 0.9988 oz. AGW   **Subject:** Mountain Skiing

Date	Mintage	F	VF	XF	Unc	BU
2010 Proof	500 Value: 1,850					

Y# 796   1000 ROUBLES
156.4000 g., 0.9990 Gold 5.0231 oz. AGW, 50 mm.   **Subject:** The Bark Sedov **Obv:** Double-headed eagle **Rev:** Four-masted sailing ship **Edge:** Reeded

Date	Mintage	F	VF	XF	Unc	BU
2001(m) Proof	250 Value: 9,000					

Y# 878   1000 ROUBLES
156.4000 g., 0.9990 Gold 5.0231 oz. AGW, 50 mm.   **Rev:** Cronstadt

Date	Mintage	F	VF	XF	Unc	BU
2003(m) Proof	250 Value: 9,000					

Y# 1037   1000 ROUBLES
1046.0000 g., 0.9250 Silver 31.106 oz. ASW, 100 mm.   **Subject:** Uglich

Date	Mintage	F	VF	XF	Unc	BU
2004 Proof	— Value: 1,750					

Y# 1045   1000 ROUBLES
1000.0000 g., 0.9990 Gold 32.117 oz. AGW, 100 mm.   **Subject:** Frigate Myr

Date	Mintage	F	VF	XF	Unc	BU
2006 Proof	— Value: 57,000					

Y# 1082   1000 ROUBLES
156.0000 g., 0.9990 Gold 5.0103 oz. AGW, 100 mm.   **Subject:** International Artic Year

Date	Mintage	F	VF	XF	Unc	BU
2007 Proof	— Value: 9,000					

Y# 1164   1000 ROUBLES
156.0000 g., 0.9990 Gold 5.0103 oz. AGW, 100 mm.   **Subject:** Russian Currency

Date	Mintage	F	VF	XF	Unc	BU
2009 Proof	— Value: 9,000					

Y# 1227   1000 ROUBLES
155.5000 g., 0.9990 Gold 4.9942 oz. AGW   **Subject:** Warship - Goto Predestination

Date	Mintage	F	VF	XF	Unc	BU
2010 Proof	— Value: 8,500					

Y# 1281   1000 ROUBLES
155.5000 g., 0.9990 Gold 4.9942 oz. AGW, 50 mm.   **Subject:** Beginning of Great Reforms - Abolition of Serfdom **Rev:** Man plowing, quill pen and signature on document

Date	Mintage	F	VF	XF	Unc	BU
2011ММД Proof	250 Value: 9,000					

Y# 1288   1000 ROUBLES
155.5000 g., 0.9990 Gold 4.9942 oz. AGW, 50 mm.   **Rev:** U.A. Gagarin in spacesuit waving

Date	Mintage	F	VF	XF	Unc	BU
2011 Proof	500 Value: 9,000					

Y# 1297   1000 ROUBLES
155.5000 g., 0.9990 Gold 4.9942 oz. AGW, 50 mm.   **Subject:** 2014 Winter Olympics - Sochi - Flora of Sochi **Rev:** Goddess Flora who's hair has plants of the Sochi region, female figure skater to right

Date	Mintage	F	VF	XF	Unc	BU
2014 (2011) Proof	600 Value: 9,000					

Y# 784   10000 ROUBLES
1001.1000 g., 0.9990 Gold 32.152 oz. AGW, 100 mm.   **Subject:** Works of Dionissy **Obv:** Double-headed eagle **Rev:** Interior view of the carved portal of the Virgin of the Nativity Church **Edge:** Reeded **Note:** Illustration reduced.

Date	Mintage	F	VF	XF	Unc	BU
2002(sp) Proof	100 Value: 57,000					

Y# 879   10000 ROUBLES
1001.1000 g., 0.9990 Gold 32.152 oz. AGW, 100 mm.   **Rev:** St. Petersburg area map

Date	Mintage	F	VF	XF	Unc	BU
2003 Proof	200 Value: 57,000					

Y# 1017   10000 ROUBLES
1000.0000 g., 0.9990 Gold 32.117 oz. AGW, 100 mm.   **Subject:** Theophanes the Greek

Date	Mintage	F	VF	XF	Unc	BU
2004 Proof	— Value: 57,000					

Y# 880   10000 ROUBLES
1001.1000 g., 0.9990 Gold 32.152 oz. AGW, 100 mm.   **Rev:** Church of the Transfiguration of the Savior, Novgorod

Date	Mintage	F	VF	XF	Unc	BU
2004 Proof	100 Value: 57,000					

Y# 1028   10000 ROUBLES
1000.0000 g., 0.9990 Gold 32.117 oz. AGW, 100 mm.   **Subject:** Reindeer

Date	Mintage	F	VF	XF	Unc	BU
2004 Proof	100 Value: 57,000					

Y# 896   10000 ROUBLES
1001.1000 g., 0.9990 Gold 32.152 oz. AGW, 100 mm.   **Subject:** 60th Anniversary - Victory Over Germany **Obv:** Double-headed eagle **Rev:** Soldiers dishonoring captured Nazi flags and standards **Edge:** Reeded **Note:** Illustration reduced.

Date	Mintage	F	VF	XF	Unc	BU
2005 Proof	250 Value: 57,000					

Y# 913   10000 ROUBLES
1001.1000 g., 0.9990 Gold 32.152 oz. AGW, 100 mm.   **Obv:** Two headed eagle **Rev:** Kazan Kremlin view **Edge:** Reeded **Note:** Illustration reduced.

Date	Mintage	F	VF	XF	Unc	BU
2005 Proof	150 Value: 57,000					

Y# 1043   10000 ROUBLES
1000.0000 g., 0.9990 Gold 32.117 oz. AGW, 100 mm. **Subject:** Parliament, 100th Anniversary

Date	Mintage	F	VF	XF	Unc	BU
2006 Proof	100				Value: 57,000	

Y# 1064   10000 ROUBLES
1000.0000 g., 0.9990 Gold 32.117 oz. AGW, 100 mm. **Subject:** Moscow's Kremlin and Red Square

Date	Mintage	F	VF	XF	Unc	BU
2006 Proof	—				Value: 57,000	

Y# 1091   10000 ROUBLES
1000.0000 g., 0.9990 Gold 32.117 oz. AGW, 100 mm. **Subject:** Andrew Rublyov

Date	Mintage	F	VF	XF	Unc	BU
2007 Proof	—				Value: 57,000	

Y# 1095   10000 ROUBLES
1000.0000 g., 0.9990 Gold 32.117 oz. AGW, 100 mm. **Subject:** Bashkiria, 450th Anniversary of Annexation by Russia

Date	Mintage	F	VF	XF	Unc	BU
2007 Proof	—				Value: 57,000	

Y# 1098   10000 ROUBLES
1000.0000 g., 0.9990 Gold 32.117 oz. AGW, 100 mm. **Subject:** Khakassia, 300th Anniversary of Annexation by Russia

Date	Mintage	F	VF	XF	Unc	BU
2007 Proof	—				Value: 57,000	

Y# 1122   10000 ROUBLES
1000.0000 g., 0.9990 Gold 32.117 oz. AGW, 100 mm. **Subject:** Udmurtiya, 450th Anniversary of Annexation into Russia

Date	Mintage	F	VF	XF	Unc	BU
2008 Proof	—	—	—	—	—	57,000

Y# 1145   10000 ROUBLES
1000.0000 g., 0.9990 Gold 32.117 oz. AGW, 100 mm. **Subject:** European Beaver

Date	Mintage	F	VF	XF	Unc	BU
2008 Proof	—				Value: 57,000	

Y# 1149   10000 ROUBLES
1000.0000 g., 0.9990 Gold 32.117 oz. AGW, 100 mm. **Subject:** Kamchatka Volcano

Date	Mintage	F	VF	XF	Unc	BU
2008 Proof	—				Value: 57,000	

Y# 1203   10000 ROUBLES
1000.0000 g., 0.9990 Gold 32.117 oz. AGW, 100 mm. **Subject:** Velikly Novgorod

Date	Mintage	F	VF	XF	Unc	BU
2009 Proof	—				Value: 57,000	

Y# 1236   10000 ROUBLES
1000.0000 g., 0.9990 Gold 32.117 oz. AGW, 100 mm. **Subject:** UNESCO Heritage Site - Yaroslav

Date	Mintage	F	VF	XF	Unc	BU
2010 Prooflike	—	—	—	—	—	57,000

Y# 1117   25000 ROUBLES
1000.0000 g., 0.9990 Gold 32.117 oz. AGW, 100 mm. **Subject:** Goznak, 190th Anniversary

Date	Mintage	F	VF	XF	Unc	BU
2008 Proof	—				Value: 57,000	

Y# 1165   25000 ROUBLES
1000.0000 g., 0.9990 Gold 32.117 oz. AGW, 100 mm. **Subject:** Russian Currency

Date	Mintage	F	VF	XF	Unc	BU
2009 Proof	—				Value: 57,000	

Y# 1231   50000 ROUBLES
5000.0000 g., 0.9990 Gold 160.58 oz. AGW **Subject:** Bank of Russia, 150th Anniversary

Date	Mintage	F	VF	XF	Unc	BU
2010 Prooflike	—	—	—	—	—	285,000

MINT SETS

KM#	Date	Mintage	Identification	Issue Price	Mkt Val
MS44	2002 (7)	—	Y#600-603, 797-799, plus mint medal	7.50	15.00

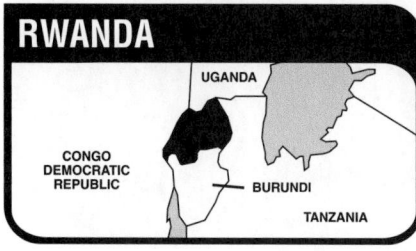

RWANDA

UGANDA
CONGO DEMOCRATIC REPUBLIC
BURUNDI
TANZANIA

The Republic of Rwanda, located in central Africa between the Republic of the Congo and Tanzania, has an area of 10,169 sq. mi. (26,340 sq. km.) and a population of 7.3 million. Capital: Kigali. The economy is based on agriculture and mining. Coffee and tin are exported.

For earlier coinage see Belgian Congo, and Rwanda and Burundi.

MINT MARKS
(a) - Paris, privy marks only
(b) - Brussels, privy marks only

MONETARY SYSTEM
100 Centimes = 1 Franc

REPUBLIC
STANDARD COINAGE

KM# 22   FRANC
0.0700 g., Aluminum, 16 mm. **Obv:** National arms **Rev:** Sorghum plant **Edge:** Plain

Date	Mintage	F	VF	XF	Unc	BU
2003	—	—	—	0.25	0.65	1.00

KM# 23   5 FRANCS
2.9600 g., Brass Plated Steel, 20 mm. **Obv:** National arms **Rev:** Coffee plant **Edge:** Plain

Date	Mintage	F	VF	XF	Unc	BU
2003	—	—	—	0.25	0.65	1.00

KM# 24   10 FRANCS
5.0000 g., Brass Plated Steel, 23.9 mm. **Obv:** National arms **Rev:** Banana tree **Edge:** Plain

Date	Mintage	F	VF	XF	Unc	BU
2003	—			0.45	1.00	1.50
2009	—			0.45	1.00	1.50

KM# 33   10 FRANCS
5.0000 g., Brass Plated Steel, 23.9 mm. **Obv:** National arms **Rev:** Banana tree **Rev. Legend:** BANKI NKURU YU RWANDA

Date	Mintage	F	VF	XF	Unc	BU
2009	—				1.00	1.50

KM# 25   20 FRANCS
3.5000 g., Nickel Plated Steel, 20 mm. **Obv:** National arms **Rev:** Coffee plant seedling **Edge:** Reeded

Date	Mintage	F	VF	XF	Unc	BU
2003	—				1.75	2.00
2009	—				1.75	2.00

KM# 26   50 FRANCS
5.8000 g., Nickel Plated Steel, 24 mm. **Obv:** National arms **Rev:** Ear of corn within husks **Edge:** Reeded

Date	Mintage	F	VF	XF	Unc	BU
2003(a)	—			—	2.50	4.00

KM# 32   100 FRANCS
Bi-Metallic Copper center in Copper-Nickel ring, 27 mm. **Obv:** National arms **Rev:** Value

Date	Mintage	F	VF	XF	Unc	BU
2007	—	—	—	—	5.00	6.50

KM# 28   200 FRANCS
1.0000 g., 0.9990 Gold 0.0321 oz. AGW, 13.9 mm. **Subject:** 75th Birthday Dian Fossey **Obv:** National arms **Obv. Legend:** BANKI NASIYONALI Y'U RWANDA **Rev:** Fossey facing holding monkey **Edge:** Plain

Date	Mintage	F	VF	XF	Unc	BU
2007 Proof	15,000				Value: 85.00	

KM# 30   500 FRANCS
22.2000 g., 0.9000 Silver 0.6423 oz. ASW **Obv:** National arms **Obv. Legend:** BANQUE NATIONALE DU RWANDA **Rev:** Stalk of bananas on leaves

Date	Mintage	F	VF	XF	Unc	BU
2002(a) Proof	500				Value: 115	

KM# 31   500 FRANCS
22.2000 g., 0.9000 Silver 0.6423 oz. ASW **Subject:** Euro Parity **Obv:** Arms **Rev:** Plant

Date	Mintage	F	VF	XF	Unc	BU
2002 Proof	500				Value: 115	

KM# 27   500 FRANCS

20.0000 g., 0.9990 Silver 0.6423 oz. ASW, 38 mm. **Subject:** Olympic Games 2008 - Peking, marathon races **Obv:** National arms **Obv. Legend:** BANKI NASIYONALI Y'U RWANDA **Rev:** Three male marathon runners, Rwanda Olympic logo at right **Rev. Legend:** JEUX OLYMPIQUES **Edge:** Plain

Date	Mintage	F	VF	XF	Unc	BU
2006 Proof	—	Value: 110				

KM# 29   1000 FRANCS

93.3000 g., 0.9990 Silver And Gold 2.9965 oz., 65 mm. **Obv:** National arms **Obv. Legend:** BANKI NASIYONALI Y'U RWANDA **Rev:** Gilt elephant family of four with diamonds inset in eyes **Rev. Legend:** AFRICAN ELEPHANT **Edge:** Plain **Note:** Illustration reduced.

Date	Mintage	F	VF	XF	Unc	BU
2007	1,500	—	—	—	—	650
2007 Proof	500	Value: 1,000				

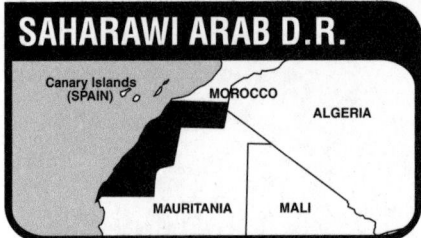

SAHARAWI ARAB D.R.

The Saharawi Arab Democratic Republic, located in northwest Africa has an area of 102,703 sq. mi. and a population (census taken 1974) of 76,425. Formerly known as Spanish Sahara, the area is bounded on the north by Morocco, on the east and southeast by Mauritania, on the northeast by Algeria, and on the west by the Atlantic Ocean. Capital: El Aaium. Agriculture, fishing and mining are the three main industries. Exports are barley, livestock and phosphates. The SADR is a "government in exile". It currently controls about 20% of its claimed territory, the former Spanish colony of Western Sahara; Morocco controls and administers the majority of the territory as its Southern Provinces. SADR claims control over a zone largely bordering Mauritania, described as "the Free Zone," although characterized by Morocco as a buffer zone.

DEMOCRATIC REPUBLIC

STANDARD COINAGE

KM# 54   1000 PESETAS

19.9400 g., 0.9990 Silver 0.6404 oz. ASW, 38.1 mm. **Obv:** National arms **Rev:** Soccer player and stadium **Edge:** Plain

Date	Mintage	F	VF	XF	Unc	BU
2002 Proof	—	Value: 35.00				

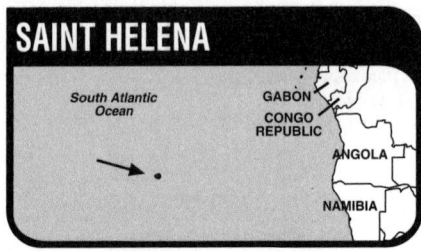

SAINT HELENA

Saint Helena, a British colony located about 1,150 miles (1,850 km.) from the west coast of Africa, has an area of 47 sq. mi. (410 sq. km.) and a population of *7,000. Capital: Jamestown. Flax, lace, and rope are produced for export. Ascension and Tristan da Cunha are dependencies of Saint Helena.

MONETARY SYSTEM
100 Pence = 1 Pound

BRITISH COLONY

STANDARD COINAGE

KM# 19   50 PENCE

38.6000 g., Copper-Nickel, 38.6 mm. **Ruler:** Elizabeth II **Subject:** 75th Birthday of Queen Elizabeth II **Obv:** Crowned bust right **Rev:** Bust facing within circle and rose sprigs **Edge:** Reeded

Date	Mintage	VG	F	VF	XF	Unc
2001	—	—	—	—	—	8.00

KM# 19a   50 PENCE

28.2800 g., 0.9250 Silver 0.8410 oz. ASW, 38.6 mm. **Ruler:** Elizabeth II **Subject:** 75th Birthday of Queen Elizabeth II **Obv:** Crowned bust right **Rev:** Bust facing within circle and rose sprigs **Edge:** Reeded

Date	Mintage	F	VF	XF	Unc	BU
2001 Proof	10,000	Value: 45.00				

KM# 19b   50 PENCE

47.5400 g., 0.9166 Gold 1.4009 oz. AGW, 38.6 mm. **Ruler:** Elizabeth II **Subject:** 75th Birthday of Queen Elizabeth II **Obv:** Crowned bust right **Rev:** Bust facing within circle and rose sprigs **Edge:** Reeded

Date	Mintage	F	VF	XF	Unc	BU
2001 Proof	75	Value: 2,250				

KM# 20   50 PENCE

28.5500 g., Copper-Nickel, 38.6 mm. **Ruler:** Elizabeth II **Subject:** Queen Victoria's Death **Obv:** Crowned bust right **Rev:** Half-length figure facing and ship within circle **Edge:** Reeded

Date	Mintage	VG	F	VF	XF	Unc
2001	—	—	—	—	—	8.00

KM# 20a   50 PENCE

28.2800 g., 0.9250 Silver 0.8410 oz. ASW, 38.6 mm. **Ruler:** Elizabeth II **Subject:** Centennial - Death of Queen Victoria **Obv:** Crowned bust right **Rev:** Half-length figure facing and ship within circle **Edge:** Reeded

Date	Mintage	F	VF	XF	Unc	BU
2001 Proof	10,000	Value: 45.00				

KM# 20b   50 PENCE

47.5400 g., 0.9166 Gold 1.4009 oz. AGW, 38.6 mm. **Ruler:** Elizabeth II **Subject:** Centennial - Death of Queen Victoria **Obv:** Crowned bust right **Rev:** Half-length figure facing and ship within circle **Edge:** Reeded

Date	Mintage	F	VF	XF	Unc	BU
2001 Proof	100	Value: 2,200				

KM# 23   50 PENCE

28.2800 g., Copper-Nickel, 38.6 mm. **Ruler:** Elizabeth II **Subject:** 50th Anniversary - Queen Elizabeth II's Accession **Obv:** Crowned bust right **Rev:** Crown on pillow within circle **Edge:** Reeded

Date	Mintage	F	VF	XF	Unc	BU
ND(2002)	—	—	—	—	8.00	10.00

KM# 23a 50 PENCE
28.2800 g., 0.9250 Silver 0.8410 oz. ASW, 38.6 mm. **Ruler:**
Elizabeth II **Subject:** 50th Anniversary - Queen Elizabeth's
Accession **Obv:** Crowned bust right **Rev:** Crown on pillow within
circle **Edge:** Reeded

Date	Mintage	F	VF	XF	Unc	BU
ND(2002) Proof	10,000	Value: 40.00				

KM# 24 50 PENCE
28.2800 g., Copper-Nickel, 38.6 mm. **Ruler:** Elizabeth II
Subject: To Celebrate a Life of Duty, Dignity and Love, 1900-
2002 **Obv:** Crowned bust right **Rev:** Conjoined busts right **Edge:**
Reeded

Date	Mintage	F	VF	XF	Unc	BU
ND(2002)	—	—	—	—	8.00	10.00

KM# 24a 50 PENCE
28.2800 g., 0.9250 Silver 0.8410 oz. ASW, 38.6 mm. **Ruler:**
Elizabeth II **Subject:** To Celebrate a Life of Duty, Dignity and
Love, 1900-2002 **Obv:** Crowned bust right **Rev:** Conjoined busts
right **Edge:** Reeded

Date	Mintage	F	VF	XF	Unc	BU
ND(2002) Proof	10,000	Value: 40.00				

KM# 25 50 PENCE
28.2800 g., Copper-Nickel, 38.6 mm. **Ruler:** Elizabeth II
Subject: 500th Anniversary - Discovery of St. Helena **Obv:**
Crowned bust right **Rev:** Half length figure right and ship above
1502 date **Edge:** Reeded

Date	Mintage	F	VF	XF	Unc	BU
ND(2002)	—	—	—	—	10.00	12.00

KM# 25a 50 PENCE
28.2800 g., 0.9250 Silver 0.8410 oz. ASW, 38.6 mm. **Ruler:**
Elizabeth II **Subject:** 500th Anniversary - Discovery of St. Helena
Obv: Crowned bust right **Rev:** Half length figure right and ship
above 1502 date **Edge:** Reeded

Date	Mintage	F	VF	XF	Unc	BU
ND(2002) Proof	5,000	Value: 50.00				

KM# 26 50 PENCE
28.2800 g., Copper-Nickel, 38.6 mm. **Ruler:** Elizabeth II **Obv:**
Crowned bust right **Rev:** Bust 1/4 left, ship HMS Paramour and
a comet **Edge:** Reeded

Date	Mintage	F	VF	XF	Unc	BU
ND(2002)	—	—	—	—	10.00	12.00

KM# 26a 50 PENCE
28.2800 g., 0.9250 Silver 0.8410 oz. ASW, 38.6 mm. **Ruler:**
Elizabeth II **Obv:** Crowned bust right **Rev:** Bust 1/4 left, ship HMS
Paramour and a comet **Edge:** Reeded

Date	Mintage	F	VF	XF	Unc	BU
ND(2002) Proof	5,000	Value: 50.00				

KM# 27 50 PENCE
28.2800 g., Copper-Nickel, 38.6 mm. **Ruler:** Elizabeth II **Obv:**
Crowned bust right **Rev:** Bust 1/4 right and the HMS Resolution
Edge: Reeded

Date	Mintage	F	VF	XF	Unc	BU
ND(2002)	—	—	—	—	10.00	12.00

KM# 27a 50 PENCE
28.2800 g., 0.9250 Silver 0.8410 oz. ASW, 38.6 mm. **Ruler:**
Elizabeth II **Obv:** Crowned bust right **Rev:** Bust 1/4 right and the
HMS Resolution **Edge:** Reeded

Date	Mintage	F	VF	XF	Unc	BU
ND(2002) Proof	5,000	Value: 50.00				

KM# 28 50 PENCE
28.2800 g., Copper-Nickel, 38.6 mm. **Ruler:** Elizabeth II **Obv:**
Crowned bust right **Rev:** Half length figure facing and the ship
HMS Northumberland **Edge:** Reeded

Date	Mintage	F	VF	XF	Unc	BU
ND(2002)	—	—	—	—	10.00	12.00

KM# 28a 50 PENCE
28.2800 g., 0.9250 Silver 0.8410 oz. ASW, 38.6 mm. **Ruler:**
Elizabeth II **Obv:** Queen Elizabeth II **Rev:** Napoleon and the ship
HMS Northumberland **Edge:** Reeded

Date	Mintage	F	VF	XF	Unc	BU
ND(2002) Proof	5,000	Value: 50.00				

KM# 29 50 PENCE
28.2800 g., Copper-Nickel, 38.6 mm. **Ruler:** Elizabeth II **Obv:**
Crowned bust right **Rev:** Four conjoined busts left plus the HMS
Vanguard **Edge:** Reeded

Date	Mintage	F	VF	XF	Unc	BU
ND(2002)	—	—	—	—	8.00	10.00

KM# 29a 50 PENCE
28.2800 g., 0.9250 Silver 0.8410 oz. ASW, 38.6 mm. **Ruler:**
Elizabeth II **Obv:** Crowned bust right **Rev:** Four conjoined busts
left plus the HMS Vanguard **Edge:** Reeded

Date	Mintage	F	VF	XF	Unc	BU
ND(2002) Proof	5,000	Value: 45.00				

KM# 30 50 PENCE
28.2800 g., Copper-Nickel, 38.6 mm. **Ruler:** Elizabeth II
Subject: 50th Anniversary of Queen Elizabeth's Coronation **Obv:**
Crowned bust right **Rev:** Crowned Queen facing with scepter and
orb **Edge:** Reeded

Date	Mintage	F	VF	XF	Unc	BU
ND(2003)	—	—	—	—	10.00	12.00

KM# 30a 50 PENCE
28.2800 g., 0.9250 Silver 0.8410 oz. ASW, 38.6 mm. **Ruler:**
Elizabeth II **Subject:** 50th Anniversary - Queen Elizabeth's
Coronation **Obv:** Crowned bust right **Rev:** Crowned Queen facing
with scepter and orb **Edge:** Reeded

Date	Mintage	F	VF	XF	Unc	BU
ND(2003) Proof	5,000	Value: 50.00				

KM# 30b 50 PENCE
39.9400 g., 0.9166 Gold 1.1770 oz. AGW, 38.6 mm. **Ruler:**
Elizabeth II **Subject:** 50th Anniversary of Queen's Coronation
Obv: Crowned bust right **Rev:** Crowned Queen facing with
scepter and orb **Edge:** Reeded

Date	Mintage	F	VF	XF	Unc	BU
ND(2003) Proof	50	Value: 2,150				

KM# 31 50 PENCE
28.2800 g., Copper-Nickel, 38.6 mm. **Ruler:** Elizabeth II
Subject: 50th Anniversary of Coronation **Obv:** Crowned bust
right **Rev:** Coronation implements **Edge:** Reeded

Date	Mintage	F	VF	XF	Unc	BU
ND(2003)	—	—	—	—	10.00	12.00

KM# 31a 50 PENCE
28.2800 g., 0.9250 Silver 0.8410 oz. ASW, 38.6 mm. **Ruler:**
Elizabeth II **Subject:** 50th Anniversary - Queen Elizabeth II's
Coronation **Obv:** Crowned bust right **Rev:** Coronation
implements **Edge:** Reeded

Date	Mintage	F	VF	XF	Unc	BU
ND(2003) Proof	5,000	Value: 50.00				

KM# 31b 50 PENCE
39.9400 g., 0.9166 Gold 1.1770 oz. AGW, 38.6 mm. **Ruler:**
Elizabeth II **Subject:** 50th Anniversary of Coronation **Obv:**
Crowned bust right **Rev:** Coronation implements **Edge:** Reeded

Date	Mintage	F	VF	XF	Unc	BU
ND(2003) Proof	50	Value: 2,150				

PIEDFORT

KM#	Date	Mintage	Identification	Mkt Val
P3	ND(2002)	500	50 Pence. 0.9250 Silver. 56.5600 g. 38.6 mm. Reeded edge. Proof.	120

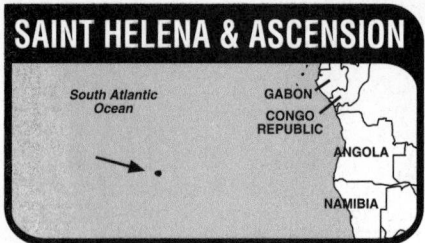

SAINT HELENA & ASCENSION

South Atlantic Ocean — GABON, CONGO REPUBLIC, ANGOLA, NAMIBIA

BRITISH OVERSEAS TERRITORY

STANDARD COINAGE

100 Pence = 1 Pound

KM# 13a PENNY
3.5000 g., Copper Plated Steel, 20.28 mm. **Ruler:** Queen Elizabeth II **Obv:** Crowned head right **Rev:** Tuna above value **Edge:** Plain

Date	Mintage	F	VF	XF	Unc	BU
2003	—	—	—	0.15	0.35	0.75

KM# 12a 2 PENCE
Copper Plated Steel, 25.9 mm. **Ruler:** Queen Elizabeth II **Obv:** Crowned head right **Rev:** Value below donkey

Date	Mintage	F	VF	XF	Unc	BU
2003	—	—	—	0.20	0.60	1.25
2006	—	—	—	0.20	0.60	1.25

KM# 22 5 PENCE
3.2500 g., Copper-Nickel, 18 mm. **Ruler:** Queen Elizabeth II **Obv:** Crowned head right **Rev:** Giant tortoise

Date	Mintage	F	VF	XF	Unc	BU
2003	—	—	—	1.00	2.50	5.00

KM# 23 10 PENCE
6.5000 g., Copper-Nickel, 24.5 mm. **Ruler:** Queen Elizabeth II **Obv:** Crowned head right **Rev:** Dolphins

Date	Mintage	F	VF	XF	Unc	BU
2003	—	—	—	2.00	4.00	6.00
2006	—	—	—	2.00	4.00	6.00

KM# 21 20 PENCE
5.0000 g., Copper-Nickel, 21.4 mm. **Ruler:** Queen Elizabeth II **Obv:** Crowned head right **Rev:** Ebony flower **Shape:** 7-sided

Date	Mintage	F	VF	XF	Unc	BU
2003	—	—	—	0.75	1.50	2.50

KM# 16 50 PENCE
13.5000 g., Copper-Nickel, 30 mm. **Ruler:** Queen Elizabeth II **Obv:** Crowned head right **Rev:** Green sea turtle **Shape:** 7-sided

Date	Mintage	F	VF	XF	Unc	BU
2003	—	—	—	1.50	4.00	6.00
2006	—	—	—	1.50	4.00	6.00

KM# 17 POUND
9.5000 g., Nickel-Brass, 22.5 mm. **Ruler:** Queen Elizabeth II **Obv:** Crowned head right **Rev:** Sooty terns (Wideawake birds)

Date	Mintage	F	VF	XF	Unc	BU
2003	—	—	—	2.25	5.00	8.00
2006	—	—	—	2.25	5.00	8.00

KM# 26 2 POUNDS
11.8100 g., Nickel-Brass, 28.3 mm. **Ruler:** Queen Elizabeth II **Obv:** Crowned head right **Rev:** National arms above value **Edge:** Reeded and lettered **Edge Lettering:** 500TH ANNIVERSARY

Date	Mintage	F	VF	XF	Unc	BU
2002	—	—	—	6.00	10.00	12.50

KM# 25 2 POUNDS
12.0000 g., Bi-Metallic Copper-Nickel center in Brass ring, 28.4 mm. **Ruler:** Queen Elizabeth II **Obv:** Crowned bust right **Rev:** National Arms **Edge:** Reeded and lettered **Edge Lettering:** LOYAL AND FAITHFUL

Date	Mintage	F	VF	XF	Unc	BU
2003	—	—	—	9.00	15.00	17.50
2006	—	—	—	9.00	15.00	17.50

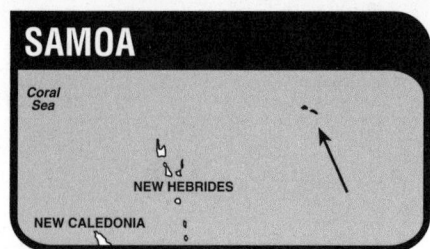

SAMOA

Coral Sea — NEW HEBRIDES, NEW CALEDONIA

The Independent State of Samoa (formerly Western Samoa), located in the Pacific Ocean 1,600 miles (2,574 km.) northeast of New Zealand, has an area of 1,097 sq. mi. (2,860 sq. km.) and a population of *182,000. Capital: Apia. The economy is based on agriculture, fishing and tourism. Copra, cocoa and bananas are exported.

Samoa is a member of the Commonwealth of Nations. The Chief Executive is Chief of State. The prime minister is the Head of Government. The present Head of State, Malietoa Tanumafili II, holds his position for life. The Legislative Assembly will elect future Heads of State for 5-year terms.

Samoa, which had used New Zealand coinage, converted to a decimal coinage in 1967.

RULER
Malietoa Tanumafili II, 1962-2007
Tuiatua Tupua Tamasese Efi, 2007-

MONETARY SYSTEM
100 Sene = 1 Tala

CONSTITUTIONAL MONARCHY
Commonwealth of Nations

STANDARD COINAGE

KM# 131 5 SENE
2.8400 g., Copper-Nickel, 19.5 mm. **Obv:** Head left **Rev:** Pineapple and value **Edge:** Reeded **Note:** "Western" dropped from country name

Date	Mintage	F	VF	XF	Unc	BU
2002	—	—	—	0.30	0.50	0.75
2006	—	—	—	0.30	0.50	0.75
2010	—	—	—	0.30	0.50	0.75

KM# 167 5 SENE
Nickel Plated Steel

Date	Mintage	F	VF	XF	Unc	BU
2010	—	—	—	—	0.50	0.75

KM# 132 10 SENE
5.6500 g., Copper-Nickel, 23.6 mm. **Obv:** Head left **Rev:** Taro leaves and value **Edge:** Reeded **Note:** "Western" dropped from country name

Date	Mintage	F	VF	XF	Unc	BU
2002	—	—	—	0.45	0.75	1.00
2006	—	—	—	0.45	0.75	1.00
2010	—	—	—	0.45	0.75	1.00

KM# 168 10 SENE
Nickel Plated Steel

Date	Mintage	F	VF	XF	Unc	BU
2010	—	—	—	—	0.75	1.00

KM# 133 20 SENE
11.4000 g., Copper-Nickel, 28.45 mm. **Obv:** Head left **Rev:** Breadfruits and value **Edge:** Reeded **Note:** "Western" dropped from country name

Date	Mintage	F	VF	XF	Unc	BU
2002	—	—	—	0.60	1.00	1.50
2006	—	—	—	0.60	1.00	1.50

KM# 169 20 SENE
Nickel Plated Steel

Date	Mintage	F	VF	XF	Unc	BU
2010	—	—	—	—	1.00	1.50

KM# 134 50 SENE
14.1300 g., Copper-Nickel, 32.3 mm. **Obv:** Head left **Rev:** Banana tree and value **Edge:** Reeded **Note:** "Western" dropped from country name

Date	Mintage	F	VF	XF	Unc	BU
2002	—	—	—	—	1.75	2.00
2006	—	—	—	—	1.75	2.00
2010	—	—	—	—	1.75	2.00

KM# 170 50 SENE
Nickel Plated Steel

Date	Mintage	F	VF	XF	Unc	BU
2010	—	—	—	—	1.75	2.00

KM# 135 TALA
9.5000 g., Brass, 30 mm. **Obv:** Head left **Rev:** National arms above value and banner flanked by sprigs **Edge:** Reeded **Note:** "Western" dropped from country name

Date	Mintage	F	VF	XF	Unc	BU
2002	—	—	—	1.50	2.50	3.00
2006	—	—	—	1.50	2.50	3.00

KM# 150 TALA
Goldine Plated Metal **Subject:** Thomas Mann **Obv:** Arms **Rev:** Bust facing

Date	Mintage	F	VF	XF	Unc	BU
2009	—	—	—	—	—	30.00

KM# 151 TALA
Goldine Plated Metal **Subject:** Hercules & Hydra

Date	Mintage	F	VF	XF	Unc	BU
2009	—	—	—	—	—	25.00

KM# 152 TALA
Goldine Plated Metal **Subject:** Alhambra

Date	Mintage	F	VF	XF	Unc	BU
2009	—	—	—	—	—	25.00

KM# 153 TALA
Goldine Plated Metal **Rev:** Golden horn

Date	Mintage	F	VF	XF	Unc	BU
2009	—	—	—	—	—	25.00

KM# 154 TALA
Goldine Plated Metal **Rev:** Sphinx

Date	Mintage	F	VF	XF	Unc	BU
2009	—	—	—	—	—	25.00

KM# 155 TALA
Goldine Plated Metal **Rev:** Kaiser Wilhelm II

Date	Mintage	F	VF	XF	Unc	BU
2009	—	—	—	—	—	25.00

KM# 156 TALA
Goldine Plated Metal **Rev:** Hagia Sophia

Date	Mintage	F	VF	XF	Unc	BU
2009	—	—	—	—	—	25.00

KM# 171 TALA
Aluminum-Bronze

Date	Mintage	F	VF	XF	Unc	BU
2010	—	—	—	—	2.50	3.00

KM# 174 TALA
0.5000 g., 0.9990 Gold 0.0161 oz. AGW, 11 mm. **Obv:** National arms **Rev:** Samoan Flying Fox (bat) in flight

Date	Mintage	F	VF	XF	Unc	BU
2010 Proof	10,000	Value: 75.00				

KM# 165 5 TALA
28.2800 g., 0.9250 Silver 0.8410 oz. ASW, 38.61 mm. **Obv:** National Arms **Rev:** Steam Locomotive centennial

Date	Mintage	F	VF	XF	Unc	BU
2007 Proof	Est. 5,000	Value: 75.00				

KM# 166 5 TALA
31.1050 g., 0.9990 Silver 0.9990 oz. ASW, 38.6 mm. **Obv:** National arms **Rev:** John Paul II at right and as figure in flames

Date	Mintage	F	VF	XF	Unc	BU
2009 Proof	Est. 2,000	Value: 85.00				

KM# 137 10 TALA
31.1000 g., 0.9990 Silver with Mother-of-Pearl insert 0.9988 oz. ASW, 40 mm. **Series:** Save the Whales **Obv:** National arms above value and banner flanked by sprigs **Obv. Legend:** SAMOA I SISIFO **Rev:** Bowhead Whale on mother-of-pearl insert **Edge:** Plain

Date	Mintage	F	VF	XF	Unc	BU
2002 Proof	2,000	Value: 85.00				

KM# 139 10 TALA
31.4700 g., 0.9250 Silver 0.9359 oz. ASW **Subject:** XXVIII Summer Olympics - Athens **Obv:** National arms **Obv. Legend:** SAMOA I SISIFO **Rev:** Swimming - two divers

Date	Mintage	F	VF	XF	Unc	BU
2003 Proof	—	Value: 60.00				

KM# 146 10 TALA
1.2300 g., Gold, 13.89 mm. **Obv:** National arms **Obv. Legend:** SAMOA SISIFO **Rev:** Bust of Fletcher Christian 3/4 left at left, sailing ship "H. M. S. Bounty" at right **Edge:** Reeded

Date	Mintage	F	VF	XF	Unc	BU
2003 Proof	—	Value: 90.00				

KM# 140 10 TALA
1.2400 g., 0.9990 Gold 0.0398 oz. AGW **Series:** World Statesmen **Subject:** Mahatma Gandhi **Obv:** National arms **Obv. Legend:** SAMOA I SISIFO

Date	Mintage	F	VF	XF	Unc	BU
2003 Proof	—	Value: 90.00				

KM# 141 10 TALA
1.2400 g., 0.9990 Gold 0.0398 oz. AGW **Series:** World Statesmen **Subject:** Konrad Adenauer **Obv:** National arms **Obv. Legend:** SAMOA I SISIFO

Date	Mintage	F	VF	XF	Unc	BU
2003 Proof	—	Value: 90.00				

KM# 159 10 TALA
1.2400 g., 0.9990 Gold 0.0398 oz. AGW, 13.92 mm. **Obv:** National arms **Rev:** Theodore Roosevelt

Date	Mintage	F	VF	XF	Unc	BU
2003 Proof	Est. 2,000	Value: 90.00				

KM# 160 10 TALA
1.2400 g., 0.9990 Gold 0.0398 oz. AGW, 13.92 mm. **Obv:** National arms **Rev:** Winston Churchill

Date	Mintage	F	VF	XF	Unc	BU
2003 Proof	Est. 2,000	Value: 90.00				

KM# 161 10 TALA
1.2400 g., 0.9990 Gold 0.0398 oz. AGW, 13.92 mm. **Obv:** National arms **Rev:** Charles de Gaulle

Date	Mintage	F	VF	XF	Unc	BU
2003 Proof	Est. 2,000	Value: 90.00				

KM# 162 10 TALA
1.2400 g., 0.9990 Gold 0.0398 oz. AGW, 13.92 mm. **Obv:** National arms **Rev:** John F. Kennedy

Date	Mintage	F	VF	XF	Unc	BU
2003 Proof	Est. 2,000	Value: 90.00				

KM# 143 10 TALA
28.5800 g., Silver, 38.61 mm. **Obv:** National arms **Obv. Legend:** SAMOA I SISIFO **Rev:** Sailing ship "La Récherche" **Rev. Legend:** JEAN FRANCOIS GALAUP - COMTE DE LA PEROUSE **Edge:** Reeded

Date	Mintage	F	VF	XF	Unc	BU
2004 Proof	—	Value: 55.00				

KM# 142 10 TALA
1.2400 g., 0.9990 Gold 0.0398 oz. AGW **Subject:** Death of Pope John-Paul II **Obv:** National arms

Date	Mintage	F	VF	XF	Unc	BU
2005	15,000	—	—	—	—	65.00
2005 Proof	3,300	Value: 90.00				

KM# 163 10 TALA
1.2400 g., 0.9990 Gold 0.0398 oz. AGW, 13.92 mm. **Obv:** National arms **Rev:** 2006 FIFA World Cup Germany logo

Date	Mintage	F	VF	XF	Unc	BU
2005 Proof	Est. 25,000	Value: 90.00				

KM# 164 10 TALA
1.2400 g., 0.9990 Gold 0.0398 oz. AGW, 13.92 mm. **Obv:** National arms **Rev:** Pope Benedict XVI in robes and mitre giving blessing

Date	Mintage	F	VF	XF	Unc	BU
2006 Proof	—	Value: 90.00				

KM# 172 10 TALA
20.0000 g., 0.9250 Silver 0.5948 oz. ASW, 38.61 mm. **Obv:** National arms **Rev:** Sailing ship Preussen

Date	Mintage	F	VF	XF	Unc	BU
2010 Proof	2,500	Value: 75.00				

KM# 173   10 TALA
25.0000 g., 0.9250 Silver 0.7435 oz. ASW, 38.61 mm. **Obv:** National arms **Rev:** Samoan Flying Fox (bat) hanging, with colored eyes

Date	Mintage	F	VF	XF	Unc	BU
2010 Proof	2,500	Value: 75.00				

SAN MARINO

The Republic of San Marino, the oldest and smallest republic in the world is located in north central Italy entirely surrounded by the Province of Emilia-Romagna. It has an area of 24 sq. mi. (60 sq. km.) and a population of *23,000. Capital: San Marino. The principal economic activities are farming, livestock raising, cheese making, tourism and light manufacturing. Building stone, lime, wheat, hides and baked goods are exported. The government derives most of its revenue from the sale of postage stamps for philatelic purposes.

San Marino has its own coinage, but Italian and Vatican City coins and currency are also in circulation.

MINT MARKS
R - Rome

MONETARY SYSTEM
100 Centesimi = 1 Lira

REPUBLIC
STANDARD COINAGE

KM# 424   10 LIRE
1.6000 g., Aluminum, 23.3 mm. **Obv:** Three towers within circle **Rev:** Wheat stalks and value **Edge:** Plain

Date	Mintage	F	VF	XF	Unc	BU
2001R	—	—	—	—	0.35	0.50

KM# 425   20 LIRE
3.6000 g., Aluminum-Bronze, 21.8 mm. **Obv:** Three towers within circle **Rev:** Two dolphins and value **Edge:** Plain

Date	Mintage	F	VF	XF	Unc	BU
2001R	—	—	—	—	1.00	2.00

KM# 426   50 LIRE
4.5000 g., Copper-Nickel, 19 mm. **Obv:** Three towers within circle **Rev:** Tree and value **Edge:** Plain

Date	Mintage	F	VF	XF	Unc	BU
2001R	—	—	—	—	0.85	1.50

KM# 427   100 LIRE
4.5000 g., Copper-Nickel, 22 mm. **Obv:** Three towers within circle **Rev:** Grasping hands and value **Edge:** Plain and reeded sections

Date	Mintage	F	VF	XF	Unc	BU
2001R	—	—	—	—	1.25	2.00

KM# 428   200 LIRE
5.0000 g., Aluminum-Bronze, 24 mm. **Obv:** Three towers within circle **Rev:** Broken chain, leaves, vines and value **Edge:** Reeded

Date	Mintage	F	VF	XF	Unc	BU
2001R	—	—	—	—	1.50	2.50

KM# 429   500 LIRE
Bi-Metallic Aluminum-Bronze center in Stainless Steel ring, 25.8 mm. **Obv:** Three towers within circle **Rev:** Three different plant stalks and value **Edge:** Segmented reeding **Note:** 6.8 grams.

Date	Mintage	F	VF	XF	Unc	BU
2001R	—	—	—	—	3.00	3.50

KM# 430   1000 LIRE
8.8000 g., Bi-Metallic Stainless-Steel center in Aluminum-Bronze ring, 27 mm. **Obv:** Three towers within circle **Rev:** Value within circle of birds **Edge:** Segmented reeding

Date	Mintage	F	VF	XF	Unc	BU
2001R	—	—	—	—	7.50	10.00

KM# 431   5000 LIRE
18.0000 g., 0.8350 Silver 0.4832 oz. ASW, 32 mm. **Obv:** Three towers within circle **Rev:** Dove on laurel branch above value **Edge:** Reeded and plain sections

Date	Mintage	F	VF	XF	Unc	BU
2001R	—	—	—	—	22.50	27.50

KM# 436   5000 LIRE
18.0000 g., 0.8350 Silver 0.4832 oz. ASW, 32 mm. **Subject:** Last Lire Coinage **Obv:** Crowned arms within sprigs **Rev:** Feather above six old coin designs with value below, all within beaded border **Edge:** Lettered

Date	Mintage	F	VF	XF	Unc	BU
2001R Proof	20,000	Value: 25.00				

KM# 432   10000 LIRE
22.0000 g., 0.8350 Silver 0.5906 oz. ASW, 34 mm. **Subject:** Ferrari **Obv:** Crowned arms within sprigs **Rev:** Race car with "FERRARI" background **Edge:** Reeded and plain sections

Date	Mintage	F	VF	XF	Unc	BU
2001R Proof	20,000	Value: 45.00				

KM# 437   10000 LIRE
22.0000 g., 0.8350 Silver 0.5906 oz. ASW, 34 mm. **Subject:** Last Lire Coinage **Obv:** Crowned arms within sprigs **Rev:** Feather above six old coin designs with value below, all within star border **Edge:** Reeded and plain sections

Date	Mintage	F	VF	XF	Unc	BU
2001R Proof	20,000	Value: 42.00				

KM# 438   10000 LIRE
22.0000 g., 0.8350 Silver 0.5906 oz. ASW, 34 mm. **Subject:** 2nd International Chambers of Commerce Convention **Obv:** Crowned arms within sprigs **Rev:** Mercury running by a computer **Edge:** Reeded and plain sections.

Date	Mintage	F	VF	XF	Unc	BU
2001R Proof	20,000	Value: 42.00				

KM# 433   1/2 SCUDO
1.6100 g., 0.9000 Gold 0.0466 oz. AGW, 13.8 mm. **Subject:** Cavaliere **Obv:** Crowned arms within sprigs **Rev:** Horse and rider **Edge:** Reeded

Date	Mintage	F	VF	XF	Unc	BU
2001R Proof	4,500	Value: 100				

KM# 434   SCUDO
3.2200 g., 0.9000 Gold 0.0932 oz. AGW, 16 mm. **Subject:** Tiziano **Obv:** Crowned arms within sprigs **Rev:** Bearded bust left **Edge:** Reeded

Date	Mintage	F	VF	XF	Unc	BU
2001R Proof	4,500	Value: 190				

KM# 435   2 SCUDI
6.4400 g., 0.9000 Gold 0.1863 oz. AGW, 21 mm. **Subject:** Flora **Obv:** Crowned arms within sprigs **Rev:** Bust 1/4 left and value **Edge:** Reeded

Date	Mintage	F	VF	XF	Unc	BU
2001R Proof	4,500	Value: 375				

KM# 457 2 SCUDI

6.4516 g., 0.9000 Gold 0.1867 oz. AGW, 21 mm. **Obv:** Crowned arms within sprigs **Rev:** Madonna and Child **Edge:** Reeded

Date	Mintage	F	VF	XF	Unc	BU
2002R Proof	3,000	Value: 375				

KM# 459 2 SCUDI

6.4516 g., 0.9000 Gold 0.1867 oz. AGW, 21 mm. **Obv:** Crowned arms within sprigs **Rev:** Nostradamus above value **Edge:** Reeded

Date	Mintage	F	VF	XF	Unc	BU
2003R Proof	7,500	Value: 375				

KM# 464 2 SCUDI

6.4516 g., 0.9000 Gold 0.1867 oz. AGW, 21 mm. **Subject:** The Domagnano Treasure **Obv:** Crowned arms within sprigs **Rev:** Gothic Eagle Brooch, 5 Mark coin of 1952 **Edge:** Reeded

Date	Mintage	F	VF	XF	Unc	BU
2004R Proof	6,500	Value: 375				

KM# 493 2 SCUDI

6.4100 g., 0.9000 Gold 0.1855 oz. AGW, 21 mm. **Subject:** Pompeo Batoni, 300th Anniversary of Brith **Obv:** Arms **Rev:** Batoni's "San Marino Risolleva la Republica"

Date	Mintage	F	VF	XF	Unc	BU
2008R Proof	2,100	Value: 375				

KM# 439 5 SCUDI

16.9655 g., 0.9166 Gold 0.4999 oz. AGW, 28 mm. **Subject:** San Marino's World Bank Membership **Obv:** Crowned arms within sprigs **Rev:** Orchid and bee within globe **Edge:** Reeded

Date	Mintage	F	VF	XF	Unc	BU
2001R Proof	4,000	Value: 950				

EURO COINAGE

KM# 440 EURO CENT

2.2700 g., Copper Plated Steel, 16.2 mm. **Obv:** "Il Montale" **Rev:** Value and globe **Edge:** Plain

Date	Mintage	F	VF	XF	Unc	BU
2002R	125,000	—	—	—	—	40.00
2003R In sets only	70,000	—	—	—	—	42.00
2004R	1,500,000	—	—	—	—	20.00
2005R In sets only	70,000	—	—	—	—	20.00
2006R	2,730,000	—	—	—	8.00	12.00
2007R	—	—	—	—	8.00	12.00
2008R	—	—	—	—	8.00	12.00
2008R Proof	13,000	Value: 10.00				
2009R	—	—	—	—	8.00	12.00
2009R Proof	13,500	Value: 10.00				
2010R	—	—	—	—	8.00	12.00
2010R Proof	8,600	Value: 10.00				
2011R	—	—	—	—	8.00	12.00
2011R Proof	8,600	Value: 10.00				
2012R	—	—	—	—	8.00	12.00

KM# 441 2 EURO CENT

3.0300 g., Copper Plated Steel, 18.7 mm. **Obv:** Stefano Gallietti, Liberty fighter **Rev:** Value and globe **Edge:** Grooved

Date	Mintage	F	VF	XF	Unc	BU
2002R	125,000	—	—	—	—	40.00
2003R In sets only	70,000	—	—	—	—	42.00
2004R	1,395,000	—	—	—	—	20.00
2005R In sets only	150,000	—	—	—	—	20.00
2006R	2,730,000	—	—	—	8.00	12.00
2007R	—	—	—	—	8.00	12.00
2008R	—	—	—	—	8.00	12.00
2008R Proof	13,000	Value: 10.00				
2009R	—	—	—	—	8.00	12.00
2009R Proof	13,500	Value: 10.00				
2010R	—	—	—	—	8.00	12.00
2010R Proof	8,600	Value: 10.00				
2011R	—	—	—	—	8.00	12.00
2011R Proof	8,600	Value: 10.00				
2012R	—	—	—	—	8.00	12.00

KM# 442 5 EURO CENT

3.8600 g., Copper Plated Steel, 21.2 mm. **Obv:** "Guaita" tower **Rev:** Value and globe **Edge:** Plain

Date	Mintage	F	VF	XF	Unc	BU
2002R	125,000	—	—	—	—	40.00
2003R In sets only	70,000	—	—	—	—	42.00
2004R	1,000,000	—	—	—	—	20.00
2005R In sets only	70,000	—	—	—	—	20.00
2006R	2,880,000	—	—	—	8.00	12.00
2007R	—	—	—	—	8.00	12.00
2008R	—	—	—	—	8.00	12.00
2008R Proof	13,000	Value: 10.00				
2009R	—	—	—	—	8.00	12.00
2009R Proof	13,500	Value: 10.00				
2010R	—	—	—	—	8.00	12.00
2010R Proof	8,600	Value: 10.00				
2011R	—	—	—	—	8.00	12.00
2011R Proof	8,600	Value: 10.00				
2012R	—	—	—	—	8.00	12.00

KM# 443 10 EURO CENT

4.0700 g., Brass, 19.7 mm. **Obv:** Building Basilica del Santo Marinus **Rev:** Map and value **Edge:** Reeded

Date	Mintage	F	VF	XF	Unc	BU
2002R	125,000	—	—	—	—	40.00
2003R In sets only	70,000	—	—	—	—	42.00
2004R	180,000	—	—	—	—	22.00
2005R In sets only	70,000	—	—	—	—	22.00
2006R In sets only	65,000	—	—	—	—	20.00
2007R	—	—	—	—	—	18.00

KM# 482 10 EURO CENT

4.0700 g., Brass, 19.7 mm. **Obv:** Basilica de Santo Marinus facade **Rev:** Relief maps of Western Europe, value and stars

Date	Mintage	F	VF	XF	Unc	BU
2008R	—	—	—	—	8.00	12.00
2008R Proof	13,000	Value: 12.00				
2009R	—	—	—	—	8.00	12.00
2009R Proof	13,500	Value: 12.00				
2010R	—	—	—	—	8.00	12.00
2010R Proof	8,600	Value: 12.00				
2011R	—	—	—	—	8.00	12.00
2011R Proof	8,600	Value: 12.00				
2012R	—	—	—	—	8.00	12.00

KM# 444 20 EURO CENT

5.7300 g., Brass, 22.1 mm. **Obv:** St. Marinus from a portrait by van Guercino **Rev:** Map and value **Edge:** Notched

Date	Mintage	F	VF	XF	Unc	BU
2002R	267,400	—	—	—	18.00	20.00
2003R	430,000	—	—	—	15.00	18.00
2004R In sets only	70,000	—	—	—	15.00	18.00
2005R	310,000	—	—	—	15.00	18.00
2006R In sets only	70,000	—	—	—	15.00	18.00
2007R	—	—	—	—	14.00	16.00

KM# 483 20 EURO CENT

5.7300 g., Brass **Obv:** Saint holding Monte Titano **Rev:** Relief map of Western Europe, value and stars

Date	Mintage	F	VF	XF	Unc	BU
2008R	—	—	—	—	8.00	12.00
2008R Proof	13,000	Value: 15.00				
2009R	—	—	—	—	8.00	12.00
2009R Proof	13,500	Value: 15.00				
2010R	—	—	—	—	8.00	12.00
2010R Proof	8,600	Value: 15.00				
2011R	—	—	—	—	8.00	12.00

Date	Mintage	F	VF	XF	Unc	BU
2011R Proof	8,600	Value: 15.00				
2012R	—	—	—	—	8.00	12.00

KM# 445 50 EURO CENT

7.8100 g., Brass, 24.2 mm. **Obv:** Fortress of San Marino **Rev:** Map and value **Edge:** Reeded

Date	Mintage	F	VF	XF	Unc	BU
2002R	230,400	—	—	—	20.00	22.50
2003R	415,000	—	—	—	17.50	20.00
2004R In sets only	70,000	—	—	—	17.50	20.00
2005R	179,000	—	—	—	17.50	20.00
2006R	343,880	—	—	—	15.00	18.00
2007R	—	—	—	—	14.00	16.00

KM# 484 50 EURO CENT

7.8000 g., Brass, 24.2 mm. **Obv:** Buildings on hill top **Rev:** Relief map of Western Europe, value and stars

Date	Mintage	F	VF	XF	Unc	BU
2008R	—	—	—	—	10.00	12.00
2008R Proof	13,000	Value: 13.00				
2009R	—	—	—	—	10.00	12.00
2009R Proof	13,500	Value: 13.00				
2010R	—	—	—	—	10.00	12.00
2010R Proof	8,600	Value: 13.00				
2011R	—	—	—	—	10.00	12.00
2011R Proof	8,600	Value: 13.00				
2012R	—	—	—	—	10.00	12.00

KM# 446 EURO

7.5000 g., Bi-Metallic Copper-Nickel center in Nickel-Brass ring, 23.25 mm. **Obv:** Crowned arms within sprigs and circle within star border **Rev:** Value and map **Edge:** Segmented reeding

Date	Mintage	F	VF	XF	Unc	BU
2002R	360,800	—	—	—	22.00	25.00
2003R In sets only	70,000	—	—	—	—	45.00
2004R	180,000	—	—	—	—	25.00
2005R In sets only	70,000	—	—	—	—	25.00
2006R In sets only	220,000	—	—	—	—	20.00
2007R	—	—	—	—	—	18.00

KM# 485 EURO

7.5000 g., Bi-Metallic Copper-Nickel center in Nickel-Brass ring, 23.25 mm. **Obv:** Covered arms within wreath and stars **Rev:** Relief map of Western Europe, value and stars **Edge:** Segmented reeding

Date	Mintage	F	VF	XF	Unc	BU
2008R	—	—	—	—	12.00	15.00
2008R Proof	13,000	Value: 15.00				
2009R	—	—	—	—	12.00	15.00
2009R Proof	13,500	Value: 15.00				
2010R	—	—	—	—	12.00	15.00
2010R Proof	8,600	Value: 15.00				
2011R	—	—	—	—	12.00	15.00
2011R Proof	8,600	Value: 15.00				
2012R	—	—	—	—	12.00	15.00

KM# 447   2 EURO

8.5000 g., Bi-Metallic Nickel-Brass center in Copper-Nickel ring, 25.75 mm. **Obv:** Government building **Rev:** Value and map **Edge:** Reeded with 2's and stars

Date	Mintage	F	VF	XF	Unc	BU
2002R	255,760	—	—	—	25.00	28.00
2003R In sets only	70,000	—	—	—	—	45.00
2004R In sets only	70,000	—	—	—	—	28.00
2005R In sets only	210,000	—	—	—	—	28.00
2006R In sets only	190,000	—	—	—	—	22.00
2007R	—	—	—	—	—	20.00

KM# 467   2 EURO

8.5000 g., Bi-Metallic Nickel-Brass center in Copper-Nickel ring, 25.75 mm. **Obv:** Crowned arms within sprigs **Rev:** Bartolomeo Borghesi **Edge:** Alternating stars and 2's

Date	Mintage	F	VF	XF	Unc	BU
2004R	110,000	—	—	—	135	150

KM# 469   2 EURO

8.5000 g., Bi-Metallic Nickel-Brass center in Copper-Nickel ring, 25.75 mm. **Obv:** Galileo Galilei at telescope

Date	Mintage	F	VF	XF	Unc	BU
2005R	130,000	—	—	—	135	150

KM# 478   2 EURO

8.5000 g., Bi-Metallic Nickel-Brass center in Copper-Nickel ring, 25.75 mm. **Subject:** Christopher Columbus, 500th Anniversary of Death **Obv:** Head of Columbus within border of stars **Rev:** Map and value

Date	Mintage	F	VF	XF	Unc	BU
2006R	120,000	—	—	—	125	100

KM# 481   2 EURO

8.5000 g., Bi-Metallic Nickel-Brass center in Copper-Nickel ring, 25.75 mm. **Subject:** Giuseppe Garibaldi, 200th Anniversary of Birth **Obv:** Half length bust facing **Rev:** Relief map of Western Europe, value and stars

Date	Mintage	F	VF	XF	Unc	BU
2007R	130,000	—	—	—	60.00	75.00

KM# 486   2 EURO

8.5000 g., Bi-Metallic Nickel-Brass center in Copper-Nickel ring,

25.75 mm. **Obv:** Palace **Rev:** Relief map of Western Europe, value and stars

Date	Mintage	F	VF	XF	Unc	BU
2008R	—	—	—	—	24.00	28.00
2008R Proof	13,000	Value: 20.00				
2009R	—	—	—	—	24.00	28.00
2009R Proof	13,500	Value: 20.00				
2010R	—	—	—	—	24.00	28.00
2010R Proof	8,600	Value: 20.00				
2011R	—	—	—	—	24.00	28.00
2011R Proof	8,600	Value: 20.00				
2012R	—	—	—	—	24.00	28.00

KM# 487   2 EURO

8.5000 g., Bi-Metallic Nickel-Brass center in Copper-Nickel ring, 25.75 mm. **Subject:** European Year of Intercultural Dialogue **Obv:** Five figures with arms outstretched, books below **Rev:** Relief map of Western Europe, value and stars

Date	Mintage	F	VF	XF	Unc	BU
2008R	130,000	—	—	—	70.00	90.00

KM# 490   2 EURO

8.5000 g., Bi-Metallic Nickel-Brass center in Copper-Nickel ring, 25.75 mm. **Subject:** Creativity and Innovation **Obv:** Chemical flasks and book

Date	Mintage	F	VF	XF	Unc	BU
2009R	—	—	—	—	45.00	55.00

KM# 494   2 EURO

8.5000 g., Bi-Metallic Nickel-Brass center in Copper-Nickel ring, 25.75 mm. **Subject:** Sandra Botticeli, 500th Anniversary of Death

Date	Mintage	F	VF	XF	Unc	BU
2010R	—	—	—	—	45.00	55.00

KM# 500   2 EURO

8.5000 g., Bi-Metallic Nickel-Brass center in Copper-Nickel ring, 25.75 mm. **Subject:** Hgiorgio Vasari, 500th Anniversary of Birth

Date	Mintage	F	VF	XF	Unc	BU
2011R	—	—	—	—	35.00	45.00

KM# 448   5 EURO

18.0000 g., 0.9250 Silver 0.5353 oz. ASW, 32 mm. **Subject:** Welcome Euro **Obv:** Three plumed towers **Rev:** Circle of roses

Date	Mintage	F	VF	XF	Unc	BU
2002R Proof	37,000	Value: 75.00				

KM# 450   5 EURO

18.0000 g., 0.9250 Silver 0.5353 oz. ASW, 32 mm. **Subject:** 1600th Anniversary of Ravenna **Obv:** National arms **Rev:** Bas-relief wall design **Edge:** Reeded

Date	Mintage	F	VF	XF	Unc	BU
2002R Proof	—	Value: 60.00				

KM# 453   5 EURO

18.0000 g., 0.9250 Silver 0.5353 oz. ASW, 32 mm. **Subject:** 2004 Olympics **Obv:** Stylized three towers **Rev:** Ancient Olympians **Edge:** Reeded

Date	Mintage	F	VF	XF	Unc	BU
2003R Proof	37,766	Value: 50.00				

KM# 452   5 EURO

18.0000 g., 0.9250 Silver 0.5353 oz. ASW, 32 mm. **Obv:** National arms **Rev:** Allegorical depiction of Independence, Tolerance and Liberty

Date	Mintage	F	VF	XF	Unc	BU
2003R	70,000	—	—	—	35.00	40.00

KM# 458   5 EURO

18.0000 g., 0.9250 Silver 0.5353 oz. ASW, 32 mm. **Obv:** National arms **Rev:** Value behind Bartolomeo Borghesi

Date	Mintage	F	VF	XF	Unc	BU
2004R	70,000	—	—	—	—	35.00

KM# 462   5 EURO

18.0000 g., 0.9250 Silver 0.5353 oz. ASW, 32 mm. **Obv:** Three stylized plumed towers **Rev:** Two soccer players

Date	Mintage	F	VF	XF	Unc	BU
2004R Proof	30,000	Value: 45.00				

KM# 468   5 EURO

18.0000 g., 0.9250 Silver 0.5353 oz. ASW, 32 mm. **Obv:** Three towers **Rev:** Antonio Onofri and value

Date	Mintage	F	VF	XF	Unc	BU
2005R	70,000	—	—	—	30.00	35.00

KM# 511   5 EURO

18.0000 g., 0.9250 Silver 0.5353 oz. ASW, 32 mm. **Subject:** Winter Olympics, Turin **Rev:** Snowflake, snowman on skies

Date	Mintage	F	VF	XF	Unc	BU
2005R Proof	26,786	Value: 50.00				

KM# 472   5 EURO

18.0000 g., 0.9250 Silver 0.5353 oz. ASW, 32 mm. **Obv:** Portrait of Melchiorie Delfico

Date	Mintage	F	VF	XF	Unc	BU
2006R	65,000	—	—	—	30.00	35.00

KM# 476   5 EURO

18.0000 g., 0.9250 Silver 0.5353 oz. ASW, 32 mm. **Subject:** Andrea Mantegna, 500th Anniversary of Death **Obv:** Three towers **Rev:** Statue of soldier and naked female

Date	Mintage	F	VF	XF	Unc	BU
2006R Proof	19,000	Value: 40.00				

KM# 473   5 EURO

18.0000 g., 0.9250 Silver 0.5353 oz. ASW, 32 mm. **Subject:** Equal Opportunity between the sexes **Obv:** Three plumed towers **Obv. Legend:** REPUBLICA DI SAN MARINO **Rev:** Nude female at left, nude male at right, ribbon across symbols within circle above, value below **Rev. Inscription:** PARI OPPORTITA **Edge:** Reeded

Date	Mintage	F	VF	XF	Unc	BU
2007R	70,000	—	—	—	30.00	35.00

KM# 474   5 EURO

18.0000 g., 0.9250 Silver 0.5353 oz. ASW, 32 mm. **Subject:** 50th Anniversary Death of Toscanini **Obv:** Stylized national arms **Obv. Legend:** REPUBBLICA DI SAN MARINO **Rev:** Head of Toscanini left **Edge:** Reeded

Date	Mintage	F	VF	XF	Unc	BU
ND(2007)R Proof	18,000	Value: 40.00				

KM# 512   5 EURO

18.0000 g., 0.9250 Silver 0.5353 oz. ASW, 32 mm. **Rev:** Winds, land, sea

Date	Mintage	F	VF	XF	Unc	BU
2008R	50,000	—	—	—	30.00	35.00

KM# 513   5 EURO

18.0000 g., 0.9250 Silver 0.5353 oz. ASW, 32 mm. **Subject:** Summer Olympics, Peking **Rev:** Ribbon Dancer

Date	Mintage	F	VF	XF	Unc	BU
2008R	21,000	—	—	—	37.50	45.00

KM# 506   5 EURO

18.0000 g., 0.9250 Silver 0.5353 oz. ASW, 32 mm. **Subject:** Kepler **Obv:** Kepler bust and globe **Rev:** Planets orbit around central sun

Date	Mintage	F	VF	XF	Unc	BU
2009R Proof	13,400	Value: 50.00				

KM# 515   5 EURO

18.0000 g., 0.9250 Silver 0.5353 oz. ASW, 32 mm. **Subject:** Year of Astronomy **Obv:** Planets in orbit **Rev:** Planets in orbit, Astrolab

Date	Mintage	F	VF	XF	Unc	BU
2009R	50,000	—	—	—	30.00	35.00

KM# 495   5 EURO

18.0000 g., 0.9250 Silver 0.5353 oz. ASW, 32 mm. **Subject:** Shanghai Expo

Date	Mintage	F	VF	XF	Unc	BU
2010R Proof	10,000	Value: 65.00				

KM# 496 5 EURO
18.0000 g., 0.9250 Silver 0.5353 oz. ASW, 32 mm. **Subject:** Michelangelo Caravaggio, 500th Anniverdary of Death

Date	Mintage	F	VF	XF	Unc	BU
2010R	48,000	—	—	—	30.00	35.00

KM# 501 5 EURO
18.0000 g., 0.9250 Silver 0.5353 oz. ASW, 32 mm. **Subject:** European Discoveries **Obv:** Crowned coat of arms **Rev:** Busts of Antonio & Roberto Pazzaglia, Mt. Everest in background

Date	Mintage	F	VF	XF	Unc	BU
2011R Proof	10,000	Value: 50.00				

KM# 502 5 EURO
18.0000 g., 0.9250 Silver 0.5353 oz. ASW, 32 mm. **Subject:** First Manned Space Flight, 50th Anniversary

Date	Mintage	F	VF	XF	Unc	BU
2011R	48,000	—	—	—	30.00	35.00

KM# 449 10 EURO
22.0000 g., 0.9250 Silver 0.6542 oz. ASW, 34 mm. **Subject:** Welcome Euro **Obv:** Three plumed towers **Rev:** Infant sleeping in flower

Date	Mintage	F	VF	XF	Unc	BU
2002R Proof	37,000	Value: 100				

KM# 451 10 EURO
22.0000 g., 0.9250 Silver 0.6542 oz. ASW, 34 mm. **Subject:** 1600th Anniversary of Ravenna **Obv:** National arms **Rev:** Wall painting

Date	Mintage	F	VF	XF	Unc	BU
2002R Proof	—	Value: 95.00				

KM# 454 10 EURO
22.0000 g., 0.9250 Silver 0.6542 oz. ASW, 34 mm. **Subject:** 2004 Olympics **Obv:** Three stylized towers **Rev:** Modern Olympians **Edge:** Segmented reeding

Date	Mintage	F	VF	XF	Unc	BU
2003R Proof	37,766	Value: 75.00				

KM# 463 10 EURO
22.0000 g., 0.9250 Silver 0.6542 oz. ASW, 34 mm. **Obv:** Three stylized plumed towers **Rev:** Two soccer players

Date	Mintage	F	VF	XF	Unc	BU
2004R Proof	30,000	Value: 70.00				

KM# 477 10 EURO
22.0000 g., 0.9250 Silver 0.6542 oz. ASW, 34 mm. **Subject:** Antonio Canova **Obv:** Three towers **Rev:** The Three Graces

Date	Mintage	F	VF	XF	Unc	BU
2006R Proof	19,000	Value: 65.00				

KM# 475 10 EURO
22.0000 g., 0.9250 Silver 0.6542 oz. ASW, 34 mm. **Subject:** 100th Anniversary - Birthday of Giosuè Carducci **Obv:** Stylized national arms **Obv. Legend:** REPUBBLICA DI SAN MARINO **Rev:** 1/2 length figure of Carducci facing with quill pen in hand at table **Rev. Legend:** CARDUCCI **Edge:** Segmented reeding

Date	Mintage	F	VF	XF	Unc	BU
ND(2007)R Proof	16,000	Value: 55.00				

KM# 514 10 EURO
22.0000 g., 0.9250 Silver 0.6542 oz. ASW, 34 mm. **Subject:** Andrea Palladio, 500th Anniversary of Birth **Rev:** Building façade

Date	Mintage	F	VF	XF	Unc	BU
2008R Proof	17,000	Value: 65.00				

KM# 516 10 EURO
22.0000 g., 0.9250 Silver 0.6542 oz. ASW, 34 mm. **Subject:** Euro, 10th Anniversary

Date	Mintage	F	VF	XF	Unc	BU
2009R Proof	12,500	Value: 60.00				

KM# 497 10 EURO
22.0000 g., 0.9250 Silver 0.6542 oz. ASW, 34 mm. **Subject:** Robert Schumann, 200th Anniversary of Birth

Date	Mintage	F	VF	XF	Unc	BU
2010R Proof	—	Value: 55.00				

KM# 517 10 EURO
22.0000 g., 0.9250 Silver 0.6542 oz. ASW, 34 mm. **Subject:** Robert Schumann, 200th Anniversary of Birth **Obv:** Crowned National arms **Rev:** Bust at right facing left

Date	Mintage	F	VF	XF	Unc	BU
2010R Proof	10,000	Value: 65.00				

KM# 503 10 EURO
22.0000 g., 0.9250 Silver 0.6542 oz. ASW, 34 mm. **Subject:** Euro Coins and Banknotes, 10th Anniversary

Date	Mintage	F	VF	XF	Unc	BU
2011R Proof	10,000	Value: 60.00				

KM# 460 20 EURO
6.4510 g., 0.9000 Gold 0.1867 oz. AGW, 21 mm. **Subject:** 1600th Anniversary of Ravenna **Obv:** National arms **Rev:** Bas-relief wall design **Edge:** Reeded

Date	Mintage	F	VF	XF	Unc	BU
2002R Proof	4,550	Value: 375				

KM# 455 20 EURO
6.4516 g., 0.9000 Gold 0.1867 oz. AGW, 21 mm. **Obv:** Three plumes **Rev:** Giotto's "Presentation of Jesus at the Temple" **Edge:** Reeded

Date	Mintage	F	VF	XF	Unc	BU
2003R Proof	7,300	Value: 375				

KM# 465 20 EURO
6.4510 g., 0.9000 Gold 0.1867 oz. AGW, 21 mm. **Obv:** Three plumes **Rev:** Marco Polo meeting Kublai Khan **Edge:** Reeded

Date	Mintage	F	VF	XF	Unc	BU
2004R Proof	7,300	Value: 375				

KM# 470 20 EURO
6.4510 g., 0.9000 Gold 0.1867 oz. AGW, 21 mm. **Subject:** International Day of Peace **Obv:** Stylized faces and leaves

Date	Mintage	F	VF	XF	Unc	BU
2005R Proof	5,300	Value: 375				

KM# 479 20 EURO
6.4500 g., 0.9000 Gold 0.1866 oz. AGW, 21 mm. **Subject:** Giovan Battista Belluzzi, 500th Birthday **Obv:** Crowned shield **Rev:** Fortification plan

Date	Mintage	F	VF	XF	Unc	BU
2006R Proof	4,500	Value: 375				

KM# 507 20 EURO
6.4510 g., 0.9000 Gold 0.1867 oz. AGW

Date	Mintage	F	VF	XF	Unc	BU
2007R Proof	—	Value: 350				

KM# 491 20 EURO
6.4500 g., 0.9000 Gold 0.1866 oz. AGW **Subject:** Roman Antiquities **Obv:** Arms **Rev:** Small statue of Mercury

Date	Mintage	F	VF	XF	Unc	BU
2008R Proof	2,100	Value: 375				

KM# 509 20 EURO
6.4510 g., 0.9000 Gold 0.1867 oz. AGW, 21 mm.

Date	Mintage	F	VF	XF	Unc	BU
2009R Proof	—	Value: 350				

KM# 498 20 EURO
6.4510 g., 0.9000 Gold 0.1867 oz. AGW, 21 mm. **Subject:** Treasurers from San Marino - Wooden bust of St. Agata

Date	Mintage	F	VF	XF	Unc	BU
2010R Proof	2,000	Value: 375				

KM# 504 20 EURO
6.4510 g., 0.9000 Gold 0.1867 oz. AGW, 21 mm. **Subject:** Treasures from San Marino

Date	Mintage	F	VF	XF	Unc	BU
2011R Proof	2,000	Value: 375				

KM# 461 50 EURO
16.1290 g., 0.9000 Gold 0.4667 oz. AGW, 28 mm. **Subject:** 1600th Anniversary of Ravenna **Obv:** National arms **Rev:** Wall painting **Edge:** Reeded

Date	Mintage	F	VF	XF	Unc	BU
2002R Proof	4,550	Value: 900				

KM# 456 50 EURO
16.1290 g., 0.9000 Gold 0.4667 oz. AGW, 28 mm. **Obv:** Three plumes **Rev:** Giotto's "The Pentecost" **Edge:** Reeded

Date	Mintage	F	VF	XF	Unc	BU
2003R Proof	7,300	Value: 900				

KM# 466 50 EURO
16.1290 g., 0.9000 Gold 0.4667 oz. AGW, 28 mm. **Obv:** Three plumes **Rev:** Marco Polo **Edge:** Reeded

Date	Mintage	F	VF	XF	Unc	BU
2004R Proof	7,300	Value: 900				

KM# 471 50 EURO
16.1290 g., 0.9000 Gold 0.4667 oz. AGW, 28 mm. **Subject:** International Day of Peace **Obv:** Group of people gathering

Date	Mintage	F	VF	XF	Unc	BU
2005R Proof	5,300	Value: 900				

KM# 480 50 EURO
16.1300 g., 0.9000 Gold 0.4667 oz. AGW, 28 mm. **Subject:** Giovan Batista Belluzzi **Obv:** Crowned shield **Rev:** Bust right

Date	Mintage	F	VF	XF	Unc	BU
2006R Proof	4,500	Value: 900				

KM# 508 50 EURO
16.1290 g., 0.9000 Gold 0.4667 oz. AGW, 28 mm.

Date	Mintage	F	VF	XF	Unc	BU
2007R Proof	—	Value: 900				

KM# 492 50 EURO
16.1300 g., 0.9000 Gold 0.4667 oz. AGW, 28 mm. **Subject:** Antiquities **Obv:** Arms **Rev:** Two bronze fibulae

Date	Mintage	F	VF	XF	Unc	BU
2008R Proof	2,100	Value: 900				

KM# 510 50 EURO
16.1300 g., 0.9000 Gold 0.4667 oz. AGW, 28 mm.

Date	Mintage	F	VF	XF	Unc	BU
2009R Proof	—	Value: 900				

KM# 499 50 EURO
16.1290 g., 0.9000 Gold 0.4667 oz. AGW, 28 mm. **Subject:** Treasurers from San Marino - Saint Marinus

Date	Mintage	F	VF	XF	Unc	BU
2010R Proof	2,000	Value: 900				

KM# 505 50 EURO
16.1290 g., 0.9000 Gold 0.4667 oz. AGW, 28 mm. **Subject:** Treasures from San Marino

Date	Mintage	F	VF	XF	Unc	BU
2011R Proof	5,000	Value: 900				

MINT SETS

KM#	Date	Mintage	Identification	Issue Price	Mkt Val
MS61	2001 (8)	2,000	KM424-431	18.00	50.00
MS62	2002 (8)	120,000	KM440 - 447	—	275
MS63	2003 (9)	—	KM440-447, 452	55.00	350
MS64	2004 (9)	—	KM440-447, 458	55.00	220
MS65	2005 (9)	—	KM440-447, 468	55.00	225
MS66	2006 (9)	65,000	KM440-447, 472	—	185
MS67	2007 (3)	—	KM443, 444, 447	27.50	55.00
MS68	2007 (9)	—	KM440-447, 473	120	160

PROOF SETS

KM#	Date	Mintage	Identification	Issue Price	Mkt Val
PS14	2001 (3)	4,500	KM433-435	179	500
PSA15	2001 (2)	—	KM436, 437	—	70.00
PS15	2002 (2)	37,000	KM448-449	—	175
PS16	2002 (2)	4,550	KM460-461	—	1,150
PS17	2003 (2)	7,300	KM455-456	—	975
PS18	2004 (2)	7,300	KM465-466	—	975
PS19	2005 (2)	5,300	KM470-471	—	1,050
PS20	2008 (8)	13,000	KM440-442, 482-486	—	135
PS21	2009 (8)	13,500	KM440-443, 482-486	—	135
PS22	2010 (8)	8,600	KM440-442, 482-486	—	135
PS23	2011 (8)	8,600	KM440-442, 482-486	—	135

SAUDI ARABIA

The Kingdom of Saudi Arabia, an independent and absolute hereditary monarchy comprising the former sultanate of Nejd, the old kingdom of Hejaz, Asir and Al Hasa, occupies four-fifths of the Arabian peninsula. The kingdom has an area of 830,000 sq. mi. (2,149,690 sq. km.) and a population of *16.1 million. Capital: Riyadh. The economy is based on oil, which provides 85 percent of Saudi Arabia's revenue.

TITLES

العربية السعودية

Al-Arabiya(t) as-Sa'udiya(t)

المملكة العربية السعودية

Al-Mamlaka(t) al-'Arabiya(t) as-Sa'udiya(t)

RULERS

al Sa'ud Dynasty

Fahad bin Abd Al-Aziz, AH1403-1426/1982-2005AD
Abdullah bin Abdul Aziz, AH1426-/2005AD

KINGDOM

REFORM COINAGE

5 Halala = 1 Ghirsh; 100 Halala = 1 Riyal

KM# 69 5 HALALA (Ghirsh)
Copper-Nickel **Ruler:** Abdullah bin Abdul Aziz AH1426-/2005-AD **Obv:** National emblem at center **Rev:** Legend above inscription in circle, dividing value, date below

Date	Mintage	F	VF	XF	Unc	BU
AH1430(2009)	—	—	0.30	0.60	1.50	2.00

KM# 62   10 HALALA (2 Ghirsh)
4.0000 g., Copper-Nickel, 21 mm. **Ruler:** Fahad Bin Abd Al-Aziz AH1403-1426/1982-2005AD **Obv:** National emblem at center, legend above and below **Rev:** Legend above inscription in circle dividing value, date below **Edge:** Reeded

Date	Mintage	F	VF	XF	Unc	BU
AH1423 (2002)	—	—	0.15	0.35	0.90	1.00

KM# 70   10 HALALA (2 Ghirsh)
Copper-Nickel **Ruler:** Abdullah bin Abdul Aziz AH1426-/2005-AD **Obv:** National emblem at center **Rev:** Legend above inscription in circle, dividing value, date below

Date	Mintage	F	VF	XF	Unc	BU
AH1430 (2009)	—	—	0.30	0.60	1.50	2.50

KM# 63   25 HALALA (1/4 Riyal)
5.0000 g., Copper-Nickel, 23 mm. **Ruler:** Fahad Bin Abd Al-Aziz AH1403-1426/1982-2005AD **Obv:** National emblem at center, legend above and below **Rev:** Legend above inscription in circle dividing value, date below **Edge:** Reeded

Date	Mintage	F	VF	XF	Unc	BU
AH1423 (2002)	—	—	0.20	0.45	1.10	1.50

KM# 71   25 HALALA (1/4 Riyal)
Copper-Nickel **Ruler:** Abdullah bin Abdul Aziz AH1426-/2005-AD **Obv:** National emblem at center **Rev:** Legend above inscription in circle, divides value, date below

Date	Mintage	F	VF	XF	Unc	BU
AH1427 (2006)	—	—	0.20	0.45	1.10	1.50
AH1430 (2009)	—	—	0.20	0.45	1.10	1.50

KM# 64   50 HALALA (1/2 Riyal)
6.5000 g., Copper-Nickel, 26 mm. **Ruler:** Fahad Bin Abd Al-Aziz AH1403-1426/1982-2005AD **Obv:** National emblem at center, legend above and below **Rev:** Legend above inscription in circle dividing value, date below **Edge:** Reeded

Date	Mintage	F	VF	XF	Unc	BU
AH1423 (2002)	—	0.15	0.30	0.75	1.50	2.00

KM# 68   50 HALALA (1/2 Riyal)
6.5000 g., Copper-Nickel, 26 mm. **Ruler:** Abdullah bin Abdul Aziz AH1426-/2005-AD **Obv:** National emblem at center **Rev:** Legend above inscription in circle, dividing value, date below **Edge:** Reeded

Date	Mintage	F	VF	XF	Unc	BU
AH1427 (2006)	—	—	0.30	0.60	1.50	2.00
AH1428 (2007)	—	—	0.30	0.60	1.50	2.00
AH1431 (2010)	—	—	0.30	0.60	1.50	2.00

KM# 72   100 HALALA (1 Riyal)
Bi-Metallic Brass center in Copper-Nickel ring, 23 mm. **Ruler:** Abdullah bin Abdul Aziz AH1426-/2005-AD **Obv:** National emblem at center **Rev:** Legend above inscription, divides value, date below **Edge:** Reeded

Date	Mintage	F	VF	XF	Unc	BU
AH1427(2006)	—	—	0.45	0.90	2.25	3.00
AH1429(2008)	—	—	0.45	0.90	2.25	3.00

SERBIA

Serbia, a former inland Balkan kingdom has an area of 34,116 sq. mi. (88,361 sq. km.). Capital: Belgrade.

MINT MARKS
A - Paris
(a) - Paris, privy mark only
H - Birmingham
V - Vienna
БП - (BP) Budapest

MONETARY SYSTEM
100 Para = 1 Dinara

DENOMINATIONS
ПАРА = Para
ДИНАР = Dinar
ДИНАРА = Dinara

REPUBLIC
STANDARD COINAGE

KM# 34   DINAR
4.3400 g., Copper-Nickel-Zinc, 20 mm. **Obv:** National Bank emblem within circle **Rev:** Bank building and value **Edge:** Reeded

Date	Mintage	F	VF	XF	Unc	BU
2003	10,326,000	—	—	0.25	1.00	1.50
2004	25,038,000	—	—	0.25	1.00	1.50

KM# 39   DINAR
4.2600 g., Nickel-Brass, 20 mm. **Obv:** Crowned and mantled arms **Rev:** National Bank and value **Edge:** Segmented reeding

Date	Mintage	F	VF	XF	Unc	BU
2005	32,452,000	—	—	0.25	1.00	1.50
2006	39,550,000	—	—	0.25	1.00	1.50
2007	20,000,000	—	—	0.25	1.00	1.50
2008	10,093,000	—	—	0.25	1.00	1.50
2009	10,008,000	—	—	0.25	1.00	1.50

KM# 48   DINAR
4.2000 g., Copper Plated Steel, 20 mm. **Obv:** Arms **Rev:** National Bank and value

Date	Mintage	F	VF	XF	Unc	BU
2009	35,750,000	—	—	—	1.00	1.50
2010	30,600,000	—	—	—	—	—
2011	24,785,000	—	—	—	—	—

KM# 54   DINAR
20.0000 g., Copper Plated Steel, 20 mm. **Obv:** Arms, flat bottom crown above shield **Rev:** National Bank building and value

Date	Mintage	F	VF	XF	Unc	BU
2011	—	—	—	—	1.00	1.50

KM# 35   2 DINARA
5.2400 g., Copper-Nickel-Zinc, 22 mm. **Obv:** National Bank emblem within circle **Rev:** Gracanica Monastery and value **Edge:** Reeded

Date	Mintage	F	VF	XF	Unc	BU
2003	15,216,000	—	—	0.50	2.00	2.50

KM# 46   2 DINARA
5.1500 g., Nickel-Brass, 22 mm. **Obv:** Crowned and mantled arms **Rev:** Gracanica Monastery and value **Edge:** Segmented reeding

Date	Mintage	F	VF	XF	Unc	BU
2006	15,385,500	—	—	0.50	2.00	2.50
2007	15,002,500	—	—	0.50	2.00	2.50
2008	10,093,000	—	—	0.50	2.00	2.50
2009	10,008,000	—	—	0.50	2.00	2.50
2010		—	—	0.50	2.00	2.50
2011		—	—	0.50	2.00	2.50

KM# 49   2 DINARA
5.0500 g., Copper Plated Steel, 22 mm. **Obv:** Arms **Rev:** Gracanica Monastery and value

Date	Mintage	F	VF	XF	Unc	BU
2009	27,845,000	—	—	0.50	2.00	2.50
2010	9,600,000	—	—	—	—	—
2011	12,400,000	—	—	—	—	—

KM# 55   2 DINARA
5.0500 g., Copper Plated Steel, 22 mm. **Obv:** Arms, flat bottom crown above shield **Rev:** Gracanica Monastery and value

Date	Mintage	F	VF	XF	Unc	BU
2011	—	—	—	—	2.00	2.50

KM# 36   5 DINARA
6.2300 g., Copper-Nickel-Zinc, 22 mm. **Obv:** National Bank emblem within circle **Rev:** Krusedol Monastery and value **Edge:** Reeded

Date	Mintage	F	VF	XF	Unc	BU
2003	15,184,000	—	0.50	1.00	2.25	3.50

KM# 40   5 DINARA
6.1300 g., Nickel-Brass, 24 mm. **Obv:** Crowned and mantled arms **Rev:** Krusedol Monastery and value **Edge:** Segmented reeding

Date	Mintage	F	VF	XF	Unc	BU
2005	5,099,500	—	—	0.75	2.00	3.50
2006	10,372,500	—	—	0.75	2.00	3.50
2007	14,998,500	—	—	0.75	2.00	3.50
2008	15,093,000	—	—	0.75	2.00	3.50
2009	9,998,500	—	—	0.75	2.00	3.50
2010	15,005,000	—	—	0.75	2.00	3.50
2011	13,626,500	—	—	0.75	2.00	3.50

KM# 56   5 DINARA
Copper Plated Steel, 24 mm. **Obv:** Arms, flat bottom crown above shield **Rev:** Krusedol Monastery

Date	Mintage	F	VF	XF	Unc	BU
2011	—	—	—	—	2.25	3.50

KM# 37   10 DINARA
7.7700 g., Copper-Nickel-Zinc, 26 mm. **Obv:** National Bank emblem within circle **Rev:** Studenica Monastery and value **Edge:** Reeded

Date	Mintage	F	VF	XF	Unc	BU
2003	15,166,500	—	0.50	1.00	2.50	3.50

KM# 41   10 DINARA
7.7700 g., Copper-Nickel-Zinc, 26 mm.   **Obv:** Crowned and mantled arms **Rev:** Studenica Monastery and value **Edge:** Segmented reeding

Date	Mintage	F	VF	XF	Unc	BU
2005	5,099,500	—	—	0.75	2.25	4.00
2006	1,019,500	—	—	0.75	2.25	4.00
2007	1,050,500	—	—	0.75	2.00	4.00
2010	500,250	—	—	1.50	3.00	5.00
2011	500,250	—	—	1.50	3.00	5.00

KM# 51   10 DINARA
7.7700 g., Copper-Nickel-Zinc, 26 mm.   **Subject:** 25th Summer Universiade, Belgrade **Obv:** Arms **Rev:** Logo

Date	Mintage	F	VF	XF	Unc	BU
2009	500,000	—	—	1.50	3.00	5.00

KM# 57   10 DINARA
7.7700 g., Copper-Nickel-Zinc, 26 mm.   **Obv:** Arms, flat bottom crown above shield **Rev:** Studenica Monastery and value

Date	Mintage	F	VF	XF	Unc	BU
2011	—	—	—	—	2.25	4.00

KM# 38   20 DINARA
9.0000 g., Copper-Nickel-Zinc, 28 mm.   **Obv:** National Bank emblem within circle **Rev:** Temple of St. Sava and value **Edge:** Reeded

Date	Mintage	F	VF	XF	Unc	BU
2003	25,497,500	—	—	0.75	2.25	4.00

KM# 42   20 DINARA
9.0000 g., Copper-Nickel-Zinc, 28 mm.   **Obv:** Crowned and mantled Serbian royal arms **Rev:** Nikola Tesla **Edge:** Segmented reeding

Date	Mintage	F	VF	XF	Unc	BU
2006	992,500	—	—	0.75	2.25	4.00

KM# 47   20 DINARA
9.0000 g., Copper-Nickel-Zinc, 28 mm.   **Subject:** Dositej Obradovic, 1742-1811 **Obv:** National arms **Obv. Legend:** РЕПУБЛИКА СРБИЈА - REPUBLIKA SRBIJA **Rev:** Bust facing slightly left **Edge:** Segmented reeding

Date	Mintage	F	VF	XF	Unc	BU
2007	1,020,000	—	—	1.00	2.50	4.50

KM# 52   20 DINARA
9.0000 g., Copper-Nickel-Zinc, 28 mm.   **Obv:** National arms **Rev:** Milutin Milankovic profile 3/4 left

Date	Mintage	F	VF	XF	Unc	BU
2009	494,500	—	—	—	2.00	3.50

KM# 53   20 DINARA
9.0000 g., Copper-Nickel-Zinc, 28 mm.   **Obv:** National arms **Rev:** Ivo Andric

Date	Mintage	Good	VG	F	VF	XF
2011	500,000	—	—	—	2.50	5.00

KM# 43   1000 DINARA
13.0000 g., 0.9250 Silver 0.3866 oz. ASW, 30 mm.   **Obv:** Crowned and mantled Serbian royal arms **Rev:** Nikola Tesla **Edge:** Segmented reeding

Date	Mintage	F	VF	XF	Unc	BU
2006 Proof	2,000	Value: 40.00				

KM# 44   5000 DINARA
3.4550 g., 0.9000 Gold 0.1000 oz. AGW, 20 mm.   **Obv:** Crowned and mantled Serbian royal arms **Rev:** Nikola Tesla

Date	Mintage	F	VF	XF	Unc	BU
2006 Proof	2,000	Value: 200				

KM# 45   10000 DINARA
8.6400 g., 0.9000 Gold 0.2500 oz. AGW, 25 mm.   **Obv:** Crowned and mantled Serbian royal arms **Rev:** Nikola Tesla

Date	Mintage	F	VF	XF	Unc	BU
2006 Proof	1,000	Value: 475				

MINT SETS

KM#	Date	Mintage	Identification	Issue Price	Mkt Val
MS1	2003 (5)	—	KM34-38	—	15.00
MS2	2005 (3)	—	KM39-41	—	10.00
MS3	2006 (5)	—	KM#39-42, 46	—	16.00

MINT SETS NON-STANDARD METALS

KM#	Date	Mintage	Identification	Issue Price	Mkt Val
MS4	2007 (5)	—	KM#39-42, 47	—	16.00

PROOF SETS

KM#	Date	Mintage	Identification	Issue Price	Mkt Val
PS1	2006 (3)	—	KM#43-45	—	725

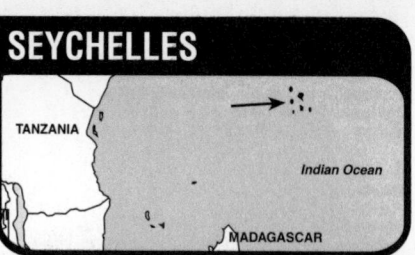

SEYCHELLES

The Republic of Seychelles, an archipelago of 85 granite and coral islands situated in the Indian Ocean 600 miles (965 km.) northeast of Madagascar, has an area of 156 sq. mi. (455 sq. km.) and a population of *70,000. Among these islands are the Aldabra Islands, the Farquhar Group, and Ile Desroches, which the United Kingdom ceded to the Seychelles upon its independence. Capital: Victoria, on Mahe. The economy is based on fishing, a plantation system of agriculture, and tourism. Copra, cinnamon and vanilla are exported.

Seychelles is a member of the Commonwealth of Nations. The president is the Head of State and of the Government.

MINT MARKS
(sa) - M in oval – South African Mint Co.
   (starting in 2000, not PM)
None - British Royal Mint

MONETARY SYSTEM
100 Cents = 1 Rupee

REPUBLIC

STANDARD COINAGE

KM# 46.2   CENT
1.4300 g., Brass, 16.03 mm.   **Obv:** Altered coat of arms **Rev:** Mud Crab **Edge:** Plain

Date	Mintage	F	VF	XF	Unc	BU
2004	—	—	—	0.15	0.25	0.35

KM# 47.2   5 CENTS
2.0000 g., Brass, 18 mm.   **Obv:** Altered coat of arms **Rev:** Tapioca plant

Date	Mintage	F	VF	XF	Unc	BU
2003	—	—	—	0.10	0.30	0.50

KM# 47a   5 CENTS
1.9700 g., Brass Plated Steel, 17.97 mm.   **Obv:** National arms **Rev:** Tapioca plant **Edge:** Plain

Date	Mintage	F	VF	XF	Unc	BU
2007PM	—	—	—	0.10	0.30	0.50

KM# 48.2   10 CENTS
3.3400 g., Brass, 21 mm.   **Obv:** Altered coat of arms **Rev:** Yellowfin tuna **Edge:** Plain

Date	Mintage	F	VF	XF	Unc	BU
2003	—	—	0.10	0.35	1.00	1.50

KM# 48a   10 CENTS
3.3700 g., Brass Plated Steel, 21 mm.   **Obv:** National arms **Rev:** Black parrot, value **Edge:** Plain

Date	Mintage	F	VF	XF	Unc	BU
2007PM	—	—	0.15	0.30	0.75	1.00

KM# 49a   25 CENTS
2.9700 g., Nickel Clad Steel, 18.9 mm.   **Obv:** National arms **Rev:** Black Parrot and value **Edge:** Plain

Date	Mintage	F	VF	XF	Unc	BU
2003PM	—	—	—	0.40	1.00	1.25
2007PM	—	—	—	0.40	1.00	1.25
2010PM	—	—	—	0.40	1.00	1.25

KM# 50.2   RUPEE
6.1800 g., Copper-Nickel, 25.46 mm.   **Obv:** Altered coat of arms **Rev:** Triton Conch Shell **Edge:** Reeded

Date	Mintage	F	VF	XF	Unc	BU
2007	—	—	—	0.45	1.10	1.50
2010PM	—	—	—	0.45	1.10	1.50

KM# 118   5 RUPEES
28.2800 g., Copper-Nickel, 38.6 mm. **Subject:** John Paul II memorial **Obv:** National Arms **Rev:** John Paul II in mitre waving

Date	Mintage	F	VF	XF	Unc	BU
2005	—	—	—	—	8.00	10.00

KM# 119   5 RUPEES
28.2800 g., Copper-Nickel, 38.6 mm. **Obv:** National Arms **Rev:** Benedict XVI blessing crowd at St. Peter's Square

Date	Mintage	F	VF	XF	Unc	BU
2005	—	—	—	—	10.00	12.00

KM# 51.2   5 RUPEES
9.0000 g., Copper-Nickel, 29 mm. **Obv:** Altered arms **Rev:** Fruit tree divides value **Edge:** Reeded

Date	Mintage	F	VF	XF	Unc	BU
2007	—	—	0.30	0.70	1.75	2.25

KM# 121   25 RUPEES
28.2800 g., 0.9250 Silver 0.8410 oz. ASW, 38.6 mm. **Obv:** National arms **Rev:** Benedict XVI blessing crowd at St. Peter's Square **Edge:** Reeded

Date	Mintage	F	VF	XF	Unc	BU
2005	—	Value: 55.00				

KM# 120   25 RUPEES
28.2800 g., 0.9250 Silver 0.8410 oz. ASW, 38.6 mm. **Obv:** National arms **Rev:** Description John Paul II in mitre waving **Edge:** Reeded

Date	Mintage	F	VF	XF	Unc	BU
2005 Proof	—	Value: 55.00				

KM# 122   250 RUPEES
6.2200 g., 0.9999 Gold 0.1999 oz. AGW, 22 mm. **Obv:** National arms **Rev:** Description John Paul II in mitre waving **Edge:** Reeded

Date	Mintage	F	VF	XF	Unc	BU
2005 Proof	—	Value: 400				

KM# 123   250 RUPEES
6.2200 g., 0.9999 Gold 0.1999 oz. AGW, 22 mm. **Obv:** National arms **Rev:** Benedict XVI blessing crowd at St. Peter's Square **Edge:** Reeded

Date	Mintage	F	VF	XF	Unc	BU
2005 Proof	—	Value: 400				

SHAWNEE TRIBAL NATION

SOVEREIGN NATION
MILLED COINAGE

KM# 1   DOLLAR
31.2000 g., 0.9999 Silver 1.0030 oz. ASW, 39 mm. **Obv:** Tribal seal **Obv. Legend:** THE SOVEREIGN NATION OF THE SHAWNEE TRIBE **Rev:** Bust of Chief Chief "Shooting Star" Tecumseh right **Edge:** Reeded

Date	Mintage	F	VF	XF	Unc	BU
2002	50,000	—	—	—	—	50.00
2002 Proof	20,000	Value: 55.00				

KM# 10   DOLLAR
124.4120 g., 0.9990 Silver 3.9958 oz. ASW

Date	Mintage	F	VF	XF	Unc	BU
2003 Proof	10,000	Value: 175				

KM# 3   DOLLAR
31.2000 g., 0.9999 Silver 1.0030 oz. ASW, 39 mm. **Obv:** Tribal seal **Obv. Legend:** THE SOVEREIGN NATION OF THE SHAWNEE TRIBE **Rev:** Lewis, Clark and Drouillard scouting **Edge:** Reeded

Date	Mintage	F	VF	XF	Unc	BU
2003	50,000	—	—	—	—	50.00
2003 Proof	20,000	Value: 55.00				

KM# 5   DOLLAR
31.2000 g., 0.9999 Silver 1.0030 oz. ASW, 39 mm. **Obv:** Tribal seal **Obv. Legend:** THE SOVEREIGN NATION OF THE SHAWNEE TRIBE **Rev:** Flag behing Indian Chief and Thomas Jefferson standing, eagle on shield at their feet **Edge:** Reeded

Date	Mintage	F	VF	XF	Unc	BU
2004	50,000	—	—	—	—	50.00
2004 Proof	20,000	Value: 55.00				

KM# 15   DOLLAR
31.3100 g., 0.9990 Silver 1.0056 oz. ASW, 40.6 mm. **Obv:** Tribal seal **Obv. Legend:** THE SOVEREIGN NATION OF THE SHAWNEE TRIBE **Rev:** Lewis, Clark, Dromillard and Sacagawea in a canoe **Rev. Legend:** EXPEDITION OF DISCOVERY **Edge:** Reeded

Date	Mintage	F	VF	XF	Unc	BU
2005	50,000	—	—	—	50.00	—
2005 Proof	20,000	Value: 55.00				

KM# 20   DOLLAR
31.2100 g., 0.9999 Silver 1.0033 oz. ASW, 40.6 mm. **Obv:** Tribal seal **Obv. Legend:** THE SOVEREIGN NATION OF THE SHAWNEE TRIBE **Rev:** 1/2 length figure of Tenskwatawa "the prophet" 3/4 left **Rev. Legend:** PROPHET TENSKWATAWA **Edge:** Reeded

Date	Mintage	F	VF	XF	Unc	BU
2006	50,000	—	—	—	—	50.00
2006 Proof	20,000	Value: 55.00				

KM# 24   DOLLAR
31.1050 g., 0.9990 Silver 0.9990 oz. ASW, 39 mm. **Subject:** Battle of the Wabash **Rev:** Indian warrior on horseback **Edge:** Reeded

Date	Mintage	F	VF	XF	Unc	BU
2007	50,000	—	—	—	—	40.00
2007 Proof	20,000	Value: 50.00				

KM# 26   DOLLAR
31.1050 g., 0.9990 Silver 0.9990 oz. ASW, 39 mm. **Subject:** Battle of Point Pleasant **Rev:** Indian warrior on horseback **Edge:** Reeded

Date	Mintage	F	VF	XF	Unc	BU
2008	50,000	—	—	—	—	40.00
2008 Proof	20,000	Value: 50.00				

KM# 28   DOLLAR
31.1050 g., 0.9990 Silver 0.9990 oz. ASW **Rev:** Battle of Fallen Timber

Date	Mintage	F	VF	XF	Unc	BU
2009	50,000	—	—	—	—	40.00
2009 Proof	20,000	Value: 50.00				

KM# 2   5 DOLLARS
6.2200 g., 0.9999 Gold 0.1999 oz. AGW, 20 mm. **Obv:** Arms **Obv. Legend:** THE SOVEREIGN NATION OF THE SHAWNEE TRIBE **Rev:** Bust of Tecumseh "Shooting Star" 3/4 left **Edge:** Reeded

Date	Mintage	F	VF	XF	Unc	BU
2002 Proof	5,000	Value: 375				

KM# 4   5 DOLLARS
6.2200 g., 0.9999 Gold 0.1999 oz. AGW, 22.5 mm. **Obv:** Arms
Obv. Legend: THE SOVEREIGN NATION OF THE SHAWNEE
TRIBE **Rev:** Bust of George Drouillard 3/4 right **Rev. Legend:**
GEORGE DROUILLARD SIGN TALKER

Date	Mintage	F	VF	XF	Unc	BU
2003 Proof	5,000	Value: 375				

KM# 6   5 DOLLARS
6.2207 g., 0.9990 Gold 0.1998 oz. AGW, 22 mm. **Obv:** Arms
Obv. Legend: THE SOVEREIGN NATION OF THE SHAWNEE
TRIBE **Rev:** Sacagawea with child and horse **Edge:** Reeded

Date	Mintage	F	VF	XF	Unc	BU
2004 Proof	5,000	Value: 375				

KM# 16   5 DOLLARS
6.3000 g., 0.9999 Gold 0.2025 oz. AGW, 22.5 mm. **Obv:** Tribal
seal **Obv. Legend:** THE SOVEREIGN NATION OF THE
SHAWNEE TRIBE **Rev:** Sacagawea with papoose on horseback
right **Rev. Legend:** EXPEDITION OF DISCOVERY **Edge:**
Reeded

Date	Mintage	F	VF	XF	Unc	BU
2005 Proof	5,000	Value: 375				

KM# 21   5 DOLLARS
6.2500 g., 0.9999 Gold 0.2009 oz. AGW, 22.5 mm. **Obv:** Tribal
seal **Obv. Legend:** THE SOVEREIGN NATION OF THE
SHAWNEE TRIBE **Rev:** Bust of Chief Tecumseh 3/4 right **Rev.
Legend:** TECVMSEH **Edge:** Reeded

Date	Mintage	F	VF	XF	Unc	BU
2006 Proof	5,000	Value: 375				

KM# 25   5 DOLLARS
6.2500 g., 0.9990 Gold 0.2007 oz. AGW **Rev:** Chief Blue Jacket

Date	Mintage	F	VF	XF	Unc	BU
2007 Proof	5,000	Value: 400				

KM# 27   5 DOLLARS
6.2500 g., 0.9990 Gold 0.2007 oz. AGW **Rev:** Chief Cornstalk

Date	Mintage	F	VF	XF	Unc	BU
2008 Proof	5,000	Value: 400				

KM# 29   5 DOLLARS
6.2500 g., 0.9990 Gold 0.2007 oz. AGW **Rev:** Chief Black-Hoof

Date	Mintage	F	VF	XF	Unc	BU
2009 Proof	5,000	Value: 400				

KM# 7   50 DOLLARS
15.5500 g., 0.9990 Gold 0.4994 oz. AGW **Rev:** George
Drouillard

Date	Mintage	F	VF	XF	Unc	BU
2003 Proof	999	Value: 800				

KM# 11   50 DOLLARS
15.5500 g., 0.9990 Gold 0.4994 oz. AGW **Rev:** Sacagawea and
child

Date	Mintage	F	VF	XF	Unc	BU
2004 Proof	—	Value: 800				

KM# 17   50 DOLLARS
15.5500 g., 0.9999 Gold 0.4999 oz. AGW, 30.1 mm. **Obv:** Tribal
seal **Obv. Legend:** THE SOVEREIGN NATION OF THE
SHAWNEE TRIBE **Rev:** Sacagawea with papoose on horseback
right **Rev. Legend:** EXPEDITION OF DISCOVERY **Edge:**
Reeded

Date	Mintage	F	VF	XF	Unc	BU
2005 Proof	999	Value: 800				

KM# 8   100 DOLLARS
30.9100 g., 0.9999 Gold 0.9936 oz. AGW, 38.9 mm. **Obv:** Tribal
seal **Obv. Legend:** THE SOVEREIGN NATION OF THE
SHAWNEE TRIBE **Rev:** Bust of "Sign Talker" 3/4 right **Rev.
Legend:** GEORGE DROILLARD "SIGN TALKER" **Edge:** Milled

Date	Mintage	F	VF	XF	Unc	BU
2003 Proof	999	Value: 1,800				

KM# 12   100 DOLLARS
31.1050 g., 0.9990 Gold 0.9990 oz. AGW **Rev:** Sacagawea and
child

Date	Mintage	F	VF	XF	Unc	BU
2004 Proof	—	Value: 1,800				

KM# 18   100 DOLLARS
31.1050 g., 0.9990 Gold 0.9990 oz. AGW **Rev:** Sacagawea and
child on horseback

Date	Mintage	F	VF	XF	Unc	BU
2005 Proof	999	Value: 1,800				

KM# 23   100 DOLLARS
62.2100 g., 0.9990 Bi-Metallic 1 oz. gold and 1 oz. silver
1.9980 oz. **Rev:** Lewis and Clark

Date	Mintage	F	VF	XF	Unc	BU
2005 Proof	500	Value: 2,500				

KM# 9   500 DOLLARS
93.5000 g., 0.9999 Gold 3.0057 oz. AGW **Obv:** Tribal seal **Obv.
Legend:** THE SOVEREIGN NATION OF THE SHAWNEE TRIBE
Rev: Lewis, Clark and Drouillard scouting **Rev. Legend:** LEWIS
• CLARK • DROUILLARD **Edge:** Reeded

Date	Mintage	F	VF	XF	Unc	BU
2003 Proof	300	Value: 5,700				

KM# 13   500 DOLLARS
15.5400 g., 0.9990 Platinum 0.4991 oz. APW, 30 mm. **Obv:**
Tribal seal **Obv. Legend:** THE SOVEREIGN NATION OF THE
SHAWNEE TRIBE **Rev:** Flag and shield between standing Chief
and Thomas Jefferson **Rev. Legend:** EXPEDITION OF
DISCOVERY **Edge:** Reeded

Date	Mintage	F	VF	XF	Unc	BU
2004 Proof	999	Value: 1,250				

KM# 23A   500 DOLLARS
15.5500 g., 0.9990 Platinum 0.4994 oz. APW **Rev:** Shawnee
Chief and Thomas Jefferson standing

Date	Mintage	F	VF	XF	Unc	BU
2005 Proof	999	Value: 1,250				

KM# 14   1000 DOLLARS
31.0000 g., 0.9999 Platinum 0.9965 oz. APW, 38.7 mm. **Obv:**
Tribal seal **Obv. Legend:** THE SOVEREIGN NATION OF THE
SHAWNEE TRIBE **Rev:** Flag and shield between standing Chief
and Thomas Jefferson **Rev. Legend:** EXPEDITION OF
DISCOVERY **Edge:** Reeded

Date	Mintage	F	VF	XF	Unc	BU
2004 Proof	300	Value: 3,000				

KM# 22   1000 DOLLARS
31.1050 g., 0.9990 Platinum 0.9990 oz. APW **Rev:** Shawnee
Chief and Thomas Jefferson standing

Date	Mintage	F	VF	XF	Unc	BU
2005 Proof	300	Value: 3,000				

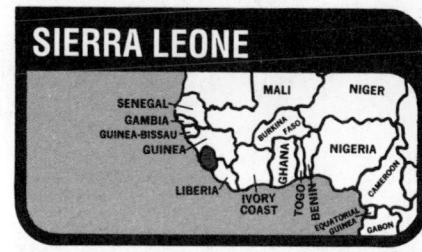

SIERRA LEONE

The Republic of Sierra Leone is located in western Africa
between Guinea and Liberia, has an area of 27,699 sq. mi.
(71,740 sq. km.) and a population of *4.1 million. Capital: Free-
town. The economy is predominantly agricultural but mining con-
tributes significantly to export revenues. Diamonds, iron ore,
palm kernels, cocoa, and coffee are exported.
Sierra Leone is a member of the Commonwealth of Nations.
The president is Chief of State and Head of Government.

MONETARY SYSTEM
100 Cents = 1 Leone

NOTE: Sierra Leone's official currency is the Leone. For previously listed Dollar Denominated Coinage, see the 5th Edition of
Unusual World Coins.

REPUBLIC
STANDARD COINAGE

KM# 295 20 LEONES
3.9200 g., Copper-Nickel, 21.7 mm. **Obv:** Value within fish and beaded circle **Rev:** Chimpanzee facing **Edge:** Plain

Date	Mintage	F	VF	XF	Unc	BU
2003	—	—	—	—	0.50	1.25

KM# 302 100 LEONES
28.2800 g., Copper-Nickel, 38.6 mm. **Subject:** 40th Anniversary - Bank of Sierra Leone **Obv:** Bank President Kabbah **Rev:** Lion **Edge:** Reeded

Date	Mintage	F	VF	XF	Unc	BU
ND (2004)PM	5,000	—	—	—	15.00	18.00

KM# 296 500 LEONES
7.2000 g., Bi-Metallic Stainless Steel center in Brass ring, 24 mm. **Obv:** Building within circle **Rev:** Bust with hat facing within circle **Edge:** Plain **Shape:** 10-sided

Date	Mintage	F	VF	XF	Unc	BU
2004	—	—	—	—	7.50	9.00

KM# 346 500 LEONES
28.2800 g., Bronze, 38.6 mm. **Subject:** 40th Anniversary - Bank of Sierra Leone **Obv:** Bank President Kabbah **Rev:** Lion, denomination as "Le 500" **Edge:** Reeded

Date	Mintage	F	VF	XF	Unc	BU
ND(2004)PM	10,000	—	—	—	15.00	18.00

DOLLAR DENOMINATED COINAGE

KM# 222 DOLLAR
28.4900 g., Copper-Nickel, 38.5 mm. **Series:** The Big Five **Obv:** National arms **Rev:** Rhino **Edge:** Reeded

Date	Mintage	F	VF	XF	Unc	BU
2001PM	—	—	—	—	12.50	15.00

KM# 225 DOLLAR
28.4900 g., Copper-Nickel, 38.6 mm. **Series:** The Big Five **Obv:** National arms **Rev:** Lion **Edge:** Reeded

Date	Mintage	F	VF	XF	Unc	BU
2001PM	—	—	—	—	10.00	15.00

KM# 228 DOLLAR
28.4900 g., Copper-Nickel, 38.6 mm. **Series:** The Big Five **Obv:** National arms **Rev:** Leopard **Edge:** Reeded

Date	Mintage	F	VF	XF	Unc	BU
2001PM	—	—	—	—	10.00	15.00

KM# 231 DOLLAR
28.4900 g., Copper-Nickel, 38.6 mm. **Series:** The Big Five **Obv:** National arms **Rev:** Elephants **Edge:** Reeded

Date	Mintage	F	VF	XF	Unc	BU
2001PM	—	—	—	—	10.00	15.00

KM# 234 DOLLAR
28.4900 g., Copper-Nickel, 38.6 mm. **Series:** The Big Five **Obv:** National arms **Rev:** Buffalo **Edge:** Reeded

Date	Mintage	F	VF	XF	Unc	BU
2001PM	—	—	—	—	10.00	15.00

KM# 237 DOLLAR
28.4900 g., Copper-Nickel, 38.5 mm. **Series:** The Big Five **Obv:** National arms **Rev:** All five animals **Edge:** Reeded

Date	Mintage	F	VF	XF	Unc	BU
2001PM	—	—	—	—	10.00	15.00

KM# 241.1 DOLLAR
28.5400 g., Copper-Nickel, 38.65 mm. **Series:** Big Cats **Obv:** National arms **Rev:** Male and female lions **Edge:** Reeded

Date	Mintage	F	VF	XF	Unc	BU
2001PM	—	—	—	—	12.50	15.00

KM# 241.2 DOLLAR
28.5400 g., Copper-Nickel, 38.65 mm. **Series:** Big Cats **Obv:** National arms **Rev:** Multi-colored male and female lions **Edge:** Reeded

Date	Mintage	F	VF	XF	Unc	BU
2001PM	—	—	—	—	15.00	17.50

KM# 242.1 DOLLAR
28.5400 g., Copper-Nickel, 38.65 mm. **Series:** Big Cats **Obv:** National arms **Rev:** Tiger **Edge:** Reeded

Date	Mintage	F	VF	XF	Unc	BU
2001PM	—	—	—	—	10.00	14.00

KM# 242.2 DOLLAR
28.5400 g., Copper-Nickel, 38.65 mm. **Series:** Big Cats **Obv:** National arms **Rev:** Multi-colored Tiger **Edge:** Reeded

Date	Mintage	F	VF	XF	Unc	BU
2001PM	—	—	—	—	15.00	17.50

KM# 243.1 DOLLAR
28.5400 g., Copper-Nickel, 38.65 mm. **Series:** Big Cats **Obv:** National arms **Rev:** Cheetah **Edge:** Reeded

Date	Mintage	F	VF	XF	Unc	BU
2001PM	—	—	—	—	12.50	15.00

KM# 243.2 DOLLAR
28.5400 g., Copper-Nickel, 38.65 mm. **Series:** Big Cats **Obv:** National arms **Rev:** Multi-colored Cheetah **Edge:** Reeded

Date	Mintage	F	VF	XF	Unc	BU
2001PM	—	—	—	—	15.00	17.50

KM# 244.1 DOLLAR
28.5400 g., Copper-Nickel, 38.65 mm. **Series:** Big Cats **Obv:** National arms **Rev:** Cougar **Edge:** Reeded

Date	Mintage	F	VF	XF	Unc	BU
2001PM	—	—	—	—	10.00	14.00

KM# 244.2 DOLLAR
28.5400 g., Copper-Nickel, 38.65 mm. **Series:** Big Cats **Obv:** National arms **Rev:** Multi-colored Cougar **Edge:** Reeded

Date	Mintage	F	VF	XF	Unc	BU
2001PM	—	—	—	—	15.00	17.50

KM# 245.1 DOLLAR
28.5400 g., Copper-Nickel, 38.65 mm. **Series:** Big Cats **Obv:** National arms **Rev:** Black panther **Edge:** Reeded

Date	Mintage	F	VF	XF	Unc	BU
2001PM	—	—	—	—	10.00	14.00

KM# 245.2 DOLLAR
28.5400 g., Copper-Nickel, 38.65 mm. **Series:** Big Cats **Obv:** National arms **Rev:** Multi-colored Black Panther **Edge:** Reeded

Date	Mintage	F	VF	XF	Unc	BU
2001PM	—	—	—	—	15.00	17.50

KM# 198 DOLLAR
28.2800 g., Copper-Nickel, 38.6 mm. **Subject:** Year of the Snake **Obv:** National arms **Rev:** Snake **Edge:** Reeded

Date	Mintage	F	VF	XF	Unc	BU
2001	—	—	—	—	10.00	14.00

KM# 206 DOLLAR
Copper-Nickel, 38.6 mm. **Subject:** P'an Ku **Obv:** National arms **Rev:** Dragon

Date	Mintage	F	VF	XF	Unc	BU
2001	—	—	—	—	10.00	14.00

KM# 214 DOLLAR
Copper-Nickel, 38.6 mm. **Subject:** P'an Ku **Obv:** National arms **Rev:** Dragon and three animals

Date	Mintage	F	VF	XF	Unc	BU
2001	—	—	—	—	10.00	14.00

KM# 256 DOLLAR
28.2800 g., Copper-Nickel, 38.6 mm. **Subject:** Year of the Horse **Obv:** National arms **Rev:** Horse **Edge:** Reeded

Date	Mintage	F	VF	XF	Unc	BU
2002	—	—	—	—	14.50	17.50

KM# 264 DOLLAR
28.2800 g., Copper-Nickel, 38.6 mm. **Subject:** RMS Titanic **Obv:** National arms **Rev:** Titanic at dock **Edge:** Reeded

Date	Mintage	F	VF	XF	Unc	BU
2002	—	—	—	—	10.00	12.00

KM# 268 DOLLAR
28.2800 g., Copper-Nickel, 38.6 mm. **Subject:** Queen's Golden Jubilee **Obv:** National arms **Rev:** Queen Elizabeth II and Prince Philip visiting blacksmiths in Sierra Leone **Edge:** Reeded

Date	Mintage	F	VF	XF	Unc	BU
2002	—	—	—	—	10.00	12.00

KM# 269 DOLLAR
28.2800 g., Copper-Nickel, 38.6 mm. **Subject:** Queen's Golden Jubilee **Obv:** National arms **Rev:** Queen, Prince Charles and Princess Anne **Edge:** Reeded

Date	Mintage	F	VF	XF	Unc	BU
2002	—	—	—	—	10.00	12.00

KM# 276 DOLLAR
28.2800 g., Copper-Nickel, 38.6 mm. **Subject:** British Queen Mother **Obv:** National arms **Rev:** Queen Mother with dog in garden **Edge:** Reeded

Date	Mintage	F	VF	XF	Unc	BU
2002	—	—	—	—	10.00	12.00

KM# 279 DOLLAR
28.2800 g., Copper-Nickel, 38.6 mm. **Subject:** Queen Mother **Obv:** National arms **Rev:** Queen Mother with daughters **Edge:** Reeded

Date	Mintage	F	VF	XF	Unc	BU
2002	—	—	—	—	10.00	12.00

KM# 282 DOLLAR
28.2800 g., Copper-Nickel, 38.6 mm. **Subject:** Queen's Golden Jubilee **Obv:** National arms **Rev:** Queen Elizabeth and a young Prince Charles **Edge:** Reeded

Date	Mintage	F	VF	XF	Unc	BU
2002	—	—	—	—	10.00	12.00

KM# 285 DOLLAR
28.2800 g., Copper-Nickel, 38.6 mm. **Subject:** Queen's Golden Jubilee **Obv:** National arms **Rev:** Queen Elizabeth and Prince Philip **Edge:** Reeded

Date	Mintage	F	VF	XF	Unc	BU
2002	—	—	—	—	10.00	12.00

KM# 288 DOLLAR
28.2800 g., Copper-Nickel, 38.6 mm. **Subject:** Olympics **Obv:** National arms **Rev:** Victory goddess Nike **Edge:** Reeded

Date	Mintage	F	VF	XF	Unc	BU
2003	—	—	—	—	10.00	12.00
2004	—	—	—	—	10.00	12.00

KM# 291 DOLLAR
28.2800 g., Copper-Nickel, 38.6 mm. **Subject:** Olympics **Obv:** National arms **Rev:** Ancient archer **Edge:** Reeded

Date	Mintage	F	VF	XF	Unc	BU
2003	—	—	—	—	10.00	12.00
2004	—	—	—	—	10.00	12.00

KM# 297 DOLLAR
28.2800 g., Copper-Nickel, 38.6 mm. **Obv:** National arms **Rev:** Nelson Mandela **Edge:** Reeded

Date	Mintage	F	VF	XF	Unc	BU
2004	—	—	—	—	15.00	16.50

KM# 300 DOLLAR
28.2800 g., Copper-Nickel, 38.6 mm. **Obv:** National arms **Rev:** Ronald Reagan **Edge:** Reeded

Date	Mintage	F	VF	XF	Unc	BU
2004	—	—	—	—	15.00	16.50

KM# 304 DOLLAR
28.4200 g., Copper-Nickel, 38.6 mm. **Obv:** National arms **Rev:** Giraffe **Edge:** Reeded

Date	Mintage	F	VF	XF	Unc	BU
2005	—	—	—	—	12.00	16.00

KM# 305 DOLLAR
28.4200 g., Copper-Nickel, 38.6 mm. **Obv:** National arms **Rev:** Crocodile **Edge:** Reeded

Date	Mintage	F	VF	XF	Unc	BU
2005	—	—	—	—	12.00	16.00

KM# 306 DOLLAR
28.4200 g., Copper-Nickel, 38.6 mm. **Obv:** National arms **Rev:** Hippo in water **Edge:** Reeded

Date	Mintage	F	VF	XF	Unc	BU
2005	—	—	—	—	12.00	16.00

KM# 345 DOLLAR
28.5000 g., Copper-Nickel, 38.58 mm. **Subject:** Death of Prince Rainier III **Obv:** National arms **Rev:** Bust left, small knight horseback right on neck **Edge:** Reeded

Date	Mintage	F	VF	XF	Unc	BU
2005	—	—	—	—	7.00	9.00

KM# 317 DOLLAR
Copper-Nickel **Series:** 60th Anniversary End of WW II **Subject:** Battle of El Alamein **Obv:** National arms **Obv. Legend:** REPUBLIC OF SIERRA LEONE **Rev:** Tank, plane and ground troops

Date	Mintage	F	VF	XF	Unc	BU
2005	—	—	—	—	10.00	12.00

KM# 316 DOLLAR
Copper-Nickel **Series:** 60th Anniversary End of WW II **Subject:** The Battle of the Atlantic **Obv:** National arms **Obv. Legend:** REPUBLIC OF SIERRA LEONE **Rev:** Plane and ship convoy

Date	Mintage	F	VF	XF	Unc	BU
2005	—	—	—	—	10.00	12.00

KM# 319 DOLLAR
Copper-Nickel **Series:** 60th Anniversary End of WW II **Subject:** The Battle of Berlin **Obv:** National arms **Obv. Legend:** REPUBLIC OF SIERRA LEONE **Rev:** Berlin city view, tank

Date	Mintage	F	VF	XF	Unc	BU
2005	—	—	—	—	10.00	12.00

KM# 315 DOLLAR
Copper-Nickel **Series:** 60th Anniversary End of WW II **Subject:** Battle of Britian **Obv:** National arms **Obv. Legend:** REPUBLIC OF SIERRA LEONE **Rev:** Planes in flight

Date	Mintage	F	VF	XF	Unc	BU
2005	—	—	—	—	10.00	12.00

KM# 318 DOLLAR
Copper-Nickel **Series:** 60th Anniversay End of WW II **Subject:** Battle of the Bulge **Obv:** National arms **Obv. Legend:** REPUBLIC OF SIERRA LEONE **Rev:** Forest battle scene

Date	Mintage	F	VF	XF	Unc	BU
2005	—	—	—	—	10.00	12.00

KM# 320 DOLLAR
Copper-Nickel **Series:** 60th Anniversary End of WW II **Subject:** The Heavy Water Raids **Obv:** National arms **Obv. Legend:** REPUBLIC OF SIERRA LEONE **Rev:** Troops on skies, factory in ruins

Date	Mintage	F	VF	XF	Unc	BU
2005	—	—	—	—	10.00	12.00

KM# 321 DOLLAR
Copper-Nickel **Obv:** National Arms **Rev:** Mountain Gorillia

Date	Mintage	F	VF	XF	Unc	BU
2005	—	—	—	—	12.00	16.00

KM# 322 DOLLAR
Copper-Nickel **Rev:** John Paul II head left, within ring of the Stations of the Cross

Date	Mintage	F	VF	XF	Unc	BU
2005	—	—	—	—	10.00	12.00

KM# 323 DOLLAR
Copper-Nickel **Rev:** Benedict XVI and St. Peter's

Date	Mintage	F	VF	XF	Unc	BU
2005	—	—	—	—	10.00	12.00

KM# 324 DOLLAR
Copper-Nickel **Obv:** National Arms **Rev:** Brontosaurus

Date	Mintage	F	VF	XF	Unc	BU
2006	—	—	—	—	14.00	16.00

KM# 308 DOLLAR
28.3700 g., Copper-Nickel, 38.5 mm. **Obv:** National arms **Rev:** Stegosaurus **Edge:** Reeded

Date	Mintage	F	VF	XF	Unc	BU
2006	—	—	—	—	14.00	16.00

KM# 309 DOLLAR
28.3700 g., Copper-Nickel, 38.5 mm. **Obv:** National arms **Rev:** Tyrannosaurus Rex **Edge:** Reeded

Date	Mintage	F	VF	XF	Unc	BU
2006	—	—	—	—	14.00	16.00

KM# 310 DOLLAR
28.3700 g., Copper-Nickel, 38.5 mm. **Obv:** National arms **Rev:** Triceratops **Edge:** Reeded

Date	Mintage	F	VF	XF	Unc	BU
2006	—	—	—	—	14.00	16.00

KM# 311 DOLLAR
28.3700 g., Copper-Nickel, 38.5 mm. **Obv:** National arms **Rev:** Lion **Edge:** Reeded

Date	Mintage	F	VF	XF	Unc	BU
2006	—	—	—	—	12.00	16.00

KM# 312 DOLLAR
28.3700 g., Copper-Nickel, 38.5 mm. **Obv:** National arms **Rev:** Dromedary Camel **Edge:** Reeded

Date	Mintage	F	VF	XF	Unc	BU
2006	—	—	—	—	12.00	16.00

KM# 313 DOLLAR
28.3700 g., Copper-Nickel, 38.63 mm. **Obv:** National arms **Rev:** Chimpanzee **Edge:** Reeded

Date	Mintage	F	VF	XF	Unc	BU
2006	—	—	—	—	12.00	16.00

KM# 314 DOLLAR
28.3700 g., Copper-Nickel, 38.5 mm. **Obv:** National arms **Rev:** Impala **Edge:** Reeded

Date	Mintage	F	VF	XF	Unc	BU
2006	—	—	—	—	12.00	16.00

KM# 326 DOLLAR
28.3700 g., Copper-Nickel, 38.5 mm. **Rev:** Cheetah

Date	Mintage	F	VF	XF	Unc	BU
2007	—	—	—	—	14.00	17.00

KM# 327 DOLLAR
28.3700 g., Copper-Nickel, 38.5 mm. **Rev:** Zebra

Date	Mintage	F	VF	XF	Unc	BU
2007	—	—	—	—	14.00	17.00

KM# 328 DOLLAR
28.3700 g., Copper-Nickel, 38.5 mm. **Rev:** Rhino

Date	Mintage	F	VF	XF	Unc	BU
2007	—	—	—	—	14.00	17.00

KM# 329 DOLLAR
28.3700 g., Copper-Nickel, 38.5 mm. **Obv:** Arms **Rev:** African elephant

Date	Mintage	F	VF	XF	Unc	BU
2007	—	—	—	—	15.00	18.00

KM# 347 DOLLAR
28.3700 g., Copper-Nickel, 38.6 mm. **Series:** Nocturnal

Creatures of Africa **Obv:** National arms **Rev:** Duiker Antelope standing left, facing **Edge:** Reeded **Note:** Blackened finish.

Date	Mintage	F	VF	XF	Unc	BU
2008	—	—	—	—	17.50	20.00

KM# 348 DOLLAR
28.3700 g., Copper-Nickel, 38.6 mm. **Series:** Nocturnal Creatures of Africa **Obv:** National arms **Rev:** Bush Baby on tree limb **Edge:** Reeded **Note:** Blackened finish.

Date	Mintage	F	VF	XF	Unc	BU
2008	—	—	—	—	17.50	20.00

KM# 349 DOLLAR
28.3700 g., Copper-Nickel, 38.6 mm. **Series:** Nocturnal Creatures of Africa **Obv:** National arms **Rev:** Honey Badger **Edge:** Reeded **Note:** Blackened finish

Date	Mintage	F	VF	XF	Unc	BU
2008	—	—	—	—	17.50	20.00

KM# 350 DOLLAR
28.3700 g., Copper-Nickel, 38.6 mm. **Series:** Nocturnal Creatures of Africa **Obv:** National arms. **Rev:** Pygmy Hippopotamus in water facing **Edge:** Reeded **Note:** Blackened finish.

Date	Mintage	F	VF	XF	Unc	BU
2008	—	—	—	—	17.50	20.00

KM# 223 10 DOLLARS
28.2800 g., 0.9250 Silver 0.8410 oz. ASW, 38.6 mm. **Series:** The Big Five **Obv:** National arms **Rev:** Rhino and value within circle **Edge:** Reeded

Date	Mintage	F	VF	XF	Unc	BU
2001 Proof	—	Value: 45.00				

KM# 226 10 DOLLARS
28.2800 g., 0.9250 Silver 0.8410 oz. ASW, 38.6 mm. **Series:** The Big Five **Obv:** National arms **Rev:** Lion head and value within circle

Date	Mintage	F	VF	XF	Unc	BU
2001 Proof	Est. 10,000	Value: 45.00				

KM# 229 10 DOLLARS
28.2800 g., 0.9250 Silver 0.8410 oz. ASW, 38.6 mm. **Series:** The Big Five **Obv:** National arms **Rev:** Leopard and value within circle

Date	Mintage	F	VF	XF	Unc	BU
2001 Proof	Est. 10,000	Value: 45.00				

KM# 232 10 DOLLARS
28.2800 g., 0.9250 Silver 0.8410 oz. ASW, 38.6 mm. **Series:** The Big Five **Obv:** National arms **Rev:** Elephants and value within circle

Date	Mintage	F	VF	XF	Unc	BU
2001 Proof	Est. 10,000	Value: 45.00				

KM# 235 10 DOLLARS
28.2800 g., 0.9250 Silver 0.8410 oz. ASW, 38.6 mm. **Series:** The Big Five **Obv:** National arms **Rev:** Buffalo and value within circle

Date	Mintage	F	VF	XF	Unc	BU
2001 Proof	Est. 10,000	Value: 45.00				

KM# 238 10 DOLLARS
28.2800 g., 0.9250 Silver 0.8410 oz. ASW, 38.6 mm. **Series:** The Big Five **Obv:** National arms **Rev:** All five animals within circle

Date	Mintage	F	VF	XF	Unc	BU
2001 Proof	Est. 10,000	Value: 45.00				

KM# 246.1 10 DOLLARS
28.2800 g., 0.9250 Silver 0.8410 oz. ASW, 38.6 mm. **Series:** Big Cats **Obv:** National arms **Rev:** Male and female lions **Edge:** Reeded

Date	Mintage	F	VF	XF	Unc	BU
2001 Proof	10,000	Value: 45.00				

KM# 246.2 10 DOLLARS
28.2800 g., 0.9250 Silver 0.8410 oz. ASW, 38.6 mm. **Series:** Big Cats **Obv:** National arms **Rev:** Multi-colored male and female lions **Edge:** Reeded

Date	Mintage	F	VF	XF	Unc	BU
2001 Proof	—	Value: 55.00				

KM# 247.1 10 DOLLARS
28.2800 g., 0.9250 Silver 0.8410 oz. ASW, 38.6 mm. **Series:** Big Cats **Obv:** National arms **Rev:** Tiger **Edge:** Reeded

Date	Mintage	F	VF	XF	Unc	BU
2001 Proof	—	Value: 45.00				

KM# 247.2 10 DOLLARS
28.2800 g., 0.9250 Silver 0.8410 oz. ASW, 38.6 mm. **Series:** Big Cats **Obv:** National arms **Rev:** Multi-colored Tiger **Edge:** Reeded

Date	Mintage	F	VF	XF	Unc	BU
2001 Proof	—	Value: 55.00				

KM# 248.1 10 DOLLARS
28.2800 g., 0.9250 Silver 0.8410 oz. ASW, 38.6 mm. **Series:** Big Cats **Obv:** National arms **Rev:** Cheetah head facing **Edge:** Reeded

Date	Mintage	F	VF	XF	Unc	BU
2001 Proof	10,000	Value: 45.00				

KM# 248.2 10 DOLLARS
28.2800 g., 0.9250 Silver 0.8410 oz. ASW, 38.6 mm. **Series:** Big Cats **Obv:** National arms **Rev:** Multi-colored Cheetah head facing **Edge:** Reeded

Date	Mintage	F	VF	XF	Unc	BU
2001 Proof	—	Value: 55.00				

KM# 249.1 10 DOLLARS
28.2800 g., 0.9250 Silver 0.8410 oz. ASW, 38.6 mm. **Series:** Big Cats **Obv:** National arms **Rev:** Cougar **Edge:** Reeded

Date	Mintage	F	VF	XF	Unc	BU
2001 Proof	10,000	Value: 45.00				

KM# 249.2 10 DOLLARS
28.2800 g., 0.9250 Silver 0.8410 oz. ASW, 38.6 mm. **Series:** Big Cats **Obv:** National arms **Rev:** Multi-colored Cougar **Edge:** Reeded

Date	Mintage	F	VF	XF	Unc	BU
2001 Proof	—	Value: 55.00				

KM# 250.1   10 DOLLARS
28.2800 g., 0.9250 Silver 0.8410 oz. ASW, 38.6 mm. **Series:**
Big Cats **Obv:** National arms **Rev:** Leopard **Edge:** Reeded

Date	Mintage	F	VF	XF	Unc	BU
2001 Proof	10,000			Value: 45.00		

KM# 199   10 DOLLARS
28.2800 g., 0.9250 Silver 0.8410 oz. ASW, 38.6 mm. **Subject:**
Year of the Snake **Obv:** National arms **Rev:** Snake on bamboo
Edge: Reeded

Date	Mintage	F	VF	XF	Unc	BU
2001 Proof	Est. 25,000			Value: 55.00		

KM# 207   10 DOLLARS
28.2800 g., 0.9250 Silver 0.8410 oz. ASW, 38.6 mm. **Subject:**
P'an Ku **Obv:** National arms **Rev:** Dragon

Date	Mintage	F	VF	XF	Unc	BU
2001 Proof	Est. 5,000			Value: 55.00		

KM# 215   10 DOLLARS
28.2800 g., 0.9250 Silver 0.8410 oz. ASW, 38.6 mm. **Subject:**
P'an Ku **Obv:** National arms **Rev:** Dragon and three animals

Date	Mintage	F	VF	XF	Unc	BU
2001 Proof	Est. 5,000			Value: 55.00		

KM# 250.2   10 DOLLARS
28.2800 g., 0.9250 Silver 0.8410 oz. ASW, 38.6 mm. **Series:**
Big Cats **Obv:** National arms **Rev:** Multi-colored Leopard **Edge:**
Reeded

Date	Mintage	F	VF	XF	Unc	BU
2001 Proof	—			Value: 55.00		

KM# 277   10 DOLLARS
28.2800 g., 0.9250 Silver Gold clad 0.8410 oz. ASW, 38.6 mm.
Subject: British Queen Mother **Obv:** National arms **Rev:** Bust
facing in garden with dog within sprigs **Edge:** Reeded

Date	Mintage	F	VF	XF	Unc	BU
2002 Proof	10,000			Value: 55.00		

KM# 280   10 DOLLARS
28.2800 g., 0.9250 Silver Gold clad 0.8410 oz. ASW, 38.6 mm.
Subject: British Queen Mother **Obv:** National arms **Rev:**
Conjoined busts facing within sprigs **Edge:** Reeded

Date	Mintage	F	VF	XF	Unc	BU
2002 Proof	10,000			Value: 55.00		

KM# 257   10 DOLLARS
28.2800 g., 0.9250 Silver 0.8410 oz. ASW, 38.6 mm. **Subject:**
Year of the Horse **Obv:** National arms **Rev:** Horse divides circle
Edge: Reeded

Date	Mintage	F	VF	XF	Unc	BU
2002 Proof	5,000			Value: 60.00		

KM# 265   10 DOLLARS
28.2800 g., 0.9250 Silver 0.8410 oz. ASW, 38.6 mm. **Subject:**
RMS Titanic **Obv:** National arms **Rev:** Titanic at dock **Edge:**
Reeded

Date	Mintage	F	VF	XF	Unc	BU
2002 Proof	10,000			Value: 55.00		

KM# 270   10 DOLLARS
28.2800 g., 0.9250 Silver Gold clad 0.8410 oz. ASW, 38.6 mm.
Subject: Queen's Golden Jubilee **Obv:** National arms **Rev:**
Queen Elizabeth II and Prince Philip visiting blacksmiths in Sierra
Leone **Edge:** Reeded

Date	Mintage	F	VF	XF	Unc	BU
2002 Proof	10,000			Value: 55.00		

KM# 271   10 DOLLARS
28.2800 g., 0.9250 Silver Gold clad 0.8410 oz. ASW, 38.6 mm.
Subject: Queen's Golden Jubilee **Obv:** National arms **Rev:**
Queen Elizabeth II, Prince Charles and Princess Anne **Edge:**
Reeded

Date	Mintage	F	VF	XF	Unc	BU
2002 Proof	10,000			Value: 52.00		

KM# 283   10 DOLLARS
28.2800 g., 0.9250 Silver Gold clad 0.8410 oz. ASW, 38.6 mm.
Subject: Queen Elizabeth's Golden Jubilee **Obv:** National arms
Rev: Queen and young Prince Charles **Edge:** Reeded

Date	Mintage	F	VF	XF	Unc	BU
2002 Proof	10,000			Value: 50.00		

KM# 286   10 DOLLARS
28.2800 g., 0.9250 Silver Gold clad 0.8410 oz. ASW, 38.6 mm.
Subject: Queen Elizabeth's Golden Jubilee **Obv:** National arms
Rev: Queen and Prince Philip **Edge:** Reeded

Date	Mintage	F	VF	XF	Unc	BU
2002 Proof	10,000			Value: 50.00		

KM# 292 10 DOLLARS
28.2800 g., 0.9250 Silver 0.8410 oz. ASW, 38.6 mm. **Subject:** Olympics **Obv:** National arms **Rev:** Ancient archer **Edge:** Reeded

Date	Mintage	F	VF	XF	Unc	BU
2003 Proof	10,000	Value: 50.00				
2004 Proof	10,000	Value: 50.00				

KM# 289 10 DOLLARS
28.2800 g., 0.9250 Silver 0.8410 oz. ASW, 38.6 mm. **Subject:** Olympics **Obv:** National arms **Rev:** Victory goddess Nike **Edge:** Reeded **Note:** The leone is the official currency of Sierra Leone

Date	Mintage	F	VF	XF	Unc	BU
2003 Proof	10,000	Value: 50.00				
2004 Proof	10,000	Value: 50.00				

KM# 298 10 DOLLARS
28.2800 g., 0.9250 Silver 0.8410 oz. ASW, 38.6 mm. **Obv:** National arms **Rev:** Nelson Mandela **Edge:** Reeded

Date	Mintage	F	VF	XF	Unc	BU
2004 Proof	10,000	Value: 55.00				

KM# 301 10 DOLLARS
28.2800 g., 0.9250 Silver 0.8410 oz. ASW, 38.6 mm. **Obv:** National arms **Rev:** Ronald Reagan **Edge:** Reeded

Date	Mintage	F	VF	XF	Unc	BU
2004 Proof	10,000	Value: 55.00				

KM# 307 10 DOLLARS
28.6200 g., 0.9250 Silver 0.8511 oz. ASW, 38.5 mm. **Obv:** National arms **Rev:** Giraffe **Edge:** Reeded

Date	Mintage	F	VF	XF	Unc	BU
2005 Proof	—	Value: 50.00				

KM# 339 10 DOLLARS
28.2800 g., 0.9250 Silver 0.8410 oz. ASW **Series:** 60th Anniversary of WW II **Subject:** Battle of Britain **Obv:** National arms **Obv. Legend:** REPUBLIC OF SIERRA LEONE **Rev:** Planes in flight

Date	Mintage	F	VF	XF	Unc	BU
2005 Proof	—	Value: 50.00				

KM# 340 10 DOLLARS
28.2800 g., 0.9250 Silver 0.8410 oz. ASW **Series:** 60th Anniversary End of WW II **Subject:** The Battle of the Atlantic **Obv:** National arms **Obv. Legend:** REPUBLIC OF SIERRA LEONE **Rev:** Plane and ship convoy

Date	Mintage	F	VF	XF	Unc	BU
2005 Proof	—	Value: 50.00				

KM# 341 10 DOLLARS
28.2800 g., 0.9250 Silver 0.8410 oz. ASW **Series:** 60th Anniversary End of WW II **Subject:** Battle of El Alamein **Obv:** National arms **Obv. Legend:** REPUBLIC OF SIERRA LEONE **Rev:** Tank, plane and ground troops

Date	Mintage	F	VF	XF	Unc	BU
2005 Proof	—	Value: 50.00				

KM# 342 10 DOLLARS
28.2800 g., 0.9250 Silver 0.8410 oz. ASW **Series:** 60th Anniversary End of WW II **Subject:** Battle of the Bulge **Obv:** National arms **Obv. Legend:** REPUBLIC OF SIERRA LEONE **Rev:** Forest battle scene

Date	Mintage	F	VF	XF	Unc	BU
2005 Proof	—	Value: 50.00				

KM# 343 10 DOLLARS
28.2800 g., 0.9250 Silver 0.8410 oz. ASW **Series:** 60th Anniversary End of WW II **Subject:** Battle of Berlin **Obv:** National arms **Obv. Legend:** REPUBLIC OF SIERRA LEONE **Rev:** Berlin city view, tank

Date	Mintage	F	VF	XF	Unc	BU
2005 Proof	—	Value: 50.00				

KM# 344 10 DOLLARS
28.2800 g., 0.9250 Silver 0.8410 oz. ASW **Series:** 60th Anniversary End of WW II **Subject:** The Heavy Water Raids **Obv:** National arms **Obv. Legend:** REPUBLIC OF SIERRA LEONE **Rev:** Troops on skies, factory in ruins

Date	Mintage	F	VF	XF	Unc	BU
2005 Proof	—	Value: 50.00				

KM# 330 10 DOLLARS
28.2800 g., 0.9250 Silver 0.8410 oz. ASW **Series:** Crown Jewels **Obv:** Arms **Obv. Legend:** REPUBLIC OF SIERRA LEONE **Rev:** Imperial State crown with ruby setting **Rev. Legend:** CROWN JEWELS **Edge:** Reeded

Date	Mintage	F	VF	XF	Unc	BU
2006 Proof	—	Value: 120				

KM# 331 10 DOLLARS
28.2800 g., 0.9250 Silver 0.8410 oz. ASW **Series:** Crown Jewels **Obv:** Arms **Obv. Legend:** REPUBLIC OF SIERRA LEONE **Rev:** Sword of State with sapphire setting **Rev. Legend:** CROWN JEWELS **Edge:** Reeded

Date	Mintage	F	VF	XF	Unc	BU
2006 Proof	—	Value: 120				

KM# 332 10 DOLLARS
28.2800 g., 0.9250 Silver 0.8410 oz. ASW **Series:** Crown Jewels **Obv:** Arms **Obv. Legend:** REPUBLIC OF SIERRA LEONE **Rev:** St. Edward's Crown with emerald setting **Rev. Legend:** CROWN JEWELS **Edge:** Reeded

Date	Mintage	F	VF	XF	Unc	BU
2006 Proof	—	Value: 120				

KM# 333 10 DOLLARS
28.2800 g., 0.9250 Silver 0.8410 oz. ASW **Series:** Crown Jewels **Obv:** Arms **Obv. Legend:** REPUBLIC OF SIERRA LEONE **Rev:** Orb and Sceptre with the cross with diamond setting **Rev. Legend:** CROWN JEWELS **Edge:** Reeded

Date	Mintage	F	VF	XF	Unc	BU
2006 Proof	—	Value: 120				

KM# 334 10 DOLLARS
Copper-Nickel **Subject:** 80th Birthday of Queen Elizabeth II **Obv:** Arms **Obv. Legend:** REPUBLIC OF SIERRA LEONE **Rev:** Elizabeth II seated giving Christmas message **Edge:** Reeded

Date	Mintage	F	VF	XF	Unc	BU
2006	—	—	—	—	16.50	18.50

KM# 334a 10 DOLLARS
28.2800 g., 0.9250 Silver 0.8410 oz. ASW **Subject:** 80th Birthday of Queen Elizabeth II **Obv:** Arms **Obv. Legend:** REPUBLIC OF SIERRA LEONE **Rev:** Elizabeth II seated giving Christmas Message **Edge:** Reeded

Date	Mintage	F	VF	XF	Unc	BU
2006 Proof	—	Value: 75.00				

KM# 335 10 DOLLARS
Copper-Nickel **Subject:** 80th Birthday of Queen Elizabeth II **Obv:** Arms **Obv. Legend:** REPUBLIC OF SIERRA LEONE **Rev:** Elizabeth II at 2002 Golden Jubilee celebrations in London, Concorde and Red Arrows doing flypass over Buckingham Palace **Edge:** Reeded

Date	Mintage	F	VF	XF	Unc	BU
2006	—	—	—	—	16.50	18.50

KM# 335a 10 DOLLARS
28.2800 g., 0.9250 Silver 0.8410 oz. ASW **Subject:** 80th Birthday of Queen Elizabeth Ii **Obv:** Arms **Obv. Legend:** REPUBLIC OF SIERRA LEONE **Rev:** Elizabeth II at 2002 Golden Jubilee celebrations in London, Concorde and Red Arrows doing flypass over Buckingham Palace **Edge:** Reeded

Date	Mintage	F	VF	XF	Unc	BU
2006 Proof	—	Value: 75.00				

KM# 336 10 DOLLARS
Copper-Nickel **Subject:** 80th Birthday of Queen Elizabeth II **Obv:** Arms **Obv. Legend:** REPUBLIC OF SIERRA LEONE **Rev:** Elizabeth II presenting 1966 Football World Cup to English team **Edge:** Reeded

Date	Mintage	F	VF	XF	Unc	BU
2006	—	—	—	—	16.50	18.50

KM# 336a 10 DOLLARS
28.2800 g., 0.9250 Silver 0.8410 oz. ASW **Subject:** 80th Birthday of Queen Elizabeth II **Obv:** Arms **Obv. Legend:** REPUBLIC OF SIERRA LEONE **Rev:** Elizabeth II presenting 1966 Football World Cup to English team **Edge:** Reeded

Date	Mintage	F	VF	XF	Unc	BU
2006 Proof	—	Value: 75.00				

KM# 337 10 DOLLARS
Copper-Nickel **Subject:** 80th Birthday of Queen Elizabeth II **Obv:** Arms **Obv. Legend:** REPUBLIC OF SIERRA LEONE **Rev:** Investiture of Charles as Prince of Wales in 1969 **Edge:** Reeded

Date	Mintage	F	VF	XF	Unc	BU
2006	—	—	—	—	16.50	18.50

KM# 337a 10 DOLLARS
0.9167 Silver **Subject:** 80th Birthday of Queen Elizabeth II **Obv:** Arms **Obv. Legend:** REPUBLIC OF SIERRA LEONE **Rev:** Investiture of Charles as Prince of Wales in 1969 **Edge:** Reeded

Date	Mintage	F	VF	XF	Unc	BU
2006 Proof	—	Value: 75.00				

KM# 338 10 DOLLARS
Copper-Nickel **Subject:** 10th Anniversary Death of Princess Diana **Obv:** Arms **Obv. Legend:** REPUBLIC OF SIERRA LEONE **Rev:** Diana with sons, Prince William and Prince Harry facing **Rev. Legend:** DIANA — PRINCESS OF WALES **Edge:** Reeded

Date	Mintage	F	VF	XF	Unc	BU
2007	—	—	—	—	16.50	18.50

KM# 338a 10 DOLLARS
28.2800 g., 0.9250 Silver 0.8410 oz. ASW **Subject:** 10th Anniversary Death of Princess Diana **Obv:** Arms **Obv. Legend:** REPUBLIC OF SIERRA LEONE **Rev:** Diana with sons, Prince William and Prince Harry facing **Rev. Legend:** DIANA — PRINCESS OF WALES **Edge:** Reeded

Date	Mintage	F	VF	XF	Unc	BU
2007 Proof	—	Value: 75.00				

KM# 200 20 DOLLARS
1.2441 g., 0.9990 Gold 0.0400 oz. AGW, 13.9 mm. **Subject:** Year of the Snake **Obv:** National arms **Rev:** Snake **Edge:** Reeded

Date	Mintage	F	VF	XF	Unc	BU
2001 Proof	Est. 50,000	Value: 85.00				

KM# 208 20 DOLLARS
1.2441 g., 0.9990 Gold 0.0400 oz. AGW, 13.9 mm. **Subject:** P'an Ku **Obv:** National arms **Rev:** Dragon

Date	Mintage	F	VF	XF	Unc	BU
2001 Proof	Est. 5,000	Value: 85.00				

KM# 216 20 DOLLARS
1.2441 g., 0.9990 Gold 0.0400 oz. AGW, 13.9 mm. **Subject:** P'an Ku **Obv:** National arms **Rev:** Dragon and three animals

Date	Mintage	F	VF	XF	Unc	BU
2001 Proof	Est. 5,000	Value: 85.00				

KM# 258 20 DOLLARS
1.2400 g., 0.9990 Gold 0.0398 oz. AGW, 13.92 mm. **Subject:** Year of the Horse **Obv:** National arms **Rev:** Horse **Edge:** Reeded

Date	Mintage	F	VF	XF	Unc	BU
2002 Proof	5,000	Value: 85.00				

KM# 272 30 DOLLARS
6.2200 g., 0.3750 Gold 0.0750 oz. AGW, 22 mm. **Subject:** Queen's Golden Jubilee **Obv:** National arms **Rev:** Queen Elizabeth II and Prince Philip **Edge:** Reeded

Date	Mintage	F	VF	XF	Unc	BU
2002 Proof	5,000	Value: 150				

KM# 273 30 DOLLARS
6.2200 g., 0.3750 Gold 0.0750 oz. AGW, 22 mm. **Subject:** Queen's Golden Jubilee **Obv:** National arms **Rev:** Queen Elizabeth II, Prince Charles and Princess Anne **Edge:** Reeded

Date	Mintage	F	VF	XF	Unc	BU
2002 Proof	5,000	Value: 150				

KM# 201 50 DOLLARS
3.1103 g., 0.9990 Gold 0.0999 oz. AGW, 18 mm. **Subject:** Year of the Snake **Obv:** National arms **Rev:** Snake **Edge:** Reeded

Date	Mintage	F	VF	XF	Unc	BU
2001 Proof	Est. 10,000	Value: 200				

KM# 209 50 DOLLARS
3.1103 g., 0.9990 Gold 0.0999 oz. AGW, 18 mm. **Subject:** P'an Ku **Obv:** National arms **Rev:** Dragon

Date	Mintage	F	VF	XF	Unc	BU
2001 Proof	Est. 5,000	Value: 200				

KM# 217 50 DOLLARS
3.1103 g., 0.9990 Gold 0.0999 oz. AGW, 18 mm. **Subject:** P'an Ku **Obv:** National arms **Rev:** Dragon and three animals

Date	Mintage	F	VF	XF	Unc	BU
2001 Proof	Est. 5,000	Value: 200				

KM# 266 50 DOLLARS
155.5500 g., 0.9999 Silver 5.0003 oz. ASW, 65 mm. **Subject:** RMS Titanic **Obv:** National arms **Rev:** Titanic at dock **Edge:** Reeded

Date	Mintage	F	VF	XF	Unc	BU
2002 Proof	2,000	Value: 220				

KM# 259 50 DOLLARS
3.1100 g., 0.9990 Gold 0.0999 oz. AGW, 18 mm. **Subject:** Year of the Horse **Obv:** National arms **Rev:** Horse **Edge:** Reeded

Date	Mintage	F	VF	XF	Unc	BU
2002 Proof	5,000	Value: 200				

KM# 202 100 DOLLARS
6.2200 g., 0.9990 Gold 0.1998 oz. AGW, 22 mm. **Subject:** Year of the Snake **Obv:** National arms **Rev:** Snake **Edge:** Reeded

Date	Mintage	F	VF	XF	Unc	BU
2001 Proof	—	Value: 380				

KM# 210 100 DOLLARS
6.2200 g., 0.9990 Gold 0.1998 oz. AGW, 22 mm. **Subject:** P'an Ku **Obv:** National arms **Rev:** Dragon

Date	Mintage	F	VF	XF	Unc	BU
2001 Proof	Est. 10,000	Value: 380				

KM# 218 100 DOLLARS
6.2200 g., 0.9990 Gold 0.1998 oz. AGW, 22 mm. **Subject:** P'an Ku **Obv:** National arms **Rev:** Dragon and three animals

Date	Mintage	F	VF	XF	Unc	BU
2001 Proof	Est. 10,000	Value: 380				

KM# 224 100 DOLLARS
6.2200 g., 0.9990 Gold 0.1998 oz. AGW, 22 mm. **Series:** The Big Five **Obv:** National arms **Rev:** Rhino **Edge:** Reeded

Date	Mintage	F	VF	XF	Unc	BU
2001 Proof	Est. 5,000	Value: 380				

KM# 227 100 DOLLARS
6.2200 g., 0.9990 Gold 0.1998 oz. AGW, 22 mm. **Series:** The Big Five **Obv:** National arms **Rev:** Lion

Date	Mintage	F	VF	XF	Unc	BU
2001 Proof	Est. 5,000	Value: 380				

KM# 230 100 DOLLARS
6.2200 g., 0.9990 Gold 0.1998 oz. AGW, 22 mm. **Series:** The Big Five **Obv:** National arms **Rev:** Leopard

Date	Mintage	F	VF	XF	Unc	BU
2001 Proof	Est. 5,000	Value: 380				

KM# 233 100 DOLLARS
6.2200 g., 0.9990 Gold 0.1998 oz. AGW, 22 mm. **Series:** The Big Five **Obv:** National arms **Rev:** Elephants

Date	Mintage	F	VF	XF	Unc	BU
2001 Proof	Est. 5,000	Value: 380				

KM# 236 100 DOLLARS
6.2200 g., 0.9990 Gold 0.1998 oz. AGW, 22 mm. **Series:** The Big Five **Obv:** National arms **Rev:** Buffalo

Date	Mintage	F	VF	XF	Unc	BU
2001 Proof	Est. 5,000	Value: 380				

KM# 239 100 DOLLARS
6.2200 g., 0.9990 Gold 0.1998 oz. AGW, 22 mm. **Series:** The Big Five **Obv:** National arms **Rev:** All five animals

Date	Mintage	F	VF	XF	Unc	BU
2001 Proof	Est. 5,000	Value: 380				

KM# 251 100 DOLLARS
6.2200 g., 0.9990 Gold 0.1998 oz. AGW, 22 mm. **Series:** Big Cats **Obv:** National arms **Rev:** Male and female lions **Edge:** Reeded

Date	Mintage	F	VF	XF	Unc	BU
2001 Proof	5,000	Value: 380				

KM# 252 100 DOLLARS
6.2200 g., 0.9990 Gold 0.1998 oz. AGW, 22 mm. **Series:** Big Cats **Rev:** Tiger **Edge:** Reeded

Date	Mintage	F	VF	XF	Unc	BU
2001 Proof	5,000	Value: 380				

KM# 253   100 DOLLARS
6.2200 g., 0.9990 Gold 0.1998 oz. AGW, 22 mm. **Series:** Big Cats **Rev:** Cheetah **Edge:** Reeded

Date	Mintage	F	VF	XF	Unc	BU
2001 Proof	5,000	Value: 380				

KM# 254   100 DOLLARS
6.2200 g., 0.9990 Gold 0.1998 oz. AGW, 22 mm. **Series:** Big Cats **Rev:** Cougar **Edge:** Reeded

Date	Mintage	F	VF	XF	Unc	BU
2001 Proof	5,000	Value: 380				

KM# 255   100 DOLLARS
6.2200 g., 0.9990 Gold 0.1998 oz. AGW, 22 mm. **Series:** Big Cats **Rev:** Black panther **Edge:** Reeded

Date	Mintage	F	VF	XF	Unc	BU
2001 Proof	5,000	Value: 380				

KM# 274   100 DOLLARS
6.2200 g., 0.9999 Gold 0.1999 oz. AGW, 22 mm. **Subject:** Queen's Golden Jubilee **Obv:** National arms **Rev:** Queen Elizabeth II and Prince Philip **Edge:** Reeded

Date	Mintage	F	VF	XF	Unc	BU
2002 Proof	2,002	Value: 380				

KM# 275   100 DOLLARS
6.2200 g., 0.9999 Gold 0.1999 oz. AGW, 22 mm. **Subject:** Queen's Golden Jubilee **Obv:** National arms **Rev:** Queen Elizabeth II, Prince Charles and Princess Anne **Edge:** Reeded

Date	Mintage	F	VF	XF	Unc	BU
2002 Proof	5,000	Value: 380				

KM# 284   100 DOLLARS
6.2200 g., 0.9999 Gold 0.1999 oz. AGW, 22 mm. **Subject:** Queen Elizabeth's Golden Jubilee **Obv:** National arms **Rev:** Queen and young Prince Charles **Edge:** Reeded

Date	Mintage	F	VF	XF	Unc	BU
2002 Proof	2,002	Value: 380				

KM# 287   100 DOLLARS
6.2200 g., 0.9999 Gold 0.1999 oz. AGW, 22 mm. **Subject:** Queen Elizabeth's Golden Jubilee **Obv:** National arms **Rev:** Queen and Prince Philip **Edge:** Reeded

Date	Mintage	F	VF	XF	Unc	BU
2002 Proof	2,002	Value: 380				

KM# 278   100 DOLLARS
6.2200 g., 0.9999 Gold 0.1999 oz. AGW, 22 mm. **Subject:** British Queen Mother **Obv:** National arms **Rev:** Queen Mother in garden with dog **Edge:** Reeded

Date	Mintage	F	VF	XF	Unc	BU
2002 Proof	2,000	Value: 380				

KM# 281   100 DOLLARS
6.2200 g., 0.9999 Gold 0.1999 oz. AGW, 22 mm. **Subject:** British Queen Mother **Obv:** National arms **Rev:** Queen Mother with daughters **Edge:** Reeded

Date	Mintage	F	VF	XF	Unc	BU
2002 Proof	2,000	Value: 380				

KM# 260   100 DOLLARS
6.2200 g., 0.9990 Gold 0.1998 oz. AGW, 22 mm. **Subject:** Year of the Horse **Obv:** National arms **Rev:** Horse **Edge:** Reeded

Date	Mintage	F	VF	XF	Unc	BU
2002 Proof	2,000	Value: 380				

KM# 290   100 DOLLARS
6.2200 g., 0.9999 Gold 0.1999 oz. AGW, 22 mm. **Subject:** Olympics **Obv:** National arms **Rev:** Victory goddess Nike **Edge:** Reeded

Date	Mintage	F	VF	XF	Unc	BU
2003 Proof	5,000	Value: 380				
2004 Proof	5,000	Value: 380				

KM# 293   100 DOLLARS
6.2200 g., 0.9999 Gold 0.1999 oz. AGW, 22 mm. **Subject:** Olympics **Obv:** National arms **Rev:** Ancient archer **Edge:** Reeded

Date	Mintage	F	VF	XF	Unc	BU
2003 Proof	5,000	Value: 380				
2004 Proof	5,000	Value: 380				

KM# 267   150 DOLLARS
1000.0000 g., 0.9999 Silver 32.146 oz. ASW, 85 mm. **Subject:** RMS Titanic **Obv:** National arms **Rev:** Titanic at dock **Edge:** Reeded

Date	Mintage	F	VF	XF	Unc	BU
2002 Proof	500	Value: 1,350				

KM# 203   250 DOLLARS
15.5118 g., 0.9990 Gold 0.4982 oz. AGW, 30 mm. **Subject:** Year of the Snake **Obv:** National arms **Rev:** Snake **Edge:** Reeded

Date	Mintage	F	VF	XF	Unc	BU
2001 Proof	Est. 5,000	Value: 950				

KM# 211   250 DOLLARS
15.5518 g., 0.9990 Gold 0.4995 oz. AGW, 30 mm. **Subject:** P'an Ku **Obv:** National arms **Rev:** Dragon **Edge:** Reeded

Date	Mintage	F	VF	XF	Unc	BU
2001 Proof	Est. 2,000	Value: 950				

KM# 219   250 DOLLARS
15.5518 g., 0.9990 Gold 0.4995 oz. AGW, 30 mm. **Subject:** P'an Ku **Obv:** National arms **Rev:** Dragon and three animals **Edge:** Reeded

Date	Mintage	F	VF	XF	Unc	BU
2001 Proof	Est. 2,000	Value: 950				

KM# 261   250 DOLLARS
15.5500 g., 0.9990 Gold 0.4994 oz. AGW, 30 mm. **Subject:** Year of the Horse **Obv:** National arms **Rev:** Horse **Edge:** Reeded

Date	Mintage	F	VF	XF	Unc	BU
2002 Proof	2,000	Value: 950				

KM# 204   500 DOLLARS
31.1035 g., 0.9990 Gold 0.9990 oz. AGW, 32.7 mm. **Subject:** Year of the Snake **Obv:** National arms **Rev:** Snake **Edge:** Reeded

Date	Mintage	F	VF	XF	Unc	BU
2001 Proof	Est. 1,000	Value: 1,850				

KM# 212   500 DOLLARS
31.1035 g., 0.9990 Gold 0.9990 oz. AGW, 32.7 mm. **Subject:** P'an Ku **Obv:** National arms **Rev:** Dragon

Date	Mintage	F	VF	XF	Unc	BU
2001 Proof	Est. 1,000	Value: 1,850				

KM# 220   500 DOLLARS
31.1035 g., 0.9990 Gold 0.9990 oz. AGW, 32.7 mm. **Subject:** P'an Ku **Obv:** National arms **Rev:** Dragon and three animals

Date	Mintage	F	VF	XF	Unc	BU
2001 Proof	Est. 1,000	Value: 1,850				

KM# 262   500 DOLLARS
31.1000 g., 0.9990 Gold 0.9988 oz. AGW, 32.7 mm. **Subject:** Year of the Horse **Obv:** National arms **Rev:** Horse **Edge:** Reeded

Date	Mintage	F	VF	XF	Unc	BU
2002 Proof	1,000	Value: 1,850				

KM# 294   500 DOLLARS
31.1000 g., 0.9990 Gold 0.9997 oz. AGW, 32.7 mm. **Obv:** National arms **Rev:** Multicolor Astro Boy cartoon **Edge:** Reeded

Date	Mintage	F	VF	XF	Unc	BU
2003 Proof	2,003	Value: 1,850				

KM# 299   500 DOLLARS
31.1035 g., 0.9999 Gold 0.9999 oz. AGW, 32.7 mm. **Obv:** National arms **Rev:** Nelson Mandela **Edge:** Reeded

Date	Mintage	F	VF	XF	Unc	BU
2004 Proof	—	Value: 1,850				

KM# 205   2500 DOLLARS
155.5175 g., 0.9990 Gold 4.9948 oz. AGW, 50 mm. **Subject:** Year of the Snake **Obv:** National arms **Rev:** Snake **Edge:** Reeded

Date	Mintage	F	VF	XF	Unc	BU
2001 Proof	Est. 250	Value: 9,250				

KM# 213   2500 DOLLARS
155.5175 g., 0.9990 Gold 4.9948 oz. AGW, 50 mm. **Subject:** P'an Ku **Obv:** National arms **Rev:** Dragon

Date	Mintage	F	VF	XF	Unc	BU
2001 Proof	Est. 250	Value: 9,250				

KM# 263   2500 DOLLARS
155.5100 g., 0.9990 Gold 4.9946 oz. AGW, 50 mm. **Subject:** Year of the Horse **Obv:** National arms **Rev:** Horse **Edge:** Reeded

Date	Mintage	F	VF	XF	Unc	BU
2002 Proof	250	Value: 9,250				

MINT SETS

KM#	Date	Mintage	Identification	Issue Price	Mkt Val
MS2	2006 (4)	—	KM# 334-337	65.00	75.00

PROOF SETS

KM#	Date	Mintage	Identification	Issue Price	Mkt Val
PS7	2006 (4)	—	KM# 330-333	450	480
PS8	2006 (4)	—	KM# 334a-337a	300	300

SINGAPORE

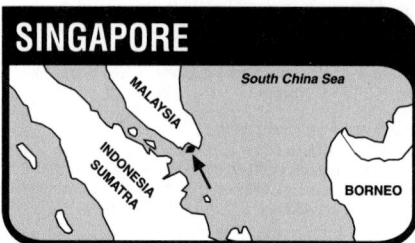

The Republic of Singapore, a member of the Commonwealth of Nations situated off the southern tip of the Malay peninsula, has an area of 224 sq. mi. (633 sq. km.) and a population of *2.7 million. Capital: Singapore. The economy is based on entrepôt trade, manufacturing and oil. Rubber, petroleum products, machinery and spices are exported.

The President is Chief of State. The prime minister is Head of Government.

MINT MARK
sm = "*sm*" - Singapore Mint monogram

MONETARY SYSTEM
100 Cents = 1 Dollar

REPUBLIC

STANDARD COINAGE

KM# 98a   CENT
1.8100 g., 0.9250 Silver 0.0538 oz. ASW, 15.9 mm. **Obv:** National arms **Rev:** Value divides plants

Date	Mintage	F	VF	XF	Unc	BU
2001sm Proof	6,000	Value: 2.50				
2002sm Proof	6,300	Value: 2.50				

KM# 98   CENT
1.2400 g., Copper Plated Zinc, 15.9 mm. **Obv:** National arms **Rev:** Value divides plants **Edge:** Plain **Note:** Similar to KM#49 but motto ribbon on arms curves down at center.

Date	Mintage	F	VF	XF	Unc	BU
2001	40,101,738	—	—	—	0.10	0.15
2002	19,003,000	—	—	—	0.10	0.15

KM# 99a   5 CENTS
2.0000 g., 0.9250 Silver 0.0595 oz. ASW, 16.75 mm. **Obv:** National arms **Rev:** Fruit salad plant

Date	Mintage	F	VF	XF	Unc	BU
2001sm Proof	6,000	Value: 2.75				
2002sm Proof	6,300	Value: 2.75				
2003sm Proof	4,900	Value: 2.75				
2004sm Proof	4,000	Value: 2.75				
2005sm Proof	3,250	Value: 2.75				

KM# 99   5 CENTS
1.5600 g., Aluminum-Bronze, 16.75 mm. **Obv:** National arms **Rev:** Fruit salad plant **Edge:** Reeded **Note:** Similar to KM#50 but motto ribbon on arms curves down at center.

Date	Mintage	F	VF	XF	Unc	BU
2001	13,101,738	—	—	—	0.20	0.30
2002	33,556,000	—	—	—	0.20	0.30
2003	16,508,980	—	—	—	0.20	0.30
2003 Proof	4,550	Value: 3.00				
2004	20,070,000	—	—	—	0.20	0.30
2004 Proof	3,500	Value: 3.00				
2005	70,061,981	—	—	—	0.20	0.30
2006 In sets only	53,214	—	—	—	0.50	—
2007	22,884,889	—	—	—	0.20	0.30
2008 In sets only	55,000	—	—	—	0.50	—
2009	19,850,000	—	—	—	0.20	0.30
2010sm	5,160,000	—	—	—	0.20	0.30
2011sm	—	—	—	—	0.20	0.30

KM# 100a   10 CENTS
3.0500 g., 0.9250 Silver 0.0907 oz. ASW, 18.5 mm. **Obv:** National arms **Rev:** Star Jasmine plant **Edge:** Reeded

Date	Mintage	F	VF	XF	Unc	BU
2001sm Proof	6,000	Value: 4.00				
2002sm Proof	6,300	Value: 4.00				
2003sm Proof	4,900	Value: 4.00				
2004sm Proof	4,000	Value: 4.00				
2005sm Proof	3,250	Value: 4.00				

KM# 100   10 CENTS
2.6000 g., Copper-Nickel, 18.5 mm. **Obv:** National arms **Rev:** Star Jasmine plant **Edge:** Reeded **Note:** Similar to KM#51 but motto ribbon on arms curves down at center.

Date	Mintage	F	VF	XF	Unc	BU
2001	70,600,000	—	—	—	0.20	0.30
2002	61,670,000	—	—	—	0.20	0.30
2003	21,578,980	—	—	—	0.20	0.30
2003 Proof	4,550	Value: 4.00				
2004	59,670,000	—	—	—	0.20	0.30
2004 Proof	3,500	Value: 4.00				
2005	50,021,981	—	—	—	0.20	0.30
2006 In sets only	53,214	—	—	—	—	0.50
2007	50,054,889	—	—	—	0.20	0.30
2008 In sets only	55,000	—	—	—	—	0.50
2009	38,790,000	—	—	—	—	0.50
2010sm In sets only	Est. 40,000	—	—	—	0.20	0.50
2011sm	—	—	—	—	0.20	0.50

KM# 101a   20 CENTS
5.2400 g., 0.9250 Silver 0.1558 oz. ASW, 21.36 mm. **Obv:** National arms **Rev:** Powder puff plant above value **Edge:** Reeded

Date	Mintage	F	VF	XF	Unc	BU
2001sm Proof	6,000	Value: 7.00				
2002sm Proof	6,300	Value: 7.00				
2003sm Proof	4,900	Value: 7.00				
2004sm Proof	4,000	Value: 7.00				
2005sm Proof	3,250	Value: 7.00				

KM# 101 20 CENTS
4.5000 g., Copper-Nickel, 21.36 mm. **Obv:** National arms **Rev:** Powder-puff plant above value **Edge:** Reeded **Note:** Similar to KM#52 but motto ribbon on arms curves down at center.

Date	Mintage	F	VF	XF	Unc	BU
2001	52,050,000	—	—	—	0.60	0.75
2002	48,120,000	—	—	—	0.60	0.75
2003	45,470,000	—	—	—	0.60	0.75
2003 Proof	4,550	Value: 5.00				
2004	44,870,000	—	—	—	0.60	0.75
2004 Proof	3,500	Value: 5.00				
2005 In sets only	61,981	—	—	—	—	1.00
2006	40,143,214	—	—	—	0.60	0.75
2007	30,144,889	—	—	—	0.60	0.75
2008 In sets only	55,000	—	—	—	—	1.00
2009	30,160,000	—	—	—	0.60	0.75
2010sm	Est. 10,030,000	—	—	—	0.60	0.75
2011sm	—	—	—	—	0.60	0.75

KM# 102a 50 CENTS
8.5600 g., 0.9250 Silver 0.2546 oz. ASW, 24.66 mm. **Obv:** National arms **Rev:** Yellow Allamanda plant above value

Date	Mintage	F	VF	XF	Unc	BU
2001sm Proof	6,000	Value: 12.00				
2002sm Proof	6,300	Value: 12.00				
2003sm Proof	4,900	Value: 12.00				
2004sm Proof	1,900	Value: 12.00				
2005sm Proof	3,250	Value: 12.00				

KM# 102 50 CENTS
7.2900 g., Copper-Nickel, 24.66 mm. **Obv:** National arms **Rev:** Yellow Allamanda plant above value **Edge Lettering:** REPUBLIC OF SINGAPORE (lion's head) **Note:** Similar to KM#53 but motto ribbon on arms curves down at center.

Date	Mintage	F	VF	XF	Unc	BU
2001	30,020,000	—	—	—	0.75	1.00
2002	27,420,000	—	—	—	0.75	1.00
2003	23,650,000	—	—	—	0.75	1.00
2003 Proof	4,550	Value: 6.00				
2004	24,640,000	—	—	—	0.75	1.00
2004 Proof	3,500	Value: 6.00				
2005	25,057,981	—	—	—	0.75	1.00
2006 In sets only	53,214	—	—	—	—	1.25
2007	28,764,889	—	—	—	0.75	1.00
2008 In sets only	55,000	—	—	—	—	1.25
2009	12,390,000	—	—	—	0.75	1.00
2010	Est. 8,270,000	—	—	—	0.75	1.00
2011	—	—	—	—	0.75	1.00

KM# 103a DOLLAR
8.0500 g., 0.9250 Silver 0.2394 oz. ASW, 22.4 mm. **Obv:** National arms **Rev:** Periwinkle flower

Date	Mintage	F	VF	XF	Unc	BU
2001sm Proof	6,000	Value: 15.00				
2002sm Proof	6,300	Value: 15.00				
2003sm Proof	4,900	Value: 15.00				
2004sm Proof	4,000	Value: 15.00				
2005sm Proof	3,250	Value: 15.00				

KM# 103 DOLLAR
6.3000 g., Aluminum-Bronze, 22.4 mm. **Obv:** National arms **Rev:** Periwinkle flower **Edge:** Reeded **Note:** Similar to KM#54 but motto ribbon on arms curves down at center.

Date	Mintage	F	VF	XF	Unc	BU
2001	40,941,738	—	—	—	1.50	2.25
2002	35,744,577	—	—	—	1.50	2.25
2003	31,968,980	—	—	—	1.50	2.25
2003 Proof	4,550	Value: 10.00				
2004	39,950,000	—	—	—	1.50	2.25
2004 Proof	3,500	Value: 10.00				
2005 In sets only	61,891	—	—	—	—	2.75
2006	63,053,214	—	—	—	1.50	2.25
2007 In sets only	54,889	—	—	—	—	2.75

Date	Mintage	F	VF	XF	Unc	BU
2008	10,375,000	—	—	—	1.50	2.25
2009	21,750,000	—	—	—	1.50	2.25
2010sm In sets only	40,000	—	—	—	—	2.75
2011sm	—	—	—	—	1.50	2.75

KM# 184a DOLLAR
8.5600 g., 0.9990 Silver 0.2749 oz. ASW, 24.7 mm. **Subject:** Old World Charm - Balestier **Obv:** Arms with supporters **Rev:** Old buildings **Note:** Colorized

Date	Mintage	F	VF	XF	Unc	BU
2004sm Proof	2,009	Value: 27.50				

KM# 190a DOLLAR
8.5600 g., 0.9990 Silver 0.2749 oz. ASW, 24.7 mm. **Subject:** Old World Charm - Jalan Besar **Note:** Colorized

Date	Mintage	F	VF	XF	Unc	BU
2004sm Proof	2,844	Value: 27.50				

KM# 191a DOLLAR
8.5600 g., 0.9990 Silver 0.2749 oz. ASW, 24.7 mm. **Subject:** Old World Charm - Joo Chiat **Note:** Colorized

Date	Mintage	F	VF	XF	Unc	BU
2004sm Proof	2,863	Value: 27.50				

KM# 184 DOLLAR
7.2900 g., Copper-Nickel, 24.7 mm. **Subject:** Old World Charm - Balestier **Obv:** Arms with supporters **Rev:** Old buildings **Edge:** Reeded

Date	Mintage	F	VF	XF	Unc	BU
2004sm Prooflike	3,486	—	—	—	—	10.00

KM# 190 DOLLAR
7.2900 g., Copper-Nickel, 24.7 mm. **Subject:** Old World Charm - Jalan Besar

Date	Mintage	F	VF	XF	Unc	BU
2004sm Prooflike	3,551	—	—	—	—	10.00

KM# 191 DOLLAR
Copper-Nickel, 24.6 mm. **Subject:** Old World Charm - Joo Chiat

Date	Mintage	F	VF	XF	Unc	BU
2004sm Prooflike	—	—	—	—	—	10.00

KM# 192 DOLLAR
7.2900 g., Copper-Nickel, 24.7 mm. **Subject:** Old World Charm - Tanjong Katong

Date	Mintage	F	VF	XF	Unc	BU
2004sm Prooflike	3,555	—	—	—	—	10.00

KM# 192a DOLLAR
0.9990 Silver, 24.7 mm. **Subject:** Old World Charm - Tanjong Katong

Date	Mintage	F	VF	XF	Unc	BU
2004sm Proof	2,263	Value: 27.50				

KM# 244 DOLLAR
18.0000 g., Copper-Nickel, 33 mm. **Series:** Urban Redevelopment **Obv:** National arms **Rev:** Anak Bukit

Date	Mintage	F	VF	XF	Unc	BU
2005sm Prooflike	2,620	Value: 12.00				

KM# 244a DOLLAR
17.3000 g., 0.9999 Silver 0.5561 oz. ASW, 33 mm. **Series:** Urban Redevelopment **Obv:** National arms **Rev:** Anak Bukit - multicolor

Date	Mintage	F	VF	XF	Unc	BU
2005sm Proof	2,450	Value: 45.00				

KM# 245 DOLLAR
18.0000 g., Copper-Nickel, 33 mm. **Series:** Urban Redevelopment **Obv:** National arms **Rev:** Coronation

Date	Mintage	F	VF	XF	Unc	BU
2005sm Prooflike	2,620	Value: 12.00				

KM# 245a DOLLAR
17.3000 g., 0.9999 Silver 0.5561 oz. ASW, 33 mm. **Series:** Urban Redevelopment **Obv:** National arms **Rev:** Coronation - multicolor

Date	Mintage	F	VF	XF	Unc	BU
2005sm Proof	790	Value: 45.00				

KM# 246 DOLLAR
18.0000 g., Copper-Nickel, 33 mm. **Series:** Urban Redevelopment **Obv:** National arms **Rev:** Jalan Leban and Casuarina Road

Date	Mintage	F	VF	XF	Unc	BU
2005sm Prooflike	2,620	Value: 12.00				

KM# 246a DOLLAR
17.0000 g., 0.9999 Silver 0.5465 oz. ASW, 33 mm. **Series:** Urban Redevelopment **Obv:** National arms **Rev:** Jalan Leban and Casuarina Road - multicolor

Date	Mintage	F	VF	XF	Unc	BU
2005sm Proof	790	Value: 45.00				

KM# 247 DOLLAR
18.0000 g., Copper-Nickel, 33 mm. **Series:** Urban Redevelopment **Obv:** National arms **Rev:** Springleaf

Date	Mintage	F	VF	XF	Unc	BU
2005sm Prooflike	2,620	Value: 12.00				

KM# 247a DOLLAR
17.3000 g., 0.9999 Silver 0.5561 oz. ASW, 33 mm. **Series:** Urban Redevelopment **Obv:** National arms **Rev:** Springleaf - multicolor

Date	Mintage	F	VF	XF	Unc	BU
2005sm Proof	2,450	Value: 45.00				

KM# 248 DOLLAR
18.0000 g., Copper-Nickel, 33 mm. **Series:** Urban Redevelopment **Obv:** National arms **Rev:** Thomson Village

Date	Mintage	F	VF	XF	Unc	BU
2005sm Prooflike	2,620	Value: 12.00				

KM# 248a DOLLAR
17.3000 g., 0.9999 Silver 0.5561 oz. ASW, 33 mm. **Series:** Urban Redevelopment **Obv:** National arms **Rev:** Thomson Village - multicolor

Date	Mintage	F	VF	XF	Unc	BU
2005sm Proof	800	Value: 45.00				

KM# 262a DOLLAR
17.3000 g., 0.9990 Silver 0.5556 oz. ASW, 33 mm. **Series:** Urban Redevelopment **Obv:** National arms **Rev:** Punggoi Point and Coney Island - multicolor

Date	Mintage	F	VF	XF	Unc	BU
2007sm Proof	2,289	Value: 32.50				

KM# 259 DOLLAR
Copper-Nickel **Series:** Urban Redevelopment **Obv:** National arms **Rev:** Changi Village - multicolor

Date	Mintage	F	VF	XF	Unc	BU
2007sm Prooflike	2,568	—	—	—	—	12.50

KM# 259a DOLLAR
17.3000 g., 0.9990 Silver 0.5556 oz. ASW, 33 mm. **Series:** Urban Redevelopment **Obv:** National arms **Rev:** Changi Village - multicolor

Date	Mintage	F	VF	XF	Unc	BU
2007sm Proof	976	Value: 37.50				

KM# 260 DOLLAR
Copper-Nickel **Series:** Urban Redevelopment **Obv:** National arms **Rev:** Pasir Ris Park - multicolor

Date	Mintage	F	VF	XF	Unc	BU
2007sm Prooflike	2,430	—	—	—	—	12.50

KM# 260a DOLLAR
17.3000 g., 0.9990 Silver 0.5556 oz. ASW, 33 mm. **Series:** Urban Redevelopment **Obv:** National arms **Rev:** Pasir Ris Park - multicolor

Date	Mintage	F	VF	XF	Unc	BU
2007sm Proof	936	Value: 37.50				

KM# 261 DOLLAR
Copper-Nickel **Series:** Urban Redevelopment **Obv:** National arms **Rev:** Pulau Ubin - multicolor

Date	Mintage	F	VF	XF	Unc	BU
2007sm Prooflike	2,408	—	—	—	—	12.50

KM# 261a DOLLAR
17.3000 g., 0.9990 Silver 0.5556 oz. ASW, 33 mm. **Series:** Urban Redevelopment **Obv:** National arms **Rev:** Pulau Ubin - multicolor

Date	Mintage	F	VF	XF	Unc	BU
2007sm Proof	2,327	Value: 32.50				

KM# 262 DOLLAR
Copper-Nickel **Series:** Urban Redevelopment **Obv:** National arms **Rev:** Punggoi Point and Coney Island - multicolor

Date	Mintage	F	VF	XF	Unc	BU
2007sm Prooflike	2,387	—	—	—	—	12.50

KM# 290 DOLLAR
Copper-Nickel **Obv:** Supported arms **Rev:** Multicolor Kent Ridge Park

Date	Mintage	F	VF	XF	Unc	BU
2008 Prooflike	2,250	Value: 10.00				

KM# 290a DOLLAR
17.3000 g., 0.9990 Silver 0.5556 oz. ASW **Obv:** Supported arms **Rev:** Multicolor Kent Ridge Park

Date	Mintage	F	VF	XF	Unc	BU
2008 Proof	850	Value: 37.50				

KM# 291 DOLLAR
Copper-Nickel **Obv:** Supported arms **Rev:** Multicolor Labrador Nature Reserve

Date	Mintage	F	VF	XF	Unc	BU
2008 Prooflike	2,250	Value: 10.00				

KM# 291a DOLLAR
17.3000 g., 0.9990 Silver 0.5556 oz. ASW **Obv:** Supported arms **Rev:** Multicolor Labrador Nature Reserve

Date	Mintage	F	VF	XF	Unc	BU
2008 Proof	850	Value: 37.50				

KM# 292 DOLLAR
Copper-Nickel **Obv:** Supported arms **Rev:** Multicolor Mount Faber Building

Date	Mintage	F	VF	XF	Unc	BU
2008 Prooflike	2,800	—	—	—	—	10.00

KM# 292a DOLLAR
17.3000 g., 0.9990 Silver 0.5556 oz. ASW **Obv:** Supported arms **Rev:** Multicolor Mount Faber Building

Date	Mintage	F	VF	XF	Unc	BU
2008 Proof	2,300	Value: 37.50				

KM# 293 DOLLAR
Copper-Nickel **Obv:** Supported arms **Rev:** Multicolor Telok Blangah Hill Park

Date	Mintage	F	VF	XF	Unc	BU
2008 Prooflike	2,300	—	—	—	—	10.00

KM# 293a DOLLAR
17.3000 g., 0.9990 Silver 0.5556 oz. ASW **Obv:** Supported arms **Rev:** Multicolor Telok Blangah Hill Park

Date	Mintage	F	VF	XF	Unc	BU
2008 Proof	2,200	Value: 37.50				

KM# 294 DOLLAR
0.3000 g., 0.9990 Gold 0.0096 oz. AGW, 7 mm. **Subject:** Year of the Ox **Obv:** Supported arms **Rev:** Ox

Date	Mintage	F	VF	XF	Unc	BU
2009	3,000	—	—	—	30.00	35.00

KM# 196 2 DOLLARS
Copper-Nickel **Subject:** Tribute to Healthcare Givers **Obv:** National arms **Rev:** Five 3/4 length people standing facing, clinic in background

Date	Mintage	F	VF	XF	Unc	BU
2003sm Prooflike	32021	—	—	—	—	15.00

KM# 196a 2 DOLLARS
0.9990 Silver **Subject:** Tribute to Healthcare Givers **Obv:** National arms **Rev:** Five 3/4 length people standing facing, clinic in background

Date	Mintage	F	VF	XF	Unc	BU
2003sm Proof	5,200	Value: 60.00				

KM# 223 2 DOLLARS
20.0000 g., 0.9990 Silver 0.6423 oz. ASW, 38.70 mm. **Series:** Lunar **Subject:** Year of the Goat **Obv:** National arms **Rev:** Stylized goat standing right facing left

Date	Mintage	F	VF	XF	Unc	BU
2003sm Proof	2,000	Value: 60.00				

KM# 229 2 DOLLARS
20.0000 g., 0.9990 Silver 0.6423 oz. ASW, 38.7 mm. **Series:** Lunar **Subject:** Year of the Monkey **Obv:** National arms **Rev:** Stylized monkey sitting left

Date	Mintage	F	VF	XF	Unc	BU
2004sm Proof	2,180	Value: 60.00				

KM# 234 2 DOLLARS
20.0000 g., Copper-Nickel, 38.7 mm. **Series:** Lunar **Subject:** Year of the Rooster **Obv:** National arms **Rev:** Rooster standing right

Date	Mintage	F	VF	XF	Unc	BU
2005sm Prooflike	79,115	—	—	—	—	15.00

KM# 242 2 DOLLARS
Copper-Nickel **Subject:** 40th National Day Parade **Obv:** National arms **Rev:** Fireworks, parade in government plaza, multicolor

Date	Mintage	F	VF	XF	Unc	BU
2005sm Prooflike	5,443	Value: 15.00				

KM# 242a 2 DOLLARS
20.0000 g., 0.9999 Silver 0.6429 oz. ASW **Subject:** 40th National Day Parade **Obv:** National arms **Rev:** Fireworks, parade in government plaza

Date	Mintage	F	VF	XF	Unc	BU
2005sm Proof	4,204	Value: 60.00				

KM# 234a 2 DOLLARS
20.0000 g., 0.9999 Silver 0.6429 oz. ASW, 38.7 mm. **Series:** Lunar **Subject:** Year of the Rooster **Obv:** National arms **Rev:** Stylized rooster standing right

Date	Mintage	F	VF	XF	Unc	BU
2005sm Proof	4,879	Value: 42.50				

KM# 250 2 DOLLARS
20.0000 g., Copper-Nickel **Series:** Lunar **Subject:** Year of the Dog **Obv:** National arms **Rev:** Stylized dog standing left

Date	Mintage	F	VF	XF	Unc	BU
2006sm Prooflike	69,552	Value: 15.00				

KM# 250a 2 DOLLARS
20.0000 g., 0.9999 Silver 0.6429 oz. ASW **Series:** Lunar **Subject:** Year of the Dog **Obv:** National arms **Rev:** Stylized dog standing left

Date	Mintage	F	VF	XF	Unc	BU
2006sm Proof	4,500	Value: 60.00				

KM# 258 2 DOLLARS
Copper-Nickel **Subject:** 41st National Day **Obv:** National arms **Rev:** People in stadium, emblem - multicolor

Date	Mintage	F	VF	XF	Unc	BU
2006sm Prooflike	4,300	Value: 15.00				

KM# 258a 2 DOLLARS
20.0000 g., 0.9990 Silver 0.6423 oz. ASW **Subject:** 41st National Day **Obv:** National arms **Rev:** People in stadium, emblem - multicolor

Date	Mintage	F	VF	XF	Unc	BU
2006sm Proof	4,100	Value: 60.00				

KM# 264 2 DOLLARS
Copper-Nickel **Series:** Lunar **Subject:** Year of the Boar **Obv:** National arms **Rev:** Stylized boar running right

Date	Mintage	F	VF	XF	Unc	BU
2007sm Prooflike	63,930	—	—	—	—	12.00

KM# 193 2 DOLLARS
20.0000 g., Copper-Nickel, 38.70 mm. **Subject:** 42nd National Day Parade **Obv:** Arms with supporters **Obv. Legend:** SINGAPURA - SINGAPORE **Rev:** Colored overlay with four children above Marina Bay floating platform **Edge:** Reeded

Date	Mintage	F	VF	XF	Unc	BU
2007 Prooflike	6,400	—	—	—	—	13.50

KM# 193a 2 DOLLARS
20.0000 g., 0.9990 Silver 0.6423 oz. ASW, 38.70 mm. **Subject:** 42nd National Day Parade **Obv:** Arms with supporters **Obv. Legend:** SINGAPURA - SINGAPORE **Rev:** Colored overlay with four children above Marina Bay floating platform **Edge:** Reeded

Date	Mintage	F	VF	XF	Unc	BU
2007 Proof	6,150	Value: 42.50				

KM# 264a 2 DOLLARS
20.0000 g., 0.9990 Silver 0.6423 oz. ASW **Series:** Lunar **Subject:** Year of the Boar **Obv:** National arms **Rev:** Stylized boar running right

Date	Mintage	F	VF	XF	Unc	BU
2007sm Proof	6,000	Value: 45.00				

KM# 270 2 DOLLARS
20.0000 g., Copper-Nickel **Series:** Lunar **Subject:** Year of the Rat **Obv:** National arms **Rev:** Stylized rat lying left

Date	Mintage	F	VF	XF	Unc	BU
2008sm Prooflike	58,637	—	—	—	—	12.50

KM# 270a 2 DOLLARS
20.0000 g., 0.9990 Silver 0.6423 oz. ASW **Series:** Lunar **Subject:** Year of the Rat **Obv:** National arms **Rev:** Stylized rat lying left

Date	Mintage	F	VF	XF	Unc	BU
2008sm Proof	5,789	Value: 45.00				

KM# 287 2 DOLLARS
Copper-Nickel, 38.7 mm. **Subject:** Formula 1 - Singapore Grand Prix **Obv:** Supported arms **Rev:** Formula 1 racecar and skyline

Date	Mintage	F	VF	XF	Unc	BU
2008 Proof	7,000	Value: 10.00				

KM# 295 2 DOLLARS
Copper-Nickel **Subject:** Year of the Ox **Obv:** Supported arms

Date	Mintage	F	VF	XF	Unc	BU
2009 Prooflike	80,000	—	—	—	—	10.00

KM# 296 2 DOLLARS
20.0000 g., 0.9990 Silver 0.6423 oz. ASW **Subject:** Year of the Ox **Obv:** Supported arms **Rev:** Ox

Date	Mintage	F	VF	XF	Unc	BU
2009 Proof	6,000	Value: 37.50				

KM# 303 2 DOLLARS
Copper-Nickel, 38.7 mm. **Subject:** Independence, 44th Anniversary **Note:** Partially colorized

Date	Mintage	F	VF	XF	Unc	BU
2009 Prooflike	6,000	—	—	—	—	15.00

KM# 303a 2 DOLLARS
20.0000 g., 0.9990 Silver 0.6423 oz. ASW, 38.7 mm. **Series:** Indpendence, 44th Anniversary **Note:** Colorized

Date	Mintage	F	VF	XF	Unc	BU
2009 Proof	5,000	Value: 40.00				

KM# 104.1a 5 DOLLARS
8.2500 g., 0.9250 Silver 0.2453 oz. ASW, 23.3 mm. **Obv:** National arms **Rev:** Vanda Miss Joaquim flower and value within beaded circle

Date	Mintage	F	VF	XF	Unc	BU
1999sm Proof	9,200	Value: 25.00				
2001sm Proof	6,000	Value: 25.00				
2000sm Proof	8,900	Value: 25.00				
2002sm Proof	6,300	Value: 25.00				

KM# 104.2a 5 DOLLARS
8.2500 g., 0.9250 Silver 0.2453 oz. ASW, 23.3 mm. **Obv:** National arms, date and BCCS logo **Rev:** Vanda Miss Joaquim flower above value **Edge:** Plain

Date	Mintage	F	VF	XF	Unc	BU
2001sm Proof	6,000	Value: 25.00				
2002sm Proof	6,300	Value: 25.00				
2003sm Proof	4,900	Value: 25.00				
2004sm Proof	4,000	Value: 25.00				
2005sm Proof	3,250	Value: 25.00				
2006sm Proof	—	Value: 25.00				

KM# 104.2 5 DOLLARS
6.7000 g., Bi-Metallic Aluminumn-Bronze center in Copper-Nickel ring, 23.3 mm. **Obv:** National arms, date and BCCS logo **Rev:** Canda Miss Joaquim flower above value **Edge:** Plain **Note:** Date in hologram

Date	Mintage	F	VF	XF	Unc	BU
2001 In sets only	101,738	—	—	—	—	12.00
2002 In sets only	84,577	—	—	—	—	12.00
2003		—	—	—	—	12.00
2004		—	—	—	—	12.00
2005		—	—	—	—	12.00
2006		—	—	—	—	12.00

KM# 177a 5 DOLLARS
20.0000 g., 0.9250 Silver 0.5948 oz. ASW, 38.6 mm. **Subject:** Productivity Movement **Obv:** Arms with supporters **Rev:** Spiral design **Edge:** Reeded

Date	Mintage	F	VF	XF	Unc	BU
2001sm Proof	5,650	Value: 50.00				

KM# 177 5 DOLLARS
20.0000 g., Copper-Nickel, 38.6 mm. **Subject:** Productivity Movement **Obv:** Arms with supporters **Rev:** Spiral design **Edge:** Reeded

Date	Mintage	F	VF	XF	Unc	BU
2001sm	5,300	—	—	—	12.50	15.00

KM# 181 5 DOLLARS
20.0000 g., Copper-Nickel, 38.7 mm. **Subject:** Esplanade Theaters on the Bay **Obv:** Arms with supporters **Rev:** Stylized symbolic design **Edge:** Reeded

Date	Mintage	F	VF	XF	Unc	BU
2002sm	7,430	—	—	—	13.50	16.50

KM# 181a 5 DOLLARS
20.0000 g., 0.9990 Silver 0.6423 oz. ASW, 38.7 mm. **Subject:** Esplanade Theaters on the Bay **Obv:** Arms with supporters **Rev:** Stylized symbolic design **Edge:** Reeded

Date	Mintage	F	VF	XF	Unc	BU
2002sm Proof	6,540	Value: 45.00				

KM# 104.3 5 DOLLARS
6.7000 g., Bi-Metallic Aluminum-Bronze center in Copper-Nickel ring, 23.3 mm. **Obv:** National arms above latent image "MAS" **Rev:** Flower and value **Shape:** Scalloped

Date	Mintage	F	VF	XF	Unc	BU
2002sm		—	—	—	—	10.00
2003sm		—	—	—	—	10.00
2003sm Proof	4,550	Value: 15.00				
2004sm		—	—	—	—	10.00
2004sm Proof	3,500	Value: 15.00				
2005sm		—	—	—	—	10.00
2006sm		—	—	—	—	10.00
2007sm		—	—	—	—	10.00
2008sm		—	—	—	—	10.00
2009sm		—	—	—	—	10.00
2010sm		—	—	—	—	10.00

KM# 104.3a 5 DOLLARS
8.2500 g., 0.9250 Silver 0.2453 oz. ASW **Obv:** National arms above latent image "MAS or date" **Rev:** Flower and value **Shape:** Scalloped

Date	Mintage	F	VF	XF	Unc	BU
2003sm Proof	4,900	Value: 25.00				
2004sm Proof	4,000	Value: 25.00				
2005sm Proof	3,250	Value: 25.00				

KM# 194 5 DOLLARS
20.0000 g., 0.9990 Silver 0.6423 oz. ASW, 38.7 mm. **Obv:** Arms with supporters **Obv. Legend:** SINGAPURA - SINGAPORE **Rev:** Multicolor Singapore's skyline above world map, golden lion symbol below pointing to location of Singapore **Rev. Legend:** BOARD OF GOVERNORS ANNUAL MEETINGS • SINGAPORE 2006 • INTERNATIONAL MONETARY FUND • WORLD BANK GROUP •

Date	Mintage	F	VF	XF	Unc	BU
2006sm Proof	5,450	Value: 60.00				

KM# 256 5 DOLLARS
20.0000 g., 0.9990 Silver 0.6423 oz. ASW **Series:** Heritage Orchids **Obv:** National arms **Rev:** Vanda Tan Chay Yan - multicolor

Date	Mintage	F	VF	XF	Unc	BU
2006sm Proof	8,000	Value: 60.00				

KM# 257 5 DOLLARS
20.0000 g., 0.9990 Silver 0.6423 oz. ASW **Series:** Heritage Orchids **Obv:** National arms **Rev:** Aranda Majula - multicolor

Date	Mintage	F	VF	XF	Unc	BU
2006sm Proof	8,000	Value: 60.00				

KM# 275 5 DOLLARS
20.0000 g., 0.9990 Silver 0.6423 oz. ASW, 38.7 mm. **Series:** Heritage Orchids **Obv:** National arms **Rev:** Dendrobium Singa Mas - multicolor

Date	Mintage	F	VF	XF	Unc	BU
2007sm Proof	8,000	Value: 45.00				

KM# 276 5 DOLLARS
20.0000 g., 0.9990 Silver 0.6423 oz. ASW, 38.7 mm. **Series:** Heritage Orchids **Obv:** National arms **Rev:** Vanda Mimi Palmer - multicolor

Date	Mintage	F	VF	XF	Unc	BU
2007sm Proof	8,000	Value: 45.00				

KM# 285 5 DOLLARS
20.0000 g., 0.9990 Silver 0.6423 oz. ASW, 38.6 mm. **Subject:** Heritage orchids **Obv:** Supported arms **Rev:** Multicolor yellow orchid - Oncidum Goldiana

Date	Mintage	F	VF	XF	Unc	BU
2008 Proof	8,000	Value: 45.00				

KM# 286 5 DOLLARS
20.0000 g., 0.9990 Silver 0.6423 oz. ASW, 38.6 mm. **Subject:** Heritage orchids **Obv:** Supported arms **Rev:** Multicolor pink orchid - Aranda Tay Swee Eng

Date	Mintage	F	VF	XF	Unc	BU
2008 Proof	8,000	Value: 45.00				

KM# 301 5 DOLLARS
20.0000 g., 0.9990 Silver 0.6423 oz. ASW **Subject:** Orchids of Singapore **Obv:** Arms **Rev:** Yellow flower - Spathoglottis Primrose

Date	Mintage	F	VF	XF	Unc	BU
2009 Proof	8,000	Value: 45.00				

KM# 302 5 DOLLARS
20.0000 g., 0.9990 Silver 0.6423 oz. ASW, 38.7 mm. **Subject:** Orchids of Singapore **Obv:** Arms **Rev:** Pink flower - Vanda Amy

Date	Mintage	F	VF	XF	Unc	BU
2009 Proof	8,000	Value: 45.00				

KM# 179   10 DOLLARS
28.0000 g., Copper-Nickel, 40.7 mm. **Series:** Lunar **Subject:** Year of the Snake **Obv:** National arms **Rev:** Stylized snake **Edge:** Reeded

Date	Mintage	F	VF	XF	Unc	BU
2001sm Prooflike	152,330	—	—	—	—	20.00

KM# 182   10 DOLLARS
28.0000 g., Copper-Nickel, 40.7 mm. **Series:** Lunar **Subject:** Year of the Horse **Obv:** National arms **Rev:** Stylized horse standing left **Edge:** Reeded

Date	Mintage	F	VF	XF	Unc	BU
2002sm Prooflike	128,666	—	—	—	—	20.00

KM# 225   10 DOLLARS
28.0000 g., Copper-Nickel, 40.7 mm. **Series:** Lunar **Subject:** Year of the Goat **Obv:** National arms **Rev:** Stylized goat standing right facing left

Date	Mintage	F	VF	XF	Unc	BU
2003sm Prooflike	103,047	—	—	—	—	20.00

KM# 187   10 DOLLARS
28.0000 g., Copper-Nickel, 40.7 mm. **Series:** Lunar **Subject:** Year of the Monkey **Obv:** National arms **Rev:** Stylized monkey sitting left **Edge:** Reeded

Date	Mintage	F	VF	XF	Unc	BU
2004sm Prooflike	100,000	—	—	—	—	20.00

KM# 189   10 DOLLARS
28.0000 g., Copper-Nickel, 40.7 mm. **Subject:** 10th Anniversary China-Singapore Suzhou Industrial Park **Obv:** National arms **Rev:** "Harmony" Sculpture **Edge:** Reeded

Date	Mintage	F	VF	XF	Unc	BU
2004sm Prooflike	3,511	—	—	—	—	20.00

KM# 189a   10 DOLLARS
20.0000 g., 0.9990 Silver 0.6423 oz. ASW, 40.7 mm. **Subject:** 10th Anniversary China-Singapore Suzhou Industrial Park **Obv:** National arms **Rev:** "Harmony" sculpture **Edge:** Reeded

Date	Mintage	F	VF	XF	Unc	BU
2004sm Proof	3,197	Value: 55.00				

KM# 240   10 DOLLARS
20.0000 g., Copper-Nickel, 40.7 mm. **Subject:** National University of Singapore **Obv:** National arms **Rev:** Person, globe and emblem

Date	Mintage	F	VF	XF	Unc	BU
2005sm Prooflike	12,264	—	—	—	—	22.50

KM# 240a   10 DOLLARS
20.0000 g., 0.9999 Silver 0.6429 oz. ASW, 38.7 mm. **Subject:** National University of Singapore **Obv:** National arms **Rev:** Person, globe and emblem

Date	Mintage	F	VF	XF	Unc	BU
2005sm Proof	5,293	Value: 60.00				

KM# 243   10 DOLLARS
31.1030 g., 0.9999 Silver with Gold 2.3g inlay 0.9998 oz. ASW **Subject:** 40th National Day parade **Obv:** National arms **Rev:** Fireworks, parade in government plaza

Date	Mintage	F	VF	XF	Unc	BU
2005sm Proof	756	Value: 245				

KM# 288   50 DOLLARS
20.0000 g., 0.9990 Silver 0.6423 oz. ASW **Subject:** Formula 1 - Singapore Grand Prix **Obv:** Supported arms **Rev:** Multicolor race car and skyline

Date	Mintage	F	VF	XF	Unc	BU
2008 Proof	5,000	Value: 40.00				

KM# 241   100 DOLLARS
31.1030 g., 0.9999 Gold 0.9998 oz. AGW, 33 mm. **Subject:** National University of Singapore **Obv:** National arms **Rev:** Person, globe and emblem

Date	Mintage	F	VF	XF	Unc	BU
2005sm Proof	244	Value: 1,850				

KM# 289   100 DOLLARS
31.0000 g., 0.2500 Gold 0.2492 oz. AGW, 38.7 mm. **Subject:** Formula 1 - Singapore Grand Prix **Obv:** Supported arms **Rev:** Formula 1 racecar and skyline

Date	Mintage	F	VF	XF	Unc	BU
2008 Proof	300	Value: 500				

BULLION COINAGE
Lunar Year Issues

KM# 212   DOLLAR
1.5550 g., 0.9999 Gold 0.0500 oz. AGW, 13.9 mm. **Series:** Lunar **Subject:** Year of the Snake **Obv:** National arms **Rev:** Stylized lion's head right, snake privy mark at lower left

Date	Mintage	F	VF	XF	Unc	BU
2001	339	—	—	—	—BV+30%	
2001sm Proof	240	BV+25%				

KM# 217   DOLLAR
1.5550 g., 0.9999 Gold 0.0500 oz. AGW, 13.9 mm. **Series:** Lunar **Subject:** Year of the Horse **Obv:** National arms **Rev:** Stylized lion's head right, horse privy mark at lower left

Date	Mintage	F	VF	XF	Unc	BU
2002	160	—	—	—	—BV+30%	
2002sm Proof	215	BV+25%				

KM# 222   DOLLAR
0.3000 g., 0.9999 Gold 0.0096 oz. AGW, 7 mm. **Series:** Lunar **Subject:** Year of the Goat **Obv:** National arms **Rev:** Stylized goat standing right facing left

Date	Mintage	F	VF	XF	Unc	BU
2003sm Prooflike	5,362	—	—	—	—	32.50

KM# 186   DOLLAR
0.3000 g., 0.9999 Gold 0.0096 oz. AGW, 7 mm. **Series:** Lunar **Subject:** Year of the Monkey **Obv:** National arms **Rev:** Stylized monkey sitting left **Edge:** Plain

Date	Mintage	F	VF	XF	Unc	BU
2004 Prooflike	3,200	—	—	—	—	32.50

KM# 233   DOLLAR
0.3000 g., 0.9999 Gold 0.0096 oz. AGW, 7 mm. **Series:** Lunar **Subject:** Year of the Rooster **Obv:** National arms **Rev:** Stylized rooster standing right

Date	Mintage	F	VF	XF	Unc	BU
2005sm Prooflike	2,817	—	—	—	—	32.50

KM# 249   DOLLAR
0.3000 g., 0.9999 Gold 0.0096 oz. AGW **Series:** Lunar **Subject:** Year of the Dog **Obv:** National arms **Rev:** Stylized dog standing left

Date	Mintage	F	VF	XF	Unc	BU
2006sm Prooflike	2,004	—	—	—	—	32.50

KM# 263   DOLLAR
0.3000 g., 0.9999 Gold 0.0096 oz. AGW **Series:** Lunar **Subject:** Year of the Boar **Obv:** National arms **Rev:** Stylized boar running right

Date	Mintage	F	VF	XF	Unc	BU
2007sm Prooflike	2,500	—	—	—	—	32.50

KM# 269   DOLLAR
0.3000 g., 0.9999 Gold 0.0096 oz. AGW **Series:** Lunar **Subject:** Year of the Rat **Obv:** National arms **Rev:** Stylized rat lying left

Date	Mintage	F	VF	XF	Unc	BU
2008sm	2,434	—	—	—	—	32.50

KM# 213   5 DOLLARS
3.1100 g., 0.9999 Gold 0.1000 oz. AGW, 17.9 mm. **Series:** Lunar **Subject:** Year of the Snake **Obv:** National arms **Rev:** Stylized lion's head right, snake privy mark at lower left

Date	Mintage	F	VF	XF	Unc	BU
2001	275	—	—	—	—BV+25%	
2001sm Proof	240	BV+20%				

KM# 218   5 DOLLARS
3.1100 g., 0.1000 Gold 0.0100 oz. AGW, 17.9 mm. **Series:** Lunar **Subject:** Year of the Horse **Obv:** National arms **Rev:** Stylized lion's head right, horse privy mark at lower left

Date	Mintage	F	VF	XF	Unc	BU
2002	200	—	—	—	—BV+25%	
2002sm Proof	215	BV+20%				

KM# 224   5 DOLLARS
7.7760 g., 0.9999 Gold 0.2500 oz. AGW, 21.9 mm. **Series:** Lunar **Subject:** Year of the Goat **Obv:** National arms **Rev:** Stylized goat standing right facing left

Date	Mintage	F	VF	XF	Unc	BU
2003sm Proof	1,000	Value: 500				

KM# 230   5 DOLLARS
7.7760 g., 0.9999 Gold 0.2500 oz. AGW, 21.9 mm. **Series:** Lunar **Subject:** Year of the Monkey **Obv:** National arms **Rev:** Stylized monkey sitting left

Date	Mintage	F	VF	XF	Unc	BU
2004sm Proof	1,426	Value: 500				

KM# 235   5 DOLLARS
7.7760 g., 0.9999 Gold 0.2500 oz. AGW, 21.9 mm. **Series:** Lunar **Subject:** Year of the Rooster **Obv:** National arms **Rev:** Stylized rooster standing right

Date	Mintage	F	VF	XF	Unc	BU
2005sm Proof	1,419	Value: 500				

KM# 251   5 DOLLARS
7.7750 g., 0.9999 Gold 0.2499 oz. AGW **Series:** Lunar **Subject:** Year of the Dog **Obv:** National arms **Rev:** Stylized dog standing left

Date	Mintage	F	VF	XF	Unc	BU
2006sm Proof	1,015	Value: 500				

KM# 265   5 DOLLARS
7.7750 g., 0.9999 Gold 0.2499 oz. AGW **Series:** Lunar **Subject:** Year of the Boar **Obv:** National arms **Rev:** Stylized boar running right

Date	Mintage	F	VF	XF	Unc	BU
2007sm Proof	1,060	Value: 500				

KM# 271   5 DOLLARS
7.7750 g., 0.9999 Gold 0.2499 oz. AGW **Series:** Lunar **Subject:** Year of the Rat **Obv:** National arms **Rev:** Stylized rat lying left

Date	Mintage	F	VF	XF	Unc	BU
2008sm Proof	1,200	Value: 500				

KM# 214   10 DOLLARS
7.7750 g., 0.9999 Gold 0.2499 oz. AGW, 21.9 mm. **Series:** Lunar **Subject:** Year of the Snake **Obv:** National arms **Rev:** Stylized lion's head right, snake privy mark at lower left

Date	Mintage	F	VF	XF	Unc	BU
2001	240	—	—	—	—BV+15%	
2001sm Proof	240	BV+10%				

KM# 179a   10 DOLLARS
62.2060 g., 0.9990 Silver 1.9979 oz. ASW, 40.7 mm. **Series:** Lunar **Subject:** Year of the Snake **Obv:** National arms **Rev:** Stylized snake **Edge:** Reeded

Date	Mintage	F	VF	XF	Unc	BU
2001sm Proof	35,000	Value: 90.00				

KM# 219   10 DOLLARS
7.7750 g., 0.9999 Gold 0.2499 oz. AGW, 21.9 mm. **Series:** Lunar **Subject:** Year of the Horse **Obv:** National arms **Rev:** Stylized lion's head right, horse privy mark at lower left

Date	Mintage	F	VF	XF	Unc	BU
2002	180	—	—	—	—	525
2002sm Proof	215	Value: 475				

KM# 182a   10 DOLLARS
62.2060 g., 0.9990 Silver 1.9979 oz. ASW, 40.7 mm. **Series:** Lunar **Subject:** Year of the Horse **Obv:** National arms **Rev:** Stylized horse standing left **Edge:** Reeded

Date	Mintage	F	VF	XF	Unc	BU
2002sm Proof	35,000	Value: 90.00				

KM# 225a   10 DOLLARS
62.2060 g., 0.9990 Silver 1.9979 oz. ASW, 40.7 mm. **Series:** Lunar **Subject:** Year of the Goat **Obv:** National arms **Rev:** Stylized goat standing right facing left

Date	Mintage	F	VF	XF	Unc	BU
2003sm Proof	35,000	Value: 90.00				

KM# 185   10 DOLLARS
31.1040 g., 0.9999 Gold 0.9999 oz. AGW, 32.1 mm. **Subject:** 10th Anniversary China-Singapore Suzhou Industrial Park **Obv:** National arms **Rev:** "Harmony" Sculpture **Edge:** Lettered edge

Date	Mintage	F	VF	XF	Unc	BU
2004sm Proof	500	Value: 1,850				

KM# 187a   10 DOLLARS
62.2060 g., 0.9990 Silver 1.9979 oz. ASW, 40.7 mm. **Series:** Lunar **Subject:** Year of the Monkey **Obv:** National arms **Rev:** Stylized monkey sitting left **Edge:** Reeded

Date	Mintage	F	VF	XF	Unc	BU
2004sm Proof	35,000	Value: 90.00				

KM# 236   10 DOLLARS
62.2060 g., 0.9999 Silver 1.9997 oz. ASW, 45 mm. **Series:** Lunar **Subject:** Year of the Rooster **Obv:** National arms **Rev:** Stylized rooster standing right

Date	Mintage	F	VF	XF	Unc	BU
2005sm Proof	30,000	Value: 90.00				

KM# 252   10 DOLLARS
62.2030 g., 0.9990 Silver 1.9978 oz. ASW **Series:** Lunar **Subject:** Year of the Dog **Obv:** National arms **Rev:** Stylized dog standing left

Date	Mintage	F	VF	XF	Unc	BU
2006sm Proof	30,000	Value: 95.00				

KM# 266   10 DOLLARS
62.2060 g., 0.9990 Silver 1.9979 oz. ASW, 45 mm. **Series:**

Lunar **Subject:** Year of the Boar **Obv:** National arms **Rev:**
Stylized pigr running right - multicolor

Date	Mintage	F	VF	XF	Unc	BU
2007sm Proof	30,000	Value: 100				

KM# 272   10 DOLLARS
62.2060 g., 0.9990 Silver 1.9979 oz. ASW **Series:** Lunar
Subject: Year of the Rat **Obv:** National arms **Rev:** Stylized rat
lying left - multicolor

Date	Mintage	F	VF	XF	Unc	BU
2008sm Proof	20,000	Value: 110				

KM# 297   10 DOLLARS
62.2000 g., 0.9990 Silver 1.9977 oz. ASW **Subject:** Year of the
Ox **Obv:** Supported arms **Rev:** Multicolor Ox

Date	Mintage	F	VF	XF	Unc	BU
2009 Proof	—	Value: 90.00				

KM# 215   20 DOLLARS
15.5520 g., 0.9999 Gold 0.4999 oz. AGW, 27 mm. **Series:** Lunar
Subject: Year of the Snake **Obv:** National arms **Rev:** Stylized
lion's head right, snake privy mark at lower left

Date	Mintage	F	VF	XF	Unc	BU
2001	169	169	—	—	—	—BV+12%
2001sm Proof	240	240	BV+12%			

KM# 220   20 DOLLARS
15.5520 g., 0.9999 Gold 0.4999 oz. AGW, 27 mm. **Series:** Lunar
Subject: Year of the Horse **Obv:** National arms **Rev:** Stylized
lion's head right, horse privy mark at lower left

Date	Mintage	F	VF	XF	Unc	BU
2002	165	—	—	—	—BV+12%	
2002sm Proof	215	BV+12%				

KM# 226   25 DOLLARS
155.5200 g., 0.9990 Silver 4.9949 oz. ASW, 65.00 mm. **Series:**
Lunar **Subject:** Year of the Goat **Obv:** National arms **Rev:**
Stylized goat standing right facing left

Date	Mintage	F	VF	XF	Unc	BU
2003sm Proof	250	Value: 300				

KM# 231   25 DOLLARS
155.5200 g., 0.9990 Silver 4.9949 oz. ASW, 65 mm. **Series:**
Lunar **Subject:** Year of the Monkey **Obv:** National arms **Rev:**
Stylized monkey sitting left

Date	Mintage	F	VF	XF	Unc	BU
2004sm Proof	250	Value: 300				

KM# 237   25 DOLLARS
155.5200 g., 0.9999 Silver 4.9994 oz. ASW, 65 mm. **Series:**
Lunar **Subject:** Year of the Rooster **Obv:** National arms **Rev:**
Stylized rooster standing right

Date	Mintage	F	VF	XF	Unc	BU
2005sm Proof	250	Value: 300				

KM# 253   25 DOLLARS
155.5150 g., 0.9990 Silver 4.9947 oz. ASW **Series:** Lunar
Subject: Year of the Dog **Obv:** National arms **Rev:** Stylized dog
standing right

Date	Mintage	F	VF	XF	Unc	BU
2006sm Proof	250	Value: 300				

KM# 267   25 DOLLARS
155.5150 g., 0.9990 Silver 4.9947 oz. ASW **Series:** Lunar
Subject: Year of the Boar **Obv:** National arms **Rev:** Stylized boar
running right

Date	Mintage	F	VF	XF	Unc	BU
2007sm Proof	250	Value: 300				

KM# 273   25 DOLLARS
155.5150 g., 0.9990 Silver 4.9947 oz. ASW **Series:** Lunar
Subject: Year of the Rat **Obv:** National arms **Rev:** Stylized rat
lying left

Date	Mintage	F	VF	XF	Unc	BU
2008sm Proof	250	Value: 300				

KM# 298   25 DOLLARS
155.5000 g., 0.9990 Silver 4.9942 oz. ASW **Subject:** Year of
the Ox **Obv:** Supported arms **Rev:** Ox

Date	Mintage	F	VF	XF	Unc	BU
2009 Proof	—	Value: 300				

KM# 216   50 DOLLARS
31.1030 g., 0.9999 Gold 0.9998 oz. AGW, 32.1 mm. **Series:**
Lunar **Subject:** Year of the Snake **Obv:** National arms **Rev:**
Stylized lion's head right, snake privy mark at lower left

Date	Mintage	F	VF	XF	Unc	BU
2001	187	—	—	—	—	BV+9%
2001sm Proof	179	BV+9%				

KM# 221   50 DOLLARS
31.1030 g., 0.9999 Gold 0.9998 oz. AGW, 32.1 mm. **Series:**
Lunar **Subject:** Year of the Horse **Obv:** National arms **Rev:**
Stylized lion's head right, horse privy mark at lower left

Date	Mintage	F	VF	XF	Unc	BU
2002	165	—	—	—	—	BV+9%
2002sm Proof	160	BV+9%				

KM# 238   100 DOLLARS
31.1030 g., 0.9999 Gold 0.9998 oz. AGW, 33 mm. **Series:** Lunar
Subject: Year of the Rooster **Obv:** National arms **Rev:** Stylized
rooster standing right

Date	Mintage	F	VF	XF	Unc	BU
2005sm Proof	1,699	BV+10%				

KM# 254   100 DOLLARS
31.1030 g., 0.9999 Gold 0.9998 oz. AGW **Series:** Lunar
Subject: Year of the Dog **Obv:** National arms **Rev:** Stylized dog
standing left

Date	Mintage	F	VF	XF	Unc	BU
2006sm Proof	1,319	BV+10%				

KM# 268   100 DOLLARS
31.1030 g., 0.9999 Gold 0.9998 oz. AGW, 33 mm. **Series:** Lunar
Subject: Year of the Boar **Obv:** National arms **Rev:** Stylized pig
running right

Date	Mintage	F	VF	XF	Unc	BU
2007sm Proof	1,220	BV+10%				

KM# 274   100 DOLLARS
31.1030 g., 0.9999 Gold 0.9998 oz. AGW **Series:** Lunar
Subject: Year of the Rat **Obv:** National arms **Rev:** Stylized rat
lying left

Date	Mintage	F	VF	XF	Unc	BU
2008sm Proof	1,153	BV+10%				

KM# 299   100 DOLLARS
31.1050 g., 0.9990 Gold 0.9998 oz. AGW **Subject:** Year of the
Ox **Obv:** Supported arms **Rev:** Ox

Date	Mintage	F	VF	XF	Unc	BU
2009 Proof	2,000	BV+10%				

KM# 239   200 DOLLARS
155.5200 g., 0.9999 Gold 4.9994 oz. AGW, 60 mm. **Series:**
Lunar **Subject:** Year of the Rooster **Obv:** National arms **Rev:**
Stylized rooster standing right

Date	Mintage	F	VF	XF	Unc	BU
2005sm Proof	84	Value: 9,500				

KM# 255   200 DOLLARS
155.1500 g., 0.9999 Gold 4.9875 oz. AGW **Series:** Lunar
Subject: Year of the Dog **Obv:** National arms **Rev:** Stylized dog
standing left

Date	Mintage	F	VF	XF	Unc	BU
2006sm Proof	50	Value: 9,500				

KM# 300   200 DOLLARS
155.5000 g., 0.9990 Gold 4.9942 oz. AGW, 60 mm. **Subject:**
Year of the Ox **Obv:** Supported arms **Rev:** Ox

Date	Mintage	F	VF	XF	Unc	BU
2009 Proof	200	Value: 9,500				

KM# 178   250 DOLLARS
31.1035 g., 0.9990 Gold 0.9990 oz. AGW, 32.1 mm. **Subject:**
Year of the Snake **Obv:** National arms **Rev:** Stylized snake **Edge:**
Reeded

Date	Mintage	F	VF	XF	Unc	BU
2001sm Proof	3,775	BV+10%				

KM# 183   250 DOLLARS
31.1035 g., 0.9999 Gold 0.9999 oz. AGW, 32.1 mm. **Subject:**
Year of the Horse **Obv:** National arms **Rev:** Horse **Edge:** Reeded

Date	Mintage	F	VF	XF	Unc	BU
2002sm Proof	3,199	BV+10%				

KM# 227   250 DOLLARS
31.1030 g., 0.9999 Gold 0.9998 oz. AGW, 32.1 mm. **Series:**
Lunar **Subject:** Year of the Goat **Obv:** National arms **Rev:**
Stylized goat standing right facing left

Date	Mintage	F	VF	XF	Unc	BU
2003sm Proof	2,390	BV+10%				

KM# 188   250 DOLLARS
31.1030 g., 0.9999 Gold 0.9998 oz. AGW, 32.1 mm. **Series:**
Lunar **Subject:** Year of the Monkey **Obv:** National arms **Rev:**
Stylized monkey sitting left **Edge:** Reeded

Date	Mintage	F	VF	XF	Unc	BU
2004sm Proof	2,535	BV+10%				

KM# 228   500 DOLLARS
155.5200 g., 0.9999 Gold 4.9994 oz. AGW, 55 mm. **Series:**
Lunar **Subject:** Year of the Goat **Obv:** National arms **Rev:**
Stylized goat standing right facing left

Date	Mintage	F	VF	XF	Unc	BU
2003sm Proof	62	Value: 9,500				

KM# 232   500 DOLLARS
155.5200 g., 0.9999 Gold 4.9994 oz. AGW, 55 mm. **Series:**
Lunar **Subject:** Year of the Monkey **Obv:** National arms **Rev:**
Stylized monkey sitting left

Date	Mintage	F	VF	XF	Unc	BU
2004sm Proof	76	Value: 9,500				

MINT SETS

KM#	Date	Mintage	Identification	Issue Price	Mkt Val
MS38A	2001 (7)	101,738	KM#98-103, 104.2	—	—
MS39	2002 (7)	84,577	KM#98-103, 104.3 Hongbao	—	15.00
MS40	2003 (6)	68,980	KM#99-103, 104.3 Hongbao	—	15.00
MS41	2004 (6)	70,000	KM#99-103, 104.3 Hongbao	—	15.00
MS42	2005 (6)	61,981	KM#99-103, 104.3 Hongbao	—	15.00
MS43	2006 (7)	53,214	KM#99-103, 104.3 Hongbao	—	15.00
MS44	2007 (6)	54,889	KM#99-103, 104.3 Hongbao	10.78	15.00
MS45	2008 (6)	55,000	KM#99-103, 104.3	—	15.00
MS46	2009 (6)	60,000	KM#99-103, 104.3	—	15.00

PROOF SETS

KM#	Date	Mintage	Identification	Issue Price	Mkt Val
PS61	2001 (2)	3,000	KM#179-180 plus copper-nickel ingot	—	115
PS62	2001 (3)	2,000	KM#178-180 plus copper-nickel ingot	—	1,625
PS63	2001 (4)	—	KM#212-215	—	1,425
PS64	2001 (6)	—	KM#212-216, plus ingot	—	3,050
PS65	2001 (2)	2,001	KM#177, 177a	—	70.00
PS66	2001 (7)	6,000	KM#98a-103a, 104.2a	—	70.00
PS67	2002 (2)	3,000	KM#182, 182a	—	115
PS68	2002 (3)	2,000	KM#182, 182a, 183	—	1,625
PS69	2002 (2)	2,001	KM#181, 181a	—	65.00
PS70	2002 (3)	2,001	KM#181, 181a, 217	—	160

KM#	Date	Mintage	Identification	Issue Price	Mkt Val
PS71	2002 (4)	—	KM#217-220	—	1,650
PS72	2002 (6)	—	KM#217-221 plus ingot	—	3,250
PS73	2002 (7)	6,300	KM#98a-103a, 104.2a	—	70.00
PS74	2003 (2)	2,003	KM#196, 196a	—	75.00
PS75	2003 (6)	4,900	KM#99a-103a, 104.3a	—	70.00
PS76	2003 (6)	1,000	KM#99a-103a, 104.3a	—	130
PS77	2003 (2)	88	KM#226, 228	—	7,800
PS78	2003 (2)	3,000	KM#225, 225a	—	115
PS79	2003 (3)	2,000	KM#225, 225a, 227	—	1,625
PS80	2004 (2)	1,000	KM#189, 189a	—	85.00
PS81	2004 (3)	88	KM#185, 189, 189a	—	1,650
PS82	2004 (6)	10,000	KM#98a-103a, 104.3a	—	70.00
PS83	2004 (2)	1,000	KM#184, 184a	—	40.00
PS84	2004 (2)	1,000	KM#190, 190a	—	40.00
PS85	2004 (2)	1,000	KM#191, 191a	—	40.00
PS86	2004 (2)	1,000	KM#192, 192a	—	40.00
PS87	2004 (4)	800	KM#184a, 190a-192a	—	110
PS88	2004 (8)	88	KM#184, 184a, 190, 190a, 191, 191a, 192, 192a	—	150
PS89	2004 (2)	80	KM#231, 232	—	9,800
PS90	2004 (2)	3,000	KM#187, 187a	—	110
PS91	2004 (3)	2,000	KM#187, 187a, 188	—	1,650
PS92	2005 (6)	3,250	KM#99a-103a, 104.3a	—	70.00
PS93	2005 (2)	3,000	KM#234, 236	—	110
PS94	2005 (2)	88	KM#237, 239	—	9,800
PS95	2005 (3)	2,000	KM#234, 236, 238	—	1,650
PS97	2006 (2)	8,000	KM#256, 257	—	120
PS99	2007 (4)	800	KM#259a-262a	—	130
PS101	2007 (2)	3,000	KM#193, 193a	65.00	65.00
PS100	2007 (2)	8,000	KM#275, 276	90.00	90.00

PROOF-LIKE SETS (PL)

KM#	Date	Mintage	Identification	Issue Price	Mkt Val
PL1	2004 (4)	800	KM#184, 190, 191, 192	—	40.00
PL2	2007 (4)	800	KM#259-262	—	50.00

SLOVAKIA

The Republic of Slovakia has an area of 18,923 sq. mi. (49,035 sq. km.) and a population of 4.9 million. Capital: Bratislava. Textiles, steel, and wood products are exported.

MINT MARK

Kremnica Mint

REPUBLIC

STANDARD COINAGE

100 Halierov = 1 Slovak Koruna (Sk)

KM# 17   10 HALIEROV
0.7200 g., Aluminum, 17 mm. **Obv:** Double cross on shield above inscription **Rev:** Church steeple **Edge:** Plain

Date	Mintage	F	VF	XF	Unc	BU
2001	20,330,000	—	—	—	0.35	—
2001 Proof	12,500	Value: 2.50				
2002	37,640,000	—	—	—	0.35	—
2002 Proof	16,100	Value: 1.50				
2003 In sets only	3,000	—	—	—	2.50	—

KM# 17a   10 HALIEROV
2.8500 g., 0.9250 Silver 0.0848 oz. ASW, 17 mm.

Date	Mintage	F	VF	XF	Unc	BU
2004	4,000	—	—	—	—	10.00
2004 Proof	2,000	Value: 15.00				

KM# 18   20 HALIEROV
0.9500 g., Aluminum, 19.5 mm. **Obv:** Double cross on shield above inscription **Rev:** Krivan Mountain and value **Edge:** Reeded

Date	Mintage	F	VF	XF	Unc	BU
2001	21,920,000	—	—	—	0.45	—
2001 Proof	12,500	Value: 2.50				

Date	Mintage	F	VF	XF	Unc	BU
2002	36,300,000	—	—	—	0.45	—
2002 Proof	16,100	Value: 1.50				
2003 In sets only	3,000	—	—	—	2.50	—

KM# 18a   20 HALIEROV
3.8700 g., 0.9250 Silver 0.1151 oz. ASW, 19.5 mm.

Date	Mintage	F	VF	XF	Unc	BU
2004	4,000	—	—	—	—	15.00
2004	2,000	Value: 20.00				

KM# 35   50 HALIEROV
2.8000 g., Copper Plated Steel, 18.75 mm. **Obv:** Double cross on shield above inscription **Rev:** Devin watch tower and value **Edge:** Segmented reeding

Date	Mintage	F	VF	XF	Unc	BU
2001	10,400,000	—	—	—	0.60	—
2001 Proof	12,500	Value: 2.50				
2002	11,000,000	—	—	—	0.60	—
2002 Proof	16,100	Value: 1.50				
2003	11,000,000	—	—	—	0.60	—
2004	16,500,000	—	—	—	0.60	—
2004 Proof	—	Value: 1.50				
2005	17,000,000	—	—	—	0.60	—
2006	22,050,000	—	—	—	0.60	—
2006 Proof	—	Value: 1.50				
2007	—	—	—	—	0.60	—
2008	—	—	—	—	0.60	—
2008 Proof	—	Value: 1.50				

KM# 12   KORUNA
3.8500 g., Bronze Plated Steel, 21 mm. **Subject:** 15th Century of Madonna and Child **Obv:** Double cross on shield above inscription **Rev:** Madonna holding child and value **Edge:** Milled

Date	Mintage	F	VF	XF	Unc	BU
2001 In sets only	12,500	—	—	—	1.50	—
2001 Proof	—	Value: 3.00				
2002	11,000,000	—	—	—	0.75	—
2002 Proof	16,100	Value: 2.50				
2003 In sets only	14,000	—	—	—	1.50	—
2004 In sets only	—	—	—	—	1.50	—
2004 Proof	—	Value: 2.50				
2005	10,000,000	—	—	—	0.75	—
2005 Proof	—	Value: 2.50				
2006	9,605,000	—	—	—	0.75	—
2006 Proof	—	Value: 2.50				
2007	—	—	—	—	0.75	—
2008	—	—	—	—	0.75	—
2008 Proof	—	Value: 2.50				

KM# 13   2 KORUNA
4.4000 g., Nickel Plated Steel, 22.5 mm. **Obv:** Double cross on shield above inscription **Rev:** Venus statue and value

Date	Mintage	F	VF	XF	Unc	BU
2001	10,668,000	—	—	—	0.85	—
2001 Proof	12,500	Value: 5.00				
2002	11,000,000	—	—	—	0.85	—
2002 Proof	16,100	Value: 2.50				
2003	11,000,000	—	—	—	0.85	—
2004 In sets only	—	—	—	—	2.00	—
2004 Proof	—	Value: 2.50				
2005 In sets only	—	—	—	—	2.00	—
2006 In sets only	—	—	—	—	2.00	—
2006 Proof	—	Value: 2.50				
2007 In sets only	—	—	—	—	2.00	—
2008 In sets only	—	—	—	—	2.00	—
2008 Proof	—	Value: 2.50				

KM# 14   5 KORUNA
5.4000 g., Nickel Plated Steel, 24.75 mm. **Obv:** Double cross on shield above inscription **Rev:** Celtic coin of BIATEC at upper left of value **Edge:** Milled

Date	Mintage	F	VF	XF	Unc	BU
2001 In sets only	—	—	—	—	2.00	—
2001 Proof	12,500	Value: 6.00				
2002 Proof	16,100	Value: 5.00				
2003 In sets only	14,000	—	—	—	2.00	—
2004 In sets only	—	—	—	—	2.00	—
2004 Proof	—	Value: 5.00				
2005 In sets only	—	—	—	—	2.00	—
2006 In sets only	—	—	—	—	2.00	—
2006 Proof	—	Value: 5.00				
2007	—	—	—	—	1.50	—
2008 In sets only	—	—	—	—	2.00	—
2008 Proof	—	Value: 5.00				

KM# 11.1   10 KORUNA
6.6000 g., Aluminum-Bronze, 26.5 mm. **Obv:** Double cross on shield above inscription **Rev:** Bronze cross and value

Date	Mintage	F	VF	XF	Unc	BU
2001 In sets only	—	—	—	—	4.00	—
2001 Proof	12,500	Value: 12.50				
2002 Proof	16,100	Value: 10.00				
2003	10,923,000	—	—	—	2.50	—
2004 In sets only	—	—	—	—	4.00	—
2004 Proof	—	Value: 10.00				
2005 In sets only	—	—	—	—	4.00	—
2006 In sets only	—	—	—	—	4.00	—
2006 Proof	—	Value: 10.00				
2007 In sets only	—	—	—	—	4.00	—
2008 In sets only	—	—	—	—	4.00	—
2008 Proof	—	Value: 10.00				

KM# 67   20 KORUN
24.4800 g., 0.9250 Silver 0.7280 oz. ASW, 27.1 x 50.6 mm. **Series:** Banknotes **Obv:** Prince Pribina (800-861) **Rev:** Nitra Castle **Edge:** Plain

Date	Mintage	F	VF	XF	Unc	BU
2003 Proof	6,000	Value: 60.00				

KM# 68   50 KORUN
26.6300 g., 0.9250 Silver 0.7919 oz. ASW, 28.2 x 52.8 mm. **Series:** Banknotes **Obv:** Saints Cyril and Methodius (814-885) **Rev:** Two hands **Edge:** Plain

Date	Mintage	F	VF	XF	Unc	BU
2003 Proof	6,000	Value: 65.00				

KM# 69 100 KORUN
28.8700 g., 0.9250 Silver 0.8585 oz. ASW, 29.3 x 55 mm.
Series: Banknotes **Obv:** The Levoca Madonna **Rev:** St. James
Church in Levoca **Edge:** Plain

Date	Mintage	F	VF	XF	Unc	BU
2003 Proof	—	Value: 75.00				

KM# 59 200 KORUN
20.0000 g., 0.7500 Silver 0.4822 oz. ASW, 34 mm. **Subject:**
Alexander Dubcek **Obv:** Double cross on shield and tree **Rev:**
Head left **Edge Lettering:** LUDSKOST SLOBODA
DEMOKRACIA

Date	Mintage	F	VF	XF	Unc	BU
2001	12,800	—	—	—	—	25.00
2001 Proof	3,000	Value: 70.00				

Note: Unc. examples without edge lettering exist. Value
$850.00.

KM# 60 200 KORUN
20.0000 g., 0.7500 Silver 0.4822 oz. ASW, 34 mm. **Subject:**
Ludovit Fulla **Obv:** Modern art **Rev:** Head facing in national
costume, value and dates **Edge:** Lettered **Note:** 1,800 pieces
melted.

Date	Mintage	F	VF	XF	Unc	BU
2002	11,300	—	—	—	—	25.00
2002 Proof	2,400	Value: 55.00				

KM# 62 200 KORUN
20.3500 g., 0.7500 Silver 0.4907 oz. ASW, 34 mm. **Subject:**
UNESCO World Heritage site - Vlkolínec **Obv:** Log building and
double cross on shield **Rev:** Wooden tower and value **Edge
Lettering:** WORLD HERITAGE PATRIMONE MONDIAL **Note:**
900 pieces melted.

Date	Mintage	F	VF	XF	Unc	BU
2002	11,500	—	—	—	—	25.00
2002 Proof	2,800	Value: 55.00				

KM# 66 200 KORUN
20.0000 g., 0.7500 Silver 0.4822 oz. ASW, 34 mm. **Subject:**
Jozef Skultety, Slovak linguist and historian **Obv:** Building below
double cross within shield **Rev:** Head facing and value **Edge
Lettering:** VYTRVALOST A VERNOST NARODNEMU IDEALU
Note: 500 pieces uncirculated melted.

Date	Mintage	F	VF	XF	Unc	BU
2003	8,800	—	—	—	—	25.00
2003 Proof	2,700	Value: 55.00				

KM# 65 200 KORUN
20.0000 g., 0.7500 Silver 0.4822 oz. ASW, 34 mm. **Subject:**
Imrich Karvas **Obv:** Building, national arms and value **Rev:**
Portrait **Edge:** Lettered **Edge Lettering:** NARODOHOSPODAR
HUMANISTA EUROPAN **Note:** 500 pieces uncirculated melted.

Date	Mintage	F	VF	XF	Unc	BU
2003	9,800	—	—	—	—	25.00
2003 Proof	3,000	Value: 50.00				

KM# 70 200 KORUN
31.2100 g., 0.9250 Silver 0.9281 oz. ASW, 30.4 x 57.2 mm.
Series: Banknotes **Obv:** Head facing and value **Rev:** 18th
Century city view and value **Edge:** Plain

Date	Mintage	F	VF	XF	Unc	BU
2003 Proof	6,000	Value: 90.00				

KM# 75 200 KORUN
20.0000 g., 0.7500 Silver 0.4822 oz. ASW, 34 mm. **Obv:**
Kempelen's Chess Machine (1770) **Rev:** Inventor Wolfgang
Kemelen (1734-1804) above Bratislava city view **Edge
Lettering:** VYNALEZCA - TECHNIK - KONSTRUKTER

Date	Mintage	F	VF	XF	Unc	BU
2004	8,000	—	—	—	—	25.00
2004 Proof	3,200	Value: 50.00				

KM# 76 200 KORUN
20.0000 g., 0.7500 Silver 0.4822 oz. ASW, 34 mm. **Obv:** Church
and town hall below double cross within shield **Rev:** Aerial view
of Bardejov circa 1768 **Edge Lettering:** WORLD HERITAGE -
PATRIMOINE MONDIAL

Date	Mintage	F	VF	XF	Unc	BU
2004	8,400	—	—	—	—	25.00
2004 Proof	3,600	Value: 50.00				

KM# 77 200 KORUN
18.0000 g., 0.9000 Silver 0.5208 oz. ASW, 34 mm. **Obv:** "The
Segner Wheel" model **Rev:** Bust with fur hat facing within circle
of designs **Edge Lettering:** VYNALEZCA - FYZIK - MATEMATIK
- PEDAGOG

Date	Mintage	F	VF	XF	Unc	BU
2004	10,500	—	—	—	—	25.00
2004 Proof	4,700	Value: 45.00				

KM# 78 200 KORUN
20.0000 g., 0.7500 Silver 0.4822 oz. ASW, 34 mm. **Subject:**
Slovakian entry into the European Union **Obv:** Circle of stars in
arch above national arms **Rev:** Map in arch above value **Edge
Lettering:** ROZSIRENIE EUROPSKEJ UNIE O DESAT KRAJIN

Date	Mintage	F	VF	XF	Unc	BU
2004	10,100	—	—	—	—	25.00
2004 Proof	4,700	Value: 45.00				

KM# 81 200 KORUN
18.0000 g., 0.9000 Silver 0.5208 oz. ASW, 34 mm. **Subject:**
Leopold I Coronation 350th Anniversary **Obv:** Value and partial
castle view **Rev:** Coin design of Leopold I in large size legend
Edge Lettering: BRATISLAVSKE KORUNOVACIE

Date	Mintage	F	VF	XF	Unc	BU
2005	8,900	—	—	—	—	25.00
2005 Proof	4,800	Value: 45.00				

KM# 82 200 KORUN
18.0000 g., 0.9000 Silver 0.5208 oz. ASW, 34 mm. **Subject:**
Treaty of Pressburg **Obv:** Primate's Palace behind French
military standard **Rev:** Napoleon and Francis I of Austria **Edge
Lettering:** 26 DECEMBER. 5 MIVOSE AN 14

Date	Mintage	F	VF	XF	Unc	BU
2005	5,100	—	—	—	—	25.00
2005 Proof	3,400	Value: 45.00				

KM# 87 200 KORUN
18.0000 g., 0.9000 Silver 0.5208 oz. ASW, 34 mm. **Subject:**
200th Anniversary Birth of Karol Kuzmány **Obv:** Small national
arms at upper left, denomination at center **Obv. Inscription:**
SLOVENSKÁ / REPUBLIKA **Rev:** Partial medallic head of
Kuzmány facing

Date	Mintage	F	VF	XF	Unc	BU
2006	—	—	—	—	—	25.00
2006 Proof	—	Value: 55.00				

KM# 105 200 KORUN
18.0000 g., 0.9000 Silver 0.5208 oz. ASW, 34 mm. **Subject:**
Josef M. Petzval, Physicist **Obv:** Lens **Rev:** Bust at left

Date	Mintage	F	VF	XF	Unc	BU
2007	2,500	—	—	—	—	25.00
2007 Proof	—	Value: 70.00				

KM# 88   200 KORUN

18.0000 g., 0.9000 Silver 0.5208 oz. ASW, 34 mm.   **Subject:**
100th Anniversary Birth of Andrej Kmet **Obv:** Small national arms
above stylized M-shaped memorial representing the Slovak
Museum. **Obv. Legend:** SLOVENSKÁ REPUBLIKA **Rev:** Head
of Kmet 3/4 left **Edge:** Lettered **Edge Lettering:** POZNÁVAJME
KRAJE SVOJE A POZNÁME SAMYCH SEBA

Date	Mintage	F	VF	XF	Unc	BU
2008	8,500	—	—	—	—	25.00
2008 Proof	3,400	Value: 75.00				

KM# 56   500 KORUN

33.6300 g., 0.9250 Silver 1.0000 oz. ASW, 40 mm.   **Subject:**
Mala Fatra National Park **Obv:** National arms center of cross
formed by beetles (Alpine Salyers) **Rev:** Orchid with mountain
background **Edge Lettering:** OCHRANA PRIRODY A KRAJINY
Note: 400 pieces uncirculated melted.

Date	Mintage	F	VF	XF	Unc	BU
2001	10,200	—	—	—	—	90.00
2001 Proof	1,800	Value: 250				

KM# 57   500 KORUN

31.1035 g., 0.9990 Silver 0.9990 oz. ASW, 45 mm.   **Subject:**
Third Millennium **Obv:** "The Universe" **Rev:** Three hands **Edge:**
Plain **Shape:** 3-sided **Note:** 400 pieces uncirculated melted.

Date	Mintage	F	VF	XF	Unc	BU
2001	13,000	—	—	—	—	55.00
2001 Proof	4,000	Value: 175				

KM# 71   500 KORUN

33.6300 g., 0.9250 Silver 1.0000 oz. ASW, 31.5 x 59.4 mm.
Series: Banknotes **Obv:** Head facing and value **Rev:** Bratislava
Castle view and value **Edge:** Plain

Date	Mintage	F	VF	XF	Unc	BU
2003 Proof	6,000	Value: 100				

KM# 85   500 KORUN

33.6300 g., 0.9250 Silver 1.0000 oz. ASW, 40 mm.   **Subject:**
Slovensky Kras National Park **Obv:** 2 Rock buntings above value
Rev: Dogs Tooth violet flowers in front of Karst cave interior view
Edge Lettering: OCHRANA PRIRODY A KRAJINY

Date	Mintage	F	VF	XF	Unc	BU
2005	8,500	—	—	—	—	45.00
2005 Proof	3,600	Value: 90.00				

KM# 84   500 KORUN

33.6300 g., 0.9250 Silver 1.0000 oz. ASW, 40 mm.   **Subject:**
Muranska Planina National Park **Obv:** Wildflowers and Muran
castle ruins **Rev:** Two wild horses **Edge Lettering:** OCHRANA
PRIRODY A KRAJINY [flower]

Date	Mintage	F	VF	XF	Unc	BU
2006	4,300	—	—	—	—	55.00
2006 Proof	2,800	Value: 200				

KM# 86   500 KORUN

33.6300 g., 0.9250 Silver 1.0000 oz. ASW, 40 mm.   **Subject:**

450th Anniversary - Construction Fortress at Komárno **Obv:** Early
ships, fortress in background, national arms at lower right **Obv.
Legend:** SLOVENSKÁ REPUBLIKA **Rev:** Layout of fortress,
horses in battle against Turks below **Rev. Legend:** PEVNOST -
KOMÁRNO **Edge Lettering:** NEC ARTE NEC MARTE -
COMORRA in relief

Date	Mintage	F	VF	XF	Unc	BU
2007	4,600	—	—	—	—	70.00
2007 Proof	2,600	Value: 250				

KM# 106   500 KORUN

33.6300 g., 0.9250 Silver 1.0000 oz. ASW, 40 mm.   **Subject:**
National Park - Low Tatra Mountains **Obv:** Mountains, flower and
shield **Rev:** Bear in pine tree

Date	Mintage	F	VF	XF	Unc	BU
2008	4,300	—	—	—	—	55.00
2008 Proof	4,800	Value: 150				

KM# 63   1000 KORUN

62.2070 g., 0.9990 Silver 1.9979 oz. ASW, 43.6 x 43.6 mm.
Subject: 10th Anniversary of Republic **Obv:** National arms
between hands **Rev:** Value above map **Edge:** Segmented
reeding **Shape:** Square

Date	Mintage	F	VF	XF	Unc	BU
2003 Proof	10,000	Value: 115				

KM# 72   1000 KORUN

43.9100 g., 0.9250 Bi-Metallic .925 Silver 43.91g planchet with
.999 Gold .28g insert 1.3058 oz., 32.6 x 61.6 mm.   **Series:**
Banknotes **Obv:** Head facing and value **Rev:** The Madonna
Protector facing and church of Liptovske Sliace **Edge:** Plain **Note:**
Illustration reduced.

Date	Mintage	F	VF	XF	Unc	BU
2003 Proof	6,000	Value: 150				

KM# 58 5000 KORUN
Tri-Metallic 31.1035, .999 Silver, 1.00 oz ASW with 6.22, .999 Gold, .20 oz AGW and .31, .999 Platinum, .10 oz. APW, 50 mm. **Series:** Third Millennium **Obv:** "The Universe" **Rev:** Three hands **Edge:** Plain **Shape:** Triangular

Date	Mintage	F	VF	XF	Unc	BU
2001 Proof	8,000	Value: 475				

KM# 61 5000 KORUN
9.5000 g., 0.9000 Gold 0.2749 oz. AGW, 26 mm. **Subject:** Vlkolinec village - UNESCO historic site **Obv:** Enclosed communal well **Rev:** Window and fence **Edge:** Reeded

Date	Mintage	F	VF	XF	Unc	BU
2002 Proof	7,200	Value: 550				

KM# 73 5000 KORUN
47.6340 g., 0.9250 Bi-Metallic .925 Silver 46.65g planchet with two .9999 Gold inserts .964g in total 1.4165 oz., 33.4 x 63.8 mm. **Series:** Banknotes **Obv:** Head facing and value **Rev:** Stefanik's grave monument **Edge:** Plain **Note:** Illustration reduced.

Date	Mintage	F	VF	XF	Unc	BU
2003 Proof	6,000	Value: 250				

KM# 80 5000 KORUN
9.5000 g., 0.9000 Gold 0.2749 oz. AGW, 26 mm. **Subject:** Bardejov - UNESCO historic site **Obv:** National arms and value

left of Town Hall **Rev:** Zachariah in window frame left of St. Aegidius Church, Bardejov **Edge:** Reeded

Date	Mintage	F	VF	XF	Unc	BU
2004 Proof	9,000	Value: 550				

KM# 83 5000 KORUN
9.5000 g., 0.9000 Gold 0.2749 oz. AGW, 26 mm. **Subject:** Leopold I Coronation **Obv:** Mounted Herald with Bratislava Castle in background **Rev:** Leopold I and Crown of St. Stephan **Edge:** Reeded

Date	Mintage	F	VF	XF	Unc	BU
2005 Proof	7,500	Value: 550				

KM# 89 5000 KORUN
9.5000 g., 0.9000 Gold 0.2749 oz. AGW, 26 mm. **Subject:** 400th Anniversary Coronation of King Matthias II **Obv:** Cathedral and Bratislava castle **Obv. Legend:** SLOVENSKÁ - REPUBLIKA **Rev:** 1/2 length figure of Matthias II left, crown in lower foreground, towers of the St. Michael's Gate and franciscan Church in Bratislava in background **Rev. Legend:** KORUNOVÁCIA MATEJA II. / BRATISLAVA **Edge:** Reeded

Date	Mintage	F	VF	XF	Unc	BU
2008 Proof	4,050	Value: 550				

KM# 64 10000 KORUN
18.8350 g., Bi-Metallic 1.555g, .999 Palladium round center in a 15.55g, .900 Gold square, 29.5 x 29.5 mm. **Subject:** 10th Anniversary of the Republic **Obv:** Young head left within circular inscription above double cross within shield **Rev:** Bratislava castle above value **Edge:** Segmented reeding **Shape:** Square

Date	Mintage	F	VF	XF	Unc	BU
2003 Proof	6,000	Value: 1,150				

KM# 79 10000 KORUN
24.8828 g., Bi-Metallic .999 Gold 12.4414g 23mm round center

in .999 Palladium 12.4414g pentagon, 40 mm. **Subject:** Slovakian entry into the European Union **Obv:** National arms above date in center **Rev:** European map with entry date **Edge:** Plain

Date	Mintage	F	VF	XF	Unc	BU
2004 Proof	7,200	Value: 1,100				

EURO COINAGE
European Union Issues

KM# 95 EURO CENT
2.3000 g., Copper Plated Steel, 16.25 mm. **Obv:** Krivan Peak in the Tatras, state emblem **Rev:** Denomination and globe

Date	Mintage	F	VF	XF	Unc	BU
2009	90,745,000	—	—	—	0.35	0.50
2009 Proof	13,300	Value: 15.00				
2010	30,000,000	—	—	—	0.35	0.50
2010 Proof	5,000	Value: 8.00				
2011	—	—	—	—	0.35	0.50
2011 Proof	6,000	Value: 6.00				
2012	—	—	—	—	—	0.50
2012 Proof	—	Value: 6.00				

KM# 96 2 EURO CENT
3.0600 g., Copper Plated Steel, 18.75 mm. **Obv:** Krivan Peak in the Tatras, state emblem **Rev:** Denomination and globe **Edge:** Grooved

Date	Mintage	F	VF	XF	Unc	BU
2009	64,387,000	—	—	—	0.50	0.65
2009 Proof	13,300	Value: 15.00				
2010	50,063,000	—	—	—	0.50	0.65
2010 Proof	5,000	Value: 8.00				
2011	—	—	—	—	0.50	0.65
2011 Proof	6,000	Value: 6.00				
2012	—	—	—	—	—	0.65
2012 Proof	—	Value: 6.00				

KM# 97 5 EURO CENT
3.9200 g., Copper Plated Steel, 21.25 mm. **Obv:** Krivan Peak in the Tatras - state emblem **Rev:** Denomination and globe

Date	Mintage	F	VF	XF	Unc	BU
2009	84,874,000	—	—	—	0.75	1.00
2009 Proof	13,300	Value: 15.00				
2010	—	—	—	—	0.75	1.00
2010 Proof	5,000	Value: 8.00				
2011	—	—	—	—	0.75	1.00
2011 Proof	6,000	Value: 6.00				
2012	—	—	—	—	0.75	1.00
2012 Proof	—	Value: 6.00				

KM# 98 10 EURO CENT
4.1000 g., Brass, 19.75 mm. **Obv:** Bratislava Castle and state emblem **Rev:** Expanded relief map of European Union at left, denomination at right **Edge:** Reeded

Date	Mintage	F	VF	XF	Unc	BU
2009	74,717,000	—	—	—	0.75	1.00
2009 Proof	13,300	Value: 15.00				
2010	—	—	—	—	0.75	1.00
2010 Proof	5,000	Value: 8.00				
2011	—	—	—	—	0.75	1.00
2011 Proof	6,000	Value: 6.00				
2012	—	—	—	—	0.75	1.00
2012 Proof	—	Value: 6.00				

KM# 99   20 EURO CENT
5.7400 g., Brass, 22.25 mm. **Obv:** Bratislava Castle and state emblem **Rev:** Expanded relief map of European Union at left, denomination at right **Edge:** Notched

Date	Mintage	F	VF	XF	Unc	BU
2009	66,519,000	—	—	—	1.00	1.25
2009 Proof	13,300	Value: 16.00				
2010	—	—	—	—	1.00	1.25
2010 Proof	5,000	Value: 10.00				
2011	—	—	—	—	1.00	1.25
2011 Proof	6,000	Value: 7.00				
2012	—	—	—	—	1.00	1.25
2012 Proof	—	Value: 7.00				

KM# 100   50 EURO CENT
7.8000 g., Brass, 24.25 mm. **Obv:** Bratislava Castle and state shield **Rev:** Expanded relief map of European Union at left, denomination at right **Edge:** Reeded

Date	Mintage	F	VF	XF	Unc	BU
2009	59,317,000	—	—	—	1.25	1.50
2009 Proof	13,300	Value: 16.00				
2010	—	—	—	—	1.25	1.50
2010 Proof	5,000	Value: 10.00				
2011	—	—	—	—	1.25	1.50
2011 Proof	6,000	Value: 7.00				
2012	—	—	—	—	1.25	1.50
2012 Proof	—	Value: 7.00				

KM# 101   EURO
7.5000 g., Bi-Metallic Copper-Nickel center in Nickel-Brass ring, 23.25 mm. **Obv:** Double cross in middle of three hills **Rev:** Value at left, expanded relief map of European Union at right **Edge:** Segmented reeding

Date	Mintage	F	VF	XF	Unc	BU
2009	46,777,000	—	—	—	2.50	2.75
2009 Proof	13,300	Value: 20.00				
2010	—	—	—	—	2.50	2.75
2010 Proof	5,000	Value: 15.00				
2011	—	—	—	—	2.50	2.75
2011 Proof	6,000	Value: 12.00				
2012	—	—	—	—	2.50	2.75
2012 Proof	—	Value: 12.00				

KM# 102   2 EURO
8.5000 g., Bi-Metallic Nickel-Brass center in Copper-Nickel ring, 25.75 mm. **Obv:** Double cross on middle of three hills **Rev:** Value at left, expanded map of European Union at left

Date	Mintage	F	VF	XF	Unc	BU
2009	35,667,000	—	—	—	5.00	6.00
2009 Proof	13,300	Value: 25.00				
2010	—	—	—	—	5.00	6.00
2010 Proof	5,000	Value: 20.00				
2011	—	—	—	—	5.00	6.00
2011 Proof	6,000	Value: 15.00				
2012	—	—	—	—	5.00	6.00
2012 Proof	—	Value: 15.00				

KM# 103   2 EURO
8.5000 g., Bi-Metallic Nickel-Brass center in Copper-Nickel ring, 25.75 mm. **Subject:** EMU 10th Anniversary **Obv:** Stick figure and large E symbol **Rev:** Expanded relief map of European Union at left, denomination at right

Date	Mintage	F	VF	XF	Unc	BU
2009	2,493,000	—	—	—	6.00	7.50
2009 Special Unc.	7,000	—	—	—	—	20.00

KM# 107   2 EURO
8.5000 g., Bi-Metallic Nickel-Brass center in Copper-Nickel ring, 25.75 mm. **Subject:** Freedom, 17 November 1989, 20th Anniversary **Obv:** Ringing Freedom bell

Date	Mintage	F	VF	XF	Unc	BU
2009	1,000,000	—	—	—	6.00	7.50
2009 Special Unc.	7,000	—	—	—	—	20.00
2009 Prooflike	1,000	—	—	—	—	175

KM# 114   2 EURO
8.5000 g., Bi-Metallic Nickel-Brass center in Copper-Nickel ring, 25.75 mm. **Subject:** Visegrad Group, 20th Anniversary

Date	Mintage	F	VF	XF	Unc	BU
2011	981,000	—	—	—	5.00	6.00
2011 Special Unc.	7,000	—	—	—	—	20.00

KM# 120   2 EURO
8.5000 g., Bi-Metallic Nickel-Brass center in Copper-Nickel ring, 25.75 mm. **Subject:** Euro coinage, 10th Anniversary **Obv:** Euro symbol on globe at center, child-like rendering around

Date	Mintage	F	VF	XF	Unc	BU
2012	1,000,000	—	—	—	6.00	8.00

KM# 108   10 EURO
18.0000 g., 0.9000 Silver 0.5208 oz. ASW, 34 mm. **Subject:** Aurel Stodola, 150th Anniversary of birth **Obv:** Turbo generator, national shield **Rev:** Portrait **Edge Lettering:** KONSTRUKTER - VYNALEZCA - PEDAGOG

Date	Mintage	F	VF	XF	Unc	BU
2009	10,100	—	—	—	—	50.00
2009 Proof	13,300	Value: 65.00				

KM# 110   10 EURO
18.0000 g., 0.9000 Silver 0.5208 oz. ASW, 34 mm. **Subject:** Wooden Churches of Carpathian Slovakia - UNESCO World Heritage site

Date	Mintage	F	VF	XF	Unc	BU
2010	—	—	—	—	—	50.00
2010 Proof	—	Value: 65.00				

KM# 111   10 EURO
18.0000 g., 0.9000 Silver 0.5208 oz. ASW, 34 mm. **Subject:** Martin Kukucin, 150th Anniversary of birth **Obv:** Landscape scene from Brac, "House on the hillside" **Rev:** Portrait facing, cuckoo, signature **Edge Lettering:** PROZAIK - DRAMATIK - PUBLICISTA

Date	Mintage	F	VF	XF	Unc	BU
2010	9,900	—	—	—	—	50.00
2010 Proof	17,325	Value: 65.00				

KM# 115   10 EURO
18.0000 g., 0.9000 Silver 0.5208 oz. ASW, 34 mm. **Subject:** Zobor Documents, 900th Anniversary **Obv:** Two scribes **Rev:** Seal and partial document text

Date	Mintage	F	VF	XF	Unc	BU
2011	—	—	—	—	—	50.00
2011 Proof	—	Value: 65.00				

KM# 116   10 EURO
18.0000 g., 0.9000 Silver 0.5208 oz. ASW, 34 mm. **Subject:** Adoption of the memorandum of the Slovak Nation, 1540th Anniversary

Date	Mintage	F	VF	XF	Unc	BU
2011	—	—	—	—	—	50.00
2011 Proof	—	Value: 65.00				

KM# 117   10 EURO
18.0000 g., 0.9000 Silver 0.5208 oz. ASW, 34 mm. **Subject:** Jan Cikker, 100th Anniversary of Birth

Date	Mintage	F	VF	XF	Unc	BU
2011	—	—	—	—	—	50.00
2011 Proof	—	Value: 65.00				

KM# 109   20 EURO
33.6300 g., 0.9250 Silver 1.0000 oz. ASW, 40 mm. **Subject:** National Park - Vel'ká Fatra **Obv:** Fora and national shield **Rev:** Falcon in flight over mountain peak **Edge Lettering:** OCHRANA PRÍRODY A KRAJINY

Date	Mintage	F	VF	XF	Unc	BU
2009	9,900	—	—	—	—	65.00
2009 Proof	12,600	Value: 75.00				

KM# 112   20 EURO
33.6300 g., 0.9250 Silver 1.0000 oz. ASW, 40 mm. **Subject:** Poloniny National Park **Obv:** Mountainside and flowers **Rev:** Two wolves

Date	Mintage	F	VF	XF	Unc	BU
2010	—	—	—	—	—	55.00
2010 Proof	—	Value: 70.00				

KM# 118   20 EURO
33.6300 g., 0.9250 Silver 1.0000 oz. ASW, 40 mm. **Subject:** Historical Sites - Trnava

Date	Mintage	F	VF	XF	Unc	BU
2011	—	—	—	—	—	55.00
2011 Proof	—	Value: 70.00				

KM# 121   20 EURO
33.6300 g., 0.9250 Silver 1.0000 oz. ASW, 40 mm. **Subject:** Historical towns - Trencin **Obv:** Castle, historical Roman inscription and National arms below **Rev:** Rendering of the Trencin historical preservation area

Date	Mintage	F	VF	XF	Unc	BU
2012	5,900	—	—	—	—	50.00
2012 Proof	7,500	Value: 60.00				

KM# 113   100 EURO
9.5000 g., 0.9000 Gold 0.2749 oz. AGW, 26 mm. **Subject:** Wooden Churches of Carpathian Slovakia - UNESCO Heritage Site **Obv:** Church of St. Francis of Assisi in Hervartov, belfry of the church in Hronsek and Church of St. Nicholas in Brodrzal **Rev:** Baroque altar of All Saints Church in Tvrdosin **Edge:** Reeded

Date	Mintage	F	VF	XF	Unc	BU
2010 Proof	Est. 7,000	Value: 550				

KM# 119   100 EURO
9.5000 g., 0.9000 Gold 0.2749 oz. AGW, 26 mm. **Subject:** Prince Pribina Nitra, 1150th Anniversary of Death

Date	Mintage	F	VF	XF	Unc	BU
2011 Proof	—	Value: 550				

MINT SETS

KM#	Date	Mintage	Identification	Issue Price	Mkt Val
MS9	2001 (7)	—	KM#11-14, 17-18, 35, plus medal	—	20.00
MS10	2002 (7)	—	KM#11-1-14, 17-18, 35, plus medal	—	17.50
MS11	2003 (7)	—	KM#11.1-14, 17-18, 35, plus medal	—	15.00
MS12	2004 (7)	—	KM#11.1-14, 17, 18, 35 plus medal	—	12.00
MS13	2005 (7)	—	KM#11.1-14, 17, 18, 35 plus medal	—	12.00
MS14	2006 (7)	—	KM#11.1-14, 17, 18, 35 plus medal	—	12.00
MS15	2007 (7)	—	KM#11.1-14, 17, 18, 35 plus medal	—	12.00
MS16	2007 (5)	—	KM11.2, 12-14, 35. National parks	—	15.00
MS17	2005 (5)	—	KM#11.1, 12-14, 35, Austrian 2005 KM#3088	—	10.00
MS18	2007 (5)	—	KM#11.1, 12-14, 35	—	12.00
MS19	2007 (5)	—	KM#11.1, 12-14, 35. National parks packaging	—	15.00
MS20	2007 (5)	—	KM#11.1, 12-14, 35 and a bimetallic medal and cd. Set to commemorate musician Gejza Dusik	—	20.00

PROOF SETS

KM#	Date	Mintage	Identification	Issue Price	Mkt Val
PS2	2001 (7)	12,500	KM#11.1-14, 17-18, 35	—	35.00
PS3	2002 (7)	16,500	KM#11.1-14, 17-18, 35	—	25.00
PS4	2004 (7)	—	KM#11.1, 12-14, 35, silver strikes of 1993, KM#17-18	—	40.00
PS5	2006 (6)	—	KM#11.1, 12-14, 35 plus medal. 2006 Torino Winter Olympics	—	45.00
PS6	2008 (6)	—	KM#11.1, 12-14, 35 plus medal. 2008 Peking Olympics	—	45.00
PS7	2009 (9)	13,300	KM#95-102 plus medal	—	125
PS8	2010 (9)	5,000	KM#95-102 plus medal	—	80.00
PS9	2011 (9)	5,000	KM#95-102 plus CN medal	—	65.00
PS10	2011 (9)	1,000	KM#95-102 plus CN medal, wood box	—	350

SLOVENIA

The Republic of Slovenia is located northwest of Yugoslavia in the valleys of the Danube River. It has an area of 7,819 sq. mi. and a population of *1.9 million. Capital: Ljubljana. Agriculture is the main industry with large amounts of hops and fodder crops grown as well as many varieties of fruit trees. Sheep raising, timber production and the mining of mercury from one of the country's oldest mines are also very important to the economy. Slovenia joined the European Union in May 2004.

MINT MARKS
Based on last digit in date.
(K) - Kremnitz (Slovakia): open 4, upturned 5
(BP) - Budapest (Hungary): closed 4, down-turned 5

REPUBLIC
STANDARD COINAGE
100 Stotinow = 1 Tolar

KM# 7   10 STOTINOV
0.5500 g., Aluminum, 16 mm. **Obv:** Value within square **Rev:** Olm salamander **Edge:** Plain **Note:** Varieties exist.

Date	Mintage	F	VF	XF	Unc	BU
2001 In sets only	1,000	—	—	—	—	3.00
2001 Proof	800	Value: 5.00				
2002 In sets only	1,000	—	—	—	—	3.00
2002 Proof	800	Value: 5.00				
2003 In sets only	1,000	—	—	—	—	3.00
2003 Proof	800	Value: 5.00				
2004 In sets only	1,000	—	—	—	—	3.00
2004 Proof	800	Value: 5.00				
2005 In sets only	3,000	—	—	—	—	2.00
2005 Proof	1,000	Value: 5.00				
2006 In sets only	4,000	—	—	—	—	2.00
2006 Proof	1,000	Value: 5.00				

KM# 8   20 STOTINOV
0.7000 g., Aluminum, 18 mm. **Obv:** Value within square **Rev:** Barn owl and value **Edge:** Plain

Date	Mintage	F	VF	XF	Unc	BU
2001 In sets only	1,000	—	—	—	—	4.00
2001 Proof	800	Value: 6.00				
2002 In sets only	1,000	—	—	—	—	4.00
2002 Proof	800	Value: 6.00				
2003 In sets only	1,000	—	—	—	—	4.00
2003 Proof	800	Value: 6.00				
2004 In sets only	1,000	—	—	—	—	4.00
2004 Proof	500	Value: 6.00				
2005 In sets only	3,000	—	—	—	—	3.00
2005 Proof	1,000	Value: 6.00				
2006 In sets only	4,000	—	—	—	—	3.00
2006 Proof	1,000	Value: 6.00				

KM# 3   50 STOTINOV
0.8500 g., Aluminum, 20 mm. **Obv:** Value within square **Rev:** Bee and value **Edge:** Plain

Date	Mintage	F	VF	XF	Unc	BU
2001 In sets only	1,000	—	—	—	—	6.00
2001 Proof	800	Value: 7.50				
2002 In sets only	1,000	—	—	—	—	6.00
2002 Proof	800	Value: 7.50				
2003 In sets only	1,000	—	—	—	—	6.00
2003 Proof	800	Value: 7.50				
2004 In sets only	1,000	—	—	—	—	6.00
2004 Proof	500	Value: 12.00				
2005 In sets only	3,000	—	—	—	—	4.00
2005 Proof	1,000	Value: 7.00				
2006 In sets only	4,000	—	—	—	—	4.00
2006 Proof	1,000	Value: 7.00				

KM# 4   TOLAR
4.5000 g., Nickel-Brass, 22 mm. **Obv:** Value within circle **Rev:** Three brown trout **Rev. Legend:** SALMO TRUTTA FARIO **Edge:** Reeded **Note:** Date varieties exist: 1994 = closed or open "4"; 1995 = serif up and serif down in "5".

Date	Mintage	F	VF	XF	Unc	BU
2001	10,001,000	—	—	—	0.75	1.25
2001 Proof	800	Value: 7.50				
2002 In sets only	1,000	—	—	—	—	5.00
2002 Proof	800	Value: 7.50				
2003 In sets only	1,000	—	—	—	—	5.00
2003 Proof	800	Value: 7.50				
2004	10,001,000	—	—	—	0.75	1.25
2004 (K) In sets only	1,000	—	—	—	—	5.00
Note: 4 open to right						
2004 Proof	500	Value: 8.50				
2005 In sets only	3,000	—	—	—	—	4.00
2005 Proof	1,000	Value: 7.50				
2006 In sets only	4,000	—	—	—	—	4.00
2006 Proof	1,000	Value: 7.50				

KM# 5   2 TOLARJA
5.4000 g., Nickel-Brass, 24 mm. **Obv:** Value within circle **Rev:** Barn swallow in flight **Rev. Legend:** HIRUNDO RUSTICA **Edge:** Reeded **Note:** Date varieties exist: 1994 = closed or open "4"; 1995 = serif up and serif down in "5".

Date	Mintage	F	VF	XF	Unc	BU
2001	10,001,000	—	—	—	0.75	1.75
2001 Proof	800	Value: 8.50				
2002 In sets only	1,000	—	—	—	—	7.00
2002 Proof	800	Value: 8.50				
2003 In sets only	1,000	—	—	—	—	7.00
2003 Proof	800	Value: 8.50				
2004	10,001,000	—	—	—	0.75	1.50
2004 Proof	500	Value: 8.50				
2005 In sets only	3,000	—	—	—	—	7.00
2005 Proof	1,000	Value: 8.50				
2006 In sets only	4,000	—	—	—	—	7.00
2006 Proof	1,000	Value: 8.50				

KM# 6   5 TOLARJEV
6.4400 g., Nickel-Brass, 26 mm. **Obv:** Value within circle **Rev:** Head and horns of ibex **Edge:** Reeded **Note:** Date varieties exist: 1994 = closed or open "4"; 1995 = serif up and serif down in "5".

Date	Mintage	F	VF	XF	Unc	BU
2001 In sets only	1,000	—	—	—	—	8.00

Date	Mintage	F	VF	XF	Unc	BU
2001 Proof	800	Value: 10.00				
2002 In sets only	1,000	—	—	—	—	8.00
2002 Proof	800	Value: 10.00				
2003 In sets only	1,000	—	—	—	—	8.00
2003 Proof	800	Value: 10.00				
2004 In sets only	1,000	—	—	—	—	8.00
2004 Proof	500	Value: 15.00				
2005 In sets only	3,000	—	—	—	—	7.00
2005 Proof	1,000	Value: 10.00				
2006 In sets only	4,000	—	—	—	—	7.00
2006 Proof	800	Value: 10.00				

KM# 41   10 TOLARJEV
5.7500 g., Copper-Nickel, 24 mm. **Obv:** Value within circle **Rev:** Stylized rearing horse **Rev. Legend:** EQUUS **Edge:** Reeded

Date	Mintage	F	VF	XF	Unc	BU
2001	29,441,000	—	—	—	2.00	3.50
2001 Proof	800	Value: 12.00				
2002	10,037,000	—	—	—	2.00	3.50
2002 Proof	800	Value: 12.00				
2003 In sets only	1,000	—	—	—	—	5.00
2003 Proof	800	Value: 12.00				
2004	10,001,000	—	—	—	2.00	3.50
2004 Proof	500	Value: 12.00				
2005	6,003,000	—	—	—	2.00	3.50
2005 Proof	1,000	Value: 12.00				
2006	6,001,000	—	—	—	2.00	3.50
2006 Proof	1,000	Value: 12.00				

KM# 51   20 TOLARJEV
6.8500 g., Copper-Nickel, 24 mm. **Obv:** Value within circle **Rev:** White Stork **Rev. Legend:** CICONIA CICONIA **Edge:** Reeded

Date	Mintage	F	VF	XF	Unc	BU
2003	10,001,000	—	—	—	3.50	5.00
2003 Proof	800	Value: 15.00				
2004	10,001,000	—	—	—	3.00	5.00
2004 Proof	500	Value: 15.00				
2005	12,003,000	—	—	—	3.50	5.00
2005 Proof	1,000	Value: 15.00				
2006	4,004,000	—	—	—	3.50	5.00
2006 Proof	1,000	Value: 15.00				

KM# 52   50 TOLARJEV
8.0000 g., Copper-Nickel, 26 mm. **Obv:** Value within circle **Rev:** Stylized bull **Rev. Legend:** TAURUS TAURUS **Edge:** Segmented reeding

Date	Mintage	F	VF	XF	Unc	BU
2003	10,001,000	—	—	—	2.50	4.50
2003 Proof	800	Value: 12.00				
2004	5,001,000	—	—	—	2.50	4.50
2004 Proof	500	Value: 15.00				
2005	8,003,000	—	—	—	2.50	4.50
2005 Proof	1,000	Value: 12.00				
2006 In sets only	4,000	—	—	—	—	6.50
2006 Proof	1,000	Value: 12.00				

KM# 42   100 TOLARJEV
9.1000 g., Copper-Nickel, 28 mm. **Subject:** 10th Anniversary of Slovenia and the Tolar **Obv:** Value **Rev:** Tree rings and inscription **Edge:** Reeded

Date	Mintage	F	VF	XF	Unc	BU
2001	500,000	—	—	—	3.00	4.00
2001 Proof	800	Value: 10.00				

KM# 45   500 TOLARJEV
8.5400 g., Bi-Metallic Copper-Nickel center in Brass ring, 28.1 mm. **Subject:** Soccer **Obv:** Value **Rev:** Soccer player and radiant sun **Edge:** Reeded

Date	Mintage	F	VF	XF	Unc	BU
2002	500,000	—	—	—	5.50	7.50
2002 Proof	800	Value: 12.50				

KM# 50   500 TOLARJEV
8.7200 g., Bi-Metallic Copper-Nickel center in Brass ring, 27.9 mm. **Subject:** European Year of the Disabled **Obv:** Stylized wheelchair **Rev:** Value **Edge:** Reeded

Date	Mintage	F	VF	XF	Unc	BU
2003	200,000	—	—	—	6.00	8.00
2003 Proof	800	Value: 13.50				

KM# 57   500 TOLARJEV
8.6000 g., Bi-Metallic Copper-Nickel center in Brass ring, 28 mm. **Obv:** Value **Rev:** Profile left looking down within mathematical graph **Edge:** Reeded

Date	Mintage	F	VF	XF	Unc	BU
2004	200,000	—	—	—	6.00	8.00
2004 Proof	500	Value: 20.00				

KM# 63   500 TOLARJEV
8.6500 g., Bi-Metallic Copper-Nickel center in Brass ring, 27.9 mm. **Obv:** Perched falcon and value **Rev:** Horizontal line in center divides partial suns **Edge:** Reeded

Date	Mintage	F	VF	XF	Unc	BU
2005	103,000	—	—	—	6.25	8.50
2005 Proof	1,000	Value: 12.00				

KM# 65   500 TOLARJEV
8.6000 g., Bi-Metallic Copper-Nickel center in Brass ring, 28 mm. **Obv:** Value **Rev:** Anton Tomaz Linhart's silhouette above life dates **Edge:** Reeded

Date	Mintage	F	VF	XF	Unc	BU
2006	104,000	—	—	—	6.00	8.00
2006 Proof	1,000	Value: 12.00				

KM# 43   2000 TOLARJEV
15.0000 g., 0.9250 Silver 0.4461 oz. ASW, 32 mm. **Subject:** 10th Anniversary of Slovenia and the Tolar **Obv:** Value **Rev:** Tree rings and inscription **Edge:** Reeded

Date	Mintage	F	VF	XF	Unc	BU
2001 Proof	3,000	Value: 35.00				

KM# 46   2500 TOLARJEV
15.0000 g., 0.9250 Silver 0.4461 oz. ASW, 32 mm. **Subject:** Soccer **Obv:** Value **Rev:** Soccer player and radiant sun **Edge:** Reeded

Date	Mintage	F	VF	XF	Unc	BU
2002 Proof	2,500	Value: 35.00				

KM# 48   2500 TOLARJEV
15.0000 g., 0.9250 Silver 0.4461 oz. ASW, 32 mm. **Subject:** 35th Chess Olympiad **Obv:** Rearing horse and reflection **Rev:** Chess pieces in starting positions and reflection **Edge:** Reeded

Date	Mintage	F	VF	XF	Unc	BU
2002 Proof	1,000	Value: 45.00				

KM# 53   2500 TOLARJEV
15.0000 g., 0.9250 Silver 0.4461 oz. ASW, 32 mm. **Subject:** European Year of the Disabled **Obv:** Value **Rev:** Stylized wheel chair **Edge:** Reeded

Date	Mintage	F	VF	XF	Unc	BU
2003 Proof	1,500	Value: 42.00				

KM# 55   5000 TOLARJEV
15.0000 g., 0.9250 Silver 0.4461 oz. ASW, 32 mm. **Subject:** 60th Anniversary of the Slovenian Assembly **Obv:** Value in partial star design **Rev:** Dates in partial star design **Edge:** Reeded

Date	Mintage	F	VF	XF	Unc	BU
2003 Proof	1,500	Value: 42.00				

KM# 58 5000 TOLARJEV
15.0000 g., 0.9250 Silver 0.4461 oz. ASW, 32 mm. **Obv:** Value **Rev:** Facial profile left looking down within mathematical graph **Edge:** Reeded

Date	Mintage	F	VF	XF	Unc	BU
2004 Proof	1,500	Value: 50.00				

KM# 60 5000 TOLARJEV
15.0000 g., 0.9250 Silver 0.4461 oz. ASW, 32 mm. **Subject:** 1000th Anniversary Town of Bled **Obv:** Value **Rev:** Castle and towers silhouette **Edge:** Reeded

Date	Mintage	F	VF	XF	Unc	BU
2004 Proof	1,500	Value: 50.00				

KM# 62 5000 TOLARJEV
15.1000 g., 0.9250 Silver 0.4490 oz. ASW, 32 mm. **Subject:** Slovenian Film Centennial **Obv:** Value above a director's clapboard **Rev:** Film segment **Edge:** Reeded

Date	Mintage	F	VF	XF	Unc	BU
2005 Proof	—	Value: 47.50				

KM# 64 5000 TOLARJEV
15.1000 g., 0.9250 Silver 0.4490 oz. ASW, 32 mm. **Obv:** Perched falcon above value **Rev:** Diagonal center line divides partial suns **Edge:** Reeded

Date	Mintage	F	VF	XF	Unc	BU
2005 Proof	—	Value: 47.50				

KM# 91 5000 TOLARJEV
15.0000 g., 0.9250 Silver 0.4461 oz. ASW, 32 mm. **Subject:** 1000th Anniversary, mention of town of Bled, 2nd issue

Date	Mintage	F	VF	XF	Unc	BU
2006 Proof	1,000	Value: 55.00				

KM# 92 5000 TOLARJEV
15.0000 g., 0.9000 Silver 0.4340 oz. ASW, 32 mm. **Subject:** Anton Tomaz Linhart, 250th Anniversary of Birth **Rev:** Bust left

Date	Mintage	F	VF	XF	Unc	BU
2006 Proof	5,000	Value: 45.00				

KM# 93 5000 TOLARJEV
15.0000 g., 0.9250 Silver 0.4461 oz. ASW, 32 mm. **Subject:** Anton Askerc, 150th Anniversary of birth **Rev:** Bust left

Date	Mintage	F	VF	XF	Unc	BU
2006 Proof	5,000	Value: 45.00				

KM# 44 20000 TOLARJEV
7.0000 g., 0.9000 Gold 0.2025 oz. AGW, 24 mm. **Subject:** 10th Anniversary of Slovenia and the Tolar **Obv:** Value **Rev:** Tree rings and inscription **Edge:** Reeded

Date	Mintage	F	VF	XF	Unc	BU
2001 Proof	1,000	Value: 400				

KM# 47 20000 TOLARJEV
7.0000 g., 0.9000 Gold 0.2025 oz. AGW, 24 mm. **Subject:** World Cup Soccer **Obv:** Value **Rev:** Soccer player and rising sun **Edge:** Reeded

Date	Mintage	F	VF	XF	Unc	BU
2002 Proof	500	Value: 400				

KM# 49 20000 TOLARJEV
7.0000 g., 0.9000 Gold 0.2025 oz. AGW, 24 mm. **Subject:** 35th Chess Olympiad **Obv:** Rearing horse and reflection **Rev:** Chess pieces in starting positions and reflection **Edge:** Reeded

Date	Mintage	F	VF	XF	Unc	BU
2002 Proof	500	Value: 400				

KM# 54 25000 TOLARJEV
7.0000 g., 0.9000 Gold 0.2025 oz. AGW, 24 mm. **Subject:** European Year of the Disabled **Obv:** Value **Rev:** Stylized wheel chair **Edge:** Reeded

Date	Mintage	F	VF	XF	Unc	BU
2003 Proof	300	Value: 400				

KM# 56 25000 TOLARJEV
7.0000 g., 0.9000 Gold 0.2025 oz. AGW, 24 mm. **Subject:** 60th Anniversary of the Slovenian Assembly **Obv:** Value in partial star design **Rev:** Dates in partial star design **Edge:** Reeded

Date	Mintage	F	VF	XF	Unc	BU
2003 Proof	300	Value: 400				

KM# 59 25000 TOLARJEV
7.0000 g., 0.9000 Gold 0.2025 oz. AGW, 24 mm. **Subject:** 250th Anniversary of Jurij Vega's Birth **Obv:** Value **Rev:** Facial profile left looking down within mathematical graph **Edge:** Reeded

Date	Mintage	F	VF	XF	Unc	BU
2004 Proof	300	Value: 400				

KM# 61 25000 TOLARJEV
7.0000 g., 0.9000 Gold 0.2025 oz. AGW, 24 mm. **Subject:** 1000th Anniversary Town of Bled **Obv:** Value **Rev:** Castle and towers silhouette **Edge:** Reeded

Date	Mintage	F	VF	XF	Unc	BU
2004 Proof	300	Value: 400				

KM# 66 25000 TOLARJEV
7.0000 g., 0.9000 Gold 0.2025 oz. AGW, 24 mm. **Subject:** Centennial of Slovene Sokol Association **Obv:** Perched falcon above value **Rev:** Rising sun and reflection **Edge:** Reeded

Date	Mintage	F	VF	XF	Unc	BU
2005 Proof	1,000	Value: 400				

KM# 67 25000 TOLARJEV
7.0000 g., 0.9000 Gold 0.2025 oz. AGW, 24 mm. **Subject:** Centennial of Slovene Film **Obv:** Value above clapboard **Rev:** Film segment **Edge:** Reeded

Date	Mintage	F	VF	XF	Unc	BU
2005 Proof	1,000	Value: 400				

KM# 83 25000 TOLARJEV
7.0000 g., 0.9000 Gold 0.2025 oz. AGW, 24 mm. **Subject:** Anton Askerc **Edge:** Reeded

Date	Mintage	F	VF	XF	Unc	BU
2006 Proof	—	Value: 400				

KM# 84 25000 TOLARJEV
7.0000 g., 0.9000 Gold 0.2025 oz. AGW, 24 mm. **Subject:** Anton Tomaz Linhart **Edge:** Reeded

Date	Mintage	F	VF	XF	Unc	BU
2006 Proof	—	Value: 400				

KM# 90 25000 TOLARJEV
7.0000 g., 0.9000 Gold 0.2025 oz. AGW, 24 mm. **Subject:** 1000th Anniversary, Town of Bled mention, 2nd issue

Date	Mintage	F	VF	XF	Unc	BU
2006 Proof	500	Value: 400				

EURO COINAGE

KM# 68 EURO CENT
2.3000 g., Copper Plated Steel, 16.25 mm. **Obv:** White Stork **Obv. Legend:** SLOVENIJA, star between each letter **Rev:** Value and globe **Edge:** Plain

Date	Mintage	F	VF	XF	Unc	BU
2007	44,700,000	—	—	—	0.25	0.35
2008		—	—	—	0.25	0.35
2008 Proof	2,000	Value: 22.00				
2009	17,900,000	—	—	—	0.25	0.35
2010		—	—	—	0.25	0.35
2010 Proof	5,000	Value: 5.00				
2011		—	—	—	0.25	0.35
2011 Proof	2,000	Value: 15.00				

KM# 69 2 EURO CENT
3.0600 g., Copper Plated Steel, 18.75 mm. **Obv:** Princely stone of power in consciousness **Obv. Legend:** SLOVENIJA, star between each letter **Rev:** Value and globe **Edge:** Grooved

Date	Mintage	F	VF	XF	Unc	BU
2007	44,250,000	—	—	—	0.50	0.65
2008		—	—	—	0.50	0.65
2008 Proof	2,000	Value: 22.00				
2009		—	—	—	0.50	0.65
2010		—	—	—	0.50	0.65
2010 Proof	5,000	Value: 5.00				
2011		—	—	—	0.50	0.65
2011 Proof	2,000	Value: 15.00				

KM# 70   5 EURO CENT

3.9200 g., Copper Plated Steel, 21.25 mm. **Obv:** Sower of Seeds - and stars **Obv. Legend:** SLOVENIJA, star between each letter **Rev:** Value and globe **Edge:** Plain

Date	Mintage	F	VF	XF	Unc	BU
2007	43,800,000	—	—	—	0.75	1.00
2008		—	—	—	0.75	1.00
2008 Proof	2,000	Value: 22.00				
2009		—	—	—	0.75	1.00
2010		—	—	—	0.75	1.00
2010 Proof	5,000	Value: 5.00				
2011		—	—	—	0.75	1.00
2011 Proof	2,000	Value: 15.00				

KM# 71   10 EURO CENT

4.1000 g., Brass, 19.75 mm. **Obv:** Plecnik's unrealised plans for Parliament building **Obv. Legend:** SLOVENIJA, star between each letter **Rev:** Value and map **Edge:** Reeded

Date	Mintage	F	VF	XF	Unc	BU
2007	42,800,000	—	—	—	1.00	1.25
2008		—	—	—	1.00	1.25
2008 Proof	2,000	Value: 22.00				
2009		—	—	—	1.00	1.25
2010		—	—	—	1.00	1.25
2010 Proof	5,000	Value: 5.00				
2011		—	—	—	1.00	1.25
2011 Proof	2,000	Value: 15.00				

KM# 72   20 EURO CENT

5.7400 g., Brass, 22.25 mm. **Obv:** Two Lipizzaner horses prancing left **Obv. Legend:** SLOVENIJA, star between each letter **Rev:** Value and map **Edge:** Notched

Date	Mintage	F	VF	XF	Unc	BU
2007	37,250,000	—	—	—	1.25	1.50
2008		—	—	—	1.25	1.50
2008 Proof	2,000	Value: 8.00				
2009		—	—	—	1.25	1.50
2010		—	—	—	1.25	1.50
2010 Proof	5,000	Value: 28.00				
2011		—	—	—	1.25	1.50
2011 Proof	2,000	Value: 18.00				

KM# 73   50 EURO CENT

7.8000 g., Brass, 24.25 mm. **Obv:** Triglav Mountain (highest peak in Slovenia) and stars **Rev:** Value and map **Edge:** Reeded

Date	Mintage	F	VF	XF	Unc	BU
2007	32,400,000	—	—	—	1.50	2.00
2008		—	—	—	1.50	2.00
2008 Proof	2,000	Value: 8.00				
2009		—	—	—	1.50	2.00
2010		—	—	—	1.50	2.00
2010 Proof	5,000	Value: 28.00				
2011		—	—	—	1.50	2.00
2011 Proof	2,000	Value: 18.00				

KM# 74   EURO

7.5000 g., Bi-Metallic Copper-Nickel center in Nickel-Brass ring, 23.25 mm. **Obv:** Bearded Primoz Trubar **Rev:** Value and map **Edge:** Segmented reeding

Date	Mintage	F	VF	XF	Unc	BU
2007	29,750,000	—	—	—	2.50	3.50
2008		—	—	—	2.50	3.50
2008 Proof	2,000	Value: 35.00				
2009		—	—	—	2.50	3.50
2010		—	—	—	2.50	3.50
2010 Proof	5,000	Value: 15.00				
2011		—	—	—	2.50	3.50
2011 Proof	2,000	Value: 22.00				

KM# 75   2 EURO

8.5000 g., Bi-Metallic Nickel-Brass center in Copper-Nickel ring, 25.75 mm. **Obv:** France Preseren silhouette and signature **Rev:** Value and map **Edge:** Reeded and lettered

Date	Mintage	F	VF	XF	Unc	BU
2007	21,250,000	—	—	—	4.00	5.00
2008		—	—	—	4.00	5.00
2008 Proof	2,000	Value: 40.00				
2009		—	—	—	4.00	5.00
2010		—	—	—	4.00	5.00
2010 Proof	5,000	Value: 20.00				
2011		—	—	—	4.00	5.00
2011 Proof	2,000	Value: 28.00				

KM# 106   2 EURO

8.5000 g., Bi-Metallic Nickel-Brass center in Copper-Nickel ring, 25.75 mm. **Subject:** Treaty of Rome, 50th Anniversary

Date	Mintage	F	VF	XF	Unc	BU
2007	399,100	—	—	—	6.50	7.50
2007 Encased in a lucite block	990	—	—	—	—	10.00

KM# 80   2 EURO

8.5000 g., Bi-Metallic Nickel-Brass center in Copper-Nickel ring, 25.75 mm. **Subject:** 500th Anniversary Birth of Primoz Tubar **Obv:** Bust of Trubar left at right **Rev:** Large "2" at left, modified map of Europe at right **Edge:** Reeded

Date	Mintage	F	VF	XF	Unc	BU
2008	950,000	—	—	—	6.00	8.00
2008 Special Unc.	10,000	—	—	—	—	32.50
2008 Proof	40,000	Value: 45.00				

KM# 82   2 EURO

8.5000 g., Bi-Metallic Nickel-Brass center in Copper-Nickel ring., 25.75 mm. **Subject:** European Monetary Union, 10th Anniversary **Obv:** Stick figure and large E symbol **Rev:** Value at left, modified map of Europe at left

Date	Mintage	F	VF	XF	Unc	BU
2009	1,000,000	—	—	—	5.00	6.00
2009 Special Unc.		—	—	—	—	32.50
2009 Proof	—	Value: 40.00				

KM# 94   2 EURO

8.5000 g., Bi-Metallic Nickel-Brass center in Copper-Nickel ring, 25.75 mm. **Subject:** Ljubljana Botanical Gardens, 200th Anniversary

Date	Mintage	F	VF	XF	Unc	BU
2010	980,000	—	—	—	8.00	10.00
2010 Proof	20,000	Value: 50.00				

KM# 100   2 EURO

8.5000 g., Bi-Metallic Nickel-Brass center in Copper-Nickel ring, 25.75 mm. **Subject:** Franc Razman, 100th Anniversary of Birth

Date	Mintage	F	VF	XF	Unc	BU
2011	486,000	—	—	—	6.00	8.00
2011 Proof	14,000	Value: 50.00				

KM# 107   2 EURO

8.5000 g., Bi-Metallic Nickel-Brass center in Copper-Nickel ring, 25.75 mm. **Subject:** Euro Coinage, 10th Anniversary **Obv:** Euro symbol on globe, child-like renderings around

Date	Mintage	F	VF	XF	Unc	BU
2012	1,000,000	—	—	—	7.00	8.00
2012 Proof	1,000	Value: 25.00				

KM# 81   3 EURO

15.0000 g., Bi-Metallic Copper-Nickel center in Aluminum-Bronze ring, 32 mm. **Subject:** Six Month Term as President of the EU 2008 **Obv:** Field of stars representing EU membership **Rev:** Pinwheel

Date	Mintage	F	VF	XF	Unc	BU
2008	348,000	—	—	—	8.00	10.00
2008 Special Unc.	148,000	—	—	—	—	20.00
2008 Proof	4,000	Value: 165				

KM# 85   3 EURO

15.0000 g., Bi-Metallic Copper-Nickel center in Aluminum-Bronze ring, 32 mm. **Subject:** First Airplane flight in Slovenia by Edvard Rusjan, 100th Anniversary

Date	Mintage	F	VF	XF	Unc	BU
2009	300,000	—	—	—	8.00	10.00

KM# 95   3 EURO

15.0000 g., Bi-Metallic Copper-Nickel center in Aluminum-Bronze ring, 32 mm. **Subject:** UNESCO - World Book Capital, Ljubljana

Date	Mintage	F	VF	XF	Unc	BU
2010	—	—	—	—	—	10.00
2010 Proof	5,000	Value: 50.00				

KM# 101   3 EURO

7.5000 g., Bi-Metallic Copper-Nickel center in Aluminum-Bronze ring, 32 mm. **Subject:** Independence, 20th Anniversary

Date	Mintage	F	VF	XF	Unc	BU
2011	5,000	—	—	—	—	15.00
2011 Proof	4,000	Value: 110				

KM# 76   30 EURO

15.0000 g., 0.9250 Silver 0.4461 oz. ASW, 32 mm. **Subject:** 250th Anniversary Birth of Valentin Vodnik **Obv:** Value **Obv. Legend:** SLOVENIJA **Rev:** Large bust of Vodnik left

Date	Mintage	F	VF	XF	Unc	BU
2008 Proof	8,000	Value: 100				

KM# 78   30 EURO

15.0000 g., 0.9250 Silver 0.4461 oz. ASW, 32 mm. **Subject:** EU President **Obv:** EU membership stars **Obv. Legend:** SLOVENIJA **Rev:** Pinwheel 5-pointed star

Date	Mintage	F	VF	XF	Unc	BU
2008 Proof	8,000	Value: 150				

KM# 86 30 EURO
15.0000 g., 0.9250 Silver 0.4461 oz. ASW, 32 mm. **Subject:**
First Airplane, 100th Anniversary

Date	Mintage	F	VF	XF	Unc	BU
2009 Proof	8,000	Value: 65.00				

KM# 88 30 EURO
15.0000 g., 0.9250 Silver 0.4461 oz. ASW, 32 mm. **Subject:**
Zoran Music, painter

Date	Mintage	F	VF	XF	Unc	BU
2009 Proof	—	Value: 70.00				

KM# 96 30 EURO
15.0000 g., 0.9250 Silver 0.4461 oz. ASW, 32 mm. **Subject:**
UNESCO - World Book Capital, Ljubljana

Date	Mintage	F	VF	XF	Unc	BU
2010 Proof	—	Value: 65.00				

KM# 98 30 EURO
15.0000 g., 0.9250 Silver 0.4461 oz. ASW, 32 mm. **Subject:**
World Ski Jumping Championships, Planica

Date	Mintage	F	VF	XF	Unc	BU
2010 Proof	—	Value: 70.00				

KM# 102 30 EURO
15.0000 g., 0.9250 Silver 0.4461 oz. ASW, 32 mm. **Subject:**
Independence, 20th Anniversary

Date	Mintage	F	VF	XF	Unc	BU
2011 Proof	—	Value: 65.00				

KM# 104 30 EURO
15.0000 g., 0.9250 Silver 0.4461 oz. ASW, 32 mm. **Series:**
World Rowing Championships

Date	Mintage	F	VF	XF	Unc	BU
2011 Proof	—	Value: 65.00				

KM# 77 100 EURO
7.0000 g., 0.9000 Gold 0.2025 oz. AGW, 24 mm. **Subject:** 250th
Anniversary Birth of Valentin Vodnik **Obv:** Value **Obv. Legend:**
SLOVENIJA **Rev:** Large bust of Vodnik left

Date	Mintage	F	VF	XF	Unc	BU
2008 Proof	5,000	Value: 425				

KM# 79 100 EURO
7.0000 g., 0.9000 Gold 0.2025 oz. AGW, 24 mm. **Subject:** EU
President **Obv:** EU membership stars **Obv. Legend:**
SLOVENIJA **Rev:** Pinwheel 5-pointed star

Date	Mintage	F	VF	XF	Unc	BU
2008 Proof	5,000	Value: 650				

KM# 87 100 EURO
7.0000 g., 0.9000 Gold 0.2025 oz. AGW, 24 mm. **Subject:** First
Airplane, 100th Anniversary

Date	Mintage	F	VF	XF	Unc	BU
2009 Proof	6,000	Value: 400				

KM# 89 100 EURO
7.0000 g., 0.9000 Gold 0.2025 oz. AGW, 24 mm. **Subject:**
Zoran Music, painter

Date	Mintage	F	VF	XF	Unc	BU
2009 Proof	—	Value: 400				

KM# 97 100 EURO
7.0000 g., 0.9000 Gold 0.2025 oz. AGW, 24 mm. **Subject:**
UNESCO - World Book Capital, Ljubljana

Date	Mintage	F	VF	XF	Unc	BU
2010 Proof	—	Value: 400				

KM# 99 100 EURO
7.0000 g., 0.9000 Gold 0.2025 oz. AGW, 24 mm. **Subject:**
World Ski Jumping Championships, Planica

Date	Mintage	F	VF	XF	Unc	BU
2010 Proof	—	Value: 400				

KM# 103 100 EURO
7.0000 g., 0.9000 Gold 0.2025 oz. AGW, 24 mm. **Subject:**
Independence, 20th Anniversary

Date	Mintage	F	VF	XF	Unc	BU
2011 Proof	—	Value: 400				

KM# 105 100 EURO
7.0000 g., 0.9000 Gold 0.2025 oz. AGW, 24 mm. **Subject:**
World Rowing Championships

Date	Mintage	F	VF	XF	Unc	BU
2011 Proof	—	Value: 400				

MINT SETS

KM#	Date	Mintage Identification	Issue Price	Mkt Val
MS10	2001 (7)	1,000 KM#3-8, 41	20.00	40.00
MS11	2002 (8)	1,000 KM#3-8, 41, 45	—	45.00
MS12	2003 (10)	1,000 KM#3-8, 41, 50-52	—	55.00
MS13	2004 (10)	1,000 KM#3-8, 41, 51, 52, 57	—	45.00
MS14	2005 (9)	3,000 KM#3-8, 41, 51, 52	25.00	45.00
MS15	2006 (10)	4,000 KM#3-8, 41, 51, 52, 65	25.00	50.00
MS16	2007 (8)	100,000 KM#68-75	—	50.00
MS17	2008 (9)	148,000 KM#68-75, 81	—	50.00
MS18	2009 (9)	100,000 KM#68-75, 85	—	50.00
MS19	2010 (10)	70,000 KM#68-75, 94, 95	—	75.00
MS20	2011 (10)	150,000 KM#68-75, 100, 101	—	100

PROOF SETS

KM#	Date	Mintage Identification	Issue Price	Mkt Val
PS13	2001 (8)	800 KM#3-8, 41, 42	—	70.00
PS14	2002 (8)	800 KM#3-8, 41, 45	—	70.00
PS15	2003 (10)	800 KM#3-8, 41, 50-52	22.50	100
PS16	2004 (10)	500 KM#3-8, 41, 51-52, 57	—	120
PS17	2005 (10)	1,000 KM#3-8, 41, 51-52, 63	—	95.00
PS18	2006 (10)	1,000 KM#3-8, 41, 51-52, 65	—	95.00
PS19	2008 (9)	2,000 KM#68-75, 81	—	350
PS20	2010 (10)	5,000 KM#68-75, 94, 95	—	215
PS21	2011 (10)	2,000 KM#68-75, 100, 101	—	315

SOLOMON ISLANDS

The Solomon Islands are made up of about 200 islands. They are located in the southwest Pacific east of Papua New Guinea, have an area of 10,983 sq. mi. (28,450 sq. km.) and a population of *552,000. Capital: Honiara. The most important islands of the Solomon chain are Guadalcanal (scene of some of the fiercest fighting of World War II), Malaitia, New Georgia, Florida, Vella Lavella, Choiseul, Rendova, San Cristobal, the Lord Howe group, the Santa Cruz islands, and the Duff group. Copra is the only important cash crop but it is hoped that timber will become an economic factor.

Solomon Islands is a member of the Commonwealth of Nations. Queen Elizabeth II is Head of State, as Queen of the Solomon Islands.

RULER
British

MONETARY SYSTEM
100 Cents = 1 Dollar

COMMONWEALTH NATION
STANDARD COINAGE

KM# 24 CENT
2.3000 g., Bronze Plated Steel, 17.53 mm. **Ruler:** Elizabeth II
Obv: Crowned head right **Obv. Legend:** ELIZABETH II -
SOLOMON ISLANDS **Rev:** Food bowl divides value **Edge:** Plain

Date	Mintage	F	VF	XF	Unc	BU
2005	—	—	—	—	0.35	0.75
2010	—	—	—	—	0.35	0.75

KM# 25 2 CENTS
Bronze Plated Steel, 21.6 mm. **Ruler:** Elizabeth II **Obv:**
Crowned head right **Obv. Legend:** ELIZABETH II - SOLOMON
ISLANDS **Rev:** Eagle spirit below value **Edge:** Plain

Date	Mintage	F	VF	XF	Unc	BU
2005	—	—	—	—	0.35	0.75
2006	—	—	—	—	0.35	0.75

KM# 26a 5 CENTS
Nickel Plated Steel, 18.40 mm. **Ruler:** Elizabeth II **Obv:**
Crowned bust right **Obv. Legend:** ELIZABETH II - SOLOMON
ISLANDS **Rev:** Value at left, native mask at center right

Date	Mintage	F	VF	XF	Unc	BU
2005	—	—	—	—	0.50	1.00

KM# 27a 10 CENTS
Nickel Plated Steel, 23.6 mm. **Ruler:** Elizabeth II **Subject:**
Ngorieru **Obv:** Crowned head right **Obv. Legend:** ELIZABETH
II - SOLOMON ISLANDS **Rev:** Sea spirit divides value **Edge:**
Reeded

Date	Mintage	F	VF	XF	Unc	BU
2005	—	—	—	—	0.65	1.00

KM# 28 20 CENTS
11.2500 g., Nickel Plated Steel, 28.5 mm. **Ruler:** Elizabeth II
Obv: Crowned head right **Obv. Legend:** ELIZABETH II -
SOLOMON ISLANDS **Rev:** Malaita pendant design within circle,
denomination appears twice in legend **Edge:** Reeded

Date	Mintage	F	VF	XF	Unc	BU
2005	—	—	—	—	0.85	1.25

KM# 29 50 CENTS
10.0000 g., Copper-Nickel, 29.5 mm. **Ruler:** Elizabeth II **Obv:**
Crowned head right **Obv. Legend:** ELIZABETH II - SOLOMON
ISLANDS **Rev:** Arms with supporters **Edge:** Plain **Shape:** 12-
sided **Note:** Circulation type.

Date	Mintage	F	VF	XF	Unc	BU
2005	—	—	—	—	2.00	3.00

KM# 72 DOLLAR
13.4500 g., Copper-Nickel, 30 mm. **Ruler:** Elizabeth II **Obv:**
Crowned head right **Obv. Legend:** ELIZABETH II - SOLOMON
ISLANDS **Rev:** Sea spirit statue divides value **Edge:** Plain
Shape: 7-sided

Date	Mintage	F	VF	XF	Unc	BU
2005	—	—	—	—	2.50	4.00

KM# 123 DOLLAR
0.5000 g., 0.9990 Gold 0.0161 oz. AGW, 11 mm. **Ruler:**
Elizabeth II **Rev:** Spotted Cuscus in tree

Date	Mintage	F	VF	XF	Unc	BU
2010 Proof	15,000	Value: 75.00				

KM# 83 2 DOLLARS
62.2700 g., 0.9990 Silver 1.9999 oz. ASW, 50.3 mm. **Subject:**

Regional Assistance Mission to Solomon Islands **Obv:** Crowned head right **Rev:** Dove outline over multicolor islands in a sea of country names **Edge:** Reeded

Date	Mintage	F	VF	XF	Unc	BU
2005 Proof	2,500	Value: 75.00				

KM# 125   5 DOLLARS
Silver partially gilt, 38.6 mm. **Ruler:** Elizabeth II **Obv:** Head crowned right **Rev:** Mace and coronation scene

Date	Mintage	F	VF	XF	Unc	BU
2002 Proof	—	Value: 50.00				

KM# 113   5 DOLLARS
Copper-Nickel **Ruler:** Elizabeth II **Rev:** Orb

Date	Mintage	F	VF	XF	Unc	BU
2002	—	—	—	—	—	15.00

KM# 113a   5 DOLLARS
28.2800 g., 0.9250 Silver partially gilt 0.8410 oz. ASW, 38.6 mm. **Ruler:** Elizabeth II **Obv:** Bust right gilt **Rev:** Orb

Date	Mintage	F	VF	XF	Unc	BU
2002 Proof	20,000	Value: 40.00				

KM# 75   5 DOLLARS
28.2800 g., Copper-Nickel, 38.6 mm. **Obv:** Crowned head right **Rev:** F-117A Nighthawk Stealth fighter plane **Edge:** Reeded

Date	Mintage	F	VF	XF	Unc	BU
2003	—	—	—	—	5.00	7.00

KM# 76   5 DOLLARS
28.2800 g., Copper-Nickel, 38.6 mm. **Obv:** Crowned head right **Rev:** Concorde supersonic airliner **Edge:** Reeded

Date	Mintage	F	VF	XF	Unc	BU
2003	—	—	—	—	5.00	7.00

KM# 84   5 DOLLARS
31.1035 g., 0.9990 Silver 0.9990 oz. ASW, 38.6 mm. **Obv:** Maklouf's portrait of Elizabeth II **Rev:** Gold plated pig **Edge:** Reeded **Note:** Year of the Pig

Date	Mintage	F	VF	XF	Unc	BU
2007	10,000	—	—	—	—	50.00

KM# 85   5 DOLLARS
31.1035 g., 0.9990 Silver 0.9990 oz. ASW, 38.6 mm. **Obv:** Maklouf's portrait of Elizabeth II **Rev:** Dark red pig and piglet **Edge:** Reeded **Note:** Year of the Pig

Date	Mintage	F	VF	XF	Unc	BU
2007	10,000	—	—	—	—	50.00

KM# 119   5 DOLLARS
0.5000 g., 0.9990 Gold 0.0161 oz. AGW, 11 mm. **Ruler:** Elizabeth II **Subject:** For World Peace **Rev:** John Paul II and Mother Theresa

Date	Mintage	F	VF	XF	Unc	BU
2010 Proof	10,000	Value: 75.00				

KM# 86   10 DOLLARS
28.3600 g., 0.9250 Silver 0.8434 oz. ASW, 38.6 mm. **Obv:** Crowned bust right **Obv. Legend:** ELIZABETH II - SOLOMON ISLANDS **Rev:** Bust of Mendana facing at left, early sailing ship at center - right **Rev. Legend:** ALVARO DE MENDANA **Edge:** Reeded

Date	Mintage	F	VF	XF	Unc	BU
2004 Proof	—	Value: 50.00				

KM# 124   10 DOLLARS
28.3600 g., 0.9250 Silver 0.8434 oz. ASW, 38.6 mm. **Ruler:** Elizabeth II **Subject:** Olumpics 2004 **Rev:** Runner, Sydney Opera House and Parthenon

Date	Mintage	F	VF	XF	Unc	BU
2004 Proof	—	Value: 50.00				

KM# 96   10 DOLLARS
1.2200 g., 0.9990 Gold 0.0392 oz. AGW, 14 mm. **Ruler:** Elizabeth II **Subject:** Wonders of the Ancient World **Obv:** Head right **Rev:** Mausoleum of Mauussollos of Halicarnassus

Date	Mintage	F	VF	XF	Unc	BU
2007 Proof	7,000	Value: 75.00				

KM# 97   10 DOLLARS
1.2200 g., 0.9990 Gold 0.0392 oz. AGW, 14 mm. **Ruler:** Elizabeth II **Subject:** Wonders of the Ancient World **Obv:** Head right **Rev:** Taj Mahal

Date	Mintage	F	VF	XF	Unc	BU
2007 7000	—	Value: 75.00				

KM# 98   10 DOLLARS
1.2200 g., 0.9990 Gold 0.0392 oz. AGW, 14 mm. **Ruler:** Elizabeth II **Subject:** Wonders of the Ancient World **Obv:** Head right **Rev:** Treasury at Petra

Date	Mintage	F	VF	XF	Unc	BU
2007 Proof	7,000	Value: 75.00				

KM# 99   10 DOLLARS
1.2200 g., 0.9990 Gold 0.0392 oz. AGW, 14 mm. **Ruler:** Elizabeth II **Subject:** Wonders of the Ancient World **Obv:** Head right **Rev:** Coliseum in Rome

Date	Mintage	F	VF	XF	Unc	BU
2007 Proof	7,000	Value: 75.00				

KM# 100   10 DOLLARS
1.2200 g., 0.9990 Gold 0.0392 oz. AGW, 14 mm. **Ruler:** Elizabeth II **Subject:** Wonders of the Ancient World **Obv:** Head right **Rev:** Inca's Machu Kicuhu

Date	Mintage	F	VF	XF	Unc	BU
2007 Proof	7,000	Value: 75.00				

KM# 101   10 DOLLARS
1.2200 g., 0.9990 Gold 0.0392 oz. AGW, 14 mm. **Ruler:** Elizabeth II **Subject:** Wonders of the Ancient World **Obv:** Head right **Rev:** Chichen Itza

Date	Mintage	F	VF	XF	Unc	BU
2007 Proof	7,000	Value: 75.00				

KM# 102   10 DOLLARS
1.2200 g., 0.9990 Gold 0.0392 oz. AGW, 14 mm. **Ruler:** Elizabeth II **Subject:** Wonders of the World **Obv:** Head right **Rev:** Great wall of China

Date	Mintage	F	VF	XF	Unc	BU
2007 Proof	7,000	Value: 75.00				

KM# 103   10 DOLLARS
1.2200 g., 0.9990 Gold 0.0392 oz. AGW, 14 mm. **Ruler:** Elizabeth II **Subject:** Wonders of the World **Rev:** Christ Statue in Rio

Date	Mintage	F	VF	XF	Unc	BU
2007 Proof	7,000	Value: 75.00				

KM# 104   10 DOLLARS
1.2200 g., Gold, 14 mm. **Ruler:** Elizabeth II **Subject:** Seven Wonders of the World **Obv:** Head right **Rev:** Giza Pyramids

Date	Mintage	F	VF	XF	Unc	BU
2009 Proof	7,500	Value: 75.00				

KM# 105   10 DOLLARS
1.2200 g., 0.9990 Gold 0.0392 oz. AGW, 14 mm. **Ruler:** Elizabeth II **Subject:** Seven Wonders of the World **Obv:** Head right **Rev:** Colossus of Rhodes

Date	Mintage	F	VF	XF	Unc	BU
2009 Proof	7,500	Value: 75.00				

KM# 106   10 DOLLARS
1.2200 g., 0.9990 Gold 0.0392 oz. AGW, 14 mm. **Ruler:** Elizabeth II **Subject:** Seven Wonders of the World **Obv:** Head right **Rev:** Statue of Zeus at Olympia

Date	Mintage	F	VF	XF	Unc	BU
2009 Proof	7,500	Value: 75.00				

KM# 107   10 DOLLARS
1.2200 g., 0.9990 Gold 0.0392 oz. AGW, 14 mm. **Ruler:** Elizabeth II **Subject:** Seven Wonders of the World **Obv:** Head right **Rev:** Temple of Artemis at Ephesus

Date	Mintage	F	VF	XF	Unc	BU
2009 Proof	7,500	Value: 75.00				

KM# 108   10 DOLLARS
1.2200 g., 0.9990 Gold 0.0392 oz. AGW, 14 mm. **Ruler:** Elizabeth II **Subject:** Seven Wonders of the World **Obv:** Head right **Rev:** Hanging Gardens of Babylon

Date	Mintage	F	VF	XF	Unc	BU
2009 Proof	7,500	Value: 75.00				

KM# 109   10 DOLLARS
1.2200 g., 0.9990 Gold 0.0392 oz. AGW, 14 mm. **Ruler:**
Elizabeth II **Subject:** Seven Wonders of the World **Obv:** Head
right **Rev:** Lighthouse at Alexandria

Date	Mintage	F	VF	XF	Unc	BU
2009 Proof	7,500			Value: 75.00		

KM# 110   10 DOLLARS
1.2200 g., 0.9990 Gold 0.0392 oz. AGW, 14 mm. **Ruler:**
Elizabeth II **Subject:** Seven Wonders of the World **Obv:** Head
right

Date	Mintage	F	VF	XF	Unc	BU
2009 Proof	7,500			Value: 75.00		

KM# 120   10 DOLLARS
20.0000 g., 0.9250 Silver 0.5948 oz. ASW, 38.61 mm. **Ruler:**
Elizabeth II **Subject:** For World Peace **Rev:** John Paul II and
Mother Theresa

Date	Mintage	F	VF	XF	Unc	BU
2010 Proof	2,500			Value: 75.00		

KM# 121   10 DOLLARS
20.0000 g., 0.9250 Silver 0.5948 oz. ASW, 38.61 mm. **Ruler:**
Elizabeth II **Rev:** S.M.S. Gneisenau under full sail

Date	Mintage	F	VF	XF	Unc	BU
2010 Proof	2,500			Value: 75.00		

KM# 122   10 DOLLARS
25.0000 g., 0.9250 Silver 0.7435 oz. ASW, 38.61 mm. **Ruler:**
Elizabeth II **Rev:** Spotted Cuscus in color with Swarovsky crystal
eyes

Date	Mintage	F	VF	XF	Unc	BU
2010 Proof	2,500			Value: 75.00		

KM# 90   25 DOLLARS
31.1050 g., 0.9990 Silver 0.9990 oz. ASW, 36.6 mm. **Ruler:**
Elizabeth II **Obv:** Head right **Rev:** Wright Brother's 1903 Flyer

Date	Mintage	F	VF	XF	Unc	BU
2003 Proof	—			Value: 42.00		

KM# 91   25 DOLLARS
31.1050 g., 0.9990 Silver 0.9990 oz. ASW, 36.6 mm. **Ruler:**
Elizabeth II **Obv:** Head right **Rev:** AN-225 Mriya

Date	Mintage	F	VF	XF	Unc	BU
2003 Proof	—			Value: 42.00		

KM# 92   25 DOLLARS
31.1050 g., 0.9990 Silver 0.9990 oz. ASW, 36.6 mm. **Ruler:**
Elizabeth II **Obv:** Head right **Rev:** Spitfire

Date	Mintage	F	VF	XF	Unc	BU
2003 Proof	—			Value: 42.00		

KM# 115   25 DOLLARS
31.1000 g., 0.9250 Silver 0.9249 oz. ASW, 38.6 mm. **Ruler:**
Elizabeth II **Obv:** Messerschmitt ME 262

Date	Mintage	F	VF	XF	Unc	BU
2003 Proof	—			Value: 42.00		

KM# 93   25 DOLLARS
31.1050 g., 0.9990 Silver 0.9990 oz. ASW **Ruler:** Elizabeth II
Subject: Trafalgar **Obv:** Head right **Rev:** H.M.S. Victory

Date	Mintage	F	VF	XF	Unc	BU
2005 Proof	—			Value: 42.00		

KM# 114   25 DOLLARS
0.9250 Silver gilt, 50 mm. **Ruler:** Elizabeth II **Rev:** Wright flier
of 1903

Date	Mintage	F	VF	XF	Unc	BU
2005 Proof	—			Value: 75.00		

KM# 95   25 DOLLARS
31.1050 g., 0.9990 Silver partially gilt 0.9990 oz. ASW, 38.6 mm.
Ruler: Elizabeth II **Obv:** Head right, partially gilt **Rev:** Queen
Elizabeth II and WWII Red Cross Nurse, gilt 80 above.

Date	Mintage	F	VF	XF	Unc	BU
2006 Proof	—			Value: 42.00		

KM# 87   25 DOLLARS
0.9250 Silver **Ruler:** Elizabeth II **Obv:** Crowned bust right **Obv.**
Legend: ELIZABETH II - SOLOMON ISLANDS **Rev:** 3/4 length
figures of Elizabeth and Prince Philip facing

Date	Mintage	F	VF	XF	Unc	BU
2006 Proof	—			Value: 45.00		

KM# 87a   25 DOLLARS
31.1050 g., 0.9990 Silver partially gilt 0.9990 oz. ASW **Ruler:**
Elizabeth II **Obv:** Head right, partially gilt **Rev:** Wedding of
Elizabeth II and Philip. Gothic window behind, gilt 80 above.

Date	Mintage	F	VF	XF	Unc	BU
2006 Proof	—			Value: 45.00		

KM# 116   25 DOLLARS
28.2800 g., 0.9250 Silver 0.8410 oz. ASW, 38.6 mm. **Ruler:**
Elizabeth II **Rev:** Press clippings, soldier standing over field cross

Date	Mintage	F	VF	XF	Unc	BU
2008 Proof	—			Value: 42.00		

KM# 117   25 DOLLARS
28.2800 g., 0.9250 Silver 0.8410 oz. ASW, 38.6 mm. **Ruler:**
Elizabeth II **Rev:** Battlefield

Date	Mintage	F	VF	XF	Unc	BU
2008 Proof	—			Value: 42.00		

KM# 118   25 DOLLARS
28.2800 g., 0.9250 Silver 0.8410 oz. ASW, 38.6 mm. **Ruler:**
Elizabeth II **Rev:** Soldier overlooking beach

Date	Mintage	F	VF	XF	Unc	BU
2008 Proof	—			Value: 42.00		

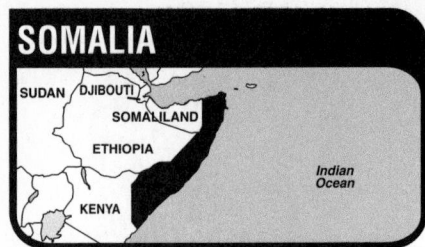

SOMALIA

SUDAN DJIBOUTI
SOMALILAND
ETHIOPIA
KENYA
Indian Ocean

The Somali Republic consists of the former Italian Somaliland and is located on the coast of the eastern projection of the African continent commonly referred to as the "Horn". It has an area of 178,201 sq. mi. (461,657 sq. km.) and a population of *8.2 million. Capital: Mogadishu. The economy is pastoral and agricultural. Livestock, bananas and hides are exported.

The Northern Somali National Movement (SNM) declared a secession of the northwestern Somaliland Republic on May 17, 1991, which is not recognized by the Somali Democratic Republic.

TITLE
Al-Jumhuriya(t)as - Somaliya(t)

REPUBLIC OF SOMALIA

STANDARD COINAGE

KM# 45   5 SHILLING / SCELLINI
1.2900 g., Aluminum, 21 mm. **Series:** F.A.O. **Obv:** Crowned arms with supporters **Rev:** Elephant **Edge:** Plain

Date	Mintage	F	VF	XF	Unc	BU
2002	—			—	1.50	1.75

KM# 159   10 SHILLINGS
25.1500 g., Copper-Nickel, 38.66 mm. **Series:** Marine Life Protection **Obv:** National arms **Rev:** Two fish multicolor **Edge:** Reeded

Date	Mintage	F	VF	XF	Unc	BU
2003 Proof	—	Value: 10.00				

KM# 46   10 SHILLINGS / SCELLINI
1.2900 g., Aluminum, 21.9 mm. **Series:** F.A.O. **Obv:** Crowned arms with supporters **Rev:** Camel **Edge:** Plain

Date	Mintage	F	VF	XF	Unc	BU
2002	—			—	2.00	2.25

KM# 175   20 SHILLINGS
0.6200 g., 0.9990 Gold 0.0199 oz. AGW **Obv:** Arms **Rev:** Mom and baby elephant

Date	Mintage	F	VF	XF	Unc	BU
2007 Proof	—	Value: 50.00				

KM# 166   25 SHILLINGS
Silver **Obv:** Arms **Rev:** Mozart, multicolor

Date	Mintage	F	VF	XF	Unc	BU
2001	—			—	—	40.00

KM# 155   25 SHILLINGS
28.1000 g., Copper-Nickel, 38.73 mm. **Subject:** The Life of Pope John-Paul II **Obv:** National arms **Obv. Legend:** SOMALI REPUBLIC **Rev:** Pope John-Paul II in window at the Vatican **Edge:** Plain

Date	Mintage	F	VF	XF	Unc	BU
2004	—			—	6.00	7.00

KM# 156   25 SHILLINGS
28.1000 g., Copper-Nickel, 38.73 mm. **Subject:** Life of Pope John Paul II **Obv:** National arms **Obv. Legend:** SOMALI REPUBLIC **Rev:** Pope traveling in special vehicle **Edge:** Plain

Date	Mintage	F	VF	XF	Unc	BU
2004	—			—	6.00	7.00

KM# 157   25 SHILLINGS
28.1000 g., Copper-Nickel, 38.73 mm. **Subject:** The Life of Pope John-Paul II **Obv:** National arms **Obv. Legend:** SOMALI REPUBLIC **Rev:** Pope blessing Mother Teresa **Edge:** Plain

Date	Mintage	F	VF	XF	Unc	BU
2004	—			—	6.00	7.00

KM# 164   25 SHILLINGS
25.8000 g., Copper-Nickel, 38.77 mm. **Obv:** National arms **Obv. Legend:** SOMALI REPUBLIC **Rev:** Black rhinoceros walking left **Edge:** Reeded

Date	Mintage	F	VF	XF	Unc	BU
2006	—			—	9.00	14.00

KM# 165   25 SHILLINGS
25.8000 g., Copper-Nickel, 38.77 mm. **Obv:** National arms **Rev:** Red Kite perched on branch **Edge:** Reeded

Date	Mintage	F	VF	XF	Unc	BU
2006	—			—	12.00	14.00

KM# 103   25 SHILLINGS / SCELLINI
4.3700 g., Brass, 21.8 mm. **Subject:** Soccer **Obv:** Crowned arms with supporters **Rev:** Soccer player **Edge:** Plain

Date	Mintage	F	VF	XF	Unc	BU
2001	—			—	1.25	1.50

KM# 111   50 SHILLINGS
3.9000 g., Nickel Clad Steel, 21.9 mm. **Obv:** Crowned arms with supporters **Rev:** Mandrill **Edge:** Plain

Date	Mintage	F	VF	XF	Unc	BU
2002	—			—	0.85	1.25

KM# 161   50 SHILLINGS
1.2000 g., 0.9990 Gold 0.0385 oz. AGW, 13.88 mm. **Subject:** Gold of the Pharaohs **Obv:** National arms **Obv. Legend:** SOMALI REPUBLIC **Rev:** King Tutankhaman's death mask **Edge:** Reeded

Date	Mintage	F	VF	XF	Unc	BU
2002 Proof	—	Value: 80.00				

KM# 109 100 SHILLINGS
10.5000 g., 0.9990 Silver 0.3372 oz. ASW, 30.1 mm. **Subject:**
Soccer **Obv:** Crowned arms with supporters **Rev:** Multicolor
soccer player and Brandenburg Gate **Edge:** Reeded

Date	Mintage	F	VF	XF	Unc	BU
2001 Proof	—	Value: 25.00				

KM# 112 100 SHILLINGS
3.5400 g., Brass, 18.8 mm. **Obv:** Crowned arms with supporters
above value **Rev:** Bust with headdress facing **Edge:** Plain

Date	Mintage	F	VF	XF	Unc	BU
2002	—	—	—	—	1.50	2.50

KM# 176 200 SHILLINGS
0.6200 g., 0.9990 Gold 0.0199 oz. AGW, 13.90 mm. **Obv:** Arms
Rev: Elephant head left

Date	Mintage	F	VF	XF	Unc	BU
2005 Proof	—	Value: 60.00				

KM# 168 250 SHILLINGS
23.0000 g., 0.9250 Silver 0.6840 oz. ASW **Obv:** Arms **Rev:**
Victoria, gothic crown

Date	Mintage	F	VF	XF	Unc	BU
2001 Proof	—	Value: 45.00				

KM# 169 250 SHILLINGS
23.0000 g., 0.9250 Silver 0.6840 oz. ASW **Obv:** Arms **Rev:**
Soccer player, Brazil

Date	Mintage	F	VF	XF	Unc	BU
2002	—	—	—	—	—	45.00

KM# 158 250 SHILLINGS
20.0500 g., Silver, 38.59 mm. **Obv:** National arms **Obv.
Legend:** SOMALI REPUBLIC **Rev:** Laureate bust of Julius
Caesar 3/4 left **Edge:** Reeded

Date	Mintage	F	VF	XF	Unc	BU
2002 Proof	—	Value: 32.00				

KM# 162 250 SHILLINGS
1.2700 g., 0.9990 Gold 0.0408 oz. AGW, 13.90 mm. **Obv:**
National arms **Obv. Legend:** SOMALI REPUBLIC **Rev:** Bust of
Hans Rühmann facing **Edge:** Reeded

Date	Mintage	F	VF	XF	Unc	BU
2002 Proof	—	Value: 80.00				

KM# 110 250 SHILLINGS
31.1050 g., 0.9990 Silver 0.9990 oz. ASW, 40 mm. **Subject:**
Queen of Sheba **Obv:** Crowned arms with supporters **Rev:**
Crowned bust 1/4 right **Edge:** Reeded

Date	Mintage	F	VF	XF	Unc	BU
2002	—	—	—	—	35.00	40.00

KM# 160 250 SHILLINGS
20.5000 g., Silver, 38.56 mm. **Subject:** Wembley Goal - England
1966 **Obv:** National arms **Obv. Legend:** SOMALI REPUBLIC
Rev: 3 soccer players at goal **Edge:** Reeded

Date	Mintage	F	VF	XF	Unc	BU
2003 Proof	—	Value: 25.00				

KM# 121 250 SHILLINGS
20.1200 g., Silver Plated Base Metal, 38.5 mm. **Obv:** Crowned
arms with supporters **Rev:** Multicolor Pope John Paul II and
mountains **Edge:** Reeded

Date	Mintage	F	VF	XF	Unc	BU
2005 Proof	—	Value: 16.50				

KM# 123 250 SHILLINGS
20.1200 g., Silver Plated Base Metal, 38.5 mm. **Obv:** Crowned
arms with supporters **Rev:** Multicolor Pope John Paul II kissing
bible **Edge:** Reeded

Date	Mintage	F	VF	XF	Unc	BU
2005 Proof	—	Value: 16.50				

KM# 125 250 SHILLINGS
20.1200 g., Silver Plated Base Metal, 38.5 mm. **Obv:** Crowned
arms with supporters **Rev:** Multicolor Pope John Paul II with
flowers **Edge:** Reeded

Date	Mintage	F	VF	XF	Unc	BU
2005 Proof	—	Value: 16.50				

KM# 127 250 SHILLINGS
20.1200 g., Silver Plated Base Metal, 38.5 mm. **Obv:** Crowned
arms with supporters **Rev:** Multicolor Pope John Paul II saying
mass **Edge:** Reeded

Date	Mintage	F	VF	XF	Unc	BU
2005 Proof	—	Value: 16.50				

KM# 129 250 SHILLINGS
20.1200 g., Silver Plated Base Metal, 38.5 mm. **Obv:** Crowned
arms with supporters **Rev:** Multicolor Pope John Paul II with
cardinals **Edge:** Reeded

Date	Mintage	F	VF	XF	Unc	BU
2005 Proof	—	Value: 16.50				

KM# 131 250 SHILLINGS
20.1200 g., Silver Plated Base Metal, 38.5 mm. **Obv:** Crowned
arms with supporters **Rev:** Pope John Paul II with red vestments
Edge: Reeded

Date	Mintage	F	VF	XF	Unc	BU
2005 Proof	—	Value: 16.50				

KM# 133 250 SHILLINGS
20.1200 g., Silver Plated Base Metal, 38.5 mm. **Obv:** Crowned
arms with supporters **Rev:** Pope John Paul II in white with skull
cap **Edge:** Reeded

Date	Mintage	F	VF	XF	Unc	BU
2005 Proof	—	Value: 16.50				

KM# 135 250 SHILLINGS
20.1200 g., Silver Plated Base Metal, 38.5 mm. **Obv:** Crowned arms with supporters **Rev:** Multicolor Pope John Paul II leaning head on staff **Edge:** Reeded

Date	Mintage	F	VF	XF	Unc	BU
2005 Proof	—	Value: 16.50				

KM# 137 250 SHILLINGS
20.1200 g., Silver Plated Base Metal, 38.5 mm. **Obv:** Crowned arms with supporters **Rev:** Multicolor Pope John Paul II with staff facing left **Edge:** Reeded

Date	Mintage	F	VF	XF	Unc	BU
2005 Proof	—	Value: 16.50				

KM# 139 250 SHILLINGS
20.1200 g., Silver Plated Base Metal, 38.5 mm. **Obv:** Crowned arms with supporters **Rev:** Multicolor Pope John Paul II with staff facing half right **Edge:** Reeded

Date	Mintage	F	VF	XF	Unc	BU
2005 Proof	—	Value: 16.50				

KM# 143 250 SHILLINGS
Copper-Nickel **Obv:** Crowned shield **Obv. Legend:** SOMALI REPUBLIC / 250 SHILLINGS **Rev:** Color applique, German Shephard **Rev. Legend:** YEAR OF THE DOG / 2006 **Edge:** Reeded

Date	Mintage	F	VF	XF	Unc	BU
2006	—	—	—	—	—	12.50

KM# 144 250 SHILLINGS
Copper-Nickel **Obv:** Crowned shield **Obv. Legend:** SOMALI REPUBLIC / 250 SHILLINGS **Rev:** Color applique, Dachsund **Rev. Legend:** YEAR OF THE DOG / 2006 **Edge:** Reeded

Date	Mintage	F	VF	XF	Unc	BU
2006	—	—	—	—	—	12.50

KM# 145 250 SHILLINGS
Copper-Nickel **Obv:** Crowned shield **Obv. Legend:** SOMALI REPUBLIC / 250 SHILLINGS **Rev:** Color applique, Yorkshire Terrier **Rev. Legend:** YEAR OF THE DOG / 2006 **Edge:** Reeded

Date	Mintage	F	VF	XF	Unc	BU
2006	—	—	—	—	—	12.50

KM# 146 250 SHILLINGS
Copper-Nickel **Obv:** Crowned shield **Obv. Legend:** SOMALI REPUBLIC / 250 SHILLINGS **Rev:** Color applique, Scottie (small white) **Rev. Legend:** YEAR OF THE DOG / 2006 **Edge:** Reeded

Date	Mintage	F	VF	XF	Unc	BU
2006	—	—	—	—	—	12.50

KM# 147 250 SHILLINGS
Copper-Nickel **Obv:** Crowned shield **Obv. Legend:** SOMALI REPUBLIC / 250 SHILLINGS **Rev:** Color applique, Wire-haired Terrier **Rev. Legend:** YEAR OF THE DOG / 2006 **Edge:** Reeded

Date	Mintage	F	VF	XF	Unc	BU
2006	—	—	—	—	—	12.50

KM# 148 250 SHILLINGS
Copper-Nickel **Obv:** Crowned shield **Obv. Legend:** SOMALI REPUBLIC / 250 SHILLINGS **Rev:** Color applique, Bulldog **Rev. Legend:** YEAR OF THE DOG / 2006 **Edge:** Reeded

Date	Mintage	F	VF	XF	Unc	BU
2006	—	—	—	—	—	12.50

KM# 149 250 SHILLINGS
Copper-Nickel **Obv:** Crowned shield **Obv. Legend:** SOMALI REPUBLIC / 250 SHILLINGS **Rev:** Color applique, Golden Retriever **Rev. Legend:** YEAR OF THE DOG **Edge:** Reeded

Date	Mintage	F	VF	XF	Unc	BU
2006	—	—	—	—	—	12.50

KM# 150 250 SHILLINGS
Copper-Nickel **Obv:** Crowned shield **Obv. Legend:** SOMALI REPUBLIC / 250 SHILLINGS **Rev:** Color applique, St. Bernard **Rev. Legend:** YEAR OF THE DOG / 2006 **Edge:** Reeded

Date	Mintage	F	VF	XF	Unc	BU
2006	—	—	—	—	—	12.50

KM# 151 250 SHILLINGS
Copper-Nickel **Obv:** Crowned shield **Obv. Legend:** SOMALI REPUBLIC / 250 SHILLINGS **Rev:** Color applique, Rottweiler **Rev. Legend:** YEAR OF THE DOG / 2006 **Edge:** Reeded

Date	Mintage	F	VF	XF	Unc	BU
2006	—	—	—	—	—	12.50

KM# 152 250 SHILLINGS
Copper-Nickel **Obv:** Crowned shield **Obv. Legend:** SOMALI REPUBLIC / 250 SHILLINGS **Rev:** Color applique, Basset Hound **Rev. Legend:** YEAR OF THE DOG / 2006 **Edge:** Reeded

Date	Mintage	F	VF	XF	Unc	BU
2006	—	—	—	—	—	12.50

KM# 153 250 SHILLINGS
Copper-Nickel **Obv:** Crowned shield **Obv. Legend:** SOMALI REPUBLIC / 250 SHILLINGS **Rev:** Color applique, Sheep Dog **Rev. Legend:** YEAR OF THE DOG / 2006 **Edge:** Reeded

Date	Mintage	F	VF	XF	Unc	BU
2006	—	—	—	—	—	12.50

KM# 154 250 SHILLINGS
Copper-Nickel **Obv:** Crowned shield **Obv. Legend:** SOMALI REPUBLIC / 250 SHILLINGS **Rev:** Color applique, Cocker Spaniel **Rev. Legend:** YEAR OF THE DOG / 2006 **Edge:** Reeded

Date	Mintage	F	VF	XF	Unc	BU
2006	—	—	—	—	—	12.50

KM# 170 250 SHILLINGS
Copper-Nickel Gilt, 38 mm. **Obv:** Arms in cartouche **Rev:** Gold mask of Tutankahamun, enameled

Date	Mintage	F	VF	XF	Unc	BU
2008	—	—	—	—	—	17.50

KM# 171 250 SHILLINGS
Copper-Nickel Gilt, 38 mm. **Obv:** Arms within cartouche **Rev:** Udjat eye, enameled

Date	Mintage	F	VF	XF	Unc	BU
2008	—	—	—	—	—	40.00

KM# 172 250 SHILLINGS
Copper-Nickel **Obv:** Arms within cartouche **Rev:** Statue of Ptah, enameled

Date	Mintage	F	VF	XF	Unc	BU
2008	—	—	—	—	—	20.00

KM# 173 250 SHILLINGS
Copper-Nickel Gilt, 38 mm. **Obv:** Arms in cartouche **Rev:** Jcarab Pectoral necklace, enameled

Date	Mintage	F	VF	XF	Unc	BU
2008	—	—	—	—	—	20.00

KM# 174 250 SHILLINGS
Copper-Nickel Gilt, 38 mm. **Obv:** Arms within cartouche **Rev:** Statue of Horus the Elder

Date	Mintage	F	VF	XF	Unc	BU
2008	—	—	—	—	—	20.00

KM# 122 500 SHILLINGS
18.8400 g., Silver Plated Base Metal, 34.1 mm. **Obv:** Crowned arms with supporters **Rev:** Multicolor Pope John Paul II and mountains **Edge:** Plain **Shape:** Square with round corners

Date	Mintage	F	VF	XF	Unc	BU
2005 Proof	—	Value: 16.50				

KM# 124 500 SHILLINGS
18.8400 g., Silver Plated Base Metal, 34.1 mm. **Obv:** Crowned arms with supporters **Rev:** Multicolor Pope John Paul II kissing bible **Edge:** Plain **Shape:** Square with round corners

Date	Mintage	F	VF	XF	Unc	BU
2005 Proof	—	Value: 16.50				

KM# 126 500 SHILLINGS
18.8400 g., Silver Plated Base Metal, 34.1 mm. **Obv:** Crowned arms with supporters **Rev:** Multicolor Pope John Paul II with flowers **Edge:** Plain **Shape:** Square with round corners

Date	Mintage	F	VF	XF	Unc	BU
2005 Proof	—	Value: 20.00				

KM# 128 500 SHILLINGS
18.1400 g., Silver Plated Base Metal, 34.1 mm. **Obv:** Crowned arms with supporters **Rev:** Multicolor Pope John Paul II saying mass **Edge:** Plain **Shape:** Square with round corners

Date	Mintage	F	VF	XF	Unc	BU
2005 Proof	—	Value: 16.50				

KM# 130 500 SHILLINGS
18.8400 g., Silver Plated Base Metal, 34.1 mm. **Obv:** Crowned arms with supporters **Rev:** Multicolor Pope John Paul II with cardinals **Edge:** Plain **Shape:** Square with round corners

Date	Mintage	F	VF	XF	Unc	BU
2005 Proof	—	Value: 16.50				

KM# 132 500 SHILLINGS
18.8400 g., Silver Plated Base Metal, 34.1 mm. **Obv:** Crowned arms with supporters **Rev:** Pope John Paul II with red vestments **Edge:** Plain **Shape:** Square with round corners

Date	Mintage	F	VF	XF	Unc	BU
2005 Proof	—	Value: 16.50				

KM# 134 500 SHILLINGS
18.8400 g., Silver Plated Base Metal, 34.1 mm. **Obv:** Crowned arms with supporters **Rev:** Pope John Paul II in white with skull cap **Edge:** Plain **Shape:** Square with round corners

Date	Mintage	F	VF	XF	Unc	BU
2005 Proof	—	Value: 16.50				

KM# 136 500 SHILLINGS
18.8400 g., Silver Plated Base Metal, 34.1 mm. **Obv:** Crowned arms with supporters **Rev:** Multicolor Pope John Paul II leaning head on staff **Edge:** Plain **Shape:** Square with round corners

Date	Mintage	F	VF	XF	Unc	BU
2005 Proof	—	Value: 16.50				

KM# 138 500 SHILLINGS
18.8400 g., Silver Plated Base Metal, 34.1 mm. **Obv:** Crowned arms with supporters **Rev:** Multicolor Pope John Paul II with staff facing left **Edge:** Plain **Shape:** Square with round corners

Date	Mintage	F	VF	XF	Unc	BU
2005 Proof	—	Value: 16.50				

KM# 140 500 SHILLINGS
18.8400 g., Silver Plated Base Metal, 34.1 mm. **Obv:** Crowned arms with supporters **Rev:** Multicolor Pope John Paul II with staff facing half right **Edge:** Plain **Shape:** Square with round corners

Date	Mintage	F	VF	XF	Unc	BU
2005 Proof	—	Value: 16.50				

KM# 181 1000 SHILLINGS
31.1050 g., 0.9990 Silver 0.9990 oz. ASW, 39 mm. **Obv:** Arms **Rev:** Heard of six elephants, multicolor

Date	Mintage	F	VF	XF	Unc	BU
2008	—	—	—	—	—	40.00

BULLION COINAGE

KM# 200 20 SHILLINGS
0.6200 g., 0.9990 Gold 0.0199 oz. AGW, 11 mm. **Rev:** Mother and baby elephant

Date	Mintage	F	VF	XF	Unc	BU
2007 Proof	20,000	Value: 50.00				

KM# 208 20 SHILLINGS
0.6200 g., 0.9990 Gold 0.0199 oz. AGW

Date	Mintage	F	VF	XF	Unc	BU
2008 Proof	20,000	Value: 50.00				

KM# 217 20 SHILLINGS
0.6200 g., 0.9990 Gold 0.0199 oz. AGW, 11 mm. **Rev:** Elephant advancing right, sunrise

Date	Mintage	F	VF	XF	Unc	BU
2009 Proof	20,000	Value: 50.00				

KM# 226 20 SHILLINGS
0.6200 g., 0.9990 Gold 0.0199 oz. AGW, 11 mm. **Rev:** Elephant advacning left, sunrise

Date	Mintage	F	VF	XF	Unc	BU
2010 Proof	20,000	Value: 50.00				

KM# 236 20 SHILLINGS
0.6200 g., 0.9990 Gold 0.0199 oz. AGW, 11 mm. **Rev:** Mother and baby elephant walking left, sun high up

Date	Mintage	F	VF	XF	Unc	BU
2011 Proof	20,000	Value: 50.00				

KM# 177 25 SHILLINGS
7.7800 g., 0.9990 Silver 0.2499 oz. ASW

Date	Mintage	F	VF	XF	Unc	BU
2007 Proof	2,000	Value: 15.00				

KM# 205 25 SHILLINGS
7.7800 g., 0.9990 Silver 0.2499 oz. ASW, 26 mm. **Rev:** Heard of six elephants

Date	Mintage	F	VF	XF	Unc	BU
2008 Proof	2,000	Value: 15.00				

KM# 214 25 SHILLINGS
7.7800 g., 0.9990 Silver 0.2499 oz. ASW, 26 mm. **Rev:** Elephant advancing right, sunrise

Date	Mintage	F	VF	XF	Unc	BU
2009 Proof	2,000	Value: 15.00				

KM# 223 25 SHILLINGS
7.7800 g., 0.9990 Silver 0.2499 oz. ASW, 26 mm. **Rev:** Elephant advacning left, sunrise

Date	Mintage	F	VF	XF	Unc	BU
2010 Proof	2,000	Value: 15.00				

KM# 232 25 SHILLINGS
7.7800 g., 0.9990 Silver 0.2499 oz. ASW, 26 mm. **Rev:** Mother and baby elephant walking left, sun high up

Date	Mintage	F	VF	XF	Unc	BU
2011	2,000	Value: 15.00				

KM# 178 50 SHILLINGS
15.5500 g., 0.9990 Silver 0.4994 oz. ASW, 32 mm.

Date	Mintage	F	VF	XF	Unc	BU
2007 Proof	2,000	Value: 30.00				

KM# 206 50 SHILLINGS
15.5500 g., 0.9990 Silver 0.4994 oz. ASW, 32 mm. **Rev:** Heard of six elephants

Date	Mintage	F	VF	XF	Unc	BU
2008 Proof	—	Value: 30.00				

KM# 209 50 SHILLINGS
1.2400 g., 0.9990 Gold 0.0398 oz. AGW, 13.92 mm. **Rev:** Heard of six elephants

Date	Mintage	F	VF	XF	Unc	BU
2008 Proof	10,000	Value: 100				

KM# 215 50 SHILLINGS
15.5500 g., 0.9990 Silver 0.4994 oz. ASW, 32 mm. **Rev:** Elephant advancing right, sunrise

Date	Mintage	F	VF	XF	Unc	BU
2009 Proof	2,000	Value: 30.00				

KM# 218 50 SHILLINGS
1.2400 g., 0.9990 Gold 0.0398 oz. AGW, 13.92 mm. **Rev:** Elephant advancing right, sunrise

Date	Mintage	F	VF	XF	Unc	BU
2009 Proof	10,000	Value: 100				

KM# 224 50 SHILLINGS
15.5500 g., 0.9990 Silver 0.4994 oz. ASW, 32 mm. **Rev:** Elephant advancing left, sunrise

Date	Mintage	F	VF	XF	Unc	BU
2010 Proof	2,000	Value: 30.00				

KM# 227 50 SHILLINGS
1.2400 g., 0.9990 Gold 0.0398 oz. AGW, 13.92 mm. **Rev:** Elephant advancing left, sunrise

Date	Mintage	F	VF	XF	Unc	BU
2010 Proof	10,000	Value: 100				

KM# 233 50 SHILLINGS
15.5500 g., 0.9990 Silver 0.4994 oz. ASW, 32 mm. **Rev:** Mother and baby elephant walking left, sun high up

Date	Mintage	F	VF	XF	Unc	BU
2011 Proof	2,000	Value: 30.00				

KM# 237 50 SHILLINGS
1.2400 g., 0.9990 Gold 0.0398 oz. AGW, 13.92 mm. **Rev:**
Mother and baby elephant walking left, sun high up

Date	Mintage	F	VF	XF	Unc	BU
2011 Proof	10,000	Value: 100				

KM# 182 100 SHILLINGS
31.1050 g., 0.9990 Silver 0.9990 oz. ASW, 39 mm. **Obv:** Arms
Rev: Mom and baby elephant

Date	Mintage	F	VF	XF	Unc	BU
2007	20,000	—	—	—	—	45.00
2007 Proof	5,000	Value: 55.00				

KM# 182a 100 SHILLINGS
31.1050 g., 0.9990 Silver partially gilt 0.9990 oz. ASW, 39 mm.
Rev: Mother and baby elephant, partially gilt

Date	Mintage	F	VF	XF	Unc	BU
2007	3,000	—	—	—	—	50.00

KM# 180 100 SHILLINGS
31.1050 g., 0.9990 Silver 0.9990 oz. ASW, 39 mm. **Rev:** Mother
and baby elephant, colored

Date	Mintage	F	VF	XF	Unc	BU
2007	5,000	—	—	—	—	50.00

KM# 203 100 SHILLINGS
31.1050 g., 0.9990 Silver 0.9990 oz. ASW, 39 mm. **Rev:** Heard
of six elephants

Date	Mintage	F	VF	XF	Unc	BU
2008	20,000	—	—	—	—	35.00
2008 Proof	5,000	Value: 55.00				

KM# 203a 100 SHILLINGS
31.1050 g., 0.9990 Silver partially gilt 0.9990 oz. ASW, 39 mm.
Obv: Arms **Rev:** Heard of six elephants

Date	Mintage	F	VF	XF	Unc	BU
2008	5,000	—	—	—	—	35.00

KM# 204 100 SHILLINGS
31.1050 g., 0.9990 Silver 0.9990 oz. ASW, 39 mm. **Rev:** Heard
of six elephants, multicolored

Date	Mintage	F	VF	XF	Unc	BU
2008	5,000	—	—	—	—	50.00

KM# 212 100 SHILLINGS
31.1050 g., 0.9990 Silver 0.9990 oz. ASW, 39 mm. **Rev:**
Elephant advancing right, sunrise

Date	Mintage	F	VF	XF	Unc	BU
2009	—	—	—	—	—	50.00
2009 Proof	5,000	Value: 55.00				

KM# 212a 100 SHILLINGS
31.1050 g., 0.9990 Silver partially gilt 0.9990 oz. ASW

Date	Mintage	F	VF	XF	Unc	BU
2009	5,000	—	—	—	—	55.00

KM# 213 100 SHILLINGS
31.1050 g., 0.9990 Silver 0.9990 oz. ASW, 39 mm. **Rev:**
Elephant advancing right, sunrise, multicolor

Date	Mintage	F	VF	XF	Unc	BU
2009	5,000	—	—	—	—	55.00

KM# 221a 100 SHILLINGS
31.1050 g., 0.9990 Silver partially gilt 0.9990 oz. ASW

Date	Mintage	F	VF	XF	Unc	BU
2010	5,000	—	—	—	—	55.00

KM# 221 100 SHILLINGS
31.1050 g., 0.9990 Silver 0.9990 oz. ASW, 39 mm. **Rev:**
Elephant advancing left, sunrise

Date	Mintage	F	VF	XF	Unc	BU
2010	—	—	—	—	—	50.00
2010 Proof	5,000	Value: 55.00				

KM# 222 100 SHILLINGS
31.1050 g., 0.9990 Silver 0.9990 oz. ASW, 39 mm. **Rev:**
Elephant advancing left, sunrise, multicolor

Date	Mintage	F	VF	XF	Unc	BU
2010	5,000	—	—	—	—	55.00

KM# 230 100 SHILLINGS
31.1050 g., 0.9990 Silver 0.9990 oz. ASW, 39 mm. **Rev:** Mother
and baby elephant walking left, sun high up

Date	Mintage	F	VF	XF	Unc	BU
2011	—	—	—	—	—	50.00
2011 Proof	5,000	Value: 55.00				

KM# 230a 100 SHILLINGS
31.1050 g., 0.9990 Silver partially gilt 0.9990 oz. ASW

Date	Mintage	F	VF	XF	Unc	BU
2011	5,000	—	—	—	—	55.00

KM# 231 100 SHILLINGS
31.1050 g., 0.9990 Silver 0.9990 oz. ASW, 39 mm. **Rev:** Mother
and baby elephant walking left, sun high up, multicolor

Date	Mintage	F	VF	XF	Unc	BU
2011	5,000	—	—	—	—	55.00

KM# 188 200 SHILLINGS
0.6200 g., 0.9990 Gold 0.0199 oz. AGW

Date	Mintage	F	VF	XF	Unc	BU
2004 Proof	—	Value: 45.00				

KM# 194 200 SHILLINGS
0.6200 g., 0.9990 Gold 0.0199 oz. AGW

Date	Mintage	F	VF	XF	Unc	BU
2005 Proof	20,000	Value: 45.00				

KM# 179   200 SHILLINGS
62.2000 g., 0.9990 Silver 1.9977 oz. ASW, 50 mm.

Date	Mintage	F	VF	XF	Unc	BU
2007 Proof	—	Value: 100				

KM# 207   200 SHILLINGS
62.2000 g., 0.9990 Silver 1.9977 oz. ASW, 50 mm. **Rev:** Heard of six elephants

Date	Mintage	F	VF	XF	Unc	BU
2008 Proof	2,000	Value: 100				

KM# 216   200 SHILLINGS
62.2000 g., 0.9990 Silver 1.9977 oz. ASW, 50 mm. **Rev:** Elephant advancing right, sunrise

Date	Mintage	F	VF	XF	Unc	BU
2009	2,000	Value: 100				

KM# 225   200 SHILLINGS
62.2000 g., 0.9990 Silver 1.9977 oz. ASW, 50 mm. **Rev:** Elephant advacning left, sunrise

Date	Mintage	F	VF	XF	Unc	BU
2010 Proof	2,000	Value: 100				

KM# 234   200 SHILLINGS
62.2000 g., 0.9990 Silver 1.9977 oz. ASW **Rev:** Mother and baby elephant walking left, sun high up **Edge Lettering:** 50

Date	Mintage	F	VF	XF	Unc	BU
2011 Proof	2,000	Value: 100				

KM# 185   250 SHILLINGS
7.7800 g., 0.9990 Silver 0.2499 oz. ASW

Date	Mintage	F	VF	XF	Unc	BU
2004 Proof	2,000	Value: 15.00				

KM# 191   250 SHILLINGS
7.7800 g., 0.9990 Silver 0.2499 oz. ASW

Date	Mintage	F	VF	XF	Unc	BU
2005 Proof	2,000	Value: 15.00				

KM# 197   250 SHILLINGS
7.7800 g., 0.9990 Silver 0.2499 oz. ASW

Date	Mintage	F	VF	XF	Unc	BU
2006 Proof	2,000	Value: 15.00				

KM# 186   500 SHILLINGS
15.5500 g., 0.9990 Silver 0.4994 oz. ASW, 32 mm. **Rev:** Elefant facing forward

Date	Mintage	F	VF	XF	Unc	BU
2004 Proof	2,000	Value: 30.00				

KM# 192   500 SHILLINGS
15.5500 g., 0.9990 Silver 0.4994 oz. ASW

Date	Mintage	F	VF	XF	Unc	BU
2005 Proof	—	Value: 30.00				

KM# 198   500 SHILLINGS
15.5500 g., 0.9990 Silver 0.4994 oz. ASW

Date	Mintage	F	VF	XF	Unc	BU
2006 Proof	2,000	Value: 30.00				

KM# 183   1000 SHILLINGS
31.1050 g., 0.9990 Silver 0.9990 oz. ASW

Date	Mintage	F	VF	XF	Unc	BU
2004	20,000	—	—	—	—	50.00
2004 Proof	5,000	Value: 55.00				

KM# 183a   1000 SHILLINGS
31.2700 g., 0.9990 Silver partially gilt 1.0043 oz. ASW, 38.54 mm. **Series:** African Wildlife **Obv:** National arms **Obv. Legend:** SOMALI REPUBLIC **Rev:** Elephant standing facing - gilt **Edge:** Reeded

Date	Mintage	F	VF	XF	Unc	BU
2004	—	—	—	—	—	55.00

KM# 184   1000 SHILLINGS
31.1050 g., 0.9990 Silver multicolored 0.9990 oz. ASW, 39 mm. **Rev:** Elephant facing forward, colored

Date	Mintage	F	VF	XF	Unc	BU
2004	5,000	—	—	—	—	55.00

KM# 189   1000 SHILLINGS
31.1050 g., 0.9990 Silver 0.9990 oz. ASW, 39 mm. **Rev:** Elephant profile left thrumpanting

Date	Mintage	F	VF	XF	Unc	BU
2005	20,000	—	—	—	—	50.00
2005 Proof	5,000	Value: 55.00				

KM# 189a   1000 SHILLINGS
31.1050 g., 0.9990 Silver partially gilt 0.9990 oz. ASW, 39 mm. **Rev:** Elephant profile left thrumpanting, partially gilt

Date	Mintage	F	VF	XF	Unc	BU
2005	3,000	—	—	—	—	55.00

KM# 190   1000 SHILLINGS
31.1050 g., 0.9990 Silver 0.9990 oz. ASW, 39 mm. **Obv:** Arms **Rev:** Elephant profile left thrumpanting, multicolor

Date	Mintage	F	VF	XF	Unc	BU
2005	5,000	—	—	—	—	45.00

KM# 195   1000 SHILLINGS
31.1050 g., 0.9990 Silver 0.9990 oz. ASW, 38 mm. **Obv:** Arms **Rev:** Elephant and mountain

Date	Mintage	F	VF	XF	Unc	BU
2006	20,000	—	—	—	—	45.00
2006 Proof	5,000	Value: 55.00				

KM# 195a 1000 SHILLINGS
31.1050 g., 0.9990 Silver partially gilt 0.9990 oz. ASW, 39 mm.
Rev: Elephant, mountain, partially gilt

Date	Mintage	F	VF	XF	Unc	BU
2006	3,000	—	—	—	—	55.00

KM# 196 1000 SHILLINGS
31.1050 g., 0.9990 Silver 0.9990 oz. ASW, 39 mm. **Obv:** Arms
Rev: Elephant, mountian in background. Multicolor

Date	Mintage	F	VF	XF	Unc	BU
2006	5,000	—	—	—	—	45.00

KM# 228 1000 SHILLINGS
31.1050 g., 0.9990 Gold 0.9990 oz. AGW, 38.6 mm. **Rev:**
Elephant advacning left, sunrise

Date	Mintage	F	VF	XF	Unc	BU
2010	—	—	—	—	—	1,850

KM# 238 1000 SHILLINGS
31.1050 g., 0.9990 Gold 0.9990 oz. AGW, 38.6 mm. **Rev:**
Mother and baby elephant walking left, sun high up

Date	Mintage	F	VF	XF	Unc	BU
2011	—	—	—	—	—	1,850

KM# 201 1500 SHILLINGS
155.5000 g., 0.9990 Gold 4.9942 oz. AGW, 65 mm. **Rev:** Mother
and baby elephant

Date	Mintage	F	VF	XF	Unc	BU
2007 Proof	99	Value: 9,250				

KM# 210 1500 SHILLINGS
155.5000 g., 0.9990 Gold 4.9942 oz. AGW, 65 mm. **Rev:** Heard
of six elephants

Date	Mintage	F	VF	XF	Unc	BU
2008 Proof	99	Value: 9,250				

KM# 219 1500 SHILLINGS
155.5000 g., 0.9990 Gold 4.9942 oz. AGW, 65 mm. **Rev:**
Elephant advancing right, sunrise

Date	Mintage	F	VF	XF	Unc	BU
2009 Proof	99	Value: 9,250				

KM# 229 1500 SHILLINGS
155.5000 g., 0.9990 Gold 4.9942 oz. AGW, 65 mm. **Rev:**
Elephant advancing left, sunrise

Date	Mintage	F	VF	XF	Unc	BU
2010 Proof	99	Value: 9,250				

KM# 239 1500 SHILLINGS
155.5000 g., 0.9990 Gold 4.9942 oz. AGW, 65 mm. **Rev:** Mother
and baby elephant walking left, sun high up

Date	Mintage	F	VF	XF	Unc	BU
2011	99	Value: 9,250				

KM# 187 2000 SHILLINGS
62.2000 g., 0.9990 Silver 1.9977 oz. ASW, 50 mm. **Rev:**
Elephant facing forward

Date	Mintage	F	VF	XF	Unc	BU
2004 Proof	2,000	Value: 100				

KM# 193 2000 SHILLINGS
62.2000 g., 0.9990 Silver 1.9977 oz. ASW

Date	Mintage	F	VF	XF	Unc	BU
2005 Proof	2,000	Value: 100				

KM# 199 2000 SHILLINGS
62.2000 g., 0.9990 Silver 1.9977 oz. ASW

Date	Mintage	F	VF	XF	Unc	BU
2006 Proof	2,000	Value: 100				

KM# 235   2000 SHILLINGS
1000.0000 g., 0.9990 Silver 32.117 oz. ASW, 100 mm. **Rev:** Mother and baby elephant walking left, sun high up

Date	Mintage	F	VF	XF	Unc	BU
2011	—	—	—	—	—	1,700

KM# 202   5000 SHILLINGS
1000.0000 g., 0.9990 Gold 32.117 oz. AGW

Date	Mintage	F	VF	XF	Unc	BU
2007 Proof	50	Value: 57,000				

KM# 211   5000 SHILLINGS
1000.0000 g., 0.9990 Gold 32.117 oz. AGW

Date	Mintage	F	VF	XF	Unc	BU
2008 Proof	50	Value: 57,000				

KM# 220   5000 SHILLINGS
1000.0000 g., 0.9990 Gold 32.117 oz. AGW **Rev:** Elephant advancing right, sunrise

Date	Mintage	F	VF	XF	Unc	BU
2009 Proof	50	Value: 57,000				

SOMALILAND

The Somaliland Republic consists of the former British Somaliland Protectorate and is located on the coast of the north-eastern projection of the African continent commonly referred to as the "Horn" on the southwestern end of the Gulf of Aden. Bordered by Ethiopia to the west and south and Somalia to the east. It has an area of 68,000* sq. mi. (176,000* sq. km). Capital: Hargeysa. It is mostly arid and mountainous except for the gulf shoreline.

The northern Somali National Movement (SNM) declared a secession of the Somaliland Republic on May 17, 1991, which is not recognized by the Somali Democratic Republic.

REPUBLIC

SHILLING COINAGE

KM# 4   5 SHILLINGS
1.4500 g., Aluminum, 21.9 mm. **Obv:** Value **Rev:** Bust of Sir Richard F. Burton - explorer, divides dates **Edge:** Plain

Date	Mintage	F	VF	XF	Unc	BU
2002	—	—	—	—	1.25	1.50

KM# 5   5 SHILLINGS
1.4500 g., Aluminum, 21.9 mm. **Obv:** Value **Rev:** Rooster **Edge:** Plain

Date	Mintage	F	VF	XF	Unc	BU
2002	—	—	—	—	1.00	1.25

KM# 19   5 SHILLINGS
1.2400 g., Aluminum, 22 mm. **Obv:** Elephant with calf walking right **Obv. Legend:** REPUBLIC OF SOMALILAND **Rev:** Value **Rev. Legend:** BAANKA SOMALILAND **Edge:** Plain

Date	Mintage	F	VF	XF	Unc	BU
2005	—	—	—	—	1.25	1.50

KM# 3   10 SHILLINGS
3.5100 g., Brass, 17.7 mm. **Obv:** Vervet Monkey **Rev:** Value **Edge:** Plain

Date	Mintage	F	VF	XF	Unc	BU
2002	—	—	—	—	0.65	1.25

KM# 7   10 SHILLINGS
4.8000 g., Stainless Steel, 24.9 mm. **Obv:** Value **Rev:** Aquarius the water carrier **Edge:** Plain

Date	Mintage	F	VF	XF	Unc	BU
2006	—	—	—	—	1.00	1.25

KM# 8   10 SHILLINGS
4.8000 g., Stainless Steel, 24.9 mm. **Obv:** Value **Rev:** Pisces the two fish **Edge:** Plain

Date	Mintage	F	VF	XF	Unc	BU
2006	—	—	—	—	1.00	1.25

KM# 9   10 SHILLINGS
4.8000 g., Stainless Steel, 24.9 mm. **Obv:** Value **Rev:** Aries the ram **Edge:** Plain

Date	Mintage	F	VF	XF	Unc	BU
2006	—	—	—	—	1.00	1.25

KM# 10   10 SHILLINGS
4.8000 g., Stainless Steel, 24.9 mm. **Obv:** Value **Rev:** Taurus the bull **Edge:** Plain

Date	Mintage	F	VF	XF	Unc	BU
2006	—	—	—	—	1.00	1.25

KM# 11   10 SHILLINGS
4.8000 g., Stainless Steel, 24.9 mm. **Obv:** Value **Rev:** Gemini twins **Edge:** Plain

Date	Mintage	F	VF	XF	Unc	BU
2006	—	—	—	—	1.00	1.25

KM# 12   10 SHILLINGS
4.8000 g., Stainless Steel, 24.9 mm. **Obv:** Value **Rev:** Cancer the crab **Edge:** Plain

Date	Mintage	F	VF	XF	Unc	BU
2006	—	—	—	—	1.00	1.25

KM# 13   10 SHILLINGS
4.8000 g., Stainless Steel, 24.9 mm. **Obv:** Value **Rev:** Leo the lion **Edge:** Plain

Date	Mintage	F	VF	XF	Unc	BU
2006	—	—	—	—	1.00	1.25

KM# 14 10 SHILLINGS
4.8000 g., Stainless Steel, 24.9 mm. **Obv:** Value **Rev:** Virgo as a winged woman **Edge:** Plain

Date	Mintage	F	VF	XF	Unc	BU
2006	—				1.00	1.25

KM# 15 10 SHILLINGS
4.8000 g., Stainless Steel, 24.9 mm. **Obv:** Value **Rev:** Libra balance scale **Edge:** Plain

Date	Mintage	F	VF	XF	Unc	BU
2006	—				1.00	1.25

KM# 16 10 SHILLINGS
4.8000 g., Stainless Steel, 24.9 mm. **Obv:** Value **Rev:** Scorpio the scorpion **Edge:** Plain

Date	Mintage	F	VF	XF	Unc	BU
2006	—				1.00	1.25

KM# 17 10 SHILLINGS
4.8000 g., Stainless Steel, 24.9 mm. **Obv:** Value **Rev:** Sagittarius the archer **Edge:** Plain

Date	Mintage	F	VF	XF	Unc	BU
2006	—				1.00	1.25

KM# 18 10 SHILLINGS
4.8000 g., Stainless Steel, 24.9 mm. **Obv:** Value **Rev:** Capricorn the goat **Edge:** Plain

Date	Mintage	F	VF	XF	Unc	BU
2006	—				1.00	1.25

KM# 6 20 SHILLINGS
3.8700 g., Stainless Steel, 21.8 mm. **Obv:** Value **Rev:** Greyhound dog **Edge:** Plain

Date	Mintage	F	VF	XF	Unc	BU
2002	—				1.00	1.50

KM# 2 1000 SHILLINGS
31.2700 g., 0.9990 Silver 1.0043 oz. ASW, 38.8 mm. **Obv:** Crowned arms with supporters **Rev:** Bust with hat 3/4 right **Edge:** Reeded

Date	Mintage	F	VF	XF	Unc	BU
2002	—				45.00	50.00

SOUTH AFRICA

The Republic of South Africa, located at the southern tip of Africa, has an area of 471,445 sq. mi. (1,221,043 sq. km.) and a population of *30.2 million. Capitals: Administrative, Pretoria; Legislative, Cape Town; Judicial, Bloemfontein. Manufacturing, mining and agriculture are the principal industries. Exports include wool, diamonds, gold, and metallic ores.

The apartheid era ended April 27, 1994 with the first democratic election for all people of South Africa. Nelson Mandela was inaugurated President May 10, 1994, and South Africa was readmitted into the Commonwealth of Nations.

South African coins and currency bear inscriptions in tribal languages, Afrikaans and English.

MONETARY SYSTEM
100 Cents = 1 Rand

MINT MARKS
GRC + paw print = Gold Reef City Mint

REPUBLIC

STANDARD COINAGE
100 Cents = 1 Rand

KM# 221 CENT
1.5000 g., Copper Plated Steel, 15 mm. **Obv:** New national arms **Obv. Legend:** ISEWULA AFRIKA **Rev:** Value divides two sparrows **Edge:** Plain

Date	Mintage	F	VF	XF	Unc	BU
2001	—			0.15	0.35	0.50
2001 Proof	3,678	Value: 5.00				

KM# 222 2 CENTS
3.0000 g., Copper Plated Steel, 18 mm. **Obv:** New national arms **Obv. Legend:** AFURIKA TSHIPEMBE **Rev:** Eagle with fish in talons divides value **Edge:** Plain

Date	Mintage	F	VF	XF	Unc	BU
2001	—				0.50	0.75
2001 Proof	3,678	Value: 6.00				

KM# 223 5 CENTS
4.4200 g., Copper Plated Steel, 21 mm. **Obv:** New national arms **Obv. Legend:** AFRIKA DZONGA **Rev:** Value and Blue crane **Edge:** Plain

Date	Mintage	F	VF	XF	Unc	BU
2001	—		0.10	0.25	0.65	1.00
2001 Proof	—	Value: 5.00				

KM# 268 5 CENTS
4.5000 g., Copper Plated Steel, 21 mm. **Obv:** New national arms **Obv. Legend:** Ningizimu Afrika **Rev:** Value and Blue crane **Edge:** Plain

Date	Mintage	F	VF	XF	Unc	BU
2002	—			0.30	0.75	1.00
2002 Proof	3,250	Value: 5.00				

KM# 324 5 CENTS
4.5000 g., Copper Plated Steel, 21 mm. **Obv:** New national arms **Obv. Legend:** Afrika Dzonga **Rev:** Blue crane and denomination **Edge:** Plain

Date	Mintage	F	VF	XF	Unc	BU
2003	—			0.30	0.75	1.00
2003 Proof	2,909	Value: 5.00				

KM# 325 5 CENTS
4.5000 g., Copper Plated Steel, 21 mm. **Obv:** New national arms **Obv. Legend:** South Africa **Rev:** Value and Blue crane **Edge:** Plain

Date	Mintage	F	VF	XF	Unc	BU
2004	—			0.20	0.50	0.75
2004 Proof	1,935	Value: 5.00				

KM# 291 5 CENTS
4.5000 g., Copper Plated Steel, 21 mm. **Obv:** New national arms **Obv. Legend:** Aforika Borwa **Rev:** Value and Blue crane **Edge:** Plain

Date	Mintage	F	VF	XF	Unc	BU
2005	—			0.20	0.50	0.75
2005 Proof	—	Value: 5.00				

KM# 486   5 CENTS
4.5000 g., Copper Plated Steel, 21 mm. **Obv:** New National arms **Obv. Legend:** Afrika Borwa **Rev:** Blue crane and value

Date	Mintage	F	VF	XF	Unc	BU
2006	—	—	—	—	0.50	0.75
2006 Proof	—	Value: 5.00					

KM# 340   5 CENTS
4.5100 g., Copper Plated Steel, 21 mm. **Obv:** New national arms **Obv. Legend:** Suid- Afrika **Rev:** Value at left, Blue Crane at right **Edge:** Plain

Date	Mintage	F	VF	XF	Unc	BU
2007	—	—	—	0.20	0.50	0.75
2007 Proof	—	Value: 5.00					

KM# 440   5 CENTS
4.5000 g., Copper Plated Steel, 21 mm. **Obv:** New National arms **Obv. Legend:** uMzantsi Afrika **Rev:** Blue crane and value

Date	Mintage	F	VF	XF	Unc	BU
2008	—	—	—	—	0.75	1.00
2008 Proof	—	Value: 5.00					

KM# 464   5 CENTS
4.5000 g., Copper Plated Steel, 21 mm. **Obv:** National arms **Rev:** Value and Blue crane

Date	Mintage	F	VF	XF	Unc	BU
2009	—	—	—	—	0.50	0.75
2009 Proof	—	Value: 5.00					

KM# 493   5 CENTS
4.5000 g., Copper Plated Steel, 21 mm. **Obv:** National arms **Rev:** Value and Blue crane

Date	Mintage	F	VF	XF	Unc	BU
2010	—	—	—	—	0.75	1.00
2010 Proof	—	Value: 5.00					

KM# 500   5 CENTS
4.5000 g., Copper Plated Steel, 21 mm. **Obv:** National arms **Rev:** Blue crane and vlaue

Date	Mintage	F	VF	XF	Unc	BU
2011	—	—	—	—	0.75	1.00
2011 Proof	—	Value: 5.00					

KM# 224   10 CENTS
2.0000 g., Bronze Plated Steel, 16 mm. **Obv:** New national arms **Obv. Legend:** AFRIKA DZONGA **Rev:** Arum Lily and value **Edge:** Reeded

Date	Mintage	F	VF	XF	Unc	BU
2001	—	—	—	0.30	0.60	1.00
2001 Proof	3,678	Value: 6.00					

KM# 269   10 CENTS
2.0000 g., Bronze Plated Steel, 16 mm. **Obv:** New national arms **Obv. Legend:** Afrika Dzonga **Rev:** Arum Lily and value **Edge:** Reeded

Date	Mintage	F	VF	XF	Unc	BU
2002	—	—	—	0.30	0.75	1.00
2002 Proof	3,250	Value: 6.00					

KM# 347   10 CENTS
2.0000 g., Bronze Plated Steel, 16 mm. **Obv:** New national arms **Obv. Legend:** South Africa **Rev:** Arum lily and value **Edge:** Reeded

Date	Mintage	F	VF	XF	Unc	BU
2003	—	—	—	0.30	0.75	1.00
2003 Proof	2,909	Value: 6.00					

KM# 326   10 CENTS
2.0000 g., Bronze Plated Steel, 16 mm. **Obv:** New national arms **Obv. Legend:** Aforika Borwa **Rev:** Arum lily and value **Edge:** Reeded

Date	Mintage	F	VF	XF	Unc	BU
2004	—	—	—	0.30	0.75	1.00
2004 Proof	1,935	Value: 6.00					

KM# 292   10 CENTS
2.0000 g., Bronze Plated Steel, 16 mm. **Obv:** New national arms **Obv. Legend:** Afrika Borwa **Rev:** Arum Lily and value **Edge:** Reeded

Date	Mintage	F	VF	XF	Unc	BU
2005	—	—	—	0.30	0.75	1.00
2005 Proof	—	Value: 6.00					

KM# 487   10 CENTS
2.0000 g., Bronze Plated Steel, 16 mm. **Obv:** National arms **Obv. Legend:** Suid-Afrika **Rev:** Arum lily and value **Edge:** Reeded

Date	Mintage	F	VF	XF	Unc	BU
2006	—	—	—	—	0.75	1.00
2006 Proof	—	Value: 6.00					

KM# 341   10 CENTS
2.0000 g., Bronze Plated Steel, 16 mm. **Obv:** New national arms **Obv. Legend:** uMzantsi - Afrika **Rev:** Alum lily and value **Edge:** Reeded

Date	Mintage	F	VF	XF	Unc	BU
2007	—	—	—	0.30	0.75	1.00
2007 Proof	—	Value: 6.00					

KM# 441   10 CENTS
2.0000 g., Bronze Plated Steel, 16 mm. **Obv:** National arms **Obv. Legend:** iNingizimu Afrika **Rev:** Arum lily and value **Edge:** Reeded

Date	Mintage	F	VF	XF	Unc	BU
2008	—	—	—	—	0.75	1.00
2008 Proof	—	Value: 8.00					

KM# 465   10 CENTS
2.0000 g., Copper Plated Steel, 16 mm. **Obv:** National arms **Rev:** Arum lily and value

Date	Mintage	F	VF	XF	Unc	BU
2009	—	—	—	—	0.75	1.00
2009 Proof	—	Value: 8.00					

KM# 494   10 CENTS
2.0000 g., Bronze Plated Steel, 16 mm. **Obv:** National arms **Rev:** Arum Lily and value

Date	Mintage	F	VF	XF	Unc	BU
2010	—	—	—	—	0.90	1.20
2010 Proof	—	Value: 7.00					

KM# 501   10 CENTS
2.0000 g., Bronze Plated Steel, 16 mm. **Obv:** National arms **Rev:** Arum lily and value

Date	Mintage	F	VF	XF	Unc	BU
2011	—	—	—	—	0.75	1.00
2011 Proof	—	Value: 6.00					

KM# 225   20 CENTS
3.5000 g., Bronze Plated Steel, 19 mm. **Obv:** New national arms **Obv. Legend:** AFERIKA BORWA **Rev:** Protea flower and value **Edge:** Reeded

Date	Mintage	F	VF	XF	Unc	BU
2001	—	—	—	0.35	0.90	1.20
2001 Proof	3,678	Value: 7.00					

KM# 270   20 CENTS
3.5000 g., Bronze Plated Steel, 19 mm. **Obv:** New national arms **Obv. Legend:** South Africa **Rev:** Protea flower and value **Edge:** Reeded

Date	Mintage	F	VF	XF	Unc	BU
2002	—	—	—	0.35	0.90	1.20
2002 Proof	3,250	Value: 7.00					

KM# 327   20 CENTS
3.5000 g., Bronze Plated Steel, 19 mm. **Obv:** New national arms **Obv. Legend:** Aforika Borwa **Rev:** Protea flower and value **Edge:** Reeded

Date	Mintage	F	VF	XF	Unc	BU
2003	—	—	—	0.35	0.90	1.20
2003 Proof	2,909	Value: 7.00					

KM# 328   20 CENTS
3.5000 g., Bronze Plated Steel, 19 mm. **Obv:** New national arms **Obv. Legend:** Afrika Borwa **Rev:** Protea flower and value **Edge:** Reeded

Date	Mintage	F	VF	XF	Unc	BU
2004	—	—	—	0.35	0.90	1.20
2004 Proof	1,935	Value: 7.00					

KM# 293   20 CENTS
3.5000 g., Bronze Plated Steel, 19 mm. **Obv:** New national arms **Obv. Legend:** Suid-Afrika **Rev:** Protea flower and value **Edge:** Reeded **Shape:** Round

Date	Mintage	F	VF	XF	Unc	BU
2005	—	—	—	0.35	0.90	1.20
2005 Proof	—	Value: 7.00					

KM# 488   20 CENTS
3.5000 g., Bronze Plated Steel, 19 mm. **Obv:** National arms **Obv. Legend:** uMzantsi Afrika **Rev:** Protea flower and value **Edge:** Reeded

Date	Mintage	F	VF	XF	Unc	BU
2006	—	—	—	—	0.90	1.20
2006 Proof	—	Value: 7.00					

KM# 342 20 CENTS
3.5000 g., Bronze Plated Steel, 19 mm. **Obv:** New national arms
Obv. Legend: iNingizimu Afrika **Rev:** Protea flower and value
Edge: Reeded

Date	Mintage	F	VF	XF	Unc	BU
2007	—	—	—	0.35	0.90	1.20
2007 Proof	—	Value: 7.00				

KM# 442 20 CENTS
3.5000 g., Bronze Plated Steel, 19 mm. **Obv:** National arms
Rev: Protea flower and value **Edge:** Reeded

Date	Mintage	F	VF	XF	Unc	BU
2008	—	—	—	—	0.90	1.20
2008 Proof	—	Value: 7.00				

KM# 466 20 CENTS
3.5000 g., Bronze Plated Steel, 19 mm. **Obv:** National arms
Rev: Protea flower and value

Date	Mintage	F	VF	XF	Unc	BU
2009	—	—	—	—	0.90	1.20
2009 Proof	—	Value: 7.00				

KM# 495 20 CENTS
3.5000 g., Bronze Plated Steel, 19 mm. **Obv:** National arms
Rev: Protea flower and vlaue

Date	Mintage	F	VF	XF	Unc	BU
2010	—	—	—	—	0.90	1.50
2010	—	Value: 7.00				

KM# 502 20 CENTS
3.5000 g., Bronze Plated Steel, 19 mm. **Obv:** National arms
Rev: Protea flower and value

Date	Mintage	F	VF	XF	Unc	BU
2011	—	—	—	—	0.90	1.20
2011 Proof	—	Value: 7.00				

KM# 226 50 CENTS
5.0000 g., Bronze Plated Steel, 22 mm. **Obv:** New national arms
Obv. Legend: AFERIKA BORWA **Rev:** Strelitzia plant, value
Edge: Reeded

Date	Mintage	F	VF	XF	Unc	BU
2001	1,152,000	—	—	0.50	1.20	1.60
2001 Proof	3,678	Value: 8.00				

KM# 271 50 CENTS
5.0000 g., Bronze Plated Steel, 22 mm. **Obv:** New national arms
Obv. Legend: Aforika Borwa **Rev:** Strelitzia plant **Edge:** Reeded

Date	Mintage	F	VF	XF	Unc	BU
2002	16,000,000	—	—	0.50	1.20	1.60
2002 Proof	3,250	Value: 8.00				

KM# 287 50 CENTS
5.0000 g., Bronze Plated Steel, 22 mm. **Obv:** New national arms
Obv. Legend: Aforika - Borwa **Rev:** Soccer player and value
Edge: Reeded

Date	Mintage	F	VF	XF	Unc	BU
2002	—	—	—	—	9.00	12.00

KM# 276 50 CENTS
5.0000 g., Bronze Plated Steel, 22 mm. **Obv:** New national arms

---

Obv. Legend: Afrika - Borwa **Rev:** Cricket player diving towards
the wicket, value below **Edge:** Reeded

Date	Mintage	F	VF	XF	Unc	BU
2003	11,749	—	—	—	9.00	12.00

KM# 329 50 CENTS
5.0000 g., Bronze Plated Steel, 22 mm. **Obv:** New national arms
Obv. Legend: Aforika Borwa **Rev:** Cricket player diving towards
the wicket **Edge:** Reeded

Date	Mintage	F	VF	XF	Unc	BU
2003	—	—	—	—	9.00	12.00
2003 Proof	—	Value: 15.00				

KM# 330 50 CENTS
5.0000 g., Bronze Plated Steel, 22 mm. **Obv:** New national arms
Obv. Legend: Afrika Borwa **Rev:** Strelitzia plant, value **Edge:**
Reeded

Date	Mintage	F	VF	XF	Unc	BU
2003	—	—	—	0.50	1.60	1.20
2003 Proof	2,909	Value: 8.00				

KM# 331 50 CENTS
5.0000 g., Bronze Plated Steel, 22 mm. **Obv:** New national arms
Obv. Legend: Suid Afrika **Rev:** Strelitzia plant, value **Edge:**
Reeded

Date	Mintage	F	VF	XF	Unc	BU
2004	—	—	—	0.50	1.20	1.60
2004 Proof	1,935	Value: 8.00				

KM# 294 50 CENTS
5.0000 g., Bronze Plated Steel, 22 mm. **Obv:** New national arms
Obv. Legend: uMzantsi Afrika **Rev:** Strelitzia plant, value **Edge:**
Reeded

Date	Mintage	F	VF	XF	Unc	BU
2005	—	—	—	0.50	1.20	1.60
2005 Proof	—	Value: 8.00				

KM# 489 50 CENTS
5.0000 g., Bronze Plated Steel, 22 mm. **Obv:** National arms
Obv. Legend: iNingizimu Afrika **Rev:** Strelitzia plant and value
Edge: Reeded

Date	Mintage	F	VF	XF	Unc	BU
2006	—	—	—	—	1.20	1.60
2006 Proof	—	Value: 8.00				

KM# 343 50 CENTS
5.0000 g., Bronze Plated Steel, 22 mm. **Obv:** National arms
Obv. Legend: iSewula Afrika **Rev:** Strelitzia plant and value
Edge: Reeded

Date	Mintage	F	VF	XF	Unc	BU
2007	—	—	—	—	1.20	1.60
2007 Proof	—	Value: 8.00				

KM# 443 50 CENTS
5.0000 g., Bronze Plated Steel, 22 mm. **Obv:** National arms
Obv. Legend: Afurika Tshipembe **Rev:** Strelitzia plant and value
Edge: Reeded

Date	Mintage	F	VF	XF	Unc	BU
2008	—	—	—	—	1.20	1.60
2008 Proof	—	Value: 8.00				

KM# 467 50 CENTS
5.0000 g., Bronze Plated Steel, 22 mm. **Obv:** National arms
Rev: Strelitzia plant

Date	Mintage	F	VF	XF	Unc	BU
2009	—	—	—	—	1.20	1.60
2009 Proof	—	Value: 8.00				

KM# 496 50 CENTS
5.0000 g., Bronze Plated Steel, 22 mm. **Obv:** National arms
Rev: Strelitzia plant

Date	Mintage	F	VF	XF	Unc	BU
2010	—	—	—	—	1.20	1.60
2010 Proof	—	Value: 8.00				

KM# 503 50 CENTS
5.0000 g., Bronze Plated Steel, 22 mm. **Obv:** National arms
Rev: Strelitzia plant and value

Date	Mintage	F	VF	XF	Unc	BU
2011	—	—	—	—	1.20	1.60
2011 Proof	—	Value: 10.00				

KM# 227 RAND
4.0000 g., Nickel Plated Copper, 20 mm. **Obv:** New national
arms **Obv. Legend:** SUID-AFRIKA **Rev:** Springbok, value **Edge:**
Segmented reeding

Date	Mintage	F	VF	XF	Unc	BU
2001	—	—	—	0.60	1.50	2.00
2001 Proof	3,678	Value: 10.00				

KM# 272 RAND
4.0000 g., Nickel Plated Copper, 20 mm. **Obv:** New national
arms **Obv. Legend:** Suid-Afrika Afrika Borwa **Rev:** Springbok,
value **Edge:** Segmented reeding

Date	Mintage	F	VF	XF	Unc	BU
2002	—	—	—	0.60	1.50	2.00
2002 Proof	3,250	Value: 10.00				

KM# 275 RAND
4.0000 g., Nickel Plated Copper, 20 mm. **Subject:**
Johannesburg World Summit on Sustainable Development **Obv:**

New national arms **Obv. Legend:** Suid-Afrika - Afrika Borwa **Rev:** World globe and logo **Edge:** Segmented reeding

Date	Mintage	F	VF	XF	Unc	BU
2002	—				12.00	18.00

KM# 332   RAND
4.0000 g., Nickel Plated Copper, 20 mm. **Obv:** New national arms **Obv. Legend:** uMzantsi Afrika Suid-Afrika **Rev:** Springbok, value **Edge:** Segmented reeding

Date	Mintage	F	VF	XF	Unc	BU
2003	—			0.60	1.50	2.00
2003 Proof	2,909	Value: 10.00				

KM# 333   RAND
4.0000 g., Nickel Plated Copper, 20 mm. **Obv:** New national arms **Obv. Legend:** iNingizimu Afrika - uMzantsi Afrika **Rev:** Springbok, value **Edge:** Segmented reeding

Date	Mintage	F	VF	XF	Unc	BU
2004	—			0.60	1.50	2.00
2004 Proof	1,935	Value: 10.00				

KM# 295   RAND
4.0000 g., Nickel Plated Copper, 20 mm. **Obv:** new national arms **Obv. Legend:** iSewula Afrika - iNingizima Afrika **Rev:** Springbok, value **Edge:** Segmented reeding **Shape:** Round

Date	Mintage	F	VF	XF	Unc	BU
2005	—			0.60	1.50	2.00
2005 Proof	—	Value: 10.00				

KM# 490   RAND
4.0000 g., Nickel Plated Copper, 20 mm. **Obv:** National arms **Obv. Legend:** Afurika Tshipembe - iSewula Afrika **Rev:** Springbok and value

Date	Mintage	F	VF	XF	Unc	BU
2006	—				1.50	2.00
2006 Proof	—	Value: 10.00				

KM# 344   RAND
3.9300 g., Nickel Plated Copper, 19.94 mm. **Obv:** Natinal arms **Obv. Legend:** Ningizimu Afrika - Afurika Tshipemba **Rev:** Springbok leaping right **Edge:** segmented reeding

Date	Mintage	F	VF	XF	Unc	BU
2007	—			0.60	1.50	2.00
2007 Proof	—	Value: 10.00				

KM# 444   RAND
4.0000 g., Nickel Plated Copper, 20 mm. **Obv:** National arms **Obv. Legend:** Afrika-Dzonga - Ningizima Afrika **Rev:** Springbok and value

Date	Mintage	F	VF	XF	Unc	BU
2008	—				2.00	2.75
2008 Proof	—	Value: 12.00				

KM# 468   RAND
4.0000 g., Nickel Plated Copper, 20 mm. **Obv:** National arms **Rev:** Spingbok

Date	Mintage	F	VF	XF	Unc	BU
2009	—				1.50	2.00
2009 Proof	—	Value: 10.00				

KM# 497   RAND
4.0000 g., Nickel Plated Copper, 20 mm. **Obv:** National arms **Rev:** Springbok right

Date	Mintage	F	VF	XF	Unc	BU
2010	—			—	1.50	2.00
2010 Proof	—	Value: 10.00				

KM# 508   RAND
3.1100 g., 0.9999 Gold 0.1000 oz. AGW, 16.5 mm. **Subject:** World Cup Soccer

Date	Mintage	F	VF	XF	Unc	BU
2010 Proof	—	Value: 200				

KM# 504   RAND
20.0000 g., Nickel Plated Copper, 20 mm. **Obv:** National arms **Rev:** Springbok and value

Date	Mintage	F	VF	XF	Unc	BU
2011	—			—	1.50	2.00
2011 Proof	—	Value: 10.00				

KM# 228   2 RAND
5.5000 g., Nickel Plated Copper, 23 mm. **Obv:** New national arms **Obv. Legend:** UMZANSTI AFRIKA **Rev:** Greater Kudu, value **Edge:** Segmented reeding

Date	Mintage	F	VF	XF	Unc	BU
2001	3,600,000	—		0.80	2.00	3.00
2001 Proof	3,678	Value: 12.00				

KM# 273   2 RAND
5.5000 g., Nickel Plated Copper, 23 mm. **Obv:** New national arms **Obv. Legend:** iNingizimu Afrika - uMzantsi Afrika **Rev:** Greater Kudu, value **Edge:** Segmented reeding

Date	Mintage	F	VF	XF	Unc	BU
2002	12,000,000	—	—	0.80	2.00	3.50
2002 Proof	3,250	Value: 12.00				

KM# 335   2 RAND
5.5000 g., Nickel Plated Copper, 23 mm. **Obv:** New national arms **Obv. Legend:** iNingizimu Afrika - iSewula Afrika **Rev:** Greater Kudu, value **Edge:** Segmented reeding

Date	Mintage	F	VF	XF	Unc	BU
2003	5,000,000	—		0.80	2.00	3.50
2003 Proof	2,909	Value: 12.00				

KM# 336   2 RAND
5.5000 g., Nickel Plated Copper, 23 mm. **Obv:** New national arms **Obv. Legend:** Afurika Tshipembe / iSewula Afrika **Rev:** Greater Kudu, value **Edge:** Segmented reeding

Date	Mintage	F	VF	XF	Unc	BU
2004	—	—	—	0.80	2.00	3.50
2004 Proof	1,935	Value: 12.00				

KM# 334   2 RAND
5.5000 g., Nickel Plated Copper, 23 mm. **Subject:** 10 Years of Freedom - 1994-2004 **Obv:** New national arms **Obv. Legend:** SOUTH / AFRICA **Rev:** Value, flag logo, people **Edge:** Segmented reeding **Note:** 5,885 issued in souvenir card.

Date	Mintage	F	VF	XF	Unc	BU
2004	—			0.80	2.00	2.75

KM# 296   2 RAND
5.5000 g., Nickel Plated Copper, 23 mm. **Obv:** New national arms **Obv. Legend:** Ningizimu Afrika - Afurika Tshipembe **Rev:** Greater Kudu, value **Edge:** Segmented reeding

Date	Mintage	F	VF	XF	Unc	BU
2005	—			0.80	2.00	2.75
2005 Proof	—	Value: 12.00				

KM# 491   2 RAND
5.5000 g., Nickel Plated Copper, 23 mm. **Obv:** National arms **Obv. Legend:** Afrika-Dzonga - Ningizimo Afrika **Rev:** Greater kudu and value

Date	Mintage	F	VF	XF	Unc	BU
2006	—	—	—	—	2.00	2.75
2006 Proof	—	Value: 12.00				

KM# 345   2 RAND
5.5000 g., Nickel Plated Copper, 23 mm. **Obv:** National arms **Rev:** Greater Kudu

Date	Mintage	F	VF	XF	Unc	BU
2007	—	—	—	0.80	2.00	3.00
2007 Proof	—	Value: 15.00				

KM# 445   2 RAND
5.5000 g., Nickel Plated Copper, 23 mm. **Obv:** National arms **Obv. Legend:** Afrika-Dzonga - South Africa **Rev:** Kudu at center left, value at right **Edge:** Segmented reeding

Date	Mintage	F	VF	XF	Unc	BU
2008	—			0.80	2.00	2.75
2008 Proof	—	Value: 12.00				

KM# 469   2 RAND
5.5000 g., Nickel Plated Copper, 22 mm. **Obv:** National arms **Rev:** Greater Kudu

Date	Mintage	F	VF	XF	Unc	BU
2009	—				2.00	2.75
2009 Proof	—	Value: 12.00				

KM# 498   2 RAND
5.5000 g., Nickel Plated Copper, 23 mm. **Obv:** National arms **Rev:** Greater Kudu

Date	Mintage	F	VF	XF	Unc	BU
2010	—				2.00	2.75
2010 Proof	—	Value: 12.00				

KM# 505   2 RAND
5.5000 g., Nickel Plated Copper, 23 mm. **Obv:** Naitonal arms
Rev: Kudo at center

Date	Mintage	F	VF	XF	Unc	BU
2011	—	—	—	—	2.00	2.75
2011 Proof	—	Value: 12.00				

KM# 229   5 RAND
7.0000 g., Nickel Plated Copper, 26 mm. **Obv:** New national arms **Obv. Legend:** ININGIZIMU AFRIKA **Rev:** Wildebeest, value **Edge:** Segmented reeding

Date	Mintage	F	VF	XF	Unc	BU
2001	2,000,000	—	—	1.20	4.50	6.00
2001 CW	779	—	—	—	67.50	90.00
2001 Proof	3,678	Value: 15.00				

KM# 274   5 RAND
7.0000 g., Nickel Plated Copper, 26 mm. **Obv:** New national arms **Obv. Legend:** Afurika Tshipembe - Isewula Afrika **Rev:** Wildebeest, value **Edge:** Segmented reeding

Date	Mintage	F	VF	XF	Unc	BU
2002	—	—	—	1.20	4.50	6.00
2002 CW	106	—	—	—	—	150
2002 Proof	3,250	Value: 15.00				

KM# 337   5 RAND
7.0000 g., Nickel Plated Copper, 26 mm. **Obv:** New national arms **Obv. Legend:** Afurika Tshipembe - Ningizimu Afrika **Rev:** Wildebeest, value **Edge:** Segmented reeding

Date	Mintage	F	VF	XF	Unc	BU
2003	—	—	—	1.20	4.50	6.00
2003 Proof	2,909	Value: 15.00				

KM# 281   5 RAND
9.5000 g., Bi-Metallic Brass center in Copper-Nickel ring, 26 mm. **Obv:** New national arms **Obv. Legend:** Afrika-Dzonga - Ningizimu Afrika **Rev:** Wildebeest, value **Edge:** Security type with lettering **Edge Lettering:** "SARB R5" repeated ten times

Date	Mintage	F	VF	XF	Unc	BU
2004	—	—	—	1.20	5.00	6.50
2004 CW	3,243	—	—	—	—	22.50
2004 Proof	1,935	Value: 15.00				

KM# 297   5 RAND
9.5000 g., Bi-Metallic Brass center in Copper-Nickel ring, 26 mm. **Obv:** New national arms **Obv. Legend:** Afrika Dzonga - South Africa **Rev:** Wildebeest, value **Edge:** Security type with lettering **Edge Lettering:** "SARB R5" repeated ten times

Date	Mintage	F	VF	XF	Unc	BU
2005	—	—	—	1.20	3.75	5.00
2005 CW	997	—	—	—	—	50.00
2005 Proof	—	Value: 15.00				

KM# 492   5 RAND
5.5000 g., Bi-Metallic Brass center in Copper-Nickel ring., 26 mm. **Obv:** National arms **Obv. Legend:** Aforika Borwa - South Africa **Rev:** Wildebeest and value

Date	Mintage	F	VF	XF	Unc	BU
2006	—	—	—	—	4.50	6.00
2006 Proof	—	Value: 12.00				

KM# 346   5 RAND
9.5000 g., Bi-Metallic Brass center in Copper-Nickel ring, 26 mm. **Obv:** National arms **Obv. Legend:** Aforika Borwa - Afrika Borwa **Rev:** Wildebeest and value **Edge:** Security type and lettered **Edge Lettering:** "SARB R5" repeated ten times

Date	Mintage	F	VF	XF	Unc	BU
2007	—	—	—	1.20	3.00	4.00
2007 CW	—	—	—	—	—	22.50
2007 Proof	—	Value: 15.00				

KM# 446   5 RAND
9.5000 g., Bi-Metallic Brass center in Copper-Nickel ring, 26 mm. **Obv:** National arms **Rev:** Wildebeest rearing left

Date	Mintage	F	VF	XF	Unc	BU
2008	—	—	—	—	3.00	4.00
2008 CW	—	—	—	—	—	22.50
2008 Proof	—	Value: 12.00				

KM# 439   5 RAND
9.5000 g., Bi-Metallic Brass center in Copper-Nickel ring, 26 mm. **Subject:** Nelson Mandella, 90th Birthday **Obv:** National arms **Rev:** Bust facing

Date	Mintage	F	VF	XF	Unc	BU
2008	—	—	—	1.20	3.75	5.00
2008 Proof	—	Value: 15.00				

KM# 470   5 RAND
9.5000 g., Bi-Metallic, 26 mm. **Obv:** National arms **Rev:** Wildebeest rearing left

Date	Mintage	F	VF	XF	Unc	BU
2009 CW	—	—	—	—	—	22.50
2009	—	—	—	—	3.00	4.00
2009 Proof	—	Value: 15.00				

KM# 499   5 RAND
9.5000 g., Bi-Metallic Brass center in Copper-Nickel ring, 26 mm. **Obv:** National arms **Rev:** Wildebeest rearing left

Date	Mintage	F	VF	XF	Unc	BU
2010	—	—	—	—	4.50	6.00
2010 CW	—	—	—	—	—	22.50
2010 Proof	—	Value: 15.00				

KM# 506   5 RAND
9.5000 g., Bi-Metallic Brass center in Copper-Nickel ring, 26 mm. **Obv:** National arms **Rev:** Wildebeest and value

Date	Mintage	F	VF	XF	Unc	BU
2011	—	—	—	—	4.50	6.00
2011 Proof	—	Value: 15.00				

KM# 507   5 RAND
9.5000 g., Bi-Metallic Brass center in Copper-Nickel ring, 26 mm. **Subject:** 90th Anniversary of the Rand **Obv:** National arms **Rev:** Old coin and bank note designs

Date	Mintage	F	VF	XF	Unc	BU
2011	—	—	—	—	4.50	7.00
2011 Proof	—	Value: 12.00				

GOLD BULLION COINAGE

KM# 105   1/10 KRUGERRAND
3.3930 g., 0.9170 Gold 0.1000 oz. AGW, 16.50 mm. **Obv:** Bust of Paul Kruger left **Rev:** Springbok walking right divides date **Edge:** Reeded **Note:** 180 edge serrations for uncirculated, 220 serrations for proof

Date	Mintage	F	VF	XF	Unc	BU
2001	17,936	—	—	—BV+15%		
2001 Proof	4,058	Value: 200				
2002	12,890	—	—	—BV+15%		
2002 Proof	3,110	Value: 200				
2003	15,893	—	—	—BV+15%		
2003 Proof	1,893	Value: 200				
2004	—	—	—	—BV+15%		
2004 Proof	3,811	Value: 200				
2005	—	—	—	—BV+15%		
2005 Proof	—	Value: 200				
2006	—	—	—	—BV+15%		
2006 Proof	—	Value: 200				
2007	—	—	—	—BV+15%		
2007 Proof	4,400	Value: 200				
2008	—	—	—	—BV+15%		
2008 Proof	4,800	Value: 200				
2009	—	—	—	—BV+15%		
2009 Proof	6,000	Value: 200				
2010	—	—	—	—BV+15%		
2010 Proof	6,000	Value: 200				

KM# 106   1/4 KRUGERRAND
8.4820 g., 0.9170 Gold 0.2501 oz. AGW, 22 mm. **Obv:** Bust of Paul Kruger left **Obv. Legend:** SUID — AFRIKA • SOUTH AFRICA **Rev:** Springbok bounding right divides date **Edge:** Reeded **Note:** 180 edge serrations for uncirculated, 220 serrations for proof

Date	Mintage	F	VF	XF	Unc	BU
2001	10,607	—	—	—BV+10%		
2001 Proof	3,841	Value: 475				
2002	10,558	—	—	—BV+10%		
2002 Proof	2,442	Value: 475				
2003	11,468	—	—	—BV+10%		
2003 Proof	2,450	Value: 475				
2004	—	—	—	—BV+10%		
2004 Proof	4,570	Value: 475				
2005	—	—	—	—BV+10%		
2005 Proof	—	Value: 475				
2006	—	—	—	—BV+10%		
2006 Proof	—	Value: 475				
2007	—	—	—	—BV+10%		
2007 Proof	4,400	Value: 475				
2008	—	—	—	—BV+10%		
2008 Proof	4,800	Value: 475				
2009	—	—	—	—BV+10%		
2009 Proof	6,000	Value: 475				
2010	—	—	—	—BV+10%		
2010 Proof	6,000	Value: 475				

KM# 107 1/2 KRUGERRAND
16.9650 g., 0.9170 Gold 0.5001 oz. AGW, 27 mm. **Obv:** Bust of Paul Kruger left **Obv. Legend:** SUID - AFRIKA - SOUTH AFRICA **Rev:** Springbok walking right divides date **Edge:** Reeded **Note:** 180 edge serrations for uncirculated, 220 serrations for proof

Date	Mintage	F	VF	XF	Unc	BU
2001	6,429	—	—	—	BV+8%	—
2001 Proof	3,696	Value: 950				
2002	—	—	—	—	BV+8%	—
2002 Proof	2,295	Value: 950				
2003	11,588	—	—	—	BV+8%	—
2003 Proof	1,285	Value: 950				
2004	—	—	—	—	BV+8%	—
2004 Proof	3,288	Value: 950				
2005	—	—	—	—	BV+8%	—
2005 Proof	—	Value: 950				
2006	—	—	—	—	BV+8%	—
2006 Proof	—	Value: 950				
2007	—	—	—	—	BV+8%	—
2007 Proof	3,400	Value: 950				
2008	—	—	—	—	BV+8%	—
2008 Proof	3,300	Value: 950				
2009	—	—	—	—	BV+8%	—
2009 Proof	2,500	Value: 950				
2010	—	—	—	—	BV+8%	—
2010 Proof	2,500	Value: 950				

KM# 73 KRUGERRAND
33.9300 g., 0.9170 Gold 1.0003 oz. AGW, 32.7 mm. **Obv:** Bust of Paul Kruger left **Obv. Legend:** SUID — AFRIKA • SOUTH AFRICA **Rev:** Springbok walking right divides date **Edge:** Reeded **Note:** 180 edge serrations for uncirculated, 220 serrations for proof

Date	Mintage	F	VF	XF	Unc	BU
2001	5,889	—	—	—	—	BV+5%
2001 Proof	5,563	Value: 1,850				
2002	16,469	—	—	—	—	BV+5%
2002 Proof	3,531	Value: 1,850				
2003	47,789	—	—	—	—	BV+5%
2003 Proof	2,136	Value: 1,850				
2004	71,269	—	—	—	—	BV+5%
2004 Proof	3,492	Value: 1,850				
2004 W/MM Proof	500	Value: 1,850				
2005	—	—	—	—	—	BV+5%
2005 Proof	—	Value: 1,850				
2006	—	—	—	—	—	BV+5%
2006 Proof	—	Value: 1,850				
2007	—	—	—	—	—	BV+5%
2007 Proof	3,400	Value: 1,850				
2008	—	—	—	—	—	BV+5%
2008 Proof	3,300	Value: 1,850				
2009	—	—	—	—	—	BV+5%
2009 Proof	2,500	Value: 1,850				
2010	—	—	—	—	—	BV+5%
2010 Proof	2,500	Value: 1,850				

SILVER BULLION NATURA COINAGE

KM# 242 2-1/2 CENTS
1.4140 g., 0.9250 Silver 0.0420 oz. ASW, 16.3 mm. **Obv:** Crowned arms **Rev:** Dolphin **Edge:** Reeded

Date	Mintage	F	VF	XF	Unc	BU
2001 Proof	—	Value: 27.50				

KM# 480 2-1/2 CENTS
1.4140 g., 0.9250 Silver 0.0420 oz. ASW, 16.3 mm. **Obv:** Flower **Rev:** Vasco de Gama's ship "Sao Gabriel"

Date	Mintage	F	VF	XF	Unc	BU
2009 Proof	3,500	Value: 15.00				

KM# 243 5 CENTS
8.4560 g., 0.9250 Silver 0.2515 oz. ASW, 26.7 mm. **Series:** Wildlife - Power **Obv:** Water buffalo's head **Rev:** Two water buffalo heads within circle below value **Edge:** Reeded

Date	Mintage	F	VF	XF	Unc	BU
2001 Proof	1,853	Value: 40.00				

KM# 351 5 CENTS
8.4560 g., 0.9250 Silver 0.2515 oz. ASW, 26.7 mm. **Series:** Wildlife - Strength **Obv:** Elephant walking, facing **Rev:** Elephant 3/4 left bathing **Edge:** Reeded

Date	Mintage	F	VF	XF	Unc	BU
2002 Proof	2,425	Value: 30.00				

KM# 355 5 CENTS
8.4560 g., 0.9250 Silver 0.2515 oz. ASW, 26.7 mm. **Series:** Wildlife - Survivor **Obv:** New national arms **Rev:** 2 White Rhinoceros drinking at stream **Edge:** Reeded

Date	Mintage	F	VF	XF	Unc	BU
2003 Proof	1,870	Value: 40.00				

KM# 359 5 CENTS
8.4560 g., 0.9250 Silver 0.2515 oz. ASW, 26.7 mm. **Series:** Wildlife - The Legend **Obv:** New national arms **Rev:** Head of Leopard right drinking **Edge:** Reeded

Date	Mintage	F	VF	XF	Unc	BU
2004 Proof	—	Value: 40.00				

KM# 320 5 CENTS
8.4560 g., 0.9250 Silver 0.2515 oz. ASW, 27.12 mm. **Series:**

Wildlife - African Wild Dog **Obv:** New national arms **Rev:** Painted Dog's head facing slightly left **Edge:** Reeded

Date	Mintage	F	VF	XF	Unc	BU
2005 Proof	1,500	Value: 40.00				

KM# 316 5 CENTS
8.4560 g., 0.9250 Silver 0.2515 oz. ASW, 27 mm. **Series:** Wildlife - Black-backed Jackal **Obv:** New national arms **Rev:** Black-backed jackal drinking **Edge:** Reeded

Date	Mintage	F	VF	XF	Unc	BU
2006 Proof	1,500	Value: 40.00				

KM# 363 5 CENTS
8.4560 g., 0.9250 Silver 0.2515 oz. ASW, 26.7 mm. **Series:** Wildlife - Kgalagadi Transfrontier Peace Park **Obv:** New national arms **Rev:** Local desert melons, value **Edge:** Reeded

Date	Mintage	F	VF	XF	Unc	BU
2007 Proof	—	Value: 40.00				

KM# 458 5 CENTS
8.4060 g., 0.9250 Silver 0.2500 oz. ASW, 27 mm. **Subject:** Richtersveld Transfrontier Park **Obv:** Arms **Rev:** Orbea Namaquensis succulant flower

Date	Mintage	F	VF	XF	Unc	BU
2008 Proof	2,200	Value: 30.00				

KM# 482 5 CENTS
8.4060 g., 0.9250 Silver 0.2500 oz. ASW, 27 mm. **Subject:** Maloti Drakensberg Transfrontier Project **Obv:** Arms **Rev:** Spiral Aloe Tree (aloe polyphylla)

Date	Mintage	F	VF	XF	Unc	BU
2009 Proof	3,700	Value: 25.00				

KM# 513 5 CENTS
8.4060 g., 0.9250 Silver 0.2500 oz. ASW, 27 mm.

Date	Mintage	F	VF	XF	Unc	BU
2011 Proof	—	Value: 40.00				

KM# 529 5 CENTS
8.4500 g., 0.9250 Silver 0.2513 oz. ASW, 27 mm. **Subject:** Great Mapungubwe Transfrontier Conservation Area **Obv:** National arms **Rev:** Baobab tree seed pod, sandstone landscape in background

Date	Mintage	F	VF	XF	Unc	BU
2012 Proof	—	Value: 25.00				

KM# 244 10 CENTS
16.8630 g., 0.9250 Silver 0.5015 oz. ASW, 32.7 mm. **Series:**
Wildlife - Power **Obv:** Water buffalo's head **Rev:** Two water
buffalo bulls fighting **Edge:** Reeded

Date	Mintage	F	VF	XF	Unc	BU
2001 Proof	1,989	Value: 65.00				

KM# 352 10 CENTS
16.8130 g., 0.9250 Silver 0.5000 oz. ASW, 38.3 mm. **Series:**
Wildlife - Strength **Obv:** Elephant walking, facing **Rev:** 2 elephant
heads facing each other **Edge:** Reeded

Date	Mintage	F	VF	XF	Unc	BU
2002 Proof	2,395	Value: 55.00				

KM# 356 10 CENTS
16.8130 g., 0.9250 Silver 0.5000 oz. ASW, 32.7 mm. **Series:**
Wildlife - Survivor **Obv:** New national arms **Rev:** 2 Black
Rhinoceros standing, facing **Edge:** Reeded

Date	Mintage	F	VF	XF	Unc	BU
2003 Proof	1,815	Value: 65.00				

KM# 360 10 CENTS
16.8130 g., 0.9250 Silver 0.5000 oz. ASW, 32.7 mm. **Series:**
Wildlife - The Legend **Obv:** New national arms **Rev:** Leopard and
impala above two leopard cubs playing **Edge:** Reeded

Date	Mintage	F	VF	XF	Unc	BU
2004 Proof	—	Value: 65.00				

KM# 321 10 CENTS
16.8130 g., 0.9250 Silver 0.5000 oz. ASW, 32.7 mm. **Series:**
Wildlife - African Wild Dog **Obv:** New national arms **Rev:** Two
Painted Dogs walking right **Edge:** Reeded

Date	Mintage	F	VF	XF	Unc	BU
2005 Proof	1,500	Value: 65.00				

KM# 317 10 CENTS
16.8630 g., 0.9250 Silver 0.5015 oz. ASW, 32.7 mm. **Series:**
Wildlife - Black-backed Jackel **Obv:** New national arms **Rev:**
Black-backed jackal chasing birds **Edge:** Reeded

Date	Mintage	F	VF	XF	Unc	BU
2006 Proof	1,500	Value: 65.00				

KM# 364 10 CENTS
16.8130 g., 0.9250 Silver 0.5000 oz. ASW, 32.7 mm. **Series:**
Wildlife - Kgaladadi Transfrontier Peace Park **Obv:** New national
arms **Rev:** Local tribe, value **Edge:** Reeded

Date	Mintage	F	VF	XF	Unc	BU
2007 Proof	—	Value: 65.00				

KM# 459 10 CENTS
16.8130 g., 0.9250 Silver 0.5000 oz. ASW, 32.7 mm. **Subject:**
Richtersveld Transfrontier Park **Obv:** Arms **Rev:** Local Nama
native and livestock

Date	Mintage	F	VF	XF	Unc	BU
2008 Proof	2,200	Value: 55.00				

KM# 483 10 CENTS
16.8130 g., 0.9250 Silver 0.5000 oz. ASW, 32.7 mm. **Subject:**
Maloti Drakensberg Transfrontier Project **Obv:** Arms **Rev:** Native
Basotho riding pony

Date	Mintage	F	VF	XF	Unc	BU
2009 Proof	3,700	Value: 45.00				

KM# 514 10 CENTS
16.8130 g., 0.9250 Silver 0.5000 oz. ASW, 32.7 mm.

Date	Mintage	F	VF	XF	Unc	BU
2011 Proof	—	Value: 65.00				

KM# 530 10 CENTS
16.8630 g., 0.9250 Silver 0.5015 oz. ASW, 32.82 mm. **Subject:**

Great Mapungubwe Transfrontier Conservation Area **Obv:**
National arms **Rev:** Golden Rhino and sandstone rock formations
in background

Date	Mintage	F	VF	XF	Unc	BU
2012 Proof	—	Value: 65.00				

KM# 245 20 CENTS
33.7260 g., 0.9250 Silver 1.0030 oz. ASW, 38.3 mm. **Series:**
Wildlife - Power **Obv:** Water buffalo's head **Rev:** Two water
buffalo heads facing **Edge:** Reeded

Date	Mintage	F	VF	XF	Unc	BU
2001 Proof	1,902	Value: 85.00				

KM# 353 20 CENTS
33.7260 g., 0.9250 Silver 1.0030 oz. ASW, 38.3 mm. **Series:**
Wildlife - Strength **Obv:** Elephant walking, facing **Rev:** Family of
four elephants **Edge:** Reeded

Date	Mintage	F	VF	XF	Unc	BU
2002 Proof	2,435	Value: 75.00				

KM# 357 20 CENTS
33.7260 g., 0.9250 Silver 1.0030 oz. ASW, 38.3 mm. **Series:**
Wildlife - Survivor **Obv:** New national arms **Rev:** White
Rhinoceros mother with an offspring **Edge:** Reeded

Date	Mintage	F	VF	XF	Unc	BU
2003 Proof	1,930	Value: 85.00				

KM# 361 20 CENTS
33.7260 g., 0.9250 Silver 1.0030 oz. ASW, 38.3 mm. **Series:**
Wildlife - The legend **Obv:** New national arms **Rev:** Leopard
looking left, cub on branch behind her **Edge:** Reeded

Date	Mintage	F	VF	XF	Unc	BU
2004 Proof	—	Value: 85.00				

KM# 322   20 CENTS
33.7500 g., 0.9250 Silver 1.0037 oz. ASW, 38.67 mm. **Series:**
Wildlife - African Wild Dog **Obv:** New National arms **Rev:** Three
Painted Dogs **Edge:** Reeded

Date	Mintage	F	VF	XF	Unc	BU
2005 Proof	1,500	Value: 85.00				

KM# 318   20 CENTS
33.7260 g., 0.9250 Silver 1.0030 oz. ASW, 38.7 mm. **Series:**
Wildlife - Black-backed Jackal **Obv:** National arms **Rev:** Two
Black-backed jackals **Edge:** Reeded

Date	Mintage	F	VF	XF	Unc	BU
2006 Proof	1,500	Value: 85.00				

KM# 365   20 CENTS
33.7260 g., 0.9250 Silver 1.0030 oz. ASW, 38.3 mm. **Series:**
Wildlife - Kgalagadi Transfrontier Peace Park **Obv:** New national
arms **Rev:** Lion's head 3/4 right at left, meerkat standing with
offspring at right, value **Edge:** Reeded

Date	Mintage	F	VF	XF	Unc	BU
2007 Proof	—	Value: 85.00				

KM# 460   20 CENTS
33.7250 g., 0.9250 Silver 1.0029 oz. ASW, 38.7 mm. **Subject:**
Richtersveld Transfrontier Park **Obv:** Arms **Rev:** Two shy
Kipspringer (Oreotragus oreotragos)

Date	Mintage	F	VF	XF	Unc	BU
2008 Proof	2,200	Value: 75.00				

KM# 484   20 CENTS
33.6200 g., 0.9250 Silver 0.9998 oz. ASW, 38.72 mm. **Subject:**
Maloti Drakensberg Transfrontier Project **Obv:** Arms **Rev:** Cape
griffon vulture

Date	Mintage	F	VF	XF	Unc	BU
2009 Proof	3,700	Value: 75.00				

KM# 531   20 CENTS
33.7260 g., 0.9250 Silver 1.0030 oz. ASW, 38.3 mm. **Subject:**
Great Mapungubwe Transfrontier Conservation Area **Obv:**
National arms **Rev:** Pel's Fishing Owl (scotopelia peli) and
standstone rock formations in background

Date	Mintage	F	VF	XF	Unc	BU
2012 Proof	—	Value: 85.00				

KM# 246   50 CENTS
76.4020 g., 0.9250 Silver 2.2721 oz. ASW, 50 mm. **Series:**
Wildlife - Power **Obv:** Water buffalo's head **Rev:** Water buffalo
head, value **Edge:** Reeded

Date	Mintage	F	VF	XF	Unc	BU
2001 Proof	1,866	Value: 110				

KM# 354   50 CENTS
76.4020 g., 0.9250 Silver 2.2721 oz. ASW, 50 mm. **Series:**
Wildlife - Strength **Obv:** Elephant walking, facing **Rev:** Elephant
right with head raised **Edge:** Reeded

Date	Mintage	F	VF	XF	Unc	BU
2002 Proof	2,318	Value: 110				

KM# 358   50 CENTS
76.4020 g., 0.9250 Silver 2.2721 oz. ASW, 50 mm. **Series:**
Wildlife - Survivor **Obv:** New national arms **Rev:** White
Rhinoceros' head 3/4 right, value **Edge:** Reeded

Date	Mintage	F	VF	XF	Unc	BU
2003 Proof	1,918	Value: 110				

KM# 362   50 CENTS
76.4620 g., 0.9250 Silver 2.2738 oz. ASW, 50 mm. **Series:**
Wildlife - The Legend **Obv:** New national arms **Rev:** Leopard
facing snarling, two leopards at lower left **Edge:** Reeded

Date	Mintage	F	VF	XF	Unc	BU
2004 Proof	—	Value: 110				

KM# 323   50 CENTS
76.8600 g., 0.9250 Silver 2.2857 oz. ASW, 50.48 mm. **Series:**
Wildlife - African Wild Dog **Obv:** New national arms **Rev:** Two
painted Dog's heads facing **Edge:** Reeded

Date	Mintage	F	VF	XF	Unc	BU
2005 Proof	1,500	Value: 110				

KM# 319   50 CENTS
76.2520 g., 0.9250 Silver 2.2676 oz. ASW, 50 mm. **Series:**
Wildlife - Black-backed Jackal **Obv:** New national arms **Rev:** Two
black-backed jackals fighting over a carcass **Edge:** Reeded

Date	Mintage	F	VF	XF	Unc	BU
2006 Proof	1,500	Value: 110				

KM# 366 50 CENTS
76.4020 g., 0.9250 Silver 2.2721 oz. ASW, 50 mm. **Series:** Wildlife - Kgalagadi Transfrontier Peace Park **Obv:** New national arms **Rev:** Antelope running right **Edge:** Reeded

Date	Mintage	F	VF	XF	Unc	BU
2007 Proof	—	Value: 110				

KM# 461 50 CENTS
76.2520 g., 0.9250 Silver 2.2676 oz. ASW, 50 mm. **Subject:** Richtersveld Transfrontier Park **Obv:** Arms **Rev:** Giant aloe pillansii tree

Date	Mintage	F	VF	XF	Unc	BU
2008 Proof	2,200	Value: 110				

KM# 485 50 CENTS
76.2520 g., 0.9250 Silver 2.2676 oz. ASW, 50 mm. **Subject:** Maloti Drakensberg Transfrontier Project **Obv:** Arms **Rev:** Amphitheatre and Trukela River

Date	Mintage	F	VF	XF	Unc	BU
2009 Proof	3,700	Value: 100				

KM# 516 50 CENTS
76.4020 g., 0.9250 Silver 2.2721 oz. ASW, 50 mm.

Date	Mintage	F	VF	XF	Unc	BU
2011 Proof	—	Value: 110				

KM# 532 50 CENTS
76.4020 g., 0.9250 Silver 2.2721 oz. ASW, 50 mm. **Subject:** Great Mapungubwe Transfrontier Conservation Area **Obv:** National Arms **Rev:** Baobab Tree and sandstone landscape in background

Date	Mintage	F	VF	XF	Unc	BU
2012 Proof	—	Value: 110				

KM# 248 2 RAND
33.6260 g., 0.9250 Silver 1.0000 oz. ASW, 38.7 mm. **Obv:** New national arms **Rev:** Dolphins **Edge:** Reeded

Date	Mintage	F	VF	XF	Unc	BU
2001 Proof	2,987	Value: 80.00				

KM# 280 2 RAND
33.6260 g., 0.9250 Silver 1.0000 oz. ASW, 38.7 mm. **Obv:** New national arms **Rev:** Southern Right Whale **Edge:** Reeded

Date	Mintage	F	VF	XF	Unc	BU
2002 Proof	1,808	Value: 85.00				

KM# 286 2 RAND
33.6260 g., 0.9250 Silver 1.0000 oz. ASW, 38.7 mm. **Obv:** New national arms **Rev:** Martial and Bateleur Eagles **Edge:** Reeded

Date	Mintage	F	VF	XF	Unc	BU
2003 Proof	2,166	Value: 75.00				

KM# 284 2 RAND
33.6260 g., 0.9250 Silver 1.0000 oz. ASW, 38.7 mm. **Obv:** New national arms **Rev:** Verreaux's Eagle Owl face and value **Edge:** Reeded

Date	Mintage	F	VF	XF	Unc	BU
2004	—	—	—	—	50.00	55.00
2004 Proof	1,752	Value: 85.00				

KM# 372 2 RAND
33.6260 g., 0.9250 Silver 1.0000 oz. ASW, 38.7 mm. **Obv:** New national arms **Rev:** Three vultures **Edge:** Reeded

Date	Mintage	F	VF	XF	Unc	BU
2005 Proof	4,000	Value: 70.00				

KM# 374 2 RAND
33.6260 g., 0.9250 Silver 1.0000 oz. ASW, 38.7 mm. **Series:** Bird of Prey **Obv:** New national arms **Rev:** Two Secretary birds **Edge:** Reeded

Date	Mintage	F	VF	XF	Unc	BU
2006 Proof	4,000	Value: 75.00				

KM# 481 2 RAND
33.6260 g., 0.9250 Silver 1.0000 oz. ASW, 38.7 mm. **Obv:** Arms and country name **Rev:** Jan van Riebeeck's ship "Drommedaries"

Date	Mintage	F	VF	XF	Unc	BU
2009 Proof	3,500	Value: 55.00				

KM# 515 20 RAND
33.7260 g., 0.9250 Silver 1.0030 oz. ASW, 38.72 mm.

Date	Mintage	F	VF	XF	Unc	BU
2011 Proof	—	Value: 85.00				

SILVER BULLION PROTEA COINAGE

KM# 282 2-1/2 CENTS
1.4140 g., 0.9250 Silver 0.0420 oz. ASW, 16.3 mm. **Obv:** Protea flower **Rev:** Southern Right Whale **Edge:** Plain

Date	Mintage	F	VF	XF	Unc	BU
2002 Proof	3,000	Value: 27.50				

KM# 285 2-1/2 CENTS
1.4140 g., 0.9250 Silver 0.0420 oz. ASW, 16.3 mm. **Obv:** Protea flower **Rev:** Martial and Bateleur Eagles **Edge:** Plain

Date	Mintage	F	VF	XF	Unc	BU
2003 Proof	—	Value: 25.00				

KM# 283 2-1/2 CENTS
1.4140 g., 0.9250 Silver 0.0420 oz. ASW, 16.3 mm. **Series:** Birds of Prey **Obv:** Protea flower **Rev:** Pearl Spotted Owlet **Edge:** Plain

Date	Mintage	F	VF	XF	Unc	BU
2004 Proof	2,000	Value: 25.00				

KM# 348   2-1/2 CENTS
1.4140 g., 0.9250 Silver 0.0420 oz. ASW, 16.3 mm. **Obv:** Protea flower **Obv. Legend:** SOUTH AFRICA **Rev:** Vulture alighting **Edge:** Plain

Date	Mintage	F	VF	XF	Unc	BU
2005 Proof	—	Value: 25.00				

KM# 349   2-1/2 CENTS
1.4140 g., 0.9250 Silver 0.0420 oz. ASW, 16.3 mm. **Obv:** Protea flower **Obv. Legend:** SOUTH AFRICA **Rev:** Head of Secretary bird **Edge:** Plain

Date	Mintage	F	VF	XF	Unc	BU
2006 Proof	—	Value: 25.00				

KM# 350   2-1/2 CENTS
1.4140 g., 0.9250 Silver 0.0420 oz. ASW, 16.3 mm. **Subject:** International Polar Year **Obv:** Protea flower **Obv. Legend:** SOUTH AFRICA **Rev:** Globe displaying South Pole **Edge:** Plain

Date	Mintage	F	VF	XF	Unc	BU
2007 Proof	—	Value: 25.00				

KM# 456   2-1/2 CENTS
1.4140 g., 0.9250 Silver 0.0420 oz. ASW, 16.3 mm. **Obv:** Flower **Rev:** Map of Antarctica

Date	Mintage	F	VF	XF	Unc	BU
2008 Proof	3,000	Value: 15.00				

KM# 231   RAND
15.0000 g., 0.9250 Silver 0.4461 oz. ASW, 32.7 mm. **Subject:** Tourism **Obv:** Protea flower **Rev:** Steam locomotive and flower **Edge:** Reeded

Date	Mintage	F	VF	XF	Unc	BU
2001	2,400	—	—	—	40.00	45.00
2001 Proof	1,784	Value: 65.00				

KM# 277   RAND
15.0000 g., 0.9250 Silver 0.4461 oz. ASW, 32.7 mm. **Subject:** Soccer **Obv:** Protea flower **Rev:** Goalkeeper in action **Edge:** Reeded

Date	Mintage	F	VF	XF	Unc	BU
2002	1,777	—	—	—	40.00	45.00
2002 Proof	1,250	Value: 65.00				

KM# 367   RAND
15.5500 g., 0.9250 Silver 0.4624 oz. ASW **Subject:** World Summit - Johannesburg **Obv:** Protea flower **Rev:** Globe **Edge:** Reeded

Date	Mintage	F	VF	XF	Unc	BU
2002	1,531	—	—	—	55.00	60.00
2002 Proof	1,413	Value: 75.00				

KM# 298   RAND
15.0500 g., 0.9250 Silver 0.4476 oz. ASW, 32.7 mm. **Obv:** Protea flower **Rev:** Cricket player **Edge:** Reeded

Date	Mintage	F	VF	XF	Unc	BU
2003	1,697	—	—	—	55.00	60.00
2003 Proof	1,250	Value: 75.00				

KM# 288   RAND
15.0000 g., 0.9250 Silver 0.4461 oz. ASW, 32.7 mm. **Subject:** 10th Anniversary of South African Democracy **Obv:** Protea flower **Rev:** Flora and fauna **Edge:** Reeded

Date	Mintage	F	VF	XF	Unc	BU
2004	3,427	—	—	—	35.00	40.00
2004 Proof	2,930	Value: 50.00				

KM# 368   RAND
15.0000 g., 0.9250 Silver 0.4461 oz. ASW, 32.7 mm. **Series:** Nobel Peace Prize Winners **Obv:** Protea flower **Rev:** Bust of Chief A. J. Luthuli facing at center, Luthuli seated at desk left at lower right **Edge:** Reeded

Date	Mintage	F	VF	XF	Unc	BU
2005	—	—	—	—	50.00	55.00
2005 Proof	—	Value: 65.00				

KM# 369   RAND
15.0000 g., 0.9250 Silver 0.4461 oz. ASW, 32.7 mm. **Series:** Nobel Peace prize Winners **Obv:** Protea flower **Rev:** 1/3 length figure of Archbishop Desmond Mpilo Tutu facing at right **Edge:** Reeded

Date	Mintage	F	VF	XF	Unc	BU
2006	—	—	—	—	60.00	65.00
2006	—	Value: 75.00				

KM# 370   RAND
15.0000 g., 0.9250 Silver 0.4461 oz. ASW, 32.7 mm. **Series:** Nobel Peace Prize Winners **Obv:** Protea flower **Rev:** Bust of De Klerk facing **Edge:** Reeded

Date	Mintage	F	VF	XF	Unc	BU
2007	—	—	—	—	55.00	60.00
2007 Proof	—	Value: 70.00				

KM# 371   RAND
15.5500 g., 0.9250 Silver 0.4624 oz. ASW, 32.7 mm. **Series:** Nobel Peace Prize Winners **Obv:** Protea flower **Rev:** Bust of Mandela facing **Edge:** Reeded

Date	Mintage	F	VF	XF	Unc	BU
2007	—	—	—	—	65.00	75.00
2007 Proof	—	Value: 95.00				

KM# 451   RAND
15.5500 g., 0.9250 Silver 0.4624 oz. ASW, 32.7 mm. **Obv:** Protea flower **Rev:** Ghandi portrait

Date	Mintage	F	VF	XF	Unc	BU
2008	—	—	—	—	—	22.00
2008 Proof	11,000	Value: 27.00				

KM# 475   RAND
15.5500 g., 0.9250 Silver 0.4624 oz. ASW, 32.7 mm. **Obv:** Protea flower **Rev:** Portraits of C. J. Langenhoven and N. L. de Villiers with musical score

Date	Mintage	F	VF	XF	Unc	BU
2009	—	—	—	—	—	20.00
2009 Proof	11,000	Value: 27.00				

SILVER BULLION CULTURE COINAGE

KM# 456   2-1/2 CENTS
1.4140 g., 0.9250 Silver 0.0420 oz. ASW, 16.3 mm. **Obv:** Flower **Rev:** Map of Antarctica

Date	Mintage	F	VF	XF	Unc	BU
2008 Proof	3,000	Value: 15.00				

KM# 373   2 RAND
33.6260 g., 0.9250 Silver 1.0000 oz. ASW, 38.7 mm. **Subject:** 2006 FIFA World Cup Soccer - Germany **Obv:** New national arms **Rev:** Soccer ball above globe **Edge:** Reeded

Date	Mintage	F	VF	XF	Unc	BU
2005 Proof	50,000	Value: 60.00				

KM# 435   2 RAND
33.6260 g., 0.9250 Silver 1.0000 oz. ASW, 38.7 mm. **Subject:** 2010 World Cup

Date	Mintage	F	VF	XF	Unc	BU
2006	25,000	—	—	—	—	50.00

KM# 376   2 RAND
33.6260 g., 0.9250 Silver 1.0000 oz. ASW, 38.7 mm. **Subject:** International Polar Year **Obv:** New national arms **Rev:** Logo above globe **Edge:** Reeded

Date	Mintage	F	VF	XF	Unc	BU
2007 Proof	6,000	Value: 70.00				

KM# 377   2 RAND
33.6260 g., 0.9250 Silver 1.0000 oz. ASW, 38.7 mm. **Subject:** 2010 FIFA World Cup Soccer - South Africa **Obv:** New national arms **Rev:** Tower at left, animal heads at top. animal at right, soccer ball ar bottom **Edge:** Reeded

Date	Mintage	F	VF	XF	Unc	BU
2007 Proof	20,000	Value: 65.00				

KM# 437   2 RAND
33.6260 g., 0.9250 Silver 1.0000 oz. ASW, 38.7 mm. **Subject:**
2010 World Cup

Date	Mintage	F	VF	XF	Unc	BU
2008 Proof	—	Value: 55.00				

KM# 457   2 RAND
33.6260 g., 0.9250 Silver 1.0000 oz. ASW, 38.7 mm. **Obv:** Arms
Rev: Polar ship "SA Sgulhas"

Date	Mintage	F	VF	XF	Unc	BU
2008 Proof	3,000	Value: 55.00				

GOLD BULLION NATURA COINAGE

KM# 517   2 RAND
7.7700 g., 0.9999 Gold 0.2498 oz. AGW, 22 mm.

Date	Mintage	F	VF	XF	Unc	BU
2011 Proof	—	Value: 450				

KM# 533   2 RAND
7.7700 g., 0.9999 Gold 0.2498 oz. AGW, 22 mm. **Subject:**
Khoisan Heritage **Obv:** National Arms **Rev:** Incuse stone carving
of an eland

Date	Mintage	F	VF	XF	Unc	BU
2012 Proof	—	Value: 450				

KM# 410   10 RAND
3.1107 g., 0.9999 Gold 0.1000 oz. AGW, 16.5 mm. **Series:**
Natura **Obv:** Cheetah's head **Rev:** Cheetah drinking water **Edge:**
Reeded

Date	Mintage	F	VF	XF	Unc	BU
2002 Proof	3,156	Value: 200				

KM# 414   10 RAND
3.1107 g., 0.9999 Gold 0.1000 oz. AGW, 16.5 mm. **Series:**
Natura **Obv:** Male and female lion's heads **Rev:** Two lioness
drinking water **Edge:** Reeded

Date	Mintage	F	VF	XF	Unc	BU
2003 Proof	4,233	Value: 200				

KM# 418   10 RAND
3.1107 g., 0.9999 Gold 0.1000 oz. AGW, 16.5 mm. **Series:**
Natura **Obv:** Caracal's head and shoulders **Rev:** Caracal drinking
water **Edge:** Reeded

Date	Mintage	F	VF	XF	Unc	BU
2004 Proof	1,809	Value: 210				

KM# 422   10 RAND
3.1107 g., 0.9999 Gold 0.1000 oz. AGW, 16.5 mm. **Series:**
Natura **Obv:** Hippopotamus 1/2 way in water **Rev:** Hippopotamus
deeply in water **Edge:** Reeded

Date	Mintage	F	VF	XF	Unc	BU
2005 Proof	—	Value: 210				

KM# 426   10 RAND
3.1107 g., 0.9999 Gold 0.1000 oz. AGW, 16.5 mm. **Series:**
Natura **Obv:** Giraffe's head and neck **Rev:** Giraffe drinking water
Edge: Reeded

Date	Mintage	F	VF	XF	Unc	BU
2006 Proof	—	Value: 200				

KM# 430   10 RAND
3.1107 g., 0.9999 Gold 0.1000 oz. AGW, 16.5 mm. **Series:**
Natura **Obv:** Forepart of Eland left **Rev:** Eland drinking water
right **Edge:** Reeded

Date	Mintage	F	VF	XF	Unc	BU
2007 Proof	—	Value: 200				

KM# 447   10 RAND
3.1100 g., 0.9990 Gold 0.0999 oz. AGW, 16.5 mm. **Obv:** Large
elephant head and elephant family below **Rev:** One elephant
eating, three elephants below

Date	Mintage	F	VF	XF	Unc	BU
2008 Proof	3,300	Value: 200				

KM# 471   10 RAND
3.1100 g., 0.9990 Gold 0.0999 oz. AGW, 16.5 mm. **Obv:** White
rhino, silouette and forepart **Rev:** Two rhino foreparts facing left
within large silouette

Date	Mintage	F	VF	XF	Unc	BU
2009 Proof	2,500	Value: 200				

KM# 509   10 RAND
3.1107 g., 0.9999 Gold 0.1000 oz. AGW, 16.5 mm.

Date	Mintage	F	VF	XF	Unc	BU
2011 Proof	—	Value: 210				

KM# 525   10 RAND
3.1170 g., 0.9999 Gold 0.1002 oz. AGW, 16.5 mm. **Subject:**
Great Mapungubwe Transfrontier Conservation Area

Date	Mintage	F	VF	XF	Unc	BU
2012 Proof	—	Value: 210				

KM# 411   20 RAND
7.7770 g., 0.9999 Gold 0.2500 oz. AGW, 22 mm. **Series:** Natura
Obv: Cheetah's head **Rev:** Cheetah family resting **Edge:** Reeded

Date	Mintage	F	VF	XF	Unc	BU
2002 Proof	2,548	Value: 500				

KM# 415   20 RAND
7.7770 g., 0.9999 Gold 0.2500 oz. AGW, 22 mm. **Series:** Natura
Obv: Male and female lion's heads **Rev:** Lion family resting **Edge:**
Reeded

Date	Mintage	F	VF	XF	Unc	BU
2003 Proof	2,799	Value: 500				

KM# 419   20 RAND
7.7770 g., 0.9999 Gold 0.2500 oz. AGW, 22 mm. **Series:** Natura
Obv: Caracal's head and shoulders **Rev:** Caracal with cub
standing right **Edge:** Reeded

Date	Mintage	F	VF	XF	Unc	BU
2004 Proof	1,407	Value: 500				

KM# 423   20 RAND
7.7770 g., 0.9999 Gold 0.2500 oz. AGW, 22 mm. **Series:** Natura
Obv: Hippopotamus 1/2 way in water **Rev:** Mother and baby
Hippopotamus grazing **Edge:** Reeded

Date	Mintage	F	VF	XF	Unc	BU
2005 Proof	—	Value: 500				

KM# 389   20 RAND
7.7770 g., 0.9999 Gold 0.2500 oz. AGW, 22 mm. **Series:** World
Heritage Site **Subject:** Mapungubwe **Obv:** New national arms
Rev: Rhinoceros standing right **Edge:** Reeded

Date	Mintage	F	VF	XF	Unc	BU
2005 Proof	1,000	Value: 500				

KM# 427   20 RAND
7.7770 g., 0.9999 Gold 0.2500 oz. AGW, 22 mm. **Series:** Natura
Obv: Giraffe's head and neck **Rev:** Mother and baby giraffes
grazing **Edge:** Reeded

Date	Mintage	F	VF	XF	Unc	BU
2006 Proof	—	Value: 500				

KM# 431   20 RAND
7.7770 g., 0.9999 Gold 0.2500 oz. AGW, 22 mm. **Series:** Natura
Obv: Forepart of Eland left **Rev:** Mother Eland and calf grazing
Edge: Reeded

Date	Mintage	F	VF	XF	Unc	BU
2007 Proof	—	Value: 500				

KM# 448   20 RAND
7.7770 g., 0.9990 Gold 0.2498 oz. AGW, 22 mm. **Obv:** Large
elephant head and elephant family below **Rev:** Two elephants
fighting, three elephants below

Date	Mintage	F	VF	XF	Unc	BU
2008 Proof	3,300	Value: 500				

KM# 455   20 RAND
7.7700 g., 0.9990 Gold 0.2496 oz. AGW, 22 mm. **Subject:**
Vredefort Dome **Obv:** Arms **Rev:** Meteorite

Date	Mintage	F	VF	XF	Unc	BU
2008 Proof	2,000	Value: 500				

KM# 472   20 RAND
7.7770 g., 0.9990 Gold 0.2498 oz. AGW, 22 mm. **Obv:** White
rhino silouette and forepart **Rev:** Two rhinos walking forward
within silhouette

Date	Mintage	F	VF	XF	Unc	BU
2009 Proof	2,500	Value: 500				

KM# 510   20 RAND
7.7700 g., 0.9999 Gold 0.2498 oz. AGW, 22 mm.

Date	Mintage	F	VF	XF	Unc	BU
2011 Proof	—	Value: 400				

KM# 526   20 RAND
7.7700 g., 0.9999 Gold 0.2498 oz. AGW, 22 mm.

Date	Mintage	F	VF	XF	Unc	BU
2012 Proof	—	Value: 400				

KM# 412   50 RAND
15.5530 g., 0.9999 Gold 0.5000 oz. AGW, 27 mm. **Series:**
Natura **Obv:** Cheetah's head **Rev:** Cheetah attacking Impala
Edge: Reeded

Date	Mintage	F	VF	XF	Unc	BU
2002 Proof	2,295	Value: 950				

KM# 416   50 RAND
15.5530 g., 0.9999 Gold 0.5000 oz. AGW, 27 mm. **Series:**
Natura **Obv:** Male and female lion's heads **Rev:** Female and male
lions playing **Edge:** Reeded

Date	Mintage	F	VF	XF	Unc	BU
2003 Proof	2,600	Value: 950				

KM# 420   50 RAND
15.5530 g., 0.9999 Gold 0.5000 oz. AGW, 27 mm. **Series:**
Natura **Obv:** Caracal's head and shoulders **Rev:** Caracal eating
prey **Edge:** Reeded

Date	Mintage	F	VF	XF	Unc	BU
2004 Proof	1,327	Value: 950				

KM# 424   50 RAND
15.5530 g., 0.9999 Gold 0.5000 oz. AGW, 27 mm. **Series:**
Natura **Obv:** Hippopotamus 1/2 way in water **Rev:** Hippopotamus
submerged in water with head raised above, mouth wide open
Edge: Reeded

Date	Mintage	F	VF	XF	Unc	BU
2005 Proof	—	Value: 950				

KM# 428   50 RAND
15.5530 g., 0.9999 Gold 0.5000 oz. AGW, 27 mm. **Series:**
Natura **Obv:** Giraffe's head and neck **Rev:** Giraffe family walking
left **Edge:** Reeded

Date	Mintage	F	VF	XF	Unc	BU
2006 Proof	—	Value: 950				

KM# 432   50 RAND
15.5530 g., 0.9999 Gold 0.5000 oz. AGW, 27 mm. **Series:**
Natura **Obv:** Forepart of eland left **Rev:** Three eland running right
Edge: Reeded

Date	Mintage	F	VF	XF	Unc	BU
2007 Proof	—	Value: 950				

KM# 449   50 RAND
15.5530 g., 0.9990 Gold 0.4995 oz. AGW, 27 mm. **Obv:** Large elephant and elephant family below **Rev:** Three elephants, one trumpeting, three elephants below

Date	Mintage	F	VF	XF	Unc	BU
2008 Proof	4,800	Value: 950				

KM# 473   50 RAND
15.5500 g., 0.9990 Gold 0.4994 oz. AGW, 27 mm. **Obv:** White rhino silhouette and forpart **Rev:** Two rhinos facing off within large silouette

Date	Mintage	F	VF	XF	Unc	BU
2009 Proof	4,000	Value: 950				

KM# 511   50 RAND
15.5530 g., Gold, 27 mm.

Date	Mintage	F	VF	XF	Unc	BU
2011 Proof	—	Value: 800				

KM# 527   50 RAND
15.5530 g., 0.9999 Gold 0.5000 oz. AGW, 27 mm.

Date	Mintage	F	VF	XF	Unc	BU
2012 Proof	—	Value: 800				

KM# 413   100 RAND
31.1070 g., 0.9999 Gold 1.0000 oz. AGW, 32.69 mm. **Series:** Natura **Obv:** Cheetah's head **Rev:** Cheetah posing **Edge:** Reeded

Date	Mintage	F	VF	XF	Unc	BU
2002 Proof	2,550	Value: 1,850				
2002 RSA logo Proof	496	Value: 1,850				

KM# 417   100 RAND
31.1070 g., 0.9999 Gold 1.0000 oz. AGW, 32.69 mm. **Series:** Natura **Obv:** Male and female lion's heads **Rev:** Snarling male and female lion's heads **Edge:** Reeded **Note:** L P RSA - LION PARK RSA.

Date	Mintage	F	VF	XF	Unc	BU
2003 Proof	2,758	Value: 1,850				
2003 L P RSA Proof	498	Value: 1,850				

KM# 421   100 RAND
31.1070 g., 0.9999 Gold 1.0000 oz. AGW, 32.69 mm. **Series:** Natura **Obv:** Caracal's head and shoulders **Rev:** Caracal crouching on branch left **Edge:** Reeded **Note:** C/C - CARACAL / CARACAL

Date	Mintage	F	VF	XF	Unc	BU
2004 Proof	1,405	Value: 1,850				
2004 C/C Proof	500	Value: 1,850				

KM# 425   100 RAND
31.1070 g., 0.9999 Gold 1.0000 oz. AGW, 32.69 mm. **Series:** Natura **Obv:** Hippopotamus 1/2 way in water **Rev:** Two hippopotami submerged in water, heads raised, mouths open faced in combat **Edge:** Reeded **Note:** MAPU - MAPUNGUBWE.

Date	Mintage	F	VF	XF	Unc	BU
2005 Proof	—	Value: 1,850				
2005 MAPU Proof	—	Value: 1,850				

KM# 429   100 RAND
31.1070 g., 0.9999 Gold 1.0000 oz. AGW, 32.69 mm. **Series:** Natura **Obv:** Giraffe's head and neck **Rev:** Head and neck view of giraffe eating tree leaves **Edge:** Reeded **Note:** lpp/EWT - lion's paw print / EWT.

Date	Mintage	F	VF	XF	Unc	BU
2006 Proof	—	Value: 1,850				
2006 lpp/EWT Proof	—	Value: 1,850				

KM# 433   100 RAND
31.1070 g., 0.9999 Gold 1.0000 oz. AGW, 32.7 mm. **Series:** Natura **Obv:** Forepart of eland left **Rev:** Eland grazing left **Edge:** Reeded

Date	Mintage	F	VF	XF	Unc	BU
2007 Proof	—	Value: 1,850				
2007 Proof	—	Value: 1,850				

KM# 450   100 RAND
31.1070 g., 0.9990 Gold 0.9991 oz. AGW, 32.69 mm. **Obv:** Large elephant head and elephant family below **Rev:** Large elephant facing, three elephants below

Date	Mintage	F	VF	XF	Unc	BU
2008 Proof	4,800	Value: 1,850				

KM# 474   100 RAND
31.1070 g., 0.9990 Gold 0.9991 oz. AGW **Obv:** White rhino silouette and forepart **Rev:** Rhino standing facing within large silouette **Shape:** 32.7

Date	Mintage	F	VF	XF	Unc	BU
2009 Proof	4,000	Value: 1,850				

KM# 512   100 RAND
31.1070 g., 0.9999 Gold 1.0000 oz. AGW, 32.7 mm.

Date	Mintage	F	VF	XF	Unc	BU
2011 Proof	—	Value: 1,750				

KM# 528   100 RAND
31.1070 g., 0.9999 Gold 1.0000 oz. AGW, 32.7 mm.

Date	Mintage	F	VF	XF	Unc	BU
2012 Proof	—	Value: 1,750				

KM# 264   1/10 OUNCE
3.1107 g., 0.9999 Gold 0.1000 oz. AGW, 16.5 mm. **Series:** Natura **Obv:** Gemsbok's upper body **Rev:** Gemsbok drinking **Edge:** Reeded

Date	Mintage	F	VF	XF	Unc	BU
2001 Proof	3,498	Value: 200				

KM# 265   1/4 OUNCE
7.7770 g., 0.9999 Gold 0.2500 oz. AGW, 22 mm. **Series:** Natura **Obv:** Gemsbok's upper body **Rev:** Two Gemsbok bulls facing off **Edge:** Reeded

Date	Mintage	F	VF	XF	Unc	BU
2001 Proof	2,904	Value: 500				

KM# 266   1/2 OUNCE
15.5530 g., 0.9999 Gold 0.5000 oz. AGW, 27 mm. **Series:** Natura **Obv:** Gemsbok's upper body **Rev:** Gemsbok family grazing **Edge:** Reeded

Date	Mintage	F	VF	XF	Unc	BU
2001 Proof	2,754	Value: 950				

KM# 267   OUNCE
31.1070 g., 0.9999 Gold 1.0000 oz. AGW, 32.69 mm. **Series:** Natura **Obv:** Gemsbok's upper body **Rev:** Gemsbok grazing **Edge:** Reeded **Note:** ghCW - Gemsbok's head CW

Date	Mintage	F	VF	XF	Unc	BU
2001 Proof	3,104	Value: 1,850				
2001 Proof	491	Value: 1,750				

GOLD BULLION CULTURE COINAGE

KM# 247   RAND
3.1103 g., 0.9999 Gold 0.1000 oz. AGW, 16.5 mm. **Series:** Cultural **Obv:** New national arms **Obv. Legend:** UMZANTSI AFRIKA - SOUTH AFRICA **Rev:** Seated Sotho figure with headdress **Edge:** Reeded

Date	Mintage	F	VF	XF	Unc	BU
2001 Proof	236	Value: 275				

KM# 378   RAND
3.1103 g., 0.9999 Gold 0.1000 oz. AGW, 16.5 mm. **Series:** Cultural **Obv:** New national arms **Obv. Legend:** UMZANTSI AFRIKA - SOUTH AFRICA **Rev:** Three Xhosa tribe members **Edge:** Reeded

Date	Mintage	F	VF	XF	Unc	BU
2001 Proof	—	Value: 675				

KM# 379   RAND
3.1103 g., 0.9999 Gold 0.1000 oz. AGW, 16.5 mm. **Series:** Cultural **Subject:** Tswana Nation **Obv:** New national arms **Obv. Legend:** Aforika Borwa - South Africa **Rev:** Four tribe people standing **Edge:** Reeded

Date	Mintage	F	VF	XF	Unc	BU
2002 Proof	300	Value: 350				

KM# 380   RAND
3.1103 g., 0.9999 Gold 0.1000 oz. AGW, 16.5 mm. **Series:** Cultural **Obv:** New national arms **Obv. Legend:** Afrika-Dzonga - South Africa **Rev:** Tsonga tribe dancer and drummer **Edge:** Reeded

Date	Mintage	F	VF	XF	Unc	BU
2003 Proof	348	Value: 350				

KM# 381   RAND
3.1103 g., 0.9999 Gold 0.1000 oz. AGW, 16.5 mm. **Series:** Cultural **Obv:** New national arms **Obv. Legend:** Afurika Tshipembe - South Africa **Rev:** Six Venda tribe members crossing bridge **Edge:** Reeded

Date	Mintage	F	VF	XF	Unc	BU
2004 Proof	380	Value: 350				

KM# 382   RAND
3.1103 g., 0.9999 Gold 0.1000 oz. AGW, 16.5 mm. **Series:** Cultural **Obv:** New national arms **Obv. Legend:** iSewula Afrika - South Africa **Rev:** Ndebele woman standing, native print in background **Edge:** Reeded

Date	Mintage	F	VF	XF	Unc	BU
2005 Proof	1,000	Value: 200				

KM# 383   RAND
3.1103 g., 0.9999 Gold 0.1000 oz. AGW, 16.5 mm. **Series:** Cultural **Obv:** New national arms **Obv. Legend:** Ningizimu Afrika - South Africa **Rev:** 1/2 length figure of Ema-Swati Chief left at right **Edge:** Reeded

Date	Mintage	F	VF	XF	Unc	BU
2006 Proof	1,000	Value: 200				

KM# 385 RAND
3.1103 g., 0.9999 Gold 0.1000 oz. AGW, 16.5 mm. **Subject:** 2010 FIFA World Cup Soccer - South Africa **Obv:** New national arms **Obv. Legend:** SOUTH AFRICA **Rev:** Bird head at left facing animal at right, soccer ball at bottom **Edge:** Reeded

Date	Mintage	F	VF	XF	Unc	BU
2007 Proof	10,000	Value: 200				

KM# 384 RAND
3.1103 g., 0.9999 Gold 0.1000 oz. AGW, 16.5 mm. **Subject:** The Afrikaner Nation **Obv:** New national arms **Obv. Legend:** SOUTH AFRIKA **Rev:** Ox drawn wagon up hillside **Edge:** Reeded

Date	Mintage	F	VF	XF	Unc	BU
2007 Proof	—	Value: 200				

KM# 454 RAND
3.1100 g., 0.9990 Gold 0.0999 oz. AGW, 16.5 mm. **Obv:** Arms

Date	Mintage	F	VF	XF	Unc	BU
2008 Proof	1,000	Value: 200				

KM# 478 RAND
3.1100 g., 0.9990 Gold 0.0999 oz. AGW, 16.5 mm. **Subject:** Northern Sotho (Bapedi) peoples **Obv:** Arms **Rev:** Woman seated, cooking

Date	Mintage	F	VF	XF	Unc	BU
2009 Proof	1,000	Value: 200				

KM# 249 2 RAND
7.7770 g., 0.9999 Gold 0.2500 oz. AGW, 22 mm. **Obv:** New national arms **Rev:** Gondwana theoretical landmass and dinosaur **Edge:** Reeded

Date	Mintage	F	VF	XF	Unc	BU
2001 Proof	558	Value: 500				

KM# 386 2 RAND
7.7770 g., 0.9999 Gold 0.2500 oz. AGW, 22 mm. **Series:** World Heritage Site **Subject:** Robben Island **Obv:** New national arms **Rev:** Carved stone, island in background **Edge:** Reeded

Date	Mintage	F	VF	XF	Unc	BU
2002 Proof	999	Value: 500				

KM# 387 2 RAND
7.7770 g., 0.9999 Gold 0.2500 oz. AGW, 22 mm. **Series:** World heritage Site **Subject:** Greater St. Lucia Wetland Park **Obv:** New national arms **Rev:** Various birds **Edge:** Reeded

Date	Mintage	F	VF	XF	Unc	BU
2003 Proof	637	Value: 500				

KM# 388 2 RAND
7.7770 g., 0.9999 Gold 0.2500 oz. AGW, 22 mm. **Series:** World Heritage Park **Subject:** "Ukhahlamba" Drakensberg Park **Obv:** New national arms **Rev:** Early painting of animal and hunters **Edge:** Reeded

Date	Mintage	F	VF	XF	Unc	BU
2004 Proof	750	Value: 500				

KM# 390 2 RAND
7.7770 g., 0.9999 Gold 0.2500 oz. AGW, 22 mm. **Subject:** 2006 FIFA World Cup Soccer - Germany **Obv:** New national arms **Rev:** Soccer ball at center above partial globe within ornate border art **Edge:** Reeded

Date	Mintage	F	VF	XF	Unc	BU
2005 Proof	—	Value: 500				

KM# 391 2 RAND
7.7770 g., 0.9999 Gold 0.2500 oz. AGW, 22 mm. **Series:** World Heritage Site **Subject:** Cradle of Mankind **Obv:** New national arms **Rev:** Early man standing at upper left, ape's head at upper right, skull at lower left, value at lower right **Edge:** Reeded

Date	Mintage	F	VF	XF	Unc	BU
2006 Proof	1,000	Value: 500				

KM# 392 2 RAND
7.7770 g., 0.9999 Gold 0.2500 oz. AGW, 22 mm. **Subject:** 2006 FIFA World Cup Soccer - Germany **Obv:** New national arms **Rev:** Logo in ornate frame **Edge:** Reeded

Date	Mintage	F	VF	XF	Unc	BU
2006 Proof	15,000	Value: 500				

KM# 393 2 RAND
7.7770 g., 0.9999 Gold 0.2500 oz. AGW, 22 mm. **Series:** World Heritage Site **Subject:** Cape Floral **Obv:** New national arms **Rev:** Bird perched on branch at left, plant at center, land in distance **Edge:** Reeded

Date	Mintage	F	VF	XF	Unc	BU
2007 Proof	—	Value: 500				

KM# 394 2 RAND
7.7770 g., 0.9999 Gold 0.2500 oz. AGW, 22 mm. **Subject:** 2010 FIFA World Cup Soccer - South Africa **Obv:** New national arms **Rev:** Animal in ornate frame at left and right, small soccer ball at bottom below value **Edge:** Reeded

Date	Mintage	F	VF	XF	Unc	BU
2007 Proof	10,000	Value: 500				

KM# 479 2 RAND
7.7700 g., 0.9990 Gold 0.2496 oz. AGW, 22 mm. **Subject:** Richtersveld Cultural and Botanical Landscape **Obv:** Arms **Rev:** Native "haru on" hut and aloe pilansil tree

Date	Mintage	F	VF	XF	Unc	BU
2009 Proof	2,000	Value: 500				

GOLD BULLION PROTEA COINAGE

KM# 395 5 RAND
3.1107 g., 0.9999 Gold 0.1000 oz. AGW, 16.5 mm. **Subject:** 10th Anniversary Soccer "Bafana Bafana" **Obv:** Protea flower **Rev:** Two players running right **Edge:** Reeded

Date	Mintage	F	VF	XF	Unc	BU
2002 Proof	386	Value: 275				

KM# 397 5 RAND
3.1107 g., 0.9999 Gold 0.1000 oz. AGW, 16.5 mm. **Subject:** World Summit on Sustainable Development **Obv:** Protea flower **Rev:** Globe featuring Africa **Rev. Inscription:** prosperity **Edge:** Reeded

Date	Mintage	F	VF	XF	Unc	BU
2002 Proof	511	Value: 225				

KM# 278 5 RAND
3.1104 g., 0.9999 Gold 0.1000 oz. AGW, 16.5 mm. **Obv:** Protea flower **Rev:** Soccer player heading the ball **Edge:** Reeded

Date	Mintage	F	VF	XF	Unc	BU
2002 Proof	—	Value: 200				

KM# 399 5 RAND
3.1107 g., 0.9999 Gold 0.1000 oz. AGW, 16.5 mm. **Subject:** Cricket World Cup **Obv:** Protea flower **Rev:** Cricket ball striking stumps **Rev. Inscription:** Protea **Edge:** Reeded

Date	Mintage	F	VF	XF	Unc	BU
2003 Proof	925	Value: 200				

KM# 289 5 RAND
3.1100 g., 0.9999 Gold 0.1000 oz. AGW, 16.5 mm. **Subject:** 10th Anniversary of South African Democracy **Obv:** Protea flower **Rev:** Inscription covered flag **Edge:** Reeded

Date	Mintage	F	VF	XF	Unc	BU
2004 Proof	1,000	Value: 200				

KM# 401 5 RAND
3.1107 g., 0.9999 Gold 0.1000 oz. AGW, 16.5 mm. **Subject:** 10th Anniversay Democracy **Obv:** Protea flower **Rev:** Flag made of constitution **Edge:** Reeded **Note:** 10YF - circular 10 YEARS FREEDOM

Date	Mintage	F	VF	XF	Unc	BU
2004 Proof	2,089	Value: 375				
2004 10YF Proof	492	Value: 600				

KM# 403 5 RAND
3.1107 g., 0.9999 Gold 0.1000 oz. AGW, 16.5 mm. **Subject:** Nobel Prize Winners **Obv:** Protea flower **Rev:** Freedom Charter, Luthuli seated left at desk at lower right **Edge:** Reeded **Note:** FR - FREEDOM

Date	Mintage	F	VF	XF	Unc	BU
2005 Proof	2,000	Value: 200				
2005 FR Proof	—	Value: 600				

KM# 405 5 RAND
3.1107 g., 0.9999 Gold 0.1000 oz. AGW, 16.5 mm. **Subject:** Nobel Prize Winners **Obv:** Protea flower **Rev:** Cross, inscription **Edge:** Reeded

Date	Mintage	F	VF	XF	Unc	BU
2006 Proof	5,600	Value: 200				
2006 logo Proof	400	Value: 500				

KM# 407 5 RAND
3.1107 g., 0.9999 Gold 0.1000 oz. AGW, 16.5 mm. **Subject:** Nobel Prize winners **Obv:** Protea flower **Rev:** Extract from de Klerk's acceptance speech **Edge:** Reeded

Date	Mintage	F	VF	XF	Unc	BU
2007 Proof	8,000	Value: 200				
2007 dove Proof	—	Value: 700				

KM# 408 5 RAND
3.1107 g., 0.9999 Gold 0.1000 oz. AGW, 16.5 mm. **Subject:** Nobel Prize Winners **Obv:** Protea flower **Rev:** Extract from Mandela's acceptance speech **Edge:** Reeded

Date	Mintage	F	VF	XF	Unc	BU
2007 Proof	—	Value: 200				
2007 dove Proof	—	Value: 700				

KM# 452 5 RAND
3.1100 g., 0.9990 Gold 0.0999 oz. AGW, 16.5 mm. **Obv:** Protea flower **Rev:** Ghandi figure at prayer

Date	Mintage	F	VF	XF	Unc	BU
2008 Proof	8,000	Value: 200				

KM# 476 5 RAND
3.1100 g., 0.9990 Gold 0.0999 oz. AGW, 16.5 mm. **Obv:** Protea flower **Rev:** Portraits of C. J. Langenhoven and M. L. de Villiers with musical score

Date	Mintage	F	VF	XF	Unc	BU
2009 Proof	8,000	Value: 200				

KM# 396 25 RAND
31.1070 g., 0.9999 Gold 1.0000 oz. AGW, 32.69 mm. **Subject:** 10th Anniversary Soccer "Bafana Bafana" **Obv:** Protea flower **Rev:** Two players running left **Edge:** Reeded

Date	Mintage	F	VF	XF	Unc	BU
2002 Proof	137	Value: 1,850				
2002 flag/CW Proof	84	Value: 2,250				

KM# 398 25 RAND
31.1070 g., 0.9999 Gold 1.0000 oz. AGW, 32.69 mm. **Subject:** World Summit on Sustainable Development **Obv:** Protea flower **Rev:** Globe featuring Africa **Edge:** Reeded

Date	Mintage	F	VF	XF	Unc	BU
2002 Proof	421	Value: 1,850				

KM# 279 25 RAND
31.1035 g., 0.9999 Gold 0.9999 oz. AGW, 32.7 mm. **Obv:** Protea flower **Rev:** Soccer player kicking ball **Edge:** Reeded

Date	Mintage	F	VF	XF	Unc	BU
2002 Proof	492	Value: 1,850				

KM# 400 25 RAND
31.1070 g., 0.9999 Gold 1.0000 oz. AGW, 32.69 mm. **Subject:** Cricket World Cup **Obv:** Protea flower **Rev:** Batsman on one knee about to sweep the ball **Rev. Legend:** PROTEA **Edge:** Reeded

Date	Mintage	F	VF	XF	Unc	BU
2003 Proof	210	Value: 1,850				
2003 ball/RSA Proof	208	Value: 1,850				

KM# 402 25 RAND
31.1070 g., 0.9999 Gold 1.0000 oz. AGW, 32.69 mm. **Subject:** 10th Anniversary Democracy **Obv:** Protea flower **Rev:** Two heads of Mandela, one left, one facing, Union building in background **Edge:** Reeded **Note:** 10FP - 10/flag, people

Date	Mintage	F	VF	XF	Unc	BU
2004 Proof	6,000	Value: 3,000				
2004 10FP Proof	492	Value: 5,400				

KM# 404 25 RAND
31.1070 g., 0.9999 Gold 1.0000 oz. AGW, 32.69 mm. **Subject:** Nobel Prize Winners **Obv:** Protea flower **Rev:** Bust of Chief Albert Luthuli facing **Edge:** Reeded **Note:** FC - FREEDOM / CHARTER / 26 JUNE 1955

Date	Mintage	F	VF	XF	Unc	BU
2005 Proof	6,000	Value: 1,850				
2005 FC Proof	—	Value: 3,750				

KM# 406 25 RAND
31.1070 g., 0.9999 Gold 1.0000 oz. AGW, 32.69 mm. **Subject:** Nobel Prize Winners **Obv:** Protea flower **Rev:** Cross, bust of Archbishop Desmond Tutu right **Edge:** Reeded

Date	Mintage	F	VF	XF	Unc	BU
2006 Proof	7,600	Value: 1,850				
2006 logo Proof	400	Value: 2,600				

KM# 409 25 RAND
31.1070 g., 0.9999 Gold 1.0000 oz. AGW, 32.69 mm. **Subject:**

Nobel Prize Winners **Obv:** Protea flower **Rev:** Busts of Mandela, de Klerk right **Edge:** Reeded **Note:** d-P - dove Peace

Date	Mintage	F	VF	XF	Unc	BU
2007 Proof	12,000	Value: 1,850				
2007 d-P Proof	—	Value: 2,750				

KM# 453   25 RAND
31.1070 g., 0.9990 Gold 0.9991 oz. AGW, 32.7 mm. **Obv:** Protea flower **Rev:** Ghandi profile at right

Date	Mintage	F	VF	XF	Unc	BU
2008 Proof	600	Value: 1,850				
2008 Proof	12,000	Value: 1,850				

KM# 477   25 RAND
31.1070 g., 0.9990 Gold 0.9991 oz. AGW, 32.7 mm. **Obv:** Protea flower **Rev:** Portraits of C. J. Langenhoven and M. L. de Villiers and musical score

Date	Mintage	F	VF	XF	Unc	BU
2009 Proof	11,000	Value: 1,850				

KM# 262   1/10 PROTEA
3.1107 g., 0.9999 Gold 0.1000 oz. AGW, 16.5 mm. **Subject:** Tourism **Obv:** Protea flower **Rev:** Lion's head facing, partial shield **Rev. Inscription:** PROTEA **Edge:** Reeded

Date	Mintage	F	VF	XF	Unc	BU
2001 Proof	1,076	Value: 200				

KM# 263   PROTEA
31.1070 g., 0.9999 Gold 1.0000 oz. AGW, 32.6 mm. **Subject:** Tourism **Obv:** Protea flower **Rev:** Child on sandy beach, Table Mountain in background, partial star at right **Rev. Inscription:** PROTEA **Edge:** Reeded

Date	Mintage	F	VF	XF	Unc	BU
2001 Proof	972	Value: 1,850				
2001 GRC(pp) Proof	196	Value: 2,000				

MINT SETS

KM#	Date	Mintage	Identification	Issue Price	Mkt Val
MS38	2002 (7)	—	KM#268-274 plus 1- and 2-cent medals	30.00	32.50
MS39	2001 (9)	5,577	KM#221-229	—	60.00
MS40	2002 (7)	3,886	KM#268-274	—	52.50
MS41	2002 (7)	1,640	KM#268-274, circulated coins	—	17.50
MS42	2003 (7)	2,602	KM#324, 327, 330, 332, 335, 337, 347	—	45.00
MS43	2003 (7)	1,380	KM#324, 327, 330, 332, 335, 337, 347, circulted coins	—	10.00
MS44	2004 (7)	1,948	KM#281, 325, 326, 328, 331, 333, 336	—	37.50
MS45	2004 (7)	1,131	KM#281, 325, 325, 328, 331, 333, 336, circulated coins	—	17.50
MS46	2004 (7)	325	KM#281, 325, 326, 328, 331, 333, 336, Baby	—	22.50
MS47	2004 (7)	23	KM#281, 325, 326, 328, 331, 333, 336, Wedding	—	22.50
MS48	2005 (7)	—	KM#291-297	—	30.00
MS49	2005 (7)	—	KM#291-297, circulated coins	—	15.00
MS50	2005 (7)	—	KM#291-297, Baby	—	23.00
MS51	2005 (7)	—	KM#291-297, Wedding	—	22.50
MS52	2006 (7)	—	KM#291-297	—	22.50
MS53	2006 (7)	—	KM#291-297, circulated coins	—	15.00
MS54	2006 (7)	—	KM#291-297, Baby	—	15.00
MS55	2006 (7)	—	KM#291-297, Wedding	—	15.00
MS56	2007 (7)	—	KM#340-346	—	22.50
MS57	2007 (7)	—	KM#340-346, circulated coins	—	15.00
MS58	2007 (7)	—	KM#340-346, baby	—	15.00
MS59	2007 (7)	—	KM#340-346, wedding	—	15.00

PIEFORT PROOF SETS (PPS)

KM#	Date	Mintage	Identification	Issue Price	Mkt Val
PS242	2007 (4)	—	KM#430-433, leatherette	—	3,000

PROOF SETS

KM#	Date	Mintage	Identification	Issue Price	Mkt Val
PS170	2002 (7)	—	KM#268-274 plus 1- and 2-cent medals	40.00	65.00
PS171	2005 (4)	1,500	KM#320-323	—	300
PS172	2001 (9)	3,678	KM#221-229	—	75.00
PS173	2001 (9)	—	KM#221-229 wedding	—	75.00
PS174	2002 (7)	—	KM#268-274	—	75.00
PS175	2002 (7)	330	KM#268-274, baby	—	75.00
PS176	2003 (7)	2,356	KM#324, 327, 330, 332, 335, 337, 347	—	65.00
PS177	2003 (7)	500	KM#324, 327, 330, 332, 335, 337, 347, baby	—	65.00
PS178	2003 (7)	53	KM#324, 327, 330, 332, 335, 337, 347, wedding	—	65.00
PS179	2004 (7)	1,935	KM#281, 325, 326, 328, 331, 333, 336	—	65.00
PS180	2004 (7)	326	KM#281, 325, 326, 328, 331, 333, 336, baby	—	65.00
PS181	2004 (7)	23	KM#281, 325, 326, 328, 331, 333, 336, wedding	—	65.00
PS182	2005 (7)	—	KM#291-297	—	65.00
PS183	2005 (7)	—	KM#291-297, baby	—	65.00
PS184	2005 (7)	—	KM#291-297, wedding	—	65.00
PS185	2006 (7)	—	KM#291-297	—	65.00
PS186	2006 (7)	—	KM#291-297, baby	—	65.00
PS187	2006 (7)	—	KM#291-297, wedding	—	65.00
PS188	2007 (7)	—	KM#340-346	—	65.00
PS189	2007 (7)	—	KM#340-346, baby	—	65.00
PS190	2007 (7)	—	KM#340-346, wedding	—	65.00
PS193	2001 (4)	411	KM#243-246, wooden case	—	375
PS194	2001 (4)	746	KM#243-246, velvet (med case)	—	300
PS195	2002 (3)	81	KM#234, 243, 351 (mixed dates)	—	110
PS196	2002 (3)	95	KM#235, 244, 352 (mixed dates)	—	185
PS197	2002 (3)	81	KM#236, 245, 353 (mixed dates)	—	250
PS198	2002 (3)	92	KM#237, 246, 354 (mixed dates)	—	335
PS199	2002 (4)	411	KM#351-354, wooden case	—	375
PS200	2002 (4)	746	KM#351-354, velvet lined case	—	275
PS201	2003 (4)	59	KM#234, 243, 351, 355 (mixed dates)	—	150
PS202	2003 (4)	47	KM#235, 244, 352, 356 (mixed dates)	—	250
PS203	2003 (4)	75	KM#236, 245, 353, 357 (mixed dates)	—	330
PS204	2003 (4)	62	KM#237, 246, 354, 358 (mixed dates)	—	450
PS205	2003 (4)	532	KM#355-358, wooden case	—	375
PS206	2003 (4)	1,029	KM#355-358, velvet lined case	—	300
PS207	2004 (5)	132	KM#234, 243, 351, 355, 359 (mixed dates)	—	200
PS208	2004 (5)	133	KM#235, 244, 352, 356, 360 (mixed dates)	—	325
PS209	2004 (5)	181	KM#236, 245, 353, 357, 361 (mixed dates)	—	450
PS210	2004 (5)	158	KM#237, 246, 354, 358, 362 (mixed dates)	—	555
PS211	2004 (4)	645	KM#359-362, wooden case	—	375
PS212	2004 (4)	454	KM#359-362, velvet lined case	—	300
PS213	2004 (4)	299	KM#359-362, plus 1/4 oz. medal	—	300
PS214	2005 (4)	—	KM#320-323, wooden case	—	300
PS215	2005 (4)	—	KM#320-323, velvet lined case	—	300
PS216	2006 (4)	—	KM#316-319, wooden case	—	300
PS217	2006 (4)	—	KM#316-319, velvet lined case	—	300
PS218	2007 (2)	—	KM#363-364, wooden case	—	150
PS219	2007 (2)	—	KM#363-364	—	105
PS223	2000 (4)	483	KM#258-261, prestige	—	3,500
PS224	2000 (4)	334	KM#258-261, leatherette	—	3,500
PS225	2001 (4)	691	KM#264-267	—	3,500
PS226	2001 (4)	985	KM#264-267, leatherette	—	3,500
PS227	2001 (4)	310	KM#264-267, special export	—	3,500
PS228	2002 (4)	698	KM#410-413, prestige	—	3,500
PS229	2002 (4)	529	KM#410-413, leatherette	—	3,500
PS230	2002 (4)	682	KM#410-413, special	—	3,500
PS231	2003 (4)	698	KM#414-417, prestige	—	3,500
PS232	2003 (4)	908	KM#414-417, leatherette	—	3,500
PS233	2003 (4)	722	KM#414-417, anniversary	—	3,500
PS234	2004 (4)	700	KM#418-421, prestige	—	3,525
PS235	2004 (4)	440	KM#418-421, leatherette	—	3,525
PS236	2004 (4)	125	KM#418-421, special export with silver African Continent	—	3,525
PS237	2005 (4)	—	KM#422-425, prestige	—	3,525
PS238	2005 (4)	—	KM#422-425, leatherette	—	3,525
PS239	2006 (4)	—	KM#426-429, prestige	—	3,500
PS240	2006 (4)	—	KM#426-429, leatherette	—	3,500
PS241	2007 (4)	—	KM#430-433, prestige	—	3,500

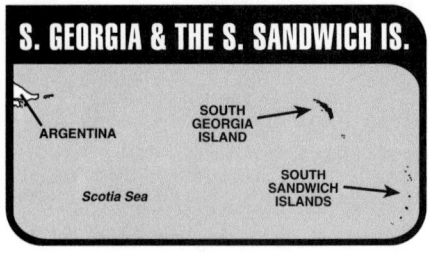

S. GEORGIA & THE S. SANDWICH IS.

South Georgia and the South Sandwich Islands are a dependency of the Falkland Islands, and located about 800 miles east of them. South Georgia is 1,450 sq. mi. (1,770 sq. km.), and the South Sandwich Islands are 120 sq. mi. (311 sq. km.) Fishing and Antarctic research are the main industries. The islands were claimed for Great Britain in 1775 by Captain James Cook.

RULER
British since 1775

BRITISH OVERSEAS TERRITORY
STANDARD COINAGE

KM# 7   2 POUNDS
28.2800 g., Copper-Nickel, 38.6 mm. **Subject:** Sir Ernest H. Shackleton **Obv:** Crowned bust right **Rev:** Bust facing and ship "Endurance" **Edge:** Reeded

Date	Mintage	F	VF	XF	Unc	BU
2001	—	—	—	—	10.00	12.00

KM# 7a   2 POUNDS
28.2800 g., 0.9250 Silver 0.8410 oz. ASW **Obv:** Crowned bust right **Rev:** Bust facing and ship "Endurance"

Date	Mintage	F	VF	XF	Unc	BU
2001 Proof	Est. 10,000	Value: 50.00				

KM# 9   2 POUNDS
Copper-Nickel **Subject:** Sir Joseph Banks **Obv:** Crowned bust right **Rev:** Cameo and ship

Date	Mintage	F	VF	XF	Unc	BU
2001	—	—	—	—	10.00	12.00

KM# 9a   2 POUNDS
28.2800 g., 0.9250 Silver 0.8410 oz. ASW   **Obv:** Crowned bust right   **Rev:** Ship and cameo

Date	Mintage	F	VF	XF	Unc	BU
2001 Proof	Est. 10,000	Value: 50.00

KM# 11   2 POUNDS
28.2800 g., Copper-Nickel, 38.6 mm.   **Subject:** Queen Elizabeth II's Golden Jubilee   **Obv:** Crowned bust right   **Rev:** Young crowned bust right   **Edge:** Reeded

Date	Mintage	F	VF	XF	Unc	BU
2002	—	—	—	—	10.00	12.00

KM# 11a   2 POUNDS
28.2800 g., 0.9250 Gold Clad Silver 0.8410 oz., 38.6 mm.   **Subject:** Queen Elizabeth II's Golden Jubilee   **Obv:** Crowned bust right   **Rev:** Young crowned bust right   **Edge:** Reeded

Date	Mintage	F	VF	XF	Unc	BU
2002 Proof	10,000	Value: 50.00

KM# 13   2 POUNDS
28.2800 g., Copper-Nickel, 38.6 mm.   **Subject:** Queen Elizabeth II's Golden Jubilee   **Obv:** Crowned bust right   **Rev:** Small crown above shield flanked by flower sprigs   **Edge:** Reeded

Date	Mintage	F	VF	XF	Unc	BU
2002	—	—	—	—	10.00	12.00

KM# 13a   2 POUNDS
28.2800 g., 0.9250 Gold Clad Silver 0.8410 oz., 38.6 mm.   **Subject:** Queen Elizabeth II's Golden Jubilee   **Obv:** Crowned bust right   **Rev:** Small crown above shield flanked by flower sprigs   **Edge:** Reeded

Date	Mintage	F	VF	XF	Unc	BU
2002 Proof	10,000	Value: 50.00

KM# 15   2 POUNDS
28.2800 g., Copper-Nickel, 38.6 mm.   **Subject:** Diana, Princess of Wales - The Work Continues   **Obv:** Crowned bust right   **Rev:** Head 1/4 left   **Edge:** Reeded

Date	Mintage	F	VF	XF	Unc	BU
2002	—	—	—	—	10.00	12.00

KM# 17   2 POUNDS
28.2800 g., Copper-Nickel, 38.6 mm.   **Subject:** Prince William's 21st Birthday   **Obv:** Crowned bust right   **Rev:** Arms of Prince William of Wales   **Edge:** Reeded

Date	Mintage	F	VF	XF	Unc	BU
2003PM	—	—	—	—	10.00	12.00

KM# 17a   2 POUNDS
28.2800 g., 0.9250 Silver 0.8410 oz. ASW, 38.6 mm.   **Subject:** Prince William's 21st Birthday   **Obv:** Crowned bust right   **Rev:** Arms of Prince William of Wales   **Edge:** Reeded

Date	Mintage	F	VF	XF	Unc	BU
2003PM Proof	—	Value: 50.00

KM# 18   2 POUNDS
28.2800 g., Copper-Nickel, 38.6 mm.   **Obv:** Crowned bust right   **Rev:** Capt. Cook, ship and map   **Edge:** Reeded

Date	Mintage	F	VF	XF	Unc	BU
2003PM	—	—	—	—	10.00	12.00

KM# 18a   2 POUNDS
28.2800 g., 0.9250 Silver 0.8410 oz. ASW, 38.6 mm.   **Obv:** Crowned bust right   **Rev:** Capt. Cook, ship and map   **Edge:** Reeded

Date	Mintage	F	VF	XF	Unc	BU
2003PM Proof	—	Value: 50.00

KM# 20   2 POUNDS
28.2800 g., Copper-Nickel, 38.6 mm.   **Obv:** Crowned bust right   **Rev:** Sir Ernest Shackleton and icebound ship   **Edge:** Reeded

Date	Mintage	F	VF	XF	Unc	BU
2004	—	—	—	—	15.00	16.50

KM# 20a   2 POUNDS
28.2800 g., 0.9250 Silver 0.8410 oz. ASW, 38.6 mm.   **Obv:** Crowned bust right   **Rev:** Sir Ernest Shackleton and icebound ship   **Edge:** Reeded

Date	Mintage	F	VF	XF	Unc	BU
2004 Proof	10,000	Value: 50.00

KM# 21   2 POUNDS
28.2800 g., Copper-Nickel, 38.6 mm.   **Subject:** Centennial of Grytviken   **Obv:** Crowned bust right   **Rev:** Portrait above ship in harbor   **Edge:** Reeded

Date	Mintage	F	VF	XF	Unc	BU
2004	—	—	—	—	15.00	16.50

KM# 21a   2 POUNDS
28.2800 g., 0.9250 Silver 0.8410 oz. ASW, 38.6 mm.   **Subject:** Centennial of Grytviken   **Obv:** Crowned bust right   **Rev:** Portrait above ship in harbor   **Edge:** Reeded

Date	Mintage	F	VF	XF	Unc	BU
2004 Proof	—	Value: 50.00

KM# 25   2 POUNDS
Copper-Nickel   **Subject:** Marriage of Charles to Parker Bowles   **Rev:** Arms of Prince of Wales

Date	Mintage	F	VF	XF	Unc	BU
2005	—	—	—	—	8.50	10.00

KM# 22   2 POUNDS
28.3700 g., Copper-Nickel, 38.5 mm.   **Obv:** Elizabeth II   **Rev:** Rockhopper Penguin and chick   **Edge:** Reeded

Date	Mintage	F	VF	XF	Unc	BU
2006	—	—	—	—	12.00	14.00

KM# 23   2 POUNDS
28.3700 g., Copper-Nickel, 38.5 mm.   **Obv:** Elizabeth II   **Rev:** Elephant Seal and cub   **Edge:** Reeded

Date	Mintage	F	VF	XF	Unc	BU
2006	—	—	—	—	10.00	12.00

KM# 24   2 POUNDS
28.3700 g., Copper-Nickel, 38.5 mm.   **Obv:** Elizabeth II   **Rev:** Humpback Whale and calf   **Edge:** Reeded

Date	Mintage	F	VF	XF	Unc	BU
2006	—	—	—	—	8.50	12.00

KM# 26   2 POUNDS
Copper-Nickel **Subject:** Queen Elizabeth's II 80th Birthday **Rev:** Queen on horseback taking part in Trouping of the Color ceremony

Date	Mintage	F	VF	XF	Unc	BU
2006	—	—	—	—	8.50	10.00

KM# 26a   2 POUNDS
28.2800 g., 0.9167 Silver 0.8334 oz. ASW **Subject:** Queen Elizabeth's II 80th Birthday **Rev:** Queen on horseback taking part in Trouping of the Color ceremony

Date	Mintage	F	VF	XF	Unc	BU
2006 Proof	25,000	Value: 75.00				

KM# 27   2 POUNDS
Copper-Nickel, 38.5 mm.   **Rev:** Pair of Grey-headed Albatros

Date	Mintage	F	VF	XF	Unc	BU
2006	—	—	—	—	8.50	12.00

KM# 28   2 POUNDS
Copper-Nickel **Subject:** Queen Elizabeth's II 80th Birthday **Rev:** 1953 Royal family

Date	Mintage	F	VF	XF	Unc	BU
2006	—	—	—	—	8.50	10.00

KM# 28a   2 POUNDS
28.2800 g., 0.9167 Silver 0.8334 oz. ASW **Subject:** Queen Elizabeth's II 80th Birthday **Rev:** 1953 Royal family

Date	Mintage	F	VF	XF	Unc	BU
2006 Proof	25,000	Value: 75.00				

KM# 29   2 POUNDS
Copper-Nickel **Subject:** Queen Elizabeth's II 80th Birthday **Rev:** Wedding of Queen Elizabeth II and Prince Philip

Date	Mintage	F	VF	XF	Unc	BU
2006	—	—	—	—	8.50	10.00

KM# 29a   2 POUNDS
28.2800 g., 0.9167 Silver 0.8334 oz. ASW **Subject:** Queen Elizabeth's 80th Birthday **Rev:** Wedding of Queen Elizabeth II and Prince Philip

Date	Mintage	F	VF	XF	Unc	BU
2006 Proof	25,000	Value: 75.00				

KM# 30   2 POUNDS
Copper-Nickel **Subject:** Queen Elizabeth's II 80th Birthday **Rev:** Queen in Robes of Garter

Date	Mintage	F	VF	XF	Unc	BU
2006	—	—	—	—	8.50	10.00

KM# 30a   2 POUNDS
28.2800 g., 0.9167 Silver 0.8334 oz. ASW **Subject:** Queen Elizabeth's II 80th Birthday **Rev:** Queen in Robes of Garter

Date	Mintage	F	VF	XF	Unc	BU
2006 Proof	25,000	Value: 75.00				

KM# 31   2 POUNDS
Copper-Nickel   **Rev:** Queen Elizabeth II 1926 (1953 portrait)

Date	Mintage	F	VF	XF	Unc	BU
2007	—	—	—	—	8.50	10.00

KM# 32   2 POUNDS
Copper-Nickel **Subject:** 25th Anniversary of Liberation **Rev:** Warship and helicopters

Date	Mintage	F	VF	XF	Unc	BU
2007	—	—	—	—	8.50	10.00

KM# 33   2 POUNDS
Copper-Nickel   **Rev:** Trans Artic Expedition

Date	Mintage	F	VF	XF	Unc	BU
2007	—	—	—	—	8.50	10.00

KM# 34   2 POUNDS
Copper-Nickel **Subject:** International Polar Year **Rev:** Shackelton Expedition

Date	Mintage	F	VF	XF	Unc	BU
2007	—	—	—	—	8.50	10.00

KM# 35   2 POUNDS
Copper-Nickel   **Rev:** Ernest Shacketon

Date	Mintage	F	VF	XF	Unc	BU
2007	—	—	—	—	8.50	10.00

KM# 36   2 POUNDS
Copper-Nickel   **Rev:** James Cook

Date	Mintage	F	VF	XF	Unc	BU
2007	—	—	—	—	8.50	10.00

KM# 37   2 POUNDS
28.2800 g., Copper-Nickel, 38.60 mm.   **Ruler:** Elizabeth II **Subject:** Diamond Wedding Anniversary **Obv:** Conjoined busts with Prince Philip right **Obv. Legend:** SOUTH GEORGIA & SOUTH SANDWICH ISLANDS **Rev:** Bust of Princess Elizabeth facing **Rev. Legend:** Diamond Wedding of H.M. Queen Elizabeth II & H.R.H. Prince Philip **Rev. Inscription:** THE BRIDE **Edge:** Reeded

Date	Mintage	F	VF	XF	Unc	BU
2007	—	—	—	—	15.00	16.50

KM# 37a   2 POUNDS
28.2800 g., 0.9167 Silver ASW 0.8335 0.8334 oz. ASW, 38.60 mm.   **Ruler:** Elizabeth II **Subject:** Diamond Wedding Anniversary **Obv:** Conjoined busts with Prince Philip right **Obv. Legend:** SOUTH GEORGIA & SOUTH SANDWICH ISLANDS **Rev:** Bust of Princess Elizabeth facing **Rev. Legend:** Diamond Wedding of H.M. Queen Elizabeth II & H.R.H. Prince Philip **Rev. Inscription:** THE BRIDE **Edge:** Reeded

Date	Mintage	F	VF	XF	Unc	BU
2007 Proof	25,000	Value: 75.00				

KM# 38   2 POUNDS
28.2800 g., Copper-Nickel, 38.60 mm.   **Ruler:** Elizabeth II **Subject:** Diamond Wedding Anniversary **Obv:** Conjoined busts with Prince Philip right **Obv. Legend:** SOUTH GEORGIA & SOUTH SANDWICH ISLANDS **Rev:** Bust of the bridegroom facing **Rev. Legend:** Diamond Wedding of H.M. Queen Elizabeth II & H.R.H. Prince Philip **Rev. Inscription:** THE BRIDEGROOM **Edge:** Reeded

Date	Mintage	F	VF	XF	Unc	BU
2007	—	—	—	—	15.00	16.50

KM# 38a   2 POUNDS
28.2800 g., 0.9167 Silver ASW 0.8335 0.8334 oz. ASW, 38.60 mm.   **Ruler:** Elizabeth II **Subject:** Diamond Wedding Anniversary **Obv:** Conjoined busts with Prince Philip right **Obv. Legend:** SOUTH GEORGIA & SOUTH SANDWICH ISLANDS **Rev:** Bust of the bridegroom facing **Rev. Legend:** Diamond Wedding of H.M. Queen Elizabeth II & H.R.H. Prince Philip **Rev. Inscription:** THE BRIDEGROOM **Edge:** Reeded

Date	Mintage	F	VF	XF	Unc	BU
2007 Proof	25,000	Value: 75.00				

KM# 39   2 POUNDS
28.2800 g., Copper-Nickel, 38.60 mm.   **Ruler:** Elizabeth II **Subject:** Diamond Wedding Anniversary **Obv:** Conjoined busts with Prince Philip right **Obv. Legend:** SOUTH GEORGIA & SOUTH SANDWICH ISLANDS **Rev:** 1/2 length figures of royal engaged couple looking at each other **Rev. Legend:** Diamond Wedding of H.M. Queen Elizabeth II & H.R.H. Prince Philip **Rev. Inscription:** ROYAL ENGAGEMENT • JULY • 10 • 1947 **Edge:** Reeded

Date	Mintage	F	VF	XF	Unc	BU
2007	—	—	—	—	15.00	16.50

KM# 39a   2 POUNDS
28.2800 g., 0.9167 Silver ASW 0.8335 0.8334 oz. ASW, 38.60 mm.   **Ruler:** Elizabeth II **Subject:** Diamond Wedding Anniversary **Obv:** Conjoined busts with Prince Philip right **Obv. Legend:** SOUTH GEORGIA & SOUTH SANDWICH ISLANDS **Rev:** 1/2 length figures of royal engaged couple looking at each other **Rev. Legend:** Diamond Wedding of H.M. Queen Elizabeth II & H.R.H. Prince Philip **Rev. Inscription:** ROYAL ENGAGEMENT • JULY • 10 • 1947 **Edge:** Reeded

Date	Mintage	F	VF	XF	Unc	BU
2007 Proof	25,000	Value: 75.00				

KM# 40   2 POUNDS
28.2800 g., Copper-Nickel, 38.60 mm.   **Ruler:** Elizabeth II **Subject:** Diamond Wedding Anniversary **Obv:** Conjoined busts with Prince Philip right **Obv. Legend:** SOUTH GEORGIA & SOUTH SANDWICH ISLANDS **Rev:** Marriage license, jubilant crowd scene **Rev. Legend:** Diamond Wedding of H.M. Queen Elizabeth II & H.R.H. Prince Philip **Rev. Inscription:** THE MARRIAGE LICENSE **Edge:** Reeded

Date	Mintage	F	VF	XF	Unc	BU
2007	—	—	—	—	15.00	16.50

KM# 40a   2 POUNDS
28.2800 g., 0.9167 Silver ASW 0.8335 0.8334 oz. ASW, 38.60 mm.   **Ruler:** Elizabeth II **Subject:** Diamond Wedding Anniversary **Obv:** Conjoined busts with Prince Philip right **Obv. Legend:** SOUTH GEORGIA & SOUTH SANDWICH ISLANDS **Rev:** Marriage license, jubilant crowd scene **Rev. Legend:** Diamond Wedding of H.M. Queen Elizabeth II & H.R.H. Prince Philip **Rev. Inscription:** THE MARRIAGE LICENSE **Edge:** Reeded

Date	Mintage	F	VF	XF	Unc	BU
2007 Proof	25,000	Value: 75.00				

KM# 41   2 POUNDS
28.3700 g., Copper-Nickel, 38.5 mm.   **Ruler:** Elizabeth II **Subject:** The Nimrod Expedition **Rev:** Sailing ship stuck in ice

Date	Mintage	F	VF	XF	Unc	BU
2009PM	—	—	—	—	—	16.50

KM# 19   10 POUNDS
155.5100 g., 0.9990 Silver 4.9946 oz. ASW, 65 mm.   **Obv:** Crowned bust right **Rev:** Capt. Cook, ship and map **Edge:** Reeded

Date	Mintage	F	VF	XF	Unc	BU
2003PM Proof	2,003	Value: 225				

KM# 8   20 POUNDS
6.2200 g., 0.9999 Gold 0.1999 oz. AGW, 22 mm.   **Obv:** Crowned bust right **Rev:** Sir Ernest H. Shackleton and ship **Edge:** Reeded

Date	Mintage	F	VF	XF	Unc	BU
2001 Proof	Est. 2,000	Value: 400				

KM# 10   20 POUNDS
6.2200 g., 0.9999 Gold 0.1999 oz. AGW   **Obv:** Crowned bust right **Rev:** Sir Joseph Banks cameo and ship

Date	Mintage	F	VF	XF	Unc	BU
2001 Proof	Est. 2,000	Value: 400				

KM# 16   20 POUNDS
6.2200 g., 0.9999 Gold 0.1999 oz. AGW, 22 mm.   **Subject:** Princess Diana **Obv:** Crowned bust right **Rev:** Diana's portrait **Edge:** reeded

Date	Mintage	F	VF	XF	Unc	BU
2002PM Proof	—	Value: 400				

KM# 12   20 POUNDS
6.2200 g., 0.9990 Gold 0.1998 oz. AGW, 22 mm.   **Subject:** Queen Elizabeth II's Golden Jubilee **Obv:** Crowned bust right **Rev:** Young crowned bust right **Edge:** Reeded

Date	Mintage	F	VF	XF	Unc	BU
2002 Proof	2,002	Value: 400				

KM# 14   20 POUNDS
6.2200 g., 0.9990 Gold 0.1998 oz. AGW, 22 mm.   **Subject:** Queen Elizabeth II's Golden Jubilee **Obv:** Crowned bust right **Rev:** National arms **Edge:** Reeded

Date	Mintage	F	VF	XF	Unc	BU
2002 Proof	2,002	Value: 400				

SPAIN

The Kingdom of Spain, forming the greater part of the Iberian Peninsula of southwest Europe, has an area of 195,988 sq. mi. (504,714 sq. km.) and a population of 39.4 million including the Balearic and the Canary Islands. Capital: Madrid. The economy is based on agriculture, industry and tourism. Machinery, fruit, vegetables and chemicals are exported.

RULER
Juan Carlos I, 1975-

MINT MARK
After 1982
(M) - Crowned "M" – Madrid

KINGDOM
1949 - Present

DECIMAL COINAGE
Peseta System

100 Centimos = 1 Peseta

KM# 832   PESETA
0.5500 g., Aluminum, 14 mm.   **Ruler:** Juan Carlos I **Obv:** Vertical line divides head left from value **Rev:** Crowned shield flanked by pillars with banner **Edge:** Plain

Date	Mintage	F	VF	XF	Unc	BU
2001	62,300,000	—	—	0.10	0.30	0.50

KM# 833 5 PESETAS
3.0000 g., Aluminum-Bronze, 17.5 mm. **Ruler:** Juan Carlos I
Obv: Stylized JC I and date **Rev:** Value above stylized sailboats
Edge: Plain

Date	Mintage	F	VF	XF	Unc	BU
2001	294,000,000	—	—	—	0.10	0.25	0.35

KM# 1013 25 PESETAS
4.2500 g., Aluminum-Bronze, 19.5 mm. **Ruler:** Juan Carlos I
Obv: Center hole divides bust left and vertical letters **Rev:**
Crowned above center hole, order collar at right, value at left
Edge: Plain

Date	Mintage	F	VF	XF	Unc	BU
2001	91,200,000	—	—	—	2.00	2.50

KM# 1016 100 PESETAS
9.2500 g., Aluminum-Bronze, 24.5 mm. **Ruler:** Juan Carlos I
Subject: 132nd Anniversary of the Peseta **Obv:** Head left **Rev:**
Seated allegorical figure from an old coin design **Edge:** Fleur-de-lis repeated

Date	Mintage	F	VF	XF	Unc	BU
2001	142,800,000	—	—	—	2.25	2.75

KM# 924 500 PESETAS
12.0000 g., Aluminum-Bronze, 28 mm. **Ruler:** Juan Carlos I **Obv:**
Conjoined heads of Juan Carlos and Sofia left **Rev:** Crowned shield
flanked by pillars with banner, vertical value at right

Date	Mintage	F	VF	XF	Unc	BU
2001	3,300,000	—	—	—	7.00	9.00

KM# 1131 500 PESETAS
6.7300 g., Silver, 26.96 mm. **Ruler:** Juan Carlos I **Obv:** Minting
equipment **Obv. Legend:** ESPAÑA **Rev:** Copy of Charles II silver
Reales coin **Rev. Legend:** CASA DE LA MONEDA DE SEGOVIA
Edge: Reeded **Note:** Aqueduct and crowned M mintmarks
appear on obverse

Date	Mintage	F	VF	XF	Unc	BU
2001 Proof	—	Value: 20.00				

KM# 1017 2000 PESETAS
18.0000 g., 0.9250 Silver 0.5353 oz. ASW, 32.9 mm. **Ruler:**
Juan Carlos I **Subject:** 132nd Anniversary of the Peseta **Obv:**
Conjoined heads left **Rev:** Seated allegorical design from the
1869 Spanish coin series **Edge:** Plain

Date	Mintage	F	VF	XF	Unc	BU
2001	1,942,835	—	—	—	30.00	35.00

KM# 1038 2000 PESETAS
27.0000 g., 0.9250 Silver 0.8029 oz. ASW, 40 mm. **Ruler:**
Juan Carlos I **Subject:** Segovia Mint's 500th Anniversary **Obv:**
Hammer coining scene within beaded circle **Rev:** Segovia Mint
8 reales coin design of 1588 **Edge:** Reeded

Date	Mintage	F	VF	XF	Unc	BU
2001 Proof	15,000	Value: 55.00				

EURO COINAGE
European Union Issues

KM# 1040 EURO CENT
2.3000 g., Copper Plated Steel, 16.3 mm. **Ruler:** Juan Carlos I
Obv: Cathedral of Santiago de Compostela **Rev:** Value and globe
Edge: Plain

Date	Mintage	F	VF	XF	Unc	BU
2001(M)	130,900,000	—	—	—	0.25	0.30
2002(M)	141,100,000	—	—	—	0.25	0.30
2002(M) Proof	35,000	Value: 10.00				
2003(M)	670,500,000	—	—	—	0.25	0.30
2003(M) Proof	20,000	Value: 10.00				
2004(M)	206,700,000	—	—	—	0.25	0.30
2005(M)	444,200,000	—	—	—	0.25	0.30
2005(M) Proof	3,000	Value: 10.00				
2006(M)	383,900,000	—	—	—	0.25	0.35
2007(M)	—	—	—	—	0.25	0.35
2007(M) Proof	5,000	Value: 10.00				
2008(M)	—	—	—	—	0.25	0.35
2008(M) Proof	5,000	Value: 10.00				
2009(M)	—	—	—	—	0.25	0.35
2009(M) Proof	5,000	Value: 10.00				

KM# 1144 EURO CENT
2.3000 g., Copper Plated Steel, 16.25 mm. **Ruler:** Juan Carlos I
Obv: Cathedral of Santiago de Compostela **Rev:** Value and globe

Date	Mintage	F	VF	XF	Unc	BU
2010	—	—	—	—	0.25	0.35
2010 Proof	—	Value: 10.00				
2011	—	—	—	—	0.25	0.35
2011 Proof	—	Value: 10.00				
2012	—	—	—	—	0.25	0.35
2012 Proof	—	Value: 10.00				

KM# 1041 2 EURO CENT
3.0600 g., Copper Plated Steel, 16.25 mm. **Ruler:** Juan Carlos I
Obv: Cathedral of Santiago de Compostela **Rev:** Value and globe
Edge: Grooved

Date	Mintage	F	VF	XF	Unc	BU
2001(M)	463,100,000	—	—	—	0.25	0.30
2002(M)	4,100,000	—	—	—	1.25	1.50
2002(M) Proof	35,000	Value: 10.00				
2003(M)	31,600,000	—	—	—	1.00	1.25
2003(M) Proof	20,000	Value: 10.00				
2004(M)	206,700,000	—	—	—	0.25	0.30
2005(M)	275,100,000	—	—	—	0.25	0.30
2005(M) Proof	3,000	Value: 10.00				
2006(M)	262,200,000	—	—	—	0.25	0.30
2007(M)	—	—	—	—	0.25	0.30
2007(M) Proof	5,000	Value: 10.00				
2008(M)	—	—	—	—	0.25	0.30
2008(M) Proof	5,000	Value: 10.00				
2009(M)	—	—	—	—	0.25	0.30
2009(M) Proof	5,000	Value: 10.00				

KM# 1145 2 EURO CENT
3.0600 g., Copper Plated Steel, 18.75 mm. **Ruler:** Juan Carlos I
Obv: Cathedral of Santiago de Compostela **Rev:** Value and globe
Edge: Grooved

Date	Mintage	F	VF	XF	Unc	BU
2010	—	—	—	—	0.25	0.30
2010 Proof	—	Value: 10.00				
2011	—	—	—	—	0.25	0.30
2011 Proof	—	Value: 10.00				
2012	—	—	—	—	0.25	0.30
2012 Proof	—	Value: 10.00				

KM# 1042 5 EURO CENT
3.9200 g., Copper Plated Steel, 21.25 mm. **Ruler:** Juan Carlos I
Obv: Cathedral of Santiago de Compostela **Rev:** Value and globe
Edge: Plain

Date	Mintage	F	VF	XF	Unc	BU
2001(M)	216,100,000	—	—	—	0.50	0.60
2002(M)	8,300,000	—	—	—	1.00	1.50
2002(M) Proof	35,000	Value: 10.00				
2003(M)	327,600,000	—	—	—	0.50	0.60
2003(M) Proof	8,904	Value: 10.00				
2004(M)	258,700,000	—	—	—	0.40	0.50
2005(M)	411,400,000	—	—	—	0.40	0.50
2005(M) Proof	3,000	Value: 10.00				
2006(M)	142,800,000	—	—	—	0.40	0.50
2007(M)	—	—	—	—	0.40	0.50
2007(M) Proof	5,000	Value: 10.00				
2008(M)	—	—	—	—	0.40	0.50
2008(M) Proof	2,000	Value: 10.00				
2009(M)	—	—	—	—	0.40	0.50
2009(M) Proof	5,000	Value: 10.00				

KM# 1146 5 EURO CENT
3.9200 g., Copper Plated Steel, 21.25 mm. **Ruler:** Juan Carlos I
Obv: Cathedral of Santiago de Compostela **Rev:** Value and globe

Date	Mintage	F	VF	XF	Unc	BU
2010	—	—	—	—	0.40	0.50
2010 Proof	—	Value: 10.00				
2011	—	—	—	—	0.40	0.50
2011 Proof	—	Value: 10.00				
2012	—	—	—	—	0.40	0.50
2012 Proof	—	Value: 10.00				

KM# 1043 10 EURO CENT
4.0700 g., Brass, 19.7 mm. **Ruler:** Juan Carlos I **Obv:** Head of
Cervantes with ruffed collar 1/4 left within star border **Rev:** Value
and map **Edge:** Reeded

Date	Mintage	F	VF	XF	Unc	BU
2001(M)	160,100,000	—	—	—	0.60	0.75
2002(M)	113,100,000	—	—	—	0.60	0.75
2002(M) Proof	35,000	Value: 10.00				
2003(M)	292,500,000	—	—	—	0.75	0.90
2003(M) Proof	20,000	Value: 10.00				
2004(M)	121,900,000	—	—	—	0.40	0.50
2005(M)	321,300,000	—	—	—	0.40	0.50
2005(M) Proof	3,000	Value: 10.00				
2006(M)	91,800,000	—	—	—	0.40	0.50

KM# 1070   10 EURO CENT
4.1000 g., Brass, 19.7 mm.   **Ruler:** Juan Carlos I   **Obv:** Cervantes   **Rev:** Relief map of Western Europe, stars, lines and value   **Edge:** Reeded

Date	Mintage	F	VF	XF	Unc	BU
2007(M)	132,058,000	—	—	—	0.75	1.00
2007(M) Proof	5,000	Value: 12.00				
2008(M)	—	—	—	—	0.75	1.00
2008(M) Proof	5,000	Value: 12.00				
2009(M)	—	—	—	—	0.75	1.00
2009(M) Proof	5,000	Value: 12.00				

KM# 1147   10 EURO CENT
4.1000 g., Brass, 19.75 mm.   **Ruler:** Juan Carlos I   **Obv:** Cervantes bust at right   **Rev:** Relief map of Western Europe, stars, lines and value   **Edge:** Reeded

Date	Mintage	F	VF	XF	Unc	BU
2010	—	—	—	—	0.75	1.00
2010 Proof	—	Value: 12.00				
2011	—	—	—	—	0.75	1.00
2011 Proof	—	Value: 12.00				
2012	—	—	—	—	0.75	1.00
2012 Proof	—	Value: 12.00				

KM# 1044   20 EURO CENT
5.6200 g., Brass, 22.2 mm.   **Ruler:** Juan Carlos I   **Obv:** Head of Cervantes with ruffed collar 1/4 left within star border   **Rev:** Value and map   **Edge:** Notched

Date	Mintage	F	VF	XF	Unc	BU
2001(M)	146,600,000	—	—	—	1.00	1.25
2002(M)	91,500,000	—	—	—	0.60	0.75
2002(M) Proof	35,000	Value: 12.00				
2003(M)	4,100,000	—	—	—	1.25	1.50
2003(M) Proof	20,000	Value: 12.00				
2004(M)	3,900,000	—	—	—	0.60	0.75
2005(M)	4,000,000	—	—	—	0.60	0.75
2005(M) Proof	3,000	Value: 12.00				
2006(M)	102,000,000	—	—	—	0.60	0.75

KM# 1071   20 EURO CENT
5.7300 g., Brass, 22.3 mm.   **Ruler:** Juan Carlos I   **Obv:** Cervantes   **Rev:** Relief map of Western Europe, stars, lines and value   **Edge:** Notched

Date	Mintage	F	VF	XF	Unc	BU
2007(M)	46,458,000	—	—	—	1.00	1.25
2007(M) Proof	5,000	Value: 12.00				
2008(M)	—	—	—	—	1.00	1.25
2008(M) Proof	2,000	Value: 12.00				
2009(M)	—	—	—	—	1.00	1.25
2009(M) Proof	5,000	Value: 12.00				

KM# 1148   20 EURO CENT
5.7400 g., Brass, 22.25 mm.   **Ruler:** Juan Carlos I   **Obv:** Cervantes bust at right   **Rev:** Relief map of Western Europe, stars, lines and value   **Edge:** Notched

Date	Mintage	F	VF	XF	Unc	BU
2010	—	—	—	—	1.00	1.25
2010 Proof	—	Value: 12.00				
2011	—	—	—	—	1.00	1.25
2011 Proof	—	Value: 12.00				
2012	—	—	—	—	1.00	1.25
2012 Proof	—	Value: 12.00				

KM# 1045   50 EURO CENT
7.8100 g., Brass, 24.2 mm.   **Ruler:** Juan Carlos I   **Obv:** Head of Cervantes with ruffed collar 1/4 left within star border   **Rev:** Value and map   **Edge:** Reeded

Date	Mintage	F	VF	XF	Unc	BU
2001(M)	351,100,000	—	—	—	1.00	1.25
2002(M)	9,800,000	—	—	—	3.00	3.50

Date	Mintage	F	VF	XF	Unc	BU
2002(M) Proof	35,000	Value: 12.00				
2003(M)	6,000,000	—	—	—	3.00	3.50
2003(M) Proof	20,000	Value: 12.00				
2004(M)	4,400,000	—	—	—	1.50	2.00
2005(M)	3,900,000	—	—	—	1.25	1.50
2005(M) Proof	3,000	Value: 12.00				
2006(M)	4,000,000	—	—	—	1.25	1.50

KM# 1072   50 EURO CENT
7.8500 g., Brass, 24.2 mm.   **Ruler:** Juan Carlos I   **Obv:** Cervantes   **Rev:** Relief map of Western Europe, stars, lines and value   **Edge:** Reeded

Date	Mintage	F	VF	XF	Unc	BU
2007(M)	3,958,000	—	—	—	1.25	1.50
2007(M) Proof	5,000	Value: 12.00				
2008(M)	—	—	—	—	1.25	1.50
2008(M) Proof	5,000	Value: 12.00				
2009(M)	—	—	—	—	1.25	1.50
2009(M) Proof	5,000	Value: 12.00				

KM# 1149   50 EURO CENT
7.8000 g., Brass, 24.25 mm.   **Ruler:** Juan Carlos I   **Obv:** Cervantes bust at right   **Rev:** Relief map of Western Europe, stars, lines and value   **Edge:** Reeded

Date	Mintage	F	VF	XF	Unc	BU
2010	—	—	—	—	1.25	1.50
2010 Proof	—	Value: 12.00				
2011	—	—	—	—	1.25	1.50
2011 Proof	—	Value: 12.00				
2012	—	—	—	—	1.25	1.50
2012 Proof	—	Value: 12.00				

KM# 1046   EURO
7.5000 g., Bi-Metallic Copper-Nickel center in Nickel-Brass ring, 23.25 mm.   **Ruler:** Juan Carlos I   **Obv:** Head 1/4 left within circle and star border   **Rev:** Value and map within circle   **Edge:** Segmented reeding

Date	Mintage	F	VF	XF	Unc	BU
2001(M)	259,100,000	—	—	—	3.00	4.00
2002(M)	335,600,000	—	—	—	2.00	2.50
2002(M) Proof	23,000	Value: 15.00				
2003(M)	297,400,000	—	—	—	2.00	2.50
2003(M) Proof	20,000	Value: 15.00				
2004(M)	9,870,000	—	—	—	2.00	2.50
2005(M)	77,800,000	—	—	—	2.00	2.50
2005(M) Proof	3,000	Value: 15.00				
2006(M)	101,600,000	—	—	—	2.00	2.50

KM# 1073   EURO
7.5000 g., Bi-Metallic Copper-Nickel center in Nickel-Brass ring, 23.25 mm.   **Ruler:** Juan Carlos I   **Obv:** King's portrait   **Rev:** Relief map of Western Europe, stars, lines and value   **Edge:** Segmented reeding

Date	Mintage	F	VF	XF	Unc	BU
2007(M)	150,558,000	—	—	—	3.00	3.50
2007(M) Proof	5,000	Value: 15.00				
2008(M)	—	—	—	—	3.00	3.50
2008(M) Proof	5,000	Value: 15.00				
2009(M)	—	—	—	—	3.00	3.50
2009(M) Proof	5,000	Value: 15.00				

KM# 1150   EURO
7.5000 g., Bi-Metallic Copper-Nickel center in Nickel-Brass ring, 23.25 mm.   **Ruler:** Juan Carlos I   **Obv:** King's portrait at right   **Rev:** Relief map of Western Europe, stars, lines and value   **Edge:** Segmented reeding

Date	Mintage	F	VF	XF	Unc	BU
2010	—	—	—	—	3.00	3.50
2010 Proof	—	Value: 15.00				
2011	—	—	—	—	3.00	3.50
2011 Proof	—	Value: 15.00				
2012	—	—	—	—	3.00	3.50
2012 Proof	—	Value: 15.00				

KM# 1047   2 EURO
8.5200 g., Bi-Metallic Brass center in Copper-Nickel ring, 25.7 mm.   **Ruler:** Juan Carlos I   **Obv:** Head 1/4 left within circle and star border   **Rev:** Value and map within circle   **Edge:** Reeded   **Edge Lettering:** 2's and stars

Date	Mintage	F	VF	XF	Unc	BU
2001(M)	140,200,000	—	—	—	4.50	5.00
2002(M)	164,000,000	—	—	—	3.50	4.00
2002(M) Proof	35,000	Value: 20.00				
2003(M)	44,500,000	—	—	—	4.50	5.00
2003(M) Proof	20,000	Value: 20.00				
2004(M)	4,100,000	—	—	—	4.50	5.00
2005(M)	4,000,000	—	—	—	4.50	5.00
2005(M) Proof	3,000	Value: 20.00				
2006(M)	4,000,000	—	—	—	4.50	5.00

KM# 1063   2 EURO
8.5200 g., Bi-Metallic Brass center in Copper-Nickel ring, 25.7 mm.   **Ruler:** Juan Carlos I   **Obv:** Stylized half length figure of Don Quixote holding spear within circle and star border   **Rev:** Value and map within circle and star border   **Edge:** Reeding over stars and 2's   **Note:** Mint mark: Crowned M.

Date	Mintage	F	VF	XF	Unc	BU
2005	8,000,000	—	—	—	5.00	6.00
2005 Proof	3,000	Value: 25.00				

KM# 1074   2 EURO
8.5000 g., Bi-Metallic Brass center in Copper-Nickel ring, 25.8 mm.   **Ruler:** Juan Carlos I   **Obv:** King's portrait   **Rev:** Relief map of Western Europe, stars, lines and value   **Edge:** Reeded   **Edge Lettering:** 2's and stars

Date	Mintage	F	VF	XF	Unc	BU
2007(M)	3,958,000	—	—	—	4.75	5.00
2007(M) Proof	5,000	Value: 20.00				
2008(M)	—	—	—	—	4.75	5.00
2008(M) Proof	5,000	Value: 20.00				
2009(M)	—	—	—	—	4.75	5.00
2009(M) Proof	5,000	Value: 20.00				

KM# 1130 2 EURO
8.5000 g., Bi-Metallic Nickel-Brass center in Copper-Nickel ring, 25.75 mm. **Ruler:** Juan Carlos I **Subject:** 50th Anniversary Treaty of Rome **Obv:** Open treaty book **Obv. Legend:** ESPAÑA **Rev:** Large value at left, modified outline of Europe at right **Edge:** Reeded with 2's and stars

Date	Mintage	F	VF	XF	Unc	BU
2007	7,935,000	—	—	—	7.00	9.00
2007(M) Special Unc.	60,000	—	—	—	—	20.00
2007(M) Proof	5,000	Value: 35.00				

KM# 1142.2 2 EURO
8.5000 g., Bi-Metallic Nickel-Brass center in Copper-Nickel ring, 25.75 mm. **Ruler:** Juan Carlos I **Subject:** European Monetary Unit, 10th Aniversary **Obv:** Stick figure and large E symbol **Edge:** Reeded with 2's and stars

Date	Mintage	F	VF	XF	Unc	BU
2009 Large Stars	—	—	—	—	40.00	45.00

KM# 1142.1 2 EURO
8.5000 g., Bi-Metallic Nickel-Brass center in Copper-Nickel ring, 25.75 mm. **Ruler:** Juan Carlos I **Subject:** European Monetary Unit, 10th Anniversary **Obv:** Stick figure and large E symbol **Rev:** Large value at left, modified map of Europe at right **Edge:** Reeded with 2's and stars

Date	Mintage	F	VF	XF	Unc	BU
2009 Small Stars	—	—	—	—	5.00	6.00
2009 Special Unc.	—	—	—	—	—	20.00
2009 Proof	—	Value: 35.00				

KM# 1151 2 EURO
8.5000 g., Bi-Metallic Nickel-Brass center in Copper-Nickel ring, 25.75 mm. **Ruler:** Juan Carlos I **Obv:** King's portrait at right **Rev:** Relief map of Western Europe, stars, lines and value **Edge:** Reeded with 2's and stars

Date	Mintage	F	VF	XF	Unc	BU
2010	—	—	—	—	4.75	5.00
2010 Proof	—	Value: 20.00				
2011	—	—	—	—	4.75	5.00
2011 Proof	—	Value: 20.00				
2012	—	—	—	—	4.75	5.00
2012 Proof	—	Value: 20.00				

KM# 1152 2 EURO
8.5000 g., Bi-Metallic Nickel-Brass center in Copper-Nickel ring, 25.75 mm. **Ruler:** Juan Carlos I **Subject:** Cordoba - UNESCO Heritage site **Edge:** Reeded with 2's and stars

Date	Mintage	F	VF	XF	Unc	BU
2010	—	—	—	—	7.00	9.00
2010 Proof	5,000	Value: 25.00				

KM# 1184 2 EURO
8.5000 g., Bi-Metallic Nickel-Brass center in Copper-Nickel ring, 25.75 mm. **Ruler:** Juan Carlos I **Subject:** UNESCO Heritage Site - Granada **Obv:** The Alhambra **Edge:** Reeded with 2's and stars

Date	Mintage	F	VF	XF	Unc	BU
2011	8,000,000	—	—	—	7.00	9.00
2011 Proof	5,000	Value: 25.00				

KM# 1252 2 EURO
8.5000 g., Bi-Metallic Nickel-Brass center in Copper-Nickel ring, 25.75 mm. **Ruler:** Juan Carlos I **Subject:** Euro coinage, 10th Anniversary **Obv:** Euro symbol on globe at center, child-like rendering around

Date	Mintage	F	VF	XF	Unc	BU
2012	8,000,000	—	—	—	6.00	8.00
2012 Proof	—	Value: 25.00				

KM# 1153 5 EURO
13.5000 g., 0.9250 Silver 0.4015 oz. ASW, 33 mm. **Ruler:** Juan Carlos I **Subject:** Almeria

Date	Mintage	F	VF	XF	Unc	BU
2010 Proof	—	Value: 45.00				

KM# 1154 5 EURO
13.5000 g., 0.9250 Silver 0.4015 oz. ASW, 33 mm. **Ruler:** Juan Carlos I **Subject:** Huesca

Date	Mintage	F	VF	XF	Unc	BU
2010 Proof	—	Value: 45.00				

KM# 1155 5 EURO
13.5000 g., 0.9250 Silver 0.4015 oz. ASW, 33 mm. **Ruler:** Juan Carlos I **Subject:** Las Palmas G.C.

Date	Mintage	F	VF	XF	Unc	BU
2010 Proof	—	Value: 45.00				

KM# 1156 5 EURO
13.5000 g., 0.9250 Silver 0.4015 oz. ASW, 33 mm. **Ruler:** Juan Carlos I **Subject:** Santander

Date	Mintage	F	VF	XF	Unc	BU
2010 Proof	—	Value: 45.00				

KM# 1157 5 EURO
13.5000 g., 0.9250 Silver 0.4015 oz. ASW, 33 mm. **Ruler:** Juan Carlos I **Subject:** Avila

Date	Mintage	F	VF	XF	Unc	BU
2010 Proof	—	Value: 45.00				

KM# 1158 5 EURO
13.5000 g., 0.9250 Silver 0.4015 oz. ASW, 33 mm. **Ruler:** Juan Carlos I **Subject:** Albacete

Date	Mintage	F	VF	XF	Unc	BU
2010 Proof	—	Value: 45.00				

KM# 1159 5 EURO
13.5000 g., 0.9250 Silver 0.4015 oz. ASW, 33 mm. **Ruler:** Juan Carlos I **Subject:** Barcelona

Date	Mintage	F	VF	XF	Unc	BU
2010 Proof	—	Value: 45.00				

KM# 1160 5 EURO
13.5000 g., 0.9250 Silver 0.4015 oz. ASW, 33 mm. **Ruler:** Juan Carlos I **Subject:** Ceuta

Date	Mintage	F	VF	XF	Unc	BU
2010 Proof	—	Value: 45.00				

KM# 1161 5 EURO
13.5000 g., 0.9250 Silver 0.4015 oz. ASW, 33 mm. **Ruler:** Juan Carlos I **Subject:** Melilla

Date	Mintage	F	VF	XF	Unc	BU
2010 Proof	—	Value: 45.00				

KM# 1162 5 EURO
13.5000 g., 0.9250 Silver 0.4015 oz. ASW, 33 mm. **Ruler:** Juan Carlos I **Subject:** Madrid

Date	Mintage	F	VF	XF	Unc	BU
2010 Proof	—	Value: 45.00				

KM# 1163 5 EURO
13.5000 g., 0.9250 Silver 0.4015 oz. ASW, 33 mm. **Ruler:** Juan Carlos I **Subject:** Pamplona

Date	Mintage	F	VF	XF	Unc	BU
2010 Proof	—	Value: 45.00				

KM# 1164 5 EURO
13.5000 g., 0.9250 Silver 0.4015 oz. ASW, 33 mm. **Ruler:** Juan Carlos I **Subject:** Alicante

Date	Mintage	F	VF	XF	Unc	BU
2010 Proof	—	Value: 45.00				

KM# 1226 5 EURO
13.5000 g., 0.9250 Silver 0.4015 oz. ASW, 33 mm. **Ruler:** Juan Carlos I **Subject:** Oviedo

Date	Mintage	F	VF	XF	Unc	BU
2011 Proof	—	Value: 45.00				

KM# 1227 5 EURO
13.5000 g., 0.9250 Silver 0.4015 oz. ASW **Ruler:** Juan Carlos I **Subject:** Palma

Date	Mintage	F	VF	XF	Unc	BU
2011 Proof	—	Value: 45.00				

KM# 1228 5 EURO
13.5000 g., 0.9250 Silver 0.4015 oz. ASW, 33 mm. **Ruler:** Juan Carlos I **Subject:** Santa Cruz

Date	Mintage	F	VF	XF	Unc	BU
2011 Proof	—	Value: 45.00				

KM# 1229 5 EURO
13.5000 g., 0.9250 Silver 0.4015 oz. ASW, 33 mm. **Ruler:** Juan Carlos I **Subject:** Teruel

Date	Mintage	F	VF	XF	Unc	BU
2011 Proof	—	Value: 45.00				

KM# 1230 5 EURO
13.5000 g., 0.9250 Silver 0.4015 oz. ASW, 33 mm. **Ruler:** Juan Carlos I **Subject:** Bilbao

Date	Mintage	F	VF	XF	Unc	BU
2011 Proof	—	Value: 45.00				

KM# 1231 5 EURO
13.5000 g., 0.9250 Silver 0.4015 oz. ASW, 33 mm. **Ruler:** Juan Carlos I **Subject:** Cadiz

Date	Mintage	F	VF	XF	Unc	BU
2011 Proof	—	Value: 45.00				

KM# 1232 5 EURO
13.5000 g., 0.9250 Silver 0.4015 oz. ASW, 33 mm. **Ruler:** Juan Carlos I **Subject:** Logrono

Date	Mintage	F	VF	XF	Unc	BU
2011 Proof	—	Value: 45.00				

KM# 1233 5 EURO
13.5000 g., 0.9250 Silver 0.4015 oz. ASW, 33 mm. **Ruler:** Juan Carlos I **Subject:** Murcia

Date	Mintage	F	VF	XF	Unc	BU
2011 Proof	—	Value: 45.00				

KM# 1234 5 EURO
13.5000 g., 0.9250 Silver 0.4015 oz. ASW, 33 mm. **Ruler:** Juan Carlos I **Subject:** Donostila

Date	Mintage	F	VF	XF	Unc	BU
2011 Proof	—	Value: 45.00				

KM# 1235 5 EURO
13.5000 g., 0.9250 Silver 0.4015 oz. ASW, 33 mm. **Ruler:** Juan Carlos I **Subject:** Zaragoza

Date	Mintage	F	VF	XF	Unc	BU
2011 Proof	—	Value: 45.00				

KM# 1236 5 EURO
13.5000 g., 0.9250 Silver 0.4015 oz. ASW, 33 mm. **Ruler:** Juan Carlos I **Subject:** A Coruna

Date	Mintage	F	VF	XF	Unc	BU
2011 Proof	—	Value: 45.00				

KM# 1237 5 EURO
13.5000 g., 0.9250 Silver 0.4015 oz. ASW, 33 mm. **Ruler:** Juan Carlos I **Subject:** Badajoz

Date	Mintage	F	VF	XF	Unc	BU
2011 Proof	—	Value: 45.00				

KM# 1238 5 EURO
13.5000 g., 0.9250 Silver 0.4015 oz. ASW, 33 mm. **Ruler:** Juan Carlos I **Subject:** Cordoba

Date	Mintage	F	VF	XF	Unc	BU
2011 Proof	—	Value: 45.00				

KM# 1239 5 EURO
13.5000 g., 0.9250 Silver 0.4015 oz. ASW, 33 mm. **Ruler:** Juan Carlos I **Subject:** Girona

Date	Mintage	F	VF	XF	Unc	BU
2011 Proof	—	Value: 45.00				

KM# 1240 5 EURO
13.5000 g., 0.9250 Silver 0.4015 oz. ASW, 33 mm. **Ruler:** Juan Carlos I **Subject:** Leon

Date	Mintage	F	VF	XF	Unc	BU
2011 Proof	—	Value: 45.00				

KM# 1241 5 EURO
13.5000 g., 0.9250 Silver 0.4015 oz. ASW, 33 mm. **Ruler:** Juan Carlos I **Subject:** Lugo

Date	Mintage	F	VF	XF	Unc	BU
2011 Proof	—	Value: 45.00				

KM# 1242 5 EURO
13.5000 g., 0.9250 Silver 0.4015 oz. ASW, 33 mm. **Ruler:** Juan Carlos I **Subject:** Burgos

Date	Mintage	F	VF	XF	Unc	BU
2011 Proof	—	Value: 45.00				

KM# 1243 5 EURO
13.5000 g., 0.9250 Silver 0.4015 oz. ASW, 33 mm. **Ruler:** Juan Carlos I **Subject:** Caceres

Date	Mintage	F	VF	XF	Unc	BU
2011 Proof	—	Value: 45.00				

KM# 1244 5 EURO
13.5000 g., 0.9250 Silver 0.4015 oz. ASW, 33 mm. **Ruler:** Juan Carlos I **Subject:** Castello

Date	Mintage	F	VF	XF	Unc	BU
2011 Proof	—	Value: 45.00				

KM# 1245 5 EURO
13.5000 g., 0.9250 Silver 0.4015 oz. ASW, 33 mm. **Ruler:** Juan Carlos I **Subject:** Ciudad Real

Date	Mintage	F	VF	XF	Unc	BU
2011 Proof	—	Value: 45.00				

KM# 1048 10 EURO
27.0000 g., 0.9250 Silver 0.8029 oz. ASW, 40 mm. **Ruler:** Juan Carlos I **Subject:** Spanish Presidency of the European Union **Obv:** Head left **Rev:** Map of Europe **Edge:** Reeded

Date	Mintage	F	VF	XF	Unc	BU
2002 Proof	30,000	Value: 55.00				

KM# 1078   10 EURO
27.0000 g., 0.9250 Silver 0.8029 oz. ASW, 40 mm.   **Ruler:** Juan Carlos I **Subject:** XIX Winter Olympics - Salt Lake City **Obv:** Head left **Obv. Legend:** JUAN CARLOS I REY DE ESPAÑA **Rev:** Cross country skier right, stylized snowflake at right **Rev. Legend:** JUEGOS OLIMPICOS DE - INVERNO 2002

Date	Mintage	F	VF	XF	Unc	BU
2002(M) Proof	30,000	Value: 60.00				

KM# 1079   10 EURO
27.0000 g., 0.9250 Silver 0.8029 oz. ASW, 40 mm.   **Ruler:** Juan Carlos I **Subject:** XVII Football World Games 2002 - South Korea and Japan **Obv. Legend:** MUNDIAL DE FUTBOL/2002 - ESPAÑA **Rev:** Football against net

Date	Mintage	F	VF	XF	Unc	BU
2002(M) Proof	25,000	Value: 60.00				

KM# 1080   10 EURO
27.0000 g., 0.9250 Silver 0.8029 oz. ASW, 40 mm.   **Ruler:** Juan Carlos I **Subject:** XVII Football World Games 2002 - South Korea and Japan **Obv. Legend:** MUNDIAL DE FUTBOL/2002 - ESPAÑA **Rev:** Glove

Date	Mintage	F	VF	XF	Unc	BU
2002(M) Proof	25,000	Value: 60.00				

KM# 1087   10 EURO
27.0000 g., 0.9250 Silver 0.8029 oz. ASW, 40 mm.   **Ruler:** Juan Carlos I **Subject:** 100th Anniversary - Birth of Luis Cernuda **Obv:** Head left

Date	Mintage	F	VF	XF	Unc	BU
2002(M) Proof	25,000	Value: 60.00				

KM# 1088   10 EURO
27.0000 g., 0.9250 Silver 0.8029 oz. ASW, 40 mm.   **Ruler:** Juan Carlos I **Subject:** 100th Anniversary - Birth of Rafael Alberti **Obv:** Head left **Obv. Legend:** JUAN CARLOS I REY DE ESPAÑA **Rev:** Bust of Alberti facing 3/4 right

Date	Mintage	F	VF	XF	Unc	BU
2002(M) Proof	25,000	Value: 60.00				

KM# 1082   10 EURO
27.0000 g., 0.9250 Silver 0.8029 oz. ASW, 40 mm.   **Ruler:** Juan Carlos I **Subject:** 150th Anniversary Birth of Antonio Gaudí **Obv:** Bust of Gaudí at right **Obv. Legend:** Año Internacional **Rev:** Casa Milà

Date	Mintage	F	VF	XF	Unc	BU
2002(M) Proof	25,000	Value: 55.00				

KM# 1083   10 EURO
27.0000 g., 0.9250 Silver 0.8029 oz. ASW, 40 mm.   **Ruler:** Juan Carlos I **Subject:** 150th Anniversary Birth of Antonio Gaudí **Obv:** Bust of Gaudí at right **Obv. Legend:** Año Internacional **Rev:** El Capricho

Date	Mintage	F	VF	XF	Unc	BU
2002(M) Proof	25,000	Value: 55.00				

KM# 1084   10 EURO
27.0000 g., 0.9250 Silver 0.8029 oz. ASW, 40 mm.   **Ruler:** Juan Carlos I **Subject:** 150th Anniversary - Birth of Antonio Gaudí **Obv:** Bust of Gaudí at right **Obv. Legend:** Año Internacional **Rev:** Parque Güell

Date	Mintage	F	VF	XF	Unc	BU
2002(M) Proof	25,000	Value: 55.00				

KM# 1089   10 EURO
27.0000 g., 0.9250 Silver 0.8029 oz. ASW, 40 mm.   **Ruler:** Juan Carlos I **Series:** Ibero-America V - ships **Obv:** Crowned arms in center circle, 10 participating country arms in outer circle **Obv. Legend:** JUAN CARLOS I REY DE ESPAÑA **Rev:** Galleon of the Spanish Armada **Rev. Legend:** ENCUENTRO DE DOS MUNDOS **Note:** Issued in 2003.

Date	Mintage	F	VF	XF	Unc	BU
2002(M) Proof	12,000	Value: 135				

KM# 1050   10 EURO
27.0000 g., 0.9250 Silver 0.8029 oz. ASW, 40 mm.   **Ruler:** Juan Carlos I **Subject:** Annexation of Minorca **Obv:** Conjoined heads left **Rev:** Uniformed equestrians shaking hands flanked by ships **Edge:** Reeded **Note:** Mint mark: Crowned M.

Date	Mintage	F	VF	XF	Unc	BU
2002 Proof	30,000	Value: 55.00				

KM# 1076   10 EURO
27.0000 g., 0.9250 Silver 0.8029 oz. ASW, 40 mm.   **Ruler:** Juan Carlos I **Subject:** FIFA World Cup **Obv:** Kings head left **Rev:** Goalie jumping for ball by net **Edge:** Reeded **Note:** Issued in 2004.

Date	Mintage	F	VF	XF	Unc	BU
2003(M) Proof	50,000	Value: 55.00				

KM# 1090   10 EURO
27.0000 g., 0.9250 Silver 0.8029 oz. ASW, 40 mm.   **Ruler:** Juan Carlos I **Obv:** Conjoined heads left **Obv. Legend:** JUAN CARLOS I Y SOFIA **Rev:** Ediface of Parliament building in Madrid **Rev. Legend:** CONSTITUCION ESPAÑOLA

Date	Mintage	F	VF	XF	Unc	BU
2003(M) Proof	30,000	Value: 60.00				

KM# 1092   10 EURO
27.0000 g., 0.9250 Silver 0.8029 oz. ASW, 40 mm.   **Ruler:** Juan Carlos I **Subject:** !st Anniversary of Euro **Obv:** Conjoined heads left **Obv. Legend:** PREMIER ANIVERSARIO EURO ? JUAN CARLOS I Y SOFIA **Rev:** Europa riding steer left

Date	Mintage	F	VF	XF	Unc	BU
2003(M) Proof	50,000	Value: 55.00				

KM# 1094   10 EURO
27.0000 g., 0.9250 Silver 0.8029 oz. ASW, 40 mm.   **Ruler:** Juan Carlos I **Subject:** World Swimming Championship Games - Barcelona 2003 **Obv:** Head left **Obv. Legend:** JUAN CARLOS I REY DE ESPAÑA **Rev:** Swimmer doing the crawl right **Rev. Legend:** X FINA CAMPEONATOS DEL MUNDO DENATACION

Date	Mintage	F	VF	XF	Unc	BU
2003(M) Proof	30,000	Value: 60.00				

KM# 1052   10 EURO
27.0000 g., 0.9250 Silver 0.8029 oz. ASW, 40 mm.   **Ruler:** Juan Carlos I **Obv:** Head left **Rev:** Sailing ship - De Eleano **Edge:** Reeded

Date	Mintage	F	VF	XF	Unc	BU
2003 Proof	50,000	Value: 55.00				

KM# 1053   10 EURO
27.0000 g., 0.9250 Silver 0.8029 oz. ASW, 40 mm.   **Ruler:** Juan Carlos I **Obv:** Juan Carlos I **Rev:** Miguel Lopez de Legazpi **Edge:** Reeded

Date	Mintage	F	VF	XF	Unc	BU
2003 Proof	25,000	Value: 55.00				

KM# 1054   10 EURO
27.0000 g., 0.9250 Silver 0.8029 oz. ASW, 40 mm.   **Ruler:** Juan Carlos I **Obv:** Head facing **Rev:** Seated female figure and Swan **Edge:** Reeded

Date	Mintage	F	VF	XF	Unc	BU
2003 Proof	25,000	Value: 60.00				

KM# 1055   10 EURO
27.0000 g., 0.9250 Silver 0.8029 oz. ASW, 40 mm.   **Ruler:** Juan Carlos I **Obv:** Head facing **Rev:** Dali's painting "El gran masturbador" of 1929 **Edge:** Reeded

Date	Mintage	F	VF	XF	Unc	BU
2004 Proof	25,000	Value: 60.00				

KM# 1056   10 EURO
27.0000 g., 0.9250 Silver 0.8029 oz. ASW, 40 mm.   **Ruler:** Juan Carlos I **Obv:** Head facing **Rev:** Dali's self portrait with bacon strip **Edge:** Reeded

Date	Mintage	F	VF	XF	Unc	BU
2004 Proof	25,000	Value: 60.00				

KM# 1059   10 EURO
27.0000 g., 0.9250 Silver 0.8029 oz. ASW, 40 mm.   **Ruler:** Juan Carlos I **Obv:** Conjoined heads left **Rev:** Bust of St. James facing **Edge:** Reeded

Date	Mintage	F	VF	XF	Unc	BU
2004 Proof	20,000	Value: 55.00				

KM# 1060   10 EURO
27.0000 g., 0.9250 Silver 0.8029 oz. ASW, 40 mm. **Ruler:**
Juan Carlos I **Obv:** Conjoined heads left within beaded circle
Rev: Bust 1/4 left within beaded circle (1451-1504) **Edge:**
Reeded

Date	Mintage	F	VF	XF	Unc	BU
2004 Proof	20,000	Value: 55.00				

KM# 1099   10 EURO
27.0000 g., 0.9250 Silver 0.8029 oz. ASW, 40 mm. **Ruler:**
Juan Carlos I **Subject:** Expansion of the European Union **Obv:**
Head left **Obv. Legend:** JUAN CARLOS I Y SOFIA **Rev:** Outlined
map of European Union

Date	Mintage	F	VF	XF	Unc	BU
2004(M) Proof	50,000	Value: 45.00				

KM# 1101   10 EURO
27.0000 g., 0.9250 Silver 0.8029 oz. ASW, 40 mm. **Ruler:**
Juan Carlos I **Subject:** XXVIII Summer Olympics - Athens 2004
Obv: Conjoined heads left **Obv. Legend:** JUAN CARLOS I Y
SOFIA **Rev:** Broad jumper, outlined world map in backgound
Rev. Legend: JUEGOS OLIMICOS

Date	Mintage	F	VF	XF	Unc	BU
2004(M) Proof	30,000	Value: 60.00				

KM# 1102   10 EURO
27.0000 g., 0.9250 Silver 0.8029 oz. ASW, 40 mm. **Ruler:**
Juan Carlos I **Subject:** XVIII World Football games - Germany
2006 **Obv:** Head left **Obv. Legend:** JUAN CARLOS I REY DE
ESPAÑA **Rev:** Goalie deflecting ball at net

Date	Mintage	F	VF	XF	Unc	BU
2004(M) Proof	50,000	Value: 60.00				

KM# 1097   10 EURO
27.0000 g., 0.9250 Silver 0.8029 oz. ASW, 40 mm. **Ruler:**
Juan Carlos I **Subject:** Wedding of Prince Philip and Letizia Ortiz
Rocasolano **Obv:** Conjoined heads left **Obv. Legend:** JUAN
CARLOS I T SOFÍA **Rev:** Busts of wedding couple facing 3/4
right, crowned shield below **Rev. Legend:** FELIPE Y LETIZIA -
22.V.2004

Date	Mintage	F	VF	XF	Unc	BU
2004(M) Proof	100,000	Value: 55.00				

KM# 1104   10 EURO
27.0000 g., 0.9250 Silver 0.8029 oz. ASW, 40 mm. **Ruler:**
Juan Carlos I **Obv:** Quixote seated reading a large book **Obv.**
Legend: ESPAÑA - IV CENTENARIO DE LA PRIMERA
EDICIÓN DE " EL QUIJOTE" **Rev:** Quixote being knocked off his
horse by windmill blade **Rev. Legend:** LA AVENTURA - DE LOS
- MOLINOS DE VIENTO

Date	Mintage	F	VF	XF	Unc	BU
2005(M) Proof	18,000	Value: 65.00				

KM# 1105   10 EURO
27.0000 g., 0.9250 Silver 0.8029 oz. ASW, 40 mm. **Ruler:**
Juan Carlos I **Obv:** Quixote seated reading a large book **Obv.**
Legend: ESPAÑA - IV CENTENARIO DE LA PREMERA
EDICIÓN DE LA "EL QUIJOTE" **Rev:** Quixote thrusting his sword
into an animal skin wine sack **Rev. Legend:** CON UNOS
CUEROS DE VINO - BATALLA

Date	Mintage	F	VF	XF	Unc	BU
2005(M) Proof	18,000	Value: 65.00				

KM# 1106   10 EURO
27.0000 g., 0.9250 Silver 0.8029 oz. ASW, 40 mm. **Ruler:**
Juan Carlos I **Obv:** Quixote seated reading a large book **Obv.**
Legend: ESPAÑA - IV CENTENARIO DE LA PRIMERA
EDICIÓN DE "EL QUIJOTE" **Rev:** Boy mounting a hobby horse
with Quixote on it **Rev. Legend:** LA VENIDA DE CLAVAILEÑO
CON...DILATADA AVENTURA

Date	Mintage	F	VF	XF	Unc	BU
2005(M) Proof	18,000	Value: 65.00				

KM# 1110   10 EURO
27.0000 g., 0.9250 Silver 0.8029 oz. ASW, 40 mm. **Ruler:**
Juan Carlos I **Rev:** Crowned shield at left, head of Prince Philip
at right **Rev. Legend:** XXV ANIVERSARIO - PREMIOS
PRÍNCIPE DE ASTURIAS

Date	Mintage	F	VF	XF	Unc	BU
2005(M) Proof	35,000	Value: 60.00				

KM# 1109   10 EURO
27.0000 g., 0.9250 Silver 0.8029 oz. ASW, 40 mm. **Ruler:**
Juan Carlos I **Series:** Ibero-America VI - Architecture **Obv:**
Crowned arms in center circle, 10 participating country arms in
outer circle **Obv. Legend:** JUAN CARLOS I REY DE ESPAÑA
Rev: General Archives building of West Indes in Seville **Rev.**
Legend: ENCUENTRO DE DOS MUNDOS

Date	Mintage	F	VF	XF	Unc	BU
2005(M) Proof	12,000	Value: 90.00				

KM# 1064   10 EURO
27.0000 g., 0.9250 Silver 0.8029 oz. ASW, 40 mm. **Ruler:**
Juan Carlos I **Subject:** 2006 Winter Olympics **Obv:** Juan Carlos
Rev: Skier **Edge:** Reeded

Date	Mintage	F	VF	XF	Unc	BU
2005 Proof	25,000	Value: 55.00				

KM# 1065   10 EURO
27.0000 g., 0.9250 Silver 0.8029 oz. ASW, 40 mm. **Ruler:**
Juan Carlos I **Subject:** European Peace and Freedom **Obv:**
Juan Carlos **Rev:** European map on clasped hands **Edge:**
Reeded

Date	Mintage	F	VF	XF	Unc	BU
2005 Proof	40,000	Value: 40.00				

KM# 1114   10 EURO
27.0000 g., 0.9250 Silver 0.8029 oz. ASW, 40 mm.   **Ruler:** Juan Carlos I **Subject:** 500th Anniversary Death of Columbus **Obv:** Bust of Columbus facing at right, astrolabe at lower left **Obv. Legend:** ESPAÑA **Rev:** Sailing ship "Santa Maria" **Rev. Legend:** CRISTOBAL COLON **Edge:** Reeded

Date	Mintage	F	VF	XF	Unc	BU
2006(M) Proof	12,000	Value: 65.00				

KM# 1115   10 EURO
27.0000 g., 0.9250 Silver 0.8029 oz. ASW, 40 mm.   **Ruler:** Juan Carlos I **Subject:** 500th Anniversary - Death of Columbus **Obv:** Bust of Columbus facing at left, astrolabe at lower right **Obv. Legend:** ESPAÑA **Rev:** Sailing ship "Pinta" **Rev. Legend:** CRISTOBAL COLON **Edge:** Reeded

Date	Mintage	F	VF	XF	Unc	BU
2006(M) Proof	12,000	Value: 65.00				

KM# 1116   10 EURO
27.0000 g., 0.9250 Silver 0.8029 oz. ASW, 40 mm.   **Ruler:** Juan Carlos I **Subject:** 500th Anniversary - Death of Columbus **Obv:** Bust of Columbus facing at right, astrolabe at lower left **Obv. Legend:** ESPAÑA **Rev:** Sailing ship "Niña" **Rev. Legend:** CRISTOBAL COLON **Edge:** Reeded

Date	Mintage	F	VF	XF	Unc	BU
2006(M) Proof	12,000	Value: 65.00				

KM# 1119   10 EURO
27.0000 g., 0.9250 Silver 0.8029 oz. ASW, 40 mm.   **Ruler:** Juan Carlos I **Subject:** 20th Anniversary of Spain and Portugal membership in European Union **Obv:** Juan Carlos I **Rev:** Outlined map of Europe, bridge below **Rev. Legend:** ADHESIÓN A LAS COMUNIDADES EUROPEAS **Rev. Inscription:** ESPAÑA - PORTUGAL

Date	Mintage	F	VF	XF	Unc	BU
2006(M) Proof	12,000	Value: 60.00				

KM# 1120   10 EURO
27.0000 g., 0.9250 Silver 0.8029 oz. ASW, 40 mm.   **Ruler:** Juan Carlos I **Rev:** Basketball player scoring in front of defender **Rev. Legend:** CAMPEONS DEL MUNDO - JAPÓN 2006

Date	Mintage	F	VF	XF	Unc	BU
2006(M) Proof	15,000	Value: 60.00				

KM# 1122   10 EURO
27.0000 g., 0.9250 Silver 0.8029 oz. ASW, 40 mm.   **Ruler:** Juan Carlos I **Obv:** Head left **Obv. Legend:** JUAN CARLOS I REY DE ESPAÑA **Rev:** Charles I (V) standing facing 3/4 right in front of portal **Rev. Legend:** CAROLVS IMPERATOR

Date	Mintage	F	VF	XF	Unc	BU
2006(M) Proof	35,000	Value: 65.00				

KM# 1124   10 EURO
27.0000 g., 0.9250 Silver 0.8029 oz. ASW, 40 mm.   **Ruler:** Juan Carlos I **Rev:** Two ornate portals **Rev. Legend:** V ANIVERSARIO DEL EURO

Date	Mintage	F	VF	XF	Unc	BU
2007 Proof	12,000	Value: 60.00				

KM# 1125   10 EURO
27.0000 g., 0.9250 Silver 0.8029 oz. ASW, 40 mm.   **Ruler:** Juan Carlos I **Rev:** Stone arch bridge **Rev. Legend:** V ANIVERSARIO DEL EURO

Date	Mintage	F	VF	XF	Unc	BU
2007 Proof	12,000	Value: 60.00				

KM# 1126   10 EURO
27.0000 g., 0.9250 Silver 0.8029 oz. ASW, 40 mm.   **Ruler:** Juan Carlos I **Rev:** Stone archway **Rev. Legend:** V ANIVERSARIO DEL EURO

Date	Mintage	F	VF	XF	Unc	BU
2007 Proof	12,000	Value: 60.00				

KM# 1132   10 EURO
27.0000 g., 0.9250 Silver 0.8029 oz. ASW, 40 mm.   **Ruler:** Juan Carlos I **Obv:** Conjoined heads left **Obv. Legend:** JUAN CARLOS I Y SOFÍA - AÑO DE ESPAÑA EN CHINA **Rev:** Early silver "Pillar" reales coin with Chinese characters to left and right of pillars **Rev. Legend:** VTRAQUE VNVM

Date	Mintage	F	VF	XF	Unc	BU
2007 Proof	20,000	Value: 55.00				

KM# 1134   10 EURO
27.0000 g., 0.9250 Silver 0.8029 oz. ASW, 40 mm.   **Ruler:** Juan Carlos I **Obv:** Head left **Obv. Legend:** JUAN CARLOS I REY DE ESPAÑA **Rev:** Basketball player shooting basket **Rev. Legend:** EUROBASKET 2007

Date	Mintage	F	VF	XF	Unc	BU
2007 Proof	12,000	Value: 65.00				

KM# 1141 10 EURO
27.0000 g., 0.9250 Silver 0.8029 oz. ASW, 40 mm. **Ruler:**
Juan Carlos I **Subject:** Zaragoza Expo 2008

Date	Mintage	F	VF	XF	Unc	BU
2007 Proof	25,000	Value: 55.00				

KM# 1135 10 EURO
27.0000 g., 0.9250 Silver 0.8029 oz. ASW, 40 mm. **Ruler:**
Juan Carlos I **Subject:** Treaty of Rome, 50th Anniversary **Obv:**
Head left **Rev:** Map of Western Europe

Date	Mintage	F	VF	XF	Unc	BU
2007 Proof	15,000	Value: 60.00				

KM# 1137 10 EURO
27.0000 g., 0.9250 Silver 0.8029 oz. ASW, 40 mm. **Ruler:**
Juan Carlos I **Subject:** El Cid 700th Anniversary **Obv:** Female
standing before arches **Rev:** Monk writing

Date	Mintage	F	VF	XF	Unc	BU
2007 Proof	12,000	Value: 65.00				

KM# 1140 10 EURO
27.0000 g., 0.9250 Silver 0.8029 oz. ASW, 40 mm. **Ruler:**
Juan Carlos I **Subject:** International Polar Year **Rev:** Ship left,
outline map of Antarctica in background

Date	Mintage	F	VF	XF	Unc	BU
2007 Proof	—	Value: 60.00				

KM# 1187 10 EURO
27.0000 g., 0.9250 Silver 0.8029 oz. ASW, 40 mm. **Ruler:**
Juan Carlos I **Subject:** Expo Zaragoza **Rev:** Bridge

Date	Mintage	F	VF	XF	Unc	BU
2007	—	Value: 60.00				

KM# 1190 10 EURO
27.0000 g., 0.9250 Silver 0.8029 oz. ASW, 40 mm. **Ruler:**
Juan Carlos I **Subject:** Velazquez

Date	Mintage	F	VF	XF	Unc	BU
2008 Proof	—	Value: 60.00				

KM# 1192 10 EURO
27.0000 g., 0.9250 Silver 0.8029 oz. ASW, 40 mm. **Ruler:**
Juan Carlos I **Subject:** Soccer, European Champions

Date	Mintage	F	VF	XF	Unc	BU
2008 Proof	—	Value: 60.00				

KM# 1194 10 EURO
27.0000 g., 0.9250 Silver 0.8029 oz. ASW, 40 mm. **Ruler:**

Juan Carlos I **Subject:** Numismatic Treasures - Hispano-Greek
Pegasus

Date	Mintage	F	VF	XF	Unc	BU
2008 Proof	—	Value: 60.00				

KM# 1196 10 EURO
27.0000 g., 0.9250 Silver 0.8029 oz. ASW, 40 mm. **Ruler:**
Juan Carlos I **Subject:** Olympic Sports - Sailing

Date	Mintage	F	VF	XF	Unc	BU
2008 Proof	—	Value: 60.00				

KM# 1199 10 EURO
27.0000 g., 0.9250 Silver 0.8029 oz. ASW, 40 mm. **Ruler:**
Juan Carlos I **Subject:** War of Independence, 200th Anniversary

Date	Mintage	F	VF	XF	Unc	BU
2008 Proof	—	Value: 60.00				

KM# 1200 10 EURO
27.0000 g., 0.9250 Silver 0.8029 oz. ASW, 40 mm. **Ruler:**
Juan Carlos I **Subject:** War of Independence, 200th Anniversary

Date	Mintage	F	VF	XF	Unc	BU
2008 Proof	—	Value: 60.00				

KM# 1201   10 EURO
27.0000 g., 0.9250 Silver 0.8029 oz. ASW, 40 mm.   **Ruler:**
Juan Carlos I **Subject:** War of Independence, 200th Anniversary

Date	Mintage	F	VF	XF	Unc	BU
2008 Proof	—				Value: 60.00	

KM# 1203   10 EURO
27.0000 g., 0.9250 Silver 0.8029 oz. ASW, 40 mm.   **Ruler:**
Juan Carlos I **Subject:** Alphonse the wise

Date	Mintage	F	VF	XF	Unc	BU
2008 Proof	—				Value: 60.00	

KM# 1143   10 EURO
27.0000 g., 0.9250 Silver 0.8029 oz. ASW, 40 mm.   **Ruler:**
Juan Carlos I **Obv:** Head left **Rev:** Soccer player, ball and net

Date	Mintage	F	VF	XF	Unc	BU
2009 Proof	12,000				Value: 55.00	

KM# 1209   10 EURO
27.0000 g., 0.9250 Silver 0.8029 oz. ASW, 40 mm.   **Ruler:**
Juan Carlos I **Subject:** Dali

Date	Mintage	F	VF	XF	Unc	BU
2009 Proof	—				Value: 60.00	

KM# 1210   10 EURO
27.0000 g., 0.9250 Silver 0.8029 oz. ASW, 40 mm.   **Ruler:**
Juan Carlos I **Subject:** Dali

Date	Mintage	F	VF	XF	Unc	BU
2009 Proof	—				Value: 60.00	

KM# 1211   10 EURO
27.0000 g., 0.9250 Silver 0.8029 oz. ASW, 40 mm.   **Ruler:**
Juan Carlos I **Subject:** Dali

Date	Mintage	F	VF	XF	Unc	BU
2009 Proof	—				Value: 60.00	

KM# 1214   10 EURO
27.0000 g., 0.9250 Silver 0.8029 oz. ASW, 40 mm.   **Ruler:**
Juan Carlos I **Subject:** Philip II

Date	Mintage	F	VF	XF	Unc	BU
2009 Proof	—				Value: 60.00	

KM# 1216   10 EURO
27.0000 g., 0.9250 Silver 0.8029 oz. ASW, 40 mm.   **Ruler:**
Juan Carlos I **Subject:** World Cup Soccer, Africa

Date	Mintage	F	VF	XF	Unc	BU
2009 Proof	—				Value: 60.00	

KM# 1165   10 EURO
27.0000 g., 0.9250 Silver 0.8029 oz. ASW, 40 mm.   **Ruler:**
Juan Carlos I **Subject:** Numismatic Treasurers - Silver Shekel
from Carthage, 3rd Century BC

Date	Mintage	F	VF	XF	Unc	BU
2010 Proof	—				Value: 70.00	

KM# 1169   10 EURO
27.0000 g., 0.9250 Silver 0.8029 oz. ASW, 33 mm.   **Ruler:**
Juan Carlos I **Subject:** Antoni Gaudi

Date	Mintage	F	VF	XF	Unc	BU
2010 Proof	—				Value: 70.00	

KM# 1171   10 EURO
27.0000 g., 0.9250 Silver 0.8029 oz. ASW, 40 mm.   **Ruler:**
Juan Carlos I **Subject:** EU Council Presidency

Date	Mintage	F	VF	XF	Unc	BU
2010 Proof	—				Value: 65.00	

KM# 1173   10 EURO
27.0000 g., 0.9250 Silver 0.8029 oz. ASW, 40 mm.   **Ruler:**
Juan Carlos I **Subject:** Holy Year 2010 - St. James the Elder

Date	Mintage	F	VF	XF	Unc	BU
2010 Proof	—				Value: 65.00	

KM# 1174   10 EURO
27.0000 g., 0.9250 Silver 0.8029 oz. ASW, 40 mm.   **Ruler:**
Juan Carlos I **Subject:** Shanghai Expo

Date	Mintage	F	VF	XF	Unc	BU
2010 Proof	—				Value: 65.00	

KM# 1175   10 EURO
27.0000 g., 0.9250 Silver 0.8029 oz. ASW, 40 mm.   **Ruler:**
Juan Carlos I **Subject:** Ibero-American Series - Historical Coins

Date	Mintage	F	VF	XF	Unc	BU
2010 Proof	—				Value: 70.00	

KM# 1176   10 EURO
27.0000 g., 0.9250 Silver 0.8029 oz. ASW, 40 mm.   **Ruler:**
Juan Carlos I **Subject:** FIFA World Cup - South Africa 2010

Date	Mintage	F	VF	XF	Unc	BU
2010 Proof	—				Value: 60.00	

KM# 1178   10 EURO
27.0000 g., 0.9250 Silver 0.8029 oz. ASW, 40 mm.   **Ruler:**
Juan Carlos I **Subject:** Francisco de Goya - The Clothed Maja

Date	Mintage	F	VF	XF	Unc	BU
2010 Proof	—				Value: 65.00	

KM# 1179   10 EURO
27.0000 g., 0.9250 Silver 0.8029 oz. ASW, 40 mm.   **Ruler:**
Juan Carlos I **Subject:** Francisco de Goya - The Grape Harvest

Date	Mintage	F	VF	XF	Unc	BU
2010 Proof	—				Value: 65.00	

KM# 1180   10 EURO
27.0000 g., 0.9250 Silver 0.8029 oz. ASW, 40 mm.   **Ruler:**
Juan Carlos I **Subject:** Francisco de Goya - Duel with Clubs

Date	Mintage	F	VF	XF	Unc	BU
2010 Proof	—				Value: 65.00	

KM# 1185   10 EURO
27.0000 g., 0.9250 Silver 0.8029 oz. ASW, 40 mm. **Ruler:**
Juan Carlos I **Subject:** International Year of Chemistry **Rev:**
Marie Curie

Date	Mintage	F	VF	XF	Unc	BU
2011 Proof	10,000	Value: 85.00				

KM# 1219   10 EURO
27.0000 g., 0.9250 Silver 0.8029 oz. ASW, 40 mm. **Ruler:**
Juan Carlos I **Subject:** Spain-Portugal

Date	Mintage	F	VF	XF	Unc	BU
2011 Proof	—	Value: 60.00				

KM# 1220   10 EURO
27.0000 g., 0.9250 Silver 0.8029 oz. ASW, 40 mm. **Ruler:**
Juan Carlos I **Subject:** Historic Spanish Coin, Ibero American
series

Date	Mintage	F	VF	XF	Unc	BU
2011 Proof	—	Value: 60.00				

KM# 1223   10 EURO
27.0000 g., 0.9250 Silver 0.8029 oz. ASW, 40 mm. **Ruler:**
Juan Carlos I **Subject:** El Greco

Date	Mintage	F	VF	XF	Unc	BU
2011 Proof	—	Value: 60.00				

KM# 1224   10 EURO
27.0000 g., 0.9250 Silver 0.8029 oz. ASW, 40 mm. **Ruler:**
Juan Carlos I **Subject:** El Greco

Date	Mintage	F	VF	XF	Unc	BU
2011 Proof	—	Value: 60.00				

KM# 1225   10 EURO
27.0000 g., 0.9250 Silver 0.8029 oz. ASW, 40 mm. **Ruler:**
Juan Carlos I **Subject:** El Greco

Date	Mintage	F	VF	XF	Unc	BU
2011 Proof	—	Value: 60.00				

KM# 1248   10 EURO
27.0000 g., 0.9250 Silver 0.8029 oz. ASW, 40 mm. **Ruler:**
Juan Carlos I **Subject:** Orellana

Date	Mintage	F	VF	XF	Unc	BU
2011 Proof	—	Value: 60.00				

KM# 1250   10 EURO
27.0000 g., 0.9250 Silver 0.8029 oz. ASW, 40 mm. **Ruler:**
Juan Carlos I **Subject:** Numismatic Treasurers - Elephant coin

Date	Mintage	F	VF	XF	Unc	BU
2011 Proof	—	Value: 60.00				

KM# 1217   10 EURO
27.0000 g., 0.9250 Silver 0.8029 oz. ASW, 40 mm. **Ruler:**
Juan Carlos I **Subject:** Spain-Russia

Date	Mintage	F	VF	XF	Unc	BU
2012 Proof	—	Value: 60.00				

KM# 1049   12 EURO
18.0000 g., 0.9250 Silver 0.5353 oz. ASW, 33 mm. **Ruler:**
Juan Carlos I **Subject:** Spanish European Union Presidency
Obv: Conjoined heads left **Rev:** Distorted star design **Edge:**
Reeded

Date	Mintage	F	VF	XF	Unc	BU
2002	1,500,000	—	—	—	22.50	25.00
2002 Special select	25,000				—	30.00
2002 Proof	50,000	Value: 50.00				

KM# 1051   12 EURO
18.0000 g., 0.9250 Silver 0.5353 oz. ASW, 33 mm. **Ruler:**
Juan Carlos I **Subject:** 25th Anniversary of Constitution **Obv:**
Conjoined heads left **Rev:** National arms above denomination
Edge: Plain

Date	Mintage	F	VF	XF	Unc	BU
2003	1,469,000	—	—	—	27.00	30.00
2003 Proof	8,904	Value: 40.00				

KM# 1069   12 EURO
18.0000 g., 0.9250 Silver 0.5353 oz. ASW, 33 mm. **Ruler:**
Juan Carlos I **Obv:** Juan Carlos and Sofia **Rev:** Felipe and Letizia

Date	Mintage	F	VF	XF	Unc	BU
2004M	—	—	—	—	27.00	30.00

KM# 1095   12 EURO
18.0000 g., 0.9250 Silver 0.5353 oz. ASW, 32.93 mm. **Ruler:** Juan Carlos I **Subject:** 500th Anniversary - Death of Isabel **Obv:** Conjoined heads left **Obv. Legend:** JUAN CARLOS I Y SOFIA **Rev:** Bust of Isabella I left **Rev. Legend:** ISABEL I DE CASTILLA / 1481-1504 **Edge:** Plain

Date	Mintage	F	VF	XF	Unc	BU
2004(M)	1,500,000	—	—	—	27.00	30.00

KM# 1096   12 EURO
18.0000 g., 0.9250 Silver 0.5353 oz. ASW, 32.94 mm. **Ruler:** Juan Carlos I **Subject:** Wedding of Prince Philip and Letizia Ortiz Rocasolano **Obv:** Conjoined heads left **Obv. Legend:** JUAN CARLOS I Y SOFIA **Rev:** Busts of wedding couple facing 3/4 right **Rev. Legend:** FELIPE Y LETIZIA - 22.V.2004 **Edge:** Plain

Date	Mintage	F	VF	XF	Unc	BU
2004(M)	4,000,000	—	—	—	25.00	28.00

KM# 1067   12 EURO
18.0000 g., 0.9250 Silver 0.5353 oz. ASW, 33 mm. **Ruler:** Juan Carlos I **Subject:** Don Quixote **Obv:** Conjoined heads left **Rev:** Man seated on books **Edge:** Reeded

Date	Mintage	F	VF	XF	Unc	BU
2005	4,000,000	—	—	—	25.00	28.00

KM# 1113   12 EURO
18.0000 g., 0.9250 Silver 0.5353 oz. ASW, 32.95 mm. **Ruler:** Juan Carlos I **Subject:** 500th Anniversary - Death of Columbus **Obv:** Conjoined heads left **Obv. Legend:** JUAN CARLOS I Y SOFIA **Rev:** Bust of Columbus facing 3/4 right, latitude and longitude lines with three small sailing ships in background **Edge:** Plain

Date	Mintage	F	VF	XF	Unc	BU
2006(M)	4,000,000	—	—	—	25.00	28.00

KM# 1129   12 EURO
18.0000 g., 0.9250 Silver 0.5353 oz. ASW, 32 mm. **Ruler:** Juan Carlos I **Rev:** Hand with pen **Rev. Legend:** 50 ANIVERSARIO • TRATADO DE ROMA **Rev. Inscription:** EUROPA

Date	Mintage	F	VF	XF	Unc	BU
2007 Proof	25,000			Value: 30.00		

KM# 1195   12 EURO
18.0000 g., 0.9250 Silver 0.5353 oz. ASW, 33 mm. **Ruler:** Juan Carlos I **Subject:** International Year of Planet Earth

Date	Mintage	F	VF	XF	Unc	BU
2008 Proof	5,000			Value: 30.00		

KM# 1212   12 EURO
18.0000 g., 0.9250 Silver 0.5353 oz. ASW, 33 mm. **Ruler:** Juan Carlos I **Subject:** European Monetary Union, 10th Anniversary

Date	Mintage	F	VF	XF	Unc	BU
2009 Proof	—			Value: 30.00		

KM# 1172   12 EURO
18.0000 g., 0.9250 Silver 0.5353 oz. ASW, 33 mm. **Ruler:** Juan Carlos I **Subject:** EU Council Presidency

Date	Mintage	F	VF	XF	Unc	BU
2010 Proof	—			Value: 30.00		

KM# 1133   20 EURO
1.2400 g., 0.9990 Gold 0.0398 oz. AGW, 13.92 mm. **Ruler:** Juan Carlos I **Obv:** National arms **Obv. Legend:** JUAN CARLOS I REY DE ESPAÑA - AÑO DE ESPAÑA EN CHINA **Rev:** Early silver "Pillar" reales coin with Chinese chopmarks

Date	Mintage	F	VF	XF	Unc	BU
2007 Proof	15,000			Value: 95.00		

KM# 1193   20 EURO
1.2400 g., 0.9990 Gold 0.0398 oz. AGW, 13.92 mm. **Ruler:** Juan Carlos I **Subject:** Numismatic Treasures - Roman Aureaus

Date	Mintage	F	VF	XF	Unc	BU
2008 Proof	—			Value: 100		

KM# 1206   20 EURO
1.2400 g., 0.9990 Gold 0.0398 oz. AGW, 13.92 mm. **Ruler:** Juan Carlos I **Subject:** Numismatic Treasurers - Spanish coin

Date	Mintage	F	VF	XF	Unc	BU
2009 Proof	—			Value: 100		

KM# 1166   20 EURO
1.2400 g., 0.9990 Gold 0.0398 oz. AGW, 13.92 mm. **Ruler:** Juan Carlos I **Subject:** Numismatic Treasurers - Tremis, King Leovigild (569-86)

Date	Mintage	F	VF	XF	Unc	BU
2010 Proof	—			Value: 100		

KM# 1177   20 EURO
1.2400 g., 0.9990 Gold 0.0398 oz. AGW, 13.92 mm. **Ruler:** Juan Carlos I **Subject:** FIFA World Cup - South Africa

Date	Mintage	F	VF	XF	Unc	BU
2010 Proof	—			Value: 100		

KM# 1183   20 EURO
18.0000 g., 0.9250 Silver 0.5353 oz. ASW, 33 mm. **Ruler:** Juan Carlos I **Subject:** FIFA World Cup Winners

Date	Mintage	F	VF	XF	Unc	BU
2010 Proof	—			Value: 100		

KM# 1218   20 EURO
1.2400 g., 0.9990 Gold 0.0398 oz. AGW **Ruler:** Juan Carlos I **Subject:** Span & Portugal **Shape:** 13.92

Date	Mintage	F	VF	XF	Unc	BU
2011 Proof	—			Value: 100		

KM# 1246   20 EURO
18.0000 g., 0.9250 Silver 0.5353 oz. ASW, 33 mm. **Ruler:** Juan Carlos I **Subject:** International Women's Day, 100th Anniversary

Date	Mintage	F	VF	XF	Unc	BU
2011 Proof	—			Value: 100		

KM# 1251   20 EURO
1.2400 g., 0.9990 Gold 0.0398 oz. AGW, 13.92 mm. **Ruler:** Juan Carlos I **Subject:** Numismatic Treasurers - Leovigild Gold

Date	Mintage	F	VF	XF	Unc	BU
2011 Proof	—			Value: 100		

KM# 1085   50 EURO
168.7500 g., 0.9250 Silver 5.0183 oz. ASW, 73 mm. **Ruler:** Juan Carlos I **Subject:** 150th Anniversary - Birth of Antonio Gaudí **Obv:** Bust of Gaudí at right **Obv. Legend:** Año Internacional **Rev:** Sagrada Familia

Date	Mintage	F	VF	XF	Unc	BU
2002(M) Proof	8,000			Value: 225		

KM# 1093   50 EURO
168.7500 g., 0.9250 Silver 5.0183 oz. ASW, 73 mm. **Ruler:** Juan Carlos I **Subject:** 1st Anniversary of Euro **Obv:** Conjoined heads left **Obv. Legend:** PREMIER ANIVERSARIO EURO • JUAN CARLOS I Y SOFÍA **Rev:** National arms at center surrounded by various items of architecture

Date	Mintage	F	VF	XF	Unc	BU
2003 Proof	20,000			Value: 250		

KM# 1057   50 EURO
168.7500 g., 0.9250 Silver with removeable gold plated silver insert 5.0183 oz. ASW, 73 mm.   **Ruler:** Juan Carlos I **Obv:** Dali's "Dream State" painting **Rev:** Dali's "Rhinocerotic Disintegration..." painting **Edge:** Reeded

Date	Mintage	F	VF	XF	Unc	BU
2004 Proof	12,000	Value: 225				

KM# 1117   50 EURO
168.7500 g., 0.9250 Silver 5.0183 oz. ASW, 73 mm.   **Ruler:** Juan Carlos I **Subject:** 500th Anniversary - Death of Columbus **Obv:** Landing party at Guanahani **Obv. Legend:** ESPAÑA **Rev:** Columbus standing facing 3/4 left with right arm outstretched standing on outline of the northern part of South America **Rev. Legend:** CRISTOBAL COLON **Edge:** Plain

Date	Mintage	F	VF	XF	Unc	BU
2006(M) Proof	6,000	Value: 245				

KM# 1189   50 EURO
168.7500 g., 0.9250 Silver 5.0183 oz. ASW, 73 mm.   **Ruler:** Juan Carlos I **Subject:** Velazquez

Date	Mintage	F	VF	XF	Unc	BU
2008 Proof	—	Value: 245				

KM# 1061   50 EURO
168.7300 g., 0.9250 Silver 5.0177 oz. ASW, 73 mm.   **Ruler:** Juan Carlos I **Obv:** Crowned bust left(1451-1504) and castle within beaded circle **Rev:** Surrender of Grenada scene within beaded circle **Edge:** Reeded

Date	Mintage	F	VF	XF	Unc	BU
2004 Proof	8,000	Value: 225				

KM# 1127   50 EURO
168.7500 g., 0.9250 Silver 5.0183 oz. ASW, 73 mm.   **Ruler:** Juan Carlos I **Rev:** Euro seated on resting bull left **Rev. Legend:** V ANIVERSARIO DEL EURO

Date	Mintage	F	VF	XF	Unc	BU
2007 Proof	6,000	Value: 245				

KM# 1198   50 EURO
168.7500 g., 0.9250 Silver 5.0183 oz. ASW, 73 mm.   **Ruler:** Juan Carlos I **Subject:** War of Independence, 200th Anniversary

Date	Mintage	F	VF	XF	Unc	BU
2008 Proof	—	Value: 225				

KM# 1205   50 EURO
168.7500 g., 0.9250 Silver 5.0183 oz. ASW, 73 mm.   **Ruler:** Juan Carlos I **Subject:** Numismatic Treasurers - Spanish real

Date	Mintage	F	VF	XF	Unc	BU
2009 Proof	—	Value: 245				

KM# 1107   50 EURO
168.7500 g., 0.9250 Silver 5.0183 oz. ASW, 73 mm.   **Ruler:** Juan Carlos I **Obv:** 1/2 length figure of Miguel de Cervantes Saavedra facing writing in manuscript with quill pen **Obv. Legend:** ESPAÑA - IV CENTENARIO DE LA PRIMERA EDICIÓN DE "EL QUIJOTE" **Rev:** Quixote

Date	Mintage	F	VF	XF	Unc	BU
2005(M) Proof	12,000	Value: 225				

KM# 1138   50 EURO
168.7500 g., 0.9250 Silver 5.0183 oz. ASW, 73 mm.   **Ruler:** Juan Carlos I **Subject:** El Cid 700th Anniversary **Obv:** Statue of Rodrigo Diaz de Vivar in Burgas **Rev:** Two seated trumpeters

Date	Mintage	F	VF	XF	Unc	BU
2007 Proof	6,000	Value: 245				

KM# 1208   50 EURO
168.7500 g., 0.9250 Silver 5.0183 oz. ASW, 73 mm.   **Ruler:** Juan Carlos I **Subject:** Dali

Date	Mintage	F	VF	XF	Unc	BU
2009 Proof	—	Value: 245				

KM# 1181   50 EURO
168.7500 g., 0.9250 Silver 5.0183 oz. ASW, 73 mm.   **Ruler:** Juan Carlos I **Subject:** Francisco de Goya - Witches' Sabbath

Date	Mintage	F	VF	XF	Unc	BU
2010 Proof	—	Value: 250				

KM# 1222 50 EURO
168.7500 g., 0.9990 Silver 5.4198 oz. ASW, 73 mm. **Ruler:** Juan Carlos I **Subject:** El Greco

Date	Mintage	F	VF	XF	Unc	BU
2011 Proof	—	Value: 250				

KM# 1077 100 EURO
6.7500 g., 0.9990 Gold 0.2168 oz. AGW, 23 mm. **Ruler:** Juan Carlos I **Obv:** Head left **Obv. Legend:** JUAN CARLOS I REY DE ESPAÑA **Rev:** Player running right kicking ball **Rev. Legend:** ALEMANIA 2006 at bottom **Note:** Issued in 2004.

Date	Mintage	F	VF	XF	Unc	BU
2003(M) Proof	25,000	Value: 425				

KM# 1103 100 EURO
6.7500 g., 0.9990 Gold 0.2168 oz. AGW, 23 mm. **Ruler:** Juan Carlos I **Subject:** XVIII World Football Games - Germany 2006 **Obv:** Head left **Obv. Legend:** JUAN CARLOS I REY DE ESPAÑA **Rev:** Goalie deflecting ball at net **Rev. Inscription:** COPA MUNDIAL DE LA FIFA

Date	Mintage	F	VF	XF	Unc	BU
2004(M) Proof	25,000	Value: 425				

KM# 1167 100 EURO
168.8800 g., 0.9250 Silver with gold plating 5.0222 oz. ASW, 73 mm. **Ruler:** Juan Carlos I **Subject:** Numismatic treasurers - The Centen, 100 Escudos, 1609

Date	Mintage	F	VF	XF	Unc	BU
2009 Proof	—	Value: 250				

KM# 1204 100 EURO
6.7500 g., 0.9990 Gold 0.2168 oz. AGW, 23 mm. **Ruler:** Juan Carlos I **Subject:** Numismatic Treasures - Spanish Escudo

Date	Mintage	F	VF	XF	Unc	BU
2009 Proof	—	Value: 425				

KM# 1215 100 EURO
6.7500 g., 0.9990 Gold 0.2168 oz. AGW, 23 mm. **Ruler:** Juan Carlos I **Subject:** World Cup Soccer, Africa

Date	Mintage	F	VF	XF	Unc	BU
2009 Proof	—	Value: 425				

KM# 1168 100 EURO
6.7500 g., 0.9990 Gold 0.2168 oz. AGW, 23 mm. **Ruler:** Juan Carlos I **Subject:** Numismatic Treasurers - Tremis, Suintila (621-31)

Date	Mintage	F	VF	XF	Unc	BU
2010 Proof	6,000	Value: 425				

KM# 1249 100 EURO
6.7500 g., 0.9990 Gold 0.2168 oz. AGW, 23 mm. **Ruler:** Juan Carlos I **Subject:** Numismatic Treasurers - Swinthila Gold

Date	Mintage	F	VF	XF	Unc	BU
2011 Proof	—	Value: 425				

KM# 1081 200 EURO
13.5000 g., 0.9990 Gold 0.4336 oz. AGW, 30 mm. **Ruler:** Juan Carlos I **Subject:** XVII Football World Games 2002 - South Korea and Japan **Obv. Legend:** MUNDIAL DE FUTBOL/2002 - ESPAÑA **Rev:** Ball hitting net

Date	Mintage	F	VF	XF	Unc	BU
2002(M) Proof	4,000	Value: 825				

KM# 1091 200 EURO
13.5000 g., 0.9990 Gold 0.4336 oz. AGW **Ruler:** Juan Carlos I **Obv:** Conjoined heads left **Obv. Legend:** JUAN CARLOS I Y SOFIA **Rev:** Ediface of Parliament Building in Madrid **Rev. Legend:** CONSTITUCION ESPANOLA

Date	Mintage	F	VF	XF	Unc	BU
2003(M) Proof	4,000	Value: 825				

KM# 1075 200 EURO
13.5000 g., 0.9990 Gold 0.4336 oz. AGW, 30 mm. **Ruler:** Juan Carlos I **Subject:** Birth of the Euro **Obv:** Spanish King and Queen left **Rev:** Mythological Europa riding on the back of a bull

Date	Mintage	F	VF	XF	Unc	BU
2003 Proof	20,000	Value: 825				

KM# 1062 200 EURO
13.5000 g., 0.9990 Gold 0.4336 oz. AGW, 30 mm. **Ruler:** Juan Carlos I **Obv:** Seated crowned figures on shield flanked by date and value **Rev:** Crowned busts facing each other on coin design **Edge:** Reeded

Date	Mintage	F	VF	XF	Unc	BU
2004 Proof	5,000	Value: 825				

KM# 1100 200 EURO
13.5000 g., 0.9990 Gold 0.4336 oz. AGW, 30 mm. **Ruler:** Juan Carlos I **Subject:** Expansion of the European Union **Obv:** Head left **Obv. Legend:** JUAN CARLOS I Y SOFIA **Rev:** Outlined map of the European Union

Date	Mintage	F	VF	XF	Unc	BU
2004(M) Proof	5,000	Value: 825				

KM# 1098 200 EURO
13.5000 g., 0.9990 Gold 0.4336 oz. AGW, 30 mm. **Ruler:** Juan Carlos I **Subject:** Wedding of Prince Philip and Letizia Ortiz Rocasolano **Obv:** Conjoined heads left **Obv. Legend:** JUAN CARLOS I Y SOFIA **Rev:** Busts of wedding couple facing 3/4 right at center left, crowned shield at right **Rev. Legend:** FELIPE Y LETIZIA - 22.V.2004

Date	Mintage	F	VF	XF	Unc	BU
2004(M) Proof	30,000	Value: 825				

KM# 1111 200 EURO
13.5000 g., 0.9990 Gold 0.4336 oz. AGW, 30 mm. **Ruler:** Juan Carlos I **Rev:** Crowned shield at left, head of Prince Philip left at right **Rev. Legend:** XXV ANIVERSAIO - PREMIOS PRÍNCIPE DE ASTURIAS

Date	Mintage	F	VF	XF	Unc	BU
2005(M) Proof	3,500	Value: 825				

KM# 1066 200 EURO
13.5000 g., 0.9990 Gold 0.4336 oz. AGW, 30 mm. **Ruler:** Juan Carlos I **Subject:** European Peace and Freedom **Obv:** Juan Carlos **Rev:** European map on clasped hands **Edge:** Reeded

Date	Mintage	F	VF	XF	Unc	BU
2005 Proof	4,000	Value: 825				

KM# 1123 200 EURO
13.5000 g., 0.9990 Gold 0.4336 oz. AGW, 30 mm. **Ruler:** Juan Carlos I **Obv:** Head left **Obv. Legend:** JUAN CARLOS I REY DE ESPAÑA **Rev:** Charles I (V) standing facing 3/4 right in front of portal **Rev. Legend:** CAROLVS IMPERATOR

Date	Mintage	F	VF	XF	Unc	BU
2006(M) Proof	5,000	Value: 825				

KM# 1136   200 EURO
13.5000 g., 0.9990 Gold 0.4336 oz. AGW, 30 mm. **Ruler:**
Juan Carlos I **Subject:** Treaty of Rome, 50th Anniversary **Obv:**
Head left **Rev:** Map of Western Europe

Date	Mintage	F	VF	XF	Unc	BU
2007 Proof	3,500	Value: 825				

KM# 1139   200 EURO
13.5000 g., 0.9990 Gold 0.4336 oz. AGW, 30 mm. **Ruler:**
Juan Carlos I **Subject:** El Cid, 700th Anniversary **Obv:** Rodrigo
Diaz de Vivar bust facing **Rev:** Knight on horseback within
rectangle

Date	Mintage	F	VF	XF	Unc	BU
2007 Proof	3,500	Value: 825				

KM# 1188   200 EURO
13.5000 g., 0.9990 Gold 0.4336 oz. AGW, 30 mm. **Ruler:**
Juan Carlos I **Subject:** Velazquez

Date	Mintage	F	VF	XF	Unc	BU
2008 Proof	—	Value: 825				

KM# 1191   200 EURO
13.5000 g., 0.9990 Gold 0.4336 oz. AGW, 30 mm. **Ruler:**
Juan Carlos I **Subject:** Soccer, European Champions

Date	Mintage	F	VF	XF	Unc	BU
2008 Proof	—	Value: 825				

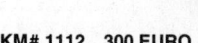

KM# 1202   200 EURO
13.5000 g., 0.9990 Gold 0.4336 oz. AGW, 30 mm. **Ruler:**
Juan Carlos I **Subject:** Alphonse the Wise

Date	Mintage	F	VF	XF	Unc	BU
2008 Proof	—	Value: 825				

KM# 1213   200 EURO
13.5000 g., 0.9990 Gold 0.4336 oz. AGW, 30 mm. **Ruler:**
Juan Carlos I **Subject:** Philip II

Date	Mintage	F	VF	XF	Unc	BU
2009 Proof	—	Value: 825				

KM# 1170   200 EURO
13.5000 g., 0.9990 Gold 0.4336 oz. AGW, 30 mm. **Ruler:**
Juan Carlos I **Subject:** Antoni Gaudi

Date	Mintage	F	VF	XF	Unc	BU
2010 Proof	—	Value: 825				

KM# 1247   200 EURO
13.5000 g., 0.9990 Gold 0.4336 oz. AGW, 30 mm. **Ruler:**
Juan Carlos I **Subject:** Orellana

Date	Mintage	F	VF	XF	Unc	BU
2011 Proof	—	Value: 825				

KM# 1112   300 EURO
Bi-Metallic .554 AGW Gold center in .343 ASW Silver ring, 40 mm.
Ruler: Juan Carlos I **Subject:** XVIII World Championship
Football Games - Germany 2006 **Obv:** Football player facing
kicking ball **Obv. Legend:** ESPAÑA **Rev:** Football player kicking
ball into net at foreground **Rev. Legend:** COPA MUNDIAL DE
LA FIFA - ALEMANIA **Shape:** 12-sided

Date	Mintage	F	VF	XF	Unc	BU
2005(M) Proof	2,006	Value: 1,000				

KM# 1121   300 EURO
Bi-Metallic .554 AGW Gold center in .343 ASW Silver ring, 40 mm.

Ruler: Juan Carlos I **Rev:** Basketball player facing tossing ball
Rev. Legend: CAMPEONES DEL MUNDO - JAPÓN 2006
Shape: 12-sided

Date	Mintage	F	VF	XF	Unc	BU
2006(M) Proof	2,000	Value: 1,000				

KM# 1086   400 EURO
27.0000 g., 0.9990 Gold 0.8672 oz. AGW, 38 mm. **Ruler:**
Juan Carlos I **Subject:** 150th Anniversary - Birth of Antonio
Gaudí **Obv:** Bust of Gaudí at right **Obv. Legend:** Año
Internacional **Rev:** Casa Batlló

Date	Mintage	F	VF	XF	Unc	BU
2002(M) Proof	3,000	Value: 1,600				

KM# 1058   400 EURO
27.0000 g., 0.9990 Gold 0.8672 oz. AGW, 38 mm. **Ruler:**
Juan Carlos I **Obv:** Bust facing **Rev:** Dali's painting "Girl at the
Window" **Edge:** Reeded

Date	Mintage	F	VF	XF	Unc	BU
2004 Proof	5,000	Value: 1,600				

KM# 1108   400 EURO
27.0000 g., 0.9990 Gold 0.8672 oz. AGW, 38 mm. **Ruler:**
Juan Carlos I **Obv:** Quixote seated reading a large book **Obv.
Legend:** ESPAÑA - IV CENTENARIO DE LA PRIMERA
EDICIÓN DE "EL QUIJOTE" **Rev:** Quixote on horseback 3/4 right
followed by his friend on a burro **Rev. Legend:** DON QUIJOTE
DE LA MANCHA SANCHO PANZA

Date	Mintage	F	VF	XF	Unc	BU
2005(M) Proof	3,000	Value: 1,600				

KM# 1118   400 EURO
27.0000 g., 0.9990 Gold 0.8672 oz. AGW, 38 mm. **Ruler:**
Juan Carlos I **Subject:** 500th Anniversary - Death of Columbus
Obv: Columbus **Rev:** Audience with Ferdinand and Isabella

Date	Mintage	F	VF	XF	Unc	BU
2006(M) Proof	3,000	Value: 1,600				

KM# 1128   400 EURO
27.0000 g., 0.9990 Gold 0.8672 oz. AGW, 38 mm.   **Ruler:** Juan Carlos I **Rev:** Large ring of stars around globe **Rev. Legend:** V ANIVERSARIO DEL EURO

Date	Mintage	F	VF	XF	Unc	BU
2007 Proof	3,000	Value: 1,600				

KM# 1197   400 EURO
27.0000 g., 0.9990 Gold 0.8672 oz. AGW, 38 mm.   **Ruler:** Juan Carlos I **Subject:** War of Independence, 200th Anniversary

Date	Mintage	F	VF	XF	Unc	BU
2008 Proof	—	Value: 1,600				

KM# 1207   400 EURO
27.0000 g., 0.9990 Gold 0.8672 oz. AGW, 38 mm.   **Ruler:** Juan Carlos I **Subject:** Dali

Date	Mintage	F	VF	XF	Unc	BU
2009 Proof	—	Value: 1,600				

KM# 1182   400 EURO
27.0000 g., 0.9990 Gold 0.8672 oz. AGW, 38 mm.   **Ruler:** Juan Carlos I **Subject:** Francisco de Goya - Volaverunt

Date	Mintage	F	VF	XF	Unc	BU
2010 Proof	—	Value: 1,600				

KM# 1221   400 EURO
27.0000 g., 0.9990 Gold 0.8672 oz. AGW, 38 mm.   **Ruler:** Juan Carlos I **Subject:** El Greco

Date	Mintage	F	VF	XF	Unc	BU
2011 Proof	—	Value: 1,600				

MINT SETS

KM#	Date	Mintage	Identification	Issue Price	Mkt Val
MS27	2000-2001 (8)	49,426	KM#832-833, 924, 991-992 (both dated 2000), 1012-1013, 1016	15.50	35.00
MS28	2002 (8)	99,301	KM#1040-1047	—	15.00
MS29	2003 (8)	149	KM#1040-1047	—	15.00
MS30	2004 (8)	43,000	KM#1040-1047	—	70.00
MS31	2005 (8)	49,923	KM#1040-1047	—	30.00
MS32	2006 (8)	49,996	KM#1040-1047	—	12.50
MS33	2007 (8)	—	KM#1040-1042, 1070-1074	—	30.00

PROOF SETS

KM#	Date	Mintage	Identification	Issue Price	Mkt Val
PS34	2002 (9)	23,000	KM#1040-1047, 1049	125	150
PS35	2003 (9)	8,904	KM#1040-1047, 1051	—	320
PS36	2005 (9)	3,000	KM#1040-1047, 1063	—	175
PS38	2007 (9)	1,800	KM#1040-1042, 1070-1074, 1130	—	150
PS39	2008 (8)	2,000	KM#1040-1042, 1070-1074	—	150
PS40	2009 (9)	5,000	KM#1040-1042, 1070-1074, 1142.1	—	150
PS41	2010 (9)	5,000	KM#1144-1150, 1152	—	150
PS42	2011 (9)	5,000	KM#1144-1151, 1184	—	150

SRI LANKA

The Democratic Socialist Republic of Sri Lanka (formerly Ceylon) situated in the Indian Ocean 18 miles (29 km.) southeast of India, has an area of 25,332 sq. mi. (65,610 sq. km.) and a population of *16.9 million. Capital: Colombo. The economy is chiefly agricultural. Tea, coconut products and rubber are exported.

Sri Lanka is a member of the Commonwealth of Nations. The president is Chief of State. The prime minister is Head of Government. The present leaders of the country have reverted the country name back to Sri Lanka.

DEMOCRATIC SOCIALIST REPUBLIC

DECIMAL COINAGE

100 Cents = 1 Rupee

KM# 141a   25 CENTS
Nickel Clad Steel **Obv:** National arms **Rev:** Denomination **Edge:** Reeded

Date	Mintage	F	VF	XF	Unc	BU
2001	10,000,000	—	—	0.10	0.25	0.45
2002	10,000,000	—	—	0.10	0.25	0.45

KM# 141.2b   25 CENTS
1.1700 g., Copper Plated Steel, 16 mm.   **Obv:** National arms **Rev:** Denomination

Date	Mintage	F	VF	XF	Unc	BU
2005	—	—	—	0.10	0.25	0.45
2006	—	—	—	0.10	0.25	0.45

KM# 135.2a   50 CENTS
Nickel Plated Steel, 21.5 mm.   **Obv:** National arms **Rev:** Value above designs within wreath **Edge:** Reeded

Date	Mintage	F	VF	XF	Unc	BU
2001	30,000,000	—	0.10	0.25	0.65	1.00
2002	10,000,000	—	0.10	0.25	0.65	1.00
2004	—	—	0.10	0.25	0.65	1.00

KM# 135.2b   50 CENTS
2.4900 g., Copper Plated Steel, 17.92 mm.   **Obv:** National arms **Rev:** Value above designs within wreath **Edge:** Reeded

Date	Mintage	F	VF	XF	Unc	BU
2005	—	—	—	0.25	0.60	1.00
2006	—	—	—	0.25	0.60	1.00
2009	—	—	—	0.25	0.60	1.00

KM# 166   RUPEE
7.1300 g., Copper-Nickel, 25.4 mm.   **Subject:** Air Force's 50th Anniversary **Obv:** Badge of the Sri Lanka Air Force **Rev:** Two jets above propeller plane within circle **Edge:** Reeded

Date	Mintage	F	VF	XF	Unc	BU
2001 Proof	2,000	Value: 100				

KM# 136a   RUPEE
Nickel Clad Steel **Obv:** National arms **Rev:** Inscription below designs within wreath **Edge:** Reeded

Date	Mintage	F	VF	XF	Unc	BU
2002	50,000,000	—	—	—	1.00	1.50
2004	—	—	—	—	1.00	1.50

KM# 136.3   RUPEE
3.6200 g., Brass Plated Steel, 20 mm.   **Obv:** National emblem **Rev:** Inscription below designs within wreath **Edge:** Segmented reeding

Date	Mintage	F	VF	XF	Unc	BU
2005	—	—	—	—	0.75	1.00
2006	—	—	—	—	0.75	1.00
2008	—	—	—	—	0.75	1.00
2009	—	—	—	—	0.75	1.00

KM# 147   2 RUPEES
8.2500 g., Copper-Nickel, 28.5 mm.   **Obv:** National arms **Rev:** Value

Date	Mintage	F	VF	XF	Unc	BU
2001	10,000,000	—	0.30	0.60	1.35	1.75
2002	40,000,000	—	0.30	0.60	1.35	1.75
2004	—	—	0.30	0.60	1.35	1.75

KM# 167   2 RUPEES
8.2500 g., Copper-Nickel, 28.5 mm.   **Subject:** Colombo Plan's

50th Anniversary **Obv:** Value within inscription above date **Rev:** Gear wheel **Edge:** Reeded

Date	Mintage	F	VF	XF	Unc	BU
2001	10,000,000	—	—	—	2.00	3.00

KM# 147a 2 RUPEES
7.0800 g., Nickel Clad Steel, 28.5 mm. **Obv:** National arms **Rev:** Value **Edge:** Reeded

Date	Mintage	F	VF	XF	Unc	BU
2005	—	—	—	0.45	1.10	1.50
2006	—	—	—	0.45	1.10	1.50
2008	—	—	—	0.45	1.10	1.50
2009	—	—	—	0.45	1.10	1.50

KM# 178 2 RUPEES
7.0000 g., Nickel Plated Steel, 28.4 mm. **Subject:** Employees Provident Fund, 50th Anniversary **Obv:** Large 2 **Rev:** Open hands with image of tea pluckers, garment workers and office worker

Date	Mintage	F	VF	XF	Unc	BU
2008	2,000,000	—	—	—	1.35	1.75

KM# 184 2 RUPEES
7.0000 g., Nickel Plated Steel, 28.5 mm. **Obv:** Large value **Rev:** Large 60, Air Force emblem and historic aircraft circling

Date	Mintage	F	VF	XF	Unc	BU
2011	3,000,000	—	—	—	2.00	—
2011 Special Unc	500	—	—	—	—	15.00

KM# 148.2 5 RUPEES
9.5000 g., Nickel-Brass, 23.5 mm. **Obv:** National arms **Rev:** Value **Edge Lettering:** C.B.S.L.

Date	Mintage	F	VF	XF	Unc	BU
2002	30,000,000	—	0.35	0.65	2.00	2.75
2004	—	—	0.35	0.65	2.00	2.75

KM# 168 5 RUPEES
9.5200 g., Aluminum-Bronze, 23.4 mm. **Subject:** 250th Annniversary of the "Upasampada" Rite **Obv:** Value **Rev:** 1/2-length figure facing divides dates

Date	Mintage	F	VF	XF	Unc	BU
2003	4,000,000	—	—	—	3.00	4.50

KM# 169 5 RUPEES
9.5200 g., Aluminum-Bronze, 23.4 mm. **Subject:** 250th Anniversary - Upasampada **Obv:** Value **Rev:** Bust facing standing behind shield **Edge:** Reeded and lettered

Date	Mintage	F	VF	XF	Unc	BU
2003	4,000,000	—	—	—	3.00	4.50

KM# 148a 5 RUPEES
7.6700 g., Brass Plated Steel, 23.49 mm. **Obv:** National arms **Rev:** Value **Edge:** Reeded and Lettered **Edge Lettering:** CBSL repeated in various languages

Date	Mintage	F	VF	XF	Unc	BU
2005	—	—	—	0.75	1.85	2.50
2006	—	—	—	0.75	1.85	2.50
2008	—	—	—	0.75	1.85	2.50
2009	—	—	—	0.75	1.85	2.50

KM# 170 5 RUPEES
7.6500 g., Brass Plated Steel, 23.5 mm. **Subject:** 2550th Anniversary of Buddha **Obv:** Value **Rev:** "Buddha Jayanthi", wheel above mountain **Edge:** Reeded and lettered

Date	Mintage	F	VF	XF	Unc	BU
2006	20,000,000	—	—	—	3.00	4.00

KM# 173 5 RUPEES
7.6500 g., Brass Plated Steel, 23.5 mm. **Subject:** Cricket World Cup

Date	Mintage	F	VF	XF	Unc	BU
2007	—	—	—	—	3.00	4.00

KM# 181 10 RUPEES
8.3600 g., Nickel Plated Steel, 26.4 mm. **Obv:** Sri Lanka ensign **Rev:** Large value **Shape:** 11-sided

Date	Mintage	F	VF	XF	Unc	BU
2009	—	—	—	—	1.50	2.50
2010	—	—	—	—	1.50	2.50

KM# 186 10 RUPEES
8.3600 g., Nickel Plated Steel, 26.4 mm. **Subject:** Sambuddhatva Jayanti 2600 **Obv:** Large value **Rev:** 24 prong DharmaChakra (wheel of dochrine) **Shape:** 11-sided

Date	Mintage	F	VF	XF	Unc	BU
2011	1,500,000	—	—	—	—	2.50

KM# 180 200 RUPEES
11.9000 g., 0.9250 Silver 0.3539 oz. ASW, 28.4 mm. **Subject:** Customs Service, 200th Anniversary **Obv:** Proposed new Customs Building **Rev:** Customs Logo

Date	Mintage	F	VF	XF	Unc	BU
2009 Proof	3,000	Value: 55.00				

KM# 174 1000 RUPEES
Nickel Plated Steel **Subject:** Cricket World Cup

Date	Mintage	F	VF	XF	Unc	BU
2007	10,000	—	—	—	12.00	15.00

KM# 179 1000 RUPEES
Nickel Plated Steel, 28.5 mm. **Subject:** Employees Provident Fund, 50th Anniversary **Obv:** Large 1000 **Rev:** Open hands with image of tea pluckers, garment workers and office worker

Date	Mintage	F	VF	XF	Unc	BU
2008 Proof	1,200	Value: 150				

KM# 182 1000 RUPEES
Copper-Nickel, 27 mm. **Subject:** Sri Lanka Army - 60th Anniversary **Obv:** Army badge above value **Rev:** Soldier standing with flag, map of Sri Lanka in background, two smaller solders at right

Date	Mintage	F	VF	XF	Unc	BU
2009	—	—	—	—	20.00	25.00

KM# 182a 1000 RUPEES
Silver, 27 mm. **Subject:** Sri Lanka Army - 60th Anniversary **Obv:** Army badge above value **Rev:** Soldier standing with flag, map of Sri Lanka in background, two smaller solders at right

Date	Mintage	F	VF	XF	Unc	BU
2009 Proof	—	Value: 50.00				

KM# 185 1000 RUPEES
28.2800 g., 38.6100 Silver 35.103 oz. ASW, 38.61 mm. **Subject:** Sambuddhatva Jayanti 2600 **Obv:** 24 prong Dharma Chakra (wheel of doctrine) **Rev:** Sri Maha Bo-Sapling bowl on a large pedistal

Date	Mintage	F	VF	XF	Unc	BU
2011 Proof	2,000	Value: 70.00				

KM# 171 1500 RUPEES
Silver **Subject:** 2550 Anniversary of Buddha

Date	Mintage	F	VF	XF	Unc	BU
2006 Proof	20,000	Value: 85.00				

KM# 172 2000 RUPEE
Silver **Subject:** 2550 Anniversary of Buddha

Date	Mintage	F	VF	XF	Unc	BU
2006 Proof	10,000	Value: 125				

KM# 183 5000 RUPEES
28.2800 g., 0.9250 Silver 0.8410 oz. ASW, 38.61 mm. **Subject:** Central Bank of Sri Lanka, 60th Anniversary **Obv:** Multicolor Central Bank crest at center **Rev:** Banyan tree **Edge:** Reeded

Date	Mintage	F	VF	XF	Unc	BU
2010 Proof	5,000	Value: 65.00				

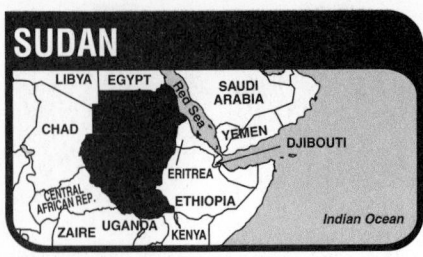

SUDAN

The Republic of the Sudan, located in northeast Africa on the Red Sea between Egypt and Ethiopia, has an area of 967,500 sq. mi. (2,505,810 sq. km.) and a population of *24.5 million. Capital: Khartoum. Agriculture and livestock raising are the chief occupations. Cotton, gum arabic and peanuts are exported.

REPUBLIC

REFORM COINAGE

100 Qurush (Piastres) = 1 Dinar
10 Pounds = 1 Dinar

KM# 119   5 DINARS
3.3500 g., Brass, 19 mm. **Obv:** Value **Rev:** Central Bank building

Date	Mintage	F	VF	XF	Unc	BU
AH1424-2003	—	—	0.75	1.50	3.00	5.00

KM# 120.1   10 DINARS
4.6800 g., Brass, 22 mm. **Rev:** Central Bank building, "a" above "n" at the left end of the Arabic inscription, 64 border beads

Date	Mintage	F	VF	XF	Unc	BU
AH1424-2003	—	—	1.00	2.00	3.50	6.00

KM# 120.2   10 DINARS
4.5600 g., Brass, 22 mm. **Obv:** Value **Rev:** Larger Central Bank building, "a" to right of "n" at the left end of the Arabic inscription, 72 border beads

Date	Mintage	F	VF	XF	Unc	BU
AH1424-2003	—	—	1.00	2.00	3.50	6.00

KM# 121   50 DINARS
Copper-Nickel, 24 mm. **Rev:** Central Bank building

Date	Mintage	F	VF	XF	Unc	BU
AH1423-2002	—	—	2.00	3.50	6.00	9.00

REFORM COINAGE

100 Piastres = 1 Pound

2005 -

KM# 126   PIASTRE (Ghirsh)
2.2500 g., Aluminum-Bronze, 16 mm. **Obv:** Clay pot **Obv. Legend:** CENTRAL BANK OF SUDAN **Rev:** Value

Date	Mintage	F	VF	XF	Unc	BU
2006	—	—	—	0.90	2.25	3.00

KM# 125   5 PIASTRES
2.8400 g., Brass, 18 mm. **Obv:** National arms **Rev:** Large value **Edge:** Reeded

Date	Mintage	F	VF	XF	Unc	BU
2006	—	—	—	1.20	3.00	4.00

KM# 122   10 PIASTRES
3.7000 g., Nickel, 20 mm. **Obv:** Pyramid **Obv. Legend:** CENTRAL BANK OF SUDAN **Rev:** Large value **Edge:** Reeded

Date	Mintage	F	VF	XF	Unc	BU
2006	—	—	—	1.25	3.00	4.00

KM# 124   20 PIASTRES
5.0000 g., Bi-Metallic Copper-Nickel center in Brass ring, 22 mm. **Obv:** Ankole Bull in right profile **Obv. Legend:** CENTRAL BANK OF SUDAN **Rev:** large value **Edge:** Reeded

Date	Mintage	F	VF	XF	Unc	BU
2006	—	—	—	1.20	3.00	4.00

KM# 123   50 PIASTRES
5.8200 g., Bi-Metallic Brass center in Copper-Nickel ring, 24 mm. **Obv:** Dove in flight **Obv. Legend:** CENTRAL BANK OF SUDAN **Rev:** Value **Edge:** Reeded

Date	Mintage	F	VF	XF	Unc	BU
2006	—	—	—	0.90	2.25	3.00

SURINAME

The Republic of Suriname also known as Dutch Guiana, located on the north central coast of South America between Guyana and French Guiana has an area of 63,037 sq. mi. (163,270 sq. km.) and a population of *433,000. Capital: Paramaribo. The country is rich in minerals and forests, and self-sufficient in rice, the staple food crop. The mining, processing and exporting of bauxite is the principal economic activity.

Lieutenants of Amerigo Vespucci sighted the Guiana coast in 1499. Spanish explorers of the 16th century, disappointed at finding no gold, departed leaving the area to be settled by the British in 1652. The colony prospered and the Netherlands acquired it in 1667 in exchange for the Dutch rights in Nieuw Nederland (state of New York). During the European wars of the 18th and 19th centuries, which were fought in part in the new world, Suriname was occupied by the British from 1781-1784 and 1796-1814. Suriname became an autonomous part of the Kingdom of the Netherlands on Dec. 15, 1954. Full independence was achieved on Nov. 25, 1975. In 1980, a coup installed a military government, which has since been dissolved.

MINT MARKS
(u) - Utrecht (privy marks only)

MONETARY SYSTEM
1 Dollar = 100 Cents

REPUBLIC

MODERN COINAGE

KM# 11b   CENT
2.5000 g., Copper Plated Steel, 18 mm. **Obv:** Arms with supporters within wreath **Rev:** Value divides date within circle **Edge:** Plain

Date	Mintage	F	VF	XF	Unc	BU
2004(u) In sets only	4,000	—	—	—	—	1.50
2005(u) In sets only	1,500	—	—	—	—	1.50
2006(u) In sets only	1,500	—	—	—	—	1.50
2007(u) In sets only	1,000	—	—	—	—	1.50
2008(u) In sets only	1,000	—	—	—	—	1.50
2009(u) In sets only	1,000	—	—	—	—	1.50
2010(u) In sets only	1,000	—	—	—	—	1.50

KM# 12.1b   5 CENTS
3.0000 g., Copper Plated Steel, 18 mm. **Obv:** Arms with supporters within circle **Rev:** Value divides date within circle **Edge:** Plain **Shape:** Square

Date	Mintage	F	VF	XF	Unc	BU
2004(u) In sets only	4,000	—	—	—	—	4.50
2005(u) In sets only	1,500	—	—	—	—	4.50
2006(u) In sets only	1,500	—	—	—	—	4.50
2007(u) In sets only	1,000	—	—	—	—	4.50
2008(u) In sets only	1,000	—	—	—	—	4.50
2009	—	—	—	0.40	1.00	2.50
2009(u) In sets only	1,000	—	—	—	—	4.50
2010(u) In sets only	1,000	—	—	—	—	4.50

KM# 13a   10 CENTS
2.0000 g., Nickel Plated Steel, 16 mm. **Obv:** Arms with supporters within wreath **Rev:** Value and date within circle **Edge:** Reeded

Date	Mintage	F	VF	XF	Unc	BU
2004(u) In sets only	4,000	—	—	—	—	4.50
2005(u) In sets only	1,500	—	—	—	—	4.50
2006(u) In sets only	1,500	—	—	—	—	4.50
2007(u) In sets only	1,000	—	—	—	—	4.50
2008(u) In sets only	1,000	—	—	—	—	4.50
2009	—	—	—	0.50	1.00	2.00
2009(u) In sets only	1,000	—	—	—	—	4.50
2010(u) In sets only	1,000	—	—	—	—	4.50

KM# 14a   25 CENTS
3.5000 g., Nickel Plated Steel, 20 mm. **Obv:** Arms with supporters within wreath **Rev:** Value and date within circle **Edge:** Reeded

Date	Mintage	F	VF	XF	Unc	BU
2004(u) In sets only	4,000	—	—	—	—	4.50
2005(u) In sets only	1,500	—	—	—	—	4.50
2006(u) In sets only	1,500	—	—	—	—	4.50
2007(u) In sets only	1,000	—	—	—	—	4.50
2008(u) In sets only	1,000	—	—	—	—	4.50
2009	—	—	—	—	1.25	2.50
2009(u) In sets only	1,000	—	—	—	—	4.50
2010(u) In sets only	1,000	—	—	—	—	4.50

KM# 23   100 CENTS
5.6500 g., Copper-Nickel, 23 mm. **Obv:** Arms with supporters within wreath **Rev:** Value and date within circle **Edge:** Reeded

Date	Mintage	F	VF	XF	Unc	BU
2004(u) In sets only	4,000	—	—	—	—	6.00
2005(u) In sets only	1,500	—	—	—	—	6.00
2006(u) In sets only	1,500	—	—	—	—	6.00
2007(u) In sets only	1,000	—	—	—	—	6.00

Date	Mintage	F	VF	XF	Unc	BU
2008(u) In sets only	1,000	—	—	—	—	6.00
2009(u) In sets only	1,000	—	—	—	—	6.00
2010(u) In sets only	1,000	—	—	—	—	6.00

KM# 24 250 CENTS
9.5700 g., Copper-Nickel, 28 mm. **Obv:** Arms with supporters within wreath **Rev:** Value and date within circle

Date	Mintage	F	VF	XF	Unc	BU
2004(u) In sets only	4,000	—	—	—	—	10.00
2005(u) In sets only	1,500	—	—	—	—	10.00
2006(u) In sets only	1,500	—	—	—	—	10.00
2007(u) In sets only	1,000	—	—	—	—	10.00
2008(u) In sets only	1,000	—	—	—	—	10.00
2009(u) In sets only	1,000	—	—	—	—	10.00
2010(u) In sets only	1,000	—	—	—	—	10.00

KM# 65 $20
1.2442 g., 0.9990 Gold 0.0400 oz. AGW, 13.92 mm. **Subject:** Antony Nesty's 1988 Gold Medal win at Seoul Olympics, 20th Anniversary **Obv:** Arms with supporters **Rev:** Nesty swimming

Date	Mintage	F	VF	XF	Unc	BU
2008 Proof	5,000	Value: 85.00				

KM# 64 400 DOLLARS
7.9800 g., 0.9160 Gold 0.2350 oz. AGW, 22 mm. **Subject:** 30 Years of Independence **Obv:** Arms with supporters **Rev:** Man kissing flag **Edge:** Reeded

Date	Mintage	F	VF	XF	Unc	BU
2005 Proof	1,000	Value: 500				

KM# 66 500 DOLLARS
7.9800 g., 0.9160 Gold 0.2350 oz. AGW, 22 mm. **Subject:** Central Bank, 50th Anniversary **Obv:** Arms with supporters **Rev:** 50 jaar Central Bank van Suriname 1957-2007

Date	Mintage	F	VF	XF	Unc	BU
2007 Proof	1,000	Value: 450				

MINT SETS

KM#	Date	Mintage	Identification	Issue Price	Mkt Val
MS1	2004 (6)	4,000	KM#11b, 12.1b, 13a, 14a, 23, 24	25.00	35.00
MS2	2005 (6)	1,500	KM#11b, 12.1b, 13a-14a, 23-24	25.00	35.00
MS3	2006 (6)	1,500	KM#11b, 12.1b, 13a-14a, 23-24	25.00	35.00
MS4	2007 (6)	1,000	KM#11b, 12.1b, 13a-14a, 23-24	27.00	27.50
MS5	2008 (6)	1,000	KM#11b, 12.1b, 13a-14a, 23-24	27.00	27.50
MS6	2009 (6)	1,000	KM#11b, 12.1b, 13a, 14a, 23, 24	27.00	27.50
MS7	2010 (6)	1,000	KM#11b, 12.1b, 13a, 14a, 23, 24	27.00	27.50

SWAZILAND

The Kingdom of Swaziland, located in southeastern Africa, has an area of 6,704 sq. mi. (17,360 sq. km.) and a population of *756,000. Capital: Mbabane (administrative); Lobamba (legislative). The diversified economy includes mining, agriculture, and light industry. Asbestos, iron ore, wood pulp, and sugar are exported.

The Kingdom is a member of the Commonwealth of Nations. King Mswati III is Head of State. The prime minister is Head of Government.

RULER
King Msawati III, 1986-

KINGDOM
DECIMAL COINAGE
100 Cents = 1 Lilangeni (plural emelangeni)

KM# 48 5 CENTS
2.1000 g., Copper-Nickel, 18.5 mm. **Ruler:** King Msawati III **Obv:** Bust 3/4 right **Rev:** Arum lily and value **Edge:** Plain **Shape:** Scalloped

Date	Mintage	F	VF	XF	Unc	BU
2001	—	—	—	—	0.50	0.75
2002	—	—	—	—	0.50	0.75
2003	—	—	—	—	0.50	0.75
2005	—	—	—	—	0.50	0.75
2006	—	—	—	—	0.50	0.75
2007	—	—	—	—	0.50	0.75
2008	—	—	—	—	0.50	0.75
2009	—	—	—	—	0.50	0.75

KM# 49 10 CENTS
3.6000 g., Copper-Nickel, 22 mm. **Ruler:** King Msawati III **Obv:** Bust 3/4 right **Rev:** Sugar cane and value **Edge:** Plain **Shape:** Scalloped

Date	Mintage	F	VF	XF	Unc	BU
2001	—	—	—	0.30	0.75	1.00
2002	—	—	—	0.30	0.75	1.00
2005	—	—	—	0.30	0.75	1.00
2006	—	—	—	0.30	0.75	1.00

KM# 50.2 20 CENTS
5.5200 g., Copper-Nickel, 25.2 mm. **Ruler:** King Msawati III **Obv:** Small bust 3/4 right **Rev:** Elephant head, value **Edge:** Plain **Shape:** Scalloped

Date	Mintage	F	VF	XF	Unc	BU
2001	—	—	—	0.35	0.90	2.25
2002	—	—	—	0.35	0.90	2.25
2003	—	—	—	0.35	0.90	2.25

KM# 52 50 CENTS
8.9000 g., Copper-Nickel, 29.45 mm. **Ruler:** King Msawati III **Obv:** Head 1/4 right **Rev:** Arms with supporters

Date	Mintage	F	VF	XF	Unc	BU
2001	—	—	—	—	3.75	4.50
2003	—	—	—	—	3.75	4.50

KM# 45 LILANGENI
9.5000 g., Brass, 22.5 mm. **Ruler:** King Msawati III **Obv:** Head 1/4 right **Rev:** Bust facing

Date	Mintage	F	VF	XF	Unc	BU
2002	—	—	—	1.50	2.75	3.50
2003	—	—	—	1.50	2.75	3.50
2005	—	—	—	1.50	2.75	3.50
2008	—	—	—	1.50	2.75	3.50

KM# 46 2 EMALANGENI
5.0000 g., Brass **Ruler:** King Msawati III **Obv:** Head 1/4 right **Rev:** Lilies and value

Date	Mintage	F	VF	XF	Unc	BU
2003 sm. bust	—	—	—	—	3.75	4.25
2005	—	—	—	—	3.75	4.25
2008	—	—	—	—	3.75	4.25
2009	—	—	—	—	3.75	4.25

KM# 47 5 EMALANGENI
7.6000 g., Brass **Ruler:** King Msawati III **Obv:** Head 1/4 right **Rev:** Arms with supporters above value that divides date

Date	Mintage	F	VF	XF	Unc	BU
2003 sm. bust	—	—	—	—	6.00	7.00

KM# 54a 5 EMALANGENI
Gold **Ruler:** King Msawati III **Subject:** 40th Anniversary of Independence **Obv:** Head 1/4 right **Rev:** National arms at center

Date	Mintage	F	VF	XF	Unc	BU
2008 Proof, rare	100	—	—	—	—	—

KM# 55a 5 EMALANGENI
Gold **Ruler:** King Msawati III **Subject:** 40th Anniversary of Independence **Obv:** Head 1/4 right **Rev:** National arms at center

Date	Mintage	F	VF	XF	Unc	BU
2008 Proof, rare	100	—	—	—	—	—

KM# 54 5 EMALANGENI
7.6000 g., Brass, 27 mm. **Ruler:** King Msawati III **Subject:** 40th Anniversary of Independence **Obv:** Head 1/4 right **Rev:** National arms at center

Date	Mintage	F	VF	XF	Unc	BU
2008	—	—	—	—	5.00	7.00

KM# 55   5 EMALANGENI
7.6000 g., Brass, 27 mm. **Ruler:** King Msawati III **Subject:** 40th Birthday of King **Obv:** Head 1/4 right **Rev:** National arms at center

Date	Mintage	F	VF	XF	Unc	BU
2008	—	—	—	—	5.00	7.00

SWEDEN

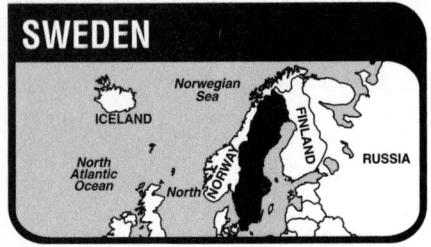

The Kingdom of Sweden, a limited constitutional monarchy located in northern Europe between Norway and Finland, has an area of 173,732 sq. mi. (449,960 sq. km.) and a population of *8.5 million. Capital: Stockholm. Mining, lumbering and a specialized machine industry dominate the economy. Machinery, paper, iron and steel, motor vehicles and wood pulp are exported.

RULER
Carl XVI Gustaf, 1973-

MINT OFFICIALS' INITIALS

Letter	Date	Name
B	1992-2005	Stefan Ingves
D	1986-2005	Bengt Dennis
SI	2006-	Stefan Ingves

MONETARY SYSTEM
100 Ore = 1 Krona

KINGDOM

REFORM COINAGE

KM# 878   50 ORE
3.7000 g., Bronze, 18.7 mm. **Ruler:** Carl XVI Gustaf **Obv:** Value **Rev:** Three crowns and date **Edge:** Reeded

Date	Mintage	F	VF	XF	Unc	BU
2001 B	30,120,532	—	—	0.10	0.15	0.25
2002 B	—	—	—	0.10	0.15	0.25
2003 H	—	—	—	0.10	0.15	0.25
2004 H	25,958,649	—	—	0.10	0.15	0.25
2005 H	—	—	—	0.10	0.15	0.25
2006 SI	—	—	—	0.10	0.15	0.25
2007 SI	—	—	—	0.10	0.15	0.25
2008 SI	—	—	—	0.10	0.15	0.25
2009 SI	—	—	—	0.10	0.15	0.25

KM# 894   KRONA
7.0000 g., Copper-Nickel, 25 mm. **Ruler:** Carl XVI Gustaf **Obv:** Head left **Rev:** Crown and value **Edge:** Reeded

Date	Mintage	F	VF	XF	Unc	BU
2001 B	23,905,454	—	—	—	0.65	1.00
2002 B	—	—	—	—	0.65	1.00
2003 H	—	—	—	—	0.65	1.00
2004 H	42,060,252	—	—	—	0.65	1.00
2005 H	—	—	—	—	0.65	1.00
2006	—	—	—	—	0.65	1.00
2007 B	—	—	—	—	0.65	1.00
2008	—	—	—	—	0.65	1.00

KM# 916   KRONA
7.0000 g., Copper-Nickel, 25 mm. **Ruler:** Carl XVI Gustaf **Subject:** Separation from Finland, 200 Anniversary **Obv:** Head left **Rev:** Horizontal sea waves **Edge:** Reeded

Date	Mintage	F	VF	XF	Unc	BU
2009	—	—	—	—	0.65	1.00

KM# 853a   5 KRONOR
9.6000 g., Copper-Nickel Clad Nickel, 28.5 mm. **Ruler:** Carl XVI Gustaf **Obv:** Crowned monogram **Rev:** Value

Date	Mintage	F	VF	XF	Unc	BU
2001 B	6,001,481	—	—	—	1.00	1.25
2002 B	—	—	—	—	1.00	1.25
2003 H	—	—	—	—	1.00	1.25
2004 H	6,732,730	—	—	—	1.00	1.25
2005 H	—	—	—	—	1.00	1.25
2006 H	—	—	—	—	1.00	1.25
2007 H	—	—	—	—	1.00	1.25
2008 H	—	—	—	—	1.00	1.25
2009 H	—	—	—	—	1.00	1.25

KM# 895   10 KRONOR
6.6000 g., Copper-Aluminum-Zinc, 20.5 mm. **Ruler:** Carl XVI Gustaf **Obv:** Head left **Rev:** Three crowns and value **Edge:** Segmented reeding

Date	Mintage	F	VF	XF	Unc	BU
2001 B	4,171,757	—	—	—	1.75	2.00
2002 B	—	—	—	—	1.75	2.00
2003 H	—	—	—	—	1.75	2.00
2004 H	9,045,581	—	—	—	1.75	2.00
2005 H	—	—	—	—	1.75	2.00
2006 SI	—	—	—	—	1.75	2.00
2007	—	—	—	—	1.75	2.00
2008	—	—	—	—	1.75	2.00
2009	—	—	—	—	1.75	2.00

KM# 910   50 KRONOR
22.0000 g., Aluminum-Bronze, 36 mm. **Ruler:** Carl XVI Gustaf **Subject:** 95th Anniversary - Birth of Astrid Lindgren **Obv:** Playful young girl **Rev:** Astrid Lindgren **Edge:** Plain

Date	Mintage	F	VF	XF	Unc	BU
ND (2002)	100,000	—	—	—	8.00	10.00

KM# 915   50 KRONOR
22.0000 g., Aluminum-Bronze, 36 mm. **Ruler:** Carl XVI Gustaf **Subject:** 150th Anniversary of Sweden's first postage stamp **Obv:** Winged letter flying over landscape **Rev:** Sweden's first postage stamp design **Edge:** Plain

Date	Mintage	F	VF	XF	Unc	BU
ND (2005)	100,000	—	—	—	8.00	10.00

KM# 896   200 KRONOR
27.2500 g., 0.9250 Silver 0.8104 oz. ASW, 36 mm. **Ruler:** Carl XVI Gustaf **Subject:** 25th Wedding Anniversary **Obv:** Conjoined busts left **Rev:** Crowned arms with supporters **Edge:** Plain

Date	Mintage	F	VF	XF	Unc	BU
ND(2001)	50,000	—	—	—	40.00	50.00

KM# 908   200 KRONOR
27.2500 g., 0.9250 Silver 0.8104 oz. ASW, 36 mm. **Ruler:** Carl XVI Gustaf **Subject:** 750th Anniversary of Stockholm **Obv:** City seal with three towers and gate **Rev:** Three towers of city hall **Edge:** Plain

Date	Mintage	F	VF	XF	Unc	BU
ND (2002) Proof	25,000	Value: 40.00				

KM# 902   200 KRONOR
27.2500 g., 0.9250 Silver 0.8104 oz. ASW **Ruler:** Carl XVI Gustaf **Subject:** 30th Anniversary of Reign

Date	Mintage	F	VF	XF	Unc	BU
2003	—	—	—	—	40.00	50.00

KM# 904   200 KRONOR
27.0000 g., 0.9250 Silver 0.8029 oz. ASW, 36 mm. **Ruler:** Carl XVI Gustaf **Subject:** 700th Anniversary, St. Birgitta **Obv:** Cross in circle above value **Rev:** St. Birgitta **Edge:** Plain

Date	Mintage	F	VF	XF	Unc	BU
ND (2003)	60,000	—	—	—	40.00	50.00

KM# 911   200 KRONOR
27.0000 g., 0.9250 Silver 0.8029 oz. ASW, 36 mm. **Ruler:** Carl XVI Gustaf **Subject:** Royal Palace in Stockholm 250th Anniversary **Obv:** Two antique keys over map **Rev:** Royal Palace in Stockholm **Edge:** Plain

Date	Mintage	F	VF	XF	Unc	BU
ND (2004) Proof	35,000	Value: 40.00				

KM# 913   200 KRONOR
27.0000 g., 0.9250 Silver 0.8029 oz. ASW, 36 mm. **Ruler:** Carl XVI Gustaf **Subject:** 100th Anniversary of Dag Hammarskjöld **Obv:** Stylized flames **Rev:** Dag Hammarskjöld **Edge:** Plain

Date	Mintage	F	VF	XF	Unc	BU
ND (2005) Proof	35,000	Value: 40.00				

KM# 906   200 KRONOR
27.0300 g., 0.9250 Silver 0.8038 oz. ASW, 36 mm. **Ruler:** Carl XVI Gustaf **Subject:** Centennial of the end of the Union between Norway and Sweden **Obv:** Split disc **Rev:** Flag on pole and two clouds

Date	Mintage	F	VF	XF	Unc	BU
2005	35,000	—	—	—	40.00	50.00

KM# 917   300 KRONOR
27.0300 g., 0.9250 Silver 0.8038 oz. ASW, 36 mm. **Ruler:** Carl XVI Gustaf **Subject:** Wedding of Princess Victoria and Daniel

Date	Mintage	F	VF	XF	Unc	BU
2010 Proof	—	Value: 50.00				

KM# 909   2000 KRONOR
12.0000 g., 0.9000 Gold 0.3472 oz. AGW, 26 mm. **Ruler:** Carl XVI Gustaf **Subject:** 750th Anniversary of Stockholm **Obv:** City seal with three towers and gate **Rev:** Three towers of city hall **Edge:** Plain

Date	Mintage	F	VF	XF	Unc	BU
ND (2002) Proof	5,000	Value: 600				

KM# 903   2000 KRONOR
12.0000 g., 0.9990 Gold 0.3854 oz. AGW **Ruler:** Carl XVI Gustaf **Subject:** 30th Anniversary of Reign

Date	Mintage	F	VF	XF	Unc	BU
2003	—	—	—	—	575	600

KM# 905   2000 KRONOR
12.0000 g., 0.9000 Gold 0.3472 oz. AGW, 26 mm. **Ruler:** Carl XVI Gustaf **Subject:** St. Birgitta's 700th Anniversary of birth **Obv:** Gothic letter B above value **Rev:** St. Birgitta **Edge:** Plain

Date	Mintage	F	VF	XF	Unc	BU
ND (2003)	8,000	—	—	—	575	600

KM# 912   2000 KRONOR
12.0000 g., 0.9000 Gold Royal Palace in Stockholm 250th Anniversary 0.3472 oz. AGW, 26 mm. **Ruler:** Carl XVI Gustaf **Subject:** Royal Palace in Stockholm **Obv:** Two antique keys over map **Edge:** Plain

Date	Mintage	F	VF	XF	Unc	BU
ND (2004) Proof	5,243	Value: 575				

KM# 914   2000 KRONOR
12.0000 g., 0.9000 Gold 0.3472 oz. AGW, 26 mm. **Ruler:** Carl XVI Gustaf **Subject:** 100th Anniversary of Dag Hammarskjöld **Obv:** Stylized flames **Rev:** Dag Hammarskjöld **Edge:** Plain

Date	Mintage	F	VF	XF	Unc	BU
ND (2005) Proof	5,000	Value: 575				

KM# 907   2000 KRONOR

12.0000 g., 0.9000 Gold 0.3472 oz. AGW, 26 mm. **Ruler:** Carl XVI Gustaf **Subject:** Centennial of the end of the Union between Norway and Sweden **Obv:** Split disc **Rev:** Flag pole dividing two clouds

Date	Mintage	F	VF	XF	Unc	BU
2005	5,000	—	—	—	515	600

KM# 918   4000 KRONOR

12.0000 g., 0.9000 Gold 0.3472 oz. AGW, 26 mm. **Ruler:** Carl XVI Gustaf **Subject:** Wedding of Princess Victoria and Daniel

Date	Mintage	F	VF	XF	Unc	BU
2010 Proof	—	Value: 625				

MINT SETS

KM#	Date	Mintage	Identification	Issue Price	Mkt Val
MS107	2002 (4)	—	KM#853a, 878, 894, 895 plus medal	—	10.00

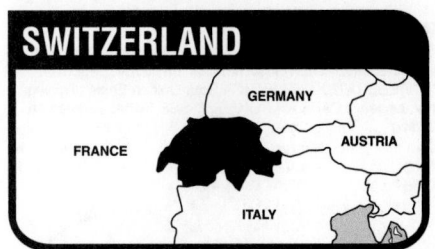

SWITZERLAND

The Swiss Confederation, located in central Europe north of Italy and south of Germany, has an area of 15,941 sq. mi. (41,290 sq. km.) and a population of *6.6 million. Capital: Bern. The economy centers about a well-developed manufacturing industry. Machinery, chemicals, watches and clocks, and textiles are exported.

The Swiss Constitutions of 1848 and 1874 established a union modeled upon that of the United States.

MINT MARK
B – Bern

MONETARY SYSTEM
100 Rappen (Centimes) = 1 Franc

CONFEDERATION
Confoederatio Helvetica

DECIMAL COINAGE

KM# 46   RAPPEN

1.5000 g., Bronze, 16 mm. **Obv:** Cross **Rev:** Value and oat sprig **Edge:** Plain

Date	Mintage	F	VF	XF	Unc	BU
2001B	1,522,000	—	—	—	0.50	1.00
2001B Proof	6,000	Value: 2.00				
2002B	2,024,000	—	—	—	0.50	1.00
2002B Proof	5,500	Value: 2.00				
2003B	1,522,000	—	—	—	0.50	1.00
2003B Proof	5,500	Value: 2.00				
2004B	1,526,000	—	—	—	0.50	1.00
2004B Proof	5,000	Value: 2.00				
2005B	1,524,000	—	—	—	0.50	1.00
2005B Proof	4,500	Value: 2.00				
2006B	26,000	—	—	—	—	135

Note: In sets only, circulation strikes not released

| 2006B Proof | 4,000 | Value: 200 | | | | |

KM# 26c   5 RAPPEN

1.8000 g., Aluminum-Bronze, 17.15 mm. **Obv:** Crowned head right **Rev:** Value within wreath **Edge:** Plain

Date	Mintage	F	VF	XF	Unc	BU
2001B	5,022,000	—	—	—	0.50	1.00
2001B Proof	6,000	Value: 2.00				
2002B	12,024,000	—	—	—	0.50	1.00
2002B Proof	6,000	Value: 2.00				
2003B	10,022,000	—	—	—	0.50	1.00
2003B Proof	5,500	Value: 2.00				
2004B	10,026,000	—	—	—	0.50	1.00
2004B Proof	5,000	Value: 2.00				
2005B	13,024,000	—	—	—	0.50	1.00
2005B Proof	4,500	Value: 2.00				
2006B	12,026,000	—	—	—	0.50	1.00
2006B Proof	4,000	Value: 2.00				
2007B	13,024,000	—	—	—	0.50	1.00

Date	Mintage	F	VF	XF	Unc	BU
2007B Proof	4,000	Value: 2.00				
2008B	40,022,000	—	—	—	0.50	1.00
2008B Proof	4,000	Value: 2.00				
2009B	45,022,000	—	—	—	0.50	1.00
2009B Proof	4,000	Value: 2.00				
2010B	Est. 41,022,000	—	—	—	0.50	1.00
2010B Proof	Est. 4,000	Value: 2.00				
2011B	Est. 50,022,000	—	—	—	0.30	1.00
2011B Proof	Est. 4,000	Value: 2.00				
2012B	—	—	—	—	0.30	1.00
2012B Proof	—	Value: 2.00				

KM# 27   10 RAPPEN

3.0000 g., Copper-Nickel, 19.15 mm. **Obv:** Crowned head right **Obv. Legend:** CONFOEDERATIO HELVETICA **Rev:** Value within wreath **Edge:** Plain

Date	Mintage	F	VF	XF	Unc	BU
2001B	7,022,000	—	—	—	0.50	1.00
2001B Proof	6,000	Value: 2.00				
2002B	15,024,000	—	—	—	0.50	1.00
2002B Proof	6,000	Value: 2.00				
2003B	12,022,000	—	—	—	0.50	1.00
2003B Proof	5,500	Value: 2.00				
2004B	5,026,000	—	—	—	0.50	1.00
2004B Proof	5,000	Value: 2.00				
2005B	7,024,000	—	—	—	0.50	1.00
2005B Proof	4,500	Value: 2.00				
2006B	2,026,000	—	—	—	0.50	1.00
2006B Proof	4,000	Value: 2.00				
2007B	18,024,000	—	—	—	0.50	1.00
2007B Proof	4,000	Value: 2.00				
2008B	35,022,000	—	—	—	0.50	1.00
2008B Proof	4,000	Value: 2.00				
2009B	35,022,000	—	—	—	0.50	1.00
2009B Proof	4,000	Value: 2.00				
2010B	Est. 42,022,000	—	—	—	0.50	1.00
2010B Proof	Est. 4,000	Value: 2.00				
2011B	Est. 35,022,000	—	—	—	0.40	1.00
2011B Proof	Est. 4,000	Value: 2.00				
2012B	—	—	—	—	0.40	1.00
2012B Proof	—	Value: 2.00				

KM# 29a   20 RAPPEN

4.0000 g., Copper-Nickel, 21.05 mm. **Obv:** Crowned head right **Rev:** Value within wreath **Edge:** Plain

Date	Mintage	F	VF	XF	Unc	BU
2001B	7,022,000	—	—	—	1.00	2.00
2001B Proof	6,000	Value: 3.00				
2002B	12,024,000	—	—	—	1.00	2.00
2002B Proof	6,000	Value: 3.00				
2003B	10,022,000	—	—	—	1.00	2.00
2003B Proof	5,500	Value: 3.00				
2004B	10,026,000	—	—	—	1.00	2.00
2004B Proof	5,000	Value: 3.00				
2005B	6,024,000	—	—	—	1.00	2.00
2005B Proof	4,500	Value: 3.00				
2006B	5,026,000	—	—	—	1.00	2.00
2006B Proof	4,000	Value: 3.00				
2007B	22,024,000	—	—	—	1.00	2.00
2007B Proof	4,000	Value: 3.00				
2008B	41,022,000	—	—	—	1.00	2.00
2008B Proof	4,000	Value: 3.00				
2009B	32,022,000	—	—	—	1.00	2.00
2009B Proof	4,000	Value: 3.00				
2010B	Est. 18,022,000	—	—	—	1.00	2.00
2010B Proof	Est. 4,000	Value: 3.00				
2011B	Est. 20,022,000	—	—	—	0.75	2.00
2011B Proof	Est. 4,000	Value: 3.00				
2012B	—	—	—	—	0.75	2.00
2012B Proof	—	Value: 3.00				

KM# 23a.3   1/2 FRANC

2.2000 g., Copper-Nickel, 18.2 mm. **Obv:** 23 Stars around figure **Rev:** Value within wreath **Edge:** Reeded

Date	Mintage	F	VF	XF	Unc	BU
2001B	6,022,000	—	—	—	2.50	3.50
2001B Proof	6,000	Value: 5.00				

Date	Mintage	F	VF	XF	Unc	BU
2002B	2,024,000	—	—	—	2.50	3.50
2002B Proof	6,000	Value: 5.00				
2003B	2,022,000	—	—	—	2.50	3.50
2003B Proof	5,500	Value: 5.00				
2004B	2,026,000	—	—	—	2.50	3.50
2004B Proof	5,000	Value: 5.00				
2005B	1,024,000	—	—	—	2.50	3.50
2005B Proof	4,500	Value: 5.00				
2006B	2,025,000	—	—	—	2.50	3.50
2006B Proof	4,500	Value: 5.00				
2007B	18,024,000	—	—	—	2.00	3.00
2007B Proof	4,000	Value: 5.00				
2008B	25,022,000	—	—	—	2.00	3.00
2008B Proof	4,000	Value: 5.00				
2009B	27,022,000	—	—	—	2.00	3.00
2009B Proof	4,000	Value: 5.00				
2010B	Est. 27,022,000	—	—	—	2.00	3.00
2010B Proof	Est. 4,000	Value: 5.00				
2011B	Est. 15,022,000	—	—	—	1.50	3.00
2011B Proof	Est. 4,000	Value: 5.00				
2012B	—	—	—	—	1.50	3.00
2012B Proof	—	Value: 5.00				

KM# 24a.3   FRANC

4.4000 g., Copper-Nickel, 23.2 mm. **Obv:** 23 Stars around figure **Rev:** Value and date within wreath **Edge:** Reeded

Date	Mintage	F	VF	XF	Unc	BU
2001B	3,022,000	—	—	—	3.00	5.00
2001B Proof	6,000	Value: 7.00				
2002B	1,024,000	—	—	—	3.00	5.00
2002B Proof	6,000	Value: 7.00				
2003B	2,022,000	—	—	—	3.00	5.00
2003B Proof	5,500	Value: 7.00				
2004B	2,026,000	—	—	—	3.00	5.00
2004B Proof	5,000	Value: 7.00				
2005B	1,024,000	—	—	—	3.00	5.00
2005B Proof	4,500	Value: 7.00				
2006B	2,026,000	—	—	—	3.00	5.00
2006B Proof	4,000	Value: 7.00				
2007B	3,024,000	—	—	—	3.00	5.00
2007B Proof	4,000	Value: 7.00				
2008B	7,022,000	—	—	—	3.00	5.00
2008B Proof	4,000	Value: 7.00				
2009B	11,022,000	—	—	—	3.00	5.00
2009B Proof	4,000	Value: 7.00				
2010B	Est. 15,022,000	—	—	—	3.00	5.00
2010B Proof	Est. 4,000	Value: 7.00				
2011B	Est. 15,022,000	—	—	—	2.50	5.00
2011B Proof	Est. 4,000	Value: 7.00				
2012B	—	—	—	—	2.50	5.00
2012B Proof	—	Value: 7.00				

KM# 21a.3   2 FRANCS

8.8000 g., Copper-Nickel, 27.4 mm. **Obv:** 23 Stars around figure **Rev:** Value within wreath **Edge:** Reeded

Date	Mintage	F	VF	XF	Unc	BU
2001B	4,022,000	—	—	—	4.00	7.00
2001B Proof	6,000	Value: 10.00				
2002B	1,024,000	—	—	—	4.50	7.50
2002B Proof	6,000	Value: 10.00				
2003B	1,022,000	—	—	2.50	4.50	7.50
2003B Proof	5,500	Value: 10.00				
2004B	1,026,000	—	—	2.50	4.50	7.50
2004B Proof	5,000	Value: 10.00				
2005B	2,024,000	—	—	—	4.50	7.50
2005B Proof	4,500	Value: 10.00				
2006B	7,026,000	—	—	—	4.50	7.50
2006B Proof	4,000	Value: 10.00				
2007B	16,024,000	—	—	—	4.50	7.50
2007B Proof	4,000	Value: 10.00				
2008B	6,022,000	—	—	—	4.50	7.50
2008B Proof	4,000	Value: 10.00				
2009B	8,022,000	—	—	—	4.50	7.50
2009B Proof	4,000	Value: 10.00				
2010B	Est. 9,022,000	—	—	—	4.50	7.97
2010B Proof	Est. 4,000	Value: 10.00				
2011B	Est. 7,022,000	—	—	—	4.00	7.50
2011B Proof	Est. 4,000	Value: 10.00				
2012B	—	—	—	—	4.00	7.50
2012B Proof	—	Value: 10.00				

KM# 40a.4   5 FRANCS

13.2000 g., Copper-Nickel, 31.45 mm. **Obv:** William Tell right **Rev:** Shield flanked by sprigs **Edge:** DOMINUS PROVIDEBIT and 13 stars raised

Date	Mintage	F	VF	XF	Unc	BU
2001B	1,022,000	—	—	—	7.00	10.00
2001B Proof	6,000	Value: 15.00				
2002B	1,024,000	—	—	—	7.00	10.00
2002B Proof	6,000	Value: 15.00				
2003B	1,022,000	—	—	—	7.00	10.00
2003B Proof	5,500	Value: 15.00				
2004B	524,000	—	—	—	7.50	11.00
2004B Proof	5,000	Value: 15.00				
2005B	524,000	—	—	—	7.50	11.00
2005B Proof	4,500	Value: 15.00				
2006B	526,000	—	—	—	7.50	11.00
2006B Proof	4,000	Value: 15.00				
2007B	524,000	—	—	—	7.50	11.00
2007B Proof	4,000	Value: 15.00				
2008B	522,000	—	—	—	7.50	11.00
2008B Proof	4,000	Value: 15.00				
2009B	2,022,000	—	—	—	7.50	11.00
2009B Proof	4,000	Value: 15.00				
2010B	Est. 5,022,000	—	—	—	7.50	11.00
2010B Proof	Est. 4,000	Value: 15.00				
2011B	Est. 3,022,000	—	—	—	7.50	11.00
2011B Proof	Est. 4,000	Value: 15.00				
2012B	—	—	—	—	7.50	11.00
2012B Proof	—	Value: 15.00				

COMMEMORATIVE COINAGE

KM# 92   5 FRANCS

15.0000 g., Bi-Metallic Nordic gold center in Copper-Nickel ring, 32.85 mm. **Subject:** Zurcher Sechselauten **Obv:** Value within circle **Rev:** Burning strawman within circle **Edge:** Reeded **Edge Lettering:** DOMINUS PROVIDEBIT (13 stars)

Date	Mintage	F	VF	XF	Unc	BU
2001B	170,000	—	—	—	8.00	12.00
2001B Proof	20,000	Value: 24.00				

KM# 98   5 FRANCS

15.0000 g., Bi-Metallic Nordic gold center in Copper-Nickel ring, 32.85 mm. **Subject:** Escalade 1602-2002 **Obv:** Value within circle **Rev:** Swirling ladders design within circle **Edge:** Reeded **Edge Lettering:** DOMINUS PROVIDEBIT (13 stars)

Date	Mintage	F	VF	XF	Unc	BU
2002B	130,000	—	—	—	8.00	12.00
2002B Proof	15,000	Value: 24.00				

KM# 103   5 FRANCS

15.0000 g., Bi-Metallic Nordic gold center in Copper-Nickel ring, 32.85 mm. **Subject:** Chalandamarz **Obv:** Value within circular inscription and designed wreath **Rev:** Boys shaking bells within 3/4 designed wreath **Edge:** Reeded **Edge Lettering:** DOMINUS PROVIDEBIT (13 stars)

Date	Mintage	F	VF	XF	Unc	BU
2003B	96,000	—	—	—	8.00	12.00
2003B Proof	12,000	Value: 24.00				

KM# 107   10 FRANCS

15.0000 g., Bi-Metallic Copper-Nickel center in Aluminum-Bronze ring, 32.85 mm. **Obv:** Value **Rev:** Matterhorn Mountain **Edge:** Segmented reeding

Date	Mintage	F	VF	XF	Unc	BU
2004B	94,976	—	—	—	—	22.00
2004B Proof	12,168	Value: 45.00				

KM# 111   10 FRANCS

15.0000 g., Bi-Metallic Copper-Nickel center in Aluminum-Bronze ring, 32.85 mm. **Obv:** Value **Rev:** Jungfrau mountain **Edge:** Segmented reeding

Date	Mintage	F	VF	XF	Unc	BU
2005B	77,791	—	—	—	—	18.00
2005B Proof	10,495	Value: 40.00				

KM# 114   10 FRANCS

15.0000 g., Bi-Metallic Copper-Nickel center in Aluminum-Bronze ring, 32.85 mm. **Obv:** Value **Rev:** Piz Bernina mountain **Edge:** Segmented reeding

Date	Mintage	F	VF	XF	Unc	BU
2006B	66,000	—	—	—	—	16.00
2006B Proof	9,000	Value: 40.00				

KM# 118   10 FRANCS

15.0000 g., Bi-Metallic Copper-Nickel center in Aluminum-Bronze ring, 32.85 mm. **Subject:** Swiss National Park **Obv:** Value **Rev:** Ibex **Edge:** Segmented reeding

Date	Mintage	F	VF	XF	Unc	BU
2007B	80,200	—	—	—	—	17.00
2007B Proof	10,300	Value: 40.00				

KM# 126   10 FRANCS

15.0000 g., Bi-Metallic Copper-Nickel center in Aluminum-Bronze ring, 32.85 mm. **Obv:** Small national arms **Obv. Legend:** CONFEDERATIO - HELVETICA **Rev:** Golden Eagle alighting **Rev. Legend:** PARK NATIONAL SUISSE **Edge:** Segmented reeding

Date	Mintage	F	VF	XF	Unc	BU
2008B	66,000	—	—	—	—	17.00
2008B Proof	10,300	Value: 40.00				

KM# 130   10 FRANCS

15.0000 g., Bi-Metallic Copper-Nickel center in Aluminum-Bronze ring, 32.85 mm. **Subject:** Swiss National Park **Obv:** Value **Rev:** Red deer

Date	Mintage	F	VF	XF	Unc	BU
2009B	Est. 95,000	—	—	—	—	17.00
2009B Proof	Est. 12,000	Value: 40.00				

KM# 134   10 FRANCS

15.0000 g., Bi-Metallic Copper-Nickel center in Aluminum-Bronze ring, 32.85 mm. **Subject:** Swiss National Park - Alpine Marmot **Obv:** Value **Rev:** Marmot

Date	Mintage	F	VF	XF	Unc	BU
2010B	Est. 94,000	—	—	—	—	17.00
2010B Proof	Est. 12,000	Value: 40.00				

KM# 138   10 FRANCS

15.0000 g., Bi-Metallic Copper-Nickel center in Aluminum-Bronze ring, 33 mm. **Subject:** Bern Onion Market **Obv:** Value **Rev:** Bear of Bern at left, woven plaits of onions at right **Edge:** Segmented reeding

Date	Mintage	F	VF	XF	Unc	BU
2011B	Est. 94,000	—	—	—	—	17.00
2011B Proof	Est. 12,000	Value: 40.00				

KM# 142   10 FRANCS
15.0000 g., Bi-Metallic Copper-Nickel center in Aluminum-Bronze ring, 33 mm. **Subject:** Bull fighting **Rev:** Two bull's heads butting

Date	Mintage	F	VF	XF	Unc	BU
2012B	94,000	—	—	—	—	17.00
2012B Proof	12,000	Value: 40.00				

KM# 93   20 FRANCS
20.0000 g., 0.8350 Silver 0.5369 oz. ASW, 32.8 mm. **Subject:** Mustair Cloister **Obv:** Church floor plan **Rev:** Cloister of Müstair **Edge Lettering:** DOMINUS PROVIDEBIT and 13 stars

Date	Mintage	F	VF	XF	Unc	BU
2001B	50,076	—	—	—	26.00	30.00
2001B Proof	15,000	Value: 55.00				

KM# 94   20 FRANCS
20.0000 g., 0.8350 Silver 0.5369 oz. ASW, 32.8 mm. **Subject:** Johanna Spyri **Obv:** Value within handwritten background **Rev:** Bust facing **Edge Lettering:** DOMINUS PROVIDEBIT (13 stars)

Date	Mintage	F	VF	XF	Unc	BU
2001B	60,364	—	—	—	26.00	30.00
2001B Proof	15,000	Value: 55.00				

KM# 99   20 FRANCS
20.0000 g., 0.8350 Silver 0.5369 oz. ASW, 32.8 mm. **Obv:** St. Gall and bear cub **Rev:** St. Gall Cloister **Edge Lettering:** DOMINUS PROVIDEBIT (13 stars)

Date	Mintage	F	VF	XF	Unc	BU
2002B	35,895	—	—	—	26.00	30.00
2002B Proof	6,250	Value: 55.00				

KM# 100   20 FRANCS
20.0000 g., 0.8350 Silver 0.5369 oz. ASW, 32.8 mm. **Subject:**

REGA **Obv:** Value, inscription and raised cross above rotating propeller **Rev:** Rescue helicopter in flight **Edge Lettering:** DOMINUS PROVIDEBIT (13 stars)

Date	Mintage	F	VF	XF	Unc	BU
2002B	37,314	—	—	—	26.00	30.00
2002B Proof	6,453	Value: 55.00				

KM# 101   20 FRANCS
20.0000 g., 0.8350 Silver 0.5369 oz. ASW, 32.8 mm. **Subject:** Expo '02 **Obv:** Value and date within circle **Rev:** Child at water's edge within beaded circle **Edge Lettering:** DOMINUS PROVIDEBIT (13 stars)

Date	Mintage	F	VF	XF	Unc	BU
2002B	51,899	—	—	—	26.00	30.00
2002B Proof	7,691	Value: 55.00				

KM# 104   20 FRANCS
19.9700 g., 0.8350 Silver 0.5361 oz. ASW, 32.8 mm. **Subject:** St. Moritz Ski Championships **Obv:** Value in snow storm **Rev:** Skier in snow storm **Edge Lettering:** DOMINUS PROVIDEBIT (13 stars)

Date	Mintage	F	VF	XF	Unc	BU
2003B	39,411	—	—	—	26.00	30.00
2003B Proof	6,471	Value: 55.00				

KM# 106   20 FRANCS
20.0000 g., 0.8350 Silver 0.5369 oz. ASW, 32.8 mm. **Subject:** Bern, Old Town **Obv:** Stylized clock tower and buildings **Rev:** Stylized aerial view of Berner Altstadt **Edge Lettering:** DOMINUS PROVIDEBIT

Date	Mintage	F	VF	XF	Unc	BU
2003B	38,644	—	—	—	26.00	30.00
2003B Proof	5,909	Value: 55.00				

KM# 108   20 FRANCS
20.0000 g., 0.8350 Silver 0.5369 oz. ASW, 32.8 mm. **Obv:** Value **Rev:** The Three Castles of Bellinzona **Edge Lettering:** DOMINUS PROVIDEBIT

Date	Mintage	F	VF	XF	Unc	BU
2004B	29,697	—	—	—	26.00	30.00
2004B Proof	5,190	Value: 55.00				

KM# 109   20 FRANCS
20.0000 g., 0.8350 Silver 0.5369 oz. ASW, 32.8 mm. **Obv:** Value **Rev:** Chillon Castle and reflection **Edge Lettering:** DOMINUS PROVIDEBIT

Date	Mintage	F	VF	XF	Unc	BU
2004B	35,133	—	—	—	26.00	30.00
2004B Proof	5,670	Value: 55.00				

KM# 121   20 FRANCS
20.0000 g., 0.8350 Silver 0.5369 oz. ASW, 32.8 mm. **Subject:** FIFA Centennial **Obv:** Soccer ball with value at left **Rev:** Flower in center of cross

Date	Mintage	F	VF	XF	Unc	BU
2004B Proof only	14,041	Value: 150				

KM# 122   20 FRANCS
20.0000 g., 0.8350 Silver 0.5369 oz. ASW, 32.8 mm. **Subject:** Chapel Bridge Lucerne **Obv:** Value **Rev:** View of Chapel Bridge **Edge Lettering:** DOMINUS PROVIDEBIT

Date	Mintage	F	VF	XF	Unc	BU
2005B	44,359	—	—	—	26.00	30.00
2005B Proof	5,998	Value: 55.00				

KM# 112   20 FRANCS
20.0000 g., 0.8350 Silver 0.5369 oz. ASW, 32.8 mm. **Subject:** Geneva Motor Show **Obv:** Value **Rev:** Partial view of prototype car **Edge Lettering:** DOMINUS PROVIDEBIT

Date	Mintage	F	VF	XF	Unc	BU
2005B	45,000	—	—	—	26.00	30.00
2005B Proof	6,000	Value: 55.00				

KM# 115   20 FRANCS
20.0000 g., 0.8350 Silver 0.5369 oz. ASW, 32.8 mm. **Obv:**

Value **Rev:** 1906 Post Bus **Edge Lettering:** DOMINUS PROVIDEBIT

Date	Mintage	F	VF	XF	Unc	BU
2006B	40,000	—	—	—	26.00	30.00
2006B Proof	6,000	Value: 55.00				

KM# 117   20 FRANCS

20.0000 g., 0.8350 Silver 0.5369 oz. ASW, 32.8 mm. **Obv:** Value and legend **Rev:** Swiss Parliament Building **Edge Lettering:** DOMINUS PROVIDEBIT (13 stars)

Date	Mintage	F	VF	XF	Unc	BU
2006B	35,000	—	—	—	25.00	30.00
2006B Proof	6,000	Value: 60.00				

KM# 119   20 FRANCS

20.0000 g., 0.8350 Silver 0.5369 oz. ASW, 32.8 mm. **Subject:** National Bank Centennial **Obv:** Value **Rev:** Partial face of Arthur Honegger (Composer) **Edge Lettering:** DOMINUS PROVIDEBIT

Date	Mintage	F	VF	XF	Unc	BU
2007B	41,747	—	—	—	25.00	30.00
2007B Proof	11,000	Value: 60.00				

KM# 124   20 FRANCS

20.0000 g., 0.8350 Silver 0.5369 oz. ASW, 32.8 mm. **Series:** Famous buildings **Subject:** Munot castle of Schaffhausen **Obv. Legend:** CONFEDERATIO - HELVETICA **Rev:** Two views of castle **Rev. Legend:** MUNOT

Date	Mintage	F	VF	XF	Unc	BU
2007B	40,000	—	—	—	25.00	30.00
2007B Proof	5,000	Value: 60.00				

KM# 127   20 FRANCS

20.0000 g., 0.8350 Silver 0.5369 oz. ASW, 32.8 mm. **Subject:** 100th Anniversary Hockey **Obv:** Small national arms **Obv. Legend:** CONFEDERATIO - HELVETICA **Rev:** Two players, one about to swing at puck **Rev. Legend:** ICE HOCKEY 1908-2008

Date	Mintage	F	VF	XF	Unc	BU
2008B	46,000	—	—	—	25.00	30.00
2008B Proof	5,500	Value: 65.00				

KM# 128   20 FRANCS

20.0000 g., 0.8350 Silver 0.5369 oz. ASW, 32.8 mm. **Subject:** Vitznau-Rigi Cog Railway **Obv:** Value **Rev:** Modern locomotive descending, early locomotive ascending (inverted)

Date	Mintage	F	VF	XF	Unc	BU
2008B	Est. 50,000	—	—	—	25.00	30.00
2008B Proof	7,000	Value: 65.00				

KM# 131   20 FRANCS

20.0000 g., 0.8350 Silver 0.5369 oz. ASW, 32.8 mm. **Subject:** Swiss Museum of Transport, 50th Anniversary **Obv:** National arms and value **Rev:** Spiral of transport vehicles **Edge:** DOMINUS PROVIDEBIT

Date	Mintage	F	VF	XF	Unc	BU
2009B	Est. 50,000	—	—	—	25.00	30.00
2009B Proof	7,000	Value: 65.00				

KM# 132   20 FRANCS

20.0000 g., 0.8350 Silver 0.5369 oz. ASW, 32.8 mm. **Subject:** Brienz-Rothorn Railway **Obv:** Value **Rev:** Locomotive and rail-car

Date	Mintage	F	VF	XF	Unc	BU
2009B	Est. 50,000	—	—	—	25.00	30.00
2009B Proof	7,000	Value: 65.00				

KM# 135   20 FRANCS

20.0000 g., 0.8350 Silver 0.5369 oz. ASW, 32.8 mm. **Subject:** 100 Years Bernina Railway **Rev:** Steam train on viaduct

Date	Mintage	F	VF	XF	Unc	BU
2010B	Est. 50,000	—	—	—	30.00	35.00
2010B Proof	Est. 7,000	Value: 50.00				

KM# 136   20 FRANCS

20.0000 g., 0.8350 Silver 0.5369 oz. ASW, 32.8 mm. **Subject:**

100 Anniversary Death of Henry Dunant (Red Cross founder) **Rev:** Bust at left, flag

Date	Mintage	F	VF	XF	Unc	BU
2010B	Est. 50,000	—	—	—	30.00	35.00
2010B Proof	Est. 7,000	Value: 50.00				

KM# 139   20 FRANCS

20.0000 g., 0.8350 Silver 0.5369 oz. ASW, 33 mm. **Subject:** Max Frisch, 100th Anniversary of Birth **Obv:** Value **Rev:** Facing portrait with pipe

Date	Mintage	F	VF	XF	Unc	BU
2011B	Est. 50,000	—	—	—	30.00	35.00
2011B Proof	Est. 7,000	Value: 50.00				

KM# 140   20 FRANCS

20.0000 g., 0.8350 Silver 0.5369 oz. ASW, 33 mm. **Subject:** Pilatus Railway **Obv:** Value, date and inscription "CONFOEDERATIO HELVETICA" **Rev:** Electric railway car climbing mountain and inscription "PILATUSBAHN" **Edge:** COMINUS PROVIDEBIT (13 stars)

Date	Mintage	F	VF	XF	Unc	BU
2011B	50,000	—	—	—	45.00	50.00
2011B Proof	7,000	Value: 95.00				

KM# 143   20 FRANCS

20.0000 g., 0.8350 Silver 0.5369 oz. ASW, 33 mm. **Subject:** Jungfrau Railway

Date	Mintage	F	VF	XF	Unc	BU
2012B	50,000	—	—	—	—	30.00
2012B Proof	7,000	Value: 65.00				

KM# 95   50 FRANCS

11.2900 g., 0.9000 Gold 0.3267 oz. AGW, 25.1 mm. **Obv:** Landscape and value **Rev:** Heidi and goat running **Edge:** Lettered **Edge Lettering:** DOMINUS PROVIDEBIT (13 stars)

Date	Mintage	F	VF	XF	Unc	BU
2001B Proof	3,967	Value: 700				

KM# 102   50 FRANCS

11.2900 g., 0.9000 Gold 0.3267 oz. AGW, 25.1 mm. **Subject:**

Expo '02 **Obv:** Value **Rev:** Aerial view of 3 lakes landscape **Edge:** Lettered **Edge Lettering:** DOMINUS PROVIDEBIT (13 stars)

Date	Mintage	F	VF	XF	Unc	BU
2002B Proof	4,856	Value: 625				

KM# 105   50 FRANCS

11.2900 g., 0.9000 Gold 0.3267 oz. AGW, 25.1 mm. **Obv:** Skier and value **Rev:** St. Moritz city view **Edge Lettering:** DOMINUS PROVIDEBIT (13 stars)

Date	Mintage	F	VF	XF	Unc	BU
2003B Proof	4,000	Value: 625				

KM# 110   50 FRANCS

11.2900 g., 0.9000 Gold 0.3267 oz. AGW, 25.1 mm. **Obv:** Value **Rev:** Matterhorn Mountain **Edge Lettering:** DOMINUS PROVIDEBIT (13 stars)

Date	Mintage	F	VF	XF	Unc	BU
2004B Proof	7,000	Value: 700				

KM# 123   50 FRANCS

11.2900 g., 0.9000 Gold 0.3267 oz. AGW, 25.1 mm. **Subject:** FIFA Centennial **Obv:** FIFA depicting Wilhelm Tell **Rev:** Soccer ball on left value on right

Date	Mintage	F	VF	XF	Unc	BU
2004B Proof	10,000	Value: 900				

KM# 113   50 FRANCS

11.2900 g., 0.9000 Gold 0.3267 oz. AGW, 25.1 mm. **Subject:** Geneva Motor Show **Obv:** Value **Rev:** Partial view of an antique car **Edge Lettering:** DOMINUS PROVIDEBIT

Date	Mintage	F	VF	XF	Unc	BU
2005B Proof	6,000	Value: 625				

KM# 116   50 FRANCS

11.2900 g., 0.9000 Gold 0.3267 oz. AGW, 25.1 mm. **Obv:** Value **Rev:** Swiss Guardsman **Edge Lettering:** DOMINUS PROVIDEBIT

Date	Mintage	F	VF	XF	Unc	BU
2006B Proof	6,000	Value: 750				

KM# 120   50 FRANCS

11.2900 g., 0.9000 Gold 0.3267 oz. AGW, 25.1 mm. **Subject:** National Bank Centennial **Obv:** Value **Obv. Legend:** CONFEDERATIO - HELVETICA **Rev:** "Lumberjack" from painting by Ferdinand Hodler **Rev. Inscription:** SNB BNS + **Edge Lettering:** DOMINUS PROVIDEBIT

Date	Mintage	F	VF	XF	Unc	BU
2007B Proof	6,000	Value: 625				

KM# 129   50 FRANCS

11.2900 g., 0.9000 Gold 0.3267 oz. AGW, 25.1 mm. **Subject:** International Year of Planet Earth **Obv:** Value **Rev:** Dancing child with 3 globes above head, in hands and standing on one globe **Rev. Inscription:** DE LA PLANETE TERRE ANNEE INTERNATIONALE **Edge:** DOMINUS PROVIDEBIT

Date	Mintage	F	VF	XF	Unc	BU
2008B Proof	6,000	Value: 625				

KM# 133   50 FRANCS

11.2900 g., 0.9000 Gold 0.3267 oz. AGW, 25.1 mm. **Subject:** Pro Patria, 100th Anniversary **Obv:** Value **Edge:** DOMINUS PROVIDEBIT

Date	Mintage	F	VF	XF	Unc	BU
2009B Proof	6,000	Value: 650				

KM# 137   50 FRANCS

11.2900 g., 0.9000 Gold 0.3267 oz. AGW, 25.1 mm. **Subject:** 100th Anniversary Death of Alber Anker (Painter)

Date	Mintage	F	VF	XF	Unc	BU
2010B Proof	6,000	Value: 650				

KM# 141   50 FRANCS

11.2900 g., 0.9000 Gold 0.3267 oz. AGW, 25.1 mm. **Subject:** Bell for Ursli **Obv:** Value, date and inscription "CONFOEDERATIO HELVETICA" **Rev:** Boy holding bell and inscription "Schellen-Ursli" **Edge:** DOMINUS PROVIDEBIT

Date	Mintage	F	VF	XF	Unc	BU
2011B Proof	6,000	Value: 650				

ESSAIS

KM#	Date	Mintage	Identification	Mkt Val
E13	2001B	600	20 Francs. 0.8350 Silver. 20.0000 g. 33 mm. KM#93	300
E14	2002B	700	5 Francs. Bi-Metallic. 15.0000 g. 33 mm. KM#98	180
E15	2003B	700	5 Francs. Bi-Metallic. 15.0000 g. 33 mm. KM#103	200
E16	2004B	700	10 Francs. Bi-Metallic. 15.0000 g. 33 mm. KM#107.	300
E19	2005B	500	20 Francs. 0.8320 Silver. 20.0000 g. 33 mm. KM#112.	285
E20	2006B	500	20 Francs. 0.8350 Silver. 20.0000 g. 33 mm. KM#117.	285
E21	2007	500	20 Francs. Silver. 20.0000 g. 33 mm. KM#119. Munot	250
E22	2008B	700	10 Francs. 33.0000 Bi-Metallic. 15.0000 g. KM#126	200
E23	2009B	500	20 Francs. 0.8350 Silver. 20.0000 g. 33mm KM#132	220
E24	2010B	700	10 Francs. Bi-Metallic. 15.0000 g. 33 mm. KM#134	200

MINT SETS

KM#	Date	Mintage	Identification	Issue Price	Mkt Val
MS35	2001 (9)	21,532	KM#21a.3, 23a.3, 24a.3, 26c, 27, 29a, 40a.4, 46, 92 Zurich Sechselauten	—	40.00
MS36	2002 (9)	17,920	KM#21a.3, 23a.3, 24a.3, 26c, 27, 29a, 40a.4, 46, 98 Escalade	—	45.00
MS37	2002 (9)	1,974	KM#21a.3, 23a.3, 24a.3, 26c, 27, 29a, 40a.4, 46, 98 Plus a medal; Baby mint set	—	220
MS38	2003 (9)	17,200	KM#21a.3, 23a.3, 24a.3, 26c, 27, 29a, 40a.4, 46, 103 Chalandamarz	—	50.00
MS39	2003 (8)	4,800	KM#21a.3, 23a.3, 24a.3, 26c, 27, 29a, 40a.2, 46 plus medal; Baby Mint Set	—	80.00
MS40	2004 (9)	16,000	KM#21a.3, 23a.3, 24a.3, 26c, 27, 29a, 40a.4, 46, 107 Matterhorn	—	80.00
MS41	2004 (8)	8,400	KM#21a.3, 23a.3, 24a.3, 26c, 27, 29a, 40a.2, 46 plus medal; Baby Mint Set	—	65.00
MS42	2005 (9)	15,279	KM#21a.3, 23a.3, 24a.3, 26c, 27, 29a, 40a.4, 46, 111 Jung Frau	—	40.00
MS43	2005 (8)	7,500	KM#21a.3, 23a.3, 24a.3, 26c, 27, 29a, 40a.2, 46 plus medal; Baby Mint Set	—	40.00
MS44	2006 (9)	16,000	KM#21a.3, 23a.3, 24a.3, 26c, 27, 29a, 40a.4, 46, 114 Piz Bernina	—	140
MS45	2006 (8)	2,000	KM#21a.3, 23a.3, 24a.3, 26c, 27, 29a, 40a.2, 46 plus medal; Jubilee Mint Set	—	450
MS46	2006 (8)	8,000	KM#21a.3, 23a.3, 24a.3, 26c, 27, 29a, 40a.2, 46 plus medal; Baby Mint Set	—	175
MS47	2007 (8)	16,000	KM#21a.3, 23a.3, 24a.3, 26c, 27, 29a, 40a.4, 118	—	45.00
MS48	2007 (7)	7,500	KM#21a.3, 23a.3, 24a.3, 26c, 27, 29a, 40a.2, plus medal; Baby Mint Set	—	45.00
MS49	2008 (8)	15,000	KM#21a.3, 23a.3, 24a.3, 26c, 27, 29a, 40a.4, 126	—	45.00
MS50	2008 (7)	7,000	KM#21a.3, 23a.3, 24a.3, 26c, 27, 29a, 40a.2, plus medal; Baby Mint Set	—	40.00
MS51	2009 (8)	14,500	KM#21a.3, 23a.3, 24a.3, 26c, 27, 29a, 40a4, 130.	—	50.00
MS52	2009 (7)	7,500	KM#21a.3, 23a.3, 24a.3, 26c, 27, 29a, 40a.2, plus medal; Baby Mint Set	—	40.00
MS53	2010 (8)	14,000	KM#21a.3, 23a.3, 24a.3, 26c, 27, 29a, 40a.2, 134	—	50.00
MS54	2010 (7)	8,000	KM#21a.3, 23a.3, 24a.3, 26c, 27, 29a, 40a.2, plus medal; Baby Mint Set	—	40.00
MS55	2011 (8)	14,000	KM#21a.3, 23a.3, 24a.3, 26c, 27, 29a, 40a.2, 138	—	50.00
MS56	2011 (7)	8,000	KM#21a.3, 23a.3, 24a.3, 26c, 27, 29a, 40a.2, plus medal; Baby Mint Set	—	40.00

PROOF SETS

KM#	Date	Mintage	Identification	Issue Price	Mkt Val
PS30	2001 (9)	5,184	KM#21a.3, 23a.3, 24a.3, 26c, 27, 29a, 40a.4, 46, 92 Zurich Sechselauten	—	75.00
PS31	2002 (9)	4,518	KM#21a.3, 23a.3, 24a.3, 26c, 27, 29a, 40a.4, 46, 98 Escalade	—	80.00
PS32	2003 (9)	4,520	KM#21a.3, 23a.3, 24a.3, 26c, 27, 29a, 40a.4, 46, 103 Chatandamarz	—	80.00
PS33	2004 (9)	4,168	KM#21a.3, 23a.3, 24a.3, 26c, 27, 29a, 40a.4, 46, 107 Matterhorn	68.00	95.00
PS34	2005 (9)	3,783	KM#21a.3, 23a.3, 24a.3, 26c, 27, 29a, 40a.4, 46, 111	68.00	90.00
PS35	2006 (9)	4,000	KM#21a.3, 23a.3, 24a.3, 26c, 27, 29a, 40a.4, 46, 114	68.00	300
PS36	2007 (8)	4,000	KM#21a.3, 23a.3, 24a.3, 26c, 27, 29a, 40a.4, 118	68.00	85.00
PS37	2008 (8)	4,000	KM#21a.3, 23a.3, 24a.3, 26c, 27, 29a, 40a.4, 126	72.00	90.00
PS38	2009 (8)	4,000	KM#21a.3, 23a.3, 24a.3, 26c, 27, 29a, 40a.4, 130	75.00	90.00
PS39	2010 (8)	4,000	KM#21a.3, 23a.3, 24a.3, 26c, 27, 29a, 40a.4, 134	75.00	90.00
PS40	2011 (8)	4,000	KM#21a.3, 23a.3, 24a.3, 26c, 27, 29a, 40a.2, 138	—	90.00

SYRIA

The Syrian Arab Republic, located in the Near East at the eastern end of the Mediterranean Sea, has an area of 71,498 sq. mi. (185,180 sq. km.) and a population of *12 million. Capital: Greater Damascus. Agriculture and animal breeding are the chief industries. Cotton, crude oil and livestock are exported.

TITLES

الجمهورية السورية

al-Jumhuriya(t) al-Suriya(t)

الجمهورية لعربية السورية

al-Jumhuriya(t) al-Arabiya(t) as-Suriya(t)

SYRIAN ARAB REPUBLIC

STANDARD COINAGE

KM# 129   5 POUNDS
7.5300 g., Nickel Clad Steel, 24.5 mm. **Obv:** National arms within design and beaded border **Rev:** Old fort and latent image above value within design and beaded border **Edge:** Reeded and lettered **Edge Lettering:** CENTRAL BANK 5 SYP

Date	Mintage	F	VF	XF	Unc	BU
AH1424-2003	—				1.25	1.75

KM# 130   10 POUNDS
9.5300 g., Copper-Nickel-Zinc, 27.4 mm. **Obv:** National arms within beaded border **Rev:** Ancient ruins with latent image within beaded border **Edge Lettering:** 10 SYRIAN POUNDS

Date	Mintage	F	VF	XF	Unc	BU
AH1424-2003	—				2.50	3.50

KM# 131   25 POUNDS
8.4000 g., Bi-Metallic Copper-Nickel center in Nickel-Brass ring, 25 mm. **Obv:** National arms within beaded border **Rev:** Building and latent image within beaded border **Edge Lettering:** CENTRAL BANK OF SYRIA 25

Date	Mintage	F	VF	XF	Unc	BU
AH1424-2003	—			1.50	3.75	5.00

TAJIKISTAN

The Republic of Tajikistan (Tadjiquistan), was formed from those regions of Bukhara and Turkestan where the population consisted mainly of Tajiks. It is bordered in the north and west by Uzbekistan and Kyrgyzstan, in the east by China and in the south by Afghanistan. It has an area of 55,240 sq. miles (143,100 sq. km.) and a population of 5.95 million. It includes 2 provinces of Khudzand and Khatlon together with the Gorno-Badakhshan Autonomous Region with a population of 5,092,603. Capital: Dushanbe. Tajikistan was admitted as a constituent republic of the Soviet Union on Dec. 5, 1929. In August 1990 the Tajik Supreme Soviet adopted a declaration of republican sovereignty, and in Dec. 1991 the republic became a member of the CIS.

After demonstrations and fighting, the Communist government was replaced by a Revolutionary Coalition Council on May 7, 1992. Following further demonstrations President Nabiev was ousted on Sept. 7, 1992. Civil war broke out, and the government resigned on Nov. 10, 1992. On Nov. 30, 1992 it was announced that a CIS peacekeeping force would be sent to Tajikistan. A state of emergency was imposed in Jan. 1993. A ceasefire was signed in 1996 and a peace agreement signed in June 1997.

MONETARY SYSTEM
100 Drams = 1 Somoni

REPUBLIC

DECIMAL COINAGE

KM# 2.1   5 DRAMS
2.0000 g., Brass Clad Steel, 16.5 mm. **Obv:** Crown within 1/2 star border **Rev:** Small value within design **Edge:** Plain

Date	Mintage	F	VF	XF	Unc	BU
2001(sp)	—				0.50	0.75
2001(sp) Proof	—	Value: 2.50				

KM# 2.2   5 DRAMS
2.0000 g., Brass Clad Steel, 16.5 mm. **Obv:** Crown with 1/2 star border **Rev:** Large value within design

Date	Mintage	F	VF	XF	Unc	BU
2006(sp)	—				0.75	1.25

KM# 3.1   10 DRAMS
2.4000 g., Brass Clad Steel, 17.5 mm. **Obv:** Crown within 1/2 star border **Rev:** Small value within design **Edge:** Plain

Date	Mintage	F	VF	XF	Unc	BU
2001(sp)	—				0.75	1.00
2001(sp) Proof	—	Value: 3.00				

KM# 3.2   10 DRAMS
2.4000 g., Brass Clad Steel, 17.5 mm. **Obv:** Crown within 1/2 star border **Rev:** Large value within design

Date	Mintage	F	VF	XF	Unc	BU
2006(sp)	—				1.00	1.50

KM# 4.1   20 DRAMS
2.7000 g., Brass Clad Steel, 18.5 mm. **Obv:** Crown within 1/2 star border **Rev:** Small value within design **Edge:** Plain

Date	Mintage	F	VF	XF	Unc	BU
2001(sp)	—				1.00	1.25
2001(sp) Proof	—	Value: 3.75				

KM# 4.2   20 DRAMS
2.7000 g., Brass Clad Steel, 18.5 mm. **Obv:** Crown within 1/2 star border **Rev:** Large value within design

Date	Mintage	F	VF	XF	Unc	BU
2006(sp)	—				1.50	2.00

KM# 5.1   25 DRAMS
2.7600 g., Brass, 19 mm. **Obv:** Crown within 1/2 star border **Rev:** Small value within design **Edge:** Plain

Date	Mintage	F	VF	XF	Unc	BU
2001(sp)	—				1.50	1.75
2001(sp) Proof	—	Value: 5.00				

KM# 5.2   25 DRAMS
2.7600 g., Brass, 19 mm. **Obv:** Crown within 1/2 star border **Rev:** Large value within design

Date	Mintage	F	VF	XF	Unc	BU
2006(sp)	—				1.75	2.50

KM# 6.1   50 DRAMS
3.6000 g., Brass, 21 mm. **Obv:** Crown within 1/2 star border **Rev:** Value within design **Edge:** Plain

Date	Mintage	F	VF	XF	Unc	BU
2001(sp)	—				2.00	3.00
2001(sp) Proof	—	Value: 7.00				

KM# 6.2   50 DRAMS
3.6000 g., Brass, 21 mm. **Obv:** Crown within 1/2 star border **Rev:** Large value within design

Date	Mintage	F	VF	XF	Unc	BU
2006(sp)	—				2.00	3.00

KM# 7   SOMONI
5.2000 g., Copper-Nickel-Zinc, 24 mm. **Obv:** King's bust 1/2 right **Rev:** Value **Edge:** Segmented reeding

Date	Mintage	F	VF	XF	Unc	BU
2001(sp)	—	—	—	—	3.50	5.00
2001(sp) Proof		Value: 12.00				

KM# 12 SOMONI
5.2000 g., Copper-Nickel-Zinc, 24 mm. **Subject:** Year of Aryan Civilization **Obv:** National arms above value **Rev:** Ancient archer in war chariot **Edge:** Segmented reeding

Date	Mintage	F	VF	XF	Unc	BU
2006(sp)	100,000	—	—	—	3.50	5.00

KM# 13 SOMONI
5.2000 g., Copper-Nickel-Zinc, 24 mm. **Subject:** Year of Aryan Civilization **Obv:** National arms above value **Rev:** Two busts left **Edge:** Segmented reeding

Date	Mintage	F	VF	XF	Unc	BU
2006(sp)	100,000	—	—	—	3.50	5.00

KM# 19 SOMONI
20.0000 g., 0.9250 Silver 0.5948 oz. ASW, 35 mm. **Subject:** Year of Aryan Civilization **Obv:** National arms above value **Rev:** Ancient archer in war chariot **Edge:** Segmented reeding

Date	Mintage	F	VF	XF	Unc	BU
2006(sp) Proof	1,500	Value: 60.00				

KM# 18 SOMONI
20.0000 g., 0.9250 Silver 0.5948 oz. ASW, 24 mm. **Subject:** Year of Aryan Civilization **Obv:** National arms above value **Rev:** Two busts left **Edge:** Segmented reeding

Date	Mintage	F	VF	XF	Unc	BU
2006 Proof	1,500	Value: 60.00				

KM# 16 SOMONI
5.2000 g., Copper-Nickel-Zinc, 24 mm. **Subject:** 800th Anniversary Birth of Jaloliddini Rumi **Obv:** Small arms above value in cartouche **Rev:** 1/2 length figure facing **Edge:** Segmented reeding

Date	Mintage	F	VF	XF	Unc	BU
2007	—	—	—	—	3.50	5.00

KM# 8 3 SOMONI
6.3000 g., Copper-Nickel-Zinc, 25.5 mm. **Obv:** National arms **Rev:** Crown above value within design **Edge:** Lettered

Date	Mintage	F	VF	XF	Unc	BU
2001(sp)	—	—	—	—	5.00	7.00
2001(sp) Proof		Value: 18.00				

KM# 10 3 SOMONI
6.3000 g., Bi-Metallic Copper-Nickel center in Brass ring, 25.5 mm. **Subject:** 80th Year - Dushanbe City **Obv:** Value below arms within circle **Rev:** Statue in arch within circle

Date	Mintage	F	VF	XF	Unc	BU
2004(sp)	—	—	—	—	6.50	9.00

KM# 10a 3 SOMONI
6.9800 g., 0.9250 Silver 0.2076 oz. ASW, 25.5 mm. **Subject:** 80th Anniversary of Republic **Obv:** Value below arms within circle **Rev:** Statue in arch within circle

Date	Mintage	F	VF	XF	Unc	BU
2004 Proof	1,000	Value: 75.00				

KM# 14 3 SOMONI
6.3000 g., Bi-Metallic Copper-Nickel center in Brass ring, 25.5 mm. **Subject:** 2700th Anniversary of Kulyab **Obv:** National arms above value **Rev:** Kulyab city arms **Edge:** Lettered

Date	Mintage	F	VF	XF	Unc	BU
2006(sp)	100,000	—	—	—	6.00	7.50

KM# 20 3 SOMONI
26.0000 g., 0.9250 Silver 0.7732 oz. ASW, 39 mm. **Subject:** 2700th Anniversary of Kulyab **Obv:** National arms above value **Rev:** Kulyab city arms

Date	Mintage	F	VF	XF	Unc	BU
2006(sp) Proof	2,000	Value: 70.00				

KM# 9 5 SOMONI
7.0000 g., Copper-Nickel-Zinc, 26.5 mm. **Obv:** Turbaned head right **Rev:** Crown above value within design **Edge:** Segmented reeding with a star

Date	Mintage	F	VF	XF	Unc	BU
2001(sp)	—	—	—	—	7.50	9.00
2001(sp) Proof		Value: 25.00				

KM# 11 5 SOMONI
6.9400 g., Bi-Metallic Copper-Nickel center in Brass ring, 26.5 mm. **Subject:** 10th Anniversary - Constitution **Obv:** Arms above value within circle **Rev:** Flag and book within circle **Edge:** Lettered

Date	Mintage	F	VF	XF	Unc	BU
2004(sp)	—	—	—	—	7.50	10.00

KM# 11a 5 SOMONI
8.5500 g., 0.9250 Silver 0.2543 oz. ASW, 26.5 mm. **Subject:** 10th Anniversary - Constitution **Obv:** Arms above value within circle **Rev:** Flag and book within circle

Date	Mintage	F	VF	XF	Unc	BU
2004 Proof	2,000	Value: 65.00				

KM# 15 5 SOMONI
7.0000 g., Bi-Metallic Copper-Nickel center in Brass ring, 26.5 mm. **Subject:** 15th Anniversary of Independence **Obv:** National arms above value **Rev:** Government building **Edge:** Lettered

Date	Mintage	F	VF	XF	Unc	BU
2006(sp)	100,000	—	—	—	7.50	10.00

KM# 21 5 SOMONI
34.0000 g., 0.9250 Silver 1.0111 oz. ASW, 42 mm. **Subject:** 15th Anniversary of Independence **Obv:** National arms above value **Rev:** Government building

Date	Mintage	F	VF	XF	Unc	BU
2006(sp) Proof	2,000	Value: 75.00				

KM# 17 5 SOMONI
7.0000 g., Bi-Metallic Copper-Nickel center in Brass ring, 26.5 mm. **Subject:** 1150th Anniversary founding of Persian (Tajik) literature by Abuabdullo Rudaki **Obv:** National arms above value **Rev:** Bust of Rudaki left, scroll, feather pen

Date	Mintage	F	VF	XF	Unc	BU
2008	—	—	—	—	7.50	10.00

KM# 22 5 SOMONI
34.0000 g., 0.9250 Silver 1.0111 oz. ASW, 42 mm. **Subject:** 1150 Anniversary founding of Persian Literature by Abuabdullo Rudaki **Obv:** National arms above value **Rev:** Bust of Rudaki left, scroll, feather pen

Date	Mintage	F	VF	XF	Unc	BU
2008(sp) Proof	1,000	Value: 115				

MINT SETS

KM#	Date	Mintage Identification	Issue Price	Mkt Val
MS1	2001 (8)	— KM#2.1-6.1, 7-9	—	30.00

PROOF SETS

KM#	Date	Mintage Identification	Issue Price	Mkt Val
PS1	2001 (8)	— KM#2.1-6.1, 7-9	—	80.00

TANZANIA

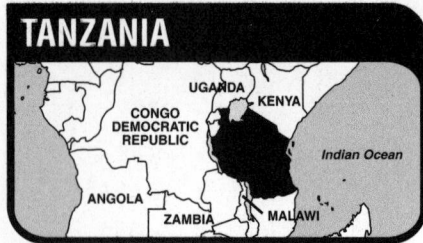

The United Republic of Tanzania, located on the east coast of Africa between Kenya and Mozambique, consists of Tanganyika and the islands of Zanzibar and Pemba. It has an area of 364,900 sq. mi. (945,090 sq. km.) and a population of *25.2 million. Capital: Dodoma. The chief exports are cotton, coffee, diamonds, sisal, cloves, petroleum products, and cashew nuts.

Tanzania is a member of the Commonwealth of Nations. The President is Chief of State.

REPUBLIC
STANDARD COINAGE

100 Senti = 1 Shilingi

KM# 34   200 SHILINGI
8.0000 g., Copper-Nickel-Zinc **Obv:** Head of Sheikh Karume 1/4 left within circle **Rev:** Two lions **Edge:** Plain and reeded sections

Date	Mintage	F	VF	XF	Unc	BU
2008	—	—	—	—	6.00	9.00

KM# 56   500 SHILLINGS
31.4600 g., 0.9250 Silver 0.9356 oz. ASW, 38.6 mm. **Obv:** Arms with supporters above value **Rev:** African dhow **Edge:** Reeded

Date	Mintage	F	VF	XF	Unc	BU
2001 Proof	—	Value: 45.00				

THAILAND

The Kingdom of Thailand (formerly Siam), a constitutional monarchy located in the center of mainland Southeast Asia between Burma and Laos, has an area of 198,457 mi. (514,000 sq. km.) and a population of *55.5 million. Capital: Bangkok. The economy is based on agriculture and mining. Rubber, rice, teakwood, tin and tungsten are exported.

The history of The Kingdom of Siam, the only country in south and Southeast Asia that was never colonized by an European power, dates from the 6th century A.D. when Thai people started to migrate into the area a process that accelerated with the Mongol invasion of China in the 13th century. After 400 years of sporadic warfare with the neighboring Burmese, King Taskin won the last battle in 1767. He founded a new capital, Dhonburi, on the west bank of the Chao Praya River. King Rama I moved the capital to Bangkok in 1782, thus initiating the so-called Bangkok Period of Siamese coinage characterized by Pot Duang money (bullet coins) stamped with regal symbols.

The Portuguese, who were followed by the Dutch, British and French, introduced the Thai to the Western world. Rama III of the present ruling dynasty negotiated a treaty of friendship and commerce with Britain in 1826, and in 1896 the independence of the kingdom was guaranteed by an Anglo-French accord.

In 1909 Siam ceded to Great Britain its suzerain rights over the dependencies of Kedah, Kelantan, Trengganu and Perlis, Malay states situated in southern Siam just north of British Malaya, which eliminated any British jurisdiction in Siam proper.

The absolute monarchy was changed into a constitutional monarchy in 1932.

On Dec. 8, 1941, after five hours of fighting, Thailand agreed to permit Japanese troops passage through the country to invade Northern British Malaysia. This eventually led to increased Japanese intervention and finally occupation of the country. On Jan. 25, 1942, Thailand declared war on Great Britain and the United States. A free Thai guerilla movement was soon organized to counteract the Japanese. In July 1943 Japan transferred the four northern Malay States back to Thailand. These were returned to Great Britain after peace treaties were signed in 1946.

DATING

Typical BE Dating

1238   **1244**

Typical CS Dating

NOTE: Sometimes the era designator *BE* or *CS* will actually appear on the coin itself.

Denomination

2-1/2 (Satang)   RS Dating

DATE CONVERSION TABLES
B.E. date - 543 = A.D. date
Ex: 2516 - 543 = 1973
R.S. date + 1781 = A.D. date
Ex: 127 + 1781 = 1908
C.S. date + 638 = A.D. date
Ex 1238 + 638 = 1876
Primary denominations used were 1 Baht, 1/4 and 1/8 Baht up to the reign of Rama IV. Other denominations are much scarcer.

KINGDOM OF THAILAND
DECIMAL COINAGE

25 Satang = 1 Salung; 100 Satang = 1 Baht

Y# 186   SATANG
0.5000 g., Aluminum, 14.58 mm. **Ruler:** Rama IX **Obv:** Head left **Rev:** Haripunchai Temple, Lumpoon province **Edge:** Plain

Date	Mintage	F	VF	XF	Unc	BU
BE2544 (2001)	50,000	—	—	—	0.75	1.00
BE2546 (2003)	10,000	—	—	—	1.50	2.00
BE2547 (2004)	20,000	—	—	—	1.25	1.75
BE2548 (2005)	10,000	—	—	—	1.50	2.00
BE2549 (2006)	3,000	—	—	—	3.00	4.00
BE2550 (2007)	10,000	—	—	—	1.50	2.00
BE2551 (2008)	10,000	—	—	—	1.50	2.00

Y# 456 SATANG
0.5000 g., Aluminum, 15 mm. **Ruler:** Rama IX **Obv:** Bust left **Rev:** Haripunchai Temple, Lumpoon province

Date	Mintage	F	VF	XF	Unc	BU
BE2552 (2009)	10,000	—	—	—	1.50	2.00
BE2553	10,000	—	—	—	1.50	2.00

Y# 208 5 SATANG
0.6000 g., Aluminum, 16 mm. **Ruler:** Rama IX **Obv:** Bust left **Rev:** Phra Patom Temple, Nakhon Pathom province **Edge:** Plain

Date	Mintage	F	VF	XF	Unc	BU
BE2544 (2001)	50,000	—	—	—	1.00	1.25
BE2546 (2003)	10,000	—	—	—	2.00	2.50
BE2547 (2004)	10,000	—	—	—	2.00	2.50
BE2548 (2005)	20,000	—	—	—	1.25	1.50
BE2549 (2006)	3,000	—	—	—	3.00	4.00
BE2550 (2007)	10,000	—	—	—	2.00	2.50

Y# 457 5 SATANG
0.6000 g., Aluminum, 16.5 mm. **Ruler:** Rama IX **Obv:** Bust left **Rev:** Phra Patom Temple, Nakhon Pathom province

Date	Mintage	F	VF	XF	Unc	BU
BE2551 (2008)	10,000	—	—	—	2.00	2.50
BE2552 (2009)	10,000	—	—	—	2.00	2.50
BE2553 (2010)	10,000	—	—	—	2.00	2.50

Y# 209 10 SATANG
0.8000 g., Aluminum, 17.5 mm. **Ruler:** Rama IX **Obv:** Young bust left **Rev:** Phra Tat Chungchum Temple, Sakon Nakhon province **Edge:** Plain

Date	Mintage	F	VF	XF	Unc	BU
BE2544 (2001)	50,000	—	—	—	1.00	1.50
BE2546 (2003)	10,000	—	—	1.00	2.00	2.50
BE2547 (2004)	20,000	—	—	—	0.75	1.75
BE2548 (2005)	10,000	—	—	1.00	2.00	2.50
BE2549 (2006)	3,000	—	—	2.00	4.00	5.00
BE2550 (2007)	10,000	—	—	1.00	2.00	2.50
BE 2551 (2008) (2008)	10,000	—	—	1.00	2.00	2.50

Y# 458 10 SATANG
0.8000 g., Aluminum, 17.5 mm. **Ruler:** Rama IX **Obv:** Bust left **Rev:** Phra Tat Chungchum Temple, Sakon Nakhon province

Date	Mintage	F	VF	XF	Unc	BU
BE2552 (2009)	10,000	—	—	1.00	2.00	2.50
BE2553 (2010)	10,000	—	—	1.00	2.00	2.50

Y# 187 25 SATANG = 1/4 BAHT
1.9000 g., Aluminum-Bronze, 16 mm. **Ruler:** Rama IX **Obv:** Head left **Rev:** Mahathat Temple, Nakhon Si Thammarat province **Edge:** Reeded

Date	Mintage	F	VF	XF	Unc	BU
BE2544 (2001)	10,000	1.00	2.00	3.00	5.00	6.00
BE2545 (2002)	141,562,000	1.00	2.00	3.00	5.00	6.00
BE2546 (2003)	82,668,000	—	—	—	0.10	0.15
BE2547 (2004)	104,830,000	—	—	—	0.10	0.15
BE2548 (2005)	95,362,000	—	—	—	0.10	0.15
BE2549 (2006)	120,003,000	—	—	—	0.10	0.15
BE2550 (2007) r	180,000,000	—	—	—	0.10	0.15
BE2551 (2008) r	255,600	—	0.50	0.75	1.00	1.50
BE2552 (2009)	30,000	—	1.00	3.00	5.00	6.00

Y# 441 25 SATANG = 1/4 BAHT
1.9000 g., Copper Plated Steel, 16 mm. **Ruler:** Rama IX **Obv:** King's portrait **Rev:** Mahathat Temple, Nakhon Si Thammarat province

Date	Mintage	F	VF	XF	Unc	BU
BE2552 (2009)v	289,995,600	—	—	—	0.10	0.15
BE2553 (2010)v	220,000,000	—	—	—	0.10	0.15
BE2554 (2011)v	—	—	—	—	0.10	0.15
BE2555 (2012)v	—	—	—	—	0.10	0.15

Y# 203 50 SATANG = 1/2 BAHT
2.4000 g., Aluminum-Bronze, 18 mm. **Ruler:** Rama IX **Obv:** Head left **Rev:** Soi Suthep Temple, Chiang Mai province

Date	Mintage	F	VF	XF	Unc	BU
BE2544 (2001)	52,738,000	—	—	—	0.10	0.15
BE2545 (2002)	102,804,000	—	—	—	0.10	0.15
BE2546 (2003)	101,200,000	—	—	—	0.10	0.15
BE2547 (2004)	79,596,000	—	—	—	0.10	0.15
BE2548 (2005)	99,920,000	—	—	—	0.10	0.15
BE2549 (2006)	130,803,000	—	—	—	0.10	0.15
BE2550 (2007)	24,905,000	—	—	—	0.10	0.15
BE2551 (2008)	27,163,509	—	—	—	0.10	0.15

Y# 442 50 SATANG = 1/2 BAHT
2.4000 g., Copper Plated Steel **Ruler:** Rama IX **Obv:** King's portrait **Rev:** Doi Suthep Temple, Chiang Mai province

Date	Mintage	F	VF	XF	Unc	BU
BE2552 (2009)v	225,000,000	—	—	—	0.10	0.15
BE2553 (2010)v	118,536,000	—	—	—	0.10	0.15
BE2554 (2011)v	—	—	—	—	0.10	0.15

Y# 183 BAHT
3.4500 g., Copper-Nickel, 20 mm. **Ruler:** Rama IX **Obv:** Head left **Rev:** Phra Kaew Temple, Bangkok **Edge:** Reeded **Note:** Varieties exist.

Date	Mintage	F	VF	XF	Unc	BU
BE2544 (2001)	385,140,000	—	—	—	0.10	0.15
BE2545 (2002)	266,025,000	—	—	—	0.10	0.15
BE2546 (2003)	236,533,000	—	—	—	0.10	0.15
BE2547 (2004)	903,964,000	—	—	—	0.10	0.15
BE2548 (2005) wg	1,137,820,000	—	—	—	0.10	0.15
BE2549 (2006) v	778,061,000	—	—	—	0.10	0.15
BE2550 (2007) wg	614,866,877	—	—	—	0.10	0.15
BE2551 (2008)	660,307,123	—	—	—	0.10	0.15

Y# 443 BAHT
3.0000 g., Nickel Plated Steel, 20 mm. **Ruler:** Rama IX **Obv:** King's portrait **Rev:** Phra Kaew Temple, Bangkok **Edge:** Reeded

Date	Mintage	F	VF	XF	Unc	BU
BE2552 (2009)v	507,250,000	—	—	—	0.10	0.15
BE2553 (2010)v	551,853,000	—	—	—	0.10	0.15
BE2554 (2011)v	—	—	—	—	0.10	0.15
BE2555 (2012)v	—	—	—	—	0.10	0.15

Y# 444 2 BAHT
4.4000 g., Nickel Plated Steel, 21.75 mm. **Ruler:** Rama IX **Obv:** King's portrait **Rev:** Saket Temple, Bangkok

Date	Mintage	F	VF	XF	Unc	BU
BE2548 (2005)wg	60,000	—	—	—	0.20	0.25
BE2549 (2006)wg	107,872,500	—	—	—	0.20	0.25
BE2550 (2007)wg	232,105,100	—	—	—	0.20	0.25
BE2552 (2009)	50,370	—	—	2.00	4.00	6.00

Y# 445 2 BAHT
4.0000 g., Aluminum-Bronze, 21.75 mm. **Ruler:** Rama IX **Obv:** King's portrait **Rev:** Saket Temple, Bangkok

Date	Mintage	F	VF	XF	Unc	BU
BE2551 (2008)	10,004,000	—	—	0.15	0.30	0.40
BE2552 (2009)	244,741,000	—	—	—	0.20	0.25
BE2553 (2010)	137,228,000	—	—	—	0.20	0.25
BE2554 (2011)	—	—	—	—	0.20	0.25
BE2555 (2012)	—	—	—	—	0.20	0.25

Y# 219 5 BAHT
7.5000 g., Copper-Nickel Clad Copper, 24 mm. **Ruler:** Rama IX **Obv:** Head left **Rev:** Benchamabophit Temple, Bangkok **Edge:** Coarse reeding

Date	Mintage	F	VF	XF	Unc	BU
BE2544 (2001)	76,566,000	—	—	—	0.50	0.75
BE2545 (2002)	29,601,500	—	—	—	0.75	1.00
BE2546 (2003)	182,000	3.00	5.00	8.00	15.00	20.00

Date	Mintage	F	VF	XF	Unc	BU
BE2547 (2004)	120,187,000	—	—	—	0.50	0.75
BE2548 (2005)	91,079,000	—	—	—	0.50	0.75
BE2549 (2006)	254,403,000	—	—	—	0.50	0.75
BE2550 (2007) dj	131,126,000	—	—	—	0.50	0.75
BE2551 (2008)	220,463,200	—	—	—	0.50	0.75

Y# 446 5 BAHT
6.0000 g., Copper-Nickel Clad Copper, 24 mm. **Ruler:** Rama IX **Obv:** King's portrait **Rev:** Benchamabophit Temp, Bangkok, Temple top does not break legend **Edge:** Coarse Reeding

Date	Mintage	F	VF	XF	Unc	BU
BE2551 (2008)	6,225,000	—	—	—	0.75	1.00
BE2552 (2009)	308,283,000	—	—	—	0.50	0.75
BE2553 (2010)	2,903,000	—	—	—	1.00	1.25
BE2554 (2011)	—	—	—	—	0.50	0.75

Y# 373 10 BAHT
8.5000 g., Bi-Metallic Aluminum-Bronze center in Copper-Nickel ring, 26 mm. **Ruler:** Rama IX **Subject:** Department of Lands, 100th Anniversary, February 17 **Obv:** Conjoined busts facing divides circle **Rev:** Department seal within circle **Edge:** Segmented reeding

Date	Mintage	F	VF	XF	Unc	BU
BE2544 (2001)	3,000,000	—	—	1.00	2.50	3.00

Y# 227 10 BAHT
8.5000 g., Bi-Metallic Aluminum-Bronze center in Copper-Nickel ring, 26 mm. **Ruler:** Rama IX **Obv:** Head left within circle **Rev:** Arun Temple (Temple of the Dawn), Bankok **Edge:** Segmented reeding **Note:** Varieties exist.

Date	Mintage	F	VF	XF	Unc	BU
BE2544 (2001)	2,060,000	—	0.75	2.00	5.00	6.00
BE2545 (2002)	61,333,000	—	—	—	2.25	2.75
BE2546 (2003)	49,292,000	—	—	—	2.25	2.75
BE2547 (2004)	62,689,000	—	—	—	2.25	2.50
BE2548 (2005)	111,491,000	—	—	—	2.00	2.50
BE2549 (2006) v	128,903,000	—	—	—	2.00	2.50
BE2550 (2007) v	130,202,000	—	—	—	2.00	2.50
BE2551 (2008)	179,165,360	—	—	—	2.00	2.50

Y# 387 10 BAHT
8.5000 g., Bi-Metallic Aluminum-Bronze center in Copper-Nickel ring, 26 mm. **Ruler:** Rama IX **Subject:** King's 75th Birthday, December 5 **Obv:** Head left **Rev:** Royal crown in radiant oval **Edge:** Segmented reeding

Date	Mintage	F	VF	XF	Unc	BU
BE2545 (2002)	7,500,000	—	—	1.00	2.00	2.75

Y# 381   10 BAHT
8.5000 g., Bi-Metallic Aluminum-Bronze center in Copper-Nickel ring, 26 mm.   **Ruler:** Rama IX **Subject:** Irrigation Department, 100th Anniversary, June 13 **Obv:** Conjoined busts facing divides circle **Rev:** Department logo **Edge:** Segmented reeding

Date	Mintage	F	VF	XF	Unc	BU
BE2545 (2002)	3,000,000	—	—	1.00	2.00	2.75

Y# 382   10 BAHT
8.5000 g., Bi-Metallic Aluminum-Bronze center in Copper-Nickel ring, 26 mm.   **Ruler:** Rama IX **Subject:** Department of Internal Trade, 60th Anniversary May 5 **Obv:** Head left **Rev:** Department logo **Edge:** Segmented reeding

Date	Mintage	F	VF	XF	Unc	BU
BE2545 (2002)	3,000,000	—	—	1.00	2.00	2.75

Y# 383   10 BAHT
8.5000 g., Bi-Metallic Aluminum-Bronze center in Copper-Nickel ring, 26 mm.   **Ruler:** Rama IX **Subject:** Highway Department, 90th Anniversary, April 1 **Obv:** Conjoined busts facing divides circle **Rev:** Highway Department logo **Edge:** Segmented reeding

Date	Mintage	F	VF	XF	Unc	BU
BE2545 (2002)	3,000,000	—	—	1.00	2.00	2.75

Y# 384   10 BAHT
8.5000 g., Bi-Metallic Aluminum-Bronze center in Copper-Nickel ring, 26 mm.   **Ruler:** Rama IX **Subject:** Vajira Medical Center, 90th Anniversary, January 2 **Obv:** Conjoined busts facing divides circle **Rev:** Hospital logo **Edge:** Segmented reeding

Date	Mintage	F	VF	XF	Unc	BU
BE2545 (2002)	3,500,000	—	—	1.00	2.00	2.75

Y# 385   10 BAHT
8.5000 g., Bi-Metallic Aluminum-Bronze center in Copper-Nickel ring, 26 mm.   **Ruler:** Rama IX **Subject:** 20th World Scouting Jamboree **Obv:** Rama IX wearing a scouting uniform **Rev:** Jamboree log **Edge:** Segmented reeding

Date	Mintage	F	VF	XF	Unc	BU
BE2546 (2003)	3,000,000	—	—	1.00	2.00	2.75

Y# 400   10 BAHT
8.5000 g., Bi-Metallic Aluminum-Bronze center in Copper-Nickel ring, 26 mm.   **Ruler:** Rama IX **Subject:** APEC 2003 Summit **Obv:** Head left **Rev:** APEC logo **Edge:** Segmented reeding

Date	Mintage	F	VF	XF	Unc	BU
BE2546-2003	1,000,000	—	—	1.00	2.25	3.00

Y# 409   10 BAHT
8.5000 g., Bi-Metallic Aluminum-Bronze center in Copper-Nickel ring, 26 mm.   **Ruler:** Rama IX **Subject:** King Rama V, 150th Anniversary **Obv:** Bust of Rama V left **Rev:** Royal crown **Edge:** Segmented reeding

Date	Mintage	F	VF	XF	Unc	BU
BE2546 (2003)	3,600,000	—	—	1.00	1.80	2.50

Y# 405   10 BAHT
8.5000 g., Bi-Metallic Aluminum-Bronze center in Copper-Nickel ring, 26 mm.   **Ruler:** Rama IX **Subject:** CITES World Meeting **Obv:** Bust 3/4 left within circle **Rev:** CITES logo **Edge:** Segmented reeding

Date	Mintage	F	VF	XF	Unc	BU
ND(2003)	Est. 3,000,000	—	—	1.00	2.00	2.75

Y# 391   10 BAHT
8.5000 g., Bi-Metallic Aluminum-Bronze center in Copper-Nickel ring, 26 mm.   **Ruler:** Rama IX **Subject:** Inspector General's Department, 100th Anniversary, May 6 **Obv:** Head left within circle **Rev:** Department seal within circle and design **Edge:** Segmented reeding

Date	Mintage	F	VF	XF	Unc	BU
BE2546 (2003)	3,000,000	—	—	1.00	1.75	2.50

Y# 392   10 BAHT
8.5000 g., Bi-Metallic Aluminum-Bronze center in Copper-Nickel ring, 26 mm.   **Ruler:** Rama IX **Subject:** Princess Galaniwattana, 80th Birthday, May 6 **Obv:** Bust 1/4 right **Rev:** Crowned emblem and value **Edge:** Alternating reeded and plain **Note:** This is the king's sister.

Date	Mintage	F	VF	XF	Unc	BU
BE2546 (2003)	2,000,000	—	—	1.00	1.75	2.50

Y# 396   10 BAHT
8.5000 g., Bi-Metallic Aluminum-Bronze center in Copper-Nickel ring, 26 mm.   **Ruler:** Rama IX **Subject:** Government Savings Bank, 90th Anniversary, April 1 **Obv:** Uniformed bust facing within circle **Rev:** Bank emblem **Edge:** Segmented reeding

Date	Mintage	F	VF	XF	Unc	BU
BE2546 (2003)	2,000,000	—	—	1.00	2.00	2.75

Y# 411   10 BAHT
8.5000 g., Bi-Metallic Aluminum-Bronze center in Copper-Nickel ring, 26 mm.   **Ruler:** Rama IX **Subject:** Royal Institute Board, 70th Anniversary **Obv:** 1/2 length civilian busts of 2 kings facing **Rev:** Royal Scholar Institute seal **Edge:** Segmented reeding

Date	Mintage	F	VF	XF	Unc	BU
BE2547 (2004)	2,000,000	—	—	1.00	1.80	2.50

Y# 412   10 BAHT
8.5000 g., Bi-Metallic Aluminum-Bronze center in Copper-Nickel ring, 26 mm.   **Ruler:** Rama IX **Subject:** Queen's 72nd Birthday **Obv:** Bust of queen facing 3/4 left **Rev:** Royal seal **Edge:** Segmented reeding

Date	Mintage	F	VF	XF	Unc	BU
BE2547 (2004)	6,000,000	—	—	1.00	1.80	2.50

Y# 413   10 BAHT
8.5000 g., Bi-Metallic Aluminum-Bronze center in Copper-Nickel ring, 26 mm.   **Ruler:** Rama IX **Subject:** IUCN World Conservation Congress **Obv:** Civilian bust 3/4 right **Rev:** IUCN logo **Edge:** Segmented reeding

Date	Mintage	F	VF	XF	Unc	BU
BE2547 (2004)	Est. 3,000,000	—	—	1.00	1.80	2.50

Y# 414   10 BAHT
8.5000 g., Bi-Metallic Aluminum-Bronze center in Copper-Nickel ring, 26 mm.   **Ruler:** Rama IX **Subject:** Anti Drug Campaign **Obv:** Civilian bust left **Rev:** Tear drop shaped logo **Edge:** Segmented reeding

Date	Mintage	F	VF	XF	Unc	BU
BE2546 (2004)	3,000,000	—	—	—	1.80	2.50

Y# 415 10 BAHT
8.5000 g., Bi-Metallic Aluminum-Bronze center in Copper-Nickel ring, 26 mm. **Ruler:** Rama IX **Subject:** King Rama IV, 200th Anniversary **Obv:** Bust of Rama IV 3/4 right **Rev:** Royal seal **Edge:** Segmented reeding

Date	Mintage	F	VF	XF	Unc	BU
BE2547 (2004)	3,500,000	—	—	1.00	1.80	2.50

Y# 410 10 BAHT
8.5000 g., Bi-Metallic Aluminum-Bronze center in Copper-Nickel ring, 26 mm. **Subject:** Thammasat University, 70th Anniversary **Obv:** Civilian bust 3/4 left **Rev:** Thammasat University seal **Edge:** Segmented reeding

Date	Mintage	F	VF	XF	Unc	BU
BE2547 (2004)	3,000,000	—	—	1.00	1.80	2.50

Y# 416 10 BAHT
8.5000 g., Bi-Metallic Aluminum-Bronze center in Copper-Nickel ring, 26 mm. **Ruler:** Rama IX **Subject:** Army Transportation Corp, 100th Anniversary **Obv:** 2 King's military busts left **Rev:** Steering wheel, badge at center **Edge:** Segmented reeding

Date	Mintage	F	VF	XF	Unc	BU
BE2548 (2005)	3,000,000	—	—	1.00	1.80	2.50

Y# 402 10 BAHT
8.5000 g., Bi-Metallic Aluminum-Bronze center in Copper-Nickel ring, 26 mm. **Ruler:** Rama IX **Subject:** Department of the Treasury, 72nd Anniversary **Obv:** Bust 1/4 left within circle **Rev:** Treasury Department seal within circle **Edge:** Segmented reeding

Date	Mintage	F	VF	XF	Unc	BU
BE2548 (2005)	3,000,000	—	—	1.00	2.50	3.25

Y# 418 10 BAHT
8.5000 g., Bi-Metallic Aluminum-Bronze center in Copper-Nickel ring, 26 mm. **Ruler:** Rama IX **Subject:** 25th Asia-Pacific Scout Jamboree **Obv:** Rama IX in scout uniform 3/4 left **Rev:** Logo **Edge:** Segmented reeding

Date	Mintage	F	VF	XF	Unc	BU
BE2548 (2005)	3,000,000	—	—	1.00	1.80	2.50

Y# 424 10 BAHT
8.5000 g., Bi-Metallic Aluminum-Bronze center in Copper-Nickel ring, 26 mm. **Ruler:** Rama IX **Subject:** Prince Jaturon Ratsamee, 150th Anniversary of Birth **Obv:** Bust of Prince facing 3/4 right **Rev:** Radiant badge **Edge:** Segmented reeding

Date	Mintage	F	VF	XF	Unc	BU
BE2549(2006)	—	—	—	1.00	2.50	3.25

Y# 417 10 BAHT
8.5000 g., Bi-Metallic Aluminum-Bronze center in Copper-Nickel ring, 26 mm. **Ruler:** Rama IX **Subject:** Princess's Royal Cradle Ceremony **Obv:** Princess's baby head 3/4 left **Rev:** 4-line inscription **Edge:** Segmented reeding

Date	Mintage	F	VF	XF	Unc	BU
BE2548 (2006)	3,000,000	—	—	1.00	1.80	2.50

Y# 406 10 BAHT
8.5000 g., Bi-Metallic Aluminum-Bronze center in Copper-Nickel ring, 26 mm. **Ruler:** Rama IX **Subject:** 60th Anniversary of Reign **Obv:** Bust 1/4 left within circle **Rev:** Royal Crown on display **Edge:** Segmented reeding

Date	Mintage	F	VF	XF	Unc	BU
BE2549 (2006)	16,000,000	—	—	1.00	2.50	3.25

Y# 428 10 BAHT
8.5000 g., Bi-Metallic Aluminum-Bronze center in Copper-Nickel ring, 26 mm. **Ruler:** Rama IX **Subject:** Secretariat of the Cabinet, 72nd Anniversary **Obv:** Military bust 3/4 right **Rev:** Royal Cabinet seal **Edge:** Segmented reeding **Note:** Minted in 2005 but released in 2006.

Date	Mintage	F	VF	XF	Unc	BU
BE2547 (2004)	Est. 3,000,000	—	—	1.00	1.80	2.50

Y# 429 10 BAHT
8.5000 g., Bi-Metallic Aluminum-Bronze center in Copper-Nickel ring, 26 mm. **Ruler:** Rama IX **Subject:** Princess Petcharat, 80th Birthday **Obv:** Bust of Princess facing **Rev:** Royal seal of Princess **Edge:** Segmented reeding

Date	Mintage	F	VF	XF	Unc	BU
BE2548 (2006)	1,000,000	—	—	1.25	2.25	2.75

Y# 430 10 BAHT
8.5000 g., Bi-Metallic Aluminum-Bronze center in Copper-Nickel ring, 26 mm. **Ruler:** Rama IX **Subject:** Budget Inspection Department, 130th Anniversary **Obv:** Conjoined kings' busts left **Rev:** Ornate scale **Edge:** Segmented reeding

Date	Mintage	F	VF	XF	Unc	BU
BE2548 (2006)	Est. 3,000,000	—	—	1.00	1.80	2.50

Y# 431 10 BAHT
8.5000 g., Bi-Metallic Aluminum-Bronze center in Copper-Nickel ring, 26 mm. **Ruler:** Rama IX **Subject:** 60th Anniversary of Reign **Obv:** Bust 3/4 right **Rev:** Royal throne **Edge:** Segmented reeding

Date	Mintage	F	VF	XF	Unc	BU
BE2549 (2006)	16,000,000	—	—	1.00	1.80	2.50

Y# 432 10 BAHT
8.5000 g., Bi-Metallic Aluminum-Bronze center in Copper-Nickel ring, 26 mm. **Ruler:** Rama IX **Subject:** Department of Judge Advocate General, 100th Anniversary **Obv:** Conjoined kings' busts left **Rev:** Military emblem with scales of justice in background **Edge:** Segmented reeding

Date	Mintage	F	VF	XF	Unc	BU
BE2549 (2006)	3,000,000	—	—	1.00	1.80	2.50

Y# 425 10 BAHT
8.5000 g., Bi-Metallic Aluminum-Bronze center in Copper-Nickel ring, 26 mm. **Ruler:** Rama IX **Subject:** Royal Calvary Division, 100th Anniversary **Obv:** Conjoined kings' busts left **Rev:** Royal crown above emblem **Edge:** Segmented reeding

Date	Mintage	F	VF	XF	Unc	BU
BE2550 (2007)	3,000,000	—	—	1.00	1.75	2.50

Y# 426 10 BAHT
8.5000 g., Bi-Metallic Aluminum-Bronze center in Copper-Nickel ring, 26 mm. **Ruler:** Rama IX **Subject:** 1st Thai Commercial Bank, 100th Anniversary **Obv:** Conjoined kings' busts left **Rev:** Garuda Bird **Edge:** Segmented reeding

Date	Mintage	F	VF	XF	Unc	BU
BE2550 (2007)	5,000,000	—	—	1.00	1.75	2.50

Y# 433 10 BAHT
8.5000 g., Bi-Metallic Aluminum-Bronze center in Copper-Nickel ring, 26 mm. **Ruler:** Rama IX **Subject:** Queen's WHO Food Safety Award **Obv:** Queen's bust 3/4 right **Rev:** WHO emblem at upper left of inscription in sprays **Edge:** Segmented reeding

Date	Mintage	F	VF	XF	Unc	BU
BE2550 (2007)	5,000,000	—	—	1.00	1.75	2.50

Y# 434   10 BAHT
8.5000 g., Bi-Metallic Aluminum-Bronze center in Copper-Nickel ring, 26 mm.   **Ruler:** Rama IX **Subject:** Medical Technology Department, 50th Anniversary **Obv:** Robed bust 3/4 right **Rev:** Oval medical seal **Edge:** Segmented reeding

Date	Mintage	F	VF	XF	Unc	BU
BE2550 (2007)	3,000,000	—	—	1.00	1.75	2.50

Y# 435   10 BAHT
8.5000 g., Bi-Metallic Aluminum-Bronze center in Copper-Nickel ring, 26 mm.   **Ruler:** Rama IX **Subject:** UNIVERSIADE 2007 - World University Games **Obv:** Civilian bust 3/4 right **Rev:** Games logo **Edge:** Segmented reeding

Date	Mintage	F	VF	XF	Unc	BU
BE2550 (2007)	5,000,000	—	—	1.00	1.75	2.50

Y# 436   10 BAHT
8.5000 g., Bi-Metallic Aluminum-Bronze center in Copper-Nickel ring, 26 mm.   **Ruler:** Rama IX **Subject:** Queen's 75th birthday **Obv:** Bust of Queen wearing tiara 3/4 left **Rev:** Queen's Royal seal **Edge:** Segmented reeding

Date	Mintage	F	VF	XF	Unc	BU
BE2550 (2007)	7,500,000	—	—	1.00	1.75	2.50

Y# 437   10 BAHT
8.5000 g., Bi-Metallic Aluminum-Bronze center in Copper-Nickel ring, 26 mm.   **Ruler:** Rama IX **Subject:** IASAJ Conference - Bangkok **Obv:** Civilian bust 3/4 left **Rev:** Oval seal with scale above conference logo **Edge:** Segmented reeding

Date	Mintage	F	VF	XF	Unc	BU
BE2550 (2007)	3,000,000	—	—	1.00	1.75	2.50

Y# 438   10 BAHT
8.5000 g., Bi-Metallic Aluminum-Bronze center in Copper-Nickel ring, 26 mm.   **Ruler:** Rama IX **Subject:** King's 80th birthday **Obv:** Royal bust 3/4 left **Rev:** Royal seal **Edge:** Segmented reeding

Date	Mintage	F	VF	XF	Unc	BU
BE2550 (2007)	18,000,000	—	—	1.00	1.75	2.50

Y# 439   10 BAHT
8.5000 g., Bi-Metallic Aluminum-Bronze center in Copper-Nickel ring, 26 mm.   **Ruler:** Rama IX **Subject:** 24th SEA Games **Obv:** Civilian bust 3/4 left **Rev:** Games logo above inscription **Edge:** Segmented reeding

Date	Mintage	F	VF	XF	Unc	BU
BE2550 (2007)	3,000,000	—	—	1.00	1.75	2.50

Y# 440   10 BAHT
8.5000 g., Bi-Metallic Aluminum-Bronze center in Copper-Nickel ring, 26 mm.   **Ruler:** Rama IX **Subject:** Siriraj Hospital, 120th Anniversary **Obv:** Conjoined kings' busts right **Rev:** Royal hospital's seal **Edge:** Segmented reeding

Date	Mintage	F	VF	XF	Unc	BU
BE2550 (2007)	—	—	—	1.00	1.75	2.50

Y# 459   10 BAHT
8.5000 g., Bi-Metallic Aluminum-Bronze center in Copper-Nickel ring, 26 mm.   **Ruler:** Rama IX **Obv:** Head left **Rev:** Arun Temple (Temple of the Dawn), Bangkok

Date	Mintage	F	VF	XF	Unc	BU
BE2551 (2008)	18,450,000	—	—	—	2.00	2.75
BE2552 (2009)	59,107,733	—	—	—	2.00	2.75
BE2553 (2010)	1,953,000	—	—	—	2.00	2.75
BE2554 (2011)	—	—	—	—	2.00	2.75
BE2555 (2012)	—	—	—	—	2.00	2.75

Y# 460   10 BAHT
8.5000 g., Bi-Metallic Aluminum-Bronze center in Copper-Nickel ring, 26 mm.   **Ruler:** Rama IX **Subject:** Thai Postal Service, 125th Anniversary **Obv:** Conjoined busts left **Rev:** Scroll with legend **Edge:** Segmented Reeding

Date	Mintage	F	VF	XF	Unc	BU
BE2551 (2008)	3,000,000	—	—	1.00	2.00	2.75

Y# 470   10 BAHT
8.5000 g., Bi-Metallic Aluminum-Bronze center in Copper-Nickel ring, 26 mm.   **Ruler:** Rama IX **Subject:** Siriraj Hospital, 120th Anniversary **Obv:** Conjoined heads right **Edge:** Segmented Reeding

Date	Mintage	F	VF	XF	Unc	BU
BE2551 (2008)	3,000,000	—	—	1.00	2.00	2.75

Y# 461   10 BAHT
8.5000 g., Bi-Metallic Aluminum-Bronze center in Copper-Nickel ring, 26 mm.   **Ruler:** Rama IX **Subject:** National Research Council, 50th Anniversary **Obv:** Bust left **Rev:** Nucleus surrounded by electrons **Edge:** Segmented Reeding

Date	Mintage	F	VF	XF	Unc	BU
BE2552 (2009)	3,000,000	—	—	—	2.00	2.75

Y# 497   10 BAHT
Bi-Metallic Aluminum-bronze center in Copper-nickel ring, 26 mm.   **Ruler:** Rama IX **Subject:** 120th Anniversary of the Department of Finance **Obv:** Conjoined heads facing left **Rev:** Seal of the Department of Finance (bird), inscription, value and date **Edge:** Segmented reeding

Date	Mintage	F	VF	XF	Unc	BU
BE2553 (2010)	1,000,000	—	—	—	2.00	2.50

Y# 498   10 BAHT
Bi-Metallic Aluminum bronze center in copper-nickel ring, 26 mm.   **Ruler:** Rama IX **Subject:** 60th Anniversary of the Office of National Economic and Social Development **Obv:** Head of King Rama IX facing 1/4 right and inscriptions **Rev:** Seal of the Office of National Economic and Social Development (statue of three people), inscription, value and date

Date	Mintage	F	VF	XF	Unc	BU
BE2553 (2010)	—	—	—	—	2.00	2.50

Y# 504   10 BAHT
8.5000 g., Bi-Metallic Aluminum-Bronze center in Copper-Nickel ring, 26 mm.   **Ruler:** Rama IX **Subject:** Princess Bejaratana, 84th Birthday **Rev:** Emblem

Date	Mintage	F	VF	XF	Unc	BU
BE2553 (2010)	—	—	—	—	2.00	2.75

KM# 505   10 BAHT
8.5000 g., Bi-Metallic Aluminum-Bronze center in Copper-Nickel ring, 26 mm.   **Ruler:** Rama IX **Subject:** Comptroller General Bureau, 120th Anniversary **Rev:** Bird in flight upward

Date	Mintage	F	VF	XF	Unc	BU
BE2554 (2011)	—	—	—	—	2.00	2.75

Y# 374   20 BAHT
15.0000 g., Copper-Nickel, 32 mm.   **Ruler:** Rama IX **Subject:** Chulalongkorn University 84th Anniversary March 26 **Obv:** Three conjoined busts right **Rev:** University emblem divides value **Edge:** Reeded

Date	Mintage	F	VF	XF	Unc	BU
BE2544 (2001)	800,040	—	—	2.00	3.50	5.00
BE2544 (2001) Proof	5,340	Value: 22.00				

Y# 375   20 BAHT
15.0000 g., Copper-Nickel, 32 mm.   **Ruler:** Rama IX **Subject:** Civil Service Comission 72nd Anniversary April 1 **Obv:** Conjoined busts left **Rev:** Civil service emblem divides value **Edge:** Reeded

Date	Mintage	F	VF	XF	Unc	BU
BE2544 (2001)	500,000	—	—	2.00	3.50	5.00
BE2544 (2001) Proof	3,340	Value: 25.00				

Y# 393   20 BAHT
15.0000 g., Copper-Nickel, 32 mm.   **Ruler:** Rama IX **Subject:** 80th Birthday of Princess Calyani Vadhani **Obv:** Bust 1/4 right **Rev:** Crowned emblem and value **Edge:** Reeded

Date	Mintage	F	VF	XF	Unc	BU
BE2546 (2003)	350,000	—	—	2.00	3.50	5.00
BE2546 (2003) Proof	3,200	Value: 17.50				

Y# 419   20 BAHT
15.0000 g., Copper-Nickel, 32 mm.   **Ruler:** Rama IX **Subject:** 50th Anniversary of Audit Department of Cooperatives **Edge:** Reeded

Date	Mintage	F	VF	XF	Unc	BU
BE2545 (2002)	300,000	—	—	2.00	3.50	5.00
BE2545 (2002) Proof	3,000	Value: 17.50				

Y# 386   20 BAHT
15.0000 g., Copper-Nickel, 32 mm.   **Ruler:** Rama IX **Subject:** Centennial of Thai Banknotes 2445-2545 **Obv:** Conjoined busts left **Rev:** Coat of arms in center of seal **Edge:** Reeded

Date	Mintage	F	VF	XF	Unc	BU
BE2545 (2002)	1,000,000	—	—	2.00	3.50	5.00
BE2545 (2002) Proof	40,000	Value: 17.50				

Y# 397   20 BAHT
15.0000 g., Copper-Nickel, 32 mm.   **Ruler:** Rama IX **Subject:** Centennial of the National Police April 19 **Obv:** Conjoined busts left **Rev:** National Police emblem above banner **Edge:** Reeded

Date	Mintage	F	VF	XF	Unc	BU
BE2545 (2002)	600,000	—	—	2.00	3.50	5.00
BE2545 (2002) Proof	5,000	Value: 17.50				

Y# 398   20 BAHT
15.0000 g., Copper-Nickel, 32 mm.   **Ruler:** Rama IX **Subject:**

50th Birthday of the Crown Prince July 28 **Obv:** Bust facing **Rev:** Crowned monogram **Edge:** Reeded

Date	Mintage	F	VF	XF	Unc	BU
BE2545 (2002)	300,000	—	—	2.00	3.50	5.00
BE2545 (2002) Proof	5,000	Value: 40.00				

Y# 388 20 BAHT
15.0000 g., Copper-Nickel, 32 mm. **Ruler:** Rama IX **Subject:** King's 75th Birthday December 5 **Obv:** Head left **Rev:** Royal crown in radiant oval **Edge:** Reeded **Note:** Minted and released in 2003.

Date	Mintage	F	VF	XF	Unc	BU
BE2545(2002)	1,200,000	—	—	2.00	3.50	5.00
BE2545(2002) Proof	16,000	Value: 17.50				

Y# 420 20 BAHT
15.0000 g., Copper-Nickel, 32 mm. **Ruler:** Rama IX **Subject:** 150th Anniversary, Birth of Rama V **Edge:** Reeded

Date	Mintage	F	VF	XF	Unc	BU
BE2546 (2003)	1,000,000	—	—	2.00	3.50	5.00
BE2546 (2003) Proof	26,000	Value: 18.00				

Y# 421 20 BAHT
15.0000 g., Copper-Nickel, 32 mm. **Ruler:** Rama IX **Subject:** Rama IV, 200th Anniversary of Birth **Obv:** King Rama IV **Edge:** Reeded

Date	Mintage	F	VF	XF	Unc	BU
BE2547 (2004)	500,000	—	—	2.00	3.50	5.00
BE2547 (2004) Proof	10,500	Value: 20.00				

Y# 422 20 BAHT
15.0000 g., Copper-Nickel, 32 mm. **Ruler:** Rama IX **Subject:** 72nd Anniversary of Queen's Birthday **Obv:** Head of Queen facing left **Edge:** Reeded

Date	Mintage	F	VF	XF	Unc	BU
BE2547 (2004)	600,000	—	—	2.00	3.50	5.00
BE2547 (2004) Proof	10,000	Value: 20.00				

Y# 462 20 BAHT
15.0000 g., Copper-Nickel, 32 mm. **Ruler:** Rama IX **Subject:** Rama IV, 200th Anniversary of Birth **Obv:** Bust 3/4 right **Rev:** Horizontal oval Royal seal **Edge:** Reeded

Date	Mintage	F	VF	XF	Unc	BU
BE2547 (2004)	500,000	—	—	2.00	4.00	6.00
BE2547 (2004) Proof	10,500	Value: 15.00				

Y# 423 20 BAHT
15.0000 g., Copper-Nickel, 32 mm. **Ruler:** Rama IX **Subject:** 50th Birthday of Princess Sirinhorn **Obv:** Head of Princess facing right **Edge:** Reeded

Date	Mintage	F	VF	XF	Unc	BU
BE2548 (2005)	650,000	—	—	2.00	4.00	6.00
BE2548 (2005) Proof	12,000	Value: 20.00				

Y# 403 20 BAHT
15.0000 g., Copper-Nickel, 32 mm. **Ruler:** Rama IX **Subject:** Department of the Treasury, 72nd Anniversary **Obv:** Bust 1/4 left **Rev:** Treasury Department seal **Edge:** Reeded

Date	Mintage	F	VF	XF	Unc	BU
BE2548 (2005)	300,000	—	—	2.00	4.00	6.00
BE2548 (2005) Proof	3,000	Value: 25.00				

Y# 471 20 BAHT
15.0000 g., Copper-Nickel, 32 mm. **Ruler:** Rama IX **Subject:** Centennial of the National Library **Obv:** Two busts, one facing left, one right **Rev:** Circle with inscription **Edge:** Reeded

Date	Mintage	F	VF	XF	Unc	BU
BE2548 (2005)	Est. 200,000	—	—	2.00	3.50	5.00

Y# 472 20 BAHT
15.0000 g., Copper-Nickel, 32 mm. **Ruler:** Rama IX **Subject:** Princess Rattana, 80th birthday **Obv:** Front facing portrait **Edge:** Reeded **Note:** Minted and released in 2006.

Date	Mintage	F	VF	XF	Unc	BU
BE2548 (2005)	200,000	—	—	2.00	3.50	5.00

Y# 474 20 BAHT
15.0000 g., Copper-Nickel, 32 mm. **Ruler:** Rama IX **Subject:** UN Development Program Award **Obv:** Head right **Rev:** Chalice on stand with legends **Edge:** Reeded

Date	Mintage	F	VF	XF	Unc	BU
BE2549 (2006)	2,200,000	—	—	2.00	3.50	5.00

Y# 407 20 BAHT
15.0000 g., Copper-Nickel, 32 mm. **Ruler:** Rama IX **Subject:** 60th Anniversary of Reign **Obv:** Head left **Rev:** Royal Crown on display **Edge:** Reeded

Date	Mintage	F	VF	XF	Unc	BU
BE2549 (2006)	5,600,000	—	—	2.00	4.00	6.00
BE2549 (2006) Proof	96,000	Value: 18.50				

Y# 473 20 BAHT
15.0000 g., Copper-Nickel, 32 mm. **Ruler:** Rama IX **Subject:** Royal Artificial Rain, 50th Anniversary **Obv:** Statue of King holding book and pencil **Rev:** Artificial rain wing symbol surrounded by rays and legend **Edge:** Reeded

Date	Mintage	F	VF	XF	Unc	BU
BE2549 (2006)	3,000,000	—	—	2.00	3.50	5.00

Y# 450 20 BAHT
15.0000 g., Copper-Nickel, 32 mm. **Ruler:** Rama IX **Subject:** King's 80th Birthday **Obv:** Bust left **Edge:** Reeded

Date	Mintage	F	VF	XF	Unc	BU
BE 2550 (2007)	5,800,000	—	—	2.00	3.50	5.00
BE 2550 (2007) Proof	95,000	Value: 15.00				

Y# 453 20 BAHT
15.0000 g., Copper-Nickel **Ruler:** Rama IX **Subject:** Queen's 75th Birthday **Obv:** Bust left **Edge:** Reeded **Shape:** 32

Date	Mintage	F	VF	XF	Unc	BU
BE 2550 (2007)	600,000	—	—	2.00	3.50	5.00
BE 2550 (2007) Proof	12,000	Value: 18.00				

Y# 475 20 BAHT
15.0000 g., Copper-Nickel, 32 mm. **Ruler:** Rama IX **Subject:** Princess Galyana Vadhana, 84th birthday **Obv:** Head left **Edge:** Reeded

Date	Mintage	F	VF	XF	Unc	BU
BE2550 (2007)	700,000	—	—	2.00	3.50	5.00
BE2550 (2007) Proof	8,400	Value: 18.00				

Y# 476 20 BAHT
15.0000 g., Copper-Nickel, 32 mm. **Ruler:** Rama IX **Subject:** Father of Thai heritage conservation **Obv:** Head left **Edge:** Reeded **Note:** Minted and released in 2008.

Date	Mintage	F	VF	XF	Unc	BU
BE2550 (2007)	500,000	—	—	2.00	3.50	5.00

Y# 495 20 BAHT
15.0000 g., Copper-Nickel, 32 mm. **Ruler:** Rama IX **Subject:** King Rama I, Father of Thai Trade **Obv:** Bust facing front and inscription **Rev:** Symbol, inscription, value and date **Edge:** Reeded **Note:** Minted and issued in BE2553

Date	Mintage	F	VF	XF	Unc	BU
BE2553 (2008)	500,000	—	—	—	3.50	4.00

Y# 464 20 BAHT
15.0000 g., Copper-Nickel, 32 mm. **Ruler:** Rama IX **Subject:** Princess Mother, 9th Cycle (108th Anniversary of Birth) **Obv:** Portrait facing left **Rev:** Emblem of Princess Mother Srinakarindra

Date	Mintage	F	VF	XF	Unc	BU
BE2551 (2008)	450,000	—	—	2.00	3.50	5.00
BE2551 (2008) Proof	5,500	Value: 20.00				

Y# 477 20 BAHT
15.0000 g., Copper-Nickel, 32 mm. **Ruler:** Rama IX **Subject:** WIPO Award **Obv:** Head left **Rev:** Award medal and legend **Edge:** Reeded **Note:** Minted and released in 2010

Date	Mintage	F	VF	XF	Unc	BU
BE2551 (2008)	500,000	—	—	2.00	3.50	5.00

Y# 499 20 BAHT
15.0000 g., Copper-Nickel, 32 mm. **Ruler:** Rama IX **Subject:** 100th Anniversary of Indra College **Obv:** Conjoined busts facing left **Rev:** Symbol, inscription, value and date **Edge:** Reeded **Note:** Minted and issued in BE2553

Date	Mintage	F	VF	XF	Unc	BU
BE2553 (2010)	500,000	—	—	—	3.50	4.00

Y# 404 50 BAHT
21.0000 g., Copper-Nickel, 36 mm. **Ruler:** Rama IX **Subject:** Air Force 50th Anniversary May 7 **Obv:** Uniformed bust facing **Rev:** Crowned wings within 3/4 wreath **Edge:** Reeded

Date	Mintage	F	VF	XF	Unc	BU
BE2546 (2003)	250,000	—	—	4.00	12.50	15.00

Y# 478 50 BAHT
21.0000 g., Copper-Nickel, 36 mm. **Ruler:** Rama IX **Subject:** National Intelligence Agency, 50th Anniversary **Obv:** Head right **Rev:** Emblem of the National Intelligence Agency **Edge:** Reeded **Note:** Minted and released in 2003.

Date	Mintage	F	VF	XF	Unc	BU
BE2547 (2004)	200,000	—	—	3.50	4.50	6.00

Y# 493 50 BAHT
Copper-Nickel, 36 mm. **Ruler:** Rama IX **Obv:** Head of infant facing right **Rev:** Design including chick, inscription, value and date **Edge:** Reeded

Date	Mintage	F	VF	XF	Unc	BU
BE2549 (2006)	450,000	—	—	—	4.50	6.00

Y# 479 50 BAHT
21.0000 g., Copper-Nickel, 36 mm. **Ruler:** Rama IX **Subject:** Technological Research **Obv:** Child's head right **Rev:** Small chicken at left, legends **Edge:** Reeded

Date	Mintage	F	VF	XF	Unc	BU
BE2549 (2006)	450,000	—	—	3.50	4.50	6.00

Y# 480 50 BAHT
21.0000 g., Copper-Nickel, 36 mm. **Ruler:** Rama IX **Subject:** Naval Academy, 100th Anniversary **Obv:** Conjoined heads left **Rev:** Symbol, inscriptions, value and date **Edge:** Reeded

Date	Mintage	F	VF	XF	Unc	BU
BE2549 (2006)	200,000	—	—	3.50	4.50	6.00

Y# 500 50 BAHT
21.0000 g., Copper-Nickel, 36 mm. **Ruler:** Rama IX **Subject:** 150th Anniversary of Thai Mint **Obv:** Conjoined busts facing 1/2 right and inscription **Rev:** Complex design, inscription, value and date **Edge:** Reeded

Date	Mintage	F	VF	XF	Unc	BU
BE2553 (2010)	150,000	—	—	—	4.50	6.00

Y# 501 50 BAHT
21.0000 g., Copper-Nickel, 36 mm. **Ruler:** Rama IX **Subject:** King's Seventh Cycle Ceremony **Obv:** Head of King facing 1/2 left **Rev:** Symbol, inscription, value and date **Edge:** Reeded

Date	Mintage	F	VF	XF	Unc	BU
BE2554 (2011)	Est. 3,000,000	—	—	—	4.50	6.00

Y# 389 600 BAHT
22.0000 g., 0.9250 Silver 0.6542 oz. ASW, 35 mm. **Ruler:** Rama IX **Subject:** King's 75th Birthday **Obv:** King's portrait **Rev:** Royal crown in radiant oval **Edge:** Reeded

Date	Mintage	F	VF	XF	Unc	BU
BE2545 (2002)	14,000	—	—	25.00	30.00	35.00
BE2545 (2002) Proof	3,000	Value: 70.00				

Y# 481 600 BAHT
22.0000 g., 0.9250 Silver 0.6542 oz. ASW, 35 mm. **Ruler:** Rama IX **Subject:** Crown Prince, 50th Birthday **Obv:** Crown Prince bust 1/4 facing left **Rev:** Crowned monogram **Edge:** Reeded

Date	Mintage	F	VF	XF	Unc	BU
BE2545 (2002)	5,000	—	—	40.00	50.00	55.00
BE2545 (2002) Proof	1,000	Value: 95.00				

Y# 394 600 BAHT
22.0000 g., 0.9250 Silver 0.6542 oz. ASW, 35 mm. **Ruler:** Rama IX **Subject:** 80th Birthday of Princess Calgani Vedhana **Obv:** Bust half right **Rev:** Crowned emblem and value **Edge:** Reeded

Date	Mintage	F	VF	XF	Unc	BU
BE2546 (2003)	4,500	—	—	35.00	45.00	50.00
BE2546 (2003) Proof	1,000	Value: 95.00				

Y# 482 600 BAHT
22.0000 g., 0.9250 Silver 0.6542 oz. ASW, 35 mm. **Ruler:** Rama V **Subject:** Rama V. 150th Anniversary of Birth **Obv:** Rama V bust left **Rev:** Royal Crown **Edge:** Reeded

Date	Mintage	F	VF	XF	Unc	BU
BE2546 (2003)	15,000	—	—	30.00	35.00	40.00
BE2546 (2003) Proof	4,600	Value: 85.00				

Y# 401 600 BAHT
22.1500 g., 0.9250 Silver 0.6587 oz. ASW, 35 mm. **Ruler:** Rama IX **Subject:** Queen's 72nd Birthday **Obv:** Crowned monogram **Rev:** Crowned bust of Queen 3/4 right **Edge:** Reeded

Date	Mintage	F	VF	XF	Unc	BU
BE2547 (2004)	12,000	—	—	30.00	35.00	40.00
BE2547(2004) Proof	3,700	Value: 85.00				

Y# 463 600 BAHT
22.0000 g., 0.9250 Silver 0.6542 oz. ASW, 35 mm. **Ruler:** Rama IX **Subject:** King Rama IV, 200th Anniversary of Birth **Obv:** Bust right **Rev:** Horizontal oval seal **Edge:** Reeded

Date	Mintage	F	VF	XF	Unc	BU
BE2547 (2004)	12,000	—	—	40.00	45.00	60.00
BE2547 (2004) Proof	3,000	Value: 95.00				

Y# 467 600 BAHT
22.1500 g., 0.9250 Silver 0.6587 oz. ASW, 35 mm. **Ruler:** Rama IX **Subject:** Princess Petcharat, 80th Birthday **Obv:** Bust facing **Rev:** Princess' emblem

Date	Mintage	F	VF	XF	Unc	BU
BE2548 (2005)	—	—	—	40.00	55.00	60.00
BE2548 (2005) Proof	—	Value: 120				

Y# 427 600 BAHT
22.1500 g., 0.9250 Silver 0.6587 oz. ASW, 35 mm. **Ruler:** Rama IX **Subject:** Princess Maha Chakri Sirindhorn's 50th Birthday **Obv:** Bust right **Rev:** Oval **Edge:** Reeded

Date	Mintage	F	VF	XF	Unc	BU
BE2548 (2005)	15,000	—	—	40.00	45.00	35.00
BE2548 (2005) Proof	4,000	Value: 85.00				

Y# 484 600 BAHT
22.0000 g., 0.9250 Silver 0.6542 oz. ASW, 35 mm. **Ruler:** Rama IX **Subject:** Princess Rattana, 80th birthday **Obv:** Bust facing of Princess **Note:** Minted and released in 2006.

Date	Mintage	F	VF	XF	Unc	BU
BE2548 (2005)	3,500	—	—	40.00	55.00	60.00

Y# 408 600 BAHT
22.1500 g., 0.9250 Silver 0.6587 oz. ASW, 35 mm. **Ruler:** Rama IX **Subject:** 60th Anniversary of Reign **Obv:** Rama IX **Rev:** Royal cypher **Edge:** Reeded

Date	Mintage	F	VF	XF	Unc	BU
BE2549 (2006)	66,000	—	—	30.00	35.00	40.00
BE2549 (2006) Proof with colored hologram	16,000	Value: 90.00				

Y# 485   600 BAHT
22.0000 g., 0.9250 Silver 0.6542 oz. ASW. **Ruler:** Rama IX **Subject:** Prince Royal Cradle Ceremony **Obv:** Prince's baby head left **Rev:** Four line legend **Edge:** Reeded

Date	Mintage	F	VF	XF	Unc	BU
BE2549 (2006)	10,000	—	—	40.00	45.00	50.00
BE2549 (2006) Proof	3,700	Value: 85.00				

Y# 502   800 BAHT
22.0000 g., 0.9250 Silver 0.6542 oz. ASW, 35 mm. **Ruler:** Rama IX **Subject:** King's 84th Birthday **Obv:** Head facing 1/4 left and inscription **Rev:** Symbol, value, date and inscription **Edge:** Reeded

Date	Mintage	F	VF	XF	Unc	BU
BE2554 (2003) Proof	100,000	Value: 55.00				

Y# 447   800 BAHT
22.0000 g., 0.9900 Silver 0.7002 oz. ASW, 35 mm. **Ruler:** Rama IX **Obv:** Bust left **Rev:** WHO logo and legend

Date	Mintage	F	VF	XF	Unc	BU
2005	Est. 6,500	—	—	—	40.00	45.00
2005 Proof	Inc. above	Value: 100				

Y# 486   800 BAHT
33.0000 g., 0.9250 Silver 0.9814 oz. ASW, 35 mm. **Ruler:** Rama IX **Subject:** King's 84th Birthday **Obv:** Head of Queen Sirikit facing right **Rev:** WHO emblem and four line English inscription **Edge:** Reeded

Date	Mintage	F	VF	XF	Unc	BU
BE2550 (2007)	6,500	—	—	—	35.00	40.00

Y# 451   800 BAHT
22.0000 g., 0.9900 Silver 0.7002 oz. ASW, 35 mm. **Ruler:** Rama IX **Subject:** King's 80th Birthday **Obv:** Bust left **Edge:** Reeded

Date	Mintage	F	VF	XF	Unc	BU
BE 2550 (2007)	80,000	—	—	—	35.00	40.00
BE 2550 (2007) Proof	28,000	Value: 75.00				

Y# 454   800 BAHT
22.0000 g., 0.9250 Silver 0.6542 oz. ASW, 35 mm. **Ruler:** Rama IX **Subject:** Queen's 75th Birthday **Obv:** Queen's bust left **Rev:** Queen's Royal Seal **Edge:** Reeded

Date	Mintage	F	VF	XF	Unc	BU
BE 2550 (2007)	12,000	—	—	—	35.00	40.00
BE 2550 (2007) Proof	4,000	Value: 75.00				

Y# 466   800 BAHT
22.0000 g., 0.9250 Silver 0.6542 oz. ASW, 35 mm. **Ruler:** Rama IX **Subject:** Princess Galyani Vadhana, 84th Birthday **Obv:** Bust facing right **Rev:** Princess' emblem

Date	Mintage	F	VF	XF	Unc	BU
BE2550 (2007)	11,500	—	—	—	35.00	40.00
BE2550 (2007) Proof	1,500	Value: 95.00				

Y# 465   800 BAHT
22.0000 g., 0.9250 Silver 0.6542 oz. ASW, 35 mm. **Ruler:** Rama IX **Subject:** Princess Mother, 9th Cycle (108th Birthday) **Obv:** Bust facing **Rev:** Princess Mother's emblem **Edge:** Reeded

Date	Mintage	F	VF	XF	Unc	BU
BE2551 (2008)	11,200	—	—	—	35.00	40.00
BE2551 (2008) Proof	1,500	Value: 95.00				

Y# 468   800 BAHT
22.0000 g., 0.9900 Silver 0.7002 oz. ASW, 35 mm. **Ruler:** Rama IX **Subject:** King's WIPO leader award **Obv:** Bust left **Rev:** Award medal and legned **Note:** Minted and released in 2010.

Date	Mintage	F	VF	XF	Unc	BU
BE2551 (2008) Proof	15,000	Value: 75.00				

Y# 469   900 BAHT
31.1050 g., 0.9990 Silver 0.9990 oz. ASW, 40.6 mm. **Ruler:** Rama IX **Subject:** UNDP Human Development Lifetime Achievement Award **Obv:** King facing in multicolor applique **Rev:** Award bowl **Edge:** Reeded

Date	Mintage	F	VF	XF	Unc	BU
BE2549 (2006) Proof	200,000	Value: 75.00				

Y# 390   7500 BAHT
15.0000 g., 0.9000 Gold 0.4340 oz. AGW, 26 mm. **Ruler:** Rama IX **Subject:** King's 75th Birthday **Obv:** King's portrait **Rev:** Royal crown in radiant oval **Edge:** Reeded

Date	Mintage	F	VF	XF	Unc	BU
BE2545(2002)	6,000	—	—	—	800	825
BE2545(2002) Proof	1,200	Value: 850				

Y# 395   9000 BAHT
15.0000 g., 0.9000 Gold 0.4340 oz. AGW, 26 mm. **Ruler:** Rama IX **Subject:** 72nd Birthday of Queen **Obv:** Bust half right **Rev:** Crowned emblem and value **Edge:** Reeded

Date	Mintage	F	VF	XF	Unc	BU
BE2546 (2004)	6,000	—	—	—	800	825
BE2546 (2004) Proof	1,600	Value: 850				

Y# 490   9000 BAHT
15.0000 g., 0.4340 Gold 0.2093 oz. AGW, 26 mm. **Ruler:** Rama IX **Subject:** 150th Aniversary of the Birth of Rama V **Obv:** Bust of Rama V facing left and inscription **Rev:** Three symbols, inscription, value and date **Edge:** Reeded

Date	Mintage	F	VF	XF	Unc	BU
BE2546 (2003)	5,000	—	—	—	800	825
BE2546 (2003) Proof	1,500	Value: 900				

Y# 491   9000 BAHT
15.0000 g., 0.9000 Gold 0.4340 oz. AGW, 26 mm. **Ruler:** Rama IX **Subject:** Queen Sirikit's 72nd Birthday **Obv:** Bust of Queen facing 1/4 left and inscription **Rev:** Symbol honoring Queen Sirikit, inscription, value and date **Edge:** Reeded

Date	Mintage	F	VF	XF	Unc	BU
BE2547 (2004)	6,000	—	—	—	800	825
BE2547 (2004) Proof	1,600	Value: 900				

Y# 492   9000 BAHT
15.0000 g., 0.9000 Gold 0.4340 oz. AGW, 26 mm. **Ruler:** Rama IX **Subject:** 200th Anniversary of the Birth of King Rama IV **Obv:** Bust of King Rama IV facing 3/4 right and inscription **Rev:** Horizontal oval royal seal, inscription, value and date **Edge:** Reeded

Date	Mintage	F	VF	XF	Unc	BU
BE2547 (2004)	3,000	—	—	—	800	825
BE2547 (2004)	1,000	Value: 900				

Y# 488   9000 BAHT
15.0000 g., 0.9000 Gold 0.4340 oz. AGW, 26 mm. **Ruler:** Rama IX **Subject:** WHO Food Safety Award to Queen Sirikit **Obv:** Bust of Queen Sirikit right **Rev:** WHO emblem and legend **Edge:** Reeded

Date	Mintage	F	VF	XF	Unc	BU
BE2550 (2007) Proof	2,800	Value: 850				

Y# 494   12,000 BAHT
15.0000 g., 0.9000 Gold 0.4340 oz. AGW, 26 mm. **Ruler:** Rama IX **Subject:** 60th Anniversary of Reign **Obv:** Framed head facing 1/4 right **Rev:** Symbol of 60th Anniversary of Reign, value and date **Edge:** Reeded

Date	Mintage	F	VF	XF	Unc	BU
BE2551 (2008)	16,000	—	—	—	800	825
BE2551 (2008) Proof	9,600	Value: 900				

Y# 448   16,000 BAHT
15.0000 g., 0.9000 Gold 0.4340 oz. AGW, 26 mm. **Ruler:** Rama IX **Obv:** Bust of Queen Sirikit, right **Rev:** WHO logo and legend **Note:** Minted and issued in BE2550

Date	Mintage	F	VF	XF	Unc	BU
BE2585 (2005)	Est. 3,000	—	—	—	800	825
BE2548 (2005) Proof	Inc. above	Value: 850				

Y# 452   16,000 BAHT
15.0000 g., 0.9900 Gold 0.4774 oz. AGW, 26 mm. **Ruler:** Rama IX **Subject:** King's 80th Birthday **Obv:** Bust left **Rev:** Symbols, inscription, value and date **Edge:** Reeded

Date	Mintage	F	VF	XF	Unc	BU
BE2550 (2007)	16,800	—	—	—	870	900
BE2550 (2007) Proof	12,800	Value: 925				

Y# 455   16,000 BAHT
15.0000 g., 0.9000 Gold 0.4340 oz. AGW, 26 mm. **Ruler:** Rama IX **Subject:** Queen's 75th Birthday **Obv:** Bust left and inscription **Rev:** Symbol, inscription, value and date **Edge:** Reeded

Date	Mintage	F	VF	XF	Unc	BU
BE2550 (2007)	5,000	—	—	—	800	825
2550 (2007) Proof	2,000	Value: 850				

Y# 496   16,000 BAHT
15.0000 g., 0.9000 Gold 0.4340 oz. AGW, 26 mm. **Ruler:** Rama IX **Subject:** 108th Aniversary of the Birth of the Princess Mother **Obv:** Head of Princess Mother facing 1/4 left **Rev:** Symbol, inscription, value and date **Edge:** Reeded

Date	Mintage	F	VF	XF	Unc	BU
BE2551 (2008)	1,200	—	—	—	800	825
BE2551 (2008) Proof	400	Value: 1,000				

Y# 489   16,000 BAHT
15.0000 g., 0.9900 Gold 0.4774 oz. AGW, 26 mm. **Ruler:** Rama IX **Subject:** World Interlectural Propery Organization Award **Obv:** Head left **Rev:** Award Medal and legend **Edge:** Reeded **Note:** Minted and released in 2010.

Date	Mintage	F	VF	XF	Unc	BU
BE2551 (2008) Proof	2,000	Value: 850				

Y# 503   16,000 BAHT
15.0000 g., 0.9650 Gold 0.4654 oz. AGW, 26 mm. **Ruler:** Rama IX **Subject:** King's Seventh Cycle Ceremony **Obv:** Head of King facing 1/2 left **Rev:** Synmbol, inscription, value and date **Edge:** Reeded

Date	Mintage	F	VF	XF	Unc	BU
BE2554 (2011) Proof	Est. 25,000	Value: 1,000				

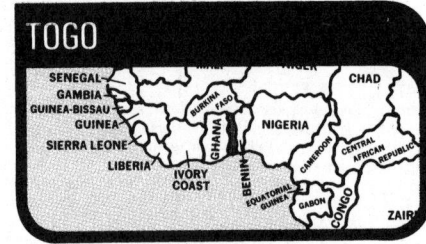

The Togolese Republic (formerly part of German Togoland), situated on the Gulf of Guinea in West Africa between Ghana and Benin, has an area of 21,622 sq. mi. (56,790 sq. km.) and a population of *3.4 million. Capital: Lome. Agriculture and herding, the production of dyewoods, and the mining of phosphates and iron ore are the chief industries. Copra, phosphates and coffee are exported.

MINT MARK
(a) - Paris, privy marks only

MONETARY SYSTEM
100 Centimes = 1 Franc

REPUBLIC
STANDARD COINAGE

100 Centimes = 1 Franc

KM# 51   100 FRANCS
26.0000 g., Copper-Nickel, 38.6 mm. **Rev:** Blue sunbird, prism technology

Date	Mintage	F	VF	XF	Unc	BU
2010 Prooflike	2,500	—	—	—	—	25.00

KM# 52   100 FRANCS
26.0000 g., Copper-Nickel, 38.6 mm. **Rev:** Green bird, prism technology

Date	Mintage	F	VF	XF	Unc	BU
2010 Prooflike	2,500	—	—	—	—	25.00

KM# 53   100 FRANCS
26.0000 g., Copper-Nickel, 38.6 mm. **Rev:** Yellow bird, prism technology

Date	Mintage	F	VF	XF	Unc	BU
2010 Prooflike	2,500	—	—	—	—	25.00

KM# 43   250 FRANCS
5.0000 g., 0.9990 Silver 0.1606 oz. ASW **Subject:** German President Horst Kohler **Obv:** National arms **Obv. Legend:** REPUBLIQUE TOGOLAISE **Rev:** Gilt figure

Date	Mintage	F	VF	XF	Unc	BU
2004 Proof	—	Value: 15.00				

KM# 29   500 FRANCS
7.0500 g., 0.9990 Silver 0.2264 oz. ASW, 30 mm. **Obv:** National arms above value **Rev:** Multicolor big cat **Edge:** Plain

Date	Mintage	F	VF	XF	Unc	BU
2001 Proof	—	Value: 35.00				

KM# 41   500 FRANCS
10.0000 g., 0.9990 Silver 0.3212 oz. ASW **Subject:** XVIII World Football Championship - Germany 2006 **Obv:** National arms **Obv. Legend:** REPUBLIQUE TOGOLAISE **Rev:** Two players, map of Germany in background

Date	Mintage	F	VF	XF	Unc	BU
2001 Proof	—	Value: 22.50				

KM# 60   500 FRANCS
15.0000 g., 0.9250 Silver 0.4461 oz. ASW, 30 mm.   **Obv:**
National arms **Rev:** Albrecht Durer portrait

Date	Mintage	F	VF	XF	Unc	BU
2003 Proof	—	Value: 25.00				

KM# 47   500 FRANCS
14.9700 g., 0.9250 Silver 0.4452 oz. ASW, 30 mm.   **Obv:** Arms
with supporters **Rev:** Full figures of Johann Wolfgang von Goethe
and Friedrich von Schiller on pedestal facing

Date	Mintage	F	VF	XF	Unc	BU
2004 Proof	—	Value: 22.50				

KM# 44   500 FRANCS
7.0000 g., 0.9990 Silver 0.2248 oz. ASW   **Subject:** German
Chancellor Helmut Schmidt **Obv:** National arms **Obv. Legend:**
REPUBLIQUE TOGOLAISE **Rev:** Gilt figue

Date	Mintage	F	VF	XF	Unc	BU
ND(2004) Proof	—	Value: 22.50				

KM# 17   1000 FRANCS
14.9500 g., 0.9990 Silver 0.4802 oz. ASW, 35 mm.   **Obv:**
National arms **Obv. Legend:** REPUBLIQUE TOGOLAISE **Rev:**
German sailing ship **Rev. Legend:** Adler von Lübeck **Edge:** Plain

Date	Mintage	F	VF	XF	Unc	BU
2001 Proof	—	Value: 50.00				

KM# 35   1000 FRANCS
14.7000 g., 0.9990 Silver 0.4721 oz. ASW, 36 mm.   **Subject:**
World Cup Soccer - Bern 1954 **Obv:** National arms **Rev:** Bust
facing and tower **Edge:** Plain

Date	Mintage	F	VF	XF	Unc	BU
2001 Proof	—	Value: 40.00				

KM# 36   1000 FRANCS
19.9100 g., 0.9990 Silver 0.6395 oz. ASW, 38.1 mm.   **Subject:**
World Cup Soccer - France 1938 **Obv:** National arms **Rev:** Eiffel
Tower behind soccer player kicking ball **Edge:** Reeded

Date	Mintage	F	VF	XF	Unc	BU
2001 Proof	—	Value: 40.00				

KM# 40   1000 FRANCS
14.9700 g., Silver, 35 mm.   **Obv:** National arms **Obv. Legend:**
REPUBLIQUE TOGOLAISE **Rev:** Imperial German sailing ship
Rev. Legend: "PREUSSEN" **Edge:** Plain

Date	Mintage	F	VF	XF	Unc	BU
2001 Proof	—	Value: 40.00				

KM# 54   1000 FRANCS
15.0000 g., 0.9990 Silver 0.4818 oz. ASW, 36 mm.   **Rev:**
Multicolor Airbus 319 right

Date	Mintage	F	VF	XF	Unc	BU
2001 Proof	—	Value: 35.00				

KM# 37   1000 FRANCS
19.9700 g., 0.9990 Silver 0.6414 oz. ASW, 40 mm.   **Subject:**
World Cup Soccer - USA 1994 **Obv:** National arms **Obv. Legend:**
REPUBLIQUE TOGOLAISE **Rev:** Soccer player kicking ball **Rev.
Legend:** COUPE MONDIALE DE FOOTBALL **Edge:** Reeded

Date	Mintage	F	VF	XF	Unc	BU
2002 Proof	—	Value: 40.00				

KM# 55   1000 FRANCS
15.0000 g., 0.9990 Silver 0.4818 oz. ASW, 36 mm.   **Rev:**
Multicolor Douglas DC-4 and NY skyline

Date	Mintage	F	VF	XF	Unc	BU
2002 Proof	—	Value: 35.00				

KM# 56   1000 FRANCS
15.0000 g., 0.9990 Silver 0.4818 oz. ASW   **Rev:** Multicolor
Caravelle SE-210 before London skyline **Shape:** 36

Date	Mintage	F	VF	XF	Unc	BU
2002 Proof	—	Value: 35.00				

KM# 57   1000 FRANCS
15.0000 g., 0.9990 Silver 0.4818 oz. ASW, 36 mm.   **Rev:**
Multicolor Convair 440 at airport

Date	Mintage	F	VF	XF	Unc	BU
2003 Proof	—	Value: 35.00				

KM# 58   1000 FRANCS
15.0000 g., 0.9990 Silver 0.4818 oz. ASW, 36 mm.   **Rev:**
Multicolor McDonnell-Douglas MD-81 right

Date	Mintage	F	VF	XF	Unc	BU
2003 Proof	—	Value: 35.00				

KM# 34   1000 FRANCS
30.9200 g., 0.9990 Silver 0.9931 oz. ASW, 39 mm.   **Obv:** Bust
with headdress left within circle **Rev:** Gold plated baboon within
circle **Edge:** Reeded **Note:** Date in Chinese numerals.

Date	Mintage	F	VF	XF	Unc	BU
2004 Proof	—	Value: 45.00				

KM# 39   1000 FRANCS

62.2400 g., 0.9999 Silver 2.0008 oz. ASW, 50 mm. **Subject:**
Year of the Monkey **Obv:** Gold plated world globe **Rev:** Gold
plated center with radiant holographic monkey within circle **Edge:**
Reeded and lettered sections **Edge Lettering:** PAN ASIA BANK
TAIWAN in English and Chinese **Note:** Date in Chinese
numerals.

Date	Mintage	F	VF	XF	Unc	BU
2004 Proof	—	Value: 115				

KM# 38   1000 FRANCS

30.7300 g., 0.9990 Silver 0.9870 oz. ASW, 39 mm. **Subject:**
Year of the Monkey **Obv:** Head with headdress 1/4 right within
circle **Rev:** Gold plated baboon within circle **Edge:** Reeded **Note:**
Note: Date in Chinese numerals.

Date	Mintage	F	VF	XF	Unc	BU
2004 Proof	—	Value: 50.00				

KM# 25   1000 FRANCS

31.1035 g., 0.9990 Silver 0.9990 oz. ASW, 40 mm. **Obv:**
National arms **Obv. Legend:** REPUBLIQUE TOGOLAISE **Rev:**
Relief rendering of statue of Princess Kyninska of Sparta
horseback right **Rev. Legend:** SPORTS - ANTIQUES **Edge:**
Plain

Date	Mintage	F	VF	XF	Unc	BU
2004	2,500	—	—	—		60.00

KM# 26   1000 FRANCS

1.2440 g., 0.9999 Gold 0.0400 oz. AGW, 13.92 mm. **Obv:**
National arms **Obv. Legend:** REPUBLIQUE TOGOLAISE **Rev:**
Convex statue of Nike **Edge:** Plain

Date	Mintage	F	VF	XF	Unc	BU
2004 Proof	5,000	Value: 75.00				

KM# 59   1000 FRANCS

15.0000 g., 0.9990 Silver 0.4818 oz. ASW, 36 mm. **Rev:**
Multicolor DeHaviland DH-89 biplane

Date	Mintage	F	VF	XF	Unc	BU
2004 Proof	—	Value: 35.00				

KM# 27   1000 FRANCS

1.2440 g., 0.9999 Gold 0.0400 oz. AGW, 13.92 mm. **Obv:**
National arms **Obv. Legend:** REPUBLIQUE TOGOLAISE **Rev:**
Concave statue of Nike **Edge:** Plain

Date	Mintage	F	VF	XF	Unc	BU
2004 Proof	5,000	Value: 75.00				

KM# 45   1000 FRANCS

Silver **Subject:** 170th Anniversary German Railroad, Nürnberg
- Fürth **Obv:** National arms **Obv. Legend:** REPUBLIQUE
TOGOLAISE **Rev:** Early steam locomotive "Adler"

Date	Mintage	F	VF	XF	Unc	BU
2005 Proof	—	Value: 55.00				

KM# 46   1000 FRANCS

1.2400 g., 0.9999 Gold 0.0399 oz. AGW **Subject:** 250th
Anniversary Birth of Wolfgang Amadeus Mozart **Obv:** National
arms **Obv. Legend:** REPUBLIQUE TOGOLAISE

Date	Mintage	F	VF	XF	Unc	BU
2006 Proof	—	Value: 85.00				

KM# 24   1000 FRANCS

31.1035 g., 0.9990 Silver 0.9990 oz. ASW, 40 mm. **Obv:**
National arms **Obv. Legend:** REPUBLIQUE TOGOLAISE **Rev:**
Incuse rendering of statue of Princess Kyninska of Sparta
horseback left **Rev. Legend:** SPORTS - ANTIQUES **Edge:** Plain

Date	Mintage	F	VF	XF	Unc	BU
2004	2,500	—	—	—	—	60.00

KM# 48   1000 FRANCS

25.0000 g., 0.9250 Silver 0.7435 oz. ASW, 38.6 mm. **Rev:** Blue
sunbird, prism technology

Date	Mintage	F	VF	XF	Unc	BU
2010 Proof	2,500	Value: 50.00				

KM# 49   1000 FRANCS

25.0000 g., 0.9250 Silver 0.7435 oz. ASW, 38.6 mm. **Rev:**
Green bird, prism technology

Date	Mintage	F	VF	XF	Unc	BU
2010 Proof	2,500	Value: 50.00				

KM# 50   1000 FRANCS

25.0000 g., 0.9250 Silver 0.7435 oz. ASW, 38.6 mm. **Rev:**
Yellow bird, prism technology

Date	Mintage	F	VF	XF	Unc	BU
2010 Proof	2,500	Value: 50.00				

KM# 61   1000 FRANCS

25.0000 g., 0.9250 Silver partially plated 0.7435 oz. ASW,
38.61 mm. **Subject:** Year of the Tiger **Obv:** National arms **Rev:**
Tiger, gilt

Date	Mintage	F	VF	XF	Unc	BU
2010 Proof	1,000	Value: 75.00				

KM# 42   2000 FRANCS

62.2000 g., 0.9990 Silver 1.9977 oz. ASW **Series:** Lunar
Subject: Year of the Monkey **Obv:** World map **Obv. Legend:**
REPUBLIQUE TOGOLAISE **Rev:** Monkey

Date	Mintage	F	VF	XF	Unc	BU
2004 Proof	—	Value: 125				

TOKELAU ISLANDS

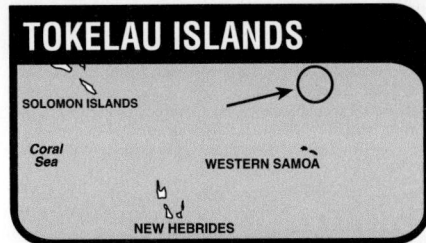

Tokelau or Union Islands, a New Zealand Territory located in the South Pacific 2,100 miles (3,379 km.) northeast of New Zealand and 300 miles (483 km.) north of Samoa, has an area of 4 sq. mi. (10 sq. km.) and a population of *2,000. Geographically, the group consists of four atolls - Atafu, Nukunono, Fakaofo and Swains – but the last belongs to American Samoa (and the United States claims the other three). The people are of Polynesian origin; Samoan is the official language. The New Zealand Minister for Foreign Affairs governs the islands; councils of family elders handle local government at the village level. The chief settlement is Fenuafala, on Fakaofo. It is connected by wireless technology with the offices of the New Zealand Administrative Center, located at Apia, Samoa. Subsistence farming and the production of copra for export are the main occupations. Revenue is also derived from the sale of postage stamps and, since 1978, coins.

Tokelau Islands issued its first coin in 1978, a "$1 Tahi Tala," Tokelauan for "One Dollar."

RULER
British

MINT MARK
PM - Pobjoy

NEW ZEALAND TERRITORY
STANDARD COINAGE

KM# 30   5 TALA
31.1000 g., 0.9990 Silver with Mother-of-Pearl inlay 0.9988 oz. ASW, 40 mm.   **Series:** Save the Whales **Obv:** Crowned head right **Obv. Legend:** TOKELAU **Rev:** Fin Whale on mother of pearl insert **Edge:** Plain

Date	Mintage	F	VF	XF	Unc	BU
2002 Proof	2,000	Value: 85.00				

KM # 32   5 TALA
31.1000 g., 0.9990 Silver 0.9988 oz. ASW, 40 mm.   **Ruler:** Elizabeth II **Obv:** Elizabeth II **Rev:** Capt. Smith and ship General Jackson **Edge:** Reeded

Date	Mintage	F	VF	XF	Unc	BU
2003 Proof	—	Value: 45.00				

KM# 47   5 TALA
Silver, 38.6 mm.   **Ruler:** Elizabeth II **Subject:** Endangered Wildlife **Obv:** Head crowned right **Rev:** Pacific Boa around a tree branch **Edge:** Reeded

Date	Mintage	F	VF	XF	Unc	BU
2003 Proof	—	Value: 50.00				

KM# 48   5 TALA
Silver, 38.6 mm.   **Ruler:** Elizabeth II **Subject:** Olympics, 2004 **Obv:** Head crowned right **Rev:** Runner, swimmer and bicyalist **Edge:** Reeded

Date	Mintage	F	VF	XF	Unc	BU
2004 Proof	—	Value: 50.00				

KM# 33   5 TALA
28.6500 g., Silver, 38.60 mm.   **Ruler:** Elizabeth II **Obv:** Crowned head right **Obv. Legend:** TOKELAU **Rev:** Sailing ship **Rev. Legend:** CUTTY SARK 1869 **Edge:** Reeded

Date	Mintage	F	VF	XF	Unc	BU
2005 Proof	—	Value: 45.00				

KM# 46   10 TALA
1.2400 g., 0.9990 Gold 0.0398 oz. AGW, 13.92 mm.   **Ruler:** Elizabeth II **Obv:** Crowned head right **Obv. Legend:** TOKELAU **Rev:** Two whales **Rev. Legend:** ENDANGERED WILDLIFE **Edge:** Reeded

Date	Mintage	F	VF	XF	Unc	BU
2003 Proof	—	Value: 85.00				

TONGA

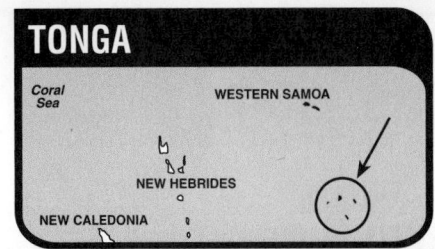

The Kingdom of Tonga (or Friendly Islands) is an archipelago situated in the southern Pacific Ocean south of Western Samoa and east of Fiji comprised of 150 islands. Tonga has an area of 270 sq. mi. (748 sq. km.) and a population of *100,000. Capital: Nuku'alofa. Primarily agricultural, the kingdom exports bananas and copra.

The monarchy is a member of the Commonwealth of Nations. King Siosa Tupou V is Head of State and Government.

RULER
King Taufa'ahau IV, 1965-2006
King Siosa Tupou V, 2006-2012

KINGDOM
DECIMAL COINAGE

100 Senti = 1 Pa'anga; 100 Pa'anga = 1 Hau

KM# 66a   SENITI
Copper Plated Steel, 17.5 mm.   **Ruler:** King Taufa'ahau Tupou IV **Series:** World Food Day **Obv:** Ear of corn **Obv. Legend:** TONGA **Rev:** Vanilla plant **Rev. Legend:** FAKALAHI ME'AKAI **Edge:** Plain

Date	Mintage	F	VF	XF	Unc	BU
2002	—	—	—	0.10	0.35	0.75
2003	—	—	—	0.10	0.35	0.75
2004	—	—	—	0.10	0.35	0.75

KM# 66   SENITI
1.8000 g., Bronze, 16.51 mm.   **Ruler:** King Taufa'ahau Tupou IV **Series:** World Food Day **Obv:** Ear of corn **Rev:** Vanilla plant **Edge:** Plain

Date	Mintage	F	VF	XF	Unc	BU
2005	—	—	—	0.10	0.35	0.75

KM# 67a   2 SENITI
Copper Plated Steel, 21 mm.   **Ruler:** King Taufa'ahau Tupou IV **Series:** World Food Day **Obv:** Taro plants **Obv. Legend:** TONGA **Rev:** Paper doll cutouts form design in center circle of sprays **Rev. Legend:** PLANNED FAMILIES • FOOD FOR ALL

Date	Mintage	F	VF	XF	Unc	BU
2002	—	—	—	0.15	0.65	1.25
2003	—	—	—	0.15	0.65	1.25
2004	—	—	—	0.15	0.65	1.25

KM# 68a   5 SENITI
2.7900 g., Nickel Plated Steel, 19.39 mm.   **Ruler:** King Taufa'ahau Tupou IV **Series:** World Food Day **Obv:** Hen with chicks **Obv. Legend:** TONGA **Rev:** Coconuts **Rev. Legend:** FAKALAHI ME'AKAI **Edge:** Reeded

Date	Mintage	F	VF	XF	Unc	BU
2002	—	—	—	0.25	0.75	1.35
2003	—	—	—	0.25	0.75	1.35
2004	—	—	—	0.25	0.75	1.35
2005	—	—	—	0.25	0.75	1.35

KM# 68   5 SENITI
2.8000 g., Copper-Nickel, 19.5 mm.   **Ruler:** King Taufa'ahau Tupou IV **Series:** World Food Day **Obv:** Hen with chicks **Rev:** Coconuts above sprig **Edge:** Reeded

Date	Mintage	F	VF	XF	Unc	BU
2005	—	0.10	0.25	0.75	1.25	

KM# 69a   10 SENITI
Nickel Plated Steel, 23.5 mm.   **Ruler:** King Taufa'ahau Tupou IV **Series:** World Food Day **Obv:** Uniformed bust facing **Obv. Legend:** F • A • O - TONGA **Rev:** Banana tree **Rev. Legend:** FAKALAHI ME'AKAI

Date	Mintage	F	VF	XF	Unc	BU
2002	—	—	—	0.30	1.00	1.75
2003	—	—	—	0.30	1.00	1.75
2004	—	—	—	0.30	1.00	1.75
2005	—	—	—	0.30	1.00	1.75

KM# 70.1 20 SENITI

11.3000 g., Nickel Plated Steel, 28.5 mm. **Ruler:**
King Taufa'ahau Tupou IV **Subject:** FAO - World Food Day **Obv:**
Uniformed bust facing **Rev:** Yams

Date	Mintage	F	VF	XF	Unc	BU
2002	—	—	0.25	0.50	1.25	2.00
2003	—	—	0.25	0.50	1.25	2.00
2004	—	—	0.25	0.50	1.25	2.00

KM# 70a 50 SENITI

14.6000 g., Nickel Plated Steel, 32.5 mm. **Ruler:**
King Taufa'ahau Tupou IV **Subject:** FAO - World Food Day **Obv:**
Uniformed bust facing **Rev:** Tomato plants **Shape:** 12-sided

Date	Mintage	F	VF	XF	Unc	BU
2002	—	—	0.45	0.75	1.50	2.50
2003	—	—	0.45	0.75	1.50	2.50
2004	—	—	0.45	0.75	1.50	2.50

KM# 178 PA'ANGA

31.1000 g., 0.9990 Silver with Mother-of-Pearl inlay 0.9988 oz.
ASW, 40 mm. **Ruler:** King Taufa'ahau Tupou IV **Series:** Save
the Whales **Obv:** Crown within wreath above national arms within
circle **Obv. Legend:** KINGDOM OF TONGA **Rev:** Right Whale
on mother of pearl insert **Edge:** Plain

Date	Mintage	F	VF	XF	Unc	BU
2002 Proof	2,000	Value: 85.00				

KM# 182 PA'ANGA

31.4700 g., 0.9250 Silver 0.9359 oz. ASW **Ruler:**
King Taufa'ahau Tupou IV **Subject:** 2004 Olympics **Obv:**
National arms **Rev:** Kayak crew seen from above

Date	Mintage	F	VF	XF	Unc	BU
2003 Proof	—	Value: 60.00				

KM# 179 2 PA'ANGA

Silver **Ruler:** King Taufa'ahau Tupou IV **Subject:** King's 85th
Birthday **Obv:** National arms

Date	Mintage	F	VF	XF	Unc	BU
2003 Proof	—	Value: 120				

TRANSNISTRIA

The Pridnestrovskaia Moldavskaia Respublica was formed
in 1990, even before the separation of Moldavia from Russia. It
has an area of 11,544 sq. mi. (29,900 sq. km.) and a population
of 555,000. Capital: Tiraspol.

Transnistria (or Transdniestra) has a president, parliament,
army and police forces, but as yet it is lacking international recognition.

MOLDAVIAN REPUBLIC

STANDARD COINAGE

1 Rublei = 100 Kopeek

KM# 50 5 KOPEEK

0.7000 g., Aluminum, 17.9 mm. **Obv:** Modified national arms
Obv. Legend: ПРИДНЕСТРОВСКАЯ МОЛДАВСКАЯ
РЕСПУБЛИКА **Rev:** Value flanked by wheat stalks. **Edge:** Plain
Note: Prev. KM#2, 16.

Date	Mintage	F	VF	XF	Unc	BU
2005	—	—	—	0.20	0.50	0.65

KM# 51 10 KOPEEK

1.0000 g., Aluminum, 20 mm. **Obv:** Modified national arms **Obv.
Legend:** ПРИДНЕСТРОВСКАЯ МОЛДАВСКАЯ РЕСПУБЛИКА
Rev: Value flanked by wheat stalks **Edge:** Plain **Note:** Prev.
KM#3, 17.

Date	Mintage	F	VF	XF	Unc	BU
2005	—	—	—	0.25	0.65	0.90

KM# 5 25 KOPEEK

2.1500 g., Aluminum-Bronze, 16.88 mm. **Obv:** National arms
Rev: Value within sprays **Edge:** Plain

Date	Mintage	F	VF	XF	Unc	BU
2002	—	—	0.15	0.35	0.90	1.20

KM# 52 25 KOPEEK

Aluminum-Bronze, 16.9 mm. **Obv:** Modified national arms **Obv.
Legend:** ПРИДНЕСТРОВСКАЯ МОЛДАВСКАЯ РЕСПУБЛИКА
Rev: Value within sprays **Edge:** Plain **Note:** Prev. KM#18.

Date	Mintage	F	VF	XF	Unc	BU
2005	—	—	0.15	0.35	0.90	1.20

KM# 52a 25 KOPEEK

2.1000 g., Bronze Plated Steel, 16.9 mm. **Obv:** Modified national
arms **Obv. Legend:** ПРИДНЕСТРОВСКАЯ МОЛДАВСКАЯ
РЕСПУБЛИКА **Rev:** Value within sprays **Edge:** Plain **Note:** Prev.
KM#5a; 18a.

Date	Mintage	F	VF	XF	Unc	BU
2005	—	—	0.15	0.35	0.90	1.20

KM# 53 50 KOPEEK

2.8000 g., Aluminum-Bronze, 19 mm. **Obv:** Modified national

arms **Obv. Legend:** ПРИДНЕСТРОВСКАЯ МОЛДАВСКАЯ
РЕСПУБЛИКА **Rev:** Value within sprays **Edge:** Plain **Note:** Prev.
KM#4a; 19.

Date	Mintage	F	VF	XF	Unc	BU
2005	—	—	0.15	0.45	1.10	1.50

KM# 53a 50 KOPEEK

Bronze Plated Steel, 19 mm. **Obv:** Modified national arms **Obv.
Legend:** ПРИДНЕСТРОВСКАЯ МОЛДАВСКАЯ
РЕСПУБЛИКА **Rev:** Value within sprays **Edge:** Plain **Note:** Prev.
KM#19a.

Date	Mintage	F	VF	XF	Unc	BU
2005	—	—	0.15	0.45	1.10	1.50

KM# 55 RUBLE

14.1400 g., 0.9250 Silver 0.4205 oz. ASW, 32 mm. **Obv:**
National Arms **Rev:** Building with dome

Date	Mintage	F	VF	XF	Unc	BU
2005 Proof	500	Value: 125				

KM# 77 RUBLE

14.1400 g., 0.9250 Silver 0.4205 oz. ASW, 32 mm. **Obv:**
National Arms **Rev:** Moth and caterpillar

Date	Mintage	F	VF	XF	Unc	BU
2006 Proof	1,000	Value: 145				

KM# 79 RUBLE

14.1400 g., 0.9250 Silver 0.4205 oz. ASW, 32 mm. **Obv:**
Olympics - Turin **Rev:** Slalom

Date	Mintage	F	VF	XF	Unc	BU
2006 Proof	500	Value: 150				

KM# 95 3 RUBLYA

8.0000 g., 0.9000 Gold 0.2315 oz. AGW, 21 mm. **Obv:** National
Arms **Rev:** Shield **Rev. Legend:** РЫБНИЦА

Date	Mintage	F	VF	XF	Unc	BU
2007 Proof	100	Value: 650				

KM# 97 3 RUBLYA

8.0000 g., 0.9000 Gold 0.2315 oz. AGW, 21 mm. **Obv:** National
Arms **Rev:** Shield **Rev. Legend:** ТНРАСПОЛЬ

Date	Mintage	F	VF	XF	Unc	BU
2007 Proof	100	Value: 650				

KM# 110 3 RUBLYA

14.1400 g., 0.9250 Silver 0.4205 oz. ASW, 32 mm. **Obv:**
National Arms **Rev:** Aquarius within zodiac emblems

Date	Mintage	F	VF	XF	Unc	BU
2007 Proof	100	Value: 650				

KM# 100 5 RUBLES

33.8500 g., 0.9250 Silver 1.0066 oz. ASW, 39 mm. **Obv:**
National Arms **Rev:** Wooley mammoth

Date	Mintage	F	VF	XF	Unc	BU
2007 Proof	500	Value: 145				

KM# 101 5 RUBLES

33.8500 g., 0.9250 Silver 1.0066 oz. ASW, 39 mm. **Obv:**
National Arms **Rev:** Moose

Date	Mintage	F	VF	XF	Unc	BU
2007 Proof	500	Value: 145				

KM# 134 5 RUBLES

33.8000 g., 0.9250 Silver 1.0052 oz. ASW, 39 mm. **Obv:**
National Arms **Rev:** Woolly Mammoth (Archidiskodon Trogrnterii)

Date	Mintage	F	VF	XF	Unc	BU
2007 Proof	500	Value: 100				

KM# 112 10 RUBLEI

14.1400 g., 0.9250 Silver 0.4205 oz. ASW, 32 mm. **Obv:**
National Arms **Rev:** Aquarius within circle of zodiac symbols

Date	Mintage	F	VF	XF	Unc	BU
2007 Proof	500	Value: 100				

KM# 102 10 RUBLEI

14.1400 g., 0.9250 Silver 0.4205 oz. ASW, 32 mm. **Obv:**
National Arms **Rev:** Multicolor sprinter

Date	Mintage	F	VF	XF	Unc	BU
2007 Proof	500	Value: 100				

KM# 103 10 RUBLEI

14.1400 g., 0.9250 Silver 0.4205 oz. ASW, 32 mm. **Obv:**
National Arms **Rev:** Multicolor female gymnast

Date	Mintage	F	VF	XF	Unc	BU
2007 Proof	500	Value: 100				

KM# 104 10 RUBLEI

14.1400 g., 0.9250 Silver 0.4205 oz. ASW, 32 mm. **Obv:**
National Arms **Rev:** Multicolor runner, sports designs

Date	Mintage	F	VF	XF	Unc	BU
2007 Proof	500	Value: 100				

KM# 105 10 RUBLEI

0.9250 Silver, 32 mm. **Obv:** National Arms **Rev:** Multicolor javlin
thrower

Date	Mintage	F	VF	XF	Unc	BU
2007 Proof	500	Value: 100				

KM# 106 10 RUBLEI

0.9250 Silver, 32 mm. **Obv:** National Arms **Rev:** Multicolor
runner breaking tape at finish line

Date	Mintage	F	VF	XF	Unc	BU
2007 Proof	500	Value: 100				

KM# 107 10 RUBLEI

14.1400 g., 0.9250 Silver 0.4205 oz. ASW, 32 mm. **Obv:**
National Arms **Rev:** Multicolor soccer player

Date	Mintage	F	VF	XF	Unc	BU
2007 Proof	500	Value: 100				

KM# 111 10 RUBLEI

14.1400 g., 0.9250 Silver 0.4205 oz. ASW, 32 mm. **Obv:**
National Arms **Rev:** Constellation ophiuchus (man grasping
serpent)

Date	Mintage	F	VF	XF	Unc	BU
2007 Proof	500	Value: 100				

KM# 125   10 RUBLEI
14.1400 g., 0.9250 Silver 0.4205 oz. ASW, 32 mm. **Obv:**
National Arms **Rev:** Sturgeon fish

Date	Mintage	F	VF	XF	Unc	BU
2008 Proof	500	Value: 150				

KM# 126   10 RUBLEI
14.1400 g., 0.9250 Silver 0.4205 oz. ASW, 32 mm. **Obv:**
National Arms **Rev:** Owl

Date	Mintage	F	VF	XF	Unc	BU
2008 Proof	500	Value: 165				

KM# 127   10 RUBLEI
14.1400 g., 0.9250 Silver 0.4205 oz. ASW, 32 mm. **Obv:**
National Arms **Rev:** Flower

Date	Mintage	F	VF	XF	Unc	BU
2008 Proof	500	Value: 185				

KM# 128   10 RUBLEI
14.1400 g., 0.9250 Silver 0.4205 oz. ASW, 32 mm. **Obv:**
National Arms **Rev:** Otter

Date	Mintage	F	VF	XF	Unc	BU
2008 Proof	500	Value: 190				

KM# 135   10 RUBLEI
14.1400 g., 0.9250 Silver 0.4205 oz. ASW, 32 mm. **Obv:**
National Arms **Rev:** Lutra otter

Date	Mintage	F	VF	XF	Unc	BU
2008 Proof	5,000	Value: 85.00				

KM# 54   15 RUBLEI
156.4000 g., 0.9990 Gold 5.0231 oz. AGW, 50 mm. **Obv:**
National Arms **Rev:** Building with dome

Date	Mintage	F	VF	XF	Unc	BU
2005 Proof, Rare	15	—	—	—	—	—

KM# 75   15 RUBLEI
156.4000 g., 0.9990 Gold 5.0231 oz. AGW, 15 mm. **Obv:**
National Arms **Rev:** Building with tower

Date	Mintage	F	VF	XF	Unc	BU
2006 Proof, Rare	15	—	—	—	—	—

KM# 17   100 RUBLEI
14.1400 g., 0.9250 Silver 0.4205 oz. ASW, 32 mm. **Obv:**
National Arms **Rev:** Cathedral of Ascension, Kitskany 1864

Date	Mintage	F	VF	XF	Unc	BU
2001 Proof	1,000	Value: 100				

KM# 10   100 RUBLEI
14.1400 g., 0.9250 Silver 0.4205 oz. ASW, 32 mm. **Obv:**
National Arms **Rev:** D. Zielinskieg, chemist

Date	Mintage	F	VF	XF	Unc	BU
2001 Proof	1,000	Value: 70.00				

KM# 11   100 RUBLEI
14.1400 g., 0.9250 Silver 0.4205 oz. ASW, 32 mm. **Obv:**
National Arms **Rev:** S. Berg, fish

Date	Mintage	F	VF	XF	Unc	BU
2001 Proof	1,000	Value: 70.00				

KM# 12   100 RUBLEI
14.1400 g., 0.9250 Silver 0.4205 oz. ASW, 32 mm. **Obv:**
National Arms **Rev:** N.F. Skilfosowskieg, portrait at right

Date	Mintage	F	VF	XF	Unc	BU
2001 Proof	1,000	Value: 70.00				

KM# 13   100 RUBLEI
14.1400 g., 0.9250 Silver 0.4205 oz. ASW, 32 mm. **Obv:**
National Arms **Rev:** M.F. Larionowa, bust, painter

Date	Mintage	F	VF	XF	Unc	BU
2001 Proof	1,000	Value: 70.00				

KM# 14   100 RUBLEI
14.1400 g., 0.9250 Silver 0.4205 oz. ASW, 32 mm. **Obv:**
National Arms **Rev:** Cathedral in Tyraspol

Date	Mintage	F	VF	XF	Unc	BU
2001 Proof	1,000	Value: 80.00				

KM# 15   100 RUBLEI
14.1400 g., 0.9250 Silver 0.4205 oz. ASW, 32 mm. **Obv:**
National Arms **Rev:** Cathedral XVII

Date	Mintage	F	VF	XF	Unc	BU
2001 Proof	1,000	Value: 100				

KM# 16   100 RUBLEI
14.1400 g., 0.9250 Silver 0.4205 oz. ASW, 32 mm. **Obv:**
National Arms **Rev:** Cathedral 1800

Date	Mintage	F	VF	XF	Unc	BU
2001 Proof	1,000	Value: 100				

KM# 18   100 RUBLEI
14.1400 g., 0.9250 Silver 0.4205 oz. ASW, 32 mm. **Obv:**
National Arms **Rev:** Cathedral 1825

Date	Mintage	F	VF	XF	Unc	BU
2001 Proof	1,000	Value: 100				

KM# 19   100 RUBLEI
14.1400 g., 0.9250 Silver 0.4205 oz. ASW, 32 mm. **Obv:**
National Arms **Rev:** Church of St. Trinity, Rashkov 1778

Date	Mintage	F	VF	XF	Unc	BU
2001 Proof	1,000	Value: 100				

KM# 20   100 RUBLEI
14.1400 g., 0.9250 Silver 0.4205 oz. ASW, 32 mm. **Obv:**
National Arms **Rev:** Cathedral XIX

Date	Mintage	F	VF	XF	Unc	BU
2001 Proof	1,000	Value: 100				

KM# 21   100 RUBLEI
14.1400 g., 0.9250 Silver 0.4205 oz. ASW, 32 mm. **Obv:**
National Arms **Rev:** Cathedral 1784

Date	Mintage	F	VF	XF	Unc	BU
2001 Proof	1,000	Value: 100				

KM# 22   100 RUBLEI
14.1400 g., 0.9250 Silver 0.4205 oz. ASW, 32 mm. **Obv:**
National Arms **Rev:** Cathedral 1854

Date	Mintage	F	VF	XF	Unc	BU
2001 Proof	1,000	Value: 100				

KM# 37   100 RUBLEI
14.0400 g., 0.9250 Silver 0.4175 oz. ASW, 32 mm. **Subject:**
10th Anniversary - Trans-Dniester Republican Bank **Obv:**
National arms **Rev:** Colorized monogram within 3/4 wreath with
"1992" at top **Edge:** Plain **Note:** Prev. KM#10.

Date	Mintage	F	VF	XF	Unc	BU
2002 Proof	500	Value: 90.00				

KM# 35   100 RUBLEI
14.1600 g., 0.9250 Silver 0.4211 oz. ASW, 32 mm. **Subject:**
City of Tiraspol **Obv:** National arms **Rev:** Statue and buildings
Edge: Plain **Note:** Prev. KM#7.

Date	Mintage	F	VF	XF	Unc	BU
2002 Proof	—	Value: 80.00				

KM# 36   100 RUBLEI
14.1600 g., 0.9250 Silver 0.4211 oz. ASW, 32 mm. **Subject:**
City of Tiraspol **Obv:** National arms **Rev:** Cameo above fortress
Edge: Plain **Note:** Prev. KM#8.

Date	Mintage	F	VF	XF	Unc	BU
2002 Proof	—	Value: 80.00				

KM# 38   100 RUBLEI
14.1600 g., 0.9250 Silver 0.4211 oz. ASW, 32 mm. **Subject:** K.
K. Gedroets **Obv:** National arms **Rev:** Bust facing flanked by
sprigs, beaker and book **Edge:** Plain **Note:** Prev. KM#9.

Date	Mintage	F	VF	XF	Unc	BU
2002 Proof	500	Value: 80.00				

KM# 40   100 RUBLEI
14.1400 g., 0.9250 Silver 0.4205 oz. ASW, 32 mm. **Obv:**
National Arms **Rev:** Shield **Rev. Legend:** ТИРАСЛОЛЬ

Date	Mintage	F	VF	XF	Unc	BU
2002 Proof	500	Value: 100				

KM# 41   100 RUBLEI
14.1400 g., 0.9250 Silver 0.4205 oz. ASW, 32 mm. **Obv:**
National Arms **Rev:** Shield **Rev. Legend:** ГРНГОРКОПОЛЛ

Date	Mintage	F	VF	XF	Unc	BU
2002 Proof	500	Value: 100				

KM# 45   100 RUBLEI
14.1400 g., 0.9250 Silver 0.4205 oz. ASW, 32 mm. **Obv:**
National Army **Rev:** Soccer Player

Date	Mintage	F	VF	XF	Unc	BU
2003 Proof	500	Value: 100				

KM# 43   100 RUBLEI
14.1400 g., 0.9250 Silver 0.4205 oz. ASW, 32 mm. **Obv:**
National arms **Rev:** Hoopoe (Upupa Epops) bird on branch **Edge:**
Plain **Note:** Prev. KM#11.

Date	Mintage	F	VF	XF	Unc	BU
2003 Proof	500	Value: 100				

KM# 42   100 RUBLEI
14.1400 g., 0.9250 Silver 0.4205 oz. ASW, 32 mm. **Obv:**
National arms **Rev:** Shield flanked by sprigs **Edge:** Plain **Note:**
Prev. KM#12.

Date	Mintage	F	VF	XF	Unc	BU
2003 Proof	500	Value: 75.00				

KM# 48   100 RUBLEI
14.1400 g., 0.9250 Silver 0.4205 oz. ASW, 32 mm. **Subject:**
80th Anniversary of Nationhood **Obv:** National arms **Rev:** Map
and multicolor flag **Edge:** Plain **Note:** Prev. KM#13.

Date	Mintage	F	VF	XF	Unc	BU
2004 Proof	500	Value: 225				

KM# 44   100 RUBLEI
14.1400 g., 0.9250 Silver 0.4205 oz. ASW, 32 mm. **Obv:**
National arms **Rev:** Doe and fawn flanked by trees **Edge:** Plain
Note: Prev. KM#14.

Date	Mintage	F	VF	XF	Unc	BU
2004 Proof	1,000	Value: 225				

KM# 46   100 RUBLEI
14.1400 g., 0.9250 Silver 0.4205 oz. ASW, 32 mm. **Obv:**
National Arms **Rev:** A.G. Rubinstein and music score

Date	Mintage	F	VF	XF	Unc	BU
2004 Proof	1,000	Value: 100				

KM# 47   100 RUBLEI
14.1400 g., 0.9250 Silver 0.4205 oz. ASW, 32 mm. **Obv:**
National Arms **Rev:** JS Grousul

Date	Mintage	F	VF	XF	Unc	BU
2004 Proof	1,000	Value: 100				

KM# 60   100 RUBLEI
14.1400 g., 0.9250 Silver 0.4205 oz. ASW, 32 mm. **Obv:**
National arms **Rev:** Eurasian Griffin bird on rock **Edge:** Plain
Note: Prev. KM#15.

Date	Mintage	F	VF	XF	Unc	BU
2005 Proof	1,000	Value: 125				

KM# 56   100 RUBLEI
14.1400 g., 0.9250 Silver 0.4205 oz. ASW, 32 mm. **Obv:**
National Arms **Rev:** Building with tower

Date	Mintage	F	VF	XF	Unc	BU
2005 Proof	500	Value: 110				

KM# 57 100 RUBLEI
14.1400 g., 0.9250 Silver 0.4205 oz. ASW, 32 mm. **Obv:** National Arms **Rev:** Zodiac - Capricorn

Date	Mintage	F	VF	XF	Unc	BU
2005 Proof	1,000	Value: 90.00				

KM# 58 100 RUBLEI
14.1400 g., 0.9250 Silver 0.4205 oz. ASW, 32 mm. **Obv:** National Arms **Rev:** Statue and long building

Date	Mintage	F	VF	XF	Unc	BU
2005 Proof	500	Value: 110				

KM# 59 100 RUBLEI
14.1400 g., 0.9250 Silver 0.4205 oz. ASW, 32 mm. **Obv:** National Arms **Rev:** Flag as book

Date	Mintage	F	VF	XF	Unc	BU
2005 Proof	500	Value: 180				

KM# 61 100 RUBLEI
14.1400 g., 0.9250 Silver 0.4205 oz. ASW, 32 mm. **Obv:** National Arms **Rev:** PP Werszygora

Date	Mintage	F	VF	XF	Unc	BU
2005 Proof	500	Value: 110				

KM# 62 100 RUBLEI
14.1400 g., 0.9250 Silver 0.4205 oz. ASW, 32 mm. **Obv:** National Arms **Rev:** Zodiac - Aquarius

Date	Mintage	F	VF	XF	Unc	BU
2005 Proof	500	Value: 90.00				

KM# 63 100 RUBLEI
14.1400 g., 0.9250 Silver 0.4205 oz. ASW, 32 mm. **Obv:** National Arms **Rev:** Zodiac - Pisces

Date	Mintage	F	VF	XF	Unc	BU
2005 Proof	500	Value: 90.00				

KM# 64 100 RUBLEI
14.1400 g., 0.9250 Silver 0.4205 oz. ASW, 32 mm. **Obv:** National Arms **Rev:** Zodiac - Aries

Date	Mintage	F	VF	XF	Unc	BU
2005 Proof	500	Value: 90.00				

KM# 65 100 RUBLEI
14.1400 g., 0.9250 Silver 0.4205 oz. ASW, 32 mm. **Obv:** National Arms **Rev:** Zodiac - Taurus

Date	Mintage	F	VF	XF	Unc	BU
2005 Proof	500	Value: 90.00				

KM# 66 100 RUBLEI
14.1400 g., 0.9250 Silver 0.4205 oz. ASW, 32 mm. **Obv:** National Arms **Rev:** Zodiac - Gemini

Date	Mintage	F	VF	XF	Unc	BU
2005 Proof	500	Value: 90.00				

KM# 67 100 RUBLEI
14.1400 g., 0.9250 Silver 0.4205 oz. ASW, 32 mm. **Obv:** National Arms **Rev:** Zodiac - Cancer

Date	Mintage	F	VF	XF	Unc	BU
2005 Proof	500	Value: 90.00				

KM# 68 100 RUBLEI
14.1400 g., 0.9250 Silver 0.4205 oz. ASW, 32 mm. **Obv:** National Arms **Rev:** Zodiac - Leo

Date	Mintage	F	VF	XF	Unc	BU
2005 Proof	500	Value: 90.00				

KM# 69 100 RUBLEI
14.1400 g., 0.9250 Silver 0.4205 oz. ASW, 32 mm. **Obv:** National Arms **Rev:** Zodiac - Virgo

Date	Mintage	F	VF	XF	Unc	BU
2005 Proof	500	Value: 90.00				

KM# 70 100 RUBLEI
14.1400 g., 0.9250 Silver 0.4205 oz. ASW, 32 mm. **Obv:** National Arms **Rev:** Zodiac - Libra

Date	Mintage	F	VF	XF	Unc	BU
2005 Proof	500	Value: 90.00				

KM# 71 100 RUBLEI
14.1400 g., 0.9250 Silver 0.4205 oz. ASW, 32 mm. **Obv:** National Arms **Rev:** Zodiac - Scorpio

Date	Mintage	F	VF	XF	Unc	BU
2005 Proof	500	Value: 90.00				

KM# 72 100 RUBLEI
14.1400 g., 0.9250 Silver 0.4205 oz. ASW, 32 mm. **Obv:** National Arms **Rev:** Zodiac - Sagittarius

Date	Mintage	F	VF	XF	Unc	BU
2005 Proof	500	Value: 90.00				

KM# 76 100 RUBLEI
0.9250 Silver, 32 mm. **Obv:** National Arms **Rev:** Lunar Year of the (fire) Dog

Date	Mintage	F	VF	XF	Unc	BU
2006 Proof	1,000	Value: 65.00				

KM# 78 100 RUBLEI
14.1400 g., 0.9250 Silver 0.4205 oz. ASW, 32 mm. **Obv:** National Arms **Rev:** Stag Beetle

Date	Mintage	F	VF	XF	Unc	BU
2006 Proof	500	Value: 285				

KM# 80 100 RUBLEI
14.1400 g., 0.9250 Silver 0.4205 oz. ASW, 32 mm. **Obv:** National Arms **Rev:** Biathlon

Date	Mintage	F	VF	XF	Unc	BU
2006 Proof	300	Value: 300				

KM# 81 100 RUBLEI
14.1400 g., 0.9250 Silver 0.4205 oz. ASW, 32 mm. **Subject:** Turin Olympics **Obv:** National Arms **Rev:** Ski Jump

Date	Mintage	F	VF	XF	Unc	BU
2006 Proof	200	Value: 325				

KM# 82 100 RUBLEI
14.1400 g., 0.9250 Silver 0.4205 oz. ASW, 32 mm. **Obv:** National Arms **Rev:** Town View - Tyraspol

Date	Mintage	F	VF	XF	Unc	BU
2006 Proof	500	Value: 110				

KM# 83 100 RUBLEI
14.1400 g., 0.9250 Silver 0.4205 oz. ASW, 32 mm. **Obv:** National Arms **Rev:** Town view Bendery

Date	Mintage	F	VF	XF	Unc	BU
2006 Proof	500	Value: 100				

KM# 84 100 RUBLEI
14.1400 g., 0.9250 Silver 0.4205 oz. ASW, 32 mm. **Obv:** Naational Arms **Rev:** Man in forest legend

Date	Mintage	F	VF	XF	Unc	BU
2006 Proof	1,000	Value: 85.00				

KM# 85 100 RUBLEI
14.1400 g., 0.9250 Silver 0.4205 oz. ASW, 32 mm. **Obv:** National Arms **Rev:** Legend - Fisherman in rowboat

Date	Mintage	F	VF	XF	Unc	BU
2006 Proof	1,000	Value: 85.00				

KM# 86 100 RUBLEI
14.1400 g., 0.9250 Silver 0.4205 oz. ASW, 32 mm. **Obv:** National Arms **Rev:** Legend dragon slayer

Date	Mintage	F	VF	XF	Unc	BU
2006 Proof	1,000	Value: 85.00				

KM# 87 100 RUBLEI
14.1400 g., 0.9250 Silver 0.4205 oz. ASW **Obv:** National Arms **Rev:** Kossak

Date	Mintage	F	VF	XF	Unc	BU
2006 Proof	500	Value: 120				

KM# 88 100 RUBLEI
14.1400 g., 0.9250 Silver 0.4205 oz. ASW, 32 mm. **Obv:** National Arms **Rev:** General Bursak

Date	Mintage	F	VF	XF	Unc	BU
2006 Proof	500	Value: 120				

KM# 89 100 RUBLEI
14.1400 g., 0.9250 Silver 0.4205 oz. ASW **Obv:** National Arms **Rev:** Multicolor baseball player hitting ball **Shape:** 32

Date	Mintage	F	VF	XF	Unc	BU
2006 Proof	500	Value: 100				

KM# 90 100 RUBLEI
14.1400 g., 0.9250 Silver 0.4205 oz. ASW, 32 mm. **Obv:** National Arms **Rev:** Cathedral of the Arch Angel Michael

Date	Mintage	F	VF	XF	Unc	BU
2006 Proof	500	Value: 100				

KM# 91 100 RUBLEI
14.1400 g., 0.9250 Silver 0.4205 oz. ASW, 32 mm. **Obv:** National Arms **Rev:** Sidor Bialy bust at right

Date	Mintage	F	VF	XF	Unc	BU
2006 Proof	300	Value: 175				

KM# 136 100 RUBLEI
14.1400 g., 0.9250 Silver 0.4205 oz. ASW, 32 mm. **Obv:** National Arms **Rev:** Monarch butterfly

Date	Mintage	F	VF	XF	Unc	BU
2006 Proof	1,000	Value: 60.00				

KM# 92 100 RUBLEI
14.1400 g., 0.9250 Silver 0.4205 oz. ASW, 32 mm. **Obv:** National Arms **Rev:** Seal impression, partially plated

Date	Mintage	F	VF	XF	Unc	BU
2006 Proof	300	Value: 175				

KM# 120 100 RUBLEI
14.1400 g., 0.9250 Silver 0.4205 oz. ASW, 32 mm. **Obv:** National Arms **Rev:** General Potiomkin

Date	Mintage	F	VF	XF	Unc	BU
2007 Proof	300	Value: 160				

KM# 96 100 RUBLEI
14.1400 g., 0.9250 Silver 0.4205 oz. ASW, 32 mm. **Obv:** National Arms **Rev:** Rybnitsa Shield **Rev. Legend:** РЫҔЦИUA

Date	Mintage	F	VF	XF	Unc	BU
2007 Proof	500	Value: 120				

KM# 113 100 RUBLEI
14.1400 g., 0.9250 Silver 0.4205 oz. ASW, 32 mm. **Obv:** National Arms **Rev:** Lunar year of the pig

Date	Mintage	F	VF	XF	Unc	BU
2007 Proof	300	Value: 160				

KM# 114 100 RUBLEI
14.1400 g., 0.9250 Silver 0.4205 oz. ASW, 32 mm. **Obv:** National Arms **Rev:** Castle view, 4 towers

Date	Mintage	F	VF	XF	Unc	BU
2007 Proof	500	Value: 120				

KM# 115 100 RUBLEI
14.1400 g., 0.9250 Silver 0.4205 oz. ASW, 32 mm. **Subject:** Soroky Fortress **Obv:** National Arms **Rev:** Castle view central tower and gate

Date	Mintage	F	VF	XF	Unc	BU
2007 Proof	500	Value: 120				

KM# 116 100 RUBLEI
14.1400 g., 0.9250 Silver 0.4205 oz. ASW, 32 mm. **Obv:** National Arms **Rev:** Zachary Czerega Kulis, ship at left

Date	Mintage	F	VF	XF	Unc	BU
2007 Proof	300	Value: 165				

KM# 117 100 RUBLEI
14.1400 g., 0.9250 Silver 0.4205 oz. ASW, 32 mm. **Subject:** Anton Goloway **Obv:** National Arms **Rev:** Bust facing

Date	Mintage	F	VF	XF	Unc	BU
2007 Proof	300	Value: 125				

KM# 118 100 RUBLEI
14.1400 g., 0.9250 Silver 0.4205 oz. ASW, 32 mm. **Obv:** National Arms **Rev:** Alexander Kuszer

Date	Mintage	F	VF	XF	Unc	BU
2007 Proof	500	Value: 115				

KM# 119 100 RUBLEI
14.1400 g., 0.9250 Silver 0.4205 oz. ASW, 32 mm. **Obv:** National Arms **Rev:** Field Marshal - Rumiancew-Zadunajski

Date	Mintage	F	VF	XF	Unc	BU
2007 Proof	300	Value: 125				

KM# 121 100 RUBLEI
14.1400 g., 0.9250 Silver 0.4205 oz. ASW, 32 mm. **Obv:** National Arms **Rev:** General Panin

Date	Mintage	F	VF	XF	Unc	BU
2007 Proof	300	Value: 125				

KM# 130 100 RUBLEI
14.4000 g., 0.9250 Silver 0.4282 oz. ASW, 32 mm. **Obv:** Naitonal Arms **Rev:** Tulip (Tulipa Biebersteiniana)

Date	Mintage	F	VF	XF	Unc	BU
2008 Proof	—	Value: 125				

KM# 131 100 RUBLEI
14.4000 g., 0.9250 Silver 0.4282 oz. ASW, 32 mm. **Obv:** National Arms **Rev:** Moldavian Metal Works shield

Date	Mintage	F	VF	XF	Unc	BU
2008 Proof	500	Value: 90.00				

KM# 132 100 RUBLEI
14.4000 g., 0.9250 Silver 0.4282 oz. ASW, 32 mm. **Obv:** National Arms **Rev:** Field Marshal Piotr Vitgenshtain

Date	Mintage	F	VF	XF	Unc	BU
2008 Proof	500	Value: 90.00				

KM# 133 100 RUBLEI
14.4000 g., 0.9250 Silver 0.4282 oz. ASW, 32 mm. **Obv:** National Arms **Rev:** Belgorod Dnestrovskaya Fortress

Date	Mintage	F	VF	XF	Unc	BU
2008 Proof	500	Value: 100				

KM# 129 100 RUBLEI
14.1600 g., 0.9250 Silver 0.4211 oz. ASW, 32 mm. **Subject:** Year of the Bull

Date	Mintage	F	VF	XF	Unc	BU
2009 Proof	500	Value: 100				

KM# 25 1000 RUBLEI
8.0000 g., 0.9000 Gold 0.2315 oz. AGW, 21 mm. **Obv:** National Arms **Rev:** 1800 Cathedral of God's Ascension

Date	Mintage	F	VF	XF	Unc	BU
2001 Proof	50	Value: 750				

KM# 23 1000 RUBLEI
8.0000 g., 0.9000 Gold 0.2315 oz. AGW, 21 mm. **Obv:** National Arms **Rev:** Church of the Blessed Virgins

Date	Mintage	F	VF	XF	Unc	BU
2001 Proof	50	Value: 750				

KM# 24 1000 RUBLEI
Gold, 21 mm. **Obv:** National Arms **Rev:** Orthodox Church of the Virgin's Assumption

Date	Mintage	F	VF	XF	Unc	BU
2001 Proof	50	Value: 750				

KM# 26 1000 RUBLEI
8.0000 g., 0.9000 Gold 0.2315 oz. AGW, 21 mm. **Obv:** National Arms **Rev:** Cathedral of the Birth of Christ

Date	Mintage	F	VF	XF	Unc	BU
2001 Proof	50	Value: 750				

KM# 27 1000 RUBLEI
8.0000 g., 0.9000 Gold 0.2315 oz. AGW, 21 mm. **Rev:** Cathedral of the Transfiguration

Date	Mintage	F	VF	XF	Unc	BU
2001 Proof	50	Value: 750				

KM# 28 1000 RUBLEI
8.0000 g., 0.9000 Gold 0.2315 oz. AGW, 21 mm. **Obv:** National Arms **Rev:** Church of the Blessed Virgin's Birth

Date	Mintage	F	VF	XF	Unc	BU
2001 Proof	50	Value: 750				

KM# 29 1000 RUBLEI
8.0000 g., 0.9000 Gold 0.2315 oz. AGW, 21 mm. **Obv:** National Arms **Rev:** Church of the Transfiguration

Date	Mintage	F	VF	XF	Unc	BU
2001 Proof	50	Value: 750				

KM# 30 1000 RUBLEI
8.0000 g., 0.9000 Gold 0.2315 oz. AGW, 21 mm. **Obv:** National Arms **Rev:** Church of the Lifegiving Trinity

Date	Mintage	F	VF	XF	Unc	BU
2001 Proof	50	Value: 750				

KM# 31 1000 RUBLEI
8.0000 g., 0.9000 Gold 0.2315 oz. AGW, 21 mm. **Obv:** National Arms **Rev:** Orthodox Church to the Serbian Paraskeva (1854)

Date	Mintage	F	VF	XF	Unc	BU
2001 Proof	50	Value: 750				

KM# 32 1000 RUBLEI
8.0000 g., 0.9000 Gold 0.2315 oz. AGW, 21 mm. **Obv:** National Arms **Rev:** Church of Michael the Arch Angel in Stoiesti

Date	Mintage	F	VF	XF	Unc	BU
2001 Proof	50	Value: 750				

MINT SETS

KM#	Date	Mintage	Identification	Issue Price	Mkt Val
MS1	2005 (4)	—	KM#50, 51, 52a, 53.	—	20.00

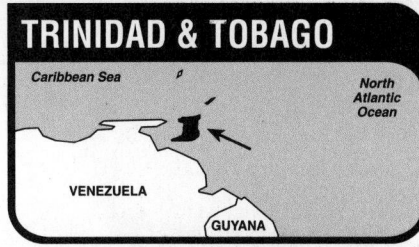

TRINIDAD & TOBAGO

Caribbean Sea — *North Atlantic Ocean* — VENEZUELA — GUYANA

The Republic of Trinidad and Tobago is situated 7 miles (11 km.) off the coast of Venezuela, has an area of 1,981 sq. mi. (5,130 sq. km.) and a population of *1.2 million. Capital: Port-of-Spain. The island of Trinidad contains the world's largest natural asphalt bog. Birds of Paradise live on little Tobago, the only place outside of their native New Guinea where they can be found in a wild state. Petroleum and petroleum products are the mainstay of the economy. Petroleum products, crude oil and sugar are exported.

Trinidad and Tobago is a member of the Commonwealth of Nations. The President is Chief of State. The Prime Minister is Head of Government.

MONETARY SYSTEM
100 Cents = 1 Dollar

REPUBLIC
STANDARD COINAGE

KM# 29 CENT
1.9500 g., Bronze, 17.76 mm. **Obv:** National arms **Rev:** Hummingbird and value **Edge:** Plain

Date	Mintage	F	VF	XF	Unc	BU
2001	—	—	—	0.10	0.30	0.40
2002	—	—	—	0.10	0.30	0.40
2003	—	—	—	0.10	0.30	0.40
2005	—	—	—	0.10	0.30	0.40
2006	—	—	—	0.10	0.30	0.40
2007	—	—	—	0.10	0.30	0.40
2008	—	—	—	0.10	0.30	0.40
2009	—	—	—	0.10	0.30	0.40
2010FM	—	—	—	0.10	0.30	0.40

KM# 30 5 CENTS
3.3100 g., Bronze, 21.2 mm. **Obv:** National arms **Rev:** Bird of paradise and value **Edge:** Plain

Date	Mintage	F	VF	XF	Unc	BU
2001	—	—	—	0.15	0.45	0.60
2002	—	—	—	0.15	0.45	0.60
2003	—	—	—	0.15	0.45	0.60
2004	—	—	—	0.15	0.45	0.60
2005	—	—	—	0.15	0.45	0.60
2006	—	—	—	0.15	0.45	0.60
2007	—	—	—	0.15	0.45	0.60
2008	—	—	—	0.15	0.45	0.60
2009FM	—	—	—	0.15	0.45	0.60
2010FM	—	—	—	0.15	0.45	0.60

KM# 31 10 CENTS
1.4000 g., Copper-Nickel, 16.2 mm. **Obv:** National arms **Rev:** Hibiscus and value **Edge:** Reeded

Date	Mintage	F	VF	XF	Unc	BU
2001	—	—	—	0.25	0.60	0.80
2002	—	—	—	0.25	0.60	0.80
2003	—	—	—	0.25	0.60	0.80
2004	—	—	—	0.25	0.60	0.80
2005	—	—	—	0.25	0.60	0.80
2006	—	—	—	0.25	0.60	0.80
2007	—	—	—	0.25	0.60	0.80
2008	—	—	—	0.25	0.60	0.80

KM# 32 25 CENTS
3.5000 g., Copper-Nickel, 20 mm. **Obv:** National arms **Rev:** Chaconia and value **Edge:** Reeded

Date	Mintage	F	VF	XF	Unc	BU
2001	—	—	—	0.30	0.75	1.00
2002	—	—	—	0.30	0.75	1.00
2003	—	—	—	0.30	0.75	1.00
2004	—	—	—	0.30	0.75	1.00
2005	—	—	—	0.30	0.75	1.00
2006	—	—	—	0.30	0.75	1.00
2007	—	—	—	0.30	0.75	1.00
2008	—	—	—	0.30	0.75	1.00

KM# 33 50 CENTS
7.0000 g., Copper-Nickel, 26 mm. **Obv:** National arms **Rev:** Kettle drums and value **Edge:** Reeded

Date	Mintage	F	VF	XF	Unc	BU
2003	—	—	—	1.00	2.00	4.00

KM# 63 10 DOLLARS
Copper-Nickel **Subject:** FIFA - XVIII World Football Championship - Soca Warriors - Germany 2006 **Obv:** Native hands playing steel drum, gilt **Rev:** Logo

Date	Mintage	F	VF	XF	Unc	BU
2006	—	—	—	5.00	12.00	35.00

KM# 64 100 DOLLARS
28.2800 g., 0.9250 Silver 0.8410 oz. ASW **Subject:** FIFA - XVIII World Football Championship - Soca Warriors - Germany 2006 **Obv:** Native hands playing steel drum, gilt **Rev:** Logo

Date	Mintage	F	VF	XF	Unc	BU
2006 Proof	—	Value: 70.00				

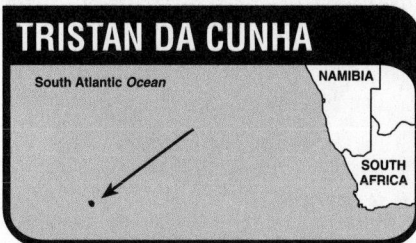

TRISTAN DA CUNHA

South Atlantic Ocean — NAMIBIA — SOUTH AFRICA

Tristan da Cunha is the principal island and group name of a small cluster of volcanic islands located in the South Atlantic midway between the Cape of Good Hope and South America, and 1,500 miles (2,414 km.) south-southwest of the British colony of St. Helena. The other islands are inaccessible, Gough, and the three Nightingale Islands. The group, which comprises a dependency of St. Helena, has a total area of 40 sq. mi. (104 sq. km.) and a population of less than 300. There is a village of 60 houses called Edinburgh. Potatoes are the staple subsistence crop.

MONETARY SYSTEM
100 Pence = 1 Pound

ST. HELENA DEPENDENCY
STANDARD COINAGE

KM# 27 1/2 PENNY
3.8300 g., Copper, 16.91 mm. **Ruler:** Elizabeth II **Obv:** Head with tiara right **Rev:** Snipe Eel **Edge:** Plain

Date	Mintage	F	VF	XF	Unc	BU
2008	—	—	—	—	0.75	1.00

KM# 28 PENNY
4.6300 g., Copper, 18.66 mm. **Ruler:** Elizabeth II **Obv:** Head with tiara right **Rev:** Crayfish **Edge:** Plain

Date	Mintage	F	VF	XF	Unc	BU
2008	—	—	—	—	1.20	1.60

KM# 29 2 PENCE
6.6000 g., Copper, 22.02 mm. **Ruler:** Elizabeth II **Obv:** Head with tiara right **Rev:** Violet Seasnail **Edge:** Plain

Date	Mintage	F	VF	XF	Unc	BU
2008	—	—	—	—	1.50	2.00

KM# 30 5 PENCE
3.7400 g., Copper-Nickel, 16.90 mm. **Ruler:** Elizabeth II **Obv:** Head with tiara right **Rev:** Sea Turtle **Edge:** Plain

Date	Mintage	F	VF	XF	Unc	BU
2008	—	—	—	—	1.80	2.40

KM# 31 10 PENCE
6.4900 g., Copper-Nickel, 22.03 mm. **Ruler:** Elizabeth II **Obv:** Head with tiara right **Rev:** Crab **Edge:** Plain

Date	Mintage	F	VF	XF	Unc	BU
2008	—	—	—	—	2.25	3.00

KM# 32 20 PENCE
6.1000 g., Aluminum-Bronze, 22.02 mm. **Ruler:** Elizabeth II **Obv:** Head with tiara right **Rev:** Orcha - Killer Whale **Edge:** Plain

Date	Mintage	F	VF	XF	Unc	BU
2008	—	—	—	—	3.00	4.00

KM# 33 25 PENCE
Bi-Metallic Aluminum-Bronze center in Copper-Nickel ring., 25.76 mm. **Ruler:** Elizabeth II **Obv:** Head with tiara right **Rev:** 2 Bottlenose Dolphins **Edge:** Plain

Date	Mintage	F	VF	XF	Unc	BU
2008	—	—	—	—	6.00	8.00

KM# 12   50 PENCE
29.1000 g., Copper-Nickel, 38.6 mm.   **Ruler:** Elizabeth II
Subject: Queen Elizabeth's 75th Birthday **Obv:** Crowned bust
right **Rev:** Crowned bust facing **Edge:** Reeded

Date	Mintage	F	VF	XF	Unc	BU
2001	—	—	—	—	7.00	8.00

KM# 13   50 PENCE
29.6000 g., Copper-Nickel, 38.7 mm.   **Ruler:** Elizabeth II
Subject: Centennial of Queen Victoria's Death **Obv:** Crowned
bust right **Rev:** Crown and veil on half-length figure of Queen
Victoria facing left within oval circle **Edge:** Reeded

Date	Mintage	F	VF	XF	Unc	BU
2001	—	—	—	—	8.00	10.00

KM# 12a   50 PENCE
28.2800 g., 0.9250 Silver 0.8410 oz. ASW, 38.6 mm.   **Ruler:**
Elizabeth II **Subject:** Queen's 75th Birthday **Obv:** Crowned bust
right **Rev:** Crowned bust facing **Edge:** Reeded

Date	Mintage	F	VF	XF	Unc	BU
2001 Proof	10,000	Value: 40.00				

KM# 12b   50 PENCE
47.5400 g., 0.9166 Gold 1.4009 oz. AGW, 38.6 mm.   **Ruler:**
Elizabeth II **Obv:** Crowned bust right **Rev:** Crowned bust facing

Date	Mintage	F	VF	XF	Unc	BU
2001 Proof	75	Value: 2,200				

KM# 13a   50 PENCE
28.2800 g., 0.9250 Silver 0.8410 oz. ASW, 38.6 mm.   **Ruler:**
Elizabeth II **Subject:** Centennial of Queen Victoria's Death **Obv:**
Crowned bust right **Rev:** Crown and veil on half-length figure of
Queen Victoria facing left within oval circle **Edge:** Reeded

Date	Mintage	F	VF	XF	Unc	BU
2001 Proof	10,000	Value: 50.00				

KM# 13b   50 PENCE
47.5400 g., 0.9166 Gold 1.4009 oz. AGW, 38.6 mm.   **Ruler:**
Elizabeth II **Subject:** Centennial of Queen Victoria's Death **Obv:**
Crowned bust right **Rev:** Crown and veil on half-length figure of
Queen Victoria facing left within oval circle **Edge:** Reeded

Date	Mintage	F	VF	XF	Unc	BU
2001 Proof	100	Value: 2,150				

KM# 41   CROWN
Copper-Nickel, 38.6 mm.   **Ruler:** Elizabeth II **Obv:** Bust crowned
right **Rev:** Conjoined busts left

Date	Mintage	F	VF	XF	Unc	BU
2005	—	—	—	—	—	20.00

KM# 43   CROWN
Copper-Nickel, 38.6 mm.   **Ruler:** Elizabeth II **Obv:** Bust in tiara
right **Rev:** Lord Nelson's bust 1/4 left

Date	Mintage	F	VF	XF	Unc	BU
2005	—	—	—	—	—	15.00

KM# 44   CROWN
Copper-Nickel, 38.6 mm.   **Ruler:** Elizabeth II **Subject:** VE-Day,
60th Anniversary **Obv:** Bust in tiara right **Rev:** Ship, tank, two
panes

Date	Mintage	F	VF	XF	Unc	BU
2005	—	—	—	—	—	15.00

KM# 14   CROWN
Copper-Nickel, 38.5 mm.   **Ruler:** Elizabeth II **Obv:** Crowned bust
right **Rev:** Pope John Paul II **Edge:** Reeded

Date	Mintage	F	VF	XF	Unc	BU
2005	—	—	—	—	8.50	12.00

KM# 14a   CROWN
24.1200 g., 0.9250 Silver 0.7173 oz. ASW, 38.5 mm.   **Ruler:**
Elizabeth II **Obv:** Crowned bust right **Rev:** Pope John Paul II
Edge: Reeded

Date	Mintage	F	VF	XF	Unc	BU
2005 Proof	—	Value: 45.00				

KM# 15   CROWN
25.0000 g., Copper-Nickel, 38.83 mm.   **Ruler:** Elizabeth II
Series: Privateering ships of the South Atlantic **Obv:** Crowned
bust right **Obv. Legend:** ELIZABETH II — TRISTAN DA CUNHA
Rev: Sailing ship "Tybalt" **Edge:** Reeded

Date	Mintage	F	VF	XF	Unc	BU
2006	—	—	—	—	8.50	12.00

KM# 16   CROWN
25.0000 g., Copper-Nickel, 38.83 mm.   **Ruler:** Elizabeth II
Series: Privateering ships of the South Atlantic **Obv:** Crowned
bust right **Obv. Legend:** ELIZABETH II — TRISTAN DA CUNHA
Rev: Sailing ship "Syren" **Edge:** Reeded

Date	Mintage	F	VF	XF	Unc	BU
2006	—	—	—	—	8.50	12.00

KM# 17   CROWN
25.0000 g., Copper-Nickel, 38.83 mm.   **Ruler:** Elizabeth II
Series: Privateering ships of the South Atlantic **Obv:** Crowned
bust right **Obv. Legend:** ELIZABETH II — TRISTAN DA CUNHA
Rev: Sailing ship "Pride of Baltimore" **Edge:** Reeded

Date	Mintage	F	VF	XF	Unc	BU
2006	—	—	—	—	8.50	12.00

KM# 18   CROWN
25.0000 g., Copper-Nickel, 38.83 mm.   **Ruler:** Elizabeth II
Series: Privateering ships of the South Atlantic **Obv:** Crowned
bust right **Obv. Legend:** ELIZABETH II — TRISTAN DA CUNHA
Rev: Sailing ship "Hornet" **Edge:** Reeded

Date	Mintage	F	VF	XF	Unc	BU
2006	—	—	—	—	8.50	12.00

KM# 19   CROWN
25.0000 g., Copper-Nickel, 38.83 mm.   **Ruler:** Elizabeth II
Series: Privateering ships of the South Atlantic **Obv:** Crowned
bust right **Obv. Legend:** ELIZABETH II — TRISTAN DA CUNHA
Rev: Sailing ship "Griffin" **Edge:** Reeded

Date	Mintage	F	VF	XF	Unc	BU
2006	—	—	—	—	8.50	12.00

KM# 20   CROWN
25.0000 g., Copper-Nickel, 38.83 mm. **Ruler:** Elizabeth II
Series: Privateering ships of the South Atlantic **Obv:** Crowned
bust right **Obv. Legend:** ELIZABETH II — TRISTAN DA CUNHA
Rev: Sailing ship "Enterprise" **Edge:** Reeded

Date	Mintage	F	VF	XF	Unc	BU
2006	—	—	—	—	8.50	12.00

KM# 21   CROWN
25.0000 g., Copper-Nickel, 38.83 mm. **Ruler:** Elizabeth II
Series: Privateering ships of the South Atlantic **Obv:** Crowned
bust right **Obv. Legend:** ELIZABETH II — TRISTAN DA CUNHA
Rev: Sailing ship "Columbus" **Edge:** Reeded

Date	Mintage	F	VF	XF	Unc	BU
2006	—	—	—	—	8.50	12.00

KM# 22   CROWN
25.0000 g., Copper-Nickel, 38.8 mm. **Ruler:** Elizabeth II **Series:**
Privateering ships of the South Atlantic **Obv:** Crowned bust right
Obv. Legend: ELIZABETH II — TRISTAN DA CUNHA **Rev:**
Sailing ship "Chausseur" **Edge:** Reeded

Date	Mintage	F	VF	XF	Unc	BU
2006	—	—	—	—	8.50	12.00

KM# 23   CROWN
25.0000 g., Copper-Nickel, 38.8 mm. **Ruler:** Elizabeth II **Series:**
Privateering ships of the South Atlantic **Obv:** Crowned bust right
Obv. Legend: ELIZABETH II — TRISTAN DA CUNHA **Rev:**
Sailing ship "Cabot" **Edge:** Reeded

Date	Mintage	F	VF	XF	Unc	BU
2006	—	—	—	—	8.50	12.00

KM# 24   CROWN
25.0000 g., Copper-Nickel, 38.8 mm. **Ruler:** Elizabeth II **Series:**
Privateering ships of the South Atlantic **Obv:** Crowned bust right
Obv. Legend: ELIZABETH II — TRISTAN DA CUNHA **Rev:**
Sailing ship "Black Prince" **Edge:** Reeded

Date	Mintage	F	VF	XF	Unc	BU
2006	—	—	—	—	8.50	12.00

KM# 25   CROWN
25.0000 g., Copper-Nickel, 38.8 mm. **Ruler:** Elizabeth II **Series:**
Privateering ships of the South Atlantic **Obv:** Crowned bust right
Obv. Legend: ELIZABETH II — TRISTAN DA CUNHA **Rev:**
Sailing ship "Argus" **Edge:** Reeded

Date	Mintage	F	VF	XF	Unc	BU
2006	—	—	—	—	8.50	12.00

KM# 26   CROWN
25.0000 g., Copper-Nickel, 38.8 mm. **Ruler:** Elizabeth II **Series:**
Privateering ships of the South Atlantic **Obv:** Crowned bust right
Obv. Legend: ELIZABETH II — TRISTAN DA CUNHA **Rev:**
Sailing ship "True Blooded Yankee" **Edge:** Reeded

Date	Mintage	F	VF	XF	Unc	BU
2006	—	—	—	—	8.50	12.00

KM# 35   CROWN
Copper-Nickel, 38.75 mm. **Ruler:** Elizabeth II **Rev:** HMS Victory

Date	Mintage	F	VF	XF	Unc	BU
2008	—	—	—	—	—	15.00

KM# 36   CROWN
25.1800 g., Copper-Nickel **Ruler:** Elizabeth II **Obv:** HMS Belfast

Date	Mintage	F	VF	XF	Unc	BU
2008	—	—	—	—	—	15.00

KM# 37   CROWN
25.1800 g., Copper-Nickel, 38.75 mm. **Ruler:** Elizabeth II **Obv:**
HMS Sceptre

Date	Mintage	F	VF	XF	Unc	BU
2008	—	—	—	—	—	15.00

KM# 38   CROWN
25.1800 g., Copper-Nickel, 38.75 mm. **Ruler:** Elizabeth II **Obv:**
HMS Beagle

Date	Mintage	F	VF	XF	Unc	BU
2008	—	—	—	—	—	15.00

KM# 39   CROWN
28.1500 g., Copper-Nickel, 38.75 mm. **Ruler:** Elizabeth II **Obv:**
HMS Dreadnought

Date	Mintage	F	VF	XF	Unc	BU
2008	—	—	—	—	—	15.00

KM# 34   CROWN
Copper-Nickel, 39 mm. **Ruler:** Elizabeth II **Obv:** Bust right **Rev:**
Two whales

Date	Mintage	F	VF	XF	Unc	BU
2008	—	—	—	—	—	15.00

KM# 34a CROWN
Copper-Nickel, 38 mm. **Ruler:** Elizabeth II **Obv:** Head with tiara right **Rev:** 2 whales, multicolor

Date	Mintage	F	VF	XF	Unc	BU
2008	—			—	8.00	15.00

KM# 40 CROWN
28.1500 g., Copper-Nickel, 38.75 mm. **Ruler:** Elizabeth II **Rev:** H.M.S. Ark Royal

Date	Mintage	F	VF	XF	Unc	BU
2008	—			—		15.00

KM# 42 5 POUNDS
Silver **Ruler:** Elizabeth II **Rev:** St. George slaying dragon

Date	Mintage	F	VF	XF	Unc	BU
2008	—			—	45.00	50.00

KM# 45 5 POUNDS
Silver, 38.6 mm. **Ruler:** Elizabeth II **Obv:** Bust in tiara right **Rev:** Titles of the Queen

Date	Mintage	F	VF	XF	Unc	BU
2008 Proof			Value: 50.00			

PIEDFORT

KM#	Date	Mintage	Identification	Mkt Val
P1	2001	500	50 Pence. 0.9250 Silver. 56.5400 g. 38.6 mm.	100
P2	2001	500	50 Pence. 0.9250 Silver. 56.5600 g. 38.6 mm. Reeded edge. Proof KM-13a.	100

GOUGH ISLAND
DEPENDANCY
DECIMAL COINAGE

KM# 1 HALFPENNY
Copper Plated Steel, 17 mm. **Ruler:** Elizabeth II **Obv:** Bust right **Obv. Legend:** GOUGH ISLAND Tristan da Cunha **Rev:** Gough moorhen **Edge:** Plain

Date	Mintage	F	VF	XF	Unc	BU
2009	—			—	0.75	1.00

KM# 2 PENNY
Copper Plated Steel, 18.5 mm. **Ruler:** Elizabeth II **Obv:** Bust right **Obv. Legend:** GOUGH ISLAND Tristan da Cunha **Rev:** Pair of Sooty Albatross **Edge:** Plain

Date	Mintage	F	VF	XF	Unc	BU
2009	—			—	1.00	1.50

KM# 3 2 PENCE
Copper Plated Steel, 22 mm. **Ruler:** Elizabeth II **Obv:** Bust right **Obv. Legend:** GOUGH ISLAND Tristan da Cunha **Rev:** Pair of Antarctic Tern **Edge:** Plain

Date	Mintage	F	VF	XF	Unc	BU
2009	—			—	1.50	2.00

KM# 4 5 PENCE
Copper-Nickel Plated Steel, 17 mm. **Ruler:** Elizabeth II **Obv:** Bust right **Obv. Legend:** GOUGH ISLAND Tristan da Cunha **Rev:** Northern Rock Hopper Penguins **Edge:** Plain

Date	Mintage	F	VF	XF	Unc	BU
2009	—			—	2.00	2.50

KM# 5 10 PENCE
Copper-Nickel Plated Steel, 22 mm. **Ruler:** Elizabeth II **Obv:** Bust right **Obv. Legend:** GOUGH ISLAND Tristan da Cunha **Rev:** Giant Petrel on water **Edge:** Plain

Date	Mintage	F	VF	XF	Unc	BU
2009	—			—	3.00	3.50

KM# 6 20 PENCE
Brass, 22 mm. **Ruler:** Elizabeth II **Obv:** Bust right **Obv. Legend:** GOUGH ISLAND Tristan da Cunha **Rev:** Antarctic Skua **Edge:** Plain

Date	Mintage	F	VF	XF	Unc	BU
2009	—			—	4.50	5.00

KM# 7 25 PENCE
Bi-Metallic Brass center in Copper-Nickel ring, 25.8 mm. **Ruler:** Elizabeth II **Obv:** Bust right **Obv. Legend:** GOUGH ISLAND Tristan da Cunha **Rev:** Barn Owl **Edge:** Plain

Date	Mintage	F	VF	XF	Unc	BU
2009	—			—	8.00	9.00

KM# 8 CROWN
Copper-Nickel, 38.8 mm. **Ruler:** Elizabeth II **Obv:** Bust right **Obv. Legend:** GOUGH ISLAND Tristan da Cunha **Rev:** Peregrine Falcon **Edge:** Plain

Date	Mintage	F	VF	XF	Unc	BU
2009	—			—	12.00	14.00

STOLTENHOFF ISLAND
DEPENCENCY
DECIMAL COINAGE

KM# 1 HALFPENNY
Copper Plated Steel, 17 mm. **Ruler:** Elizabeth II **Obv:** Bust right **Rev:** Small sailboat - West Riding Tragedy Longboat

Date	Mintage	F	VF	XF	Unc	BU
2008	—			—	0.75	1.00

KM# 2 PENNY
Copper Plated Steel **Ruler:** Elizabeth II **Obv:** Bust right **Rev:** 18th century sailing ship - Portuguese Carrack type

Date	Mintage	F	VF	XF	Unc	BU
2008	—			—	1.00	1.50

KM# 3 2 PENCE
Copper Plated Steel, 21.5 mm. **Ruler:** Elizabeth II **Obv:** Bust right **Rev:** Three masted sailing ship - HMS Julia

Date	Mintage	F	VF	XF	Unc	BU
2008	—			—	1.50	2.00

KM# 4 5 PENCE
Copper-Nickel Plated Steel, 16 mm. **Ruler:** Elizabeth II **Obv:**
Bust right **Rev:** Two masted sailing ship - HMS Beagle

Date	Mintage	F	VF	XF	Unc	BU
2008	—				2.00	2.50

KM# 5 10 PENCE
Copper-Nickel Plated Steel, 21.5 mm. **Ruler:** Elizabeth II **Obv:**
Bust right **Rev:** Three masted sailing ship - Blenden Hall

Date	Mintage	F	VF	XF	Unc	BU
2008	—				3.00	3.50

KM# 6 20 PENCE
Brass, 21.5 mm. **Ruler:** Elizabeth II **Obv:** Bust right **Rev:** Two
masted sailing ship - HMS Satellite

Date	Mintage	F	VF	XF	Unc	BU
2008	—				4.50	5.00

KM# 7 25 PENCE
Bi-Metallic Brass center in Copper-Nickel ring, 25 mm. **Ruler:**
Elizabeth II **Obv:** Bust right **Rev:** Sailing ship - Iron Barque West
Riding

Date	Mintage	F	VF	XF	Unc	BU
2008	—				7.00	8.00

KM# 8 CROWN
Copper-Nickel, 39 mm. **Ruler:** Elizabeth II **Obv:** Bust right **Rev:**
Sailing ship L'Heure du Berger

Date	Mintage	F	VF	XF	Unc	BU
2008	—				10.00	12.00

TUNISIA

The Republic of Tunisia, located on the northern coast of
Africa between Algeria and Libya, has an area of 63,170sq. mi.
(163,610 sq. km.) and a population of *7.9 million. Capital: Tunis.
Agriculture is the backbone of the economy. Crude oil, phosphates, olive oil, and wine are exported.

TITLES

المملكة التونسية

al-Mamlaka al-Tunisiya

الجمهورية التونسية

al-Jumhuriya al-Tunisiya

al-Amala al-Tunisiya
  (Tunisian Protectorate)

REPUBLIC

DECIMAL COINAGE
1000 Millim = 1 Dinar

KM# 348 5 MILLIM
1.4900 g., Aluminum, 24 mm. **Obv:** Oak tree and dates **Rev:**
Value within sprigs

Date	Mintage	F	VF	XF	Unc	BU
AH1425-2004	—				0.50	—
AH1426-2005	—				0.50	—

KM# 306 10 MILLIM
3.5000 g., Brass, 19 mm. **Obv:** Inscription and dates within inner
circle of design **Rev:** Value in center of design **Edge:** Reeded

Date	Mintage	F	VF	XF	Unc	BU
AH1425-2004	—	—	0.15	0.25	0.50	—
AH1426-2005	—	—	0.15	0.25	0.50	—
AH1429-2008	—	—	0.15	0.25	0.50	—
AH1432-2011	—	—	0.15	0.25	0.50	—

KM# 307 20 MILLIM
4.5000 g., Brass, 22 mm. **Obv:** Inscription and dates within
center circle of design **Rev:** Value within center of design

Date	Mintage	F	VF	XF	Unc	BU
AH1425-2004	—	—	—	0.50	0.80	—
AH1426-2005	—	—	—	0.50	0.80	—
AH1428-2007	—	—	—	0.50	0.80	—
AH1430-2009	—	—	—	0.50	0.80	—
AH1432-2011	—	—	—	0.50	0.80	—

KM# 308 50 MILLIM
6.0000 g., Brass, 25 mm. **Obv:** Inscription and dates within
center circle of design **Rev:** Value in center of design

Date	Mintage	F	VF	XF	Unc	BU
AH1425-2004	—	—	0.65	0.85	1.25	—
AH1426-2005	—	—	0.65	0.85	1.25	—
AH1428-2007	—	—	0.65	0.85	1.25	—

KM# 309 100 MILLIM
7.5000 g., Brass, 27 mm. **Obv:** Inscription and dates within
center circle of design **Rev:** Value in center of design

Date	Mintage	F	VF	XF	Unc	BU
AH1425-2004	—	—	1.25	1.50	2.00	—
AH1426-2005	—	—	1.25	1.50	2.00	—
AH1427-2006	—	—	1.25	1.50	2.00	—
AH1429-2008	—	—	1.25	1.50	2.00	—
AH1432-2011	—	—	1.25	1.50	2.00	—

KM# 346 1/2 DINAR
Copper-Nickel **Obv:** Shield within circle **Rev:** 2 hands with fruit
and wheat sprig **Note:** Rim width varieties exist.

Date	Mintage	F	VF	XF	Unc	BU
AH1426-2005	—	—	1.00	2.50	4.50	—
AH1428-2007	—	—	1.00	2.50	4.50	—
AH1430-2009	—	—	1.00	2.50	4.50	—
AH1432-2011	—	—	1.00	2.50	4.50	—

KM# 347 DINAR
10.1000 g., Copper-Nickel, 28 mm. **Series:** F.A.O. **Obv:** Shield
within circle **Rev:** Female half figure right

Date	Mintage	F	VF	XF	Unc	BU
AH1428-2007	—	—	2.00	4.00	7.50	—
AH1430-2009	—	—	2.00	4.00	7.50	—
AH1432-2011	—	—	2.00	4.00	7.50	—

KM# 330 5 DINARS
9.4060 g., 0.9000 Gold 0.2722 oz. AGW **Subject:** Anniversary
of 7 Nov 1987 **Obv:** Shield **Rev:** Upstretched hand, flag **Note:**
Arabic legends vary by year.

Date	Mintage	F	VF	XF	Unc	BU
2001-1421	40	—	—	—	650	700

KM# 329 5 DINARS
9.4060 g., 0.9000 Gold 0.2722 oz. AGW **Subject:** Anniversary
of 7 Nov 1987 **Obv:** Shield **Rev:** Upstretched hand, flag **Note:**
French legends vary by year.

Date	Mintage	F	VF	XF	Unc	BU
2001-1422	40	—	—	—	650	700

KM# 435   5 DINARS
9.4800 g., 0.9000 Gold 0.2743 oz. AGW, 22 mm. **Subject:** 7 November 1987, 15th Anniversary **Obv:** Shield **Rev:** Stylized dove **Note:** Arabic legends

Date	Mintage	F	VF	XF	Unc	BU
AH1423-2002 Proof	40	Value: 750				

KM# 436   5 DINARS
9.4800 g., 0.9000 Gold 0.2743 oz. AGW, 22 mm. **Subject:** 7 November 1987, 15th Anniversary **Obv:** Shield **Rev:** Stylized dove **Note:** French legends

Date	Mintage	F	VF	XF	Unc	BU
AH1423-2002 Proof	40	Value: 750				

KM# 443   5 DINARS
Bi-Metallic Silver center in Gold ring, 29 mm. **Subject:** 2nd Anniversary of Death **Obv:** Shield **Rev:** Head left

Date	Mintage	F	VF	XF	Unc	BU
AH1423-2002 Proof	750	Value: 275				

KM# 444   5 DINARS
10.0000 g., Bi-Metallic Copper-Nickel center in Copper ring, 29 mm. **Obv:** Shield **Rev:** Head left

Date	Mintage	F	VF	XF	Unc	BU
AH1423-2002	20,275,000	—	—	—	8.00	10.00

KM# 350   5 DINARS
10.0000 g., Bi-Metallic Copper-Nickel center in Aluminum-Bronze ring, 29 mm. **Obv:** National arms **Rev:** Former President Habib Bourguiba **Edge:** Segmented reeding **Shape:** 12-sided

Date	Mintage	F	VF	XF	Unc	BU
AH1423-2002	—	—	—	—	6.50	8.00

KM# 350a   5 DINARS
Bi-Metallic .925 Silver center in .900 gold ring, 29 mm. **Obv:** National arms **Rev:** Former President Habib Bourguiba **Edge:** 6 reeded and 6 plain sections **Shape:** 12-sided

Date	Mintage	F	VF	XF	Unc	BU
AH1423-2002 Proof	—	Value: 350				

KM# 445   5 DINARS
9.4800 g., 0.9000 Gold 0.2743 oz. AGW, 22 mm. **Subject:** 7 November 1987, 16th Anniversary **Obv:** Shield **Rev:** Hand with UN logo **Note:** Arabic legends

Date	Mintage	F	VF	XF	Unc	BU
AH1424-2003 Proof	40	Value: 750				

KM# 446   5 DINARS
9.4800 g., 0.9000 Gold 0.2743 oz. AGW, 22 mm. **Subject:** 7 November 1987, 16th Anniversary **Obv:** Shield **Rev:** Hand with UN logo **Note:** French legend

Date	Mintage	F	VF	XF	Unc	BU
AH1424-2003 Proof	40	Value: 750				

KM# 456   5 DINARS
9.4000 g., 0.9000 Gold 0.2720 oz. AGW, 22 mm. **Subject:** 7 November 1987, 17th Anniversary - Elections **Obv:** Shield **Rev:** Star and crescent and stylized flame **Note:** French legend

Date	Mintage	F	VF	XF	Unc	BU
AH1425-2004 Proof	40	Value: 750				

KM# 455   5 DINARS
9.4000 g., 0.9000 Gold 0.2720 oz. AGW, 22 mm. **Subject:** 7 November 1987, 17th Anniversary - Elections **Obv:** Shield **Rev:** Star and crescent and stylized flame **Note:** Arabic legend

Date	Mintage	F	VF	XF	Unc	BU
AH1425-2004 Proof	40	Value: 750				

KM# 465   5 DINARS
9.4000 g., 0.9000 Gold 0.2720 oz. AGW, 22 mm. **Subject:** 7 November 1987, 18th Anniversary **Obv:** Shield **Rev:** Globe in stylized ship **Note:** Arabic legend

Date	Mintage	F	VF	XF	Unc	BU
AH1426-2005 Proof	40	Value: 750				

KM# 466   5 DINARS
9.4000 g., 0.9000 Gold 0.2720 oz. AGW, 22 mm. **Subject:** 7 November 1987, 18th Anniversary **Obv:** Shield **Rev:** Globe in stylized ship **Note:** French legend

Date	Mintage	F	VF	XF	Unc	BU
AH1426-2005 Prook	40	Value: 750				

KM# 479   5 DINARS
9.4000 g., 0.9000 Gold 0.2720 oz. AGW, 22 mm. **Subject:** 7 November 1987, 19th Anniversary **Obv:** Shield **Rev:** Dove and atom **Note:** French legend

Date	Mintage	F	VF	XF	Unc	BU
AH1427-2006 Proof	40	Value: 750				

KM# 472   5 DINARS
24.0000 g., 0.9000 Silver 0.6944 oz. ASW, 35 mm. **Subject:** 50th Anniversary **Obv:** Shield **Rev:** Logo **Note:** Arabic legend

Date	Mintage	F	VF	XF	Unc	BU
AH1427-2006 Proof	900	Value: 125				

KM# 478   5 DINARS
9.4000 g., 0.9000 Gold 0.2720 oz. AGW, 22 mm. **Subject:** 7 November 1987, 19th Anniversary **Obv:** Shield **Rev:** Dove and atom **Note:** Arabic legends

Date	Mintage	F	VF	XF	Unc	BU
AH1427-2006 Proof	40	Value: 750				

KM# 473   5 DINARS
24.0000 g., 0.9000 Silver 0.6944 oz. ASW, 35 mm. **Subject:** 50th Anniversary **Obv:** Shield **Rev:** Logo **Note:** French legends

Date	Mintage	F	VF	XF	Unc	BU
AH1427-2006 Proof	100	Value: 225				

KM# 491   5 DINARS
9.4000 g., 0.9000 Gold 0.2720 oz. AGW, 22 mm. **Subject:** 7 November 1987, 20th Anniversary **Obv:** Head of Zine el Abidine Ben Ali right **Rev:** Two profiles, keyboard, satellite receiver **Note:** French legends

Date	Mintage	F	VF	XF	Unc	BU
AH1428-2007 Proof	40	Value: 750				

KM# 486   5 DINARS
24.0000 g., 0.9000 Silver 0.6944 oz. ASW, 35 mm. **Subject:** 50th Anniversary **Obv:** Shield **Rev:** Ship, scales of Justice **Note:** Arabic legend

Date	Mintage	F	VF	XF	Unc	BU
AH1428-2007 Proof	900	Value: 125				

KM# 490   5 DINARS
9.4000 g., 0.9000 Gold 0.2720 oz. AGW, 22 mm. **Subject:** 7

November 1987, 20th Anniversary **Obv:** Head of Zine el Abidne Ben Ali right **Rev:** Two profiles, keyboard, satellite receiver **Note:** Arabic legend

Date	Mintage	F	VF	XF	Unc	BU
AH1428-2007 Proof	43	Value: 750				

KM# 487   5 DINARS
24.0000 g., 0.9000 Silver 0.6944 oz. ASW, 35 mm. **Subject:** 50th Anniversary **Obv:** Shield **Rev:** Ship, scales of Justice **Note:** French legend

Date	Mintage	F	VF	XF	Unc	BU
AH1428-2007 Proof	100	Value: 225				

KM# 378   10 DINARS
38.0000 g., 0.9000 Silver 1.0995 oz. ASW **Subject:** 14th Anniversary 7 Nov and 19th Mediterranean Games **Edge:** Reeded

Date	Mintage	F	VF	XF	Unc	BU
AH1422-2001	—	—	—	—	275	—

KM# 341   10 DINARS
18.7700 g., 0.9000 Gold 0.5431 oz. AGW **Subject:** Anniversary - 7 Nov 1987 **Obv:** Shield **Rev:** Upstretched hand, flag **Note:** Arabic legends vary by year.

Date	Mintage	F	VF	XF	Unc	BU
2001-1422	40	—	—	—	1,025	1,050

KM# 430   10 DINARS
38.0000 g., 0.9000 Silver 1.0995 oz. ASW, 40 mm. **Subject:** 7 November 1987, 14th Anniversary **Obv:** Shield **Rev:** Open door **Note:** French legend

Date	Mintage	F	VF	XF	Unc	BU
AH1422-2001 Proof	400	Value: 150				

KM# 340   10 DINARS
18.7700 g., 0.9000 Gold 0.5431 oz. AGW **Subject:** Anniversary - 7 Nov 1987 **Obv:** Shield **Rev:** Upstretched hand, flag **Note:** French legends vary by year.

Date	Mintage	F	VF	XF	Unc	BU
2001-1422	40	—	—	—	1,025	1,050

KM# 438   10 DINARS
18.8000 g., 0.9000 Gold 0.5440 oz. AGW, 28 mm. **Subject:** 7 November 1987, 15th Anniversary **Obv:** Shield **Rev:** Stylized dove **Note:** French legends

Date	Mintage	F	VF	XF	Unc	BU
AH1423-2002 Proof	40	Value: 1,000				

KM# 379   10 DINARS
38.0000 g., 0.9000 Silver 1.0995 oz. ASW **Subject:** 15th Anniversary 7 Nov 1987 **Obv:** National arms **Edge:** Reeded

Date	Mintage	F	VF	XF	Unc	BU
AH1423-2002	—	—	—	—	275	—

KM# 433   10 DINARS
38.0000 g., 0.9000 Silver 1.0995 oz. ASW, 40 mm. **Subject:** 7 November 1987, 15th Anniversary **Obv:** Shield **Rev:** Stylized dove **Note:** Arabic legends

Date	Mintage	F	VF	XF	Unc	BU
AH1423-2002 Proof	490	Value: 150				

KM# 437   10 DINARS
18.8000 g., 0.9000 Gold 0.5440 oz. AGW, 28 mm. **Subject:** 7 November 1987, 15th Anniversary **Obv:** Shield **Rev:** Stylized dove **Note:** Arabic legends

Date	Mintage	F	VF	XF	Unc	BU
AH1423-2002 Proof	40	Value: 1,000				

KM# 380   10 DINARS
38.0000 g., 0.9000 Silver 1.0995 oz. ASW **Subject:** 16th Anniversary 7 Nov 1987 plus International Solidarity Fund **Obv:** National arms **Rev:** Large 16 with hands holding globe within the 6, banner which says International Solidarity Fund **Edge:** Reeded

Date	Mintage	F	VF	XF	Unc	BU
AH1424-2003	—	—	—	—	250	—
AH1424-2003 Proof	—	Value: 300				

KM# 452   10 DINARS
38.0000 g., 0.9000 Silver 1.0995 oz. ASW, 40 mm. **Subject:** 7 November 1987, 16th Anniversary **Obv:** Shield **Rev:** Large 16 and globe

Date	Mintage	F	VF	XF	Unc	BU
AH1423-2003 Proof	24	Value: 225				

KM# 447   10 DINARS
18.1800 g., 0.9000 Gold 0.5260 oz. AGW, 28 mm. **Subject:** 7 November 1987, 16th Anniversary **Obv:** Shield **Rev:** Hand with UN logo **Note:** Arabic legend

Date	Mintage	F	VF	XF	Unc	BU
AH1424-2003 Proof	40	Value: 1,000				

KM# 448   10 DINARS
18.1800 g., 0.9000 Gold 0.5260 oz. AGW, 28 mm. **Subject:** 7 November 1987, 16th Anniversary **Obv:** Shield **Rev:** Hand with UN logo **Note:** French legends

Date	Mintage	F	VF	XF	Unc	BU
AH1424-2003 Proof	40	Value: 1,000				

KM# 454   10 DINARS
38.0000 g., 0.9000 Silver 1.0995 oz. ASW, 40 mm. **Subject:** 7 November 1987, 17th Anniversary - Elections **Obv:** Shield **Rev:** Star and crescent and stylized flame **Note:** French legends

Date	Mintage	F	VF	XF	Unc	BU
AH1425-2004 Proof	24	Value: 225				

KM# 458   10 DINARS
18.8000 g., 0.9000 Gold 0.5440 oz. AGW, 28 mm. **Subject:** 7 November 1987, 17th Anniversary - Elections **Obv:** Shield **Rev:** Star and crescent adn stylized flame **Note:** French legend

Date	Mintage	F	VF	XF	Unc	BU
AH1425-2004 Proof	40	Value: 1,000				

KM# 457   10 DINARS
18.8000 g., 0.9000 Gold 0.5440 oz. AGW, 28 mm. **Subject:** 7 November 1987, 17th Anniversary - Elections **Obv:** Shield **Rev:** Star and crescent and stylized flame **Note:** Arabic legend

Date	Mintage	F	VF	XF	Unc	BU
AH1425-2004 Proof	40	Value: 1,000				

KM# 381   10 DINARS
38.0000 g., 0.9000 Silver 1.0995 oz. ASW **Subject:** 17th Anniversary of 7 Nov 1987 plus Elections of President and Parliament **Obv:** National arms **Edge:** Reeded

Date	Mintage	F	VF	XF	Unc	BU
AH1425-2004	—	—	—	—	275	—

KM# 453   10 DINARS
38.0000 g., 0.9000 Silver 1.0995 oz. ASW, 40 mm. **Subject:** 7 November 1987, 17th Anniversary - Elections **Obv:** Shield **Rev:** Star and crescent and stylized flame **Note:** Arabic legends

Date	Mintage	F	VF	XF	Unc	BU
AH1425-2004 Proof	375	Value: 150				

KM# 467 10 DINARS
18.8000 g., 0.9000 Gold 0.5440 oz. AGW **Subject:** 7 November 1987, 18th Anniversary **Obv:** Shield **Rev:** Globe in stylized ship **Shape:** 28 **Note:** Arabic legends

Date	Mintage	F	VF	XF	Unc	BU
AH1426-2005 Proof	40	Value: 1,000				

KM# 382 10 DINARS
38.0000 g., 0.9000 Silver 1.0995 oz. ASW **Subject:** 18th Anniversary of 7 Nov 1987 and Conference on Information in Tunis 2005 **Edge:** Reeded

Date	Mintage	F	VF	XF	Unc	BU
AH1426-2005	—	—	—	—	275	—

KM# 464 10 DINARS
38.0000 g., 0.9000 Silver 1.0995 oz. ASW, 40 mm. **Subject:** 7 November 1987, 18th Anniversary **Obv:** Shield **Rev:** Globe in stylized ship **Note:** Arabic legend

Date	Mintage	F	VF	XF	Unc	BU
AH1426-2005 Proof	431	Value: 150				

KM# 468 10 DINARS
18.8000 g., 0.9000 Gold 0.5440 oz. AGW, 28 mm. **Subject:** 7 November 1987, 18th Anniversary **Obv:** Shield **Rev:** Globe in stylized ship **Note:** French legend

Date	Mintage	F	VF	XF	Unc	BU
AH1426-2005 Proof	40	Value: 1,000				

KM# 463 10 DINARS
38.0000 g., 0.9000 Silver 1.0995 oz. ASW, 40 mm. **Subject:** 7 November 1987, 18th Anniversary **Obv:** Shield **Rev:** Globe in stylized ship **Note:** French legends

Date	Mintage	F	VF	XF	Unc	BU
AH1426-2005 Proof	50	Value: 175				

KM# 475 10 DINARS
18.8000 g., 0.9000 Gold 0.5440 oz. AGW, 28 mm. **Subject:** 50th Anniversary **Obv:** Shield **Rev:** Logo **Note:** French legends

Date	Mintage	F	VF	XF	Unc	BU
AH1427-2006 Proof	200	Value: 1,000				

KM# 477 10 DINARS
38.0000 g., 0.9000 Silver 1.0995 oz. ASW, 40 mm. **Subject:** 7 November 1987, 19th Anniversary **Obv:** Shield **Rev:** Dove and atom **Note:** French legend

Date	Mintage	F	VF	XF	Unc	BU
AH1427-2006 Proof	30	Value: 225				

KM# 481 10 DINARS
18.8000 g., 0.9000 Gold 0.5440 oz. AGW, 28 mm. **Subject:** 7 November 1987, 19th Anniversary **Obv:** Shield **Rev:** Dove and atom **Note:** French legend

Date	Mintage	F	VF	XF	Unc	BU
AH1427-2006 Proof	40	Value: 1,000				

KM# 476 10 DINARS
38.0000 g., 0.9000 Silver 1.0995 oz. ASW, 40 mm. **Subject:** 7 November 1987, 19th Anniversary **Obv:** Shield **Rev:** Dove and atom **Note:** Arabic legend

Date	Mintage	F	VF	XF	Unc	BU
AH1427-2006 Proof	300	Value: 150				

KM# 480 10 DINARS
18.8000 g., 0.9000 Gold 0.5440 oz. AGW, 28 mm. **Subject:** 7 November 1987, 19th Anniversary **Obv:** Shield **Rev:** Dove and atom **Note:** Arabic legend

Date	Mintage	F	VF	XF	Unc	BU
AH1427-2006 Proof	40	Value: 1,000				

KM# 383 10 DINARS
38.0000 g., 0.9000 Silver 1.0995 oz. ASW **Subject:** 50th Anniversary of Independence (12.3.1956) **Obv:** National arms **Rev:** Stylized bird, "50", crescent moon with stars

Date	Mintage	F	VF	XF	Unc	BU
AH1427-2006	—	—	—	—	275	—

KM# 383a 10 DINARS
19.0000 g., 0.9000 Gold 0.5498 oz. AGW **Subject:** 50th Anniversary of Independence

Date	Mintage	F	VF	XF	Unc	BU
AH1427-2006 Proof	600	Value: 1,000				

KM# 474 10 DINARS
18.8000 g., 0.9000 Gold 0.5440 oz. AGW, 28 mm. **Subject:** 50th Anniversary **Obv:** Shield **Rev:** Logo **Note:** Arabic legends

Date	Mintage	F	VF	XF	Unc	BU
AH1427-2006 Proof	1,800	Value: 950				

KM# 488 10 DINARS
18.8000 g., 0.9000 Gold 0.5440 oz. AGW, 28 mm. **Subject:** 50th Anniversary **Obv:** Shield **Rev:** Ship, scales of Justice **Note:** Arabic legend

Date	Mintage	F	VF	XF	Unc	BU
AH1428-2007 Proof	450	Value: 975				

KM# 492 10 DINARS
18.8000 g., 0.9000 Gold 0.5440 oz. AGW, 28 mm. **Subject:** 7 November 1987, 20th Anniversary **Obv:** Head of Zine El abidine Ben Ali right **Rev:** Two profiles, keyboard, satellite receiver **Note:** Arabic legend

Date	Mintage	F	VF	XF	Unc	BU
AH1428-2007 Proof	42	Value: 1,000				

KM# 489 10 DINARS
18.8000 g., 0.9000 Gold 0.5440 oz. AGW, 28 mm. **Subject:** 50th Anniversary **Obv:** Shield **Rev:** Ship, scales of Justice **Note:** French legend

Date	Mintage	F	VF	XF	Unc	BU
AH1428-2007 Proof	50	Value: 1,000				

KM# 493 10 DINARS
18.8000 g., 0.9000 Gold 0.5440 oz. AGW, 28 mm. **Subject:** 7 November 1987, 20th Anniversary **Obv:** Head of Zine El Abidine Ben Ali right **Rev:** Two profiles, keyboard, satellite receiver **Note:** French legends

Date	Mintage	F	VF	XF	Unc	BU
AH1428-2007 Proof	40	Value: 1,000				

KM# 396 50 DINARS
21.0000 g., 0.9000 Gold 0.6076 oz. AGW, 34 mm. **Subject:** 14th Anniversary 7 Nov 1987 and 19th Mediterranean Games **Edge:** Reeded **Note:** Arabic legends.

Date	Mintage	F	VF	XF	Unc	BU
AH1422-2001 Proof	—	Value: 1,200				

KM# 431 50 DINARS
21.0000 g., 0.9000 Gold 0.6076 oz. AGW, 34 mm. **Subject:** 7 November 1987, 14th Anniversary **Obv:** Shield **Rev:** Open door **Note:** French legends

Date	Mintage	F	VF	XF	Unc	BU
AH1422-2001 Proof	150	Value: 1,150				

KM# 397 50 DINARS
21.0000 g., 0.9000 Gold 0.6076 oz. AGW, 34 mm. **Subject:** 15th Anniversary of 7 Nov 1987 **Edge:** Reeded

Date	Mintage	F	VF	XF	Unc	BU
AH1423-2002 Proof	—	Value: 1,200				

KM# 440 50 DINARS
21.0000 g., 0.9000 Gold 0.6076 oz. AGW, 21 mm. **Subject:** 7 November 1987, 15th Anniversary **Obv:** Shield **Rev:** Stylized dove

Date	Mintage	F	VF	XF	Unc	BU
AH1423-2002 Proof	80	Value: 1,250				

KM# 439 50 DINARS
21.0000 g., 0.9000 Gold 0.6076 oz. AGW, 34 mm. **Subject:** 7 November 1987, 15th Anniversary **Obv:** Shield **Rev:** Stylized dove **Note:** Arabic legend

Date	Mintage	F	VF	XF	Unc	BU
AH1423-2002 Proof	580	Value: 1,100				

KM# 450 50 DINARS
21.0000 g., 0.9000 Gold 0.6076 oz. AGW, 34 mm. **Subject:** 7 November 1987, 16th Anniversary **Obv:** Shield **Rev:** Hand with UN logo **Note:** French legends

Date	Mintage	F	VF	XF	Unc	BU
AH1424-2003 Proof	55	Value: 1,250				

KM# 449 50 DINARS
21.0000 g., 0.9000 Gold 0.6076 oz. AGW, 34 mm. **Subject:** 7 November 1987, 16th Anniversary **Obv:** Shield **Rev:** Hand with UN logo **Note:** Arabic legends

Date	Mintage	F	VF	XF	Unc	BU
AH1424-2003 Proof	545	Value: 1,100				

KM# 459 50 DINARS
21.0000 g., 0.9000 Gold 0.6076 oz. AGW, 34 mm. **Subject:** 7 November 1987, 17th Anniversary - Elections **Obv:** Shield **Rev:** Star and crescent and stylized flame **Note:** Arabic legend

Date	Mintage	F	VF	XF	Unc	BU
AH1425-2004 Proof	379	Value: 1,100				

KM# 398 50 DINARS
21.0000 g., 0.9000 Gold 0.6076 oz. AGW, 34 mm. **Subject:** 17th Anniversary of 7 Nov 1987 plus Elections of President and Parliament **Edge:** Reeded

Date	Mintage	F	VF	XF	Unc	BU
AH1425-2004 Proof	—	Value: 1,250				

KM# 460 50 DINARS
21.0000 g., 0.9000 Gold 0.6076 oz. AGW, 34 mm. **Subject:** 7 November 1987, 17th Anniversary - Elections **Obv:** Shield **Rev:** Star and crescent and stylized flame **Note:** French legend

Date	Mintage	F	VF	XF	Unc	BU
AH1425-2004 Proof	28	Value: 1,250				

KM# 470 50 DINARS
21.0000 g., 0.9000 Gold 0.6076 oz. AGW, 34 mm. **Subject:** 7 November 1987, 18th Anniversary **Obv:** Shield **Rev:** Globe and stylized ship **Note:** French legend

Date	Mintage	F	VF	XF	Unc	BU
AH1426-2005 Proof	45	Value: 1,250				

KM# 482 50 DINARS
21.0000 g., 0.9000 Gold 0.6076 oz. AGW, 34 mm. **Subject:** 7 November 1987, 19th Anniversary **Obv:** Shield **Rev:** Dove and atom **Note:** Arabic legend

Date	Mintage	F	VF	XF	Unc	BU
AH1427-2006 Proof	183	Value: 1,200				

KM# 483 50 DINARS
21.0000 g., 0.9000 Gold 0.6076 oz. AGW, 34 mm. **Subject:** 7 November 1987, 19th Anniversary **Obv:** Shield **Rev:** Dove and atom **Note:** French legends

Date	Mintage	F	VF	XF	Unc	BU
AH1427-2006 Proof	23	Value: 1,250				

KM# 432 100 DINARS
38.0000 g., 0.9000 Gold 1.0995 oz. AGW, 43 mm. **Subject:** 7 November 1987, 14th Anniversary **Obv:** Shield **Rev:** Open door **Note:** Arabic legend

Date	Mintage	F	VF	XF	Unc	BU
AH1422-2001 Proof	375	Value: 1,750				

KM# 412 100 DINARS
38.0000 g., 0.9000 Gold 1.0995 oz. AGW, 40 mm. **Subject:** 14th Anniversary of 7 Nov 1987 and 19th Mediterranean Games **Obv:** National arms **Rev:** Olympic rings divide 2 portals **Edge:** Reeded

Date	Mintage	F	VF	XF	Unc	BU
AH1422-2001 Proof	—	Value: 1,900				

KM# 441 100 DINARS
38.0000 g., 0.9000 Gold 1.0995 oz. AGW, 43 mm. **Subject:** 7 November 1987, 15th Anniversary **Obv:** Shield **Rev:** Stylized dove **Note:** Arabic legends

Date	Mintage	F	VF	XF	Unc	BU
AH1423-2002 Proof	380	Value: 1,750				

KM# 442 100 DINARS
38.0000 g., 0.9000 Gold 1.0995 oz. AGW, 43 mm. **Subject:** 7 November 1987, 15th Anniversary **Obv:** Shield **Rev:** Stylized dove **Note:** French legend

Date	Mintage	F	VF	XF	Unc	BU
AH1423-2002 Proof	110	Value: 1,800				

KM# 352 100 DINARS
38.0000 g., 0.9000 Gold 1.0995 oz. AGW, 40 mm. **Subject:** United Nations **Obv:** National arms above value **Rev:** UN logo on stylized hand **Edge:** Reeded

Date	Mintage	F	VF	XF	Unc	BU
AH1424-2003 Proof	—	Value: 1,900				

KM# 451   100 DINARS
38.0000 g., 0.9000 Gold 1.0995 oz. AGW, 43 mm. **Subject:** 7 November 1987, 16th Anniversary **Obv:** Shield **Rev:** Hand with UN logo **Note:** French text

Date	Mintage	F	VF	XF	Unc	BU
AH1424-2003 Proof	53	Value: 1,850				

KM# 462   100 DINARS
38.0000 g., 0.9000 Gold 1.0995 oz. AGW, 43 mm. **Subject:** 7 November 1987, 17th Anniversary - Elections **Obv:** Shield **Rev:** Star and crescent and stylized flame **Note:** French legends

Date	Mintage	F	VF	XF	Unc	BU
AH1425-2004 Proof	44	Value: 1,850				

KM# 461   100 DINARS
38.0000 g., 0.9000 Gold 1.0995 oz. AGW, 43 mm. **Subject:** 7 November 1987, 17th Anniversary - Elections **Obv:** Shield **Rev:** Star and crescent and stylized flame **Note:** Arabic legend

Date	Mintage	F	VF	XF	Unc	BU
AH1425-2004 Proof	385	Value: 1,750				

KM# 469   100 DINARS
21.0000 g., 0.9000 Gold 0.6076 oz. AGW, 34 mm. **Subject:** 7 November 1987, 18th Anniversary **Obv:** Shield **Rev:** Globe in stylized ship **Note:** Arabic legend

Date	Mintage	F	VF	XF	Unc	BU
AH1426-2005 Proof	390	Value: 1,100				

KM# 413   100 DINARS
38.0000 g., 0.9000 Gold 1.0995 oz. AGW **Subject:** 18th Anniversary of 7 Nov 1987 and Conference on Information in Tunis 2005 **Edge:** Reeded

Date	Mintage	F	VF	XF	Unc	BU
AH1426-2005 Proof	—	Value: 1,900				

KM# 471   100 DINARS
38.0000 g., 0.9000 Gold 1.0995 oz. AGW, 43 mm. **Subject:** 7 November 1987, 18th Anniversary **Obv:** Shield **Rev:** Globe in stylized ship **Note:** French legends

Date	Mintage	F	VF	XF	Unc	BU
AH1426-2005 Proof	45	Value: 1,850				

KM# 485   100 DINARS
38.0000 g., 0.9000 Gold 1.0995 oz. AGW, 43 mm. **Subject:** 7 November 1987, 19th Anniversary **Obv:** Shield **Rev:** Dove and atom **Note:** French legend

Date	Mintage	F	VF	XF	Unc	BU
AH1427-2006 Proof	23	Value: 2,000				

KM# 484   100 DINARS
38.0000 g., 0.9000 Gold 1.0995 oz. AGW, 43 mm. **Subject:** 7 November 1987, 19th Anniversary **Obv:** Shield **Rev:** Dove and atom **Note:** Arabic legend

Date	Mintage	F	VF	XF	Unc	BU
AH1427-2006 Proof	212	Value: 1,800				

TURKEY

The Republic of Turkey, a parliamentary democracy of the Near East located partially in Europe and partially in Asia between the Black and the Mediterranean Seas, has an area of 301,382 sq. mi. (780,580 sq. km.) and a population of *55.4 million. Capital: Ankara. Turkey exports cotton, hazelnuts, and tobacco, and enjoys a virtual monopoly in meerschaum.

RULER
Republic, AH1341/AD1923-

Mint mark
"d" for darphane (meaning mint) is used on coins for overseas market.

REPUBLIC

DECIMAL COINAGE
Western numerals and Latin alphabet

40 Para = 1 Kurus; 100 Kurus = 1 Lira

KM# 1104   25000 LIRA (25 Bin Lira)
2.7000 g., Brass, 17 mm. **Obv:** Head left **Rev:** Value **Edge:** Plain

Date	Mintage	F	VF	XF	Unc	BU
2001	—	—	—	—	2.00	—
2002	—	—	—	—	2.00	—
2003	—	—	—	—	2.00	—

KM# 1105   50000 LIRA (50 Bin Lira)
3.2000 g., Copper-Nickel-Zinc, 17.75 mm. **Obv:** Head left within circle **Rev:** Value **Edge:** Plain

Date	Mintage	F	VF	XF	Unc	BU
2001	—	—	—	—	0.50	—
2002	—	—	—	—	0.50	—
2003	—	—	—	—	0.50	—
2004	—	—	—	—	0.50	—

KM# 1106   100000 LIRA (100 Bin Lira)
4.6000 g., Copper-Nickel-Zinc, 21 mm. **Obv:** Head with hat right within circle **Rev:** Value **Edge:** Plain

Date	Mintage	F	VF	XF	Unc	BU
2001	—	—	—	—	0.75	1.25
2002	—	—	—	—	0.75	1.25
2003	—	—	—	—	0.75	1.25
2004	—	—	—	—	0.75	1.25

KM# 1137   250000 LIRA
6.4200 g., Copper-Nickel-Zinc, 23.4 mm. **Obv:** Bust facing within circle **Rev:** Value **Edge Lettering:** "T.C." six times dividing reeded sections

Date	Mintage	F	VF	XF	Unc	BU
2002	—	—	—	—	1.00	1.50
2003	—	—	—	—	1.00	1.50
2004	—	—	—	—	1.00	1.50

KM# 1161 500000 LIRA
4.6000 g., Copper-Nickel, 21 mm. **Obv:** Value and date within sprigs **Rev:** One sheep **Edge:** Plain

Date	Mintage	F	VF	XF	Unc	BU
2002	—	—	—	—	2.00	3.00

KM# 1162 750000 LIRA
6.4000 g., Copper-Nickel, 23.5 mm. **Obv:** Value and date within sprigs **Rev:** Angora Ram **Edge:** Plain

Date	Mintage	F	VF	XF	Unc	BU
2002	—	—	—	—	3.00	4.00

KM# 1163 1000000 LIRA
12.0000 g., Copper-Nickel, 31.9 mm. **Obv:** Value and date within sprigs **Rev:** Turbaned bust 1/4 left divides dates **Edge:** Reeded

Date	Mintage	F	VF	XF	Unc	BU
2002	—	—	—	—	5.00	6.00

KM# 1170 1000000 LIRA
31.4200 g., 0.9250 Silver 0.9344 oz. ASW, 38.6 mm. **Subject:** Mevlana Celaleddin-I Rumi **Obv:** Value and date in wreath **Rev:** Turbaned bust **Edge:** Reeded

Date	Mintage	F	VF	XF	Unc	BU
2002 Proof	—	Value: 40.00				

KM# 1139.1 1000000 LIRA
11.8700 g., Bi-Metallic Brass center in Copper-Nickel ring, 32.1 mm. **Subject:** Foundation of the Mint **Obv:** Building and value within circle **Rev:** Legend and date inscription **Edge:** Plain **Note:** This coin type is produced by a machine outside the money museum at the Istanbul Mint. Visitors pay 1 mio lira, press a button and strike a coin with the actual date of their visit. Many other dates exist in unknown and unregistered quantities. Only Turkish months are on struck coins.

Date	Mintage	F	VF	XF	Unc	BU
Mayis 2002	—	—	—	—	5.00	6.00
Haziran 2002	—	—	—	—	5.00	6.00
Temmuz 2002	—	—	—	—	5.00	6.00
Agostos 2002	—	—	—	—	5.00	6.00
Eylul 2002	—	—	—	—	5.00	6.00
Ekim 2002	—	—	—	—	5.00	6.00
Kasim 2002	—	—	—	—	5.00	6.00
Aralik 2002	—	—	—	—	5.00	6.00

KM# 1139.2 1000000 LIRA
Bi-Metallic Brass center in Copper-Nickel ring., 32.1 mm. **Subject:** Foundation of the Mint **Obv:** Building and value within circle **Rev:** Legend and date inscription **Edge:** Plain **Note:** This coin type is produced by a machine outside the money museum at the Istanbul Mint. Visitors pay 1 mio lira, press a button and strike a coin with the actual date of their visit. Many other dates exist in unknown and unregistered quantities. The months are listed in both Turkish and English on struck coins.

Date	Mintage	F	VF	XF	Unc	BU
Ocak/January 2003	—	—	—	—	5.00	6.00
Subat/February 2003	—	—	—	—	5.00	6.00
Mart/March 2003	—	—	—	—	5.00	6.00
Nisan/April 2003	—	—	—	—	5.00	6.00
Mayis/May 2003	—	—	—	—	5.00	6.00
Haziran/June 2003	—	—	—	—	5.00	6.00
Temmuz/July 2003	—	—	—	—	5.00	6.00
Agostos/August 2003	—	—	—	—	5.00	6.00
Eylul/September 2003	—	—	—	—	5.00	6.00
Ekim/October 2003	—	—	—	—	5.00	6.00
Kasim/November 2003	—	—	—	—	5.00	6.00
Aralik/December 2003	—	—	—	—	5.00	6.00

KM# 1107 3000000 LIRA
31.4700 g., 0.9250 Silver 0.9359 oz. ASW, 38.6 mm. **Series:** Olympics **Obv:** Value and date within wreath **Rev:** Long jumper and logo **Edge:** Reeded

Date	Mintage	F	VF	XF	Unc	BU
2002 Proof	—	Value: 42.50				

KM# 1110 5000000 LIRA
67.0000 g., Bronze, 50 mm. **Subject:** Children's Day **Obv:** Legend and inscription **Rev:** Dancing children **Edge:** Plain

Date	Mintage	F	VF	XF	Unc	BU
2001 Matte	1,583	—	—	—	35.00	—

KM# 1142 7500000 LIRA
31.2500 g., 0.9250 Silver 0.9293 oz. ASW, 38.5 mm. **Subject:** Cahit Arf, Turkish mathematician (1910-1997) **Obv:** Mathematical formula within circle **Rev:** 1/2-length figure facing **Edge:** Reeded

Date	Mintage	F	VF	XF	Unc	BU
2001 Proof	—	Value: 45.00				

KM# 1143 7500000 LIRA
31.2500 g., 0.9250 Silver 0.9293 oz. ASW, 38.5 mm. **Obv:** Ornamented circle design **Rev:** 1/2-length bust facing **Edge:** Reeded

Date	Mintage	F	VF	XF	Unc	BU
2001 Proof	—	Value: 45.00				

KM# 1144 7500000 LIRA
31.2500 g., 0.9250 Silver 0.9293 oz. ASW, 38.5 mm. **Subject:** Koca Yusuf Baspehlivan **Obv:** Two figures wrestling **Rev:** Portrait on circular background **Edge:** Reeded

Date	Mintage	F	VF	XF	Unc	BU
2001 Proof	—	Value: 42.50				

KM# 1120 7500000 LIRA
15.4000 g., 0.9250 Silver 0.4580 oz. ASW **Subject:** Bird Series - Saz Horozu **Obv:** Value and date within sprigs **Rev:** Purple swamphen on ground **Edge:** Plain **Shape:** 4-sided **Note:** 28.1 x 28.1mm

Date	Mintage	F	VF	XF	Unc	BU
2001 Proof	—	Value: 35.00				

KM# 1121 7500000 LIRA
15.4000 g., 0.9250 Silver 0.4580 oz. ASW **Subject:** Bird Series - Toy **Obv:** Value and date within sprigs **Rev:** Greater Bustard on ground **Edge:** Plain **Shape:** 4-sided **Note:** 28.1 x 28.1mm

Date	Mintage	F	VF	XF	Unc	BU
2001 Proof	—	Value: 35.00				

KM# 1122 7500000 LIRA
15.4000 g., 0.9250 Silver 0.4580 oz. ASW **Subject:** Bird Series - Yaz Ordegi **Obv:** Value and date within sprigs **Rev:** White-headed Duck on ground **Edge:** Plain **Shape:** 4-sided **Note:** 28.1 x 28.1mm

Date	Mintage	F	VF	XF	Unc	BU
2001 Proof	—	Value: 35.00				

KM# 1123 7500000 LIRA
15.4000 g., 0.9250 Silver 0.4580 oz. ASW **Subject:** Bird Series - Dikkuyruk **Obv:** Value and date within sprigs **Rev:** Marbled teal on water **Edge:** Plain **Shape:** 4-sided **Note:** 28.1 x 28.1mm

Date	Mintage	F	VF	XF	Unc	BU
2001 Proof	—	Value: 35.00				

KM# 1124 7500000 LIRA
15.4000 g., 0.9250 Silver 0.4580 oz. ASW **Subject:** Bird Series
- Yesil Arikusu **Obv:** Value and date within sprigs **Rev:** Bee-eater
on branch **Edge:** Plain **Shape:** 4-sided **Note:** 28.1 x 28.1mm

Date	Mintage	F	VF	XF	Unc	BU
2001 Proof	—	Value: 35.00				

KM# 1125 7500000 LIRA
15.4000 g., 0.9250 Silver 0.4580 oz. ASW **Subject:** Bird Series
- Kucuk Karabatak **Obv:** Value and date within sprigs **Rev:** Three
pygmy cormorants **Edge:** Plain **Shape:** 4-sided **Note:** 28.1 x
28.1mm

Date	Mintage	F	VF	XF	Unc	BU
2001 Proof	—	Value: 35.00				

KM# 1126 7500000 LIRA
15.4000 g., 0.9250 Silver 0.4580 oz. ASW **Subject:** Bird Series
- Kizil Akbaba **Obv:** Value and date within sprigs **Rev:** Eurasian
griffon **Edge:** Plain **Shape:** 4-sided **Note:** 28.1 x 28.1mm

Date	Mintage	F	VF	XF	Unc	BU
2001 Proof	—	Value: 35.00				

KM# 1127 7500000 LIRA
15.4000 g., 0.9250 Silver 0.4580 oz. ASW **Subject:** Bird Series
- Sah Kartal **Obv:** Value and date within sprigs **Rev:** Eagles **Edge:**
Plain **Shape:** 4-sided **Note:** 28.1 x 28.1mm

Date	Mintage	F	VF	XF	Unc	BU
2001 Proof	—	Value: 35.00				

KM# 1128 7500000 LIRA
15.4000 g., 0.9250 Silver 0.4580 oz. ASW **Subject:** Bird Series
- Ala Sigireik **Obv:** Value and date within sprigs **Rev:** Rosy starling
on ground **Edge:** Plain **Shape:** 4-sided **Note:** 28.1 x 28.1mm

Date	Mintage	F	VF	XF	Unc	BU
2001 Proof	—	Value: 35.00				

KM# 1129 7500000 LIRA
15.4000 g., 0.9250 Silver 0.4580 oz. ASW **Subject:** Bird Series
- Izmir Yalicapkini **Obv:** Value and date within sprigs **Rev:** White-
throated kingfisher on stump **Edge:** Plain **Shape:** 4-sided **Note:**
28.1 x 28.1mm

Date	Mintage	F	VF	XF	Unc	BU
2001 Proof	—	Value: 35.00				

KM# 1130 7500000 LIRA
15.4000 g., 0.9250 Silver 0.4580 oz. ASW **Subject:** Bird Series -
Turac **Obv:** Value and date within sprigs **Rev:** Black francolin birds
on the ground **Edge:** Plain **Shape:** 4-sided **Note:** 28.1 x 28.1mm

Date	Mintage	F	VF	XF	Unc	BU
2001 Proof	—	Value: 35.00				

KM# 1131 7500000 LIRA
15.4000 g., 0.9250 Silver 0.4580 oz. ASW **Subject:** Bird Series
- Kelaynak **Obv:** Value and date within sprigs **Rev:** Two Bald Ibis
birds on ground **Edge:** Plain **Shape:** 4-sided **Note:** 28.1 x 28.1mm

Date	Mintage	F	VF	XF	Unc	BU
2001 Proof	—	Value: 35.00				

KM# 1132 7500000 LIRA
15.4000 g., 0.9250 Silver 0.4580 oz. ASW **Subject:** Bird Series
- Sakalli Akbaba **Obv:** Value and date within sprigs **Rev:** Bearded
vulture **Edge:** Plain **Shape:** 4-sided **Note:** 28.1 x 28.1mm

Date	Mintage	F	VF	XF	Unc	BU
2001 Proof	—	Value: 35.00				

KM# 1133 7500000 LIRA
15.4000 g., 0.9250 Silver 0.4580 oz. ASW **Subject:** Bird Series
- Tepeli Pelikan **Obv:** Value and date within sprigs **Rev:**
Dalmatian pelican on rock **Edge:** Plain **Shape:** Square **Note:**
28.1 x 28.1mm

Date	Mintage	F	VF	XF	Unc	BU
2001 Proof	—	Value: 35.00				

KM# 1134 7500000 LIRA
15.4000 g., 0.9250 Silver 0.4580 oz. ASW **Subject:** Bird Series
- Ishakkusu **Obv:** Value and date within sprigs **Rev:** European
scops owl on branch **Edge:** Plain **Shape:** Square **Note:** 28.1 x
28.1mm

Date	Mintage	F	VF	XF	Unc	BU
2001 Proof	—	Value: 35.00				

KM# 1117 7500000 LIRA
31.4700 g., 0.9250 Silver 0.9359 oz. ASW **Subject:** Iznik Tabak
Obv: Two peacocks within circle **Rev:** Iznik Tabak (Nicean
pottery) 1570; Circle of flowers at center

Date	Mintage	F	VF	XF	Unc	BU
2001 Proof	1,349	Value: 50.00				

KM# 1135 7500000 LIRA
31.0300 g., 0.9250 Silver 0.9228 oz. ASW, 38.5 mm. **Subject:**
Mevlana Celaleddin-i Rumi **Obv:** Dancer within circle **Rev:**
Turbaned bust 3/4 right above dates **Edge:** Reeded

Date	Mintage	F	VF	XF	Unc	BU
2001 Proof	—	Value: 45.00				

KM# 1145 7500000 LIRA
15.6100 g., 0.9250 Silver 0.4642 oz. ASW, 27.9 x 38.6 mm.
Series: Flowers **Obv:** Value and date within sprigs **Rev:** Paeonia
turcica **Edge:** Reeded **Shape:** Oval

Date	Mintage	F	VF	XF	Unc	BU
2002 Proof	—	Value: 28.00				

KM# 1146 7500000 LIRA
15.6100 g., 0.9250 Silver 0.4642 oz. ASW, 27.9 x 38.6 mm.
Series: Flowers **Obv:** Value and date within sprigs **Rev:** Orchis
anatolica **Edge:** Reeded **Shape:** Oval

Date	Mintage	F	VF	XF	Unc	BU
2002 Proof	—	Value: 28.00				

KM# 1147 7500000 LIRA
15.6100 g., 0.9250 Silver 0.4642 oz. ASW, 27.9 x 38.6 mm.
Series: Flowers **Obv:** Value and date within sprigs **Rev:** Iris
pamphylica **Edge:** Reeded **Shape:** Oval

Date	Mintage	F	VF	XF	Unc	BU
2002 Proof	—	Value: 28.00				

KM# 1148 7500000 LIRA
15.6100 g., 0.9250 Silver 0.4642 oz. ASW, 27.9 x 38.6 mm.
Series: Flowers **Obv:** Value and date within sprigs **Rev:**
Gladiolus anatolicus **Edge:** Reeded **Shape:** Oval

Date	Mintage	F	VF	XF	Unc	BU
2002 Proof	—	Value: 28.00				

KM# 1149 7500000 LIRA
15.6100 g., 0.9250 Silver 0.4642 oz. ASW, 27.9 x 38.6 mm.
Series: Flowers **Obv:** Value and date within sprigs **Rev:** Crocus
sativus **Edge:** Reeded **Shape:** Oval

Date	Mintage	F	VF	XF	Unc	BU
2002 Proof	—	Value: 28.00				

KM# 1150 7500000 LIRA
15.6100 g., 0.9250 Silver 0.4642 oz. ASW, 27.9 x 38.6 mm.
Series: Flowers **Obv:** Value and date within sprigs **Rev:**
Campanula betulifolia **Edge:** Reeded **Shape:** Oval

Date	Mintage	F	VF	XF	Unc	BU
2002 Proof	—	Value: 28.00				

KM# 1151 7500000 LIRA
15.6100 g., 0.9250 Silver 0.4642 oz. ASW, 27.9 x 38.6 mm.
Series: Flowers **Obv:** Value and date within sprigs **Rev:**
Centaurea tchihatcheffii **Edge:** Reeded **Shape:** Oval

Date	Mintage	F	VF	XF	Unc	BU
2002 Proof	—	Value: 28.00				

KM# 1152 7500000 LIRA
15.6100 g., 0.9250 Silver 0.4642 oz. ASW, 27.9 x 38.6 mm.
Series: Flowers **Obv:** Value and date within sprigs **Rev:**
Tchihatchewia isatidea **Edge:** Reeded **Shape:** Oval

Date	Mintage	F	VF	XF	Unc	BU
2002 Proof	—	Value: 28.00				

KM# 1153 7500000 LIRA
15.6100 g., 0.9250 Silver 0.4642 oz. ASW, 27.9 x 38.6 mm.
Series: Flowers **Obv:** Value and date within sprigs **Rev:** Linum
anatolicum **Edge:** Reeded **Shape:** Oval

Date	Mintage	F	VF	XF	Unc	BU
2002 Proof	—	Value: 28.00				

KM# 1154 7500000 LIRA
15.6100 g., 0.9250 Silver 0.4642 oz. ASW, 27.9 x 38.6 mm.
Series: Flowers **Obv:** Value and date within sprigs **Rev:**
Cyclamen trochopteranthum **Edge:** Reeded **Shape:** Oval

Date	Mintage	F	VF	XF	Unc	BU
2002 Proof	—	Value: 28.00				

KM# 1155 7500000 LIRA
15.6100 g., 0.9250 Silver 0.4642 oz. ASW, 27.9 x 38.6 mm.
Series: Flowers **Obv:** Value and date within sprigs **Rev:** Tulipa
orphanidea **Edge:** Reeded **Shape:** Oval

Date	Mintage	F	VF	XF	Unc	BU
2002 Proof	—	Value: 28.00				

KM# 1156 7500000 LIRA
15.6100 g., 0.9250 Silver 0.4642 oz. ASW, 27.9 x 38.6 mm.
Obv: Value and date within sprigs **Rev:** Stenbergia candida
Edge: Reeded **Shape:** Oval

Date	Mintage	F	VF	XF	Unc	BU
2002 Proof	—	Value: 28.00				

Date	Mintage	F	VF	XF	Unc	BU
2005	148,419,560	—	—	—	0.15	0.20
2006	9,002,010	—	—	—	0.15	0.20
2007	5,357,000	—	—	—	0.15	0.20
2008	—	—	—	—	0.15	0.20

KM# 1157 7500000 LIRA
15.6100 g., 0.9250 Silver 0.4642 oz. ASW, 27.9 x 38.6 mm.
Series: Flowers **Obv:** Value and date within sprigs **Rev:** Arum maculatum **Edge:** Reeded **Shape:** Oval

Date	Mintage	F	VF	XF	Unc	BU
2002 Proof	—	Value: 28.00				

KM# 1118 10000000 LIRA
31.4700 g., 0.9250 Silver 0.9359 oz. ASW, 38.6 mm. **Subject:** Divrigi Ulu Camii **Obv:** Artwork within circle **Rev:** Ornate door at the Divrigi ulu Camii (Divrigi Great Mosque) built 1228 in Sivas Province **Edge:** Reeded

Date	Mintage	F	VF	XF	Unc	BU
2001 Matte	15,000	—	—	—	40.00	—

KM# 1159 10000000 LIRA
31.4200 g., 0.9250 Silver 0.9344 oz. ASW, 38.6 mm. **Subject:** Bogazici'nde Yalilar **Obv:** Value and date within sprigs **Rev:** Waterfront buildings **Edge:** Reeded

Date	Mintage	F	VF	XF	Unc	BU
2001 Proof	4,458	Value: 40.00				

KM# 1160 10000000 LIRA
31.4200 g., 0.9250 Silver 0.9344 oz. ASW, 38.6 mm. **Obv:** Turkish mint symbol within circle **Rev:** Mosque within surrounding buildings **Edge:** Reeded

Date	Mintage	F	VF	XF	Unc	BU
2002 Proof	2,106	Value: 45.00				

KM# 1140 10000000 LIRA
31.4600 g., 0.9250 Silver 0.9356 oz. ASW, 38.6 mm. **Subject:** 75th Anniversary of TRT (Türkiye Radyo Televizyon) **Obv:** Large mint mark and design within circle **Rev:** Radio microphone **Edge:** Reeded

Date	Mintage	F	VF	XF	Unc	BU
2002 Proof	—	Value: 45.00				

KM# 1265 150000000 LIRA
31.4900 g., 0.9250 Silver 0.9365 oz. ASW, 38.61 mm. **Subject:** 2006 FIFA World Cup **Obv:** Value within wreath **Rev:** Two scoccer players and globe **Edge:** Reeded

Date	Mintage	F	VF	XF	Unc	BU
2003 Proof	Est. 5,000	Value: 50.00				

REFORM DECIMAL COINAGE
2005

100,000 Old Lira = 1 New Lira

KM# 1239 KURUS
Copper Plated Steel **Obv:** Head of Ataturk left **Rev:** Plant and value

Date	Mintage	F	VF	XF	Unc	BU
2009	—	—	—	—	0.30	0.50
2010	—	—	—	—	0.30	0.50
2011	—	—	—	—	0.30	0.50
2012	—	—	—	—	0.30	0.50

KM# 1164 NEW KURUS
2.7200 g., Aluminum-Bronze, 17 mm. **Obv:** Head of Atatürk left within circle **Rev:** Value **Edge:** Plain

KM# 1240 5 KURUS
Brass **Obv:** Head of Ataturk left **Rev:** Value and traditional embroidery pattern

Date	Mintage	F	VF	XF	Unc	BU
2009	—	—	—	—	0.30	0.50
2010	—	—	—	—	0.30	0.50
2011	—	—	—	—	0.30	0.50
2012	—	—	—	—	0.30	0.50

KM# 1165 5 NEW KURUS
2.9500 g., Copper-Nickel-Zinc, 17.1 mm. **Obv:** Head of Atatürk left within circle **Rev:** Value **Edge:** Plain

Date	Mintage	F	VF	XF	Unc	BU
2005	203,339,160	—	—	0.10	0.25	0.35
2006	202,253,310	—	—	0.10	0.25	0.35
2007	122,090,000	—	—	0.10	0.25	0.35

KM# 1241 10 KURUS
Brass **Obv:** Head of Ataturk left **Rev:** Value

Date	Mintage	F	VF	XF	Unc	BU
2009	—	—	—	—	0.30	0.50
2010	—	—	—	—	0.30	0.50
2011	—	—	—	—	0.30	0.50

KM# 1166 10 NEW KURUS
3.8300 g., Copper-Nickel-Zinc, 19.4 mm. **Obv:** Head of Atatürk with hat right within circle **Rev:** Value **Edge:** Plain

Date	Mintage	F	VF	XF	Unc	BU
2005	261,538,050	—	—	0.20	0.45	0.60
2006	196,717,510	—	—	0.20	0.45	0.60
2007	134,104,000	—	—	0.20	0.45	0.60

KM# 1242 25 KURUS
Copper-Nickel **Obv:** Head of Ataturk left **Rev:** Value

Date	Mintage	F	VF	XF	Unc	BU
2009	—	—	—	—	0.50	0.75
2010	—	—	—	—	0.50	0.75
2011	—	—	—	—	0.50	0.75

KM# 1167 25 NEW KURUS
5.3000 g., Copper-Nickel-Zinc, 21.5 mm. **Obv:** Bust of Atatürk facing within circle **Rev:** Value **Edge:** Reeded

Date	Mintage	F	VF	XF	Unc	BU
2005	173,705,760	—	—	0.25	0.60	0.80
2006	67,803,010	—	—	0.30	0.75	1.00
2007	33,463,500	—	—	0.25	0.60	0.80

KM# 1243   50 KURUS
Bi-Metallic Brass center in Copper-Nickel ring   **Obv:** Head of Atatürk left **Rev:** Value above suspension bridge

Date	Mintage	F	VF	XF	Unc	BU
2009	—	—	—	—	0.75	1.00
2010	—	—	—	—	0.75	1.00
2011	—	—	—	—	0.75	1.00

KM# 1168   50 NEW KURUS
7.0000 g., Bi-Metallic Copper-Nickel center in Nickel-Brass ring, 23.8 mm.   **Obv:** Head of Atatürk right within circle **Rev:** Value within circle **Edge:** Reeded

Date	Mintage	F	VF	XF	Unc	BU
2005	203,749,569	—	—	0.60	1.50	2.00
2006	45,089,010	—	—	0.60	1.50	2.00
2007	21,946,500	—	—	0.50	1.20	1.60

KM# 1244   LIRA
Bi-Metallic Copper-Nickel center in Brass ring   **Obv:** Head of Atatürk left **Rev:** Value

Date	Mintage	F	VF	XF	Unc	BU
2009	—	—	—	—	3.00	5.00
2010	—	—	—	—	3.00	5.00
2011	—	—	—	—	3.00	5.00
2012	—	—	—	—	3.00	5.00

KM# 1169   NEW LIRA
8.5000 g., Bi-Metallic Nickel-Bronze center in Copper-Nickel-Zinc ring, 26 mm.   **Obv:** Bust of Atatürk 3/4 left within circle **Rev:** Value within circle **Edge:** Segmented reeding

Date	Mintage	F	VF	XF	Unc	BU
2005	305,235,560	—	—	—	2.25	3.00
2006	69,247,010	—	—	—	2.25	3.00
2007	56,498,200	—	—	—	2.25	3.00
2008	—	—	—	—	2.25	3.00

KM# 1171   5 NEW LIRA
12.0000 g., Bi-Metallic Brass center in Copper-Nickel ring, 32 mm.   **Subject:** 23rd Universiade in red holder **Obv:** Stylized bird within circle **Rev:** Logo within circle

Date	Mintage	F	VF	XF	Unc	BU
ND (2005)	2,957	—	—	—	22.00	25.00

KM# 1172   5 NEW LIRA
12.0000 g., Bi-Metallic Copper-Nickel center in Brass ring, 32 mm.   **Subject:** 23rd Universiade in blue holder **Obv:** Stylized bird within circle **Rev:** Logo within circle

Date	Mintage	F	VF	XF	Unc	BU
ND (2005)	2,900	—	—	—	22.00	25.00

KM# 1195   15 NEW LIRA
1.2400 g., 0.9990 Gold 0.0398 oz. AGW, 13.92 mm.   **Subject:** Nemrud **Obv:** Value within wreath **Rev:** Two large statue heads **Note:** Dated 2003 but released in 2005

Date	Mintage	F	VF	XF	Unc	BU
2003	1,820	Value: 75.00				

KM# 1193   15 NEW LIRA
15.5500 g., 0.9250 Silver 0.4624 oz. ASW, 32 mm.   **Obv:** Bird **Rev:** Logo

Date	Mintage	F	VF	XF	Unc	BU
2005 Proof	1,237	Value: 40.00				

KM# 1203   15 NEW LIRA
31.4700 g., 0.9250 Silver 0.9359 oz. ASW, 38.6 mm.   **Subject:** Scouting in Turkey, 100th Anniversary **Obv:** Scout emblem, multicolor **Rev:** Flag, Scouts saluting, camp scene

Date	Mintage	F	VF	XF	Unc	BU
2007 Proof	1,414	Value: 50.00				

KM# 1180.1   20 NEW LIRA
23.5000 g., 0.9250 Silver 0.6988 oz. ASW, 38.6 mm.   **Obv:** Value within sprigs and circle **Rev:** Angora Cat with plain eyes **Edge:** Reeded

Date	Mintage	F	VF	XF	Unc	BU
2005 Proof	5,000	Value: 60.00				

KM# 1180.2   20 NEW LIRA
23.5000 g., 0.9250 Silver 0.6988 oz. ASW, 38.6 mm.   **Obv:** Value within sprigs and circle **Rev:** Angora cat with mismatched colored eyes **Edge:** Reeded

Date	Mintage	F	VF	XF	Unc	BU
2005 Proof	—	Value: 65.00				

KM# 1173   20 NEW LIRA
31.3600 g., 0.9250 Silver 0.9326 oz. ASW, 38.6 mm.   **Obv:** Value within sprigs and circle **Rev:** Aegean Carpet **Edge:** Reeded

Date	Mintage	F	VF	XF	Unc	BU
2005 Proof	1,195	Value: 70.00				

KM# 1174   20 NEW LIRA
31.4300 g., 0.9250 Silver 0.9347 oz. ASW, 38.6 mm.   **Obv:** Value within sprigs and circle **Rev:** Mostar Bridge **Edge:** Reeded

Date	Mintage	F	VF	XF	Unc	BU
2005 Proof	1,592	Value: 75.00				

KM# 1175   20 NEW LIRA
23.4500 g., 0.9250 Silver 0.6974 oz. ASW, 38.6 mm.   **Obv:** Value within sprigs and circle **Rev:** Angora Goat **Edge:** Reeded

Date	Mintage	F	VF	XF	Unc	BU
2005 Proof	898	Value: 60.00				

KM# 1176   20 NEW LIRA
23.4600 g., 0.9250 Silver 0.6977 oz. ASW, 38.6 mm.   **Obv:** Value within sprigs and circle **Rev:** Long-eared Desert Hedgehog **Edge:** Reeded

Date	Mintage	F	VF	XF	Unc	BU
2005 Proof	744	Value: 60.00				

KM# 1177   20 NEW LIRA
23.4100 g., 0.9250 Silver 0.6962 oz. ASW, 38.6 mm.   **Obv:** Value within sprigs and circle **Rev:** Anatolian Mouflon **Edge:** Reeded

Date	Mintage	F	VF	XF	Unc	BU
2005 Proof	779	Value: 60.00				

KM# 1178   20 NEW LIRA
23.4300 g., 0.9250 Silver 0.6968 oz. ASW, 38.6 mm.   **Obv:** Value within sprigs and circle **Rev:** Striped Hyena **Edge:** Reeded

Date	Mintage	F	VF	XF	Unc	BU
2005 Proof	778	Value: 60.00				

KM# 1179 20 NEW LIRA
23.4300 g., 0.9250 Silver 0.6968 oz. ASW, 38.6 mm. **Obv:** Value within sprigs and circle **Rev:** Hazel Dormouse **Edge:** Reeded

Date	Mintage	F	VF	XF	Unc	BU
2005 Proof	744	Value: 60.00				

KM# 1181 20 NEW LIRA
23.3700 g., 0.9990 Silver 0.7506 oz. ASW, 38.6 mm. **Obv:** Value within sprigs and circle **Rev:** Anatolian Leopard **Edge:** Reeded

Date	Mintage	F	VF	XF	Unc	BU
2005 Proof	855	Value: 60.00				

KM# 1182 20 NEW LIRA
23.2500 g., 0.9250 Silver 0.6914 oz. ASW, 38.6 mm. **Obv:** Value within sprigs and circle **Rev:** Turkish Kangal Dog **Edge:** Reeded

Date	Mintage	F	VF	XF	Unc	BU
2005 Proof	1,128	Value: 60.00				

KM# 1183 20 NEW LIRA
23.4600 g., 0.9250 Silver 0.6977 oz. ASW, 38.6 mm. **Obv:** Value within sprigs and circle **Rev:** Five-toed Jerboa **Edge:** Reeded

Date	Mintage	F	VF	XF	Unc	BU
2005 Proof	746	Value: 60.00				

KM# 1184 20 NEW LIRA
23.2600 g., 0.9250 Silver 0.6917 oz. ASW, 38.6 mm. **Obv:** Value within sprigs and circle **Rev:** Brown Bear **Edge:** Reeded

Date	Mintage	F	VF	XF	Unc	BU
2005 Proof	802	Value: 60.00				

KM# 1185 20 NEW LIRA
23.5300 g., 0.9250 Silver 0.6997 oz. ASW, 38.6 mm. **Obv:** Value within sprigs and circle **Rev:** Desert Monitor **Edge:** Reeded

Date	Mintage	F	VF	XF	Unc	BU
2005 Proof	753	Value: 60.00				

KM# 1188 20 NEW LIRA
31.4700 g., 0.9250 Silver 0.9359 oz. ASW, 38.6 mm. **Subject:** Edirne Selimiye Mosque **Obv:** Value within wreath **Rev:** Mosque

Date	Mintage	F	VF	XF	Unc	BU
2005 Proof	1,660	Value: 55.00				

KM# 1189 20 NEW LIRA
31.4700 g., 0.9250 Silver 0.9359 oz. ASW, 38.6 mm. **Obv:** Crescent and star **Rev:** Large 85 above building

Date	Mintage	F	VF	XF	Unc	BU
2005 Proof	1,216	Value: 55.00				

KM# 1190 20 NEW LIRA
31.4600 g., 0.9250 Silver 0.9359 oz. ASW, 38.6 mm. **Subject:** Galatasaray Spor **Obv:** 100 above team mascot **Rev:** GS monogram

Date	Mintage	F	VF	XF	Unc	BU
2005 Proof	2,828	Value: 55.00				

KM# 1194 20 NEW LIRA
31.4700 g., 0.9250 Silver 0.9359 oz. ASW, 38.6 mm. **Subject:** Belt Maglova Cultural Heritage site **Obv:** Value within wreath **Rev:** Aqueduct

Date	Mintage	F	VF	XF	Unc	BU
2005 Proof	1,250	Value: 55.00				

KM# 1191 25 NEW LIRA
31.4700 g., 0.9250 Silver 0.9359 oz. ASW, 38.6 mm. **Subject:** Galatasaray Spor **Obv:** 100 above team mascot **Rev:** GS monogram, colored

Date	Mintage	F	VF	XF	Unc	BU
2005 Proof	1,250	Value: 85.00				

KM# 1196 25 NEW LIRA
31.4700 g., 0.9250 Silver 0.9359 oz. ASW, 38.6 mm. **Subject:** 800 year of Medical Education in Turkey **Obv:** Two snakes **Rev:** Figure

Date	Mintage	F	VF	XF	Unc	BU
2006 Proof	1,650	Value: 60.00				

KM# 1198 25 NEW LIRA
31.4700 g., 0.9250 Silver 0.9359 oz. ASW, 38.6 mm. **Subject:** Nevruz of Hatira **Obv:** Flower and rays **Rev:** Statue holding flames

Date	Mintage	F	VF	XF	Unc	BU
2006 Proof	1,300	Value: 85.00				

KM# 1199 25 NEW LIRA
31.4700 g., 0.9250 Silver 0.9359 oz. ASW, 38.6 mm. **Subject:** Hattat Hamid Aytac **Obv:** Design **Rev:** Bust facing

Date	Mintage	F	VF	XF	Unc	BU
2006 Proof	1,301	Value: 75.00				

KM# 1200 25 NEW LIRA
31.4700 g., 0.9250 Silver 0.9359 oz. ASW, 38.6 mm. **Subject:** T.C. Devlet Demiryollari, 150th Anniversary **Obv:** 150 above laural **Rev:** Building

Date	Mintage	F	VF	XF	Unc	BU
2006 Proof	1,950	Value: 55.00				

KM# 1201 25 NEW LIRA
31.4700 g., 0.9250 Silver 0.9359 oz. ASW, 38.6 mm. **Subject:** Mehmet Ersoy Akif, 70th Anniversary of death **Obv:** Scroll **Rev:** Linear portrait facing

Date	Mintage	F	VF	XF	Unc	BU
2006 Antiqued	1,500	—	—	—	55.00	—

KM# 1211 25 NEW LIRA
15.5500 g., 0.9250 Silver 0.4624 oz. ASW, 38.6x28 mm. **Obv:** Legend **Rev:** Zodiac - Pisces **Shape:** Oval

Date	Mintage	F	VF	XF	Unc	BU
2008 Proof	—	Value: 45.00				

KM# 1212 25 NEW LIRA
15.5500 g., 0.9250 Silver 0.4624 oz. ASW, 38.6x28 mm. **Obv:** Text **Rev:** Zodiac - Aquarius **Shape:** Oval

Date	Mintage	F	VF	XF	Unc	BU
2008 Proof	—	Value: 45.00				

KM# 1213 25 NEW LIRA
15.5500 g., 0.9250 Silver 0.4624 oz. ASW, 38.6x28 mm. **Obv:** Text **Rev:** Zodiac - Capricorn **Shape:** Oval

Date	Mintage	F	VF	XF	Unc	BU
2008 Proof	—	Value: 45.00				

KM# 1214 25 NEW LIRA
15.5500 g., 0.9250 Silver 0.4624 oz. ASW, 38.6x28 mm. **Obv:** Text **Rev:** Zodiac - Sagittarius **Shape:** Oval

Date	Mintage	F	VF	XF	Unc	BU
2008 Proof	—	Value: 45.00				

KM# 1215 25 NEW LIRA
15.5500 g., 0.9250 Silver 0.4624 oz. ASW, 38.6x28 mm. **Obv:** Text **Rev:** Zodiac - Libra **Shape:** Oval

Date	Mintage	F	VF	XF	Unc	BU
2008 Proof	—	Value: 45.00				

KM# 1216 25 NEW LIRA
15.5500 g., 0.9250 Silver 0.4624 oz. ASW, 38.6x28 mm. **Obv:** Text **Rev:** Zodiac - figure **Shape:** Oval

Date	Mintage	F	VF	XF	Unc	BU
2008 Proof	—	Value: 45.00				

KM# 1217 25 NEW LIRA
15.5500 g., 0.9250 Silver 0.4624 oz. ASW, 38.6x28 mm. **Obv:** Text **Rev:** Zodiac - Leo **Shape:** Oval

Date	Mintage	F	VF	XF	Unc	BU
2008 Proof	—	Value: 45.00				

KM# 1218 25 NEW LIRA
15.5500 g., 0.9250 Silver 0.4624 oz. ASW, 38.6x28 mm. **Obv:** Text **Rev:** Zodiac - Virgo **Shape:** Oval

Date	Mintage	F	VF	XF	Unc	BU
2008 Proof	—	Value: 45.00				

KM# 1219 25 NEW LIRA
15.5500 g., 0.9250 Silver 0.4624 oz. ASW, 38.6x28 mm. **Obv:** Text **Rev:** Zodiac - Gemeni **Shape:** Oval

Date	Mintage	F	VF	XF	Unc	BU
2008 Proof	—	Value: 45.00				

KM# 1220 25 NEW LIRA
15.5500 g., 0.9250 Silver 0.4624 oz. ASW, 38.6x28 mm. **Obv:** Text **Rev:** Zodiac - Taurus **Shape:** Oval

Date	Mintage	F	VF	XF	Unc	BU
2008 Proof	—	Value: 45.00				

KM# 1192 30 NEW LIRA
31.4700 g., 0.9250 Silver 0.9359 oz. ASW, 38.6 mm. **Subject:** Galatasaray Spor **Obv:** 100 above team mascot **Rev:** GS monogram colored and selective gold plating

Date	Mintage	F	VF	XF	Unc	BU
2005 Proof	1,106	Value: 55.00				

KM# 1197 30 NEW LIRA
23.3300 g., 0.9250 Silver partially gold plated 0.6938 oz. ASW, 38.61 mm. **Subject:** Solar Eclipse **Obv:** Turkey map with route of the eclipse **Rev:** Sun, gilt

Date	Mintage	F	VF	XF	Unc	BU
2006 Proof	2,475	Value: 100				

KM# 1204 30 NEW LIRA
31.4700 g., 0.9250 Silver 0.9359 oz. ASW, 38.6 mm. **Subject:** Bank of Sarfanbolu **Obv:** Building **Rev:** Landscape

Date	Mintage	F	VF	XF	Unc	BU
2007 Proof	1,312	Value: 70.00				

KM# 1205 30 NEW LIRA
31.4700 g., 0.9250 Silver 0.9359 oz. ASW, 38.6 mm. **Obv:** Crescent and star at center of four objects **Rev:** Knotted fabric pattern

Date	Mintage	F	VF	XF	Unc	BU
2007 Proof	1,210	Value: 55.00				

KM# 1206 30 NEW LIRA
31.4700 g., 0.9250 Silver 0.9359 oz. ASW, 38.6 mm. **Obv:** Crescent and star within four objects **Rev:** Twirling Dirvishes

Date	Mintage	F	VF	XF	Unc	BU
2007 Proof	1,224	Value: 55.00				

KM# 1207 30 NEW LIRA
31.4700 g., 0.9250 Silver 0.9359 oz. ASW, 38.6 mm. **Obv:** Crescent and star within four designs **Rev:** Twirling Dirvish and town facades around

Date	Mintage	F	VF	XF	Unc	BU
2007 Proof	1,179	Value: 55.00				

KM# 1208 30 NEW LIRA
31.4700 g., 0.9250 Silver 0.9359 oz. ASW, 38.6 mm. **Obv:** Mosque **Rev:** Entranceway arch

Date	Mintage	F	VF	XF	Unc	BU
2007 Proof	1,222	Value: 70.00				

KM# 1222   30 NEW LIRA
10.0000 g., 0.9250 Silver 0.2974 oz. ASW, 22 mm. **Obv:** Seal within border **Rev:** Large seal rendering

Date	Mintage	F	VF	XF	Unc	BU
2008 Proof	—	Value: 30.00				

KM# 1210   35 NEW LIRA
23.2300 g., 0.9250 Silver 0.6908 oz. ASW, 38.6 mm. **Subject:** Antikabir, 70th Anniversary **Obv:** Value within wreath **Rev:** Antikabir building

Date	Mintage	F	VF	XF	Unc	BU
2008 Proof	3,000	Value: 40.00				

KM# 1232   35 NEW LIRA
23.3300 g., 0.9250 Silver 0.6938 oz. ASW, 38.6 mm. **Obv:** Value within wreath **Rev:** Bust at left

Date	Mintage	F	VF	XF	Unc	BU
2008 Proof	—	Value: 40.00				

KM# 1233   35 NEW LIRA
23.3300 g., 0.9250 Silver 0.6938 oz. ASW, 38.6 mm. **Obv:** Classical design **Rev:** Mahmud of Kashgar at right

Date	Mintage	F	VF	XF	Unc	BU
2008 Proof	—	Value: 40.00				

KM# 1238   35 NEW LIRA
23.3300 g., 0.9250 Silver 0.6938 oz. ASW, 38.6 mm. **Obv:** Value within wreath **Rev:** Sultan on horseback

Date	Mintage	F	VF	XF	Unc	BU
2008 Proof	—	Value: 45.00				

KM# 1202   40 NEW LIRA
31.4700 g., 0.9250 Silver 0.9359 oz. ASW, 38.6 mm. **Subject:** Troy **Obv:** Linear design **Rev:** Stylized Trojan Horse

Date	Mintage	F	VF	XF	Unc	BU
2007 Proof	1,500	Value: 50.00				

KM# 1224   40 NEW LIRA
31.4700 g., 0.9990 Silver 1.0107 oz. ASW, 38.6 mm. **Obv:** Historic map **Rev:** Kyrgyzstan building

Date	Mintage	F	VF	XF	Unc	BU
2008 Antiqued	—	—	—	—	80.00	

KM# 1225   40 NEW LIRA
31.4700 g., 0.9250 Silver 0.9359 oz. ASW, 38.6 mm. **Obv:** Village scene **Rev:** Large classical figure

Date	Mintage	F	VF	XF	Unc	BU
2008 Proof	—	Value: 80.00				

KM# 1227   40 NEW LIRA
31.4700 g., 0.9250 Silver 0.9359 oz. ASW, 38.6 mm. **Obv:** Building **Rev:** Seated figure

Date	Mintage	F	VF	XF	Unc	BU
2008 Proof	—	Value: 45.00				

KM# 1228   40 NEW LIRA
31.4700 g., 0.9250 Silver 0.9359 oz. ASW, 38.6 mm. **Obv:** Classical intricate design **Rev:** Mosque

Date	Mintage	F	VF	XF	Unc	BU
2008 Proof	—	Value: 45.00				

KM# 1229   40 NEW LIRA
31.4700 g., 0.9250 Silver 0.9359 oz. ASW, 38.6 mm. **Obv:** Head left above school building **Rev:** Monogram at center

Date	Mintage	F	VF	XF	Unc	BU
2008 Proof	—	Value: 45.00				

KM# 1230   40 NEW LIRA
31.4700 g., 0.9250 Silver 0.9359 oz. ASW, 38.6 mm. **Obv:** Large tower and acqueduct **Rev:** Classical scene

Date	Mintage	F	VF	XF	Unc	BU
2008 Proof	—	Value: 45.00				

KM# 1231   40 NEW LIRA
31.4700 g., 0.9250 Silver 0.9359 oz. ASW, 38.6 mm. **Obv:** Tortoise, seal and lighthouse in distance **Rev:** Lighthouse

Date	Mintage	F	VF	XF	Unc	BU
2008 Proof	—	Value: 45.00				

KM# 1234   40 NEW LIRA
23.3300 g., 0.9250 Silver 0.6938 oz. ASW, 38.6 mm. **Subject:** Vefs Sports Club, 100th Anniversary **Obv:** Club seal multicolor **Rev:** Large 100 and logo

Date	Mintage	F	VF	XF	Unc	BU
2008 Proof	—	Value: 45.00				

KM# 1235   40 NEW LIRA
31.4700 g., 0.9250 Silver 0.9359 oz. ASW, 38.6 mm. **Obv:** Ancient craft items **Rev:** Cave paintings

Date	Mintage	F	VF	XF	Unc	BU
2008 Proof	—	Value: 45.00				

KM# 1236   40 NEW LIRA
31.4700 g., 0.9250 Silver 0.9359 oz. ASW, 38.6 mm. **Obv:** Ancient map **Rev:** Uzbekistan mosque

Date	Mintage	F	VF	XF	Unc	BU
2008 Antiqued	—	—	—	—	40.00	45.00

KM# 1237   40 NEW LIRA
31.4700 g., 0.9250 Silver 0.9359 oz. ASW **Obv:** Tower **Rev:** Tower **Shape:** 38.6

Date	Mintage	F	VF	XF	Unc	BU
2008 Proof	—	Value: 45.00				

KM# 1209   60 NEW LIRA
1.5000 g., 0.9160 Gold 0.0442 oz. AGW, 13.95 mm. **Obv:** Text **Rev:** Ancient pottery

Date	Mintage	F	VF	XF	Unc	BU
2007 Proof	1,925	Value: 70.00				

KM# 1223   100 NEW LIRA
7.2160 g., 0.9160 Gold 0.2125 oz. AGW, 22 mm. **Obv:** Seal within border **Rev:** Large seal

Date	Mintage	F	VF	XF	Unc	BU
2008 Proof	—	Value: 425				

KM# 1226   100 NEW LIRA
7.2160 g., 0.9160 Gold 0.2125 oz. AGW, 22 mm. **Obv:** Village scene **Rev:** Large classical figure

Date	Mintage	F	VF	XF	Unc	BU
2008 Proof	—	Value: 425				

REFORM DECIMAL COINAGE
2009

KM# 1249   LIRA
6.4000 g., Copper-Nickel, 23.5 mm. **Obv:** Lammergeier standing on rock **Rev:** Two eagles

Date	Mintage	F	VF	XF	Unc	BU
2009	120,000	—	—	—	4.50	6.00

KM# 1263   LIRA
8.3000 g., Bi-Metallic Copper-Nickel center in Brass ring, 26.15 mm. **Obv:** Value within wreath **Rev:** Elephant and calf

Date	Mintage	F	VF	XF	Unc	BU
2009	5,000	—	—	—	7.50	10.00

KM# 1264   LIRA
8.3000 g., Bi-Metallic Copper-Nickel center in Brass ring, 26.15 mm. **Obv:** Value within wreath **Rev:** Sea tortoise

Date	Mintage	F	VF	XF	Unc	BU
2009	5,000	—	—	—	7.50	10.00

KM# 1250   10 LIRA
23.3300 g., Bronze, 38.6 mm. **Obv:** Scroll and inkwell **Rev:** Child's story **Edge:** Reeded

Date	Mintage	F	VF	XF	Unc	BU
2009 Antiqued	—	—	—	—	15.00	—

KM# 1258   20 LIRA
27.5000 g., Copper-Nickel, 38.6 mm. **Subject:** Year 1430 **Obv:** Inscription within rose wreath **Rev:** Interior of the Grand Mosque in Mecca

Date	Mintage	F	VF	XF	Unc	BU
2009 Antiqued	—	—	—	—	35.00	—

KM# 1221   25 NEW LIRA
15.5500 g., 0.9250 Silver 0.4624 oz. ASW, 38.6x28 mm. **Obv:** Text **Rev:** Zodiac sign **Shape:** Oval

Date	Mintage	F	VF	XF	Unc	BU
2008 Proof	—	Value: 45.00				

KM# 1257   50 LIRA
36.0800 g., 0.9250 Silver 1.0730 oz. ASW, 38.6 mm. **Obv:**
Eastern Hemisphere logo **Rev:** Female face with hair forming
waves and vine

Date	Mintage	F	VF	XF	Unc	BU
2009 Proof	—	Value: 55.00				

KM# 1255   50 LIRA
36.0800 g., 0.9250 Silver 1.0730 oz. ASW, 38.6 mm. **Subject:**
Sunlight **Obv:** Eastern Hemisphere logo **Rev:** Eastern
Hemisphere in Sun

Date	Mintage	F	VF	XF	Unc	BU
2008 Proof	—	Value: 55.00				

KM# 1253   50 LIRA
36.0800 g., 0.9250 Silver 1.0730 oz. ASW, 38.6 mm. **Subject:**
IMF Meeting, Istanbul **Obv:** Istanbul Skyline **Rev:** World Bank
Group logo, multicolor

Date	Mintage	F	VF	XF	Unc	BU
2009 Proof	—	Value: 55.00				

KM# 1247   50 LIRA
36.0000 g., 0.9250 Silver 1.0706 oz. ASW, 38.6 mm. **Obv:**
Value within wreath **Rev:** Samsun 90th Anniversary

Date	Mintage	F	VF	XF	Unc	BU
2009 Proof	3,000	Value: 55.00				

KM# 1251   50 LIRA
36.0800 g., 0.9250 Silver 1.0730 oz. ASW, 38.6 mm. **Obv:** Scroll
and inkwell **Rev:** Children's story character

Date	Mintage	F	VF	XF	Unc	BU
2009 Proof	—	Value: 40.00				

KM# 1254   50 LIRA
36.0800 g., 0.9250 Silver 1.0730 oz. ASW, 38.6 mm. **Subject:**
Water, source of life **Obv:** Eastern Hemisphere logo **Rev:** Clock
hands, small amount of water, cracked and dried earth in rest of
area

Date	Mintage	F	VF	XF	Unc	BU
2009 Proof	—	Value: 55.00				

KM# 1259   50 LIRA
36.0000 g., 0.9250 Silver 1.0706 oz. ASW, 38.6 mm. **Subject:**
Year 1430 **Obv:** Inscription within rose wreath **Rev:** Interior
courtyard of Grand Mosque in Mecca

Date	Mintage	F	VF	XF	Unc	BU
2009 Proof	2,500	Value: 70.00				

KM# 1256   50 LIRA
36.0800 g., 0.9250 Silver 1.0730 oz. ASW, 38.6 mm. **Obv:**
Eastern Hemisphere logo **Rev:** Small seedling within light blue
colored water droplet, dried earth background

Date	Mintage	F	VF	XF	Unc	BU
2009 Antiqued	—	—	—	—	55.00	—

KM# 1261   50 LIRA
36.0000 g., 0.9250 Silver 1.0706 oz. ASW, 38.6 mm. **Subject:**
150th Anniversary **Obv:** Multicolor shield and text **Rev:** Building
facade

Date	Mintage	F	VF	XF	Unc	BU
2009 Proof	5,000	Value: 45.00				

KM# 1252   50 LIRA
36.0800 g., 0.9250 Silver 1.0730 oz. ASW, 38.6 mm. **Subject:**
Frederic Chopin, 200th Anniversary **Obv:** Piano and map of
Europe **Rev:** Chopin's bust at left, piano at right, score in
background

Date	Mintage	F	VF	XF	Unc	BU
2009	—	Value: 70.00				

KM# 1262   50 LIRA
36.0000 g., 0.9250 Silver 1.0706 oz. ASW, 38.6 mm.   **Subject:** Chalabi clerks **Obv:** Symbol **Rev:** Classical figure seated

Date	Mintage	F	VF	XF	Unc	BU
2009 Proof	3,000	Value: 55.00				

KM# 1245   50 NEW LIRA
36.0800 g., 0.9250 Silver 1.0730 oz. ASW, 38.6 mm.   **Obv:** US and Turkish flags **Rev:** Barak Obama portrait facing

Date	Mintage	F	VF	XF	Unc	BU
2009 Proof	3,000	Value: 55.00				

KM# 1248   100 LIRA
1.5000 g., 0.9160 Gold 0.0442 oz. AGW, 13.95 mm.   **Obv:** Classical orniament **Rev:** Hittite artifacts

Date	Mintage	F	VF	XF	Unc	BU
2009 Proof	—	Value: 95.00				

KM# 1246   200 LIRA
36.0800 g., 0.9160 Gold 1.0625 oz. AGW, 38.6 mm.   **Obv:** US and Turkish flags **Rev:** Barak Obama portrait facing

Date	Mintage	F	VF	XF	Unc	BU
2009 Proof	1,000	Value: 1,650				

KM# 1260   200 LIRA
36.0000 g., 0.9160 Gold 1.0602 oz. AGW, 38.6 mm.   **Obv:** Inscription within rose wreath **Rev:** Central courtyard of the Grand Mosque in Mecca

Date	Mintage	F	VF	XF	Unc	BU
2009 Proof	1,500	Value: 1,650				

GOLD BULLION COINAGE

Since 1943, the Turkish government has issued regular and deluxe gold coins in five denominations corresponding to the old traditional 25, 50, 100, 250, and 500 Kurus of the Ottoman period. The regular coins are all dated 1923, plus the year of the republic (e.g. 1923/40 = 1963), de Luxe coins bear actual AD dates. For a few years, 1944-1950, the bust of Ismet Inonu replaced that of Kemal Ataturk.

KM# 851   25 KURUSH
1.8041 g., 0.9170 Gold 0.0532 oz. AGW   **Obv:** Head of Ataturk left **Rev:** Legend and date within wreath

Date	Mintage	F	VF	XF	Unc	BU
1923/78	—	—	—	BV	105	120
1923/79	—	—	—	BV	105	120
1923/70	—	—	—	BV	105	120
1923/71	—	—	—	BV	105	120
1923/72	—	—	—	BV	105	120
1923/73	—	—	—	BV	105	120
1923/74	—	—	—	BV	105	120
1923/75	—	—	—	BV	105	120
1923/76	—	—	—	BV	105	120
1923/77	—	—	—	BV	105	120

KM# 870   25 KURUSH
1.7540 g., 0.9170 Gold 0.0517 oz. AGW   **Series:** Monnaie de Luxe **Obv:** Head of Ataturk left **Rev:** Country name and date in ornate monogram within circle of stars, floral border surrounds

Date	Mintage	F	VF	XF	Unc	BU
2001	—	—	—	BV	105	120
2002	—	—	—	BV	105	120
2003	—	—	—	BV	105	120
2004	—	—	—	BV	105	120
2005	—	—	—	BV	105	120
2006	—	—	—	BV	105	120
2007	—	—	—	BV	105	120
2008	—	—	—	BV	105	120
2009	—	—	—	BV	105	120
2010	—	—	—	BV	105	120

KM# 853   50 KURUSH
3.6083 g., 0.9170 Gold 0.1064 oz. AGW   **Obv:** Head of Ataturk left **Rev:** Legend and date within wreath

Date	Mintage	F	VF	XF	Unc	BU
1923/78	—	—	—	BV	200	225
1923/79	—	—	—	BV	200	225
1923/80	—	—	—	BV	200	225
1923/81	—	—	—	BV	200	225
1923/82	—	—	—	BV	200	225
1923/83	—	—	—	BV	200	225
1923/84	—	—	—	BV	200	225
1923/85	—	—	—	BV	200	225
1923/86	—	—	—	BV	200	225
1923/87	—	—	—	BV	200	225

KM# 871   50 KURUSH
3.5080 g., 0.9170 Gold 0.1034 oz. AGW   **Series:** Monnaie de Luxe **Obv:** Head of Kemal Ataturk left within circle of stars, wreath surrounds **Rev:** Country name and date in ornate monogram within circle of stars, floral border surrounds

Date	Mintage	F	VF	XF	Unc	BU
2001	—	—	—	BV	200	225
2002	—	—	—	BV	200	225
2003	—	—	—	BV	200	225
2004	—	—	—	BV	200	225
2005	—	—	—	BV	200	225
2006	—	—	—	BV	200	225
2007	—	—	—	BV	200	225
2008	—	—	—	BV	200	225
2009	—	—	—	BV	200	225
2010	—	—	—	BV	200	225

KM# 855   100 KURUSH
7.2160 g., 0.9170 Gold 0.2127 oz. AGW   **Obv:** Head of Ataturk left **Rev:** Legend and date within wreath

Date	Mintage	F	VF	XF	Unc	BU
1923/78	—	—	—	BV	400	425
1923/79	—	—	—	BV	400	425
1923/80	—	—	—	BV	400	425
1923/81	—	—	—	BV	400	425
1923/82	—	—	—	BV	400	425
1923/83	—	—	—	BV	400	425
1923/84	—	—	—	BV	400	425
1923/85	—	—	—	BV	400	425
1923/86	—	—	—	BV	400	425
1923/87	—	—	—	BV	400	425

KM# 872   100 KURUSH
7.0160 g., 0.9170 Gold 0.2068 oz. AGW   **Series:** Monnaie de Luxe **Obv:** Head of Ataturk left within circle of stars, wreath surrounds **Rev:** Country name and date in ornate monogram within circle of stars, floral border surrounds

Date	Mintage	F	VF	XF	Unc	BU
2001	—	—	—	BV	300	320
2002	—	—	—	BV	300	320
2003	—	—	—	BV	300	320
2004	—	—	—	BV	300	320
2005	—	—	—	BV	300	320
2006	—	—	—	BV	300	320
2007	—	—	—	BV	300	320
2008	—	—	—	BV	300	320
2009	—	—	—	BV	300	320
2010	—	—	—	BV	300	320

KM# 857   250 KURUSH
18.0400 g., 0.9170 Gold 0.5318 oz. AGW   **Obv:** Head of Ataturk left **Rev:** Legend and date within wreath

Date	Mintage	F	VF	XF	Unc	BU
1923/78	—	—	—	BV	1,025	1,075
1923/79	—	—	—	BV	1,025	1,075
1923/80	—	—	—	BV	1,025	1,075
1923/81	—	—	—	BV	1,025	1,075
1923/82	—	—	—	BV	1,025	1,075
1923/83	—	—	—	BV	1,025	1,075
1923/84	—	—	—	BV	1,025	1,075

Date	Mintage	F	VF	XF	Unc	BU
1923/85	—	—	—	BV	1,025	1,075
1923/86	—	—	—	BV	1,025	1,075
1923/87	—	—	—	BV	1,025	1,075

KM# 873 250 KURUSH
17.5400 g., 0.9170 Gold 0.5171 oz. AGW **Series:** Monnaie de Luxe **Obv:** Head of Atatürk left within circle of stars, wreath surrounds **Rev:** Country name and date in ornate monogram within circle of stars, floral border surrounds

Date	Mintage	F	VF	XF	Unc	BU
2001	—	—	—	BV	1,000	1,050
2002	—	—	—	BV	1,000	1,050
2003	—	—	—	BV	1,000	1,050
2004	—	—	—	BV	1,000	1,050
2005	—	—	—	BV	1,000	1,050
2006	—	—	—	BV	1,000	1,050
2007	—	—	—	BV	1,000	1,050
2008	—	—	—	BV	1,000	1,050
2009	—	—	—	BV	1,000	1,050
2010	—	—	—	BV	1,000	1,050

KM# 859 500 KURUSH
36.0800 g., 0.9170 Gold 1.0637 oz. AGW **Obv:** Head of Atatürk left **Rev:** Legend and date within wreath

Date	Mintage	F	VF	XF	Unc	BU
1923/78	—	—	—	BV	1,950	2,000
1923/79	—	—	—	BV	1,950	2,000
1923/80	—	—	—	BV	1,950	2,000
1923/81	—	—	—	BV	1,950	2,000
1923/82	—	—	—	BV	1,950	2,000
1923/83	—	—	—	BV	1,950	2,000
1923/84	—	—	—	BV	1,950	2,000
1923/85	—	—	—	BV	1,950	2,000
1923/86	—	—	—	BV	1,950	2,000
1923/87	—	—	—	BV	1,950	2,000

KM# 874 500 KURUSH
35.0800 g., 0.9170 Gold 1.0342 oz. AGW **Series:** Monnaie de Luxe **Obv:** Head of Atatürk left within circle of stars, wreath surrounds **Rev:** Country name and date in ornate monogram within circle of stars, floral border surrounds

Date	Mintage	F	VF	XF	Unc	BU
2001	—	—	—	BV	1,950	2,000
2002	—	—	—	BV	1,950	2,000
2003	—	—	—	BV	1,950	2,000
2004	—	—	—	BV	1,950	2,000
2005	—	—	—	BV	1,950	2,000
2006	—	—	—	BV	1,950	2,000
2007	—	—	—	BV	1,950	2,000
2008	—	—	—	BV	1,950	2,000
2009	—	—	—	BV	1,950	2,000
2010	—	—	—	BV	1,950	2,000

Turkmenistan, (formerly the Turkmen Soviet Socialist Republic) covers the territory of the Trans-Caspian Region of Turkestan, the Charjiui Vilayet of Bukhara and the part of Khiva located on the right bank of the Oxus. Bordered on the north by the Autonomous Kara-Kalpak Republic (a constituent of Uzbekistan), by Iran and Afghanistan on the south, by the Usbek Republic on the east and the Caspian Sea on the west. It has an area of 186,400 sq. mi. (488,100 sq. km.) and a population of 3.5 million. Capital: Ashkhabad (formerly Poltoratsk). Main occupation is agricultural products including cotton and maize. It is rich in minerals, oil, coal, sulphur and salt and is also famous for its carpets, Turkoman horses and Karakui sheep.

The Turkomans arrived in Trancaspia as nomadic Seluk Turks in the 11th century. It often became subjected to one of the neighboring states. Late in the 19th century the Czarist Russians invaded with their first victory at Kyzyl Arvat in 1877, arriving in Ashkhabad in 1882 resulting in submission of the Turkmen tribes. By March 18,1884 the Transcaspian province of Russian Turkestan was formed. During WW I the Czarist government tried to conscript the Turkmen; this led to a revolt in Oct. 1916 under the leadership of Aziz Chapykov. In 1918 the Turks captured Baku from the Red army and the British sent a contingent to Merv to prevent a German-Turkish offensive toward Afghanistan and India. In mid-1919 a Bureau of Turkestan Moslem Communist Organization was formed in Moscow hoping to develop one large republic including all surrounding Turkic areas within a Soviet federation. A Turkestan Autonomous Soviet Socialist Republic was formed and plans to partition Turkestan into five republics according to the principle of nationalities was quickly implemented by Joseph Stalin. On Oct. 27, 1924 Turkmenistan became a Soviet Socialist Republic and was accepted as a member of the U.S.S.R. on Jan. 29, 1925. The Bureau of T.M.C.O. was disbanded in 1934. In Aug. 1990 the Turkmen Supreme Soviet adopted a declaration of sovereignty followed by a declaration of independence in Oct. 1991 joining the Commonwealth of Independent States in Dec. A new constitution was adopted in 1992 providing for an executive presidency.

REPUBLIC
STANDARD COINAGE
100 Tenge = 1 Manat

KM# 25 500 MANAT
28.2800 g., 0.9250 Silver 0.8410 oz. ASW, 38.5 mm. **Subject:** 10th Anniversary of Independence **Obv:** Head of President Saparmyrat Nyyazow left within circle **Rev:** Monument divides dates within circle **Edge:** Reeded

Date	Mintage	F	VF	XF	Unc	BU
ND(2001) Proof	5,000	Value: 60.00				

KM# 41 500 MANAT
28.2800 g., 0.9250 Silver 0.8410 oz. ASW **Subject:** President's 61st Birthday **Obv:** National Flag

Date	Mintage	F	VF	XF	Unc	BU
2001	2,000	—	—	—	—	55.00

KM# 42 500 MANAT
28.2800 g., 0.9250 Silver 0.8410 oz. ASW **Subject:** President's 61st Birthday **Rev:** State arms

Date	Mintage	F	VF	XF	Unc	BU
2001	2,000	—	—	—	—	55.00

KM# 43 500 MANAT
28.2800 g., 0.9250 Silver 0.8410 oz. ASW **Subject:** Historical leaders **Rev:** Artogrul Grazy Turkmen (1191-1281)

Date	Mintage	F	VF	XF	Unc	BU
2001	100	—	—	—	—	55.00

KM# 44 500 MANAT
28.2800 g., 0.9250 Silver 0.8410 oz. ASW **Subject:** Historical leaders **Rev:** Oguz Khan Turkmen

Date	Mintage	F	VF	XF	Unc	BU
2001	1,000	—	—	—	—	55.00

KM# 45 500 MANAT
28.2800 g., 0.9250 Silver 0.8410 oz. ASW **Subject:** Historical leaders **Rev:** Gara Yusup Beg Turkmen

Date	Mintage	F	VF	XF	Unc	BU
2001	1,000	—	—	—	—	55.00

KM# 46 500 MANAT
28.2800 g., 0.9250 Silver 0.8410 oz. ASW **Subject:** Historical leaders **Rev:** Keymir Kor Turkmen

Date	Mintage	F	VF	XF	Unc	BU
2001	—	—	—	—	—	65.00

KM# 47 500 MANAT
28.2800 g., 0.9250 Silver 0.8410 oz. ASW **Subject:** Historical leaders **Rev:** Uzun Khasan Beg Turkmen

Date	Mintage	F	VF	XF	Unc	BU
2001	1,000	—	—	—	—	55.00

KM# 48 500 MANAT
28.2800 g., 0.9250 Silver 0.8410 oz. ASW **Subject:** Historical leaders **Rev:** Gorogly Beg Turkmen

Date	Mintage	F	VF	XF	Unc	BU
2001	1,000	—	—	—	—	55.00

KM# 49 500 MANAT
28.2800 g., 0.9250 Silver 0.8410 oz. ASW **Subject:** Historical leader **Rev:** Gorkut Ata Turkmen

Date	Mintage	F	VF	XF	Unc	BU
2001	1,000	—	—	—	—	55.00

KM# 50 500 MANAT
28.2800 g., 0.9250 Silver 0.8410 oz. ASW **Subject:** Historical leaders **Rev:** Muhammet Togrul Beg Turkmen

Date	Mintage	F	VF	XF	Unc	BU
2001	1,000	—	—	—	—	55.00

KM# 51 500 MANAT
Silver **Subject:** Historical leaders **Rev:** Muhammet Bayram Khan Turkmen

Date	Mintage	F	VF	XF	Unc	BU
2001	1,000	—	—	—	—	55.00

KM# 52 500 MANAT
28.2800 g., 0.9250 Silver 0.8410 oz. ASW **Subject:** Historical leaders **Rev:** Soltan Sawjar Turkmen

Date	Mintage	F	VF	XF	Unc	BU
2001	1,000	—	—	—	—	55.00

KM# 53 500 MANAT
28.2800 g., 0.9250 Silver 0.8410 oz. ASW, 46 mm. **Subject:** Historical writers **Obv:** State emblem **Rev:** Bust and Laurel branch **Rev. Legend:** Seyitnazar Seydi (1760-1830)

Date	Mintage	F	VF	XF	Unc	BU
2003	—	—	—	—	—	65.00

KM# 54 500 MANAT
28.2800 g., 0.9250 Silver 0.8410 oz. ASW **Subject:** Historical authors **Obv:** State emblem **Rev:** Bust and Laurel branch **Rev. Legend:** Mammetweli Kemine (1770-1840)

Date	Mintage	F	VF	XF	Unc	BU
2003	—	—	—	—	—	65.00

KM# 55 500 MANAT
28.2800 g., 0.5000 Silver 0.4546 oz. ASW, 46 mm. **Subject:** State emblem **Rev:** Bust and Laurel branch **Rev. Legend:** Mollanepes (1810-1862)

Date	Mintage	F	VF	XF	Unc	BU
2003	—	—	—	—	—	50.00

KM# 56 500 MANAT
28.2800 g., 0.9250 Silver 0.8410 oz. ASW, 46 mm. **Subject:** Historical authors **Obv:** State emblem **Rev:** Bust and Laurel branch **Rev. Legend:** Annagylyc Mataji (1824-1882)

Date	Mintage	F	VF	XF	Unc	BU
2003	—	—	—	—	—	65.00

KM# 62 500 MANAT
28.2800 g., 0.9250 Silver 0.8410 oz. ASW **Obv:** Bust left **Rev:** Wheat ears as rays

Date	Mintage	F	VF	XF	Unc	BU
2004	—	—	—	—	—	65.00

KM# 64   500 MANAT
28.2800 g., 0.9250 Silver 0.8410 oz. ASW **Obv:** Bust left **Rev:** Wheat ears forming rays

Date	Mintage	F	VF	XF	Unc	BU
2004	1,000	—	—	—	—	55.00

KM# 66   500 MANAT
28.2800 g., 0.9250 Silver 0.8410 oz. ASW **Subject:** 60th Anniversary of WWII **Obv:** State emblem **Rev:** Soldier standing, rays behind

Date	Mintage	F	VF	XF	Unc	BU
2005	1,000	—	—	—	—	65.00

KM# 68   500 MANAT
28.2800 g., 0.9250 Silver 0.8410 oz. ASW, 75 mm. **Subject:** President Nijazov, 60th Birthday **Obv:** State emblem **Rev:** Head left above tree design

Date	Mintage	F	VF	XF	Unc	BU
2005	—	—	—	—	—	65.00

KM# 40   1000 MANAT
7.9800 g., 0.9160 Gold 0.2350 oz. AGW, 28.28 mm. **Obv:** President Nyyazow **Rev:** Monument

Date	Mintage	F	VF	XF	Unc	BU
2001	1,000	—	—	—	—	1,800

KM# 57   1000 MANAT
47.6400 g., 0.9160 Gold 1.4029 oz. AGW, 46 mm. **Subject:** Historical authors **Obv:** State emblem **Rev:** Bust and Laurel branch **Rev. Legend:** Seyitnazar Seydi (1760-1830)

Date	Mintage	F	VF	XF	Unc	BU
2003	—	—	—	—	—	2,250

KM# 58   1000 MANAT
47.6400 g., 0.9160 Gold 1.4029 oz. AGW, 46 mm. **Subject:** Historical authors **Obv:** State arms **Rev:** Bust and laurel branch **Rev. Legend:** Mammetweli Kemine

Date	Mintage	F	VF	XF	Unc	BU
2003	—	—	—	—	—	2,250

KM# 59   1000 MANAT
47.6400 g., 0.9250 Gold 1.4167 oz. AGW, 46 mm. **Subject:** Historical authors **Obv:** State emblem **Rev:** Bust and laurel branch **Rev. Legend:** Mollanepes (1810-1862)

Date	Mintage	F	VF	XF	Unc	BU
2003	—	—	—	—	—	2,250

KM# 60   1000 MANAT
47.6400 g., 0.9160 Gold 1.4029 oz. AGW, 46 mm. **Subject:** Historical authors **Obv:** State emblem **Rev:** Bust and laurel branch **Rev. Legend:** Annagylyc Mataji (1824-1882)

Date	Mintage	F	VF	XF	Unc	BU
2003	—	—	—	—	—	2,250

KM# 61   1000 MANAT
28.2800 g., 0.9250 Silver 0.8410 oz. ASW **Subject:** 10th Anniversary of Reform

Date	Mintage	F	VF	XF	Unc	BU
2003	—	—	—	—	—	85.00

KM# 63   1000 MANAT
7.9800 g., 0.9160 Gold 0.2350 oz. AGW **Subject:** 100th Anniversary **Obv:** Bust left **Rev:** Wheat ears forming rays above

Date	Mintage	F	VF	XF	Unc	BU
2004	—	—	—	—	—	1,550

KM# 65   1000 MANAT
7.9800 g., 0.9160 Gold 0.2350 oz. AGW **Obv:** Bust left **Rev:** Wheat ears forming rays

Date	Mintage	F	VF	XF	Unc	BU
2004	250	—	—	—	—	1,550

KM# 67   1000 MANAT
47.5400 g., 0.9160 Gold 1.4000 oz. AGW **Subject:** 60th Anniversary of WWII **Obv:** State arms **Rev:** Soldier standing, rays behind

Date	Mintage	F	VF	XF	Unc	BU
2005	—	—	—	—	—	2,250

KM# 69   1000 MANAT
155.5000 g., 0.9990 Gold 4.9942 oz. AGW, 75 mm. **Subject:** President Nijazov Goth **Obv:** State emblem **Rev:** Head left above tree

Date	Mintage	F	VF	XF	Unc	BU
2005	—	—	—	—	—	8,000

KM# 70   1000 MANAT
28.2800 g., 0.9250 Silver 0.8410 oz. ASW **Subject:** Writings of President Nijazov

Date	Mintage	F	VF	XF	Unc	BU
2006	—	—	—	—	—	85.00

KM# 71   1000 MANAT
28.2800 g., 0.9250 Silver 0.8410 oz. ASW **Subject:** Writings of President Nijazov

Date	Mintage	F	VF	XF	Unc	BU
2006	—	—	—	—	—	85.00

KM# 72   1000 MANAT
28.2800 g., 0.9250 Silver 0.8410 oz. ASW **Subject:** Writings of President Nijazov

Date	Mintage	F	VF	XF	Unc	BU
2006	—	—	—	—	—	85.00

KM# 73   1000 MANAT
28.2800 g., 0.9250 Silver 0.8410 oz. ASW **Subject:** Writings of President Nijazov

Date	Mintage	F	VF	XF	Unc	BU
2006	—	—	—	—	—	85.00

KM# 74   1000 MANAT
28.2800 g., 0.9250 Silver 0.8410 oz. ASW **Subject:** Writings of President Nijazov

Date	Mintage	F	VF	XF	Unc	BU
2006	—	—	—	—	—	85.00

KM# 75   1000 MANAT
28.2800 g., 0.9250 Silver 0.8410 oz. ASW **Subject:** Writings of President Nijazov

Date	Mintage	F	VF	XF	Unc	BU
2006	—	—	—	—	—	85.00

REFORM COINAGE
January 1, 2009 - 5000 Old Manat = 1 New Manat

100 Tenge = 1 Manat

KM# 95   TENGE
Nickel Plated Steel, 16 mm. **Obv:** Spire over country map **Rev:** Denomination and date

Date	Mintage	F	VF	XF	Unc	BU
2009	—	—	—	—	0.50	0.75

KM# 96   2 TENGE
Nickel Plated Steel, 18 mm. **Obv:** Spire over country map **Rev:** Denomination and date

Date	Mintage	F	VF	XF	Unc	BU
2009	—	—	—	—	0.75	1.00

KM# 97   5 TENGE
Nickel Plated Steel, 20 mm. **Obv:** Spire over country map **Rev:** Denomination and date

Date	Mintage	F	VF	XF	Unc	BU
2009	—	—	—	—	1.00	1.25

KM# 98   10 TENGE
Brass, 22 mm. **Obv:** Spire over country map **Rev:** Denomination and date

Date	Mintage	F	VF	XF	Unc	BU
2009	—	—	—	—	1.50	1.75

KM# 99   20 TENGE
Brass, 23 mm. **Obv:** Spire over country map **Rev:** Denomination and date

Date	Mintage	F	VF	XF	Unc	BU
2009	—	—	—	—	2.50	3.00

KM# 100   50 TENGE
Brass, 26 mm. **Obv:** Spire over country map **Rev:** Denomination and date

Date	Mintage	F	VF	XF	Unc	BU
2009	—	—	—	—	3.00	3.50

KM# 103   MANAT
9.3000 g., Bi-Metallic Stainless-steel center in Brass ring, 27 mm. **Obv:** Spire over country map **Rev:** Denomination and date

Date	Mintage	F	VF	XF	Unc	BU
2010	—	—	—	—	—	4.00

KM# 104   2 MANAT
10.4000 g., Bi-Metallic Brass center in copper-nickel ring **Obv:** Spire over country map **Rev:** Value and date

Date	Mintage	F	VF	XF	Unc	BU
2010	—	—	—	—	—	7.50

TURKS & CAICOS ISLANDS

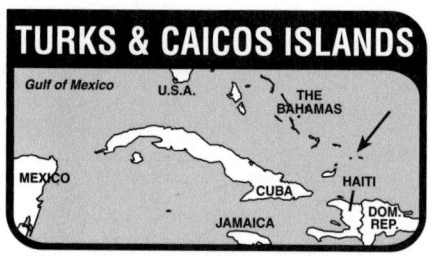

The Colony of the Turks and Caicos Islands, a British colony situated in the West Indies at the eastern end of the Bahama Islands, has an area of 166 sq. mi. (430 sq.km.) and a population of *10,000. Capital: Cockburn Town, on Grand Turk. The principal industry of the colony is the production of salt, which is gathered by raking. Salt, crayfish, and conch shells are exported.

RULER
British

MONETARY SYSTEM
1 Crown = 1 Dollar U.S.A.

BRITISH COLONY
STANDARD COINAGE

KM# 233   5 CROWNS
26.4300 g., Copper-Nickel, 39.2 mm. **Ruler:** Elizabeth II **Subject:** Royal Navy Submarines **Obv:** Head with tiara right **Rev:** Old and modern submarines **Edge:** Reeded

Date	Mintage	F	VF	XF	Unc	BU
2001	—	—	—	6.00	10.00	12.00

KM# 236 20 CROWNS
31.2000 g., 0.9990 Silver 1.0021 oz. ASW, 38.9 mm. **Obv:**
Crowned head right **Rev:** Bust right facing divides dates **Edge:**
Reeded

Date	Mintage	F	VF	XF	Unc	BU
2001 Proof	—	Value: 50.00				

KM# 245 20 CROWNS
31.1600 g., 0.9990 Silver 1.0008 oz. ASW, 39 mm. **Obv:**
Crowned head right **Rev:** Richard II (1377-1399) **Edge:** Reeded

Date	Mintage	F	VF	XF	Unc	BU
2002 Proof	—	Value: 50.00				

KM# 246 20 CROWNS
Hafnium, 38.6 mm. **Ruler:** Elizabeth II **Subject:** H.M. Queen
Elizabeth, The Queen Mother **Obv:** Crowned head right **Rev:**
Crowned bust right within circle **Edge:** Reeded

Date	Mintage	F	VF	XF	Unc	BU
2002 Proof	—	Value: 145				

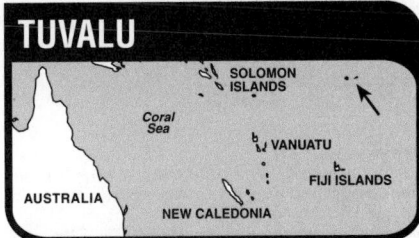

TUVALU

SOLOMON
ISLANDS

Coral
Sea

VANUATU

FIJI ISLANDS

AUSTRALIA

NEW CALEDONIA

Tuvalu (formerly the Ellice or Lagoon Islands of the Gilbert
and Ellice Islands), located in the South Pacific north of the Fiji
Islands, has an area of 10 sq. mi. (26 sq.km.) and a population
of *9,000. Capital: Funafuti. The independent state includes the
islands of Nanumanga, Nanumea, Nui, Niutao, Viatupa, Funafuti,
Nukufetau, Nukulailai and Nurakita. The latter four islands were
claimed by the United States until relinquished by the Feb. 7,
1979, Treaty of Friendship signed by the United States and
Tuvalu. The principal industries are copra production and phosphate mining.

Tuvalu is a member of the Commonwealth of Nations. Elizabeth II is Head of State as Queen of Tuvalu.

RULER
British, until 1978

MONETARY SYSTEM
100 Cents = 1 Dollar

CONSTITUTIONAL
MONARCHY WITHIN
THE COMMONWEALTH

STANDARD COINAGE

KM# 168 50 CENTS
15.5900 g., 0.9990 Silver 0.5007 oz. ASW, 36.6 mm. **Ruler:**
Elizabeth II **Rev:** Two doves tying pink ribbon heart

Date	Mintage	F	VF	XF	Unc	BU
2011 Proof	2,500	Value: 50.00				

KM# 191 50 CENTS
15.5910 g., 0.9999 Silver 0.5012 oz. ASW, 36.6 mm. **Ruler:**
Elizabeth II **Subject:** Forever Love **Rev:** Two koalas framed by
heart shaped gum leaves and blossoms

Date	Mintage	F	VF	XF	Unc	BU
2012P Proof	7,500	Value: 60.00				

KM# 193 50 CENTS
15.5500 g., 0.9990 Silver 0.4994 oz. ASW, 30.6 mm. **Ruler:**
Elizabeth II **Rev:** Baby dragon in color

Date	Mintage	F	VF	XF	Unc	BU
2012P Proof	—	Value: 60.00				

KM# 40 DOLLAR
20.0000 g., Brass, 38.7 mm. **Ruler:** Elizabeth II **Subject:**
Dinosaurs **Obv:** Crowned head right **Rev:** Giganotosaurus **Edge:**
Reeded **Note:** See KM#49.

Date	Mintage	F	VF	XF	Unc	BU
2002	50,000	—	—	—	18.00	22.00

KM# 41 DOLLAR
20.0000 g., Brass, 38.7 mm. **Ruler:** Elizabeth II **Subject:**
Dinosaurs **Obv:** Crowned head right **Rev:** Dromaeosaurus **Edge:**
Reeded **Note:** See KM#50.

Date	Mintage	F	VF	XF	Unc	BU
2002	50,000	—	—	—	18.00	22.00

KM# 43 DOLLAR
20.0000 g., Brass, 38.7 mm. **Ruler:** Elizabeth II **Subject:**
Dinosaurs **Obv:** Crowned head right **Rev:** Stegosaurus **Edge:**
Reeded **Note:** See KM#51.

Date	Mintage	F	VF	XF	Unc	BU
2002	50,000	—	—	—	18.00	22.00

KM# 42 DOLLAR
20.0000 g., Brass, 38.7 mm. **Ruler:** Elizabeth II **Subject:**
Dinosaurs **Obv:** Crowned head right **Rev:** Seismosaurus **Edge:**
Reeded **Note:** See KM#52.

Date	Mintage	F	VF	XF	Unc	BU
2002	50,000	—	—	—	18.00	22.00

KM# 149 DOLLAR
31.1030 g., 0.9990 Silver 0.9989 oz. ASW, 40.7 mm. **Ruler:**
Elizabeth II **Subject:** Harry Potter **Rev:** Multicolor dementor

Date	Mintage	F	VF	XF	Unc	BU
2004	—	—	—	—	—	42.00

KM# 150 DOLLAR
31.1030 g., 0.9990 Silver 0.9989 oz. ASW, 40.7 mm. **Ruler:**
Elizabeth II **Subject:** Harry Potter **Rev:** Multicolor owl

Date	Mintage	F	VF	XF	Unc	BU
2004	—	—	—	—	—	42.00

KM# 151 DOLLAR
31.1030 g., 0.9990 Silver 0.9989 oz. ASW, 40.7 mm. **Ruler:**
Elizabeth II **Subject:** Harry Potter **Rev:** Multicolor color Harry
Potter chasing snitch

Date	Mintage	F	VF	XF	Unc	BU
2004	—	—	—	—	—	42.00

KM# 53 DOLLAR
Silver **Ruler:** Elizabeth II **Obv:** Crowned head right **Rev:** 1955
Mercedes Benz 300 SL Gullwing

Date	Mintage	F	VF	XF	Unc	BU
2006 Proof	—	Value: 55.00				

KM# 54 DOLLAR
Silver **Ruler:** Elizabeth II **Obv:** Crowned head right **Rev:** 1963
Jaguar E-Type colorized

Date	Mintage	F	VF	XF	Unc	BU
2006 Proof	—	Value: 55.00				

KM# 55 DOLLAR
Silver **Ruler:** Elizabeth II **Obv:** Crowned head right **Rev:** 1969
Datsun 240Z

Date	Mintage	F	VF	XF	Unc	BU
2006 Proof	—	Value: 65.00				

KM# 58   DOLLAR
31.3100 g., 0.9990 Silver enameled 1.0056 oz. ASW, 40.51 mm. **Ruler:** Elizabeth II **Subject:** 400th Anniversary of First European Sighting of Australia **Obv:** Crowned bust right **Obv. Legend:** QUEEN ELIZABETH II **Rev:** Bust of Captain James Cook at left, his ship; "H.M.S. Endeavor" within ship's wheel **Rev. Inscription:** 1770 DISCOVERY - EASTERN AUSTRALIA **Edge:** Reeded

Date	Mintage	F	VF	XF	Unc	BU
2006 Proof	—	Value: 85.00				

KM# 59   DOLLAR
31.3100 g., 0.9990 Silver enameled 1.0056 oz. ASW, 40 mm. **Ruler:** Elizabeth II **Subject:** 400th Anniversary of First European Sighting of Australia **Obv:** Crowned bust right **Obv. Legend:** QUEEN ELIZABETH II **Rev:** Bust of Abel Jansoon Tasman at left, his Dutch ship within compass rose **Rev. Legend:** 1642 DISCOVERY OF VAN DIEMAN'S LAND **Edge:** Reeded

Date	Mintage	F	VF	XF	Unc	BU
2006 Proof	—	Value: 85.00				

KM# 60   DOLLAR
31.1050 g., 0.9990 Silver enameled 0.9990 oz. ASW, 40 mm. **Ruler:** Elizabeth II **Subject:** 400th Anniversary of First European Sighting of Australia **Obv:** Crowned bust right **Obv. Legend:** QUEEN ELIZABETH II **Rev:** Bust of William Dampier at right, his ship within wreath **Rev. Legend:** 1688 BRITISH DISCOVERY OF AUSTRALIA **Edge:** Reeded

Date	Mintage	F	VF	XF	Unc	BU
2006 Proof	—	Value: 85.00				

KM# 61   DOLLAR
31.3100 g., 0.9990 Silver enameled 1.0056 oz. ASW, 40 mm. **Ruler:** Elizabeth II **Subject:** 400th Anniversary of First European Sighting of Australia **Obv:** Crowned bust right **Obv. Legend:** QUEEN ELIZABETH II **Rev:** Dutch ship "Duyfken" within compass rose **Rev. Legend:** 1606 FIRST EUROPEAN DISCOVERY AUSTRALIA **Edge:** Reeded

Date	Mintage	F	VF	XF	Unc	BU
2006 Proof	—	Value: 85.00				

KM# 68   DOLLAR
31.1030 g., 0.9990 Silver 0.9989 oz. ASW, 40 mm. **Ruler:** Elizabeth II **Obv:** Crowned bust right **Obv. Legend:** QUEEN ELIZABETH II - TUVALU **Rev:** Red-back Spider, multicolor

Date	Mintage	F	VF	XF	Unc	BU
2006 Proof	5,000	Value: 275				

KM# 170   DOLLAR
31.1050 g., 0.9990 Silver 0.9990 oz. ASW, 40.6 mm. **Ruler:** Elizabeth II **Rev:** Lamborghini in color

Date	Mintage	F	VF	XF	Unc	BU
2006 Proof	—	Value: 65.00				

KM# 171   DOLLAR
31.1050 g., 0.9990 Copper Plated Silver 0.9990 oz., 40.6 mm. **Ruler:** Elizabeth II **Rev:** 1923 1/2 Penny of Australia, reverse

Date	Mintage	F	VF	XF	Unc	BU
2006 Proof	—	Value: 90.00				

KM# 62   DOLLAR
31.1035 g., 0.9990 Silver 0.9990 oz. ASW, 40.51 mm. **Ruler:**

Elizabeth II **Obv:** Crowned bust right **Obv. Legend:** ELIZABETH II **Rev:** Multicolor Great White Shark **Edge:** Reeded

Date	Mintage	F	VF	XF	Unc	BU
2007 Proof	5,000	Value: 145				

KM# 63   DOLLAR
0.9990 Silver, 40 mm. **Ruler:** Elizabeth II **Series:** Fighting Ships of WW II **Obv:** Crowned bust right **Obv. Legend:** QUEEN ELIZABETH II - TUVALU **Rev:** USSR Sevastopol, multicolor water

Date	Mintage	F	VF	XF	Unc	BU
2007 Proof	1,500	Value: 75.00				

KM# 64   DOLLAR
0.9990 Silver, 40 mm. **Ruler:** Elizabeth II **Series:** Fighting Ships of WW II **Obv:** Crowned bust right **Obv. Legend:** QUEEN ELIZABETH II - TUVALU **Rev:** HMS Hood, multicolor water and smoke

Date	Mintage	F	VF	XF	Unc	BU
2007 Proof	1,500	Value: 75.00				

KM# 65   DOLLAR
0.9990 Silver, 40 mm. **Ruler:** Elizabeth II **Series:** Fighting Ships of WW II **Obv:** Crowned bust right **Obv. Legend:** QUEEN ELIZABETH II - TUVALU **Rev:** Bismarck, multicolor water and gun flashes

Date	Mintage	F	VF	XF	Unc	BU
2007 Proof	1,500	Value: 75.00				

KM# 66   DOLLAR
0.9990 Silver, 40 mm. **Ruler:** Elizabeth II **Series:** Fighting Ships of WW II **Obv:** Crowned bust right **Obv. Legend:** QUEEN ELIZABETH II - TUVALU **Rev:** IJN Yamato, multicolor water and rising sun

Date	Mintage	F	VF	XF	Unc	BU
2007 Proof	1,500	Value: 75.00				

KM# 67   DOLLAR
0.9990 Silver, 40 mm. **Ruler:** Elizabeth II **Series:** Fighting Ships of WW II **Obv:** Crowned bust right **Obv. Legend:** QUEEN ELIZABETH II - TUVALU **Rev:** USS Missouri

Date	Mintage	F	VF	XF	Unc	BU
2007 Proof	1,500	Value: 75.00				

KM# 75   DOLLAR
31.1030 g., 0.9990 Silver 0.9989 oz. ASW, 40.6 mm. **Ruler:** Elizabeth II **Subject:** Early Governors of Australia **Obv:** Head right **Rev:** Multicolor Lahlan Macquarie

Date	Mintage	F	VF	XF	Unc	BU
2008 Proof	1,808	Value: 90.00				

KM# 71   DOLLAR
31.1030 g., 0.9990 Silver 0.9989 oz. ASW, 40.6 mm. **Ruler:** Elizabeth II **Subject:** Early Governors of Austrialia **Obv:** Head right **Rev:** Multicolor Arthur Phillip **Edge:** Reeded

Date	Mintage	F	VF	XF	Unc	BU
2008 Proof	1,808	Value: 90.00				

KM# 72 DOLLAR
31.1030 g., 0.9990 Silver 0.9989 oz. ASW, 40.6 mm. **Ruler:** Elizabeth II **Subject:** Early Governors of Australia **Obv:** Head right **Rev:** Multicolor John Hunter **Edge:** Reeded

Date	Mintage	F	VF	XF	Unc	BU
2008 Proof	1,808	Value: 90.00				

KM# 73 DOLLAR
31.1030 g., 0.9990 Silver 0.9989 oz. ASW, 40.6 mm. **Ruler:** Elizabeth II **Subject:** Early Governors of Australia **Obv:** Head right **Rev:** Multicolor Philip G. King

Date	Mintage	F	VF	XF	Unc	BU
2008 Proof	1,808	Value: 90.00				

KM# 74 DOLLAR
31.1030 g., 0.9990 Silver 0.9989 oz. ASW, 40.6 mm. **Ruler:** Elizabeth II **Subject:** Early Governors of Australia **Obv:** Head right **Rev:** Multicolor William Bligh **Edge:** Reeded

Date	Mintage	F	VF	XF	Unc	BU
2008 Proof	1,808	Value: 90.00				

KM# 76 DOLLAR
37.1080 g., 0.9990 Silver 1.1918 oz. ASW, 40.6 mm. **Ruler:**

Elizabeth II **Obv:** Head right **Rev:** Multicolor Australian Lesser Blue-ringed Octopus **Edge:** Reeded

Date	Mintage	F	VF	XF	Unc	BU
2008 Proof	5,000	Value: 200				

KM# 81 DOLLAR
31.1050 g., 0.9990 Silver 0.9990 oz. ASW **Ruler:** Elizabeth II **Subject:** Motorcycles **Rev:** Indian Chief

Date	Mintage	F	VF	XF	Unc	BU
2008 Proff	—	Value: 70.00				

KM# 82 DOLLAR
31.1050 g., 0.9990 Silver 0.9990 oz. ASW **Ruler:** Elizabeth II **Subject:** Motorcycles **Rev:** BMW R12

Date	Mintage	F	VF	XF	Unc	BU
2008 Proof	—	Value: 70.00				

KM# 83 DOLLAR
31.1050 g., 0.9990 Silver 0.9990 oz. ASW **Ruler:** Elizabeth II **Subject:** Motorcycles **Rev:** BSA Gold Star DBD34

Date	Mintage	F	VF	XF	Unc	BU
2008 Proof	—	Value: 70.00				

KM# 84 DOLLAR
31.1050 g., 0.9990 Silver 0.9990 oz. ASW **Ruler:** Elizabeth II **Subject:** Motorcycles **Rev:** Norton - Commando 750

Date	Mintage	F	VF	XF	Unc	BU
2008 Proof	—	Value: 70.00				

KM# 85 DOLLAR
31.1050 g., 0.9990 Silver 0.9990 oz. ASW **Ruler:** Elizabeth II **Subject:** Motorcycles **Rev:** Honda CB760

Date	Mintage	F	VF	XF	Unc	BU
2008 Proof	—	Value: 70.00				

KM# 162 DOLLAR
31.1050 g., 0.9990 Silver 0.9990 oz. ASW, 40 mm. **Ruler:** Elizabeth II **Rev:** Charles Darwin, youthful multicolor portrait, older man portrait, ship Beagle.

Date	Mintage	F	VF	XF	Unc	BU
2009 Proof	—	Value: 75.00				

KM# 80 DOLLAR
31.1050 g., 0.9990 Silver 0.9990 oz. ASW **Ruler:** Elizabeth II **Subject:** Barbie, 50th Anniversary **Rev:** Barbie doll and drawing

Date	Mintage	F	VF	XF	Unc	BU
2009 Proof	20,000	Value: 65.00				

KM# 87 DOLLAR
31.1050 g., 0.9990 Silver 0.9990 oz. ASW, 40 mm. **Ruler:** Elizabeth II **Rev:** Saltwater Crocodile

Date	Mintage	F	VF	XF	Unc	BU
2009 Proof	—	Value: 150				

KM# 88 DOLLAR
31.1050 g., 0.9990 Silver 0.9990 oz. ASW. **Ruler:** Elizabeth II
Subject: Battle of Hastings **Rev:** Battle scene in multicolor

Date	Mintage	F	VF	XF	Unc	BU
2009 Proof	—	Value: 70.00				

KM# 89 DOLLAR
31.1050 g., 0.9990 Silver 0.9990 oz. ASW, 40.6 mm. **Ruler:**
Elizabeth II **Subject:** Battle of Cannae, 216 BC **Rev:** Battlefield
scene, multicolor

Date	Mintage	F	VF	XF	Unc	BU
2009 Proof	5,000	Value: 70.00				

KM# 90 DOLLAR
31.1050 g., 0.9990 Silver 0.9990 oz. ASW **Ruler:** Elizabeth II
Subject: Battle of Gettysburg **Rev:** Battlefield scene, multicolor

Date	Mintage	F	VF	XF	Unc	BU
2009 Proof	—	Value: 70.00				

KM# 91 DOLLAR
31.1050 g., 0.9990 Silver 0.9990 oz. ASW **Ruler:** Elizabeth II
Subject: Battle of Balaklava, 1854 **Rev:** Battle scene, multicolor

Date	Mintage	F	VF	XF	Unc	BU
2009 Proof	—	Value: 70.00				

KM# 92 DOLLAR
31.1050 g., 0.9990 Silver 0.9990 oz. ASW **Ruler:** Elizabeth II
Subject: Poltava, Peter the Great's 300th Anniversary **Rev:**
Statue of Peter on horseback, multicolor battle scene

Date	Mintage	F	VF	XF	Unc	BU
2009 Proof	—	Value: 70.00				

KM# 94 DOLLAR
31.1050 g., 0.9990 Silver 0.9990 oz. ASW, 40.6 mm. **Ruler:**
Elizabeth II **Subject:** Transformers **Rev:** Optimus Prime,
multicolor

Date	Mintage	F	VF	XF	Unc	BU
2009 Proof	5,000	Value: 75.00				

KM# 95 DOLLAR
31.1050 g., 0.9990 Silver 0.9990 oz. ASW, 40.6 mm. **Ruler:**
Elizabeth II **Subject:** Transformers **Rev:** Megatron, multicolor

Date	Mintage	F	VF	XF	Unc	BU
2009 Proof	5,000	Value: 75.00				

KM# 96 DOLLAR
31.1050 g., 0.9990 Silver 0.9990 oz. ASW, 40.6 mm. **Ruler:**
Elizabeth II **Subject:** Fall of the Berlin Wall, 20th Anniversary
Rev: Brandenburg gate, multicolor

Date	Mintage	F	VF	XF	Unc	BU
2009 Proof	5,000	Value: 65.00				

KM# 97 DOLLAR
31.1050 g., 0.9990 Silver 0.9990 oz. ASW, 40.6 mm. **Ruler:**
Elizabeth II **Subject:** Golden Age of Piracy - Black Bart **Obv:**
Head right **Rev:** Black Bart at left, multicolor treasure items at right

Date	Mintage	F	VF	XF	Unc	BU
2009 Proof	1,500	Value: 80.00				

KM# 98 DOLLAR
31.1050 g., 0.9990 Silver 0.9990 oz. ASW, 40.6 mm. **Ruler:**
Elizabeth II **Subject:** Golden Age of Piracy - Black Beard **Obv:**
Head right **Rev:** Black Beard at left, multicolor treasure chest at
right

Date	Mintage	F	VF	XF	Unc	BU
2009 Proof	1,500	Value: 80.00				

KM# 99 DOLLAR
31.1050 g., 0.9990 Silver 0.9990 oz. ASW, 40.6 mm. **Ruler:**
Elizabeth II **Subject:** Golden Age of Piracy - William Kidd **Obv:**
Head right **Rev:** William Kidd at left, multicolor pistol and treasure
map at right

Date	Mintage	F	VF	XF	Unc	BU
2009 Proof	1,500	Value: 80.00				

KM# 100 DOLLAR
31.1050 g., 0.9990 Silver 0.9990 oz. ASW, 40.6 mm. **Ruler:**
Elizabeth II **Subject:** Golden Age of Piracy - Henry Morgan **Obv:**
Head right **Rev:** Henry Morgan at left, multicolor kegs at right

Date	Mintage	F	VF	XF	Unc	BU
2009 Proof	1,500	Value: 80.00				

KM# 101 DOLLAR
31.1050 g., 0.9990 Silver 0.9990 oz. ASW, 40.6 mm. **Ruler:**
Elizabeth II **Subject:** Golden Age of Piracy - Calico Jack **Obv:**
Head right **Rev:** Calico jack at left, multicolor pirate flag at right

Date	Mintage	F	VF	XF	Unc	BU
2009 Proof	1,500	Value: 80.00				

KM# 102 DOLLAR
31.1050 g., 0.9990 Silver 0.9990 oz. ASW, 40.6 mm. **Ruler:**
Elizabeth II **Subject:** Nikolai Gogol, 200th Anniversary of Birth
Obv: Head right **Rev:** Bust at left, multicolor

Date	Mintage	F	VF	XF	Unc	BU
2009 Proof	6,000	Value: 60.00				

KM# 122 DOLLAR
31.1350 g., 0.9990 Silver 1.0000 oz. ASW, 40.6 mm. **Ruler:**
Elizabeth II **Subject:** Mendelssohn

Date	Mintage	F	VF	XF	Unc	BU
2009P Proof	5,000	Value: 80.00				

KM# 123 DOLLAR
31.1350 g., 0.9990 Silver 1.0000 oz. ASW, 40.6 mm. **Ruler:**
Elizabeth II **Subject:** Chopin

Date	Mintage	F	VF	XF	Unc	BU
2009P Proof	5,000	Value: 80.00				

KM# 133 DOLLAR
31.1350 g., 0.9990 Silver 1.0000 oz. ASW, 40.6 mm. **Ruler:**
Elizabeth II **Subject:** Battle fo Poltava, 300th Anniversary **Rev:**
Rearing horse

Date	Mintage	F	VF	XF	Unc	BU
2009P Proof	—	Value: 75.00				

KM# 93 DOLLAR
62.2100 g., 0.9990 Silver 1.9980 oz. ASW **Ruler:** Elizabeth II
Subject: Battle of Marathon **Rev:** Pheidippides' run

Date	Mintage	F	VF	XF	Unc	BU
2010 Proof	5,000	Value: 100				

KM# 103 DOLLAR
31.1050 g., 0.9990 Silver 0.9990 oz. ASW, 40.6 mm. **Ruler:**
Elizabeth II **Subject:** Anton Chekhov, 150th Anniversary of Birth
Obv: Head right **Rev:** Chekhov multicolor portrait at left, comedy
and tragedy masks at right

Date	Mintage	F	VF	XF	Unc	BU
2010 Proof	6,000	Value: 60.00				

KM# 104 DOLLAR
31.1050 g., 0.9990 Silver 0.9990 oz. ASW, 40 mm. **Ruler:**
Elizabeth II **Subject:** Great River Journeys - The Rhine **Obv:**
Head right **Rev:** Tour boat, color castle in background

Date	Mintage	F	VF	XF	Unc	BU
2010 Proof	1,500	Value: 90.00				

KM# 105 DOLLAR
31.1050 g., 0.9990 Silver 0.9990 oz. ASW, 40 mm. **Ruler:**
Elizabeth II **Subject:** Great River Journeys - Volga **Obv:** Head
right **Rev:** Tour boat and color river front view

Date	Mintage	F	VF	XF	Unc	BU
2010 Proof	1,500	Value: 90.00				

KM# 106 DOLLAR
31.1050 g., 0.9990 Silver 0.9990 oz. ASW, 40 mm. **Ruler:**
Elizabeth II **Subject:** Great River Journeys - Yangtzee **Obv:**
Head right **Rev:** Sail boat and color river gorge

Date	Mintage	F	VF	XF	Unc	BU
2010 Proof	1,500	Value: 90.00				

KM# 107 DOLLAR
31.1050 g., 0.9990 Silver 0.9990 oz. ASW, 40 mm. **Ruler:**
Elizabeth II **Subject:** Great River Journeys - Mississippi **Obv:**
Head right **Rev:** Delta Queen and multicolor New Orleans skyline

Date	Mintage	F	VF	XF	Unc	BU
2010 Proof	1,500	Value: 90.00				

KM# 108 DOLLAR
31.1050 g., 0.9990 Silver 0.9990 oz. ASW, 40 mm. **Ruler:**
Elizabeth II **Subject:** Great River Journeys - The Nile **Obv:** Head
right **Rev:** Dhow, classical sculpture, multicolor sandscape

Date	Mintage	F	VF	XF	Unc	BU
2010 Proof	1,500	Value: 90.00				

KM# 109 DOLLAR
31.1050 g., 0.9990 Silver 0.9990 oz. ASW, 40 mm. **Ruler:**
Elizabeth II **Subject:** Ned Kelly - Outlaw **Obv:** Head right **Rev:**
Ned Kelly multicolor - Reward Poster

Date	Mintage	F	VF	XF	Unc	BU
2010 Proof	1,880	Value: 90.00				

KM# 110 DOLLAR
31.1050 g., 0.9990 Silver 0.9990 oz. ASW, 40 mm. **Ruler:**
Elizabeth II **Subject:** Ned Kelly - Armour **Obv:** Head right **Rev:**
Ned Kelley's helmet in multicolor

Date	Mintage	F	VF	XF	Unc	BU
2010 Proof	1,880	Value: 90.00				

KM# 111 DOLLAR
31.1050 g., 0.9990 Silver 0.9990 oz. ASW, 40 mm. **Ruler:**
Elizabeth II **Subject:** Ned Kelly - Siege **Obv:** Head right **Rev:**
Ned Kelly in shoutout, multicolor

Date	Mintage	F	VF	XF	Unc	BU
2010 Proof	1,880	Value: 90.00				

KM# 112 DOLLAR
31.1050 g., 0.9990 Silver 0.9990 oz. ASW, 40 mm. **Ruler:**
Elizabeth II **Subject:** Ned Kelly - Gallows **Obv:** Head right **Rev:**
Ned Kelly standing at the gallows, multicolor

Date	Mintage	F	VF	XF	Unc	BU
2010 Proof	1,880	Value: 90.00				

KM# 113 DOLLAR
25.0000 g., 0.9250 Silver 0.7435 oz. ASW **Ruler:** Elizabeth II
Rev: Sea horse facing left, Swarovski crystal chip eye **Shape:**
38.61

Date	Mintage	F	VF	XF	Unc	BU
2010 Proof	2,500	Value: 65.00				

KM# 114 DOLLAR
0.5000 g., 0.9990 Gold 0.0161 oz. AGW, 11 mm. **Ruler:**
Elizabeth II **Rev:** Sea horse facing right

Date	Mintage	F	VF	XF	Unc	BU
2010 Proof	15,000	Value: 50.00				

KM# 115 DOLLAR
25.0000 g., 0.9250 Silver 0.7435 oz. ASW, 38.6 mm. **Ruler:**
Elizabeth II **Subject:** Marine Life **Rev:** Hawksbill sea turtle,
multicolor

Date	Mintage	F	VF	XF	Unc	BU
2010 Proof	2,500	Value: 50.00				

KM# 117 DOLLAR
31.1350 g., 0.9990 Silver 1.0000 oz. ASW, 40.6 mm. **Ruler:**
Elizabeth II **Subject:** Ballet - Don Quixote **Rev:** Multicolor
windmill scene

Date	Mintage	F	VF	XF	Unc	BU
2010P Proof	2,500	Value: 80.00				

KM# 118 DOLLAR
31.1350 g., 0.9990 Silver 1.0000 oz. ASW, 40.6 mm. **Ruler:**
Elizabeth II **Subject:** Ballet - Sleeping Beauty **Rev:** Multicolor
castle scene

Date	Mintage	F	VF	XF	Unc	BU
2010P Proof	2,500	Value: 80.00				

KM# 119 DOLLAR
31.1350 g., 0.9990 Silver 1.0000 oz. ASW, 40.6 mm. **Ruler:**
Elizabeth II **Subject:** Ballet - Nutcracker **Rev:** Multicolor snow
scene

Date	Mintage	F	VF	XF	Unc	BU
2010P Proof	2,500	Value: 80.00				

KM# 120 DOLLAR
31.1350 g., 0.9990 Silver 1.0000 oz. ASW, 40.6 mm. **Ruler:**
Elizabeth II **Subject:** Ballet - Swan Lake **Rev:** Multicolor swan
and lake scene

Date	Mintage	F	VF	XF	Unc	BU
2010P Proof	2,500	Value: 80.00				

KM# 121 DOLLAR
31.1350 g., 0.9990 Silver 1.0000 oz. ASW, 40.6 mm. **Ruler:**
Elizabeth II **Subject:** Ballet - Cinderella **Rev:** Multicolor pumpkin
coach scene

Date	Mintage	F	VF	XF	Unc	BU
2010P Proof	2,500	Value: 80.00				

KM# 124 DOLLAR
31.1350 g., 0.9990 Silver 1.0000 oz. ASW, 40.6 mm. **Ruler:**
Elizabeth II **Subject:** Robert Schumann **Rev:** Bust, G-cleff and
score

Date	Mintage	F	VF	XF	Unc	BU
2010P Proof	5,000	Value: 80.00				

KM# 125   DOLLAR
31.1350 g., 0.9990 Silver 1.0000 oz. ASW, 40.6 mm.   **Ruler:**
Elizabeth II **Subject:** Gustav Mahler

Date	Mintage	F	VF	XF	Unc	BU
2010P Proof	5,000	Value: 80.00				

KM# 127   DOLLAR
31.1350 g., 0.9990 Silver 1.0000 oz. ASW, 40.6 mm.   **Ruler:**
Elizabeth II **Subject:** Warrior - Legionary **Rev:** Multicolor Roman
Legionary soldier standing

Date	Mintage	F	VF	XF	Unc	BU
2010P Proof	—	Value: 80.00				

KM# 128   DOLLAR
31.1350 g., 0.9990 Silver 1.0000 oz. ASW, 40.6 mm.   **Ruler:**
Elizabeth II **Subject:** Warrior - Viking **Rev:** Multicolor Viking

Date	Mintage	F	VF	XF	Unc	BU
2010P Proof	—	Value: 80.00				

KM# 129   DOLLAR
31.1350 g., 0.9990 Silver 1.0000 oz. ASW, 40.6 mm.   **Ruler:**
Elizabeth II **Subject:** Warrior - Knight **Rev:** Multicolor Knight

Date	Mintage	F	VF	XF	Unc	BU
2010P Proof	—	Value: 80.00				

KM# 130   DOLLAR
31.1350 g., 0.9990 Silver 1.0000 oz. ASW, 40.6 mm.   **Ruler:**
Elizabeth II **Subject:** Warrior - Samurai **Rev:** Multicolor Samurai

Date	Mintage	F	VF	XF	Unc	BU
2010P Proof	—	Value: 80.00				

KM# 131   DOLLAR
31.1350 g., 0.9990 Silver 1.0000 oz. ASW, 40 mm.   **Ruler:**
Elizabeth II **Subject:** "Banjo" Paterson Ballard - Man from Snowy
River **Rev:** Multicolor cowboy chasing two horses

Date	Mintage	F	VF	XF	Unc	BU
2010P Proof	—	Value: 80.00				

KM# 134   DOLLAR
31.1350 g., 0.9990 Silver 1.0000 oz. ASW, 40.6 mm.   **Ruler:**
Elizabeth II **Rev:** Multicolor brown snake

Date	Mintage	F	VF	XF	Unc	BU
2010P Proof	—	Value: 165				

KM# 135   DOLLAR
31.1350 g., 0.9990 Silver 1.0000 oz. ASW, 40.6 mm.   **Ruler:**
Elizabeth II **Subject:** German Unification, 20th Anniversary **Rev:**
Large 20, statues on Brandenburg gate

Date	Mintage	F	VF	XF	Unc	BU
2010P Proof	5,000	Value: 75.00				

KM# 136   DOLLAR
31.1350 g., 0.9990 Silver 1.0000 oz. ASW, 40.6 mm.   **Ruler:**
Elizabeth II **Subject:** Sir Charles Kingsford

Date	Mintage	F	VF	XF	Unc	BU
2010P Proof	—	Value: 75.00				

KM# 137   DOLLAR
31.1350 g., 0.9990 Silver 1.0000 oz. ASW, 40.6 mm.   **Ruler:**
Elizabeth II **Subject:** Working dogs **Rev:** Multicolor golden
retreiver pups

Date	Mintage	F	VF	XF	Unc	BU
2010P Proof	—	Value: 75.00				

KM# 138   DOLLAR
31.1350 g., 0.9990 Silver 1.0000 oz. ASW, 40.6 mm.   **Ruler:**
Elizabeth II **Subject:** Man from Snowy River **Rev:** Multicolor
group of horsemen

Date	Mintage	F	VF	XF	Unc	BU
2010P Proof	—	Value: 75.00				

KM# 139   DOLLAR
31.1350 g., 0.9990 Silver 1.0000 oz. ASW, 40.7 mm.   **Ruler:**
Elizabeth II **Subject:** Trucks - W900 **Rev:** Truck cab

Date	Mintage	F	VF	XF	Unc	BU
2010P Proof	—					

KM# 140   DOLLAR
31.1350 g., 0.9990 Silver 1.0000 oz. ASW, 40.6 mm.   **Ruler:**
Elizabeth II **Subject:** Trucks - Cascadia **Rev:** Multicolor truck cab

Date	Mintage	F	VF	XF	Unc	BU
2010P Proof	—	Value: 75.00				

KM# 141   DOLLAR
31.1350 g., 0.9990 Silver 1.0000 oz. ASW, 40.6 mm.   **Ruler:**
Elizabeth II **Subject:** Trucks - R500 **Rev:** Multicolor truck cab

Date	Mintage	F	VF	XF	Unc	BU
2010P Proof	—	Value: 75.00				

KM# 142   DOLLAR
31.1350 g., 0.9990 Silver 1.0000 oz. ASW, 40.6 mm.   **Ruler:**
Elizabeth II **Subject:** Trucks - GiGamax **Rev:** Multicolor truck cab

Date	Mintage	F	VF	XF	Unc	BU
2010P Proof	—	Value: 75.00				

KM# 143   DOLLAR
31.1350 g., 0.9990 Silver 1.0000 oz. ASW, 40.7 mm.   **Ruler:**
Elizabeth II **Subject:** Tanks - A22 Churchill **Rev:** Multicolor tank

Date	Mintage	F	VF	XF	Unc	BU
2010P Proof	—	Value: 75.00				

KM# 144 DOLLAR
31.1350 g., 0.9990 Silver 1.0000 oz. ASW **Ruler:** Elizabeth II
Subject: Tanks - M-4 Sherman **Rev:** Multicolor tank **Shape:** 40.6

Date	Mintage	F	VF	XF	Unc	BU
2010P Proof	—	Value: 75.00				

KM# 145 DOLLAR
31.1350 g., 0.9990 Silver 1.0000 oz. ASW, 40.6 mm. **Ruler:**
Elizabeth II **Subject:** Tanks - Type 97 Chi-Ha **Rev:** Multicolor tank

Date	Mintage	F	VF	XF	Unc	BU
2010P Proof	—	Value: 75.00				

KM# 146 DOLLAR
31.1350 g., 0.9990 Silver 1.0000 oz. ASW, 40.6 mm. **Ruler:**
Elizabeth II **Subject:** Tanks - T-34 **Rev:** Multicolor tank

Date	Mintage	F	VF	XF	Unc	BU
2010P Proof	—	Value: 75.00				

KM# 147 DOLLAR
31.1350 g., 0.9990 Silver 1.0000 oz. ASW, 40.6 mm. **Ruler:**
Elizabeth II **Subject:** Tanks - PzK pfw VI Tiger 1 **Rev:** Multicolor
tank

Date	Mintage	F	VF	XF	Unc	BU
2010P Proof	—	Value: 75.00				

KM# 148 DOLLAR
13.9000 g., Aluminum-Bronze, 30.6 mm. **Ruler:** Elizabeth II
Rev: Blackbeard standing, treasure chest at right

Date	Mintage	F	VF	XF	Unc	BU
2010P	—	—	—	—	—	15.00

KM# 126 DOLLAR
31.1350 g., 0.9990 Silver 1.0000 oz. ASW, 40.6 mm. **Ruler:**
Elizabeth II **Subject:** Franz List

Date	Mintage	F	VF	XF	Unc	BU
2011P Proof	5,000	Value: 80.00				

KM# 163 DOLLAR
31.1350 g., 0.9990 Silver 1.0000 oz. ASW, 40.6 mm. **Ruler:**
Elizabeth II **Subject:** Australia's extinct animals - Thylacine **Obv:**
Head in diadem right **Rev:** Thylacine - Tasmanian tiger in
multicolor

Date	Mintage	F	VF	XF	Unc	BU
2011P Proof	5,000	Value: 175				

KM# 165 DOLLAR
31.1050 g., 0.9990 Silver 0.9990 oz. ASW, 40.6 mm. **Ruler:**
Elizabeth II **Obv:** Head with tiara right **Rev:** Australia's Box
Jellyfish in color **Edge:** Reeded

Date	Mintage	F	VF	XF	Unc	BU
2011 Proof	5,000	Value: 100				

KM# 172 DOLLAR
31.1050 g., 0.9990 Silver 0.9990 oz. ASW, 40.6 mm. **Ruler:**
Elizabeth II **Subject:** Franz Lizst, 200th anniversary of birth **Rev:**
Lizst at left, G-cleft, 4 lines of score

Date	Mintage	F	VF	XF	Unc	BU
2011 Proof	—	Value: 80.00				

KM# 177 DOLLAR
13.8000 g., Aluminum-Bronze, 30.6 mm. **Ruler:** Elizabeth II
Subject: Henry Morgan **Rev:** Morgan, ship, chest and barrels

Date	Mintage	F	VF	XF	Unc	BU
2011P	—	—	—	—	—	15.00

KM# 178 DOLLAR
13.8000 g., Aluminum-Bronze, 30.8 mm. **Ruler:** Elizabeth II
Subject: Calico Jack **Rev:** Jack standing, ship, Skull and
crossed-swords flag

Date	Mintage	F	VF	XF	Unc	BU
2011P	—	—	—	—	—	15.00

KM# 179 DOLLAR
13.8000 g., Aluminum-Bronze, 30.8 mm. **Ruler:** Elizabeth II
Subject: Black Bart **Rev:** Bart at left, ship and cross

Date	Mintage	F	VF	XF	Unc	BU
2011P	—	—	—	—	—	15.00

KM# 180 DOLLAR
13.8000 g., Aluminum-Bronze, 30.8 mm. **Ruler:** Elizabeth II
Subject: William Kidd **Rev:** Bust at left, ship, pistol and map

Date	Mintage	F	VF	XF	Unc	BU
2011P	—	—	—	—	—	15.00

KM# 181 DOLLAR
31.1350 g., 0.9990 Silver 1.0000 oz. ASW, 40.6 mm. **Ruler:**
Elizabeth II **Subject:** Ships that changed the World **Rev:** Santa
Maria under sail

Date	Mintage	F	VF	XF	Unc	BU
2011P Proof	5,000	Value: 75.00				

KM# 182   DOLLAR
31.1350 g., 0.9990 Silver 1.0000 oz. ASW, 40.6 mm.   **Ruler:**
Elizabeth II **Subject:** Ships that changed the World **Rev:** Golden
Hind under sail

Date	Mintage	F	VF	XF	Unc	BU
2011P Proof	5,000	Value: 75.00				

KM# 183   DOLLAR
31.1350 g., 0.9990 Silver 1.0000 oz. ASW, 40.6 mm.   **Ruler:**
Elizabeth II **Subject:** Heroes and Villains **Rev:** Holmes and
Moriarty

Date	Mintage	F	VF	XF	Unc	BU
2011P Proof	1,500	Value: 75.00				

KM# 184   DOLLAR
31.1350 g., 0.9990 Silver 1.0000 oz. ASW, 40.6 mm.   **Ruler:**
Elizabeth II **Subject:** Heroes and Villains **Rev:** van Helsing and
Dracula

Date	Mintage	F	VF	XF	Unc	BU
2011P Proof	1,500	Value: 75.00				

KM# 185   DOLLAR
31.1350 g., 0.9990 Silver 1.0000 oz. ASW, 40.6 mm.   **Ruler:**
Elizabeth II **Subject:** Heroes and Villains **Rev:** Robin Hood and
the Sherif

Date	Mintage	F	VF	XF	Unc	BU
2011P Proof	1,500	Value: 75.00				

KM# 186   DOLLAR
31.1350 g., 0.9990 Silver 1.0000 oz. ASW, 40.6 mm.   **Ruler:**
Elizabeth II **Subject:** Heros and Villains **Rev:** Peter Pan and
Captain Hook

Date	Mintage	F	VF	XF	Unc	BU
2011P Proof	1,500	Value: 75.00				

KM# 187   DOLLAR
31.1350 g., 0.9990 Silver 1.0000 oz. ASW, 40.6 mm.   **Ruler:**
Elizabeth II **Subject:** Heroes and Villains **Rev:** Dr. Jeckel and
Mr. Hyde

Date	Mintage	F	VF	XF	Unc	BU
2011P Proof	1,500	Value: 75.00				

KM# 188   DOLLAR
31.1350 g., 0.9990 Silver 1.0000 oz. ASW, 40.6 mm.   **Ruler:**
Elizabeth II **Subject:** Ships that changed the World **Rev:**
Mayflower at sail

Date	Mintage	F	VF	XF	Unc	BU
2012P Proof	5,000	Value: 100				

KM# 189   DOLLAR
31.1350 g., 0.9990 Silver 1.0000 oz. ASW, 40.6 mm.   **Ruler:**
Elizabeth II **Subject:** Ships that changed the World **Rev:** U.S.S.
Constitution in sea battle

Date	Mintage	F	VF	XF	Unc	BU
2012P Proof	5,000	Value: 100				

KM# 190   DOLLAR
13.8000 g., Aluminum-Bronze, 30.6 mm.   **Ruler:** Elizabeth II
Subject: Year of the Dragon **Rev:** Baby Dragon in color

Date	Mintage	F	VF	XF	Unc	BU
2012	10,000	—	—	—	—	15.00

KM# 192   DOLLAR
31.1350 g., 0.9990 Silver 1.0000 oz. ASW, 40.6 mm.   **Ruler:**
Elizabeth II **Rev:** R.M.S. Titanic sailing forward, tug at side

Date	Mintage	F	VF	XF	Unc	BU
2012P Proof	5,000	Value: 100				

KM# 194   DOLLAR
31.1350 g., 0.9990 Silver 1.0000 oz. ASW   **Ruler:** Elizabeth II
Subject: Wildlife in Need **Obv:** Head with tiara right **Rev:** Black
rhinoceros and calf in color **Edge:** Reeded

Date	Mintage	F	VF	XF	Unc	BU
2012P Proof	5,000	Value: 100				

KM# 173   2 DOLLARS
Silver, 38.6 mm.   **Ruler:** Elizabeth II **Subject:** Year of the Goat
Obv: Head crowned right **Rev:** Two goats

Date	Mintage	F	VF	XF	Unc	BU
2003 Proof	—	Value: 50.00				

KM# 175   2 DOLLARS
31.1050 g., 0.9990 Silver 0.9990 oz. ASW, 38.6 mm.   **Ruler:**
Elizabeth II **Obv:** Head crowned right **Rev:** Harry Potter with
wand raised, being followed by Dementor

Date	Mintage	F	VF	XF	Unc	BU
2004 Proof	—	Value: 50.00				

KM# 116   2 DOLLARS
1.2400 g., 0.9990 Gold 0.0398 oz. AGW, 13.92 mm.   **Ruler:**
Elizabeth II **Rev:** Los Reyes sailing ship

Date	Mintage	F	VF	XF	Unc	BU
2010 Proof	15,000	Value: 80.00				

KM# 169   2 DOLLARS
Gold, 13.9 mm.   **Ruler:** Elizabeth II **Subject:** Marine life **Rev:**
Sea horse

Date	Mintage	F	VF	XF	Unc	BU
2010 Proof	—	Value: 75.00				

KM# 174   3 DOLLARS
1.2240 g., 0.9990 Gold 0.0393 oz. AGW, 13.9 mm.   **Ruler:**
Elizabeth II **Subject:** Year of the Horse **Rev:** Horse galloping right

Date	Mintage	F	VF	XF	Unc	BU
2002 Proof	—	Value: 115				
2008 Proof	—	Value: 115				

KM# 158   3 DOLLARS
1.2240 g., 0.9990 Gold 0.0393 oz. AGW, 13.9 mm.   **Ruler:**
Elizabeth II **Rev:** Australian owl

Date	Mintage	F	VF	XF	Unc	BU
2005 Proof	—	Value: 85.00				
2006 Proof	—	Value: 85.00				
2007 Proof	—	Value: 85.00				

KM# 152   3 DOLLARS
1.2240 g., 0.9990 Gold 0.0393 oz. AGW, 13.9 mm.   **Ruler:**
Elizabeth II **Rev:** Multicolor mouse with heart

Date	Mintage	F	VF	XF	Unc	BU
2008	—	—	—	—	—	95.00

KM# 49 5 DOLLARS
62.5000 g., 0.9990 Silver 2.0073 oz. ASW, 49.9 mm. **Ruler:** Elizabeth II **Subject:** Dinosaurs **Obv:** Crowned head right **Rev:** Giganotosaurus **Edge:** Reeded

Date	Mintage	F	VF	XF	Unc	BU
2002 Proof	1,000	Value: 90.00				

KM# 50 5 DOLLARS
62.5000 g., 0.9990 Silver 2.0073 oz. ASW, 49.9 mm. **Ruler:** Elizabeth II **Subject:** Dinosaurs **Obv:** Crowned head right **Rev:** Dromaeosaurus **Edge:** Reeded

Date	Mintage	F	VF	XF	Unc	BU
2002 Proof	1,000	Value: 90.00				

KM# 51 5 DOLLARS
62.5000 g., 0.9990 Silver 2.0073 oz. ASW, 49.9 mm. **Ruler:** Elizabeth II **Subject:** Dinosaurs **Obv:** Crowned head right **Rev:** Stegosaurus **Edge:** Reeded

Date	Mintage	F	VF	XF	Unc	BU
2002 Proof	1,000	Value: 90.00				

KM# 52 5 DOLLARS
62.5000 g., 0.9990 Silver 2.0073 oz. ASW, 49.9 mm. **Ruler:** Elizabeth II **Subject:** Dinosaurs **Obv:** Crowned head right **Rev:** Seismosaurus **Edge:** Reeded

Date	Mintage	F	VF	XF	Unc	BU
2002 Proof	1,000	Value: 90.00				

KM# 159 15 DOLLARS
3.1110 g., 0.9990 Gold 0.0999 oz. AGW, 17.95 mm. **Ruler:** Elizabeth II **Rev:** Australian owl

Date	Mintage	F	VF	XF	Unc	BU
2005 Proof	—	Value: 175				
2006 Proof	—	Value: 175				
2007 Proof	—	Value: 175				

KM# 153 15 DOLLARS
3.1110 g., 0.9990 Gold 0.0999 oz. AGW, 17.95 mm. **Ruler:** Elizabeth II **Rev:** Multicolor mouse and golden egg

Date	Mintage	F	VF	XF	Unc	BU
2008	—	—	—	—	—	235

KM# 132 25 DOLLARS
7.7700 g., 0.9990 Gold 0.2496 oz. AGW, 22.6 mm. **Ruler:** Elizabeth II **Subject:** Ned Kelly **Rev:** Multicolor gun slinger and steel helmet

Date	Mintage	Good	VG	F	VF	XF
2010P Proof	1,000	Value: 600				

KM# 160 30 DOLLARS
6.2220 g., 0.9990 Gold 0.1998 oz. AGW, 21.95 mm. **Ruler:** Elizabeth II **Rev:** Australian owl

Date	Mintage	F	VF	XF	Unc	BU
2005 Proof	—	Value: 350				
2006 Proof	—	Value: 350				
2007 Proof	—	Value: 350				

KM# 176 30 DOLLARS
6.2200 g., 0.9990 Platinum 0.1998 oz. APW, 21.95 mm. **Ruler:** Elizabeth II **Subject:** Year of the Horse **Obv:** Head crowned right **Rev:** Horse galloping right

Date	Mintage	F	VF	XF	Unc	BU
2008 Proof	—	Value: 400				

KM# 154 30 DOLLARS
15.5540 g., 0.9990 Gold 0.4996 oz. AGW, 21.95 mm. **Ruler:** Elizabeth II **Rev:** Multicolor mouse and money bag

Date	Mintage	F	VF	XF	Unc	BU
2008	—	—	—	—	—	950

KM# 167 30 DOLLARS
6.2200 g., 0.9995 Platinum 0.1999 oz. APW **Ruler:** Elizabeth II **Rev:** Horse galloping right

Date	Mintage	F	VF	XF	Unc	BU
2008 Proof	—	Value: 500				

KM# 155 30 DOLLARS
6.2200 g., 0.9990 Gold 0.1998 oz. AGW, 21.95 mm. **Ruler:** Elizabeth II **Rev:** Cow seated with fans above

Date	Mintage	F	VF	XF	Unc	BU
2009	—	—	—	—	—	320

KM# 156 30 DOLLARS
6.2200 g., 0.9990 Gold 0.1998 oz. AGW, 21.95 mm. **Ruler:** Elizabeth II **Rev:** Cow standing with success symbol

Date	Mintage	F	VF	XF	Unc	BU
2009	—	—	—	—	—	320

KM# 157 30 DOLLARS
6.2200 g., 0.9990 Gold 0.1998 oz. AGW, 21.95 mm. **Ruler:** Elizabeth II **Rev:** Cow standing next to money bag

Date	Mintage	F	VF	XF	Unc	BU
2009	—	—	—	—	—	320

KM# 164 30 DOLLARS
6.2200 g., 0.9990 Gold 0.1998 oz. AGW **Ruler:** Elizabeth II **Obv:** Head crowned right **Rev:** Horse running right

Date	Mintage	F	VF	XF	Unc	BU
2010 Proof	—	Value: 350				

KM# 166 30 DOLLARS
6.2200 g., 0.9995 Gold 0.1999 oz. AGW **Ruler:** Elizabeth II **Rev:** Horse galloping right

Date	Mintage	F	VF	XF	Unc	BU
2010 Proof	—	Value: 400				

KM# 161 50 DOLLARS
15.5540 g., 0.9990 Gold 0.4996 oz. AGW, 30 mm. **Ruler:** Elizabeth II **Rev:** Australiam owl

Date	Mintage	F	VF	XF	Unc	BU
2005 Proof	—	Value: 800				
2006 Proof	—	Value: 800				
2007 Proof	—	Value: 800				

KM# 69 100 DOLLARS
Gold **Ruler:** Elizabeth II **Obv:** Crowned head right **Rev:** Red 1963 Corvette Sting Ray

Date	Mintage	F	VF	XF	Unc	BU
2006 Proof	250	Value: 1,600				

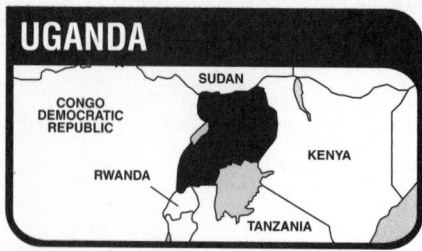

UGANDA

The Republic of Uganda, a former British protectorate located astride the equator in east-central Africa, has an area of 91,134 sq. mi. (236,040 sq. km.) and a population of *17 million. Capital: Kampala. Agriculture, including livestock, is the basis of the economy; there is some mining of copper, tin, gold and lead. Coffee, cotton, copper and tea are exported.

Uganda is a member of the Commonwealth of Nations. The president is Chief of State and Head of Government.

For earlier coinage refer to East Africa.

MONETARY SYSTEM
100 Cents = 1 Shilling

REPUBLIC

STANDARD COINAGE

KM# 66   50 SHILLINGS
4.0000 g., Nickel Plated Steel **Obv:** National arms **Rev:** Antelope head facing

Date	Mintage	F	VF	XF	Unc	BU
2003	—	—	—	—	1.00	1.25
2007	—	—	—	—	1.00	1.25

KM# 67   100 SHILLINGS
7.0000 g., Copper-Nickel, 26.9 mm. **Obv:** National arms **Rev:** African bull **Edge:** Reeded

Date	Mintage	F	VF	XF	Unc	BU
2003	—	—	—	—	1.50	1.75
2007	—	—	—	—	1.50	1.75
2008	—	—	—	—	1.50	1.75

KM# 129   100 SHILLINGS
3.5400 g., Stainless Steel, 23.98 mm. **Series:** Zodiac **Obv:** National arms **Rev:** Monkey with elf-like ears **Edge:** Plain

Date	Mintage	F	VF	XF	Unc	BU
2004	—	—	—	—	1.50	2.50

KM# 135   100 SHILLINGS
3.5400 g., Steel, 23.98 mm. **Series:** Zodiac **Obv:** National arms **Rev:** Ox **Edge:** Plain

Date	Mintage	F	VF	XF	Unc	BU
2004	—	—	—	—	1.50	2.50

KM# 136   100 SHILLINGS
3.5400 g., Steel, 23.98 mm. **Series:** Zodiac **Obv:** National arms **Rev:** Goat **Edge:** Plain

Date	Mintage	F	VF	XF	Unc	BU
2004	—	—	—	—	1.50	2.50

KM# 137   100 SHILLINGS
3.5400 g., Steel, 23.98 mm. **Series:** Zodiac **Obv:** National arms **Rev:** Horse **Edge:** Plain

Date	Mintage	F	VF	XF	Unc	BU
2004	—	—	—	—	1.50	2.50

KM# 138   100 SHILLINGS
3.5400 g., Steel, 23.98 mm. **Series:** Zodiac **Obv:** National arms **Rev:** Dragon **Edge:** Plain

Date	Mintage	F	VF	XF	Unc	BU
2004	—	—	—	—	1.50	2.50

KM# 139   100 SHILLINGS
3.5400 g., Steel, 23.98 mm. **Series:** Zodiac **Obv:** National arms **Rev:** Dog **Edge:** Plain

Date	Mintage	F	VF	XF	Unc	BU
2004	—	—	—	—	1.50	2.50

KM# 140   100 SHILLINGS
3.5400 g., Steel, 23.98 mm. **Series:** Zodiac **Obv:** National arms **Rev:** Tiger **Edge:** Plain

Date	Mintage	F	VF	XF	Unc	BU
2004	—	—	—	—	1.50	2.50

KM# 141   100 SHILLINGS
3.5400 g., Steel, 23.98 mm. **Series:** Zodiac **Obv:** National arms **Rev:** Snake **Edge:** Plain

Date	Mintage	F	VF	XF	Unc	BU
2004	—	—	—	—	1.50	2.50

KM# 142   100 SHILLINGS
3.5400 g., Steel, 23.98 mm. **Series:** Zodiac **Obv:** National arms **Rev:** Rooster **Edge:** Plain

Date	Mintage	F	VF	XF	Unc	BU
2004	—	—	—	—	1.50	2.50

KM# 143   100 SHILLINGS
3.5400 g., Steel, 23.98 mm. **Series:** Zodiac **Obv:** National arms **Rev:** Rabbit **Edge:** Plain

Date	Mintage	F	VF	XF	Unc	BU
2004	—	—	—	—	1.50	2.50

KM# 144   100 SHILLINGS
3.5400 g., Steel, 23.98 mm. **Series:** Zodiac **Obv:** National arms **Rev:** Rat **Edge:** Plain

Date	Mintage	F	VF	XF	Unc	BU
2004	—	—	—	—	1.50	2.50

KM# 145   100 SHILLINGS
3.5400 g., Steel, 23.98 mm. **Series:** Zodiac **Obv:** National arms **Rev:** Pig **Edge:** Plain

Date	Mintage	F	VF	XF	Unc	BU
2004	—	—	—	—	1.50	2.50

KM# 130   100 SHILLINGS
Steel, 23 mm. **Rev:** Type I of five different monkeys

Date	Mintage	F	VF	XF	Unc	BU
2004	—	—	—	—	1.75	2.75

KM# 131   100 SHILLINGS
Steel, 23 mm. **Rev:** Type II of five different monkeys

Date	Mintage	F	VF	XF	Unc	BU
2004	—	—	—	—	1.75	2.75

KM# 132   100 SHILLINGS
Steel, 23 mm. **Rev:** Type III of five different monkeys

Date	Mintage	F	VF	XF	Unc	BU
2004	—	—	—	—	1.75	2.75

KM# 133   100 SHILLINGS
Steel, 23 mm. **Rev:** Type IV of five different monkys

Date	Mintage	F	VF	XF	Unc	BU
2004	—	—	—	—	1.50	2.75

KM# 134   100 SHILLINGS
Steel, 23 mm. **Rev:** Type V of five different monkeys

Date	Mintage	F	VF	XF	Unc	BU
2004	—	—	—	—	1.75	2.75

KM# 188   100 SHILLINGS
3.5300 g., Nickel Plated Steel, 24 mm. **Series:** Zodiac **Obv:** National arms **Obv. Legend:** BANK OF UGANDA **Rev:** Head of a rat **Rev. Legend:** BANK OF UGANDA **Edge:** Plain

Date	Mintage	F	VF	XF	Unc	BU
2004	—	—	—	—	1.75	2.75

KM# 189   100 SHILLINGS
3.5300 g., Nickel Plated Steel, 24 mm. **Series:** Zodiac **Obv:** National arms **Obv. Legend:** BANK OF UGANDA **Rev:** Head of an ox **Rev. Legend:** BANK OF UGANDA **Edge:** Plain

Date	Mintage	F	VF	XF	Unc	BU
2004	—	—	—	—	1.75	2.75

KM# 190   100 SHILLINGS
3.5300 g., Nickel Plated Steel, 24 mm. **Series:** Zodiac **Obv:** National arms **Obv. Legend:** BANK OF UGANDA **Rev:** Head of a tiger **Rev. Legend:** BANK OF UGANDA **Edge:** Plain

Date	Mintage	F	VF	XF	Unc	BU
2004	—	—	—	—	1.75	2.75

KM# 191   100 SHILLINGS
3.5300 g., Nickel Plated Steel, 24 mm. **Series:** Zodiac **Obv:** National arms **Obv. Legend:** BANK OF UGANDA **Rev:** Head of a rabbit **Rev. Legend:** BANK OF UGANDA **Edge:** Plain

Date	Mintage	F	VF	XF	Unc	BU
2004	—	—	—	—	1.75	2.75

KM# 192   100 SHILLINGS
3.5300 g., Nickel Plated Steel, 24 mm. **Series:** Zodiac **Obv:** National arms **Obv. Legend:** BANK OF UGANDA **Rev:** Head of a dragon **Rev. Legend:** BANK OF UGANDA **Edge:** Plain

Date	Mintage	F	VF	XF	Unc	BU
2004	—	—	—	—	1.75	2.75

KM# 193   100 SHILLINGS
3.5300 g., Nickel Plated Steel, 24 mm. **Series:** Zodiac **Obv:** National arms **Obv. Legend:** BANK OF UGANDA **Rev:** Head and hood of Cobra snake **Rev. Legend:** BANK OF UGANDA **Edge:** Plain

Date	Mintage	F	VF	XF	Unc	BU
2004	—	—	—	—	1.75	2.75

KM# 194   100 SHILLINGS
3.5300 g., Nickel Plated Steel, 24 mm. **Series:** Zodiac **Obv:** National arms **Obv. Legend:** BANK OF UGANDA **Rev:** Head of a horse **Rev. Legend:** BANK OF UGANDA **Edge:** Plain

Date	Mintage	F	VF	XF	Unc	BU
2004	—	—	—	—	1.75	2.75

KM# 195   100 SHILLINGS
3.5300 g., Nickel Plated Steel, 24 mm. **Series:** Zodiac **Obv:** National arms **Obv. Legend:** BANK OF UGANDA **Rev:** Head of a goat **Rev. Legend:** BANK OF UGANDA **Edge:** Plain

Date	Mintage	F	VF	XF	Unc	BU
2004	—	—	—	—	1.75	2.75

KM# 196   100 SHILLINGS
3.5300 g., Nickel Plated Steel, 24 mm. **Series:** Zodiac **Obv:** National arms **Obv. Legend:** BANK OF UGANDA **Rev:** Head of a monkey **Rev. Legend:** BANK OF UGANDA **Edge:** Plain

Date	Mintage	F	VF	XF	Unc	BU
2004	—	—	—	—	1.75	2.75

KM# 197   100 SHILLINGS
3.5300 g., Nickel Plated Steel, 24 mm. **Series:** Zodiac **Obv:** National arms **Obv. Legend:** BANK OF UGANDA **Rev:** Forepart of a rooster **Rev. Legend:** BANK OF UGANDA **Edge:** Plain

Date	Mintage	F	VF	XF	Unc	BU
2004	—	—	—	—	1.75	2.75

KM# 198   100 SHILLINGS
3.5300 g., Nickel Plated Steel, 24 mm. **Series:** Zodiac **Obv:** National arms **Obv. Legend:** BANK OF UGANDA **Rev:** Head of a dog **Rev. Legend:** BANK OF UGANDA **Edge:** Plain

Date	Mintage	F	VF	XF	Unc	BU
2004	—	—	—	—	1.75	2.75

KM# 199   100 SHILLINGS
3.5300 g., Nickel Plated Steel, 24 mm. **Series:** Zodiac **Obv:** National arms **Obv. Legend:** BANK OF UGANDA **Rev:** Head of a pig **Rev. Legend:** BANK OF UGANDA **Edge:** Plain

Date	Mintage	F	VF	XF	Unc	BU
2004	—	—	—	—	1.75	2.75

KM# 200   100 SHILLINGS
Copper-Nickel **Subject:** Year of the Monkey **Obv. Legend:** BANK OF UGANDA **Rev:** Monkey swinging right

Date	Mintage	F	VF	XF	Unc	BU
2004	—	—	—	—	2.00	3.00

KM# 201   100 SHILLINGS
Copper-Nickel **Subject:** Year of the Monkey **Obv. Legend:** BANK OF UGANDA

Date	Mintage	F	VF	XF	Unc	BU
2004	—	—	—	—	2.00	3.00

KM# 202   100 SHILLINGS
Copper-Nickel **Subject:** Year of the Monkey **Obv. Legend:** BANK OF UGANDA **Rev:** Monkey right on all fours

Date	Mintage	F	VF	XF	Unc	BU
2004	—	—	—	—	2.00	3.00

KM# 203   100 SHILLINGS
Copper-Nickel **Subject:** Year of the Monkey **Obv. Legend:** BANK OF UGANDA **Rev:** Monkey seated left

Date	Mintage	F	VF	XF	Unc	BU
2004	—	—	—	—	2.00	3.00

KM# 204   100 SHILLINGS
Copper-Nickel **Subject:** Year of the Monkey **Obv. Legend:** BANK OF UGANDA **Rev:** Monkeys seated right, looking left over his shoulder

Date	Mintage	F	VF	XF	Unc	BU
2004	—	—	—	—	2.00	3.00

KM# 67a   100 SHILLINGS
Nickel Plated Steel, 26.9 mm. **Obv:** National arms **Rev:** African bull

Date	Mintage	F	VF	XF	Unc	BU
2007	—	—	—	—	1.00	1.75
2008	—	—	—	—	1.00	1.75

KM# 68   200 SHILLINGS
8.0500 g., Copper-Nickel, 24.9 mm. **Obv:** National arms **Rev:** Cichlid fish above value and date **Edge:** Plain

Date	Mintage	F	VF	XF	Unc	BU
2003	—	—	—	—	2.00	3.00
2008	—	—	—	—	2.00	3.00

KM# 68a   200 SHILLINGS
8.0500 g., Nickel Plated Steel, 24.9 mm. **Obv:** National arms **Rev:** Cichlid fish above value and date

Date	Mintage	F	VF	XF	Unc	BU
2007	—	—	—	—	2.00	3.00
2008	—	—	—	—	2.00	3.00

KM# 69 500 SHILLINGS
9.0000 g., Nickel-Brass, 23.5 mm. **Obv:** National arms **Rev:** East African crowned crane head left **Edge:** Reeded

Date	Mintage	F	VF	XF	Unc	BU
2003	—	—	—	—	3.50	4.50
2008	—	—	—	—	3.50	4.50

KM# 77 1000 SHILLINGS
19.8400 g., Copper-Nickel, 38.6 mm. **Subject:** Colourful Big Five of Africa **Obv:** Arms with supporters **Rev:** Multicolor rhinocerous within stamp design in front of outlined African map **Edge:** Reeded

Date	Mintage	F	VF	XF	Unc	BU
2001 Proof	—	Value: 22.50				

KM# 78 1000 SHILLINGS
19.8400 g., Copper-Nickel, 38.6 mm. **Subject:** Colourful Big Five of Africa **Obv:** Arms with supporters **Rev:** Multicolor lion within stamp design in front of outlined African map **Edge:** Reeded

Date	Mintage	F	VF	XF	Unc	BU
2001 Proof	—	Value: 22.50				

KM# 79 1000 SHILLINGS
19.8400 g., Copper-Nickel, 38.6 mm. **Subject:** Coulourful Big Five of Africa **Obv:** Arms with supporters **Rev:** Multicolor water buffalo within stamp design in front of outlined African map **Edge:** Reeded

Date	Mintage	F	VF	XF	Unc	BU
2001 Proof	—	Value: 22.50				

KM# 80 1000 SHILLINGS
19.8400 g., Copper-Nickel, 38.6 mm. **Subject:** Colourful Big Five of Africa **Obv:** Arms with supporters **Rev:** Multicolor leopard within stamp design in front of outlined map **Edge:** Reeded

Date	Mintage	F	VF	XF	Unc	BU
2001 Proof	—	Value: 22.50				

KM# 81 1000 SHILLINGS
19.8400 g., Copper-Nickel, 38.6 mm. **Subject:** Colourful Big Five of Africa **Obv:** Arms with supporters **Rev:** Multicolor elephant within stamp design in front of outlined map **Edge:** Reeded

Date	Mintage	F	VF	XF	Unc	BU
2001 Proof	—	Value: 22.50				

KM# 173 1000 SHILLINGS
Silver **Subject:** XVII World Football Championship Games - Korea and Japan **Obv. Legend:** BANK OF UGANDA **Rev:** Football - gilt

Date	Mintage	F	VF	XF	Unc	BU
2001 Proof	—	Value: 27.50				

KM# 82 1000 SHILLINGS
24.8300 g., 0.9990 Silver 0.7975 oz. ASW, 38.6 mm. **Subject:** World of Football **Obv:** Arms with supporters **Rev:** Soccer ball globe **Edge:** Reeded

Date	Mintage	F	VF	XF	Unc	BU
2002 Proof	—	Value: 35.00				

KM# 83 1000 SHILLINGS
24.8300 g., 0.9990 Silver 0.7975 oz. ASW, 38.6 mm. **Subject:** World of Football **Obv:** Arms with supporters **Rev:** Soccer ball in net **Edge:** Reeded

Date	Mintage	F	VF	XF	Unc	BU
2002 Proof	—	Value: 32.50				

KM# 84 1000 SHILLINGS
24.8300 g., 0.9990 Silver 0.7975 oz. ASW, 38.6 mm. **Subject:** World of Football **Obv:** Arms with supporters **Rev:** Goalie catching ball, red kicker insert at right **Edge:** Reeded

Date	Mintage	F	VF	XF	Unc	BU
2002 Proof	—	Value: 32.50				

KM# 85 1000 SHILLINGS
24.8300 g., 0.9990 Silver 0.7975 oz. ASW, 38.6 mm. **Subject:** World of Football **Obv:** Arms with supporters **Rev:** Two players going after the ball, red runner insert at left **Edge:** Reeded

Date	Mintage	F	VF	XF	Unc	BU
2002 Proof	—	Value: 32.50				

KM# 86 1000 SHILLINGS
24.8300 g., 0.9990 Silver 0.7975 oz. ASW, 38.6 mm. **Subject:** World of Football **Obv:** Arms with supporters **Rev:** Player kicking ball, blue kicker insert at right **Edge:** Reeded

Date	Mintage	F	VF	XF	Unc	BU
2002 Proof	—	Value: 32.50				

KM# 101 1000 SHILLINGS
29.4400 g., Silver Plated Bronze (Specific gravity 8.8675), 38.5 mm. **Series:** Gorillas of Africa **Obv:** National arms **Rev:** Seated gorilla **Edge:** Reeded

Date	Mintage	F	VF	XF	Unc	BU
2002 Proof	—	Value: 12.50				
2003 Proof	—	Value: 12.00				

KM# 102 1000 SHILLINGS
29.4400 g., Silver Plated Bronze (Specific gravity 8.8675),
38.5 mm. **Series:** Gorillas of Africa **Obv:** National arms **Rev:**
Gorilla eating **Edge:** Reeded

Date	Mintage	F	VF	XF	Unc	BU
2002 Proof	—	Value: 12.50				
2003 Proof	—	Value: 10.00				

KM# 103 1000 SHILLINGS
29.4400 g., Silver Plated Bronze (Specific gravity 8.8675),
38.5 mm. **Series:** Gorillas of Africa **Obv:** National arms **Rev:**
Gorilla on all fours **Edge:** Reeded

Date	Mintage	F	VF	XF	Unc	BU
2002 Proof	—	Value: 12.50				
2003 Proof	—	Value: 10.00				

KM# 104 1000 SHILLINGS
29.4400 g., Silver Plated Bronze (Specific gravity 8.8675),
38.5 mm. **Series:** Gorillas of Africa **Obv:** National arms **Rev:**
Gorilla female with infant **Edge:** Reeded

Date	Mintage	F	VF	XF	Unc	BU
2002 Proof	—	Value: 12.50				
2003 Proof	—	Value: 10.00				

KM# 106 1000 SHILLINGS
29.1600 g., Silver Plated Bronze (Specific gravity 8.8096),
38.6 mm. **Subject:** Marine Life **Obv:** Arms with supporters **Rev:**
Multicolor sea horses **Edge:** Reeded

Date	Mintage	F	VF	XF	Unc	BU
2002 Proof	—	Value: 22.00				

KM# 107 1000 SHILLINGS
29.1600 g., Silver Plated Bronze (Specific gravity 8.8096),
38.6 mm. **Subject:** Marine Life **Obv:** Arms with supporters **Rev:**
Multicolor Hammerhead sharks **Edge:** Reeded

Date	Mintage	F	VF	XF	Unc	BU
2002 Proof	—	Value: 22.00				

KM# 108 1000 SHILLINGS
29.1600 g., Silver Plated Bronze (Specific gravity 8.8096),
38.6 mm. **Subject:** Marine Life **Obv:** Arms with supporters **Rev:**
Multicolor Stingray **Edge:** Reeded

Date	Mintage	F	VF	XF	Unc	BU
2002 Proof	—	Value: 22.00				

KM# 109 1000 SHILLINGS
29.1600 g., Silver Plated Bronze (Specific gravity 8.8096),
38.6 mm. **Subject:** Marine Life **Obv:** Arms with supporters **Rev:**
Multicolor Seal **Edge:** Reeded

Date	Mintage	F	VF	XF	Unc	BU
2002 Proof	—	Value: 22.00				

KM# 110 1000 SHILLINGS
29.1600 g., Silver Plated Bronze (Specific gravity 8.8096),
38.6 mm. **Subject:** Marine Life **Obv:** Arms with supporters **Rev:**
Multicolor sea turtle **Edge:** Reeded

Date	Mintage	F	VF	XF	Unc	BU
2002 Proof	—	Value: 22.00				

KM# 111 1000 SHILLINGS
29.1600 g., Silver Plated Bronze (Specific gravity 8.8096),
38.6 mm. **Subject:** Marine Life **Obv:** Arms with supporters **Rev:**
Multicolor dolphins **Edge:** Reeded

Date	Mintage	F	VF	XF	Unc	BU
2002 Proof	—	Value: 22.00				

KM# 112 1000 SHILLINGS
29.1600 g., Silver Plated Bronze (Specific gravity 8.8096),
38.6 mm. **Subject:** Marine Life **Obv:** Arms with supporters **Rev:**
Multicolor octopus **Edge:** Reeded

Date	Mintage	F	VF	XF	Unc	BU
2002 Proof	—	Value: 22.00				

KM# 113 1000 SHILLINGS
29.1600 g., Silver Plated Bronze (Specific gravity 8.8096),
38.6 mm. **Subject:** Marine Life **Obv:** Arms with supporters **Rev:**
Multicolor red fish **Edge:** Reeded

Date	Mintage	F	VF	XF	Unc	BU
2002 Proof	—	Value: 22.00				

KM# 114 1000 SHILLINGS
29.1600 g., Silver Plated Bronze (Specific gravity 8.8096),
38.6 mm. **Subject:** Marine Life **Obv:** Arms with supporters **Rev:**
Multicolor black fish with white dots **Edge:** Reeded

Date	Mintage	F	VF	XF	Unc	BU
2002 Proof	—	Value: 22.00				

KM# 115 1000 SHILLINGS
29.1600 g., Silver Plated Bronze (Specific gravity 8.8096),
38.6 mm. **Subject:** Marine Life **Obv:** Arms with supporters **Rev:**
Multicolor yellow and black striped fish **Edge:** Reeded

Date	Mintage	F	VF	XF	Unc	BU
2002 Proof	—	Value: 22.00				

KM# 240 1000 SHILLINGS
Silver **Obv:** Arms **Rev:** Pope John Paul II bust facing

Date	Mintage	F	VF	XF	Unc	BU
2003 Proof	—	Value: 75.00				

KM# 105 1000 SHILLINGS
29.2000 g., Silver Plated Bronze (Specific gravity 9.0123),
38.6 mm. **Subject:** Pope John Paul II **Obv:** Arms with supporters
Rev: Pope saying mass, design of Zambian 1000 Kwacha KM-
160 **Edge:** Reeded **Note:** Muling error

Date	Mintage	F	VF	XF	Unc	BU
2003 Proof	—	Value: 300				

KM# 216 1000 SHILLINGS
Bronze **Subject:** Christmas **Obv: Legend:** BANK OF UGANDA
Rev: Peace on Earth

Date	Mintage	F	VF	XF	Unc	BU
2004	500	—	—	—	—	50.00

KM# 75 2000 SHILLINGS
49.9000 g., 0.9990 Silver 1.6027 oz. ASW, 50 mm. **Subject:**
Illusion: "Spirit of the Mountain" **Obv:** Crowned head right divides
date above arms with supporters **Rev:** Landscape and tree that
looks like a male portrait **Edge:** Reeded

Date	Mintage	F	VF	XF	Unc	BU
2001 Proof	—	Value: 75.00				

KM# 121 2000 SHILLINGS
25.0000 g., 0.9250 Silver 0.7435 oz. ASW, 38.6 mm. **Subject:**
Queen Elizabeth's 75th Birthday **Obv:** Arms with supporters
above crowned head right **Rev:** Queen accepting flowers from
children **Edge:** Reeded

Date	Mintage	F	VF	XF	Unc	BU
2001 Proof	2,000	Value: 35.00				

KM# 100   2000 SHILLINGS
31.4000 g., 0.9990 Silver 1.0085 oz. ASW, 38.8 mm. **Obv:** Crowned head right divides date above arms with supporters **Rev:** Bust of Henry M. Stanley facing **Edge:** Reeded

Date	Mintage	F	VF	XF	Unc	BU
2002	—	—	—	—	40.00	45.00

KM# 177   2000 SHILLINGS
15.5500 g., 0.9990 Silver 0.4994 oz. ASW **Series:** Famous Places in China **Subject:** Mount Huangshan - Anhwei **Obv:** Two dragons **Obv. Legend:** BANK OF UGANDA

Date	Mintage	F	VF	XF	Unc	BU
2003 Proof	3,000	Value: 35.00				

KM# 178   2000 SHILLINGS
15.5500 g., 0.9990 Silver 0.4994 oz. ASW **Series:** Famous Places in China **Subject:** Zhangjiajie - Hunan **Obv:** Two dragons **Obv. Legend:** BANK OF UGANDA

Date	Mintage	F	VF	XF	Unc	BU
2003 Proof	3,000	Value: 35.00				

KM# 179   2000 SHILLINGS
15.5500 g., 0.9990 Silver 0.4994 oz. ASW **Series:** Famous Places in China **Subject:** Stone Forest - Yunnan **Obv:** Two dragons **Obv. Legend:** BANK OF UGANDA

Date	Mintage	F	VF	XF	Unc	BU
2003 Proof	3,000	Value: 35.00				

KM# 180   2000 SHILLINGS
15.5500 g., 0.9990 Silver 0.4994 oz. ASW **Series:** Famous Places in China **Subject:** Potala Palace - Lhasa, Tibet **Obv:** Two dragons **Obv. Legend:** BANK OF UGANDA

Date	Mintage	F	VF	XF	Unc	BU
2003 Proof	3,000	Value: 35.00				

KM# 181   2000 SHILLINGS
15.5500 g., 0.9990 Silver 0.4994 oz. ASW **Series:** Famous Places inChina **Subject:** Yangtse River Gorges **Obv:** Two dragons **Obv. Legend:** BANK OF UGANDA

Date	Mintage	F	VF	XF	Unc	BU
2003 Proof	3,000	Value: 35.00				

KM# 182   2000 SHILLINGS
31.1000 g., 0.9990 Silver 0.9988 oz. ASW **Series:** Chinese symbolism **Subject:** Harmony **Obv. Legend:** BANK OF UGANDA **Rev:** Dragon and phoenix

Date	Mintage	F	VF	XF	Unc	BU
2003 Proof	3,000	Value: 60.00				

KM# 183   2000 SHILLINGS
31.1000 g., 0.9990 Silver 0.9988 oz. ASW **Series:** Chinese symbolism **Subject:** Happiness **Obv. Legend:** BANK OF UGANDA **Rev:** Unicorn

Date	Mintage	F	VF	XF	Unc	BU
2003 Proof	3,000	Value: 60.00				

KM# 184   2000 SHILLINGS
31.1000 g., 0.9990 Silver 0.9988 oz. ASW **Series:** Chinese symbolism **Subject:** Health and long life **Obv. Legend:** BANK OF UGANDA **Rev:** Two cranes

Date	Mintage	F	VF	XF	Unc	BU
2003 Proof	3,000	Value: 60.00				

KM# 185   2000 SHILLINGS
31.1000 g., 0.9990 Silver 0.9988 oz. ASW **Series:** Chinese symbolism **Subject:** Success **Obv. Legend:** BANK OF UGANDA **Rev:** Carp

Date	Mintage	F	VF	XF	Unc	BU
2003 Proof	3,000	Value: 60.00				

KM# 186   2000 SHILLINGS
31.1000 g., 0.9990 Silver 0.9988 oz. ASW **Series:** Chinese symbolism **Subject:** Wealth **Obv. Legend:** BANK OF UGANDA **Rev:** Toad

Date	Mintage	F	VF	XF	Unc	BU
2003 Proof	3,000	Value: 60.00				

KM# 175   2000 SHILLINGS
15.5500 g., 0.9990 Silver 0.4994 oz. ASW **Series:** Famous Places in China **Subject:** Yugan Garden - Shanghai **Obv:** Two dragons **Obv. Legend:** BANK OF UGANDA

Date	Mintage	F	VF	XF	Unc	BU
2003 Proof	3,000	Value: 35.00				

KM# 176   2000 SHILLINGS
15.5500 g., 0.9990 Silver 0.4994 oz. ASW **Series:** Famous Places in China **Subject:** Tiger Hill Pagoda - Jiangsu **Obv:** Two dragons **Obv. Legend:** BANK OF UGANDA

Date	Mintage	F	VF	XF	Unc	BU
2003 Proof	3,000	Value: 35.00				

KM# 187   2000 SHILLINGS
4.0000 g., 0.9999 Gold 0.1286 oz. AGW **Series:** Guanyin **Subject:** Fulun **Obv:** Lotus blossom **Obv. Legend:** BANK OF UGANDA

Date	Mintage	F	VF	XF	Unc	BU
2003 Proof	—	Value: 200				

KM# 205   2000 SHILLINGS
Silver **Subject:** XXVIII Summer Olympics - Athens 2004 **Obv. Legend:** BANK OF UGANDA **Rev:** Sprinter

Date	Mintage	F	VF	XF	Unc	BU
2003 Proof	500	Value: 60.00				

KM# 210   2000 SHILLINGS
31.1000 g., 0.9990 Silver 0.9988 oz. ASW **Series:** Chinese symbolic floral New Year paintings **Subject:** Happiness **Obv. Legend:** BANK OF UGANDA **Rev:** Multicolor

Date	Mintage	F	VF	XF	Unc	BU
2004 Proof	2,000	Value: 60.00				

KM# 211   2000 SHILLINGS
31.1000 g., 0.9990 Silver 0.9988 oz. ASW **Series:** Chinese Dieties **Subject:** Happiness **Obv. Legend:** BANK OF UGANDA **Rev:** Fú - multicolor

Date	Mintage	F	VF	XF	Unc	BU
2004 Proof	2,000	Value: 60.00				

KM# 212   2000 SHILLINGS
31.1000 g., 0.9990 Silver 0.9988 oz. ASW **Series:** Chinese Dieties **Subject:** Prosperity **Obv. Legend:** BANK OF UGANDA **Rev:** Lù - multicolor

Date	Mintage	F	VF	XF	Unc	BU
2004 Proof	2,000	Value: 60.00				

KM# 213   2000 SHILLINGS
31.1000 g., 0.9990 Silver 0.9988 oz. ASW **Series:** Chinese Dieties **Subject:** Health and Long Life **Obv. Legend:** BANK OF UGANDA **Rev:** Shòu - multicolor

Date	Mintage	F	VF	XF	Unc	BU
2004 Proof	2,000	Value: 60.00				

KM# 206   2000 SHILLINGS
31.1000 g., 0.9990 Silver 0.9988 oz. ASW **Series:** Chinese symbolic floral New Year paintings **Obv. Legend:** BANK OF UGANDA **Rev:** Carp and Lotus blossom - multicolor

Date	Mintage	F	VF	XF	Unc	BU
2004 Proof	2,000	Value: 60.00				

KM# 207   2000 SHILLINGS
31.1000 g., 0.9990 Silver 0.9988 oz. ASW **Series:** Chinese symbolic floral New Year paintings **Obv. Legend:** BANK OF UGANDA **Rev:** Deer - multicolor

Date	Mintage	F	VF	XF	Unc	BU
2004 Proof	2,000	Value: 60.00				

KM# 208   2000 SHILLINGS
31.1000 g., 0.9990 Silver 0.9988 oz. ASW **Series:** Chinese symbolic floral New Year paintings **Subject:** Abundance **Obv. Legend:** BANK OF UGANDA **Rev:** Fruit - multicolor

Date	Mintage	F	VF	XF	Unc	BU
2004 Proof	2,000	Value: 60.00				

KM# 209   2000 SHILLINGS
31.1000 g., 0.9990 Silver 0.9988 oz. ASW **Series:** Chinese symbolic floral New Year paintings **Subject:** Peace and prosperity **Obv. Legend:** BANK OF UGANDA **Rev:** Multicolor

Date	Mintage	F	VF	XF	Unc	BU
2004 Proof	2,000	Value: 60.00				

KM# 221   2000 SHILLINGS
Silver Plated Bronze **Series:** XIX World Football Championship - South Africa 2010 **Obv:** National arms **Obv. Legend:** BANK OF UGANDA **Rev:** Player about to kick

Date	Mintage	F	VF	XF	Unc	BU
2005 Proof	10,000	Value: 15.00				

KM# 222   2000 SHILLINGS
Silver Plated Bronze **Series:** XIX World Football Championship - South Afrika 2010 **Obv:** National arms **Obv. Legend:** BANK OF UGANDA **Rev:** Ball in net

Date	Mintage	F	VF	XF	Unc	BU
2005 Proof	10,000	Value: 15.00				

KM# 223   2000 SHILLINGS
Silver Plated Bronze **Series:** XIX World Football Championship - South Afrika 2010 **Obv:** National arms **Obv. Legend:** BANK OF UGANDA **Rev:** Player, map of Afrika

Date	Mintage	F	VF	XF	Unc	BU
2005 Proof	10,000	Value: 15.00				

KM# 224   2000 SHILLINGS
Silver Plated Bronze **Series:** XIX World Football Championship - South Afrika 2010 **Obv:** National arms **Obv. Legend:** BANK OF UGANDA **Rev:** Goalkeeper with ball

Date	Mintage	F	VF	XF	Unc	BU
2005 Proof	10,000	Value: 15.00				

KM# 225   2000 SHILLINGS
Silver Plated Bronze **Series:** XIX World Football Championship - South Afrika 2010 **Obv:** National arms **Obv. Legend:** BANK OF UGANDA **Rev:** Player and ball

Date	Mintage	F	VF	XF	Unc	BU
2005 Proof	10,000	Value: 15.00				

KM# 217   2000 SHILLINGS
31.1000 g., 0.9990 Silver 0.9988 oz. ASW **Obv:** Lotus blossom **Obv. Legend:** BANK OF UGANDA **Rev:** Guanyin - multicolor

Date	Mintage	F	VF	XF	Unc	BU
2005 Proof	2,000	Value: 75.00				

KM# 226   2000 SHILLINGS
40.0000 g., Bronze Gilt **Series:** Zodiac **Subject:** Year of the Dog **Obv:** Two dragons **Obv. Legend:** BANK OF UGANDA **Rev:** Three dogs - multicolor

Date	Mintage	F	VF	XF	Unc	BU
2006 Proof	—	Value: 45.00				

KM# 227   2000 SHILLINGS
40.0000 g., Bronze Gilt **Series:** Zodiac **Subject:** Year of the Dog **Obv:** Archaic Chinese characters **Obv. Legend:** BANK OF UGANDA **Rev:** Two dogs - multicolor

Date	Mintage	F	VF	XF	Unc	BU
2006 Proof	—	Value: 45.00				

KM# 227a   2000 SHILLINGS
31.1000 g., 0.9990 Silver 0.9988 oz. ASW **Series:** Zodiac **Subject:** Year of the Dog **Obv:** Archaic Chinese characters **Obv. Legend:** BANK OF UGANDA **Rev:** Two dogs - multicolor

Date	Mintage	F	VF	XF	Unc	BU
2006 Proof	3,000	Value: 75.00				

KM# 234   2000 SHILLINGS
31.1000 g., 0.9990 Silver 0.9988 oz. ASW **Series:** Zodiac **Subject:** Year of the Dog **Obv. Legend:** BANK OF UGANDA **Rev:** Tibet Terrier with pup surrounded by 10 symbols

Date	Mintage	F	VF	XF	Unc	BU
2006 Proof	3,000	Value: 75.00				

KM# 237   2000 SHILLINGS
31.1000 g., 0.9990 Silver 0.9988 oz. ASW **Series:** Zodiac **Subject:** Year of the Dog **Obv:** National arms **Obv. Legend:** BANK OF UGANDA **Rev:** Chow-chow as watchdog, gold bars, bat and flower

Date	Mintage	F	VF	XF	Unc	BU
2006 Proof	—	Value: 60.00				

KM# 172   5000 SHILLINGS
4.0000 g., 0.9999 Gold 0.1286 oz. AGW **Series:** Guanyin **Subject:** Chilian **Obv:** Lotus blossom **Obv. Legend:** BANK OF UGANDA

Date	Mintage	F	VF	XF	Unc	BU
2001 Proof	—	Value: 200				

KM# 87   5000 SHILLINGS
33.7300 g., 0.8500 Silver 0.9217 oz. ASW, 38.65 mm. **Subject:** "The Big Five" **Obv:** Arms with supporters **Rev:** Rhinoceros **Edge:** Reeded

Date	Mintage	F	VF	XF	Unc	BU
2002 Proof	—	Value: 65.00				

KM# 88   5000 SHILLINGS
33.7300 g., 0.8500 Silver 0.9217 oz. ASW, 38.65 mm. **Subject:** "The Big Five" **Obv:** Arms with supporters **Rev:** Lion **Edge:** Reeded

Date	Mintage	F	VF	XF	Unc	BU
2002 Proof	—	Value: 65.00				

KM# 89   5000 SHILLINGS
33.7300 g., 0.8500 Silver 0.9217 oz. ASW, 38.65 mm. **Subject:** "The Big Five" **Obv:** Arms with supporters **Rev:** Cape Buffalo **Edge:** Reeded

Date	Mintage	F	VF	XF	Unc	BU
2002 Proof	—	Value: 50.00				

KM# 90   5000 SHILLINGS
33.7300 g., 0.8500 Silver 0.9217 oz. ASW, 38.65 mm. **Subject:** "The Big Five" **Obv:** Arms with supporters **Rev:** Leopard **Edge:** Reeded

Date	Mintage	F	VF	XF	Unc	BU
2002 Proof	—	Value: 65.00				

KM# 91   5000 SHILLINGS
33.7300 g., 0.8500 Silver 0.9217 oz. ASW, 38.65 mm. **Subject:** "The Big Five" **Obv:** Arms with supporters **Rev:** Elephant **Edge:** Reeded

Date	Mintage	F	VF	XF	Unc	BU
2002 Proof	—	Value: 65.00				

KM# 96   5000 SHILLINGS
31.1035 g., 0.9990 Silver 0.9990 oz. ASW, 40.6 mm. **Subject:** Matthew Flinders **Obv:** Arms with supporters below crowned head right dividing date **Rev:** Multicolor bust half left at right with ship and harbor scene at left **Edge:** Plain **Shape:** Continent of Australia

Date	Mintage	F	VF	XF	Unc	BU
2002 Proof	2,500	Value: 55.00				

KM# 97   5000 SHILLINGS
31.1035 g., 0.9990 Silver 0.9990 oz. ASW, 40.6 mm. **Subject:** Matthew Flinders - H. M. S. Investigator **Obv:** Crowned head right

divides date above arms with supporters **Rev:** Multicolor cameo at upper right of ship **Edge:** Plain **Shape:** Continent of Australia

Date	Mintage	F	VF	XF	Unc	BU
2002 Proof	2,500	Value: 55.00				

KM# 98   5000 SHILLINGS
31.1035 g., 0.9990 Silver 0.9990 oz. ASW, 40.6 mm. **Subject:** Matthew Flinders - Meeting at Encounter Bay **Obv:** Crowned head right divides date above arms with supporters **Rev:** Date and inscription divides multicolor busts facing **Edge:** Plain **Shape:** Continent of Australia

Date	Mintage	F	VF	XF	Unc	BU
2002 Proof	2,500	Value: 55.00				

KM# 99   5000 SHILLINGS
31.1035 g., 0.9990 Silver 0.9990 oz. ASW, 40.6 mm. **Subject:** Matthew Flinders - First Circumnavigation of Terra Australia - 1802 **Rev:** Multicolor bust right on Australian map showing his route around Australia **Edge:** Plain **Shape:** Continent of Australia

Date	Mintage	F	VF	XF	Unc	BU
2002 Proof	2,500	Value: 55.00				

KM# 174   5000 SHILLINGS
4.0000 g., 0.9999 Gold 0.1286 oz. AGW **Series:** Guanyin **Subject:** Fuyu **Obv:** Lotus blossom **Obv. Legend:** BANK OF UGANDA

Date	Mintage	F	VF	XF	Unc	BU
2002 Proof	—	Value: 200				

KM# 214   5000 SHILLINGS
4.0000 g., 0.9999 Gold 0.1286 oz. AGW **Series:** Guanyin **Subject:** Shile **Obv:** Lotus blossom **Obv. Legend:** BANK OF UGANDA

Date	Mintage	F	VF	XF	Unc	BU
2004 Proof	—	Value: 200				

KM# 220   5000 SHILLINGS
4.0000 g., 0.9999 Gold 0.1286 oz. AGW **Series:** Guanyin **Subject:** Songjing **Obv:** Lotus blossom **Obv. Legend:** BANK OF UGANDA

Date	Mintage	F	VF	XF	Unc	BU
2005 Proof	—	Value: 200				

KM# 235   6000 SHILLINGS
3.1100 g., 0.9999 Gold 0.1000 oz. AGW **Series:** Zodiac **Subject:** Year of the Dog **Obv. Legend:** BANK OF UGANDA **Rev:** Tibet Terrier with pup surrounded by 10 symbols

Date	Mintage	F	VF	XF	Unc	BU
2006 Proof	—	Value: 165				

KM# 228   6000 SHILLINGS
4.0000 g., 0.9999 Gold 0.1286 oz. AGW **Series:** Zodiac **Subject:** Year of the Dog **Obv:** Archaic Chinese characters **Obv. Legend:** BANK OF UGANDA **Rev:** Yorkshire Terrier and "Fú" - Happiness

Date	Mintage	F	VF	XF	Unc	BU
2006 Proof	14,000	Value: 225				

KM# 229   6000 SHILLINGS
4.0000 g., 0.9999 Gold 0.1286 oz. AGW **Series:** Zodiac **Subject:** Year of the Dog **Obv:** Archaic Chinese characters **Obv. Legend:** BANK OF UGANDA **Rev:** Yorkshire Terrier and "Lù" - Prosperity

Date	Mintage	F	VF	XF	Unc	BU
2006 Proof	14,000	Value: 225				

KM# 230   6000 SHILLINGS
4.0000 g., 0.9999 Gold 0.1286 oz. AGW **Series:** Zodiac **Subject:** Year of the Dog **Obv:** Archaic Chinese characters **Obv. Legend:** BANK OF UGANDA **Rev:** Yorkshire Terrier and "Shòu" - Health and Long Life

Date	Mintage	F	VF	XF	Unc	BU
2006 Proof	14,000	Value: 225				

KM# 238   6000 SHILLINGS
3.1100 g., 0.9999 Gold 0.1000 oz. AGW **Series:** Zodiac **Subject:** Year of the Dog **Obv:** National arms **Obv. Legend:** BANK OF UGANDA **Rev:** Chow-chow as watchdog, gold bars, bat and flower

Date	Mintage	F	VF	XF	Unc	BU
2006 Proof	—	Value: 165				

KM# 231   8000 SHILLINGS
8.0000 g., 0.9999 Gold 0.2572 oz. AGW **Series:** Zodiac **Subject:** Year of the Dog **Obv:** Archaic Chinese characters **Obv. Legend:** BANK OF UGANDA **Rev:** Yorkshire Terrier and "Fú" - Happiness

Date	Mintage	F	VF	XF	Unc	BU
2006 Proof	1,000	Value: 400				

KM# 232   8000 SHILLINGS
8.0000 g., 0.9999 Gold 0.2572 oz. AGW **Series:** Zodiac **Subject:** Year of the Dog **Obv:** Archaic Chinese characters **Obv. Legend:** BANK OF UGANDA **Rev:** Yorkshire Terrier and "Lù" - Prosperity

Date	Mintage	F	VF	XF	Unc	BU
2006 Proof	1,000	Value: 400				

KM# 215   10000 SHILLINGS
10.0000 g., 0.9999 Gold 0.3215 oz. AGW **Obv:** Lotus blossom **Obv. Legend:** BANK OF UGANDA **Rev:** Buddha

Date	Mintage	F	VF	XF	Unc	BU
2004 Proof	3,000	Value: 700				

KM# 76   12000 SHILLINGS
6.2207 g., 0.9999 Gold 0.2000 oz. AGW, 22 mm. **Subject:** Illusion: "Spirit of the Mountain" **Obv:** Crowned head right divides date above arms with supporters **Rev:** Landscape and tree that looks like a male portrait **Edge:** Reeded

Date	Mintage	F	VF	XF	Unc	BU
2001 Proof	—	Value: 325				

KM# 236   20000 SHILLINGS
15.5500 g., 0.9999 Gold 0.4999 oz. AGW **Series:** Zodiac **Subject:** Year of the Dog **Obv. Legend:** BANK OF UGANDA **Rev:** Tibet Terrier with pup surrounded by 10 symbols

Date	Mintage	F	VF	XF	Unc	BU
2006 Proof	—	Value: 775				

KM# 239   20000 SHILLINGS
15.5500 g., 0.9999 Gold 0.4999 oz. AGW **Series:** Year of the Dog **Obv:** National arms **Obv. Legend:** BANK OF UGANDA **Rev:** Chow-chow as watchdog, gold bars, bat and flower

Date	Mintage	F	VF	XF	Unc	BU
2006 Proof	—	Value: 775				

UKRAINE

Ukraine (formerly the Ukrainian Soviet Socialist Republic) is bordered by Russia to the east, Russia and Belarus to the north, Poland, Slovakia and Hungary to the west, Romania and Moldova to the southwest and in the south by the Black Sea and the Sea of Azov. It has an area of 233,088 sq. mi. (603,700 sq. km.) and a population of 51.9 million. Capital: Kyiv (Kiev). Coal, grain, vegetables and heavy industrial machinery are major exports.

Ukraine is a charter member of the United Nations and has inherited the third largest nuclear arsenal in the world.

MONETARY SYSTEM
(1) Kopiyka
(2) Kopiyky KOKH
(5 and up) Kopiyok KOIOK
100 Kopiyok = 1 Hrynia PBEH
100,000 Karbovanetsiv = 1 Hryni or Hryven)

REPUBLIC

REFORM COINAGE
September 2, 1996

100,000 Karbovanets = 1 Hryvnia; 100 Kopiyok = 1 Hryvnia; The Kopiyok has replaced the Karbovanet

KM# 6   KOPIYKA
1.5000 g., Stainless Steel, 16 mm. **Obv:** National arms **Rev:** Value within wreath **Edge:** Plain

Date	Mintage	F	VF	XF	Unc	BU
2001	—	—	—	0.35	0.75	—
2002	—	—	—	0.35	0.75	—
2003	—	—	—	0.35	0.75	—
2004	—	—	—	0.35	0.75	—
2005	—	—	—	0.35	0.75	—
2006	—	—	—	0.35	0.75	—

Date	Mintage	F	VF	XF	Unc	BU
2007	—	—	—	0.35	0.75	—
2008	—	—	—	0.35	0.75	—
2008 Prooflike	5,000	—	—	—	—	1.50
2009	—	—	—	0.35	0.75	—
2010	—	—	—	0.35	0.75	—
2011	—	—	—	0.35	0.75	—
2011 Prooflike	5,000	—	—	—	—	1.50

KM# 4b   2 KOPIYKY

1.8000 g., Stainless Steel, 17.3 mm. **Obv:** National arms **Rev:** Value within wreath **Edge:** Plain

Date	Mintage	F	VF	XF	Unc	BU
2001	—	—	0.20	0.50	1.00	—
2002	—	—	0.20	0.50	1.00	—
2003	Est. 5,000	—	—	—	—	300
2004	—	—	0.20	0.50	1.00	—
2005	—	—	0.20	0.50	1.00	—
2006	—	—	—	0.50	1.00	—
2007	—	—	—	0.50	1.00	—
2008	—	—	—	0.50	1.00	—
2008 Prooflike	5,000	—	—	—	—	2.00
2009	—	—	—	0.50	1.00	—
2010	—	—	—	0.50	1.00	—
2011	—	—	—	0.50	1.00	—
2011 Prooflike	5,000	—	—	—	—	1.50

KM# 7   5 KOPIYOK

4.3000 g., Stainless Steel, 23.91 mm. **Obv:** National arms **Rev:** Value within wreath **Edge:** Reeded

Date	Mintage	F	VF	XF	Unc	BU
2001 In sets only	10,000	—	—	—	—	10.00
2003	—	—	—	0.50	1.00	—
2004	—	—	—	0.50	1.00	—
2005	—	—	—	0.50	1.00	—
2006	—	—	—	0.50	1.00	—
2007	—	—	—	0.50	1.00	—
2008	—	—	—	0.50	1.00	—
2008 Prooflike	5,000	—	—	—	—	2.50
2009	—	—	—	0.50	1.00	—
2010	—	—	—	0.50	1.00	—
2011	—	—	—	5.00	1.00	—
2011 Prooflike	5,000	—	—	—	—	2.00

KM# 1.1b   10 KOPIYOK

1.7000 g., Aluminum-Bronze, 16.24 mm. **Obv:** National arms **Rev:** Value within wreath **Edge:** Reeded

Date	Mintage	F	VF	XF	Unc	BU
2001 In sets only	10,000	—	—	—	—	7.50
2002	—	—	0.60	1.25	2.50	—
2003	—	—	0.50	1.00	2.25	—
2004	—	—	0.50	1.00	2.25	—
2005	—	—	—	1.00	2.25	—
2006	—	—	—	1.00	2.25	—
2007	—	—	—	1.00	2.25	—
2008	—	—	—	1.00	2.25	—
2008 Prooflike	5,000	—	—	—	—	5.00
2009	—	—	—	1.00	2.00	—
2010	—	—	—	1.00	2.00	—
2011	—	—	—	1.00	2.00	—
2011 Prooflike	5,000	—	—	—	—	5.00

KM# 2.1b   25 KOPIYOK

2.9000 g., Aluminum-Bronze, 20.8 mm. **Obv:** National arms **Rev:** Value within wreath **Edge:** Segmented reeding

Date	Mintage	F	VF	XF	Unc	BU
2001	—	—	0.80	3.00	6.00	—
2003 Prooflike	Est. 5,000	—	—	—	—	300
2006	—	—	0.80	2.00	4.00	—
2007	—	—	0.80	2.00	4.00	—
2008	—	—	—	2.00	4.00	—
2008 Prooflike	5,000	—	—	—	—	8.00
2009	—	—	—	2.00	3.50	—
2010	—	—	—	2.00	3.50	—
2011	—	—	—	2.00	3.50	—
2011 Prooflike	5,000	—	—	—	—	8.00

KM# 3.3b   50 KOPIYOK

4.2000 g., Aluminum-Bronze, 23 mm. **Obv:** National arms **Rev:** Five dots grouped in wreath to right of final letter 'K' in value **Edge:** Segmented reeding

Date	Mintage	F	VF	XF	Unc	BU
2001 In sets only	—	—	—	—	10.00	—
2003	Est. 5,000	—	—	—	300	—
2006	—	—	1.00	2.00	4.00	—
2007	—	—	1.00	2.00	4.00	—
2008	—	—	—	2.00	4.00	—
2008 Prooflike	5,000	—	—	—	—	8.00
2009	—	—	—	2.00	4.00	—
2010	—	—	—	2.00	4.00	—
2011	—	—	—	2.00	4.00	—
2011 Prooflike	5,000	—	—	—	—	8.00

KM# 8b   HRYVNIA

6.9000 g., Aluminum-Bronze, 26 mm. **Obv:** National arms **Rev:** Value, sprigs and designs **Edge:** Lettered

Date	Mintage	F	VF	XF	Unc	BU
2001	—	—	—	2.50	4.50	—

KM# 8b.1   HRYVNIA

7.1000 g., Aluminum-Bronze, 26 mm. **Obv:** National arms **Rev:** Value, sprigs and designs **Edge:** Lettered

Date	Mintage	F	VF	XF	Unc	BU
2002	—	—	—	3.50	6.50	—
2003	—	—	—	2.50	4.50	—

KM# 208   HRYVNIA

6.8000 g., Aluminum-Bronze, 26 mm. **Subject:** 60th Anniversary - Victory over the Nazis **Obv:** National arms above value **Rev:** Uniform lapel with Soviet military medals group **Edge:** Lettered **Edge Lettering:** Date and denomination

Date	Mintage	F	VF	XF	Unc	BU
2004	5,000,000	—	—	—	5.00	—

KM# 209   HRYVNIA

6.7400 g., Aluminum-Bronze, 26 mm. **Obv:** National arms above value **Rev:** Half length figure of Volodymyr the Great facing holding church model building and staff **Edge:** Lettered **Edge Lettering:** Date and denomination

Date	Mintage	F	VF	XF	Unc	BU
2004	10,000,000	—	—	—	4.00	—
2005	—	—	—	—	3.00	—
2006	—	—	—	—	3.00	—
2008 Prooflike	5,000	—	—	—	—	12.50
2010	—	—	—	—	3.00	—
2011	—	—	—	—	3.00	—
2011 Prooflike, in sets only	5,000	—	—	—	—	12.50

KM# 228   HRYVNIA

6.8000 g., Aluminum-Bronze, 26 mm. **Subject:** WW II Victory 60th Anniversary **Obv:** Value **Rev:** Soldiers in a "V" of search lights **Edge:** Reeded

Date	Mintage	F	VF	XF	Unc	BU
2005	5,000,000	—	—	—	5.00	—

KM# 634   HRYVNIA

16.8200 g., 0.9250 Silver 0.5002 oz. ASW, 33 mm. **Subject:** Mykhailo Yangel, 100th Anniversary of Birth **Obv:** Kosmos launch and satellite, earth in background **Rev:** Yangel portrait

Date	Mintage	F	VF	XF	Unc	BU
2011 Proof	5,000	Value: 90.00				

KM# 654   HRYVNIA

31.1050 g., 0.9999 Silver 0.9999 oz. ASW, 38.6 mm. **Obv:** Logo of the Ukraine National Bank **Rev:** Archangel Michael

Date	Mintage	F	VF	XF	Unc	BU
2011	10,000	—	—	—	—BV+10%	

KM# 106   2 HRYVNI

12.8000 g., Copper-Nickel-Zinc, 31 mm. **Series:** Olympics - Salt Lake City, 2002 **Obv:** National arms, value and designs **Rev:** Stylized ice dancing couple **Edge:** Reeded

Date	Mintage	F	VF	XF	Unc	BU
2001	30,000	—	—	—	25.00	—

KM# 133   2 HRYVNI

12.8000 g., Copper-Nickel-Zinc, 31 mm. **Subject:** Kindness to Children **Obv:** National arms above value flanked by sprigs and doves **Rev:** Two children frolicking under fountain of knowledge **Edge:** Reeded

Date	Mintage	F	VF	XF	Unc	BU
2001	100,000	—	—	—	12.00	—

KM# 134   2 HRYVNI

12.8000 g., Copper-Nickel-Zinc, 31 mm. **Subject:** 5th Anniversary of Constitution **Obv:** National arms above value flanked by sprigs **Rev:** Building above book flanked by sprigs **Edge:** Reeded

Date	Mintage	F	VF	XF	Unc	BU
2001	30,000	—	—	—	25.00	—

KM# 111   2 HRYVNI

12.8000 g., Copper-Nickel-Zinc, 31 mm. **Series:** Flora and Fauna **Obv:** National arms and date divides wreath, value within **Rev:** Lynx and offspring **Edge:** Reeded

Date	Mintage	F	VF	XF	Unc	BU
2001	30,000	—	—	—	50.00	—

KM# 136   2 HRYVNI

12.8000 g., Copper-Nickel-Zinc, 31 mm. **Subject:** Mykolaiv Zoo **Obv:** Man running alongside large cat **Rev:** Twelve animals **Edge:** Reeded

Date	Mintage	F	VF	XF	Unc	BU
2001	30,000	—	—	—	37.50	—

KM# 137   2 HRYVNI
12.8000 g., Copper-Nickel-Zinc, 31 mm.   **Subject:** Mykhailo
Ostrohradskiy (Mathematician) **Obv:** National arms divides date
and value divided by wavy line graph **Rev:** Head 1/4 left **Edge:**
Reeded

Date	Mintage	F	VF	XF	Unc	BU
2001	30,000	—	—	—	12.00	—

KM# 138   2 HRYVNI
12.8000 g., Copper-Nickel-Zinc, 31 mm.   **Subject:** Larix
Polonica **Obv:** Value within wreath **Rev:** Pine branch with cone
Edge: Reeded

Date	Mintage	F	VF	XF	Unc	BU
2001	30,000	—	—	—	40.00	—

KM# 139   2 HRYVNI
12.8000 g., Copper-Nickel-Zinc, 31 mm.   **Subject:** Volodymyr
Dal **Obv:** Books **Rev:** Head right **Edge:** Reeded

Date	Mintage	F	VF	XF	Unc	BU
2001	30,000	—	—	—	12.00	—

KM# 147   2 HRYVNI
12.8000 g., Copper-Nickel-Zinc, 31 mm.   **Series:** Olympics - Salt
Lake City, 2002 **Obv:** National arms and value on ice design **Rev:**
Stylized hockey player **Edge:** Reeded

Date	Mintage	F	VF	XF	Unc	BU
2001	30,000	—	—	—	20.00	—

KM# 149   2 HRYVNI
12.8000 g., Copper-Nickel-Zinc, 31 mm.   **Subject:** Mykhailo
Drahomanov (Historian, Politician, etc.) **Obv:** National arms and
value **Rev:** Bust right **Edge:** Reeded

Date	Mintage	F	VF	XF	Unc	BU
2001	30,000	—	—	—	12.00	—

KM# 150   2 HRYVNI
12.8000 g., Copper-Nickel-Zinc, 31 mm.   **Series:** Olympics - Salt
lake City, 2002 **Obv:** National arms and value on ice design **Rev:**
Speed skater **Edge:** Reeded

Date	Mintage	F	VF	XF	Unc	BU
2002	30,000	—	—	—	18.00	—

KM# 155   2 HRYVNI
12.8000 g., Copper-Nickel-Zinc, 31 mm.   **Series:** Flora and
Fauna **Obv:** National arms and date divides wreath, value within
Rev: Eurasian Eagle Owl **Edge:** Reeded

Date	Mintage	F	VF	XF	Unc	BU
2002	30,000	—	—	—	60.00	—

KM# 156   2 HRYVNI
12.8000 g., Copper-Nickel-Zinc, 31 mm.   **Subject:** Olympics -

Athens, 2004 **Obv:** Two ancient figures above value **Rev:**
Swimmer **Edge:** Reeded

Date	Mintage	F	VF	XF	Unc	BU
2002	30,000	—	—	—	18.00	—

KM# 166   2 HRYVNI
12.8000 g., Copper-Nickel-Zinc, 31 mm.   **Subject:** Leonid
Glibov, writer (1827-1893) **Obv:** National arms and value within
scroll and wreath **Rev:** 1/2-length bust right **Edge:** Reeded

Date	Mintage	F	VF	XF	Unc	BU
2002	30,000	—	—	—	12.00	—

KM# 154   2 HRYVNI
12.8000 g., Copper-Nickel-Zinc, 31 mm.   **Subject:** Mykola
Lysenko (composer) **Obv:** Musical score and value **Rev:** Head
1/4 right **Edge:** Reeded

Date	Mintage	F	VF	XF	Unc	BU
2002	30,000	—	—	—	12.00	—

KM# 167   2 HRYVNI
12.8000 g., Copper-Nickel-Zinc, 31 mm.   **Series:** Flora and
Fauna **Obv:** National arms and date divides wreath, value within
Rev: European Bison **Edge:** Reeded

Date	Mintage	F	VF	XF	Unc	BU
2003	50,000	—	—	—	30.00	—

KM# 168   2 HRYVNI
12.8000 g., Copper-Nickel-Zinc, 31 mm.   **Obv:** National arms
and date divides wreath, value within **Rev:** Long-snouted Sea
Horse **Edge:** Reeded

Date	Mintage	F	VF	XF	Unc	BU
2003	50,000	—	—	—	25.00	—

KM# 169   2 HRYVNI
12.8000 g., Copper-Nickel-Zinc, 31 mm.   **Subject:** Volodymyr
Vernadskyi (academic) **Obv:** National arms, value and world
globe **Rev:** Head on hand looking down **Edge:** Reeded

Date	Mintage	F	VF	XF	Unc	BU
2003	30,000	—	—	—	12.00	—

KM# 170   2 HRYVNI
12.8000 g., Copper-Nickel-Zinc, 31 mm.   **Subject:** Volodymyr
Korolenko (writer) **Obv:** National arms above book and value
Rev: Bearded head 1/4 right above dates **Edge:** Reeded

Date	Mintage	F	VF	XF	Unc	BU
2003	30,000	—	—	—	12.00	—

KM# 171   2 HRYVNI
12.8000 g., Copper-Nickel-Zinc, 31 mm.   **Subject:** Viacheslav
Chornovil (politician) **Obv:** Arms with supporters within beaded
circle **Rev:** Head 1/4 left **Edge:** Reeded

Date	Mintage	F	VF	XF	Unc	BU
2003	30,000	—	—	—	30.00	—

KM# 178   2 HRYVNI
1.2400 g., 0.9999 Gold 0.0399 oz. AGW, 13.92 mm.   **Obv:**
National arms flanked by dates within beaded circle **Rev:** Spotted
Salamander divides beaded circle **Edge:** Plain

Date	Mintage	F	VF	XF	Unc	BU
2003	10,000	—	—	—	—	220

KM# 179   2 HRYVNI
12.8000 g., Copper-Nickel-Zinc, 31 mm.   **Subject:** Singer Boris
Gmyrya **Obv:** Value, arms ,date and musical symbol **Rev:** Head
1/4 left and dates **Edge:** Reeded

Date	Mintage	F	VF	XF	Unc	BU
2003	30,000	—	—	—	12.00	—

KM# 180   2 HRYVNI
12.8000 g., Copper-Nickel-Zinc, 31 mm.   **Subject:** 70th
Anniversary National Aviation University **Obv:** World globe
behind national arms, value and date **Rev:** Wright Brothers
biplane **Edge:** Reeded

Date	Mintage	F	VF	XF	Unc	BU
2003	30,000	—	—	—	20.00	—

KM# 181   2 HRYVNI
12.8000 g., Copper-Nickel-Zinc, 31 mm.   **Subject:** Ostap Veresay (musician) **Obv:** Musical stringed instrument and ornamental design **Rev:** Bust facing playing stringed instrument **Edge:** Reeded

Date	Mintage	F	VF	XF	Unc	BU
2003	30,000	—	—	—	13.00	—

KM# 202   2 HRYVNI
12.8000 g., Copper-Nickel-Zinc, 31 mm.   **Subject:** Football World Cup - 2006 **Obv:** Soccer ball in net **Rev:** Two soccer players **Edge:** Reeded

Date	Mintage	F	VF	XF	Unc	BU
2004	50,000	—	—	—	15.00	—

Kotsyubynsky (writer) **Obv:** Two reclining figures **Rev:** Head 1/4 right **Edge:** Reeded

Date	Mintage	F	VF	XF	Unc	BU
2004	30,000	—	—	—	12.00	—

KM# 182   2 HRYVNI
12.8000 g., Copper-Nickel-Zinc, 31 mm.   **Subject:** Olympics **Obv:** Two ancient women with seedlings **Rev:** Boxer **Edge:** Reeded

Date	Mintage	F	VF	XF	Unc	BU
2003	30,000	—	—	—	20.00	—

KM# 203   2 HRYVNI
12.8000 g., Copper-Nickel-Zinc, 31 mm.   **Subject:** Serhiy Lyfar (ballet artist) **Obv:** Stylized dancer **Rev:** Head right **Edge:** Reeded

Date	Mintage	F	VF	XF	Unc	BU
2004	30,000	—	—	—	13.00	—

KM# 214   2 HRYVNI
12.8000 g., Copper-Nickel-Zinc, 31 mm.   **Subject:** Maria Zankovetska (actress) **Obv:** National arms, value and drawn curtain **Rev:** Hooded head 1/4 left **Edge:** Reeded

Date	Mintage	F	VF	XF	Unc	BU
2004	30,000	—	—	—	12.00	—

KM# 183   2 HRYVNI
12.8000 g., Copper-Nickel-Zinc, 31 mm.   **Subject:** Vasyl Sukhomlynski (teacher) **Obv:** Children, books, value and national arms **Rev:** Head 1/4 right **Edge:** Reeded

Date	Mintage	F	VF	XF	Unc	BU
2003	30,000	—	—	—	13.00	—

KM# 210   2 HRYVNI
12.8000 g., Copper-Nickel-Zinc, 31 mm.   **Subject:** 170 Years of the Kyiv National University **Obv:** National arms in center above value dividing scientific items **Rev:** University building main entrance **Edge:** Reeded

Date	Mintage	F	VF	XF	Unc	BU
2004	50,000	—	—	—	11.00	—

KM# 215   2 HRYVNI
12.8000 g., Copper-Nickel-Zinc, 31 mm.   **Subject:** Mykhailo Maksymovych (historian, archaeologist) **Obv:** National arms above building and value **Rev:** Bust left **Edge:** Reeded

Date	Mintage	F	VF	XF	Unc	BU
2004	30,000	—	—	—	12.00	—

KM# 184   2 HRYVNI
12.8000 g., Copper-Nickel-Zinc, 31 mm.   **Subject:** Andriy Malyshko (poet) **Obv:** Ornamental shawl, national arms and value **Rev:** Head 1/4 right flanked by radiant sun and tree **Edge:** Reeded

Date	Mintage	F	VF	XF	Unc	BU
2003	30,000	—	—	—	13.00	—

KM# 211   2 HRYVNI
12.8000 g., Copper-Nickel-Zinc, 31 mm.   **Subject:** Oleksander Dovzhenko (movie producer, writer) **Obv:** Boy standing in small boat **Rev:** Head facing **Edge:** Reeded

Date	Mintage	F	VF	XF	Unc	BU
2004	30,000	—	—	—	12.00	—

KM# 216   2 HRYVNI
12.8000 g., Copper-Nickel-Zinc, 31 mm.   **Subject:** Mykhailo Deregus (painter) **Obv:** National arms and value on artists palette **Rev:** Head right **Edge:** Reeded

Date	Mintage	F	VF	XF	Unc	BU
2004	30,000	—	—	—	12.00	—

KM# 212   2 HRYVNI
12.8000 g., Copper-Nickel-Zinc, 31 mm.   **Subject:** Mykola Bazhan (poet, translator) **Obv:** Winged pens and value **Rev:** Head 1/4 left **Edge:** Reeded

Date	Mintage	F	VF	XF	Unc	BU
2004	30,000	—	—	—	12.00	—

KM# 201   2 HRYVNI
12.8000 g., Copper-Nickel-Zinc, 31 mm.   **Subject:** Azov Dolphin **Obv:** National arms and date divides wreath, value within **Rev:** Harbor Porpoises **Edge:** Reeded

Date	Mintage	F	VF	XF	Unc	BU
2004	30,000	—	—	—	50.00	—

KM# 213   2 HRYVNI
12.8000 g., Copper-Nickel-Zinc, 31 mm.   **Subject:** Mykhailo

KM# 217   2 HRYVNI
12.8000 g., Copper-Nickel-Zinc, 31 mm.   **Subject:** Nuclear Power Engineering of Ukraine **Obv:** National arms and value in atomic design **Rev:** Nuclear reactor **Edge:** Reeded

Date	Mintage	F	VF	XF	Unc	BU
2004	30,000	—	—	—	18.00	—

KM# 227   2 HRYVNI
1.2400 g., 0.9999 Gold 0.0399 oz. AGW, 13.92 mm.   **Obv:** National arms divides dates within beaded circle **Rev:** Flying White Stork divides beaded circle **Edge:** Plain

Date	Mintage	F	VF	XF	Unc	BU
2004	10,000	—	—	—	—	220

KM# 330   2 HRYVNI
12.8000 g., Copper-Nickel-Zinc, 31 mm. **Subject:** 200th Anniversary of Kharkiv University **Obv:** National arms and atom **Rev:** University building and reflection **Edge:** Reeded

Date	Mintage	F	VF	XF	Unc	BU
2004	50,000	—	—	—	11.00	—

KM# 331   2 HRYVNI
12.8000 g., Copper-Nickel-Zinc, 31 mm. **Subject:** Ukraine National Academy of Law named after Yaroslav the Wise **Obv:** National arms above National Academy of Law arms and date **Rev:** Building **Edge:** Reeded

Date	Mintage	F	VF	XF	Unc	BU
2004	30,000	—	—	—	20.00	—

KM# 332   2 HRYVNI
12.8000 g., Copper-Nickel-Zinc, 31 mm. **Subject:** Yurii Fedkovych (poet, writer) **Obv:** National arms, value and man on horse **Rev:** Bust 1/4 right and dates **Edge:** Reeded

Date	Mintage	F	VF	XF	Unc	BU
2004	30,000	—	—	—	12.00	—

KM# 346   2 HRYVNI
12.8000 g., Copper-Nickel-Zinc, 31 mm. **Subject:** Boris Liatoshynsky (composer) **Obv:** Musical G Clef symbol and value below national arms **Rev:** Head 1/4 left **Edge:** Reeded

Date	Mintage	F	VF	XF	Unc	BU
2005	20,000	—	—	—	13.00	—

KM# 347   2 HRYVNI
12.8000 g., Copper-Nickel-Zinc, 31 mm. **Subject:** Volodymyr Filatov (surgeon) **Obv:** Light passing through the lens of an eye **Rev:** Head with cap facing **Edge:** Reeded

Date	Mintage	F	VF	XF	Unc	BU
2005	20,000	—	—	—	13.00	—

KM# 348   2 HRYVNI
12.8000 g., Copper-Nickel-Zinc, 31 mm. **Obv:** Books between stylized horsemen **Rev:** Ulas Samchuk **Edge:** Reeded

Date	Mintage	F	VF	XF	Unc	BU
2005	20,000	—	—	—	13.00	—

KM# 349   2 HRYVNI
12.8000 g., Copper-Nickel-Zinc, 31 mm. **Subject:** Pavlo Virsky (ballet artist) **Obv:** National arms in flower circle **Rev:** Bust right **Edge:** Reeded

Date	Mintage	F	VF	XF	Unc	BU
2005	20,000	—	—	—	13.00	—

KM# 350   2 HRYVNI
12.8000 g., Copper-Nickel-Zinc, 31 mm. **Obv:** Roses and grapes **Rev:** Poet Maksym Rylsky **Edge:** Reeded

Date	Mintage	F	VF	XF	Unc	BU
2005	20,000	—	—	—	13.00	—

KM# 351   2 HRYVNI
1.2400 g., 0.9999 Gold 0.0399 oz. AGW, 13.9 mm. **Obv:** National arms within beaded circle **Rev:** Scythian horseman depicted on golden plaque **Edge:** Plain

Date	Mintage	F	VF	XF	Unc	BU
2005	15,000	—	—	—	200	220

KM# 352   2 HRYVNI
12.8000 g., Copper-Nickel-Zinc, 31 mm. **Subject:** Serhiy Vsekhsviatsky (astronomer) **Obv:** "Solar Wind" depiction **Rev:** Head right **Edge:** Reeded

Date	Mintage	F	VF	XF	Unc	BU
2005	20,000	—	—	—	13.00	—

KM# 353   2 HRYVNI
12.8000 g., Copper-Nickel-Zinc, 31 mm. **Subject:** 50 Years of Kyivmiskbud **Obv:** National arms **Rev:** Buildings **Edge:** Reeded

Date	Mintage	F	VF	XF	Unc	BU
2005	20,000	—	—	—	18.00	—

KM# 354   2 HRYVNI
12.8000 g., Copper-Nickel-Zinc, 31 mm. **Subject:** 75 Years of Zhukovsky Aerospace University in Kharkiv **Obv:** Building divides book outline **Rev:** Airplane, computer monitor and books **Edge:** Reeded

Date	Mintage	F	VF	XF	Unc	BU
2005	30,000	—	—	—	18.00	—

KM# 356   2 HRYVNI
12.8000 g., Copper-Nickel-Zinc, 31 mm. **Subject:** Oleksander Korniychuk (writer, playright) **Obv:** Theatrical masks and feather **Rev:** Bust 1/4 right **Edge:** Reeded

Date	Mintage	F	VF	XF	Unc	BU
2005	20,000	—	—	—	13.00	—

KM# 357   2 HRYVNI
12.8000 g., Copper-Nickel-Zinc, 31 mm. **Obv:** National arms and date divides wreath, value within **Rev:** Sandy Mole Rat **Edge:** Reeded

Date	Mintage	F	VF	XF	Unc	BU
2005	60,000	—	—	—	15.00	—

KM# 359   2 HRYVNI
12.8000 g., Copper-Nickel-Zinc, 31 mm. **Obv:** National arms **Rev:** Tairov Wine Institute building and cameo **Edge:** Reeded

Date	Mintage	F	VF	XF	Unc	BU
2005	20,000	—	—	—	20.00	—

KM# 360   2 HRYVNI
12.8000 g., Copper-Nickel-Zinc, 31 mm. **Subject:** 300 Years to David Guramishvili (poet) **Obv:** Georgian and Ukrainian style ornamentation **Rev:** Head right **Edge:** Reeded

Date	Mintage	F	VF	XF	Unc	BU
2005	30,000	—	—	—	11.00	—

KM# 361 2 HRYVNI
12.8000 g., Copper-Nickel-Zinc, 31 mm. **Subject:** Dmytro Yavornytsky (historian, archaeologist, writer) **Obv:** National arms **Rev:** Bust 3/4 right **Edge:** Reeded

Date	Mintage	F	VF	XF	Unc	BU
2005	30,000	—	—	—	11.00	—

KM# 375 2 HRYVNI
12.8000 g., Copper-Nickel-Zinc, 31 mm. **Subject:** Oleksiy Alchevsky (banker) **Obv:** Steam train, factory, National arms and value **Rev:** Head with beard 1/4 right **Edge:** Reeded

Date	Mintage	F	VF	XF	Unc	BU
2005	20,000	—	—	—	20.00	—

KM# 376 2 HRYVNI
12.8000 g., Copper-Nickel-Zinc, 31 mm. **Subject:** Illia Mechnikov (biologist, Nobel prize laureate) **Obv:** Amoeba and National arms **Rev:** Bust with beard facing **Edge:** Reeded

Date	Mintage	F	VF	XF	Unc	BU
2005	20,000	—	—	—	20.00	—

KM# 377 2 HRYVNI
12.8000 g., Copper-Nickel-Zinc, 31 mm. **Subject:** Vsevolod Holubovych (politician) **Obv:** National arms **Rev:** Head 1/4 left **Edge:** Reeded

Date	Mintage	F	VF	XF	Unc	BU
2005	20,000	—	—	—	18.00	—

KM# 378 2 HRYVNI
12.8000 g., Copper-Nickel-Zinc, 31 mm. **Subject:** Volodymyr Vynnychenko (writer, politician) **Obv:** National arms **Rev:** Head facing **Edge:** Reeded

Date	Mintage	F	VF	XF	Unc	BU
2005	20,000	—	—	—	15.00	—

KM# 383 2 HRYVNI
12.8000 g., Copper-Nickel-Zinc, 31 mm. **Subject:** Kyiv National University of Economics **Obv:** National arms, value and graph **Rev:** University building **Edge:** Reeded

Date	Mintage	F	VF	XF	Unc	BU
2006	60,000	—	—	—	12.00	—

KM# 384 2 HRYVNI
12.8000 g., Copper-Nickel-Zinc, 31 mm. **Subject:** Viacheslav Prokopovych (historian, publist) **Obv:** National arms **Rev:** Bust facing **Edge:** Reeded

Date	Mintage	F	VF	XF	Unc	BU
2006	30,000	—	—	—	12.00	—

KM# 385 2 HRYVNI
12.8000 g., Copper-Nickel-Zinc, 31 mm. **Subject:** Heorhii Narbut (artist) **Obv:** Peasant couple **Rev:** Silhouette of standing figure on one leg facing right **Edge:** Reeded

Date	Mintage	F	VF	XF	Unc	BU
2006	30,000	—	—	—	12.00	—

KM# 386 2 HRYVNI
12.8000 g., Copper-Nickel-Zinc, 31 mm. **Subject:** Oleh Antonov (aircraft engineer) **Obv:** Large jet plane **Rev:** Bust 1/4 right **Edge:** Reeded

Date	Mintage	F	VF	XF	Unc	BU
2006	45,000	—	—	—	15.00	—

KM# 391 2 HRYVNI
12.8000 g., Copper-Nickel-Zinc, 31 mm. **Obv:** National arms

above value in wreath **Rev:** Bush Katydid Grasshopper **Edge:** Reeded

Date	Mintage	F	VF	XF	Unc	BU
2006	60,000	—	—	—	18.00	—

KM# 398 2 HRYVNI
12.8000 g., Copper-Nickel-Zinc, 31 mm. **Subject:** Mykhailo Hrushevskyi **Obv:** National arms and value **Edge:** Reeded

Date	Mintage	F	VF	XF	Unc	BU
2006	45,000	—	—	—	12.00	—

KM# 408 2 HRYVNI
1.2400 g., 0.9999 Gold 0.0399 oz. AGW, 13.92 mm. **Subject:** Hedgehog **Obv:** National arms **Edge:** Plain

Date	Mintage	F	VF	XF	Unc	BU
2006	10,000	—	—	—	150	200

KM# 399 2 HRYVNI
12.8000 g., Copper-Nickel-Zinc, 31 mm. **Subject:** Serhii Ostapenko **Obv:** National arms **Edge:** Reeded

Date	Mintage	F	VF	XF	Unc	BU
2006	30,000	—	—	—	12.00	—

KM# 401 2 HRYVNI
12.8000 g., Copper-Nickel-Zinc, 31 mm. **Subject:** Economic University of Kharkiv

Date	Mintage	F	VF	XF	Unc	BU
2006	30,000	—	—	—	12.00	—

KM# 393 2 HRYVNI
12.8000 g., Copper-Nickel-Zinc, 31 mm. **Subject:** Mykola Strazhesko **Obv:** National arms and value **Edge:** Reeded

Date	Mintage	F	VF	XF	Unc	BU
2006	45,000	—	—	—	12.00	—

KM# 394   2 HRYVNI
12.8000 g., Copper-Nickel-Zinc, 31 mm. **Subject:** Volodymyr
Chekhivsky **Obv:** National arms and value **Edge:** Reeded

Date	Mintage	F	VF	XF	Unc	BU
2006	30,000	—	—	—	12.00	—

KM# 395   2 HRYVNI
12.8000 g., Copper-Nickel-Zinc, 31 mm. **Subject:** Mykola
Vasylenko **Obv:** National arms and value **Edge:** Reeded

Date	Mintage	F	VF	XF	Unc	BU
2006	30,000	—	—	—	13.00	—

KM# 396   2 HRYVNI
12.8000 g., Copper-Nickel-Zinc, 31 mm. **Subject:** Ivan Franko
Obv: National arms and value **Edge:** Reeded

Date	Mintage	F	VF	XF	Unc	BU
2006	45,000	—	—	—	12.00	—

KM# 397   2 HRYVNI
12.8000 g., Copper-Nickel-Zinc, 31 mm. **Subject:** Dmytro
Lutsenko **Obv:** National arms and value **Edge:** Reeded

Date	Mintage	F	VF	XF	Unc	BU
2006	30,000	—	—	—	12.00	—

KM# 400   2 HRYVNI
12.8000 g., Copper-Nickel-Zinc, 31 mm. **Subject:** Mykhailo
Lysenko **Obv:** National arms and value **Edge:** Reeded

Date	Mintage	F	VF	XF	Unc	BU
2006	35,000	—	—	—	12.00	—

KM# 403   2 HRYVNI
1.2400 g., 0.9999 Gold 0.0399 oz. AGW, 13.92 mm. **Subject:**
Ram **Obv:** National arms **Edge:** Plain

Date	Mintage	F	VF	XF	Unc	BU
2006	10,000	—	—	—	140	200

KM# 404   2 HRYVNI
1.2400 g., 0.9999 Gold 0.0399 oz. AGW, 13.92 mm. **Subject:**
Bull **Obv:** National arms **Edge:** Plain

Date	Mintage	F	VF	XF	Unc	BU
2006	10,000	—	—	—	140	200

KM# 406   2 HRYVNI
1.2400 g., 0.9999 Gold 0.0399 oz. AGW, 13.92 mm. **Subject:**
The Twins **Obv:** National arms **Edge:** Plain

Date	Mintage	F	VF	XF	Unc	BU
2006	10,000	—	—	—	140	200

KM# 428   2 HRYVNI
12.8000 g., Copper-Nickel-Zinc, 31 mm. **Subject:** Serhii
Koroljov **Obv:** National arms **Edge:** Reeded

Date	Mintage	F	VF	XF	Unc	BU
2007	35,000	—	—	—	—	20.00

KM# 429   2 HRYVNI
12.8000 g., Copper-Nickel-Zinc, 31 mm. **Subject:** Les Kurbas
Obv: National arms **Edge:** Reeded

Date	Mintage	F	VF	XF	Unc	BU
2007	35,000	—	—	—	—	12.00

KM# 430   2 HRYVNI
12.8000 g., Copper-Nickel-Zinc, 31 mm. **Subject:** Olexander
Liapunov **Obv:** Small national arms above geometrical depiction
of celestial mechanics graphics **Rev:** Large bust facing **Edge:**
Reeded

Date	Mintage	F	VF	XF	Unc	BU
2007	35,000	—	—	—	—	12.00

KM# 431   2 HRYVNI
1.2400 g., 0.9999 Gold 0.0399 oz. AGW, 13.92 mm. **Subject:**
Steppe Marmot **Obv:** National arms **Edge:** Plain

Date	Mintage	F	VF	XF	Unc	BU
2007	10,000	—	—	—	150	200

KM# 440   2 HRYVNI
12.8000 g., Copper-Nickel-Zinc, 31 mm. **Subject:** Ivan Ohienko
Obv: Cross **Rev:** Head and hands clasped at prayer **Edge:**
Reeded

Date	Mintage	F	VF	XF	Unc	BU
2007	35,000	—	—	—	—	12.00

KM# 441   2 HRYVNI
12.8000 g., Copper-Nickel-Zinc, 31 mm. **Subject:** Oleh Olzhych
Obv: Chestnut leaf and stone path **Rev:** Bust facing **Edge:**
Reeded

Date	Mintage	F	VF	XF	Unc	BU
2007	35,000	—	—	—	—	12.00

KM# 442   2 HRYVNI
12.8000 g., Copper-Nickel-Zinc, 31 mm. **Subject:** Donetsk
Region 75th Anniversary **Obv:** Miner's lamp illuminating industrial
plants **Rev:** Flag and 75 **Edge:** Reeded

Date	Mintage	F	VF	XF	Unc	BU
2007	35,000	—	—	—	—	20.00

KM# 443   2 HRYVNI
12.8000 g., Copper-Nickel-Zinc, 31 mm. **Subject:** Olena Teliha
Obv: Scorched cherry blossom **Rev:** Bust facing **Edge:** Reeded

Date	Mintage	F	VF	XF	Unc	BU
2007	35,000	—	—	—	—	12.00

KM# 444   2 HRYVNI
12.8000 g., Copper-Nickel-Zinc, 31 mm. **Subject:** Orienteering
Obv: Compass, star and benchmarks **Rev:** Runner **Edge:**
Reeded

Date	Mintage	F	VF	XF	Unc	BU
2007	35,000	—	—	—	—	14.00

KM# 445   2 HRYVNI
12.8000 g., Copper-Nickel-Zinc, 31 mm. **Subject:** Ivan Bahrianji
Obv: Book edge **Rev:** Bust facing, book edge **Edge:** Reeded

Date	Mintage	F	VF	XF	Unc	BU
2007	35,000	—	—	—	—	12.00

KM# 446 2 HRYVNI
12.8000 g., Copper-Nickel-Zinc, 31 mm. **Subject:** Petro Hryhorenko **Obv:** Sprout squeezing brick wall **Rev:** Head right **Edge:** Reeded

Date	Mintage	F	VF	XF	Unc	BU
2007	35,000	—	—	—	—	13.00

KM# 447 2 HRYVNI
12.8000 g., Copper-Nickel-Zinc, 31 mm. **Subject:** 90th Anniversary of 1st Government **Obv:** Parts of early 20th century bank notes and industrial elements **Rev:** Volodymyr Vynnychenko and ornamentation **Edge:** Reeded

Date	Mintage	F	VF	XF	Unc	BU
2007	35,000	—	—	—	—	13.00

KM# 448 2 HRYVNI
1.2400 g., 0.9990 Gold 0.0398 oz. AGW, 13.9 mm. **Subject:** Capricorn **Obv:** Elements of earth, air, water and fire **Rev:** Zodiac sign

Date	Mintage	F	VF	XF	Unc	BU
2007	35,000	—	—	—	140	200

KM# 450 2 HRYVNI
1.2400 g., 0.9990 Gold 0.0398 oz. AGW, 13.9 mm. **Subject:** Pisces **Obv:** Elements of earth, air, water and fire **Rev:** Zodiac sign, two fish

Date	Mintage	F	VF	XF	Unc	BU
2007	10,000	—	—	—	140	200

KM# 449 2 HRYVNI
1.2400 g., 0.9990 Gold 0.0398 oz. AGW, 13.9 mm. **Subject:** Aquarius **Obv:** Elements of earth, air, water and fire **Rev:** Zodiac sign, man pouring water

Date	Mintage	F	VF	XF	Unc	BU
2007	10,000	—	—	—	140	200

KM# 451 2 HRYVNI
1.2400 g., 0.9990 Gold 0.0398 oz. AGW, 13.9 mm. **Subject:** Scorpion **Obv:** Elements of earth, air, water and fire **Rev:** Zodiac sign

Date	Mintage	F	VF	XF	Unc	BU
2007	10,000	—	—	—	140	200

KM# 452 2 HRYVNI
1.2400 g., 0.9990 Gold 0.0398 oz. AGW, 13.9 mm. **Subject:** Sagitarius **Obv:** Elements of earth, air, water & fire **Rev:** Zodiac sign, archer

Date	Mintage	F	VF	XF	Unc	BU
2007	10,000	—	—	—	140	200

KM# 433 2 HRYVNI
12.8000 g., Copper-Nickel-Zinc, 31 mm. **Obv:** Small national arms at top, value in sprays with bird at left, butterfly at right **Rev:** Cinereous Vulture perched on nest with chick **Rev. Legend:** AEGYPIUS MONACHUS - ГРИФ ЧОРНИЙ **Edge:** Reeded

Date	Mintage	F	VF	XF	Unc	BU
2008	45,000	—	—	—	—	20.00

KM# 475 2 HRYVNI
12.8000 g., Copper-Nickel-Zinc, 31 mm. **Subject:** Vasyl Stus, Poet **Edge:** Reeded

Date	Mintage	F	VF	XF	Unc	BU
2008	35,000	—	—	—	—	12.00

KM# 476 2 HRYVNI
12.8000 g., Copper-Nickel-Zinc, 31 mm. **Subject:** Leo Landau **Edge:** Reeded

Date	Mintage	F	VF	XF	Unc	BU
2008	35,000	—	—	—	—	12.00

KM# 477 2 HRYVNI
12.8000 g., Copper-Nickel-Zinc, 31 mm. **Subject:** Sydir Holubovych **Edge:** Reeded

Date	Mintage	F	VF	XF	Unc	BU
2008	35,000	—	—	—	—	12.00

KM# 478 2 HRYVNI
12.8000 g., Copper-Nickel-Zinc, 31 mm. **Subject:** Kyiv Zoo, 100th Anniversary **Edge:** Reeded

Date	Mintage	F	VF	XF	Unc	BU
2008	50,000	—	—	—	—	15.00

KM# 479 2 HRYVNI
12.8000 g., Copper-Nickel-Zinc, 31 mm. **Subject:** Yevhen Petrushevych **Edge:** Reeded

Date	Mintage	F	VF	XF	Unc	BU
2008	35,000	—	—	—	—	12.00

KM# 481 2 HRYVNI
12.8000 g., Copper-Nickel-Zinc, 31 mm. **Subject:** Heorhii Voronyi **Edge:** Reeded

Date	Mintage	F	VF	XF	Unc	BU
2008	35,000	—	—	—	—	12.00

KM# 482 2 HRYVNI
1.2400 g., 0.9990 Gold 0.0398 oz. AGW, 13.9 mm. **Subject:** Skythian Gold (Goddess Api)

Date	Mintage	F	VF	XF	Unc	BU
2008	10,000	—	—	—	140	200

KM# 483 2 HRYVNI
1.2400 g., 0.9990 Gold 0.0398 oz. AGW, 13.9 mm. **Subject:** Zodiac **Rev:** Cancer

Date	Mintage	F	VF	XF	Unc	BU
2008	10,000	—	—	—	140	200

KM# 484 2 HRYVNI
1.2400 g., 0.9990 Gold 0.0398 oz. AGW, 13.9 mm. **Subject:** Zodiac **Rev:** Leo

Date	Mintage	F	VF	XF	Unc	BU
2008	10,000	—	—	—	140	200

KM# 485 2 HRYVNI
1.2400 g., 0.9990 Gold 0.0398 oz. AGW **Subject:** Virgo

Date	Mintage	F	VF	XF	Unc	BU
2008	10,000	—	—	—	140	200

KM# 486 2 HRYVNI
1.2400 g., 0.9990 Gold 0.0398 oz. AGW, 13.9 mm. **Subject:** Libra

Date	Mintage	F	VF	XF	Unc	BU
2008	—	—	—	—	140	200

KM# 487 2 HRYVNI
12.8000 g., Copper-Nickel-Zinc, 31 mm. **Subject:** Nataliia Vzhvii **Edge:** Reeded

Date	Mintage	F	VF	XF	Unc	BU
2008	35,000	—	—	—	—	12.00

KM# 488 2 HRYVNI
12.8000 g., Copper-Nickel-Zinc, 31 mm. **Subject:** Hryhorii Kvitka - Osnovianenko **Edge:** Reeded

Date	Mintage	F	VF	XF	Unc	BU
2008	35,000	—	—	—	—	12.00

KM# 489 2 HRYVNI
12.8000 g., Copper-Nickel-Zinc, 31 mm. **Subject:** Western Ukraine People's Republic, 90th Anniversary **Edge:** Reeded

Date	Mintage	F	VF	XF	Unc	BU
2008	35,000	—	—	—	—	12.00

KM# 490 2 HRYVNI
12.8000 g., Copper-Nickel-Zinc, 31 mm. **Subject:** Vasyl Symonenko **Edge:** Reeded

Date	Mintage	F	VF	XF	Unc	BU
2008	35,000	—	—	—	—	12.00

KM# 533 2 HRYVNI
12.8000 g., Copper-Nickel-Zinc, 31.0 mm. **Subject:** Pavlo Chubynskyi **Obv:** Folk music instruments **Obv. Legend:** НАЦІОНАЛЬНИЙ БАНК УКРА?НИ - 2 / ГРИВНІ / 2009 **Rev:** Chubynskyi's portrait **Rev. Legend:** ПАВЛО ЧУБИНСЬКИЙ - 1839-1884 **Edge:** Reeded

Date	Mintage	F	VF	XF	Unc	BU
2009	35,000	—	—	—	—	12.00

KM# 534 2 HRYVNI
12.8000 g., Copper-Nickel-Zinc, 31.0 mm. **Subject:** Andrii Livytskyi **Obv:** National Arms and value **Obv. Legend:** НАЦІОНАЛЬНИЙ БАНК УКРА?НИ - ДВІ ГРИВНІ **Rev:** Livytskyi's portrait **Rev. Legend:** АНДРІЙ ЛІВИЦЬКИЙ - 1879/1954 - ПРЕЗИДЕНТ УНР В ЕКЗИЛІ **Edge:** Reeded

Date	Mintage	F	VF	XF	Unc	BU
2009	35,000	—	—	—	—	12.00

KM# 535 2 HRYVNI
1.2400 g., 0.9990 Gold 0.0398 oz. AGW, 13.92 mm. **Subject:** Ukraine Fauna **Obv:** National Arms, value **Obv. Legend:** НАЦІОНАЛЬНИЙ БАНК УКРА?НИ - 2 ГРИВНІ **Rev:** Turtle **Rev. Legend:** ЧЕРЕПАХА - TESTUDINES

Date	Mintage	F	VF	XF	Unc	BU
2009	10,000	—	—	—	200	140

KM# 536 2 HRYVNI
12.8000 g., Copper-Nickel-Zinc, 31.0 mm. **Subject:** Borys Martos **Obv:** National Arms and value **Obv. Legend:** НАЦІОНАЛЬНИЙ БАНК УКРА?НИ - ДВІ ГРИВНІ **Rev:** Martos's portrait **Rev. Legend:** БОРИС МАРТОС **Edge:** Reeded

Date	Mintage	F	VF	XF	Unc	BU
2009	35,000	—	—	—	—	12.00

KM# 537 2 HRYVNI
12.8000 g., Copper-Nickel-Zinc, 31.0 mm. **Subject:** General Symon Petliura **Obv:** Two Military men holding wreath of a woman's profile **Obv. Legend:** НАЦІОНАЛЬНИЙ БАНК УКРА?НИ - 2 ГРИВНІ **Rev:** Petliura's portrait **Rev. Legend:** СИМОН ПЕТЛЮРА **Edge:** Reeded

Date	Mintage	F	VF	XF	Unc	BU
2009	35,000	—	—	—	—	15.00

KM# 538 2 HRYVNI
12.8000 g., Copper-Nickel-Zinc, 31 mm. **Subject:** Igor Sikorskyi, 100th Anniversary of birth **Obv:** Aircraft, National Arms, value **Obv. Legend:** НАЦІОНАЛЬНИЙ БАНК УКРА?НИ - 2 ГРИВНІ **Rev:** Sikorskyi portrait as an airman, Da Vinci drawing **Rev. Legend:** ІГОР СІКОРСЬКИЙ **Edge:** Reeded

Date	Mintage	F	VF	XF	Unc	BU
2009	35,000	—	—	—	—	15.00

KM# 539 2 HRYVNI
12.8000 g., Copper-Nickel-Zinc, 31 mm. **Subject:** Mykola Bogolijubov, physicist, 100th Anniversary of birth **Obv:** Diagram and formula, National Arms, value **Rev:** Bogolijubov's portrait **Edge:** Reeded

Date	Mintage	F	VF	XF	Unc	BU
2009	35,000	—	—	—	—	12.00

KM# 540 2 HRYVNI
12.8000 g., Copper-Nickel-Zinc, 31 mm. **Subject:** Volodymyr Ivasiuk, poet and singer **Obv:** Flower of Chervona Ruta, electrical musical instruments **Obv. Legend:** НАЦІОНАЛЬНИЙ БАНК УКРА?НИ - 2 / ГРИВНІ / 2009 **Rev:** Ivasiuk's portrait **Rev. Legend:** ВОЛОДИМИР ІВАСЮК **Edge:** Reeded

Date	Mintage	F	VF	XF	Unc	BU
2009	35,000	—	—	—	—	12.00

KM# 541 2 HRYVNI
12.8000 g., Copper-Nickel-Zinc, 31.0 mm. **Subject:** Bohdan-Igor Antonych, poet **Obv:** Figurative interpretation of Antonych's poetry **Obv. Legend:** НАЦІОНАЛЬНИЈ БАНК УКРА?НИ - 2 / ГРИВНІ **Rev:** Antonych's portrait **Rev. Legend:** БОГДАН-ІГОР АНТОНИЧ **Edge:** Reeded

Date	Mintage	F	VF	XF	Unc	BU
2009	35,000	—	—	—	—	12.00

KM# 542 2 HRYVNI
12.8000 g., Copper-Nickel-Zinc, 31.0 mm. **Subject:** Kost Levytskyi **Obv:** State Coat of Arms, issue year **Obv. Legend:** НАЦІОНАЛЬНИЙ БАНК УКРАЇНИ - ДВІ ГРИВНІ **Rev:** Levytskyi bust **Rev. Legend:** КОСТЬ ЛЕВИЦЬКИЈ

Date	Mintage	F	VF	XF	Unc	BU
2009	35,000	—	—	—	—	12.00

KM# 551 2 HRYVNI
12.8000 g., Copper-Nickel-Zinc, 31.0 mm. **Subject:** Carpatho-Ukraine Republic, 70th Anniversary **Obv:** Carpathian ornamentation patterns, National Arms, value **Obv. Legend:** НАЦІОНАЛЬНИЈ БАНК УКРАЇНИ - 2 / ГРИВНІ **Rev:** Transcarpathian holding flag with arms of Carpatho-Ukraine **Rev. Legend:** 70 / РОКІВ - ПРОГОЛОШЕННЯ КАРПАТСЬКОІ УКРАЇНИ **Edge:** Reeded

Date	Mintage	F	VF	XF	Unc	BU
2009	35,000	—	—	—	—	14.00

KM# 571 2 HRYVNI
1.2400 g., 0.9990 Gold 0.0398 oz. AGW, 13.92 mm. **Subject:** Skythian Gold **Obv:** National Arms **Rev:** Scythian boar figure

Date	Mintage	F	VF	XF	Unc	BU
2009 Special Unc.	10,000	—	—	—	140	200

KM# 578 2 HRYVNI
12.8000 g., Copper-Nickel-Zinc, 31 mm. **Subject:** Zaporizhzhia Oblast **Obv:** Zaporizhzhia Arms **Rev:** Stone bana, Dnieper's waves and Dniporhes dam **Edge:** Reeded

Date	Mintage	F	VF	XF	Unc	BU
2009	45,000	—	—	—	—	13.00

KM# 572 2 HRYVNI
1.2400 g., 0.9990 Gold 0.0398 oz. AGW, 13.92 mm. **Obv:** National Arms **Rev:** Bee **Edge:** Plain

Date	Mintage	F	VF	XF	Unc	BU
2010 Special Unc.	10,000	—	—	—	140	200

KM# 576 2 HRYVNI
12.8000 g., Copper-Nickel-Zinc, 31 mm. **Subject:** Ukraine Ice Hockey, 100th Anniversary **Obv:** Golie before net, National Arms **Rev:** Old time and modern hockey players **Edge:** Reeded

Date	Mintage	F	VF	XF	Unc	BU
2010	35,000	—	—	—	—	13.00

KM# 580 2 HRYVNI
12.8000 g., Copper-Nickel-Zinc, 31 mm. **Subject:** Ivan Kozhedub **Obv:** La-7 aircraft in two searchlight beams **Rev:** Kozhedub's portrait and airfield **Edge:** Reeded

Date	Mintage	F	VF	XF	Unc	BU
2010	35,000	—	—	—	—	13.00

KM# 581 2 HRYVNI
12.8000 g., Copper-Nickel, 31 mm. **Subject:** Lviv Polytechnic National University, 165th Anniversary **Obv:** Arts and Sciences sculptures from main building **Rev:** University building façade

Date	Mintage	F	VF	XF	Unc	BU
2010	45,000	—	—	—	—	13.00

KM# 583 2 HRYVNI
12.8000 g., Copper-Nickel, 31 mm. **Subject:** Kharkiv Polytechnic Institute, 125th Anniversary **Obv:** Radio telescope and open book **Rev:** University building at right, symbols of science at left, oval portrait of V.L. Kyrpychov

Date	Mintage	F	VF	XF	Unc	BU
2010	50,000	—	—	—	—	13.00

KM# 585 2 HRYVNI
12.8000 g., Copper-Nickel, 31 mm. **Subject:** Ukraine Sovereignty, 20th Anniversary **Obv:** National flag in enamel within viburnum wreath **Rev:** Ukraine map within uneven background **Edge:** Reeded

Date	Mintage	F	VF	XF	Unc	BU
2010	35,000	—	—	—	—	18.00

KM# 593 2 HRYVNI
12.8000 g., Copper-Nickel, 31 mm. **Subject:** Flora and fauna **Obv:** National Arms and wreath **Rev:** Stipa Ucrainica, feather grass

Date	Mintage	F	VF	XF	Unc	BU
2010	35,000	—	—	—	—	13.00

KM# 603 2 HRYVNI
1.2400 g., 0.9990 Gold 0.0398 oz. AGW, 13.92 mm. **Obv:** National Arms **Rev:** Cranberry bush branch **Edge:** Plain

Date	Mintage	F	VF	XF	Unc	BU
2010	10,000	—	—	—	140	200

KM# 608 2 HRYVNI
12.8000 g., Copper-Nickel, 31 mm. **Subject:** Ukranian Medical Association, 100th Anniversary **Obv:** UMA Shield within wreath **Rev:** UMA in Lviv emblem (lion on cross) **Edge:** Reeded

Date	Mintage	F	VF	XF	Unc	BU
2010	35,000	—	—	—	—	15.00

KM# 612 2 HRYVNI
12.8000 g., Copper-Nickel-Zinc, 31 mm. **Subject:** Ivan Franko National University, Lviv, 350th Anniversary **Obv:** National arms, Statuary group, value **Rev:** Main University building facade

Date	Mintage	F	VF	XF	Unc	BU
2011	45,000	—	—	—	—	12.00

KM# 624 2 HRYVNI
1.2400 g., 0.9999 Gold 0.0399 oz. AGW, 13.92 mm. **Subject:** Scythian Gold **Obv:** National arms **Rev:** Scythian jewlery, gilt deer

Date	Mintage	F	VF	XF	Unc	BU
2011	10,000	—	—	—	—	100

KM# 636 2 HRYVNI
12.8000 g., Copper-Nickel-Zinc, 31 mm. **Subject:** CIS, 20th Anniversary **Obv:** National flag in color **Rev:** Commonwealth of Independent States emblem

Date	Mintage	F	VF	XF	Unc	BU
2011	30,000	Value: 15.00				

KM# 107 5 HRYVEN
9.4000 g., Bi-Metallic Brass center in Copper-Nickel ring, 28 mm. **Subject:** New Millennium **Obv:** Spiral design within circle **Rev:** Mother and child within circle **Edge:** Segmented reeding

Date	Mintage	F	VF	XF	Unc	BU
2001	50,000	—	—	—	32.00	—

KM# 112 5 HRYVEN
16.5400 g., Copper-Nickel-Zinc, 35 mm. **Subject:** Ostrozhska Academy **Obv:** Value, old writing and printing artifacts **Rev:** Seated figures, partial building and crowned arms with supporters **Edge:** Reeded

Date	Mintage	F	VF	XF	Unc	BU
2001	30,000	—	—	—	30.00	—

KM# 129 5 HRYVEN
16.5400 g., Copper-Nickel-Zinc, 35 mm. **Subject:** 10th Anniversary - National Bank **Obv:** National arms between two arches **Rev:** Large building central entrance **Edge:** Reeded

Date	Mintage	F	VF	XF	Unc	BU
2001	50,000	—	—	—	17.50	—

KM# 132 5 HRYVEN
16.5400 g., Copper-Nickel-Zinc, 35 mm. **Subject:** 10th Anniversary - National Independence **Obv:** Arms with supporters within beaded circle **Rev:** Building on map within beaded circle **Edge:** Reeded

Date	Mintage	F	VF	XF	Unc	BU
2001	100,000	—	—	—	15.00	—

KM# 135 5 HRYVEN
16.5400 g., Copper-Nickel-Zinc, 35 mm. **Subject:** 1100th Anniversary - Poltava **Obv:** National arms above value flanked by flower sprigs **Rev:** Buildings above shield **Edge:** Reeded

Date	Mintage	F	VF	XF	Unc	BU
2001	50,000	—	—	—	20.00	—

KM# 140 5 HRYVEN
9.4000 g., Bi-Metallic Brass center in Copper-Nickel ring, 28 mm. **Subject:** 10th Anniversary of Military forces **Obv:** Crossed maces, arms and date within wreath and circle **Rev:** Circle in center of cross within wreath and circle **Edge:** Reeded and plain sections

Date	Mintage	F	VF	XF	Unc	BU
2001	30,000	—	—	—	100	—

KM# 148 5 HRYVEN
16.5400 g., Copper-Nickel-Zinc, 35 mm. **Subject:** 400 Years of Krolevets **Obv:** National arms above gateway and value **Rev:** Krolivets city arms flanked by designs **Edge:** Reeded

Date	Mintage	F	VF	XF	Unc	BU
2001	30,000	—	—	—	30.00	—

KM# 151 5 HRYVEN
16.5400 g., Copper-Nickel-Zinc, 35 mm. **Subject:** City of Khotyn **Obv:** Value within arch above military fittings **Rev:** Castle below crowned shield **Edge:** Reeded

Date	Mintage	F	VF	XF	Unc	BU
2002	30,000	—	—	—	40.00	—

KM# 152 5 HRYVEN
16.5400 g., Copper-Nickel-Zinc, 35 mm. **Obv:** Sun and flying geese divides beaded circle **Rev:** "AN-225 Mrija" cargo jet divide beaded circle **Edge:** Reeded

Date	Mintage	F	VF	XF	Unc	BU
2002	30,000	—	—	—	80.00	—

KM# 158 5 HRYVEN
9.4300 g., Bi-Metallic Brass center in Copper-Nickel ring, 28 mm. **Subject:** 70th Anniversary of Dnipro Hydroelectric Power Station **Obv:** Turbine within circle **Rev:** Large dam within circle **Edge:** Reeded and plain sections

Date	Mintage	F	VF	XF	Unc	BU
2002	30,000	—	—	—	50.00	—

KM# 159 5 HRYVEN
16.5400 g., Copper-Nickel-Zinc, 35 mm. **Obv:** Arms with supporters within beaded circle **Rev:** Battle scene around Batig in 1652 divides beaded circle **Edge:** Reeded

Date	Mintage	F	VF	XF	Unc	BU
2002	30,000	—	—	—	30.00	—

KM# 163 5 HRYVEN
16.5400 g., Copper-Nickel-Zinc, 35 mm. **Subject:** Christmas **Obv:** National arms in star above value flanked by designed sprigs **Rev:** Christmas pageant scene **Edge:** Reeded

Date	Mintage	F	VF	XF	Unc	BU
ND(2002)	30,000	—	—	—	100	—

KM# 157 5 HRYVEN
16.5400 g., Copper-Nickel, 35 mm. **Subject:** 1100th

Anniversary - City of Romny **Obv:** Sprigs divide national arms and value **Rev:** City view **Edge:** Reeded

Date	Mintage	F	VF	XF	Unc	BU
2002	30,000	—	—	—	40.00	—

KM# 200 5 HRYVEN
9.4000 g., Bi-Metallic Brass center in Copper-Nickel ring, 28 mm. **Obv:** Bandura strings over ornamental design **Rev:** Bandura divides circle and wreath **Edge:** Segmented reeding

Date	Mintage	F	VF	XF	Unc	BU
2003	30,000	—	—	—	20.00	—

KM# 172 5 HRYVEN
16.5400 g., Copper-Nickel-Zinc, 35 mm. **Subject:** Easter **Obv:** Circle of Easter eggs, national arms in center above value **Rev:** Religious celebration **Edge:** Reeded

Date	Mintage	F	VF	XF	Unc	BU
2003	50,000	—	—	—	45.00	—

KM# 173 5 HRYVEN
16.5400 g., Copper-Nickel-Zinc, 35 mm. **Subject:** Antonov AN-2 Biplane **Obv:** National arms sun face and flying geese divide beaded circle **Rev:** World's largest biplane divides beaded circle **Edge:** Reeded

Date	Mintage	F	VF	XF	Unc	BU
2003	50,000	—	—	—	25.00	—

KM# 185 5 HRYVEN
9.4000 g., Bi-Metallic Brass center in Copper-Nickel ring, 28 mm. **Subject:** 150th Anniversary of the Central Ukrainian Archives **Obv:** Value, signature and seal **Rev:** Hourglass divides books and circle **Edge:** Segmented reeding

Date	Mintage	F	VF	XF	Unc	BU
2003	30,000	—	—	—	15.00	—

KM# 186 5 HRYVEN
16.5400 g., Copper-Nickel-Zinc, 35 mm. **Subject:** 2500th Anniversary of the City of Yevpatoria **Obv:** National arms, date and value with partial sun background **Rev:** Ancient amphora and modern city view **Edge:** Reeded

Date	Mintage	F	VF	XF	Unc	BU
2003	30,000	—	—	—	35.00	—

KM# 187 5 HRYVEN
16.5400 g., Copper-Nickel-Zinc, 35 mm. **Subject:** 60th Anniversary - Liberation of Kiev **Obv:** Eternal flame monument **Rev:** Battle scene and map of the offense **Edge:** Reeded

Date	Mintage	F	VF	XF	Unc	BU
2003	30,000	—	—	—	20.00	—

KM# 204 5 HRYVEN
16.5400 g., Copper-Nickel-Zinc, 35 mm. **Subject:** 50th Anniversary - Pivdenne Space Design Office **Obv:** Satellite orbiting Earth **Rev:** Satellite above moonscape **Edge:** Reeded

Date	Mintage	F	VF	XF	Unc	BU
2004	30,000	—	—	—	17.00	—

KM# 205 5 HRYVEN
16.5400 g., Copper-Nickel-Zinc, 35 mm. **Subject:** 2500 Anniversary City of Balaklava **Obv:** National arms between two ancient ships **Rev:** Harbor view above pillar **Edge:** Reeded

Date	Mintage	F	VF	XF	Unc	BU
2004	30,000	—	—	—	20.00	—

KM# 218 5 HRYVEN
16.9400 g., 0.9250 Silver 0.5038 oz. ASW, 33 mm. **Obv:** National arms, value and atom **Rev:** Kharkiv University building **Edge:** Reeded

Date	Mintage	F	VF	XF	Unc	BU
2004 Proof	7,000	Value: 60.00				

KM# 219　5 HRYVEN
16.9400 g., 0.9250 Silver 0.5038 oz. ASW, 33 mm. **Obv:**
National arms above value dividing scientific items **Rev:** Kiev
University building main entrance **Edge:** Reeded

Date	Mintage	F	VF	XF	Unc	BU
2004 Proof	7,000	Value: 60.00				

KM# 220　5 HRYVEN
9.4300 g., Bi-Metallic BRASS center in COPPER-NICKEL ring,
28 mm. **Subject:** 50 Years of Ukraine's Membership in UNESCO
Obv: National arms in center of sprigs and circle **Rev:** Building
within sprigs and circle **Edge:** Segmented reeding

Date	Mintage	F	VF	XF	Unc	BU
2004	50,000	—	—	—	15.00	—

KM# 221　5 HRYVEN
16.5400 g., Copper-Nickel-Zinc, 35 mm. **Subject:** Ice Breaker
"Captain Belousov" **Obv:** National arms on ship's wheel and
anchor **Rev:** Ice breaker ship **Edge:** Reeded

Date	Mintage	F	VF	XF	Unc	BU
2004	30,000	—	—	—	16.00	—

KM# 222　5 HRYVEN
16.5400 g., Copper-Nickel-Zinc, 35 mm. **Subject:** Whit Sunday
Obv: National arms in flower wreath above value flanked by
sprigs **Rev:** Four dancing women and child **Edge:** Reeded

Date	Mintage	F	VF	XF	Unc	BU
2004	50,000	—	—	—	18.00	—

KM# 333　5 HRYVEN
9.4000 g., Bi-Metallic Brass center in Copper-Nickel ring, 28 mm.
Obv: Horizontal lines across flowery design **Rev:** Cossack-style
lyre within circle and wreath **Edge:** Segmented reeding

Date	Mintage	F	VF	XF	Unc	BU
2004	30,000	—	—	—	18.00	—

KM# 334　5 HRYVEN
16.5400 g., Copper-Nickel-Zinc, 35 mm. **Subject:** 250th
Anniversary of Kirovohrad **Obv:** National arms above crossed
cannons and value **Rev:** Arms with supporters above city view
Edge: Reeded

Date	Mintage	F	VF	XF	Unc	BU
2004	30,000	—	—	—	16.00	—

KM# 335　5 HRYVEN
16.5400 g., Copper-Nickel-Zinc, 35 mm. **Subject:** 350 Years to
Kharkiv **Obv:** Assumption Cathedral, value and national arms
Rev: Kharkiv State Industrial Building complex **Edge:** Reeded

Date	Mintage	F	VF	XF	Unc	BU
2004	30,000	—	—	—	25.00	—

KM# 336　5 HRYVEN
9.4000 g., Bi-Metallic Brass center in Copper-Nickel ring, 28 mm.
Subject: 50th Anniversary of Crimean Union With Ukraine **Obv:**
National arms on wheat sheaf on map **Rev:** Crowned lion on
shield flanked by pillars within rope wreath **Edge:** Segmented
reeding

Date	Mintage	F	VF	XF	Unc	BU
2004	30,000	—	—	—	18.00	—

KM# 337　5 HRYVEN
16.5400 g., Copper-Nickel-Zinc, 35 mm. **Obv:** National arms on
sun, flying geese divide beaded circle **Rev:** AN-140 Airliner
divides beaded circle **Edge:** Reeded

Date	Mintage	F	VF	XF	Unc	BU
2004	50,000	—	—	—	15.00	—

KM# 362　5 HRYVEN
16.5400 g., Copper-Nickel-Zinc, 35 mm. **Obv:** National arms on

sun with flying geese divide beaded circle **Rev:** AN-124 jet divides
beaded circle **Edge:** Reeded

Date	Mintage	F	VF	XF	Unc	BU
2005	60,000	—	—	—	—	15.00

KM# 364　5 HRYVEN
16.5400 g., Copper-Nickel-Zinc, 35 mm. **Subject:** City of
Korosten 1300th Anniversary **Obv:** National arms **Rev:** Ancient
earring below modern building and bridge **Edge:** Reeded

Date	Mintage	F	VF	XF	Unc	BU
2005	30,000	—	—	—	—	16.00

KM# 365　5 HRYVEN
16.5400 g., Copper-Nickel-Zinc, 35 mm. **Subject:** City of Sumy
350th Anniversary **Obv:** National arms **Rev:** City view behind city
arms **Edge:** Reeded

Date	Mintage	F	VF	XF	Unc	BU
2005	30,000	—	—	—	—	16.00

KM# 366　5 HRYVEN
16.5400 g., Copper-Nickel-Zinc, 35 mm. **Subject:** The
Protection of the Virgin **Obv:** National arms on Cossack regalia
Rev: Wedding scene **Edge:** Reeded

Date	Mintage	F	VF	XF	Unc	BU
2005	45,000	—	—	—	—	16.00

KM# 368　5 HRYVEN
16.5400 g., Copper-Nickel-Zinc, 35 mm. **Subject:** Sorochynsky
Fair **Obv:** Busts facing each other flanked by sprigs **Rev:** Farmer
with family in ox cart **Edge:** Reeded

Date	Mintage	F	VF	XF	Unc	BU
2005	60,000	—	—	—	—	16.00

KM# 379 5 HRYVEN
16.5400 g., Copper-Nickel-Zinc, 35 mm. **Subject:** 500th Anniversary - Kalmiuska Palanqua Cossack Settlement **Obv:** Cossack in ornamental frame and national arms **Rev:** Soldiers **Edge:** Reeded

Date	Mintage	F	VF	XF	Unc	BU
2005	30,000	—	—	—	—	17.00

KM# 380 5 HRYVEN
16.5400 g., Copper-Nickel-Zinc, 35 mm. **Subject:** Sviatohirsky Assumption Monastery **Obv:** Madonna and child flanked by angels **Rev:** Hillside monastery **Edge:** Reeded

Date	Mintage	F	VF	XF	Unc	BU
2005	45,000	—	—	—	—	16.00

KM# 387 5 HRYVEN
16.5400 g., Copper-Nickel-Zinc, 35 mm. **Subject:** Vernadsky Antarctic Station **Obv:** Flag and buildings **Rev:** Antarctica map within compass face **Edge:** Reeded

Date	Mintage	F	VF	XF	Unc	BU
2006	60,000	—	—	—	—	15.00

KM# 388 5 HRYVEN
16.9300 g., 0.9250 Silver 0.5035 oz. ASW, 33 mm. **Subject:** Year of the Dog **Obv:** Value on textile art **Rev:** Stylized dog **Edge:** Reeded

Date	Mintage	F	VF	XF	Unc	BU
2006 Proof	12,000	Value: 200				

KM# 389 5 HRYVEN
16.9300 g., 0.9250 Silver 0.5035 oz. ASW, 33 mm. **Subject:** Zodiac - Ram **Obv:** Sun face **Rev:** Ram **Edge:** Reeded

Date	Mintage	F	VF	XF	Unc	BU
2006 Proof	10,000	Value: 100				

KM# 390 5 HRYVEN
16.9300 g., 0.9250 Silver 0.5035 oz. ASW, 33 mm. **Subject:** Kyiv National University of Economics **Obv:** National arms, graph above value **Rev:** University building within circle **Edge:** Reeded

Date	Mintage	F	VF	XF	Unc	BU
2006 Proof	5,000	Value: 80.00				

KM# 402 5 HRYVEN
9.4200 g., Bi-Metallic Brass center in Copper-Nickel ring, 28 mm. **Obv:** Symbolic sound of music **Rev:** Tsimbal stringed musical instrument **Edge:** Segmented reeding

Date	Mintage	F	VF	XF	Unc	BU
2006	100,000	—	—	—	—	13.00

KM# 409 5 HRYVEN
16.5400 g., Copper-Nickel-Zinc, 35 mm. **Subject:** 10 Years of the Constitution of Ukraine **Obv:** National arms **Edge:** Reeded

Date	Mintage	F	VF	XF	Unc	BU
2006	30,000	—	—	—	—	20.00

KM# 411 5 HRYVEN
16.5400 g., Copper-Nickel-Zinc, 35 mm. **Subject:** 15 Years of Ukraine Independence **Obv:** National arms **Edge:** Reeded

Date	Mintage	F	VF	XF	Unc	BU
2006	75,000	—	—	—	—	13.00

KM# 413 5 HRYVEN
16.5400 g., Copper-Nickel-Zinc, 35 mm. **Subject:** 10 Years to the Currency Reform in Ukraine **Obv:** National arms **Edge:** Reeded

Date	Mintage	F	VF	XF	Unc	BU
2006	45,000	—	—	—	—	15.00

KM# 405 5 HRYVEN
16.8200 g., 0.9250 Silver 0.5002 oz. ASW, 33 mm. **Subject:** Bull **Obv:** National arms

Date	Mintage	F	VF	XF	Unc	BU
2006 Proof	10,000	Value: 100				

KM# 415 5 HRYVEN
16.5400 g., Copper-Nickel-Zinc, 35 mm. **Subject:** 750 Years of the City of L'viv **Obv:** National arms **Edge:** Reeded

Date	Mintage	F	VF	XF	Unc	BU
2006	60,000	—	—	—	—	15.00

KM# 416 5 HRYVEN
16.8200 g., 0.9250 Silver 0.5002 oz. ASW, 33 mm. **Subject:** Mykhailo Hrushevskyi **Obv:** National arms

Date	Mintage	F	VF	XF	Unc	BU
2006 Proof	5,000	Value: 80.00				

KM# 417 5 HRYVEN
16.8200 g., 0.9250 Silver 0.5002 oz. ASW, 33 mm. **Subject:** Dmytro Lutsenko **Obv:** National arms

Date	Mintage	F	VF	XF	Unc	BU
2006 Proof	3,000	Value: 95.00				

KM# 418 5 HRYVEN
16.8200 g., 0.9250 Silver 0.5002 oz. ASW, 33 mm. **Subject:** Ivan Franko **Obv:** National arms

Date	Mintage	F	VF	XF	Unc	BU
2006 Proof	5,000	Value: 80.00				

KM# 407 5 HRYVEN
16.8200 g., 0.9250 Silver 0.5002 oz. ASW, 33 mm. **Subject:** Gemini **Obv:** National arms

Date	Mintage	F	VF	XF	Unc	BU
2006 Proof	10,000	Value: 120				

KM# 420 5 HRYVEN
16.5400 g., Copper-Nickel-Zinc, 35 mm. **Subject:** Epiphany **Obv:** National arms **Edge:** Reeded

Date	Mintage	F	VF	XF	Unc	BU
2006	75,000	—	—	—	—	15.00

KM# 422 5 HRYVEN
16.5400 g., Copper-Nickel-Zinc, 35 mm. **Subject:** Saint Kyryl Church **Obv:** National arms

Date	Mintage	F	VF	XF	Unc	BU
2006	45,000	—	—	—	—	15.00

KM# 432 5 HRYVEN
16.5400 g., Copper-Nickel-Zinc, 35 mm. **Subject:** 100th Anniversary of "Motor Sich" **Obv:** Small national arms above falcon in flight with two globes in background **Rev:** Jet engine **Edge:** Reeded

Date	Mintage	F	VF	XF	Unc	BU
2007	45,000	—	—	—	—	15.00

KM# 419 5 HRYVEN
16.8200 g., 0.9250 Silver 0.5002 oz. ASW, 33 mm. **Subject:** Year of the Pig **Obv:** National arms **Edge:** Reeded

Date	Mintage	F	VF	XF	Unc	BU
2007 Proof	15,000	Value: 100				

KM# 453 5 HRYVEN
9.4000 g., Bi-Metallic Brass center in copper-nickel ring, 28 mm. **Subject:** Pure water is the source of life **Obv:** Drop of water in pond **Rev:** Man taking drink at waterfall

Date	Mintage	F	VF	XF	Unc	BU
2007	50,000	—	—	—	—	15.00

KM# 455 5 HRYVEN
9.4000 g., Bi-Metallic Brass center in copper-nickel ring, 28 mm. **Subject:** Organization Safety and Cooperation, 16th Annual Meeting **Obv:** State emblem and ornamentation **Rev:** Parliamentary Assemby Building in Kyiv

Date	Mintage	F	VF	XF	Unc	BU
2007	35,000					17.00

KM# 456 5 HRYVEN
16.5000 g., Copper-Nickel-Zinc, 35 mm. **Subject:** Odessa National Opera and Ballet, 120th Anniversary **Obv:** Ballet scene in oval **Rev:** Opera house in Odessa **Edge:** Reeded

Date	Mintage	F	VF	XF	Unc	BU
2007	35,000					15.00

KM# 457 5 HRYVEN
16.5000 g., Copper-Nickel-Zinc, 35 mm. **Subject:** Chernihiv, 1100th Anniversary **Obv:** Sword hilts and slate fragment **Rev:** Town view and open book **Edge:** Reeded

Date	Mintage	F	VF	XF	Unc	BU
2007	45,000					16.00

KM# 458 5 HRYVEN
9.4000 g., Bi-Metallic Brass center in copper-nickel ring, 28 mm. **Subject:** Buhai **Obv:** Sound waves as a baroque ornament **Rev:** Drum-like musical instrument

Date	Mintage	F	VF	XF	Unc	BU
2007	50,000					14.50

KM# 459 5 HRYVEN
16.5400 g., Copper-Nickel-Zinc, 35 mm. **Subject:** The Famine, Genocide of the Ukranian People **Obv:** Girl standing on fallow ground **Rev:** Stork within cross, candles in background **Edge:** Reeded

Date	Mintage	F	VF	XF	Unc	BU
2007	75,000	—	—	—	—	13.00

KM# 460 5 HRYVEN
16.5400 g., Copper-Nickel-Zinc, 35 mm. **Subject:** Crimean Resorts, 200th Anniversary **Obv:** Seaside Resort **Rev:** Felix De Searr and well **Edge:** Reeded

Date	Mintage	F	VF	XF	Unc	BU
2007	35,000	—	—	—	—	15.00

KM# 461 5 HRYVEN
15.5500 g., 0.9250 Silver 0.4624 oz. ASW, 33 mm. **Subject:** Capricorn **Obv:** Sun and seasons **Rev:** Zodiac sign

Date	Mintage	F	VF	XF	Unc	BU
2007 Proof	15,000	Value: 80.00				

KM# 462 5 HRYVEN
16.8200 g., 0.9250 Silver 0.5002 oz. ASW, 33 mm. **Subject:** Aquarius **Obv:** Sun and seasons **Rev:** Zodiac sign, man pouring water

Date	Mintage	F	VF	XF	Unc	BU
2007 Proof	15,000	Value: 80.00				

KM# 463 5 HRYVEN
16.8200 g., 0.9250 Silver 0.5002 oz. ASW, 33 mm. **Subject:** Pisces **Obv:** Sun and seasons **Rev:** Zodiac sign, two fish

Date	Mintage	F	VF	XF	Unc	BU
2007 Proof	15,000	Value: 80.00				

KM# 464 5 HRYVEN
16.8200 g., 0.9250 Silver 0.5002 oz. ASW, 33 mm. **Subject:** Scorpion **Obv:** Sun and seasons **Rev:** Zodiac sign, scorpion **Edge:** Reeded

Date	Mintage	F	VF	XF	Unc	BU
2007 Proof	15,000	Value: 80.00				

KM# 465 5 HRYVEN
16.8200 g., 0.9250 Silver 0.5002 oz. ASW, 33 mm. **Subject:** Sagittarius **Obv:** Sun and seasons **Rev:** Zodiac sign, archer

Date	Mintage	F	VF	XF	Unc	BU
2007 Proof	15,000	Value: 80.00				

KM# 531 5 HRYVEN
16.5400 g., Copper-Nickel, 35 mm. **Subject:** 1100th Aniversary of Perejaslav-Khmelnytskyi **Obv:** Parchment. **Obv. Legend:** НАЦІОНАЛЬНИЙ БАНК УКРА?НИ - 5 ГРИВЕНЬ / 2007 **Rev:** Old Rus cathedral, old Rus and Cossacks. **Rev. Legend:** ПЕРЕЯСЛАВ-ХМЕЛЬНИЦЬКИJ - 1100

Date	Mintage	F	VF	XF	Unc	BU
2007	45,000	—	—	—	—	15.00

KM# 511 5 HRYVEN
16.5400 g., Copper-Nickel-Zinc, 35 mm. **Subject:** Rivne, 725th Anniversary **Edge:** Reeded

Date	Mintage	F	VF	XF	Unc	BU
2008	45,000	—	—	—	—	15.00

KM# 500 5 HRYVEN
16.5000 g., Copper-Nickel-Zinc, 35 mm. **Subject:** The Annunciation **Edge:** Reeded

Date	Mintage	F	VF	XF	Unc	BU
2008	45,000	—	—	—	—	15.00

KM# 501 5 HRYVEN
16.5000 g., Copper-Nickel-Zinc, 35 mm. **Subject:** Chernivtsi, 600th Anniversary **Edge:** Reeded

Date	Mintage	F	VF	XF	Unc	BU
2008	45000	—	—	—	—	15.00

KM# 502 5 HRYVEN
16.5000 g., Copper-Nickel-Zinc, 35 mm. **Subject:** Sniatyn, 850th Anniversary **Edge:** Reeded

Date	Mintage	F	VF	XF	Unc	BU
2008	45,000	—	—	—	—	15.00

KM# 503 5 HRYVEN
16.8200 g., 0.9250 Silver 0.5002 oz. ASW, 33 mm. **Subject:** Year of the Rat **Rev:** Rat, diamond insert eye **Edge:** Reeded

Date	Mintage	F	VF	XF	Unc	BU
2008 Proof	15,000	Value: 100				

KM# 504 5 HRYVEN
16.8200 g., 0.9250 Silver 0.5002 oz. ASW, 33 mm. **Subject:** Cancer **Edge:** Reeded

Date	Mintage	F	VF	XF	Unc	BU
2008 Proof	15,000	Value: 80.00				

KM# 505 5 HRYVEN
16.8200 g., 0.9250 Silver 0.5002 oz. ASW, 33 mm. **Subject:** Roman Shukhevich, General **Edge:** Reeded

Date	Mintage	F	VF	XF	Unc	BU
2008 Proof	3,000	Value: 250				

KM# 506 5 HRYVEN
16.8200 g., 0.9250 Silver 0.5002 oz. ASW, 33 mm. **Subject:** Leo **Edge:** Reeded

Date	Mintage	F	VF	XF	Unc	BU
2008 Proof	15,000	Value: 80.00				

KM# 507 5 HRYVEN
16.8200 g., 0.9250 Silver 0.5002 oz. ASW, 33 mm. **Subject:** Virgo **Edge:** Reeded

Date	Mintage	F	VF	XF	Unc	BU
2008 Proof	15,000	Value: 80.00				

KM# 508 5 HRYVEN
16.8200 g., 0.9250 Silver 0.5002 oz. ASW, 33 mm. **Subject:** Libra **Edge:** Reeded

Date	Mintage	F	VF	XF	Unc	BU
2008 Proof	15,000	Value: 80.00				

KM# 509 5 HRYVEN
16.5400 g., Copper-Nickel-Zinc, 35 mm. **Subject:** State Arboretum "Trostianet-s", 175th Anniversary **Edge:** Reeded

Date	Mintage	F	VF	XF	Unc	BU
2008	45,000	—	—	—	—	15.00

KM# 510 5 HRYVEN
16.5400 g., Copper-Nickel-Zinc, 35 mm. **Subject:** Kievan Rus **Edge:** Reeded

Date	Mintage	F	VF	XF	Unc	BU
2008	45,000	—	—	—	—	15.00

KM# 512   5 HRYVEN
16.5400 g., Copper-Nickel-Zinc, 35 mm. **Subject:** Bohuslav, 975th Anniversary **Edge:** Reeded

Date	Mintage	F	VF	XF	Unc	BU
2008	45,000	—	—	—	—	14.00

KM# 513   5 HRYVEN
9.4000 g., Bi-Metallic Brass center in copper-nickel ring, 28 mm. **Subject:** Taras Shevchenko "Prosvita Society" 140th Anniversary

Date	Mintage	F	VF	XF	Unc	BU
2008	45,000	—	—	—	—	14.00

KM# 514   5 HRYVEN
16.8200 g., 0.9250 Silver 0.5002 oz. ASW, 33 mm. **Subject:** Mariya Prymachenko

Date	Mintage	F	VF	XF	Unc	BU
2008 Proof	5,000	Value: 80.00				

KM# 530   5 HRYVEN
16.8200 g., 0.9250 Silver 0.5002 oz. ASW, 33 mm. **Subject:** Year of the Ox **Obv:** National Arms and value **Rev:** Ox, rubies in eyes **Edge:** Reeded

Date	Mintage	F	VF	XF	Unc	BU
2009 Proof	20,000	Value: 80.00				

KM# 543   5 HRYVEN
16.8200 g., 0.9250 Silver 0.5002 oz. ASW, 33.0 mm. **Subject:** Nikolai Gogol **Obv:** Compositions of two main subjects of Gogol's work, National Arms, value **Obv. Legend:** НАЦІОНАЛЬНИЙ БАНК УКРАЇНИ - 5 ГРИВЕНЬ / 2009 **Rev:** Nikolai's portrait **Rev. Legend:** МИКОЛА ГОГОЛЬ

Date	Mintage	F	VF	XF	Unc	BU
2009 Proof	5,000	Value: 80.00				

KM# 544   5 HRYVEN
16.8200 g., 0.9250 Silver 0.5002 oz. ASW, 33.0 mm. **Subject:** Sholem Aleichem **Obv:** Conventionalized composition, book sheets, Aleichem's signet **Obv. Legend:** НАЦІОНАЛЬНИЙ БАНК УКРАЇНИ - 5 ГРИВЕНЬ / 2009 **Rev:** Aleichem's portrait **Rev. Legend:** МИР ВАМ – ШОЛОМ-АЛЕЙХЕМ - РАБИНОВИЧ ШОЛОМ

Date	Mintage	F	VF	XF	Unc	BU
2009 Proof	5,000	Value: 80.00				

KM# 545   5 HRYVEN
16.5400 g., Copper-Nickel-Zinc, 35.0 mm. **Subject:** Simferopol, 225th Anniversary **Obv:** Main railway station, National Arms **Obv. Legend:** НАЦІОНАЛЬНИЙ БАНК УКРАЇНИ - 5 ГРИВЕНЬ 2009 **Rev:** City Coat of Arms, Architectural elements **Rev. Legend:** 225 / РОКІВ - СІМФЕРОПОЛЬ **Edge:** Reeded

Date	Mintage	F	VF	XF	Unc	BU
2009	45,000	—	—	—	—	16.00

KM# 546   5 HRYVEN
16.8200 g., 0.9250 Silver 0.5002 oz. ASW, 33 mm. **Subject:** Ivan Kotljarevskyi **Obv:** National Arms, boat, column and helmet **Obv. Legend:** НАЦІОНАЛЬНИЙ БАНК УКРАЇНИ - П'ЯТЬ ГРИВЕНЬ **Rev:** Kotljarevskyi's portrait **Rev. Legend:** ...ПОКИ СОНЦЕ З НЕБА СЯЄ, ТЕБЕ НЕ ЗАБУДУТЬ! - ІВАН КОТЛЯРЕВСЬКИЙ

Date	Mintage	F	VF	XF	Unc	BU
2009 Proof	5,000	Value: 80.00				

KM# 547   5 HRYVEN
16.5400 g., Copper-Nickel-Zinc, 35 mm. **Subject:** Mykolaiv,

---

220th Anniversary **Obv:** Varvarivskyi Bridge, gull, ship, anchor **Obv. Legend:** НАЦІОНАЛЬНИЙ БАНК УКРА?НИ - П'ЯТЬ ГРИВЕНЬ **Rev:** Frigate Saint Nicholas, Architecture of Mykolaiv **Rev. Legend:** МИКОЛА?В - РІК ЗАСНУВАННЯ / 1789 **Edge:** Reeded

Date	Mintage	F	VF	XF	Unc	BU
2009	45,000	—	—	—	—	16.00

KM# 548   5 HRYVEN
9.4000 g., Bi-Metallic Brass center in Copper-Nickel ring, 28 mm. **Subject:** Council of Europe, 60th Anniversary **Obv:** Stars, map of Europe **Obv. Legend:** НАЦІОНАЛЬНИЙ БАНК УКРА?НИ - П'ЯТЬ ГРИВЕНЬ **Rev:** Council of Europe logo, stars **Rev. Legend:** COUNCIL OF EUROPE, CONSEIL DE EUROPE, РАДА ?ВРОПИ

Date	Mintage	F	VF	XF	Unc	BU
2009	45,000	—	—	—	—	15.00

KM# 549   5 HRYVEN
16.8200 g., 0.9250 Silver 0.5002 oz. ASW, 33.0 mm. **Subject:** Lviv National Medical University, 225th Anniversary **Obv:** Hippocratic Oath in Latin, National Arms, value **Obv. Legend:** НАЦІОНАЛЬНИЙ БАНК УКРАЇНИ - 5 / ГРИВЕНЬ **Rev:** University building **Rev. Legend:** 225/ РОКІВ - ІМЕНІ / ДАНИЛА / ГАЛИЦЬКОГО - ЛЬВІВСЬКИЙ НАЦІОНАЛЬНИЙ МЕДИЧНИЙ УНІВЕРСИТЕТ

Date	Mintage	F	VF	XF	Unc	BU
2009 Proof	7,000	Value: 80.00				

KM# 550   5 HRYVEN
16.5400 g., Copper-Nickel-Zinc, 35 mm. **Subject:** T. H. Shevchenko National Museum, 60th Anniversary **Obv:** Kateryna painting, bandura, National Arms, value **Rev:** Museum bulding and portrait **Edge:** Reeded

Date	Mintage	F	VF	XF	Unc	BU
2009	30,000	—	—	—	—	15.00

KM# 553   5 HRYVEN
16.5400 g., Copper-Nickel-Zinc, 35 mm. **Subject:** Pysanka - Easter Egg decorating **Obv:** Easter eggs, National Arms, value **Rev:** Easter bread, eggs. **Edge:** Reeded

Date	Mintage	F	VF	XF	Unc	BU
2009	50,000	—	—	—	—	16.00

KM# 555   5 HRYVEN
16.5000 g., Copper-Nickel, 35 mm. **Subject:** Folk crafts of the Ukraine - Bokorash (Raftsmen) **Obv:** Two birds, Carpathian landscape, trees, cottages, logs **Obv. Legend:** НАЦІОНАЛЬНИЙ БАНК УКРА?НИ - 5 / ГРИВЕНЬ, 2009 **Rev:** Bokorash directing raft **Rev. Legend:** БОКОРАШ **Edge:** Reeded

Date	Mintage	F	VF	XF	Unc	BU
2009	45,000	—	—	—	—	14.00

KM# 557   5 HRYVEN
16.5400 g., Copper-Nickel, 35.0 mm. **Subject:** International Year of Astronomy **Obv:** Urania, planets, stars, solar system, National Arms, value **Obv. Legend:** НАЦІОНАЛЬНИЙ БАНК УКРА?НИ - 5 ГРИВЕНЬ **Rev:** Yurii Drohobych, International Year of Astronomy logo, artifacts **Rev. Legend:** МІЖНАРОДНИЙ / РІК / АСТРОНОМІ? **Edge:** Reeded

Date	Mintage	F	VF	XF	Unc	BU
2009	45,000	—	—	—	—	14.00

KM# 573   5 HRYVEN
16.5000 g., Copper-Nickel-Zinc, 35 mm. **Subject:** Ukrainian Folk crafts - Cartwright **Obv:** Wood cart and wheels **Rev:** Woodcraftsman hewing wood to make cart detail **Edge:** Reeded

Date	Mintage	F	VF	XF	Unc	BU
2009	45,000	—	—	—	—	14.00

KM# 567   5 HRYVEN
16.8200 g., 0.9250 Silver 0.5002 oz. ASW, 33 mm. **Subject:** Yevhen Paton **Obv:** Paton Bridge and the footbridge over Petrovska Alley **Rev:** Paton's portrait

Date	Mintage	F	VF	XF	Unc	BU
2010 Proof	5,000	—	—	—	—	80.00

KM# 566   5 HRYVEN
16.8200 g., 0.9250 Silver 0.5002 oz. ASW, 33 mm. **Subject:** Ivan Puliui **Obv:** X-ray of jewelry portrait **Rev:** Puliui portrait and text

Date	Mintage	F	VF	XF	Unc	BU
2010 Proof	5,000	Value: 80.00				

KM# 568   5 HRYVEN
16.8200 g., 0.9250 Silver 0.5002 oz. ASW, 33 mm. **Subject:** Oksana Petrusenko **Obv:** Poppy flower and musical notation **Rev:** Bust facing

Date	Mintage	F	VF	XF	Unc	BU
2010 Proof	5,000	Value: 80.00				

KM# 569   5 HRYVEN
16.8200 g., 0.9250 Silver 0.5002 oz. ASW, 33 mm. **Subject:** Mykola Ivanovych Pyrohov, scientist and surgeon **Obv:** Sepulchral church erected over scientist's tomb **Rev:** Half length figure in apron holding surgical instruments

Date	Mintage	F	VF	XF	Unc	BU
2010 Proof	5,000	Value: 80.00				

KM# 577   5 HRYVEN
16.8200 g., 0.9250 Silver 0.5002 oz. ASW, 33 mm. **Subject:** Year of the tiger **Obv:** Vegitable ornamention pattern, National Arms **Rev:** Stylized playful tiger **Edge:** Reeded

Date	Mintage	F	VF	XF	Unc	BU
2010 Proof	20,000	Value: 80.00				

KM# 579 5 HRYVEN
16.5400 g., Copper-Nickel-Zinc, 35 mm. **Subject:** Kyiv National University Astronomical Observatory, 165th Anniversary **Obv:** Observatory building **Rev:** Telescope and night sky **Edge:** Reeded

Date	Mintage	F	VF	XF	Unc	BU
2010	45,000	—	—	—	—	14.50

KM# 582 5 HRYVEN
16.8200 g., 0.9250 Silver 0.5002 oz. ASW, 33 mm. **Subject:** Lviv Polytechnic National University, 165th Anniversary **Obv:** Arts and Science sculpture from main building **Rev:** University building façade

Date	Mintage	F	VF	XF	Unc	BU
2010 Proof	5,000	Value: 80.00				

KM# 584 5 HRYVEN
15.5500 g., 0.9250 Silver 0.4624 oz. ASW, 33 mm. **Subject:** Kharkiv Polytechnic Institute, 125th Anniversary **Obv:** Radio telescope and open book **Rev:** University building and oval portrait of V.L. Kyrpychov

Date	Mintage	F	VF	XF	Unc	BU
2010 Proof	5,000	Value: 80.00				

KM# 587 5 HRYVEN
16.5000 g., Copper-Nickel, 35 mm. **Subject:** Folk Crafts - Weaver **Obv:** Spinning wheel and weaving products **Rev:** Woman working on a loom **Edge:** Reeded

Date	Mintage	F	VF	XF	Unc	BU
2010	45,000	—	—	—	—	14.00

KM# 589 5 HRYVEN
16.5000 g., Copper-Nickel, 35 mm. **Subject:** UKranian spas **Obv:** Two cornucopiae and the Savior's Feast **Rev:** Peasants getting food gifts blessed **Edge:** Reeded

Date	Mintage	F	VF	XF	Unc	BU
2010	45,000	—	—	—	—	14.00

KM# 592 5 HRYVEN
16.5000 g., Copper-Nickel, 35 mm. **Subject:** Lutsk, 925th Anniversary **Obv:** Entrance tower to town's castle **Rev:** City view from tower top, city carms above **Edge:** Reeded

Date	Mintage	F	VF	XF	Unc	BU
2010	45,000	—	—	—	—	13.00

KM# 598 5 HRYVEN
16.8200 g., 0.9250 Silver 0.5002 oz. ASW, 33 mm. **Subject:** Johann Georg Pinzel **Obv:** Buchach City hall **Rev:** Sculptor and angel

Date	Mintage	F	VF	XF	Unc	BU
2010 Proof	5,000	Value: 80.00				

KM# 599 5 HRYVEN
16.8200 g., 0.9250 Silver 0.5002 oz. ASW, 33 mm. **Subject:** Ivan Fedorov **Obv:** Apostol book page and large quill pin **Rev:** Ivan Fedorov portrait facing

Date	Mintage	F	VF	XF	Unc	BU
2010 Proof	5,000	Value: 80.00				

KM# 601 5 HRYVEN
16.5400 g., Copper-Nickel, 35 mm. **Subject:** Maritime History **Obv:** Banner seperating compas rose and seal of the Zaporohian Host **Rev:** Cossack boat of the 18th century

Date	Mintage	F	VF	XF	Unc	BU
2010	45,000	—	—	—	—	14.00

KM# 604 5 HRYVEN
16.5000 g., Copper-Nickel, 35 mm. **Subject:** Folk Crafts - Potter **Obv:** Pottery flanking central pattern **Rev:** Potter at wheel **Edge:** Reeded

Date	Mintage	F	VF	XF	Unc	BU
2010	4,500	—	—	—	—	13.00

KM# 607 5 HRYVEN
16.8200 g., 0.9250 Silver 0.5002 oz. ASW, 33 mm. **Subject:** Year of the cat (rabbit, hare) **Obv:** National Arms above artistic pattern **Rev:** Cat, crystals in eyes

Date	Mintage	F	VF	XF	Unc	BU
2010 Proof	20,000	Value: 80.00				

KM# 611 5 HRYVEN
16.8200 g., 0.9250 Silver 0.5002 oz. ASW, 33 mm. **Subject:** Pavlo Tychyna **Obv:** View of family homestead, mallow flowers, national arms **Rev:** Portrait with books **Edge:** lettered, incuse **Edge Lettering:** .925 15.55

Date	Mintage	F	VF	XF	Unc	BU
2011 Proof	5,000	Value: 80.00				

KM# 610 5 HRYVEN
16.8200 g., 0.9250 Silver 0.5002 oz. ASW, 33 mm. **Subject:** Year of the Cat **Obv:** National arms, value and dloral design **Rev:** Playful cat with green alpinites in eyes **Edge:** Reeded

Date	Mintage	F	VF	XF	Unc	BU
2011 Proof	20,000	Value: 80.00				

KM# 613 5 HRYVEN
16.8200 g., 0.9250 Silver 0.5002 oz. ASW, 33 mm. **Subject:** Ivan Franko National University, Lviv, 350th Anniversary **Obv:** National arms, statuary group, value **Rev:** Main Building façade **Edge Lettering:** .925 15.55 (Mint logo)

Date	Mintage	F	VF	XF	Unc	BU
2011 Proof	7,000	Value: 80.00				

KM# 615 5 HRYVEN
16.5400 g., Copper-Nickel-Zinc, 35 mm. **Obv:** Blacksmith items, two birds **Rev:** Blacksmith at work **Edge:** Reeded

Date	Mintage	F	VF	XF	Unc	BU
2011	45,000	—	—	—	—	11.00

KM# 618 5 HRYVEN
16.8200 g., 0.9250 Silver 0.5002 oz. ASW, 33 mm. **Subject:** Heorhii Berehovyi **Obv:** Spacecraft launch, in orbit, sun **Rev:** Bust facing

Date	Mintage	F	VF	XF	Unc	BU
2011 Proof	5,000	Value: 90.00				

KM# 619 5 HRYVEN
16.5400 g., Copper-Nickel-Zinc, 35 mm. **Subject:** Taras Shevchenko, 150th Anniversary of Death **Obv:** Shevchenko's monument **Rev:** Portrait **Edge:** Reeded

Date	Mintage	F	VF	XF	Unc	BU
2011	35,000	—	—	—	—	11.00

KM# 620 5 HRYVEN
16.8200 g., 0.9250 Silver 0.5002 oz. ASW, 33 mm. **Subject:** Okeksandr Bohomolets **Obv:** Hands of an adult and child **Rev:** Portrait of Bohomolets

Date	Mintage	F	VF	XF	Unc	BU
2011 Proof	5,000	Value: 80.00				

KM# 621 5 HRYVEN
16.5400 g., Copper-Nickel-Zinc, 35 mm. **Subject:** Taras Shevchenko National Prize of Ukraine, 50th Anniversary **Obv:** Open book, quill, palette, brushes and National Arms **Rev:** Shevchenko Portrait

Date	Mintage	F	VF	XF	Unc	BU
2011	35,000	—	—	—	—	11.00

KM# 622 5 HRYVEN
16.5400 g., Copper-Nickel-Zinc, 35 mm. **Subject:** Constitution, 15th Anniversary **Obv:** National flag in color within wreath **Rev:** Book of the Constitution and Verkhjovna Rada building

Date	Mintage	F	VF	XF	Unc	BU
2011	30,000	—	—	—	—	15.00

KM# 623 5 HRYVEN
16.5400 g., Copper-Nickel-Zinc, 35 mm. **Subject:** Zbarazh, 800th Anniversary **Obv:** Jerusalem cross on wall of Our Saviour's Transfiguration Church **Rev:** Gate of the Zbarazh Castle

Date	Mintage	F	VF	XF	Unc	BU
2011	35,000	—	—	—	—	15.00

KM# 625 5 HRYVEN
16.5400 g., Copper-Nickel-Zinc, 35 mm. **Obv:** Baroque design from Church **Rev:** St. Andrew's Church

Date	Mintage	F	VF	XF	Unc	BU
2011	45,000	—	—	—	—	15.00

KM# 627 5 HRYVEN
16.5400 g., Copper-Nickel-Zinc, 35 mm. **Obv:** Couple in a dance **Rev:** Hopak folk dance

Date	Mintage	F	VF	XF	Unc	BU
2011	45,000	—	—	—	—	15.00

KM# 629 5 HRYVEN
16.5400 g., Copper-Nickel-Zinc, 35 mm. **Subject:** Independence, 20th anniversary **Obv:** National arms, rushnyks and portraits **Rev:** Legend

Date	Mintage	F	VF	XF	Unc	BU
2011	45,000	—	—	—	—	15.00

KM# 635 5 HRYVEN
16.8200 g., 0.9250 Silver 0.5002 oz. ASW, 33 mm. **Subject:** Liudmyla Vasylevska, 150th Anniversary of Birth **Obv:** Girl near the sea **Rev:** Vasylevska portrait

Date	Mintage	F	VF	XF	Unc	BU
2011 Proof	5,000	Value: 80.00				

KM# 638 5 HRYVEN
9.4000 g., Bi-Metallic, 28 mm. **Subject:** International year of Forests **Obv:** Conceptual tree **Rev:** Tree in leaf **Edge:** Segmented reeding

Date	Mintage	F	VF	XF	Unc	BU
2011	30,000	—	—	—	—	15.00

KM# 639 5 HRYVEN
16.8200 g., 0.9250 Silver 0.5002 oz. ASW, 33 mm. **Subject:** International Year of Forests **Obv:** Two birds sitting on branches **Rev:** Hand-like branches extended to the Sun

Date	Mintage	F	VF	XF	Unc	BU
2011 Antique finish	3,000	Value: 100				

KM# 645 5 HRYVEN
16.8200 g., 0.9250 Silver 0.5002 oz. ASW, 33 mm. **Subject:** Year of the Dragon **Obv:** National arms **Rev:** Dragon with orange zirconia crystals in eyes

Date	Mintage	F	VF	XF	Unc	BU
2011 Proof	20,000	Value: 80.00				

KM# 647 5 HRYVEN
16.5400 g., Copper-Nickel-Zinc, 35 mm. **Subject:** UEFA Euro 2012 Final Tournament **Obv:** Players superimposed on large 2012 in background **Rev:** UEFA logo and map of europe

Date	Mintage	F	VF	XF	Unc	BU
2011	100,000	—	—	—	—	15.00

KM# 648 5 HRYVEN
16.5400 g., 0.9250 Copper-Nickel-Zinc 0.4919 oz., 35 mm.
Subject: UEFA Euro 2012 Final Tournament **Obv:** Two players within stadium **Rev:** Logo and map of Ukraine

Date	Mintage	F	VF	XF	Unc	BU
2011	100,000	—	—	—	—	15.00

KM# 649 5 HRYVEN
16.5400 g., Copper-Nickel-Zinc, 35 mm. **Subject:** UEFA Euro 2012 Final Tournament **Obv:** UEFA logo and map of the Ukraine **Rev:** Soccer plater and Lviv stadium

Date	Mintage	F	VF	XF	Unc	BU
2011	100,000	—	—	—	—	15.00

KM# 650 5 HRYVEN
16.5400 g., Copper-Nickel-Zinc, 35 mm. **Subject:** UEFA Euro 2012 Final Tournament **Obv:** UEFA logo and map of the Ukraine **Rev:** Two soccer players and Metalist Stadium, Kharkiv

Date	Mintage	F	VF	XF	Unc	BU
2011	100,000	—	—	—	—	15.00

KM# 651 5 HRYVEN
16.5400 g., Copper-Nickel-Zinc, 35 mm. **Subject:** UEFA Euro 2012 Final Tournament **Obv:** UEFA logo and map of the Ukraine **Rev:** Soccer player and Donbass Arena, Donetsk

Date	Mintage	F	VF	XF	Unc	BU
2011	100,000	—	—	—	—	15.00

KM# 653 5 HRYVEN
7.7800 g., 0.9999 Gold 0.2501 oz. AGW, 20 mm. **Obv:** Logo of the Ukraine National Bank **Rev:** Archangel Michael

Date	Mintage	F	VF	XF	Unc	BU
2011	3,000	—	—	—	—	500

KM# 655 5 HRYVEN
16.8200 g., 0.9250 Silver 0.5002 oz. ASW, 33 mm. **Subject:** Eugene Grebinka **Obv:** Cossack horseman **Rev:** Grebinka portrait

Date	Mintage	F	VF	XF	Unc	BU
2011 Proof	3,000	Value: 85.00				

KM# 515 10 HRYVNI
33.6220 g., 0.9250 Silver 0.9999 oz. ASW, 38.6 mm. **Subject:** The Annunciation **Edge:** Reeded

Date	Mintage	F	VF	XF	Unc	BU
2008 Proof	8,000	Value: 95.00				

KM# 113 10 HRYVEN
33.6220 g., 0.9250 Silver 0.9999 oz. ASW, 38.61 mm. **Subject:** Ivan Mazepa (Cossack leader) **Obv:** Arms with supporters within beaded circle **Rev:** Half figure divides beaded circle flanked by palace and oval shield **Edge:** Reeded

Date	Mintage	F	VF	XF	Unc	BU
2001 Proof	5,000	Value: 200				

KM# 114 10 HRYVEN
33.6220 g., 0.9250 Silver 0.9999 oz. ASW, 38.61 mm. **Subject:** Great Prince Yaroslav the Wise **Obv:** Value within grape wreath **Rev:** Mosaic head facing, half length figure facing holding scroll and dome building **Edge:** Reeded

Date	Mintage	F	VF	XF	Unc	BU
2001 Proof	3,000	Value: 1,400				

KM# 115 10 HRYVEN
33.6220 g., 0.9250 Silver 0.9999 oz. ASW, 38.61 mm. **Series:** Ukranian Flora and Fauna **Obv:** National arms and date divides wreath, value within **Rev:** Lynx with offspring **Edge:** Reeded

Date	Mintage	F	VF	XF	Unc	BU
2001 Proof	3,000	Value: 475				

KM# 130 10 HRYVEN
33.6220 g., 0.9250 Silver 0.9999 oz. ASW, 38.61 mm. **Subject:** 10th Anniversary - National Bank **Obv:** National arms and value between arches **Rev:** Large building entrance **Edge:** Reeded

Date	Mintage	F	VF	XF	Unc	BU
2001 Proof	3,000	Value: 250				

KM# 131 10 HRYVEN
33.6220 g., 0.9250 Silver 0.9999 oz. ASW, 38.61 mm. **Series:** Olympics **Obv:** National arms and value on ice **Rev:** Stylized ice dancing couple **Edge:** Reeded

Date	Mintage	F	VF	XF	Unc	BU
2001 Proof	15,000	Value: 100				

KM# 141 10 HRYVEN
33.6220 g., 0.9250 Silver 0.9999 oz. ASW, 38.61 mm. **Subject:** Flora and Fauna **Obv:** National arms and date divides wreath, value within **Rev:** Pine branch with cone **Edge:** Reeded

Date	Mintage	F	VF	XF	Unc	BU
2001 Proof	3,000	Value: 350				

KM# 142 10 HRYVEN
33.6220 g., 0.9250 Silver 0.9999 oz. ASW, 38.61 mm. **Subject:** Khan Palace in Bakhchisarai **Obv:** Value in arch **Rev:** Courtyard view **Edge:** Reeded

Date	Mintage	F	VF	XF	Unc	BU
2001 Proof	3,000	Value: 400				

KM# 143 10 HRYVEN
4.3110 g., 0.9000 Gold 0.1247 oz. AGW, 16 mm. **Subject:** 10 Years Independence **Obv:** National arms **Rev:** Parliament building on map **Edge:** Plain

Date	Mintage	F	VF	XF	Unc	BU
2001 Proof	3,000	Value: 1,100				

KM# 165 10 HRYVEN
33.6220 g., 0.9250 Silver 0.9999 oz. ASW, 38.61 mm. **Subject:** Olympics **Obv:** National arms and value on ice **Rev:** Stylized hockey player **Edge:** Reeded

Date	Mintage	F	VF	XF	Unc	BU
2001 Proof	15,000	Value: 100				

KM# 229 10 HRYVEN
33.6220 g., 0.9250 Silver 0.9999 oz. ASW, 38.61 mm. **Obv:** National arms and date divides wreath, value within **Rev:** Eurasian Eagle Owl on branch **Edge:** Reeded

Date	Mintage	F	VF	XF	Unc	BU
2002 Proof	3,000	Value: 650				

KM# 145 10 HRYVEN
33.6220 g., 0.9250 Silver 0.9999 oz. ASW, 38.61 mm. **Subject:** Ivan Sirko **Obv:** Arms with supporters within beaded circle **Rev:** Cossack battle scene divides beaded circle **Edge:** Reeded

Date	Mintage	F	VF	XF	Unc	BU
2002 Proof	3,000	Value: 400				

KM# 146   10 HRYVEN
33.6220 g., 0.9250 Silver 0.9999 oz. ASW, 38.61 mm. **Obv:**
National arms and value on ice **Rev:** Stylized speed skater **Edge:**
Reeded

Date	Mintage	F	VF	XF	Unc	BU
2002 Proof	3,000	Value: 150				

KM# 160   10 HRYVEN
33.9500 g., 0.9250 Silver 1.0096 oz. ASW, 38.61 mm. **Obv:**
Value encircled by angels flanked by stars **Rev:** Steepled church
and tower **Edge:** Reeded

Date	Mintage	F	VF	XF	Unc	BU
2002 Proof	3,000	Value: 375				

KM# 161   10 HRYVEN
33.6220 g., 0.9250 Silver 0.9999 oz. ASW, 38.61 mm. **Subject:**
Grand Prince Vladimir Monomakh **Obv:** Value within jewelry
design **Rev:** Bust holding book flanked by buildings and St.
George **Edge:** Reeded

Date	Mintage	F	VF	XF	Unc	BU
2002 Proof	3,000	Value: 550				

KM# 162   10 HRYVEN
33.6220 g., 0.9250 Silver 0.9999 oz. ASW, 38.61 mm. **Subject:**
Prince Svyatoslav **Obv:** Value in ornate design **Rev:** Armored
half length figure facing **Edge:** Reeded

Date	Mintage	F	VF	XF	Unc	BU
2002 Proof	3,000	Value: 550				

KM# 164   10 HRYVEN
33.6220 g., 0.9250 Silver 0.9999 oz. ASW, 38.61 mm. **Subject:**
Christmas **Obv:** National arms within star above value **Rev:**
Christmas pageant scene **Edge:** Reeded

Date	Mintage	F	VF	XF	Unc	BU
2002 Proof	3,000	Value: 600				

KM# 176   10 HRYVEN
33.6220 g., 0.9250 Silver 0.9999 oz. ASW, 38.61 mm. **Subject:**
Olympics **Obv:** Two ancient women with seedlings **Rev:**
Swimmer **Edge:** Reeded

Date	Mintage	F	VF	XF	Unc	BU
2002 Proof	15,000	Value: 100				

KM# 177   10 HRYVEN
33.6220 g., 0.9250 Silver 0.9999 oz. ASW, 38.61 mm. **Subject:**
Hetman Pylyp Orlik 1672-1742 **Obv:** Arms with supporters within
beaded circle **Rev:** Standing figure facing holding scroll flanked
by other standing figures **Edge:** Reeded

Date	Mintage	F	VF	XF	Unc	BU
2002 Proof	3,000	Value: 350				

KM# 198   10 HRYVEN
33.6220 g., 0.9250 Silver 0.9999 oz. ASW, 38.61 mm. **Obv:**
National arms and date divides wreath, value within **Rev:**
European bison **Edge:** Reeded

Date	Mintage	F	VF	XF	Unc	BU
2003 Proof	2,000	Value: 600				

KM# 189   10 HRYVEN
33.6220 g., 0.9250 Silver 0.9999 oz. ASW, 38.61 mm. **Subject:**
Olympics **Obv:** Two ancient women with seedlings **Rev:** Boxer
Edge: Reeded

Date	Mintage	F	VF	XF	Unc	BU
2003 Proof	15,000	Value: 100				

KM# 190   10 HRYVEN
33.6220 g., 0.9250 Silver 0.9999 oz. ASW, 38.61 mm. **Obv:**
Fancy art work and sculpture **Rev:** Livadia Palace view **Edge:**
Reeded

Date	Mintage	F	VF	XF	Unc	BU
2003 Proof	3,000	Value: 300				

KM# 191   10 HRYVEN
33.6220 g., 0.9250 Silver 0.9999 oz. ASW, 38.61 mm. **Obv:**
National arms on sun, flying geese divides beaded circle **Rev:**
Antonov AN-2 biplane divides beaded circle **Edge:** Reeded

Date	Mintage	F	VF	XF	Unc	BU
2003 Proof	3,000	Value: 320				

KM# 192   10 HRYVEN
33.6220 g., 0.9250 Silver 0.9999 oz. ASW, 38.61 mm. **Obv:**
Easter eggs around arms above value **Rev:** Easter celebration
Edge: Reeded

Date	Mintage	F	VF	XF	Unc	BU
2003 Proof	3,000	Value: 500				

KM# 193   10 HRYVEN
33.6220 g., 0.9250 Silver 0.9999 oz. ASW, 38.61 mm. **Obv:**

Angels, national arms and value **Rev:** The protection of the Virgin Mary over the Pochayiv Lavra (Monastery) **Edge:** Reeded

Date	Mintage	VF	XF	Unc	BU
2003 Proof	Est. 8,000	Value: 300			

KM# 194   10 HRYVEN
33.6220 g., 0.9250 Silver 0.9999 oz. ASW, 38.61 mm. **Obv:** National arms and date divide wreath, value within **Rev:** Long-snouted seahorse **Edge:** Reeded

Date	Mintage	F	VF	XF	Unc	BU
2003 Proof	2,000	Value: 750				

KM# 195   10 HRYVEN
33.6220 g., 0.9250 Silver 0.9999 oz. ASW, 38.61 mm. **Subject:** Kyrylo Rozumovskyi (Cossack leader) **Obv:** Arms with supporters within beaded circle **Rev:** Half length figure 1/4 left within beaded circle **Edge:** Reeded

Date	Mintage	F	VF	XF	Unc	BU
2003 Proof	3,000	Value: 350				

KM# 196   10 HRYVEN
33.6220 g., 0.9250 Silver 0.9999 oz. ASW, 38.61 mm. **Subject:** Pavlo Polubotok (Cossack leader) **Obv:** Arms with supporters within beaded circle **Rev:** Half length figure within beaded circle **Edge:** Reeded

Date	Mintage	F	VF	XF	Unc	BU
2003 Proof	3,000	Value: 375				

KM# 197   10 HRYVEN
33.6220 g., 0.9250 Silver 0.9999 oz. ASW, 38.61 mm. **Obv:** Map, national arms and value **Rev:** Genoese Fortress in Sudak **Edge:** Reeded

Date	Mintage	F	VF	XF	Unc	BU
2003 Proof	3,000	Value: 300				

KM# 206   10 HRYVEN
33.9100 g., 0.9250 Silver 1.0084 oz. ASW, 38.61 mm. **Subject:** Azov Dolphin **Obv:** National arms and date divides wreath, value within **Rev:** Harbor Porpoises **Edge:** Reeded

Date	Mintage	F	VF	XF	Unc	BU
2004 Proof	8,000	Value: 150				

KM# 207   10 HRYVEN
33.9100 g., 0.9250 Silver 1.0084 oz. ASW, 38.61 mm. **Subject:** Football World Cup - 2006 **Obv:** Soccer ball in net **Rev:** Two soccer players **Edge:** Reeded

Date	Mintage	F	VF	XF	Unc	BU
2004 Proof	50,000	Value: 200				

KM# 223   10 HRYVEN
33.9100 g., 0.9250 Silver 1.0084 oz. ASW, 38.61 mm. **Obv:** National arms on sun, flying geese and value divides beaded circle **Rev:** AH-140 Airliner divides beaded circle **Edge:** Reeded

Date	Mintage	F	VF	XF	Unc	BU
2004 Proof	10,000	Value: 170				

KM# 224   10 HRYVEN
33.9100 g., 0.9250 Silver 1.0084 oz. ASW, 38.61 mm. **Subject:** Ice Breaker "Captain Belousov" **Obv:** National arms on ship's wheel and anchor **Rev:** Ice breaker ship **Edge:** Reeded

Date	Mintage	F	VF	XF	Unc	BU
2004 Proof	10,000	Value: 100				

KM# 225   10 HRYVEN
33.6220 g., 0.9250 Silver 0.9999 oz. ASW, 38.61 mm. **Subject:** Whit Sunday **Obv:** National arms within wreath above value flanked by sprigs **Rev:** Four women folk dancers and child **Edge:** Reeded

Date	Mintage	F	VF	XF	Unc	BU
2004 Proof	10,000	Value: 300				

KM# 339   10 HRYVEN
33.6220 g., 0.9250 Silver 0.9999 oz. ASW, 38.61 mm. **Subject:** Ostrozhsky Family **Obv:** Our Lady of Duben and Elias Icon **Rev:** Three cameos above crowned shield **Edge:** Reeded

Date	Mintage	F	VF	XF	Unc	BU
2004 Proof	3,000	Value: 270				

KM# 340   10 HRYVEN
33.6220 g., 0.9250 Silver 0.9999 oz. ASW, 38.61 mm. **Subject:** St. Yura Cathedral **Obv:** Statue of St. George on horse killing dragon **Rev:** Cathedral **Edge:** Reeded

Date	Mintage	F	VF	XF	Unc	BU
ND (2004) Proof	8,000	Value: 110				

KM# 342   10 HRYVEN
33.6220 g., 0.9250 Silver 0.9999 oz. ASW, 38.61 mm. **Subject:** Defense of Sevastopol 1854-56 **Obv:** National arms and value above fortifications map **Rev:** Cannon and ships **Edge:** Reeded

Date	Mintage	F	VF	XF	Unc	BU
2004 Proof	10,000	Value: 110				

KM# 343   10 HRYVEN
33.6220 g., 0.9250 Silver 0.9999 oz. ASW, 38.61 mm. **Subject:** Perejaslav Cossack Rada of 1654 **Obv:** National arms above value **Rev:** Standing figures facing **Edge:** Reeded

Date	Mintage	F	VF	XF	Unc	BU
2004 Proof	8,000	Value: 160				

KM# 358   10 HRYVEN
33.6220 g., 0.9250 Silver 0.9999 oz. ASW, 38.61 mm. **Subject:** Spalax Arenarius Reshetnik **Obv:** National arms and date divides wreath, value within **Rev:** Sandy mole rat **Edge:** Reeded

Date	Mintage	F	VF	XF	Unc	BU
2005 Proof	8,000	Value: 110				

KM# 367   10 HRYVEN
33.6220 g., 0.9250 Silver 0.9999 oz. ASW, 38.61 mm. **Subject:** The Protection of the Virgin **Obv:** National arms on Cossack regalia **Rev:** Wedding scene **Edge:** Reeded

Date	Mintage	F	VF	XF	Unc	BU
2005 Proof	8,000	Value: 150				

KM# 370   10 HRYVEN
33.6220 g., 0.9250 Silver 0.9999 oz. ASW, 38.61 mm. **Subject:** 60 Years UN Membership **Obv:** National arms, value and olive branch **Rev:** UN logo above partial globe **Edge:** Reeded

Date	Mintage	F	VF	XF	Unc	BU
2005 Proof	5,000	Value: 100				

KM# 371   10 HRYVEN
33.6220 g., 0.9250 Silver 0.9999 oz. ASW, 38.61 mm. **Subject:** National Anthem **Obv:** Musical score, national arms, value and date **Rev:** Coiled legend around holographic flower **Edge:** Reeded

Date	Mintage	F	VF	XF	Unc	BU
2005 Proof	3,000	Value: 300				

KM# 372   10 HRYVEN
33.6220 g., 0.9250 Silver 0.9999 oz. ASW, 38.61 mm. **Subject:** 100 Years of Olga Kobylianska Music and Drama Theatre in Chernivtsi **Obv:** Statue **Rev:** Theater **Edge:** Reeded

Date	Mintage	F	VF	XF	Unc	BU
2005 Proof	5,000	Value: 100				

KM# 373   10 HRYVEN
33.6220 g., 0.9250 Silver 0.9999 oz. ASW, 38.61 mm. **Subject:** Sviatohirsky Lavra Monastery **Obv:** Madonna and child flanked by angels **Rev:** Monastery on river bank **Edge:** Reeded

Date	Mintage	F	VF	XF	Unc	BU
2005 Proof	8,000	Value: 120				

KM# 381   10 HRYVEN
33.8600 g., 0.9250 Silver 1.0069 oz. ASW, 38.61 mm. **Subject:** Baturyn Hetman Capital City **Obv:** National arms within sun rays, value flanked by standing figures **Rev:** Four cameos and banner above city view **Edge:** Reeded

Date	Mintage	F	VF	XF	Unc	BU
2005 Proof	5,000	Value: 120				

KM# 382   10 HRYVEN
33.8600 g., 0.9250 Silver 1.0069 oz. ASW, 38.61 mm. **Subject:** Symyrenko Family **Obv:** Country name below national arms within sprigs **Rev:** Family tree **Edge:** Reeded

Date	Mintage	F	VF	XF	Unc	BU
2005 Proof	5,000	Value: 100				

KM# 392   10 HRYVEN
33.6220 g., 0.9250 Silver 0.9999 oz. ASW, 38.61 mm. **Obv:** National arms above value in wreath **Rev:** Grasshopper **Edge:** Reeded

Date	Mintage	F	VF	XF	Unc	BU
2006 Proof	8,000	Value: 140				

KM# 424   10 HRYVEN
33.6221 g., 0.9250 Silver 0.9999 oz. ASW, 38.61 mm. **Subject:** Chyhyryn **Obv:** National arms

Date	Mintage	F	VF	XF	Unc	BU
2006 Proof	5,000	Value: 120				

KM# 425   10 HRYVEN
33.6220 g., 0.9250 Silver 0.9999 oz. ASW, 38.61 mm. **Subject:** 10 Years of the Clearing House **Obv:** National arms

Date	Mintage	F	VF	XF	Unc	BU
2006 Proof	5,000	Value: 100				

KM# 410   10 HRYVEN
33.6220 g., 0.9250 Silver 0.9999 oz. ASW, 38.61 mm. **Subject:** 10 Years of the Constitution of Ukraine **Obv:** National arms

Date	Mintage	F	VF	XF	Unc	BU
2006 Proof	5,000	Value: 100				

KM# 421   10 HRYVEN
33.6200 g., 0.9250 Silver 0.9998 oz. ASW, 38.61 mm. **Subject:**
Epiphany **Obv:** National arms **Edge:** Reeded

Date	Mintage	F	VF	XF	Unc	BU
2006 Proof	10,000	Value: 120				

KM# 423   10 HRYVEN
33.6220 g., 0.9250 Silver 0.9999 oz. ASW, 38.61 mm. **Subject:**
Saint Kyryl Church **Obv:** National arms **Edge:** Reeded

Date	Mintage	F	VF	XF	Unc	BU
2006 Proof	8,000	Value: 110				

KM# 427   10 HRYVEN
33.6220 g., 0.9250 Silver 0.9999 oz. ASW, 38.61 mm. **Subject:**
Twentieth Winter Olympic Games of 2006 **Obv:** National arms
Edge: Reeded

Date	Mintage	F	VF	XF	Unc	BU
2006 Proof	5,000	Value: 100				

KM# 466   10 HRYVEN
33.6220 g., 0.9250 Silver 0.9999 oz. ASW, 38.6 mm. **Subject:**
Odessa National Opera and Ballet, 120th Anniversary **Obv:**
Interior view from stage **Rev:** Opera house in Odessa **Edge:**
Reeded

Date	Mintage	F	VF	XF	Unc	BU
2007 Proof	5,000	Value: 100				

KM# 467   10 HRYVEN
33.6220 g., 0.9250 Silver 0.9999 oz. ASW, 38.61 mm. **Subject:**
Ivan Bohun **Edge:** Reeded

Date	Mintage	F	VF	XF	Unc	BU
2007 Proof	5,000	Value: 110				

KM# 516   10 HRYVEN
33.6220 g., 0.9250 Silver 0.9999 oz. ASW, 38.61 mm. **Subject:**
Black Griffin **Edge:** Reeded

Date	Mintage	F	VF	XF	Unc	BU
2008 Proof	7,000	Value: 120				

KM# 517   10 HRYVEN
33.6220 g., 0.9250 Silver 0.9999 oz. ASW, 38.61 mm. **Subject:**
Sevastopol, 225th Anniversary **Edge:** Reeded

Date	Mintage	F	VF	XF	Unc	BU
2008 Proof	5,000	Value: 100				

KM# 518   10 HRYVEN
33.6220 g., 0.9250 Silver 0.9999 oz. ASW, 38.61 mm. **Subject:**
Swallow's Nest **Edge:** Reeded

Date	Mintage	F	VF	XF	Unc	BU
2008 Proof	5,000	Value: 110				

KM# 519   10 HRYVEN
33.6220 g., 0.9250 Silver 0.9999 oz. ASW, 38.61 mm. **Subject:**
Tereschenko Family **Edge:** Reeded

Date	Mintage	F	VF	XF	Unc	BU
2008 Proof	7,000	Value: 95.00				

KM# 520   10 HRYVEN
33.6220 g., 0.9250 Silver 0.9999 oz. ASW, 38.61 mm. **Subject:**
Ukranian Swedish Alliances XVII-XVIII Century **Edge:** Reeded

Date	Mintage	F	VF	XF	Unc	BU
2008 Proof	5,000	Value: 95.00				

KM# 521   10 HRYVEN
33.6220 g., 0.9250 Silver 0.9999 oz. ASW, 38.61 mm. **Subject:**
Hlukhiv **Edge:** Reeded

Date	Mintage	F	VF	XF	Unc	BU
2008 Proof	7,000	Value: 100				

KM# 522   10 HRYVEN
33.6220 g., 0.9250 Silver 0.9999 oz. ASW, 38.61 mm. **Subject:**
UNESCO World Heritage Site - LVIV **Edge:** Reeded

Date	Mintage	F	VF	XF	Unc	BU
2008 Proof	5,000	Value: 120				

KM# 523   10 HRYVEN
33.6220 g., 0.9250 Silver 0.9999 oz. ASW, 38.61 mm. **Subject:** Cathedral in Buky Village **Edge:** Reeded

Date	Mintage	F	VF	XF	Unc	BU
2008 Proof	5,000	Value: 150				

KM# 532   10 HRYVEN
33.6220 g., 0.9250 Silver 0.9999 oz. ASW, 38.61 mm. **Subject:** Annunciation **Obv:** Conventionalized setting of the Gospel, lilies. **Obv. Legend:** НАЦІОНАЛЬНИЙ БАНК УКРАЇНИ - 10 ГРИВЕНЬ **Rev:** Annunciation scene. **Rev. Legend:** БЛАГОВІЩЕННЯ **Edge:** Reeded

Date	Mintage	F	VF	XF	Unc	BU
2008 Proof	8,000	Value: 100				

KM# 556   10 HRYVEN
33.6220 g., 0.9250 Silver 0.9999 oz. ASW, 38.61 mm. **Subject:** Folk Crafts of the Ukraine - Bokorash (Raftsmen) **Obv:** Two birds, Carpathian landscape, trees, cottages, logs **Obv. Legend:** НАЦІОНАЛЬНИЙ БАНК УКРА?НИ - 10 / ГРИВЕНЬ / 2009 **Rev:** Bokorash directing raft **Rev. Legend:** БОКОРАШ

Date	Mintage	F	VF	XF	Unc	BU
2009 Proof	Est. 10,000	Value: 95.00				

KM# 559   10 HRYVEN
33.6220 g., 0.9250 Silver 0.9999 oz. ASW, 38.61 mm. **Subject:** Surb Khach Monastery **Obv:** National Arms, vegitation ornament pattern **Obv. Legend:** НАЦІОНАЛЬНИЙ БАНК УКРАЇНИ - ДЕСЯТЬ ГРИВЕНЬ **Rev:** Monastery buildings **Rev. Legend:** СТАРИЙ КРИМ - ВІРМЕНСЬКИЙ МОНАСТИР XIV СТ. - СУРБ ХАЧ **Edge:** Segmented reeding

Date	Mintage	F	VF	XF	Unc	BU
2009 Proof	Est. 10,000	Value: 95.00				

KM# 560   10 HRYVEN
33.6220 g., 0.9250 Silver 0.9999 oz. ASW, 38.61 mm. **Subject:** Battle of Konotop, 350th Anniversary **Obv:** Hetman's Insignia, Cossack arms and bandura, National Arms. **Obv. Legend:** НАЦІОНАЛЬНИЙ БАНК УКРАЇНИ - 10 **Rev:** Ivan Vyhovskyi with sabre, Cossacks, Konotop fortifications, banners. **Rev. Legend:** ПЕРЕМОГА В КОНОТОПСЬКІЙ БИТВІ - 350 РОКІВ

Date	Mintage	F	VF	XF	Unc	BU
2009 Proof	8,000	Value: 95.00				

KM# 561   10 HRYVEN
33.6220 g., 0.9250 Silver 0.9999 oz. ASW, 38.61 mm. **Subject:** Church of the Holy Spirit in Rogatyn **Obv:** Church Icon with candelabra flanking, National Arms **Rev:** Church facade

Date	Mintage	F	VF	XF	Unc	BU
2009 Proof	Est. 10,000	Value: 100				

KM# 562   10 HRYVEN
33.6220 g., 0.9250 Silver 0.9999 oz. ASW, 38.61 mm. **Subject:** Famous Ukranian Families - Galagan Family **Obv:** The family estate, National Arms, value **Rev:** Galagan's College building and three portraits

Date	Mintage	F	VF	XF	Unc	BU
2009 Proof	7,000	Value: 95.00				

KM# 563   10 HRYVEN
33.6220 g., 0.9250 Silver 0.9999 oz. ASW, 38.61 mm. **Subject:** Kiev Academy of Operatta Theater, 75th Anniversary **Obv:** Dance scene, National Arms, value **Obv. Legend:** НАЦІОНАЛЬНИЙ БАНК УКРАЇНИ - 10 / ГРИВНЬ / 2009 **Rev:** Theater building, operetta character silhouettes. **Rev. Legend:** КІВСЬКИЙ АКАДЕМІЧНИЙ ТЕАТР ОПЕРЕТИ - 75/РОКІВ

Date	Mintage	F	VF	XF	Unc	BU
2009 Proof	5,000	Value: 95.00				

KM# 574   10 HRYVEN
31.1000 g., 0.9250 Silver 0.9249 oz. ASW, 38.61 mm. **Subject:** Ukrainian folk craft - Cartwright **Obv:** Wagon and wheels **Rev:** Woodcraftsman hewing wood to make a cart detail **Edge:** Reeded

Date	Mintage	F	VF	XF	Unc	BU
2009	10,000	—	—	—	—	95.00

KM# 570   10 HRYVEN
31.1000 g., 0.9250 Silver 0.9249 oz. ASW, 38.6 mm. **Subject:** Pulyp Oriyk Constitution, 300th Anniversary **Obv:** Hetman and Cossack officials **Rev:** Pylyp Orlyk, quill pen and constitution

Date	Mintage	F	VF	XF	Unc	BU
2010 Proof	7,000	Value: 95.00				

KM# 575   10 HRYVEN
31.1000 g., 0.9250 Silver 0.9249 oz. ASW, 38.61 mm. **Subject:** Vancouver Winter Olympics **Obv:** Winter scene **Rev:** Snowflake, sport figures, downhill skier at left

Date	Mintage	F	VF	XF	Unc	BU
2010 Proof	8,000	Value: 95.00				

KM# 586   10 HRYVEN
31.1000 g., 0.9250 Silver 0.9249 oz. ASW, 38.61 mm. **Obv:** Icon of Our Lady of Zarvanytsia **Rev:** Cathedral of Our Lady of Zarvanytsia

Date	Mintage	F	VF	XF	Unc	BU
2010	7,000	Value: 95.00				

KM# 588   10 HRYVEN
31.1000 g., 0.9250 Silver 0.9249 oz. ASW, 38.61 mm. **Subject:** Folk Crafts - Weaving **Obv:** Spinning wheel and weaving products **Rev:** Woman working at a loom

Date	Mintage	F	VF	XF	Unc	BU
2010 Proof	10,000	Value: 95.00				

KM# 590   10 HRYVEN
31.1000 g., 0.9250 Silver 0.9249 oz. ASW, 38.61 mm. **Subject:** Ukraine Spas **Obv:** Two cornucopiae and Savior's fest **Rev:** Peasants getting food gifts blessed

Date	Mintage	F	VF	XF	Unc	BU
2010 Proof	—	Value: 95.00				

KM# 594   10 HRYVEN
31.1000 g., 0.9250 Silver 0.9249 oz. ASW, 38.61 mm. **Subject:** Flora and Fauna **Obv:** National Arms and wreath **Rev:** Stipa Ucrainica, feather grass

Date	Mintage	F	VF	XF	Unc	BU
2010 Proof	8,000	Value: 95.00				

KM# 600   10 HRYVEN
31.1000 g., 0.9250 Silver 0.9249 oz. ASW, 38.61 mm. **Subject:** Hetman Danylo Apostol **Obv:** National arms, Archangel Michael and Crowned lion (Symbols of Kyiv and Lviv) **Rev:** Danylo Apostol half length figure holding scep-tre

Date	Mintage	F	VF	XF	Unc	BU
2010 Proof	8,000	Value: 95.00				

KM# 605 10 HRYVEN
31.1000 g., 0.9250 Silver 0.9249 oz. ASW, 38.61 mm. **Subject:** Folk Crafts - Potter **Obv:** Pottery flanking central design **Rev:** Potter at wheel

Date	Mintage	F	VF	XF	Unc	BU
2010 Proof	10,000				Value: 95.00	

KM# 606 10 HRYVEN
31.1000 g., 0.9250 Silver 0.9249 oz. ASW, 38.6 mm. **Subject:** Tarnovskyi Family **Obv:** Mansion in Kachanivka, Chernihiv oblast **Rev:** Vasyl Tarnovskyi standing and oval portraits of Hryhorii and Vasyl.

Date	Mintage	F	VF	XF	Unc	BU
2010 Proof	10,000	—	—	—	—	95.00

KM# 616 10 HRYVEN
33.6230 g., 0.9250 Silver 0.9999 oz. ASW, 38.61 mm. **Obv:** Blacksmith items, two little birds **Rev:** Blacksmith at work

Date	Mintage	F	VF	XF	Unc	BU
2011 Antique finish	10,000	—	—	—	—	110

KM# 626 10 HRYVEN
33.6230 g., 0.9250 Silver 0.9999 oz. ASW, 38.61 mm. **Obv:** Baroque element from the Church **Rev:** St. Andrew's Church

Date	Mintage	F	VF	XF	Unc	BU
2011 Proof	8,000	Value: 110				

KM# 628 10 HRYVEN
33.6230 g., 0.9250 Silver 0.9999 oz. ASW, 38.61 mm. **Obv:** Hopak dance **Rev:** Dancing Cossack

Date	Mintage	F	VF	XF	Unc	BU
2011 Proof	7,000	Value: 110				

KM# 632 10 HRYVEN
33.6230 g., 0.9250 Silver 0.9999 oz. ASW, 38.61 mm. **Subject:** Hryhorovych-Barskyi family **Obv:** Samson fountain in Kyiv **Rev:** Arms of the family

Date	Mintage	F	VF	XF	Unc	BU
2011 Proof	5,000	Value: 110				

KM# 641 10 HRYVEN
33.6230 g., 0.9250 Silver 0.9999 oz. ASW, 38.61 mm. **Subject:** UEFA Euro 2012 Final Tournament **Obv:** UEFA logo hologram and map of the Ukraine **Rev:** Two players, Olympic Stadium, Kyiv and city view

Date	Mintage	F	VF	XF	Unc	BU
2011 Proof	15,000	Value: 110				

KM# 642 10 HRYVEN
33.6230 g., 0.9250 Silver 0.9999 oz. ASW, 38.61 mm. **Subject:** UEFA Euro 2012 Final Tornament **Obv:** UEFA Euro 2012 Logo and map **Rev:** Player, city view and Livi Stadium

Date	Mintage	F	VF	XF	Unc	BU
2011 Proof	15,000	Value: 110				

KM# 643 10 HRYVEN
33.6230 g., 0.9250 Silver 0.9999 oz. ASW, 38.61 mm. **Subject:** UEFA Euro 2012 Final Tournament **Obv:** UEFA logo hologram and Map of Ukraine **Rev:** City view with two players

Date	Mintage	F	VF	XF	Unc	BU
2011 Proof	15,000	Value: 110				

KM# 644 10 HRYVEN
33.6230 g., 0.9250 Silver 0.9999 oz. ASW, 38.61 mm. **Subject:** UEFA Euro 2012 Final Tournament **Obv:** UEFA logo hologram and map of Ukraine **Rev:** Player with ball, Donbass Arena

Date	Mintage	F	VF	XF	Unc	BU
2011 Proof	15,000	Value: 110				

KM# 144 20 HRYVEN
67.2400 g., 0.9250 Silver 1.9996 oz. ASW, 50 mm. **Subject:** 10 Years Independence **Obv:** National arms **Rev:** Parliament building on map within beaded circle **Edge:** Segmented reeding

Date	Mintage	F	VF	XF	Unc	BU
2001 Proof	1,000	Value: 4,000				

KM# 174 20 HRYVEN
14.7000 g., Bi-Metallic .916 Gold center in .925 silver ring, 31 mm. **Subject:** "Kyiv Rus" Culture **Obv:** Old arms of Ukraine, Prince and a cathedral model in his hand and princess **Rev:** Old Rus earring **Edge:** Reeded and plain sections

Date	Mintage	F	VF	XF	Unc	BU
2001 Proof	2,000	Value: 1,000				

KM# 175 20 HRYVEN
14.7000 g., Bi-Metallic .916 Gold center in .925 Silver ring, 31 mm. **Subject:** Scythian Culture **Obv:** Warrior with a bowl in his hand and to the right, a Queen of Scythia **Rev:** Stylized horse flanked by pegasists **Edge:** Reeded and plain sections

Date	Mintage	F	VF	XF	Unc	BU
2001 Proof	2,000	Value: 1,200				

KM# 153 20 HRYVEN
67.2400 g., 0.9250 Silver 1.9996 oz. ASW, 50 mm. **Obv:** National arms on sun and flying geese divides beaded circle **Rev:** "AN-225 Mrija" cargo jet divides beaded circle **Edge:** Reeded and plain sections

Date	Mintage	F	VF	XF	Unc	BU
2002 Proof	2,002	Value: 1,200				

KM# 188 20 HRYVEN
67.2400 g., 0.9250 Silver 1.9996 oz. ASW, 50 mm. **Subject:** 60th Anniversary - Liberation of Kiev **Obv:** Eternal flame monument **Rev:** Map and battle scene **Edge:** Segmented reeding

Date	Mintage	F	VF	XF	Unc	BU
2003 Proof	2,000	Value: 400				

KM# 226 20 HRYVEN
67.2440 g., 0.9250 Silver 1.9997 oz. ASW, 50 mm. **Subject:** "Our Souls Do Not Die" **Obv:** National arms above value **Rev:** Bust of Taras Shevchenko facing flanked by standing figures **Edge:** Segmented reeding

Date	Mintage	F	VF	XF	Unc	BU
2004 Proof	4,000	Value: 250				

KM# 344   20 HRYVEN
67.2440 g., 0.9250 Silver 1.9997 oz. ASW, 50 mm.   **Subject:**
2006 Olympic Games **Obv:** Woman holding flame and branch
Rev: Six athletes around flame within square design **Edge:**
Segmented reeding

Date	Mintage	F	VF	XF	Unc	BU
2004 Proof	5,000			Value: 200		

KM# 374   20 HRYVEN
67.2440 g., 0.9250 Silver 1.9997 oz. ASW, 50 mm.   **Subject:**
60th Anniversary of Victory in WWII **Obv:** Flying cranes divides
value, date and national arms **Rev:** V-shaped searchlight beams
filled with soldiers, order of the Patriotic War at bottom left **Edge:**
Segmented reeding

Date	Mintage	F	VF	XF	Unc	BU
2005 Proof	5,000			Value: 200		

KM# 470   20 HRYVEN
67.2500 g., 0.9250 Silver 1.9999 oz. ASW, 50 mm.   **Subject:**
The Famine, Genocide of the Ukranina People **Obv:** Girl standing
on fallow ground, small green plant at left **Rev:** Swan at center
of cross, candles in background

Date	Mintage	F	VF	XF	Unc	BU
2007 Antique finish	10,000	—	—	—	200	

KM# 363   20 HRYVEN
67.2440 g., 0.9250 Silver 1.9997 oz. ASW, 50 mm.   **Obv:**
National arms on sun with flying geese divides beaded circle **Rev:**
AN-124 jet plane divides beaded circle **Edge:** Segmented reeding

Date	Mintage	F	VF	XF	Unc	BU
2005 Proof	5,000			Value: 200		

KM# 412   20 HRYVEN
67.2500 g., 0.9250 Silver 1.9999 oz. ASW, 50 mm. **Subject:** 15
Years of Ukraine Independency **Obv:** National arms

Date	Mintage	F	VF	XF	Unc	BU
2006 Proof	7,000			Value: 200		

KM# 524   20 HRYVEN
67.2500 g., 0.9250 Silver 1.9999 oz. ASW, 50 mm.   **Subject:**
Kyiv, 1000th Anniversary of minting

Date	Mintage	F	VF	XF	Unc	BU
2008 Proof	5,000			Value: 250		

KM# 552   20 HRYVEN
67.2500 g., 0.9250 Silver 1.9999 oz. ASW, 50.0 mm.   **Subject:**
Republic of Carpatho-Ukraine - 70th Anniversary of proclamation
Obv: Carpathian ornament patterns, National Arms, value **Obv.
Legend:** НАЦІОНАЛЬНИЈ БАНК УКРАЇНИ - 20 / ГРИВНЬ **Rev:**
Transcarpathian holding flag with the arms of the Carpatho-
Ukraine **Rev. Legend:** 70 / РОКІВ - ПРОГОЛОШЕННЯ
КАРПАТСЬКОЇ УКРАЇНИ

Date	Mintage	F	VF	XF	Unc	BU
2009 Proof	3,000			Value: 300		

KM# 554   20 HRYVEN
67.2500 g., 0.9250 Silver 1.9999 oz. ASW, 50 mm.   **Subject:**
Pysanka - Easter Egg decorating **Obv:** Ukrainian embroidered
towels, eggs, Naitonal Arms, value **Rev:** Female pysanka maker
ornamenting egg, young girl watching

Date	Mintage	F	VF	XF	Unc	BU
2009 Proof	8,000			Value: 250		

KM# 468   20 HRYVEN
14.2300 g., Silver, 31 mm.   **Subject:** Pure water is source of life
Obv: Drop of water in pond **Rev:** Man taking drink from waterfall
Edge: Segmented reeding

Date	Mintage	F	VF	XF	Unc	BU
2007 Prooflike	3,000	—	—	—	—	600

KM# 369   20 HRYVEN
67.2440 g., 0.9250 Silver 1.9997 oz. ASW, 50 mm.   **Subject:**
Sorochynsky Fair **Obv:** Busts facing each other flanked by flower
sprigs **Rev:** Farmer leading family in ox cart **Edge:** Segmented
reeding

Date	Mintage	F	VF	XF	Unc	BU
2005 Proof	5,000			Value: 250		

KM# 469   20 HRYVEN
67.2600 g., 0.9250 Silver 2.0002 oz. ASW, 50 mm.   **Subject:**
Chumaky's Way **Obv:** Hologram wheel at center of fiery spiral
Rev: Merchant's carts under night sky

Date	Mintage	F	VF	XF	Unc	BU
2007 Proof	5,000			Value: 350		

KM# 591   20 HRYVEN
62.2000 g., 0.9250 Silver partially gilt 1.8497 oz. ASW, 50 mm.
Subject: Zymne Cloister **Obv:** Madonna icon partially gilt **Rev:**
Zymne Cloister

Date	Mintage	F	VF	XF	Unc	BU
2010 Proof	5,000	—	—	—	—	250

KM# 596   20 HRYVEN
62.2000 g., 0.9250 Silver 1.8497 oz. ASW, 50 mm.   **Subject:** Battle of Grunwald, 600th Anniversary **Obv:** Value within wreath, three armored hands holding horizontal sword **Rev:** Knights with spears on horseback in battle

Date	Mintage	F	VF	XF	Unc	BU
2010 Proof	5,000	Value: 200				

KM# 602   20 HRYVEN
62.2000 g., 0.9250 Silver 1.8497 oz. ASW, 50 mm.   **Subject:** Maritime History **Obv:** Banner, compass rose and seal of Zaporozhin host **Rev:** Cossack boat of the 18th century

Date	Mintage	F	VF	XF	Unc	BU
2010 Proof	5,000	Value: 200				

KM# 614   20 HRYVEN
67.2500 g., 0.9250 Silver 1.9999 oz. ASW, 50 mm.   **Subject:** Lesya Ukrainka's "The Forest Song" **Obv:** Portrait **Rev:** Girl holding willow branch, boy in distance

Date	Mintage	F	VF	XF	Unc	BU
2011 Proof	4,000	Value: 200				

KM# 617   20 HRYVEN
67.2500 g., 0.9250 Silver 1.9999 oz. ASW, 50 mm.   **Subject:** Peresopnytsia Gospels **Obv:** Gospel maker icon **Rev:** Four miniatures of the initial illustrations of each Gospel

Date	Mintage	F	VF	XF	Unc	BU
2011 Special Unc.	4,000	—	—	—	—	200

KM# 637   20 HRYVEN
67.2820 g., 0.9250 Silver 2.0008 oz. ASW, 50 mm.   **Subject:** Ukrainian Railroads, 150th Anniversary **Obv:** Modern high-speed train **Rev:** Ukrainian railways logo, gilt

Date	Mintage	F	VF	XF	Unc	BU
2011 Proof	4,000	Value: 200				

KM# 640   20 HRYVEN
67.2820 g., 0.9250 Silver 2.0008 oz. ASW, 62.2 mm.   **Subject:** UEFA Euro 2012 Final Tournament **Obv:** Holographic images of UEFA Euro 2012 logo **Rev:** Stadium

Date	Mintage	F	VF	XF	Unc	BU
2011 Proof	15,000	Value: 200				

KM# 652   20 HRYVEN
31.1050 g., 0.9999 Gold 0.9999 oz. AGW, 32 mm.   **Subject:** Archangel Michael **Obv:** Logo of the Ukraine National Bank **Rev:** Archangel Michael **Edge:** Segmented reeding

Date	Mintage	F	VF	XF	Unc	BU
2011	1,500	Value: 2,000				

KM# 426   50 HRYVEN
17.6300 g., 0.9000 Gold 0.5101 oz. AGW, 25 mm.   **Subject:** Nestor - The Chronicler **Obv:** National arms

Date	Mintage	F	VF	XF	Unc	BU
2006 Proof	5,000	Value: 1,400				

KM# 525   50 HRYVEN
17.6300 g., 0.9000 Gold 0.5101 oz. AGW, 25 mm.   **Subject:** Swallow's Nest Castle **Edge:** Plain

Date	Mintage	F	VF	XF	Unc	BU
2008 Proof	4,000	Value: 1,400				

KM# 526   50 HRYVEN
500.0000 g., 0.9999 Silver 16.073 oz. ASW   **Subject:** Visit of Ecumenical Patriarch Bartholomew I

Date	Mintage	F	VF	XF	Unc	BU
2008 Proof	1,000	Value: 2,200				

KM# 564   50 HRYVEN
500.0000 g., 0.9990 Silver 16.058 oz. ASW, 85 mm.   **Subject:** Mykola Hohol's stories - Evenings on a farm near Dykanka **Obv:** Hohol's portrait with quill, National arms, value **Rev:** Christmas star with yellow sapphire

Date	Mintage	F	VF	XF	Unc	BU
2009 Proof	Est. 1,500	Value: 2,500				

KM# 595   50 HRYVEN
17.6300 g., 0.9000 Gold 0.5101 oz. AGW, 25 mm.   **Subject:** Ukrainian ballet **Obv:** Ballet shoes **Rev:** Ballet couple **Edge:** Plain

Date	Mintage	F	VF	XF	Unc	BU
2010 Proof	4,000	Value: 1,300				

KM# 609   50 HRYVEN
500.0000 g., 0.9990 Silver 16.058 oz. ASW, 85 mm.   **Subject:** Cradle of the Ukrainian Cossacks **Obv:** Zaporizka Sich, historic site, shield and swords below **Rev:** Dovbysh (Cossack drummer) beating kettle drums, ornamental pattern

Date	Mintage	F	VF	XF	Unc	BU
2010 Proof	Est. 1,500	Value: 2,250				

KM# 631   50 HRYVEN
500.0000 g., 0.9990 Silver 16.058 oz. ASW, 85 mm.   **Subject:** Independence, 20th Anniversary **Obv:** National arms, rushnyks, portraits **Rev:** Legend within wreath

Date	Mintage	F	VF	XF	Unc	BU
2011	1,000				—	1,500

KM# 633   50 HRYVEN
500.0000 g., 0.9990 Silver 16.058 oz. ASW, 85 mm.   **Subject:** St. Sophia Cathedral, 1000th Anniversary **Obv:** St. Sophia Cathedral cupolas, model of XI century design **Rev:** Altar mural mosaics

Date	Mintage	F	VF	XF	Unc	BU
2011	1,000	—	—	—	—	1,500

KM# 199   100 HRYVEN
31.1000 g., 0.9000 Gold 0.8999 oz. AGW, 32 mm.   **Subject:** Ancient Scythian Culture **Obv:** National arms above ornamental design and value within rope wreath **Rev:** Ancient craftsmen and jewelry **Edge:** Reeded

Date	Mintage	F	VF	XF	Unc	BU
2003 Proof	1,500	Value: 7,500				

KM# 345   100 HRYVEN
34.5594 g., 0.9000 Gold 1.0000 oz. AGW, 32 mm.   **Subject:** The Golden Gate **Obv:** National arms above value between two stylized cranes **Rev:** Riders approaching castle gate **Edge:** Segmented reeding

Date	Mintage	F	VF	XF	Unc	BU
2004 Proof	2,000	Value: 5,000				

KM# 414   100 HRYVEN
1000.0000 g., 0.9990 Silver 32.117 oz. ASW, 100 mm.   **Subject:** 10 Years to the Currency Reform in Ukraine **Obv:** National arms **Note:** Illustration reduced.

Date	Mintage	Good	VG	F	VF	XF
2006 Proof	1,501	Value: 6,500				

KM# 471   100 HRYVEN
34.5600 g., 0.9000 Gold 1.0000 oz. AGW, 32 mm.   **Subject:** The Ostroh Bible **Obv:** Part of illumination on page **Rev:** Ivan Fedorov and Kostiantyn of Ostroth holding open bible

Date	Mintage	F	VF	XF	Unc	BU
2007 Proof	4,000	Value: 3,000				

KM# 527 100 HRYVEN
1000.0000 g., 0.9990 Silver 32.117 oz. ASW **Subject:** Kievan Rus

Date	Mintage	F	VF	XF	Unc	BU
2008 Proof	800	Value: 4,500				

KM# 558 100 HRYVEN
1000.0000 g., 0.9990 Silver 32.117 oz. ASW, 100 mm. **Subject:** International Year of Astronomy **Obv:** Solar System, armillary sphere, stars. **Obv. Legend:** НАЦІОНАЛЬНИЙ БАНК УКРАЇНИ - 100 / ГРИВНЬ **Rev:** Galileo, stars, telescope, galaxies, observatory, Saturn (as the letter O). **Rev. Legend:** МІЖНАРОДНИЙ РІК АСТРОНОМІЇ

Date	Mintage	F	VF	XF	Unc	BU
2009 Proof	Est. 700	Value: 4,000				

KM# 565 100 HRYVEN
34.5700 g., 0.9000 Gold 1.0003 oz. AGW, 32 mm. **Subject:** Ancient Site - Chersonesos Taurica **Obv:** Ancient ruins, coins, Naitonal Arms **Rev:** Ruins of ancient Chersonesos **Edge:** Segmented reeding

Date	Mintage	F	VF	XF	Unc	BU
2009 Proof	4,000	Value: 2,950				

KM# 597 100 HRYVEN
31.1000 g., 0.9000 Gold 0.8999 oz. AGW, 32 mm. **Subject:** Bosporan Kingdom **Obv:** Panticapaeum runins: classical columns, winged animals **Rev:** Panticapaeum stater, buildings, ancient sailing vessel

Date	Mintage	F	VF	XF	Unc	BU
2010 Proof	3,000	Value: 2,950				

KM# 630 100 HRYVEN
34.5600 g., 0.9000 Gold 1.0000 oz. AGW, 32 mm. **Subject:** Independence, 20th Anniversary **Obv:** National arms in center of rushnyks, Portraits around **Rev:** Legend within wreath

Date	Mintage	F	VF	XF	Unc	BU
2011 Proof	1,000	Value: 4,000				

MINT SETS

KM#	Date	Mintage	Identification	Issue Price	Mkt Val
MS2	2001 (8)	5,000	KM#1.1b, 2.1b, 3.3b, 4b, 6, 7, 8b, 129	—	130
MS3	2006 (8)	5,000	KM#1.1b, 2.1b, 3.3b, 4b, 6, 7, 8b, 411	—	30.00
MS4	2008 (7)	5,000	KM#1.1b, 2.1b, 3.3b, 4b, 6, 7, 209, prooflike	—	50.00
MS5	2011 (7)	5,000	KM#1.1b, 2.1b, 3.3b, 4b, 6, 7, 209. Prooflike	—	45.00

UNITED ARAB EMIRATES

The seven United Arab Emirates (formerly known as the Trucial Sheikhdoms or States), located along the southern shore of the Persian Gulf, are comprised of the Sheikhdoms of Abu Dhabi, Dubai, al-Sharjah, Ajman, Umm al Qaiwain, Ras al-Khaimah and al-Fujairah. They have a combined area of about 32,000 sq. mi. (83,600 sq. km.) and a population of *2.1 million. Capital: Abu Zaby (Abu Dhabi). Since the oil strikes of 1958-60, the economy has centered about petroleum.

TITLES

الامارات العربية المتحدة

al-Imara(t) al-Arabiya(t) al-Muttahida(t)

UNITED EMIRATES
STANDARD COINAGE

KM# 2.2 5 FILS
Bronze **Series:** F.A.O. **Obv:** Value **Rev:** Fish above dates **Note:** Reduced size.

Date	Mintage	F	VF	XF	Unc	BU
AH1422-2001	—	—	—	0.15	0.30	1.00
AH1426-2005	—	—	—	0.15	0.30	1.00

KM# 3.2 10 FILS
Bronze, 19 mm. **Obv:** Value **Rev:** Arab dhow above dates **Note:** Reduced size.

Date	Mintage	F	VF	XF	Unc	BU
AH1422-2001 (2001)	—	—	0.20	0.35	0.80	1.20
AH1425-2005 (2005)	—	—	0.20	0.35	0.80	1.20

KM# 4 25 FILS
3.5000 g., Copper-Nickel, 20 mm. **Obv:** Value **Rev:** Gazelle above dates **Edge:** Reeded

Date	Mintage	F	VF	XF	Unc	BU
AH1425-2005	—	—	—	0.40	0.75	1.00
AH1428-2007	—	—	—	0.40	0.75	1.00
AH1428-2008	—	—	—	0.40	0.75	1.00
AH1432-2011	—	—	—	0.40	0.75	1.00

KM# 16 50 FILS
4.3000 g., Copper-Nickel, 21 mm. **Obv:** Value **Rev:** Oil derricks above dates **Shape:** 7-sided **Note:** Reduced size.

Date	Mintage	F	VF	XF	Unc	BU
AH1425-2005	—	—	—	0.45	1.35	1.85
AH1428-2007	—	—	—	0.45	1.35	1.85
AH1428-2008	—	—	—	0.45	1.35	1.85

KM# 49 DIRHAM
6.4000 g., Copper-Nickel, 24 mm. **Subject:** 25th Anniversary - Armed Forces Unification **Obv:** Value **Rev:** Heraldic eagle within rope wreath **Edge:** Reeded

Date	Mintage	F	VF	XF	Unc	BU
ND(2001) (2001)	250,000	—	—	—	3.50	5.00

KM# 51 DIRHAM
6.3300 g., Copper-Nickel, 24 mm. **Subject:** 50 Years of Formal Education **Obv:** Value **Rev:** Symbolic design **Edge:** Reeded

Date	Mintage	F	VF	XF	Unc	BU
ND (2003)	—	—	—	—	3.50	5.00

KM# 52 DIRHAM
6.4000 g., Copper-Nickel, 24 mm. **Subject:** Abu Dhabi National Bank 35th Anniversary **Obv:** Value **Rev:** Bank building tower divide dates within circle **Edge:** Reeded

Date	Mintage	F	VF	XF	Unc	BU
ND (2003)	—	—	—	—	3.50	4.00

KM# 54 DIRHAM
6.4000 g., Copper-Nickel, 24 mm. **Subject:** 40th Anniversary of Crude Oil Exports **Obv:** Value **Rev:** "ADCO" logo **Edge:** Reeded

Date	Mintage	F	VF	XF	Unc	BU
ND (2003)	—	—	—	—	3.50	5.00

KM# 73 DIRHAM
6.4000 g., Copper-Nickel, 23.93 mm. **Subject:** WBG & IMF meeting in Dubai 2003 **Obv:** Denomination **Rev:** Mosaic arc **Edge:** Reeded

Date	Mintage	F	VF	XF	Unc	BU
2003	250,000	—	—	—	4.00	5.00

KM# 74 DIRHAM
6.4000 g., Copper-Nickel, 24 mm. **Subject:** First Gulf Bank 25th Anniversary **Obv:** Value **Rev:** Bank logo **Edge:** Reeded

Date	Mintage	F	VF	XF	Unc	BU
ND(2004)	—	—	—	—	4.00	5.00

KM# 83 DIRHAM
6.4700 g., Copper-Nickel, 24.02 mm. **Subject:** Honoring Mother of Nations **Obv:** Large value **Rev:** Inscription in flower bud at center **Rev. Legend:** Sheikha Fatima Bint Mubarak **Edge:** Reeded

Date	Mintage	F	VF	XF	Unc	BU
2005	—	—	—	—	4.00	5.00

KM# 6.2 DIRHAM
6.4000 g., Copper-Nickel, 24 mm. **Obv:** Value **Rev:** Jug above dates **Edge:** Reeded **Note:** Reduced size.

Date	Mintage	F	VF	XF	Unc	BU
AH1425-2005	—	—	0.35	0.65	1.85	2.25
AH1428-2007	—	—	0.35	0.65	1.85	2.25

KM# 78 DIRHAM
6.4000 g., Copper-Nickel, 24 mm. **Obv:** Value **Obv. Legend:** UNITED ARAB EMIRATES **Rev:** Police badge in center **Rev. Legend:** DUABI POLICE GOLDEN JUBILEE **Edge:** Reeded

Date	Mintage	F	VF	XF	Unc	BU
ND(2006)	—	—	—	—	3.50	5.00

KM# 77 DIRHAM
6.3000 g., Copper-Nickel, 24 mm. **Obv:** Value **Rev:** Zakum Development Co. logo **Edge:** Reeded

Date	Mintage	F	VF	XF	Unc	BU
ND(2007)	—	—	—	—	3.50	5.00

KM# 76 DIRHAM
6.4000 g., Copper-Nickel, 24 mm. **Subject:** Sharjah International Airport, 75th Anniversary **Obv:** Value **Obv. Legend:** UNITED ARAB EMIRATES **Rev:** Three birds in flight under arc **Edge:** Reeded

Date	Mintage	F	VF	XF	Unc	BU
ND(2007)	—	—	—	—	3.00	4.00

KM# 96 DIRHAM
6.4000 g., Copper-Nickel, 24 mm. **Subject:** U.A.E. Boy Scouts, 50th Anniversary **Obv:** Value at center **Rev:** Scout Fleur-de-lis within rope circle

Date	Mintage	F	VF	XF	Unc	BU
2007	—	—	—	—	3.50	5.00

KM# 84 DIRHAM
6.4000 g., Copper-Nickel, 24 mm. **Subject:** 10th Anniversary of the Hamdan Bin Rashed Award for Distinguished Academic

Performance **Obv:** Large value **Rev:** 10 below pen with tip touching star **Edge:** Reeded

Date	Mintage	F	VF	XF	Unc	BU
ND(2007)	—	—	—	—	4.00	5.00

KM# 79 DIRHAM
6.4300 g., Copper-Nickel, 24.03 mm. **Obv:** Value **Obv. Legend:** UNITED ARAB EMIRATES **Rev:** Large "30" and logo **Rev. Legend:** 30TH ANNIVERSARY OF THE 1ST LNG SHIPMENT **Rev. Inscription:** ADGAS **Edge:** Reeded

Date	Mintage	F	VF	XF	Unc	BU
ND(2007)	—	—	—	—	3.50	5.00

KM# 85 DIRHAM
6.4000 g., Copper-Nickel **Subject:** National Bank of Abu Dhabi, 40th Anniversary **Obv:** Large value **Obv. Legend:** UNITED ARAB EMIRATES **Rev:** Large stylized "40" **Edge:** Reeded

Date	Mintage	F	VF	XF	Unc	BU
ND(2008)	—	—	—	—	3.00	4.00

KM# 47 50 DIRHAMS
40.2200 g., 0.9250 Silver 1.1961 oz. ASW, 40 mm. **Subject:** 25th Anniversary - Women's Union (1975-2000) **Obv:** Bust of President H. H. Sheikh Zayed bin Sultan Al Nahyan 7/8 right **Rev:** Stylized gazelle **Edge:** Reeded

Date	Mintage	F	VF	XF	Unc	BU
ND(2001) Proof	5,000	Value: 80.00				

KM# 59 50 DIRHAMS
40.0000 g., 0.9250 Silver 1.1895 oz. ASW, 40 mm. **Subject:** 25th Anniversary - Arab Bank of Investment and Foreign Trade **Edge:** Reeded

Date	Mintage	F	VF	XF	Unc	BU
ND(2001) Proof	2,000	Value: 100				

KM# 60 50 DIRHAMS
40.0000 g., 0.9250 Silver 1.1895 oz. ASW, 40 mm. **Subject:** 25th Anniversary - Armed Forces Unification **Edge:** Reeded

Date	Mintage	F	VF	XF	Unc	BU
ND(2001) Proof	10,000	Value: 75.00				

KM# 61 50 DIRHAMS
40.0000 g., 0.9250 Silver 1.1895 oz. ASW, 40 mm. **Subject:** 30th Anniversary - Al-Ain National Museum **Edge:** Reeded

Date	Mintage	F	VF	XF	Unc	BU
ND(2001) Proof	5,000	Value: 85.00				

KM# 62 50 DIRHAMS
40.0000 g., 0.9250 Silver 1.1895 oz. ASW, 40 mm. **Subject:** 25th Anniversary - University of the U.A.E. **Obv:** Bust of President H. H. Sheikh Zayed bin Sultan Al Nahyan 7/8 right **Rev:** Inscriptions **Edge:** Reeded

Date	Mintage	F	VF	XF	Unc	BU
ND(2002) Proof	5,000	Value: 85.00				

KM# 63 50 DIRHAMS
40.0000 g., 0.9250 Silver 1.1895 oz. ASW, 40 mm. **Subject:** Etisalat - Emirates Telecommunications, 25th Anniversary **Obv:** Value **Rev:** Stylized 25 **Edge:** Reeded

Date	Mintage	F	VF	XF	Unc	BU
ND(2002) Proof	5,000	Value: 85.00				

KM# 64 50 DIRHAMS
40.0000 g., 0.9250 Silver 1.1895 oz. ASW, 40 mm. **Subject:** Sheikh Hamdan bin Rashid al Maktoum Award for Medical Sciences **Obv:** Value **Rev:** Sheikh Hamdan bin Rashid al Maktoum bust 3/4 left **Edge:** Reeded

Date	Mintage	F	VF	XF	Unc	BU
ND(2002) Proof	2,000	Value: 100				

KM# 65 50 DIRHAMS
40.0000 g., 0.9250 Silver 1.1895 oz. ASW, 40 mm. **Subject:** Al Ahmadia School, 90th Anniversary **Obv:** Sheikh Rashid bin Saaed al Maktoum 3/4 left **Rev:** School building **Edge:** Reeded

Date	Mintage	F	VF	XF	Unc	BU
ND(2002) Proof	5,000	Value: 85.00				

KM# 67 50 DIRHAMS
40.0000 g., 0.9250 Silver 1.1895 oz. ASW, 40 mm. **Subject:** Administrative Development Institute, 20th Anniversary **Obv:** Sheikh Zayed bin Sultan al Nahyan bust 3/4 right **Rev:** Eagle **Edge:** Reeded

Date	Mintage	F	VF	XF	Unc	BU
ND(2002) Proof	2,000	Value: 100				

KM# 68   50 DIRHAMS
40.0000 g., 0.9250 Silver 1.1895 oz. ASW, 40 mm. **Subject:**
U.A.E. Central Bank, 30th Anniversary **Obv:** Sheikh Zayed bin
Sultan al Nahyan bust 3/4 right **Rev:** Sheikh Maktoum bin Rashid
al Maktoum bust 3/4 right **Edge:** Reeded

Date	Mintage	F	VF	XF	Unc	BU
ND(2003) Proof	5,000	Value: 85.00				

KM# 69   50 DIRHAMS
40.0000 g., 0.9250 Silver 1.1895 oz. ASW, 40 mm. **Subject:**
58th Annual Meeting of the World Bank Group and the Int'l Money
Fund **Obv:** Colored dots **Edge:** Reeded

Date	Mintage	F	VF	XF	Unc	BU
ND(2003) Proof	10,000	Value: 75.00				

KM# 50   50 DIRHAMS
40.0000 g., 0.9250 Silver 1.1895 oz. ASW, 40 mm. **Obv:** Value
Rev: FIFA 2003 World Youth Soccer Championship **Edge:**
Reeded

Date	Mintage	F	VF	XF	Unc	BU
ND(2003) Proof	—	Value: 85.00				

KM# 66   50 DIRHAMS
40.0000 g., 0.9250 Silver 1.1895 oz. ASW, 40 mm. **Subject:**
Ministry of Finance and Industry ISO Certification **Obv:** Value
Rev: Eagle at center **Edge:** Reeded

Date	Mintage	F	VF	XF	Unc	BU
ND(2003) Proof	3,000	Value: 95.00				

KM# 70   50 DIRHAMS
40.0000 g., 0.9250 Silver 1.1895 oz. ASW, 40 mm. **Subject:**
40th Anniversary - First Oil Export from Abu Dhabi Onshore Oil
Fields (ADCO) **Obv:** Bust of President H. H. Sheikh Zayed bin
Sultan Al Nayhan 3/4 right **Rev:** Logo **Edge:** Reeded

Date	Mintage	F	VF	XF	Unc	BU
ND(2004) Proof	—	Value: 300				

KM# 71   50 DIRHAMS
40.0000 g., 0.9250 Silver 1.1895 oz. ASW, 40 mm. **Subject:**
25th Anniversary - Sharjah City for Humanitarian Services
(SCHS) **Edge:** Reeded

Date	Mintage	F	VF	XF	Unc	BU
ND(2005) Proof	—	Value: 85.00				

KM# 87   50 DIRHAMS
40.0000 g., 0.9250 Silver 1.1895 oz. ASW, 40 mm. **Subject:**
Mother of the Nation - Seikha Fatima Bint Mubarak

Date	Mintage	F	VF	XF	Unc	BU
2005 Proof	—	Value: 85.00				

KM# 98   50 DIRHAMS
40.0000 g., 0.9250 Silver 1.1895 oz. ASW, 40 mm. **Subject:**
Sheikha Fatima Birt Mubarak, Mother of the Nation

Date	Mintage	F	VF	XF	Unc	BU
2005 Proof	—	Value: 85.00				

KM# 82   50 DIRHAMS
40.0000 g., 0.9250 Silver 1.1895 oz. ASW, 40 mm. **Subject:**
25th Anniversary Emirates Banks Association **Obv:** Value **Obv.
Legend:** UNITED ARAB EMIRATES **Rev:** Logo **Edge:** Reeded

Date	Mintage	F	VF	XF	Unc	BU
ND(2007) Proof	—	Value: 90.00				

KM# 95   50 DIRHAMS
40.0000 g., 0.9250 Silver 1.1895 oz. ASW, 40 mm. **Subject:**
Hamdan Bin Rashed Award for Distinguished Academic
Performance **Obv:** Denomination, legend above **Rev:** Pen with
tip touching star, legend above **Edge:** Reeded **Note:** Issued 10th
Anniversary of the Award

Date	Mintage	F	VF	XF	Unc	BU
ND(2008) Proof	—	Value: 600				

KM# 80   100 DIRHAMS
60.0000 g., 0.9250 Silver 1.7843 oz. ASW, 50 mm. **Obv:** Sheikh
Zayed bin Sultan **Rev:** Sheikh Zayed Mosque

Date	Mintage	F	VF	XF	Unc	BU
2004 Proof	—	Value: 120				

KM# 97   100 DIRHAMS
60.0000 g., 0.9250 Silver 1.7843 oz. ASW, 50 mm. **Subject:**
Sheikh Khalifa Ben Zayed, 1st Anniversary **Rev:** Emir's Palace

Date	Mintage	F	VF	XF	Unc	BU
2005 Proof	—	Value: 120				

UNITED STATES OF AMERICA

The United States of America as politically organized, under the Articles of Confederation consisted of the 13 original British-American colonies; New Hampshire, Massachusetts, Rhode Island, Connecticut, New York, New Jersey, Pennsylvania, Delaware, Virginia, North Carolina, South Carolina, Georgia and Maryland. Clustered along the eastern seaboard of North America between the forests of Maine and the marshes of Georgia. Under the Article of Confederation, the United States had no national capital: Philadelphia, where the "United States in Congress Assembled", was the "seat of government". The population during this political phase of America's history (1781-1789) was about 3 million, most of whom lived on self-sufficient family farms. Fishing, lumbering and the production of grains for export were major economic endeavors. Rapid strides were also being made in industry and manufacturing by 1775, the (then) colonies were accounting for one-seventh of the world's production of raw iron.

On the basis of the voyage of John Cabot to the North American mainland in 1497, England claimed the entire continent. The first permanent English settlement was established at Jamestown, Virginia, in 1607. France and Spain also claimed extensive territory in North America. At the end of the French and Indian Wars (1763), England acquired all of the territory east of the Mississippi River, including East and West Florida. From 1776 to 1781, the States were governed by the Continental Congress. From 1781 to 1789, they were organized under the Articles of Confederation, during which period the individual States had the right to issue money. Independence from Great Britain was attained with the American Revolution in 1776. The Constitution organized and governs the present United States. It was ratified on Nov. 21, 1788.

MINT MARKS
D – Denver, CO, 1906-present
P – Philadelphia, PA, 1793-present
S – San Francisco, CA, 1854-present
W – West Point, NY, 1984-present

BULLION COINS
Silver Eagle = $1.00
Gold 1/10 Ounce = $5.00
Gold ¼ Ounce = $10.00
Gold ½ Ounce = $25.00
Gold Ounce = $50.00
Platinum 1/10 Ounce = $10.00
Platinum ¼ Ounce = $25.00
Platinum ½ Ounce = $50.00
Platinum Ounce = $100.00

CIRCULATION COINAGE

CENT

Lincoln Cent

Lincoln Memorial reverse

KM# 201b • **Copper Plated Zinc**, 19 mm. • **Notes:** MS60 prices are for brown coins and MS65 prices are for coins that are at least 90% original red.

Date	Mintage	XF-40	MS-65	Prf-65
2001	4,959,600,000	—	.25	—
2001D	5,374,990,000	—	.25	—
2001S	3,099,096	—	—	4.00
2002	3,260,800,000	—	.25	—
2002S	3,157,739	—	—	4.00
2002D	4,028,055,000	—	.25	—
2003	3,300,000,000	—	.25	—
2003D	3,548,000,000	—	.25	—
2003S	3,116,590	—	—	4.00
2004	3,379,600,000	—	.25	—
2004D	3,456,400,000	—	.25	—
2004S	2,992,069	—	—	4.00
2005	3,935,600,000	—	.25	—
2005D	3,764,450,000	—	.25	—
2005S	3,273,000	—	—	4.00
2006	4,290,000,000	—	.25	—
2006D	3,944,000,000	—	.25	—
2006S	2,923,105	—	—	4.00
2007	—	—	1.50	—
2007D	—	—	1.50	—
2007S	—	—	—	4.00
2008	—	—	1.50	—
2008D	—	—	1.50	—
2008S	—	—	—	4.00

Lincoln Bicentennial

Bust right obverse   Log cabin reverse

KM# 441 • 2.5000 g., **Copper Plated Zinc**, 19 mm. • **Rev. Designer:** Richard Masters and James Licaretz

Date	Mintage	XF-40	MS-65	Prf-65
2009P	284,400,000	—	1.50	—
2009D	350,400,000	—	1.50	—

KM# 441a • 3.3100 g., **Brass** • **Rev. Designer:** Richard Masters and James Licaretz

Date	Mintage	XF-40	MS-65	Prf-65
2009S	—	—	—	4.00

Lincoln seated on log reverse

KM# 442 • 2.5000 g., **Copper Plated Zinc**, 19 mm. • **Rev. Designer:** Charles Vickers

Date	Mintage	XF-40	MS-65	Prf-65
2009P	376,000,000	—	1.50	—
2009D	363,600,000	—	1.50	—

KM# 442a • 3.1100 g., **Brass**, 19 mm. • **Rev. Designer:** Charles Vickers

Date	Mintage	XF-40	MS-65	Prf-65
2009S	—	—	—	4.00

Lincoln standing before Illinois Statehouse reverse

KM# 443 • 2.5000 g., **Copper Plated Zinc**, 19 mm. • **Rev. Designer:** Joel Ishowitz and Don Everhart

Date	Mintage	XF-40	MS-65	Prf-65
2009P	316,000,000	—	1.50	—
2009D	336,000,000	—	1.50	—

KM# 443a • 3.1100 g., **Brass**, 19 mm. • **Rev. Designer:** Joel Iskowitz and Don Everhart

Date	Mintage	XF-40	MS-65	Prf-65
2009S	—	—	—	4.00

Capitol Building reverse

KM# 444 • 2.5000 g., **Copper Plated Zinc** • **Rev. Designer:** Susan Gamble and Joseph Menna

Date	Mintage	XF-40	MS-65	Prf-65
2009P	129,600,000	—	1.50	—
2009D	198,000,000	—	1.50	—

KM# 444a • 3.1100 g., **Brass**, 19 mm. • **Rev. Designer:** Susan Ganmble and Joseph Menna

Date	Mintage	XF-40	MS-65	Prf-65
2009S	—	—	—	4.00

Shield reverse

KM# 468 • 2.5000 g., **Copper Plated Zinc**, 19 mm. • **Obv. Designer:** Victor D. Brenner **Rev. Designer:** Lyndall Bass and Joseph Menna

Date	Mintage	XF-40	MS-65	Prf-65
2010P	—	—	1.50	—
2010D	—	—	1.50	—
2010S	—	—	—	4.00
2011P	—	—	1.50	—
2011D	—	—	1.50	—
2011S	—	—	—	4.00
2012P	—	—	1.50	—
2012D	—	—	1.50	—
2012S	—	—	—	4.00

5 CENTS

Jefferson Nickel

KM# A192 • 5.0000 g., **Copper-Nickel**, 21.2 mm. • **Designer:** Felix Schlag **Edge Desc:** Plain

Date	Mintage	XF-40	MS-65	Prf-65
2001P	675,704,000	—	.50	—
2001D	627,680,000	—	.50	—
2001S	3,099,096	—	—	4.00
2002P	539,280,000	—	.50	—
2002D	691,200,000	—	.50	—
2002S	3,157,739	—	—	2.00
2003P	441,840,000	—	.50	—
2003D	383,040,000	—	.50	—
2003S	3,116,590	—	—	2.00

Jefferson - Westward Expansion - Lewis & Clark Bicentennial

Jefferson era peace medal design: two clasped hands, pipe and hatchet reverse

KM# 360 • 5.0000 g., **Copper-Nickel**, 21.2 mm. • **Obv. Designer:** Felix Schlag **Rev. Designer:** Norman E. Nemeth

Date	Mintage	MS65	PRF65
2004P	361,440,000	1.50	—
2004D	372,000,000	1.50	—
2004S	—	—	10.00

Lewis and Clark's Keelboat reverse

KM# 361 • 5.0000 g., **Copper-Nickel**, 21.2 mm. • **Obv. Designer:** Felix Schlag **Rev. Designer:** Al Maletsky

Date	Mintage	MS65	PRF65
2004P	366,720,000	1.50	—
2004D	344,880,000	1.50	—
2004S	—	—	10.00

American Bison right reverse

KM# 368 • 5.0000 g., **Copper-Nickel**, 21.2 mm. • **Obv. Designer:** Joe Fitzgerald and Don Everhart II **Rev. Designer:** Jamie Franki and Norman E. Nemeth

Date	Mintage	MS65	PRF65
2005P	448,320,000	1.50	—
2005D	487,680,000	1.50	—
2005S	—	—	6.50

Pacific coastline reverse

KM# 369 • 5.0000 g., **Copper-Nickel**, 21.2 mm. • **Obv. Designer:** Joe Fitzgerald and Don Everhart **Rev. Designer:** Joe Fitzgerald and Donna Weaver

Date	Mintage	MS65	PRF65
2005P	394,080,000	1.25	—
2005D	411,120,000	1.25	—
2005S	—	—	5.50

Jefferson large facing portrait - Enhanced Monticello Reverse

KM# 381 • 5.0000 g., **Copper-Nickel**, 21.2 mm. • **Obv. Designer:** Jamie N. Franki and Donna Weaver **Rev. Designer:** Felix Schlag and John Mercanti

Date	Mintage	MS65	PRF65
2006P	693,120,000	2.50	—
2006P Satin finish	—	4.00	—
2006D	809,280,000	2.50	—
2006D Satin finish	—	4.00	—

Date	Mintage	MS65	PRF65
2006S	—	—	5.00
2007P	—	2.50	—
2007P Satin finish	—	4.00	—
2007D	—	2.50	—
2007D Satin finish	—	4.00	—
2007S	—	—	4.00
2008P	—	2.50	—
2008P Satin finish	—	4.00	—
2008D	—	2.50	—
2008D Satin finish	—	4.00	—
2008S	—	—	4.00
2009P	—	2.50	—
2009P Satin finish	—	4.00	—
2009D	—	2.50	—
2009D Satin finish	—	4.00	—
2009S	—	—	3.00
2010P	—	2.50	—
2010P Satin finish	—	4.00	—
2010D	—	2.50	—
2010D Satin finish	—	4.00	—
2010S	—	—	3.00
2011P	—	2.50	—
2011D	—	2.50	—
2011S	—	—	3.00
2012P	—	2.50	—
2012D	—	2.50	—
2012S	—	—	3.00

DIME

Roosevelt Dime

Mint mark 1968- present   1982 No mint mark

KM# 195a • 2.2680 g., **Copper-Nickel Clad Copper**, 17.91 mm. • **Designer:** John R. Sinnock **Notes:** The 1979-S and 1981-S Type II proofs have clearer mint marks than the Type I proofs of those years. On the 1982 no-mint-mark variety, the mint mark was inadvertently left off.

Date	Mintage	MS65	PRF65
2001P	1,369,590,000	2.75	—
2001D	1,412,800,000	2.75	—
2001S	2,249,496	—	3.75
2002P	1,187,500,000	2.75	—
2002D	1,379,500,000	3.00	—
2002S	2,268,913	—	2.50
2003P	1,085,500,000	3.00	—
2003D	986,500,000	3.00	—
2003S	2,076,165	—	2.60
2004P	1,328,000,000	3.00	—
2004D	1,159,500,000	3.00	—
2004S	1,804,396	—	4.75
2005P	1,412,000,000	2.75	—
2005P Satin Finish	—	4.00	—
2005D	1,423,500,000	2.75	—
2005D Satin Finish	—	4.00	—
2005S	—	—	2.60
2006P	1,381,000,000	2.50	—
2006P Satin Finish	—	4.00	—
2006D	1,447,000,000	2.50	—
2006D Satin Finish	—	4.00	—
2006S	—	—	2.50
2007P	—	2.00	—
2007P Satin Finish	—	3.00	—
2007D	—	2.00	—
2007D Satin Finish	—	3.00	—
2007S	—	—	2.50
2008P	—	1.25	—
2008 Satin Finish	—	2.50	—
2008D	—	1.25	—
2008 Satin Finish	—	2.50	—
2008S	—	—	2.50
2009P	—	1.25	—
2009 Satin Finish	—	1.00	—
2009D	—	1.25	—
2009 Satin Finish	—	1.00	—
2009S	—	—	2.50
2010P	—	4.00	—
2010P Satin Finish	—	2.00	—
2010D	—	4.00	—
2010D Satin Finish	—	2.00	—
2010S	—	—	2.50
2011P	—	4.00	—
2011P Satin Finish	—	2.00	—
2011D	—	4.00	—
2011D Satin Finish	—	2.00	—
2011S	—	—	2.50

Date	Mintage	MS65	PRF65
2012P	—	4.00	—
2012 Satin Finish	—	2.00	—
2012D	—	4.00	—
2012D Satin Finish	—	2.00	—
2012S	—	—	2.50

Roosevelt Dime

KM# 195b • 2.5000 g., 0.9000 **Silver**, 0.0723 oz. ASW, 17.9 mm. • **Designer:** John R. Sinnock

Date	Mintage	Prf-65
2001S	849,600	5.00
2002S	888,826	5.00
2003S	1,090,425	4.75
2004S	—	5.00
2005S	—	5.00
2006S	—	4.50
2007S	—	6.00
2008S	—	6.50
2009S	—	6.75
2010S	—	6.75
2011S	—	6.75

QUARTER

50 State Quarters

Kentucky

KM# 322 • 5.6700 g., **Copper-Nickel Clad Copper** •

Date	Mintage	MS-63	MS65	PRF65
2001P	353,000,000	1.00	6.50	—
2001D	370,564,000	1.00	7.00	—
2001S	3,094,140	—	—	4.00

KM# 322a • 6.2500 g., 0.9000 **Silver**, 0.1808 oz. ASW •

Date	Mintage	MS-63	MS65	PRF65
2001S	889,697	—	—	11.00

New York

KM# 318 • 5.6700 g., **Copper-Nickel Clad Copper** •

Date	Mintage	MS-63	MS-65	Prf-65
2001P	655,400,000	.80	5.50	—
2001D	619,640,000	.80	5.50	—
2001S	3,094,140	—	—	4.00

KM# 318a • 6.2500 g., 0.9000 **Silver**, 0.1808 oz. ASW •

Date	Mintage	MS-63	MS-65	Prf-65
2001S	889,697	—	—	11.00

North Carolina

KM# 319 • 5.6700 g., **Copper-Nickel Clad Copper** •

Date	Mintage	MS-63	MS-65	Prf-65
2001P	627,600,000	1.00	5.50	—
2001D	427,876,000	1.00	6.50	—
2001S	3,094,140	—	—	4.00

KM# 319a • 6.2500 g., 0.9000 **Silver**, 0.1808 oz. ASW •

Date	Mintage	MS-63	MS-65	Prf-65
2001S	889,697	—	—	11.00

Rhode Island

KM# 320 • 5.6700 g., **Copper-Nickel Clad Copper** •

Date	Mintage	MS-63	MS-65	Prf-65
2001P	423,000,000	.80	5.50	—
2001D	447,100,000	.80	6.00	—
2001S	3,094,140			4.00

KM# 320a • 6.2500 g., 0.9000 **Silver**, 0.1808 oz. ASW •

Date	Mintage	MS-63	MS-65	Prf-65
2001S	889,697	—	—	11.00

Vermont

KM# 321 • 5.6700 g., **Copper-Nickel Clad Copper** •

Date	Mintage	MS-63	MS-65	Prf-65
2001P	423,400,000	.80	6.50	—
2001D	459,404,000	.80	6.50	—
2001S	3,094,140	—	—	4.00

KM# 321a • 6.2500 g., 0.9000 **Silver**, 0.1808 oz. ASW •

Date	Mintage	MS-63	MS-65	Prf-65
2001S	889,697	—	—	11.00

Indiana

KM# 334 • 5.6700 g., **Copper-Nickel Clad Copper** •

Date	Mintage	MS-63	MS-65	Prf-65
2002P	362,600,000	.80	5.00	—
2002D	327,200,000	.80	5.00	—
2002S	3,084,245			2.30

KM# 334a • 6.2500 g., 0.9000 **Silver**, 0.1808 oz. ASW •

Date	Mintage	MS-63	MS-65	Prf-65
2002S	892,229	—	—	9.00

Louisiana

KM# 333 • 5.6700 g., **Copper-Nickel Clad Copper** •

Date	Mintage	MS-63	MS-65	Prf-65
2002P	362,000,000	.80	5.50	—
2002D	402,204,000	.80	6.00	—
2002S	3,084,245			2.30

KM# 333a • 6.2500 g., 0.9000 **Silver**, 0.1808 oz. ASW •

Date	Mintage	MS-63	MS-65	Prf-65
2002S	892,229	—	—	9.00

Mississippi

KM# 335 • 5.6700 g., **Copper-Nickel Clad Copper** •

Date	Mintage	MS-63	MS-65	Prf-65
2002P	290,000,000	.80	5.00	—
2002D	289,600,000	.80	5.00	—
2002S	3,084,245			2.30

KM# 335a • 6.2500 g., 0.9000 **Silver**, 0.1808 oz. ASW •

Date	Mintage	MS-63	MS-65	Prf-65
2002S	892,229	—	—	9.00

Ohio

KM# 332 • 5.6700 g., **Copper-Nickel Clad Copper** •

Date	Mintage	MS-63	MS-65	Prf-65
2002P	217,200,000	.80	5.50	—
2002D	414,832,000	.80	5.50	—
2002S	3,084,245			2.30

KM# 332a • 6.2500 g., 0.9000 **Silver**, 0.1808 oz. ASW •

Date	Mintage	MS-63	MS-65	Prf-65
2002S	892,229	—	—	9.00

Tennessee

KM# 331 • 5.6700 g., **Copper-Nickel Clad Copper** •

Date	Mintage	MS-63	MS-65	Prf-65
2002P	361,600,000	1.40	6.50	—
2002D	286,468,000	1.40	7.00	—
2002S	3,084,245			2.30

KM# 331a • 6.2500 g., 0.9000 **Silver**, 0.1808 oz. ASW •

Date	Mintage	MS-63	MS-65	Prf-65
2002S	892,229	—	—	9.00

Alabama

KM# 344 • 5.6700 g., **Copper-Nickel Clad Copper** •

Date	Mintage	MS-63	MS-65	Prf-65
2003P	225,000,000	.65	5.00	—
2003D	232,400,000	.65	5.00	—
2003S	3,408,516			2.30

KM# 344a • 6.2500 g., 0.9000 **Silver**, 0.1808 oz. ASW •

Date	Mintage	MS-63	MS-65	Prf-65
2003S	1,257,555	—	—	9.00

Arkansas

KM# 347 • 5.6700 g., **Copper-Nickel Clad Copper** •

Date	Mintage	MS-63	MS-65	Prf-65
2003P	228,000,000	.65	5.00	—
2003D	229,800,000	.65	5.00	—
2003S	3,408,516			2.30

KM# 347a • 6.2500 g., 0.9000 **Silver**, 0.1808 oz. ASW •

Date	Mintage	MS-63	MS-65	Prf-65
2003S	1,257,555	—	—	9.00

Illinois

KM# 343 • 5.6700 g., **Copper-Nickel Clad Copper** •

Date	Mintage	MS-63	MS-65	Prf-65
2003P	225,800,000	1.10	5.00	—
2003D	237,400,000	1.10	5.00	—
2003S	3,408,516			2.30

KM# 343a • 6.2500 g., 0.9000 **Silver**, 0.1808 oz. ASW •

Date	Mintage	MS-63	MS-65	Prf-65
2003S	1,257,555	—	—	9.00

Maine

KM# 345 • 5.6700 g., **Copper-Nickel Clad Copper** •

Date	Mintage	MS-63	MS-65	Prf-65
2003P	217,400,000	.65	5.00	—
2003D	213,400,000	.65	5.00	—
2003S	3,408,516			2.30

KM# 345a • 6.2500 g., 0.9000 **Silver**, 0.1808 oz. ASW •

Date	Mintage	MS-63	MS-65	Prf-65
2003S	1,257,555	—	—	9.00

Missouri

KM# 346 • **Copper-Nickel Clad Copper** •

Date	Mintage	MS-63	MS-65	Prf-65
2003P	225,000,000	.65	5.00	—
2003D	228,200,000	.65	5.00	—
2003S	3,408,516			2.30

KM# 346a • 6.2500 g., 0.9000 **Silver**, 0.1808 oz. ASW •

Date	Mintage	MS-63	MS-65	Prf-65
2003S	1,257,555	—	—	9.00

Florida

KM# 356 • 5.6700 g., **Copper-Nickel Clad Copper** •

Date	Mintage	MS-63	MS-65	Prf-65
2004P	240,200,000	.65	5.00	—
2004D	241,600,000	.65	5.00	—
2004S	2,740,684	—	—	2.30

KM# 356a • 6.2500 g., 0.9000 **Silver**, 0.1808 oz. ASW •

Date	Mintage	MS-63	MS-65	Prf-65
2004S	1,775,370	—	—	9.00

Iowa

KM# 358 • 5.6700 g., **Copper-Nickel Clad Copper** •

Date	Mintage	MS-63	MS-65	Prf-65
2004P	213,800,000	.65	5.00	—
2004D	251,800,000	.65	5.00	—
2004S	2,740,684	—	—	2.30

KM# 358a • 6.2500 g., 0.9000 **Silver**, 0.1808 oz. ASW •

Date	Mintage	MS-63	MS-65	Prf-65
2004S	—	—	—	9.00

Michigan

KM# 355 • 5.6700 g., **Copper-Nickel Clad Copper** •

Date	Mintage	MS-63	MS-65	Prf-65
2004P	233,800,000	.65	5.00	—
2004D	225,800,000	.65	5.00	—
2004S	2,740,684	—	—	2.30

KM# 355a • 6.2500 g., 0.9000 **Silver**, 0.1808 oz. ASW •

Date	Mintage	MS-63	MS-65	Prf-65
2004S	1,775,370	—	—	9.00

Texas

KM# 357 • 5.6700 g., **Copper-Nickel Clad Copper** •

Date	Mintage	MS-63	MS-65	Prf-65
2004P	278,800,000	.65	5.00	—
2004D	263,000,000	.65	5.00	—
2004S	2,740,684	—	—	2.30

KM# 357a • 6.2500 g., 0.9000 **Silver**, 0.1808 oz. ASW •

Date	Mintage	MS-63	MS-65	Prf-65
2004S	1,775,370	—	—	9.00

Wisconsin

KM# 359 • 5.6700 g., **Copper-Nickel Clad Copper** •

Date	Mintage	MS-63	MS-65	Prf-65
2004P	226,400,000	.65	5.00	—
2004D	226,800,000	.65	5.00	—
2004D Extra Leaf Low	Est. 9,000	175	275	—
2004D Extra Leaf High	Est. 3,000	200	400	—
2004S		—	—	2.30

KM# 359a • 6.2500 g., 0.9000 **Silver**, 0.1808 oz. ASW •

Date	Mintage	MS-63	MS-65	Prf-65
2004S	1,775,370	—	—	9.00

California

KM# 370 • 5.6700 g., **Copper-Nickel Clad Copper** •

Date	Mintage	MS-63	MS-65	Prf-65
2005P	257,200,000	.65	5.00	—
2005P Satin Finish	Inc. above	2.00	4.50	—
2005D	263,200,000	.65	5.00	—
2005D Satin Finish	Inc. above	2.00	4.50	—
2005S	3,262,960	—	—	2.30

KM# 370a • 6.2500 g., 0.9000 **Silver**, 0.1808 oz. ASW •

Date	Mintage	MS-63	MS-65	Prf-65
2005S	1,679,600	—	—	9.00

Kansas

KM# 373 • 5.6700 g., **Copper-Nickel Clad Copper** •

Date	Mintage	MS-63	MS-65	Prf-65
2005P	263,400,000	.65	5.00	—
2005P Satin Finish	Inc. above	2.00	4.50	—
2005D	300,000,000	.65	5.00	—
2005D Satin Finish	Inc. above	2.00	4.50	—
2005S	3,262,960	—	—	2.30

KM# 373a • 6.2500 g., 0.9000 **Silver**, 0.1808 oz. ASW •

Date	Mintage	MS-63	MS-65	Prf-65
2005S	1,679,600	—	—	9.00

Minnesota

KM# 371 • 5.6700 g., **Copper-Nickel Clad Copper** •

Date	Mintage	MS-63	MS-65	Prf-65
2005P	226,400,000	.65	5.00	—
2005P Satin Finish	Inc. above	2.00	4.50	—
2005D	226,800,000	.65	5.00	—
2005D Satin Finish	Inc. above	2.00	4.50	—
2005S	3,262,960	—	—	2.30

KM# 371a • 6.2500 g., 0.9000 **Silver**, 0.1808 oz. ASW •

Date	Mintage	MS-63	MS-65	Prf-65
2005S	1,679,600	—	—	9.00

Oregon

KM# 372 • 5.6700 g., **Copper-Nickel Clad Copper** •

Date	Mintage	MS-63	MS-65	Prf-65
2005P	316,200,000	.65	5.00	—
2005P Satin Finish	Inc. above	2.00	4.50	—
2005D	404,000,000	.65	5.00	—
2005D Satin Finish	Inc. above	2.00	4.50	—
2005S	3,262,960	—	—	2.30

KM# 372a • 6.2500 g., 0.9000 **Silver**, 0.1808 oz. ASW •

Date	Mintage	MS-63	MS-65	Prf-65
2005S	1,679,600	—	—	9.00

West Virginia

KM# 374 • 5.6700 g., **Copper-Nickel Clad Copper** •

Date	Mintage	MS-63	MS-65	Prf-65
2005P	365,400,000	.65	5.00	—
2005P Satin Finish	Inc. above	2.00	4.50	—
2005D	356,200,000	.65	5.00	—
2005D Satin Finish	Inc. above	2.00	4.50	—
2005S	3,262,960	—	—	2.30

KM# 374a • 6.2500 g., 0.9000 **Silver**, 0.1808 oz. ASW •

Date	Mintage	MS-63	MS-65	Prf-65
2005S	1,679,600	—	—	6.00

Colorado

KM# 384 • 5.7100 g., **Copper-Nickel Clad Copper**, 24.2 mm. •

Date	Mintage	MS-63	MS-65	Prf-65
2006P	274,800,000	.65	5.00	—
2006P Satin Finish	Inc. above	2.00	4.50	—
2006D	294,200,000	.65	5.00	—
2006D Satin Finish	Inc. above	2.00	4.50	—
2006S	2,862,078	—	—	2.30

KM# 384a • 6.2500 g., 0.9000 **Silver**, 0.1808 oz. ASW •

Date	Mintage	MS-63	MS-65	Prf-65
2006S	1,571,839	—	—	9.00

Nebraska

KM# 383 • 5.6700 g., **Copper-Nickel Clad Copper** •

Date	Mintage	MS-63	MS-65	Prf-65
2006P	318,000,000	.65	5.00	—
2006P Satin Finish	Inc. above	2.00	4.50	—
2006D	273,000,000	.65	5.00	—
2006D Satin Finish	Inc. above	2.00	4.50	—
2006S	2,862,078	—	—	2.30

KM# 383a • 6.2500 g., 0.9000 **Silver**, 0.1808 oz. ASW •

Date	Mintage	MS-63	MS-65	Prf-65
2006S	1,571,839	—	—	9.00

Nevada

KM# 382 • 5.6700 g., Copper-Nickel Clad Copper •

Date	Mintage	MS-63	MS-65	Prf-65
2006P	277,000,000	.65	5.00	—
2006P Satin Finish	Inc. above	2.00	4.50	—
2006D	312,800,000	.65	5.00	—
2006D Satin Finish	Inc. above	2.00	4.50	—
2006S	2,862,078	—	—	2.30

KM# 382a • 6.2500 g., 0.9000 Silver, 0.1808 oz. ASW •

Date	Mintage	MS-63	MS-65	Prf-65
2006S	1,571,839	—	—	9.00

Montana

KM# 396 • 5.6700 g., Copper-Nickel Clad Copper •

Date	Mintage	MS-63	MS-65	Prf-65
2007 Satin Finish	—	—	—	—
2007 Satin Finish	—	—	—	—
2007P	257,000,000	.65	8.00	—
2007D	256,240,000	.65	5.00	—
2007S	2,374,778	—	—	2.30

KM# 396a • 6.2500 g., 0.9000 Silver, 0.1808 oz. ASW •

Date	Mintage	MS-63	MS-65	Prf-65
2007S	1,299,878	—	—	9.00

Alaska

KM# 424 • 5.6700 g., Copper-Nickel Clad Copper •

Date	Mintage	MS-63	MS-65	Prf-65
2008P	251,800,000	.65	5.00	—
2008P Satin finish	—	2.00	4.50	—
2008D	254,000,000	.65	5.00	—
2008D Satin finish	—	2.00	4.50	—
2008S	2,100,000	—	—	2.30

KM# 424a • 6.2500 g., 0.9000 Silver, 0.1808 oz. ASW •

Date	Mintage	MS-63	MS-65	Prf-65
2008S	1,200,000	—	—	9.00

North Dakota

KM# 385 • 5.7200 g., Copper-Nickel Clad Copper, 24.2 mm. •

Date	Mintage	MS-63	MS-65	Prf-65
2006P	305,800,000	.65	5.00	—
2006P Satin Finish	Inc. above	2.00	4.50	—
2006D	359,000,000	.65	5.00	—
2006D Satin Finish	Inc. above	2.00	4.50	—
2006S	2,862,078	—	—	2.30

KM# 385a • 6.2500 g., 0.9000 Silver, 0.1808 oz. ASW •

Date	Mintage	MS-63	MS-65	Prf-65
2006S	1,571,839	—	—	9.00

Utah

KM# 400 • Copper-Nickel Clad Copper •

Date	Mintage	MS-63	MS-65	Prf-65
2007P	255,000,000	.65	5.00	—
2007P Satin finish	—	2.00	4.50	—
2007D	253,200,000	.65	5.00	—
2007CC Satin finish	—	2.00	4.50	—
2007S	2,374,778	—	—	2.30

KM# 400a • 6.2500 g., 0.9000 Silver, 0.1808 oz. ASW •

Date	Mintage	MS-63	MS-65	Prf-65
2007S	1,299,878	—	—	9.00

Arizona

KM# 423 • 5.6700 g., Copper-Nickel Clad Copper •

Date	Mintage	MS-63	MS-65	Prf-65
2008P	244,600,000	.65	5.00	—
2008P Satin finish	—	2.00	4.50	—
2008D	265,000,000	.65	5.00	—
2008D Satin finish	—	2.00	4.50	—
2008S	2,100,000	—	—	2.30

KM# 423a • 6.2500 g., 0.9000 Silver, 0.1808 oz. ASW •

Date	Mintage	MS-63	MS-65	Prf-65
2008S	1,200,000	—	—	9.00

South Dakota

KM# 386 • 5.6500 g., Copper-Nickel Clad Copper, 24.3 mm. •

Date	Mintage	MS-63	MS-65	Prf-65
2006P	245,000,000	.65	5.00	—
2006P Satin Finish	Inc. above	2.00	4.50	—
2006D	265,800,000	.65	5.00	—
2006D Satin Finish	Inc. above	2.00	4.50	—
2006S	2,862,078	—	—	2.30

KM# 386a • 6.2500 g., 0.9000 Silver, 0.1808 oz. ASW •

Date	Mintage	MS-63	MS-65	Prf-65
2006S	1,571,839	—	—	9.00

Washington

 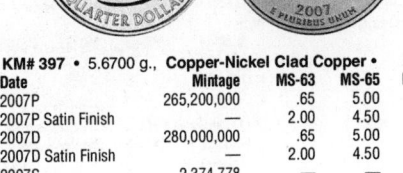

KM# 397 • 5.6700 g., Copper-Nickel Clad Copper •

Date	Mintage	MS-63	MS-65	Prf-65
2007P	265,200,000	.65	5.00	—
2007P Satin Finish	—	2.00	4.50	—
2007D	280,000,000	.65	5.00	—
2007D Satin Finish	—	2.00	4.50	—
2007S	2,374,778	—	—	2.30

KM# 397a • 6.2500 g., 0.9000 Silver, 0.1808 oz. ASW •

Date	Mintage	MS-63	MS-65	Prf-65
2007S	1,299,878	—	—	9.00

Hawaii

KM# 425 • 5.6700 g., Copper-Nickel Clad Copper •

Date	Mintage	MS-63	MS-65	Prf-65
2008P	254,000,000	.65	5.00	—
2008P Satin finish	—	2.00	4.50	—
2008D	263,600,000	.65	5.00	—
2008D Satin finish	—	2.00	4.50	—
2008S	2,100,000	—	—	2.30

KM# 425a • 6.2500 g., 0.9000 Silver, 0.1808 oz. ASW •

Date	Mintage	MS-63	MS-65	Prf-65
2008S	1,200,000	—	—	9.00

Idaho

KM# 398 • 5.6700 g., Copper-Nickel Clad Copper •

Date	Mintage	MS-63	MS-65	Prf-65
2007P	294,600,000	.65	5.00	—
2007P Satin finish	—	2.00	4.50	—
2007D	286,800,000	.65	5.00	—
2007D Satin finish	—	2.00	4.50	—
2007S	2,374,778	—	—	2.30

KM# 398a • 6.2500 g., 0.9000 Silver, 0.1808 oz. ASW •

Date	Mintage	MS-63	MS-65	Prf-65
2007S	1,299,878	—	—	9.00

Wyoming

KM# 399 • 5.6700 g., Copper-Nickel Clad Copper •

Date	Mintage	MS-63	MS-65	Prf-65
2007P	243,600,000	.65	5.00	—
2007P Satin finish	—	2.00	4.50	—
2007D	320,800,000	.65	5.00	—
2007 Satin finish	—	2.00	4.50	—
2007S	2,374,778	—	—	2.30

KM# 399a • 6.2500 g., 0.9000 Silver, 0.1808 oz. ASW •

Date	Mintage	MS-63	MS-65	Prf-65
2007S	1,299,878	—	—	9.00

New Mexico

KM# 422 • 5.6700 g., Copper-Nickel Clad Copper •

Date	Mintage	MS-63	MS-65	Prf-65
2008P	244,200,000	.65	5.00	—
2008P Satin finish	—	2.00	4.50	—
2008D	244,400,000	.65	5.00	—
2008D Satin finish	—	2.00	4.50	—
2008S	2,100,000	—	—	2.30

KM# 422a • 6.2500 g., 0.9000 Silver, 0.1808 oz. ASW •

Date	Mintage	MS-63	MS-65	Prf-65
2008S	1,200,000	—	—	9.00

Oklahoma

KM# 421 • 5.6700 g., **Copper-Nickel Clad Copper** •

Date	Mintage	MS-63	MS-65	Prf-65
2008P	222,000,000	.65	5.00	—
2008P Satin finish	—	2.00	4.50	—
2008D	194,600,000	.65	5.00	—
2008D Satin finish	—	2.00	4.50	—
2008S	2,100,000	—	—	2.30

KM# 421a • 6.2500 g., 0.9000 **Silver**, 0.1808 oz. ASW •

Date	Mintage	MS-63	MS-65	Prf-65
2008S	1,200,000	—	—	9.00

DC and Territories

American Samoa

KM# 448 • 5.6700 g., **Copper-Nickel Clad Copper**, 24 mm. •
Rev. Designer: Charles Vickers

Date	Mintage	MS-63	MS-65	Prf-65
2009P	42,600,000	.75	5.00	—
2009D	39,600,000	.75	5.00	—
2009S	—	—	—	3.75

KM# 448a • 6.2500 g., 0.9000 **Silver**, 0.1808 oz. ASW, 24 mm. •

Date	Mintage	MS-63	MS-65	Prf-65
2009S	—	—	—	7.75

District of Columbia

KM# 445 • 5.6700 g., **Copper-Nickel Clad Copper**, 24 mm. •
Rev. Designer: Don Everhart

Date	Mintage	MS-63	MS-65	Prf-65
2009P	83,600,000	.75	5.00	—
2009D	88,800,000	.75	5.00	—
2009S	—	—	—	3.75

KM# 445a • 6.2500 g., 0.9000 **Silver**, 0.1808 oz. ASW, 24 mm. •

Date	Mintage	MS-63	MS-65	Prf-65
2009S	—	—	—	7.75

Guam

KM# 447 • 5.6700 g., **Copper-Nickel Clad Copper**, 24 mm. •
Rev. Designer: James Licaretz

Date	Mintage	MS-63	MS-65	Prf-65
2009P	45,000,000	.75	5.00	—
2009D	42,600,000	.75	5.00	—
2009S	—	—	—	3.75

KM# 447a • 6.2500 g., 0.9000 **Silver**, 0.1808 oz. ASW, 24 mm. •

Date	Mintage	MS-63	MS-65	Prf-65
2009S	—	—	—	7.75

Northern Mariana Islands

KM# 466 • 5.6700 g., **Copper-Nickel Clad Copper** • **Rev. Designer:** Pheve Hemphill

Date	Mintage	MS-63	MS-65	Prf-65
2009P	35,200,000	.75	5.00	—
2009D	37,600,000	.75	5.00	—
2009S	—	—	—	3.75

KM# 466a • 6.2500 g., 0.9000 **Silver**, 0.1808 oz. ASW •

Date	Mintage	MS-63	MS-65	Prf-65
2009S	—	—	—	7.75

Puerto Rico

KM# 446 • 5.6700 g., **Copper-Nickel Clad Copper**, 24 mm. •
Rev. Designer: Joseph Menna

Date	Mintage	MS-63	MS-65	Prf-65
2009P	53,200,000	.75	5.00	—
2009D	86,000,000	.75	5.00	—
2009S	—	—	—	3.75

KM# 446a • 6.2500 g., 0.9000 **Silver**, 0.1808 oz. ASW, 24 mm. •

Date	Mintage	MS-63	MS-65	Prf-65
2009S	—	—	—	7.75

US Virgin Islands

KM# 449 • 5.6700 g., **Copper-Nickel Clad Copper**, 24 mm. •
Rev. Designer: Joseph Menna

Date	Mintage	MS-63	MS-65	Prf-65
2009P	41,000,000	.75	5.00	—
2009D	41,000,000	.75	5.00	—
2009S	—	—	—	3.75

KM# 449a • 6.2500 g., 0.9000 **Silver**, 0.1808 oz. ASW, 24 mm. •

Date	Mintage	MS-63	MS-65	Prf-65
2009S	—	—	—	7.75

America the Beautiful

Grand Canyon National Park

KM# 472 • 5.6700 g., **Copper-Nickel Clad Copper**, 24.3 mm. •

Date	Mintage	MS-63	MS-65	Prf-65
2010P	—	.75	5.00	—
2010D	—	.75	5.00	—
2010S	—	—	—	3.75

KM# 472a • 6.2500 g., 0.9000 **Silver**, 0.1808 oz. ASW •

Date	Mintage	MS-63	MS-65	Prf-65
2010	—	—	—	7.75

Hot Springs, Ark.

KM# 469 • 5.6700 g., **Copper-Nickel Clad Copper**, 24.3 mm. •

Date	Mintage	MS-63	MS-65	Prf-65
2010P	—	.75	5.00	—
2010D	—	.75	5.00	—
2010S	—	—	—	3.75

KM# 469a • 6.2500 g., 0.9000 **Silver**, 0.1808 oz. ASW •

Date	Mintage	MS-63	MS-65	Prf-65
2010S	—	—	—	7.75

Mount Hood National Park

KM# 473 • 5.6700 g., **Copper-Nickel Clad Copper** •

Date	Mintage	MS-63	MS-65	Prf-65
2010P	—	.75	5.00	—
2010D	—	.75	5.00	—
2010S	—	—	—	3.75

KM# 473a • 6.2500 g., 0.9000 **Silver**, 0.1808 oz. ASW •

Date	Mintage	MS-63	MS-65	Prf-65
2010	—	—	—	7.75

Yellowstone National Park

KM# 470 • 5.6700 g., **Copper-Nickel Clad Copper**, 24.3 mm. •

Date	Mintage	MS-63	MS-65	Prf-65
2010P	—	.75	5.00	—
2010D	—	.75	5.00	—
2010S	—	—	—	3.75

KM# 470a • 6.2500 g., 0.9000 **Silver**, 0.1808 oz. ASW •

Date	Mintage	MS-63	MS-65	Prf-65
2010	—	—	—	7.75

Yosemite National Park

KM# 471 • 5.6700 g., **Copper-Nickel Clad Copper**, 24.3 mm. •

Date	Mintage	MS-63	MS-65	Prf-65
2010P	—	.75	5.00	—
2010D	—	.75	5.00	—
2010S	—	—	—	3.75

KM# 471a • 6.2500 g., 0.9000 **Silver**, 0.1808 oz. ASW •

Date	Mintage	MS-63	MS-65	Prf-65
2010	—	—	—	7.75

Chickasaw National Recreation Area

KM# 498 • 5.6700 g., **Copper-Nickel Clad Copper**, 24 mm. •

Date	Mintage	MS-63	MS-65	Prf-65
2011P	—	.75	5.00	—
2011D	—	.75	5.00	—
2011S	—	—	—	3.75

KM# 498a • 6.2500 g., 0.9000 **Silver**, 0.1808 oz. ASW •

Date	Mintage	MS-63	MS-65	Prf-65
2011S	—	—	—	7.75

Gettysburg National Military Park

KM# 494 • 5.6700 g., **Copper-Nickel Clad Copper**, 24 mm. •

Date	Mintage	MS-63	MS-65	Prf-65
2011P	—	.75	5.00	—
2011D	—	.75	5.00	—
2011S	—	—	—	3.75

KM# 494a • 6.2500 g., 0.9000 **Silver**, 0.1808 oz. ASW •

Date	Mintage	MS-63	MS-65	Prf-65
2011S	—	—	—	7.75

Glacier National Park

KM# 495 • 5.6700 g., **Copper-Nickel Clad Copper**, 24 mm. •

Date	Mintage	MS-63	MS-65	Prf-65
2011P	—	.75	5.00	—
2011D	—	.75	5.00	—
2011S	—	—	—	3.75

KM# 495a • 6.2500 g., 0.9000 **Silver**, 0.1808 oz. ASW •

Date	Mintage	MS-63	MS-65	Prf-65
2011S	—	—	—	7.75

Olympic National Park

KM# 496 • 5.6700 g., **Copper-Nickel Clad Copper**, 24 mm. •

Date	Mintage	MS-63	MS-65	Prf-65
2011P	—	.75	5.00	—
2011D	—	.75	5.00	—
2011S	—	—	—	3.75

KM# 496a • 6.2500 g., 0.9000 **Silver**, 0.1808 oz. ASW •

Date	Mintage	MS-63	MS-65	Prf-65
2011S	—	—	—	7.75

Vicksburg National Military Park

KM# 497 • 5.6700 g., **Copper-Nickel Clad Copper**, 24 mm. •

Date	Mintage	MS-63	MS-65	Prf-65
2011P	—	.75	5.00	—
2011D	—	.75	5.00	—
2011S	—	—	—	3.75

KM# 497a • 6.2500 g., 0.9000 **Silver**, 0.1808 oz. ASW •

Date	Mintage	MS-63	MS-65	Prf-65
2011S	—	—	—	7.75

Acadia National Park

KM# 521 • 5.6700 g., **Copper-Nickel Clad Copper**, 24.3 mm. •

Date	Mintage	MS-63	MS-65	Prf-65
2012P	—	.75	5.00	—
2012D	—	.75	5.00	—
2012S	—	—	—	3.75

KM# 521a • 6.2500 g., 0.9000 **Silver**, 0.1808 oz. ASW, 24.3 mm. •

Date	Mintage	MS-63	MS-65	Prf-65
2012S	—	—	—	7.75

Chaco Culture National Historic Park

KM# 520 • 5.7100 g., **Copper-Nickel Clad Copper**, 24.3 mm. •

Date	Mintage	MS-63	MS-65	Prf-65
2012P	—	.75	8.00	—
2012D	—	.75	8.00	—
2012S	—	—	—	4.00

KM# 520a • 6.2500 g., 0.9000 **Silver**, 0.1808 oz. ASW, 24.3 mm. •

Date	Mintage	MS-63	MS-65	Prf-65
2012	—	—	—	7.75

Denali National Park

KM# 523 • 5.6700 g., **Copper-Nickel Clad Copper**, 24.3 mm. •

Date	Mintage	MS-63	MS-65	Prf-65
2012P	—	.75	5.00	—
2012D	—	.75	5.00	—
2012S	—	—	—	3.75

KM# 523a • 6.2500 g., 0.9000 **Silver**, 0.1808 oz. ASW, 24.3 mm. •

Date	Mintage	MS-63	MS-65	Prf-65
2012	—	—	—	7.75

El Yunque National Forest

KM# 519 • 5.6700 g., **Copper-Nickel Clad Copper**, 24.3 mm. •

Date	Mintage	MS-63	MS-65	Prf-65
2012P	—	.75	5.00	—
2012D	—	.75	5.00	—
2012S	—	—	—	3.75

KM# 519a • 6.2500 g., 0.9000 **Silver**, 0.1808 oz. ASW, 24.3 mm. •

Date	Mintage	MS-63	MS-65	Prf-65
2012S	—	—	—	7.75

Hawai'i Volcanoes National Park

KM# 522 • 5.6700 g., **Copper-Nickel Clad Copper**, 24.3 mm. •

Date	Mintage	MS-63	MS-65	Prf-65
2012P	—	.75	5.00	—
2012D	—	.75	5.00	—
2012S	—	—	—	3.75

KM# 522a • 6.2500 g., 0.9000 **Silver**, 0.1808 oz. ASW, 24.3 mm. •

Date	Mintage	MS-63	MS-65	Prf-65
2012	—	—	—	7.75

HALF DOLLAR

Kennedy Half Dollar

KM# A202b • 11.1000 g., **Copper-Nickel Clad Copper**, 30.4 mm. • **Edge Desc:** Reeded **Notes:** KM#202b design and composition resumed. The 1979-S and 1981-S Type II proofs have clearer mint marks than the Type I proofs of those years.

Date	Mintage	MS65	PRF65
2001P	21,200,000	10.00	—
2001D	19,504,000	9.00	—
2001S	2,235,000	—	5.00
2002P	3,100,000	10.00	—
2002D	2,500,000	10.50	—
2002S	2,268,913	—	5.00
2003P	2,500,000	6.00	—
2003D	2,500,000	6.00	—
2003S	2,076,165	—	5.00
2004P	2,900,000	4.50	—
2004D	2,900,000	4.50	—
2004S	1,789,488	—	6.00
2005P	3,800,000	6.00	—
2005P Satin finish	1,160,000	8.00	—
2005D	3,500,000	5.00	—
2005D Satin finish	1,160,000	10.00	—
2005S	2,275,000	—	5.00
2006P	2,400,000	4.50	—
2006P Satin finish	847,361	12.00	—
2006D	2,000,000	4.50	—
2006D Satin finish	847,361	14.00	—
2006S	1,934,965	—	6.00
2007P	—	4.50	—
2007P Satin finish	—	8.00	—
2007D	—	4.50	—
2007D Satin finish	—	8.00	—
2007S	—	—	6.00
2008P	—	4.50	—
2008P Satin finish	—	8.50	—
2008D	—	4.50	—
2008D Satin finish	—	8.50	—
2008S	—	—	9.00
2009P	—	4.50	—
2009P Satin finish	—	8.50	—
2009D	—	4.50	—
2009D Satin finish	—	8.50	—
2009S	—	—	6.00
2010P	—	4.50	—
2010P Satin finish	—	8.50	—
2010D	—	4.50	—
2010D Satin finish	—	8.50	—
2010S	—	—	13.00
2011P	—	4.50	—
2011P Satin finish	—	8.50	—
2011D	—	4.50	—
2011D Satin finish	—	8.50	—
2011S	—	—	9.00
2012P	—	4.50	—
2012P Satin finish	—	8.50	—
2012D	—	4.50	—
2012D Satin finish	—	8.50	—
2012S	—	—	—

KM# A202c • 12.5000 g., 0.9000 **Silver**, 0.3617 oz. ASW, 30.6 mm. • **Designer:** Gilroy Roberts

Date	Mintage	Prf-65
2001S	849,600	14.00
2002S	888,816	14.00
2003S	1,040,425	14.00
2004S	1,175,935	14.00
2005S	1,069,679	15.00
2006S	988,140	15.00
2007S	1,384,797	16.50
2008S	620,684	15.00
2009S	—	14.00
2010S	—	15.00
2011S	—	15.00

DOLLAR

Sacagawea Dollar

Eagle in flight left reverse

KM# 310 • 8.0700 g., Copper-Zinc-Manganese-Nickel Clad Copper, 26.5 mm. •

Date	Mintage	MS65	PRF65
2001P	62,468,000	2.00	
2001D	70,939,500	2.00	
2001S	3,190,000	—	100.00
2002P	3,865,610	2.00	
2002D	3,732,000	2.00	
2002S	3,210,000	—	28.50
2003P	3,080,000	3.00	
2003D	3,080,000	3.00	
2003S	3,300,000	—	20.00
2004P	2,660,000	2.50	
2004D	2,660,000	2.50	
2004S	2,965,000	—	22.50
2005P	2,520,000	2.50	
2005D	2,520,000	2.50	
2005S	3,273,000	—	22.50
2006P	4,900,000	2.50	
2006D	2,800,000	5.00	
2006S	3,028,828	—	22.50
2007P	3,640,000	2.50	
2007D	3,920,000	2.50	
2007S	2,563,563	—	22.50
2008P	9,800,000	2.50	
2008D	14,840,000	2.50	
2008S	—	—	22.50

Native American female planting corn, beans and squash reverse

KM# 467 • 8.0700 g., Copper-Zinc-Manganese-Nickel Clad Copper, 26.5 mm. • **Edge Lettering:** E PLURIBUS UNUM, date, mint mark **Notes:** Date and mint mark on edge

Date	Mintage	MS65	PRF65
2009P	37,380,000	2.00	
2009D	33,880,000	2.00	
2009S	—	—	22.50

Hiawatha belt and bundle of five arrows reverse

KM# 474 • 8.0700 g., Copper-Zinc-Manganese-Nickel Clad Copper, 26.5 mm. • **Edge Lettering:** E PLURIBUS UNUM, date, mint mark **Notes:** Date and mint mark on edge

Date	Mintage	MS65	PRF65
2010P	—	2.00	

Date	Mintage	MS65	PRF65
2010D	—	2.00	
2010S	—	—	22.50

Hands passing peace pipe reverse

KM# 503 • 8.0700 g., Copper-Zinc-Manganese-Nickel Clad Copper, 26.5 mm. • **Obv. Designer:** Glenna Goodacre **Rev. Designer:** Richard Masters and Joseph Menna **Edge Lettering:** E PLURIBUS UNUM, date, mint mark **Notes:** Date and mint mark on edge

Date	Mintage	MS65	PRF65
2011P	—	2.00	
2011D	—	2.00	
2011S	—	—	8.00

Horse and Native American profile facing left reverse

KM# 528 • 8.0700 g., Copper-Zinc-Manganese-Nickel Clad Copper, 26.5 mm. • **Edge Lettering:** E PLURIBUS UNUM, date, mint mark **Notes:** Date and mint mark on edge

Date	Mintage	MS65	PRF65
2012P	—	2.00	
2012D	—	2.00	
2012S	—	—	8.00

Presidents

George Washington

KM# 401 • 8.0700 g., Copper-Zinc-Manganese-Nickel Clad Copper, 26.5 mm. • **Edge Lettering:** IN GOD WE TRUST date, mint mark E PLURIBUS UNUM **Notes:** Date and mint mark incuse on edge.

Date	Mintage	MS-63	MS-65	Prf-65
2007P	176,680,000	2.00	5.00	
(2007) Plain edge error	Inc. above	75.00	—	
2007D	163,680,000	2.00	5.00	
2007S	3,883,103	—	—	5.00

James Madison

KM# 404 • 8.0700 g., Copper-Zinc-Manganese-Nickel Clad Copper, 26.5 mm. • **Edge Lettering:** IN GOD WE TRUST date, mint mark E PLURIBUS UNUM **Notes:** Date and mint mark incuse on edge.

Date	Mintage	MS-63	MS-65	Prf-65
2007P	84,560,000	2.00	5.00	
2007D	87,780,000	2.00	5.00	
2007S	3,876,829	—	—	5.00

John Adams

KM# 402 • 8.0700 g., Copper-Zinc-Manganese-Nickel Clad Copper, 26.5 mm. • **Edge Lettering:** IN GOD WE TRUST date, mint mark E PLURIBUS UNUM **Notes:** Date and mint mark incuse on edge.

Date	Mintage	MS-63	MS-65	Prf-65
2007P	112,420,000	2.00	5.00	
2007P Double edge lettering	Inc. above	250	—	
2007D	112,140,000	2.00	5.00	
2007S	3,877,409	—	—	5.00

Thomas Jefferson

KM# 403 • 8.0700 g., Copper-Zinc-Manganese-Nickel Clad Copper, 26.5 mm. • **Edge Lettering:** IN GOD WE TRUST date, mint mark E PLURIBUS UNUM **Notes:** Date and mint mark incuse on edge.

Date	Mintage	MS-63	MS-65	Prf-65
2007P	100,800,000	2.00	5.00	
2007D	102,810,000	2.00	5.00	
2007S	3,877,573	—	—	5.00

Andrew Jackson

KM# 428 • 8.0700 g., Copper-Zinc-Manganese-Nickel Clad Copper, 26.5 mm. • **Edge Lettering:** IN GOD WE TRUST date, mint mark E PLURIBUS UNUM **Notes:** Date and mint mark incuse on edge.

Date	Mintage	MS-63	MS-65	Prf-65
2008P	61,180,000	2.00	5.00	
2008D	61,070,000	2.00	5.00	
2008S	3,000,000	—	—	5.00

James Monroe

KM# 426 • 8.0700 g., Copper-Zinc-Manganese-Nickel Clad Copper, Date and mint mark incuse on edge., 26.5 mm. • **Edge Lettering:** IN GOD WE TRUST date, mint mark E PLURIBUS UNUM

Date	Mintage	MS-63	MS-65	Prf-65
2008P	64,260,000	2.00	5.00	
2008D	60,230,000	2.00	5.00	
2008S	3,000,000	—	—	5.00

John Quincy Adams

KM# 427 • 8.0700 g., **Copper-Zinc-Manganese-Nickel Clad Copper**, 26.5 mm. • **Edge Lettering:**IN GOD WE TRUST date, mint mark E PLURIBUS UNUM **Notes:** Date and mint mark incuse on edge.

Date	Mintage	MS-63	MS-65	Prf-65
2008P	57,540,000	2.00	5.00	—
2008D	57,720,000	2.00	5.00	—
2008S	3,000,000	—	—	5.00

Martin van Buren

KM# 429 • 8.0700 g., **Copper-Zinc-Manganese-Nickel Clad Copper**, 26.5 mm. • **Edge Lettering:**IN GOD WE TRUST date, mint mark E PLURIBUS UNUM **Notes:** Date and mint mark incuse on edge.

Date	Mintage	MS-63	MS-65	Prf-65
2008P	51,520,000	2.00	5.00	—
2008D	50,960,000	2.00	5.00	—
2008S	3,000,000	—	—	5.00

James K. Polk

KM# 452 • 8.0700 g., **Copper-Zinc-Manganese-Nickel Clad Copper**, 26.5 mm. • **Edge Lettering:**E PLURIBUS UNUM, date, mint mark **Notes:** Date and mint mark on edge

Date	Mintage	MS-63	MS-65	Prf-65
2009P	46,620,000	2.00	5.00	—
2009D	41,720,000	2.00	5.00	—
2009S	—	—	—	5.00

John Tyler

KM# 451 • 8.0700 g., **Copper-Zinc-Manganese-Nickel Clad Copper**, 26.5 mm. • **Edge Lettering:**E PLURIBUS UNUM, date, mint mark **Notes:** Date and mint mark on edge.

Date	Mintage	MS-63	MS-65	Prf-65
2009P	43,540,000	2.00	5.00	—
2009D	43,540,000	2.00	5.00	—
2009S	—	—	—	5.00

William Henry Harrison

KM# 450 • 8.0700 g., **Copper-Zinc-Manganese-Nickel Clad Copper**, 26.5 mm. • **Edge Lettering:**E PLURIBUS UNUM, date, mint mark **Notes:** Date and mint mark on edge

Date	Mintage	MS-63	MS-65	Prf-65
2009P	43,260,000	2.00	5.00	—
2009D	55,160,000	2.00	5.00	—
2009S	—	—	—	5.00

Zachary Taylor

KM# 453 • 8.0700 g., **Copper-Zinc-Manganese-Nickel Clad Copper**, 26.5 mm. • **Edge Lettering:**E PLURIBUS UNUM, date, mint mark **Notes:** Date and mint mark on edge.

Date	Mintage	MS-63	MS-65	Prf-65
2009P	41,580,000	2.00	5.00	—
2009D	36,680,000	2.00	5.00	—
2009S	—	—	—	5.00

Abraham Lincoln

KM# 478 • 8.0700 g., **Copper-Zinc-Manganese-Nickel Clad Copper**, 26.5 mm. • **Edge Lettering:**E PLURIBUS UNUM, date, mint mark **Notes:** Date and mint mark on edge.

Date	Mintage	MS-63	MS-65	Prf-65
2010P	—	2.00	5.00	—
2010D	—	2.00	5.00	—
2010S	—	—	—	5.00

Franklin Pierce

KM# 476 • 8.0700 g., **Copper-Zinc-Manganese-Nickel Clad Copper**, 26.5 mm. • **Edge Lettering:**E PLURIBUS UNUM, date, mint mark **Notes:** Date and mint mark on edge.

Date	Mintage	MS-63	MS-65	Prf-65
2010P	—	2.00	5.00	—
2010D	—	2.00	5.00	—
2010S	—	—	—	5.00

James Buchanan

KM# 477 • 8.0700 g., **Copper-Zinc-Manganese-Nickel Clad Copper**, 26.5 mm. • **Edge Lettering:**E PLURIBUS UNUM, date, mint mark **Notes:** Date and mint mark on edge.

Date	Mintage	MS-63	MS-65	Prf-65
2010P	—	2.00	5.00	—
2010D	—	2.00	5.00	—
2010S	—	—	—	5.00

Millard Filmore

KM# 475 • 8.0700 g., **Copper-Zinc-Manganese-Nickel Clad Copper**, 26.5 mm. • **Edge Lettering:**E PLURIBUS UNUM, date, mint mark **Notes:** Date and mint mark on edge.

Date	Mintage	MS-63	MS-65	Prf-65
2010P	—	2.00	5.00	—
2010D	—	2.00	5.00	—
2010S	—	—	—	5.00

Andrew Johnson

KM# 499 • 8.0700 g., **Copper-Zinc-Manganese-Nickel Clad Copper**, 26.5 mm. • **Edge Lettering:**E PLURIBUS UNUM, date, mint mark **Notes:** Date and mint mark on edge.

Date	Mintage	MS-63	MS-65	Prf-65
2011P	—	2.00	5.00	—
2011D	—	2.00	5.00	—
2011S	—	—	—	5.00

James Garfield

KM# 502 • 8.0700 g., **Copper-Zinc-Manganese-Nickel Clad Copper**, 26.5 mm. • **Edge Lettering:**E PLURIBUS UNUM, date, mint mark **Notes:** Date and mint mark on edge.

Date	Mintage	MS-63	MS-65	Prf-65
2011P	—	2.00	5.00	—
2011D	—	2.00	5.00	—
2011S	—	—	—	5.00

Rutherford B. Hayes

KM# 501 • 8.0700 g., **Copper-Zinc-Manganese-Nickel Clad Copper**, 26.5 mm. • **Edge Lettering:** E PLURIBUS UNUM, date, mint mark **Notes:** Date and mint mark on edge.

Date	Mintage	MS-63	MS-65	Prf-65
2011P	—	2.00	5.00	—
2011D	—	2.00	5.00	—
2011S	—	—	—	5.00

Ulysses S. Grant

KM# 500 • 8.0700 g., **Copper-Zinc-Manganese-Nickel Clad Copper**, 26.5 mm. • **Edge Lettering:** E PLURIBUS UNUM, date, mint mark **Notes:** Date and mint mark on edge.

Date	Mintage	MS-63	MS-65	Prf-65
2011P	—	2.00	5.00	—
2011D	—	2.00	5.00	—
2011S	—	—	—	5.00

Benjamin Harrison

KM# 526 • 8.0700 g., **Copper-Zinc-Manganese-Nickel Clad Copper**, 26.5 mm. • **Edge Lettering:** E PLURIBUS UNUM, date, mintmark **Notes:** Date at mint mark on edge

Date	Mintage	MS-63	MS-65	Prf-65
2012P	—	2.00	5.00	—
2012D	—	2.00	5.00	—
2012S	—	—	—	5.00

Chester A. Arthur

KM# 524 • 8.0700 g., **Copper-Zinc-Manganese-Nickel Clad Copper**, 26.5 mm. • **Edge Lettering:** E PLURIBUS UNUM, date, mintmark **Notes:** Date and mintmark on edge

Date	Mintage	MS-63	MS-65	Prf-65
2012P	—	2.00	5.00	—
2012D	—	2.00	5.00	—
2012S	—	—	—	5.00

Grover Cleveland, first term

KM# 525 • 8.0700 g., **Copper-Zinc-Manganese-Nickel Clad Copper**, 26.5 mm. • **Edge Lettering:** E PLURIBUS UNUM, date, mintmark **Notes:** Date and mint mark on edge

Date	Mintage	MS-63	MS-65	Prf-65
2012P	—	2.00	5.00	—
2012D	—	2.00	5.00	—
2012S	—	—	—	5.00

Grover Cleveland, second term

KM# 527 • 8.0700 g., **Copper-Zinc-Manganese-Nickel Clad Copper**, 26.5 mm. • **Edge Lettering:** E PLURIBUS UNUM, date, mintmark **Notes:** Date and mint mark on edge

Date	Mintage	MS-63	MS-65	Prf-65
2012P	—	2.00	5.00	—
2012D	—	2.00	5.00	—
2012S	—	—	—	5.00

COMMEMORATIVE COINAGE

1982-PRESENT

All commemorative silver dollar coins of 1982-present have the following specifications: diameter — 38.1 millimeters; weight — 26.7300 grams; composition — 0.9000 silver, 0.7736 ounces actual silver weight. All commemorative $5 coins of 1982-present have the following specificiations: diameter — 21.6 millimeters; weight — 8.3590 grams; composition: 0.9000 gold, 0.242 ounces actual gold weight.

Note: In 1982, after a hiatus of nearly 20 years, coinage of commemorative half dollars resumed. Those designated with a 'W' were struck at the West Point Mint. Some issues were struck in copper-nickel. Those struck in silver have the same size, weight and composition as the prior commemorative half-dollar series.

HALF DOLLAR

U. S. CAPITOL VISITOR CENTER. KM# 323 Copper-Nickel Clad Copper 0 oz. 11.3400 g. **Obverse:** Capitol sillouete, 1800 structure in detail **Reverse:** Legend within circle of stars **Obv. Designer:** Dean McMullen **Rev. Designer:** Alex Shagin and Marcel Jovine

Date	Mintage	MS65	PRF65
2001P	99,157	14.50	—
2001P	77,962	—	15.50

FIRST FLIGHT CENTENNIAL. KM# 348 Copper-Nickel Clad Copper 0 oz. 11.3400 g. **Obverse:** Wright Monument at Kitty Hawk **Reverse:** Wright Flyer in flight **Obv. Designer:** John Mercanti **Rev. Designer:** Donna Weaver

Date	Mintage	MS65	PRF65
2003P	57,726	15.00	—
2003P	111,569	—	17.00

AMERICAN BALD EAGLE. KM# 438 Copper-Nickel Clad Copper 0 oz. 30.6 mm. 11.3400 g. **Obverse:** Two eaglets in nest with egg **Reverse:** Eagle Challenger facing right, American Flag in background **Obv. Designer:** Susan Gamble and Joseph Menna **Rev. Designer:** Donna Weaver and Charles Vickers

Date	Mintage	MS65	PRF65
2008S	120,180	12.50	—
2008S	222,577	—	14.00

U.S. ARMY. KM# 506 Copper-Nickel Clad Copper 0 oz. 30.6 mm. 11.3400 g. **Obverse:** Army contributions during peacetime, surveying, building a flood wall and space exploration **Reverse:** Continental soldier with musket **Obv. Designer:** Donna Weaver and Charles L. Vickers **Rev. Designer:** Thomas Cleveland and Joseph Menna

Date	Mintage	MS65	PRF65
2011D	39,461	69.00	—
2011	68,349	—	35.00

DOLLAR

CAPITOL VISITOR CENTER. KM# 324 Obv. Designer: Marika Somogyi **Rev. Designer:** John Mercanti **Obverse:** Original and current Capital facades **Reverse:** Eagle with sheild and ribbon

Date	Mintage	MS65	PRF65
2001P	66,636	40.80	—
2001P	143,793	—	40.80

NATIVE AMERICAN - BISON. KM# 325 Designer: James E. Fraser. **Obverse:** Native American bust right **Reverse:** Bison standing left

Date	Mintage	MS65	PRF65
2001D	197,131	165	—
2001P	272,869	—	169

2002 WINTER OLYMPICS - SALT LAKE CITY. KM# 336 Obv. Designer: John Mercanti **Rev. Designer:** Donna Weaver **Obverse:** Salt Lake City Olympic logo **Reverse:** Stylized skyline with mountains in background

Date	Mintage	MS65	PRF65
2002P	35,388	40.80	—
2002P	142,873	—	38.30

U.S. MILITARY ACADEMY AT WEST POINT-BICENTENNIAL.
KM# 338 Obv. Designer: T. James Ferrell **Rev. Designer:** John Mercanti **Obverse:** Cadet Review flagbearers, Academy buildings in background **Reverse:** Academy emblems - Corinthian helmet and sword

Date	Mintage	MS65	PRF65
2002W	103,201	38.30	—
2002W	288,293	—	39.80

FIRST FLIGHT CENTENNIAL. KM# 349 Obv. Designer: T. James Ferrell **Rev. Designer:** Norman E. Nemeth **Obverse:** Orville and Wilbur Wright busts left **Reverse:** Wright Flyer over dunes

Date	Mintage	MS65	PRF65
2003P	53,761	40.80	—
2003P	193,086	—	46.80

LEWIS AND CLARK CORPS OF DISCOVERY BICENTENNIAL. KM# 363 Designer: Donna Weaver. **Obverse:** Lewis and Clark standing **Reverse:** Jefferson era clasped hands peace medal

Date	Mintage	MS65	PRF65
2004P	90,323	40.80	—
2004P	288,492	—	46.80

THOMAS A. EDISON - ELECTRIC LIGHT 125TH ANNIVERSARY. KM# 362 Obv. Designer: Donna Weaver **Rev. Designer:** John Mercanti **Obverse:** Edison half-length figure facing holding light bulb **Reverse:** Light bulb and rays

Date	Mintage	MS65	PRF65
2004P	68,031	40.80	—
2004P	213,409	—	41.80

JOHN MARSHALL, 250TH BIRTH ANNIVERSARY. KM# 375 Obv. Designer: John Mercanti **Rev. Designer:** Donna Weaver **Obverse:** Marshall bust left **Reverse:** Marshall era Supreme Court Chamber

Date	Mintage	MS65	PRF65
2005P	48,953	37.30	—
2005P	141,993	—	35.80

U.S. MARINE CORPS, 230TH ANNIVERSARY. KM# 376 Obv. Designer: Norman E. Nemeth **Rev. Designer:** Charles Vickers **Obverse:** Flag Raising at Mt. Suribachi on Iwo Jima **Reverse:** Marine Corps emblem

Date	Mintage	MS65	PRF65
2005P	130,000	48.00	—
2005P	370,000	—	52.50

BENJAMIN FRANKLIN, 300TH BIRTH ANNIVERSARY. KM# 387 Obv. Designer: Norman E. Nemeth **Rev. Designer:** Charles Vickers **Obverse:** Youthful Franklin flying kite **Reverse:** Revolutionary era "JOIN, or DIE" snake cartoon illustration

Date	Mintage	MS65	PRF65
2006P	58,000	40.80	—
2006P	142,000	—	45.00

BENJAMIN FRANKLIN, 300TH BIRTH ANNIVERSARY. KM# 388 Obv. Designer: Don Everhart II **Rev. Designer:** Donna Weaver **Obverse:** Bust 3/4 right, signature in oval below **Reverse:** Continental Dollar of 1776 in center

Date	Mintage	MS65	PRF65
2006P	58,000	40.80	—
2006P	142,000	—	51.00

SAN FRANCISCO MINT MUSEUM. KM# 394 Obv. Designer: Sherl J. Winter **Rev. Designer:** George T. Morgan **Obverse:** 3/4 view of building **Reverse:** Reverse of 1880s Morgan silver dollar

Date	Mintage	MS65	PRF65
2006S	65,609	40.80	—
2006S	255,700	—	40.80

CENTRAL HIGH SCHOOL DESEGREGATION. KM# 418 Obv. Designer: Richard Masters and Charles Vickers **Rev. Designer:** Don Everhart II **Obverse:** Children's feet walking left with adult feet in military boots **Reverse:** Little Rock's Central High School

Date	Mintage	MS65	PRF65
2007P	66,093	40.80	—
2007P	124,618	—	43.00

JAMESTOWN - 400TH ANNIVERSARY. KM# 405 Obv. Designer: Donna Weaver and Don Everhart II **Rev. Designer:** Susan Gamble and Charles Vickers **Obverse:** Two settlers and Native American **Reverse:** Three ships

Date	Mintage	MS65	PRF65
2007P	79,801	40.80	—
2007P	258,802	—	38.30

AMERICAN BALD EAGLE. KM# 439 Obv. Designer: Joel Iskowitz and Don Everhart II **Rev. Designer:** James Licaretz **Obverse:** Eagle with flight, mountain in background at right **Reverse:** Great Seal of the United States

Date	Mintage	MS65	PRF65
2008P	110,073	44.00	—
2008P	243,558	—	38.30

LINCOLN BICENTENNIAL. KM# 454 Obv. Designer: Justin Kunz and Don Everhart II **Rev. Designer:** Phebe Hemphill **Obverse:** 3/4 portrait facing right **Reverse:** Part of Gettysburg Address within wreath

Date	Mintage	MS65	PRF65
2009P	125,000	55.00	—
2009P	375,000	—	55.00

LOUIS BRAILLE BIRTH BICENTENNIAL. KM# 455 Obv. Designer: Joel Iskowitz and Phebe Hemphill **Rev. Designer:** Susan Gamble and Joseph Menna **Obverse:** Louis Braille bust facing **Reverse:** School child reading book in Braille, BRL in Braille code above

Date	Mintage	MS65	PRF65
2009P	82,639	38.50	—
2009P	135,235	—	38.30

AMERICAN VETERANS DISABLED FOR LIFE. KM# 479 Obv. Designer: Don Everhart II **Rev. Designer:** Thomas Cleveland and Joseph Menna **Obverse:** Soldier's feet, crutches **Reverse:** Legend within wreath

Date	Mintage	MS65	PRF65
2010W	77,859	40.80	—
2010W	189,881	—	42.30

BOY SCOUTS OF AMERICA, 100TH ANNIVERSARY. KM# 480 Obv. Designer: Donna Weaver **Rev. Designer:** Jim Licaretz **Obverse:** Cub Scout, Boy Scout and Venturer saluting **Reverse:** Boy Scouts of America logo

Date	Mintage	MS65	PRF65
2010P		38.50	—
2010P		—	42.00

MEDAL OF HONOR. KM# 504 Obv. Designer: James Licaretz **Rev. Designer:** Richard Masters and Phebe Hemphill **Obverse:** Medal of Honor designs for Army, Navy and Air Force awards **Reverse:** Army infantry doldier carrying another to safety

Date	Mintage	MS65	PRF65
2011S	44,769	46.50	—
2011S	112,850	—	43.50

U.S. ARMY. KM# 507 Obv. Designer: Richard Masters and Michael Gaudioso **Rev. Designer:** Susan Gamble and Don Everhart, II **Obverse:** Male and femlae soldier heads looking outward **Reverse:** Seven core values of the Army, Eagle from the great seal

Date	Mintage	MS65	PRF65
2011S		45.00	—
2011S		—	43.50

$5 (HALF EAGLE)

CAPITOL VISITOR CENTER. KM# 326 Designer: Elizabeth Jones. **Obverse:** Column at right **Reverse:** First Capital building

Date	Mintage	MS65	PRF65
2001W	6,761	1,750	—
2001W	27,652	—	442

2002 WINTER OLYMPICS. KM# 337 Designer: Donna Weaver. **Obverse:** Salt Lake City Olympics logo **Reverse:** Stylized cauldron

Date	Mintage	MS65	PRF65
2002W	10,585	452	—
2002W	32,877	—	442

SAN FRANCISCO MINT MUSEUM. KM# 395 Obv. Designer: Charles Vickers and Joseph Menna **Rev. Designer:** Christian Gobrecht **Obverse:** Front entrance façade **Reverse:** Eagle as on 1860's $5. Gold

Date	Mintage	MS65	PRF65
2006S	16,230	442	—
2006S	41,517	—	442

JAMESTOWN - 400TH ANNIVERSARY. KM# 406 Obv. Designer: John Mercanti **Rev. Designer:** Susan Gamble and Norman Nemeth **Obverse:** Settler and Native American **Reverse:** Jamestown Memorial Church ruins

Date	Mintage	MS65	PRF65
2007W	18,843	442	—
2007W	47,050	—	442

AMERICAN BALD EAGLE. KM# 440 Obv. Designer: Susan Gamble adn Phebe Hemphill **Rev. Designer:** Don Everhart II **Obverse:** Two eagles on branch **Reverse:** Eagle with shield

Date	Mintage	MS65	PRF65
2008W	13,467	457	—
2008W	59,269	—	442

MEDAL OF HONOR. KM# 505 Obv. Designer: Joseph Menna **Rev. Designer:** Joel Iskowitz and Michael Gaudioso **Obverse:** 1861 Medal of Honor design for the Navy **Reverse:** Minerva standing with shield and Union flag, field artillery canon flanking

Date	Mintage	MS65	PRF65
2011S	8,251	585	—
2011S	18,012	—	500

U.S. ARMY. KM# 508 Obv. Designer: Joel Iskowitz and Phebe Hemphill **Rev. Designer:** Joseph Menna **Obverse:** Five Soldiers of different eras **Reverse:** Elements from the Army's emblem

Date	Mintage	MS65	PRF65
2011P	8,062	585	—
2011P	17,173	—	495

$10 (EAGLE)

FIRST FLIGHT CENTENNIAL. KM# 350 0.9000 Gold 0.4837 oz. AGW. 16.7180 g. **Obverse:** Orvile and Wilbur Wright busts facing **Reverse:** Wright flyer and eagle **Obv. Designer:** Donna Weaver **Rev. Designer:** Norman Nemeth

Date	Mintage	MS65	PRF65
2003P	10,129	1,050	—
2003P	21,846	—	893

$20 (DOUBLE EAGLE)

KM# 464 0.9990 Gold 0 oz. AGW. 27 mm. **Obverse:** Ultra high relief Liberty holding torch, walking forward **Reverse:** Eagle in flight left, sunrise in background **Designer:** Augustus Saint-Gaudens

Date	Mintage	MS65	PRF65
2009	115,178	—	3,150

AMERICA THE BEAUTIFUL SILVER BULLION

SILVER QUARTER

KM#489 0.9990 SILVER 4.9958 oz. ASW. 155.5500 g. **Rev. Designer:** Don Everhart II and Joseph Menna

Date	Mintage	MS65	PRF65
2010	33,000	290	—
2010P Special "Vapor Blast" finish	27,000	—	250

KM# 490 0.9990 SILVER 4.9958 oz. ASW. 155.5500 g. **Rev. Designer:** Don Everhart II

Date	Mintage	MS65	PRF65
2010	33,000	275	—
2010P Special "Vapor Blast" finish	27,000	—	240

KM# 491 0.9990 SILVER 4.9958 oz. ASW. 155.5500 g. **Rev. Designer:** Joseph Menna and Phebe Hemphill

Date	Mintage	MS65	PRF65
2010	33,000	275	—
2010P Special "Vapor blast" finish	27,000	—	225

KM# 492 0.9990 SILVER 4.9958 oz. ASW. 155.5500 g. **Rev. Designer:** Phebe Hemphill

Date	Mintage	MS65	PRF65
2010	33,000	250	—
2010P Special "Vapor blast" finish	26,019	—	225

KM# 493 0.9990 SILVER 4.9958 oz. ASW. 155.5500 g. **Rev. Designer:** Phebe Hemphill

Date	Mintage	MS65	PRF65
2010	33,000	275	—
2010P Special "Vapor blast" finish	25,318	—	200

KM# 513 0.9990 SILVER 4.9958 oz. ASW. 155.5500 g. **Rev. Designer:** Joel Iskowitz and Phebe Hemphill

Date	Mintage	MS65	PRF65
2011	126,700	200	—
2011P Special "Vapor blast" finish	15,243	—	—

KM# 514 0.9990 SILVER 4.9958 oz. ASW. 155.5500 g. **Rev. Designer:** Barbara Fox and Charles L. Vickers

Date	Mintage	MS65	PRF65
2011	126,700	200	—
2011P Special "Vapor blast" finish	12,209	—	190

KM# 515 0.9990 SILVER 4.9958 oz. ASW. 155.5500 g. **Rev. Designer:** Susan Gambel and Michael Gaudioso

Date	Mintage	MS65	PRF65
2011	—	200	—
2011P Special "Vapor blast" finish	—	—	190

KM# 516 0.9990 SILVER 4.9958 oz. ASW. 155.5500 g. **Rev. Designer:** Thomas Cleveland and Joseph menna

Date	Mintage	MS65	PRF65
2011	—	200	—
2011P Special "Vapor blast" finish	—	—	190

KM# 517 0.9990 SILVER 4.9958 oz. ASW. 155.5500 g. **Rev. Designer:** Donna Weaver and James Licaretz

Date	Mintage	MS65	PRF65
2011	—	200	—
2011P Special "Vapor blast" finish	—	—	190

KM# 536 0.9990 SILVER 4.9958 oz. ASW. 155.5500 g.

Date	Mintage	MS65	PRF65
2012	—	—	—
2012P Special "Vapor blast" finish	—	—	—

KM# 537 0.9990 SILVER 4.9949 oz. ASW. 155.5200 g.

Date	Mintage	MS65	PRF65
2012	—	—	—
2012P Vapor blast finish	—	—	—

KM# 538 0.9990 SILVER 4.9949 oz. ASW. 155.5200 g.

Date	Mintage	MS65	PRF65
2012	—	—	—
2012P Special "Vapor blast" finish	—	—	—

KM# 539 0.9990 SILVER 4.9949 oz. ASW. 155.5200 g.

Date	Mintage	MS65	PRF65
2012	—	—	—
2012P Special "Vapor blast" finish	—	—	—

KM# 540 0.9990 SILVER 4.9959 oz. ASW. 155.5520 g.

Date	Mintage	MS65	PRF65
2012	—	—	—
2012P Special "Vapor blast" finish	—	—	—

AMERICAN EAGLE BULLION COINS

SILVER DOLLAR

KM#273 0.9993 SILVER 0.9993 oz. ASW. 40.6mm. 31.1050 g. **Obv. Designer:** Adolph A. Weinman **Rev. Designer:** John Mercanti

Date	Mintage	MS65	PRF65
2001	9,001,711	37.60	—
2001W	746,398	—	74.10
2002	10,539,026	37.60	—
2002W	647,342	—	74.10
2003	8,495,008	37.60	—
2003W	747,831	—	74.10
2004	8,882,754	37.60	—
2004W	801,602	—	74.10
2005	8,891,025	37.60	—
2005W	816,663	—	74.10
2006	10,676,522	39.90	—
2006W	1,093,600	—	74.10
2006P Reverse Proof	—	—	195
2006W Burnished Unc.	468,000	75.00	—
2006 20th Aniv. 3 pc. set	—	—	355
2007	9,028,036	37.90	—
2007W	821,759	—	74.10
2007W Burnished Unc.	690,891	43.60	—
2008	20,583,000	37.60	—
2008W Reverse of '07, U in United with rounded bottom.	—	420	—
2008	713,353	—	79.00
2008W Burnished Unc.	—	36.50	—
2009	30,459,000	37.60	—
2010	34,764,500	37.60	—
2010	—	—	74.10
2011	—	37.60	—
2011P Reverse Proof	100,000	—	335
2011S Unc.	100,000	275	—
2011W Burnished Unc.	100,000	65.00	—
2011W Proof	100,000	—	74.10
2012	—	37.60	—

GOLD $5

KM# 216 0.9167 GOLD 0.1000 oz. AGW. 16.5mm. 3.3930 g. **Obv. Designer:** Augustus Saint-Gaudens **Rev. Designer:** Miley Busiek

Date	Mintage	MS65	PRF65
2001	269,147	201	—
2001W	37,530	—	201
2002	230,027	201	—
2002W	40,864	—	201
2003	245,029	201	—
2003W	40,027	—	201
2004	250,016	201	—
2004W	35,131	—	201
2005	300,043	201	—
2005W	49,265	—	201
2006	285,006	201	—
2006W	47,277	—	201
2006W Burnished Unc.	20,643	175	—
2007	190,010	201	—
2007W	58,553	—	216
2007W Burnished Unc.	22,501	175	—
2008	305,000	211	—
2008W	—	—	216
2008W Burnished Unc.	12,657	330	—
2009	27,000	145	—
2010	—	—	—
2010W	—	—	201
2011W	5,000	—	201
2011	—	201	—

GOLD $10

KM# 217 0.9167 GOLD 0.2500 oz. AGW. 22mm. 8.4830 g. **Obv. Designer:** Augustus Saint-Gaudens **Rev. Designer:** Miley Busiek

Date	Mintage	MS65	PRF65
2001	71,280	496	—
2001W	25,613	—	583
2002	62,027	496	—
2002W	29,242	—	583
2003	74,029	496	—
2003W	30,292	—	583
2004	72,014	496	—
2004W	28,839	—	583
2005	72,015	496	—
2005W	37,207	—	583
2006	60,004	496	—
2006W	36,127	—	583
2006W Burnished Unc.	15,188	785	—
2007	34,004	496	—
2007W	46,189	—	488
2007W Burnished Unc.	12,786	990	—
2008	—	496	—
2008W	28,000	—	488
2008W Burnished Unc.	8,883	1,750	—
2009	27,500	496	—
2010	—	—	—
2010W	—	—	583
2011W	4,000	—	583
2011	—	496	—

GOLD $25

KM# 218 0.9167 GOLD 0.5000 oz. AGW. 27mm. 16.9660 g. **Obv. Designer:** Augustus Saint-Gaudens **Rev. Designer:** Miley Busiek

Date	Mintage	MS65	PRF65
2001	48,047	900	—
2001W	23,240	—	995

Date	Mintage	MS65	PRF65
2002	70,027	957	—
2002W	26,646	—	995
2003	79,029	957	—
2003W	28,270	—	995
2004	98,040	957	—
2004W	27,330	—	995
2005	80,023	957	—
2005W	34,311	—	995
2006	66,004	960	—
2006W	34,322	—	995
2006W Burnished Unc.	15,164	1,600	—
2007	47,002	991	—
2007W	44,025	—	995
2007W Burnished Unc.	11,458	2,150	—
2008	61,000	960	—
2008W	27,800	—	995
2008W Burnished Unc.	15,683	1,750	—
2009	55,000	960	—
2010	—	—	—
2010W	—	—	995
2011W	2,000	—	995
2011	—	957	—

GOLD $50

KM# 219　0.9167 **GOLD** 100000 oz. AGW. 32.7mm. 33.9310 g.　**Obv. Designer:** Augustus Saint-Gaudens　**Rev. Designer:** Miley Busiek

Date	Mintage	MS65	PRF65
2001	143,605	1,829	—
2001W	24,555	—	1,870
2002	222,029	1,829	—
2002W	27,499	—	1,870
2003	416,032	1,829	—
2003W	28,344	—	1,870
2004	417,149	1,829	—
2004W	28,215	—	1,870
2005	356,555	1,829	—
2005W	35,246	—	1,870
2006	237,510	1,829	—
2006W	47,000	—	1,870
2006W Reverse Proof	10,000	—	2,200
2006W Burnished Unc.	45,912	1,575	—
2007	140,016	1,846	—
2007W	51,810	—	1,870
2007W Burnished Unc.	18,609	1,980	—
2008W	710,000	1,829	—
2008W Proof	29,000	—	1,870
2008W Burnished Unc.	11,908	—	2,100
2008W Reverse of '07	—	—	—
2009	122,000	1,829	—
2010	—	1,829	—
2010W	—	—	1,870
2011	—	1,829	—
2011W	—	—	1,870
2012	—	1,829	—

PLATINUM $10

KM# 327　0.9995 **PLATINUM** 0.0999 oz. 17mm. 3.1100 g.　**Obv. Designer:** John Mercanti

Date	Mintage	MS65	PRF65
2001W	12,174	—	237

KM# 283　0.9995 **PLATINUM** 0.0999 oz. 17mm. 3.1100 g.　**Obv. Designer:** John Mercanti　**Rev. Designer:** Thomas D. Rogers Sr

Date	Mintage	MS65	PRF65
2001	52,017	189	—
2002	23,005	189	—
2003	22,007	189	—

Date	Mintage	MS65	PRF65
2004	15,010	189	—
2005	14,013	189	—
2006	11,001	189	—
2006W Burnished Unc.	—	425	—
2007	13,003	280	—
2007W Burnished Unc.	—	189	—
2008	17,000	189	—
2008 Burnished Unc.	—	210	—

KM# 339　0.9995 **PLATINUM** 0.0999 oz. 17mm. 3.1100 g.　**Obv. Designer:** John Mercanti

Date	Mintage	MS65	PRF65
2002W	12,365	—	237

KM# 351　0.9995 **PLATINUM** 0.0999 oz. 17mm. 3.1100 g.　**Obv. Designer:** John Mercanti　**Rev. Designer:** Al Maletsky

Date	Mintage	MS65	PRF65
2003W	9,534	—	242

KM# 364　0.9995 **PLATINUM** 0.0999 oz. 17mm. 3.1100 g.　**Obv. Designer:** John Mercanti

Date	Mintage	MS65	PRF65
2004W	7,161	—	535

KM# 377　0.9995 **PLATINUM** 0.0999 oz. 17mm. 3.1100 g.　**Obv. Designer:** John Mercanti　**Rev. Designer:** Donna Weaver

Date	Mintage	MS65	PRF65
2005W	8,104	—	265

KM# 389　0.9995 **PLATINUM** 0.0999 oz. 17mm. 3.1100 g.　**Obv. Designer:** John Mercanti

Date	Mintage	MS65	PRF65
2006W	10,205	—	237

KM# 414　0.9995 **PLATINUM** 0.0999 oz. 17mm. 3.1100 g.　**Obv. Designer:** John Mercanti

Date	Mintage	MS65	PRF65
2007W	8,176	—	237

KM# 434　0.9995 **PLATINUM** 0.0999 oz. 17mm. 3.1100 g.　**Obv. Designer:** John Mercanti

Date	Mintage	MS65	PRF65
2008W	8,176	—	585

KM# 460　0.9995 **PLATINUM** 0.0999 oz. 17mm. 3.1100 g.　**Obv. Designer:** John Mercanti

Date	Mintage	MS65	PRF65
2009W	5,600	—	585

PLATINUM $25

KM# 328　0.9995 **PLATINUM** 0.2502 oz. 22mm. 7.7857 g.　**Obv. Designer:** John Mercanti

Date	Mintage	MS65	PRF65
2001W	8,847	—	470

KM# 284　0.9995 **PLATINUM** 0.2502 oz. 22mm. 7.7857 g.　**Obv. Designer:** John Mercanti　**Rev. Designer:** Thomas D. Rogers Sr

Date	Mintage	MS65	PRF65
2001	21,815	459	—
2002	27,405	459	—
2003	25,207	459	—
2004	18,010	459	—
2005	12,013	459	—
2006	12,001	459	—
2006W Burnished Unc.	—	585	—
2007	8,402	476	—
2007W Burnished Unc.	—	459	—
2008	22,800	459	—
2008 Burnished Unc.	—	665	—
2009	—	—	—

KM# 340　0.9995 **PLATINUM** 0.2502 oz. 22mm. 7.7857 g.　**Obv. Designer:** John Mercanti

Date	Mintage	MS65	PRF65
2002W	9,282	—	470

KM# 352　0.9995 **PLATINUM** 0.2502 oz. 22mm. 7.7857 g.　**Obv. Designer:** John Mercanti　**Rev. Designer:** Al Maletsky

Date	Mintage	MS65	PRF65
2003W	7,044	—	470

KM# 365　0.9995 **PLATINUM** 0.2502 oz. 22mm. 7.7857 g.　**Obv. Designer:** John Mercanti

Date	Mintage	MS65	PRF65
2004W	5,193	—	1,075

KM# 378　0.9995 **PLATINUM** 0.2502 oz. 22mm. 7.7857 g.　**Obv. Designer:** John Mercanti　**Rev. Designer:** Donna Weaver

Date	Mintage	MS65	PRF65
2005W	6,592	—	595

KM# 390　0.9995 **PLATINUM** 0.2502 oz. 22mm. 7.7857 g.　**Obv. Designer:** John Mercanti

Date	Mintage	MS65	PRF65
2006W	7,813	—	445

KM# 415　0.9995 **PLATINUM** 0.2502 oz. 22mm. 7.7857 g.　**Obv. Designer:** John Mercanti

Date	Mintage	MS65	PRF65
2007W	6,017	—	440

KM# 435　0.9995 **PLATINUM** 0.2502 oz. 22mm. 7.7857 g.　**Obv. Designer:** John Mercanti

Date	Mintage	MS65	PRF65
2008W	6,017	—	985

KM# 461　0.9995 **PLATINUM** 0.2502 oz. 22mm. 7.7857 g.　**Obv. Designer:** John Mercanti

Date	Mintage	MS65	PRF65
2009W	3,800	—	985

PLATINUM $50

KM# 329 0.9995 **PLATINUM** 0.4997 oz. 27mm. 15.5520 g.
Obv. Designer: John Mercanti

Date	Mintage	MS65	PRF65
2001W	8,254	—	940

KM# 285 0.9995 **PLATINUM** 0.4997 oz. 27mm. 15.5520 g.
Obv. Designer: John Mercanti **Rev. Designer:** Thomas D. Rogers Sr

Date	Mintage	MS65	PRF65
2001	12,815	919	—
2002	24,005	919	—
2003	17,409	919	—
2004	13,236	919	—
2005	9,013	919	—
2006	9,602	919	—
2006W Burnished Unc.	—	1,050	—
2007	7,001	952	—
2007W Burnished Unc.	—	919	—
2008	14,000	919	—
2008W Burnished Unc.	—	1,200	—
2009		919	—

KM# 341 0.9995 **PLATINUM** 0.4997 oz. 27mm. 15.5520 g.
Obv. Designer: John Mercanti

Date	Mintage	MS65	PRF65
2002W	8,772	—	940

KM# 353 0.9995 **PLATINUM** 0.4997 oz. 27mm. 15.5520 g.
Obv. Designer: John Mercanti **Rev. Designer:** Al Maletsky

Date	Mintage	MS65	PRF65
2003W	7,131	—	940

KM# 366 0.9995 **PLATINUM** 0.4997 oz. 27mm. 15.5520 g.
Obv. Designer: John Mercanti

Date	Mintage	MS65	PRF65
2004W	5,063	—	1,750

KM# 379 0.9995 **PLATINUM** 0.4997 oz. 27mm. 15.5520 g.
Obv. Designer: John Mercanti **Rev. Designer:** Donna Weaver

Date	Mintage	MS65	PRF65
2005W	5,942	—	1,175

KM# 391 0.9995 **PLATINUM** 0.4997 oz. 27mm. 15.5520 g.
Obv. Designer: John Mercanti

Date	Mintage	MS65	PRF65
2006W	7,649	—	940

KM# 416 0.9995 **PLATINUM** 0.4997 oz. 27mm. 15.5520 g.
Obv. Designer: John Mercanti

Date	Mintage	MS65	PRF65
2007W	22,873	—	940
2007W Reverse Proof	16,937	—	940

KM# 436 0.9995 **PLATINUM** 0.4997 oz. 27mm. 15.5520 g.
Obv. Designer: John Mercanti

Date	Mintage	MS65	PRF65
2008W	22,873	—	1,600

KM# 462 0.9995 **PLATINUM** 0.4997 oz. 27mm. 15.5520 g.
Obv. Designer: John Mercanti

Date	Mintage	MS65	PRF65
2009	3,600		

PLATINUM $100

KM# 330 0.9995 **PLATINUM** 0.9995 oz. 33mm. 31.1050 g.
Obv. Designer: John Mercanti

Date	Mintage	MS65	PRF65
2001W	8,969	—	1,879

KM# 286 0.9995 **PLATINUM** 0.9995 oz. 33mm. 31.1050 g.
Obv. Designer: John Mercanti **Rev. Designer:** Thomas D. Rogers Sr

Date	Mintage	MS65	PRF65
2001	14,070	1,838	—
2002	11,502	1,838	—
2003	8,007	1,838	—
2004	7,009	1,838	—
2005	6,310	1,838	—
2006	6,000	1,838	—
2006W Burnished Unc.		1,986	—
2007	7,202	1,887	—
2007W Burnished Unc.		1,838	—
2008	21,800	1,838	—
2008W Burnished Unc.		1,986	—
2009		—	—
2011	10,299	—	—

KM# 342 0.9995 **PLATINUM** 0.9995 oz. 33mm. 31.1050 g.
Obv. Designer: John Mercanti

Date	Mintage	MS65	PRF65
2002W	9,834	—	1,897

KM# 354 0.9995 **PLATINUM** 0.9995 oz. 33mm. 31.1050 g.
Obv. Designer: John Mercanti **Rev. Designer:** Al Maletsky

Date	Mintage	MS65	PRF65
2003W	8,246	—	1,897

KM# 367 0.9995 **PLATINUM** 0.9995 oz. 33mm. 31.1050 g.
Obv. Designer: John Mercanti **Rev. Designer:** Donna Weaver

Date	Mintage	MS65	PRF65
2004W	6,007	—	2,175

KM# 380 0.9995 **PLATINUM** 0.9995 oz. 33mm. 31.1050 g.
Obv. Designer: John Mercanti **Rev. Designer:** Donna Weaver

Date	Mintage	MS65	PRF65
2005W	6,602	—	2,400

KM# 392 0.9995 **PLATINUM** 0.9995 oz. 33mm. 31.1050 g.
Obv. Designer: John Mercanti

Date	Mintage	MS65	PRF65
2006W	9,152	—	1,879

KM# 417 0.9995 **PLATINUM** 0.9995 oz. 33mm. 31.1050 g.
Obv. Designer: John Mercanti

Date	Mintage	MS65	PRF65
2007W	8,363	—	1,838

KM# 437   0.9995 **PLATINUM** 0.9995 oz. 33mm. 31.1050 g.
Obv. Designer: John Mercanti

Date	Mintage	MS65	PRF65
2008/4	8,363	—	2,825

KM# 463   0.9995 **PLATINUM** 0.9994 oz. 33mm. 31.1020 g.
Obv. Designer: John Mercanti

Date	Mintage	MS65	PRF65
2009W Proof	4,900	—	2,600

KM# 488   0.9990 **PLATINUM** 0.9990 oz. 33mm. 31.1050 g.
Obv. Designer: John Mercanti

Date	Mintage	MS65	PRF65
2010W	—	—	2,200

KM# 518   0.9995 **PLATINUM** 0.9995 oz. 33mm. 31.1050 g.

Date	Mintage	MS65	PRF65
2011W	—	—	2,200

KM# 541   0.9995 **PLATINUM** 0.9995 oz. 31.1050 g.

Date	Mintage	MS65	PRF65
2012	—	—	2,200

BISON BULLION COINAGE

GOLD $5

KM# 411   0.9999 **GOLD** 0.1000 oz. AGW. 3.1100 g.

Date	Mintage	MS65	PRF65
2008W	19,300	—	660
2008W	19,000	555	—

GOLD $10

KM# 412   0.9999 **GOLD** 0.2503 oz. AGW. 7.7857 g.

Date	Mintage	MS65	PRF65
2008W	13,900	—	1,550
2008W	10,500	1,375	—

GOLD $25

KM# 413   0.9990 **GOLD** 0.4995 oz. AGW. 15.5520 g.

Date	Mintage	MS65	PRF65
2008W	12,500	—	1,650
2008W	17,000	1,325	—

GOLD $50

KM# 393   0.9999 **GOLD** 0.9999 oz. AGW. 32mm. 31.1050 g.   **Designer:** James E. Fraser

Date	Mintage	MS65	PRF65
2006W	246,267	—	1,854
2006W	337,012	1,829	—
2007W	136,503	1,829	—
2007W	58,998	—	1,864
2008W	189,500	1,829	—
2008W	19,500	—	2,950
2008W Moy Family Chop	—	3,700	—
2009W	—	1,829	—
2009W	—	—	1,854

Date	Mintage	MS65	PRF65
2010W	49,374	—	1,904
2011W	—	—	1,904
2012W	—	—	1,904

FIRST SPOUSE GOLD COINAGE

GOLD $10

KM# 407   0.9999 **GOLD** 0.4999 oz. AGW. 23.5mm. 15.5520 g. **Obv. Desc.:** Bust 3/4 facing right **Rev. Desc.:** Martha Washington seated sewing **Obv. Designer:** Joseph Menna   **Rev. Designer:** Susan Gamble and Don Everhart

Date	Mintage	MS65	PRF65
2007W	20,000	1,065	—
2007W	20,000	—	940

KM# 408   0.9999 **GOLD** 0.4999 oz. AGW. 26.5mm. 15.5520 g.   **Obv. Desc.:** Bust 3/4 facing **Rev. Desc.:** Abigail Adams seated at desk writing to John during the Revolutionary War **Obv. Designer:** Joseph Menna **Rev. Designer:** Thomas Cleveland and Phebe Hemphill

Date	Mintage	MS65	PRF65
2007W	20,000	1,065	—
2007W	20,000	—	940

KM# 409   0.9999 **GOLD** 0.4999 oz. AGW. 26.5mm. 15.5520 g. **Obv. Desc.:** Bust design from coinage **Rev. Desc.:** Jefferson's tombstone **Obv. Designer:** Robert Scot and Phebe Hemphill   **Rev. Designer:** Charles Vickers

Date	Mintage	MS65	PRF65
2007W	20,000	1,065	—
2007W	20,000	—	940

KM# 410   0.9999 **GOLD** 0.4999 oz. AGW. 26.5mm. 15.5520 g. **Obv. Desc.:** Bust 3/4 facing **Rev. Desc.:** Dolley standing before painting of Washington, which she saved from the White House **Obv. Designer:** Don Everhart   **Rev. Designer:** Joel Iskowitz and Don Everhart

Date	Mintage	MS65	PRF65
2007W	12,500	940	—
2007W	18,300	—	940

KM# 430   0.9990 **GOLD** 0.4995 oz. AGW. 26.5mm. 15.5520 g.   **Obv. Desc.:** Bust 3/4 facing right **Rev.**

Desc.: Elizabeth standing before mirror **Obv. Designer:** Joel Iskowitz and Don Everhart   **Rev. Designer:** Donna Weaver and Charles Vickers

Date	Mintage	MS65	PRF65
2008W	4,500	1,275	—
2008W	7,900	—	1,375

KM# 431   0.9990 **GOLD** 0.4995 oz. AGW. 26.5mm. 15.5520 g. **Obv. Desc.:** Bust 3/4 facing right **Rev. Desc.:** Lousia and son Charles before entrance **Obv. Designer:** Susan Gamble and Phebe Hemphill   **Rev. Designer:** Joseph Menna

Date	Mintage	MS65	PRF65
2008W	4,200	1,275	—
2008W	7,400	—	1,350

KM# 432   0.9990 **GOLD** 0.4995 oz. AGW. 26.5mm. 15.5520 g. **Obv. Desc.:** Capped and draped bust left **Rev. Desc.:** Andrew Jackson on horseback right **Obv. Designer:** John Reich **Rev. Designer:** Justin Kunz and Don Everhart

Date	Mintage	MS65	PRF65
2008W	4,800	1,750	—
2008W	7,800	—	1,550

KM# 433   0.9990 **GOLD** 0.4995 oz. AGW. 26.5mm. 15.5520 g. **Obv. Desc.:** Seated Liberty with shiled **Rev. Desc.:** Youthful van Buren seated under tree, family tavern in distance **Obv. Designer:** Christian Gobrecht **Rev. Designer:** Thomas Cleveland and James Licaretz

Date	Mintage	MS65	PRF65
2008W	15,000	1,875	—
2008W	Inc. above	—	1,700

KM# 456   0.9990 **GOLD** 0.4995 oz. AGW. 15.5520 g. **Obv. Desc.:** Bust 3/4 left **Rev. Desc.:** Anna reading to her three children **Obv. Designer:** Donna Weaver and Joseph Menna **Rev. Designer:** Thomas Cleveland and Charles Vickers

Date	Mintage	MS65	PRF65
2009W	15,000	1,425	—
2009W	Inc. above	—	1,325

KM# 457   0.9990 **GOLD** 0.4995 oz. AGW. 15.5520 g. **Obv. Desc.:** Bust facing **Rev. Desc.:** Letitia and two children playing outside of Cedar Grove Plantation **Obv. Designer:** Phebe Hemphill   **Rev. Designer:** Susan Gamble and Norm Nemeth

Date	Mintage	MS65	PRF65
2009W	15,000	1,675	—
2009W	Inc. above	—	1,450

KM# 458 0.9990 **GOLD** 0.4995 oz. AGW. 15.5520 g.
Obv. Desc.: Bust facing **Rev. Desc.:** **Designer:** Joel
Iskowitz and Don Everhart Julia and John Tyler dancing

Date	Mintage	MS65	PRF65
2009W	15,000	1,800	—
2009W	Inc. above	—	1,900

KM# 459 0.9990 **GOLD** 0.4995 oz. AGW. 15.5520 g.
Obv. Desc.: Bust 3/4 right **Rev. Desc.:** **Designer:**
Phebe Hemphill Sarah seated at desk as personal
secretary to James Polk

Date	Mintage	MS65	PRF65
2009W	3,501	1,500	—
2009W	5,157	—	1,250

KM# 465 0.9990 **GOLD** 0.4995 oz. AGW. 15.5520 g.
Obv. Desc.: Bust 3/4 left **Rev. Desc.:** Margaret Taylor
nurses wounded soldier during the Seminole War **Obv.
Designer:** Phebe Hemphill and Charles Vickers **Rev.
Designer:** Mary Beth Zeitz and James Licaretz

Date	Mintage	MS65	PRF65
2009W	3,430	1,165	—
2009W	4,787	—	1,350

KM# 481 0.9990 **GOLD** 0.4985 oz. AGW. 15.5200 g.
Rev. Desc.: Abigail Filmore placing books on library
shelf **Obv. Designer:** Phebe Hemphill **Rev. Designer:**
Susan Gamble and Joseph Menna

Date	Mintage	MS65	PRF65
2010W	15,000	1,450	—
2010W	Inc. above	—	1,125

KM# 482 0.9990 **GOLD** 0.4985 oz. AGW. 15.5200 g.
Rev. Desc.: Jane Pierce seated on porch **Obv.
Designer:** Donna Weaver and Don Everhart **Rev.
Designer:** Donna Weaver and Charles Vickers

Date	Mintage	MS65	PRF65
2010W	3,333	1,100	—
2010W	4,843	—	1,350

KM# 483 0.9990 **GOLD** 0.4985 oz. AGW. 26.5mm.
15.5200 g. **Rev. Desc.:** Buchanan as clerk **Obv.**

Designer: Christian Gobrecht **Rev. Designer:** Joseph
Menna

Date	Mintage	MS65	PRF65
2010W	5,348	1,065	—
2010W	7,304	—	1,100

KM# 484 0.9990 **GOLD** 0.4985 oz. AGW. 15.5200 g.
Rev. Desc.: Mary Lincoln visiting soldiers at hospital
Obv. Designer: Phebe Hemphill **Rev. Designer:** Joel
Iskowitz and Pheve Hemphill

Date	Mintage	MS65	PRF65
2010W	3,760	1,100	—
2010W	6,904	—	1,100

KM# 509 0.9990 **GOLD** 0.4994 oz. AGW. 15.5500 g.
Obv. Desc.: Bust of Eliza Johnson

Date	Mintage	MS65	PRF65
2011W	15,000	1,100	—
2011W	Inc. above	—	1,100

KM# 510 0.9990 **GOLD** 0.4995 oz. AGW. 26.5mm.
15.5520 g. **Obv. Desc.:** Bust of Julia Grant

Date	Mintage	MS65	PRF65
2011W	15,000	1,100	—
2011W	Inc. above	—	1,100

KM# 511 0.9990 **GOLD** 0.4995 oz. AGW. 15.5520 g.
Obv. Desc.: Bust of Lucy Hayes

Date	Mintage	MS65	PRF65
2011W	15,000	1,100	—
2011W	Inc. above	—	1,100

KM# 512 0.9990 **GOLD** 0.4995 oz. AGW. 15.5520 g.
Obv. Desc.: Bust of Lucretia Garfield

Date	Mintage	MS65	PRF65
2011W	15,000	1,100	—
2011W	Inc. above	—	1,100

KM# 532 0.9990 **GOLD** 0.4995 oz. AGW. 15.5520 g.
Obv. Desc.: Alice Paul, suffragist

Date	Mintage	MS65	PRF65
2012W	—	—	—
2012W	—	—	—

KM# 533 0.9990 **GOLD** 0.4995 oz. AGW. 15.5520 g.
Obv. Desc.: Francis Cleveland (first term)

Date	Mintage	MS65	PRF65
2012W	—	—	—
2012W	—	—	—

KM# 534 0.9990 **GOLD** 0.4995 oz. AGW. 15.5520 g.
Obv. Desc.: Caroline Harrison

Date	Mintage	MS65	PRF65
2012W	—	—	—
2012W	—	—	—

KM# 535 0.9990 **GOLD** 0.4995 oz. AGW. 15.5520 g.
Obv. Desc.: Francis Cleveland (second term)

Date	Mintage	MS65	PRF65
2012	—	—	—
2012	—	—	—

MINT SETS

Mint, or uncirculated, sets contain one uncirculated coin
of each denomination from each mint produced for circulation that year. Values listed here are only for those sets sold
by the U.S. Mint. Sets were not offered in years not listed.
In years when the Mint did not offer the sets, some private
companies compiled and marketed uncirculated sets. Mint
sets from 1947 through 1958 contained two examples of
each coin mounted in cardboard holders, which caused the
coins to tarnish. Beginning in 1959, the sets have been
packaged in sealed Pliofilm packets and include only one
specimen of each coin struck for that year (both P & D
mints). Listings for 1965, 1966 and 1967 are for "special
mint sets," which were of higher quality than regular mint
sets and were prooflike. They were packaged in plastic cases. The 1970 large-date and small-date varieties are distinguished by the size of the date on the coin. The 1976 three-
piece set contains the quarter, half dollar and dollar with the
Bicentennial design. The 1971 and 1972 sets do not include a dollar coin; the 1979 set does not include an S-mint-
marked dollar. Mint sets issued prior to 1959 were double
sets (containing two of each coin) packaged in cardboard
with a paper overlay. Origional sets will always be toned
and can bring large premiums if nicely preserved with good
color.

Date	Sets Sold	Issue Price	Value
2001	1,066,900	14.95	9.65
2002	1,139,388	14.95	10.75
2003	1,002,555	14.95	8.80
2004	844,484	16.95	13.75
2005	—	16.95	8.50
2006	—	16.95	12.25
2007	—	—	17.60

Date	Sets Sold	Issue Price	Value
2008	—	—	61.00
2009 18 pieces clad	—	—	25.50
2010 28 piece clad coin set	—	—	—
2010S 18 piece clad	—	—	33.00

MODERN COMMEMORATIVE COIN SETS

American Buffalo

Date	Price
2001 2 coin set: 90% silver unc. & proof $1.; KM325.	330
2001 coin & currency set 90% unc. dollar & replicas of 1899 $5 silver cert.; KM325.	180

Capitol Visitor Center

Date	Price
2001 3 coin set: proof half, silver dollar, gold $5; KM323, 324, 326.	495

Winter Olympics - Salt Lake City

Date	Price
2002 2 coin set: proof 90% silver dollar KM336 & $5.00 Gold KM337.	465
2002 4 coin set: 90% silver unc. & proof $1, KM336 & unc. & proof gold $5, KM337.	925

Thomas Alva Edison

Date	Price
2004 Uncirculated silver dollar and light bulb.	55.00

Lewis and Clark Bicentennial

Date	Price
2004 Coin and pouch set.	65.00
2004 coin and currency set: Uncirculated silver dollar, two 2005 nickels, replica 1901 $10 Bison note, silver plated peace medal, three stamps & two booklets.	58.00
2004 Westward Journey Nickel series coin and medal set: Proof Sacagawea dollar, two 2005 proof nickels and silver plated peace medal.	40.00

Chief Justice John Marshall

Date	Price
2005 Coin and Chronicles set: Uncirculated silver dollar, booklet and BEP intaglio portrait.	57.00

U.S. Marine Corps.

Date	Price
2005 Uncirculated silver dollar and stamp set.	63.00

Benjamin Franklin Tercentennary

Date	Price
2006 Coin and Chronicles set: Uncirculated "Scientist" silver dollar, four stamps, Poor Richards Almanac and intaglio print.	49.00

Central High School Desegregation

Date	Price
2007 Little Rock Dollar and medal set, KM#418	47.80

American Bald Eagle

Date	Price
2008 Proof half dollar, dollar and $5 gold, KM438, KM439, KM440	490
2008 Bald Eagle young collector's set; Half Dollar, KM#438	23.00

Louis Braille

Date	Price
Braille Education set, KM#455	43.50

PROOF SETS

Proof coins are produced through a special process involving specially selected, highly polished planchets and
dies. They usually receive two strikings from the coin press
at increased pressure. The result is a coin with mirrorlike
surfaces and, in recent years, a cameo effect on its raised
design surfaces. Proof sets have been sold off and on by
the U.S. Mint since 1858. Listings here are for sets from
what is commonly called the modern era, since 1936. Values for earlier proofs are included in regular date listings.
Sets were not offered in years not listed. Since 1968, proof
coins have been produced at the San Francisco Mint; before that they were produced at the Philadelphia Mint. In
1942 the five-cent coin was struck in two compositions.
Some proof sets for that year contain only one type (five-
coin set); others contain both types. Two types of packaging were used in 1955 -- a box and a flat, plastic holder. The
1960 large-date and small-date sets are distinguished by
the size of the date on the cent. Some 1968 sets are missing the mint mark on the dime, the result of an error in the
preparation of an obverse die. The 1970 large-date and
small-date sets are distinguished by the size of the date on
the cent. Some 1970 sets are missing the mint mark on the
dime, the result of an error in the preparation of an obverse
die. Some 1971 sets are missing the mint mark on the five-

cent piece, the result of an error in the preparation of an obverse die. The 1976 three-piece set contains the quarter, half dollar and dollar with the Bicentennial designs. The 1979 and 1981 Type II sets have clearer mint marks than the Type I sets for those years. Some 1983 sets are missing the mint mark on the dime, the result of an error in the preparation of an obverse die. Prestige sets contain the five regular-issue coins plus a commemorative silver dollar from that year. Sets issued prior to 1956 came in transparent envelopes stapled together in a small square box. In mid 1955 sets were changed to a flat clear cellophane envelope. In 1968 sets were changed to a clear hard plastic case as they still are currently issued.

Date	Sets Sold	Issue Price	Value
2001S 10 piece	2,249,498	19.95	12.25
2001S 5 quarter set	774,800	13.95	8.00
2001S Silver	849,600	31.95	57.30
2002S 10 piece	2,319,766	19.95	12.25
2002S 5 quarter set	764,419	13.95	5.00
2002S Silver	892,229	31.95	53.40
2003 X#207, 208, 209.2	—	44.00	28.75
2003S 10 piece	2,175,684	16.75	7.20
2003S 5 quarter set	1,225,507	13.95	3.60
2003S Silver	1,142,858	31.95	52.40
2004S 11 piece	1,804,396	22.95	8.25
2004S 5 quarter set	987,960	23.95	3.75
2004S Silver 11 piece	1,187,673	37.95	52.40
2004S Silver 5 quarter set	594,137	—	33.50
2005S American Legacy	—	—	77.00
2005S 11 piece	—	22.95	5.50
2005S 5 quarter set	—	15.95	3.35
2005S Silver 11 piece	—	37.95	53.40
2005S Silver 5 quarter set	—	23.95	33.50
2005S American Legacy	—	—	77.00
2006S 10 piece clad	—	22.95	8.50
2006S 5 quarter set	—	15.95	5.00
2006S Silver 10 piece	—	37.95	53.40
2006S Silver 5 quarter set	—	23.95	33.50
2006S American Legacy	—	—	71.50
2007S 5 quarter set	—	13.95	4.50
2007S Silver 5 quarter set	—	22.95	35.40
2007S 14 piece clad	—	—	13.75
2007S Silver 14 piece	—	—	62.30
2007S Presidental $ set	—	—	6.00
2007S American Legacy	—	—	125
2008 14 pieces clad	—	—	75.00
2008S Silver 14 piece	734,045	—	73.00
2008S Presidental $ set	—	—	12.25
2008S American Legacy	—	—	132
2008S 5 quarter set	—	22.95	29.50
2008S Silver 5 quarter set	—	—	35.40
2009S 18 coin clad set	1,477,967	—	21.00
2009S Silver 18 coin set	694,406	—	66.00
2009S Presidential $ set	627,925	—	6.60
2009S Lincoln Chronicle	—	—	127
2009S Lincoln 4 piece	—	—	15.50
2009S 6 quarter set	—	—	9.50
2009S Silver 6 quarter set	—	—	40.60
2010S 14 coin clad set	1,103,950	—	44.00
2010S 14 coin silver set	583,912	—	70.00
2010S Presidential $ set	535,463	—	14.00
2010S 5 Quarter clad set	276,335	—	—
2010S 5 Quarter silver set	274,003	—	—
2010S 6 Quarter silver set	—	—	41.00
2010S 6 Quarter clad set	—	—	14.00

UNCIRCULATED ROLLS

Listings are for rolls containing uncirculated coins. Large date and small date varieties for 1960 and 1970 apply to the one cent coins.

Date	Cents	Nickels	Dimes	Quarters	Halves
2001P	3.75	4.75	7.75	—	16.50
2001D	2.00	6.50	7.25	—	16.00
2002P	2.00	4.00	7.25	—	20.00
2002D	3.25	4.10	7.25	—	20.00
2003P	3.35	7.50	7.00	—	22.50
2003D	2.00	3.50	7.00	—	19.50
2004P Peace Medal Nickel	1.75	6.75	7.00	—	30.00
2004D Peace Medal Nickel	2.50	7.00	7.00	—	30.00
2004P Keelboat Nickel	—	4.00	—	—	—
2004D Keelboat Nickel	—	3.50	—	—	—
2005P Bison Nickel	1.75	3.25	7.00	—	21.00
2005D Bison Nickel	2.75	3.25	7.00	—	21.00
2005P Ocean in view Nickel	—	3.25	—	—	—
2005D Ocean in view Nickel	—	3.25	—	—	—
2006P	2.75	3.25	8.50	—	29.00
2006D	1.75	3.25	8.50	—	29.00
2007P	1.75	3.50	8.00	—	21.00
2007D	1.75	3.50	7.75	—	21.00
2008P	1.75	3.75	8.00	—	24.50
2008D	1.75	3.75	7.50	—	25.50
2009P Log Cabin	2.00	23.00	13.50	—	18.50
2009D Log Cabin	2.15	13.50	13.50	—	18.50
2009P Log Splitter	1.75	—	—	—	—
2009D Log Splitter	1.75	—	—	—	—
2009P Professional	—	1.75	—	—	—
2009D Professional	1.75	—	—	—	—
2009P President	2.00	—	—	—	—
2009D President	2.00	—	—	—	—

Date	Cents	Nickels	Dimes	Quarters	Halves
2009 DC	18.00	15.50	—	—	—
2009 Puerto Rico	15.00	15.50	—	—	—
2009 Guam	15.00	16.50	—	—	—
2009 American Samoa	15.00	15.00	—	—	—
2009 Virgin Islands	15.00	15.00	—	—	—
2009 Marianna Islands	15.00	15.00	—	—	—

URUGUAY

The Oriental Republic of Uruguay (so called because of its location on the east bank of the Uruguay River) is situated on the Atlantic coast of South America between Argentina and Brazil. This South American country has an area of 68,536 sq. mi. (176,220 sq. km.) and a population of *3 million. Capital: Montevideo. Uruguay's chief economic asset is the rich, rolling grassy plains. Meat, wool, hides and skins are exported.

MINT MARKS
 (ba) – Buenos Aires
 (br) – Acunaciones Espanolas S.A., Barcelona
 (k) – Kremnica (Slovakia)
 (m) - Madrid
 Mo, (mo) and Mx - Mexico City
 (p) – thunderbolt: Poissy, France
 (rcm) – Royal Canadian Mint
 (rj) – Rio de Janeiro
 (sa) – Pretoria, South Africa
 So, (so) – Santiago (Small o above S); (except 2007 2 Pesos Uruguayos)

REPUBLIC

REFORM COINAGE
March 1993

1,000 Nuevos Pesos = 1 Uruguayan Peso;
100 Centesimos = 1 Uruguayan Peso (UYP)

KM# 106   50 CENTESIMOS
3.0000 g., Stainless Steel, 21 mm. **Obv:** Bust of Artigas right **Obv. Legend:** REPUBLICA ORIENTAL DEL URUGUAY **Rev:** Value, date and sprig **Edge:** Plain **Note:** Coin rotation.

Date	Mintage	F	VF	XF	Unc	BU
2002(sa)	10,000,000	—	—	0.35	0.75	1.00
2005(m)	15,000,000	—	—	0.35	0.75	1.00
2008(k)	35,000,000	—	—	0.35	0.75	1.00
2009	—	—	—	0.35	0.75	1.00

KM# 103.2   UN PESO URUGUAYO
3.5000 g., Aluminum-Bronze, 20 mm. **Obv:** Bust of Artigas right **Obv. Legend:** REPUBLICA ORIENTAL DEL URUGUAY **Rev:** Value and date **Edge:** Plain **Note:** Medal rotation; left point of bust shoulder points at "P" in Republic.

Date	Mintage	F	VF	XF	Unc	BU
2005So	40,000,000	—	—	—	0.50	0.75
2007So	25,000,000	—	—	—	0.50	0.75

KM# 135   UN PESO URUGUAYO
3.5000 g., Brass Plated Steel, 20 mm. **Obv:** Arms in circle, date below **Obv. Legend:** REPUBLICA ORIENTAL DEL URUGUAY **Rev:** Mulita, armadillo **Edge:** Plain

Date	Mintage	F	VF	XF	Unc	BU
2011(m)	20,000,000	—	—	—	0.50	0.60

KM# 104.2   2 PESOS URUGUAYOS
4.5000 g., Aluminum-Bronze, 23 mm. **Obv:** Bust of Artigas right **Obv. Legend:** REPUBLICA ORIENTAL DEL URUGUAY **Rev:** Value and date **Edge:** Plain **Note:** Medal rotation. Left point of bust shoulder points at "P" in "Republic".

Date	Mintage	F	VF	XF	Unc	BU
2005So	—	—	—	0.75	1.50	2.00
2007So	25,000,000	—	—	0.75	1.50	2.00

Note: Minted at Paris with the So mintmark.

KM# 136   2 PESOS URUGUAYOS
4.5000 g., Brass Plated Steel, 23 mm. **Obv:** Arms in circle, date below **Obv. Legend:** REPUBLICA ORIENTAL DEL URUGUAY **Rev:** Carpincho **Edge:** Plain

Date	Mintage	F	VF	XF	Unc	BU
2011(m)	20,000,000	—	—	—	0.75	0.90

KM# 137   2 PESOS URUGUAYOS
6.4000 g., Brass Plated Steel, 25.5 mm. **Obv:** Arms in circle, date below **Obv. Legend:** REPUBLICA ORIENTAL DEL URUGUAY **Rev:** Nandu **Edge:** Palin

Date	Mintage	F	VF	XF	Unc	BU
2011(l)	10,000,000	—	—	—	1.25	1.50

KM# 120.2   5 PESOS URUGUAYOS
6.3000 g., Aluminum-Bronze, 26 mm. **Obv:** Bust of Antigas right **Obv. Legend:** REPUBLICA ORIENTAL DEL URUGUAY • **Rev:** Value, date **Note:** Left point of bust shoulder points at "P" in "Republic".

Date	Mintage	F	VF	XF	Unc	BU
2003So	—	—	—	—	2.50	3.00
2005So	30,000,000	—	—	—	2.50	3.00
2008So	20,000,000	—	—	—	2.50	3.00

KM# 120.1   5 PESOS URUGUAYOS
6.3000 g., Aluminum-Bronze, 26 mm. **Obv:** Bust of Antigas right **Obv. Legend:** REPUBLICA ORIENTAL DEL URUGUAY **Rev:** Value **Edge:** Plain **Note:** Left point of bust shoulder points at "U" in "Republic".

Date	Mintage	F	VF	XF	Unc	BU
2003(ba)	15,150,000	—	—	—	2.50	3.00

KM# 121   10 PESOS URUGUAYOS
10.4000 g., Bi-Metallic Aluminum-Bronze center in Stainless Steel ring, 28 mm. **Obv:** Artigas head right within circle **Rev:** Value above signature within circle **Edge:** Plain

Date	Mintage	F	VF	XF	Unc	BU
2000 (rcm)	40,000,000	—	—	—	3.50	5.00

Note: 5-pointed star on each side of date, issued 2006

KM# 134   10 PESOS URUGUAYOS
10.4000 g., Bi-Metallic Brass center, 28 mm. **Obv:** Oval arms, country name and date **Rev:** Puma walking left, sunrise in background and value

Date	Mintage	F	VF	XF	Unc	BU
2011(l)	10,000,000	—	—	—	2.00	2.50

KM# 139   50 PESOS URUGUAYOS
Copper Plated Steel, 28 mm. **Subject:** Bicentennial of Uruguayan Independence **Obv:** Portrait of General Jose Artigas, country name and value **Rev:** Sun and rays and inscriptions "BICENTENARIO DE LOS HECHOS HISTORICOS" and "1811-2011" **Edge:** Reeded

Date	Mintage	F	VF	XF	Unc	BU
2011(k)	10,000,000	—	—	—	4.00	4.50

KM# 133   500 PESOS URUGAUAYOS
12.5000 g., 0.9000 Silver 0.3617 oz. ASW, 33 mm. **Subject:** Salto, 250th Anniversary **Obv:** Uruguay map with City of Salto location **Rev:** Emblem of the Department of Salto

Date	Mintage	F	VF	XF	Unc	BU
2006(u) Proof	10,000	Value: 25.00				

KM# 122 1000 PESOS URUGUAYOS
27.0000 g., 0.9250 Silver 0.8029 oz. ASW, 40 mm. **Subject:** XVIII World Championship Football - Germany 2006 **Obv:** National arms **Obv. Legend:** REPUBLICA ORIENTAL DEL URUGUAY **Rev:** Soccer player and value **Edge:** Reeded

Date	Mintage	F	VF	XF	Unc	BU
2003(m) Proof	—	Value: 50.00				

KM# 123 1000 PESOS URUGUAYOS
27.0000 g., 0.9250 Silver 0.8029 oz. ASW, 40 mm. **Subject:** XVIII World Championship Football - Germany 2006 **Obv:** National arms above date **Obv. Legend:** REPUBLICA ORIENTAL DEL URUGUAY **Rev:** Stylized soccer player and value **Edge:** Reeded

Date	Mintage	F	VF	XF	Unc	BU
2004(m) Proof	—	Value: 50.00				

KM# 125 1000 PESOS URUGUAYOS
27.0000 g., 0.9250 Silver 0.8029 oz. ASW, 40 mm. **Subject:** 100th Anniversary FIFA - 1930 Championship **Obv:** Football before net **Obv. Legend:** REPUBLICA ORIENTAL DEL URUGUAY **Rev:** Sun of national flag **Edge:** Reeded

Date	Mintage	F	VF	XF	Unc	BU
2004(m) Proof	—	Value: 45.00				

KM# 124 1000 PESOS URUGUAYOS
27.0000 g., 0.9250 Silver 0.8029 oz. ASW, 40 mm. **Subject:** XVIII World Championship Football - Germany 2006 **Obv:** National arms above date **Obv. Legend:** REPUBLICA ORIENTAL DEL URUGUAY **Rev:** FIFA trophy **Edge:** Reeded

Date	Mintage	F	VF	XF	Unc	BU
2005(m) Proof	—	Value: 50.00				

KM# 140 1000 PESOS URUGUAYOS
25.0000 g., 0.9000 Silver 0.7234 oz. ASW, 37 mm. **Subject:** Bicentennial of Uruguayan Independence **Obv:** Painting by Juan Luis Blanes of the surrender of Posadas at the battle of Las Piedras on May 18, 1811, country name and value **Rev:** Sun and rays and inscription "BICENTENARIO DE LOS HECHOS HISTORICOS" and "1811-2011" **Edge:** Reeded

Date	Mintage	F	VF	XF	Unc	BU
2011(k) Proof	5,000	Value: 80.00				

KM# 126 5000 PESOS URUGUAYOS
6.7500 g., 0.9250 Gold 0.2007 oz. AGW, 23 mm. **Subject:** 100th Anniversary FIFA - 1930 Championship **Obv:** Football **Obv. Legend:** REPUBLICA ORIENTAL DEL URUGUAY **Rev:** Tower of Homage in Montevideo **Edge:** Reeded

Date	Mintage	F	VF	XF	Unc	BU
2004(m) Proof	—	Value: 375				

KM# 127 5000 PESOS URUGUAYOS
6.7500 g., 0.9250 Gold 0.2007 oz. AGW, 23 mm. **Subject:** XVIII World Championship Football - Germany 2006 **Obv:** National arms **Obv. Legend:** REPUBLICA ORIENTAL DEL URUGUAY **Rev:** Stylized player and value **Edge:** Reeded

Date	Mintage	F	VF	XF	Unc	BU
2004(m) Proof	—	Value: 500				

MINT SETS

KM#	Date	Mintage	Identification	Issue Price	Mkt Val
MS5	1994-2003 (7)	—	KM#102, 105 (1994), 103.2, 104.2 (1998), 106 (2002), 120.1 (2003, 121 (2000)	—	15.00

UZBEKISTAN

The Republic of Uzbekistan (formerly the Uzbek S.S.R.), is bordered on the north by Kazakhstan, to the east by Kirghizia and Tajikistan, on the south by Afghanistan and on the west by Turkmenistan. The republic is comprised of the regions of Andizhan, Bukhara, Dzhizak, Ferghana, Kashkadar, Khorezm (Khiva), Namangan, Navoi, Samarkand, Surkhan-Darya, Syr-Darya, Tashkent and the Karakalpak Autonomous Republic. It has an area of 172,741 sq. mi. (447,400 sq. km.) and a population of 20.3 million. Capital: Tashkent. Crude oil, natural gas, coal, copper, and gold deposits make up the chief resources, while intensive farming, based on artificial irrigation, provides an abundance of cotton.

MONETARY SYSTEM
100 Tiyin = 1 Som

REPUBLIC

STANDARD COINAGE

KM# 13 5 SOM
3.3500 g., Brass Plated Steel, 21.2 mm. **Obv:** National arms **Rev:** Value and map **Edge:** Plain

Date	Mintage	F	VF	XF	Unc	BU
2001	—				1.35	1.75

Note: 2 reverse map varieties known

KM# 14 10 SOM
2.7100 g., Nickel Clad Steel, 19.75 mm. **Obv:** National arms **Rev:** Value and map **Edge:** Plain

Date	Mintage	F	VF	XF	Unc	BU
2001	—				2.00	2.50

Note: 2 reverse map varieties exist

KM# 15 50 SOM
8.0000 g., Nickel Clad Steel, 26.2 mm. **Obv:** National arms **Rev:** Value and map **Edge:** Segmented reeding

Date	Mintage	F	VF	XF	Unc	BU
2001	—			1.20	3.00	4.00

KM# 16 50 SOM
7.9000 g., Nickel Clad Steel, 26.3 mm. **Subject:** 2700th Anniversary of Shahrisabz Town **Obv:** National arms **Rev:** Statue and ruins above value **Edge:** Segmented reeding

Date	Mintage	F	VF	XF	Unc	BU
2002	—			1.00	2.50	3.50

KM# 20 100 SOM
31.1000 g., 0.9990 Silver 0.9988 oz. ASW **Obv:** National arms **Obv. Legend:** O'ZBEKISTON MARKAZIY BANKI **Rev:** Amir-Timur Museum

Date	Mintage	F	VF	XF	Unc	BU
2001 Proof	1,000	Value: 225				

KM# 21 100 SOM
31.1000 g., 0.9990 Silver 0.9988 oz. ASW **Obv:** National Arms **Obv. Legend:** O'BEKISTON MARKAZIY BANKI **Rev:** Toskent town hall

Date	Mintage	F	VF	XF	Unc	BU
2001 Proof	1,000	Value: 225				

KM# 22 100 SOM
31.1000 g., 0.9990 Silver 0.9988 oz. ASW **Obv:** National arms **Obv. Legend:** O'ZBEKISTON MARKAZIY BANKI **Rev:** World

Date	Mintage	F	VF	XF	Unc	BU
2001 Proof	1,000	Value: 225				

KM# 18 100 SOM
Bronze **Subject:** 500th Anniversary Death of 'Aliser Navoi **Obv:** National arms **Obv. Legend:** O'ZBEKISTON MARKAZIY BANKI **Rev:** 'Aliser Navoi

Date	Mintage	F	VF	XF	Unc	BU
2001	—	—	—		15.00	18.00

KM# 19 100 SOM
31.1000 g., 0.9990 Silver 0.9988 oz. ASW **Obv:** National arms **Obv. Legend:** O'ZBEKISTON MARKAZIY BANKI **Rev:** Parliament building in Toskent

Date	Mintage	F	VF	XF	Unc	BU
2001 Proof	1,000	Value: 225				

KM# 23 100 SOM
31.1000 g., 0.9990 Silver 0.9988 oz. ASW **Obv:** National arms **Obv. Legend:** O'ZBEKISTON MARKAZIY BANKI **Rev:** Football player

Date	Mintage	F	VF	XF	Unc	BU
2001 Proof	1,000	Value: 225				

KM# 24   100 SOM
31.1000 g., 0.9990 Silver 0.9988 oz. ASW **Obv:** National arms
Obv. Legend: O'BEKISTON MARKAZIY BANKI **Rev:** Track
runner

Date	Mintage	F	VF	XF	Unc	BU
2001 Proof	1,000	Value: 225				

KM# 25   100 SOM
31.1000 g., 0.9990 Silver 0.9988 oz. ASW **Obv:** National arms
Obv. Legend: O'ZBEKISTON MARKAZIY BANKI **Rev:** Judo
expert

Date	Mintage	F	VF	XF	Unc	BU
2001 Proof	1,000	Value: 225				

KM# 26   100 SOM
31.1000 g., 0.9990 Silver 0.9988 oz. ASW **Obv:** National arms
Obv. Legend: O'ZBEKISTON MARKAZIY BANKI **Rev:** Tennis
player

Date	Mintage	F	VF	XF	Unc	BU
2001 Proof	1,000	Value: 225				

KM# 27   100 SOM
31.1000 g., 0.9990 Silver 0.9988 oz. ASW **Obv:** National arms
Obv. Legend: O'ZBEKISTON MARKAZIY BANKI **Rev:** Lenk
monument in Timur

Date	Mintage	F	VF	XF	Unc	BU
2001 Proof	1,000	Value: 225				

KM# 28   100 SOM
31.1000 g., 0.9990 Silver 0.9988 oz. ASW **Obv:** National arms
Obv. Legend: O'ZBEKISTON MARKAZIY BANKI **Rev:** Aliser
Navoi monument

Date	Mintage	F	VF	XF	Unc	BU
2001 Proof	1,000	Value: 225				

KM# 29   100 SOM
31.1000 g., 0.9990 Silver 0.9988 oz. ASW **Obv:** National arms
Obv. Legend: O'ZBEKISTON MARKAZIY BANKI **Rev:** Registan
in Samarkand

Date	Mintage	F	VF	XF	Unc	BU
2001 Proof	1,000	Value: 225				

KM# 30   100 SOM
31.1000 g., 0.9990 Silver 0.9988 oz. ASW **Obv:** National arms
Obv. Legend: O'BEKISTON MARKAZIY BANKI **Rev:** Bell tower
in Toskent

Date	Mintage	F	VF	XF	Unc	BU
2001 Proof	1,000	Value: 225				

KM# 17   100 SOM
7.9200 g., Nickel Plated Steel, 26.95 mm. **Subject:** 10th
Annniversary State Currency **Obv:** National arms **Obv. Legend:**
O'ZBEKISTON MARKAZIV BANKI **Rev:** Sun rays over outlined
map and value **Rev. Legend:** O'BEKISTON MILLIY
VALYUTASIGA **Edge:** Lettered

Date	Mintage	F	VF	XF	Unc	BU
2004	—			—	12.50	15.00

KM# 31   100 SOM
7.9200 g., Nickel Plated Steel, 26.95 mm. **Subject:** Tashkent,
2200th Anniversary of settlement **Obv:** National arms **Rev:** Linear
archway and monument in background

Date	Mintage	F	VF	XF	Unc	BU
2009	—	—	—	—	3.50	5.00

KM# 32   100 SOM
7.9200 g., Nickel Plated Steel, 26.95 mm. **Subject:** Tashkent,
2200th Anniversary of settlement **Obv:** National arms **Rev:**
Monument

Date	Mintage	F	VF	XF	Unc	BU
2009	—	—	—	—	3.50	5.00

VANUATU

The Republic of Vanuatu, formerly New Hebrides Condominium, a group of islands located in the South Pacific 500 miles
(800 km.) west of Fiji, were under the joint sovereignty of Great
Britain and France. The islands have an area of 5,700 sq. mi.
(14,760 sq. km.) and a population of 165,000, mainly Melane-
sians of mixed blood. Capital: Port-Vila. The volcanic and coral
islands, while malarial land subject to frequent earthquakes, are
extremely fertile, and produce copra, coffee, tropical fruits and
timber for export.

The New Hebrides were discovered by Portuguese navigator Pedro de Quiros (sailing under orders by the King of Spain)
in 1606, visited by French explorer Bougainville in 1768, and
named by British navigator Capt. James Cook in 1774. Ships of
all nations converged on the islands to trade for sandalwood,
prompting France and Britain to relinquish their individual claims
and declare the islands a neutral zone in 1878. The New Hebrides
were placed under the control of a mixed Anglo-French commission of naval officers during the native uprisings of 1887, and
established as a condominium under the joint sovereignty of
France and Great Britain in 1906.

Vanuatu became an independent republic within the Commonwealth in July 1980. A president is Head of State and the
Prime Minister is Head of Government.

MONETARY SYSTEM
Vatu to Present

REPUBLIC
STANDARD COINAGE

KM# 3   VATU
1.9900 g., Nickel-Brass, 16.95 mm. **Obv:** National arms **Rev:**
Shell and value **Edge:** Plain

Date	Mintage	F	VF	XF	Unc	BU
2002	—			0.15	0.50	0.75

KM# 4   2 VATU
3.0000 g., Nickel-Brass, 20 mm. **Obv:** National arms **Rev:** Shell
and value **Edge:** Plain

Date	Mintage	F	VF	XF	Unc	BU
2002	—	—	—	0.25	0.85	1.50

KM# 5   5 VATU
4.1000 g., Nickel-Brass, 23.5 mm. **Obv:** National arms **Rev:**
Shell and value **Edge:** Plain

Date	Mintage	F	VF	XF	Unc	BU
2002	—	—	—	—	1.00	1.75
2009	—	—	—	—	1.00	1.75

KM# 45   10 VATU
Copper-Nickel silver plated **Obv:** Arms **Rev:** Multicolor butterfly
(Papilio Toboroi)

Date	Mintage	F	VF	XF	Unc	BU
2006	2,500	—	—	—	—	32.00

KM# 50   10 VATU
Copper-Nickel silver plated **Obv:** Arms **Rev:** Multicolor butterfly
(Delias Sagessa)

Date	Mintage	F	VF	XF	Unc	BU
2006	2,500	—	—	—	—	32.00

KM# 46   10 VATU
Copper-Nickel silver plated **Obv:** Arms **Rev:** Multicolor butterfly
(Taenaris Catops)

Date	Mintage	F	VF	XF	Unc	BU
2006	2,500	—	—	—	—	32.00

KM# 47   10 VATU
Copper-Nickel silver plated **Obv:** Arms **Rev:** Multicolor Butterfly
(Ornithoptera Priamus Urvillianus)

Date	Mintage	F	VF	XF	Unc	BU
2006	2,500	—	—	—	—	32.00

KM# 48   10 VATU
Copper-Nickel silver plated **Obv:** Arms **Rev:** Multicolor butterfly
(Ornithoptera Paradisea)

Date	Mintage	F	VF	XF	Unc	BU
2006	2,500	—	—	—	—	32.00

KM# 49   10 VATU
Copper-Nickel silver plated **Obv:** Arms **Rev:** Multicolor butterfly
(Cethosia Cydippe)

Date	Mintage	F	VF	XF	Unc	BU
2006	2,500	—	—	—	—	32.00

KM# 6   10 VATU
6.1000 g., Copper-Nickel, 23.95 mm. **Obv:** National arms **Rev:**
Crab and value, palm trees **Edge:** Plain

Date	Mintage	F	VF	XF	Unc	BU
2009	—	—	—	0.35	1.25	2.80

KM# 51   10 VATU
Copper-Nickel **Subject:** Barack Obama **Obv:** National arms
Rev: Profile right

Date	Mintage	F	VF	XF	Unc	BU
2009	—	—	—	—	—	14.00

KM# 8   50 VATU
15.0000 g., Copper-Nickel, 32.9 mm. **Series:** F.A.O. **Obv:**
National arms **Rev:** Tubers encircled by leafy vines, value above

Date	Mintage	F	VF	XF	Unc	BU
2002	—	—	—	—	2.00	3.00
2009	—	—	—	—	2.00	3.00

KM# 53   50 VATU
Silver, 38.6 mm. **Subject:** Olympics, 2004 **Obv:** National
emblem **Rev:** Athlethe with torch, large torch, fragment of ancient
vase

Date	Mintage	F	VF	XF	Unc	BU
2003 Proof	—	Value: 50.00				

KM# 38   50 VATU
28.3200 g., 0.9250 Silver 0.8422 oz. ASW, 38.6 mm. **Obv:**
National arms **Obv. Legend:** RIPABLIK / VANUATU **Rev:** Early
sailing ship center - left, stylized compass at right **Rev. Legend:**
HISTORY OF SEAFARING / PEDRO FERNANDEZ DE QUIRÓS
Edge: Reeded

Date	Mintage	F	VF	XF	Unc	BU
2005 Proof	—	Value: 45.00				

KM# 41   50 VATU
25.0000 g., 0.9000 Silver 0.7234 oz. ASW **Series:** Protection
of Marine Life **Obv:** National arms **Rev:** Tiger Shark - multicolor

Date	Mintage	F	VF	XF	Unc	BU
2005 Proof	—	Value: 75.00				

KM# 54   50 VATU
Silver, 38.6 mm. **Obv:** National emblem **Rev:** Two soccer
players with large globe in background

Date	Mintage	F	VF	XF	Unc	BU
2006 Proof	—	Value: 50.00				

KM# 42   50 VATU
25.0000 g., 0.9000 Silver 0.7234 oz. ASW **Series:** Protection
of Marine Life **Obv:** National arms **Rev:** Sea Turtle - multicolor

Date	Mintage	F	VF	XF	Unc	BU
2006 Proof	—	Value: 75.00				

KM# 43   50 VATU
25.0000 g., 0.9000 Silver 0.7234 oz. ASW **Series:** Protection
of Marine Life **Obv:** National arms **Rev:** Sea Horse - multicolor

Date	Mintage	F	VF	XF	Unc	BU
2006 Proof	—	Value: 75.00				

KM# 52   50 VATU
Silver **Subject:** 2006 World Cup - Germany **Obv:** National arms
Rev: 2 soccer players and globe

Date	Mintage	F	VF	XF	Unc	BU
2006 Proof	—	Value: 35.00				

KM# 9   100 VATU
9.5500 g., Nickel-Brass, 23.9 mm. **Obv:** National arms **Rev:**
Sprouting bulbs

Date	Mintage	F	VF	XF	Unc	BU
2002	—	—	—	—	3.00	4.00
2008	—	—	—	—	3.00	4.00

VATICAN CITY

The State of the Vatican City, a papal state on the right bank
of the Tiber River within the boundaries of Rome, has an area of
0.17 sq. mi. (0.44 sq. km.) and a population of *775. Capital: Vatican City.

Today the Pope exercises supreme legislative, executive
and judicial power within the Vatican City, and the State of the
Vatican City is recognized by many nations as an independent
sovereign state under the temporal jurisdiction of the Pope, even
to the extent of ambassadorial exchange. The Pope is of course,
the head of the Roman Catholic Church.

PONTIFFS
John Paul II, 1978-2005
  Sede Vacante, April 2 - 19, 2005
Benedict XVI, 2005-

MINT MARK
R – Rome

MONETARY SYSTEM
100 Centesimi = 1 Lira (thru 2002)
100 Euro Cent = 1 Euro

DATING
Most Vatican coins indicate the regnal year of the pope preceded by the word *Anno* (or an abbreviation), even if the *anno
domini* date is omitted.

CITY STATE

DECIMAL COINAGE
100 Centesimi = 1 Lira

KM# 331   10 LIRE
1.6000 g., Aluminum, 23.2 mm. **Ruler:** John Paul II **Obv:** Bust
left **Rev:** Papal arms **Edge:** Plain

Date	Mintage	F	VF	XF	Unc	BU
2001/XXIII	—	—	0.50	1.00	3.00	—

KM# 331a   10 LIRE
Gold, 23.2 mm. **Ruler:** John Paul II **Obv:** Benedict XV bust left
Rev: Papal arms **Note:** Struck in 2007.

Date	Mintage	F	VF	XF	Unc	BU
2001R Proof	499	—	—	—	—	—

KM# 332   20 LIRE
3.5700 g., Brass, 21.2 mm. **Ruler:** John Paul II **Obv:** Bust left
Rev: Papal arms **Edge:** Plain

Date	Mintage	F	VF	XF	Unc	BU
2001/XXIII	—	—	0.50	1.00	3.00	—

KM# 332a   20 LIRE
Gold, 21.2 mm. **Ruler:** John Paul II **Obv:** Pius XI bust left **Rev:**
Papal arms **Note:** Struck in 2007.

Date	Mintage	F	VF	XF	Unc	BU
2001R Proof	499	—	—	—	—	—

KM# 333 50 LIRE
4.5000 g., Copper-Nickel, 19.2 mm. **Ruler:** John Paul II **Obv:** Pius XII bust left **Rev:** Papal arms **Edge:** Plain

Date	Mintage	F	VF	XF	Unc	BU
2001/XXIII	—	—	0.50	1.00	3.00	—

KM# 333a 50 LIRE
Gold, 19.2 mm. **Ruler:** John Paul II **Obv:** Pius XII bust left **Rev:** Papal arms **Note:** Struck in 2007.

Date	Mintage	F	VF	XF	Unc	BU
2001R Proof	499	—	—	—	—	—

KM# 334 100 LIRE
4.5000 g., Copper-Nickel, 22 mm. **Ruler:** John Paul II **Obv:** Bust left **Rev:** Papal arms within circle **Edge:** Reeded and plain sections

Date	Mintage	F	VF	XF	Unc	BU
2001/XXIII	—	—	0.50	1.00	3.00	—

KM# 334a 100 LIRE
Gold, 22 mm. **Ruler:** John Paul II **Obv:** John XXIII bust left **Rev:** Papal arms **Note:** Struck in 2007.

Date	Mintage	F	VF	XF	Unc	BU
2001R Proof	499	—	—	—	—	—

KM# 335 200 LIRE
5.0000 g., Brass, 22 mm. **Ruler:** John Paul II **Obv:** Bust right **Rev:** Papal arms within circle **Edge:** Reeded

Date	Mintage	F	VF	XF	Unc	BU
2001/XXIII	—	—	0.50	1.00	3.00	—

KM# 335a 200 LIRE
Gold, 22 mm. **Ruler:** John Paul II **Obv:** Paul VI bust right **Rev:** Papal arms **Note:** Struck in 2007.

Date	Mintage	F	VF	XF	Unc	BU
2001R Proof	499	—	—	—	—	—

KM# 336 500 LIRE
6.7700 g., Bi-Metallic Aluminum-Bronze center in Stainless steel ring, 25.7 mm. **Ruler:** John Paul II **Obv:** John Paul I head left **Rev:** Papal arms within circle **Edge:** Segmented reeding

Date	Mintage	F	VF	XF	Unc	BU
2001/XXIII	—	—	—	3.50	7.00	—

KM# 336a 500 LIRE
Gold, 25.7 mm. **Ruler:** John Paul II **Obv:** John Paul I bust left **Rev:** Papal arms

Date	Mintage	F	VF	XF	Unc	BU
2001R Proof	499	—	—	—	—	—

KM# 337 1000 LIRE
8.8500 g., Bi-Metallic Copper-Nickel center in Brass ring, 26.9 mm. **Ruler:** John Paul II **Obv:** John Paul II bust left **Rev:** Papal arms **Edge:** Segmented reeding

Date	Mintage	F	VF	XF	Unc	BU
2001/XXIII	—	—	—	5.50	9.00	—

KM# 337a 1000 LIRE
Gold, 26.9 mm. **Ruler:** John Paul II **Obv:** John Paul II bust left **Rev:** Papal arms

Date	Mintage	F	VF	XF	Unc	BU
2001R Proof	499	—	—	—	—	—

KM# 338 1000 LIRE
14.6000 g., 0.8350 Silver 0.3919 oz. ASW, 31.4 mm. **Ruler:** John Paul II **Subject:** Peace **Obv:** Stylized dove in front of globe **Rev:** Crowned shield **Edge Lettering:** +++ TOTVSTVVS +++ MMI

Date	Mintage	F	VF	XF	Unc	BU
2001/XXIII	—	—	—	20.00	40.00	—

KM# 338a 1000 LIRE
Gold, 31.4 mm. **Ruler:** John Paul II **Obv:** Stylized dove in front of globe **Rev:** Crowned arms

Date	Mintage	F	VF	XF	Unc	BU
2001R Proof	499	—	—	—	—	—

KM# 339 2000 LIRE
16.0000 g., 0.8350 Silver 0.4295 oz. ASW, 31.4 mm. **Ruler:** John Paul II **Subject:** Dialog for Peace **Obv:** Bust right holding crozier **Rev:** Dove above crowd **Edge:** Reeded

Date	Mintage	F	VF	XF	Unc	BU
2001/XXIII	16,000	—	—	25.00	40.00	—
2001/XXIII Proof	8,000	Value: 45.00				

KM# 340 5000 LIRE
18.0000 g., 0.8350 Silver 0.4832 oz. ASW, 32 mm. **Ruler:** John Paul II **Subject:** Easter **Obv:** Kneeling Pope praying **Rev:** Standing figure flanked by clouds below dove **Edge:** Reeded and plain sections

Date	Mintage	F	VF	XF	Unc	BU
2001	—	—	—	30.00	45.00	—
2001/XXIII Proof	16,000	Value: 35.00				

KM# 390 50000 LIRE
7.5000 g., 0.9170 Gold 0.2211 oz. AGW, 23 mm. **Ruler:** John Paul II **Subject:** Religious symbols **Obv:** Bust right **Rev:** Cross

Date	Mintage	F	VF	XF	Unc	BU
2001R	—	—	—	—	800	—
2001//XXIIIR Proof	6,000	Value: 550				

KM# 391 100000 LIRE
15.0000 g., 0.9170 Gold 0.4422 oz. AGW, 28 mm. **Ruler:**

John Paul II **Subject:** Religious symbols **Obv:** Bust right **Rev:** Chi rho with Alpha and Omega letters

Date	Mintage	F	VF	XF	Unc	BU
2001R	—	—	—	—	1,000	—
2001//XXIIIR Proof	6,000	Value: 800				

EURO COINAGE
John Paul II

KM# 341 EURO CENT
2.3000 g., Copper Plated Steel, 16.25 mm. **Ruler:** John Paul II **Obv:** Bust 1/4 left **Rev:** Value and globe **Edge:** Plain

Date	Mintage	F	VF	XF	Unc	BU
2002R	80,000	—	—	—	115	—
2002R Proof	9,000	Value: 175				
2003R In sets only	65,000	—	—	—	55.00	—
2003R Proof	13,000	Value: 145				
2004R In sets only	65,000	—	—	—	25.00	—
2004R Proof	13,000	Value: 145				
2005R In sets only	85,000	—	—	—	25.00	—
2005R Proof	16,000	Value: 140				

KM# 342 2 EURO CENT
3.0600 g., Copper Plated Steel, 18.75 mm. **Ruler:** John Paul II **Obv:** Bust 1/4 left **Rev:** Value and globe **Edge:** Grooved

Date	Mintage	F	VF	XF	Unc	BU
2002R	80,000	—	—	—	115	—
2002R Proof	9,000	Value: 175				
2003R In sets only	65,000	—	—	—	55.00	—
2003R Proof	13,000	Value: 145				
2004R In sets only	65,000	—	—	—	25.00	—
2004R Proof	13,000	Value: 145				
2005R In sets only	85,000	—	—	—	25.00	—
2005R Proof	16,000	Value: 140				

KM# 343 5 EURO CENT
3.9200 g., Copper Plated Steel, 21.25 mm. **Ruler:** John Paul II **Obv:** Bust 1/4 left **Rev:** Value and globe **Edge:** Plain

Date	Mintage	F	VF	XF	Unc	BU
2002R	80,000	—	—	—	115	—
2002R Proof	9,000	Value: 175				
2003R In sets only	65,000	—	—	—	55.00	—
2003R Proof	13,000	Value: 145				
2004R In sets only	65,000	—	—	—	28.00	—
2004R Proof	13,000	Value: 145				
2005R In sets only	85,000	—	—	—	28.00	—
2005R Proof	16,000	Value: 140				

KM# 344 10 EURO CENT
4.1000 g., Brass, 19.75 mm. **Ruler:** John Paul II **Obv:** Bust 1/4 left **Edge:** Reeded

Date	Mintage	F	VF	XF	Unc	BU
2002R	80,000	—	—	—	115	—
2002R Proof	9,000	Value: 175				
2003R In sets only	65,000	—	—	—	55.00	—
2003R Proof	13,000	Value: 145				
2004R In sets only	65,000	—	—	—	35.00	—
2004R Proof	13,000	Value: 145				
2005R In sets only	85,000	—	—	—	35.00	—
2005R Proof	16,000	Value: 140				

KM# 345 20 EURO CENT
5.7400 g., Brass, 22.25 mm. **Ruler:** John Paul II **Obv:** Bust 1/4 left **Rev:** Map and value **Edge:** Notched

Date	Mintage	F	VF	XF	Unc	BU
2002R	80,000	—	—	—	115	—
2002R Proof	9,000	Value: 175				
2003R In sets only	65,000	—	—	—	55.00	—
2003R Proof	13,000	Value: 145				
2004R In sets only	65,000	—	—	—	38.00	—
2004R Proof	13,000	Value: 145				
2005R In sets only	85,000	—	—	—	38.00	—
2005R Proof	16,000	Value: 140				

KM# 346 50 EURO CENT
7.8000 g., Brass, 24.25 mm. **Ruler:** John Paul II **Obv:** Bust 1/4 left **Rev:** Map and value **Edge:** Reeded

Date	Mintage	F	VF	XF	Unc	BU
2002R	80,000	—	—	—	115	—
2002R Proof	9,000	Value: 175				
2003R In sets only	65,000	—	—	—	55.00	—
2003R Proof	13,000	Value: 145				
2004R In sets only	65,000	—	—	—	42.00	—
2004R Proof	13,000	Value: 145				
2005R In sets only	85,000	—	—	—	42.00	—
2005R Proof	16,000	Value: 140				

KM# 347 EURO
7.5000 g., Bi-Metallic Copper-Nickel center in Nickel-Brass ring, 23.25 mm. **Ruler:** John Paul II **Obv:** Bust 1/4 left **Rev:** Value and map **Edge:** Segmented reeding

Date	Mintage	F	VF	XF	Unc	BU
2002R	80,000	—	—	—	100	—
2002R Proof	9,000	Value: 185				
2003R In sets only	65,000	—	—	—	75.00	—
2003R Proof	13,000	Value: 145				
2004R In sets only	65,000	—	—	—	60.00	—
2004R Proof	13,000	Value: 145				
2005R In sets only	85,000	—	—	—	60.00	—
2005R Proof	16,000	Value: 140				

KM# 348 2 EURO
8.5000 g., Bi-Metallic Nickel-Brass center in Copper-Nickel ring, 25.75 mm. **Ruler:** John Paul II **Obv:** Bust 1/4 left **Rev:** Value and map **Edge:** Reeded with 2's and stars

Date	Mintage	F	VF	XF	Unc	BU
2002R	80,000	—	—	—	165	—
2002R Proof	9,000	Value: 215				

Date	Mintage	F	VF	XF	Unc	BU
2003R In sets only	65,000	—	—	—	100	—
2003R Proof	13,000	Value: 185				
2004R In sets only	65,000	—	—	—	80.00	—
2004R Proof	13,000	Value: 185				
2005R In sets only	85,000	—	—	—	80.00	—
2005R Proof	16,000	Value: 180				

KM# 358 2 EURO
8.5000 g., Bi-Metallic Nickel-Brass center in Copper-Nickel ring, 25.75 mm. **Ruler:** John Paul II **Subject:** 75th Anniversary of the Founding of the Vatican City State **Obv:** St. Peter's Square within city walls, dates 1929-2004 **Rev:** Value and map **Edge:** Reeded with 2's and stars

Date	Mintage	F	VF	XF	Unc	BU
2004R	85,000	—	—	—	25.00	—

KM# 349 5 EURO
18.0000 g., 0.8350 Silver 0.4832 oz. ASW, 32 mm. **Ruler:** John Paul II **Subject:** 24th Anniversary of Reign **Obv:** Bust 1/4 left **Rev:** Allegorical female and bridge **Edge:** Lettered **Edge Lettering:** +++ TOTUS TUUS +++ MMII

Date	Mintage	F	VF	XF	Unc	BU
2002R Proof	10,000	Value: 125				

KM# 354 5 EURO
18.0000 g., 0.9250 Silver 0.5353 oz. ASW, 34 mm. **Ruler:** John Paul II **Subject:** Year of the Rosary **Obv:** Pope praying the rosary **Rev:** "Our Lady of Pompei" presenting rosaries to Saints Dominic and Catherine **Edge:** Reeded

Date	Mintage	F	VF	XF	Unc	BU
2003R Proof	10,000	—	—	—	65.00	—

KM# 359 5 EURO
18.0000 g., 0.9250 Silver 0.5353 oz. ASW, 32 mm. **Ruler:** John Paul II **Subject:** 150th Anniversary of the Proclamation of the Dogma of the Immaculate Conception **Obv:** Virgin Mary **Rev:** Two Papal coat of arms **Edge:** Reeded and plain sections

Date	Mintage	F	VF	XF	Unc	BU
2004R	13,000	—	—	—	60.00	—

KM# 350 10 EURO
22.0000 g., 0.8350 Silver 0.5906 oz. ASW, 34 mm. **Ruler:** John Paul II **Subject:** 24th Anniversary of Reign **Obv:** Pope holding crucifix **Rev:** Risen Christ (Message of peace) **Edge:** Reeded

Date	Mintage	F	VF	XF	Unc	BU
2002R Proof	10,000	Value: 80.00				

KM# 355 10 EURO
22.0000 g., 0.9250 Silver 0.6542 oz. ASW, 34 mm. **Ruler:** John Paul II **Subject:** 25th Anniversary of Reign **Obv:** Pope praying **Rev:** St. Peter receiving the keys of Earth and Heaven **Edge:** Reeded

Date	Mintage	F	VF	XF	Unc	BU
2003R Proof	10,000	Value: 80.00				

KM# 360 10 EURO
22.0000 g., 0.9250 Silver 0.6542 oz. ASW, 34 mm. **Ruler:** John Paul II **Obv:** Pope praying for peace **Rev:** Tree of Life rooted in virtues **Edge:** Reeded and plain sections

Date	Mintage	F	VF	XF	Unc	BU
2004R	13,000	—	—	—	90.00	—

KM# 361 20 EURO
6.0000 g., 0.9170 Gold 0.1769 oz. AGW **Ruler:** John Paul II **Subject:** Roots of Faith **Rev:** Noah's Ark

Date	Mintage	F	VF	XF	Unc	BU
2002	2,800	Value: 1,200				

KM# 351 20 EURO
6.0000 g., 0.9166 Gold 0.1768 oz. AGW, 21 mm. **Ruler:** John Paul II **Rev:** Moses being found in floating basket **Edge:** Reeded

Date	Mintage	F	VF	XF	Unc	BU
2003R Proof	2,800	Value: 1,300				

KM# 363 20 EURO
6.0000 g., 0.9170 Gold 0.1769 oz. AGW, 21 mm. **Ruler:** John Paul II **Rev:** David slaying Goliath

Date	Mintage	F	VF	XF	Unc	BU
2004/XXVIIR Proof	3,050	Value: 1,200				

KM# 362 50 EURO
15.0000 g., 0.9170 Gold 0.4422 oz. AGW **Ruler:** John Paul II **Subject:** Roots of Faith **Rev:** Sacrifice of Abraham

Date	Mintage	F	VF	XF	Unc	BU
2002 Proof	2,800	Value: 2,200				

KM# 352 50 EURO
15.0000 g., 0.9166 Gold 0.4420 oz. AGW, 28 mm. **Ruler:** John Paul II **Rev:** Moses receiving the Ten Commandments **Edge:** Reeded

Date	Mintage	F	VF	XF	Unc	BU
2003R Proof	2,800	Value: 2,200				

KM# 364 50 EURO
15.0000 g., 0.9170 Gold 0.4422 oz. AGW **Ruler:** John Paul II **Rev:** Judgement of Solomon

Date	Mintage	F	VF	XF	Unc	BU
2004/XXVIIR Proof	3,050	Value: 2,200				

Sede Vacante

KM# 365 EURO CENT
2.3000 g., Copper Plated Steel, 16.25 mm. **Ruler:** Sede Vacante **Obv:** Arms of Cardinal Eduardo Martinez Somalo **Rev:** Value and globe

Date	Mintage	F	VF	XF	Unc	BU
MMV (2005)R In sets only	60,000	—	—	—	45.00	

KM# 366 2 EURO CENT
3.0600 g., Copper Plated Steel, 18.75 mm. **Ruler:** Sede Vacante **Obv:** Arms of Cardinal Eduardo Martinez Somalo **Rev:** Value and globe **Edge:** Grooved

Date	Mintage	F	VF	XF	Unc	BU
MMV (2005)R In sets only	60,000	—	—	—	42.00	

KM# 367 5 EURO CENT
3.9200 g., Copper Plated Steel, 21.25 mm. **Ruler:** Sede Vacante **Obv:** Arms of Cardinal Eduardo Martinez Somalo **Rev:** Value and globe

Date	Mintage	F	VF	XF	Unc	BU
MMV (2005)R In sets only	60,000	—	—	—	45.00	

KM# 368 10 EURO CENT
4.1000 g., Brass, 19.75 mm. **Ruler:** Sede Vacante **Obv:** Arms of Cardinal Eduardo Martinez Somalo **Rev:** Map and value **Edge:** Reeded

Date	Mintage	F	VF	XF	Unc	BU
MMV (2005)R In sets only	60,000	—	—	—	48.00	

KM# 369 20 EURO CENT
5.7400 g., Brass, 22.25 mm. **Ruler:** Sede Vacante **Obv:** Arms of Cardinal Eduardo Martinez Somalo **Rev:** Map and value **Edge:** Notched

Date	Mintage	F	VF	XF	Unc	BU
MMV (2005)R In sets only	60,000	—	—	—	50.00	

KM# 370 50 EURO CENT
7.8000 g., Brass, 24.25 mm. **Ruler:** Sede Vacante **Obv:** Arms of Cardinal Eduardo Martinez Somalo **Rev:** Map and value **Edge:** Reeded

Date	Mintage	F	VF	XF	Unc	BU
MMV (2005)R In sets only	60,000	—	—	—	—	55.00

KM# 371 EURO
7.5000 g., Bi-Metallic Copper-Nickel center in Nickel-Brass ring, 23.25 mm. **Ruler:** Sede Vacante **Obv:** Arms of Cardinal Eduardo Martinez Somalo **Rev:** Value and map **Edge:** Segmented reeding

Date	Mintage	F	VF	XF	Unc	BU
MMV (2005)R In sets only	60,000	—	—	—	—	70.00

KM# 372 2 EURO
8.5000 g., Bi-Metallic Nickel-Brass center in Copper-Nickel ring, 25.75 mm. **Ruler:** Sede Vacante **Obv:** Arms of Cardinal Eduardo Martinez Somalo **Rev:** Map and value **Edge:** Reeded with 2's and stars

Date	Mintage	F	VF	XF	Unc	BU
MMV (2005)R In sets only	60,000	—	—	—	—	75.00

KM# 373 5 EURO
18.0000 g., 0.9250 Silver 0.5353 oz. ASW, 32 mm. **Ruler:** Sede Vacante **Obv:** Dove within square **Rev:** Arms of Cardinal Jorge Arturo Medina Estevez **Edge:** Reeded

Date	Mintage	F	VF	XF	Unc	BU
MMV (2005)R Proof	13,440	Value: 200				

Benedict XVI

KM# 375 EURO CENT
2.3000 g., Copper Plated Steel, 16.25 mm. **Ruler:** Benedict XVI **Obv:** Pope's bust facing 3/4 right **Obv. Legend:** CITTA' DEL VATICANO **Rev:** Value and globe **Edge:** Plain

Date	Mintage	F	VF	XF	Unc	BU
2006R In sets only	85,000	—	—	—	—	12.00
2006R Proof	16,000	Value: 18.00				
2007R In sets only	85,000	—	—	—	—	12.00
2007R Proof	16,000	Value: 18.00				
MMVIII (2008)R In sets only	85,000	—	—	—	—	12.00
MMVIII (2008)R Proof	16,000	Value: 18.00				
2009R In sets only	85,000	—	—	—	—	12.00
2009R Proof	16,000	Value: 18.00				
2010R In sets only	94,000	—	—	—	—	12.00
2010R Proof	15,000	Value: 18.00				
2011R	—	—	—	—	—	12.00
2011R Proof	—	Value: 18.00				

KM# 376 2 EURO CENT
3.0600 g., Copper Plated Steel, 18.75 mm. **Ruler:** Benedict XVI **Obv:** Pope's bust facing 3/4 right **Obv. Legend:** CITTA' DEL VATICANO **Rev:** Value and globe **Edge:** Grooved

Date	Mintage	F	VF	XF	Unc	BU
2006R In sets only	85,000	—	—	—	—	15.00
2006R Proof	16,000	Value: 20.00				
2007R In sets only	85,000	—	—	—	—	15.00
2007R Proof	16,000	Value: 20.00				
MDVIII (2008)R In sets only	85,000	—	—	—	—	15.00
MDVIII (2008)R Proof	16,000	Value: 20.00				
2009R In sets only	85,000	—	—	—	—	15.00
2009R Proof	16,000	Value: 20.00				
2010R In sets only	94,000	—	—	—	—	15.00
2010R Proof	15,000	Value: 20.00				
2011R	—	—	—	—	—	15.00
2011R Proof	—	Value: 20.00				

KM# 377 5 EURO CENT
3.9200 g., Copper Plated Steel, 21.25 mm. **Ruler:** Benedict XVI **Obv:** Pope's bust facing 3/4 right **Obv. Legend:** CITTA' DEL VATICANO **Rev:** Value and globe **Edge:** Plain

Date	Mintage	F	VF	XF	Unc	BU
2006R In sets only	85,000	—	—	—	—	16.50
2006R Proof	16,000	Value: 22.50				

Date	Mintage	F	VF	XF	Unc	BU
2007R In sets only	85,000	—	—	—	—	16.50
2007R Proof	16,000	Value: 22.50				
MDVIII (2008)R In sets only	85,000	—	—	—	—	16.50
MDVIII (2008)R Proof	16,000	Value: 22.50				
2009R In sets only	85,000	—	—	—	—	16.50
2009R Proof	16,000	Value: 22.50				
2010R In sets only	94,000	—	—	—	—	16.50
2010R Proof	15,000	Value: 22.50				
2011R	—	—	—	—	—	16.50
2011R Proof	—	Value: 22.50				

KM# 378   10 EURO CENT
4.1000 g., Brass, 19.75 mm. **Ruler:** Benedict XVI **Obv:** Pope's bust facing 3/4 right **Obv. Legend:** CITTA' DEL VATICANO **Rev:** Map and value **Edge:** Reeded

Date	Mintage	F	VF	XF	Unc	BU
2006R In sets only	85,000	—	—	—	—	17.50
2006R Proof	16,000	Value: 25.00				
2007R In sets only	85,000	—	—	—	—	17.50
2007R Proof	16,000	Value: 25.00				

KM# 385   10 EURO CENT
4.1000 g., Brass, 19.75 mm. **Ruler:** Benedict XVI **Rev:** Relief map of Western Europe, stars, lines and value **Edge:** Reeded

Date	Mintage	F	VF	XF	Unc	BU
MMVIII (2008)R In sets only	85,000	—	—	—	—	17.50
MMVIII (2008)R Proof	16,000	Value: 25.00				
2009R In sets only	85,000	—	—	—	—	17.50
2009R Proof	16,000	Value: 25.00				
2010R In sets only	91,400	—	—	—	—	17.50
2010R Proof	15,000	Value: 25.00				
2011R	—	—	—	—	—	17.50
2011R	—	Value: 25.00				

KM# 379   20 EURO CENT
5.7400 g., Brass, 22.25 mm. **Ruler:** Benedict XVI **Obv:** Pope's bust facing 3/4 right **Obv. Legend:** CITTA' DEL VATICANO **Rev:** Map and value **Edge:** Notched

Date	Mintage	F	VF	XF	Unc	BU
2006R In sets only	85,000	—	—	—	—	18.00
2006R Proof	16,000	Value: 28.00				
2007R In sets only	85,000	—	—	—	—	18.00
2007R Proof	16,000	Value: 28.00				

KM# 386   20 EURO CENT
5.7400 g., Brass, 22.25 mm. **Ruler:** Benedict XVI **Rev:** Relief map of Western Europe, stars, lines and value **Edge:** Notched

Date	Mintage	F	VF	XF	Unc	BU
MMVIII (2008)R In sets only	85,000	—	—	—	—	18.00
MMVIII (2008)R Proof	16,000	Value: 28.00				
2009R In sets only	85,000	—	—	—	—	18.00
2009R Proof	16,000	Value: 28.00				
2010R In sets only	94,000	—	—	—	—	18.00
2010R Proof	15,000	Value: 28.00				
2011R	—	—	—	—	—	18.00
2011R Proof	—	Value: 28.00				

KM# 380   50 EURO CENT
7.8000 g., Brass, 24.25 mm. **Ruler:** Benedict XVI **Obv:** Pope's bust facing 3/4 right **Obv. Legend:** CITTA' DEL VATICANO **Rev:** Map and value **Edge:** Reeded

Date	Mintage	F	VF	XF	Unc	BU
2006R In sets only	85,000	—	—	—	—	22.50
2006R Proof	16,000	Value: 35.00				
2007R In sets only	85,000	—	—	—	—	22.50
2007R Proof	16,000	Value: 35.00				

KM# 387   50 EURO CENT
7.8000 g., Brass, 24.25 mm. **Ruler:** Benedict XVI **Rev:** Relief map of Western Europe, stars, lines and value **Edge:** Reeded

Date	Mintage	F	VF	XF	Unc	BU
MMVIII (2008)R In sets only	85,000	—	—	—	—	32.50
MMVIII (2008)R Proof	16,000	Value: 40.00				
2009R In sets only	85,000	—	—	—	—	32.50
2009R Proof	16,000	Value: 40.00				
2010R In sets only	94,000	—	—	—	—	32.50
2010R Proof	15,000	Value: 40.00				
2011R	—	—	—	—	—	32.50
2011R Proof	—	Value: 40.00				

KM# 381   EURO
7.5000 g., Bi-Metallic Copper-Nickel center in Nickel-Brass ring., 23.25 mm. **Ruler:** Benedict XVI **Obv:** Pope's bust facing 3/4 right **Obv. Legend:** CITTA' - DEL VATICANO **Rev:** Value and map **Edge:** Segmented reeding

Date	Mintage	F	VF	XF	Unc	BU
2006R In sets only	85,000	—	—	—	—	25.00
2006R Proof	16,000	Value: 40.00				
2007R In sets only	85,000	—	—	—	—	25.00
2007R Proof	16,000	Value: 40.00				

KM# 388   EURO
7.5000 g., Bi-Metallic Copper-Nickel center in Nickel-Brass ring, 23.25 mm. **Ruler:** Benedict XVI **Rev:** Relief map of Western Europe, stars, lines and value **Edge:** Segmented reeding

Date	Mintage	F	VF	XF	Unc	BU
MMVIII (2008)R In sets only	85,000	—	—	—	—	25.00
MMVIII (2008)R Proof	16,000	Value: 40.00				
2009R In sets only	85,000	—	—	—	—	25.00
2009R Proof	16,000	Value: 40.00				
2010R In sets only	94,000	—	—	—	—	25.00
2010R Proof	15,000	Value: 40.00				
2011R	—	—	—	—	—	25.00
2011R Proof	—	Value: 40.00				

KM# 374   2 EURO
8.5000 g., Bi-Metallic Nickel-Brass center in Copper-Nickel ring, 25.75 mm. **Ruler:** Benedict XVI **Subject:** World Youth Day **Obv:** Cologne Cathedral **Rev:** Value and Euro map **Edge:** Reeded with 2's and stars

Date	Mintage	F	VF	XF	Unc	BU
2005R	—	—	—	—	90.00	—

KM# 382   2 EURO
8.5000 g., Bi-Metallic Nickel-Brass center in Copper-Nickel ring, 25.75 mm. **Ruler:** Benedict XVI **Obv:** Pope's bust facing 3/4 right **Obv. Legend:** CITTA' - DEL VATICANO **Rev:** Value and map **Edge:** Reeded with 2's and stars

Date	Mintage	F	VF	XF	Unc	BU
2006R In sets only	85,000	—	—	—	—	28.00
2006R Proof	16,000	Value: 50.00				
2007R In sets only	85,000	—	—	—	—	28.00
2007R Proof	16,000	Value: 50.00				

KM# 394   2 EURO
8.5000 g., Bi-Metallic Nickel-Brass center in Copper-Nickel ring, 25.75 mm. **Ruler:** Benedict XVI **Subject:** Swiss guards, 500th Anniversary **Obv:** Swiss guard taking oath on flag **Rev:** Map and value **Edge:** Reeded with 2's and stars

Date	Mintage	F	VF	XF	Unc	BU
ND (2006)R	100,000	—	—	—	80.00	—

KM# 399   2 EURO
8.5000 g., Bi-Metallic Nickel-Brass center in Copper-Nickel ring, 25.75 mm. **Ruler:** Benedict XVI **Subject:** Pope Benedict's 80th Birthday **Obv:** Bust left **Rev:** Map and value **Edge:** Reeded with 2's and stars

Date	Mintage	F	VF	XF	Unc	BU
2007R	100,000	—	—	—	50.00	—

KM# 389   2 EURO
8.5000 g., Bi-Metallic Nickel-Brass center in Copper-Nickel ring, 25.75 mm. **Ruler:** Benedict XVI **Rev:** Relief map of Western Europe, stars, lines and value **Edge:** Reeded with 2's and stars

Date	Mintage	F	VF	XF	Unc	BU
MMVIII (2008)R In sets only	85,000	—	—	—	—	28.00
MMVIII (2008)R Proof	16,000	Value: 50.00				
2009R In sets only	85,000	—	—	—	—	28.00
2009R Proof	16,000	Value: 50.00				
2010R In sets only	94,000	—	—	—	—	28.00
2010R Proof	15,000	Value: 50.00				
2011R	—	—	—	—	—	28.00
2011R Proof	—	Value: 50.00				

KM# 404   2 EURO
8.5000 g., Bi-Metallic Nickel-Brass center in Copper-Nickel ring, 25.75 mm. **Ruler:** Benedict XVI **Obv:** St. Paul being blinded on reary horse **Rev:** Map and value **Edge:** Reeded with 2's and stars

Date	Mintage	F	VF	XF	Unc	BU
ND (2008)R	106,084	—	—	—	25.00	—

KM# 410 2 EURO
8.5000 g., Bi-Metallic Nickel-Brass center in Copper-Nickel ring, 25.75 mm. **Ruler:** Benedict XVI **Subject:** International Year of Astronomy **Rev:** Map and value **Edge:** Reeded with 2's and stars

Date	Mintage	F	VF	XF	Unc	BU
2009R	100,000	—	—	—	25.00	—

KM# 420 2 EURO
8.5000 g., Bi-Metallic Nickel-Brass center in Copper-Nickel ring, 25.75 mm. **Ruler:** Benedict XVI **Subject:** Year of the Priest **Edge:** Reeded with 2's and stars

Date	Mintage	F	VF	XF	Unc	BU
2010R	115,000	—	—	—	20.00	25.00

KM# 426 2 EURO
8.5000 g., Bi-Metallic Nickel-Brass center in Copper-Nickel ring, 25.75 mm. **Ruler:** Benedict XVI **Subject:** 26th World Youth Day **Obv:** Youth with Vatican City flags **Edge:** Reeded with 2's and stars

Date	Mintage	F	VF	XF	Unc	BU
2011R	98,000	—	—	—	—	20.00
2011R Special Unc.	11,500	—	—	—	—	28.00

KM# 383 5 EURO
18.0000 g., 0.9250 Silver 0.5353 oz. ASW **Ruler:** Benedict XVI **Subject:** Life reborn **Obv:** Bust left **Rev:** Children playing among branches of an olive tree

Date	Mintage	F	VF	XF	Unc	BU
2005R Proof	13,000	Value: 100				

KM# 395 5 EURO
18.0000 g., 0.9250 Silver 0.5353 oz. ASW, 32 mm. **Ruler:** Benedict XVI **Subject:** World Day of Peace **Obv:** Half-length figure Benedict right in vestments with crozier **Rev:** St. Benedict of Nursia seated

Date	Mintage	F	VF	XF	Unc	BU
MMVI (2006)R Proof	14,160	Value: 90.00				

KM# 400 5 EURO
18.0000 g., 0.9250 Silver 0.5353 oz. ASW, 32 mm. **Ruler:** Benedict XVI **Subject:** World Day of Peace **Obv:** 1/2 length figure kneeling in prayer **Rev:** Standing St. Francis of Assisi, rays in background

Date	Mintage	F	VF	XF	Unc	BU
MMVII (2007)R Proof	13,693	Value: 55.00				

KM# 406 5 EURO
18.0000 g., 0.9250 Silver 0.5353 oz. ASW, 32 mm. **Ruler:** Benedict XVI **Subject:** World Youth Day - Sydney **Obv:** Pope right, blessing **Rev:** Sydney Harbor sites

Date	Mintage	F	VF	XF	Unc	BU
MMVIII (2008)R Proof	9,600	Value: 60.00				

KM# 415 5 EURO
18.0000 g., 0.9250 Silver 0.5353 oz. ASW, 32 mm. **Ruler:** Benedict XVI **Subject:** World day of Peace **Obv:** Bust right in prayer **Rev:** Candle, family

Date	Mintage	F	VF	XF	Unc	BU
2009R Proof	9,600	Value: 60.00				

KM# 421 5 EURO
18.0000 g., 0.9250 Silver 0.5353 oz. ASW, 32 mm. **Ruler:** Benedict XVI **Subject:** Migrants and Refugees **Obv:** Benedict standing facing in vestments and mitre **Rev:** Family scene

Date	Mintage	F	VF	XF	Unc	BU
2010R Proof	9,998	Value: 75.00				

KM# 427 5 EURO
18.0000 g., 0.9250 Silver 0.5353 oz. ASW, 32 mm. **Ruler:** Benedict XVI **Subject:** 44the World day of Peace **Obv:** Bust left **Rev:** Female standing

Date	Mintage	F	VF	XF	Unc	BU
2011R Proof	7,998	Value: 80.00				

KM# 429 5 EURO
18.0000 g., 0.9250 Silver 0.5353 oz. ASW, 32 mm. **Ruler:** Benedict XVI **Subject:** John Paul II beautification **Obv:** Bust facing of John Paul II **Rev:** Cherubs elevating Papal Arms of John Paul II

Date	Mintage	F	VF	XF	Unc	BU
2011R Proof	9,500	Value: 75.00				

KM# 384 10 EURO
22.0000 g., 0.9250 Silver 0.6542 oz. ASW **Ruler:** Benedict XVI **Subject:** Disciples of Emanaus **Obv:** Bust left **Rev:** Three men seated at table

Date	Mintage	F	VF	XF	Unc	BU
2006R Proof	13,000	Value: 215				

KM# 396 10 EURO
22.0000 g., 0.9250 Silver 0.6542 oz. ASW, 34 mm. **Ruler:** Benedict XVI **Subject:** St. Peter's Collonade, 350th Anniversary **Obv:** Collonade & Pope Benedict **Rev:** Collonade Schematics

Date	Mintage	F	VF	XF	Unc	BU
AN II MMVI (2006)R Proof	14,160	Value: 90.00				

KM# 401 10 EURO
22.0000 g., 0.9250 Silver 0.6542 oz. ASW, 34 mm. **Ruler:** Benedict XVI **Subject:** World Mission Day **Obv:** Bust right in ermine cape **Rev:** Blessed Mother Theresa of Calcutta and child

Date	Mintage	F	VF	XF	Unc	BU
AN III MVII (2007)R Proof	13,694	Value: 80.00				

KM# 407 10 EURO
22.0000 g., 0.9250 Silver 0.6542 oz. ASW, 34 mm. **Ruler:** Benedict XVI **Subject:** World Day of Peace **Obv:** Pope seated on chair in full robes and miter **Rev:** The Holy Family - Jesus, Mary, Joseph

Date	Mintage	F	VF	XF	Unc	BU
A VI MMVIII (2008)R Proof	9,602	Value: 95.00				

KM# 417 10 EURO
22.0000 g., 0.9250 Silver 0.6542 oz. ASW, 22 mm. **Ruler:** Benedict XVI **Subject:** Lateran Treaty, 80th Anniversary **Obv:** Bust right **Rev:** Rolled treaty with seal

Date	Mintage	F	VF	XF	Unc	BU
2009R Proof	9,602	Value: 95.00				

KM# 422 10 EURO
22.0000 g., 0.9250 Silver 0.6542 oz. ASW, 34 mm. **Ruler:** Benedict XVI **Subject:** 43rd World day of Peace **Obv:** Bust left **Rev:** Three figures

Date	Mintage	F	VF	XF	Unc	BU
2010R Proof	9,998	Value: 80.00				

KM# 428 10 EURO
22.0000 g., 0.9250 Silver 0.6542 oz. ASW, 34 mm. **Ruler:** Benedict XVI **Subject:** Benedict XVI's 60th Anniversary of Ordination **Obv:** Bust right **Rev:** Two fishermen hauling in net

Date	Mintage	F	VF	XF	Unc	BU
2011R Proof	7,998	Value: 90.00				

KM# 392 20 EURO
6.0000 g., 0.9160 Gold 0.1767 oz. AGW, 21 mm. **Ruler:** Benedict XVI **Subject:** Christian Initiation - Baptism **Obv:** Pope seated **Rev:** Fountain

Date	Mintage	F	VF	XF	Unc	BU
AN I MMV (2005)R Proof	3,046	Value: 600				

KM# 397 20 EURO
6.0000 g., 0.9160 Gold 0.1767 oz. AGW, 21 mm. **Ruler:** Benedict XVI **Subject:** Christian Initiation - Confirmation **Obv:** Bust right **Rev:** Bishop confirming three

Date	Mintage	F	VF	XF	Unc	BU
AN II MMVI (2006)R Proof	3,326	Value: 600				

KM# 402 20 EURO
6.0000 g., 0.9160 Gold 0.1767 oz. AGW, 21 mm. **Ruler:** Benedict XVI **Subject:** Christain Initiation - Eucharist **Obv:** Bust left in ermine cape **Rev:** Basket of fish and bread

Date	Mintage	F	VF	XF	Unc	BU
AN III (2007)R Proof	3,426	Value: 600				

KM# 408 20 EURO
6.0000 g., 0.9170 Gold 0.1769 oz. AGW, 21 mm. **Ruler:** Benedict XVI **Subject:** Vatican sculpture **Obv:** Pope right in mitre **Rev:** Torso of Belvedere

Date	Mintage	F	VF	XF	Unc	BU
AN IV MMVIII (2008)R Proof	2,930	Value: 500				

KM# 416 20 EURO
6.0000 g., 0.9170 Gold 0.1769 oz. AGW, 21 mm. **Ruler:** Benedict XVI **Subject:** Masterworks in the Vatican Collection **Rev:** Christ and the Lamb

Date	Mintage	F	VF	XF	Unc	BU
2009R Proof	2,934	Value: 550				

KM# 423 20 EURO
6.0000 g., 0.9170 Gold 0.1769 oz. AGW **Ruler:** Benedict XVI **Subject:** Vatican Sculpture - Apollo Belvedere **Obv:** Large head profile left **Rev:** Statue of Apollo Belvedere

Date	Mintage	F	VF	XF	Unc	BU
2010R Proof	3,050	Value: 500				

KM# 431 20 EURO
6.0000 g., 0.9170 Gold 0.1769 oz. AGW, 21 mm. **Ruler:** Benedict XVI **Subject:** Pauline Chapel restoration **Obv:** Bust left **Rev:** Head

Date	Mintage	F	VF	XF	Unc	BU
2011R Proof	3,050	Value: 450				

KM# 393 50 EURO
15.0000 g., 0.9160 Gold 0.4417 oz. AGW, 28 mm. **Ruler:** Benedict XVI **Subject:** Christian Initiation - Baptism **Obv:** Pope seated **Rev:** John baptising Christ

Date	Mintage	F	VF	XF	Unc	BU
AN I MMV (2005)R Proof	3,044	Value: 1,500				

KM# 398 50 EURO
15.0000 g., 0.9160 Gold 0.4417 oz. AGW, 28 mm. **Ruler:** Benedict XVI **Subject:** Christian Initiation - Confirmation **Obv:** Bust right **Rev:** Tongues of fire decending on Apostles

Date	Mintage	F	VF	XF	Unc	BU
AN II MMVI (2006)R Proof	3,324	Value: 1,500				

KM# 403 50 EURO
15.0000 g., 0.9160 Gold 0.4417 oz. AGW, 28 mm. **Ruler:** Benedict XVI **Subject:** Christian Initiation - Eucharist **Obv:** Bust left in ermine cape **Rev:** Scene of the Last Supper

Date	Mintage	F	VF	XF	Unc	BU
ANIII MMVII (2007)R Proof	—	Value: 1,500				

KM# 409 50 EURO
15.0000 g., 0.9170 Gold 0.4422 oz. AGW, 28 mm. **Ruler:** Benedict XVI **Subject:** Vatican sculpture **Obv:** Pope right in mitre **Rev:** The Pieta

Date	Mintage	F	VF	XF	Unc	BU
AN IV MMVIII (2008)R Proof	—	Value: 1,000				

KM# 418 50 EURO
15.0000 g., 0.9170 Gold 0.4422 oz. AGW **Ruler:** Benedict XVI **Subject:** Masterworks in the Vatican Collection **Rev:** Hercules statue group **Edge:** 28

Date	Mintage	F	VF	XF	Unc	BU
2009R Proof	2,930	Value: 1,200				

KM# 424 50 EURO
15.0000 g., 0.9170 Gold 0.4422 oz. AGW, 28 mm. **Ruler:** Benedict XVI **Subject:** Vatican Sculpture - Augustus of Prima **Obv:** Large head profile left **Rev:** Statue of Augustus

Date	Mintage	F	VF	XF	Unc	BU
2010R Proof	3,050	Value: 1,200				

KM# 432 50 EURO
15.0000 g., 0.9170 Gold 0.4422 oz. AGW, 28 mm. **Ruler:** Benedict XVI **Subject:** Pauline Chapel restoration **Obv:** Bust left **Rev:** Cruxifiction of St. Peter

Date	Mintage	F	VF	XF	Unc	BU
2011R Proof	2,700	Value: 900				

KM# 405 100 EURO
30.0000 g., 0.9170 Gold 0.8844 oz. AGW, 35 mm. **Ruler:** Benedict XVI **Obv:** Bust left **Rev:** The Creator from the Sistine Chapel ceiling

Date	Mintage	F	VF	XF	Unc	BU
AN IV MMVIII (2008)R Proof	960	Value: 1,700				

KM# 419 100 EURO
30.0000 g., 0.9170 Gold 0.8844 oz. AGW, 35 mm. **Ruler:** Benedict XVI **Subject:** Sistine Chapel - Banishment from Eden

Date	Mintage	F	VF	XF	Unc	BU
2009R Proof	—	Value: 1,700				

KM# 425 100 EURO
30.0000 g., 0.9170 Gold 0.8844 oz. AGW, 35 mm. **Ruler:** Benedict XVI **Subject:** Sistine Chapel - Last Judgement **Obv:** Bust left **Rev:** Detail of the painting

Date	Mintage	F	VF	XF	Unc	BU
2010R Proof	1,100	Value: 1,750				

KM# 430 100 EURO
30.0000 g., 0.9170 Gold 0.8844 oz. AGW, 35 mm. **Ruler:** Benedict XVI **Subject:** Raffaell painting **Obv:** Bust left in vestments and mitre **Rev:** Horseman and captive

Date	Mintage	F	VF	XF	Unc	BU
2011R Proof	1,100	Value: 1,650				

MINT SETS

KM#	Date	Mintage	Identification	Issue Price	Mkt Val
MS107	2001 (8)	26,000	KM#331-338	21.25	200
MS108	2002 (8)	65,000	KM#341-348	12.00	975
MS109	2003 (8)	65,000	KM#341-348	15.00	500
MS110	2004 (8)	85,000	KM#341-348	16.50	335
MS111	2005 (8)	85,000	KM#341-348.	32.50	335
MS112	MMV (2005) (8)	60,000	KM#365-372 Sede Vacante	—	435
MS113	2006 (8)	—	KM#375-382	—	210
MS114	2007 (8)	—	KM#375-382	—	230
MS115	2008 (8)	85,000	KM#375-377, 385-389	45.00	165
MS116	2009 (8)	91,400	KM#375-377, 385-389	30.00	165
MS117	2010 (8)	94,000	KM#375-377, 385-389	30.00	150

PROOF SETS

KM#	Date	Mintage	Identification	Issue Price	Mkt Val
PS13	2001 (2)	—	KM#390, 391	—	1,350
PS15	2002 (8)	9,000	KM#341-348	75.00	1,450
PS16	2003 (8)	13,000	KM#341-348	78.00	1,200
PS17	2004 (8)	13,000	KM#341-348	—	1,200
PS18	2005 (8)	16,000	KM#341-348 plus silver medal	150	1,175
PS19	2006 (8)	16,000	KM#375-382 plus silver medal	—	375
PS20	2007 (8)	16,000	KM#375-382 plus silver medal	—	315
PS21	2008 (8)	16,000	KM#375-377, 385-389 plus silver medal	195	250
PS22	2009 (8)	15,000	KM#375-377, 385-389 plus silver medal	195	250
PS23	2010 (8)	15,000	KM#375-377, 385-389 plus silver medal	195	240
PS24	2010 (8)	300	KM#375-377, 385-389 plus gold medal	2,100	2,250

VENEZUELA

The Bolivarian Republic of Venezuela ("Little Venice"), located on the northern coast of South America between Colombia and Guyana, has an area of 352,145 sq. mi. (912,050 sq. km.) and a population of 20 million. Capital: Caracas. Petroleum and mining provide a significant portion of Venezuela's exports. Coffee, grown on 60,000 plantations, is the chief crop. Metalurgy, refining, oil, iron and steel production are the main employment industries.

GOVERNMENT
Republic, 1823-2000
Republic Bolivarian, 2000-

MINT MARKS
Maracay

REPUBLIC
Bolivariana

REFORM COINAGE
1896; 100 Centimos = 1 Bolivar

Y# 80   10 BOLIVARES
2.3300 g., Nickel Clad Steel, 17 mm. **Obv:** National arms left of denomination **Obv. Legend:** REPÚBLICA BOLIVARIANA DE VENEZUELA **Rev:** Head of Bolívar left in 7-sided outline **Rev. Legend:** BOLÍVAR - LIBERTADOR **Edge:** Reeded

Date	Mintage	F	VF	XF	Unc	BU
2001	—	—	—	—	0.25	0.50
2002	—	—	—	—	0.25	0.50

Y# 80a   10 BOLIVARES
1.7390 g., Aluminum-Zinc, 16.92 mm. **Obv:** National arms and value **Obv. Legend:** REPÚBLICA BOLIVARIANA DE VENEZUELA **Rev:** Head of Bolívar left in 7-sided outline **Rev. Legend:** BOLÍVAR - LIBERTADOR **Edge:** Reeded

Date	Mintage	F	VF	XF	Unc	BU
2001	—	—	—	0.15	0.45	0.60
2002	—	—	—	0.15	0.45	0.60
2004	—	—	—	0.15	0.45	0.60

Y# 81   20 BOLIVARES
4.3200 g., Nickel Clad Steel, 20 mm. **Obv:** National arms left of denomination **Obv. Legend:** REPÚBLICA BOLIVARIANA DE VENEZUELA **Rev:** Head of Bolivar left in 7-sided outline **Rev. Legend:** BOLÍVAR - LIBERTADOR **Edge:** Plain

Date	Mintage	F	VF	XF	Unc	BU
2001	—	—	—	—	0.25	0.50
2002	—	—	—	—	0.25	0.50

Y# 81a.1   20 BOLIVARES
3.2650 g., Aluminum-Zinc, 20 mm. **Obv:** National arms and value with wavy based "2" **Obv. Legend:** REPÚBLICA BOLIVARIANA DE VENEZUELA **Rev:** Head of Bolívar left in 7-sided outline **Rev. Legend:** BOLÍVAR - LIBERTADOR **Edge:** Plain

Date	Mintage	F	VF	XF	Unc	BU
2001	—	—	—	—	0.65	1.00

Y# 81a.2   20 BOLIVARES
3.2400 g., Aluminum-Zinc, 20 mm. **Obv:** National arms and value with flat based "2" **Obv. Legend:** REPÚBLICA BOLIVARIANA DE VENEZUELA **Rev:** Head of Bolívar left in 7-sided outline **Rev. Legend:** BOLÍVAR - LIBERTADOR **Edge:** Plain

Date	Mintage	F	VF	XF	Unc	BU
2002	—	—	—	0.25	0.60	0.80
2004	—	—	—	0.25	0.60	0.80

Y# 82   50 BOLIVARES
6.5800 g., Nickel Clad Steel, 23 mm. **Obv:** National arms left of denomination **Obv. Legend:** REPÚBLICA BOLIVARIANA DE VENEZUELA **Rev:** Head of Bolívar left in 7-sided outline **Rev. Legend:** BOLÍVAR - LIBERTADOR **Edge:** Reeded

Date	Mintage	F	VF	XF	Unc	BU
2001	—	—	—	0.30	0.75	1.00
2002	—	—	—	0.30	0.75	1.00
2004	—	—	—	0.30	0.75	1.00

Y# 83   100 BOLIVARES
6.8200 g., Nickel Clad Steel, 25 mm. **Obv:** National arms and value **Obv. Legend:** REPÚBUBLICA BOLIVARIANA DE VENEZUELA **Rev:** Head of Bolívar left in 7-sided ouline **Rev. Legend:** BOLÍVAR - LIBERTADO **Edge:** Plain

Date	Mintage	F	VF	XF	Unc	BU
2001	—	—	—	0.45	1.10	1.50
2002	—	—	—	0.45	1.10	1.50
2004	—	—	—	0.45	1.10	1.50

Y# 94   500 BOLIVARES
8.5000 g., Nickel Plated Steel, 28.4 mm. **Obv:** National arms and denomination **Obv. Legend:** REPÚBLICA BOLIVARIANA DE VENEZUELA **Rev:** Head of Bolívar left in 7-sided outline **Rev. Legend:** BOLÍVAR - LIBERTADOR **Edge:** Segmented reeding

Date	Mintage	F	VF	XF	Unc	BU
2004	—	—	—	0.60	1.50	2.00

Y# 85   1000 BOLIVARES
8.3500 g., Bi-Metallic Copper-Nickel center in Brass ring, 24 mm. **Obv:** National arms and value in center **Obv. Legend:** REPÚBLICA BOLIVARIANA DE VENEZUELA **Rev:** Head of Bolívar left **Rev. Legend:** BOLÍVAR - LIBERTADOR **Edge:** Lettered **Edge Lettering:** "BCV 1000" four times

Date	Mintage	F	VF	XF	Unc	BU
2005	9,000,000	—	—	0.90	2.25	3.00

REFORM COINAGE
2007-

1000 Bolivares = 1 Bolivar Fuerte

Y# 87   CENTIMO
1.3600 g., Copper Plated Steel, 14.9 mm. **Obv:** National arms **Obv. Legend:** REPÚBLICA BOLIVARIANA DE VENEZUELA **Rev:** Eight stars at left, large value at right **Edge:** Reeded

Date	Mintage	F	VF	XF	Unc	BU
2007	—	—	—	—	0.25	0.35
	Note: Many die rotation varieties exist.					
2009	—	—	—	—	0.25	0.35

Y# 88   5 CENTIMOS
2.0300 g., Copper Plated Steel, 16.9 mm. **Obv:** National arms **Obv. Legend:** REPÚBLICA BOLIVARIANA DE VENEZUELA **Rev:** Eight stars at left, large value at right **Edge:** Plain

Date	Mintage	F	VF	XF	Unc	BU
2007	—	—	—	—	0.50	0.75
2009	—	—	—	—	0.50	0.75

Y# 89   10 CENTIMOS
2.6200 g., Nickel Plated Steel, 18 mm. **Obv:** National arms **Obv. Legend:** REPÚBLICA BOLIVARIANA DE VENEZUELA **Rev:** Eight stars at left, large value at right **Edge:** Reeded

Date	Mintage	F	VF	XF	Unc	BU
2007	—	—	—	—	0.75	1.00
2009	—	—	—	—	0.75	1.00

Y# 90   12-1/2 CENTIMOS
3.9300 g., Nickel Plated Steel, 23 mm. **Obv:** National arms **Obv. Legend:** REPÚBLICA BOLIVARIANA DE VENEZUELA **Rev:** Large value, eight stars below in sprays **Edge:** Plain

Date	Mintage	F	VF	XF	Unc	BU
2007	—	—	—	—	1.50	1.75

Y# 91   25 CENTIMOS
3.8600 g., Nickel Plated Steel, 20 mm. **Obv:** National arms **Obv. Legend:** REPÚBLICA BOLIVARIANA DE VENEZUELA **Rev:** Eight stars at left, large value at center right **Edge:** Plain

Date	Mintage	F	VF	XF	Unc	BU
2007	—	—	—	—	2.00	2.50
2009	—	—	—	—	2.00	2.50

Y# 99   25 CENTIMOS
3.8600 g., Nickel Plated Steel, 20 mm. **Subject:** Independence, 200th Anniversary **Obv:** Legend **Rev:** Large value

Date	Mintage	F	VF	XF	Unc	BU
2010	—	—	—	—	2.50	3.00

Y# 92   50 CENTIMOS
4.3000 g., Nickel Plated Steel, 21.9 mm. **Obv:** National arms **Obv. Legend:** REPÚBLICA BOLIVARIANA DE VENEZUELA **Rev:** Eight stars at left, large value at center right **Edge:** Segmented reeding

Date	Mintage	F	VF	XF	Unc	BU
2007	—	—	—	—	3.00	3.50
2009	—	—	—	—	3.00	3.50

Y# 100   50 CENTIMOS
4.3000 g., Nickel Plated Steel, 21.9 mm. **Subject:** Banco Central, 70th Anniversary **Obv:** Legend **Rev:** Large vlaue

Date	Mintage	F	VF	XF	Unc	BU
2010	—	—	—	—	3.50	4.00

Y# 93   BOLIVAR
8.0400 g., Bi-Metallic Copper-Nickel center in Aluminum-Bronze ring, 24 mm. **Obv:** Eight stars at left of national arms, large value at right **Obv. Legend:** REPÚBLICA BOLIVARIANA DE VENEZUELA **Rev:** Head of Bolívar left **Edge:** Lettered **Edge Lettering:** "BCV 1" repeated

Date	Mintage	F	VF	XF	Unc	BU
2007	—	—	—	—	5.00	6.00
2009	—	—	—	—	5.00	6.00

Y# 101   50 BOLIVARES
31.1000 g., 0.9990 Silver 0.9988 oz. ASW, 38.6 mm. **Subject:**

Banco Central, 70th Anniversary **Obv:** Legned **Rev:** Banco Central building

Date	Mintage	F	VF	XF	Unc	BU
2010 Proof	3,000	Value: 65.00				

Y# 102   50 BOLIVARES
0.9990 Gold **Subject:** Banco Central, 70th Anniversary **Obv:** Legend **Rev:** Banco Central building

Date	Mintage	F	VF	XF	Unc	BU
2010 Proof	—	Value: 1,650				

Y# 95   200 BOLIVARES
0.9990 Silver **Obv:** Flag **Rev:** Crowd outside building

Date	Mintage	F	VF	XF	Unc	BU
2010 Proof	—	Value: 75.00				

Y# 96   200 BOLIVARES
0.9990 Gold **Obv:** Flag **Rev:** Crowd before building

Date	Mintage	F	VF	XF	Unc	BU
2010 Proof	—	Value: 1,700				

Y# 97   200 BOLIVARES
0.9990 Silver **Obv:** Flag **Rev:** Francisco de Marianda

Date	Mintage	F	VF	XF	Unc	BU
2010 Proof	—	Value: 75.00				

Y# 98   200 BOLIVARES
0.9990 Gold **Obv:** Flag **Rev:** Francisco de Marianda

Date	Mintage	F	VF	XF	Unc	BU
2010 Proof	—	Value: 1,700				

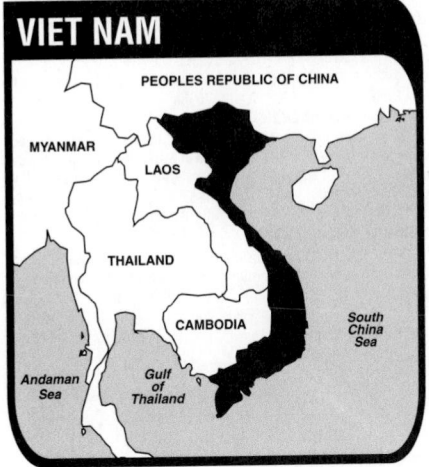

VIET NAM

PEOPLES REPUBLIC OF CHINA
MYANMAR
LAOS
THAILAND
CAMBODIA
South China Sea
Andaman Sea
Gulf of Thailand

The Socialist Republic of Viet Nam, located in Southeast Asia west of the South China Sea, has an area of 127,300 sq. mi. (329,560 sq. km.) and a population of *66.8 million. Capital: Hanoi. Agricultural products, coal, and mineral ores are exported.

The activities of Communists in South Viet Nam led to the second Indochina war which came to a brief halt in 1973 (when a cease-fire was arranged and U.S. forces withdrew), but it didn't end until April 30, 1975 when South Viet Nam surrendered unconditionally. The two Viet Nams were reunited as the Socialist Republic of Viet Nam on July 2, 1976.

NOTE: For earlier coinage refer to French Indo-China or Tonkin.

SOCIALIST REPUBLIC
STANDARD COINAGE

KM# 71   200 DONG
3.1000 g., Nickel Clad Steel, 20.75 mm. **Obv:** National emblem **Rev:** Denomination

Date	Mintage	F	VF	XF	Unc	BU
2003	125,000,000	0.15	0.20	0.35	0.75	0.50

KM# 74   500 DONG
4.5000 g., Nickel Clad Steel, 21.86 mm. **Obv:** National emblem **Rev:** Denomination **Edge:** Segmented reeding

Date	Mintage	F	VF	XF	Unc	BU
2003	175,000,000	0.15	0.25	0.50	0.75	1.00

KM# 72   1000 DONG
3.7000 g., Brass Plated Steel, 19 mm. **Obv:** National emblem **Rev:** Bat De Pagoda in Hanoi **Edge:** Reeded

Date	Mintage	F	VF	XF	Unc	BU
2003	250,000,000	0.20	0.35	0.60	0.80	1.50

KM# 75   2000 DONG
5.0000 g., Brass Plated Steel, 23.5 mm. **Obv:** National emblem **Rev:** Highland Stilt House in Tay Nguyen above value **Edge:** Segmented reeding

Date	Mintage	F	VF	XF	Unc	BU
2003	—	—	—	—	2.25	2.75

KM# 64   5000 DONG
1.2441 g., 0.9999 Gold 0.0400 oz. AGW, 13.92 mm. **Subject:** Year of the Snake **Obv:** State emblem **Rev:** Sea snake **Edge:** Reeded

Date	Mintage	F	VF	XF	Unc	BU
2001	—	—	—	—	65.00	75.00

KM# 67   5000 DONG
1.2441 g., 0.9999 Gold 0.0400 oz. AGW, 13.9 mm. **Subject:** Year of the Horse **Obv:** State emblem **Rev:** Horse **Edge:** Reeded

Date	Mintage	F	VF	XF	Unc	BU
2002	28,000	—	—	—	60.00	70.00

KM# 73   5000 DONG
7.6000 g., Brass, 25 mm. **Obv:** National emblem **Rev:** Chua Mot Cot Pagoda in Hanoi

Date	Mintage	F	VF	XF	Unc	BU
2003	500,000,000	0.50	0.75	1.00	1.25	2.50

KM# 57   10000 DONG
20.0000 g., 0.9250 Silver 0.5948 oz. ASW, 38.7 mm. **Subject:** Year of the Snake **Obv:** State emblem above value **Obv. Legend:** "CONG HOA XA HOI CHU NGHIA VIET NAM" **Rev:** Sea snake **Rev. Legend:** "...VIET NAM" **Edge:** Reeded

Date	Mintage	F	VF	XF	Unc	BU
2001(S) Proof	3,500	Value: 85.00				

KM# 58   10000 DONG
20.0000 g., 0.9250 Silver 0.5948 oz. ASW **Subject:** Year of the Snake **Obv:** State emblem above value **Obv. Legend:** "CONG HOA XA HOI CHU NGHIA VIET NAM" **Rev:** Bamboo viper **Rev. Legend:** "...VIET NAM"

Date	Mintage	F	VF	XF	Unc	BU
2001(S) Proof	3,500	Value: 85.00				

KM# 59   10000 DONG
20.0000 g., 0.9250 Silver 0.5948 oz. ASW **Subject:** Year of the Snake **Obv:** State emblem above value **Obv. Legend:** "CONG HOA XA HOI CHU NGHIA VIET NAM" **Rev:** Multicolor holographic, cobra in center **Rev. Legend:** "...VIET NAM"

Date	Mintage	F	VF	XF	Unc	BU
2001(S) Proof	3,500	Value: 80.00				

KM# 61   10000 DONG
20.0000 g., 0.9990 Silver 0.6423 oz. ASW, 38.7 mm. **Subject:** Year of the Horse **Obv:** State emblem **Rev:** Horse with octagonal latent image **Edge:** Reeded

Date	Mintage	F	VF	XF	Unc	BU
2001 Proof	3,800	Value: 65.00				

Note: In proof set only

KM# 62   10000 DONG
20.0000 g., 0.9990 Silver 0.6423 oz. ASW, 38.7 mm. **Subject:** Year of the Horse **Obv:** State emblem **Rev:** Horse with multicolor accoutrements **Edge:** Reeded

Date	Mintage	F	VF	XF	Unc	BU
2001 Proof	3,800	Value: 75.00				

Note: In proof set only

KM# 63   10000 DONG
20.0000 g., 0.9990 Silver 0.6423 oz. ASW, 38.7 mm. **Subject:** Year of the Horse **Obv:** State emblem **Rev:** Multicolor holographic horse in center **Edge:** Reeded

Date	Mintage	F	VF	XF	Unc	BU
2001 Proof	3,800	Value: 75.00				

Note: In proof set only

KM# 76   10000 DONG
20.0000 g., 0.9990 Silver 0.6423 oz. ASW, 38.7 mm. **Obv:** State emblem **Rev:** Multicolored Grey-shanked Douc Langur monkey **Edge:** Reeded

Date	Mintage	F	VF	XF	Unc	BU
2004 Proof	6,200	Value: 70.00				

KM# 65   20000 DONG
7.7759 g., 0.9999 Gold 0.2500 oz. AGW, 22 mm. **Subject:** Year of the Snake **Obv:** State emblem **Rev:** Sea snake **Edge:** Reeded

Date	Mintage	F	VF	XF	Unc	BU
2001(S) Proof	—	Value: 425				

Note: Issued in a replica Faberge egg

KM# 68   20000 DONG
7.7759 g., 0.9999 Gold 0.2500 oz. AGW, 22 mm. **Subject:** Year of the Horse **Obv:** State emblem **Rev:** Horse **Edge:** Reeded

Date	Mintage	F	VF	XF	Unc	BU
2002 Proof	1,800	Value: 400				

KM# 66   50000 DONG
15.5518 g., 0.9999 Gold 0.4999 oz. AGW, 27 mm. **Subject:** Year of the Snake **Obv:** State emblem **Rev:** Multicolor holographic King Cobra **Edge:** Reeded

Date	Mintage	F	VF	XF	Unc	BU
2001(S) Proof	3,200	Value: 825				

KM# 69   50000 DONG
15.5518 g., 0.9999 Gold 0.4999 oz. AGW, 27 mm. **Subject:** Year of the Horse **Obv:** State emblem **Rev:** Multicolor holographic horse **Edge:** Reeded

Date	Mintage	F	VF	XF	Unc	BU
2002 Proof	3,800	Value: 800				

PROOF SETS

KM#	Date	Mintage	Identification	Issue Price	Mkt Val
PS4	2001(S) (3)	3,500	KM#57-59	120	250
PS5	2001(S) (2)	—	KM#59, 66	—	925
PS6	2001(S) (2)	—	KM#65-66	—	1,250
PS7	2002 (3)	3,800	KM#61-63	—	225

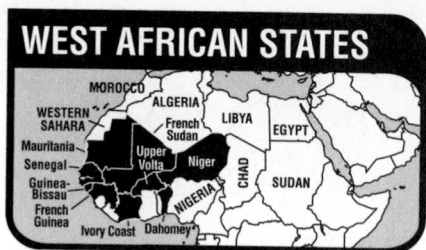

WEST AFRICAN STATES

The West African States, a former federation of eight French colonial territories on the northwest coast of Africa, has an area of 1,831,079 sq. mi. (4,742,495 sq. km.) and a population of about 17 million. Capital: Dakar. The constituent territories were Mauritania, Senegal, Dahomey, French Sudan, Ivory Coast, Upper Volta, Niger and French Guinea.

The members of the federation were overseas territories within the French Union until Sept. of 1958 when all but French Guinea approved the constitution of the Fifth French Republic, thereby electing to become autonomous members of the new French Community. French Guinea voted to become the fully independent Republic of Guinea. The other seven attained independence in 1960. The French West Africa territories were provided with a common currency, a practice which was continued as the monetary union of the West African States which provides a common currency to the autonomous republics of Dahomey (now Benin), Senegal, Upper Volta (now Burkina Faso), Ivory Coast, Mali, Togo, Niger, and Guinea-Bissau.

For earlier coinage refer to Togo, and French West Africa.

MINT MARK
(a)- Paris, privy marks only

MONETARY SYSTEM
100 Centimes = 1 Franc

FEDERATION

STANDARD COINAGE

KM# 8   FRANC
1.6000 g., Steel **Obv:** Taku - Ashanti gold weight **Rev:** Value and date

Date	Mintage	F	VF	XF	Unc	BU
2001(a)	—	—	—	0.10	0.35	0.60
2002(a)	—	—	—	0.10	0.35	0.60

KM# 2a   5 FRANCS
3.0000 g., Aluminum-Nickel-Bronze, 20 mm. **Obv:** Taku - Ashanti gold weight divides value **Rev:** Gazelle head facing

Date	Mintage	F	VF	XF	Unc	BU
2001(a)	—	—	0.10	0.20	0.40	0.60
2002(a)	—	—	0.10	0.20	0.40	0.60
2003(a)	—	—	0.10	0.20	0.40	0.60
2004(a)	—	—	0.10	0.20	0.40	0.60
2005(a)	—	—	0.10	0.20	0.40	0.60
2006(a)	—	—	0.10	0.20	0.40	0.60
2007(a)	—	—	—	0.20	0.40	0.60
2008(a)	—	—	—	0.20	0.40	0.60
2009(a)	—	—	—	0.20	0.40	0.60
2010(a)	—	—	—	0.20	0.40	0.60

KM# 10   10 FRANCS
4.0400 g., Brass, 23.4 mm. **Series:** F.A.O. **Obv:** Taku - Ashanti gold weight divides value **Rev:** People getting water

Date	Mintage	F	VF	XF	Unc	BU
2002(a)	—	—	0.25	0.50	1.25	1.50
2003(a)	—	—	0.25	0.50	1.25	1.50
2004(a)	—	—	0.25	0.50	1.00	1.50
2005(a)	—	—	0.25	0.50	1.00	1.50
2006(a)	—	—	0.25	0.50	1.00	1.50
2007(a)	—	—	—	0.50	1.00	1.50
2008(a)	—	—	—	0.50	1.00	1.50
2009(a)	—	—	—	0.50	1.00	1.50

KM# 9   25 FRANCS

7.9500 g., Aluminum-Bronze, 27 mm. **Series:** F.A.O. **Obv:** Taku - Ashanti gold weight divides value **Rev:** Figure filling tube **Note:** Mint mark position varieties exist.

Date	Mintage	F	VF	XF	Unc	BU
2001(a)	—	—	0.25	0.75	1.75	2.00
2002(a)	—	—	0.25	0.75	1.75	2.00
2003(a)	—	—	0.25	0.75	1.75	2.00
2004(a)	—	—	0.25	0.75	1.50	2.00
2005(a)	—	—	0.25	0.75	1.50	2.00
2006(a)	—	—	—	0.75	1.50	2.00
2007(a)	—	—	—	0.75	1.50	2.00
2008(a)	—	—	—	0.75	1.50	2.00
2009(a)	—	—	—	0.75	1.50	2.00

KM# 6   50 FRANCS

5.0900 g., Copper-Nickel, 22 mm. **Series:** F.A.O. **Obv:** Taku - Ashanti gold weight **Rev:** Value within mixed beans, grains and nuts

Date	Mintage	F	VF	XF	Unc	BU
2001(a)	—	—	0.35	0.50	1.25	1.50
2002(a)	—	—	0.35	0.50	1.25	1.50
2003(a)	—	—	0.35	0.50	1.25	1.50
2004(a)	—	—	0.35	0.50	1.25	1.50
2005(a)	—	—	0.35	0.50	1.25	1.50
2006(a)	—	—	—	0.50	1.25	1.50
2007(a)	—	—	—	0.50	1.25	1.50
2009(a)	—	—	—	0.50	1.25	1.50
2010(a)	—	—	—	0.50	1.25	1.50

KM# 4   100 FRANCS

7.0700 g., Nickel, 26 mm. **Obv:** Taku - Ashanti gold weight **Rev:** Value within flowers **Edge:** Reeded

Date	Mintage	F	VF	XF	Unc	BU
2001(a)	—	—	0.60	0.85	2.25	2.75
2002(a)	—	—	0.60	0.85	2.25	2.75
2003(a)	—	—	0.60	0.85	2.25	2.75
2004(a)	—	—	0.60	0.75	2.00	2.75
2005(a)	—	—	0.60	0.75	2.00	2.75
2006(a)	—	—	0.60	0.75	2.00	2.75
2009(a)	—	—	0.60	0.75	2.00	2.75

KM# 14   200 FRANCS

6.9000 g., Bi-Metallic Brass center in Copper-Nickel ring, 24.4 mm. **Obv:** Taku - Ashanti gold weight **Rev:** Agricultural produce and value **Edge:** Segmented reeding

Date	Mintage	F	VF	XF	Unc	BU
2003	—	—	—	1.60	4.00	6.00
2004(a)	—	—	—	1.60	4.00	6.00
2005(a)	—	—	—	1.60	4.00	6.00
2010(a)	—	—	—	1.60	4.00	6.00

KM# 15   500 FRANCS

10.6000 g., Bi-Metallic Copper-Nickel center in Brass ring, 27.9 mm. **Obv:** Taku - Ashanti gold weight **Rev:** Agricultural produce and value **Edge:** Segmented reeding

Date	Mintage	F	VF	XF	Unc	BU
2003	—	—	2.25	4.00	10.00	14.00
2004(a)	—	—	2.25	4.00	10.00	12.00
2005(a)	—	—	2.25	4.00	10.00	12.00

KM# 16   1000 FRANCS

22.2000 g., 0.9000 Silver 0.6423 oz. ASW **Obv:** Taku - Ashanti gold weight **Rev:** Agricultural produce above sprays surrounded by names of member countries

Date	Mintage	F	VF	XF	Unc	BU
2002(a) Proof	500	Value: 125				

KM# 17   1000 FRANCS

22.2000 g., 0.9000 Silver 0.6423 oz. ASW **Subject:** FIFA World Championship Football - Germany 2006 **Obv:** Player kicking ball, tree in background **Obv. Legend:** COUPE DU MONDE DE LA FIFA - ALLEMAGNE **Rev:** Agricultural produce above sprays surrounded by names of member countries

Date	Mintage	F	VF	XF	Unc	BU
2004(a) Proof	50,000	Value: 75.00				

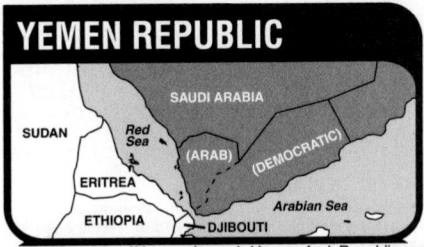

YEMEN REPUBLIC

The Republic of Yemen, formerly Yemen Arab Republic and Peoples Democratic Republic of Yemen, is located on the southern coast of the Arabian Peninsula. It has an area of 205,020 sq. mi. (531,000 sq. km.) and a population of 12 million. Capital: San'a. The port of Aden is the main commercial center and the area's most valuable natural resource. Recent oil and gas finds and a developing petroleum industry have improved their economic prospects. Agriculture and local handicrafts are the main industries. Cotton, fish, coffee, rock salt and hides are exported.

On May 22, 1990, the Yemen Arab Republic (North Yemen) and Peoples Democratic Republic of Yemen (South Yemen) merged into a unified Republic of Yemen. Disagreements between the two former governments simmered until civil war erupted in 1994, with the northern forces of the old Yemen Arab Republic eventually prevailing.

TITLES

المملكة المتوكلية اليمنية

al-Mamlaka(t) al-Mutawakkiliya(t) al-Yamaniya(t)

REPUBLIC

MILLED COINAGE

KM# 26   5 RIYALS

4.5000 g., Stainless Steel, 22.9 mm. **Obv:** Denomination within circle **Rev:** Building **Shape:** 21-sided

Date	Mintage	F	VF	XF	Unc	BU
AH1421-2001	—	—	—	—	1.75	2.25
AH1425-2004	—	—	—	—	1.75	2.25

KM# 27   10 RIYALS

6.0500 g., Stainless Steel, 26 mm. **Obv:** Denomination within circle **Rev:** Bridge at Shaharah

Date	Mintage	F	VF	XF	Unc	BU
AH1424-2003	—	—	—	—	2.75	3.50
AH1430-2009	—	—	—	—	2.75	3.50

KM# 29   20 RIYALS

7.1000 g., Bi-Metallic Brass plated Steel center in Stainless Steel ring, 29.85 mm. **Obv:** Value within circle **Rev:** Tree within circle **Edge:** Reeded

Date	Mintage	F	VF	XF	Unc	BU
AH1425-2004	—	—	—	—	4.00	5.00

KM# 29a   20 RIYALS

Stainless Steel, 29.85 mm. **Obv:** Value within circle **Rev:** Tree within circle **Edge:** Reeded

Date	Mintage	F	VF	XF	Unc	BU
AH1427-2006	—	—	—	—	4.00	5.00

KM# 30   500 RIALS

21.2500 g., Copper-Nickel-Zinc, 35.2 mm. **Subject:** City of San'a **Obv:** Value **Rev:** City gate below artwork **Edge:** Reeded

Date	Mintage	F	VF	XF	Unc	BU
AH1425-2004	—	—	—	—	30.00	40.00

KM# 32   500 RIALS

13.0000 g., Copper-Nickel gilt, 30 mm. **Subject:** City of San'a as Arab Cultural Capital **Note:** Pin added to reverse

Date	Mintage	F	VF	XF	Unc	BU
2004	—	—	—	—	40.00	50.00

KM# 31   1000 RIALS
73.3000 g., Pewter Antique silver finish, 60.3 mm. **Subject:** City of San'a **Obv:** Value **Rev:** City gate below artwork **Edge:** Plain **Note:** Illustration reduced.

Date	Mintage	F	VF	XF	Unc	BU
AH1425-2004	—	—	—	—	70.00	80.00

KM# 33   5000 RIALS
22.2000 g., 0.9000 Silver 0.6423 oz. ASW, 37 mm. **Subject:** President Ali Abdullah Saleh

Date	Mintage	F	VF	XF	Unc	BU
AH1424-2003	—	—	—	—	50.00	60.00

YUGOSLAVIA

The Federal Republic of Yugoslavia, formerly the Socialist Federal Republic of Yugoslavia, a Balkan country located on the east shore of the Adriatic Sea, has an area of 39,450 sq. mi. (102,173 sq. km.) and a population of 10.5 million. Capital: Belgrade. The chief industries are agriculture, mining, manufacturing and tourism. Machinery, nonferrous metals, meat and fabrics are exported.

The name Yugoslavia appears on the coinage in letters of the Cyrillic alphabet alone until formation of the Federated Peoples Republic of Yugoslavia in 1953, after which both the Cyrillic and Latin alphabets are employed. From 1965, the coin denomination appears in the 4 different languages of the federated republics in letters of both the Cyrillic and Latin alphabets.

MONETARY SYSTEM
100 Para = 1 Dinar

FEDERAL REPUBLIC
STANDARD COINAGE

KM# 180   DINAR
4.4000 g., Copper-Nickel-Zinc, 20 mm. **Obv:** National arms within circle **Rev:** Building **Edge:** Reeded

Date	Mintage	F	VF	XF	Unc	BU
2002	60,780,000	—	—	—	0.25	0.45

KM# 181   2 DINARA
5.2000 g., Copper-Nickel-Zinc, 21.9 mm. **Obv:** National arms within circle **Rev:** Church **Edge:** Reeded

Date	Mintage	F	VF	XF	Unc	BU
2002	71,053,000	—	—	—	0.30	0.50

KM# 182   5 DINARA
6.3000 g., Copper-Nickel-Zinc, 24 mm. **Obv:** National arms **Rev:** Domed building, denomination and date at left **Edge:** Reeded

Date	Mintage	F	VF	XF	Unc	BU
2002	30,966,000	—	—	—	1.25	1.50

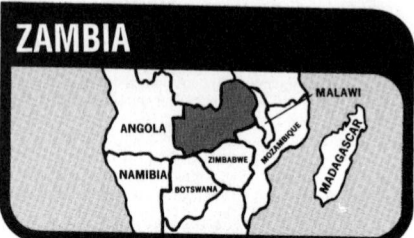

ZAMBIA

The Republic of Zambia (formerly Northern Rhodesia), a landlocked country in south-central Africa, has an area of 290,586 sq. mi. (752,610 sq. km.) and a population of 7.9 million. Capital: Lusaka. The economy of Zambia is based principally on copper, of which Zambia is the world's third largest producer. Copper, zinc, lead, cobalt and tobacco are exported. Zambia is a member of the Commonwealth of Nations. The President is the Head of State and the Head of Government.

REPUBLIC
DECIMAL COINAGE
100 Ngwee = 1 Kwacha

KM# 156   500 KWACHA
15.0000 g., 0.9990 Silver 0.4818 oz. ASW, 34.2 mm. **Subject:** Football World Champion - 1954 Germany **Obv:** Crowned head right within circle above arms with supporters and value **Rev:** Soccer game scene in front of Berlin Wall **Edge:** Plain

Date	Mintage	F	VF	XF	Unc	BU
2001 Proof	—	Value: 35.00				

KM# 174   500 KWACHA
15.0000 g., 0.9990 Silver 0.4818 oz. ASW, 34.2 mm. **Subject:** 1972 Munich Olympics **Obv:** Crowned head right above arms with supporters **Rev:** Torch runner in stadium **Edge:** Reeded

Date	Mintage	F	VF	XF	Unc	BU
2002 Proof	—	Value: 28.00				

KM# 87   1000 KWACHA
28.9100 g., Copper-Nickel, 38 mm. **Series:** Patrons of the Ocean **Obv:** Arms with supporters above crowned head right within circle **Rev:** Loggerhead sea turtle **Edge:** Reeded

Date	Mintage	F	VF	XF	Unc	BU
2001 Proof	—	Value: 17.00				

KM# 88   1000 KWACHA
28.9100 g., Copper-Nickel **Series:** Patrons of the Ocean **Obv:** Arms with supporters above crowned head right within circle **Rev:** Coelacanth

Date	Mintage	F	VF	XF	Unc	BU
2001 Proof	—	Value: 17.00				

KM# 89   1000 KWACHA
28.9100 g., Copper-Nickel **Series:** Patrons of the Ocean **Obv:** Arms with supporters above crowned head right within circle **Rev:** Sea horse and fish

Date	Mintage	F	VF	XF	Unc	BU
2001 Proof	—	Value: 17.00				

KM# 90   1000 KWACHA
28.9100 g., Copper-Nickel **Series:** Patrons of the Ocean **Obv:** Arms with supporters above crowned head right within circle **Rev:** Two dolphins

Date	Mintage	F	VF	XF	Unc	BU
2001 Proof	—	Value: 17.00				

KM# 181   1000 KWACHA
20.0300 g., Silver **Subject:** 75th Birthday Queen Elizabeth II **Obv:** Crowned head of Elizabeth II in circle, national arms below **Obv. Legend:** BANK OF ZAMBIA **Rev:** Bust of Elizabeth II facing wearing tiara **Edge:** Reeded

Date	Mintage	F	VF	XF	Unc	BU
2001 Proof	—	Value: 30.00				

KM# 74   1000 KWACHA
29.0000 g., Copper-Nickel, 40 mm. **Obv:** Crowned head right above arms with supporters divides date **Rev:** Dated calendar within circular design **Shape:** 7-sided

Date	Mintage	F	VF	XF	Unc	BU
2002 Proof-like	—	—	—	—	—	12.50
2003 Proof-like	—	—	—	—	—	12.50
2004 Proof-like	—	—	—	—	—	12.50

KM# 159   1000 KWACHA
31.2200 g., 0.9990 Silver 1.0027 oz. ASW, 38.6 mm. **Obv:** Crowned head right divides date above arms with supporters **Rev:** Bust 1/4 left **Edge:** Reeded

Date	Mintage	F	VF	XF	Unc	BU
2002	—	—	—	—	42.50	45.00

KM# 167   1000 KWACHA
25.0000 g., Copper-Nickel, 38.6 mm. **Subject:** 50th Anniversary of Elizabeth II's Coronation **Obv:** Crowned head right above arms with supporters **Rev:** Crown on pillow above crossed scepters **Edge:** Reeded

Date	Mintage	F	VF	XF	Unc	BU
ND(2003)	—	—	—	—	8.50	10.00

KM# 169   1000 KWACHA
25.0000 g., Copper-Nickel, 38.6 mm. **Obv:** Crowned head right above arms with supporters **Rev:** Prince William on jet ski **Edge:** Reeded

Date	Mintage	F	VF	XF	Unc	BU
2003	—	—	—	—	8.50	10.00

KM# 171   1000 KWACHA
25.0000 g., Copper-Nickel, 38.6 mm. **Obv:** Crowned head right above arms with supporters **Rev:** Crowned bust facing **Edge:** Reeded

Date	Mintage	F	VF	XF	Unc	BU
ND(2003)	—	—	—	—	8.50	10.00

KM# 172   1000 KWACHA
25.0000 g., 0.9250 Silver 0.7435 oz. ASW, 38.6 mm. **Obv:** Crowned head right above arms with supporters **Rev:** Crowned bust facing **Edge:** Reeded

Date	Mintage	F	VF	XF	Unc	BU
ND(2003) Proof	5,000	Value: 45.00				

KM# 160   1000 KWACHA
29.3000 g., Silver Plated Bronze (Specific gravity 9.099), 38.6 mm. **Subject:** Pope John Paul II **Obv:** National arms **Rev:** Pope saying mass **Edge:** Reeded **Note:** Specific gravity 9.099

Date	Mintage	F	VF	XF	Unc	BU
2003 Proof	—	Value: 20.00				

KM# 183   1000 KWACHA
7.7700 g., 0.9990 Silver 0.2496 oz. ASW, 26 mm. **Rev:** Elephant pair

Date	Mintage	F	VF	XF	Unc	BU
2003 Proof	2,000	Value: 18.00				

KM# 199   1000 KWACHA
Silver, 38 mm. **Subject:** Deadly Bugs **Obv:** National arms **Rev:** Harvest Ant in colored insert

Date	Mintage	F	VF	XF	Unc	BU
2010 Proof	—	Value: 40.00				

KM# 200   1000 KWACHA
Silver, 38 mm. **Subject:** Deadly Bugs **Obv:** National arms **Rev:** Giant Hornet in colored insert

Date	Mintage	F	VF	XF	Unc	BU
2010 Proof	—	Value: 40.00				

KM# 201   1000 KWACHA
Silver, 38 mm. **Subject:** Deadly Bugs **Obv:** National arms **Rev:** Mosquito in multicolor insert

Date	Mintage	F	VF	XF	Unc	BU
2010 Proof	—	Value: 40.00				

KM# 202   1000 KWACHA
Silver, 38 mm. **Subject:** Deadly Bugs **Obv:** National arms **Rev:** Scorpion

Date	Mintage	F	VF	XF	Unc	BU
2010 Proof	—	—	—	—	40.00	

KM# 203   1000 KWACHA
Silver, 38 mm. **Subject:** Deadly Bugs **Obv:** National arms **Rev:** Tsetse Fly

Date	Mintage	F	VF	XF	Unc	BU
2010 Proof	—	Value: 40.00				

KM# 118   2000 KWACHA
31.1035 g., 0.9990 Silver 0.9990 oz. ASW, 38.6 mm. **Subject:** Centennial of the Anglo-Japanese Alliance **Obv:** Queen Elizabeth **Rev:** Fantasy Japanese coin design **Edge:** Reeded

Date	Mintage	F	VF	XF	Unc	BU
2002	500	—	—	—	80.00	85.00

KM# 184   2000 KWACHA
15.1500 g., 0.9990 Silver 0.4866 oz. ASW **Rev:** Elephant pair

Date	Mintage	F	VF	XF	Unc	BU
2003 Proof	2,000	Value: 30.00				

KM# 166   4000 KWACHA
25.0000 g., 0.9250 Silver 0.7435 oz. ASW, 38.6 mm. **Subject:** Queen Elizabeth's 75th Birthday **Obv:** Crowned head right above arms with supporters **Rev:** Bust with hat facing **Edge:** Reeded

Date	Mintage	F	VF	XF	Unc	BU
2001 Proof	2,000	Value: 40.00				

KM# 85   4000 KWACHA
25.1000 g., 0.9250 Silver 0.7464 oz. ASW, 37.9 mm. **Series:** Wildlife Protection **Obv:** Crowned head right below arms **Rev:** Lion head hologram **Edge:** Reeded **Note:** Lighter weight and smaller diameter than official specifications

Date	Mintage	F	VF	XF	Unc	BU
2001 Proof	—	Value: 60.00				

KM# 110   4000 KWACHA
20.0000 g., 0.9990 Silver 0.6423 oz. ASW, 37.9 mm. **Series:** Patrons of the Ocean **Obv:** Crowned head right within circle below arms with supporters **Rev:** Loggerhead sea turtle **Edge:** Reeded

Date	Mintage	F	VF	XF	Unc	BU
2001 Proof	—	Value: 32.00				

KM# 111   4000 KWACHA
20.0000 g., 0.9990 Silver 0.6423 oz. ASW **Series:** Patrons of the Ocean **Obv:** Crowned head right divides date below arms with supporters **Rev:** Coelacanth fish

Date	Mintage	F	VF	XF	Unc	BU
2001 Proof	—	Value: 38.00				

KM# 112   4000 KWACHA
20.0000 g., 0.9990 Silver 0.6423 oz. ASW **Series:** Patrons of the Ocean **Obv:** Crowned head right divides date below arms with supporters **Rev:** Sea horse and fish

Date	Mintage	F	VF	XF	Unc	BU
2001 Proof	—	Value: 35.00				

KM# 113   4000 KWACHA
20.0000 g., 0.9990 Silver 0.6423 oz. ASW **Series:** Patrons of the Ocean **Obv:** Crowned head right divides date below arms with supporters **Rev:** Two dolphins

Date	Mintage	F	VF	XF	Unc	BU
2001 Proof	—	Value: 38.00				

KM# 114   4000 KWACHA
50.0000 g., 0.9990 Silver 1.6059 oz. ASW **Subject:** Illusion **Obv:** Arms with supporters below crowned head right **Rev:** Cat within window **Edge:** Plain **Note:** 50x50mm

Date	Mintage	F	VF	XF	Unc	BU
2001 Proof	5,000	Value: 85.00				

KM# 175   4000 KWACHA
23.0000 g., 0.9990 Silver 0.7387 oz. ASW, 40 mm. **Obv:** Head with tiara right divides date above arms **Rev:** Dated calendar **Shape:** Seven-sided

Date	Mintage	F	VF	XF	Unc	BU
2002 Prooflike	—	—	—	—	—	45.00
2003 Prooflike	15,000	—	—	—	—	45.00
2004 Prooflike	5,000	—	—	—	—	45.00

KM# 168   4000 KWACHA
25.0000 g., 0.9250 Silver 0.7435 oz. ASW, 38.6 mm. **Subject:** 50th Anniversary of Elizabeth II's Coronation **Obv:** Crowned head right above arms with supporters **Rev:** Crown on pillow above crossed scepters **Edge:** Reeded

Date	Mintage	F	VF	XF	Unc	BU
ND(2003) Proof	5,000	Value: 45.00				

KM# 170   4000 KWACHA
25.0000 g., 0.9250 Silver 0.7435 oz. ASW, 38.6 mm. **Obv:** Crowned head right above arms with supporters **Rev:** Prince William on jet ski **Edge:** Reeded

Date	Mintage	F	VF	XF	Unc	BU
2003 Proof	5,000	Value: 45.00				

KM# 117   5000 KWACHA
31.3000 g., 0.9990 Silver 1.0053 oz. ASW, 38.6 mm. **Subject:** African Wildlife **Obv:** Arms with supporters **Rev:** Elephant mother and calf grazing on grass **Edge:** Reeded

Date	Mintage	F	VF	XF	Unc	BU
2001 Matte	—	—	—	—	42.00	45.00
2001 Proof	—	Value: 45.00				
Note: 50						

KM# 143   5000 KWACHA
28.8600 g., 0.9990 Silver 0.9269 oz. ASW, 38.5 mm. **Subject:** African Wildlife **Obv:** Arms with supporters **Rev:** Elephant **Edge:** Reeded

Date	Mintage	F	VF	XF	Unc	BU
2002 Matte	—	—	—	—	42.00	45.00
2002 Proof	—	Value: 50.00				

KM# 142   5000 KWACHA
28.6400 g., 0.9990 Silver 0.9198 oz. ASW, 38.5 mm. **Subject:** African Wildlife **Obv:** Queen Elizabeth's portrait above national arms and denomination **Rev:** Adult and juvenile elephants **Edge:** Reeded

Date	Mintage	F	VF	XF	Unc	BU
2002 Matte	—	—	—	—	42.00	45.00
2002 Proof	—	Value: 50.00				

KM# 165   5000 KWACHA
31.1000 g., 0.9990 Silver 0.9988 oz. ASW, 38.5 mm. **Obv:** Crowned bust right divides date **Rev:** Two African elephants **Edge:** Reeded

Date	Mintage	F	VF	XF	Unc	BU
2003 Matte	—	—	—	—	42.00	45.00
2003 Proof	—	Value: 50.00				

KM# 185   5000 KWACHA
31.1050 g., 0.9990 Silver 0.9990 oz. ASW **Rev:** Elephant pair

Date	Mintage	F	VF	XF	Unc	BU
2003 Proof	2,000	Value: 55.00				

KM# 186 5000 KWACHA
31.1050 g., 0.9990 Silver 0.9990 oz. ASW **Obv:** Head right **Rev:** Multicolor elephant pair

Date	Mintage	F	VF	XF	Unc	BU
2003 Proof	—	Value: 42.00				

KM# 187 5000 KWACHA
31.1050 g., 0.9990 Silver partially gilt 0.9990 oz. ASW, 40 mm. **Rev:** Elephant pair, partially gilt

Date	Mintage	F	VF	XF	Unc	BU
2003 Proof	—	Value: 50.00				

KM# 188 10000 KWACHA
62.2100 g., 0.9990 Silver 1.9980 oz. ASW, 50 mm. **Rev:** Two elephants

Date	Mintage	F	VF	XF	Unc	BU
2003 Proof	2,000	Value: 125				

KM# 94 40000 KWACHA
31.1035 g., 0.9999 Gold 0.9999 oz. AGW, 37.9 mm. **Series:** Wildlife Protection **Obv:** Arms with supporters above crowned head right **Rev:** Holographic lion head **Edge:** Reeded

Date	Mintage	F	VF	XF	Unc	BU
2001 Proof	—	Value: 1,550				

KM# 153.1 40000 KWACHA
47.5400 g., 0.9166 Gold 1.4009 oz. AGW, 39 mm. **Subject:** Queen Victoria **Obv:** Crowned head right within ornate frame divides date above arms with supporters **Rev:** Crowned veiled bust of Queen Victoria left **Edge:** Reeded

Date	Mintage	F	VF	XF	Unc	BU
2001 Proof	1	—	—	—	—	—

Note: Medallic die alignment

KM# 153.2 40000 KWACHA
47.5400 g., 0.9166 Gold 1.4009 oz. AGW, 39 mm. **Subject:** Queen Victoria **Obv:** Crowned head right within ornate frame divides date above arms with supporters **Rev:** Crowned veiled bust of Queen Victoria left **Edge:** Reeded

Date	Mintage	F	VF	XF	Unc	BU
2001 Matte	1	—	—	—	—	—

Note: Coin die alignment

KM# 154.1 40000 KWACHA
47.5400 g., 0.9166 Gold 1.4009 oz. AGW, 39 mm. **Subject:** Edward VII **Obv:** Crowned head right within ornate frame divides date above arms with supporters **Rev:** Crowned bust of King Edward VII right **Edge:** Reeded

Date	Mintage	F	VF	XF	Unc	BU
2001 Proof	1	—	—	—	—	—

Note: Medallic die alignment

KM# 154.2 40000 KWACHA
47.5400 g., 0.9166 Gold 1.4009 oz. AGW, 39 mm. **Subject:** Edward VII **Obv:** Crowned head right within ornate frame divides date above arms with supporters **Rev:** Crowned bust of King Edward VII right **Edge:** Reeded

Date	Mintage	F	VF	XF	Unc	BU
2001 Matte	1	—	—	—	—	—

Note: Coin die alignment

ZIMBABWE

The Republic of Zimbabwe (formerly the Republic of Rhodesia or Southern Rhodesia), located in the east-central part of southern Africa, has an area of 150,804 sq. mi. (390,580 sq. km.) and a population of *10.1 million. Capital: Harare (formerly Salisbury). The economy is based on agriculture and mining. Tobacco, sugar, asbestos, copper, chrome, ore and coal are exported.

On April 18, 1980 pursuant to an act of the British Parliament, the colony of Southern Rhodesia became independent as the Republic of Zimbabwe, a member of the Commonwealth of Nations, until recently suspended.

MONETARY SYSTEM
100 Cents = 1 Dollar

MINT
Harare

REPUBLIC

DECIMAL COINAGE

KM# 3a 10 CENTS
Nickel Plated Steel, 20 mm. **Obv:** National emblem **Rev:** Baobab tree, value **Edge:** Plain **Mint:** Harare

Date	Mintage	F	VF	XF	Unc	BU
2001	—	—	0.15	0.30	0.75	1.00
2002	—	—	0.15	0.30	0.75	1.00
2003	—	—	0.15	0.30	0.75	1.00

KM# 4a 20 CENTS
Nickel Plated Steel, 23 mm. **Obv:** National emblem **Rev:** Birchenough Bridge over the Sabi River, value below **Edge:** Plain **Mint:** Harare

Date	Mintage	F	VF	XF	Unc	BU
2001	—	—	0.20	0.40	1.25	1.50
2002	—	—	0.20	0.40	1.25	1.50
2003	—	—	0.20	0.40	1.25	1.50

KM# 5a 50 CENTS
Nickel Plated Steel, 26 mm. **Obv:** National emblem **Rev:** Radiant sun rising, symbolic of independence, value **Edge:** Plain **Mint:** Harare

Date	Mintage	F	VF	XF	Unc	BU
2001	—	—	0.40	1.00	1.75	2.00
2002	—	—	0.40	1.00	1.75	2.00
2003	—	—	0.40	1.00	1.75	2.00

KM# 6a DOLLAR
Nickel Plated Steel, 29 mm. **Obv:** National emblem **Rev:** Zimbabwe ruins amongst trees, value **Edge:** Reeded **Mint:** Harare

Date	Mintage	F	VF	XF	Unc	BU
2001	—	—	1.00	1.50	2.50	3.00
2002	—	—	1.00	1.50	2.50	3.00
2003	—	—	1.00	1.50	2.50	3.00

KM# 12a 2 DOLLARS
Brass Plated Steel, 24.5 mm. **Obv:** National emblem **Rev:** Pangolin below value **Edge:** Reeded **Mint:** Harare

Date	Mintage	F	VF	XF	Unc	BU
2001	—	—	1.25	2.25	4.00	5.00
2002	—	—	1.25	2.25	4.00	5.00
2003	—	—	1.25	2.25	4.00	5.00

KM# 13 5 DOLLARS
9.0500 g., Bi-Metallic Nickel-plated-Steel center in Brass ring, 27.4 mm. **Obv:** National emblem **Rev:** Rhinoceros standing right **Edge:** Reeded **Mint:** Harare

Date	Mintage	F	VF	XF	Unc	BU
2001	—	—	—	—	5.00	6.00
2002	—	—	—	—	5.00	6.00
2003	—	—	—	—	5.00	6.00

KM# 14 10 DOLLARS
5.2000 g., Nickel Plated Steel, 21.5 mm. **Obv:** National emblem **Rev:** Water buffalo **Edge:** Reeded **Mint:** Harare

Date	Mintage	F	VF	XF	Unc	BU
2003	—	—	—	1.50	2.50	3.50

KM# 15 25 DOLLARS
7.3300 g., Nickel Plated Steel, 24.5 mm. **Obv:** National emblem **Rev:** Military monument **Edge:** Segmented reeding **Mint:** Harare

Date	Mintage	F	VF	XF	Unc	BU
2003	—	—	—	1.75	3.00	4.00

STANDARD CATALOGS
TO ~~EDITION~~ ON

Standard Catalog of
WORLD COINS
1601-1700   5th Editio~~n~~
GEORGE S. CUHAJ, EDITOR • THOMAS MICHAEL, MARKET ANALYS~~T~~

22,000 Actual-Size Illustrations

kp The World's Best-Selling Coin Books

item# X9654

Standard Catalog of
WORLD COINS
1701-1800   5th Edition
GEORGE S. CUHAJ, EDITOR • THOMAS MICHAEL, MARKET ANALYST

18,500 Actual-Size Illustrations

kp The World's Best-Selling Coin Books

item# Z8041

~~Sta~~ndard Catalog of°
WORLD COINS
1801-1900   6th Edition
GEORGE S. CUHAJ, EDITOR • THOMAS MICHAEL, MARKET ANALYST

27,500 Actual-Size Illustrations

kp The World's Best-Selling Coin Books

item# Z3655

2013 Standard Catalog of°
WORLD COINS
1901-2000   40th Editio~~n~~
GEORGE S. CUHAJ, EDITOR • THOMAS MICHAEL, MARKET ANALYST

60,000 Actual-Size Illustrations

kp The World's Best-Selling Coin Books

item# W7382

2013 Standard Catalog of°
WORLD COINS
2001-Date   7th Edition
GEORGE S. CUHAJ, EDITOR • THOMAS MICHAEL, MARKET ANALYST

12,500 Actual-Size Illustrations

kp The World's Best-Selling Coin Books

item# W7385

Every Standard Catalog contains:

- **Tens of thousands of current coin values, in multiple condition grades**
- **Key details for identifying coins: weight, diameter, year of issue, metal composition**
- **Thousands of actual-size illustrations of coins (front and back images)**
- **Alphabetical by country organization of coin listings**